BLACKSTONE'S
CRIMINAL
PRACTICE

BLACKSTONE'S

CRIMINAL PRACTICE

2000

Editor-in-Chief

Peter Murphy MA, LLB

of the Middle Temple, Barrister
and of the California and Texas Bars
Professor of Law, South Texas College of Law at Houston
Sometime Principal Lecturer, Inns of Court School of Law

Consultant Editor

His Honour

Eric Stockdale MSc, LLM, PhD, Hon. LLD

formerly a Circuit Judge; Visiting Professor, University of Hertfordshire

Authors

Diane Birch, Christopher J. Emmins, Peter Fortune, Marianne Giles,
Michael J. Gunn, Michael Hirst, Adrian Keane, Leonard Leigh, Richard McMahon,
John Sprack, Richard D. Taylor, Martin Wasik

BLACKSTONE
PRESS LIMITED

First published in Great Britain 1991 by Blackstone Press Limited
Aldine Place, London W12 8AA. Telephone (020) 8740 2277
www.blackstonepress.com

© Blackstone Press Limited, 1991

First edition, reprinted 1991 twice
Second edition, 1992
Third edition, 1993
Reprinted 1993
Fourth edition, 1994
Fifth edition, 1995
Sixth edition, 1996
Seventh edition, 1997
Eighth edition, 1998
Ninth edition, 1999
Tenth edition, 2000

ISBN: 1 84174 100 0
ISSN: 1355–347X

British Library Cataloguing in Publication Data
A CIP catalogue record for this book is available from the British Library

Typeset by Style Photosetting Limited, Mayfield, East Sussex.
Printed by Bath Press Limited, Bath.

PREFACE

In keeping with the seemingly universal resolve that the year 2000, rather than the mathematically correct 2001, is to be hailed as marking the beginning of the New Millennium, I now have the honour of writing the preface for the last edition of *Blackstone's Criminal Practice* of the 20th Century. Many of the developments of the last year seem appropriate to the occasion. The joint venture between Blackstone and Butterworths which resulted in *Crime Online* is surely one of the hallmarks of the approaching new era, an era in which legal research is taking on a new face. The new era practitioner expects to have (literally) at his or her fingertips, not only a basic statement of the law, but also a continually updated access to new and emerging law from all sources. *Crime Online*, a research engine of technological excellence, provides not only the annually revised text of *Blackstone*, but also a constant stream of the highest quality supplemental material and analysis by our authors, who are some of the most highly regarded experts in their respective fields. All of us who have been associated with this project are proud of this contribution to the needs of contemporary lawyers and judges. We feel that we have taken our work to a new level consistent with the demands of the new era.

Another sign of the times, reflecting a rapidly shrinking world, is the further, and this time fundamental, erosion of the cherished principle that the administration of the Common Law of England ends at the Cliffs of Dover. It has long been a truism that no man is an island. It is now becoming clear that the same applies to countries. Recent events in Europe have demonstrated that traditional concepts of sovereignty and national boundaries of laws are being replaced by an as yet uncertain concept of international responsibility for justice. Legal insularity and isolationism are on the decline. Perhaps the most obvious indication of this in terms of English law is the persistent intrusion of the European Convention on Human Rights into our domestic criminal law, evidence and procedure. Regardless of the implementation of the Human Rights Act 1998, the impact of the Convention is being felt in many areas of the law. There can be little doubt that, welcome to all or not, this is a development which is here to stay, and it has been given its due importance in this edition.

As always, we have sought to bring the work up to date in all respects. Among the new statutes dealt with are the Youth and Criminal Evidence Act 1999, the Access to Justice Act 1999, and the Football (Offences and Disorder) Act 1999. The implementation of older provisions, including some introduced by the Criminal Procedure and Investigations Act 1996, the Criminal Justice Act 1993, and the Knives Act 1997, is noted. Among the important developments affecting practice, we have dealt with the new PACE Code of Practice on Stopping and Searching, and the Practice Direction on Skeleton Arguments.

The significant new cases reviewed include: *Booth* (conspiracy and acquittal); *Richardson* (intoxication); *Emmett* (consent); *Drew* (conspiracy and drugs); *Vehicle Inspectorate v Nuttall* (meaning of 'permitting'); *Hinks* (gifts and theft); *DPP, ex parte Kebilene* (terrorism); *DPP v Jones* (trespassory assembly); *DPP v Spurrier* (intoximeters); *Manchester Crown Court, ex parte Rogers* (privilege); *Desmond* (imputations on character); *Derodra* (inferences from silence); *Kelly* (automatic life sentences); *Medway Youth Court, ex parte A* (maximum youth court sentence); *Popat and Popat (No. 2)* (identification parades); and *Kaur* (sureties).

As always, it is a pleasure to acknowledge the tireless efforts of our publishers, Blackstone Press Limited, in particular Alistair MacQueen and Heather Saward, and our most able editorial coordinator, Laurence Eastham, who, as so often in the past, has held together a complex and intensely demanding enterprise with an unfailing thoroughness and expertise.

We have tried to state the law as at 1 December 1999.

Peter Murphy
Editor-in-Chief
December, 1999

PREFACE TO THE FIRST EDITION

The last time it happened, George IV was on the throne, and Great Britain still harboured lingering pretensions to sovereignty over the United States. The Judicature Act 1875 was still over a half-century away, the common-law courts sat in Westminster Hall, imprisonment was a remedy for debt and Doctors' Commons was a flourishing institution. Felonies were capital offences, yet the accused enjoyed no right to counsel and was not permitted to testify in his own defence. Times have changed, and even given the conservative attitude of lawyers to innovation, it is time it happened again.

The 'it' referred to is the publication of a wholly new work in the field of criminal law dealing as comprehensively as practicable with all the law, evidence and procedure practitioners need to know. It was in 1822 that J. F. Archbold first published his celebrated work. The editors of its 43rd edition, published 166 years later, in announcing that it had 'exploded' into two volumes, recalled that the original was some 440 pages long, and that its author claimed to have 'taken infinite pains . . . to compress the whole into the smallest possible compass consistent with perspicuity'. It is no criticism of the stalwart efforts of those editors, or those of their many equally distinguished predecessors, that there is now a clear and widely recognised need for a new work that returns to J. F.'s elegant aspiration.

Blackstone's Criminal Practice is designed to fill, in the later years of the 20th century, the need that J. F.'s prototype was designed to fill in the earlier years of the 19th. Its constitution is, we hope, simple and apt to the work of both branches of our legal profession in the field of modern criminal law. The principal articles of that constitution are:

A single volume of manageable size and expense.

An annual edition, giving up-to-date service without the cost and inconvenience of supplements.

In areas of general principle, writing of uncompromising and rigorous scholarly quality.

In more specific areas, meticulous attention to detail.

Everywhere, emphasis on the practice of the courts.

Critical scrutiny of content to promote maximum utility and minimum confusion.

The pursuit of these ideals has led us to some novel approaches. An early decision was that *Blackstone's Criminal Practice* would not attempt to be a portable library. No one book can contain the whole of the law and practice in any field without imitating those stars whose own density causes them to collapse inwards. It is neither necessary nor desirable, in these days of increasingly available and convenient research tools, to give new meaning to the expression 'the weight of authority' by trying to compress the totality of information within the framework of a single treatise. Such lack of discrimination would be apt to produce a work both physically and professionally unmanageable.

We have striven to include everything reasonably necessary from a practical perspective to the everyday work of the practitioner. But we have omitted, without apology, certain obsolete, rarely encountered or antiquated offences and materials of minor importance. Among the casualties are the form of indictment for keeping a puma and two male leopards on the highway to the terror and alarm of the Queen's subjects, and the finer points of assaulting a clergyman of the established Church in the performance of divine worship. These must be sought elsewhere. We have also omitted some areas of law of a more specialised nature, such as offences under the Factories Acts, licensing laws and immigration statutes, the attempted inclusion of which in a general work on criminal law might prove simply to be a disservice.

This selectivity is not, however, entirely exclusive in character. On the contrary, it has created space for the most thorough treatment in a single, well cross-referenced volume of all the material which is truly essential to criminal practice, and much besides that is useful and informative. It is designed to be useful to solicitors as well as barristers, to practitioners in the magistrates' courts as well as those in the Crown Court, to those who prosecute as well as those who defend. This is accomplished by a division of the book into six well defined parts, each consisting of thoughtfully constructed sections.

Part A contains a treatise on the general principles of criminal law. In this part, we have unashamedly requested our authors to write a rigorous and challenging scholarly work that will equip the reader for argument before even the most demanding of appellate tribunals, and will commend itself to the profession as a leading source of academic criticism and opinion.

In part B of the book, which deals with the substantive criminal law, all important criminal offences are fully dealt with and analysed. Due regard is paid to summary offences. The substantive offences are helpfully classified into sections by subject-matter. Each indictable offence is then described, as appropriate, in relation to its definition, applicable procedural rules, range of sentence and any sentencing guidelines, form of indictment, alternative verdicts, elements and defences.

The most significant summary offences in each section are dealt with alongside the indictable offences. A separate part of the book, part C, covers all the most important road traffic offences.

Parts D, E and F deal respectively with criminal procedure, sentencing and evidence, providing a thorough and detailed treatment of the realities of practice, both at the trial level and at the appellate level, and in relation both to summary trial and trial on indictment. The procedural material runs the whole gamut, beginning with police investigative powers, and ending with exhaustion of the final appeal. As mentioned above, this is in addition to the relevant procedural, evidential and sentencing material appended to the treatment of the individual substantive offences.

The authors and editors of this work are a select group and represent the accumulated experience of the Bench, the Bar, the solicitors' profession and the academic world. They have produced a work of high and enduring quality. Tragically, two of those who contributed most to this work will not share the joy of holding it in their hands in its completed form. Within the space of just a few weeks, death claimed both Chris Emmins and Pat Brown while the book was still in preparation.

As a lecturer at the Council of Legal Education, and as a practitioner at the criminal Bar, Christopher Emmins established himself as the undisputed master of criminal procedure. His book *A Practical Approach to Criminal Procedure* was, at the time of his death, pre-eminent in its field. Chris possessed the rare gift of being able to write with the same clarity with which he thought. He was responsible for almost all the material in this work on procedure. Reading his manuscript as editor-in-chief was a delight comparable to that of a conductor pondering the perfection of a score of Bach or Mozart. Thorough yet readable, complex yet comprehensible, methodical yet imaginative, diverse yet harmonious, the love for the subject and for the work unmistakable. Chris was also the most likeable, modest and unassuming of men, and the most conscientious.

It is typical of the man that he had taken manuscript with him to revise even on the holiday during which he met his death.

Pat Brown brought to her work as an editor not only a keen eye for detail and an innate feel for the overall needs and appearance of a book, but also an infectious and distinctive sense of humour and zest for life. This editor-in-chief will always be in her debt for her contributions to his other writings as well as to this work, both of which are immeasurable.

On behalf of the authors, the editor-in-chief extends heartfelt thanks to the publishing team of Blackstone Press Ltd, in particular Alistair MacQueen, Heather Saward (who lent her name as well as her marvellous talent and energy to *Operation Heather*) and Jonathan Harris. Their vision, creativity, determination and patience are surely unrivalled in their profession. Despite sometimes almost unassailable logistical problems and the many human frailties of authors and editors, they have persevered purposefully, and have not wavered in their faith in us. We hope they feel that that faith has been justified.

On his own behalf, the editor-in-chief is greatly indebted to his administrative assistant, Lee McInnis, whom he believes to possess supernatural powers, and to the world's three greatest future lawyers, Marty Orozco, Edward 'Nick' Nicholas and Dara Bloom, who probably had no idea that the world contained paper in such quantity as was hurled at them to copy, organise, file and dispatch. Without their competence, cheerful good humour and often unspoken reminders of what is truly important in life, the thousands of pages of manuscript would have been literally overwhelming.

And so, after much time, dedication and effort, to which it sometimes seemed there would be no end, *Operation Heather* is complete. *Blackstone's Criminal Practice* is ready to begin its journey. There is no better way to launch it on its path than with words penned by Sir William Blackstone himself in his preface to the *Commentaries on the Laws of England*:

> If, in the pursuit of these inquiries, the author hath been able to rectify any errors which either himself or others may have heretofore imbibed, his pains will be sufficiently answered: and, if in some points he is still mistaken, the candid and judicious reader will make due allowances for the difficulties of a search so new, so extensive, and so laborious.

Peter Murphy
Editor-in-Chief
March, 1991

ACKNOWLEDGEMENTS

The publishers would again like to thank the many practitioners who were kind enough to write and make suggestions for ways in which we might improve this edition. The letters were overwhelmingly positive and constructive, and we feel sure this edition has greatly benefited from those suggestions.

Particular thanks are due to the editorial coordinator, Laurence Eastham. Without his administrative and editorial skills this new edition would not have progressed as smoothly as it has. Thanks are also due to Moira Greenhalgh for the preparation of the index, to Mandy Preece for her diligent proof reading and to Ray Constant for his continued skill and efficiency.

The Code for Crown Prosecutors in appendix 4 is reproduced with the permission of the Crown Prosecution Service.

ABREVIATIONS

The following abbreviations have been used in this edition:

A-G	Attorney-General
A-G's Ref	Attorney-General's Reference
BA 1976	Bail Act 1976
CDA 1998	Crime and Disorder Act 1998
CJA	Criminal Justice Act (dates vary)
CJPO 1994	Criminal Justice and Public Order Act 1994
CPIA 1996	Criminal Procedure and Investigations Act 1996
CPS	Crown Prosecution Service
C(S)A 1997	Crime (Sentences) Act 1997
CYPA	Children and Young Persons Act (dates vary)
DPP	Director of Public Prosecutions
DTA 1994	Drug Trafficking Act 1994
FA 1968	Firearms Act 1968
F(A)A	Firearms (Amendment) Act (dates vary)
MCA 1980	Magistrates' Courts Act 1980
MDA 1971	Misuse of Drugs Act 1971
OAPA 1861	Offences Against the Person Act 1861
PACE 1984	Police and Criminal Evidence Act 1984
PCCA 1973	Powers of Criminal Courts Act 1973
POA	Public Order Act (dates vary)
PT(TP)A	Prevention of Terrorism (Temporary Provisions) Act (dates vary)
RTA	Road Traffic Act (dates vary)
RTOA 1988	Road Traffic Offenders Act 1988
RTRA	Road Traffic Regulation Act (dates vary)
SOA	Sexual Offences Act (dates vary)
TA	Theft Act (dates vary)
YJCEA 1999	Youth Justice and Criminal Evidence Act 1999

CONTENTS

CONTENTS

CONTENTS

CONTENTS

CONTENTS

CONTENTS

CONTENTS

CONTENTS

CONTENTS

TABLE OF CASES

TABLE OF STATUTES

Where a reference is underlined, the relevant material is reproduced at that reference.

TABLE OF STATUTORY INSTRUMENTS

Where a reference is underlined, the relevant material is reproduced at that reference.

TABLE OF CODES OF PRACTICE, PRACTICE DIRECTIONS ETC.

Where a reference is underlined, the relevant material is reproduced at that reference.

PART A

GENERAL PRINCIPLES OF CRIMINAL LAW

Leonard Leigh, PhD, Barrister

Commission Member, Criminal Cases Review Commission
Formerly Professor of Criminal Law in the University of London
London School of Economics and Political Science

Richard D. Taylor, MA, LLM, Barrister

Professor of English Law and Head of School, Lancashire Law School,
University of Central Lancashire

Michael Hirst, LLB, LLM

Professor of Criminal Justice, De Montfort University, Leicester

SECTION A1: *ACTUS REUS*: THE EXTERNAL ELEMENTS OF AN OFFENCE

It is customary, for analytical purposes, to separate the essential elements of a crime into **A1.1** two main elements: (1) the prohibited act, omission, consequence or state-of-affairs (the *actus reus*); and (2) any fault element, such as intent or recklessness, required in respect of it (the *mens rea*). Smith & Hogan (*Criminal Law*, 9th ed.) define the *actus reus* as including 'all the elements in the definition of the crime except the accused's mental element'. It represents the external manifestation of the offence.

THE NATURE OF AN *ACTUS REUS*

Conduct Crimes and Result Crimes

Criminal conduct frequently causes undesirable consequences, but the consequences **A1.2** of such conduct are not necessarily included within the definition of the offence in question. Blackmail, for example, is committed where D makes an unwarranted demand with menaces, with a view to gain or with a view to causing loss to another (Theft Act 1968, s. 21). The making of such a demand is in itself a sufficient *actus reus*, whether or not it enables D to gain (or cause loss) in accordance with his intentions. Moreover, the House of Lords held in *Treacy* v *DPP* [1971] AC 537 that a demand can be 'made' without necessarily being communicated to its intended victim (or indeed to anyone else). Posting of a blackmail demand may suffice, even if it is then lost or intercepted in the post (see **B5.86**). Blackmail can thus be described as a 'conduct crime' in which problems of causation or effect can never arise. In contrast, liability for obtaining property by deception (Theft Act 1968, s. 15) can be established only where someone is proved to have been deceived by D *and* where it is proved that property was obtained by him as a result of that deception. The s. 15 offence can thus be defined as a 'result crime'. More specifically, it is a 'double result' crime: deception and consequent obtaining each being essential elements of the *actus reus*. See *Miller* (1992) 95 Cr App R 421 at **B5.10**.

The classification of offences into 'conduct crimes' and 'result crimes' can be a relatively crude process, and may not always be particularly helpful. Rape, for example, does not really lend itself to analysis in such terms. Nevertheless, it is always necessary to identify the constituent elements of an offence, and the classification can sometimes highlight essential differences between two alternative charges. Thus, the Vagrancy Act 1824, s. 4, creates an offence of indecent exposure 'with intent to insult a female', but does not require that any female should either see the exposure or feel insulted by it. It accordingly creates a conduct crime, which may be contrasted with the offence created by the Town Police Clauses Act 1847, s. 28, under which the prosecution must prove that D's indecent exposure caused someone to be 'annoyed, obstructed or endangered'.

The distinction between conduct crimes and result crimes may also be important in determining jurisdiction over cross-frontier offences. The general rule is that jurisdiction over a conduct crime depends on proof that some part of the relevant conduct occurred within England or Wales, whereas jurisdiction over a result crime ordinarily depends on at least some part of the proscribed result taking place there (see *Secretary of State for Trade* v *Markus* [1976] AC 35, *per* Lord Diplock at p. 61 and *Harden* [1963] 1 QB 8. Cases involving international fraud may now fall within part I of the CJA 1993 (see **D1.75**). If so, jurisdiction may arise where any element of the offence occurs within England or Wales.

RELATIONSHIP BETWEEN *ACTUS REUS* AND *MENS REA*

A1.3   The general rule, expressed in the maxim, *actus non facit reum nisi mens sit rea*, is that an offence can be committed only where criminal conduct is accompanied by some element of fault, the precise fault element required depending upon the particular offence involved. There are nevertheless many offences of strict liability, in which no fault element need be proved (see **A4**). In such cases, one can therefore have an *actus reus* without any corresponding *mens rea*.

In theory, there can be no criminal liability based on *mens rea* alone, but if the *actus reus* element of a crime is defined very widely (as is sometimes the case) a 'guilty mind' may turn an objectively innocent act into the *actus reus* of that offence. Thus, a witness who tells the court something that he believes to be untrue is guilty of perjury, even if his evidence turns out, to his surprise, to be true after all (see **B14.9**); and a shopper who openly selects goods in a self-service store, whilst secretly nursing a dishonest intention to avoid paying for them, is regarded as committing theft at the moment he first selects them, even though he may have done nothing objectively wrong at that stage. The *actus reus* of perjury involves nothing more than giving material evidence in court; and the concept of appropriation, which lies at the heart of the *actus reus* of theft, has been defined so widely in cases such as *Gomez* [1993] AC 442 as to strip it of any special significance. Almost any form of dealing with another person's property, legitimate or otherwise, must now be regarded as an appropriation of it: the *actus reus* of theft (see generally **B4.25** *et seq*.).

A person can meanwhile be guilty of a criminal attempt by doing an entirely lawful thing in the mistaken belief that he is doing something different, which would indeed have been criminal. If, for example, D imports a harmless vegetable powder mistakenly believing it to be heroin, he may be guilty of attempting to import a controlled drug, contrary to s. 1 of the Criminal Attempts Act 1981. The objectively lawful importation of the powder becomes the *actus reus* of the criminal attempt (*Shivpuri* [1987] AC 1; see **A6.40**).

A Mental Element in the *Actus Reus*?

A1.4   The usual distinction between the mental element and the external manifestation of a crime can be difficult to apply in cases where the crime is one of 'possessing', 'permitting', 'keeping', 'appropriating', etc, because these terms simultaneously import both mental and physical elements. A person may, for example, possess a controlled drug without realising what it is that he possesses, but he does not possess something which, unknown to him, has become stuck to the sole of his shoe or the blade of his penknife (*Warner* v *Metropolitan Police Commissioner* [1969] 2 AC 256; *Marriott* [1971] 1 WLR 187). It might therefore be argued that there is a mental element implicit in the *actus reus* of any offence of unlawful possession. From a strictly theoretical viewpoint, this cannot be correct. The correct analysis must be that the legal concept of possession involves both the *actus reus* element of physical possession and a state of mind, the *animus possidendi*, which can only be a part of the requisite *mens rea*. Nevertheless, it may be convenient in practice to treat the *animus possidendi* as if it were an *actus reus* element, because it must always be proved by the prosecution, even where, as in drug possession cases, the burden of proof in respect of other *mens rea* elements is placed on the defence (see **B20.10** *et seq*.).

Contemporaneity of *Actus Reus* and *Mens Rea*

A1.5   The general rule is that, to be guilty of a criminal offence requiring *mens rea*, an accused must possess that *mens rea* when performing the act or omission in question, and it must relate to that particular act or omission. If, for example, D accidentally kills his wife in a car crash on Monday, the fact that he was planning to cut her throat on Tuesday does not make him guilty of her murder, even if he was thinking about the planned murder at the time of the accident, and even if he is subsequently delighted to find that his wife has died. The general rule as to contemporaneity must nevertheless be qualified in certain respects.

First, D's *mens rea* need not last beyond the moment at which he causes the *actus reus* to occur. He will not be excused merely because he abandons it before that *actus reus* is complete. After inflicting a fatal injury on V with murderous intent, D may repent of his actions and may even do his utmost to save V's life; but if V dies he will be guilty of murder (*Jakeman* (1983) 76 Cr App R 223, *per* Wood J at p. 228). In *Jakeman*, J booked suitcases containing drugs onto a series of flights terminating in London. She abandoned them in Paris, allegedly because she no longer intended to import them, but the cases were sent on to London where the drugs were discovered. The Court of Appeal held that J's loss of *mens rea* came too late to prevent her being guilty of an importation offence.

Secondly, the *actus reus* of a crime may consist of an extended or ongoing course of conduct, rather than one that occurs at one instant in time. The *actus reus* of rape, for example, extends from the moment of initial non-consensual penetration to the moment at which the penis is withdrawn. If D has no *mens rea* at the moment of penetration, but later becomes aware of the absence of consent, he may commit rape by not withdrawing immediately thereafter (*Kaitamaki* v *The Queen* [1985] AC 147). Consent may even be withdrawn after initial penetration, and rape may therefore be committed if, for example, D pays no heed when V protests that he should stop because he is hurting her.

A controversial example of the 'continuous act' principle can be found in *Fagan* v *Metropolitan Police Commissioner* [1969] 1 QB 439, where F was directed by a police officer to park his vehicle by the kerb, and drove it right onto the officer's foot. There was no proof that he did so deliberately, but it was clear that he deliberately left it there after the officer told him what he had done. His conviction for assaulting the officer was upheld by the Divisional Court on the basis that there was on ongoing act, which became a criminal assault once F became aware of it. James J said:

> It is not necessary that *mens rea* should be present at the inception of the *actus reus*; it can be superimposed on an existing act. On the other hand, the subsequent inception of *mens rea* cannot convert an act which has been completed without *mens rea* into an assault.

Thirdly, the courts may extend the above principle by treating a series of different actions culminating in the *actus reus* of a crime as if they were a single, extended or continuous course of conduct. It will then be sufficient if the accused possessed the requisite *mens rea* at any point during that course of conduct. If, for example, D attempts to murder V by beating him to death, and believes that he has done so, but actually kills V by burying or dismembering what he assumes to be his corpse, D will still be guilty of murder. As Lord Reid said in *Thabo Meli* v *The Queen* [1954] 1 WLR 228:

> It is much too refined a ground of judgment to say that, because the appellants were under a misapprehension at one stage and thought that their guilty purpose had been achieved before, in fact, it was achieved, therefore they are to escape the penalties of the law.

This principle has subsequently been applied, not only in cases where there was a pre-arranged plan, of which disposal of the body was a part (as in *Moore* [1975] Crim LR 229), but also in cases where there was no such plan. In *Church* [1966] 1 QB 59, C struck a woman and panicked because he mistakenly thought he had killed her. He threw her into a river, where she drowned. Edmund Davies J, giving the judgment of the Court of Criminal Appeal, held that, '. . . if a killing by the first act would have been manslaughter, a later destruction of the supposed corpse should also be manslaughter'.

Church was followed and extended in *Le Brun* [1992] QB 61, where B struck his wife in the course of an argument outside their house, after she had refused to enter it with him. The blow left her unconscious. He then tried to drag her into the house. As he did so, her head struck the pavement, fracturing her skull and killing her. The case differed from *Church* in that the fatal impact was accidental, whereas Church's disposal of the 'body' was deliberate, but the Court of Appeal nevertheless upheld a conviction for manslaughter by identifying a continuous course of unlawful conduct. In attempting to drag his unconscious wife indoors, B was either trying to conceal his initial assault on her, or forcing her to enter the house against her wishes (this being the original reason for the assault). The trial judge had directed the jury to acquit if they concluded that B had been trying to aid or assist his wife when he attempted to move her, and the Court of Appeal agreed that this would have broken the essential nexus between the two halves of the incident.

A further difficulty arose in *A-G's Ref (No. 4 of 1980)* [1981] 1 WLR 705 where, in the course of a struggle, D pushed his girlfriend V over a landing rail onto the floor below and then, believing her dead, cut her throat and dismembered her in the bath so as to dispose of her body. It was impossible to establish whether V died in the original fall or whether he killed her (as in *Church*) by his subsequent actions. The Court of Appeal held that a manslaughter conviction was possible, despite uncertainty as to the actual cause of death, but only if it could be proved that each of D's acts was performed with the requisite *mens rea* for that offence. Since the initial fall may well have killed V, it would not suffice to establish *mens rea* (such as gross negligence) only in the subsequent act of disposal: the prosecution also had to disprove D's claim that he had merely pushed her away in a 'reflex action' when she dug her nails into him in the struggle on the upstairs landing.

VOLUNTARY AND INVOLUNTARY CONDUCT

A1.6   The vast majority of criminal offences require acts or omissions on the defendant's part, and these acts or omissions must ordinarily be willed or 'voluntary'. D does not therefore commit criminal damage if his enemies throw him from an upstairs window onto the roof of a car below. Nor is this merely because he lacks the requisite *mens rea* for that offence. It is because involuntary movements cannot ordinarily constitute the *actus reus* of any offence, not even one of strict liability. As Ashworth explains, 'It is not merely a denial of fault. It is more a denial of authorship . . . in these circumstances, it is fair to say that this was not D's act, but something which happened to D' (*Principles of Criminal Law*, 2nd ed., pp. 96–97).

Physical compulsion is merely one possible cause of involuntary conduct. Such conduct may also be caused by uncontrollable reflex actions or by a physical collapse brought on by injury or illness. If, for example, D suffers a sudden and unforeseen stroke or blackout whilst driving his car, which then careers through a red traffic light and collides with another vehicle, no offence is committed by him. The same rule would apply if D loses control of his car when attacked by a swarm of bees (an example suggested by Devlin J in *Hill* v *Baxter* [1958] 1 QB 277).

'Involuntary' conduct in this context does not include acts done by reason of duress, necessity or coercion (as to which, see **A3.19 *et seq*.**) because such acts are still conscious, willed and rational; but it may include acts 'committed' by D when in a state of automatism: i.e. when not consciously in control of his own mind or body. A condition of automatism can arise where D is suffering from concussion, where he is a diabetic who suffers an attack of hypoglycaemia (very low blood sugar) after taking insulin (see *Quick* [1973] QB 910) or, arguably, where he commits the *actus reus* whilst in a somnambulistic trance induced by hypnotism.

Limitations on the Defence of Automatism

Although involuntariness or automatism is ordinarily a complete defence to any criminal **A1.7** charge, the use of that defence is limited by a number of considerations. These are more fully explained at **A3.7** *et seq*. It must suffice to note at this point that the defence may be rendered invalid where D was culpable for falling into such a condition, as for example by driving whilst suffering from exhaustion (*Kay* v *Butterworth* (1945) 173 LT 191) or by abusing alcohol or drugs (*Lipman* [1970] 1 QB 152). It is also unavailable where the cause of the condition is a 'defect of reason arising from a disease of the mind', because this amounts in law to insanity. The term 'disease of the mind' embraces both organic and functional disorders of the mind, but excludes external causes, such as drugs, hypnosis or concussion. Epilepsy is in this sense a disease of the mind (*Sullivan* [1984] AC 156) as is a brain tumour (*Kemp* [1957] 1 QB 399) or even hyperglycaemia (excessive blood sugar) which may occur naturally in a diabetic (*Hennessy* [1989] 1 WLR 287). Sleepwalking was regarded in *Bratty* v *A-G for Northern Ireland* [1963] AC 386 as a classic example of non-insane automatism, but sleep-associated automatism may be caused by functional disorders of the mind and in *Burgess* [1991] 1 QB 92 the Court of Appeal held that any such condition which manifests itself in violence must be treated as one of insanity. Finally, the defence of automatism appears to be unavailable where D has some, albeit impaired, control over his actions (*Broome* v *Perkins* [1987] Crim LR 272; *A-G's Ref (No. 2 of 1992)* [1994] QB 91).

The Burden of Proof

Where the defence raise a defence of non-insane automatism, this must be disproved by **A1.8** the prosecution (in contrast to a defence of insanity, which must be proved by the defence) but there is always an evidential burden on the defence, who must produce some evidence of automatism before the prosecution can be required to address it (*Hill* v *Baxter* [1958] 1 QB 277; *Bratty* v *A-G for Northern Ireland* [1963] AC 386). See further, **F3.10**.

Situational Liability

It may be that voluntary conduct need not always be proved in cases where D is charged **A1.9** with a strict liability offence in which the *actus reus* takes the form not of a prohibited act or omission but of a prohibited state of affairs. Authority for this proposition can be found in *Larsonneur* (1933) 24 Cr App R 74 and *Winzar* v *Chief Constable of Kent* (1983) *The Times*, 28 March 1983. In the former case, L, a French citizen, visited the United Kingdom for the purpose of entering into a marriage of convenience. The police prevented this marriage and an order was served on her requiring her to leave and not re-enter the country. Instead of returning to France, L travelled to Ireland, whence she was deported in the custody of the Irish police, and handed over to the British police in Holyhead. They arrested her under the Aliens Order 1920 for 'being found in the United Kingdom' in breach of the original order excluding her. It was argued on L's behalf that she had returned to the United Kingdom only involuntarily, under physical compulsion, but the Court of Criminal Appeal held that the circumstances under which she was returned were 'perfectly immaterial'. All that mattered was that she was found in the United Kingdom on the occasion in question. Whether this reasoning would be followed today is open to question, and it is likely that any prosecution based on such facts would now be stayed as an abuse of process (see **D7.5** and **D9.41**).

Somewhat different considerations arguably applied in *Winzar*, where the charge was one of being 'found drunk on a highway', contrary to the Licensing Act 1872, s. 12. W had originally been found drunk in a hospital and asked to leave. When he failed to do so, police officers removed him to their patrol car, which was parked on the highway outside, and then charged him with the offence in question. Upholding the conviction,

Goff LJ pointed out that a distinction would otherwise have to be drawn between the drunk who leaves a restaurant when asked to do so and the drunk who is forcibly ejected after refusing to leave. If both are arrested in the street shortly afterwards, it would be wrong for the courts to regard the former as guilty and the latter as not. It is submitted, however, that the position must be different if the police were to drag a person from his own bed and into the street before charging him with being found drunk on a highway; that would undoubtedly involve an abuse of process.

OMISSION TO ACT

A1.10   Most criminal offences require the defendant to carry out some positive act before liability can be imposed. There can ordinarily be no liability for failure (or omission) to act, unless the law specifically imposes such a duty upon a particular person. The general rule is illustrated by this example from Stephen's *Digest of the Criminal Law* (3rd ed., 1887):

> A sees B drowning and is able to save him by holding out his hand. A abstains from doing so in order that B may be drowned, and B is drowned. A has committed no offence.

Although A may have failed to save B, he did no positive act to cause B's death. In some jurisdictions, A would always be under a duty to act in such a situation, at least where he does not have to put his own life in danger. Under English law, however, such a duty arises only in certain specific situations, and there are several offences (such as assaults or battery) which can be committed only through positive acts (see **A1.20**).

Where Statute Imposes a Specific Duty to Act

A1.11   There are many statutory provisions (mostly regulatory) which specifically impose duties on particular persons to act in particular ways and which impose criminal sanctions for failure or omission to act. A failure to keep proper accounts or business records, where these are required by law, may for example lead to criminal liability under the Companies Act 1985, the Insolvency Act 1986 or the Value Added Tax Act 1994. Road traffic law provides many further examples, including the offences of failing to stop after an accident and failing to provide a breath sample or a specimen for analysis.

Failure to Prevent or Report Criminal Conduct

A1.12   Failure to prevent or report the criminal activities of other persons is not ordinarily an offence. The offence of misprision of felony was abolished in 1967, but failure to report a known act of treason still amounts to misprision of treason and it also remains an offence at common law to refuse to assist a constable who calls for assistance in dealing with a breach of the peace (*Brown* (1841) Car & M 314; *Waugh* (1976) *The Times*, 1 October 1976). Modern legislation has added new offences of failure to disclose knowledge or suspicion of financial assistance being provided for terrorism (see **B10.63** *et seq.*) and failure to disclose knowledge or suspicion of money laundering in connection with drug trafficking (see **B20.115** *et seq.*). As to the position of police officers who fail to act in accordance with their duty, see **A1.15**.

Duty Arising from Special Relationships

A1.13   ***Care or Control of Children***   If persons are in a close or special relationship to one another, the law may impose on one a duty to act on behalf of the other. Under the CYPA 1933, s. 1 (see **B2.101** *et seq.*), a parent or any other person over the age of 16 years who has responsibility for a child under that age may incur liability for any wilful neglect of that child that was likely to cause unnecessary suffering or injury to health. This specifically includes failure by a parent etc. to provide or obtain adequate food, clothing or medical care but could also include other forms of neglect, such as failure to rescue from drowning in circumstances of the kind described at **A1.10**. Neglect leading to death may lead to liability for manslaughter by gross negligence (*Downes* (1875) 13 Cox CC 111; *Lowe* [1973] QB 702). The wilful neglect of a child contrary to s. 1 of the 1933 Act does not automatically give rise to liability for manslaughter merely because death results (*Lowe*), but it may sometimes do so if, for example, there is proof of an intent to harm the child through such neglect. Indeed, a parent who deliberately starves a child to death may be guilty of murder (*Gibbins* (1918) 13 Cr App R 134).

Assumption of Care for Another The CYPA 1933, s. 1, has no statutory **A1.14** counterpart in cases where the person in need of care or assistance is over the age of 16. In *Shepherd* (1862) 9 Cox CC 123 it was held that the parents of an 18-year-old and 'entirely emancipated' daughter were under no special duty to care for her. The common law nevertheless recognises that such a duty may arise in the context of a family relationship, as for example where a couple live together as husband and wife, or where a child continues to live with (and be dependent upon) his parents even after becoming an adult (see *Chattaway* (1922) 17 Cr App R 7).

If a person voluntarily undertakes to care for another who is unable to care for himself as a result of age, illness or other infirmity, he may thereby incur a duty to discharge that undertaking, at least until such time as he hands it over to someone else. In *Instan* [1893] 1 QB 450, D lived with her aunt, who was suddenly taken ill with gangrene in her leg and became unable either to feed herself or to call for help. D did not give her any food, nor did she call for medical help, even though she remained in the house and continued to eat her aunt's food. She was convicted of manslaughter. The principle laid down in *Instan* was applied and extended in *Stone* [1977] QB 354. Stone's sister, Fanny, came to live with him and his mistress, Dobinson. Fanny was suffering from anorexia, but was initially able to look after herself. Gradually, however, her condition deteriorated, until she became bed-ridden. She needed medical help, but none was summoned and she eventually died in squalor, covered in bed sores and filth. Stone and Dobinson were each convicted of her manslaughter and the Court of Appeal upheld their convictions. Because they had taken Fanny into their home, they had assumed a duty of care for her and had been grossly negligent in the performance of that duty. The fact that Fanny was Stone's sister was merely incidental to this.

Official, Contractual or Public Duties A person may in some cases incur criminal **A1.15** liability through failure to discharge his official duties or contractual obligations. A typical example is provided by *Pittwood* (1902) 19 TLR 37, in which P was employed to operate a level-crossing on a railway but omitted to close the crossing gates when a train was signalled. A cart was crossing the railway through the open gates when the train struck it and killed one of the carters. P was convicted of gross negligence manslaughter. In one sense this was based on his breach of contractual duty, but the victim was not, of course, a party to the contract, and P's liability can more accurately be based on the breach of a duty of care to users of the crossing, which his employers paid him to discharge, and on which the users of the crossing relied. In the absence of such a duty, it is doubtful whether any criminal liability could have arisen, whatever his contractual position with his employers (cf. *Smith* (1869) 11 Cox CC 210).

Neglect of duty by a police officer was examined by the Court of Appeal in *Dytham* [1979] QB 722. D, whilst on duty, stood aside and watched as a man was beaten to death outside a nightclub. He then left the scene, without calling for assistance or summoning an ambulance. For this, he was convicted of the common-law offence of wilful misconduct in public office. Lord Widgery CJ said (at p. 727):

> The allegation was not one of mere non-feasance, but of deliberate failure and wilful neglect. This involves an element of culpability which is not restricted to corruption or dishonesty, but which must be of such a degree that the misconduct impugned is calculated to injure the public interest so as to call for condemnation and punishment.

Although D was not charged with manslaughter, it is submitted that a conviction for manslaughter might be possible on such facts, if it were proved that the accused's inaction was a factor contributing to the death of the deceased. It was not clear in *Dytham* that D could have saved the deceased even if he had tried to do so.

Duty to Avert a Danger of One's Own Making

A1.16   If a person creates a dangerous situation through his own fault, he may be under a duty to take reasonable steps to avert that danger, and may therefore incur criminal liability for failing to do so. In *Miller* [1983] 2 AC 161, M was 'sleeping rough' in a building, and fell asleep on his mattress while smoking a cigarette. When he awoke, he saw that his mattress was smouldering but, instead of calling for help, he simply moved into another room, thereby allowing the fire to flare up and spread. He was convicted of arson, not for starting the fire but for failing to do anything about it. Lord Diplock said (at p. 176):

> . . . I see no rational ground for excluding from conduct capable of giving rise to criminal liability, conduct which consists of failing to take measures that lie within one's power to counteract a danger that one has oneself created, if at the time of such conduct one's state of mind is such as constitutes a necessary ingredient of the offence.

In *Khan* [1998] Crim LR 830, the Court of Appeal considered the *Miller* principle in the context of manslaughter. The appellants had supplied a girl with heroin on which she accidentally overdosed, and then left her to die. It was held that the trial judge should first have ruled on whether there was evidence on which the jury could find that a duty of care (and thus a duty to act) had arisen. He should then have directed the jury to decide whether that duty had been breached.

Failure to Provide Medical Treatment

A1.17   ***Refusal of Consent to Treatment***   Doctors and hospital authorities have a duty to provide medical care for their patients, and an omission to discharge that duty may sometimes involve criminal liability (e.g., for manslaughter or, in the case of a patient under 16, for wilful neglect under the CYPA 1933, s. 1), although this duty may be terminated if the patient refuses to accept medical treatment. If, for example, an adult hospital patient refuses his consent to a life-saving amputation or transfusion, the medical staff, far from being under a duty to provide that treatment, would ordinarily be acting unlawfully if they ignored his wishes (*Re C (Adult: Refusal of Treatment)* [1994] 1 WLR 290).

Refusal of consent is not always decisive in such cases. Where minors are concerned, the High Court may exercise its wardship jurisdiction so as to override parental refusal of consent (*Re B (A Minor) (Wardship: Medical Treatment)* [1981] 1 WLR 1421) or refusal of consent by the minor himself (*Re W (A Minor) (Medical Treatment: Court's Jurisdiction)* [1993] Fam 64). Even in respect of adults, the court may sometimes hold that a refusal of consent to treatment is vitiated by lack of capacity or by undue influence (*Re T (Adult: Refusal of Treatment)* [1993] Fam 95) and doctors must then provide treatment, in accordance with that patient's best interests. In acute emergencies, where doctors have no time in which to appeal to the courts, they may sometimes need to act without consent. If, for example, Jehovah's Witnesses refuse to consent to the administration of an urgent blood transfusion to their child, doctors may need to act against their wishes, or risk prosecution (together with the parents) for manslaughter (cf. *Senior* [1899] 1 QB 283).

A1.18   ***Withholding Treatment in the Best Interests of the Patient***   If a patient is incapable of communicating his wishes, the doctor's normal duty is to do everything that he reasonably can to keep the patient alive. In certain circumstances, however, a doctor may be absolved of this duty, as the House of Lords recognised in *Airedale*

National Health Service Trust v *Bland* [1993] AC 789. This case concerned a patient who had survived for three years in a 'persistent vegetative state' after suffering irreversible brain damage in the Hillsborough disaster. He continued to breathe normally, but was kept alive only by being fed through tubes. The NHS Trust sought a declaration from the courts that it might lawfully discontinue this artificial feeding and allow him to die with dignity and minimum distress. The House of Lords held that treatment could properly be withdrawn in such circumstances, because the best interests of the patient did not involve him being kept alive at all costs. Lord Goff nevertheless drew a fundamental distinction between acts and omissions in this context (at p. 865):

> . . . the law draws a crucial distinction between cases in which a doctor decides not to provide, or to continue to provide, for his patient treatment or care which could or might prolong his life, and those in which he decides, for example by administering a lethal drug, actively to bring his patient's life to an end . . . the former may be lawful, either because the doctor is giving effect to his patient's wishes . . . or even in certain circumstances in which . . . the patient is incapacitated from stating whether or not he gives his consent. But it is not lawful for a doctor to administer a drug to his patient to bring about his death, even though that course is prompted by a humanitarian desire to end his suffering, however great that suffering may be: see *Cox* (unreported) 18 September 1992 . . . So to act is to cross the Rubicon which runs between on the one hand the care of the living patient and on the other hand euthanasia.

See also *Frenchay Healthcare National Health Service Trust* v *S* [1994] 1 WLR 601. Similar issues can arise in respect of the very elderly or in respect of babies born with very severe mental or physical handicaps, especially where major (and possibly repeated) surgery would be needed to keep them alive (see *Re J* [1991] 2 WLR 140).

Practical and Financial Considerations   Even apart from the question of whether **A1.19** treatment would be in the patient's best interests, it is recognised that financial or manpower constraints on the health service must come into consideration. It is clearly not practicable for the NHS to provide intensive forms of medical care (such as major surgery) to every patient, of whatever age, whose life might possibly be prolonged by it.

Offences for which Omissions cannot be the Basis of Liability

Some offences appear to be capable of commission only by positive acts. The offence of **A1.20** acting with intent to prevent the apprehension of an offender, contrary to the Criminal Law Act 1967, s. 4, is an example (see **B14.38** *et seq.*). Crimes of assault or battery arguably come into this category. This was at least the view of the Divisional Court in *Fagan* v *Metropolitan Police Commissioner* [1969] 1 QB 439 (see **A1.5**) although F's conviction was upheld on the basis that his conduct amounted to a continuing act, rather than an innocent act followed by a deliberate omission to rectify it. See further **B2.4**.

It has also been held that omissions cannot be the basis of liability for 'doing acts' likely to interfere with the peace and comfort of a residential occupier, contrary to the Protection from Eviction Act 1977 (*Ahmad* (1986) 84 Cr App R 64; and see **B13.15**) but the courts have not been consistent in interpreting references to 'acts' as necessarily excluding omissions. In *Speck* [1977] 2 All ER 859, for example, it was held that an omission could amount to an 'act' of gross indecency with a child, contrary to the Indecency with Children Act 1960, s. 1 (see **B3.114** *et seq.*). See also *Yuthiwattana* (1984) 80 Cr App R 55, in which it was held that a landlord's omission to replace a lost key could be an 'act' of harassment against a tenant.

CAUSATION

Introduction

Causation issues appear to feature most frequently in homicide cases, but they can arise **A1.21** in respect of any 'result crime' (see, for example, **B5.10**, concerning causation issues in the context of deception offences under the Theft Acts). In order to establish whether a defendant can be guilty of a given result crime, one must first establish a factual link between his conduct and the result he is alleged to have caused. Once this has been established, a second and more difficult question must be considered, namely whether that conduct was a sufficient cause in law. This is sometimes called the question of 'imputability' or 'legal causation'. It involves issues of value-judgment and the allocation of responsibility for what has occurred.

Factual Causation

A1.22   The importance of proving factual causation is illustrated by *White* [1910] 2 KB 124. W put potassium cyanide in his mother's bedtime drink. When she was found dead the next morning, he was charged with her murder, but it was eventually established that his mother had consumed very little of the poison. She had died, coincidentally, of natural causes. W's conduct had not in any sense contributed to this. He was therefore guilty only of attempting to murder her.

It may also be necessary to prove a link between the proscribed result and a particular aspect of the defendant's conduct, such as his negligence. In *Dalloway* (1847) 2 Cox CC 273, D was charged with manslaughter after his cart had struck and killed a girl who ran out in front of him. D had not been holding the horse's reins at the time, but Erle J directed the jury that they could convict D of manslaughter only if they were satisfied that D could have avoided the accident had he been holding the reins correctly.

Factual causation is sometimes referred to as 'but for' (or *sine qua non*) causation, because it can be established only where the alleged result would not have occurred, or would not have occurred at the time or in the way it did, 'but for' the defendant's act or culpable omission. The only qualification to this basic rule involves cases of complicity or joint venture, under which a defendant may incur liability for encouraging or assisting the principal offender, even where it is proved that his conduct made no difference to the outcome. Procuring appears to be the only form of secondary participation that requires a causal link between the participation and the crime. See **A5.1**.

Legal or Imputable Causation

A1.23   Legal causation is a narrower and more subjective concept than factual causation. Not every cause in fact is a cause in law. To be so, it must be adjudged an 'operating and substantial' cause of the consequence in issue (*Smith* [1959] 2 QB 35) albeit that it does not have to be the only or even the principal such cause. The isolation of a legal cause from amongst a possible multitude of factual causes is a process involving subjective common sense rather than objectively measurable criteria, but when seeking to apportion possible criminal responsibility in this way, one must in practice look for some kind of abnormal and culpable behaviour. The logic behind such reasoning is explained by Hart and Honore, *Causation in the Law* (2nd ed., 1985):

> The notion that a cause is essentially something which interferes with or intervenes in the course of events which would normally take place, is central to our common-sense concept of cause . . .

> In distinguishing between causes and conditions, two contrasts are of prime importance. These are the contrasts between what is abnormal and what is normal in relation to any given thing or subject-matter, and between a free deliberate human action and all other conditions . . .

> In the case of a building destroyed by fire, 'mere conditions' will be factors such as the oxygen in the air, the presence of combustible material or the dryness of the building . . . which are present alike both . . . where such accidents occur and . . . where they do not . . . Such factors do not 'make the difference' between disaster and normal functioning, as . . . the dropping of a lighted cigarette does. . . .

Multiple Causes and Multiple Blame

A defendant may be guilty of causing something to happen even if his conduct was not **A1.24**
the only legal cause of it. In *Hennigan* [1971] 3 All ER 133, H argued that he was not
guilty of causing death by dangerous driving, because another driver was more to blame
than him. The Court of Appeal replied that, as long as H's contribution was substantial,
he could be held accountable. Without purporting to lay down any precise limits, the
court suggested that, even if just 20 per cent of the blame could be attributed to H, that
would suffice. *Hennigan* was followed in *Notman* [1994] Crim LR 518, where it was
stated that anything more than a *de minimis* contribution could suffice.

Indirect Causation

Although legal causation must be 'operative and substantial', it need not necessarily be **A1.25**
a direct cause of the proscribed result. In *McKechnie* (1992) 94 Cr App R 51, M inflicted
serious head injuries on V. These were not in themselves fatal, but they prevented
doctors from operating on V's duodenal ulcer, and V died when the ulcer burst. M was
held to have caused his death. Not all indirect causes will be sufficiently proximate to
the result; questions of fact and degree may be crucial, and it is therefore impossible to
formulate any universal rule in such cases. Indirect causation may also be the basis of
liability in cases involving crimes other than homicide. See for example *Roberts* (1971)
56 Cr App R 95 (see **A1.30**) and *Miller* (1992) 95 Cr App R 421 (see **B5.10**).

The 'Eggshell Skull' Rule

In criminal cases, as in tort, D must ordinarily take his victim as he finds him. If, for **A1.26**
example, the victim of his assault is unusually vulnerable to physical injury as a result of
an existing medical condition or old age, D must accept liability for any unusually
serious consequences which result. In *Hayward* (1908) 21 Cox CC 692, H was seen to
chase his wife into the road, threatening her with violence. She then collapsed and died
as a result of a long-standing heart condition and H was held liable for her manslaughter.
This principle was extended in *Blaue* [1975] 1 WLR 1411. B stabbed a woman. A blood
transfusion would have saved her life, but she was a Jehovah's witness and refused to
accept one. B was convicted of her manslaughter (on grounds of diminished
responsibility) and this verdict was upheld by the Court of Appeal. Lawton LJ said at p.
1415):

> It has long been the policy of the law that those who use violence on other people must take
> their victims as they find them. This in our judgment means the whole man, not just the
> physical man. It does not lie in the mouth of the assailant to say that the victim's religious
> beliefs which inhibited him from accepting certain kinds of treatment were unreasonable.

One possible qualification to this general rule may need to be noted. Where the victim
of a crime dies of heart failure etc., resulting from stress or fright, the charge is likely to
be one of manslaughter, and it would then have to be proved that D's unlawful conduct
was obviously dangerous, in the sense of being likely to cause some kind of injury. Where
blows are struck, this is unlikely to be a problem, but what of cases in which the victim
proved unusually vulnerable to injury caused by fear or stress? In *Dawson* (1985) 81 Cr
App R 150 the Court of Appeal quashed D's conviction for the manslaughter of V, a
60-year-old petrol station attendant, who had died of a heart attack after being
threatened with a replica gun. The court held that the trial judge had misdirected the
jury by (*inter alia*) inviting them to take account of V's heart condition when deciding
whether D's conduct had been obviously dangerous. D could not in fact have known of
V's heart condition at the time. At first sight, *Dawson* may seem inconsistent with the
eggshell skull rule, but it is probably wrong to regard it as a causation case at all. It merely
decides that it was unfair to judge the dangerousness of D's conduct as if V's heart defect
was already obvious to everyone concerned. It is submitted that the jury should instead

have been directed to consider whether the act of threatening an elderly man (of unknown health) with a replica gun involved an obvious danger of shock-induced injury. The answer to that question would surely have been 'yes', and the eggshell skull rule could then have been applied. See also *Watson* [1989] 1 WLR 684 discussed at **B1.36**.

NOVUS ACTUS INTERVENIENS

Introduction

A1.27 A defendant will not be regarded as having caused the consequence for which it is sought to make him liable if there was a *novus actus interveniens* (or new intervening act) sufficient to break the chain of causation between his original action and the consequence in question. Although his original act may remain a factual cause, but for which the consequence would never have occurred, the intervening act may supplant it as the imputable or legal cause for the purpose of criminal liability. This intervening act may be the act of a third party, an act of the victim or an unforeseeable natural event, sometimes called an 'act of God'. These three variants will be considered in turn, but one general point may be made at the outset: no such intervening act can break the chain of causation if it merely complements or aggravates the ongoing effects of the defendant's initial conduct. Suppose, for example, that D attacks V, inflicting grave injuries, and that V later suffers further injuries, caused by his own foolishness, or by E's misconduct, or by some natural disaster. If V eventually dies of his *cumulative* injuries, there can be no question of the chain of causation being broken. The chain of causation can be broken only where the effect of the intervening act is so overwhelming that any initial injuries are relegated to the status of mere historical background. The detailed application of this principle will be explored in the specific contexts within which it may arise, but the basic principle is the same in each case.

If the aggravation of injuries cannot break the chain of causation, then *a fortiori* an omission to treat those initial injuries cannot do so, even if such neglect results in relatively minor injuries becoming fatal (*Holland* (1841) 2 Mood & R 351). As Lawton LJ said in *Blaue* [1975] 1 WLR 1411, where V refused a life-saving blood transfusion on religious grounds:

> The question for decision is what caused [V's] death. The answer is the stab wound. The fact that [V] refused to stop this end coming about did not break the causal connection between the act and death.

It can make no difference whether the omission is that of the victim (as in *Blaue*) or of a third party, such as a doctor. It may even be the result of an unforeseen natural event, such as a flood which prevents medical assistance from reaching the victim.

Acts of Third Parties

A1.28 ***Deliberate, Informed and Unforeseeable Acts*** The subsequent intervention of a third party (other than one acting in concert with the accused) may break the chain of causation if it is free, deliberate and informed (*Pagett* (1983) 76 Cr App R 279; *Latif* [1996] 1 WLR 104, per Lord Steyn at p. 115). In *Latif*, L and S were involved in a plan to smuggle heroin into Britain. The heroin was delivered by S to a supposed accomplice in Pakistan, who was in fact an undercover operative of the U.S. Drug Enforcement Agency. It was then flown into Britain by a British customs officer, technically without lawful authority, whilst L and S were lured to a meeting in London, where they were arrested. It was held that the importation by the customs officer, whilst unlawful, was a deliberate third-party act for which S was not responsible, although S could still be convicted of being concerned in an *attempt* to import it, contrary to the Customs and Excise Management Act 1979, s. 170(2) (see **B17.15** *et seq*.). In contrast, the actions of an innocent agent, who is unaware of the true facts, cannot break the chain of causation. Had the case containing the heroin been forwarded by airline officials as lost luggage (as in *Jakeman* (1983) 76 Cr App R 223: see **A1.5**), S would have been held responsible for their actions.

In *Pagett*, P used his pregnant girlfriend, V, against her will, as a 'human shield' in a confused shoot-out with police officers. V was killed by bullets from officers returning his fire. He was convicted of her manslaughter. The Court of Appeal reasoned that the officers had not acted freely, but had acted 'involuntarily' in taking reasonable measures for the purpose of self-preservation and in the performance of their legal duty to apprehend P, and there was of course no suggestion that they shot V deliberately. Whether the police acted reasonably is in fact open to question (indeed, they were subsequently ordered to pay damages to V's mother for their negligent handling of the incident). It is nevertheless submitted that P's conviction was correct. He created a situation in which V was clearly endangered and over which she had no control. Even if the police officers involved were themselves at fault, it was entirely foreseeable that such an accident might happen, and it is doubtful whether any clearly foreseeable event, other than the free and deliberate act of the victim himself, will suffice to break the chain of causation. Suppose, for example, that D forces V to cross a street, knowing that a concealed gunman is shooting everyone who attempts to do so. V is shot and killed, just as D hoped she would be. Is D not guilty of murder?

The effect of deliberate third-party interventions has been considered in a number of water pollution cases. In *Impress (Worcester) Ltd v Rees* [1971] 2 All ER 357 it was held that the owners of a fuel tank did not cause pollution when vandals opened a valve releasing the fuel; but as Lord Wilberforce warned in *Alpahacell Ltd v Woodward* [1972] AC 824, this 'should not be regarded as a decision that in every case the act of a third person necessarily interrupts the chain of causation . . . The answer to such questions is one of degree and depends upon a proper attribution of responsibility for the flow of polluting matter'. Similarly, in *National Rivers Authority v Wright Engineering Ltd* [1994] Crim LR 453, Buckley J stated that foreseeability was a factor to be considered in applying common sense to the question of who or what caused the result under consideration. Where there is a known vandalism problem, but nothing is done to safeguard vital valves, etc., from interference, it might be open to a court to conclude that the operators (as well as the vandals) cause any such pollution.

Medical Intervention   It is foreseeable that the victim of an attack or accident may **A1.29** require medical treatment, but it is also foreseeable that his injuries may be misdiagnosed or that treatment may not be performed correctly. This is one reason why incorrect medical treatment is hardly ever categorised by the courts as amounting to a *novus actus interveniens*. An equally valid reason, in many cases, is that failure to provide proper treatment for an initial injury rarely amounts to an independent cause of death or injury: it is far more likely that such failure will merely aggravate the original injury, or that it will allow the original injury to take its natural course. In particular, the 'switching off' of a life support system, even if wrongful, will never break the chain of causation flowing from the original injury (see *Malcherek* [1981] 1 WLR 690). Even where incorrect treatment leads to death or more serious injury, it will only break the chain of causation if it is (a) unforeseeably bad, and (b) the sole significant cause of the death (or more serious injury) with which the accused is charged.

An exceptional case in which palpably wrong medical treatment was held to have broken the chain of causation was *Jordan* (1956) 40 Cr App R 152. J stabbed B, who was taken to hospital, where he died. J was initially convicted of his murder, but on appeal new evidence was admitted. This showed that at the time of B's death his wound had almost totally healed and that he had died as a result of a mix-up in which he was given antibiotics to which he had already proved highly allergic. The Court of Criminal Appeal concluded that, if the jury had heard this new evidence, they would have concluded that it was the medical treatment which had caused death and not the stab wound.

Smith [1959] 2 QB 35 is clearly distinguishable from *Jordan*. S stabbed his fellow soldier, C, with a bayonet during a barrack brawl. Other soldiers carried C to the camp medical centre, dropping him twice on the way. An overworked army doctor failed to notice that one of C's lungs had been pierced and the treatment given to him was described at the trial as 'thoroughly bad . . . it might well have affected his chances of recovery'. This did not however break the chain of causation. According to the Courts-Martial Appeals Court:

> If at the time of death the original wound is still an operating cause and a substantial cause, then the death can properly be said to be the result of the wound, albeit that some other cause of death is also operating. Only if it can be said that the original wounding is merely the setting in which another cause operates can it be said that the death did not result from the wound. Putting it another way, only if the second cause is so overwhelming as to make the original wound merely part of the history can it be said that the death does not flow from the wound.

C's death was therefore a case of death by multiple causes, and the stab wound was one of those causes. In contrast, the wound inflicted on B in *Jordan* had largely healed, and so the hospital treatment was in effect the sole cause of B's death. Furthermore, the mistreatment was so bizarre as to be unforeseeable. Had B died as a result of the first routine dose of antibiotics, J's murder conviction would almost certainly have been upheld. This is apparent from the later case of *Cheshire* [1991] 1 WLR 844, in which C shot V, who later died as a result of unfortunate medical complications arising from an tracheotomy he had undergone as part of his emergency treatment. The gunshot wounds had actually healed at the time of death, but the Court of Appeal upheld C's conviction on the grounds that the complications were still a natural consequence of his acts. After careful consideration of existing authorities, including *Jordan*, *Smith* and *Malcherek*, Beldam LJ concluded (at pp. 851–2):

> . . . when the victim of a criminal act is treated for wounds or injuries by a doctor or other medical staff attempting to repair the harm done, it will only be in the most extraordinary and unusual case that such treatment can be said to be so independent of the acts of the defendant that it could be regarded in law as a cause of the victim's death to the exclusion of the defendant's acts . . .

> Even though negligence in the treatment of the victim was the immediate cause of his death, the jury should not regard it as excluding the responsibility of the accused unless the negligent treatment was so independent of his acts, and in itself so potent in causing death, that they regard the contribution made by his acts as insignificant.

Cheshire was followed by the Court of Appeal in *Mellor* [1996] 2 Cr App R 245.

Acts of the Victim

A1.30   In many cases, the *actus reus* of a crime is completed, not by an act of the offender, but by an act of his victim. An obvious example is the victim of fraud, who is deceived into making a payment into the deceiver's account. Another is where V injures himself in a fall whilst attempting to escape from an attack by D, the latter may be regarded as having caused that injury. In *Roberts* (1971) 56 Cr App R 95, R was convicted of an assault causing actual bodily harm to a young woman who was injured jumping from his moving car after he had sexually assaulted her in that car. See also *DPP* v *Daley* [1980] AC 237, *Mackie* (1973) 57 Cr App R 453 and *Corbett* [1996] Crim LR 594.

A clear direction of causation is essential in such cases. In *Williams* [1992] 1 WLR 380, Stuart-Smith LJ stated that the question is whether the victim's behaviour in fleeing was 'within a range of responses which might be anticipated from a victim in his situation' or whether it was 'so daft as to make it his own voluntary act which amounted to a *novus actus interveniens*'. The jury should be directed to 'bear in mind any particular characteristic of the victim and the fact that in the agony of the moment a victim may act without thought and deliberation'.

Conversely, D cannot be held responsible for causing the voluntary and deliberate acts of V, merely because they were foreseeable consequences of his own actions. A person who provides drugs to assist or procure the suicide of another, contrary to the Suicide Act 1961, s. 2, would otherwise be guilty of murder, and one who supplies heroin with which a drug user later overdoses himself would invariably be guilty of manslaughter. This is manifestly not the law (see *Dalby* [1982] 1 WLR 425, *Armstrong* [1989] Crim LR 149 and *Khan* [1998] Crim LR 830). The distinction between such cases and those, such as *Roberts*, in which the victim is injured or killed in flight is that the drug supplier, however despicable he may be, does not force his customers to do anything. They exercise free will and cause their injuries entirely by their own acts. The Court of Appeal in *Kennedy* [1999] Crim LR 65 held that *Dalby* could be distinguished where the accused not only supplied the drug but prepared it for use, and in effect encouraged the user to inject himself with it. K's conviction for manslaughter was upheld on that basis. With respect, however, this attempt to distinguish *Dalby* is unconvincing, because the act of injection was still a voluntary act of the user; and if assisting or encouraging deliberate suicide is not manslaughter, how can it be manslaughter where death is not intended? This is not to say that a drug dealer can never be guilty of causing the death of his customer. Supplying heroin to a child who knows little or nothing about the dangers or about the 'correct' dosage might indeed give rise to liability for manslaughter.

As explained at **A1.27**, a victim's aggravation or neglect of his injuries is most unlikely to affect the chain of causation. In *Wall* (1802) 28 St Tr 51, W was found guilty of murdering a soldier, S, whom he had subjected to an illegal flogging, notwithstanding that S subsequently aggravated his condition by drinking spirits to ease the pain. A similar principle was applied more recently in *Dear* [1996] Crim LR 595, where D alleged that V, who had been slashed by D with a Stanley knife, caused his own wounds to re-open, so that he bled to death. However unwise or perverse V's actions had been, it was still the knife wounds that killed him, and D's appeal against his conviction for murder was dismissed.

Unforeseeable Natural Events

An 'act of God' or other natural event may break the chain of causation leading from **A1.31** the accused's initial act, if it was not reasonably foreseeable and if it was also the sole immediate cause of the consequence in question. The event must be 'of so powerful a nature that the conduct of the defendant was not a cause at all, but was merely a part of the surrounding circumstances' (*Southern Water Authority v Pegrum* [1989] Crim LR 442). If D attacks V and leaves him dying of his injuries, the chain of causation may thus be broken if V is ultimately killed by a lightning bolt or a falling tree. On the other hand, foreseeable natural hazards, such as seasonal floods or cold winter nights, cannot have such an effect. The borderline between what is reasonably foreseeable and what is not must ultimately be one of fact and degree, for the court or jury to decide.

SECTION A2: *MENS REA*

THE MENTAL ELEMENT GENERALLY

A2.1   In addition to proving that the accused satisfied the definition of the *actus reus* of the particular crime charged, the prosecution must also prove *mens rea*, i.e. that the accused had the necessary mental state or degree of fault at the relevant time. Lord Hailsham of St Marylebone said in *DPP* v *Morgan* [1976] AC 182 at p. 213: 'The beginning of wisdom in all the "*mens rea*" cases . . . is, as was pointed out by Stephen J in *Tolson* (1889) 23 QBD 168 at p. 185, that "*mens rea*" means a number of quite different things in relation to different crimes'. Thus one must turn to the definition of particular crimes to ascertain the precise *mens rea* required for specific offences. Nevertheless, there are a number of recurrent concepts (such as intention, recklessness etc.) which can usefully be examined here. There are some general points which can be made which ought to be borne in mind when looking at the definition of any individual crime. Some of these general points (such as the question of transferred *mens rea*) are best looked at after examining the meaning of particular concepts such as intention etc. but by way of introduction it is useful to point out the varied ways in which the individual concepts may be used.

Criminal offences vary in that some may require intention as the *mens rea*, some require only recklessness or some other state of mind and some are even satisfied by negligence. The variety in fact goes considerably further than this in that not only do different offences make use of different types of mental element, but also they utilise those elements in different ways. Compare, for example, assault occasioning actual bodily harm (OAPA 1861, s. 47) and criminal damage contrary to the Criminal Damage Act 1971, s. 1(1). Both are in one sense crimes of recklessness (see *Venna* [1976] QB 421 for assault, and the Criminal Damage Act 1971, s. 1(1), itself for criminal damage) but the *extent* to which they apply this concept is quite different. It has been confirmed that the mental element in assault occasioning actual bodily harm only extends to the element of 'assault' and not to the element of 'occasioning actual bodily harm'. In *Roberts* (1971) 56 Cr App Rep 95, the accused was liable even though he did not intend or foresee any actual bodily harm and this case was approved by the House of Lords in *Savage* [1992] 1 AC 699. In contrast, in relation to damaging any property belonging to another; the mental element applies not only to the elements of 'damaging' and 'property' but also to the element of 'belonging to another'. So in *Smith* [1974] QB 354, the accused was not guilty because he intended to damage only his own property, not property belonging to another. Thus the *range of application* of the concept of recklessness has been wider in relation to criminal damage than in relation to assault occasioning actual bodily harm.

This 'range of application' should be contrasted with the *scope of meaning* of recklessness. It now seems clear (following *Spratt* [1990] 1 WLR 1073) that recklessness should have a different (exclusively subjective) meaning in relation to assault than in relation to criminal damage where it is governed by the House of Lords decision in *Metropolitan Police Commissioner* v *Caldwell* [1982] AC 341. Thus recklessness differs in both its range (of application) and its scope (of meaning) as between the two different offences. This also appears to be the case with the offence of rape as compared with criminal damage. The Court of Appeal said in *S (Satnam)* (1983) 78 Cr App R 149 that:

> *Metropolitan Police Commissioner* v *Caldwell* [1982] AC 341 [and] *Lawrence* [1982] AC 510 . . . were concerned with recklessness in a different context and under a different statute.

The word 'reckless' in relation to rape involves a different concept to its use in relation to malicious damage or, indeed, in relation to offences against the person. In the latter cases the foreseeability, or possible foreseeability, is as to the consequences of the criminal act. In the case of rape, the foreseeability is as to the state of mind of the victim.

Thus, in considering the mental element of any particular crime one has to consider not only the *scope* (of meaning) of that element and its *range* (of application) but also the *context* of its use which may itself influence the scope of meaning to be adopted. Finally, the position of the word expressly requiring the mental element may be significant. Staying with the example of rape, under the Sexual Offences Act 1956, s. 1(2), a man commits rape if:

> (a) he has sexual intercourse with a person (whether vaginal or anal) who at the time of the intercourse does not consent to it; and
> (b) at the time he knows that the person does not consent to the intercourse or he is reckless as to whether that person consents to it.

Rape is thus clearly a crime of recklessness in one sense but the recklessness is expressly made relevant only to the element of the other person's consent rather than to the element of sexual intercourse. In relation to the element of sexual intercourse, it is left to the courts to imply an appropriate mental element which could of course again be recklessness but which in fact seems to be intention (see *Khan* [1990] 1 WLR 813). Thus in relation to rape it would seem that the *position* of the word 'reckless' means that its *range* of application is limited to the victim's lack of consent, and the *context* means that its *scope* of meaning is different to that laid down in *Metropolitan Police Commissioner v Caldwell* in relation to criminal damage.

An interesting, though less satisfactory, example of the interplay between these various factors can be seen in the House of Lords decision in *Wings Ltd v Ellis* [1985] AC 272. The case turned on the interpretation of the Trade Descriptions Act 1968, s. 14(1), which reads as follows:

> It shall be an offence for any person in the course of any trade or business—
>
> (a) to make a statement which he knows to be false; or
> (b) recklessly to make a statement which is false.

The House was concerned with s. 14(1)(a) and held that the requirement of knowledge applied only to the element of the falsity of the statement and not to the act of making the statement in the first place. Thus Wings Ltd was convicted in relation to a statement in a brochure which was initially made innocently and which the company attempted to withdraw as soon as its falsity was realised. The statement was regarded as being made when a customer read it and booked a holiday and Wings Ltd was liable since by then the statement was known to the company to be false even though it was not known that the statement was being made. The decision is not beyond criticism (see G. Stephenson and R. Taylor (1985) 48 MLR 340) but the contrast in wording between paras (a) and (b) of s. 14(1) and the respective positioning of the words requiring *mens rea* help to explain the decision. The adverb 'recklessly' is right at the start of paragraph (b) so that it can naturally refer to both the act of making a statement and the requirement of its falsity whereas para. (a), instead of referring to 'knowingly making a false statement', which would be more consistent with para. (b), merely refers to making 'a statement which he knows to be false'. Thus the *range* of application of the concept of knowledge was restricted by the *position* of the word in the section.

Having made these preliminary remarks about the way in which *mens rea* concepts are utilised by Parliament and the courts, we can now turn to the more commonly found mental elements themselves and examine the scope of their meaning.

INTENTION

A2.2   'Intention' is a word that is usually used in relation to consequences. A person clearly intends a consequence if he wants that consequence to follow from his action. This is so whether the consequence is very likely or very unlikely to result. Thus an accused who shoots at another wanting to kill him, intends to kill whether the intended victim is 2 metres away and an easy target or whether he is 200 metres away and it would have taken an exceptionally good shot to hit him. In either case, even if the accused misses, he will be liable for a crime requiring intention to kill, such as attempted murder.

The meaning of 'intention' is not restricted to consequences which are wanted or desired (sometimes referred to as 'direct' intent) but includes consequences which an accused might not want to follow but which he knows are virtually certain to do so (sometimes referred to as 'oblique' or 'indirect' intent). At one point it seemed that there was support in the House of Lords for a very wide view of oblique intent, i.e. that it included a state of not wanting a consequence to occur while knowing that it was 'highly probable' or even just 'probable' or 'likely' (*Hyam* v *DPP* [1975] AC 55 and see also per Lord Diplock in *Lemon* [1979] AC 617 at p. 638). This was regarded as too wide by the Court of Appeal in *Mohan* [1976] QB 1 in relation to attempt and in *Belfon* [1976] 1 WLR 741 in relation to wounding with intent to cause grievous bodily harm under the OAPA 1861, s. 18. It seemed possible that intention might mean different things in different offences but much of the uncertainty appeared to have been resolved by the decisions of the House of Lords in *Moloney* [1985] AC 905 and *Hancock* [1986] AC 455, although further refinements have been added by yet another House of Lords case *Woollin* [1999] AC 82.

The most important principles to emerge from *Moloney* were that (a) intention should have the same meaning throughout the criminal law (see per Lord Bridge of Harwich at p. 920F), although Lord Steyn appears to have cast doubt upon this in *Woollin*, and (b) the foresight of the probability of a consequence does not of itself amount to intention but may be evidence of it. Unfortunately the guidelines laid down in that case for directing a jury on this issue (essentially that the jury could, but would not be obliged to, infer that a person intended a consequence if he foresaw it as a 'natural' consequence of his action) were subsequently found by the House of Lords in *Hancock* to be 'unsafe and misleading'. Lord Scarman said ([1986] AC 455 at p. 473):

> [The guidelines] require a reference to probability. They also require an explanation that the greater the probability of a consequence the more likely it is that the consequence was foreseen and that if that consequence was foreseen the greater the probability is that that consequence was also intended. But juries also require to be reminded that the decision is theirs to be reached upon a consideration of all the evidence.

The result seemed to be that:

(a)   Where there is clear evidence that the accused desired the consequence to occur, the question of whether the accused intended that consequence can be left to the jury without further elaboration.

(b)   Where the accused may not have desired the consequence but may have foreseen it as a by-product of his action, a more detailed direction may be necessary.

(c)   Such a direction would emphasise that 'the probability, however high, of a consequence is only a factor, though it may in some cases be a very significant factor, to be considered with all the other evidence in determining whether the accused intended to bring it about' (Lord Scarman in *Hancock* at p. 474).

The first two principles (paras (a) and (b)) continue to apply following *Woollin*, whether the charge be murder or any other offence requiring intention. In the light of *Woollin*, para. (c) now seems to be potentially too broad, in relation to murder at least, since only foresight of a virtual certainty entitles a jury to find intention (in the absence of desire) on a murder charge (see further **B1.11**). Given the statement of Lord Steyn in *Woollin* (at p. 96) that 'it does not follow that "intent" necessarily has precisely the same meaning in every context in the criminal law', it remains possible that lower levels of foresight could still be a sufficient basis for a legitimate inference in relation to other offences requiring intention. In either case, the effect of para. (c) seems to be that a discretion is conferred on the jury because the core notion of intention which they are inferring is left undefined (even after *Woollin* in which Lord Steyn confirmed that 'the decision is for the jury upon a consideration of all the evidence in the case'). For more detailed discussion of intent in relation to murder see **B1.11** and, in relation to wounding with intent to cause grievous bodily harm, see *Bowden* [1993] Crim LR 379, which reiterates that foresight of 'virtual certainty' or at least 'a very high degree of probability' is required.

RECKLESSNESS

Recklessness Generally

Essentially concerned with unjustified risk-taking, the precise meaning of the term **A2.3** 'recklessness' has been the subject of great controversy and will no doubt continue to be so. The reason for this is that recklessness has come to be the touchstone of criminal responsibility for a large number of criminal offences. For many offences, the precise boundaries of the concept of intention are not in themselves crucial as recklessness constitutes an alternative and sufficient *mens rea* and one which it is easier to prove. For example, under the Criminal Damage Act 1971, s. 1(1), a person has the requisite *mens rea* if he acts 'intending to destroy or damage any property or being reckless as to whether any property would be destroyed or damaged'.

If an accused threw a stone which damaged X's window and is charged under s. 1(1), he may plausibly be able to say, for example, that he was aiming for the dog in front of the window and that he did not *intend* to damage the window. There would be little point here trying to argue that the accused realised that the probability was that he would miss the dog and break the window from which the jury should infer an intention to break the window. There would be a much greater chance of success in relying on recklessness which equally suffices for liability. The issue of foresight of probability as intention need only be explained in crimes such as murder or attempt where intention alone suffices for liability.

The relationship between intention and recklessness, and indeed the debate about the scope of recklessness itself, can be seen more clearly from the following list:

(a) Consequence desired: intention.
(b) Consequence foreseen as virtually certain: intention *may* be found.
(c) Consequence foreseen as probable: typically recklessness (subjective).
(d) Consequence foreseen as possible: typically recklessness (subjective).
(e) Consequence not foreseen but ought to have been: negligence (objective recklessness).
(f) Consequence even reasonable man would not foresee: strict liability.

The central case of intention is situation (a) although the jury may still find intention in situation (b) and possibly, although not in murder cases, even in (c). However, (b) and (c) are more appropriately and easily dealt with as recklessness where this will suffice for liability. Situation (d) is also capable of being within recklessness as is category (e). The difference between (d) and (e) essentially represents the distinction between the narrower subjective '*Cunningham*' recklessness (*Cunningham* [1957] 2 QB 396) and the wider objective '*Caldwell*' recklessness (*Metropolitan Police Commissioner* v *Caldwell* [1982] AC 341) favoured by the House of Lords in that decision. Category (f), of course, is not a culpable state of mind and would not normally give rise to criminal responsibility except in relation to crimes of strict liability.

Subjective *Cunningham* Recklessness

A2.4 Before discussing objective *Caldwell* recklessness (*Metropolitan Police Commissioner* v *Caldwell* [1982] AC 341), it is best to clarify some aspects of so-called *Cunningham* subjective recklessness (*Cunningham* [1957] 2 QB 396) which is covered by categories (b), (c) and (d) in the list in **A2.3**. The first point is that these states of mind equally qualify as recklessness under the *Caldwell* test. *Metropolitan Police Commissioner* v *Caldwell* merely *adds* category (e) to the scope of recklessness.

The second point is that the *degree* of foresight of risk that constitutes subjective recklessness is not fixed but variable. This can be illustrated by reference to the Law Commission's Draft Criminal Code (Law Com. No. 177), cl. 18(c), definition of (subjective) recklessness: a person acts recklessly '. . . when he is aware of a risk . . . and it is, in the circumstances known to him, unreasonable to take the risk'.

The degree of foreseen risk which would make one reckless depends therefore on the reasonableness or otherwise of the risk. At one end of the scale, a surgeon operating on a critically ill patient may knowingly run a very high risk of his patient's death, but if the patient is even more likely to die if the operation is not attempted then it would be a reasonable risk to run and no one would describe the operation as reckless. There is a very strong justification which makes the operation reasonable. On the other hand, if one offers another a chocolate from a box containing 50, just one of which the offeror knows to contain arsenic, the offeror is clearly acting recklessly. The risk is a relatively low one (one in 50, or 2 per cent), but since there is no justification for running the risk, it is an unreasonable one to take and the offeror is reckless. Thus in some circumstances, to run a very high risk may not be reckless and yet in others it may be reckless to run a relatively low risk. In the context of alleged criminal offences there will often be no plausible justification for running the risk (e.g., of wounding someone) and so often the foresight of *any* degree of risk, of the mere possibility of injury, may be sufficient. The greater the justification for running a risk, the higher the degree of foreseen risk which will be required to constitute recklessness. In *Reid* [1992] 1 WLR 793, their lordships commented (at pp. 806, 813 and 819) that taking a justified risk to avert an emergency would not be regarded as reckless.

Objective *Caldwell* Recklessness

A2.5 It is now clear that in some contexts (although not in connection with offences requiring malice or, it would appear, other offences under the Offences against the Person Act 1861), a person may be 'reckless', even though he is not subjectively aware of a risk, if he has failed to consider an obvious risk. This is the effect of the House of Lords decision in *Metropolitan Police Commissioner* v *Caldwell* [1982] AC 341, which extends the scope of recklessness to situation (e) in the list in **A2.3** and in which Lord Diplock gave (at p. 354) the following model direction for the purposes of the offence of criminal damage:

> . . . a person charged with an offence under section 1(1) of the Criminal Damage Act 1971 is 'reckless as to whether any such property would be destroyed or damaged' if (1) he does an act which in fact creates an obvious risk that property will be destroyed or damaged and (2) when he does the act he either has not given any thought to the possibility of there being any such risk or has recognised that there was some risk involved and has nonetheless gone on to do it.

Thus it is not sufficient for an accused to say (as did Caldwell himself) that he was not aware of the relevant risk (in his case the risk of endangering life under the Criminal

Damage Act 1971, s. 1(2)) because it had never occurred to him. The failure to consider an obvious risk is a sufficient form of recklessness and an alternative to actual subjective appreciation of the risk. Lord Diplock took this wider view of recklessness, embodying the two alternative states of mind, for the following reasons (at p. 352):

> Neither state of mind seems to me to be less blameworthy than the other; but if the difference between the two constituted the distinction between what does and what does not in legal theory amount to a guilty state of mind for the purposes of a statutory offence of damage to property, it would not be a practicable distinction for use in a trial by jury.

The *Caldwell* approach to recklessness was clearly not intended to be restricted to offences under the Criminal Damage Act 1971 as it was reiterated in relation to reckless driving in *Lawrence* [1982] AC 510 on the very same day. Here again Lord Diplock said:

> . . . an appropriate instruction to the jury on what is meant by driving recklessly would be that they must be satisfied of two things:

> *First*, that the defendant was in fact driving the vehicle in such a manner as to create an obvious and serious risk of causing physical injury to some other person . . . or of doing substantial damage to property; and

> *Second*, that in driving in that manner the defendant did so without having given any thought to the possibility of there being any such risk or, having recognised there was some risk involved, had nonetheless gone on to take it.

This differs from the *Caldwell* definition only in that the risk is required to be 'serious' as well as 'obvious' and is in all other relevant respects identical.

The meaning of recklessness discussed above does not affect crimes of malice under the OAPA 1861 (see *Savage* [1992] 1 AC 699) since these are not in express terms crimes requiring recklessness and Lord Diplock specifically distinguished them in the course of his opinion in *Metropolitan Police Commissioner* v *Caldwell*. The closely related offence of assault was originally the subject of some uncertainty. However, the Court of Appeal has since stated in *Spratt* [1990] 1 WLR 1073 that assault is not affected by *Metropolitan Police Commissioner* v *Caldwell* and requires subjective recklessness and on this point, at least, *Spratt* has been implicitly approved by the House of Lords in *Savage*. (See also *Paine* [1998] 1 Cr App R 36, requiring subjective recklessness for the offence of causing annoyance by flying.)

Furthermore, the Court of Appeal has held in *S (Satnam)* (1983) 78 Cr App R 149 that *Metropolitan Police Commissioner* v *Caldwell* does not apply to the offence of rape since the recklessness there applies to one of the circumstances of the offence (the state of mind of the victim) rather than to a consequence and, although this seems a somewhat arbitrary and illogical distinction, it can no doubt be used by those opposed to the width of *Caldwell* recklessness and applied to other crimes involving recklessness as to a circumstance, such as reckless deception under the Theft Act 1968, s. 15(4). The meaning of 'recklessness' for the offence of rape seems to be neither as objective as *Caldwell* recklessness nor as subjective as so-called *Cunningham* recklessness (see **A2.6**).

Indeed, the House of Lords has now recognised in *Reid* [1992] 1 WLR 793 that 'words such as reckless or recklessly, which can be used in a number of different contexts, may not necessarily be expected to bear the same meaning in all statutory provisions in which they are found' (per Lord Ackner at p. 807). Their lordships approved the decision in *Lawrence* as far as the offence of reckless driving was concerned although it would not always be necessary or appropriate to use the *ipsissma verba* of Lord Diplock's suggested direction and a number of their lordships were careful to confine their remarks to offences involving reckless driving which have now been replaced (see, in particular, Lord Browne-Wilkinson at p. 817).

Relationship between Subjective and Objective Recklessness

A2.6   Proponents of a more subjective approach to criminal responsibility have attempted to reintroduce subjective considerations by arguing that even if a person can be regarded as reckless if he fails to consider an obvious risk of which he is not subjectively aware, the risk must be obvious in the sense that it would have been obvious *to him* if *he* had stopped to think and that it is not sufficient that it would have been obvious to the reasonable man. This is the so-called 'conditionally subjective' approach and differs from the normal subjective approach in that one is not concerned with whether the accused was *actually* aware of the risk but with whether he had the *capacity to make himself aware*. However, the Divisional Court in *Elliott* v *C* [1983] 1 WLR 939 reluctantly (but, it is submitted, rightly as a matter of strict interpretation) felt constrained by *Metropolitan Police Commissioner* v *Caldwell* [1982] AC 341 and *Lawrence* [1982] AC 510 to reject this conditionally subjective test. Thus in *Elliott* v *C*, a 14-year-old girl who was of below-average intelligence and who had been out at night until the early hours of the morning was regarded as reckless in respect of a risk which the magistrates had found she would not have appreciated even had she considered the matter. This is indeed a harsh result of the *Caldwell* approach but it was confirmed by the Court of Appeal in *R (Stephen Malcolm)* (1984) 79 Cr App R 334 where it was held (in respect of a 15-year-old accused) that the test is whether the risk would have been obvious to the ordinary prudent man. The House of Lords decision in *DPP* v *Camplin* [1978] AC 705 (see **B1.20**) has no application to this rule and the accused's age or other characteristics which might affect his ability to appreciate the risk were held to be irrelevant. The cases of *Elliot* v *C* and *R (Stephen Malcolm)* were followed and applied by the Court of Appeal in *Coles* [1995] 1 Cr App R 157.

Paradoxically, although it is no defence that the accused did not consider the risk because he personally was not capable of appreciating the risk anyway (contrast *Stephenson* [1979] QB 695, schizophrenic incapable of appreciating an obvious risk not *subjectively* reckless), it may be a defence to say that one *did actually consider the question of whether there was any risk* but concluded (mistakenly) that there was none. This is the possible lacuna of ruling out the risk which may allow an accused who has run an obvious risk to escape from the almost inevitable conclusion that he was reckless. If the risk was obvious it would at first sight seem inevitable that he has either failed to consider it or has been aware of it and chosen to take it, but if he has considered the risk and ruled it out as non-existent then it would appear he is not within either limb of *Caldwell* recklessness. He has neither failed to consider the risk – he has considered it – nor has he recognised the risk and gone on to take it – he thinks there is no risk (see *Chief Constable of Avon and Somerset Constabulary* v *Shimmen* (1986) 84 Cr App R 7 at **A3.3**). As Lord Diplock himself put it in *Lawrence* [1982] AC 510 at p. 527:

> If satisfied that an obvious and serious risk was created by the manner of the defendant's driving, the jury are entitled to infer that he was in one or other of the states of mind required to constitute the offence and will probably do so; but regard must be given to any explanation he gives as to his state of mind which may displace the inference.

The paradox referred to above would be even more striking in the case of an offence such as rape where the defence of mistake (which is similar to the notion of ruling out the risk) is clearly established and important. This may explain why the Court of Appeal has chosen not to apply *Metropolitan Police Commissioner* v *Caldwell* directly to rape and to apply a slightly different test. It may also help to understand in what respect this test differs from that in *Metropolitan Police Commissioner* v *Caldwell*.

It is submitted that in relation to rape the Court of Appeal has not returned to the purely subjective *Cunningham* test of recklessness since it has not required actual subjective appreciation or consideration of the risk of lack of consent, it being sufficient that the defendant's *attitude* is one of 'couldn't care less'. Much of the argument in *S (Satnam)* (1983) 78 Cr App R 149 concerned the question (raised by *Elliott* v *C* [1983] 1 WLR 939) of the obviousness of the risk – obvious to whom? It was really that decision that the Court of Appeal was seeking to distinguish and it can be argued that recklessness in rape differs from *Caldwell* recklessness principally in that the conditionally subjective test *is* applicable to the offence of rape. In other words, an accused is not guilty if *he* would not have realised the risk even had he considered it, in much the same way that an accused is not guilty if he *does* consider the risk and decides that there is none, i.e. makes a genuine mistake (even if it is an unreasonable one). In neither case would his attitude appear to be one of 'couldn't care less'. See **B3.8** for further discussion of cases on the mental element for rape.

To sum up, it appears now that the *Caldwell* test of recklessness will be applied only to offences expressly defined by statute in terms of recklessness as to a consequence. (See *Data Protection Registrar* v *Amnesty International* [1995] Crim LR 633 for an application of *Caldwell/Lawrence* recklessness in a case concerning the Data Protection Act 1984, s. 5(5). Contrast *Paine* [1998] 1 Cr App R 36.) In applying that test, the first question is whether the risk of the consequence would have been obvious to the ordinary prudent individual. A slightly different test applies to rape and to other offences involving recklessness as to a circumstance, such as indecent assault (see *Kimber* [1983] 1 WLR 1118) or obtaining by deception (cf. *Staines* (1974) 60 Cr App R 160), in relation to which it seems the risk must be one that the accused must have been *able* to appreciate personally, although it is not necessarily required that he should *actually* have considered it on the particular occasion in question. Neither of these approaches is applicable to offences requiring 'malice' (or, indeed other offences under the OAPA 1861 such as assault) which, although traditionally explained in terms of recklessness, now have to be regarded as a distinct category requiring actual awareness of the risk being run.

MALICE

Many provisions of the OAPA 1861, notably ss. 18, 20, 23 and 24, define offences in **A2.7** terms of 'maliciously' performing an act and it is now well established that this word is not to be understood in the sense of 'wickedly' or 'with ill will' but as requiring either actual intention to cause the relevant harm or at least foresight of the risk of causing the particular type of harm. The classic formulation was given by the Court of Appeal in *Cunningham* [1957] 2 QB 396 where it was said:

> . . . malice must be taken . . . as requiring either (1) An actual intention to do the . . . harm . . .; or (2) recklessness as to whether such harm should occur or not (i.e., the accused has foreseen that the particular type of harm might be done and yet has gone on to take the risk of it).

The case of *W (A Minor)* v *Dolbey* (1983) 88 Cr App R 1 made it clear (as had Lord Diplock himself in *Metropolitan Police Commissioner* v *Caldwell* [1982] AC 341) that this meaning of malice 'as a term of art' was unaffected by the *Caldwell* definition of recklessness. In *W (A Minor)* v *Dolbey*, the magistrates had convicted, of malicious wounding, a juvenile who had fired at his friend an air rifle, which he believed not to be loaded. This was on the basis of *Caldwell* recklessness (though arguably he was not even *Caldwell* reckless if he had ruled out the risk of causing harm). The Divisional Court quashed the conviction since the juvenile did not foresee the risk of any harm to his friend. The Court of Appeal adopted a similar approach in quashing a conviction in *Morrison* (1988) 89 Cr App R 17, which was certainly not a case of ruling out the risk but of an accused not thinking about the risk to others in seeking to avoid arrest. The subjective meaning of malice has now been confirmed by the House of Lords in *Savage* [1992] 1 AC 699 (see **B2.34**). It is, however, sufficient for the accused to foresee that the harm 'might' or 'may' occur; it is not necessary that the accused foresees that it definitely would occur (*Rushworth* (1992) 95 Cr App R 252).

WILFULLY

A2.8 'Wilfully', which has some similarities with 'malice' since it dates from an earlier legislative vocabulary, should not be understood merely in its most obvious or literal sense of 'deliberately' or 'voluntarily'. It is now taken as a composite word to cover both intention and a type of recklessness. It differs from malice, however, in that it is not restricted to subjective recklessness but includes, apparently, *Caldwell* recklessness or something very similar to it, such as the 'couldn't care less' approach taken in rape cases. The leading case is *Sheppard* [1981] AC 394, which in many ways was the precursor of the decision in *Metropolitan Police Commissioner* v *Caldwell* [1982] AC 341. In *Sheppard*, Lord Diplock provided a model direction as follows:

> . . . on a charge of wilful neglect of a child under section 1 of the CYPA 1933 by failing to provide adequate medical aid, . . . the jury must be satisfied (1) that the child did in fact need medical aid at the time at which the parent is charged with failing to provide it (the *actus reus*) and (2) either that the parent was aware at that time that the child's health might be at risk if it were not provided with medical aid, or that the parent's unawareness of this fact was due to his not caring whether his child's health were at risk or not (the *mens rea*).

As Lord Diplock himself commented, this last state of mind 'imports the concept of recklessness which is a common concept in *mens rea* in the criminal law' and the model direction, though not identical, is remarkably similar in structure and effect to that subsequently laid down for recklessness in *Caldwell*.

A similar approach to the meaning of wilfulness was taken by the Court of Appeal in *Newington* (1990) 91 Cr App R 247 in interpreting the Mental Health Act 1983, s. 127, under which it is an offence 'for any individual to ill-treat or wilfully to neglect a mentally disordered patient who is for the time being . . . in his custody or care'. In *Newington* Watkins LJ had to consider the *mens rea* for ill-treatment rather than wilful neglect but despite the absence of the word 'wilfully' from the former of these two forms of the offence, his lordship implied the same sort of *mens rea* requirement. His lordship said (at p. 254) that what was required was 'a guilty mind involving either an appreciation by the appellant at the time that she was inexcusably ill-treating a patient or that she was reckless as to whether she was inexcusably acting in that way'.

The above cases seem to indicate that wilfulness requires basic *mens rea* in the sense of either intention or recklessness, and that even in the absence of the word 'wilfully', this is the *mens rea* which will normally be implied by the courts for serious criminal offences in the absence of any other factors indicating a wider or narrower basis of liability. It is important to remember, however, the point made earlier about the range of application of *mens rea* to the different elements of an offence and how this may be affected by the positioning of a word requiring *mens rea*. In *Maidstone Borough Council* v *Mortimer* [1980] 3 All ER 552, the accused was convicted of wilfully destroying a tree in contravention of a tree preservation order even though he thought permission had been given to fell the tree and was unaware that the order had been made. The word 'wilfully' was in effect restricted to the element of destroying the tree and held inapplicable to the element of there being a preservation order in force. 'Wilfully' is also used, in combination with the word 'knowingly', in the Perjury Act 1911, s. 5, in relation to the making of 'a statement false in a material particular'. In *Sood* [1998] 2 Cr App R 355 it was held that, whilst this required an intention to do the proscribed act with knowledge of the material circumstances which rendered it an offence, it did not imply any further mental element such as an intention to deceive. Similarly, but more restrictively, in *Dodman* [1998] 2 Cr App R 338 the Courts-Martial Appeal Court made it clear that if the basic *mens rea* required by the offence charged was made out (doing an act, which was in fact, prejudicial to good order and Air Force discipline), there was no requirement of proof of any additional 'blameworthiness' or knowledge of 'wrongfulness' in any wider sense. These cases may be contrasted with *Lalani* [1999] 1 Cr App R 481, where merely proving the basic intention to do the acts which had a tendency to pervert the course of justice was not sufficient since the offence charged specifically required an intention to pervert the course of justice by improperly influencing a juror, a result which it had not been proved the accused had intended or contemplated.

KNOWLEDGE

'Knowledge' can be seen in many ways as playing the same role in relation to **A2.9** circumstances as intention plays in relation to consequences. One knows something if one is absolutely sure that it is so although, unlike intention, it is of no relevance whether one wants or desires the thing to be so. Since it is difficult ever to be absolutely certain of anything, it has to be accepted that a person who feels 'virtually certain' about something can equally be regarded as knowing it. See *Dunne* (1998) 162 JP 399 for confirmation of this approach. On the other hand, one may feel entirely sure and yet be proved wrong, in which case it is difficult to say that one 'knew'. For example, perjury involves making a statement in a judicial proceeding which, *inter alia*, one knows to be false. If the accused gave evidence which he felt absolutely sure was false but it turns out that he inadvertently told the truth, it cannot accurately be said that he 'knew' that his evidence was false. In fact, he can still be convicted of perjury since the offence also applies to statements which one does not believe to be true.

BELIEF

The concept of belief could be interpreted as differing from knowledge merely in the **A2.10** respect adumbrated in **A2.9**, i.e. that beliefs can turn out to be mistaken whereas knowledge implies correctness of belief. The degree of certainty or conviction required to be experienced by the accused would on this view be the same for both belief and knowledge. This is almost, in effect, how belief has been interpreted in the context of handling stolen goods under the Theft Act 1968, s. 22, where the courts have stressed the need to distinguish belief from recklessness or suspicion and have held that it is not of itself sufficient that an accused believed it to be more probable than not that the goods were stolen. However, it has also been said that:

> Belief, of course, is something short of knowledge. It may be said to be the state of mind of a person who says to himself: 'I cannot say I know for certain that these goods are stolen, but there can be no other reasonable conclusion in the light of all the circumstances, in the light of all that I have heard and seen'. (Boreham J in *Hall* (1985) 81 Cr App R 260 at p. 264.)

The problem with this approach is that, even in the absence of the word 'belief', a court would no doubt hold that someone who felt that the only reasonable conclusion was that the goods were stolen, where the goods did indeed turn out to be stolen, could be said to know that fact. One is left therefore with the impression that the concept of belief adds little in this context to the requirement of knowledge.

Wilful blindness (deliberately shutting one's eyes to the truth) is sometimes said to be equivalent to knowledge (see per Lord Reid in *Warner* v *Metropolitan Police Commissioners* [1969] 2 AC 256 at p. 279G) but where an offence expressly requires knowledge or belief the better view seems to be that this may merely be regarded as evidence from which knowledge or belief may be inferred but should not be automatically equated with it (*Griffiths* (1974) 60 Cr App R 14).

NEGLIGENCE

A2.11   Some would exclude negligence from a discussion of *mens rea* on semantic grounds, i.e. on the basis that *mens rea* is concerned with states of mind and negligence is not a state of mind but is rather a failure to comply with the standards of the reasonable man. However, *mens rea* is here being used in the wider sense of the fault element required for liability, and although the required fault is, at least as regards the more serious offences, usually defined in terms of a state of mind, it is not exclusively so. Indeed, for the majority of criminal offences (the less serious ones), proof of *mens rea* in the sense of proof of a state of mind in relation to all the elements of the *actus reus* would be an unaffordable luxury. One alternative to requiring a mental state to be proved is to abandon the requirement of fault altogether and say that the only concern is whether the accused's conduct actually satisfies the *actus reus* of the offence charged. This is the solution of strict liability (see **A2.12**). To base liability on negligence is a less extreme and, to many, a more attractive solution which switches attention away from the accused's state of mind towards whether he has complied with the standards of the reasonable man.

Despite the potential appeal of the compromise of negligence, offences are rarely defined expressly in terms of negligence. Manslaughter is the one exception at common law but here the negligence has to be 'gross' (see **B1.37** to **B1.39**). Nor do statutory offences themselves normally expressly employ the words 'negligence' or 'negligently' but they do in effect often impose liability for negligence (i.e. for failure to comply with the standards of the reasonable man) through the following mechanisms:

   (a)   By express use of words equivalent to 'negligence' in the definition of the offence. The most obvious example is driving without due care and attention under the Road Traffic Act 1988, s. 3 (see **C5.1** to **C5.8**). Perhaps a less well known illustration is provided by the Intoxicating Substances (Supply) Act 1985, s. 1(1), which is as follows:

> It is an offence for a person to supply or offer to supply a substance other than a controlled drug—
>   (a)   to a person under the age of 18 whom he knows, or has reasonable cause to believe, to be under that age; or
>   (b)   to a person—
>   (i)   who is acting on behalf of a person under that age; and
>   (ii)   whom he knows, or has reasonable cause to believe, to be so acting,
> if he knows or has reasonable cause to believe that the substance is, or its fumes are, likely to be inhaled by the person under the age of 18 for the purpose of causing intoxication.

The minimum fault element running throughout this offence is 'reasonable cause to believe'. It matters not what the accused actually believes, it is what the reasonable man in the circumstances would have believed which counts and therefore the mimimum basis of liability is negligence. The prosecution are not required to prove a state of mind, although the accused's knowledge of facts (e.g., that pupils from a particular school rather than others in the area are habitually involved in glue sniffing) may be a relevant circumstance in determining whether he had reasonable cause to believe that a particular purchaser was likely to inhale a substance for the purposes of intoxication.

   (b)   By judicial decision that the offence is still committed if the accused has made an unreasonable mistake of fact (see, e.g, *King* [1964] 1 QB 285, unreasonable mistake that first marriage void no defence to bigamy; *Phekoo* [1981] 1 WLR 1117, mistake under Protection from Eviction Act 1977 (harassment of residential occupiers) required to be reasonable). The accused is convicted despite his innocent state of mind because he is negligent in believing that the facts are such that he is committing no offence. The reasonable man would not have made the same mistake. Negligence is not here expressly made part of the definition of the offence but is introduced as a limit on what might otherwise be a defence with similar effect (cf. the discussion of mistake in **A3.4**).

(c)   By Parliament expressly requiring a mistaken belief to be based on reasonable grounds, e.g., the 'young man's' defence under the Sexual Offences Act 1956, s. 6(3) (unlawful sexual intercourse with a girl under 16) whereby it is a defence for a person under 24 not previously having being charged with a similar offence if he 'believes her to be of the age of 16 or over and has reasonable cause for the belief'.

Other statutes provide 'no-negligence' defences of not dissimilar effect by means of different formulations, often putting the burden of proof on the accused, e.g., Trade Descriptions Act 1968, s. 24 ('took all reasonable precautions and exercised all due diligence') and Misuse of Drugs Act 1971, s. 28(2) ('. . . it shall be a defence for the accused to prove that he neither knew of nor suspected nor had reason to suspect the existence of some fact alleged by the prosecution which it is necessary for the prosecution to prove').

It is worth reiterating at this stage the point made earlier about the range of application of fault concepts to different elements of the *actus reus*. The fact that an offence is effectively satisfied by negligence as to one element does not mean that negligence will suffice for all the other elements. To return to the example of the Trade Descriptions Act 1968, s. 14(1), and *Wings Ltd* v *Ellis* [1985] AC 272 discussed in **A2.1**, that offence expressly requires knowledge as to the falsity of the statement but, as a result of the no-negligence defence in the Trade Descriptions Act 1968, s. 24 (on which the accused in *Wings Ltd* v *Ellis* chose not to rely), it is an offence satisfied by negligence in other respects, e.g., as to whether a particular statement is being made.

STRICT LIABILITY

The point just made is particularly important in connection with offences of so-called   **A2.12** strict liability. The term 'strict liability' is sometimes loosely explained as meaning 'liability without fault' but this is misleading insofar as it suggests that no mental or fault element whatsoever is required. Strict-liability offences are normally those where no fault element is required in relation to one (perhaps crucial) element of the *actus reus* but where *mens rea* is required in relation to other aspects. The classic example is *Prince* (1875) LR 2 CCR 154 where the accused was convicted of taking a girl under the age of 16 out of the possession and against the will of her father. The accused's reasonable belief that she was over 16 was no defence, so even negligence was not required in relation to the element of her being over the age of 16. However, *mens rea* was required in relation to other elements of the offence, e.g., in relation to whether the taking was against the will of the father. As Bramwell B put it: 'If the taker believed he had the father's consent, though wrongly, he would have no *mens rea*'. (See Brooke LJ in *B (A Minor)* v *DPP* [1999] 3 WLR 116 for a critical analysis of the influence of the decision in *Prince*.)

Thus, rather than talking of an offence as a whole being one of strict liability, it is more accurate to speak of it being an offence of strict liability with respect to a particular element or elements. Of course, the element in respect of which liability is strict may be the only element which has any possible criminal connotation, the remaining elements as to which some mental element is required being by contrast mundane and, in themselves, non-criminal in character. For example, in *Parker* v *Alder* [1899] 1 QB 20, the defendant was convicted of selling adulterated milk when the adulteration took place after the milk had left his control and was *en route* by rail to the purchaser. The offence was therefore of strict liability as regards the milk being adulterated and the only element left was the act of selling. To say that the offence requires *mens rea* in respect of this element, that it requires 'an intention to sell milk', has a hollow ring about it since that is not an intention which is in any way culpable. By contrast with *Prince* then, this is an example of an offence where the imposition of strict liability in relation to the one significant aspect of the *actus reus* effectively means that the offence can indeed give rise to liability without fault. At the other end of the scale, assault occasioning actual bodily harm could be regarded as an offence of strict liability as far as relates to the requirement of actual bodily harm since the only *mens rea* required relates to the assault and not to the element of actual bodily harm. However a person who intends to assault is clearly culpable and no one would describe this offence as giving rise to liability without fault.

On the other hand, a large number of regulatory offences are traditionally referred to as strict liability offences since, as with the case of *Parker* v *Alder* discussed above, no fault or mental element is required in respect of those features of the *actus reus* which give the offence its criminal character. The circumstances under which the courts will impose strict liability in respect of a particular statutory offence are difficult to predict and regard must be had to the authority (if any) on the individual statutory provision in question. The general approach of the courts is discussed in **A4.1** and **A4.2**.

TRANSFERRED *MENS REA*

A2.13 Transferred *mens rea* is often referred to as 'transferred malice' since the principal illustration is found in the case of *Latimer* (1886) 17 QBD 359 which was concerned with malicious wounding under the OAPA 1861, s. 20. The accused struck with his belt at C but missed and accidentally cut open the face of R. The Court for Crown Cases Reserved upheld the conviction. Lord Coleridge CJ pointed out that the section referred to wounding 'any other person'. This underlines the point that it is a question of interpreting the particular mental element required for the particular offence. The identity of the victim is not a material detail as far as most offences against the person are concerned, and therefore the accused's intention to injure A can be transferred so as to make the accused liable for an injury accidentally inflicted on B. The principle was applied more recently to the offence of manslaughter in *Mitchell* [1983] QB 741 where the accused assaulted A, aged 72, causing him to fall on to the even more elderly B (aged 89) ultimately causing her death. The Court of Appeal upheld the conviction for her manslaughter, Staughton J saying: 'We can see no reason of policy for holding that an act calculated to harm A cannot be manslaughter if it in fact kills B'. A more restrictive approach to the doctrine of transferred malice was taken by the House of Lords in *A-G's Ref (No. 3 of 1994)* [1998] AC 245. Lord Mustill (at p. 261) recognised the doctrine only as an '"arbitrary exception to general principles" . . . useful enough to yield rough justice in particular cases . . . [which] could sensibly be retained not withstanding its lack of any sound intellectual basis'. However, it could not be extended to create liability for murder from an intentional infliction of grievous bodily harm on a pregnant woman which later resulted in the death of the child *in utero* subsequent to it having been born alive. Such a situation could give rise to liability for manslaughter, apparently without the need of the doctrine of transferred malice, but it was not murder. The decision seems to be influenced as much by the desire not to build any further on the grievous bodily harm/murder rule as by any deficiency in the transferred *mens rea* rule explained above. The logic of the decision would not necessarily preclude liability for murder of the child where the initial attack on the mother was with intent to *kill* her. More difficult would be the case where the attack was done with intent to destroy the foetus which resulted in a live birth followed by death. This would appear to be attempted child destruction (and possibly manslaughter) rather than murder.

This last point is further exemplified by the rule that the *mens rea* for one offence cannot be transferred so as to make an accused liable for a different offence even if the two offences happen to share similar terminology in their definition. This is illustrated by the case of *Pembliton* (1874) LR 2 CCR 119 where the accused threw a stone at a crowd of people but missed and broke a glass window behind them. The jury found that he intended to hit the people but not the window. Although he could have been convicted of malicious wounding, had he injured someone, the Court for Crown Cases Reserved quashed his conviction for malicious damage since that was a separate offence with its own separate *mens rea* requiring foresight of damage to property rather than foresight of injury to a person. Lord Coleridge CJ observed that it would have been different if 'the jury had found that the prisoner had been guilty of throwing the stone recklessly, knowing that there was a window near which it might probably hit' for then he would have had the separate *mens rea* of the independent offence of malicious damage. If two separate offences have *precisely* the same *mens rea* then the problem disappears. Proof of the *mens rea* of one automatically involves proof of the *mens rea* of the other. This principle was applied in *Ellis* (1986) 84 Cr App R 235, in which it was held that an intention to import a prohibited substance is the *mens rea* sufficient both for importing a controlled drug of class A and also for the separate offence (cf. *Courtie* [1984] AC 463) of importing a controlled drug of class B. Thus if an accused believed he was importing a class B drug but was in fact importing a class A drug, he can be convicted of the latter offence since he had the necessary *mens rea* of an intention to import a prohibited substance. His mistake might be relevant in determining the sentence. Similarly, he could be convicted of importing a controlled drug even if he believed he was importing material prohibited under some other enactment, e.g., pornographic material.

The issue in the above cases ultimately hinges on precisely what is required by the *mens rea* of the particular offence charged. This is an important point in relation to the liability of accessories (see **A5.2**) for an accessory must know or at least contemplate what it is the principal is going to do, and if the principal does something outside the scope of that contemplation, the accessory will not be liable. Thus if the accessory encourages violence against a *particular* victim and the principal deliberately chooses another victim not contemplated by the accessory, the accessory will not be liable (see *Saunders* (1573) 2 Plow 473). However, if the principal tries to carry out the agreed plan but it accidentally misfires and victim B rather than victim A is injured, then the doctrine of transferred intention applies to the accessory too and he will remain liable because the principal has at least tried to do what the accessory contemplated: the principal's acts, although perhaps not their consequences, are within the accessory's contemplation and *mens rea*.

PROOF OF *MENS REA*

The various mental states discussed in this section undeniably present courts and juries **A2.14** with difficult practical problems since even when one is clear about the precise meaning of the mental state to be proved, it is not easy to be sure whether that corresponds to what actually went on in the accused's mind. Even in apparently clear cases, the accused's denial may raise a doubt in the minds of the jury. If a man shoots at another at point-blank range with a revolver it may seem easy to infer that he intended to kill or at least injure that other but an accused may seek to deny this by asserting that he believed the revolver was not loaded or was merely a harmless imitation. In the absence of such an explanation, of course, a jury will doubtless infer that he intended the natural and probable result of his action, i.e. death or injury to the other. Apart from admissions from the accused, this is indeed the most obvious way to ascertain his state of mind. Thus juries will probably infer that the accused intended or at least foresaw the natural and probable consequences of his actions. This is unexceptionable as a purely factual inference. Problems have arisen, however, when courts have sought to elevate such an inference to the status of an irrebuttable presumption. In the light of one such decision, *DPP* v *Smith* [1961] AC 290, Parliament intervened to ensure that it remains open to the jury to find that the accused did not intend or foresee the consequences (see also *Frankland* v *The Queen* [1987] AC 576). The CJA 1967, s. 8, provides:

A court or jury, in determining whether a person has committed an offence,—

(a) shall not be bound in law to infer that he intended or foresaw a result of his actions by reason only of its being a natural and probable consequence of those actions; but
(b) shall decide whether he did intend or foresee that result by reference to all the evidence, drawing such inferences from the evidence as appear proper in the circumstances.

Although this section makes it clear that there is no irrebuttable presumption, the concluding words of para. (b) equally mean that a jury *may* infer that a person intended or foresaw the natural and probable consequences of his actions if this seems appropriate on all the evidence, for example, in the absence of any evidence explaining why the accused did not intend or foresee that consequence. (For further discussion of s. 8 and the relationship between foresight and intention in murder, see **B1.11**.)

The CJA 1967, s. 8, can apply only where the prosecution are seeking to prove that the accused intended or foresaw something. Therefore whilst it can apply to the proof of intention in murder or to the proof of foresight in, for example, crimes of malice, it cannot apply where the definition of the offence does not require intention or foresight. Thus it is of no relevance to the element of manslaughter that requires the accused's act to be likely to cause bodily harm since that is a purely objective element which does not require any intent or foresight on the part of the accused (see *Lipman* [1970] 1 QB 152).

Similarly, s. 8 is of only limited relevance to *Caldwell* recklessness (see **A2.5**) since such recklessness can be established without proving any actual foresight on the part of the accused (if the accused has failed to consider an obvious risk). On the other hand it is not totally irrelevant since the allegation might be not that the accused failed to consider the risk but that he actually foresaw the possible consequence. The problem for the accused is that if the consequence is the natural and probable result of his act then the jury will be likely to conclude either that he did in fact foresee it (as s. 8 entitles but does not oblige them to do) or alternatively that, although he did not actually foresee it, this was only because he failed to consider it and he was therefore reckless on that score. It will only avail the accused to show that he did not foresee the natural and probable result of his action because he had 'ruled out the risk' (see **A2.5**) of that result and positively believed it would not occur rather than because he had failed to give the matter any thought.

Section 8 is concerned with proof of intention and foresight in relation to consequences but a similar problem arises in relation to circumstances. Again, a reasonable prima facie rule is to assume that the accused was aware of facts of which the reasonable man would have been aware provided one is prepared to adjust that conclusion in the face of credible evidence from the accused as to why he was not actually aware of it. This will often take the form of a defence of mistake. The former requirement that such mistakes had always, as a matter of law, to be based on reasonable grounds was, in effect, an irrebuttable presumption that the accused was aware of facts of which the reasonable man would be aware. The House of Lords in *DPP* v *Morgan* [1976] AC 182, in abandoning this rule for crimes requiring subjective *mens rea*, performed a similar function in this area as the CJA 1967, s. 8, performed in relation to foresight of consequences. The reasonableness or otherwise of a mistake is certainly an important factor in deciding whether the accused actually made that mistake but the court must look at all the evidence in order to decide on the accused's actual state of mind. The similarity of this approach to s. 8 can be seen from the wording of the Sexual Offences (Amendment) Act 1976, s. 1(2), which confirmed this aspect of the decision in *DPP* v *Morgan* as far as the offence of rape itself is concerned:

It is hereby declared that if at a trial for a rape offence the jury has to consider whether a man believed that a woman or man was consenting to sexual intercourse, the presence or absence of reasonable grounds for such a belief is a matter to which the jury is to have regard, in conjunction with any other relevant matters, in considering whether he so believed.

This principle should not be restricted to the offence of rape (see, e.g., for indecent assault, *Kimber* [1983] 1 WLR 1118). On the other hand, just as the CJA 1967, s. 8, applies only to crimes requiring subjective foresight, the principle only applies to crimes for which a genuine mistake is inconsistent with the *mens rea* (this probably includes *Caldwell* recklessness, see **A2.5**), and does not apply to crimes which are in effect satisfied by negligence in this respect, for example, bigamy (see the comments of the Law Lords on *Tolson* (1889) 23 QBD 168 in *DPP* v *Morgan* itself).

SECTION A3: GENERAL DEFENCES

CATEGORIES OF GENERAL DEFENCE

A3.1 This section deals with defences which are available in relation to a range of offences rather than those which are only available in relation to a single crime. Particular defences to particular crimes (such as provocation in relation to murder) are dealt with in the section of this work dealing with the particular offence. The expression 'general defences' suggests something positive that must be put forward on behalf of the accused, but in truth it is more accurate to regard these defences as circumstances where the prosecution have been unable to prove all the requirements of liability beyond reasonable doubt. This is most obviously true of defences that consist of showing that the mental element of the offence charged may be missing (as with the defence of mistake) but it is also true of defences such as duress where the burden is not on the accused to show affirmatively that he was acting under duress but rather on the prosecution (once there is evidence before the court capable of supporting duress) to prove that the accused was not acting under duress. Nevertheless, it is still possible and helpful to divide general defences into two categories:

(a)   those which involve a denial of the basic requirements of *mens rea* and voluntary conduct (the defences of mistake and automatism are best regarded in this way), and

(b)   those which do not deny these basic requirements but which rely on other circumstances of excuse or justification, as in the defences of duress and self-defence.

These two categories will be examined in turn.

DEFENCES DENYING BASIC ELEMENTS OF LIABILITY

Mistake and Inadvertence: Offences Requiring Intention or Foresight

A3.2 Because the defences of mistake and inadvertence consist of a denial of the *mens rea* of the particular crime charged, the nature and the availability of the defences will vary from offence to offence but it is possible to identify categories of offences for which consistent principles can be formulated. The first category consists of offences requiring subjective fault (e.g., crimes requiring intention or malice). For this category of offences it is clear that either a mistake (i.e. a positive belief) that a particular ingredient of the offence charged is lacking or, alternatively, a simple failure to appreciate the presence of the same ingredient will operate as a defence. For example, A, out in open country, shoots V dead with a crossbow at a range of 200 metres. A has a defence if he thinks that V is a scarecrow (mistake) or, alternatively, if it has never occurred to him that V or anybody else might be so foolish as to traverse that part of the countryside selected by A to practise his archery (inadvertence). In either case A would lack the necessary *mens rea* for murder, the intention to kill or cause grievous bodily harm, although he may well be liable for other offences. Similarly, the offence of malicious wounding (OAPA 1861, s. 20) requires subjective awareness at least of the risk of wounding, and either mistake or inadvertence will suffice for a defence. See, for example, *W (A Minor)* v *Dolbey* (1983) 88 Cr App R 1, in which the Divisional Court held that the accused's belief that his air rifle was unloaded was a defence to a charge under s. 20. (This case also illustrates the artificiality and difficulty in many cases of distinguishing between mistake and inadvertence since the accused was also described as ignoring the risk that the gun might be unloaded. Fortunately, at least in this category of offences, it is not a distinction which needs to be made, a defence of lack of *mens rea* being present in either case.) See also *Morrison* (1988) Cr App R 17.

It should be stressed that because this category of offences requires subjective fault, the test of mistake (and of inadvertence) is also a subjective one; there is no requirement that the mistake be one which a reasonable man would have made (or that a reasonable man would have failed to appreciate that which the accused failed to appreciate). The traditional requirement that, as a matter of law, mistakes have to be reasonable was emphatically refuted by the House of Lords in *DPP* v *Morgan* [1976] AC 182, although it will naturally be more difficult to persuade a jury to accept that an accused genuinely made an unreasonable mistake. (The House of Lords upheld the convictions in *DPP* v *Morgan* itself on the basis that the accused had not actually held any mistaken belief.)

The important point is that the courts regard the rule that mistakes do not have to be reasonable in this context as a logical one which flows from the nature of the mental element required for this category of offences (see especially the speech of Lord Hailsham of St Marylebone in *DPP* v *Morgan*). Thus one can generalise that wherever an offence requires subjective awareness of a particular element, a genuine mistake that such an element is absent will be a defence.

The logic of this rule is unassailable as applied to crimes requiring intention. If a man believes he is shooting at an inanimate object such as a scarecrow, he cannot at the same time by that very act intend to kill. The same is true where knowledge is required. A person who believes that the goods he buys are not stolen cannot at the same time know (or even believe) that the goods are stolen – the two states of mind are logically inconsistent with one another. However, with crimes satisfied by foresight or awareness of risk (i.e. crimes satisfied by malice or subjective recklessness) the logic is somewhat flawed. D can believe that his partner is consenting to sexual intercourse and yet at the same time be aware that there is a risk (an infinitesimally small one) that she is not consenting. Similarly, one can believe that the stone one throws in the open country is not going to injure someone whilst still recognising that there is a risk that someone lying out of sight might be injured. The point is that beliefs are not usually absolute and are not inconsistent with the recognition of the possibility of a contrary state of affairs (whereas a belief *is* inconsistent with *knowledge* of a contrary state of affairs). Of course, in most cases the belief will be sufficiently strong to leave only the faintest possibility (if any at all) in the believer's mind that he may be wrong and this small degree of possibility would not be sufficient to amount to recklessness or malice. It does, however, depend on what one means by 'belief' and also on what the jury understand by that term. Although it is no longer proper for juries to be told that a belief has to be based on reasonable grounds, it might be appropriate in some cases to direct them that the belief must be held reasonably strongly.

Mistake and Inadvertence: Offences Satisfied by Objective Recklessness

It is clear that inadvertence is no defence to an offence satisfied by objective recklessness **A3.3** given that failure to consider an obvious risk is at the core of the meaning of recklessness under *Metropolitan Police Commissioner* v *Caldwell* [1982] AC 341 (see **A2.5**). It ought to be equally clear that a positive mistake can be a defence and indeed this is supported by *S* (*Satnam*) (1983) 78 Cr App R 149 as far as the offence of rape is concerned. Nevertheless, the Court of Appeal in that case found it necessary to distinguish the *Caldwell* meaning of recklessness from that applicable to the offence of rape. This could be taken to have the implication that for offences where the *Caldwell* meaning of recklessness is applicable without modification, the defence of mistake is not available. The point does not often arise directly since the crimes governed by *Metropolitan Police Commissioner* v *Caldwell* tend to be crimes involving consequences rather than circumstances, and it is in respect of the latter that it is more natural to talk about mistakes. Indeed the basis of the Court of Appeal's distinction of recklessness in rape from *Caldwell* recklessness was that *Caldwell* recklessness deals with consequences whereas with rape one is dealing with recklessness in relation to circumstances. This distinction, however, is neither convincing nor, it is submitted, material, and it is contended that a mistake about whether or not a consequence will follow from an action should be treated in just the same way as a mistake about whether certain circumstances are present during an action. In fact, the question of mistake in relation to consequences has come to be considered under the heading of 'ruling out the risk', and the leading case is now *Chief Constable of Avon and Somerset Constabulary* v *Shimmen* (1986) 84 Cr App R 7 where the accused claimed to have ruled out the risk of causing damage to a window when he aimed a martial-art-style kick in its direction, basing his view on his faith in his own prowess as an exponent of the Korean art of self-defence. In other words, he claimed to believe that no damage would result from his action (the subsequent shattering of the window revealing this belief to be a sadly mistaken one). The Divisional Court remitted the case to the magistrates with a direction to convict since the evidence did not show that the accused had ruled out all the risk (hence he was still reckless in consciously running a small risk). But the court also expressly left open the possibility that an accused who rules out *any* risk would not be reckless (since he has neither failed to consider the risk nor consciously run it). Thus the case is somewhat inconclusive (and also perhaps rather restrictive in requiring the risk to be totally ruled out, which is akin to the court saying that mistaken beliefs have to be held with a degree of conviction equal to certainty and admitting of no doubts). In the current state of the authorities it would seem that the position as regards mistake in crimes of recklessness can best be summarised as follows. A genuine mistake is a defence to rape (*S* (*Satnam*) (1983) 78 Cr App R 149) and indecent assault (*Kimber*) [1983] 1 WLR 1118) and to any other crime of recklessness not governed by *Metropolitan Police Commissioner* v *Caldwell*. Crimes requiring *Caldwell* recklessness appear to be governed by a harsher rule that the accused has a defence only if he has totally ruled out the risk of the relevant consequence occurring, although there were a number of obiter comments in the House of Lords in *Reid* [1992] 1 WLR 793 which showed their lordships to be reasonably receptive to defences based on mistake. If the risk is ruled out to the extent that all that remains is a risk that 'an ordinary prudent individual would feel justified in treating . . . as negligible', that should, in principle, be sufficient. (See also the discussion of manslaughter at **B1.38**). However, in *Merrick* [1996] 1 Cr App R 130, the Court of Appeal continued to speak of 'preventing the risk [from arising] at all'. It was not sufficient to remedy a risk that the accused had already created as opposed to preventing the risk from arising in the first place. Only the latter would take the accused outside the *Caldwell* definition.

Mistake and Inadvertence: Offences Satisfied by Negligence

A3.4   It is clear that inadvertence is no defence to a crime of negligence. (This assumes that the risk of which the accused was unaware was one of which a reasonable man would have been aware. Strictly speaking, of course, inadvertence is wide enough to cover failure to consider non-obvious risks but the normal context of the use of the word 'inadvertence' is one whereby it is assumed that the risk is one of which a reasonable man would have been aware.)

Equally clearly, mistake can be a defence to crimes of negligence subject to the important qualification that the mistake must be a reasonable one since an unreasonable mistake itself supplies the negligence which is the sufficient basis of liability. The House of Lords in *DPP* v *Morgan* [1976] AC 182 specifically stated that the old requirement of reasonableness still applies to offences not requiring full *mens rea*. The Law Lords deliberately refrained from overruling *Tolson* (1889) 23 QBD 168 which required a mistaken belief in the death of a spouse in the offence of bigamy to be based on reasonable grounds. As Lord Fraser of Tullybelton put it ([1976] AC 182 at p. 238):

> . . . bigamy was an absolute offence, except for one defence set out in a proviso, and it is clear that the mental element in bigamy is quite different from that in rape. In particular,

bigamy does not involve any intention except the intention to go through a marriage ceremony, unlike rape in which I have already considered the mental element. So, if a defendant charged with bigamy believes that his spouse is dead, his belief does not involve the absence of any intent which forms an essential ingredient in the offence.

Thus, the logical argument that even an unreasonable mistake must deny the mental element, and so be a defence, does not apply to bigamy, and the offence is in effect interpreted as one satisfied by negligence as to whether the spouse is still alive. The courts sometimes adopt this approach in relation to other statutory offences as, for example, in *Phekoo* [1981] 1 WLR 1117 in relation to the offence of harassment of a residential occupier under the Protection from Eviction Act 1977, s. 1(3). The Court of Appeal held that a belief that a person was not a residential occupier had to be reasonable to afford a defence. This is entirely consistent with the House of Lords comments on *Tolson* in *DPP* v *Morgan*.

Treating the offence as one of negligence is at least a more sensitive approach than imposing strict liability (whereby even a reasonable mistake would be no defence) and again is in line with the sentiments expressed by Lord Diplock in *Sweet* v *Parsley* [1970] AC 132 where he said (at pp. 163–4):

> . . . had the significance of *Tolson* been appreciated here, as it was in the High Court of Australia, our courts, too, would have been less ready to infer an intention of Parliament to create offences for which an honest and reasonable mistake was no excuse.

See *B (A Minor)* v *DPP* [1999] 3 WLR 116 for a recent example. Brooke LJ clearly felt uneasy at not being able to follow the *Tolson* approach.

The case of *Lamb* [1967] 2 QB 981 provides an unusual example of a defence of mistake succeeding in relation to an offence involving negligence (manslaughter). The accused had 'jokingly' pointed and fired a revolver containing two live bullets at his best friend, thereby killing him. His mistake was in believing that, because the bullets were not in the firing position, the gun could not fire when in fact, unknown to him, pulling the trigger caused the cylinder to rotate and, in this case, placed one of the bullets in the firing position. The trial judge in effect directed the jury that the accused's beliefs were irrelevant, as was the evidence called on his behalf to show that this was a mistake that the ordinary man might make. The Court of Appeal quashed the conviction commenting (at p. 990):

> . . . it would, of course, have been fully open to a jury, if properly directed, to find the defendant guilty because they considered his view as to there being no danger was formed in a criminally negligent way. But he was entitled to a direction that the jury should take into account the fact that he had undisputedly formed that view and that there was expert evidence as to this being an understandable view.

Thus an 'understandable' (reasonable) mistake could be a defence but a criminally negligent (unreasonable) one would not be.

Mistake and Inadvertence: Offences of Strict Liability

Even a reasonable mistake is no defence to an offence of strict liability, although many **A3.5** so-called offences of strict liability now have statutory defences available based on particular types of reasonable mistake, the burden of proof of such defences being put on the accused. See, for example, Misuse of Drugs Act 1971, s. 28.

Mistake of Law

Whilst the maxim 'Ignorance of the law is no excuse' generally holds good in English **A3.6** law, it is no more than a broad generalisation and is subject to exceptions. These exceptions are really no more than an illustration of the general theme already expounded – that where the accused lacks the *mens rea* required for the offence charged, he has a defence. Since *mens rea* generally relates to facts, it is mistake or ignorance of facts that is usually the basis of a denial of *mens rea*. However, in some offences the requirement of *mens rea* includes legal concepts and a mistake about that legal concept can mean that the accused lacks *mens rea*. Thus in *Smith* [1974] QB 354 the conviction of the accused for criminal damage was quashed on the basis of a mistaken belief that the property damaged was still his own property and was therefore not property 'belonging to another'. It was the accused's ignorance of the civil law on the question of when property belongs to another (in particular, the law relating to a landlord's fixtures) which caused him to mistakenly believe that the property did not belong to the landlord. He thus lacked the *mens rea* of the offence because of his ignorance of law, and this was relevant because the offence required *mens rea* in relation to the civil-law concept of ownership (belonging to another).

It should be stressed that the mistake must be one of civil law rather than about the ambit or meaning of a criminal provision. This precludes not only defences such as 'I didn't think burglary included breaking into houses during the day' but also, for example, a defence to theft of a wild creature based on a belief that a wild creature is not 'property'. The Theft Act 1968, s. 4(4), specifically states that wild creatures are property for the purpose of theft (although there are restrictions on the circumstances when they can be the subject of a charge of theft) and this is a matter of the criminal law rather than whether wild creatures are property in any other branch of the law. Similarly, on a charge of handling stolen goods, it would be no defence to say that one did not know that goods obtained by deception count as 'stolen' since this too is a matter of criminal rather than civil law (see Theft Act 1968, s. 24(4)). The point can be further illustrated by reference to *Johnson* v *Youden* [1950] 1 KB 544. It was an offence under the Building Materials and Housing Act 1945, s. 7, to sell a house in excess of the prescribed price. The defendant solicitor knew that an extra £250 was being paid to the builder in a separate account to be spent on possible future work which might be done to the house by the builder. Even if the solicitor genuinely believed that this was not part of the price under the Act his mistake was merely one of criminal law since s. 7(5) specifically stated that associated transactions had to be included in calculating the price.

Some offences expressly make the accused's beliefs about the legality of his action relevant and in these cases there can be no question that a mistake of law can be relevant. The most obvious example is the Theft Act 1968, s. 2(1), under which a person is not to be regarded as dishonest: '(a) if he appropriates the property in the belief that he has in law the right to deprive the other of it'. A less obvious example is provided by *Secretary of State for Trade and Industry* v *Hart* [1982] 1 WLR 481 which concerned the statutory offence of acting as auditor of a company 'at a time when he knows that he is disqualified'. As a director of the company Hart was disqualified but he did not know of the quite separate statutory provision which so provided. Thus, although he knew the facts (that he was a director of the company), he did not know that he was disqualified (as the offence specifically required). Contrast *A-G's Ref (No. 1 of 1995)* [1996] 1 WLR 970, where the offence did not require any specific knowledge that deposit-taking had to be licensed by the Bank of England.

By the Statutory Instruments Act 1946, s. 3, it is a defence to prove that a relevant statutory instrument had not been issued at the time of the alleged offence although it is open to the Crown to prove that reasonable steps had been taken to bring it to the attention of relevant persons. However, it should be remembered that the *ultra vires* and unlawful nature of subordinate legislation or administrative decisions may be raised as a defence to a criminal charge (*Boddington* v *British Transport Police* [1998] 2 WLR 639).

Automatism

A3.7   The defence of automatism arises where the accused's conduct lacks the basic requirement of being voluntary (see **A1.2** and **A1.4**).

The defence is limited to cases where there is a total destruction of voluntary control; impaired or reduced control is not enough (*A-G's Ref (No. 2 of 1992)* [1994] QB 91). Where the accused is conscious, automatism will be rare but possible (e.g., reflex actions when startled by a sudden loud noise or when stung by a swarm of bees while driving: see *Hill* v *Baxter* [1958] 1 QB 277 and *Burns* v *Bidder* [1967] 2 QB 227 at p. 240). Where the accused has acted in a state of unconsciousness, it is easier to conclude that he could not have acted otherwise, and in principle he should have the defence of automatism. The law imposes serious restrictions on such a defence, however, through the rules on voluntary intoxication and insanity to be discussed in **A3.9** to **A3.18**. The question which remains for discussion here is whether, even where the automatism is not caused by insanity or voluntary intoxication, there is some further restriction or requirement that the automatism should not be self-induced.

Such a requirement seemed to be suggested by the Court of Appeal in *Quick* [1973] QB 910 even though in that case it quashed the conviction of the appellant for assault. The alleged assault had taken place whilst the appellant (a diabetic) had been in a state of hypoglycaemia (low blood sugar) which the trial judge had (wrongly, in the view of the Court of Appeal) ruled amounted to insanity. The defence of (non-insane) automatism was thus never put to the jury, but Lawton LJ had the following to say (at pp. 922–3) about such a defence:

> A self-induced incapacity will not excuse . . . nor will one which could have been reasonably foreseen as a result of either doing, or omitting to do something, as, for example, taking alcohol against medical advice after using certain prescribed drugs, or failing to have regular meals while taking insulin . . . .

> Had the defence of automatism been left to the jury, a number of questions of fact would have had to be answered. . . . to what extent had he brought about his condition by not following his doctor's instructions about taking regular meals? Did he know that he was getting into a hypoglycaemic episode? If yes, why did he not use the antidote of eating a lump of sugar as he had been advised to do? On the evidence which was before the jury Quick might have had difficulty in answering these questions in a manner which would have relieved him of responsibility for his act.

It thus appeared after *Quick* that, even where automatism was not caught by the rules on insanity and intoxication, it was not available if it could be said to be self-induced. Thus in *Bailey* [1983] 1 WLR 760 a similar defence based on automatism caused by hypoglycaemia was held by the trial judge to be unavailable (on charges under the OAPA 1861, ss. 18 and 20) since it was self-induced. The Court of Appeal (whilst dismissing the appeal on the basis that no miscarriage of justice had actually occurred) held that this was too absolute a rule:

> In our judgment, self-induced automatism, other than that due to intoxication from alcohol or drugs, may provide a defence to crimes of basic intent. The question in each case will be whether the prosecution have provided the necessary element of recklessness. In cases of assault, if the accused knows that his actions or inaction are likely to make him aggressive, unpredictable or uncontrolled with the result that he may cause some injury to others and he persists in the action or takes no remedial action when he knows it is required, it will be open to the jury to find that he was reckless.

The result of these authorities would seem to be that the fact that automatism is self-induced is a bar to the defence only if the accused was at fault (to the degree required by the particular offence charged). A diabetic falling into a state of hypoglycaemia is not inevitably at fault since it is not common knowledge, even among diabetics, that a failure to take food after an insulin injection may lead to aggressive, unpredictable and uncontrolled conduct. What is more, the limitation on self-induced automatism as a defence could not apply at all to the offence under the OAPA 1861, s. 18, since even self-induced intoxication by drink or drugs would be a defence to such a charge, the offence being one, as will be seen, of specific intent. (Another way of looking at this would be to say that since *intent* to cause grievous bodily harm is required for this offence, the accused would have to *intend* to become violent through failure to take food in order to be deprived of the defence of automatism, cf. the Dutch courage rule in relation to intoxication discussed in **A3.11**.)

Intoxication: General Rule

A3.8   Intoxication is not a defence as such. It is, for example, no defence to say (as is undoubtedly true in many cases) that the accused would not have acted as he did but for the fact that his inhibitions were reduced due to the effect of alcohol which he had consumed. On the contrary, intoxication operates so as to restrict what would otherwise be valid defences of mistake, inadvertence or automatism. However, intoxication provides very credible evidence of the fact that the accused did in fact make the mistake he alleges or that he did in fact fail to foresee the obvious risk he was running or that he was indeed in a state of automatism. The restrictions which the law imposes on defences caused by voluntary intoxication are a response to the evidential power of intoxication in supporting such defences and to the frequency and ease with which such defences could be put forward.

Intoxication: Voluntary and Involuntary

A3.9   The restrictive rules apply only where the accused's intoxication is voluntary. This is satisfied if the accused knowingly takes alcohol or other intoxicating drugs (save under medical supervision or direction) and it is immaterial that the accused may have misjudged the degree to which he would become intoxicated (see *Allen* [1988] Crim LR 698). On the other hand, a person who thought he was drinking only orange juice but who was in fact drinking orange juice spiked with quantities of vodka would not be regarded as being voluntarily intoxicated and would have any defence that his resultant state of mind warranted on ordinary principles (e.g., lack of *mens rea*). However, just as with voluntary intoxication, if despite or because of his involuntary intoxication the accused forms the necessary *mens rea* for the crime, there is no separate defence of involuntary intoxication recognised by the law — see the fully reasoned decision of the House of Lords in *Kingston* [1995] 2 AC 355, which reversed the decision of the Court of Appeal and restored the trial judge's ruling that involuntary intoxication provided no defence where the accused (with the necessary *mens rea*) indecently assaulted a boy pursuant to an intent induced by the influence of drugs administered secretly to the accused by a third party. Thus, the only advantage of a finding that the intoxication was involuntary is that it avoids the application of the restrictive rules discussed at **A3.10**.

What counts as an intoxicating drug for the purposes of the restrictive rules governing voluntary intoxication has been discussed by the courts in two cases, *Bailey* [1983] 1 WLR 760 and *Hardie* [1985] 1 WLR 64. In *Bailey*, the Court of Appeal talked about the intoxication rules being applicable to 'dangerous drugs', i.e. those where it is 'common knowledge' that the taker 'may become aggressive or do dangerous or unpredictable things' (amphetamines and LSD being obvious examples). In the second case the court had to consider an accused, charged with an offence under the Criminal Damage Act 1971, s. 1(2), who had taken a number of Valium tablets (which were prescribed for someone else) and held that this did not necessarily amount to voluntary intoxication.

> [Valium is] wholly different in kind from drugs which are liable to cause unpredictability or aggressiveness. . . . if the effect of a drug is merely soporific or sedative the taking of it, even in some excessive quantity, cannot in the ordinary way raise a *conclusive* presumption against the admission of proof of intoxication for the purpose of disproving *mens rea*. . . .
>
> [The jury] should have been directed that if they came to the conclusion that, as a result of the Valium, the appellant was, at the time, unable to appreciate the risks to property and

persons from his actions they should then consider whether the taking of the Valium was itself reckless.

Thus it would seem that there are two categories of drugs: 'dangerous' and 'non-dangerous', LSD being an obvious example of the former category and Valium being an example of the latter. Knowingly taking a 'dangerous' drug counts as voluntary intoxication whereas taking a 'non-dangerous' drug is governed by a similar rule to that discussed in relation to self-induced automatism (see **A3.7**) and depends on the actual knowledge of the offender as to the likely effects of the drug. Classification by the courts of various drugs into dangerous and non-dangerous is now awaited.

Intoxication: Specific and Basic Intent

The principal restriction imposed on defences based on intoxication is that voluntary **A3.10** intoxication can only give rise to a defence to crimes of specific rather than basic intent. The precise nature of the distinction between these two categories of offence has been shrouded in obscurity ever since Lord Birkenhead used the phrase 'specific intent' in *DPP* v *Beard* [1920] AC 479. Matters are perhaps a little clearer today, although Lord Mustill in *Kingston* [1995] 2 AC 355 (at p. 369) guardedly reserved his position as to whether a line could definitively be drawn between offences of 'specific' and 'basic' intent. Nevertheless it would appear that any offence for which only intention will suffice as the mental element can be regarded as an offence of specific intent. Thus murder, theft, robbery, wounding with intent, burglary under the Theft Act 1968, s. 9(1)(a), and any offence of attempt would all appear to be crimes of specific intent and it is open to the accused to adduce evidence that he lacked the specific intent required by these offences due to voluntary intoxication. Certain other offences which do not specifically require intention but which require other special mental states such as dishonesty would also seem to be governed by the same rule, e.g., handling stolen goods (*Durante* [1972] 1 WLR 1612). So too with criminal damage where the indictment restricts the allegation against the accused to intention as opposed to recklessness (see *Metropolitan Police Commissioner* v *Caldwell* [1982] AC 341 at p. 356).

Subject to a possible exception to be discussed below in relation to *Caldwell* recklessness, all offences other than those of specific intent can be regarded as crimes of basic intent and the accused will not be allowed to show that he lacked the *mens rea* or was in a state of automatism due to voluntary intoxication. Crimes of basic intent clearly include manslaughter, rape, malicious wounding, all forms of assault (except those requiring a specific intent such as assault with intent to rob), and taking a conveyance contrary to the Theft Act 1968, s. 12. Thus, in these cases, even the fact that the accused has 'completely blacked out', as was alleged in the leading House of Lords case of *DPP* v *Majewski* [1977] AC 443, will provide no defence, nor will the fact that he is hallucinating that he is fighting snakes at the centre of the earth, as was alleged in the Court of Appeal case of *Lipman* [1970] 1 QB 152. The rule applies not only to the person who is so intoxicated that he cannot remember anything of the offence (as in *Woods* (1981) 74 Cr App R 312) but also where the accused makes a mistake about a particular aspect of his actions as in *Fotheringham* (1988) 88 Cr App R 206 where, on a charge of rape, the accused claimed he believed he was having intercourse with his wife rather than with the babysitter. This latter decision is in fact rather difficult to reconcile with the earlier Court of Appeal decision in *Cogan* [1976] QB 217 where Cogan's conviction for rape was quashed because he had an honest, albeit unreasonable and drunken, belief in consent.

However, where a defence of honest mistake is specifically provided in a statute, then it appears that even an intoxicated mistake may suffice. In *Jaggard* v *Dickinson* [1981] QB 527, the Divisional Court held that the defence of belief in the owner's consent under the Criminal Damage Act 1971, s. 5(2), was still available even though the defendant was drunk. The court seems to have been particularly impressed by the fact that s. 5(3) specifically provides that: 'For the purposes of this section it is immaterial whether a belief is justified or not if it is honestly held'. The decision must, regrettably, be regarded as confined to defences under the Criminal Damage Act 1971, s. 5, although the same sort of issue could arise, for example, in relation to the defence of mistaken belief under the Theft Act 1968, s. 12(6). Certainly the Court of Appeal was not prepared to allow, in relation to self-defence, a drunken mistake by the accused that he was being attacked (*O'Grady* [1987] QB 995 – see further **A3.36**).

Various justifications for the basic intent rule have been put forward, but none of them are particularly convincing, and the Australian courts have refused to adopt it (see *O'Connor* (1980) 146 CLR 64). At root the rule seems to be one of legal policy – that an intoxicated offender should have a potential defence to the most serious offences such as murder or wounding with intent but should remain liable for an appropriate lesser offence of basic intent such as manslaughter or malicious wounding. The policy is embodied in both the Criminal Law Revision Committee's recommendations (14th Report, 1980, Cmnd 7844) and the Law Commission's Draft Criminal Code Bill (Law Commission No. 177), cl. 22. Although a Law Commission Consultation Paper (No. 127, 1993) proposed abolition of the basic intent rule, the final report (No. 229, 1995) reverted to recommending the retention of the rule in codified form.

Although the policy is clear, some of the basic technicalities are less so. Previous editions of this work have, in common with many other commentators, followed the words of Lord Elwyn Jones in *DPP* v *Majewski* which state that evidence of intoxication 'supplies the evidence of *mens rea*, of guilty mind, certainly sufficiently for crimes of basic intent' and therefore suggested that to proffer such evidence would seem to discharge the prosecution from the burden of showing that the accused had the *mens rea* or was acting voluntarily.

The alternative view is that evidence of intoxication is simply irrelevant and has to be ignored on the question of whether the accused has the *mens rea* of a basic intent crime but that the jury have to answer the hypothetical question of whether the accused would have had the *mens rea* if, contrary to the facts, he had not been intoxicated. This was the approach favoured by the Court of Appeal in *Richardson* [1999] 1 Cr App R 392 but it is an approach not without difficulties, especially in cases where the intoxication has reduced the accused to a state of automatism or something close to it. In most cases of course, either approach will yield the same result since, in the absence of any other special factor apart from intoxication, the jury will assume that the accused would have foreseen the natural and probable consequence of his actions if not intoxicated. The actual decision to quash the convictions in *Richardson* is strange since the only other factor mentioned by the Court of Appeal was the fact that the appellants were university students (who are surely able to appreciate the natural and probable consequences of their actions, at least in their occasional sober moments, despite the fallibility sometimes revealed in their examination scripts) and the Court actually stated that the 'reason they did not [appreciate the risk] was the amount of drink they had consumed'. Despite this, *Richardson* usefully suggests an opportunity for the defence to raise the issue that there was some exculpatory or innocent cause of the accused's mistake or inadvertence, other than voluntary intoxication, even though it is difficult to discern such a cause on the facts of *Richardson* itself.

Richardson also unfortunately clouds another issue, that of the effect of intoxication on mistaken belief in the victim's consent, on which issue the Court of Appeal said that evidence of intoxication should be taken into account. This is inconsistent with all bar one of the cases on intoxicated mistake cited above and is surely wrong unless *Jaggard* v *Dickinson* is to be elevated from an exception based on a particular statutory provision to a general principle governing beliefs in consent of any variety. Such a principle, though attractive to some, would still be anomalous and inconsistent with the general approach to intoxication in basic intent crimes.

A special rule for intoxication is required only because of the evidentiary power of intoxication in showing that the accused lacked the subjective *mens rea* required for most offences. In relation to reckless criminal damage, Lord Diplock took a different approach in *Metropolitan Police Commissioner* v *Caldwell* [1982] AC 341 and denied the effect of the accused's intoxication by defining recklessness in a wider manner. Caldwell's plea that, due to intoxication, it never occurred to him that anyone's life might be endangered became *logically* not just *legally* irrelevant once recklessness was widened to include the person who fails to consider an obvious risk. Indeed, to say that the risk never occurred to him amounted to an admission rather than a denial of recklessness. Thus Lord Diplock felt able to dispense with the policy-based basic intent rule saying (at p. 356):

> . . . classification into offences of 'specific' and 'basic' intent is irrelevant where being reckless as to whether a particular harmful consequence will result from one's act is a sufficient alternative *mens rea*.

Lord Diplock appears to have overlooked the intoxicated defendant who does consider but wrongly rules out the risk (analogous to an intoxicated mistake rather than inadvertence). Such a defendant's intoxication is not *logically* irrelevant even to the wider version of recklessness approved in *Metropolitan Police Commissioner* v *Caldwell* (see **A2.5**) and might conceivably succeed as a defence if one can take Lord Diplock literally in saying that reckless criminal damage is not an offence of basic intent. However, the courts would probably be quick to close this lacuna created by oversight and would no doubt point to the more categorical answer given (at p. 356) by Lord Diplock to the second certified question in *Caldwell*:

> If the charge is, or includes, a reference to his 'being reckless as to whether the life of another would thereby be endangered', evidence of self-induced intoxication is not relevant.

Furthermore, to allow a defence of intoxicated ruling out of the risk or of intoxicated mistake to *Caldwell* recklessness would be at odds with (arguably regrettable) decisions such as *Fotheringham* (1988) 88 Cr App R 206 denying the relevance of intoxicated mistake in crimes requiring subjective recklessness. The safest conclusion is probably that reckless criminal damage, not being an offence of specific intent, will continue to be treated as an offence of basic intent and the accused will not be allowed to show he falls outside the *Caldwell* definition of recklessness due to self-induced intoxication. (See also *Cullen* [1993] Crim LR 936 and **B8.8**.) It would however seem to follow from *Richardson* that, if the accused could point to some reason or factor (other than intoxication) which might have caused him, independently of the intoxication, to rule out the risk and thus fall outside the definition of recklessness, then that reason or other factor should be a defence.

Intoxication: the Dutch Courage Rule

The so-called Dutch courage rule is more important in principle than in practice. A **A3.11** person who deliberately makes himself intoxicated in order to commit a crime cannot raise a defence based on such intoxication, even to a crime of specific intent (*A-G for Northern Ireland* v *Gallagher* [1963] AC 349, per Lord Denning). The rule is eminently sensible but not necessarily applicable even to the facts of *A-G for Northern Ireland* v *Gallagher* itself and there seem to be no reported cases of it being applied since. The principle, however, is effectively the same as that laid down by the courts in relation to 'non-dangerous' drugs (see **A3.9**) – that if the accused has the fault element of the offence in becoming intoxicated, the lack of the fault element at the time of the offence due to such intoxication is irrelevant.

Insanity: General Principles: the M'Naghten Rules

A3.12   The defence of insanity is still governed by the M'Naghten rules (*M'Naghten's Case* (1843) 10 Cl & F 200), which today operate largely as a restriction on what might otherwise be a complete defence based on lack of *mens rea* or automatism. Only where the accused falls under that limb of the rules which requires him not to know that his act is 'wrong' do the rules provide any defence additional to that which would be available under the above general principles. Until recently, even this possibility was a largely theoretical one since the consequences of an insanity verdict were so unattractive that seldom would an accused wish to seek one. The 'special verdict' of 'not guilty by reason of insanity' is provided for in the Trial of Lunatics Act 1883, s. 2, and is one that is required to be returned by a jury rather than simply as a result of the accused's plea (see *Crown Court at Maidstone, ex parte Harrow LBC* [1999] 3 All ER 542). Where a special verdict is returned, the Criminal Procedure (Insanity) Act 1964, s. 5, previously required a court to make an order that the accused be admitted to such hospital as may be specified by the Secretary of State but, since 1991 under the amended version of s. 5, the court now has a range of orders from which to choose (see **D10.9**). These include an order for admission to hospital (whether with or without a restriction as to time), but also a guardianship order, a supervision and treatment order, and even an absolute discharge. The defence of insanity is therefore now much more attractive to an accused and is likely to be relied on more frequently (see Mackay and Kearns [1999] Crim LR 714 for an account of the relatively slow progress in this respect). However, the above flexibility does not apply where the offence to which the special verdict relates is murder or any other offence for which the sentence is fixed by law; in such a case the court must order admission to hospital without limit of time (see also the unsuccessful attempt in *Antoine* [1999] 2 Cr App R 225, a fitness to plead case, to reduce the charge to manslaughter on the grounds of diminished responsibility).

Whilst the burden of proving insanity is on the accused on the balance of probabilities (see **A3.13**), for a special verdict to be returned the prosecution must prove that the accused 'did the act or made the omission charged' (Trial of Lunatics Act 1883, s. 2(1)), otherwise the defendant is entitled to a complete acquittal on the ground of lack of an *actus reus*, despite any insanity. It was confirmed in *A-G's Ref (No. 3 of 1998)* [1999] 3 All ER 40 that this does not involve proving *mens rea* (doubting *Egan* [1997] Crim LR 225, another fitness to plead case) but did require proof of 'the ingredients which constitute the *actus reus* of the crime' which seems to include the circumstances (other than *mens rea*) whose presence or absence render the act or omission criminally unlawful (such as, for example, on appropriate facts, the absence of legitimate grounds for self-defence).

Even before the disincentives to plead insanity were reduced, the scope of the M'Naghten rules had remained important. Once the defence put the accused's state of mind in issue, it was open to the prosecution to argue (see Lord Denning in *Bratty* v *A-G for Northern Ireland* [1963] AC 386) and to the trial judge to rule (see, for example, *Sullivan* [1984] AC 156) that the defence really amounted to insanity (see also the Criminal Procedure (Insanity) Act 1964, s. 6). The rules in effect marked out one boundary of the defences of automatism (as in *Sullivan*) or lack of *mens rea* (see, for example, *Clarke* [1972] 1 All ER 219 where, however, the accused was found on appeal not to be within the M'Naghten rules and thus had a complete defence of lack of *mens rea*). The rules still retain this definitional function but the consequences of having one's defence fall within the rules are no longer automatically so severe. The accused will now be able to put his state of mind in issue more readily with less fear (murder cases apart) of the court having to make an inappropriate order if it finds the accused to be within the rules.

It should be noted that the above discussion relates to trials on indictment and that s. 2 of the Trial of Lunatics Act 1883 is inapplicable to trial in magistrates' courts. That the defence of insanity is available in magistrates' courts and that it leads to a complete acquittal rather than the special verdict was fully explained by White in his article at [1991] Crim LR 501 and this has now been confirmed by the Divisional Court in *Horseferry Road Magistrates' Court, ex parte K* [1997] QB 23. Whilst magistrates have a power to make a hospital order under the Mental Health Act 1983, s. 37(3), even though the accused is not convicted, there is no power to commit to the Crown Court for a restriction order to be made under s. 41 of that Act. The significance of the availability of the defence of insanity in the magistrates' court will be considerably reduced if *DPP v H* [1997] 1 WLR 1406 is followed. In that case the Divisional Court followed the intimation given in *Ex parte K* that insanity could be a defence only in relation to crimes requiring *mens rea* or where *mens rea* was in issue. This decision may represent a pragmatic limitation on the availability of the insanity defence in summary trials (and in triable either way cases a plea of insanity is likely to result in the case being committed to the Crown Court as in *Ex parte K*). It is, however, open to criticism on the grounds that, as has already been pointed out, the defence of insanity can go beyond a mere denial of *mens rea*. This is true both in the sense that insanity may extend to automatism, i.e. a denial of voluntariness (which is normally a requirement even of crimes of strict liability) and also in that the defence may apply where the accused 'does not know that his act is wrong'. See also the commentary on *Ex parte K* at [1997] Crim LR 132 and the article by Ward at p. 796.

The status of the M'Naghten rules in terms of the doctrine of precedent is somewhat anomalous but they have long been treated as authoritative, a treatment confirmed by the House of Lords in *Sullivan* in 1983. In *M'Naghten's Case* (1843) 10 Cl & F 200, the crucial passage (at p. 210) in the response given by Tindal CJ (on behalf of all the other judges save Maule J) reads as follows (emphasis added):

> . . . the jurors ought to be told in all cases that *every man is to be presumed to be sane*, and to possess a sufficient degree of reason to be responsible for his crimes, *until the contrary be proved to their satisfaction*; and that to establish a defence on the ground of insanity, it must be clearly proved that, *at the time of the committing of the act*, the party accused was labouring under such a *defect of reason, from disease of the mind, as not to know the nature and quality of the act he was doing*; or, if he did know it, *that he did not know he was doing what was wrong*.

The emphasis has been added and each emphasised phrase will now be explained in turn.

'. . . every man is to be presumed to be sane . . . until the contrary be proved to [the jury's] satisfaction'   A3.13   This is the basis on which, exceptionally, the burden of proof in establishing the defence is placed on the accused but it is established that the proof need only be on the balance of probabilities (*Sodeman* v *The King* [1936] 2 All ER 1138, and see **F3.3**). This exception to the general rule on burden of proof is particularly problematical where the accused puts forward both insanity and non-insane automatism as in *Bratty* v *A-G for Northern Ireland* [1963] AC 386. The solution seems to lie in remembering that, just as with intoxication, the principal utility of evidence of insanity to an accused is that the insanity is itself explanatory evidence of why the accused was not conscious of his actions (or of their obvious results). Other evidence of automatism, such as, for example, a blow on the head causing concussion, need only raise a doubt in the minds of the jury as to whether the accused's act was involuntary, but insofar as the evidence consists of evidence of insanity, the jury must be convinced on a balance of probabilities that the act was involuntary. The result may be, as was possibly the case in *Bratty*, that a jury convicts even though they entertain some doubt as to whether the accused's act was voluntary because the only evidence causing that doubt is evidence of insanity and it is not sufficiently strong to convince them on a balance of probabilities. This may appear to be anomalous but it should be noted that in *Woolmington* v *DPP* [1935] AC 462, Lord Sankey said: '. . . it is the duty of the prosecution to prove the

prisoner's guilt *subject to what I have already said as to the defence of insanity*' (emphasis added).

A3.14 *'. . . at the time of the committing of the act'*   The M'Naghten rules, in common with the other defences discussed in this section, are concerned with the accused's state of mind at the time of the alleged offence. The sanity or otherwise of the accused at other times may be relevant in other ways, not by way of defence but, for example, in relation to whether he is fit to plead (see **D10.6** *et seq*.) or in relation to the type of sentence or order to be passed. Such issues relating to the sanity of the accused at the time of the trial or the time of sentencing can arise whether or not the accused was sane or not at the time of the alleged offence.

A3.15 *'. . . a defect of reason'*   This is a central notion in the rules even though it is not the concept around which most of the case law turns. It is the basic reason why irresistible impulse and other emotional or volitional defects or disorders are not within the rules, since they are not defects of reason. Rationality is the litmus test of criminal responsibility, and defects of will are regarded either as non-existent or as irrelevant. In this respect, the defence of diminished responsibility is potentially much more liberal. However, given the way in which insanity can operate as a restriction on other defences, the requirement of a defect of reason may sometimes come to the defendant's aid. See *Clarke* [1972] 1 All ER 219 where the Court of Appeal held that even if the other elements of the rules were satisfied, there was no *defect* of reason but at most a mere absent-minded failure to use the powers of reasoning that the accused undoubtedly still possessed and thus the accused was entitled to have the simple defence of lack of *mens rea* considered by the jury rather than the defence of insanity.

A3.16 *'. . . from disease of the mind'*   The defect of reason must be caused by a disease of the mind (rather than by, for example, intoxication, which is probably the best explanation for the decision in *Thomas* [1995] Crim LR 314). It is the meaning of this concept around which most of the recent case law turns as it is this which primarily distinguishes insane automatism (a defence of insanity leading to the special verdict) from non-insane automatism (a defence of simple automatism leading to a complete acquittal).

The meaning of 'disease of the mind' is a legal question for the judge to decide rather than a medical one, even though the evidence of medical experts is required by the Criminal Procedure (Insanity and Unfitness to Plead) Act 1991, s. 1. In *Sullivan* [1984] AC 156, two medical experts in the course of their testimony stated that they would not regard something as a disease of the mind unless it produced a disorder of brain functions for a prolonged period – in the case of one witness for more than a day and in the case of the other for more than a month. It was therefore argued that the relatively short period over which an epileptic seizure takes place meant that epilepsy was not a disease of the mind. Lord Diplock emphatically rejected this argument noting (at p. 172) that:

> The nomenclature adopted by the medical profession may change from time to time. . . . But the meaning of the expression 'disease of the mind' as the cause of 'a defect of reason' remains unchanged for the purposes of the application of the M'Naghten rules. . . . 'mind' in the M'Naghten rules is used in the ordinary sense of the mental faculties of reason, memory and understanding. If the effect of a disease is to impair these faculties so severely as to have either of the consequences referred to in the latter part of the rules, it matters not whether the aetiology of the impairment is organic, as in epilepsy, or functional, or whether the impairment itself is permanent or is transient and intermittent, provided that it subsisted at the time of commission of the act.

The relevance of the medical evidence seems to be limited to showing that the impairment of the mental faculties did in fact take place and what in fact was the cause. The classification of that impairment and its cause (whether or not it is a defect of reason from disease of the mind), is then purely a matter of law for the judge. It can also be seen that to a large extent, whether something is a disease *of the mind* depends on the consequences it produces – impairment of the faculties of reason, memory and understanding. The disease certainly need not be one primarily located in the brain if it produces the relevant consequences there. Thus arteriosclerosis (hardening of the arteries) causing temporary loss of consciousness is a disease of the mind for these purposes even though it is of physical rather than mental origin (see per Devlin J in *Kemp* [1957] 1 QB 399 at p. 408).

However, not every cause of an impairment of these mental faculties is a *disease* of the mind. A disease is something *internal* to the accused and so:

> A malfunctioning of the mind of transitory effect caused by the application to the body of some *external* factor such as violence, drugs, including anaesthetics, alcohol and hypnotic influences cannot fairly be said to be due to disease (per Lawton LJ in *Quick* [1973] QB 910 at p. 922, emphasis added).

Quick's condition of hypoglycaemia was held not to have been due to a disease of the mind since it was attributable to an external factor – his use of insulin prescribed by his doctor:

> Such malfunctioning of his mind as there was, was caused by an external factor and not by a bodily disorder in the nature of a disease which disturbed the working of his mind (ibid. at pp. 922–3).

Treating the insulin, rather than the diabetes which necessitated the insulin, as the cause of the malfunctioning enabled the court in *Quick* to keep the case outside the M'Naghten rules. However, this course was not available in *Hennessy* [1989] 1 WLR 287, which again concerned a diabetic, this time suffering from the opposite condition of hyperglycaemia (excessive blood sugar) which is directly caused by the diabetes when uncorrected by the administration of insulin. It was thus the *absence* of an external factor which allowed the disease of diabetes to produce the malfunctioning and, given this effect of the disease, the Court of Appeal felt constrained to classify it as a disease of the mind. See also *Bingham* [1991] Crim LR 433.

The Court of Appeal in *Hennessy* also rejected the argument that the accused's anxiety and depression due to his marital problems constituted an external factor (even though there was medical evidence that anxiety and depression could contribute to an increased blood-sugar level). See also the Canadian case of *Rabey* (1977) 79 DLR (3d) 414, in which the Ontario Court of Appeal said (at p. 435) that 'the ordinary stresses and disappointments of life which are the common lot of mankind do not constitute an external cause'. This was subsequently approved by the English Court of Appeal in *Burgess* [1991] 1 QB 92. In this case, the court held that violence whilst sleepwalking or 'sleep associated automatism' was due to an internal factor and was therefore within the M'Naghten rules.

'. . . *as not to know the nature and quality of the act he was doing*' This refers **A3.17** to the physical rather than moral quality of the act (per Lord Reading CJ in *Codere* (1916) 12 Cr App R 21) and according to Lord Diplock in *Sullivan* [1984] AC 156 at p. 173: 'Addressed to an audience of jurors in the 1980s it might more aptly be expressed as "He did not know what he was doing"'. Clearly this would be satisfied if the accused was unconscious at the time or, even if conscious, thought, to adopt an example quoted by Lord Denning in another context, that he was throwing a log rather than the baby on the fire. Equally clearly, the accused would have a defence of automatism or lack of *mens rea* respectively in these two situations, and this underlines the point previously made that the M'Naghten rules generally merely qualify what would otherwise be a complete defence.

A3.18 '. . . *or . . . that he did not know he was doing what was wrong*' This is an alternative to not knowing the nature and quality of the act and is the only sense in which an insane person is given a defence where none would be available to the sane (knowledge of moral or legal wrongness, as opposed to knowledge of the facts which render it wrong, being generally irrelevant to criminal responsibility). The major question debated here is whether 'wrong' means legally wrong or morally wrong. It is suggested that the key to a proper understanding of this question is to recognise that the question is a negative one. If the accused *does* know *either* that his act is *morally* wrong (according to the ordinary standard adopted by reasonable men, per Lord Reading in *Codere* (1916) 12 Cr App R 21) *or* that it is *legally* wrong then it cannot be said that he does *not* know he was doing what was wrong. In the only two English decisions on the matter (*Codere* (1916) 12 Cr App R 21 and *Windle* [1952] 2 QB 826), it was only necessary to hold that it was correct to tell the jury that the accused could not rely on the defence if he knew that his act was legally wrong. Both were murder cases and it was not seriously suggested in either that the accused did not know his act was legally wrong and yet knew that it was morally wrong. (On the contrary, Windle thought he was morally right to kill his suicidal wife and yet knew it was legally wrong since he said, 'I suppose they will hang me for this'.) Despite the blunt *obiter dictum* in *Windle* (at p. 834) that ' "wrong" means contrary to law', it seems to be the better view that in the case of an accused who does not appreciate that his act is legally wrong but who does realise that it is morally wrong, the defence would not be made out.

DEFENCES INVOLVING OTHER EXCUSES AND JUSTIFICATIONS

Introduction

A3.19 To treat certain defences as excuses or justifications and to deal with them separately from defences which deny the basic elements of liability is in one sense artificial since it can be pointed out, for example, that no one commits any offence unless he acts unlawfully and, if the accused has a defence of justification available, then he has not acted unlawfully and one of the basic elements of liability is missing. Equally, it can be pointed out that the defences treated here as a denial of the elements of liability, such as mistake of fact, may be also properly classified as excuses. In the end all classifications are somewhat artificial and are really made for convenience and ease of understanding and exposition. On these grounds it seems sensible to separate out defences where the accused admits that he has voluntarily committed what is prima facie a crime with the state of mind normally sufficient for that offence but at the same time asserts some *special* circumstances which he claims excuse or justify his actions. As Lord Wilberforce said of duress in *DPP for Northern Ireland* v *Lynch* [1975] AC 653 (at pp. 679–80):

> [It] is something which is superimposed upon the other ingredients which by themselves would make up an offence, i.e., upon act and intention. . . . the victim completes the act and knows that he is doing so; but the addition of the element of duress prevents the law from treating what he has done as a crime.

Duress by Threats: General Principles

A3.20 There has been a great deal of development since the 1960s in the defence of duress by threats. Its basis seems to be excuse rather than justification. The details of the defence can conveniently be considered under three headings: the type of threat necessary, the required cogency of the threat, and the offences and persons excluded from the defence.

A3.21 *The Type of Threat Required* All the decisions recognising duress as a defence have concerned threats of death or grievous bodily harm although in *Steane* [1947] KB 997, Lord Goddard CJ, *obiter*, included fear of imprisonment which has not been ruled out by the plethora of more recent authorities – see, e.g., Lord Lane CJ in *Graham* [1982]

1 WLR 294 leaving open the question of whether false imprisonment could be relied on. It would seem from *Baker* [1997] Crim LR 497 that a threat of serious psychological injury will not suffice. Another open question is whether the threat has to be directed at the accused or whether threats to third parties, especially close relatives, can suffice. There seems to be more consensus on this point and certainly in principle threats to third parties should be *capable* of constituting duress since even the bravest man may be prepared to risk his own neck whilst flinching at subjecting his loved ones to serious peril. Indeed there is Australian authority (*Hurley* [1967] VR 526) recognising threats to the accused's common-law wife, and in *Ortiz* (1986) 83 Cr App R 173 threats to the accused's wife or family appear to have been considered to be sufficient.

The Cogency of the Threat   The fact that the accused believes that a threat of death **A3.22** or grievous bodily harm will be carried out if he does not commit the offence is not of itself sufficient 'if a person of reasonable firmness sharing the characteristics of the defendant would not have given way to the threats' (third certified question in *Howe* [1987] AC 417). In other words, the threat is only sufficiently cogent, and the accused will only be excused, if a person of reasonable firmness might have done the same thing. This objective approach was most clearly articulated by Lord Lane CJ in *Graham* [1982] 1 WLR 294 in a suggested direction (at p. 300) later approved by the House of Lords in *Howe*:

> (1) Was the defendant, or may he have been, impelled to act as he did because, as a result of what he reasonably believed [the threatener] had said or done, he had good cause to fear that if he did not so act [the threatener] would kill him or . . . cause him serious physical injury? (2) If so, have the prosecution made the jury sure that a sober person of reasonable firmness, sharing the characteristics of the defendant, would not have responded to whatever he reasonably believed [the threatener] said or did by taking part [in the offence].

It would seem that not all the elements of this direction will always be necessary. For example, the reference to 'what he reasonably believed the threatener had said or done' would be unnecessary if there was no dispute about what threats had been made and it would be simpler for a jury to consider the question in terms of what was actually said or done. As to the requirement of reasonableness, see the discussion of *DPP* v *Rogers* [1998] Crim LR 202 at the end of **A3.28**. Similarly, the reference to 'sharing the characteristics of the defendant' would be otiose if there was no evidence of the defendant having any unusual characteristics which would affect the gravity of the threats.

This point was emphasised in *Bowen* [1997] 1 WLR 372, where Stuart-Smith LJ, in denying the relevance of low IQ, derived a number of principles from the case law of which the seventh and last was as follows (at p. 380):

> In the absence of some direction from the judge as to what characteristics are capable of being regarded as relevant, we think that the direction approved in [*Graham*] without more will not be as helpful as it might be, since the jury may be tempted, especially if there is evidence, as there was in this case, relating to suggestibility and vulnerability, to think that these are relevant. *In most cases it is probably only the age and sex of the defendant that is capable of being relevant. If so, the judge should . . . confine the characteristics in question to these.* (emphasis added)

For the majority of cases, this is, it is respectfully suggested, a useful working rule, and confirms earlier cases such as *Horne* [1994] Crim LR 584 and *Hegarty* [1994] Crim LR 353, which excluded psychiatric or medical evidence to the effect that the accused was unusually pliable or vulnerable to pressure or emotionally unstable or in a 'grossly elevated neurotic state'. There remains the difficult question of what characteristics other than age and sex can exceptionally be relevant. In *Bowen* Stuart-Smith LJ gave some examples in his second principle (at p. 379) including 'pregnancy, where there is added fear for the unborn child; serious physical disability, which may inhibit self protection'. The true relevance of these, it is submitted, by analogy with the objective test for provocation, lies in the fact that they increase the gravity of the threat rather than reducing the courage or steadfastness of the accused. A threat of physical violence to a pregnant woman is much more serious because of the vulnerability of the child in the womb. Similarly, physical violence to a physically disabled person is more serious and likely to result in more serious harm if there is reduced ability to defend oneself or ward off blows. On this basis the further example of 'recognised mental illness or psychiatric condition', which seems to refer to conditions rendering sufferers 'more susceptible to pressure and threats' (see the fifth principle described in the judgment of Stuart-Smith LJ at p. 379) seems questionable since it contradicts the basic premise of the objective test of a person of reasonable firmness. See also the criticism of this aspect of the decision at [1996] Crim LR 579.

The reference to a 'sober' person of reasonable firmness makes it plain that intoxication cannot be a relevant characteristic. Intoxication is of course normally self-induced (quaere whether involuntary intoxication might be relevant) and in *Flatt* [1996] Crim LR 576 it was held that other self-induced conditions, such as being a drug addict, are excluded.

The immediacy of the threat and the possibility of seeking official protection are matters which the Court of Appeal said, in *Hurst* [1995] 1 Cr App R 82, require more attention to be paid to them. These matters were considered in *Hudson* [1971] 2 QB 202 and the court there declined to lay down any hard and fast rules other than to say that:

> It is essential to the defence of duress that the threat shall be effective at the moment when the crime is committed. The threat must be a 'present' threat in the sense that it is effective to neutralise the will of the accused at that time.

> . . . the existence at that moment of threats sufficient to destroy his will ought to provide him with a defence even though the threatened injury may not follow instantly, but after an interval. . . .

> In the present case [of perjury] the threats . . . were likely to be no less compelling, because their execution could not be effected in the court room, if they could be carried out in the streets of Salford the same night.

Whether the accused could be expected to take any opportunity of rendering the threat ineffective in the meantime by, for example, seeking police protection was a matter for the jury and:

> In deciding whether such an opportunity was reasonably open to the accused the jury should have regard to his age and circumstances, and to any risks to him which may be involved.

Whilst a low IQ is not relevant to this question (see *Bowen* [1997] 1 WLR 37), this does clearly allow the jury to take into account the fact that such police protection may be ineffective. It should be noted that the Law Commission (Law Com. No. 83) originally recommended that this question of ineffectiveness should be made irrelevant but cl. 25 of their Draft Criminal Law Bill (Law Com. No. 218) demonstrates the Commission's latest thinking. In fact, both the question of the immediacy of the threat and the question of any opportunity to render it ineffective appear to be subsumed under the question of whether under the *Graham* test a person of reasonable firmness would have responded to the threat by committing the offence and it is submitted that even the person of reasonable firmness would take account of the likely effectiveness or otherwise of police protection before deciding whether to avail himself of it (see also Law Com. No. 218, para. 29.3–29.7).

The approach in *Hudson* was followed in *Abdul-Hussain* [1999] Crim LR 570, a duress of circumstances case.

Duress by Threats: Excluded Offences and Persons

Although duress has now been recognised as available on a wide range of charges (and **A3.23** is available in contempt proceedings, see *K* (1983) 78 Cr App R 82) and is to that extent a general defence, there have always been doubts about whether it extends to murder or certain types of treason.

Murder In *Howe* [1987] AC 417, the House of Lords unequivocally held that the **A3.24** defence of duress is *not* available on a murder charge either to a principal offender or to a secondary party, and in so doing declined to follow its own previous decision in *DPP for Northern Ireland* v *Lynch* [1975] AC 653. Singling out murder in this way does itself raise some anomalies, particularly in that duress appears still to be a defence to wounding with intent under the OAPA 1861, whereas if the victim should die the intent to cause grievous bodily harm is sufficient to found a murder charge and the defence suddenly becomes unavailable. The exclusion of duress applies equally on a charge of attempted murder (see *Gotts* [1992] 2 AC 412).

Treason Duress, or something akin to it, seems to have been recognised as a defence **A3.25** to certain forms of treason both as long ago as 1419 (*Oldcastle's Case* (1419) 1 Hale PC 50) and as relatively recently as 1945 in *Purdy* (1945) 10 JCL 182 (although see per Lord Goddard CJ in *Steane* [1947] KB 997 at p. 1005). Writers such as Hale and Stephen have doubted whether duress applies to the more serious forms of treason and the judges have traditionally reserved their opinion as to the extent to which duress is available (see, for example, Lord Brandon in *Howe* [1987] AC 417 at p. 438). Given the decision in *Howe*, the courts may well be unwilling to allow a plea of duress where the particular act of treason would inevitably lead to the deaths of identifiable individuals, even if it would be difficult or impossible to bring a murder charge in relation to those deaths.

Excluded Persons It is now clear that a person cannot rely on the defence of duress **A3.26** if he has voluntarily and knowingly exposed himself to the risk of such duress by joining a criminal organisation or gang. One of the earlier illustrations of this principle was in the Northern Ireland case of *Fitzpatrick* [1977] NI 20 where the accused had voluntarily joined the IRA and was therefore unable to plead duress based on threats from that organisation as a defence to, *inter alia*, armed robbery carried out on its behalf. The restriction on the defence was supported by dicta of members of the House of Lords in *DPP for Northern Ireland* v *Lynch* [1975] AC 653 and by provisions of various Commonwealth codes and has been applied by the English Court of Appeal in *Sharp* [1987] QB 853. Sharp was a member of a gang which had carried out a series of armed robberies. He sought to plead duress as a defence to manslaughter when a sub-postmaster was shot dead by the gang leader during the course of the last robbery. Sharp alleged that he had sought to withdraw from this robbery when he saw the guns being put into the car but that a gun had then been pointed at him and a threat made 'to blow his head off' if he did not participate. Lord Lane CJ said (at p. 861):

> . . . where a person has voluntarily, and with knowledge of its nature, joined a criminal organisation or gang which he knew might bring pressure on him to commit an offence and was an active member when he was put under such pressure, he cannot avail himself of the defence of duress.

It is clear from this statement that the organisation or gang must be one likely to exercise duress and the accused must be aware of this when he joins. In *Shepherd* (1987) 86 Cr App R 47, the accused, a member of a shoplifting gang, claimed that he found the experience unnerving and that he had only taken part in a subsequent burglary because of threats of violence to himself and his family. The Court of Appeal quashed the conviction for burglary as the trial judge had wrongly withdrawn the defence of duress from the jury purely on the basis that the accused had voluntarily joined a criminal organisation. Mustill LJ said (at p. 51):

. . . the concerted shoplifting enterprise did not involve violence to the victim either in anticipation or in the way it was actually put into effect. The members of the jury have had to ask themselves whether the appellant could be said to have taken the risk of P's violence simply by joining a shoplifting gang.

The precise ambit of the accused's knowledge (see also *Ali* [1995] Crim LR 303) has been at issue in a couple of recent cases involving duress exercised in furtherance of debts run up for the illegal supply of drugs. In *Baker* [1999] 2 Cr App R 335, the Court of Appeal ordered a retrial and spoke, surely correctly, of a requirement that the accused should know of the risk of compulsion *to commit offences* (although it is submitted that the precise offence envisaged to be committed, except as it bears on the level of threat anticipated, should not of itself be important). However, this decision was commented on restrictively in *Heath* (1999) *The Times*, 15 October 1999, where it seemed to be enough for the Court of Appeal that the accused knew that violence is used in the drugs world to enforce debts. There seemed to be no requirement in *Heath* of knowledge that the violence would be used to compel the accused *to commit an offence or offences* (although on the facts it would have been easy to find such awareness once the accused returned for further drugs after the initial demand and threat was made) and in that respect *Heath* seems unduly broad.

Necessity

A3.27   It has long been unclear whether a general defence of necessity exists in English law. Very recently, however, the courts have started to recognise a defence of duress of circumstances that would achieve many of the same results. It is first necessary to examine the nature of, and the authorities concerning, necessity in order to appreciate the more recent cases on duress of circumstances.

Necessity differs from duress in that it is generally conceived of not as a concession to human frailty, i.e. as an excuse, but rather as a *justified* choice between two evils – the evil represented by committing the offence is outweighed by the greater evil which would ensue if the offence were not to be committed. This difference is often lost sight of because cases where necessity is raised also tend to be cases where there is an arguable case for excusing the accused.

The leading case of *Dudley* (1884) 14 QBD 273 is a good example which is complicated by the fact that it was a murder charge (and involved cannibalism). (As with duress, the courts are reluctant to widen the range of available defences in such cases.) The two accused had found themselves adrift in a small boat on the high seas with another man and the young cabin boy. They had had virtually no food or water for 20 days and had been reduced, for example, to drinking their own urine. Finally they killed and ate the cabin-boy who was likely anyway to have been the first to die and without this deed they would probably themselves not have survived the further four days which elapsed before they were rescued. In rejecting any defence of necessity on these facts, Lord Coleridge CJ constantly switched from the language of justification to that of excuse, but it was the notion of justification which appears to have been dominant. On that basis, the defence was probably doomed on the facts since the jury had found that there was no greater necessity for killing the boy than any of the others. The case has set the tone whereby English courts have generally rejected a defence of necessity even where the balance of evils points much more clearly in favour of committing the offence. Thus in *Buckoke* v *Greater London Council* [1971] Ch 655 (a civil case concerning the legality of instructions issued to drivers of fire-engines), Lord Denning MR (at p. 668) accepted as correct the proposition that a driver would have no defence if he proceeded through a red light to save a man in imminent peril in a blaze 200 yards away (regulations passed since would now permit this), '. . . nevertheless such a man should not be prosecuted. He should be congratulated.'

The defence is denied in law but the realities are recognised in practice by exercising discretion in prosecuting or sentencing. (The two accused in *Dudley* were sentenced to death but their sentences were later commuted to six months' imprisonment.)

So it seems that necessity as a justification is not recognised by English law (but see the dicta of Lord Brandon and Lord Goff in *F* v *West Berkshire Health Authority* [1990] 2 AC 1) as a general defence although *particular* offences may be defined in such a way as to make such a defence available. For example, the presence of the word 'unlawfully' in the OAPA 1861, s. 58, was used in *Bourne* [1939] 1 KB 687 to show that some abortions must be lawful and that that included one performed in good faith for the purpose of preserving the life of the mother (see now the Abortion Act 1967). Other statutes have more obvious specific defences such as that of lawful excuse in the Criminal Damage Act 1971 (see **B8.9**). The reluctance of the courts to recognise a *general* defence of necessity (as a justification) perhaps reflects sentiments similar to those expressed by Dickson J in the Supreme Court of Canada in *Perka* (1984) 13 DLR (4th) 1 where he said (at p. 14):

> It is still my opinion that, 'No system of positive law can recognise any principle which would entitle a person to violate the law because on his view the law conflicted with some higher social value' [*Morgentaler* v *The Queen* (1985) 53 DLR (3d) 161 at p. 209]. The Criminal Code has specified a number of identifiable situations in which an actor is justified in committing what would otherwise be a criminal offence. To go beyond that and hold that ostensibly illegal acts can be validated on the basis of their expediency, would import an undue subjectivity into the criminal law. It would invite the courts to second-guess the legislature and to assess the relative merits of social policies underlying criminal prohibitions.

Similar considerations influenced the Law Commission in once recommending (Law Com. No. 83 – but see now Law Com. No. 218, para. 35.7) that any general defence of necessity that might exist should be abolished. This proposal would have presented the apparent anomaly that a man who committed an offence in response to threats would have the defence of duress whereas if the pressure were created by some natural emergency or surrounding circumstances, no defence would be available. As will be seen in **A3.28**, the courts (and indeed the Law Commission — see Law Com. No. 218, para. 35.1) are now addressing this anomaly by recognising, as an excuse rather than as a justification, the defence of duress of circumstances which, again in the words of Dickson J in *Perka* is:

> much less open to criticism. It rests on a realistic assessment of human weakness, recognising that a liberal and humane criminal law cannot hold people to the strict obedience of laws in emergency situations where normal human instincts, whether of self-preservation or of altruism, overwhelmingly impel disobedience. The objectivity of the criminal law is preserved; such acts are still wrongful, but in the circumstances they are excusable. Praise is indeed not bestowed, but pardon is, when one does a wrongful act under pressure.

Duress of Circumstances

The early authorities on the defence of duress of circumstances were a series of cases **A3.28** dealing with road traffic offences, but in *Pommell* [1995] 2 Cr App R 607 the Court of Appeal has confirmed that the defence applies to all crimes except murder, attempted murder and some forms of treason. The first case was *Willer* (1986) 83 Cr App R 225 where the accused drove his car on to the pavement and into (and back out of) a shopping precinct to escape from a gang of youths bent on attacking himself and his passengers. At his trial for reckless driving, the judge refused to put the defence of necessity to the jury, but the Court of Appeal thought that 'a very different defence', that of duress, should have been available. According to Watkins LJ (at p. 227 emphasis added) the question then would be:

whether or not upon the outward or the return journey, or both, the appellant was wholly driven *by force of circumstance* into doing what he did and did not drive the car otherwise than under that form of compulsion.

It should be noted that although there were, in a sense, threats to the accused in this case, it was not a case of duress *by threats* as traditionally understood since in such a case the accused commits in order to *comply* with the threatener's demands rather than merely to *escape* from the threats. On the distinction between the two types of duress, see *Cole* [1994] Crim LR 582.

Willer was followed and applied in *Conway* [1989] QB 290, another reckless driving case, in which the Court of Appeal quashed the conviction, saying (at p. 297) 'it is still not clear whether there is a general defence of necessity' and 'necessity can only be a defence to a charge of reckless driving where the facts establish "duress of circumstances"'. See also *DPP v Harris* [1995] 1 Cr App R 170 for discussion of whether 'necessity of circumstances' can be a defence to a charge of driving without due care and attention for a police driver going through a red light. In *Backshall* [1998] 1 WLR 1506 the Court of Appeal confirmed that the defence is indeed available on a charge of driving without due care, a conclusion consistent with that in *Pommell* that the defence is of general application.

In *Martin* [1989] 1 All ER 652, duress of circumstances was recognised as a potential defence to driving while disqualified. According to Simon Brown J, it could arise from 'objective dangers threatening the accused or others' but 'the defence is available only if, from an objective standpoint, the accused can be said to be acting reasonably and proportionately in order to avoid a threat of death or serious injury'. The questions for the jury would then be virtually identical to that in relation to duress by threats (see **A3.20** to **A3.23**):

> . . . first, was the accused, or may he have been, impelled to act as he did because as a result of what he reasonably believed to be the situation he had good cause to fear that otherwise death or serious physical injury would result; second, if so, would a sober person of reasonable firmness, sharing the characteristics of the accused, have responded to that situation by acting as the accused acted?

The reference to the sober person of reasonable firmness shows that, as with duress by threats, the crucial question is not so much whether the accused was justified as whether he can be excused on the grounds that a reasonable person would have felt impelled to act in the same way.

The circumstances impelling the accused to act must be external to himself, so that the suicidal thoughts of life sentence prisoners could not of themselves amount to relevant circumstances excusing the offence of prison breaking according to the Court of Appeal in *Rodger* [1998] 1 Cr App R 143. The suicidal thoughts were 'a purely subjective element' (cf. the discussion of the cases of *Bowen* [1997] 1 WLR 372, *Horne* [1994] Crim LR 584 and *Hegarty* [1994] Crim LR 353 at **A3.22**).

Duress of circumstances has also been allowed by the Divisional Court on a charge of driving with excess alcohol in *DPP v Bell* [1992] RTR 335, where the accused, because of his terror of his pursuers, ran back to his car and drove off some distance down the road. The fact he did not continue to drive all the way home supported the finding that he was driving because of his fear and not because of any prior intention to use his car to get home even if intoxicated. This contrasted with the earlier case of *DPP v Jones* [1990] RTR 33 where a similar defence failed because the accused drove the two miles home without even bothering to check whether he was still being pursued. *DPP v Davis* [1994] Crim LR 600 is to similar effect and reflects an increasingly restrictive attitude to both types of duress pending statutory clarification of the details of the defences, although the case of *Pommell* [1995] 2 Cr App R 607 seems quite generous on the facts and *Abdul-Hussain* [1999] Crim LR 570 shows that even with an offence as serious as hijacking an aircraft duress may be an issue that has to go to the jury.

The restrictive approach was again evident in *DPP* v *Rogers* [1998] Crim LR 202, where the Court of Appeal commented that it was 'an extremely rare and exceptional case in which the defence would be available'. Unfortunately, Brooke LJ cast doubt on the requirement that the accused's belief, concerning the factual dangers with which he is confronted, should be based on reasonable grounds (paradoxically thereby seeming to widen the scope of the defence). Making an honest but unreasonable belief as to the facts sufficient (whilst maintaining a requirement of reasonableness in the response to those facts) might well be an improvement on the current law, but it is merely what the Law Commission has recommended should become the law and is inconsistent with previous Court of Appeal and House of Lords authority, as is pointed out in the commentary to the case at [1998] Crim LR 204–5. Until Parliament acts on the Law Commission recommendations or the previous authorities are overruled in the House of Lords, it is submitted (with some regret) that the defence still requires the accused's belief in the facts to be a reasonable one, a formulation again utilised by the Court of Appeal in *Cairns* [1999] 2 Cr App R 137.

Marital Coercion

At common law there was a rebuttable presumption that a wife who committed an **A3.29** offence (except murder or treason) in the presence of her husband did so under coercion and that she should be acquitted. The presumption was abolished by the CJA 1925, s. 47, which nevertheless went on to provide that:

> on a charge against a wife for any offence other than treason or murder it shall be a good defence to prove that the offence was committed in the presence of, and under the coercion of, the husband.

Clearly this section imposes a legal burden of proof on the wife, but it has not been clear what exactly constitutes coercion and in what sense it differs from duress. Coercion is presumably wider than duress since otherwise the defence is otiose, the wife having to prove duress *plus* the actual presence of her husband. It seems that it is wider in that there is no need for threats of death or serious injury, it being sufficient that the wife acted because of the dominating influence of her husband, her will being 'overborne by the wishes of her husband' so that 'she was forced unwillingly to participate' (see *Shortland* [1996] 1 Cr App R 116, following *Richman* [1982] Crim LR 507). The defence may be thought to be either an anachronism or a defence that, on the grounds of sexual equality, ought to be extended to husbands acting under the dominating influence of their wives. The Law Commission has recommended its abolition (Law Com. No. 83 and Law Com. No. 218, para. 32.6).

Self-Defence, Prevention of Crime, and Related Defences Generally

These defences are generally regarded as matters of justification rather than excuse. It **A3.30** is perhaps stretching matters a little to say that they are general defences since it seems that they are only available as defences to crimes committed by the use of force (see *Renouf* [1986] 1 WLR 522, where reckless driving was regarded as involving force where the only relevant evidence of reckless driving was the 'forcing' of another car off the road). Nevertheless, they are undoubtedly available to a wide range of offences. Where there is evidence 'which if accepted could raise a prima facie case of self-defence, this should be left to the jury even if the accused has not formally relied upon self-defence' (*DPP (Jamaica)* v *Bailey* [1995] 1 Cr App R 257). Where self-defence is not available because the offence charged does not involve the use of force, duress of circumstances may equally be available (see *Symonds* [1998] Crim LR 280).

Self-defence, defence of property and defence of another (sometimes referred to collectively as 'private defence') are still governed by the common law whereas the law on prevention of crime is now contained in the Criminal Law Act 1967, s. 3(1), which provides that:

> A person may use such force as is reasonable in the circumstances in the prevention of crime, or in effecting or assisting in the lawful arrest of offenders or suspected offenders or of persons unlawfully at large.

The criterion of 'such force as is reasonable in the circumstances' differs slightly from traditional formulations of the common-law rule for self-defence which usually also include some reference to necessity. See, for example, per Lord Lane CJ in *Williams* [1987] 3 All ER 411 at p. 414: 'the exercise of any necessary and reasonable force to protect himself'.

Some of the restrictive rules that applied at common law could be attributed to this reference to necessity but the modern trend seems to be to adopt a more flexible approach (as with the former so-called duty to retreat which, as will be seen, has now been abandoned). Given the fact that in most cases where the accused is acting in self-defence he will also be acting to prevent a crime being committed by his aggressor, it would seem sensible for the tests for self-defence and prevention of crime to be identical. Even though the courts do not always formulate the test for self-defence in the exact words used in the Criminal Law Act 1967, s. 3, for prevention of crime, there is no evidence from any of the cases that any such differences are matters of substance. Indeed in *Beckford* v *The Queen* [1988] AC 130, Lord Griffiths said (at p. 145) that: 'the test to be applied for self-defence is that a person may use such force as is reasonable in the circumstances as he honestly believes them to be in the defence of himself or another'. Whilst his lordship was primarily concerned with the question of mistaken belief in this case, his dictum supports the view that the rules governing the use of force in self-defence and prevention of crime are now identical (see also *Clegg* [1995] 1 AC 482). If this is correct, the law can be formulated quite simply and neatly along the following lines:

A person may use such force as is reasonable in the circumstances for the purposes of:

(a)   self-defence or
(b)   defence of another or
(c)   defence of property or
(d)   prevention of crime or
(e)   lawful arrest.

Although this formulation makes no express mention of any requirement that the use of force should be necessary (neither does the Criminal Law Act 1967, s. 3), it should be remembered that if the use of force is clearly unnecessary (e.g., because the initial aggressor has started to retreat – see *Priestnall* v *Cornish* [1979] Crim LR 310) it will not be 'reasonable in the circumstances' to use force.

A3.31   ***Self-Defence and Pre-emptive Strikes***   A person can use force to ward off an anticipated attack provided that it is anticipated as 'imminent' (*Chisam* (1963) 47 Cr App R 130). In *Beckford* v *The Queen* [1988] AC 130, Lord Griffiths said (at p. 144) 'a man about to be attacked does not have to wait for his assailant to strike the first blow or fire the first shot; circumstances may justify a pre-emptive strike'. However, if a threat of force may be expected to deter the attacker, it may be difficult to convince the jury that it was reasonable to use actual force (cf. *Cousins* [1982] QB 526).

A3.32   ***Scope of Defence of Another***   Given the overlap already referred to between, e.g., self-defence and prevention of crime, the precise boundaries of the individual defences are not always clear. Thus it is unclear whether defence of another is restricted to defence of a relative (and if so, how close) or extends to anyone with a sufficient nexus with the defender (*Devlin* v *Armstrong* [1971] NI 13) or to anyone at all. In *Duffy* [1967] 1 QB 63 the Court of Appeal found it unnecessary to decide whether defence of another extended to defence of a sister since what was done could be justified on the alternative basis of prevention of crime. The only case where this might not be so would be where the defender knows that the attacker is, for example, insane, so that it cannot be said that he is acting 'in the prevention of crime'. In such a case one would need to determine whether the person being attacked has a sufficient nexus with the defender to be within the scope of defence of another. In order to prevent anomalies, the better view is surely that no such nexus should be required and that one can act in defence of any other person (as recommended by the Criminal Law Revision Committee (14th Report)) provided, as always, that the use of force is reasonable in the circumstances.

Scope of Defence of Property　As with defence of another, it is unclear to what extent　**A3.33** defending property of other persons is a justification for committing a crime, but the arguments in favour of having no restrictions are the same. In relation to defence of one's own home, it should be noted that the statement approved in *Hussey* (1924) 18 Cr App R 160 that: 'In defence of a man's house, the owner or his family may kill a trespasser who would forcibly dispossess him of it' is of debatable authority today. It is difficult to imagine circumstances today where it would be reasonable to kill such a trespasser (unless he was also offering very serious personal violence). Forceful resistance would no doubt be in order (which might unintentionally cause death) but deliberate killing would be hard to justify given the availability of legal remedies against unlawful eviction.

No Duty to Retreat per se　The statement approved in *Hussey* (1924) 18 Cr App R　**A3.34** 160 and quoted in **A3.33** went on to say of the defender that '. . . in defending his home he need not retreat, as in other cases of self-defence, for that would be giving up his house to his adversary'. There is no longer any duty to retreat in any category of private defence. The duty was first watered down in *Julien* [1969] 1 WLR 839 where it was said (at p. 843) that 'what is necessary is that he should demonstrate by his actions that he does not want to fight'. Even this was subsequently held, in *Bird* [1985] 1 WLR 816, to be too restrictive. It is not 'necessary' to demonstrate by one's actions an unwillingness to fight. That is merely one way of negativing any suggestion that the defendant was the attacker or was acting out of motives of retaliation or revenge rather than self-defence, but it is by no means the only method of doing that. The denial of the duty to retreat underlines the shift away from formulating the defence as being the *necessary* use of force towards the use of force which is reasonable in the circumstances. If it is *possible* to retreat then the use of force is in one sense unnecessary but the real question is whether the accused acted reasonably in using force rather than retreating. As Edmund Davies LJ said in *McInnes* [1971] 1 WLR 1600 at p. 1607: 'We prefer the view expressed by the Full Court of [South] Australia [in *Howe* [1958] SASR 95] that a failure to retreat is only an *element* in the consideration upon which the reasonableness of an accused's conduct is to be judged'. Similarly, there is no hard and fast rule that a person who initiates a confrontation cannot rely on self-defence (*Balogun* [1999] All ER (D) 916, unreported in printed form).

The Degree of Force Permitted　The degree of force used by an accused will not be　**A3.35** regarded as reasonable unless the accused believed that it was necessary to use that degree of force – it is unreasonable to use force that one knows to be unnecessary. However, necessity is not enough – fatal force may be the only way of stopping a starving man trying to steal a loaf of bread but that does not make killing in such circumstances justified: it is not reasonable in the circumstances.

The traditional view was that if the accused misjudges the degree of force permissible and uses excessive force, he is deprived of the defence. Although this may appear harsh on an accused who has genuinely tried to use only a reasonable degree of force but who has in fact overreacted, the courts apply the rule in a manner which takes account of the motives of the accused and which is no longer wholly objective. Thus in *Palmer* v *The Queen* [1971] AC 814, Lord Morris of Borth-y-Gest said (at p. 832):

> . . . it will be recognised that a person defending himself cannot weigh to a nicety the exact measure of his necessary defensive action. If a jury thought that in a moment of unexpected anguish a person attacked had only done what he honestly and instinctively thought was necessary that would be most potent evidence that only reasonable defensive action had been taken. A jury will be told that the defence of self-defence, where the evidence makes its raising possible, will only fail if the prosecution show beyond doubt that what the accused did was not by way of self-defence.

This approach was described by Ormrod LJ in *Shannon* (1980) 71 Cr App R 192 at p. 194 as:

> a bridge between what is sometimes referred to as 'the objective test', that is what is reasonable judged from the viewpoint of an outsider looking at a situation quite dispassionately, and 'the subjective test', that is the viewpoint of the accused himself with the intellectual capabilities of which he may in fact be possessed and with all the emotional strains and stresses to which at the moment he may be subjected.

The Court of Appeal in this case quashed the conviction because the judge had ignored the subjective aspect of the question and put the question to the jury purely as: 'Did the appellant use more force than was necessary in the circumstances?' whereas the real question, according to Ormrod LJ (at p. 197), was:

> Was this stabbing within the conception of necessary self-defence judged by the standards of common sense, bearing in mind the position of the appellant at the moment of the stabbing, or was it a case of angry retaliation or pure aggression on his part?

It would seem that the reasonableness of the degree of force used is coming close to being treated as merely evidence of whether the accused was genuinely motivated by self-defence or whether he was in fact acting with some other illegitimate motive, excessive force being evidence that self-defence was not the accused's real purpose. In *Whyte* [1987] 3 All ER 416, the facts were said not to warrant a reference to the subjective aspect of the test as the accused had used an already open knife. However, in *Scarlett* [1993] 4 All ER 629, the failure of the trial judge to mention the subjective perspective caused the conviction to be quashed. Indeed the Court of Appeal in this case came very close to rendering the test a wholly subjective one by saying that provided the accused 'believed that the circumstances called for the degree of force used, he was not to be convicted even if his belief was unreasonable'. A restrictive interpretation of *Scarlett* was taken in *Owino* [1996] 2 Cr App R 128, but this was technically *obiter* as it was a case where the conviction was upheld on the grounds that the trial judge, in saying that the prosecution must prove that the accused did not believe that he was using reasonable force, went further in the defence's favour than the law required. The Court of Appeal took the view that it was certainly not incumbent on the judge to go further and state that the test of what force was reasonable was subjective. The move back towards the objective test has been further underlined by the Court of Appeal in *DPP* v *Armstrong-Braun* [1999] Crim LR 417. The circumstances of this case however seem to be a long way from the 'moment of unexpected anguish' envisaged in *Palmer*. Even under Art. 2 of the European Convention on Human Rights (which permits deadly force only where 'absolutely necessary'), some allowance appears to be made for 'heat of the moment' reactions (see *Andronicou* v *Cyprus* (1998) 25 EHRR 491).

Where the charge is murder, there is no rule whereby, if the defence fails because of the use of excessive force, it can have the effect of reducing the conviction to manslaughter (*McInnes* [1971] 1 WLR 1600, confirmed in *Clegg* [1995] 1 AC 482). Such a rule was applied in Australia for some years (see *Howe* (1958) 100 CLR 448) but even there has been abrogated (*Zecevic* v *DPP (Victoria)* (1987) 162 CLR 645). If excessive force were to be treated *purely* as an evidential factor in determining whether the accused intended to act in self-defence, there would be little or no scope for such a rule anyway but it should be noted that the Criminal Law Revision Committee (14th Report, para. 288) were in favour of the adoption of the Australian approach and this was embodied in the Draft Criminal Code Bill, cl. 59 (Law Com. No. 177). As things stand, however, the defence either succeeds, in which case the accused is acquitted, or it fails, in which case the accused will be convicted of murder.

Mistakes of Fact and Self-Defence

An accused who mistakenly believes he is being attacked may still be able to rely on the **A3.36** defence of self-defence. Even where the main defence is that the accused was *actually* under attack, the judge may be under a duty to direct the jury on the defence of mistake if there is evidence capable of supporting such a defence (*Oatridge* (1991) 94 Cr App R 367).

Traditionally, the accused's belief had to be a reasonable one but the Court of Appeal relaxed this requirement in *Williams* [1987] 3 All ER 411, by analogy with the House of Lords decision in *DPP* v *Morgan* [1976] AC 182. The Criminal Law Revision Committee's recommendation that a person may use such force as is reasonable in the circumstances *as he believes them to be* was adopted by Lord Lane CJ as representing the law. This approach was approved and followed by the Privy Council in *Beckford* v *The Queen* [1988] AC 130, where the appeal was allowed because the trial judge had directed the jury that a reasonable belief was required. Under Art. 2 of the European Convention on Human Rights, a more demanding standard of honest belief 'for good reasons' may be required — certainly as far as trained law enforcement officers are concerned (see *Andronicou* v *Cyprus* (1998) 25 EHRR 491).

The more subjective approach to mistake does not apply where the accused's mistake was due to voluntary intoxication (*O'Grady* [1987] QB 995). Although the actual conviction in this case was for manslaughter (a basic intent offence), the Court of Appeal seemed clear in the view that an intoxicated mistake could not be relied upon even in relation to a crime of specific intent such as murder. Lord Lane CJ said (at p. 999):

> We do not consider that any distinction should be drawn on this aspect of the matter between offences involving what is called specific intent, such as murder, and offences of so-called basic intent, such as manslaughter. . . . the question of mistake can and ought to be considered separately from the question of intent.

To deny the relevance of intoxication even to a specific intent crime is very difficult to reconcile with *DPP* v *Majewski* [1977] AC 443. The last part of the above quotation from Lord Lane's judgment contrasts sharply with his lordship's own approach in *Williams*, where mistakes of fact were admitted even if unreasonable precisely because they can be said to negative the intent to act unlawfully. *O'Grady* has been criticised insofar as it applies to crimes of specific intent, but it was followed in *O'Connor* [1991] Crim LR 135 although in that case the conviction was reduced to manslaughter on the separate ground that the intoxication might have prevented the formation of the specific intention to cause grievous bodily harm.

Unknown Circumstances Justifying Force in Self-Defence etc.

The converse of mistaken belief in the need for self-defence is the use of force in **A3.37** circumstances where, unknown to the accused, the facts would in fact justify the use of force. The case of *Dadson* (1850) 2 Den CC 35 has long been thought to hold that no defence is available in these circumstances. Dadson shot and wounded a fleeing thief, but this degree of force was only permissible, even at that time, in the prevention of crime if the offence being committed amounted to a felony. The particular form of theft involved was only a felony if the thief had two previous convictions for the offence. Although this condition was in fact satisfied in this case, Dadson was unaware of this fact when he shot. His conviction was upheld. Although this case may be taken to lay down the general principle, it is modified in relation to force used to effect an arrest by the PACE 1984, s. 24. It may be argued that since, under s. 24, an arrest of a person is lawful if *in fact* he is, e.g., 'in the act of committing an arrestable offence' (s. 24(4)(a)), the use of force in such circumstances is also lawful under the Criminal Law Act 1967, s. 3. This argument appears to be compelling, though it would apply only to force used in effecting arrest, not self-defence or prevention of crime. However, s. 3 itself permits 'such force as is reasonable in the circumstances'. If the circumstances include the accused's state of mind (cf. *Williams* [1987] 3 All ER 411) it could be said that it is not *reasonable* to use force where the accused lacks any knowledge of the lawfulness of the arrest. Since an arrest can be effected without any force at all being used, the fact that the arrest itself is lawful under the PACE 1984 does not automatically validate the use of force, the reasonableness of which is a distinct question.

Infancy

A3.38   Prior to the commencement of the CDA 1998, s. 34 (30 September 1998), children fell into one of three age groups for the purposes of criminal responsibility. Once a child has reached the age of 14, no special defence based on his or her age was or is available. Children aged under 10 were (and still are) irrebuttably presumed to be incapable of criminal responsibility (*doli incapax*) by virtue of the CYPA 1933, s. 50, but in relation to children aged 10, 11, 12 or 13 there was formerly a rebuttable presumption of *doli incapax* which could be rebutted if the prosecution proved that the child had 'mischievous discretion', i.e. knew that what he or she did was 'seriously' wrong, not just naughty or mischievous (*JM* v *Runeckles* (1984) 79 Cr App R 255). In *C (A Minor)* v *DPP* [1996] AC 1 the Divisional Court had boldly decided that the rebuttable presumption no longer formed part of English law since it had become outdated in the changed conditions of society; this decision had however been promptly reversed in the House of Lords (also [1996] AC 1), where it was held that such a change could only be made by statute. Section 34 of the CDA 1998 now effects that change by declaring that the 'rebuttable presumption of criminal law that a child aged 10 or over is incapable of committing an offence is hereby abolished'. It is only children under 10 therefore who are now specifically exempted from the criminal law on account of their age, the irrebuttable presumption in their case being unaffected, thus producing a clear line with responsibility commencing at the relatively young age of 10.

As far as children between 10 and 14 are concerned, the CDA 1998 would appear to leave them to be treated as equally responsible as adults since the *via media* of reversing rather than abolishing the presumption, which would have expressly permitted the defence to prove that the child did not understand that what he or she had done was seriously wrong, was argued for in Parliament but not accepted by the Government. The brief wording of s. 34 only expressly abolishes the rebuttable presumption in favour of the child, it does not expressly preclude the child from positively proving that he or she was incapable of committing an offence but, in view of the legislative history of s. 34, it would be a brave court that would interpret the section effectively to have merely reversed the burden of proof.

However, in the light of the very young age of responsibility now created, the courts may well be receptive to exculpatory arguments on behalf of young children in appropriate cases. The age of the accused, whether over or under 14, is clearly a factor to be taken into account in assessing the reasonableness of the accused's conduct under the defences of provocation (see *DPP* v *Camplin* [1978] AC 705 at **B1.21**), duress (*Bowen*

[1997] 1 WLR 372 at **A3.22**) and arguably self-defence (see **A3.35**). In crimes requiring subjective recklessness and *a fortiori* intention, the age of the accused may also be a relevant factor in assessing whether the accused did in fact foresee what might seem to be (to an adult) the obvious consequences of his actions or whether the accused was aware of the relevant circumstances (e.g., lack of consent in sexual cases). Such considerations were perhaps less acute under the old law since children who lacked an understanding of the likely consequences or full circumstances of their actions were likely to argue first that the prosecution had not discharged the burden of rebutting the presumption of *doli incapax* but, in the absence of the rebuttable presumption, arguments based on lack of *mens rea* may need to be pressed into service more often. Similarly, if a child can be shown by the defence not to be of normal development for his age (proving normal development was previously a common means for the prosecution to reverse the presumption of *doli incapax*), this could arguably be brought within the phrase 'retarded development of mind' in the Homicide Act 1957, s. 2, and thus open up the possibility of diminished responsibility on a murder charge. Arguments such as these will turn on the precise *mens rea* to be proved for the individual offence or the terms of a particular defence and will clearly not be available in relation to crimes governed by *Caldwell* recklessness such as criminal damage, in the light of the decision of the Divisional Court in *Elliot* v *C* [1983] 1 WLR 939 (see **A2.6**) that the age of the accused is not a relevant factor in assessing the obviousness of the risk.

SECTION A4: STRICT LIABILITY AND VICARIOUS LIABILITY

STRICT LIABILITY GENERALLY

A4.1   Some offences do not require proof of *mens rea* in respect of one or more elements of *actus reus*. In respect of these elements, the offence is one of strict liability. Most such offences are statutory but some common-law offences, such as public nuisance (*Stephens* (1866) LR 1 QB 702), criminal libel and blasphemous libel (*Lemon* [1979] AC 617), are offences of strict liability, at least in part.

Strict liability in statutory offences usually arises under regulatory legislation, but there are examples which are not of this genre. One such is *Prince* (1875) LR 2 CCR 154 where, in respect of the offence of taking an unmarried girl under 16 out of the possession of her parent (now contained in Sexual Offences Act 1956, s. 20, see **B3.15** to **B3.19**), strict liability was held to apply in relation to the girl's age. Another is *Bishop* (1880) 5 QBD 259 where it was held that the accused might be convicted of receiving two or more lunatics into an unlicensed house, although the accused honestly and reasonably believed that the persons whom she received were not lunatics. If there is a common thread uniting cases of this sort, it is perhaps that strict liability is most likely to be applied where, from the acts performed, it would be difficult if not impossible for the court to infer that the accused acted with fault, be it intention or recklessness, advertently or, today, inadvertently (*Bradish* [1990] 1 QB 981).

Many of the enactments apply to particular trades, for example, the sale of food and drink, or medicines, or if of general application apply to few activities. Many presuppose the carrying on of a business where continuous attention to standards is important. Many of the enactments are new and represent an adaptation to an impersonal market economy. It is sometimes said that these are not 'real' crimes, but mere civil matters, prohibited under a penalty (*Sherras* v *De Rutzen* [1895] 1 QB 918). Such statements give no more than a rough indication of the sorts of activities to which strict liability is most likely to be applied. They do not serve as precise principles of demarcation, nor do they, as such, serve as tests for the imposition of strict liability.

TESTS FOR STRICT LIABILITY

A4.2   As Lord Reid noted in *Sweet* v *Parsley* [1970] AC 132, in cases where Parliament has not made it clear that strict liability is intended, the courts, in construing criminal legislation, start from the presumption that Parliament did not intend to punish a blameless individual and therefore that words importing *mens rea* must be read into the statute. Lord Reid also recognised, however, that strict liability is often applied to a class of quasi-criminal offences, those referred to by Wright J in *Sherras* v *De Rutzen* [1895] 1 QB 918 as acts which are not criminal in the real sense but which are prohibited, by a penalty, in the public interest. The question is, within this broad context, whether the danger to be guarded against is of such importance that strict liability is required (*Kirkland* v *Robinson* (1987) 151 JP 377). Within this broad category, courts must also inquire whether the imposition of strict liability would promote the objects of the legislation (*Lim Chin Aik* v *The Queen* [1963] AC 160). Whether a statutory offence falls within the category to which strict liability applies involves both a question of characterisation for courts, which are influenced by the sorts of generalisation noted above, and an inquiry into the likely efficacy of imposing strict liability. Thus, in

Gammon (Hong Kong) Ltd v *A-G of Hong Kong* [1985] AC 1, a case involving breaches of building regulations, the Privy Council stressed that the matter was one of social concern, and that strict liability could be shown to promote the objects of the statute and, in particular, greater vigilance in the carrying out of works. In *Wings Ltd* v *Ellis* [1985] AC 272, the House of Lords relied upon the proposition that a requirement of full *mens rea* would stultify enforcement of the legislation. A recent case of this sort is *Torbay District Council, ex parte Singh (Satnam)* (1999) *The Times*, 5 July 1999, where it was pointed out, in upholding strict liability, that a requirement that the prosecution prove that a small trader knew of the existence of a registered trade mark would stultify enforcement of the offence under the Trade Marks Act 1994, s. 92(1) of exposing goods for sale which bear a mark corresponding to a registered trade mark.

Other criteria include the question of penalty. The circumstance that the likely penalty is pecuniary favours the imposition of strict liability (*Customs and Excise Commissioners, ex parte Claus* (1987) 86 Cr App R 189). This applies even though the maximum fine may be heavy (*Gammon (Hong Kong) Ltd* v *A-G of Hong Kong*). This is not an absolute principle: some offences bearing a heavy pecuniary penalty and even in theory a penalty of imprisonment attract strict liability (*Pharmaceutical Society of Great Britain* v *Storkwain Ltd* [1986] 1 WLR 903; *Blake* [1997] 1 WLR 1167). Allied to this is the mode of trial: where, as in *Ex parte Claus*, the offence is triable only summarily, strict liability will be more readily inferred than if the offence is triable either way or on indictment. Modern cases tend to stress the need for *mens rea* in serious offences (*Sheppard* [1981] AC 394). This is, however, a point of emphasis only and courts give considerable weight to the nature of the social danger involved, the context of the legislation as regulating a particular trade or business and, above all, the exigencies of successful enforcement.

The use of words importing *mens rea* elsewhere in a statute regulating a trade, profession or industry is often treated as an indication that an offence which uses no such words is intended to convey strict liability (*Pharmaceutical Society of Great Britain* v *Storkwain Ltd*; *Gammon (Hong Kong) Ltd* v *A-G of Hong Kong*; *Kirkland* v *Robinson* (1987) 151 JP 377). In this context, it should be noted that whilst some words such as 'intentionally' always convey *mens rea*, other words, referable to knowledge rather than to purpose, sometimes do not do so. In general, such words as 'permitting' convey the need to prove *mens rea* (*Sweet* v *Parsley* [1970] AC 132; *Reynolds* v *G.H. Austin & Sons Ltd* [1951] 2 KB 135). On some occasions they have been held not to do so (*Browning* v *J.W.H. Watson (Rochester) Ltd* [1953] 1 WLR 1172). The context in which a word is used may be significant and so too may be the use of the passive voice (*Cheshire County Council* v *Clegg* (1991) 89 LGR 600; *Cheshire County Council Trading Standards Dept, ex parte Alan Helliwell & Sons (Bolton) Ltd* [1991] Crim LR 210). 'Knowingly permitting' imports a requirement of *mens rea* into the statute (*Westminster City Council* v *Croyalgrange Ltd* [1986] 1 WLR 674; *Thomas* (1976) 63 Cr App R 65).

The position of the word 'knowingly' in a statutory offence may be crucial. In *Wings Ltd* v *Ellis* the offence of making a statement known to be false in a material particular contrary to the Trade Descriptions Act 1968, s. 14(1)(a) (see **B6.125**), was construed to require that the accused knew that the particular statement complained of was false, but not that the accused knowingly made a false statement. Wings Ltd was therefore convicted for unknowingly making a statement containing matter which was, to its knowledge, false. Apart from questions of effective enforcement, noted above, the House of Lords also relied on the literal and natural meaning of the words used and this of course was affected by their order in the subsection.

'Causing' poses difficulties both in respect of the necessary mental element and in respect of what may be regarded as having caused a prohibited phenomenon. 'Causing' is neutral as to whether *mens rea* is required (*Alphacell Ltd* v *Woodward* [1972] AC 824).

As to what may be regarded as 'causing', regard must be had to the terms in which the statutory duty is imposed. In connection with the offence of causing polluting matter to enter controlled waters contrary to the Water Resources Act 1991, s. 15(1), the prosecution need not prove that the defendant person or entity did an affirmative act which caused the pollution. A person who, for example, stores polluting material on land which he occupies in a state where it may readily be released by a third party may be convicted of causing pollution where the act of such a party releases the substance provided that the act is not unnatural, extraordinary or unusual. If the event was a matter of ordinary occurrence it will not negative the causal effect of the defendant's acts even if it was not foreseeable that it could happen to that particular defendant or take that particular form (*Environment Agency* v *Empress Car Co. (Abertillery) Ltd* [1999] 2 AC 22).

Various meanings have been given to the term 'possession'. In *Warner* v *Metropolitan Police Commissioner* [1969] 2 AC 256, in connection with drug offences, the House of Lords held that a person may be said to 'possess' prohibited drugs if he knows that he possesses drugs, even though he is unaware of their precise characteristics. Yet in *Ashwell* (1885) 16 QBD 190 it was held that a man could not be said to 'possess' a sovereign when he thought he had received a shilling. In *Warner* v *Metropolitan Police Commissioner*, since rendered otiose by the Misuse of Drugs Act 1971, Lords Pearce, Wilberforce and Reid (dissenting) sought a construction which would require the prosecution to prove some element of knowledge of the thing in possession, but not so particular a degree of knowledge as to stultify enforcement of the legislation. The decision has been construed as meaning that one possesses an article of a dangerous sort provided that one has possession of a packet containing it (*Boyesen* [1982] AC 768). In the context of offensive weapons this means that it is not a defence for an accused person to show on a balance of probabilities that he did not know and could not be expected to know that the article was an offensive weapon (*Bradish* [1990] 1 QB 981; *Waller* [1991] Crim LR 381; *Steele* [1993] Crim LR 298).

Where a due-diligence or no-negligence defence applies to a prohibition apparently cast in absolute terms, the courts are likely to hold that the offence is one of strict liability (*Wings Ltd* v *Ellis*; *Kirkland* v *Robinson*; *Bradish*; *Cheshire County Council* v *Clegg*). Courts will ask whether strict liability promotes the purposes of the enactment and whether it is unduly burdensome to expose the accused to liability, leaving it to him to establish such a defence (*Davidson* v *Strong* (1997) *The Times*, 20 March 1997). The absence of such a defence does not, however, necessarily imply that *mens rea* is to be presumed (*Alphacell Ltd* v *Woodward*).

APPLICABILITY OF GENERAL DEFENCES TO OFFENCES OF STRICT LIABILITY

A4.3   Liability is in general strict, not absolute. General defences to crime therefore, with rare exceptions, apply to such offences.

In general, strict-liability offences involve proof that the accused voluntarily acted or omitted to act. This requirement may be displaced by the words of the statute. In *Larsonneur* (1933) 24 Cr App R 74, a French citizen who was deported from the Irish Free State to the United Kingdom against her will was convicted of being an alien 'found within' the United Kingdom in breach of immigration legislation. In *Winzar* v *Chief Constable of Kent* (1983) *The Times*, 28 March 1983, the accused was convicted of being found drunk on a highway even though his presence there was attributable to the police who took him from a hospital corridor to the highway and then drove him to the police station. It is, with respect, surprising that a requirement of voluntariness was not implied in the legislation in the above cases. Dicta in *Alphacell Ltd* v *Woodward* [1972] AC 824 at pp. 834, 845, 846 and 847 imply that this may properly be done.

It does, however, seem both from *Alphacell Ltd* v *Woodward* and from *Southern Water Authority* v *Pegrum* [1989] Crim LR 442 that act of God will amount to a defence. So too will automatism, provided that the degree of impairment is virtually absolute (*A-G's Ref (No. 2) of 1992*) [1994] QB 91). Insanity which does not amount to automatism is, however, a defence only to a crime requiring *mens rea* (*DPP* v *H* [1997] 1 WLR 1406. In *Burns* v *Bidder* [1967] 2 QB 227, the accused was acquitted of failing to accord precedence to a pedestrian when his brakes failed suddenly, but absence of fault is not a fully articulated defence in English law. Duress and duress of circumstances should apply to negate offences of strict liability since they represent independent circumstances of excuse. Mistake on the other hand, will not serve as a defence to the extent that its effect is to negate *mens rea* which, *ex hypothesi*, is not applicable here (*DPP* v *Morgan* [1976] AC 182 per Lord Hailsham of St Marylebone). Even a mistake on reasonable grounds would not serve as a defence.

Many, perhaps most, statutory offences to which strict liability applies contain special defences, though this is not always the case. In pollution legislation particularly, because of the supposed ease of fabricating defences, no possibility is afforded to the accused to show that a matter arose without his fault.

Statutory defences generally require that the infraction be the fault of another person and that the accused has exercised due diligence to prevent the infraction. There is considerable variation in the way in which such defences are drafted but the principles noted above generally apply. Variations in drafting can cause problems of interpretation, in particular in determining whether a corporation may defend itself by showing that it installed a system to prevent infraction or whether the relevant state of mind is that of an employee performing a function such as sale (*Tesco Stores Ltd* v *Brent London Borough Council* [1993] 1 WLR 1037). The leading modern examples of such defences are the Weights and Measures Act 1985, the Food Safety Act 1990 and the Trade Descriptions Act 1968. The onus of proving the defence lies on the accused (*Tesco Supermarkets Ltd* v *Nattrass* [1972] AC 153). The presence of such a defence is taken as an indication that liability is strict subject to making the defence out (*Bradish* [1990] 1 QB 981; *Waller* [1991] Crim LR 381).

VICARIOUS LIABILITY

Certain offences are treated as imposing a regime of vicarious liability. Most **A4.4** vicarious-liability offences are in fact also offences of strict liability but there is no perfect coincidence between the two, partly because some few *mens rea* offences attract vicarious liability and partly because some strict-liability offences may be cast in terms which are not apt to impose vicarious liability.

The general rule is that criminal liability is personal, not vicarious (*Huggins* (1730) 2 Ld Raym 1574). A person may, of course, implicate himself in the crime of another through doctrines of complicity.

Care must be taken to distinguish between those situations which attract liability through doctrines of vicarious liability and those where the duty upon the employer is personal. In relation, for example, to an employer's duty to conduct his enterprise in such a way as to ensure the safety of his employee or not to expose to risk a person not employed by him (under the Health and Safety at Work etc. Act 1974, ss. 2(1) and 3(1)) the duty is personal to the employer. It follows that the employer's duty is defined, in the latter case, by reference to the undertaking and not the precise relationship between the entrepreneur and the employee or independent contractor as the case may be (*Associated Octel Co. Ltd* [1996] 1 WLR 1543). The effect, in the context of the Health and Safety At Work etc. Act 1974, s. 3, for example, is that if a person who is not an employee of the employer is exposed to health risks by the conduct of the employer's undertaking, the employer will be liable unless he can prove on the balance of probability that all that was reasonably practicable had been done by him or on his behalf to ensure against exposure to such risks. The question of what is reasonably practicable is one for the jury. The fact that an employee in carrying out work did so carelessly or omitted to take a necessary precaution does not of itself preclude the employer from establishing that he had done everything practicable to avoid risk. The employer need not be held liable even for an isolated act of negligence by the employee performing the work. The employer's duty to take all reasonably practicable steps includes ensuring that employees have the requisite level of skills and instruction, have had safe systems of work laid down for them, have been subjected to adequate supervision, and have been provided with safe plant and equipment (*Nelson Group Services (Maintenance) Ltd* [1999] 1 WLR 1526; *Gateway Foodmarkets Ltd* [1997] 3 All ER 78).

The accepted formula, which applies both to *mens rea* offences and to those of strict liability is the following dictum of Atkin J in *Mousell Brothers Ltd* v *London and North-Western Railway Co.* [1917] 2 KB 836 at p. 845):

> . . . while prima facie a principal is not to be made criminally responsible for the acts of his servants, yet the legislature may prohibit an act or enforce a duty in such words as to make the prohibition or the duty absolute; in which case the principal is liable if the act is in fact done by his servants. To ascertain whether a particular Act of Parliament has that effect or not regard must be had to the object of the statute, the words used, the nature of the duty laid down, the person upon whom it is imposed, the person by whom it would in ordinary circumstances be performed, and the person upon whom the penalty is imposed.

It is important to note that the duty is imposed in respect of a servant. Thus a licensee who is the joint proprietor of a shop cannot be held liable for the act of supplying liquor to a minor where the act of supply is that of an unlicensed co-proprietor because the latter is not her servant and, rather than serving her, is serving on her behalf (*Boucher* v *DPP* (1996) 160 JP 650).

While a duty imposed by a statute may appear to be imposed upon any person, an act such as sale or supply will often be done by an employee on behalf of an employer. Where a duty is imposed in terms of taking all steps to guard against harm which it is reasonable for an employer to take, the duty, and the liability in respect of any failure, will be personal (*Seaboard Offshore Ltd* v *Secretary of State for Transport* [1994] 1 WLR 541; *Associated Octel Co. Ltd* [1996] 1 WLR 1543; *Westminster City Council* v *Blenheim Leisure (Restaurants) Ltd* (1999) 163 JP 401).

The test of whether a duty to regulate should be imposed on an employer is essentially whether the employer is best placed through discipline, training, supervision and maintenance standards to ensure compliance with legislation (*National Rivers Authority* v *Alfred McAlpine Homes (East) Ltd* [1994] 4 All ER 286). The nexus is essentially that of control, which will usually be satisfied by a course-of-employment formula but which sometimes, and in particular in relation to *mens rea* offences, is satisfied by the notion of delegation.

In respect of *mens rea* offences, vicarious liability may be imposed because the statutory command is addressed to a particular person such as a licensee, whilst the business may be carried on for periods of time by his delegate. In such a case, unless vicarious liability can be imposed, premises may well fall outside the ambit of a regulatory statute simply because the licensee, if not present, commits no offence, and his delegate is not made personally responsible under the statute.

The licensee cases ought to be considered anomalous. This was certainly the view of Lord Reid both in *Vane* v *Yiannopoullos* [1965] AC 486 and in *Tesco Supermarkets Ltd* v

Nattrass [1972] AC 153 at p. 169. In the former case his lordship concluded that the existing ambit of vicarious liability ought to be upheld, but certainly not extended. According to Lords Reid and Evershed, the licensee could not be held vicariously liable when, he being on the premises, a *mens rea* offence was committed by his employee without his knowledge. Lords Donovan and Morris took a different view. The Court of Appeal in *Winson* [1969] 1 QB 371 concluded that such liability applied only where the statute was specifically addressed to the licensee and he had entirely delegated the management of his premises. Rather surprisingly, the Divisional Court in *Howker* v *Robinson* [1973] QB 178 concluded that vicarious liability for a *mens rea* offence was possible under the Licensing Act 1964, s. 169, which provides that the holder of a licence or his servant shall not knowingly sell intoxicating liquor to a person under 18. The effect of the altered wording was said not to exclude vicarious liability, but simply to add the servant as an additional target fit for prosecution. This is, of course, to ignore the entire basis in policy for vicarious responsibility in the licensee cases, though it can be brought within Atkin J's formulation in *Mousell Brothers Ltd* v *London and North-Western Railway Co.* [1917] 2 KB 836. It is submitted that *Howker* v *Robinson* ought to be regarded as wrongly decided; it is inconsistent with the tenor of their lordships' speeches in *Vane* v *Yiannopoullos* and it cannot be reconciled with *Winson*.

The requisite nexus is sometimes course of employment and sometimes delegation. These formulations are properly regarded as overlapping, not conflicting. Delegation is, however, the appropriate test under the licensee cases for obvious reasons; the courts devised liability in such cases in order to ensure that an absentee licensee would not be able to insulate himself from liability in respect of the premises.

So far as the employment relationship is concerned, the liability of the employer extends, it is clear, to acts which he did not authorise and, indeed, forbade (e.g., *Canadian Pacific Railway Co.* v *Lockhart* [1942] AC 591; *Ward* v *W.H. Smith & Son* [1913] 3 KB 154; *Griffiths* v *Studebakers Ltd* [1924] 1 KB 102; *Anderton* v *Rodgers* [1981] Crim LR 404; *Piggly Wiggly Canadian Ltd* [1933] 4 DLR 491; cf. *Anglo-American Oil Co. Ltd* v *Manning* [1908] 1 KB 536).

Vicarious liability is usually but not always imposed in the case of strict liability offences. *Seaboard Offshore Ltd* v *Secretary of State for Transport* [1994] 1 WLR 541 illustrates the exceptional case. Section 100 of the Merchant Shipping Act 1995 imposes a duty on the owner of a ship to ensure that it is operated in a safe manner. The offence of failing to do so is a strict but not vicarious liability offence first because a wide range of omissions could constitute a failure to take reasonable steps, and secondly, because a wide range of persons might make an omission. This, together with other contextual evidence, led the court to conclude that the duty and the liability are personal to the owner.

Criminal liability is not to be imposed in every instance where an employer would be vicariously liable civilly. *Portsea Island Mutual Co-operative Society Ltd* v *Leyland* [1978] ICR 1195 illustrates the point. A milk roundsman hired a boy to assist him. The act was done by the roundsman for his employer's business and with intent to benefit the employer, but it was done contrary to the employer's instructions. The company did not employ the boy; it could only be held liable where it employed him either directly or through a properly authorised agent. The fact that a company might, on similar facts, be civilly liable to a lad who suffered injuries while accompanying the roundsman was irrelevant (*Rose* v *Plenty* [1976] 1 WLR 141). There is earlier authority to the same effect (*Star Cinema (Shepherd's Bush) Ltd* v *Baker* (1921) 126 LT 506).

The formulae of employment and delegation overlap (*Barker* v *Levinson* [1951] 1 KB 342). However, it has been said that delegation does not mean the same thing as employment. Thus Wrottesley LJ, in a civil action (*Gallagher* v *Dorman, Long and Co. Ltd* [1947] 2 All ER 38), stated (at p. 41): 'An employer does not, merely by employing his servant to work a crane, delegate to him the statutory duty of seeing that the crane is not overloaded'.

Delegation, surely, involves a bestowal of managerial functions. It is thus the right word to describe the licensee cases, but hardly the ordinary sale cases. The courts in the general run of cases have continued to use the notion of course of employment to describe the requisite nexus (e.g., *Winter* v *Hinckley and District Industrial Co-operative Society Ltd* [1959] 1 WLR 182; *Tesco Supermarkets Ltd* v *Nattrass* [1972] AC 153; *Winson* [1969] 1 QB 371; *Anderton* v *Rodgers* [1981] Crim LR 404). Furthermore, there is no reason to suppose that delegation and course of employment are the only nexuses available. A partner may be held liable for the acts of his fellow partner (*Clode* v *Barnes* [1974] 1 WLR 544). A licensee will be liable for an unlawful act of sale by his staff even though they are not his employees but those of the owner, since the licensee is alone responsible for ensuring adherence to licensing legislation (*Goodfellow* v *Johnson* [1966] 1 QB 83). The ultimate question ought to be whether the proprietor has control over the actions of the other, and there seems no reason to insist that such control be contractual in character.

The courts have interpreted the legislation in this sense, and they have not allowed themselves to be seduced by a nexus argument which would defeat enforcement of the legislation. Nor have they excused an employer whose servant intended to benefit himself. It has been suggested, it is submitted wrongly, that there ought not to be liability where the servant, in committing the infraction, acted in his own interests and not in the purported interests of the master (*Navarro* v *Moregrand Ltd* [1951] 2 TLR 674 at p. 681 per Denning LJ). The suggestion is clearly inconsistent with *ICR Haulage Ltd* [1944] KB 551 which, although on corporate liability, is permeated with vicarious liability concepts. Vicarious liability exists in order to ensure that employers and others to whom it applies will police their businesses. The question of whom the offender intended to benefit is irrelevant viewed from that perspective. This is even clearer when the positive defences discussed above are considered; whether a defence is available or not depends upon, and only upon, whether the particular steps outlined in the legislation are followed. The question of intent to benefit does not appear in the schemes.

SECTION A5: PARTIES TO OFFENCES

LIABILITY OF PRINCIPALS AND ACCESSORIES GENERALLY

Responsibility for a criminal offence may be incurred either as a principal offender or as **A5.1** an accessory. Liability as an accessory applies to all offences (including statutory ones) unless it is expressly excluded by statute (*Jefferson* [1994] 1 All ER 270). A principal offender is the actual perpetrator of the offence, the person whose individual conduct satisfied the definition of the particular offence in question, whilst an accessory is one who aids, abets, counsels or procures the commission of the offence. For indictable offences, the Accessories and Abettors Act 1861, s. 8, provides that such an accessory 'shall be liable to be tried, indicted, and punished as a principal offender'. The MCA 1980, s. 44(1), is of similar effect as far as summary offences are concerned.

The distinction between an accessory and a principal offender is thus in many cases of little importance. Indeed a person charged as a principal may be convicted even though the real case against him was that he was an accessory, although it is preferable that the particulars of the offence be drawn 'in such a way as to disclose with greater clarity the real nature of the case that the accused has to answer' (per Lord Hailsham of St Marylebone in *DPP for Northern Ireland* v *Maxwell* [1978] 1 WLR 1350 at p. 1357D). If this is not done and if the prosecution do not make plain in presenting the case to the jury that joint enterprise is one of the alleged bases of liability, it may be a misdirection for the judge to introduce it in summing up (see *Taylor* [1998] Crim LR 582).

The phrase 'aid, abet, counsel and procure' may be, and generally is, used as a whole even though the accused's conduct may be properly described only by one of the four constituent words (*Re Smith* (1858) 3 H & N 227). Partly for this reason, the precise meaning of each constituent word has not been authoritatively determined, but 'aid' and 'abet' are generally considered to cover, respectively, assistance and encouragement given at the time of the offence, whereas 'counsel' and 'procure' are more apt to describe advice and assistance given at an earlier stage. Individual words are occasionally the subject of judicial discussion, as in *A-G's Ref (No. 1 of 1975)* [1975] QB 773, where the accused had laced the drinks of a friend with alcohol knowing that he would soon be driving home. As a result the friend drove with an excess quantity of alcohol in his body and was convicted as principal. The accused was then charged with aiding, abetting, counselling and procuring that offence but the trial judge took the view that, since there was not the usual shared intention or meeting of minds between the principal and alleged accessory, the accused could not be said to be an accessory. The Court of Appeal took the view that – whilst that might be right for aiding, abetting and counselling – procuring did not require any sort of conspiracy or common purpose and therefore the accused could properly have been convicted. The court said (at p. 779F): 'To procure means to produce by endeavour'. And at p. 780B: 'You cannot procure an offence unless there is a causal link between what you do and the commission of the offence'.

By way of contrast, counselling does not require any causal link (see *Calhaem* [1985] QB 808), and as long as the advice or encouragement of the accessory comes to the attention of the principal offender, it does not matter that he would have committed the offence anyway, even if not encouraged by the accessory (see *A-G* v *Able* [1984] QB 795 at p. 812). The result of all the above seems to be that common purpose and causal link are alternative requirements for liability as an accessory. Where, as in the typical case, the accessory cannot be said to have caused the offence, a common purpose will be required (though not necessarily a prearranged plan, see *Mohan* v *The Queen* [1967] 2

AC 187 where the two accused, without prior arrangement, were jointly intent on inflicting grievous bodily harm). Where there is no such common purpose, procuring becomes the crucial concept and the establishment of a causal link is required.

Before leaving the question of terminology it is worth pointing out that much of the ancient nomenclature in this area has relatively recently become redundant. Before the abolition (by the Criminal Law Act 1967, s. 1) of the distinction between felonies and misdemeanours, it was necessary to distinguish, as far as felonies were concerned, between principals in the first degree (now simply principals), principals in the second degree (roughly corresponding to aiders and abettors, now simply accessories) and accessories before the fact (roughly counsellors and procurers, again now simply accessories). Such distinctions are today otiose and any last remaining significance was, it is hoped, removed by the House of Lords in *Howe* [1987] AC 147, disapproving the Court of Appeal decision in *Richards* [1974] QB 776, which had seemed to perpetuate these archaic distinctions for certain purposes (see **A5.6**). The only distinction which now needs to be made is between a principal offender and an accessory.

In the light of the Accessories and Abettors Act 1861, s. 8, even this distinction will not often be of significance, the accessory's liability being identical with that of the principal. The availability of duress on a murder charge used to depend on whether the accused was in truth a principal or merely an accessory, but that distinction also was removed by the House of Lords decision in *Howe* [1987] AC 417. The most important distinction which remains between the liability of any accessory and that of a principal lies in the mental element required for an accessory (the other main difference relates solely to the doctrine of vicarious responsibility – see *Ferguson* v *Weaving* [1951] 1 KB 814).

THE MENTAL ELEMENT FOR ACCESSORIES

A5.2   The *actus reus* of an accessory involves two concepts: (a) aiding, abetting, counselling and procuring (b) an offence. The *mens rea* can also be expected to relate to these two concepts. The mental element for an accessory is generally considerably narrower and more demanding than that required for the principal offender in that intention or knowledge rather than recklessness or negligence or any other less culpable state of mind is required. The classic statement of the *mens rea* for an accessory is that of Lord Goddard CJ in *Johnson* v *Youden* [1950] 1 KB 544 at p. 546 that: 'Before a person can be convicted of aiding and abetting the commission of an offence, he must at least know the essential matters which constitute that offence'.

The Requirement of Knowledge

A5.3   This applies even where the principal offence is one of strict liability as in *Callow* v *Tillstone* (1900) 83 LT 411 where a vet negligently certified meat as sound and fit for sale, and a butcher was convicted of the strict-liability offence of exposing for sale meat which was unsound and unfit for human consumption. The vet's conviction for aiding and abetting was quashed since negligence was not sufficient for this form of liability even though the butcher's liability as principal offender was not dependent on proof of any degree of fault whatsoever.

The importance of this principle can be further seen in *Smith* v *Mellors* (1987) 84 Cr App R 279 where Mellors and Soar were both charged under the Road Traffic Act 1972, s. 6(1)(a) (driving with excess alcohol, now Road Traffic Act 1988, s. 5(1)(a)). The prosecution were unable to prove who was the driver and who was the passenger. Nor could they prove that each defendant was aware that the other was over the limit. The magistrates ruled that there was no case to answer. The Divisional Court affirmed their decision whilst pointing out that, in the light of the MCA 1980, s. 44 (see **A5.1**), it was not always necessary to determine who was the accessory and who the principal.

However, it was necessary where, as in this case, there was a material difference between the liability of the principal and the accessory. The Road Traffic Act 1972, s. 6(1)(a), created an offence of strict liability for the principal but the accessory could be liable only if he knew the facts. Only if both knew that the other was over the limit could both be convicted without proof of who was driving. Presumably, if it is proved that one party had the requisite knowledge, he, though not the other, could be convicted since in that case he would be liable whether or not he was the driver. Croom-Johnson LJ stated (at p. 284), 'It might be that an aider and abettor would be an aider and abettor if he was simply reckless as to whether or not the driver had the requisite amount of alcohol in his blood'. Whilst this statement might find some suppport in the earlier case of *Carter* v *Richardson* [1974] RTR 314, the better view seems to be that recklessness is not sufficient. In *Giorgianni* v *The Queen* (1985) 156 CLR 473, the Australian High Court, having discussed at length the English authorities, held that recklessness was not sufficient for an accessory to an offence of causing death by culpable (reckless) driving. The owner of a lorry involved in a fatal crash was not guilty as accessory unless he knew or was wilfully blind to the brake defect in the lorry. In *Blakely* v *DPP* [1991] Crim LR 763, which was more concerned with intention to aid (see **A5.4**) than with knowledge of circumstances, the Divisional Court was reluctant to countenance recklessness as sufficient *mens rea* for complicity, at least in relation to counselling or procuring. It also said that insofar as recklessness might have a role to play in complicity, it would be subjective rather than *Caldwell* recklessness which would be relevant. See also *Roberts* [1997] RTR 462.

Intention to Aid

Lord Goddard's statement in *Johnson* v *Youden* [1950] 1 KB 544 (see **A5.2**) that the **A5.4** accessory 'must at least know the essential matters which constitute the offence' is not, and does not purport to be, a complete definition of the mental element because *inter alia*, it relates only to part (b) of the *actus reus* as set out in **A5.2**, i.e. the principal offence. It says nothing about the intention to 'aid, abet, counsel and procure'. As Devlin J put it in *National Coal Board* v *Gamble* [1959] 1 QB 11 (at p. 20):

> . . . aiding and abetting is a crime that requires proof of *mens rea*, that is to say, of intention to aid as well as of knowledge of the circumstances.

However, as Devlin J went on to point out, at p. 23, intention to aid does not require that the accused's purpose or motive must be that the principal offence should be committed:

> If one man deliberately sells to another a gun to be used for murdering a third, he may be indifferent about whether the third man lives or dies and interested only in the cash profit to be made out of the sale, but he can still be an aider and abettor. To hold otherwise would be to negative the rule that *mens rea* is a matter of intent only and does not depend on desire or motive.

Thus in *DPP for Northern Ireland* v *Lynch* [1975] AC 653 the accused's alleged opposition to the principal offence did not preclude a finding that he intended to aid. It is submitted that the question of intention to aid is now governed by the decisions in *Moloney* [1985] AC 905 and *Hancock* [1986] AC 455 discussed in **A2.2** and that where the accused does not actually desire to assist or encourage the commission of an offence, but knows that his actions are extremely likely or virtually certain to have that result, then the question is one for the jury to infer whether or not he has the requisite intent. If *Woollin* [1999] AC 82 were to be applied beyond the context of the meaning of intention for murder, only foresight of a virtual certainty would entitle the jury to find intention. *Gillick* v *West Norfolk and Wisbech Area Health Authority* [1986] AC 112 is an example of a type of case where the uncertainties of the precise meaning of intention effectively confer a perhaps welcome discretion on whether to impose responsibility.

That case concerned, *inter alia*, the question of whether a doctor giving contraceptive advice or treatment to a girl under the age of 16 could be liable as accessory to a subsequent offence of unlawful sexual intercourse committed by the girl's sexual partner. The House of Lords held that generally this would not be the case (the action was a civil one for a declaration) since the doctor would lack the necessary intention (even though he realised that his actions would facilitate such intercourse). One rationale for the decision would be that a jury would not infer intention in such circumstances if they thought that the doctor was acting in what he considered to be the girl's best interests.

Similar reasoning could be applied to a troublesome group of cases involving the supply of articles for use in crime which the recipient already has some sort of civil right to receive. The general position seems to be that this is not aiding and abetting (see, for example, *Lomas* (1913) 9 Cr App R 220 concerning the return of a jemmy to its owner) because the alleged accessory does not intend to aid the offence but rather merely to comply with his supposed civil-law duties. Critics of this general position rightly point out that it can hardly apply to a person returning a revolver to its owner knowing that he is then going to use it to carry out a murder. But here a jury probably would infer intention to aid from the accused's knowledge of the effects of his action, and the flexibility of the notion of intention enables an appropriate solution to be found to situations for which it is difficult to formulate precise rules in advance.

It is particularly important to stress the need for an intention to aid where the accused may not personally appreciate the natural and probable consequences of his action as in *Clarkson* [1971] 1 WLR 1402 where there was 'at least the possibility that a drunken man with his self-discipline loosened by drink . . . might not intend that his presence should offer encouragement to rapers; . . . he might not realise that he was giving encouragement' (at p. 1406). The reference to intoxication underlines the fact that complicity normally requires intention rather than recklessness (*Blakely* v *DPP* [1991] Crim LR 763) and that, for the purposes of the *Majewski* rule (*DPP* v *Majewski* [1977] AC 443: see **A3.10**), complicity can be regarded as requiring specific intent.

The Scope of the Joint Venture

A5.5   The test of 'knowledge of the essential matters constituting the offence' needs some further elucidation since a strict requirement of knowledge is inappropriate or unworkable in certain situations, notably where the offence is to be committed in the future or by a person of whose precise intentions the accused cannot be certain in advance. A relatively simple case is where the accused knows that, for example, a burglary is to be committed and provides equipment to be used in the burglary. He is guilty even if he does not know of the precise time, date or place of the proposed offence. Provided that he knows the type of crime, i.e. that it will be a burglary, it does not matter that he does not know the details of the particular crime in the sense of a particular date at particular premises (see *Bainbridge* [1960] 1 QB 129 esp. at pp. 133–4). In some cases an accused may be convicted even though he is not sure whether the offence is to be burglary or some other type of crime such as handling or robbery. In *Maxwell* [1978] 1 WLR 1363, the accused had driven his car so as to guide a following car out to a remote public house into which a bomb was thrown from the second car. He argued that since he did not know exactly what type of offence was to be committed (it was obviously a terrorist attack of some sort but it was unclear whether it was to be a bombing or a shooting) he did not know the essential matters constituting the offences with which he was charged (under the Explosive Substances Act 1883). Nevertheless, Lowry CJ upheld the conviction of the accused in relation to the bombing saying (at pp. 1374–5):

> His guilt springs from the fact that he contemplates the commission of one (or more) of a number of crimes by the principal and he intentionally lends his assistance in order that such a crime will be committed. . . .

The relevant crime must be within the contemplation of the accomplice and only exceptionally would evidence be found to support the allegation that the accomplice had given the principal a completely blank cheque.

[He] must . . . have contemplated the bombing of the Crosskeys Inn as not the only possibility but one of the most obvious possibilities among the jobs which the principals were likely to be undertaking.

Thus the test in this sort of case is not so much knowledge (the accused cannot 'know' things in advance) as contemplation. It is capable of application in a wide range of situations including:

that of two persons who agree to rob a bank on the understanding, either express or implied from conduct (such as the carrying of a loaded gun by one person with the knowledge of the other), that violence *may* be resorted to. The accomplice knows, not that the principal *will* shoot the cashier, but that he may do so; and if the principal does shoot him, the accomplice will be guilty of murder. (Ibid.)

This type of case has been the subject of a long line of authorities including the leading case of *Anderson* [1966] 2 QB 110, where the principal (Anderson) armed himself with a knife unknown to the accessory (Morris) who was nevertheless convicted of manslaughter (Anderson was convicted of murder). A five-judge Court of Criminal Appeal quashed Morris's conviction, Lord Parker CJ (at p. 118F–G) accepting as correct the following principles put forward on his behalf:

where two persons embark on a joint enterprise, each is liable for the acts done in pursuance of that joint enterprise, . . . that includes liability for unusual consequences if they arise from the execution of the agreed joint enterprise.

Thus Morris would have been responsible for the sort of attack he had contemplated (i.e. one without a knife and without an intent to kill) and if death had happened to result he would have been liable for manslaughter: 'but . . . if one of the adventurers goes beyond what has been tacitly agreed as part of the common enterprise, his co-adventurer is not liable for the consequences of that unauthorised act' (p. 118G). See *Mahmood* [1995] RTR 48 for a recent case where the accessory contemplated reckless driving but not the unusual form of reckless driving concerned, and was therefore not responsible for that driving or the consequences.

The above principles have been further developed and applied in a series of decisions commencing with that of the Privy Council in *Chan Wing-Siu* v *The Queen* [1985] AC 168. In *Chan Wing-Siu*, the three appellants had broken into the victim's flat armed with knives to commit robbery. In the course of the robbery, the victim was stabbed to death. The trial judge directed the jury: 'You may convict . . . of murder if you come to the conclusion . . . that the accused contemplated that either of his companions might use a knife to cause serious bodily injury on any one or more of the occupants of that flat'. The Privy Council upheld the convictions for murder based upon this direction.

Although some difficulties were initially experienced (see *Barr* (1986) 88 Cr App R 362) in reconciling this approach (based on contemplation) with the test for intention laid down in *Moloney* [1985] AC 905 and *Hancock* [1986] AC 455 (see **A2.2**), the Court of Appeal in *Slack* [1989] QB 775 subsequently adopted a similar, though logically distinguishable, approach. The court (at p. 781E–G) made the important point that the *mens rea* required of the accessory is not necessarily the same as that of the principal offender:

A [the principal offender] must be proved to have intended to kill or do serious harm at the time he killed. B [the accessory] may not be present at the killing; he may be a distance away, for example, waiting in the get-away car; he may be in another part of the house; he may not know that A has killed; he may have hoped, and probably did hope, that A would not kill or do serious injury. If however as part of their joint plan it was understood between them expressly or tacitly that if necessary one of them would kill or do serious harm as part of their common enterprise, then B is guilty of murder.

In *Hyde* [1991] 1 QB 134 it was made clear that foresight of what the principal may do is sufficient *mens rea* for the accessory even if there is not actual agreement between them. This point was confirmed by the Privy Council in *Hui Chi-ming* [1992] 1 AC 34 and has now been put beyond all doubt by the House of Lords in *Powell* [1997] 3 WLR 959 where the certified question was as follows (at p. 967):

> Is it sufficient to found a conviction for murder for a secondary party to a killing to have realised that the primary party might kill with intent to do so or must the secondary party have held such an intention himself?

The House answered, in accordance with previous Court of Appeal authorities, that the first part of the certified question was sufficient, i.e. the secondary party need only realise that the primary party might kill with intent to do so (or with intent to cause grievous bodily harm) and the secondary party did not himself need to have the intention to kill; hence *Moloney* and *Hancock* did not apply directly to the *mens rea* of the secondary party.

However, the House of Lords at the same time also dealt with the case of *English* [1997] 3 WLR 959 where the first certified question (at p. 968) was identical with that in *Powell* except that it expressly included an intention to cause grievous bodily harm. The House of Lords answer to the certified question, including this alternative state of mind on the part of the principal, was made subject to the qualification that, where the particular weapon used by the principal or the manner of its use was different from that contemplated by the accessory, that may take the killing outside the scope of the joint venture and the accessory may not be liable. In *English*, the accessory contemplated the intentional infliction of grievous bodily harm with a wooden post but the principal used a knife which on the evidence the jury could have found was unknown and unforeseen by the accessory. The trial judge had told the jury in effect that they could convict, even if the accessory did not know of the knife, if he nevertheless knew that there was a substantial risk that the principal might cause grievous bodily harm with the wooden post. This part of the direction was held to be defective and the conviction for murder quashed.

Lord Hutton was anxious to make it clear, however, that a difference in the weapon used would not always exempt the accessory 'if the weapon used by the principal is different to, but as dangerous as, the weapon which the secondary party contemplated he might use . . . for example, if he foresaw that the primary party might use a gun to kill and the latter used a knife to kill, or vice versa' (at p. 981). This observation is clearly correct although it is submitted that one aspect of the reason is that in such a case, as formulated, the accessory contemplates an act done with intent to kill and that is precisely what the principal does, the difference in weapon being relatively immaterial. The more difficult case is where the accessory contemplates merely an act done with intent to cause grievous bodily harm where the type of weapon may be highly material in determining the type of grievous bodily harm contemplated and in particular its propensity to cause death, a phrase also utilised in *Uddin* [1999] QB 431. In such a case it is much more difficult to equate different types of weapons and in principle one should revert to the issue of whether the actual weapon used was within the range of contemplation of the accessory. A jury might more readily accept that a knife was within the range of contemplation of an accused who was primarily thinking of a gun than of an accused thinking primarily of a weapon such as a wooden post but at the end of the day it would be a question of fact for the jury. In *Uddin* a retrial was ordered so that the jury could focus on this question.

In *English*, the accessory was not proved to have contemplated an intention to kill as opposed to an intention to cause grievous bodily harm nor, more significantly, was he proved to have foreseen the weapon used by the principal and hence he did not contemplate the principal's act for which he therefore bore no responsibility. His conviction for murder was therefore quashed and he was not even liable for manslaughter. English did contemplate the relevant minimum degree of *mens rea*, an intention to cause grievous bodily harm, but not the act or type of weapon used. *English* was followed in *Greatrex* [1998] Crim LR 733, where the Court of Appeal stressed the need for serious alternative offences to be included in the indictment.

Difficult questions can arise where the difference between the two parties lies not so much in the act or weapon contemplated but more in the degree of *mens rea*, i.e. the accessory does not contemplate the degree of *mens rea* (e.g., intention to cause grievous bodily harm or to kill) with which the principal acts. The accessory is clearly not liable for the offence committed by the principal (e.g., murder), but does the accessory remain liable for the consequences of the principal's act by means of a lesser crime according to his own *mens rea* (e.g., manslaughter)? According to a line of authorities commencing with *Anderson* [1966] 2 QB 110 through *Lovesey* [1970] 1 QB 352, *Dunbar* [1988] Crim LR 693, *Wan* [1995] Crim LR 296 and *Perman* [1995] Crim LR 736 the answer appeared to be no. However another line of authorities (*Betty* (1963) 48 Cr App R 6, *Reid* (1975) 62 Cr App R 109 and most recently *Stewart* [1995] 3 All ER 159), seems to suggest that the answer may be yes. Aspects of the latter case are trenchantly and convincingly criticised by Sir John Smith at [1995] Crim LR 296 and [1995] Crim LR 422, but his conclusion that there is no room for reconciliation between the two approaches is debatable. As was concluded in *Stewart*, the fundamental question is whether what was done by the principal is within the scope of the joint venture contemplated by the accessory. The principal's *mens rea* will in some cases change the nature of his act and take it outside the joint venture just as much as if he had suddenly produced a weapon unforeseen by the accessory. However, in other cases, the fact that the principal does precisely the act contemplated by the accessory but with a more serious *mens rea* will not change the nature of the act nor take it outside the scope of the joint venture.

Suppose P and A agree that P will post a specific incendiary device to V, A contemplating only superficial injuries to V when he opens it but P foreseeing and hoping that the injuries will be serious or fatal. If V is killed as a result, P will clearly be guilty of murder, A is clearly not guilty of murder as an accessory but should be guilty of manslaughter because the act done by P is precisely what was envisaged. The fact that P happens also to have the *mens rea* of murder is irrelevant because it does not change the nature of the act that he does or the manner in which he does it. Suppose in contrast that P and A agree that P shall assault V with an iron bar, A contemplating that P will act only with intent to cause actual bodily harm as opposed to grievous bodily harm. If P uses the bar with intent to kill or cause grievous bodily harm, there must come a point where P's intent changes the nature of the assault on V and the manner in which he does it (e.g, in the number or severity of the blows) so as to take what he does outside the scope of the joint venture. *Stewart* seems to be a case where the Court of Appeal, perhaps somewhat harshly, took the view that that particular line had not been crossed, that the accessory knew that an iron bar might be used and that the actual manner of its use was not beyond the scope of the joint venture. The point was not specifically put to the jury, but it is submitted that the best approach would be to ask the jury to consider whether the principal's act (causing death) *and the manner of its doing* was within the contemplation of the accessory and thus within the scope of the joint venture (cf. the reference to 'the manner in which a particular weapon is used' at the end of Lord Hutton's speech in *English*). Depending on the answer to this question, the accessory may or may not be liable for the consequences of the act even though the principal's *mens rea* makes him liable for a more serious offence such as murder.

Lord Hutton in *English* agreed with the Privy Council in *Chan Wing-Siu* v *The Queen* that the realisation by the accessory of a fleeting risk which is then dismissed as altogether negligible is not sufficient, although the Court of Appeal in *Roberts* [1993] 1 All ER 583 said that to distinguish expressly between this and the continuing realisation of a real risk will, in most cases, be unnecessary, and would only serve to complicate directions and lead to confusion. Contemplation or foresight of a real or serious risk is clearly sufficient and it is immaterial whether the secondary party is present at the scene of the crime or lends assistance or encouragement in advance (*Rook* [1993] 1 WLR 1005).

Liability of Accessory where There Is No Principal

5.6　A person can be liable as an accessory even though the principal offender cannot be identified or has been acquitted in a previous trial (*Hui Chi-ming* [1992] 1 AC 34) or even earlier in the same trial (see *Hughes* (1860) Bell CC 242), although in this latter case such a result would only be justified where there was evidence admissible against the accessory but not against the alleged principal (see *Humphreys* [1965] 3 All ER 689). Where the same evidence is admissible against both it would normally be inconsistent for the same jury to acquit the principal and yet convict the accessory of a crime which it has already found has not been committed by the principal.

Nevertheless, in a number of cases the Court of Appeal has upheld convictions of accessories whilst recognising that the principal offender would have a valid defence. Thus in *Bourne* (1952) 36 Cr App R 125, a husband's conviction for aiding and abetting his wife to commit buggery with a dog was upheld even though it was recognised that the wife could not have been convicted as principal (she was not in fact charged) since she was acting under duress from her husband. In *Cogan* [1976] QB 217, Leak's terrified wife had intercourse with Cogan (who had allegedly been told by Leak that she would consent) because of her fear of her husband. Cogan's conviction for rape was quashed because the jury had been told that his alleged belief that Mrs Leak was consenting had to be reasonable whereas it was possible that his belief was genuinely held, but Leak's conviction as accessory was upheld. The Court of Appeal pointed out (at p. 223) that:

> . . . one fact is clear – the wife had been raped. Cogan had had sexual intercourse with her without her consent. The fact that Cogan was innocent of rape because he believed that she was consenting does not affect the position that she was raped.

The court then pointed out (at pp. 223–4) that Leak could have been guilty as a principal acting through an innocent agent:

> Had Leak been indicted as a principal offender, the case against him would have been clear beyond argument. Should he be allowed to go free because he was charged with 'being aider and abettor to the same offence'? If we are right in our opinion that the wife had been raped (and no one outside a court of law would say that she had not been), then the particulars of offence accurately stated what Leak had done, namely, he had procured Cogan to commit the offence.

There has been some debate over the precise principle involved in these cases but everyone agrees that the result is just. To say that the liability is really that of a principal acting through an innocent agent can cause problems where the accused lacks some characteristic essential for liability as a principal, for example, if in *Cogan* it had been a woman, rather than Mrs Leak's husband, who had terrorised her into submitting to intercourse. The definition of rape in the Sexual Offences Act 1956, s. 1, requires it to be committed by a man, whereas there is no problem in convicting a person as accessory to an offence which he or she cannot commit as principal (see *Ram* (1893) 17 Cox CC 609, woman as accessory to rape). Thus it is probably preferable to adopt the principle that an accessory can be liable provided that there is the *actus reus* of the principal offence even if the principal offender is entitled to be acquitted because of some defence personal to himself.

It may well be, however, that this principle is limited to cases where the accessory has procured the *actus reus* (i.e. has caused it to be committed as was the case in both *Bourne* and *Cogan*). This would also be consistent with the position stated above (see **A5.1**) that procuring does not need a common intention between the accessory and the principal whereas other forms of aiding and abetting generally do. If the principal lacks the *mens rea* of the offence there can hardly be a common intention that it should be committed, but this is not required for procuring.

The above two paragraphs were specifically approved by the Court of Appeal in *Millward* [1994] Crim LR 527 as correctly stating the law. The accessory in that case was convicted on the basis of procuring the offence of causing death by reckless driving even though the actual driver (his employee) did not know of the defect in the vehicle and was not therefore personally reckless. The case is not an easy one in which to apply the current principles because of the peculiar difficulties in defining the *actus reus* of (causing death by) reckless driving which was nevertheless, in the view of the Court of Appeal, to be found in 'the taking of the vehicle in the defective condition on to the road so as to cause the death of the little boy'; the accessory, 'being aware of the defects, . . . had procured the offence by the giving of instructions to . . . his employee'. *Millward* was approved in *Wheelhouse* [1994] Crim LR 756 and was followed in *DPP* v *K and B* [1997] 1 Cr App R 36, where two girls were convicted of procuring the rape of another teenage girl by an unknown boy even though the boy may not have had the *mens rea* of rape and in any event had to be assumed not to be responsible under the rebuttable presumption of *doli incapax* (abolished by the CDA 1998, s. 34). It would apparently have been different if the boy had been shown to be under the age of 10, although the logic behind this last conclusion is not particularly compelling.

Of course, if not even the *actus reus* is committed there can be no liability. The situation in *Millward* would now be governed by the offence of dangerous rather than reckless driving, as is illustrated by *Loukes* [1996] 1 Cr App R 444. There is room for debate over how the *actus reus* of the old offence of reckless driving should be defined, but under the new offence the test of whether a person is driving dangerously is satisfied if 'it would be obvious to a competent and careful driver that driving the vehicle in its current state would be dangerous' (Road Traffic Act 1988, s. 2A(2)). If it would not be so obvious *to the driver*, and the driver is acquitted on that ground (as in *Loukes*) then, according to the Court of Appeal in that case, there is not even the *actus reus* as no-one has driven the vehicle dangerously. Therefore, in accordance with *Thornton* v *Mitchell* [1940] 1 All ER 339, the person responsible for maintaining the vehicle and sending it out on the road cannot be liable even as an accessory, a result described by the Court of Appeal as an 'injustice'. The same result was nevertheless reached in *Roberts* [1997] Crim LR 209.

The situation in *Thornton* v *Mitchell*, in which a bus driver was acquitted of driving without due care and attention, was somewhat simpler and clearer. The driver had had to rely on signals from his conductor in reversing the bus. Because of the conductor's negligence, two pedestrians were injured, one of them fatally. The conductor's conviction for aiding and abetting had to be quashed because clearly there was no principal offence of driving without due care to which he could be accessory. The driver had driven *with* due care rather than without it, so there was not even the *actus reus* of that offence. On the other hand, there was the *actus reus* of homicide (the causing of the death of the pedestrian). It may be that the conductor could have been liable for manslaughter (as might the employer in *Millward*), if his negligence were sufficiently gross, though only on the basis that the conductor was the principal (whose own conduct caused the death) since liability as an accessory requires intention or knowledge rather than negligence or recklessness (see **A5.3**).

An analogous problem arises where there are two or more offences which share the same *actus reus*, for example, murder and manslaughter, or the offences under the OAPA

1861, ss. 18 and 20. If the principal offender commits the *actus reus* but with only the *mens rea* for the less serious of the two possible offences, can the accessory nonetheless be convicted of the more serious offence if he has sufficient *mens rea*? The Court of Appeal in *Richards* [1974] QB 776 appeared to make the answer depend on whether the accessory was present at the scene of the crime or not. However, this case almost certainly no longer represents the law following the House of Lords decision in *Howe* [1987] AC 417, where it was indicated that *Richards* should not be followed (see at pp. 436B and 457–8) and having regard to *Millward*, where it was immaterial that the procurer was not present. The issue cannot be regarded as finally settled as the question certified for the House in *Howe* was in the following terms:

> Can one who incites or procures by duress another to kill or to be a party to a killing be convicted of murder if that other is acquitted by reason of duress?

This differs from the *Richards* question in that (a) the alleged principal is not guilty of *any* crime and (b) his defence is duress rather than lack of *mens rea*. In fact the certified question in *Howe* really raises the same question as in *Bourne* (1952) 36 Cr App R 125 and the affirmative answer given by the House of Lords to the question can be regarded as confirmation of that decision. It would be extremely odd if an accessory could be convicted where the principal is acquitted altogether but could not be convicted if the principal happens to be guilty of some lesser offence. *Richards* can perhaps safely be regarded as no longer stating the law. However, just as with the principle following from *Bourne* and *Cogan*, it may be that the *mens rea* of the accessory can only be linked with the *actus reus* of the principal where the accessory can be said to have procured or caused the *actus reus*.

Such a limitation, however, would not apply to the Homicide Act 1957, s. 2(4), whereby 'The fact that one party to a killing is by virtue of this section [diminished responsibility] not liable to be convicted of murder shall not affect the question whether the killing amounted to murder in the case of any other party to it'. In other words an accessory with sufficient *mens rea* can be convicted of murder even though the principal offender is convicted only of manslaughter because of diminished responsibility.

Presence at the Scene of the Crime: Omissions

A5.7   Neither mere presence at the scene of a crime nor a failure to prevent an offence will generally give rise to liability. However, presence at the scene of a crime is *capable* of constituting encouragement (see *Jefferson* [1994] 1 All ER 270 for a recent example and contrast *Coney* (1882) 8 QBD 534 – spectators at illegal prize fight, conviction quashed since jury directed that presence was *conclusive* evidence of encouragement). If the accused is present in pursuance of a prior agreement with the principal, that will normally amount to aiding and abetting, but if the accused is only accidentally present then he must know that his presence is actually encouraging the principal(s) (see *Allan* [1965] 1 QB 130, in which it was held that a secret intention to join in if required was not of itself sufficient); there must be both actual encouragement and also awareness of that fact (see *Allan* and *Tate* [1993] Crim LR 538). *Wilcox* v *Jeffery* [1951] 1 All ER 464 was a case where there was ample evidence to draw the inference of intentional encouragement from the presence of a spectator at an illegal saxophone performance (by an American forbidden to take employment in this country). The defendant had not only paid for a ticket at the performance (thus his presence was not accidental) but had reported the arrival of the American at the airport in his magazine, *Jazz Illustrated*, and subsequently wrote a laudatory review of the concert.

Where the accused is present and has both the right and ability to control the principal offender, his failure to exercise that right of control may make him liable as an accomplice. Thus in *Rubie* v *Faulkner* [1940] 1 KB 571 a learner driver was convicted of driving without due care and attention in that he overtook on a bend, and the defendant who was supervising him was convicted of aiding and abetting him by failing to exercise his right of control. Similarly, in *Tuck v Robson* [1970] 1 WLR 741, a publican was held liable for aiding and abetting his customers to commit the offence of drinking after hours by failing to collect the customers' glasses or to eject them from the premises. See also *National Coal Board v Gamble* [1959] 1 QB 11, in which Slade J said: 'Mere passive acquiescence is sufficient only, I think, where the alleged aider and abettor has the power to control the offender *and is actually present when the offence is committed*' (emphasis added). Presence in this sort of case is arguably significant not only as evidence of encouragement but also as evidence that the accused has the knowledge that the offence is being committed and the opportunity to exercise control. In *J. F. Alford Transport Ltd* [1997] 2 Cr App R 326, the convictions of managers of a company for the offence of aiding and abetting the making of false tachograph records by the company's drivers were quashed because there was no evidence of knowledge in relation to any specific count. If such knowledge could have been proved, irrespective it was said of whether the accused was present when the offence was committed, the ability to control the action of the offender coupled with a decision to refrain from doing so would have been sufficient. Proof of encouragement and of knowledge of the facts may however be difficult to achieve where the accused is not present.

Withdrawal

There is often an interval between the act of the accessory and the completion of the **A5.8** offence by the principal offender. In some circumstances, a change of heart by the accessory coupled with steps to withdraw from participation in the offence can remove his responsibility for the completed offence (although he may remain liable for any completed offence of incitement or conspiracy). Precisely what is required for an effective withdrawal will vary from case to case. It may depend on how imminent the completed offence is at the time of the attempted withdrawal by the accomplice and also on the nature of assistance and encouragement already given by the accessory. Thus in *Becerra* (1975) 62 Cr App R 212, A1 gave A2 a knife to use if they were disturbed during the course of a burglary. When A1 heard the tenant coming he called to A2: 'There's a bloke coming. Let's go' and jumped out of a window and fled. A2, however, stabbed and killed the tenant. Both A1 and A2 were convicted of murder. A1's application for leave to appeal on the grounds that he should have been allowed the defence of withdrawal was refused since, according to Roskill LJ at p. 219 (emphasis added):

> if [he] wanted to withdraw *at that stage*, he would have to 'countermand', to use the word that is used in some of the cases or 'repent' to use another word so used, in some manner vastly different and vastly more effective than merely to say 'Come on, let's go' and go out through the window.

Similarly, leave to appeal against a conviction for murder was refused in *Baker* [1994] Crim LR 444, where the Court of Appeal was sceptical as to whether, even on D's version of events, he could be regarded as having effectively withdrawn from the joint enterprise. D inflicted three knife wounds, passed the knife to another, saying 'I'm not doing it', moved a few feet away and turned his back whilst others inflicted further wounds: the Court of Appeal considered that this constituted far from unequivocal notice that D was wholly disassociating himself from the entire enterprise. The words were quite capable of meaning no more than 'I will not myself strike any more blows'.

In *Becerra*, the court left open the question whether it was necessary to take all reasonable steps to prevent the commission of the crime which he had agreed the others should commit. As a minimum however, the accessory must communicate his intention to withdraw to the other parties; it is not sufficient merely to fail to turn up as arranged (*Rook* [1993] 1 WLR 1005). Such communication was found to be a sufficient withdrawal from a proposed burglary on the facts of *Whitefield* (1983) 79 Cr App R 36. The failure of the trial judge to put the defence of withdrawal to the jury was one of the grounds for the Court of Appeal quashing the conviction of Derek Bentley for murder, 45 years after he was hanged, following a reference by the Criminal Cases Review Commission (*Bentley* [1999] Crim LR 330).

In *Mitchell* (1999) 163 JP 75, the Court of Appeal drew a distinction between pre-planned and spontaneous violence. With the latter, the issue was not whether there had been communication of withdrawal but whether the original joint venture was still continuing at the time of the principal's act.

Victims Not Regarded as Accessories

A5.9 Where an offence is designed to protect a particular class of persons, a member of that class, i.e. a 'victim' of the offence, cannot be convicted as accessory even though the offence takes place with his or her voluntary assistance. The principle is most likely to arise in the context of sexual offences where the offence takes place despite the victim's consent. The classic illustration is *Tyrrell* [1894] 1 QB 710, in which it was held that a girl under 16 cannot be guilty of aiding and abetting an offence of unlawful carnal knowledge of her (now unlawful sexual intercourse under the Sexual Offences Act 1956, s. 6) since the offence was created for the protection of the girl. The principle can sometimes rebound so that it results in the acquittal of some other party who is not a victim, as in *Whitehouse* [1977] QB 868 where a father was acquitted of inciting his 15-year-old daughter to commit incest with him. The girl was regarded as within the class of persons the offence was designed to protect and if the girl herself could not be liable, even as an accessory, her father could not be liable for inciting her to do something which was not a crime. A special offence of incitement in these particular circumstances has since been created by the Criminal Law Act 1977, s. 54, but the general principle still remains. See *Pickford* [1995] QB 203 for a related problem.

VICARIOUS LIABILITY

A5.10 Other than where the accused has aided, abetted, counselled or procured the act of another, the general principle is that one cannot be held criminally responsible as a result of the act of another. Public nuisance and criminal libel were the only exceptions at common law. There are, however, two further exceptions to this principle in relation to statutory offences involving strict liability:

(a) where the words of the statute are apt to describe not only the physical perpetrator of an act but also some other person, typically his employer;
(b) where the statute casts some special duty on a person, typically a licensee of a public house, which he delegates to another (the delegation principle).

This aspect of vicarious liability is dealt with in **A4.4**.

CORPORATE LIABILITY

A5.11 An incorporated company is a legal person and can therefore be liable for strict-liability offences defined in such a way that the company satisfies the definition of the offence. Thus in *Alphacell Ltd* v *Woodward* [1972] AC 824 a company which owned a factory from which polluted matter entered a river had its conviction, for causing polluting matter to enter a stream contrary to the Rivers (Prevention of Pollution) Act 1951, upheld by the House of Lords. Similarly, in *Atkinson* v *Sir Alfred McAlpine & Son Ltd* (1974) 16 KIR 220, a company was held liable for failure to give written notice or provide protective clothing as required by the Asbestos Regulations 1969 (SI 1969 No. 690). Neither of these are cases of being held responsible for a particular act of an employee of the company but companies are also liable for acts done by individual employees to the same extent as are human employers (see **A4.4**), i.e. where the definition of the offence is equally capable of applying to the employer as well as to the employee. See *Green* v *Burnett* [1955] 1 QB 78 – employer (limited company) 'using' a vehicle through its employee.

The principles stated so far are only of any use in relation to offences that do not require proof of a state of mind. The personality of a company is a legal fiction and a company does not itself have a mind. However, a company can sometimes be guilty of an offence requiring a state of mind under a principle which identifies the acts and state of mind of a senior employee or officer of the company with the company itself. Under this principle a company can even be liable for a common-law offence, such as conspiracy to defraud, where the mental element is central to liability, as in *ICR Haulage Ltd* [1944] KB 551, where the agreement and intention of the managing director were regarded as those of the company. (There were ten other parties to the conspiracy in *ICR Haulage Ltd*, but a company cannot create a conspiracy with just a single director as at least two distinct minds are required for a conspiracy – see *McDonnell* [1966] 1 QB 233.) Precisely which employees or officers are identified with the company for these purposes is a matter of some debate. In the leading case of *Tesco Supermarkets Ltd* v *Nattrass* [1972] AC 153, a branch manager employed by the national chain of supermarkets was held not to be so identified. He was therefore another person so that the company could successfully rely on the defence under the Trade Descriptions Act 1968, s. 24(1). Contrast the result in *Tesco Stores Ltd* v *Brent London Borough Council* [1993] 1 WLR 1037, where the knowledge of, and information available to, a sales assistant was sufficient to prevent the company from being able to rely on the defence in the Video Recordings Act 1984, s. 11(2). Leaving such special defences aside, it seems that it will normally only be senior persons at or close to board level who will normally be identified with the company although in *DPP* v *Kent and Sussex Contractors Ltd* [1944] KB 146 the intention of the company's transport manager was treated as the company's intention. More typically, in *John Henshall (Quarries) Ltd* v *Harvey* [1965] 2 QB 233, a weighbridge operator was not identified with the company. In *National Coal Board* v *Gamble* [1959] 1 QB 11, the National Coal Board waived the point that their weighbridge operator was much too junior to be identified with the company but Slade J was dubious about the propriety of the court accepting jurisdiction on those terms.

However, hard and fast rules about which employees are identified cannot be laid down as, 'a board of directors can delegate part of their functions of management so as to make their delegate an embodiment of the company within the sphere of the delegation' (per Lord Reid in *Tesco Supermarkets Ltd* v *Nattrass* [1972] AC 53 at pp. 174–5). This is perhaps the best explanation of *DPP* v *Kent and Sussex Contractors Ltd* [1944] KB 146, whereas in *Tesco Supermarkets Ltd* v *Nattrass*, Lord Reid said (at p. 175) that:

> . . . the board never delegated any part of their functions. They set up a chain of command through regional and district supervisors, but they remained in control. The shop managers had to obey their general directions and also take orders from their superiors. The acts or omissions of shop managers were not acts of the company itself.

Lord Reid also said (at p. 170) that:

> It must be a question of law whether, once the facts have been ascertained, a person in doing particular things is to be regarded as the company or merely as the company's servant or agent.

Where the offence is a statutory one, the Privy Council has taken the view, in *Meridian Global Funds Management Asia Ltd* v *Securities Commission* [1995] 2 AC 500, that it is a question of construction of the particular statutory provisions.

Although there seems to be no decision directly in point, it seems to be generally accepted that a company would only be identified with an act done by one of its officers within 'the scope of his office', to use the expression adopted in the Law Commission's Draft Criminal Code (Law Com. No. 177), cl. 30(2). For example, if a director driving to a board meeting causes death by his dangerous driving, the company would not be liable for the statutory offence, or for manslaughter, since the director was not exercising his managerial functions whilst driving, even though he was on his way to a place where he would exercise those functions. On the other hand, if the acts done are within the scope of his office, as with the false purchase tax returns made by the company secretary in *Moore* v *I. Bresler Ltd* [1944] 2 All ER 515, it does not matter that they are done to conceal a fraud on the company. (See the Law Commission's Draft Criminal Code Bill (Law Com. No. 177), cl. 30(6), for a proposal to reverse this case – the individual employee or director would, of course, remain liable.)

The only offences of which it appears a company cannot be convicted are murder and treason since these are not punishable by a fine which is the only possible strictly penal sanction against a company. There are many other offences for which it is difficult to see how a company could be convicted as principal, rape and bigamy being obvious examples where a company would lack a basic qualification for liability. However, there seems no reason in principle why a company should not, just like a human person, be liable as an accessory to offences such as these for which it could not be liable as a principal. *Mens rea* is, of course, required for liability as an accessory but a company was convicted of aiding and abetting causing death by dangerous driving in *Robert Millar* (*Contractors*) *Ltd* [1970] 2 QB 54 where a director knew the relevant facts. Although it was held in *Cory Bros & Co. Ltd* [1927] 1 KB 810 that a company could not, *inter alia*, be guilty of manslaughter, the opposite view was taken in *Coroner for East Kent, ex parte Spooner* (1987) 88 Cr App R 10, and by Turner J in *P&O European Ferries (Dover) Ltd* (1991) 93 Cr App R 72, a case which nevertheless illustrates the considerable practical problems involved in obtaining a conviction of a company for such an offence under the present law. See further the proposals of the Law Commission in their Report No. 237 Involuntary Manslaughter (HC 171 (1996)).

However, on 8 December 1994, a company, OLL Ltd, was convicted of manslaughter and fined £60,000 at Winchester Crown Court (Ognall J) following the deaths of four sixth-formers in the Lyme Bay canoe tragedy. The managing director was also convicted and sentenced to three years' imprisonment. In contrast, the prosecution of Great Western Trains for gross negligence manslaughter failed because no relevant individual could be shown to have the requisite fault; that ruling is to be subject to an Attorney-General's reference (CPS Press Release, 25 July 1999).

The liability of a company for an offence is, as has already been mentioned, additional to the liability of the individual employee, but the fact that the company is liable may also have the effect of casting the net of individual responsibility rather more widely. This is due to the fact that many statutes (see, e.g., Trade Descriptions Act 1968, s. 20) now contain a section imposing liability on any 'director, manager, secretary or other similar officer' with whose 'consent or connivance' the offence has been committed or to whose 'neglect' it is attributable. In many cases such a person would be liable on normal principles as an accessory. However, the reference to 'neglect' means the liability is wider than that for accessories for whom negligence is not normally sufficient (see **A5.3**). On the other hand, for an accused to be a manager within the meaning of provisions of the above kind requires that he has a position of real authority with both the power and responsibility to decide corporate policy. He must perform a governing role in respect of the affairs of the company rather than merely a day-to-day management function (see *Boal* [1992] 1 QB 591).

In some statutes, the reference to 'neglect' is omitted (see, e.g., Theft Act 1968, s. 18; Public Order Act 1986, s. 28; Copyright, Designs and Patents Act 1988, s. 110) and the prosecution have to rely on connivance or consent, both of which would appear to require the same degree of knowledge as aiding and abetting. Even here, though, the liability is potentially wider than that of an accessory since a positive act of aiding and abetting is not necessarily required. A conscious failure to prevent or report a fellow director committing an offence would seem to be enough, even though there is not a sufficiently clear or immediate right of control over the fellow director to give rise to liability as an accessory.

SECTION A6: INCHOATE OFFENCES

INCITEMENT

Definition

A6.1 Incitement is primarily a common law offence, but there are also several statutory offences of incitement, notably under the OAPA 1861, s. 4 (solicitation of murder: see **B1.83**); the Incitement to Mutiny Act 1797, s. 1 (see **B9.92**); the Official Secrets Act 1920, s. 7 (see **B9.14**, **B9.19**, **B9.26** and **B9.31**) and the Misuse of Drugs Act 1971, s. 19 (see **B20.75**). The following discussion concerns incitement at common law, but the statutory offences are governed by similar principles. Incitement involves soliciting, encouraging or pressurising another person to commit an offence. The offence incited may be summary or indictable, but need not be committed by the person incited. Where it is committed, the inciter becomes a secondary party to that offence (see **A5.1**).

Indictment

A6.2 Statement of Offence

Incitement to theft contrary to common law

Particulars of Offence

A on or about the . . . day of . . . at . . . unlawfully incited P to steal a ruby ring belonging to V

Jurisdiction and Procedure

A6.3 The mode of trial for incitement is the same as for the offence incited. Thus, incitement to commit a summary offence is triable only summarily and incitement to commit an offence triable either way is triable either way (MCA 1980, s. 45 and sch. 1, para. 35).

Jurisdiction over incitement in cases involving extra-territorial elements is largely governed by the same principles as apply to attempt (see **D1.73**). In respect of incitement to commit 'Group A' offences (such as theft, forgery, etc.) under the CJA 1993 and the special provisions introduced by the Sexual Offences (Conspiracy and Incitement) Act 1996 to combat international paedophile tourism, see **D1.75** *et seq*.

Sentence

A6.4 The maximum penalty following conviction on indictment is at the discretion of the court, although judges must have regard to the penalties applicable in respect of the offence incited. The maximum penalty on summary conviction is the same as that for the offence incited (Criminal Law Act 1977, s. 28(1) and s. 30(4)).

Actus Reus

A6.5 'A person may incite another to do an act by threatening or by pressure, as well as persuasion' (*Race Relations Board* v *Applin* [1973] QB 815, per Lord Denning MR at p. 825; *Evans* [1986] Crim LR 470). Incitement may also be implicit, as in *Invicta Plastics Ltd* v *Clare* [1976] RTR 251, where a 'Radatec' device was advertised in a motoring magazine, illustrated with a picture in which it was being used to detect police radar traps, contrary to the Wireless Telegraphy Act 1949. As Park J said, 'it is plain that readers were . . . incited to use the Radatec device.' A small printed warning, to the effect that such use was illegal, did not change the thrust of the advertisement.

Although incitement can be committed even where the person incited flatly refuses to commit the offence, failure to communicate with that person, as where the incitement is contained in a letter intercepted by the police, probably only amounts to an attempt to incite (*Ransford* (1874) 13 Cox CC 9; *Krause* (1902) 66 JP 121).

Offences that Cannot be Incited

An accused cannot properly be charged with inciting X to aid, abet, counsel or procure **A6.6** an offence by Y which Y does not ultimately commit (*Bodin* [1979] Crim LR 176, a decision at first instance); nor is it an offence to incite another person to commit statutory or common-law conspiracy (Criminal Law Act 1977, s. 5(7)); but it may be an offence to incite X to incite Y to commit an offence, as long as this would not inevitably involve X conspiring with Y (*Sirat* (1986) 83 Cr App R 41; *Evans* [1986] Crim LR 470).

It is not an offence for a girl under 16 to incite or abet a man to have unlawful intercourse with her, because the law prohibiting such intercourse exists for her protection (*Tyrrell* [1894] QB 710). The common-law offence of incitement cannot apply to a man who incites a girl under 16 to have unlawful or incestuous intercourse with him, because she would commit no offence in so doing (*Whitehouse* [1977] QB 868); but see the offences of incitement to incest under the Criminal Law Act 1977, s. 54 (see **B3.62**), and incitement to indecency under the Indecency with Children Act 1960, s. 1 (see **B3.111**).

Mens Rea

To be guilty of incitement, one must ordinarily intend that the offence incited will be **A6.7** committed, although, as with attempt, recklessness as to circumstances may sometimes suffice (see **A6.36**). The accused must therefore intend or assume that the person he incites will act with the *mens rea* required for that offence. The terrorist who conceals a bomb in a postal packet does not incite postal workers to commit an offence under the Explosive Substances Acts, but uses them as his innocent agents. Insofar as *Curr* [1968] 2 QB 944 appears to require proof that persons incited actually possess such *mens rea*, it is manifestly erroneous; a person incited need not actually commit the offence at all, so it cannot be necessary to prove his *mens rea*. See *DPP* v *Armstrong* [1999] All ER (D) 1228 (unreported in printed form).

The decision in *Shaw* [1994] Crim LR 365 must also be considered erroneous. S incited K to authorise payment by his employers on the basis of forged invoices. He was charged with inciting K to obtain property by deception, but argued that he was not dishonest because his purpose was to expose the laxity of his employers' security arrangements. The Court of Appeal accepted that, if true, this was a valid defence, but with respect it should not have done. S was guilty as long as he intended that K would dishonestly commit the offence incited (cf. *Smith* [1960] 2 QB 423 at **B15.7**).

Impossibility

Impossibility in relation to incitement remains governed by the same principles that **A6.8** formerly applied to conspiracy and attempt (*Fitzmaurice* [1983] QB 1083). D cannot therefore be guilty of inciting another to commit a crime that it is, in the circumstances, impossible to commit. He cannot, for example, be convicted of inciting X to handle goods that are not proved to be stolen, nor can he be guilty of inciting Y to extract cocaine from a substance which contains none (cf. *DPP* v *Nock* [1978] AC 979). A child under the age of 10 is conclusively presumed incapable of committing an offence; inciting such a child to do so must accordingly be deemed impossible (see *Pickford* [1995] QB 203: a case involving the now-abandoned presumption that a boy under 14 was incapable of sexual intercourse).

The borderline between what is impossible and what is not may be difficult to draw. In *Fitzmaurice*, F was duped by his father into recruiting three other men for the supposed purpose of robbing a woman carrying wages from a bank in Bow. His father had meanwhile informed the police that a gang was lying in wait there for a raid on a security van, and the three men were arrested. It was argued that in the circumstances the proposed robbery was impossible, but the Court of Appeal disagreed. The offence incited by F was one of 'robbing a woman at Bow' and 'by no stretch of the imagination was that an impossible offence to carry out'. See also *DPP* v *Armstrong* [1999] All ER (D) 1228 (unreported in printed form).

CONSPIRACY GENERALLY

A6.9   At common law, conspiracy was originally defined as an agreement between two or more persons to do an unlawful act, or to do a lawful act by unlawful means (*Mulcahy* (1868) LR 3 HL 306). The unlawful act did not have to be a criminal offence. The Criminal Law Act 1977, s. 5, abolished most (but not all) forms of common-law conspiracy, whilst s. 1 of the Act created a new statutory offence in their place.

Common Law and Statutory Conspiracies

A6.10   There are now at least two distinct forms of conspiracy under English law, namely common-law conspiracy to defraud, which was preserved by the Criminal Law Act 1977, s. 5(2), and conspiracy to commit a criminal offence (i.e. statutory conspiracy) contrary to s. 1 of the 1977 Act. These two forms overlap, and many conspiracies to defraud also amount to statutory conspiracies, in which case the CJA 1987, s. 12, allows the prosecution to charge either offence (see **A6.25**). Two other possible forms of common-law conspiracy require brief consideration, namely conspiracy to corrupt public morals and conspiracy to outrage public decency; but the continued existence of these forms of conspiracy at common law is extremely doubtful. Section 5(3) of the 1977 Act purports to preserve such conspiracies as common law offences, but only:

> if and in so far as [they] may be committed by entering into an agreement to engage in conduct which—
> (a)   tends to corrupt public morals or outrages public decency; but
> (b)   would not amount to or involve the commission of an offence if carried out by a single person otherwise than in pursuance of an agreement.

If, in other words, a conspiracy to outrage public decency involves an agreement to commit a substantive criminal offence, it can *only* be charged as a statutory conspiracy under s. 1 of the Act. No overlap with the common-law offence is possible. When the 1977 Act was drafted, it was considered unclear whether any substantive offences of outraging public decency or corrupting public morals existed, and s. 5(3) was intended to preserve the effect of the notorious decisions of the House of Lords in *Shaw* v *DPP* [1962] AC 220 and *Knuller (Publishing, Printing and Promotions) Ltd* v *DPP* [1973] AC 435, lest statutory conspiracy failed to cover conduct of the kind dealt with in those cases. It is now clear that outraging public decency is indeed a substantive offence at common law (see **B3.120** *et seq*. and **B19.18**). Agreements to do acts amounting to that offence must accordingly be charged as statutory conspiracies. The only way in which the common law form of conspiracy might survive would be if the concept of outraging public decency were deemed to be wider in the context of conspiracy than in the context of the substantive offence. There is no good reason why such a distinction should be made, and it therefore appears that this form of conspiracy has been subsumed within the statutory variant.

Authority in respect of corrupting public morals is sparse, but the Court of Criminal Appeal in *Shaw* held that it did indeed exist as a substantive common-law offence, and the House of Lords did not reject that view (although it did not form part of their *ratio decidendi*). It seems probable, therefore, that this form of common law conspiracy has also been subsumed within the statutory offence, and that nothing at all has been preserved by s. 5(3). In any event, there has been no reported prosecution for this form of conspiracy since the 1977 Act came into force, and it does not warrant further discussion here.

STATUTORY CONSPIRACY

Definition

Criminal Law Act 1977, s. 1   **A6.11**

(1)   Subject to the following provisions of this part of this Act, if a person agrees with any other person or persons that a course of conduct will be pursued which, if the agreement is carried out in accordance with their intentions, either—

(a)   will necessarily amount to or involve the commission of any offence or offences by one or more of the parties to the agreement; or

(b)   would do so but for the existence of facts which render the commission of the offence or any of the offences impossible,

he is guilty of conspiracy to commit the offence or offences in question.

(2)   Where liability for any offence may be incurred without knowledge on the part of the person committing it of any particular fact or circumstance necessary for the commission of the offence, a person shall nevertheless not be guilty of conspiracy to commit that offence by virtue of subsection (1) above unless he and at least one other party to the agreement intend or know that the fact or circumstance shall or will exist at the time when the conduct constituting the offence is to take place.

(3)   [Repealed.]

(4)   In this part of this Act 'offence' means an offence triable in England and Wales.

Agreements relating to acts involving summary offences not punishable by imprisonment must be disregarded if the acts are to be done in contemplation or furtherance of a trade dispute (Trade Union and Labour Relations (Consolidation) Act 1992, s. 242).

Indictment

Statement of Offence   **A6.12**

Conspiracy to commit criminal damage contrary to section 1(1) of the Criminal Law Act 1977

Particulars of Offence

A [and B] on or about the . . . day of . . . conspired together [and/or with persons unknown] to damage the braking systems on two heavy goods vehicles belonging to V plc, with intent to endanger life, contrary to s. 1(2) of the Criminal Damage Act 1971

A single agreement (and thus a single count of conspiracy) may embrace a course of conduct involving a number of different offences, without being bad for duplicity (*Roberts* [1998] 1 Cr App R 441; see also *Greenfield* [1973] 1 WLR 1151 and **D9.16**). It has been suggested (*obiter*) by the Court of Appeal in *Roberts* that, if a single count alleges an agreement to commit more than one offence, each part of the agreement becomes an essential element of the conspiracy, so that failure to prove the conspiracy in respect of any one of those offences may be fatal to the charge as a whole. This seems, with respect, to be highly questionable (contrast *Fussell* [1997] Crim LR 812) but it is 'quite plain', according to the Court of Appeal in *Roberts*, that a conspiracy must at least be proved in respect of the most serious of the alleged ulterior offences, since that offence governs the maximum penalty which may be imposed for the conspiracy.

It may therefore be prudent to charge such a conspiracy by means of two or more separate counts. The Court of Appeal in *Roberts* endorsed the following statement by Lord Bridge in *Cooke* [1986] AC 909:

> A single agreement to pursue a course of conduct which involves the commission of two different specific offences could perfectly properly be charged in two counts alleging two different conspiracies, e.g. a conspiracy to steal a car and a conspiracy to obtain money by deception by selling the car with false registration plates and documents.

Whether an indictment for conspiracy alleges one ulterior offence or several, it is important that it properly identifies each of the individual offences in question, in accordance with the Indictments Act 1915, s. 3(1), and the Indictments Rules 1971, r. 6 (*Roberts* [1998] 1 Cr App R 441 at pp. 449–450). Where, for example, an indictment charges a conspiracy to commit criminal damage, it should make it clear whether this refers to the basic offence (contrary to the Criminal Damage Act 1971, s. 1(1)) or to the aggravated offence (contrary to s. 1(2)). See also *Booth* [1999] Crim LR 144 (arson).

An indictment for conspiracy must not be misleading. An indictment alleging that the defendants conspired to supply drugs to 'another' cannot sensibly apply to a case in which the intended recipient was one of the conspirators (*Jackson* (1999) *The Times*, 13 May 1999; *Drew* [1999] Crim LR 581).

A conspiracy count may be joined to substantive counts in an indictment where the facts warrant it and the interests of justice demand it, but see *Practice Direction (Crime: Conspiracy)* [1977] 1 WLR 537 and **D9.33** generally.

Procedure and Sentencing

A6.13 Conspiracy is triable only on indictment, even where it relates to a summary offence; but under the Criminal Law Act 1977, s. 4(1), proceedings for conspiracy to commit summary offences may not be instituted except by or with the consent of the DPP. Where a prosecution for a substantive offence may only be brought by or with leave of the DPP or A-G, this is also required in respect of a charge of conspiracy to commit it (s. 4(2) and (3)). Where the time limit for prosecuting a summary offence has expired, s. 4(4) provides that a prosecution for conspiracy is also barred, but this rule applies only where the substantive offence has been committed. As to the power of local authorities to prosecute for conspiracy (e.g. in trade descriptions cases), see *Jarrett* [1987] Crim LR 517 and *Richards* [1999] Crim LR 598.

By the Criminal Law Act 1977, s. 3, a person guilty of conspiracy to commit murder, any offence for which the maximum penalty is life imprisonment, or any indictable offence punishable with imprisonment where no maximum term is specified is subject to a maximum penalty of life imprisonment. The maximum for other statutory conspiracies is the same as the maximum provided for the completed offence.

Agreement

A6.14 Agreement is the essence of conspiracy. There is no conspiracy if negotiations fail to result in firm agreement between the parties (*Walker* [1962] Crim LR 458) nor is there a conspiracy between A and B merely because each has conspired separately with C (*Griffiths* [1966] 1 QB 589). It is possible, however, to have conspiracies in which some parties never meet others. These include 'chain' and 'wheel' conspiracies. In a chain conspiracy, A agrees with B, B agrees with C, C agrees with D, etc. In a wheel conspiracy, A, at the 'hub', recruits B, C and D to his scheme (*Ardalan* [1972] 2 All ER 257). In either case, however, the alleged conspirators must each be shown to be party to a common design, and they must be aware that there is a larger scheme to which they are attaching themselves (*Meyrick* (1929) 21 Cr App R 94; *Chrastny* [1991] 1 WLR 1381; *Barratt* [1996] Crim LR 495). If B and C each believe they have their own individual agreements with A, there are two separate conspiracies, and a single count will not be valid, even if B and C are aware that A is making similar agreements with others (*Griffiths*).

Where a series of offences are committed by a group of persons over a period of months or years, the prosecution may be tempted to proceed on the basis of a single conspiracy count, in preference to several substantive counts; but this tactic may be misconceived, because such offences are more likely in practice to be the product of a series of different agreements, and a single count of conspiracy may be impossible to prove (see *Barratt*).

Parties to Conspiracies and Acquittal of Other Alleged Conspirators

At least two persons must agree in order for there to be a conspiracy, although a single **A6.15** accused may be charged and convicted, even if the identities of his fellow conspirators remain unknown. Furthermore, the Criminal Law Act 1977, s. 5(8), confirms the principle established in *DPP* v *Shannon* [1975] AC 717, namely that acquittal of the only other alleged parties to a conspiracy (whether in the current trial or at a previous trial) need not prevent the conviction of the remaining accused, 'unless under all the circumstances of the case his conviction is inconsistent with the acquittal of the other person or persons in question'. Conviction of A and acquittal of B would be inconsistent if B is acquitted on the basis of a defence which, if true, must exonerate both, or if the evidence against each is the same (*Longman* (1980) 72 Cr App R 121); but it may be permissible to convict A on the basis of a pre-trial confession or other evidence which is not admissible against B or which does not incriminate him (cf. *Roberts* (1983) 78 Cr App R 41). As to the position where only one conspirator actually intended the agreed crime to be committed, see **A6.20**.

A corporation may be a party to a conspiracy (*ICR Haulage Ltd* [1944] KB 551), but a company and one of its directors cannot be the only parties to it because there can be no meeting of minds in such circumstances (*McDonnell* [1966] 1 QB 233). Certain other combinations are excluded under the Criminal Law Act 1977, s. 2(2), which provides that a person cannot be convicted of statutory conspiracy if the only person(s) with whom he agrees (initially and during the currency of the agreement) are (a) his spouse; (b) children under the age of 10; and (c) intended victims of the relevant offences. If, however, a husband and wife conspire with a third person who does not fall within categories (b) or (c), all three may be liable to conviction (*Chrastny* [1991] 1 WLR 1381; cf. *Lovick* [1993] Crim LR 890).

Intended victims are exempt from liability for statutory conspiracy (s. 2(1)). This appears designed to apply the principle established in *Tyrell* [1894] QB 710 in respect of laws prohibiting intercourse with underaged girls, etc. (see **A6.6**), but might also apply to terminally ill persons who agree to their own mercy killing, or even to a man who pays a prostitute in return for her agreement to whip him. In contrast, the fact that A may be incapable of committing the substantive offence as a principal offender does not prevent him incurring liability for conspiracy with B, if they agree that B will commit that offence (*Duguid* (1906) 21 Cox CC 200; *Burns* (1984) 79 Cr App R 173; *Sherry* [1993] Crim LR 536).

Agreement to Engage in Criminal Conduct

To amount to a conspiracy under the Criminal Law Act 1977, s. 1, an agreement must **A6.16** propose that a course of conduct be pursued which would necessarily involve the commission, by one or more of the parties, of a substantive offence which would itself be triable in England and Wales. A few substantive offences may be triable in England and Wales even if committed abroad, but conspiracies in England or Wales to commit acts abroad which are punishable *only* under the relevant foreign law must be dealt with under s. 1A. See further **A6.23** and **D1.75**.

To be the subject of a conspiracy, the course of conduct proposed must be something that will be done by one or more of the parties to the agreement. An agreement to procure the commission of a murder by a third party (e.g. to contact and hire a professional 'hit man') is not, in itself, a conspiracy to murder, even though anyone hiring such an assassin would become a secondary party to murder once he does his job. In other words, a conspiracy to aid, abet or procure an offence is not indictable under the Criminal Law Act 1977. This at least was the view of the Court of Appeal in *Hollinshead* [1985] 1 All ER 850, approving a passage to such effect in *Smith and Hogan*. The appellants in *Hollinshead* conspired to market devices for use by third parties, which would falsify electricity meter readings and enable users to avoid paying for electricity used. The court held that this did not amount to a conspiracy to commit offences under the Theft Act 1978, s. 2, even though the users would indeed commit such offences. The House of Lords in *Hollinshead* [1985] AC 975 did not dissent from this view, although they did not expressly decide the point.

Conditional Agreements and Contingencies

A6.17   Problems may also arise where agreements could be carried out without committing the alleged substantive offence, or where the parties recognise that it might not prove necessary to carry out the agreement itself. On the face of it, the first kind of agreement falls outside the definition of a conspiracy. In *Reed* [1982] Crim LR 819, the Court of Appeal stated that, if A and B agree to drive from London to Edinburgh in a time which might or might not be achievable without breaking speed limits, depending on the traffic conditions, they do not thereby agree that they will *necessarily* commit any offence and are not therefore guilty of conspiracy. The Court of Appeal subsequently approved this dictum in *Jackson* [1985] Crim LR 442, whilst purporting to distinguish it on the facts before them. The appellants in *Jackson* agreed with one W, who was on trial for burglary, that he would be shot in the leg so as to induce the court to treat him leniently, should he be convicted. They were charged with conspiracy to pervert the course of justice, but argued that, when the agreement was made, it was not known whether W would be convicted. Thus, the planned shooting would not necessarily have interfered with the course of justice. Rejecting this argument, the court replied that 'contingency planning' could amount to conspiracy:

> 'Necessarily' is not to be held to mean that there must inevitably be the carrying out of an offence, it means, if the agreement is carried out in accordance with the plan, there must be the commission of the offence referred to in the conspiracy count.

With respect, the agreed course of conduct (the shooting of W) was not contingent on the outcome of the trial: indeed, it was carried out before the trial ended. It was the effect of that conduct on the future course of justice that was uncertain. The convictions in *Jackson* can better be justified on the basis that the appellants conspired (unconditionally) to commit an act which was intended (conditionally on the outcome of the trial) to pervert the course of justice; and an act committed with such an intent is sufficient to amount to the substantive offence of perverting the course of justice (see **B14.30**). If, however, planning for a contingency can indeed amount to conspiracy, motorists who agree to break speed limits, if necessary, in order to get to Edinburgh on time must after all be guilty, and robbers who agree to 'shoot to kill' if challenged must be guilty of conspiracy to murder. The law is unfortunately far from clear in this respect. What is clear, however, is that agreement forms the basis of liability in conspiracy. Neither abandonment of the agreement, nor failure to carry out its terms, can affect such liability once it has been incurred (see *Bolton* (1991) 94 Cr App R 74).

Agreement Without Real Intent

A6.18   If the *actus reus* of conspiracy is agreement, the *mens rea* is harder to identify. The concept of agreement does not necessarily import an intent by each party to carry out that agreement, but such an intent was (and still is) required in respect of conspiracy at common law (*Thomson* (1965) 50 Cr App R 1; *Yip Chieu-Chung* v *The Queen* [1995] 1

AC 111) whilst there are references in the Criminal Law Act 1977, s. 1(1) and 1(4), to agreements being carried out in accordance with the intentions of the parties. The issue of intent may become problematic where one or more of the parties does not intend to keep his part of the agreement, as where a hired assassin agrees to commit a murder for which he is engaged, but intends only to make off with his advance fee, or where the supposed assassin is working undercover for the police, and intends only to collect evidence against those who hired him. Is the dishonest assassin or undercover officer guilty of conspiracy to murder. If not, where does that leave the other parties to the supposed agreement?

The House of Lords considered such questions in a slightly different context in *Anderson* [1986] AC 27. The appellant was charged with conspiracy to effect a convicted prisoner's escape from jail. He had agreed to such a plan and had supplied the other conspirators with diamond cutting wire in furtherance of it, but claimed that he had never believed the jailbreak could succeed, and was concerned only to obtain the money he had been promised for the wire. One possible answer to this supposed defence was that it amounted to an admission of complicity in the conspiracy as a secondary party. This answer found favour with the Court of Appeal in *Anderson,* but the House of Lords left it unconsidered and preferred to categorise the appellant as a principal offender. Lord Bridge, with whom the other members of the appellate committee agreed, said:

> I . . . reject any construction of the statutory language which would require the prosecution to prove an intention on the part of each conspirator that the criminal offence or offences . . . should in fact be committed. . . .
>
> . . . [b]eyond the mere fact of agreement, the necessary *mens rea* of the crime is . . . established if, and only if . . . the accused . . . intended to play some part in the agreed course of conduct in furtherance of the criminal purpose which the agreed course of conduct was intended to achieve. Nothing less will suffice; nothing more is required.

Lord Bridge went on to emphasise that a person, such as an undercover agent, 'ostensibly agreeing [but] with the purpose of exposing and frustrating the purpose of the other parties' cannot be guilty of conspiracy. This must be correct, but the earlier excerpts from his speech are problematic in a number of respects, and much of what he said is now widely considered to have been wrong. To begin with, his ruling that a conspirator need not intend the offence in question to be committed does violence to the wording of the Criminal Law Act 1977, s. 1(1), is difficult to reconcile with s.1(2) (see **A6.21**), and invokes bizarre visions of conspiracies in which *none* of the parties actually intends to carry out the supposed agreement. It is doubtful whether Lord Bridge could have meant this to be the law, however, because he refers to 'the criminal purpose which the agreed course of conduct was *intended* to achieve . . .'. Furthermore, earlier in his speech he had said, '[it] is, of course, necessary that any party to the agreement shall have assented to play his part . . . knowing that the part to be played by one or more of the others will amount to or involve the commission of an offence.'

On that basis, the fraudulent hit-man who intends only to make off with his advance fee cannot be guilty of conspiracy to murder, because he knows that without him the plan must fail. Similarly, fraudulent drug dealers who intend to supply their customers with harmless powder cannot be regarded as having conspired to supply drugs. Their plan is in fact to obtain property from the customers by deception. This interpretation makes far more sense and appears to have been accepted by the Court of Appeal in *Edwards* [1991] Crim LR 352 and by the Northern Ireland Court of Appeal in *McPhillips* (1990 unreported). See also *Yip Chieu-Chung* v *The Queen* [1995] 1 AC 111 (see **A6.20**).

Active and Passive Conspirators

A second problem with Lord Bridge's ruling in *Anderson* [1986] AC 27 is that it appears **A6.19** to require each conspirator to intend playing some active part in furtherance of the conspiracy. If so, it is an astonishing proposition, for which there is no basis either in the Criminal Law Act 1977 or in any cases decided before or after it. In *Siracusa* (1989) 90 Cr App R 340, the Court of Appeal concluded that Lord Bridge could not have meant what he said. 'He cannot have been intending' said O'Connor LJ, 'that the organiser of a crime, who recruited others to carry it out, would not himself be guilty of conspiracy. . . . Participation in a conspiracy is infinitely variable: it can be active or passive'.

Where Only One Conspirator is Genuine

A6.20   A cannot be guilty of conspiracy if B (the only other party to the supposed agreement) intends to frustrate or sabotage it. This issue did not arise in *Anderson* [1986] AC 27, but the Privy Council were required to consider it in *Yip Chieu-Chung* v *The Queen* [1995] 1 AC 111, where N, the appellant's only fellow conspirator in a plan to smuggle heroin out of Hong Kong, was an undercover agent working with the knowledge of the authorities. In an opinion delivered by Lord Griffiths, the Privy Council held that, if N's purpose had been to prevent the heroin being smuggled, no indictable conspiracy would have existed:

> The crime of conspiracy requires an agreement between two or more persons to commit an unlawful act with the intention of carrying it out. It is the intention to carry out the crime that constitutes the necessary *mens rea* for the offence. As Lord Bridge pointed out [in *Anderson*] an undercover agent who has no intention of committing the crime lacks the necessary *mens rea* to be a conspirator.

Conspiracy under Hong Kong law remains a common-law offence, but Lord Griffiths did not seek to distinguish in this respect between common-law and statutory conspiracy. He was, however, able to uphold the appellant's conviction on the basis that N had intended to smuggle the heroin out of Hong Kong as agreed. The trap was to be sprung later, when the heroin arrived in Australia. The fact that the Hong Kong authorities acquiesced in this plan did not prevent it from being a criminal act. Both parties were therefore guilty, albeit that N would never be prosecuted.

Mens Rea as to Circumstances

A6.21   At common law, a person could be guilty of conspiracy only if he and at least one other conspirator knew of any relevant circumstances necessary for the commission of the offence (*Churchill* v *Walton* [1967] 2 AC 224). Thus, it is a strict liability offence to sell or advertise goods which bear a false trade description, but there could not be a conspiracy to commit this offence unless the parties to the alleged conspiracy knew or intended that the goods were falsely described. The Criminal Law Act 1977, s. 1(2) (see **A6.11**), was clearly intended to maintain this rule in relation to statutory conspiracies. It does not expressly state that knowledge or intent must be proved in conspiracy cases where it would have to be proved in relation to the substantive offences agreed upon, but this must surely be regarded as implicit in the provision, because any other interpretation would give rise to absurd distinctions. On the other hand, knowledge of the relevant law which makes the proposed conduct illegal need not be proved (*Broad* [1997] Crim LR 666).

It was held in *Khan* [1990] 1 WLR 813 that a person may attempt to commit rape, being reckless whether the victim consents (see **A6.36**), but s. 1(2) appears to preclude such liability in cases of conspiracy to rape.

Impossibility

A6.22   At common law it was a defence to a charge of conspiracy that the object of the conspiracy was impossible to achieve. One could not, for example, be guilty of a conspiracy to extract cocaine from a substance which proved not to contain any cocaine (*DPP* v *Nock* [1978] AC 979). The Criminal Law Act 1977, s.1(1), was amended by the Criminal Attempts Act 1981, so as largely to eliminate defences based on impossibility. If A and B wrongly believe that cocaine can be extracted from a given substance, they may now commit an indictable conspiracy or attempt to do so. They may also enter into an indictable conspiracy to murder someone who turns out to be dead already or to handle goods which they wrongly believe to have been stolen. On the other hand, an agreement to pursue a course of conduct which the parties wrongly believe to be criminal, because they have misunderstood the law, cannot be indictable as a conspiracy (cf. *Taaffe* [1984] AC 539).

Jurisdiction Over Statutory Conspiracy

Conspiracy under the Criminal Law Act 1977 must involve an agreement to commit an **A6.23** offence triable under English law (s. 1(4)) and this usually means an offence which is to be committed within England and Wales or aboard a British ship or aircraft. A number of offences can however be tried under English law even if committed abroad (e.g., offences under the Aviation Security Act 1982 (see **B10.79 *et seq.***) or murder/ manslaughter committed by a British citizen on land outside the United Kingdom. Persons who conspire in England or Wales to commit such crimes abroad are therefore indictable under s. 1.

Persons who conspire in England or Wales to commit acts outside the United Kingdom, which are criminal under the law of the foreign state concerned and would be crimes under English law if committed in England or Wales, may now be indicted under the Criminal Law Act 1977, s. 1A (as inserted by the Criminal Justice (Terrorism and Conspiracy) Act 1998, s. 5). Note however that there is no overlap between s. 1 and s. 1A: if the proposed conduct would amount to an extraterritorial offence under English law, the conspiracy must be charged under s. 1, and not under s. 1A.

Conspiracy to commit a 'cross frontier' offence of fraud or dishonesty which would itself be triable in England or Wales as a Group A offence under part I of the CJA 1993 must likewise be indicted under the Criminal Law Act 1977, s. 1, rather than s. 1A. A person may be guilty of conspiracy to commit such an offence whether or not any act or omission in relation to that offence occurred in England or Wales (CJA 1993, s. 3(2); and see further **D1.75**).

Even in cases not covered by the CJA 1993, conspirators who, whilst abroad, plot the commission of a crime within England or Wales, may be indicted under English law, at least where one or more of them enters the jurisdiction to further that conspiracy (*DPP v Doot* [1973] AC 807) and probably even if none of them do so. See *Sansom* (1991) 92 Cr App R 115; *Manning* [1998] 2 Cr App R 461; and **D1.73**.

Evidential Issues

There are no special evidential rules peculiar to conspiracy. In *Murphy* (1837) 8 C & P **A6.24** 297, proof of conspiracy was said to be generally 'a matter of inference deduced from certain criminal acts of the parties accused', but there is no actual need for any such acts, and conspiracies may also be proved, *inter alia*, by direct testimony, secret recordings or confessions, subject only to the proviso that A's pre-trial confession cannot ordinarily be evidence against B. The acts and statements of one conspirator may be given in evidence against both him and his fellow conspirators, provided they were done or said in furtherance of their common purpose, but that rule is not confined to conspiracies. See further **F16.48 *et seq***.

CONSPIRACY TO DEFRAUD

Definition

The common law offence of conspiracy to defraud is expressly preserved by the Criminal **A6.25** Law Act 1977, s. 5(2), as amended by the CJA 1987, s. 12. There are two principal variants of this offence, although these are not mutually exclusive. The first is defined in the leading case of *Scott* v *Metropolitan Police Commissioner* [1975] AC 819, where Viscount Dilhorne said:

> . . . an agreement by two or more [persons] by dishonesty to deprive a person of something which is his or to which he is or would be or might be entitled [or] an agreement by two or more by dishonesty to injure some proprietary right of his suffices to constitute the offence . . .

There may or may not be an intent to deceive in such cases, and there may or may not be an intent to cause economic or financial loss to the proposed victim or victims, but it suffices if there is a dishonest agreement to expose the proposed victim to some form of economic risk or disadvantage to which he would not otherwise be exposed.

The second variant was also recognised in *Scott*, but has been more fully considered by the Privy Council in *Wai Yu-tsang* v *The Queen* [1992] AC 269. In this variant, there must be a dishonest agreement by two or more persons to 'defraud' another, by deceiving him into acting contrary to his duty. There is some doubt as to the exact scope of this offence. It was suggested (*obiter*) in *DPP* v *Withers* [1975] AC 842 that the person deceived must be a public official, and this was also the view of Lord Diplock in *Scott*, but the opinion of the Privy Council in *Wai Yu-tsang* was that it suffices if any person is deceived into acting contrary to the duty he owes to his clients or employers. The Privy Council approved and adopted the concept of 'intent to defraud' previously expounded by Lord Denning and Lord Radcliffe in *Welham* v *DPP* [1961] AC 103. *Welham* involved an alleged offence under the Forgery Act 1913, s. 6 (since repealed), rather than an alleged conspiracy, but the concept of 'intent to defraud' appears to be similar in each case. Lord Denning held in *Welham* that to defraud means 'to practise a fraud' and need not necessarily involve causing any form of economic loss or prejudice.

Either variant of conspiracy to defraud is capable of overlapping with the offence of statutory conspiracy under the Criminal Law Act 1977, s. 1 (see **A6.10** *et seq.*). Such overlap will occur wherever the course of action agreed on would necessarily involve the commission of any offence or offences by one or more of the parties to the conspiracy if carried out in accordance with their intentions and would also involve a fraud being practised on another person. In such circumstances, the prosecution has a choice as to which kind of charge to prefer (CJA 1987, s. 12(1)). A charge of conspiracy to defraud may be advantageous from the prosecution viewpoint in cases where there is doubt as to which, if any, substantive offences would be involved.

Indictment, Sentence and Procedure

A6.26 Conspiracy to defraud is triable only on indictment, and is punishable by up to 10 years' imprisonment or a fine or both (CJA 1987, s. 12(3)). For trial purposes, it is a class 4 offence (see **D12.1**). An indictment for conspiracy to defraud should not lack particularity and should enable the defence and the judge to know precisely the nature of the prosecution's case (*Landy* [1981] 1 WLR 355). This prevents the prosecution from shifting their ground during the trial, unless they obtain leave of the judge and amend the indictment itself (*Landy*).

Statement of Offence

Conspiracy to defraud contrary to common law

Particulars of Offence

A and B on divers days between . . . and . . . conspired together [and with . . .] to defraud the C Bank plc and its existing and potential shareholders, creditors and depositors

    (i)   by dishonestly concealing in the accounts of the C Bank the dishonouring of cheques in the sum of £50 million drawn on the account of D Ltd with the E Bank Inc, such cheques having been purchased by the C Bank

    (ii)   [etc.]

As to the power of local authorities to prosecute for conspiracy to defraud (e.g. in trade descriptions cases), see *Jarrett* [1997] Crim LR 517 and *Richards* [1999] Crim LR 598.

Actus Reus

As in cases of statutory conspiracy, there must always be an agreement (see **A6.14**). The **A6.27** agreement may however be wider in certain respects than that required in respect of the statutory offence. It need not be an agreement that would necessarily involve the commission of a substantive offence if carried out (*Scott* v *Metropolitan Police Commissioner* [1975] AC 819; *Cooke* [1986] AC 909) and it need not necessarily be envisaged that the fraud will be perpetrated by the conspirators themselves. In *Hollinshead* [1985] AC 975, the appellants agreed to market devices designed to falsify gas or electricity meters, which would enable customers (who were not themselves party to the conspiracy) to defraud their gas and electricity suppliers. The appellants had no intention of using the devices themselves, but they were nevertheless guilty of conspiracy to defraud.

Other reported illustrations of agreements amounting to conspiracy to defraud include: agreement to conceal a bank's losses or liabilities from its shareholders, creditors and depositors (*Wai Yu-tsang* v *The Queen* [1992] AC 269); agreement by company directors to conceal secret profits from the company, where the company would be entitled to demand that the profits be accounted for (*Adams* v *The Queen* [1995] 1 WLR 52); agreement by British Rail catering staff to sell their own refreshments to customers whilst on duty, thereby depriving British Rail of profits from legitimate sales (*Cooke* [1986] AC 909); agreement to falsify hire-purchase or credit applications, so as to induce credit companies or other lenders to make loans they might not otherwise be willing to make (*Allsop* (1976) 64 Cr App R 29); and agreement to make pirate copies of films, etc., thereby depriving the makers and distributors of legitimate profits (*Scott* v *Metropolitan Police Commissioner*).

As to the position where only one of the supposed conspirators really intends to proceed with or carry out the conduct agreed upon, see **A6.20**.

Mens Rea

To be guilty of conspiracy to defraud, D must be dishonest (in the *Ghosh* sense, as to **A6.28** which see **B4.34**) and must intend to defraud the proposed victim, in one or other of the senses explained at **A6.25**; but an intent to deceive is necessary only in respect of the second of the two variants of the offence. In *A-G's Ref (No. 1 of 1982)* [1983] QB 751, it was held that there can be no conspiracy to defraud where the defrauding would be a mere side-effect (rather than the 'true object') of the scheme agreed to, but this is now generally thought to be wrong, and has not been followed in subsequent cases. The correct position must be that D intends to defraud V wherever he is aware that the successful implementation of his plan will result in V being defrauded (cf. *McPherson* [1985] Crim LR 508).

Jurisdiction over Conspiracy to Defraud

In *Board of Trade* v *Owen* [1957] AC 602, the House of Lords held that jurisdiction over **A6.29** conspiracy to defraud was governed by the same principles as conspiracy to commit a crime. In other words, a conspiracy abroad to defraud a victim within England and Wales may be indictable here, but no indictment will lie where the victim is to be defrauded abroad. Lord Tucker said:

> A conspiracy to commit a crime abroad is not indictable in this country unless the contemplated crime is one for which an indictment would lie here . . . It necessarily follows that a conspiracy of the nature of that charged in count 3 [i.e. a conspiracy to defraud a West German government department] — which in my view was a conspiracy to attain a lawful object by unlawful means, rather than to commit a crime — is not triable in this

country, since the unlawful means and the ultimate object were both outside the jurisdiction.

See also *A-G's Ref (No. 1 of 1982)* [1983] QB 751 and *Naini* [1999] 7 Arch News 1, and **D1.73**. The position is now different in respect of things done on or after 1 June 1999. Section 5(3) of the CJA 1993, which came into force on that date, provides that various acts done or omitted within England and Wales, whether by a conspirator or by someone acting as his agent, may bring all the conspirators within English jurisdiction, even if the defrauding was intended to occur abroad. Conspirators may even be liable on the basis of acts previously done in England and Wales, before the conspiracy was formed.

Impossibility

A6.30 The abolition of the defence of impossibility in respect of attempts and statutory conspiracies has not affected the operation of that defence in the context of conspiracy to defraud or the common law offence of incitement. See generally **A6.8** and **A6.22**.

ATTEMPT

Definition

A6.31 The law relating to attempts is primarily governed by the Criminal Attempts Act 1981.

Criminal Attempts Act 1981, s. 1

(1)   If, with intent to commit an offence to which this section applies, a person does an act which is more than merely preparatory to the commission of the offence, he is guilty of attempting to commit the offence.

[(1A) and (1B) deal with attempts in England or Wales to commit acts abroad which would amount to offences of computer misuse (see **B18**) if committed in England and Wales.]

(2)   A person may be guilty of attempting to commit an offence to which this section applies even though the facts are such that the commission of the offence is impossible.

(3)   In any case where—

(a)   apart from this subsection a person's intention would not be regarded as having amounted to an intent to commit an offence; but

(b)   if the facts of the case had been as he believed them to be, his intention would be so regarded,

then for the purpose of subsection (1) above, he shall be regarded as having had an intent to commit that offence.

(4)   This section applies to any offence which, if it were completed, would be triable in England and Wales as an indictable offence, other than—

(a)   conspiracy (at common law or under section 1 of the Criminal Law Act 1977);

(b)   aiding, abetting, counselling, procuring or suborning the commission of an offence;

(c)   offences under section 4(1) (assisting offenders) or 5(1) (accepting or agreeing to accept consideration for not disclosing information about an arrestable offence) of the Criminal Law Act 1967.

Where an offence is triable only summarily, it cannot be the object of a criminal attempt under s.1, but provisions creating summary offences sometimes create matching offences of attempt: see for example the Road Traffic Act 1988, ss. 4 and 5, which create summary offences of driving *or attempting to drive* when unfit through drink or drugs or when over the prescribed limit for alcohol (see **C5.9 *et seq*.**). The Criminal Attempts Act 1981, s. 3, provides that 'attempts under special statutory provisions' shall be governed by rules which mirror those in s. 1(1)-(3).

Section 1(4)(b) does not preclude charges of attempt in relation to substantive offences of 'procuring' (e.g. under the Sexual Offences Act 1956, ss. 2 or 3) or charges of attempting to abet another person's suicide, contrary to the Suicide Act 1961 (*McShane*

(1977) 66 Cr App R 97); nor does anything in s. 1(4) preclude a charge of attempting to incite the commission of a criminal offence.

Indictment

Statement of Offence

A6.32

Attempted murder contrary to section 1(1) of the Criminal Attempts Act 1981

Particulars of Offence

A on or about the . . . day of . . . attempted to murder V

A person charged on indictment with an attempt to commit an offence can be convicted on that charge, notwithstanding any evidence proving that he has actually committed the substantive offence (Criminal Law Act 1967, s. 6(4)). The same rule applies to summary trials. Thus, in *Webley* v *Buxton* [1977] QB 481, the Divisional Court held that justices had properly convicted the appellant of an attempt to take a conveyance contrary to the Theft Act 1968, s. 12 (which at that time was an offence triable either way) notwithstanding that the evidence proved him to have committed the full offence. This rule is unaltered by the Criminal Attempts Act 1981.

Evidence, Procedure and Sentencing

Criminal Attempts Act 1981, s. 2

A6.33

(1) Any provision to which this section applies shall have effect with respect to an offence under section 1 above of attempting to commit an offence as it has effect with respect to the offence attempted.

(2) This section applies to provisions of any of the following descriptions made by or under any enactment (whenever passed)—

(a) provisions whereby proceedings may not be instituted or carried on otherwise than by, or on behalf or with the consent of, any person (including any provisions which also make other exceptions to the prohibition);

(b) provisions conferring power to institute proceedings;

(c) provisions as to the venue of proceedings;

(d) provisions whereby proceedings may not be instituted after the expiration of a time limit;

(e) provisions conferring a power of arrest or search;

(f) provisions conferring a power of seizure and detention of property;

(g) provisions whereby a person may not be convicted or committed for trial on the uncorroborated evidence of one witness (including any provision requiring the evidence of not less than two credible witnesses);

(h) provisions conferring a power of forfeiture, including any power to deal with anything liable to be forfeited;

(i) provisions whereby, if an offence committed by a body corporate is proved to have been committed with the consent or connivance of another person, that person also is guilty of the offence.

An attempt to commit an offence which is triable only on indictment is itself triable only on indictment, whilst an attempt to commit an offence triable either way is triable either way (Criminal Attempts Act 1981, s. 4(1)).

By the Criminal Attempts Act 1981, s. 4, the maximum penalty for attempted murder is life imprisonment. Other indictable offences are subject to the same maximum as applies on conviction on indictment for the offence attempted, and if the offence is triable either way the maximum penalty on summary conviction is the same as the maximum penalty available for that offence tried summarily. By s. 4(5) these provisions are made subject to anomalous provisions in the Sexual Offences Act 1956, s. 37 and sch. 2, which specify a maximum sentence of two years' imprisonment for attempted incest by a man with a female over 13 and for attempted incest by a woman (where the maximum penalty in each case for the full offence is seven years) and a maximum sentence of seven years for attempted unlawful sexual intercourse by a man with a girl under 13 (where the maximum for the full offence is life imprisonment). The Court of Appeal in *Robson* (1974) CSP A1-4B01 indicated that it would be 'at least unusual that an attempt should be visited with punishment to the maximum extent that the law permits in respect of a completed offence'. It is submitted that the sentence for a given attempt should almost always be less than the sentence which would have been imposed if that offence been completed, but clearly much will depend on the stage at which the attempt failed, and the reason(s) for its non-completion. On the other hand, within an offence category, some examples of attempt may merit more severe punishment than some examples of the completed offence. See further *Billam* [1986] 1 WLR 349, on sentencing for attempted rape (at **B3.5**).

Actus Reus

A6.34   Section 1(1) of the Criminal Attempts Act 1981 requires the accused to have committed an act which is 'more than merely preparatory' to the offence attempted. Where trial is on indictment, it is for the judge to determine whether there is evidence on which a jury could properly find that the accused's actions did go beyond mere preparation, but it is then for the jury to decide that question as one of fact (s. 4(3); and see also *DPP* v *Stonehouse* [1978] AC 55).

At common law, acts amounting to attempts were distinguished from mere preparatory acts by the concept of 'proximity'. An example of the proximity test was provided in *Robinson* [1915] 2 KB 342, in which a jeweller clumsily faked a robbery at his premises with a view to making a fraudulent insurance claim in respect of his supposed loss. It was held that his conviction for attempting to obtain money from his insurers by false pretences could not stand, because he had been arrested before he could send any claim to his insurers. As it was not a decision under the 1981 Act, *Robinson* cannot be a binding authority on its interpretation, but it is unlikely that such a case would be decided differently under the Act. Indeed, a similar approach was adopted in *Campbell* [1991] Crim LR 268, where the appellant armed himself with an imitation gun, approached to within a yard of a post office which he intended to rob, but never drew his weapon; it was held that there was no evidence on which the jury could properly have concluded that his acts went beyond mere preparation. See also *Widdowson* (1985) 82 Cr App R 314. In *Gullefer* [1990] 1 WLR 1063, Lord Lane CJ stated that the crucial question was whether the accused had 'embarked upon the crime proper', but that it was not necessary, as some earlier cases had suggested, that the accused should have reached a 'point of no return' in respect of the full offence. This view was echoed in *A-G's Ref (No.1 of 1992)* [1993] Crim LR 274, in which it was held that attempted rape may be committed without the accused having physically attempted to penetrate his victim.

In *Jones* [1990] 1 WLR 1057, the appellant was charged with attempted murder. He climbed into his victim's car and drew a loaded gun with the intention of killing him, but was disarmed in a struggle that followed. The Court of Appeal held it was open to the jury to regard this as attempted murder and in his judgment Taylor LJ provided useful guidance as to the distinction between preparation and attempts:

> The question for the judge in the present case was whether there was evidence from which a reasonable jury, properly directed, could conclude that the appellant had done acts which were more than merely preparatory. Clearly his actions in obtaining the gun, in shortening it, in loading it, in putting on his disguise and going to the [ambush point] could only be regarded as preparatory acts. But . . . once he had got into the car, taken out the loaded gun and pointed it at the victim with the intention of killing him, there was sufficient evidence for the consideration of the jury on the charge of attempted murder. It was a matter for them to decide whether they were sure those acts were more than merely preparatory.

The question will often be essentially one of degree (*Tosti* [1997] Crim LR 746; *Geddes* [1996] Crim LR 894; *Toothill* [1998] Crim LR 876). It may be necessary to identify the essential elements of the crime allegedly attempted, in order to determine whether D got beyond mere preparation. In *Nash* [1999] Crim LR 308, the Court of Appeal appears to have construed 'attempting to procure an act of gross indecency' as if it meant '*inciting* an act of gross indecency'; but procuring requires the commission of the offence procured (*Johnson* [1964] 2 QB 404) and it would seem, with respect, that the wrong test was applied.

Mens Rea

Intent is the essence of any crime of attempt under the 1981 Act, as it was at common **A6.35** law (*Pearman* (1984) 80 Cr App R 259). The prosecution must ordinarily prove that D acted with a specific intent to commit the particular crime attempted, even if the full offence is one of strict liability, or one in which the *mens rea* required falls short of the *actus reus*. Thus, although murder may be committed by someone who intends only to cause grievous bodily harm, attempted murder requires nothing less than an intent to kill (*Whybrow* (1951) 35 Cr App R 141). Note, however, an important qualification to the general rule, explained at **A6.36**.

'Intent' in this context bears the meaning laid down in *Moloney* [1985] AC 905 (see **A2.2**) and *Nedrick* [1986] 1 WLR 1025. In most cases, however, a full *Nedrick* direction (see **B1.11**) would be unnecessary and potentially confusing. On a charge of attempted murder by shooting, for example, it may suffice to direct the jury to decide: (a) whether D shot V deliberately; and (b) if so, whether D was 'shooting to kill' (*Fallon* [1994] Crim LR 519).

In *Walker* (1989) 90 Cr App R 226, the defendants were convicted of attempted murder. They had hurled their victim from a third-floor balcony, but he had somehow survived the fall. After correctly directing the jury to decide whether the defendants were 'trying to kill him', the trial judge elaborated by suggesting that such an intent may sometimes be inferred in cases where there is a 'very high degree of probability' that death will result. The Court of Appeal upheld the convictions, but doubted whether any such elaboration was called for on the facts of the case. Although the judge's suggestion was perfectly correct, there was a danger of confusing the jury into thinking that foresight of high probability could be equated with intention.

Mens Rea as to Circumstances

Although the Criminal Attempts Act 1981, s. 1(1), specifies that the accused must act **A6.36** 'with intent to commit an offence to which this section applies', the Court of Appeal has qualified this principle by holding that, whilst intent is required as to any specified consequences of the accused's conduct, something less may suffice in respect of any relevant circumstances. In *Khan* [1990] 1 WLR 813, it was held that, since recklessness as to the victim's lack of consent suffices in relation to the full offence of rape, the offence of attempted rape is committed where an accused intends (but fails) to have intercourse with a woman and is reckless as to her lack of consent. In *A-G's Ref (No. 3 of 1992)* [1994] 1 WLR 409, the court held that an acccused is guilty of an attempt to commit a criminal offence if he is in one of the states of mind required for the full offence and he does his best, so far as he can, to supply what is missing from the completion of the full offence. A person who attempts to set fire to property, being reckless as to whether life would be endangered, may accordingly be convicted of an attempt to commit an offence under the Criminal Damage Act 1971, s. 1(2).

The rule as formulated in *A-G's Ref (No. 3 of 1992)* would appear to extend to offences in which liability as to circumstances is strict. A man who attempts to have intercourse with a girl whom he believes (on reasonable grounds) to be aged over 16, but who is in fact under 16, may thus be guilty of an attempt to commit an offence under the Sexual Offences Act 1956, s. 6; and whereas a man aged under 24 may be able to raise a statutory defence of 'reasonable belief' when charged with the full offence, it is not obvious that such a defence would be available if he were charged with a mere attempt.

Conditional Intent

A6.37   Problems of conditional intent in attempts seldom arise otherwise than in relation to theft and related offences. A would-be thief may not know what he will find when searching through another person's property, and may not even be sure what he is hoping to find. In *Husseyn* (1978) 67 Cr App R 131, the accused dishonestly opened the door of a van, but were challenged just as they were about to examine a holdall lying inside the van. The holdall contained valuable scuba-diving equipment, but it was held that they could not be convicted on an indictment alleging that they attempted to steal that equipment. They did not even know what the holdall contained. Although much criticised, *Husseyn* remains good law under the 1981 Act, but it need not cause any real difficulties, provided care is taken in drafting the relevant information or indictment.

The Court of Appeal in *Husseyn* suggested that the accused could properly have been charged with an attempt to steal 'some or all of the contents' of the holdall but, following the abrogation of the rule in *Haughton* v *Smith* [1975] AC 476 (see **A6.40**), it would now be preferable simply to charge 'an attempt to steal from' the holdall or van. It would not then matter whether the holdall or van contained anything which the accused might want to steal, or indeed any property at all.

Attempts with a Foreign Element

A6.38   The Criminal Attempts Act 1981, s. 1(4) (see **A6.31**), restates the common-law rule that conduct cannot amount to a criminal attempt under English law unless it is directed towards the commission of a substantive offence which would itself be indictable under English law. An attempt in England and Wales to publish an obscene article in Scotland is not, for example, indictable under English law, because the ulterior offence would not be. Attempts to commit offences of fraud or dishonesty (if perpetrated on or after 1 June 1999) are now covered by part I of the CJA 1993 (see **D1.75**). An attempt in England and Wales to commit a 'Group A' offence (such as theft, forgery, etc.) abroad would be triable under the Criminal Attempts Act 1981, s. 1, because a Group A offence is triable under English law where any 'relevant event' concerning it takes place in England or Wales.

The CJA 1993 inserts a new s. 1A into the Criminal Attempts Act 1981, supposedly to cover cases where the accused in England and Wales attempts to commit abroad something which *would* be a Group A offence, but for the fact that it is not triable under English law. This provision is fundamentally at odds with itself. If a Group A offence is instigated by conduct within England and Wales, that offence will inevitably be triable under English law. Section 1A is merely a trap for unwary prosecutors, who may be tempted to use it instead of s. 1.

Where an attempt to commit an offence within England and Wales is instigated from abroad, the general rule is that such conduct does amount to an offence under s. 1; this is certainly true where some effect of that attempt is felt within the jurisdiction, and probably even if it is not (*Baxter* [1972] 1 QB 1; *DPP* v *Stonehouse* [1978] AC 55; *Latif* [1996] 1 WLR 104). As far as attempts to commit Group A offences are concerned, the position is put beyond doubt by the CJA 1993, s. 3(3).

Withdrawal

A6.39   There is no recognised defence of voluntary withdrawal in English law. If the accused has not progressed beyond the stage of mere preparatory acts (see **A6.34**) he can avoid incurring liability by refraining from further acts but, once he has gone beyond that stage, withdrawal will be irrelevant as far as his liability for attempt is concerned.

Impossibility

At common law, no offence of attempt could be committed where it would have been **A6.40** impossible (even in theory) for the accused to succeed in committing the substantive offence. Thus, the accused could not be guilty of attempting to steal from a bag or pocket which was empty, and he could not be guilty of attempting to handle stolen goods if the goods in question had been recovered by the police and had accordingly ceased to be stolen (*Haughton* v *Smith* [1975] AC 476). This rule was abrogated by the Criminal Attempts Act 1981, s. 1(2), but the precise effect of that provision was for a time uncertain. In *Anderton* v *Ryan* [1985] AC 560, the House of Lords held that a distinction had to be drawn between the person who attempts to commit a crime but fails because the crime is impossible (the 'empty pocket' kind of case) and the person who succeeds in doing an 'objectively innocent' act but labours under a mistaken view of the facts or circumstances, and wrongly believes that he is committing an offence.

Anderton v *Ryan* was thought to be an example of the latter type of case. R bought a video recorder in suspicious circumstances, firmly believing it to be stolen. There was, however, no evidence to prove that it was stolen, and the House of Lords held she could not be guilty even of an attempt to handle stolen goods. The decision was much criticised, and in *Shivpuri* [1987] AC 1 the House of Lords acknowledged that their earlier decision was wrong. Lord Bridge said:

> I am satisfied . . . that the concept of 'objective innocence' is incapable of sensible application in relation to the law of criminal attempts . . . Any attempt to commit an offence which . . . for any reason fails, so that in the event no offence is committed must, *ex hypothesi*, from the point of view of the criminal law, be objectively innocent. What turns what would otherwise . . . be an innocent act into a crime is the intent of the actor to commit an offence.

In *Shivpuri*, S was charged with an attempt to commit an offence under the Misuse of Drugs Act 1971, s. 3(1). He confessed to acting as a recipient and distributor of what he assumed to be an illegally imported drug. It transpired (to his surprise) that the substance was not a drug at all but he was still guilty of an attempt to commit the s. 3(1) offence.

If, however, the accused is not mistaken as to the facts, but wrongly believes that his actions amount to a criminal offence (i.e. as a result of his mistaken view of the law), this mistake cannot make him guilty of any criminal attempt. Section 1(2) does not apply in such cases (cf. *Taaffe* [1984] AC 539).

Interfering with Vehicles

Where the accused is seen interfering with a vehicle or trailer, it is often difficult to prove **A6.41** which of a number of possible offences he is trying to commit. A charge of attempt under the Criminal Attempts Act 1981, s. 1, may therefore be impossible to prove, but see the specific offence of interference with vehicles created by s. 9 (see **B4.107** *et seq.*).

PART B
OFFENCES

Leonard Leigh, PhD, Barrister

Commission Member, Criminal Cases Review Commission
Formerly Professor of Criminal Law in the University of London
London School of Economics and Political Science

Marianne Giles, LLB, BCL

Formerly Lecturer in Law, University of Kent

Michael J. Gunn, LLB

Professor of Law and Head of the Department of Academic Legal Studies,
The Nottingham Trent University

Michael Hirst, LLB, LLM

Professor of Criminal Justice, De Montfort University, Leicester

Richard D. Taylor, MA, LLM, Barrister

Professor of English Law and Head of School, Lancashire Law School,
University of Central Lancashire

Martin Wasik, LLB, MA, Barrister

Professor of Law, Manchester University
Chairman, Sentencing Advisory Panel

SECTION B1: HOMICIDE AND RELATED OFFENCES

MURDER

Definition

Murder is when a [person] . . . unlawfully killeth . . . any reasonable creature *in rerum natura* **B1.1**
under the Queen's peace, with malice aforethought . . . (Derived from *Coke's Institutes*, 3
Co Inst 47)

Procedure

Murder is triable only on indictment. It is a class 1 offence. **B1.2**

Indictment

Statement of Offence **B1.3**

Murder

Particulars of Offence

A on or about the . . . day of . . . murdered V

Alternative Verdicts

Criminal Law Act 1967, s. 6 **B1.4**

   (2)   On an indictment for murder a person found not guilty of murder may be found
guilty—
      (a)   of manslaughter, or of causing grievous bodily harm with intent to do so; or
      (b)   of any offence of which he may be found guilty under an enactment specifically
so providing, or under section 4(2) of this Act [assisting offenders]; or
      (c)   of an attempt to commit murder, or of an attempt to commit any other offence of
which he might be found guilty;
but may not be found guilty of any offence not included above.

The major enactments specifically providing for an alternative verdict within s. 6(2)(b)
are as follows:

   (a)   Suicide Act 1961, s. 2(2) (aiding and abetting suicide, see **B1.91**);
   (b)   Infant Life (Preservation) Act 1929, s. 2(2) (child destruction, see **B1.52** to
B1.60);
   (c)   Infanticide Act 1938, s. 2(2) (infanticide, see **B1.42** to **B1.51**).

To these alternative verdicts must be added:

   (d)   manslaughter;
   (e)   wounding with intent (under the Criminal Law Act 1967, s. 6(2)(a));
   (f)   assisting (contrary to the Criminal Law Act 1967, s. 4(1)) anyone guilty of any
of the above offences; and
   (g)   attempting to commit any of the above offences.

Murder is specifically excluded from the general rule on alternative verdicts laid down
in the Criminal Law Act 1967, s. 6(3) (see **D16.23**).

Although s. 6(2)(a) refers to a person being 'found not guilty of murder', a person can
still, under the common law, irrespective of s. 2, be found guilty of manslaughter as an
alternative verdict where the jury are unable to agree and are discharged by the judge
from returning a verdict on the charge of murder (*Saunders* [1988] AC 148).

It is now permissible to include other counts in an indictment for murder (see *Connelly v DPP* [1964] AC 1254; as to joinder of counts generally, see, **D9.24** to **D9.28**).

Sentence

B1.5   The penalty for murder is as follows:

Murder: Life imprisonment (mandatory sentence) (Murder (Abolition of Death Penalty) Act 1965, s. 1(1)).
Murder by a person aged 18 but under 21: Custody for life (mandatory sentence) (CJA 1982, s. 8(1)).
Murder by person aged under 18: Detention during Her Majesty's pleasure (CYPA 1933, s. 53(1)).

See further **E1.21**, **E3.9** and **E3.11**.

Elements

B1.6   The definition set out at **B1.1** is often condensed to the form 'unlawful killing with malice aforethought', to be contrasted with those forms of manslaughter which consist of unlawful killing without malice aforethought. This contrast emphasises the point that the principal distinguishing feature of murder is malice aforethought, the *mens rea*, which can now be confidently stated to be an intention to kill or to cause grievous bodily harm. Since the *actus reus* of murder also governs both manslaughter and infanticide and affects certain other offences too, it is doubly important to clarify the longer definition given by Coke.

B1.7   ***Unlawful Killing***   The word 'unlawfully' can be taken to exclude killings for which the accused has a complete and valid justification, such as killing (reasonably) in self-defence (see **A3.32** to **A3.37**) or in pursuance of a lawful order of execution. See also *Airedale NHS Trust* v *Bland* [1993] AC 789 for the distinction between (lawful) withdrawal of treatment supporting life and (unlawful) active termination of a patient's life. 'Killeth' or 'kills' means 'causes the death of', and reference should be made to the discussion of causation in **A1.22** to **A1.30** (most of the cases there discussed being homicide cases). It should also be noted that murder is a result crime for the purposes of the rule laid down by the House of Lords in *Miller* [1983] 2 AC 161 in relation to the duty to act in the face of a danger one has created oneself (see **A1.14**).

B1.8   ***Any Reasonable Creature in Rerum Natura***   This can be safely shortened to 'any human being', provided that expression is understood as being limited to one who is born alive, i.e. when it is fully expelled from its mother's body (*Poulton* (1832) 5 C & P 329) with an existence independent of its mother. Although there are difficulties about identifying the precise time at which this occurs (Criminal Law Revision Committee, 14th Report, paras 33–37), if death is caused before the child has an existence independent of its mother, the jury can convict of the offence of child destruction (see **B1.52** to **B1.60**). The accused's act may take place before the birth of the victim if it causes the victim to die after having been born alive but liability for murder or manslaughter will depend on the precise intention with which the act is done. The House of Lords decided in *A-G's Ref (No. 3 of 1994)* [1998] AC 245 that the child in utero is not simply a part of its mother as the Court of Appeal ([1996] QB 581) had held but that they are distinct organisms between which, however, the doctrine of transferred malice does not fully apply (see **A2.13**). An intention to inflict grievous bodily harm on the mother cannot ground liability for murder in respect of the subsequent live-birth-then-death of the child (although this can be manslaughter). It may however still be the case that there could be liability for the murder of the child if the intention was to kill the mother and certainly if it was intended to cause the child to die after having been born alive.

Under the Queen's Peace The original significance of this expression is somewhat **B1.9** unclear (see *Page* [1954] 1 QB 170), but the only killings it would now seem to exclude are those in the actual heat and exercise of war or in putting down a rebellion. Otherwise, the killing of aliens, whether within the jurisdiction or outside it, can amount to murder (or manslaughter) and is triable in England. Any doubts about the precise position in Coke's time in relation to killings taking place outside the jurisdiction (see *Page* [1954] 1 QB 170) are now resolved by the OAPA 1861, s. 9 (murder or manslaughter abroad), which provides as follows:

Offences against the Person Act 1861, s. 9

Where any murder or manslaughter shall be committed on land out of the United Kingdom, whether within the Queen's dominions or without, and whether the person killed were a subject of Her Majesty or not, every offence committed by any subject of Her Majesty in respect of any such case, whether the same shall amount to the offence of murder or manslaughter, . . . may be dealt with, inquired of, tried, determined, and punished . . . in England or Ireland.

The section deals with the case where the whole of the *actus reus* takes place abroad, i.e. both the act causing death and the death itself. Section 10 of the 1861 Act is a similar provision which caters for cases where one of these two elements takes place inside, and the other outside, the juridiction.

Offences against the Person Act 1861, s. 10

Where any person being criminally stricken, poisoned, or otherwise hurt upon the sea, or at any place out of England or Ireland, shall die of such stroke, poisoning, or hurt in England or Ireland, or, being criminally stricken, poisoned or otherwise hurt in any place in England or Ireland, shall die of such stroke, poisoning, or hurt upon the sea, or at any place out of England or Ireland, every offence committed in respect of any such case, whether the same shall amount to the offence of murder or of manslaughter, . . . may be dealt with, inquired of, tried, determined, and punished . . . in England or Ireland.

It will be noticed that under this section, as contrasted with s. 9, there is no express limitation on the offence requiring it to be committed 'by any subject of Her Majesty', since at least part of the *actus reus* has taken place within the jurisdiction. Nevertheless, in *Lewis* (1857) Dears & B 182, the Court for Crown Cases Reserved held that the predecessor of s. 10 (9 Geo. IV c. 34 s. 8) did not apply to a blow struck out of the jurisdiction by a foreigner which resulted in death within the jurisdiction. But it does not necessarily follow that in the case of a blow inflicted by a foreigner within the jurisdiction, but resulting in death outside it, there would not be an offence of murder triable here. Two of the points mentioned by the court in *Lewis* were that:

(a) it is impossible to say that the blow by a foreigner out of the jurisdiction was done 'feloniously' (now 'criminally' as a result of the Criminal Law Act 1967) as required by the section; and

(b) the killing should only be triable here if it could have been triable here had the death occurred at the place where the blow was given.

In our converse case of a blow inflicted within the jurisdiction causing death outside it, these objections are not applicable, since:

(a) the blow would be inflicted 'feloniously' or 'criminally' (even without an ensuing death it would constitute an assault or an unlawful wounding) since it was given within the jurisdiction; and

(b) if the death occurred here, the killing would clearly be triable here.

Thus it is submitted that, even accepting the authority of *Lewis*, s. 10 can apply to a foreigner inflicting injury in this country which results in death abroad.

The effect of all the above is that the killing of *anyone* by a British subject anywhere in the world (except, it would seem, in Scotland — see Hirst, M. at [1995] CLJ 488 and the words 'on land out of the United Kingdom' in s. 9) is triable here, and the killing of anyone by an alien is also triable here, if at least the accused's act, even if not the actual death, took place within the jurisdiction. By way of exception to all this, under the War Crimes Act 1991, certain killings in Germany or German Occupied Territory during the Second World War can be prosecuted in the United Kingdom irrespective of the nationality of the accused at the time of the alleged offence. (For offences committed on a British ship or aircraft, terrorist offences and jurisdictional questions generally, see **D1.72** *et seq.*).

B1.10   ***Abolition of Death within a Year and a Day Rule***   The former limitation that death had to occur within a year and a day of the infliction of injury was abolished, in relation to acts or omissions on or after 17 June 1996, by s. 1 of the Law Reform (Year and a Day Rule) Act 1996. The abolition is 'for all purposes' and thus affects not only murder and manslaughter but also infanticide, aiding and abetting suicide, a coroner's verdict of suicide and any statutory offences of causing death such as causing death by dangerous driving.

However, by s. 2 of the 1996 Act, the A-G's consent is required before proceedings can be instituted for a 'fatal offence' where either:

> (a)   the injury alleged to have caused the death was sustained more than three years before the death occurred, or
> (b)   the person has previously been convicted of an offence committed in circumstances alleged to be connected with the death.

It may be noted that the three-year period is expressed to run from the date that the injury is sustained rather than the date of the accused's act or omission, which may in some cases be earlier.

B1.11   ***Malice Aforethought***   Malice aforethought, the *mens rea* for murder, is now considerably clearer and rather narrower than it has been in the past, the major remaining uncertainty relating to precisely how or when a jury should infer intention from foresight (see **A2.2**), a problem which is not confined to the offence of murder. Contrary to what may be suggested by the ancient term itself, neither ill will nor premeditation is *required*, and malice aforethought is satisfied by either:

> (a)   an intention to kill; or
> (b)   an intention to cause grievous bodily harm.

Care has to be taken when referring to any cases prior to 1957, since before s. 1 of the Homicide Act of that year, an intention to further any felony was also sufficient (the so-called felony-murder or constructive malice rule). Although it was clear that constructive malice was abolished by that Act, it has taken six House of Lords decisions, and further statutory intervention, to establish the following propositions:

(a)   Murder requires intention, and nothing less (e.g., wicked recklessness as in Scotland) will suffice, i.e. it is a crime requiring specific intent, and, while foresight of virtual certainty may be evidence of intention, it is not to be equated with it (*Moloney* [1985] AC 905, explaining *Hyam* v *DPP* [1975] AC 55; see further **A2.2**).

(b)   Grievous bodily harm should be given its ordinary and natural meaning, i.e. really serious bodily harm (*DPP* v *Smith* [1961] AC 290), and is not restricted to harm likely to endanger life (*Cunningham* [1982] AC 566). As Lord Edmund-Davies commented in that case (at pp. 582–3) 'I find it passing strange that a person can be convicted of murder if death results from, say, his intentional breaking of another's arm, an action, which, while calling for severe punishment, would in most cases be unlikely to kill.' His lordship went on to recognise, however, that any change in the law on this matter was a task for Parliament.

(c)   Murder, like any other crime requiring proof of intention, involves proof of a subjective state of mind on the part of the accused.

Criminal Justice Act 1967, s. 8

A court or jury, in determining whether a person has committed an offence,—

(a)   shall not be bound in law to infer that he intended or foresaw a result of his actions by reason only of its being a natural and probable consequence of those actions; but

(b)   shall decide whether he did intend or foresee that result by reference to all the evidence, drawing such inferences from the evidence as appear proper in the circumstances.

(This reversed the effect of *DPP* v *Smith* [1961] AC 290, which had appeared to lay down an irrebuttable presumption that a man intends the natural and probable consequences of his actions, but had subsequently been said by the Privy Council in *Frankland* v *The Queen* [1987] AC 576 never to have accurately represented the common law of England.)

Thus, where an accused, as in *DPP* v *Smith* itself, does something of which the natural and probable result is death or grievous bodily harm, e.g., as in that case, driving at high speed in an erratic manner with a police officer clinging to the car, the logical processes available to the jury would appear to be as follows:

(a)   They may, but do not have to, infer that death or grievous bodily harm was *intended* (CJA 1967, s. 8).

(b)   They may, but do not have to, infer that death or grievous bodily harm was *foreseen* (CJA 1967, s. 8) *from which* they may, but do not have to, infer that death or grievous bodily harm was *intended* (*Moloney* [1985] AC 905, *Hancock* [1986] AC 455, and *Nedrick* [1986] 1 WLR 1025, and see **A2.2**).

(c)   They may, in the light of all the evidence, decide not to draw the inferences in (a) or (b) above, and conclude that the accused lacked the *mens rea* for murder.

The difference between (a) and (b) is that in (a) the inference of intention is made directly, whereas in (b) it is made indirectly via foresight (of a virtual certainty, see *Nedrick* below). Process (a) seems to be where the jury conclude from all the evidence that the accused intended death etc., in the sense that he desired to cause it, and process (b) appears to be where a jury conclude that the accused intended death etc., even though he did not necessarily desire to cause it.

Both the Court of Appeal and the House of Lords have clearly indicated that, normally, there will be no necessity to refer expressly to the accused's foresight (see *Fallon* [1994] Crim LR 519 for an example of a direction being needlessly complicated). In the words of Lord Lane CJ in *Nedrick* [1986] 1 WLR 1025 at pp. 1027–8:

> [The jury] simply has to decide whether the defendant intended to kill or do serious bodily harm. In order to reach that decision the jury must pay regard to all the relevant circumstances, including what the defendant himself said and did.

> In the great majority of cases a direction to that effect will be enough, particularly where the defendant's actions amounted to a direct attack upon his victim, because in such cases the evidence relating to the defendant's desire or motive will be clear and his intent will have been the same as his desire or motive. But in some cases, of which this is one, the defendant does an act which is manifestly dangerous and as a result someone dies. The primary desire or motive of the defendant may not have been to harm that person, or indeed anyone. In that situation what further directions should a jury be given? . . .

> Where the charge is murder and in the rare cases where the simple direction is not enough, the jury should be directed that they are not entitled to infer the necessary intention, unless they feel sure that death or serious bodily harm was a virtual certainty (barring some unforeseen intervention) as a result of the defendant's actions and that the defendant appreciated that such was the case.

109

Lord Lane CJ used the words 'virtual certainty', but in *Walker* (1990) 90 Cr App R 226, the Court of Appeal, while obviously preferring this phrase, held that it was not a misdirection to instruct a jury in terms of 'a very high degree of probability'. This was permissible provided that the dividing line between intention and recklessness was not blurred as the House of Lords held had occurred in *Woollin* [1999] AC 82 through reference to foresight of 'a substantial risk'. Lord Steyn emphasised that the *Nedrick* direction was a 'tried and tested formula' which trial judges should continue to use. This was subject to, apparently for the purposes of clarity, the substitution of the words 'to find' for the words 'to infer'.

It is instructive to look at the actual facts of *Nedrick*, as these illustrate the narrowing of the scope of malice aforethought in recent years. The appellant poured paraffin through the front door of a house and set it alight, claiming that he wished to frighten the occupant but had no desire to kill or inflict grievous bodily harm. These facts are to all intents and purposes identical with those in *Hyam* v *DPP* [1975] AC 55, and in each case the death or deaths of child occupants were caused. Whereas the House of Lords in *Hyam* v *DPP* upheld a conviction for murder based on a direction that equated foresight of a high probability with intent, the same direction was held to be a misdirection in *Nedrick*. The conviction for murder was quashed and a verdict of manslaughter substituted.

It seems in such a case that the jury, if they accept the accused's evidence that he did not want to cause death or grievous bodily harm, would only be *entitled* to convict (and even then they would not be *compelled* to do so: see *Scalley* [1995] Crim LR 504 and the final observation of Lord Steyn in *Woollin*) if they felt sure that the accused foresaw death or grievous bodily harm as a 'virtual certainty'.

Special Defences Generally

B1.12   There are three special defences to murder — diminished responsibility, provocation, and killing in pursuance of a suicide pact. All three are partial defences, reducing the offence from murder to manslaughter rather than leading to an outright acquittal, and all three are governed by the Homicide Act 1957. They are needed principally because the mandatory life sentence for murder does not leave any discretion to the judge in sentencing whereby he can take account of factors such as provocation, as he would normally be able to do on lesser charges where the sentence is not fixed by law. There is, however, a consensus that, even if the mandatory penalty were to be abolished, these defences should be retained as serving 'the valuable function of removing certain specific categories of acts from the stigma attaching to a conviction for murder and of ensuring that the facts were determined after a proper hearing before a jury' (House of Lords Select Committee on Murder and Life Imprisonment 1989, para. 82).

Before turning to the three special defences in more detail, it should also be noted that the offence of infanticide (see **B1.42** to **B1.51**) also reduces the stigma and introduces discretion as to sentence in relation to what would otherwise be murder. The difference is, however, that infanticide is an independent offence, which can be charged from the outset, whereas manslaughter on the basis of diminished responsibility or provocation arises only by way of defence. Infanticide is, however, an alternative verdict to murder (as, of course, is manslaughter) (see **B1.4**).

DIMINISHED RESPONSIBILITY

Basis of Defence

B1.13   This defence is purely statutory, having been introduced for the first time into English law (it had long been known to the Scottish courts) by the Homicide Act 1957, s. 2.

Homicide Act 1957, s. 2

(1) Where a person kills or is party to the killing of another, he shall not be convicted of murder if he was suffering from such abnormality of mind (whether arising from a condition of arrested or retarded development of mind or any inherent causes or induced by disease or injury) as substantially impaired his mental responsibility for his acts or omissions in doing or being a party to the killing.

(2) On a charge of murder, it shall be for the defence to prove that the person charged is by virtue of this section not liable to be convicted of murder.

(3) A person who but for this section would be liable, whether as principal or as accessory, to be convicted of murder shall be liable instead to be convicted of manslaughter.

(4) The fact that one party to a killing is by virtue of this section not liable to be convicted of murder shall not affect the question whether the killing amounted to murder in the case of any other party to it.

Section 2(2) puts the burden of proof on the defence, although this burden is only required to be on the balance of probabilities rather than beyond reasonable doubt (*Dunbar* [1958] 1 QB 1, and see generally **F3.4** and **F3.18**). Technically, the prosecution are allowed to allege diminished responsibility where the accused puts forward a defence of insanity (Criminal Procedure (Insanity) Act 1964, s. 6), and in such a case (which it is difficult to imagine arising very often, but see *Nott* (1958) 43 Cr App R 8) the prosecution must satisfy the normal burden of proof beyond a reasonable doubt.

The defence of diminished responsibility has largely replaced the insanity defence in murder cases. However, it is not available on a charge of attempted murder (*Campbell* [1997] Crim LR 495) nor under the Criminal Procedure (Insanity) Act 1964, s. 4A(2), following a finding of unfitness to plead (*Antoine* [1999] 2 Cr App R 225). The courts have interpreted and applied the defence in a fairly flexible manner to enable it to reduce a wide range of killings, where there are compelling mitigating circumstances, from murder to manslaughter. Nevertheless, some supporting medical evidence will invariably be required, and the court must formally be satisfied of the following ingredients.

Abnormality of Mind It is clear from the leading case of *Byrne* [1960] 2 QB 396 that **B1.14** this is much wider than 'defect of reason' within the M'Naghten Rules (see **A3.15**). In the words of Lord Parker CJ (at p. 403), abnormality of mind means:

> a state of mind so different from that of ordinary human beings that the reasonable man would term it abnormal. It appears to us to be wide enough to cover the mind's activities in all its aspects, not only the perception of physical acts and matters, and the ability to form a rational judgment as to whether an act is right or wrong, but also the ability to exercise willpower to control physical acts in accordance with that rational judgment.

Thus, there was ample evidence that Byrne, as a sexual psychopath who found it difficult, if not impossible, to control his perverted sexual desires, and who had horrifyingly mutilated the body of a young woman after strangling her, came within s. 2, and his appeal was allowed.

The broad meaning of 'abnormality of mind' should be pointed out to the jury (*Brown* [1993] Crim LR 961) and then the matter is one for them. As to medical evidence, Lord Parker CJ in *Byrne* continued:

> medical evidence is no doubt of importance, but the jury are entitled to take into consideration all the evidence, including the acts or statements of the accused and his demeanour. They are not bound to accept the medical evidence if there is other material before them which, in their good judgment, conflicts with it and outweighs it.

In this case however, 'Properly directed, we do not think that the jury could have come to any other conclusion than that the defence . . . was made out' (ibid., at p. 405).

However, if the Court of Appeal feels that the jury have been properly directed and that they have perversely rejected the medical evidence 'with no facts and no circumstances shown before them which throw doubt upon the medical evidence', then it may itself substitute a verdict of manslaughter (see *Matheson* [1958] 1 WLR 474 and *Bailey* (1961) 66 Cr App R 31 n). On the other hand, the Privy Council in *Walton* v *The Queen* [1978] AC 788 refused to interfere with a verdict of murder, even though there was medical evidence from the defence supporting diminished responsibility and no contradictory medical evidence from the prosecution. The jury were entitled to consider the 'quantity and weight' of the medical evidence and 'to consider not only the medical evidence but the evidence on the whole facts and circumstances of the case', and to conclude that 'the defence on a balance of probabilities had not been established'. The approach in *Walton* has recently been followed in *Sanders* (1991) 93 Cr App R 245.

B1.15   ***Substantial Impairment of Mental Responsibility***   Abnormality of mind is not in itself sufficient, it must be such as to 'substantially impair' the accused's 'mental responsibility'. Whether it does so:

> is a question of degree and essentially one for the jury. Medical evidence is, of course, relevant, but the question involves a decision not merely as to whether there was some impairment of the mental responsibility of the accused for his acts but whether such impairment can properly be called 'substantial', a matter upon which juries may quite legitimately differ from doctors. (*Byrne* [1960] 2 QB 396, per Lord Parker CJ at p. 404)

Lord Parker went on to refer with apparent approval to the practice (borrowed from Scotland) of referring to the requisite degree of impairment as established where there was in popular language 'partial or borderline insanity'. However, in *Seers* (1984) 79 Cr App 261 the Court of Appeal held that while this test may not have been inappropriate on the facts of *Byrne*, it was not helpful in a case such as *Seers*, where the accused was suffering from a depressive illness which the jury would clearly not regard as giving rise to partial or borderline insanity. Since the jury had been directed solely in terms of partial or borderline insanity, the conviction for murder was reduced to one of manslaughter, a verdict which, on the evidence, the jury would have been justified in returning. The Court of Appeal in *Egan* [1992] 4 All ER 470 said that explicit guidance should be given to the jury as to the meaning of 'substantial'. This should be done by adopting one of the two meanings approved in *Lloyd* [1967] 1 QB 175, namely that the jury should approach the word in a broad common-sense way, or 'that the word meant more than some trivial degree of impairment but less than total impairment'. However, in *Mitchell* [1995] Crim LR 506, the Court of Appeal declined to hold that such guidance was essential.

Although medical evidence is not conclusive on this issue, it is clearly desirable from the accused's point of view. Medical witnesses feel uneasy about testifying to a non-medical but rather legal or moral concept such as responsibility, but are generally prepared (and allowed by the court) to do so in order to make the defence workable. In *Campbell* (1986) 84 Cr App R 255 it was held that the judge rightly did not put the defence of diminished responsibility to the jury, where the medical witness's evidence (given primarily in support of a plea of provocation) was capable of showing an abnormality of mind but never addressed the question of substantial impairment. Even if the evidence had been relevant to that issue, it was said that since the burden of proof is on the defence, the judge's duty would merely be to draw the attention of defence counsel to the possible defence rather than raise it with the jury of his own accord.

B1.16   ***Causes of Abnormality of Mind***   Under the Homicide Act 1957, s. 2, this may be due to 'a condition of arrested or retarded development of mind or any inherent causes or induced by disease or injury'. These possible causes have been fairly liberally interpreted. In *Vinagre* (1979) 69 Cr App R 104 the accused was said by the medical witnesses to be suffering from 'Othello syndrome', i.e. unfounded suspicion that his wife was having an affair, and successfully pleaded diminished responsibility, much to the apparent distaste of Lawton LJ in the Court of Appeal, who nevertheless felt unable to interfere with the verdict. It seems, however, that if the wife had *in fact* been having an affair, that would merely be a case of a jealous killing which the various causes in s. 2 were designed to exclude. It would then have been merely an abnormality of mind caused by jealousy rather than by the 'disease' of 'Othello syndrome'. Even then, evidence that the well-founded jealousy caused depression or some other condition that might be described as a disease would no doubt make a successful plea possible. Less controversially, post-natal depression and premenstrual tension can constitute a disease for these purposes and so give rise to diminished responsibility (see *Reynolds* [1988] Crim LR 679) as can battered woman's syndrome (*Ahluwalia* [1992] 4 All ER 889; *Hobson* [1998] 1 Cr App R 31). 'Mercy killing' can also be dealt with as manslaughter, where the dilemma which has caused the accused to kill can be said to have given rise to depression or some other medically recognised disorder which can be said to be the cause of an abnormality of mind (see, e.g., *Price* (1971) *The Times*, 22 December 1971 (news item)).

Relevance of Intoxication

Voluntary intoxication is not an acceptable cause of the abnormality. In *Tandy* [1989] 1 **B1.17** WLR 350, the accused was an alcoholic who strangled her 11-year-old daughter after drinking nine-tenths of a bottle of vodka and upon learning that her daughter had been sexually abused. She was clearly suffering from an abnormality of mind at the time of the killing, and the amount of alcohol in her bloodstream would have been lethal for most people. However, the Court of Appeal upheld the conviction for murder based on the trial judge's direction that, for the defence to succeed, the abnormality had to be caused by the disease of alcoholism rather than by the voluntary ingestion of alcohol on the particular occasion. This would be the case 'If the alcoholism had reached the level at which her brain had been injured by the repeated insult from intoxicants so that there was gross impairment of her judgment and emotional responses' (per Watkins LJ, at p. 356).

Even if this was not the case (as the jury must have found by their verdict), the alcoholism might still found a defence if it meant that the intoxication was not voluntary, i.e. if 'she was no longer able to resist the impulse to drink'. Although the defence medical witnesses testified to this effect, the prosecution witness was of the view that 'the appellant had control over whether she had the first drink of the day, but once she had had the first drink she was no longer in control' (ibid., at p. 354), and the Court of Appeal said (at p. 357) that 'the judge was correct in telling the jury that, if the taking of the first drink was not involuntary, then the whole of the drinking [on that day] was not involuntary'.

Tandy was followed in *Inseal* [1992] Crim LR 35, where the Court of Appeal approved of the trial judge's direction only in terms of this second issue of whether the drinking had become involuntary, since no medical evidence had been given on the first question of whether the brain had been 'injured by the repeated insults from intoxicants'.

The relevance in *Tandy* of the distinction between voluntary and involuntary intoxication is in answering the question of whether the abnormality of mind is caused by disease, i.e. alcoholism. If the intoxication is voluntary, then it constitutes a *novus actus interveniens* and breaks the causal link between the alcoholism and the abnormality of mind. If it is involuntary, in the sense that the accused's alcoholism meant she was no longer able to resist the impulse to take (even the first) drink, then the actual intoxication is not a *novus actus* but part of the causal chain between the alcoholism and the abnormality of mind. As Watkins LJ put it (ibid., at p. 356), 'if her drinking was involuntary then her abnormality of mind at the time of the act of strangulation was induced by her condition of alcoholism'.

If this is correct, then logically an alcoholic (or anybody else for that matter) whose orange juice, for example, is surreptitiously laced with vodka by another, might have difficulty relying on diminished responsibility. Even though his abnormality of mind is caused by involuntary intoxication, it would appear that it is not induced by disease. This seems rather harsh but a possible answer is that the abnormality might be said to be due to one of the other causes specified in s. 2(1), i.e. 'injury'. The spiker of the drinks could be said to be inflicting an injury via the alcohol on the accused's brain, just as much as if he clubbed him over the head, and thus the abnormality could be said to be induced by 'injury'. However, in *Di Duca* (1959) 43 Cr App R 167, the court was 'very doubtful' as to whether the transient effect of drink could amount to an injury and in *O'Connell* [1997] Crim LR 683 similar doubts were expressed in respect of the transient effects of voluntarily ingested Halcion (a sleeping drug). These doubts can be explained on the grounds that the courts were speaking of cases of *voluntary* intoxication. Rather than deny that the transient effect of drink or drugs can ever constitute an injury, it would be better merely to exclude voluntarily self-inflicted injuries (including the effects of voluntary intoxication) from the meaning of 'injury' within s. 2(1). Their exclusion can be justified on the grounds that, being voluntarily self-inflicted, they are not capable of substantially impairing responsibility within the meaning of the section. (See also Mackay, R.D. 'The Abnormality of Mind Factor in Diminished Responsibility' [1999] Crim LR 117.)

A slightly different problem arises where there are two independent possible causes of the abnormality of mind, one of which *is* an allowable cause within s. 2(1) (e.g., a depressive illness) and the other of which is voluntary intoxication (which is clearly not allowable). This was essentially the situation in *Gittens* [1984] QB 698, where the judge told the jury to consider which was the substantial cause of the abnormality of mind, the accused's illness or the alcohol. The Court of Appeal held that this was a misdirection. The real question was not the relative strength of the contribution of the two causes but whether, whatever the contribution made by drink, there was an abnormality of mind, *due to causes specified in s. 2(1)*, which substantially impaired the accused's responsibility for the killing. The effect of this was summed up by Professor Smith in [1984] Crim LR 553–4 (in a passage approved by the Court of Appeal in *Atkinson* [1985] Crim LR 314 and again in *Egan* [1992] 4 All ER 470) as follows:

> the two questions for the jury, in logical sequence, would seem to be: 'Have the defence satisfied you on the balance of probabilities — that if the defendant had not taken drink — (i) he would have killed as he in fact did? And (ii) he would have been under diminished responsibility when he did so?'

Essentially it seems that the jury have to decide whether there is a *sufficient* abnormality of mind *caused by permissible factors* such as substantially to impair his responsibility, irrespective of the fact that the accused's abnormality may in fact have been accentuated even further by the ingestion of alcohol.

Accepting Plea of Diminished Responsibility

B1.18 It has already been noted that one cannot initially charge manslaughter on the basis of diminished responsibility, and so the accused has to be indicted for murder no matter how clearly he appears to come within the terms of the Homicide Act 1957, s. 2(1). In some cases the prosecution may be able to accept a plea of manslaughter to an indictment for murder. In *Cox* [1968] 1 WLR 308, Winn LJ said (at p. 310):

> that there are cases where, on an indictment for murder, it is perfectly proper, where the medical evidence is plainly to this effect, to treat the case as one of substantially diminished responsibility and accept, if it be tendered, a plea to manslaughter on that ground, and avoid a trial for murder.

However, the Court of Appeal in *Vinagre* (1979) 69 Cr App R 104 warned (in the context of the acceptance of a plea based on the 'Othello syndrome') that:

it was never intended that pleas should be accepted on flimsy grounds [but only] when there is clear evidence of mental imbalance. We do not consider that in this case there was clear evidence of mental imbalance. There was clear evidence of killing by a jealous husband which, until modern times, no one would have thought was anything else but murder. (per Lawton LJ, at pp. 106–7)

Thus, in a novel or borderline sort of case, the plea ought not to be accepted but the evidence presented to a jury for their determination. The public interest may demand this in a notorious case such as that of the 'Yorkshire Ripper' (*The Times*, 23 May 1981). This was a striking case, in the sense that the prosecution were prepared to accept the plea in the light of unanimous psychiatric reports that the accused, Sutcliffe, was a paranoid schizophrenic, but the judge insisted that there should be a trial before a jury who convicted of murder. The nub of the problem is that, however unanimous the medical witnesses may be about there being an abnormality of mind, the question of whether that abnormality 'substantially impaired responsibility' is ultimately not a medical question but one for the jury. Thus, as a general rule, the prosecution should only accept a plea (and the judge should only approve that acceptance) where there is clear and convincing evidence of diminished responsibility. Of course, there may be exceptional cases where it is desirable to accept a plea on the basis of less convincing evidence because a trial is undesirable for other reasons, e.g., the accused is himself seriously and terminally ill.

PROVOCATION

Basis of Defence

Unlike diminished responsibility, provocation was recognised at common law as a **B1.19** partial defence to murder long before the Homicide Act 1957, and is further distinguishable in that the burden of proof is not on the defence, i.e. the jury must clearly be told that, once there is evidence capable of supporting a finding that the accused was provoked, the burden is on the prosecution to prove beyond reasonable doubt that the case is not one of provocation. (See *Cascoe* [1970] 2 All ER 833.) Provocation is not available on a charge of attempted murder (*Bruzas* [1972] Crim LR 367) since it can be taken account of in sentencing, although to some it seems anomalous that a person can be convicted of attempted murder where he might only have been convicted of manslaughter had he succeeded. However, the position is the same for diminished responsibility (*Campbell* [1997] Crim LR 495).

The classic test of provocation at common law was that given by Devlin J in *Duffy* [1949] 1 All ER 932n and approved by the Court of Criminal Appeal in that case:

> Provocation is some act, or series of acts, done by the dead man to the accused which would cause in any reasonable person, and actually causes in the accused, a sudden and temporary loss of self-control, rendering the accused so subject to passion as to make him or her for the moment not master of his mind.

Although this passage has been approved again since 1957 in *Ibrams* (1981) 74 Cr App R 154, it has to be read in the light of the Homicide Act 1957, s. 3, which does not provide a complete definition of provocation, but provides as follows:

Homicide Act 1957, s. 3

> Where on a charge of murder there is evidence on which a jury can find that the person charged was provoked (whether by things done or by things said or by both together) to lose his self-control, the question whether the provocation was enough to make a reasonable man do as he did shall be left to be determined by the jury; and in determining that question the jury shall take into account everything both done and said according to the effect which, in their opinion, it would have on a reasonable man.

Inherent in both Devlin J's definition at common law and the above statutory provision is the requirement of two conditions to be satisfied for the defence to be made out, namely:

(a)   the 'subjective' condition that the accused was actually provoked so as to lose his self-control; and

(b)   the 'objective' condition that the reasonable man would have done so.

Section 3 has effected subtle but significant changes to the way in which both these conditions operate.

B1.20   ***The Subjective Condition***   The most obvious result of the Homicide Act 1957, s. 3, is that it is only on this issue that the judge can withdraw the defence of provocation from the jury on the ground that there is no evidence capable of supporting it. If there is any evidence capable of satisfying this subjective condition (whether from the accused or from the surrounding circumstances: see *Rossiter* (1992) 95 Cr App R 326 and *Cambridge* [1994] 1 WLR 971 and contrast *Wellington* [1993] Crim LR 616 and *Walch* [1993] Crim LR 714), the questions of whether the accused did in fact lose self control and whether the objective condition is satisfied have to be left to the jury. (Strictly speaking, the issue is whether the prosecution have proved beyond a reasonable doubt that the objective condition (or, alternatively, the subjective condition) is *not* satisfied.) As Lord Tucker put it in *Bullard* v *The Queen* [1957] AC 635 (at p. 642 emphasis added):

> It has long been settled law that if on the evidence, whether of the prosecution or of the defence, there is any evidence of provocation fit to be left to a jury, and whether or not this issue has been specifically raised at the trial by counsel for the defence and whether or not the accused has said in terms that he was provoked, it is the duty of the judge, after a proper direction, to leave it open to the jury to return verdict of manslaughter *if they are not satisfied beyond reasonable doubt that the killing was unprovoked.*

The above is true whatever the main defence run by the accused, whether it be one such as accident, self-defence, lack of intent or diminished responsibility which acknowledges that the accused caused the death or whether it be one such as alibi or act of another which denies even that the accused caused the death (see Lord Taylor CJ in *Cambridge* [1994] 1 WLR 971 at p. 976). It even appears to be true where counsel for the accused has indicated to the judge that provocation should not be put to the jury (*Burgess* [1995] Crim LR 425 and *Dhillon* [1997] 2 Cr App R 104). Where the judge has, as a matter of law, to leave the issue of provocation to the jury, he should indicate to them, unless it is obvious (see *Scott* [1997] Crim LR 597), what evidence might support the conclusion that the accused had lost self-control. It is particulary important that the judge does so where counsel has not raised the issue at all (*Stewart* [1995] 4 All ER 999), and this includes identifying the evidence of what was specifically said or done to constitute the provocation. Otherwise the jury will find it impossible to assess, under the second objective question, whether the reasonable man would have reacted, to what was done or said, in the way that the accused did (see the Court of Appeal judgment in *Acott* [1996] 4 All ER 443). An issue of provocation could arise only if the judge considered that there was some evidence of a specific act or words of provocation resulting in a loss of self-control. Loss of self-control caused by other factors such as fear, panic or circumstances was not enough nor was a mere speculative possibility of provocation in the absence of any actual evidence of acts or words of provocation (see the House of Lords' judgment in *Acott* [1997] 1 WLR 306).

In addition to regulating the respective roles of judge and jury, s. 3 incidentally affects the question of what is capable of constituting provocation and what is capable of satisfying the subjective condition.

First, provocation is no longer restricted to 'some act, or series of acts', since s. 3, by its use of the phrase 'whether by things done or by things said or by both together', clearly envisages that words alone can constitute provocation (see *DPP* v *Camplin* [1978] AC 705 per Lord Diplock at p. 716). The acts, words, or indeed sounds, may even be perfectly lawful or commonplace ones as, for example, the crying of a young baby in *Doughty* (1986) 83 Cr App R 319 (see **B1.27**).

Secondly, it appears it no longer need be, although it generally will be, 'something done by the dead man to the accused'. It may be something done *by* a third person in some way connected with the victim (see *Davies* [1975] QB 691, conduct by wife's lover relevant to whether husband provoked to kill his wife). Alternatively it may be something done *to* a third person, such as the child, spouse or, as in *Pearson* [1992] Crim LR 193, the brother of the accused. Some people may retain self-control if attacked personally but understandably lose it in the face of an attack on a vulnerable loved one. On the other hand, provocation does seem to require conduct on the part of someone (things done or things said), and there is no such thing as provocation by circumstances, e.g., D in anguish at seeing his wife or children killed by a bolt of lightning runs wild in his car killing innocent pedestrians (see the example given by Steyn LJ in *Acott* [1997] 1 WLR 306 at p. 312 of a slowdown of traffic due to snow).

A third possible, but not yet fully accepted, candidate for modification is the rule that provocation must result in a 'sudden and temporary loss of self-control'. The practice of trial judges in domestic killings has sometimes been to allow the defence of provocation to go to the jury even where there has been an interval between the last act which might be relied upon as provocation and the actual killing (see for example *Pearson*). However, where the trial judge rules that the time gap is such that there is no evidence that the accused was in fact provoked to lose his self-control, and withdraws the defence from the jury, the Court of Appeal has at times shown itself not to be prepared to interfere and has applied the strict letter of the law. This is illustrated in *Ibrams* (1981) 74 Cr App R 154, where the last instance of provocation, consisting of 'gross bullying and terrorising', had taken place seven days before the accused's planned, pre-emptive and fatal attack. The Court of Appeal cited with approval the passage from the judgment of Devlin J (as he then was) in *Duffy* [1949] 1 All ER 932n, quoted at **B1.19**. The court also approved the following statement:

> circumstances which induce a desire for revenge are inconsistent with provocation, since the conscious formulation of a desire for revenge means that the person has had time to think, to reflect, and that would negative a sudden temporary loss of self-control, which is of the essence of provocation.

Subsequently in *Ahluwalia* [1992] 4 All ER 889, one of a number of cases of long term domestic violence and abuse where provocation has been in issue, the Court of Appeal regarded itself as still bound by this approach stating that 'important considerations of public policy would be involved should provocation be re-defined so as possibly to blur the distinction between sudden loss of self-control and deliberate retribution'. However, Lord Taylor CJ also made it clear that, provided there was a sudden loss of control, the interval between the provocation and that loss of control was a matter to be taken in account in assessing the evidence on the facts of the case and did not give rise to a rule of law:

> It is open to the judge, when deciding whether there is any evidence of provocation to be left to the jury, and open to the jury when considering such evidence, to take account of the interval between the provocative conduct and the reaction of the defendant to it. In some cases the interval between the provocative conduct and the defendant's reaction might wholly undermine the defence of provocation. However, that depends entirely on the facts of the individual case and was not a principle of law.

Their lordships accepted that the subjective element in that defence would not as a matter of law be negatived simply because of the delayed reaction in cases of women subjected frequently over a period to violent treatment, provided that there was at the time of the killing a sudden and temporary loss of self-control.

Thus the loss of self-control has to be sudden and temporary in that it comes over the accused quickly (whether or not it does so instantly after the provocation) and departs reasonably quickly as opposed to being a planned or premeditated killing. Such a killing will not give rise to a defence of provocation even if it follows a long history of serious abuse by the victim (although this might be relevant to a defence of diminished responsibility, as was eventually successful in *Ahluwalia* itself.)

Cases of planned killings after a long period of provocation should be distinguished from cases of cumulative provocation, where the last instance of provocation closest to the time of an unplanned killing is relatively minor but is 'the straw that breaks the camel's back' or, as in *Humphreys* [1995] 4 All ER 1008, 'the trigger which caused the appellant's self-control to snap'. Here there is no reason why the defence of provocation should not succeed, even though the last instance of provocation would not on its own have been sufficient to make the accused (or the reasonable man) lose self-control. The provocation adjacent to the time of the killing must obviously be viewed in the light of past history (see *Pearson* [1992] Crim LR 193). However, there must be evidence that the accused did actually lose self-control. This appeared to be lacking in *Thornton* [1992] 1 All ER 306 (but see the retrial ordered by the Court of Appeal following a reference by the Home Secretary: *Thornton (No. 2)* [1996] 1 WLR 1174 and also in *Cocker* [1989] Crim LR 740, in which the accused calmly and quietly killed his chronically ill wife after repeated entreaties by her to do so, and the Court of Appeal said that his evidence showed not that he had lost self-control but merely that he had finally acceded to his wife's wishes.

B1.21 ***The Objective Condition*** As a result of the Homicide Act 1957, s. 3, the judge can no longer withdraw the defence from the jury on the grounds that the reasonable man would not have done as the accused did. That is now solely an issue for the jury. The evidence of witnesses as to how the reasonable man would react is not admissible, but the judge should direct the jury as to the meaning of the reasonable man test and *may* suggest considerations which might influence them in coming to their conclusion. But it must be emphasised that the issue is ultimately one for the jury alone (see *DPP* v *Camplin* [1978] AC 705, per Lord Diplock at p. 716).

Formerly, juries were told that the reasonable man shared none of the peculiarities of the accused. Thus, understandably, drunkenness and excitability or irascibility were not relevant characteristics. But neither, unfortunately, was a characteristic such as impotence, even where the provocation consisted, in part, of taunts about the accused's impotence, as in the much criticised decision of the House of Lords in *Bedder* v *DPP* [1954] 1 WLR 1119. However, *Bedder* is no longer authoritative, in view of s. 3 and the House of Lords decision in *DPP* v *Camplin*. Now that words alone can constitute provocation it would not make sense totally to exclude the characteristics of the accused, because:

> the gravity of verbal provocation may well depend upon the particular characteristics or circumstances of the person to whom a taunt or insult is addressed. To taunt a person because of his race, his physical infirmities or some shameful incident in his past may well be considered by the jury to be more offensive to the person addressed, however equable his temperament, if the facts on which the taunt is founded are true than it would be if they were not. (*DPP* v *Camplin* [1978] AC 705 per Lord Diplock at p. 717)

Thus, today:

> a proper direction to a jury on the question left to their exclusive determination by section 3 of the Act of 1957 would be on the following lines. The judge should state what the question is using the very terms of the section. He should then explain to them that the

reasonable man referred to in the question is *a person having the power of self-control to be expected of an ordinary person of the sex and age of the accused, but in other respects sharing such of the accused's characteristics as they think would affect the gravity of the provocation to him*; and that the question is not merely whether such a person would in like circumstances be provoked to lose his self-control but also whether he would react to the provocation as the accused did. (ibid., per Lord Diplock at p. 718 emphasis added)

It is not possible to draw up a list of relevant or permissible characteristics, since this depends on whether the characteristic is one which affects the gravity of the provocation, and that will depend on the nature of the provocation in the particular case. Thus, chronic alcoholism was held not to be a relevant characteristic in *Newell* (1980) 71 Cr App R 31, since the provocation consisted of taunts about the accused's former girlfriend. The fact that he was a chronic alcoholic did not affect the gravity of those taunts, although no doubt it may have affected his powers of self-control. On the other hand, had he been taunted about the fact that he was a chronic alcoholic, the characteristic would have been relevant since it would affect the gravity of the taunts. In *Roberts* [1990] Crim LR 122, deafness was a relevant characteristic since it affected the gravity of the provocation. On the other hand, evidence that persons with the accused's characteristics were subject to irrational explosions of violence was irrelevant since it related to powers of self-control, not the gravity of the provocation.

The Court of Appeal in *Newell* seemed to doubt whether chronic alcoholism was of sufficient significance or permanence to constitute a 'characteristic', although they were prepared to assume it was for the purpose of the appeal. The court was clear, however, that the fact that the accused had:

> taken an overdose of drugs and written a suicide note a few days previously, his grief at the defection of his girlfriend, and so on, are none of them matters which can properly be described as characteristics. ((1980) 71 Cr App R 331 at p. 340)

Previous editions of this work expressed the opinion that this was an unduly narrow view, since Lord Diplock in *DPP* v *Camplin* [1978] AC 705 considered that a shameful incident in the past might be relevant to the gravity of a taunt about that incident. Furthermore, it was difficult to see why a transient, as opposed to a permanent, characteristic should not be relevant if the provocation is directed towards it. Indeed, it seems particularly harsh on the facts of *Newell* that his grief at recently losing his girlfriend should be excluded when the provocation consisted of derogatory remarks about her. As Lord Diplock put it in *DPP* v *Camplin* (at p. 717 emphasis added):

> It would stultify much of the mitigation of the previous harshness of the common law in ruling out verbal provocation . . . if the jury could not take into consideration *all those factors* which in their opinion would affect the gravity of taunts and insults when applied to the person to whom they are addressed.

The decision in *Newell* (1980) 71 Cr App R 331 unfortunately fastened on the word 'characteristic' in Lord Diplock's suggested direction, and treated it as though it were a word in a statute, when in fact Lord Diplock was using it as one (perhaps the most common) example of the types of *factor* which could affect the gravity of provocation. Indeed, the Court of Appeal based its decision on the New Zealand case of *McGregor* [1962] NZLR 1069 which *was* a decision on the meaning of the word 'characteristic' in a statute and about which reservations have more recently been expressed by the New Zealand Court of Appeal (see *McCarthy* [1992] 2 NZLR 550).

Such criticisms of *Newell* and of its reliance on *McGregor* have now been accepted by the House of Lords in *Morhall* [1996] AC 90, where the accused's addiction to glue sniffing was accepted as a relevant characteristic in assessing the gravity of provocation consisting of taunts about the addiction. The earlier exclusion of such addictions and other undesirable or discreditable characteristics by the Court of Appeal as being inconsistent with the concept of the reasonable man was rejected by Lord Goff. On the other hand, the current state of being intoxicated due to glue or from some other cause, as opposed to the fact of one's addiction, would not be relevant since that would not affect the gravity of the provocation but rather the accused's powers of self-control, which are required to come up to the standard of the ordinary reasonable man. Although some recent decisions of the Court of Appeal in cases, such as *Humphreys* [1995] 4 All ER 1008, *Dryden* [1995] 4 All ER 987 and *Thornton (No. 2)* [1996] 1 WLR 1174, may appear to have weakened somewhat the distinction between characteristics or factors relevant to the gravity of the provocation and those relevant to powers of self-control, the importance of the distinction was re-iterated by the Privy Council in *Luc Thiet Thuan v The Queen* [1997] AC 131. Lord Goff, in giving the judgment of the majority, followed consistently the logic of the decision in *Morhall*, this time to *deny* the relevance to the objective test of a characteristic such as mental infirmity which, on the facts, merely affected powers of self-control rather than the gravity of the provocation.

Unfortunately, some doubt has been cast on the authority of *Luc Thiet Thuan* by some *obiter* statements of the Court of Appeal in *Campbell* [1997] 1 Cr App R 199 where Lord Bingham CJ was of the view that 'unless and until the previous decisions of this court are authoritatively overruled, our duty and that of trial judges bound by the decisions of this court is to apply the principles which those cases lay down'. The problem with this statement is that it interprets the decisions of the Court of Appeal as allowing to be taken into account mental characteristics which do not affect the gravity of the provocation and is thus inconsistent with two decisions of the House of Lords, *Camplin* and *Morhall*. The dicta in *Campbell* were recently applied by the Court of Appeal in *Parker* [1997] Crim LR 760. The defence had sought to introduce evidence that D was a chronic alcoholic with some brain damage which rendered him more susceptible to provocation. The trial judge purported to follow *Luc Thiet Thuan* and refused to admit the evidence; the Court of Appeal quashed the conviction for murder since it regarded itself as bound to follow the Court of Appeal authorities in preference to *Luc Thiet Thuan*.

However, a better explanation of the Court of Appeal cases such as *Thornton (No. 2)*, *Humphreys* and *Dryden* is that the characteristic of the accused in each case was relevant not as affecting the degree of self-control to be expected of the accused but as affecting the gravity of the provocation. Thus an instance of abuse of a woman with battered woman's syndrome can be regarded as more provocative than abuse of one not suffering from such a syndrome and a threat to evict a person who is obsessive about his land may be more provocative than it would be to an ordinary person, even though each person would be expected to exercise the same level of self-control to a given level of gravity of provocation. The same point can be made about *Parker*. Increased susceptibility to provocation can be interpreted as meaning the provocation would seem more grave to the accused whereas in *Luc Thiet Thuan* the evidence was put forward simply on the basis that the mental deficiency reduced the powers of self-control. In other words, the evidence could have been allowed in *Parker* without necessarily casting doubt on *Luc Thiet Thuan*. However, *Parker* was followed in *Smith* [1998] 4 All ER 387, where the Court of Appeal, exceptionally, itself granted leave to appeal to the House of Lords, certifying the following point of law: 'Are characteristics other than age and sex, attributable to the reasonable man, for the purpose of section 3 of the Homicide Act 1957, relevant not only to the gravity of the provocation to him but also to the standards of self-control to be expected'.

It was held in *Ali* [1989] Crim LR 736 that on the particular facts it was not necessary to draw the jury's attention to the age of the 20-year-old accused. It is submitted, however, that the safest course is to follow Lord Diplock's formula of referring to an ordinary person of the sex and age of the accused. These characteristics may be relevant as affecting powers of self-control, whether or not they affect the gravity of the provocation.

Relationship between Provocation and Accused's Retaliation

Although provocation can now clearly be constituted by words alone, more commonly **B1.22** and more cogently it will consist of a physical attack. In this context, too, the Homicide Act 1957, s. 3, has worked a change. There is no longer any hard and fast rule that 'the mode of resentment must bear a reasonable relationship to the provocation', as had been laid down by the House of Lords in *Mancini* v *DPP* [1942] AC 1 at p. 9 in approving the trial judge's decision not to put the defence of provocation to the jury where the only acceptable evidence of provocation was an *unarmed* attack by the deceased to which the accused responded with a knife. (The jury in rejecting self-defence were regarded as having thereby rejected Mancini's story that the victim had himself attacked him with a knife.) Following the Homicide Act of 1957 (assuming there is some evidence that the accused actually was provoked to lose self-control) the judge is obliged to leave the question to the jury 'whether the provocation was enough to make the reasonable man do as the [accused] did'. The relationship between the provocation and what the accused did is certainly not an irrelevant factor for the jury in answering that question. It is, however, no longer 'a rule of law which they are bound to follow, but merely a consideration which may or may not commend itself to them' (*Phillips* v *The Queen* [1969] 2 AC 130 per Lord Diplock at p. 138).

According to the less than convincing decision of the Court of Appeal in *Clarke* [1991] Crim LR 383, in considering whether the provocation was enough to make the reasonable man do as the accused did, the jury are not restricted to the accused's acts causing death but can also consider other acts done by the accused provided they are not too remote. The accused had strangled his victim and then placed live electric wires in her mouth. Even if she was already dead before the electrocution, the jury could consider whether the reasonable man would have been provoked to carry out the electrocution rather than merely the strangulation.

Self-induced Provocation

An accused may be able to rely on provocation which he is partially responsible for **B1.23** bringing about. In *Edwards* v *The Queen* [1973] AC 648 the accused was blackmailing his victim, who had the temerity to swear at him and attack him with a knife. The accused then disarmed him and stabbed him 27 times. The Privy Council noted (at p. 658) that:

> the person sought to be blackmailed, did go to extreme lengths, in that he made a violent attack on the appellant with a knife, inflicting painful wounds and putting the appellant's life in danger. There was evidence of provocation and it was fit for consideration by the jury.

However, if the blackmail victim's reaction had not been so extreme, but had merely been a predictable, hostile reaction, such as 'vituperative words and even . . . blows from a fist,' then the blackmailer would not be able to 'rely on the predictable results of his own blackmailing conduct' (ibid., at p. 658).

To reconcile this approach with the words of the Homicide Act 1957, s. 3, one has to treat the Privy Council as merely laying down factors (such as the predictability of the victim's reaction) which the judge should take into account in deciding whether there is any real evidence that the subjective condition was satisfied and that the accused actually lost self-control. The reference to 'evidence fit for consideration by the jury' confirms that this was the Privy Council's intention. Certainly, to inflict 27 stab wounds was at least consistent with loss of control. This is preferable to saying that the reasonable man would not be provoked by the predictable results of his own wrongdoing, an approach which would be unsound, given the fact that the reaction of the reasonable man is now purely a matter for the jury. Thus in *Johnson* [1989] 1 WLR 740, the Court of Appeal substituted a verdict of manslaughter where the trial judge refused to leave provocation to the jury on the ground that the provocation was to some extent the result of the accused's own conduct. Since there was evidence that the accused was in fact provoked to lose his self-control, the defence had to be put to the jury.

The Court of Appeal does not now encourage artificial rules about what can or cannot constitute provocation in order to retain the control over the defence that used to be exercised prior to the Homicide Act 1957, under the guise of the former rules about the reactions of the reasonable man. The case of *Doughty* (1986) 83 Cr App R 319 is another example of their willingness to leave the issue to the jury as intended by the Act. The Court of Appeal rejected the trial judge's ruling that the perfectly natural crying of a 17-day-old baby could not constitute provocation even so as to satisfy the subjective condition, saying (at p. 326):

> We . . . feel that reliance can be placed upon the common sense of juries upon whom the task of deciding the issue is imposed by section 3 and that that common sense will ensure that only in cases where the facts fully justified it would their verdict be likely to be that they would hold that a defendant's act in killing a crying child would be the response of a reasonable man.

The same sentiments are no doubt appropriate to a jury's reaction to a case of self-induced provocation which is actually left to them.

KILLING IN PURSUANCE OF SUICIDE PACT

Homicide Act 1957, s. 4

B1.24   (1)   It shall be manslaughter, and shall not be murder, for a person acting in pursuance of a suicide pact between him and another to kill the other or be a party to the other being killed by a third person.

The burden of proof that he was acting in pursuance of a suicide pact is placed on the accused by s. 4(2).

'Suicide pact' is defined in s. 4(3) as:

> a common agreement between two or more persons having for its object the death of all of them, whether or not each is to take his own life, but nothing done by a person who enters into a suicide pact shall be treated as done by him in pursuance of the pact unless it is done while he has the settled intention of dying in pursuance of the pact.

Thus the burden of proof on the accused involves not only proof that there was in fact a suicide pact, but also that at the time of the killing the accused still had the intention of dying himself.

Killing in pursuance of a suicide pact is closely related to the offence of aiding and abetting suicide under the Suicide Act 1961, s. 2(1) (see **B1.88**). Section 2(2) provides that, if on an indictment for murder or manslaughter it is proved that the accused aided and abetted, counselled or procured the suicide of the person in question, the jury may find him guilty of that offence. If, on the other hand, the accused aided and abetted a killing by a third person, that is still potentially murder, but will be reduced to manslaughter under the Homicide Act 1957, s. 4, if it was done in pursuance of a suicide pact.

MANSLAUGHTER GENERALLY

Voluntary and Involuntary Manslaughter

B1.25   Manslaughter can be classified as either voluntary or involuntary. Voluntary manslaughter has in effect already been considered, since it consists of those killings which would be murder (because the accused has the relevant *mens rea* — hence the label *voluntary* manslaughter) but which are reduced to manslaughter because of one of the three special defences provided for by the Homicide Act 1957, discussed at **B1.13** to **B1.17**. Voluntary manslaughter is not an offence one can be indicted for, but rather is a verdict which can result from an initial indictment for murder. The actual verdict, however, will be simply 'manslaughter' without the label of 'voluntary'.

Involuntary manslaughter, on the other hand, refers to those types of manslaughter which can be charged in their own right and where the accused lacks the *mens rea* for murder, although equally they can result from an indictment for murder where the prosecution fail to prove the *mens rea*.

The fact that a verdict of manslaughter can reflect a number of different views of the facts taken by the jury (or by different members of the same jury) can lead to difficulties in sentencing and in relation to the normal rule requiring unanimity of verdicts (*cf* **D15.16**). It was said by the Court of Criminal Appeal in *Larkin* [1943] KB 174 that it was 'most undesirable' that the jury should be asked to explain the basis of their verdict. However, in *Matheson* [1958] 1 WLR 474 the Court of Criminal Appeal said (at p. 480) that if diminished responsibility and some other ground such as provocation are left to the jury, the judge may, and generally should, ask the jury whether the verdict was based on diminished responsibility, or on the other ground or on both. This matter has been further considered in *Jones* (1999) *The Times*, 17 February 1999 (where neither of the above cases was referred to). The Court of Appeal made it clear that there is no obligation on the judge to ask any such question (of which advance warning should in any event be given), it being 'a matter entirely for him or her in the exercise of his or her discretion'. Neither is there any obligation on the jury to give an answer if asked, any such answer being merely additional information to help with sentence:

> . . . provided that the jury are agreed that the defendant is guilty of manslaughter, in the sense that they are sure that he perpetrated an unlawful act which caused the death of the accused, it is unnecessary that there be any unanimity by the jury as to the route by which that verdict is achieved.

This seems right on the facts of the case and for those cases (the majority) where the offence is at least manslaughter and may be murder if malice aforethought can be established and if provocation and diminished responsibility (if in issue) can be negatived. The prosecution has to prove causation and the unlawful act (such as an intentional assault), and negative complete defences such as self-defence if in issue, but the different possible reasons for an offence being manslaughter rather than murder are negative ones (reasonable doubt by the jury as to whether malice aforethought has been proved or whether diminished responsibility or provocation has been negatived). It is not a question of the prosecution having to prove any of these things for manslaughter; manslaughter is merely the residual verdict for any one of these reasons. It is submitted however that it would be different if manslaughter is alleged on two fundamentally separate grounds: unlawful act and gross negligence. It should not be sufficient that six jurors thought that the accused's act causing death was unlawful but not grossly negligent and the other six thought it was grossly negligent but not unlawful. Here the prosecution have not proved either of the two forms of manslaughter beyond reasonable doubt; it is quite different from a case where what would otherwise be murder has been proved and the jurors merely differ as to the reason for *reducing* the offence to manslaughter.

Definition of Involuntary Manslaughter

Superficially, this is the same as the definition for murder (see **B1.1**) without the **B1.26** requirement of malice aforethought. This is only helpful in that it emphasises that requirements such as that the victim be a fully born human being are equally part of the offence of manslaughter. It is more common to refer to manslaughter as 'unlawful killing without malice aforethought', but this is not particularly helpful, because it does not indicate which killings will be regarded as unlawful in the absence of malice aforethought. In fact there now appear to be two main categories of killing without malice aforethought which are regarded as unlawful and hence amount to manslaughter:

(a)   killing by an unlawful act likely to cause bodily harm — often called 'unlawful act manslaughter' or 'constructive manslaughter'; and
(b)   killing grossly negligently.

Procedure

B1.27   Manslaughter is triable only on indictment. It is a class 2 offence.

Indictment

B1.28   Statement of Offence

Manslaughter

                                        Particulars of Offence

A on or about the . . . day of . . . , unlawfully killed V

Alternative Verdicts

B1.29   These include:

(a)   child destruction (Infant Life (Preservation) Act 1929, s. 2(2)), see **B1.52** to **B1.60**).
(b)   abortion (Infant Life (Preservation) Act 1929, s. 2(3)), see **B1.61** to **B1.69**).
(c)   complicity in suicide (Suicide Act 1961, s. 2(2)), see **B1.88** to **B1.93**).
(d)   assisting an offender (Criminal Law Act 1967, s. 4(2)).

By way of exception to the general rule, there appears to be no such verdict as attempted manslaughter (see *Bruzas* [1972] Crim LR 367 and *Campbell* [1997] Crim LR 495).

Sentencing Guidelines: Diminished Responsibility

B1.30   The maximum penalty is life imprisonment (OAPA 1861, s. 5).

> In diminished responsibility cases there are various courses open to a judge. His choice of the right course will depend on the state of the evidence and the material before him. If the psychiatric reports recommend and justify it, and there are no contrary indications, he will make a hospital order. Where a hospital order is not recommended, or is not appropriate, and the defendant constitutes a danger to the public for an unpredictable period of time, the right sentence will, in all probabilities, be one of life imprisonment.

> In cases where the evidence indicates that the accused's responsibility for his acts was so grossly impaired that his degree of responsibility for them was minimal, then a lenient course will be open to the judge. Provided there is no danger of repetition of violence, it will usually be possible to make such an order as will give the accused his freedom, possibly with some supervision.

> There will however be cases in which there is no proper basis for a hospital order; but in which the accused's degree of responsibility is not minimal. In such cases the judge should pass a determinate sentence of imprisonment, the length of which will depend on two factors: his assessment of the degree of the accused's responsibility and his view as to the period of time, if any, for which the accused will continue to be a danger to the public. (*Chambers* (1983) 5 Cr App R (S) 190, per Leonard J at pp. 193-4)

An example of a case falling within the first category in *Chambers* is *Courtney* (1987) 9 Cr App R (S) 404. In that case the offender pleaded guilty to the manslaughter of his wife, whom he had strangled after a domestic argument. He immediately tried to revive her and to summon help. The offender had been undergoing treatment for depression and the medical witnesses agreed that the offender was suffering from depression to a degree which warranted his detention in hospital for treatment. The Court of Appeal, taking account of the medical advice that the offender did not represent a risk to other members of the public and that his depression could be cured within a year, varied a restriction order under the Mental Health Act 1983, s. 41, to a hospital order under s. 37 of that Act. See further the decision in *Birch* (1989) 11 Cr App R (S) 202, where the criteria for deciding between a hospital order, a life sentence and a determinate custodial sentence were discussed (see **E24.6 *et seq*.**). A life sentence was upheld in *Sanderson* (1994) 15 Cr App R (S) 263, where the offender was a man with a long history of drug addiction and violence towards women. He had battered his girlfriend to death. The period specified under the CJA 1991, s. 34, was eight years.

In the second category of case is *Sangha* [1997] 1 Cr App R (S) 262, where the offender had suffered physical and mental cruelty and abuse from her husband over a period of 22 years. She had made several attempts at suicide. After she discovered that her husband had been having an affair, she took an overdose, but subsequently discharged herself from hospital and the following day stabbed her husband. He died four days later during which time the offender stabbed herself, causing minor injury. The medical evidence was that she was suffering from depressive illness and was subject to acute stress reaction. A sentence of 18 months' imprisonment was varied by the Court of Appeal to a probation order for three years, although by that time the offender had served five months of her sentence.

An example of the third type of case is *Leggett* [1996] 2 Cr App R (S) 77, where the appellant pleaded guilty to the manslaughter of her 14-month-old child. Psychiatric reports indicated that the offender had an immature personality disorder and that at the time of the killing she was in a state of emotional turmoil brought about by her separation from the child's father and her irrational fear that the child would be taken from her, together with the fact that the child would not stop crying. The medical advice was that the offender was unlikely to reoffend and that detention in a psychiatric institution might not alleviate her condition. The Court of Appeal regretted that a hospital order could not be made, but said that since the offender retained a degree of responsibility for the killing there had to be an element of retribution and deterrence. A prison sentence of four years was upheld. See also *Yeomans* (1988) 10 Cr App R (S) 63 (eight years' imprisonment reduced to five where a man drowned his 18-month-old daughter in the sea while suffering from acute reactive depression), *Michael* (1993) 15 Cr App R (S) 265 and *Bourne* (1994) 16 Cr App R (S) 237.

Sentencing Guidelines: Provocation

The maximum penalty is life imprisonment (OAPA 1861, s. 5).   **B1.31**

The sentencing bracket for offences of manslaughter committed after provocation has normally been set at a period between three and seven years, although longer sentences have occasionally been upheld. In *A-G's Ref (No. 33 of 1996)* [1997] 2 Cr App R (S) 10, however, the Court of Appeal accepted that in cases where an offender carries a knife as a weapon and uses it to cause death, even where there is provocation, a sentence of seven years is too low and that henceforth the appropriate sentence in a contested case would be between 10 and 12 years. This decision was followed in *A-G's Ref (No. 2 of 1997)* [1998] 1 Cr App R (S) 27 where, following a period of animosity between the offender and the deceased, the offender obtained a revolver, went to the victim's house and shot him in the head. The Court of Appeal said that the sentence of seven years' imprisonment was unduly lenient and that the lowest sentence which the sentencer could properly have passed was 10 years.

The appropriate punishment in these cases seems to turn upon the amount of provocation, the 'cooling-off' time, the extent to which the offender was at fault in bringing about the situation in the first place, and the means used to kill the victim. According to Shaw LJ in *Bancroft* (1981) 3 Cr App R (S) 119, (at p. 120):

> notwithstanding that a man's reason might be unseated on the basis that the reasonable man would have found himself out of control, there is still in every human being a residual capacity for self-control, which the exigencies of a given situation may call for. That must be the justification for passing a sentence of imprisonment, to recognise that there is still left some degree of culpability . . .

In *Taylor* (1987) 9 Cr App R (S) 175, the offender stabbed and killed the woman with whom he had been living, after a domestic quarrel following heavy drinking. In reducing the sentence from seven years' imprisonment to five years, Lord Lane CJ commented that:

> sentencing in these circumstances is an almost impossible task . . . There are two objects in view which the sentencer must have in mind: first of all the necessity to ensure that the criminal expiates his offence. For that of course a term of imprisonment is almost always necessary. Secondly, although to some extent where there is provocation it may seem illogical, it has got to be a lesson to other people that they should keep their tempers and not be provoked in such circumstances. Bearing those two matters in mind, the judge then has to determine what the least period is which will reflect those two matters.

Much shorter sentences may be appropriate in exceptional cases, e.g., 18 months in *Dimasi* (1981) 3 Cr App R (S) 146, where a man of exemplary character killed his daughter after intervening in a domestic argument and under severe provocation. In *Gardner* (1993) 14 Cr App R (S) 364 a woman suffering from 'battered woman syndrome', in consequence of years of abuse and violence from her husband, appealed against a sentence of five years' imprisonment for manslaughter of the husband, after stabbing him with a kitchen knife. The Court of Appeal varied the sentence to a probation order, saying that the offender posed no risk to society and had already served several months in prison.

Sentencing Guidelines: Killing in Pursuance of Suicide Pact

B1.32 The maximum penalty is life imprisonment (OAPA 1861, s. 5).

The offender in *Sweeney* (1986) 8 Cr App R (S) 419 pleaded guilty to the manslaughter of his wife. He was prone to depression and had married the deceased when she was suffering from advanced muscular dystrophy. They decided to commit suicide together by taking tablets and then setting fire to their car when they were inside it. Once the fire started both tried to escape, but the wife was killed. The offender suffered serious burns. The Court of Appeal reduced a four-year prison term to one of two years, that being 'sufficient, in our judgment, to mark the seriousness of this matter'. See also *England* (1990) 12 Cr App R (S) 98.

Sentencing Guidelines: Involuntary Manslaughter

B1.33 The maximum penalty is life imprisonment (OAPA 1861, s. 5).

Such offences vary very widely in culpability and circumstances.

In manslaughter arising from *fights*, according to Cumming-Bruce LJ in *Stuart* (1979) 1 Cr App R (S) 228 (at p. 230), 'English law has always regarded causing of the death of a man as an offence of great gravity, although the circumstances in which death is caused are manifestly relevant to assessing the degree of criminal responsibility and wickedness.' A sentence of four years was reduced to two years in that case, where the offender, in the course of a fight, had pushed the victim down some steps where he had fallen and fractured his skull. In *Cenci* (1989) 11 Cr App R (S) 199, following an incident of domestic violence between a man and a woman living together, the woman climbed out of a window to escape, but fell to her death. Ten years' imprisonment was reduced to five. Some general indications on sentencing in this type of case, following a review of the earlier authorities, were given in *Coleman* (1991) 95 Cr App R 159. Lord Lane CJ said that in a case of involuntary manslaughter where the victim was felled by a blow, cracked his head on the floor or pavement, suffered a skull fracture and died, the starting point for sentence on a plea of guilty was 12 months. Relevant mitigating factors would be absence of premeditation, the fact that the injury resulted from a single blow of moderate force, remorse, and an immediate admission of guilt. Aggravating factors would include a history of violent behaviour on the part of the offender, the fact that the assault was gratuitous or unprovoked and the fact that more than one blow had been struck. Cases where there was an accidental fall resulting in a fracture of the skull had to be sharply distinguished from more serious cases where a victim on the ground had been kicked about the head, or cases where a weapon had been used. In *Shelton* (1979) 1 Cr App R (S) 202, an exceptional case, the Court of Appeal said that a custodial sentence should not have been imposed where two brothers, both in their sixties, had fought following a family quarrel. The offender had fallen on the victim, injuring him with his knee. The victim failed to take medical advice and died three days later.

In cases of manslaughter involving *firearms*, again much depends on the circumstances, particularly the degree of planning in the use of the firearm. In *O'Mahoney* (1980) 2 Cr App R (S) 57, a sentence of 15 years was upheld. The offender and two other men had set out to find a fourth man to give him a beating, having first obtained a pistol and some ammunition. Although they did not find the man they were looking for, the pistol was subsequently fired on two occasions on that same day, and then a completely innocent man was shot in the chest at close range and killed after an argument at a club. Eveleigh J said that it was proper to take account of the whole day's events in fixing the sentence: 'This is not the case of a man who, having taken drink, is suddenly in possession of a firearm and then carelessly, because of drink, fires it.' This may be compared with *Wesson* (1989) 11 Cr App R (S) 161, where a sentence of seven years was reduced to two years in a case where the offender had been cleaning his shotgun, waving it about but saying that it was unloaded, and it had discharged, killing his wife. See further **B1.31**.

In cases where manslaughter is committed in the *course of the commission of another offence*, such as burglary, robbery or arson, the Court of Appeal has held that the sentence should not be the same as would have been imposed for the lesser offence, and 'however unintended that killing may be, the sentence should reflect the gravity of the fact that death has been caused' (*Paget* (1982) 4 Cr App R (S) 399, per Robert Goff LJ). Again, a great deal depends on the precise circumstances of the killing. In *Cook* (1982) 4 Cr App R (S) 237, where a manslaughter by stabbing in the course of a burglary was described as 'close to being accidental', a six-year sentence was appropriate, while a 10-year sentence was proper in *Wood* (1984) 6 Cr App R (S) 139, where the offenders had broken into the home of an elderly lady and had left her with her eyes and mouth covered with sticking plaster and had tied her to the bed. See also *Brophy* (1995) 16 Cr App R (S) 652.

Manslaughter of a *young child* normally attracts a custodial sentence between two and eight years, depending upon the degree of culpability. A sentence at the top end of the range was upheld in *Ali* (1988) 10 Cr App R (S) 59, where the four-year-old child had been maltreated over a lengthy period, died of a fractured skull, and was found to have had a number of other fractures caused on various other occasions. In *Bashford* (1988) 10 Cr App R (S) 359, the child died from being shaken violently after persistent crying, and there was no evidence of violence used on any other occasion. Stocker LJ, upholding a two year sentence, commented (at p. 362), 'it is not really disputed that a custodial sentence, and an immediate one, was the only course open . . . The sentence appears to be, if anything, at the bottom limit.' See also *Staynor* [1996] 1 Cr App R (S) 376.

There are few appellate cases dealing with *reckless or gross negligence manslaughter*, rather than killing by an unlawful act. One example is *Morgan* (1990) 12 Cr App R (S) 504. The offender, an engine driver, inexplicably ignored yellow and red track warning signals, with the result that his train crashed into another. Five people were killed and 87 were injured. He pleaded guilty, was a person of good character and there was no suggestion that he had been drinking at the time of the crash. The Court of Appeal, attempting to 'reconcile the irreconcilable' (at p. 508) by balancing the need to express public disapproval with the reality that prison could achieve nothing in this case and that the crime would trouble the offender's conscience for the rest of his life, reduced a sentence of 18 months' imprisonment, with six months to serve and the balance suspended, to four months' imprisonment. Another example is *Saha* (1994) 15 Cr App R (S) 342, where a sentence of 21 months' imprisonment was upheld on a doctor who recklessly prescribed, over a ten-day period, increasing doses of largactil and methadone, causing the death of a patient in his care. A third is *Kite* [1996] 2 Cr App R (S) 295, where the offender was the manager of a company organising leisure activities for young people, four of whom were drowned while taking part in a canoeing trip. The defendant was convicted of manslaughter by gross negligence, on the basis that he had failed to establish adequate safety procedures. Two years' imprisonment was imposed.

CONSTRUCTIVE MANSLAUGHTER (KILLING BY AN UNLAWFUL ACT LIKELY TO CAUSE BODILY HARM)

The Unlawful Act

B1.34   The accused's act must be unlawful, in that it constitutes a criminal offence in its own right (independently of the fact that it has caused death). See *Franklin* (1883) 15 Cox CC 163, where the fact that the accused had committed a tort did not make his act an unlawful one for the purposes of manslaughter, although it should be noted that the accused was nonetheless convicted on the ground of gross negligence. Typically the unlawful act will be an assault (see, e.g., *Larkin* [1943] KB 174) or some other offence against the person such as administering a noxious thing under the OAPA 1861, s. 23 (see *Cato* [1976] 1 WLR 110 where the Court of Appeal seemed to think the act was unlawful *even if* the offence under s. 23 was not made out).

It now seems clear that the offence need not be directed against the person; an offence of arson or criminal damage can supply the required element of unlawfulness (*Goodfellow* (1986) 83 Cr App R 23).

The unlawful act must be an act which is unlawful in itself rather than one which is unlawful because of the negligent manner of its performance. Thus, driving without due care and attention does not count as an unlawful act for these purposes (see *Andrews* v *DPP* [1937] AC 576, per Lord Atkin at p. 585), otherwise unlawful act manslaughter would swallow up both the statutory offence of causing death by dangerous driving and also killing by gross negligence in the context of road traffic deaths. Perhaps a better way of excluding driving without due care and attention would be to say that the unlawful act must be an offence which requires the proof of full *mens rea* in the sense of intention or recklessness or some equally culpable state of mind. This would have the merit of also clearly excluding offences of strict liability (e.g., under health and safety legislation) which happen to result in death. Such situations should only be capable of amounting to manslaughter (and are only so treated) if they come within the gross negligence head discussed at **B1.37** to **B1.40**.

The phrase 'unlawful act' connotes, an act as opposed to an omission, so that the fact that the accused has committed the offence of wilful neglect of a child under the CYPA 1933, s. 1, does not supply the unlawful act required (*Lowe* [1973] QB 702). The facts may, however, justify a verdict of manslaughter on some other ground such as gross negligence.

The *Mens Rea* of the Unlawful Act

Although a person accused of manslaughter by definition lacks the *mens rea* for murder, **B1.35** the prosecution must normally prove that he has the *mens rea* appropriate to the unlawful act which caused the victim's death, a point well illustrated by the case of *Lamb* [1967] 2 QB 981, where the accused 'in jest' pointed a loaded revolver at his friend and pulled the trigger, believing that it was safe to do so because neither of the two bullets in the gun was in a chamber opposite the barrel. What neither the appellant nor his friend (who was similarly treating the incident as a joke) appreciated was that pulling the trigger rotated the cylinder so as to place one of the bullets opposite the barrel, and hence in the firing position. The Court of Appeal quashed the conviction for manslaughter on the ground that there was not proved 'the element of intent without which there can be no assault'. It would have been different had Lamb intended to frighten his friend (for then he would have had the *mens rea* of an unlawful act) – see *Ball* [1989] Crim LR 730. Since the decision in *Lamb* [1967] 2 QB 981, it has been confirmed that recklessness is sufficient *mens rea* for assault (*Venna* [1976] QB 421). However, it is subjective recklessness which applies (*Spratt* [1990] 1 WLR 1073) so Lamb would still lack the necessary *mens rea*. See also *Slingsby* [1995] Crim LR 570, where vigorous consensual sexual activity did not amount to a battery or other unlawful act since there was no intention to cause, or foresight of, harm.

The accused cannot, however, rely on his lack of *mens rea* induced by voluntary intoxication, as manslaughter is a crime of basic intent (see *Lipman* [1970] 1 QB 152). This was an extreme case in many ways, in which the accused killed his girlfriend whilst suffering LSD-induced hallucinations that he was at the centre of the earth being attacked by snakes. If the unlawful act alleged were to be a crime of specific intent, then the accused's intoxication *should* be relevant, but such situations are likely to be rare (see, however, *Watson* [1989] 1 WLR 684, burglary with intent to steal).

Likely to Cause Bodily Harm

The classic formulation of this requirement, sometimes referred to as the requirement **B1.36** that the unlawful act be 'dangerous', is that of Edmund Davies J in *Church* [1966] 1 QB 59, where he said (at p. 70):

> the unlawful act must be such as all sober and reasonable people would inevitably recognise must subject the other person to, at least, the risk of some harm resulting therefrom, albeit not serious harm.

This formulation has the merit that it emphasises that the test is an objective one, which depends not on the accused's appreciation of likely harm but on what the sober and reasonable person would appreciate. The objective nature of the test was confirmed by the House of Lords in *DPP* v *Newbury* [1977] AC 500, where two youths pushed a paving stone off the parapet of a bridge into the path of an approaching train, thereby killing the guard. The House upheld the convictions for manslaughter and answered yes to the certified question, 'Can a defendant be properly convicted of manslaughter, when his mind is not affected by drink or drugs, if he did not foresee harm to another?'

On the other hand, the defendant's foresight of harm may be relevant to the separate question of whether he has the *mens rea* of the unlawful act if the unlawful act is an offence against the person. The House of Lords in *DPP* v *Newbury* [1977] AC 500 did not make it clear what the unlawful act was, and indeed appeared to be rather dismissive of the requirement of *mens rea* for the unlawful act. However, it now seems clear in the light of *Goodfellow* (1986) 83 Cr App R 23 (see **B1.34**) that criminal damage would be the obvious and sufficient unlawful act in *Newbury*, and that the two accused were reckless in the *Caldwell* sense, so that they did have the *mens rea* for an unlawful act even if they did not foresee harm to another. Even where the unlawful act is an assault, the *mens rea* need not relate to harm; an intention to put in fear is sufficient. Thus the following dictum of Lord Denning MR in *Gray* v *Barr* [1971] 2 QB 554, at p. 568, on which doubt was cast by Lord Salmon in *Newbury*, is perfectly sound in the context of a case where the unlawful act is an assault: 'the accused must do a dangerous act with the *intention* of frightening or harming someone, or with the *realisation* that it is likely to frighten or harm someone'. Lord Denning was not casting doubt on the requirement that the act be *objectively* likely to cause bodily harm (he refers to a 'dangerous' act), but was making the important and separate point that the accused must be shown to have the *mens rea* for whatever is alleged to be the unlawful act. See also *Jennings* [1990] Crim LR 588 and *Scarlett* [1993] 4 All ER 629.

The harm *likely* to result from the act must be physical harm. Emotional harm will not suffice, even though physical harm (and death) does in fact result from the foreseeable emotional harm: see *Dawson* (1985) 81 Cr App R 150, where the fact that a robbery of a petrol station was likely to cause emotional disturbance to the attendant was held not to be sufficient, even though the attendant, who had a weak heart, suffered a heart attack and died. The heart attack did constitute physical harm but the reasonable man would not have *foreseen* such physical harm as likely to result. The reasonable man is to be regarded as having the knowledge of facts that the accused has, and the accused in this case did not know that the attendant had a weak heart. In *Watson* [1989] 1 WLR 684, however, the unlawful act was burglary under the Theft Act 1968, s. 9(1)(a), which allegedly caused the elderly occupier (again with a weak heart) to suffer a heart attack and die. The Court of Appeal held (at p. 867) that, although the appellant did not know the age or physical condition of the occupier at the point of entry,

> the jury were entitled to ascribe to the bystander the knowledge which the appellant gained during the whole of his stay in the house . . . The unlawful act in the present circumstances comprised the whole of the burglarious intrusion and did not come to an end on the appellant's foot crossing the threshold . . .

The statement about the duration of the unlawful act seems, with respect, to stretch the definition of the offence under s. 9(1)(a) and can be regarded as *obiter*, since the conviction was quashed on another ground. However, the case is a useful illustration of the proposition that if the accused knows of the victim's susceptibility to physical harm, then that knowledge can be ascribed to the reasonable man and the accused's act can be regarded as 'likely to cause bodily harm'.

On the other hand, the reasonable man does not share the accused's mistaken beliefs. In *Ball* [1989] Crim LR 730, the accused mistakenly believed he had loaded his gun with blank cartridges but the reasonable bystander, not sharing that belief, would have considered the act of firing the gun dangerous.

A further limitation on the type of harm required was suggested in *Dalby* [1982] 1 WLR 425, where the Court of Appeal quashed a conviction for manslaughter based on the accused unlawfully supplying his friend with drugs, which his friend subsequently injected into himself with fatal consequences. Waller LJ said that the act had to be 'directed at the victim and likely to cause *immediate* injury, however slight' (emphasis added). The harm (or injury) in this case was caused by the deceased's own act of injecting the drugs. The mere supply of the drug was not dangerous in the sense that it was likely to cause *immediate* injury. The qualification suggested in *Dalby* is capable of restricting the scope of constructive manslaughter in a number of ways but it has been distinguished in subsequent cases.

In *Mitchell* [1983] QB 741 the accused assaulted X, causing him to fall on top of an elderly woman who died as a result. The Court of Appeal quite rightly had no difficulty in dismissing the argument that the accused's act was directed at X rather than at the deceased, saying that in *Dalby* [1982] 1 WLR 425 the court had been concerned with 'the quality of the act rather than the identity of the victim'. This is no real restriction on *Dalby* and is similar to the familiar transferred *mens rea* rule (see **A2.13**). In *Pagett* (1983) 76 Cr App R 279, the accused, at the end of a police siege, held the victim (a girl pregnant by him) in front of him as a shield while he fired at the police. The police fired back, in what the jury found to be a lawful manner, but unfortunately killed the girl. Pagett was convicted of manslaughter. The Court of Appeal was principally concerned with the question of whether the acts of the police in firing back constituted a *novus actus interveniens* (see **A1.27** to **A1.30**), which it held it was not because the police had been acting lawfully. However, the court briefly referred to the elements of unlawful act manslaughter and said (at p. 291):

> [the accused] committed not one but two unlawful acts, both of which were dangerous — the act of firing at the police, and the act of holding Gail Kinchen as a shield in front of him when the police might well fire shots in his direction in self-defence.

No mention was made of the *Dalby* requirement of 'directed at the victim' or 'likely to cause immediate injury'. However, the facts can be accommodated within the *Dalby* test, although with more difficulty than in *Mitchell* [1988] QB 741. Firing at the police certainly was directed at *a* victim and likely to cause immediate injury (at least to the police). Holding the girl as a shield was an act directed at her and in the circumstances likely to cause immediate harm to her, given that bullets were likely to be fired in the accused's direction as a result of the accused's own act.

The decision in *Goodfellow* (1986) 83 Cr App R 23 moves more clearly away from the limitation suggested in *Dalby* [1982] 1 WLR 425. The accused, wishing to be rehoused, set fire to his council house. The fire spread more rapidly than he had anticipated, and his wife and child, and another woman were killed in the blaze. The Court of Appeal upheld the conviction for manslaughter, even though the accused's acts were not directed at a victim but rather against property. Lord Lane CJ said (at p. 27) that all that had been intended to be said in *Dalby* was that 'there must be no fresh intervening cause between the act and the death'. His lordship went on:

> The questions which the jury have to decide on the charge of manslaughter of this nature are: (1) Was the act intentional? (2) Was it unlawful? (3) Was it an act which any reasonable person would realise was bound to subject some other human being to the risk of physical harm, albeit not necessarily serious harm? (4) Was that act the cause of death?

The *Dalby* limitation of 'likely to cause immediate injury' seems then to have been abandoned, regrettably perhaps, inasmuch as on facts such as *Goodfellow*, as Lord Lane CJ himself recognised, gross negligence manslaughter would appear to be available. It should also be noted that, in a case such as *Lamb* [1967] 2 QB 981 (see **B1.35**), Lord Lane's second question for the jury would need to be amplified in order to stress that an act is only unlawful if the accused has the *mens rea* for the particular unlawful act alleged. To ask, Was the act intentional? is not sufficient, since that can be interpreted merely as referring to voluntariness, e.g., on the facts of *Lamb*, as asking Did the accused intend to pull the trigger? rather than Did he intend to assault his friend? On the facts of *Goodfellow* (1986) 83 Cr App R 23, the problem does not really arise, because the accused clearly had the *mens rea* for criminal damage.

The essential requirement from *Dalby* that 'there must be no intervening cause' between the accused's act and death was unfortunately glossed over in the case of *Kennedy* [1999] Crim LR 65, where the accused supplied a prepared syringe of heroin with which the deceased voluntarily injected himself. The Court of Appeal upheld a conviction for manslaughter but did not convincingly answer the question of why the deceased's own voluntary act did not break the chain of causation between the unlawful act of supply and the death. The Court found the degree of encouragement to be the crucial aspect but if the encouragement to inject rather than the supply was the cause of death, it is to say the least unclear in what sense that encouragement constituted an unlawful act and, even then, the deceased's own voluntary decision to inject surely still broke the chain of causation.

MANSLAUGHTER BY GROSS NEGLIGENCE

Basis of Liability

B1.37 Manslaughter has traditionally been the one offence at common law in which negligence is expressly recognised as a sufficient basis of liability, but even here the negligence has to be 'gross'. Defining the precise degree of negligence required has always been problematical, and ultimately the question, being one of degree, has been one for the jury. This is evident from the following test laid down by Lord Hewart CJ in *Bateman* (1925) 19 Cr App R 8, at pp. 11–12:

> the facts must be such that, in the opinion of the jury, the negligence of the accused went beyond a mere matter of compensation between subjects and showed such disregard for the life and safety of others as to amount to a crime against the State and conduct deserving punishment.

In *Andrews* v *DPP* [1937] AC 576, at p. 583, Lord Atkin said that whilst this was:

> not . . . a precise definition of the crime . . . the substance of the judgment is most valuable, and in my opinion is correct. In practice it has generally been adopted by judges in charging juries in all cases of manslaughter by negligence.

Lord Atkin went on to say that in summarising the very high degree of negligence required:

> Probably of all the epithets that can be applied 'reckless' most nearly covers the case . . . but it is probably not all-embracing, for 'reckless' suggests an indifference to risk, whereas the accused may have appreciated the risk and intended to avoid it and yet shown such a high degree of negligence in the means adopted to avoid as would justify a conviction. (ibid., at p. 583)

Nevertheless, judges have often used the word 'reckless' to sum up to the jury the degree of fault required without making it clear how, if at all, this differs from the concept of gross negligence. This lack of clarity was perhaps inevitable while the meaning of 'reckless' in the criminal law generally was unclear. But after the authoritative House of Lords decisions on the meaning of recklessness in *Metropolitan Police Commissioner* v *Caldwell* [1982] AC 341 and *Lawrence* [1982] AC 510 (see A2.5), the issue became very difficult to ignore. In *Adomako* [1995] 1 AC 171 the House of Lords has restored gross negligence rather than recklessness as the essential basis of liability, but to understand the current statement of the law it is necessary to outline the somewhat chequered history of this variety of manslaughter over the previous decade.

Gross Negligence as Opposed to Recklessness

B1.38 In *Seymour* [1983] 2 AC 493, the accused, having recently quarrelled with the woman with whom he lived, was involved in a minor collision between his 11-ton lorry and her car. The woman got out of the car, but was crushed between the lorry and her own car as the accused tried, allegedly, to shunt her car out of the way (moving it 10 to 20 feet and forcing a tyre off in the process). Rather than charge the statutory offence of causing death by reckless driving, the prosecution took the view (rightly in the view of the House of Lords) that this was such a bad case that the offence of common-law manslaughter was appropriate. Nevertheless, in referring to the fault element required, the judge directed the jury in terms of recklessness as defined by the House of Lords in *Lawrence* [1982] AC 510 in relation to the statutory offence (see **A2.5**), save only that he omitted any reference to a risk of damage to property and limited the risk to 'an obvious and serious risk of causing physical harm'. Seymour appealed on the grounds that the *Lawrence* meaning of 'recklessness' was not applicable to common-law manslaughter, and that a more subjective meaning should be applied. The House of Lords dismissed the appeal and said that the *Lawrence* direction was appropriate (though without the reference to damage to property), the legal ingredients of the statutory offence and of common-law manslaughter being the same.

The decision raised many difficult issues including the question whether the *Lawrence* test of recklessness could be said to have completely supplanted the test of gross negligence in manslaughter.

Clarification of this question appeared to come in the Privy Council decision in *Kong Cheuk Kwan* v *The Queen* (1985) 82 Cr App R 18. This case arose out of a collision in perfect weather between two hydrofoils in Hong Kong harbour, which resulted in the deaths of two passengers. The trial judge gave a direction which reflected what the Privy Council called the 'confusion' in *Archbold* between unlawful act manslaughter and various pronouncements in the cases of *Metropolitan Police Commissioner* v *Caldwell* [1982] AC 341, *Lawrence* [1982] AC 510 and *Bateman* (1925) 19 Cr App R 8. Lord Roskill, in allowing the appeal, remarked (82 Cr App R 18 at p. 23): 'The Court of Appeal [of Hong Kong] . . . felt . . . able to conclude that other later passages in the summing-up, including repeated references to "gross negligence" put the matter sufficiently right'. However, his lordship went on to observe that 'from beginning to end of the summing-up neither the word "reckless" nor the word "recklessness" ever appears'.

His lordship thought that here, too, a proper direction should have been based on *Lawrence*-type recklessness and appeared to confirm that the test is recklessness rather than gross negligence. Indeed Lord Roskill approved the comments of Watkins LJ in the Court of Appeal in *Seymour* (1983) 76 Cr App R 211, where he said (at p. 216): 'it is no longer necessary or helpful to make reference to compensation and negligence'.

However, in *Prentice* [1994] QB 302 the Court of Appeal made it clear that gross negligence had by no means been totally supplanted by recklessness. Indeed it was of the view that, 'leaving motor manslaughter aside, the proper test in manslaughter based on breach of duty was the gross negligence test and that the *Lawrence/Caldwell* recklessness test was . . . inappropriate in the present class of case'. One of the appellants (Adomako) appealed to the House of Lords which also considered these issues.

In *Adomako* [1995] 1 AC 171, the House was able to go further than the Court of Appeal and hold that the *Bateman/Andrews* gross negligence test was of general application and that there should be no separate test for motor manslaughter.

> . . . the law as stated in *Seymour* . . . should no longer apply since the underlying statutory provisions on which it rested have not been repealed by the Road Traffic Act 1991. It may be that cases of involuntary motor manslaughter will as a result become rare but I consider it unsatisfactory that there should be any exception to the generality of the statement which I have made . . . (per Lord Mackay LC at p. 187).

It is not immediately apparent why the reversion from *Lawrence* recklessness to gross negligence should make convictions for involuntary motor manslaughter any more rare (they have not exactly been common in the past). Part of the explanation may lie in the fact that in the Court of Appeal the convictions of Prentice and Sulman for manslaughter (not of the motorised variety) had been quashed because the direction in terms of *Lawrence* recklessness had failed to leave it open to the jury to take account of the excuses or mitigating circumstances that might have been relevant to the issue of gross negligence. Lord Mackay and the Court of Appeal may have regarded gross negligence as a narrower basis of liability than *Lawrence* recklessness; this is surprising in the light of Lord Atkin's comments in *Andrews* v *DPP* [1937] AC 576 (at p. 583) that 'reckless suggests an indifference to risk whereas the accused may have appreciated the risk and intended to avoid it and yet shown such a high degree of negligence in the means adopted to avoid the risk as would justify the conviction'. This seems more consistent with the view that gross negligence is *wider* than recklessness, particularly in the sense that 'ruling out the risk' may negative recklessness but not necessarily gross negligence.

Whatever the explanation, Lord Mackay went on to answer the certified question before the House of Lords in *Adomako* (at p. 188):

> In cases of criminal negligence involving a breach of duty it is a sufficient direction to the jury to adopt the gross negligence test . . . it is not necessary to refer to the definition of recklessness in *Lawrence* [1982] AC 510, although it is perfectly open to the trial judge to use the word 'reckless' in its ordinary meaning as part of his exposition of the law if he deems it appropriate in the circumstances of the particular case.

His lordship emphasised that whilst a judge *may* feel it to be so appropriate to use the word reckless as indicating the extent to which a defendant's conduct must deviate from a proper standard of care, it would not be right 'to *require* that this should be done and certainly not right that it should incorporate the full detail required in *Lawrence*'.

Nature of Gross Negligence

B1.39   Running throughout Lord Mackay's judgment in *Adomako* [1995] 1 AC 171 is a concern that directions should be 'comprehensible to an ordinary member of the public who is called to sit on a jury' and he was therefore reluctant 'to state the law more elaborately' as had perhaps been attempted by the Court of Appeal. Nevertheless it is necessary to investigate a little more closely the essentials of gross negligence manslaughter. *Bateman* (1925) 19 Cr App R 8 and *Andrews* v *DPP* [1937] AC 576 are not necessarily all that helpful since they say little more than that the negligence must go beyond that required for civil liability, which is a question of degree for the jury; if matters had been entirely clear from those two cases, there would not have since been the many conflicting appellate pronouncements on the issue. Having expressed his approval of those two cases, Lord Mackay set out what he regarded as the essentials of gross negligence (at p. 187):

> . . . in my opinion the ordinary principles of the law of negligence apply to ascertain whether or not the defendant has been in breach of a duty of care towards the victim who has died. If such a breach of duty is established the next question is whether that breach of duty caused the death of the victim. If so, the jury must go on to consider whether that breach of duty should be characterised as gross negligence and therefore as a crime. This will depend on the seriousness of the breach of duty committed by the defendant in all the circumstances in which the defendant was placed when it occurred . . .
>
> . . . The essence of the matter which is supremely a jury question is whether, having regard to the risk of death involved, the conduct of the defendant was so bad in all the circumstances as to amount in their judgment to a criminal act or omission.

Two particular aspects of the above explanation are worthy of comment. The first is the re-introduction of the ordinary principles of negligence to decide whether there is a breach of a duty of care. This is not necessarily a simple matter especially if the factual situation is one where policy factors might impinge see, for example, *Ancell* v *McDermott* [1993] 4 All ER 355. Is it envisaged that the types of arguments raised by that sort of case could be relevant to whether a person is guilty of manslaughter and might need to be rehearsed in a criminal prosecution? Even if this hurdle is overcome (and the question of whether there is or can be a duty seems to be a question of law: *Khan* [1998] Crim LR 830 and *Singh* [1999] Crim LR 582), one is still faced with the second issue, foreseeability of what type of risk? The nature of the risk was problematical under the *Lawrence/Seymour* approach and indeed before those cases. Lord Mackay speaks above of the jury 'having regard to the risk of death involved' but he also later referred approvingly to the formulation in *Stone* [1977] QB 354 and *West London Coroner, ex parte Gray* [1988] QB 467, which was in terms of a risk of injury to the 'health and welfare' of an infirm person. Reference to the civil law of negligence is especially dangerous here given the egg-shell skull rule and cases such as *Smith* v *Leech Brain & Co. Ltd* [1962] 2 QB 405. If D in a grossly careless manner causes a relatively minor burn to V's lip and V subsequently dies of cancer because of the pre-malignant condition of the lip, can D really be guilty of manslaughter by gross negligence? It is submitted that the duty of care arises only if serious injury is foreseeable and that references to risks to the health and welfare of infirm people are explicable on the basis that such risks are inevitably serious because of the precariousness of their health to start with. This would be consistent with the reference of Lord Hewart CJ in *Bateman* (1925) 19 Cr App R 8 (at p. 12) to 'disregard for the life and safety of others' where it is strongly arguable that his lordship was referring to safety from serious injury, not absolute safety from any degree of minor injury.

If this could be clarified, there could at least be some degree of symmetry between the law of murder and that of manslaughter so that it would be murder to cause death intending to cause death or serious bodily harm and it would be manslaughter, *inter alia*, to cause death being grossly negligent in respect of a risk of death or grievous bodily harm. Such a conclusion may or may not be premature at the moment (see *Singh* [1999] Crim LR 582, where a risk of death was required), but would be consistent with the proposals of the Law Commission in Report No. 237, Involuntary Manslaughter (HC 171: 1996). For a recent example of the application of the gross negligence test, see *Litchfield* [1998] Crim LR 507.

Sentencing Guidelines

See **B1.33**.   **B1.40**

MOTOR MANSLAUGHTER AND ROAD TRAFFIC ACT OFFENCES

Until the coming into force of the Road Traffic Act 1991, s. 1, there appeared to be a **B1.41** complete overlap between (reckless) motor manslaughter and the statutory offence of causing death by reckless driving (see *Seymour* [1983] 2 AC 493). The 1991 Act replaced the offence of causing death by reckless driving in the Road Traffic Act 1988, s. 1, by the offence of causing death by dangerous driving and s. 2A of the 1988 Act defines the meaning of dangerous driving in a way which has echoes of the *Lawrence* definition of recklessness but is not identical with it; indeed it is somewhat wider in its scope. There has thus ceased to be a complete overlap with motor manslaughter but it seems that manslaughter should still be reserved for the very worst cases. If a charge of manslaughter is being considered rather than the new statutory offence, it should be borne in mind that causing death by dangerous driving is not an alternative verdict to manslaughter. Furthermore, Lord Roskill stated in *Seymour* (at p. 507) that it was not permissible to allow a trial to proceed on two separate counts, one statutory and the other at common law, and the same is likely to be true in relation to the new offence. One should also bear in mind the comments of Lord Mackay LC in *Adomako* [1995] 1 AC 171 (see **B1.38**) that cases of involuntary motor manslaughter are likely to become rare following the re-establishment of gross negligence rather than recklessness. (See further **C3.3** and **C3.9** *et seq.*)

INFANTICIDE

Definition

B1.42   **Infanticide Act 1938, s. 1**

(1)   Where a woman by any wilful act or omission causes the death of her child being a child under the age of 12 months, but at the time of the act or omission the balance of her mind was disturbed by reason of her not having fully recovered from the effect of giving birth to the child or by reason of the effect of lactation consequent upon the birth of the child, then, notwithstanding that the circumstances were such that but for this Act the offence would have amounted to murder, she shall be guilty of [an offence], to wit of infanticide, and may for such offence be dealt with and punished as if she had been guilty of the offence of manslaughter of the child.

Procedure

B1.43   Infanticide is triable only on indictment. It is a class 2 offence.

Indictment

B1.44   Statement of Offence

Infanticide contrary to section 1(1) of the Infanticide Act 1938

Particulars of Offence

A on or about the . . . day of . . . did cause the death of her child V aged under 12 months by a wilful act [or omission], namely, smothering him with a pillow [failing to . . .], but at a time when the balance of her mind was disturbed by reason of the fact that she had not fully recovered from the effect of giving birth to V [and/or from the effect of lactation consequent on giving birth to V]

Alternative Verdicts

B1.45   Child destruction (Infant Life (Preservation) Act 1929, s. 2(2)), see **B1.52**.

Sentencing Guidelines

B1.46   The maximum sentence is life imprisonment (Infanticide Act 1938, s. 1).

The proper approach for sentencing in cases of infanticide was considered by the Court of Appeal in *Sainsbury* (1989) 11 Cr App R (S) 533. The offender had become pregnant at the age of 15. She did not tell anyone about this, and gave birth to the baby without medical assistance in the bathroom of her boyfriend's flat. The baby was then wrapped in a blanket, taken some distance away and drowned in a river. The sentencer accepted that the balance of the offender's mind was disturbed by the effect of giving birth and that she was very immature, but did not accept that her responsibility was removed altogether. He imposed a sentence of 12 months' detention in a young offender institution. The Court of Appeal, however, having regard to statistics which indicated that in 59 cases of infanticide dealt with between 1979 and 1988 there had been no custodial sentences, all offenders having been dealt with by way of probation, supervision or hospital orders, decided that although the offence was serious the mitigating factors were overwhelming, and varied the sentence to probation. See also *Lewis* (1989) 11 Cr App R (S) 457.

Elements Generally

B1.47   The offence predates the introduction of the defence of diminished responsibility, and is designed to serve a similar role in relation to killings of very young children by their mothers in circumstances where the mothers are not fully responsible for their actions. It differs from diminished responsibility (and thus has survived the introduction of that defence) in that it can be charged from the outset and can be used (in appropriate cases) to avoid charging a woman with the offence of murder in relation to her own child. Under s. 1(2), it can also be returned as an alternative verdict to murder, although s. 1(3) makes it clear that that is without prejudice to the jury's power on an indictment for murder to return a verdict of manslaughter or not guilty by reason of insanity. The offence covers a narrower range of circumstances than diminished responsibility, as the disturbance of the mother's mind must be due either to 'her not having fully recovered from the effect of giving birth' or to 'the effect of lactation consequent upon the birth of the child'. However, a legal burden of proof is placed on the defence in a case of diminished responsibility, where the prosecution are alleging the offence amounts to murder, the burden of proving that it is not a case of infanticide remains on the prosecution.

Meaning of 'Wilful'

As to the meaning of 'wilfully' generally, see **A2.8**. There appears to be no authority on the meaning of 'wilful' in this particular offence. It could be interpreted to mean merely 'voluntary', but that would raise the possibility that the offence could be committed even though the mother did not intend to cause death or serious bodily harm to the child. This could be avoided by reading the phrase 'notwithstanding that the circumstances were such that but for this Act the offence would have amounted to murder' as meaning 'notwithstanding *and provided that* etc.'. This reading seems unlikely, and would strictly mean that the elements of murder ought to be alleged in the indictment. Alternatively, 'wilful' could be given a similar interpretation to that adopted in relation to 'wilfully' in *Sheppard* [1981] AC 394, i.e., as requiring intention or recklessness in relation to the child's death. This would mean that the offence would cover a wider range of cases than just those where the offence would otherwise be murder, and would overlap with cases that would in any case only be manslaughter. This is probably not what was intended, but seems to be the result of how the offence is defined (murder was itself a wider offence in 1938 when the definition of infanticide was put on the statute book, and that definition has not changed even though the scope of the offence of murder has narrowed). The problem is not acute, since in practice it seems that the offence will only be charged where there is evidence that the mother did intend serious bodily harm or death, even though this is not necessarily an element of the offence which strictly has to be proved. **B1.48**

Act or Omission which Causes Death

See **A1.10** to **A1.20** for liability for omissions. See **A1.13** for the duty of parents to preserve the life of their children; essentially, parents have a duty to take any reasonable steps lying within their power to prevent harm to their child. See **A1.21** *et seq*. for the principles of causation. **B1.49**

'Of Her Child under the Age of 12 Months'

If the mother kills the child of another, even if it is in the course of killing her own child, then the killing of that other cannot amount to infanticide. If the mother intended to kill or cause grievous bodily harm, it would prima facie be murder but might be brought within the defence of diminished responsibility. Strictly speaking, the same principles apply if the mother kills, say, her own 11-month-old child as a result of giving birth to another child later in the same year, since the disturbance of her mind has to be due to the effects of the birth of the child which is killed. **B1.50**

The offence cannot apply once the child has reached the age of 12 months, but again, diminished responsibility would be the appropriate defence to consider. If, at the other end of the scale, the child has not been fully born before the mother kills it, the offence is not infanticide but child destruction (see **B1.52** to **B1.60**) and, by virtue of the Infant Life (Preservation) Act 1929, s. 2(2), child destruction is an alternative verdict to infanticide.

Complicity and Attempt

B1.51   Where a mother aids and abets the killing of her child by another (e.g., the father) but cannot be said to cause its death, it would appear that infanticide is inapplicable, and again, diminished responsibility would have to be relied on. If a third person (including, e.g., the father) aids and abets the mother to commit what is (for her) only infanticide, it would seem likely that, by analogy with the Homicide Act 1957, s. 2(4) (see **B1.13**), that third person should still be guilty of murder if he or she has the appropriate *mens rea*.

Some doubts have been expressed whether attempted infanticide is an offence known to the law, but such an indictment was approved in *Smith* [1983] Crim LR 789.

CHILD DESTRUCTION

Definition

B1.52   Infant Life (Preservation) Act 1929, s. 1

(1)   Subject as hereinafter in this subsection provided, any person who, with intent to destroy the life of a child capable of being born alive, by any wilful act causes a child to die before it has an existence independent of its mother, shall be guilty of [an offence], to wit, of child destruction, and shall be liable on conviction thereof on indictment to life imprisonment:

Provided that no person shall be found guilty of an offence under this section unless it is proved that the act which caused the death of the child was not done in good faith for the purpose only of preserving the life of the mother.

Procedure

B1.53   Child destruction is triable only on indictment. It is a class 2 offence.

Indictment

B1.54   Statement of Offence

Child destruction contrary to section 1(1) of the Infant Life (Preservation) Act 1929

Particulars of Offence

A on or about the . . . day of . . ., with intent to destroy the life of a child capable of being born alive, did cause the death of the child of V, before it had an existence independent of the said V, by means of a wilful act, namely . . .

Alternative Verdict

B1.55   Abortion contrary to the OAPA 1861, s. 58 (Infant Life (Preservation) Act 1929, s. 2(3)).

Sentencing

B1.56   The maximum sentence is life imprisonment (Infant Life (Preservation) Act 1929, s. 1).

Relationship with Other Offences

B1.57   This offence was created to fill the gap between murder (which, as noted at **B1.1** and **B1.8**, requires a live birth) and abortion (which requires an attempt to procure a miscarriage, see **B1.61** to **B1.69**). A child killed in the process of being born would not be murdered, because there would be no live birth, and it would not be abortion since there was no miscarriage. The offence, however, overlaps with abortion, as it is not restricted to acts done while the child is in the process of being born and also covers the causing of miscarriage of a child 'capable of being born alive'. Abortion is an alternative verdict to child destruction (Infant Life (Preservation) Act 1929, s. 2(3)).

Meaning of 'Capable of Being Born Alive'

Infant Life (Preservation) Act 1929, s. 1   **B1.58**

> (2)   For the purposes of this Act, evidence that a woman had at any material time been pregnant for a period of 28 weeks or more shall be prima facie proof that she was at that time pregnant of a child capable of being born alive.

In addition to this statutory presumption, it is open to the prosecution to try to prove that a particular child was capable of being born alive even though it has not reached the relevant number of weeks gestation. In a civil case, *C* v *S* [1988] QB 135, the Court of Appeal held that a child between 18 and 21 weeks was not capable of being born alive, as it could not breathe. On the other hand, in *Rance* v *Mid-Downs Health Authority* [1991] 1 QB 587, Brooke J held that a child of 26 or 27 weeks gestation, who could have breathed unaided for two to three hours at least, was capable of being born alive.

Meaning of 'Wilful Act'

In contrast to the offence of infanticide discussed at **B1.42** to **B1.51**, the definition   **B1.59** requires a positive act and an omission will not suffice. 'Wilful' seems here to mean merely 'voluntary', as the *mens rea* of an 'intent to destroy the life of a child capable of being born alive' is separately stated. For the meaning of wilfulness generally, see **A2.8**. Recklessness is clearly insufficient.

Special Defences

Under the proviso to the Infant Life (Preservation) Act 1929, s. 1(1), 'no person shall   **B1.60** be found guilty . . . unless it is proved that the act which caused the death of the child was not done in good faith for the purpose only of preserving the life of the mother'. Thus, the burden is on the prosecution to negate this defence, whether or not, it would seem, the accused adduces any evidence to raise the issue. The only cases relating to the scope of this defence are first instance rulings of trial judges, and even these were prosecutions for abortion under the OAPA 1861, s. 58, where the court implied a similar defence by analogy with the proviso currently under discussion. A fairly flexible view of the meaning of 'preserving the life of the mother' was taken in these cases. In *Bourne* [1939] 1 KB 687, at p. 694, Macnaghten J took the view that the jury could properly conclude that the accused was acting in good faith to preserve the life of the mother if he believed 'that the probable consequence of the continuance of the pregnancy will be to make the woman a physical or mental wreck'. In *Newton* [1958] Crim LR 469, Ashworth J referred to 'preserving the life or health of the woman . . . not only her physical health but also her mental health'.

The Abortion Act 1967, s. 5(1), provides a defence to a charge of child destruction as follows:

> No offence under the Infant Life (Preservation) Act 1929 shall be committed by a registered medical practitioner who terminates a pregnancy in accordance with the provisions of this Act.

The offence of child destruction and the presumption that a child is capable of being born alive at 28 weeks gestation no longer therefore represent one of the limits on the lawfulness of abortions under the 1967 Act. If the provisions of the 1967 Act (see below) are complied with, an act is neither abortion nor child destruction.

ABORTION

Definition

B1.61   **Offences against the Person Act 1861, s. 58**

Every woman, being with child, who, with intent to procure her own miscarriage, shall unlawfully administer to herself any poison or other noxious thing, or shall unlawfully use any instrument or other means whatsoever with the like intent, and whosoever, with intent to procure the miscarriage of any woman, whether she be or be not with child, shall unlawfully administer to her or cause to be taken by her any poison or other noxious thing, or shall unlawfully use any instrument or other means whatsoever with the like intent, shall be guilty of [an offence], and being convicted thereof shall be liable to [imprisonment] for life.

Procedure

B1.62   Abortion is triable only on indictment. It is a class 2 offence.

Indictment

B1.63   Statement of Offence (1)

Administering poison with intent to procure miscarriage contrary to section 58 of the Offences against the Person Act 1861

Particulars of Offence

A on or about the . . . day of . . . did unlawfully administer [or cause to be administered] to V a poison or other noxious thing, namely . . . , with intent to procure her miscarriage

Statement of Offence (2)

Using an instrument or other means with intent to procure miscarriage contrary to section 58 of the Offences against the Person Act 1861

Particulars of Offence

A on or about the . . . day of . . . did unlawfully use the following means, namely . . . , with intent to procure the miscarriage of V

Sentencing Guidelines

B1.64   The maximum penalty is life imprisonment (OAPA 1861, s. 58).

Sentences of three years' imprisonment were upheld on offenders in *Scrimaglia* (1971) 55 Cr App R 280, who pleaded guilty to using an instrument to procure a miscarriage. Lord Parker CJ endorsed the trial judge's comment that 'Now that abortions can be performed legally either under the National Health Service or at the patient's own expense, operations such as yours, carried out at a cut price and in disgraceful, insanitary and even dangerous conditions, are totally unnecessary apart from being against the law'.

Elements Generally

B1.65   Given the large number of abortions now carried out legally under the provisions of the Abortion Act 1967 (see **B1.69**), the offence is comparatively rarely prosecuted. There are two peculiar features to note about the definition of the offence. First, it is in the nature of a statutory attempt. The *actus reus* does not require the actual procuring of a miscarriage, but rather an act done with the intention of procuring that result. Secondly, the requirements of the offence differ according to whether it is the (pregnant) woman herself or another person who is charged. In the case of the woman herself she must indeed be pregnant, whereas in the case of others, it is sufficient if she is believed to be pregnant and there is thus an intention to procure her miscarriage. This latter distinction is now almost redundant, because:

(a)   if a non-pregnant woman is helped by another, she can be convicted either of aiding and abetting (*Sockett* (1908) 1 Cr App R 101) or conspiring with (*Whitchurch* (1890) 24 QBD 42) that other; and

(b)   even if she is acting alone, she would appear to be guilty of an attempt to commit the offence under s. 58 as a result of the Criminal Attempts Act 1981, s. 1(2) (see **A6.31** *et seq*.).

In practice, the woman herself is not prosecuted today, and the offence is aimed principally at third parties operating outside the terms of what is permitted under the Abortion Act 1967 and exploiting the woman's predicament for financial gain.

Intention to Procure Miscarriage

For the meaning of 'intention', see **A2.2**. What stage of a pregnancy has to be reached **B1.66** before it is possible to 'miscarry' is a matter of some controversy. Is it as soon as the ovum is fertilised, or only when the fertilised ovum is implanted in the womb some 10 days later? If it were the former, then some types of so-called contraceptives, such as 'the morning-after' pill, would be technically illegal under the OAPA 1861, s. 58. The current practice is not to regard these methods of halting pregnancy at a very early stage as criminal, but technical advances are likely to mean that ultimately a decision will have to be made as to precisely where the line between contraception and abortion is to be drawn. It should be remembered that the question is not so much at what point the pregnancy *was* halted (as noted at **B1.65**, it is not always essential that there is a pregnancy in the first place), but rather at what point did the accused intend the pregnancy to halt. That may well depend on the extent of (or lack of) understanding of the mechanics of the situation on the part of the accused.

'Poison or other Noxious Thing . . . Instrument or Other Means'

If the indictment alleges the administration of a poison or noxious thing, it must either **B1.67** be a 'recognised poison' or, to be a noxious thing, some substance which is either harmful in itself or administered in such a quantity as to be harmful (*Cramp* (1880) 5 QBD 307) though not necessarily abortifacient (see *Marlow* (1964) 49 Cr App R 49). However, it may be that a practical way out of the difficulty, if there is any doubt about whether the substance administered constitutes a poison or noxious thing, would be to utilise that form of the offence that can be committed by 'any means whatsoever', and to frame the indictment accordingly as in Statement of Offence (2) at **B1.63**.

Special Defences

It was held in *Bourne* [1939] 1 KB 687 that, by analogy to the proviso to the Infant Life **B1.68** (Preservation) Act 1929, s. 1(1), an act was not unlawful within s. 58 of the 1861 Act if it was done in good faith for the purpose only of preserving the life of the mother. This defence now seems to be entirely supplanted by the provision in the Abortion Act 1967, s. 5, that anything done with intent to procure a woman's miscarriage is unlawfully done unless authorised by s. 1 of the 1967 Act (see **B1.69**).

Abortion Act 1967, ss. 1 and 5

Abortion Act 1967, ss. 1 and 5   **B1.69**

1.—(1)   Subject to the provisions of this section, a person shall not be guilty of an offence under the law relating to abortion when a pregnancy is terminated by a registered medical practitioner if two registered medical practitioners are of the opinion, formed in good faith—

(a)   that the pregnancy has not exceeded its twenty-fourth week and that the continuance of the pregnancy would involve risk, greater than if the pregnancy were terminated, of injury to the physical or mental health of the pregnant woman or any existing children of her family; or

    (b)   that the termination is necessary to prevent grave permanent injury to the physical or mental health of the pregnant woman; or

    (c)   that the continuance of the pregnancy would involve risk to the life of the pregnant woman, greater than if the pregnancy were terminated; or

    (d)   that there is a substantial risk that if the child were born it would suffer from such physical or mental abnormalities as to be seriously handicapped.

    (2)   In determining whether the continuance of a pregnancy would involve such risk of injury to health as is mentioned in paragraph (a) or (b) of subsection (1) of this section, account may be taken of the pregnant woman's actual or reasonably foreseeable environment.

    (3)   Except as provided by subsection (4) of this section, any treatment for the termination of pregnancy must be carried out in a hospital vested in the Minister of Health or the Secretary of State under the National Health Service Acts, or in a place for the time being approved for the purposes of this section by the said Minister or the Secretary of State.

    (3A)   The power under subsection (3) of this section to approve a place includes power, in relation to treatment consisting primarily in the use of such medicines as may be specified in the approval and carried out in such manner as may be so specified, to approve a class of places.

    (4)   Subsection (3) of this section, and so much of subsection (1) as relates to the opinion of two registered medical practitioners, shall not apply to the termination of a pregnancy by a registered medical practitioner in a case where he is of the opinion, formed in good faith, that the termination is immediately necessary to save the life or to prevent grave permanent injury to the physical or mental health of the pregnant woman.

5.—(1)   No offence under the Infant Life (Preservation) Act 1929 shall be committed by a registered medical practitioner who terminates a pregnancy in accordance with the provisions of this Act.

    (2)   For the purposes of the law relating to abortion, anything done with intent to procure a woman's miscarriage (or, in the case of a woman carrying more than one foetus, her miscarriage of any foetus) is unlawfully done unless authorised by section 1 of this Act and, in the case of a woman carrying more than one foetus, anything done with intent to procure her miscarriage of any foetus is authorised by that section if—

    (a)   the ground for termination of the pregnancy specified in subsection (1)(d) of that section applies in relation to any foetus and the thing is done for the purpose of procuring the miscarriage of the foetus, or

    (b)   any of the other grounds for termination of the pregnancy specified in that section applies.

One of the significant changes caused by the amendment of ss. 1 and 5 by the Human Fertilisation and Embryology Act 1990, s. 37, was that the legality of abortions ceased to be limited by the presumption in the Infant Life (Preservation) Act 1929 (see **B1.58**) that a child of 28 weeks' gestation is capable of being born alive; under the Abortion Act 1967, s. 5(1), compliance with the provisions of the Abortion Act is also a defence to a charge of child destruction. Instead there is now a fixed time-limit of 24 weeks for abortions under s. 1(1)(a) of the 1967 Act, but no time-limit at all (up to the point of a live birth) under s. 1(1)(b), (c) or (d). Section 1(3A) is intended to cater for drugs such as RU 486 (mifepristone) being used in places other than National Health Service hospitals or approved nursing homes. Section 5(2) makes it clear that selective reduction (procuring the miscarriage of one or more, but not all, of the foetuses in a multiple pregnancy) may in appropriate cases be authorised by s. 1.

Section 1 was considered by the House of Lords in *Royal College of Nursing of the United Kingdom* v *Department of Health and Social Security* [1981] AC 800, in which Lord Diplock said (at p. 828):

> Subsection 1 although it is expressed to apply only 'when a pregnancy is terminated by a registered medical practitioner' . . . also appears to contemplate treatment that is in the nature of a team effort and to extend its protection to all those who play a part in it.

Thus, methods of abortion, such as induction of premature delivery by means of prostaglandin drip, which involve nurses (or others) playing a substantial role, are covered, and all the participants are exempted provided that a registered medical practitioner accepts (loc. cit.):

> responsibility for all stages of the treatment for the termination of the pregnancy. The particular method to be used should be decided by the doctor in charge of the treatment for termination of the pregnancy; he should carry out any physical acts, forming part of the treatment, that in accordance with accepted medical practice are done only by qualified medical practitioners, and should give specific instructions as to the carrying out of such parts of the treatment as in accordance with accepted medical practice are carried out by nurses or other members of the hospital staff without medical qualifications. To each of them, the doctor, or his substitute, should be available to be consulted or called on for assistance from beginning to end of the treatment.

Although s. 1 refers to when 'a pregnancy *is* terminated', its protection also extends to cases where the attempt to terminate is unsuccessful (see *Royal College of Nursing* v *DHSS* [1981] AC 800, per Lord Diplock at p. 828), a not insignificant point, since the offence under the Offences against the Person Act 1861, s. 58, is committed irrespective of whether a miscarriage is actually procured.

The precise scope of the grounds for abortion enumerated in s. 1 are likely to continue to escape detailed interpretation by the courts, since the question is not whether these grounds actually exist but whether 'two registered medical practitioners are of the opinion, formed in good faith' that they exist. It was said in *Smith* [1973] 1 WLR 1510 that a conviction of a doctor without evidence as to professional practice and the medical probabilities was likely to be unsafe, but it was stressed that the question of good faith is a matter for the jury to be determined by reference to all the evidence (and the appeal in that case was dismissed).

Although under the Abortion Act 1967, s. 1(3), the termination must normally be carried out in a National Health Service hospital or an approved clinic, under s. 1(4) this requirement does not apply if just one registered medical practitioner 'is of the opinion, formed in good faith, that the termination is immediately necessary to save the life or to prevent grave permanent injury to the physical or mental health of the pregnant woman'. Although, as noted at **B1.68**, s. 5 makes compliance with the Act the sole test of unlawfulness for the purposes of the law of abortion, it is possible that this does not exclude a general defence such as duress of circumstances (see **A3.28** and also the Canadian case of *Morgentaler* v *The Queen* (1975) 53 DLR (3d) 161 discussed in L.H. Leigh, 'Necessity and the case of Dr Morgentaler' [1978] Crim LR 151), e.g., where a competent medical student finds himself, rather than a registered medical practitioner, in the sort of emergency situation outlined in s. 1(4).

Regulations have been made under s. 2(1) of the 1967 Act relating to the form of certificates of opinions, requiring notifications etc. of terminations and prohibiting disclosure of information in such notifications etc. Under s. 2(3) of the Act, contravention of the regulations is a summary offence, but would not appear to render an abortion illegal if the provisions of s. 1 of the Act are complied with. However, absence of the proper certificates may make it more difficult to show that the relevant opinion(s) had indeed been formed in good faith.

SUPPLYING OR PROCURING MEANS FOR ABORTION

Definition

Offences against the Person Act 1861, s. 59   B1.70

> Whoever shall unlawfully supply or procure any poison or other noxious thing, or any instrument or thing whatsoever, knowing that the same is intended to be unlawfully used

or employed with intent to procure the miscarriage of any woman, whether she be or be not with child, shall be guilty of [an offence], and being convicted thereof shall be liable . . . to imprisonment . . . for any term not exceeding five years.

Procedure

B1.71 Supplying or procuring means for abortion is triable only on indictment. It is a class 3 offence.

Indictment

B1.72

Statement of Offence

Supplying [or procuring] the means to procure a miscarriage contrary to section 59 of the Offences against the Person Act 1861

Particulars of Offence

A on or about the . . . day of . . . unlawfully supplied [or procured] a poison or other noxious thing, namely . . . , knowing that it was intended to be unlawfully used with intent to procure the miscarriage of V

Sentence

B1.73 The maximum sentence is five years (OAPA 1861, s. 59).

Elements

B1.74 'Supply' obviously means supply to another, and conversely 'procure' (any poison etc.) means procure *from* another, i.e. 'get possession of something of which you do not have possession already' (*Mills* [1963] 1 QB 522). Thus, the offence is not committed merely by producing the instrument or noxious thing etc. from one's cupboard (although the offence clearly is committed if it is then supplied, with the necessary knowledge, to another).

Although s. 59 refers to the accused's *knowledge* of the intentions of others, such old authorities as there are interpret this in effect as *belief* that the others intend unlawfully to use the poison etc. with intent to procure a miscarriage (*Hillman* (1863) Le & Ca 343; *Titley* (1880) 14 Cox CC 502) — i.e. the accused can be convicted even if in actual fact the other or others do not intend so to use it unlawfully. The effect of the Criminal Attempts Act 1981, s. 1(3) (see **A6.31** *et seq*.), is probably that, quite apart from these decisions, the accused could now be convicted of attempt in these circumstances.

Special Defences

B1.75 The exemption from liability provided by the Abortion Act 1967, s. 1, is equally applicable to this offence, as s. 6 of the Act defines 'the law relating to abortion' as meaning, 'sections 58 and 59 of the OAPA 1861 and any rule of law relating to the procurement of abortion'.

CONCEALMENT OF BIRTH

Definition

B1.76

Offences against the Person Act 1861, s. 60

If any woman shall be delivered of a child, every person who shall, by any secret disposition of the dead body of the said child, whether such child died before, at, or after its birth, endeavour to conceal the birth thereof, shall be guilty of [an offence], and being convicted thereof shall be liable, at the discretion of the court, to be imprisoned for any term not exceeding two years.

Procedure

Concealing the birth of a child is triable either way. When tried on indictment it is a class **B1.77**
4 offence.

Indictment

Statement of Offence **B1.78**

Endeavouring to conceal birth contrary to section 60 of the Offences against the Person Act
1861

Particulars of Offence

A on or about the . . . day of . . . endeavoured to conceal the birth of a child of which V had
been delivered by a secret disposition of the dead body of that child

Alternative Verdicts

There are no alternative verdicts. It should also be noted that as a result of the Criminal **B1.79**
Law Act 1967, sch. 2, it is no longer possible to convict of this offence on an indictment
for murder, infanticide or child destruction. Other offences which should be borne in
mind include the common-law misdemeanours of disposing of or destroying a dead
body with intent to prevent an inquest being held (*Stephenson* (1884) 13 QBD 331) and
preventing the burial of a body (see *Hunter* [1974] QB 95). See also **B14.37**.

Sentence

The maximum penalty is two years (Offences against the Person Act 1861, s. 60). **B1.80**

Meaning of 'child'

In *Berriman* (1854) 6 Cox CC 388, Erle J said (at p. 390) that the child must have: **B1.81**

> arrived at that stage of maturity at the time of birth, that it might have been a living child.
> . . . No specific limit can be assigned to the period when the chance of life begins, but it
> may, perhaps, be safely assumed that under seven months the great probability is that the
> child would not be born alive.

However, in *Colmer* (1864) 9 Cox CC 506, a child of just four or five months' gestational
age, about the length of a man's finger, was said by Martin B at first instance to be within
the definition. The decision has been doubted, and indeed the jury acquitted. The
meaning given to 'child' in *Berriman* is probably preferable and would make the offence
consistent with that of child destruction. The qualifying words 'capable of being born
alive' in the Infant Life (Preservation) Act 1929 (see **B1.58**), although in one sense
somewhat otiose if 'child' itself is given the more limited *Berriman* meaning, could be
regarded as clarifying the ambiguity already demonstrated in these cases.

Secret Disposition

This is satisfied by putting the dead body in a place where it is unlikely to be found, even **B1.82**
though the body is not concealed in the sense that it is completely hidden from view (see
Brown (1870) LR 1 CCR 244). Conversely, hiding the body from view is not sufficient
if it is in such a manner that the body is nevertheless likely to be found (see *George* (1868)
11 Cox CC 41). The accused's act must be done in relation to a dead body, so that the
offence is not committed where the accused conceals a living child which later dies (*May*
(1867) 10 Cox CC 448). However, there is almost certain to be liability for murder or
manslaughter in this situation (or at least for attempt to commit an offence under the
Offences against the Person Act 1861, s. 60, where the accused believes the child is
already dead). In *Hughes* (1850) 4 Cox CC 447, the accused concealed a living child,
returned and found it dead, and replaced the covers which were concealing it. This was

held to be an offence within a predecessor of s. 60 (9 Geo. 4 c. 31, s. 14), and to be a disposition of the dead body. An alternative and more appropriate charge would appear to be some form of homicide in relation to the initial act of concealing the living child which led to its death.

SOLICITATION OF MURDER

Definition

B1.83   **Offences against the Person Act 1861, s. 4**

Whosoever shall solicit, encourage, persuade or endeavour to persuade, or shall propose to any person, to murder any other person, whether he be a subject of Her Majesty or not, and whether he be within the Queen's dominions or not, shall be guilty of [an offence], and being convicted thereof shall be liable to imprisonment for life.

Procedure

B1.84   Solicitation of murder is triable only on indictment. It is a class 1 offence.

Indictment

B1.85   Statement of Offence

Soliciting to commit murder contrary to section 4 of the Offences against the Person Act 1861

Particulars of Offence

A on or about the . . . day of . . . , solicited [or encouraged etc.] X to murder V

Sentencing Guidelines

B1.86   The maximum penalty is life imprisonment (OAPA 1861, s. 4).

In *Kayani* [1997] 2 Cr App R (S) 313 a sentence of 12 years' imprisonment was upheld on an offender convicted for soliciting the murder of his niece and her husband. He was arrested by an undercover police officer posing as a contract killer, to whom payment of £20,000 was tendered partly in cash and partly in heroin. The offender received concurrent sentences for supplying heroin. In *Raw* (1983) 5 Cr App R (S) 229, where the offender attempted to contact someone who would murder his wife for a fee of £2,000, the Court of Appeal said that a prison sentence of seven years was 'the minimum sentence, regardless of the fact of the personality and circumstances of the appellant, that would constitute a proper deterrent'. This case was followed in *Peatfield* (1985) 7 Cr App R (S) 132, where a 10-year prison sentence was upheld on an offender who offered to pay a man £5,000 to murder his wife and 10-year-old daughter. In *Adamthwaite* (1994) 15 Cr App R (S) 241, however, where the offender had met with an undercover police officer and agreed to pay £5,000 for the murder of the offender's wife, the sentence of six years on a guilty plea was said to be 'on the high side' and was reduced to four years by the Court of Appeal. See also *A-G's Ref (No. 43 of 1996)* [1997] 1 Cr App R (S) 378.

Elements

B1.87   The phrase 'whether he be a subject of Her Majesty or not, and whether he be within the Queen's dominions or not' refers to the person to be murdered rather than to the persons doing the soliciting or being solicited, who themselves are governed by the normal rules on jurisdiction (see **D1.72** *et seq.*). The encouragement does not have to be directed to a particular individual — see *Most* (1881) 7 QBD 244, where the offence was committed by means of a newspaper article. The offence is not complete until someone is in receipt of the solicitation, although the act of sending it can constitute an attempt (*Krause* (1902) 66 JP 121). It does not matter that the recipient is not in fact influenced, although in this case it might be prudent to allege an 'endeavour to persuade' in the particulars. Encouraging a pregnant woman to kill her child in the future, after it shall have been born alive, is an offence within the section (*Shephard* [1919] 2 KB 125). See *Tait* [1990] 1 QB 290 and **B1.98**. The principles relating to the inchoate offence of incitement (see **A6.1** to **A6.8**) will generally be applicable to this offence.

COMPLICITY IN SUICIDE

Definition

Suicide Act 1961, s. 2

B1.88

(1)   A person who aids, abets, counsels or procures the suicide of another, or an attempt by another to commit suicide, shall be liable on conviction on indictment to imprisonment for a term not exceeding 14 years.

Procedure

Complicity in suicide is triable only on indictment. It is a class 3 offence. The consent of the DPP is required to initiate proceedings for this offence (Suicide Act 1961, s. 2(4)).

B1.89

Indictment

Statement of Offence

B1.90

Aiding, abetting, counselling or procuring suicide contrary to section 2(1) of the Suicide Act 1961

Particulars of Offence

A on or about the . . . day . . . did aid, abet, counsel or procure V to commit suicide

Alternative Verdicts

There are no alternative verdicts specifically provided for. The offence is itself an alternative verdict to murder or manslaughter (Suicide Act 1961, s. 2(2)).

B1.91

Sentencing Guidelines

The maximum penalty is 14 years' imprisonment (Suicide Act 1961, s. 2).

B1.92

In *Hough* (1984) 6 Cr App R (S) 406, Lord Lane CJ commented that this crime could vary 'from the borders of cold-blooded murder down to the shadowy area of mercy killing or common humanity'. In that case a nine-month prison term was upheld on a 60-year-old woman of unblemished character who had been a regular visitor to an 84-year-old woman who was partly blind, partly deaf, and suffered from arthritis. The old lady had persisted in various statements to the effect that she intended to take her own life, and the offender eventually supplied her with tablets. When she became unconscious, the offender placed a plastic bag over her head. In *Wallis* (1983) 5 Cr App R (S) 342, a sentence of 12 months' imprisonment was described by the Court of Appeal as 'at the extreme of leniency' in a case where the offender pleaded guilty to aiding the suicide of a 17-year-old flatmate by buying her tablets and alcohol, sitting with her while she took the tablets, and not calling an ambulance until she was dead. *Sweeney* (1986) 8 Cr App R (S) 419 and *England* (1990) 12 Cr App R (S) 98 were both cases involving suicide pacts. In the former, the facts of which were given at **B1.32**, a sentence of four years' imprisonment on the survivor was reduced to two years and, in the latter, a sentence of five years' imprisonment was reduced to three years.

Elements

The offence would seem to be governed by the normal rules applicable to aiding and abetting crime (see **A5.1** to **A5.9**), this special statutory version having been created

B1.93

because the substantive offence of suicide was abolished by the Suicide Act 1961, s. 1. However, although aiding and abetting normally requires that the substantive offence be committed, or at least attempted, and there is usually no such thing as an attempt to aid and abet (see Criminal Attempts Act 1981, s. 1(4)), it is possible to convict of an attempt to commit the offence under s. 2(1). The person doing the aiding and abetting etc. is in this case the principal offender. This effectively extends the ambit of the offence to incitement to commit suicide, so that there can be liability even if the person encouraged does not in fact commit or attempt to commit suicide (see *McShane* (1977) 66 Cr App R 97). The accused must, of course, intend that someone commit or attempt to commit suicide (*A-G* v *Able* [1984] 1 QB 795). Similarly, despite the confusion over whether there can generally be a conspiracy to aid and abet (see **A6.16**), there can be liability for conspiracy to aid and abet an offence under s. 2(1) (*Reed* [1982] Crim LR 819).

THREATS TO KILL

Definition

B1.94 **Offences against the Person Act 1861, s. 16**

> A person who without lawful excuse makes to another a threat, intending that that other would fear it would be carried out, to kill that other or a third person shall be guilty of an offence and liable on conviction on indictment to imprisonment for a term not exceeding 10 years.

Procedure

B1.95 Threatening to kill is triable either way. When tried on indictment it is a class 4 offence.

Indictment

B1.96 Statement of Offence

Making a threat to kill contrary to section 16 of the Offences against the Person Act 1861

Particulars of Offence

> A on or about the . . . day of . . . , without lawful excuse, threatened V that he would kill him [or that he would kill X] intending that V would fear that the said threat would be carried out

Sentencing Guidelines

B1.97 The maximum penalty is 10 years' imprisonment (Criminal Law Act 1977, sch. 12, replacing OAPA 1861, s. 16).

Sentences approved by the Court of Appeal for this offence range downwards from the five years' imprisonment imposed in *Bowden* (1986) 8 Cr App R (S) 155, where the offender, under treatment for alcoholism, went to the home of a woman with whom he had formerly lived, and threatened her with a sword. The woman barricaded herself in the bedroom and the police had to force their way into the house to arrest the offender. The court heard evidence that the offender had a large collection of weapons which he intended to use against a list of people, headed by his ex-girlfriend. The Court of Appeal agreed that the trial judge's duty was to protect the public; in the absence of any evidence of mental disorder, the custodial sentence was proper. See also *Perry* (1986) 8 Cr App R (S) 132, a case where the offender issued threats against his ex-wife, whom he had already seriously injured in the past, where a four-year sentence was upheld. In *Martin* (1993) 14 Cr App R (S) 645, four years' imprisonment was reduced to three years in a case where the offender sent two anonymous notes, stained with blood. In *Gaskin* (1996) *The Times*, 15 August 1996, Judge Allen in the Court of Appeal noted that cases of making threats to kill posed difficult sentencing problems, since they ranged from threats made in the heat of the moment to cases where the victim continued to fear for the future as well as having suffered short-term terror. In recognising that the instant appeal was a case of the latter type, the Court of Appeal upheld a prison sentence of four years. In *Choudhury* [1997] 2 Cr App R (S) 300 the offender, after being released on bail for a public order offence, made repeated threats to kill the police officer who had arrested him and also threatened the officer's family. Although the case had been contested, the Court of Appeal noted that the threats had been made while the offender was in an agitated state, and so reduced the prison sentence from three years to two years.

Elements

The words 'without lawful excuse' in the OAPA 1861, s. 16, would exempt, for example, **B1.98** a threat made reasonably in self-defence to deter an apprehended attack or to prevent crime (see *Cousins* [1982] QB 526). An implied threat will suffice (see the facts of *Solanke* [1970] 1 WLR 1), as will a threat that is only to be carried out at some time in the future, although it would seem that it has to be one that will be carried out by the accused, or at least under his instructions. It is the person to whom the threat is made, rather than the person to be killed, who must fear that the threat will be carried out, although often these two will be one and the same person. A threat to a pregnant woman in respect of her unborn child is not sufficient if the threat is to kill it before its birth. But if it is a threat to kill the child after its birth, then that would appear to be within the section (*Tait* [1990] 1 QB 290).

SECTION B2: NON-FATAL OFFENCES AGAINST THE PERSON

ASSAULT AND BATTERY

Definition

B2.1   Strictly speaking, assault and battery are separate summary offences. An assault is committed when the accused intentionally or recklessly causes another to apprehend immediate and unlawful violence. A battery is committed when the accused intentionally or recklessly inflicts unlawful force. A battery may, but does not inevitably, follow an assault. Despite this technical difference, the term 'assault', or 'common assault', has been generally used, both in cases (*Fagan* v *Metropolitan Police Commissioner* [1969] 1 QB 439) and in statutes (OAPA 1861, ss. 38, 42, 47), to cover either an assault or a battery.

It is now necessary to be more specific when laying an information. The Divisional Court in *DPP* v *Taylor* [1992] QB 645 has held that all common assaults and batteries are now offences contrary to the CJA 1988, s. 39, and that the information must include a reference to that section. An information would be bad for duplicity if the phrase 'assault and battery' were used; the court suggested that 'assault by beating' was the appropriate wording. Despite this guidance, the point is not always picked up. In *Notman* [1994] Crim LR 518 (see **A1.29**) the Court of Appeal made no comment on just such a duplicitous charge.

The CDA 1998, s. 29, creates a racially aggravated form of this offence which carries a higher maximum penalty. For the meaning of 'racially aggravated', see **B11.154**.

Procedure

B2.2   Common assault and battery are generally triable only summarily (CJA 1988, s. 39). However, a count for common assault may be included in an indictment in the circumstances prescribed by the CJA 1988, s. 40, dealt with in detail at **D9.6** (see also **D3.20**). Common assault under s. 40 has the ordinary everyday meaning of that word, including battery (*Lynsey* [1995] 3 All ER 654). For powers of committal for trial to the Crown Court, see the CJA 1988, s. 41, dealt with in detail at **D7.23**.

The racially aggravated form of the offence is triable either way.

Sentencing Guidelines

B2.3   The maximum penalties for common assault and battery are six months' imprisonment, a fine not exceeding level 5 on the standard scale, or both (CJA 1988, s. 39). The maximum for the racially aggravated form of the offence is two years' imprisonment, a fine or both on indictment; six months, a fine not exceeding the statutory maximum or both summarily (CDA 1998, s. 29(3)).

The Magistrates' Association Guidelines (1997) indicate the following:

Aggravating Factors ⊕
For example racial motivation; group action; offender in position of authority; premeditated; injury; weapon; victim particularly vulnerable; victim public servant; offence committed on bail; previous convictions and failures to respond to previous sentences, if relevant.

Mitigating Factors ⊖
For example impulsive; minor injury; provocation; single blow.

Guideline: Is it serious enough for a community penalty?

In *Fenton* (1994) 15 Cr App R (S) 682 the offender pleaded guilty to common assault (charges of assault occasioning actual bodily harm and dangerous driving were not proceeded with). In the course of an altercation between two motorists, the offender pushed the victim in the chest. The Court of Appeal said that almost all cases of violence between motorists would be so serious that only custody could be justified. The appropriate sentence was seven days' imprisonment. See also *Ross* (1994) 15 Cr App R (S) 384.

Actus Reus of Assault

An assault requires conduct which causes the victim to apprehend the imminent **B2.4** application of unlawful force upon him (*Ireland* [1998] AC 147, per Lord Steyn at p. 161). A fear of *possible* violence may suffice (*Ireland*) and it may also suffice where the victim is unsure as to when exactly the threatened attack may occur; but as the Court of Appeal pointed out in *Constanza* [1997] 2 Cr App R 492, the conduct in question must at least provoke a fear of violence 'at some time not excluding the immediate future'. A threat of violence only in the more distant future cannot suffice. As to what may amount to unlawful force, see **B2.5** and **B2.7** to **B2.9**. An omission to act probably cannot amount to an assault, or indeed a battery, but see **B2.5**.

The relevant conduct in cases of assault may take the form of threatening acts or gestures, as for example where D brandishes a weapon at V or fires a shot in his direction; but it may also take the form of threatening words, or it may involve acts and words together. It may even involve a series of acts (*Cox* [1998] Crim LR 810). It was at one time thought that words alone, whether written or spoken, could never amount to an assault (*Meade and Belt* (1823) 1 Lew CC 184; *Russell on Crime*, 4th ed. 1865) but this view has now been rejected, both by the Court of Appeal in *Constanza* (a case involving the sending of threatening letters) and by the House of Lords in *Ireland* (a case involving telephone calls). Giving the judgment of the House of Lords in *Ireland*, Lord Steyn said:

> The proposition that a gesture may amount to an assault, but that words can never suffice, is unrealistic and indefensible. A thing said is also a thing done. There is no reason why something said should be incapable of causing an apprehension of immediate personal violence . . . I would, therefore, reject the proposition that an assault can never be committed by words.

One of the appellants in *Ireland* made 'silent' telephone calls to a number of women, and it was held that such conduct could amount to the *actus reus* of assault if it caused the victims to fear that physical violence might be used against them in the immediate future. It may suffice for this purpose if it causes the victim to fear the mere *possibility* of imminent violence, but it cannot suffice if the victim fears only the prospect of receiving further calls (*Ireland*, per Lord Hope at p. 166), nor can it suffice if it is clear to the victim that the accused or his friends can do nothing to harm her in the immediate future.

The concept of immediacy has nevertheless been interpreted with some flexibility, and there have been a number of recent cases in which 'stalkers' have been prosecuted for assault on that basis. In *Smith* v *Chief Superintendent, Woking Police Station* (1983) 76 Cr App R 234, the Divisional Court held that a threat of violence could be considered immediate, even though the accused was still outside the victim's home, looking in at her through a window, and would have needed to force an entry before he could attack her. In *Ireland,* the House of Lords adopted an even more flexible approach, stating (at p. 162) that 'there is no reason why a telephone caller who says to a woman in a menacing way, "I will be at your door in a minute or two" may not be guilty of an assault'. Such conduct may alternatively, and perhaps more appropriately, be prosecuted under the Protection from Harassment Act 1997 (see **B11.77** *et seq.*).

Words used by the accused may indicate that no attack is threatened, even where the circumstances might otherwise suggest that one is. Thus, in *Tuberville* v *Savage* (1669) 1 Mod 3, T, in the course of a quarrel with S, placed his hand on the hilt of his sword (an act which might ordinarily have been construed as an assault) and exclaimed, 'If it were not assize time, I would not take such language from you'. This was held to be no assault, 'for the declaration of [T] was that he would not assault [S], the judges being in town'.

A 'conditional' threat of unlawful violence may amount to an assault, even though the victim is told that he may avoid such violence by complying with the defendant's conditions. Thus, in the civil case of *Read* v *Coker* (1853) 13 CB 850, the plaintiff successfully sued for assault on the basis that the defendant and his men had surrounded him and threatened to 'break his neck' if he refused to leave the defendant's premises. See also *Ansell* v *Thomas* [1974] Crim LR 31.

Although an assault may take the form of a 'failed battery', as where D's blow fails to connect with V, assault is always a result crime (see **A1.2**). No assault can be committed unless the threats are actually perceived by the victim. There is no assault if a stone thrown by D sails past V's head without him noticing (although D may have attempted to commit an offence under the OAPA 1861, s. 47). If, however, D threatens V with an imitation firearm, this will indeed amount to an assault, unless V knows that the weapon cannot fire (*Logdon* v *DPP* [1976] Crim LR 121). If V does apprehend the threat of imminent violence, it does not matter whether he is frightened by it. He may relish the opportunity to teach D a lesson, and yet still be regarded as the victim of D's assault.

Actus Reus of Battery

B2.5   A battery requires the unlawful application of force upon the victim. It cannot include the circumstances of a telephone caller who thereby causes his victim's psychiatric injury (*Ireland* [1998] AC 147 at p. 161); but as to assault see **B2.4** and **B2.19**; and as to liability under the Protection from Harassment Act 1997, see **B11.77** *et seq.*).

Battery need not necessarily be preceded by any assault. A blow may, for example, be struck from behind, without warning. Nor need a battery involve any serious violence. Any unlawful touching of another may be classed as a battery. As Goff LJ stated in *Collins* v *Wilcock* [1984] 3 All ER 374 (at p. 378), 'everybody is protected, not only against physical injury, but against any form of physical molestation'. The ordinary everyday jostling that one must expect on crowded pavements, corridors or trains cannot be considered unlawful unless it is excessive and unreasonable (*Wilson* v *Pringle* [1986] 2 All ER 440) and even where it is objected to, a mere technical battery is unlikely to be prosecuted; but difficulties have sometimes arisen where persons are touched by police officers against their will, because even a trivial technical assault or battery by a police officer takes that officer outside the scope of his duty, and prevents him from qualifying as the victim of any offence under the Police Act 1996, s. 89 (see **B2.23**).

It is submitted that a battery must take the form of a positive act, rather than a mere omission, and that it must involve a *direct* application of force upon the victim. V might, for example, suffer pain or injury if he slips on a patch of oil which D has previously spilled and omitted to clear up, but it is very doubtful whether D can thereby be said to have battered him, even if the spillage of the oil was deliberate. The need for a positive act was emphasised by the Divisional Court in *Fagan* v *Metropolitan Police Commissioner* [1969] 1 QB 439 (as to which, see **A1.5**). If *Fagan* is correct, it would appear that there is no room in assault or battery cases for application of the *Miller* principle (see *Miller* [1983] 2 AC 161 explained at **A1.16**). Battery suggests some kind of attack, and it is submitted that one cannot attack another person through mere inaction.

The question whether a battery must involve a direct application of unlawful force to the victim is a matter of some controversy, but the balance of authority suggests that it must.

In *Metropolitan Police Commissioner* v *Wilson* [1984] AC 242, the House of Lords held (albeit by implication) that *indirect* violence, such as the setting of a trap into which P falls, may not amount to a battery, although it may involve the unlawful 'infliction' of harm, for the purpose of liability under the OAPA 1861, s. 20, and that view has been reiterated by the House of Lords, both in *Savage* [1992] 1 AC 699 and in *Ireland* [1998] AC 147 at p. 160. *Martin* (1881) 8 QBD 54 is often said to be authority to the contrary, but that case merely decided that M's conduct in barring the doors to a theatre and putting out the lights could make him liable for the s. 20 'infliction' of grievous bodily harm upon a number of persons who were crushed in the ensuing panic. *Martin* is thus consistent with what was said in *Wilson* and has no bearing on the law of assault or battery.

There is one case which supports the concept of indirect battery. In *DPP* v *K* [1990] 1 WLR 1067, the Divisional Court held that K, a schoolboy, was guilty of an offence under the OAPA 1861, s. 47, when he poured acid into a warm-air drier in his school cloakroom, causing injury to the next pupil who used it. This appears to have been a decision *per incuriam*, however, because no account was taken of *Wilson*. See Hirst, 'Assault, Battery and Indirect Violence' [1999] Crim LR 557.

The administering of a poison or noxious substance can only rarely involve a battery (e.g., where it is sprayed directly into the victim's face, as in *Gillard* (1988) 87 Cr App R 189: see **B2.54**). In contrast, setting one's dog on another person involves a direct use of force, because the dog is used as a weapon.

Mens Rea of Assault or Battery

An assault or battery must be committed intentionally or recklessly. Recklessness, in this **B2.6** context, means subjective or *Cunningham* recklessness. As explained at **A2.5**, the courts (notably in *Spratt* [1990] 1 WLR 1073 and *Savage* [1992] 1 AC 699) have held that objective (or *Caldwell*) recklessness is not a sufficient basis for liability in cases where assault or battery must be established. This is true both of common assault and of aggravated assaults under the OAPA 1861, s. 47, or the Police Act 1996, s. 89. Evidence of voluntary intoxication can never assist the defence in respect of such offences because they do not require 'specific intent' (see **A3.10**).

Lawful and Unlawful Force

Assault or battery must involve the use or threat of unlawful force. The use or threat of **B2.7** force is not always unlawful. In particular, it may be justified on the basis of actual or implied consent; on the basis of self-defence, crime prevention or crowd control; or on the basis that it involved the lawful correction of a child.

Self-defence and related justifications for the use or threat of force are considered in section **A3** and in particular at **A3.30**. The concepts of consent and lawful correction are considered below at **B2.8** and **B2.9**.

Consent   Where consent is in issue, the burden of disproving it must always lie on the **B2.8** prosecution (*Donovan* [1934] 2 KB 498). The two principal questions which arise in this context are (1) Did the alleged victim indeed consent (expressly or by implication) to the physical contact or force complained of; and (2) if so, is that consent deemed to be valid in the circumstances?

As to (1), this is usually a simple question of fact, but a person may be 'deemed' to consent to harmless or unavoidable everyday contacts with his fellow citizens, which for that reason cannot be unlawful (see **B2.5**). Issue (2) is more problematic. Consent may be invalid where the person giving it has no real understanding of what he is consenting to (*Burrell* v *Harmer* [1967] Crim LR 169; *D* [1984] AC 778) but cf. *Clarence* (1888) 22

QBD 23, *Richardson* [1998] 2 Cr App R 200 and *Bolduc* (1967) 63 DLR (2d) 82, which make clear that, as long as V understands what he is consenting to, that consent is not invalidated by fraud as to the circumstances or as to D's motives (the same rule applies in cases of alleged rape: see **B3.7**). Furthermore, where actual bodily harm (or worse) is intended or inflicted, consent to it will ordinarily be deemed invalid on grounds of public policy, even if V knows exactly what he is consenting to.

In *Brown* [1994] 1 AC 212, the House of Lords upheld convictions for offences under ss. 20 and 47 of the OAPA 1861 in respect of a group of homosexual sado-masochists, who had engaged in acts of consensual torture with each other for the purpose of sexual gratification. Lord Templeman said (at pp. 231, 234 and 236):

> In some circumstances violence is not punishable under the criminal law. When no actual bodily harm is caused, the consent of the person affected precludes him from complaining. There can be no conviction for the summary offence of common assault if the victim has consented. . . . Even when violence is intentionally inflicted and results in . . . wounding or serious bodily harm the accused is entitled to be acquitted if the injury was a foreseeable incident of a lawful activity in which the person injured was participating. Surgery . . . is a lawful activity. . . . ritual [*male*] circumcision, tattooing, ear piercing and violent sports including boxing are lawful activities.

> . . . The question whether the defence of consent should be extended to the consequences of sado-masochistic encounters can only be decided by consideration of policy and public interest.

> . . . The violence of sado-masochistic encounters involves the indulgence of cruelty by sadists and the degradation of victims. Such violence is injurious to the participants and unpredictably dangerous. I am not prepared to invent a defence of consent for sado-masochistic encounters which breed and glorify cruelty and result in offences under sections 47 and 20 of the Act of 1861.

The defendants in *Brown* sought redress from the European Court of Human Rights (*Laskey* v *United Kingdom* (1997) 24 EHRR 39) but the court ruled that state interference in this aspect of their private lives could be justified on the basis of 'protection of health'.

The approach adopted in *Brown* is consistent with earlier decisions and dicta of the Court of Appeal and Court of Criminal Appeal. Thus, in *Donovan* [1934] 2 KB 498, it was stated that a 17-year-old girl could not give valid consent to a sado-masochistic caning; and in *A-G's Ref (No. 6 of 1980)* [1981] QB 715 Lord Lane CJ held that it would not be in the public interest to allow a defence of consent in the context of a fist-fight where actual bodily harm was intended and/or caused for no good reason ('minor struggles' being excepted).

A number of further qualifications to the basic rule have been identified by the Court of Appeal. One concerns 'rough and undisciplined horseplay'. In *Jones* (1986) 83 Cr App R 375, a group of youths tossed other youths into the air and let them fall to the ground. One of the victims suffered a ruptured spleen and another suffered a broken arm. The trial judge refused to allow the issue of consent to be raised, owing to the serious nature of the injuries, but the Court of Appeal held that the defence should (for what it was worth) have been left to the jury. This ruling was approved in *Brown* and followed in *Aitken* [1992] 1 WLR 1006, but its proper limits must be understood. Individuals may lawfully engage in rough horseplay only where there is at least a genuine belief that the 'victim' consents, and only where no injury is intended. In *A-G's Ref (No. 6 of 1980)*, Lord Lane CJ also identified an exception covering 'dangerous exhibitions'. The knife-thrower who accidentally injures his assistant with a badly aimed blade would thus appear to be innocent of any battery or wounding.

A further limitation has subsequently been identified in *Wilson* [1996] 2 Cr App R 241, in which the Court of Appeal held that nothing said in *Brown* prevented a wife from validly consenting to the branding of her husband's initials on her buttocks. The branding was said to be more akin to tattooing than to any act of sado-masochism (whereas sado-masochistic branding was one of the acts declared criminal in *Brown*). Furthermore, 'Consensual activity between husband and wife in the privacy of the matrimonial home is not, in our judgment, normally a proper matter for criminal investigation, let alone criminal prosecution'.

Wilson must now be followed by trial courts, even if it appears to modify the law as stated in *Brown*, but it is not entirely clear how far its effects extend, especially since the view of the court was that the law should be left to develop on a case-by-case basis. Some clarification has now been provided by *Emmett* (1999) *The Times*, 15 October 1999, in which the Court of Appeal held that dangerous and damaging sado-masochistic games (involving suffocation and burning) were not exempted by the *Wilson* principle, even where carried out consensually in what was effectively a husband and wife relationship.

The law concerning the limits and effectiveness of consent to medical treatment is a highly specialised subject which cannot be covered in detail here; but the basic issues are examined at **A1.17**.

Lawful Correction or Chastisement At common law, a parent or any other person **B2.9** acting *in loco parentis* may use reasonable force to control the behaviour of a child in his care. This may extend to the infliction of reasonable corporal punishment, but 'if the punishment is administered for the gratification of passion or rage, or if it be immoderate or excessive in its nature or degree . . . it is unlawful' (*Hopley* (1860) 2 F & F 202 per Cockburn CJ at p. 206). The limits of what may be considered reasonable have narrowed in recent years. Caning, for example, is unlikely to be considered acceptable, and has been held to be 'inhuman and degrading treatment' by the European Court of Human Rights (see *A v United Kingdom* (1999) 27 EHRR 611). The reasonableness (and thus legality) of parental chastisement nevertheless remains a question of fact for the court or jury, the members of whom are likely to have differing views on what 'reasonable punishment' may involve.

The law governing the infliction of punishment in schools is the Education Act 1996, s. 548, as substituted by the School Standards and Framework Act 1998, s. 131 (in force 1 September 1999). This removes the right of any teacher at any school (state or private sector) to administer corporal punishment to any pupil 'by virtue of his position as such'. This effectively abolishes all corporal punishment in British schools.

It is also unlawful for a teacher to throw an object (such as a blackboard duster) at a pupil, even if that pupil is misbehaving (*Taylor* (1983) *The Times*, 28 December 1983), but teachers or other staff in schools may use reasonable force to restrain pupils who are violent or disruptive (Education Act 1996, s. 550A). Corporal punishment does not include things done to avert immediate danger of personal injury or damage to property (s. 548(5)).

ASSAULT WITH INTENT TO RESIST OR PREVENT ARREST

Definition

Offences against the Person Act 1861, s. 38 **B2.10**

> Whosoever . . . shall assault any person with intent to resist or prevent the lawful apprehension or detainer of himself or of any other person for any offence, shall be guilty of [an offence], and being convicted thereof shall be liable, at the discretion of the court, to be imprisoned for any term not exceeding two years . . .

Procedure

B2.11 Assault with intent to resist or prevent arrest is triable either way. When tried on indictment it is a class 4 offence.

Indictment

B2.12
Statement of Offence

Assault with intent to resist arrest, contrary to section 38 of the Offences against the Person Act 1861

Particulars of Offence

A on or about the . . . day of . . . assaulted X with intent to resist or prevent the lawful apprehension of A [or another] for the commission of an offence

Sentence

B2.13 The maximum penalty is two years (OAPA 1861, s. 38). As to sentencing considerations, see those applicable to assault occasioning actual bodily harm, at **B2.16**.

Elements

B2.14 The *actus reus* is the same as that for assault (see **B2.4**). As well as the *mens rea* for assault (see **B2.6**), a further specific intent is required for this offence. Because this is an offence of specific intent, only intention to cause the relevant consequence will suffice.

There must be proved an intent to resist or prevent the lawful arrest of a person, and the requirements relevant to such an intent in the context of s. 18 of the 1861 Act are also applicable here. In particular, the requirement that the intent be to resist or prevent the *lawful* arrest means that a subjective realisation of the lawfulness of the arrest must be proved. The Court of Appeal in *Brightling* [1991] Crim LR 364 held that the issue in respect of the Offences against the Person Act 1861, s. 38, was that a genuine mistake as to the identity of the victim was relevant to the defendant's intent. The court noted the distinction between s. 38 and what is now the Police Act 1996, s. 89(2) (see **B2.28**). For the purposes of s. 38, the person attempting to make an arrest does not have to be a police constable, and to that extent the defendant's belief that such person was not a police constable does not automatically exculpate him. He may realise that a lawful citizen's arrest is being attempted.

The arrest (or apprehension of detainer) must be lawful, bearing in mind that different powers are available under statute to constables and private citizens (see **D1.3** *et seq*. and *Self* [1992] 1 WLR 657).

The wording in s. 38 is in contrast to the wording in the Police Act 1996, s. 89(2); the latter uses the word 'obstruct', s. 38 refers to resisting or preventing. Resisting might be taken to imply some kind of physical action, but preventing can be said to have a much wider meaning; an intent to prevent an arrest should be easier to prove.

<h2>ASSAULT OCCASIONING ACTUAL BODILY HARM</h2>

Definition

B2.15
Offences against the Person Act 1861, s. 47

Whosoever shall be convicted upon an indictment of any assault occasioning actual bodily harm shall be liable . . . to [imprisonment for five years].

The CDA 1998, s. 29, creates a racially aggravated form of this offence which carries a higher maximum penalty. For the meaning of 'racially aggravated', see **B11.154**.

Procedure

Assault occasioning actual bodily harm is triable either way. When tried on indictment it **B2.16** is a class 4 offence. The racially aggravated form of the offence is also triable either way. *Practice Note* (*Mode of Trial: Guidelines*) (1995) (see **D3.7**) states the following in relation to determining mode of trial for the basic offence:

> Cases should be tried summarily unless the court considers that one or more of the following features is present in the case *and* that its sentencing powers are insufficient.
> 1.   The use of weapon of a kind likely to cause serious injury.
> 2.   A weapon is used and serious injury is caused.
> 3.   More than minor injury is caused by kicking, head-butting or similar forms of assault.
> 4.   Serious violence is caused to those whose work has to be done in contact with the public or who are likely to face violence in the course of their work.
> 5.   Violence to vulnerable people (e.g. the elderly and infirm).
> The same considerations apply to cases of domestic violence.

Indictment

Statement of Offence   **B2.17**

Assault occasioning actual bodily harm, contrary to section 47 of the Offences against the Person Act 1861

Particulars of Offence

A on or about the . . . day of . . . assaulted V thereby causing him actual bodily harm

Sentencing Guidelines

The maximum penalty is five years (OAPA 1861, s. 47) on indictment; six months, or **B2.18** a fine not exceeding level 5, or both, summarily. The maximum for the racially aggravated form of the offence is seven years, a fine or both on indictment; six months, a fine not exceeding the statutory maximum or both summarily (CDA 1998, s. 29(2)).

The Magistrates' Association Guidelines (1997) indicate the following:

Aggravating Factors ⊕
For example racial motivation; deliberate kicking or biting; extensive injuries (may be psychiatric); group action; offender in position of authority; premeditated; victim particularly vulnerable; victim serving public; weapon; offence committed on bail; previous convictions and failures to respond to previous sentences, if relevant.

Mitigating Factors ⊖
For example impulsive; minor injury; provocation; single blow.

Guideline: Is it so serious that only custody is appropriate?

In *Audit* (1994) 15 Cr App R (S) 36 the offender, after drinking heavily, assaulted another man by punching him in the face, causing a cut to the eyebrow which needed stitches and bruising to the face and jaw. The Court of Appeal said that a custodial sentence of three months was appropriate. In *Graham* [1993] Crim LR 628, the female offender, after an argument in a restaurant, assaulted a woman who had called her names, by hitting her in the face. She suffered black eyes and a swollen nose. Six months' imprisonment was reduced to 28 days. Four months' imprisonment was the appropriate sentence in *Marples* [1998] 1 Cr App R (S) 335 where, in the course of an altercation in a taxi queue, the defendant struck the victim in the face, breaking his nose.

Heavier sentences will be imposed where the assault was committed against a police officer or involved a vulnerable victim. In *Leather* (1993) 14 Cr App R (S) 736 a custodial sentence of eight months was upheld on a 17-year-old woman who had seized a police officer by the testicles, in order to prevent the officer arresting her boyfriend. Nine months' imprisonment was upheld in *Fletcher* [1998] 1 Cr App R (S) 7, the defendant being convicted after a trial of assault occasioning actual bodily harm. Police officers had been engaged in towing away a car, which had been illegally parked. The car owner returned, punched one of the officers, then got into his car and drove at the officer, striking him with the wing mirror. The officer received a fracture at the base of his spine and was unable to work for four months. If it is not proved that the offender knew that the victim was a police officer, then the heavier sentence will not be appropriate (*Stosiek* (1982) 4 Cr App R (S) 205). In *Glover* (1993) 14 Cr App R (S) 261 a sentence of four months' detention in a young offender institution was varied to a probation order where a 20-year-old woman, described as immature and of limited intelligence, had slapped her three-year-old son in the face, causing a swollen and bruised cheek and a bruise inside the mouth, but in *Barnes* (1993) 14 Cr App R (S) 547 a custodial sentence was upheld, though reduced from 6 months to 28 days, where a man left in charge of the 10-month-old daughter of the woman with whom he was living, slapped the child in the face causing bruising.

Longer sentences will also be proper, *inter alia*, where a weapon is used by the offender, or the assault is committed upon a public servant (*Foster* (1982) 4 Cr App R (S) 101, where six months' detention was ordered for an assault by a youth on a bus conductor, who had been cut on the head, and see also *Tremlett* (1983) 5 Cr App R (S) 199); where the assault is committed at a football match, particularly against someone not themselves involved in violence (*Birkin* (1988) 10 Cr App R (S) 303, *Wood* (1984) 6 Cr App R (S) 2). Racial motivation is an important aggravating factor (*Earley* [1998] 2 Cr App R (S) 158). There is no reason to treat an assault committed by one motorist upon another after a road accident or dispute as any less serious than an assault committed in other circumstances (*Arnold* [1996] 1 Cr App R (S) 115, where six months imprisonment was upheld for headbutting the victim, causing a broken nose). *Arnold* was followed and applied in *Maben* [1997] 2 Cr App R (S) 341. Nor should assaults between spouses receive more lenient treatment than other assaults (*Nicholas* (1994) 15 Cr App R (S) 381, where three years' imprisonment was appropriate for serious and repeated assaults by a man on his wife, even after she had obtained a non-molestation injunction against him). An offender convicted of assault committed by 'stalking' the victim over a four-year period received a sentence of 21 months' imprisonment in *Smith* [1998] 1 Cr App R (S) 138.

Actus Reus

B2.19 An offence under the OAPA 1861, s. 47, must involve an assault or battery (as to which see **B2.4** *et seq.*) and it must be established that this assault or battery occasioned (i.e. caused) the victim actual bodily harm. Such injury cannot ordinarily be consented to (see **B2.8**). As to the position where bodily harm results from the cumulative effect of a series of separate incidents, see *Cox* [1998] Crim LR 810. As long as there was a direct assault or battery, it does not matter if the bodily harm was suffered indirectly. In *Roberts* (1971) 56 Cr App R 95, R assaulted a young woman in his car, and frightened her to the extent that she leaped from it to escape whilst it was still in motion; she suffered injuries as a result. R was convicted of a s. 47 offence. Stephenson LJ said:

> The test is: was [her injury] the natural result of what [R] said and did, in the sense that it was something that could reasonably have been foreseen as the consequence of what he was saying or doing.

'Actual bodily harm' has been defined as any injury which is 'calculated to interfere with the health or comfort of the [victim]' (*Miller* [1954] 2 QB 282, per Lynskey J at p. 292). Minor cuts and bruises may satisfy this test, although the Charging Standards agreed between the police and the CPS do not endorse the bringing of s. 47 charges in the absence of more serious injuries, such as broken teeth, extensive bruising or cuts etc., which require medical treatment.

Psychiatric injury (going beyond mere fear or anxiety) may be a form of actual (or even grievous) bodily harm (*Chan-Fook* [1994] 1 WLR 689; *Ireland* [1998] AC 147) and will typically be caused by assault, rather than by any battery. Where such injury is alleged, it must be proved by expert psychiatric evidence (*Chan-Fook*) and there must also be expert evidence to prove that the defendant's assault was the cause of that injury. In the absence of such evidence, there may be no case to leave to the jury (*Morris* [1998] 1 Cr App R 386).

Mens Rea

The *mens rea* of a s. 47 offence is no different from that required in respect of a common **B2.20** assault or battery (see **B2.6**). Although the causing of actual bodily harm is an additional *actus reus* element, no *mens rea* as to it is required. If injury is caused, it need not even be proved that the injury was foreseeable, because this element of the offence is one of strict liability. This is now clear from the decision of the House of Lords in *Savage* [1992] 1 AC 699, in which S aimed to throw the contents of a beer glass over B, but inadvertently allowed the glass to slip from her hand and break, with the result that B was injured by it. It was held that a conviction for malicious wounding could not be sustained in the absence of proof that S had at least foreseen the possibility of injury to B, but a conviction for an offence under s. 47 could be substituted, because throwing beer over B was an intentional assault (indeed a battery) and that same assault had resulted in B's injury. Similarly, in a case such as *Ireland* [1998] AC 147, where threats are made by letter or by telephone etc., *mens rea* for a s. 47 offence can be established if D intends or foresees that V may be frightened into apprehending immediate violence. He need not intend or foresee (nor even have any reason to foresee) that V will suffer psychiatric injury.

ASSAULT ON CONSTABLE IN EXECUTION OF DUTY

Definition

Police Act 1996, s. 89   **B2.21**

(1)   Any person who assaults a constable in the execution of his duty, or a person assisting a constable in the execution of his duty, shall be guilty of an offence and liable on summary conviction to imprisonment for a term not exceeding six months or to a fine not exceeding level 5 on the standard scale, or to both.

Procedure and Sentencing

This offence is triable only summarily.   **B2.22**

The maximum penalties are six months' imprisonment, a fine not exceeding level 5, or both (Police Act 1996, s. 89(1)). The Magistrates' Association Guidelines (1997) indicate the following:

Aggravating Factors ⊕
   For example any injuries caused; gross disregard for police authority; group action; premeditated; offence committed on bail; previous convictions and failures to respond to previous sentences, if relevant.

Mitigating Factors ⊖
   For example impulsive; unaware that the person was a police officer.

   Guideline: Is it so serious that only custody is appropriate?

See also the sentencing considerations for assault occasioning actual bodily harm, at **B2.18**.

Actus Reus

An offence under the Police Act 1996, s. 89, must involve an assault or battery (as **B2.23** defined in **B2.4** *et seq.*) and it must be proved that the victim was a police or prison officer (of any rank) acting in the execution of his duty, or a person assisting such an officer. An off-duty police officer may act in the course of duty if a breach of the peace or other incident occurs which justifies immediate action on his part (see *Albert* v *Lavin* [1982] AC 546) but it is essential in all cases that the officer is shown to have been acting lawfully, because even a minor, technical and inadvertent act of unlawfulness on his part will mean that he cannot have been acting in the execution of his duty (*Riley* v *DPP* (1989) 91 Cr App R 14; *Kerr* v *DPP* [1995] Crim LR 394). A violent assault in response to a trivial act of unlawfulness on the part of a police officer may be punishable on some other basis (e.g., as a common assault or battery, or as assault occasioning actual bodily harm), but although common assault is necessarily included within any s. 89 assault, courts of summary jurisdiction have no power to convict of included offences, and it may therefore be desirable to draft alternative charges in cases where the legality of the officer's conduct is in doubt (*Kerr* v *DPP; Bentley* v *Brudzinski* (1982) 75 Cr App R 217).

The precise limits of a constable's duty remain undefined. It is clear, however, that a police officer may be acting in the execution of his duty, even where he is doing more than the minimum which the law requires of him (*Waterfield* [1964] 1 QB 164; *Coffin* v *Smith* (1980) 71 Cr App R 221). It is also clear that any action amounting to assault, battery, unlawful arrest or trespass to property takes the officer outside the course of his duty (*Davis* v *Lisle* [1936] 2 KB 434). Some of the most difficult cases in this area concern the power of a police officer to touch or take hold of an individual (without arresting him) in order to speak with or restrain him. As the Divisional Court held in *Donnelly* v *Jackman* [1970] 1 WLR 562, it is not every interference with a citizen's liberty that will amount to a course of conduct sufficient to take the officer out of the execution of his duty; but how far an officer may go in attracting or retaining the citizen's attention appears to be largely a question of fact. In *Collins* v *Wilcock* [1984] 1 WLR 1172, a police officer was held to have committed a battery when, without purporting to exercise any lawful power of arrest, she held a woman by the arm in order to question her, whereas in *Mepstead* v *DPP* (1996) 160 JP 475, it was held to be lawful for a police officer to take hold of a person's arm in order to attract his attention and calm him down. Police powers are more fully examined in **D1**.

Mens Rea

B2.24 The *mens rea* required in respect of this offence is no different from that required in respect of common assault or battery. The defendant need not know, or even have reason to suspect, that his victim is a police officer or that the officer is acting in the execution of his duty (*Forbes* (1865) 10 Cox CC 362; *Blackburn* v *Bowering* [1994] 1 WLR 1324). In this respect, the offence is one of strict liability. In *Albert* v *Lavin* [1982] AC 546, D unlawfully assaulted a man who attempted to prevent him from causing a breach of the peace. He claimed not to know that this man was a police officer, but the House of Lords held that his alleged mistake was irrelevant. He would have been guilty of an assault or battery even if the man had not been a police officer, because the officer had been doing only what any citizen would have had the right to do in the circumstances. In contrast, if D honestly believes that he is being attacked or kidnapped by criminals, and uses force to resist them, he will not be guilty of a s. 89 offence, even though the 'criminals' prove to be police officers who were acting lawfully at the time. D's honest belief in his need to act in self-defence would negative any *mens rea* for assault (*Kenlin* v *Gardiner* [1967] 2 QB 510; *Blackburn* v *Bowering;* and see generally **A3.36**).

RESISTING OR WILFULLY OBSTRUCTING CONSTABLE

Definition

B2.25   **Police Act 1996, s. 89**

(2)   Any person who resists or wilfully obstructs a constable in the execution of his duty, or a person assisting a constable in the execution of his duty, shall be guilty of an offence and

liable on summary conviction to imprisonment for a term not exceeding one month or to a fine not exceeding level 3 on the standard scale, or to both.

Procedure

This offence is triable only summarily (Police Act 1996, s. 89(2)). **B2.26**

Sentencing Guidelines

The maximum penalties are 1 month imprisonment, a fine not exceeding level 3, or both **B2.27**
(Police Act 1996, s. 89(2)). The Magistrates' Association Guidelines (1997) indicate the following:

Aggravating Factors ⊕
For example racial motivation; group action; premeditated; offence committed on bail; previous convictions and failures to respond to previous sentences, if relevant.

Mitigating Factors ⊖
For example genuine misjudgment; impulsive action; minor obstruction.

Guideline: Is compensation, discharge or fine appropriate?

The guideline fine is £90 (low income), £225 (average income) or £540 (high income).

Elements

A defendant obstructs a police constable if he makes it more difficult for him to carry **B2.28**
out his duty (*Hinchcliffe* v *Sheldon* [1955] 1 WLR 1207, *obiter*). While 'resisting' implies some physical action, no physical act is necessary to constitute obstruction. Simple refusal to answer questions does not constitute an obstruction (*Rice* v *Connolly* [1966] 2 QB 414), neither does advising another person not to answer questions (*Green* v *DPP* (1991) 155 JP 816). Answering questions incorrectly may, however, amount to obstruction, although the distinction is not always clear (see *Ledger* v *DPP* [1991] Crim LR 439).

A person may obstruct by omission, provided that such a person is under an initial duty to act (*Lunt* v *DPP* [1993] Crim LR 534). There is also a common-law offence of refusing to aid a constable who is attempting to prevent or to quell a breach of the peace and who calls for assistance (*Waugh* (1986) *The Times*, 1 October 1986).

In *Green* v *Moore* [1982] QB 1044 the court held that a tip-off to persons who were preparing to commit an offence, and who as a result of the tip-off decided not to commit such an offence, could amount to an obstruction. Police could still be said to be acting in execution of their duty even if only making general inquiries before an offence was committed. The court admitted that this was a difficult situation, since the result of the tip-off was in fact the prevention of crime. Liability would turn, however, on the *mens rea* and the question of whether the defendant's intent was to assist the potential criminal or to assist the police.

A constable is not acting in the course of his duty, and a person cannot therefore be liable for obstructing him in the course of such action, if what he is doing is carrying out an arrest which is in fact unlawful (*Edwards* v *DPP* (1993) 97 Cr App R 301).

If obstruction (rather than resistance) is alleged, it must be proved to have been wilful. The defendant does not commit wilful obstruction if he tries to help the police, even if he actually makes their job more difficult (*Wilmott* v *Atack* [1977] QB 498) nor can he be guilty if he is unaware that he is obstructing police officers at all (*Ostler* v *Elliott* [1980] Crim LR 584), but if the defendant deliberately obstructs the police, it will be no defence to argue that he was merely trying to prevent the arrest of a person he believed to be innocent (*Lewis* v *Cox* [1985] QB 509).

WOUNDING OR INFLICTING GRIEVOUS BODILY HARM

Definition

B2.29   **Offences against the Person Act 1861, s. 20**

Whosoever shall unlawfully and maliciously wound or inflict any grievous bodily harm upon any other person, either with or without any weapon or instrument, shall be guilty of [an offence], and being convicted thereof shall be liable to [imprisonment for not more than five years].

The CDA 1998, s. 29, creates a racially aggravated form of this offence which carries a higher maximum penalty. For the meaning of 'racially aggravated', see **B11.154**.

Procedure

B2.30   Wounding or inflicting grievous bodily harm is triable either way. When tried on indictment it is a class 4 offence. The racially aggravated form of the offence is also triable either way. The considerations relevant to determining mode of trial for the basic offence given in *Practice Note (Mode of Trial: Guidelines)* (1995) (see **D3.7**) are the same as for assault occasioning actual bodily harm (see **B2.16**).

Indictment

B2.31   Statement of Offence

Unlawful wounding, contrary to section 20 of the Offences against the Person Act 1861

Particulars of Offence

A on or about the . . . day of . . . unlawfully and maliciously wounded [or inflicted grievous bodily harm on] V

Alternative Verdicts

B2.32   A verdict of assault occasioning actual bodily harm under the OAPA 1861, s. 47, can be returned. (See Criminal Law Act 1967, s. 6(3).)

Sentencing Guidelines

B2.33   The maximum penalty is five years (OAPA 1861, s. 20; Penal Servitude Act 1891, s. 1; CJA 1948, s. 1) on indictment; six months, a fine not exceeding level 5, or both, summarily (MCA 1980, s. 32(1)). The maximum for the racially aggravated form of the offence is seven years, a fine or both on indictment; six months, a fine not exceeding the statutory maximum or both summarily (CDA 1998, s. 29(2)).

When dealt with summarily, the Magistrates' Association Guidelines (1997) indicate the following:

Aggravating Factors ⊕
  For example racial motivation; deliberate kicking/biting; extensive injuries; group action; offender in position of authority; premeditated; victim particularly vulnerable; victim serving public; weapon; offence committed on bail; previous convictions and failures to respond to previous sentences, if relevant.

Mitigating Factors ⊖
  For example single blow; minor wound; impulse; provocation.

Guideline: Is it so serious that only custody is appropriate?

Sentences of up to three years for this offence have been upheld by the Court of Appeal where aggravating factors have been present, or where the offence has been close to the borderline with the offence of wounding with intent; such sentences will be imposed where the assault was committed against a police officer or other public servant or against a child.

A sentence of three years' imprisonment was upheld in *Moore* (1991) 13 Cr App R (S) 130 where, after an altercation with another man over the use of a telephone box, the offender was seen to kick the victim about the head and body as he lay unconscious on the ground. The victim suffered serious facial injuries and was detained in hospital for two weeks. In *Ambrose* [1997] 1 Cr App R (S) 404, the 22 year-old offender came across the victim, a man who had molested him some years before. After a degree of further provocation from the victim, the offender punched him in the face, causing him to fall and strike his head. The victim suffered multiple cerebral haemorrhage, and was in a confusional state from which it was uncertain whether he would recover. The Court of Appeal reduced a sentence of three and a half years' imprisonment to one of 18 months. Rougier J commented that the original sentence was out of line with other cases and that, given the decision in *Coleman* (1991) 95 Cr App R 159 (see **B1.33**), if the victim had died it was unlikely that the sentence would have been as long as three and a half years. See also *McCarthy* (1995) 16 Cr App R (S) 1038. In *Fox* (1980) 2 Cr App R (S) 188 the offender, a bouncer at a club, lost his temper with a man who refused to leave and struck him in the face causing 'considerable injury'. Sentence was reduced from three years to 12 months. An unprovoked assault in a public house, by a man of previous good character on a man wearing glasses, thereby causing severe cuts in the region of his eye, merited six months' imprisonment in *Martin* (1981) 3 Cr App R (S) 39. In *Rogers* (1993) 15 Cr App R (S) 393 the offender head-butted an opposing player in the course of an amateur soccer match, causing a displaced fracture of the cheekbone. A sentence of nine months' imprisonment was reduced to four months. See also *Goodwin* (1995) 16 Cr App R (S) 885.

The use of a weapon is an important aggravating feature. What was described as 'a disgraceful and unprovoked incident of racial violence' attracted a sentence of 18 months' detention in a young offender institution in *Bray* (1992) 13 Cr App R (S) 5, notwithstanding the 20 year-old offender's previous good character. The offender had got out of his car armed with a metal bar and, together with a co-defendant who was armed with a billiard cue, attacked a passer-by, inflicting a deep head wound upon him which required four stitches. A sentence of four years was reduced to 30 months on appeal in *Simpson* [1998] 1 Cr App R (S) 197, where the offender had made an unprovoked attack on a stranger, stabbing him in the arm with a chisel. A plea of guilty to unlawful wounding had been accepted on the basis that the offender had at the time been too drunk to form the necessary intent for an offence of wounding with intent. In *Bayes* (1994) 16 Cr App R (S) 290, after a driving incident, the offender attacked the driver of the other vehicle, punching him in the face and striking him on the back with a hammer, causing superficial bruising and cuts. Fifteen months' imprisonment was reduced to nine months to take account of personal mitigation and remorse.

Reported cases involving 'glassing' include *Jones* (1984) 6 Cr App R (S) 55, where the offender hit the victim on the side of the head with a glass and then pushed the edge of the glass into the victim's face, causing probable loss of sight in one eye. A sentence of two years' imprisonment was upheld. More recently, in *Robertson* [1998] 1 Cr App R (S) 21, the Court of Appeal noted that, in the light of earlier authorities, any sentence of more than two years' imprisonment for unlawful wounding required careful scrutiny to see if it was justified on the facts. In that case the offender had been drinking in a public house and had thrust a beer glass into another man's face, causing wounds to his face. A sentence of 30 months was reduced to two years. Two years was also appropriate in *Singleton* [1998] 1 Cr App R (S) 199, a very similar case but where the injuries were more severe, the victim remaining at risk of visual loss or possible blindness. In *Marsden* (1993) 15 Cr App R (S) 177, the offender became involved in an argument in a public house and, after having been asked to leave, threw a glass across the room. It hit the victim and caused a cut to the head which required hospital treatment. A sentence of 12 months' imprisonment was upheld. See also **B2.39**.

Elements

B2.34 The *actus reus* of an offence under the OAPA 1861, s. 20, may involve either unlawful wounding or the infliction of grievous bodily harm. Wounding requires the breaking of the continuity of the whole of the skin (dermis and epidermis) or the breaking of the inner skin within the cheek, lip or urethra (*Smith* (1837) 8 C & P 173; *Waltham* (1849) 3 Cox 442). It does not include the rupturing of internal blood vessels (*J.J.C. (A Minor)* v *Eisenhower* [1983] 3 All ER 230). In theory, even trivial wounds may qualify, but the Charging Standards agreed between the police and the CPS urge that minor wounds should not in practice be charged under s. 20. Where, however, there is evidence of a serious wound, this ought generally to be charged as wounding, rather than as inflicting grievous bodily harm (*McReady* [1978] 1 WLR 1376).

Grievous bodily harm is not defined in the 1861 Act, but has been interpreted as meaning no more and no less than really serious harm (*DPP* v *Smith* [1961] AC 290; *Cunningham* [1982] AC 566; cf. *Saunders* [1985] Crim LR 230). There is no definitive list of the kind of injuries that may be considered really serious, but where the seriousness of an injury is questionable, a trial judge may withdraw a charge of grievous bodily harm from the jury. The CPS Charging Standards list examples of injuries which may be considered sufficiently serious, but this list can at best be of persuasive value in court. Psychiatric injury or illness may involve really serious harm (*Ireland* [1998] AC 147) but its cause and effect will need to be proved by expert psychiatric evidence, as in cases of alleged psychiatric injury brought under s. 47 (see **B2.19**).

Section 20 refers to the 'infliction' of grievous bodily harm. The meaning of this term was once a matter of some uncertainty and debate, but appears to have been largely resolved by the recent decision of the House of Lords in *Ireland* [1998] AC 147, where Lord Steyn, in giving the majority judgment, held (at p. 160) that harm could be inflicted without the need for an assault, and that in the context of the 1861 Act, there was no radical divergence between the meanings of the words 'cause' and 'inflict' (see also *Salisbury* [1976] VR 452; *Wilson* [1984] AC 242). Grievous bodily harm within the meaning of s. 20 could thus be inflicted by means of menacing telephone calls which gave rise to serious psychiatric injury, whether or not the injury was caused by fear of imminent physical attack.

On the other hand, Lord Steyn later denied that the words 'cause' and 'inflict' were exactly synonymous, and this point was developed by Lord Hope, who said that, although there was no real practical difference between the two words, the word 'inflict' invariably implies detriment to the victim of some kind. Lord Steyn and Lord Hope both appear to have stopped just short of overruling the authority of *Clarence* (1888) 22 QBD 23, in which it was held that grievous bodily harm was caused, *but not inflicted*, where C enjoyed consensual sexual intercourse with his wife, without warning her that he was infected with a venereal disease, which she then contracted. The authority and rationale of *Clarence* was nevertheless gravely damaged by what was said and decided in *Ireland* and it is submitted that it can no longer safely be relied upon.

A s. 20 offence must be committed 'maliciously'. Maliciousness requires *either* an intent to do some kind of bodily harm to another person *or* recklessness (in the subjective or *Cunningham* sense) as to whether any such harm might be caused. The harm intended or foreseen by the defendant need not amount to a wound or grievous bodily harm: an intent to cause minor injury, which inadvertently results in the infliction of a wound or serious injury, is sufficient to found liability under s. 20 (*Mowatt* [1968] 1 QB 421; *Sullivan* [1981] Crim LR 46). On the other hand, there cannot ordinarily be liability under s. 20 if the defendant was unaware that his conduct might cause any injury at all (*Savage* [1992] 1 AC 699). The only qualification to this rule concerns cases of voluntary intoxication: such intoxication cannot be relied upon by a defendant in order to negative *mens rea* under s. 20, because it is not a crime of 'specific intent' (see **A3.10**).

The Court of Appeal held in *Beeson* [1994] Crim LR 190 that it was unnecessary to direct the jury on the meaning of the word 'maliciously'; but whilst such an omission may have been unimportant on the facts of that particular case (where the only real issue was self-defence), there will be many cases in which careful guidance on its meaning must be vital. The concept of maliciousness is further explained at **A2.7**.

WOUNDING OR CAUSING GRIEVOUS BODILY HARM WITH INTENT

Definition

Offences against the Person Act 1861, s. 18   **B2.35**

Whosoever shall unlawfully and maliciously by any means whatsoever wound or cause any grievous bodily harm to any person with intent to do some grievous bodily harm to any person, or with intent to resist or prevent the lawful apprehension or detainer of any person, shall be guilty of [an offence], and being convicted thereof shall be liable to [imprisonment] for life.

Procedure

Wounding or causing grievous bodily harm with intent is triable on indictment only. It **B2.36** is a class 4 offence.

Indictment

Statement of Offence   **B2.37**

Wounding [or causing grievous bodily harm] with intent, contrary to section 18 of the Offences against the Person Act 1861

Particulars of Offence

A on or about the . . . day of . . . unlawfully and maliciously wounded [or caused grievous bodily harm to] V with intent to do him grievous bodily harm [or to prevent the lawful apprehension of X]

As to the proper form of indictment in a 'transferred malice' case, where it is alleged that the accused wounded the victim whilst intending to do grievous bodily harm to another, see *Monger* [1973] Crim LR 301, *Slimmings* [1999] Crim LR 69.

Alternative Verdicts

This subject is complex, and is dealt with in detail at **D16.18** *et seq*. and **D16.30**. Where **B2.38** wounding is alleged in a count under the OAPA 1861, s. 18, then wounding under s. 20 and s. 47 assault are possible alternative verdicts. If, however, the s. 18 count alleges the causing of grievous bodily harm only, the situation is more complex. Problems have arisen in recent cases where an alternative count of inflicting grievous bodily harm under s. 20 has not been specified, and the alternative verdict of *causing* grievous bodily harm under s. 20 has been accepted. Strictly speaking, this is an offence unknown to law, given the use of the term 'inflicting' in the offence created by s. 20.

The House of Lords in *Mandair* [1995] 1 AC 208, overruling the previous decision on the point by the Court of Appeal in *Field* (1993) 97 Cr App R 357, has held that a judge is entitled under the Criminal Law Act 1967, s. 6(3), to leave to a jury a conviction under s. 20 as an alternative to s. 18 because the term 'causing' is wide enough to include 'inflicting' (see *Metropolitan Police Commissioner* v *Wilson* [1984] AC 242). Even though in *Mandair* the word 'inflicting' was not used, the meaning is clear given the context of the direction in the case and the wording of the verdict. A verdict of 'causing grievous bodily harm contrary to s. 20' can only mean causing grievous bodily harm by inflicting it, as that is the particular method referred to in s. 20. Therefore the jury had not returned a verdict unknown to law. The case was remitted to the Court of Appeal for a decision on a further point it had not considered. *Mandair* was applied in *White* [1995] Crim LR 393.

Although it is now clear that an alternative verdict can be considered following an oral direction, the House of Lords in *Mandair* re-affirmed the point that it is preferable to add an alternative specific count using the correct wording of the statute. Normally, if the accused is acquitted under s. 18 without an alternative indictment under s. 20, a later prosecution under s. 20 cannot be brought, but in circumstances where the accused was for some reason not in jeopardy of a s. 20 conviction in the first trial, a later prosecution can arguably be brought. See *Old Street Magistrates' Court, ex parte Davies* [1995] Crim LR 629, and *Brookes* [1995] Crim LR 630, where the initial charge was under s. 20, and the subsequent charge was under s. 18.

Sentencing Guidelines

B2.39   The maximum penalties for this offence and related offences are:

Wounding or causing grievous bodily harm with intent to do grievous bodily harm: life imprisonment (OAPA 1861, s. 18);

Wounding or causing grievous bodily harm with intent to resist arrest: life imprisonment (OAPA 1861, s. 18);

Attempting to choke, suffocate or strangle with intent: life imprisonment (OAPA 1861, s. 21);

Throwing corrosive fluid: life imprisonment (OAPA 1861, s. 29).

A custodial sentence will almost always be required for this offence (*A-G's Ref (No. 33 of 1997)* [1998] 1 Cr App R (S) 352). The normal sentencing bracket is in the range of three to eight years, although sentences over eight years are upheld in particularly grave cases. Relevant aggravating factors include the extent of the injuries, the degree of premeditation, racial motivation, use of a weapon, and kicking or stamping on the victim. Mitigating factors such as a plea of guilty and the previous good character of the offender may be of little weight in very serious cases, but significant provocation is to be taken into account.

In a case involving *stabbing*, the Court of Appeal upheld an eight-year sentence in *Gilmore* (1980) 2 Cr App R (S) 201. The offender, a man of previous good character, after having been told that the woman with whom he had been having an affair had decided to return to her husband, arranged a meeting with him and stabbed him three times with a kitchen knife he had taken with him, almost killing the victim. A seven-year term was upheld on a 19-year-old in *Robinson* (1980) 2 Cr App R (S) 193, where the offender had accosted an older man and threatened him with a knife. When he refused to hand over any money, he was stabbed twice with almost fatal consequences. Nine years was upheld in *Pollin* [1997] 2 Cr App R (S) 356, where the victim was stabbed numerous times with a kitchen knife.

The use of other weapons will attract comparable sentences, depending upon the extent of the injuries, taken together with relevant mitigating and aggravating factors. In *Chesterman* (1984) 6 Cr App R (S) 151, a 12-year sentence was upheld on an offender who fired a shotgun twice at a police officer. The officer was permanently blinded and suffered other injuries. The offender was acquitted of attempted murder, but the case was described as 'at the very top of the scale for offences of causing grievous bodily harm with intent'. See, however, *Sullivan* (1987) 9 Cr App R (S) 196, where 15 years was upheld for a carefully planned shooting of the victim in both legs, resulting in very serious injury and the necessary amputation of one leg. In *Craney* [1996] 2 Cr App R (S) 336 sentences of 11 years were proper in a case where an unprovoked and racially motivated attack by two youths using a torch and an iron bar left the victim with severe head injuries inducing a coma, requiring him to be placed on a life-support machine, and a badly broken leg resulting from the victim's attempts to flee from his attackers.

The Court of Appeal has considered cases of '*glassing*' on several occasions. A sentence of five years was upheld in *James* (1981) 3 Cr App R (S) 233, where the offender attacked a shopkeeper with two broken milk bottles, pushing them into his face and cutting him very badly. The court described this as 'about as bad a case of . . . glassing as it is possible to imagine,' though presumably causing loss of the victim's sight would merit a longer sentence still. In *Harwood* (1979) 1 Cr App R (S) 354, Lord Lane CJ said (at p. 355) that 'one cannot really recognise anything less than three years as being right for deliberate glassing,' and exactly that sentence was upheld in the case of an 18-year-old who had been involved in a fight in a public house and had pushed a broken bottle into the victim's face. In *A-G's Ref (No. 23 of 1990)* (1990) 12 Cr App R (S) 575, the offender, at a New Year's Eve party in a public house, struck the victim on the back of the head with a bottle, and then pushed the broken bottle into his cheek and towards his neck. A sentence of 18 months' imprisonment was said by the Court of Appeal (at p. 578) to be 'undoubtedly excessively lenient'. The minimum appropriate sentence on the facts was said to be four years, and the sentence was so increased, though Lord Lane CJ noted that something less than four years might have been proper if the offender had pleaded guilty. See also *Martin* (1992) 13 Cr App R (S) 303.

It is clear that where an offender causes grievous bodily harm by kicking or stamping on the victim's head while the latter is on the ground, he should receive a substantial custodial term. In *Ivey* (1981) 3 Cr App R (S) 185 a man of previous good character became caught up in a fracas at a club, during the course of which he knocked a man to the ground and stamped on his head, inflicting grave injuries to his face and skull. A four-year sentence was upheld, Griffiths LJ explaining (at p. 186) that, 'The degree of injury likely to be caused by kicking a man in the head when he is down is of a wholly different degree to that which is likely to be suffered in the course of a fist fight. . . . The injuries thereby inflicted are often appalling.' *Ivey* has been followed and applied in several cases, including *A-G's Ref (No. 59 of 1996)* [1997] 2 Cr App R (S) 250. See also *Legge* (1988) 10 Cr App R (S) 208, where the victim was stripped and subjected to various indignities, as well as being severely beaten and kicked: seven years upheld. Eighteen months' imprisonment was upheld in *Lloyd* (1989) 11 Cr App R (S) 36, where the deliberate kicking was inflicted by a rugby player on a member of the opposition during a match, the victim suffering a fractured cheekbone. Four years' imprisonment was upheld in *Alleyne* (1995) 16 Cr App R (S) 506, where the offender bit off part of the victim's ear.

In cases where corrosive fluid is thrown, lengthy terms will be appropriate. In *Radford* (1986) 8 Cr App R (S) 60, five years was upheld where the offender squirted a corrosive substance into the victim's face, causing substantial loss of vision in one eye. The offender in *Carrington* [1999] 2 Cr App R (S) 206 threw some liquid containing sulphuric acid into the face of his former girlfriend. The victim received prompt first aid treatment, and fortunately suffered no long-term damage. In light of the fact that the attack was premeditated and that the offender had contested the case and had shown no remorse, a sentence of six years' imprisonment was upheld.

Elements

An offence under the OAPA 1861, s. 18, may take one of four different forms, namely: **B2.40**

    (a)   wounding with intent to do grievous bodily harm;
    (b)   causing grievous bodily harm with intent to do so;
    (c)   maliciously wounding with intent to resist or prevent the lawful apprehension
etc. of any person; or

(d)   maliciously causing grievous bodily harm with intent to resist or prevent lawful apprehension etc. of any person.

As to the meaning of the terms 'wound' and 'grievous bodily harm', see **B2.34**. Following the decision of the House of Lords in *Ireland* [1998] AC 147, it now seems unlikely that anything of significance turns on the supposed difference between 'causing' injury in cases under s. 18 and 'inflicting' injury in cases under s. 20 (but see further **B2.34**). This means that the *actus reus* elements of the two offences are for most purposes the same. The difference lies in the specific intent required under s. 18.

If the defendant is alleged to have acted with intent to do grievous bodily harm, the concept of maliciousness is rendered otiose and need not be examined (*Mowatt* [1968] 1 QB 421). Where, in contrast, it is alleged that the defendant merely intended to resist arrest etc., maliciousness becomes an important further element to be proved. If, for example, D tries to pull free from the officer arresting him and quite unforeseeably injures the officer in the process, he could not be considered to have acted maliciously and could not therefore be convicted of an offence under s. 18. If, however, he intended or foresaw that he would cause some minor injury, he could indeed be adjudged malicious.

Where it is alleged that the accused acted with intent to avoid or resist the lawful apprehension of any person, it may be his own arrest or that of another that he resisted, but the lawfulness of that arrest or detention must in either event be proved by the prosecution (*Howarth* (1828) 1 Mood 207). It does not follow that the accused must be proved to have known that the arrest etc. was lawful, but in a case such as *Kenlin* v *Gardiner* [1967] 2 QB 510, where the accused mistook arresting officers for kidnappers, mistaken self-defence may be raised by the defence in accordance with the principles established in *Williams* [1987] 3 All ER 411. See generally **A3.30**.

TORTURE

Definition

B2.41   **Criminal Justice Act, 1988, s. 134**

(1)   A public official or person acting in an official capacity, whatever his nationality, commits the offence of torture if in the United Kingdom or elsewhere he intentionally inflicts severe pain or suffering on another in the performance or purported performance of his official duties.

(2)   A person not falling within subsection (1) above commits the offence of torture, whatever his nationality, if—

(a)   in the United Kingdom or elsewhere he intentionally inflicts severe pain or suffering on another at the instigation or with the consent or acquiescence—

(i)   of a public official; or

(ii)   of a person acting in an official capacity; and

(b)   the official or other person is performing or purporting to perform his official duties when he instigates the commission of the offence or consents to or acquiesces in it.

(3)   It is immaterial whether the pain or suffering is physical or mental and whether it is caused by an act or omission.

Procedure

B2.42   Proceedings for an offence under the CJA 1988, s. 134, may be begun only by or with the consent of the A-G (CJA 1988, s. 135). The offence is triable only on indictment (CJA 1988, s. 134(6)). It is a class 3 offence.

The offence may be prosecuted in England, wherever committed and regardless of the nationality of the accused. Section 137(1) of the Act provides that the offence of torture shall be deemed to be included in the list of extradition crimes contained in sch. 1 to the Extradition Act 1870. The remaining subsections of s. 137 provide for extradition arrangements in cases not covered by the Extradition Act 1870. The territorial jurisdiction and extradition provisions of the Act are in furtherance of the adherence of the United Kingdom to the Convention against Torture and Other Cruel, Inhuman or Degrading Treatment or Punishment adopted by the General Assembly of the United Nations on 10 December 1984.

Indictment

Statement of Offence

B2.43

Torture, contrary to section 134(1) of the Criminal Justice Act 1988

Particulars of Offence

D on or about the . . . day of . . . being a public official, that is to say . . . , [or: a person acting in an official capacity, that is to say . . .] intentionally inflicted severe pain or suffering on V in the performance or purported performance of his official duties

Sentence

The maximum penalty is life imprisonment (CJA 1988, s. 134(6)).   **B2.44**

Public Official or Person Acting in Official Capacity in Performance etc. of Official Duties

The offence of torture is meant to be confined to the abuse of power by persons in **B2.45** positions of public authority, acting under colour of that authority. There is no definition in the statutory provisions creating the offence of 'public official' or 'official duties', but it seems clear that members of the armed forces, police officers and prison officers, while acting or purporting to act as such, would be covered. The inclusion of the phrase 'purported performance' would appear to indicate that a person may commit the offence of torture while committing acts which might have been disapproved of or even forbidden by his superiors, had they known of them, or which have actually been disapproved of or forbidden. The perpetrator must, however, appear, to all intents and purposes, to be acting in his official capacity, as opposed to acting as a private individual.

Section 134(2) of the CJA 1988 extends liability for the offence to a person who commits torture at the instigation of, or with the consent or acquiescence of, a public official or person acting in an official capacity, and who therefore makes himself part of the official conduct. In this case, although the Act does not address the point, there would seem to be no reason why the instigating, consenting or acquiescing official may not be charged as an aider and abettor, counsellor or procurer. This may give rise to a difficulty of application of the defence of lawful authority etc. in some instances (see **B2.48**).

Where the perpetrator cannot be proved to have been acting under colour of his office as provided for by the Act, he may, of course, be charged with causing grievous bodily harm with intent, or other appropriate offence, including, in a proper case, attempted murder. However, regard must be had to the usual territorial jurisdiction rules in such a case (see **D1.72** *et seq.*).

Severe Pain or Suffering

The phrase 'severe pain or suffering' is not defined by the statutory provisions creating **B2.46** the offence of torture. It would appear that, as in the case of the concept of grievous bodily harm (see **B2.31**), it may safely be left to the jury to determine what amounts to severe pain or suffering. There is no reason to suppose, however, that the meaning of 'severe pain or suffering' should be equated with that of grievous bodily harm, actual bodily harm or any standard measured by degree of injury. Indeed, the provision of the CJA 1988, s. 134(3), that the pain or suffering may be purely mental militates against any such construction. It is the severity of the pain rather than whether or not identifiable injury results that should be considered, though no doubt evidence of injury would be admissible evidence of the severity of the pain.

Mens Rea

B2.47 Nothing less than the specific intention to inflict severe pain will suffice. As to intention generally, see **A2.2**.

Specific Defence

B2.48
Criminal Justice Act 1988, s. 134

(4)   It shall be a defence for a person charged with an offence under this section in respect of any conduct of his to prove that he had lawful authority, justification or excuse for that conduct.

(5)   For the purposes of this section 'lawful authority, justification or excuse' means—

(a)   in relation to pain or suffering inflicted in the United Kingdom, lawful authority, justification or excuse under the law of the part of the United Kingdom where it was inflicted;

(b)   in relation to pain or suffering inflicted outside the United Kingdom—

(i)   if it was inflicted by a United Kingdom official acting under the law of the United Kingdom or by a person acting in an official capacity under that law, lawful authority, justification or excuse under that law;

(ii)   if it was inflicted by a United Kingdom official acting under the law of any part of the United Kingdom or by a person acting in an official capacity under such law, lawful authority, justification or excuse utnder the law of the part of the United Kingdom under whose law he was acting; and

(iii)   in any other case, lawful authority, justification or excuse under the law of the place where it was inflicted.

The effect of this provision is that the law of the relevant part of the United Kingdom is to govern pain or suffering inflicted in the United Kingdom by any official, of whatever nationality, and the infliction of pain or suffering by a United Kingdom official, regardless of where the pain or suffering was inflicted. In two circumstances, however, it may be necessary for the court to consider whether lawful authority, justification or excuse was provided by relevant foreign law. These are: (a) where pain or suffering is inflicted by a foreign official outside the United Kingdom, and (b) where a person other than a public official etc. inflicts pain or suffering outside the United Kingdom at the instigation or with the consent or acquiescence of a United Kingdom official. The latter case may be somewhat anomalous, and may lead to difficulties where the law of the United Kingdom differs materially from the relevant foreign law, and where the official and the person inflicting the pain are tried together.

ADMINISTERING POISON ETC. SO AS TO ENDANGER LIFE ETC.

Definition

B2.49
Offences against the Person Act 1861, s. 23

Whosoever shall unlawfully and maliciously administer to or cause to be administered to or taken by any other person any poison or other destructive or noxious thing, so as thereby to endanger the life of such person, or so as thereby to inflict upon such person any grievous bodily harm, shall be guilty of [an offence], and being convicted thereof shall be liable . . . to [imprisonment] for any term not exceeding 10 years.

Procedure

B2.50 An offence under the OAPA 1861, s. 23, is triable only on indictment. It is a class 3 offence.

Indictment

Statement of Offence

B2.51

Administering poison so as to endanger life [or so as to cause grievous bodily harm], contrary to section 23 of the Offences against the Person Act 1861

Particulars of Offence

A on or about the . . . day of . . . unlawfully and maliciously administered to V a poison, namely . . . , so as thereby to endanger the life of the said V [or so as to inflict on the said V grievous bodily harm]

Alternative Verdicts

Under the OAPA 1861, s. 25, if a jury are not satisfied that a person charged under s. 23 **B2.52** is guilty of that offence but they are satisfied that he is guilty of an offence under s. 24 (see **B2.56** to **B2.61**), then they can acquit under s. 23 and return a verdict of guilty under s. 24, and the accused will be sentenced as if he had been tried on indictment under s. 24.

Sentence

The maximum penalty for administering any poison or noxious thing, so as to endanger **B2.53** life or inflict grievous bodily harm is 10 years (OAPA 1861, s. 23).

Actus Reus

The *actus reus* under the OAPA 1861, s. 23, involves administering or causing to be **B2.54** administered a particular substance. The accused's act can therefore be direct or indirect, and may even consist of causing the victim to administer the substance to himself (*Harley* (1830) 4 C & P 369).

The most recent case on the meaning of 'administer' is *Gillard* (1988) 87 Cr App R 189, although the discussion there was in the context of an s. 24 offence (see **B2.56** to **B2.61**). The Court of Appeal held that the word 'administer' includes conduct which brings the noxious thing into contact with the body, whether directly or indirectly. The accused had sprayed noxious gas into the victim's face, and the question at issue was whether this was an assault rather than an administering. The court's wide definition of the term 'administer' meant that the accused's action did come within the section, and although the court agreed that an assault could have been charged, it was felt that such a charge would have been misleading and that s. 24 was more appropriate.

In interpreting the word 'administer' the Court of Appeal was not prepared to treat it as an ordinary everyday word of the English language, but held that it was a matter of law and construction of that particular section of the statute. 'Administer' was used in the section as an alternative to 'take', and therefore meant something different from that word. The word 'take' implied ingestion of the substance, and therefore the word 'administer' was held not to be limited to ingestion of a substance. *Dones* [1987] Crim LR 682 was held to have been wrong in its interpretation of the word.

The administering must be unlawful. In *Hill* (1985) 81 Cr App R 206 the court pointed out that consent will normally negative unlawfulness, unless the victim is too young to give valid consent or the act is one which cannot be consented to.

The substance administered has to be noxious. In *Marcus* [1981] 1 WLR 774 where the accused put sleeping pills into her neighbour's milk, the question was held to be one of both quantity and quality. Something which is harmless in small doses can be noxious in larger doses. Its effect on the victim is what is important. A noxious substance was held to be different in quality from and of less importance than a poisonous substance, and the court referred to the dictionary definition of 'noxious' as 'injurious, hurtful, harmful, unwholesome'. Neither does it necessarily import a direct physical effect. The court held that the word in its weakest sense could also apply to objectionable or obnoxious substances, although the potential of such a wide definition is much greater in s. 24 of the 1861 Act, where no consequence is required. In s. 23, the consequence of endangering life or inflicting grievous bodily harm is required, and that will almost inevitably mean that the substance or thing is noxious in one of the more serious senses of the word. The use of the word 'inflict' would imply that the same interpretation of it could be used, and the same case law applied, as under s. 20 of the Act.

Mens Rea

B2.55 The word 'maliciously' is used in the OAPA 1861, s. 23, and the same meaning attributed to it as in s. 20 (see **B2.34**). This means that *Cunningham* or subjective recklessness is required as to the administering, and presumably also as to the circumstance that the thing is 'noxious'. Once again problems arise in respect of *mens rea* as to consequences. The requisite consequence is either endangering life or inflicting grievous bodily harm. In *Cato* [1976] 1 WLR 110 the Court of Appeal applied the malice requirement only to the act of administering the heroin by injection. No foresight of consequences was required. There are two alternative explanations. One is that liability is strict in respect of this element, and no consequence need be foreseen or intended. The wording of s. 23, 'so as thereby to . . . ', in comparison with s. 24, which creates an offence of specific intent, might imply that all that need be proved is a causal connection. The other alternative, by analogy with s. 20, is that the accused must foresee the risk of some harm, though not necessarily serious harm or danger to life. This was the implication in *Cunningham* [1957] 2 QB 396, confirmed by the House of Lords in *Savage* [1992] 1 AC 699. In *Cunningham* [1957] 2 QB 396, the court held that the word 'malicious' in a statute postulated foresight of consequence, but went on to describe such foresight in an offence under s. 23 as foresight of some injury. The Court of Appeal in *Cato* [1976] 1 WLR 110 distinguished *Cunningham* on the basis that the injury was indirectly caused in that case. The implication, however, that in cases where a consequence is directly caused there is no need to prove foresight of consequence, appears dangerously close to contravening the CJA 1967, s. 8, which provides that a jury shall not be bound to infer that a person 'foresaw a result of his actions by reason only of its being a natural and probable consequence of those actions'.

ADMINISTERING POISON ETC. WITH INTENT

Definition

B2.56 **Offences against the Person Act 1861, s. 24**

Whosoever shall unlawfully and maliciously administer to or cause to be administered to or taken by any other person any poison or other destructive or noxious thing, with intent to injure, aggrieve, or annoy such person, shall be guilty of [an offence] and being . . . convicted thereof shall be liable to [imprisonment for a term not exceeding five years].

Procedure

B2.57 Administering poison etc. with intent is triable only on indictment. It is a class 3 offence.

Indictment

B2.58 Statement of Offence

Administering poison with intent, contrary to section 24 of the Offences against the Person Act 1861

Particulars of Offence

D on or about the . . . day of . . . unlawfully and maliciously administered to V a poison, namely . . . with intent to injure, aggrieve or annoy the said V

Alternative Verdicts

See **B2.52**.   **B2.59**

Sentence

The maximum penalty is five years (OAPA 1861, s. 24). In *Jones* (1990) 12 Cr App R   **B2.60**
(S) 233, Glidewell LJ accepted that the appropriate sentencing bracket for this offence
was equivalent to that for an offence of wounding or inflicting grievous bodily harm
under the OAPA 1861, s. 20 (see **B2.33**), or a serious example of an offence of assault
occasioning actual bodily harm under the OAPA 1861, s. 47 (see **B2.18**), on the basis
that the maximum penalty available for each of the three offences is five years. Nine
months was said to be the correct sentence in *Hogan* (1994) 15 Cr App R (S) 834, where
the offender gave to a woman a drink which contained a large quantity of a Class C drug.
It caused her to fall into a deep sleep for a day. The same sentence was appropriate in
Hunt [1997] 1 Cr App R (S) 414 where, following a minor traffic incident, the offender
sprayed another driver with de-icing fluid, some of which got into his eyes.

Elements

The *actus reus* of the OAPA 1861, s. 24, is the same as that for s. 23, with the exception   **B2.61**
of the consequences. No consequence is required under s. 24, although there must be
an intent to cause one; it is a conduct crime.

The same requirement as to malice applies in respect of administering the noxious thing,
but there is a further or ulterior intent, namely to injure, aggrieve or annoy, which must
additionally be proved.

The leading case is *Hill* (1985) 81 Cr App R 206, where the accused administered
slimming pills to young boys in order to keep them awake. The Court of Appeal held
that, in order to decide whether there was an intent to injure, it was necessary to look at
the accused's whole object in acting as he had done. This seems to allow motive to
become relevant, and restrict unduly the meaning of 'intent'. The example given in the
case makes the matter a little clearer, distinguishing between the person who administers
a sleeping pill to allow someone to sleep, and a person who administers the same dose
to the same person with an intent to facilitate theft or rape, for example. The Court of
Appeal considered that the latter instance would be an offence under s. 24, although it
declined to give any general definition of the phrase 'with intent to injure', preferring
rather to give examples of instances which would come within it. Given that the
examples indicate a very wide interpretation of the phrase, particularly in respect of the
causal link between the administering and the injuring, and given that the alternatives
of intending to aggrieve or annoy are also very wide, this is potentially an offence of very
great breadth. The limit placed upon it is that it is an offence of specific intent, and
recklessness is not sufficient.

FALSE IMPRISONMENT

Definition

False imprisonment is a common-law offence, but is not often charged. It is much more   **B2.62**
common as a civil action in tort. The overlap with kidnapping (see **B2.68** to **B2.73**) and
child abduction (see **B2.74** to **B2.86**) means that those offences are more likely to be
charged than a simple false imprisonment.

The case of *Rahman* (1985) 81 Cr App R 349 provides the following definition (at p.
353): 'False imprisonment consists in the unlawful and intentional or reckless restraint
of a victim's freedom of movement from a particular place.'

Procedure

B2.63 False imprisonment is triable only on indictment. It is a class 3 offence.

Indictment

B2.64

Statement of Offence

False imprisonment

Particulars of Offence

D on divers days between the . . . day of . . . and the . . . day of . . . falsely imprisoned V and detained the said V against his will

Sentencing Guidelines

B2.65 The maximum penalty is at large (common-law offence). For indications of appropriate sentencing, see those applicable to kidnapping at **B2.71**.

Actus Reus

B2.66 This consists of preventing the victim's freedom of movement. The victim may be restrained physically or by deliberate intimidation (*James* (1997) *The Times*, 2 October 1997). A victim might be detained in a building or vehicle, or simply prevented from going on his way. In *Bird* v *Jones* (1845) 7 QB 742, a civil case, the victim was prevented from going in one particular direction in which he wished to go, but there was an alternative route available to him; this did not constitute a false imprisonment.

The *actus reus* is the imprisoning without lawful excuse, and there seems no logical reason for requiring that the victim realise this is the case. No such realisation is necessary in the tort of false imprisonment (*Meering* v *Grahame White Aviation Co. Ltd* (1919) 122 LT 44).

The imprisonment must be unlawful. Two main situations arise where this can be problematic. One is in respect of a parent restraining a child. In *Rahman* (1985) 81 Cr App R 349 the question arose of the limits of a parent's right to lawfully restrain a child. The defendant had taken his 15-year-old daughter from her foster parents against her will. He was convicted and appealed. The court held that it was a question of fact in each case whether a parent had overstepped the limits of lawful correction and restraint. Whether the child's lack of consent was relevant must also be a question of fact depending on the circumstances of a particular case. In this case the appellant's appeal was dismissed. He had overstepped his right as a parent to exercise normal parental control. (See also kidnapping at **B2.68** to **B2.73** and child abduction at **B2.74** to **B2.86**.)

The other main situation in the context of which false imprisonment can arise is where an arrest is carried out by either a constable or a private citizen, which turns out to be unlawful. The lawfulness of an arrest is to be decided by reference to the general law, including the PACE 1984, s. 24. See, as to lawful and unlawful arrests, **D1.3** to **D1.8**. If the arrest is unlawful, the *actus reus* of the offence will have been committed.

Mens Rea

B2.67 *Rahman* (1985) 81 Cr App R 349 states that the *mens rea* for false imprisonment is intention or recklessness. Recklessness here means subjective or *Cunningham* recklessness (*James* (1997) *The Times*, 2 October 1997).

The offence is one of basic intent, and therefore evidence of the accused's voluntary intoxication is irrelevant. This was recently confirmed in *Hutchins* [1988] Crim LR 379, which case also emphasised the overlap and analogy with kidnapping.

In that case the accused, having taken drugs at a party, took a neighbour hostage. He was charged with both kidnapping and false imprisonment. It was confirmed that his intoxication was irrelevant, and the court took the opportunity to define both 'false imprisonment' and 'kidnapping'. It emphasised that in kidnapping the taking must be by force or fraud, and that the definition was in terms of 'taking or carrying away' rather than a mere detaining, which would suffice for false imprisonment.

KIDNAPPING

Definition

Kidnapping is a common-law offence. It overlaps partly with false imprisonment (see **B2.62** to **B2.67**) and partly with child abduction (see **B2.74** to **B2.86**).   **B2.68**

The offence has been defined and explained most recently by the House of Lords in *D* [1984] AC 778. It consists of the taking or carrying away of one person by another by force or by fraud, without the consent of that person and without lawful excuse.

Procedure

Kidnapping is triable only on indictment. It is a class 3 offence.   **B2.69**

Indictment

Statement of Offence   **B2.70**

Kidnapping

Particulars of Offence

A on or about the . . . day of . . . unlawfully took and carried away V against his will

Despite the acknowledged overlap between the offences of kidnapping and statutory abduction, an indictment should not contain counts for both offences (*C* (1990) *The Times*, 9 November 1990).

Sentencing Guidelines

The maximum penalty is at large (common-law offence).   **B2.71**

Some general observations on sentencing for this offence were provided in *Spence* (1983) 5 Cr App R (S) 413, where Lord Lane CJ said (at p. 416):

> there is a wide possible variation in seriousness between one instance of the crime and another. At the top of the scale of course, come the carefully planned abductions where the victim is used as a hostage or where ransom money is demanded. Such offences will seldom be met with less than eight years' imprisonment or thereabouts. Where violence or firearms are used, or there are other exacerbating features such as detention of the victim over a long period of time, then the proper sentence will be very much longer than that. At the other end of the scale are those offences which can perhaps scarcely be classed as kidnapping at all. They very often arise as a sequel to family tiffs or lovers' disputes, and they seldom require anything more than 18 months' imprisonment, and sometimes a great deal less.

In *Brown* (1985) 7 Cr App R (S) 15, a case of unpremeditated kidnapping and false imprisonment of a young woman by forcing her into her car and causing her minor injuries in an ensuing struggle, sentences of five years concurrent were imposed on the kidnapping and false imprisonment counts. In *Karunaratne* (1983) 5 Cr App R (S) 2, an 11-year-old child was abducted and ransom demands made. Sentences of 12 years and 10 years were imposed on the offenders for offences of kidnapping, false imprisonment and blackmail. Kidnapping was employed for political ends in *Barak* (1985) 7 Cr App R (S) 404, where sentences varying between 10 and 14 years were imposed on the offenders involved. See also *Bond* (1994) 15 Cr App R (S) 196.

Actus Reus

B2.72   The elements of the *actus reus* are the taking or carrying away, and the circumstances of lack of consent, lack of lawful excuse and the use of either force or fraud.

The requirement of taking or carrying away distinguishes the offence from that of false imprisonment (see **B2.62** to **B2.67**) for which detention or prevention of free movement is sufficient. Lawful excuse has the same meaning as in false imprisonment. The issue was considered in detail in *D* [1984] AC 778, in particular with regard to the question of whether a parent could be held criminally liable for kidnapping his child. The House of Lords held that a parent who took custody of a child in contravention of a court order could be guilty of kidnapping, and a majority held that the rule was more general, and that parents could be acting without lawful excuse in some circumstances by taking their children even where there was no court order. It will be a question of fact whether or not a parent has a lawful excuse to exercise such physical control over the whereabouts of the child. It is submitted that, even where one parent has no more than *de facto* control of the child, it may amount to kidnapping for the other to 'snatch' the child for the purpose of abusing or intimidating that parent. Similarly, there may be liability where a parent removes a child from care, from foster parents or grandparents, or from other relatives with whom the child lives.

The kidnapping must be without the consent, or in the context of fraud without the true consent of the victim. This presents particular difficulties with very young children not capable of giving consent. The House of Lords emphasised that it is the consent of the victim which is relevant, but it may be that this misunderstands the nature of kidnapping in such cases, because in reality it is the consent of the parents which is relevant. Even if one assumes, in the case of a child too young to give valid independent consent, that there is no valid consent, it may prove difficult to show force or fraud, if the child is simply picked up and taken. In such circumstance a charge under the Child Abduction Act 1984 may be more appropriate. If a person initially consents to being taken away, the offence will nevertheless be committed if that consent is later withdrawn and force is used to maintain a kidnapping (*Lewis* (22 March 1993 unreported)).

Mens Rea

B2.73   The *mens rea* is not specifically discussed in *D* [1984] AC 778, but the Court of Appeal in *Hutchins* [1988] Crim LR 379 pointed out the close analogy between false imprisonment and kidnapping, the differences being in the *actus reus*. This indicates that the *mens rea* is likely to be the same as that for false imprisonment (see **B2.67**).

CHILD ABDUCTION

Abduction by Person Connected with Child: Definition

B2.74   Child Abduction Act 1984, s. 1

(1)   Subject to subsections (5) and (8) below, a person connected with a child under the age of 16 commits an offence if he takes or sends the child out of the United Kingdom without the appropriate consent.

(2)   A person is connected with a child for the purposes of this section if—

   (a)   he is a parent of the child; or

   (b)   in the case of a child whose parents were not married to each other at the time of his birth, there are reasonable grounds for believing that he is the father of the child; or

   (c)   he is a guardian of the child; or

   (d)   he is a person in whose favour a residence order is in force with respect to the child; or

   (e)   he has custody of the child.

(3)   In this section 'the appropriate consent', in relation to a child, means—

(a)   the consent of each of the following—
    (i)   the child's mother;
    (ii)   the child's father, if he has parental responsibility for him;
    (iii)   any guardian of the child;
    (iv)   any person in whose favour a residence order is in force with respect to the child;
    (v)   any person who has custody of the child; or
(b)   the leave of the court granted under or by virtue of any provision of part II of the Children Act 1989; or
(c)   if any person has custody of the child, the leave of the court which awarded custody to him.

(4)   A person does not commit an offence under this section by taking or sending a child out of the United Kingdom without obtaining the appropriate consent if—
(a)   he is a person in whose favour there is a residence order in force with respect to the child, and
(b)   he takes or sends him out of the United Kingdom for a period of less than one month.

(4A)   Subsection (4) above does not apply if the person taking or sending the child out of the United Kingdom does so in breach of an order under part II of the Children Act 1989.

(5)   A person does not commit an offence under this section by doing anything without the consent of another person whose consent is required under the foregoing provisions if—
(a)   he does it in the belief that the other person—
    (i)   has consented; or
    (ii)   would consent if he was aware of all the relevant circumstances; or
(b)   he has taken all reasonable steps to communicate with the other person but has been unable to communicate with him; or
(c)   the other person has unreasonably refused to consent.

(5A)   Subsection (5)(c) above does not apply if—
(a)   the person who refused to consent is a person—
    (i)   in whose favour there is a residence order in force with respect to the child; or
    (ii)   who has custody of the child; or
(b)   the person taking or sending the child out of the United Kingdom is, by so acting, in breach of an order made by a court in the United Kingdom.

(6)   Where, in proceedings for an offence under this section, there is sufficient evidence to raise an issue as to the application of subsection (5) above, it shall be for the prosecution to prove that that subsection does not apply.

(7)   For the purposes of this section—
(a)   'guardian of a child', 'residence order' and 'parental responsibility' have the same meaning as in the Children Act 1989; and
(b)   a person shall be treated as having custody of a child if there is in force an order of a court in the United Kingdom awarding him (whether solely or jointly with another person) custody, legal custody or care and control of the child.

(8)   This section shall have effect subject to the provisions of the schedule to this Act in relation to a child who is in the care of a local authority, detained in a place of safety, remanded to local authority accommodation or the subject of proceedings or an order relating to adoption.

Abduction by Person Connected with Child: Procedure

The consent of the DPP is required before a prosecution under s. 1 of the Act can be **B2.75**
brought (Child Abduction Act 1984, s. 4(2)). The offence is triable either way (s. 4(1)).
When tried on indictment it is a class 4 offence.

Abduction by Person Connected with Child: Indictment

Statement of Offence **B2.76**

Child abduction by person connected with child contrary to section 1 of the Child Abduction Act 1984

Particulars of Offence

A on or about the . . . day of . . . , being a parent of V, a child under the age of 16 years, unlawfully took the said V out of the United Kingdom, to wit to Dallas, Texas, in the United States of America, without the consent of . . .

Abduction by Person Connected with Child: Sentence

B2.77   The maximum penalty is seven years (Child Abduction Act 1984, s. 4(1)) on indictment; six months, a fine not exceeding level 5 or both, summarily. In *Downes* (1994) 15 Cr App R (S) 435 three years' imprisonment was upheld on a father who abducted his two-year-old daughter in defiance of a court order denying him access to the child, and took her abroad. In *Holland* [1996] 1 Cr App R (S) 368, 18 months' imprisonment was upheld for the abduction by a father of his daughter who was in the care of foster parents by order of a court. See also *Taylor* [1997] 1 Cr App R (S) 329.

Abduction by Person Connected with Child: *Actus Reus*

B2.78   The offence can only be committed by a person 'connected with' the child, and this is defined in the Child Abduction Act 1984, s. 1(2) (see **B2.74**).

Such a person must either take, or be responsible for sending, the child out of the United Kingdom himself. This offence is not committed by holding the child within the jurisdiction. The meanings of 'taking' and of 'sending' are set out in s. 3 of the Act, and include causing a child to be taken, inducing a child to accompany the accused or any other person, and causing a child to be sent.

Lack of appropriate consent is a necessary circumstance which must be established. Consent of each of the persons mentioned in s. 1(3)(a) is required, or if there is a custody order in force the court's permission must be sought. Alternatively, the leave of the court under part II of the Children Act 1989 will suffice.

Abduction by Person Connected with Child: *Mens Rea*

B2.79   No *mens rea* is specified in the definition of the offence, but it can be deduced from the 'defences' available under the Child Abduction Act 1984, s. 1(5), at least in respect of the circumstance of lack of appropriate consent (see **B2.80**).

Abduction by Person Connected with Child: Defences

B2.80   Under the Child Abduction Act 1984, s. 1(5), an accused will not be liable if he acts in the belief that the appropriate person has consented, or would have done so if he had known the relevant circumstances. There is no requirement that such belief be reasonable, and the test is therefore subjective.

There is an additional objectively based defence if either the accused has taken all reasonable steps to communicate with the appropriate person, or if the consent has been unreasonably withheld. Magistrates, or on indictment the jury, would decide the issue of reasonableness as one of fact. If the consent needed is that of the court, then, under s. 1(5A), the provision concerning unreasonably withheld consent does not apply.

Once the accused provides prima facie evidence of any such defence, then the burden is on the prosecution to disprove it.

Abduction of Child by Other Persons: Definition

B2.81   Under the Child Abduction Act 1984, s. 2, a separate offence is created to cover the situation where someone other than a parent or other person connected to the child takes the child, although it may apply to the child's father where he was not married to the mother at the time of the child's birth (but see **B2.86**). It solves some of the problems inherent in the offence of kidnapping arising from the issue of consent (see **B2.72**), because, as with s. 1, the offence seems to be based on lack of parental or other appropriate consent.

Child Abduction Act 1984, s. 2

(1) Subject to subsection (3) below, a person, other than one mentioned in subsection (2) below, commits an offence if, without lawful authority or reasonable excuse, he takes or detains a child under the age of 16—

(a) so as to remove him from the lawful control of any person having lawful control of the child; or

(b) so as to keep him out of the lawful control of any person entitled to lawful control of the child.

(2) The persons are—

(a) where the father and mother of the child in question were married to each other at the time of his birth, the child's father and mother;

(b) where the father and mother of the child in question were not married to each other at the time of his birth, the child's mother; and

(c) any other person mentioned in section 1(2)(c) to (e) above.

(3) In proceedings against any person for an offence under this section, it shall be a defence for that person to prove—

(a) where the father and mother of the child in question were not married to each other at the time of his birth—

(i) that he is the child's father; or

(ii) that, at the time of the alleged offence, he believed, on reasonable grounds, that he was the child's father; or

(b) that, at the time of the alleged offence, he believed that the child had attained the age of sixteen.

Abduction by Other Persons: Procedure

This offence is triable either way. When tried on indictment it is a class 4 offence. Unlike **B2.82** the s. 1 offence committed by persons connected with the child, under the Child Abduction Act 1984, s. 2, there is no requirement of obtaining the consent of the DPP.

Abduction by Other Persons: Indictment

Statement of Offence   **B2.83**

Child abduction contrary to section 2 of the Child Abduction Act 1984

Particulars of Offence

A on or about the . . . day of . . . without lawful authority or reasonable excuse detained V, a child under the age of 16 years, so as to keep him out of the lawful control of X, a person entitled to lawful control of V

Abduction by Other Persons: Sentence

As for s. 1, see **B2.77**. In *Cooper* (1994) 15 Cr App R (S) 470 a sentence of 18 months **B2.84** was upheld where the offender had taken a baby from a pram outside a shop and kept it for four hours. In *Whitlock* (1994) 15 Cr App R (S) 146 the offender had induced a 13-year-old boy to get off the school bus and spend the morning with him. Three years' imprisonment was reduced to two years. Four years' imprisonment was upheld in *Parsons* [1996] 1 Cr App R (S) 36, where a man with a record of sexual offences attempted to abduct a 13-year-old child by offering her a lift in his car.

Abduction by Other Persons: Elements

The accused must take or detain the child so as to remove or keep him from lawful **B2.85** control. 'Detaining' is defined in the Child Abduction Act 1984, s. 3, to include causing the child to be detained or inducing the child to remain with the accused or another person. 'Taking' is defined in s. 3 to include causing or inducing the child to accompany the accused or any other person or causing the child to be taken. A child can be removed from lawful control without necessarily being taken to another place. It may suffice if the child is deflected into some unauthorised activity induced by the accused (see *Leather* (1993) 98 Cr App R 179, where children were persuaded by L to go with him to look for a 'missing bicycle'). Nor need the accused's conduct be the sole cause of the abduction, as long as it was more than merely peripheral. It is no defence that another cause may be the child's own decision or state of mind *(A (Child abduction)* (1999) *The Times*, 15 October 1999).

The words, 'so as to' import *mens rea*; no offence is therefore committed unless the accused intends to interfere with another person's lawful control or entitlement *(Re Owens* [1999] All ER (D) 827, unreported in printed form). The consent of that person would amount to 'lawful authority', but the consent of the child is irrelevant. This distinguishes the offence from that of kidnapping, as does the absence of any requirement of force or fraud (see **B2.68** *et seq.*).

The burden of proving that the taking or detention is without lawful authority or reasonable excuse rests with the Crown. Thus an honest but mistaken belief (for example, that the child in question was the daughter of the accused) would afford a defence on the basis that it is capable of amounting to a reasonable excuse *(Berry* [1996] 2 Cr App R 226).

Abduction by Other Persons: Defences

B2.86 Section 2(3)(a) provides a defence only if the parents of the child were not married at the time the child was born and the accused is, in fact, the father of the child *(Berry* [1996] 2 Cr App R 226). The decision in *Berry* appears to contradict the apparent intention of the draftsman to make the defence available to any person and is perhaps best explained on the basis that s. 2(1) is more favourable to the accused both as to the burden of proof and the subjective assessment of what constitutes a reasonable excuse.

Section 2(3)(b) provides a defence for any accused who proves that at the time of the offence he believed the child had attained the age of 16.

TAKING OF HOSTAGES

Definition

B2.87   Taking of Hostages Act 1982, s. 1

(1)   A person, whatever his nationality, who, in the United Kingdom or elsewhere—
(a)   detains any other person ('the hostage'), and
(b)   in order to compel a State, international governmental organisation, or person to do or abstain from doing any act, threatens to kill, injure or continue to detain the hostage, commits an offence.

Procedure

B2.88 The consent of the A-G is required before a prosecution can be brought under the Taking of Hostages Act 1982, s. 1. Taking hostages is triable only on indictment. It is a class 3 offence.

Indictment

B2.89   Statement of Offence

Hostage taking contrary to section 1 of the Taking of Hostages Act 1982

Particulars of Offence

A on divers days between the . . . day of . . . and the . . . day of . . . , detained V, and in order to compel the Government of the United Kingdom to release from prison certain convicted offenders, threatened to kill the said V

Sentence

The maximum penalty is life imprisonment (Taking of Hostages Act 1982, s. 1(2)). **B2.90**

Elements

The *actus reus* consists of detaining any person, and making threats to kill, injure or **B2.91** continue to detain that person.

The *mens rea* defined is in terms of the purpose for which the act and threat take place, and in that respect the accused's motive is relevant. The offence could therefore be seen as one of further or ulterior intent to cause the doing or abstaining from any act, and such intent or purpose must be proved, although it does not have to be achieved.

BIGAMY

Definition

Offences against the Person Act 1861, s. 57   **B2.92**

Whosoever, being married, shall marry any other person during the life of the former husband or wife, whether the second marriage shall have taken place in England or Ireland or elsewhere, shall be guilty of [an offence], and being convicted thereof shall be liable to [imprisonment] for any term not exceeding seven years . . . : Provided, that nothing in this section contained shall extend to any second marriage contracted elsewhere than in England and Ireland by any other than a subject of Her Majesty, or to any person marrying a second time whose husband or wife shall have been continually absent from such person for the space of seven years then last past, and shall not have been known by such person to be living within that time, or shall extend to any person who, at the time of such second marriage, shall have been divorced from the bond of the first marriage, or to any person whose former marriage shall have been declared void by the sentence of any court of competent jurisdiction.

Procedure

Bigamy is triable either way (MCA 1980, s. 17 and sch. 1). When tried on indictment **B2.93** it is a class 4 offence.

Indictment

Statement of Offence   **B2.94**

Bigamy contrary to section 57 of the Offences against the Person Act 1861

Particulars of Offence

A on or about the . . . day of . . . married V during the life of his wife, W

Sentencing Guidelines

The maximum penalty is seven years, a fine, or both, on indictment (OAPA 1861, s. 57); **B2.95** six months, a fine not exceeding the statutory maximum, or both, summarily.

There are very few Court of Appeal decisions on the proper approach to sentencing for this offence. According to Waller LJ in *Crowhurst* (1978) CSP B9-43A01:

It appears to this court that the sentence for bigamy must vary very much with the particular circumstances of the case. In many cases of bigamy it is possible to deal with the case by some sentence which does not involve deprivation of liberty. In other cases there may be a clear deception which has resulted in some injury to the woman concerned; in which an immediate custodial sentence must be passed, and the length of that sentence must depend greatly on the seriousness of the injury that has been done.

On the facts of the particular case, where the marriage was not consummated and lasted only a week, but where the woman's evidence was that she would not have married the offender had she known that he was still married, a short custodial sentence was held to be proper. The Court of Appeal reduced an 18-month sentence, which was 'wholly out of proportion to the gravity of this offence', to one of four months. *Crowhurst* was followed and applied in *Smith* (1994) 15 Cr App R (S) 407. In *Cairns* [1997] 1 Cr App R (S) 118, the offender entered a sham marriage to a Zimbabwean national and then went through a marriage ceremony with a Nigerian national, in both cases to evade immigration control. He received payment from the women. There was no deception on the woman concerned, but there was an intended deception on the state. A sentence of 15 months' imprisonment for bigamy was reduced to nine months on appeal.

Actus Reus

B2.96   The *actus reus* consists of marrying, in certain circumstances. Those circumstances are first, that the accused was already married at the time of the ceremony leading to the offence; secondly, that the new 'marriage' takes place within the lifetime of the first husband or wife; and thirdly, in respect of some categories of person, that the second marriage has taken place in England or Ireland or a Commonwealth country (see **B2.97**). There is one true proviso to this, which provides that no offence is committed where the first husband or wife has been missing for seven years or more (see **B2.100**). The other provisos are strictly unnecessary, because they refer to situations where the accused cannot be said to be 'married' already, because he has been validly divorced or had his marriage validly annulled.

There are problems with each aspect of the *actus reus*.

B2.97   ***The Act of 'Marrying'***   Although the OAPA 1861, s. 57, uses the term 'marry', it is the essence of the offence that this purported marriage is invalid because of an existing valid marriage, and therefore, strictly speaking, the accused does not marry at all. Section 57 has been interpreted as meaning 'shall go through the form of ceremony of marriage with another person' (*Allen* (1872) LR 1 CCR 367), but even this does not resolve all the difficulties inherent in the wording.

The term cannot be taken to refer to a marriage which would be valid but for the former marriage, because it is clear that even where there are other reasons for invalidity than the existence of a prior marriage, such as lack of age or capacity (see *Allen*), the second 'marriage' will nevertheless be a basis for a charge of bigamy.

Another problem which may arise is the question of the status of a second polygamous marriage validly contracted in another country. In some circumstances such a marriage may be recognised as valid by the civil courts in this country, but the position in respect of the criminal courts is as yet unclear. It is submitted that the criminal courts should adhere to the view taken by the civil courts, so that no offence would be committed where there is a second marriage recognised as valid by the civil courts.

It seems, therefore, that the term 'marries' in this context means to go through a form of ceremony of marriage with another person which is capable in normal circumstances of constituting a valid marriage within the normal understanding of that concept in this country.

The words 'or elsewhere' refer to anywhere in the world. Therefore, if the accused is a British citizen it is irrelevant where the second marriage takes place; an offence is committed if it is celebrated anywhere in the world (*Earl Russell* [1901] AC 446). If the accused is an alien, the second marriage is a basis for liability only if it takes place in England and Wales or Northern Ireland.

B2.98   ***'Being Married'***   A part of the *actus reus* of bigamy is that there must be a valid subsisting prior marriage when the purported ceremony takes place. The burden is on the prosecution to prove beyond reasonable doubt, as part of the *actus reus*, both that the accused was validly married on an earlier occasion and that the marriage was still subsisting at the time of the second ceremony. The latter is established by proof that the first husband or wife is still alive, which circumstance is also specifically required by the OAPA 1861, s. 57. The former is established by production of a certified copy of the relevant entry in the Register of Marriages (as to the admissibility of which, see **F16.2 *et seq*.** and **F16.25 *et seq*.**), together with evidence of the identity of the parties to the marriage. This second requirement must not be overlooked (*Tolson* (1864) 4 F & F 103; *Birtles* (1911) 6 Cr App R 177). In the case of a marriage celebrated abroad, expert evidence of validity is also admissible (*Sussex Peerage Case* (1844) 11 Cl & F 85; and see **F10.4 *et seq*.**). For discussion of presumptions of marriage, see **F3.33**.

If the accused is alleging that the supposed prior marriage is invalid for a particular reason, for example because it is void or has been annulled, then he need do no more than raise the issue, and the burden will then be on the prosecution to establish its validity (*Kay* (1887) 16 Cox CC 292). The presumption of validity applicable in civil cases has no application in a prosecution for bigamy, though in *Shaw* (1943) 60 TLR 344, where the ceremony alone was proved and the accused did not give evidence, the Court of Criminal Appeal held that evidence to be sufficient in law to sustain a conviction; *sed quaere*. An admission of validity by the accused is admissible as to an English marriage, but not otherwise (*Naguib* [1917] 1 KB 359; *Flaherty* (1847) 2 Car & Kir 782). But the weight of such evidence may not be great, and it would be unwise for the prosecution to rely on it.

A marriage which is void has never been a valid marriage and no court order would be necessary in order that the marriage be held to be invalid. If a marriage is voidable, it remains a valid marriage until a decree of nullity is awarded by a court, after which time there is no longer an existing marriage. This is covered by a proviso in s. 57 itself. In such circumstances, an element of the *actus reus* is not established and there can therefore be no liability. If there has been a decree of nullity, or a decree of divorce, where similarly there would be no existing marriage, this is also covered by a proviso within s. 57 (*Thomson* (1905) 70 JP 6).

It is now clear that the existing valid marriage which is the basis of the offence must be a monogamous marriage, and not one celebrated under a lawful system of polygamy (*Sagoo* [1975] QB 885). However, provided the marriage is recognised by English law as a valid marriage, it is irrelevant where it takes place.

Mens Rea

There is no specific mention of the requisite *mens rea* for the offence in the OAPA 1861, s. 57, itself. This is unlikely to cause any problems in respect of proving an intent to do the act, the going through a ceremony of marriage, but the relevant *mens rea* in respect of the circumstances has caused difficulty. In other sections of the 1861 Act strict liability has been applied to certain circumstances of an offence (see *Prince* (1875) LR 2 CCR 154), and the absence of the word 'malicious' from some sections, as compared to its presence in other sections, has created problems for the judiciary in deciding whether subjective recklessness, objective recklessness or negligence is the requisite *mens rea* applicable.

B2.99

The leading case on the *mens rea* for bigamy, relating particularly to the circumstance of being already married, is *Tolson* (1889) 23 QBD 168. In that case the accused had honestly and reasonably, but mistakenly, believed that her first husband was dead. The court held that an honest and reasonable mistake of this kind would exculpate. The same argument would also apply if the accused honestly and reasonably believed that he was validly divorced, or that his first marriage was void or had been annulled, because equally he would not have the necessary *mens rea* (negligence) in respect of the circumstance of being already married. The situation is slightly different as regards the proviso in the section relating to seven years' absence of the first spouse (see **B2.100**).

Tolson, and its explanation of this objective element of the *mens rea* requirement, was confirmed by the Court of Appeal in *Gould* [1968] 2 QB 65, which in turn was confirmed, albeit *obiter*, by the House of Lords in *DPP* v *Morgan* [1976] AC 182.

This last decision is particularly important. In *Morgan* itself an unreasonable but honest mistake was held to exculpate, although in the context of a different offence (see **A3.2**), and the decision has been treated as the basis of a general development away from any requirement that mistakes about *actus reus* must be reasonable. Indeed, this has been the case with other offences (see more generally **A3.2** to **A3.6**), but the fact that the *Tolson* test was confirmed in *DPP* v *Morgan* [1976] AC 182 undermines any such argument and is a particularly strong confirmation of the present law requiring the mistake in cases of bigamy to be both honest and reasonable. The other possible argument, although a tenuous one, is that it is now clear that the word 'malicious' does not have to be included in a particular section of the 1861 Act for there to be a requirement of subjective recklessness (see *Spratt* [1990] 1 WLR 1073). It is unlikely, however, that such a well-settled rule would be displaced.

A mistaken belief as to the death of a spouse is unlikely to be held to be reasonable unless the accused made reasonable inquiries before embarking on the second marriage. See, e.g., *Thomson* (1905) 70 JP 6; *Tolson* (1889) 23 QBD 168.

Continual Absence of First Spouse for Seven Years

B2.100 As mentioned at **B2.96** the parts of the proviso in s. 57 referring to being divorced from the bond of the first marriage and to a marriage declared void by a court of competent jurisdiction are strictly unnecessary as defences, because their effect is to defeat the *actus reus* requirement. The only proviso which provides a true defence is that which refers to a person 'whose husband or wife shall have been continually absent from such person for the space of seven years then last past'. This defence is only likely to be relevant if the prosecution have proved, as set out in the section, that the second marriage has taken place within the lifetime of the former husband or wife.

To establish the defence, the accused must adduce some evidence of the continual absence for the seven years. The prosecution must then prove beyond reasonable doubt either that there was no such continual absence, or that the accused knew the spouse to be alive at some time during that period (*Curgerwen* (1865) LR 1 CCR 1). In some older cases the defence was applied very liberally in favour of the accused. Proof of actual knowledge that the spouse was alive was generally required, even evidence that the means of discovering the truth were available to the accused being sufficient (see, e.g., *Jones* (1842) C & Mar 614; *Briggs* (1856) Dears & B 98). But it is by no means certain that in these days of better communications, the same approach would now be adopted. (As to knowledge, belief and 'wilful blindness' generally, see **A2.9** and **A2.10**.)

CHILD CRUELTY

Definition

B2.101   **Children and Young Persons Act 1933, s. 1**

(1) If any person who has attained the age of sixteen years and has responsibility for any child or young person under that age, wilfully assaults, ill-treats, neglects, abandons, or exposes him, or causes or procures him to be assaulted, ill-treated, neglected, abandoned, or exposed, in a manner likely to cause him unnecessary suffering or injury to health (including injury to or loss of sight, or hearing, or limb, or organ of the body, and any mental derangement), that person shall be guilty of [an offence], and shall be liable—

(a)   on conviction on indictment, to a fine or alternatively, or in addition thereto, to imprisonment for any term not exceeding ten years;

(b)   on summary conviction, to a fine not exceeding the prescribed sum, or alternatively or in addition thereto, to imprisonment for any term not exceeding six months.

(2)   For the purposes of this section—

(a)   a parent or other person legally liable to maintain a child or young person or the legal guardian of a child or young person shall be deemed to have neglected him in a manner likely to cause injury to his health if he has failed to provide adequate food, clothing, medical aid or lodging for him, or if, having been unable otherwise to provide such food, clothing, medical aid or lodging, he has failed to take steps to procure it to be provided under the enactments applicable in that behalf;

(b)   where it is proved that the death of an infant under three years of age was caused by suffocation (not being suffocation caused by disease or the presence of any foreign body in the throat or air passages of the infant) while the infant was in bed with some other person who has attained the age of sixteen years, that other person shall, if he was, when he went to bed, under the influence of drink, be deemed to have neglected the infant in a manner likely to cause injury to its health.

(3)   A person may be convicted of an offence under this section—

(a)   notwithstanding that actual suffering or injury to health, or the likelihood of actual suffering or injury to health, was obviated by the action of another person;

(b)   notwithstanding the death of the child or young person in question.

Indictment

Statement of Offence

B2.102

Cruelty to a person under the age of 16, contrary to s. 1(1) of the Children and Young Persons Act 1933

Particulars of Offence

A, between the . . . day of . . . and the . . . day of . . ., being a person who had attained the age of 16 and having responsibility for V, a child under that age, wilfully neglected the said V in a manner likely to cause her unnecessary suffering or injury to her health by failing to provide medical aid for her

The drafting of indictments for offences under this section may be complicated by the fact that the offence can be committed in several different ways. As to the importance of identifying the appropriate form of allegation in a given case, see *Hayles* [1969] 1 QB 364 and *Beard* (1987) 85 Cr App R 395.

Procedure

The offence is triable either way. When tried on indictment, it is a class 4 offence. Where **B2.103** an alleged offence is tried summarily, the CYPA 1933, s. 14 has effect.

Children and Young Persons Act 1933, s. 14

(1)   Where a person is charged with committing any of the offences mentioned in the first Schedule to this Act in respect of two or more children or young persons, the same information or summons may charge the offence in respect of all or any of them, but the person charged shall not, if he is summarily convicted, be liable to a separate penalty in respect of each child or young person except upon separate informations.

(2)   The same information or summons may charge him with the offence of assault, ill-treatment, neglect, abandonment, or exposure, together or separately, and may charge him with committing all or any of those offences in a manner likely to cause unnecessary suffering or injury to health, alternatively or together, but when those offences are charged together, the person charged shall not, if he is summarily convicted, be liable to a separate penalty for each.

Sentencing Guidelines

The maximum penalty on conviction on indictment is 10 years' imprisonment. The **B2.104** maximum penalty on summary conviction is six months' imprisonment, or a fine not exceeding the prescribed sum, or both.

A distinction is drawn in the cases between instances of violent assault, where the victim is a child, and cases of cruelty or neglect. In the former cases, a more usual charge is assault occasioning actual bodily harm or, where appropriate, a more serious offence against the person, but sometimes a prosecution under the CYPA 1933, s. 1 will be brought instead. A second distinction which is generally drawn is between those cases where there has been deliberate infliction of injury, of a serious nature, perhaps on more than one occasion, where a lengthy custodial sentence will be upheld, and one-off cases of less serious injury which have taken place in a context of very considerable economic or domestic pressure, where a rather lower custodial sentence is the norm.

In *Bacon* [1997] 1 Cr App R (S) 335, parents had disciplined their 15-year-old son for misbehaviour in a cruel and brutal manner, which involved pouring paint thinners over the victim, forcing him to eat cigarettes and chaining him up in the garage. A sentence of three years' imprisonment imposed on the father was reduced to 18 months on appeal, in the light of personal mitigation.

In *Smith* (1984) 6 Cr App R (S) 174, a father pleaded guilty to the offence of cruelty to his four-month-old mentally handicapped baby, whose arm he had broken by biting it. A sentence of 18 months' imprisonment was reduced on appeal to nine months. May LJ commented that a distinction had to be drawn between cases of 'deliberate wickedness' and cases 'which can really be described as disasters, which have come not only upon the child, but also upon the child's parents, largely due to the latter's inability to cope with an infant, sometimes in circumstances of unemployment, sometimes in circumstances of inadequate housing'. Whilst holding that the instant case was of the latter type, the court nevertheless felt that a custodial sentence was inevitable, given the injury which had been inflicted. In *Oates* (1991) 12 Cr App R (S) 742, the offender pleaded guilty to cruelty to the 11-month-old child of the woman with whom he was cohabiting. He smacked the child in the chest and grabbed it at the back of the ears causing a fingernail injury. The child was found to be suffering from a number of bruises when taken to hospital. The Court of Appeal reduced the sentence of nine months' imprisonment to four months, on the basis that the injury had been caused by a 'momentary reaction to exasperation', the injuries were not serious and that the offender had desisted from his attack very quickly, had shown remorse and had pleaded guilty at the first opportunity.

Most of the reported cases on cruelty or neglect (as opposed to infliction of an injury) arise from the offender's culpable failure to summon medical assistance for a child. In *Taggart* [1999] 2 Cr App R (S) 68 the offender's child aged three and a half suffered severe scalding while in the bath. It was accepted that the scalding had been accidental, but the offender pleaded guilty to cruelty on the basis of his failure to summon medical attention until more than 24 hours later. The appropriate sentence was 30 months' imprisonment.

A case of more general neglect is *Harvey* (1987) 9 Cr App R (S) 524. A mother was convicted of four counts of cruelty to her four children aged between four and eight years. The mother was frequently drunk, the living accommodation was dirty, pornographic material was left lying about and the children were not kept clean and were denied affection; there was one instance of a failure to arrange medical attention when it was needed. A sentence of nine months' imprisonment was upheld. See also *Crank* [1996] 2 Cr App R (S) 363 and *Weaver* [1998] 2 Cr App R (S) 56.

In *Colwell* (1994) 15 Cr App R (S) 323 the offender admitted that over a period of about a year she had left her daughter, aged three, at home on her own all day while she went out to work. The Court of Appeal said that a custodial sentence was appropriate in such a case but, in light of the financial problems the mother faced in bringing up her child alone, the adverse impact on the child of the mother's imprisonment and the fact that

Colwell had served one month in custody prior to the appeal, the sentence was varied from six months' imprisonment to a probation order. In *A-G's Ref (No. 57 of 1995)* [1996] 2 Cr App R (S) 159 a conditional discharge was held to have been an unduly lenient sentence where an eight-year-old child who was already ill suffered hypothermia as a result of being left alone in a car in cold weather for half an hour.

Another category of neglect is where injury has been inflicted upon the offender's child by another person with the offender's knowledge. In *Pelling* (1988) 10 Cr App R (S) 185, the offender's cohabitee had treated the offender's three-year-old daughter with such violence over a three month period that the child had died. The offender's sentence of 18 months' imprisonment, imposed on the basis that she had failed to take any steps to prevent the violence, was upheld on appeal. Similar cases are *Simpson* (1990) 12 Cr App R (S) 431 and *Camille* (1993) 14 Cr App R (S) 296.

Actus Reus: Age and Responsibility

To be guilty of an offence under the CYPA 1933, s. 1, an accused must have been over **B2.105** the age of 16 at the time of the offence, and must have 'had responsibility' for the child or young person in question. If proof of the defendant's or victim's ages is an issue, reference may be made to the CYPA 1933, s. 99, which provides (s. 99(2)) that, where in such a case the person by or in respect of whom the offence was allegedly committed 'appears to the court to have been at the date of the alleged offence a child or young person or to have been under or to have attained a particular age, as the case may be, he shall . . . be presumed to have been under or to have attained that age, as the case may be, unless the contrary is proved'. Where this presumption applies, the defence may have the burden of proving that the young person in question was in fact over the age of 16 (s. 99(4)).

'Responsibility' in this context may be shared by more than one person, and it may involve questions both of fact and law (*Liverpool Society for the Prevention of Cruelty to Children* v *Jones* [1914] 3 KB 813). Any person who has parental responsibility or who has any other legal liability to maintain a child or young person will be 'presumed' to have responsibility for him under the Act and 'shall not be taken to have ceased to be responsible for him by reason of the fact that he does not have care of him' (CYPA 1933, s. 17(1)(a) and (2)); but other persons, such as baby-sitters or teachers, may also have responsibility whilst a child or young person is in their care (s. 17(1)(b)).

Actus Reus: Conduct

Although the CYPA 1933, s. 1, creates just one offence, it may take a number of different **B2.106** forms (*Hayles* [1969] 1 QB 364; *Harding* [1997] Crim LR 815). It may take the form of positive abuse (assault, ill-treatment, abandonment or exposure) or of mere neglect, or it may take the form of causing or procuring abuse or neglect. The abuse or neglect in question must be committed 'in a manner likely to cause unnecessary suffering or injury to health' (as to which see s. 1(1)); but the offence is essentially a conduct crime rather than a result crime. It need not therefore be shown that any such injury was caused, and indeed it is no defence to show that any suffering of or danger to the victim was obviated by the action of another person (s. 1(3)(a)).

'Assault' in this context will usually mean a battery, as to which see **B2.5** *et seq*. Ill-treatment is self-explanatory in the context of the requirement that it must be likely to cause unnecessary suffering or injury (see below). In *Boulden* (1957) 41 Cr App R 105, the Court of Appeal considered a case of abandonment in which a father of five children had left them and travelled to Scotland. Although the evidence was somewhat contradictory, the court found sufficient evidence to show that he had 'washed his hands' of his children, and had 'left them to their fate'; this was sufficient proof of abandonment.

The offence of exposing a child in a manner likely to cause unnecessary suffering or injury has had little consideration in case law. Exposure to bad weather in itself would not be enough, given the second limb of the *actus reus* (*Williams* (1910) 4 Cr App R 89, a case concerning the Children Act 1908).

Cases of neglect have received frequent attention in the courts. The requisite neglect will be deemed to have occurred, and therefore need not be proved, in the circumstances set out in s. 1(2)(a) and (b), although the Court of Appeal in *Wills* [1990] Crim LR 714 stressed that even where neglect is deemed the *mens rea* element of the offence must be proved (see below). Where s. 1(2)(a) applies, it may be the basis for proving neglect; in any event, it gives a general indication of what constitutes neglect. For example, a relative who was not the legal guardian of, or legally liable to maintain, a child, but who was looking after him for several weeks, might be under a duty to act (see **A1.13 *et seq*.**). Such a person would then be expected to provide care of the kind mentioned in s. 2(1)(a).

The Court of Appeal in *S and M* [1995] Crim LR 486 explained 'neglecting' in the context of failing to obtain medical help. Either S the parent or M the boyfriend assaulted the child, who had bruising to the spine and buttocks. There was then further neglect in the failure to get medical help. The argument that there was no neglect because there was nothing a doctor could have done, was rejected. The Court of Appeal held that S or M had neglected the child within the meaning of the statute by refraining from seeking medical help, being reckless as to whether the child might need such help. There are difficulties not addressed in this case concerning the burden of proof, given that it was clear that one party had committed the assault but it was not clear which. However, there is clearly an argument that both were liable for neglect, both being under a duty to act.

The Court of Appeal in *Wills* were concerned with the meaning of the phrase 'in a manner likely to cause unnecessary suffering or injury to health' and more particularly the exact meaning of the word 'likely'. The trial judge had relied on remarks of Lord Diplock in *Sheppard* [1981] AC 394, that 'likely' was simply meant to exclude what was highly unlikely. Although the Court of Appeal agreed that these remarks were *obiter dicta*, it found that Lord Diplock had properly construed the word in the context of this statute, given the difficulties for parents in deciding how serious an injury is, and the possible grave consequences of lack of treatment. The court went on to point out however that, because of the 'deeming' provision under s. 1(2)(a) of the Act, it was unnecessary for the court to come to a decision about the meaning of the word, and these remarks too were *obiter*. In the context of interpreting s. 1(2)(a), it was held that medical aid included medical supervision or medical care in the sense of observation to discover the gravity of any particular injury. The deeming provision was also relevant in *Sheppard* and was explained by Lord Diplock as follows:

> Did the parents fail to provide . . . in the period before [the child's] death medical aid that was in fact adequate in view of his actual state of health at the relevant time? This, as it seems to me, is a pure question of objective fact to be determined in the light of what has become known by *the date of the trial* to have been the child's actual state of health at the relevant time. It does not depend upon whether a reasonably careful parent, with knowledge of those facts only which such a parent might reasonably be expected to observe for himself, would have thought it prudent to have recourse to medical aid.

The requisite *mens rea* must still be proved, even when the deeming provisions apply.

Mens Rea

B2.107 The *mens rea* of this offence is defined as 'wilfully' carrying out any of the various modes of the *actus reus*. *Sheppard* [1981] AC 394 is the leading case on the interpretation of the word in this context, and although it was decided only in the context of the neglect provision, there is no reason why it should not apply equally to all the positive modes of committing the offence.

In *Sheppard*, a child aged 16 months died of hypothermia following severe gastro-enteritis. The parents were poor and of low intelligence, and had not appreciated the seriousness of his condition. They were convicted under s. 1 on the basis of an objective test. The House of Lords in *Sheppard* allowed the defendants' appeal, and Lord Diplock explained the *mens rea* requirement as follows:

> The proper direction to be given to a jury on a charge of wilful neglect of a child under section 1 of the Children and Young Persons Act 1933 by failing to provide adequate medical aid, is that the jury must be satisfied (1) that the child did in fact need medical aid at the time at which the parent is charged with failing to provide it (the actus reus) and (2) either that the parent was aware at the time that the child's health might be at risk if it were not provided with medical aid, or that the parent's unawareness of this fact was due to his not caring whether the child's health was at risk or not (the *mens rea*).

This has been interpreted by some commentators to convey *Caldwell* recklessness (*Metropolitan Police Commissioner* v *Caldwell* [1982] AC 343: see **A2.4**) in the light of Lord Diplock's very similar judgment in that case, following shortly after *Sheppard* but objective recklessness has been interpreted since *Caldwell* as based on the reasonable man's ability to see the risk, and not on the defendant's ability to do so (had he considered the matter) (see *Elliott* v *C* [1983] 1 WLR 939 and **A2.6**). This is difficult to reconcile with the concept of 'not caring', and also in contrast to comments of Lord Diplock in *Sheppard* that he did not think the concept of what the reasonable parent would observe and understand had any part to play in the *mens rea* of this offence. Furthermore, in order to show that a parent did not care whether his child's health was at risk, it must be shown that he gave some thought to the possibility, however generally, as 'not caring' indicates a positive state of mind.

General

A defendant can be charged under the CYPA 1933, s. 1, even if death occurs (s. 1(3)(b)). **B2.108**

Liability is subject to the right of any parent or other person having lawful control or charge of a child or young person to administer punishment (see **B2.8**).

SECTION B3: SEXUAL OFFENCES

RAPE

Definition

B3.1 Rape formerly consisted of a male having sexual intercourse with a female without her consent. The old law will apply to cases arising before the coming into force of the CJPO 1994, s. 142 (3 November 1994), and reference may be made to the 1994 edition of this work. Rape is now a statutory offence which can be committed by a man upon a woman or another man.

Sexual Offences Act 1956, ss. 1 and 44

1.—(1) It is an offence for a man to rape a woman or another man.

(2) A man commits rape if—

(a) he has sexual intercourse with a person (whether vaginal or anal) who at the time of the intercourse does not consent to it; and

(b) at the time he knows that the person does not consent to the intercourse or is reckless as to whether that person consents to it.

(3) A man also commits rape if he induces a married woman to have sexual intercourse with him by impersonating her husband.

(4) Subsection (2) applies for the purpose of any enactment.

44. Where, on the trial of any offence under this Act, it is necessary to prove sexual intercourse (whether natural or unnatural), it shall not be necessary to prove the completion of the intercourse by the emission of seed, but the intercourse shall be deemed complete upon proof of penetration only.

Sexual Offences (Amendment) Act 1976, s. 1

(2) It is hereby declared that if at a trial for a rape offence the jury has to consider whether a man believed that a woman or man was consenting to sexual intercourse, the presence or absence of reasonable grounds for such a belief is a matter to which the jury is to have regard, in conjunction with any other relevant matters, in considering whether he so believed.

Procedure

B3.2 Rape is triable only on indictment. It is a class 2 offence. Formerly it was presumed that a boy under the age of 14 was incapable of sexual intercourse. This rule has been abolished both in respect of natural and unnatural intercourse (SOA 1993, s. 1).

As to reporting restrictions to protect the anonymity of the complainant in a rape case, see the Sexual Offences (Amendment) Act 1976, s. 4, and generally **D2.52**.

Indictment

B3.3 Statement of Offence

Rape contrary to section 1(1) of the Sexual Offences Act 1956

Particulars of Offence

A on or about the . . . day of . . . had sexual intercourse with V without her consent and knowing that she did not consent

Alternative Verdicts

B3.4 See the SOA 1956, sch. 2.

(a)   Attempted rape, where actual penetration cannot be proved (see **B3.9**). There is no longer a common-law offence of assault with intent to rape (*P* [1990] Crim LR 323).

(b)   Procurement of a woman by threats (SOA 1956, s. 2).

(c)   Procurement of a woman by false pretences (SOA 1956, s. 3).

(d)   Administering drugs to facilitate intercourse (SOA 1956, s. 4).

(e)   Where the accused is acquitted of rape on the basis of the victim's consent, but the victim was under 16 years of age at the material time, it would be open to the jury to convict of indecent assault (SOA 1956, s. 14), because any charge of rape necessarily includes the elements of indecent assault, and the consent of a person under 16 would afford no defence to the latter charge (*Hodgson* [1973] QB 565). It would seem preferable, however, to add a specific count for indecent assault, because the age of the victim is not a necessary averment either for rape or indecent assault, and it may be unfair to the defence to leave indecent assault to the jury purely as an alternative in some circumstances.

Unlawful sexual intercourse with a girl under 16 (SOA 1956, s. 6) is not, however, an alternative verdict on a charge of rape since the enactment of the Criminal Law Act 1967, sch. 3, repealing part of the SOA 1956, sch. 2.

Sentencing Guidelines

The maximum penalty for rape is life imprisonment (SOA 1956, s. 37 and sch. 2). The **B3.5** maximum penalty for attempted rape is life imprisonment (SOA 1956, s. 37 and sch. 2).

The guideline case on this offence where heterosexual rape is concerned is *Billam* [1986] 1 WLR 349. Lord Lane CJ said (at pp. 350–52):

> This court emphasised in *Roberts* [1982] 1 WLR 133, that rape is always a serious crime which calls for an immediate custodial sentence other than in wholly exceptional circumstances . . .

> The variable factors in cases of rape are so numerous that it is difficult to lay down guidelines as to the proper length of sentence in terms of years. That aspect of the problem was not considered in *Roberts*. There are however many reported decisions of the court which give an indication of what current practice ought to be and it may be useful to summarise their general effect.

> For rape committed by an adult without any aggravating or mitigating features, a figure of five years should be taken as the starting point in a contested case. Where a rape is committed by two or more men acting together, or by a man who has broken into or otherwise gained access to a place where the victim is living, or by a person who is in a position of responsibility towards the victim, or by a person who abducts the victim and holds her captive, the starting-point should be eight years.

> At the top of the scale comes the defendant who has carried out what might be described as a campaign of rape, committing the crime upon a number of different women or girls. He represents a more than ordinary danger and a sentence of 15 years or more may be appropriate.

> Where the defendant's behaviour has manifested perverted or psychopathic tendencies or gross personality disorder, and where he is likely, if at large, to remain a danger to women for an indefinite time, a life sentence will not be inappropriate.

> The crime should in any event be treated as aggravated by any of the following factors: (1) violence is used over and above the force necessary to commit the rape; (2) a weapon is used to frighten or wound the victim; (3) the rape is repeated; (4) the rape has been carefully planned; (5) the defendant has previous convictions for rape or other serious offences of a violent or sexual kind; (6) the victim is subjected to further sexual indignities or perversions; (7) the victim is either very old or very young; (8) the effect upon the victim, whether

physical or mental, is of special seriousness. Where any one or more of these aggravating features are present, the sentence should be substantially higher than the figure suggested as the starting point.

The extra distress which giving evidence can cause to a victim means that a plea of guilty, perhaps more so than in other cases, should normally result in some reduction from what would otherwise be the appropriate sentence. The amount of such reduction will of course depend on all the circumstances, including the likelihood of a finding of not guilty had the matter been contested.

The fact that the victim may be considered to have exposed herself to danger by acting imprudently (as for instance by accepting a lift in a car from a stranger) is not a mitigating factor; and the victim's previous sexual experience is equally irrelevant. But if the victim has behaved in a manner which was calculated to lead the defendant to believe that she would consent to sexual intercourse, then there should be some mitigation of the sentence. Previous good character is of only minor relevance.

The starting point for attempted rape should normally be less than for the completed offence, especially if it is desisted at a comparatively early stage. But . . . attempted rape may be made by aggravating features into an offence even more serious than some examples of the full offence.

At the top end of the scale of seriousness, a life sentence for rape was upheld in *Arnold* [1998] 1 Cr App R (S) 416, where the defendant pleaded guilty to two counts of rape, three of robbery and two of indecent assault, most of the offences being committed at knifepoint. The defendant had many previous convictions since the age of eleven, and represented a grave risk to women. The period specified for the purposes of the CJA 1991, s. 34 (now the C(S)A 1997, s. 28: see **E1.27**) was 10 years. Other recent cases in which life sentences for rape have been upheld by the Court of Appeal are *Brandy* [1997] 1 Cr App R (S) 38, *Razzaque* [1997] 1 Cr App R (S) 154 and *Rodwell* [1998] 2 Cr App R (S) 1.

An example of a case of rape where aggravating features referred to in *Billam* were present is *Malcolm* (1987) 9 Cr App R (S) 487. The offender pleaded guilty to false imprisonment and rape. The victim was dragged to the offender's flat, threatened with a knife, forced to participate in oral sex and raped twice. The sentencer imposed 12 years for the rape, with five years concurrent for the false imprisonment. He also stated that he regarded public awareness that a rape victim may contract AIDS as being a general aggravating feature in rape cases. The Court of Appeal reduced the sentence to 10 years, taking 12 years from *Billam* [1986] 1 WLR 349 as a starting point and reducing it by two years for the guilty plea. It was also said that AIDS would justify a heavier sentence only where the victim had a valid reason for believing that she had contracted it from the offender, or where that had actually happened. Fifteen years was reduced to 12 years to take account of a guilty plea and the offender's earlier efforts to rehabilitate himself in *Hawkins* (1986) 8 Cr App R (S) 181, where the offender had broken into the victim's home at 5 a.m., threatened her with a weapon, forced her to take part in oral sex, and then raped her. In *Henry* (1988) 10 Cr App R (S) 327, the offender pleaded guilty to five counts of rape, one of attempted rape, one of indecent assault, one of robbery and two of theft. Over a period of 14 months he had committed a series of rapes on women between the ages of 15 and 23. In some cases a knife was produced, and most of the attacks occurred in the early evening when the victims were on their way home. The Court of Appeal imposed an 18-year sentence, commenting that, if the case had been contested, a sentence of 20 years or thereabouts would have been proper. In *A-G's Ref (No. 1 of 1991)* (1992) 13 Cr App R (S) 134, the victim, a woman in her mid-sixties, worked as a bereavement counsellor and had invited the offender, who posed as a distressed widower, to her home. He made sexual advances to her and, when these were resisted, he pushed her into the bedroom and raped her several times. The sentence of five years' imprisonment was said by the Court of Appeal to be 'inordinately low' in light of the *Billam* guidelines. The aggravating features present in the case, and the absence of credit to be derived from a guilty plea, required a minimum sentence of eight years.

A case without the aggravating features cited in the preceding paragraph is *Harvey* (1987) 9 Cr App R (S) 124, where the victim had known the offender for about a year. She went to his home looking for her friend, the offender's cousin. When the victim rejected his sexual advances, the offender raped her. He had previous convictions for indecent assault on a young boy and for incest. Lord Lane CJ described the case as 'a typical *Billam* case', where five years was the appropriate starting point. The sentence of seven years was reduced to six, the year additional to the baseline of five being sufficient to take account of the related previous convictions. Four years' imprisonment was appropriate for a rape with few aggravating features in *Ford* [1998] 2 Cr App R (S) 74. The 29-year-old offender had met a 17-year-old girl who had left home after an argument with her parents. The offender ingratiated himself with her and then took advantage of her vulnerability to have sexual intercourse with her against her will. There was no use of gratuitous violence, the offender pleaded guilty, and the Court of Appeal accepted that this was not a breach of trust case in the sense envisaged in the guideline authorities. In *Sellars* [1998] 1 Cr App R (S) 117, the offender pleaded guilty to raping a 16-year-old girl, who treated him as a family friend. After drinking some wine the victim fell asleep and the offender had intercourse with her while she was asleep. A sentence of eight years' imprisonment was reduced to six years on appeal, the Court of Appeal noting that there was no violence over and above the rape itself, and that some credit should be given for the guilty plea, albeit tendered only at the start of the trial when the complainant had fully expected to have to give evidence. In *Greaves* [1999] 1 Cr App R (S) 319 a sentence of 42 months for rape was reduced on appeal to 18 months. Sexual intimacy took place with the complainant's consent but, after the offender had begun to have sexual intercourse with the complainant, she asked him to stop. He did not stop and the intercourse was completed. The offender had no relevant previous convictions, but tendered his guilty plea only when the jury had been sworn in and the trial was about to start.

In *A-G's Ref (No. 7 of 1989)* (1990) 12 Cr App R (S) 1, the offender was convicted of raping a woman with whom he had lived for about 18 months and had regular sexual intercourse. The offence took place three months after the relationship had ended. The offender invited the complainant to visit his flat, which she did. He then pushed her across the room, dragged her to the bed and removed her clothes before raping her. A sentence of two years' imprisonment was increased on appeal to four and a half years. Lord Lane CJ observed (at p. 6) that previous cohabitation 'does not license the man once that cohabitation or sexual intercourse has ceased to have sexual intercourse with the girl willy nilly. It is however a factor to which some weight can be given . . .'. The key reason for regarding the original sentence as too low was that the defendant contested the case, which does 'deprive the defendant of one of the most powerful points in mitigation which he has'. See also *Collier* (1992) 13 Cr App R (S) 33.

The appropriate sentence for rape committed by a man upon his wife was considered in *Stephen W* (1993) 14 Cr App R (S) 256. The offender and his wife had been married for three years and were living together. After an argument the offender forced his wife to have sexual intercourse. He threatened her with a knife, ordered her to suck his penis and then forcibly raped her twice. A sentence of five years' imprisonment was upheld. The Court of Appeal said that it should not be thought that a lower scale of sentencing than that set out in *Billam* applied to rape by a husband. All would depend on the circumstances of the case. Where the parties were cohabiting normally and the husband insisted on intercourse against his wife's will, but without violence or threats, the existence of the previous consensual sexual relationship would be an important factor in reducing the level of sentence. A subsequent example is *Paul Richard M* (1995) 16 Cr App R (S) 770. Where, however, the conduct was gross and did involve threats or violence, the facts of marriage, long cohabitation and that the offender was no stranger to the victim were of little significance. The instant case fell at the grave end of the scale and the offender had contested the case. See also *Edward James K* [1997] 1 Cr App R (S) 251, *Michael H* [1997] 2 Cr App R (S) 339 and *Marc Anthony W* [1998] 1 Cr App R (S) 375.

Where the victim of rape is a prostitute, the Court of Appeal said in *Cole* (1993) 14 Cr App R (S) 764 that the harm suffered by the victim may be different and perhaps somewhat less than that suffered by other victims of the offence. On the other hand prostitutes are entitled to say 'No' to sexual intercourse and are entitled to expect protection from the courts. In *Masood* [1997] 2 Cr App R (S) 137, where the 16-year-old victim was held captive in the offender's car for four hours, was subjected to a series of violent attacks and was forced to have unprotected sexual intercourse, the Court of Appeal said that the fact that the victim was a prostitute was largely irrelevant to sentence. A sentence of nine years' imprisonment was not manifestly excessive. See also *A-G's Ref (No. 28 of 1996)* [1997] 2 Cr App R (S) 206.

In *Taylor* (1983) 5 Cr App R (S) 241 a sentence of three years was varied to a probation order where the offender, who was mentally retarded, pleaded guilty to rape of a 19-year-old girl suffering from Down's syndrome and who attended the same special school as the offender. The Court of Appeal justified the exceptional sentence on the grounds of the nature of the sexual act itself (some degree of sexual penetration, but in the nature of sexual exploration with no real understanding), the mental deficiency of the offender (described as on the borderline between low intelligence and mental handicap), and the inability of the victim to communicate any effective protest at the conduct.

Cases of non-consensual anal intercourse, whether committed on a woman or on a man, will now be charged as rape (see **B3.1**). There is no guideline decision of the Court of Appeal on the new form of the offence of rape, but earlier decisions relating to forcible buggery of women and of men can be taken to provide some guide to the appropriate sentencing bracket. In *Mendez* (1992) 13 Cr App R (S) 94, the offender attacked the female victim when she was walking home, pushed her into an alleyway and twice committed forcible buggery on her. In the Court of Appeal Glidewell LJ made reference to the *Billam* guidelines on rape and said that 'In our view forcible buggery of a woman is equivalent to rape but worse than normal vaginal rape'. A prison sentence of five years was upheld. His lordship's comment has been relied upon in later cases, such as *A-G's Ref (No. 15 of 1992)* (1993) 15 Cr App R (S) 324, where the Court of Appeal increased a suspended sentence of nine months to immediate imprisonment of four years in respect of a husband who pleaded guilty to five counts of non-consensual buggery upon his wife committed over a six-year period, and *A-G's Ref (No. 25 of 1994)* (1995) 16 Cr App R (S) 562, where a sentence of 30 months' imprisonment imposed for buggery committed by a stepfather on his 17-year-old stepdaughter without her consent, was increased to five years. See also *T* [1997] 1 Cr App R (S) 196.

Actus Reus

B3.6 Sexual intercourse is required for rape. This means anal penetration or penetration *per vaginam*; it does not include oral sex (*Gaston* (1981) 73 Cr App R 164). The slightest degree of penetration will suffice (*Stanton* (1844) 1 Car & Kir 415; *Nicholls* (1846) 2 Car & Kir 246). The hymen need not be ruptured (*Hughes* (1841) 9 C & P 752). No emission of seed is required (SOA 1956, s. 44).

While rape is complete upon penetration it has been held that the act of intercourse is regarded as continuing until withdrawal. In the case of heterosexual rape a man commits rape where he remains in the body of a woman who, having initially consented, withdraws her consent (*Kaitamaki* v *The Queen* [1985] AC 147; *Cooper* [1994] Crim LR 531). It is submitted that the same principle applies to homosexual rape; an act which began as lawful buggery can become rape if the active partner remains in the body of the pathic after withdrawal of consent.

In *R* [1992] 1 AC 599, the House of Lords held in categoric terms that a husband may be guilty of raping his wife where he forces intercourse on her with the requisite *mens rea*. A wife is fully protected by the law of rape even though no formal steps have been taken to end the marriage or to end cohabitation, and even though the parties are still cohabiting. It is, however, submitted that the fact that the parties have not ceased cohabitation may be of evidential value on the question whether the wife consented or not. Whether its value be slight or more substantial will presumably depend on the history of the relationship between the parties.

It has never been doubted that a husband can be liable as a party to the rape of his wife by another (*Cogan* [1976] QB 217). Further, whilst other forms of intercourse such as fellatio are not rape they may, unless consented to, amount to indecent assault (*Kowalski* (1987) 86 Cr App R 339).

Consent

Except in the case of personation, rape requires that the intercourse be without the **B3.7** consent of the other party. The question of whether that person consented is one of fact for the jury. There is no requirement that the complainant demonstrate or communicate a lack of consent to the accused. There must, however, be some evidence to be put before the jury of lack of consent and the nature of that evidence depends on the circumstances of the case (*Malone* [1998] 2 Cr App R 447). The law does not require a woman to have resisted physically (*Olugboja* [1982] QB 320; *Howard* [1965] 1 WLR 13 is no longer good law on the point) and it is submitted that no such resistance is required as a matter of law on the part of a male victim and that the limits to consent as a defence apply equally to male as to female victims. It is, accordingly, submitted that it need not be proved that the victim's submission was induced by force, fear or fraud, although one or more of these factors will be present in most cases of rape (*Olugboja*). A man cannot claim that consent by a woman, or it is submitted a man, whom he has made drunk, is valid (*Camplin* (1845) 1 Cox CC 220). A complainant may well be incapable of consenting due to the influence of drink or drugs, and it would not seem to matter whether she became intoxicated on her own initiative (*Malone*, disapproving *Lang* (1975) 62 Cr App R 50). A sleeping victim is not deemed to have consented (*Mayers* (1872) 12 Cox CC 311), nor is one who is too young to be regarded as able to give a valid consent. In this respect it will be noted that the age for giving consent to buggery is now 18. A person who is mentally defective may be held incapable of giving a valid consent, depending on the severity of the person's condition (*Barratt* (1873) LR 2 CCR 81; *Pressy* (1876) 10 Cox CC 635).

It is unclear how far threats not involving violence or the fear of it will be held to negate consent. In *Olugboja* [1982] QB 320, the court left open the question what coercion would suffice, noting only that in the less common cases, not involving threats of physical violence or physical constraint, the judge's direction will have to be a full one, and will have to concentrate on the victim's state of mind. In particular, the jury will have to address their minds to the difficult distinction between submission and consent. It may be, for example, that in some cases economic coercion, e.g., the threat of dismissal from employment, will suffice. It is for the jury to decide whether or not there is consent. Provided that the judge directs the jury fully on 'consent' and 'submission', he need not spell out the possibility of reluctant acquiescence (*McAllister* [1997] Crim LR 233).

Consent procured by fraud will not negate rape where the fraud is as to whether the man is the victim's husband (SOA 1956, s. 1(3)) or, more broadly it would seem, as to his identity where identity is material (*Linekar* [1995] QB 250; *Elbekkay* [1995] Crim LR 163, but see doubts expressed in the note to that case). Moreover, a deception as to the nature of the sexual act itself will not give rise to valid consent (*Williams* [1923] 1 KB 340; *Flattery* (1877) 2 QBD 410). In *Williams*, a man who had intercourse with a girl after falsely pretending that his acts were a method of training her voice was properly convicted of rape.

Frauds other than those specified above do not invalidate consent so as to constitute rape. A man who has intercourse with another knowing, but not disclosing, that he suffers from venereal disease cannot be convicted of rape. A man cannot be convicted of raping a woman with whom he has intercourse after a bigamous marriage ceremony, nor can a man be so convicted where he seduces a woman under promise of marriage, or induces a woman to engage in an act of prostitution under promise of payment (*Clarence* (1888) 22 QBD 23; *Papadimitropoulos* (1957) 98 CLR 249, where the history of the rule is traced). In such a case, consensus as to act precludes rape (*Linekar*).

Mens Rea

B3.8   Rape requires that a man intends to have intercourse with another and that the man knows that the other person does not consent to intercourse or is reckless as to whether that other consents or not (SOA 1956, s. 2(2)). Section 1(2) of the Sexual Offences (Amendment) Act 1976 provides that a jury may take into account the presence or absence of reasonable grounds for belief in determining whether a man actually did believe that the other person was consenting. In this context a man is reckless where he is aware that the other party may not be consenting but proceeds to have intercourse with the other party either knowing that that party was not consenting or not caring whether the other party consented or not (*Khan* [1990] 1 WLR 13; *S (Satnam)* (1984) 78 Cr App R 149; *Breckenridge* (1983) 79 Cr App R 244; see *Pigg* [1982] 1 WLR 762, which must now be taken to have been wrongly decided).

Section 1(2) of the Sexual Offences (Amendment) Act 1976 confirms that in rape cases the question is whether the accused was actually mistaken as to consent. The jury must be directed that the Crown must disprove a defence of mistaken belief in consent where that is raised. Absence of belief in consent equates to recklessness (*Gardiner* [1994] Crim LR 455). The reasonableness or otherwise of the man's belief provides evidence on this issue, but reasonableness of belief is not itself necessary to the defence. In referring both to the presence or absence of reasonable grounds and to 'other relevant matters' the legislation permits the jury to consider, *inter alia*, the whole of the accused's conduct towards the complainant, for example whether the complainant was subjected to duress before intercourse took place (*McFall* [1994] Crim LR 226).

A man who is honestly but unreasonably mistaken concerning the other person's consent cannot therefore be convicted of rape. A jury may, however, as noted, take the circumstances into account in determining whether he may have held such a belief. Furthermore, where a man's mistake is attributable to voluntary intoxication, he may not rely on it (*O'Grady* [1987] QB 995; *Woods* (1981) 74 Cr App R 312); *Fotheringham* (1988) 88 Cr App R 206 and see **A3.10**.

Mens rea in relation to consent can arise after initial penetration. A man who persists in intercourse after he comes to realise that the other has withdrawn consent, has been held to commit rape (*Kaitamaki* v *The Queen* [1985] AC 147; *Cooper* [1994] Crim LR 531).

Attempted Rape

B3.9   Attempted rape is governed by the principles of the law of attempts generally (see **A6.31** *et seq.*). Attempted rape may be charged as such, or may be an alternative verdict on a charge of rape where the evidence does not disclose that the accused achieved sexual intercourse (see **B3.6**) with the victim. There is an obvious overlap with indecent assault.

The mental element in attempted rape is the same as that required for the full offence, namely, an intent to have sexual intercourse coupled with, at least, awareness that the the other may not be consenting (*Khan* [1990] 1 WLR 813). It is not necessary to prove that the accused had gone so far as to attempt physical penetration of the vagina or anus. It suffices if acts be proved which the jury could regard as more than merely preparatory (*A-G's Ref (No. 1 of 1992)* [1993] 1 WLR 274).

PROCURATION BY THREATS OR FALSE PRETENCES

Definitions

Sexual Offences Act 1956, ss. 2 and 3   **B3.10**

2.—(1) It is an offence for a person to procure a woman, by threats or intimidation, to have sexual intercourse in any part of the world.

3.—(1) It is an offence for a person to procure a woman, by false pretences or false representations, to have sexual intercourse in any part of the world.

Procedure

Triable only on indictment. Both offences are class 3 offences.   **B3.11**

Indictment

Statement of Offence   **B3.12**

Procuration contrary to section 2(1) of the Sexual Offences Act 1956

Particulars of Offence

A on or about the . . . day of . . . procured V, a woman, to have unlawful sexual intercourse with him by threats, namely threatening to disclose her past employment as a prostitute to X, her current employer.

Statement of Offence

Procuration contrary to section 3(1) of the Sexual Offences Act 1956

Particulars of Offence

A on or about the . . . day of . . . procured V, a woman, to have sexual intercourse with him by false pretences, namely by falsely pretending that it would improve her singing voice.

Sentencing Guidelines

The maximum penalty for procuration of a woman by threats is two years' imprison- **B3.13** ment (SOA 1956, sch. 2).

The maximum penalty for procuration of a woman by false pretences is two years' imprisonment (SOA 1956, sch. 2).

There are very few reported sentencing cases. In *Harold* (1984) 6 Cr App R (S) 30, the offender telephoned a woman whom he knew to have once been a prostitute, and threatened to disclose that fact to her employers unless she had sexual intercourse with him. A sentence of 12 months' imprisonment, with four to serve and eight suspended, was imposed for the attempt to procure sexual intercourse by threats and was upheld by the Court of Appeal for a 'nasty, mean offence'.

Elements

B3.14   The offences lie in the procuring, which must occur in England, although the intercourse can take place anywhere. They can be committed by a person of either sex. 'Procurement' cannot be said to be complete until the desired goal is actually achieved (*Johnson* [1964] 2 QB 404). It consists of persuasion by one means or another, which actually induces the woman to have sexual intercourse with the accused or another person (*Williams* [1923] 1 KB 340). If the woman consents voluntarily, there is no procurement (*Christian* (1913) 23 Cox CC 541; cf. *A-G's Ref* (*No. 1 of 1975*) [1975] QB 773).

TAKING OUT OF POSSESSION

Definitions

B3.15   **Sexual Offences Act 1956, ss. 17, 19, 20, and 21**

17.—(1)   It is [an offence] for a person to take away or detain a woman against her will with the intention that she shall marry or have unlawful sexual intercourse with that or any other person, if she is so taken away or detained either by force or for the sake of her property or expectations of property.

(2)   In the foregoing subsection, the reference to a woman's expectations of property relates only to property of a person to whom she is next of kin or one of the next of kin, and 'property' includes any interest in property.

19.—(1)   It is an offence, subject to the exception mentioned in this section, for a person to take an unmarried girl under the age of 18 out of the possession of her parent or guardian against his will, if she is so taken with the intention that she shall have unlawful sexual intercourse with men or with a particular man.

(2)   A person is not guilty of an offence under this section because he takes such a girl out of the possession of her parent or guardian as mentioned above, if he believes her to be of the age of 18 or over and has reasonable cause for the belief.

(3)   In this section 'guardian' means any person having parental responsibility for or care of the girl.

20.—(1)   It is an offence for a person acting without lawful authority or excuse to take an unmarried girl under the age of 16 out of the possession of her parent or guardian against his will.

(2)   In the foregoing subsection 'guardian' means any person having parental responsibility for or care of the girl.

21.—(1)   It is an offence, subject to the exception mentioned in this section, for a person to take a woman who is a defective out of the possession of her parent or guardian against his will, if she is so taken with the intention that she shall have unlawful sexual intercourse with men or with a particular man.

(2)   A person is not guilty of an offence under this section because he takes such a woman out of the possession of her parent or guardian as mentioned above, if he does not know and has no reason to suspect her to be a defective.

(3)   In this section 'guardian' means any person having parental responsibility for or care of the woman.

Procedure

B3.16   Abduction is triable only on indictment. These are class 3 offences.

Indictment

B3.17   Statement of Offence

Abduction of an unmarried girl under the age of 18 contrary to section 19(1) of the Sexual Offences Act 1956

Particulars of Offence

A on or about the . . . day of . . . took V, an unmarried girl under the age of 18, out of the possession of her parent, X, against his will and with the intention that she should have unlawful sexual intercourse with men [or with M]

Sentence

The maximum penalty is two years' imprisonment (SOA 1956, s. 37 and sch. 2).   **B3.18**

Elements

A series of cases deals with what must be shown in respect of taking out of possession. **B3.19** In brief, it must first be shown that a girl is in the possession of her parent as distinct from leading an independent life (*Henkers* (1887) 16 Cox CC 257). Several decisions, all of some antiquity, hold that a girl, though absent from her father's house, may yet be in his constructive possession, provided that she intends to return home (*Mycock* (1871) 12 Cox CC 28; *Olifier* (1866) 10 Cox CC 402). Then, it must be shown that there was a taking. This involves the accused having assisted or persuaded the girl to leave her home, an active taking or keeping away (*Alexander* (1912) 7 Cr App R 110). Blandishments will suffice (*Jarvis* (1903) 20 Cox CC 249). It is not enough simply to persuade young girls to go for a walk, even though the actor does so in order to indecently assault them. The accused's conduct must amount to a substantial interference with the possessory relationship of mother and child (*Jones* [1973] Crim LR 621).

In offences under s. 20, it is not a defence that the accused acted from good motives. The accused must show that he had a lawful excuse, which is not the same thing, and the burden of proving this lies with him (*Packer* (1886) 16 Cox CC 57). A putative father may thus not take a child out of the possession of her mother, nor may a person take a child from its parent in order to save the child from influences which he considers to be undesirable (*Tegerdine* (1982) 75 Cr App R 298; *Booth* (1872) 12 Cox CC 231). Sections 19 and 21 each provide a defence based upon lack of guilty knowledge, as to which the accused bears the burden of proof (SOA 1956, s. 47).

It is clear from the wording of ss. 19 and 21, that the offence can be committed by a person of either sex. The offences do not require that the accused intend to cause the woman to engage in prostitution, though they require an intention that she shall have extra-marital intercourse (see *Chapman* [1959] 1 QB 100). The taking of such a woman with intent to marry her or to cause her to marry would fall outside these sections, but may amount to an offence under s. 17, if she is taken away or detained by force, or for the sake of her property or expectations of property.

PROCURATION OF PROSTITUTION OR UNLAWFUL SEXUAL INTERCOURSE

Definitions

Sexual Offences Act 1956, ss. 22 and 23   **B3.20**

22.—(1)   It is an offence for a person—
    (a)   to procure a woman to become, in any part of the world, a common prostitute; or
    (b)   to procure a woman to leave the United Kingdom, intending her to become an inmate of or frequent a brothel elsewhere; or
    (c)   to procure a woman to leave her usual place of abode in the United Kingdom, intending her to become an inmate of or frequent a brothel in any part of the world for the purposes of prostitution.

23.—(1)   It is an offence for a person to procure a girl under the age of 21 to have unlawful sexual intercourse in any part of the world with a third person.

Procedure

B3.21 These offences are triable only on indictment. They are class 3 offences.

Indictment

B3.22   Statement of Offence

Procuring a woman to become a common prostitute contrary to section 22(1)(a) of the Sexual Offences Act 1956

Particulars of Offence

A on or about the . . . day of . . . at . . . procured V, a woman, to become a common prostitute

Sentence

B3.23 The maximum penalty is two years' imprisonment (SOA 1956, s. 37, and sch. 2).

Elements

B3.24 The offence under the SOA 1956, s. 22, will apply to procuration of a woman to perform acts of lewdness for payment. It is not necessary that she be induced to engage in full sexual intercourse (*Webb* [1964] 1 QB 357). 'Procure' means the same as it does under ss. 2 and 3 (see **B3.14**) (*Broadfoot* [1976] 3 All ER 753). Thus any offer of money in return for services may amount to procuration (*Morris-Lowe* [1985] 1 WLR 29). A man cannot be convicted of this offence or of attempting it if he believes that the woman already is a common prostitute (*Brown* [1984] 1 WLR 1211).

Section 23 of the Act makes it an offence for a person to procure a girl under 21 to have intercourse with a third person anywhere in the world. The intercourse must be 'unlawful' (*Chapman* [1959] 1 QB 100); cf. ss. 19 to 21 (see **B3.19**).

CAUSING OR ENCOURAGING PROSTITUTION

Definitions

B3.25   **Sexual Offences Act 1956, ss. 28, 29 and 24**

28.—(1)   It is an offence for a person to cause or encourage the prostitution of, or the commission of unlawful sexual intercourse with, or of an indecent assault on, a girl under the age of 16 for whom he is responsible.

(2)   Where a girl has become a prostitute, or has had unlawful sexual intercourse, or has been indecently assaulted, a person shall be deemed for the purposes of this section to have caused or encouraged it, if he knowingly allowed her to consort with, or to enter or continue in the employment of, any prostitute or person of known immoral character.

(3)   The persons who are to be treated for the purposes of this section as responsible for a girl are (subject to subsection (4) of this section)—

(a)   her parents;

(b)   any person who is not a parent of hers but who has parental responsibility for her; and

(c)   any person who has care of her.

(4)   An individual falling within subsection 3(a) or (b) of this section is not to be treated as responsible for a girl if—

(a)   a residence order under the Children Act 1989 is in force with respect to her and he is not named in the order as the person with whom she is to live; or

(b)   a care order under that Act is in force with respect to her.

(5)   If, on a charge of an offence against a girl under this section, the girl appears to the court to have been under the age of 16 at the time of the offence charged, she shall be presumed for the purposes of this section to have been so, unless the contrary is proved.

29.—(1)   It is an offence, subject to the exception mentioned in this section, for a person to cause or encourage the prostitution in any part of the world of a woman who is a defective.

(2)   A person is not guilty of an offence under this section because he causes or encourages the prostitution of such a woman, if he does not know and has no reason to suspect her to be a defective.

24.—(1)   It is an offence for a person to detain a woman against her will on any premises with the intention that she shall have unlawful sexual intercourse with men or with a particular man, or to detain a woman against her will in a brothel.

(2)   Where a woman is on any premises for the purpose of having unlawful sexual intercourse or is in a brothel, a person shall be deemed for the purpose of the foregoing subsection to detain her there if, with the intention of compelling or inducing her to remain there, he either withholds from her her clothes or any other property belonging to her or threatens her with legal proceedings in the event of her taking away clothes provided for her by him or on his directions.

(3)   A woman shall not be liable to any legal proceedings, whether civil or criminal, for taking away or being found in possession of any clothes she needed to enable her to leave premises on which she was for the purpose of having unlawful sexual intercourse or to leave a brothel.

Procedure

These offences are triable only on indictment. They are class 3 offences.   **B3.26**

Indictment

Statement of Offence   B3.27

Causing or encouraging the prostitution of [or the commission of unlawful sexual intercourse with, or the commission of an indecent assault on] a girl contrary to section 28 of the Sexual Offences Act 1956

Particulars of Offence

A on or about the . . . day of . . . at . . . caused or encouraged the prostitution of [or the commission of unlawful sexual intercourse with, or an indecent assault on] V, a girl under the age of 16 for whom A is responsible

Statement of Offence

Detaining a woman against her will for unlawful sexual intercourse [or in a brothel] contrary to section 24 of the Sexual Offences Act 1956

Particulars of Offence

A on or about the . . . day of . . . detained V, a woman, against her will at . . . intending her to have unlawful sexual intercourse with men [or detained V, a woman, at . . . , a brothel]

Sentence

The maximum penalty is two years' imprisonment in respect of each offence.   **B3.28**

Elements

Under the SOA 1956, s. 28, where any of the three developments specified in the section **B3.29** has occurred, a person who has permitted the girl to consort with or be in the employment of a prostitute or person of known immoral character is deemed to have caused or encouraged such prostitution etc. If a person is present and knows that his acts are encouraging indecency, and is in control of the situation and knows that indecency is likely to occur, then that is capable of being encouragement (*Ralphs* (1913) 9 Cr App R 86). Thus, a man who plies a girl with alcohol, knowing that that will enable another person to engage in familiarities with her, is held to encourage the resulting indecent assault (*Drury* (1974) 60 Cr App R 195). Those persons responsible are a parent or legal guardian, or a person having actual possession or control of the girl, or into whose charge a parent or guardian has committed her, or any person who has the custody, charge or care of her (s. 28(3) and (4)). Whether a person has such custody, charge or care is a question of fact for the jury (*Drury*). There is a presumption as to age based on the youthful appearance of the girl to the trial court (s. 28(5)).

The question arose in *Gillick* v *West Norfolk and Wisbech Area Health Authority* [1986] AC 112 of whether a doctor who prescribes contraceptive advice or treatment to a girl under 16 commits the offence under s. 28. The answer is in the negative. First, as Woolf J pointed out at trial ([1984] QB 581, at p. 593) the girl is not in the *ad hoc* care of the doctor. This point was approved by Lord Bridge in [1986] AC 112, at p. 194. Secondly, the bona fide exercise of clinical judgment is inconsistent with the presence of a guilty mind (per Lord Scarman at p. 190, per Lord Fraser of Tullybelton at p. 175). Thirdly, Woolf J held ([1984] QB 581 at p. 595) that the doctor will not have the particularity of knowledge required to make him a party to the offence.

Detention of a woman in a brothel or other premises for the purpose of sexual intercourse is also an offence. Where a woman is on such premises, a person is deemed to detain her there if he withholds her clothes or other property or threatens her with legal proceedings if she takes away clothing which he provides. A woman who takes away such clothing for the purposes of escape is not liable in criminal or civil proceedings in respect of such taking (SOA 1956, s. 24(3)).

In respect of the offence under s. 29, a person is not guilty of the offence if he does not know, and has no reason to suspect, that the woman whose prostitution he causes or encourages is a defective (s. 29(2)). The burden of proving this lies upon him (s. 47).

ADMINISTRATION OF DRUGS SO AS TO ENABLE UNLAWFUL SEXUAL INTERCOURSE

Definition

B3.30   **Sexual Offences Act 1956, s. 4**

4.—(1)   It is an offence for a person to apply or administer to, or cause to be taken by, a woman any drug, matter or thing with intent to stupefy or overpower her so as thereby to enable any man to have unlawful sexual intercourse with her.

Procedure

B3.31   This offence is triable only on indictment. It is a class 3 offence.

Indictment

B3.32   Statement of Offence

Administering a drug to obtain sexual intercourse contrary to section 4 of the Sexual Offences Act 1956

Particulars of Offence

A on or about the . . . day of . . . administered to V, a woman, a drug, namely . . . , with intent to stupefy or overpower the said V so as to enable X [or men] to have unlawful sexual intercourse with her

Sentence

B3.33   The maximum penalty is two years' imprisonment (SOA 1956, s. 37, and sch. 2).

Elements

B3.34   This is an offence which formerly could not be committed by a husband who proposes to have intercourse with his wife himself but see now *R* [1992] 1 AC 599, the logic of which suggests that a husband can commit it. He could be guilty of an offence of administration with intent to enable another to have intercourse, since this would be unlawful intercourse in any event. The essence of the offence lies in the administering of the drug, and not in the number of persons who seek to take advantage of it in order to have intercourse (*Shillingford* [1968] 1 WLR 566).

SEXUAL INTERCOURSE WITH GIRL UNDER 13

Definition

Sexual Offences Act 1956, s. 5   **B3.35**

5.   It is [an offence] for a man to have unlawful sexual intercourse with a girl under the age of 13.

Procedure

This offence is triable only on indictment. It is a class 2 offence.   **B3.36**

Indictment

Statement of Offence   **B3.37**

Sexual intercourse with a girl under 13 contrary to section 5 of the Sexual Offences Act 1956

Particulars of Offence

A on or about the . . . day of . . . had sexual intercourse with V, a girl under 13 years of age

Alternative Verdicts

Indecent assault. This is necessarily contained within the allegation of unlawful sexual **B3.38** intercourse, and may be left to the jury wherever confirmed by the evidence (*McCormack* [1969] 2 QB 442). As to the position when rape of a girl under 16 is alleged, see **B3.4**. See generally **D16.18** *et seq*.

Sentencing Guidelines

The maximum penalty for sexual intercourse with a girl under 13 is life imprisonment. **B3.39** The maximum penalty for the attempted offence is seven years' imprisonment (SOA 1956, s. 37 and sch. 2).

A number of cases illustrate the sentencing bracket for the offence of unlawful sexual intercourse with a girl under 13. In *Upfield* (1984) 6 Cr App R (S) 63, the offender pleaded guilty to one offence of unlawful sexual intercourse with a girl of 12. The offender had a long-standing relationship with the girl's mother and often acted as a baby-sitter for the daughter. The Court of Appeal said that the offence was 'a gross breach of trust' and a three-year sentence was upheld. In *Polley* [1997] 2 Cr App R (S) 144, a sentence of 30 months' imprisonment was appropriate where a man aged 45 with no previous convictions pleaded guilty to having sexual intercourse with a girl of 12 who was described as 'alert, precocious and sexually experienced'. The girl absconded from care and stayed at the offender's flat. A large quantity of alcohol was consumed and intercourse took place at the girl's request. In *Luff* (1986) 8 Cr App R (S) 318, the offender committed a series of indecent assaults and unlawful sexual intercourse on his stepdaughter, starting when she was aged nine. The Court of Appeal said that there was no error in principle with a sentence of six years' imprisonment for the unlawful sexual intercourse and three years concurrent for the indecent assault, though it was a 'sentence at the top of the appropriate range, perhaps very near the top of it'. In *Robertson* (1988) 10 Cr App R (S) 183, however, a total of 10 years' imprisonment was upheld on an offender who was convicted, after a trial, of four counts of indecent assault and one of unlawful sexual intercourse committed on his two stepdaughters, with whom the offender had sexual intercourse on several occasions over a period of years, threatening them with being taken into a home if they told their mother. Hazan J in the Court of Appeal, said (at p. 185):

This Court approaches its task in this case only too conscious of the increase of sexual child abuse, especially within the home and the concern that is felt about that matter and the need to protect children not only from physical injury but from appalling psychological damage which may blight their lives as they grow from adolescence into adulthood.

In *A-G's Ref (No. 4 of 1991)* (1992) 13 Cr App R (S) 182, the Court of Appeal said that the most useful guide for sentencing in a case of unlawful sexual intercourse on a girl aged under 13 committed by her stepfather were the guidelines for cases of incest given in *A-G's Ref (No. 1 of 1989)* [1989] 1 WLR 1117 (see **B3.66**). In *Brough* [1997] 1 Cr App R (S) 55 a sentence of two years' imprisonment for unlawful sexual intercourse with a girl of 12 was reduced to 15 months on a guilty plea where the offender, a man of 22, had a mild to borderline learning disability. See also *B* (1993) 14 Cr App R (S) 482 and *Bulmer* (1989) 11 Cr App R (S) 586.

Elements

B3.40   The offence is one of strict liability as to age (*Prince* (1875) LR 2 CCR 154). The offence does not require an absence of consent, but if the girl does not consent either this offence or rape may be charged (*Howard* [1966] 1 WLR 13; *Ratcliffe* (1882) 10 QBD 74). For the meaning of 'sexual intercourse', see **B3.6**.

The age of the child at the date of the alleged intercourse must be strictly proved. This may be done by the evidence of a parent or by production of a certified copy of the birth certificate, together with evidence of identity (*Cox* [1898] 1 QB 179; *Weaver* (1873) LR 2 CCR 85; *Bellis* (1911) 6 Cr App R 283; see also **F16.32**). As to the competence of a child of tender years to give evidence, see **F4.15**.

SEXUAL INTERCOURSE WITH GIRL UNDER 16

Definition

B3.41   **Sexual Offences Act 1956, s. 6**

(1)   It is an offence, subject to the exceptions mentioned in this section, for a man to have unlawful sexual intercourse with a girl under the age of 16.

(2)   Where a marriage is invalid under section two of the Marriage Act 1949 or section one of the Age of Marriage Act 1929 (the wife being a girl under the age of 16), the invalidity does not make the husband guilty of an offence under this section because he has sexual intercourse with her, if he believes her to be his wife and has reasonable cause for the belief.

(3)   A man is not guilty of an offence under this section because he has unlawful sexual intercourse with a girl under the age of 16, if he is under the age of 24 and has not previously been charged with a like offence, and he believes her to be of the age of 16 or over and has reasonable cause for the belief.

In this subsection, 'a like offence' means an offence under this section or an attempt to commit one . . .

Procedure

B3.42   Unlawful sexual intercourse with a girl under 16 is triable either way. When tried on indictment it is a class 4 offence. The offence (or an attempt to commit it) must be prosecuted within 12 months of the act complained of (SOA 1956, s. 37 and sch. 2). See also **B3.36**.

The guidelines for determining mode of trial for unlawful sexual intercourse (*Practice Note (Mode of Trial: Guidelines)* (1995): see **D3.7**) are that cases should be tried summarily unless the court considers that one or more of the following features is present *and* that its sentencing powers are insufficient:

1.   Wide disparity of age.
2.   Breach of position of trust.
3.   The victim is particularly vulnerable.

Indictment

B3.43

Statement of Offence

Sexual intercourse with a girl under 16 contrary to section 6 of the Sexual Offences Act 1956

Particulars of Offence

A on or about the . . . day of . . . had unlawful sexual intercourse with V, a girl under 16 years of age

Alternative Verdicts

See **B3.38**.

B3.44

Sentencing Guidelines

The maximum penalty on indictment is two years' imprisonment; summarily, it is six **B3.45** months' imprisonment and/or a fine to the statutory maximum (SOA 1956, s. 37 and sch. 2; MCA 1980, s. 32).

The guideline case on sentencing for unlawful sexual intercourse with a girl under 16 is *Taylor* [1977] 1 WLR 612. According to Lawton LJ (at p. 615):

> At one end of [the] spectrum is the youth who stands in the dock, maybe 16, 17 or 18, who has had what started off as a virtuous friendship with a girl under the age of 16. That virtuous friendship has ended with their having sexual intercourse with one another. At the other end of the spectrum is the man in a supervisory capacity, a schoolmaster or social worker, who sets out deliberately to seduce a girl under the age of 16 who is in his charge. The penalties appropriate for the two types of case to which I have just referred are very different indeed. Nowadays, most judges would take the view, and rightly take the view, that when there is a virtuous friendship which ends in unlawful sexual intercourse, it is inappropriate to pass sentences of a punitive nature. What is required is a warning to the youth to mend his ways. At the other end, a man in a supervisory capacity who abuses his position of trust for his sexual gratification, ought to get a sentence somewhere near the maximum allowed by law, which is two years' imprisonment. In between there come many degrees of guilt. A common type of offender is the youth who picks up a girl of loose morals at a dance, takes her out in to the local park and, behind the bushes, has sexual intercourse with her. That is the kind of offence which normally is dealt with by a fine. When an older man in his twenties, or older, goes off to a dance and picks up a young girl, he can expect to get a much stiffer fine, and if the girl is under 15 he can expect to go to prison for a short time. A young man who deliberately sets out to seduce a girl under the age of 16 can expect to go to detention. The older man who deliberately so sets out can expect to go to prison. Such is the wide variety of penalties which can be applied in this class of case.

In *Goy* (1986) 8 Cr App R (S) 40 the offender pleaded guilty to two counts of unlawful sexual intercourse and admitted having sexual intercourse with his stepdaughter on four occasions. A sentence of two years' imprisonment was upheld. Fifteen months was upheld in *Dewar* (1986) 8 Cr App R (S) 311, where the victim was the 14-year-old stepsister of the offender's wife, who was spending the night at their house. The victim had been drinking during the evening, and in the night the offender, aged 30, went to her room and had sexual intercourse with her. In *Carter* [1997] 1 Cr App R (S) 434 a 32-year-old man pleaded guilty to having sexual intercourse on one occasion with a 14-year-old girl who was the daughter of a neighbour. She became pregnant and gave birth to a child. A sentence of six months' imprisonment was appropriate. See also *Palmer* (1995) 16 Cr App R (S) 642.

Elements

See **B3.40**, dealing with sexual intercourse with girls under 13. This offence also is one **B3.46** of strict liability as to age (*Prince* (1875) LR 2 CCR 154). To this, however, there are the following exceptions, applicable to the offence with a girl under 16:

(a)   Where a marriage is invalid by reason of the wife being under the age of 16, the invalidity does not render the husband guilty of the offence, provided that he believes the girl to be his wife and has reasonable cause for the belief (SOA 1956, s. 6(2)). Such a 'marriage' would be void in law (Marriage Act 1949, s. 2).

(b)   A man who is under the age of 24, who has not previously been charged with the like offence (e.g., an offence or attempted offence under this section), and who believes the girl to be aged 16 or over, and who has reasonable grounds for this belief, is not guilty of the offence. It should be noted that the availability of the defence is premised upon the accused not having been previously charged with a like offence, rather than convicted of it.

Because s. 6 is directed towards the protection of young girls, an under-age girl cannot be convicted of aiding and abetting the man to commit the offence (*Tyrrell* [1894] 1 QB 710).

PERMITTING GIRLS TO USE PREMISES FOR UNLAWFUL SEXUAL INTERCOURSE

Definitions

B3.47   **Sexual Offences Act 1956, ss. 25 and 26**

25.   It is [an offence] for a person who is the owner or occupier of any premises, or who has, or acts or assists in, the management or control of any premises, to induce or knowingly suffer a girl under the age of 13 to resort to or be on those premises for the purpose of having unlawful sexual intercourse with men or with a particular man.

26.   It is an offence for a person who is the owner or occupier of any premises, or who has, or acts or assists in, the management or control of any premises, to induce or knowingly suffer a girl under the age of 16, to resort to or be on those premises for the purpose of having unlawful sexual intercourse with men or with a particular man.

Procedure

B3.48   An offence under the SOA 1956, s. 25, is triable only on indictment. It is a class 3 offence. An offence under s. 26 is triable either way. When tried on indictment it is a class 4 offence.

Indictment

B3.49   Statement of Offence

Inducing a girl under the age of 13 to use premises for unlawful sexual intercourse contrary to section 25 of the Sexual Offences Act 1956

Particulars of Offence

A on or about the . . . day of . . . at . . . , being the owner or occupier [or having, or acting or assisting in, the management or control] of premises, namely . . . , induced or knowingly suffered V, a girl under the age of 13, to resort to or be on the said premises for the purpose of having unlawful sexual intercourse with men [or with M, a man]

Statement of Offence

Permitting a girl aged between 13 and 16 to use premises for unlawful sexual intercourse contrary to section 26 of the Sexual Offences Act 1956

Particulars of Offence

A on or about the . . . day of . . . at . . . , being the owner or occupier [or having, or acting or assisting in, the management or control] of premises, namely . . . , induced or knowingly suffered V, a girl aged between 13 and 16, to resort to or be on the said premises for the purpose of having unlawful sexual intercourse with men [or with M, a man]

Sentence

The maximum penalty for an offence under the SOA 1956, s. 25, is life imprisonment. **B3.50**
The maximum penalty for an offence under s. 26 is two years' imprisonment on
indictment; six months' imprisonment and/or a fine to the statutory maximum
summarily. (SOA 1956, s. 37 and sch. 2; MCA 1980, s. 32.)

Elements

The words 'knowingly suffer' require that the prosecution prove that the accused knew **B3.51**
of the girl's purpose in resorting to the premises. A person is said to suffer a girl to be on
premises for the purpose of engaging in unlawful sexual intercourse where he or she
knows why the girl has resorted to the premises, and having the power to prevent such
acts occurring, fails to do so (*Webster* (1885) 16 QBD 134).

SEXUAL INTERCOURSE WITH AND PROCUREMENT
OF MENTAL DEFECTIVES

Definitions

Sexual Offences Act 1956, ss. 7, 9, and 27   **B3.52**

7.—(1)   It is an offence, subject to the exception mentioned in this section, for a man to
have unlawful sexual intercourse with a woman who is defective.
  (2)   A man is not guilty of an offence under this section because he has unlawful sexual
intercourse with a woman if he does not know and has no reason to suspect her to be a
defective.

9.—(1)   It is an offence, subject to the exception mentioned in this section, for a person to
procure a woman who is a defective to have unlawful sexual intercourse in any part of the
world.
  (2)   A person is not guilty of an offence under this section because he procures a
defective to have unlawful sexual intercourse, if he does not know and has no reason to
suspect her to be a defective.

27.—(1)   It is an offence, subject to the exception mentioned in this section, for a person
who is the owner or occupier of any premises, or who has, or acts or assists in, the
management or control of any premises, to induce or knowingly suffer a woman who is a
defective to resort to or be on those premises for the purpose of having unlawful sexual
intercourse with men or with a particular man.
  (2)   A person is not guilty of an offence under this section because he induces or
knowingly suffers a defective to resort to or be on any premises for the purpose mentioned,
if he does not know and has no reason to suspect her to be a defective.

Procedure

These offences are triable only on indictment. They are class 3 offences.   **B3.53**

Indictment

Statement of Offence   **B3.54**

Sexual intercourse with a woman who is defective contrary to section 7 of the Sexual
Offences Act 1956

Particulars of Offence

A on or about the . . . day of . . . at . . . had unlawful sexual intercourse with V, a woman
who is defective

Statement of Offence

Procuring a woman who is a defective to have unlawful sexual intercourse conrary to section
9 of the Sexual Offences Act 1956

Particulars of Offence

A on or about the . . . day of . . . procured V, a woman who is defective, to have unlawful sexual intercourse

Sentence

B3.55 The maximum penalty is two years' imprisonment in each case (SOA 1956, s. 37 and sch. 2).

Elements

B3.56 'Defective', for the purposes of the SOA 1956, means a person suffering from a state of arrested or incomplete development of mind, which includes severe impairment of intelligence and social functioning (s. 46). Severe impairment is to be measured against the standard of the normal person (*Hall* (1987) 86 Cr App R 159). The consent of such a woman is not a defence. On the other hand, the man does have a defence if he does not know, and has no reason to suspect, that the woman is a defective. This defence also applies to s. 9 of the Act. The accused must, by reason of s. 47, prove this defence. The offence of procuration by false pretences under s. 3 may, furthermore, apply where the woman is not so mentally defective as to fall within s. 9, but is more readily open to persuasion because of her mental condition.

SEXUAL INTERCOURSE WITH PATIENTS

Definitions

B3.57   **Mental Health Act 1959, s. 128**

(1)   Without prejudice to section 7 of the Sexual Offences Act 1956, it shall be an offence, subject to the exception mentioned in this section,—

(a)   for a man who is an officer on the staff of or is otherwise employed in, or is one of the managers of, a hospital or mental nursing home to have unlawful sexual intercourse with a woman who is for the time being receiving treatment for mental disorder in that hospital or home, or to have such intercourse on the premises of which the hospital or home forms part with a woman who is for the time being receiving such treatment there as an out-patient;

(b)   for a man to have unlawful sexual intercourse with a woman who is a mentally disordered patient and who is subject to his guardianship under the Mental Health Act 1983 or is otherwise in his custody or care under the Mental Health Act 1983 or in pursuance of arrangements under part III of the National Assistance Act 1948 or the National Health Service Act 1977, or as a resident in a residential care home within the meaning of part I of the Registered Homes Act 1984.

(2)   It shall not be an offence under this section for a man to have sexual intercourse with a woman if he does not know and has no reason to suspect her to be a mentally disordered patient.

(3)   Any person guilty of an offence under this section shall be liable on conviction on indictment to imprisonment for a term not exceeding two years.

(4)   No proceedings shall be instituted for an offence under this section except by or with the consent of the Director of Public Prosecutions.

(5)   This section shall be construed as one with the Sexual Offences Act 1956; and section 47 of that Act (which relates to the proof of exceptions) shall apply to the exception mentioned in this section.

Sexual Offences Act 1967, s. 1

(4)   Section 128 of the Mental Health Act 1959 (prohibition on men on the staff of a hospital, or otherwise having responsibility for mental patients, having sexual intercouse with women patients) shall have effect as if any reference therein to having unlawful sexual intercourse with a woman included a reference to committing buggery or an act of gross indecency with another man.

Procedure

This offence is triable only on indictment. It is a class 3 offence. Proceedings may be **B3.58** instituted only by or with the consent of the DPP.

Indictment

Statement of Offence   **B3.59**

Sexual intercourse with a patient contrary to section 128 of the Mental Health Act 1959

Particulars of Offence

A on or about the . . . of . . . at . . . , being an officer on the staff of [or an employee of, or a manager of] . . . , a hospital [or mental nursing home], had unlawful sexual intercourse with V, a woman who was receiving treatment

Sentence

The maximum penalty is two years' imprisonment (Mental Health Act 1959, s. 128(3)). **B3.60** The maximum sentence was upheld in *Goodwin* (1995) 16 Cr App R (S) 144, where a psychiatric nurse was convicted on two counts of sexual intercourse with a patient, displaying a gross and deliberate breach of trust.

Elements

A man who does not know and who does not suspect a woman to be a defective does **B3.61** not commit an offence under the Mental Health Act 1959, s. 128 (s. 128(2)). The section provides that he must, however, by reason of the SOA 1956, s. 47, prove this defence. Note that the SOA 1967, s. 1(4) requires s. 128 of the 1959 Act to be construed to include sexual acts with male patients, such acts being excluded from the legalisation of homosexual acts between consenting adults committed in private.

INCEST

Definitions

Sexual Offences Act 1956, ss. 10 and 11   **B3.62**

10.—(1) It is an offence for a man to have sexual intercourse with a woman whom he knows to be his granddaughter, daughter, sister or mother.

(2) In the foregoing subsection 'sister' includes half-sister, and for the purposes of that subsection any expression importing a relationship between two people shall be taken to apply notwithstanding that the relationship is not traced through lawful wedlock.

11.—(1) It is an offence for a woman of the age of 16 or over to permit a man whom she knows to be her grandfather, father, brother or son to have sexual intercourse with her by her consent.

(2) In the foregoing subsection 'brother' includes half-brother, and for the purposes of that subsection any expression importing a relationship between two people shall be taken to apply notwithstanding that the relationship is not traced through lawful wedlock.

Criminal Law Act 1977, s. 54

(1) It is an offence for a man to incite to have sexual intercourse with him a girl under the age of 16 whom he knows to be his granddaughter, daughter or sister.

(2) In the preceding subsection 'man' includes boy, 'sister' includes half-sister, and for the purposes of that subsection any expression importing a relationship between two people shall be taken to apply notwithstanding that the relationship is not traced through lawful wedlock.

(3) The following provisions of section 1 of the Indecency with Children Act 1960, namely—

subsection (3) (references in Children and Young Persons Act 1933 to the offences mentioned in Schedule 1 to that Act to include offences under that section);

subsection (4) (offences under that section to be deemed offences against the person for the purpose of section 3 of the Visiting Forces Act 1952),

shall apply in relation to offences under this section.

(4)   A person guilty of an offence under this section shall be liable—

(a)   on summary conviction, to imprisonment for a term not exceeding six months or to a fine not exceeding the prescribed sum, or both;

(b)   on conviction on indictment, to imprisonment for a term not exceeding two years.

Procedure

B3.63   Offences under the SOA 1956, ss. 10 and 11, are triable only on indictment. Offences under the Criminal Law Act 1977, s. 54, are triable either way.

Offences under the SOA 1956, ss. 10 and 11, are class 3 offences (except where the female is under 13, when they are within class 2), and proceedings for them may be instituted only by or with the consent of the DPP. An offence under the Criminal Law Act 1977, s. 54, is a class 4 offence when tried on indictment.

Indictment

B3.64

Statement of Offence

Incest by a man contrary to section 10(1) of the Sexual Offences Act 1956

Particulars of Offence

A on or about the . . . of . . . , being a man, had sexual intercourse with V, a woman [or a girl under the age of 13] whom he knew to be his granddaughter [or daughter, sister or mother]

Statement of Offence

Incest by a woman contrary to section 11(1) of the Sexual Offences Act 1956

Particulars of Offence

A on or about the . . . of . . . , being a woman aged . . . , with her consent permitted M, a man whom she knew to be her grandfather [or father, brother or son] to have sexual intercourse with her

Statement of Offence

Incitement to incest contrary to section 54 of the Criminal Law Act 1977

Particulars of Offence

A on or about the . . . of . . . at . . . , being a man, incited V, a girl under the age of 16, whom he knew to be his granddaughter [or daughter or sister] to have sexual intercourse with him

Alternative Verdicts

B3.65   On a charge of incest by a man under the SOA 1956, s. 10, the jury may convict of unlawful sexual intercourse either under s. 5 or under s. 6, as appropriate (see generally, **B3.35** *et seq.*; **B3.41** *et seq.*), or, where the female is under 16, indecent assault (SOA 1956, s. 37 and sch. 2; *Rogina* (1975) 64 Cr App R 79 n; and see **B3.4** and **B3.38**). Indecent assault is presumably also an alternative on a charge under s. 11 of the 1956 Act where the boy is under 16.

Sentencing Guidelines

B3.66   The maximum penalties are as follows.

Incest by a man with a girl under 13: Life imprisonment (SOA 1956, s. 37 and sch. 2).
Incest by a man with a female over 13: Seven years (SOA 1956, s. 37 and sch. 2).
Incest by a woman: Seven years (SOA 1956, s. 37 and sch. 2).

Attempted incest by a man with a girl under 13: Seven years (SOA 1956, s. 37 and sch. 2).

Attempted incest by a man with a female over 13: Two years (SOA 1956, s. 37 and sch. 2).

Attempted incest by a woman: Two years (SOA 1956, s. 37 and sch. 2).

Incitement by a man of a girl under 16 whom he knows to be his granddaughter, daughter or sister to have sexual intercourse with him: Two years on indictment; six months or a fine not exceeding the statutory maximum, or both, summarily (Criminal Law Act 1977, s. 54(4)).

The guideline case is *A-G's Ref (No. 1 of 1989)* [1989] 1 WLR 1117. The guidelines also apply to cases where the victim stands in a family relationship with the offender which is too remote to make the case one of incest (*A-G's Ref (No. 4 of 1991)* (1992) 13 Cr App R (S) 182). According to Lord Lane CJ in *A-G's Ref (No. 1 of 1989)*:

> . . . it is stating the obvious to say that the gravity of the offence of incest varies greatly according, primarily, to the age of the victim and the related matter, namely, the degree of coercion or corruption.

> At one end of the scale is incest committed by a father with a daughter in her late teens or older who is a willing participant and indeed may be the instigator of the offences. In such a case the court usually need do little more than mark the fact that there has been a breach of the law and little, if anything, is required in the way of punishment.

> The next class of case is that where the girl has achieved the age of 13, which in most cases will mean that she has achieved puberty. This of course is the demarcation line chosen in the Sexual Offences Act 1956. . . .

> The last and much the most difficult area is that involving girls under the age of 13. As in the case of those between 13 and 16, sexual intercourse is an offence, quite apart from the parental relationship. For victims under the age of 13 however a further factor comes into play. Although the girl may 'consent' to the act of intercourse in such a way as to render a charge of rape inappropriate, the girl is from the very relationship in a particularly vulnerable position, which the father is in a position to exploit due to her dependence and inexperience and possibly fear. . . .

> . . . we venture to make the following suggestions as a broad guide to the level of sentence for various categories of the crime of incest. All are on the assumption that there has been no plea of guilty.

> (1) *Where the girl is over 16*
> Generally speaking a range from three years' imprisonment down to a nominal penalty will be appropriate depending in particular on the one hand on whether force was used, and upon the degree of harm, if any, to the girl, and on the other the desirability where it exists of keeping family disruption to a minimum. The older the girl the greater the possibility that she may have been willing or even the instigating party to the liaison, a factor which will be reflected in the sentence. In other words, the lower the degree of corruption, the lower the penalty.

> (2) *Where the girl is aged from 13 to 16*
> Here a sentence between about five years and three years seems on the authorities to be appropriate. Much the same principles will apply as in the case of a girl over 16, though the likelihood of corruption increases in inverse proportion to the age of the girl. Nearly all the cases in this and in other categories have involved pleas of guilty and the sentences in this category seem to range between about two and four years, credit having been given for the plea.

> (3) *Where the girl is under 13*
> It is here that the widest range of sentence is likely to be found. If one can properly describe any case of incest as the 'ordinary' type of case, it will be one where the sexual relationship between husband and wife has broken down; the father has probably resorted to excessive drinking and the eldest daughter is gradually, by way of familiarities, indecent acts and

suggestions made the object of the father's frustrated sexual inclinations. If the girl is not far short of her thirteenth birthday and there are no particularly adverse or favourable features on a not guilty plea, a term of about six years on the authorities would seem to be appropriate. It scarcely needs to be stated that the younger the girl when the sexual approach is started, the more likely it will be that the girl's will was overborne and accordingly the more serious would be the crime.

Other aggravating factors, whatever the age of the girl may be, are (*inter alia*) as follows:

(1) If there is evidence that the girl has suffered physically or psychologically from the incest.
(2) If the incest has continued at frequent intervals over a long period of time.
(3) If the girl has been threatened or treated violently by or was terrified of the father.
(4) If the incest has been accompanied by perversions abhorrent to the girl, e.g., buggery or fellatio.
(5) If the girl has become pregnant by reason of the father failing to take contraceptive measures.
(6) If the defendant has committed similar offences against more than one girl.

Possible mitigating features are (*inter alia*) the following:

(1) A plea of guilty. It is seldom that such a plea is not entered, and it should be met by an appropriate discount, depending on the usual considerations, that is to say how promptly the defendant confessed and his degree of contrition and so on.
(2) If it seems that there was a genuine affection on the part of the defendant rather than the intention to use the girl simply as an outlet for his sexual inclinations.
(3) Where the girl has had previous sexual experience.
(4) Where the girl has made deliberate attempts at seduction.
(5) Where, as very occasionally is the case, a shorter term of imprisonment for the father may be of benefit to the victim and the family. (per Lord Lane CJ, at pp. 412-14)

Cases of incest by a father with a daughter under the age of 13 are *Hardcastle* (1985) 7 Cr App R (S) 270 (seven years' imprisonment), *Palmer* (1988) 10 Cr App R (S) 179 (10 years upheld), and *Meggs* (1989) 11 Cr App R (S) 96 (sentences reduced to total of seven years and six months); with a daughter aged between 13 and 16, *Martin* (1988) 10 Cr App R (S) 367 (sentence reduced to three years), and *Jones* (1987) 9 Cr App R (S) 130 (sentence reduced to three years); and with a daughter aged over 16, *White* (1989) 11 Cr App R (S) 186 (sentence reduced to 18 months). A case of incest committed by brother and sister is *Harding* (1989) 11 Cr App R (S) 190, where the brother admitted that incest had occurred on about 50 occasions over a period of time between when he was aged 13 and 20. The sister was three years younger than he. A sentence of three years was reduced to 18 months.

A 'wholly exceptional' case is *A-G's Ref No. 4 of 1989* (1989) 11 Cr App R (S) 517. The Court of Appeal, in a case where the father had committed incest with his 15-year-old daughter, varied a suspended sentence to a probation order for three years with requirements of residence and compliance with treatment and counselling. The court paid close attention to the complex family relationships involved, the best interests of the victim and the rest of the family, a range of relevant mitigating factors and the counselling and social work which was taking place within the family since the offences had come to light.

In *Richard Stephen C* (1990) 12 Cr App R (S) 292, the point was made that where a father had been convicted of rape of his daughter, the appropriate guidelines were those given in *Billam* [1986] 1 WLR 349 (set out at **B3.5**) and not the incest guidelines.

Elements

B3.67 Incest applies only to acts of sexual intercourse and not to other indecent acts within the familial relationship. A boy aged under 14 is now capable of committing the offence. Formerly he was not, and therefore could not be incited to commit incest. The principle will continue to be important in respect of cases arising before the law was reformed (*Pickford* [1994] 3 WLR 1022). As to the meaning of 'sexual intercourse', see **B3.6**. A man who has intercourse with a non-consenting woman within the categories mentioned may be convicted of rape as well as incest. 'Brother' and 'sister' extend to half-blood relationships, but the relationships do not include step-parents (*Gedderson* (1906) 25 NZLR 323). Adoptive parents are not included, but the law of incest applies to subsequent sexual relationships between the adopted child and members of his original family (Adoption Act 1976, s. 47(1)). The relationship between the accused and the sexual partner need not be traced through lawful wedlock, so that illegitimate relationships are included. The offences require *mens rea*, inasmuch as the accused must know of the relationship. Obviously, this will usually be the case. But see, as to the defences of mistake and intoxication, **A3.2** and **A3.8** *et seq.*

BUGGERY

Definition

Sexual Offences Act 1956, ss. 12 and 16

B3.68

12.—(1)   It is [an offence] for a person to commit buggery with another person otherwise than in the circumstances described in subsection (1A) below.

(1A)   The circumstances referred to in subsection (1) are that the act of buggery takes place in private and both parties have attained the age of eighteen.

(1B)   An act of buggery by one man with another shall not be treated as taking place in private if it takes place—

(a)   when more than two persons take part or are present; or

(b)   in a lavatory to which the public have or are permitted to have access, whether on payment or otherwise.

(1C)   In any proceedings against a person for buggery with another person it shall be for the prosecutor to prove that the act of buggery took place otherwise than in private or that one of the parties to it had not attained the age of eighteen.

16.   It is an offence for a person to assault another person with intent to commit buggery.

Sexual Offences Act 1967, ss. 1, 4, 7, and 8

1.—(1)   Notwithstanding any statutory or common-law provision, a homosexual act in private shall not be an offence provided that the parties consent thereto and have attained the age of 18 years.

(2)   An act which would otherwise be treated for the purposes of this Act as being done in private shall not be so treated if done—

(a)   when more than two persons take part or are present; or

(b)   in a lavatory to which the public have or are permitted to have access, whether on payment or otherwise.

(3)   A man who is suffering from severe mental handicap cannot in law give any consent which, by virtue of subsection (1) of this section, would prevent a homosexual act from being an offence, but a person shall not be convicted, on account of the incapacity of such a man to consent, of an offence consisting of such an act if he proves that he did not know and had no reason to suspect that man to be suffering from severe mental handicap.

(3A)   In subsection (3) of this section 'severe mental handicap' means a state of arrested or incomplete development of mind which includes severe impairment of intelligence and social functioning.

(4)   Section 128 of the Mental Health Act 1959 (prohibition on men on the staff of a hospital, or otherwise having responsibility for mental patients, having sexual intercourse with women patients) shall have effect as if any reference therein to having unlawful sexual intercourse with a woman included a reference to committing buggery or an act of gross indecency with another man.

(5)   [Repealed.]

(6)   It is hereby declared that where in any proceedings it is charged that a homosexual act is an offence the prosecutor shall have the burden of proving that the act was done

otherwise than in private or otherwise than with the consent of the parties or that any of the parties had not attained the age of 18 years.

(7)   For the purposes of this section a man shall be treated as doing a homosexual act if, and only if, he commits buggery with another man or commits an act of gross indecency with another man or is a party to the commission by a man of such an act.

4.—(1)   A man who procures another man to commit with a third man an act of buggery which by reason of section 1 of this Act is not an offence shall be liable on conviction on indictment to imprisonment for a term not exceeding two years.

(2)   . . .

(3)   It shall not be an offence under section 13 of the Act of 1956 for a man to procure the commission by another man of an act of gross indecency with the first-mentioned man which by reason of section 1 of this Act is not an offence under the said section 13.

7.—(1)   No proceedings for an offence to which this section applies shall be commenced after the expiration of 12 months from the date on which that offence was committed.

(2)   This section applies to—

(a)   any offence under section 13 of the Act of 1956 (gross indecency between men);
(b)   . . .
(c)   any offence of buggery by a man with another man not amounting to an assault on that other man and not being an offence by a man with a boy under the age of 16.

8.   No proceedings shall be instituted except by or with the consent of the DPP against any man for the offence of buggery with, or gross indecency with, another man, or for aiding, abetting, counselling, procuring or commanding its commission where either of those men was at the time of its commission under the age of 21.

Procedure

B3.69   This offence is triable only on indictment. It is a class 3 offence.

Proceedings for an offence of buggery by a man with another man not amounting to an assault, other than an offence by a man with a boy under the age of 16, are subject to a time-limit – proceedings must be commenced within 12 months of the commission of the offence (SOA 1967, s. 7). Proceedings for any offence of buggery, either as a principal or an accessory, by a man with another man, where either man was under 16 at the time of the commission of the offence, may be instituted only by or with the consent of the DPP (SOA 1967, s. 8).

Indictment

B3.70   Statement of Offence

Buggery contrary to section 12 of the Sexual Offences Act 1956

Particulars of Offence

A on the . . . day of . . . committed buggery with V, a male person under the age of 18 years, namely 16 years of age

As to the drafting of indictments for buggery, see *Courtie* [1984] AC 463 at **B3.72**.

Alternative Verdicts

B3.71   Where the accused's sexual partner is under 16, indecent assault (SOA 1956, ss. 14 and 15: see **B3.79** *et seq*.).

Sentencing Guidelines

B3.72   The maximum penalties are as follows:

Buggery: If with a person under the age of 16 or with an animal: Life imprisonment; if the accused is of or over the age of 21 and the other person is under the age of 18, five years, but otherwise two years (SOA 1956, sch. 2).

Attempted buggery: If with a person under the age of 16 or with an animal: Life imprisonment; if the accused is of or over the age of 21 and the other person is under the age of 18, five years, but otherwise two years (SOA 1956, sch. 2, as amended).

Where buggery of a male or a female victim is committed without consent on or after 3 November 1994, the offence will be charged as rape (see **B3.1**). For such an offence committed before that date the maximum sentences formerly available (10 years in the case of a male victim and life imprisonment in respect of a female victim) will still apply. If an offender is convicted of buggery, it is no longer open to the sentencer to pass sentence on the basis that the buggery was non-consensual (*Davies* [1998] 1 Cr App R (S) 380). According to the Court of Appeal in that case, it is clearly not permissible for a person convicted of buggery to be sentenced on the basis that he has committed rape.

The guideline case is *Willis* [1975] 1 WLR 292, which dealt with buggery committed between an adult and a partner under the age of 16. Lawton LJ said that, in the absence of strong mitigating factors, the offence should result in immediate custody; should there be neither aggravating nor mitigating factors, the correct bracket was three to five years, with placement in the bracket depending on the age, intelligence and education of the offender. Aggravating factors include:

(a)   physical injury to the boy, whether by the penetration itself or by the use of force to overcome his resistance;
(b)   emotional and psychological damage to the victim;
(c)   moral corruption (use of gifts to corrupt boys);
(d)   abuse of authority or trust.

Mitigating factors include:

(e)   the offender having been in a state of emotional stress; or
(f)   suffering from mental illness.

Where the offender is suffering from a personality disorder which does not justify a hospital order, Lawton LJ advised that a probation order with a condition of psychiatric treatment might be appropriate, but if the offender represented a danger to boys if at liberty, a lengthy custodial sentence was necessary to protect other victims.

In *A-G's Ref (No. 43 of 1994)* (1995) 16 Cr App R (S) 815, the Court of Appeal noted that, for cases involving significant aggravating features (such as a sustained course of conduct against a number of boys) or where there had been gross breach of trust and authority, a sentence significantly longer than the five years referred to in *Willis* would be appropriate, somewhere between six and 10 years. Recent decisions in which the guidelines in *Willis* have been followed and applied include *Malloy* [1997] 1 Cr App R (S) 189, where seven years' imprisonment was reduced to five years for a single count of buggery on a boy aged 15 where the offender had contested the case and had shown no remorse for what he had done, and *A-G's Ref (No. 31 of 1996)* [1997] 1 Cr App R (S) 308, where a sentence of two years' imprisonment together with an order under the CJA 1991, s. 44, was increased to three and a half years' imprisonment on an offender who pleaded guilty to one count of buggery with a boy aged 13, to whom he had paid £10. The sentence would have been somewhat longer in this case without the element of double jeopardy involved in re-sentencing the offender. In *Bradley* [1998] 1 Cr App R (S) 432, the offender, a man of 24, pleaded guilty to buggery of a boy aged 15. They had met at a club which was a meeting place for homosexuals and the boy stayed at the offender's flat for two nights. Buggery took place on one occasion. The Court of Appeal said that the appropriate sentence was 18 months' imprisonment, which was 'at the lower end of the range'. See also *Wells* [1999] 1 Cr App R (S) 320.

Where consenting parties to a homosexual act are both over 18, but the act is still a criminal offence because of its taking place in a cubicle in a public lavatory, a custodial sentence is wrong in principle (*Tosland* (1981) 3 Cr App R (S) 364). The case was followed in *Bedborough* (1984) 6 Cr App R (S) 98 and *Dighton* (1983) 5 Cr App R (S) 233. In both cases the Court of Appeal said that the proper sentence would have been a fine.

In one case involving buggery of a dog, *Higson* (1984) 6 Cr App R (S) 20, a probation order was substituted for a two-year prison term by the Court of Appeal, on the basis that 'it is the appellant, and indeed his wife, and not the dog, who need help'. A custodial sentence of three months was imposed in *Tierney* (1991) 12 Cr App R (S) 216 where the defendant had persuaded his wife to commit sexual acts with their dog. Photographs of the incident were later seen by staff at a processing laboratory. In *P* (1992) 13 Cr App R (S) 369 the defendant pleaded guilty to attempted buggery with a dog, a video recording of the incident later being sent to the woman's employer by the man she was living with, who had persuaded her to commit the offence. Three months' imprisonment was varied to allow the woman's immediate release from prison.

Elements

B3.73 The effect of the substantial amendments made to the SOA 1956, s. 12, by the CJPO 1994, s. 143, is that buggery between males or between a man and a woman is no longer an offence provided that there is consent and provided that the conduct takes place in private. If there is no consent, the offence will be rape whether it takes place in private or not. This follows from the revised wording of the SOA 1956, s. 1. If there is consent but the conduct takes place otherwise than in private, the offence will continue to be buggery, as it will if committed with an animal.

Buggery is defined by the common law as carnal copulation against nature by human beings with each other or with a beast (1 East PC 480). Both partners, active and passive, are liable for the offence. The intercourse against nature consists of anal intercourse by a man with another or with a woman (*Wiseman* (1718) Fort 91). It also comprehends anal or vaginal intercourse by a man or a woman with an animal, e.g., a dog (*Bourne* (1952) 36 Cr App R 125), an ewe (*Cozins* (1834) 6 C & P 351), or a duck or fowl (*Brown* (1889) 24 QBD 357). It does not comprehend oral intercourse (*Jacobs* (1817) Russ & Ry 331). A husband can commit buggery upon his wife (*Jellyman* (1838) 8 C & P 604). Penetration must be proved, but by the SOA 1956, s. 44, the emission of seed need not be proved.

Notwithstanding the amendments to the SOA 1956, s. 12, a wide range of homosexual acts will still constitute one or other criminal offences. A defence of consent applies in respect of such activities. The SOA 1967, s. 1(1), provides that a homosexual act in private shall not be an offence, provided that it takes place between consenting males, each of whom has attained the age of 18 years. This exemption applies as between men and not as respects an act of buggery or gross indecency committed by a man with a woman. This follows from the SOA 1967, s. 1(7), which has not been repealed and which specifies that a man shall be treated as doing a homosexual act if, and only if, his actions are with another man (see definition at **B3.68**). It follows that consensual buggery as between man and man and man and woman is not an offence where it takes place in private (by reason of the amendments to the SOA 1956, s. 12, and the instant provision). Gross indecency between men is, by the force of the instant provision, not an offence where it is committed in private. Indecent conduct between man and woman is not an offence under the SOA 1956, s. 13 (see **B3.74**). 'Man' means biological man and does not include a person who has undergone a sex change operation (*Tan* [1983] QB 1053). 'Private place' is not defined in the statute: the question is one of fact in the light of the surrounding circumstances, the time, the place, the lighting, and the likelihood of a third party coming on the scene (*Reakes* [1974] Crim LR 615). There is strict liability as to age for the defence to apply; the parties must actually be of the requisite age — mistaken belief as to age, however reasonable, will not suffice (*Prince* (1875) LR 2 CCR 154).

The decriminalisation of consensual homosexual acts does not limit or affect the right of the competent authority to discharge any person serving in HM forces or on merchant ships who, but for the provisions of the CJPO 1994, s. 146, would have been guilty of a criminal offence.

A person suffering from a severe mental handicap cannot give an effective consent for the purposes of the section (SOA 1967, s. 1(3)). An accused person has a defence if he proves that he did not know, and had no reason to suspect, that the other party so suffered.

By the SOA 1967, s. 4, it is an offence to procure a man to commit with another man an act of buggery which would not otherwise be an offence because of the exemption from liability of homosexual acts between consenting male adults in private. It is also an offence for a person to assault another with intent to commit buggery (SOA 1956, s. 16(1)).

GROSS INDECENCY

Definitions

Sexual Offences Act 1956, s. 13   B3.74

It is an offence for a man to commit an act of gross indecency with another man, whether in public or private, or to be a party to the commission by a man of an act of gross indecency with another man, or to procure the commission by a man of an act of gross indecency with another man.

This is no longer generally an offence if committed in private by consenting persons over the age of 18 (SOA 1967, ss. 1 and 4(3)).

Procedure

This offence is triable either way. It is a class 4 offence. Proceedings for this offence may **B3.75** not be commenced after the expiration of 12 months from the commission of the offence (SOA 1967, s. 7). Where either man was under 21 years of age at the time of commission, proceedings may be instituted only by or with the consent of the DPP (s. 8).

Indictment

Statement of Offence   B3.76

Gross indecency between men contrary to section 13 of the Sexual Offences Act 1956

Particulars of Offence

A on the . . . day of . . . at . . . committed [or was a party to the commission by M, a man, of] [or procured the commission by M, a man, of] an act of gross indecency with V, a man

As to the desirability of alleging the age of the person with whom the offence is committed, see *Courtie* [1984] AC 463 at **B3.72**.

Sentencing Guidelines

The maximum penalties are as follows: **B3.77**

Gross indecency between men: If by a man of or over the age of 21 with a man under the age of 18, five years; otherwise two years, on indictment; six months, a fine not exceeding the statutory maximum, or both, summarily (SOA 1956, sch. 2).

An attempt to procure the commission by a man of an act of gross indecency with another man: same penalties as for indecency between men.

The guideline case on the offence of gross indecency between men is *Morgan* (1978) CSP B4–9.2(B), where the offenders, aged 61 and 39, had been seen committing an act of gross indecency in a public lavatory. Lawton LJ said:

> In general first offenders using public lavatories and behaving in this sort of way in them do not get sent to prison. They are generally fined. On occasions they may be put on probation or some other non-custodial order is made . . . Occasionally those who are convicted persist in this kind of behaviour and when they do, prison sentences may be appropriate.

See also *Clayton* (1981) 3 Cr App R (S) 67. In a case of importuning for an immoral purpose, *Gray* (1981) 3 Cr App R (S) 363, a fine was also held to be the appropriate sentence.

Elements

B3.78   Consenting males over 18 who act in private do not commit the offence (SOA 1967, ss. 1 and 4(3)). Section 4(3) is in contrast to the corresponding situation of procuration of buggery (s. 4(1) and **B3.68**), which remains an offence even where the act itself is not criminal. The two men involved in the act must be acting in concert, and there must be at least some participation and cooperation by both (*Preece* [1977] QB 370), but actual physical contact between them is not necessary (*Hornby* [1946] 2 All ER 487). The acquittal of one accused is no bar to the conviction of the other, whether they are charged in the same count or separate counts (*Jones* [1896] 1 QB 4; *Pearce* [1951] 1 All ER 493).

INDECENT ASSAULT

Definitions

B3.79   **Sexual Offences Act 1956, ss. 14 and 15**

> **14.**—(1)   It is offence, subject to the exception mentioned in subsection (3) of this section, for a person to make an indecent assault on a woman.
>   (2)   A girl under the age of 16 cannot in law give any consent which would prevent an act being an assault for the purposes of this section.
>   (3)   Where a marriage is invalid under section 2 of the Marriage Act 1949 or section 1 of the Age of Marriage Act 1929 (the wife being a girl under the age of 16), the invalidity does not make the husband guilty of any offence under this section by reason of her incapacity to consent while under that age, if he believes her to be his wife and has reasonable cause for the belief.
>   (4)   A woman who is a defective cannot in law give any consent which would prevent an act being an assault for the purposes of this section, but a person is only to be treated as guilty of an indecent assault on a defective by reason of that incapacity to consent, if that person knew or had reason to suspect her to be a defective.
>
> **15.**—(1)   It is an offence for a person to make an indecent assault on a man.
>   (2)   A boy under the age of 16 cannot in law give any consent which would prevent an act being an assault for the purposes of this section.
>   (3)   A man who is a defective cannot in law give any consent which would prevent an act being an assault for the purposes of this section, but a person is only to be treated as guilty of an indecent assault on a defective by reason of that incapacity to consent, if that person knew or had reason to suspect him to be a defective.

Procedure

B3.80   Indecent assault is triable either way (MCA 1980, s. 17(1) and sch. 1). When tried on indictment it is a class 4 offence.

The guidelines for determining mode of trial for indecent assault (*Practice Note (Mode of Trial: Guidelines)* (1995): see **D3.7**) are that cases should be tried summarily unless the court considers that one or more of the following features is present *and* that its sentencing powers are insufficient.

 1. Substantial disparity in age between victim and defendant, and the assault is more than trivial.
 2. Violence or threats of violence.
 3. Relationship of trust or responsibility between defendant and victim.
 4. Several similar offences, and the assaults are more than trivial.
 5. The victim is particularly vulnerable.
 6. Serious nature of the assault.

Indictment

Statement of Offence

                         B3.81

Indecent assault on a woman contrary to section 14(1) of the Sexual Offences Act 1956

Particulars of Offence

A on or about the . . . day of . . . indecently assaulted V, a woman

This form may readily be adapted for offences under s. 15.

Alternative Verdicts

Common assault (*Bostock* (1893) 17 Cox CC 700). Pursuant to the CJA 1988, s. 40, a **B3.82** count for common assault may also be added to the indictment. See **D8.6**.

Sentencing Guidelines

The maximum penalties are as follows: **B3.83**

 Indecent assault on a female: 10 years on indictment; six months, a fine not exceeding the statutory maximum or both, summarily (SOA 1956, s. 37 and sch. 2).
 Indecent assault on a male: 10 years on indictment; six months, a fine not exceeding the statutory maximum or both, summarily (SOA 1956, s. 37 and sch. 2).

When dealt with summarily, the Magistrates' Association Guidelines (1997) indicate the following:

 Aggravating Factors ⊕
 For example vulnerable victim; breach of trust; age differential; injury (may be psychiatric); very young victim; offence committed on bail; previous convictions and failures to respond to previous sentences, if relevant.

 Mitigating Factors ⊖
 For example slight contact.

 Guideline: Is it so serious that only custody is appropriate?

Where the indecent assault has been committed on a person who is a mental defective, the sentencer should bear in mind that the maximum penalty for unlawful sexual intercourse with such a person is two years' imprisonment (see **B3.55**). Sentence was reduced from four years' imprisonment to 21 months in *Blair* [1996] 1 Cr App R (S) 336 partly for that reason. See also *Phillips* [1996] 1 Cr App R (S) 339.

For a very serious case of indecent assault, a sentence approaching the maximum will be approved. In *Sheen* (1987) 9 Cr App R (S) 164, the offender pleaded guilty to false imprisonment, indecent assault and assault occasioning actual bodily harm. The offender accosted a young woman, grabbed her by the hair and forced her into his car. He then indecently assaulted her in various ways, including ejaculating into her mouth. She eventually escaped. The offender had previous convictions for indecent assault. A sentence of eight years was upheld. Four years' imprisonment was upheld in *Pike* [1996]

1 Cr App R (S) 4, where the offender carried out internal examinations on a woman on the pretext that they were necessary for medical treatment. In *Currie* (1988) 10 Cr App R (S) 85 the offender attacked a woman who was walking to her car at a station car park, late at night. He seized her breast and attempted to pull off her clothing. Thirty months' imprisonment was upheld.

General guidance on the less serious offences of indecent assault may be derived from *Bibi* [1980] 1 WLR 1193, where Lord Lane CJ said (at p. 1195) that 'Many offenders can be dealt with equally justly and effectively by a sentence of six or nine months' imprisonment as by one of 18 months or three years. We have in mind . . . the minor cases of sexual indecency'. In *Neem* (1993) 14 Cr App R (S) 18, a sentence of 28 days' imprisonment was said to be wrong in principle, and was reduced to a fine of £300, where a man of previous good character indecently assaulted a young woman by pressing against her while standing in a London Underground train. *Neem* was followed in *Chagan* (1995) 16 Cr App R (S) 15 but doubted in *Tanyildiz* [1998] 1 Cr App R (S) 362. In *A-G's Ref (No. 25 of 1997)* [1998] 1 Cr App R (S) 310, the offender, who owned a pet-shop business, had sexually harassed a 15-year-old girl who spent time in the shop on work placement. He was convicted of two counts of indecent assault, in relation to occasions when he had touched her sexually through her clothing and had persisted in that behaviour despite her protests. The Court of Appeal said that the £500 fine which had been imposed by the sentencer was unduly lenient, and that the proper penalty would have been 12 months' imprisonment. A case where a non-custodial sentence was approved is *W* [1999] 1 Cr App R (S) 488, where the 13-year-old offender was convicted of indecent assault on a 12-year-old girl. He put his hand inside the girl's clothes, to which she objected. He then followed her, tripped her up and lay on top of her, simulating sexual intercourse. The Court of Appeal noted that such a case was 'extremely difficult to deal with', but concluded that the original sentence of eight months' detention under CYPA 1933, s. 53(3), was incorrect, and substituted a supervision order.

Many of the reported cases concern acts of indecency committed against children, often by offenders who were in some position of authority in respect to them. In *A-G's Ref (No. 34 of 1997)* [1998] 1 FLR 515, the Court of Appeal noted that the public rightly and strongly condemned offences of indecent assault committed on children. The Court held that a suspended sentence passed on an offender who had pleaded guilty to six counts of indecent assault on three boys aged between six and eleven by touching their genitalia under their clothing, in incidents spanning a period of two and a half years, was an unduly lenient sentence. The boys had been left in his charge as friends of his own children. The proper sentence in a contested case would have been in the range of 30 months' to three years' imprisonment and, after a guilty plea, between 18 months and two years. Personal circumstances, such as that the offender had himself suffered abuse as a child, that his marriage was undergoing difficulties, and that he had voluntarily sought psychiatric help and was responding to it, were frequently encountered in such cases and could not be regarded as 'exceptional', so as to justify suspension of the sentence. See also *A-G's Ref (No. 61 of 1998)* [1999] 2 Cr App R (S) 226. *Cook* (1988) 10 Cr App R (S) 42 is perhaps the most serious of all the reported cases, where the offender pleaded guilty to eight counts of indecent assault and one of buggery, committed against his four stepchildren, as part of a pattern of offending which took place over a nine-year period, the offences not coming to light until the children had become adults. Sentences totalling 11 years were upheld in this 'dreadful case' by the Court of Appeal. In *Lennon* [1999] 1 Cr App R (S) 19 the offender was acquitted of rape but convicted of indecent assault. He had masturbated in the presence of his partner's nine-year-old daughter, and had pulled off her trousers and knickers. A sentence of two years' imprisonment was upheld, the Court of Appeal rejecting the argument that there was a tariff of between 13 and 18 months' imprisonment in cases of this kind. The Court further observed that care must be taken if relying on cases sentenced before 1985, since a much lower maximum penalty for the offence existed at that time. *Lennon* was followed and approved in *Wellman* [1999] 2 Cr App R (S) 162. Cases involving indecent assaults committed on young boys include *Roe* (1988) 10 Cr App R (S) 435 (series of offences committed by a man of previous good character on two boys aged 14, involving mutual masturbation and oral sex; the boys were given small sums of money, but no coercion involved: 30 months appropriate) and *Connery* (1989) 11 Cr App R (S) 76 (indecent assault committed on three boys aged between eight and 12, apparently on about 500 occasions over three years, involving masturbation, photographing the boys and showing them pornographic pictures: six years reduced to four and a half years on appeal).

In *Allen* [1996] 2 Cr App R (S) 36, a 20-year-old woman committed a number of indecent assaults (which included digitally penetrating the vagina) on a girl aged 13, who was a willing participant throughout. The Court of Appeal intimated that, in a case where the defendant pleaded guilty and where no force or coercion was used, a custodial sentence of 15 months' imprisonment was appropriate.

Elements

Common to all these offences is the requirement that what is done amount to an assault. **B3.84** As to the elements of assault generally, see **B2.4** to **B2.9**. This requires an application of force or the threat of force by the accused to the person of the victim. Where, therefore, a child is invited to commit an indecent act and does so, there is no assault (*Fairclough* v *Whipp* [1951] 2 All ER 834). If there is a touching in circumstances of indecency, the child's consent will not prevent the act from being an indecent assault. If there is no indecency, the child's consent will preclude any finding of assault. If the child be 14 years of age or under, the accused may be charged under the Indecency with Children Act 1960 (*Sutton* [1977] 1 WLR 1086, and see **B3.111** *et seq.*). If the child is over 14, no offence is committed in such circumstances. Thus, it is not an offence of indecent assault for a woman simply to have sexual intercourse with a boy aged over 14 (*Mason* (1968) 53 Cr App R 12).

Subject to the provisions of the SOA 1956, ss. 14 and 15, dealing with persons under 16 and defectives, consent will be a defence to the same extent as in cases of common assault, provided that the hurt was merely transient or trifling (see **B2.8**). The latter phrase must be read in the light of contemporary attitudes, which probably accept a higher degree of vigour in sexual relations than formerly and therefore the voluntarily accepted risk of incurring some injury is probably higher than it formerly was (*Boyea* (1992) 156 JP 505). However, the classic formula (that in order to negate consent the harm need not be permanent but must be more than transient or trifling) still applies and was applied with some strictness in *Brown* [1994] 1 AC 212, where it was held that sado-masochistic acts which occurred in private and which were consented to could found charges under the OAPA 1861, ss. 20 and 47, if the injuries, though not permanent, were neither transient nor trifling. It mattered not that the participants took care not to inflict or sustain injuries of a serious character. It is for the prosecution to prove lack of consent. Actual belief in consent will be a defence (*Kimber* [1983] 1 WLR 1118; and see generally **B2.6** and **B2.8**).

In relation to indecent assault upon a woman, where a marriage is invalid on the ground that the woman is under the age of consent to marry, the man does not commit this offence if he believes the woman to be his wife and has reasonable cause for the belief (SOA 1956, s. 14(1) and (3)). A girl under 16 cannot give a valid consent which would prevent the act from being an assault, nor can a mental defective. In the latter case the person may only be convicted if that person knew, or had reason to suspect, the other of being a defective (s. 14(2) and (4)). In relation to indecent assault on a man (SOA 1956, s. 15), provisions similar to those under s. 14 above apply in relation to the age of consent and the special position of mental defectives.

The test for indecent assault is primarily objective. An indecent assault is defined as an assault committed in circumstances of indecency. Circumstances of indecency need not involve any indecent touching of the victim or a threat of indecent touching. The assault or the circumstances accompanying it must, however, be capable of being considered by right-minded persons as indecent (*Sargeant* (1997) 161 JP 127). Spoken words may constitute circumstances of indecency on the part of the person using them. If the circumstances of the assault are incapable of being regarded as indecent, the assault cannot become indecent because of some secret motive of the accused. Where the assault is indecent in itself, the basic intent needed to establish assault is enough; whether or not the accused was drunk at the time is irrelevant (*Culyer* (1992) *The Times*, 17 April 1992). Where the circumstances are such that the assault could be considered indecent, it must at least be proved that the accused intentionally assaulted the victim with knowledge of the indecent circumstances or being reckless as to the existence of them (*Court* [1989] AC 28). This means intention or recklessness with regard to circumstances which are shown to contravene standards of decent behaviour with regard to sexual modesty or privacy. Whether or not the victim appreciates the fact of the indecency is irrelevant. So, in a sense, is the accused's motive for his act, though evidence of this may be admitted (as it was in *Court*, where the accused had told the police he had a 'buttock fetish').

It has not been decided whether 'reckless' in this sense means knowing of the possibility that certain circumstances exist and that they could be regarded as indecent, or whether it means that if thought were given to the matter by the accused he would have realised that circumstances exist and that they could be thought to be indecent, or knowledge that circumstances exist where if thought had been given to the question of indecency the accused would have realised that they could be so considered. In *Court* [1988] 2 WLR 1071 some light is perhaps thrown on the issue by the court's intimation that a person who uses words in a foreign language without knowing their meaning and without recklessness could not be said to commit an indecent assault, whatever the victim's view of their effect. This perhaps suggests that the accused must at least contemplate that the words could amount to an affront to modesty. That in turn would suggest that advertent recklessness is required.

LIVING ON EARNINGS OF PROSTITUTION

Definitions

B3.85

Sexual Offences Act 1956, s. 30

(1)   It is an offence for a man knowingly to live wholly or in part on the earnings of prostitution.

(2)   For the purposes of this section a man who lives with or is habitually in the company of a prostitute, or who exercises control, direction or influence over a prostitute's movements in a way which shows that he is aiding, abetting or compelling her prostitution with others, shall be presumed to be knowingly living on the earnings of prostitution, unless he proves the contrary.

Sexual Offences Act 1967, s. 5

(1)   A man or woman who knowingly lives wholly or in part on the earnings of prostitution of another man shall be liable—

(a)   on summary conviction to imprisonment for a term not exceeding six months; or

(b)   on conviction on indictment to imprisonment for a term not exceeding seven years.

(2)   . . .
(3)   Anyone may arrest without a warrant a person found committing an offence under this section.

Procedure

Both offences are triable either way. When tried on indictment they are class 4 offences. **B3.86**
The offence under the SOA 1967, s. 5, does not contain a presumption akin to that in the SOA 1956, s. 30(2).

Indictment

Statement of Offence **B3.87**

Living on the earnings of prostitution, contrary to section 30 of the Sexual Offences Act 1956

Particulars of Offence

A, a man, on the . . . day of . . ., and other days between that date and the . . . day of . . ., knowingly lived wholly or in part on the earnings of prostitution of P

Note that an indictment may be laid as living on the earnings of one day only (*Hill* [1914] 2 KB 386).

Sentencing Guidelines

The maximum penalty for offences under the SOA 1956, s. 30, is seven years on **B3.88**
indictment; six months and/or a fine not exceeding the statutory maximum, summarily (SOA 1956, s. 37 and sch. 2). The maximum penalty for offences under the SOA 1967, s. 5, is the same as under s. 30 of the 1956 Act (s. 5(1)).

In the case of *Farrugia* (1979) 69 Cr App R 108, Lawton LJ said that the crucial factor in sentencing in cases of living on immoral earnings is whether there is any evidence of coercion, whether physical or mental, of the prostitutes involved, or of corruption. A sentence exceeding two years should, he said, be reserved for cases where there is such coercion or corruption. The case was applied in *Smyle* (1990) 12 Cr App R (S) 258, where the offender had received £10,000 over 14 months from an established prostitute, using the money to feed his addiction to drugs, but where there was no physical oppression or corruption and in *Dixon* (1995) 16 Cr App R (S) 779. In *Thomas* (1983) 5 Cr App R (S) 138 the Court of Appeal said that a three-year sentence was proper, despite exceeding Lawton LJ's guidelines, since the offender had a history of similar offending. See also *Smith* (1995) 16 Cr App R (S) 1026, where the offender lived for two months with a woman who was a prostitute, receiving money from her; 10 months' imprisonment was appropriate.

Other cases concern the running of 'escort agencies' or 'massage parlours'. In *El-Gazzar* (1986) 8 Cr App R (S) 182, a sentence of 12 months for living on the earnings of prostitution was upheld on an offender who operated an escort agency. The approach taken in *Farrugia* (1979) 69 Cr App R 108 was approved. *Martin* (1988) 10 Cr App R (S) 33 was a case where the offender was convicted of keeping a disorderly house, where various sexual activities were offered for payment. No other prostitute was involved. The offender had previously been fined for a similar offence. A nine-month sentence was reduced to three months, to take account of the small scale of the activity. In contrast, in *Malik* [1998] 1 Cr App R (S) 115, a sentence of two years was upheld on a man who maintained premises for the use of prostitutes, who paid him a daily rent. Forty prostitutes were involved, operating from four premises owned by the offender who had thereby received about £89,000 over a 21-month period. There was no suggestion of violence or corruption.

Meaning of 'Prostitution'

B3.89 In the case of the offence under the SOA 1956, s. 30, the woman must be a prostitute, but she need not be a 'common prostitute'. The latter term refers to a woman who is a prostitute and who engages for reward in acts of lewdness with all and sundry (*Morris-Lowe* [1985] 1 WLR 29). Prostitution does not necessarily involve that the woman (or under the SOA 1967, s. 5, the man) offer full sexual intercourse or intend to perform her (or his) part of any bargain. It is the making of the offer which is immoral (*McFarlane* [1994] QB 419). A person who, for example, masturbates clients falls within the definition. Nor is prostitution confined to the case where the person offers his or her body passively (*Morris-Lowe*; *De Munck* [1918] 1 KB 635; *Webb* [1964] 1 QB 357). The breadth of this definition brings proprietors of massage parlours where sexual indecencies are practised, and escort agencies where such practices are encouraged, within the section.

Living on Earnings

B3.90 Taken at their widest, the wording of both offences would be apt to incriminate any person whose livelihood depends in any measure upon the earnings of a prostitute or prostitutes. The effect of such an interpretation would be to cast a net more widely than the policy of the law warrants. While it is not easy to state definitively what the policy underlying the legislation is, it may at least be said that it is not intended to deny the necessaries of life to a prostitute. A grocer, a lawyer or a doctor who provides goods or services to a prostitute fall outside the section. So, too, does a landlord, unless there is a factor pertaining to the landlord-tenant relationship which is apt to colour the legal litmus paper (*Shaw* v *DPP* [1962] AC 220, per Viscount Simonds at pp. 263–4, per Lord Reid at pp. 269–71). Positively, in words which have been cited in later decisions, Lord Reid characterised the essence of the mischief as that of men who live parasitically on prostitutes and their earnings, for example touts and protectors, who would not have an occupation if the women were not prostitutes (ibid., at p. 270). This factor is also referred to with approval by Viscount Simonds (at p. 264), who further holds that a person may be said to be living in whole or in part on the earnings of prostitution if he is paid by prostitutes for goods and services which he would not have supplied but for the fact that they are prostitutes. The concepts involved are slippery, and the contexts in which they arise differ considerably. It is not surprising that a later court has doubted whether a sufficiently close definition to cover all cases could be provided (*Stewart* (1986) 83 Cr App R 327).

The following propositions are stated in, or can be deduced from, the cases:

(a) There must be a close connection between the receipt of money and the trade before the offence is committed (*Stewart* (1986) 83 Cr App R 327), and the clearest case is where the service is referable to prostitution and nothing else (*Shaw* v *DPP* [1962] AC 220 per Viscount Simonds).

(b) It is not necessary that there be something in the nature of a joint venture between the accused and the prostitute since, by the SOA 1956, s. 30(2), a man who lives with a prostitute or is supported by her is living on the earnings, even though he plays no part in the running of her trade (*Stewart* (1986) 83 Cr App R 327).

(c) Subject to this reservation, an approach which will often be useful is to identify for the jury the flavour of the words 'living on', and then to express this general concept in the shape of guidance more directly referable to the case in hand: 'parasite' provides a useful starting-point (*Stewart*; *Shaw* v *DPP*).

(d) Where an accused supplies goods or services to a prostitute, a good working test sufficient to deal with many cases is whether the fact of supply means that the supplier and the prostitute were engaged in business together (*Stewart*). The fact of supply will include the scale of supply, the price charged, and the nature of the goods and services.

(e)   It cannot be said in advance that certain services must necessarily either be outside or within the section (*Stewart*). As Lord Reid put it in *Shaw* (at p. 152), it might in some cases be difficult to point to items which an honest woman would not require, since simple eccentricity is always possible.

The idea of participation in a prostitute's business will enable the jury to distinguish readily between, say, a supplier of groceries and the publisher of prostitute's advertisements. The formula adopted by Lord Goddard CJ in *Calvert* v *Mayes* [1954] 1 QB 342, and approved by Viscount Simonds in *Shaw* v *DPP* [1962] AC 220, of trading in prostitution may be helpful in some cases but not necessarily in all (*Ansell* [1975] QB 215, per Roskill LJ).

Most cases require only a simple direction that a person may fairly be said to be living in whole or in part on the earnings if he is paid by prostitutes for goods or services which are supplied by him to them for the purposes of their prostitution and which he could not supply but for the fact that they are prostitutes. A person who makes a business of accepting advertisements from prostitutes for reward knowingly lives on the earnings of prostitution (*Howard* (1990) 92 Cr App R 223). The use of a large number of different expressions such as 'joint venture' or 'exploitation' only serve to confuse; a person who is paid for supplying advertising cards and stickers to prostitutes clearly lives on the earnings of prostitution (*Howard* (1991) 94 Cr App R 89).

Letting of Premises to Prostitutes and 'Living on Earnings'

The most difficult problems arise in relation to the letting of premises to prostitutes. **B3.91** Here, the following principles apply:

(a)   It is not an offence to let premises to a prostitute, even though she may carry on some part or all of her business from them. A prostitute must have somewhere to live, and it is not the policy of the law to deny her accommodation (*Shaw* v *DPP* [1962] AC 220). However, it should be noted that it may be a separate offence to let premises knowingly for use as a brothel (SOA 1956, ss. 34 and 35; **B3.98 *et seq*.**).

(b)   A test, but not the exclusive test, for determining whether a letting is such as to constitute a living on the earnings is to ask whether the landlord and the prostitute are engaged in a joint venture (*Stewart* (1986) 83 Cr App R 327). The test is not exclusive, since in certain cases the relationship may be better described as parasitic or exploitative than as a joint venture. In *Shaw* v *DPP* Viscount Simonds notes that the words 'coadjutor' or 'joint venturer' do not denote a precise legal relationship in this context. The words used are impressionistic, and may indeed be conclusory in nature.

(c)   Where a very high rent is charged, it may be easy for the jury to determine that there is an element of 'living on' in the case. This is because in some cases the margin between actual and market rents may be considered to be the accused's profit margin relative to the element of joint venture (*Stewart*; *Calderhead* (1978) 68 Cr App R 37). Alternatively, it is submitted, it may be looked upon as the product of exploitation and parasitic in that sense.

(d)   It is submitted, on the authority of *Stewart* and of a Scots case (*Soni* v *HM Advocate* 1970 SLT 275), that the same element of joint venture may be shown, and more clearly, where a landlord lets premises intending that the business of prostitution shall be carried on there, and does acts which facilitate this, such as adapting them for the purpose, installing a telephone, and advising the prostitute against involvement with the police. Among other relevant factors may be the nature and location of the premises, the duration of the letting, the hours of occupation, the method of payment of rent, the presence or absence of a personal relationship between lessor and lessee, the steps taken by the landlord to remove prostitutes from the premises, and any steps taken by the lessor to disguise his relationship with the premises and persons working there. Again, this may amount to an offence under the SOA 1956, s. 34 or s. 35 (see **B3.98 *et seq*.**).

(e)   It may be possible to conclude that there is an element of 'living on' even where a moderate rent is demanded (*Stewart* (1986) 83 Cr App R 327, *Calderhead* (1978) 68 Cr App R 37). The requisite mental element is obscure. Clearly, where it can be shown, perhaps by reference to some or all of the factors in (d) above, that the lessor intends that prostitution be carried on in the premises, the charge will be made out (*Thomas* [1957] 1 WLR 747, where, however, a high rent was demanded). It will not be made out where no more can be proven than that a woman conducts herself to the lessor's knowledge as a prostitute in premises which she occupies (*Shaw* v *DPP* [1962] AC 220, per Viscount Simonds at pp. 265–6, per Lord Reid at p. 271). Without the presence of such factors it may well be impossible to prove an element of joint adventure, and in such a case no element of exploitation could be indicated. It may, in any event, be impossible to prove a case less than intent or purpose where a normal rent is demanded. Where an exorbitant rent is demanded it would seem too narrow to put the test in terms of purpose; it should, it is submitted, be enough that the accused was prepared to share in the proceeds of prostitution, knowing that such proceeds would, or would probably, accrue from activities carried on in the premises.

Receipt of Payment by Accused

B3.92   Whatever may be the mode of 'living on', the prosecution is not required to prove that direct payment was made by the prostitute to the accused (*Farrugia* (1979) 69 Cr App R 108; *Calvert* v *Mayes* [1954] 1 QB 342). It must, however, be established that what the accused received was earned by a prostitute or from prostitution. The mere fact that money comes from a prostitute does not establish that it is money earned by prostitution, but where a person exercises direction, influence or control over a prostitute, it may be inferred that any payment made to him represents the earnings of prostitution (*Farrugia*, explaining *Ansell* (1974) 60 Cr App R 45). Furthermore, where sums are paid by men to the accused for introducing men to prostitutes, the offence is made out, even though no payment is received from the women (*Ansell*).

Presumption of Living on Earnings of Prostitution

B3.93   In certain cases the accused is presumed to be knowingly living on the earnings of (female) prostitution (SOA 1956, s. 30(2)). These are cases where there is an element of direction, control or influence over the movements of the woman or women in question.

There are three separate and distinct foundations upon which the prosecution can rely in order to raise the presumption:

(a)   proof that the accused was living with a prostitute;
(b)   proof that he was at the material time in her company;
(c)   proof that he exercised control, direction or influence over her movements in such a way as to show him to be aiding and abetting her prostitution.

Once evidence giving rise to the presumption has been led, it is presumed both that the accused was living on the proceeds of prostitution and that he was doing so knowingly (*Clarke* [1976] 2 All ER 696; *Lawrence* (1963) 47 Cr App R 72). The onus then shifts to the man to prove on a balance of probabilities that he was not living wholly or partly on the earnings of a woman whom he knew to be a prostitute (*Ptohopoulos* (1967) 52 Cr App R 47). Whether proof sufficient to raise the presumption has been adduced is a question of fact for the jury. Such proof may be made from evidence of conversation between a man and a prostitute, of numbers of men visiting a flat, or of the services offered (*Ptohopoulos*; *Wilson* (1983) 78 Cr App R 247).

The words 'living together' may well not present much difficulty to a jury, nor, surely, does the notion of being habitually in the company of a prostitute. The words 'control, direction or influence' have been widely construed. Taxi drivers who habitually drove prostitutes to assignations have been said to exercise direction and influence over their movement, aiding and abetting their prostitution (*Calvert v Mayes* [1954] 1 QB 342, per Barry and Sellars JJ; *Farrugia* (1979) 69 Cr App R 108, where the drivers collected cab fare from the prostitutes and an agency fee from the male customers). Wide as these cases undoubtedly are, there seems to be no authoritative definition of control, direction and influence.

Woman Exercising Control over Prostitute

By the SOA 1956, s. 31, it is also an offence for a woman for purposes of gain to exercise **B3.94** control, direction or influence over a prostitute's movements in a way which shows she is aiding, abetting or compelling her prostitution.

This offence is triable either way, and is punishable on indictment by a maximum of seven years, or summarily by six months and/or the statutory maximum (SOA 1956, s. 37 and sch. 2).

The terms 'control, direction or influence' are used disjunctively. They represent a descending level of seriousness. Compulsion or persuasion may be a necessary ingredient of control and possibly direction. Depending on the circumstances, compulsion or persuasion may be an ingredient of influence but neither is a necessary ingredient of influence. From this it follows that a person who operates a call-girl service outwith the brothel-keeping provisions of s. 31 may be convicted of this offence (*A-G's Ref (No. 2 of 1995)* [1996] 3 All ER 860).

KEEPING BROTHEL AND RELATED OFFENCES

Definitions

Sexual Offences Act 1956, ss. 33, 34, 35, and 36 **B3.95**

33. It is an offence for a person to keep a brothel, or to manage, or act or assist in the management of, a brothel.

34. It is an offence for the lessor or landlord of any premises or his agent to let the whole or part of the premises with the knowledge that it is to be used, in whole or in part, as a brothel, or, where the whole or part of the premises is used as a brothel, to be wilfully a party to that use continuing.

35.—(1) It is an offence for the tenant or occupier, or person in charge, of any premises knowingly to permit the whole or part of the premises to be used as a brothel.

(2) Where the tenant or occupier of any premises is convicted . . . of knowingly permitting the whole or part of the premises to be used as a brothel, the first schedule to this Act shall apply to enlarge the rights of the lessor or landlord with respect to the assignment or determination of the lease or other contract under which the premises are held by the person convicted.

(3) Where the tenant or occupier of any premises is so convicted . . . and either—

(a) the lessor or landlord, after having the conviction brought to his notice, fails or failed to exercise his statutory rights in relation to the lease or contract under which the premises are or were held by the person convicted; or

(b) the lessor or landlord, after exercising his statutory rights so as to determine that lease or contract, grants or granted a new lease or enters or entered into a new contract of tenancy of the premises to, with or for the benefit of the same person, without having all reasonable provisions to prevent the recurrence of the offence inserted in the new lease or contract;

then, if subsequently an offence under this section is committed in respect of the premises during the subsistence of the lease or contract referred to in paragraph (a) of this subsection or (where paragraph (b) applies) during the subsistence of the new lease or contract, the lessor or landlord shall be deemed to be a party to that offence unless he shows that he took all reasonable steps to prevent the recurrence of the offence.

References in this subsection to the statutory rights of a lessor or landlord refer to his rights under the First Schedule to this Act . . .

36. It is an offence for the tenant or occupier of any premises knowingly to permit the whole or part of the premises to be used for the purposes of habitual prostitution.

Sexual Offences Act 1967, s. 6

Premises shall be treated for purposes of sections 33 to 35 of the Act of 1956 as a brothel if people resort to it for the purpose of lewd homosexual practices in circumstances in which resort thereto for lewd heterosexual practices would have led to its being treated as a brothel for the purposes of those sections.

Procedure

B3.96 These offences are triable summarily only. Brothel keeping may be regarded as a single continuing transaction, and therefore an information charging the offence over a period of time is not void for duplicity (*Anderton v Cooper* (1980) 72 Cr App R 232).

Sentence

B3.97 Under each section, for an offence committed after a previous conviction for the same or a related offence, the maximum penalty is six months or a fine not exceeding level 4 on the standard scale, or both; otherwise three months or a fine not exceeding level 3 on the standard scale, or both (SOA 1956, s. 37 and sch. 2).

Meaning of 'Brothel'

B3.98 A brothel is defined as a place where people are permitted to resort for the purposes of unlawful sexual intercourse (*Winter v Woolfe* [1931] 1 KB 549, per Avory J). It is not necessary that full sexual intercourse be offered there. A massage parlour where masturbation and other acts of indecency are offered by more than one woman for the sexual gratification of men is a brothel. Nor, *semble*, is it necessary that payment for such services be made (*Kelly v Purvis* [1983] AC 663). By the SOA 1967, s. 6, premises may be a brothel if people resort to them for the purposes of lewd homosexual practices.

A brothel may be a house, or a room, or a set of rooms kept for the purposes of prostitution. A place which is used by one woman for the purposes of her own prostitution is not a brothel (*Stevens v Christy* (1987) 85 Cr App R 249). Problems can arise where ostensibly separate units in a building in multiple occupation are used for prostitution. Whether such premises constitute a brothel is a question of fact and degree. The court may, from such factors as whether the original lettings were independent, the pattern of user and the sharing of facilities, be able to conclude that such premises constitute a 'nest' of prostitutes and therefore a brothel, even though each unit is separately occupied by one prostitute, and where the facts clearly show that a 'nest' of prostitutes operates from premises, the fact that the lettings were originally independent carries no weight at all (*Donovan v Gavin* [1965] 2 QB 648, *Abbott v Smith* [1965] 2 QB 662n, explaining *Strath v Foxon* [1956] 1 QB 67, *Singleton v Ellison* [1895] 1 QB 607). It should further be noted that premises may be a brothel even though, on any one day, only one prostitute was present (*Stevens v Christy* (1987) 85 Cr App R 249). The same case holds that the offence is not dependent upon any element of nuisance. Police witnesses may describe women in the premises as known to them to be common prostitutes. Such evidence is probative and its prejudicial effect is said to be minimal (*Korie* [1966] 1 All ER 50).

Keeping Brothel

B3.99 One mode of commission of the offence under the SOA 1956, s. 33, is to keep a brothel. A woman who uses premises exclusively for her own prostitution does not keep a brothel

(*Stevens* v *Christy* (1987) 85 Cr App R 249). A landlord who lets flats to tenants, but who does not retain a part of the house in which the flats are located and who has no control over it, does not keep a disorderly house (*Stannard* (1863) 9 Cox CC 405), nor does he become liable simply because he has not given his tenants notice to quit (*Barrett* (1862) 9 Cox CC 255). Such a person may, however, become liable either for living on the earnings of prostitution (see **B3.85 *et seq*.**), or, if a landlord, for letting premises for use as a brothel (SOA 1956, s. 34) or, if a tenant or occupier, for permitting premises to be used as a brothel (SOA 1956, s. 35) or for the purposes of habitual prostitution (SOA 1956, s. 36). These offences are dealt with at **B3.102 *et seq*.**

Managing etc. Brothel

Other modes of commission of the offence under the SOA 1956, s. 33, are to manage, or to **B3.100** act or assist in the management of, a brothel. A person may be guilty of assisting in the management even though he or she acts in a menial capacity, such as a receptionist (*Stevens* v *Christy* (1987) 85 Cr App R 249). A person who keeps an appointments system, answers the telephone, decides to a large extent on the price of the services, pays the rent and opens and locks the premises thus assists in management even though she is primarily a prostitute rather than a manager (*DPP* v *Curley* [1991] COD 186). Statements in earlier cases that something more than menial or routine duties are required must be understood subject to the above; it would seem that a person may be convicted even though he or she lacks any element of managerial discretion (see *Gorman* v *Standen* [1964] 1 QB 294). It is, however, submitted that a purely menial servant, such as a cleaner, who neither admits nor denies admission to others does not assist in the management (*Abbott* v *Smith* [1965] 2 QB 662n). In *Jones* v *DPP* (1992) 96 Cr App R 130 the Divisional Court held that it need not be shown that the person exercised control over management, nor need it be shown that there was a specific act of management, for that would be acting in the management. Within those limits the question of whether a person assisted in the management of a brothel was a question of fact. In *Jones*, the accused had taken advertisements to the post office and paid for them; this was said to constitute a clear offence under s. 33.

Keeping Brothel: Requirement of Knowledge

This has not proved problematic. It is submitted that a person cannot keep a brothel **B3.101** unless he knows both that the premises are used for the purposes of prostitution in the wide sense noted at **B3.98**, and that they are not used simply by one woman for the purposes exclusively of her own prostitution.

Landlord Letting Premises as Brothel

The requisite elements are set out in the SOA 1956, s. 34. Knowledge of intended user **B3.102** or of continued user is required, since otherwise the defendant in the latter case cannot be said to act wilfully.

In determining whether premises are let to be used as a brothel, it is relevant, but not conclusive, that the original lettings were independent and not a subterfuge (*Donovan* v *Gavin* [1965] 2 QB 648). The status of the original tenancy would, it is submitted, only be relevant on a charge of being wilfully a party to such an user of premises, on the evidentiary question whether knowledge on the part of the defendant is made out.

Tenant Permitting Premises to be Used as Brothel

The offence under the SOA 1956, s. 35, has attracted little case law. It is apt to **B3.103** incriminate a person such as a lessee who sublets premises and who is not a landlord for the purposes of s. 34 (*Siviour* v *Napolitano* [1931] 1 KB 636).

Where a person is convicted of an offence under the Act, the rights of the lessor or landlord to terminate the lease are enhanced (s. 35(2)). Where a person is convicted and the lessor or landlord, after having the conviction brought to his notice, fails to exercise his statutory rights against the accused person, or grants a new tenancy to or for the benefit of the same person without inserting provisions to protect himself against the like conduct, in respect of any further offence he is deemed to be a party to that offence, unless he shows that he took all reasonable steps to prevent recurrence (s. 35(3)).

Tenant Permitting Premises to be Used for Prostitution

B3.104 It should be noted that under the SOA 1956, s. 36, the premises need not be used as a brothel. It is enough if they are used by a single prostitute for the purposes of his or her habitual prostitution. The prostitute does not commit an offence under the section by using her own premises for the purpose of habitual prostitution, but a tenant or occupier who permits a prostitute to use premises of which he is the lessee or occupier commits the offence.

Keeping Disorderly House

B3.105 It is an indictable offence at common law for a person to keep a disorderly house. As a common-law offence, punishment is at large by imprisonment and fine.

While a brothel is undoubtedly a disorderly house at common law, other premises also fall within the definition. In *Berg* (1927) 20 Cr App R 38, the court did not dissent from counsel's observation based on *Stephen's Digest*, 7th ed. (1926), art. 258, that disorderly houses are common betting houses, common gaming houses, and disorderly places of entertainment. The court made clear, however, that *Stephen's* capitulation is not exhaustive. The breadth of the offence is justified by the consideration that such houses present temptations to idleness, and the drawing together of numbers of disorderly persons (*Rogier* (1823) 1 B & C 272).

In *Tan* [1983] QB 1053 the court summed up the elements of the offence thus:

    (a)   there must be some element of keeping open house;
    (b)   the house must not be regulated by the restraints of morality, or must be unchaste or of bad repute; and
    (c)   it must be so conducted as to violate law and good order.

In *Moores* v *DPP* [1992] QB 125, it was held that there must also be knowledge that the house is so used.

There is no requirement that any indecency or disorderly conduct be perceptible from outside the house. The offence is thus not premised on nuisance (*Brady* [1964] 3 All ER 616; *Rice* (1866) LR 1 CCR 21). An element of persistent use is required: a single indecent performance is not enough to constitute the offence (*Moores* v *DPP*).

Quite how open the house must be is unclear. The house need not be open to the public at large (*Berg* (1927) 20 Cr App R 38), but there must, as noted, be an element of open house about it (*Tan* [1983] QB 1053).

As to the third requirement, that the conduct violate law and good order, what passes in the house need not be a criminal offence on the part of any participant. It may, for example, consist in an indecent performance. In *Quinn* [1962] 2 QB 245 the court expressed itself particularly widely, noting that a house could be a disorderly house where a performance takes place which amounts to an outrage to public decency, or tends to deprave and corrupt, or is otherwise calculated to injure the public interest so as to call for condemnation and punishment. In *Tan*, it was held that the jury must be directed to consider whether the services provided at such a house amount to an outrage to public decency or are otherwise calculated to injure the public interest to such an extent as to call for condemnation and punishment. Clearly, an evaluative judgment on the part of the jury is required, since the morality involved is that of the person in the jury-box, and it is impossible to set abstract limits to the offence (*Quinn*).

The Disorderly Houses Act 1751 provides that 'any person acting or appearing as the master or mistress or having the care of management of any such house' should be deemed the owner, and be liable to prosecution as such, even if not the real keeper thereof.

SOLICITING

Definitions

Street Offences Act 1959, s. 1   B3.106

(1)   It shall be an offence for a common prostitute to loiter or solicit in a street or public place for the purpose of prostitution.

(2)   A person guilty of an offence under this section shall be liable on summary conviction to a fine of an amount not exceeding level 2 on the standard scale, as defined in section 75 of the Criminal Justice Act 1982, or, for an offence committed after a previous conviction, to a fine of an amount not exceeding level 3 on that scale.

(3)   A constable may arrest without warrant anyone he finds in a street or public place and suspects, with reasonable cause, to be committing an offence under this section.

(4)   For the purposes of this section 'street' includes any bridge, road, lane, footway, subway, square, court, alley or passage, whether a thoroughfare or not, which is for the time being open to the public; and the doorways and entrances of premises abutting on a street (as hereinbefore defined), and any ground adjoining and open to a street, shall be treated as forming part of the street.

Sexual Offences Act 1985, ss. 1, 2, and 4

1.—(1)   A man commits an offence if he solicits a woman (or different women) for the purpose of prostitution—

(a)   from a motor vehicle while it is in a street or public place; or

(b)   in a street or public place while in the immediate vicinity of a motor vehicle that he has just got out of or off,

persistently or in such manner or in such circumstances as to be likely to cause annoyance to the woman (or any of the women) solicited, or nuisance to other persons in the neighbourhood.

(2)   A person guilty of an offence under this section shall be liable on summary conviction to a fine not exceeding level 3 on the standard scale.

(3)   In this section 'motor vehicle' has the same meaning as in the Road Traffic Act 1988.

2.—(1)   A man commits an offence if in a street or public place he persistently solicits a woman (or different women) for the purpose of prostitution.

(2)   A person guilty of an offence under this section shall be liable on summary conviction to a fine not exceeding level 3 on the standard scale.

4.—(1)   References in this Act to a man soliciting a woman for the purpose of prostitution are references to his soliciting her for the purpose of obtaining her services as a prostitute.

(2)   The use in any provision of this Act of the word 'man' without the addition of the word 'boy' shall not prevent the provision applying to any person to whom it would have applied if both words had been used, and similarly with the words 'woman' and 'girl'.

(3)   Paragraphs (a) and (b) of section 6 of the Interpretation Act 1978 (words importing the masculine gender to include the feminine, and vice versa) do not apply to this Act.

(4)   For the purposes of this Act 'street' includes any bridge, road, lane, footway, subway, square, court, alley or passage, whether a thoroughfare or not, which is for the time being open to the public; and the doorways and entrances of premises abutting on a street (as hereinbefore defined), and any ground adjoining and open to a street, shall be treated as forming part of the street.

Sexual Offences Act 1956, s. 32

It is an offence for a man persistently to solicit or importune in a public place for immoral purposes.

Procedure

B3.107 The offence under the SOA 1956 is triable either way. When tried on indictment it is a class 4 offence. The offences under the SOA 1985 and the Street Offences Act 1959 are triable summarily only.

Sentence

B3.108 The maximum penalties are as follows:

Solicitation by a man (SOA 1956, s. 32): On indictment, two years; summarily, six months and/or a fine to the statutory maximum (SOA 1956, s. 37 and sch. 2).

Loitering for the purposes of prostitution under the Street Offences Act 1959: A fine not exceeding level 2 on the standard scale, or for an offence committed after a previous conviction, a fine not exceeding level 3 (Street Offences Act 1959, s. 1(2)).

Persistent soliciting of women under the SOA 1985, s. 1 or s. 2: A fine not exceeding level 3 on the standard scale (SOA 1985, s. 1(2), s. 2(2)).

Loitering or Soliciting for Purposes of Prostitution

B3.109 Solicitation may consist of any conduct by a woman, but not by a man, which invites or importunes another to engage in an act of prostitution (*DPP* v *Bull* [1995] QB 88). Solicitation by a common prostitute may be active or passive. (The term common prostitute refers to a woman who is a prostitute and who engages for reward in acts of lewdness with all and sundry: *Morris-Lowe* [1985] 1 WLR 29.) A prostitute who was observed sitting in the downstairs bay window of a house illuminated by a red light and dressed in a low-cut top and mini skirt, and who received men for the purposes of prostitution, was held to have solicited within the meaning of the Act (*Behrendt* v *Burridge* [1977] 1 WLR 29). It follows from this and earlier cases that the woman need not actually be in the street or a public place, provided that her solicitation is projected there (*Smith* v *Hughes* [1960] 1 WLR 830). On the other hand, the woman soliciting must be physically present at the time. An advertisement speaking for her in her absence is insufficient (*Weisz* v *Monahan* [1962] 1 WLR 262; *Burge* v *DPP* [1962] 1 WLR 265). 'Loitering' means lingering with no intent to move on, and may be engaged in while in a vehicle as well as on foot (*Bridge* v *Campbell* (1947) 177 LT 444; see *Williamson* v *Wright* 1924 JC 57).

The phrase 'public place' is not defined in s. 1. In general, a place does not cease to be a place of public resort either because the public have to pay to go there or because the occupier reserves the right to refuse admission. The question is one of degree. If, for example, entry is allowed only to a limited class of persons, the place may well not be one of public resort (*Glynn* v *Simmonds* [1952] 2 All ER 47). An inn car park where a licensee invites customers to park their cars, and a field to which the public is invited have both been held to be public places, albeit under different (road traffic) legislation (*Elkins* v *Cartlidge* [1947] 1 All ER 829; *Collinson* (1931) 23 Cr App R 49). The term 'street' is widely defined by the Street Offences Act 1959, s. 1(4) (see **B3.106**).

The immoral conduct contemplated by the SOA 1956, s. 32, is immoral sexual activity and the importuning must be for an immoral sexual purpose (*Kirkup* [1993] 1 WLR 774). This need not be criminal as such (*Goddard* (1990) 92 Cr App R 185). Whether a particular form of sexual activity is immoral is for the jury. It is assumed that importuning males for a homosexual activity would be immoral but there is no per se category of such acts. Again, it is for the jury to determine whether soliciting women in public for sexual intercourse is immoral and the jury must consider the circumstances in which overtures were made and the nature of those overtures. The fact that an approach is offensive does not necessarily mean that it is for an immoral purpose (*Kirkup*, where the authorities are fully reviewed).

Kerb-crawling and Persistent Soliciting by Man

In respect of the offence of 'kerb-crawling', it is not necessary to require persons to be **B3.110** present witnessing the incident for the offence to be made out. It is sufficient if there was a likelihood of nuisance to other persons in the neighbourhood. In determining that issue, the justices are entitled to use their local knowledge of the area, its frequentation by prostitutes, and its population density and residential character (*Paul* v *DPP* (1989) 90 Cr App R 173).

In respect of offences of persistent soliciting, the prosecution must prove more than one act of soliciting. Two invitations to the same person may amount to persistence and *a fortiori* when the conduct is unpleasant, disturbing and offensive (*Darroch* v *DPP* (1990) 91 Cr App R 78; *Goddard* (1991) 92 Cr App R 185). In essence, there must be a degree of repetition – more than one invitation to one person or invitations to different people (*Tuck* [1994] Crim LR 375). Where such conduct as beckoning is alleged, evidence that the accused had earlier been seen in the company of a prostitute in that area may be relevant to rebut an allegation that there was an innocent motive for beckoning (*Darroch* v *DPP*).

The term 'street' is defined for the purposes of the SOA 1985, ss. 1 and 2, by s. 4(4) of that Act in language identical to that of the Street Offences Act 1959, s. 1(4) (see **B3.106**). However, again, there is no statutory definition of 'public place'.

INDECENCY WITH CHILDREN

Definition

Indecency with Children Act 1960, s. 1   **B3.111**

    (1)   Any person who commits an act of gross indecency with or towards a child under the age of 14, or who incites a child under that age to such an act with him or another, shall be liable on conviction on indictment to imprisonment for a term not exceeding ten years, or on summary conviction to imprisonment for a term not exceeding six months, to a fine not exceeding the prescribed sum, or to both.
    (2)   . . .
    (3)   References in the Children and Young Persons Act 1933, to the offences mentioned in the first schedule to that Act shall include offences under this section.
    (4)   Offences under this section shall be deemed to be offences against the person for the purpose of section 3 of the Visiting Forces Act 1952 (which restricts the trial by the United Kingdom courts of offenders connected with visiting forces).

Procedure

This offence is triable either way. When tried on indictment it is a class 4 offence.   **B3.112**

Sentence

The maximum penalty on indictment is ten years' imprisonment, although where the **B3.113** offence was committed before 1 October 1997 the maximum is two years; on summary conviction, six months and/or a fine to the prescribed sum (Indecency with Children Act 1960, s. 1, as amended by the C(S)A 1997, s. 52). See **B3.83** for relevant sentencing guidelines.

Elements

The Indecency with Children Act 1960 creates only one offence, the committing of an **B3.114** act of gross indecency involving a child. The offence is one of strict liability as to the age of the child (*B (A Minor)* v *DPP* [1999] 3 WLR 116. The words 'with or towards a child' are to be read as a phrase, because it is impossible to say definitely in any particular case whether it involves conduct with, rather than towards, a child. The alternative offence of inciting is inciting *with* and not towards (*DPP* v *Burgess* [1971] 1 QB 432). The offence of committing an act of gross indecency may be committed by inactivity, provided that the child, if not actually invited to join in grossly indecent conduct, is at least invited in some form to continue with it (*Morley* [1989] Crim LR 566). A case of inactivity amounting to the offence is that of *Speck* [1977] 2 All ER 859, where the accused allowed a child's hand to remain on his penis while he had an erection. However, the offence was not made out where the accused, a homosexual, at a boy's request described the nature of various homosexual practices and later slept in the same bed as the boy (with a duvet between them) and repelled sexual advances by the boy concerned (*B* [1999] Crim LR 594).

In the case of *Francis* (1988) 88 Cr App R 127, the issue was whether the accused, who apparently masturbated in the presence of young boys, acted indecently towards them. The court distinguished between a person who masturbates in the presence of children believing that they are unaware of his actions, in which case no offence under the statute is committed, and a person who knows that they are watching him, whether he attracted their attention or not, in which case he commits the offence. No actual physical contact with the child is required for the offence, but the acts must in some way be directed towards the children, at the very least by the accused deriving satisfaction from the knowledge that the children are watching what he is doing.

INDECENT PHOTOGRAPHS OF CHILDREN

Definitions

B3.115

Protection of Children Act 1978, s. 1

(1)   It is an offence for a person—
    (a)   to take, or permit to be taken or to make, any indecent photograph or pseudo-photograph of a child; or
    (b)   to distribute or show such indecent photographs or pseudo-photographs; or
    (c)   to have in his possession such indecent photographs or pseudo-photographs, with a view to their being distributed or shown by himself or others; or
    (d)   to publish or cause to be published any advertisement likely to be understood as conveying that the advertiser distributes or shows such indecent photographs or pseudo-photographs, or intends to do so.

Criminal Justice Act 1988, s. 160

(1)   It is an offence for a person to have any indecent photograph or pseudo-photograph of a child in his possession.
(2)   Where a person is charged with an offence under subsection (1) above, it shall be a defence for him to prove—
    (a)   that he had a legitimate reason for having the photograph or pseudo-photograph in his possession; or
    (b)   that he had not himself seen the photograph or pseudo-photograph and did not know, nor had any cause to suspect, it to be indecent; or
    (c)   that the photograph or pseudo-photograph was sent to him without any prior request made by him or on his behalf and that he did not keep it for an unreasonable time.

Procedure

B3.116   Offences under the Protection of Children Act 1978, s. 1, are triable either way. When tried on indictment they are class 4 offences. The offence under the CJA 1988, s. 160(1), is triable summarily only. By s. 1(3) of the 1978 Act and s. 160(4) of the 1988 Act, proceedings for any such offences may be instituted only by or with the consent of the DPP.

Sentence

The maximum penalty for an offence under the Protection of Children Act 1978, s. 1, **B3.117** is three years on indictment; six months and/or a fine to the statutory maximum on summary conviction (Protection of Children Act 1978, s. 6; MCA 1980, s. 32). In *McGuigan* [1996] 2 Cr App R (S) 253 a sentence of 12 months' imprisonment was appropriate in respect of a 'small-scale commercial pornographer' who pleaded guilty to six counts of possessing indecent photographs of a child with a view to distribution. An order for forfeiture of the material and other equipment was upheld. Thirty months' imprisonment was appropriate in *Caley* [1999] 2 Cr App R (S) 154 where the offender had downloaded indecent images of children from the Internet, and had stored these on disk with a view to distribution and commercial gain.

The maximum penalty for an offence under the CJA 1988, s. 160, is six months' imprisonment or a fine not exceeding level 5 on the standard scale, or both.

Elements

A person cannot be convicted of showing an indecent photograph of a child where he **B3.118** proposes to show it only to himself, nor can he be convicted of possession with intent to show such a photograph where he possesses the photograph only with intent to show it to himself (*E.T.* (1999) 163 JP 349). 'Pseudo-photographs' are defined as an image, whether made by computer graphics or otherwise, which appears to be a photograph. The offences of distribution and showing, of having in possession and of publication also extend to pseudo-photographs. In general, throughout the Act, pseudo-photographs are placed on the same footing as actual photographs. The effect of this, taken with interpretation provisions, is that while 'child' will continue to refer to a person under the age of 16, it will be possible to convict a person of making a pseudo-photograph where the dominant impression conveyed is that the person shown is a child, notwithstanding that some of the physical characteristics shown are those of an adult.

References to a photograph include both the negative and the positive version and data stored on a computer disk or by other electronic means which is capable of conversion into a photograph.

The Protection of Children Act 1978, s. 2(3), provides that a person is to be taken as having been a child at any material time if it appears, from the evidence as a whole, that he was then under the age of 16.

Note that by s. 1(2), a person is to be regarded as distributing an indecent photograph if he parts with possession of it to, or exposes or offers it for acquisition by, any person. In respect of the offences of distribution and possession only, s. 1(4) gives a defence to an accused who proves that he had a legitimate reason for distributing or showing the photographs or having them in his possession; or that he had not himself seen the photographs, and neither knew nor had any reason to suspect them to be indecent. Section 4 of the Act provides powers of entry, search and seizure with respect to indecent photographs of children. Section 5 provides for forfeiture of such photographs. Photographs include indecent films and video recordings, and are 'of' children if they show children and are indecent (s. 7).

Possession of Indecent Photograph

The CJA 1988, s. 160, penalises possession, even though the possessor does not intend **B3.119** that the photograph or pseudo-photograph be distributed.

A defendant has a defence to a charge under s. 160 if he can prove that he had a legitimate reason for having the photograph in his possession, or that he had not himself seen the photograph, and neither knew nor had any reason to suspect that it was indecent, or that the photograph was sent to him without any prior request by him, and that he did not keep it for an unreasonable time. Presumably, a reasonable time is that which is required to determine that a photograph is indecent, and that possession of it cannot be justified by any legitimate purpose of the defendant. It is not clear what matters come within the notion of legitimate purpose, but presumably possession of photographs collected for forensic teaching purposes, for example, would be regarded as legitimate.

OUTRAGING PUBLIC DECENCY: INDECENT EXPOSURE

Definition

B3.120 At common law it is an indictable offence of outraging public decency to expose the person or to engage in or simulate a sexual act. Under the Vagrancy Act 1824, s. 4, it is an offence, *inter alia*, for any person wilfully, openly, lewdly and obscenely to expose his person with intent to insult any female. Under the Town Police Clauses Act 1847, s. 28, it is an offence for a person indecently to expose himself to the annoyance of passengers.

As to the offence of outraging public decency by way of obscene publications, see **B19.18**.

Procedure

B3.121 The common-law offence is triable only on indictment. It is a class 3 offence. The offences under the Vagrancy Act 1824, s. 4, and the Town Police Clauses Act 1847, s. 28, are triable summarily only.

Indictment

B3.122   Statement of Offence

Outraging public decency

Particulars of Offence

A on or about the . . . day of . . . outraged public decency, namely by publicly, to wit in the street at . . . , having sexual intercourse with X, within the sight and to the outrage of other persons then present

Sentence

B3.123 The maximum penalty for the common-law offence is imprisonment and/or a fine at large. The maximum penalty for the summary offence under the Vagrancy Act 1824, s. 4, is three months' imprisonment, or a fine not exceeding level 3 on the standard scale or both; on a second conviction and commitment to the Crown Court for sentence, it is 12 months.

Elements

B3.124 The existence of the common-law offence was confirmed in *Mayling* [1963] 3 QB 717 and in *Knuller (Publishing, Printing and Promotions) Ltd* v *DPP* [1973] AC 435.

The act itself must be lewd or obscene. Evidence of intention or motive cannot be adduced to supply the element of lewdness or obscenity (*Rowley* [1991] 1 WLR 1020).

In these offences the 'person' means the penis, and under both the common-law offence and that under the Vagrancy Act 1824, there must be an intent to insult or annoy (*Evans* v *Ewels* [1972] 1 WLR 671). More than one person must be able to see the indecency complained of, but it is not necessary to prove that an observer was in fact disgusted or annoyed (*Mayling* above and *May* (1989) 91 Cr App R 157). The act must be committed where a real possibility existed that the general public might witness it (*Walker* [1996] 1 Cr App R 111). In any event, the offence under the Vagrancy Act 1824 does not require that the exposure be in a public place.

Under the common-law offence, police officers whose duty it is to watch out for acts of public indecency are members of the public who are capable of being annoyed by such actions. Where the acts complained of are plainly indecent and likely to disgust or annoy, the jury are entitled to infer such disgust and annoyance without affirmative evidence that anyone was in fact disgusted or annoyed (*Lunderbech* [1991] Crim LR 784). In that case, the offence is distinguished from that of indecent exposure to the annoyance of passengers contrary to the Town Police Clauses Act 1847, s. 28. In *Cheeseman* v *DPP* [1991] 2 WLR 1105, the court held that police officers keeping watch in a public lavatory are not passengers, but the reasoning is not applicable to the offence of outraging public decency.

It is not necessary to convict for the common-law offence that the accused should stand and expose his person in a public place. It is enough if he be in a place where a number of persons can, and do, see the exposure (*Thallman* (1863) 9 Cox CC 388). The common-law offence may thus be committed in any place to which the public resorts, whether as of right or not (*Wellard* (1884) 15 Cox CC 559). An accused cannot set up a customary right, for example, to nude bathing in a given location, as a defence to either offence (*Reed* (1871) 12 Cox CC 1; *Crumden* (1809) 2 Camp 89).

SECTION B4: THEFT, HANDLING STOLEN GOODS AND RELATED OFFENCES

THEFT

Definition

B4.1

Theft Act 1968, s. 1

(1) A person is guilty of theft if he dishonestly appropriates property belonging to another with the intention of permanently depriving the other of it; and 'thief' and 'steal' shall be construed accordingly.

Procedure

B4.2 Theft is triable either way (MCA 1980, s. 17 and sch. 1, para. 28). When tried on indictment it is a class 4 offence. *Practice Note (Mode of Trial: Guidelines)* (1995) (see **D3.7**) states that theft should be tried summarily unless the court considers that one or more of the following features is present in the case *and* that its sentencing powers are insufficient:

(a) Breach of trust by a person in a position of substantial authority, or in whom a high degree of trust is placed.
(b) Theft which has been committed or disguised in a sophisticated manner.
(c) Theft committed by an organised gang.
(d) The victim is particularly vulnerable to theft (e.g., the elderly or infirm).
(e) The unrecovered property is of high value (at least £10,000).

There are important issues in relation to territorial jurisdiction over theft, but as some of these issues involve a deeper analysis of the definition of theft, they are dealt with later in this section (see **B4.45**).

Indictment

B4.3

Statement of Offence

Theft contrary to section 1(1) of the Theft Act 1968

Particulars of Offence

A on or about the . . . day of . . . stole a pearl necklace belonging to V

It is proper to allege in a single count the theft of an aggregate sum of money or items of property where the evidence does not disclose the precise dates and amounts of each individual transaction, provided that the conduct of the accused amounted to a continuous offence over a period of time. Such an allegation is usually referred to as theft of a 'general deficiency'. Thus it would be proper to indict for theft of the total sum missing on a day on which the accused was bound to account for it, even though he clearly took it in instalments (*Balls* (1871) LR 1 CCR 328) or theft of all items stolen from a department store on one day, even though the various articles emanated from different departments of the store (*Wilson* (1979) 69 Cr App R 83; *Heaton* v *Costello* (1984) 148 JP 688). A count drafted in this way is not bad for duplicity. This principle also applies where 'money' was in different forms and it could not be said whether what was stolen was a debt, cash drawn from a bank account or cash disposed of otherwise and representing funds provided by clients of financial advisers (*Hallam* [1995] Crim LR 323). The elements of the offence must exist throughout, otherwise there would be a lack of coincidence (see **B4.27**). As to indictments for continuous offences generally, see *DPP* v *Merriman* [1973] AC 584; **D9.16** to **D9.20**.

Not all the items mentioned in an information or count do have to be proved to have been stolen (*Machent* v *Quinn* [1970] 2 All ER 255), provided it is proved that the accused stole one of the articles. However, there will be cases where the prosecution should not include in a single count more than one allegation of theft, for example where several items are alleged to have been stolen from an employer on different days (*Jackson* (1991) *The Guardian*, 20 November 1991). Some property must be specified in the indictment or information.

As to the relevance of conditional intention in drafting an indictment, see **B4.44**. As to the relationship between theft and handling, see **B4.139**.

Alternative Verdicts

In addition to the general power under the Criminal Law Act 1967, s. 6(3), the TA 1968,   **B4.4** s. 12(4), provides that, as an alternative to a conviction of theft, the jury may on a trial on indictment for theft find the accused guilty of an offence under s. 12(1) (taking a motor vehicle or other conveyance without authority etc.; see **B4.90** to **B4.98**). He is liable then as he would have been liable under s. 12(2) on summary conviction (s. 12(4): see **B4.92**).

Sentencing Guidelines: Offences of Theft Generally

The maximum penalty is seven years (TA 1968, s. 1(7)) on indictment; six months or a   **B4.5** fine not exceeding the statutory maximum, or both, summarily.

Theft is such a wide offence that no general sentencing guideline can be given. In *Upton* (1980) 2 Cr App R (S) 132, in which the offender was convicted of theft of goods worth £5 from the supermarket of which he was deputy manager, Lord Lane CJ said:

> This was petty theft and in ordinary circumstances it would, and should, not have attracted any immediate sentence of imprisonment.

> . . . non-violent petty offenders should not be allowed to take up what has become valuable space in prison. If there really is no alternative . . . to an immediate prison sentence, then it should be as short as possible . . . a prison sentence, however short, is a very unpleasant experience indeed for the inmates.

When dealt with summarily, the Magistrates' Association Guidelines (1997) indicate the following:

Aggravating Factors ⊕
For example high value; planned; sophisticated; adult involving children; organised team; related damage; vulnerable victim; offence committed on bail; previous convictions and failures to respond to previous sentences, if relevant.

Mitigating Factors ⊖
For example impulsive action; low value.

Guideline: Is compensation, discharge or fine appropriate? The guideline fine is £135 (low income), £340 (average income) or £810 (high income).

Sentencing Guidelines: Shoplifting

Court of Appeal decisions indicate that shoplifting should not attract a custodial   **B4.6** sentence, unless the offender has a record of similar offending or the shoplifting was carefully planned and executed or there were other aggravating features. A fine is the usual sentence. In *Ball* (1981) 3 Cr App R (S) 283 a suspended sentence for shoplifting a small quantity of children's clothes was quashed, the offender being an 18-year-old single woman with one child, living on social security benefit, who was in breach of a conditional discharge imposed for handling stolen goods. That was her only previous conviction. Holding that 'This was not the sort of case which merited imprisonment at all, whether suspended or immediate', and accepting advice from the social inquiry report that the offender was not in need of supervision, the Court of Appeal substituted a small fine with six months in which to pay as being 'the least wrong course which is open to us'. In *Bond* (1994) 15 Cr App R (S) 430 the offender pleaded guilty in a magistrates' court to theft of a packet of gammon steaks, worth £3.50, from a shop. The Court of Appeal said that the offence 'came nowhere near the threshold of seriousness to justify a custodial sentence'.

Where a custodial sentence is imposed for shoplifting, it will generally be very short. In *Roth* (1980) 2 Cr App R (S) 65 a one-month prison sentence was regarded as being a proper disposal for a man aged 58 who, together with his wife, committed a carefully planned theft from a shop involving goods to the value of £91. See also *MacLeod* (1981) 3 Cr App R (S) 247 (planned shoplifting of £100 worth of drink from supermarket; six weeks' imprisonment upheld). Much longer custodial sentences will be upheld where 'professional' shoplifters are at work (e.g., *Jones* (1979) 1 Cr App R (S) 136: four years upheld on offenders with 'lamentable' criminal histories who stole £300 worth of records by use of a specially made box for concealing them). Taking young children along when shoplifting is regarded by the courts as a serious aggravating feature (*Moss* (1986) 8 Cr App R (S) 276).

When dealt with summarily, the relevant Magistrates' Association Guidelines (1997) are those set out at **B4.5**.

Sentencing Guidelines: Theft from the Person

B4.7 This category covers the taking of articles from handbags, shopping bags and the activities of pickpockets. While the majority of such cases are dealt with by non-custodial sentences, particularly fines, custodial sentences have been upheld by the Court of Appeal for deterrent reasons, particularly in cases where the offender has a record of similar offending (e.g., *O'Rourke* (1994) 15 Cr App R (S) 650: three years upheld where stealing women's handbags had become the offender's speciality), and cases of 'professional' pickpocketing (e.g., *Wilson* (1981) 3 Cr App R (S) 102: three years upheld on offenders who worked as a team, one distracting the victim while the other stole from the victim's bag, and who had numerous previous convictions for similar offending). In *Masagh* (1990) 12 Cr App R (S) 568, Lloyd LJ stressed that while heavy custodial sentences were appropriate for systematic pickpocketing, particularly by offenders with records, they were quite wrong for isolated offences committed by an individual.

When dealt with summarily, the relevant Magistrates' Association Guidelines (1997) are those set out at **B4.5**.

Sentencing Guidelines: Theft in Breach of Trust

B4.8 When dealt with summarily, the Magistrates' Association Guidelines (1997) for 'theft in breach of trust' indicate the following:

Aggravating Factors ⊕
   For example casting suspicion on others; committed over a period; high value; organised team; planned; senior employee; sophisticated; vulnerable victim; offence committed on bail; previous convictions and failures to respond to previous sentences, if relevant.

Mitigating Factors ⊖
   For example impulsive action; low value; previous inconsistent attitude by employer; single item; unsupported junior.

Guideline: Is it so serious that only custody is appropriate?

The guideline case of *Barrick* (1985) 81 Cr App R 78 is concerned with serious cases where:

> a person in a position of trust, for example, an accountant, solicitor, bank employee or postman, has used that privileged and trusted position to defraud his partners or clients or employers or the general public of sizeable sums of money. He will usually, as in this case, be a person of hitherto impeccable character. It is practically certain, again as in this case, that he will never offend again and, in the nature of things, he will never again in his life be able to secure similar employment with all that that means in the shape of disgrace for himself and hardship for himself and also his family.

The guidelines indicate that such a case will attract immediate custody, save in very exceptional circumstances or where the sum involved is small. Where the amount involved is less than £10,000, terms of imprisonment ranging from the very short up to about 18 months are appropriate. Where the sum is between £10,000 and £50,000, the term should be about two or three years. Where greater sums are involved a term of $3\frac{1}{2}$ to 4 years may be appropriate. These figures assume that the case is contested. In the event of a guilty plea, an appropriate discount should be given. Other matters to be taken into account by the court, apart from the size of the sum involved, are (a) the quality and degree of trust reposed in the offender, (b) the period over which the thefts were committed, (c) the use to which the money was put, (d) the effect upon the victim, (e) the impact on the public and public confidence, (f) effect upon fellow employees or business partners, (g) effect on the offender, (h) his own history, (i) matters of mitigation special to himself, (j) any help given by him to the police.

The Court of Appeal in *Clark* [1998] 2 Cr App R (S) 95, indicated that the sentencing brackets set out in *Barrick* now required revision because of the impact of inflation upon the figures there referred to, the effect of the *Practice Statement (Crime: Sentencing)* [1992] 1 WLR 948 (see **E1.20**), and the reduction in the maximum sentence for theft from ten years to seven years. In the light of these changes, their lordships made the following suggestions, stressing that they were guidelines only and that many factors other than the amount involved might affect the sentence:

> Where the amount stolen was not small but was less than £17,500, terms of imprisonment from the very short up to 21 months would be appropriate; cases involving sums between £17,500 and £100,000 would merit two to three years; cases involving sums between £100,000 and £250,000 would merit between three to four years; cases involving £250,000 to £1 million would merit between five and nine years; cases involving £1 million or more would merit ten years or more. Those terms were appropriate for contested cases. Pleas of guilty would attract an appropriate discount. Where the sums involved were exceptionally large and not stolen on a single occasion, or the dishonesty was directed at more than one victim or group of victims, consecutive sentences might be called for.

It should be noted that all the following examples relate to the sentencing brackets as originally established in *Barrick*. Appropriate adjustments should now be made in the light of the guidance in *Clark*.

Examples of cases where immediate custody was avoided are *Kirk* (1984) 6 Cr App R (S) 231, a case decided before *Barrick* but followed in *Boggs* (1990) 12 Cr App R (S) 39, where a hotel cashier stole £316 over a period of six weeks in small amounts of cash, covering this up by voiding entries in the cash register. A sentence of two months' imprisonment suspended for 12 months was regarded as appropriate by the Court of Appeal. In *Boggs*, an identical sentence was given in respect of a theft of £439 by a person employed in a kiosk who was responsible for banking the takings. In both cases a compensation order in the sum taken was also imposed.

Cases illustrative of the sentencing bracket below £10,000 are *Chatfield* (1985) 7 Cr App R (S) 262 (four months appropriate for honorary booking secretary of a community centre who stole £350 over 2½ years); *Patel* (1986) 8 Cr App R (S) 67 (12 months proper for accounts clerk who stole £9,000 over three months) and *Ross-Goulding* [1997] 2 Cr App R (S) 348 (15 months upheld for the theft of £8,000 by a care assistant from a disabled person by forging her signature and withdrawing the cash from a building society account). Cases falling in the bracket between £10,000 and £50,000 are *Davies* (1986) 8 Cr App R (S) 25 (two years upheld in respect of a bank clerk who opened various accounts in false names and transferred to them £15,000 from the bank's account) and *Brown* (1987) 9 Cr App R (S) 266 (security officer responsible for delivering sums in cash to various companies who hid an extra bag containing £25,000 loaded by mistake and later spent the money: three years upheld). Examples of cases falling in the bracket over £100,000 are *Miller* (1985) 7 Cr App R (S) 318 (three years proper for a chief cashier responsible for loss of more than £300,000) and *Offord* (1985) 7 Cr App R (S) 327 (five years reduced to three years in light of personal mitigation where the offender, acting as a solicitor while unqualified, defrauded clients and others of £242,000).

Elements

B4.9   It has been said that theft consists of four elements: '(i) a dishonest (ii) appropriation (iii) of property belonging to another (iv) with the intention of permanently depriving the owner of it' (*Lawrence* [1971] 1 QB 373 at p. 376 per Megaw LJ, approved, in the House of Lords (sub nom. *Lawrence* v *Metropolitan Police Commissioner*) [1972] AC 626 at p. 632, per Viscount Dilhorne). A more accurate description is that theft consists of five elements, since it may be important to separate consideration of the meaning of 'property' from consideration of whether that property 'belongs to another'. Further, theft can be committed against other people than the 'owner' of it.

Meaning of 'Property'

B4.10   It cannot be said that theft has been committed unless some form of property has been dealt with in such a way as to comply with the other elements of the offence. 'Property' is partially defined in the TA 1968, s. 4, as follows:

> (1)   'Property' includes money and all other property, real or personal, including things in action and other intangible property.
> (2)   A person cannot steal land, or things forming part of land and severed from it by him or by his directions, except in the following cases, that is to say—
> (a)   when he is a trustee or personal representative, or is authorised by power of attorney, or as liquidator of a company, or otherwise, to sell or dispose of land belonging to another, and he appropriates the land or anything forming part of it by dealing with it in breach of the confidence reposed in him; or
> (b)   when he is not in possession of the land and appropriates anything forming part of the land by severing it or causing it to be severed, or after it has been severed; or
> (c)   when, being in possession of the land under a tenancy, he appropriates the whole or part of any fixture or structure let to be used with the land.
> For purposes of this subsection 'land' does not include incorporeal hereditaments; 'tenancy' means a tenancy for years or any less period and includes an agreement for such a tenancy, but a person who after the end of a tenancy remains in possession as statutory tenant or otherwise is to be treated as having possession under the tenancy, and 'let' shall be construed accordingly.
> (3)   A person who picks mushrooms growing wild on any land, or who picks flowers, fruit or foliage from a plant growing wild on any land, does not (although not in possession of the land) steal what he picks, unless he does it for reward or for sale or other commercial purpose.
> For purposes of this subsection 'mushroom' includes any fungus, and 'plant' includes any shrub or tree.
> (4)   Wild creatures, tamed or untamed, shall be regarded as property; but a person cannot steal a wild creature not tamed nor ordinarily kept in captivity, or the carcase of any

such creature, unless either it has been reduced into possession by or on behalf of another person and possession of it has not since been lost or abandoned, or another person is in course of reducing it into possession.

Money   It is clear that coins and banknotes are property which may, therefore, be **B4.11** stolen (see, for example, *Davis* (1988) 88 Cr App R 347). 'Money' does not cover accounts held with banks and building societies, even though a colloquial meaning of the term might cover such accounts. A bank or building society account may be property which may be stolen by virtue of its being a thing in action.

Real Property   Despite the apparently comprehensive reference to 'real property' in **B4.12** the TA 1968, s. 4(1), land cannot, in general, be stolen (s. 4(2)). It may, however, form the basis of an offence of obtaining property by deception contrary to the TA 1968, s. 15, or some other offence, such as criminal damage. There is, however, a theft of land when a person who is a trustee or personal representative, or who is authorised by power of attorney, or as liquidator of a company, or otherwise, to sell or dispose of land *belonging to another* appropriates the land or anything forming part of it by dealing with it in breach of the confidence reposed in him (s. 4(2)(a)).

It is theft for a person who is not in possession of land (which includes a person occupying the land under a licence as opposed to a tenancy) to appropriate something forming part of the land, by severing it or causing it to be severed, or after it has been severed (s. 4(2)(b)), though picking wild mushrooms or the flowers, fruit or foliage of wild plants is not theft unless done for reward or for sale or other commercial purpose (s. 4(3)). 'Mushroom' includes any fungus and 'plant' includes any shrub or tree (ibid.).

It is not theft for someone in possession of land to appropriate something forming part of the land, by severing it or causing it to be severed or after it has been severed, unless the occupation is under a tenancy and the thing appropriated is the whole or part of a fixture or structure let to be used with the land (s. 4(2)(c)). 'Tenancy' is defined in s. 4(2) to mean a tenancy for years or any less period and includes an agreement for such a tenancy. A person in possession as a statutory tenant or otherwise in possession after the end of a tenancy is to be treated as in possession under the tenancy.

Whilst land may not generally be stolen, incorporeal hereditaments may be stolen, since s. 4(2) specifically excludes incorporeal hereditaments from the meaning of 'land'. Incorporeal hereditaments, i.e., intangible real property, include easements, profits à prendre and rentcharges.

Personal Property   Personal property includes tangible personal property, which **B4.13** might also be described as 'things in possession', 'choses in possession', 'chattels' or 'goods'. In addition to such things as cars, televisions and handbags, personal property refers to the piece of printed paper upon which a cheque is written (a cheque form) and the piece of paper upon which an examination or other confidential information is written.

Personal property also includes things in action and other intangible property; 'things in action' are otherwise known as 'choses in action'.

> 'Chose in action' is a known legal expression used to describe all personal rights of property which can only be claimed or enforced by action, and not by taking physical possession. (*Torkington* v *Magee* [1902] 2 KB 427 at p. 430, per Channell J quoted in *Kohn* (1979) 69 Cr App R 395 at p. 404)

A debt for a liquidated, or known, sum is a common form of thing in action. The term also includes shares in a company. In *Marshall* [1998] 2 Cr App R 282, the Court of Appeal, having noted the definition provided in *Torkington* v *Magee* [1902] 2 KB 427, stated, *obiter*, that, because the issuing of a ticket resulted in the creation of a contract between the customer and London Underground, the contractual rights arising were enforceable by action:

> Therefore it is arguable, we suppose, that by the transaction each party has acquired a chose in action. On the side of the purchaser it is represented by a right to use the ticket to the extent which it allows travel on the underground system. On the side of London Underground Limited it encompasses the right to insist that the ticket is used by no one other than the purchaser. It is that right which is disregarded when the ticket is acquired by the appellant and sold on.

Whether this supposition is correct is a matter open to considerable debate. Ordinarily, choses in action have been thought to have rather more limited application than this case would suggest. It suggests that any contractual right gives rise to a chose in action, but this rather seems to slide over the requirement in the definition that there must be a personal right of property, which does not necessarily arise in all contracts. Indeed, the contract in this case is not about any property rights but is about acquiring the right to travel by the purchaser, within the limitations set by London Underground (and general passenger carriage rules). This seems insufficient, it is submitted, to give rise to a chose in action.

'Other intangible property' includes patents (Patents Act 1977, s. 30), copyright (Copyright, Designs and Patents Act 1988, s. 1) and design rights (Copyright, Designs and Patents Act 1988, s. 213). The Privy Council held in *A-G of Hong Kong* v *Nai-Keung* [1987] 1 WLR 1339 that export quotas for textiles in Hong Kong are a form of 'other intangible property', on the basis that such quotas may be freely bought and sold. However, confidential information is not a form of intangible property (see *Oxford* v *Moss* (1978) 68 Cr App R 183). Thus a student was not guilty of theft for copying the questions from an examination paper and then returning the paper. If the student had intended to keep the paper itself, he could have been charged with theft of the piece of paper. It might have been theft even if the examination paper had been returned if it was no longer the same thing, by analogy with *Downes* (1983) 77 Cr App R 260 (see **B4.38**). The tax vouchers belonging to the Inland Revenue which were stolen in *Downes* are best described as 'other intangible property', since the Court of Appeal was not interested in the vouchers as pieces of paper, and they could not be a thing in action since no one could sue on them.

Subsequent to *Preddy* [1996] AC 815 (see **B4.28** and **B5.117** *et seq*.), Professor Sir John Smith has argued that a valuable security as defined in s. 20(3) of the TA 1968 (see **B5.43** and **B5.47**) is property for the purposes of s. 4 (see, e.g., the commentary to *Horsman* [1998] QB 531 which appears in [1998] Crim LR 128). That there is considerable merit in the point has been recognised by the Court of Appeal on one occasion (but not in all cases), see *Arnold* [1997] 4 All ER 1. Whilst the argument is primarily made in the context of offences contrary to s. 15, the argument clearly also applies to theft.

B4.14 ***Cheques and Bank Accounts*** A cheque as a piece of paper, i.e. as a cheque form, is a form of personal property and may be stolen, regardless of the state of the account upon which the cheque is drawn (*Duru* [1974] 1 WLR 2; *Kohn* (1979) 69 Cr App R 395). This proposition is not affected by the decision in *Preddy* [1996] AC 815 and its reliance upon *Danger* (1857) Dears & B 307 since, as Professor Sir John Smith has made clear (see, e.g., the commentary to *Horsman* [1998] QB 531), that is concerned with the fact that the cheque represents the chose in action, e.g., the account held by a customer at his bank, and not with the piece of paper or the cheque as a valuable security (see **B4.13**).

An account held at a bank or a building society provides the account holder with a thing in action. Provided the account is in credit, the relationship of debtor and creditor exists between the bank and the customer. The debt cannot be physically handled or possessed, but it can be enforced by action and is a thing in action which may be stolen

(*Kohn* (1979) 69 Cr App Rep 395 at p. 404; see also, e.g., *Chan Man-sin* v *The Queen* [1988] 1 WLR 196; *Wille* (1987) 86 Cr App R 296; *Preddy* [1996] AC 815 at p. 825).

The Court of Appeal went further in *Kohn* in saying that if the account is within the agreed limits of an overdraft facility, there is an obligation on the bank to meet cheques drawn on that account. This is an obligation which may be enforced by action and so constitutes a right of property which may properly be described as a thing in action (*Kohn* (1979) 69 Cr App R 395 at p. 407). Although, strictly speaking, the thing in action is the benefit of the contractual arrangement with the bank, the Privy Council in *Chan Man-sin* v *The Queen* [1988] 1 WLR 196 (at p. 198E) accepted the statement in *Kohn*.

There is not even a notional relationship of debtor and creditor when the account is overdrawn and not within the limit of an overdraft facility. The bank may decline to honour a cheque drawn on an account in that state. If it does honour such a cheque, it does so only as a matter of honour and not as the consequence of an obligation. Thus where the account is overdrawn, there is no thing in action capable of being stolen (*Kohn* (1979) 69 Cr App R 395 at p. 408).

It is important to be aware that what really matters is whether the property belongs to another (*Preddy* [1996] AC 815 (at p. 834) and see **B4.19** to **B4.21**).

Wild Creatures   All wild creatures are property, but where a wild creature is not either **B4.15** tamed or ordinarily kept in captivity or is the carcase of such a creature, it can be stolen only if it has either (a) been reduced into possession by or on behalf of another person and possession of it has not since been lost or abandoned, or (b) another person is in the course of reducing it into possession (TA 1968, s. 4(4)).

Things that Cannot Be Stolen

Electricity cannot be stolen (see *Low* v *Blease* [1975] Crim LR 513) but it is an offence **B4.16** to abstract electricity contrary to the TA 1968, s. 13 (see **B4.111** *et seq.*).

The Court of Appeal has recently affirmed the view that human bodies (or parts thereof) cannot be stolen as, without more, they are not capable of being property protected by rights (*Kelly* [1998] 3 All ER 741, following *Sharpe* (1857) Dears & B 160). Parts of a corpse are capable of being property 'if they have acquired different attributes by virtue of the application of skill, such as dissection or preservation techniques, for exhibition or teaching purposes' (*Kelly* at pp. 749–750, following *Doodeward* v *Spence* (1907) 6 CLR 406 and *Dobson* v *North Tyneside Health Authority* [1997] 1 WLR 596 at p. 601). It follows that, e.g., Egyptian mummies in museums can be stolen in view of the preservation techniques used to ensure that they can be displayed. In *Kelly* the court indicated potential future developments in the law when it said, at p. 750:

> It may be that if . . . the question arises, the courts will hold that human body parts are capable of being property for the purposes of [TA 1968, s. 4], even without the acquisition of different attributes, if they have a use or significance beyond their mere existence. This may be so if, for example, they are intended for use in an organ transplant operation, for the extraction of DNA or, for that matter, as an exhibit in a trial.

Whether human gametes or embryos can be protected by the law of theft remains to be seen, but there is a natural reluctance to engage in property based discussions when discussing material that has the potential for human life. There are offences in relation to human corpses created by the Human Tissue Act 1961 and the Anatomy Act 1984, and the Human Fertilisation and Embryology Act 1990, s. 41 makes breach of various provisions of the Act an offence. It remains to be considered whether certain items, less controversial, can be stolen even if they are simply removed from the body, but it is submitted that it is clear that they should be regarded as property. Examples include hair (in particular, hair of a loved one offered as a present even if not displayed in a casket or brooch) and toenails and fingernails (for those keen to collect them, so the artist who retained a collection of such nails and of her own pubic hair should be regarded as having property rights in them even before she used them in some of her work for the Edinburgh Festival 1998). Some indication that there is no doubt that these items would be property is provided by the Court of Appeal's failure to comment on the conviction when reducing the sentence (on an appeal against sentence) of a driver for theft when he poured a sample of urine away (see *Welsh* [1974] RTR 478).

Meaning of 'Belonging to Another'

B4.17   The TA 1968, s. 5, provides assistance in determining to whom property belongs:

Theft Act 1968, s. 5

> (1)   Property shall be regarded as belonging to any person having possession or control of it, or having in it any proprietary right or interest (not being an equitable interest arising only from an agreement to transfer or grant an interest).
>
> (2)   Where property is subject to a trust, the persons to whom it belongs shall be regarded as including any person having a right to enforce the trust, and an intention to defeat the trust shall be regarded accordingly as an intention to deprive of the property any person having that right.
>
> (3)   Where a person receives property from or on account of another, and is under an obligation to the other to retain and deal with that property or its proceeds in a particular way, the property or proceeds shall be regarded (as against him) as belonging to the other.
>
> (4)   Where a person gets property by another's mistake, and is under an obligation to make restoration (in whole or in part) of the property or its proceeds or of the value thereof, then to the extent of that obligation the property or proceeds shall be regarded (as against him) as belonging to the person entitled to restoration, and an intention not to make restoration shall be regarded accordingly as an intention to deprive that person of the property or proceeds.
>
> (5)   Property of a corporation sole shall be regarded as belonging to the corporation notwithstanding a vacancy in the corporation.

The identity of the 'other' is generally irrelevant. All that is required is that the property belong to someone other than the accused.

Ownership, Possession or Control

B4.18   In the classic case, theft is perpetrated against the owner of property, who need not be in possession, whether actual or constructive (*Hancock* [1990] 2 QB 242). However, it can be perpetrated against people with lesser interests in the property, as the TA 1968, s. 5(1), makes clear. A person may be in control of property, even though unaware of its presence, since the general principle is that control of a site by excluding others from it is prima facie control of articles on the site (*Woodman* [1974] QB 754 at p. 758, where the site owner was in control of scrap metal which, unknown to him, had been left after the site's clearance).

If the interest of a person satisfies s. 5(1), the property belongs to that person for the purposes of the TA 1968. In *Turner (No. 2)* [1971] 1 WLR 901, the Court of Appeal held that an owner of property can steal that property from someone else with a sufficient interest, including mere possession through a bailment. The owner of a car had thus stolen it from a garage proprietor who had been undertaking work on it. The trial judge had directed that the garage proprietor had no lien over the car, which seems to have been an incorrect application of the civil law. The Court of Appeal had to decide whether the conviction could be upheld on the basis that there was no lien. This the court surprisingly did, even though the owner could easily have regained possession in a more usual fashion than driving it away furtively at night. Nevertheless it is accurate to say that the garage proprietor had possession of the car, which is sufficient for it to belong to another under s. 5(1). However, mere possession by the police of an impounded car has been held by a Crown Court judge not to be sufficient to enable the owner to be guilty of theft by retaking it (*Meredith* [1973] Crim LR 253).

The other to whom the property belongs need not be an individual, but may be a corporation such as a company incorporated by registration under the Companies Act 1985. Such a company is a legal entity separate from its members (shareholders) and directors. It can own money, things in action and other property which may be stolen from it by persons who are in total control of it by reason of shareholding and directorships (*A-G's Ref (No. 2 of 1982)* [1984] QB 624; *Philippou* (1989) 89 Cr App R 290). In cases where persons in control of a company are accused of theft of the company's property, issues may arise relating to other aspects of the offence of theft, including appropriation (see **B4.25**), dishonesty (see **B4.34** to **B4.37**) and intention permanently to deprive (see **B4.38** to **B4.44**).

The Crown has a prerogative right in royal fish (whale and sturgeon caught within territorial waters) and wild swans, preserved by the Wild Creatures and Forest Laws Act 1971. Under the Treasure Act 1996, s. 4(1), when treasure is found, it vests, subject to prior interests and rights, in the franchisee (if there is one) and otherwise in the Crown; 'treasure' is defined in s. 1 of the Act, 'prior interests or rights' in s. 2, and 'franchisee' in s. 5.

Proprietary Right or Interest

For the purposes of the TA 1968, property 'belongs' to any person who has any **B4.19** proprietary right or interest in it other than an equitable interest arising only from an agreement to transfer or grant an interest (s. 5(1)). A partner, who has a proprietary interest in partnership property, may steal it, as his copartners also have such an interest (*Bonner* [1970] 1 WLR 838). In *Goodwin* [1996] Crim LR 262, the Court of Appeal held, on a charge of going equipped to steal (see **B4.118** *et seq.*), that the coins and tokens in a gaming machine belonged to another even when a player inserted Kenyan shillings (worth less than the equivalently sized and shaped 50 pence piece) and so they could be stolen. This result involves no contravention of the gaming legislation, which was important to the result in *Gilks* [1972] 1 WLR 1341, see **B4.24**. In *Marshall* [1998] 2 Cr App R 282, the appellant had purchased from travellers tickets and travel cards that had not been fully used up and sold them on. The Court of Appeal was of the view that the property 'belongs to London Underground'. The trial judge's ruling was that 'although the tickets had passed into the possession and control of the customers, London Underground retained a proprietary right or interest in the tickets which were to be regarded therefore as the property of London Underground pursuant to section 5(1) of the Act'. Quite on what basis London Underground retained a proprietary interest in the tickets and travel cards is not clear.

If it is established that one person has handed to another property under a trust, the giver retains a beneficial interest in that property, which is a proprietary interest for the purposes of s. 5(1) and (2) (see *Clowes (No. 2)* [1994] 2 All ER 316 and *Wain* [1995] 2 Cr App R 660). It is, therefore, not necessary to use s. 5(3). In practice, it is most likely that s. 5(3) will continue to be used to avoid intricate discussions of the law of trusts, although the requirement that the obligation be a legal one under s. 5(3) may give rise to the necessity to deal with exactly the same issues. One view is that s. 5(3) is, in fact, more difficult to satisfy, see the discussion of *Wain* at (1994) 1 Arch News 5.

A bank account (i.e. the debt owed by the bank to the account holder) belongs to the customer (*Kohn* (1979) 69 Cr App R 395). When a thing in action is created by the writing of a cheque, the only person to whom it can belong is the payee. Thus he cannot steal a thing in action when a cheque is written in his favour (*Davies* (1988) 88 Cr App R 347 at p. 351). The Court of Appeal in *Shadrokh-Cigari* [1988] Crim LR 465 appears to have thought that banker's drafts created by the Midland Bank to the credit of the payee could be property belonging to another as against the payee. That, however, can only be the case with regard to the drafts as pieces of paper, but not with regard to the drafts as things in action.

Trust property 'belongs' to the trustee who has legal title to it and also to 'any person having a right to enforce the trust' (s. 5(2)), that is, any beneficiary of the trust or, in the case of a charitable trust, the A-G (Charities Act 1993, s. 33). A trustee who appropriates trust property with the intention of defeating the trust is to be regarded as intending to deprive the person who has the right to enforce the trust of property (TA 1968, s. 5(2)). A solicitor is required by Law Society Rules to hold client money in a separate bank account. Any money paid in, and the thing in action representing that money, is held by the solicitor satisfying s. 5(2), so that transferring funds to a business account is theft (see *Hedworth* (1998 unreported)).

However, it seems that property subject to a constructive trust does not 'belong', for the purposes of the TA 1968, to the person for whose benefit the trust was imposed. In *A-G's Ref (No. 1 of 1985)* [1986] QB 491, a publican sold his own beer in a tied house, keeping the profit for himself. The Court of Appeal, at p. 503, took the view that s. 5(2) does not import the constructive trust into the TA 1968, and so the profit was the property of the publican and did not 'belong' to the brewery. To include constructive trusts, according to the court, would have made criminal a whole area of behaviour which had previously not been considered to be criminal. Such a change would demand more explicit wording. Similar sentiments were expressed in *Governor of Pentonville Prison, ex parte Tarling* (1978) 70 Cr App R 77. Further, the Court of Appeal in *A-G's Ref (No. 1 of 1985)* decided that there was no identifiable trust property which could form the subject-matter of a theft charge. The obligation of the publican was only to account for the profit being made, until, if ever, that profit was identified as a separate piece of property, which then could provide the basis for a theft charge. However, this situation can often be dealt with under the TA 1968, s. 5(3) (see **B4.17**).

It is clear from the decision of the Divisional Court in *Powell* v *MacRae* [1977] Crim LR 571 that a bribe received by an employee does not 'belong' to the employer and therefore the employee does not commit theft when he keeps it as against the employer.

Property Belonging to Another: Equitable Proprietary Interests

B4.20   The TA 1968 deals with two instances where property appears to have been transferred but is nevertheless to be regarded as belonging to another so that the recipient may be guilty of theft: s. 5(3) (see **B4.23**) and s. 5(4) (see **B4.24**). There is an argument that these sections were unnecessary since the owner of the property may have an equitable proprietary interest in the property that is no longer in his possession or apparently ownership. If he does retain such an interest, it is sufficient to satisfy s. 5(1). Indeed, there is a view that s. 5(1) ought to be used more often so as to avoid the complexities of s. 5(3) (see *Wakeman* v *Farrar* [1974] Crim LR 136). Where there is an obligation to retain and deal with the property it would not be necessary to rely upon s. 5(3) but it would be right to argue both points. In *Hallam* [1995] Crim LR 323, the Court of Appeal held that the clients of financial advisers, having paid cheques in the expectation that investments would be made on their behalf, retained an equitable interest in the cheques, their proceeds and any balance in accounts operated by the accused or the company through which they operated to which the payment could be traced. It was immaterial whether the property was regarded as belonging to another through s. 5(1) or (3). See also *Governor of Brixton Prison, ex parte Levin* [1997] AC 741.

There are two situations where s. 5(3) must be utilised. One is where there is a constructive trust (see **B4.19**), which will satisfy s. 5(3). The second is where there is no legal or equitable interest in the property, but s. 5(3), as a deeming provision, regards the property for the purposes of the law of theft as belonging to another (*Smith* (1997 unreported); *Klineberg* [1999] 1 Cr App R 427; and *Floyd* v *DPP* [1999] All ER (D) 1190, unreported in printed form). It may be advisable therefore for reliance to be placed, in criminal courts, on s. 5(3), rather than on the complex, and probably narrower, civil law rules.

An equitable proprietary interest may be retained where the criteria for the application of s. 5(4) are satisfied, that is, e.g., money is paid over on the basis of a mistake. This appeared to be the implication of *Chase Manhattan Bank NA* v *Israel-British Bank (London) Ltd* [1981] Ch 105 (see *Shadrokh-Cigari* [1988] Crim LR 465). However, this is a highly controversial decision which has been severely criticised in subsequent decisions (see *Re Goldcorp Exchange Ltd* [1995] 1 AC 74 and *Westdeutsche Landesbank Girozentrale* v *Islington LBC* [1996] AC 669) to the point that it would appear to be inadvisable for a criminal court to rely on the principle rather than making use of s. 5(4).

Requirement that Property Must Exist and Belong to Another at the Time it Is Appropriated

At the time of the appropriation, there must be property belonging to another in **B4.21** existence. There was no theft where a person decided not to pay for a meal after he had eaten it (*Corcoran* v *Whent* [1977] Crim LR 52; see also *Stuart* (1982) *The Times*, 14 December 1982). It is particularly important when considering charges related to intangible property that, first, the type of property be identified, and, then, that those to whom it belongs be identified, as is exemplified by *Preddy* [1996] AC 815 (see **B5.16**).

A chose, or thing, in action is, for example, created by a cheque. This chose in action can only ever belong to the payee. He cannot steal it because he is the only person to whom it ever belongs. Another chose in action exists, which is the debt owed by the bank to the account holder who wrote the cheque. However, this thing in action (or part of it, assuming that the cheque would not extinguish the account) is never acquired by the payee. He gets a thing in action representing the thing in action (or part of it) that the account holder has with the bank. For the purposes of theft, there are a number of ways around this '*Preddy*' problem. First, the accused need not acquire anything for theft. Rather, he must appropriate it, which includes destruction or, presumably, reduction of the property (see **B4.28**). Secondly, TA 1968, s. 5(3), may apply to make the property apparently belonging to the accused actually, for the purposes only of theft, belong to another (see **B4.23**). Finally, the person for whom a thing in action is created (the accused payee) may hold it as a trustee for its creator; whether this argument is viable remains to be determined (see *Nathan* [1997] Crim LR 835). Whilst any of these arguments may assist with a conviction for theft, they do not operate where the charge is obtaining property by deception (see **B5.16**).

The act of appropriation may coincide with the transfer of ownership in that property. For example the alleged act of appropriation may be the pouring of petrol into the car's tank at a self-service station. This is also the moment of transfer of ownership (Sale of Goods Act 1979, s. 18). It had been assumed that there could not be theft in this instance. However, *Gomez* [1993] AC 442 has decided that consent of the owner is irrelevant in deciding whether there has been an appropriation (see **B4.29**). Therefore, the only question in the example is whether the property belonged to another. It appears to be consistent with the decision in *Gomez* that theft has been committed in this example, provided the *mens rea* is present. Whilst the House of Lords did not approve the judgment of Bingham LJ in *Dobson* v *General Accident Fire and Life Assurance Corporation plc* [1990] 1 QB 274, the solution which he accepted may resolve the current problem. He assumed that the question is whether the property belonged to another immediately before the alleged act of appropriation, on which basis any transfer of ownership by the alleged act of appropriation would not prevent theft being committed. This would certainly be consistent with the decision of the Court of Appeal in *Lawrence* [1971] 1 QB 373, but it is unclear whether the House of Lords in that case ([1972] AC 626, at p. 632) accepted the view of the Court of Appeal. The decision of the House of Lords in *Lawrence*, at least with regard to the point about consent, has been approved in *Gomez*.

It follows that complicated issues of civil law do not have to be considered when the alleged act of appropriation is coincidental with transfer of ownership. That is consistent with Lord Roskill in *Morris* [1984] AC 320, where he indicated that difficult questions of whether contracts were void or voidable on the ground of mistake or fraud or whether any mistake is sufficiently fundamental to vitiate a contract should, so far as possible, be confined to those fields of law to which they are immediately relevant. This view was quoted with approval by Parker LJ in *Dobson*, and this portion of the judgment of Parker LJ was approved by Lord Keith in *Gomez*.

The stricture against becoming involved in the intricacies of the civil law cannot apply in all circumstances since it is sometimes not possible to ignore it. For example, it may be necessary to determine to whom property belongs well before, rather than immediately before, any alleged act of appropriation. So it was essential in *Walker* [1984] Crim LR 112 to consider the civil law. Walker had sold a video cassette recorder to a customer who had returned it for repair. Walker then sold the recorder and was charged with stealing it from the customer. Walker's defence was that under the law on sale of goods, the customer had rejected the recorder (so that ownership of it had reverted to Walker) by suing Walker for the price of it. Dunn LJ, giving the judgment of the Court of Appeal, stated that 'a careful direction as to the law relating to the passing of property and rejection of goods under the provisions of the Sale of Goods Act [1979] was plainly required' and that 'there is no distinction between the civil law and the criminal law'.

In *Edwards* v *Ddin* [1976] 1 WLR 942, the Divisional Court applied rule 5(1) of what is now the Sale of Goods Act 1979, s. 18, to hold that the accused became the owner of petrol when it was poured into his car by a garage attendant. Driving off later without paying could not be theft. It is unlikely that there was an appropriation at an earlier time. (In such a situation it may be that a deception offence or the offence of making off without payment is committed: see **B5.68**.)

The civil law has also been applied with regard to theft in supermarkets. The Divisional Court in *Davies* v *Leighton* (1978) 68 Cr App R 4 decided that ownership of goods in a supermarket does not pass until they are paid for at the checkout. Shoppers, therefore, do not become the owners of goods which they pick from the shelves or have handed to them by a shop assistant in the shop; whilst in the shop, the shopper merely has possession of the goods and presents himself at the checkout where he makes an offer to buy which the cashier may accept. The goods are appropriated when removed from the shelves (see **B4.26**), so theft is committed if the necessary *mens rea* is present.

The Court of Appeal in *Wheeler* (1991) 92 Cr App R 279 was obliged to examine the intricacies of the Sale of Goods Act 1979, s. 22, in determining the liability of the defendant not only for theft, but also for obtaining property by deception (see **B5.23**).

Abandoned Goods

B4.22   In *Small* (1988) 86 Cr App R 170 the Court of Appeal, in considering whether a person is dishonest if he has a belief that property has been abandoned, referred to *White* (1912) 7 Cr App R 266 and *Ellerman's Wilson Line Ltd* v *Webster* [1952] 1 Lloyd's Rep 179 and implicitly assumed that the proposition from those cases that one cannot steal abandoned property remains correct.

Obligation to Retain and Deal with Property or Proceeds as Property Belonging to Another

Section 5(3) of the TA 1968 provides: **B4.23**

> Where a person receives property from or on account of another, and is under an obligation to the other to retain and deal with that property or its proceeds in a particular way, the property or proceeds shall be regarded (as against him) as belonging to the other.

See **B4.20** for consideration of the circumstances in which the retention of an equitable proprietary interest means that a sufficient interest is maintained in the property for it to belong to another, and thus there may be no need for recourse to s. 5(3).

The obligation in s. 5(3) is on the receiver of property to retain and deal with it, or its proceeds, in a particular way. The obligation must be a legal one; and a moral or social obligation is not sufficient (*Hall* [1973] QB 126; *Wakeman* v *Farrar* [1974] Crim LR 136; *Meech* [1974] QB 549; *Mainwaring* (1981) 74 Cr App R 99; *Davidge* v *Bunnett* [1984] Crim LR 297; *DPP* v *Huskinson* (1988) 152 JP 582; *Breaks* [1998] Crim LR 349; *Smith* (1997 unreported); *Klineberg* [1999] 1 Cr App R 427; *Floyd* v *DPP* [1999] All ER (D) 1190, unreported in printed form: cf. *Hayes* (1976) 64 Cr App R 82). The Court of Appeal in *Arnold* [1997] 4 All ER 1 has said that what needs to be identified is an obligation 'which clearly requires the recipient of the property to retain and deal with that property or its proceeds in a particular way for the benefit of the transferor [of the bill of exchange]' and 'no words of limitation in relation to the interest of the transferor's interest' should be introduced over and above those demanded by s. 5(3). This is the case even where the transferor is the 'true owner' but he has recognised by agreement an obligation sufficient to satisfy s. 5(3).

A defendant need not have been under an obligation to deal with the particular monies or property handed over: 'It is sufficient that he is under an obligation to keep in existence a fund equivalent to that which he has received' (J. C. Smith, *The Law of Theft*, 6th ed., para. 73, approved in *Lewis* v *Lethbridge* [1987] Crim LR 59). The courts' approach in identifying whether there is a legal obligation is consistent with relevant civil law principles. Whether an agent is obliged to keep his principal's money or property separate from his own or whether the relationship is merely that of creditor and debtor will depend upon their intentions. Civil law principles were applied in *Williams* [1995] Crim LR 77, where the accused acted as a solicitor in a client's property transaction. After completion of the transaction, he retained £3,000 which should have been used to pay the mortgagee. The accused was held to be under a separate obligation to the bank, which was more than merely a commercial undertaking, even though the client was the owner and legal recipient of the money to whom the accused also owed an obligation.

An obligation will normally arise where, for example, a person receives money from sponsors for onward transmission to a charity, either because the charity imposes such an obligation as a condition of involvement or because the sponsors impose such an obligation, at least implicitly, in handing over the money (see J. C. Smith, *The Law of Theft*, 6th ed., pp. 38–39, approved in *Wain* [1995] 2 Cr App R 660). Thus where the money, or its equivalent, is not then handed over to the charity, that money belongs to another and, provided the other elements of the offence are satisfied (in particular dishonesty), a conviction for theft may follow (see *Wain*, overruling any suggestions to the contrary in *Lewis* v *Lethbridge*). Indeed, in such a situation, the defendant may have had a trust imposed upon him sufficient to satisfy s. 5(2) (which seems to be the explanation for the sentence in *Wain* at p. 665f).

The express contractual term to deal with investors' money in a particular way in *Smith* (1997 unreported) meant that the necessary obligation existed. As theft was alleged to be from the resulting company rather than the investors, the allegation of theft was upheld. In *Klineberg*, the allegation was that the money was stolen from intending purchasers of timeshares rather than from the company established to sell the timeshares. This meant that the necessary obligation had to be established with regard to each of the intending purchasers. This could be established on the facts (taking particular account of the element of the scheme whereby investors' money would be safeguarded by a trusteeship pending completion of the purchase) and, where it could be established that the money had not been used properly, theft convictions were upheld.

It is not sufficient that a duty to account arises (*Powell* v *MacRae* [1977] Crim LR 571; *A-G's Ref (No. 1 of 1985)* [1986] QB 491). Nor is it sufficient to establish the relationship of debtor and creditor. In *Hall* [1973] QB 126, a travel agent received money from customers as deposits and payments for air flights which were never provided nor was any of the money refunded. However, the accused's only obligation in relation to the money was as a debtor to the customers; he was not obliged to retain and deal with the money in a particular way. It might have been possible to make special arrangements which would have satisfied s. 5(3), but this would have required the creation of something akin to a separate fund out of which only the flight tickets for these particular customers could have been purchased. It is unlikely that such an arrangement will exist in such circumstances.

It would seem to be implicit, at least in the requirement that the obligation be a legal one, that it must also be one which is legally enforceable. Two cases cause some problems with regard to this requirement. To the extent that these cases run contrary to the clear requirement that the obligation must be a legal one, they must be regarded as highly questionable. In *Cullen* (1974 unreported) the Court of Appeal held that theft was committed when a man gave his mistress some money to buy food and pay certain domestic debts but she spent it on herself. The problem is that it is usually thought that the parties to 'domestic arrangements' about housekeeping do not intend to create legally enforceable obligations (*Balfour* v *Balfour* [1919] 2 KB 571) and yet Roskill LJ (giving the judgment of the court) stated that there was a legal obligation to deal with the money as the man directed and it did not cease to be such an obligation simply because the accused was his mistress at the time.

In *Meech* [1974] QB 549, the Court of Appeal was satisfied that there was an obligation to deal with money in a particular way, even though it was plainly unenforceable. McCord had obtained a cheque by fraud and given it to Meech to cash. Before Meech cashed the cheque he discovered the fraud. Meech, with Parslow and Jolliffe, staged a fake robbery in which the money, the proceeds of the cheque, was appropriated. It was held that Meech's obligation to deal with the proceeds in a particular way, though unenforceable, was sufficient to bring s. 5(3) into operation.

The courts have made clear that whether an obligation sufficient to satisfy s. 5(3) arises depends upon the particular facts of the case (see *Hall* and *McHugh* (1993) 97 Cr App R 335). Whether the facts actually give rise to a situation such that an obligation arises is a matter, on trial on indictment, for the jury to determine, after an appropriate direction from the judge. The functions of judge and jury were described as follows in *Mainwaring*, at p. 107 (approved in *Dubar* [1994] 1 WLR 1484 and *Breaks* [1998] Crim LR 349):

> Whether or not an obligation arises is a matter of law, because an obligation must be a legal obligation. But a legal obligation arises only in certain circumstances, and in many cases the circumstances cannot be known until the facts have been established. It is for the jury, not the judge, to establish the facts, if they are in dispute.

> What, in our judgment, a judge ought to do is this: if the facts relied upon by the prosecution are in dispute he should direct the jury to make their findings on the facts, and then say to them: 'If you find the facts to be such-and-such, then I direct you as a matter of law that a legal obligation arose to which section 5(3) applies.

If the facts are not in dispute, it may be appropriate for the judge to direct the jury that an obligation had been undertaken by the person receiving the property.

According to *McHugh*, the obligation must be understood by both parties. However, it is submitted that the crucial factor is only that the accused be aware of it. There might be circumstances where the accused knows that an obligation is imposed upon him, but the other person concerned is ignorant of this obligation. This should be sufficient for liability. The accused must know of the obligation (*Wills* (1991) 92 Cr App R 297), but for such knowledge it is not necessary that he understand that an obligation existed, rather he must appreciate the necessary facts which, as a matter of law, amount to an obligation (*Dubar*).

Obligation to Make Restoration of Property as Property Belonging to Another

The TA 1968, s. 5(4), deals with the case where ownership in property is passed by **B4.24** mistake to another who is under an obligation to return the property or its proceeds. Section 5(4) covers both tangible and intangible property. The property is regarded, as against the recipient, as belonging to the person entitled to restoration:

> Where a person gets property by another's mistake, and is under an obligation to make restoration (in whole or in part) of the property or its proceeds or of the value thereof, then to the extent of that obligation the property or proceeds shall be regarded (as against him) as belonging to the person entitled to restoration, and an intention not to make restoration shall be regarded accordingly as an intention to deprive that person of the property or proceeds.

As the Court of Appeal recognised in *Gilks* [1972] 1 WLR 1341, s. 5(4) was enacted to deal with the mischief of the decision in *Moynes* v *Cooper* [1956] 1 QB 439. Moynes was overpaid in his weekly wages, having received an advance payment which was not then deducted from his pay packet at the end of the week. Moynes was not guilty of an offence under the Larceny Act 1916 because, *inter alia*, he was the only person with a legal interest in the money. The TA 1968, s. 5(4), would now apply to such a case: Moynes had clearly 'got' tangible property in that he had received coins and notes.

In *A-G's Ref (No. 1 of 1983)* [1985] QB 182, s. 5(4) was applied to intangible property. A policewoman had been mistakenly credited with wages and overtime for a day which she had not worked. Her bank account was credited by credit transfer with £74.74. The Court of Appeal was satisfied that she had got property, since she had acquired a thing in action against her bank, that is, a right to sue the bank for the debt which it owed to her. This is clearly a form of property (see **B4.14**). See also *Stalham* [1993] Crim LR 310.

Not only does 'property' have a wide meaning, but so also does the word 'got'. It is about as wide a word as could possibly have been adopted (*A-G's Ref (No. 1 of 1983)*). Consequently, it would not only cover the handing over of coins and notes as in *Moynes* v *Cooper*, but also the crediting of a bank account by credit transfer.

Section 5(4) applies only where some error has been made by the giver of the property which amounts to a mistake. In *Moynes* v *Cooper* the mistake was the error of the wages clerk in believing that M was entitled to his full wages, whereas there should have been a deduction to account for the money received in advance. In *A-G's Ref (No. 1 of 1983)* the mistake was the belief that the policewoman had worked on a particular day and was entitled to wages and overtime, when in fact she had not so worked.

Section 5(4) does not apply unless the obligation to make restoration is a legal obligation (*Gilks* [1972] 1 WLR 1341). Gilks placed a bet on a horse called Flying Scot. The race was won by Flying Taff. The relief manager paid out to Gilks as if he had backed the winning horse and so Gilks was overpaid by £106.63. Gilks knew that a mistake had been made, but decided to keep the money. The Court of Appeal held that Gilks did not owe a legal obligation to return the money because the bookmaker could not have sued on a gaming transaction (*Morgan* v *Ashcroft* [1938] 1 KB 490). The court held further that s. 5(4) did not apply to the moral or social obligation of Gilks to return the money.

In *A-G's Ref (No. 1 of 1983)* [1985] QB 182 the Court of Appeal decided that 'restoration' has the same meaning as 'restitution'. Consequently, it has to be established that the recipient of the property is under an obligation within the general principles of restitution. The Court of Appeal went on to say that a recipient of property is obliged to pay for a benefit received when it has been given under a mistake on the part of the giver about a material fact. The mistake has to be about a fundamental or essential fact and the payment must have been induced by the mistaken fact (*Norwich Union Fire Insurance Society Ltd* v *Wm H. Price Ltd* [1934] AC 455). Consequently, not everyone who receives property under a mistake sufficient to satisfy the first element of s. 5(4) will, as a result of that mistake, be under an obligation to make restoration.

In an *obiter* statement the Court of Appeal in *Davis* (1988) 88 Cr App R 347 indicated that the 'language of quasi-contract and of other parts of the civil law' are 'unwelcome visitors to a statute which is supposed to furnish lay juries with tests which they can readily grasp and apply'. It is submitted that the solution must be not a refusal to make use of the law of quasi-contract or restitution, but rather that care should be taken in directions given to juries such that the jury are clear that if they find certain facts then an obligation to restore has been established. This approach is consistent with that to be used when directing juries with regard to s. 5(3) as laid down in *Mainwaring* (1981) 74 Cr App R 99 (see **B4.23**).

'Appropriation'

B4.25   'Appropriation' is defined in the TA 1968, s. 3:

> (1)   Any assumption by a person of the right of an owner amounts to an appropriation, and this includes, where he has come by the property (innocently or not) without stealing it, any later assumption of a right to it by keeping or dealing with it as owner.
> (2)   Where property or a right or interest in property is or purports to be transferred for value to a person acting in good faith, no later assumption by him of rights which he believed himself to be acquiring shall, by reason of any defect in the transferor's title, amount to theft of the property.

The meaning of 'appropriation' has been considered in three House of Lords cases: *Lawrence* v *Metropolitan Police Commissioner* [1972] AC 626; *Morris* [1984] AC 320 and *Gomez* [1993] AC 442. In *Gomez* three members of the House of Lords (Lords Jauncey, Browne-Wilkinson and Slynn) agreed with the speech of Lord Keith. Lord Lowry dissented. Lord Browne-Wilkinson also delivered a speech which considered some of the ramifications of Lord Keith's speech.

In *Gomez* the House of Lords approved the decision in *Morris* that it is unnecessary to prove that an accused assumed all of another's rights over the property alleged to have been stolen. It is sufficient to prove the assumption of *any* of the rights of an owner, see **B4.26** and **B4.28**. 'Appropriation' does not entail that a 'taking' is required; the decision of the Court of Appeal in *Gallasso* (1993) 98 Cr App R 284 is wrong (so, contrary to the view expressed by the Court of Appeal in *Ngan* [1998] 1 Cr App R 331, the owner need not be deprived of property; see also **B4.31**). The main issue in *Gomez* concerned the role of consent in appropriation. Their lordships decided, first, that *Lawrence* makes it clear that consent to or authorisation by the owner of the taking by the rogue is irrelevant and, secondly, that *Morris* was erroneous, although the decision on the facts was correct. There is still an apparent tendency in some decisions to look for something that seems similar to the requirement in *Morris* of an adverse interference or usurpation of the rights of the owner (see, e.g., *Ngan*, where the court talks of the need for the 'assertion of a right adverse to' the owner; see also *Marshall* [1998] 2 Cr App R 282). This is no longer good law.

It should be noted that appropriation can occur through an innocent agent's acts, as where the accused, by signing false invoices, sets in motion a chain of events which will result in the company's account being debited (*Stringer* (1992) 94 Cr App R 13).

Assumption of One or More of the Rights of An Owner

In *Gomez* [1993] AC 442, Lord Keith stated, approving *Morris* [1984] AC 320 on this **B4.26** point, that on a charge of theft, and in order to prove an appropriation, it is sufficient for the prosecution to prove the assumption by the accused of any of the rights of the owner. It followed that 'the removal of an article from the shelf [of a supermarket] and the changing of the price label on it constituted an assumption of one of the rights of the owner and hence an appropriation'. Lord Keith further stated that 'the switching of price labels on the article is in itself an assumption of one of the rights of the owner, whether or not it is accompanied by some other act such as removing the article from the shelf and placing it in a basket or trolley' because 'no one but the owner has the right to remove a price label from an article or to place a price label upon it'. Thus the practical joker, a person first considered by Lord Roskill in *Morris*, appropriates each and every item the price label of which he alters, but commits theft only if he also has the *mens rea* of theft, that is dishonesty (see **B4.34**) and an intention permanently to deprive (see **B4.38**). There was an appropriation which satisfies this test where an accused tugged at a lady's handbag causing her to release it, even though the accused never obtained complete control over the bag (*Corcoran* v *Anderton* (1980) 71 Cr App R 104).

Appropriation is a relatively easy concept to understand and to prove (a full and rigorous examination of the rights of an owner does not have to be undertaken), but it is nevertheless controversial (see e.g., J. C. Smith, *The Law of Theft*, 8th ed, at paras 2–04 and 2–49 and E. J. Griew, *The Theft Acts 1968 and 1978*, at paras 2–65 to 2–67). Further, it may present particular problems with 'consecutive' or 'continuing' appropriations (see **B4.27**).

The approach to appropriation in *Gomez* has particular significance when considering theft and cheques. The writing of a cheque appears to be, at least arguably, a sufficient act. The writing of the cheque is an assumption of one of the rights of the owner of the thing or chose in action (the debt of the bank owed to the customer, which exists when either the account is in credit or within the overdraft limit, such that the legal obligation to honour the cheques arises: see *Kohn* (1979) 69 Cr App R 395). There is, of course, an alternative view which is that the cheque must have been presented to a bank for there to be an act of appropriation. In *Kohn* Lord Lane CJ went further when he said, 'the completion of the theft does not take place until the transaction has gone through to completion', which, as Professor Sir John Smith points out (*Law of Theft*, 8th ed, para. 2–108), must mean the debiting of the account. That observation, however, was *obiter* as Lord Lane himself made clear in *Navvabi* [1986] 1 WLR 1311. Recently, the Court of Appeal in *Ngan* [1998] 1 Cr App R 331 has considered this issue. Leggatt LJ said (at pp. 335–6):

> the act of theft itself was the presentation of the cheque. Until then no right as against the Bank had been exercised . . . In [*Governor of Pentonville Prison, ex parte Osman* [1990] 1 WLR 277] the Divisional Court held that appropriation occurs when a cheque is presented. We agree; but it does not follow that it cannot occur earlier . . . In one sense the very act of signing each cheque might be regarded as an assumption of a right. But it must be remembered that the right assumed is not to the cheque, but to the property or chose in action, that is, to the debt mistakenly due from the Bank. . . . [*Gomez*] has no application here, because until on each occasion a cheque was presented for payment there was no dealing with any of [the other's] rights to the balance mistakenly standing to the credit of

the appellant. Her acts of signing the cheques and sending them to her sister were preparatory acts, and more needed to be done by or on behalf of the appellant before [the other] could be deprived of their property.

The Court of Appeal appears to be in favour of a late act (i.e. presentation rather than actual debiting of an account) being an appropriation, but is mindful of the decision of the House of Lords in *Gomez*, believing that it does not apply. Whether any 'dealing' with the property is required under *Gomez* is open to doubt, as also therefore is this view of the Court of Appeal. One further difficulty with these statements is that *Ex parte Osman* is used as support for them. However, it is not authority for that point as the Divisional Court actually alighted on the issuing of a cheque (the first delivery of a cheque, complete in form, to a person who takes it as holder: Bills of Exchange Act 1882, s. 2) as being the act of appropriation (*Ex parte Osman* at p. 295, see also Smith, *The Law of Theft*, 8th ed, para. 2–108). In *Ex parte Osman*, the court made the helpful observation that there is a difference between when theft was complete in law (upon issuing of the cheque) and when it was complete in fact (upon actual debiting of the account).

It may be argued that if an accused has forged a cheque on another person's bank account there has been no appropriation of the other person's rights against the bank because a bank is not entitled to debit a customer with the amount of a forged cheque. In *Chan Man-sin* v *The Queen* [1988] 1 WLR 196, Lord Oliver of Aylmerton (delivering the advice of the Privy Council) said (at p. 199):

> . . . it is, in their lordship's view, beyond argument that one who draws, presents and negotiates a cheque on a particular bank account is assuming the rights of the owner of the credit in the account or (as the case may be) of the pre-negotiated right to draw on the account up to the agreed figure. Ownership, of course, consists of a bundle of rights and it may well be that there are other rights which an owner could exert over the chose in action in question which are not trespassed upon by the particular dealing which the thief chooses to assume. In [*Morris*] [1984] AC 320, however, the House of Lords decisively rejected a submission that it was necessary, in order to constitute an appropriation as defined by section 3(1) of the [TA 1968], to demonstrate an assumption by the accused of all the rights of an owner.

In *Wille* (1987) 86 Cr App R 296, W, a director of a company had issued numerous cheques on the company's bank account (which was at all times in credit) for his own benefit. Each cheque was signed by himself alone and had been honoured by the bank despite the fact that the mandate from the company authorised it to honour only cheques bearing two signatures. Accordingly the bank was not entitled to debit the amounts of the cheques to the company's account. Nevertheless, W was rightly convicted of stealing the debts owed by the bank to the company. Woolf LJ said (at p. 302):

> When what the appellant did in this case is considered, it is hard to see what more he could do to assume the rights of the owner in respect of the account at Barclays Bank to the extent of the amount for which the cheques were drawn, than to draw a cheque, issue the cheque, and then take steps which were designed to achieve that the account of the company at the bank was debited with the amount of the cheque. . . . The fact that the company may still have rights against the bank for the amounts of those cheques is . . . irrelevant to the issues with which the jury were concerned.

In both *Wille* and *Chan Man-sin* v *The Queen*, the cheques were honoured by the banks (see also **B4.28**). If the cheques had not been honoured, there might still have been an appropriation following the discussion above.

More Than One Appropriation of the Same Property

B4.27   It appears to follow from *Gomez* [1993] AC 442 that one item may be appropriated on a number of occasions (see also **B4.28**). If this were right it would be for the prosecution to choose which act of appropriation it was going to concentrate upon, choosing the act in relation to which it was easiest to prove the other elements of theft. Alternatively, it might be that only the first act of appropriation may be considered, on the basis that a person may not steal an item which he has already stolen. The relevance of the second part of the TA 1968, s. 3(1), to this issue remains to be clarified. It provides that a person who has 'come by the property (innocently or not) *without stealing it*' (emphasis supplied) may appropriate it by a specified later act (see **B4.32**). This might mean that the label switcher in a supermarket cannot be guilty of theft if charged for his actions at the cash desk (trying to pay less than he should), because he will already have stolen the item by the switching of a label. The Court of Appeal in *Atakpu* [1994] QB 69 has confirmed that 'if goods have once been stolen . . . they cannot be stolen again by the same thief'. It is submitted that the best point to consider whether theft has been committed is at the cash desk, taking account of what has gone before as evidence of the crime. So the solution is to consider what is the complete activity, which may be spread over a period of time. In *Atakpu*, the Court of Appeal decided that *Gomez* should not be interpreted so as to rule out appropriation as a continuous course of action; it preferred 'to leave it for the commonsense of the jury to decide that the appropriation can continue for so long as the thief can sensibly be regarded as in the act of stealing or, in more understandable words, so long as he is "on the job" as the editors of Smith and Hogan . . . suggest the test should be'. This *obiter* statement appears to support the position prior to the decision in *Gomez* when careful thought had to be given to three Court of Appeal decisions (*Hale* (1978) 68 Cr App R 415, *Gregory* (1981) 77 Cr App R 41 and *Pitham* (1977) 65 Cr App R 45). *Hale* and *Gregory* support the proposition that appropriation is a continuing act.

In *Hale*, a decision which remains good law (*Lockley* [1995] Crim LR 656), the Court of Appeal stated that the 'act of appropriation does not suddenly cease. It is a continuous act and it is a matter for the jury to decide whether or not the act of appropriation has finished'. Consequently, Hale's conviction for robbery could be upheld, because the view was taken that the act of appropriation was continuing so as to coincide with the use of force after the jewellery box had been seized. A similar approach was taken in *Gregory*, thus enabling a burglary conviction to be upheld, because the view was taken that the act of appropriation was a 'continuing process'. In *Pitham*, however, it was decided that the act of appropriation was complete upon an offer to sell furniture, so that handling convictions could be upheld.

In *Hallam* [1995] Crim LR 323, it was not possible to identify whether the defendants stole a chose in action or the proceeds of it, but they had failed to account for the sums received. It was held that, provided the other elements of theft are present, a conviction is possible in such circumstances without identifying which form of property was stolen, since there was property throughout which did always belong to another (see **B4.20**; cf. *Caresana* [1996] Crim LR 667).

It is important to note that an item may be stolen, whether once or more than once, only if all the elements of theft are present. In particular, it may be essential to determine whether the property concerned does still belong to another, see **B4.21**.

Identifying an Act of Appropriation

The lesson of *Preddy* [1996] AC 815 (see **B5.17** *et seq.*) is that it is essential that the **B4.28** property belonging to another be accurately and carefully identified (see also **B4.13** and **B4.21**). It must be established, for TA 1968, s. 15, whether it has been obtained by the defendant by deception, whereas for theft it has to be established whether the defendant has appropriated it. This is a critical difference, which means that *Preddy* has had a less dramatic effect on the law of theft than on the deception offences. For theft the defendant does not have to get anything, whereas in deception he must obtain something. Indeed, it has been re-emphasised that causing the destruction of property can be theft, thus confirming that aspect of the decision of the Court of Appeal in *Kohn* (1979) 69 Cr App R 395. In the addendum to the Court of Appeal's judgment in *Graham* [1997] 1 Cr App R 302, Lord Bingham CJ said:

> We wish to make it clear that nothing we said was intended to cast doubt upon the principle that theft of a chose in action may be committed when a chose in action belonging to another is destroyed by the defendant's act of appropriation as defined by section 3(1) of the Act.

It should be remembered that, where the property is destroyed but there is an obligation on the bank to restore so that the transaction may be a legal nullity, there can still be an appropriation and an intention permanently to deprive, as decided in *Chan Man-sin* v *R* [1988] 1 All ER 1, which was confirmed in *Wille* (1989) 86 Cr App R 296 (see also **B4.26**, **B4.31** and **B4.39**).

What must, therefore, be looked for is an act which can be regarded as an appropriation that takes place when the identified property exists and belongs to another (see, e.g., *Forsyth* [1997] 2 Cr App R 299). For the position where cheques are involved, see **B4.26**. Where the property is a bank account, but the activity controlling it is not a cheque, great care must be taken to determine whether there is an act of appropriation. So in *Naviede* [1997] Crim LR 662, the Court of Appeal said:

> We are not satisfied that a misrepresentation which persuades the account holder to direct payment out of his account is an assumption of the rights of the account holder as owner such as to amount to an appropriation of his rights within section 3(1) of the 1968 Act.

This is the same point as that propounded by Professor Sir John Smith (see commentary to *Naviede* [1997] Crim LR 665–6) who comments as follows:

> I distinguished the case where D induces V to make a telegraphic transfer from that where D dishonestly presents a cheque drawn on V's account causing it to be debited. This, it is submitted, does amount to an appropriation of the thing in action belonging to V. . . . In the telegraphic case it is true that D procures the whole course of events resulting in V's account being debited; but the telegraphic transfer is initiated by V and his voluntary intervening acts break the chain of causation. It is the same as if V is induced by deception to take money out of his safe to pay to D. D does not at that moment 'appropriate' it — V is not acting as his agent. D commits theft only if and when the money is put into his hands.

It is important to emphasise that this is an issue about identifying what amounts to an act of appropriation, and is a separate and subsequent issue to that of assessing what is the property that might be appropriated. It is a matter of importance, and is also of a technical nature. It is perhaps not surprising that the Court of Appeal in *Hilton* [1997] 2 Cr App R 445 had some difficulty with understanding the point (as is noted by Smith in the commentary to *Naviede* at p. 666). In fact, the Court of Appeal in *Hilton* does appear to have grasped the point, since it endeavoured to determine what was the property, and whether it was appropriated by an act of the defendant. Smith's point is that, in some cases, it is difficult to identify what is the act of the defendant that may be termed an appropriation. Where the defendant signs a cheque for an improper purpose or forges a cheque or issues instructions to a bank, an appropriation may be identified, because those acts are 'the key' to the property. Where the defendant's act is more remote or where it induces the victim to do an act which acts as the key to the property, Smith states that it is not possible to identify the defendant's act that can be termed an appropriation.

Whether the courts follow the logical demands of Smith's point remains to be seen, but there will be difficulties if an act of appropriation is not carefully identified. It is not sufficient that the thing in action has been reduced or destroyed (which may be an assumption of the rights of the owner), but it must also be the case that the defendant did that act himself or through innocent agents. If only the outcome is considered, a defendant may be regarded as having assumed the rights of an owner where he has done nothing himself or through innocent agents which may properly be described as an act. On the other hand, it might successfully be argued that the defendant has done something because it is his instructions or requests that have set in motion a chain of events that results in an outcome which has the effect that can be termed as an appropriation, thus the activity dismissed by Smith as being sufficient for an act of appropriation (see the following paragraph) might, in fact, be sufficient.

As Smith points out, there was an act of appropriation in *Hilton,* because 'There, D had direct control of a bank account belonging to a charity. He caused payments to be made from that account to settle his personal debts. That was a completely straightforward case of theft of the thing in action belonging to another'. This, he goes on to say, is a very different scenario from that appertaining in cases such as *Carasena* [1996] Crim LR 67, *Preddy* [1996] AC 815, *Graham* [1997] 1 Cr App R 302, *Cooke* [1997] Crim LR 436 and *Naviede* which 'were all concerned with the situation where D by deception induces V to initiate a transaction whereby V's bank account is debited and D's is credited' (commentary to *Naviede* at p. 666).

This issue is also of importance in jurisdictional terms. An act of the defendant must be identified as the appropriation. It can then be determined whether that act was done within the jurisdiction or, for the purposes of extradition, was done within the jurisdiction of the requesting state, which must be assessed on the basis of assuming, for the purposes of argument, that the requesting state is England and Wales (see *Roberts* [1991] RTR 361 and *Morgan* [1991] RTR 365). In *Governor of Pentonville Prison, ex parte Osman* [1990] 1 WLR 277, the Divisional Court held that the issuing of the telex instruction in Hong Kong (or England and Wales, as it was an extradition case), which had an effect in New York was a sufficient act, in Hong Kong, to amount to an act of appropriation. Contrast *Governor of Brixton Prison, ex parte Levin* [1997] QB 65, where no instructions could be given without first gaining entry to Citibank's computer based in the United States (or in England and Wales as it was an extradition case), and D was operating in St. Petersburg. The following comments were made (at p. 81):

> No doubt there was an appropriation of the right of the client to gain access to the computer but that is a different right of property which on [K]'s evidence had been appropriated by the applicant many times before he actually set about entering the computer for the purpose of giving any instructions. We see no reason why the appropriation of the client's right to give instructions should not be regarded as having taken place in the computer. Lloyd LJ [in *Ex parte Osman*] did not rule out the possibility that a crime could have a dual location.

As regards the operation of a computer that can have almost instantaneous effect even if the keyboard and mainframe are thousands of miles apart:

> It seems to us artificial to regard the act as having been done in one rather than the other place. But, in the position of having to choose on the facts of this case whether, after entering the computer in Parsipenny, the act of appropriation by inserting instructions on the disk occurred there or in St. Petersburg, we would opt for Parsipenny. The fact that the applicant was physically in St. Petersburg is of far less significance than the fact that he was looking at and operating on magnetic disks located in Parsipenny. The essence of what he was doing was done there . . . In the case of a virtually instantaneous instruction intended to take effect where the computer is situated it seems to us artificial to regard the insertion of an instruction onto the disk as having been done only at the remote place where the keyboard is situated.

This clearly reflects the choice which may be available to the court (but cf. the approach of the Court of Appeal in *Atakpu* [1994] QB 69 at **B4.27**), and that choice might be determined upon a basis that is difficult to predict, unless an approach akin to that propounded by Professor Sir John Smith or some other clearer basis is accepted.

Some of the difficulties are apparent when *Thompson* [1984] 1 WLR 962 is considered. This case concerned an offence contrary to s. 15 but the issues are relevant to a discussion in the context of theft. T programmed a computer in Kuwait to credit his Kuwaiti account with funds from other customers' accounts. When in England, after opening accounts, he instructed the Kuwaiti bank to transfer his credit balance to his English account. The Court of Appeal held that there was an act that meant that the 'relevant sums of money' were obtained by the deception in England, and so the case was triable in England. However, the only property that belonged to another did so when T was in Kuwait; the account in England only ever belonged to T. The acts which he performed first were performed in Kuwait, then his acts in England were instructions which had their impact in Kuwait on property which belonged to him. Thus, whilst the instructions might have been sufficient to amount to an act of appropriation, there was no property belonging to another which was being appropriated by them. The only acts of theft occurred outside the jurisdiction.

In *Ngan* [1998] 1 Cr App R 331, the Court of Appeal had to address the jurisdiction question in considering whether an act of appropriation had taken place in Scotland or England. The presentation of the cheque was identified as the act of appropriation, with the signing of the cheques being regarded as merely a preparatory act; this view must be open to some doubt in the light of the interpretation of appropriation in *Morris* [1984] AC 320 and *Gomez* [1993] AC 442, though the approach of the Court of Appeal in *Atakpu* [1994] QB 69 may force the court or the jury to look for the important act (see **B4.27** and, more generally on *Ngan*, **B4.26**).

The difficulties associated with identifying the act of appropriation would suggest that this is a matter worthy of further consideration. Should an act of appropriation be regarded as continuous leaving the jury to decide when the defendant was 'on the job' or should it be possible for the prosecution or extradition agency to choose one of a number of possible options as the most suitable moment to identify an act of appropriation? (see **B4.27**). The difficulties encountered are exacerbated by the wide range of activities that may be identified as an appropriation after the interpretation of that phrase by the House of Lords in *Morris* and *Gomez* (see **B4.26**).

Consent or Authority of Owner

B4.29 It is now abundantly clear that 'consent to or authorisation by the owner of the taking by the rogue is irrelevant' per Lord Keith in *Gomez* [1993] AC 442 at p. 464. In reaching this conclusion, the House of Lords in *Gomez* approved the decision of *Lawrence* v *Metropolitan Police Commissioner* [1972] AC 626 and decided that, on this point, the decision of the House of Lords in *Morris* [1984] AC 320 was erroneous.

In *Lawrence* v *Metropolitan Police Commissioner* [1972] AC 626 the House of Lords decided that on a charge of theft it is unnecessary for the prosecution to prove that the appropriation was without the consent of the owner. The House of Lords was asked to consider the question 'Whether section 1(1) of the TA 1968 is to be construed as though it contained the words "without the consent of the owner" or words to that effect'. In a speech with which the other Law Lords agreed, Viscount Dilhorne said (at pp. 631–2):

> I see no ground for concluding that the omission of the words 'without the consent of the owner' was inadvertent and not deliberate, and to read the subsection as if they were included is, in my opinion, wholly unwarranted. Parliament by the omission of these words has relieved the prosecution of the burden of establishing that the taking was without the owner's consent. That is no longer an ingredient of the offence.

In *Lawrence* v *Metropolitan Police Commissioner* the defendant was a taxi-driver who picked up Mr Occhi, an Italian, at an airport. The proper fare for the journey was 10*s*. 6*d*. (52.5p). Mr Occhi offered a £1 note, but this was rejected by Lawrence. Mr Occhi offered his wallet, and Lawrence took out of it another £1 note and a £5 note. The House of Lords was satisfied that Lawrence had dishonestly appropriated property belonging to another and so upheld the theft conviction. Whilst they were asked to consider the issue of consent and provided the answer already alluded to, Viscount Dilhorne, stated (at p. 631) that '. . . the facts of this case . . . fall far short of establishing that Mr Occhi had so consented'.

The House of Lords in *Gomez* also decided (at p. 460) that no 'sensible distinction can be made in this context between consent and authorisation'; thus, whilst an act by way of adverse interference with or usurpation of the rights of an owner (see Lord Roskill in *Morris* at p. 332) does amount to an appropriation, the concept is not limited to such acts. In arriving at this view, their lordships accepted that the decision of the Court of Appeal (Civil Division) in *Dobson* v *General Accident Fire and Life Assurance Corporation plc* [1990] 1 QB 274 was correct, and Lord Keith found himself in full agreement with the judgment of Parker LJ in that case.

In *Gomez*, G's conviction for theft was upheld. G, an assistant manager of an electrical shop, had obtained the consent or authorisation of the manager to allowing goods to be delivered to others against two building society cheques which G knew to be stolen. The manager had consented because G told him that the bank had indicated that the cheques were acceptable and that such a cheque was as good as cash.

The House of Lords in *Gomez* accepted that it follows from the decision that *Lawrence* is correct and *Morris* erroneous and that the cases of *Skipp* [1975] Crim LR 114 and *Fritschy* [1985] Crim LR 745, where the courts decided that there was no theft because the act of appropriation was done with the consent of the owner of the property, are wrong. In *Skipp* it seems that there was an appropriation each time a load was put on to Skipp's lorry, not only when either all the loads were on the lorry or when it deviated from its authorised route. In *Fritschy* there was an appropriation by taking possession of the kruggerrands and not only when Fritschy deviated from the owner's authority to deliver them to the proper bank account in Switzerland. Whether theft is committed in a similar case depends upon whether the other elements of the offence are present. In addition to *Skipp* and *Fritschy*, which were specifically referred to in *Gomez*, it would seem, as a matter of logic that the following cases were also wrongly decided: *Meech* [1974] QB 549 (where it might now be decided that an appropriation took place when M resolved to deprive another of the proceeds of a cheque the other had obtained as a result of forgery and not only at the later time of the fake robbery); *Hircock* (1978) 67 Cr App R 278 (where it would now be decided that there was an appropriation when H got the car on a hire-purchase agreement and not only later when he sold it); *Eddy* v *Niman* (1981) 73 Cr App R 237 (where it would now be decided that an appropriation was committed when a shopper put goods into a wire basket provided by the supermarket); *McPherson* [1973] Crim LR 191 (where it would now be decided that M appropriated the whiskey bottles when she removed them from the shelves). Whether theft was committed in cases similar to these depends upon the existence of the other elements of theft. In particular, having regard to Lord Roskill's concern about the honest customer in a supermarket, the honest customer does appropriate the goods he removes from the shelves, but does not commit theft because he is not dishonest. As Lord Browne-Wilkinson puts it in *Gomez* (at p. 495), appropriation is an 'objective description of the act done irrespective of the mental state of either the owner or the accused'. The mental state of the owner is irrelevant, and the mental state of the accused arises only in relation to the questions of dishonesty and intention permanently to deprive.

It follows from the decision of the House of Lords in *Gomez* that there will be considerable overlap between the offence of theft and the offence of obtaining property by deception contrary to the TA 1968, s. 15 (see **B5.14 *et seq*.**). Lord Browne-Wilkinson accepted that this would be the case, and expressed little concern, but pointed out as an example of the difference that land can rarely be stolen but can always be obtained by deception. In *Gomez* their lordships declined to consider the Eighth Report of the Criminal Law Revision Committee (1966) Cmnd. 2977, which preceded the TA 1968 and which might have influenced the House to reach a different decision, as indeed it did Lord Lowry, who dissented.

Despite the apparent clarity of the decision in *Gomez*, it is now clear that the decision will present considerable problems. The Court of Appeal in *Gallasso* (1993) 98 Cr App R 284, decided at the time of *Gomez*, was concerned about its implications; it took the view that affirming another's ownership rights is not an appropriation.

In *Mazo* [1997] 2 Cr App R 518, the Court of Appeal may be interpreted as thinking that the House of Lords went too far in *Gomez*. In *Mazo*, the Court of Appeal said that it was 'clear that a transaction may be a theft . . . notwithstanding that it was done with the owner's consent if it was induced by fraud, deception or a false representation'. Certainly this point was made in the question of public importance addressed to the House of Lords, but it did not expressly form part of the decision in the way that their lordships stated it. The Court of Appeal in *Mazo* went on to assert that 'the receiver of a valid gift, *inter vivos*, could not be the subject of a conviction for theft'. The Court of Appeal in *Kendrick* [1997] 2 Cr App R 524 thought that the court in *Mazo* had introduced a gloss on the decision in *Gomez*. There are two potential strands to this concern.

First, that in *Mazo* the Court of Appeal introduced an after the event interpretation of the *ratio decidendi* of *Gomez* by limiting it to the terms of the question of public importance and the facts of the particular decision. Thereby it is asserted that there is an appropriation and so theft is committed where there is the consent or authority of the owner only if that consent has been obtained by fraud, deception or a false representation. There is considerable attraction in this approach. Where there is consent not so obtained, it prevents there being an appropriation and so there is no theft. In view of the many Court of Appeal decisions pre-dating *Gomez* in which consent was thought to prevent an appropriation, this might be thought to be a good solution that will satisfy the innate concern that those who acquire property with consent should not be regarded as thieves as, if nothing else, it offends common sense to convict them of theft. The weakness in this view is that this does not appear to be the basis upon which *Gomez* was decided as there is no explicit limitation in what is said on the basis of the means whereby that consent was obtained. In *Kendrick*, there is some evidence that the Court of Appeal was concerned about this aspect of the decision in *Mazo*. Certainly, the court took the view that the words 'without the consent of the owner' could not be read into s. 1 and this suggests that the distinction just propounded was not one with which it was happy.

Secondly, prosecution counsel in *Mazo* conceded that there cannot be theft where there was a valid gift and so it was necessary for a judge to direct the jury as to the validity of gifts. There is some evidence that the Court of Appeal accepted that view. It was not accepted by the Court of Appeal in *Kendrick*, where the Court was particularly concerned about whether the defendant was dishonest, as well as affirming the clear law that the words 'without the consent of the owner' cannot be read into TA 1968, s. 1(1). The Court of Appeal in *Hinks* [1998] Crim LR 904 had to consider the relevance of a valid gift to a charge of theft. It affirmed that 'appropriation for the purpose of the Theft Act 1968 does not depend on the consent of the owner'. The issue 'is not whether there has been a gift, valid or otherwise, but whether there has been an appropriation. But a jury should not . . . be asked to consider whether a gift has been validly made because, first, that is not what section 1 of the Theft Act requires; secondly, such an approach is inconsistent with *Lawrence* and *Gomez* and, thirdly, the state of mind of a donor is irrelevant to appropriation. . . .' This decision must be correct. However, there are two ways in which the validity of the gift might be relevant. First, as the trial judge properly directed in *Kendrick*, the accused may not be dishonest by operation of s. 2 (in particular if he believes that he has a claim of right: s. 2(1)(a), but also if he believes that he has the other's consent: s. 2(1)(b)) or by application of the general test in *Ghosh* [1982] QB 1053 (see **B4.35** and **B4.36**). Secondly, the property may not have belonged to another but to the defendant at the time of the appropriation. In this case, it will be necessary to identify the time of the appropriation and the moment in time that ownership passed to the defendant. If the transfer of ownership precedes the act of appropriation, the defendant is not appropriating property belonging to another (see **B4. 21**). In examining the validity of a gift in either case, it will be necessary to consider the donor's state of mind.

Appropriation and Company Controllers

In *Gomez* [1993] AC 442 Lord Browne-Wilkinson, following the general approach **B4.30** propounded by Lord Keith, considered the position of people in de facto control of a company and charged with theft from it. He decided (at p. 496) that the decision of their lordships meant that:

> the whole question of consent by the company [is] irrelevant. Whether or not those controlling the company consented or purported to consent to the abstraction of the company's property by the accused, he will have appropriated the property of the company. The question will be whether the other necessary elements are present, viz. was such appropriation dishonest and was it done with the intention of permanently depriving the company of such property?

Lord Browne-Wilkinson, therefore, disapproved *McHugh* (1988) 88 Cr App R 385, and approved the decisions in *A-G's Ref (No. 2 of 1982)* [1984] QB 624 and *Philippou* (1989) 89 Cr App R 290.

Where the authorised signatory is the sole proprietor of the company, the Court of Appeal in *A-G's Ref (No. 2 of 1982)* took the view that an appropriation is committed, though the case is mainly concerned with the question of dishonesty. This approach was followed in *Philippou*. Indeed, the Court of Appeal said (at pp. 299–300):

> [Lord Roskill] cannot be understood as saying that the prosecution must prove that the appropriation alleged was without the authority of the owner, or that would be directly contrary to what was said in *Lawrence* v *Metropolitan Police Commissioner*. We think it obvious that the House of Lords in *Morris* was not inserting into the definition of theft in section 1(1) after the word 'appropriates' the words 'without the authority of the owner'.

In addition, Lord Browne-Wilkinson indicated in *Gomez* that the acts and intentions of the directing minds of a company are not to be attributed to that company where the directing minds are themselves committing a crime against the company. It would therefore seem clear that the company controllers and the company are to be regarded as separate entities, and that a company is not to be presumed to intend that which the controller intends where there is a conflict of interest involving a direct effect upon the assets of the company.

The approach outlined here is subject to the application of the decision in *Mazo* [1997] 2 Cr App R 518, discussed at **B4.29**.

Appropriation without Loss to the Owner

Since an appropriation may occur even though not all the rights of an owner are **B4.31** assumed, it follows that the owner need not necessarily lose his property. In *Chan Man-sin* v *The Queen* [1988] 1 WLR 196, C, an accountant, forged company cheques to his own benefit. The company would lose nothing, since a forged cheque is a nullity once discovered, and so it is entitled to have the initial debit in its account reversed. It was held that, although the company lost nothing, C had appropriated property belonging to another and since he had the requisite *mens rea* his conviction for theft was upheld.

Appropriation after Innocent Acquisition by Later Assumption of Rights

B4.32   Section 3(1) of the TA 1968 provides not only a non-exhaustive definition of appropriation but also that an accused appropriates property in the following situation:

> . . . where he has come by the property (innocently or not) without stealing it, any later assumption of a right to it by keeping it or dealing with it as owner [is an appropriation].

For this provision to operate, it must be proved that the accused has 'come by the property' by some means, whether innocent or not, 'without stealing it'. The obvious interpretation that if the accused has got the property by stealing it, whatever he later does with it cannot constitute an appropriation and, therefore, theft. Since *Gomez* [1993] AC 442 this interpretation may present particular problems which are considered at **B4.27**.

In order to have appropriated property of which he already has possession, an alleged thief must have later assumed a right of an owner, but only by keeping it or dealing with it as owner. The latter may cause no problems. However, it may not always be easy to establish that a person has kept property as owner. In *Broom* v *Crowther* (1984) 148 JP 592, the defendant had come into possession of a theodolite by purchasing it. Once he became aware that it was stolen, he kept it in his possession, but he had not come to any decision as to what to do with it. This finding of fact by the magistrates was inconsistent with an inference that he was keeping the theodolite as owner. The Divisional Court decided that he had not assumed a right to the theodolite by keeping it as owner and quashed the conviction for theft. The Court indicated that the factors relevant in determining the matter were that he had not kept the theodolite for a long time (he had had it for between four and five months), he had not attempted to dispose of it and had not even used it. It simply remained in his bedroom.

Appropriation: Purchaser in Good Faith of Stolen Goods

B4.33   **Theft Act 1968, s. 3(2)**

> Where property or a right or interest in property is or purports to be transferred for value to a person acting in good faith, no later assumption by him of rights which he believed himself to be acquiring shall, by reason of any defect in the transferor's title, amount to theft of the property.

Ordinarily a person who has gained possession of property appropriates that property if he then keeps or deals with it as owner (TA 1968, s. 3(1); see **B4.32**). However, s. 3(2) provides an exception, which is fairly limited. The defendant must, first, have given value for property in which he consequently appears to gain an interest. It is irrelevant that the civil law would say, on the facts of a particular instance, that he does not actually gain any such interest. Secondly, the defendant must have initially acted in good faith. It was the defendant's failure to act in good faith in *Broom* v *Crowther* (1984) 148 JP 592 (see **B4.32**) that led to a conviction for theft when purchasing a theodolite. That conviction was quashed, however, because, whilst s. 3(2) might not have been satisfied by the defendant so as to avoid conviction, he had not kept the property as owner, so he had committed no later assumption of the property. The two conditions called for by s. 3(2) were presumed, it would appear correctly, to have been satisfied by the accused in *Bloxham* [1983] 1 AC 109, which explains why he was charged with handling stolen goods by the later sale of them, and not with theft. Bloxham had purchased a car while unaware of the fact that it had been stolen. He then sold the car to a third party who was unknown to the prosecution. The prosecution must have rejected the possibility of charging him with theft because he had given value for the car and had acted in good faith. If so, his later assumption of the car by dealing with it as owner when he sold it on to a third party could not be an appropriation because of the provisions of s. 3(2). (See also *Wheeler* (1991) 92 Cr App R 279.) As regards the words 'rights which he believed himself to be acquiring', the relevant time at which the belief must be held is the moment when the receiver purchased for value (*Adams* [1993] Crim LR 72).

Meaning of 'Dishonesty'

The concept of 'dishonesty', like the concept of 'intention permanently to deprive', is a **B4.34** question of the state of the accused's mind, part of the *mens rea* of theft. Consequently, inferences may be drawn from his conduct, even though conduct is not determinative of *mens rea*, see *Ingram* [1975] Crim LR 457 and *Boggeln* v *Williams* [1978] 1 WLR 873.

The TA 1968 provides a partial definition of 'dishonesty'. A general definition has been provided by the Court of Appeal in *Ghosh* [1982] QB 1053. The decision whether somebody is 'dishonest' is one for either the jury or the magistrates.

Circumstances in which Appropriation is Not to Be Regarded as Dishonest

Theft Act 1968, s. 2 **B4.35**

(1)   A person's appropriation of property belonging to another is not to be regarded as dishonest—
    (a)   if he appropriates the property in the belief that he has in law the right to deprive the other of it, on behalf of himself or a third person; or
    (b)   if he appropriates the property in the belief that he would have the other's consent if the other knew of the appropriation and the circumstances of it; or
    (c)   (except where the property came to him as trustee or personal representative) if he appropriates the property in the belief that the person to whom the property belongs cannot be discovered by taking reasonable steps.
(2)   A person's appropriation of property belonging to another may be dishonest notwithstanding that he is willing to pay for the property.

The TA 1968, s. 2(1)(a), requires only that it be shown that the accused had an honest belief that he was entitled to take the property. It is not necessary to show that he had an honest belief that he was entitled to take it in the way that he did (*Robinson* [1977] Crim LR 173, following the decision on the earlier law in *Skivington* [1968] 1 QB 166). However, the accused's method of taking property may render him liable for some other offence. The issue of the reasonableness of the belief is relevant only in considering whether the accused had an honest belief (*Holden* [1991] Crim LR 478).

The importance of drawing the jury's attention to the provisions of s. 2(1)(a) was emphasised by the Court of Appeal in *Falconer-Atlee* (1973) 58 Cr App R 348. The Court of Appeal held in *Wootton* [1990] Crim LR 201 that a trial judge should direct the jury on s. 2(1)(a) whenever a claim of right is raised, even though a direction in accordance with *Ghosh* [1982] QB 1053 (see **B4.34**) is likely to cover all the occasions when s. 2(1)(a) might be applicable. See also *Forrester* [1992] Crim LR 793.

The Court of Appeal had to consider s. 2(1)(a) and (b) in *A-G's Ref (No. 2 of 1982)* [1984] QB 624. The court held that persons who between them represent the directing mind and will of a company cannot rely on s. 2(1)(b) to negate the dishonesty of their appropriation of the company's property if the only consent they can allege is the consent of themselves which they say should be deemed to be the company's consent by virtue of the doctrine that their minds are the minds of the company (the identification theory) for in those circumstances there is no consent by an 'other', only their own consent. Whether or not such persons could establish a defence under

s. 2(1)(a) would depend on whether or not the prosecution could prove that they did not honestly believe that they were entitled to do what they did. The court disagreed 'entirely' that in such a situation the jury is bound to be directed that, when all the members and directors of a company act in concert in appropriating the property of their company, they cannot, as a matter of law, be held to have acted dishonestly; or that, on such facts, any reasonable jury is bound to reach this conclusion. Although this point was not discussed in detail by Lord Browne-Wilkinson in *Gomez* [1993] AC 442 it would appear that he approved of this approach.

Dishonesty notwithstanding Willingness to Pay

B4.36   The Divisional Court in *Boggeln* v *Williams* [1978] 1 WLR 873 stressed the word 'may' in the TA 1968, s. 2(2), because, although a person may be guilty of dishonesty even though he is willing to pay, nevertheless it is in each case a question of fact for the tribunal of fact whether the accused is guilty of dishonesty or not.

Meaning of 'Dishonesty' According to *Ghosh*

B4.37   The Court of Appeal in *Ghosh* [1982] QB 1053 established two principles which apply whether or not the statutory provisions are under consideration. Although the case is actually concerned with offences contrary to the TA 1968, ss. 15 and 20, the decision clearly applies to the law of theft. The two principles are, first, that the question of deciding whether the accused was dishonest in his appropriation of property belonging to another is for the jury to decide. Secondly, 'dishonesty is something in the mind of the accused' (p. 1064A). Consequently, '. . . if the mind of the accused is honest, it cannot be deemed dishonest merely because members of the jury would have regarded it as dishonest to embark on that course of conduct' (p. 1064A).

According to the Court of Appeal in *Ghosh* (at p. 1064D–E), if the TA 1968, s. 2, is of no assistance or relevance, the jury should determine whether the accused was acting dishonestly in two stages:

> [1.] . . . a jury must first of all decide whether according to the ordinary standards of reasonable and honest people what was done was dishonest. If it was not dishonest by those standards, that is the end of the matter and the prosecution fails.

> If it was dishonest by those standards, then the jury must consider [the second question].

> [2] . . . the jury must consider whether the defendant himself must have realised that what he was doing was by [the standards of reasonable and honest people] dishonest.

The questions must be asked in the indicated order; to reverse them is confusing (*Green* [1992] Crim LR 292). The Court of Appeal in *Ghosh* gave further explanation of the second question when it said (at p. 1064E–G):

> In most cases, where the actions are obviously dishonest by ordinary standards, there will be no doubt about it. It will be obvious that the defendant himself knew that he was acting dishonestly. It is dishonest for a defendant to act in a way which he knows ordinary people consider to be dishonest, even if he asserts or genuinely believes that he is morally justified in acting as he did. For example, Robin Hood or those ardent anti-vivisectionists who remove animals from vivisection laboratories are acting dishonestly, even though they may consider themselves to be morally justified in doing what they do, because they know that ordinary people would consider these actions to be dishonest.

In some cases a 'full *Ghosh* direction' is not necessary. Where it is necessary, the exact words in *Ghosh* should be followed (*Hyam* [1997] Crim LR 439). The Court of Appeal has recognised that in many cases it will be obvious that the defendant knew he was acting dishonestly. In *Roberts* (1985) 84 Cr App R 117, a decision concerned with handling stolen goods, the Court of Appeal indicated that a full *Ghosh* direction would not be necessary unless the defendant raised the issue by, for example, suggesting that he did not know that anybody would regard his actions as dishonest. Further, in *Price* (1989) 90 Cr App R 409, a decision concerned with the TA 1978, ss. 1 and 2, the Court of Appeal, following *Roberts*, said (at p. 411):

> ... it is by no means in every case involving dishonesty that a *Ghosh* direction is necessary. Indeed in the majority of such cases, of which this was one, it is unnecessary and potentially misleading to give such a direction. It need only be given in cases where the defendant might have believed that what he is alleged to have done was in accordance with the ordinary person's idea of honesty.

In consequence Price's convictions were upheld when the judge had not given a *Ghosh* direction, since the only question relevant to dishonesty was whether the defendant honestly believed that he was the beneficiary of a trust fund or not (see also *Buzalek* [1991] Crim LR 130 (a fraudulent trading case), *Brennen* [1990] Crim LR 118 (a handling case) and *Green* [1992] Crim LR 292 (a s. 20 case)). But in other cases failure to direct on *Ghosh* could be fatal to a conviction, see e.g., *Clarke* [1996] Crim LR 824.

In *Clowes (No. 2)* [1994] 2 All ER 316, the Court of Appeal approved the approach established by the same court in *Lightfoot* (1992) 97 Cr App R 24 that, on the question of dishonesty, the defendant's knowledge of the law, whether the criminal or civil law, is irrelevant. What matters is whether the *Ghosh* test is satisfied. In some cases of theft, however, it is more likely that a defendant will be found to be dishonest if he does have an appreciation of the relevant civil law.

It is clear that the meaning of dishonesty provided by the Court of Appeal in *Ghosh* [1982] QB 1053 applies to obtaining property by deception (*Ghosh* and *Woolven* (1983) 77 Cr App R 231), to procuring the execution of a valuable security by deception (*Ghosh*), to handling stolen goods (*Roberts* (1985) 84 Cr App R 117), to obtaining services by deception (*Price* (1989) 90 Cr App R 410), and to evasion of liability by deception (*Price*). It is therefore proper to state that it applies to 'dishonesty' wherever it appears in the Theft Acts 1968 and 1978 and possibly in other contexts as well.

Intention Permanently to Deprive

On a charge of theft the prosecution must prove that the accused had an intention **B4.38** permanently to deprive another of property at the time that property was appropriated. The fact that the accused later returns the property does not negate the intention present at the time of the appropriation (*McHugh* (1993) 97 Cr App R 335). Nothing less than an intention permanently to deprive will do (*Warner* (1970) 55 Cr App R 93 at p. 96; *Cocks* (1976) 63 Cr App R 79 at p. 81). The TA 1968, s. 6, may assist in establishing whether or not there is such an intention. In most cases, though, s. 6 will not need to be referred to because there will be no factors in the case which demand consideration of the special circumstances covered by that section. Section 6 should be referred to 'in exceptional cases only' (*Lloyd* [1985] QB 829; *Coffey* [1987] Crim LR 498).

In *Duru* [1974] 1 WLR 2 it was held that there was an intention permanently to deprive where a stolen cheque is inevitably returned to the bank on which it is drawn as a paid cheque is not the same thing as that which was stolen. However, this has been overruled by the decision of the House of Lords in *Preddy* [1996] AC 815, where it was said that 'there can have been no intention on the part of the payee permanently to deprive the drawer of the cheque form, which would on presentation of the cheque for payment be returned to the drawer via his bank'. Their Lordships then said that *Duru* had 'to this extent been wrongly decided'. This then must create doubt about the decision in *Downes* (1983) 77 Cr App R 260 in which the stolen property was vouchers which self-employed individuals could present to persons for whom they worked to establish their right to receive payments without deduction of PAYE income tax. The vouchers when used were returned to the Inland Revenue. The fact that they had been used and could not be reused made them different things from the stolen vouchers. The argument relied upon *Duru*, and so the case must be regarded as wrong. However, in neither case did the court rely upon s. 6 (although some consideration was given to it in *Downes*). In *Marshall* [1998] 2 Cr App R 282, the Court of Appeal relied upon s. 6 in a similar type of case to uphold a conviction for theft (see **B4.39**).

Intention to Treat Property as one's Own to Dispose of, Regardless of Another's Rights

B4.39   **Theft Act 1968, s. 6**

(1)   A person appropriating property belonging to another without meaning the other permanently to lose the thing itself is nevertheless to be regarded as having the intention of permanently depriving the other of it if his intention is to treat the thing as his own to dispose of regardless of the other's rights; and a borrowing or lending of it may amount to so treating it if, but only if, the borrowing or lending is for a period and in circumstances making it equivalent to an outright taking or disposal.

(2)   Without prejudice to the generality of subsection (1) above, where a person, having possession or control (lawfully or not) of property belonging to another, parts with the property under a condition as to its return which he may not be able to perform, this (if done for purposes of his own and without the other's authority) amounts to treating the property as his own to dispose of regardless of the other's rights.

The Court of Appeal in *Lloyd* [1985] QB 829 observed (at p. 834B) that s. 6 of the TA 1968 means that there are circumstances where a defendant is 'deemed to have the intention permanently to deprive, even though he may intend the owner eventually to get back the object which has been taken'.

Different approaches have been taken to the interpretation of s. 6. In *Lloyd* [1985] QB 829 the Court of Appeal, relying on the judgment of Edmund Davies LJ in *Warner* (1970) 55 Cr App R 93, indicated that it would try to interpret s. 6 'in such a way as to ensure that nothing is construed as an intention permanently to deprive which would not prior to the 1968 Act have been so construed'. On the other hand, the Court of Appeal in *Downes* (1983) 77 Cr App R 260 was desirous of giving the words of s. 6 their normal meaning.

The latter view, meaning that it is not essential to consider the law prior to the TA 1968, appears to be the view more likely to be accepted by future courts. Acceptance of that view is supported by the approaches taken to s. 6 by the Court of Appeal in *Duru* [1974] 1 WLR 2 (the reliability of this decision in relation to the intention permanently to deprive someone of the cheque form has been undermined by the statement in *Preddy* [1996] AC 815 (at p. 837) that the case was wrongly decided), the Privy Council in *Chan Man-sin* v *The Queen* [1988] 1 WLR 196 and the Divisional Court in *Governor of Pentonville Prison, ex parte Osman* [1990] 1 WLR 277. Further, Edmund Davies LJ in *Warner* (1970) 55 Cr App R 93 did not say that the pre-existing law should determine the meaning of s. 6, but that its aim was to prevent specious pleas which might have succeeded previously. The Court of Appeal in *Bagshaw* [1988] Crim LR 321 said that the observations of the Court of Appeal in *Lloyd* were *obiter* 'and that there may be other occasions on which the section applies'. Finally, the Court of Appeal in *Fernandes* [1996] 1 Cr App R 175 made clear that s. 6(1) is not limited to the illustrations given in *Lloyd* (see also *Marshall* [1998] 2 Cr App R 282).

That s. 6 generally and s. 6(1) specifically should not be interpreted narrowly is supported by the decision in *Chan Man-sin* v *The Queen* [1988] 1 WLR 196. The Privy Council briefly referred to the Hong Kong equivalent of s. 6(1) and said that even if it were possible that the fraud practised by the accused would be discovered there would be an intention permanently to deprive, since the defendant was 'purporting to deal with the companies' property without regard to their rights'. The defendant had forged cheques belonging to a company for which he was the accountant. He may well have known that once the fraud was discovered these cheques would have no effect and thus the companies would lose nothing. The critical notion in s. 6(1) is the 'intention to treat the thing as his own to dispose of regardless of the other's rights' and so s. 6(1) should not be artificially limited in its scope (*Fernandes* [1996] 1 Cr App R 175, and see *Marshall*).

In *Marshall*, tickets and travel cards had been acquired by the appellants from travellers and sold on because they had not been used up. They were returned to London Underground eventually. The Court of Appeal held that the appellants had an intention permanently to deprive London Underground of its property even though 'its usefulness or virtue [was] exhausted' because s. 6(1) applied. This may be the approach to upholding convictions in cases such as *Duru* [1974] 1 WLR 2 and *Downes* (1983) 77 Cr App R 260 in the future (for the problem presented by *Preddy* [1996] 2 AC 815, see **B4.38**). In *Downes*, this approach was considered since the Court of Appeal took the view, *obiter*, that the first part of s. 6(1) would clearly cover the facts of the case. The court, adopting the approach of giving the words of the section their ordinary meaning, was not convinced of the view submitted by counsel for the appellant that the first part of s. 6(1) was confined to only one case, that is, where the property is taken from its owner and then sold back to him. The Court of Appeal in *Coffey* [1987] Crim LR 498 was satisfied that a situation in which property was held to ransom would be a clear case for the application of s. 6(1). Where the judge must direct the jury on the first part of s. 6(1), it is important for him to draw the jury's attention to all the requisite elements. It is a material misdirection to fail to give adequate guidance as to the effect of the words 'to dispose of' (*Cahill* [1993] Crim LR 141), but a narrow dictionary definition should not be taken to that phrase *DPP* v *Lavender* [1994] Crim LR 297).

Borrowing or Lending In *Velumyl* [1989] Crim LR 299, the Court of Appeal **B4.40** rejected an argument that a person who borrowed money from his employer expecting to return an equivalent sum had no intention permanently to deprive the employer of that money, because he had no intention to return the objects that he had taken.

In *Bagshaw* [1988] Crim LR 321, the Court of Appeal said, *obiter*, 'that it would be open to the judge to leave to the jury . . . the question whether it was Bagshaw's intention to keep the "borrowed" cylinders until there was no more gas in them, by which time all their "virtue" would have gone, before returning them in one way or another to BOC'. In *Coffey* [1987] Crim LR 498, Coffey had been convicted of obtaining property by deception. He had been in dispute with Hodkinson and decided to exert pressure on him by obtaining from him baking equipment and keeping it until the dispute was resolved. It was not entirely clear what Coffey would do if he did not achieve his purpose. The Court of Appeal said that if the jury might have thought that the defendant 'intended to return the goods even if Hodkinson did not do what he wanted, they would not convict unless they were sure that he intended that the period of detention should be so long as to amount to an outright taking'. These cases appear to be suggesting that an intention to borrow or lend property can only amount to an intention permanently to deprive when almost all, if not all, the 'virtue' in the property has gone. In *Coffey* the court also said that 'the reference in section 6(1) to "borrowing" (plainly used in a loose sense to denote non-consensual assumption of possession coupled with an intention ultimately to restore the object taken) shows that the "deprivation" can be "permanent" even if it is meant to be temporary'. Further, the court pointed out that 'the reference to "the thing itself" in s. 6(1) indicates that the question of deprivation will not always be confined to the tangible object itself'. The object may be returned after 'its useful qualities have been exhausted' and there may nevertheless be an intention permanently to deprive, as in *Downes* (1983) 77 Cr App 260 and *Duru* [1974] 1 WLR 2.

B4.41 ***Parting with Property on a Condition which the Accused May Not Be Able to Perform*** The TA 1968, s. 6(2) clearly covers such instances as a person pawning the property of another, hoping that he will be able to redeem the property at the appropriate time.

B4.42 ***Trust Property*** In relation to trust property, s. 5(2) of the TA 1968 provides that 'an intention to defeat the trust shall be regarded accordingly as an intention to deprive of the property any person having that right'. The right referred to is the right to enforce the trust and 'that person' is the person to whom the trust property belongs (see **B4.20**). Section 5(2) states only that the intention to defeat the trust is an intention to deprive. It must still be established whether there was an intention to deprive permanently.

B4.43 ***Property Got by another's Mistake*** Section 5(4) of the TA 1968 provides that 'an intention not to make restoration shall be regarded accordingly as an intention to deprive that person of the property or proceeds'. 'That person' is the person who is entitled to restoration (see **B4.25**). Section 5(4) states only that the intention not to make restoration is an intention to deprive. It must still be established whether there was an intention to deprive permanently.

B4.44 ***Conditional Intention*** There has been a problem of 'conditional intention' in relation to attempted theft when nothing has been taken and it is argued for the accused that he had not decided to take anything but was simply ascertaining whether there was something worth taking. In *Easom* [1971] 2 QB 315 the Court of Appeal said that 'a conditional appropriation will not do'. So rummaging through a handbag with that intention was not sufficient. In *Husseyn* (1977) 67 Cr App R 131, the Court of Appeal followed *Easom* and so held that the accused was not guilty of attempted theft of some sub-aqua equipment from a holdall, because he had not yet looked into the bag and decided whether there was anything worth stealing. The solution to this problem is the same as in burglary (see **B4.68**). If the indictment is drafted generally (e.g., an attempt to steal some or all of the contents of the handbag or the holdall) the prosecution do not have to prove that the accused intended to steal the specific item present, but simply that he did intend to steal anything worth stealing (*A-G's Ref (Nos 1 and 2 of 1979* [1980] QB 180).

Territorial Jurisdiction

B4.45 For the general principles of territorial jurisdiction, see **D1.72**. For discussion in the context of theft, see **B4.28**.

Theft Act 1968, s. 14

(1) Where a person—

(a) steals or attempts to steal any mailbag or postal packet in the course of transmission as such between places in different jurisdictions in the British postal area, or any of the contents of such a mailbag or postal packet, or

(b) in stealing or with intent to steal any such mailbag or postal packet or any of its contents, commits any robbery, attempted robbery or assault with intent to rob;

then, notwithstanding that he does so outside England and Wales, he shall be guilty of committing or attempting to commit the offence against this Act as if he had done so in England or Wales, and he shall accordingly be liable to be prosecuted, tried and punished in England and Wales without proof that the offence was committed there.

(2) In subsection (1) above the reference to different jurisdictions in the British postal area is to be construed as referring to the several jurisdictions of England and Wales, of Scotland, of Northern Ireland, of the Isle of Man and of the Channel Islands.

(3) For the purposes of this section 'mailbag' includes any article serving the purpose of a mailbag.

There are specific offences concerned with mail thefts: it is an offence, contrary to the Post Office Act 1953, s. 53, unlawfully to take away or open a mailbag; it is an offence, contrary to the Post Office Act 1953, s. 56, wilfully and maliciously, with intent to injure any other person, to open or divert postal packets; and it is an offence, contrary to the Post Office Act 1953, s. 57, to secrete a postal packet.

ROBBERY

Definition

Theft Act 1968, s. 8

B4.46

> (1) A person is guilty of robbery if he steals, and immediately before or at the time of doing so, and in order to do so, he uses force on any person or puts or seeks to put any person in fear of being then and there subjected to force.
> (2) A person guilty of robbery, or of an assault with intent to rob, shall on conviction on indictment be liable to imprisonment for life.

Procedure

Robbery and assault with intent to rob are triable only on indictment. They are class 4 offences.

B4.47

Indictment

Statement of Offence

B4.48

Robbery contrary to section 8(1) of the Theft Act 1968

Particulars of Offence

A on the . . . day of . . . robbed V of a gold watch

As to the practice of including a count for an offence contrary to the Firearms Act 1968, see *French* (1982) **75** Cr App R 1 per Lord Lane CJ.

Alternative Verdicts

Theft is the obvious alternative verdict by the application of the Criminal Law Act 1967, s. 6(3). The House of Lords in *Maxwell* [1990] 1 WLR 401 has held that the trial judge is only obliged to leave such a lesser alternative verdict to the jury if necessary in the interests of justice, for example, if the question of force was in doubt but there was substantial evidence of theft.

B4.49

The decision in *Tennant* [1976] Crim LR 133, that it is not possible under the Criminal Law Act 1967, s. 6(3), to convict a person of an assault on an indictment charging robbery, needs to be reconsidered in the light of *Metropolitan Police Commissioner* v *Wilson* [1984] AC 242. It may be that an allegation of robbery can in many cases impliedly include an allegation of an assault, because most uses of force will involve an assault, even though it is not possible exactly to assimilate 'force' as required for robbery (see below) with 'assault'.

Sentencing Guidelines

The maximum penalty for robbery is life imprisonment (TA 1968, s. 8(2)). The maximum penalty for assault with intent to rob is life imprisonment (TA 1968, s. 8(2)).

B4.50

The combination of violence and theft makes robbery the most serious of the common offences of dishonesty. The great majority of offenders convicted of robbery receive custodial sentences. The guideline cases are *Turner* (1975) 61 Cr App R 67, *Daly* (1981) 3 Cr App R (S) 340 and *Gould* (1983) 5 Cr App R (S) 72.

In *Turner* there were 19 appellants, members of a gang which, over a four-year period had carried out 20 armed robberies on banks and security vans, netting over £1 million at 1975 values. Firearms and ammonia were carried, but used only to frighten, and injuries inflicted were slight. Lawton LJ said (at p. 91) that the normal starting-point for sentence for anyone taking part in a bank robbery or in the hold-up of a security or a Post Office van should be 15 years, if firearms were carried and no serious injury done. The lack of a previous criminal record is not, he said, to be regarded as a powerful mitigating matter. In *Daly*, Lord Lane CJ indicated that in a bank-robbery type of case, the most serious features calling for heavy sentences are:

> . . . detailed planning, use of loaded firearms or ammonia, where a number of men execute a planned attack on a bank or a similar target in the hope of stealing substantial sums of money, where the participants are masked and armed either with guns, handguns or sawn-off shotguns, or sometimes with ammonia, and squirt ammonia into the faces of clients or staff of the bank in order to overpower resistance. In such cases, as Lawton LJ in *Turner* (of which everyone is aware) has rightly said that a starting-point of 15 years is correct. It may be, and no doubt will in nearly every case where there has been a plea of guilty, possible to reduce that term in the light of the plea and in the light of the assistance given to the police and other mitigating factors. It may be necessary on the other hand in some cases to increase the starting number of years because of the number of offences which the particular defendant has commited during the course of his depredation.

In *Gould* Lord Lane CJ confirmed that the *Turner* guidelines remained the basis for sentencing in armed robbery offences. He also added:

> Some of the features likely to mitigate an offence are, a plea of guilty, the youth of the offender, a previously clean record, the fact that the defendant had no companion when committing the offence and the fact that no one was injured. On the other hand the fact that a real rather than imitation weapon was used, that it was discharged, that violence was used upon the victim, that a number of men took part in the attack, that careful reconnaissance and planning were involved, that there was more than one offence committed by the offender, are all matters which the court must put into the balance on the other side of the scale when determining the correct sentence for any particular offender. These considerations are of course not exhaustive and are not intended so to be.

For robberies in the so-called 'first division', which are the subject of the guideline cases of *Turner*, *Daly* and *Gould*, the normal starting-point is 15 years. Sentences of 18 years and 17 years were imposed in *Knight* (1981) 3 Cr App R (S) 211 and *Reed* (1988) 10 Cr App R (S) 243 respectively. Wholly abnormal crimes, such as the Great Train Robbery will attract sentence in excess of 18 years (*Wilson* [1965] 1 QB 408). The 'irreducible minimum' in such cases is said to be 11 years (*Davis* (1980) 2 Cr App R (S) 168).

Robberies at sub-post offices, shops and similar premises will also attract substantial custodial sentences, though generally in a bracket below the first division for the offence. The relevant aggravating and mitigating factors appear to be very similar to those cited in that context. In *Stanford* (1988) 10 Cr App R (S) 222 the offenders, aged between 20 and 22, pleaded guilty to two counts of robbery, two of attempted robbery and two of taking a conveyance. In the robberies, they had entered post offices, threatened the owners with an imitation firearm and demanded money. A sentence of seven years was upheld on the offender who 'was the front man with the gun'. Sentences on the others were reduced to five years to take account of the facts that no actual violence was used and that the offenders gave up their attempts very easily when meeting any resistance, their guilty pleas, previous good characters and ages. In *A-G's Ref (No. 3 of 1990 and others)* (1991) 92 Cr App R 166, the Court of Appeal dealt with four separate references and increased custodial sentences on seven offenders involved in robberies of small shops, off-licences and similar premises, in each case to sentences of between three and a half and six years. In *A-G's Ref (Nos 26 and 27 of 1996)* [1997] 1 Cr App R (S) 243 sentences of four and a half years' detention in a young offender institution for two robberies at building society branches in the course of which imitation firearms were brandished and a hostage was taken were increased to seven and a half years by the Court of Appeal. See also *Loughlin* [1997] 1 Cr App R (S) 277.

A third category of robbery is street robbery or 'mugging'. The Court of Appeal's approved tariff seems to be from two to five years, though it appears that some less serious cases of mugging are dealt with by shorter terms or non-custodial sentences. Community sentences were held to have been unduly lenient disposals in *A-G's Ref (No. 44 of 1997)* [1998] 2 Cr App R (S) 105, a violent mugging where the victim was lured into a park, pulled to the ground and kicked about the head and body by two offenders, who then stole his wallet. The Court of Appeal indicated that on these facts custodial sentences in the order of three years would have been appropriate for an adult on a plea of guilty. The mugging of a female victim at night attracted a sentence of three years in *Byfield* (1994) 15 Cr App R (S) 674. A female mugger received 30 months in *Williams* (1982) 4 Cr App R (S) 156.

Where victims are attacked in their own homes, sentence varies according to the degree of violence used and the value of the property taken. A six-year sentence was upheld in *Waddingham* (1983) 5 Cr App R (S) 66 where the victim was threatened with a knife and then tied to the bed. In *Skilton* (1982) 4 Cr App R (S) 339 a sentence of $3\frac{1}{2}$ years was held to be proper where the offenders tricked their way into the home of a blind man, tied him up and then made off with his £28 social security payment.

A case towards the lower end of the scale of seriousness is *Golding* (1992) 13 Cr App R (S) 142. A sentence of six months' detention in a young offender institution was upheld where an 18-year-old youth had accosted a 16-year-old, and threatened to beat him up if he did not hand over his bicycle. Notwithstanding the guilty plea and the offender's good record, it was held that this offence of robbery was so serious that a non-custodial sentence could not be justified. See also *A-G's Ref (No. 39 of 1996)* [1997] 1 Cr App R (S) 355.

Actus Reus: Requirement of Theft

'Steal' in the TA 1968, s. 8(1), must refer to theft contrary to s. 1 (but note that the Court **B4.51** of Appeal surprisingly treated this matter as open in *Forrester* [1992] Crim LR 793). Thus in *Robinson* [1977] Crim LR 173 it was held that as there was no dishonesty there was no theft and, therefore, no robbery.

Actus Reus: Use of Force or Fear of Subjection to Force in Order to Steal

It is possible for the theft and the assault or force to be separate. Robbery links them. It **B4.52** is therefore necessary for there to be a careful direction on this point, following the words of the statute (*James* [1997] Crim LR 598). In *Dawson* (1976) 64 Cr App R 170 the Court of Appeal said that the use of the word 'force' in the TA 1968, s. 8(1), was deliberate: it is a word in ordinary use, which juries understand. The jury were entitled to arrive at the conclusion that force was used in the instant case. The defendants stood around the victim, one of them nudged him and his wallet was stolen.

Whether the force has been used on a person (or someone has been put in fear of the use of force) is a question for the jury to consider, and it appears that they may conclude that force has been used when it is used indirectly. So in *Clouden* [1987] Crim LR 56 the Court of Appeal dismissed an appeal against a conviction for robbery when the defendant had wrenched the victim's shopping basket from her hand and run off with it. This also appears to have been the view of the Divisional Court in *Corcoran v Anderton* (1980) 71 Cr App R 104.

In *Shendley* [1970] Crim LR 49 the trial judge had directed the jury as follows: '. . . if you come to the conclusion that the violence was unconnected with the stealing but you are satisfied there was a stealing it does not mean that is an acquittal because it would be open to you to find [him] guilty of robbery, that is, robbery without violence'. The Court of Appeal held that that direction was wrong. Robbery is committed when theft is carried out by a person using force in order to steal. The court substituted a conviction of theft for that of robbery.

Force must be used immediately before or at the time of stealing. Consequently, it is important to know whether or not the theft is complete (see **B4.27**).

Mens Rea

B4.53   Clearly the *mens rea* for theft is required. This indicates dishonesty (see **B4.34** to **B4.37**) and intention permanently to deprive (see **B4.38** to **B4.44**). It is also arguable that there must be intention or at least recklessness as to the use of force. Certainly it would seem that some accidental use of force during the course of an ordinary theft would not suffice since the accused must use the force in order to steal.

BURGLARY

Definition

B4.54   **Theft Act 1968, s. 9**

(1)   A person is guilty of burglary if—
(a)   he enters any building or part of a building as a trespasser and with intent to commit any such offence as is mentioned in subsection (2) below; or
(b)   having entered any building or part of a building as a trespasser he steals or attempts to steal anything in the building or that part of it or inflicts or attempts to inflict on any person therein any grievous bodily harm.
(2)   The offences referred to in subsection (1)(a) above are offences of stealing anything in the building or part of a building in question, of inflicting on any person therein any grievous bodily harm or raping any person therein, and of doing unlawful damage to the building or anything therein.

Section 9 creates two groups of offences: one of entering a building (or part of a building) as a trespasser with the requisite intent, contrary to s. 9(1)(a); the other of having entered a building (or part of a building) as a trespasser and committing one of the four specified offences, contrary to s. 9(1)(b). In each case there are two offences dependent upon whether the building is a dwelling. The different sentence provisions (see **B4.58**) mean that, under *Courtie* [1984] AC 463, there are two offences in each group.

Procedure

B4.55   By virtue of the MCA 1980, s. 17 and sch. 1, para. 28, most forms of burglary are triable either way. When tried on indictment, burglary is a class 4 offence. However,

(a)   if the burglary comprises the commission of, or an intention to commit, an offence which is triable only on indictment, then the burglary is also triable only on indictment (sch. 1, para. 28(b));
(b)   if the burglary is in a dwelling-house and any person in the dwelling was subjected to violence or the threat of violence, the offence is triable only on indictment (sch. 1, para. 28(c)).

Burglary triable only on indictment is a class 3 offence.

In the *Practice Note (Mode of Trial: Guidelines)* (1995) (see **D3.7**), separate guidelines are given for burglary at a dwelling-house and burglary at non-dwellings. The guidelines for burglary from a dwelling-house state that cases should be tried summarily unless the court considers that one or more of the following features is present *and* that its sentencing powers are insufficient:

(a)   Entry in the daytime when the occupier (or another) is present.

(b)   Entry at night of a house which is normally occupied, whether or not the occupier (or another) is present.

(c)   The offence is alleged to be one of a series of similar offences.

(d)   When soiling, ransacking, damage or vandalism occurs.

(e)   The offence has professional hallmarks.

(f)   The unrecovered property is of high value (at least £10,000).

The guidelines for burglary from non-dwellings state that cases should be tried summarily unless the court considers that one or more of the following features is present *and* that its sentencing powers are insufficient:

(a)   Entry of a pharmacy or doctor's surgery.

(b)   Fear is caused or violence is done to anyone lawfully on the premises (e.g., nightwatchman; security guard).

(c)   The offence has professional hallmarks.

(d)   Vandalism on a substantial scale.

(e)   The unrecovered property is of high value (at least £10,000).

Indictment

Statement of Offence   **B4.56**

Burglary with intent contrary to section 9(1)(a) of the TA 1968

Particulars of Offence

A, on or about the . . . day of . . . entered a dwelling [or part of a dwelling, or a building or part of a building], namely . . ., as a trespasser with intent to steal therein [or inflict grievous bodily harm upon a person therein, or to rape a person therein, or to do unlawful damage to the building or anything therein]

Statement of Offence

Burglary contrary to section 9(1)(b) of the TA 1968

Particulars of Offence

A on or about the . . . day of . . ., having entered a dwelling [or part of a dwelling, or a building or part of a building], namely . . ., as a trespasser, stole therein [or attempted to steal therein, or inflicted grievous bodily harm upon . . . therein]

In *Machent* v *Quinn* [1970] 2 All ER 255 the Divisional Court decided that it is unnecessary for the prosecution to prove that all the articles mentioned in an information or an indictment have been stolen. Proof that the accused stole any one of those articles is sufficient.

As to the relevance of conditional intention in drafting an indictment, see **B4.68**.

Alternative Verdicts

By virtue of the Criminal Law Act 1967, s. 6(3), on a charge of burglary contrary to the **B4.57** TA 1968, s. 9(1)(b), the accused may be convicted of the underlying offence that the court alleges he committed in the building (*Lillis* [1972] 2 QB 236). There is no express provision separate from the Criminal Law Act 1967, s. 6(3), but that section has been applied with important consequences in the offence of burglary. The House of Lords in *Metropolitan Police Commissioner* v *Wilson* [1984] AC 242 considered the meaning of 'inflicts grievous bodily harm' and also considered what alternative verdicts might generally be available and, specifically, whether a conviction under the OAPA 1861, s. 47, could be an alternative verdict to burglary under the TA 1968, s. 9(1)(b). The House decided that that was possible, having ruled on the meaning of the Criminal Law

Act 1967, s. 6(3). Whether a conviction under the OAPA 1861, s. 47, is an alternative verdict depends upon whether one of the four options envisaged by the Criminal Law Act 1967, s. 6(3), is satisfied:

> First, the allegation in the indictment expressly amounts to an allegation of another offence. Secondly, the allegation in the indictment impliedly amounts to an allegation of another offence. Fourthly, the allegation in the indictment impliedly includes an allegation of another offence. (per Lord Roskill at p. 258)

A charge of burglary with intent to inflict grievous bodily harm impliedly includes an allegation of an offence contrary to the OAPA 1861, s. 47, since an assault may be alleged by the charge, although it is not an essential element to that offence. Consequently, there will be some cases where an assault offence is possible as an alternative verdict to burglary.

The approach in *Wilson* has been applied in *Whiting* (1987) 85 Cr App R 78. The Court of Appeal decided that it is possible that a person may be found guilty of burglary under the TA 1968, s. 9(1)(a) on a charge of burglary under s. 9(1)(b), because s. 9(1)(b) impliedly includes an allegation of an offence contrary to s. 9(1)(a). Of course, such an alternative verdict can be arrived at in some, but not all cases, since these two offences are essentially quite different in certain respects (see below).

Sentencing Guidelines

B4.58   The maximum penalty which may be imposed for burglary, and the penalty likely to be imposed in a particular case, varies according to whether the burglary is in respect of a dwelling or in respect of premises other than a dwelling.

The maximum penalty for burglary of a building or part of a building which is a dwelling is 14 years' imprisonment on indictment, six months or a fine not exceeding the statutory maximum, or both, summarily (TA 1968, s. 9(4)).

Where an offence of burglary is committed in relation to a dwelling, and the offence is tried summarily, the Magistrates' Association Guidelines (1997) indicate the following:

> **Aggravating Factors** ⊕
> For example racial motivation; deliberately frightening occupants; group offence; people in house; professional operation; forcible entry; soiling, ransacking, damage; offence committed on bail; previous convictions and failures to respond to previous sentences, if relevant.
>
> **Mitigating Factors** ⊖
> For example low value; nobody frightened; no damage or disturbance; no forcible entry; opportunist.
>
> *Guideline*: Is it so serious that only custody is appropriate?

In respect of burglaries from dwellings, in *Brewster* [1998] 1 Cr App R 220 the Lord Chief Justice issued the following sentencing guidance.

> Domestic burglary is, and always has been, regarded as a very serious offence. It may involve considerable loss to the victim. Even where it does not, the victim may lose possessions of particular value to him or her. To those who are insured, the receipt of financial compensation does not replace what is lost. But many victims are uninsured; because they may have fewer possessions, they are the more seriously injured by the loss of those they do have.
>
> The loss of material possessions is, however, only part (and often a minor part) of the reason why domestic burglary is a serious offence. Most people, perfectly legitimately, attach importance to the privacy and security of their own homes. That an intruder should break in or enter, for his own dishonest purposes, leaves the victim with a sense of violation and insecurity. Even where the victim is unaware, at the time, that a burglar is in the house, it

can be a frightening experience to learn that a burglary has taken place; and it is all the more frightening if the victim confronts or hears the burglar. Generally speaking, it is more frightening if the victim is in the house when the burglary takes place, and if the intrusion takes place at night; but that does not mean that the offence is not serious if the victim returns to an empty house during the daytime to find that it has been burgled.

The seriousness of the offence can vary almost infinitely from case to case. It may involve an impulsive act involving an object of little value (reaching through a window to take a bottle of milk, or stealing a can of petrol from an outhouse). At the other end of the spectrum it may involve a professional, planned organisation, directed at objects of high value. Or the offence may be deliberately directed at the elderly, the disabled or the sick, and it may involve repeated burglaries of the same premises. It may sometimes be accompanied by acts of wanton vandalism.

The record of the offender is of more significance in the case of domestic burglary than in the case of some other crimes. There are some professional burglars whose records show that from an early age they have behaved as predators preying on their fellow citizens, returning to their trade almost as soon as each prison sentence has been served. Such defendants must continue to receive substantial terms of imprisonment. There are, however, other domestic burglars whose activities are of a different character, and whose careers may lack any element of persistence or deliberation. They are entitled to more lenient treatment.

It is common knowledge that many domestic burglars are drug addicts who burgle and steal in order to raise money to satisfy their craving for drugs. This is often an expensive craving, and it is not uncommon to learn that addicts commit a burglary, or even several burglaries, each day, often preying on houses in less affluent areas of the country. But to the victim of burglary the motivation of the burglar may well be of secondary interest. Self-induced addiction cannot be relied on as mitigation. The courts will not be easily persuaded that an addicted offender is genuinely determined and able to conquer his addiction.

Generally speaking, domestic burglaries are the more serious if they are of occupied houses at night; if they are the result of professional planning, organisation or execution; if they are targeted at the elderly, the disabled and the sick; if there are repeated visits to the same premises; if they are committed by persistent offenders; if they are accompanied by vandalism or any wanton injury to the victim; if they are shown to have a seriously traumatic effect on the victim; if the offender operates as one of a group; if goods of high value (whether actual or sentimental) are targeted or taken; if force is used or threatened; if there is a pattern of repeat offending. It mitigates the seriousness of an offence if the offender pleads guilty, particularly if the plea is indicated at an early stage and there is hard evidence of genuine regret and remorse.

Lord Bingham CJ stated that, overall, the cases showed that:

(a)   burglary of a dwelling-house, occupied or unoccupied, is not necessarily and in all cases an offence of such seriousness that a non-custodial sentence cannot be justified;

(b)   the decision whether a custodial sentence is required, and if so the length of such sentence, is heavily dependent on the aggravating and mitigating features mentioned above and, usually to a lesser extent, the personal circumstances of the offender;

(c)   the courts, particularly the higher courts, have generally reflected in their sentences the abhorrence with which the public regard those who burgle the houses of others.

This guidance may be regarded as superseding that which had earlier been provided by the Court of Appeal in *Mussell* [1991] 1 WLR 187 and in *Edwards* (1996) *The Times*, 1 July 1996. In respect of the latter case, Lord Bingham CJ commented that the decision had sought to establish clear sentencing brackets for the offence where it was not possible or desirable to do so, and that it had placed too much emphasis upon a distinction between burglary of occupied and unoccupied houses.

Decisions of the Court of Appeal on house burglary reflect the balance of considerations outlined by Lord Bingham CJ in *Brewster*. Towards the top of the sentencing scale are cases involving 'professional' burglars with substantial records. In *Whittaker* [1998] 1 Cr App R (S) 172, sentences totalling ten years' imprisonment were upheld for a series of burglaries targeting the homes of elderly people, although no deliberate violence was used against the occupiers. A second pair of offences was committed while the offender had been on bail in respect of two others. The Court of Appeal said that it had been correct to impose consecutive sentences in such a case, and that the overall term was not excessive. See also *Brewster* (1980) 2 Cr App R (S) 191, where a sentence of 10 years was upheld on an offender who had convictions for 57 burglaries in the previous ten years and had committed two more while on parole. In *Henry* [1998] 1 Cr App R (S) 289, a sentence of five years' imprisonment was upheld on an offender who distracted the attention of a woman aged 93 while his co-defendant entered her flat and stole items of jewellery. In the Court of Appeal, Potter LJ referred to Henry as a 'dyed-in-the-wool social menace, preying on old people over a period of ten years . . . every type of sentence, custodial and non-custodial, has been tried and failed'.

A more typical case is *Kyle* (1993) 14 Cr App R (S) 613, where the offender, aged 20, had broken into a house while the occupiers were away on holiday. He was apprehended quickly and all property taken was recovered. A sentence of 12 months' detention in a young offender institution was reduced to nine months by the Court of Appeal. In *Lewis* (1993) 14 Cr App R (S) 744 a sentence of 18 months' imprisonment for the burglary of the home of a recently deceased person was upheld by the Court of Appeal. Lewis, together with a co-defendant, had forced open the rear door of the house and loaded property worth at least £5,000 into a van. When arrested, Lewis was found to have in his possession a paper containing the names and addresses of persons whose death notices had recently appeared in the newspapers, and it was clear that the offender was targeting these homes for burglary. In *Russell* (1994) 15 Cr App R (S) 41, sentences of nine months' imprisonment were upheld on women aged 27 and 23 who had burgled a flat during the day equipped with a jemmy, an iron bar and other housebreaking tools. The offenders were detained by the occupiers and nothing was taken. In *Herridge* (1994) 15 Cr App R (S) 648 the offender pleaded guilty to two counts of burglary, having gained access to the houses of two elderly ladies by pretending to be a council official and stealing £130 and other items from one victim and £55 from the other. The Court of Appeal said that three and a half years' imprisonment was the proper sentence. See also *Tucker* [1997] 1 Cr App R (S) 337.

Custody was held to be inappropriate in *Suker* (1990) 12 Cr App R (S) 290, where a 19-year-old, affected by drink and looking for money to pay his taxi fare home, attempted to climb through the bathroom window of a house in the early hours of the morning and was detained by the householder. See also *Finney* [1998] 2 Cr App R (S) 239.

Burglary committed in relation to premises other than a dwelling is regarded as somewhat less serious than the previous category. The maximum penalty for burglary other than from a dwelling is ten years' imprisonment on indictment, six months or a fine not exceeding the statutory maximum, or both, summarily (TA 1968, s. 9(4)). When an offence of 'non-dwelling' burglary is committed, and the offence is dealt with summarily, the Magistrates' Association Guidelines (1997) indicate the following:

Aggravating Factors ⊕
For example racial motivation; deliberately frightening occupants; group offence; night time; professional operation; forcible entry; soiling, ransacking, damage, serious harm to business; offence committed on bail; previous convictions and failures to respond to previous sentences, if relevant.

Mitigating Factors ⊖

For example low value; nobody frightened; no damage or disturbance; no forcible entry.

Guideline: Is it serious enough for a community penalty?

Decisions of the Court of Appeal indicate that some cases of 'non-dwelling' burglary will be regarded as so serious that only a custodial sentence can be justified.

An example is *Dorries* (1993) 14 Cr App R (S) 608, where the offenders pleaded guilty to burglary of a shop. They had been seen in the vicinity of the shop and, when the police arrived, they drove away. Entry had been effected by removing bricks from a wall, and property worth £600 had been taken. A hammer, crowbar and radio scanner were found in their car. The Court of Appeal agreed with the sentencer that only a custodial sentence could be justified, but reduced the sentence from ten months to six months. In contrast to *Dorries*, the Court of Appeal held in *Tetteh* (1994) 15 Cr App R (S) 46 that the offence did not pass the threshold of seriousness. The offender had forced open the spirits store at a YMCA club and the drayman's entry cover had been opened to give access to the street. Nothing had been taken however, and it was an opportunistic rather than a planned offence. The Court of Appeal said that a community sentence would have been the proper sentence. See also *Carlton* (1994) 15 Cr App R (S) 335.

Where the offence is an isolated one committed by a younger offender with a good record, a community order is the preferred sentence. In *Lawrence* (1982) 4 Cr App R (S) 69 the offender, aged 23, together with three others had taken a conveyance, driven to another town, broken the window of a shop and stolen television sets, video recorders and tape recorders. A sentence of 18 months was varied to 150 hours' community service (this took account of a period in custody; otherwise 190 hours would have been proper). Lord Lane CJ said that the offender 'has all the marks of someone who, at this stage in his life, is capable of settling down'. Lawrence had two previous convictions for dishonesty but none since 1976.

Some other specific types of burglary have been the subject of comment by the Court of Appeal. In *Hunter* (1994) 15 Cr App R (S) 530, a case involving 'ram-raiding', the Court of Appeal upheld sentences of five years in respect of two offenders and four years in respect of a third. The first two offenders had, on separate occasions, reversed a van through the door of an electrical shop and driven a car into the window of a clothing shop. Goods had been stolen and damage caused totalling nearly £12,000. The third offender had been involved only in the second incident, at the scene of which all three had been arrested. In *Larcher* (1979) 1 Cr App R (S) 137 the offender admitted a series of burglaries of doctors' premises and chemists' shops in order to obtain drugs. Although he had not served a custodial sentence before, five years was imposed by the Court of Appeal. Sentences of five years were also approved in two cases of burglary with intent to rape. In *Staunton* (1981) 3 Cr App R (S) 375 the offender went to a house occupied by a widow and her 15-year-old daughter, forced entry to the house and ripped out the telephone wires. He subsequently fled after waking some dogs and being seen by the widow. In *Bolland* (1988) 10 Cr App R (S) 129 the offender entered at night the house of a woman known to him, assaulted her and threatened her with a knife.

Elements Common to Both s. 9(1)(a) and s. 9(1)(b)

Despite the fact that s. 9(1)(a) and s. 9(1)(b) of the TA 1968 create separate offences, **B4.59** there are a number of elements which are common to both and which can, therefore, be examined together. A 'building or part of a building' must be or have been 'entered' as 'a trespasser' in order for burglary to have been committed. The trespassory entry requirement demands a consideration not only of whether the entry was trespassory, but also whether the defendant knew that it was trespassory, or was reckless. The difference lies in s. 9(1)(a) with the need for an intention to commit certain offences and in

s. 9(1)(b) with the need to do certain things in the building (see, e.g., *O'Leary* (1986) 82 Cr App R 341 at p. 343).

B4.60 **Meaning of 'Building'** In *B* v *Leathley* [1979] Crim LR 314, the Crown Court (on an appeal from magistrates) held that the defendants had committed burglary. They had stolen some meat from a freezer container in a farmyard. The freezer was 25 feet long with 7 feet square cross-section, weighing about three tons and had been in place for two or three years. The freezer was, therefore, 'a structure of considerable size and intended to be permanent or at least to endure for a considerable period', that is, the court were satisfied that the test of Byles J in *Stevens* v *Gourley* (1859) CBNS 99 at p. 112 was fulfilled. In addition its doors were equipped to keep trespassers out and it was connected to an outside source of electricity. The court concluded that it was a building for the purposes of the offence of burglary. In *Norfolk Constabulary* v *Seekings* [1986] Crim LR 167 it was decided that a disconnected freezer trailer was not a building. Something will not qualify as a 'building' unless it has some degree of permanence, which would appear to exclude a tent, and the freezer trailer in *Norfolk Constabulary* v *Seekings*. In *Manning* (1871) LR 1 CCR 338 it was decided that a building does not have to be complete. In that case the building was a house which was very nearly complete, but the court was satisfied that structures not as complete could also be 'buildings'.

The meaning of 'building' is extended by s. 9(3):

> References in subsections (1) and (2) above to a building shall apply also to an inhabited vehicle or vessel, and shall apply to any such vehicle or vessel at times when the person having a habitation in it is not there as well as at times when he is.

Since a person need enter only a part of a building as a trespasser to be a burglar, it would be possible for a person lawfully on premises to become a burglar by entering another part of the building to which he was not entitled to enter. In *Walkington* [1979] 1 WLR 1169, the Court of Appeal decided that it is for the jury to decide whether an area physically marked out is sufficiently segregated to amount to a 'part of a building'. Walkington had gone behind the sales counter in a large store. The counter was movable, but occupied a clearly identified area. In the circumstances, the court took the view that there was evidence on which the jury could conclude that there was a separate part of the building identified by the counter area, since there was a physical partition and the management impliedly prohibited customers from entering the area.

B4.61 **Meaning of 'Entry'** In *Collins* [1973] QB 100, the Court of Appeal decided (at p. 106) that the accused has to make 'an effective and substantial entry into' a building or part of a building. This phrase was considered by the Court of Appeal in *Brown* [1985] Crim LR 212 and it took the view that the important point was whether the entry was 'effective'. A person could, therefore, enter a building when only part of the body is actually within it, so B had entered where the top half of his body was leaning into a shop window. The prosecution does not have to prove that the person was capable of stealing when only partially in a building. The issue is whether the partial entry was capable of constituting entry, as it was where the accused was stuck in an open window; the matter is then for the tribunal of fact to decide (*Ryan* (1996) 160 JP 610).

It was said in *Collins*, that entry must be 'deliberate'. Consequently, it cannot be shown that this element of the crime has been satisfied if the entry is accidental, which it might be, for example, if boundaries of private land are unclear or obstructed by snow.

B4.62 **Meaning of 'as a Trespasser'** It is important that at the time the accused entered the building, his entry was as a trespasser (see *Laing* [1995] Crim LR 395). A trespasser is someone who does not have permission, express or implied, to be on the premises. Since this is an aspect of the criminal law, it must be shown that there was a trespassory entry, and also that the person entered with *mens rea* (i.e. he either knew that he was entering as a trespasser or was reckless as to whether this was so).

Adequate permission can be given by someone other than the householder. In *Collins* [1973] QB 100, the accused went past a house where he knew a young lady lived. He climbed a ladder up to her window and peered in. She was lying naked on the bed, which was near the window. Collins descended the ladder, took off all his clothes, except his socks, and climbed back up the ladder. As he reached the window, the young lady woke up and, thinking he was her boyfriend, invited him in; they then had sexual intercourse. She then realised that it was not her boyfriend. Collins was convicted of burglary. His appeal against that conviction succeeded because the jury had not been asked to consider the vital question whether he had entered the building as a trespasser and whether he knew or was reckless as to whether he was entering as a trespasser. It was accepted by the Court of Appeal that an invitation from the young lady would have been sufficient to make Collins's entry not trespassory and so consideration should have been given to when her invitation was made, that is, whether he was outside the building at that time or not. Presumably such permission could be overridden by someone with a greater interest in the building in question.

The court expressed its view on *mens rea* as follows (at p. 105E):

> . . . there cannot be a conviction for entering premises 'as a trespasser' within the meaning of section 9 of the TA [1968] unless the person entering does so knowing that he is a trespasser and nevertheless deliberately enters, or, at the very least, is reckless as to whether or not he is entering the premises of another without the other party's consent.

The matter will not always be a simple one of deciding whether at the time the accused entered, permission had been granted. Permission, specific or general, may be exceeded. It is then to be determined whether that makes the entry trespassory. In *Jones* [1976] 1 WLR 672, the Court of Appeal upheld a conviction of burglary contrary to the TA 1968, s. 9(1)(b). Smith and Jones entered the house of Smith's father. They entered with the intention of taking, and did take, two television sets. The question for the court was whether the entry was trespassory, and whether they had the necessary *mens rea*. The court said:

> . . . it is our view that a person is a trespasser for the purpose of section 9(1)(b) of the TA 1968 if he enters premises of another knowing that he is entering in excess of the permission that has been given to him, or being reckless as to whether he is entering in excess of the permission that has been given to him to enter. Provided the facts are known to the accused which enable him to realise that he is acting in excess of the permission given or that he is acting recklessly as to whether he exceeds that permission, then that is sufficient for the jury to decide that he is in fact a trespasser.

Since the jury were, in the instant case, satisfied that Smith and Jones entered against the consent or in excess of the consent that had been given by Mr Smith to his son, the conviction was upheld. The same principle would apply to a charge under s. 9(1)(a).

It is essential, therefore, for the person entering to know that entry is prohibited, or at least be advertently reckless as to the prohibition. In *Walkington* [1979] 1 WLR 1169 (see **B4.60**) the Court of Appeal emphasised that it was necessary in order for a conviction to be sustained that the defendant knew that he was not supposed to enter the counter area.

It is possible to suggest that *Collins* [1973] QB 100 and *Jones* [1976] 1 WLR 672 are inconsistent or, rather, that one factor was not considered in *Collins*. If Collins all along intended to have sexual intercourse with the young lady, should it have been considered whether or not he was exceeding the permission she gave when she invited him in? (It is possible, however, that she invited him in for sexual intercourse as she saw 'a naked male with an erect penis'. It is questionable whether this would have afforded a defence if Collins had realised her mistake about his identity.)

'. . . the common-law doctrine of trespass *ab initio* has no application to burglary under the TA 1968'. (*Collins* [1973] QB 100 at p. 107.)

Burglary with Intent (s. 9(1)(a)): Proof of Intent

B4.63   On a charge of burglary with intent contrary to the TA 1968, s. 9(1)(a), it must be shown that, at the time of the entry (not before and not after), the accused intended to commit the offences listed in s. 9(2). As to intention generally, see **A2.2**.

B4.64   *Intent to Commit an Offence of Stealing*   'Stealing' is defined in the TA 1968, s. 1, see **B4.1**. It is not burglary to enter a building with intent to abstract electricity because abstracting electricity is not stealing (*Low* v *Blease* [1975] Crim LR 513). In *Gregory* (1981) 77 Cr App R 41, the Court of Appeal said (at p. 46):

> In a case of burglary of a dwelling-house and before any property is removed from it, it may consist of a continuing process and involve either a single appropriation by one or more persons or a number of appropriations of the property in the house by several persons at different times during the same incident. . . . Thus a person who may have more the appearance of a handler than the thief can nevertheless still be convicted of theft, and thus of burglary, if the jury are satisfied that with the requisite dishonest intent he appropriated, or took part in the appropriation, of another person's goods.

As to the question whether, in theft and therefore burglary, an appropriation is instantaneous or continuing, see **B4.28**.

B4.65   *Intent to Commit an Offence of Inflicting Grievous Bodily Harm*   In order to prove an intention to commit grievous bodily harm on a charge of burglary with intent it is unnecessary to prove an assault (*Metropolitan Police Commissioner* v *Wilson* [1984] AC 242). As to the meaning of 'grievous bodily harm', see generally **B2.34**.

In *O'Neill* (1986) *The Times*, 17 October 1986 the Court of Appeal appears to have decided, presumably on the facts of the particular case in question, that charges of burglary by entering a building with intent to inflict grievous bodily harm should not have been left to the jury because there was no specific express evidence of such intent. No weapons had been carried by the defendants and no grievous bodily harm had been committed, even though two persons on the premises had been assaulted. The offence is committed by intending, at the time of entering premises as a trespasser, to inflict grievous bodily harm, and the fact that no grievous bodily harm is actually inflicted does not affect liability, though it may make it very difficult to prove the intent.

B4.66   *Intent to Commit an Offence of Rape*   As to the offence of rape, see **B3.1** to **B3.9**.

B4.67   *Intent to Commit an Offence of Doing Unlawful Damage*   It is to be presumed that this phrase refers to what is now criminal damage, see **B8.1** to **B8.24**.

B4.68   *Conditional Intent*   At one stage it was thought that a 'burglar's charter' had been created by the case of *Husseyn* (1977) 67 Cr App R 131. The argument was that if a person only intended to steal that which he found worth stealing then there was no intention to steal, since it was conditional on his finding something worth stealing, which might not be the case. The solution to this problem was found by the Court of Appeal in *Walkington* [1979] 1 WLR 1169 and adopted by the Court of Appeal in *A-G's Refs (Nos 1 and 2 of 1979)* [1980] QB 180. If a person is charged with burglary, contrary to s. 9(1)(a) of the TA 1968, by entering a building as a trespasser with intent to steal therein, and there is no reference to the stealing of specific items, that person is guilty if he has an intention to steal anything in the building and the fact that there was nothing in the building worth his stealing is immaterial. The problem is identical to that which may arise on a charge of theft: see **B4.44**.

Burglary (s. 9(1)(b)): Proof of Stealing or Grievous Bodily Harm

On a charge of burglary contrary to the Theft Act 1968, s. 9(1)(b), the prosecution must **B4.69** establish that the accused either stole or attempted to steal in the building or part of a building, or inflicted or attempted to inflict on any person in the building or part of a building any grievous bodily harm. For the meaning of 'steal' and 'inflict grievous bodily harm', see **B4.1** and **B2.34**. For the law of attempts, see **A6.31** *et seq*. It is not burglary under s. 9(1)(b) either to rape a woman or to cause unlawful damage, though intent to commit those offences is relevant to burglary with intent contrary to s. 9(1)(a).

AGGRAVATED BURGLARY

Definition

Theft Act 1968, s. 10 **B4.70**

(1)   A person is guilty of aggravated burglary if he commits any burglary and at the time has with him any firearm or imitation firearm, any weapon of offence, or any explosive.

Procedure

Aggravated burglary is triable only on indictment. It is a class 3 offence. **B4.71**

Indictment

Statement of Offence **B4.72**

Aggravated burglary contrary to section 10(1) of the Theft Act 1968

Particulars of Offence

A on or about the . . . day of . . . having entered a dwelling [or part of a dwelling, or a building or part of a building], namely . . . , as a trespasser stole therein [or attempted to steal therein, or inflicted grievous bodily harm upon . . . therein] and at the time had with him a firearm [or an imitation firearm, or a weapon of offence or an explosive], namely . . .

See also **B4.56**.

Alternative Verdicts

Burglary contrary to either s. 9(1)(a) or s. 9(1)(b) of the Theft Act 1968 (by virtue of the **B4.73** Criminal Law Act 1967, s. 6(3)). See also **B4.57**.

Sentencing Guidelines

The maximum penalty is: life imprisonment (Theft Act 1968, s. 10(2)). **B4.74**

Towards the top of the scale of seriousness is *O'Driscoll* (1986) 8 Cr App R (S) 121, where the offender gained access to the home of an elderly man and struck him a number of blows with a hammer. The victim was also threatened with a lighted gas poker, tied up with wire and gagged. A sentence of 15 years was upheld. Subsequent decisions which treat *O'Driscoll* as a guideline case include *A-G's Refs (Nos 32 and 33 of 1995)* [1996] 2 Cr App R (S) 345 and *Eastap* [1997] 2 Cr App R (S) 55. In *A-G's Ref (No. 24 of 1997)* [1998] 1 Cr App R (S) 319 a sentence of two years' detention under the CYPA 1933, s. 53(3), was increased to three and a half years where a 16-year-old offender targeted the home of an elderly lady and entered her bedroom in the early hours of the morning armed with a knife. When the lady woke up and screamed he fled. The Court of Appeal indicated that the right sentence on the facts would have been four years' detention without the element of double jeopardy involved in the offender being sentenced twice. In *A-G's Ref (No. 10 of 1996)* [1997] 1 Cr App R (S) 76 the offender, a man with a long criminal record, together with three friends all armed with baseball bats, staged a revenge attack at the home of a man the offender believed to have stolen property from him. The offender beat the victim with a bat, causing a depressed fracture of the skull and other injuries. A sentence of 15 months' imprisonment was increased to four years on appeal, with an unspecified allowance for the element of double jeopardy. In *A-G's Ref (No. 16 of 1994)* (1995) 16 Cr App R (S) 629, the offender, who had a record of violent offences and was armed with a baseball bat, went to the flat of a man he knew. He used the bat to smash property in the flat, thereby frightening the female occupant. A sentence of 18 months' imprisonment was increased to three years.

Meaning of 'Firearm', 'Imitation Firearm', 'Weapon of Offence', 'Explosive'

B4.75 **Theft Act 1968, s. 10**

(1) . . . and for this purpose—

(a) 'firearm' includes an airgun or air pistol, and 'imitation firearm' means anything which has the appearance of being a firearm, whether capable of being discharged or not, and

(b) 'weapon of offence' means any article made or adapted for use for causing injury to or incapacitating a person, or intended by the person having it with him for such use; and

(c) 'explosive' means any article manufactured for the purpose of producing a practical effect by explosion, or intended by the person having it with him for that purpose.

B4.76 *Paragraph (a)* Whilst a definition of 'imitation firearm' is provided, there is no definition of 'firearm', except to make clear that it includes airguns and air pistols. It may be that the general definition of 'firearm' in the Firearms Act 1968 is appropriate (see **B12.4**).

B4.77 *Paragraph (b)* In *Stones* [1989] 1 WLR 156, approved in *Kelly* (1992) 97 Cr App R 245, the Court of Appeal said (at p. 160):

It is not necessary to prove the intention to use the [weapon] to cause injury etc. during the course of the burglary.

. . . The mischief at which the section is clearly aimed is that if a burglar has a weapon which he intends to use to injure some person unconnected with the premises burgled [as in the instant case], he may nevertheless be tempted to use it if challenged during the course of the burglary and put under sufficient pressure.

The court also drew attention to the similarity between this paragraph and the provisions of the Prevention of Crime Act 1953, s. 1, concerned with the possession of offensive weapons. Whilst the two provisions are not identical since the phrase 'incapacitating a person' does not appear in s. 1 of the 1953 Act, some assistance may be obtained from the cases concerned with possession of offensive weapons. The defence of lawful authority or reasonable excuse for the possession of an offensive weapon (see **B12.86** to **B12.88**) does not appear to apply to aggravated burglary.

B4.78 *Paragraph (c)* The definition of 'explosive' for the purposes of aggravated burglary is narrower than that to be found in the Explosive Substances Act 1883, but that Act may be of assistance in determining the meaning of the TA 1968, s. 10(1)(c).

Relevant Time

B4.79 The gravamen of the offence is entry into a building with a weapon. It is intended to deter people taking weapons into buildings whilst committing burglary. Therefore, one of the entrants to the building must have the weapon with him (*Klass* [1998] 1 Cr App R 453). The time a person must have a weapon of offence (or other relevant article) with him depends upon the form of aggravated burglary with which he is charged. If, as in *O'Leary* (1986) 82 Cr App R 341, a person is charged with aggravated burglary under the TA 1968, s. 10 and s. 9(1)(b), it follows that, according to the Court of Appeal in that case (at p. 343):

. . . the time at which the defendant must be proved to have had with him a weapon of offence to make him guilty of aggravated burglary was the time at which he actually stole. . . .

> The judge ruled, as this court has indicated he should have ruled, namely that the material time in this charge for the possession of the weapon was the time when he confronted the householders and stole.

O'Leary had confronted the householders of a building which he had entered as a trespasser and demanded their cash and jewellery, which was the theft, and at the time he still had a kitchen knife in his hand which he had obtained downstairs in the same house. See also *Kelly* (1992) 97 Cr App R 245.

A conviction under s. 9(1)(a) could not have been upheld in *O'Leary* because it would have been necessary to prove an intention to steal at the time of entry and possession of the weapon of offence at that time. This follows from the decision of the Court of Appeal in *Francis* [1982] Crim LR 363 where, according to the report in the *Criminal Law Review*, it was decided that:

> if a person entered a building as a trespasser with intent to steal, he was guilty of burglary under section 9(1)(a) and if at the time of entry he had with him a weapon of offence, he was guilty of aggravated burglary; and that if a person entered a building as a trespasser and stole under section 9(1)(b) he committed burglary at the moment when he stole and he committed aggravated burglary only if he had with him a weapon of offence at the time when he stole.

The convictions for aggravated burglary had to be replaced by convictions for burglary since the defendants discarded their weapons of offence, which they had used to persuade the occupier to permit them to enter, either before they entered or shortly thereafter and the judge had directed the jury that all that needed to be proved was that the defendants were armed when they entered the house as trespassers.

Meaning of 'Has with Him'

There is a requirement for a degree of immediate control of the weapon of offence or other **B4.80** article (*Kelt* [1977] 1 WLR 1365 and *Pawlicki* [1992] 1 WLR 827). Indeed, 'the word will normally mean "carrying"' (*Kelt* and *Klass* [1998] 1 Cr App R 453). The cases decided on the Prevention of Crime Act 1953, s. 1 (possession of offensive weapons) are of no assistance because of the different purposes of the two offence-creating sections (*Kelly* (1992) 97 Cr App R 245). Since a dictum in *Stones* [1989] 1 WLR 156 at p. 160, it has been unclear whether the prosecution must prove that the accused knew he had a weapon of offence with him or knew he had something with him which was, in fact, a weapon of offence. It is submitted that the latter is to be preferred. It is more consistent with the general approach to this type of offence. For the comparable offence contrary to the Firearms Act 1968, s. 19, see **B12.64**. For the related offence contrary to the Firearms Act 1968, s. 1, see **B12.21**. For the decision on the drugs legislation that lies at the heart of many of these decisions, see **B20.13**. This issue has also recently arisen for decision under the Prevention of Crime Act 1953, s. 1 where the matter is controversial (see **B12.92**). The offence contrary to the Firearms Act 1968, s. 18 explicitly requires knowledge (see **B12.63**).

REMOVAL OF ARTICLES FROM PLACES OPEN TO THE PUBLIC

Definition

Theft Act 1968, s. 11 **B4.81**

> (1) Subject to subsections (2) and (3) below, where the public have access to a building in order to view the building or part of it, or a collection or part of a collection housed in it, any person who without lawful authority removes from the building or its grounds the whole or part of any article displayed or kept for display to the public in the building or that part of it or in its grounds shall be guilty of an offence.

Procedure

Removal of an article from a place open to the public is triable either way (MCA 1980, **B4.82** s. 17 and sch. 1, para. 28). When tried on indictment it is a class 4 offence.

Indictment

B4.83

Statement of Offence

Removing an article from a place open to the public contrary to section 11 of the Theft Act 1968

Particulars of Offence

A on or about the . . . day of . . . without lawful authority removed from the V art gallery, being a place to which the public then had access in order to view an art collection therein, a painting, namely *Portrait of the Madonna* by von Klomp

Sentence

B4.84 The maximum penalty is five years on indictment (TA 1968, s. 11(4)); six months and/or a fine not exceeding the statutory maximum summarily. No sentencing guidelines are reported for this offence.

Purpose for which the Public Have Access

B4.85 An offence under the TA 1968, s. 11(1), can be committed only in relation to a building to which the public have access for the purpose of viewing the building (or a part of it) or a collection (or part of a collection). It is the purpose of the inviter in granting access that matters (*Barr* [1978] Crim LR 244).

Meaning of 'Collection'

B4.86

Theft Act 1968, s. 11

(1)   For this purpose, 'collection' includes a collection got together for a temporary purpose, but references in this section to a collection do not apply to a collection made or exhibited for the purpose of effecting sales or other commercial dealings.

Time of Public Access

B4.87

Theft Act 1968, s. 11

(2)   It is immaterial for purposes of subsection (1) above, that the public's access to a building is limited to a particular period or particular occasion; but where anything removed from a building or its grounds is there otherwise than as forming part of, or being on loan for exhibition with, a collection intended for permanent exhibition to the public, the person removing it does not thereby commit an offence under this section unless he removes it on a day when the public have access to the building as mentioned in subsection (1) above.

If an art gallery, for example, is usually open it is possible for an offence under s. 11(1) to be committed on a day when the gallery is closed by removing an item which is part of a collection intended for permanent exhibition, whether it is actually on display or kept in store and exhibited on a rota basis (*Durkin* [1973] QB 786).

Meaning of 'Displayed or Kept for Display'

B4.88 Whether an article is displayed, or kept for display, depends upon the intention of the person setting out the articles. For example, in *Barr* [1978] Crim LR 244 it was found that a cross and ewer in a church were not on display but were intended to be aids to worship and devotion.

Belief in Lawful Authority

B4.89

Theft Act 1968, s. 11

(3)   A person does not commit an offence under this section if he believes that he has lawful authority for the removal of the thing in question or that he would have it if the person entitled to give it knew of the removal and the circumstances of it.

It is submitted that, if an accused raises the issue of his belief, it is then for the prosecution to prove beyond reasonable doubt that he had no such belief (compare the position under s. 12 of the Act, see **B4.96**). As to the defence of mistake generally, see **A3.2** to **A3.6**.

TAKING CONVEYANCE WITHOUT AUTHORITY

Definition

Theft Act 1968, s. 12   **B4.90**

(1)   Subject to subsections (5) and (6) below, a person shall be guilty of an offence if, without having the consent of the owner or other lawful authority, he takes any conveyance for his own or another's use or, knowing that any conveyance has been taken without such authority, drives it or allows himself to be carried in or on it.

Procedure

An offence under the TA 1968, s. 12(1), is triable only summarily. However, a count for **B4.91** such an offence may be included in an indictment for another offence in the circumstances set out in the CJA 1988, s. 40 (see **D9.6**). On the trial of an indictment for theft, the jury may find the accused guilty of an offence under s. 12(1) as an alternative verdict (TA 1968, s. 12(4)).

Sentencing Guidelines

The maximum penalty for taking a conveyance without authority is six months and/or **B4.92** a fine not exceeding level 5 (TA 1968, s. 12(2)). Additionally, for the offence or an attempt to commit it in respect of a motor vehicle, there is discretionary disqualification (Road Traffic Offenders Act 1988, sch. 2). The same maximum penalty and liability for disqualification applies in relation to the offence of driving or allowing oneself to be carried in or on a conveyance taken without authority.

The Magistrates' Association Guidelines (1997) indicate the following:

Aggravating Factors ⊕
For example group action; premeditated; related damage; professional hallmarks; vulnerable victim; offence committed on bail; previous convictions and failures to respond to previous sentences, if relevant.

Mitigating Factors ⊖
For example misunderstanding with owner; soon returned; vehicle belonging to family or friend.

Guideline: Is it serious enough for a community penalty?

In *Bushell* (1987) 9 Cr App R (S) 537 the offender, aged 17 and with no previous convictions, took a friend's car without permission, and subsequently crashed it, damaging it beyond repair. A sentence of 180 hours' community service, together with a disqualification for one year, was upheld by the Court of Appeal. Where the offence is combined with other offences arising out of the same circumstances, an immediate custodial sentence may be appropriate. Thus in *Jeary* (1986) 8 Cr App R (S) 491 the offender, aged 18, and with one previous finding of guilt for assault occasioning actual bodily harm, pleaded guilty to two counts of taking a conveyance, two counts of theft, and asked for two other offences to be taken into consideration. He was involved with others in taking several cars in the course of an evening and driving them at high speed in a city centre 'just as a bit of fun'. Three cars were damaged, one beyond repair. The offender also admitted taking property from the cars, though most of that was recovered. The Court of Appeal agreed with the sentencer's view that the offences were so serious that a non-custodial sentence could not be justified because, in addition to the unlawful taking, the cars had been deliberately damaged. Four months' detention was upheld.

Meaning of 'Conveyance'

B4.93 Whilst the marginal note to the TA 1968, s. 12, uses the phrase 'motor vehicle or other conveyance', the section itself refers only to a 'conveyance'. A definition of 'conveyance' is to be found in s. 12(7)(a):

> 'conveyance' means any conveyance constructed or adapted for the carriage of a person or persons whether by land, water or air, except that it does not include a conveyance constructed or adapted for use only under the control of a person not carried in or on it, and 'drive' shall be construed accordingly.

This definition would ordinarily include a pedal cycle, but s. 12(5), which creates a separate offence (see **B4.106**), makes clear that the offence under s. 12(1) does not apply in relation to pedal cycles. Otherwise, it is a very wide definition. In *Neal* v *Gribble* (1978) 68 Cr App R 9, the Divisional Court had to consider whether a horse was a conveyance within the meaning of s. 12. The court was of the view that it was not such a conveyance, since the definition in s. 12(7)(a) 'seems to be directed towards artefacts rather than towards animals'.

Taking for his Own or Another's Use

B4.94 It is essential that a conveyance be moved in order for it to be taken, however small that movement may be. Merely trying to start the engine of a motor vehicle without moving the vehicle does not amount to taking it (*Bogacki* [1973] QB 832). Attempt is not available as an alternative offence (Criminal Attempts Act 1981, s. 1(1) and (4)). On a charge of taking it is not necessary that the accused used the conveyance to convey himself, merely that he 'took' it. In *Pearce* [1973] Crim LR 321 an appeal against conviction was dismissed where the accused had placed the conveyance, an inflatable rubber dinghy, on a trailer and drove away with it.

On a charge of taking, the prosecution must prove that the accused took the conveyance 'for his own or another's use'. In *Bow* (1976) 64 Cr App R 54, it was argued that the accused had not taken the conveyance 'for his own use' when he got into a Land Rover which was obstructing his way and released its handbrake and let it coast for about 200 yards. The Court of Appeal said (at p. 58):

> The short answer . . . is that where as here, a conveyance is taken and moved in a way which necessarily involves its use as a conveyance, the taker cannot be heard to say that the taking was not for that use. If he has in fact taken the conveyance and used it as such, his motive in so doing is . . . quite immaterial.

In *Stokes* [1983] RTR 59, the accused and two others pushed a car round a corner as a practical joke. The conviction could not be upheld because the judge failed specifically to emphasise the importance of establishing that someone was being conveyed inside the car or riding on it, i.e. failed clearly to require a finding that the car was being taken for use as a conveyance, rather than merely that it was 'taken'.

Pearce, *Bow* and *Stokes* were further explained by the Court of Appeal in *Marchant* (1984) 80 Cr App R 361. Robert Goff LJ, giving the judgment of the court, stated that 'to be guilty of the offence, the accused must have both taken the vehicle, i.e. have taken control of it and caused it to be moved, and he must have done so for his own or another's use'. That phrase requires that it be taken *for use as* a conveyance, which is satisfied provided that is why the conveyance was taken, rather than that it must have been taken *as* a conveyance. For example, if a person takes a car by pushing it around a corner and leaving it, he satisfies the first element of this requirement. If, at the time he moves it, he intends to get it going after he has returned to it, his purpose is plain: it was for use as a conveyance and the offence has been committed. In *Pearce* the dinghy was clearly taken and the accused's purpose was to use it as a dinghy, that is, as a conveyance. In

Bow the defendant actually used the Land Rover as a conveyance whilst taking it. In *Stokes* the accused did take the conveyance, but his purpose was not to use it as a conveyance and so the offence was not committed.

Once a vehicle has been taken, it cannot be taken again by the same accused, but, where a first taker abandons a vehicle, that same vehicle may be taken by another (*DPP* v *Spriggs* [1994] RTR 1).

Without the Consent of the Owner or Other Lawful Authority

On a charge of taking a conveyance without authority, the prosecution must prove that **B4.95** the taking was actually without the owner's consent or other lawful authority (*Ambler* [1979] RTR 217 and *Sturrock* v *DPP* [1996] RTR 216). 'Owner' is defined by the TA 1968, s. 12(7)(b), in relation to a conveyance which is the subject of a hiring agreement or hire-purchase agreement, as meaning the person in possession of the conveyance under that agreement.

In *Whittaker* v *Campbell* [1984] QB 318 the two defendants, neither of whom had a driving licence, had come by Dunn's licence. They hired a van, using that acquired licence by pretending that one of them was Dunn. They paid the appropriate hire charge and drove the van away. The Divisional Court was asked to consider the effect of the false representation on the consent that was obtained as a consequence. It stated that there is no general principle of law that fraud vitiates consent. The court took the view that where force is used, it is possible to distinguish between consent and mere submission, but that when the factor being exercised was fraud and not force, no such sensible distinction can be drawn. In common-sense terms, the owner has consented and, despite the fraud, that means that no offence is committed.

In *Peart* [1970] 2 QB 672, the Court of Appeal quashed a conviction where the accused had falsely represented to the owner of a car that he needed it to drive from Bedlington to Alnwick to sign a contract. The owner let him have the vehicle, provided he returned it that day. As he all along intended he drove the car instead to Burnley in the evening. The court reserved the question whether a fundamental misrepresentation can vitiate consent (according to the Divisional Court in *Whittaker* v *Campbell* it would appear that it does not), but decided that the sort of false pretence in the particular case did not vitiate the consent, and the activity involved was not the type of activity with which the TA 1968, s. 12, was concerned.

In *Phipps* (1970) 54 Cr App R 300 the Court of Appeal approved a direction by the trial judge that if, after a lawful purpose had been fulfilled, the accused then did not return the car but drove it off on his own business, the offence was committed. It is not clear whether a deception was practised upon the owner, and the decision of the Court of Appeal does not raise the issue of such a deception. It may, therefore, be that this case can be regarded as consistent with *Peart* and *Whittaker* v *Campbell* since in *Phipps* there may well have been no question of consent obtained by fraud or a false representation. Rather it seems that it was a case of the accused clearly going beyond what were the known and actual limits of the consent that had been given by the owner of the car (see also *McKnight* v *Davies* [1974] RTR 4).

Mens Rea of Offence of Taking

There are two aspects to the mental element of the offence of taking a conveyance **B4.96** without authority.

First, the taking must be intentional. In *Blayney* v *Knight* (1974) 60 Cr App R 269, Lord Widgery CJ, in a judgment with which the other members of the Divisional Court agreed, stated, 'I do not see how anybody could be charged with taking a motor car because of the fact that the car accidentally moves forward'.

Secondly, the TA 1968, s. 12(6), provides:

> A person does not commit an offence under this section by anything done in the belief that he has lawful authority to do it or that he would have the owner's consent if the owner knew of his doing it and the circumstances of it.

It is essential that this belief exist at the time of the taking. It is not enough if the owner says, later, that he would have consented had he known (*Ambler* [1979] RTR 217). This question is one for the magistrates to decide and they may well take into account a factor such as the likelihood of a person genuinely believing that an owner would authorise another to drive a car when uninsured. Clearly an owner could provide such an authorisation (*Clotworthy* [1981] RTR 477). An example of what might amount to 'unlawful authority' is given by *Briggs* [1987] Crim LR 708, where the defendant claimed that he was repairing the motor cycle for a friend. Since the judge had not focused the attention of the jury on this matter, the conviction was quashed by the Court of Appeal.

The onus of proof of this matter lies on the prosecution (*MacPherson* [1973] RTR 157; *Gannon* (1987) 87 Cr App R 254) but before that stage is reached, it is for the accused to raise the issue. That means that he must call evidence or point to some evidence which tends to show that he did hold the necessary belief (*Gannon*).

It is not possible to argue that simply because the accused was drunk he must have believed or may have believed that the car was his. That would amount in effect to replacing the defence provide by s. 12(6) by some simple defence of drunkenness (*Gannon*). This offence is one of basic intent for the purposes of the defence of intoxication (*MacPherson*). As to intoxication as a defence, see **A3.8** to **A3.11**.

Driving or Allowing himself to be Carried

B4.97   Section 12(7)(a) of the TA 1968 indicates that 'drive' is to be construed in accordance with the meaning of 'conveyance' (see **B4.92**) and therefore includes 'driving' not only motor vehicles, but any land, water or air conveyance. The meaning of 'drives' is considered generally at **C1.8**.

On a charge of allowing himself to be carried in or on a conveyance taken without authority, it is not enough for the prosecution to prove that the accused was in or on the conveyance, there must have been some movement of the conveyance (*Miller* [1976] Crim LR 417; *Diggin* (1980) 72 Cr App R 204). If a taker of a motor vehicle offers a person a lift and he gets into the seat next to the driver, the person is not allowing himself to be driven before the driver turns on the ignition switch (*Diggin*).

Mens Rea of Offence of Driving or Allowing himself to be Carried

B4.98   On a charge of driving or allowing himself to be carried in or on a conveyance taken without authority, it must be proved that the accused knew that the conveyance had been taken without lawful authority (*Diggin* (1980) 72 Cr App R 204 and *Boldizsar* v *Knight* [1980] Crim LR 653). As to the meaning of these terms, see **B4.93** to **B4.96**. It seems that the accused need not be aware that the taker took the conveyance for his own or another's use, though no doubt ordinarily he will know this. As to knowledge generally, see **A2.9**.

The TA 1968, s. 12(6), applies to the offence of driving or allowing oneself to be carried in or on a conveyance taken without consent (see **B4.96**).

AGGRAVATED VEHICLE-TAKING

B4.99   The Aggravated Vehicle-Taking Act 1992 created aggravated forms of the offence contrary to the TA 1968, s. 12(1) (see **B4.90** to **B4.98**), through the TA 1968, s. 12A.

Theft Act 1968, s. 12A

(1)   Subject to subsection (3) below, a person is guilty of aggravated taking of a vehicle if—
    (a)   he commits an offence under section 12(1) above (in this section referred to as a 'basic offence') in relation to a mechanically propelled vehicle; and
    (b)   it is proved that, at any time after the vehicle was unlawfully taken (whether by him or another) and before it was recovered, the vehicle was driven, or injury or damage was caused, in one or more of the circumstances set out in paragraphs (a) to (d) of subsection (2) below.
(2)   The circumstances referred to in subsection (1)(b) above are—
    (a)   that the vehicle was driven dangerously on a road or other public place;
    (b)   that, owing to the driving of the vehicle, an accident occurred by which injury was caused to any person;
    (c)   that, owing to the driving of the vehicle, an accident occurred by which damage was caused to any property, other than the vehicle;
    (d)   that damage was caused to the vehicle.

Since the maximum penalty is greater where death is caused (see **B4.102**), the House of Lords decision in *Courtie* [1984] AC 403 establishes that s. 12A creates two offences (see *Sherwood* [1995] RTR 60).

Procedure

The offences are triable either way. When tried on indictment it is a class 4 offence.   **B4.100**

The accused has no right to elect trial on indictment where the only allegation is of damage to the vehicle or other property or both and the total value of the damage alleged to have been caused is less than the 'relevant sum' (i.e. £5,000) (MCA 1980, ss. 22 and 33 and sch. 2: see **D3.12**).

Alternative Verdict

Under the TA 1968, s. 12A(5), where a person charged with either of these offences is   **B4.101** found not guilty, he may be convicted of the basic offence, contrary to the TA 1968, s. 12(1) (see **B4.90** *et seq.*). If convicted of the basic offence at the Crown Court, that court has the same powers and duties as a magistrates' court would have had on convicting him of such an offence (s. 12A(6)) (see **B4.92**).

Sentence

The maximum penalty is, on indictment, two years or a fine or both. The maximum   **B4.102** penalty, on indictment, is increased to five years where it is proved that, in circumstances falling within the TA 1968, s. 12A(2)(b), the accident caused the death of the person concerned (TA 1968, s. 12A(4) and Aggravated Vehicle-Taking Act 1992, s. 1(2)(a)).

The maximum penalty on summary conviction is a term of imprisonment not exceeding six months or a fine not exceeding the statutory maximum or both. The limit on penalties imposed by the MCA 1980, s. 33(1), with regard to an offence tried summarily in pursuance of the MCA 1980, s. 22, does not apply where the offence is aggravated vehicle-taking (MCA 1980, s. 33(3)).

By virtue of the Road Traffic Offenders Act 1988, ss. 28, 96, 97 and sch. 2, part II, where a person is convicted of aggravated vehicle-taking, disqualification from driving is obligatory, endorsement of licence is obligatory and the penalty points which may be imposed for the offence are 3 to 11. As to disqualification, endorsement of licence and penalty points, see **part C**. The fact that the defendant did not drive the vehicle at any particular time or at all is not a special reason to avoid obligatory disqualification (Road Traffic Offenders Act 1988, s. 34).

When tried summarily, the Magistrates' Association Guidelines (1997) indicate the following:

Aggravating Factors ⊕

For example avoiding detection or apprehension; competitive driving, racing, showing off; disregard of warnings e.g. from passengers or others in the vicinity; group action, premeditated, serious injury/damage; serious risk; offence committed on bail; previous convictions and failures to respond to previous sentences, if relevant.

Mitigating Factors ⊖

For example impulsive; no competitiveness/racing; passenger only; single incident of bad driving; speed not excessive; very minor injury/damage.

Guideline: Is it so serious that only custody is appropriate?

In *Bird* (1993) 14 Cr App R (S) 343, the Court of Appeal said that when sentencing for this offence, relevant aggravating features would be related to the overall culpability of the driver: how bad the driving was and for how long it had lasted and, to a lesser extent, how much injury or damage had been caused. Drink would affect the assessment of culpability, but where drink was a major factor in the case it would be the subject of a separate charge. Mitigation might be found in a guilty plea showing contrition, but the youth of the offender would be of less significance in this type of case than in others, since the offence was aimed primarily at young offenders. See also *Evans* (1994) 15 Cr App R (S) 137, *Sealey* (1994) 15 Cr App R (S) 189, *Robinson* (1994) 15 Cr App R (S) 452 and *Frostick* [1998] 1 Cr App R (S) 257.

Actus Reus

B4.103 The offences of aggravated vehicle-taking are committed only if, first, an offence under the TA 1968, s. 12(1) (see **B4.90** to **B4.98**), is committed in relation to a mechanically propelled vehicle (s. 12A(1)(a)); 'mechanically propelled vehicle' is defined in the Road Traffic Act 1988, s. 185 (see **C1.14**). Secondly, the prosecution must prove that, at any time after the vehicle was taken and before it was recovered, one or more of the circumstances in s. 12A(2)(a) to (d) occurred (s. 12A(1)(b)). All that the prosecution has to prove is that the circumstances occurred, it does not have to prove that the defendant was the cause of them (see *Dawes v DPP* [1995] 1 Cr App R 65); it is for the defendant to prove one of the specific defences if he is to avoid conviction (see **B4.105**).

The circumstances of aggravation in s. 12A(2) are listed at **B4.99**. The phrase 'driven dangerously', which occurs in s. 12A(2)(a), is defined in s. 12A(7) in identical terms to the definition which applies to the offence of dangerous driving (see **C3.9**). Whilst the vehicle must be driven dangerously for s. 12A(2)(a) to apply, there is no such requirement in s.12A(2)(b) or (c), so the simple fact that the vehicle is being driven, without fault, is sufficient (*Marsh* [1997] 1 Cr App R 67, in which M was guilty under s. 12A(2)(b) when he drove a vehicle without permission and knocked a pedestrian down despite driving apparently carefully). The question is whether the driving was the cause of the accident. It is, of course, not necessary that the defendant be the driver or even that he be in or near the car. None of the other phrases used in s. 12A(2) are specifically defined, but for 'accident', see **C1.1**, for 'driving', see **C1.8**, and for 'damage', see **B8.5**.

An offence under s. 12A may be committed only in the period after the vehicle is taken and before it is recovered. A vehicle is recovered when it is restored to its owner or other lawful possession or custody (s. 12A(8)); a similar concept is used in the offence of handling stolen goods, see **B4.134**. 'Owner' has the same meaning as in s. 12 (s. 12A(8)) (see **B4.95**).

Mens Rea

B4.104 *Mens rea* has to be established with regard to the first element of an offence of aggravated vehicle-taking, that is the *mens rea* of the basic offence (see **B4.96** and **B4.98**). No *mens* *rea* need be shown with regard to the second element, the circumstances of aggravation: the offences are offences of strict liability in that regard.

Specific Defence

Theft Act 1968, s. 12A   **B4.105**

(3)   A person is not guilty of an offence under this section if he proves that, as regards any such proven driving, injury or damage as is referred to in subsection (1)(b) above, either—
(a)   the driving, accident or damage referred to in subsection (2) above occurred before he committed the basic offence; or
(b)   he was neither in nor in the immediate vicinity of the vehicle when that driving, accident or damage occurred.

TAKING OR RIDING A PEDAL CYCLE WITHOUT AUTHORITY

It is an offence, contrary to the TA 1968, s. 12(5), and subject to s. 12(6) (see **B4.96**), **B4.106** for a person, without having the consent of the owner or other lawful authority, to take a pedal cycle for his own or another's use, or ride a pedal cycle knowing it to have been taken without such authority. In *Sturrock* v *DPP* [1996] RTR 216, it was held that it is not necessary to have a formal statement of ownership from the owner of a cycle where the primary facts permit the inference that the cycle had not been abandoned and had an owner. The offence is punishable on summary conviction with a fine not exceeding level 3 on the standard scale.

INTERFERENCE WITH VEHICLES

Definition

Criminal Attempts Act 1981, s. 9   **B4.107**

(1)   A person is guilty of the offence of vehicle interference if he interferes with a motor vehicle or trailer or with anything carried in or on a motor vehicle or trailer with the intention that an offence specified in subsection (2) below shall be committed by himself or some other person.
(2)   The offences mentioned in subsection (1) above are—
(a)   theft of the motor vehicle or trailer or part of it;
(b)   theft of anything carried in or on the motor vehicle or trailer; and
(c)   an offence under section 12(1) of the Theft Act 1968 (taking and driving away without consent);
and, if it is shown that a person accused of an offence under this section intended that one of those offences should be committed, it is immaterial that it cannot be shown which it was.

Procedure

The offence is triable summarily only (Criminal Attempts Act 1981, s. 9(3)).   **B4.108**

Sentence

The maximum penalty is imprisonment for a term not exceeding three months or a fine **B4.109** not exceeding level 4 on the standard scale or both (Criminal Attempts Act 1981, s. 9(3)).

The Magistrates' Association Guidelines (1997) indicate the following:

Aggravating Factors ⊕
For example group action; planned; related damage; offence committed on bail; previous convictions and failures to respond to previous sentences, if relevant.

Mitigating Factors ⊖
For example impulsive action.

Guideline: Is it serious enough for a community penalty?

Elements

B4.110   As to theft, see **B4.1** *et seq*. As to the offence under the TA 1968, s. 12(1), see **B4.90** *et seq*.

There is no definition of 'interference'. Clearly there has to be interference as well as intention. Merely looking into cars is probably not an act of interference whereas opening doors and putting pressure on the door handles is an act of interference. However, whether placing a hand on a door handle is an act of interference is not clear, nor was it clarified in the Crown Court case of *Reynolds and Warren* v *Metropolitan Police* [1982] Crim LR 831.

'Motor vehicle' and 'trailer', by virtue of s. 9(5), have the same meaning as in the Road Traffic Act 1988, s. 185(1):

> 'motor vehicle' means, subject to section 20 of the Chronically Sick and Disabled Persons Act 1970 (which makes special provision about invalid carriages, within the meaning of that Act), a mechanically propelled vehicle intended or adapted for use on roads, and
> 'trailer' means a vehicle drawn by a motor vehicle.

ABSTRACTING ELECTRICITY

Definition

B4.111   **Theft Act 1968, s. 13**

> A person who dishonestly uses without due authority, or dishonestly causes to be wasted or diverted, any electricity shall [be guilty of an offence].

Procedure

B4.112   Abstracting electricity is triable either way (MCA 1980, s. 17 and sch. 1, para. 28). When tried on indictment it is a class 4 offence.

Indictment

B4.113   Statement of Offence

> Abstracting electricity contrary to section 13 of the Theft Act 1968

                          Particulars of Offence

> A on or about the . . . day of . . . dishonestly and without due authority used [or dishonestly caused to be wasted or diverted] a quantity of electricity

Sentencing Guidelines

B4.114   The maximum penalty is five years (TA 1968, s. 13) on indictment; six months or a fine not exceeding the statutory maximum, or both, summarily.

In *Hodkinson* (1980) 2 Cr App R (S) 331, the offender pleaded guilty to abstracting electricity, in that he had fitted a device to the electricity meter at his home, which caused the meter to give a false reading. Bristow J commented that:

> In the judgment of this court deliberately stealing electricity in this way is an offence which calls for deterrent treatment when caught. In the circumstances of this case this court has come to the conclusion that the necessary deterrent element would be sufficiently dealt with by a sentence of one month's immediate imprisonment, accompanied by a fine of £750.

See also *Western* (1987) 9 Cr App R (S) 6.

Actus Reus

Electricity cannot be property and so when electricity is 'obtained' the only available **B4.115**
offence is the present one (*Low* v *Blease* [1975] Crim LR 513).

Any use, waste or diversion of electricity will suffice (*Low* v *Blease*), so a meter does not
have to be tampered with (*McCreadie* (1992) 96 Cr App R 143). Electricity is abstracted
where the electricity supply to a house is reconnected without the consent of the
electricity supplier (*Boggeln* v *Williams* [1978] 1 WLR 873). It is also abstracted where
the electricity supply to a house is caused not to be registered by the meter (*Collins* v
DPP (1987) *The Times*, 20 October 1987). It may well be an abstraction of electricity to
make a call from a telephone belonging to another person (*Low* v *Blease*).

Mens Rea

Abstracting electricity is an offence of dishonesty to which the definition provided by the **B4.116**
Court of Appeal in *Ghosh* [1982] QB 1053 applies (see **B4.37**). This is so even though
the Court of Appeal in *Boggeln* v *Williams* [1978] 1 WLR 873 took the view that
'dishonesty' was to be approached as a subjective concept in s. 13.

FRAUDULENT USE OF TELECOMMUNICATION SYSTEMS
AND FRAUDULENT RECEIPT OF PROGRAMMES

It is an offence triable either way, contrary to the Telecommunications Act 1984, s. 42, **B4.117**
dishonestly to obtain a service provided by means of a telecommunication system
licensed under s. 7 of the Act. It is also an offence, triable either way, for a person, who
has in his custody anything which may be used for the purpose of obtaining, or for a
purpose connected with the obtaining of, a service to which s. 42 applies, to intend (a)
to use it to obtain such a service dishonestly or for a purpose connected with the
dishonest obtaining of such a service, (b) dishonestly to allow the thing to be used to
obtain such a service, or (c) to allow the thing to be used for a purpose connected with
the dishonest obtaining of such a service (Telecommunications Act 1984, s. 42A(1) and
(2)). A similar offence arises where a person supplies or offers to supply anything which
may be used for the purpose of obtaining, or for a purpose connected with the obtaining
of, such a service (s. 42A(3) and (4)).

It is a summary offence, contrary to the Copyright, Designs and Patents Act 1988,
s. 297(1), dishonestly to receive a programme included in a broadcasting or cable
programme service provided from a place in the United Kingdom with intent to avoid
payment of any charge applicable to the reception of the programme.

In *Nadig* (1993) 14 Cr App R (S) 49 the offender was convicted of fraudulent use of a
telecommunications system. He used a tone-dialling device to make calls from a
telephone box without paying. A suspended sentence was held to be wrong in principle
for an isolated offence. Auld J, in the Court of Appeal, said that the preferred sentence
was a fine, and that comparison between sentencing for this offence and sentencing for
abstracting electricity (see **B4.114**) would be helpful only where the fraudulent use of
the telephone had taken place over a period of time. See also *Adewale* (1994) 15 Cr App
R (S) 790 and *Aslam* [1996] 2 Cr App R 377.

GOING EQUIPPED

Definition

Theft Act 1968, s. 25   **B4.118**

(1)   A person shall be guilty of an offence if, when not at his place of abode, he has with
him any article for use in the course of or in connection with any burglary, theft or cheat.

(2)   A person guilty of an offence under this section shall on conviction on indictment be liable to imprisonment for a term not exceeding three years.

(3)   Where a person is charged with an offence under this section, proof that he had with him any article made or adapted for use in committing a burglary, theft or cheat shall be evidence that he had it with him for such use.

(4)   Any person may arrest without warrant anyone who is, or whom he, with reasonable cause, suspects to be, committing an offence under this section.

(5)   For purposes of this section an offence under section 12(1) of this Act of taking a conveyance shall be treated as theft, and 'cheat' means an offence under section 15 of this Act.

Procedure

B4.119   Going equipped for stealing is triable either way (MCA 1980, s. 17 sch. 1, para. 28). When tried on indictment it is a class 4 offence.

Indictment

B4.120

Statement of Offence

Going equipped for burglary [or theft, or cheat] contrary to section 25 of the Theft Act 1968

Particulars of Offence

A on or about the . . . day of . . . , not being at his place of abode, had with him articles, namely a jemmy and a kitchen knife, for use in the course of or in connection with burglary [or theft, or cheat]

Sentence

B4.121   The maximum penalty is three years (TA 1968, s. 25(2)) on indictment; six months or a fine not exceeding the statutory maximum, or both, summarily. If committed with reference to the theft or taking of motor vehicles, disqualification is discretionary (Road Traffic Offenders Act 1988, sch. 2). There are no reported sentencing guidelines for this offence, but in *Ferry* [1997] 2 Cr App R (S) 42 a sentence of 12 months' imprisonment was upheld where the offenders, found in possession of a cordless drill, screwdrivers, surgical gloves and a map, were targeting a series of telephone boxes in a rural area.

When dealt with summarily, the Magistrates' Association Guidelines (1997) indicate the following:

Aggravating Factors ⊕
For example premeditated; group action; sophisticated; specialised equipment; number of items; people put in fear; offence committed on bail; previous convictions and failures to respond to previous sentences, if relevant.

Mitigating Factors ⊖
None.

Guideline: Is it serious enough for a community penalty? Consider forfeiture of equipment.

Relation to Other Offences

B4.122   It is not an offence under the TA 1968, s. 25, to keep or possess articles intended for use in theft, burglary etc. as long as those articles are kept at home. An individual who has been found to possess a jemmy or similar implement at his place of abode may, however, be charged under the Criminal Damage Act 1971, s. 3, if it appears that the thing in question might be used to damage windows, locks etc. in the course of forcing an entry for the purpose of theft or burglary. Firearms or imitation firearms kept for the purpose of a robbery or aggravated burglary come within the scope of the TA 1968, s. 25, but more obviously come within the provisions of the Firearms Act 1968.

When not at his Place of Abode

'Place of abode' is not defined in the TA 1968. It could include a caravan or motor **B4.123**
vehicle, but in *Bundy* [1977] 1 WLR 914, the Court of Appeal held that a vehicle is not
to be regarded as a place of abode unless parked at a site where the accused abides or
intends to abide. If a traveller keeps housebreaking tools in his vehicle, he will therefore
commit an offence under the TA 1968, s. 25, whenever he drives his vehicle away from
that site.

Meaning of 'Has with Him'

This phrase in the TA 1968, s. 25, must bear the same meaning as in s. 10 of the Act **B4.124**
(see **B4.80**) and implies a degree of immediate control (*Kelt* [1977] 1 WLR 1365). It
would suffice if the accused had the article in his car or bag, at his place of work, or on
his person. In *Re McAngus* [1994] Crim LR 602 the Divisional Court held, in relation
to extradition proceedings, that a s. 25 offence could be made out where the applicant
showed undercover agents counterfeit shirts stored in a bonded warehouse.

Any Article for Use in the Course of or in Connection with any Burglary, Theft or Cheat

The connection between the articles and the proposed theft etc. must not be too remote. **B4.125**
In *Mansfield* [1975] Crim LR 101, the accused was charged under the TA 1968, s. 25,
with possessing another person's driving licence, with intent to use this to obtain
employment, in the course of which he would have an opportunity to steal. Not
surprisingly, the Court of Appeal quashed his conviction.

As to the offences which may be intended, see the TA 1968, s. 25(5). Although the taking
of pedal cycles contrary to s. 12(5) of the Act is not one of those offences, the possession
of bolt-cutters etc. for cutting cycle locks could readily be interpreted as intended for
use in theft. Burglary includes burglary with intent to rape etc. under s. 9(1)(a) and theft
includes theft with force which would amount to robbery.

The most ordinary of articles, including footwear and clothing, could be used in the
course of such crimes, but in practice s. 25 is used only in connection with articles which
seem intended to play a prominent or obvious role: something which the accused would
not have with him if he was not intending to commit such a crime. Coshes, masks,
jemmies, glass-cutters and skeleton keys are obvious examples; less obvious perhaps are
credit cards stolen or illicitly borrowed from their real owners (see also *Re McAngus*
[1994] Crim LR 602: counterfeit clothing). This does not mean that apparently
innocuous articles cannot be within the scope of the section. Bottles of wine were found
to constitute such articles in *Doukas* [1978] 1 WLR 372, where D had apparently
brought the wine to the hotel where he worked as a waiter in order dishonestly to sell it
to his employer's customers, who would be deceived (contrary to s. 15 of the Act) into
thinking that they were buying wine from the employer. In *Rashid* [1977] 1 WLR 298,
the Court of Appeal indicated, *obiter*, that a British Rail steward should not be regarded
as guilty under s. 25 for having introduced his own food on to the train on which he was
working with the intention of making and selling his own sandwiches to passengers
instead of those supplied by his employer. The court seems to have based this view on
its doubt that any obtaining by deception had occurred. This is probably the point of
distinction from *Doukas*.

The article need not be intended for use that day, nor for use by the accused himself,
but it must be intended for *future* use. The possession of articles that *have been used* in
theft etc. with a view to disposing of them is not an offence under s. 25, although a charge
under the Criminal Law Act 1967, s. 4, may be appropriate (*Ellames* [1974] 1 WLR
1391).

In the absence of a confession or other self-incriminating behaviour by the accused, it may sometimes be difficult to prove that the article was indeed intended for use in the course of or in connection with burglary, theft or cheat, and proof of intent is needed: it is not sufficient to show that the accused merely contemplated possible use (*Hargreaves* [1985] Crim LR 243). Section 25(3) is of very limited use in this respect, since it only states the obvious. If the accused was found to be carrying a jemmy or a bunch of skeleton keys, a court or jury would in any case consider this to be evidence (and possibly sufficient proof) of intent to commit burglary. Possession of a torch or screwdriver would be less likely to be considered evidence of such intent, and here s. 25(3) is of no help at all (*Harrison* [1970] Crim LR 415).

HANDLING STOLEN GOODS

Definition

B4.126

Theft Act 1968, s. 22

(1) A person handles stolen goods if (otherwise than in the course of the stealing) knowing or believing them to be stolen goods he dishonestly receives the goods, or dishonestly undertakes or assists in their retention, removal, disposal or realisation by or for the benefit of another person, or if he arranges to do so.

(2) A person guilty of handling stolen goods shall on conviction on indictment be liable to imprisonment for a term not exceeding 14 years.

Procedure

B4.127 The offence is triable either way (MCA 1980, s. 17 and sch. 1, para. 28). When tried on indictment it is a class 4 offence. It is a Group A offence for jurisdiction purposes under the CJA 1993, part I (see **D1.75**).

According to *Practice Note* (*Mode of Trial: Guidelines*) (1995) (see **D3.7**), cases of handling should be tried summarily unless the court considers that one or more of the following features is present in the case *and* that its sentencing powers are insufficient:

(a) Dishonest handling of stolen property by a receiver who has commissioned the theft.

(b) The offence has professional hallmarks.

(c) The property is of high value (at least £10,000).

Indictment

B4.128

First Count

Statement of Offence

Handling stolen goods contrary to section 22(1) of the TA 1968

Particulars of Offence

A on or about the . . . day of . . . dishonestly received stolen goods, namely a pearl necklace belonging to V, knowing or believing the same to be stolen goods

Second Count

Statement of Offence

Handling stolen goods contrary to section 22(1) of the TA 1968

Particulars of Offence

A on or about the . . . day of . . . dishonestly undertook or assisted in the retention, removal, disposal or realisation of stolen goods, namely a pearl necklace belonging to V, by or for the benefit of B, or dishonestly arranged to do so, knowing or believing the same to be stolen goods

It may be prudent to include both counts unless there is clear evidence of one particular form of handling and the prosecution intend to present the case exclusively in those terms. See further *Deakin* [1972] 1 WLR 1618.

The general deficiency principle applies to counts for handling stolen goods (for the application of this principle to theft, see **B4.3**, and for the drafting of counts for continuous offences generally, see **D9.10**). It is, therefore, proper to indict for the handling of a total amount of money if the evidence does not precisely disclose the date or amount of each dishonest transaction but the transactions are so closely linked as to be, in effect, a continuous transaction (*Cain* [1983] Crim LR 802). However, if the accused is charged with handling items of property which are clearly the proceeds of different thefts, burglaries or robberies, and which are received or dealt with on separate occasions, there should be a separate count of handling for each occasion (*Smythe* (1980) 72 Cr App R 8).

Theft Act 1968, s. 27

(1) Any number of persons may be charged in one indictment, with reference to the same theft, with having at different times or at the same time handled all or any of the stolen goods, and the persons so charged may be tried together.

(2) On the trial of two or more persons indicted for jointly handling any stolen goods the jury may find any of the accused guilty if the jury are satisfied that he handled all or any of the stolen goods, whether or not he did so jointly with the other accused or any of them.

The TA 1968, s. 27(2), arguably goes further than the general rule, established in *DPP* v *Merriman* [1973] AC 584, that a person jointly indicted for an offence may be convicted of committing it independently of the others. The TA 1968, s. 27(2), also covers cases in which two co-accused handle goods on separate occasions (*French* [1973] Crim LR 632).

Sentencing Guidelines

The maximum penalty is 14 years (TA 1968, s. 22(2)) on indictment; six months or a **B4.129** fine not exceeding the statutory maximum, or both, summarily.

When dealt with summarily, the Magistrates' Association Guidelines (1997) indicate the following:

Aggravating Factors ⊕
For example adult involving children; high value; organiser or distributor; offence committed on bail; previous convictions and failures to respond to previous sentences, if relevant.

Mitigating Factors ⊖
For example for personal use; impulsive action; low value, no financial gain; not part of a sophisticated operation; single item.

Guideline: Is it serious enough for a community penalty?

The maximum penalty available for handling stolen goods is significantly higher than that available for theft, reflecting the view that some cases of handling are intrinsically more serious than any case of simple theft. Long custodial sentences are, however, rare, being reserved for cases where the handler was closely involved in a large-scale criminal enterprise. In *Patel* (1984) 6 Cr App R (S) 191 a sentence of four years was upheld on a man who received 660 cartons of cigarettes, worth £160,000, part of a larger consignment worth £1 million which had been stolen from a manufacturer's depot. The offender had previously served a six-year term for importing drugs. Lord Lane CJ said:

. . . proper penalties for cases of handling will vary enormously according to the circumstances. At the top end of the scale come the cases where the handler provides an outlet for the proceeds of very substantial thefts or robberies, where the advantages to the thief of having such an outlet are very great and where accordingly the receiver or handler is indirectly encouraging the thefts to take place, and where also the profits to the handler are likewise very great, as plainly they were going to be here.

See also *Hutchings* (1994) 15 Cr App R (S) 498, *Shearer* [1997] 1 Cr App R (S) 159, and *Davies* [1998] 2 Cr App R (S) 193.

Where a 'fence' deals directly with thieves or burglars, and provides a regular outlet for whatever property they may steal, sentences in the two to four-year bracket will be appropriate. In *Byrne* (1994) 15 Cr App R (S) 34 a sentence of 15 months was upheld for handling stolen computers worth £48,000. See also *Amlani* (1995) 16 Cr App R (S) 339. Most handlers receive non-custodial sentences. For the 'one-off', opportunistic offence, the Court of Appeal has indicated that a fine will often be the correct penalty. In *Khemlani* (1981) 3 Cr App R (S) 208 the offender was a young businessman running a cash and carry store. He bought 350 watches, which were part of a stolen consignment, at an undervalue from an unnamed person. He was of previous good character and pleaded guilty. A sentence of three months' imprisonment was quashed and a fine of £1,000 substituted. A suspended sentence was varied to a fine in *Murray* [1983] Crim LR 203 where the offender, who had no previous convictions, assisted a motor-cycle thief to change parts on the cycle so as to disguise it. The Court of Appeal said that the case was properly dealt with by way of a £60 fine.

Meaning of 'Goods', 'Stolen Goods', 'Theft' etc.

B4.130   Sections 22 to 24 of the TA 1968 deal with what are referred to therein as 'stolen goods' but the combined effect of ss. 24 and 34(2)(b) ensures that the provisions apply to a wider range of property than the ordinary meaning of that term might suggest.

Theft Act 1968, s. 34(2)(b)

'goods', except insofar as the context otherwise requires, includes money and every other description of property except land, and includes things severed from the land by stealing.

A credit balance in a bank account might be regarded as stolen goods if it directly or indirectly represents the proceeds of theft etc. (s. 24(2); *Forsyth* [1997] 2 Cr App R 299: but see **B4.147**). As to things severed from land see **B4.13**.

The concept of stolen goods has an extended meaning by statute.

Theft Act 1968, ss. 24 and 24A

24.—(1)   The provisions of this Act relating to goods which have been stolen shall apply whether the stealing occurred in England or Wales or elsewhere, and whether it occurred before or after the commencement of this Act, provided that the stealing (if not an offence under this Act) amounted to an offence where and at the time when the goods were stolen; and references to stolen goods shall be construed accordingly.

(2)   For purposes of those provisions references to stolen goods shall include, in addition to the goods originally stolen and parts of them (whether in their original state or not),—

(a)   any other goods which directly or indirectly represent or have at any time represented the stolen goods in the hands of the thief as being the proceeds of any disposal or realisation of the whole or part of the goods stolen or of goods so representing the stolen goods; and

(b)   any other goods which directly or indirectly represent or have at any time represented the stolen goods in the hands of a handler of the stolen goods or any part of them as being the proceeds of any disposal or realisation of the whole or part of the stolen goods handled by him or of goods so representing them.

(3)   But no goods shall be regarded as having continued to be stolen goods after they have been restored to the person from whom they were stolen or to other lawful possession or custody, or after that person and any other person claiming through him have otherwise ceased as regards those goods to have any right to restitution in respect of the theft.

(4)   For purposes of the provisions of this Act relating to goods which have been stolen (including subsections (1) to (3) above) goods obtained in England or Wales or elsewhere either by blackmail or in the circumstances described in section 15(1) of this Act shall be regarded as stolen; and 'steal', 'theft' and 'thief' shall be construed accordingly.

24A.—(8)   References to stolen goods include money which is dishonestly withdrawn from an account to which a wrongful credit has been made, but only to the extent that the money derives from the credit.

If the property in question appears to represent the proceeds of an offence that falls outside the scope of the TA 1968, s. 24 or s. 24A(8) it may be possible to consider charges under the 'money laundering' provisions inserted into the CJA 1988 by the CJA 1993, part III (as to which, see **B22**). These provisions overlap significantly with the offence of handling, and, even where the goods concerned are stolen, the prosecution may in some cases find it easier to charge one or more of the offences they create in preference to handling. As to the handling of dishonestly obtained money transfers, see the TA 1968, s. 24A, discussed at **B4.144** *et seq*.

Goods Obtained by Blackmail or Deception   The TA 1968, s. 24(4) governs **B4.131** s. 24(1) to (3) and extends the meaning of 'stolen goods' to cover the fruits or proceeds of offences under s. 15(1) (obtaining property by deception) and s. 21 (blackmail). No mention of burglary or robbery is needed, because any property obtained by such means must necessarily have been obtained by theft.

Goods Stolen outside England and Wales   TA 1968 offences (other than theft of **B4.132** mails under s. 14 and offences on British ships etc.) do not ordinarily apply to conduct taking place outside England or Wales (see generally **B4.45** and **D1.72** *et seq*.) but s. 24(1), read in conjunction with s. 24(4), ensures that property obtained outside the jurisdiction, by what would in England have been regarded as theft, blackmail or deception, will be regarded as stolen property within the jurisdiction if either:

(a)   the stealing etc. was (exceptionally) punishable as an extraterritorial offence under English law (for example, where the thief was a British subject aboard a foreign ship to which he did not belong: Merchant Shipping Act 1995, s. 281); or
(b)   the stealing was punishable under the law then in force where it took place.

Thus, if a thief stole property in Spain, and the accused received it (or its proceeds) in England, knowing of the circumstances, the accused may be guilty of handling under s. 22, but it must be proved that the conduct of the thief was, at the time of the theft, punishable under Spanish law. It is not possible to rely on any presumption that foreign law will be similar to English law, nor can judicial notice be taken of foreign law for such a purpose (*Ofori* (1994) 99 Cr App R 223). See also **F10.9** for the general rules on evidence of foreign law.

Theft, blackmail, handling and obtaining property by deception are all Group A offences under the CJA 1993, part I, and will therefore be punishable under English law if any essential element of the offence occurs within England and Wales. See further **D1.75**.

Fruits and Proceeds of Stolen Goods   Although wide-ranging, the TA 1968, **B4.133** s. 24(2), is significantly narrower than the corresponding provision in the Larceny Act 1916, which it replaced. The old law failed to distinguish between the proceeds of stolen goods in the hands of a thief or receiver of stolen goods, and such proceeds in the hands of an innocent person. Thus, anything purchased with, or exchanged for, stolen goods or the proceeds thereof would itself become categorised as stolen goods, even if it had never itself been possessed by either the thief or a receiver. In theory, the potential spread of the contagion was almost limitless.

The present position is that property is categorised as stolen only if it is the original property stolen, or something that has at some time represented the proceeds thereof in the hands of the original thief or of a dishonest handler. For example, if a person innocently acquires a stolen bicycle and then (still innocently) part-exchanges it for a new one, the new cycle cannot be categorised as stolen goods; but it would be otherwise if he knew the original one was stolen.

It may be difficult to determine whether property subsequently acquired by the thief or by an alleged handler represents the proceeds of a disposal of the original stolen goods. Classification may be particularly problematic where bank accounts are involved. A thief (A) may for example pay into his account both legitimately obtained moneys (such as his salary) and the proceeds of his thefts. He may then buy goods with funds drawn from that account, or arrange for funds to be transferred to other accounts. In *A-G's Ref (No. 4 of 1979)* [1981] 1 WLR 667, the Court of Appeal held in such a case that any credit balance in A's account constitutes, in part, stolen goods and that funds withdrawn from that account by A may also constitute stolen goods, to the extent that they derive from the original theft, etc. If the withdrawal involves a sum greater than the amount covered by 'legitimate' funds in the account, it must necessarily represent (at least in part) the proceeds of theft; but in other cases, it must be proved that A intended the withdrawal to represent such proceeds, as where his intention is to settle up with an accomplice to whom he 'owes' part of the proceeds. Note that it is A's intention which matters. The recipient's belief that this is what the withdrawal represents cannot suffice (*ibid.*).

If A withdraws money (i.e. cash) from his account, and hands this to B as B's share of the proceeds of theft, B undoubtedly receives stolen goods (TA 1968, s. 24A(8): see **B4.130**). If, however, A arranges for funds to be transferred from his account to an account operated by B, then, for reasons which are explained in **B4.147**, B cannot be guilty of handling the chose in action thereby created in his favour. The proper charge would be one of dishonestly retaining a wrongful credit, contrary to the TA 1968, s. 24A (see **B4.144** *et seq.*) or one of knowingly acquiring or possessing the proceeds of criminal conduct, contrary to the CJA 1988, s. 93B (see **B4.149** and **B22.10**).

B4.134 ***Goods Restored to Owner etc.*** As to what amounts to restoration to lawful possession, see *Haughton* v *Smith* [1975] AC 476 and *A-G's Ref (No. 1 of 1974)* [1974] QB 744. In the latter case, a police officer immobilised a parked car he suspected to contain stolen goods, and apprehended the accused when he attempted to start it. The question arose whether the accused could be guilty of handling at the time of his arrest, or whether the goods had already been taken into lawful police custody. It was held by the Court of Appeal that, if the police officer had already resolved to prevent the removal of the goods under any circumstances, they would indeed have ceased to be stolen; but if he had remained in doubt, and had resolved only to seek a satisfactory explanation before deciding whether or not to take charge of them, then they would remain stolen.

On somewhat different facts, the Divisional Court in *Metropolitan Police Commissioner* v *Streeter* (1980) 71 Cr App R 113 held that stolen goods were not taken into lawful custody merely because they had been marked for later identification and followed in the thief's possession to a rendezvous with the handler.

If there is any doubt about the status of such property when received, it may sometimes be desirable to charge theft (since receiving will usually amount to appropriation of property belonging to another), or it may be easier to prove that the accused arranged to receive the goods before they ceased to be stolen. Other possibilities are attempt (now that *Haughton* v *Smith* is no longer good law) and conspiracy.

'Loss of right to restitution' is a matter determined by the civil law. Briefly, this right will be lost where a stolen cheque or other negotiable instrument is acquired by a person who can establish title to it as a holder in due course (see Bills of Exchange Act 1882, s. 29). See also the Factors Act 1889, s. 2 (theft by mercantile agent and sale to bona fide purchaser) and the Hire Purchase Act 1964, s. 27.

Goods which are 'stolen' in the sense of being the proceeds of deception, rather than theft, may have become in law the property of the obtainer, albeit subject to the victim's right to rescind for fraud. In such a case, any bona fide purchaser may acquire good title to them (Sale of Goods Act 1979, s. 23). Property obtained by blackmail will sometimes give the blackmailer voidable title (as with deception); but since some kinds of blackmail are analogous to robbery, there will be cases in which no title passes, because the victim never 'consented' to parting with it. Loss to right to restitution of the original property need not usually prevent any proceeds from continuing to be classed as stolen goods.

Actus Reus: Goods Must Be Stolen

However dishonest the accused may be, there can be no conviction for handling stolen **B4.135** goods unless the prosecution prove that the goods in question were in fact stolen goods at the time of the alleged handling. However, a person who has done an act which would be a sufficient act of handling, intended to handle, was dishonest and believed the goods to be stolen will be liable for an attempt to handle if the goods were not stolen (Criminal Attempts Act 1981, s. 1(2) and (3); *Shivpuri* [1987] AC 1; see generally **A6.40**). The cases of *Haughton* v *Smith* [1975] AC 476 and *Anderton* v *Ryan* [1985] AC 560, which were formerly authority for the contrary proposition, are no longer good law.

Proof that handled goods were stolen may be facilitated by the TA 1968, s. 27(4), which provides for the use, in theft or handling cases, of statutory declarations by witnesses to loss of goods in transit where the accused is notified and does not require personal attendance of the witnesses.

Theft Act 1968, s. 27

(4) In any proceedings for the theft of anything in the course of transmission (whether by post or otherwise), or for handling stolen goods from such a theft, a statutory declaration made by any person that he dispatched or received or failed to receive any goods or postal packet, or that any goods or postal packet when dispatched or received by him were in a particular state or condition, shall be admissible as evidence of the facts stated in the declaration, subject to the following conditions:—

(a) a statutory declaration shall only be admissible where and to the extent to which oral evidence to the like effect would have been admissible in the proceedings: and

(b) a statutory declaration shall only be admissible if at least seven days before the hearing or trial a copy of it has been given to the person charged, and he has not, at least three days before the hearing or trial or within such further time as the court may in special circumstances allow, given the prosecutor written notice requiring the attendance at the hearing or trial of the person making the declaration.

(5) This section is to be construed in accordance with section 24 of this Act; and in subsection (3)(b) above the reference to handling stolen goods shall include any corresponding offence committed before the commencement of this Act.

Actus Reus: The Forms of Handling

The TA 1968, s. 22, must be read in conjunction with s. 24 (see **B4.130**). The term **B4.136** 'handling' is a form of shorthand embracing the several forms of dealing in the property specified in s. 22(1). In *Bloxham* [1983] 1 AC 109, Lord Bridge of Harwich stated, *obiter*, that s. 22 creates two distinct offences: receiving (or arranging to receive) being one and the various other forms being different variants of the other; but as most commentators have been quick to point out, this is, strictly speaking, incorrect. There is only one offence (*Griffiths* v *Freeman* [1970] 1 WLR 659), and an indictment alleging 'handling' without specifying the form is not therefore bad for duplicity (*Nicklin* [1977] 1 WLR 403). On the other hand, Lord Bridge's dictum has been accepted as a good indication of proper practice. An indictment should indicate which of the two main forms of handling is alleged, and if both are alleged there should be separate counts. A person cannot be accused of one and convicted on the basis of the other (*Nicklin*).

Except in cases of receiving or arranging to receive, it must be both alleged and proved that the accused assisted, or acted for the benefit of, another person: this is the main difference between receiving etc. and the other variants of the offence.

Receiving and Arranging to Receive

B4.137 The TA 1968 does not define 'receiving', but cases on receiving decided under the Larceny Act 1916, s. 33, defined it as involving the taking of possession or control of property, either jointly, or exclusively (*Frost* (1964) 48 Cr App R 284). Possession does not necessarily require physical handling, nor indeed would such handling suffice in the absence of any intent to possess or control the goods (*Hobson* v *Impett* (1957) 41 Cr App R 138). It is sufficient that the goods were handled by the accused's agents on his behalf (*Miller* (1854) 6 Cox CC 353). Things in action, which are not capable of physical handling, can certainly be received, as where the proceeds of a stolen cheque are credited to a bank account.

Arranging to receive is a substantive offence which may consist of the kind of preparatory arrangements that would fall short of constituting an attempt to receive, or of arrangements with an innocent party, so that there would be no conspiracy. It is not enough, however, for arrangements to be made for receipt of goods that have yet to be stolen. This might be conspiracy to steal and to handle stolen goods, but cannot be a full s. 22 offence (*Park* (1987) 87 Cr App R 164).

Undertaking or Assisting in Retention, Removal, Disposal or Realisation by or for the Benefit of Another Person

B4.138 In *Bloxham* [1983] 1 AC 109, the accused innocently purchased a car which he later came to realise must have been stolen. He sold it to an unidentified person at a knock-down price, and it was alleged that this amounted to realisation for the benefit of that unidentified purchaser. The House of Lords disagreed, on the basis that the sale (realisation) was for the benefit of the accused himself, and Lord Bridge of Harwich added (at pp. 113–14):

> The offence can be committed in relation to any one of [four named] activities in one or other of two ways. First, the offender may himself undertake the activity *for the benefit of* another person. Secondly, the activity may be undertaken *by* another person and the offender may assist him. . . . the category of other persons contemplated by the subsection is subject to the same limitations in whichever way the offence is committed. Accordingly, a purchaser, as such, of stolen goods, cannot . . . be 'another person' within the subsection, since his act of purchase could not sensibly be described as a disposal or realisation of the stolen goods *by* him. . . . therefore, even if the sale to him could be described as a disposal or realisation for his benefit, the transaction is not . . . within the ambit of the subsection.

See also *Gingell* (1999) 163 JP 648 and *Tokeley-Parry* [1999] Crim LR 578.

Assisting in the retention of stolen goods requires active assistance to be given to the other person. Accommodating or banking the stolen property would suffice (*Pitchley* (1972) 57 Cr App R 30); but mere failure to cooperate with the police during a search for stolen goods would not (*Brown* [1970] 1 QB 105). It is not necessary that the assistance should be successful; an attempt to deceive the police during such a search will amount to the complete offence under the TA 1968, s. 22 (*Kanwar* [1982] 1 WLR 845).

Disposing of or assisting in the disposal or realisation of stolen goods typically means moving the property from one place to another or converting it from one form into another (*Forsyth* [1997] 2 Cr App R 299 at p. 317). This may be a continuing offence and may therefore be committed in England even where part of the relevant conduct occurs abroad (*Forsyth*). Cases of 'money laundering', or other cases in which arrangements are made for the transfer, concealment or investment of the proceeds of crime, are now covered by a range of provisions inserted into the CJA 1988 by the CJA 1993, part III (see **B22**). There is a considerable overlap between the offences created by these provisions and offences of handling stolen goods, and the newer offences will in some cases be easier to prove.

Relationship between Handling and Theft

The TA 1968, s. 22, stipulates that the offence of handling may only be committed **B4.139** 'otherwise than in the course of the stealing'. The stealing referred to is the crime whereby the goods become 'stolen' in the first place. (This may, under s. 24(4), take the form of an obtaining by blackmail or deception: see **B4.130**). The stipulation prevents thieves or blackmailers etc. becoming handlers whilst still participating in the original offence, which may take the form of a continuous or on-going series of acts (see **B4.27**). Where, for example, burglar A passes the items he steals to his accomplice, burglar B, who carries them out to the get-away car, B might otherwise become a handler through 'receiving' stolen goods. It may therefore be necessary for the prosecution to prove, in appropriate cases, that the original stealing had been completed prior to the alleged act of handling and was not still in progress at the time. This was the issue in *Pitham* (1976) 65 Cr App R 45, where the appellants were invited by one M to pay him for furniture belonging to another man, who was in prison at the time. They agreed a price with M and removed the furniture, and were indicted on those facts with alternative counts of burglary and handling. (As to the joinder of 'mutually destructive' counts within a single indictment, see *Bellman* [1989] AC 836 and **D9.25**.) The appellants were convicted of handling and their convictions were upheld on appeal; Lawton LJ took the view that the jury were fully justified in finding that the appellants had dealt with the furniture only after M had stolen it by assuming the right to dispose of it. They had either helped M to steal the goods or M had stolen them and got rid of them by sale to the appellants; but the jury had, by their verdict, rejected the former possibility.

It does not follow that the prosecution must affirmatively prove every alleged handler to be innocent of the original theft, blackmail or deception. The courts have refused to place such a burden on the prosecution where there is no evidence to suggest that the accused was anything other than a handler (*Cash* [1985] QB 801). Problems may however arise where the evidence is ambiguous, as where property that has been stolen in a burglary is discovered a day later, hidden in D's attic. Under the doctrine of recent possession (see **F3.28**), the court or jury may legitimately infer, in the absence of any alternative explanation, that D must either have been the burglar or have dishonestly received the property knowing it to be stolen; but unless there is some further evidence to indicate which of the two offences D committed, it would appear to be impossible for them to draw one inference rather than the other.

The problem in such cases would not be solved merely by treating the words 'otherwise than in the course of the stealing' as a proviso or qualification to the general words of s. 22, and thus as a matter to be raised and proved by the defence under the rule as to the burden of proof which was affirmed by the House of Lords in *Hunt* [1987] AC 352 (see **F3.5**). The prosecution would still have to prove that D 'received the goods, knowing or believing them to be stolen', D would not have done so if he had appropriated them as the original burglar. Nor is it permissible for the court or jury to convict D of whichever offence appears, on balance, to be the more likely possibility. They must be sure that D is guilty of the specific offence of which they convict him (*A-G of Hong Kong* v *Yip Kai-foon* [1988] AC 642; cf. *Bellman* [1989] AC 836, per Lord Griffiths at p. 838).

It does not follow that D must be acquitted in such circumstances. The courts have recognised two possible solutions to the problem, each of which enables a conviction to be recorded. The first, and preferable, solution is for the prosecution to compromise by seeking a conviction for theft. Although a thief or burglar cannot become guilty of handling in the course of the original stealing, the offences of theft and handling are not mutually exclusive. Receiving property stolen or obtained in an earlier, completed theft must invariably involve a further appropriation of it, and it follows that a dishonest receiver of such goods must be a thief as well (*Stapylton* v *O'Callaghan* [1973] 2 All ER 782). It is accordingly open to the prosecution to include within the indictment a count for theft, drawn sufficiently widely to cover an appropriation of the property on any date between that of the original theft or burglary etc. and the date on which the property was found in D's possession (*More* [1987] 1 WLR 1578). This count may be additional to more specific counts, such as for handling or burglary, or it may stand alone; but the prosecution should in either case be able to prove that D stole the property at some point, and it need not matter if they cannot prove whether it was theft by burglary or theft by receiving (*Shelton* (1986) 83 Cr App R 379).

In *Shelton* the Court of Appeal offered the following advice (at pp. 384–5).

> As we have been asked by counsel to do so, for the guidance of judges and counsel we make the following comments. First that the long established practice of charging theft and handling as alternatives should continue whenever there is a real possibility, not a fanciful one, that at trial the evidence might support one rather than the other. Secondly, that there is a danger that juries may be confused by reference to second or later appropriations since the issue in every case is whether the defendant has in fact appropriated property belonging to another. If he has done so, it is irrelevant how he came to make the appropriation provided it was in the course of theft. Thirdly, that a jury should be told that a handler can be a thief, but he cannot be convicted of being both a thief and a handler. Fourthly, that handling is the more serious offence, carrying a heavier penalty because those who knowingly have dealings with thieves encourage stealing. Fifthly, in the unlikely event of the jury not agreeing amongst themselves whether theft or handling has been proved, they should be discharged. Finally, and perhaps most importantly, both judges and counsel when directing and addressing juries should avoid intellectual subtleties which some jurors may have difficulty in grasping; the golden rule should be 'Keep it short and simple'.

The second possible solution to the problem has the support of the Privy Council in *A-G of Hong Kong* v *Yip Kai-foon* [1988] AC 642 and that of the Court of Appeal in *Foreman* [1991] Crim LR 702, but is, with respect, based on doubtful logic. In *Yip Kai-foon*, the Privy Council took the view that, where the evidence was equally consistent with robbery or handling, and the jury was accordingly unable to convict the accused of robbery, it would then be open to them to rely upon his 'innocence' of that offence as proof that he must have committed handling. This is objectionable, in that it can lead to a conviction for handling being recorded when the jury think it more likely that the accused committed robbery, burglary or simple theft (see Sir John Smith's commentary on *Ryan* v *DPP* [1994] Crim LR 457). It is accordingly submitted that a widely drawn count for theft offers a more logical solution to cases in which it is unclear how the accused acquired the stolen property.

Mens Rea: Dishonesty

B4.140 Dishonesty must bear the same meaning as it does in deception cases and (save for the fact that the TA 1968, s. 2, is not directly applicable) in theft. In other words, it is dishonesty in the *Ghosh* sense (*Ghosh* [1982] QB 1053, see **B4.37**). As to the possible relationship between knowledge and dishonesty, see **B4.141**.

Mens Rea: Knowledge or Belief that the Goods are Stolen

B4.141 On a charge of handling stolen goods, it must be proved that the accused actually knew that the goods were stolen, or correctly believed that they were. This knowledge or belief must correspond in time with the *actus reus* (*Williams* [1994] Crim LR 934). In cases of handling by receiving, this means the moment of receipt or acquisition. If the defendant only later becomes aware that the goods are stolen, this will not suffice, even if his retention of them is clearly dishonest (*Brook* [1993] Crim LR 455). On the other hand, dishonest retention in such circumstances may sometimes amount to theft (subject to the TA 1968, s. 3(2), which precludes such liability in cases where the property was acquired bona fide and for value); or it may amount to an offence under the CJA 1988, s. 93B (as to which, see **B22.10**).

Knowledge of the circumstances which make the goods stolen will generally suffice for liability in cases of alleged handling whether or not the accused appreciated the legal consequences of those circumstances. An accused's belief that the proceeds of blackmail are something different from stolen goods will accordingly be no defence. Nor should it be any defence for an accused to argue that he believed the goods to be the proceeds of theft, when they are in fact the proceeds of blackmail or deception. In either event, the goods are stolen, and his belief is not incorrect in any material sense.

Another immaterial error would be one about the precise identity of the goods. It would be no defence for an accused to argue that he thought a container held stolen whisky, when in fact it contained stolen cigars (*McCullum* (1973) 57 Cr App R 645).

An accused's ignorance of the law may prevent him from being considered dishonest. For example, a person may know that certain property indirectly represents the proceeds of the sale, by a thief or handler, of the original stolen goods, but may not realise that these proceeds are accordingly 'stolen goods' within the meaning of the TA 1968, s. 24. Not realising the legal position, he is perhaps unlikely to realise that his handling of them would be considered dishonest according to the standards of reasonable and honest people.

Belief that goods are stolen is an alternative *mens rea* to knowledge of that fact. It is not of course an alternative to the goods actually *being* stolen (*Haughton* v *Smith* [1975] AC 485 at p. 503). If the goods are not in fact stolen, there may be an attempt to handle stolen goods (see **B4.135**) or he may actually steal them himself, but he cannot be guilty of handling.

The distinction between knowledge and belief is not crucial in this context, since either state of mind may suffice for liability. In *Hall* (1985) 81 Cr App R 260, the Court of Appeal nevertheless attempted to distinguish between the two concepts. The court suggested that a person 'knows' that goods are stolen if someone with first-hand knowledge (such as the thief) has told him so; whereas he 'believes' that fact if he does not know it for certain, but realises that there is no other reasonable conclusion to be drawn in the light of all the circumstances. With respect, however, a person cannot properly be said to 'know' a fact merely because someone else has told him about it. He can only know a fact (or indeed testify as to such a fact at a criminal trial) if he himself has first-hand knowledge of it, as for example where he personally witnesses the theft taking place or where he positively identifies property which he knows to have been stolen (cf. *Overington* [1978] Crim LR 692; *Hulbert* (1979) 69 Cr App R 243). Failing this, he can at most 'believe' the goods to be stolen.

The critical distinction in handling cases is that between knowledge or belief, on the one hand, and suspicion, on the other, because it has been held on many occasions that suspicion, even grave suspicion accompanied by dishonesty and a wilful failure to make reasonable enquiries, cannot suffice for liability (*Griffiths* (1974) 60 Cr App R 14; *Pethick* [1980] Crim LR 242; *Moys* (1984) 79 Cr App R 72; *Forsyth* [1997] 2 Cr App R 299). The Court of Appeal in *Hall* suggested that a person may believe goods to be stolen where he 'refuses to believe what his brain tells him is obvious', but this suggestion has rightly been rejected as potentially confusing (*Forsyth*). A person cannot sensibly be said to believe what he refuses to believe, and the test must be a subjective one, rather than an objective test based on what the defendant ought to have realised. In *Forsyth*, the Court of Appeal defined belief as 'the mental acceptance of a fact as true or existing', and suggested that juries might be directed in the following terms, as previously suggested by Lord Lane CJ in *Moys*:

> . . . it must be proved that the defendant was aware of the theft or that he believed the goods to be stolen. Suspicion that they were stolen, even coupled with the fact that he shut his eyes to the circumstances, is not enough, although these matters may be taken into account . . . in deciding whether or not the necessary knowledge or belief existed.

This is certainly preferable to the definition attempted in *Hall*, but the definition of belief remains imprecise. Does belief on balance of probabilities suffice, or must the defendant have felt sure of it, beyond reasonable doubt? In *Forsyth*, the Court of Appeal merely observed, rather unhelpfully, that 'between suspicion and belief there may be a range of awareness' and it would therefore be safer to assume that the stricter concept of belief applies. In other words, a person believes that goods are stolen only if he harbours no serious or substantial doubt as to that fact.

A person who is invited to deal with goods which he suspects *may* be stolen and who deliberately asks no questions might sometimes be considered dishonest, but is not guilty of handling. Dealers in second-hand goods know that from time to time they may be offered goods which turn out to be stolen, but cannot cross-examine their suppliers every time they buy. On the other hand, a person who has already concluded that the goods he is being offered *must* be stolen (for example, because the serial number has been removed from the car stereo he is being offered for a knock-down price by the man in the pub, and he knows that there is no other explanation for it) cannot set up his failure to ask questions as a defence. He is in fact only pretending to be blind to the truth. See *Griffiths* (1974) 60 Cr App R 14. See also **F3.28**.

Similar Facts and Previous Convictions

B4.142   On a charge of handling, the TA 1968, s. 27(3), makes evidence of previous convictions for theft or handling, or previous dealings in stolen goods, admissible in certain circumstances for the limited purpose of proving the accused's knowledge or belief that the goods were stolen on the present occasion. That provision, and its relationship with the similar fact rule at common law, is dealt with at **F12.24** *et seq*. For similar fact evidence generally, see **F12.3** *et seq*.

Effect of Conviction or Acquittal of the Alleged Thief

B4.143   A conviction for handling stolen goods does not depend on the conviction of the alleged thief (or blackmailer etc.), nor is it even necessary to identify him in every case. It follows that there is nothing necessarily inconsistent in the acquittal of the alleged thief and the conviction at the same trial of the alleged handler. It may be, for example, that the handler is convicted on the basis of a confession that is not admissible against his co-accused. On the other hand, acquittal of the alleged thief could sometimes be inconsistent with conviction of the handler at the same trial. The tribunal of fact must be satisfied that the goods are stolen, and this would not, for example, be consistent with acquittal of a child who is alleged to have been the thief, but who is found to be under the age of criminal responsibility (cf. *Walters* v *Lunt* [1951] 2 All ER 645).

At the trial of a person for handling stolen goods, conviction, by a court in, or by a Service court outside, the United Kingdom, of another person for stealing those goods is admissible evidence that that person did commit the theft. If the alleged handler wishes to argue that the goods were not stolen, he will have to prove it on balance of probabilities (PACE 1984, s. 74; see *Barnes* [1991] Crim LR 132 and **F11.3**). Conviction of the alleged thief by a foreign court is not, however, admissible as evidence that he committed the theft. This may hamper the use of the TA 1968, s. 24(1) (see **B4.130**), somewhat, although it does not preclude expert evidence that an act would have been an offence under foreign law.

DISHONESTLY RETAINING A WRONGFUL CREDIT

Definition

Theft Act 1968, s. 24A   B4.144

(1)   A person is guilty of an offence if—
   (a)   a wrongful credit has been made to an account kept by him or in respect of which he has any right or interest;
   (b)   he knows or believes that the credit is wrongful; and
   (c)   he dishonestly fails to take such steps as are reasonable in the circumstances to secure that the credit is cancelled.
(2)   References to a credit are to a credit of an amount of money.
(3)   A credit to an account is wrongful if it is the credit side of a money transfer obtained contrary to section 15A of this Act.
(4)   A credit to an account is also wrongful to the extent that it derives from—
   (a)   theft;
   (b)   an offence under section 15A of this Act;
   (c)   blackmail; or
   (d)   stolen goods.
(5)   In determining whether a credit to an account is wrongful, it is immaterial (in particular) whether the account is overdrawn before or after the credit is made.
(6)   A person guilty of an offence under this section shall be liable on conviction on indictment to imprisonment for a term not exceeding ten years.
(7)   Subsection (8) below applies for purposes of provisions of this Act relating to stolen goods (including subsection (4) above).
(8)   References to stolen goods include money which is dishonestly withdrawn from an account to which a wrongful credit has been made, but only to the extent that the money derives from the credit.
(9)   In this section, 'account' and 'money' shall be construed in accordance with section 15B of this Act.

For the TA 1968, ss. 15A and 15B, see **B5.30**.

Procedure and Sentence

An offence under s. 24A is triable either way (MCA 1980, s. 17 and sch. 1, para. 28). **B4.145** When tried on indictment, it is a class 4 offence. It is a Group A offence for jurisdiction purposes under the CJA 1993, part I (see **D1.75**).

The maximum penalty is 10 years (TA 1968, s. 24A(6)) on indictment; six months and/or a fine not exceeding the statutory maximum on summary conviction. There are no reported sentencing guidelines for this offence.

Indictment

Statement of Offence   B4.146

Dishonestly retaining a wrongful credit, contrary to section 24A(1) of the Theft Act 1968

Particulars of Offence

A between the . . . day of . . . and the . . . day of . . . knowing or believing that a wrongful credit, namely a transfer of £20,000 obtained by B from Abbey National plc, contrary to section 15A of the TA 1968, had been made to a current account (no. . . . .) kept jointly by A and B at Barclays Bank plc, dishonestly failed to take such steps as were reasonable in the circumstances to secure that the credit was cancelled.

Wrongful Credits and Stolen Goods

B4.147 One (at least arguable) side-effect of the decision of the House of Lords in *Preddy* [1996] AC 815 (see **B5.17**) is that, where D dishonestly obtains a money transfer from V, the sum thereby credited to D's account can no longer be categorised as stolen goods. This indeed was the view of the Law Commission when reviewing the impact of *Preddy*. Furthermore, even where A pays stolen bank notes directly into his account, the proceeds of a subsequent transfer from that account to an account held by B cannot be classed as stolen goods, because any credit balance thereby created in B's account is an entirely different chose in action from the credit balance which previously represented the stolen money in A's account. B's credit balance admittedly represents the proceeds of A's original crime, but it has never done so in the hands of the original thief, and any argument that it does so in the hands of a handler of the stolen property (i.e. B) is circular, because that presupposes the very point it seeks to establish, namely that the funds in B's account are stolen goods. In *A-G's Ref (No. 4 of 1979)* [1981] 1 WLR 667, it was held that B may be guilty of handling in such circumstances; but this cannot stand with *Preddy* on that particular issue.

The TA 1968, s. 24A addresses the problem in three ways. First, s. 24A(3) deals with cases in which a wrongful credit is made to the accused's account as a result of a s. 15A offence. If it is clear that the accused was himself responsible for the s. 15A offence, there would be little sense in charging him with a s. 24A offence as well, but there may be cases in which it is easier to prove that he became aware of the wrongful credit than that he was implicated in its obtaining. Secondly, s. 24A(4) extends the ambit of s. 24A to cases in which the accused dishonestly retains a credit which he knows or correctly believes derives from theft, blackmail, a s. 15A offence or stolen goods. If, for example, A pays stolen money into his account and transfers the funds from that account to an account owned by B, a wrongful credit has been made to B's account, and B may commit a s. 24A offence if he dishonestly retains it, knowing or believing it to be derived from one or other of those offences. Lastly, s. 24A(8) provides that any *money* dishonestly withdrawn from an account to which a wrongful credit has been made can be classed as stolen goods, subject to the principles explained in **B4.133** in respect of withdrawals from accounts into which both 'clean' and 'dirty' money has been paid. It may seem strange that the proceeds of A's original theft can be classed as stolen goods when paid into A's own bank account, cease to be so classified when effectively 'transferred' to B's account, and yet revert to being stolen goods when dishonestly withdrawn as cash by B; but such is now the law.

Dishonesty, Omissions and Bona Fide Purchasers

B4.148 The offence created by s. 24A(1) is one of dishonest omission. Dishonesty must bear the same meaning as in offences of handling or deception (i.e. the test set out in *Ghosh* [1982] QB 1053: see **B4.37**, **B4.140** and **B.141**), but knowledge cannot always be equated with dishonesty. A may discover that B has caused the payment of a wrongful credit into their joint account. It may be difficult for her to insist on the cancellation of this credit, unless she is prepared to inform on B, but would a court or jury necessarily categorise her inactivity as dishonest? Similarly, although the bona fide purchaser of a credit is not exempted from liability under s. 24A where he retains the credit after belatedly discovering it to have been a wrongful one (contrast the TA 1968, s. 3(2)) it may be very difficult to persuade a jury that such a person acted dishonestly.

Wrongful Credits and the Proceeds of Criminal Conduct

B4.149 The CJA 1988, s. 93B (see **B22.10**), creates an offence of knowingly acquiring, using or possessing property which directly or indirectly represents another person's proceeds of criminal conduct. Dishonesty need not be proved. Where a money transfer is made, e.g., from a thief's account to an account held by A, the money credited to A's account represents the proceeds of the thief's original crime, and (in contrast to the position under the TA 1968, s. 22) it does not matter for this purpose that it was never held by the thief himself. *Preddy* [1996] AC 815, in other words, does not affect the operation of s. 93B. Since the TA 1968, s. 24A, applies only to wrongful credits made on or after 18 December 1996 (Theft (Amendment) Act 1996, s. 2(2)), s. 93B may be of great value to prosecutors in respect of earlier transactions.

ADVERTISING REWARDS FOR RETURN OF GOODS STOLEN OR LOST

Definition

Theft Act 1968, s. 23

B4.150

Where any public advertisement of a reward for the return of any goods which have been stolen or lost uses any words to the effect that no questions will be asked, or that the person producing the goods will be safe from apprehension or inquiry, or that any money paid for the purchase of the goods or advanced by way of loan on them will be repaid, the person advertising the reward and any person who prints or publishes the advertisement shall on summary conviction be liable to a fine not exceeding level 3 on the standard scale.

Elements

The TA 1968, s. 23, does not necessarily forbid the offering of rewards for the return of **B4.151** stolen goods, nor does it necessarily prohibit advertisements promising that 'no questions will be asked'. What it prohibits are public advertisements which *combine* an offer of a reward with a promise that no questions will be asked or that immunity will be granted. It does not matter if the advertiser is uncertain whether the goods were lost or stolen; he may even be confident that they were only lost.

The printing or publishing of an offending advertisement is an offence of strict liability (*Denham v Scott* (1984) 77 Cr App R 210).

For the meaning of 'goods', 'stolen goods', 'theft' etc., see **B4.130**.

SECTION B5: DECEPTION AND BLACKMAIL

OFFENCES INVOLVING DECEPTION UNDER THE THEFT ACTS 1968 AND 1978

B5.1　The Theft Acts 1968 and 1978 create a number of deception offences, which deal with situations in which something is obtained, secured or procured, or in which some liability is evaded, as a result of the successful and dishonest deception of another person.

The relevant offences in the 1968 Act are those created by s. 15 (obtaining property), s. 15A (obtaining a money transfer), s. 16 (obtaining a pecuniary advantage) and s. 20(2) (procuring the execution of a valuable security). The 1978 Act, in replacing one troublesome provision of the 1968 Act (namely, s. 16(2)(a), which was repealed by s. 5(5) of the 1978 Act), added the offences of obtaining services (TA 1978, s. 1), securing remission of an existing liability (TA 1978, s. 2(1)(a)), inducing a creditor to wait for or forgo payment (s. 2(1)(b)) and obtaining exemption from, or abatement of, liability to make a payment (s. 2(1)(c)). Two other closely related offences under the 1968 Act, making off without payment (TA 1968, s. 3) and suppression of documents (s. 20(1)), are also dealt with in this section. See further **B5.14** *et seq*.

DECEPTION GENERALLY

Definition

B5.2　The TA 1968, s. 15(4), provides a partial definition of the concept of deception. It applies to the offences under ss. 15, 15A, 16 and 20(2) of the 1968 Act and also, by virtue of the TA 1978, s. 5(1), to offences under the 1978 Act.

Theft Act 1968, s. 15

> (4) . . . 'deception' means any deception (whether deliberate or reckless) by words or conduct as to fact or as to law, including a deception as to the present intentions of the person using the deception or any other person.

This does not really attempt to explain what a deception is; it merely indicates that a deception under the Theft Acts 1968 and 1978 may possess certain characteristics which might have precluded convictions for offences involving false representation under the Larceny Act 1916. (For example, it was not previously an offence to deceive another by making a false statement as to one's present intentions, or as to a point of law.)

The best known judicial definition of deception is that of Buckley J in *Re London and Globe Finance Corporation Ltd* [1903] 1 Ch 728 at p. 732:

> To deceive is . . . to induce a man to believe that a thing is true which is false.

This was quoted with approval in *DPP* v *Ray* [1974] AC 370 and is consistent with the normal dictionary meaning of the term, but does not quite tell the full story, because more recent cases, notably *Metropolitan Police Commissioner* v *Charles* [1977] AC 177 and *Lambie* [1982] AC 449, appear to establish that it is deception falsely to persuade someone that something only *may* be true. See **B5.9**.

Reckless Deception

B5.3　It is submitted that, in this context, *Caldwell* recklessness (see **A2.5**) cannot be applicable, because all the deception offences require proof of dishonesty, and a person can hardly be considered dishonest if it has never occurred to him that he may be deceiving someone. *Cunningham* recklessness (see **A2.4**) is therefore the relevant concept. See *Large* v *Mainprize* [1989] Crim LR 213, *Feeny* (1991) 94 Cr App R 1 and *Goldman* [1997] Crim LR 894.

Deception and Machines

In the absence of any clear authority (the point being left open in *Davies* v *Flackett* [1973] **B5.4** RTR 8), commentators have always taken the view that offences of actual or intended deception can only be practised against some other living person. A person who uses another's personal identification number to access a computer or to withdraw cash from a bank's automatic service till would not therefore be regarded as obtaining either services or property by deception. In the latter case he might of course be guilty of theft, as if he had used that other's key to open a safe.

Deception of a Person Other than the Victim

A deception need not necessarily be practised against the ultimate victim of the offence **B5.5** concerned. Where, for example, a retailer is deceived into accepting payment by a cheque supported by a guarantee card that is used in excess of authority, a conviction for obtaining a pecuniary advantage (namely borrowing by way of overdraft from the bank) by deception (TA 1968, s. 16(1)(b)) may still be imposed, even though the bank itself has not been deceived (*Kovacks* [1974] 1 WLR 370; *Smith* v *Koumourou* [1979] Crim LR 116; *Metropolitan Police Commissioner* v *Charles* [1977] AC 177).

On the other hand, it was held in *Rozeik* [1996] 1 WLR 159 that, where D was charged with obtaining cheques from finance companies by deception, convictions could not be justified unless it was proved that branch managers or employees who had signed the relevant cheques had been deceived, rather than having acted as parties to the fraud. If two such persons had signed a relevant cheque, it would have to be proved that at least one of them had been deceived. It would not be enough to prove that other employees, such as those who had prepared the blank cheque forms, had been deceived.

A further qualification must be added in respect of offences under the TA 1978, ss. 1 and 2. The s. 2(1)(b) offence in particular cannot be committed without the deception operating on the mind of the creditor or his agent (see *Gee* [1999] Crim LR 397).

Deception and False Representations

Because the relevant offences under the Theft Acts 1968 and 1978 are not expressed in **B5.6** terms of making false statements or representations, there is arguably no reason why a deception offence need involve the making of any such things. The courts sometimes go to great lengths to find 'implied representations' when the better view is that none are necessary. It is submitted that it suffices if the accused 'by words or conduct' induces a false belief in the other person's mind. If, on the other hand, it is alleged that the accused deceived his victim (or another) with a number of false representations, a court or jury should convict only if collectively satisfied as to the falsity of at least one of those representations. It will not suffice if half the jury are satisfied as to the falsity of one and half as to the falsity of another (*Brown* (1983) 79 Cr App R 115), unless they can agree that *some* at least of the representations must have been false, or that their cumulative effect was misleading, and that the other person was thereby deceived (*Agbim* [1979] Crim LR 171). See also *Price* [1991] Crim LR 465.

Deception by Conduct

Examples of deception by conduct are provided by *DPP* v *Stonehouse* [1978] AC 55, and **B5.7** *Williams* [1980] Crim LR 589. In *Williams*, the accused dishonestly presented obsolete Yugoslavian banknotes at a bureau de change, and asked for them to be exchanged for sterling. The counter staff assumed, as he had hoped, that the notes were current, and he made a handsome profit. He never said that the notes were current, but his conduct certainly implied it, and the Court of Appeal therefore opined that a charge of obtaining property by deception should have been put to the jury. This must surely be correct: if a false representation is needed, then one was implicit in his conduct; but a better way of explaining it is that he deliberately deceived the counter staff into making the false assumption.

In *DPP* v *Stonehouse*, the accused left his clothes on a beach in Miami, and slipped out of the USA under a false name, in the hope that insurance companies in England would be deceived into thinking him drowned, and thus into paying out on life assurance policies in favour of his wife. The scheme failed, but he was found guilty of an attempt to commit offences under the TA 1968, s. 15. See also *Hamilton* (1990) 92 Cr App R 54.

Dishonest overcharging for goods or services in situations where the purchaser trusts or relies upon the provider to charge a fair and reasonable price has been held to be capable of giving rise to liability for obtaining property by deception (see *Silverman* (1988) 86 Cr App R 214 and *Jones* (1993) *The Times*, 15 February 1993).

Deception by Omission

B5.8   It is clear that the courts are prepared to construe misleading omissions as deceptions in appropriate cases. A good illustration of this approach is provided by *Firth* (1989) 91 Cr App R 217, in which a consultant obstetrician omitted to inform his hospital that certain of his patients were being treated privately, with the result that no charge was made to him or to them for use of National Health Service beds and facilities. It could no doubt have been argued that he had impliedly represented the women in question to have been National Health Service patients, but the Court of Appeal held instead that 'it mattered not whether it was an act of commission or omission'. See also *Rai* (1999) *The Times*, 10 November 1999.

Deception, Uncertainty and Indifference

B5.9   There has been difficulty in deciding whether there is a deception where the accused made a false representation to a person who remained unconvinced of its truth, or who was not particularly concerned to verify it, but who was prepared to give the accused the property or advantage sought as long as he did not know for a fact that the representation was false.

This problem might arise where a person tells a false 'hard luck' story, and is given money on the basis that the story might be true and that he should have the benefit of the doubt. More significantly, it will arise where a cheque guarantee card or credit card is used to make a payment. Tendering the card is a representation that the person tendering it is authorised to use it, but the person taking the payment need not concern himself whether that is so. As long as the card is current, certain formalities are correctly attended to, and the signature corresponds with that on the card, then the bank or card company can be relied upon to pay, even if the tenderer has exceeded his authority, and even (depending on the exact conditions of use relating to the particular card) if he has stolen the card. The person taking the payment may, therefore, take the view that the correctness of the representation is of no concern to him. A third type of situation is a tender of a forged or invalid ticket, which the person to whom it is tendered, although both concerned and suspicious, accepts because he does not feel that he can prove what he suspects.

The leading cases on this question were concerned with cheque cards and credit cards but indicate that a deception would be committed in all three situations. In *Metropolitan Police Commissioner* v *Charles* [1977] AC 177, a gaming club accepted the accused's cheques because they were backed by a valid guarantee card. The club took the view that if the accused was exceeding his authority from his bank (as indeed he was), this was no concern of theirs, but the manager added in the course of his testimony that the position would have been different had the club possessed actual knowledge of the accused's lack of authority. On these facts, the House of Lords found that there had been a deception for the purposes of the TA 1968, s. 16(2)(b).

Metropolitan Police Commissioner v *Charles* was followed in *Lambie* [1982] AC 449, where goods had been purchased with a credit card which the accused knew she had no right to use. Both cases have attracted hostile academic comment, but it is submitted that the practical consequences would have been most unfortunate had their lordships reached any other interpretation. In contrast, a sales assistant or shopkeeper is unlikely to be concerned with matters such as the customer's ability to pay off his credit card account, or whether the customer was entirely honest when applying for the card in the first place. If the customer is currently authorised to use the card, that is probably all that concerns him. See *Nabina* [1999] All ER (D) 733 (unreported in printed form), [1999] 7 Arch News 2.

A person who persuades someone to draw a cheque in his favour and use a cheque card to guarantee it, even though both know that this would be in excess of authority, may also be guilty of a deception of the bank, which would presumably honour the cheque in the mistaken belief that the payee had relied on the card in good faith. Alternatively, both could be charged with conspiracy to defraud the bank.

Relationship of Deception to Consequences

To constitute one of the offences dealt with in this section the obtaining, procuring, **B5.10** evasion etc. must be a consequence (albeit perhaps not solely a consequence) of the deception. If a person tells a false 'hard luck' story to someone who gives him money despite being completely uninterested in the truth or otherwise of the story (a different situation from that where he considers that it might not be true but gives the deceiver the benefit of the doubt), there is only an attempt to deceive (*Hensler* (1870) 22 LT 691). A motorist who had already filled his car's tank with petrol before practising a deception on the attendant cannot be guilty of obtaining that petrol by deception (*Collis-Smith* [1971] Crim LR 716; *Coady* [1996] Crim LR 518). Furthermore, the deception must not be too remote from the obtaining. If a person deceives someone into allowing him to bet on a horse, and the horse wins, then the deceiver may be guilty of an offence under the TA 1968, s. 16(2)(c) (see **B5.35** to **B5.42**), but is probably not guilty of obtaining the winnings by that deception, because the immediate cause of his obtaining those winnings is not the deception, but is the fact that his horse has won (*Clucas* [1949] 2 KB 226).

Clucas was distinguished by the Court of Appeal in *Miller* (1992) 95 Cr App R 421, where M, posing as a taxi driver, picked up foreign visitors at London airports and then charged them up to ten times the proper fare. He was convicted of obtaining property by deception, and appealed on the ground that all his victims had realised that they were being cheated by the time they came to hand over the excessive fares demanded. It appeared that they paid so as to avoid trouble or because they were afraid of losing their luggage. The Court of Appeal nevertheless upheld his conviction as there was ample evidence on which a jury could conclude that the initial deception of his victims was the effective cause of the losses they suffered.

Evidence from the alleged victim of the deception may sometimes be the only satisfactory way of proving that he was indeed deceived and that it was because of the deception that he let the accused obtain the property etc. There will be few circumstances in which the prosecution can safely dispense with such evidence (*Tirado* (1974) 59 Cr App R 80); but see *Etim* v *Hatfield* [1975] Crim LR 234, where the Divisional Court was satisfied that the defendant could not possibly have obtained a social security payment to which he was not entitled, had the unidentified Post Office employee responsible not been deceived by his falsified order book. See also *Doukas* [1978] 1 WLR 372; *Hamilton* (1990) 92 Cr App R 54; and *Modupe* [1991] Crim LR 530.

Deception as to the Future; Worthless Cheques

B5.11 For a deception to be an offence under the Theft Acts 1968 or 1978, it must be a deception as to existing facts, or as to law. A representation that something will happen in the future will not suffice. It therefore will not do to argue that, when one person issues a worthless cheque to another, he has deceived the other into thinking that it will be honoured. For similar reasons, if a person falsely promises to perform a service for someone in the future, it cannot be argued that the person to whom the promise was made has been deceived into thinking that the service will be performed. There may indeed have been a criminal deception, but in either case, the deception must be expressed in terms of present fact.

The key to the problem is to be found in the TA 1968, s. 15(4), itself. As this makes clear, a deception may relate to the present intentions of the deceiver or of anyone else. These are 'as much a fact as the state of his digestion' (*Edgington* v *Fitzmaurice* (1885) 29 ChD 459). The person who was promised the service may have been deceived into thinking that the promisor intended to perform the promised service. The person who received the worthless cheque may have been deceived into thinking that the issuer of the cheque intended or believed it would be honoured.

In *Gilmartin* [1983] QB 953, the Court of Appeal held that a person who issues a cheque impliedly represents that the existing circumstances are such that in the ordinary course of events one would expect the cheque to be honoured. He does not necessarily represent that there are already sufficient funds in the account: there will not ordinarily be any deception if the issuer of a cheque is expecting sufficient funds to be credited to the account in time to meet the cheque on presentation; but see *Greenstein* [1975] 1 WLR 1353 (see **B5.12**).

Other Deceptions Involving Cheques

B5.12 The express or implied representations associated with issuing a cheque may be somewhat different from those envisaged in *Gilmartin* [1983] QB 953 (see **B5.11**). The issuer may, for example, indicate that he is unsure about the adequacy of his current account, but that he will indemnify the holder in the event of dishonour. *Gilmartin* would not then be applicable.

There may also be special circumstances in which a person might be guilty of a dishonest deception even where he expects the cheque to be honoured on presentation as where a cheque guarantee card is used (see **B5.9**). A further example is provided by *Greenstein* [1975] 1 WLR 1353, where the appellants drew cheques for sums vastly exceeding their credit limits in order to subscribe for the largest possible number of shares in oversubscribed company flotations. They relied on being allocated only a small percentage of the shares applied for, and on the issuing houses' refund cheques arriving in time to ensure their own cheques would be honoured. They had been warned that such tactics were considered improper, and in some cases had given an express undertaking that their cheques would be honoured on first presentation (something of which they could not in fact be sure and which did not always happen). In those circumstances they were held to have deceived the issuing houses, and to have committed offences under the TA 1968, s. 15.

Dishonesty

B5.13 Relatively little need be added here to what has been said about dishonesty in theft (see **B4.35 et seq.**); indeed it should be remembered that *Ghosh* [1982] QB 1053 is itself a deception case. Certain distinctions must, however, be noted.

The most important distinction is that the TA 1968, s. 2 is not directly applicable to any of the deception offences. This means, for example, that it is not necessarily impossible for a person to be guilty of an offence of obtaining a thing by deception when he believes himself to have a legal right to the thing in question (cf. s. 2(1)(a)). In practice, however, this distinction is probably of limited significance, because the *Ghosh* test of dishonesty, although less precise on this point, is likely to be more generous to an accused than s. 2 itself. Belief in a moral claim of right might suffice under *Ghosh*, but it would not suffice under s. 2 alone. See also *Woolven* (1983) 77 Cr App R 231, *Melwani* [1989] Crim LR 565 and *Lightfoot* (1993) 97 Cr App R 24.

When considering the issue of dishonesty, it would be wrong to assume that proof of an intention to deceive must *ipso facto* prove dishonesty (*Potger* (1970) 55 Cr App R 42; *O'Connell* (1991) 94 Cr App R 39; *Clarke* [1996] Crim LR 824). The jury should be warned against any such assumption.

Selection of Charges Generally

The deception offences overlap extensively. If a person deceives someone into accepting **B5.14** a cheque backed by a cheque guarantee card he has no right to use, he may thereby obtain property or services contrary to the TA 1968, s. 15, or the TA 1978, s. 1. He may also force his bank to honour the cheque, and to grant him an increased overdraft contrary to the TA 1968, s. 16(2)(b). (It matters not that only the payee of the cheque was deceived: see **B5.5**.) The position is complicated by the fact that, in many deception offences, false instruments are made or used, contrary to the Forgery and Counterfeiting Act 1981, s. 1 or s. 3.

In some respects, this kind of overlap can work to the advantage of the prosecution, since they may be able to succeed on one count of an indictment even if they fail on others; but there is at the same time added scope for error and confusion, and multiple counts may not always be advisable. Considerable care should therefore be taken in selecting the most suitable charges. It is not practicable to provide guidance here on the most appropriate charge in every possible situation, but the following general points may assist.

What has been Obtained? If goods, cash or other kinds of property (within the **B5.15** meaning of the TA 1968, s. 4(1)) appear to have been acquired as a result of the alleged deception, then a charge under the TA 1968, s. 15 (see **B5.23** *et seq*.), should ordinarily be brought in preference to other possible deception charges arising from the same facts. Where, however, D deceives V into drawing a cheque or draft in D's favour, or into transferring funds into D's account, a charge brought under s. 15 may be impossible to establish and alternative charges must be considered. See generally **B5.17**.

Deception and Theft Following the decision of the House of Lords in *Gomez* [1993] **B5.16** AC 442 (see **B4.25** *et seq*.), most cases in which property has been acquired by deception will now be chargeable as theft, which may be easier to prove. Conviction in a s. 15 prosecution requires proof not only that the property in question was obtained dishonestly and with intent to permanently deprive the person to whom it belonged, but also that it was obtained as a result of a successful deception of the victim or some other person. In contrast, a charge of theft merely requires proof of a dishonest appropriation coupled with an intent to permanently deprive. If for example D dishonestly selects goods in a self-service shop, intending to pay for them with a stolen credit card or cheque, his selection of the goods will in itself have amounted to theft, without the need for proof that the intended deception was successful. It does not follow that charges of theft should necessarily be preferred in such cases. If the deception can be proved, then it may be felt that a charge under s. 15 would better reflect the gravamen of the case against the defendant. In very serious fraud cases, the longer maximum sentence available under s. 15 may also be a relevant consideration.

B5.17 *Loans, Cheques and Money Transfers*   Where D deceives V into making a loan or advance, whether by way of mortgage or otherwise, this will only rarely involve the direct provision of cash. More commonly, V will issue D with a cheque or draft for the sum agreed, or will arrange for that sum to be credited electronically to D's account. Where a cheque or draft is issued to D, the latter acquires both the piece of paper on which it is printed and the chose in action it represents, namely the payee's right to enforce it. Where funds are credited to D's account, any credit balance thereby created is again a chose in action (although if the account remains overdrawn, D acquires no chose in action at all). A chose in action is a form of property within the meaning of the TA 1968, s. 4, but in each case it is a new chose in action rather than one which ever belonged to V; and this precludes any charge of obtaining that chose in action by deception (see *Preddy* [1996] AC 815, overruling *Duru* [1974] 1 WLR 2; and see also **B4.14**). The position is not significantly altered where the initial transfer is made to a firm of solicitors acting in the transaction (*Preddy* per Lord Goff at pp. 837–8 and see also *Nathan* [1997] Crim LR 835).

If a loan or advance is provided in the form of a cheque or banker's draft, a charge of obtaining the instrument itself (i.e. the completed form) by deception ought in principle to be viable, since the instrument is a valuable security; but in *Preddy* Lord Goff assumed that D could have no intent to permanently deprive the drawer of the instrument, because 'a cheque on presentation for payment is returned to the drawer via his bank' (at p. 836). In the case of a cheque, Lord Goff's assumption is largely false, because as a general rule banks no longer return cancelled cheques to the drawers; and in those cases where they still do so, the piece of paper that is returned is no longer a valuable security (cf. *Duru*). If on the other hand D obtains a banker's draft from V Bank, which is to be presented to V Bank itself for payment, an intention to permanently deprive V Bank of the draft may indeed be impossible to establish.

A number of other charges may, however, be considered. Where the alleged offence was committed on or after 18 December 1996, the obvious charge is one of obtaining a money transfer by deception, contrary to the TA 1968, s. 15A (see **B5.30** *et seq.*). In other cases, the prosecution may be able to prove a conspiracy to defraud at common law (see **A6.17** *et seq.*). Where a cheque or draft is issued to D, either by V or by an innocent solicitor to whom funds have been transferred electronically, D may be guilty of procuring the execution of a valuable security by deception contrary to the TA 1968, s. 20(2) (see *Cooke* [1997] Crim LR 436, *Aston* [1998] Crim LR 498 and **B5.43** *et seq.*). Such a charge may (at least arguably) be brought in respect of the authorisation of a CHAPS order, for the reasons given by the Court of Appeal in *King* [1992] QB 20 (see **B5.43**). The Court of Appeal in *Bolton* (1991) 94 Cr App R 74 suggested that an alternative charge would be one of procuring the execution of the mortgage deed by deception, but this will not work where the mortgage deed is executed by the borrower himself, nor will charges of conspiracy or attempt to procure execution of a cheque or CHAPS authorisation succeed unless it can be proved that the accused intended his deception would result in the execution of such a security (see *Mensah-Lartey* [1996] 1 Cr App R 143).

A charge of obtaining services by deception was for many years precluded by the decision of the Court of Appeal in *Halai* [1983] Crim LR 624, in which it was held that the provision of a mortgage advance was not a service for the purposes of the TA 1978, s. 1 (see **B5.52**). *Halai* has been widely condemned. It was not overruled in *Preddy*, but the Court of Appeal has repeatedly declared it to have been decided *per incuriam* on that point (see *Graham* [1997] 1 Cr App R 302; *Cooke* [1997] Crim LR 436 and *Cummings-John* [1997] Crim LR 660). In respect of offences committed on or after 18 December 1996, the Theft (Amendment) Act 1996 inserted a new s. 1(3) into the TA 1978, so as to make it clear that the obtaining of a loan is indeed an obtaining of services.

B5.18 *Jurisdictional Issues*   The selection of charges in cases with a foreign or 'cross-frontier' element may be influenced by jurisdictional considerations, especially where the alleged acts or events took place before 1 June 1999, which is the date on which the CJA 1993, part I was brought into force. The deception offences are all 'Group A' offences for the purpose of jurisdiction under part I. This means that they can be tried in England and Wales if any 'relevant event' (i.e. any essential element of the offence) takes place there on or after that date (see **D1.75** *et seq*.). Where, however, the acts or events in question occurred prior to that date, jurisdiction generally depends on where the actual obtaining took place. A deception practised from England would not be an offence if the obtaining took place abroad (see *Harden* [1963] 1 QB 8, *Tirado* (1974) 59 Cr App R 80 and *Manning* [1998] 2 Cr App R 461). A contrary view adopted by the Court of Appeal in *Smith* [1996] 2 Cr App R 1 appears to be wrong and was disapproved in *Manning*.

Purpose and Effect The prosecution must carefully consider what exactly the **B5.19** deception in question has achieved, and what it was intended to achieve. If for example the accused has paid a hotelier with a stolen cheque for services already provided, this cannot in itself amount to an offence under the TA 1978, s. 1, because the services have already been obtained (*Collis-Smith* [1971] Crim LR 716; *Coady* [1996] Crim LR 518). If an offence under s. 1 has been committed, it can only be on the basis of some deception practised before the services were provided, and that might depend on whether the accused intended to practise this trick from the start.

The TA 1978, s. 2(1)(b), might be more appropriate in such a case; but a charge under this provision would fail if the accused misused his own cheque card or credit card, knowing that the bank concerned would have to pay. The accused could not then be regarded as intending to make permanent default on his liability to pay. A charge under the TA 1968, s. 16(2)(b) might be the only effective one on such facts.

Forgery and Deception Charges of making or using a false instrument may have **B5.20** considerable advantages over deception offences where such instruments have been made or used for fraud. The complete offence may be committed without any successful deception, and without the obtaining or procuring of any benefit by the accused. He must of course intend to deceive ('induce somebody to accept [the falsified instrument] as genuine'), and thereby induce the person deceived to act to his own or another's prejudice, but the accused need not have succeeded in this object, and it is not necessary to prove he has been dishonest (*Campbell* (1984) 80 Cr App R 47). On the other hand, an instrument may be deceptive for the purpose of offences under the TA 1968 without being 'false' within the meaning of the Forgery and Counterfeiting Act 1981 (*More* [1987] 1 WLR 1578). See further **B6.2**.

Going Equipped Another possible charge in cases where a successful deception **B5.21** cannot be proved is one under the TA 1968, s. 25 (going equipped for a cheat); but it must be proved that the accused 'had with him' something which he intended should be used for an offence under s. 15: an intent to misuse a credit card in order to obtain services would not suffice. See further **B4.118** *et seq*.

Specialised Legislation Deception offences under the Theft Acts 1968 and 1978 **B5.22** may sometimes be less appropriate and harder to prove than offences under the Companies Act 1985 or other specialised enactments. See generally **B7**.

OBTAINING PROPERTY BY DECEPTION

Definition

Theft Act 1968, s. 15   **B5.23**

(1) A person who by any deception dishonestly obtains property belonging to another, with the intention of permanently depriving the other of it, shall on conviction on indictment be liable to imprisonment for a term not exceeding 10 years.

(2)   For purposes of this section a person is to be treated as obtaining property if he obtains ownership, possession or control of it, and 'obtain' includes obtaining for another or enabling another to obtain or to retain.

(3)   Section 6 above shall apply for purposes of this section, with the necessary adaptation of the reference to appropriating, as it applies for purposes of section 1.

(4)   For purposes of this section 'deception' means any deception (whether deliberate or reckless) by words or conduct as to fact or as to law, including a deception as to the present intentions of the person using the deception or any other person.

Procedure and Jurisdiction

B5.24   The offence is triable either way (MCA 1980, s. 17 and sch. 1, para. 28). When tried on indictment it is a class 4 offence. It is a Group A offence for jurisdiction purposes under the CJA 1993, part I (see **D1.75**).

Practice Note (Mode of Trial: Guidelines) (1995) (see **D3.7**) states that fraud should be tried summarily unless the court considers that one or more of the following features is present in the case *and* that its sentencing powers are insufficient:

(a)   Breach of trust by a person in a position of substantial authority, or in whom a high degree of trust is placed.

(b)   Fraud which has been committed or disguised in a sophisticated manner.

(c)   Fraud committed by an organised gang.

(d)   The victim is particularly vulnerable to fraud (e.g., the elderly or infirm).

(e)   The unrecovered property is of high value (at least £10,000).

In addition, the practice note states that social security fraud should be tried summarily unless the court considers that one or more of the following features is present in the case *and* that its sentencing powers are insufficient:

(a)   Organised fraud on a large scale.

(b)   The frauds are substantial and carried out over a long period of time.

For the liability of officers of a company for an offence committed by the company, see the TA 1968, s. 18, and **B5.67**.

Indictment

B5.25   Statement of Offence

Obtaining property by deception contrary to section 15(1) of the Theft Act 1968

Particulars of Offence

A on or about the . . . day of . . . dishonestly obtained from V a pearl necklace, with intent to deprive the said V of it permanently, by deception, namely by falsely representing that he was an employee of a jewellery restorer who had sent him to collect the said necklace for restoration

Sentencing Guidelines

B5.26   The maximum penalty is 10 years (TA 1968, s. 15(1)) on indictment; six months, or a fine not exceeding the statutory maximum, or both, summarily.

When dealt with summarily, the Magistrates' Association Guidelines (1997) indicate the following:

Aggravating Factors ⊕
For example committed over a lengthy period; large sums or valuable goods; two or more involved; victim particularly vulnerable; offence committed on bail; previous convictions and failures to respond to previous sentences, if relevant.

Mitigating Factors ⊖
For example impulsive action; short period; small sum.

Guideline: Is it serious enough for a community penalty?

The sentencing pattern for this and related offences of deception overlaps substantially with that for theft (see **B4.5** to **B4.8**). Since the offence varies so widely, there is no guideline judgment, save perhaps the general comments of Lord Lane CJ in *Bibi* [1980] 1 WLR 1193, where it was said that shorter sentences would be appropriate for the more petty frauds where small amounts of money are involved. The appropriate sentencing bracket for frauds committed by professional persons was reconsidered in *Barrick* (1985) 81 Cr App R 78, which is discussed in **B4.8**. Large-scale commercial frauds will attract lengthy custodial sentences. In *Copeland* (1982) 4 Cr App R (S) 110 the offender was involved in a well organised scheme by which cheque-books and cheque cards were stolen in Britain, passports were obtained in the names of the losers, and teams of two went to the Continent, using the passports, and obtained money by means of the stolen cheque-books and cards. Each trip netted about £15,000 and the scheme had been in operation for a considerable time. The offender had several previous convictions for dishonesty resulting in prison terms of up to three years. The Court of Appeal reduced the sentence for the present offences from six years to 4½ years. In *Griffiths* (1989) 11 Cr App R (S) 216 the offender, an 'intelligent and resourceful man', pleaded guilty to 23 counts of deception relating to a total of 93 multiple applications for shares. He made a profit of £5,000, but if all the applications had been successful he would have made £64,000. The Court of Appeal said that an immediate custodial sentence was appropriate, varying the original sentence of 12 months, with six to serve and six suspended, to an immediate term of six months. A striking case illustrating what the Court of Appeal described as 'a classic sentencing problem' is *Jackson* (1992) 13 Cr App R (S) 22. The offenders were husband and wife. They each pleaded guilty to three counts of obtaining property by deception and asked for similar offences, 31 and 47 respectively, to be taken into consideration. The offenders, who found themselves in severe financial difficulties, had bought a number of stolen store credit cards and had used them to obtain clothing and other items from various shops to the value of about £4,000, of which £1,000 was recovered. Sentences of 15 months' imprisonment in each case were reduced by the Court of Appeal to community service orders in the light of the offenders' previous good records and other strong personal mitigation. In *Stevens* (1993) 14 Cr App R (S) 372, the Court of Appeal noted that various forms of mortgage fraud had become more prevalent in recent years. Relevant factors in sentencing such offences were the degree of involvement of the individual offender, the duration of the fraud, the personal benefit derived and whether the offender was a professional person. A sentence of three years on an offender who was involved in 14 transactions and had recruited others to the fraud was upheld.

In contrast to these frauds are what may be described as the activities of 'con men'. Non-custodial sentences will often be appropriate but, once again, much turns on the sum involved. Also relevant is the method of deception ('callous' deception of the elderly, for example, will attract a more severe sentence) and the previous record of the offender. In *Hafeez* [1998] 1 Cr App R (S) 276, the offender pleaded guilty to conspiring to obtain by deception, by carrying out repair work on cars which was not needed, or by charging customers for repair work which had not been done. A sentence of three years' imprisonment on the defendant, who had organised the 'cynical and deeply dishonest' deception, was upheld, while a second defendant who was more peripherally involved, received 12 months. A sentence of five years was reduced to three years. In *Williams* (1983) 5 Cr App R (S) 244 the offender, 'a confidence trickster, especially of gullible women', who had a record of dishonesty over 15 years, had obtained £300 and £175 from different women by telling false hard luck stories. A sentence of 15 months was reduced to nine months.

Most cases involving the dishonest obtaining of social security benefits or payments are dealt with summarily under the Social Security Administration Act 1992, s. 110 (see **B16.10**). More serious cases will be prosecuted under the TA 1968, s. 15. A number of social security and other benefit frauds have reached the Court of Appeal. In *Stewart* (1987) 9 Cr App R (S) 135 Lord Lane CJ provided the following important guidance for Crown Court sentencers:

> . . . only a small proportion of offences of this nature . . . are dealt with in the Crown Court. . . . If prosecuted at all, the run of the mill offence is almost certain to be before the magistrates.

> . . . These offences involve the dishonest abstraction of honest taxpayers' money, and are not to be treated lightly. They are easy to commit and difficult and expensive to track down. However it must be remembered that they are non-violent, non-sexual and non-frightening crimes.

> In some cases immediate unsuspended imprisonment (or youth custody) is unavoidable. At the top of the range, requiring substantial sentences, perhaps of $2\frac{1}{2}$ years' imprisonment and upwards, are the carefully organised frauds on a large scale in which considerable sums of money are obtained. . . . These offenders are in effect professional fraudsmen, as is often apparent from their previous records. . . .

> As to the remainder, who form the great majority of those appearing in the Crown Court, the sentence will depend on an almost infinite variety of factors, only some of which it is possible to forecast. It may well be advisable as a first precaution for the court to enquire what steps the department proposes to take to recover their loss from the offender. Counsel for the Crown should be equipped to assist the court on this aspect of the matter. . . .

> Other considerations which may affect the decision of the court are: (i) a guilty plea; (ii) the amount involved and the length of time over which the defalcations were persisted in (bearing in mind that a large total may in fact represent a very small amount weekly), (iii) the circumstances in which the offence began (e.g. there is a plain difference between a legitimate claim which becomes false owing to a change of situation and on the other hand a claim which is false from the very beginning); (iv) the use to which the money is put (the provision of household necessities is more venial than spending the money on unnecessary luxury); (v) previous character; (vi) matters special to the offender, such as illness, disability, family difficulties, etc.; (vii) any voluntary repayment of the amounts overpaid.

> If immediate imprisonment is necessary, a short term of up to about 9 or 12 months will usually be sufficient in a contested case where the overpayment is less than, say, £10,000 . . .

> So far as compensation is concerned, we would add this. Where no immediate custodial sentence is imposed, and the amount of overpayment is below, say, £1,000 or thereabouts, a compensation order is often of value. This will usually only be the case where the defendant is in work.

> . . . we do not think that the element of deterrence should play a large part in the sentencing of this sort of case.

The guidelines in *Stewart* (1987) 9 Cr App R (S) 135 were applied to bring sentences within the 'normal' nine to 12-month range in *Graham* (1988) 10 Cr App R (S) 352 and *Miah* (1989) 11 Cr App R (S) 163. In *McDonagh* (1989) 11 Cr App R (S) 94, however, two years was upheld in respect of a 'deliberate, ingenious and calculated course of conduct' and three years was upheld in *Perry* (1989) 11 Cr App R (S) 58 where there was 'persistent deliberation' and a total of more than £44,000 obtained by deception. More than £100,000 was obtained in *Adewuyi* [1997] 1 Cr App R (S) 254, a case of 'exceptional seriousness', where a sentence of four years' imprisonment was approved by the Court of Appeal.

Actus Reus: **Property Belonging to Another**

B5.27 'Property', in the TA 1968, s. 15(1), bears the same meaning as it does in theft cases. The definition provided in s. 4(1) (see **B4.10** to **B4.15**) applies by virtue of s. 34(1). Subsections (2) to (4) of s. 4 are not mentioned in s. 34, and do not therefore apply to any offences other than theft (see s. 1(3)). This means that there are no special rules precluding or restricting charges of obtaining land by deception.

The term 'belonging to another' likewise bears the same basic meaning as it does in relation to theft (see **B4.17**), s. 5(1) also being of general application by virtue of s. 34(1). However, as with s. 4, it is only s. 5(1) that applies in respect of offences other than theft, and subsections (2) to (5) cannot be relied upon for these purposes.

Cheques involve special considerations. If one person tricks another into negotiating to him a cheque of which the other is presently the payee or holder, he may be regarded as obtaining both the cheque itself and the chose in action it represents (i.e. the right to enforce it against the drawer and endorsers in the event of it being dishonoured). Both are forms of property belonging to the other person within the TA 1968, ss. 4(1) and 5(1). However, deceiving someone into *issuing* a cheque involves no obtaining of another person's chose in action, because there was no right to enforce the cheque before it was issued. The prosecution may be able to charge the accused with an offence under s. 15A (see **B5.30**) or with procuring the execution of a valuable security contrary to the TA 1968, s. 20(2) (see **B5.43**).

Actus Reus: **The Obtaining**

As to the need to prove a causative connection between the deception and the obtaining, see **B5.10**. 'Obtaining' is defined widely in the TA 1968, s. 15(2), so that an offence under s. 15(1) may be committed when and where the deceiver obtains possession or control of the property in question, even if he does not obtain ownership (and vice versa). This raises the question of whether the deceiver can be guilty of obtaining the same property more than once. Can an offence involving only the obtaining of ownership be followed by a further offence involving the obtaining of physical possession or control? Since property can be regarded as 'belonging to another' in any of these three senses, the logical answer would appear to be 'yes', and it would also appear to be possible for a thief to follow up his initial appropriation of physical possession with a deceptive obtaining of legal title. The position is now complicated, however, by *Atakpu* [1994] QB 69, in which the Court of Appeal held that there cannot ordinarily be successive thefts of the same property by the same thief. Most cases of obtaining property by deception also amount to theft (see *Gomez* [1993] AC 442 at **B4.21** *et seq.*), and it could be argued that much of the reasoning adopted in *Atakpu* is applicable to both offences, but *Atakpu* was not concerned with cases in which ownership and possession are obtained or appropriated in separate transactions, and does not necessarily apply to them. *Atakpu* is considered, insofar as it deals with theft, at **B4.27**.

If the property obtained by a deception was obtained for a person other than the deceiver then that other person may be a party to the offence, but need not be (*Duru* [1974] 1 WLR 2; *DPP* v *Stonehouse* [1978] AC 55).

Curiously, enabling another person to *retain* property can be an offence under the TA 1968, s. 15, whereas enabling oneself to retain property cannot be.

Mens Rea

On a charge of obtaining property by deception contrary to the TA 1968, s. 15(1), the prosecution must prove that the accused acted dishonestly and with the intention of permanently depriving of the property. As to dishonesty, see **B5.13**. As to intention permanently to deprive, the whole of the definition of this concept in the TA 1968, s. 6, is applicable to s. 15 by virtue of s. 15(3). Section 6 is discussed at **B4.38** to **B4.41**.

B5.28

B5.29

OBTAINING A MONEY TRANSFER BY DECEPTION

Definition

Theft Act 1968, s. 15A

B5.30

(1)   A person is guilty of an offence if by any deception he dishonestly obtains a money transfer for himself or another.

(2) A money transfer occurs when—
    (a) a debit is made to one account,
    (b) a credit is made to another, and
    (c) the credit results from the debit or the debit results from the credit.
(3) References to a credit and to a debit are to a credit of an amount of money and to a debit of an amount of money.
(4) It is immaterial (in particular)—
    (a) whether the amount credited is the same as the amount debited;
    (b) whether the money transfer is effected on presentation of a cheque or by another method;
    (c) whether any delay occurs in the process by which the money transfer is effected;
    (d) whether any intermediate credits or debits are made in the course of the money transfer;
    (e) whether either of the accounts is overdrawn before or after the money transfer is effected.
(5) A person guilty of an offence under this section shall be liable on conviction on indictment to imprisonment for a term not exceeding ten years.

Procedure, Jurisdiction and Sentence

B5.31 An offence under the TA 1968, s. 15A, is triable either way (MCA 1980, s. 17 and sch. 1, para. 28). When tried on indictment, it is a class 4 offence. It is a Group A offence for jurisdiction purposes under the CJA 1993, part I (see **D1.75**). As to the circumstances in which summary trial of fraud cases may be inappropriate, see **D3.7** and **B5.24**.

The maximum penalty is 10 years on indictment (TA 1968, s. 15A(5)); six months and/or a fine not exceeding the statutory maximum on summary conviction. This is the same as for offences under s. 15. For sentencing guidelines in s. 15 cases, see **B5.26**.

Indictment

B5.32

Statement of Offence

Obtaining a money transfer by deception, contrary to section 15A(1) of the Theft Act 1968

Particulars of Offence

A on the . . . day of . . . dishonestly obtained from Abbey National plc a money transfer, namely the crediting of an unsecured loan of £5,000 to his current account at Abbey National plc, by deception, namely by falsely representing that he was in paid employment at that time.

Elements

B5.33 In a typical mortgage or loan transaction, an account held by the borrower or by someone acting on his behalf is credited with a sum of money, and an account held by the lending institution is debited as a result. The ambit of the TA 1968, s. 15A, is confined to such cases (s. 15A(2) and (3)). An account for the purpose of s. 15A must be kept with a bank or with a person carrying on business in which money received by way of deposit is lent to others or in which any other activity of the business is financed, to any material extent, out of the capital of or out of the interest on money received by way of deposit (s. 15B(3) and (4)).

Deception has the same meaning in s. 15A as in s. 15 (s. 15B(2)). As to this meaning, see **B5.2** *et seq*. Dishonesty is not defined, but clearly bears the same meaning as in other deception offences (see **B5.13**). An intent permanently to deprive need not be proved.

Relationship to Other Offences

B5.34 Although *Preddy* [1996] AC 815 decided that fraudulently obtained money transfers are not obtained from the lender in contravention of the TA 1968, s. 15, a number of other offences may be committed in the course of such frauds (see **B5.17**). These may have to be relied upon in cases where the conduct in question occurred before s. 15A became law.

OBTAINING A PECUNIARY ADVANTAGE BY DECEPTION

Definition

Theft Act 1968, s. 16

B5.35

(1)   A person who by any deception dishonestly obtains for himself or another any pecuniary advantage shall on conviction on indictment be liable to imprisonment for a term not exceeding five years.

(2)   The cases in which a pecuniary advantage within the meaning of this section is to be regarded as obtained for a person are cases where—

(a)   [repealed]

(b)   he is allowed to borrow by way of overdraft, or to take out any policy of insurance or annuity contract, or obtains an improvement of the terms on which he is allowed to do so; or

(c)   he is given the opportunity to earn remuneration or greater remuneration in an office or employment, or to win money by betting.

(3)   For purposes of this section 'deception' has the same meaning as in section 15 of this Act.

Procedure and Jurisdiction

The offence is triable either way (MCA 1980, s. 17 and sch. 1, para. 28). When tried on   B5.36 indictment it is a class 4 offence. It is a Group A offence for jurisdiction purposes under the CJA 1993, part I (see **D1.75**). For the provisions of *Practice Note (Mode of Trial: Guidelines)* (1995) relating to fraud generally, see **B5.24**.

For the liability of officers of a company for an offence committed by the company, see the TA 1968, s. 18, and **B5.67**.

Indictment

Statement of Offence

B5.37

Obtaining a pecuniary advantage by deception contrary to section 16(1) of the Theft Act 1968

Particulars of Offence

A on or about the . . . day of . . . dishonestly obtained for himself a pecuniary advantage, namely being allowed to borrow by way of overdraft from the V Bank, by deception, namely by falsely representing that he was then entitled to use a cheque guarantee card when issuing a cheque numbered . . . drawn on account number . . . at the said V Bank

Sentence

The maximum penalty is five years (TA 1968, s. 16(1)) on indictment; six months, a   B5.38 fine not exceeding the statutory maximum, or both, summarily. There is no guideline judgment reported for an offence under the TA 1968, s. 16(1). For sentencing guidelines for offences of deception generally, see **B5.26**. For sentencing guidelines for theft offences, see **B4.5** to **B4.8**.

Elements

Some of the terms used in the TA 1968, s. 16(1), have already been explained.   B5.39 'Deception' and 'dishonestly' bear the same meanings as in s. 15 (see **B5.2** to **B5.13**) but 'obtaining a pecuniary advantage' is a mere term of art, which has no meaning save that given to it in s. 16. As the House of Lords held in *DPP* v *Turner* [1974] AC 537, if the accused's deception has produced any of the consequences specified in s. 16(2) then a pecuniary advantage 'is to be regarded as obtained'. There cannot then be any room for argument about whether the accused (or another) actually derived any real profit from the transaction. Conversely, if the accused has profited in some way *not* covered by s. 16(2), there can be no question of liability under s. 16(1): some other charge would have to be considered (e.g., under the TA 1978).

Pecuniary Advantage: Being Allowed to Borrow by Way of Overdraft etc.

B5.40   As well as being an offence under the TA 1968, s. 16(1), borrowing cash could involve a more serious offence under s. 15, as could the use of a cheque-book and cheque guarantee card to buy goods in circumstances where the bank has no choice but to honour cheques on an overdrawn account. To this extent, the two provisions overlap, since the bank does (albeit unwillingly) 'allow' the overdraft, and the offences are committed even though it was not the bank that was deceived but someone else (*Waites* [1982] Crim LR 369 and see **B5.5**). The offence created by s. 16(2)(b) has the advantage from the prosecution viewpoint of being complete as soon as overdraft facilities have been granted, even if they have not been used (*Watkins* [1976] 1 All ER 578) but it has a limited ambit: a bank loan is not the same as an overdraft, nor can an overdraft be incurred by misuse of a credit card. Section 16(2)(b) is equally inapt where the accused has misused cheques stolen from another person. See further *Metropolitan Police Commissioner* v *Charles* [1977] AC 177; *Bevan* (1986) 84 Cr App R 143; *Kovacs* [1974] 1 WLR 370.

Pecuniary Advantage: Opportunity to Earn Remuneration etc.

B5.41   The essence of the offence defined in the TA 1968, s. 16(2)(c), is the obtaining of the opportunity: it does not matter whether the accused (or anyone else for whom he has acted) has earned any remuneration or won his bet. In respect of betting, this provision filled the gap in the old law apparently revealed in *Clucas* [1949] 2 KB 226: see **B5.10**.

As to the meaning of 'opportunity to earn remuneration in an office or employment', see *McNiff* [1986] Crim LR 57, and *Callender* [1993] QB 303, where it was held that s. 16(2)(c) covered the case of a self-employed accountant who obtained work from clients by falsely claiming to hold CIMA qualifications.

Relationship between s. 16(2)(b) and s. 16(2)(c)

B5.42   The TA 1968, s. 16, apparently creates only one offence, but a conviction on an indictment alleging an offence under s. 16(2)(b) cannot be supported when the evidence points only to an offence under s. 16(2)(c) (cf. *Aston* (1970) 55 Cr App R 48).

PROCURING EXECUTION OF A VALUABLE SECURITY BY DECEPTION

Definition

B5.43   **Theft Act 1968, s. 20**

(2)   A person who dishonestly, with a view to gain for himself or another or with intent to cause loss to another, by any deception procures the execution of a valuable security shall on conviction on indictment be liable to imprisonment for a term not exceeding seven years; and this subsection shall apply in relation to the making, acceptance, endorsement, alteration, cancellation or destruction in whole or in part of a valuable security, and in relation to the signing or sealing of any paper or other material in order that it may be made or converted into, or used or dealt with as, a valuable security, as if that were the execution of a valuable security.

(3)   For purposes of this section 'deception' has the same meaning as in section 15 of this Act, and 'valuable security' means any document creating, transferring, surrendering or releasing any right to, in or over property, or authorising the payment of money or

delivery of any property, or evidencing the creation, transfer, surrender or release of any such right, or the payment of money or delivery of any property, or the satisfaction of any obligation.

This offence is frequently of significance in deception cases where cheques and similar instruments are involved, and not only where they have been executed in favour of the accused.

The concepts of dishonesty and deception bear the same meanings as in s. 15 of the Act (see **B5.2** to **B5.13**).

Procedure and Jurisdiction

The offence is triable either way (MCA 1980, s. 17 and sch. 1, para. 28). When tried on **B5.44** indictment it is a class 4 offence. It is a Group A offence for jurisdiction purposes under the CJA 1993, part I (see **D1.75**). For the provisions of *Practice Note (Mode of Trial: Guidelines)* (1995) relating to fraud generally, see **B5.24**.

For the liability of officers of a company for an offence committed by the company, see the TA 1968, s. 18, and **B5.67**.

Indictment

Statement of Offence

B5.45

Procuring the execution of a valuable security by deception contrary to section 20(2) of the Theft Act 1968

Particulars of Offence

A on or about the . . . day of . . . , with a view to gain for himself, dishonestly procured V to execute a valuable security, namely a cheque for £10,000, by deception, namely by falsely representing to the said V that goods of that value had been supplied to V's account

Sentence

The maximum penalty is seven years (TA 1968, s. 20(2)) on indictment; six months, a **B5.46** fine not exceeding the statutory maximum, or both, summarily. There is no guideline judgment reported for an offence under the TA 1968, s. 20(2). For sentencing guidelines for offences of deception generally, see **B5.26**. For sentencing guidelines for theft offences, see **B4.5** to **B4.8**.

Actus Reus: Meaning of 'Valuable Security'

The definition of the term 'valuable security' provided in the TA 1968, s. 20(3), clearly **B5.47** embraces cheques, bills of exchange and banker's drafts, all of which authorise the payment of money. Share certificates, irrevocable letters of credit (*Benstead* (1982) 75 Cr App R 276), bills of lading and vouchers evidencing credit card sales also come within the definition, even if they are forgeries (*Beck* [1985] 1 WLR 22). In *King* [1992] 1 QB 20, the Court of Appeal held that a clearing house automated payment system (or CHAPS) order is also a valuable security in that, once signed, it is a document transferring rights over a thing in action, namely the bank credit created by that order. A telex document, in contrast, does no such thing. Even if it could be regarded as a valuable security, in the sense of being an authority to pay money, it is not signed and cannot be 'executed' (*Johl* [1994] Crim LR 522). See also *Cooke* [1997] Crim LR 436.

Meaning of 'Execution'

Execution is partly defined within the TA 1968, s. 20(2) itself, but the definition has **B5.48** proved capable of differing interpretations. Should terms such as 'acceptance' be construed in their technical sense (as where the bank on which a bill is drawn signs its acceptance of liability on that instrument) or should they be construed in a wider sense, as they are used in ordinary language?

In a number of Court of Appeal decisions on the meaning of 'execution', notably *Beck* [1985] 1 WLR 22, it was formerly held that 'execution' for the purposes of s. 20(2) bore the wider meaning, and extended to any act giving effect to or carrying out the terms of the security in question. Payment of a cheque was thus regarded as a form of execution; but doubts were raised as to the correctness of this non-technical interpretation and in *Kassim* [1992] 1 AC 9, the House of Lords concluded that *Beck* was wrongly decided. Lord Ackner said that s. 20(2) contemplates acts being done to or in connection with bills of exchange and other such instruments but does not contemplate, and accordingly is not concerned with, giving effect to the documents by the carrying out of the instructions which they may contain, such as the delivery of goods or the payment of money. Section 20(2) nevertheless provides that some actions which do not amount to execution in the strict sense shall be treated as if they were acts of execution. Thus, the signing of any paper 'in order that it may be . . . dealt with as a valuable security' will be treated as equivalent to execution, and this extension of the concept of execution was relied upon by the Court of Appeal in *King* [1992] 1 QB 20 (see **B5.17**).

'Procuring'

B5.49 In *Beck* [1985] 1 WLR 22, Watkins LJ stated that 'procuring' is a word in common usage, meaning 'to cause or bring about'. This interpretation has more recently been followed in *Aston* [19981 Crim LR 498, in which the Court of Appeal also approved a passage from Professor Sir John Smith's *Law of Theft* (8th ed at para. 6–18), to the effect that D must be proved to have at least been reckless as to the possibility that his deception would lead to the execution of some type of valuable security. D need not specifically have intended that he would receive a valuable security rather than (say) cash, although a specific intent of this kind may have to be proved if the charge is one of conspiracy or attempt to procure one (see *Mensah-Lartey* [1996] 1 Cr App R 143). A further qualification has been added by the House of Lords in *Kassim* [1992] 1 AC 9, in which it was held that D cannot be regarded as procuring any form of execution (such as the cancellation of the security) which takes place only after his fraudulent plans have already succeeded. To hold otherwise would involve 'confusing consequences with intention'.

Mens Rea: With a View to Gain or with Intent to Cause Loss

B5.50 The TA 1968, s. 20(2) specifies an ulterior intent, and the full offence may be committed without either consequence actually occurring. 'Gain' and 'loss' are defined (as for blackmail and false accounting) in s. 34(2)(a) of the 1968 Act:

> 'gain' and 'loss' are to be construed as extending only to gain or loss in money or other property, but as extending to any such gain or loss whether temporary or permanent; and—
>> (i) 'gain' includes a gain by keeping what one has, as well as a gain by getting what one has not; and
>> (ii) 'loss' includes a loss by not getting what one might get, as well as a loss by parting with what one has.

In a false-accounting case (*Eden* (1971) 55 Cr App R 193) it was emphasised that an intent to gain or lose on a temporary basis may suffice under s. 34(2)(a); but contrast *Golechha* [1989] 1 WLR 1050, where the Court of Appeal adopted a very restrictive view of s. 34(2) and held that falsification made with intent to postpone the enforcement of a debt by the creditor was not made with a view to gain by keeping money or other property. See also *Lee Cheung Wing* v *The Queen* [1992] Crim LR 440 at **B6.13**.

OBTAINING SERVICES BY DECEPTION

Definition

B5.51   **Theft Act 1978, s. 1**

(1) A person who by any deception dishonestly obtains services from another shall be guilty of an offence.

(2)   It is an obtaining of services where the other is induced to confer a benefit by doing some act, or causing or permitting some act to be done, on the understanding that the benefit has been or will be paid for.

(3)   Without prejudice to the generality of subsection (2) above, it is an obtaining of services where the other is induced to make a loan, or to cause or permit a loan to be made, on the understanding that any payment (whether by way of interest or otherwise) will be or has been made in respect of the loan.

Procedure and Jurisdiction

The offence is triable either way (TA 1978, s. 4(1)). When tried on indictment it is a **B5.52** class 4 offence. It is a Group A offence for jurisdiction purposes under the CJA 1993, part I (see **D1.75**). For the provisions of *Practice Note (Mode of Trial: Guidelines)* (1995) relating to fraud generally, see **B5.24**.

For the liability of officers of a company for an offence committed by the company, see the TA 1968, s. 18 (which is applied to the TA 1978, s. 1, by s. 5(1) of the 1978 Act), and **B5.67**.

Indictment

Statement of Offence   **B5.53**

Obtaining services by deception contrary to section 1(1) of the TA 1978

Particulars of Offence

A on or about the . . . day of . . . dishonestly obtained from V services, namely the preparation of A's will, by deception, namely by falsely representing to the said V that a cheque in the sum of . . . numbered . . . and drawn on the X Bank, was a good and valid payment for V's professional fees

Sentence

The maximum penalty is five years (TA 1978, s. 4(2)(a)) on indictment; six months, a **B5.54** fine not exceeding the statutory maximum, or both, summarily. There is no guideline judgment reported for an offence under the TA 1978, s. 1. In *Takyi* [1998] 1 Cr App R (S) 372, the offender attempted to board an international flight using a passport which belonged to someone else. He pleaded guilty to attempting to obtain services by deception, the Court of Appeal reducing his prison sentence from nine months to three months on appeal. For sentencing guidelines for offences of deception generally, see **B5.25**. For sentencing guidelines for theft offences, see **B4.5** to **B4.8**.

Relationship with Other Offences

The TA 1978, s. 1, together with s. 2 and (less directly) s. 3 of the 1978 Act, replaced **B5.55** s. 16(2)(a) of the TA 1968, which had been described as 'a judicial nightmare' (*Royle* [1971] 1 WLR 1764 per Edmund Davies LJ).

There is some overlap between this provision and other deception offences. In particular, an obtaining of services might also result in the execution of a valuable security or the obtaining of an unauthorised overdraft, and the same deception could be responsible for both. There will be some circumstances in which an obtaining of property might also be described as an obtaining of services, as where goods are obtained on hire-purchase or some kind of leasing arrangement (*Widdowson* (1985) 82 Cr App R 314).

Deception, Dishonesty and Obtaining

'Deception' in the TA 1978, s. 1, bears the same meaning as in the TA 1968, s. 15, and **B5.56** other deception offences (TA 1978, s. 5(1)), and the concept of dishonesty is likewise identical. For discussion of these concepts, see **B5.2** to **B5.13**. It would seem from the TA 1978, s. 1(2), that, in contrast to the offences under the 1968 Act, the person from whom the services are obtained must himself be a victim of the deception; he must be 'induced' to provide them, and this presumably means induced by the deception. As far as the obtaining is concerned, there is no mention in s. 1(2) of 'obtaining for another or enabling another to obtain' (contrast s. 15(2) of the 1968 Act and s. 2(4) of the 1978 Act) but in *Nathan* [1997] Crim LR 835 the Court of Appeal could see no justification for restricting the ambit of the offence so as to exclude such conduct. Nor need the deception relate to the prospect of payment (*Naviede* [1997] Crim LR 662).

Meaning of 'Services'

B5.57   The TA 1978, s. 1(2), defines 'services' in terms of benefits (which would include accommodation, travel, education, medical care etc.), but excludes benefits which are provided gratuitously. In *Halai* [1983] Crim LR 624, the Court of Appeal held that a building society had not provided services merely by allowing the accused to open a savings account because building societies do not charge any fees for such accounts. The position would be different if the accused practices his deception in order to open a current account with a bank which charges for services provided to such accounts (*Shortland* [1995] Crim LR 893). It was also held in *Halai* that a mortgage advance falls outside the definition of 'services', but this ruling was widely criticised and has been abrogated (in respect of matters occurring on or after 18 December 1996) by the TA 1978, s. 1(3), which was inserted by the Theft (Amendment) Act 1996, s. 4, in response to such criticism. Even in respect of matters occurring before that date, it has been held on several occasions that *Halai* should no longer be followed (see *Graham* [1997] 1 Cr App R 302; *Cooke* [1997] Crim LR 436 and *Cummings-John* [1997] Crim LR 660). In *Naviede* [1997] Crim LR 662, the Court of Appeal preferred to distinguish *Halai* on the basis that the case before them involved the dishonest obtaining of revolving credit facilities, whilst *Halai* concerned a mortgage, but their lordships nevertheless indicated that they would have refused to follow *Halai* in any event.

If one person deceives another into providing free benefits which the other would normally have charged for then there can be no offence under the TA 1978, s. 1, though there may be an offence under s. 2(1)(c).

A typical offence under the TA 1978, s. 1, will involve the accused deceiving someone into thinking that the accused would pay him for the benefit provided, when the accused had no intention of so paying. However, an offence may be committed under this section involving a deception that has nothing to do with intent to pay. If the service is only available to qualified persons, or is available to some at a lower price than others, then a deception as to status may be sufficient. (See *Adams* [1993] Crim LR 525.) If a person claims to be a paid-up member of a club, and thus entitled to use club facilities free of further charge, the club may thereby be deceived into providing a benefit on the understanding that it *has been* paid for (via the membership fee).

EVASION OF LIABILITY BY DECEPTION

Definition

B5.58   **Theft Act 1978, s. 2**

    (1)   Subject to subsection (2) below, where a person by any deception—
      (a)   dishonestly secures the remission of the whole or part of any existing liability to make a payment, whether his own liability or another's; or
      (b)   with intent to make permanent default in whole or in part on any existing liability to make a payment, or with intent to let another do so, dishonestly induces the creditor or any person claiming payment on behalf of the creditor to wait for payment (whether or not the due date for payment is deferred) or to forgo payment; or

(c)   dishonestly obtains any exemption from or abatement of liability to make a payment;

he shall be guilty of an offence.

(2)   For purposes of this section 'liability' means legally enforceable liability; and subsection (1) shall not apply in relation to a liability that has not been accepted or established to pay compensation for a wrongful act or omission.

(3)   For purposes of subsection (1)(b) a person induced to take in payment a cheque or other security for money by way of conditional satisfaction of a pre-existing liability is to be treated not as being paid but as being induced to wait for payment.

(4)   For purposes of subsection (1)(c) 'obtains' includes obtaining for another or enabling another to obtain.

'Deception' in the TA 1978, s. 2, bears the same meaning as in the TA 1968, s. 15, and other deception offences (TA 1978, s. 5(1)), and the concept of dishonesty is likewise identical. For discussion of these concepts, see **B5.2** to **B5.13**.

Procedure and Jurisdiction

The offences are triable either way (TA 1978, s. 4(1)). When tried on indictment they **B5.59** are class 4 offences. These are Group A offences for jurisdiction purposes of the CJA 1993, part I (see **D1.75**). For the provisions of *Practice Note (Mode of Trial: Guidelines)* (1995) relating to fraud generally, see **B5.24**.

For the liability of officers of a company for an offence committed by the company, see the TA 1968, s. 18 (which is applied to the TA 1978, s. 2, by s. 5(1) of the 1978 Act), and **B5.67**.

Indictment

Statement of Offence   B5.60

Evasion of liability by deception contrary to section 2(1)(a) of the Theft Act 1978

Particulars of Offence

A on or about the . . . day of . . . dishonestly secured the remission of the whole of an existing liability to make a payment to V for a quantity of petrol, by deception, namely by falsely representing to the said V that he (A) was then entitled to use a credit card issued by the X Oil Company and that V would receive payment for the said petrol from the X Oil Company

Sentence

The maximum penalty is five years (TA 1978, s. 4(2)(a)) on indictment; six months, a **B5.61** fine not exceeding the statutory maximum, or both, summarily. There is no guideline judgment reported for an offence under the TA 1978, s. 2. For sentencing guidelines for offences of deception generally, see **B5.26**. For sentencing guidelines for theft offences, see **B4.5** to **B4.8**.

Relationship with Other Offences

Whereas the TA 1978, s. 1, penalises the dishonest obtaining of services, this provision **B5.62** generally confines itself to the dishonest evasion of a pre-existing liability to pay for something. There is nevertheless some degree of overlap between s. 1 and s. 2(1)(c), either or both of which could apply where a person dishonestly deceives another into providing him with some benefit at a reduced price. Further overlaps exist between the three distinct offences created by paragraphs (a) to (c) of s. 2(1). See *Sibartie* [1983] Crim LR 470.

There may be some overlap between offences under s. 2 and the offence of making off without payment under s. 3 of the 1978 Act (see **B5.68** to **B5.75**), for example, where a person tricks another into waiting for him to 'fetch his cheque-book from the car' and then simply drives off (cf. *DPP* v *Ray* [1974] AC 370).

What if a person deceives another into taking a worthless cheque, and then makes off? It could be argued that he has not 'made payment as required', so that an offence under s. 3 has been committed; but on such facts s. 2(1)(b) provides the more obvious charge and also avoids arguments about whether 'making off' necessarily involves leaving without the consent of the person to whom the payment is owed (see *Hammond* [1982] Crim LR 611).

Liability to Make a Payment

B5.63   The concept of a liability to make a payment is common to all three offences under the TA 1978, s. 2(1), and is explained in s. 2(2). It must in every case be a liability which is legally enforceable. It is possible to commit an offence under the TA 1978, s. 1, or the TA 1968, s. 16(2)(c), by deceiving someone into providing a service or accepting a bet under an unlawful or unenforceable contract, but one cannot commit an offence under the TA 1978, s. 2, by practising a deception in order to avoid paying an unenforceable debt, nor can it be an offence under s. 2(1)(c) to obtain an unlawful service free of the usual charge. In contrast, the fact that liability may be enforceable only when a court order has been obtained does not prevent it from being an existing liability for the purposes of s. 2(1) (*Modupe* [1991] Crim LR 530).

Special provision is made in the TA 1978, s. 2(2), for liabilities arising out of allegedly wrongful acts or omissions. The subsection provides that it can be an offence to evade such a liability only if the liability has been accepted or established. There are doubtless good policy reasons for excluding cases in which the existence of liability is still disputed, but the effect of this rule may be surprising. Thus, a person would commit no offence under the TA 1978 by brazenly denying responsibility for damage he knows he has caused to another's property, but he will risk prosecution if he admits causing the damage but gives a false name and address 'to which the bill may be sent'. It is submitted that if there is an informal admission of liability which is later retracted then liability can no longer be treated as having been accepted or established.

Securing Remission of an Existing Liability

B5.64   'Remission' means release. The offence under the TA 1978, s. 2(1)(a), is therefore committed where a person has deceived another into releasing him (or a third party) from all or part of an existing liability to pay. It is not committed where another is deceived into thinking that no liability exists, nor where he is deceived into extending the deadline for payment (though there may then be an offence under s. 2(1)(b)).

The Court of Appeal held in *Jackson* [1983] Crim LR 617 that the accused was properly convicted of an offence under s. 2(1)(a) where he had induced another to accept a stolen credit card in payment for petrol previously supplied. The other's acceptance of the card meant that he would henceforward look to the card issuer for payment.

The position is arguably similar where a person, by deception, dishonestly induces another person to accept a cheque in payment of a liability, even if the cheque is not backed by a guarantee card. The TA 1978, s. 2(3), which provides that, for the purposes of s. 2(1)(b), inducing someone to accept payment by cheque constitutes an inducement to wait for payment, is not applicable to the offence under s. 2(1)(a), and a person who takes a cheque in such circumstances takes it in substitution (albeit conditional substitution) for payment in cash. Having accepted it, he cannot ordinarily sue for the debt without making any effort to present the cheque for payment. In the event of dishonour, he could choose to sue either on the cheque or for the original debt; but even though the remission of the debt is thus conditional (*Gunn v Bolckow, Vaughan & Co.* (1875) LR 10 Ch App 491), it could still be within the scope of s. 2(1)(a), which says nothing about remission having to be unconditional.

Nevertheless, it would be better to rely on s. 2(1)(b) in any case where it can be proved that the accused passed a worthless cheque with intent to make permanent default in payment. It is in cases where the accused was only stalling for time that the point becomes significant.

Inducement of a creditor to accept less than the full amount of a debt in full satisfaction of the debt may be more problematic because, unless the creditor gives a deed of release or joins with other creditors in agreeing to a compromise, the balance of the debt may still be sued for, there being no valid consideration for the release (*D & C Builders Ltd* v *Rees* [1966] 2 QB 617). So it would seem there has not been a remission of liability within s. 2(1)(a). A better charge would be one brought under s. 2(1)(b), assuming that an intent to make permanent default can be proved.

Inducing a Creditor to Wait for or Forgo Payment

The TA 1978, s. 2(3), applies to the offence under s. 2(1)(b). The need to prove an **B5.65** intent to make permanent default distinguishes s. 2(1)(b) from the other two s. 2 offences, but in other respects it is wider than the others, since the creditor or his agents need not grant either exemption from or remission of any liability to pay. It will suffice if they are deceived into doing without payment, either permanently or (as they imagine) temporarily (for example, if a person falsely tells a creditor that he has no money on him, and the creditor has no choice but to wait). If the deceiver is indeed granted remission of or exemption from an existing liability, this may also involve the creditor forgoing payment, and the deceiver may also be guilty of an offence under s. 2(1)(b) (*Holt* [1981] 1 WLR 1000). Note that the deception must be practised against the creditor or some person claiming payment on his behalf (*Gee* [1999] Crim LR 397).

As to the meaning of the words, 'or with intent to let another do so; see *Attewell-Hughes* [1991] 1 WLR 955.

Obtaining Exemption from or Abatement of Liability

Exemption from liability under the TA 1978, s. 2(1)(c), includes exemption from either **B5.66** an existing or a freshly created liability (*Firth* (1989) 91 Cr App R 217). In this respect its scope is wider than that of the other s. 2 offences. In *Sibartie* [1983] Crim LR 470 it was held that the offence could be committed through use of an invalid season ticket. Most commentators have taken the view that this was overextending the meaning of s. 2(1)(c) and that a better charge would have been one under s. 2(1)(b), but *Sibartie* perhaps indicates that the judges prefer not to draw too rigid a distinction between the different s. 2 offences.

LIABILITY OF COMPANY OFFICERS FOR OFFENCES OF DECEPTION COMMITTED BY THE COMPANY

Theft Act 1968, s. 18   **B5.67**

(1)   Where an offence committed by a body corporate under section 15, 16 or 17 of this Act is proved to have been committed with the consent or connivance of any director, manager, secretary or other similar officer of the body corporate, or any person who was purporting to act in any such capacity, he as well as the body corporate shall be guilty of that offence, and shall be liable to be proceeded against and punished accordingly.

(2)   Where the affairs of a body corporate are managed by its members, this section shall apply in relation to the acts and defaults of a member in connection with his functions of management as if he were a director of the body corporate.

The TA 1978, s. 5(1), applies this provision to offences under ss. 1 and 2 of the TA 1978. Section 18 is nevertheless a provision of limited scope and importance.

As to the limitations on the scope of s. 18, see the discussion of *Boal* [1992] 1 QB 591 at **A5.11**. As to the limitations on the importance of s. 18, offences to which it applies can only be committed by corporations if the persons who control them possess the requisite *mens rea*, which can then be imputed to the corporation. Such persons will necessarily be guilty as joint perpetrators or as accessories under the general law governing complicity in offences, without any need for reference to s. 18. Any junior manager or officer who knowingly assists in the commission of such an offence by his company will similarly incur secondary liability.

This leaves s. 18 with one significant function. It may apply to senior officers or directors who knowingly consent to the commission of relevant offences, without themselves doing any acts that could result in liability as accessories under the general law (see further **A5.11**).

MAKING OFF WITHOUT PAYMENT

Definition

B5.68   **Theft Act 1978, s. 3**

> (1)   Subject to subsection (3) below, a person who, knowing that payment on the spot for any goods supplied or service done is required or expected from him, dishonestly makes off without having paid as required or expected and with intent to avoid payment of the amount due shall be guilty of an offence.
> (2)   For purposes of this section 'payment on the spot' includes payment at the time of collecting goods on which work has been done or in respect of which service has been provided.
> (3)   Subsection (1) above shall not apply where the supply of the goods or the doing of the service is contrary to law, or where the service done is such that payment is not legally enforceable.
> (4)   Any person may arrest without warrant anyone who is, or whom he, with reasonable cause, suspects to be, committing or attempting to commit an offence under this section.

Procedure

B5.69 Making off without payment is triable either way (TA 1978, s. 4(1)). When tried on indictment it is a class 4 offence. For the provisions of *Practice Note (Mode of Trial: Guidelines)* (1995) relating to fraud generally, see **B5.24**.

Indictment

B5.70   Statement of Offence

Making off without payment contrary to section 3(1) of the Theft Act 1978

Particulars of Offence

A on or about the . . . day of . . . , knowing that payment on the spot of £. . . was required of him for petrol supplied to him by V, dishonestly made off without having paid the amount due as so required and with intent to avoid payment thereof

Sentence

B5.71 The maximum penalty is two years (TA 1978, s. 4(2)(b)) on indictment; six months, a fine not exceeding the statutory maximum, or both, summarily. There is no guideline judgment reported for an offence under the TA 1978, s. 3, when tried on indictment. For sentencing guidelines for offences of deception generally, see **B5.26**. For sentencing guidelines for theft offences, see **B4.5** to **B4.8**.

When dealt with summarily, the Magistrates' Association Guidelines (1997) indicate the following:

Aggravating Factors ⊕
For example deliberate plan; high value, two or more involved; victim particularly vulnerable; offence committed on bail; previous convictions and failures to respond to previous sentences, if relevant.

Mitigating Factors ⊖
For example impulsive; low value.

Guideline: Is compensation, discharge or fine appropriate?

The guideline fine is £90 (low income), £225 (average income) or £540 (high income).

In *Foster* (1994) 15 Cr App R (S) 340 the Court of Appeal upheld a sentence of three months' imprisonment on an offender convicted of four counts of making off without payment. He had engaged taxis to take him on trips resulting in fares between £37 and £63 and had disappeared without paying. The offences were planned, and the offender was at the time subject to a suspended sentence of nine months imposed for offences of conspiracy to burgle and theft. That sentence was activated consecutively, making 12 months' imprisonment in all.

Overlap with Other Offences under the Theft Acts 1968 and 1978

A possible overlap between making off without payment and evasion of a liability by **B5.72** deception is considered at **B5.62**. Because of the relative ease with which the offence of making off without payment can be proved, it may be charged in circumstances where a more serious charge of theft or of obtaining etc. might otherwise have been pressed. If, for example, it is clear that the accused dishonestly made off without paying for his meal, or for the petrol which has been put into his car's tank, the TA 1978, s. 3, provides the obvious charge. It may be that the accused never intended to pay, and therefore committed theft or an offence under the TA 1968, s. 15, but this will be far harder to prove in the absence of a confession or other evidence of the accused's state of mind at the time of the original obtaining.

Payment on the Spot for Goods Supplied or Service Done

The phrase 'payment on the spot' used in the TA 1978, s. 3(1) is partially explained in **B5.73** s. 3(2). The 'spot' in question is the place where payment is required etc., and this will usually be the premises where the transaction takes place, but it may sometimes mean something narrower (see **B5.74**).

Under the TA 1978, s. 5(2), 'goods' in s. 3(1) is to be interpreted in accordance with the TA 1968, s. 34(2)(b), and it can be assumed that 'service' bears the same meaning as in s. 1 of the 1978 Act (see **B5.57**).

The required payment must be one which is legally enforceable (TA 1978, s. 3(3)). It is possible to commit an offence of obtaining property or services by deception by tricking another person into entering into a legally unenforceable transaction; but the evasion of an unenforceable obligation, whether by deception or by making off, cannot be an offence.

Meaning of 'Making Off'

In *Brooks* (1982) 76 Cr App R 66, the Court of Appeal said that the words 'dishonestly **B5.74** makes off' are easily understandable by a jury, and in the majority of cases require no elaboration in a summing-up. If, however, a person who should pay for goods or a service uses deception as a result of which the person to whom payment is due allows him to leave, it may be doubted whether this is properly called 'making off'. A charge of evading liability by deception may be more appropriate here. See *Hammond* [1982] Crim LR 611.

'Making off' ordinarily means leaving the place or premises concerned, so that if a person who is leaving premises without paying is stopped at the exit he will usually have committed only an attempt to commit this offence (*McDavitt* [1981] Crim LR 843), but this must largely be a question of fact. If, for example, the accused ran away from the top-floor restaurant in a department store, without paying for his meal at the counter, and was caught on the ground floor before leaving the building, there can be little doubt that he has made off within the meaning of the section (cf. *Brooks* (1982) 76 Cr App R 66). A person who gets out of a taxi and dishonestly disappears into the night without paying has clearly committed the offence; the 'spot' is where the taxi is standing after the journey. If a passenger travels on a public transport system without a ticket and dishonestly makes off when required to produce one, it will be no defence to argue that payment should have been made before the journey began (*Moberley* v *Alsop* (1991) 156 JP 514); an honest passenger inadvertently travelling without a ticket would of course be expected to pay during or after the journey. See also *Aziz* [1993] Crim LR 708.

Mens Rea: Dishonesty and Intent to Avoid Payment

B5.75 On a charge of making off without payment the prosecution must prove that the accused intended to make permanent default (*Allen* [1985] AC 1029). If the accused made off, but intended to pay later, or knew he would have to do so (because the person to whom payment was due knew his address), he will not be guilty.

As to the meaning of 'dishonesty', see *Ghosh* [1982] QB 1053 and **B4.38**. The issue of dishonesty may arise where the accused walked out of a restaurant in protest at poor service or poor food. If he considered himself to be acting reasonably, and thought that ordinary honest people would agree, then he should not be considered dishonest.

SUPPRESSION OF DOCUMENTS

Definition

B5.76 **Theft Act 1968, s. 20**

(1)   A person who dishonestly, with a view to gain for himself or another or with intent to cause loss to another, destroys, defaces or conceals any valuable security, any will or other testamentary document or any original document of or belonging to, or filed or deposited in, any court of justice or any government department shall on conviction on indictment be liable to imprisonment for a term not exceeding seven years.

Procedure

B5.77 Suppression of documents is triable either way (TA 1978, s. 4(1)). When tried on indictment it is a class 4 offence. For the provisions of *Practice Note* (*Mode of Trial: Guidelines*) (1995) relating to fraud generally, see **B5.24**.

Indictment

B5.78 Statement of Offence

Destroying a valuable security contrary to section 20(1) of the Theft Act 1968

Particulars of Offence

A on or about the . . . day of . . . , dishonestly and with a view to gain for himself, destroyed a deed of trust executed by V

Sentence

B5.79 The maximum penalty is seven years (TA 1968, s. 20(1)) on indictment; six months, a fine not exceeding the statutory maximum, or both, summarily. There is no guideline judgment reported for an offence under the TA 1968, s. 20(1). For sentencing guidelines for offences of deception generally, see **B5.26**. For sentencing guidelines for theft offences, see **B4.5** to **B4.8**.

Elements

The TA 1968, s. 20(1), is little used, perhaps because offences involving the destruction **B5.80** or concealment of wills etc. are difficult to detect. The defacing of such instruments may sometimes amount to forgery if intended to deceive, and destruction etc. might in many cases be charged as theft or criminal damage.

Most of the terms used in this provision have been discussed elsewhere. The meaning of 'dishonesty' is discussed in **B4.35** *et seq*. and **B5.13**. The definition of 'view to gain' etc. in s. 34(2)(a) is discussed at **B5.50**. 'Valuable security' is defined in s. 20(3) (see **B5.43** and **B5.49**).

BLACKMAIL

Definition

Theft Act 1968, s. 21   **B5.81**

(1) A person is guilty of blackmail if, with a view to gain for himself or another or with intent to cause loss to another, he makes any unwarranted demand with menaces; and for this purpose a demand with menaces is unwarranted unless the person making it does so in the belief—

(a) that he has reasonable grounds for making the demand; and

(b) that the use of the menaces is a proper means of reinforcing the demand.

(2) The nature of the act or omission demanded is immaterial, and it is also immaterial whether the menaces relate to action to be taken by the person making the demand.

(3) A person guilty of blackmail shall on conviction on indictment be liable to imprisonment for a term not exceeding 14 years.

Procedure and Jurisdiction

The offence is triable only on indictment (TA 1968, s. 21(3); MCA 1980, s. 17 and sch. **B5.82** 1, para. 28). It is a class 3 offence. It is a Group A offence for jurisdiction purposes under the CJA 1993, part I (see **D1.75**).

Indictment

Statement of Offence   **B5.83**

Blackmail contrary to section 21(1) of the Theft Act 1968

Particulars of Offence

A on or about the . . . day of . . . , with a view to gain for himself, made an unwarranted demand for £1,000 from V with menaces

Sentencing Guidelines

The maximum penalty is 14 years (TA 1968, s. 21(3)).   **B5.84**

In *Witchelo* (1992) 13 Cr App R (S) 371 the offender received a sentence of 13 years after conviction of six offences of blackmail. He had written to food producers and threatened to contaminate their products. Some food was contaminated, and the offender obtained £32,000. He received a further four years for related offences. See also *Telford* (1992) 13 Cr App R (S) 676, where eight years was appropriate and *Riolfo* [1997] 1 Cr App R (S) 57, where a sentence of six years was substituted.

Sentences of six years and five years were reduced to four years and three years in *Cox* (1979) 1 Cr App R (S) 190, where the offenders removed discs and tapes from their employer and demanded £275,000 as the price for returning them. Three years was said to be appropriate in *Stone* (1989) 11 Cr App R (S) 176, where the offender took part in homosexual activities with the victim and then demanded sums of money under the threat of disclosing the victim's behaviour to the police. See also *Hadjou* (1989) 11 Cr App R (S) 29 and *Hollingworth* (1994) 15 Cr App R (S) 258. In a 'wholly exceptional' case, where the claim which was made was on the fact of it warranted, but improper means were used to enforce the claim (threat to publish nude photographs of the victim) a sentence of six months' imprisonment, suspended for two years was imposed (*Helal* (1980) 2 Cr App R (S) 383). See also *West* (1985) 7 Cr App R (S) 46.

View to Gain or Intent to Cause Loss

B5.85   Demands reinforced by improper threats do not necessarily constitute blackmail, which can only be committed 'with a view to gain . . . or intent to cause loss' (TA 1968, s. 21(1)). The concepts of gain and loss are defined in s. 34(2)(a) of the Act (see **B5.50**) as extending only to gain or loss, temporary or permanent, in money or other property. 'Gain' includes keeping what one has; 'loss' includes not getting what one might have got; and it is certainly possible to commit blackmail by using improper menaces in the course of demanding money or other property to which one is legally entitled (*Lawrence* (1971) 57 Cr App R 64); but merely seeking sexual favours or political advantage is not blackmail, though procuring sexual intercourse by threats etc. may amount to an offence under the Sexual Offences Act 1956, s. 2 (see **B3.10** to **B3.14**), and may even amount to rape if the woman concerned is found to have submitted without genuinely consenting (see *Olugboja* [1982] QB 320 and **B3.7**).

A blackmailer need not be seeking any kind of material profit. In *Bevans* (1987) 87 Cr App R 64, the accused used menaces in order to obtain a pain-killing injection from a doctor; this was held to be blackmail as the drug involved was a form of property.

Meaning of 'Making a Demand'

B5.86   The definition of the offence of blackmail in the TA 1968, s. 21, is deliberately drafted in such a way as to penalise the making of the demand, rather than the obtaining of property or the intimidation of the victim. In other words, it is a 'conduct crime', in which the effectiveness of the accused's behaviour is irrelevant (whether for jurisdictional or any other purpose), and in which the results thereof form no constituent part of the offence.

'Demands' are not defined in the Act. Earlier authorities established that a demand need not be expressed openly. As was pointed out in *Studer* (1915) 85 LJ KB 1017, 'it may be in language only a request'; and indeed it need not even be that, if the context makes the blackmailer's meaning clear. The kidnapper who writes to the child's parents, asking them whether they regard the child as being worth £10,000, would clearly be regarded as having 'demanded' that sum. Similarly, there would be a demand where a man offers to sell a victim his 'protection' whilst his friends demonstrate their willingness to wreck the victim's premises in the event of the offer being declined (*Colister* (1955) 39 Cr App R 100).

The earlier authorities did not provide any definite answer to the question whether a demand could be 'made' without successful communication to the intended recipient; but the question came before the House of Lords in *Treacy* v *DPP* [1971] AC 537, where the accused had posted his blackmail demand from England to a victim in West Germany. If receipt of the demand was regarded as an essential part of its 'making' then the blackmail would have been completed (and thus committed, for jurisdictional purposes) in West Germany, beyond the territorial ambit of the TA 1968; but it was held that the demand was made earlier, and within the jurisdiction, when the letter was posted.

Since *Treacy* thus relegates communication of the demand to a non-essential element in the offence, it is not clear whether the receipt of a demand by a victim in England renders an overseas blackmailer liable to conviction under English law. The point was left open in *Treacy*, although it was suggested that the concept of a 'continuing demand' might possibly be a basis for claiming jurisdiction, and it appears (quite inadvertently) to have been left open under the CJA 1993, part I (see **D1.75**). Section 4(b) of that Act provides that there is a communication of a demand within the jurisdiction if it is sent from England or Wales to a place elsewhere, or sent from elsewhere to a place in England or Wales. Section 2(1) provides that a person may be guilty of a Group A offence, such as blackmail, if any 'relevant event' occurs in England or Wales. Relevant events are defined in s. 2(2) as events which must be proved as essential ingredients in the offence concerned; but communication of a blackmail demand is not, according to *Treacy* such an event.

Attempted Blackmail

B5.87 It follows from the way blackmail is defined that offences of attempted blackmail must be unlikely occurrences. One could perhaps have such an offence where a telephone call is cut off just as the caller is starting to present his demand, or where a letter containing demands is seized just as the demander is about to post it; but in other circumstances it would seem that either the full offence is committed or only preparatory acts, which would not suffice for liability under the Criminal Attempts Act 1981.

Meaning of 'Menaces'

B5.88 In drafting the proposals which later became incorporated into the TA 1968, s. 21, the Criminal Law Revision Committee adopted the term 'menaces' in preference to 'threats', on the basis that the latter term might possibly be too wide. As the Court of Appeal later said in *Clear* [1968] 1 QB 670:

> Words or conduct which would not intimidate or influence anyone to respond to the demand would not be menaces . . . , but threats and conduct of such a nature and extent that the mind of an ordinary person of normal stability and courage might be influenced or made apprehensive so as to accede unwillingly to the demand would be sufficient for a jury's consideration.

Menaces are therefore serious or significant threats; but since blackmail cases rarely involve any dispute about whether the alleged threats, if proved, were serious, there is generally no need for a trial judge to define the term for the jury. (See *Lawrence* (1971) 57 Cr App R 64; and *Garwood* [1987] 1 WLR 319, in which it was said, somewhat questionably, that the term 'menaces' is an ordinary English word which any jury can be expected to understand.)

Nevertheless, there are at least two situations in which it is recognised that the jury may need guidance:

(a)   A threat which one person would find trivial may be one which another would find terrifying. Some people are more timid than others, and fear is not always rational, even in people who may otherwise be very brave. If a demander knows that his victim suffers from arachnophobia, his threat to drop a large spider down the victim's back would obviously be calculated to have at least the same impact as a threat of serious violence. In *Garwood* [1987] 1 WLR 319, it was recognised that the victim's 'unusual timidity' could be taken into account, provided the accused knew of it; and it is submitted that it should suffice if the accused merely hoped to discover such weakness (for example, where he mistakenly believed the victim suffers from such a phobia).

(b)   In the converse situation, where an apparently serious threat failed to intimidate the victim at all (perhaps because he knew something the blackmailer did not), the jury should be told that liability may still be incurred (*Clear* [1968] 1 QB 670).

Meaning of 'Unwarranted Demands'

B5.89 A demand with menaces will be unwarranted unless the demander genuinely believes both that he has reasonable grounds for making the demand, and that it is proper to reinforce it with those particular menaces. Note that he need not have reasonable grounds for his belief: it is a subjective test of what he thinks is reasonable and proper. Once the issue is raised, the prosecution will have the burden of proving that the accused had no such belief.

A menace may be considered improper without necessarily being a threat to do anything improper. Publicising a person's scandalous behaviour may in itself be perfectly legitimate: threatening him with such publicity in order to extract money from him would clearly be a classic case of blackmail.

In *Harvey* (1980) 72 Cr App R 139, the Court of Appeal stated that one cannot believe a threat to be proper if one knows it would be unlawful (i.e. criminal) to carry it out. This seemingly conflicts with the later pronouncement of the Court of Appeal in *Cousins* [1982] QB 526 that a threat to kill might sometimes be lawful where the killing threatened would not be; but the dicta in *Harvey* clearly indicate a link between legality and propriety. A fanatic might believe that he would be *justified* in killing or threatening to kill for the sake of his cause, but it seems that he cannot argue that he believes such threats to be *proper* when he knows that what he threatens would be criminal (*Harvey* (1980) 72 Cr App R 139 at p. 142).

In this respect, blackmail can be contrasted with robbery. A person who takes back property borrowed from him by another, believing that he is entitled to recover the property, cannot be guilty of stealing it, and thus cannot be guilty of robbery if he threatens violence in order to recover it; but since he can hardly believe his threats of violence are proper, he will almost certainly be guilty of blackmail (*Lawrence* (1971) 57 Cr App R 64; *Harvey* (1980) 72 Cr App R 139).

HARASSMENT OF DEBTORS

B5.90   ### Administration of Justice Act 1970, s. 40

(1)   A person commits an offence if, with the object of coercing another person to pay money claimed from the other as a debt due under a contract, he—

(a)   harasses the other with demands for payment which, in respect of their frequency or the manner or occasion of making any such demand, or of any threat or publicity by which any demand is accompanied, are calculated to subject him or members of his family or household to alarm, distress or humiliation;

(b)   falsely represents, in relation to the money claimed, that criminal proceedings lie for failure to pay it;

(c)   falsely represents himself to be authorised in some official capacity to claim or enforce payment; or

(d)   utters a document falsely represented by him to have some official character or purporting to have some official character which he knows it has not.

(2)   A person may be guilty of an offence by virtue of subsection (1)(a) above if he concerts with others in the taking of such action as is described in that paragraph, notwithstanding that his own course of conduct does not by itself amount to harassment.

(3)   Subsection (1)(a) above does not apply to anything done by a person which is reasonable (and otherwise permissible in law) for the purpose—

(a)   of securing the discharge of an obligation due, or believed by him to be due, to himself or to persons for whom he acts, or protecting himself or them from future loss; or

(b)   of the enforcement of any liability by legal process.

(4)   A person guilty of an offence under this section shall be liable on summary conviction to a fine of not more than level 5 on the standard scale.

The overlap between this summary offence and blackmail is clearly significant. If a person acts for the purpose of coercing another person into paying money, he necessarily acts 'with a view to gain', and some at least of the tactics proscribed by paras (a) to (d) of the Administration of Justice Act 1970, s. 40(1), could well amount to the use of menaces. The most significant distinction between the two offences (insofar as they both apply to debt-collection) is that a threatener's beliefs about the propriety of his threats may be crucial in a blackmail prosecution, but largely irrelevant on a charge of harassment.

OTHER OFFENCES INVOLVING THREATS OR DEMANDS

The use of threats to procure sexual intercourse with a woman is considered at **B3.10** **B5.91** to **B3.14**. Threats to kill, whether or not amounting to blackmail, may be punishable under the OAPA 1861, s. 16 (see **B1.94** to **B1.98**. Threats of immediate violence may be punished as assault (see **B2.1** to **B2.9**) or under the Public Order Act 1986; and if done for the purposes of theft may amount to robbery or assault with intent to rob (see **B4.47** *et seq*.). Threats to damage property may be covered by the Criminal Damage Act 1971, s. 2 (see **B8.25** to **B8.29**). Threats of violence for the purpose of securing entry to premises may be covered by the Criminal Law Act 1977, s. 6(1) (see **B13.22** to **B13.28**). The Criminal Law Act 1977, s. 51, deals with bomb hoaxes (see **B11.104** *et seq*.), which may or may not be made with a view to gain etc. Contamination of goods (often connected with blackmail of the manufacturers or suppliers) is punishable under the Public Order Act 1986, s. 38 (see **B11.109** *et seq*.).

The demanding of payment for unsolicited goods may be an offence under the Unsolicited Goods and Services Act 1972, s. 2(1), and if supported by threats, it may be a more serious (but still only summary) offence under s. 2(2) of the Act.

Sending threatening letters is covered by the Malicious Communications Act 1988, s. 1 (see **B19.41**). As to the offences under the Protection from Harassment Act 1997, see **B11.77** *et seq*.

SECTION B6: FALSIFICATION, FORGERY AND COUNTERFEITING

FALSIFICATION

Falsity and Deception

B6.1 Where false representations or deceptions are successfully used in order to obtain property, services or financial advantages, charges under ss. 15, 16 or 20(2) of the TA 1968 or ss. 1 or 2 of the TA 1978 will usually be appropriate. These are considered in **B5**. If the intended deception proves ineffective, it may be that a charge of attempt could still succeed; but in many cases the prosecution might be better advised to consider alternative charges based on the making of false or misleading statements, or on the making or use of false instruments or falsified records.

Apart from the obvious consideration that they are 'conduct crimes', which may be committed without necessarily resulting in either deception or the obtaining of any advantage, these offences usually differ from true deception offences in terms of *mens rea*. Dishonesty remains a requisite element in offences under the TA 1968, s. 17, but is not strictly required in most other cases; and there are some relevant offences for which no true *mens rea* need be proved at all. Most offences under the Trade Descriptions Act 1968 come within this category. If a car dealer offers to sell a vehicle which has a falsified odometer reading, this may, without more, involve prima facie liability under the Trade Descriptions Act 1968, s. 1. In contrast, a charge under the TA 1968, s. 15, would require proof of the accused's dishonesty, and of his knowledge or recklessness as to the falsity of the odometer reading. Without this, the accused could not even be convicted of an attempted s. 15 offence. The full s. 15 offence would additionally require proof that a buyer was deceived and that he was influenced by the deception when buying. For these reasons, it may sometimes be better to charge an offence under the Trade Descriptions Act 1968 (see **B6.99** *et seq.*) rather than the TA 1968, even where there is some evidence of fraud.

Falsification, False Statements and False Instruments

B6.2 The concept of falsity, as applied to documents or instruments, is not always the same as that of falsity in statements. A lie is a false statement, but documents containing lies or false statements are not always regarded as false instruments.

As far as offences under the Forgery and Counterfeiting Act 1981 are concerned, an instrument is only false if it purports to be something it is not, or if it 'tells a lie' about its own authorship, origins or history. Conversely, such an instrument might be false in one or more of those respects, despite being a true and accurate statement of the matters with which it deals (as where an exact copy of a genuine document purports to be the original). See further, s. 9 of the Act (see **B6.23** to **B6.26**), which provides an exhaustive definition of falsity for those purposes.

For most purposes a document is not regarded as 'falsified' unless it has been fraudulently altered or interfered with. Such a document will usually be rendered 'false' for the purposes of the Forgery and Counterfeiting Act 1981, even if falsified by the same person who made it in the first place (see s. 9(1)(g) of the Act); but the concept of falsification would not necessarily extend to the inclusion of false statements in an original document or record. For example, the offence of falsification by a bankrupt of his papers (Insolvency Act 1986, s. 355(2)(b)) would not be committed where the bankrupt merely enters incorrect details when drawing up his accounts; the correct charge would be one of making false entries, contrary to s. 355(2)(c) (see **B7.76**).

There are few decided cases on the meaning of 'falsification', but the issue arose in *Edwards* v *Toombs* [1983] Crim LR 43, where it was held that an act which interferes with a mechanical (or presumably electronic) recording device (in that case a turnstile meter at a soccer stadium) can amount to falsification of the record, for the purpose of liability under the TA 1968, s. 17(1)(a).

Falsification is 'deemed' to bear a further meaning in the TA 1968, s. 17, by virtue of s. 17(2), but this has no wider application, and is therefore dealt with in the analysis of that provision at **B6.10** and **B6.11**.

FALSE ACCOUNTING

Definition

Theft Act 1968, s. 17   **B6.3**

(1) Where a person dishonestly, with a view to gain for himself or another or with intent to cause loss to another,—

(a) destroys, defaces, conceals or falsifies any account or any record or document made or required for any accounting purpose; or

(b) in furnishing information for any purpose produces or makes use of any account, or any such record or document as aforesaid, which to his knowledge is or may be misleading, false or deceptive in a material particular;

he shall, on conviction on indictment, be liable to imprisonment for a term not exceeding seven years.

(2) For purposes of this section a person who makes or concurs in making in an account or other document an entry which is or may be misleading, false or deceptive in a material particular, or who omits or concurs in omitting a material particular from an account or other document, is to be treated as falsifying the account or document.

Procedure and Jurisdiction

The offence is triable either way (MCA 1980, s. 17 and sch. 1, para. 28). When tried on **B6.4** indictment it is a class 4 offence. It is a Group A offence for jurisdiction purposes under the CJA 1993, part I (see **D1.75**). For the provisions of *Practice Note (Mode of Trial: Guidelines)* (1995) relating to fraud generally, see **B5.24**.

For the liability of officers of a company for an offence committed by the company, see the TA 1968, s. 18, **B5.67** and **A5.11**.

Indictment

Statement of Offence   **B6.5**

False accounting contrary to section 17(1)(a) of the Theft Act 1968

Particulars of Offence

A on or about the . . . day of . . . dishonestly and with a view to gain for himself [or for X] [or with intent to cause loss to Y] falsified a document required for an accounting purpose, namely a ledger, by making therein an entry which was misleading, false or deceptive in a material particular in that it falsely purported to show that A had received the sum of £10,000 from Z in payment for services rendered

Statement of Offence

Furnishing false information contrary to section 17(1)(b) of the Theft Act 1968

Particulars of Offence

A on or about the . . . day of . . . dishonestly and with a view to gain for himself, in furnishing information to Q for accounting purposes, produced to the said Q a ledger, knowing that an entry therein, namely an entry purporting to show that A had received the sum of £10,000 from Z in payment for services rendered, was misleading, false or deceptive in a material particular, namely in falsely purporting to show that A had received the said sum from Z

Sentence

B6.6 The maximum penalty is seven years (TA 1968, s. 17(1)) on indictment; six months, a fine not exceeding the statutory maximum, or both, summarily. There is no guideline judgment reported for an offence under the TA 1968, s. 17(1), but in *Smith* (1994) 15 Cr App R (S) 145 30 months' imprisonment was upheld for false accounting, where the offender had obtained a book of Inland Revenue vouchers, and used them falsely so as to cause a loss to the Revenue of £50,000. For sentencing guidelines for offences of deception generally, see **B5.26**. For sentencing guidelines for theft offences, see **B4.5** to **B4.8**.

Scope of Offence

B6.7 The TA 1968, s. 17, creates two distinct offences: destruction, concealment or falsification etc. (s. 17(1)(a)) and using false or misleading documents etc. in furnishing information (s. 17(1)(b)). The user of falsified accounts may well be the person who falsified them, but this is not necessarily so. A person does not, however, commit an offence under s. 17(1)(b) unless he knows of the misleading, false or deceptive nature of the documents in question. Section 17(2) seems incapable of applying to s. 17(1)(b) because it deals only with falsification — the subject-matter of s. 17(1)(a).

Relationship to Other Offences

B6.8 There is clearly a potential overlap between the falsification of accounts or records under the TA 1968, s. 17(1)(a), and the offence of forgery under the Forgery and Counterfeiting Act 1981, s. 1, and a similar overlap may occur between the TA 1968, s. 17(1)(b), and the offence of using a false instrument under s. 3 of the 1981 Act. Nevertheless it would be quite wrong to suggest that any case of false accounting must necessarily involve forgery (*Dodge* [1972] 1 QB 416). As explained in **B6.2**, the concept of falsity in the 1981 Act is a narrow one, and does not generally extend to the making of false or misleading entries when compiling a document, or to the destruction (as opposed to the falsification) of documents or records.

A further area of significant overlap involves documents relating to the affairs of companies or bankrupts. See Companies Act 1985, s. 450; Insolvency Act 1986, ss. 209 and 355(2) (see **B7.11**, **B7.49** and **B7.62**).

Cases of false accounting are often closely associated with various other offences under the TA 1968. The falsification or concealment may be a cover for past, contemporaneous or future offences under ss. 1 or 15 of the 1968 Act, and it is not unusual for an indictment to include counts for both false accounting and theft. In *Eden* (1971) 55 Cr App R 193, the Court of Appeal expressed the view that the inclusion of parallel counts of this kind should be discouraged if they would both stand or fall by the same evidence; but the inclusion of both counts was at the same time recognised as prudent in a situation where (as in *Eden* itself) theft might be harder to prove.

False accounting and theft are not always clearly distinguishable from each other. The courts appear prone at times to confuse the appropriation of money or choses in action (such as debts) with the falsification or misuse of documents or records relating to them. *Monaghan* [1979] Crim LR 673 is an example of this. The accused's dishonest failure to record a payment of £3.99 on the supermarket till she was operating, with a view to taking an equivalent sum from the till later in the day, was held to amount to theft, even though the cash was properly placed in the till, where it belonged, and even though the accused would no doubt have taken different notes and coins anyway. Even after *Gomez*

[1993] AC 442 (see **B4.25 *et seq*.**), the better view must be that she had done nothing more than falsify the till roll; but if *Monaghan* is indeed correct, the overlap between the TA 1968, s. 17, and theft must be very substantial.

Accounts, Records and Documents

The word 'account' must be given the meaning it bears in normal English usage **B6.9** (*Scot-Simmonds* [1994] Crim LR 933). A record or account need not necessarily be a document. In *Edwards* v *Toombs* [1983] Crim LR 43 it was held that a turnstile meter at a soccer stadium was a record, and thus within the scope of the section. See also *Solomons* [1909] 2 KB 980 (taximeter). Conversely, a document or record need not be an account, as long as it is made or required for an accounting purpose, either by the accused or by another person. This purpose need not be anything more than a secondary or incidental one; thus in *A-G's Ref (No. 1 of 1980)* [1981] 1 WLR 34 it was held that loan proposal forms, which would eventually be used by the loan company for an accounting purpose, could be the subject of an offence under the TA 1968, s. 17 (see also *Cummings-John* [1997] Crim LR 660). Whether a document is one required for an accounting purpose is a question of fact and will ordinarily need to be proved by the prosecution. See *Okanta* [1997] Crim LR 451, *Osinuga* v *DPP* [1998] Crim LR 216, *Sundhers* [1998] Crim LR 497 and *Manning* [1998] 2 Cr App R 461.

Extended Meaning of Falsification under Theft Act 1968, s. 17(2)

The TA 1968, s. 17(2), gives 'falsification' a specially extended meaning for the **B6.10** purposes of s. 17(1)(a). It clearly embraces the preparation of false accounts as well as the falsification of existing ones (*Scot-Simmonds* [1994] Crim LR 933). It does not, however, purport to provide an exhaustive definition of the concept, and it was held in *Edwards* v *Toombs* [1983] Crim LR 43 that anything amounting to falsification within the ordinary meaning of the term (see **B6.2**) would equally amount to falsification for s. 17 purposes.

Falsification by Omission

The TA 1968, s. 17(2), expressly provides that the omission of material information **B6.11** from a document etc. can have the effect of falsifying it. In *Shama* [1990] 1 WLR 661 the Court of Appeal upheld the conviction of a telephone operator who had failed even to start filling out standard forms provided by his employer for the recording of international calls. He was held to have falsified the forms by leaving them unmarked. A statement or record with material omissions may be misleading for purposes of s. 17(1)(b) even if it contains no outright lies; there is authority to the effect that such statements may also be regarded as being 'false in a material particular' (*Lord Kylsant* [1932] 1 KB 442) but it would not be necessary to rely thereon.

Meaning of 'Material'

Falsity etc. is not a basis of liability under the TA 1968, s. 17, unless it is falsity 'in a **B6.12** material particular'. The meaning of this concept was examined in *Mallett* [1978] 1 WLR 820, where the Court of Appeal rejected the argument that the falsity etc. must be material in the sense of being directly connected with the accuracy etc. of an accounting process. In *Mallett* the accused had furnished false information to a finance company concerning the status of a potential customer. The falsity was material to the company's decision to finance the transaction, and the form containing the false information was required for accounting purposes. It was held that the accused had been rightly convicted even though no accounts had been rendered inaccurate by his supply of false information.

Mens Rea

In false accounting there need be no proof of any intent to permanently deprive another **B6.13** person of his property. What is needed is dishonesty (in the *Ghosh* [1982] QB 1053 sense, see **B4.37**) coupled with a 'view to gain' or 'intent to cause loss'; and in *Eden* (1971) 55 Cr App R 193 it was said that this might involve nothing more than an intent to gain or avoid loss on a temporary basis, perhaps in order to play for time, whilst losses caused by honest incompetence are made good. In *Lee Cheung Wing* v *The Queen* [1992] Crim LR 440, falsified documents were used by securities dealers to mask withdrawals of unauthorised profits from accounts they had kept secret from their employers. The Privy Council held that the falsification of these documents had been made with a view to gain and constituted an offence under equivalent legislation in Hong Kong.

As to the meaning of 'gain' and 'loss', see the TA 1968, s. 34(2)(a), and *Golechha* [1989] 1 WLR 1050 (see **B5.50**).

FALSE STATEMENTS BY OFFICERS OF COMPANY OR ASSOCIATION

Definition

B6.14   **Theft Act 1968, s. 19**

(1)   Where an officer of a body corporate or unincorporated association (or person purporting to act as such), with intent to deceive members or creditors of the body corporate or association about its affairs, publishes or concurs in publishing a written statement or account which to his knowledge is or may be misleading, false or deceptive in a material particular, he shall on conviction on indictment be liable to imprisonment for a term not exceeding seven years.

(2)   For purposes of this section a person who has entered into a security for the benefit of a body corporate or association is to be treated as a creditor of it.

(3)   Where the affairs of a body corporate or association are managed by its members, this section shall apply to any statement which a member publishes or concurs in publishing in connection with his functions of management as if he were an officer of the body corporate or association.

Procedure and Jurisdiction

B6.15   The offence is triable either way (MCA 1980, s. 17 and sch. 1, para. 28). When tried on indictment it is a class 4 offence. It is a Group A offence for jurisdiction purposes under the CJA 1993, part I (see **D1.75**). For the provisions of *Practice Note (Mode of Trial: Guidelines)* (1995) relating to fraud generally, see **B5.24**.

Indictment

B6.16   Statement of Offence

Publishing a false statement contrary to section 19(1) of the Theft Act 1968

Particulars of Offence

A on or about the . . . day of . . . , being a director of a body corporate, namely X plc, with intent to deceive the members or creditors or the said X plc, published a written statement about the affairs of the said X plc which to his knowledge was misleading, false or deceptive in a material particular in that it falsely stated that X plc then had no contingent liabilities

Sentence

B6.17   The maximum penalty is seven years (TA 1968, s. 19(1)) on indictment; six months, a fine not exceeding the statutory maximum, or both, summarily. There is no guideline judgment reported for an offence under the TA 1968, s. 19(1). For sentencing guidelines for offences of deception generally, see **B5.26**. For sentencing guidelines for theft offences, see **B4.5** to **B4.8**.

Relationship to Other Offences

B6.18   The commission of an offence under the TA 1968, s. 19(1), by a company director may be in circumstances in which the company itself commits an offence under s. 17 or possibly ss. 15 or 16 for which the director may be liable under s. 18. There is clearly some overlap between such liability and possible liability under s. 19(1), subject to the consideration that under s. 19(1) there need be no successful deception, no proof of dishonesty and no need for the statement to be made or required for any accounting purpose, but, insofar as the s. 19 offence can be committed by officers of an unincorporated association, its scope is nevertheless wider than that of s. 18.

Meaning of 'Officer of a Body Corporate or Unincorporated Association'

In relation to registered companies, the term 'officer' includes a director, manager or **B6.19** secretary (Companies Act 1985, s. 744), and an auditor may also be considered to be an officer (*Shacter* [1960] 2 QB 252). As to the meaning of manager, see the discussion of *Boal* [1992] 1 QB 591 at **A5.11**.

In relation to unincorporated associations, treasurers, secretaries and chairmen would be considered to be officers; as would any partner publishing or concurring in the publication of an offending statement in connection with his firm's affairs. Where the affairs of a company or association are managed by its members, a member may commit this offence (TA 1968, s. 19(3)).

Intent to Deceive Members or Creditors

A statement published with intent to deceive only prospective members or creditors **B6.20** would not appear to come within the ambit of this offence, but would be likely to fall within the Financial Services Act 1986, s. 47 (see **B7.35**). The TA 1968, s. 19(2), provides that for the purposes of s. 19, a person who has entered into a security for the benefit of a body corporate or association is to be treated as a creditor of it. This seems to refer to a guarantor, though the precise scope of the subsection is unclear.

FORGERY AND KINDRED OFFENCES: GENERAL CONSIDERATIONS

Offences and Penalties under Part I of the Forgery and Counterfeiting Act 1981

The Forgery and Counterfeiting Act 1981, s. 30, together with the schedule to that Act, **B6.21** repealed a number of older statutory offences of forgery, and s. 13 abolished the offence of forgery at common law. In their place, part I (ss. 1 to 13) of the Act created the following offences:

   (a)   making a false instrument (s. 1);
   (b)   copying a false instrument (s. 2);
   (c)   using a false instrument (s. 3);
   (d)   using a copy of a false instrument (s. 4);
   (e)   having custody or control of specified kinds of false instrument (s. 5(1)); and
   (f)   making or having custody etc. or machines, paper etc. for making false instruments of that kind (s. 5(3));

These offences all require proof of an 'intention to induce somebody to accept the instrument as genuine' (or as a copy of a genuine instrument) and 'by reason of so accepting it to do or not to do some act to his own or any other person's prejudice'. They are punishable following conviction on indictment with up to 10 years' imprisonment under s. 6(2) and (3) of the Act.

In addition, subsections (2) and (4) of s. 5 create two further, less serious, offences, which do not require proof of this ulterior intent, but which are otherwise comparable to the offences created by s. 5(1) and (3) respectively. These are punishable with up to two years' imprisonment under s. 6(4).

On summary conviction, all eight offences attract up to six months' imprisonment and/or a fine not exceeding the statutory maximum (s. 6(1)).

The above offences all use certain key terms, the meanings of which are defined in ss. 8 to 10 of the Act.

Meaning of 'Instrument'

B6.22   **Forgery and Counterfeiting Act 1981, s. 8**

(1)   Subject to subsection (2) below, in this part of this Act 'instrument' means—
(a)   any document, whether of a formal or informal character;
(b)   any stamp issued or sold by the Post Office;
(c)   any Inland Revenue stamp; and
(d)   any disc, tape, soundtrack or other device on or in which information is recorded or stored by mechanical, electronic or other means.

(2)   A currency note within the meaning of part II of this Act is not an instrument for the purposes of this part of this Act.

(3)   A mark denoting payment of postage which the Post Office authorise to be used instead of an adhesive stamp is to be treated for the purposes of this part of this Act as if it were a stamp issued by the Post Office.

It had been recognised that one of the many difficulties surrounding the old Forgery Act 1913 was uncertainty about what kinds of article fell within the scope of the offences it created. The fact that it referred to 'documents', without providing any definition of that term, meant, *inter alia*, that doubts surrounded things such as wrappers on goods or the signatures on paintings or other works of art (*Closs* (1857) Dears & B 460; *Smith* (1858) Dears & B 566; *Douce* [1972] Crim LR 105). In proposing the new legislation, the Law Commission advocated the adoption of the term 'instrument' instead, on the basis that forgery and its kindred offences should apply only to those documents, such as cheques, which create rights and duties, or which give directions that are to be accepted and acted upon. This proposal was seemingly rejected; the term 'instrument' has indeed been adopted in the Act, but it has been defined in such a way that it includes any document (still without defining that term!) and several things that might not otherwise have been thought of as documents at all. The only documents excluded are currency notes, which are covered by the counterfeiting offences in part II of the Act.

Electronic impulses representing passwords for accessing computers are too ephemeral to be instruments (*Gold* [1988] AC 1063) though the misuse of such a password may be an offence under the Computer Misuse Act 1990 (see **B18**).

Meaning of 'False' and 'Making'

B6.23   **Forgery and Counterfeiting Act 1981, s. 9**

(1)   An instrument is false for the purposes of this part of this Act—
(a)   if it purports to have been made in the form in which it is made by a person who did not in fact make it in that form; or
(b)   if it purports to have been made in the form in which it is made on the authority of a person who did not in fact authorise its making in that form; or
(c)   if it purports to have been made in the terms in which it is made by a person who did not in fact make it in those terms; or
(d)   if it purports to have been made in the terms in which it is made on the authority of a person who did not in fact authorise its making in those terms; or
(e)   if it purports to have been altered in any respect by a person who did not in fact alter it in that respect; or
(f)   if it purports to have been altered in any respect on the authority of a person who did not in fact authorise the alteration in that respect; or
(g)   if it purports to have been made or altered on a date on which, or at a place at which, or otherwise in circumstances in which, it was not in fact made or altered; or
(h)   if it purports to have been made or altered by an existing person but he did not in fact exist.

(2)   A person is to be treated for the purposes of this part of this Act as making a false instrument if he alters an instrument so as to make it false in any respect (whether or not it is false in some other respect apart from that alteration).

As was the position at common law and under the earlier legislation, a false statement in a document or instrument does not ordinarily make that instrument a forgery; a false instrument is one which purports to be something which it is not (*Re Windsor* (1865) 10 Cox CC 118; *Warneford* [1994] Crim LR 753).

The Forgery and Counterfeiting Act 1981, s. 9(1), lists the ways in which an instrument may be false. It is an exhaustive list: an instrument cannot be regarded as false on any alternative basis. On the other hand, an indictment does not need to specify the exact ground on which an instrument is alleged to be false.

Falsity as to Authorship (s. 9(1)(a), (c) or (h))   An instrument will be false if the supposed maker did not make it at all, or if it has been altered since he made it. The obvious example of such falsity would be where one person forges another's signature on a cheque (*Lack* (1986) 84 Cr App R 342). **B6.24**

The concept might appear to be a simple one, but is not always so. In *Macer* [1979] Crim LR 659, decided under earlier, but essentially similar, provisions, it was held *not* to be forgery for a person to sign his own name on a cheque, but with a different signature from his normal one, with a view to later denying its authenticity. It was said that the cheque did not 'purport' to have been signed by any other person. On such facts, it would be better to charge an offence, or attempted offence, of evading a liability by deception under the TA 1978, s. 2.

Another difficulty concerns the use of assumed names. There is generally no law against the use of assumed names. An instrument signed in a false name is not necessarily a forgery, even if the false name has been used for dishonest purposes (*More* [1987] 1 WLR 1578). However, assuming the name of another person in the pretence of being that other person may constitute forgery. In *More*, the accused stole a cheque and paid it into a building society account opened in the same name as the payee. He later withdrew the proceeds, using withdrawal forms signed in that same name, and was charged, *inter alia*, with forgery of those forms. The House of Lords held that the forms were not forgeries: they purported to have been signed by the person who had opened the account, as indeed they had been, and (crucially) did not refer back to the original cheque.

Falsification by Alteration (s. 9(1)(e))   Alteration of an instrument so as to change its value or terms would come within paragraph (c) of the Forgery and Counterfeiting Act 1981, s. 9(1), if the alteration is intended to pass undetected. Paragraph (e) of s. 9(1) covers alterations which purport to be those of someone other than the person who made, or authorised the making of, the instrument, even an alteration which purports to be unauthorised (done, for example, for the purpose of falsely accusing someone else of forgery). If the person purportedly responsible for the alteration did not really exist then the instrument would be false by virtue of s. 9(1)(h). **B6.25**

Falsity as to Date, Place or Circumstances (s. 9(1)(g))   An instrument which is dated otherwise than with the date on which it is made is not necessarily false, because in some cases it is recognised that the date indicates, not the date of making, but the date at which the instrument becomes enforceable (as with a postdated cheque). An antedated cheque is more problematic. It is not uncommon for a shop selling goods for a value exceeding the amount covered by a cheque guarantee card to ask the customer for two cheques, one of which is to be antedated, so as to deceive the bank into thinking that the cheques relate to two different transactions. It will be for the jury to decide whether this amounts to dishonesty for the purpose of deception offences under the TA 1968, but forgery does not require dishonesty, and it might be argued that an antedated cheque purports to have been drawn no later than the date it bears. **B6.26**

Paragraph (g) of the Forgery and Counterfeiting Act 1981, s. 9(1), is the 'sweeping-up' provision, and is potentially very wide-ranging. In some circumstances, the concept of falsity in this paragraph can be hard to distinguish from that of mere false statements which, as explained at **B6.2**, fall outside the scope of the Act.

In *Donnelly* [1984] 1 WLR 1017, the Court of Appeal held that a jeweller's certificate purporting to value jewellery that did not exist was a forgery. Had the certificate merely lied about the value of items inspected, it could not possibly have been so categorised; and the decision has attracted forceful academic criticism on the basis that there is no real difference between a certificate relating to real items and one relating to fictional items. It has also been argued that *Donnelly* cannot stand with *More* [1987] 1 WLR 1578 (discussed in **B6.24**), but it is submitted that the decision was correct. The certificate did not just tell lies; it was not just an inaccurate valuation; it purported to be something it was not: a valuation made after inspection of the jewellery.

Donnelly was firmly approved by the Court of Appeal in *Jeraj* [1994] Crim LR 595, but a differently constituted court subsequently held it to be wrongly decided and inconsistent with *More* (*Warneford* [1994] Crim LR 753). The judges who decided *Warneford* were apparently unaware of the recent decision in *Jeraj*; but it is submitted that the facts of *Warneford* were in any case clearly distinguishable from those of *Donnelly* and fell outside the scope of s. 9(1)(g). The case involved a reference which falsely stated that a certain person had been employed by the appellant. As such, it told a lie, but the person concerned did indeed exist, and only on the broadest possible interpretation of s. 9(1)(g) could the reference be said to tell a lie about itself.

Meaning of 'Prejudice' and 'Induce'

B6.27   **Forgery and Counterfeiting Act 1981, s. 10**

(1)   Subject to subsections (2) and (4) below, for the purposes of this part of this Act an act or omission intended to be induced is to a person's prejudice if, and only if, it is one which if it occurs—
   (a)   will result—
      (i)   in his temporary or permanent loss of property; or
      (ii)   in his being deprived of an opportunity to earn remuneration or greater remuneration; or
      (iii)   in his being deprived of an opportunity to gain a financial advantage otherwise than by way of remuneration; or
   (b)   will result in somebody being given an opportunity—
      (i)   to earn remuneration or greater remuneration from him; or
      (ii)   to gain a financial advantage from him otherwise than by way of remuneration; or
   (c)   will be the result of his having accepted a false instrument as genuine, or a copy of a false instrument as a copy of a genuine one, in connection with his performance of any duty.
(2)   An act which a person has an enforceable duty to do and an omission to do an act which a person is not entitled to do shall be disregarded for the purposes of this part of this Act.
(3)   In this part of this Act references to inducing somebody to accept a false instrument as genuine, or a copy of a false instrument as a copy of a genuine one, include references to inducing a machine to respond to the instrument or copy as if it were a genuine instrument or, as the case may be, a copy of a genuine one.
(4)   Where subsection (3) above applies, the act or omission intended to be induced by the machine responding to the instrument or copy shall be treated as an act or omission to a person's prejudice.
(5)   In this section 'loss' includes not getting what one might get as well as parting with what one has.

The Forgery and Counterfeiting Act 1981, s. 10, provides an exhaustive definition of the concept of 'prejudice' for the purposes of the six offences which require an intent to induce another person to act or omit to act to his own or another's prejudice (see **B6.21**). 'Inducing' is only defined to the extent that it applies to machines.

To be guilty of one of these offences, an accused need not have induced any reaction at all: it is a matter of ulterior intent, rather than of *actus reus* (*Ondhia* [1998] 2 Cr App R 150). It would not however suffice that the accused was merely aware that prejudice might result (*Garcia* [1988] Crim LR 115).

Section 10(1)(a) covers situations in which acceptance of a false instrument would result in loss, or loss of potential profit; s. 10(1)(b) covers situations where actual loss might be difficult to identify, but where someone might be able to obtain a pecuniary advantage from the person induced; and the broad scope of s. 10(1)(c) is illustrated by *Campbell* (1984) 80 Cr App R 47, in which it was held that a bank would be prejudiced if it was induced to pay or collect payment on a forged cheque, whether or not it suffered financially by so doing, and whether or not anyone profited thereby. Another illustration is provided by *Utting* [1987] 1 WLR 1375, where, but for a defective indictment, the accused might have been convicted of forging an instrument in order to induce the police to act to their prejudice by not prosecuting him.

The effect of s. 10(2) is that it cannot be an offence under the Act to make or use a false instrument in order to secure or protect one's lawful rights against anyone it is intended to deceive; but in the case of cheques and other instruments covered by s. 5, s. 10(2) and (4) might still apply.

Subsections (3) and (4) of s. 10 ensure, *inter alia*, that the use of a forged card in an automatic service till could be an offence under s. 3, and making such a forged card could be an offence under s. 1. In contrast, the obtaining of cash using such a device would not be regarded as a deception offence under the TA 1968 or TA 1978, both of which lack any provisions akin to these (see **B5.4**). The correct charge in such a case would be theft. Subsections (3) and (4) would also apply where forged identification cards are used in computers etc., but not where hackers merely transmit or key in false user identification numbers, these being too ephemeral to constitute 'instruments' under s. 8 (*Gold* [1988] AC 1063). Similar considerations would apply to the misuse of another person's card and personal identification number in a bank automatic service till. Misuse of a user identification may, however, be an offence under the Computer Misuse Act 1990 (see **B18**).

FORGERY

Definition

Forgery and Counterfeiting Act 1981, s. 1   **B6.28**

A person is guilty of forgery if he makes a false instrument, with the intention that he or another shall use it to induce somebody to accept it as genuine, and by reason of so accepting it to do or not to do some act to his own or any other person's prejudice.

Procedure and Jurisdiction

The offence is triable either way (Forgery and Counterfeiting Act 1981, s. 6). When tried **B6.29** on indictment it is a class 4 offence. It is a Group A offence for jurisdiction purposes under the CJA 1993, part I (see **D1.75**).

Indictment

Statement of Offence   **B6.30**

Forgery contrary to section 1 of the Forgery and Counterfeiting Act 1981

Particulars of Offence

A on or about the . . . day of . . . made a false instrument, namely a document purporting to be the will of X, with the intention of using it to induce Y to accept it as genuine and by reason of so accepting to give A a Ming vase forming part of the estate of X to the prejudice of the beneficiaries under the true will of X

Sentence

B6.31   The maximum sentence is 10 years on indictment; six months or a fine not exceeding the statutory maximum or both summarily (Forgery and Counterfeiting Act 1981, s. 6). There is no guideline judgment reported for this offence but in *Lincoln* (1994) 15 Cr App R 333, where the offender forged the signature of his estranged wife on a contract for sale of a house and a Land Registry transfer, it was held that the proper sentence was six months' imprisonment.

Elements

B6.32   Most of the key terms used in the Forgery and Counterfeiting Act 1981, s. 1, are considered in **B6.22** to **B6.27**. By virtue of s. 9(2), 'making' a false instrument includes falsifying an existing one; but however it is made, it must be proved that it was made with the specified 'double intention': it must be proved that the accused intended both that the instrument would be accepted as genuine and that someone would therefore act to his own or another's prejudice. It is a specific intent; recklessness or foresight will not suffice (*Garcia* [1988] Crim LR 115). In *Ondhia* [1998] 2 Cr App R 150, O created a false 'copy bill of lading', not for the purpose of using it directly to deceive any other person, but for the purpose of feeding it into his fax machine, so that the recipient of his call would receive the facsimile copy thereby created. This was held to amount to an offence of forgery under s. 1. No doubt O would also have been guilty of copying a false instrument, contrary to s. 2 of the Act, but overlapping offences are common in English law, and there is nothing artificial or unnatural in the argument that a person who faxes a forged document to another 'uses' that document for the purpose of inducing that other (or indeed a third party) to accept it as genuine. A person who relies upon a facsimile of a bill of lading will recognise it to be a facsimile; and if he is deceived by the facsimile, he is deceived by the original from which it was made.

On the other hand, dishonesty is not an essential ingredient in this or any other offences under the Act (*Campbell* (1984) 80 Cr App R 47; *Winston* [1999] 1 Cr App R 337), and the intent is ulterior, so that actual inducement or prejudice need not be proved, and need not even be intended to take place within the jurisdiction (cf. *Treacy* v *DPP* [1971] AC 537; *Berry* [1985] AC 246).

COPYING A FALSE INSTRUMENT

Definition

B6.33   **Forgery and Counterfeiting Act 1981, s. 2**

> It is an offence for a person to make a copy of an instrument which is, and which he knows or believes to be, a false instrument, with the intention that he or another shall use it to induce somebody to accept it as a copy of a genuine instrument, and by reason of so accepting it to do or not to do some act to his own or any other person's prejudice.

Procedure and Jurisdiction

B6.34   The offence is triable either way (Forgery and Counterfeiting Act 1981, s. 6). When tried on indictment it is a class 4 offence. It is a Group A offence for jurisdiction purposes under the CJA 1993, part I (see **D1.75**).

Indictment

B6.35   Statement of Offence

Copying a false instrument contrary to section 2 of the Forgery and Counterfeiting Act 1981

Particulars of Offence

A on or about the . . . day of . . . made a copy of an instrument, namely a document purporting to be the will of X, which was and which he knew to be a false instrument, with the intention of using it to induce Y to accept it as genuine and by reason of so accepting to give A a Ming vase forming part of the estate of X to the prejudice of the beneficiaries under the true will of X

Sentence

The maximum sentence is 10 years on indictment; six months or a fine not exceeding **B6.36** the statutory maximum or both summarily (Forgery and Counterfeiting Act 1981, s. 6).

Elements

The Forgery and Counterfeiting Act 1981, s. 2, does not deal with copies which are **B6.37** intended to be passed off as originals, even if they are themselves copies of copies, nor does it deal with instruments which purport to be copies of originals which do not in fact exist. (The correct charge for making such copies is one of forgery under s. 1.) This provision aims instead at copies (particularly photocopies) which purport to be true copies of original instruments, but which are not, either because the original has been falsified prior to photocopying etc., or because the original was a complete forgery from the start.

It might be argued that there is really no need for such a provision, since a document which purports to be a photocopy of a genuine instrument, but which is in fact a copy of a forgery, would *ipso facto* be false under s. 9(1)(g) (and see *Utting* [1987] 1 WLR 1375). This might be true where the original is a total forgery; but difficulties could arise in other circumstances. If, for example, an individual is required to send to some person a copy of his birth certificate, and takes a photocopy for that purpose, knowing that the original was falsified in some way by his father 10 years before, it could be argued that the photocopy is a true copy of the certificate, and thus not false within s. 9 at all. Section 2, however, would clearly apply in such circumstances.

USING A FALSE INSTRUMENT: USING COPY OF FALSE INSTRUMENT

Definitions

Forgery and Counterfeiting Act 1981, ss. 3 and 4   B6.38

3. It is an offence for a person to use an instrument which is, and which he knows or believes to be, false, with the intention of inducing somebody to accept it as genuine, and by reason of so accepting it to do or not to do some act to his own or any other person's prejudice.

4. It is an offence for a person to use a copy of an instrument which is, and which he knows or believes to be, a false instrument, with the intention of inducing somebody to accept it as a copy of a genuine instrument, and by reason of so accepting it to do or not to do some act to his own or any other person's prejudice.

Procedure and Jurisdiction

Both offences are triable either way (Forgery and Counterfeiting Act 1981, s. 6). When **B6.39** tried on indictment they are class 4 offences. It is a Group A offence for jurisdiction purposes under the CJA 1993, part I (see **D1.75**).

Indictment

Statement of Offence   **B6.40**

Using a false instrument contrary to section 3 of the Forgery and Counterfeiting Act 1981

Particulars of Offence

A on or about the . . . day of . . . used an instrument, namely a document purporting to be the will of X, which was and which he knew to be false, with the intention of inducing Y to accept it as genuine and by reason of so accepting to give A a Ming vase forming part of the estate of X to the prejudice of the beneficiaries under the true will of X

This form may easily be adapted for a charge under s. 4.

Sentence

B6.41 The maximum sentence is 10 years on indictment; six months or a fine not exceeding the statutory maximum or both summarily (Forgery and Counterfeiting Act 1981, s. 6). There are no guideline judgments reported for these offences. In *Singh* [1999] 1 Cr App R (S) 490, the Court of Appeal upheld a sentence of eight months' imprisonment on an offender who had pleaded guilty to an offence under s. 3, in that he had attempted to use a false British passport at Gatwick Airport in order to travel to Canada. After reviewing a number of authorities involving the misuse of passports, Rose LJ explained that a deterrent custodial sentence within the range of six to nine months would usually be merited. A guilty plea would always attract an appropriate discount, but previous good character and personal mitigation were of very limited value.

Elements

B6.42 Whereas the Forgery and Counterfeiting Act 1981, s. 1, penalises the making of a false instrument, even if it is never used for its intended purpose or intended for use outside the jurisdiction, s. 3 strikes at the use of such an instrument, even if it was not originally made to be used in a way prohibited by s. 3, or made outside the jurisdiction. The same 'double intention' is required as in s. 1: see **B6.32** and *Tobierre* [1986] 1 WLR 125.

Section 4 relates to s. 2 as s. 3 relates to s. 1. Like s. 2 it does not apply to copies which purport to be originals; and like s. 3 it does not matter who made the copy, or for what purpose it was made.

'Using' is not defined in the Act. Previous legislation used the term 'uttering', and using was the principal form of uttering (*Harris* [1966] 1 QB 184). 'Use' must presumably bear its ordinary meaning: 'to put into action or service: avail oneself of: . . . to carry out a purpose or action by means of' (*Webster's Ninth New Collegiate Dictionary*). However, the use need not be successful: the full offence may be committed even if the instrument is at once recognised as a forgery.

OFFENCES RELATING TO STAMPS, SHARE CERTIFICATES, PASSPORTS ETC.

Definitions

B6.43   **Forgery and Counterfeiting Act 1981, s. 5**

   (1)   It is an offence for a person to have in his custody or under his control an instrument to which this section applies which is, and which he knows or believes to be, false, with the intention that he or another shall use it to induce somebody to accept it as genuine, and by reason of so accepting it to do or not to do some act to his own or any other person's prejudice.

   (2)   It is an offence for a person to have in his custody or under his control, without lawful authority or excuse, an instrument to which this section applies which is, and which he knows or believes to be, false.

   (3)   It is an offence for a person to make or to have in his custody or under his control a machine or implement, or paper or any other material, which to his knowledge is or has been specially designed or adapted for the making of an instrument to which this section applies, with the intention that he or another shall make an instrument to which this section applies which is false and that he or another shall use the instrument to induce somebody

to accept it as genuine, and by reason of so accepting it to do or not to do some act to his own or any other person's prejudice.

(4)   It is an offence for a person to make or to have in his custody or under his control any such machine, implement, paper or material, without lawful authority or excuse.

(5)   The instruments to which this section applies are—
- (a)   money orders;
- (b)   postal orders;
- (c)   United Kingdom postage stamps;
- (d)   Inland Revenue stamps;
- (e)   share certificates;
- (f)   passports and documents which can be used instead of passports;
- (g)   cheques;
- (h)   travellers' cheques;
- (i)   cheque cards;
- (j)   credit cards;
- (k)   certified copies relating to an entry in a register of births, adoptions, marriages or deaths and issued by the Registrar-General, the Registrar-General for Northern Ireland, a registration officer or person lawfully authorised to register marriages; and
- (l)   certificates relating to entries in such registers.

(6)   In subsection (5)(e) above 'share certificate' means an instrument entitling or evidencing the title of a person to a share or interest—
- (a)   in any public stock, annuity, fund or debt of any government or State, including a State which forms part of another State; or
- (b)   in any stock, fund or debt of a body (whether corporate or unincorporated) established in the United Kingdom or elsewhere.

Procedure and Jurisdiction

Offences under the Forgery and Counterfeiting Act 1981, s. 5, are triable either way **B6.44** (Forgery and Counterfreiting Act 1981, s. 6). When tried on indictment they are class 4 offences. These are Group A offences for jurisdiction purposes under the CJA 1993, part I (see **D1.75**).

Indictment

Statement of Offence **B6.45**

Having custody or control of a false instrument contrary to section 5(1) of the Forgery and Counterfeiting Act 1981

Particulars of Offence

A on or about . . . day of . . . had in his custody or under his control an instrument, namely a purported United Kingdom 'penny black' postage stamp, knowing the same to be false, with the intention of using it to induce V to accept it as genuine and by reason of so accepting to act to his prejudice by purchasing it from A as if genuine

This form may easily be adapted for a charge under s. 5(2), (3) or (4).

Alternative Verdicts

Based on the usual principles of law governing alternative verdicts (Criminal Law Act **B6.46** 1967, s. 6(3): see **D16.18** to **D16.31**), it is submitted that on an indictment for an offence under the Forgery and Counterfeiting Act 1981, s. 5(1), the jury may return a verdict of guilty of an offence under s. 5(2); and that on an indictment for an offence under s. 5(3) the jury may return a verdict of guilty under s. 5(4). It may, nevertheless, be prudent to add alternative counts.

Sentence

The maximum sentence for an offence under s. 5(1) or 5(3) of the Forgery and **B6.47** Counterfeiting Act 1981 is 10 years on indictment; six months or a fine not exceeding the statutory maximum or both summarily (Forgery and Counterfeiting Act 1981, s. 6).

The maximum sentence for an offence under s. 5(2) or 5(4) of the Forgery and Counterfeiting Act 1981 is two years on indictment; six months or a fine not exceeding the statutory maximum or both summarily (Forgery and Counterfeiting Act 1981, s. 6).

Elements

B6.48 It is not generally an offence merely to have custody or control of false instruments, or materials etc. for making them, even if the instruments or materials are intended for some unlawful purpose (though having such items with one when not at one's place of abode and for use in the course of or in connection with any cheat may be an offence under the Theft Act 1968, s. 25: see **B4.118** to **B4.125**). The instruments listed in the Forgery and Counterfeiting Act 1981, s. 5(5), have been singled out for protection, as have those to which the Mental Health Act 1983, s. 126, applies (specified documents relating to mental health).

Most of the terms used in the Forgery and Counterfeiting Act 1981, s. 5, are considered in **B6.22** to **B6.27**, but the concepts of 'custody or control' and 'lawful authority or excuse' require some comment.

B6.49 *Custody or Control*   The offences in the Forgery and Counterfeiting Act 1981, s. 5, are not limited to having the offending items on one's person, or even 'with' one in the sense required for liability under comparable legislation dealing with offensive weapons or theft etc. (e.g., TA 1968, ss. 10 and 25; see **B4.80** and **B4.124**). It will suffice if they are kept in one's home, garage, car or workplace. Problems of liability based on 'innocent possession', such as sometimes arise in other offences (e.g., possession of drugs or firearms) should not be a problem, because the prosecution must prove the accused's knowledge of the falsity and, in cases under s. 5(1) or 5(3), his ulterior intent. One might perhaps know of the falsity etc. without knowing one had custody or control (cf. *Wings Ltd* v *Ellis* [1985] AC 272), but such a case would be most unusual, and it is doubtful whether strict liability would be imposed even then.

B6.50 *Lawful Authority or Excuse*   In the absence of any definition in the Forgery and Counterfeiting Act 1981 itself, the concept of lawful excuse must presumably extend to any recognised general defences, and would also cover possession with intent to hand the relevant items to the police or other authorities at the first reasonable opportunity (*Wuyts* [1969] 2 QB 474; *Sunman* [1995] Crim LR 569). It would seem that the burden of proving lawful authority or excuse must only be evidential: contrast s. 17(4) of the Act (making or having implements etc. for counterfeiting protected coins), where the legal burden of proof is expressly placed on the accused. If this is correct, then once the accused raises the issue of lawful authority or excuse, the prosecution must disprove it beyond reasonable doubt. (As to the legal and evidential burdens of proof in relation to the accused generally, see **F3.1** *et seq*. and **F3.18**.)

ACKNOWLEDGING RECOGNISANCE, BAIL ETC. IN THE NAME OF ANOTHER

Definition

B6.51   **Forgery Act 1861, s. 34**

> Whosoever, without lawful authority or excuse (the proof whereof shall lie on the party accused), shall, in the name of any other person, acknowledge any recognisance or bail, or any *cognovit actionem* or judgment, or any deed or other instrument, before any court, judge, or other person lawfully authorised in that behalf, being convicted thereof shall be liable to imprisonment for any term not exceeding seven years.

Procedure

B6.52 Offences under the Forgery Act 1861, s. 34, are triable only on indictment. They are class 3 offences.

Indictment

Statement of Offence **B6.53**

Acknowledging recognisance in the name of another contrary to section 34 of the Forgery Act 1861

Particulars of Offence

A on or about the . . . day of . . . , without lawful authority or excuse, acknowledged before the Bow Street Magistrates' Court, in the name of X, a recognisance lawfully required of X as a condition of the admission to bail by the said court of one Y

Sentence

The maximum sentence for an offence under the Forgery Act 1861, s. 34, is seven years. **B6.54**

Elements

There is clearly a significant overlap between the Forgery Act 1861, s. 34, and the **B6.55** Forgery and Counterfeiting Act 1981. If, for example, a man forges his wife's acknowledgement or consent on a form in connection with divorce proceedings between them, this would be an offence under both Acts, assuming that he acted with the double intent required under the 1981 Act (see **B6.32**). On the other hand, no ulterior intent is required under the 1861 Act, and the burden of proving lawful authority or excuse is placed fully on the defence (in contrast to the mere evidential burden arising under the 1981 Act; see **B6.50**).

The reference to '*cognovit actionem*' is obsolete; but a court order made by consent would be within the scope of the section as a species of 'other instrument'.

Any recognisance etc. must be a valid one. A person who is improperly required to enter into one cannot be guilty of using a false name when so doing (*McKenzie* [1971] 1 All ER 729).

FORGERY, FALSIFICATION ETC. OF REGISTERS, CERTIFICATES OR CERTIFIED COPIES

Forgery Act 1861

Under the Forgery Act 1861, ss. 36 and 37, it is an offence, punishable with a maximum **B6.56** penalty of life imprisonment, unlawfully to destroy, deface, injure etc. any register of births, baptisms, marriages, deaths or burials; to cause or permit such damage; or knowingly to make, sign or permit the making of false entries or insertions in such registers or in copies thereof, or knowingly to issue false certificates or copies.

These provisions overlap with those of the Forgery and Counterfeiting Act 1981, but deal with acts of damage and destruction as well as with falsification.

Other Provisions Relating to Registers and Certificates

As to the falsification of birth or death certificates, see the Births and Deaths Registration **B6.57** Act 1953, s. 37. As to the making of false statements and the use of false certificates in connection with births and deaths, see the Perjury Act 1911, s. 4 (see **B14.21**). Various non-parochial registers deposited with the Registrar-General are protected under the Non-parochial Registers Act 1840, s. 8.

As to the falsification of entries under the Land Registration Act 1925, see ss. 116 and 117 of that Act. See also s. 115 (suppression of facts or documents with intent to substantiate false claims etc.).

The falsification of any pedigree upon which title to land (or some interest therein) depends, with intent to defraud a purchaser who might thereby be induced to accept the title offered, is punishable with up to two years' imprisonment and/or a fine under the Law of Property Act 1925, s. 183. The A-G must give leave before any prosecution is commenced.

As to falsification of entries in the register of trade marks, see the Trade Marks Act 1994, s. 94. As to forgery of a county court summons or other process of a county court, see the County Courts Act 1984, s. 135.

COUNTERFEITING AND KINDRED OFFENCES

Introduction

B6.58 The counterfeiting of currency notes and 'protected coins' is dealt with in part II (ss. 14 to 28) of the Forgery and Counterfeiting Act 1981; the counterfeiting of hallmarks and dies etc. is protected under the Hallmarking Act 1973, s. 6; as to 'counterfeit goods' to which false trade marks are applied, so as to imitate the products of leading manufacturers, see the Trade Marks Act 1994, ss. 92 and 97 (see **B6.92** to **B6.98**).

Scope of Offences under Part II of the Forgery and Counterfeiting Act 1981

B6.59 Part II of the Forgery and Counterfeiting Act 1981 applies only in respect of currency notes and protected coins, as defined in s. 27.

Forgery and Counterfeiting Act 1981, s. 27

(1)   In this part of this Act—
'currency note' means—
(a)   any note which—
(i)   has been lawfully issued in England and Wales, Scotland, Northern Ireland, any of the Channel Islands, the Isle of Man or the Republic of Ireland: and
(ii)   is or has been customarily used as money in the country where it was issued: and
(iii)   is payable on demand: or
(b)   any note which—
(i)   has been lawfully issued in some country other than those mentioned in paragraph (a)(i) above: and
(ii)   is customarily used as money in that country: and
'protected coin' means any coin which—
(a)   is customarily used as money in any country: or
(b)   is specified in an order made by the Treasury for the purposes of this part of this Act.
(2)   The power to make an order conferred on the Treasury by subsection (1) above shall be exercisable by statutory instrument.
(3)   A statutory instrument containing such an order shall be laid before Parliament after being made.

British or Irish notes come within the Act even if no longer customarily used as money (s. 27(1)(a)); but foreign or Commonwealth notes must be in current use (s. 27(1)(b)). Neither kind need ever have been legal tender: Scottish notes, for example, are not legal tender even in Scotland (and see also s. 28(3)).

Coins must either be in current use or be specified by the Treasury for the purpose of this Act. The following coins have been so specified: sovereigns, half-sovereigns, krugerrands, coins which are denominated in fractions of krugerrands, Maria-Theresia thalers dated 1780 and euro-coins (Forgery and Counterfeiting (Protected Coins) Orders 1981 and 1999 (SI 1981 No. 1505 and 1999 No. 2095)). The counterfeiting of ancient coins *not* specified for these purposes cannot be an offence under this Act, however dishonest the motives.

Meaning of 'Counterfeit'

Forgery and Counterfeiting Act 1981, s. 28   **B6.60**

(1)   For the purposes of this part of this Act a thing is a counterfeit of a currency note or of a protected coin—

(a)   if it is not a currency note or a protected coin but resembles a currency note or protected coin (whether on one side only or on both) to such an extent that it is reasonably capable of passing for a currency note or protected coin of that description: or

(b)   if it is a currency note or protected coin which has been so altered that it is reasonably capable of passing for a currency note or protected coin of some other description.

(2)   For the purposes of this part of this Act—

(a)   a thing consisting of one side only of a currency note, with or without the addition of other material, is a counterfeit of such a note:

(b)   a thing consisting—

(i)   of parts of two or more currency notes: or

(ii)   of parts of a currency note, or of parts of two or more currency notes, with the addition of other material,

is capable of being a counterfeit of a currency note.

(3)   References in this part of this Act to passing or tendering a counterfeit of a currency note or a protected coin are not to be construed as confined to passing or tendering it as legal tender.

It is not possible to argue that a one-sided note or coin is *ipso facto* incapable of passing for a genuine one, but in other respects the question of what kind of imitation can amount to a counterfeit is one of fact. An incompetent counterfeiter whose notes would fool nobody can be guilty of an attempt to counterfeit or of an offence under s. 17 of the Act (making or having custody of materials etc. for counterfeiting; see **B6.84** to **B6.89**).

Section 19 of the Act (imitation coins produced for promotional purposes) appears to assume that a coin may imitate a British coin in size, shape and substance, without necessarily being a counterfeit. Since any such coins could, in some circumstances, be confused with the real thing (e.g., when mixed in a handful of change in poor light), it would seem that a counterfeit must be 'reasonably capable' of bearing some direct scrutiny, if not perhaps close or careful scrutiny.

Sentencing Guidelines

The maximum penalties for the various offences are set out in the sections dealing with **B6.61** them below. The following notes refer to counterfeiting generally.

In *Crick* (1981) 3 Cr App R (S) 275, a case where the offender pleaded guilty to possessing a press for making silver coins, and to making counterfeit 50 pence coins, which he had used to obtain goods from vending machines, Mustill J made the following general remarks about the offences of counterfeiting notes or coinage:

> Coining is a serious offence. It was rightly treated as such by the learned judge, who correctly took the view that it called for an immediate custodial sentence. It must, however, be recognised that not all such offences are of the same gravity. At one extreme is the professional forger, with carefully prepared plates, and elaborate machinery, who manufactures large quantities of banknotes and puts them into circulation. A long sentence of imprisonment is appropriate in such a case. Here the offence is at the other end of the scale. The tools used to make the blanks were primitive, and were not acquired specially for the purpose; the techniques used were amateurish, and there was little real attempt to make the blanks a facsimile of a 50 pence piece. The coins were not, and could not have been, put into general circulation.

A three-year sentence was, accordingly, reduced to one of nine months.

Longer sentences will be upheld for production of banknotes, but much depends on the sophistication of the enterprise and the success of the offenders. Sentences of nine years were reduced to seven years in *Barry* (1983) 5 Cr App R (S) 11, where the offenders had obtained printing machinery and counterfeited £5 notes. See also *Allyson* (1989) 11 Cr App R (S) 60 and *Britton* (1994) 15 Cr App R (S) 482.

In *Howard* (1985) 82 Cr App R 262, the Court of Appeal laid down guidelines for sentencing in cases involving counterfeit notes. It was said that a custodial sentence would be required in nearly all cases where counterfeit notes have been passed, and that possession of large quantities of notes, indicating proximity to the counterfeiters, would be a most important consideration in determining the severity of the sentence.

In *Everett* (1983) 5 Cr App R (S) 207 the offender had bought two counterfeit £20 notes for £4 each and changed them at a club. Whilst the offence was a 'one-off', the offender had previous convictions for dishonesty, and a sentence of 12 months was upheld. In *Shah* (1987) 9 Cr App R (S) 167 the offender, while on bail in relation to unrelated charges, attempted to purchase a record using a counterfeit £50 note. The defendant had previous convictions, but of a nature different to the current offence. There was no evidence of dealing in counterfeit currency, and the offender contested the case on the ground that he had not realised the note to be counterfeit. Steyn J said that while this case was at the lower end of the spectrum of seriousness, 'in the absence of exceptional circumstances an immediate custodial sentence is necessary in all cases involving the tendering or passing of forged banknotes'. A 12-month prison sentence, suspended for two years, together with a supervision order, was upheld.

COUNTERFEITING NOTES OR COINS

Definition

B6.62   **Forgery and Counterfeiting Act 1981, s. 14**

(1)   It is an offence for a person to make a counterfeit of a currency note or of a protected coin, intending that he or another shall pass or tender it as genuine.
(2)   It is an offence for a person to make a counterfeit of a currency note or of a protected coin without lawful authority or excuse.

Procedure

B6.63   Offences under the Forgery and Counterfeiting Act 1981, s. 14, are, by s. 22 of the Act, triable either way. When tried on indictment they are class 4 offences.

Indictment

B6.64   Statement of Offence

Counterfeiting contrary to section 14(1) of the Forgery and Counterfeiting Act 1981

Particulars of Offence

A on or about the . . . day of . . . made a counterfeit of a currency note, namely a Bank of England £5 note, intending to pass or tender the same as genuine

Alternative Verdicts

B6.65   It is submitted that, on an indictment for an offence under the Forgery and Counterfeiting Act 1981, s. 14(1), it is open to the jury to return a verdict of guilty of the offence under s. 14(2) (see generally the Criminal Law Act 1967, s. 3, and **D16.18** to **D16.31**). It may, however, be prudent to add an alternative count.

Sentence

B6.66   The Forgery and Counterfeiting Act 1981, s. 22, prescribes the maximum penalties. For an offence under s. 14(1), 10 years and/or a fine on indictment; six months and/or a fine not exceeding the statutory maximum summarily. For an offence under s. 14(2), two years and/or a fine on indictment; six months and/or a fine not exceeding the statutory maximum summarily. For sentencing guidelines, see **B6.61**.

Elements

In the Forgery and Counterfeiting Act 1981, s. 14, a distinction is drawn (as in s. 5 of **B6.67** the Act: see **B6.43** to **B6.50**) between cases in which there is proof of an intent that the fake item shall be passed as genuine (s. 14(1)) and cases in which there is not (s. 14(2)). In the latter kind of case counterfeiting is still an offence (albeit a less serious one), unless the maker has lawful authority or excuse. The reason for this is that even the honest manufacture of realistic fakes carries risks of confusion or subsequent misuse (see *Heron* [1982] 1 WLR 451, decided under the Coinage Offences Act 1936, in which the making of counterfeit coins was held to be an offence without proof of any intent to deceive: and see also *Selby* v *DPP* [1972] AC 515).

The intent specified in the Forgery and Counterfeiting Act 1981, s. 14(1), is ulterior. The actual passing of the counterfeit need never happen, and it would suffice even if it was intended to happen outside the jurisdiction, as long as the counterfeiting itself was committed within it. In contrast to ss. 1 to 4 and s. 5(1) of the Act, there is no need to prove an intent to induce someone to act to his own or another's prejudice.

PASSING, TENDERING OR DELIVERING COUNTERFEIT NOTES OR COINS

Definitions

Forgery and Counterfeiting Act 1981, s. 15

B6.68

   (1)   It is an offence for a person—
      (a) to pass or tender as genuine any thing which is, and which he knows or believes to be, a counterfeit of a currency note or of a protected coin; or
      (b) to deliver to another any thing which is, and which he knows or believes to be, such a counterfeit, intending that the person to whom it is delivered or another shall pass or tender it as genuine.
   (2)   It is an offence for a person to deliver to another, without lawful authority or excuse, any thing which is, and which he knows or believes to be, a counterfeit of a currency note or of a protected coin.

Procedure

Offences under the Forgery and Counterfeiting Act 1981, s. 15, are, by s. 22 of the Act, **B6.69** triable either way. When tried on indictment they are class 4 offences.

Indictment

Statement of Offence

B6.70

Passing a counterfeit note contrary to section 15(1) of the Forgery and Counterfeiting Act 1981

Particulars of Offence

A on or about the . . . day of . . . passed to V a counterfeit of a currency note, namely a Bank of England £5 note, knowing or believing the same to be counterfeit

Alternative Verdicts

It is submitted that, on an indictment for an offence under the Forgery and **B6.71** Counterfeiting Act 1981, s. 15(1)(b), it is open to the jury to return a verdict of guilty of the offence under s. 15(2) (see generally the Criminal Law Act 1967, s. 3, and **D16.18** to **D16.31**). It may, however, be prudent to add an alternative count.

Sentence

B6.72 The Forgery and Counterfeiting Act 1981, s. 22, prescribes the maximum penalties. For an offence under s. 15(1)(a) or (b), 10 years and/or a fine on indictment; six months and/or a fine not exceeding the statutory maximum summarily. For an offence under s. 15(2), two years and/or a fine on indictment; six months and/or a fine not exceeding the statutory maximum summarily. For sentencing guidelines, see **B6.61**.

Scope of Offence

B6.73 The Forgery and Counterfeiting Act 1981, s. 15, follows the same pattern as s. 14 (see **B6.62** to **B6.67**), in that it distinguishes between cases in which a counterfeit is passed as genuine or delivered to another with intent that he should so pass it, and cases in which it is merely 'delivered', perhaps expressly described as a reproduction (see *Selby* v *DPP* [1972] AC 515). The latter kind of case attracts less serious penalties, but is still regarded as dangerous and undesirable.

Meaning of 'Passing' and 'Tendering'

B6.74 'Passing' suggests acceptance by the person to whom the thing is given, but a counterfeit may be *tendered* as genuine, even if it is at once rejected, and an offence may be committed even where the item in question is not passed or tendered as legal tender (Forgery and Counterfeiting Act 1981, s. 28(3)). Many forms of notes etc. used as money are not legal tender (e.g., Scottish notes), and many protected coins have a collectors' value exceeding any nominal value as currency.

Knowledge and Belief

B6.75 It would not be an offence under the Forgery and Counterfeiting Act 1981, s. 15, to pass or tender a note etc. which one suspects *may* be a counterfeit, even if the suspicion is a strong one. The section requires knowledge or belief, as in handling stolen goods under the Theft Act 1968, s. 22 (see **B4.135**), and those terms must presumably bear the same meanings as under that provision.

Meaning of 'Delivering'

B6.76 'Delivering', in the Forgery and Counterfeiting Act 1981, s. 15(1)(b) and (2), need not involve any intent to deceive as to the nature of the thing delivered, but the more serious offence under s. 15(1)(b) may be committed if it is intended that the counterfeits should eventually be tendered as genuine, by the recipient or some other person.

Lawful Authority or Excuse

B6.77 An obvious example of lawful delivery, which would not be an offence under the Forgery and Counterfeiting Act 1981, s. 15(2), would be where the counterfeits are handed over to the police; but lawful excuse could extend to general defences, such as mistake or duress. In view of the contrast with s. 17(4) (see **B6.89**), in which the legal burden of proof is expressly placed on the accused, it seems clear that the defence have only an evidential burden to discharge under s. 15(2). If the issue is raised by evidence, the prosecution must disprove the existence of lawful authority or excuse (see generally **F3.1** *et seq.* and **F3.6** *et seq.*), but if there is no evidence capable of supporting such a defence, the judge need not leave it to the jury (*Sunman* [1995] Crim LR 569).

CUSTODY OR CONTROL OF COUNTERFEIT NOTES OR COINS

Definitions

B6.78   **Forgery and Counterfeiting Act 1981, s. 16**

(1)   It is an offence for a person to have in his custody or under his control any thing which is, and which he knows or believes to be, a counterfeit of a currency note or of a

protected coin, intending either to pass or tender it as genuine or to deliver it to another with the intention that he or another shall pass or tender it as genuine.

(2) It is an offence for a person to have in his custody or under his control, without lawful authority or excuse, any thing which is, and which he knows or believes to be, a counterfeit of a currency note or of a protected coin.

(3) It is immaterial for the purposes of subsections (1) and (2) above that a coin or note is not in a fit state to be passed or tendered or that the making or counterfeiting of a coin or note has not been finished or perfected.

Procedure

Offences under the Forgery and Counterfeiting Act 1981, s. 16, are, by s. 22 of the Act, **B6.79** triable either way. When tried on indictment they are class 4 offences.

Indictment

Statement of Offence   **B6.80**

Having custody or control of a counterfeit note contrary to section 16(1) of the Forgery and Counterfeiting Act 1981

Particulars of Offence

A on or about the . . . day of . . . had in his custody or under his control a counterfeit of a currency note, namely a Bank of England £5 note, knowing or believing the same to be counterfeit and intending to pass or tender it as genuine [or to deliver it to X with the intention that X should pass or tender it as genuine]

Alternative Verdicts

It is submitted that on an indictment for an offence under the Forgery and **B6.81** Counterfeiting Act 1981, s. 16(1), it is open to the jury to return a verdict of guilty of the offence under s. 16(2) (see generally the Criminal Law Act 1967, s. 3, and **D16.18** to **D16.31**). It may, however, be prudent to add an alternative count.

Sentence

The Forgery and Counterfeiting Act 1981, s. 22, prescribes the maximum penalties. For **B6.82** an offence under s. 16(1), 10 years and/or a fine on indictment; six months and/or a fine not exceeding the statutory maximum summarily. For an offence under s. 16(2), two years and/or a fine on indictment; six months and/or a fine not exceeding the statutory maximum summarily. For sentencing guidelines, see **B6.61**.

Elements

Section 16 of the Forgery and Counterfeiting Act 1981 follows the same format as ss. **B6.83** 14 and 15 (see **B6.62** to **B6.77**). Section 16 serves the same kind of function as that served by s. 5(1) and (2) in relation to forgery offences (see **B6.43** to **B6.50**). As to the meaning of 'custody and control' in this context, see the discussion of s. 5 at **B6.49**.

OFFENCES RELATING TO MATERIALS AND IMPLEMENTS FOR COUNTERFEITING

Definitions

Forgery and Counterfeiting Act 1981, s. 17   **B6.84**

(1) It is an offence for a person to make, or to have in his custody or under his control, any thing which he intends to use, or permit any other person to use, for the purpose of making a counterfeit of a currency note or of a protected coin with the intention that it be passed or tendered as genuine.

(2) It is an offence for a person without lawful authority or excuse—

   (a)   to make; or
   (b)   to have in his custody or under his control,
any thing which, to his knowledge, is or has been specially designed or adapted for the making of a counterfeit of a currency note.
   (3)   Subject to subsection (4) below, it is an offence for a person to make, or to have in his custody or under his control, any implement which, to his knowledge, is capable of imparting to any thing a resemblance—
   (a)   to the whole or part of either side of a protected coin: or
   (b)   to the whole or part of the reverse of the image on either side of a protected coin.
   (4)   It shall be a defence for a person charged with an offence under subsection (3) above to show—
   (a)   that he made the implement or, as the case may be, had it in his custody or under his control, with the written consent of the Treasury; or
   (b)   that he had lawful authority otherwise than by virtue of paragraph (a) above, or a lawful excuse, for making it or having it in his custody or under his control.

Procedure

B6.85   Offences under the Forgery and Counterfeiting Act 1981, s. 17, are, by s. 22 of the Act, triable either way. When tried on indictment they are class 4 offences.

Indictment

B6.86
Statement of Offence

Having custody or control of thing intended for use in making a counterfeit, with intent, contrary to section 17(1) of the Forgery and Counterfeiting Act 1981

Particulars of Offence

A on or about the . . . day of . . . had in his custody or under his control a press and a quantity of inks intending to use the same to make a counterfeit of a currency note, namely a Bank of England £5 note, with the intention that such note be passed or tendered as genuine

Sentence

B6.87   The Forgery and Counterfeiting Act 1981, s. 22, prescribes the maximum penalties. For an offence under s. 17(1), 10 years and/or a fine on indictment; six months and/or a fine not exceeding the statutory maximum summarily. For an offence under s. 17(2) or (3), two years and/or a fine on indictment; six months and/or a fine not exceeding the statutory maximum summarily. For sentencing guidelines, see **B6.61**.

Scope of Offence

B6.88   The Forgery and Counterfeiting Act 1981, s. 17, serves the same kind of function as that served by s. 5(3) and (4) in relation to forgery offences (see **B6.43** to **B6.50**), and it follows s. 5 in distinguishing between cases where there is proof of an intent to pass false items as genuine and cases where there is not. Subsection (1) of s. 17 deals with the more serious kind of case; subsections (2) and (3) deal with the less serious kind. Either subsection may apply, not only to essential counterfeiting materials such as inks, but also to optional 'quality-control' devices such as chromolins (*Maltman* [1995] 1 Cr App R 239).

Lawful Authority or Excuse

B6.89   Subsection (3) of the Forgery and Counterfeiting Act 1981, s. 17 is subject to subsection (4), which expressly places the burden of proving lawful authority or excuse on the defence. However, subsection (2) is not subject to subsection (4). This indicates that the legal burden lies on the prosecution to disprove beyond reasonable doubt defences of lawful excuse etc. under s. 17(2), and indeed under all other provisions in the Act except s. 17(3). See generally **F3.1** *et seq*. and **F3.6** *et seq*.

IMPORTATION AND EXPORTATION OF COUNTERFEIT NOTES OR COINS

Forgery and Counterfeiting Act 1981, ss. 20 and 21   **B6.90**

20. The importation, landing or unloading of a counterfeit of a currency note or of a protected coin without the consent of the Treasury is hereby prohibited.

21.—(1) The exportation of a counterfeit of a currency note or of a protected coin without the consent of the Treasury is hereby prohibited.

(2) A counterfeit of a currency note or of a protected coin which is removed to the Isle of Man from the United Kingdom shall be deemed to be exported from the United Kingdom—

(a) for the purposes of this section: and

(b) for the purposes of the customs and excise Acts, in their application to the prohibition imposed by this section.

The relevant offences are under ss. 50 and 68 of the Customs and Excise Management Act 1979. As to acquisition with intent to evade the prohibition, see s. 170 of that Act (**B17.15** to **B17.21**).

POWERS OF SEARCH, SEIZURE AND FORFEITURE

Powers of search and seizure in relation to false instruments and the means of their **B6.91** production are contained in the Forgery and Counterfeiting Act 1981, s. 7(1). Broadly similar powers in relation to counterfeiting are contained in s. 24(1) of that Act.

An order for the forfeiture, destruction or disposal of such objects may be obtained from a magistrates' court, if it is satisfied that the order is conducive to the public interest; but anyone claiming a proprietary right or other interest in the objects concerned must be given the opportunity to 'show cause why the order should not be made' (ss. 7(4) and 24(4)). Where convictions are imposed under the Act, the court concerned may order the destruction or forfeiture of any object which has been shown to relate to the offence, or it may order it to be dealt with in such other manner as it thinks fit (ss. 7(3) and 24(3)). Any applicant claiming an interest in the object concerned must be given the opportunity to oppose the order under ss. 7(4) or 24(4).

FALSE APPLICATION OR USE OF TRADE MARKS

Definitions

Trade Marks Act 1994, s. 92   **B6.92**

(1) A person commits an offence who with a view to gain for himself or another, or with intent to cause loss to another, and without the consent of the proprietor—

(a) applies to goods or their packaging a sign identical to, or likely to be mistaken for, a registered trade mark, or

(b) sells or lets for hire, offers or exposes for sale or hire or distributes goods which bear, or the packaging of which bears, such a sign, or

(c) has in his possession, custody or control in the course of a business any such goods with a view to the doing of anything, by himself or another, which would be an offence under paragraph (b).

(2) A person commits an offence who with a view to gain for himself or another, or with intent to cause loss to another, and without the consent of the proprietor—

(a) applies a sign identical to, or likely to be mistaken for, a registered trade mark to material intended to be used—

(i) for labelling or packaging goods,

(ii) as a business paper in relation to goods, or

(iii) for advertising goods, or

(b)   uses in the course of a business material bearing such a sign for labelling or packaging goods, as a business paper in relation to goods, or for advertising goods, or

(c)   has in his possession, custody or control in the course of a business any such material with a view to the doing of anything, by himself or another, which would be an offence under paragraph (b).

(3)   A person commits an offence who with a view to gain for himself or another, or with intent to cause loss to another, and without the consent of the proprietor—

(a)   makes an article specifically designed or adapted for making copies of a sign identical to, or likely to be mistaken for, a registered trade mark, or

(b)   has such an article in his possession, custody or control in the course of a business, knowing or having reason to believe that it has been, or is to be, used to produce goods, or material for labelling or packaging goods, as a business paper in relation to goods, or for advertising goods.

Sentence and Procedure

B6.93   Offences under the Trade Marks Act 1994, s. 92, are punishable on indictment with a fine and/or a maximum of 10 years' imprisonment; on summary conviction with imprisonment for six months and/or a fine not exceeding the statutory maximum (s. 92(6)). Relevant sentencing decisions are *Kelly* [1996] 1 Cr App R (S) 61, *Yanko* [1996] 1 Cr App R (S) 217 and *Bhad* [1999] 2 Cr App R (S) 139. Proceedings for offences committed by partnerships must be brought against the partnership in the name of the firm, and not that of the partners (s. 101(1)). As to the liability of individual partners, see **B6.97**.

Local weights and measures authorities are responsible for the enforcement of s. 92, and for this purpose are vested with the same powers to make test purchases, enter premises, seize goods and documents, etc., as under the Trade Descriptions Act 1968, ss. 27 to 29 and 33 (Trade Marks Act 1994, s. 93).

Requirement for Specific Offence

B6.94   Although commercial activities involving trade in counterfeit goods will often involve the commission of offences under the Trade Descriptions Act 1968 (see **B6.99 *et seq.***), and in some cases offences under the TA 1968, it was felt that a set of specific offences should exist to combat this trade. Such offences were originally introduced by s. 58A of the Trade Marks Act 1938, inserted by s. 300 of the Copyright, Designs and Patents Act 1988. The Trade Marks Act 1994, s. 92, repeals and replaces these offences with broadly similar, but not identical, provisions.

Scope of Offences under Trade Marks Act 1994, s. 92

B6.95   The offences created by the Trade Marks Act 1994, s. 92(1) to (3), deal only with the infringement, etc., of registered trade marks in respect of goods. A trade mark is defined in s. 1 of the 1994 Act as any sign capable of being represented graphically which is capable of distinguishing goods or services of one undertaking from those of other undertakings. It may consist of words, names, designs, letters, numerals or the shape of goods or their packaging. Registration gives the owner a property right in it, which is protected under the 1994 Act (s. 2). Section 92 does not, however, apply to infringement of trade marks in respect of services. Furthermore, s. 92(4) provides that no offence can be committed under s. 92 unless the goods involved are goods in respect of which the trade mark has been registered, or the use of the counterfeit mark, etc., would take unfair advantage of, or be detrimental to the distinctive character or reputation of, a trade mark that has a reputation in the United Kingdom.

Mens Rea and Defences

B6.96   The accused must in all cases be shown to have acted with a view to gain or with an intent to cause loss to another. This is the same ulterior intent that is required under the TA 1968, ss. 17 and 21, and it must have the same meaning as it bears there (see **B5.50**).

This may not necessarily mean, however, that the accused acted dishonestly, knowingly or fraudulently. Any trader who offers or exposes goods for sale does so with a view to gain, and traders may sometimes be unaware that the goods are counterfeit or unaware that the relevant trade mark has been registered (*Torbay District Council, ex parte Singh* (1999) *The Times*, 5 July 1999).

Under s. 92(5) it is a defence for the accused to prove that he believed on reasonable grounds that the use or proposed use of the offending sign concerned was not an infringement of the registered trade mark. Where a partnership is adjudged guilty of an offence, every individual partner is then guilty, unless he can prove that he was ignorant of, or attempted to prevent, the commission of the offence (s. 101(4)).

Offences Committed by Bodies Corporate

Directors, managers or other officers of a body corporate who connive at or consent to the commission of an offence by that body will be guilty of the same offence (s. 101(5)). As to the meaning of the term 'manager', see *Boal* [1992] 1 QB 591 and **A5.11**. **B6.97**

Forfeiture Provisions

The Trade Marks Act 1994, s. 97, provides for the making of forfeiture orders in relation to counterfeit goods or packaging (or articles used in their production, etc.) seized in connection with the investigation or prosecution of an offence under s. 92, an offence under the Trade Descriptions Act 1968, or an offence of dishonesty or deception. Such orders may be sought either from the court before which relevant criminal proceedings have been brought or, where no such application has been made, by way of complaint to a magistrates' court (s. 97(2)). **B6.98**

If satisfied that a relevant offence has been committed in relation to the goods, etc. (or other goods which are representative of them), the court may order that they be destroyed in accordance with its directions, or that they be released to a specified person, on condition (a) that he causes offending signs to be removed or obliterated and (b) that any order against him to pay costs in those proceedings is complied with (s. 97(7)).

FALSE TRADE DESCRIPTIONS IN RESPECT OF GOODS

Definition

Trade Descriptions Act 1968, s. 1   B6.99

(1) Any person who, in the course of a trade or business—
   (a) applies a false trade description to any goods; or
   (b) supplies or offers to supply any goods to which a false trade description is applied;
shall, subject to the provisions of this Act, be guilty of an offence.
(2) Sections 2 to 6 of this Act shall have effect for the purposes of this section and for the interpretation of expressions used in this section, wherever they appear in this Act.

Procedure and Enforcement

Except where otherwise specified, all offences under the Trade Descriptions Act 1968 are triable either way. When tried on indictment, they are class 4 offences. Enforcement of the Act is primarily the responsibility of local weights and measures authorities. In practice, this means the trading standards department of the relevant local authority. Authorised officers have the power to make test purchases, and may in certain circumstances enter premises to inspect and seize goods and documents for the purpose of determining whether offences are being committed (Trade Descriptions Act 1968, ss. 27 to 28). As to offences involving the obstruction of trading standards officers or the provision of false information, see s. 29 (see **B6.117**). **B6.100**

No prosecution for an offence under the Act may be commenced after the expiration of three years from its commission, or one year from its discovery by the prosecutor, whichever is the earlier (s. 19(1); and see **D1.87**). In *Beaconsfield Justices, ex parte Johnston & Sons Ltd* (1985) 149 JP 535, it was held that a prosecuting authority 'discovers' an offence as soon as it becomes aware of it, even if it does not collect enough admissible evidence to bring a prosecution until a later date. The time limits set under s. 19 also apply to charges of conspiracy to contravene the Act (*Pain* [1986] BTCL 142). Section 19(2) and (4) contain further provisions concerning time-limits for summary prosecutions under the Act, but these are negated, as far as either way offences are concerned, by the MCA 1980, s. 127(2). Summary trials for s. 1 offences are therefore governed by the time-limits imposed by s. 19(1).

Indictment

B6.101

Statement of Offence

Applying a false trade description to goods, contrary to section 1(1)(a) of the Trade Descriptions Act 1968

Particulars of Offence

A on a day unknown between . . . and . . . in the course of a trade or business, namely . . . falsified the odometer reading on a Ford Fiesta motor car, registration no. . . ., so as to indicate that the said car had covered 12,050 miles, whereas the true figure was in excess of 35,000 miles.

Sentence

B6.102 The penalty on summary conviction is a fine not exceeding £5,000; on conviction on indictment, the penalty is a fine and/or imprisonment for up to two years (Trade Descriptions Act 1968, s. 18). There are a number of reported decisions of the Court of Appeal which provide guidance on sentencing for the offences under s. 1. No material difference appears to have been drawn between s. 1(1)(a) and s. 1(1)(b) for sentencing purposes. It should always be borne in mind when sentencing for offences involving strict liability that, if the offender denies knowledge of material matters, the prosecution is required to establish fault at the sentencing stage beyond reasonable doubt, even after a guilty plea (see *Lester* (1975) 63 Cr App R 144). For observations on sentencing under this Act, as compared to the Trade Marks Act 1994, see *Bhad* [1999] 2 Cr App R (S) 139.

In *Gupta* (1985) 7 Cr App R (S) 172 Lawton LJ observed that 'clocking' of motor cars was 'all too prevalent from one end of England and Wales to the other'. He noted that very often dishonest second-hand car dealers were punished by way of fine, but said that the proper sentence in many such cases was a custodial sentence together with a fine to remove the profit which had been made. Subsequent cases involving 'clocking' of cars are *Davies* (1992) 13 Cr App R (S) 459, where the offender (a man 'who had dabbled in criminal activities in motor cars on previous occasions') was convicted of 28 offences and a sentence of nine months' imprisonment was upheld, and *Waring* (1994) 15 Cr App R (S) 371, where four offences were admitted and a sentence of six months' imprisonment together with compensation orders of £990 were upheld. Examples of sentencing in respect of goods other than cars are provided by *Ahmadi* (1994) 15 Cr App R (S) 254, where the offender had been re-cycling toner cartridges for photocopying machines and passing them off as new ones, six months' imprisonment being upheld on appeal, and *Foster* [1992] 12 Cr App R (S) 394 where the offender marketed a slimming diet in respect of which false claims were made. The Court of Appeal accepted that, although the offender had contested the case, imposition of the maximum sentence of two years' imprisonment was inappropriate in light of mitigation, and reduced the term to one of 18 months.

Elements

Section 1 of the Trade Descriptions Act 1968 creates two distinct offences, the offence **B6.103** under s. 1(1)(a) and the offence under s. 1(1)(b). They are each offences of strict liability, subject to possible 'no fault' defences under s. 24 or s. 25 of the Act (see **B6.111** *et seq.*). No intent to deceive need be proved, nor need the defendant be proved to know the falsity of the description (*Swithland Motors Ltd v Peck* [1991] RTR 322 at p. 328). There is some tentative authority to the effect that the defendant must at least know that the trade description has been applied to the goods (*Cottee v Douglas Seaton (Used Cars)* [1972] 1 WLR 1408) but this cannot be correct, because it is clear from s. 24(3) of the Act that the prosecution do not have to prove the existence of such knowledge. On the contrary, it is for the defence to prove that the defendant did not know (*and* could not with reasonable diligence have ascertained) that the description had been applied to the goods. As to other fundamental distinctions between trade description offences and deception offences under the Theft Acts, see **B6.1**.

The Course of Trade or Business

It is essential for the prosecution to prove either that a false trade description was applied in **B6.104** the course of a trade or business (Trade Descriptions Act 1968, s. 1(1)(a)), or that goods to which such a description had been applied were supplied or offered for supply in the course of a trade or business (s. 1(1)(b)). No immediate offence is committed under the Act where a private individual falsely describes goods he is selling, either to another private individual or to someone acting in the course of a trade or business (cf. *John v Matthews* [1970] 2 QB 443). It is possible, however, for a private individual to be held responsible for the falsity of a subsequent trade description, as for example where a private car owner falsifies the mileage recorded on his car's odometer before selling it to a dealer, who then offers it for sale in the course of his business, without realising that the odometer has been falsified. Section 23 of the Act enables prosecutions to be brought against both persons in cases such as this, or (using the 'by-pass procedure') against the private car owner alone (see **B6.115**).

Persons working in professional practice (lawyers, veterinary surgeons, etc.) act in the course of a trade or business (*Roberts v Leonard* (1995) 94 LGR 284), and although the Trade Descriptions Act 1968 is usually considered to be a 'consumer protection' statute, it is clear that transactions between traders, businessmen or professionals also fall within its scope. A business may be a sideline (*Fletcher v Sledmore* [1973] RTR 371) but must be more than a self-financing hobby (cf. *Blakemore v Bellamy* [1983] RTR 303).

Problems can arise in respect of activities which are peripheral or incidental to the accused's trade, business or profession. In *Havering LBC v Stevenson* [1970] 1 WLR 1375, S operated a car-hire business. He regularly traded in his cars for new models once they had been used for two years. He sold one such car on which the odometer reading had been falsified. This was held to be an offence under s. 1(1)(b), even though his business was not one of dealing in cars. He had sold the car 'in the course of business', because such sales were a regular, if peripheral, part of his business and the proceeds were used by him as a regular source of business finance.

Stevenson must be contrasted with *Davies v Sumner* [1984] 1 WLR 1301, in which D was a self-employed courier who used his car to transport films, videos and other material throughout Wales. He eventually traded it to a dealer in part exchange for a new one, but the odometer reading of 18,000 miles was found to be false. The true mileage covered was over 100,000. The House of Lords distinguished this case from *Stevenson* on the basis, *inter alia*, that D's sale of his car could only be classed as being made in the course of his business if he conducted such transactions with some regularity. He had not, however, carried out any previous transactions of that kind, nor was it clear that he had planned to carry out more in future.

Trade Descriptions in Respect of Goods

B6.105 **Trade Descriptions Act 1968, s. 2**

(1)   A trade description is an indication, direct or indirect, and by whatever means given, of any of the following matters with respect to any goods or parts of goods, that is to say—

(a)   quantity, size or gauge;

(b)   method of manufacture, production, processing or reconditioning;

(c)   composition;

(d)   fitness for purpose, strength, performance, behaviour or accuracy;

(e)   any physical characteristics not included in the preceding paragraphs;

(f)   testing by any person and results thereof;

(g)   approval by any person or conformity to a type approved by any person;

(h)   place or date of manufacture, production, processing or reconditioning;

(i)   person by whom manufactured, produced, processed or reconditioned;

(j)   other history, including previous ownership or use.

(2)   The matters specified in subsection (1) of this section shall be taken—

(a)   in relation to any animal, to include sex, breed or cross, fertility and soundness;

(b)   in relation to any semen, to include the identity and characteristics of the animal from which it was taken and measure of dilution.

(3)   In this section, 'quantity' includes length, width, height, area, volume, capacity, weight and number.

(4) and (5)   [Detailed provisions as to agricultural produce, seeds, food and drugs.]

'Goods' are defined in s. 39 as including ships, aircraft, things attached to land and growing crops. The country of origin of goods is deemed to be that in which they last underwent a treatment or process resulting in a substantial change (s. 36).

Section 2 is definitive, rather than merely illustrative, and some descriptions (e.g., concerning the availability of after-sales service) may fall through the net it casts. The list is also confined to matters of fact. Statements of opinion cannot therefore be trade descriptions within the meaning of s. 2, but the dividing line between fact and opinion is not always clear. For example, to describe a television as having 'superb' picture quality would ordinarily be seen as mere opinion; but such a description must at least indicate (as a fact) that a reasonable picture can be obtained from the set. Similarly, a car cannot be in 'good condition' if it is not even in working order (cf. *Robertson* v *Dicicco* [1972] RTR 431 and *Furniss* v *Scholes* [1974] RTR 133). See also s. 3(3) to (4) of the Act (see **B6.107**) as to matters which are not strictly trade descriptions, but which may be may be deemed to be false trade descriptions under that section.

An odometer reading is a trade description within s. 2(1)(j) (*Hammertons Cars Ltd* [1976] 1 WLR 1243). A dealer's statement that a car has a valid MOT certificate is clearly a trade description within s. 2(1)(f), but the mileage etc. recorded on such a certificate is deemed not to be (*Corfield* v *Sevenways Garage Ltd* [1985] RTR 109; cf. *Coventry Justices, ex parte Farrand* [1988] RTR 273) .

A representation to the effect that particular goods are of a type tested or approved by a particular person (such as a famous sportsman) may come within s. 2(1)(f) or (g), but offences created by the Trade Descriptions Act 1968, ss. 12 and 13 may in some cases be more apposite. The s. 12(1) offence is one of falsely representing that a person supplies goods or services to members of the Royal Family; the s. 12(2) offence is one of using, without authorisation, an emblem or device suggesting receipt of the Queen's Award to Industry; and the s. 13 offence is one of representing that goods or services are of a kind supplied to any person. These offences are subject to the same procedures and penalties as offences under s. 1. See *Wall* v *Rose and Sargent* (1998) 162 JP 38.

Falsity in Trade Descriptions

B6.106 **Trade Descriptions Act 1968, s. 3**

(1)   A false trade description is a trade description which is false to a material degree.

(2)   A trade description which, though not false, is misleading, that is to say, likely to be taken for an indication of any of those matters specified in section 2 of this Act as would be false to a material degree, shall be deemed to be a false trade description.

(3)   Anything which, though not a trade description, is likely to be taken for an indication of any of those matters and, as such an indication, would be false to a material degree, shall be deemed to be a false trade description.

(4)   A false indication, or anything which is likely to be taken as an indication which would be false, that any goods comply with a standard specified or recognised by any person or implied by the approval of any person shall be deemed to be a false trade description, if there is no such person or no standard so specified, recognised or implied.

The question whether a trade description is false to a material degree is largely one of fact. Some cases suggest that a description should not be considered materially false if it could not be expected to mislead anyone. In *Donnelly* v *Rowlands* [1970] 1 WLR 1600, a dairyman sold milk in a bottle embossed with the name of another dairy, but sealed with his own silver cap. It was held that there was no false trade description, because the correctly labelled cap made it clear that the milk was his produce, and that only the bottle containing it belonged to the other dairy. It has also been held that the *de minimis* rule applies, so that insignificant or purely technical inaccuracies do not make a trade description false to a material degree (*Ford Motor Co. Ltd* [1974] 1 WLR 1220).

A trade description may be literally correct, but misleading because of what it omits. Under s. 3(2), it may then be treated as if it were a false trade description. An example is provided by *Inner London Justices, ex parte Wandsworth Borough Council* [1983] RTR 425, in which a dealer described a car as having had 'one previous owner', whilst omitting to point out that this owner was a car leasing company. This was deemed to be a false trade description by virtue of s. 3(2).

Section 3(3) deals with things which are likely to be taken for trade descriptions, but which do not strictly speaking fall within any of the categories listed in s. 2(1). Its possible effect was illustrated in *Holloway* v *Cross* [1981] 1 All ER 1012, in which a dealer acquired a car which had obviously exceeded the very low mileage shown on its odometer. He described it to a customer as having covered an 'estimated' 45,000 miles, but it was proved that the car must have covered some 70,000 miles, and he was prosecuted under s. 1(1)(b). The justices who heard his case held that his estimate was a mere opinion, and thus not an 'indication of . . . history or use' within s. 2(1)(j); but they nevertheless convicted him on the basis that it would be taken by the non-expert customer to be just such an indication. The Divisional Court upheld his conviction, their only doubt being whether it was absolutely necessary to rely on s. 3(3) rather than on s. 2(1) itself.

The unauthorised use of a trade mark does not necessarily involve the application of a false trade description, unless it is thereby implied that the goods were manufactured, distributed, processed or approved of by the owner of that trade mark, which is a question of fact that depends upon all the circumstances of the case. It may, for example, be clear that the goods are being supplied as cheap imitations, rather than being passed off as the genuine article (see *Veys* (1992) 157 JP 567 and *Kent County Council* v *Price* (1993) 157 JP 1161). The sale or supply of counterfeit goods may be more appropriately dealt with under the Trade Marks Act 1994, s. 92 (see **B6.92** *et seq.*).

Application of Description to Goods

Trade Descriptions Act 1968, s. 4   B6.107

(1)   A person applies a trade description to goods if he—
  (a)   affixes or annexes it to or in any manner marks it on or incorporates it with—
    (i)   the goods themselves, or
    (ii)   anything in, on or with which, the goods are supplied; or

(b) places the goods in, on or with anything which the trade description has been affixed or annexed to, marked on or incorporated with, or places any such thing with the goods; or

(c) uses the trade description in any manner likely to be taken as referring to the goods.

(2) An oral statement may amount to the use of a trade description.

(3) Where goods are supplied in pursuance of a request in which a trade description is used and circumstances are such as to make it reasonable to infer that the goods are supplied as goods conforming to that trade description, the person supplying the goods shall be deemed to have applied the trade description to the goods.

The methods of application listed in s. 4 are definitive, rather than merely illustrative, but nothing in s. 4 (or in s. 1) requires that a trade description must be applied by a person selling or supplying the goods. It may accordingly be applied by a trade buyer, as for example where a used car dealer falsely states that the vehicle offered to him is good only for scrap (*Fletcher* v *Budgen* [1974] 1 WLR 1056) or where an antique dealer falsely states that a Chippendale chair offered for sale to him is a modern reproduction. On the other hand, although s. 4 is silent on the point, it has been held that a description first applied by a dealer only after the completion of a sale cannot come within the proper scope of the Act, since it cannot influence the transaction in question (*Hall* v *Wickens Motors (Gloucester) Ltd* [1972] 1 WLR 1418).

A trade description may be applied by mere implication, and may even be applied secretly. In *Cottee* v *Douglas Seaton (Used Cars)* [1972] 1 WLR 1408, it was held that a false trade description was secretly applied to a car when serious rust defects in its bodywork (and previous amateur repairs) were concealed with paint.

One effect of s. 4(3) is that the delivery of goods which fail to meet a previously agreed contractual specification may involve an offence under s. 1(1)(b) (see *Shropshire County Council* v *Simon Dudley Ltd* (1997) 161 JP 224).

Advertisements

B6.108   **Trade Descriptions Act 1968, s. 5**

(1) The following provisions of this section shall have effect where in an advertisement a trade description is used in relation to any class of goods.

(2) The trade description shall be taken as referring to all goods of the class, whether or not in existence at the time the advertisement is published—

(a) for the purpose of determining whether an offence has been committed under paragraph (a) of section 1(1) of this Act; and

(b) where goods of the class are supplied or offered to be supplied by a person publishing or displaying the advertisement, also for the purpose of determining whether an offence has been committed under paragraph (b) of the said section 1(1).

(3) In determining for the purposes of this section whether any goods are of a class to which a trade description used in an advertisement relates regard shall be had not only to the form and content of the advertisement but also to the time, place, manner and frequency of its publication and all other matters making it likely or unlikely that a person to whom the goods are supplied would think of the goods as belonging to the class in relation to which the trade description is used in the advertisement.

This provision supplements s. 4 (see **B6.107**) by clarifying the circumstances in which an advertisement shall be taken to apply to particular goods. A manufacturer or distributor who falsely describes goods in an advertisement to potential customers commits an offence under s. 1(1)(a), even if the goods have already been supplied to the retailers. Furthermore, the retailers may themselves be guilty of supplying goods to which the false trade description has been applied, subject however to a possible defence under s. 24 (see **B6.111**). Section 39 of the Act provides that 'advertisements' include catalogues, circulars and price lists, but the section does not purport to give an exhaustive definition.

Offers to Supply

Trade Descriptions Act 1968, s. 6   **B6.109**

> A person exposing goods for supply or having goods in his possession for supply shall be deemed to offer to supply them.

Section 6 ensures that traders who display falsely described goods in their shops or showrooms are covered by s. 1(1)(b). From a strict contractual position, such displays are mere invitations to treat (*Fisher* v *Bell* [1961] 1 QB 394). In *Stainthorpe* v *Bailey* [1980] RTR 7, a motor dealer was held to have offered to supply a vehicle with a falsified odometer even though it was kept at his home rather than his business premises. It had been advertised for sale and a trading standards officer posing as a prospective purchaser was invited to inspect it.

The term, 'supply' is not defined in the Act, but must include dispositions by way of sale, leasing, hire-purchase or even promotional gift (see *Cahalne* v *Croydon London Borough Council* (1985) 149 JP 561 at p. 565). In *Formula One Autocentres* v *Birmingham City Council* [1999] RTR 195, it was held that the return of a car to a customer after a service constitutes a 'supply' of that car to the customer. Since the supposed service had not been carried out as specified in that case, it amounted to an offence under s. 1. This saved the respondent authority from having to prove *mens rea* under s. 14 (see **B6.118** *et seq.*) but the decision seems, with respect, to impose strict liability where Parliament did not intend it.

Disclaimers

The Trade Descriptions Act 1968 makes no express reference to disclaimers, but in **B6.110** some areas of trade and business the practice has developed of relying on disclaimers wherever it is feared that trade descriptions may not be accurate. The purpose of such disclaimers is to displace or negate any false impression that a doubtful trade description might otherwise create (*Hammertons Cars* [1976] 1 WLR 1243; *Wandsworth London Borough Council* v *Bentley* [1980] RTR 429). Disclaimer cases can therefore be distinguished from defences under s. 24 of the Act (see **B6.111**) which operate on the basis that the *actus reus* of the offence has indeed been committed. It has been held that in order to be effective disclaimers must be 'as bold, precise and compelling as the trade description itself' (*Norman* v *Bennett* [1974] 1 WLR 229, per Lord Widgery CJ at p. 232). Disclaimers in small print or on obscure notices cannot therefore suffice (*Waltham Forest London Borough Council* v *TG Wheatley (Central Garage) Ltd* [1978] RTR 157), nor may a disclaimer itself be phrased misleadingly or ambiguously (as in *Corfield* v *Starr* [1981] RTR 380, where a notice next to a car's odometer stated that the 'Customer's Protection Act' (*sic*) precluded the dealers from verifying the accuracy of the mileage recorded — this might have given the impression that, but for this fictitious statute, the dealers would have been able to verify the recorded mileage, whereas the dealers knew it to be incorrect). Oral disclaimers may in theory be effective, but in practice are unlikely to provide full protection, if only because the offence may be complete before the oral disclaimer is made (*Lewin* v *Fuell* (1991) 155 JP 206).

Most reported cases on disclaimers involve vehicle odometers. Dealers are frequently unable to verify the recorded mileages on used vehicles acquired by them, and may know in some cases that the readings cannot possibly be correct. A clear and prominent disclaimer placed next to (or across) the suspect odometer display will suffice to avoid liability under s. 1(1)(b) (*Ealing London Borough Council* v *Taylor* (1995) 159 JP 460).

It has been stated in a number of cases (including *Southwood* [1987] 1 WLR 1361, *Southend Borough Council* v *White* (1991) 156 JP 463 and (*obiter*) in *Shrewsbury Crown Court, ex parte Venables* [1994] Crim LR 61) that disclaimers cannot be relied upon in cases where false trade descriptions have been applied by the defendant himself, contrary to s. 1(1)(a). Where a disclaimer is added only after the application of a false trade description, it will come too late to avoid liability that has already been incurred (*Newman v Hackney London Borough Council* [1982] RTR 296); and the courts are rightly unwilling to assist dishonest dealers who deliberately falsify odometers etc., but it is clear that cases can arise in which the application of a false trade description is not dishonest and is accompanied by a contemporaneous disclaimer. *Bull* [1997] RTR 123 was such a case. B, a car dealer, displayed for sale a car bearing an odometer reading he rightly regarded as suspect. He placed a clearly worded disclaimer over the odometer itself, thereby avoiding any liability under s. 1(1)(b), but at the moment of sale he entered the false odometer reading on the invoice, subject again to a clear disclaimer, which stated that the mileage could not be verified and 'must be considered incorrect'. This led to a conviction under s. 1(1)(a), but his conviction was quashed by the Court of Appeal, on the basis that the disclaimer was attached to the invoice in such a way as to prevent it from ever being false. *Newman* was distinguished on that basis and *Southwood* was not discussed, but it is submitted that *Bull* is rightly decided on its facts and that disclaimers may, in appropriate cases, prevent liability from being incurred under s. 1(1)(a).

Defence of Mistake, Accident, etc.

B6.111
Trade Descriptions Act 1968, s. 24

(1) In any proceedings for an offence under this Act it shall, subject to subsection (2) of this section, be a defence for the person charged to prove—

(a) that the commission of the offence was due to a mistake or to reliance on information supplied to him or to the act or default of another person, an accident or some other cause beyond his control; and

(b) that he took all reasonable precautions and exercised all due diligence to avoid the commission of such an offence by himself or any person under his control.

(2) If in any case the defence provided by the last foregoing subsection involves the allegation that the commission of the offence was due to the act or default of another person or to reliance on information supplied by another person, the person charged shall not, without leave of the court, be entitled to rely on that defence unless, within a period ending seven clear days before the hearing, he has served on the prosecutor a notice in writing giving such information identifying or assisting in the identification of that other person as was then in his possession.

(3) In any proceedings for an offence under this Act of supplying or offering to supply goods to which a false trade description is applied it shall be a defence for the person charged to prove that he did not know, and could not with reasonable diligence have ascertained, that the goods did not conform to the description or that the description had been applied to the goods.

'Good intentions and mistake do not by themselves constitute a defence. The accused must plead and prove the circumstances specified in s. 24' (*Wings Ltd v Ellis* [1985] AC 272, per Lord Templeman). A defendant must prove at least one of the five specific elements mentioned in s. 24(1)(a) *and* satisfy the reasonable precautions/due diligence test in s. 24(1)(b) in order to succeed in the defence. 'Reasonable diligence' is also central to the separate defence under s. 24(3).

Where mistake is pleaded, this must be the defendant's own mistake and not, for example, that of an employee (*Birkenhead and District Co-operative Society Ltd v Roberts* [1970] 1 WLR 1497). A mistake by an employee may be pleaded as the act or default of another person (*Tesco Supermarkets Ltd v Nattrass* [1972] AC 153) but must then be notified in advance of the trial, in accordance with s. 24(2). Where a corporate defendant is involved, the acts or defaults of the board of directors, managing director, etc., must be treated as those of the defendant itself, but the acts of middle ranking officers or branch managers are treated as those of third parties (*Tesco Supermarkets Ltd v Nattrass*).

Third parties allegedly responsible must be identified, wherever possible, in accordance with s. 24(2).

Due (or Reasonable) Diligence under s. 24   What amounts to 'due diligence' **B6.112** under s. 24(1) or 'reasonable diligence' under s. 24(3) must largely be a question of fact. The two expressions mean much the same thing (*Texas Homecare v Stockport Metropolitan Borough Council* (1988) 152 JP 83). In the case of used motor vehicles, it has been held that dealers should be careful to disclaim the accuracy of an odometer reading, unless they can verify it from the vehicle's log book or service record, from previous owners (*Simmons v Potter* [1975] RTR 347) or from a careful examination of the vehicle's age and condition (*Naish v Gore* [1971] 3 All ER 737). It is clearly not enough for a dealer to rely on information as to mileage or roadworthiness provided by an MOT certificate (*Barker v Hargreaves* [1981] RTR 197) but there is no rule of law to the effect that particular precautions must always be taken in particular cases (*Ealing London Borough Council v Taylor* (1995) 159 JP 460).

Where it is alleged that employees were to blame, the defendant must be able to show that a satisfactory system of training, supervision and inspection was provided (*Tesco Supermarkets v Nattrass* [1972] AC 153). Where goods are sold in large quantities, samples should be examined to ensure that they conform to any trade description applied to them. The adequacy of any system of sampling must be assessed as a question of fact. In *Rotherham Metropolitan Borough Council v Raysun (UK) Ltd* (1988) *The Times*, 27 April 1988, 100,000 packets of 'poisonless' crayons were imported from Hong Kong, but only one packet was tested for toxicity by the defendants and it was not clear whether any tests had been carried out in Hong Kong. It was held that the due diligence test under s. 24(1) had not been satisfied.

Defences to Charges under s. 1(1)(a)   The Court of Appeal held in *Southwood* **B6.113** [1987] 1 WLR 1361 that a person who deliberately falsifies a car odometer cannot rely on any s. 24 defence. As Lord Lane CJ pointed out in that case, 'by falsifying the instrument, he has disqualified himself from asserting that he has taken any precautions, let alone reasonable precautions'. That does not, however, preclude reliance on s. 24(1) in cases where the defendant has mistakenly, and despite taking all reasonable care, applied a false trade description to goods (cf. *Bull* [1997] RTR 123).

Innocent Publication of Advertisement

Trade Descriptions Act 1968, s. 25   **B6.114**

> In proceedings for an offence under this Act committed by the publication of an advertisement it shall be a defence for the person charged to prove that he is the person whose business it is to publish or arrange for the publication of advertisements and that he received the advertisement for publication in the ordinary course of business and did not know and had no reason to suspect that its publication would amount to an offence under this Act.

This defence is additional to the ones provided in s. 24 (see **B6.111**). It does not assist persons whose business is not one of publishing advertisements or who do not publish the offending advertisement in the ordinary course of their business, but it is submitted that a shopkeeper who places an advertisement in his window may argue that such advertising is an ordinary (if only a peripheral) part of his business (see the cases discussed at **B6.104**).

Offences Due to the Act or Default of Another Person

Trade Descriptions Act 1968, s. 23   **B6.115**

> Where the commission by any person of an offence under this Act is due to the act or default of some other person that other person shall be guilty of the offence, and a person may be

charged with and convicted of the offence by virtue of this section whether or not proceedings are taken against the first-mentioned person.

Section 23 is usually referred to as the 'by-pass' provision, although it does not always operate in that way. It may equally operate so as to enable the 'other person' to be joined as a co-defendant. The drafting of the provision is faulty, since it suggests that proof of the guilt of the first person is an essential pre-requisite for the conviction of the 'other person'; and yet the first person may well be able to escape liability under s. 24(1) for the very reason that the offence was caused by the act or default of the other person. In *Coupe* v *Guyett* [1973] 1 WLR 669, the Divisional Court resolved this problem by holding that a s. 23 prosecution may succeed in cases where it is proved that the 'first person' *would* have been guilty, but for the fact that he has a s. 24 defence. This interpretation is in fact consistent with the wording of s. 24(1)(a). This also refers to the 'commission of the offence', even though it actually provides defendants with a complete defence.

In cases where the 'other person' was himself acting in the course of a trade or business, it is unlikely that resort to s. 23 would ever be strictly necessary. If, for example, Dealer 1 falsifies the mileage recorded on the odometer of a car, and sells it through the trade to Dealer 2, who is prosecuted for an offence under s. 1(1)(b), it would be possible to prosecute Dealer 1 under s. 23, but it would usually be easier to prosecute him under s. 1(1)(a), for applying the false trade description in the first place. Section 23 may, however, be useful where it is desired to prosecute a private individual, who has 'clocked' his car before selling it to the trade, but who cannot be prosecuted directly under s. 1 (see *Olgeirsson* v *Kitching* [1986] 1 WLR 304).

Directors and Officers of Corporations

B6.116 Where offences committed by corporations are proved to have been committed with the consent and connivance of a director or other officer of the corporation, or any person acting in that capacity (or to have been attributable to neglect on the part of any such person), he may also be convicted of the offence (Trade Descriptions Act 1968, s. 20).

Obstruction of Authorised Officers

B6.117   **Trade Descriptions Act 1968, s. 29**

(1)   Any person who—
(a)   wilfully obstructs an officer of a local weights and measures authority or of a government department acting in pursuance of this Act; or
(b)   wilfully fails to comply with any requirement properly made to him by such an officer under section 28 of this Act; or
(c)   without reasonable cause fails to give such an officer so acting any other assistance or information which he may reasonably require of him for the purpose of the performance of his functions under this Act,
shall be guilty of an offence and liable on conviction to a fine not exceeding level 3 on the standard scale.
(2)   If any person, in giving any such information as is mentioned in the preceding subsection, makes any statement which he knows to be false, he shall be guilty of an offence.
(3)   Nothing in this section shall be construed as requiring a person to answer any question or give any information if to do so might incriminate him.

Section 28 gives authorised officers the power, in specified circumstances, to enter premises and inspect and seize goods and documents, but no solicitor can be compelled to produce privileged documents etc. under that section (s. 28(7)). An offence under s. 29(2), which is triable either way and subject to the same penalties as an offence under s. 1, can be committed even during an interview under caution, in which the suspect has the right to remain silent (*Page* [1996] Crim LR 439). It follows that a s. 29(2) offence may also be committed where D has the right to remain silent under s. 29(3).

FALSE TRADE DESCRIPTIONS IN RESPECT OF SERVICES, ACCOMMODATION OR FACILITIES

Definition

Trade Descriptions Act 1968, s. 14

B6.118

(1)   It shall be an offence for any person in the course of any trade or business—

(a)   to make a statement which he knows to be false; or

(b)   recklessly to make a statement which is false;

as to any of the following matters, that is to say,—

(i)   the provision in the course of any trade or business of any services, accommodation or facilities;

(ii)   the nature of any services, accommodation or facilities provided in the course of any trade or business;

(iii)   the time at which, manner in which or persons by whom any services, accommodation or facilities are so provided;

(iv)   the examination, approval or evaluation by any person of any services, accommodation or facilities so provided; or

(v)   the location or amenities of any accommodation so provided.

(2)   For the purposes of this section—

(a)   anything (whether or not a statement as to any of the matters specified in the preceding subsection) likely to be taken as a statement as to any of those matters as would be false shall be deemed to be a false statement as to that matter; and

(b)   a statement made regardless of whether it is true or false shall be deemed to be made recklessly, whether or not the person making it had reasons for believing that it might be false.

(3)   In relation to any services consisting of or including the application of any treatment or process or the carrying out of any repair, the matters specified in subsection (1) of this section shall be taken to include the effect of the treatment, process or repair.

(4)   In this section, 'false' means false to a material degree and 'services' does not include anything done under a contract of service.

Procedure and Enforcement

The position is the same as for offences under the Trade Descriptions Act 1968, s. 1 (see **B6.100**). **B6.119**

Indictment

Statement of Offence

B6.120

Recklessly making a false statement, contrary to section 14(1)(b) of the Trade Descriptions Act 1968

Particulars of Offence

A Ltd on or about the . . . day of . . . in the course of their trade or business, recklessly stated that the Hotel . . . in . . . provided air conditioned accommodation in all rooms, whereas the said hotel was not equipped with air-conditioning.

In *Piper* (1996) 160 JP 116 the Court of Appeal offered guidance on the framing of charges for offences contrary to the Trade Descriptions Act 1968, s. 14(1). Subparagraphs (i) to (v) of section 14(1)(b) overlap, and there may be cases in which the facts potentially fall within more than one of them. It is therefore inadvisable to specify any of these sub-paragraphs. The particulars of the offence should be limited to identifying the offending statement and the way in which it is alleged to have been false. Further particulars may be provided, by order if appropriate, if the defence are embarrassed by insufficient knowledge of the allegation they have to meet.

Sentence

B6.121 The penalty on summary conviction is a fine not exceeding £5,000; on conviction on indictment, the penalty is a fine and/or imprisonment for up to two years (Trade Descriptions Act 1968, s. 18). In *Burridge* (1985) 7 Cr App (S) 125 the offender pleaded guilty to four offences of making false statements as to the nature of services provided. He was the director of a small company which repaired washing machines, and on the occasions in question invoices had been submitted to customers even though the specified work had not been carried out. A sentence of nine months' imprisonment was imposed, with three months to serve and the balance suspended. Lord Lane CJ said that the sentence was, 'if anything, on the light side'.

Elements

B6.122 The two offences created by the Trade Descriptions Act 1968, s. 14(1), have some elements in common with offences under s. 1, but differ in a number of important respects, notably in that the s. 14 offences each require proof of *mens rea*: knowledge of the falsity of the statement, in the case of offences under s. 14(1)(a); and recklessness as to its falsity, in the case of offences under s. 14(1)(b). This does not mean that strict liability has no role to play in respect of offences under s. 14(1) (see *Wings Ltd v Ellis* [1985] AC 272 at **B6.125**).

The Course of Trade or Business

B6.123 The concept of a trade or business must have broadly the same meaning as it has in respect of offences under the Trade Descriptions Act 1968, s. 1 (see **B6.104**); and see also *Breeze* [1973] 1 WLR 994, in which it was held to be an offence under s. 14 for a person who was not a qualified architect to offer his services, commercially, on the basis that he was so qualified. *Breeze* was decided before *Roberts v Leonard* (1995) 94 LGR 284, in which it was finally decided that the business activities of professional men are performed in the course of a trade or business.

Where A, in the course of a trade or business, makes a false statement as to the provision of services, etc. by B, this must mean services, etc. provided (or supposedly provided) by B in the course of a trade or business.

False Statements under s. 14

B6.124 As is the case under the Trade Descriptions Act 1968, s. 1, a false statement under s. 14 must be false to a material degree (s. 14(4)). Section 14(2)(a) serves the same function in respect of s. 14(1) as s. 3(2) and (3) serve in relation to s. 1 (see **B6.106**). This means that misleading statements or indications, even if technically correct, may involve offences under s. 14.

In contrast to the position under s. 1, it has been held that offences under s. 14 can be committed, even where the offending statement is made after the transaction to which it relates has been completed. In *Breed v Cluett* [1970] 2 QB 459, a s. 14 offence was committed by a builder who falsely stated, after completing the sale of a bungalow, that the building was covered by a ten-year NHBRC guarantee. It has also been held that s. 14 can apply to statements concerning services which have already been provided. In *Bevelectric Ltd* (1992) 157 JP 323, the defendants, who carried on a washing machine repair business, always told customers that their machines needed new motors, regardless of whether this was the case. They were charged with offences under s. 14(1)(b), on the basis that their statements falsely indicated that genuine assessments had been made of the condition of the machines. Upholding their convictions, Staughton LJ stated that 'a false statement about services already provided is within the section if it is connected or associated with the supply of the services in question'.

A statement which is not false at the time it is made does not become so, merely because the defendant or a third party subsequently fails to provide services, etc. in accordance with that statement (*Sunair Holidays Ltd* v *Dodd* [1970] 1 WLR 1037; *Sunair Holidays Ltd* [1973] 1 WLR 1105). It does not, for example, criminalise a failure to fulfil a contractual obligation which the defendant entered into in good faith; but a promise as to the future may involve representations of present fact (e.g., as to the maker's present intentions or policies) and may thus come within the scope of s. 14 (cf. *British Airways Board* v *Taylor* [1976] 1 WLR 13).

Mens Rea

The offence created by the Trade Descriptions Act 1968, s. 14(1)(a), was surely meant **B6.125** to be a full *mens rea* offence. To commit it, the defendant must 'make a statement which he knows to be false' and the draftsman no doubt assumed that this meant the same thing as 'knowingly making a false statement'. In *Wings Ltd* v *Ellis* [1985] AC 272, however, the House of Lords held that the offence was one of 'partially strict' liability, because the defendant need not know he is making the statement, as long as he knows that some part of it is false. In that case, W published a holiday brochure which they found to contain inaccurate information concerning accommodation provided at a hotel in Sri Lanka. They tried to ensure that this faulty information was not communicated to potential customers, but unknown to them a travel agent subsequently provided a customer with an uncorrected copy of the brochure, which he read. W argued that they did not know of the error in the brochure when it was printed, and did not know that the customer would be shown an uncorrected copy once the error had been discovered. They did not therefore knowingly make a false statement concerning the hotel. The House of Lords held that this did not matter. When the brochure was read by the customer, W already knew the statement was false, and the offence was therefore made out.

'Recklessness' under s. 14(1)(b) must be construed in accordance with s. 14(2)(b), and is a wider concept than recklessness in Theft Act deception cases (see **B5.2** and **B5.3**). It is sufficient if the defendant 'did not have regard to the truth or falsity of his advertisement, even though it cannot be shown that he was deliberately closing his eyes to the truth or that he had any kind of dishonest mind' (*MFI Warehouses Ltd* v *Nattrass* [1973] 1 WLR 307 per Lord Widgery CJ at p. 313). See also *Dixons Ltd* v *Roberts* (1984) 148 JP 513.

As to circumstances in which *mens rea* can be attributed to a corporation, see **A5.11**. As to the liability of directors or officers, see the Trade Descriptions Act 1968, s. 20 at **B6.116**.

Services, Accommodation and Facilities

The provision of services, accommodation or facilities for the purposes of the Trade **B6.126** Descriptions Act 1968, s. 14, must ordinarily involve something different from the supply of goods (*Newell* v *Hicks* [1984] RTR 135; *Westminster City Council* v *Ray Alan (Manshops) Ltd* [1982] 1 WLR 383), but a guarantee relating to goods may involve the promise of a service (*Ashley* v *Sutton London Borough Council* (1994) 159 JP 631; cf. *Breed* v *Cluett* [1970] 2 QB 459 — NHBRC guarantee on bungalow). Repair, servicing, insurance, parking or credit arrangements for purchasers or prospective purchasers of goods may be classed as services or facilities, but may also involve the supply of goods (see *Formula One Autocentres* v *Birmingham City Council* [1999] RTR 195 at **B6.109**).

'Accommodation' clearly includes hotel rooms and holiday lettings, and 'services' include house builders' guarantees and the professional services of architects, etc., but s. 14 does not appear to cover false or misleading statements concerning residential or commercial property sales or lettings. These are covered by the Property Misdescriptions Act 1991, s. 1 (see **B6.129**).

It is not necessary for an information or indictment to specify whether an allegedly false trade description refers to services, facilities or accommodation, as long as it identifies the offending statement and the sense in which it is alleged to be false (see *Piper* (1996) 160 JP 116 at **B6.120**).

Defences, Disclaimers and By-pass Procedures

B6.127   The rules governing the use of disclaimers for the purpose of nullifying potential misdescriptions under the Trade Descriptions Act 1968, s. 1, would appear to be equally applicable to cases under s. 14 (see for example *Clarksons Holidays Ltd* (1972) 57 Cr App R 38). The same is true of third-party or by-pass prosecutions under s. 23 (see **B6.115**). The s. 24(1) defence (see **B6.111**) can be pleaded in s. 14 cases (*Wings Ltd* v *Ellis* [1985] AC 272) but the *mens rea* elements required for offences under s. 14 make it less likely that defendants will need to have recourse to that defence.

MISLEADING PRICES AND PROPERTY MISDESCRIPTIONS

Misleading Price Indications

B6.128   Misleading price indications as to goods (but not services, etc.) were once covered, somewhat unsatisfactorily, by the Trade Descriptions Act 1968, s. 11. The Consumer Protection Act 1987, part III, now deals more comprehensively with misleading price indications as to goods, services, accommodation or facilities. It is supplemented by the Code of Practice for Traders on Price Indications, issued and approved by the Secretary of State under s. 25 of the Act (see SI 1988/2078) and by regulations which make specific provision for price indications in respect of methods of payment (credit cards, etc.), bureaux de change and ticket resales. The Code of Practice does not have direct legal effect, but conformity to it (or contraventions of it) may be relied upon evidentially in determining whether an offence has been committed under s. 20 (s. 25(2)). For an example of the effect of the Code of Practice, see *Mirror Group Newspapers* v *Northants County Council* [1997] Crim LR 882.

In brief, the Consumer Protection Act 1987, s. 20, makes it an offence:

    (a)   for a person acting in the course of any business of his to give any consumers a misleading indication as to the price at which goods, services, accommodation or facilities are available; or

    (b)   for such a person to fail to take all reasonable steps to prevent consumers from relying on an indication which was correct when first given, but which has become incorrect thereafter.

The scope of these offences is in some respects narrower than that of Trade Descriptions Act offences, in that the indication must be given to consumers (defined in s. 20(6) of the 1987 Act) and must be made by someone acting in the course of his own business, thus excluding the acts of mere employees (see *Warwickshire County Council, ex parte Johnson* [1993] AC 583). Senior officers of a corporation may however incur liability for acts committed through their default etc. under s. 40(2).

A number of specific defences are provided by s. 24 of the 1987 Act, and s. 39 provides a more general 'due diligence' defence. Where this defence is applicable, s. 40(1) permits prosecutions to be brought against responsible third parties. In contrast to the position under the Trade Descriptions Act 1968, s. 23 (see **B6.115**), a third party can be prosecuted under s. 40(1) only if he was acting in the course of any business of his at the relevant time. Private individuals cannot be prosecuted under the 1987 Act.

In all other respects, the rules governing procedures, time limits, enforcement, modes of trial and penalties are the same as for 'either way' offences under the Trade Descriptions Act 1968 (see **B6.100** and **B6.102**).

Property Misdescriptions

As previously explained (see **B6.126**), the Trade Descriptions Act 1968 does not appear **B6.129** to cover false or misleading statements concerning residential or commercial property sales or lettings. These may, however, be covered by the Property Misdescriptions Act 1991, s. 1, which applies to false or misleading statements concerning 'prescribed matters' and made in the course of an estate agency business or property development business (otherwise than in the course of providing conveyancing services). The Property Misdescriptions (Prescribed Matters) Order 1992 (SI 1992/2834) provides a list of 'prescribed matters'. The list includes: physical or structural characteristics, location, aspect, view, proximity to facilities, accommodation, measurements, survey reports, guarantees, history, length of time for sale, price, tenure/estate, council tax classification and planning permission status.

Liability is strict, subject to proof of a due diligence defence under s. 2 (see *Enfield London Borough Council* v *Castles Estate Agents Ltd* (1996) 160 JP 618). Employees of estate agents etc. can be convicted where the misdescription results from their acts or defaults, whether or not proceedings are taken against the employer (s. 1(2)). Offences are triable either way and punishable on summary conviction with a fine not exceeding £5,000 or by an unlimited fine following conviction on indictment. They are not punishable by imprisonment.

In other respects, the rules governing procedures, time limits and enforcement (set out in s. 5 and in the schedule to the Act) are the same as for 'either way' offences under the Trade Descriptions Act 1968 (see **B6.100** and **B6.102**).

SECTION B7: COMPANY, INVESTMENT AND INSOLVENCY OFFENCES

OFFENCES UNDER THE COMPANIES ACT 1985: GENERAL

Scope of the Companies Act 1985

B7.1 The Companies Act 1985 contains nearly 150 offence-creating provisions, many of which must be read in conjunction with various other provisions which do not themselves create offences. Some of the offences relate only to minor, regulatory, defaults or irregularities; others may involve serious acts of fraud. The distinction is not, however, clear-cut, because minor defaults and irregularities will often be associated with more serious offences, as, for example, where improperly maintained accounts or records are used to conceal fraudulent trading or unlawful loans to directors. In such cases, an indictment may include counts alleging fraud offences and counts alleging lesser defaults and irregularities, many of which are triable either way.

A general work on criminal law cannot attempt to cover all possible offences under the Companies Act 1985 or to investigate the relationship between the offence-creating provisions and the rest of the Act. Readers requiring such coverage must therefore refer to specialised works on company law. This section will concentrate instead on the principal fraud (or fraud-related) offences under the Act. A complete table of offences under the Act, together with provisions relating to mode of trial and penalties, is contained in sch. 24 to the Act, and part of this schedule is reproduced at **B7.2**.

Schedule of Offences under the Companies Act 1985

B7.2 **Companies Act 1985, sch. 24, Abridged**

Some regulatory offences are omitted.

Section of Act creating offence	General nature of offence	Mode of prosecution	Punishment
95(6)	Knowingly or recklessly authorising or permitting misleading, false or deceptive material in statement by directors under section 95(5).	1. On indictment. 2. Summary.	Two years or a fine; or both. Six months or the statutory maximum; or both.
110(2)	Making misleading, false or deceptive statement in connection with valuation under section 103 or 104.	1. On indictment. 2. Summary.	Two years or a fine; or both. Six months or the statutory maximum; or both.
114	Contravention of any of the provisions of sections 99 to 104, 106.	1. On indictment. 2. Summary.	A fine. The statutory maximum.

Section of Act creating offence	General nature of offence	Mode of prosecution	Punishment
143(2)	Company acquiring its own shares in breach of section 143.	1. On indictment.	In the case of the company, a fine. In the case of an officer of the company who is in default. two years or a fine; or both.
		2. Summary.	In the case of the company, the statutory maximum. In the case of an officer of the company who is in default, six months or the statutory maximum; or both.
151(3)	Company giving financial assistance towards acquisition of its own shares.	1. On indictment.	Where the company is convicted, a fine. Where an officer of the company is convicted, two years or a fine; or both.
		2. Summary.	Where the company is convicted, the statutory maximum. Where an officer of the company is convicted, six months or the statutory maximum; or both.
156(7)	Director making statutory declaration under section 155, without having reasonable grounds for opinion expressed in it.	1. On indictment. 2. Summary.	Two years or a fine; or both. Six months or the statutory maximum; or both.
173(6)	Director making statutory declaration under section 173 without having reasonable grounds for the opinion expressed in the declaration.	1. On indictment. 2. Summary.	Two years or a fine; or both. Six months or the statutory maximum; or both.
210(3)	Failure to discharge obligation of disclosure under part VI; other forms of non-compliance with that part.	1. On indictment. 2. Summary.	Two years or a fine; or both. Six months or the statutory maximum; or both.
216(3)	Failure to comply with company notice under section 212; making false statement in response, etc.	1. On indictment. 2. Summary.	Two years or a fine; or both. Six months or the statutory maximum; or both.
221(5) or 222(4)	Company failing to keep accounting records (liability of officers).	1. On indictment. 2. Summary.	Two years or a fine; or both. Six months or the statutory maximum; or both.
222(6)	Officer of company failing to secure compliance with, or intentionally causing default under section 222(5) (preservation of accounting records for requisite number of years).	1. On indictment. 2. Summary.	Two years or a fine; or both. Six months or the statutory maximum; or both.
233(5)	Approving defective accounts.	1. On indictment. 2. Summary.	A fine. The statutory maximum.

Section of Act creating offence	General nature of offence	Mode of prosecution	Punishment
234(5)	Non-compliance with part VII, as to directors' report and its content; directors individually liable.	1. On indictment. 2. Summary.	A fine. The statutory maximum.
238(5)	Failing to send company's annual accounts, directors' report and auditors' report to those entitled to receive them.	1. On indictment. 2. Summary.	A fine. The statutory maximum.
317(7)	Director failing to disclose interest in contract.	1. On indictment. 2. Summary.	A fine. The statutory maximum.
323(2)	Director dealing in options to buy or sell company's listed shares or debentures.	1. On indictment. 2. Summary.	Two years or a fine; or both. Six months or the statutory maximum; or both.
324(7)	Director failing to notify interest in company's shares; making false statement in purported notification.	1. On indictment. 2. Summary.	Two years or a fine; or both. Six months or the statutory maximum; or both.
326(2), (3), (4), (5)	Various defaults in connection with company register of directors' interests.	Summary.	One-fifth of the statutory maximum. [Daily default fine: Except in the case of s. 326(5), one-fiftieth of the statutory maximum.]
328(6)	Director failing to notify company that members of his family have, or have exercised, options to buy shares or debentures; making false statement in purported notification.	1. On indictment. 2. Summary.	Two years or a fine; or both. Six months or the statutory maximum; or both.
329(3)	Company failing to notify investment exchange of acquisition of its securities by a director.	Summary.	One-fifth of the statutory maximum. [Daily default fine: One-fiftieth of the statutory maximum.]
342(1)	Director of relevant company authorising or permitting company to enter into transaction or arrangement, knowing or suspecting it to contravene section 330.	1. On indictment. 2. Summary.	Two years or a fine; or both. Six months or the statutory maximum; or both.
342(2)	Relevant company entering into transaction or arrangement for a director in contravention of section 330.	1. On indictment. 2. Summary.	Two years or a fine; or both. Six months or the statutory maximum; or both.
342(3)	Procuring a relevant company to enter into transaction or arrangement known to be contrary to section 330.	1. On indictment. 2. Summary.	Two years or a fine; or both. Six months or the statutory maximum; or both.
343(8)	Company failing to maintain register of transactions, etc., made with and for directors and not disclosed in company accounts; failing to make register available at registered office or at company meeting.	1. On indictment. 2. Summary.	A fine. The statutory maximum.

Section of Act creating offence	General nature of offence	Mode of prosecution	Punishment
389A(2)	Officer of company making false, misleading or deceptive statement to auditors.	1. On indictment. 2. Summary.	Two years or a fine; or both. Six months or the statutory maximum; or both.
429(6)	Offeror failing to send copy of notice or making statutory declaration knowing it to be false, etc.	1. On indictment. 2. Summary.	Two years or a fine; or both. Six months or the statutory maximum; or both. [Daily default fine: One-fiftieth of the statutory maximum.]
430A(6)	Offeror failing to give notice of rights to minority shareholder.	1. On indictment. 2. Summary.	A fine. The statutory maximum. [Daily default fine: One-fiftieth of the statutory maximum.]
444(3)	Failing to give Secretary of State, when required to do so, information about interests in shares, etc.; giving false information.	1. On indictment. 2. Summary.	Two years or a fine; or both. Six months or the statutory maximum; or both.
447(6)	Failure to comply with requirement to produce documents imposed by Secretary of State under section 447.	1. On indictment. 2. Summary.	A fine. The statutory maximum.
448(7)	Obstructing the exercise of any rights conferred by a warrant or failing to comply with a requirement imposed under subsection (3)(d).	1. On indictment. 2. Summary.	A fine. The statutory maximum.
449(2)	Wrongful disclosure of information or document obtained under section 447 or 448.	1. On indictment. 2. Summary.	Two years or a fine; or both. Six months or the statutory maximum; or both.
450	Destroying or mutilating company documents; falsifying such documents or making false entries; parting with such documents or altering them or making omissions.	1. On indictment. 2. Summary.	Seven years or a fine; or both. Six months or the statutory maximum; or both.
451	Making false statement or explanation in purported compliance with section 447.	1. On indictment. 2. Summary.	Two years or a fine; or both. Six months or the statutory maximum; or both.
458	Being a party to carrying on company's business with intent to defraud creditors, or for any fraudulent purpose.	1. On indictment. 2. Summary.	Seven years or a fine; or both. Six months or the statutory maximum; or both.

Scope of Offences under the Companies Act 1985

Although the Companies Act 1985 is primarily concerned with registered companies as **B7.3** defined in s. 735 (i.e. those registered under this and former Companies Acts), some of the provisions have a wider ambit. Thus, many provisions of part XIV (company investigations) apply equally to certain unregistered companies and to companies incorporated outside Great Britain which are or have been carrying on business in Great

Britain (s. 453 and sch. 22). A full list of provisions applicable to unregistered companies is contained in sch. 22 to the Act.

Procedural Provisions in Respect of Summary Proceedings

B7.4   Companies Act 1985, s. 731

(1)   Summary proceedings for any offence under the Companies Acts may (without prejudice to any jurisdiction exercisable apart from this subsection) be taken against a body corporate at any place at which the body has a place of business, and against any other person at any place at which he is for the time being.

(2)   Notwithstanding anything in section 127(1) of the Magistrates' Courts Act 1980, an information relating to an offence under the Companies Acts which is triable by a magistrates' court in England and Wales may be so tried if it is laid at any time within three years after the commission of the offence and within 12 months after the date on which evidence sufficient in the opinion of the Director of Public Prosecutions or the Secretary of State (as the case may be) to justify the proceedings comes to his knowledge.

(3)   [Applies only to Scotland.]

(4)   For purposes of this section, a certificate of the Director of Public Prosecutions . . . or the Secretary of State (as the case may be) as to the date on which such evidence as is referred to above came to his knowledge is conclusive evidence.

This provision has no effect in relation to the summary trial of offences triable either way (*Thames Metropolitan Stipendiary Magistrate, ex parte Horgan* [1998] QB 719).

OPTION DEALINGS BY DIRECTORS AND THEIR FAMILIES

B7.5   The offence of insider dealing is covered at **B7.18 *et seq*.** Directors and other individuals who have access to inside information concerning companies and their securities are not ordinarily prohibited from acquiring or disposing of such securities. Indeed, it is considered right and proper for directors to invest in the companies for which they work. They are prohibited from dealing in shares or other securities only when in possession of certain specified inside information which has not been made public and which would have a significant effect on prices if published (CJA 1993, s. 52).

In contrast, dealings by directors or certain members of their families in options to buy or sell 'relevant' shares or debentures are totally prohibited at all times, whether or not the persons concerned hold any such unpublished information. Trading in options is a form of speculation rather than of investment, and involves something akin to gambling on the future value of the securities concerned. Directors are clearly likely to hold some kind of inside information, and this is the rationale behind the prohibition, but possession of such information is not a requisite element of the offence.

Companies Act 1985, ss. 323 and 327

Prohibition on directors dealing in share options

323.—(1)   It is an offence for a director of a company to buy—

(a)   a right to call for delivery at a specified price and within a specified time of a specified number of relevant shares or a specified amount of relevant debentures; or

(b)   a right to make delivery at a specified price and within a specified time of a specified number of relevant shares or a specified amount of relevant debentures; or

(c)   a right (as he may elect) to call for delivery at a specified price and within a specified time or to make delivery at a specified price and within a specified time of a specified number of relevant shares or a specified amount of relevant debentures.

(2)   A person guilty of an offence under subsection (1) is liable to imprisonment or a fine, or both.

(3)   In subsection (1)—

(a)   'relevant shares', in relation to a director of a company, means shares in the company or in any other body corporate, being the company's subsidiary or holding company, or a subsidiary of the company's holding company, being shares as respects which there has been granted a listing on a stock exchange (whether in Great Britain or elsewhere);

    (b)   'relevant debentures', in relation to a director of a company, means debentures of the company or of any other body corporate, being the company's subsidiary or holding company or a subsidiary of the company's holding company, being debentures as respects which there has been granted such a listing; and

    (c)   'price' includes any consideration other than money.

    (4)   This section applies to a shadow director as to a director.

    (5)   This section is not to be taken as penalising a person who buys a right to subscribe for shares in, or debentures of, a body corporate or buys debentures of a body corporate that confer upon the holder of them a right to subscribe for, or to convert the debentures (in whole or in part) into, shares of that body.

Extension of s. 323 to spouses and children

327.—(1)   Section 323 applies to—

    (a)   the wife or husband of a director of a company (not being herself or himself a director of it), and

    (b)   an infant son or infant daughter of a director (not being himself or herself a director of the company),

as it applies to the director; but it is a defence for a person charged by virtue of this section with an offence under section 323 to prove that he (she) had no reason to believe that his (her) spouse or, as the case may be, parent was a director of the company in question.

    (2)   For purposes of this section—

    (a)   'son' includes stepson, and 'daughter' includes stepdaughter ('parent' being construed accordingly),

    (b)   'infant' means, in relation to Scotland, pupil or minor, and

    (c)   a shadow director of a company is deemed a director of it.

For procedural and sentencing provisions, see **B7.2** and **B7.4**.

Option dealings by the friends or unmarried partners of directors, or by other members of their families, are not caught by these provisions; but if the director can be proved to have encouraged or procured such dealings whilst in possession of unpublished inside information, or if such information has been disclosed to the persons who deal, liability may arise under the CJA 1993, part V (see **B7.18** *et seq*.).

PROHIBITED TRANSACTIONS INVOLVING LOANS ETC. TO DIRECTORS AND CONNECTED PERSONS

Definition

There is a grave danger that loan or other credit transactions between a company and **B7.6** one of its directors will be entered into on terms or in circumstances which are not in the company's best interests; and in extreme cases there is a danger that the loans etc. will merely be a cover for the fraudulent abstraction of company money, or the means of funding an illegal share support operation. The Companies Act 1985, s. 330, accordingly prohibits various kinds of loans and credit transactions, subject to exceptions contained in ss. 332 to 338, which relate to transactions (mostly, but not all, minor) that are not perceived to be deserving of prohibition.

There is an important distinction between 'relevant companies' and others. Relevant companies are defined in s. 331 as public companies and companies which are in the same group as a public company (e.g., subsidiaries of public companies). The distinction is important for two reasons. First, the prohibitions contained in s. 330 itself all apply to relevant companies, but those contained in s. 330(3) and (4) do not apply to other companies. Secondly, contraventions of s. 330 by relevant companies or their directors may lead to criminal penalties under s. 342, as well as civil remedies under s. 341, whereas contraventions by other companies or their directors can lead only to civil remedies.

Companies Act 1985, ss. 330, 331, 342 and 346

General restriction on loans etc. to directors and persons connected with them
330.—(1)   The prohibitions listed below in this section are subject to the exceptions in sections 332 to 338.

(2)   A company shall not—

(a)   make a loan to a director of the company or of its holding company;

(b)   enter into any guarantee or provide any security in connection with a loan made by any person to such a director.

(3)   A relevant company shall not—

(a)   make a quasi-loan to a director of the company or of its holding company;

(b)   make a loan or a quasi-loan to a person connected with such a director;

(c)   enter into a guarantee or provide any security in connection with a loan or quasi-loan made by any other person for such a director or a person so connected.

(4)   A relevant company shall not—

(a)   enter into a credit transaction as creditor for such a director or a person so connected;

(b)   enter into any guarantee or provide any security in connection with a credit transaction made by any other person for such a director or a person so connected.

(5)   For purposes of sections 330 to 346, a shadow director is treated as a director.

(6)   A company shall not arrange for the assignment to it, or the assumption by it, of any rights, obligations or liabilities under a transaction which, if it had been entered into by the company, would have contravened subsection (2), (3) or (4); but for the purposes of sections 330 to 347 the transaction is to be treated as having been entered into on the date of the arrangement.

(7)   A company shall not take part in any arrangement whereby—

(a)   another person enters into a transaction which, if it had been entered into by the company, would have contravened any of subsections (2), (3), (4) or (6); and

(b)   that other person, in pursuance of the arrangement, has obtained or is to obtain any benefit from the company or its holding company or a subsidiary of the company or its holding company.

Definitions for ss. 330
331.—(1)   The following subsections apply for the interpretation of sections 330 to 346.

(2)   'Guarantee' includes indemnity, and cognate expressions are to be construed accordingly.

(3)   A quasi-loan is a transaction under which one party ('the creditor') agrees to pay, or pays otherwise than in pursuance of an agreement, a sum for another ('the borrower') or agrees to reimburse, or reimburses otherwise than in pursuance of an agreement, expenditure incurred by another party for another ('the borrower')—

(a)   on terms that the borrower (or a person on his behalf) will reimburse the creditor; or

(b)   in circumstances giving rise to a liability on the borrower to reimburse the creditor.

(4)   Any reference to the person to whom a quasi-loan is made is a reference to the borrower; and the liabilities of a borrower under a quasi-loan include the liabilities of any person who has agreed to reimburse the creditor on behalf of the borrower.

(5)   [Repealed.]

(6)   'Relevant company' means a company which—

(a)   is a public company, or

(b)   is a subsidiary of a public company, or

(c)   is a subsidiary of a company which has as another subsidiary a public company, or

(d)   has a subsidiary which is a public company.

(7)   A credit transaction is a transaction under which one party ('the creditor')—

(a)   supplies any goods or sells any land under a hire-purchase agreement or a conditional sale agreement;

(b)   leases or hires any land or goods in return for periodical payments;

(c)   otherwise disposes of land or supplies goods or services on the understanding that payment (whether in a lump sum or instalments or by way of periodial payments or otherwise) is to be deferred.

(8) 'Services' means anything other than goods or land.

(9) A transaction or arrangement is made 'for' a person if—

(a) in the case of a loan or a quasi-loan, it is made to him;

(b) in the case of a credit transaction, he is the person to whom goods or services are supplied, or land is sold or otherwise disposed of, under the transaction;

(c) in the case of a guarantee or security, it is entered into or provided in connection with a loan or quasi-loan made to him or a credit transaction made for him;

(d) in the case of an arrangement within subsection (6) or (7) of section 330, the transaction to which the arrangement relates was made for him; and

(e) in the case of any other transaction or arrangement for the supply or transfer of, or of any interest in, goods, land or services, he is the person to whom the goods, land or services (or the interest) are supplied or transferred.

(10) 'Conditional sale agreement' means the same as in the Consumer Credit Act 1974.

Criminal penalties for breach of s. 330

342.—(1) A director of a relevant company who authorises or permits the company to enter into a transaction or arrangement knowing or having reasonable cause to believe that the company was thereby contravening section 330 is guilty of an offence.

(2) A relevant company which enters into a transaction or arrangement for one of its directors or for a director of its holding company in contravention of section 330 is guilty of an offence.

(3) A person who procures a relevant company to enter into a transaction or arrangement knowing or having reasonable cause to believe that the company was thereby contravening section 330 is guilty of an offence.

(4) A person guilty of an offence under this section is liable to imprisonment or a fine, or both.

(5) A relevant company is not guilty of an offence under subsection (2) if it shows that, at the time the transaction or arrangement was entered into, it did not know the relevant circumstances.

'Connected persons', etc.

346.—(1) This section has effect with respect to references in this part to a person being 'connected' with a director of a company, and to a director being 'associated with' or 'controlling' a body corporate.

(2) A person is connected with a director of a company if, but only if, he (not being himself a director of it) is—

(a) that director's spouse, child or stepchild; or

(b) except where the context otherwise requires, a body corporate with which the director is associated; or

(c) a person acting in his capacity as trustee of any trust the beneficiaries of which include—

(i) the director, his spouse or any children or stepchildren of his, or

(ii) a body corporate with which he is associated,

or of a trust whose terms confer a power on the trustees that may be exercised for the benefit of the director, his spouse, or any children or stepchildren of his, or any such body corporate; or

(d) a person acting in his capacity as partner of that director or of any person who, by virtue of paragraph (a), (b) or (c) of this subsection, is connected with that director; or

(e) a Scottish firm in which—

(i) that director is a partner,

(ii) a partner is a person who, by virtue of paragraph (a), (b) or (c) above, is connected with that director, or

(iii) a partner is a Scottish firm in which that director is a partner or in which there is a partner who, by virtue of paragraph (a), (b) or (c) above, is connected with that director.

(3) In subsection (2)—

(a) a reference to the child or stepchild of any person includes an illegitimate child of his, but does not include any person who has attained the age of 18; and

(b) paragraph (c) does not apply to a person acting in his capacity as trustee under an employees' share scheme or a pension scheme.

(4)   A director of a company is associated with a body corporate if, but only if, he and the persons connected with him, together—

(a)   are interested in shares comprised in the equity share capital of that body corporate of a nominal value equal to at least one-fifth of that share capital; or

(b)   are entitled to exercise or control the exercise of more than one-fifth of the voting power at any general meeting of that body.

(5)   A director of a company is deemed to control a body corporate if, but only if—

(a)   he or any person connected with him is interested in any part of the equity share capital of that body or is entitled to exercise or control the exercise of any part of the voting power at any general meeting of that body; and

(b)   that director, the persons connected with him and the other directors of that company, together, are interested in more than one-half of that share capital or are entitled to exercise or control the exercise of more than one-half of that voting power.

(6)   For purposes of subsections (4) and (5)—

(a)   a body corporate with which a director is associated is not to be treated as connected with that director unless it is also connected with him by virtue of subsection (2)(c) or (d); and

(b)   a trustee of a trust the beneficiaries of which include (or may include) a body corporate with which a director is associated is not to be treated as connected with a director by reason only of that fact.

(7)   The rules set out in part I of schedule 13 apply for the purposes of subsections (4) and (5).

(8)   References in those subsections to voting power the exercise of which is controlled by a director include voting power whose exercise is controlled by a body corporate controlled by him; but this is without prejudice to other provisions of subsections (4) and (5).

For procedural and sentencing provisions, see **B7.2** and **B7.4**.

Scope of the s. 330 Prohibitions

B7.7   The scope of the Companies Act 1985, s. 330, can be illustrated by the following examples:

(a)   A relevant company loans money, or guarantees a loan made by a bank or other lender, to one of its own directors, or to a director of its holding company, or to the spouse or minor child of either such director, or to another company with which such a director is 'associated' within the meaning of s. 346(4). Any such transactions may involve contraventions of s. 330(2) or (3), with the result that the directors responsible for making the loan or guarantee may be liable under s. 342(1). The prosecution would have to prove that they at least had reasonable cause to believe a breach of s. 330 was involved; but this would be self-evident, unless, perhaps, in the case of the loan to the company associated with a director, they were unaware of the association, in which case that director might himself be liable under s. 317 for not having declared his interest. The recipient could be liable on the same basis, if he (or it) procured the transaction (s. 342(3)); but the relevant company itself would face strict liability, unless it was able to prove that it (i.e., its controlling directors: see **A5.11**) did not know the circumstances (s. 342(5)).

(b)   A relevant company sells goods on credit to another company, which is 'associated' (as defined in s. 346(4)) with one of its own directors, or with a director of its holding company, or it offers a guarantee or security to procure a credit transaction on that company's behalf. This may involve a breach of s. 330(4) (consequences as in (a) above) unless the transaction is a minor or business transactions exempted by s. 335 (see **B7.8**).

(c)   Another person loans money to a director of a relevant company or to a connected person, and the company, as part of that arrangement, provides some benefit or service to the lender. A back-to-back arrangement of this kind is caught by s. 330(7). Alternatively, a simple assignment to the company of the creditor's rights etc. may fall foul of s. 330(6).

Summary of Permitted Transactions

The following transactions are not prohibited by the Companies Act 1985, s. 330: **B7.8**

(a)   Short-term quasi-loans which have to be reimbursed within two months may be permitted up to a total value of £5,000 (s. 332). This permits, *inter alia*, use of company credit cards etc. (but only by directors personally, not by connected persons).

(b)   Intercompany loans etc. within the same group may be permitted under s. 333, if they would otherwise be prohibited *only* by the fact that a director of one company is associated with another. See also s. 336, below.

(c)   Small loans totalling no more than £5,000, which would otherwise come within s. 330(2)(a), may be permitted under s. 334.

(d)   Credit transactions (otherwise caught by s. 330(4)) may be permitted under s. 335 if they do not total more than £10,000, or if made on ordinary credit terms as might reasonably be given to unconnected persons.

(e)   Various transactions made by a subsidiary company at the behest of its holding company are exempted under s. 336.

(f)   Loans etc. made to fund a director's expenditure on behalf of the company, or to enable him to perform his duties, may be permitted under s. 337, up to a limit of £20,000, subject to a requirement that they are either approved in advance by a general meeting of the company (after full disclosure), or made conditional on approval at or before the next annual general meeting. Failing such approval, they must be repaid within six months of that meeting.

(g)   Under s. 338, loans, quasi-loans and guarantees totalling up to £100,000 may be made to any director or connected person by a money-lending company on normal terms and in the ordinary course of its business; and for these purposes loans etc. to a company 'associated' with a director are not counted towards that aggregate, unless he 'controls' that company within the meaning of s. 346(5). If the money-lending company is a banking company, there is no restriction on the amounts involved; and if the loan is made for the purpose of facilitating the purchase or improvement of a director's main residence, a director of a money-lending company may be given the same favourable terms as company employees, up to a limit of £100,000.

Complicated provisions for calculating the totals of relevant amounts and the value of transactions are contained in ss. 339 and 340.

FINANCIAL ASSISTANCE PROVIDED BY COMPANIES IN CONNECTION WITH THE ACQUISITION OF THEIR OWN SHARES

Some of the most scandalous offences in the field of company fraud have involved the **B7.9** activities of 'asset strippers' who, having acquired control of companies with the aid of loans or other credit, used that control to make the company reimburse their creditors. Companies with large liquid assets are always a tempting target for such exploitation. In other cases, loans or other forms of financial assistance from the company may be arranged by the outgoing directors whose shares are being purchased. In a third type of case, loans may be made to enable 'insiders' to purchase shares prior to an anticipated surge in their market value. In many such cases, the sums loaned etc. are never repaid. See *Re VGM Holdings Ltd* [1942] Ch 235; *Selangor United Rubber Estates Ltd* v *Cradock (No. 3)* [1968] 1 WLR 1555; *Wallersteiner* v *Moir* [1974] 1 WLR 991. A somewhat different type of abuse is a 'share support' operation, as to which see *Saunders* [1996] 1 Cr App R 463 and **B7.37**.

Enactments prohibiting the provision of such assistance have existed since 1929, but until 1981 they were highly unsatisfactory in many respects, rendering many perfectly harmless transactions illegal, whilst providing wholly inadequate criminal penalties for serious fraud. The most significant sanctions were civil; in particular, the courts developed the doctrine of constructive trust in this area, and this remains important as a means of recovering company money etc., even though the criminal law has now been strengthened. The 1981 provisions have become ss. 151 to 158 of the Companies Act 1985. Of these, ss. 155 to 158 are concerned with special procedures which may be followed by private companies seeking to provide financial assistance within the law, and these provisions fall outside the scope of this work.

Companies Act 1985, s. 151

151.—(1)   Subject to the following provisions of this chapter [i.e. ss. 151 to 158] where a person is acquiring or is proposing to acquire shares in a company, it is not lawful for the company or any of its subsidiaries to give financial assistance directly or indirectly for the purpose of that acquisition before or at the same time as the acquisition takes place.

(2)   Subject to those provisions, where a person has acquired shares in a company and any liability has been incurred (by that or any other person), for the purpose of that acquisition, it is not lawful for the company or any of its subsidiaries to give financial assistance directly or indirectly for the purpose of reducing or discharging the liability so incurred.

(3)   If a company acts in contravention of this section, it is liable to a fine, and every officer of it who is in default is liable to imprisonment or a fine, or both.

For procedural and sentencing provisions, see **B7.2** and **B7.4**.

Financial assistance is defined in s. 152(1) as meaning assistance given by way of gift, guarantee, security, release, waiver loan or indemnity (other than indemnity in respect of the indemnifier's own neglect or default); or by way of certain transactions analogous to loans; or by way of the assignment of rights under loans or analogous transactions; or in any other way which materially reduces the net assets of the company; or financial assistance given by a company without net assets. Assistance given to the acquirer for the purpose of discharging his liabilities includes assistance given for the purpose of restoring him to his previous financial position (s. 152(3)).

Section 151 covers both assistance given in order to facilitate acquisition (s. 151(1)) and assistance given in order to discharge liabilities incurred in previous acquisitions (s. 151(2)). It may be direct, as where a gift or loan is made to the purchaser, or indirect, as where transactions are entered into with other persons (perhaps other companies controlled by the purchaser) and moneys paid over in accordance with these other transactions are ultimately passed to, or used for the benefit of, the purchaser (cf. *Wallersteiner* v *Moir* [1974] 1 WLR 991, in which Lord Denning MR said that payments to companies controlled by Dr Wallersteiner should be treated as payments made to him). Section 151 has no extraterritorial effect. In *Arab Bank plc* v *Mercantile Holdings Ltd* [1994] Ch 71 it was held that it did not prohibit a company registered in Gibraltar from providing financial assistance for the acquisition of shares in its English holding company.

In many cases, the question whether financial assistance has been provided will largely be one of fact (*Charterhouse Investment Trust Ltd* v *Tempest Diesels Ltd* [1986] BCLC 1).

A loan to a director or connected person may also fall foul of s. 330 (see **B7.6** to **B7.8**).

Permitted Transactions

B7.10   Certain transactions that would otherwise be prohibited by s. 151 are nevertheless permitted under s. 153. These include, cases in which the assistance is unintended or incidental to some larger purpose and is given in good faith in the interests of the company (s. 153(1) and (2)); cases in which it takes the form of a lawful dividend or bonus share issue (s. 153(3)); cases in which money is loaned in the course of a money-lending company's ordinary business (s. 153(4)(a)); and cases in which such assistance is provided as part of a bona fide share-owning scheme or arrangement for employees, former employees or their families (s. 153(4)(b) and (c)). Public companies may take advantage of s. 153(4) only if they have net assets which are not thereby reduced or if the assistance is provided out of distributable profits (s. 154(1)).

As to the problems of interpretation which may be raised by the 'principal purpose' doctrine, see *Brady* v *Brady* [1989] AC 755.

DESTRUCTION, MUTILATION OR FALSIFICATION OF COMPANY DOCUMENTS

Companies Act 1985, s. 450   B7.11

> (1)   An officer of a company or of an insurance company to which part II of the Insurance Companies Act 1982 applies, who—
> (a)   destroys, mutilates or falsifies, or is privy to the destruction, mutilation or falsification of a document affecting or relating to the company's property or affairs, or
> (b)   makes, or is privy to the making of, a false entry in such a document,
> is guilty of an offence, unless he proves that he had no intention to conceal the state of affairs of the company or to defeat the law.
> (2)   Such a person as above mentioned who fraudulently either parts with, alters or makes an omission in any such document or is privy to fraudulent parting with, fraudulent altering or fraudulent making of an omission in, any such document, is guilty of an offence.
> (3)   A person guilty of an offence under this section is liable to imprisonment or a fine, or both.
> (4)   Sections 732 (restriction on prosecutions), 733 (liability of individuals for corporate default) and 734 (criminal proceedings against unincorporated bodies) apply to an offence under this section.
> (5)   In this section 'document' includes information recorded in any form.

For procedural and sentencing provisions, see **B7.2** and **B7.4**.

This is one of the most serious offences under the Companies Act 1985, being punishable by up to seven years' imprisonment in addition to any fine. Clearly, such conduct (which might take the form of deleting computer files as well as interference with conventional documents) may be designed to remove evidence of serious company frauds. It may, in particular, be designed to frustrate or hinder an investigation into the company's affairs under part XIV (ss. 431 to 453) of the Act; but the offence may be committed whether or not any such investigation is in prospect.

FRAUDULENT TRADING

Definition

Companies Act 1985, s. 458   B7.12

> If any business of a company is carried on with intent to defraud creditors of the company or creditors of any other person, or for any fraudulent purpose, every person who was knowingly a party to the carrying on of the business in that manner is liable to imprisonment or a fine, or both.
> This applies whether or not the company has been, or is in the course of being, wound up.

For procedural and sentencing provisions see **B7.2** and **B7.4**. For disqualification orders see **E23.3**. The Court of Appeal provided guidance on sentencing in cases of fraudulent trading in *Smith* [1997] 2 Cr App R (S) 167, where the offenders had admitted using misleading accounts and false invoices to maintain the credit of a marketing company which had eventually failed, with losses of £520,000. Neither offender had previous convictions, the offence had taken place six years ago, and the offenders and their families had suffered considerably as a result of the offence. Sentences of three years' imprisonment were reduced to 18 months. Disqualifications for five years under the Company Directors Disqualification Act 1986 were upheld. In the Court of Appeal, Potter LJ observed that this case lay towards the lower end of a wide spectrum of offences covered by the offence of fraudulent trading. At one extreme there may have been deliberate reckless trading on a large scale aimed at a rapid return, with no genuine intention to discharge the company's debts but simply to milk creditors and line the directors' pockets. At the other end of the scale there may have been a properly funded business which has run into financial problems, where the directors have attempted to trade in order to save their own and their employees' jobs, but come to a point where they should have faced up to reality and ceased to trade. His lordship observed that the amount of loss involved and the level of criminality of the offender were important considerations in sentencing but that, broadly speaking, a charge of fraudulent trading resulting in loss to creditors is somewhat less seriously regarded than a charge of theft or fraud of the same amount. Credit should be given for personal mitigation, including a timely guilty plea and the tendering of full assistance to the receiver. In *Cook* (1995) 16 Cr App R (S) 917 a sentence of 12 months' imprisonment was upheld on the offender, who was a company secretary. The company had continued to trade for ten months while insolvent, during which time the offender received payment of £10,000. The company was wound up with debts of more than £286,000. *Cook* was followed and applied in *Thobani* [1998] 1 Cr App R (S) 227.

Fraudulent trading features both in the criminal law and in the civil law. The Insolvency Act 1986, s. 213, now provides that persons who were knowingly parties to such conduct may be required to contribute to the assets of the company concerned in the course of its winding up. Unlike the criminal provision in the Companies Act 1985, s. 458, the civil provision has no application unless the company goes into liquidation. In other respects, however, the civil courts apply exactly the same tests in defining the concept, and it may be appropriate to refer to their decisions when determining the scope of the criminal offence.

A conviction for fraudulent trading would be admissible evidence in any later civil proceedings (Civil Evidence Act 1968, s. 11) and the convicted person would be taken to have engaged in such conduct unless the contrary could be proved (ibid.), but the converse is not true: a finding of liability in civil proceedings would not be admissible evidence in later criminal proceedings (see **F11.1 *et seq*.**).

Indictment

B7.13

Statement of Offence

Fraudulent trading contrary to section 458 of the Companies Act 1985

Particulars of Offence

A between the . . . day of . . . and the . . . day of . . . was knowingly a party to the carrying on of certain business of a company called . . . with intent to defraud creditors of the said company [or with intent to defraud creditors of . . .] [or for a fraudulent purpose, namely . . .]

Carrying on the Business of the Company

B7.14   The wording of the Companies Act 1985, s. 458, might appear to suggest that it applies only where the whole business is fraudulently conducted. This is not the way that the provision has been construed. In *Re Gerald Cooper Chemicals Ltd* [1978] Ch 262, Templeman J said (at p. 267) that a single transaction could suffice:

> It does not matter . . . that only one creditor was defrauded, and by one transaction, provided that the transaction can properly be described as a fraud on a creditor perpetrated in the course of carrying on business.

See also *Lockwood* (1985) 2 BCC 99, 333. In *Philippou* (1989) 89 Cr App R 290 it was held that the fraudulent obtaining of an air travel organiser's licence from the Civil Aviation Authority involved carrying on a business for a fraudulent purpose, as the licence was essential to that business.

Intent to Defraud

Although the concept of intent to defraud was defined in *Welham* v *DPP* [1961] AC 103 **B7.15** in a way which appeared to include no specific requirement of dishonesty, so that certain kinds of conduct would, as a matter of law, fall within its scope, it is now clear that dishonesty (in the *Ghosh* [1982] QB 1053 sense: see **B4.37**) is an essential element both in fraudulent trading and in other fraud offences involving similar terminology. See *Cox* (1982) 75 Cr App R 291. The extent to which a jury need be directed on the meaning of dishonesty varies from case to case. A full *Ghosh* direction would not be appropriate in a case where the accused denies any knowledge of the allegedly fraudulent activities, whereas such a direction might be essential where he admits the facts and claims that he regarded them as normal business practice. See *Miles* [1992] Crim LR 657 and **B4.37**; and see also *Goldman* [1997] Crim LR 894.

Welham v *DPP* remains significant insofar as it establishes that there need not be any intent to cause financial loss to another person. Deliberately and dishonestly putting another person's property or financial interests in jeopardy may suffice (*Allsop* (1977) 64 Cr App R 29; *Wai Yu-Tsang* v *The Queen* [1992] 1 AC 269), whether or not there is any deception (*Scott* v *Metropolitan Police Commissioner* [1975] AC 819), and it may be fraud to deceive public officers into failing to perform their duty (*Welham* v *DPP*; cf. *Philippou* (1989) 89 Cr App R 290 at **B7.14**).

Frauds on Creditors and Other Fraudulent Purposes

A typical example of fraudulent trading involves a company which has lapsed into **B7.16** insolvency but which continues to obtain credit in circumstances where its directors know that there can be little if any chance of the creditors being paid. It would probably not be considered dishonest for debts to be incurred in the expectation that they could be repaid shortly after they fall due, because most debts are paid at least a few days or weeks late; but a jury may well consider it dishonest for debts to be incurred when they could at best be repaid months late (*Grantham* [1984] QB 675).

It was argued for a time that the words 'any fraudulent purpose' should be construed *eiusdem generis* with defrauding creditors, and that defrauding customers etc. should not e regarded as falling within the scope of this provision (see *Re Gerald Cooper Chemicals Ltd* [1978] Ch 226). This argument has been rejected. In *Kemp* [1988] QB 645 the Court of Appeal held that the mischief aimed at is fraudulent trading generally, and not just insofar as it affects creditors; whilst in *Philippou* (1989) 89 Cr App R 290, the fraudulent obtaining of an air travel organiser's licence was held to have involved fraudulent trading. This latter case perhaps stretches the meaning of 'purpose', because the licence was obtained as a means to an end, rather than as an end in itself; but it signals a clear rejection of any attempt to restrict the offence to frauds on creditors or potential creditors. As to the meaning of 'creditors' under s. 458, see *Smith* [1996] 2 Cr App R 1.

It is not necessarily fraudulent trading for a holding company to issue letters of comfort in respect of a subsidiary which it later allows to go into insolvent liquidation, though it would largely depend on whether the holding company was sincere at the time the letters were issued (*Re Augustus Barnett & Son Ltd* [1986] BCLC 170). Preference of one creditor over another may be open to attack in the civil courts under the Insolvency Act 1986, but is unlikely to be deemed fraudulent trading (*Re Sarflax Ltd* [1979] Ch 592).

Persons who May Be Liable for Fraudulent Trading

B7.17 The Court of Appeal held in *Miles* [1992] Crim LR 657 that the offence of fraudulent trading can be committed only by persons who exercise some kind of controlling or managerial function within the company. Employees who exercise no such function (and this includes junior managers and managers of local branches) are not regarded, for this purpose, as being party to the carrying on of the company's business.

This narrow interpretation of the Companies Act 1985, s. 458, leaves open the possibility of employees incurring liability as secondary parties to offences committed by the company's directors or senior managers. Persons holding no formal position within the company could meanwhile incur liability for fraudulent trading if they exercise *de facto* managerial powers, as where the directors bow to the will of a majority shareholder (a 'shadow director') who thereby determines company policy.

In *Maidstone Buildings Provisions Ltd* [1971] 1 WLR 1085 it was said that mere acquiescence on the part of a company secretary would make him liable under s. 458. Some positive action on his part would be needed. Passivity on the part of an executive director might be different, but *mens rea* would be needed in any event.

INSIDER DEALING

Scope of the Criminal Justice Act 1993, part V

B7.18 The law governing insider dealing was recast by the CJA 1993, part V, which implemented reforms required by Council Directive 89/592/EEC and replaced the Company Securities (Insider Dealing) Act 1985. The most significant difference from the old law lies in the wider range of securities to which the legislation applies. Gilts and debt securities issued by local authorities or other public sector bodies (British or overseas) are now included, whereas the old legislation covered only company securities and their derivatives, such as contracts for differences by reference to company share prices. The structure of the new legislation is also very different from the old. There is just one short offence-creating section (s. 52) which is drafted widely enough to cover all kinds of insider dealing. Improper disclosure of inside information is classed for these purposes as a form of insider dealing, as are the actions of an insider who encourages others to deal in circumstances proscribed under the Act. Section 52 is followed by 12 further sections and two schedules, which provide essential definitions, prescribe penalties and create specific defences, rather in the manner of the Theft Act 1968, ss. 2 to 7.

The protection of markets is the primary concern of the new legislation, as it was with the old. Private off-market deals therefore remain largely unaffected, but off-market dealing may be covered if it involves a professional intermediary.

Definition of the Offence of Insider Dealing

B7.19   **Criminal Justice Act 1993, s. 52**

(1)   An individual who has information as an insider is guilty of insider dealing if, in the circumstances mentioned in subsection (3), he deals in securities that are price-affected securities in relation to the information.

(2)   An individual who has information as an insider is also guilty of insider dealing if—

(a)   he encourages another person to deal in securities that are (whether or not that other knows it) price-affected securities in relation to the information, knowing or having reasonable cause to believe that the dealing would take place in the circumstances mentioned in subsection (3); or

(b)   he discloses the information, otherwise than in the proper performance of the functions of his employment, office or profession, to another person.

(3)   The circumstances referred to above are that the acquisition or disposal in question occurs on a regulated market, or that the person dealing relies on a professional intermediary or is himself acting as a professional intermediary.

(4)   This section has effect subject to section 53.

Section 53 contains special defences and is reproduced at **B7.32**.

Procedure

Insider dealing is triable either way (CJA 1993, s. 61). Prosecutions may be brought only **B7.20** by or with the consent of the Secretary of State or DPP (s. 61(2)).

Indictment

Statement of Offence   **B7.21**

Insider dealing contrary to section 52(1) of the Criminal Justice Act 1993

Particulars of Offence

A on the . . . day of . . ., being an individual who had information as an insider, namely information acquired by him through being a director of X plc relating to undisclosed losses incurred by X plc, dealt on a regulated market in securities of X plc, namely by procuring the disposal by B of 5,000 X plc ordinary shares on the London Stock Exchange, knowing them to be price-affected securities in relation to that information

Sentence

The penalty for insider dealing following conviction on indictment is imprisonment for **B7.22** a term not exceeding seven years, or a fine or both. On summary conviction, the penalty is up to six months imprisonment and/or a fine not exceeding the statutory maximum (CJA 1993, s. 61(1)). See *Stebbing* (1992) 14 Cr App R (S) 68.

For disqualification orders, see **B7.34** and **E23.3**.

Elements of the Offence

The principal offender in any case of insider dealing under the CJA 1993, s. 52, must be **B7.23** an individual, but persons encouraged to deal and persons to whom information is wrongly disclosed may be either individuals or corporations, and corporations may in some cases incur liability as secondary parties at common law. Furthermore, the definition of 'dealing' provided in s. 55 (see **B7.25**) is wide enough to cover cases in which the principal offender procures another person to acquire or dispose of the securities in question.

The concept of 'encouragement' of another person (s. 52(2)(a)) must be different from that of procuring, which is itself a form of dealing under s. 52(1). One difference is that dealing is procured only if it actually takes place, whereas encouragement is merely a form of incitement and need not be successful.

Improper disclosure of information (s. 52(2)(b)) need not be proved to have been committed with any improper intent. If the disclosure was a bona fide error or indiscretion, it will be for the defendant to prove this under s. 53(3) (see **B7.32**).

In a prosecution for insider dealing under s. 52(1), the following elements must be proved:

(a)   that the securities concerned were ones to which part V of the Act applies;

(b)   that the accused dealt in those securities;

(c)   that he had information as an insider;

(d)   that the securities were price affected in relation to that information; and

(e)   that he acquired or disposed of the securities on a regulated market (or as or in reliance on a professional intermediary).

The prosecution must also be able to prove a sufficient territorial connection with the United Kingdom under s. 62 of the Act. Only then may it be necessary for the accused to rely on the special defences created by s. 53 and sch. 1.

B7.24   *Securities to which part V Applies*   By virtue of s. 54 of the CJA 1993, part V applies to any security which falls within any paragraph of sch. 2 and which satisfies any conditions applied to it by the Insider Dealing (Securities and Regulated Markets) Order 1994 (SI 1994 No. 187)).

The following types of security are listed in sch. 2 (read in conjunction with s. 60 of the Act): company shares and stock (including those of unincorporated and foreign companies); debt securities and bonds issued by companies or public sector bodies (including the British Government and the Bank of England, other national governments or central banks, local authorities in Britain or elsewhere and some international organisations); share warrants or other rights to subscribe for shares or debt securities; rights under depository receipts; options to acquire or dispose of securities; contractual rights under which relevant securities are to be acquired or disposed of at a future date and at a pre-determined price ('futures'); and 'contracts for differences', by reference to fluctuations in share prices, market indices or interest rates for money placed on deposit.

The Insider Dealing (Securities and Regulated Markets) Order 1994, art. 4, restricts the application of sch. 2 to securities which are officially listed in a state within the European Economic Area (the European Community, Finland, Iceland, Norway and Leichtenstein) or admitted to dealing or quoted on or under the rules of a regulated market (as to which, see **B7.28**). Warrants, depository receipts, options, futures and contracts for differences may alternatively include those which relate to other securities that fall within the terms of art. 4.

Dealing in Securities

B7.25   **Criminal Justice Act 1993, s. 55**

   (1)   For the purposes of this part, a person deals in securities if—
      (a)   he acquires or disposes of the securities (whether as principal or agent); or
      (b)   he procures, directly or indirectly, an acquisition or disposal of the securities by any other person.
   (2)   For the purposes of this part, 'acquire', in relation to a security, includes—
      (a)   agreeing to acquire the security; and
      (b)   entering into a contract which creates the security.
   (3)   For the purposes of this part 'dispose', in relation to a security, includes—
      (a)   agreeing to dispose of the security; and
      (b)   bringing to an end a contract which created the security.
   (4)   For the purposes of subsection (1), a person procures an acquisition or disposal of a security if the security is acquired or disposed of by a person who is—
      (a)   his agent,
      (b)   his nominee, or
      (c)   a person who is acting at his direction,
in relation to the acquisition or disposal.
   (5)   Subsection (4) is not exhaustive as to the circumstances in which one person may be regarded as procuring an acquisition or disposal of securities by another.

B7.26   *Having Information as an Insider*   The basic definition of a person who has information as an insider is provided by the CJA 1993, s. 57; but some of the terms used in s. 57 must themselves be defined by reference to s. 56(1) and some of the terms used in s. 56 are in turn defined by s. 58 and by s. 60(4).

Criminal Justice Act 1993, ss. 56, 57 and 58

56.—(1)   For the purposes of this section and section 57 'inside information' means information which—
    (a)   relates to particular securities or to a particular issuer of securities or to particular issuers of securities and not to securities generally or to issuers of securities generally;
    (b)   is specific or precise;
    (c)   has not been made public; and
    (d)   if it were made public would be likely to have a significant effect on the price of any securities.

57.—(1)   For the purposes of this part, a person has information as an insider if and only if—
    (a)   it is, and he knows that it is, inside information, and
    (b)   he has it, and knows that he has it, from an inside source.
    (2)   For the purposes of subsection (1), a person has information from an inside source if and only if—
    (a)   he has it through—
      (i)   being a director, employee or shareholder of an issuer of securities; or
      (ii)   having access to the information by virtue of his employment, office or profession; or
    (b)   the direct or indirect source of his information is a person within paragraph (a).

58.—(1)   For the purposes of section 56 'made public', in relation to information, shall be construed in accordance with the following provisions of this section; but those provisions are not exhaustive as to the meaning of that expression.
    (2)   Information is made public if—
    (a)   it is published in accordance with the rules of a regulated market for the purpose of informing investors and their professional advisers;
    (b)   it is contained in records which by virtue of any enactment are open to inspection by the public;
    (c)   it can be readily acquired by those likely to deal in any securities—
      (i)   to which the information relates, or
      (ii)   of an issuer to which the information relates; or
    (d)   it is derived from information which has been made public.
    (3)   Information may be treated as made public even though—
    (a)   it can be acquired only by persons exercising diligence or expertise;
    (b)   it is communicated to a section of the public and not to the public at large;
    (c)   it can be acquired only by observation;
    (d)   it is communicated only on payment of a fee; or
    (e)   it is published only outside the United Kingdom.

Section 60(4) provides that information is to be treated as relating to an issuer of securities which is a company not only where the information is about the company but also where it may affect the company's business prospects.

It is no longer necessary to prove (as under the old law) that the information concerned was of a confidential nature. Section 58 ensures that information derived from expert analysis of information that has been made public will not be regarded as inside information, even if the analyst is the only person who appreciates its significance. The position of those whose only inside information is 'market information', as defined in sch. 1, para. 2, is protected by the special defence contained within sch. 1, although this defence must be proved by an accused. See **B7.32**.

Price-Affected Securities

Criminal Justice Act 1993, s. 56   **B7.27**

    (2)   For the purposes of this part, securities are 'price-affected securities' in relation to inside information, and inside information is 'price-sensitive information' in relation to securities, if and only if the information would, if made public, be likely to have a significant effect on the price of the securities.
    (3)   For the purpose of this section 'price' includes value.

As to the need for prompt publication of price-sensitive information, see the Traded Securities (Disclosure) Regulations 1994 (SI 1994 No. 188).

B7.28   ***Dealing on a Regulated Market***   Regulated markets are defined by the Insider Dealing (Securities and Regulated Markets) Order 1994 (SI 1994 No. 187) and are effectively confined to exchanges in the European Economic Area (see **B7.24**).

Professional Intermediaries

B7.29   Criminal Justice Act 1993, s. 59

(1)   For the purposes of this part, a 'professional intermediary' is a person—
   (a)   who carries on a business consisting of an activity mentioned in subsection (2) and who holds himself out to the public or any section of the public (including a section of the public constituted by persons such as himself) as willing to engage in any such business; or
   (b)   who is employed by a person falling within paragraph (a) to carry out any such activity.
(2)   The activities referred to in subsection (1) are—
   (a)   acquiring or disposing of securities (whether as principal or agent); or
   (b)   acting as an intermediary between persons taking part in any dealing in securities.
(3)   A person is not to be treated as carrying on a business consisting of an activity mentioned in subsection (2)—
   (a)   if the activity in question is merely incidental to some other activity not falling within subsection (2); or
   (b)   merely because he occasionally conducts one of those activities.
(4)   For the purposes of section 52, a person dealing in securities relies on a professional intermediary if and only if a person who is acting as a professional intermediary carries out an activity mentioned in subsection (2) in relation to that dealing.

Under the old law, off-market dealing was covered if it involved advertised securities and if the transaction was carried out as or through a market maker in those securities. Certain kinds of 'over the counter' transaction could be caught in this way. Section 59 gives the new legislation a much wider scope. A sale of shares in a private family company could be covered if the services of a professional intermediary are involved but, under s. 52(3), only if an accused himself acts as a professional intermediary or relies on such an intermediary.

Jurisdictional Limitations

B7.30   Criminal Justice Act 1993, s. 62

(1)   An individual is not guilty of an offence falling within subsection (1) of section 52 unless—
   (a)   he was within the United Kingdom at the time when he is alleged to have done any act constituting or forming part of the alleged dealing;
   (b)   the regulated market on which the dealing is alleged to have occurred is one which, by an order made by the Treasury, is identified (whether by name or by reference to criteria prescribed by the order) as being, for the purposes of this part, regulated in the United Kingdom; or
   (c)   the professional intermediary was within the United Kingdom at the time when he is alleged to have done anything by means of which the offence is alleged to have been committed.
(2)   An individual is not guilty of an offence falling within subsection (2) of section 52 unless—
   (a)   he was within the United Kingdom at the time when he is alleged to have disclosed the information or encouraged the dealing; or
   (b)   the alleged recipient of the information or encouragement was within the United Kingdom at the time when he is alleged to have received the information or encouragement.

For the purposes of s. 62(1)(b) the regulated markets in question are defined by the Insider Dealing (Securities and Regulated Markets) Order 1994 (SI 1994 No. 187) as those established under the rules of the London Stock Exchange Ltd, OMLX, LIFFE and Tradepoint Financial Networks plc.

Other Limitations

Criminal Justice Act 1993, s. 63   B7.31

(1) Section 52 does not apply to anything done by an individual acting on behalf of a public sector body in pursuit of monetary policies or policies with respect to exchange rates or the management of public debt or foreign exchange reserves.

(2) No contract shall be void or unenforceable by reason only of section 52.

Defences

Criminal Justice Act 1993, s. 53   B7.32

(1) An individual is not guilty of insider dealing by virtue of dealing in securities if he shows—

(a) that he did not at the time expect the dealing to result in a profit attributable to the fact that the information in question was price-sensitive information in relation to the securities, or

(b) that at the time he believed on reasonable grounds that the information had been disclosed widely enough to ensure that none of those taking part in the dealing would be prejudiced by not having the information, or

(c) that he would have done what he did even if he had not had the information.

(2) An individual is not guilty of insider dealing by virtue of encouraging another person to deal in securities if he shows—

(a) that he did not at the time expect the dealing to result in a profit attributable to the fact that the information in question was price-sensitive information in relation to the securities, or

(b) that at the time he believed on reasonable grounds that the information had been or would be disclosed widely enough to ensure that none of those taking part in the dealing would be prejudiced by not having the information, or

(c) that he would have done what he did even if he had not had the information.

(3) An individual is not guilty of insider dealing by virtue of a disclosure of information if he shows—

(a) that he did not at the time expect any person, because of the disclosure, to deal in securities in the circumstances mentioned in subsection (3) of section 52; or

(b) that, although he had such an expectation at the time, he did not expect the dealing to result in a profit attributable to the fact that the information was price-sensitive information in relation to the securities.

. . .

(6) In this section references to a profit include references to the avoidance of a loss.

Section 53 also provides that the special defences in sch. 1 are to have effect.

Criminal Justice Act 1993, sch. 1

Market makers

1.—(1) An individual is not guilty of insider dealing by virtue of dealing in securities or encouraging another person to deal if he shows that he acted in good faith in the course of—

(a) his business as a market maker, or

(b) his employment in the business of a market maker.

(2) A market maker is a person who—

(a) holds himself out at all normal times in compliance with the rules of a regulated market or an approved organisation as willing to acquire or dispose of securities; and

(b) is recognised as doing so under those rules.

(3) In this paragraph 'approved organisation' means an international securities self-regulating organisation approved under paragraph 25B of schedule 1 to the Financial Services Act 1986.

Market information

2.—(1)   An individual is not guilty of insider dealing by virtue of dealing in securities or encouraging another person to deal if he shows that—

   (a)   the information which he had as an insider was market information; and

   (b)   it was reasonable for an individual in his position to have acted as he did despite having that information as an insider at the time.

(2)   In determining whether it is reasonable for an individual to do any act despite having market information at the time, there shall, in particular, be taken into account—

   (a)   the content of the information;

   (b)   the circumstances in which he first had the information and in what capacity; and

   (c)   the capacity in which he now acts.

3.   An individual is not guilty of insider dealing by virtue of dealing in securities or encouraging another person to deal if he shows—

   (a)   that he acted—

     (i)   in connection with an acquisition or disposal which was under consideration or the subject of negotiation, or in the course of a series of such acquisitions or disposals; and

     (ii)   with a view to facilitating the accomplishment of the acquisition or disposal or the series of acquisitions or disposals; and

   (b)   that the information which he had as an insider was market information arising directly out of his involvement in the acquisition or disposal or series of acquisitions or disposals.

4.   For the purposes of paragraphs 2 and 3 market information is information consisting of one or more of the following facts—

   (a)   that securities of a particular kind have been or are to be acquired or disposed of, or that their acquisition or disposal is under consideration or the subject of negotiation;

   (b)   that securities of a particular kind have not been or are not to be acquired or disposed of;

   (c)   the number of securities acquired or disposed of or to be acquired or disposed of or whose acquisition or disposal is under consideration or the subject of negotiation;

   (d)   the price (or range of prices) at which securities have been or are to be acquired or disposed of or the price (or range of prices) at which securities whose acquisition or disposal is under consideration or the subject of negotiation may be acquired or disposed of;

   (e)   the identity of the persons involved or likely to be involved in any capacity in an acquisition or disposal.

Price stabilisation

5.—(1)   An individual is not guilty of insider dealing by virtue of dealing in securities or encouraging another person to deal if he shows that he acted in conformity with the price stabilisation rules.

(2)   [Defines 'price stabilisation rules'.]

It is clear that the legal burden of proving any of the above defences lies on the accused. In contrast, the wording of the equivalent provisions under the Company Securities (Insider Dealing) Act 1985 was at best ambiguous, and arguably inconsistent with the interpretation placed on them by the courts (see *Cross* (1990) 91 Cr App R 115).

The new defences differ from the old in several other respects. The specific defence (or 'presumption of propriety') available to trustees or personal representatives under the old law has not been retained, nor has the specific defence relating to acts done for the purpose of facilitating takeovers or similar transactions between companies. The new version of the 'market maker' defence (CJA 1993, sch. 1, para. 1) is wider than its predecessor in that it is no longer confined to cases in which the information concerned was of a kind that the market maker could reasonably be expected to obtain in the ordinary course of his business; and the defence of not expecting to make a profit attributable to the inside information (CJA 1993, s. 53(1)) differs from the old defence of not acting *with a view* to profiting thereby.

Investigations

The Financial Services Act 1986, s. 177, empowers the Secretary of State to appoint **B7.33**
inspectors where it appears to him that there are circumstances suggesting possible
offences under the CJA 1993, part V.

Under the Financial Services Act 1986, s. 178, refusal to cooperate with the inspectors
may be referred to the court (i.e. a court having jurisdiction to wind up the company),
which, if satisfied that a person refused to cooperate 'without reasonable excuse' may
punish him as if guilty of contempt, or direct that the Secretary of State may exercise his
powers under s. 178(3) to remove or restrict any authorisation he may have under the
Act (i.e. so as to disqualify him from practising in the investment business).

As to the factors to be taken into account in deciding whether an alleged offender had
'reasonable excuse' for his behaviour, see *Re An Inquiry under the Company Securities
(Insider Dealing) Act 1985* [1988] AC 660. As to the admissibility of self-incriminating
statements obtained under s. 177, see **F9.14**.

The deliberate or reckless furnishing of false or misleading information in relation to
such an investigation is punishable under the Financial Services Act 1986, s. 200(1).

Disqualification of Directors

Disqualification under the Company Directors Disqualification Act 1986 may be **B7.34**
imposed either under s. 2 of that Act following conviction for insider dealing etc.
(*Goodman* [1993] 2 All ER 789) or under s. 8 of that Act following an investigation under
the Financial Services Act 1986, s. 177. See **E23.3**.

FALSE OR MISLEADING STATEMENTS AND PRACTICES IN THE CONDUCT OF INVESTMENT BUSINESS

Financial Services Act 1986, s. 47   B7.35

(1)   Any person who—
    (a)   makes a statement, promise or forecast which he knows to be misleading, false or
deceptive or dishonestly conceals any material facts; or
    (b)   recklessly makes (dishonestly or otherwise) a statement, promise or forecast
which is misleading, false or deceptive,
is guilty of an offence if he makes the statement, promise or forecast or conceals the facts
for the purpose of inducing, or is reckless as to whether it may induce, another person
(whether or not the person to whom the statement, promise or forecast is made or from
whom the facts are concealed) to enter or offer to enter into, or to refrain from entering or
offering to enter into, an investment agreement or to exercise, or refrain from exercising,
any rights conferred by an investment.
    (2)   Any person who does any act or engages in any course of conduct which creates a
false or misleading impression as to the market in or the price or value of any investments
is guilty of an offence if he does so for the purpose of creating that impression and of thereby
inducing another person to acquire, dispose of, subscribe for or underwrite those
investments or to refrain from doing so or to exercise, or refrain from exercising, any rights
conferred by those investments.
    (3)   In proceedings brought against any person for an offence under subsection (2)
above it shall be a defence for him to prove that he reasonably believed that his act or
conduct would not create an impression that was false or misleading as to the matters
mentioned in that subsection.
    (4)   Subsection (1) above does not apply unless—
    (a)   the statement, promise or forecast is made in or from, or the facts are concealed
in or from, the United Kingdom;
    (b)   the person on whom the inducement is intended to or may have effect is in the
United Kingdom; or

(c)   the agreement is or would be entered into or the rights are or would be exercised in the United Kingdom.

(5)   Subsection (2) above does not apply unless—

(a)   the act is done or the course of conduct is engaged in in the United Kingdom; or

(b)   the false or misleading impression is created there.

(6)   A person guilty of an offence under this section shall be liable—

(a)   on conviction on indictment, to imprisonment for a term not exceeding seven years or to a fine or to both;

(b)   on summary conviction, to imprisonment for a term not exceeding six months or to a fine not exceeding the statutory maximum or to both.

Prosecutions may be instituted only by or with the consent of the Secretary of State or the DPP (Financial Services Act 1986, s. 201). Where an offence committed by a body corporate is proved to have been committed with the consent or connivance of a director or other officer, or is attributable to his neglect, he may also be prosecuted for that offence (s. 202(1)).

Making False and Misleading Statements

B7.36   The Financial Services Act 1986, s. 47(1), creates only 'conduct crimes', the gist of which lies in the making of the false statements etc., or in the concealment of material facts. It must be proved that an accused intended, or in some cases was reckless as to, the effect this might have on inducing other persons to invest etc.; but this is only a matter of *mens rea*, and not part of the *actus reus* of the offence.

Offences under the Financial Services Act 1986, s. 47(1), can be committed in several different ways, and with different forms of *mens rea*. The concealment of material (i.e., significant) facts must be done dishonestly. Dishonesty is not defined in the Act, and must be presumed to bear the same meaning as it bears in relation to deception offences under the Theft Acts 1968 and 1978 (see *Ghosh* [1982] QB 1053 discussed in **B4.37**).

In contrast, dishonesty is not required in respect of false, deceptive or misleading statements, promises or forecasts. These may be made knowingly or recklessly, and since it is expressly provided that a person may be reckless without being dishonest, *Caldwell* recklessness (i.e. failure to consider an obvious risk of someone being misled etc.) would appear to suffice. As to this kind of recklessness, see **A2.5**.

Recklessness (presumably in the same *Caldwell* sense) will equally suffice in relation to the possible consequences of deception or dishonest concealment. These are only possible consequences, and not part of the *actus reus*, so a person may be guilty even though he neither misleads, nor intends to mislead, anyone at all.

A false or misleading promise must be one which is false or misleading when made (e.g., because the promisor never has any intention or expectation that it will or can ever be kept). It is not enough that the promise is ultimately unfulfilled (cf. *Re Augustus Barnett & Son Ltd* [1986] BCLC 170, discussed in **B7.16**, which deals with broken promises in the context of offences under the Companies Act 1985, s. 458).

Where several false or misleading statements are alleged, they may be included in a single count (*Linnell* [1969] 1 WLR 1514), but the judge must be careful to warn the jury that they cannot convict merely because some jurors are satisfied as to the falsity etc. of one statement and the rest are satisfied as to the falsity etc. of another. The jury must agree about one at least (*Brown* (1983) 79 Cr App R 115).

Conduct Creating False or Misleading Impression

B7.37   At common law, measures taken to 'rig the market', by circulating false rumours or by engaging in artificial transactions for the purpose of creating a false impression of demand, could be prosecuted as conspiracies to defraud (since such measures almost always require collaboration between several persons). See *De Berenger* (1814) 3 M & S 67; *Scott* v *Brown Doering McNab & Co.* [1892] 2 QB 724. For conspiracy to defraud, see **A6.25** *et seq*.

The Financial Services Act 1986, s. 47(2), goes further. No conspiracy is needed, nor need the fraud relate to the securities markets. False information concerning the value of a private company, circulated with intent to persuade any person to invest in such a company, would come within its scope. It applies to improper 'share support' operations, in which a company bidding to take over another company engages in artificial practices designed to boost the current market value of its own shares, so as to make these more attractive to shareholders in the target company, to whom they would be offered in exchange. If these practices involve the bidding company offering financial assistance, directly or indirectly, to persons who then buy its shares in order to stimulate further demand and push up prices, liability may also arise under the Companies Act 1985, s. 151 (see **B7.9** and **B7.10**). Section 47(2) does not however apply to anything done in conformity with the Financial Services (Stabilisation) Order 1988 (SI 1988 No. 717) and s. 48(7) of the Act.

The Financial Services Act 1986, s. 133, creates a broadly similar offence in respect of misleading statements as to insurance contracts.

In *A-G's Ref (Nos 14, 15 and 16 of 1995)* (1997) *The Times*, 10 April 1997, the Court of Appeal stated that offenders who took part in conspiracy to defraud involving the creation of false share markets to influence the fate of takeovers would ordinarily receive custodial sentences. Deterrent sentences were appropriate since creating false share markets could lead both to a fraud on shareholders and to considerable damage to the City of London.

INSOLVENCY OFFENCES: GENERAL

The law relating to personal and corporate insolvency has been consolidated in the **B7.38** Insolvency Act 1986. The principal offences under the Act are contained in part IV, chapter X (in relation to company insolvency), and part IX, chapter VI (in respect of bankruptcy of individuals). Some serious offences are created by the Insolvency Rules 1986 (SI 1986 No. 1925).

As with the Companies Act 1985, the scale, complexity and specialised subject-matter of this legislation precludes comprehensive coverage of its offences within a general work on criminal law. This section accordingly covers only the principal offences; for information concerning minor and regulatory offences, a specialist work on insolvency must be consulted.

Retrospective Liability

Many insolvency offences are unusual, in that they may criminalise acts which were not **B7.39** criminal when originally performed. It is not, for example, an offence to gamble recklessly with one's own money nor is it an offence for an individual trader to fail to keep proper business accounts; but in the event of bankruptcy following within two years, liability may retrospectively arise under the Insolvency Act 1986, ss. 361 and 362. The offences relating to corporate insolvency acknowledge the retrospective nature of this liability by 'deeming' offences to have been committed; the bankruptcy provisions, derived from a different source, do not.

Penalties

Penalties for offences under the Insolvency Act 1986, together with brief descriptions of **B7.40** the offences and details of modes of trial, are set out in sch. 10. This is reproduced in abridged form at **B7.75**.

OFFENCES CONCERNING COMPANY INSOLVENCY AND LIQUIDATION

Procedure in Summary Proceedings

B7.41   **Insolvency Act 1986, s. 431**

(1)   Summary proceedings for any offence under any of parts I to VII of this Act may (without prejudice to any jurisdiction exercisable apart from this subsection) be taken against a body corporate at any place at which the body has a place of business, and against any other person at any place at which he is for the time being.

(2)   Notwithstanding anything in section 127(1) of the Magistrates' Courts Act 1980, an information relating to such an offence which is triable by a magistrates' court in England and Wales may be so tried if it is laid at any time within 3 years after the commission of the offence and within 12 months after the date on which evidence sufficient in the opinion of the Director of Public Prosecutions or the Secretary of State (as the case may be) to justify the proceedings comes to his knowledge.

(3)   [Applies only to Scotland.]

(4)   For purposes of this section, a certificate of the Director of Public Prosecutions, the Lord Advocate or the Secretary of State (as the case may be) as to the date on which such evidence as is referred to above came to his knowledge is conclusive evidence.

Insolvency and Winding Up

B7.42   Companies which are put into liquidation are not always insolvent, and the offences contained within the Insolvency Act 1986 are often capable of applying to the winding up of solvent companies. In practice, however, prosecutions under the relevant parts of the Act will almost invariably be concerned with the winding up of insolvent companies.

The date at which winding up commences is often crucial to the application of the relevant law. Under s. 86, a voluntary winding up commences when the resolution for winding up is passed, and, under s. 129, this remains the relevant date even when a winding-up order is later made in respect of that company. In other cases, the relevant date is the date on which the winding-up petition was presented (s. 129(2)).

False Declarations of Solvency in Voluntary Liquidations

B7.43   **Insolvency Act 1986, s. 89**

(1)   Where it is proposed to wind up a company voluntarily, the directors (or, in the case of a company having more than two directors, the majority of them) may at a directors' meeting make a statutory declaration to the effect that they have made a full inquiry into the company's affairs and that, having done so, they have formed the opinion that the company will be able to pay its debts in full, together with interest at the official rate (as defined in section 251), within such period, not exceeding 12 months from the commencement of the winding up, as may be specified in the declaration.
. . .
(4)   A director making a declaration under this section without having reasonable grounds for the opinion that the company will be able to pay its debts in full, together with interest at the official rate, within the period specified is liable to imprisonment or a fine, or both.

(5)   If the company is wound up in pursuance of a resolution passed within 5 weeks after the making of the declaration, and its debts (together with interest at the official rate) are not paid or provided for in full within the period specified, it is to be presumed (unless the contrary is shown) that the director did not have reasonable grounds for his opinion.

This section now applies, subject to modifications, to friendly societies (Friendly Societies Act 1992, s. 23 and sch. 10).

For procedural provisions, see **B7.41**; for sentencing provisions, see **B7.75** and **B7.76**.

The importance of the declaration is that it determines whether the winding up will be a members' or a creditors' winding up (s. 90). In the latter, it is an offence under s. 166 for any liquidator nominated by the members to dispose of company property (except perishables and other goods likely to diminish in value) unless and until his status is confirmed by a creditors' meeting. In this way, the Act prohibits the once prevalent practice of 'Centrebinding', in which assets of insolvent companies were sold to the directors or other persons associated with the company at knock-down prices without the creditors being warned or consulted (see *Re Centrebind Ltd* [1967] 1 WLR 377).

Fraud etc. in Anticipation of Winding Up

Insolvency Act 1986, s. 206   **B7.44**

    (1)   When a company is ordered to be wound up by the court, or passes a resolution for voluntary winding up, any person, being a past or present officer of the company, is deemed to have committed an offence if, within the 12 months immediately preceding the commencement of the winding up, he has—

    (a)   concealed any part of the company's property to the value of £500 or more, or concealed any debt due to or from the company, or

    (b)   fraudulently removed any part of the company's property to the value of £500 or more, or

    (c)   concealed, destroyed, mutilated or falsified any book or paper affecting or relating to the company's property or affairs, or

    (d)   made any false entry in any book or paper affecting or relating to the company's property or affairs, or

    (e)   fraudulently parted with, altered or made any omission in any document affecting or relating to the company's property or affairs, or

    (f)   pawned, pledged or disposed of any property of the company which has been obtained on credit and has not been paid for (unless the pawning, pledging or disposal was in the ordinary way of the company's business).

    (2)   Such a person is deemed to have committed an offence if within the period above mentioned he has been privy to the doing by others of any of the things mentioned in paragraphs (c), (d) and (e) of subsection (1); and he commits an offence if, at any time after the commencement of the winding up, he does any of the things mentioned in paragraph (a) to (f) of that subsection, or is privy to the doing by others of any of the things mentioned in paragraphs (c) to (e) of it.

    (3)   For purposes of this section, 'officer' includes a shadow director.

    (4)   It is a defence—

    (a)   for a person charged under paragraph (a) or (f) of subsection (1) (or under subsection (2) in respect of the things mentioned in either of those two paragraphs) to prove that he had no intent to defraud, and

    (b)   for a person charged under paragraph (c) or (d) of subsection (1) (or under subsection (2) in respect of the things mentioned in either of those two paragraphs) to prove that he had no intent to conceal the state of affairs of the company or to defeat the law.

    (5)   Where a person pawns, pledges or disposes of any property in circumstances which amount to an offence under subsection (1)(f), every person who takes in pawn or pledge, or otherwise receives, the property knowing it to be pawned, pledged or disposed of in such circumstances, is guilty of an offence.

For procedural provisions, see **B7.41**; for sentencing provisions, see **B7.75** and **B7.76**.

It will be observed that fraud is a definitional element in the offences under s. 206(1)(b) and (e), and must therefore be proved by the prosecution. In the case of other offences under s. 206(1), liability is strict, unless an accused can prove a defence (on balance of probabilities) under s. 206(4) (see *Lusty* [1964] 1 WLR 606). Section 206 does not refer to any presumption of fraud in such cases, but it might be perceived as having a similar effect.

The combined effect of s. 206(1) and (2) is that offences can be committed before or after commencement of winding up. Offences under s. 206(1)(c) to (e) can be committed by officers who are 'privy' to the acts of others; these others need not themselves be officers nor need they be guilty of any offence.

Subsections (1) and (2) create separate offences; a charge cannot be brought under s. 206(1) in respect of things done after the commencement of the winding up.

B7.45 **Fraudulent Conduct and Intent to Defraud**   References to fraudulent conduct in the Insolvency Act 1986, s. 206(1), and to 'intent to defraud' in s. 206(4)(a), must be concerned with the same concept (for further discussion of this in the context of fraudulent trading, see **B7.15**). It must, in other words, involve dishonesty, but need not involve deceit.

B7.46 **Receipt of Property Disposed of Contrary to s. 206(1)(f) etc.**   The wording of the Insolvency Act 1986, s. 206(5), leaves much to be desired, and seems open to two possible interpretations. One possibility is that the recipient need know only of the circumstances specified in s. 206(1)(f), and that knowledge of whether the person disposing of the property could establish a defence under s. 206(4) is irrelevant; fraud is not, after all, a definitional element in an offence under s. 206(1)(f). The other possibility is that the prosecution must prove the recipient's knowledge of the disposer's guilt, and that that guilt arises only where the disposer is unable to prove a defence under s. 206(4); the recipient would therefore need to know that no such defence could be established, in other words, he must be shown to know that the disposer is acting fraudulently. It is submitted that the latter interpretation is the correct one; the former could lead to cases in which the recipient is convicted despite the acquittal of the disposer and would be in marked contrast to the position under the corresponding bankruptcy provision (Insolvency Act 1986, s. 359 — see **B7.65**). In contrast, there is nothing illogical in a rule under which conviction of the disposer is made easier than conviction of the recipient.

An example of disposal otherwise than in the ordinary course of business is provided by *Bolus* (1870) 23 LT 339. In that case, a tool manufacturer disposed of six tons of unworked steel, which had been delivered on credit as raw material. Purchase of such steel was within the ordinary course of the toolmaker's business; sale was not. See also *Thomas* (1870) 22 LT 138.

Transactions in Fraud of Creditors

B7.47   **Insolvency Act 1986, s. 207**

(1)   When a company is ordered to be wound up by the court or passes a resolution for voluntary winding up, a person is deemed to have committed an offence if he, being at the time an officer of the company—

(a)   has made or caused to be made any gift or transfer of, or charge on, or has caused or connived at the levying of any execution against, the company's property, or

(b)   has concealed or removed any part of the company's property since, or within 2 months before, the date of any unsatisfied judgment or order for the payment of money obtained against the company.

(2)   A person is not guilty of an offence under this section—

(a)   by reason of conduct constituting an offence under subsection (1)(a) which occurred more than 5 years before the commencement of the winding up, or

(b)   if he proves that, at the time of the conduct constituting the offence, he had no intent to defraud the company's creditors.

For procedural provisions, see **B7.41**; for sentencing provisions, see **B7.75** and **B7.76**.

Although the ambit of s. 207(1)(a) seems extremely wide, its effect is in practice heavily curtailed by s. 207(2). The overall effect achieved is the same as if an intent to defraud creditors were specified, but with the existence of such intent being presumed unless the contrary was proved on balance of probabilities.

There is old authority to the effect that any intent to defraud creditors must refer to creditors at the time of the action concerned (*Hopkins* [1896] 1 QB 652), but this seems doubtful on principle, and would produce very unsatisfactory results where the company has a long-term debt problem, but a series of short-term creditors (see *Seillon* [1982] Crim LR 676).

A person 'causes' a thing to be done when he orders or directs it to be done (*Houston* v *Buchanan* [1940] 2 All ER 179).

Misconduct in the Course of Winding Up

Insolvency Act 1986, s. 208   **B7.48**

(1)   When a company is being wound up, whether by the court or voluntarily, any person, being a past or present officer of the company, commits an offence if he—

(a)   does not to the best of his knowledge and belief fully and truly discover to the liquidator all the company's property, and how and to whom and for what consideration and when the company disposed of any part of that property (except such part as has been disposed of in the ordinary way of the company's business), or

(b)   does not deliver up to the liquidator (or as he directs) all such part of the company's property as is in his custody or under his control, and which he is required by law to deliver up, or

(c)   does not deliver up to the liquidator (or as he directs) all books and papers in his custody or under his control belonging to the company and which he is required by law to deliver up, or

(d)   knowing or believing that a false debt has been proved by any person in the winding up, fails to inform the liquidator as soon as practicable, or

(e)   after the commencement of the winding up, prevents the production of any book or paper affecting or relating to the company's property or affairs.

(2)   Such a person commits an offence if after the commencement of the winding up he attempts to account for any part of the company's property by fictitious losses or expenses; and he is deemed to have committed that offence if he has so attempted at any meeting of the company's creditors within the 12 months immediately preceding the commencement of the winding up.

(3)   For the purposes of this section, 'officer' includes a shadow director.

(4)   It is a defence—

(a)   for a person charged under paragraph (a), (b) or (c) of subsection (1) to prove that he had no intent to defraud, and

(b)   for a person charged under paragraph (e) of that subsection to prove that he had no intent to conceal the state of affairs of the company or to defeat the law.

For procedural provisions, see **B7.41**; for sentencing provisions, see **B7.75** and **B7.76**.

No proof of fraud is necessary in respect of any of the offences under s. 208. As with many other insolvency offences, it is natural to think of a 'presumption of fraud' in such cases, and this is re-inforced by the 'no fraud' defences provided by s. 208(4); but strictly speaking there is no such presumption. Fraud is not a definitional element in the offences, nor is it necessary for the liquidator to have demanded the specific property in question. There is accordingly a continuing duty to disclose and deliver any valuable items of which the liquidator may be unaware (*McCredie* (1999) *The Times*, 5 October 1999).

The offences contained within s. 208(1)(d) and s. 208(2) do not allow for the proving of any special defences. Under s. 208(2), full and frank disclosure to the liquidator does not excuse previous lies told to creditors, and under s. 208(1)(d) mere hesitation in disclosing a false claim may be sufficient.

Falsification of Company Books

Insolvency Act 1986, s. 209   **B7.49**

(1)   When a company is being wound up, an officer or contributory of the company commits an offence if he destroys, mutilates, alters or falsifies any books, papers or

securities, or makes or is privy to the making of any false or fraudulent entry in any register, book of account or document belonging to the company with intent to defraud or deceive any person.

For procedural provisions, see **B7.41**; for sentencing provisions, see **B7.75** and **B7.76**.

Section 209(1) is not clearly worded, but appears to divide into two distinct halves. Destroying, mutilating altering or falsifying books, papers or securities forms the first half, and making false or fraudulent entries in company documents etc. forms the second. If this interpretation is correct, certain important consequences follow.

First, the phrase 'belonging to the company' appears to govern only the latter half of s. 209(1), as does the phrase 'with intent to defraud or deceive'. This means that the destruction or falsification of papers or securities belonging to another person would suffice (as where D destroys P's bill of exchange or debenture certificate, on which the company would be liable), and it also follows that fraud or deceit need not be proved by the prosecution in such cases.

Secondly, 'documents' are defined in the Insolvency Act 1986, s. 436, as including computer records and other non-documentary records. This means, for example, that the fraudulent insertion of false entries on a company computer record would be an offence under s. 209(1) if the insertion is made with intent to defraud or deceive. On the other hand, it would seem that the destruction or mutilation of such records could not be an offence within s. 209(1) (i.e. the first part thereof), unless the records could be regarded as 'books, papers or securities'. It might be better to consider charges under the Companies Act 1985, s. 450, in such cases (see **B7.11**).

Material Omissions from Statements Relating to the Company's Affairs

B7.50   **Insolvency Act 1986, s. 210**

   (1)   When a company is being wound up, whether by the court or voluntarily, any person, being a past or present officer of the company, commits an offence if he makes any material omission in any statemet relating to the company's affairs.
   (2)   When a company has been ordered to be wound up by the court, or has passed a resolution for voluntary winding up, any such person is deemed to have committed that offence if, prior to the winding up, he has made any material omission in any such statement.
   (3)   For the purposes of this section, 'officer' includes a shadow director.
   (4)   It is a defence for a person charged under this section to prove that he had no intent to defraud.

For procedural provisions, see **B7.41**; for sentencing provisions, see **B7.75** and **B7.76**.

This provision purports to create an offence of enormous width, but s. 210(4) goes some way towards keeping it within reasonable bounds. Unlike the equivalent provision in respect of bankruptcy (Insolvency Act 1986, s. 356(1), see **B7.62**), it is not necessary that the material omission be made in a statement under any provision of the Act; any statement, oral or written, would seem to be within its scope, whether made during winding up or prior to it. Arlidge & Parry (*Fraud*, para. 9.14) suggest that the offence should be confined to statements which become misleading owing to the material omission (cf. *Lord Kylsant* [1932] 1 KB 442), but this does some violence to the wording of the section. The better view would seem to be that any material (i.e. significant) omission could suffice; if that omission was understandable in the circumstances (as where the statement was informal and unrehearsed), it would be relatively easy to prove that there was no intent to defraud. In practice, it is unlikely that the offence will be charged unless there is evidence suggesting fraud.

False Representations to Creditors

B7.51   **Insolvency Act 1986, s. 211**

   (1)   When a company is being wound up, whether by the court or voluntarily, any person, being a past or present officer of the company—

(a)   commits an offence if he makes any false representation or commits any other fraud for the purpose of obtaining the consent of the company's creditors or any of them to an agreement with reference to the company's affairs or to the winding up, and

(b)   is deemed to have committed that offence if, prior to the winding up, he has made any false representation, or committed any other fraud, for that purpose.

(2)   For purposes of this section, 'officer' includes a shadow director.

For procedural provisions, see **B7.41**; for sentencing provisions, see **B7.75** and **B7.76**.

In view of the fact that s. 211 makes no provision for an accused to prove that he acted without fraudulent intent, and in view of the references to false representations 'or any other fraud', it is submitted that the offence of making false representations should be construed as requiring the prosecution to prove fraud. This interpretation gains some support from *Cherry* (1871) 12 Cox 32, in which it was said (in relation to bankruptcy provisions) that, in this context, 'false' means 'fraudulent'.

Fraudulent Trading and Wrongful Trading

Sections 213 and 214 of the Insolvency Act 1986 deal with fraudulent trading and wrongful trading prior to the liquidation of a company, but do not create criminal offences. Fraudulent trading as a criminal offence is dealt with by the Companies Act 1985, s. 458 (see **B7.12**), and need not necessarily be connected with winding up or insolvency. Wrongful trading is not a criminal matter, although any attempt to avoid civil liability for fraudulent or wrongful trading (e.g., by false representations or falsification of records) could lead to criminal liability under the Insolvency Act 1986, ss. 209 to 211. **B7.52**

Re-Use of Company Names

Insolvency Act 1986, s. 216   **B7.53**

(1)   This section applies to a person where a company ('the liquidating company') has gone into insolvent liquidation on or after the appointed day and he was a director or shadow director of the company at any time in the period of 12 months ending with the day before it went into liquidation.

(2)   For the purposes of this section, a name is a prohibited name in relation to such a person if—

(a)   it is a name by which the liquidating company was known at any time in that period of 12 months, or

(b)   it is a name which is so similar to a name falling within paragraph (a) as to suggest an association with that company.

(3)   Except with leave of the court or in such circumstances as may be prescribed, a person to whom this section applies shall not at any time in the period of 5 years beginning with the day on which the liquidating company went into liquidation—

(a)   be a director of any other company that is known by a prohibited name, or

(b)   in any way, whether directly or indirectly, be concerned or take part in the promotion, formation or management of any such company, or

(c)   in any way, whether directly or indirectly, be concerned or take part in the carrying on of a business carried on (otherwise than by a company) under a prohibited name.

For procedural provisions, see **B7.41**; for sentencing provisions, see **B7.75** and **B7.76**.

Section 216 deals with one aspect of the so-called 'Phoenix Syndrome', in which companies would go into insolvent liquidation only to re-appear, with almost identical names, businesses and directors, a few months later. The re-born companies would in law be new enterprises, unfettered by the unpaid debts of the previous ones, but would, to outside appearances, be the same as before, and they often acquired assets cheaply from the liquidator of the previous company. The prohibition of 'Centrebinding' (see **B7.43**) and the tighter regulation of insolvency practitioners has done much to eliminate such practices, but re-use of a familiar name was considered worthy of proscription in its own right. The court which may give leave under s. 216(3) is the court having jurisdiction to wind up companies, and a company is regarded as going into insolvent liquidation if its assets are insufficient to meet its liabilities and the expenses of the winding up (s. 216(5) and (7)). References, in relation to a time, to a name by which a company is known are to the name of the company at that time or to any name under which the company carries on business at that time (s. 216(6)).

Contravention of s. 216 may involve civil liability under s. 217, as well as the criminal penalties prescribed in sch. 10. The offence created by s. 216 is one of strict liability (*Cole* [1998] BCC 87).

False Representations under the Insolvency Rules 1986

B7.54   The provisions of the Insolvency Rules 1986 generally fall outside the scope of this work, but the provisions of r. 1.30 should be particularly noted.

Insolvency Rules 1986, r. 1.30

(1)   A person being a past or present officer of a company commits an offence if he makes any false representation or commits any other fraud for the purpose of obtaining the approval of the company's members or creditors to a proposal for a voluntary arrangement under part I of the Act.

(2)   For this purpose 'officer' includes a shadow director.

This offence is triable either way. On conviction on indictment, the maximum penalty is seven years' imprisonment; on summary conviction, it is six months' imprisonment and/or a fine. See also r. 12.18 (**B7.72**).

BANKRUPTCY OFFENCES

B7.55   The provisions of the Insolvency Act 1986, part IX, chapter VI, which deal with the principal bankruptcy offences, are in many respects similar, but by no means identical, to the provisions dealing with offences concerning company insolvency and liquidation.

Scheme of Chapter VI

B7.56   **Insolvency Act 1986, s. 350**

(1)   Subject to section 360(3) below, this chapter applies where the court has made a bankruptcy order on a bankruptcy petition.

(2)   This chapter applies whether or not the bankruptcy order is annulled, but proceedings for an offence under this chapter shall not be instituted after the annulment.

(3)   Without prejudice to his liability in respect of a subsequent bankruptcy, the bankrupt is not guilty of an offence under this chapter in respect of anything done after his discharge; but nothing in this group of parts prevents the institution of proceedings against a discharged bankrupt for an offence committed before his discharge.

(4)   It is not a defence in proceedings for an offence under this chapter that anything relied on, in whole or in part, as constituting that offence was done outside England and Wales.

(5)   Proceedings for an offence under this chapter or under the rules shall not be instituted except by the Secretary of State or by or with the consent of the Director of Public Prosecutions.

(6)   A person guilty of any offence under this chapter is liable to imprisonment or a fine, or both.

Penalties for offences under chapter VI (ss. 353 to 362) are prescribed by sch. 10, the relevant parts of which are printed at **B7.75**.

Definitions

Insolvency Act 1986, ss. 351 and 381

B7.57

351. In the following provisions of this chapter—

(a) references to property comprised in the bankrupt's estate or to property possession of which is required to be delivered up to the official receiver or the trustee of the bankrupt's estate include any property which would be such property if a notice in respect of it were given under section 307 (after-acquired property) or 308 (personal property and effects of bankrupt having more than replacement value);

(b) 'the initial period' means the period between the presentation of the bankruptcy petition and the commencement of the bankruptcy; and

(c) a reference to a number of months or years before petition is to that period ending with the presentation of the bankruptcy petition.

381.—(1) 'Bankrupt' means an individual who has been adjudged bankrupt, and, in relation to a bankruptcy order, it means the individual adjudged bankrupt by that order.

(2) 'Bankruptcy order' means an order adjudging an individual bankrupt.

(3) 'Bankruptcy petition' means a petition to the court for a bankruptcy order.

Under s. 307, the bankrupt's trustee may by notice in writing claim for his estate property acquired or devolved upon the bankrupt since commencement of his bankruptcy; and under s. 308 he may similarly claim tools of trade, household effects etc., which would not ordinarily be claimed, but which appear to have a realisable value exceeding the cost of reasonable replacements. The precise details and conditions involved fall outside the scope of this work.

Further definitions (not printed in this work) are to be found in ss. 382 to 385, and are mentioned where relevant in the context of particular offences.

Defence of Innocent Intention

Insolvency Act 1986, s. 352

B7.58

Where in the case of an offence under any provision of this chapter it is stated that this section applies, a person is not guilty of the offence if he proves that, at the time of the conduct constituting the offence, he had no intent to defraud or to conceal the state of his affairs.

Proof of no intent to defraud or conceal the state of the bankrupt's affairs must be established on the balance of probabilities, as with any such defence burden. It would not be strictly correct to refer to a 'presumption of fraud' which the accused must defeat in order to avoid conviction, because the correct position is that fraud need neither be proved nor presumed in such cases. In practice, however, some of the relevant offences may be perceived as involving such a presumption.

Offences of Non-Disclosure

Insolvency Act 1986, s. 353

B7.59

(1) The bankrupt is guilty of an offence if—

(a) he does not to the best of his knowledge and belief disclose all the property comprised in his estate to the official receiver or the trustee, or

(b) he does not inform the official receiver or the trustee of any disposal of any property which but for the disposal would be so comprised, stating how, when, to whom and for what consideration the property was disposed of.

(2) Subsection (1)(b) does not apply to any disposal in the ordinary course of a business carried on by the bankrupt or to any payment of the ordinary expenses of the bankrupt or his family.

(3) Section 352 applies to this offence.

For procedural provisions, see **B7.56**; for sentencing provisions, see **B7.75** and **B7.76**. As to the meaning of 'property' see **B7.57**. Section 353(1)(b) is primarily concerned with property which the bankrupt has had at some time and which the trustee might be able to trace and reclaim through exercise of his powers under the Act.

As to what might or might not amount to disposal 'in the ordinary course of business', see **B7.46**, *Bolus* (1870) 23 LT 339 and *Thomas* (1870) 22 LT 138.

Concealment of Property and Failure to Account for Losses

B7.60   **Insolvency Act 1986, s. 354**

(1) The bankrupt is guilty of an offence, if—

(a) he does not deliver up possession to the official receiver or trustee, or as the official receiver or trustee may direct, of such part of the property comprised in his estate as is in his possession or under his control, and possession of which he is required by law so to deliver up,

(b) he conceals any debt due to or from him or conceals any property the value of which is not less than the prescribed amount and possession of which he is required to deliver up to the official receiver or trustee, or

(c) in the 12 months before petition, or in the initial period, he did anything which would have been an offence under paragraph (b) above if the bankruptcy order had been made immediately before he did it.

Section 352 applies to this offence.

(2) The bankrupt is guilty of an offence if he removes, or in the initial period removed, any property the value of which was not less than the prescribed amount and possession of which he has or would have been required to deliver up to the official receiver or the trustee.

Section 352 applies to this offence.

(3) The bankrupt is guilty of an offence if he without reasonable excuse fails, on being required to do so by the official receiver or the court—

(a) to account for the loss of any substantial part of his property incurred in the 12 months before petition or in the initial period, or

(b) to give a satisfactory explanation of the manner in which such a loss was incurred.

For procedural provisions, see **B7.56**; for sentencing provisions, see **B7.75** and **B7.76**. For the defence under s. 352 (lack of fraudulent intent), see **B7.58**. The 'prescribed amount' for the purposes of s. 354 is fixed by the Insolvency Proceedings (Monetary Limits) Order 1986 (SI 1986 No. 1996) at £500.

The offence contained within s. 354(3) differs from those contained within the preceding subsections in that it is absolute, and does not allow for any possible defence under s. 352. As Sachs LJ said in *Salter* [1968] 2 QB 793 (in relation to a similarly worded offence under the Bankruptcy Act 1914) at p. 798:

A jury should be directed that if they are satisfied as regards the total sum of money constituting 'the loss of any substantial part of his estate' the bankrupt had not at the time of the alleged failure given with such reasonable detail as was appropriate in the circumstances an explanation which is both reasonably clear and true of how such sum was made up (for the loss may be composed of more than one component), of how it came to be lost, and of where the money has gone, then the offence has been committed. The degree of particularity required of the bankrupt may vary greatly according to the facts of the case: sums which are really small in relation to 'the substantial part of the estate' need not of course be traced, but an explanation unsupported by sufficient detail can be very unsatisfactory indeed. [The provision] intends to and does, in the interests of the business community as a whole, put in peril the man who goes bankrupt without having so conducted his affairs as to be able satisfactorily to explain why some substantial loss has been incurred. It is as well to make it plain that, as the offence is absolute, it follows that, once a prosecution has been initiated, no issue arises before verdict as to the reasons why the failure has occurred or as to any motive which led to that failure.

An explanation, if clear and true, need not also be 'satisfactory' in the sense of clearing the bankrupt of blame. If the explanation reveals heavy gambling losses, this may be satisfactory for the purposes of s. 354, even though it may lead to prosecution under s. 362 (see **B7.71**).

Concealment or Falsification of Books and Papers

Insolvency Act 1986, s. 355　　　　　　　　　　　　　　　**B7.61**

(1)　The bankrupt is guilty of an offence if he does not deliver up possession to the official receiver or the trustee, or as the official receiver or trustee may direct, of all books, papers and other records of which he has possession or control and which relate to his estate or his affairs.
Section 352 applies to this offence.

(2)　The bankrupt is guilty of an offence if—

(a)　he prevents, or in the initial period prevented, the production of any books, papers or records relating to his estate or affairs;

(b)　he conceals, destroys, mutilates or falsifies, or causes or permits the concealment, destruction, mutilation or falsification of, any books, papers or other records relating to his estate or affairs.

(c)　he makes or causes or permits the making of, any false entries in any book, document or record relating to his estate or affairs; or

(d)　in the 12 months before petition, or in the initial period, he did anything which would have been an offence, under paragraph (b) or (c) above if the bankruptcy order had been made before he did it.
Section 352 applies to this offence.

(3)　The bankrupt is guilty of an offence if—

(a)　he disposes of, or alters or makes any omission in, or causes or permits the disposal, altering or making of any omission in, any book, document or record relating to his estate or affairs, or

(b)　in the 12 months before petition, or in the initial period, he did anything which would have been an offence under paragraph (a) if the bankruptcy order had been made before he did it.
Section 352 applies to this offence.

For procedural provisions, see **B7.56**; for sentencing provisions, see **B7.75** and **B7.76**. For the meaning of 'the initial period', see **B7.57**. For the defence under s. 352 (lack of fraudulent intent), see **B7.58**.

'Causing' an act means ordering or directing it, and 'permitting' it means allowing it to happen (*Houston* v *Buchanan* [1940] 2 All ER 179). It is not always clear whether an accused must be proved to know the circumstances which make the act criminal although, in this context, it is unlikely that such proof would be required. Where an accused has, for example, permitted his secretary to clear out old files in his office, and it transpires that these included papers relating to his estate or affairs, it is submitted that his only possible defence to a charge under s. 355(2)(b) would be that provided by s. 352.

For persons who engage in business, the scope of s. 355(2)(d) and (3)(b) is modified by s. 361(4), so that concealment, falsification or disposal etc. of accounting records within two years before petition may be an offence. See further **B7.70**.

The offences under s. 355(2) and (3) overlap with the Theft Act 1968, s. 17 (see **B6.3**), and the Forgery and Counterfeiting Act 1981, s. 1 (see **B6.28**), but, under those provisions, the burden of proof rests on the prosecution.

False Statements

Insolvency Act 1986, s. 356　　　　　　　　　　　　　　　**B7.62**

(1)　The bankrupt is guilty of an offence if he makes or has made any material omission in any statement made under any provision in this group of parts and relating to his affairs.
Section 352 applies to this offence.

(2)   The bankrupt is guilty of an offence if—

(a)   knowing or believing that a false debt has been proved by any person under the bankruptcy, he fails to inform the trustee as soon as practicable; or

(b)   he attempts to account for any part of his property by fictitious losses or expenses; or

(c)   at any meeting of his creditors in the 12 months before petition or (whether or not at such a meeting) at any time in the initial period, he did anything which would have been an offence under paragraph (b) if the bankruptcy order had been made before he did it; or

(d)   he is, or at any time has been, guilty of any false representation or other fraud for the purpose of obtaining the consent of his creditors, or any of them, to an agreement with reference to his affairs or to his bankruptcy.

For procedural provisions, see **B7.56**; for sentencing provisions, see **B7.75** and **B7.76**. For the defence under s. 352 (lack of fraudulent intent), see **B7.58**.

Section 356(1) differs from its equivalent company liquidation offence (s. 210) in that the statement concerned must be one made under relevant provisions of the Act. This might be a 'statement of affairs' under s. 288 or a statement made in purported compliance with s. 333 or any other relevant provision.

The defence under s. 352 applies only to s. 356(1); the offences under s. 356(2) require proof of knowledge or belief. Thus, proof of the inaccuracy of a bankrupt's account would not suffice to prove an offence under s. 366(2)(b): it must also be proved to be fictitious (i.e. that the inaccuracy is deliberate). In respect of s. 356(2)(d), fraud must be proved (see the analysis of the equivalent provision in s. 211 at **B7.51**). In respect of the other offences under s. 356(2), the requisite *mens rea* need not necessarily involve fraud, which thus becomes wholly irrelevant to the issue of guilt: the prosecution need not prove it, and it will not avail the defence to prove its absence.

Fraudulent Disposal or Concealment of Property

B7.63   **Insolvency Act 1986, s. 357**

(1)   The bankrupt is guilty of an offence if he makes or causes to be made, or has in the period of 5 years ending with the commencement of the bankruptcy made or caused to be made, any gift or transfer of, or any charge on, his property.
Section 352 applies to this offence.

(2)   The reference to making a transfer of or charge on any property includes causing or conniving at the levying of any execution against the property.

(3)   The bankrupt is guilty of an offence if he conceals or removes, or has at any time before the commencement of the bankruptcy concealed or removed, any part of his property after, or within 2 months before, the date on which a judgment or order for the payment of money has been obtained against him, being a judgment or order which was not satisfied before the commencement of the bankruptcy.
Section 352 applies to this offence.

For procedural provisions, see **B7.56**; for sentencing provisions, see **B7.75** and **B7.76**; for definitions, see **B7.57**. Section 357(1) is basically similar to the companies offence contained within s. 207 (see **B7.47**) and, like s. 207, would be of very wide application but for the defence provided under s. 352 (see **B7.58**). A bankrupt who commits an offence under s. 357 can expect to receive a custodial sentence, even if of previous good character (*Mungroo* [1998] BPIR 784).

The Debtors Act 1869, s. 13(3), creates an offence similar in form to the Insolvency Act 1986, s. 357(3), but it does not require there to be a bankruptcy, and places the burden of proving fraud on the prosecution. The Debtors Act 1869, s. 13(2), creates an offence of making gifts etc. with intent to defraud creditors; again this is not dependent on bankruptcy.

Absconding with Property

Insolvency Act 1986, s. 358   **B7.64**

The bankrupt is guilty of an offence if—
    (a)   he leaves, or attempts or makes preparations to leave, England and Wales with any property the value of which is not less than the prescribed amount and possession of which he is required to deliver up to the official receiver or the trustee, or
    (b)   in the 6 months before the petition, or in the initial period, he did anything which would have been an offence under paragraph (a) if the bankruptcy order had been made immediately before he did it.
Section 352 applies to this offence.

For procedural provisions, see **B7.56**; for sentencing provisions, see **B7.75** and **B7.76**; for definitions, see **B7.57**. The 'prescribed amount' is fixed by the Insolvency Proceedings (Monetary Limits) Order 1986 at £500.

If the bankrupt has done nothing worse than travel abroad with property (e.g., his car) with which he has later returned, it may well be easy for him to show that he had no intent to defraud and thus take advantage of the defence under s. 352 (see **B7.58**).

Fraudulent Dealing with Property Obtained on Credit

Insolvency Act 1986, s. 359   **B7.65**

    (1)   The bankrupt is guilty of an offence if, in the 12 months before petition, or in the initial period, he disposed of any property which he had obtained on credit and, at the time he disposed of it, had not paid for.
Section 352 applies to this offence.
    (2)   A person is guilty of an offence if, in the 12 months before petition or in the initial period, he acquired or received property from the bankrupt knowing or believing—
    (a)   that the bankrupt owed money in respect of the property, and
    (b)   that the bankrupt did not intend, or was unlikely to be able, to pay the money he so owed.
    (3)   A person is not guilty of an offence under subsection (1) or (2) if the disposal, acquisition or receipt of the property was in the ordinary course of a business carried on by the bankrupt at the time of the disposal, acquisition or receipt.
    (4)   In determining for the purposes of this section whether any property is disposed of, acquired or received in the ordinary course of a business carried on by the bankrupt, regard may be had, in particular, to the price paid for the property.
    (5)   In this section references to disposing of property include pawning or pledging it; and references to acquiring or receiving property shall be read accordingly.

For procedural provisions, see **B7.56**; for sentencing provisions, see **B7.75** and **B7.76**. For definitions, see **B7.57**. For the defence of no intent under s. 352, see **B7.58**.

The mischief against which s. 359 strikes is that of obtaining goods on credit, and then selling or otherwise disposing of them, often on disadvantageous terms or for inadequate consideration, as a method of raising cash which may be unobtainable by more conventional means. Such tactics are generally resorted to only by persons who are already in serious financial difficulties, and prejudice the interests of the unpaid suppliers.

As to what may amount to disposal 'otherwise than in the ordinary course of business', see **B7.46**.

Obtaining Credit: Engaging in Business

Insolvency Act 1986, s. 360   **B7.66**

    (1)   The bankrupt is guilty of an offence if—
    (a)   either alone or jointly with any other person, he obtains credit to the extent of the prescribed amount or more without giving the person from whom he obtains it the relevant information about his status; or

(b)   he engages (whether directly or indirectly) in any business under a name other than that in which he was adjudged bankrupt without disclosing to all persons with whom he enters into any business transaction the name in which he was so adjudged.

(2)   The reference to the bankrupt obtaining credit includes the following cases—

(a)   where goods are bailed to him under a hire-purchase agreement, or agreed to be sold to him under a conditional sale agreement, and

(b)   where he is paid in advance (whether in money or otherwise) for the supply of goods or services.

(3)   A person whose estate has been sequestrated in Scotland, or who has been adjudged bankrupt in Northern Ireland, is guilty of an offence if, before his discharge, he does anything in England and Wales which would be an offence under subsection (1) if he were an undischarged bankrupt and the sequestration of his estate or the adjudication in Northern Ireland were an adjudication under this part.

(4)   For the purposes of subsection (1)(a), the relevant information about the status of the person in question is the information that he is an undischarged bankrupt or, as the case may be, that his estate has been sequestrated in Scotland and that he has not been discharged.

For procedural provisions, see **B7.56**; for sentencing provisions, see **B7.75** and **B7.76**.

Section 360 is not subject to the defence of innocent intention s. 352. The offences, re-enacted in s. 360 have always been regarded as absolute. Thus, in *Duke of Leinster* [1924] 1 KB 311, it was held that D committed the offence even though his agent had been instructed to inform the creditor of D's status and had failed to do so. See also *Dyson* [1894] 2 QB 176.

B7.67   ***Credit to the Extent of the Prescribed Amount***   The amount prescribed by the Insolvency Proceedings (Monetary Limits) Order 1986 (SI 1986 No. 1996) for the purposes of the Insolvency Act 1986, s. 360, is £250. This limit governs the aggregate of the credit obtained, and it cannot be circumvented merely by ensuring that no one transaction exceeds the limit (*Juby* (1886) 16 Cox 160; *Hartley* [1972] 2 QB 1). It seems to have been assumed in *Hartley* that the prescribed amount nevertheless refers to the aggregate obtained from any one creditor. If this is correct, it would be no offence for a bankrupt to obtain £249 worth of credit from each of four different persons without admitting to being a bankrupt. This proposition is of doubtful validity, for, although the section refers in the singular to 'the person' from whom credit is obtained, there would not seem to be any obvious rejection therein of the general principle that the singular includes the plural (Interpretation Act 1978, s. 6(c)). On the other hand, it might be argued that the purpose of the provision is to protect unwary creditors from the risk of substantial losses, and that as long as no one creditor is unknowingly exposed to a potential loss of £250 or more the bankrupt's conduct is unobjectionable. It is far from obvious that this is the sole purpose of the provision and, in any event, the risk of loss to each is increased by the increase in the aggregate of the bankrupt's debt.

B7.68   ***Obtaining***   Any obtaining must be of credit given to the bankrupt himself. Credit given to him jointly with another is expressly included, but cases where credit is obtained by the bankrupt as agent for another person to whom the creditor looks for payment would not be covered (*Godwin* (1980) 71 Cr App R 97). 'Obtaining' has a narrower meaning for the purposes of s. 360 than it has, for example, in respect of insider dealing; it must involve 'some conduct, either by words or otherwise . . . which amounts to an obtaining' (*Hayat* (1976) 63 Cr App R 181). There may not necessarily have been any 'obtaining' in this sense where the bankrupt's bank account becomes overdrawn as a result of the dishonouring of certain incoming cheques and the honouring of certain cheques drawn by him on that account; it will be a question of fact for the jury (*Hayat*). There is no obtaining of credit where the bankrupt defaults on an existing hire-purchase obligation and thereby becomes liable to pay the arrears (*Miller* [1977] 1 WLR 1129) nor where funds are received from a business partner in the course of a joint venture. It makes no difference if the bankrupt intends to default on his side of the bargain: 'It is the nature of the agreement which determines whether or not credit has been obtained, not the intention of the defendant.' (*Ramzan* [1998] 2 Cr App R 328, per Ebsworth J at p. 334.)

Credit is 'obtained' where any goods or monies concerned are received (*Ellis* [1899] 1 QB 230), but the Insolvency Act 1986, s. 350(4) (see **B7.56**), ensures that the provisions of chapter VI have extraterritorial effect, and so it will be no defence to argue that credit was obtained abroad.

Engaging in Business A bankrupt may engage in business without necessarily **B7.69** disclosing his status, although he cannot become a company director, manager or promoter without leave of the court (see the Company Directors Disqualification Act 1986, ss. 11 and 13 at **B7.73**). He must not hide his bankruptcy by using a different name. The reference in the Insolvency Act 1986, s. 360(1)(b), to indirectly engaging in business is designed to deal with bankrupts who procure some other persons to 'front' businesses effectively controlled by themselves.

Failure to Keep Proper Business Accounts

Insolvency Act 1986, s. 361   **B7.70**

  (1) Where the bankrupt has been engaged in any business for any of the period of 2 years before petition, he is guilty of an offence if he—

    (a) has not kept proper accounting records throughout that period and throughout any part of the initial period in which he was so engaged, or

    (b) has not preserved all the accounting records which he has kept.

  (2) The bankrupt is not guilty of an offence under subsection (1)—

    (a) if his unsecured liabilities at the commencement of the bankruptcy did not exceed the prescribed amount, or

    (b) if he proves that in the circumstances in which he carried on business the omission was honest and excusable.

  (3) For the purposes of this section a person is deemed not to have kept proper accounting records if he has not kept such records as are necessary to show or explain his transactions and financial position in his business, including—

    (a) records containing entries from day to day, in sufficient detail, of all cash paid and received,

    (b) where the business involved dealings in goods, statement of annual stock-takings, and

    (c) except in the case of goods sold by way of retail trade to the actual customer, records of all goods sold and purchased showing the buyers and sellers in sufficient detail to enable the goods and the buyers and sellers to be identified.

  (4) In relation to any such records as are mentioned in subsection (3), subsections (2)(d) and (3)(b) of section 355 apply with the substitution of 2 years for 12 months.

For procedural provisions, see **B7.56**; for sentencing provisions, see **B7.75** and **B7.76**; for definitions, see **B7.57**. For the provisions of s. 355(2)(d) and (3)(b), see **B7.61**. The 'prescribed amount' for the purposes of s. 361(2)(a) is fixed by the Insolvency Proceedings (Monetary Limits) Order 1986 (SI 1986 No. 1996) at £20,000. The defence under s. 352 (lack of fraudulent intent) does not apply in respect of s. 361, but s. 361(2)(b) does allow for proof that the omission was both honest and excusable. What is excusable is of course a question of fact in each case, but sloppiness and inefficiency may well be regarded as inexcusable even though honest (see *Dandridge* (1931) 22 Cr App R 156). As Brett MR said in *Re Wallace, ex parte Campbell* (1885) 15 QBD 213:

> The not keeping of books is one of the greatest offences which can be committed by a trader . . . You may be almost certain that a trader who does not keep books will sooner or later become a bankrupt.

Gambling or Rash and Hazardous Speculations

B7.71   **Insolvency Act 1986, s. 362**

(1)   The bankrupt is guilty of an offence if he has—
(a)   in the 2 years before petition, materially contributed to, or increased the extent of, his insolvency by gambling or by rash and hazardous speculations, or
(b)   in the initial period, lost any part of his property by gambling or by rash and hazardous speculations.
(2)   In determining for the purposes of this section whether any speculations were rash and hazardous, the financial position of the bankrupt at the time when he entered into them shall be taken into consideration.

For procedural provisions, see **B7.56**; for sentencing provisions, see **B7.75** and **B7.76**. For the meaning of the 'initial period', see **B7.57**.

A distinction must be drawn between gambling losses on the one hand and rash and hazardous speculation on the other. The bankrupt's financial position at the time of any speculation is expressly made relevant to the question whether such speculation was rash and hazardous (s. 362(2)). A calculated risk for a man who is wealthy at the time might be considered a rash and hazardous one for a man already staring bankruptcy in the face. The position in respect of gambling losses is different. Liability is automatic in respect of any losses at all during the 'initial period' following presentation of the petition, and losses in the two years prior to this will also give rise to liability unless they were so small, relative to the bankrupt's overall losses, that their contribution to his insolvency was not material.

Where, during the initial period, the loss of some part of the bankrupt's property is counterbalanced or exceeded by gains elsewhere, as where one gamble fails and another pays off, it is by no means clear that he would escape liability under s. 362(1)(b).

Offences under the Insolvency Rules 1986

B7.72   The Insolvency Rules 1986 (SI 1986 No. 1925) generally fall outside the scope of this work, but the following provisions should be noted.

Insolvency Rules 1986, rr. 5.30 and 12.18

5.30—(1)   The debtor commits an offence if he makes any false representation or commits any other fraud for the purpose of obtaining the approval of his creditors to a proposal for a voluntary arrangement under part VIII of the Act.
12.18—(1)   Where the rules provide for creditors, members of a company or contributories in a company's winding up a right to inspect any documents, whether on the court's file or in the hands of a responsible insolvency practitioner or other person, it is an offence for a person, with the intention of obtaining a sight of documents which he has not under the rules any right to inspect, falsely to claim a status which would entitle him to inspect them.

These offences are triable either way. On conviction on indictment for an offence contrary to r. 5.30, the maximum penalty is seven years' imprisonment and/or a fine; on summary conviction, it is six months' imprisonment and/or a fine of the statutory maximum. On conviction on indictment for an offence contrary to r. 12.18, the maximum penalty is two years' imprisonment and/or a fine; on summary conviction, it is six months' imprisonment and/or a fine of the statutory maximum.

Disqualification from Company Management etc.

B7.73   **Company Directors Disqualification Act 1986, s. 11**

(1)   It is an offence for a person who is an undischarged bankrupt to act as director of, or directly or indirectly to take part in or be concerned in the promotion, formation or management of, a company, except with the leave of the court.

(2) 'The court' for this purpose is the court by which the person was adjudged bankrupt or, in Scotland, sequestration of his estates was awarded.

(3) In England and Wales, the leave of the court shall not be given unless notice of intention to apply for it has been served on the official receiver; and it is the latter's duty, if he is of opinion that it is contrary to the public interest that the application should be granted, to attend on the hearing of the application and oppose it.

This offence is triable either way. On conviction on indictment, the maximum penalty is two years' imprisonment and/or a fine; on summary conviction, it is six months' imprisonment and/or a fine of the statutory maximum (Company Directors Disqualification Act 1986, s. 13). Liability is strict; it is no defence that the accused honestly believed that his bankruptcy had been discharged at the relevant time (*Brockley* [1994] Crim LR 671).

Note that the directors of companies which have been wound up as insolvent, unlike bankrupts, will not be disqualified in this way unless a court order is made to that effect. The scope of the prohibition is illustrated by *Campbell* (1983) 78 Cr App R 95, where it was held that a disqualified person could commit the offence by advising on financial matters and on company restructuring as a 'management consultant'.

Disqualification is clearly to be taken seriously and enforced strictly. Deliberate or reckless infringement will accordingly merit a custodial sentence in the absence of mitigating circumstances (*Theivendran* (1992) 13 Cr App R (S) 601).

Disqualification under the Insolvency Act 1986

It is an offence under the Insolvency Act 1986, s. 31, for an undischarged bankrupt to act as a receiver or manager on behalf of debenture holders, unless appointed by the court, and since such a person is also disqualified from acting as an insolvency practitioner (Insolvency Act 1986, s. 390(4)), it follows that he commits an offence under s. 389 if he acts as a liquidator, administrator, or trustee in bankruptcy. **B7.74**

SCHEDULE OF OFFENCES UNDER THE INSOLVENCY ACT 1986

Insolvency Act 1986, sch. 10, Abridged   B7.75

A number of minor regulatory offences are omitted.

Section	General nature of offence	Mode of prosecution	Punishment
30	Body corporate acting as receiver.	1. On indictment. 2. Summary.	A fine. The statutory maximum.
31	Undischarged bankrupt acting as receiver or manager.	1. On indictment. 2. Summary.	Two years or a fine; or both. Six months or the statutory maximum; or both.
89(4)	Director making statutory declaration of company's solvency without reasonable grounds for his opinion.	1. On indictment. 2. Summary.	Two years or a fine; or both. Six months or the statutory maximum; or both.
206(1)	Fraud, etc. in anticipation of winding up.	1. On indictment. 2. Summary.	Seven years or a fine; or both. Six months or the statutory maximum; or both.
206(2)	Privity to fraud in anticipation of winding up; fraud, or privity to fraud, after commencement of winding up.	1. On indictment. 2. Summary.	Seven years or a fine; or both. Six months or the statutory maximum; or both.
206(5)	Knowingly taking in pawn or pledge, or otherwise receiving, company property.	1. On indictment. 2. Summary.	Seven years or a fine; or both. Six months or the statutory maximum; or both.

Section	General nature of offence	Mode of prosecution	Punishment
207	Officer of company entering into transaction in fraud of company's creditors.	1. On indictment. 2. Summary.	Two years or a fine; or both. Six months or the statutory maximum; or both.
208	Officer of company misconducting himself in course of winding up.	1. On indictment. 2. Summary.	Seven years or a fine; or both. Six months or the statutory maximum; or both.
209	Officer or contributory destroying, falsifying, etc. company's books.	1. On indictment. 2. Summary.	Seven years or a fine; or both. Six months or the statutory maximum; or both.
210	Officer of company making material omission from statement relating to company's affairs.	1. On indictment. 2. Summary.	Seven years or a fine; or both. Six months or the statutory maximum; or both.
211	False representation or fraud for purpose of obtaining creditors' consent to an agreement in connection with winding up.	1. On indictment. 2. Summary.	Seven years or a fine; or both. Six months or the statutory maximum; or both.
216(4)	Contravening restrictions on re-use of name of company in insolvent liquidation.	1. On indictment. 2. Summary.	Two years or a fine; or both. Six months or the statutory maximum; or both.
353(1)	Bankrupt failing to disclose property or disposals to official receiver or trustee.	1. On indictment. 2. Summary.	Seven years or a fine; or both. Six months or the statutory maximum; or both.
354(1)	Bankrupt failing to deliver property to, or concealing property from, official receiver or trustee.	1. On indictment. 2. Summary.	Seven years or a fine; or both. Six months or the statutory maximum; or both.
354(2)	Bankrupt removing property which he is required to deliver to official receiver or trustee.	1. On indictment. 2. Summary.	Seven years or a fine; or both. Six months or the statutory maximum; or both.
354(3)	Bankrupt failing to account for loss of substantial part of property.	1. On indictment. 2. Summary.	Two years or a fine; or both. Six months or the statutory maximum; or both.
355(1)	Bankrupt failing to deliver books, papers and records to official receiver or trustee.	1. On indictment. 2. Summary.	Seven years or a fine; or both. Six months or the statutory maximum; or both.
355(2)	Bankrupt concealing, destroying etc. books, papers or records, or making false entries in them.	1. On indictment. 2. Summary.	Seven years or a fine; or both. Six months or the statutory maximum; or both.
355(3)	Bankrupt disposing of, or altering, books, papers or records relating to his estate or affairs.	1. On indictment. 2. Summary.	Seven years or a fine; or both. Six months or the statutory maximum; or both.
356(1)	Bankrupt making material omission in statement relating to his affairs.	1. On indictment. 2. Summary.	Seven years or a fine; or both. Six months or the statutory maximum; or both.
356(2)	Bankrupt making false statement, or failing to inform trustee, where false debt proved.	1. On indictment. 2. Summary.	Seven years or a fine; or both. Six months or the statutory maximum; or both.
357	Bankrupt fraudulently disposing of property.	1. On indictment. 2. Summary.	Two years or a fine; or both. Six months or the statutory maximum; or both.

Section	General nature of offence	Mode of prosecution	Punishment
358	Bankrupt absconding with property he is required to deliver to official receiver or trustee.	1. On indictment. 2. Summary.	Two years or a fine; or both. Six months or the statutory maximum; or both.
359(1)	Bankrupt disposing of property obtained on credit and not paid for.	1. On indictment. 2. Summary.	Seven years or a fine; or both. Six months or the statutory maximum; or both.
359(2)	Obtaining property in respect of which money is owed by a bankrupt.	1. On indictment. 2. Summary.	Seven years or a fine; or both. Six months or the statutory maximum; or both.
360(1)	Bankrupt obtaining credit or engaging in business without disclosing his status or name in which he was made bankrupt.	1. On indictment. 2. Summary.	Two years or a fine; or both. Six months or the statutory maximum; or both.
360(3)	Person made bankrupt in Scotland or Northern Ireland obtaining credit, etc. in England and Wales.	1. On indictment. 2. Summary.	Two years or a fine; or both. Six months or the statutory maximum; or both.
361(1)	Bankrupt failing to keep proper accounting records.	1. On indictment. 2. Summary.	Two years or a fine; or both. Six months or the statutory maximum; or both.
362	Bankrupt increasing extent of insolvency by gambling.	1. On indictment. 2. Summary.	Two years or a fine; or both. Six months or the statutory maximum; or both.
389	Acting as insolvency practitioner when not qualified.	1. On indictment. 2. Summary.	Two years or a fine; or both. Six months or the statutory maximum; or both.
429(5)	Contravening s. 429 in respect of disabilities imposed by county court on revocation of administration order.	1. On indictment. 2. Summary.	Two years or a fine; or both. Six months or the statutory maximum; or both.

SENTENCING: INSOLVENCY AND BANKRUPTCY OFFENCES

There are relatively few reported sentencing decisions on insolvency and bankruptcy **B7.76** offences. In *Thievendran* (1992) 13 Cr App R (S) 601, the offender pleaded guilty to eight offences contrary to s. 360(1) of the Insolvency Act 1986. Although he had been made bankrupt in 1980, the offender for several years continued to act as a director of a group of companies which he had set up. The companies traded honestly, but were later wound up. The offender was sentenced to nine months' imprisonment and was disqualified from acting as a company director for ten years. The Court of Appeal found that while there had been a 'plain flouting of the order' in this case, no dishonesty had been established. The prison term was accordingly reduced to six months and suspended for two years; the disqualification period was halved. In contrast, in *Vanderwell* [1998] 1 Cr App R (S) 439, the offender pleaded guilty to two counts of being concerned in the management of a company while an undischarged bankrupt, one count of obtaining credit as a bankrupt, one of obtaining by deception, one of failing to keep proper business accounts and one of concealment of debts. The offender had been made bankrupt in 1978 and again in 1986. He was sentenced to imprisonment in 1990 and disqualified from acting as a company director. On his release he again started trading and accumulated debts of £25,000. The Court of Appeal accepted that the offender was 'thoroughly dishonest', and upheld a total prison sentence of four years and three months, together with a company director disqualification for 15 years. See also *Thompson* (1992) 14 Cr App R (S) 89, *Teece* (1993) 15 Cr App R (S) 302, *Dawes* [1997] 1 Cr App R (S) 149 and *Ashby* [1998] 2 Cr App R (S) 37. In *Mungroo* [1998] BPIR 784, the Court of Appeal stated that a bankrupt offender, against whom a judgment debt had been entered, who concealed assets and used them to pay personal debts, could expect to receive a custodial sentence, even if of previous exemplary character.

SECTION B8: DAMAGE TO PROPERTY

SIMPLE CRIMINAL DAMAGE

Definition

Criminal Damage Act 1971, s. 1   **B8.1**

(1)   A person who without lawful excuse destroys or damages any property belonging to another intending to destroy or damage any such property or being reckless as to whether any such property would be destroyed or damaged shall be guilty of an offence.

The CDA 1998, s. 30, creates a racially aggravated form of this offence which carries a higher maximum penalty. For the meaning of racially aggravated, see **B11.154**.

Procedure

Criminal damage is, subject to an important caveat, triable either way (MCA 1980, s. 17   **B8.2** and sch. 1, para. 29). When tried on indictment it is a class 4 offence. However, where the value of the property alleged to have been destroyed or the value of the alleged damage is not more than £5,000 (unless the destruction or damage was by fire and thus constitutes arson, see **B8.19** to **B8.24**), criminal damage is treated as if it were triable only summarily (MCA 1980, s. 22 and sch. 2). This does not convert it into a summary offence for all purposes and thus there can still be an attempt to commit low value criminal damage even though only an attempt to commit an indictable offence is caught by the Criminal Attempts Act 1981, s. 1(4) (*Bristol Magistrates' Court, ex parte E* [1998] 3 All ER 798). For consideration of the mode of trial for criminal damage, including the method of determining the value involved, see **D3.12** and **D3.13**. Even if the value involved is not more than £5,000, a count for criminal damage may be included in an indictment for another offence in the circumstances set out in the CJA 1988, s. 40 (see **D9.6**).

The guidelines in *Practice Note (Mode of Trial: Guidelines)* (1995) (see **D3.7**), which apply where the value involved is more than £5,000, state that, in general, cases should be tried summarily unless the court considers that one or more of the following features is present in the case *and* that its sentencing powers are insufficient:

(a)   Deliberate fire-raising (an offence under the Criminal Damage Act, s. 1(1), committed by destroying or damaging property by fire is charged as arson – see **B8.19** to **B8.24**).
(b)   Committed by a group.
(c)   Damage of a high value (at least £10,000).
(d)   The offence has clear racial motivation.

The racially aggravated form of the offence is triable either way, irrespective of the value of the damage.

Indictment

Statement of Offence   **B8.3**

Criminal damage contrary to section 1(1) of the Criminal Damage Act 1971

Particulars of Offence

A on or about the . . . day of . . . did without lawful excuse damage [or destroy] a glass window, having a value of £120, belonging to V intending to damage [or destroy] such property or being reckless as to whether such property would be damaged [or destroyed]

Sentence

B8.4   For the maximum penalty and for sentencing guidelines, see **B8.35** to **B8.38**.

Meaning of 'Damage'

B8.5   'Damage' is left undefined in the Criminal Damage Act 1971. The courts have construed the term liberally. Criminal damage is not limited to permanent damage, so smearing mud on the walls of a police cell may be criminal damage. See *Roe* v *Kingerlee* [1986] Crim LR 735, where it was also said that: 'What constitutes criminal damage is a matter of fact and degree and it is for the justices, applying their common sense, to decide whether what occurred was damage or not'.

Older (persuasive) authorities under pre-1971 enactments further illustrate the breadth of the notion of damage: see, for example, *Roper* v *Knott* [1898] 1 QB 868 (milk damaged by adulteration with water) and *Tacey* (1821) Russ & Ry 452 (machine damaged by removal of essential part, although if the constituent part or parts are not themselves damaged it is important to charge damage to the machine, i.e., to the whole rather than to the parts – see *Woolcock* [1977] Crim LR 104 and 161). *Hardman* v *Chief Constable of Avon and Somerset* [1986] Crim LR 330 is a more modern illustration of the scope of the meaning of 'damage', in which water-soluble pavement paintings were held to constitute damage to the pavement.

The damage need not be tangible or visible if it affects the value or performance of the property: see *Cox* v *Riley* (1986) 83 Cr App R 54, where a plastic circuit card for controlling a computerised saw was held to have been damaged by the erasure of the programs electronically written on it. Nor did it matter that the damage was not permanent in that it could be remedied, as restoring the programs necessitated 'time, labour and expense'. See now *Whiteley* (1991) 93 Cr App R 25, where a computer disk was held to be damaged by the addition and deletion of files. The interference with the disk amounted to an 'impairment of the value or usefulness of the disk to the owner'. These two decisions remain significant for the general meaning of damage but are overtaken as regards their own particular facts by the Computer Misuse Act 1990, s. 3(6), which restricts the meaning of damage where it is done by 'the modification of the contents of a computer' (see further **B18.3**).

Meaning of 'Property'

B8.6   **Criminal Damage Act 1971, s. 10**

>   (1)   In this Act 'property' means property of a tangible nature, whether real or personal, including money and—
>   (a)   including wild creatures which have been tamed or are ordinarily kept in captivity . . .; but
>   (b)   not including mushrooms growing wild on any land or flowers, fruit or foliage or a plant growing wild on any land.

This definition of property is wider than that in the Theft Act 1968, s. 4 (see **B4.10** to **B4.16**), in that it lacks the restrictions on stealing land in that section, but, on the other hand, is narrower in that it does not include 'things in action and other intangible property'. Thus, land can be damaged by, e.g., dumping on it, even though it cannot be stolen (see discussion in *Cox* v *Riley* (1986) 83 Cr App 54 and **B8.5**). However, a copyright cannot be damaged by infringing it (contrast the offences under the Copyright, Designs and Patents Act 1988, s. 107), even though it can in theory be stolen. In *Cox* v *Riley*, even though the erased program might be said to be 'intangible property', the property alleged to be damaged was the circuit card and not the erased program itself. See also *Whiteley* (1991) 93 Cr App R 25, discussed in **B8.5**. (Note that both *Whiteley* and *Cox* v *Riley* have now to be read in the light of the Computer Misuse Act 1990, s. 3(6); see **B18.3**).

Meaning of 'Belonging to Another'

Criminal Damage Act 1971, s. 10

B8.7

(2) Property shall be treated for the purposes of this Act as belonging to any person—
    (a) having the custody or control of it;
    (b) having in it any proprietary right or interest (not being an equitable interest arising only from an agreement to transfer or grant an interest); or
    (c) having a charge on it.

The effect of this provision (as with theft, see **B4.17** to **B4.23**) is that an owner can be guilty of criminal damage to his own property if at the same time it belongs to someone else within the extended meaning of s. 10.

Mens Rea

This is satisfied by either intention or recklessness, and it is the latter, wider concept **B8.8** which has proved crucial. It is now clear following *Metropolitan Police Commissioner* v *Caldwell* [1982] AC 341 that recklessness in this context does not require subjective appreciation of the risk of causing damage, but is also satisfied by a failure to consider an obvious risk. In *Metropolitan Police Commissioner* v *Caldwell* Lord Diplock gave the following model direction (at p. 354):

> . . . a person charged with an offence under section 1(1) of the Criminal Damage Act 1971 is 'reckless as to whether any such property would be destroyed or damaged' if (1) he does an act which in fact creates an obvious risk that property will be destroyed or damaged and (2) when he does the act he either has not given any thought to the possibility of there being any such risk or has recognised that there was some risk involved and has nonetheless gone on to do it.

The risk need only be obvious in the sense that it would have been obvious to the reasonable man, not to the accused if he or she had stopped to think (*Elliott* v *C* [1983] 1 WLR 939), nor to a person of the age of the accused or sharing the accused's characteristics (*R (Stephen Malcolm)* (1984) 79 Cr App R 334; *Miller* [1983] 2 AC 161). These cases were recently confirmed and followed in *Coles* [1995] 1 Cr App R 157.

In *Metropolitan Police Commissioner* v *Caldwell* [1982] AC 341, Lord Diplock said that it is unnecessary to classify the offence as one of specific or basic intent, since, as far as recklessness is concerned, evidence of intoxication is logically irrelevant and therefore no defence anyway. If this had been borne in mind in *Cullen* [1993] Crim LR 936, the difficulties encountered would never have arisen — see the commentary on p. 938. On the other hand, if the accused, influenced by alcohol, decides positively that there is no risk of damage, i.e., rules out the risk, evidence of his intoxication does seem to be *logically* relevant and perhaps could ground a defence, although in such a case the courts might revert to saying that the offence is one of basic intent. The Divisional Court in *Chief Constable of Avon and Somerset* v *Shimmen* (1986) 84 Cr App R 7 (see **A3.3**) was at least prepared to countenance this sort of defence where the accused had been drinking. Certainly where the intoxication contributes to a belief in lawful excuse under the Criminal Damage Act 1971, s. 5 (see **B8.9**), rather than negativing recklessness, it can form the basis of a defence (see *Jaggard* v *Dickinson* [1981] QB 527).

Meaning of 'Without Lawful Excuse'

The meaning of 'lawful excuse' is specially provided for in relation to this offence in the **B8.9** Criminal Damage Act 1971, s. 5 (which, however, is not applicable to the aggravated offence of criminal damage under s. 1(2) – see **B8.10** to **B8.18**).

Criminal Damage Act 1971, s. 5

(2) A person charged with an offence to which this section applies shall, whether or not he would be treated for the purposes of this Act as having a lawful excuse apart from this subsection, be treated for those purposes as having a lawful excuse—

(a)   if at the time of the act or acts alleged to constitute the offence he believed that the person or persons whom he believed to be entitled to consent to the destruction of or damage to the property in question had so consented, or would have so consented to it if he or they had known of the destruction or damage and its circumstances; or

(b)   if he destroyed or damaged or threatened to destroy or damage the property in question or, in the case of a charge of an offence under section 3 above, intended to use or cause or permit the use of something to destroy or damage it, in order to protect property belonging to himself or another or a right or interest in property which was or which he believed to be vested in himself or another, and at the time of the act or acts alleged to constitute the offence he believed—

(i)   that the property, right or interest was in immediate need of protection; and

(ii)   that the means of protection adopted or proposed to be adopted were or would be reasonable having regard to all the circumstances.

(3)   For the purposes of this section it is immaterial whether a belief is justified or not if it is honestly held.

(4)   For the purposes of subsection (2) above a right or interest in property includes any right or privilege in or over land, whether created by grant, licence or otherwise.

(5)   This section shall not be construed as casting doubt on any defence recognised by law as a defence to criminal charges.

The words in s. 5(2) 'whether or not he would be treated for the purposes of this Act as having a lawful excuse apart from this subsection' together with s. 5(5), indicate that the section is not intended to be an exhaustive account of the circumstances of lawful excuse. Thus, general defences such as duress or prevention of crime are not excluded (cf. *Baker* [1997] Crim LR 497). However, a motorist who damages a wheel clamp to free his car, having parked on another's property knowing of the risk of being clamped, does not have a lawful excuse (*Lloyd* v *DPP* [1992] 1 All ER 982: contrast the entirely different approach to wheel clamping in the Scottish case *Black* v *Carmichael* (1992) *The Times*, 25 June 1992).

Section 5 does specifically cover, however, two alternative types of belief which are outlined in more detail in s. 5(2):

(a)   belief in consent; or

(b)   belief in the immediate necessity to protect property.

Section 5(3) emphasises that the question is the purely subjective one of whether the belief is honestly held, not whether it is justified or reasonable. In *Jaggard* v *Dickinson* [1981] QB 527, the accused, due to intoxication, mistakenly believed she would have had the owner's consent to breaking a window in order to gain access to a house (unfortunately she tried to break into the wrong house). The Divisional Court quashed her conviction, saying (per Mustill J, at pp. 531–2): '. . . the court is required by section 5(3) to focus on the existence of the belief, not its intellectual soundness; and a belief can be just as much honestly held if it is induced by intoxication, as if it stems from stupidity, forgetfulness or inattention'.

Although the test under s. 5(2)(b)(ii) is clearly *subjective* and the question is not whether the accused's action is *in fact* reasonable but whether the accused *believed* it to be reasonable, whether an accused is acting 'in order to protect property' under s. 5(2)(b) does seem to have an objective aspect. In *Hunt* (1977) 66 Cr App R 105, the accused set fire to bedding to draw attention to a defective fire alarm in old people's accommodation which the court ruled was not 'in order to protect property', despite the accused's belief that it would ultimately have that effect. See further *Hill* (1988) 89 Cr App R 74, where the accused's beliefs about the ultimate effects of damaging perimeter fencing at a United States naval base were held not to amount to a purpose of protecting property, or to a belief that property was in *imminent* need of protection under s. 5(2)(b)(i). See however *Chamberlain* v *Lindon* [1998] 1 WLR 1252 for a case where these two requirements were satisfied.

If the accused does hold a belief provided for in s. 5, it is immaterial as far as his liability for criminal damage is concerned that he has some ulterior fraudulent or criminal purpose. Thus, in *Denton* [1981] 1 WLR 1446, the accused set fire to the cotton mill where he worked, because he believed he had been asked to do so by his employer with a view to gaining the insurance money on the property. The Court of Appeal quashed his conviction for criminal damage, pointing out that if the owner himself had caused the damage he would have committed no offence (under s. 1(1), though other charges might be possible), since he was not damaging property 'belonging to another', and hence the accused, who believed he was acting on behalf of the owner and with his consent, should be in no worse position. In fact, the 'employer' (an individual) in this case was not strictly the owner of the property, which legally belonged to the company, a separate legal entity. This did not particularly matter on the facts, since it was conceded that the accused honestly believed that his 'employer' was the person 'entitled to consent' within s. 5(2)(a). Contrast *Appleyard* (1985) 81 Cr App R 319, where a managing director was convicted of destroying the company's store, and was not allowed to claim that he himself was the person entitled to consent to the damage. It would seem, therefore, that the belief under s. 5(2)(a) must relate to some other person having the right to consent and not to the accused himself. If a person mistakenly believes he is the actual owner (as opposed to being merely the person entitled to consent), then he has a defence, not under s. 5(2) but because he lacks *mens rea* (see *Smith* [1974] QB 354).

AGGRAVATED CRIMINAL DAMAGE

Definition

Criminal Damage Act 1971, s. 1   **B8.10**

    (2)   A person who without lawful excuse destroys or damages any property, whether belonging to himself or another—
      (a)   intending to destroy or damage any property or being reckless as to whether any property would be destroyed or damaged; and
      (b)   intending by the destruction or damage to endanger the life of another or being reckless as to whether the life of another would be thereby endangered;
shall be guilty of an offence.

Procedure

Aggravated criminal damage is triable only on indictment. It is a class 3 offence.   **B8.11**

Indictment

Statement of Offence   **B8.12**

Destroying [or damaging] property with intent to endanger life [or being reckless as to whether life would be endangered] contrary to section 1(2) of the Criminal Damage Act 1971

Particulars of Offence

A on or about the . . . day of . . . did without lawful excuse damage [or destroy] a motor vehicle belonging to V, intending to damage [or destroy] such vehicle or being reckless as to whether such vehicle would be damaged [or destroyed] and intending by such damage [or destruction] to endanger the life of V or being reckless as to whether the life of V would be thereby endangered

Alternative Verdicts

It is submitted that in some cases, on an indictment for aggravated criminal damage, it   **B8.13** may be possible for the jury to return an alternative verdict of simple criminal damage, pursuant to the Criminal Law Act 1967, s. 3 (**D16.18** to **D16.31**). However, this is problematic in that it will be possible only where:

(a)   it is specifically alleged that the property in question belonged not to the accused but to another (which is not an essential averment under the Criminal Damage Act 1971, s. 1(2), but is under s. 1(1)); and

(b)   there is no issue as to lawful excuse (the meaning of which differs as between the two offences, inasmuch as the provisions of the Criminal Damage Act 1971, s. 5, do not apply to offences under s. 1(2)).

It is therefore always appropriate to add an alternative count (which may be done even where the value of the property is less than £5,000 – see CJA 1988, s. 40, and **D9.6**). In the absence of such an alternative count, trial judges may be reluctant to leave the alternative to the jury (see generally **D16.30**).

Sentence

B8.14   For the maximum penalty and for sentencing guidelines, see **B8.35** to **B8.38**.

Relationship to Simple Criminal Damage

B8.15   Aggravated criminal damage is identical with the offence under the Criminal Damage Act 1971, s. 1(1), as far as relates to the meaning of damage and property (see **B8.5** and **B8.6**), but differs in three main respects:

(a)   The presence of the aggravating ulterior *mens rea* of intention to endanger life or recklessness as to whether life would be endangered.

(b)   The fact that the offence can be committed irrespective of whether the property 'belongs to another'.

(c)   The inapplicability of s. 5 of the Act to the meaning of 'lawful excuse'.

B8.16   ***Mens Rea***   The *Caldwell* definition of recklessness (see **B8.8** and generally **A2.5** *et seq*.) is again clearly applicable as it was this offence which was in issue on the facts of *Metropolitan Police Commissioner* v *Caldwell* [1982] AC 341 itself. The test is therefore the objective one of whether the risk of endangering life would have been obvious to the ordinary prudent bystander. In *Sangha* [1988] 1 WLR 519 the appellant set fire to furniture in a house, which at the time was unoccupied and which was constructed in such a way that the fire would not spread to neighbouring houses. Although, in fact, no one's life was endangered, the conviction was upheld, since the ordinary prudent bystander, not blessed with hindsight or any special knowledge, at the time the fire was started would have thought there was such a risk. See also *Parker* [1993] Crim LR 856.

In the case of attempt to commit an offence under the Criminal Damage Act 1971, s. 1(2), *Caldwell* recklessness as to life being endangered will suffice even though a specific intent to cause damage is also required (*A-G's Ref (No. 3 of 1992)* [1994] 1 WLR 409, which followed the principle established in the attempted rape case *Khan* [1990] 1 WLR 813 (see **A6.36**)).

B8.17   ***Requirement that Danger to Life Result from Damage Intended***   The accused must be at least reckless as to causing damage, as to endangering life and also as to whether life would be endangered *as a result of the damage*. The offence was thus not made out in *Steer* [1988] AC 111, where the accused shot through a window behind which two people were standing. Although the accused was reckless as to whether life would be endangered, the danger to life was not caused by the damage to the window but by the firing of the bullet. Compare *Webster* [1995] 2 All ER 168, where damaging the windscreen of a moving car or ramming the car was held to be capable of endangering life as a result of the damage. Furthermore, it is the damage which the accused intended, or as to which he was reckless, which is relevant, rather than the actual damage which happens to be caused. See *Dudley* [1989] Crim LR 57, where only trivial damage, not likely to endanger life, was *actually* caused, but the appellant's conviction was upheld since he created a *risk* of much more serious damage which was capable of endangering life.

Meaning of 'Without Lawful Excuse' The partial definition of 'lawful excuse' in **B8.18** the Criminal Damage Act 1971, s. 5, is not applicable, because belief in the owner's consent or of the immediate need to protect *property* cannot justify the endangering of human life. However, 'without lawful excuse' in any other sense remains part of the definition of the offence so that, e.g., damaging property in lawful self-defence would not be criminal even if it endangers the aggressor's (or possibly even a third party's) life, provided that it was reasonable to do so.

ARSON

Definition

Criminal Damage Act 1971, s. 1   B8.19

(3)   An offence committed under this section by destroying or damaging property by fire shall be charged as arson.

Procedure

Simple arson contrary to the Criminal Damage Act 1971, s. 1(1) and (3), is triable either **B8.20** way (MCA 1980, s. 17 and sch. 1, para. 29). When tried on indictment it is a class 4 offence. For the guidelines for determining mode of trial see **B8.2**. The value involved in simple arson does not cause the MCA 1980, s. 22, to restrict the mode of trial because arson is, by sch. 2 to the MCA 1980, not an offence to which s. 22 applies.

Aggravated arson contrary to the Criminal Damage Act 1971, s. 1(2) and (3), is triable only on indictment. It is a class 3 offence.

Indictment

The wording of the Criminal Damage Act 1971, s. 1(3) (see **B8.19**), is mandatory. A **B8.21** charge of criminal damage 'contrary to s. 1(1) plus (3) of the Act' is a nullity (*Booth* [1999] Crim LR 144).

Statement of Offence

Arson contrary to section 1(1) and (3) of the Criminal Damage Act 1971

Particulars of Offence

A on or about the . . . day of . . . did without lawful excuse damage by fire a motor vehicle, having a value of £3,500, belonging to V intending to damage such vehicle by fire or being reckless as to whether such vehicle would be damaged by fire

An offence under s. 1(2) by fire must also be charged as arson. In such a case there should be separate counts of arson with intent to endanger life and arson being reckless as to whether life would be endangered (see *Hoof* (1980) 72 Cr App 126; *sed quaere,* the two forms of *mens rea* do not mean that the section creates two offences, and, of course, the maximum penalty is the same).

First Count

Statement of Offence

Arson contrary to section 1(2) and (3) of the Criminal Damage Act 1971

Particulars of Offence

A on or about the . . . day of . . . did without lawful excuse damage by fire a motor vehicle, having a value of £3,500, belonging to V intending to damage such vehicle by fire and intending by such damage to endanger the life of V

Second Count

As above, but alleging instead of the intent to endanger life: '. . . and being reckless as to whether the life of V would thereby be endangered'

431

Alternative Verdicts

B8.22 See **B8.13**. On indictment for arson under the Criminal Damage Act 1971, s. 1(1) and (3) or s. 1(2) and (3), it is submitted that the jury should not be invited to return an alternative verdict of guilty of criminal damage other than by fire, even under the corresponding subsection of s. 1, because of the different nature of the *actus reus*. In the unlikely event of doubt as to the method of causing the damage, an alternative count should be added.

Sentence

B8.23 For the maximum penalty and for sentencing guidelines, see **B8.35** to **B8.38**.

Elements

B8.24 Arson differs from simple or aggravated criminal damage only in that the destruction or damage to the property must be 'by fire'. *Quaere* whether this might extend to damage caused, for example, by water in saving the property from imminent destruction by the fire, or by a fall resulting from the collapse due to fire of a structure on which the property had stood.

THREATS TO DESTROY OR DAMAGE PROPERTY

Definition

B8.25   **Criminal Damage Act 1971, s. 2**

> A person who without lawful excuse makes to another a threat, intending that that other would fear it would be carried out,—
> (a)   to destroy or damage any property belonging to that other or a third person; or
> (b)   to destroy or damage his own property in a way which he knows is likely to endanger the life of that other or a third person;
> shall be guilty of an offence.

Procedure

B8.26 A threat to destroy or damage property is triable either way (MCA 1980, s. 17 and sch. 1, para. 29). When tried on indictment it is a class 4 offence.

Indictment

B8.27   Statement of Offence

Threatening to destroy property contrary to section 2(a) of the Criminal Damage Act 1971

Particulars of Offence

A on or about the . . . day of . . . did without lawful excuse make a threat to V to destroy a motor vehicle belonging to V [or X] intending that V would fear that the threat would be carried out

Sentence

B8.28 For the maximum penalty see **B8.35**.

Elements

B8.29 For the meaning of 'without lawful excuse', see **B8.9**, but note that by virtue of the Criminal Damage Act 1971, s. 5(1), the partial definition of 'lawful excuse' does not apply where the accused knows that the threatened damage is likely to endanger life. This is no doubt for the same sorts of reasons that s. 5 does not apply to aggravated criminal damage under s. 1(2).

There is no requirement that the threat be carried out or be capable of being carried out immediately, or that the accused intended to carry it out or that the person threatened *actually* fears that it will be carried out, provided that the accused *intends* that there should be such fear.

POSSESSION WITH INTENT TO DESTROY OR DAMAGE PROPERTY

Definition

Criminal Damage Act 1971, s. 3

B8.30

A person who has anything in his custody or under his control intending without lawful excuse to use it or cause or permit another to use it—
    (a)   to destroy or damage any property belonging to some other person; or
    (b)   to destroy or damage his own or the user's property in a way which he knows is likely to endanger the life of some other person;
shall be guilty of an offence.

Procedure

Possession of an article with intent to destroy or damage property is triable either way B8.31 (MCA 1980, s. 17 and sch. 1, para. 29). When tried on indictment it is a class 4 offence.

Indictment

Statement of Offence

B8.32

Possession of an article with intent to destroy [or damage] property contrary to section 3 of the Criminal Law Act 1971

Particulars of Offence

A on or about the . . . day of . . . did have in his custody [or under his control] a can of spray paint intending without lawful excuse to use it [or cause or permit X to use it] to damage a motor vehicle belonging to V

Sentence

For the maximum penalty, see **B8.35**.
B8.33

Elements

The essence of the offence is the intention to use the article, *any article,* or to cause or B8.34 permit it to be used, to cause damage. A conditional intention to so use it if given circumstances arise will suffice (*Buckingham* (1976) 63 Cr App R 159).

The partial definition of 'lawful excuse' in the Criminal Damage Act 1971, s. 5, is applicable only to the form of the offence in s. 3(a) and not to that in s. 3(b), although it is still open to the accused to put forward a lawful excuse independently of s. 5.

The Criminal Damage Act 1971, s. 6, enables the police to search for articles used, or intended to be used, to cause criminal damage.

Criminal Damage Act 1971, s. 6

    (1)   If it is made to appear by information on oath before a justice of the peace that there is reasonable cause to believe that any person has in his custody or under his control or on his premises anything which there is reasonable cause to believe has been used or is intended for use without lawful excuse—
    (a)   to destroy or damage property belonging to another; or
    (b)   to destroy or damage any property in a way likely to endanger the life of another,
the justice may grant a warrant authorising any constable to search for and seize that thing.

(2)   A constable who is authorised under this section to search premises for anything, may enter (if need be by force) and search the premises accordingly and may seize anything which he believes to have been used or to be intended to be used as aforesaid.

(3)   The Police (Property) Act 1897 (disposal of property in the possession of the police) shall apply to property which has come into the possession of the police under this section as it applies to property which has come into the possession of the police in the circumstances mentioned in that Act.

SENTENCING: OFFENCES INVOLVING DAMAGE TO PROPERTY

Maximum Penalties

B8.35   Criminal damage, with intent to endanger life or recklessness whether life is endangered: Life imprisonment (Criminal Damage Act 1971, s. 4(1)).

Criminal damage: 10 years (Criminal Damage Act 1971, s. 4(2)) on indictment; six months or a fine not exceeding the statutory maximum, or both, summarily. If, however, damage is quantified at less than £5,000, so that the offence is treated as triable summarily only: three months, a fine not exceeding level 4 on the standard scale, or both.

Racially aggravated criminal damage: 14 years on indictment (CDA 1998, s. 30(2)); six months or a fine not exceeding the statutory maximum, or both, summarily.

Arson (where either of the above offences is committed by fire): Life imprisonment (Criminal Damage Act 1971, s. 4(1)) on indictment; where criminal damage by fire, but not criminal damage with intent or recklessness whether life is endangered, six months or a fine not exceeding the statutory maximum, or both, summarily.

Threat to destroy or damage property: 10 years (Criminal Damage Act 1971, s. 4(2)) on indictment; six months or a fine not exceeding the statutory maximum, or both, summarily.

Possessing article with intent to destroy or damage property: 10 years (Criminal Damage Act 1971, s. 4(2)) on indictment; six months or a fine not exceeding the statutory maximum, or both, summarily.

General Sentencing Guidelines

B8.36   Where tried summarily, the Magistrates' Association Guidelines (1997) indicate the following:

Aggravating Factors ⊕
For example racial motivation; deliberate; group offence; serious damage; offence committed on bail; previous convictions and failures to respond to previous sentences, if relevant.

Mitigating Factors ⊖
For example impulsive action; minor damage; provocation.

Guideline: Is compensation, discharge or fine appropriate?

The guideline fine is £135 (low income), £340 (average income) or £810 (high income).

B8.37   Sentencing Guidelines: Criminal Damage

In *Dodd* [1997] 1 Cr App R (S) 127, the offender pleaded guilty to damaging property being reckless whether life was endangered, and to driving while disqualified. He had driven his car, at between 35 and 40 mph through the glass-fronted doors of Plymouth Magistrates' Court and through inner doors, the car coming to rest against the rear wall of the building, causing £34,000 worth of damage. Nobody was injured. A sentence of four years' imprisonment for the criminal damage offence was upheld by the Court of Appeal. In *Kavanagh* [1998] 1 Cr App R (S) 241 the offender, after an argument with his partner, released gas from a gas fire and threatened to blow up their flat. The police were called and the threat was not carried out. A sentence of four years' imprisonment was reduced to three years on appeal.

There are few Court of Appeal decisions relating to simple criminal damage. In *Bowles* (1988) 10 Cr App R (S) 146, a sentence of 14 days' imprisonment was upheld in a case where the offender daubed paint over the door and surrounding walls of South Africa House, as a political protest. In *Toomey* (1993) 14 Cr App R (S) 42, the offender smashed the windows and door of a restaurant after an argument with the owner. Customers were in the restaurant at the time and over £2,000 worth of damage was done. Eighteen months' imprisonment was reduced to 12 months on appeal. In *Ward* (1997) 161 JP 297, the Court of Appeal upheld sentences of 12, 15 and 18 months on offenders sentenced for conspiracy to commit criminal damage. The defendants, wearing Nazi-style armbands and emblems, had set out to damage gravestones in a Jewish cemetery but were prevented from doing so by the police.

Sentencing Guidelines: Arson

The CJA 1991, s. 31(1), provides that any offence which is required to be charged as **B8.38** arson is included within the meaning of the term 'violent offence', whether or not it would otherwise fall within the definition having effect for part I of that Act (see **E1.10**). The Court of Appeal cases taken together indicate that there should be a psychiatric report available on the offender in cases of arson, and that where there is appropriate psychiatric evidence, a medical disposal, such as probation order with a condition of psychiatric treatment or a hospital order, may be passed. Minor cases can be dealt with by non-custodial sentences. Otherwise, in the absence of mitigation, a custodial sentence will generally be appropriate. Longer custodial sentences are appropriate where substantial damage has been caused, or where death or serious injury has been risked by the offender.

In *Cheeseborough* (1982) 4 Cr App R (S) 394, the offender went to the house of a man with whom his wife had formed an attachment and, after cutting the telephone wires, poured petrol through the letter-box and set fire to it. The three people in the house escaped and the fire was put out before extensive structural damage was done to the house. A sentence of seven years was said to be proper by the Court of Appeal. Although the act was deliberate (the sentencer regarded it as being close to attempted murder), the offender was not regarded by the court as representing a general danger to the public. Revenge attacks, where there is no evidence of mental disorder, attract custodial sentences. A sentence of three years was upheld in *Downey* (1986) 8 Cr App R (S) 168, where the offender caused £53,000 worth of damage by setting fire to a barn and its contents. Four years was held to be appropriate in *Elliot* (1989) Cr App R (S) 67, where the offender set fire to a depot where he had formerly been employed, causing damage to the extent of £1,811,000.

A combination order was held to have been an unduly lenient sentence in *A-G's Ref (No. 35 of 1996)* [1997] 1 Cr App R (S) 350, where the offender, who had fallen into rent arrears, started a fire in his flat which caused £2,000 worth of damage. The Court of Appeal stated that a sentence of three years' imprisonment would normally be appropriate for such an offence. A probation order was held to have been an unduly lenient sentence for arson being reckless whether life was endangered in *A-G's Ref (No. 61 of 1996)* [1997] 2 Cr App R (S) 316. The offender, in a jealous rage, set light to some of his girlfriend's clothes in the bedroom of their terraced house. He then maimed her dog with a sledgehammer, locked the door and left the fire burning. The fire was seen by police officers and extinguished before it spread to the next-door house. A sentence of two years' imprisonment was substituted by the Court of Appeal, the sentence being discounted for an unspecified period by virtue of the offender being sentenced twice for the offence. See also *A-G's Ref (No. 5 of 1993)* (1994) 15 Cr App R (S) 201, *Sparkes* (1995) 16 Cr App R (S) 393 and *Potts* [1996] 2 Cr App R (S) 291.

SECTION B9: OFFENCES AFFECTING SECURITY

ACTS PREJUDICIAL TO SAFETY OR INTERESTS OF STATE ('SPYING')

Definition

B9.1
Official Secrets Act 1911, s. 1

(1) If any person for any purpose prejudicial to the safety or interests of the State—

(a) approaches, inspects, passes over or is in the neighbourhood of, or enters any prohibited place within the meaning of this Act, or
(b) makes any sketch, plan, model, or note which is calculated to be or might be or is intended to be directly or indirectly useful to an enemy; or
(c) obtains, collects, records, or publishes, or communicates to any other person any secret official code word or pass word, or any sketch, plan, model, article, or note, or other document or information which is calculated to be or might be or is intended to be directly or indirectly useful to an enemy;
he shall be guilty of [an offence].

Procedure

B9.2   This offence is triable only on indictment. It is a class 1 offence.

Official Secrets Act 1911, s. 8

A prosecution for an offence under this Act shall not be instituted except by or with the consent of the Attorney-General.

By virtue of the Official Secrets Act 1911, s. 10(1) and (2), and the Official Secrets Act 1920, s. 8(3), a competent British court in the place where the offence was committed has jurisdiction to try a person, and a court in England has jurisdiction to try a person alleged to have committed the instant offence, even though the offence was committed elsewhere. The Official Secrets Act 1911 contains the basic provisions, the 1920 Act amplifies them by making clear that a person commits the offence, for the purposes of trial, either where it was committed, or, if that is outside the jurisdiction of the English courts, where he was found. As to territorial jurisdiction generally, see **D1.72** *et seq*.

In addition to general powers (see **D2.47** to **D2.56**), the Official Secrets Act 1920, s. 8(4), permits the court, on the application of the prosecution, on grounds of national safety to exclude all or some of the public from a trial, except for the sentencing of the person once found guilty. This power not only applies to the offences under the 1911 and 1920 Acts, but also to the offences under the Official Secrets Act 1989, except those created by s. 8.

The Official Secrets Act 1911, s. 10(3), limits the courts outside the United Kingdom which may try such offences to those which may impose the greatest punishment allowed by law. It also provides that a sheriff court in Scotland cannot try such offences.

Indictment

B9.3
Statement of Offence

Entering a prohibited place contrary to section 1(1)(a) of the Official Secrets Act 1911

Particulars of Offence

A on or about the . . . day of . . ., for a purpose prejudicial to the safety or interests of the State, namely . . ., entered a prohibited place, namely . . .

Sentencing Guidelines

A person guilty of an offence under the Official Secrets Act 1911, s. 1, is liable to **B9.4** imprisonment for a term not exceeding 14 years (Official Secrets Act 1920, s. 8(1)).

Offences committed under the Official Secrets Act 1911, s. 1, will inevitably attract a lengthy custodial sentence. In *Prime* (1983) 5 Cr App R (S) 127, the offender pleaded guilty to two indictments. On the first, he admitted seven offences against the Official Secrets Acts. The offender had been employed for nine years in the Government Communications Service, where he had access to highly sensitive intelligence information of importance to national security. During that period he passed on information to the Soviet Union. On the second indictment he pleaded guilty to counts of indecent assault against young girls. For the espionage offences, he received consecutive terms of 14, 14, and seven years' imprisonment. For the indecent assault offences he received a further three years, consecutive, a total of 38 years. These sentences were upheld on appeal. In *Schulze* (1986) 8 Cr App R (S) 463, the offenders' home was found to contain spying equipment, forged documents and radio receiving equipment. They were convicted of doing acts preparatory to the commission of an offence under s. 1 of the Act. Sentences of 10 years were upheld in each case.

Offence not limited to 'Spying'

The Official Secrets Act 1911, s. 1, is stated in the marginal note as being concerned with **B9.5** 'penalties for spying'. The offence is, however, not limited to 'spying' (*Chandler* v *DPP* [1964] AC 763). Lord Reid (at p. 789–90) was of the view that the marginal note could not affect the obvious meaning of the section, which clearly covered sabotage and temporary sabotage.

Mens Rea: Purpose Prejudicial to the Safety or Interests of the State

An offence under the Official Secrets Act 1911, s. 1(1), may be committed in a number **B9.6** of ways, which must be considered separately. However, one element is common to each paragraph of s. 1(1), and that is the *mens rea* requirement that a person act with a 'purpose prejudicial to the safety or interests of the State'.

Consideration of this aspect of the offence demands both a consideration of the Official Secrets Act 1911, s. 1(2), and of the decision of the House of Lords in *Chandler* v *DPP* [1964] AC 763. The Act deals with some particular aspects of how the necessary purpose can be established. First, it makes clear that it is not necessary to establish an act on the part of the accused which would show the requisite purpose. Secondly, it establishes circumstances, including his conduct and his known character as proved, from which it is possible to infer that the accused's purpose was a purpose prejudicial to the interests of the State. Thirdly, it makes clear that it will be deemed that a sketch, plan, model etc. made, obtained, collected, recorded, published or communicated by a person not acting under lawful authority is made etc. for a purpose prejudicial to the interests of the State, but the contrary may be proved.

In *Chandler* v *DPP* [1964] AC 763 it was essential to consider what is 'a purpose prejudicial to the safety or interests of the State', because the claim of the co-accused, who were members of CND, was that their objective was to prevent aircraft taking off from an American airbase for six hours. They claimed that the aircraft used nuclear bombs, and that it was not in the interests of the State to have such aircraft armed at an airbase. Thus it was beneficial to the interests of the State to immobilise these aircraft. These arguments failed. The fact that the offences in question were not the substantive offence, but conspiracy to incite or commit it, is irrelevant. The House made a number of points of considerable importance in rejecting the arguments of the co-accused:

(a)   'Purpose' includes the state of mind shown by the co-accused in this case, that is, an intention and desire to immobilise the base for a time. Whatever their motive, they did have as their purpose the immobilisation of the base (see per Lord Reid at p. 790, per Viscount Radcliffe at p. 795).

(b)   As regards the phrase 'prejudicial to the safety or interests of the State':

(i)   'State' does not mean the government or the executive, or the individuals who inhabit these islands. The country or the realm are good synonyms. As good a definition as any would be 'the organised community' (per Lord Reid at p. 790 and per Lord Hodson at p. 801) or 'the organs of government of a national community' (per Lord Devlin at p. 807).

(ii)   Whether a person's purpose is prejudicial to the safety or interests of the State is a matter for the jury to decide, on the basis that it is for the Crown to decide what is for the safety or interests of the State and that decision of the Crown is not challengeable (see Lord Reid at pp. 790–2, Viscount Radcliffe at pp. 796–8, Lord Hodson at pp. 799–801, Lord Pearce at pp. 813–14). The function of the jury is (according to Lord Reid at p. 792), to decide whether the purpose of the accused 'was to interfere to a material extent' with the airfield (or to obstruct it, see e.g., Viscount Radcliffe at p. 795), in which case the purpose was one which was prejudicial to the safety or interests of the State. Thus, the opinion of the accused as to what is in the safety or interests of the State is irrelevant (see *Bettaney* [1985] Crim LR 104).

Approaching, etc. Prohibited Place

B9.7   'Prohibited place' is defined by the Official Secrets Act 1911, s. 3.

Official Secrets Act 1911, ss. 3 and 12

3.   For the purposes of this Act, the expression 'prohibited place' means—

(a)   any work of a defence, arsenal, naval or air force establishment or station, factory, dockyard, mine, minefield, camp, ship, or aircraft belonging to or occupied by or on behalf of His Majesty, or any telegraph, telephone, wireless or signal station, or office so belonging or occupied, and any place belonging to or occupied by or on behalf of His Majesty and used for the purpose of building, repairing, making, or storing any munitions of war, or any sketches, plans, models, or documents relating thereto, or for the purpose of getting any metals, oil, or minerals of use in time of war;

(b)   any place not belonging to His Majesty where any munitions of war, or any sketches, models, plans or documents relating thereto, are being made, repaired, gotten or stored under contract with, or with any person on behalf of, His Majesty, or otherwise on behalf of His Majesty; and

(c)   any place belonging to or used for the purposes of His Majesty which is for the time being declared by order of a Secretary of State to be a prohibited place for the purposes of this section on the ground that information with respect thereto, or damage thereto, would be useful to an enemy; and

(d)   any railway, road, way, or channel, or other means of communication by land or water (including any works or structures being part thereof or connected therewith), or any place used for gas, water, or electricity works or other works for purposes of a public character, or any place where any munitions of war, or any sketches, models, plans or documents relating thereto, are being made, repaired, or stored otherwise than on behalf of His Majesty, which is for the time being declared by order of a Secretary of State to be a prohibited place for the purposes of this section, on the ground that information with respect thereto, or the destruction or obstruction thereof, or interference therewith, would be useful to an enemy.

12.   In this Act, unless the context otherwise requires,—

Any reference to a place belonging to His Majesty includes a place belonging to any department of the Government

. . . whether the place is or is not actually vested in His Majesty; . . .

The expression 'document' includes part of a document;

The expression 'model' includes design, pattern and specimen;

The expression 'sketch' includes any photograph or other mode of representing any place or thing;

The expression 'munitions of war' includes the whole or any part of any ship, submarine, aircraft, tank or similar engine, arms and ammunition, torpedo, or mine, intended or adapted for use in war, and any other article, material, or device, whether actual or proposed, intended for such use; . . .

The Official Secrets (Prohibited Places) Orders 1955 and 1994 (SI 1955 No. 1497 and 1994 No. 968), which are made under s. 3(c), provide that the works and offices of the UKAEA at Dounreay, the BNF sites at Sellafield and Capenhurst, the Urenco site at Capenhurst and the UKAEA sites at Harwell and Windscale are prohibited places. Further, any place used by the Civil Aviation Authority is a place belonging to Her Majesty under s. 3(c) (Civil Aviation Act 1982, s. 18(2) to (4)); and any telecommunications station or office belonging to, or occupied by, a public telecommunications operator is a prohibited place (Telecommunications Act 1984, s. 109 and sch. 4, para. 12(2)).

Making Sketches etc. Useful to Enemy

For the definitions of 'sketch' and 'model' in the Official Secrets Act 1911, s. 12, see **B9.8**
B9.7.

As to the meaning of the word 'enemy', Phillimore J, giving the judgment of the Court of Criminal Appeal in *Parrott* (1913) 8 Cr App R 186, said (at p. 192): 'When the statute uses the word "enemy" it does not mean necessarily some one with whom this country is at war, but a potential enemy with whom we might some day be at war'.

Obtaining or Communicating Sketches etc. Useful to Enemy

A partial definition of the words 'obtains' and 'communicates' is provided by the Official **B9.9**
Secrets Act 1911, s. 12:

Official Secrets Act 1911, s. 12

Expressions referring to communicating include any communicating, whether in whole or in part, and whether the sketch, plan, model, article, note, document, or information itself or the substance, effect, or description thereof only be communicated; expressions referring to obtaining or retaining any sketch, plan, model, article, note, or document, include the copying or causing to be copied the whole or any part of any sketch, plan, model, article, note, or document, and expressions referring to the communication of any sketch, plan, model, article, note or document include the transfer or transmissions of the sketch, plan, model, article, note or document.

For the definitions of 'sketch', 'model' and 'enemy', see **B9.7** and **B9.8**.

The Official Secrets Act 1920, s. 2(1), provides that communication with a foreign agent is to be evidence that the accused has obtained or communicated information useful to an enemy with a purpose prejudicial to the safety or interests of the State. Section 2(2)(a) lays down the circumstances in which a person is deemed to have been in communication with a foreign agent, unless he proves the contrary. They are:

(a)   he has, either within or without the United Kingdom, visited the address of a foreign agent or consorted or associated with a foreign agent; or

(b)   either within or without the United Kingdom, the name or address of, or any other information regarding a foreign agent has been found in his possession, or has been supplied by him to any other person, or has been obtained by him from any other person.

'Foreign agent' is defined by s. 2(2)(b) as including any person who is, or has been, or is reasonably suspected of being or having been employed by a foreign power either directly or indirectly for the purpose of committing an act, either within or without the United Kingdom, prejudicial to the safety or interests of the State, or who has, or is reasonably suspected of having, either within or without the United Kingdom, committed, or attempted to commit, such an act in the interests of a foreign power. Finally, s. 2(2)(c) provides that an address, whether or not in the United Kingdom, is deemed to be the address of a foreign agent, and communications to that address deemed to be communications with a foreign agent, if the address is reasonably suspected of being an address for the receipt of communications or where he resides, or resorts for giving or receiving communications or carries on a business.

Related Offences

B9.10   (a)   A duty to give information about the commission of an offence under the Official Secrets Act 1911, s. 1(1), may be imposed by a chief officer of police acting under the Official Secrets Act 1920, s. 6. It is an offence to fail to provide such information. A person guilty of this offence is liable, on conviction on indictment, to imprisonment for a term not exceeding two years or a fine or both, or, on summary conviction, to a term of imprisonment not exceeding three months or a fine not exceeding the prescribed sum or both (Official Secrets Act 1920, s. 8(2)).

(b)   The Official Secrets Act 1920, s. 7, makes it an offence to attempt, solicit or endeavour to persuade, or to aid and abet or do an act preparatory to, an offence under the Official Secrets Act 1911, s. 1(1) or the Official Secrets Act 1920, s. 6. The penalty for this offence is the same as for the substantive offence.

(c)   It is an offence, contrary to the Official Secrets Act 1989, s. 5(6), for a person to disclose any information, document or other article which he knows, or has reasonable cause to believe, to have come into his possession as a result of a contravention of the Official Secrets Act 1911, s. 1.

(d)   The European Communities Act 1972, s. 11(2), protects Euratom secrets. It creates an offence which is to be regarded as an offence under the 1911 Act, and thus the provision in relation to restriction on prosecution (see **B9.2**) applies.

European Communities Act 1972, s. 11

(2)   Where a person (whether a British subject or not) owing either—
(a)   to his duties as a member of any Euratom institution or committee, or as an officer or servant of Euratom; or
(b)   to his dealings in any capacity (official or unofficial) with any Euratom institution or installation or with any Euratom joint enterprise;
has occasion to acquire, or obtain cognisance of, any classified information, he shall be guilty of [an offence] if, knowing or having reason to believe that it is classified information, he communicates it to any unauthorised person or makes any public disclosure of it, whether in the United Kingdom or elsewhere and whether before or after the termination of those duties or dealings.

Sections 10 and 11 of the 1911 Act, dealing with the extent of the Act and the place of trial of the offence, and saving for laws of British possessions, do not apply to this offence.

This offence is triable either way, but it may be dealt with summarily only with the consent of the A-G. A person guilty of the offence is liable on conviction on indictment to imprisonment for a term not exceeding two years or a fine or both, or, on summary conviction, to a term of imprisonment not exceeding three months or a fine not exceeding the prescribed sum or both.

'Classified information' means any facts, information, knowledge, documents or objects that are subject to the security rules of a member State or any Euratom institution (European Communities Act 1972, s. 11(2)).

HARBOURING 'SPIES'

Definition

Official Secrets Act 1911, s. 7   **B9.11**

If any person knowingly harbours any person whom he knows, or has reasonable grounds for supposing, to be a person who is about to commit or who has committed an offence under this Act, or knowingly permits to meet or assemble in any premises in his occupation or under his control any such persons, or if any person having harboured any such person, or permitted to meet or assemble in any premises in his occupation or under his control any such persons, wilfully omits or refuses to disclose to a superintendent of police any information which it is in his power to give in relation to any such person he shall be guilty of [an offence].

Procedure

As to the restriction on prosecutions, requiring the consent of the A-G, see **B9.2**.   **B9.12**

The offence is triable either way, subject to the proviso to the Official Secrets Act 1920, s. 8(2), which provides that the offence may be dealt with summarily only with the consent of the A-G. When tried on indictment it is a class 4 offence.

Indictment

Statement of Offence   **B9.13**

Harbouring an offender contrary to section 7 of the Official Secrets Act 1911

Particulars of Offence

A on or about the . . . day of . . . harboured O whom he knew or had reasonable grounds for supposing was about to commit [or had committed] an offence under the Official Secrets Act 1911, namely [state the offence]

Sentence

The maximum penalty is: on conviction on indictment, imprisonment for a term not **B9.14** exceeding two years or a fine or both; on summary conviction, a term of imprisonment not exceeding three months or a fine not exceeding the prescribed sum or both (Official Secrets Act 1920, s. 8(2)).

Offence not Limited to Harbouring 'Spies'

The offence is not limited to harbouring 'spies', since the person being harboured must **B9.15** simply have committed an 'offence under this Act', which means any act, omission, or other thing which is punishable under the 1911 Act (Official Secrets Act 1911, s. 12).

Meaning of 'Superintendent of Police'

Official Secrets Act 1911, s. 12   **B9.16**

In this Act, unless the context otherwise requires,—
    . . .
    The expression 'superintendent of police' includes any police officer of a like or superior rank and any person upon whom the powers of a superintendent of police are for the purposes of this Act conferred by a Secretary of State.

Related Offences

The Official Secrets Act 1920, s. 7, makes it an offence to attempt, solicit or endeavour **B9.17** to persuade, or to aid and abet or do an act preparatory to, an offence under the Official Secrets Act 1911, s. 7.

GAINING ACCESS TO PROHIBITED PLACES

Definition

B9.18

Official Secrets Act 1920, s. 1

(1)   If any person for the purpose of gaining admission, or of assisting, any other person to gain admission, to a prohibited place, within the meaning of the Official Secrets Act 1911 . . . , or for any other purpose prejudicial to the safety or interests of the State within the meaning of the said Act—

(a)   uses or wears, without lawful authority, any naval, military, air-force, police, or other official uniform, or any uniform so nearly resembling the same as to be calculated to deceive, or falsely represents himself to be a person who is or has been entitled to use or wear any such uniform; or

(b)   orally, or in writing in any declaration or application, or in any document signed by him or on his behalf, knowingly makes or connives at the making of any false statement or any omission; or

(c)   tampers with any passport or naval, military, air-force, police, or other official pass, permit, certificate, licence, or other document of a similar character (hereinafter in this section referred to as an official document), or has in his possession any forged, altered, or irregular official document; or

(d)   personates, or falsely represents himself to be a person holding, or in the employment of a person holding office under His Majesty, or to be or not to be a person to whom an official document or secret official code word or pass word has been duly issued or communicated, or with intent to obtain an official document, secret official code word or pass word, whether for himself or any other person, knowingly makes any false statement; or

(e)   uses, or has in his possession or under his control, without the authority of the Government Department or the authority concerned, any die, seal, or stamp of or belonging to, or used, made or provided by any Government Department, or by any diplomatic, naval, military, or air force authority appointed by or acting under the authority of His Majesty, or any die, seal or stamp so nearly resembling any such die, seal or stamp as to be calculated to deceive, or counterfeits any such die, seal or stamp, or uses, or has in his possession, or under his control, any such conterfeited die, seal or stamp;

he shall be guilty of [an offence].

Procedure

B9.19   As to the restriction on prosecutions requiring the consent of the A-G, see **B9.2**.

The offence is triable either way, subject to the proviso to the Official Secrets Act 1920, s. 8(2), which provides that the offence may be dealt with summarily only with the consent of the A-G. When tried on indictment it is a class 4 offence.

As to the special provisions in relation to a trial, relating to territorial jurisdiction, excluding the public from the trial and offences tried outside the United Kingdom, see **B9.2**.

Indictment

B9.20

Statement of Offence

Unlawfully wearing a uniform for the purpose of gaining access to a prohibited place contrary to section 1(1) of the Official Secrets Act 1920

Particulars of Offence

A on or about the . . . day of . . ., for the purpose of gaining admission to a prohibited place, namely . . ., wore a naval [or military etc.] uniform without lawful authority

Sentence

B9.21   The maximum penalty is: on conviction on indictment, imprisonment for a term not exceeding two years or a fine or both; on summary conviction, a term of imprisonment not exceeding three months or a fine not exceeding the prescribed sum or both (Official Secrets Act 1920, s. 8(2)).

Elements

For the meaning of 'prohibited place', see **B9.7**. For the meaning of 'purpose prejudicial **B9.22** to the safety or interests of the State', see **B9.6**.

By virtue of the Official Secrets Act 1911, s. 12, 'office under His Majesty' includes any office or employment in or under any department of the government of the United Kingdom, or of any British possession. A police officer is in employment under Her Majesty (see *Lewis* v *Cattle* [1938] 2 KB 454). This phrase also includes the Parliamentary Commissioner for Administration and his officers, by virtue of the Parliamentary Commissioner Act 1967, s. 11(1).

Related Offences

The Official Secrets Act 1920, s. 7, makes it an offence to attempt, solicit or endeavour **B9.23** to persuade, or to aid and abet or do an act preparatory to, an offence under the Official Secrets Act 1920, s. 1(1).

RETENTION AND POSSESSION OF OFFICIAL DOCUMENTS ETC.

Definition

Official Secrets Act 1920, s. 1 **B9.24**

(2) If any person—
  (a) retains for any purpose prejudicial to the safety or interests of the State any official document, whether or not completed or issued for use, when he has no right to retain it, or when it is contrary to his duty to retain it, or fails to comply with any directions issued by any government department or any person authorised by such department with regard to the return or disposal thereof, or
  (b) allows any other person to have possession of any official document issued for his use alone, or communicates any secret official code word or pass word so issued, or, without lawful authority or excuse, has in his possession any official document or secret official code word or pass word issued for the use of some person other than himself, or on obtaining possession of any official document by finding or otherwise, neglects or fails to restore it to the person or authority by whom or for whose use it was issued, or to a police constable; or
  (c) without lawful authority or excuse, manufactures or sells, or has in his possession for sale any such die, seal or stamp as aforesaid;
he shall be guilty of [an offence].

Procedure

As to the restriction on prosecutions requiring the consent of the A-G, see **B9.2**. **B9.25**

The offence is triable either way, subject to the proviso to the Official Secrets Act 1920, s. 8(2), which provides that the offence may be dealt with summarily only with the consent of the A-G. When tried on indictment it is a class 4 offence.

As to the special provisions in relation to a trial, relating to territorial jurisdiction, excluding the public from the trial and offences tried outside the United Kingdom, see **B9.2**.

Indictment

Statement of Offence **B9.26**

Retaining an official document contrary to section 1(2) of the Official Secrets Act 1920

Particulars of Offence

A on or about the . . . day of . . ., for a purpose prejudicial to the safety or interests of the State, namely . . ., retained an official document, namely . . ., when he had no right to retain it [or when it was contrary to his duty to retain it]

Sentence

B9.27 The maximum penalty is: on conviction on indictment, imprisonment for a term not exceeding two years or a fine or both; on summary conviction, a term of imprisonment not exceeding three months or a fine not exceeding the prescribed sum or both (Official Secrets Act 1920, s. 8(2)).

Elements

B9.28 For the meaning of 'official document', see the Official Secrets Act 1920, s. 1(1)(c) at **B9.18**. For the meaning of 'die, seal or stamp', see s. 1(1)(e) of that Act. For the meaning of 'communicate', see **B9.9**.

For the meaning of 'purpose prejudicial to the safety or interests of the State', see **B9.6**.

Related Offences

B9.29 The Official Secrets Act 1920, s. 7, makes it an offence to attempt, solicit or endeavour to persuade, or to aid and abet or do an act preparatory to, an offence under the Official Secrets Act 1920, s. 1(2).

INTERFERING WITH OFFICERS OF POLICE OR MEMBERS OF ARMED FORCES IN VICINITY OF PROHIBITED PLACE

Definition

B9.30 **Official Secrets Act 1920, s. 3**

No person in the vicinity of any prohibited place shall obstruct, knowingly mislead or otherwise interfere with or impede, the chief officer or a superintendent or other officer of police, or any member of His Majesty's forces engaged on guard, sentry, patrol, or other similar duty in relation to the prohibited place, and, if any person acts in contravention of, or fails to comply with, this provision, he shall be guilty of [an offence].

Procedure

B9.31 As to the restriction on prosecutions requiring the consent of the A-G, see **B9.2**.

This offence is triable either way, subject to the proviso to the Official Secrets Act 1920, s. 8(2), which provides that the offence may be dealt with summarily only with the consent of the A-G. When tried on indictment it is a class 4 offence.

As to the special provisions relating to territorial jurisdiction, excluding the public from the trial and offences tried outside the United Kingdom see **B9.2**.

Sentence

B9.32 The maximum penalty is: on conviction on indictment, imprisonment for a term not exceeding two years or a fine or both; on summary conviction, a term of imprisonment not exceeding three months or a fine not exceeding the prescribed sum or both (Official Secrets Act 1920, s. 8(2)).

Elements

B9.33 For the meaning of 'prohibited place', see **B9.7**.

In *Adler* v *George* [1964] 2 QB 7 it was held that the phrase 'in the vicinity of' in the Official Secrets Act 1920, s. 3, is to be interpreted as 'in or in the vicinity of' so that obstruction of someone at an airbase could constitute an offence under the section.

The word 'obstruct' presumably has the same meaning as in the offence of obstruction of a police officer in the execution of his duty (see **B2.25** to **B2.28**). The meaning of 'superintendent' is considered at **B9.16**.

Related Offences

The Official Secrets Act 1920, s. 7, makes it an offence to attempt, solicit or endeavour **B9.34** to persuade, or to aid and abet or do an act preparatory to, an offence under the Official Secrets Act 1920, s. 3. As to the offences of assaulting and obstructing a police officer in the execution of his duty, see **B2.21** to **B2.28**.

DISCLOSURE OF SECURITY AND INTELLIGENCE INFORMATION

Definition

Official Secrets Act 1989, s. 1   **B9.35**

(1)   A person who is or has been—
    (a)   a member of the security and intelligence services; or
    (b)   a person notified that he is subject to the provisions of this subsection,
shall be guilty of an offence if without lawful authority he discloses any information, document or other article relating to security or intelligence which is or has been in his possession by virtue of his position as a member of any of those services or in the course of his work while the notification is or was in force.

Procedure

Official Secrets Act 1989, ss. 9, 11, and 15   **B9.36**

9.—(1)   Subject to subsection (2) below, no prosecution for an offence under this Act shall be instituted in England and Wales or in Northern Ireland except by or with the consent of the Attorney-General or, as the case may be, the Attorney-General for Northern Ireland.
(2)   Subsection (1) above does not apply to an offence in respect of any such information, document or article as is mentioned in section 4(2) above but no prosecution for such an offence shall be instituted in England and Wales or in Northern Ireland except by or with the consent of the Director of Public Prosecutions or, as the case may be, the Director of Public Prosecutions for Northern Ireland.

11.—(5)   Proceedings for an offence under this Act may be taken in any place in the United Kingdom.

15.—(1)   Any act—
    (a)   done by a British citizen or Crown servant; or
    (b)   done by any person in any of the Channel Islands or the Isle of Man or any colony,
shall, if it would be an offence by that person under any provision of this Act other than section 8(1), (4) or (5) when done by him in the United Kingdom, be an offence under that provision.

This offence is triable either way (Official Secrets Act 1989, s. 10(1)). When tried on indictment it is a class 4 offence.

The power to exclude the public under the Official Secrets Act 1920, s. 8(4), applies to the instant offence by virtue of the Official Secrets Act 1989, s. 11(4) (see **B9.2**).

Indictment

Statement of Offence   **B9.37**

Unlawful disclosure of information contrary to section 1(1) of the Official Secrets Act 1989

Particulars of Offence

A on or about the . . . day of . . ., being a person notified that he was subject to the provisions of section 1 of the Official Secrets Act 1989, without lawful authority disclosed to P a document, namely . . ., which related to security or intelligence and which the said A had in his possession in the course of his work while the said notification was in force

Sentence

B9.38   The maximum penalty is: on conviction on indictment, imprisonment for a term not exceeding two years or a fine or both; on summary conviction, imprisonment for a term not exceeding six months or a fine not exceeding the statutory maximum or both (Official Secrets Act 1989, s. 10(1)).

Persons who Can Commit Offence

B9.39   An offence under the Official Secrets Act 1989, s. 1(1), can be committed by either a person who is or has been a member of the security and intelligence services, or someone who is or has been a notified person (i.e. notified that he is subject to s. 1 of the Act).

Official Secrets Act 1989, s. 1

(6)   Notification that a person is subject to subsection (1) above shall be effected by a notice in writing served on him by a Minister of the Crown; and such a notice may be served if, in the Minister's opinion, the work undertaken by the person in question is or includes work connected with the security and intelligence services and its nature is such that the interests of national security require that he should be subject to the provisions of that subsection.

(7)   Subject to subsection (8) below, a notification for the purposes of subsection (1) above shall be in force for the period of five years beginning with the day on which it is served but may be renewed by further notices under subsection (6) above for periods of five years at a time.

(8)   A notification for the purposes of subsection (1) above may at any time be revoked by a further notice in writing served by the Minister on the person concerned; and the Minister shall serve such a further notice as soon as, in his opinion, the work undertaken by that person ceases to be such as is mentioned in subsection (6) above.

Meaning of 'Security' and 'Intelligence'

B9.40   #### Official Secrets Act 1989, s. 1

(9)   In this section 'security or intelligence' means the work of, or in support of, the security and intelligence services or any part of them, and references to information relating to security or intelligence include references to information held or transmitted by those services or by persons in support of, or of any part of, them.

The security service has now been placed on a statutory basis (see the Security Service Act 1989).

Disclosure of Information

B9.41   #### Official Secrets Act 1989, ss. 1 and 13

1.—(2)   The reference in subsection (1) above to disclosing information relating to security or intelligence includes a reference to making any statement which purports to be a disclosure of such information or is intended to be taken by those to whom it is addressed as being such a disclosure.

13.—(1)   In this Act—
'disclose' and 'disclosure', in relation to a document or other article, include
   parting with possession of it.

Meaning of 'Without Lawful Authority'

B9.42   The Official Secrets Act 1989, s. 1(1), applies only to unauthorised disclosures. The Official Secrets Act 1989, s. 7, provides for the only circumstances in which a disclosure may be made 'with lawful authority'. Only s. 7(1) applies to s. 1(1), since the offence applies only to the limited range of Crown servants who work for the security and intelligence services, or who are notified as being covered by the provisions of s. 1(1).

Official Secrets Act 1989, s. 7

(1)   For the purposes of this Act a disclosure by—

(a)   a Crown servant; or

(b)   a person, not being a Crown servant or government contractor, in whose case a notification for the purposes of section 1(1) above is in force,

is made with lawful authority if, and only if, it is made in accordance with his official duty.

As to the broader provisions relating, generally, to authorised disclosures, see **B9.52**.

Specific Defences

Official Secrets Act 1989, ss. 1 and 7   **B9.43**

1.—(5)   It is a defence for a person charged with an offence under this section to prove that at the time of the alleged offence he did not know, and had no reasonable cause to believe, that the information, document or article in question related to security or intelligence.

7.—(4)   It is a defence for a person charged with an offence under any of the foregoing provisions of this Act to prove that at the time of the alleged offence he believed that he had lawful authority to make the disclosure in question and had no reasonable cause to believe otherwise.

The wording of these subsections makes it clear that in each case, the legal burden of proving the defences lies on the accused. The burden may be discharged on the balance of probabilities. See generally, **F3.4** and **F3.18**.

Related Offences

It is an offence, contrary to the Official Secrets Act 1989, s. 1(3), for a Crown servant or **B9.44** government contractor to make a damaging disclosure of security or intelligence information (see **B9.45** to **B9.54**).

DAMAGING DISCLOSURE OF SECURITY AND INTELLIGENCE INFORMATION

Definition

Official Secrets Act 1989, s. 1   **B9.45**

(3)   A person who is or has been a Crown servant or government contractor shall be guilty of an offence if without lawful authority he makes a damaging disclosure of any information, document or other article relating to security or intelligence which is or has been in his possession by virtue of his position as such but otherwise than as mentioned in subsection (1) above.

Procedure

As to the requirement of consent of the A-G, see the Official Secrets Act 1989, s. 9(1), **B9.46** and **B9.36**.

The offence is triable either way (Official Secrets Act 1989, s. 10(1)). When tried on indictment it is a class 4 offence.

As to provisions relating to place of trial, territorial jurisdiction and excluding the public from the trial, see **B9.36**.

Indictment

Statement of Offence   **B9.47**

Unlawfully making a damaging disclosure of information relating to security [or intelligence] contrary to section 1(3) of the Official Secrets Act 1989

Particulars of Offence

A on or about the . . . day of . . ., being then [or having been] a Crown servant [or government contractor], without lawful authority disclosed to P information relating to security [or intelligence], namely . . ., which was in his possession by virtue of his position as a Crown servant [or government contractor], which disclosure caused [or disclosure of which would have been likely to cause] damage to the work of the security and intelligence services [or the work of . . ., being part of the security and intelligence services]

Sentence

B9.48 The maximum penalty is: on conviction on indictment, imprisonment for a term not exceeding two years or a fine or both; on summary conviction, imprisonment for a term not exceeding six months or a fine not exceeding the statutory maximum or both (Official Secrets Act 1989, s. 10(1)).

Meaning of 'Security', 'Intelligence', 'Disclosure', 'Damaging Disclosure'

B9.49 For the meaning of 'security' and 'intelligence' see **B9.40**. For the meaning of 'disclosure', see **B9.41**. The words 'damaging disclosure' are defined by the Official Secrets Act 1989, s. 1(4).

Official Secrets Act 1989, s. 1

(4)   For the purposes of subsection (3) above a disclosure is damaging if—
(a)   it causes damage to the work of, or of any part of, the security and intelligence services; or
(b)   it is of information or a document or other article which is such that its unauthorised disclosure would be likely to cause such damage or which falls within a class or description of information, documents or articles the unauthorised disclosure of which would be likely to have that effect.

This offence is committed whether or not the information disclosed was secret or confidential, and whether or not the disclosure was damaging to national interests (*A-G* v *Blake* [1997] Ch 84 (per Sir Richard Scott (*obiter*)).

Meaning of 'Crown Servant'

B9.50   **Official Secrets Act 1989, s. 12**

12.—(1)   In this Act 'Crown servant' means—
(a)   a Minister of the Crown;
(b)   [repealed]
(c)   any person employed in the civil service of the Crown, including Her Majesty's Diplomatic Service, Her Majesty's Overseas Civil Service, the civil service of Northern Ireland and the Northern Ireland Court Service;
(d)   any member of the naval, military or air forces of the Crown, including any person employed by an association established for the purposes of part XI of the Reserve Forces Act 1996;
(e)   any constable and any other person employed or appointed in or for the purposes of any police force (including a police force within the meaning of the Police Act (Northern Ireland) 1998) or of the National Criminal Intelligence Service or the National Crime Squad;
(f)   any person who is a member or employee of a prescribed body or a body of a prescribed class and either is prescribed for the purposes of this paragraph or belongs to a prescribed class of members or employees of any such body;
(g)   any person who is the holder of a prescribed office or who is an employee of such a holder and either is prescribed for the purposes of this paragraph or belongs to a prescribed class of such employees.

The Official Secrets Act 1989 (Prescription) Order 1990 (SI 1990 No. 200), art. 2, prescribes that the following classes of members or employees of certain bodies are 'Crown servants' for the purpose of s. 12(1)(f):

Official Secrets Act 1989 (Prescription) Order 1990, sch. 1

PRESCRIPTIONS: SECTION 12(1)(f)

British Nuclear Fuels plc	The employees of the Company
The Board of the above	The members of the Board
The United Kingdom Atomic Energy Authority	The members, officers and employees of the Authority
Urenco Limited	The employees of the Company
The Board of the above	The members of the Board
Urenco (Capenhurst) Limited	The employees of the Company
The Board of the above	The members of the Board

The Official Secrets Act 1989 (Prescription) Order 1990 (SI 1990 No. 200), art. 3, prescribes that the following classes of members or employees of certain bodies are 'Crown servants' for the purpose of s. 12(1)(g):

Official Secrets Act 1989 (Prescription) Order 1990, sch. 2

PRESCRIPTIONS: SECTION 12(1)(g)

Comptroller and Auditor General	–
Member of staff of the National Audit Office	–
Comptroller and Auditor General for Northern Ireland	–
Member of staff of the Northern Ireland Audit Office	–
Auditor General for Scotland	–
Parliamentary Commissioner for Administration	The officers of the Commissioner who are not otherwise Crown servants
Officer of the Health Service Commissioner for England or Scotland or Wales being an officer who is authorised by the Parliamentary Commissioner for Administration to perform any of his functions and who is not otherwise a Crown Servant	–
Northern Ireland Parliamentary Commissioner for Administration	The officers of the Commissioner who are not otherwise Crown servants
A private secretary to the Sovereign	–

The 1989 Act applies to the First Minister and deputy First Minister in Northern Ireland and Northern Ireland Ministers and junior Ministers in the same way as it applies to Crown servants (Official Secrets Act 1989, s. 12(5)). The Auditor General of Wales is a Crown servant for the purposes only of the 1989 Act (Government of Wales Act 1998, s. 90(7)).

Meaning of 'Government Contractor'

Official Secrets Act 1989, ss. 12 and 13   B9.51

12.—(2)   In this Act 'government contractor' means, subject to subsection (3) below, any person who is not a Crown servant but who provides, or is employed in the provision of, goods or services—

(a)   for the purposes of any Minister of the Crown or person mentioned in paragraph (a) or (b) of subsection (1) above, of any of the services, forces or bodies mentioned in that subsection or of the holder of any office prescribed under that subsection; or

(aa)   for the purposes of the National Assembly for Wales;

(b)   under an agreement or arrangement certified by the Secretary of State as being one to which the government of a State other than the United Kingdom or an international organisation is a party or which is subordinate to, or made for the purposes of implementing, any such agreement or arrangement.

(3)   Where an employee or class of employees of any body, or of any holder of an office, is prescribed by an order made for the purposes of subsection (1) above—

(a)   any employee of that body, or the holder of that office who is not prescribed or is not within the prescribed class; and

(b)   any person who does not provide, or is not employed in the provision of, goods or services for the purposes of the performance of those functions of the body or the holder of the office in connection with which the employee or prescribed class of employees is engaged,

shall not be a government contractor for the purposes of this Act.

13.—(1)   In this Act—

. . .

'international organisation' means, subject to subsections (2) and (3) below, an organisation of which only States are members and includes a reference to any organ of such an organisation;

. . .

'State' includes the government of a State and any organ of its government and references to a State other than the United Kingdom include references to any territory outside the United Kingdom.

(2)   In section 12(2)(b) above the reference to an international organisation includes a reference to any such organisation whether or not one of which only States are members and includes a commercial organisation.

(3)   In determining for the purposes of subsection (1) above whether only States are members of an organisation, any member which is itself an organisation of which only States are members, or which is an organ of such an organisation, shall be treated as a State.

'Without Lawful Authority'

B9.52   An offence under the Official Secrets Act 1989, s. 1(3), is committed only if the disclosure is 'without lawful authority'. The only circumstances in which a disclosure is made with lawful authority are to be found in s. 7:

Official Secrets Act 1989, s. 7

(1)   For the purposes of this Act a disclosure by—

(a)   a Crown servant; or

(b)   a person, not being a Crown servant or government contractor, in whose case a notification for the purposes of section 1(1) above is in force,

is made with lawful authority if, and only if, it is made in accordance with his official duty.

(2)   For the purposes of this Act a disclosure by a government contractor is made with lawful authority if, and only if, it is made—

(a)   in accordance with an official authorisation; or

(b)   for the purposes of the functions by virtue of which he is a government contractor and without contravening an official restriction.

(3)   For the purposes of this Act a disclosure made by any other person is made with lawful authority if, and only if, it is made—

(a)   to a Crown servant for the purposes of his functions as such; or

(b)   in accordance with an official authorisation.

. . .

(5)   In this section 'official authorisation' and 'official restriction' mean, subject to subsection (6) below, an authorisation or restriction duly given or imposed by a Crown servant or government contractor or by or on behalf of a prescribed body or a body of a prescribed class.

Certain bodies have been prescribed by the Official Secrets Act 1989 (Prescription) Order 1990 (SI 1990 No. 200), art. 4 and sch. 3, for the purpose of s. 7(5) so as to enable them to give official authorisations or restrictions.

Official Secrets Act 1989 (Prescription) Order 1990, sch. 3

PRESCRIPTIONS: SECTIONS 7(5) AND 8(9)

The Civil Aviation Authority	Sections 7(5) and 8(9)
The Tribunal established under section 7 of the Interception of Communications Act 1985	Section 7(5)
The Tribunal established under section 5 of the Security Service Act 1989	Section 7(5)

Specific Defences

The defence of having no knowledge or reasonable cause to believe that information **B9.53** related to security or intelligence, created by the Official Secrets Act 1989, s. 1(5), applies to this offence, and is considered at **B9.43**. The defence that the accused believed that he had lawful authority for disclosure, created by the Official Secrets Act 1989, s. 7(4), also applies to this offence, and is considered at **B9.43**.

Related Offences

It is an offence, contrary to the Official Secrets Act 1989, s. 1(1), for a present or past **B9.54** member of the security and intelligence services or a notified person to make a disclosure of security or intelligence information (see **B9.35** to **B9.44**).

DAMAGING DISCLOSURE OF DEFENCE INFORMATION

Definition

Official Secrets Act 1989, s. 2   B9.55

(1) A person who is or has been a Crown servant or government contractor shall be guilty of an offence if without lawful authority he makes a damaging disclosure of any information, document or other article relating to defence which is or has been in his possession by virtue of his position as such.

Procedure

As to the requirement of consent of the A-G, see **B9.36**. The offence is triable either way **B9.56** (Official Secrets Act 1989, s. 10(1)). When tried on indictment it is a class 4 offence.

As to provisions relating to place of trial, territorial jurisdiction and excluding the public from the trial, see **B9.36**.

Indictment

Statement of Offence   B9.57

Unlawfully making a damaging disclosure of information relating to defence contrary to section 2(1) of the Official Secrets Act 1989

Particulars of Offence

A on or about the . . . day of . . ., being then [or having been] a Crown servant [or government contractor], without lawful authority disclosed to P information relating to defence, namely . . ., which was in his possession by virtue of his position as a Crown servant [or government contractor], which disclosure prejudiced [or disclosure of which would have been likely to prejudice] the capability of the armed forces of the Crown to carry out their tasks [or other form of damage specified in s. 2(2): see **B9.59**]

Sentence

The maximum penalty is: on conviction on indictment, imprisonment for a term not **B9.58** exceeding two years or a fine or both; on summary conviction, imprisonment for a term not exceeding six months or a fine not exceeding the statutory maximum or both.

Elements

B9.59   The meaning of 'disclosure' is considered at **B9.41**.

Official Secrets Act 1989, s. 2

(2)   For the purposes of subsection (1) above a disclosure is damaging if—
(a)   it prejudices the capability of, or any part of, the armed forces of the Crown to carry out their tasks or leads to loss of life or injury to members of those forces or serious damage to the equipment or installations of those forces; or
(b)   otherwise than in paragraph (a) above, it endangers the interests of the United Kingdom abroad, seriously obstructs the promotion or protection by the United Kingdom of those interests or endangers the safety of British citizens abroad; or
(c)   it is of information or of a document or article which is such that its unauthorised disclosure would be likely to have any of those effects.
. . .
(4)   In this section 'defence' means—
(a)   the size, shape, organisation, logistics, order of battle, deployment, operations, state of readiness and training of the armed forces of the Crown;
(b)   the weapons, stores or other equipment of those forces and the invention, development, production and operation of such equipment and research relating to it;
(c)   defence policy and strategy and military planning and intelligence;
(d)   plans and measures for the maintenance of essential supplies and services that are or would be needed in time of war.

The meanings of 'Crown servant' and 'government contractor' are considered at **B9.50** and **B9.51**. As to the meaning of 'without lawful authority', see s. 7 of the Act, at **B9.52**. As to the only circumstances in which a disclosure is made with lawful authority, see **B9.52**.

Specific Defences

B9.60   Official Secrets Act 1989, s. 2

(3)   It is a defence for a person charged with an offence under this section to prove that at the time of the alleged offence he did not know, and had no reasonable cause to believe, that the information, document or article in question related to defence or that its disclosure would be damaging within the meaning of subsection (1) above.

The accused has the burden of proving this defence on the balance of probabilities (see generally, **F3.4** and **F3.18**).

The defence that the accused believed that he had lawful authority for disclosure, created by the Official Secrets Act 1989, s. 7(4), also applies to this offence, and is considered at **B9.43**.

DAMAGING DISCLOSURE OF INTERNATIONAL RELATIONS INFORMATION

Definition

B9.61   Official Secrets Act 1989, s. 3

(1)   A person who is or has been a Crown servant or government contractor shall be guilty of an offence if without lawful authority he makes a damaging disclosure of—
(a)   any information, document or other article relating to international relations; or
(b)   any confidential information, document or other article which was obtained from a State other than the United Kingdom or an international organisation,
being information or a document or article which is or has been in his possession by virtue of his position as a Crown servant or government contractor.

Procedure

As to the requirement of the A-G's consent, see **B9.36**. The offence is triable either way **B9.62** (Official Secrets Act 1989, s. 10(1)). When tried on indictment it is a class 4 offence.

As to provisions relating to place of trial, territorial jurisdiction and excluding the public from the trial, see **B9.36**.

Indictment

B9.63

Statement of Offence

Unlawfully making a damaging disclosure of information relating to international relations contrary to section 3(1) of the Official Secrets Act 1989

Particulars of Offence

A on or about the . . . day of . . ., being then [or having been] a Crown servant [or government contractor], without lawful authority disclosed to P information relating to international relations, namely . . ., which was in his possession by virtue of his position as a Crown servant [or government contractor], which disclosure endangered [or disclosure of which would have been likely to endanger] the interests of the United Kingdom abroad [or other form of damage specified in s. 3(2): see **B9.65**]

Sentence

The maximum penalty is: on conviction on indictment, imprisonment for a term not **B9.64** exceeding two years or a fine or both; on summary conviction, imprisonment for a term not exceeding six months or a fine not exceeding the statutory maximum or both (Official Secrets Act 1989, s. 10(1)).

Elements

The meaning of 'disclosure' is considered at **B9.41**. **B9.65**

The phrases 'damaging disclosure', 'international relations' and 'confidential information' are defined by the Official Secrets Act 1989, s. 3.

Official Secrets Act 1989, s. 3

(2) For the purposes of subsection (1) above a disclosure is damaging if—
    (a) it endangers the interests of the United Kingdom abroad, seriously obstructs the promotion or protection by the United Kingdom of those interests or endangers the safety of British citizens abroad; or
    (b) it is of information or of a document or article which is such that its unauthorised disclosure would be likely to have any of those effects.
(3) In the case of information or a document or article within subsection (1) above—
    (a) the fact that it is confidential, or
    (b) its nature or contents,
may be sufficient to establish for the purposes of subsection (2)(b) above that the information, document or article is such that its unauthorised disclosure would be likely to have any of the effects there mentioned.
(5) In this section 'international relations' means the relations between States, between international organisations or between one or more States and one or more such organisations and includes any matter relating to a State other than the United Kingdom or to an international organisation which is capable of affecting the relations of the United Kingdom with another State or with an international organisation.
(6) For the purposes of this section any information, document or article obtained from a State or organisation is confidential at any time while the terms on which it was obtained require it to be held in confidence or while the circumstances in which it was obtained make it reasonable for the State or organisation to expect that it would be so held.

Section 13 of the Act defines 'State and international organisation' (see **B9.51**). The meanings of 'Crown servant' and 'government contractor' are considered at **B9.50** and **B9.51**. The phrase 'without lawful authority' is defined by s. 7 of the Act (see **B9.52**).

Specific Defences

B9.66   **Official Secrets Act 1989, s. 3**

> (4)   It is a defence for a person charged with an offence under this section to prove that
> at the time of the alleged offence he did not know, and had no reasonable cause to believe,
> that the information, document or article in question was such as is mentioned in subsection
> (1) above or that its disclosure would be damaging within the meaning of that subsection.

The accused has the burden of proving this defence on the balance of probabilities (see
generally **F3.4** and **F3.18**).

The defence that the accused believed that he had lawful authority for disclosure,
created by s. 7(4) of the Act, applies to this offence (see **B9.43**).

DISCLOSURE OF INFORMATION RELEVANT TO CRIMINAL INVESTIGATIONS

Definition

B9.67   **Official Secrets Act 1989, s. 4**

> (1)   A person who is or has been a Crown servant or government contractor is guilty of
> an offence if without lawful authority he discloses any information, document or other
> article to which this section applies and which is or has been in his possession by virtue of
> his position as such.

(As to the materials referred to, see s. 4(2) and (3), at **B9.71**.)

Procedure

B9.68   As to the requirement of the consent of the A-G, see **B9.36**. This offence is triable either
way (Official Secrets Act 1989, s. 10(1)). When tried on indictment it is a class 4 offence.

As to provisions relating to the place of trial, territorial jurisdiction and excluding the
public from the trial, see **B9.36**.

Indictment

B9.69   Statement of Offence

> Unlawful disclosure of information resulting in the commission of an offence contrary to
> section 4(1) of the Official Secrets Act 1989

                            Particulars of Offence

> A on or about the . . . day of . . ., being then [or having been] a Crown servant [or government
> contractor], without lawful authority disclosed to P information, which was such that its
> unauthorised disclosure resulted in the commission of an offence, namely . . .

Sentence

B9.70   The maximum penalty is: on conviction on indictment, imprisonment for a term not
exceeding two years or a fine or both; on summary conviction, imprisonment for a term
not exceeding six months or a fine not exceeding the statutory maximum or both
(Official Secrets Act 1989, s. 10(1)).

Elements

B9.71   **Official Secrets Act 1989, s. 4**

> (2)   This section applies to any information, document or other article—
>   (a)   the disclosure of which—
>   (i)   results in the commission of an offence; or

(ii)   facilitates an escape from legal custody or the doing of any other act prejudicial to the safekeeping of persons in legal custody; or

(iii)   impedes the prevention or detection of offences or the apprehension or prosecution of suspected offenders; or

(b)   which is such that its unauthorised disclosure would be likely to have any of those effects.

(3)   This section also applies to—

(a)   any information obtained by reason of the interception of any communication in obedience to a warrant issued under section 2 of the Interception of Communications Act 1985, any information relating to the obtaining of information by reason of any such interception and any document or other article which is or has been used or held for use in, or has been obtained by reason of, any such interception; and

(b)   any information obtained by reason of action authorised by a warrant issued under section 3 of the Security Service Act 1989, any information relating to the obtaining of information by reason of any such action and any document or other article which is or has been used or held for use in, or has been obtained by reason of, any such action.

. . .

(6)   In this section 'legal custody' includes detention in pursuance of any enactment or any instrument made under an enactment.

The meaning of 'discloses' has been considered at **B9.41**. With regard to the meaning of 'without lawful authority', see s. 7 of the Act, at **B9.52**.

Specific Defences

Official Secrets Act 1989, s. 4   B9.72

(4)   It is a defence for a person charged with an offence under this section in respect of a disclosure falling within subsection (2)(a) above to prove that at the time of the alleged offence he did not know, and had no reasonable cause to believe, that the disclosure would have any of the effects there mentioned.

(5)   It is a defence for a person charged with an offence under this section in respect of any other disclosure to prove that at the time of the alleged offence he did not know, and had no reasonable cause to believe, that the information, document or article in question was information or a document or article to which this section applies.

The accused has the burden of proving these defences on the balance of probabilities (see generally, **F3.4** and **F3.18**).

The defence that the accused believed that he had lawful authority for disclosure, created by s. 7(4) of the Act, applies to this offence (see **B9.43**).

OTHER OFFENCES RELATING TO UNAUTHORISED DISCLOSURE OF INFORMATION

Other offences dealing with the unauthorised disclosure of information are listed below. **B9.73** Those offences created by the Official Secrets Act 1989 are subject to the same procedural rules governing consent for commencement of proceedings, mode of trial, place of trial, territorial jurisdiction and exclusion of the public from the trial as the offence under s. 1(1) of the Act (see Official Secrets Act 1989, ss. 9, 11 and 15, and **B9.36**). As to sentence, see s. 10 of the Act.

The terms 'disclose', 'Crown servant', 'government contractor', 'State', 'international organisation' and 'without lawful authority' have the same meanings as elsewhere in the Act (see **B9.41; B9.50; B9.51;** and **B9.52**).

The other offences created by the Official Secrets Act 1989 are:

(a)   Disclosure of information resulting from unauthorised disclosures or entrusted in confidence (Official Secrets Act 1989, s. 5(1) and (2)). This offence provides additional protection for information 'protected against disclosure' (for the meaning of which, see s. 5(5)).

(b)   Disclosure of information possessed in contravention of the Official Secrets Act 1911, s. 1 (Official Secrets Act 1989, s. 5(6)). For s. 1 of the 1911 Act, see **B9.1** to **B9.10**.

(c)   Disclosure of information entrusted in confidence to other states or an international organisation (Official Secrets Act 1989, s. 6(1) and (2)). Under this provision, a disclosure is to be regarded as 'damaging' if it would be so regarded in relation to an offence under ss. 1(3), 2(1) or 3(1) (Official Secrets Act 1989, s. 6(4)). For the meaning of 'damaging disclosure' under those provisions, see **B9.49**; **B9.59**; and **B9.65**.

(d)   Disclosure of official information which can be used for gaining access to protected information (Official Secrets Act 1989, s. 8(6)). For the meaning of 'disclosure of official information, see s. 8(7).

The CJA 1991, s. 91, creates an offence of wrongful disclosure of information by a person employed in pursuance of prison escort arrangements. The offence is triable either way. On conviction on indictment, the maximum penalty is imprisonment for a term not exceeding two years or a fine, or both; on summary conviction, the maximum penalty is imprisonment for a term not exceeding six months or a fine not exceeding the statutory maximum, or both. The CJPO 1994, s. 14, creates a similar offence in respect of the wrongful disclosure of information relating to offenders detained at secure training centres.

FAILURE TO SAFEGUARD INFORMATION

Definition

B9.74   The Official Secrets Act 1989, s. 8, creates three offences concerned with failure to safeguard information:

(a)   Section 8(1) makes it an offence for a Crown servant or government contractor to fail to safeguard certain information.

(b)   Section 8(4) makes it an offence for a person with information as a consequence of an unauthorised disclosure or entrusted in confidence to fail to safeguard it.

(c)   Section 8(5) makes it an offence for a person with information entrusted in confidence to States or international organisations to fail to safeguard it.

Official Secrets Act 1989, s. 8

(1)   Where a Crown servant or government contractor, by virtue of his position as such, has in his possession or under his control any document or other article which it would be an offence under any of the foregoing provisions of this Act for him to disclose without lawful authority he shall be guilty of an offence if—

(a)   being a Crown servant, he retains the document or article contrary to his official duty; or

(b)   being a government contractor, he fails to comply with an official direction for the return or disposal of the document or article,

or if he fails to take such care to prevent the unauthorised disclosure of the document or article as a person in his position may reasonably be expected to take.

. . .

(4)   Where a person has in his possession or under his control any document or other article which it would be an offence under section 5 above for him to disclose without lawful authority, he shall be guilty of an offence if—

(a)   he fails to comply with an official direction for its return or disposal; or

(b)   where he obtained it from a Crown servant or government contractor on terms requiring it to be held in confidence or in circumstances in which that servant or contractor could reasonably expect that it would be so held, he fails to take such care to prevent its unauthorised disclosure as a person in his position may reasonably be expected to take.

(5)   Where a person has in his possession or under his control any document or other article which it would be an offence under section 6 above for him to disclose without lawful authority, he shall be guilty of an offence if he fails to comply with an official direction for its return or disposal.

Procedure

As to the requirement of consent of the A-G, see **B9.36**. These offences are triable summarily only (Official Secrets Act 1989, s. 10(2)). Section 11(5) (place of trial) applies to these offences (see **B9.36**).   **B9.75**

Sentence

The maximum penalty on summary conviction is imprisonment for a term not exceeding three months or a fine not exceeding level 5 on the standard scale or both (Official Secrets Act 1989, s. 10(2)).   **B9.76**

Common Elements

Certain elements are common to all three offences: **B9.77**

The terms 'possession' and 'control' are not defined by the Act, but 'possession' appears as an essential requirement in a number of criminal offences, and, it is submitted, should be interpreted in the same way as in relation to, e.g., dangerous drugs (see **B20.10**). The meaning of the word 'disclose' is considered at **B9.41**.

As to the meaning of 'official direction', the Official Secrets Act 1989, s. 8(9), provides that 'official direction' means a direction duly given by a Crown servant or government contractor or by or on behalf of a prescribed body or a body of a prescribed class. The making of such an order has to comply with the Official Secrets Act 1989, s. 14, the provisions of which are set out at **B9.50**.

The Official Secrets Act 1989 (Prescription) Order (SI 1990 No. 200), art. 4, provides that the body referred to in sch. 4, that is the Civil Aviation Authority, has the power to impose official restrictions for the purpose of s. 8(9).

As to the only circumstances in which a disclosure is made with lawful authority, see s. 7 of the Act and **B9.52**.

Elements Specific to s. 8(1) and (4)

The meanings of 'Crown servant' and 'government contractor' are considered at **B9.59** and **B9.51**. However, for the purposes of this offence, the Official Secrets Act 1989, s. 8(3), provides that 'Crown servant' includes a person notified within the meaning of s. 1(1), who is not otherwise either a Crown servant or a government contractor (see **B9.39**).   **B9.78**

Elements Specific to s. 8(5)

The information protected by this offence is that which it would be an offence to disclose under s. 6 of the Act. As to such information, see s. 6(1).   **B9.79**

Specific Defences

The accused's belief that he had lawful authority for the disclosure is a defence to all three charges under the Official Secrets Act 1989, s. 8. As to this defence, see s. 7(4) of the Act and **B9.43**.   **B9.80**

In relation to the offence under s. 8(1) only, the Official Secrets Act 1989, s. 8(2), provides that it is a defence for a Crown servant to prove that at the time of the alleged offence he believed that he was acting in accordance with his official duty and had no reasonable cause to believe otherwise. The legal burden of proving this defence lies on the accused on the balance of probabilities. See generally, **F3.4** and **F3.18**.

PROHIBITION ON INTERCEPTION OF COMMUNICATIONS

Definition

B9.81 **Interception of Communications Act 1985, s. 1**

(1) Subject to the following provisions of this section, a person who intentionally intercepts a communication in the course of its transmission by post or by means of a public telecommunication system shall be guilty of an offence.

Procedure

B9.82 **Interception of Communications Act 1985, s. 1**

(4) No proceedings in respect of an offence under this section shall be instituted—
    (a) in England and Wales, except by or with the consent of the Director of Public Prosecutions; . . .

This offence is triable either way (Interception of Communications Act 1985, s. 1(1)). When tried on indictment it is a class 4 offence.

Special provision is made, under Interception of Communications Act 1985, s. 9, to restrict the adduction of evidence or cross-examination which tends to suggest that an offence has been committed under s. 1.

Indictment

B9.83 Statement of Offence

Intentionally intercepting a communication contrary to section 1 of the Interception of Communications Act 1985

Particulars of Offence

A on or about the . . . day of . . . intentionally intercepted a communication, namely . . ., in the course of its transmission by post [or by means of a public telecommunication system]

Sentence

B9.84 The maximum penalty is: on summary conviction, a fine not exceeding the statutory maximum; on conviction on indictment, imprisonment for a term not exceeding two years or to a fine or to both (Interception of Communications Act 1985, s. 1(1)). In *Winton* [1996] 1 Cr App R (S) 382, the offender, who ran a detective agency, received 12 months' imprisonment for conspiracy to intercept a communication by attaching a tape recorder to a telephone line.

Elements

B9.85 The phrase 'public telecommunication system' has the same meaning as in the Telecommunications Act 1984; the Secretary of State designates telecommunications systems which are authorised to run by a licence under s. 8 of that Act as 'public' (s. 9). The phrase 'telecommunications system' is widely defined in s. 4 of that Act to include systems for the transmission of speech, music and other sounds, visual images and other signals by electric, magnetic, electromagnetic, electrochemical or electromechanical energy means. The Secretary of State has made more than 100 designating orders.

What must be intercepted is a 'communication in the course of commission' and that communication must be over a public system, either the post or a public telecommunication system. Thus, the place where an interception is made is crucial in deciding whether the offence (assuming no warrant is in operation) has been committed. The legislative intent was the protection of the public system (*Taylor-Sabori* [1999] 1 WLR 858). The Court of Appeal in *Ahmed* [1995] Crim LR 246 held that an interception takes place when, and at the place where, the electrical impulse or signal (the message) passing along the telephone lines is intercepted in fact. The electrical impulse or signal is the 'communication', which does not mean the whole of a transmission or message. So, where calls made from a pay telephone in a police station were routed to the internal switchboard before being connected to the public system, there was no unlawful interception of a communication because the interception device was attached to the private system. The public system ends at a junction box, for example the telephone socket in domestic systems, where it is connected to the subscriber's private system, and so, beyond that point, there is no system 'comprised in' a public telecommunications system. This was approved by the House of Lords in *Effik* [1995] 1 AC 309, where it was decided that intercepting a message between a cordless telephone and its base unit did not involve intercepting anything in a public system. The Court of Appeal in *Taylor-Sabari* applied this approach in deciding that an interception of messages between a pager terminal and a pager (achievable because the police had a pager that received messages on the same frequency as that of the defendant) did not fall within the Act.

Where there is an international element to the communication, account must be taken of the Interception of Communications Act 1985, s. 10(2), which has proved particularly difficult for the courts:

Interception of Communications Act 1985, s. 10

(2) For the purposes of this Act a communication which is in the course of its transmission otherwise than by means of a public telecommunication system is deemed to be in the course of its transmission by means of such a system if its mode of transmission identifies it as a communication which—

(a) is to be or has been transmitted by means of such a system; and

(b) has been sent from, or is to be sent to, a country or territory outside the British Islands.

This section requires three elements be satisfied: (i) there is or has been a communication via a public telecommunications system as understood elsewhere in the Act; (ii) that it came from or will be sent to somewhere outside the British Islands; and (iii) that its mode of transmission identifies it as a communication satisfying both (a) and (b). The Court of Appeal in *Taylor-Sabari* reviewed the law on s. 10(2) relying not only on *Ahmed* and *Effik*, but also on *Governor of Belmarsh Prison, ex parte Martin* [1995] 1 WLR 412 and *Aujla* [1998] 2 Cr App R 16. A wide reading of s. 10(2) was rejected. In *Taylor-Sabari* the Court concluded that:

s. 10(2) was there to bridge the gap between a message leaving the protected public system of the foreign state (at its borders) and coming within our protected public system (at our borders). Thus, if the message is transferred from border to border, for example by satellite, the satellite used (the mode of transmission) will identify the communication as coming from the Dutch public system for connection with ours.

The Court, therefore, concluded that the transmission of a message originating in Holland from the pager terminal in the British Islands to the accused's pager did not fall within s. 10(2). A broader view of s. 10(2) is possible. Adopting that view, the message sent from Holland to the BT Pager Service in the British Islands clearly satisfies elements (i) and (ii), the only problem would be whether the mode of transmission (the radio message as received by the pager) identified that it was a message that had originated outside the British Islands. If it did not do that (e.g., by revealing the originating telephone number), it could not satisfy element (iii). However, the weight of the courts is against such an extended view of s. 10(2). Thus the police interception of the pager message did not fall within the Act as it was not covered by the usual definition nor by the extended definition provided by s.10(2).

'British Islands' means the United Kingdom, the Channel Islands and the Isle of Man (Interpretation Act 1978, sch. 1). By virtue of the Interception of Communications Act

1985, s. 10(1), 'person' includes any organisation and any association or combination of persons.

Specific Defences

B9.86   **Interception of Communications Act 1985, s. 1**

(2)   A person shall not be guilty of an offence under this section if—
(a)   the communication is intercepted in obedience to a warrant issued by the Secretary of State under section 2 below; or
(b)   that person has reasonable grounds for believing that the person to whom, or the person by whom, the communication is sent has consented to the interception.

Warrants for interception may be issued by the Secretary of State in accordance with the Interception of Communications Act 1985, s. 2. For the power of the Secretary of State to grant such warrants, see **D1.51**.

Interception of Communications Act 1985, s. 1

(3)   A person shall not be guilty of an offence under this section if—
(a)   the communication is intercepted for purposes connected with the provisions of postal or public telecommunication services or with the enforcement of any enactment relating to the use of those services, or
(b)   the communication is being transmitted by wireless telegraphy and is intercepted, with the authority of the Secretary of State, for purposes connected with the issue of licences under the Wireless Telegraphy Act 1949 or the prevention or detection of interference with wireless telegraphy.

Section 10 of the Act provides that 'public telecommunications service' means a telecommunication service provided by means of a telecommunication system, as to which see **B9.85**. 'Telecommunication service' has the same meaning as in the Telecommunications Act 1984; 'wireless telegraphy' has the same meaning as in the Wireless Telegraphy Act 1949.

Related Provision

B9.87   The Official Secrets Act 1920, s. 5, requires persons carrying on the business of receiving for reward postal packets for delivery and forwarding to register with the chief officer of police. It is a summary offence to fail to register or comply with s. 5 (s. 5(4)).

DISCLOSURE OF TELECOMMUNICATION MESSAGES

Definition

B9.88   **Telecommunications Act 1984, s. 45**

(1)   A person engaged in the running of a public telecommunication system who otherwise than in the course of his duty intentionally discloses to any person—
(a)   the contents of any message which has been intercepted in the course of its transmission by means of that system; or
(b)   any information concerning the use made of telecommunication services provided for any other person by means of that system,
shall be guilty of an offence.

For the meaning of 'public telecommunications system', see **B9.85**.

Procedure

B9.89   This offence is triable either way (Telecommunications Act 1984, s. 45(4)). When tried on indictment it is a class 4 offence.

Sentence

The maximum penalty is: on summary conviction, a fine not exceeding the statutory **B9.90** maximum; on conviction on indictment, a fine (Telecommunications Act 1984, s. 45(4)).

Specific Defences

Telecommunications Act 1984, s. 45   B9.91

(2) Subsection (1) above does not apply to—

(a) any disclosure which is made for the prevention or detection of crime or for the purposes of any criminal proceedings;

(b) any disclosure of matter falling within paragraph (a) of that subsection which is made in obedience to a warrant issued by the Secretary of State under section 2 of the Interception of Communications Act 1985 or in pursuance of a requirement imposed by the Commissioner under section 8(3) of that Act, or

(c) any disclosure of matter falling within paragraph (b) of that subsection which is made in the interests of national security or in pursuance of the order of a court.

(3) For the purposes of subsection 2(c) above a certificate signed by a Minister of the Crown who is a Member of the Cabinet, or by the Attorney-General or the Lord Advocate, certifying that a disclosure was made in the interests of national security shall be conclusive evidence of that fact, and a document purporting to be such a certificate shall be received in evidence and deemed to be such a certificate unless the contrary is proved.

As to warrants issued by the Secretary of State, see **D1.49**.

INCITEMENT TO MUTINY AND DISAFFECTION

Definitions

Incitement to Mutiny Act 1797, s. 1   B9.92

. . . any person who shall maliciously and advisedly endeavour to seduce any person or persons serving in His Majesty's forces, by sea or land from his or their duty and allegiance to His Majesty, or to incite or stir up any such person or persons to commit any act of mutiny, or to make or endeavour to make any mutinous assembly, or to commit any traitorous or mutinous practice whatsoever, shall, on being legally convicted of such offence be adjudged guilty.

As to efforts to seduce persons serving in the Royal Air Force, the section is extended by the Air Force (Application of Enactments) (No. 2) Order 1918, made pursuant to the Air Force (Constitution) Act 1917, s. 13.

Incitement to Disaffection Act 1934, ss. 1 and 2

1. If any person maliciously and advisedly endeavours to seduce any member of His Majesty's forces from his duty or allegiance to His Majesty, he shall be guilty of an offence under this Act.

2.—(1) If any person, with intent to commit or to aid, abet, counsel, or procure the commission of an offence under section 1 of this Act, has in his possession or under his control any document of such a nature that the dissemination of copies thereof among members of His Majesty's forces would constitute such an offence, he shall be guilty of an offence under this Act.

As to armed forces discipline, see the Army Act 1955, the Air Force Act 1955 and the Naval Discipline Act 1957.

Police Act 1996, s. 91

(1) Any person who causes, or attempts to cause, or does any act calculated to cause, disaffection amongst the members of any police force, or induces or attempts to induce, or

does any act calculated to induce, any member of a police force to withhold his services, shall be guilty of an offence. . .

(2)   This section applies to special constables appointed for a police area as it applies to members of a police force.

Procedure

B9.93   **Incitement to Disaffection Act 1934, s. 3**

(2)   No prosecution in England under this Act shall take place without the consent of the DPP.

(3)   Where a prosecution under this Act is being carried on by the Director of Public Prosecutions, a court of summary jurisdiction shall not deal with the case summarily without the consent of the Director.

The offence under the Incitement to Mutiny Act 1797, s. 1, is triable only on indictment. It is a class 2 offence. The offences under the Incitement to Disaffection Act 1934 and the Police Act 1996 are triable either way. When tried on indictment they are class 4 offences.

Sentence

B9.94   The maximum penalties are:

Incitement to Mutiny Act 1797, s. 1: Life imprisonment (Punishment of Offences Act 1837, s. 1).

Incitement to Disaffection Act 1934, s. 1: on indictment, two years and/or a fine; summarily, four months and/or a fine not exceeding the statutory maximum (Incitement to Disaffection Act 1934, s. 3(1)). The court also has power to order the destruction or other disposal of any documents connected with the offence after conviction of the accused and after expiration of the time during which an appeal may be lodged (Incitement to Disaffection Act 1934, s. 3(4)).

Police Act 1996, s. 91: on indictment, two years and/or a fine; summarily, six months and/or a fine not exceeding the statutory maximum.

Elements

B9.95   It is not necessary to show that any particular individual was the object of the attempted seduction. It suffices if the attempt was directed to members of the armed forces, or a police force generally (*Bowman* (1912) 76 JP 271). However, if the allegation is that the attempt was to seduce particular individuals, the status of any such particular individual as a serving member of the force at the time of the offence must be proved. It also appears necessary that the accused had the *mens rea* of knowing that the person concerned was such a serving member, though this may be proved circumstantially, for example by evidence that the offence was committed at a military establishment or police station, or that the person concerned was in uniform. See *Fuller* (1797) 2 Leach 790.

The method of attempted seduction, whether by written or oral communication, is irrelevant, though circumstances such as the offering of an inducement or the use of threats or blackmail will no doubt affect sentence.

SECTION B10: TERRORISM, PIRACY AND HIJACKING

MEMBERSHIP OF, SUPPORT FOR ETC., PROSCRIBED ORGANISATIONS

Definition

Prevention of Terrorism (Temporary Provisions) Act 1989, s. 2   B10.1

(1) Subject to subsection (3) below, a person is guilty of an offence if he—
    (a) belongs or professes to belong to a proscribed organisation;
    (b) solicits or invites support for a proscribed organisation other than support with money or other property; or
    (c) arranges or assists in the arrangement or management of, or addresses, any meeting of three or more persons (whether or not it is a meeting to which the public are admitted) knowing that the meeting is—
        (i) to support a proscribed organisation;
        (ii) to further the activities of such an organisation; or
        (iii) to be addressed by a person belonging or professing to belong to such an organisation.

Procedure and Evidence

The main provisions of the PT(TP)A 1989 must be renewed by Parliament at least on **B10.2** an annual basis, and expire unless continued in force by order of the Secretary of State. The Prevention of Terrorism (Temporary Provisions) Act 1989 (Continuance) Order 1999 (SI 1999 No. 906) did not continue in force part IVA of the Act (as had also been the case under the (Continuance) Order 1998 (SI 1998 No. 768)). However, parts IVA and IVB of the Act have been revived as from 25 June 1999 by the Prevention of Terrorism (Temporary Provisions) Act 1989 (Revival of Parts IVA and IVB) Order 1999 (SI 1999 No. 1813). The offences contrary to ss. 16A (see **B10.40**) and 16B (see **B10.45**) are, therefore, in force.

Prevention of Terrorism (Temporary Provisions) Act 1989, s. 19

(1) Proceedings shall not be instituted—
    (a) in England and Wales for an offence under section 2, 3, 8, 9, 10, 11, 17, 18 or 18A above or schedule 7 to this Act except by or with the consent of the Attorney-General;
    (aa) in England and Wales for an offence under section 13A, 16A or 16B except by or with the consent of the Director of Public Prosecutions; or
    (b) in Northern Ireland for an offence under section 8, 9, 10, 11, 17, 18 or 18A above or schedule 7 to this Act except by or with the consent of the Attorney-General for Northern Ireland.

The offence is triable either way (PT(TP)A 1989, s. 2(2)). When tried on indictment it is a class 4 offence.

Prevention of Terrorism (Temporary Provisions) Act 1989, s. 19

(2) Any document purporting to be an order, notice or direction made or given by the Secretary of State for the purposes of any provision of this Act and to be signed by him or on his behalf shall be received in evidence, and shall, until the contrary is proved, be deemed to be made or given by him.

(3) A document bearing a certificate purporting to be signed by or on behalf of the Secretary of State and stating that the document is a true copy of such an order, notice or direction shall, in any legal proceedings, be evidence, and in Scotland sufficient evidence, of the order, notice or direction.

Prevention of Terrorism (Temporary Provisions) Act 1989, ss. 2A and 2B

2A.—(1) This section applies where a person is charged with an offence under section 2(1)(a) above; and references here to a specified organisation must be construed in accordance with section 2B below.

(2) Subsection (3) below applies if a police officer of or above the rank of superintendent states in oral evidence that in his opinion the accused—

(a) belongs to an organisation which is specified, or

(b) belonged at a particular time to an organisation which was then specified.

(3) If this subsection applies—

(a) the statement shall be admissible as evidence of the matter stated, but

(b) the accused shall not be committed for trial in England and Wales, or be found to have a case to answer or be convicted, solely on the basis of the statement.

(4) Subsection (6) below applies if evidence is given that—

(a) at any time before being charged with the offence the accused, on being questioned under caution by a constable, failed to mention a fact which is material to the offence and which he could reasonably be expected to mention, and

(b) before being questioned he was permitted to consult a solicitor.

(5) Subsection (6) below also applies if evidence is given that—

(a) on being charged with the offence or informed by a constable that he might be prosecuted for it the accused failed to mention a fact which is material to the offence and which he could reasonably be expected to mention, and

(b) before being charged or informed he was permitted to consult a solicitor.

(6) If this subsection applies—

(a) the court or jury, in considering any question whether the accused belongs or belonged at a particular time to a specified organisation, may draw from the failure inferences relating to that question, but

(b) the accused shall not be committed for trial in England and Wales, or be found to have a case to answer or be convicted, solely on the basis of the inferences.

(7) Subject to any directions by the court, evidence tending to establish the failure may be given before or after evidence tending to establish the fact which the accused is alleged to have failed to mention.

(8) This section does not—

(a) prejudice the admissibility of evidence admissible apart from this section;

(b) preclude the drawing of inferences which could be drawn apart from this section;

(c) prejudice an enactment providing (in whatever words) that an answer or evidence given by a person in specified circumstances is not admissible in evidence against him or some other person in any proceedings or class of proceedings (however described, and whether civil or criminal).

(9) In subsection (8)(c) above the reference to giving evidence is a reference to giving it in any manner (whether by giving information, making discovery or disclosure, producing documents or otherwise).

(10) [Scotland.]

(11) In this section 'police officer' means a member of—

(a) a police force within the meaning of the Police Act 1996 or the Police (Scotland) Act 1967, or

(b) the Royal Ulster Constabulary.

(12) This section does not apply to a statement made or failure occurring before the day on which the Criminal Justice (Terrorism and Conspiracy) Act 1998 was passed.

2B.—(1) For the purposes of section 2A above an organisation is specified at a particular time if at that time—

(a) it is specified under section 3(8) of the Northern Ireland (Sentences) Act 1998 or under subsection (2) below, and

(b) it is, or forms part of, an organisation which is proscribed for the purposes of this Act.

(2) If the condition in subsection (3) below is satisfied the Secretary of State may by order specify an organisation which is not specified under section 3(8) of the Northern Ireland (Sentences) Act 1998.

(3)   The condition is that the Secretary of State believes that the organisation—
  (a)   is concerned in terrorism connected with the affairs of Northern Ireland, or in promoting or encouraging it, and
  (b)   has not established or is not maintaining a complete and unequivocal ceasefire.

Indictment

Statement of Offence

B10.3

Belonging to a proscribed organisation contrary to section 2(1) of the Prevention of Terrorism (Temporary Provisions) Act 1989

Particulars of Offence

A, between . . . and . . ., was a member of a proscribed organisation, namely . . .

Sentence

The maximum penalty is: on conviction on indictment, imprisonment for a term not exceeding 10 years or a fine or both; on summary conviction, imprisonment for a term not exceeding six months or a fine not exceeding the statutory maximum or both (PT(TP)A 1989, s. 2(2)). A forfeiture order may be made if the Criminal Justice (Terrorism and Conspiracy) Act 1998, s. 4, is satisfied. **B10.4**

Meaning of 'Proscribed Organisation'

The PT(TP)A 1989, s. 1, provides that any organisation for the time being specified in sch. 1 to the Act is a proscribed organisation, and that any organisation which passes under a name mentioned in sch. 1 is to be treated as proscribed, whatever relationship, if any, it has to any other organisation of the same name. **B10.5**

The Secretary of State may by order made by statutory instrument add to or remove an organisation from sch. 1 (s. 1(2)). The only organisations proscribed at present are the Irish Republican Army and the Irish National Liberation Army. It should be noted that more organisations are proscribed under the Northern Ireland (Emergency Provisions) Act 1996 (see **B10.33**).

Specific Defences

Prevention of Terrorism (Temporary Provisions) Act 1989, s. 2

B10.6

(3)   A person belonging to a proscribed organisation is not guilty of an offence under this section if he shows—
  (a)   that he became a member when it was not a proscribed organisation under the current legislation; and
  (b)   that he has not since he became a member taken part in any of its activities at any time while it was a proscribed organisation under that legislation.
(4)   In subsection (3) above 'the current legislation', in relation to any time, means whichever of the following was in force at that time—
  (a)   the Prevention of Terrorism (Temporary Provisions) Act 1974;
  (b)   the Prevention of Terrorism (Temporary Provisions) Act 1976;
  (a)   the Prevention of Terrorism (Temporary Provisions) Act 1984; or
  (d)   this Act.
(5)   The reference in subsection (3) above to a person becoming a member of an organisation is a reference to the only or last occasion on which he became a member.

DISPLAY OF SUPPORT IN PUBLIC FOR PROSCRIBED ORGANISATIONS

Definition

Prevention of Terrorism (Temporary Provisions) Act 1989, s. 3

B10.7

(1)   Any person who in a public place—

    (a)   wears any item of dress; or
    (b)   wears, carries or displays any article,
in such a way or in such circumstances as to arouse reasonable apprehension that he is a member or supporter of a proscribed organisation, is guilty of an offence.

Procedure

B10.8 As to the requirement that proceedings be brought by or with the consent of the A-G, see **B10.2**. The offence is triable summarily only (PT(TP)A 1989, s. 3(1)).

The special evidential provisions relating to orders, notices or directions made or given by the Secretary of State are set out in the PT(TP)A 1989, s. 19(1) and (2), and are dealt with at **B10.2**.

Sentence

B10.9 The maximum penalty on summary conviction is imprisonment for a term not exceeding six months or a fine not exceeding level 5 on the standard scale or both (PT(TP)A 1989, s. 3(1)).

Elements

B10.10 As to 'proscribed organisation', see **B10.5**.

As to the meaning of 'public place', the PT(TP)A 1989, s. 3(3), provides that it includes any highway and any premises to which at the material time the public have, or are permitted to have, access, whether on payment or otherwise. 'Premises' is defined in s. 20 as including any place, and in particular includes:

    (a)   any vehicle, vessel or aircraft;
    (b)   any offshore intallation as defined in the Mineral Workings (Offshore Installations) Act 1971, s. 1; and
    (c)   any tent or movable structure.

'Vehicle' includes a train and carriages forming part of a train.

Related Offence

B10.11 As to the offence under the Public Order Act 1936, relating to the wearing of uniforms, see **B11.11** to **B11.16**.

FAILING TO COMPLY WITH EXCLUSION ORDERS ETC.

Definitions

B10.12   **Prevention of Terrorism (Temporary Provisions) Act 1989, s. 8**

    (1)   A person who is subject to an exclusion order is guilty of an offence if he fails to comply with the order at a time after he has been, or become liable to be, removed under Schedule 2 to this Act.
    (2)   A person is guilty of an offence—
    (a)   if he is knowingly concerned in arrangements for securing or facilitating the entry into Great Britain, Northern Ireland or the United Kingdom of a person whom he knows; or has reasonable grounds for believing, to be an excluded person; or
    (b)   if he knowingly harbours such a person in Great Britain, Northern Ireland or the United Kingdom.

Procedure

B10.13 As to the requirement that proceedings be brought by or with the consent of the A-G, see **B10.2**. These offences are triable either way. When tried on indictment they are class 4 offences.

The provisions of the PT(TP)A 1989, s. 19(1) and (2), apply to these offences (see **B10.2**).

Sentence

The maximum penalty is: on conviction on indictment, imprisonment for a term not **B10.14** exceeding five years or a fine or both; on summary conviction, imprisonment for a term not exceeding six months or a fine not exceeding the statutory maximum or both (PT(TP)A 1989, s. 8(4)).

Elements

Prevention of Terrorism (Temporary Provisions) Act 1989, s. 8   **B10.15**

(3)   In subsection (2) above 'excluded person' means—
    (a)   in relation to Great Britain, a person subject to an exclusion order made under section 5 above who has been, or has become liable to be, removed from Great Britain under Schedule 2 to this Act;
    (b)   in relation to Northern Ireland, a person subject to an exclusion order made under section 6 above who has been, or has become liable to be, removed from Northern Ireland under that Schedule; and
    (c)   in relation to the United Kingdom, a person subject to an exclusion order made under section 7 above who has been, or has become liable to be, removed from the United Kingdom under that Schedule.

Thus, the making of exclusion orders and consequent removal directions are essential elements in the instant offences. There are three types of exclusion orders, dependent on the part of the United Kingdom from which a person is to be excluded.

Prevention of Terrorism (Temporary Provisions) Act 1989, s. 5

(1)   If the Secretary of State is satisfied that any person—
    (a)   is or has been concerned in the commission, preparation or instigation of acts of terrorism to which this Part of this Act applies; or
    (b)   is attempting or may attempt to enter Great Britain with a view to being concerned in the commission, preparation or instigation of such acts of terrorism, the Secretary of State may make an exclusion order against him.
(2)   An exclusion order under this section is an order prohibiting a person from being in, or entering, Great Britain.
(3)   In deciding whether to make an exclusion order under this section against a person who is ordinarily resident in Great Britain, the Secretary of State shall have regard to the question whether that person's connection with any country or territory outside Great Britain is such as to make it appropriate that such an order should be made.
(4)   An exclusion order shall not be made under this section against a person who is a British citizen and who—
    (a)   is at the time ordinarily resident in Great Britain and has then been ordinarily resident in Great Britain throughout the last three years; or
    (b)   is at the time subject to an order under section 6 below.

Sections 6 and 7 of the Act make corresponding provision for the exclusion of persons from Northern Ireland and the United Kingdom respectively.

Related Offences

(a)   Person failing to comply with removal directions (i.e. directions used to enforce **B10.16** an exclusion order).

Prevention of Terrorism (Temporary Provisions) Act 1989, sch. 2, para. 6(8)

Any person who without reasonable excuse fails to comply with directions given to him under [para. 6] is guilty of an offence and is liable on summary conviction to imprisonment for a term not exceeding three months or a fine not exceeding level 4 on the standard scale or both.

(b)   Enforcement of detention pending removal:

Prevention of Terrorism (Temporary Provisions) Act 1989, sch. 2, para. 7

(4)   The captain of a ship or aircraft who fails to take reasonable steps to comply with a requirement imposed under subparagraph (3) above is guilty of an offence and liable on summary conviction to imprisonment for a term not exceeding six months or a fine not exceeding level 4 on the standard scale or both.

The requirement is for such a captain to prevent a person subject to a removal direction who has been placed on board the ship or aircraft from disembarking.

(c)   Enforcement of port and border controls:

Prevention of Terrorism (Temporary Provisions) Act 1989, sch. 5, para. 11

A person who knowingly contravenes any prohibition or fails to comply with any duty or requirement imposed by or under this schedule is guilty of an offence and liable on summary conviction to imprisonment for a term not exceeding three months or a fine not exceeding level 4 on the standard scale or both.

Schedule 5 is concerned with the imposition of port and border controls, and the offence in para. 11 supports the powers created for that purpose.

INVOLVEMENT WITH CONTRIBUTIONS INTENDING THEY BE USED FOR TERRORISM

Definition

B10.17   **Prevention of Terrorism (Temporary Provisions) Act 1989, s. 9**

(1)   A person is guilty of an offence if he—
(a)   solicits or invites any other person to give, lend or otherwise make available, whether for consideration or not, any money or other property;
(b)   receives or accepts from any other person, whether for consideration or not, any money or other property; or
(c)   uses or has possession of, whether for consideration or not, any money or other property,
intending that it shall be applied or used for the commission of, or in furtherance of or in connection with, acts of terrorism to which this section applies or having reasonable cause to suspect that it may be so used or applied.

Procedure

B10.18 As to the requirement that proceedings be brought by or with the consent of the A-G, see **B10.2**. The offence is triable either way. When tried on indictment it is a class 4 offence.

Indictment

B10.19   Statement of Offence

Soliciting [or inviting etc.] [or receiving etc.] money [or property] with intent contrary to section 9(1) of the Prevention of Terrorism (Temporary Provisions) Act 1989

Particulars of Offence

A on or about the . . . day of . . . solicited from X [or invited to give . . .] [or received from X] money [or property] intending that the same be applied or used for the commission of [or in the furtherance of] [or in connection with] acts of terrorism in Northern Ireland, namely . . .

Sentence

The maximum penalty is: on conviction on indictment, imprisonment for a term not **B10.20** exceeding 14 years or a fine or both; on summary conviction, a term of imprisonment not exceeding six months or a fine not exceeding the statutory maximum or both (PT(TP)A 1989, s. 13(1)).

The court has a power to order forfeiture of any money or other property, in accordance with s. 13 of and sch. 4 to the Act.

Prevention of Terrorism (Temporary Provisions) Act 1989, s. 13

(2)   Subject to the provisions of this section, the court by or before which a person is convicted of an offence under section 9(1) . . . above may order the forfeiture of any money or other property—
(a)   which, at the time of the offence, he had in his possession or under his control; and
(b)   which, at that time—
(i)   in the case of an offence under subsection (1) of section 9, he intended should be applied or used, or had reasonable cause to suspect might be applied or used as mentioned in that subsection; . . .
(5)   The court shall not under this section make an order forfeiting any money or other property unless the court considers that the money or property may, unless forfeited, be applied or used as mentioned in section 9(1) above but the court may, in the absence of evidence to the contrary, assume that any money or property may be applied or used as there mentioned.
(6)   Where a person other than the convicted person claims to be the owner of or otherwise interested in anything which can be forfeited by an order under this section, the court shall, before making such an order in respect of it, give him an opportunity to be heard.

Detailed provisions relating to forfeiture orders are contained in sch. 4.

Acts of Terrorism to which Section Applies

Prevention of Terrorism (Temporary Provisions) Act 1989, s. 9   B10.21

(3)   The acts of terrorism to which this section applies are—
(a)   acts of terrorism connected with the affairs of Northern Ireland; and
(b)   subject to subsection (4) below, acts of terrorism of any other description except acts connected solely with the affairs of the United Kingdom or any part of the United Kingdom other than Northern Ireland.
(4)   Subsection (3)(b) above does not apply to an act done or to be done outside the United Kingdom unless it constitutes or would constitute an offence triable in the United Kingdom.
(5)   In proceedings against a person for an offence under this section in relation to an act within subsection (3)(b) above done or to be done outside the United Kingdom—
(a)   the prosecution need not prove that that person knew or had reasonable cause to suspect that the act constituted or would constitute such an offence as is mentioned in subsection (4) above; but
(b)   it shall be a defence to prove that he did not know and had no reasonable cause to suspect that the facts were such that the act constituted or would constitute such an offence.

The word 'terrorism' is defined in s. 20 of the Act as meaning the use of violence for political ends, and includes any use of violence for the purpose of putting the public or any section of the public in fear.

Application to Crown Servants

By virtue of the PT(TP)A 1989, s. 19A, and Prevention of Terrorism (Temporary **B10.22** Provisions) Act 1989 (Crown Servants and Regulators, etc.) Regulations 1994 (SI 1994 No. 1758), reg. 3, offences contrary to ss. 9, 10, 11, 17 and 18A of the PT(TP)A 1989 apply to the Director of Savings and any person employed or otherwise engaged in his service in circumstances where the Director or any such person is carrying on relevant financial business as defined in the Money Laundering Regulations 1993 (SI 1993 No. 1933), reg. 4.

Meaning of 'Property'

B10.23 By the PT(TP)A 1989, s. 20, the word 'property' includes property wherever situated, and whether real or personal, heritable or moveable, and things in action and other intangible or incorporeal property.

Specific Defences

B10.24 As stated at **B10.21**, where relevant acts of terrorism are those defined in the PT(TP)A 1989, s. 9(3)(b) and (4), the prosecution do not have to prove that the accused knew or had reasonable cause to suspect that the act assisted by his actions constituted such an offence (s. 9(5)(a)), but it is a defence within s. 9(5)(b) 'to prove that he did not know and had no reasonable cause to suspect that the facts were such that the act constituted or would constitute such an offence'. The burden of proving such defence lies on the accused on the balance of probabilities (see **F3.4** and **F3.18**).

The PT(TP)A 1989, s. 12, removes restrictions on the disclosure of information and provides a number of defences relating to disclosure or other forms of co-operation with the proper authorities.

Prevention of Terrorism (Temporary Provisions) Act 1989, s. 12

(1)   A person may notwithstanding any restriction on the disclosure of information imposed by statute or otherwise disclose to a constable a suspicion or belief that any money or other property is or is derived from terrorist funds or any matter on which such a suspicion or belief is based.

(2)   A person who enters into or is otherwise concerned in any such transaction or arrangement as is mentioned in section 9, 10 or 11 above does not commit an offence under that section if he is acting with the express consent of a constable or if—

(a)   he discloses to a constable his suspicion or belief that the money or other property concerned is or is derived from terrorist funds or any matter on which such a suspicion or belief is based; and

(b)   the disclosure is made after he enters into or otherwise becomes concerned in the transaction or arrangement in question but is made on his own initiative and as soon as it is reasonable for him to make it,

but paragraphs (a) and (b) above do not apply in a case where, having disclosed any such suspicion, belief or matter to a constable and having been forbidden by a constable to enter into or otherwise be concerned in the transaction or arrangement in question, he nevertheless does so.

(2A)   For the purposes of subsection (2) above a person who uses or has possession of money or other property shall be taken to be concerned in a transaction or arrangement.

(3)   In proceedings against a person for an offence under section 9(1)(b) or (c) or (2), 10(1)(b) or (c) or 11 above it is a defence to prove—

(a)   that he intended to disclose to a constable such a suspicion, belief or matter as is mentioned in paragraph (a) of subsection (2) above; and

(b)   that there is a reasonable excuse for his failure to make the disclosure as mentioned in paragraph (b) of that subsection.

(4)   In the case of a person who was in employment at the relevant time, subsections (1) to (3) above shall have effect in relation to disclosures, and intended disclosures, to the appropriate person in accordance with the procedures established by his employer for the making of such disclosures as they have effect in relation to disclosures, and intended disclosures, to a constable.

(5)   No constable or other person shall be guilty of an offence under section 9(1)(b) or (c) or 10(1)(b) or (c) above in respect of anything done by him in the course of acting in connection with the enforcement, or intended enforcement, of any provision of this Act or of any other enactment relating to terrorism or the proceeds or resources of terrorism.

(6) For the purposes of subsection (5) above, having possession of any property shall be taken to be doing an act in relation to it.

INVOLVEMENT WITH CONTRIBUTIONS KNOWING OR REASONABLY SUSPECTING USE FOR TERRORISM

Definition

Prevention of Terrorism (Temporary Provisions) Act 1989, s. 9   B10.25

(2) A person is guilty of an offence if he—
    (a) gives, lends or otherwise makes available to any other person, whether for consideration or not, any money or other property, or
    (b) enters into or is otherwise concerned in an arrangement whereby money or other property is or is to be made available to another person,
knowing or having reasonable cause to suspect that it will or may be applied or used as mentioned in subsection (1) above.

Procedure

As to the requirement that proceedings be brought by or with the consent of the A-G, see B10.26
B10.2. This offence is triable either way (PT(TP)A 1989, s. 13(1)). When tried on indictment it is a class 4 offence.

Sentence

The maximum penalty is: on conviction on indictment, imprisonment for a term not B10.27
exceeding 14 years or a fine or both; on summary conviction, a term of imprisonment not exceeding six months or a fine not exceeding the statutory maximum or both (PT(TP)A 1989, s. 13(1)).

The court has a power to order forfeiture of any money or other property in accordance with s. 13 and sch. 4. It should be noted that the forfeiture power where the offence is that contrary to s. 9(2)(a) is to be found in s. 13(2), whereas where the offence is that contrary to s. 9(2)(b) it is to be found in s. 13(3). See **B10.20**.

Elements

The meaning of 'property' is considered at **B10.22**.   B10.28

It is necessary for the accused to know or have reasonable cause to suspect that the money or other property will or may be used as mentioned in s. 9(1), which may be a matter of inference from all the circumstances, including the accused's conduct.

The accused must know or have reasonable cause to suspect that the money or other property will or may be applied or used for the commission of, or in furtherance of or in connection with, acts of terrorism to which s. 9 applies. The meaning of the phrase 'acts of terrorism to which this section applies' is dealt with at **B10.21**.

As to the application of this offence to certain Crown servants, see **B10.22**.

Specific Defences

See **B10.24**.   B10.29

INVOLVEMENT IN CONTRIBUTIONS TO PROSCRIBED ORGANISATIONS

Definition

Prevention of Terrorism (Temporary Provisions) Act 1989, s. 10   B10.30

(1) A person is guilty of an offence if he—

    (a)   solicits or invites any other person to give, lend or otherwise make available, whether for consideration or not, any money or other property for the benefit of a proscribed organisation;

    (b)   gives, lends or otherwise makes available or receives or accepts or uses or has possession of, whether for consideration or not, any money or other property for the benefit of such an organisation; or

    (c)   enters into or is otherwise concerned in an arrangement whereby money or other property is or is to be made available for the benefit of such an organisation.

Procedure

B10.31 As to the requirement that proceedings be brought by or with the consent of the A-G, see **B10.2**. This offence is triable either way (PT(TP)A 1989, s. 13(1)). When tried on indictment it is a class 4 offence.

Sentence

B10.32 The maximum penalty is: on conviction on indictment, imprisonment for a term not exceeding 14 years or a fine or both; on summary conviction, a term of imprisonment not exceeding six months or a fine not exceeding the statutory maximum or both (PT(TP)A 1989, s. 13(1)).

The court has a power to order forfeiture of any money or other property. The forfeiture power that it may exercise depends upon of which offence the accused has been convicted. If the offence is s. 10(1)(a) or (b), the forfeiture power is found in s. 13(2), whereas if the offence is s. 10(1)(c), the forfeiture power is found in s. 13(3). In whichever provision the forfeiture power is to be found, the supplementary provisions, that is s. 13(5), (6), and (8), are the same. See **B10.20**.

Elements

B10.33 The meaning of 'property' is considered at **B10.22**.

The general meaning of the phrase 'proscribed organisation' is considered at **B10.5**. For the purposes of s. 10, and ss. 11 and 13, the PT(TP)A 1989, s. 10(3), provides that 'proscribed organisation' includes a proscribed organisation for the purposes of the Northern Ireland (Emergency Provisions) Act 1996, s. 30, that is, The Irish Republican Army, Cumann na mBan, Fianna na-Eireann, The Red Hand Commando, Saor Eire, The Ulster Freedom Fighters, The Ulster Volunteer Force, The Irish National Liberation Army, The Irish People's Liberation Organisation, The Ulster Defence Association.

As to the application of this offence to certain Crown servants, see **B10.22**.

Specific Defences

B10.34   **Prevention of Terrorism (Temporary Provisions) Act 1989, s. 10**

    (2)   In proceedings against a person for an offence under subsection (1)(b) above it is a defence to prove that he did not know and had no reasonable cause to suspect that the money or property was for the benefit of a proscribed organisation; and in proceedings against a person for an offence under subsection (1)(c) above it is a defence to prove that he did not know and had no reasonable cause to suspect that the arrangement related to a proscribed organisation.

The burden of proving these defences lies on the accused on the balance of probabilities (see generally, **F3.4** and **F3.18**).

As to defences concerned with disclosure of information about terrorist funds, see **B10.24**.

ASSISTING IN RETENTION OR CONTROL OF TERRORIST FUNDS

Definition

Prevention of Terrorism (Temporary Provisions) Act 1989, s. 11   **B10.35**

(1)   A person is guilty of an offence if he enters into or is otherwise concerned in an arrangement whereby the retention or control by or on behalf of another person of terrorist funds is facilitated, whether by concealment, removal from the jurisdiction, transfer to nominees or otherwise.

Procedure

As to the requirement that proceedings be brought by or with the consent of the A-G, see   **B10.36** **B10.2**. This offence is triable either way (PT(TP)A 1989, s. 13(1)). When tried on indictment it is a class 4 offence.

Sentence

The maximum penalty is: on conviction on indictment, imprisonment for a term not   **B10.37** exceeding 14 years or a fine or both; on summary conviction, a term of imprisonment not exceeding six months or a fine not exceeding the statutory maximum or both (PT(TP)A 1989, s. 13(1)).

The court has a power to order forfeiture of any money or other property in accordance with s. 13 and sch. 4. The forfeiture power that it may exercise is to be found in s. 13(3). See **B10.20**.

Elements

Prevention of Terrorism (Temporary Provisions) Act 1989, s. 11   **B10.38**

(3)   In this section and section 12 below 'terrorist funds' means—
    (a)   funds which may be applied or used for the commission of, or in furtherance of or in connection with, acts of terrorism to which section 9 above applies;
    (b)   the proceeds of the commission of such acts of terrorism or of activities engaged in in furtherance of or in connection with such acts; and
    (c)   the resources of a proscribed organisation.
(4)   Paragraph (b) of subsection (3) includes any property which in whole or in part directly or indirectly represents such proceeds as are mentioned in that paragraph; and paragraph (c) of that subsection includes any money or other property which is or is to be applied or made available for the benefit of a proscribed organisation.

The 'acts of terrorism to which section 9 above applies' are considered at **B10.21**, and the meaning of 'proscribed organisation' is considered at **B10.5**.

As to the application of this offence to certain Crown servants, see **B10.22**.

Specific Defences

Prevention of Terrorism (Temporary Provisions) Act 1989, s. 11   **B10.39**

(2)   In proceedings against a person for an offence under this section it is a defence to prove that he did not know and had no reasonable cause to suspect that the arrangement related to terrorist funds.

The burden of proving the defence in s. 11(2) lies on the accused on the balance of probabilities (see generally **F3.4** and **F3.18**).

As to defences concerned with disclosure of information about terrorist funds, see **B10.24**.

473

POSSESSION OF ARTICLES FOR SUSPECTED TERRORIST OFFENCES

Definition

B10.40   **Prevention of Terrorism (Temporary Provisions) Act 1989, s. 16A**

(1)   A person is guilty of an offence if he has any article in his possession in circumstances giving rise to a reasonable suspicion that the article is in his possession for a purpose connected with the commission, preparation or instigation of acts of terrorism to which this section applies.

(2)   The acts of terrorism to which this section applies are —

(a)   acts of terrorism connected with the affairs of Northern Ireland; and

(b)   acts of terrorism of any other description except acts connected solely with the affairs of the United Kingdom or any part of the United Kingdom other than Northern Ireland.

For the meaning of 'terrorism', see **B10.21**.

Procedure

B10.41   As to the requirement that proceedings be brought by or with the consent of the A-G, see **B10.2**. This offence is triable either way (PT(TP)A 1989, s. 16A(5)).

Sentence

B10.42   The maximum penalty is: on conviction on indictment, imprisonment for a term not exceeding 10 years or a fine or both; on summary conviction, a term of imprisonment not exceeding six months or a fine not exceeding the statutory maximum or both (PT(TP)A 1989, s. 16A(5)).

Possession

B10.43   Where a person is charged with an offence under s. 16A and it is proved that at the time of the alleged offence he and that article were both present in any premises or the article was in premises of which he was the occupier or which he habitually used otherwise than as a member of the public, the court may accept the fact proved as sufficient evidence of his possessing that article at that time unless it is further proved that he did not at that time know of its presence in the premises in question or, if he did know, that he had no control over it (PT(TP)A 1989, s. 16A(4)). (The general rules as to the meaning of 'possession' apply; as to the term's meaning in drugs offences, see **B20.10**.)

The term 'premises' is not defined but the offence applies also to vessels, aircraft and vehicles (s. 16A(6)).

Compliance with European Convention on Human Rights

B10.44   In *DPP, ex parte Kebilene* [1999] 3 WLR 175, the applicants challenged the decision of the DPP to consent to prosecutions under PT(TP)A 1989, ss. 16A and 16B (see **B10.45**). Their argument was that these two offences contravened Art. 6(2) of the European Convention on Human Rights (see **appendix 7**), which provides:

Everyone charged with a criminal offence shall be presumed innocent until proved guilty according to law.

In part the case is concerned with challenging the discretion of the DPP by way of judicial review.

In considering the compliance of the offences with the Convention, the Divisional Court could not determine that the offences could be reconciled with the Convention. The initial views of Lord Bingham CJ and Laws LJ were that there would be difficulty in such a reconciliation. Lord Bingham took the following view:

> on their face, both sections undermine, in a blatant and obvious way, the presumption of innocence. . . . Under section 16A a defendant could be convicted even if the jury entertained a reasonable doubt whether he knew that the items were in his premises and whether he had the items for a terrorist purpose. Under section 16B a defendant could be convicted even if the jury entertained a reasonable doubt whether the information had been collected or was possessed for any terrorist purpose. In both sections the presumption of innocence is violated.

Having been addressed on the practical need for such offences in the fight against terrorism, Lord Bingham accepted that such matters deserved careful attention, but they were not sufficient to 'dissuade me from the conclusion already expressed'. He also took into account the substantial maximum penalty for the offences.

It is indeed clear that Art. 6(2) is relevant to the question of whether these offences comply with the Convention. Harris, D.J., O'Boyle, M. and Warbrick, C., *Law of the European Convention on Human Rights* state (at pp. 243 and 244, with footnotes removed) as follows:

> Although the burden of proof must fall on the prosecution, it may be transferred to the accused when he is seeking to establish a defence. Similarly, Article 6(2) does not prohibit presumptions of fact or of law that may operate against the accused. However, it does require that states confine such presumptions 'within reasonable limits which take into account the importance of what is at stake and maintain the rights of the defence.' . . . Article 6(2) does not prohibit offences of strict liability, which are a common feature of the criminal law of the Convention parties. An offence may thus be committed, consistently with Article 6(2), on the basis that a certain act has been committed, without it being necessary to prove *mens rea*. Provided a state respects the rights protected by the Convention, it is free to punish any kind of activity as criminal and to establish elements of the offence in its discretion, including any requirement of *mens rea*.

The leading case on Art. 6(2) is *Salabiaku* v *France* (1988) 13 EHRR 379. Mr Salabiaku was concerned about an 'almost irrebuttable' presumption against him. The French Government took the view that the presumption of guilt (in relation to the importation of drugs) was 'a rebuttable presumption of fact and liability . . . strictly defined by the case law and justified by the very nature of the subject-matter of the law in question. This implied no more than a sharing of the burden of proof and not its reversal'. The European Court of Human Rights made clear that it is possible for strict liability to be the basis for criminal liability. However, the Court recognised that Mr Salabiaku:

> Was not convicted for mere possession of unlawfully imported prohibited goods. [Under the relevant provision,] a conclusion is drawn from a simple fact, which in itself does not necessarily constitute a petty or a more serious offence, but that the 'criminal liability' for the unlawful importation of goods lies with the person in whose possession they are found. It infers therefrom a legal presumption on the basis of which the [French courts] found the applicant 'guilty . . . of smuggling prohibited goods,' a customs offence for whose commission possession is not essential. . . . This shift from the idea of accountability in criminal law to the notion of guilt shows the very relative nature of such a distinction. It raises a question with regard to Article 6 para. 2. . . . Presumptions of facts or of law operate in every legal system. Clearly the Convention does not prohibit such presumptions in principle. It does, however, require the Contracting States to remain within certain limits. . . . [Article 6(2)] requires States to confine [presumptions of fact or of law] within reasonable limits which take into account the importance of what is at stake and maintain the rights of the defence.

Article 6(2) was not contravened in *Salabiaku* because the applicant had a *force majeure* defence which counteracted the presumption of the *actus reus* of the smuggling offence. This might well be compared with the position with regard to s. 16B and perhaps suggest that it is not so obvious that it falls foul of Art. 6(2).

The guidance from the European Court of Human Rights, therefore, will not be easy to apply in any given case. It is entirely possible that, despite the pressures that terrorism and its control produces, the Divisional Court was right in thinking that ss. 16A and 16B had gone too far, especially noting that there was no derogation from Art. 6 under Art. 15. The offences are committed by the doing of an apparently innocent act which, in the case of s. 16A, gives rise to a mere 'reasonable suspicion' of terrorist activity. This is very different from many other circumstances where there are presumptions of law or fact or where the burden of proof of a defence lies on the defence (see, e.g., *Hunt* [1987] AC 352 and **F3.5**) and it would seem unlikely that they fall foul of Art. 6(2). Further, there is nothing in the jurisprudence to suggest that offences of strict liability fall foul of Art. 6(2). The dividing line between that which falls foul of Art. 6(2) and that which does not is, it is submitted, a difficult one to draw or to predict.

On appeal to the House of Lords *DPP, ex parte Kebilene* [1999] 3 WLR 972), primary focus was upon the question of whether the DPP's decision to consent to a prosecution was amenable to judicial review. Little attention, therefore, was given to the compliance of the Prevention of Terrorism (Temporary Provisions) Act 1989, s. 16A, with the European Convention. The exception to this was Lord Hope of Craighead, because the Scotland Act 1998, s. 29(2)(d), means that legislation is outside the competence of the Scottish Parliament if it is incompatible with any Convention right. His approach underlines the view expressed above, that predicting compatibility is no easy task. Lord Hope engaged in a summary of the law in relation to the presumption of innocence and the burden of proof in criminal trials. Lord Hope took the view that s. 16A(3) imposed, upon the accused, a persuasive burden of proof, on a balance of probabilities, that the article was not in his possession for a purpose connected with terrorism. If not discharged, there is a mandatory presumption that the article was in the accused's possession for a purpose connected with terrorism. There is only a discretionary presumption arising under s. 16A(4). Lord Hope felt that these techniques were not unique to the 1989 Act. Lord Hope was not convinced that s. 16A and Art. 6(2) are incompatible, especially taking into account the 'question of balance, as to the interests of the individual as against those of society. The Convention jurisprudence and that which is to be found from the cases decided in other jurisdictions suggests that account may legitimately be taken, in striking the right balance, of the problems which the legislation was designed to address.' This balance would be assessed by addressing it through the three questions suggested by counsel, i.e. '(1) what does the prosecution have to prove in order to transfer the onus to the defence? (2) what is the burden on the accused — does it relate to something which is likely to be difficult for him to prove, or does it relate to something which is likely to be within his knowledge or . . . to which he readily has access? (3) what is the nature of the threat faced by society which the provision is designed to combat?' Lord Hope applied those questions to s. 16A. He concluded, first, that the prosecution must 'prove beyond reasonable doubt (a) that the accused had the article in his possession and (b) that it was in his possession in circumstances giving rise to a reasonable suspicion that it was in his possession for a purpose connected with terrorism. . . . It should not be thought that proof [of possession] to this standard will be a formality.' Secondly, the onus of proving the 'defence', as Lord Hope calls it, in s. 16A(3) is on the accused. Lord Hope does not accept that this imposes an unreasonable burden upon the accused. Account would have to be taken of various facts about the individual case, and also about 'the nature of the threat which terrorism poses to a free and democratic society. . . . Society has a strong interest in preventing acts of terrorism before they are perpetrated'. Whilst not determining the matter, Lord Hope concluded that it 'is a question which is still open to argument'.

Specific Defence

B10.45 Under the PT(TP)A 1989, s. 16A(3), it is a defence for a person charged with this offence to prove that at the time of the alleged offence the article in question was not in his possession for a purpose mentioned in s. 16A(1).

UNLAWFUL COLLECTION, ETC. OF INFORMATION

Definition

Prevention of Terrorism (Temporary Provisions) Act 1989, s. 16B **B10.46**

(1)   No person shall, without lawful authority or reasonable excuse (the proof of which lies on him)—
    (a)   collect or record any information which is of such a nature as is likely to be useful to terrorists in planning or carrying out any act of terrorism to which this section applies; or
    (b)   have in his possession any record or document containing any such information as is mentioned in paragraph (a) above.

The acts of terrorism to which s. 16B applies are those specified in s. 16B(2), which is in identical terms to s. 16A(2) (see **B10.40**).

Procedure

As to the requirement that proceedings be brought by or with the consent of the A-G, see **B10.47** **B10.2**. This offence is triable either way (PT(TP)A 1989, s. 16B(4)).

Sentence

The maximum penalty is: on conviction on indictment, imprisonment for a term not **B10.48** exceeding 10 years or a fine or both; on summary conviction, a term of imprisonment not exceeding six months or a fine not exceeding the statutory maximum or both (PT(TP)A 1989, s. 16B(4)). The court by or before which a person is convicted may order the forfeiture of any record or document mentioned in s. 16B(1) which is found in his possession (s. 16B(5)).

Recording Information

By virtue of the PT(TP)A 1989, s. 16B(3), the reference to recording information in **B10.49** s. 16B(1) includes a reference to recording it by means of photography or by any other means.

PREJUDICING OR OTHERWISE INTERFERING WITH INVESTIGATION OF TERRORIST ACTIVITIES

Definition

Prevention of Terrorism (Temporary Provisions) Act 1989, s. 17 **B10.50**

(2)   A person is guilty of an offence if, knowing or having reasonable cause to suspect that a constable is acting, or is proposing to act, in connection with a terrorist investigation which is being, or is about to be, conducted, he—
    (a)   discloses to any other person information or any other matter which is likely to prejudice the investigation or proposed investigation, or
    (b)   falsifies, conceals or destroys or otherwise disposes of, or causes or permits the falsification, concealment, destruction or disposal of, material which is or is likely to be relevant to the investigation, or proposed investigation.
(2A)   A person is guilty of an offence if, knowing or having reasonable cause to suspect that a disclosure ('the disclosure') has been made to a constable under section 12, 18 or 18A of this Act, he—
    (a)   discloses to any other person information or any other matter which is likely to prejudice any investigation which might be conducted following the disclosure; or
    (b)   falsifies, conceals or destroys or otherwise disposes of, or causes or permits the falsification, concealment, destruction or disposal of, material which is or is likely to be relevant to any such investigation.
(2B)   A person is guilty of an offence if, knowing or having reasonable cause to suspect that a disclosure ('the disclosure') of a kind mentioned in section 12(4) or 18A(5) of this Act has been made, he—

(a)   discloses to any person information or any other matter which is likely to prejudice any investigation which might be conducted following the disclosure; or

(b)   falsifies, conceals or destroys or otherwise disposes of, or causes or permits the falsification, concealment, destruction or disposal of, material which is or is likely to be relevant to any such investigation.

Procedure

B10.51   As to the requirement that proceedings be brought by or with the consent of the A-G, see **B10.2**. The offence is triable either way (PT(TP)A 1989, s. 17(5)). When tried on indictment it is a class 4 offence.

Sentence

B10.52   The maximum penalty is: on conviction on indictment, imprisonment for a term not exceeding five years or a fine or both; on summary conviction, imprisonment for a term not exceeding six months or a fine not exceeding the statutory maximum or both (PT(TP)A 1989, s. 17(5)).

Elements

B10.53   These offences deal with improper interference in terrorist investigations. The powers of the security forces with regard to such investigations are contained the PT(TP)A 1989, sch. 7. A 'terrorist investigation' is defined in s. 17(1).

Prevention of Terrorism (Temporary Provisions) Act 1989, s. 17

(1)   Schedule 7 to this Act shall have effect for conferring powers to obtain information for the purposes of terrorist investigations, that is to say—

(a)   investigations into—

(i)   the commission, preparation or instigation of acts of terrorism to which section 14 above applies; or

(ii)   any other act which appears to have been done in furtherance of or in connection with such acts of terrorism, including any act which appears to constitute an offence under section 2, 9, 10, 11, 18 or 18A of this Act or section 29 or 30 of the Northern Ireland (Emergency Provisions) Act 1996; or

(iii)   without prejudice to subparagraph (ii) above, the resources of a proscribed organisation within the meaning of this Act or a proscribed organisation for the purposes of section 30 of the said Act of 1996; and

(b)   investigations into whether there are grounds justifying the making of an order under section 1(2)(a) above or section 30(3) of that Act.

Insofar as s. 17(1) applies in relation to any offence under s. 18 or 18A of the Act, 'act' includes omission (s. 17(6)). As to the application of this offence to certain Crown servants, see **B10.22**.

Specific Defences

B10.54   Section 17 of the PT(TP)A 1989 makes provision for five specific defences. The burden of proving these defences lies on the accused on the balance of probabilities (see generally, **F3.4** and **F3.18**).

B10.55   *Lack of Knowledge or Suspicion of Investigation*   It is a defence for a person to prove, in proceedings for an offence under the PT(TP)A 1989, s. 17(2)(a), (2A)(a) or (2B)(a), that he did not know and had no reasonable cause to suspect that the disclosure was likely to prejudice the investigation or proposed investigation (s. 17(3)(a) and (3A)(a)).

B10.56   *Lawful Authority or Reasonable Excuse*   It is a defence for a person to prove, in proceedings for an offence under the PT(TP)A 1989, s. 17(2)(a), (2A)(a) or (2B)(a), that he had lawful authority or reasonable excuse for making the disclosure (s. 17(3)(b) and (3A)(b)).

No Intention to Conceal Information It is a defence for a person to prove, in **B10.57** proceedings for an offence under the PT(TP)A 1989, s. 17(2)(b), that he had no intention of concealing any information carried in the material in question from any person conducting, or likely to be conducting, the investigation or proposed investigation (s. 17(4)).

It is a defence for a person to prove, in proceedings for an offence under s. 17(2A)(b) or (2B)(b), that he had no intention of concealing any information carried in the material in question from any person who might carry out the investigation in question (s. 17(4)).

Professional Legal Advisers Except where information is disclosed with a view to **B10.58** furthering any criminal purpose, the PT(TP)A 1989, s. 17(2) to (2B), do not make it an offence for a professional legal adviser to disclose any information or other matter:

(a) to, or to a representative of, his client or in connection with the giving by the adviser of legal advice to the client; or
(b) to any person in contemplation of, or in connection with, legal proceedings, and for the purpose of those proceedings (s. 17(2C) and (2D)).

Acting in Connection with Enforcement or Intended Enforcement No con- **B10.59** stable or other person commits an offence under the PT(TP)A 1989, s. 17, in respect of anything done by him in the course of acting in connection with the enforcement, or intended enforcement, of any provision of the Act or of any other enactment relating to terrorism or the proceeds or resources of terrorism (s. 17(2E)).

FAILURE TO DISCLOSE INFORMATION ABOUT ACTS OF TERRORISM

Definition

Prevention of Terrorism (Temporary Provisions) Act 1989, s. 18   **B10.60**

(1) A person is guilty of an offence if he has information which he knows or believes might be of material assistance—
(a) in preventing the commission by any other person of an act of terrorism connected with the affairs of Northern Ireland; or
(b) in securing the apprehension, prosecution or conviction of any other person for an offence involving the commission, preparation or instigation of such an act,
and fails without reasonable excuse to disclose that information as soon as reasonably practicable—
(i) in England and Wales, to a constable;
(ii) in Scotland, to a constable or the procurator fiscal; or
(iii) in Northern Ireland, to a constable or a member of Her Majesty's Forces.

Procedure

As to the requirement that proceedings be brought by or with the consent of the A-G, see **B10.61** **B10.2**. The offence is triable either way. When tried on indictment it is a class 4 offence.

Prevention of Terrorism (Temporary Provisions) Act 1989, s. 18

(3) Proceedings for an offence under this section may be taken, and the offence may for the purposes of those proceedings be treated as having been committed, in any place where the person to be charged is or has at any time been since he first knew or believed that the information might be of material assistance as mentioned in subsection (1) above.

Sentence

The maximum penalty is: on conviction on indictment, imprisonment for a term not **B10.62** exceeding five years or a fine or both; on summary conviction, imprisonment for a term not exceeding six months or a fine not exceeding the statutory maximum or both (PT(TP)A 1989, s. 18(2)).

Elements

B10.63 As to the meaning of 'terrorism', see **B10.21**.

FAILURE TO DISCLOSE KNOWLEDGE OR SUSPICION OF FINANCIAL ASSISTANCE FOR TERRORISM

Definition

B10.64 **Prevention of Terrorism (Temporary Provisions) Act 1989, s. 18A**

(1) A person is guilty of an offence if—
(a) he knows, or suspects, that another person is providing financial assistance for terrorism;
(b) the information, or other matter, on which that knowledge or suspicion is based came to his attention in the course of his trade, profession, business or employment; and
(c) he does not disclose the information or other matter to a constable as soon as is reasonably practicable after it comes to his attention.

Procedure

B10.65 As to the requirement that proceedings be brought by or with the consent of the A-G, see **B10.2**. The offence is triable either way. When tried on indictment it is a class 4 offence.

Sentence

B10.66 The maximum penalty is: on conviction on indictment, imprisonment for a term not exceeding five years or a fine or both; on summary conviction, imprisonment for a term not exceeding six months or a fine not exceeding the statutory maximum or both (PT(TP)A 1989, s. 18A(11)).

Elements

B10.67 The term 'providing financial assistance for terrorism' means doing any act which constitutes an offence under the PT(TP)A 1989, s. 9, 10 or 11, or, in the case of an act which is not done in the United Kingdom, which would have constituted such an offence if done in the United Kingdom (s. 18A(7)). Having possession of any property is taken as doing an act in relation to it (s. 18A(8)). As indicated at **B10.22** this offence applies to certain Crown servants. Further, the Prevention of Terrorism (Temporary Provisions) Act 1989 (Crown Servants and Regulators, etc.) Regulations 1994 (SI 1994 No. 1758), reg. 4, provides that this offence does not apply, as regards England and Wales, to the following organisations and bodies or persons employed by or otherwise engaged in their service: the Bank of England, the Building Societies Commission, a designated agency, self-regulating organisation, recognised professional body, transferee body or recognised self-regulating organisation for friendly societies within the meaning of the Financial Services Act 1986, the Council of Lloyd's, the Friendly Societies Commission, and the Central Office of the Registry of Friendly Societies.

Effect of Disclosure to Constable

B10.68 Disclosure to a constable is not a breach of any restriction imposed by statute or otherwise where what is disclosed is a person's suspicion or belief that another person is providing financial assistance for terrorism, or is any information or other matter on which that suspicion or belief is based (PT(TP)A 1989, s. 18A(4)).

Specific Defences

B10.69 Under the PT(TP)A 1989, s. 18A(3), it is a defence to a charge under s. 18A 'that the person charged had a reasonable excuse for not disclosing the information or other matter in question'.

In addition s. 18A provides defences applicable only to professional legal advisers and employees.

Professional Legal Adviser It is not 'an offence for a professional legal adviser to fail **B10.70** to disclose any information or other matter which has come to him in privileged circumstances' (PT(TP)A 1989, (s. 18A(2)). Such privileged circumstances arise where the information or other matter is communicated or given to the professional legal adviser:

(a) by, or by a representative of, his client in connection with the adviser giving legal advice to the client;

(b) by, or by a representative of, a person seeking legal advice from him; or

(c) by any person in contemplation of, or in connection with, legal proceedings, and for the purpose of those proceedings (s. 18A(9)).

No information or matter is covered by the privilege if it is communicated or given with a view to furthering any criminal purpose (s. 18A(10)).

Disclosure by Employee to Appropriate Person Under the PT(TP)A 1989, **B10.71** s. 18A(5), and without prejudice to s. 18A(3) or (4), 'in the case of a person who was in employment at the relevant time, it is a defence to a charge of committing an offence under [s. 18A] that he disclosed the information or other matter in question to the appropriate person in accordance with the procedure established by his employer for the making of such disclosures'. Any such disclosure is not a breach of any restriction imposed by statute or otherwise (s. 18A(6)).

NUCLEAR MATERIAL OFFENCES

The Nuclear Material (Offences) Act 1983 implements the Convention on the Physical Protection of Nuclear Material 1980 (Cmnd. 8112).

Definition

Nuclear Material (Offences) Act 1983, s. 2 **B10.72**

(1) If a person, whatever his nationality, in the United Kingdom or elsewhere contravenes subsection (2), (3) or (4) below he shall be guilty of an offence.

(2) A person contravenes this subsection if he receives, holds or deals with nuclear material—

(a) intending, or for the purpose of enabling another, to do by means of that material an act which is an offence mentioned in paragraph (a) or (b) of subsection (1) of section 1 above; or

(b) being reckless as to whether another would do such an act.

(3) A person contravenes this subsection if he—

(a) makes to another person a threat that he or any other person will do by means of nuclear material such an act as is mentioned in paragraph (a) of subsection (2) above; and

(b) intends that the person to whom the threat is made shall fear that it will be carried out.

(4) A person contravenes this subsection if, in order to compel a State, international governmental organisation or person to do, or abstain from doing, any act, he threatens that he or any other person will obtain nuclear material by an act which is an offence mentioned in paragraph (c) of subsection (1) of section 1 above.

'Act' includes omission (s. 1(2)). The acts referred to in s. 2(2) and (3) are the offences of murder and manslaughter, offences under the OAPA 1861, ss. 18 and 20, offences under the Criminal Damage Act 1971, s. 1, and certain Scottish offences. The acts referred to in s. 2(4) are theft, robbery, assault with intent to rob, burglary, aggravated burglary and certain Scottish offences (ss. 1(1) and 2(2), (3), (4) and (7)).

Procedure

B10.73 Proceedings for such an offence cannot be instituted except by, or with the consent of, the A-G (s. 3(1)). The offence is triable on indictment only. It is a class 3 offence.

Sentence

B10.74 The maximum penalty is a term of imprisonment which must not exceed 14 years and also must not exceed the term of imprisonment to which a person would be liable for the offence constituted by doing the 'contemplated act' at the place where the conviction occurs and at the time of the offence to which the conviction relates (s. 2(5)). 'Contemplated act' means, by virtue of s. 2(6):

(a) where the conviction relates to an offence under s. 2(2), the act intended or as to the doing of which the person convicted was reckless, as the case may be; and
(b) where the conviction relates to an offence under s. 2(3) or (4), the act threatened.

Elements

B10.75 The Act defines nuclear material in terms identical to those contained in the Convention. There is no definition of 'peaceful purposes' within the Act, but a certificate issued by or under the authority of the Secretary of State and stating that the material was, or was not, used for peaceful purposes at a time specified in the certificate is conclusive of the question whether any material was used for peaceful purposes (s. 6(2)).

Section 1 extends the scope of certain offences to permit trial in the United Kingdom of crimes related to nuclear material committed outside the United Kingdom.

PIRACY

Piracy *Iure Gentium*

B10.76 Piracy is a crime against the law of nations, and is referred to as piracy *iure gentium*. There is no tribunal or procedure for the trial of criminal offences internationally, so the procedure and trial of offences of piracy *iure gentium* are entrusted to the domestic law of sovereign states. The relevant provisions of the United Nations Convention on the Law of the Sea 1982 are treated as part of the law of nations for the purposes of any proceedings before a United Kingdom court (Merchant Shipping and Maritime Security Act 1997, s. 26(1)). Piracy is defined in the Convention, which is to be found in the Merchant Shipping and Maritime Security Act 1997, sch. 5. The Article numbers are those of the United Nations Convention. This is the only extant form of piracy.

Merchant Shipping and Maritime Security Act 1997, sch. 5

Article 101 Piracy consists of any of the following acts:
    (a) any illegal acts of violence or detention, or any act of depredation, committed for private ends by the crew or the passengers of a private ship or a private aircraft, and directed—
        (i) on the high seas, against another ship or aircraft, or against persons or property on board such ship or aircraft;
        (ii) against a ship, aircraft, persons or property in a place outside the jurisdiction of any State;
    (b) any act of voluntary participation in the operation of a ship or of an aircraft with knowledge of facts making it a pirate ship or aircraft;
    (c) any act of inciting or of intentionally facilitating an act described in subparagraph (a) or (b).

Article 102 The acts of piracy, as defined in article 101, committed by a warship, government ship or government aircraft whose crew has mutinied and taken control of the ship or aircraft are assimilated to acts committed by a private ship or aircraft.

Article 103   A ship or aircraft is considered a pirate ship or aircraft if it is intended by the persons in dominant control to be used for the purpose of committing one of the acts referred to in article 101. The same applies if the ship or aircraft has been used to commit any such act, so long as it remains under the control of the persons guilty of that act.

The 'high seas' are taken to include all waters beyond the territorial sea of the United Kingdom or any other State (s. 26(2)).

Procedure

Piracy is defined so as to require that it be committed either on the high seas or in a place   **B10.77** outside the jurisdiction of any State. It is clear that the normal rules of territorial jurisdiction do not apply (see **D1.72** *et seq*.). Prior to the adoption of the definitions within the United Nations Convention on the Law of the Sea 1982 by the Merchant Shipping and Maritime Security Act 1997, the true jurisdictional test was whether the ship was 'at sea' within the normal meaning of that expression, or was in a geographical position in which an attack on her could properly be described as a maritime offence (see *Athens Maritime Enterprises Corporation* v *Hellenic Mutual War Risks Association (Bermuda) Ltd* [1983] QB 647 per Staughton J). But this view must be open to challenge in view of the new definitions applying under the 1997 Act and the UN Convention.

The jurisdiction of the court is not affected by the fact that the co-accused may be foreign nationals. Although as a matter of international law any State may assume jurisdiction of an offence of piracy *iure gentium*, the scant authority suggests that English courts will be slow to assume jurisdiction where there is no real connection with England (see e.g., *Republic of Bolivia* v *Indemnity Mutual Marine Assurance Co. Ltd* [1909] 1 KB 785). It is submitted that the true test is whether the geographical circumstances, the nationality or identity of the offenders, victims and vessel, and other factors suggest the propriety of assuming jurisdiction; or whether the offence has security or defence implications or may otherwise affect the national interest of the United Kingdom, the European Union or a friendly State. In cases where there is no real connection with England, and no other factors conducive to assuming jurisdiction, the possibility of extradition to a State with a more compelling interest should be considered.

Piracy *iure gentium* is triable only on indictment. It is a class 2 offence.

Aviation Security Act 1982, s. 5

(1)   Any court in the United Kingdom having jurisdiction in respect of piracy committed on the high seas shall have jurisdiction in respect of piracy committed by or against an aircraft, wherever that piracy is committed.

Sentence

Piracy Act 1837, s. 2   **B10.78**

Whosoever, with intent to commit or at the time of or immediately before or immediately after committing the crime of piracy in respect of any ship or vessel, shall assault, with intent to murder, any person being on board of or belonging to such ship or vessel, or shall stab, cut or wound any such person, or unlawfully do any act, by which the life of such person may be endangered, shall be guilty of [an offence], and being convicted thereof shall be liable to imprisonment for life.

An act of piracy *iure gentium* committed without the aggravating acts set out in this provision is a non-capital offence punishable by imprisonment and a fine at large at common law, although it is difficult to envisage circumstances in which the life of a person is not endangered by an act of piracy. Any specific offences committed during the piracy would also be punishable as if committed on land (Offences at Sea Act 1799).

Related Offences

B10.79 Other relevant specific offences, some of which would cover what used to be piracy, include the hijacking of aircraft contrary to the Aviation Security Act 1982 (see **B10.81**), the hijacking of ships contrary to the Aviation and Maritime Security Act 1990 (see **B10.108**), and hostage-taking contrary to the Taking of Hostages Act 1982 (see **B2.87**).

HIJACKING OF AIRCRAFT AND SHIPS AND RELATED OFFENCES

B10.80 The Aviation Security Act 1982 (as amended by the Aviation and Maritime Security Act 1990) creates a number of offences with respect to the safety of aircraft. The Aviation and Maritime Security Act 1990 in giving effect to the Rome Convention 1988 and the Fixed Platforms Protocol 1988 creates a number of offences concerned with the safety of ships and fixed platforms. These offences are dealt with below. In addition, these two Acts make further provision in relation to the protection of aircraft, aerodromes and air navigation installations against acts of violence (see the Aviation Security Act 1982, part II); with regard to the policing of airports (see the Aviation Security Act 1982, part III); and in relation to the protection of ships and harbour areas against acts of violence (see the Aviation and Maritime Security Act 1990, part II).

HIJACKING OF AIRCRAFT

Definition

B10.81

Aviation Security Act 1982, s. 1

> (1) A person on board an aircraft in flight who unlawfully, by the use of force or by threats of any kind, seizes the aircraft or exercises control of it commits the offence of hijacking, whatever his nationality, whatever the State in which the aircraft is registered and whether the aircraft is in the United Kingdom or elsewhere . . ..

Procedure

B10.82 Although generally there is no jurisdictional restriction in respect of this offence, the Aviation Security Act 1982, s. 1(2), provides that if the aircraft is used in military, customs or police service, or both the place of take-off and the place of landing are in the territory of the State in which the aircraft is registered, s. 1(1) does not apply unless:

> (a) the person seizing or exercising control of the aircraft is a United Kingdom national;
> (b) his act is committed in the United Kingdom; or
> (c) the aircraft is registered in the United Kingdom or is used in the United Kingdom's military or customs service or in the service of any United Kingdom police force.

The territory of a State includes its territorial water (s. 1(5)).

Proceedings for such an offence cannot be instituted in England and Wales except by, or with the consent of, the A-G (s. 8(1)). The offence is triable on indictment only (s. 1(3)). It is a class 3 offence.

Indictment

B10.83

Statement of Offence

Hijacking contrary to s. 1(1) of the Aviation Security Act 1982

Particulars of Offence

A, on the . . . day of . . ., unlawfully issued a threat, namely that he would kill V and others, while on board an aircraft in flight, namely British Airways flight no. . . . . from London to Paris, and thereby exercised control of that aircraft

Sentence

The maximum penalty is life imprisonment (Aviation Security Act 1982, s. 1(3)).   **B10.84**

Elements

An aircraft is in flight during any period from the moment when all its external doors **B10.85** are closed following embarkation until the moment when any such door is opened for disembarkation, and, in the case of a forced landing, any period until the competent authorities take over responsibility for the aircraft and for persons and property on board (Aviation Security Act 1982, s. 38(3)(a)).

The Secretary of State may, by order, declare that an organisation or agency operating aircraft has been established by two or more States and that one of the States has been designated as exercising the powers of the State of registration. In such a case, the designated State shall be deemed to be the State in which the aircraft is registered, but in relation to s. 1(2)(b), that provision has effect as if it referred to the territory of any of the States named in the order (s. 1(4)).

Section 38 defines 'military service' as including naval and air force service, and 'United Kingdom national' as meaning an individual who is (a) a British citizen, a British Dependent Territories citizen or a British overseas citizen, (b) a person who is a British subject under the British Nationality Act 1981, or (c) a British protected person.

Offences by Bodies Corporate

Aviation Security Act 1982, s. 37   **B10.86**

(1)   Where an offence under this Act . . . has been committed by a body corporate and is proved to have been committed with the consent or connivance of, or to be attributable to any neglect on the part of, any director, manager, secretary or other similar officer of the body corporate, or any person who was purporting to act in any such capacity, he as well as the body corporate shall be guilty of that offence and shall be liable to be proceeded against and punished accordingly.

(2)   Where the affairs of a body corporate are managed by its members, subsection (1) above shall apply in relation to the acts and defaults of a member in connection with his functions of management as if he were a director of the body corporate.

Related Offences

Ancillary Offences under s. 6(1)   Without prejudice to the jurisdiction provisions of **B10.87** the Civil Aviation Act 1982, s. 92 and the Aviation Security Act 1982, s. 2(1)(b), where a person (of whatever nationality) does on board any aircraft (wherever registered) and while outside the United Kingdom any act which, if done in the United Kingdom, would constitute the offence of murder, attempted murder, manslaughter, culpable homicide or assault, or an offence under the OAPA 1861, ss. 18, 21, 22, 23, 24, 28 or 29, or the Explosive Substances Act 1883, s. 2, his act constitutes that offence if it is done in connection with the offence of hijacking committed or attempted by him on board that aircraft. This offence may not be prosecuted except by, or with the consent of, the A-G (Aviation Security Act 1982, s. 8(1)).

Inducing or Assisting the Commission of ss. 1, 2 or 3   It is an offence for any **B10.88** person in the United Kingdom to induce or assist in the commission outside the United Kingdom of any act which would, but for the Aviation Security Act 1982, ss. 1(2), 2(4), 3(5) or (6), be an offence under ss. 1, 2 or 3 (s. 6(2)). The offence is triable on indictment only and is punishable with life imprisonment (s. 6(3)). It may not be prosecuted except by, or with the consent of, the A-G (s. 8(1)).

DESTROYING, DAMAGING OR ENDANGERING SAFETY OF AIRCRAFT

Definition

B10.89   **Aviation Security Act 1982, s. 2**

(1)   It shall, subject to subsection (4) below, be an offence for any person unlawfully and intentionally—

(a)   to destroy an aircraft in service or so to damage such an aircraft as to render it incapable of flight or as to be likely to endanger its safety in flight; or

(b)   to commit on board an aircraft in flight any act of violence which is likely to endanger the safety of the aircraft.

(2)   It shall also, subject to subsection (4) below, be an offence for any person unlawfully and intentionally to place, or cause to be placed, on an aircraft in service any device or substance which is likely to destroy the aircraft, or is likely so to damage it, as to render it incapable of flight or as to be likely to endanger its safety in flight; but nothing in this subsection shall be construed as limiting the circumstances in which the commission of any act—

(a)   may constitute an offence under subsection (1) above, or

(b)   may constitute attempting or conspiring to commit, or aiding, abetting, counselling or procuring, or being art and part in, the commission of such an offence.

Procedure

B10.90 Generally, the offences under the Aviation Security Act 1982, s. 2, apply whether any act covered is committed in the United Kingdom or elsewhere, whatever the nationality of the person committing the act and whatever the State in which the aircraft is registered (s. 2(3)). However, the offences do not apply to any act committed in relation to an aircraft used in military, customs or police service unless (a) the act is committed in the United Kingdom, or (b) where the act is committed outside the United Kingdom, the person committing it is a United Kingdom national (s. 2(4)).

Proceedings for such an offence cannot be instituted in England and Wales except by, or with the consent of, the A-G (s. 8(1)). The offence is triable on indictment only (s. 2(5)). It is a class 3 offence.

Sentence

B10.91 The maximum penalty is life imprisonment (Aviation Security Act 1982, s. 2(5)).

Elements

B10.92 Section 2(6) of the Aviation Security Act 1982 defines unlawfully for the purpose of the offence under s. 2(1). In relation to the commission of an act in the United Kingdom, it means so as (apart from the Act) to constitute an offence under the law of the part of the United Kingdom in which the act is committed. In relation to the commission of an act outside the United Kingdom, unlawfully means so that the commission of the act would (apart from the Act) have been an offence under the law of England and Wales or Scotland if it had been committed there.

'Act of violence' is defined in s. 2(7) as meaning (a) any act done in the United Kingdom which constitutes the offence of murder, attempted murder, manslaughter, culpable homicide or assault, or an offence under the Offences against the Person Act 1861, ss. 18, 20, 21, 22, 23, 24, 28, or 29, or under the Explosive Substances Act 1883, s. 2, and (b) any act done outside the United Kingdom which, if done in the United Kingdom, would be such an offence.

Section 38(3)(b) provides that an aircraft is to be taken to be in service during the whole of the period which begins with the pre-flight preparation of the aircraft for a flight and ends 24 hours after the aircraft lands having completed that flight, and also at any time (not falling within that period) while the aircraft is in flight. For the meaning of 'aircraft in flight' and 'United Kingdom national', see **B10.85**.

Related Offences

For the related offence of inducing or assisting the commission of an offence under the **B10.93** Aviation Security Act 1982, s. 2, see **B10.88**.

OTHER ACTS ENDANGERING OR LIKELY TO ENDANGER SAFETY OF AIRCRAFT

Definition

Aviation Security Act 1982, s. 3 **B10.94**

(1)   It shall, subject to subsections (5) and (6) below, be an offence for any person unlawfully and intentionally to destroy or damage any property to which this subsection applies, or to interfere with the operation of any such property, where the destruction, damage or interference is likely to endanger the safety of the aircraft in flight.

(2)   Subsection (1) above applies to any property used for the provision of air navigation facilities, including any land, building or ship so used, and including any apparatus or equipment so used, whether it is on board an aircraft or elsewhere.

(3)   It shall also, subject to subsections (4) and (5) below, be an offence for any person intentionally to communicate any information which is false, misleading or deceptive in a material particular, where the communication of the information endangers the safety of an aircraft in flight or is likely to endanger the safety of aircraft in flight.

Procedure

Proceedings for such an offence cannot be instituted in England and Wales except by, **B10.95** or with the consent of, the A-G (Aviation Security Act 1982, s. 8(1)). The offence is triable on indictment only (s. 2(5)). It is a class 3 offence.

Section 3(5) and (6) makes provision as to jurisdiction.

Aviation Security Act 1982, s. 3

(5)   Subsections (1) and (3) above shall not apply to the commission of any act unless either the act is committed in the United Kingdom or, where it is committed outside the United Kingdom—

(a)   the person committing it is a United Kingdom national; or

(b)   the commission of the act endangers or is likely to endanger the safety in flight of civil aircraft registered in the United Kingdom or chartered by demise to a lessee whose principal place of business, or (if he has no place of business) whose permanent residence, is in the United Kingdom; or

(c)   the act is committed on board a civil aircraft which is so registered or so chartered; or

(d)   the act is committed on board a civil aircraft which lands in the United Kingdom with the person who committed the act still on board.

(6)   Subsection (1) above shall also not apply to any act committed outside the United Kingdom and so committed in relation to property which is situated outside the United Kingdom and is not used for the provision of air navigation facilities in connection with international air navigation, unless the person committing the act is a United Kingdom national.

Sentence

The maximum penalty is life imprisonment (Aviation Security Act 1982, s. 3(7)). **B10.96**

Elements

'Property', by virtue of the Aviation Security Act 1982, s. 38(1), includes any land, **B10.97** buildings or works, any aircraft or vehicle and any baggage, cargo or other article of any description. 'Civil aircraft' means any aircraft other than an aircraft used in military, customs or police service (s. 3(8)).

'Unlawfully' has the same meaning as in s. 2, see **B10.78**. For the meaning of 'aircraft in flight' and 'United Kingdom national', see **B10.85**.

Specific Defence to Charge under s. 3(3)

B10.98

Aviation Security Act 1982, s. 3

(4)   It shall be a defence for a person charged with an offence under subsection (3) above to prove—
(a)   that he believed, and had reasonable grounds for believing, that the information was true; or
(b)   that, when he communicated the information, he was lawfully employed to perform duties which consisted of or included the communication of information and that he communicated the information in good faith in the performance of those duties.

Related Offence

B10.99   For the related offence of inducing or assisting the commission of an offence under the Aviation Security Act 1982, s. 3, see **B10.88**.

OFFENCES IN RELATION TO CERTAIN DANGEROUS ARTICLES

Definition

B10.100

Aviation Security Act 1982, s. 4

(1)   It shall be an offence for any person without lawful authority or reasonable excuse (the proof of which shall lie on him) to have with him—
(a)   in any aircraft registered in the United Kingdom, whether at a time when the aircraft is in the United Kingdom or not, or
(b)   in any other aircraft at a time when it is in, or in flight over, the United Kingdom or
(c)   in any part of an aerodrome in the United Kingdom, or
(d)   in any air navigation installation in the United Kingdom which does not form part of an aerodrome,
any article to which this section applies.

For the articles to which this section applies, see **B10.103**.

Procedure

B10.101   The offence is triable either way (Aviation Security Act 1982, s. 4(4)). It is a class 4 offence when tried on indictment.

Sentence

B10.102   The maximum penalty on conviction on indictment is imprisonment for a term not exceeding five years or a fine or both; on summary conviction, it is imprisonment for a term not exceeding three months, a fine not exceeding the statutory maximum or both (Aviation Security Act 1982, s. 4(4)).

Elements

B10.103   The articles to which the Aviation Security Act, s. 4, applies are specified in s. 4(2):
(a)   any firearm, or any article having the appearance of being a firearm, whether capable of being discharged or not;
(b)   any explosive, any article manufactured or adapted (whether in the form of a bomb, grenade or otherwise) so as to have the appearance of being an explosive, whether it is capable of producing a practical effect by explosion or not, or any article marked or labelled so as to indicate that it is or contains an explosive; and

(c) any article (not falling within either of the preceding paragraphs) made or adapted for use for causing injury to or incapacitating a person or for destroying or damaging property, or intended by the person having it with him for such use, whether by him or by any other person.

'Explosive' means any article manufactured for the purpose of producing a practical effect by explosion, or intended for that purpose by a person having the article with him. Firearm includes an airgun or air pistol (s. 38(1)).

Assistance in the interpretation of the phrase 'have with him' is provided by s. 4(3), which is not to be regarded as limiting it (s. 4(5)).

Aviation Security Act 1982, s. 4

(3)   For the purposes of this section a person who is for the time being in an aircraft, or in part of an aerodrome, shall be treated as having with him in an aircraft, or in that part of the aerodrome, as the case may be, an article to which this section applies if—
(a)   where he is in an aircraft, the article, or an article in which it is contained, is in the aircraft and has been caused (whether by him or by any other person) to be brought there as being, or as forming part of, his baggage on a flight in the aircraft, or has been caused by him to be brought there as being, or as forming part of, any other property to be carried on such a flight, or
(b)   where he is in part of an aerodrome (otherwise than in an aircraft), the article, or an article in which it is contained, is in that or any other part of the aerodrome and has been caused (whether by him or by any other person) to be brought into the aerodrome as being, or as forming part of, his baggage on a flight from that aerodrome or has been caused by him to be brought there as being, or as forming part of, any other property to be carried on such a flight on which he is also to be carried,
notwithstanding that the circumstance may be such that (apart from this subsection) he would not be regarded as having the article with him in the aircraft or in a part of the aerodrome, as the case may be.

For the meaning of 'aircraft in flight' and 'United Kingdom national', see **B10.85**. Section 38(1) provides that:

'air navigation installation' means any building, works, apparatus or equipment used wholly or mainly for the purpose of assisting air traffic control or as an aid to air navigation, together with any land contiguous or adjacent to any such building, works, apparatus or equipment and used wholly or mainly for purposes connected therewith.

ENDANGERING SAFETY AT AERODROMES

Definition

Aviation and Maritime Security Act 1990, s. 1   B10.104

(1)   It is an offence for any person by means of any device, substance or weapon intentionally to commit at an aerodrome serving international civil aviation any act of violence which—
(a)   causes or is likely to cause death or serious personal injury, and
(b)   endangers or is likely to endanger the safe operation of the aerodrome or the safety of persons at the aerodrome.
(2)   It is also, subject to subsection (4) below, an offence for any person by means of any device, substance or weapon unlawfully and intentionally—
(a)   to destroy or seriously to damage—
(i)   property used for the provision of any facilities at an aerodrome serving international civil aviation (including any apparatus or equipment so used), or
(ii)   any aircraft which is at such aerodrome but is not in service, or
(b)   to disrupt the services of such an aerodrome,
in such a way as to endanger or be likely to endanger the safe operation of the aerodrome or the safety of persons at the aerodrome.

As to s. 1(4), see **B10.105**.

Procedure

B10.105 Generally, the offences under the Aviation Security Act 1982, s. 1, apply whether any act covered by them is committed in the United Kingdom or elsewhere and whatever the nationality of the person committing the act (s. 1(3)). In the case of s. 1(2)(a)(ii), the offence does not apply to any act committed in relation to an aircraft used in military, customs or police service unless the act is committed in the United Kingdom or, where the act is committed outside the United Kingdom, the person committing it is a United Kingdom national (s. 1(4)).

Proceedings for such an offence cannot be instituted except by, or with the consent of, the A-G (s. 1(7)). The offence is triable on indictment only (s. 1(5)). It is a class 3 offence.

Sentence

B10.106 The maximum penalty is life imprisonment (Aviation and Maritime Security Act 1990, s. 1(5)).

Elements

B10.107 'Act of violence' means (a) any act done in the United Kingdom which constitutes the offence of murder, attempted murder, manslaughter, culpable homicide or assault, or an offence under the OAPA 1861, ss. 18, 20, 21, 22, 23, 24, 28, or 29, or an offence under the Explosive Substances Act 1883, s. 2, and (b) any act done outside the United Kingdom which, if done in the United Kingdom, would constitute such an offence (Aviation Security Act 1982, s. 1(9)). 'Aerodrome', by virtue of s. 1(9), has the same meaning as in the Civil Aviation Act 1982:

Civil Aviation Act 1982, s. 105(1)

'aerodrome' means any area of land or water designed, equipped, set apart or commonly used for affording facilities for the landing and departure of aircraft and includes any area or space, whether on the ground, on the roof of a building or elsewhere, which is designed, equipped or set apart for affording facilities for the landing and departure of aircraft capable of descending or climbing vertically.

By virtue of s. 1(9), 'United Kingdom national', 'unlawfully' and 'aircraft in service' have the same meaning as in the Aviation Security Act 1982 (see **B10.85** and **B10.92**).

HIJACKING OF SHIPS

Definition

B10.108
Aviation and Maritime Security Act 1990, s. 9

(1)   A person who unlawfully, by the use of force or threats of any kind, seizes a ship or exercises control of it, commits the offence of hijacking a ship, whatever his nationality and whether the ship is in the United Kingdom or elsewhere, but subject to subsection (2) below.

For s. 9(2), see **B10.109**.

Procedure

B10.109 Section 9(1) of the Aviation and Maritime Security Act 1990 has no jurisdictional boundaries except where the ship involved is a warship or any other ship used as a naval auxiliary or in customs or police service, in which case the offence can only be committed if (a) the person seizing or exercising control of the ship is a United Kingdom national, or (b) his act is committed in the United Kingdom, or (c) the ship is used in the naval or customs service of the United Kingdom or in the service of any police force in the United Kingdom (s. 9(2)).

Proceedings for such an offence cannot be instituted except by, or with the consent of, the A-G (s. 16(1)). The offence is triable on indictment only (s. 9(3)). It is a class 3 offence.

Sentence

The maximum penalty is life imprisonment (Aviation and Maritime Security Act 1990, **B10.110** s. 9(3)).

Elements

'Ship' is defined as meaning any vessel (including hovercraft, submersible craft and **B10.111** other floating craft) other than one which permanently rests on, or is permanently attached to, the seabed, or has been withdrawn from navigation or laid up (Aviation and Maritime Security Act 1990, s. 17(1)). 'Naval service' includes military and air force service (s. 17(1)).

By virtue of s. 17(2), 'United Kingdom national' has the same meaning as in the Aviation Security Act 1982 (see **B10.85**).

Offences by Bodies Corporate

Aviation and Maritime Security Act 1990, s. 50   B10.112

(1) Where an offence under this Act . . . has been committed by a body corporate and is proved to have been committed with the consent or connivance of, or to be attributable to any neglect on the part of, any director, manager, secretary or other similar officer of the body corporate, or any person who was purporting to act in any such capacity, he as well as the body corporate shall be guilty of that offence and shall be liable to be proceeded against and punished accordingly.

(2) Where the affairs of a body corporate are managed by its members, subsection (1) above shall apply in relation to the acts and defaults of a member in connection with his functions of management as if he were a director of the body corporate.

Related Offences

Proceedings for the following offences may be instituted only by, or with the consent of, **B10.113** the A-G (Aviation and Maritime Security Act 1990, s. 16(1)).

Ancillary Offences under s. 14(1) Where a person (of whatever nationality) does **B10.114** outside the United Kingdom any act which, if done in the United Kingdom, would constitute an offence of murder, attempted murder, manslaughter, culpable homicide or assault, or an offence under the OAPA 1861, ss. 18, 20, 21, 22, 23, 28 and 29, or an offence against the Explosive Substances Act 1883, s. 2, his act constitutes that offence if it is done in connection with an offence under the Aviation and Maritime Security Act 1990, ss. 9, 10, 11, or 12 committed or attempted by him (s. 14(1) and (2)). These provisions are without prejudice to the jurisdiction clauses of the Merchant Shipping Act 1995, ss. 281 and 282 or the Oil and Gas (Enterprise) Act 1982, s. 22 (Aviation and Maritime Security Act 1990, s. 14(3)).

Inducing or Assisting in Commission of s. 9 It is an offence for any person in the **B10.115** United Kingdom to induce or assist the commission outside the United Kingdom of any act which would, but for the Aviation and Maritime Security Act 1990, s. 9(2), be an offence under s. 9 (s. 14(4)(a)). The offence is triable on indictment only and the maximum penalty is life imprisonment (s. 14(5)).

Master's Power of Delivery

Section 15 of the Aviation and Maritime Security Act 1990 provides the master of a ship **B10.116** with the power to deliver a person to an appropriate officer in the United Kingdom or any other Rome Convention country where he has reasonable grounds to believe that

that person has (a) committed an offence under ss. 9, 11, 12 or 13, (b) attempted to commit such an offence, or (c) aided, abetted, counselled, procured or incited, been art and part in, the commission of such an offence.

OTHER OFFENCES UNDER THE AVIATION AND MARITIME SECURITY ACT 1990

B10.117 The Aviation and Maritime Security Act 1990 creates further offences under s. 10 (seizing or exercising control of fixed platforms), s. 11 (destroying ships or fixed platforms or endangering their safety), s. 12 (other acts endangering or likely to endanger safe navigation), and s. 13 (offences involving threats). All these offences are triable only on indictment and may be instituted only by or with the consent of the A-G. All carry a maximum penalty of life imprisonment.

Aviation and Maritime Security Act 1990, ss. 10, 11, 12, and 13

10.—(1)   A person who unlawfully, by the use of force or by threats of any kind, seizes a fixed platform or exercises control of it, commits an offence, whatever his nationality and whether the fixed platform is in the United Kingdom or elsewhere.

11.—(1)   Subject to subsection (5) below, a person commits an offence if he unlawfully and intentionally—
    (a)   destroys a ship or a fixed platform,
    (b)   damages a ship, its cargo or a fixed platform so as to endanger, or to be likely to endanger, the safe navigation of the ship, or as the case may be, the safety of the platform, or
    (c)   commits on board a ship or on a fixed platform an act of violence which is likely to endanger the safe navigation of the ship, or as the case may be, the safety of the platform.
    (2)   Subject to subsection (5) below, a person commits an offence if he unlawfully and intentionally places, or causes to be placed, on a ship or fixed platform any device or substance which—
    (a)   in the case of a ship, is likely to destroy the ship or is likely so to damage it or its cargo as to endanger its safe navigation, or
    (b)   in the case of a fixed platform, is likely to destroy the fixed platform or so to damage it as to endanger its safety.

12.—(1)   Subject to subsection (6) below, it is an offence for any person unlawfully and intentionally—
    (a)   to destroy or damage any property to which this subsection applies, or
    (b)   seriously to interfere with the operation of any such property.
where the destruction, damage or interference is likely to endanger the safe navigation of any ship.
    (3)   Subject to subsection (6) below, it is also an offence for any person intentionally to communicate any information which he knows to be false in a material particular, where the communication of the information endangers the safe navigation of any ship.

13.—(1)   A person commits an offence if—
    (a)   in order to compel any other person to do or abstain from doing any act, he threatens that he or some other person will do in relation to any ship or fixed platform an act which is an offence by virtue of section 11(1) of this Act, and
    (b)   the making of that threat is likely to endanger the safe navigation of the ship or, as the case may be, the safety of the fixed platform.
    (2)   . . . a person commits an offence if—
    (a)   in order to compel any other person to do or abstain from doing any act, he threatens that he or some other person will do an act which is an offence by virtue of section 12(1) of this Act, and
    (b)   the making of that threat is likely to endanger the safe navigation of any ship.

SECTION B11: OFFENCES AFFECTING PUBLIC ORDER

INTRODUCTION

The POA 1986 abolished a number of common-law offences, including riot, unlawful **B11.1** assembly and affray, replacing them with statutory offences of riot, violent disorder, affray, threatening behaviour etc. and disorderly conduct. It extended controls over processions and created controls over open-air assemblies. It expanded the law relating to incitement to racial hatred and provided for exclusion of certain offenders from sporting events, notably association football matches. This section also deals with surviving offences under the POA 1936 and the Unlawful Drilling Act 1819 and the common-law offence of public nuisance.

PROHIBITION OF QUASI-MILITARY ORGANISATIONS

Definition

Public Order Act 1936, s. 2   B11.2

(1)   If the members or adherents of any association of persons, whether incorporated or not, are—
  (a)   organised or trained or equipped for the purpose of enabling them to be employed in usurping the functions of the police or of the armed forces of the Crown; or
  (b)   organised and trained or organised and equipped either for the purpose of enabling them to be employed for the use or display of physical force in promoting any political object, or in such manner as to arouse reasonable apprehension that they are organised and either trained or equipped for that purpose;
then any person who takes part in the control or management of the association, or in so organising or training as aforesaid any members or adherents thereof, shall be guilty of an offence under this section.

Procedure

Offences under the POA 1936, s. 2, are triable either way (POA 1936, s. 7(1)). When **B11.3** tried on indictment they are class 4 offences. By virtue of s. 2(2), no prosecution shall be instituted without the consent of the A-G.

Public Order Act 1936, s. 2

(4)   In any criminal or civil proceedings under this section proof of things done or of words written, spoken or published (whether or not in the presence of any party to the proceedings) by any person taking part in the control or management of an association or in organising, training or equipping members or adherents of an association shall be admissible as evidence of the purposes for which, or the manner in which, members or adherents of the association (whether those persons or others) were organised, or trained, or equipped.

Indictment

Statement of Offence   B11.4

Taking part in the control or management [or organising or training members or adherents] of an association contrary to section 2(1)(a) of the Public Order Act 1936

Particulars of Offence

A between the . . . day of . . . and the . . . day of . . . took part in the management or control [or organising or training members or adherents] of an association, namely . . ., whose

493

members or adherents were organised, trained or equipped for the purpose of enabling them to be employed in usurping the functions of the police or the armed forces of the Crown

Sentence

B11.5   The maximum penalty is two years or a fine or both on indictment; six months or a fine not exceeding the prescribed sum or both summarily (POA 1936, s. 7(1)).

Specific Defences

B11.6   **Public Order Act 1936, s. 2**

> Provided that in any proceedings against a person charged with the offence of taking part in the control or management of such an association as aforesaid it shall be a defence to that charge to prove that he neither consented to nor connived at the organisation, training, or equipment of members or adherents of the association in contravention of the provisions of this section.

Furthermore, s. 2(6) provides that s. 2 does not prohibit the employment of a reasonable number of people as stewards to assist in the preservation of order at a public meeting held on private premises, or the making of arrangements for that purpose or the instruction of people to be so employed in their lawful duties as such stewards, or their being furnished with badges or other distinguishing signs.

Powers of High Court in Relation to Quasi-Military Organisations

B11.7   **Public Order Act 1936, s. 2**

> (3)   If upon application being made by the Attorney-General it appears to the High Court that any association is an association of which members or adherents are organised, trained, or equipped in contravention of the provisions of this section, the court may make such order as appears necessary to prevent any disposition without the leave of the court of property held by or for the association and in accordance with rules of court may direct an inquiry and report to be made as to any such property as aforesaid and as to the affairs of the association and make such further orders as appear to the court to be just and equitable for the application of such property in or towards the discharge of the liabilities of the association lawfully incurred before the date of the application or since that date with the approval of the court, in or towards the repayment of moneys to persons who became subscribers or contributors to the association in good faith and without knowledge of any such contravention as aforesaid, and in or towards any costs incurred in connection with any such inquiry and report as aforesaid or in winding-up or dissolving the association, and may order that any property which is not directed by the court to be so applied as aforesaid shall be forfeited to the Crown.

Under s. 2(5) a High Court judge may grant a search warrant with a view to seizing evidence of the commission of an offence under s. 2. The judge must be satisfied on information under oath that there is reasonable ground for believing that an offence under s. 2 has been committed, and that evidence of it may be found at the place specified in the information. Application must be made by a police officer of a rank not lower than inspector.

PROHIBITION OF UNLAWFUL DRILLING

Definition

B11.8   **Unlawful Drilling Act 1819, s. 1**

All meetings and assemblies of persons for the purpose of training or drilling themselves, or of being trained or drilled, to the use of arms of for the purpose of practising military exercise, movements or evolutions, without any lawful authority from Her Majesty or a

Secretary of State . . . shall be and the same are hereby prohibited and every person who shall be present at or attend any such meeting or assembly for the purpose of training or drilling any other person or persons to the use of arms or the practice of military exercise, movements or evolutions or who shall train or drill any other person or persons to the use of arms or the practice of military exercise, movements or evolutions, or who shall aid and assist therein, being legally convicted thereof, shall be liable to be imprisoned for any term not exceeding seven years . . . and every person who shall attend or be present at any such meeting or assembly as aforesaid, for the purpose of being, or who shall at any such meeting or assembly be trained or drilled to the use of arms, or the practice of military exercise, movements or evolutions, being legally convicted thereof, shall be liable to be punished by fine and imprisonment not exceeding two years.

Procedure

Offences under the Unlawful Drilling Act 1819, s. 1, are triable only on indictment. **B11.9** They are class 3 offences. Proceedings must be commenced within six calendar months after commission of the offence (Unlawful Drilling Act 1819, s. 7).

Sentence

The maximum penalties prescribed by the Unlawful Drilling Act 1819, s. 1, for offences **B11.10** under the section are:

(a)   for persons who have attended or been present for the purpose of training or drilling any other person or persons, or who have trained or drilled any other person or persons, or who have aided or assisted in the training or drilling of others: seven years;

(b)   for persons who have attended or been present for the purpose of being trained or drilled, or who have been trained or drilled: two years.

PROHIBITION OF UNIFORMS IN CONNECTION WITH POLITICAL OBJECTS

Definition

Public Order Act 1936, s. 1   **B11.11**

(1)   Subject as hereinafter provided, any person who in any public place or at any public meeting wears uniform signifying his association with any political organisation or with the promotion of any political object is guilty of an offence:

Provided that, if the chief officer of police is satisfied that the wearing of any such uniform as aforesaid on any ceremonial, anniversary, or other special occasion will not be likely to involve risk of public disorder, he may, with the consent of a Secretary of State, by order permit the wearing of such uniform on that occasion either absolutely or subject to such conditions as may be specified in the order.

Procedure

An offence under the POA 1936, s. 1(1), is triable only summarily (POA 1936, s. 7(2)). **B11.12**

Public Order Act 1936, s. 1

(2)   Where any person is charged before any court with an offence under this section, no further proceedings in respect thereof shall be taken against him without the consent of the Attorney-General except such as are authorised by [section 25 of the Prosecution of Offences Act 1985], so, however, that if that person is remanded in custody he shall, after the expiration of a period of eight days from the date on which he was so remanded, be entitled to be released on bail without sureties unless within that period the Attorney-General has consented to such further proceedings as aforesaid.

Sentence

The maximum penalty is three months or a fine not exceeding level 4 (POA 1936, **B11.13** s. 7(2)).

Uniform Signifying Association with a Political Organisation etc.

B11.14   In *O'Moran* v *DPP* [1975] QB 864 the Divisional Court held that the defendant was wearing a uniform when wearing a black beret, because that beret was worn by each member of the group to signify that he was a member of a group in association with others. The court took the view that the wearing of a uniform signifying the requisite association may be proved either by evidence showing that that uniform has been used in the past as that of a political organisation, in which case it is sufficient to show that it is associated with an organisation even if it is not possible to show exactly which organisation that uniform is to be identified with, or by evidence showing that the group in question assembled together wearing the uniform so as to indicate an association with each other and that, further, by their conduct it was indicated that the uniform associated them with political activity.

Meaning of 'Public Place' and 'Public Meeting'

B11.15   The concept of 'public place' in the POA 1936 was frequently litigated. All that litigation is relevant to the instant offence and also to the POA 1986, and probably also all other legislation in which a similar concept plays an important part.

Public Order Act 1936, s. 9

> (1)   In this Act the following expressions have the meanings hereby respectively assigned to them, that is to say:—
> . . .
> 'Public place' includes any highway and any other premises or place to which at the material time the public have or are permitted to have access, whether on payment or otherwise.

This is an incomplete definition. The question of whether a particular place is a 'public place' depends upon a number of factors as decided by a series of cases on the since repealed s. 5 of the POA 1936. (See also **B12.93**.)

Whether a place is a public place depends upon an assessment of the factual position at 'the material time'. Consequently, the Divisional Court decided in *Marsh* v *Arscott* (1982) 75 Cr App Rep 211 that a shop car park could not be a public place at 11.30 p.m. when the shop was shut. If at the material time, the public do have access as members of the public rather than under any other provision of law, s. 9 means that that place is a public place even if entry may be refused to certain people. Accordingly a public house was held to be a public place by the Divisional Court in *Lawrenson* v *Oxford* [1982] Crim LR 185. On the other hand the Court of Appeal in *Edwards* (1978) 67 Cr App R 228 held that the front garden of a house was not a public place because people have access only on an individual basis as lawful visitors. The Divisional Court in *Cawley* v *Frost* [1976] 1 WLR 1207 held that a place is a 'public place' even if the public are denied access to parts of it. Consequently, a football ground is a public place, even though members of the public are permitted only to go to certain areas and are denied access to other private areas.

Public Order Act 1936, s. 9

> (1)   In this Act the following expressions have the meanings hereby respectively assigned to them, that is to say:—
> . . .
> 'Meeting' means a meeting held for the purpose of the discussion of matters of public interest or for the purpose of the expression of views on such matters; . . .
> 'Public meeting' includes any meeting in a public place and any meeting which the public or any section thereof are permitted to attend, whether on payment or otherwise.

Related Offences

It is an offence, contrary to the Uniforms Act 1894, s. 3, to wear or to employ someone **B11.16** to wear, without permission, the uniform or other dress bearing any of the regimental or other distinctive marks of such uniform of Her Majesty's naval or military forces or the Air Force. The offence is punishable on summary conviction with imprisonment for a term not exceeding one month or a fine not exceeding level 3.

It is an offence, contrary to the Merchant Shipping Act 1970, s. 87(3), to wear the merchant navy uniform or any part of it or something resembling such uniform. The offence is punishable on summary conviction with a fine not exceeding level 3. There are, however, no regulations prescribing what the merchant navy uniform is.

It is an offence, contrary to the Police Act 1996, s. 90(2), for someone who is not a police officer to wear any article of police uniform, which includes distinctive badges, marks and documents, where it gives that person an appearance so resembling a member of a police force that it is calculated to deceive. The offence is punishable on summary conviction with a fine not exceeding level 3.

For offences relating to the use of uniforms to gain access to prohibited places (Official Secrets Act, 1920, s. 1(1)), see **B9.18** to **B9.23**.

RIOT

Definition

Public Order Act 1986, s. 1 **B11.17**

> (1) Where 12 or more persons who are present together use or threaten unlawful violence for a common purpose and the conduct of them (taken together) is such as would cause a person of reasonable firmness present at the scene to fear for his personal safety, each of the persons using unlawful violence for the common purpose is guilty of riot.
> (2) It is immaterial whether or not the 12 or more use or threaten unlawful violence simultaneously.
> (3) The common purpose may be inferred from conduct.
> (4) No person of reasonable firmness need actually be, or be likely to be, present at the scene.
> (5) Riot may be committed in private as well as in public places.

Procedure

Riot is triable only on indictment (POA 1986, s. 1(6)). It is a class 3 offence. A **B11.18** prosecution for riot or incitement to riot may be commenced only by, or with the consent of, the DPP (POA 1986, s. 7(1)).

Indictment

Statement of Offence **B11.19**

Riot contrary to section 1 of the Public Order Act 1986

Particulars of Offence

A on or about the . . . day of . . ., being one of 12 or more persons present together at . . . and using [or threatening] unlawful violence for a common purpose, namely . . ., used unlawful violence for the said common purpose by assaulting members of the public, the conduct of the 12 or more persons aforesaid, taken together, being such as would cause a person of reasonable firmness present at the scene to fear for his personal safety.

This form of indictment was approved by the Court of Appeal in *Tyler* (1992) 96 Cr App R 332 and *Jefferson* [1994] 1 All ER 270.

As to the importance of alleging the presence of the required 12 persons, see by analogy *Mahroof* (1989) 88 Cr App R 317 (a case concerned with violent disorder: see **B11.31** and **B11.34**). See also *Fleming* (1989) 153 JP 517; *Worton* (1989) 154 JP 201.

The POA 1986, s. 7(2), declares that for the purposes of the rules against charging more than one offence in the same count, each of sections 1 to 5 of the Act creates one offence.

Alternative Verdicts

B11.20   The POA 1986, s. 7(3), provides for alternative verdicts on charges under the Act without mentioning s. 1. However, the Criminal Law Act 1967, s. 6(3) (see **D16.18** to **D16.31**), would allow the jury on an indictment for riot to return an alternative verdict of guilty of violent disorder under the POA 1986, s. 2, or of affray under s. 3 (see also **B11.32**). It may, however, be prudent to add alternative counts.

Sentencing Guidelines

B11.21   The maximum penalty is 10 years or a fine or both (POA 1986, s. 1(6)).

Some general guidance on the gravity of public order offences, including riot, is to be found in *Caird* (1970) 54 Cr App R 499, a case, like several others cited below, decided in respect of common-law offences of public order which have been replaced by the statutory scheme in the POA 1986. In *Caird*, Sachs LJ said (at pp. 506–8) that:

> When there is wanton and vicious violence of gross degree the court is not concerned with whether it originates from gang rivalry or from political motives. It is the degree of mob violence that matters and the extent to which the public peace is being broken. . . .
>
> It has been suggested that there is something wrong in giving an appropriate sentence to one convicted of an offence because there are considerable numbers of others who were at the same time committing the same offence, some of whom indeed, if identified and arrested and established as having taken a more serious part, could have received heavier sentences. This is a plea which is almost invariably put forward where the offence is one of those classed as disturbances of the public peace — such as riots, unlawful assemblies and affrays. It indicates a failure to appreciate that on these confused and tumultuous occasions each individual who takes an active part by deed or encouragement is guilty of a really grave offence by being one of the number engaged in a crime against the peace. . . .
>
> In the view of this court, it is a wholly wrong approach to take the acts of any individual participator in isolation. They were not committed in isolation and, as already indicated, it is that very fact that constitutes the gravity of the offence.

In *Muranyi* (1986) 8 Cr App R (S) 176, the offender pleaded guilty to riot. He had been concerned in planning and instigating a number of attacks on football supporters. Between 30 and 150 people attacked visiting football supporters, a number of whom suffered serious injuries, including one who was stabbed in the neck with a bottle which severed an artery. Five years' imprisonment was upheld on appeal. Leggatt J, in the Court of Appeal, dealt with the argument that Muranyi had not been seen with a weapon on these occasions by saying that: 'He plainly was leading others who to his knowledge were equipped with the assortment of weapons to which we have referred'. In *Pilgrim* (1983) 5 Cr App R (S) 140, three offenders had been involved in a riot in which 100 youths, equipped with various weapons, had attacked a public house frequented by members of an opposing group, and subsequently attacked a number of people who were unconnected with the event, one of whom was killed. The first offender was convicted of manslaughter in respect of that, and received sentences totalling eight years. The other two received sentences of five years and three years respectively. The Court of Appeal upheld the sentences, Lord Lane CJ saying that:

> What the court has to pay regard to is the level of violence used, the scale of the riot or affray as described by the witnesses, the extent to which it is premeditated, or on the other hand spontaneously arises, and finally the number of people who are engaged in its execution. . . .

This case . . . is as good an example as any of how mob violence feeds upon itself, and how it is apt to, and very frequently does, end in catastrophic events, as the death of May indicates in the present case.

The case of *Sallis* (1994) 15 Cr App R (S) 281, which involved prisoners who took part in a riot at a remand centre, during which a prison officer was injured and the establishment was damaged to the extent of £1.3 million, illustrates the continuing importance of the sentencing principles stated above. Sentences of four and a half and five years were imposed on two of those involved.

Twelve or More Persons Present Using or Threatening Violence for a Common Purpose

It is immaterial whether or not the 12 or more use or threaten unlawful violence **B11.22** simultaneously (POA 1986, s. 1(2)). It is also immaterial (by s. 6(7)) whether all of the 12 or more intend to use violence or are aware that their conduct may be violent (the mental element in the offence of riot: see **B11.27**). In other words, a person may be guilty of riot even if some of the 12 or more co-rioters are not guilty of riot (or of violent disorder or affray) because of lack of *mens rea* (see **B11.34**). Common purpose may be inferred from the conduct of the rioters (POA 1986, s. 1(3)) together with such circumstances as the carrying of banners, shouting of slogans, threats and the like.

Defendant Must Use Violence

Each accused must use, rather than merely threaten, unlawful violence to be guilty (see **B11.23** *Jefferson* [1994] 1 All ER 270).

Meaning of 'Unlawful Violence'

Public Order Act 1986, s. 8   **B11.24**

In this part—
  . . .
    'violence' means any violent conduct, so that—
      (a)   except in the context of affray, it includes violent conduct towards property as well as violent conduct towards persons, and
      (b)   it is not restricted to conduct causing or intended to cause injury or damage but includes any other violent conduct (for example, throwing at or towards a person a missile of a kind capable of causing injury which does not hit or falls short).

As to the meaning of 'unlawful', see **B11.42**.

Consequences of the Use or Threat of Violence

Under the POA 1986, s. 1(1), riot occurs where a person of reasonable firmness present **B11.25** at the scene *would* be caused, not *was* caused, to fear for his personal safety. Further, s. 1(4) provides that: 'No person of reasonable firmness need actually be, or be likely to be, present at the scene' (see **B11.43**).

Place of Commission

Riot may occur in private as well as in public places (POA 1986, s. 1(5)).   **B11.26**

Mens Rea

A person is guilty of riot only if he intends to use violence or is aware that his conduct **B11.27** may be violent (POA 1986, s. 6(1)).

Effect of Voluntary, Self-induced Intoxication on *Mens Rea*

The POA 1986, s. 6, deals with the problem of whether a person's intoxication should **B11.28** be taken into account when determining that of which a defendant was aware.

Consequently, the problems encountered with the defence of self-induced intoxication (see **A3.9** to **A3.11**) and the effect of intoxication on mistakes which a person makes are of no direct concern in the offence of riot.

Public Order Act 1986, s. 6

(5) For the purposes of this section a person whose awareness is impaired by intoxication shall be taken to be aware of that of which he would be aware if not intoxicated, unless he shows either that his intoxication was not self-induced or that it was caused solely by the taking or administration of a substance in the course of medical treatment.

(6) In subsection (5) 'intoxication' means any intoxication, whether caused by drink, drugs or other means, or by a combination of means.

VIOLENT DISORDER

Definition

B11.29

Public Order Act 1986, s. 2

(1) Where three or more persons who are present together use or threaten unlawful violence and the conduct of them (taken together) is such as would cause a person of reasonable firmness present at the scene to fear for his personal safety, each of the persons using or threatening unlawful violence is guilty of violent disorder.

(2) It is immaterial whether or not the three or more use or threaten unlawful violence simultaneously.

(3) No person of reasonable firmness need actually be, or be likely to be, present at the scene.

(4) Violent disorder may be committed in private as well as in public places.

Procedure

B11.30 Violent disorder is triable either way (POA 1986, s. 2(5)). However, according to the *Practice Note (Mode of Trial: Guidelines)* (1995) (see **D3.7**), 'Cases of violent disorder should generally be committed for trial'. When tried on indictment, violent disorder is a class 4 offence.

Indictment

B11.31

Statement of Offence

Violent disorder contrary to section 2(1) of the Public Order Act 1986

Particulars of Offence

A on or about the . . . day of . . ., being one of three or more persons present together at . . . and using [or threatening] unlawful violence used [or threatened to use] unlawful violence by assaulting members of the public, the conduct of the three or more persons aforesaid, taken together, being such as would cause a person of reasonable firmness present at the scene to fear for his personal safety.

The POA 1986, s. 7(2), declares that for the purposes of the rules against charging more than one offence in the same count, each of sections 1 to 5 of the Act creates one offence.

Violent disorder is not committed unless there are three or more persons together. In *Mahroof* (1988) 88 Cr App R 317, the jury had acquitted two of the accused named in the indictment, but had convicted Mahroof. The Court of Appeal decided that there was a sufficient allegation in the indictment, even though no other persons were named, 'subject to two *very important* qualifications':

(a) 'that there is evidence before the jury that there were three people involved in the criminal behaviour, though not necessarily those named in the indictment', and

(b) 'that the defence are apprised of what it is they have to meet'.

The court made clear that the best way, and generally the only way, of satisfying the second qualification is by putting it in the indictment. This could be done by adding the phrase, after naming certain individuals, 'and others', which could have been pursued in this case by the defence seeking particulars, which would have led to the provision of information about two other people who were known about. In *Mahroof*, qualification (b) was not satisfied. This decision was followed in *Fleming* (1989) 153 JP 517 and was followed and applied by the Court of Appeal in *Worton* (1989) 154 JP 201, although the court seems to have been satisfied, perhaps too easily, that the defence was sufficiently apprised of the matter. It seems unsatisfactory that qualification (b) should be satisfied by the evidence given by the prosecution at the trial, rather than information provided in advance of the trial.

If one or more of the defendants may lack the *mens rea* for the offence, the determination of numbers is not affected (see **B11.34**).

Alternative Verdicts

Public Order Act 1986, s. 7   **B11.32**

    (3)   If on the trial on indictment of a person charged with violent disorder . . . the jury find him not guilty of the offence charged, they may (without prejudice to section 6(3) of the Criminal Law Act 1967) find him guilty of an offence under section 4.
    (4)   The Crown Court has the same powers and duties in relation to a person who is by virtue of subsection (3) convicted before it of an offence under section 4 as a magistrates' court would have on convicting him of the offence.

As to the operation of the POA 1986, s. 7(3), see *Mahroof* (1988) 88 Cr App R 317 and *Worton* (1989) 154 JP 201. Section 7(3) applies only where the jury has found the defendant not guilty, whether as a result of its own deliberations or as a result of following the judge's proper direction (*Carson* (1990) 92 Cr App R 236). The Criminal Law Act 1967, s. 6(3) (see **D16.18** to **D16.31**), may be resorted to where the defendant on arraignment pleads not guilty to an offence contrary to the POA 1986, s. 2 or 3, but wishes to plead guilty to an offence contrary to s. 4 (*O'Brien* (1992) 156 JP 925). The operation of the 1967 Act is unaffected by the POA 1986, so, on a charge of violent disorder, it is possible, provided the elements of the offence are established, to substitute a conviction, for example, of affray under s. 3 (see *Fleming* (1989) 153 JP 517). Particular attention must be paid to matters such as the different meanings of 'violence' in the offences (see *McGuigan* [1991] Crim LR 719 and see **B11.35** and **B11.43**). The same principles apply to finding a person guilty of an offence contrary to s. 4 in the alternative.

Sentencing Guidelines

The maximum penalty is five years, a fine or both, on indictment (POA 1986, s. 2(5));   **B11.33** six months, a fine not exceeding the statutory maximum, or both, summarily.

When dealt with summarily, the Magistrates' Association Guidelines (1997) indicate the following:

    Aggravating Factors ⊕
      For example racial motivation; busy public place; fighting between rival groups; large group; people actually put in fear; planned; vulnerable victims; weapon; offence committed on bail; previous convictions and failures to respond to previous sentences, if relevant.

    Mitigating Factors ⊖
      For example impulsive; nobody actually afraid; provocation.

    Guideline: Is it so serious that only custody is appropriate?

In *Cotter* (1989) 11 Cr App R (S) 102, the offenders were aged 21 and 19 and had been involved with about 150 youths causing a disturbance. Cotter also kicked out the window of a police van. Cotter had one previous finding of guilt and three previous convictions, whilst Farrell had one previous finding of guilt and one previous conviction. Sentences of 18 months' imprisonment and 18 months' detention in a young offender institution were reduced on appeal to four months' imprisonment and three months' detention, since the offenders had been sentenced on the basis that they had kicked a police officer, but that fact had never been clearly established. Custodial sentences were proper, however, since the offences were too serious to be dealt with by non-custodial penalties. Sentences of two years and 12 months were upheld in *Vanes* (1989) 11 Cr App R (S) 147, where the offenders had taken part in a fight in a public house between members of two families, one group having sought out and challenged the other. Between 10 and 15 men were involved, variously armed with pickaxe handles, the legs of stools and glasses. Damage to the value of £800 was done. See also *Alderson* (1989) 11 Cr App R (S) 301, where a sentence of 30 months was upheld in respect of a racially motivated attack by the offender, who had seven previous convictions, mainly for dishonesty, and three other men, upon a group of Jordanian students, who were punched, kicked, butted and struck with a chair. Eighteen months' imprisonment was upheld on three offenders of previous good character in *Watson* (1990) 12 Cr App R (S) 477. One of the offenders, who had witnessed the stabbing of a workmate, who eventually died from his wound, met co-defendants and went to the scene of the stabbing, the premises of a taxi firm, to exact revenge. They broke in and attacked a taxi driver and a 17-year-old female controller, who were unconnected with the stabbing incident. See also *Sturton* (1992) 13 Cr App R (S) 116, *Betts* (1995) 16 Cr App R (S) 436 and *Green* [1997] 2 Cr App R (S) 191.

Actus Reus

B11.34 ***Three or More People Present Together Using or Threatening Violence*** It is immaterial whether or not the three or more use or threaten unlawful violence simultaneously (POA 1986, s. 2(2)).

As stated at **B11.31**, it is essential to establish that three or more people were together using or threatening violence. In *Fleming* (1989) 153 JP 517, the Court of Appeal made it clear that a jury should be directed that 'if it cannot be sure that three or more of the defendants were using or threatening violence, then it should acquit every defendant, even if satisfied that one or more particular defendants were unlawfully fighting'. See also *McGuigan* [1991] Crim LR 719.

Usually, therefore, when only three are named in the indictment, the jury must acquit all three if they acquit one. This is not the case where the jury is satisfied that others not charged were taking part in the violent disorder in which case the jury may convict (*Worton* (1989) 154 JP 201). Account can be taken of such others only if the requirements established in *Mahroof* (1988) 88 Cr App R 317 (see **B11.31**) are satisfied.

Further, where one (or more) defendant is acquitted as a result of lack of *mens rea* (see **B11.36**), the determination of the number of persons is unaffected (POA 1986, s. 6(7)). Thus if one (or more) of the named defendants is found not guilty because he lacks *mens rea*, the remaining defendants may be found guilty, even if there are only two of them.

B11.35 ***Other Elements*** Unlike the offence of riot, it is not part of the definition of violent disorder that those present have a common purpose.

For the elements of unlawful violence, producing fear in a person of reasonable firmness, and place of commission, see the discussion of those elements in the offence of riot at **B11.24** to **B11.26**.

Mens Rea

Public Order Act 1986, s. 6   **B11.36**

(2)   A person is guilty of violent disorder . . . only if he intends to use or threaten violence or is aware that his conduct may be violent or threaten violence.

The *mens rea* is subjective, see **B11.69**. For the effect of voluntary, self-induced intoxication on *mens rea*, see the discussion in relation to the offence of riot at **B11.28**.

AFFRAY

Definition

Public Order Act 1986, s. 3   **B11.37**

(1)   A person is guilty of affray if he uses or threatens unlawful violence towards another and his conduct is such as would cause a person of reasonable firmness present at the scene to fear for his personal safety.

(2)   Where two or more persons use or threaten the unlawful violence, it is the conduct of them taken together that must be considered for the purposes of subsection (1).

(3)   For the purposes of this section a threat cannot be made by the use of words alone.

(4)   No person of reasonable firmness need actually be, or be likely to be, present at the scene.

(5)   Affray may be committed in private as well as in public places.

(6)   A constable may arrest without warrant anyone he reasonably suspects is committing affray.

Procedure

Affray is triable either way (POA 1986, s. 3(7)). According to the *Practice Note (Mode of* **B11.38** *Trial: Guidelines)* (1995) (see **D3.7**), cases of affray should be tried summarily unless the court considers that one or more of the following features is present in the case *and* that its sentencing powers are insufficient:

(a)   Organised violence or use of weapons.

(b)   Significant injury or substantial damage.

(c)   The offence has clear racial motivation.

(d)   An attack upon police officers, prison officers, ambulance men, firemen and the like.

When tried on indictment, affray is a class 4 offence.

Prosecutions for affray should be instituted only where the incident gives rise to serious disturbance to public order (Law Commission Report No. 123, para. 3.38, referred to in *Davison* [1992] Crim LR 31).

Indictment

Statement of Offence   **B11.39**

Affray contrary to section 3(1) of the Public Order Act 1986

Particulars of Offence

A on or about the . . . day of . . . used [or threatened] violence towards one V, the conduct of A being such as to cause a person of reasonable firmness present at the scene to fear for his personal safety

The POA 1986, s. 7(2), declares that for the purpose of the rules against charging more than one offence in the same count, each of sections 1 to 5 of the Act creates one offence.

Alternative Verdicts

B11.40   **Public Order Act 1986, s. 7**

    (3)   If on the trial on indictment of a person charged with . . . affray the jury find him not guilty of the offence charged, they may (without prejudice to section 6(3) of the Criminal Law Act 1967) find him guilty of an offence under section 4.

    (4)   The Crown Court has the same powers and duties in relation to a person who is by virtue of subsection (3) convicted before it of an offence under section 4 as a magistrates' court would have on convicting him of the offence.

It is important that the jury be properly directed as to the lesser offence, which it should consider only if it is unsure that affray has been committed (*Stanley* [1993] Crim LR 618). The differences between the offences may be crucial (see *Va Kun Hau* [1990] Crim LR 518, where s. 4 was not available because the act took place in a dwelling house).

As to the interrelationship between s. 7(3) and the Criminal Law Act 1967, s. 6(3), see **B11.32**.

Sentencing Guidelines

B11.41   The maximum penalty is three years, a fine, or both, on indictment (POA 1986, s. 3(7)); six months, a fine not exceeding the statutory maximum, or both, summarily.

When dealt with summarily, the Magistrates' Association Guidelines (1997) indicate the following:

Aggravating Factors ⊕
For example racial motivation; busy public place; group action; people actually put in fear; vulnerable victim(s); offence committed on bail; previous convictions and failures to respond to previous sentences, if relevant.

Mitigating Factors ⊖
For example offender acting alone; provocation; did not start the trouble; stopped as soon as the police arrived.

Guideline: Is it so serious that only custody is appropriate?

In *Holmes* [1999] 2 Cr App R (S) 100 two offenders, after an evening of heavy drinking, started a fight with another customer in a fish and chip shop, in which the victim was punched and kicked. They pleaded guilty in the magistrates' court to affray, and were committed for sentence. In light of personal mitigation, custodial sentences were reduced from 15 months to nine months by the Court of Appeal. In *Oliver* [1999] 1 Cr App R (S) 394, 12 months was appropriate for a man who admitted creating a disturbance on a transatlantic flight. He assaulted his wife, was abusive to a steward and behaved in a threatening manner. It was accepted that the offender had been under stress at the time, but the sentencer was right to take account of concern over the prevalence of such incidents. In *Williams* [1997] 2 Cr App R (S) 97, the affray took the form of a racially motivated disturbance involving a large number of men who had been drinking heavily after the Cup Final. There was a lot of shouting and bottles were thrown in the vicinity of a shop owned by an Asian family. Abusive racist remarks were made, but no physical injury was caused. A sentence of 12 months' imprisonment was appropriate.

Meaning of 'Threat' and 'Unlawful Violence'

B11.42   The essential elements of affray, according to the Court of Appeal, are '(a) the use or threat of violence by the defendant; (b) to another person; which (c) would cause a third person to fear for his or her own safety' (*Thind* [1999] Crim LR 842). For (a) and (b), see below. For (c), see **B11.43**. Lord Bingham CJ has described affray in *Smith* [1997] 1 Cr App R 14 at p. 16:

It typically involves a group of people who may well be shouting, struggling, threatening, waving weapons, throwing objects, exchanging and threatening blows and so on. Again, typically, it involves a continuous course of conduct, the criminal character of which depends on the general nature and effect of the conduct as a whole and not on particular incidents and events which may take place in the course of it. Where reliance is placed on such a continuous course of conduct, it is not necessary for the Crown to identify and prove particular incidents.

These 'typical activities' must amount to the use or threat of unlawful violence (POA 1986, s. 3(1)). The definition of 'violence' in affray is different from its definition for other purposes in POA 1986. By s. 8, violence, for affray, does not include violent conduct towards property. It is, therefore, limited to violent conduct towards persons. Otherwise, s. 8 provides:

> 'violence' means any violent conduct, so that—
> . . .
>
> (b)   it is not restricted to conduct causing or intended to cause injury or damage but includes any other violent conduct (for example, throwing at or towards a person a missile of a kind capable of causing injury which does not hit or falls short).

In *Rothwell* [1993] Crim LR 626, it was held that the word 'unlawful' is intended to ensure that defences such as self-defence apply to offences under the POA 1986 (see also *Key* (24 November 1992 unreported), *Afzal* [1993] Crim LR 791 and *Pulham* [1995] Crim LR 296).

Since a threat cannot be made by words alone (POA 1986, s. 3(3)), there must be conduct on the part of the accused; the fact that the experience was frightening does not make aggressive words sufficient (*Robinson* [1993] Crim LR 581). However, in *Dixon* [1993] Crim LR 579, ordering a dog to attack was sufficient to constitute a threat, because there was conduct, the dog being used as a weapon. Since the dog did attack, it is arguable that there was conduct but, had the dog not attacked, what would have been the conduct sufficient to satisfy s. 3(3)?

Whether there is a threat of unlawful violence is a question of fact. The mere possession of petrol bombs was capable of amounting to such a threat, but there would have to be threatening circumstances so that the simple possession of a weapon is not sufficient. The threatening circumstances might be, for example, having the weapons as a show of force or as a threatening spectacle (*M v DPP* [1999] All ER (D) 604, unreported in printed form).

The usage or threat of violence must be to someone (which could include police officers called to the scene) at or in the vicinity to whom the threat of violence could be directed even if they were of unknown identity (*M v DPP*). Only in this way is the requirement in s. 3(1) of 'another person' satisfied (see *Thind*).

The Test for Conduct Causing Fear

The test, as for riot and violent disorder, is whether a person of reasonable firmness **B11.43** present at the scene *would* be caused, not *was* caused, to fear for his personal safety. No person of reasonable firmness need actually be, or be likely to be, present at the scene (POA 1986, s. 3(4)).

In *Davison* [1992] Crim LR 31, the Court of Appeal, taking account of Law Commission Report No. 123, decided that the conduct to be considered is that of the defendant. Its consequences are judged by an objective standard, i.e. whether the hypothetical bystander of reasonable firmness (not the person assaulted) would be put in fear of his personal safety if he was there. Account may be taken of the nature of the premises and scene where the incident actually took place, and of the fact that the violence was limited to those involved and that others present were not afraid (*DPP* v *Cotcher* (1992) *The Times*, 29 December 1992). In *Sanchez* (1996) 160 JP 321, the Divisional Court approved the commentary of Professor Sir John Smith to *Davison* as being the correct approach: 'the question in the present case was not whether a person of reasonable firmness in [the victim's] shoes would have feared for his personal safety but whether [the] hypothetical person, present in the room and seeing [the accused's] conduct towards [the victim] would have so feared . . . [The offence] is designed for the protection of the bystander. It is a public order offence. There are other offences for the protection of persons at whom the violence is aimed'. The court commented that it thought that, even though the instant case might fit s. 3 (where S had lunged at V with a knife in a car parked in a car park in the middle of the night), it was not the most appropriate charge.

Mens Rea

B11.44

Public Order Act 1986, s. 6

(2)   A person is guilty of . . . affray only if he intends to use or threaten violence or is aware that his conduct may be violent or threaten violence.

The *mens rea* is subjective, see **B11.72**. For the effect of voluntary, self-induced intoxication on *mens rea*, see the discussion in relation to the offence of riot at **B11.28**.

FEAR OR PROVOCATION OF VIOLENCE

Definition

B11.45

Public Order Act 1986, s. 4

(1)   A person is guilty of an offence if he—
(a)   uses towards another person threatening, abusive or insulting words or behaviour, or
(b)   distributes or displays to another person any writing, sign or other visible representation which is threatening, abusive or insulting,
with intent to cause that person to believe that immediate unlawful violence will be used against him or another by any person, or to provoke the immediate use of unlawful violence by that person or another, or whereby that person is likely to believe that such violence will be used or it is likely that such violence will be provoked.
(2)   An offence under this section may be committed in a public or a private place, except that no offence is committed where the words or behaviour are used, or the writing, sign or other visible representation is distributed or displayed, by a person inside a dwelling and the other person is also inside that or another dwelling.
(3)   A constable may arrest without warrant anyone he reasonably suspects is committing an offence under this section.

Procedure

B11.46   An offence under the POA 1986, s. 4(1), is, by s. 4(4) of the Act, triable summarily only. The racially aggravated form of the offence is triable either way.

The POA 1986, s. 7(2), declares that for the purposes of the rules against charging more than one offence in the same information, each of ss. 1 to 5 of the Act creates one offence. The offence under s. 4 may be committed in one of four ways (*Winn* v *DPP* (1992) 156 JP 881, and see **B11.48**). Care must be taken in formulating the charge so that the way of committing the offence reflects the facts of the case, otherwise there may be unjustifiable variance between the charge and the particulars alleged. More than one way of committing the offence may be included and amendment is possible if necessary (*Winn* v *DPP*; *Loade* v *DPP* [1990] 1 QB 1052: for amendment, see Magistrates' Courts Rules 1981, r. 100 and **D19.7**).

The person towards whom threatening, abusive or insulting words or behaviour are used can be held to perceive the threatening words or behaviour when he does not give evidence at the trial (*Swanston* v *DPP* (1997) 161 JP 203). Of course, there must be other evidence, as there was in *Swanston* in view of the small area in which the incidents took place, and the evidence of the police constable.

Sentence

The maximum penalty is six months or a fine not exceeding level 5 or both (POA 1986, **B11.47** s. 4(4)).

The Magistrates' Association Guidelines (1997) indicate the following:

> **Aggravating Factors** ⊕
> For example group action; people put in fear; vulnerable victims; offence committed on bail; previous convictions and failures to respond to previous sentences, if relevant.

> **Mitigating Factors** ⊖
> For example minor matter; short duration.

> *Guideline*: Is it serious enough for a community penalty?

The Four Ways of Committing an Offence under s. 4

Common to all four ways of committing an offence under the POA 1986, s. 4, are (i) the **B11.48** use of threatening words or behaviour or the distribution or display of threatening, abusive or insulting writing etc. (see **B11.50** to **B11.53**) and (ii) the requirement as to *mens rea* in s. 6(3) (see **B11.54**). The four ways, as indicated in *Winn* v *DPP* (1992) 156 JP 881, are:

(a) the defendant must 'intend the person against whom the conduct is directed to believe that immediate unlawful violence will be used against him or another by [any] person' — as McCowan LJ put it in *Swanston* v *DPP* (1997) 161 JP 203, 'It is a vital component of the offence that it does not have to be shown that the other person believed: it has to be shown that the [accused] had the intention to cause that person to believe' that immediate unlawful violence would be used against him;

(b) the defendant must 'intend to provoke the immediate use of unlawful violence by that person or another';

(c) 'the person against whom [the words, behaviour, distribution or display] are directed is likely to believe that such violence will be used' (note that the person who must be caused to believe that violence will be used or threatened is the person to whom the words, behaviour, distribution or display are directed, see *Loade* v *DPP* [1990] 1 QB 1052);

(d) 'it is likely that such violence will be provoked'.

In paragraphs (c) and (d) above, 'such violence' means 'immediate unlawful violence' (see *Horseferry Road Metropolitan Stipendiary Magistrate, ex parte Siadatan* [1991] 1 QB 260).

Uses Towards

The Divisional Court in *Atkin* v *DPP* (1989) 89 Cr App R 199 held that the phrase 'uses **B11.49** towards' in the POA 1986, s. 4(1)(a), connotes the physical presence of the person to whom the words were used. That other person must perceive with his own senses the threatening words or behaviour (see also **B11.43**). In *Atkin* the conviction had to be quashed, since the person outside the dwelling was only aware of the threat because it was relayed to him by a Customs and Excise officer.

Threatening, Abusive or Insulting

B11.50 The phrase 'threatening, abusive or insulting words or behaviour' used in the POA 1986, s. 4(1)(a), is not defined in the Act. However, 'threatening, abusive or insulting' was used with reference to words or behaviour in the POA 1936, s. 5, and the Metropolitan Police Act 1839, s. 54(13).

The House of Lords in *Brutus* v *Cozens* [1973] AC 854 decided that 'insulting' is to be given its ordinary meaning and the question whether words or behaviour are insulting is a question of fact. The same approach is adopted with regard to the words 'threatening' and 'abusive' and the courts have adopted this approach in interpretation of the 1986 Act (*DPP* v *Clarke* (1991) 94 Cr App R 359, a decision on s. 5). In *Ambrose* (1973) 57 Cr App R 538, the Court of Appeal said that rude or offensive words were not necessarily insulting. The Divisional Court in *Masterson* v *Holden* [1986] 1 WLR 101 seems to have thought that conduct was insulting if it was unacceptable in public, so that it was able to uphold the conviction of two men for an offence under the Metropolitan Police Act 1839, s. 54(13), who had been kissing and cuddling each other at a bus stop on Oxford Street. Many people may find such conduct objectionable and even offensive, but it must be doubted whether, on its ordinary meaning, it can be described as insulting (or threatening or abusive). The Divisional Court in *Parkin* v *Norman* [1983] QB 92 held that masturbating in a public lavatory in the sight of a stranger, in this case a police officer, is conduct capable of being insulting because the stranger might be a heterosexual who would be insulted by such homosexual conduct. It must again be questioned whether such conduct is accurately described as insulting (or threatening or abusive) or whether the most accurate description might be that it is offensive, which is not sufficient to found a conviction under s. 4. However, the *Concise Oxford Dictionary* includes in its definition of 'insult', 'offend the self-respect or modesty of', and it may be that it is the affront to modesty which constituted the insult in *Masterson* v *Holden* and *Parkin* v *Norman*. In *Vigon* v *DPP* (1998) 162 JP 115, it was held that secretly filming people in a changing area where they tried on swimwear could amount to insulting behaviour. Whether such behaviour can properly be described as 'insulting' must again be questioned — it would seem better to have described it as a nuisance (although such behaviour falls outside the Act).

Meaning of 'Writing' and 'Display'

B11.51 'Writing' includes typing, printing, lithography, photography and other modes of representing or reproducing words in a visible form (Interpretation Act 1978, s. 5 and sch. 1). As to 'display', see **B11.69**.

Meaning of 'Immediate Unlawful Violence' and 'Violence'

B11.52 The Divisional Court in *Horseferry Road Metropolitan Stipendiary Magistrate, ex parte Siadatan* [1991] 1 QB 260 decided that it is not sufficient that conduct was likely to lead to violence at some unspecified time in the future. On the other hand, the court decided that 'immediate' does not mean 'instantaneous', so a relatively short time interval may elapse between the act and the violence. Further, the court decided that 'immediate' connotes proximity in both time and causation, that is, that the violence must result within a relatively short period of time without any other intervening occurrence. The court dismissed an application for judicial review of a refusal to issue a summons against Penguin Viking Books Ltd in connection with the publication of *The Satanic Verses* since it was not contended that immediate unlawful violence was thereby provoked. The Divisional Court held in *Valentine* v *DPP* [1997] COD 339 that the justices were entitled to find the defendant guilty where his threats caused a woman to fear 'immediate' violence the next time she went to work, but only because she might have gone to work the same night that the threat was made. As to the concept of immediacy in assault, see **B2.4**. As to the definition of 'violence' in the POA 1986, s. 8, see **B11.24**.

Place of Commission

Public Order Act 1986, ss. 4 and 8

B11.53

4.—(2)   An offence under this section may be committed in a public or a private place, except that no offence is committed where the words or behaviour are used, or the writing, sign or other visible representation is distributed or displayed, by a person inside a dwelling and the other person is also inside that or another dwelling.

8.   In this part—
   'dwelling' means any structure or part of a structure occupied as a person's home or as other living accommodation (whether the occupation is separate or shared with others) but does not include any part not so occupied, and for this purpose 'structure' includes a tent, caravan, vehicle, vessel or other temporary or movable structure.

'The other person' referred to in s. 4(2) is the same person as is referred to as 'another person' in s. 4(1)(a). Thus the offence is not committed in a dwelling if the only person to whom the words or behaviour are used, etc. (see **B11.49**) is also in that or another dwelling (*Atkin* v *DPP* (1989) 89 Cr App R 199). It appears to follow that the offence can be committed by the use of telephones and fax machines.

Where common parts (a communal landing) were the means of access to living accommodation, they were not part of a dwelling, even though access was via an entry phone system, and were not part of the living area or home (*Rukwira* v *DPP* [1993] Crim LR 882).

Mens Rea

The intention with which the defendant must act is to be found in s. 4(1) (see **B11.45**)   B11.54
as explained further at **B11.48**. Thus, the *mens rea* that must be proved is dependent upon which form of the offence is charged.

For all four forms of the offence, the following applies.

Public Order Act 1986, s. 6

   (3)   A person is guilty of an offence under section 4 only if he intends his words or behaviour, or the writing, sign or other visible representation, to be threatening, abusive or insulting, or is aware that it may be threatening, abusive or insulting.

Since the POA 1986, s. 6, deals with intoxication when determining that of which a defendant was aware, the general problems encountered with self-induced intoxication (see **A3.9** to **A3.11**), and the effect of intoxication on mistakes, are of no direct concern in this offence.

Racially Aggravated Offence

CDA 1998, s. 31, created a racially aggravated form of this offence. For the meaning of **B11.55**
'racially aggravated', see **B11.155**. The maximum penalty is raised, on trial on indictment, to a term of imprisonment for a maximum of two years or a fine or both, and, on summary trial, to a term of imprisonment for a maximum of six months or a fine not exceeding the statutory maximum or both (s. 31(4)). If, on trial on indictment, the jury find the defendant not guilty, it may find him guilty of the basic offence (s. 31(6)). As to the power of arrest, see s. 31(2). For sentencing in respect of this offence, see *Miller* [1999] 2 Cr App R (S) 392.

INTENTIONALLY CAUSING HARASSMENT, ALARM OR DISTRESS

Definition

Public Order Act 1986, s. 4A

B11.56

   (1)   A person is guilty of an offence if, with intent to cause a person harassment, alarm or distress, he—

(a)   uses threatening, abusive or insulting words or behaviour, or disorderly behaviour, or

(b)   displays any writing, sign or other visible representation which is threatening, abusive or insulting,

thereby causing that or another person harassment, alarm or distress.

Procedure and Sentence

B11.57   The offence is triable summarily only (POA 1986, s. 4A(5)). The racially aggravated form of the offence is triable either way.

The maximum penalty is a term of imprisonment not exceeding six months or a fine not exceeding level 5 on the standard scale or both (s. 4A(5)).

The Magistrates' Association Guidelines (1997) indicate the following:

Aggravating Factors ⊕
For example racial motivation; group action; victims specially targetted; high degree of planning; night time offence; weapon; offence committed on bail; previous convictions and failures to respond to previous sentences, if relevant.

Mitigating Factors ⊖
For example short duration.

Guideline: Is it so serious that only custody is appropriate?

Meaning of 'Harassment, Alarm or Distress' etc.

B11.58   Harassment, alarm or distress have not been defined, but it is assumed that they are ordinary words of the English language unless and until a definition is provided. The guidance on these words under the POA 1986, s. 5, supports this approach, see **B11.70**.

For the meaning of the phrase 'threatening, abusive or insulting', see **B11.50**. For the meaning of 'disorderly behaviour', see **B11.67**. For the meaning of 'writing', see **B11.51**. For the meaning of 'display' in the POA 1986, s. 5, see **B11.69**.

Place of Commission of Offence

B11.59   **Public Order Act 1986, s. 4A**

(2)   An offence under this section may be committed in a public or a private place, except that no offence is committed where the words or behaviour are used, or the writing, sign or other visible representation is displayed, by a person inside a dwelling and the person who is harassed, alarmed or distressed is also inside that or another dwelling.

As to the consideration of the similar provision in s. 5(2), see **B11.71**.

Mens Rea

B11.60   This is an offence requiring proof of an intention to cause harassment, alarm or distress (POA 1986, s. 4A(1)). As to the meaning of 'intention', see **A2.2**. For the effect of voluntary, self-induced intoxication on *mens rea*, see the discussion in relation to the offence of riot at **B11.28**.

Specific Defence

B11.61   **Public Order Act 1986, s. 4A**

(3)   It is a defence for the accused to prove—
(a)   that he was inside a dwelling and had no reason to believe that the words or behaviour used, or the writing, sign or other visible representation displayed, would be heard or seen by a person outside that or any other dwelling; or
(b)   that his conduct was reasonable.

Power of Arrest

B11.62   A constable may arrest without warrant anyone he reasonably suspects is committing this offence (POA 1986, s. 4A(4)).

Racially Aggravated Offence

CDA 1998, s. 31, created a racially aggravated form of this offence. For the meaning of **B11.63** 'racially aggravated', see **B11.155**. The maximum penalty is raised, on trial on indictment, to a term or imprisonment for a maximum of two years or a fine or both, and, on summary trial, to a term of imprisonment for a maximum of six months or a fine not exceeding the statutory maximum or both (s. 31(4)). If, on trial on indictment, the jury find the defendant not guilty, it may find him guilty of the basic offence (s. 31(6)). As to the power of arrest, see s. 31(2).

Alternative Offence

It is a summary offence, contrary to the CJA 1967, s. 91, where a person in any public **B11.64** place is, while drunk, of disorderly behaviour (see **B11.178**).

HARASSMENT, ALARM OR DISTRESS

Definition

Public Order Act 1986, s. 5

B11.65

> (1) A person is guilty of an offence if he—
> (a) uses threatening, abusive or insulting words or behaviour, or disorderly behaviour, or
> (b) displays any writing, sign or other visible representation which is threatening, abusive or insulting,
> within the hearing or sight of a person likely to be caused harassment, alarm or distress thereby.
> [(2) and (3) concern the place of commission of the offence and a specific defence.]
> (4) A constable may arrest a person without warrant if—
> (a) he engages in offensive conduct which a constable warns him to stop, and
> (b) he engages in further offensive conduct immediately or shortly after the warning.
> (5) In subsection (4) 'offensive conduct' means conduct the constable reasonably suspects to constitute an offence under this section, and the conduct mentioned in paragraph (a) and the further conduct need not be of the same nature.

Procedure

An offence under the POA 1986, s. 5(1), is, by s. 5(6) of the Act, triable summarily only. **B11.66** The racially aggravated form of the offence is also triable only summarily.

The POA 1986, s. 7(2), declares that for the purposes of the rules against charging more than one offence in the same information, each of sections 1 to 5 of the Act creates one offence.

Sentence

The maximum penalty is a fine not exceeding level 3 (POA 1986, s. 5(6)). **B11.67**

The Magistrates' Association Guidelines (1997) indicate the following:

Aggravating Factors ⊕
For example racial motivation; group action; vulnerable victim; offence committed on bail; previous convictions and failures to respond to previous sentences, if relevant.

Mitigating Factors ⊖
For example stopped as soon as police arrived; trivial incident.

Guideline: Is compensation, discharge or fine appropriate?

The guideline fine is £90 (low income), £225 (average income) or £540 (high income).

Threatening, Abusive or Insulting Words or Behaviour; Disorderly Behaviour; Writing

B11.68 For the meaning of the phrase 'threatening, abusive or insulting', see **B11.50**. This element of the offence and that of causing harassment, alarm or distress are separate and different; the two must not be equated. The approach in *Brutus* v *Cozens* [1973] AC 854 (i.e. that words should be given their ordinary meaning: see **B11.50**) should be adopted in considering the meaning of disorderly behaviour. The disorderly behaviour need not be threatening, abusive or insulting nor is it necessary to prove any feeling of insecurity in an apprehensive sense (*Chambers* v *DPP* [1995] Crim LR 896). For the meaning of 'writing', see **B11.51**.

Display

B11.69 The Divisional Court in *Chappell* v *DPP* (1988) 89 Cr App R 82 held that magistrates were correct to decide that the posting of an envelope, with writing containing abusive or insulting words concealed inside it, through a letter box could not amount to a 'display'. This approach might apply to envelopes containing threatening, abusive or insulting material even in public.

Person Likely to Be Caused Harassment, Alarm or Distress

B11.70 Harassment, alarm and distress are alternatives . 'Harassment' does not demand any element of apprehension about personal safety (*Chambers* v *DPP* [1995] Crim LR 896).

In *Lodge* v *DPP* (1988) *The Times*, 26 October 1988, the Divisional Court decided that whether a person was likely to be caused harassment, alarm or distress is a matter of fact to be determined by the magistrates. The court indicated that it is sufficient if the other person in question, in that case a police officer, feels alarm (or harassment or distress) for someone else, for example a child.

In *DPP* v *Orum* [1989] 1 WLR 88, the Divisional Court decided that, where the only people present were the defendant, his girlfriend with whom he was having an argument and two police officers, a police officer can be a person likely to be caused harassment, alarm or distress. However, if an officer is the only other person present and he is not likely to be caused harassment, alarm or distress, no offence is committed, because the element of causation is lacking. However, the Court of Appeal in *Ball* (1989) 90 Cr App R 378, without reference to *Orum*, was of the opinion that in such circumstances a police officer could arrest the person because he could have reasonable cause to suspect that an offence had been committed, since the conduct in s. 5 does not have to be directed towards another person.

Place of Commission of Offence

B11.71   **Public Order Act 1986, s. 5**

   (2)   An offence under this section may be committed in a public or a private place, except that no offence is committed where the words or behaviour are used, or the writing, sign or other visible representation is displayed, by a person inside a dwelling and the other person is also inside that or another dwelling.

The Divisional Court in *Chappell* v *DPP* (1988) 89 Cr App R 82 held that the delivery of a letter to a person within his or her own home, where he or she reads it and is alarmed or distressed by its contents, cannot be an offence under s. 5. Such conduct would constitute an offence contrary to the Malicious Communications Act 1988, s. 1(1).

Mens Rea

B11.72   **Public Order Act 1986, s. 6**

   (4)   A person is guilty of an offence under section 5 only if he intends his words or behaviour, or the writing, sign or other visible representation, to be threatening, abusive or insulting, or is

aware that it may be threatening, abusive or insulting or (as the case may be) he intends his behaviour to be or is aware that it may be disorderly.

Whether the defendant had the intention or awareness is to be tested subjectively in the light of the whole evidence, the burden of proof beyond a reasonable doubt lying upon the prosecution (*DPP* v *Clarke* (1991) 94 Cr App R 359). The defendant must intend the behaviour to be disorderly or be aware that it might be disorderly (*Chambers* v *DPP* [1995] Crim LR 896).

For the effect of voluntary, self-induced intoxication on *mens rea*, see the discussion in relation to the offence of riot at **B11.28**.

Specific Defence

Public Order Act 1986, s. 5	**B11.73**

(3)   It is a defence for the accused to prove—
   (a)   that he had no reason to believe that there was any person within hearing or sight who was likely to be caused harassment, alarm or distress, or
   (b)   that he was inside a dwelling and had no reason to believe that the words or behaviour used, or the writing, sign or other visible representation displayed, would be heard or seen by a person outside that or any other dwelling, or
   (c)   that his conduct was reasonable.

The burden of proving this defence lies on the defendant on the balance of probabilities (see **F3.4** and **F3.18**). An objective test must be used to assess the conduct referred to in s. 5(3)(c) (*DPP* v *Clarke* (1991) 94 Cr App R 359; *Kwasi Poku* v *DPP* [1993] Crim LR 705; *Morrow* v *DPP* [1994] Crim LR 58; *Lewis* v *DPP* (1996 unreported).

Power of Arrest

To amount to a warning, the police officer's instruction must convey the idea that, **B11.74** should the conduct be repeated or continued, the offender would be breaking the law. Whether a warning was given is decided as a matter of common sense taking account of all the relevant circumstances (*Groom* v *DPP* [1991] Crim LR 713).

Racially Aggravated Offence

CDA 1998, s. 31 created a racially aggravated form of this offence. For the meaning of **B11.75** 'racially aggravated', see **B11.155**. This definition has effect as if the person likely to be caused harassment, alarm or distress were the victim of the offence (s. 31(7)). The maximum penalty is raised to a fine not exceeding level 4 (s. 31(5)). As to the power of arrest, see s. 31(3).

Alternative Offence

See **B11.64**.   **B11.76**

PUTTING PEOPLE IN FEAR OF VIOLENCE

Definition

Protection from Harassment Act 1997, s. 4	**B11.77**

(1)   A person whose course of conduct causes another to fear, on at least two occasions, that violence will be used against him is guilty of an offence if he knows or ought to know that his course of conduct will cause the other so to fear on each of those occasions.

The CDA 1998, s. 32 creates a racially aggravated form of this offence which carries a higher maximum penalty. For the meaning of 'racially aggravated', see **B11.155**.

Procedure

B11.78 The offence is triable either way (Protection from Harassment Act 1997, s. 4(4)) and, when tried on indictment, is a class 4 offence. The racially aggravated form of the offence is also triable either way.

Section 4(5) provides that if, on trial on indictment for this offence, a person is found not guilty, the jury may find him guilty of the offence under s. 2 (see **B11.85** *et seq.*). If convicted of the offence under s. 2, the Crown Court has the same powers and duties in relation to that person as a magistrates' court would have on convicting him of the offence (s. 4(6)).

Sentence

B11.79 The maximum penalty is five years, a fine or both on indictment; six months, a fine not exceeding the statutory maximum or both summarily (Protection from Harassment Act 1997, s. 4(4)). In *Liddle* [1999] Crim LR 754, the Court of Appeal considered the approach to sentence for breach of a restraining order imposed by a court under s. 5 of the 1997 Act, following conviction under s. 4 or s. 2. Curtis J observed that relevant sentencing factors would be the relative seriousness and persistence of the offender's conduct, whether there was a history of disobedience to court orders, and the actual impact of harassment on the victim. The attitude of the offender was also relevant, such as where he had pleaded guilty, expressed remorse, and was willing to receive appropriate treatment or help.

Course of Conduct

B11.80   **Protection from Harassment Act 1997, s. 7**

> (3)   A 'course of conduct' must involve conduct on at least two occasions.
> (4)   'Conduct' includes speech.

How separate the two occasions must be remains to be seen. The nature of stalking, the activity which primarily created the need for the new offences, might mean that the occasions are likely to be on separate days, although it may be possible to differentiate activities on one day where they can be viewed as not being continuous. The further apart the incidents, the less likely it is that they will be regarded as a course of conduct.

'Conduct' would appear to allow different events to occur, but nevertheless may be regarded as contributing to a course of conduct.

As to the general approach to interpretation of this statute, see **B11.88**.

Violence

B11.81 'Violence' is not defined in the Protection from Harassment Act 1997. As to the similar, though not identical, concept defined for the purposes of the POA 1986, see **B11.24** and **B11.42**.

Mens Rea

B11.82   **Protection from Harassment Act 1997, s. 4**

> (2)   For the purposes of this section, the person whose course of conduct is in question ought to know that it will cause another to fear that violence will be used against him on any occasion if a reasonable person in possession of the same information would think the course of conduct would cause the other so to fear on that occasion.

Defences

B11.83   **Protection from Harassment Act 1997, ss. 4 and 12**

> 4.—(3)   It is a defence for a person charged with an offence under this section to show that—

(a) his course of conduct was pursued for the purpose of preventing or detecting crime,

(b) his course of conduct was pursued under any enactment or rule of law or to comply with any condition or requirement imposed by any person under any enactment, or

(c) the pursuit of his course of conduct was reasonable for the protection of himself or another or for the protection of his or another's property.

12.—(1) If the Secretary of State certifies that in his opinion anything done by a specified person on a specified occasion related to—

(a) national security,

(b) the economic well-being of the United Kingdom, or

(c) the prevention or detection of serious crime,

and was done on behalf of the Crown, the certificate is conclusive evidence that this Act does not apply to any conduct of that person on that occasion.

In s. 12, 'specified' means specified in the certificate in question (s. 12(2)). A document purporting to be such a certificate is to be received in evidence and, unless the contrary is proved, treated as being such a certificate (s. 12(3)). For consideration of when the course of conduct may be reasonable, see **B11.90**.

Racially Aggravated Offence

CDA 1998, s. 32, created a racially aggravated form of this offence. For the meaning of **B11.84** 'racially aggravated', see **B11.155**. The maximum penalty is raised, on trial on indictment, to a term or imprisonment for a maximum of seven years or a fine or both, and, on summary trial, to a term of imprisonment for a maximum of six months or a fine not exceeding the statutory maximum or both (s. 32(4)). If, on trial on indictment, the jury find the defendant not guilty, it may find him guilty of racially aggravated harassment (s. 32 (6)). A restraining order under PHA 1997, s. 5, may be made (s. 32(7)).

OFFENCE OF HARASSMENT

Definition

Protection from Harassment Act 1997, ss. 1 and 2   **B11.85**

1.—(1) A person must not pursue a course of conduct—

(a) which amounts to harassment of another, and

(b) which he knows or ought to know amounts to harassment of the other.

2.—(1) A person who pursues a course of conduct in breach of section 1 is guilty of an offence.

See **B11.79** for the definition of 'course of conduct'.

Procedure

The offence is triable summarily only (Protection from Harassment Act 1997, s. 2(2)). **B11.86** The racially aggravated form of the offence is triable either way.

Sentence

The maximum penalty is a term of imprisonment not exceeding six months or a fine not **B11.87** exceeding level 5 on the standard scale or both (Protection from Harassment Act 1997, s. 2(2)). See further **B11.79**.

Harassment

Protection from Harassment Act 1997, s. 7   **B11.88**

(1) References to harassing a person include alarming the person or causing the person distress.

For concepts similar to, if not identical with, 'harassment', 'alarm' and 'distress' in the 1997 Act, see the POA 1986, ss. 4A and 5 and **B11.58** and **B11.70**. The courts, in view of the individual's right to protest and demonstrate about issues of public interest, will resist any attempts to interpret the statute widely (*Huntingdon Life Sciences Ltd* v *Curtin* (1997) *The Times*, 11 December 1997). However, 'whatever may have been the purpose behind [the Act], its words are clear, and it can cover harassment of any sort' (*DPP* v *Moseley* [1999] All ER (D) 587, unreported in printed form, per Collins J). This is subject to the defences mentioned at **B11.90**, one of which was the issue in *Moseley*.

Mens Rea

B11.89 The *mens rea* for this offence, as defined in the Protection from Harassment Act 1997, s. 1(1)(b), is that the accused know or ought to know that the course of conduct amounts to harassment of the other. Assistance in understanding, and thus determining, when a defendant ought so to know is provided by s. 1(2).

Protection from Harassment Act 1997, s. 1

(2)   For the purposes of this section, the person whose course of conduct is in question ought to know that it amounts to harassment of another if a reasonable person in possession of the same information would think the course of conduct amounted to harassment of the other.

Lawful Courses of Conduct

B11.90 #### Protection from Harassment Act 1997, s. 1

(3)   Subsection (1) does not apply to a course of conduct if the person who pursued it shows—
(a)   that it was pursued for the purpose of preventing or detecting crime;
(b)   that it was pursued under any enactment or rule of law or to comply with any condition or requirement imposed by any person under any enactment, or
(c)   that in the particular circumstances the pursuit of the course of conduct was reasonable.

It would appear not to be sufficient for the defendant to show that it was either his opinion that one of these conditions was satisfied or that it was reasonable to believe that one of these conditions was satisfied, although reasonableness may enter the calculation through the requirements needed to satisfy s. 1(3)(a) and (b) (see, e.g., the Criminal Law Act 1967, s. 3(1), and the PACE 1984, s. 24). Further, the requirement of reasonableness in pursuing the course of conduct is likely to amount to the same thing as the defendant having a reasonable belief, although it is technically a distinct requirement.

In *DPP* v *Moseley* [1999] All ER (D) 587, unreported in printed form, the Divisional Court considered the relevance of an injunction to the question of whether the course of conduct being pursued by M and S was reasonable. The injunction was in force against S (and others), but not against M. The terms of the injunction were crucial. It endeavoured to prevent harassment (defined as in the 1997 Act) of H and his family. Thus it was difficult to see how the course of conduct in contravention of the injunction and being harassment could be reasonable. There might be circumstances in which it was necessary for those covered by the injunction to go on to the other's land, but to make this of relevance they would have to explain away a course of conduct and not merely one emergency entry on to that land. In the case of M, it was not sufficient to be aware of the existence of the injunction. M would have to be aware of its specific terms. M was not sufficiently aware, and so the defence of reasonableness of the course of conduct was open for consideration. In the balancing exercise to determine reasonableness, the existence, in general terms, of the injunction would be relevant, though it would have little impact. On a more general level, when engaging in the balancing of different interests (such as the right of peaceful protest and the right to quiet enjoyment of property) the courts may have to get involved in the same sort of exercise as occurs when considering the exercise of the police powers to prevent a breach of the peace. It does not follow that it is always the first party's rights that are protected (e.g., to process). They may, in effect, be held responsible for the reaction of the other party. Priority will, however, always be given, where possible, to lawful activity that is not (deliberately) provocative. For a recent consideration of this problem, see *Redmond-Bate* v *DPP* (1999) *The Times*, 28 July 1999). See **B11.121**.

For the special defence to national security etc., see s. 12 at **B11.83**.

Power of Arrest

This offence is specifically made into an arrestable offence within the meaning of the **B11.91** PACE 1984, s. 24 (PACE 1984, s. 24(2)(n), inserted by the Protection from Harassment Act 1997, s. 2(3)).

Racially Aggravated Offence

CDA 1998, s. 32, created a racially aggravated form of this offence. For the meaning of **B11.92** 'racially aggravated', see **B11.155**. The maximum penalty is raised, on trial on indictment, to a term or imprisonment for a maximum of two years or a fine or both, and, on summary trial, to a term of imprisonment for a maximum of six months or a fine not exceeding the statutory maximum or both (s. 32(3)). If, on trial on indictment, the jury find the defendant not guilty it may find him guilty of the basic offence (s. 32(5)). This offence is an arrestable offence within the meaning of the PACE 1984, s. 24 (PACE 1984, s. 24(2)(p)). A restraining order under PHA 1997, s. 5, may be made (s. 32(7)).

Related Offence

The Protection from Harassment Act 1997, s. 3(6), makes it an offence, where the High **B11.93** Court or a county court has granted an injunction under s. 3(3)(a) (which may be imposed to restrain the defendant in a claim in civil proceedings by a person who is the victim of harassment within s. 1 from pursuing any conduct which amounts to harassment), for a person, without reasonable excuse, to do anything which he is prohibited from doing by such an injunction. Such conduct is not punishable as a contempt of court (s. 3(7)) nor can a person be convicted of this offence for any conduct which has been punished as a contempt of court (s. 3(8)). A person guilty of this offence is liable, on conviction on indictment, to imprisonment for a term not exceeding five years or a fine or both; and, on summary conviction, to imprisonment for a term not exceeding six months or a fine not exceeding the statutory maximum or both (s. 3(9)).

PUBLIC NUISANCE

Definition

In recent times, the Court of Appeal has expressed approval of the following definitions **B11.94** of public nuisance:

> A common nuisance is an act not warranted by law or an omission to discharge a legal duty, which act or omission obstructs or causes inconvenience or damage to the public in the exercise of rights common to all of His Majesty's subjects. (*Stephen's Digest of Criminal Law*, confirmed in *A-G* v *PYA Quarries Ltd* [1957] 2 QB 169, per Romer LJ, *Madden* [1975] 1 WLR 1379 and *Shorrock* [1994] QB 279.)

> Nuisance, nocumentum, or annoyance, signifies anything that worketh hurt, inconvenience, or damage. And nuisances are of two kinds; public or common nuisances, which affect the public, and are an annoyance to all the King's subjects; for which reason we must refer them to the class of public wrongs, or crimes and misdemeanours; and private

nuisances, which are the objects of our present consideration, and may be defined, anything done to the hurt or annoyance of the lands, tenements or hereditaments of another. (*Blackstone's Commentaries*, confirmed in *A-G* v *PYA Quarries Ltd* [1957] 2 QB 169 and quoted, with apparent approval, in *Shorrock* [1994] QB 279.)

Procedure

B11.95 It is a common-law offence, triable either way, for a person to cause a public nuisance. When tried on indictment, it is a class 4 offence.

Sentence

B11.96 On conviction on indictment, the maximum sentence is at the discretion of the court. On summary conviction, the statutory maxima apply. Reported sentencing cases indicate a range of circumstances in which the offence of public nuisance has been charged in the past. In *Millward* (1986) 8 Cr App R (S) 209, a sentence of 30 months' imprisonment was upheld by the Court of Appeal in a case of harassment by persistent telephoning of a woman. The offender had been placed on probation three times and had received several suspended and immediate custodial sentences, but after each one he reverted to the same behaviour. No suitable psychiatric treatment could be recommended. In *Ruffell* (1992) 13 Cr App R (S) 204, the offender organised an 'acid house' party in unsuitable premises which was attended by a large number of people. A road leading to the site was blocked by traffic, local residents were disturbed by noise throughout the night, and litter and excrement were deposited in adjoining woodlands. A 12-month suspended prison sentence was upheld by the Court of Appeal but a fine imposed in addition was quashed because of the offender's lack of means. See also *Taylor* (1992) 13 Cr App R (S) 466, a comparable case, where the Court of Appeal quashed a suspended sentence and said that the proper penalty was a fine of £5,000.

Private and Public Nuisance

B11.97 The torts and the crime are closely connected: 'public nuisance is defined by reference to private nuisance and as differing from private nuisance only in the range of its effect' (*Shorrock* [1994] QB 279). A further difference appears in the judgment of Denning LJ in *A-G* v *PYA Quarries Ltd* [1957] 2 QB 169 (at p. 192): 'I quite agree that a private nuisance always involves some degree of repetition or continuance . . . But an isolated act may amount to a public nuisance if it is done under such circumstances that the public right to condemn it should be vindicated'.

Where someone suffers particular damage as a result of a public nuisance they may sue in tort for public nuisance.

Nuisance

B11.98 There must be conduct by the accused which 'renders the enjoyment of life and property uncomfortable' (*White* (1775) 1 Burr 333, per Lord Mansfield) or 'materially affects the reasonable comfort and convenience of a class of Her Majesty's subjects' (*A-G* v *PYA Quarries Ltd* [1957] 2 QB 169, approved by the Court of Appeal in *Johnson* [1996] 2 Cr App R 434).

Professor Sir John Smith has stated that 'the interference with the public's rights must be substantial and unreasonable ' (*Smith and Hogan on Criminal Law* (9th ed., 1999) at p. 755). Thus, as he points out, not all obstructions of the highway amount to a public nuisance (see, e.g., *Dwyer* v *Mansfield* [1946] KB 437 and *DPP* v *Jones* [1999] 2 AC 240).

Criminal convictions have for example been successful in the following circumstances:

(a) the accused was responsible for a house which was ruinous and likely to fall down thus endangering people using the highway (*Watts* (1757) 1 Salkeld 357);

(b)   the accused carried her child whilst infected with smallpox along the public highway, thus incurring the risk of infecting others (*Vantandillo* (1815) 4 M & S 73);

(c)   the accused took a horse infected with a contagious disease along the highway thus risking infecting others (*Henson* (1852) Dears 24);

(d)   the accused sold meat unfit for human consumption (*Stephens* (1866) LR 1 QB 702);

(e)   the accused caused 30 houses and the highway to be affected by dust and noise from its quarry (*A-G* v *PYA Quarries Ltd* [1957] 2 QB 169);

(f)   the accused sniffed glue in a school playground when staff and pupils were absent (*Sykes* v *Homes* [1985] Crim LR 791, holding that it was a nuisance within the Local Government (Miscellaneous Provisions) Act 1982, s. 40 — whether it would be a public nuisance would depend upon the public nature of the nuisance);

(g)   the accused allowed a rave to take place in his field (*Shorrock* [1994] QB 279);

(h)   the accused made hundreds of telephone calls to at least 13 women in South Cumbria (*Johnson* [1996] 2 Cr App R 434).

Act or Omission

It is clear that a public nuisance may be caused by either an act (see, e.g., *Vantandillo* **B11.99** (1815) 4 M & S 73 and *A-G* v *PYA Quarries Ltd* [1957] 2 QB 169) or an omission (see, e.g., *Watts* (1757) 1 Salkeld 357 and *Shorrock* [1994] QB 279; see also *A-G* v *Tod Heatley* [1897] 1 Ch 560, where it was held that it was the duty of the owner of land to prevent it from being used as a dumping ground which caused a public nuisance).

The Public Nature of the Nuisance

In order to establish that a crime has been committed, it is necessary to establish the **B11.100** essential public nature of the nuisance. It is clear that not all the public need be affected. But it must be established that the act or omission was sufficiently widespread or indiscriminate as to amount to a public rather than a private nuisance. In *A-G* v *PYA Quarries Ltd* [1957] 2 QB 169, Romer LJ stated:

> any nuisance is 'public' which materially affects the reasonable comfort and convenience of life of a class of Her Majesty's subjects. The sphere of the nuisance may be described generally as 'the neighbourhood'; but the question whether the local community within that sphere comprises sufficient number of persons to constitute a class of the public is a question of fact in every case. It is not necessary, in my judgment, to prove that every member of the class has been injuriously affected; it is sufficient to show that a representative cross-section of the class has been so affected for an injunction to issue.

In the same case, Denning LJ said, 'a public nuisance is a nuisance which is so widespread in its range or so indiscriminate in its effect that it would not be reasonable to expect one person to take proceedings on his own responsibility to put a stop to it, but that it should be taken on the responsibility of the community at large'. In that case, there was a public nuisance where 30 houses and the highway were affected by dust and noise from the workings of a quarry (see also *Mutters* (1864) Le & Ca 491).

In *Johnson* [1996] 2 Cr App R 434, the Court of Appeal took the view that, provided the scale of the undoubted nuisance is sufficient, it is capable of constituting a public nuisance. In that case it was accepted that the making of hundreds of telephone calls to at least 13 women in South Cumbria, who had been indiscriminately selected by the defendant, was capable of amounting to a public nuisance. The court said that whether there was a sufficient number of persons complaining about the calls to amount to a public nuisance was a question for the jury to decide following proper directions, as given in that case. In *Madden* [1975] 1 WLR 1379, however, the court decided that a bomb hoax call could not amount to a public nuisance because it affected only one factory and eight security officers (for the bomb hoax offence, see **B11.104**). A similar problem lead to the acquittal of the defendant in *Lloyd, ex parte Allen* (1802) 4 Esp 200, where Lord Ellenborough decided that the fact that the nuisance affected only three members of Clifford's Inn was insufficient to support the required public nature of the nuisance.

Mens Rea

B11.101 The 'requirement as to the accused's state of mind is the same whether the proceedings brought be civil or criminal. Actual knowledge of the nuisance need not be established'. The *mens rea*, therefore, is that the defendant is 'guilty of the offence charged if either he knew or he ought to have known, in the sense that the means of knowledge were available to him, that there was a real risk that the consequences of the licence granted by [the accused] in respect of his field [on which a rave took place] would be to create the sort of nuisance that in fact occurred' (*Shorrock* [1994] QB 279). It remains to be seen whether the objective mental element identified in this passage is open to challenge.

Vicarious Liability

B11.102 For the ordinary rules relating to vicarious liability, see **A4.4**. However, a master may be liable for a public nuisance even if the act of the servant is contrary to the master's orders (see *Stephens* (1866) LR 1 QB 702 and *Smith and Hogan on Criminal Law* (9th ed., 1999), p. 757). The decision in *Stephens* was doubted in *Chisholm v Doulton* (1889) 22 QBD 736. It remains to be seen whether such a rule will continue to apply and, if so, if it will apply consistently to all forms of public nuisance (a view the decision in *Shorrock* [1994] QB 279 may be interpreted as implicitly supporting, see *Smith and Hogan on Criminal Law*, p. 757).

Defences

B11.103 Statutory authorisation is a defence to public nuisance, provided that the statute covers that which is done (see *Hammersmith and City Railway Company v Brand and Louisa* (1868) LR 4 QB 171, *Managers of the Metropolitan Asylum District v Hill* (1881) LR 6 AC 193, *London, Brighton and South Coast Railway v Truman* (1885) LR 11 AC 45 and *Saunders v Holborn District Board of Works* [1895] 1 QB 64).

BOMB HOAXES

Definition

B11.104   **Criminal Law Act 1977, s. 51**

    (1)   A person who—
        (a)   places any article in any place whatever; or
        (b)   dispatches any article by post, rail or any other means whatever of sending things from one place to another,
with the intention (in either case) of inducing in some other person a belief that it is likely to explode or ignite and thereby cause personal injury or damage to property is guilty of an offence.
    In this subsection 'article' includes substance.
    (2)   A person who communicates any information which he knows or believes to be false to another person with the intention of inducing in him or any other person a false belief that a bomb or other thing liable to explode or ignite is present in any place or location whatever is guilty of an offence.

Procedure

B11.105 Offences under the Criminal Law Act 1977, s. 51, are triable either way. When tried on indictment they are class 4 offences.

Indictment

B11.106

First Count
Statement of Offence

Perpetrating bomb hoax contrary to section 51(1) of the Criminal Law Act 1977

Particulars of Offence

A on or about the . . . day of . . . placed an article, namely a parcel, in [or: dispatched by post (or rail etc.) an article, namely a parcel, to] the Dead Parrot Public House at . . . with the intention of inducing in V, the manager of the said house, a belief that the said parcel was likely to explode or ignite and thereby cause personal injury or damage to property therein

Second Count
Statement of Offence

Perpetrating bomb hoax contrary to section 51(2) of the Criminal Law Act 1977

Particulars of Offence

A on or about the . . . day of . . . communicated to V the information that a parcel containing a bomb liable to explode or ignite was present on the premises of the Dead Parrot Public House at . . ., knowing or believing the said information to be false and with the intention of inducing in V the false belief that it was true

Sentencing Guidelines

The maximum penalty is seven years on indictment; six months, a fine not exceeding the **B11.107** statutory maximum, or both, summarily (Criminal Law Act 1977, s. 51(4)).

In *Harrison* [1997] 2 Cr App R (S) 174, a sentence of four years' imprisonment was upheld on an offender who made a series of telephone calls to a theatre saying that a bomb had been planted. The offender had previous convictions for similar offences and was said to be suffering from a personality disorder but not mental illness. In *Dunbar* (1987) 9 Cr App R (S) 393, the offenders pleaded guilty to communicating a bomb hoax. They telephoned the police to say that incendiary devices had been placed in various stores, apparently in order to cause financial loss to the stores. Sentences of 12 months' imprisonment were upheld by the Court of Appeal, Leggatt J commenting that:

> A bomb hoax of this kind, as this court has had occasion to say in the past, is a public nuisance, and it is important not to underrate the anxiety and apprehension that this kind of behaviour engenders. The public rightly expect judges to pass severe sentences as a mark of public disapprobation of this kind of offence.

The Court of Appeal in *Wilburn* (1992) 13 Cr App R (S) 309 held that placing an imitation bomb in a department store, which resulted in evacuation of the store, full scale mobilisation of the emergency services and a trading loss of over £21,000, was an offence so serious that a non-custodial sentence for it could not be justified. A sentence of two years' detention in a young offender institution was upheld on a 17-year-old offender with a clean record.

Elements

A call stating 'there is a bomb' is sufficient to comprise the offence, even though there **B11.108** is no reference to a place or location (*Webb* (1995) *The Times*, 19 June 1995).

By the Criminal Law Act 1977, s. 51(3), for a person to be guilty of an offence under s. 51(1) or (2), it is not necessary for him to have any particular person in mind as the person in whom he intends to induce the belief mentioned in the relevant subsection.

CONTAMINATION OF OR INTERFERENCE WITH GOODS

Definition

B11.109
Public Order Act 1986, s. 38

(1) It is an offence for a person, with the intention—

    (a) of causing public alarm or anxiety, or

    (b) of causing injury to members of the public consuming or using the goods, or

    (c) of causing economic loss to any person by reason of the goods being shunned by members of the public, or

    (d) of causing economic loss to any person by reason of steps taken to avoid such alarm or anxiety, injury or loss,

to contaminate or interfere with goods, or make it appear that goods have been contaminated or interfered with, or to place goods which have been contaminated or interfered with, or which appear to have been contaminated or interfered with, in a place where goods of that description are consumed, used, sold or otherwise supplied.

(2) It is also an offence for a person, with any such intention as is mentioned in paragraph (a), (c) or (d) of subsection (1), to threaten that he or another will do, or claim that he or another has done, any of the acts mentioned in that subsection.

(3) It is an offence for a person to be in possession of any of the following articles with a view to the commission of an offence under subsection (1)—

    (a) materials to be used for contaminating or interfering with goods or making it appear that goods have been contaminated or interfered with, or

    (b) goods which have been contaminated or interfered with, or which appear to have been contaminated or interfered with.

Procedure

B11.110 Offences under the POA 1986, s. 38, are triable either way (s. 38(4)). When tried on indictment they are class 4 offences.

Indictment (for an Offence Contrary to s. 38(1)(a))

B11.111
Statement of Offence

Contamination of goods contrary to section 38(1)(a) of the Public Order Act 1986

Particulars of Offence

A on or about the . . . day of . . . with the intention of causing public alarm or anxiety, placed certain goods, namely 100 jars of . . . brand honey which had been contaminated by the insertion of fragments of broken glass therein, in a place where goods of that description are sold to the public, namely V's department store, . . .

Sentence

B11.112 The maximum penalty is 10 years, a fine or both, on indictment (POA 1986, s. 38(4)); six months, a fine not exceeding the statutory maximum, or both, summarily. In *Smith* (1994) 15 Cr App R (S) 106 the offender had told a journalist that certain products in a warehouse had been contaminated. The offender was arrested shortly afterwards and admitted that the story was an invention. The Court of Appeal, taking account of the fact that Smith had been working alone and that there had been no disruption to trade and no publicity, reduced the sentence imposed from three years' imprisonment to 18 months. This case may be contrasted with *Witchelo* (1992) 13 Cr App R (S) 371, considered at **B5.84**.

Meaning of 'Goods'

B11.113 In the POA 1986, s. 38 'goods' includes substances whether natural or manufactured and whether or not incorporated in or mixed with other goods (s. 38(5)).

Meaning of 'Claim' that Acts Have Been Committed

The reference in the POA 1986, s. 38(2), to a person claiming that certain acts have been **B11.114** committed does not include a person who in good faith reports or warns that such acts have been, or appear to have been, committed (s. 38(6)).

PRISON MUTINY

The Prison Security Act 1992 created the offence of prison mutiny. For offences relating **B11.115** to the escape of prisoners, see **B14.54** *et seq*.

Prison Security Act 1992, s. 1

    (1)   Any prisoner who takes part in a prison mutiny shall be guilty of an offence and liable, on conviction on indictment, to imprisonment for a term not exceeding ten years or to a fine or to both.

    (2)   For the purposes of this section there is a prison mutiny where two or more prisoners, while on the premises of any prison, engage in conduct which is intended to further a common purpose of overthrowing lawful authority in that prison.

    (3)   For the purposes of this section the intentions and common purpose of prisoners may be inferred from the form and circumstances of their conduct and it shall be immaterial that conduct falling within subsection (2) above takes a different form in the case of different prisoners.

    (4)   Where there is a prison mutiny, a prisoner who has or is given a reasonable opportunity of submitting to lawful authority and fails, without reasonable excuse, to do so shall be regarded for the purposes of this section as taking part in the mutiny.

    (5)   Proceedings for an offence under this section shall not be brought except by or with the consent of the Director of Public Prosecutions.

    (6)   In this section—
'conduct' includes acts and omissions;
'prison' means any prison, young offender institution or remand centre which is under the general superintendence of, or is provided by, the Secretary of State under the Prison Act 1952, including a contracted out prison within the meaning of part IV of the Criminal Justice Act 1991;
'prisoner' means any person for the time being in a prison as a result of any requirement imposed by a court or otherwise that he be detained in legal custody.

In *Mitchell* (1995) 16 Cr App R (S) 924, custodial sentences of five years were upheld in respect of two offenders convicted of prison mutiny. They had taken a leading part in an incident involving 120 remand prisoners which had caused extensive damage at Reading prison.

CONTROL OF PROCESSIONS, ASSEMBLIES AND MEETINGS

Advance Notice of Public Procession

It is an offence, contrary to the POA 1986, s. 11(7), for a person organising a public **B11.116** procession to fail to satisfy the requirements in s. 11 concerning the giving of notice of the procession to the police. Having given notice, an organiser commits an offence if the date when the procession is held, the time when it starts or its route differ from the date, time or route specified in the notice. The offence is triable only summarily and is punishable with a fine not exceeding level 3.

It is a defence, under s. 11(8), for the defendant to prove that he did not know of, and neither suspected nor had reason to suspect, the failure to satisfy the requirements or (as the case may be) the difference of date, time or route. It is also a defence, under s. 11(9), when the offence turns on a difference of date, time or route, for the defendant to prove that the difference arose from circumstances beyond his control or from something done with the agreement of a police officer or by his direction.

Failure to Comply with Conditions Imposed on Public Procession

B11.117 Under the POA 1986, s. 12, conditions may be imposed on public processions. Conditions may be imposed either in advance or at the time of the procession by the senior police officer acting under s. 12(1) to (3). It is an offence, triable only summarily:

(a)   for a person who organises a public procession knowingly to fail to comply with a condition (s. 12(4)) (see *DPP* v *Baillie* [1995] Crim LR 426);

(b)   for a person who takes part in such a procession knowingly to fail to comply with a condition (s. 12(5));

(c)   for a person to incite another to commit an offence under s. 12(5) (s. 12(6)).

In the case of the organiser's offence and the offence committed by a person taking part, it is a defence to prove that the failure to comply with a condition arose from circumstances beyond the defendant's control.

The maximum penalty for the organiser's offence and the inciter's offence is imprisonment for a term not exceeding three months or a fine not exceeding level 4 or both. A person who commits an offence by taking part in a procession is liable to a fine not exceeding level 3.

Contravening Prohibition of Public Procession

B11.118 Under the POA 1986, s. 13, a public procession may be prohibited. Where the procession is to take place outside the City of London or the metropolitan police district, it is the district council, on application from the chief officer of police and with the approval of the Secretary of State, which may make a procession prohibition order (s. 13(1) to (3)). In the City of London or the metropolitan police district, it is the relevant Commissioner, with the approval of the Secretary of State, who may make a procession prohibition order (s. 13(4)).

It is an offence, triable only summarily:

(a)   for a person to organise a public procession the holding of which he knows to be prohibited (s. 13(7));

(b)   for a person to take part in a public procession the holding of which he knows to be prohibited (s. 13(8));

(c)   for a person to incite another to commit an offence under s. 13(8) (s. 13(9)).

The maximum penalty for the organiser's offence and the inciter's offence is imprisonment for a term not exceeding three months or a fine not exceeding level 4 or both. A person who commits an offence by taking part in a procession is liable to a fine not exceeding level 3.

Failure to Comply with Conditions Imposed on Public Assembly

B11.119 Under the POA 1986, s. 14, conditions may be imposed on public assemblies. Conditions may be imposed either in advance or at the time of the assembly by the senior police officer acting under s. 14(1) to (3). It is an offence, triable only summarily:

(a)   for a person who organises a public assembly knowingly to fail to comply with a condition (s. 14(4)) (see *DPP* v *Baillie* [1995] Crim LR 426);

(b)   for a person who takes part in such an assembly knowingly to fail to comply with a condition (s. 14(5));

(c)   for a person to incite another to commit an offence under s. 14(5) (s. 14(6)).

The term 'public assembly' means an assembly of 20 or more persons in a public place which is wholly or partly open to the air (s. 16).

In the case of the organiser's offence and the offence committed by a person taking part, it is a defence to prove that the failure to comply with a condition arose from circumstances beyond the defendant's control.

The maximum penalty for the organiser's offence and the inciter's offence is imprisonment for a term not exceeding three months or a fine not exceeding level 4 or both. A person who commits an offence by taking part in an assembly is liable to a fine not exceeding level 3.

Contravention of Prohibition of Trespassory Assembly

Under the POA 1986, s. 14A, the chief officer of police has the power, if he reasonably **B11.120** believes that it is intended to hold a trespassory assembly which may result in serious disruption to the life of the community or significant damage to the land, building or monument which is of historical, archaeological or scientific importance, to apply to the district council for an order prohibiting for a specified period the holding of all trespassory assemblies in the district or part of it, but the order must not last for more than four days and must not apply to an area greater than that represented by a circle of five miles radius from a specified centre. The council must receive the consent of the Secretary of State for the making of such an order. The Metropolitan Police Commissioner or the Commissioner of the City of London Police may make such an order with the consent of the Secretary of State.

It is an offence, triable only summarily:

(a) for a person to organise an assembly which he knows is prohibited by an order under s. 14A (s. 14B(1));
(b) for a person to take part in an assembly which he knows is prohibited by such an order (s. 14B(2));
(c) for a person to incite another to commit an offence under s. 14B(2) (s. 14B(3)).

An assembly is not trespassory where the user of the highway is reasonable. This is determined by the ordinary law. Use of the highway is not restricted to the right of passage and matters incidental or ancillary to it. The public has the right to use the public highway for any reasonable and usual mode, including peaceful assembly on the highway, as is consistent with and does not obstruct the general public's primary right of passage. Further the use of the highway must not amount to a public or private nuisance (*DPP* v *Jones* [1999] 2 AC 240).

The maximum penalty for the organiser's offence and the inciter's offence (notwithstanding the MCA 1980, s. 45(3), which sets the offence for incitement as the same as for the substantive offence) is imprisonment for a term not exceeding three months or a fine not exceeding level 4 on the standard scale or both (s. 14B(5) and (7)). A person who commits an offence by taking part is liable to a fine not exceeding level 3 on the standard scale (s. 14B(6)). A constable in uniform may arrest without warrant anyone he reasonably suspects to be committing an offence under s. 14B (s. 14B(4)).

A constable in uniform has power, which may be exercised only within the area to which an order under s. 14A applies, to stop someone he reasonably believes to be on his way to an assembly prohibited by an order under s. 14A and to direct him not to proceed in the direction of the assembly (s. 14C(1) and (2)). A person who fails to comply with such a direction which he knows has been given commits a summary offence punishable with a fine not exceeding level 3 on the standard scale (s. 14C(3) and (5)). The constable has a power of arrest (s. 14C(4)).

Endeavouring to Break up a Public Meeting

It is an offence, contrary to the Public Meeting Act 1908, s. 1(1), for a person at a lawful **B11.121** public meeting to act in a disorderly manner for the purpose of preventing the transaction of the business for which the meeting was called together. The offence is triable summarily only. A person guilty of the offence is liable to imprisonment for a term not exceeding six months or to a fine not exceeding level 5 or to both.

There is no definition of either 'meeting' or 'public meeting' in the Public Meeting Act 1908 though there is in the POA 1936, s. 9. The case law that exists is concerned with whether the public meeting is lawful or not and indicates that a lawful meeting may be held on a highway, even if it might amount to an obstruction of that highway (*Burden* v *Rigler* [1911] 1 KB 337). Further, a public meeting does not cease to be lawful just because there is disorderly opposition from other persons (*Beatty* v *Gillbanks* (1882) 9 QBD 308, the authority of which does not, on this point, seem to be doubted by the Divisional Court in *Duncan* v *Jones* [1936] 1 KB 218). See **B11.90**.

It is an offence, contrary to the Public Meeting Act 1908, s. 1(2), to incite another person to commit an offence under s. 1; the offence is subject to similar punishment.

Failure to Comply with Constable's Request with Regard to Public Meeting

B11.122   It is an offence, contrary to the Public Meeting Act 1908, s. 1(3), for a person to refuse or fail to declare his name and address when asked to do so by a constable who reasonably suspects the person of committing an offence under the Public Meeting Act 1908, s. 1(1) or s. 1(2) (see **B11.121**) if the constable has been requested to ask for them by the chairman of the meeting. It is an offence to give a false name and address in such circumstances. A person guilty of the offence is liable to a fine not exceeding level 1.

Illegal Electoral Practice with Regard to Public Meeting

B11.123   It is one of the illegal electoral practices, contrary to the Representation of the People Act 1983, s. 97(1), for a person at a lawful public meeting to act, or incite others to act, in a disorderly manner for the purpose of preventing the transaction of the business for which the meeting was called together. The offence is triable summarily only. It is punishable on summary conviction with a fine not exceeding level 5.

'Lawful public meeting' in this offence means a political meeting held in any constituency between the date of the issue of the writ for the return of a Member of Parliament for the constituency and the date at which a return to the writ is made, or a meeting held with reference to a local government election in the electoral area for that election in the period beginning with the last date on which notice of the election may be published in accordance with the local government election rules and ending with the day of the election (Representation of the People Act 1983, s. 97(2)).

OFFENCES UNDER THE FOOTBALL (OFFENCES) ACT 1991

B11.124   The Football (Offences) Act 1991 creates three offences: throwing of missiles (s. 2), indecent or racialist chanting (s. 3) and going onto the playing area (s. 4).

Football (Offences) Act 1991, ss. 2, 3, and 4

2.   It is an offence for a person at a designated football match to throw anything at or towards—
   (a)   the playing area, or any area adjacent to the playing area to which spectators are not generally admitted, or
   (b)   any area in which spectators or other persons are or may be present, without lawful authority or lawful excuse (which shall be for him to prove).

3.—(1)   It is an offence to engage or take part in chanting of an indecent or racialist nature at a designated football match.
   (2)   For this purpose—
   (a)   'chanting' means the repeated uttering of any words or sounds (whether alone or in concert with one or more others); and
   (b)   'of racialist nature' means consisting of or including matter which is threatening, abusive or insulting to a person by reason of his colour, race, nationality (including citizenship) or ethnic or national origins.

4. It is an offence for a person at a designated football match to go onto the playing area, or any area adjacent to the playing area to which spectators are not generally admitted, without lawful authority of lawful excuse (which shall be for him to prove).

Procedure

All the offences are triable summarily only.   **B11.125**

Sentence

The maximum penalty is a fine not exceeding level 3 on the standard scale (s. 5(2)).   **B11.126**

Elements

A 'designated football match' is an association football match designated, or of a **B11.127** description designated, for the purposes of the Act by the Secretary of State. The Football (Offences) (Designation of Football Matches) Order 1999 (SI 1999 No. 2462) has been made, under the Football Spectators Act 1989, for this purpose. It designates association football matches in which one or more of the participating teams represents a club which is for the time being a member (whether a full or associate member) of the Football League or the Football Association Premier League, or represents a club, country or territory outside England and Wales; and which is played at a sports ground which is designated under the Safety of Sports Grounds Act 1975 or registered with the Football League or the Football Association Premier League as the home ground of a club which is a member of the Football League or the Football Association Premier League at the time when the match is played.

References to things done at a designated football match include anything done at the ground:

(a)   within the period beginning two hours before the start of the match or (if earlier) two hours before the time at which it is advertised to start and ending one hour after the end of the match,

(b)   where the match is advertised to start at a particular time on a particular day but does not take place, within the period beginning two hours before and ending one hour after the advertised starting time (s. 1(2)).

OFFENCES UNDER THE FOOTBALL SPECTATORS ACT 1989

The Football Spectators Act 1989 was designed to control the admission of spectators at **B11.128** designated football matches and provided for the making of restriction orders on persons convicted of offences of violence or disorder at, or in connection with, such matches. In the light of the Taylor Report on the deaths which occurred at Hillsborough, many of its provisions, particularly those relating to a national football membership scheme, have not been, and are not likely to be, brought into force. However, the majority of the provisions relating to the grant of licences to admit spectators and the whole of part II (which concerns football matches taking place outside England and Wales) are in force.

Under s. 9, it is an offence to admit spectators to watch a designated football match unless it is played at licensed premises. By virtue of s. 10(13), it is a summary offence for any responsible person to contravene any term or condition of a licence granted to admit spectators to any premises for the purpose of watching any designated football match played there. It is a defence, in accordance with s. 10(14), for an accused to prove that the contravention took place without his consent and that he took all reasonable precautions and exercised all due diligence to avoid the commission of such an offence. The relevant licences are those issued by the Football Licensing Authority under the Football Spectators (Seating) Order 1994 (SI 1994 No. 1666). The Football Spectators (Designation of Football Matches in England and Wales) Order 1999 (SI 1999 No.

2461) designates matches for the purposes of the Act. It is in the same terms as that which applies for the purposes of the Football (Offences) Act 1991 (see **B11.127**).

As to banning orders and other powers to exclude persons from football matches, see **E23.2**.

TICKET TOUTS

Definition

B11.129   **Criminal Justice and Public Order Act 1994, s. 166**

    (1)   It is an offence for an unauthorised person to sell, or offer or expose for sale, a ticket for a designated football match in any public place or place to which the public has access or, in the course of a trade or business, in any other place.

Procedure

B11.130 The offence is triable summarily (CJPO 1994, s. 166(3)).

Sentence

B11.131 The maximum sentence is a fine not exceeding level 5 on the standard scale (CJPO 1994, s. 166(3)).

Elements

B11.132 A person is 'an unauthorised person' unless he is authorised in writing to sell tickets for the match by the home club or by the organisers of the match; 'ticket' means anything which purports to be a ticket (CJPO 1994, s. 166(2)). For the meaning of 'designated football match', see **B11.127**.

Power of Arrest and Search of Person and Premises

B11.133 The PACE 1984, s. 24(2)(h), has been inserted by the CJPO 1994, s. 166(4), to make an offence under s. 166 an arrestable offence and the PACE 1984, s. 32, has effect in relation to such an offence as if the power conferred on a constable to enter and search any vehicle extended to any vehicle which the constable has reasonable grounds for believing was being used for any purpose connected with the offence (CJPO 1994, s. 166(5)).

OFFENCES IN CONNECTION WITH ALCOHOL ON COACHES AND TRAINS

Definition

B11.134   **Sporting Events (Control of Alcohol etc.) Act 1985, s. 1**

    (2)   A person who knowingly causes or permits intoxicating liquor to be carried on a vehicle to which this section applies is guilty of an offence—
    (a)   if the vehicle is a public service vehicle and he is the operator of the vehicle or the servant or agent of the operator, or
    (b)   if the vehicle is a hired vehicle and he is the person to whom it is hired or the servant or agent of that person.
    (3)   A person who has intoxicating liquor in his possession while on a vehicle to which this section applies is guilty of an offence.
    (4)   A person who is drunk on a vehicle to which this section applies is guilty of an offence.

Procedure

B11.135 Offences under the Sporting Events (Control of Alcohol etc.) Act 1985, s. 1, are, by s. 8 of the Act, triable summarily only.

Sentence

Sporting Events (Control of Alcohol etc.) Act 1985, s. 8   **B11.136**

A person guilty of an offence under this Act shall be liable on summary conviction—
    (a)   in the case of an offence under section 1(2) . . ., to a fine not exceeding level 4 on the standard scale,
    (b)   in the case of an offence under section 1(3), . . . to a fine not exceeding level 3 on the standard scale or to imprisonment for a term not exceeding three months or both,
    (c)   in the case of an offence under section 1(4), . . . to a fine not exceeding level 2 on the standard scale.

Meaning of 'Vehicle'

Sporting Events (Control of Alcohol etc.) Act 1985, s. 1   **B11.137**

    (1)   This section applies to a vehicle which—
    (a)   is a public service vehicle or railway passenger vehicle, and
    (b)   is being used for the principal purpose of carrying passengers for the whole or part of a journey to or from a designated sporting event.
. . .
    (5)   In this section 'public service vehicle' and 'operator' have the same meaning as in the Public Passenger Vehicles Act 1981.

Meaning of 'Designated Sporting Event'

Sporting Events (Control of Alcohol etc.) Act 1985, s. 9   **B11.138**

    (3)   'Designated sporting event'—
    (a)   means a sporting event or proposed sporting event for the time being designated, or of a class designated, by order made by the Secretary of State, and
    (b)   includes a designated sporting event within the meaning of part II of the Criminal Law (Consolidation) (Scotland) Act 1995;
and an order under this subsection may apply to events or proposed events outside Great Britain as well as those in England and Wales.

See the Sports Grounds and Sporting Events (Designation Order) 1985 (SI 1985 No. 1151).

OFFENCES IN CONNECTION WITH ALCOHOL, CONTAINERS ETC. AT SPORTS GROUNDS

Definition

Sporting Events (Control of Alcohol etc.) Act 1985, s. 2   **B11.139**

    (1)   A person who has intoxicating liquor or an article to which this section applies in his possession—
    (a)   at any time during the period of a designated sporting event when he is in any area of a designated sports ground from which the event may be directly viewed, or
    (b)   while entering or trying to enter a designated sports ground at any time during the period of a designated sporting event at that ground,
is guilty of an offence.
    (2)   A person who is drunk in a designated sports ground at any time during the period of a designated sporting event at that ground or is drunk while entering or trying to enter such a ground at any time during the period of a designated sporting event at that ground is guilty of an offence.

Procedure

Offences under the Sporting Events (Control of Alcohol etc.) Act 1985, s. 2, are, by s. 8 **B11.140** of the Act, triable summarily only.

Sentence

B11.141   **Sporting Events (Control of Alcohol etc.) Act 1985, s. 8**

A person guilty of an offence under this Act shall be liable on summary conviction—

...

(b)   in the case of an offence under section . . . 2(1), . . . to a fine not exceeding level 3 on the standard scale or to imprisonment for a term not exceeding three months or both,

(c)   in the case of an offence under section . . . 2(2), to a fine not exceeding level 2 on the standard scale.

Meaning of Terms Used in Defining Offence

B11.142   For the meaning of 'designated sporting event', see **B11.103**.

Sporting Events (Control of Alcohol etc.) Act 1985, s. 9

(2)   'Designated sports ground' means any place—

(a)   used (wholly or partly) for sporting events where accommodation is provided for spectators, and

(b)   for the time being designated, or of a class designated, by order made by the Secretary of State;

and an order under this subsection may include provision for determining for the purposes of this Act the outer limit of any designated sports ground.

...

(4)   The period of a designated sporting event is the period beginning two hours before the start of the event or (if earlier) two hours before the time at which it is advertised to start and ending one hour after the end of the event, but—

(a)   where an event advertised to start at a particular time on a particular day is postponed to a later day, the period includes the period in the day on which it is advertised to take place beginning two hours before and ending one hour after that time, and

(b)   where an event advertised to start at a particular time on a particular day does not take place, the period is the period referred to in paragraph (a) above.

The articles to which s. 2 applies are defined in s. 2(3):

This section applies to any article capable of causing injury to a person struck by it, being—

(a)   a bottle, can or other portable container (including such an article when crushed or broken) which—

(i)   is for holding any drink, and

(ii)   is of a kind which, when empty, is normally discarded or returned to, or left to be recovered by, the supplier, or

(b)   part of an article falling within paragraph (a) above;

but does not apply to anything that is for holding any medicinal product (within the meaning of the Medicines Act 1968).

INTIMIDATION OR ANNOYANCE BY VIOLENCE OR OTHERWISE

Definition

B11.143   **Trade Union and Labour Relations (Consolidation) Act 1992, s. 241**

(1)   A person commits an offence who, with a view to compelling another person to abstain from doing or to do any act which that person has a legal right to do or abstain from doing, wrongfully and without legal authority—

(a)   uses violence to or intimidates that person or his wife or children, or injures his property,

(b)   persistently follows that person about from place to place,

(c)   hides any tools, clothes or other property owned or used by that person, or deprives him of or hinders him in the use thereof,

(d)   watches or besets the house or other place where that person resides, works, carries on business or happens to be, or the approach to any such house or place, or

  (e) follows that person with two or more other persons in a disorderly manner in or through any street or road.

  (2) A person guilty of an offence under this section is liable on summary conviction to imprisonment for a term not exceeding six months or a fine not exceeding level 5 on the standard scale, or both.

  (3) A constable may arrest without warrant anyone he reasonably suspects is committing an offence under this section.

Procedure

An offence under the Trade Union and Labour Relations (Consolidation) Act 1992, **B11.144** s. 241, is triable summarily only.

Sentence

The maximum penalty is six months and/or a fine not exceeding level 5 (Trade Union **B11.145** and Labour Relations (Consolidation) Act 1992, s. 241(2)).

Elements

It has been made clear by the Divisional Court in *Todd* v *DPP* [1996] Crim LR 344 that the **B11.146** offence is not limited to trade disputes. It can, therefore, apply to someone engaged in an anti-roads protest (as in *Todd*) and might apply, for example, to stalking (see also Professor Sir John Smith at [1996] Crim LR 345). The general elements of the offence are, first, the *mens rea*, which is dealt with below and, secondly, the requirements that the act be done 'wrongfully' and 'without lawful authority'. No special consideration has been given to the phrase 'without lawful authority' apart from the creation of a defence for trade unions acting in contemplation or furtherance of a dispute, which is treated as a defence, below.

Meaning of 'Wrongfully' Scott J in *Thomas* v *National Union of Mineworkers (South* **B11.147** *Wales Area)* [1986] Ch 20 decided that the authorities established that conduct must, in order to be an offence under what was, prior to consolidation, the Conspiracy, and Protection of Property Act 1875, s. 7, be tortious (at p. 61). This approach to the question of whether there is a wrongful act does indeed seem to be consistent with the existing case law. The Court of Appeal in *Ward, Lock & Co. Ltd* v *Operative Printers' Assistants' Society* (1906) 22 TLR 327 clearly took the view that s. 7 (now the Trade Union and Labour Relations (Consolidation) Act 1992, s. 241) was concerned only to provide a criminal remedy to what was already recognised as being a civil wrong. Thus in order for the criminal remedy to be available, it had to be established that what was done was a civil wrong, without reference to the provisions of the Act.

Intimidates The Court of Appeal in *Jones* (1974) 59 Cr App R 120, whilst not **B11.148** wishing to define 'intimidation' exhaustively, said that:

> . . . 'intimidate' in this section includes putting persons in fear by the exhibition of force or violence or the threat of force or violence, and there is no limitation restricting the meaning to cases of violence or threats of violence to the person.

In *Connor* v *Kent* [1891] 2 QB 545, the court also did not want to attempt an exhaustive definition of the word, preferring instead to make clear (at p. 559) that 'intimidate' is 'a word of common speech and everyday use; and it must receive, therefore, a reasonable and sensible interpretation according to the circumstances of the cases as they arise from time to time'. Further assistance may be gleaned from the decision of Stuart-Smith J in *News Group Newspapers Ltd* v *SOGAT 82 (No. 2)* [1987] ICR 181, at pp. 204–5, considering the related tort of intimidation.

Persistently Follows In *Smith* v *Thomasson* (1890) 62 LT 68, Hawkins J stated that: **B11.149** 'It is impossible to define generally what is 'persistently following'. However, it was held dogging of a workman's footsteps could amount to 'persistently following' him. See also *Elsey* v *Smith* 1982 SCCR 218.

B11.150 ***Deprivation of Property*** The Court of Appeal in *Fowler* v *Kibble* [1922] 1 Ch 487 made clear the significance of the requirement that the activity must be wrongful separately from a consideration of the section creating the offence. Thus there could be no offence where a workman did not let miners who were not members of a particular union have safety lamps because such an act of deprivation was not unlawful.

B11.151 ***Watches or Besets*** In general, it would seem that the words 'watch' and 'beset' are viewed as words of the ordinary English language, see, e.g., *J. Lyons & Sons* v *Wilkins* [1899] 1 Ch 811 and *Ward, Lock & Co. Ltd* v *Operative Printers' Assistants' Society* (1906) 22 TLR 327. The High Court of Justiciary in *Gatt* v *Philp* 1983 JC 51 took the view that the essence of the offence comprised preventing access to and egress from somewhere. Thus a sit-in satisfied this element of the offence.

The watching and besetting must be 'wrongful', that is, unlawful without reference to s. 241. Thus, e.g., in *J. Lyons & Sons* v *Wilkins* [1899] 1 Ch 811, careful consideration was given to the question of whether the activity amounted to a nuisance and was therefore 'wrongful' and within the ambit of the section. The length of time the people were present was relevant, since that would help determine whether there was a nuisance. Consequently, lawful picketing is not 'watching and besetting' unless it amounts to a nuisance, or some other tort or other wrong such as obstruction of the highway (see, e.g., *News Group Newspapers Ltd* v *SOGAT 82 (No. 2)* [1987] ICR 181 and *Walters* v *Green* [1899] 2 Ch 696; see also *Bonsall* [1985] Crim LR 150).

In *Charnock* v *Court* [1899] 2 Ch 35 and *Farmer* v *Wilson* (1900) 69 LJ QB 496, it was made clear that the offence is committed when any place where the person happens to be is watched and beset, whether or not such persons are in the service or employment of any person. This latter point in *Farmer* v *Wilson* makes clear that the offence is not solely concerned with employment disputes.

B11.152 ***Following in a Disorderly Manner*** Whether the following is in a disorderly manner is a question of fact in each case, and therefore will depend upon the conduct of the defendant and all the circumstances of the particular case, see *McKenzie* [1892] 2 QB 519 and *Elsey* v *Smith* 1982 SCCR 218.

Mens Rea: With a View to Compel Any Other Person

B11.153 This is a *mens rea* requirement importing not motive but purpose according to the Divisional Court in *DPP* v *Fidler* [1992] 1 WLR 91, explaining *J. Lyons & Sons* v *Wilkins* [1899] 1 Ch 255. The Divisional Court stated that purpose is a more objective concept not concerned with the different motives with which members of the group might have joined, for example, a demonstration. The court also decided that the defendant's purpose must be one to compel and not merely to persuade (see also *Bonsall* [1985] Crim LR 150 and *McKenzie* [1892] 2 QB 519). It is not necessary to show that the compulsion was in any way effective (*Agnew* v *Munro* (1891) 18 R (J) 22). The phrase 'such other person' refers back to the person whom the defendant has a view to compel to abstain from doing or to do something (*J. Lyons & Sons* v *Wilkins* [1899] 1 Ch 811).

Application to Trade or Employment Disputes

B11.154 **Trade Union and Labour Relations (Consolidation) Act 1992, s. 220**

> (1) It shall be lawful for a person in contemplation or furtherance of a trade dispute to attend—
> (a) at or near his own place of work, or
> (b) if he is an official of a trade union, at or near the place of work of a member of that union whom he is accompanying and whom he represents,
> for the purpose only of peacefully obtaining or communicating information, or peacefully persuading any person to work or abstain from working.

(2)   If a person works or normally works—
   (a)   otherwise than at any one place, or
   (b)   at a place the location of which is such that attendance there for a purpose mentioned in subsection (1) above is impracticable,
his place of work for the purposes of that subsection shall be any premises of his employer from which he works or from which his work is administered.
(3)   In the case of a worker who is not in employment where—
   (a)   his last employment was terminated in connection with a trade dispute, or
   (b)   the termination of his employment was one of the circumstances giving rise to a trade dispute,
in relation to that dispute his former place of work shall be treated for the purposes of subsection (1) as being his place of work.
(4)   A person who is an official of a trade union by virtue only of having been elected or appointed to be a representative of some of the members of the union shall be regarded for the purposes of subsection (1) above as representing only those members; but otherwise an official of a trade union shall be regarded for those purposes as representing all its members.

RACIALLY AGGRAVATED OFFENCES

The CDA 1998 has introduced a series of racially aggravated offences, i.e. existing offences which are racially aggravated according to the definition in s. 28.   **B11.155**

Crime and Disorder Act 1998, s. 28

(1)   An offence is racially aggravated for the purposes of sections 29 to 32 below if—
   (a)   at the time of committing the offence, or immediately before or after doing so, the offender demonstrates towards the victim of the offence hostility based on the victim's membership (or presumed membership) of a racial group; or
   (b)   the offence is motivated (wholly or partly) by hostility towards members of a racial group based on their membership of that group.
(2)   In subsection (1)(a) above—
'membership', in relation to a racial group, includes association with members of that group;
'presumed' means presumed by the offender.
(3)   It is immaterial for the purposes of paragraph (a) or (b) of subsection (1) above whether or not the offender's hostility is also based, to any extent, on—
   (a)   the fact or presumption that any person or group of persons belongs to any religious group; or
   (b)   any other factor not mentioned in that paragraph.
(4)   In this section 'racial group' means a group of persons defined by reference to race, colour, nationality (including citizenship) or ethnic or national origins.

The offences which may be racially aggravated are an offence contrary to the OAPA 1861, ss. 20 and 47 and common assault (CDA 1998, s. 29: see **B2.1**, **B2.15** and **B2.29**), criminal damage (CDA 1998, s. 30: see **B8.1**), offences contrary to the POA 1986, ss. 4, 4A and 5 (CDA 1998, s. 31: see **B11.45**, **B11.56** and **B11.65**) and harassment contrary to the Protection from Harassment Act 1997, ss. 2 and 4 (CDA 1998, s. 32: see **B11.77** and **B11.85**). The racially aggravated form of each offence carries a higher maximum penalty than the ordinary form of the offence.

The concept, 'racial group', is the same as that which appears in the POA 1986, s. 17, and is similar to that in the Race Relations Act 1976, see **B11.160**.

USING WORDS OR BEHAVIOUR OR DISPLAYING WRITTEN MATERIAL STIRRING UP RACIAL HATRED

Definition

Public Order Act 1986, s. 18   **B11.156**

(1)   A person who uses threatening, abusive or insulting words or behaviour, or displays any written material which is threatening, abusive or insulting, is guilty of an offence if—

    (a)   he intends thereby to stir up racial hatred, or
    (b)   having regard to all the circumstances racial hatred is likely to be stirred up
thereby.

Procedure

B11.157 An offence under the POA 1986, s. 18, is triable either way. When tried on indictment
it is a class 4 offence. No proceeding may be instituted except by, or with the consent
of, the A-G (POA 1986, s. 27(3)).

For the liability of corporate officers, see **B11.166**.

Indictment

B11.158
Statement of Offence

Displaying threatening, abusive or insulting material with intent to stir up racial hatred
contrary to section 18 of the Public Order Act 1986

Particulars of Offence

A on or about the . . . day of . . . at . . . displayed certain threatening, abusive or insulting
materials, namely a quantity of pamphlets entitled . . . with intent thereby to stir up racial
hatred

The POA 1986, s. 27(2), declares that for the purposes of the rules against charging
more than one offence in the same count, each of sections 18 to 23 of the Act creates
one offence.

Sentencing Guidelines

B11.159 The maximum penalty is two years' imprisonment, a fine, or both, on indictment (POA
1986, s. 27(3)); six months, a fine not exceeding the statutory maximum, or both,
summarily.

In *Relf* (1979) 1 Cr App R (S) 111, the offenders were convicted of publishing leaflets
containing derogatory remarks about West Indians, the leaflets being displayed in public
places. The conduct did not lead to disorder. The Court of Appeal agreed with the trial
judge that an immediate custodial penalty was necessary for Relf, but reduced the
sentence from 15 months to nine. The co-accused, more peripherally involved in the
offence, received a nine-month prison sentence, suspended, together with a fine of
£250. In *Edwards* (1983) 5 Cr App R (S) 145, the offender had drawn a comic strip to
be published in a magazine intending to stir up racial hatred, received a 12-month
sentence. Lawton LJ, in the Court of Appeal, said that sentence 'was not a day too long',
since the offender's conduct had been 'intended to prejudice children against Jews,
Asians and people of coloured blood'.

The court also has a power to order forfeiture where the accused is convicted of
displaying written material.

Public Order Act 1986, s. 25

    (1)   A court by or before which a person is convicted of—
      (a)   an offence under section 18 relating to the display of written material, or
      (b)   an offence under section 19, 21 or 23,
shall order to be forfeited any written material. . . produced to the court and shown to its
satisfaction to be written material. . . to which the offence relates.
    (2)   An order made under this section shall not take effect—
      (a)   in the case of an order made in proceedings in England and Wales, until the expiry
of the ordinary time within which an appeal may be instituted or, where an appeal is duly
instituted, until it is finally decided or abandoned. . . .
    (3)   For the purposes of subsection (2)(a)—

(a) an application for a case stated or for leave to appeal shall be treated as the institution of an appeal, and

(b) where a decision on appeal is subject to a further appeal, the appeal is not finally determined until the expiry of the ordinary time within which a further appeal may be instituted or, where a further appeal is duly instituted, until the further appeal is finally decided or abandoned.

Meaning of 'Racial Hatred'

The essence of the offence under the POA 1986, s. 18, lies in the use of words or **B11.160** behaviour or the display of material either when the defendant intends to stir up racial hatred (s. 18(1)(a)) or where racial hatred is, in the circumstances, likely to be stirred up (s. 18(1)(b)). The concept of 'racial hatred' is therefore central to the offence.

Public Order Act 1986, s. 17

In this part [i.e. ss. 17 to 29] 'racial hatred' means hatred against a group of persons in Great Britain defined by reference to colour, race, nationality (including citizenship) or ethnic or national origins.

In the Race Relations Act 1976, 'racial group' is defined as meaning 'a group of persons defined by reference to colour, race, nationality or ethnic or national origins'. In *Mandla v Dowell Lee* [1983] 2 AC 548, it was necessary to determine whether the Sikhs are a 'racial group' for the purposes of the 1976 Act. The House of Lords was satisfied that it was necessary to determine whether Sikhs are a group defined by ethnic origins, since none of the other descriptions would distinguish them from at least some other groups of people. In holding that Sikhs are an ethnic group, Lord Fraser of Tullybelton said (at pp. 562D–563A):

For a group to constitute an ethnic group in the sense of the Act of 1976, it must, in my opinion, regard itself, and be regarded by others, as a distinct community by virtue of certain characteristics. Some of these characteristics are essential; others are not essential but one or more of them will commonly be found and will help to distinguish the group from the surrounding community. The conditions which appear to me to be essential are these: (1) a long shared history, of which the group is conscious as distinguishing it from other groups, and the memory of which it keeps alive; (2) a cultural tradition of its own, including family and social customs and manners, often but not necessarily associated with religious observance. In addition to those two essential characteristics the following characteristics are, in my opinion, relevant; (3) either a common geographical origin, or descent from a small number of common ancestors; (4) a common language, not necessarily peculiar to the group; (5) a common literature peculiar to the group; (6) a common religion different from that of neighbouring groups or from the general community surrounding it; (7) being a minority or being an oppressed or a dominant group within a larger community, for example a conquered people (say the inhabitants shortly after the Norman conquest) and their conquerors might both be ethnic groups.

A group defined by reference to enough of these characteristics would be capable of including converts, for example, people who marry into the group, and of excluding apostates. Provided a person who joins the group feels himself or herself to be a member of it, and is accepted by other members, then he is, for the purposes of the Act, a member. . . . In my opinion, it is possible for a person to fall into a particular racial group either by birth or by adherence, and it makes no difference, so far as the Act of 1976 is concerned, by which route he finds his way into the group.

Lord Templeman, taking a similar approach to that of Lord Fraser, said (at p. 569E):

In my opinion, for the purposes of the Race Relations Act a group of persons defined by reference to ethnic origins must possess some of the characteristics of a race, namely group descent, a group of geographical origin and a group history.

Lord Fraser also approved the decision of the New Zealand Court of Appeal in *King-Ansell v Police* [1979] 2 NZLR 531 that Jews form a group with common ethnic origins within the New Zealand Race Relations Act 1971. In the course of his judgment, Richardson J said (at p. 543):

> . . . a group is identifiable in terms of its ethnic origins if it is a segment of the population distinguished from others by a sufficient combination of shared customs, beliefs, traditions and characteristics derived from a common or presumed common past, even if not drawn from what in biological terms is a common racial stock. It is that combination which gives them an historically determined social identity in their own eyes and in the eyes of those outside the group. They have a distinct social identity based not simply on group cohesion and solidarity but also on their belief as to their historical antecedents.

Gypsies properly so called, rather than 'travellers', are capable of being a racial group on the basis of their ethnic origin (*Commission for Racial Equality* v *Dutton* [1989] QB 783). Following the test in *Mandla* v *Dowell Lee*, the Court of Appeal held that Rastafarians are not members of an ethnic group separate from the rest of the Afro-Caribbean community (*Dawkins* v *Crown Suppliers (Property Services Agency)* (1993) *The Times*, 4 February 1993).

Threatening, Abusive or Insulting

B11.161   For discussion of the phrase 'threatening, abusive or insulting', see **B11.50**.

Meaning of 'Written Material'

B11.162   In the POA 1986, ss. 17 to 29, 'written material' includes any sign or other visible representation (s. 29). For the meaning of 'writing', see **B11.51**.

Mens Rea

B11.163   For the offence under the POA 1986, s. 18(1)(a), an intention to stir up racial hatred is required. The *mens rea* of the offence under s. 18(1)(b) is established by reference to s. 18(5):

> A person who is not shown to have intended to stir up racial hatred is not guilty of an offence under this section if he did not intend his words or behaviour, or the written material, to be, and was not aware that it might be, threatening, abusive or insulting.

Place of Commission

B11.164   **Public Order Act 1986, s. 18**

> (2)   An offence under this section may be committed in a public or a private place, except that no offence is committed where the words or behaviour are used, or the written material is displayed, by a person inside a dwelling and are not heard or seen except by other persons in that or another dwelling.
>
> (4)   In proceedings for an offence under this section it is a defence for the accused to prove that he was inside a dwelling and had no reason to believe that the words or behaviour used, or the written material displayed, would be heard or seen by a person outside that or any other dwelling.

Section 29 provides that, in ss. 17 to 29:

> 'dwelling' means any structure or part of a structure occupied as a person's home or other living accommodation (whether the occupation is separate or shared with others) but does not include any part not so occupied; and for this purpose 'structure' includes a tent, caravan, vehicle, vessel or other temporary or movable structure.

Offence Does Not Apply to Broadcasts or Cable Programme Services

B11.165   The POA 1986, s. 18, does not (by s. 18(6)) apply to words or behaviour used, or written material displayed, solely for the purpose of being included in a programme service. Such activity is controlled by s. 22 of the Act, see **B11.176**.

Liability of Corporate Officers

Public Order Act 1986, s. 28   **B11.166**

(1)   Where a body corporate is guilty of an offence under this part and it is shown that the offence was committed with the consent or connivance of a director, manager, secretary or other similar officer of the body, or a person purporting to act in any such capacity, he as well as the body corporate is guilty of the offence and liable to be proceeded against and punished accordingly.

(2)   Where the affairs of a body corporate are managed by its members, subsection (1) applies in relation to the acts and defaults of a member in connection with his functions of management as it applies to a director.

As to corporate liability generally, and the liability of corporate officers in the light of the case of *Boal* [1992] QB 591, see **A5.11**.

Defence for Reports of Parliamentary and Judicial Proceedings

Public Order Act 1986, s. 26   **B11.167**

(1)   Nothing in this part applies to a fair and accurate report of proceedings in Parliament.

(2)   Nothing in this part applies to a fair and accurate report of proceedings publicly heard before a court or tribunal exercising judicial authority where the report is published contemporaneously with the proceedings or, if it is not reasonably practicable or would be unlawful to publish a report of them contemporaneously, as soon as publication is reasonably practicable and lawful.

This and the general defences (see **A3**) are the only defences available to an accused. The truth of material, or belief in its truth, is not a defence (*Birdwood* (11 April 1995 unreported).

PUBLISHING OR DISTRIBUTING WRITTEN MATERIAL STIRRING UP RACIAL HATRED

Definition

Public Order Act 1986, s. 19   **B11.168**

(1)   A person who publishes or distributes written material which is threatening, abusive or insulting is guilty of an offence if—
    (a)   he intends thereby to stir up racial hatred, or
    (b)   having regard to all the circumstances racial hatred is likely to be stirred up thereby.

Procedure

An offence under the POA 1986, s. 19, is, by s. 27(3) of the Act, triable either way. When   **B11.169** tried on indictment it is a class 4 offence. No proceeding may be instituted except by, or with the consent of, the A-G (POA 1986, s. 27(3)).

The POA 1986, s. 27(2), declares that for the purposes of the rules against charging more than one offence in the same count or information, each of ss. 18 to 23 of the Act creates one offence.

For the liability of corporate officers, see **B11.166**.

Sentence

The maximum penalty for an offence under the POA 1986, s. 19, is, by s. 27(3) of the   **B11.170** Act, two years' imprisonment or a fine or both, on indictment; six months, a fine not exceeding the statutory maximum or both, summarily. The court also has a power under s. 25 to order forfeiture where the accused is convicted of displaying written material (see **B11.156**).

Meaning of Terms Used in Defining the Offence

B11.171   For the meaning of 'racial hatred' see **B11.160**. For the meaning of 'threatening, abusive or insulting', see **B11.50**. For the meaning of 'written material', see **B11.162**.

References in the POA 1986, ss. 17 to 29, to the publication or distribution of written material are, by s. 19(3) of the Act, to the publication or distribution of that material to the public or a section of the public.

Defences

B11.172   In proceedings for an offence under the POA 1986, s. 19, it is, by virtue of s. 19(2), a defence for an accused who is not shown to have intended to stir up racial hatred to prove that he was not aware of the content of the material and did not suspect, and had no reason to suspect, that it was threatening, abusive or insulting. The burden of proof of this defence lies on the accused on the balance of probabilities (see generally **F3.4** and **F3.18**). The defence in the POA 1986, s. 26 (savings for reports of parliamentary and judicial proceedings: see **B11.167**), applies to s. 19.

These and the general defences (see **A3**) are the only offences available to an accused. The truth of the material, or a belief in its truth, is not a defence (*Birdwood* (11 April 1995 unreported)).

PUBLIC PERFORMANCE, BROADCASTING AND POSSESSION OF MATERIALS STIRRING UP RACIAL HATRED

General Provisions

B11.173   Sections 20 to 23 of the POA 1986 deal with the public performance, broadcasting and possession of materials intended to, or likely to, stir up racial hatred. The offences created are triable either way, and the following general provisions of part III of the Act apply:

(a)   Prosecution may only be by, or with the consent of, the A-G (s. 27(1)).
(b)   Each section creates one offence (s. 27(2)).
(c)   The maximum penalty is two years and/or a fine, on indictment; six months and/or a fine not exceeding the statutory maximum, summarily (s. 27(3)).
(d)   There is a saving for fair and accurate reports of parliamentary or judicial proceedings (see **B11.167**).
(e)   For the liability of corporate officers, see **B11.166**.

For the meaning of 'racial hatred' see **B11.160**. For the meaning of 'threatening, abusive or insulting', see **B11.50**. For the meaning of 'written material', see **B11.161**.

References in the POA 1986, ss. 17 to 29, to the publication or distribution of written material are, by s. 19(3) of the Act, to the publication or distribution of that material to the public or a section of the public. References to the distribution, showing or playing of a recording are, by s. 21(2), to the distribution, showing or playing of the recording to the public or a section of the public. 'Recording' means any record from which visual images or sounds may, by any means, be reproduced (s. 21(2)).

As to the limited defences available and that the truth of material, or a belief in its truth, is not a defence, see *Birdwood* (11 April 1995 unreported).

Public Performance of Play Stirring up Racial Hatred

Public Order Act 1986, s. 20

(1)   If a public performance of a play is given which involves the use of threatening, abusive or insulting words or behaviour, any person who presents or directs the performance is guilty of an offence if—

(a)   he intends thereby to stir up racial hatred, or

(b)   having regard to all the circumstances (and, in particular, taking the performance as a whole) racial hatred is likely to be stirred up thereby.

Section 20(5) of the POA 1986 provides that the words 'play' and 'public performance' in s. 20 have the same meaning as in the Theatres Act 1968.

Theatres Act 1968, s. 18

In this Act—

. . .

'play' means—

(a)   any dramatic piece, whether involving improvisation or not, which is given wholly or in part by one or more persons actually present and performing and in which the whole or a major proportion of what is done by the person or persons performing, whether by way of speech, singing or acting, involves the playing of a role; and

(b)   any ballet given wholly or in part by one or more persons actually present and performing, whether or not it falls within paragraph (a) of this definition;

. . .

'public performance' includes any performance in a public place within the meaning of the Public Order Act 1936 and any performance which the public or any section thereof are permitted to attend, whether on payment or otherwise.

The meaning of 'public place' in the POA 1936 is considered at **B11.15**.

Public Order Act 1986, s. 20

(2)   If a person presenting or directing the performance is not shown to have intended to stir up racial hatred, it is a defence for him to prove—

(a)   that he did not know and had no reason to suspect that the performance would involve the use of the offending words or behaviour, or

(b)   that he did not know and had no reason to suspect that the offending words or behaviour were threatening, abusive or insulting, or

(c)   that he did not know and had no reason to suspect that the circumstances in which the performance would be given would be such that racial hatred would be likely to be stirred up.

(3)   This section does not apply to a performance given solely or primarily for one or more of the following purposes—

(a)   rehearsal,

(b)   making a recording of the performance, or

(c)   enabling the performance to be included in a programme service,

but if it is proved that the performance was attended by persons other than those directly concerned with the giving of the performance or the doing in relation to it of the things mentioned in paragraph (b) or (c), the performance shall, unless the contrary is shown, be taken not to have been given solely for the purposes mentioned above.

(4)   For the purposes of this section—

(a)   a person shall not be treated as presenting a performance of a play by reason only of his taking part in it as a performer,

(b)   a person taking part as a performer in a performance directed by another shall be treated as a person who directed the performance if without reasonable excuse he performs otherwise than in accordance with that person's direction, and

(c)   a person shall be taken to have directed a performance of a play given under his direction notwithstanding that he was not present during the performance;

and a person shall not be treated as aiding or abetting the commission of an offence under this section by reason only of his taking part in a performance as a performer.

Distributing, Showing or Playing a Recording Stirring up Racial Hatred

B11.175   **Public Order Act 1986, s. 21**

(1)   A person who distributes, or shows or plays, a recording of visual images or sounds which are threatening, abusive or insulting is guilty of an offence if—

(a)   he intends thereby to stir up racial hatred, or

(b)   having regard to all the circumstances racial hatred is likely to be stirred up thereby.

(3)   In proceedings for an offence under this section it is a defence for an accused who is not shown to have intended to stir up racial hatred to prove that he was not aware of the content of the recording and did not suspect, and had no reason to suspect, that it was threatening, abusive or insulting.

(4)   This section does not apply to the showing or playing of a recording solely for the purpose of enabling the recording to be included in a programme service.

Broadcasting Programme Stirring up Racial Hatred

B11.176   **Public Order Act 1986, s. 22**

(1)   If a programme involving threatening, abusive or insulting visual images or sounds is included in a programme service, each of the persons mentioned in subsection (2) is guilty of an offence if—

(a)   he intends to stir up racial hatred, or

(b)   having regard to all the circumstances racial hatred is likely to be stirred up thereby.

(2)   The persons are—

(a)   the person providing the programme service,

(b)   any person by whom the programme is produced or directed, and

(c)   any person by whom offending words or behaviour are used.

(3)   If the person providing the service, or a person by whom the programme was produced or directed, is not shown to have intended to stir up racial hatred, it is a defence for him to prove that—

(a)   he did not know and had no reason to suspect that the programme would involve the offending material, and

(b)   having regard to the circumstances in which the programme was included in a programme service, it was not reasonably practicable for him to secure the removal of the material.

(4)   It is a defence for a person by whom the programme was produced or directed who is not shown to have intended to stir up racial hatred to prove that he did not know and had no reason to suspect—

(a)   that the programme would be included in a programme service, or

(b)   that the circumstances in which the programme would be so included woud be such that racial hatred would be likely to be stirred up.

(5)   It is a defence for a person by whom offending words or behaviour were used and who is not shown to have intended to stir up racial hatred to prove that he did not know and had no reason to suspect—

(a)   that a programme involving the use of the offending material would be included in a programme service, or

(b)   that the circumstances in which a programme involving the use of the offending material would be so included, or in which a programme so included would involve the use of the offending material, would be such that racial hatred would be likely to be stirred up.

(6)   A person who is not shown to have intended to stir up racial hatred is not guilty of an offence under this section if he did not know, and had no reason to suspect, that the offending material was threatening, abusive or insulting.

Possession of Written Material or Recording Stirring up Racial Hatred

B11.177   **Public Order Act 1986, s. 23**

(1)   A person who has in his possession written material which is threatening, abusive or insulting, or a recording of visual images or sounds which are threatening, abusive or insulting, with a view to—

    (a) in the case of written material, its being displayed, published, distributed, or included in a programme service, whether by himself or another, or

    (b) in the case of a recording, its being distributed, shown, played, or included in a programme service, whether by himself or another,

is guilty of an offence if he intends racial hatred to be stirred up thereby or, having regard to all the circumstances, racial hatred is likely to be stirred up thereby.

    (2) For this purpose regard is to be had to such display, publication, distribution, showing, playing, or inclusion in a programme service as he has, or it may reasonably be inferred that he has, in view.

    (3) In proceedings for an offence under this section it is a defence for an accused who is not shown to have intended to stir up racial hatred to prove that he was not aware of the content of the written material or recording and did not suspect, and had no reason to suspect, that it was threatening, abusive or insulting.

DRUNK AND DISORDERLY

Offence, Procedure and Sentence

It is a summary offence, contrary to the CJA 1967, s. 91(1), where 'Any person who in **B11.178** any public place is guilty, while drunk, of disorderly behaviour . . .'. The maximum penalty for the offence is a fine not exceeding level 3 on the standard scale. The Magistrates' Association Guidelines (1997) indicate the following:

Aggravating Factors ⊕
    For example offensive language or behaviour; with group; offence committed on bail; previous convictions and failures to respond to previous sentences, if relevant.

Mitigating Factors ⊖
    For example induced by others; no significant disturbance; not threatening.

    Guideline: Is compensation, discharge or fine appropriate?

The guideline fine is £45 (low income), £115 (average income) and £270 (high income).

Drunk

It was held by the Divisional Court in *Neale* v *R.M.J.E. (a minor)* (1984) 80 Cr App R **B11.179** 20 that the natural and ordinary meaning of the word 'drunk' in this statutory context is that it is limited to cases of drunkenness induced by alcohol. It is not, therefore, committed where the state of the accused is a product of glue-sniffing. The Divisional Court took into account, first, the statutory context, and its history in deriving from the Licensing Act 1872, s. 12, which was clearly concerned with the regulation of the sales of intoxicating liquor, and secondly the primary dictionary meanings which were limited to alcohol-induced states. This decision was followed by the Divisional Court in *Lanham* v *Rickwood* (1984) 148 JP 737, a decision on the meaning of the word 'drunk' in the Licensing Act 1872, s. 12, which states: 'Every person found drunk in any highway or other public place, whether building or not, or on any licensed premises, shall be liable to a penalty'. In both of these decisions, the different approach of the Divisional Court in *Bradford* v *Wilson* (1983) 147 JP 573 was rejected because it was, clearly, of no assistance. In that case it had been held that the offence of driving whilst unfit through drink or drugs contrary to the Road Traffic Act 1972, s. 5(2), was committed where someone was unfit through glue-sniffing.

In *Lanham* v *Rickwood* it was also decided that the condition in which the accused was found does not have to be solely attributable to alcohol:

    In each case, the magistrates have to ask themselves, no doubt as a matter of simple common sense, whether a person's loss of self-control is attributable to his having indulged in an excessive consumption of intoxicating liquor. If the evidence before them is that he has indulged both in an excessive consumption of intoxicating liquor and also in some other form of activity, such as glue-sniffing, which may also have affected his self-control, they have to decide, as a matter of common sense, whether they are satisfied that, apart from the glue-sniffing, he has consumed intoxicating liquor to an extent which affects his steady self-control.

This decision is important not only on multiple causes of a condition, but also because it gives an indication of what is meant by 'drunk'. In *Neale* v *R.J.M.E. (a minor)* Robert Goff LJ made the same point about the meaning of drunkenness: 'the word "drunk", in ordinary common speech, . . . refers to someone who has taken intoxicating liquor to an extent which affects his steady self control'. Note that a person may be in a condition which can be described as 'drunk' but that need not be the same condition as that necessary to raise the defence of intoxication.

Disorderly Behaviour

B11.180 There appear to have been no reported decisions concerned with this concept. It is to be assumed that the words will be regarded as words of the ordinary English language having no special meaning. Thus reliance may be placed upon a dictionary meaning and the understanding of the magistrates.

Public Place

B11.181 The CJA 1967, s. 91(4), provides that, in s. 91, '"public place" includes any highway and any other premises or place to which at the material time the public have or are permitted to have access, whether on payment or otherwise'.

Power of Arrest and Taking to Treatment Centre

B11.182 A person who 'is guilty, while drunk, of disorderly behaviour' may be arrested without warrant (CJA 1967, s. 91(1)). There is no provision for the exercise of reasonable suspicion. Thus, if the person arrested was not drunk or the person's behaviour was not disorderly, it is submitted that the arrest would be unlawful. This power of arrest was not repealed by the PACE 1984 (*DPP* v *Kitching* (1989) 154 JP 293).

Under the CJA 1972, s. 34(1), where a constable arrests a person for an offence contrary to either the Licensing Act 1872, s. 12, or the CJA 1967, s. 91(1), he may, if he thinks fit, take that person to any place approved for the purposes as a treatment centre for alcoholics; while a person is being so taken he shall be deemed to be in lawful custody'. It is to be presumed that this provision is an exception to the generally applicable obligation in the PACE 1984, s. 30, to take an arrested person to a police station 'as soon as practicable after the arrest'. A person taken to an approved centre under the CJA 1972, s. 34(1), is not thereby liable to be detained in such a centre (s. 34(2)). The exercise of the power under s. 34 does not preclude the person being charged with any offence (s. 34(2)).

Related Offences

B11.183 *Found Drunk in Public* It is an offence, contrary to the Licensing Act 1872, s. 12, where a person is 'found drunk in any highway or other public place, whether a building or not, or on any licensed premises'. An offender is liable to a fine not exceeding level 1 on the standard scale. Where the person, whilst drunk, is guilty of disorderly behaviour, the CJA 1967, s. 91, has replaced this offence. The fact that the person's presence in the highway (or public place) is momentary and/or involuntary is irrelevant (*Winzar* v *Chief Constable of Kent* (1983) *The Times*, 28 March 1983). In that case, W, when found to be drunk, was told to leave hospital, having been taken there on a stretcher. The police were called when he was found slumped on a chair in a corridor. The police took him to a police car on the highway outside the hospital. He was 'found to be drunk' because he was 'perceived to be drunk', which meant 'to become aware of'. Although the police were aware that he was drunk in the hospital, he was found to be drunk in the highway, even though the only reason he was in the highway was because the police had taken him there. The Licensing Act 1902, s. 8, defines 'public place' as including 'any place to which the public have access, whether on payment or otherwise'. A person 'found drunk in any highway or other public place, whether a building or not, or on any licensed premises' may be arrested where he 'appears to be incapable of taking care of himself' (Licensing Act 1902, s. 1). The expression 'licensed premises' includes any place where intoxicating liquor is sold under an occasional licence (Licensing Act 1964, s. 200(2)).

Drunk in a Late Night Refreshment House It is a summary offence, contrary to **B11.184** the Late Night Refreshment Houses Act 1969, s. 9(4), where a 'person who is drunk, riotous, quarrelsome or disorderly in a late night refreshment house licensed under this Act refuses or neglects to leave on being requested to do so by the manager or occupier, or his agent or servant, or by any constable'. He is liable, on conviction, to a fine not exceeding level 1 on the standard scale.

Drunk while in Charge of a Child It is a summary offence, contrary to the Licensing **B11.185** Act 1902, s. 2(1), where a 'person is found drunk in any highway or other public place, whether a building or not, or on any licensed premises, while having the charge of a child apparently under the age of seven years'. He is liable, on conviction, to a fine not exceeding level 2 on the standard scale or to a term of imprisonment not exceeding one month. If the child appears to the court to be under the age of seven, the child is deemed to be under that age unless the contrary is proved (s. 2(2)). The person so found may be apprehended (s. 2(1)).

Drunk and in Charge of a Carriage, etc. It is an offence, contrary to the Licensing **B11.186** Act 1872, s. 12, where a person is drunk 'while in charge on any highway or other public place of any carriage, horse, cattle, or steam engine'. An offender is liable to a fine not exceeding level 1 on the standard scale or to a term of imprisonment not exceeding one month. There is power to apprehend an offender. The term 'carriage' includes a motor vehicle or trailer (Road Traffic Act 1988, s. 191) and a bicycle, whether ridden or pushed (*Corkery* v *Carpenter* [1951] 1 KB 102). 'Cattle' includes pigs and sheep (*Child* v *Hearns* (1874) LR 9 Exch 176).

A person liable to be charged with an offence under s. 3A, 4, 5, 7 or 30 of the Road Traffic Act 1988 is not liable to be charged under s. 12 of the Licensing Act 1872 (Road Traffic Act 1988, s. 5). As to the relevant road traffic offences, see **C5.9** *et seq*.

It is an offence, contrary to the Town Police Clauses Act 1847, s. 61, to be intoxicated while driving a hackney carriage; a person found guilty is liable to a penalty not exceeding level 1 on the standard scale. It is also an offence, contrary to the London Hackney Carriages Act 1843, s. 28, to be drunk during employment as a driver of a hackney carriage, or as a driver or conductor of a stage carriage in the Metropolitan Police District.

Drunk and in Possession of Loaded Firearm It is an offence, contrary to the **B11.187** Licensing Act 1872, s. 12, where a person is drunk when in possession of any loaded firearms. An offender is liable to a fine not exceeding level 1 on the standard scale or to a term of imprisonment not exceeding one month. There is power to apprehend an offender. As to firearms offences, see **B12**.

Drunk on Passenger Steamers It is an offence, contrary to the Merchant Shipping **B11.188** Act 1995, s. 101, to be drunk and persisting, after being refused admission on that account, in attempting to enter a passenger steamer and also to be drunk on board a passenger steamer, and refusing to leave such steamer when requested.

B11.189 ***Habitual Drunkard Purchasing Liquor*** Where a person is convicted of one of the offences mentioned in the Inebriates Act 1898, sch. 1, and that person in the previous 12 months has been convicted on three occasions of one of those offences, the court may order that notice of the conviction be sent to the police authority for the police area where the court is situated (Licensing Act 1902, s. 6(1)). The offences mentioned in the Inebriates Act 1898, sch. 1 are: offences contrary to the Licensing Act 1872, ss. 12 and 18, the Refreshment Houses Act 1860, s. 41, the Town Police Clauses Act 1847, s. 61, the London Hackney Carriages Act 1843, s. 28 and the Merchant Shipping Act 1995, s. 101. Such an habitual drunkard commits a summary offence if, within three years of the conviction, he 'purchases or obtains, or attempts to purchase or obtain, any intoxicating liquor at any premises licensed for the sale of intoxicating liquor by retail, or at the premises of any club registered' under the Licensing Act 1902, part III. An offender is liable to a fine not exceeding level 1 on the standard scale.

B11.190 ***Drunken Post Office Worker*** It is a summary offence, contrary to the Post Office Act 1953, s. 59(b), where a person is 'guilty of an act of drunkenness' when 'employed to convey or deliver a mail bag, or a postal packet in course of transmission by post, or to perform any other duty in respect of a mail bag or such a postal packet'. An offender is liable to a fine not exceeding level 2 on the standard scale.

B11.191 ***Offences Committed by Licensees*** A number of offences relating to drunkenness may be committed by licensees. In particular, a licensee may commit an offence by selling to an habitual drunkard (Licensing Act 1902, s. 6(2)(b)), by permitting drunkenness or violent quarrelsome or riotous conduct or by selling liquor to a drunken person (Licensing Act 1964, s. 172) or for a licensee of a late night refreshment house knowingly to permit drunken and disorderly persons to assemble at his premises (Late Night Refreshment Houses Act 1969, s. 9(1)).

SECTION B12: OFFENCES RELATING TO WEAPONS

FIREARMS OFFENCES GENERALLY

The Firearms Acts 1968 to 1997 control the possession etc. of firearms by dividing such **B12.1** weapons into a number of different categories namely firearms, firearms within s. 1 of the FA 1968, prohibited weapons, shotguns and air weapons. The F(A)A 1988, s. 8, introduced a provision relating to the deactivation of a weapon thus taking it out of a category into which it would otherwise have fallen (see **B12.9**). Many of the offences control ammunition as well as firearms. The two important concepts are ammunition generally, and ammunition to which s. 1 of the FA 1968 applies. The Firearms Acts have different approaches to whether a particular offence deals with imitation firearms (see **B12.12** and **B12.14**).

Council Directive 91/477/EEC (the European weapons directive) was brought into force by the Firearms Act (Amendment) Regulations 1992 (SI 1992 No. 2823). This introduced changes to the FA 1968 and the F(A)A 1988 in order to recognise the problems presented by development of the internal market of the European Communities.

General Procedural Provisions

Section 51(1) to (3) of the FA 1968 provides that the mode of trial, maximum **B12.2** punishments and powers of convicting courts with respect to offences created by that Act shall be as set out in sch. 6 to that Act, which is reproduced at **B12.3**.

Firearms Act 1968, s. 51

(4)   Notwithstanding section 127(1) of the Magistrates' Courts Act 1980 or section 136 of the Criminal Procedure (Scotland) Act 1995 (limitation of time for taking proceedings) summary proceedings for an offence under this Act, other than an offence under section 22(3) or an offence relating specifically to air weapons, may be instituted at any time within four years after the commission of the offence:
Provided that no such proceedings shall be instituted in England after the expiration of six months after the commission of the offence unless they are instituted by, or by the direction of, the Director of Public Prosecutions.

Sections 46 to 49 of the FA 1968 provide for powers of search, demand by a constable for production of certificates and police powers in relation to arms traffic.

Powers of forfeiture exercisable by a convicting court may be found in two places. Part II of sch. 6 to the FA 1968 (**B12.3**) provides certain specific powers. Section 52 provides generally for forfeiture and disposal of firearms and for cancellation of certificates.

Firearms Act 1968, s. 52

(1)   Where a person—
(a)   is convicted of an offence under this Act (other than an offence under section 22(3) or an offence relating specifically to air weapons) or is convicted of a crime for which he is sentenced to imprisonment, or detention in a detention centre or in a young offenders' institution in Scotland or is subject to a secure training order; or
(b)   has been ordered into a recognizance to keep the peace or to be of good behaviour, a condition of which is that he shall not possess, use or carry a firearm; or
(c)   is subject to a probation order containing a requirement that he shall not possess, use or carry a firearm; or
(d)   [applies to Scotland only]

the court by or before which he is convicted, or by which the order is made, may make such order as to the forfeiture or disposal of any firearm or ammunition found in his possession as the court thinks fit and may cancel any firearm certificate or shot gun certificate held by him.

(2)   Where the court cancels a certificate under this section—

(a)   the court shall cause notice to be sent to the chief officer of police by whom the certificate was granted; and

(b)   the chief officer of police shall by notice in writing require the holder of the certificate to surrender it; and

(c)   it is an offence for the holder to fail to surrender the certificate within 21 days from the date of the notice given him by the chief officer of police.

(3)   A constable may seize and detain any firearm or ammunition which may be the subject of an order for forfeiture under this section.

(4)   A court of summary jurisdiction or, in Scotland, the sheriff may, on the application of the chief officer of police, order any firearm or ammunition seized and detained by a constable under this Act to be destroyed or otherwise disposed of.

Section 52(1)(a) is amended by the CDA 1998, sch. 8, to take account of the introduction of detention and training orders and to replace secure training orders. The amendment is not yet in force.

Firearms Act 1968, Schedule 6

B12.3

Firearms Act 1968, sch. 6

PART I
TABLE OF PUNISHMENTS

Section of this Act creating offence	General nature of offence	Mode of prosecution	Punishment	Additional provisions
Section 1(1)	Possessing etc. firearm or ammunition without certificate.	(a) Summary	6 months or a fine of the prescribed sum; or both.	
		(b) On indictment	(i) where the offence is committed in an aggravated form within the meaning of section 4(4) of this Act, 7 years, or a fine; or both. (ii) in any other case, 5 years or a fine; or both.	[Applies to Scotland only.]
Section 1(2)	Non-compliance with condition of firearm certificate.	Summary	6 months or a fine of level 5 on the standard scale; or both.	
Section 2(1)	Possessing, etc. shot gun without shot gun certificate.	(a) Summary	6 months or the statutory maximum or both.	
		(b) On indictment	5 years or a fine or both.	[Applies to Scotland only.]
Section 2(2)	Non-compliance with condition of shot gun certificate.	Summary	6 months or a fine of level 5 on the standard scale; or both.	
Section 3(1)	Trading in firearms without being registered as firearms dealer.	(a) Summary	6 months or a fine of the prescribed sum; or both.	
		(b) On indictment	5 years or a fine; or both.	[Applies to Scotland only.]
Section 3(2)	Selling firearm to person without a certificate.	(a) Summary	6 months or a fine of the prescribed sum, or both.	
		(b) On indictment.	5 years or a fine; or both.	
Section 3(3)	Repairing, testing etc. firearm for person without a certificate.	(a) Summary	6 months or a fine of the prescribed sum; or both.	
		(b) On indictment	5 years or a fine; or both.	

Section of this Act creating offence	General nature of offence	Mode of prosecution	Punishment	Additional provisions
Section 3(5)	Falsifying certificate, etc. with view to acquisition of firearm.	(a) Summary	6 months or a fine of the prescribed sum; or both.	
		(b) On indictment	5 years or a fine; or both.	
Section 3(6)	Pawnbroker taking firearm in pawn.	Summary	3 months or a fine of level 3 on the standard scale; or both.	
Section 4(1) (3)	Shortening a shot gun; conversion of firearms.	(a) Summary	6 months or a fine of the prescribed sum; or both.	
		(b) On indictment	7 years or a fine; or both.	
Section 5(1)	Possessing or distributing prohibited weapons or ammunition.	(a) Summary	6 months or a fine of the prescribed sum; or both.	
		(b) On indictment	10 years or a fine; or both.	
Section 5(1A)	Possessing or distributing other prohibited weapons or ammunition.	(a) Summary	6 months or a fine of the statutory maximum; or both.	
		(b) On indictment	10 years or a fine; or both.	
Section 5(5)	Non-compliance with condition of Defence Council authority.	Summary	6 months or a fine of level 5 on the standard scale; or both.	
Section 5(6)	Non-compliance with requirement to surrender authority to possess, etc. prohibited weapon or ammunition.	Summary	A fine of level 3 on the standard scale.	
Section 6(3)	Contravention of order under s. 6 (or corresponding Northern Irish order) restricting removal of arms.	Summary	3 months or, for each firearm or parcel of ammunition in respect of which the offence is committed, a fine of level 3 on the standard scale; or both.	Para. 2 of part II of this schedule applies.
Section 7(2)	Making false statement in order to obtain police permit.	Summary	6 months or a fine of level 5 on the standard scale; or both.	

Section 9(3)	Making false statement in order to obtain permit for auction of firearms etc.	Summary	6 months or a fine not exceeding level 5 on the standard scale; or both.	
Section 13(2)	Making false statement in order to obtain permit for removal of signalling apparatus.	Summary	6 months or a fine of level 5 on the standard scale; or both.	
Section 16	Possession of firearm with intent to endanger life or injure property.	On indictment	Life imprisonment or a fine; or both.	
Section 16A	Possession of firearm or imitation firearm with intent to cause fear of violence.	On indictment	10 years or a fine, or both.	
Section 17(1)	Use of firearm or imitation firearm to resist arrest.	On indictment	Life imprisonment or a fine; or both.	Paras 3 to 5 of part II of this schedule apply.
Section 17(2)	Possessing firearm or imitation firearm while committing an offence in schedule 1 or, in Scotland, an offence specified in schedule 2.	On indictment	Life imprisonment or a fine; or both.	Paras 3 and 6 of part II of this schedule apply.
Section 18(1)	Carrying firearm or imitation firearm with intent to commit indictable offence (or, in Scotland, an offence specified in schedule 2) or to resist arrest.	On indictment	Life imprisonment or a fine; or both.	
Section 19	Carrying loaded firearm in public place.	(a) Summary (b) On indictment (but not if the firearm is an air weapon).	6 months or a fine of the prescribed sum; or both. 7 years or a fine; or both.	
Section 20(1)	Trespassing with firearm or imitation firearm in a building.	(a) Summary (b) On indictment (but not in the case of an imitation firearm or if the firearm is an air weapon).	6 months or a fine of the prescribed sum; or both. 7 years or a fine; or both.	

Section of this Act creating offence	General nature of offence	Mode of prosecution		Punishment	Additional provisions
Section 20(2)	Trespassing with firearm or imitation firearm on land.	Summary		3 months or a fine of level 4 on the standard scale; or both.	
Section 21(4)	Contravention of provisions denying firearms to ex-prisoners and the like.	(a)	Summary	6 months or a fine of the prescribed sum; or both.	
Section 21(5)	Supplying firearms to person denied them under section 21.	(b) (a)	On indictment Summary	5 years or a fine; or both. 6 months or a fine of the prescribed sum; or both.	
Section 22(1)	Person under 17 acquiring firearm.	(b) Summary	On indictment	5 years or a fine; or both. 6 months or a fine of level 5 on the standard scale; or both.	
Section 22(1A)	Person under 18 using certificated firearm for unauthorised purpose.	Summary		3 months or a fine of level 5 on the standard scale or both.	
Section 22(2)	Person under 14 having firearm in his possession without lawful authority.	Summary		6 months or a fine of level 5 on the standard scale; or both.	
Section 22(3)	Person under 15 having with him a shot gun without adult supervision.	Summary		A fine of level 3 on the standard scale.	Para. 8 of part II of this schedule applies.
Section 22(4)	Person under 14 having with him an air weapon or ammunition therefor.	Summary		A fine of level 3 on the standard scale.	Paras 7 and 8 of part II of this schedule apply.
Section 22(5)	Person under 17 having with him an air weapon in a public place.	Summary		A fine of level 3 on the standard scale.	Paras 7 and 8 of part II of this schedule apply.
Section 23(1)	Person under 14 making improper use of air weapon when under supervision; person supervising him permitting such use.	Summary		A fine of level 3 on the standard scale.	Paras 7 and 8 of part II of this schedule apply.

Section	Offence	Mode	Punishment	Notes
Section 24(1)	Selling or letting on hire a firearm to person under 17.	Summary	6 months or a fine of level 5 on the standard scale; or both.	Para. 9 of part II of this schedule applies.
Section 24(2)	Supplying firearm or ammunition (being of a kind to which section 1 of this Act applies) to person under 14.	Summary	6 months or a fine of level 5 on the standard scale; or both.	Paras 7 and 8 of part II of this schedule apply.
Section 24(3)	Making gift of shot gun to person under 15.	Summary	A fine of level 3 on the standard scale.	
Section 24(4)	Supplying air weapon to person under 14.	Summary	A fine of level 3 on the standard scale.	
Section 25	Supplying firearm to person drunk or insane.	Summary	3 months or a fine of level 3 on the standard scale; or both.	
Section 26(5)	Making false statement in order to procure grant or renewal of a firearm or shot gun certificate.	Summary	6 months or a fine of level 5 on the standard scale; or both.	
Section 29(3)	Making false statement in order to procure variation of a firearm certificate.	Summary	6 months or a fine of level 5 on the standard scale; or both.	
Section 30D(3)	Failing to surrender certificate on revocation.	Summary	A fine of level 3 on the standard scale.	
Section 32B(5)	Failure to surrender expired European firearms pass.	Summary	A fine of level 3 on the standard scale.	
Section 32C(6)	Failure to produce European firearms pass or Article 7 authority for variation or cancellation etc.; failure to notify loss or theft of firearm identified in pass or to produce pass for endorsement.	Summary	3 months or a fine of level 5 on the standard scale; or both.	

Section of this Act creating offence	General nature of offence	Mode of prosecution	Punishment	Additional provisions
Section 38(8)	Failure to surrender certificate of registration [or register of transactions] on removal of firearms dealer's name from register.	Summary	A fine of level 3 on the standard scale.	
Section 39(1)	Making false statement in order to secure registration or entry in register of a place of business.	Summary	6 months or a fine of level 5 on the standard scale; or both.	
Section 39(2)	Registered firearms dealer having place of business not entered in the register.	Summary	6 months or a fine of level 5 on the standard scale; or both.	
Section 39(3)	Non-compliance with condition of registration.	Summary	6 months or a fine of level 5 on the standard scale; or both.	
Section 40(5)	Non-compliance by firearms dealer with provisions as to register of transactions; making false entry in register.	Summary	6 months or a fine of level 5 on the standard scale; or both.	
Section 42A	Failure to report transaction authorised by visitor's shot gun permit.	Summary	3 months or a fine of level 5 on the standard scale or both.	
Section 46	Obstructing constable or civilian officer in exercise of search powers.	Summary	6 months or a fine of level 5 on the standard scale; or both.	
Section 47(2)	Failure to hand over firearm or ammunition on demand by constable.	Summary	3 months, or a fine of level 4 on the standard scale; or both.	
Section 48(3)	Failure to comply with requirement of a constable that a person shall declare his name and address.	Summary	A fine of level 3 on the standard scale.	

Section 48A(4)	Failure to produce firearms pass issued in another Member State.	Summary	A fine of level 3 on the standard scale.	Para. 2 of part II of this schedule applies.
Section 49(3)	Failure to give constable facilities for examination of firearms in transit, or to produce papers.	Summary	3 months or, for each firearm or parcel of ammunition in respect of which the offence is committed, a fine of level 3 on the standard scale; or both.	
Section 52(2)(c)	Failure to surrender firearm or shot gun certificate cancelled by court on conviction.	Summary	A fine of level 3 on the standard scale.	

PART II

1.   [Applies to Scotland only.]

2.   In the case of an offence against section 6(3) or 49(3) of this Act, the court before which the offender is convicted may, if the offender is the owner of the firearms or ammunition, make such order as to the forfeiture of the firearms or ammunition as the court thinks fit.

3.—(1)   Where in England or Wales a person who has attained the age of seventeen is charged before a magistrates' court with an offence triable either way listed in schedule 1 to the Magistrates' Courts Act 1980 ('the listed offence') and is also charged before that court with an offence under section 17(1) or (2) of this Act, the following provisions of this paragraph shall apply.

   (2)   Subject to the following subparagraph the court shall proceed as if the listed offence were triable only on indictment and sections 18 to 23 of the said Act of 1980 (procedure for determining mode of trial of offences triable either way) shall not apply in relation to that offence.

   (3)   If the court determines not to commit the accused for trial in respect of the offence under section 17(1) or (2), or if proceedings before the court for that offence are otherwise discontinued, the preceding subparagraph shall cease to apply as from the time when this occurs and—

   (a)   if at that time the court has not yet begun to inquire into the listed offence as examining justices, the court shall, in the case of the listed offence, proceed in the ordinary way in accordance with the said sections 18 to 23, but

   (b)   if at that time the court has begun so to inquire into the listed offence, those sections shall continue not to apply and the court shall proceed with its inquiry into that offence as examining justices, but shall have power in accordance with section 25(3) and (4) of the said Act of 1980 to change to summary trial with the accused's consent.

4.   Where a person commits an offence under section 17(1) of this Act in respect of the lawful arrest or detention of himself for any other offence committed by him, he shall be liable to the penalty provided by part I of this schedule in addition to any penalty to which he may be sentenced for the other offence.

5.   If on the trial of a person for an offence under section 17(1) of this Act the jury are not satisfied that he is guilty of that offence but are satisfied that he is guilty of an offence under section 17(2), the jury may find him guilty of the offence under section 17(2) and he shall then be punishable accordingly.

6.   The punishment to which a person is liable for an offence under section 17(2) of this Act shall be in addition to any punishment to which he may be liable for the offence first referred to in section 17(2).

7.   The court by which a person is convicted of an offence under section 22(4) or (5), 23(1) or 24(4) of this Act may make such order as it thinks fit as to the forfeiture or disposal of the air weapon or ammunition in respect of which the offence was committed.

8.   The court by which a person is convicted of an offence under section 22(3), (4) or (5), 23(1) or 24(4) may make such order as it thinks fit as to the forfeiture or disposal of any firearm or ammunition found in his possesssion.

9.   The court by which a person is convicted of an offence under section 24(3) of this Act may make such order is it thinks fit as to the forfeiture or disposal of the shotgun or ammunition in respect of which the offence was committed.

Meaning of 'Firearm'

B12.4   **Firearms Act 1968, s. 57**

   (1)   In this Act, the expression 'firearm' means a lethal barrelled weapon of any description from which any shot, bullet or other missile can be discharged, and includes—
   (a)   any prohibited weapon, whether it is such a lethal weapon as aforesaid or not; and
   (b)   any component part of such a lethal or prohibited weapon; and
   (c)   any accessory to any such weapon designed or adapted to diminish the noise or flash caused by firing the weapon.

The meaning of 'prohibited weapon' is considered at **B12.38** *et seq*. It is not a generally relevant concept. The crucial concept is that of a 'lethal barrelled weapon'. There is no statutory definition. The Divisional Court in *Grace* v *DPP* (1989) 153 JP 491 held that the prosecution has the obligation to prove the following in order to satisfy the definition:

(a)   whether the weapon was one from which any shot, bullet or other missile could be discharged or whether it could be adapted so as to be made capable of discharging such a missile (see also *Freeman* [1970] 1 WLR 788, where a starting pistol was capable of discharging bullets since the barrel had been partially drilled), and

(b)   if so satisfied, whether it was a lethal barrelled weapon.

In determining the second question, the Divisional Court in *Read* v *Donovan* [1947] KB 326 established a test, which has been consistently followed, that a weapon is lethal if it is capable of causing injury, regardless of the maker's intentions. In that case a signal pistol capable of killing at short range was a lethal weapon. In *Cafferata* v *Wilson* [1936] 3 All ER 149, it was held that a dummy revolver which could be converted into a weapon capable of killing a man at a range of five feet by drilling it in the appropriate fashion was a lethal weapon. In *Moore* v *Gooderham* [1960] 1 WLR 1308, an air gun which was capable of causing injury from which death might result if it was misused was held to be a lethal weapon. In *Thorpe* [1987] 1 WLR 383 (applying *Read* v *Donovan* and *Moore* v *Gooderham*), an air pellet revolver was held to be a lethal weapon since it was capable of causing injury from which death could result if misused. In *Castle* v *DPP* (1998) *The Times*, 3 April 1998, the Divisional Court decided that justices were entitled to conclude that two air rifles suitable for shooting small vermin and two air rifles suitable for target practice were 'lethal barrelled weapons' on the basis that they 'could cause injury from which death might result if fired at point blank range at a vulnerable part of the body'.

However, it does not follow as a matter of law that the devices considered in these cases are lethal barrelled weapons. In *Grace* v *DPP* (1989) 153 JP 491, the Divisional Court, in explaining what was said in *Moore* v *Gooderham* held that whether the definition of 'lethal weapon' is satisfied is a question to be dealt with and established on the basis of the evidence in the particular case. Evidence that the gun is working and of its impact is necessary, but expert evidence of its potential impact is not essential. The necessary evidence was supplied in *Castle* v *DPP* by the salesman. He stated that the guns were working and for what purpose they would be suitable; it was from that evidence that the magistrates were able to draw the inference that the guns were lethal barrelled weapons. The correct approach, according to the Court of Appeal in *Singh* [1989] Crim LR 724, is for a judge to determine whether the device, in this case a hand-held signalling discharger, is capable of amounting to a firearm. Then he should leave to the jury the question of whether it actually is a lethal weapon. In the instant case, the judge had correctly left the jury to decide the matter where there was a dispute between expert witnesses as to whether the device had a barrel.

Firearms within the Firearms Act 1968, s. 1

The term 'firearms' has a meaning more limited than that considered above. It applies   **B12.5** to the offence contrary to the FA 1968, s. 1, and to a number of other offences; it applies to all firearms except shotguns and certain air weapons (the meaning of which is considered at **B12.7** and **B12.8**). However, sawn-off shotguns and air weapons declared to be 'specially dangerous' are firearms to which s. 1 applies. An air weapon is specially dangerous if it is declared to be so by the Secretary of State.

Firearms (Dangerous Air Weapons) Rules 1969 (SI 1969 No. 47), rr. 2 and 3

2.—(1)   Subject to paragraph (2) below, rule 3 of these rules applies to an air weapon (that is to say, an air rifle, air gun or air pistol)—

(a)   which is capable of discharging a missile so that the missile has, on being discharged from the muzzle of the weapon, kinetic energy in excess, in the case of an air pistol of 6ft lb or, in the case of an air weapon other than an air pistol, of 12 ft lb.

(b)   which is disguised as another object.

(2)   Rule 3 of these rules does not apply to a weapon which only falls within paragraph (1)(a) above and which is designed for use only when submerged in water.

3.   An air weapon to which this rule applies is hereby declared to be specially dangerous.

The FA 1968, s. 57(1), means that it is not only the weapon itself which is a firearm to which s. 1(3) applies, but also components of, and accessories to, such firearms. Consequently, the components of, and accessories to, shotguns, other than those with a shortened barrel, and air weapons, other than those declared to be specially dangerous, are also not included in the phrase 'firearms to which s. 1 of the FA 1968 applies'.

The F(A)A 1988, s. 7(2), makes it clear that the conversion of a weapon into a shotgun or air weapon does not affect its classification as a firearm to which s. 1 applies. This section provides:

Firearms (Amendment) Act 1988, s. 7

(2)   Any weapon which—

(a)   has at any time since the coming into force of section 2 . . . been a weapon to which section 1 of the principal Act applies; or

(b)   would at any previous time have been such a weapon if those sections had then been in force, shall if it has, or at any time has had, a rifled barrel less than 24 inches in length, be treated as a weapon to which section 1 of the principal Act applies notwithstanding anything done for the purpose of converting it into a shotgun or an air weapon.

(3)   For the purposes of subsection (2) above there shall be disregarded the shortening of a barrel by a registered firearms dealer for the sole purpose of replacing part of it so as to produce a barrel not less than 24 inches in length.

Meaning of 'Prohibited Weapon'

B12.6   The FA 1968, s. 57(4), makes it clear that 'prohibited weapon' has the meaning assigned to it by s. 5(2). This provision is considered further at **B12.38** *et seq.* below. The F(A)A 1988, s. 7(1), which is also dealt with below at **B12.41**, makes it clear that conversion of a weapon does not affect its classification as a prohibited weapon.

Meaning of 'Shotgun'

B12.7   'Shotgun' is defined in the FA 1968, s. 57(4), as having the meaning assigned to it by s. 1(3)(a).

Firearms Act 1968, s. 1

(3)   This section applies to every firearm except—

(a)   a shotgun within the meaning of this Act, that is to say a smooth-bore gun (not being an airgun) which—

(i)   has a barrel not less than 24 inches in length and does not have any barrel with a bore exceeding 2 inches in diameter;

(ii)   either has no magazine or has a non-detachable magazine incapable of holding more than two cartridges; and

(iii)   is not a revolver gun. . . .

(3A)   A gun which has been adapted to have such a magazine as is mentioned in subsection (3)(a)(ii) above shall not be regarded as falling within that provision unless the magazine bears a mark approved by the Secretary of State for denoting that fact and that mark has been made, and the adaptation has been certified in writing as having been carried out in a manner approved by him, either by one of the two companies mentioned in section 58(1) of this Act or by such other person as may be approved by him for that purpose.

The companies mentioned in s. 58(1) are the Society of the Mystery of Gunmakers of the City of London and the Birmingham proof house.

The length of the barrel of a firearm shall be measured from the muzzle to the point at which the charge is exploded on firing (s. 57(6)(a)). 'Revolver', in relation to a smooth-bore gun, means a gun containing a series of chambers which revolve when the gun is fired (s. 57(2B)).

Meaning of 'Air Weapon'

The FA 1968, s. 57(4), provides that 'air weapon' has the meaning assigned to it by **B12.8** s. 1(3)(b), 'that is to say an air rifle, airgun or air pistol' and this includes 'a reference to a rifle, pistol or gun powered by compressed carbon dioxide' (F(A)A 1997, s. 48). The Court of Appeal in *Thorpe* [1987] 1 WLR 383 held that it is essential that the propulsion of the bullet, shot or other missile be caused by or derived from the use of air. The weapon in question was not an air weapon, since the propulsion was provided by the release of carbon dioxide from a disposable cylinder in the butt of a revolver firing air pellets.

Deactivated Weapons

Any firearm may be deactivated and so cease to be a firearm.   **B12.9**

Firearms (Amendment) Act 1988, s. 8

For the purposes of the principal Act and this Act it shall be presumed, unless the contrary is shown, that a firearm has been rendered incapable of discharging any shot, bullet or other missile, and has consequently ceased to be a firearm within the meaning of those Acts, if—

(a) it bears a mark which has been approved by the Secretary of State for denoting that fact and which has been made either by one of the two companies mentioned in section 58(1) of the principal Act or by such other person as may be approved by the Secretary of State for the purposes of this section; and

(b) that company or person has certified in writing that work has been carried out on the firearm in a manner approved by the Secretary of State for rendering it incapable of discharging any shot, bullet or other missile.

As to s. 58(1), see **B12.7**.

Meaning of 'Ammunition'

The FA 1968, s. 58(3), makes clear that control over ammunition is in addition to and **B12.10** not in derogation of any enactment relating to the keeping and sale of explosives. Section 57(2) provides a general definition of 'ammunition'.

Firearms Act 1968, s. 57

(2) In this Act, the expression 'ammunition' means ammunition for any firearm and includes grenades, bombs and other like missiles, whether capable of use with a firearm or not, and also includes prohibited ammunition.

Ammunition to which the Firearms Act 1968, s. 1, applies

Section 1 applies to all ammunition except that excluded by s. 1(4).   **B12.11**

Firearms Act 1968, s. 1

(4) This section applies to any ammunition for a firearm, except the following articles, namely—

(a) cartridges containing five or more shot, none of which exceeds 0.36 inch in diameter;

(b) ammunition for an airgun, air rifle or air pistol; and

(c) blank cartridges not more than one inch in diameter measures immediately in front of the rim or cannelure of the base of the cartridge.

Paragraph (c) does not exclude a primed cartridge, that is one without gunpowder. Since such a cartridge is capable of producing an explosive effect, it is ammunition (*Stubbings* [1990] Crim LR 811).

APPLICATION OF OFFENCES TO IMITATION FIREARMS

There are three categories into which firearms offences can be placed for the purposes of considering the extension of a relevant offence to an imitation firearm.

Offences Applying to Imitation Firearms by Virtue of the Wording of the Section

B12.12 Some offences, by their definition, apply to 'imitation firearms', see, for example, the offence contrary to the FA 1968, s. 17(1). If this is the case 'imitation firearm' has the following definition, according to s. 57(4).

Firearms Act 1968, s. 57

(4) ... 'imitation firearms' means any thing which has the appearance of being a firearm (other than such a weapon as is mentioned in section 5(1)(b) of this Act) whether or not it is capable of discharging any shot, bullet or other missile.

Weapons in s. 5(1)(b) are one category of prohibited weapons, that is, a weapon designed or adapted for the discharge of any noxious liquid, gas or other thing, see **B12.38** to **B12.45**.

The essential element in determining whether an article is an imitation firearm is whether it had the appearance of a firearm when the offence was committed. The evidence of witnesses who saw the article is relevant. In addition, the jury, in deciding this question, may see the article itself (*Morris* (1984) 79 Cr App R 104). The Court of Appeal considered a British Columbian decision, *Sloan* (1974) 19 CCC (2d) 190, where it was decided that the article must be an instrument of some sort in order to amount to an imitation firearm, and thus a finger could not be an imitation firearm.

Offences Applying to Imitation Firearms by Virtue of the Firearms Act 1982

B12.13 Offences which do not fall within **B12.12** may nevertheless extend to imitation firearms if the FA 1982 covers the offence in question. In brief, the following steps have to be considered to determine whether an offence falls within the FA 1982, and thus extends to an imitation firearm:

(a) The FA 1982 applies to any firearm which has the appearance of being a firearm to which the FA 1968, s. 1, applies and is readily convertible into such a firearm (FA 1982, s. 1(1)). For the purpose of an imitation firearm all air weapons are covered, whether or not they are specially dangerous (s. 1(4)(a)). However, the definition does not apply to component parts and accessories (s. 1(4)(b)).

(b) This definition of imitation firearm applies to all offences which are concerned with a firearm to which the FA 1968, s. 1, applies (FA 1982, s. 1(2)), except ss. 4(3) and (4), 16 to 20 and 47 of the FA 1968 (FA 1982, s. 2(2)(a) and (b) and (3)).

Firearms Act 1982, ss. 1 and 2

1.—(1) This Act applies to an imitation firearm if—

(a) it has the appearance of being a firearm to which section 1 of the 1968 Act (firearms requiring a firearm certificate) applies; and

(b) it is so constructed or adapted as to be readily convertible into a firearm to which that section applies.

(2) Subject to section 2(2) of this Act and the following provisions of this section, the 1968 Act shall apply in relation to an imitation firearm to which this Act applies as it applies in relation to a firearm to which section 1 of that Act applies.

(3) Subject to the modifications in subsection (4) below, any expression given a meaning for the purposes of the 1968 Act has the same meaning in this Act.

(4) For the purposes of this section and the 1968 Act, as it applies by virtue of this section—

(a) the definition of air weapon in section 1(3)(b) of that Act (air weapons excepted from requirement of firearm certificate) shall have effect without the exclusion of any type declared by rules made by the Secretary of State under section 53 of that Act to be specially dangerous; and

(b) the definition of firearm in section 57(1) of that Act shall have effect without paragraphs (b) and (c) of that subsection (component parts and accessories).

. . .

(6) For the purposes of this section an imitation firearm shall be regarded as readily convertible into a firearm to which section 1 of the 1968 Act applies if—

(a) it can be so converted without any special skill on the part of the person converting it in the construction or adaptation of firearms of any description; and

(b) the work involved in converting it does not require equipment or tools other than such as are in common use by persons carrying out works of construction and maintenance in their own homes.

. . .

2.—(2) The following provisions of the 1968 Act do not apply by virtue of this Act to an imitation firearm to which this Act applies, that is to say—

(a) section 4(3) and (4) . . . ; and

(b) the provisions of that Act which relate to, or to the enforcement of control over, the manner in which a firearm is used or the circumstances in which it is carried;

but without prejudice, in the case of the provisions mentioned in paragraph (b) above, to the application to such an imitation firearm of such of those provisions as apply to imitation firearms apart from this Act.

(3) The provisions referred to in subsection (2)(b) are sections 16 to 20 and section 47.

If the FA 1982 does apply, a special defence is introduced by s. 1(5):

Firearms Act 1982, s. 1

(5) In any proceedings brought by virtue of this section for an offence under the 1968 Act involving an imitation firearm to which this Act applies, it shall be a defence for the accused to show that he did not know and had no reason to suspect that the imitation firearm was so constructed or adapted as to be readily convertible into a firearm to which section 1 of that Act applies.

Section Creating the Offence Not Applying to Imitation Firearm

If the section does not fall into either **B12.12** or **B12.13**, it is a section which does not **B12.14** apply to an imitation firearm, however that phrase is defined.

POSSESSING ETC. FIREARM OR AMMUNITION WITHOUT FIREARM CERTIFICATE

Definition

Firearms Act 1968, s. 1   B12.15

(1) Subject to any exemption under this Act, it is an offence for a person—

(a) to have in his possession, or to purchase or acquire, a firearm to which this section applies without holding a firearm certificate in force at the time, or otherwise than as authorised by such a certificate;

(b) to have in his possession, or to purchase or acquire, any ammunition to which this section applies without holding a firearm certificate in force at the time, or otherwise than as authorised by such a certificate, or in quantities in excess of those so authorised.

The aggravated form of the offence is to be found in the FA 1968, s. 4(4):

Firearms Act 1968, s. 4

(4)   A person who commits an offence under section 1 of this Act by having in his possession, or purchasing or acquiring, a shotgun which has been shortened contrary to subsection (1) [of section 4] or a firearm which has been converted as mentioned in subsection (3) [of section 4] (whether by a registered firearms dealer or not), without holding a firearm certificate authorising him to have it in his possession, or to purchase or acquire it, shall be treated for the purposes of provisions of this Act relating to the punishment of offences as committing that offence in an aggravated form.

As to procedure and sentence, see the FA 1968, ss. 51 and 52 and sch. 6 at **B12.2** and **B12.3**. As to those firearms and ammunition to which the FA 1968, s. 1, applies, see **B12.5** and **B12.11**.

Extension to Imitation Firearms

B12.16 The FA 1982, applies to the FA 1968, s. 1, thus extending it to imitation firearms, as defined in the FA 1982, see **B12.13**.

Indictment (for Offence under the FA 1968, s. 1(1)(a))

B12.17   Statement of Offence

Possessing a firearm without holding a current firearm certificate contrary to section 1(1)(a) of the Firearms Act 1968

Particulars of Offence

A on or about the . . . day of . . . was in possession of [or: purchased (or acquired)] a firearm to which section 1 of the Firearms Act 1968 applies, namely a . . . , without holding a firearm certificate in force at that time

Firearm Certificate

B12.18 A person does not commit the offence if he has a firearm certificate which is defined by the FA 1968, s. 57(4), as being a certificate granted by a chief officer of police under s. 26. A firearm certificate is a public document. In *Paul* [1999] Crim LR 79 the Court of Appeal rejected the possibility of allowing the jury to approach the words in a firearm certificate as those of the ordinary English language (as in *Brutus* v *Cozens* [19973] AC 854):

If [a firearm certificate] is to fulfil the clear statutory objective of providing a certain and effective system of control of particular firearms it is obvious and a matter of common-sense that it should have a certain and consistent meaning. That can only be achieved by trial judges determining the meaning as a matter of law, leaving it to the jury in each case to determine . . . whether the physical attributes of the firearm in question bring it within that meaning.

The trial judge in *Paul*, therefore, had to decide what the words 'humane killer' in the certificate meant and it would be for the jury to decide whether they covered the revolver in question, a Ruger .357. In doing this, it is not the intention of the possessor/transferor or transferee that matters, but the physical characteristics of the weapon that matter. The judge, thus, took the correct approach, and his definition was also approved. He correctly drew on the definition of 'slaughtering instrument' in s. 57(4) in defining 'humane killer' as meaning 'a firearm specially designed or adapted for instantaneous slaughter of animals . . .'.

Section 1(2) makes it an offence to fail to comply with the conditions subject to which a firearm certificate is held. As to procedure and sentence see **B12.2** and **B12.3**. As to possession authorised in accordance with a European firearms pass or other documents for European purposes, see the FA 1968, ss. 32A to 32C.

Firearms certificates are issued in accordance with the provisions of the Firearms Acts 1968 to 1997, provisions which have been significantly amended by the F(A)A 1997, see the Firearms Rules 1998 (SI 1998 No. 1941). Conditions may be imposed by the grant of a certificate on the use of a firearm, and certain conditions are statutorily imposed, for example, that any rifle or muzzle-loading pistol, which is not a prohibited weapon (see **B12.38** *et seq*.) and is covered by a certificate, may be used only for target shooting and that the certificate holder must be a member of an approved rifle or muzzle-loading pistol club (F(A)A 1997, s. 44(1)).

Meaning of 'Acquire'

The FA 1968, s. 57(4), provides that 'acquire' means 'hire, accept as a gift or borrow' **B12.19** and that 'acquisition' is to be construed accordingly.

Possession Generally

In *Sullivan* v *Earl of Caithness* [1976] QB 966, the Divisional Court held that an owner **B12.20** of firearms is in possession of them even if they are kept in another's custody. Physical custody of a firearm is, therefore, not necessary in order for someone to be in possession of it. The Divisional Court decided in *Hall* v *Cotton* [1987] QB 504 that a person does not have to have physical control of the firearms nor does he have to be present in the place where the firearms are kept in order to be in possession of them. The court made clear that whether a person is in possession of firearms is a question to be decided on the facts of the particular case in question. Custodial possession and physical possession of firearms can reside in different people. In *Woodage* v *Moss* [1974] 1 WLR 411, the Divisional Court held that the defendant was in possession of a firearm when he was handed it by an unknown person to deliver it to a dealer as a surrendered weapon.

Possession and *Mens Rea*

The offences contrary to the FA 1968, ss. 1 and 19 (see **B12.15** and **B12.64**), are both **B12.21** absolute offences, a principle drawn from a line of cases commencing with the possession of drugs case, *Warner* v *Metropolitan Police Commissioner* [1969] 2 AC 256 (see **B20.13**). The Court of Appeal in *Hussain* [1981] 1 WLR 416, in considering s. 1, held that it is an absolute offence, except for the requirement that the defendant must know that he is in possession of something which is, in fact, a firearm. See also *Howells* [1977] QB 614 (also on s. 1). The Court of Appeal in *Waller* [1991] Crim LR 381 held that the offence contrary to s. 1 is committed even where the defendant does not know there is a firearm in the container which he possesses (cf. the position with regard to drugs at **B20.13**). In *Steele* [1993] Crim LR 298 where it was recognised that the approach is Draconian.

Hussain was followed in *Vann* [1996] Crim LR 52, a case on s. 19, where the Court of Appeal held that a person does not have to know that the item which he has with him is a firearm, so no *mens rea* is required except insofar as is necessary to establish that the defendant has the article with him. There was no justification for reviewing the cases leading to this principle under *Pepper* v *Hart* [1993] AC 593. In any case, there was no argument on the basis of the report in *Hansard*, and in the light of Parliament's failure to amend the rule in the 1988 Act, that full *mens rea* should apply to either offence. The Court of Appeal appeared to reject what it called the 'halfway house', that is that the 'offence would not be proved if the defendant was unaware of the nature of the article he was holding, or the contents of the container, and he had no reasonable opportunity of discovering what it was or what they were', although subsequent comments lack clarity. It expressed no view as to whether the 'halfway house' defence could arise under the reasonable excuse defence applicable to s. 19 (see **B12.64**).

In *Harrison* [1996] 1 Cr App R 138, a case concerned with s. 19, the Court of Appeal, following *Waller*, held that, if a person claims that he was mistaken as to whether what he possessed was a loaded shotgun or loaded air weapon, his argument will not avail, provided he knowingly had possession of the item. So although H knowingly had possession of a shotgun, but claimed that he was not aware that it was loaded, his argument failed and his conviction was upheld. In *Price* v *DPP* (1996 unreported), the Divisional Court held, following *Bradish* [1990] 1 QB 981 (see **B12.45**), *Waller*, *Steele* and *Harrison*, that a person was in possession of the contents of a rucksack (ammunition) when he had knowledge of possession of the rucksack, but had no idea of its contents (and was indeed mistaken as to whom it belonged, and as to its nature and quality).

EXEMPTIONS AND DEFENCES

B12.22 The FA 1968, s. 1(1), indicates that the offence is 'subject to any exemption under this Act'. The relevant exemptions are listed in **B12.22** to **B12.35** inclusive.

Holders of Police Permits

A person may have a permit from the chief officer of police, under the FA 1968, s. 7(1) (and see the Firearms Rules 1998 (SI 1998 No. 1941)), which allows him to have in his possession, without a certificate, a firearm and or ammunition in accordance with the terms of the permit. It is a summary offence, contrary to s. 7(2), for a person knowingly or recklessly to make a statement which is false in any material particular for the purpose of procuring, whether for himself or another, the grant of a permit under s. 7(1). As to procedure and sentence, see **B12.2** and **B12.3**.

Authorised Dealers

B12.23 The FA 1968, s. 8(1), allows a registered firearms dealer, or a servant, to have in his possession, or purchase or acquire, without a certificate, a firearm or ammunition in the ordinary course of that business. This exemption applies even if the firearm or ammunition is in the possession of, or acquired by, the dealer or his servant at a place which is not his place of business (s. 8(1A)). A registered firearms dealer is defined by s. 57(4) as a person who, by way of trade or business, manufactures, sells, transfers, repairs, tests or proves firearms or ammunition to which s. 1 applies, or shotguns. A person is so registered in Great Britain under s. 33 and see the Firearms Rules 1998 (SI 1998 No. 1941).

Auctioneers, Carriers and Warehousemen

B12.24 An auctioneer, carrier or warehouseman, or a servant, may, under the FA 1968, s. 9(1), have in his possession, without a certificate, a firearm or ammunition in the ordinary course of business. It is a summary offence, contrary to the F(A)A 1988, s. 14(1), for an auctioneer, carrier or warehouseman (a) to fail to take reasonable precautions for the safe custody of any firearm or ammunition which, by virtue of the FA 1968, s. 9(1), he or any servant of his has in his possession without holding a certificate; or (b) to fail to report forthwith to the police the loss or theft of any such firearm or ammunition. The offence is punishable with a term of imprisonment not exceeding six months, or a fine not exceeding level 5 on the standard scale, or both.

Licensed Slaughterers

B12.25 A licensed slaughterer may, under the FA 1968, s. 10, have in his possession, without a certificate, a slaughtering instrument (see *Paul* [1999] Crim LR 79) or ammunition in any slaughterhouse or knacker's yard in which he is employed. Further, the person in charge of storing such instruments at the slaughterhouse or knacker's yard may have them in his possession, without a certificate, for that purpose. (As to the European weapons directive, see **B12.44**.)

Possession, etc. in Connection with Rifle or Pistol Clubs, Sports, Athletics and other Approved Activities

B12.26 The FA 1968, s. 11, and the F(A)A 1988, s. 15, provide a number of exemptions:

(a) a person borrowing a firearm or ammunition from someone who has a certificate may have the same in his possession for sporting purposes only (FA 1968, s. 11(1));

(b)   a person, without a certificate, may have a firearm in his possession at an athletic meeting to start races (s. 11(2));

(c)   a person in charge of a miniature rifle range may have in his possession, or purchase or acquire without a certificate, miniature rifles and ammunition suitable for the range; a person may use these at such a range without a certificate (s. 11(4));

(d)   a member of an approved rifle club, miniature rifle club or pistol club may have in his possession without a certificate, a firearm or ammunition when engaged as a club member in target practice (F(A)A 1988, s. 15(1)).

Approval is granted by the Secretary of State; see s. 15. As to the European weapons directive, see **B12.44**.

Possession etc. in Connection with the Theatre or Films

A person taking part in a theatrical performance or rehearsal or the production of a film **B12.27** may, under the FA 1968, s. 12, have a firearm in his possession, without a certificate, but only during and for the purpose of the performance, rehearsal or production.

Possession etc. as Equipment for Ship, Aircraft or Aerodrome

A person may, under the FA 1968, s. 13(1), without holding a certificate: **B12.28**

(a)   have in his possession a firearm, signalling apparatus or ammunition on board a ship or aircraft or at an aerodrome, provided it is equipment for same;

(b)   remove signalling apparatus or ammunition, if it is aircraft equipment, from one aircraft to another at an aerodrome or into or from storage and keep such equipment in storage at an aerodrome;

(c)   if he has a permit from a constable, remove a firearm, signalling apparatus or ammunition to or from a ship or aircraft at an aerodrome to or from a place specified in the permit.

It is an offence, contrary to s. 13(2), for a person knowingly or recklessly to make a statement which is false in any material particular for the purpose of procuring, either for himself or another person, the grant of a permit under s. 13(1)(c). As to procedure and sentence, see **B12.2** and **B12.3** above.

Persons in the Service of the Crown

By virtue of the FA 1968, s. 54(1), the possession of firearms by persons in the service **B12.29** of the Crown is not covered by the FA 1968. Section 54 applies only to a person in possession of a firearm when in his capacity as a servant of Her Majesty or a police officer, otherwise a firearm certificate is necessary. See *Heritage* v *Claxon* (1941) 85 SJ 323 and *Tarttelin* v *Bowen* [1947] 2 All ER 837.

The instant offence does apply insofar as it relates to the purchase and acquisition of firearms subject to s. 54(2) which provides a person in the service of the Crown with a defence if he is duly authorised in writing to purchase or acquire firearms and ammunition for public service without a certificate, and a person in the naval, military or air services, provided the chief officer of police is satisfied that he must purchase a firearm or ammunition, is entitled to a certificate without any payment. The Atomic Energy Authority (Special Constables) Act 1976 extends this provision to special constables nominated by the United Kingdom Atomic Energy Authority. This provision also extends to members of a visiting force and headquarters, see the Visiting Forces and International Headquarters (Application of Law) Order 1965 (SI 1965 No. 1536), Arts 3 and 12 and schs 2 and 3.

For the purposes of s. 54, certain persons are deemed to be in Her Majesty's naval, military or air service, insofar as they are not otherwise in, or treated as being in, any such service (FA 1968, s. 54(4)). Such persons are:

    (a) the members of any foreign force when they are serving with any of Her Majesty's naval, military or air forces;

    (b) members of any cadet corps approved by the Secretary of State when

        (i) they are engaged as members of the corps in, or in connection with, drill or target shooting; and

        (ii) in the case of possession of prohibited weapons or prohibited ammunition when engaged in target shooting, they are on service premises; and

    (c) persons providing instruction to any members of such a cadet corps (s. 54(5)).

'Foreign force' and 'service premises' are defined in s. 54(6).

A person under the supervision of a member of the armed forces may, without holding a certificate or obtaining the Secretary of State's authority under s. 5, have in his possession a firearm and ammunition on service premises (F(A)A 1988, s. 16A(1)). However, this provision does not apply to persons engaged in providing security protection of service premises, so it does not extend to civilian guards (F(A)A 1988, s. 16A(2)). 'Armed forces' and 'service premises' are defined in s. 16A(3).

Proof Houses of the Societies and Small Heath Rifle Range

B12.30 By virtue of the FA 1968, s. 58(1), the proof houses of the Master, Wardens and Society of the Mystery of Gunmakers of the City of London and the guardians of the Birmingham proof house or the rifle range at Small Heath in Birmingham are exempt from the provisions of that Act insofar as they would interfere with functions under the Gun Barrel Proof Act 1868 and any other Act. This protection extends to people carrying firearms to or from such places.

Antique Firearm sold or Purchased as a Curiosity or Ornament

B12.31 By virtue of the FA 1968, s. 58(2), the offence does not apply to an antique firearm which is sold, transferred, purchased, acquired or possessed as a curiosity or ornament. The Divisional Court in *Richards* v *Curwen* [1977] 1 WLR 747 and *Bennett* v *Brown* (1980) 71 Cr App R 109 has decided that whether a firearm is an antique firearm is a question of fact and degree. Consequently, as made clear by the Court of Appeal in *Burke* (1978) 67 Cr App R 220, it is a question for the jury to decide. It is not sufficient for the defendant honestly and reasonably to believe that the firearm is an antique firearm; it must actually be so (see *Howells* [1977] QB 614).

Borrowed Rifle on Private Premises

B12.32 By virtue of the F(A)A 1988, s. 16, a person who is at least 17 may, without holding a certificate, borrow a rifle from the occupier of private premises and use it on those premises in the presence of either the occupier or a servant, provided the occupier holds a certificate and the borrower's possession and use of it comply with any conditions in the certificate. In addition the borrower may purchase or acquire ammunition for the rifle, if the certificate authorises the purchase of ammunition and the borrower's possession and use of the ammunition complies with any conditions in the certificate.

Holders of Visitors' Permits

B12.33 By virtue of the F(A)A 1988, s. 17(1), the holder of a visitor's permit, granted by a chief officer of police under s. 17(2)–(9), may have in his possession, without a certificate, a firearm or ammunition to which the FA 1968, s. 1, applies and the Firearms Rules 1998 (SI 1998 No. 1941). But a visitor's shotgun permit does not authorise the purchase or acquisition of any shotgun with a magazine, except where s. 17(1A)(a)–(d) applies (s. 17(1A). No visitor's permit will be issued unless the visitor produces a European firearms pass (see **B12.18**) and satisfies other criteria (s. 17(3A)). It is an offence, contrary to the F(A)A 1988, s. 17(10), for a person (a) to make any statement which he knows to be false for the purpose of procuring the grant of a permit under this section; or (b) to fail to comply with a condition subject to which such a permit is held by him. The offence is punishable on summary conviction with imprisonment for a term not exceeding six months, or a fine not exceeding level 5 on the standard scale, or both. As to the extension of the usual time period within which summary proceedings must be instituted, see **B12.2** above.

Firearms Acquired for Export

See **B12.77** *et seq*. This defence is primarily concerned with the acquisition of firearms   **B12.34** for export, but must also cover their possession for that purpose.

Possession of a Museums Firearms Licence

By virtue of the F(A)A 1988, s. 19 and sch., a person involved with the management of   **B12.35** certain museums may, if he has a museums firearms licence, without a certificate, have in his possession, and purchase or acquire, for the purposes of the museum, firearms and ammunition which are or are to be normally exhibited or kept on its premises or on such of them as are specified in the licence. Certain specific museums are listed in the schedule, para. 5, but the paragraph also provides that similar museums, maintained wholly or mainly out of money provided by Parliament or a local authority, are also covered. Further, any museum or similar institution which is for the time being fully registered with the Museums and Galleries Commission is also covered (Firearms (Museums) Order 1997) (SI 1997 No. 1692).

The following two offences exist in relation to museums firearms licences. The offences are summary and so as to the extension of the usual time period within which summary proceedings must be instituted, see **B12.2**. In relation to both offences there is express provision dealing with offences committed by bodies corporate, see the F(A)A 1988, sch., paras 5 and 6.

(a) It is an offence, contrary to para. 4(1) of the schedule,

(i) for a person to make any statement which he knows to be false for the purpose of procuring the grant, renewal or variation of a licence;

(ii) for the person or any of the persons responsible for the management of a museum to fail to comply or to cause or permit another person to fail to comply with any condition specified in the licence held in respect of that museum.

The offence is triable summarily and is punishable with imprisonment for a term not exceeding six months or a fine not exceeding level 5 on the standard scale, or both. It is a defence for a person proceeded against under para. 4(1)(b) to prove that he took all reasonable precautions and exercised all due diligence to avoid the commission of the offence (para. 4(4)).

(b) It is an offence, contrary to para. 4(3) of the schedule, for a person to fail to comply with a notice under para. 2(4) from the Secretary of State requiring the surrender of a revoked licence. The offence is triable summarily and is punishable with a fine not exceeding level 3 on the standard scale.

Where the firearm is an imitation firearm there is a special defence under the FA 1982, s. 1(5); see **B12.13** above.

OFFENCES RELATING TO SHOTGUNS

Possessing etc. Shotgun without Shotgun Certificate

Firearms Act 1968, s. 2   **B12.36**

(1) Subject to any exemption under this Act, it is an offence for a person to have in his possession, or to purchase or acquire, a shotgun without holding a certificate under this Act authorising him to possess shotguns.

As to procedure and sentence, see **B12.2** and **B12.3**. The meaning of 'shotgun' is considered at **B12.7**. This is a section which does not extend to imitation firearms, see **B12.12** to **B12.14**. The term 'shotgun certificate' is defined by the FA 1968, s. 57(4) as 'a certificate granted by a chief officer of police . . . authorising a person to possess shotguns'. Such certificates are issued by chief officers of police under the FA 1968, s. 26, the related provisions in part II and the Firearms Rules 1998 (SI 1998 No. 1941).

The meaning of 'acquire' is considered at **B12.20** above.

The exemptions applicable in the case of firearms from liability under the FA 1968, s. 1, also apply to this offence. See **B12.20** to **B12.35** above. In addition, holders of certificates granted in Northern Ireland are exempt (FA 1968, s. 15).

Failure to Comply with Condition of Shotgun Certificate

B12.37   **Firearms Act 1968, s. 2**

>   (2)   It is an offence for a person to fail to comply with a condition subject to which a shotgun certificate is held by him.

This is a summary offence. For procedure and sentence, see **B12.2** and **B12.3**. The meaning of 'shotgun certificate' is considered at **B12.36**. The meaning of 'shotgun' is considered at **B12.7**.

POSSESSING OR DISTRIBUTING PROHIBITED WEAPONS OR AMMUNITION

Definition

B12.38   **Firearms Act 1968, s. 5**

>   (1)   A person commits an offence if, without the authority of the Secretary of State, he has in his possession, or purchases, or acquires, or manufactures, sells or transfers—
>   (a)   any firearm which is so designed or adapted that two or more missiles can be successively discharged without repeated pressure on the trigger;
>   (ab)   any self-loading or pump-action rifled gun other than one which is chambered for 0.22 rim-fire cartridges;
>   (aba)   any firearm which either has a barrel less than 30 centimetres in length or is less than 60 centimetres in length overall, other than an air weapon, a muzzle-loading gun or a firearm designed as signalling apparatus;
>   (ac)   any self-loading or pump-action smooth-bore gun which is not an air weapon or chambered for 0.22 rim-fire cartridges and either has a barrel less than 24 inches in length or is less than 40 inches in length overall;
>   (ad)   any smooth-bore revolver gun other than one which is chambered for 9 mm rim-fire cartridges or a muzzle-loading gun;
>   (ae)   any rocket launcher, or any mortar, for projecting a stabilised missile, other than a launcher or mortar designed for line-throwing or pyrotechnic purposes or as signalling apparatus;
>   (b)   any weapon of whatever description designed or adapted for the discharge of any noxious liquid, gas or other thing;
>   (c)   any cartridge with a bullet designed to explode on or immediately before impact, any ammunition containing or designed or adapted to contain any such noxious thing as is mentioned in paragraph (b) above and, if capable of being used with a firearm of any description, any grenade, bomb (or other like missile), or rocket or shell designed to explode as aforesaid.
>   (1A)   Subject to section 5A of this Act, a person commits an offence if, without the authority of the Secretary of State, he has in his possession, or purchases or acquires, or sells or transfers—
>   (a)   any firearm which is disguised as another object;
>   (b)   any rocket or ammunition not falling within paragraph (c) of subsection (1) of this section which consists in or incorporates a missile designed to explode on or immediately before impact and is for military use;

(c)   any launcher or other projecting apparatus not falling within paragraph (ae) of that subsection which is designed to be used with any rocket or ammunition falling within paragraph (b) above or with ammunition which would fall within that paragraph but for its being ammunition falling within paragraph (c) of that subsection;

(d)   any ammunition for military use which consists in or incorporates a missile designed so that a substance contained in the missile will ignite on or immediately before impact;

(e)   any ammunition for military use which consists in or incorporates a missile designed, on account of its having a jacket and hard-core, to penetrate armour plating, armour screening or body armour;

(f)   any ammunition which incorporates a missile designed or adapted to expand on impact;

(g)   anything which is designed to be projected as a missile from any weapon and is designed to be, or has been, incorporated in—

(i)   any ammunition falling within any of the preceding paragraphs; or

(ii)   any ammunition which would fall within any of those paragraphs but for its being specified in subsection (1) of this section.

(2)   The weapons and ammunition specified in subsections (1) and (1A) of this section (including, in the case of ammunition, any missiles falling within subsection (1A)(g) of this section) are referred to in this Act as 'prohibited weapons' and 'prohibited ammunition' respectively.

As to procedure and sentence, see ss. 51, 52 and sch. 6 at **B12.2** and **B12.3**.

Meaning of 'Prohibited Weapon' and 'Prohibited Ammunition'

These phrases are defined in the FA 1968, s. 5(2), see **B12.38**. The amendments **B12.39** introduced by the F(A)A 1988 have not overruled all decisions under the unamended section.

In *Law* [1999] Crim LR 837, the Court of Appeal held that a weapon satisfies s. 5(1)(a) if it is capable of burst fire, this makes it a weapon from which 'two or more missiles can be successively discharged'. This will be the case even if a weapon has been adapted and only experts would be able to make it operate as an automatic weapon.

In *Flack* v *Baldry* [1988] 1 WLR 393, the House of Lords decided that a 'Lightening Strike', a hand-held device from which electricity is emitted, was a prohibited weapon within s. 5(1)(b), because electricity is a noxious thing in view of the stunning effect it has on its victims and it is discharged from the device. The Court of Appeal decided in *Formosa* [1991] 2 QB 1 that an empty bottle of washing-up liquid is not a weapon, so filling it with hydrochloric acid does not make it a prohibited weapon. Further, merely to fill a bottle does not 'adapt' it within s. 5(1)(b). The court approved *Titus* [1971] Crim LR 279, where it was held that a water pistol is not a prohibited weapon even when used to discharge a noxious liquid.

A person is in possession of a prohibited weapon even when it is in parts (*Pannell* (1982) 76 Cr App R 53, the defendant had possession of all the parts). A weapon may be a prohibited weapon even if one essential element is missing, such as the trigger (*Clarke* [1986] 1 WLR 209). These decisions were followed in *Brown* (1992) *The Times*, 27 March 1992, where the Divisional Court held that a stun gun which did not work because of some unknown fault, and was not proved ever to have worked, was a prohibited weapon. Further, in *Clarke*, the Court of Appeal made clear that 'firearm' in s. 5(1)(a) is defined in s. 57(1) and, therefore, includes the component parts of a firearm.

Statutory Definition of Terms

Firearms Act 1968, ss. 5 and 57   B12.40

5.—(7)   For the purposes of this section and section 5A of this Act—

    (a)   any rocket or ammunition which is designed to be capable of being used with a military weapon shall be taken to be for military use;

    (b)   references to a missile designed so that a substance contained in the missile will ignite on or immediately before impact include references to any missile containing a substance that ignites on exposure to air; and

    (c)   references to a missile's expanding on impact include references to its deforming in any predictable manner on or immediately after impact.

    (8)   For the purposes of subsection (1)(aba) and (ac) above, any detachable, folding, retractable or other movable butt-stock shall be disregarded in measuring the length of any firearm.

    (9)   Any reference in this section 5 to a muzzle-loading gun is a reference to a gun which is designed to be loaded at the muzzle end of the barrel or chamber with a loose charge and a separate ball (or other missile).

57.—(2A)   In this Act 'self-loading' and 'pump-action' in relation to any weapon mean respectively that it is designed or adapted (otherwise than as mentioned in section 5(1)(a)) so that it is automatically reloaded or that it is so designed or adapted that it is reloaded by the manual operation of the fore-end or forestock of the weapon.

    (2B)   In this Act 'revolver', in relation to a smooth-bore gun, means a gun containing a series of chambers which revolve when the gun is fired.

  . . .

    (6)   For purposes of this Act—

    (a)   the length of the barrel of a firearm is measured from the muzzle to the point at which the charge is exploded on firing.

  . . .

Conversion Not to Affect Classification as Prohibited Weapon

B12.41 The F(A)A 1988 introduced an important change into the law as regards the conversion of weapons. Consequently, care needs to be taken in reading cases on the unamended s. 5 of the FA 1968, insofar as they are concerned with the conversion of weapons.

Firearms (Amendment) Act 1988, s. 7

    (1)   Any weapon which—

    (a)   has at any time (whether before or after the passing of this Act) been a weapon of a kind described in section 5(1) of the principal Act as amended by or under section 1 . . . ; and

    (b)   is not a self-loading or pump-action smooth-bore gun which has at any such time been such a weapon by reason only of having had a barrel of less than 24 inches in length, shall be treated as a prohibited weapon notwithstanding anything done for the purpose of converting it into a weapon of a different kind.

As to the deactivation of firearms, see **B12.9**.

Imitation Firearms

B12.42 Since a prohibited weapon is a form of 'firearm to which s. 1 of the FA 1968, applies' (see **B12.5**), this section may apply to imitation firearms. In any case possession etc. of an imitation prohibited weapon would be an offence contrary to s. 1.

Amending the List of Prohibited Weapons and Prohibited Ammunition

B12.43 Under the F(A)A 1988, s. 1(4) and (5), the Secretary of State may amend the list of prohibited weapons and prohibited ammunition.

Authority of the Secretary of State or under the European Weapons Directive

B12.44 The Secretary of State may grant an authority permitting possession of a prohibited weapon or ammunition.

Firearms Act 1968, s. 5

(3)   An authority given to a person by the Defence Council under this section shall be in writing and be subject to conditions specified therein.

(4)   The conditions on the authority shall include such as the Defence Council, having regard to the circumstances of each particular case, think fit to impose for the purpose of securing that the prohibited weapon or ammunition to which the authority relates shall not endanger the public safety or the peace.

The functions of the Defence Council are performed by the Secretary of State (Transfer of Functions (Prohibited Weapons) Order 1968 (SI 1968 No. 1200)). It is an offence to fail to comply with a condition of an authority (s. 5(5)). An authority may be revoked at any time by notice (s. 5(6)). As to procedure and sentence, see **B12.2** and **B12.3**.

The Secretary of State may, under s. 12(2), not only authorise a person in charge of a theatrical performance or rehearsal or the production of a cinematograph film to have possession of a prohibited weapon if it is required for the purpose of the performance, rehearsal or production, but also authorise such other person as he may select to have possession of it while taking part in the performance, rehearsal or production.

Section 5A(1) provides six exemptions to the obligation to have the authority of the Secretary of State under s. 5(1A), which arise from the European weapons directive and are concerned with possession or dealing with weapons in different situations.

Firearms Act 1968, s. 5A

(1)   Subject to subsection (2) below, the authority of the Secretary of State shall not be required by virtue of subsection (1A) of section 5 of this Act for any person to have in his possession, or to purchase, acquire, sell or transfer, any prohibited weapon or ammunition if he is authorised by a certificate under this Act to possess, purchase or acquire that weapon or ammunition subject to a condition that he does so only for the purpose of it being kept or exhibited as part of a collection.

(2)   No sale or transfer may be made under subsection (1) above except to a person who—

(a)   produces the authority of the Secretary of State under section 5 of this Act for his purchase or acquisition; or

(b)   shows that he is, under this section or a licence under the schedule to the Firearms (Amendment) Act 1988 (museums etc.) entitled to make the purchase or acquisition without the authority of the Secretary of State.

(3)   The authority of the Secretary of State shall not be required by virtue of subsection (1A) of section 5 of this Act for any person to have in his possession, or to purchase or acquire, any prohibited weapon or ammunition if his possession, purchase or acquisition is exclusively in connection with the carrying on of activities in respect of which—

(a)   that person; or

(b)   the person on whose behalf he has possession, or makes the purchase or acquisition,

is recognised, for the purposes of the law of another member State relating to firearms, as a collector of firearms or a body concerned in the cultural or historical aspects of weapons.

(4)   The authority of the Secretary of State shall not be required by virtue of subsection (1A) of section 5 of this Act for any person to have in his possession, or to purchase or acquire, or to sell or transfer, any expanding ammunition or the missile for any such ammunition if—

(a)   he is authorised by a firearm certificate or a visitor's firearm permit to possess, purchase or acquire, any expanding ammunition; and

(b)   the certificate or permit is subject to a condition restricting the use of any expanding ammunition to use in connection with any one or more of the following, namely—

(i)   the lawful shooting of deer;

(ii)   the shooting of vermin or, in the course of carrying on activities in connection with the management of any estate, other wildlife;

(iii)　the humane killing of animals;

(iv)　the shooting of animals for the protection of other animals or humans.

(5)　The authority of the Secretary of State shall not be required by virtue of subsection (1A) of section 5 of this Act for any person to have in his possession any expanding ammunition or the missile for any such ammunition if—

(a)　he is entitled, under section 10 of this Act, to have a slaughtering instrument and the ammunition for it in his possession; and

(b)　the ammunition or missile in question is designed to be capable of being used with a slaughtering instrument.

(6)　The authority of the Secretary of State shall not be required by virtue of subsection (1A) of section 5 of this Act for the sale or transfer of any expanding ammunition or the missile for any such ammunition to any person who produces a certificate by virtue of which he is authorised under subsection (4) above to purchase or acquire it without the authority of the Secretary of State.

(7)　The authority of the Secretary of State shall not be required by virtue of subsection (1A) of section 5 of this Act for a person carrying on the business of a firearms dealer, or any servant of his, to have in his possession, or to purchase, acquire, sell or transfer, any expanding ammunition or the missile for any such ammunition in the ordinary course of that business.

(8)　In this section—

(a)　references to expanding ammunition are references to any ammunition which incorporates a missile which is designed to expand on impact; and

(b)　references to the missile for any such ammunition are references to anything which, in relation to any such ammunition, falls within section 5(1A)(g) of this Act.

Section 57(4A) provides that the European weapons directive is to be taken as authorising the use of a firearm or ammunition as or with a slaughtering instrument and the use of a firearm and ammunition (a) for sporting purposes, (b) for the shooting of vermin or, in the course of carrying on activities in connection with the management of any estate, of other wildlife, and (c) for competition purposes and target shooting outside competitions.

Mens Rea

B12.45　The instant offence is an offence of strict liability. This was held by the Court of Appeal in *Bradish* [1990] 1 QB 981, following *Howells* [1977] QB 614 and *Hussain* [1981] 1 WLR 416 (see **B12.21**), and distinguishing *Warner* v *Metropolitan Police Commissioner* [1969] 2 AC 256. All that the prosecution have to prove, in addition to actual possession, is that the accused knowingly had in his possession an article which was in fact a prohibited weapon. The court distinguished *Warner* v *Metropolitan Police Commissioner* [1969] 2 AC 256 insofar as it dealt with the 'container' cases. It was submitted that the weapon of which the defendant was in possession was a spray canister containing CS gas and, therefore, he was not in possession of the contents of the container if he could show that he neither knew nor could reasonably have been expected to know that it was a prohibited weapon. The court rejected this submission (for the reasoning, see *Bradish* [1990] 1 QB 981 at pp. 991–3). The court thought that *Bradish* was not a 'container' case. This was a prohibited weapon because of the combination of the canister itself and its contents. The 'container' was, therefore, an essential part of the weapon.

Firearms Control: Small Firearms

B12.46　The firearms legislation was amended twice in 1997. It was amended, first, by the F(A)A 1997 which, whilst extending the limitations on firearms ownership, exempted small-calibre pistols. That exemption was removed by the Firearms (Amendment) (No. 2) Act 1997. The central provision is to be found in the FA 1968, s. 5(1)(aba) (as amended) (see **B12.38**) to which special exemptions have been provided as listed at **B12.47**.

Small Firearms: Special Exemptions

The special exemptions created by the F(A)A 1997 and the Firearms (Amendment) **B12.47** (No. 2) Act 1997 provide that, in the following situations, the authority of the Secretary of State is not required to avoid liability for the offence contrary to s. 5(1)(aba) of the FA 1968 (see **B12.38**).

Slaughtering Instruments A person may have in his possession, purchase or acquire, or sell or transfer 'a slaughtering instrument if he is authorised by a firearm certificate to have the instrument in his possession, or to purchase or acquire it' (F(A)A 1997, s. 2(a)). A person may have in his possession 'a slaughtering instrument if he is entitled, under section 10 of the 1968 Act, to have it in his possession without a firearm certificate' (s. 2(b)). As to s. 10 of the 1968 Act, see **B12.25**.

Firearms Used for the Humane Killing of Animals A person may have in his possession, purchase or acquire, or sell or transfer 'a firearm if he is authorised by a firearm certificate to have the firearm in his possession, or to purchase or acquire it, subject to a condition that it is only for use in connection with the humane killing of animals' (F(A)A 1997, s. 3).

Shot Pistols used for Shooting Vermin A person may have in his possession, purchase or acquire, or sell or transfer 'a shot pistol if he is authorised by a firearm certificate to have the shot pistol in his possession, or to purchase or acquire it, subject to a condition that it is only for use in connection with the shooting of vermin' (F(A)A 1997, s. 4(1)). 'Shot pistol' means a smooth-bored gun which is chambered for .410 cartridges or 9mm rim-fire cartridges (s. 4(2)).

Races at Athletic Meetings A person may 'have a firearm in his possession at an athletic meeting for the purpose of starting races at that meeting' (F(A)A 1997, s. 5(1)).

A person may have in his possession, purchase or acquire, or sell or transfer 'a firearm if he is authorised by a firearm certificate to have the firearm in his possession, or to purchase or acquire it, subject to a condition that it is only for use in connection with starting races at athletic meetings' (F(A)A 1997, s. 5(2)).

Trophies of War A person may have in his possession 'a firearm which was acquired as a trophy of war before 1st January 1946 if he is authorised by a firearm certificate to have it in his possession' (F(A)A 1997, s. 6).

Firearms of Historic Interest The following provisions have effect without prejudice to s. 58(2) of the 1968 Act which is concerned with antique firearms, and which is an additional exception (F(A)A 1997, s. 7(4)). For s. 58(2) of the 1968 Act, see **B12.31**.

(a) A person may have in his possession, purchase or acquire, or sell or transfer, a firearm which was manufactured before 1 January 1919; and (b) is of a specified description, 'if he is authorised by a firearm certificate to have the firearm in his possession, or to purchase or acquire it, subject to a condition that he does so only for the purpose of its being kept or exhibited as part of a collection' (s. 7(1)). The Secretary of State may specify descriptions of firearms for the purposes of s. 7(1) if it appears to him that firearms of that description were manufactured before 1 January 1919 and ammunition for firearms of that type is not readily available (s. 7(2)). The Firearms (Amendment) Act 1997 (Firearms of Historic Interest) Order 1997 (SI 1997 No. 1537) has been made in exercise of that power.

(b) A person may have in his possession, or may purchase or acquire, or sell or transfer 'a firearm which is of particular rarity, aesthetic quality or technical interest, or is of historical importance, if he is authorised by a firearm certificate to have the firearm in his possession subject to a condition requiring it to be kept and used only at a designated place (s. 7(3)). Places will be designated by the Secretary of State (s. 7(3)). Insofar as this exemption relates to large-calibre handguns, it applies only until 1 July 1998 or such earlier date as may be notified by the Secretary of State to the person in question (Firearms (Amendment) Act 1997 (Transitional Provisions and Savings) Regulations 1997 (SI 1997 No. 1538)).

Weapons and Ammunition used for Treating Animals This special exception applies not only to the offence contrary to s. 5(1)(aba) but also any offence contrary to s. 5(1)(b) or 5(1)(c) (see **B12.38**).

A person may have in his possession, purchase or acquire, or sell or transfer 'any firearm, weapon or ammunition designed or adapted for the purpose of tranquillising or otherwise treating any animal, if he is authorised by a firearm certificate to possess, or to purchase or acquire, the firearm, weapon or ammunition subject to a condition restricting its use in connection with the treatment of animals' (F(A)A 1997, s. 8).

Disabled Persons The authority of the Secretary of State is not required under the FA 1968, s. 5(1)(aba) for a registered disabled person with a physical disability approved by the Secretary of State to 'have in his possession or to purchase, acquire, sell or transfer a pistol chambered for 0.22 or smaller rim-fire cartridges if he is authorised under the Act to possess, purchase or acquire that weapon subject to a [relevant] condition' (Firearms (Amendment) (No. 2) Act 1997, s. 2(1) and (2)). The certificate granted for that purpose must be subject to the condition that the weapon is stored and used only at designated premises and possession of the weapon outside such designated premises is permitted only for transfer to and use at premises at which a shooting competition is taking place on specified conditions (s. 2(3)).

POSSESSION OF FIREARM WITH INTENT TO ENDANGER LIFE

Definition

B12.48

Firearms Act 1968, s. 16

> It is an offence for a person to have in his possession any firearm or ammunition with intent by means thereof to endanger life or to enable another person by means thereof to endanger life whether any injury has been caused or not.

As to procedure and sentence, see ss. 51, 52 and sch. 6; **B12.2** and **B12.3**.

Indictment

B12.49

Statement of Offence

> Having a firearm in possession with intent to endanger life, contrary to section 16 of the Firearms Act 1968

Particulars of Offence

> A on or about the . . . day of . . . at . . . had in his possession a firearm, namely . . . , with intent by means thereof to endanger life

No Extension to Imitation Firearms

B12.50 'Firearm' carries the general meaning provided by the FA 1968, s. 57(1), see **B12.4**. The section does not extend to imitation firearms, because there is no express reference to such firearms, and because subsections (2) and (3) of the FA 1982, s. 2, make clear that that Act does not extend to this section.

Intent to Endanger Life

B12.51 The test is proof of intention to behave in such a way as will in fact, to the accused's knowledge, endanger life (*Brown* [1995] Crim LR 328) disapproving the dictum in *East*

[1990] Crim LR 413). The person whose life it is intended to endanger need not be in the United Kingdom (*El-Hakkoui* [1975] 1 WLR 396) and the intent need not be an immediate or unconditional one, although it is necessary that the accused have possession of a firearm or ammunition with a view to using them if and when the occasion arises (*Bentham* [1973] QB 357 and *Jones* [1997] QB 798). The life that the accused intends to endanger must be someone else's and not his own (*Norton* [1977] Crim LR 478). Where the charge is of possessing a firearm or ammunition with intent to enable another to endanger life, it must be proved that the possessor had an intention that life be endangered by the firearm or ammunition (*Jones*).

The Court of Appeal in *Georgiades* [1989] 1 WLR 759 held that it is possible for a defendant to intend to endanger life for a lawful purpose, as when raising the defence of self-defence. Cases where such a defence could be successfully raised must be very rare. However, in the instant case, the conviction under the FA 1968, s. 16, had to be quashed because the question of whether the intention to endanger life might have been a lawful one was not left to the jury.

POSSESSION OF FIREARM OR IMITATION FIREARM WITH INTENT TO CAUSE FEAR OF VIOLENCE

Definition

Firearms Act 1968, s. 16A   B12.52

It is an offence for a person to have in his possession any firearm or imitation firearm with intent—
(a) by means thereof to cause, or
(b) to enable another person by means thereof to cause,
any person to believe that unlawful violence will be used against him or another person.

As to procedure and sentence, see **B12.2** and **B12.3**.

Indictment

Statement of Offence   B12.53

Having a firearm in possession with intent to cause a person to believe that unlawful violence will be used against him or another, contrary to section 16A of the Firearms Act 1968

Particulars of Offence

A on or about the . . . day of . . . had in his possession a firearm, namely . . ., with intent by means thereof to cause V, to believe that unlawful violence would be used against him or another

Elements

For the meaning of 'firearm', see **B12.4**; for the meaning of 'imitation firearm', see **B12.54** **B12.12**. For the meaning of 'possession', see **B12.19**. As to the meaning of 'unlawful violence', see **B11.42**.

USE OF FIREARM TO RESIST ARREST

Definition

Firearms Act 1968, s. 17   B12.55

(1) It is an offence for a person to make or attempt to make any use whatsoever of a firearm or imitation firearm with intent to resist or prevent the lawful arrest or detention of himself or another person.

As to sentence, see ss. 51 and 52 and sch. 6, and **B12.3**.

Procedure

B12.56 The FA 1968, sch. 6, part II, para. 3, deals with the position where in England and Wales a person who is aged seventeen is charged before a magistrates' court with an offence triable either way listed in the MCA 1980, sch. 1 (the 'listed offence') and is also charged before that court with an offence under the FA 1968, s. 17(1) or (2). In that case para. 3(2) provides, generally, that the court is to proceed as if the listed offence were triable only on indictment. That provision does not apply, according to para. 3(3), if the court determines not to commit the accused for trial in respect of the offence under s. 17(1) or (2), or proceedings before the court for that offence are otherwise discontinued. In those circumstances if the court has not begun to inquire into the listed offence as examining justices, the court proceeds, in the case of the listed offence, in the ordinary way. If the court has begun to inquire, however, into the listed offence, the court proceeds with its inquiry into that offence as examining justices, but has power to change to summary trial with the accused's consent. For sch. 6, see **B12.3**.

Indictment

B12.57
Statement of Offence

Using firearm with intent to resist [or: prevent] arrest, contrary to section 17(1) of the Firearms Act 1968

Particulars of Offence

A on or about the . . . day of . . . at . . . used a firearm, namely . . . with intent to resist his lawful arrest or detention [or: to prevent the lawful arrest or detention of X]

Alternative Verdicts

B12.58
Firearms Act 1968, sch. 6, part II, para. 5

If on the trial of a person for an offence under section 17(1) of this Act the jury are not satisfied that he is guilty of that offence but are satisfied that he is guilty of an offence under section 17(2), the jury may find him guilty of the offence under section 17(2) and he shall then be punishable accordingly.

As to the offence under s. 17(2), see **B12.60** to **B12.62**.

Firearms and Imitation Firearms

B12.59 By virtue of the FA 1968, s. 17(4), a limited version of the definition of 'firearm' provided by s. 57(1) applies. The definition is that considered at **B12.4** above, except that component parts of and accessories to such firearms are not part of the definition for the purposes of the instant offence (i.e. the definition in s. 57(1), except for paras (b) and (c)). Since s. 17 specifically refers to 'imitation firearm', it is the definition in the FA 1968, s. 57(1), as applied by s. 17(4) that is relevant (see **B12.12**). The FA 1982 is not relevant to this offence.

POSSESSING FIREARM WHILE COMMITTING AN OFFENCE IN THE FIREARMS ACT 1968, SCHEDULE 1

Definition

B12.60
Firearms Act 1968, s. 17

(2) If a person, at the time of his committing or being arrested for an offence specified in schedule 1 to this Act, has in his possession a firearm or imitation firearm, he shall be guilty of an offence under this subsection unless he shows that he had it in his possession for a lawful object.

As to procedure and sentence, see ss. 51, 52 and sch. 6, and **B12.2** and **B12.3**. See also **B12.56** and **B12.58**.

Firearm and Imitation Firearm

As to the meaning of 'firearm' and 'imitation firearm' in the FA 1968, s. 17, generally, **B12.61**
see **B12.59**.

Offences Specified in the Firearms Act 1968, sch. 1

The offences specified in sch. 1 are: **B12.62**

offences under the Criminal Damage Act 1971, s. 1;
offences under the OAPA 1861, ss. 20 to 22, 30, 32, 38, 47;
offences under part I of the Child Abduction Act 1984;
theft, robbery, burglary, blackmail and any offence under the Theft Act 1968, s. 12(1);
offences under the Police Act 1996, s. 89(1), or the Police (Scotland) Act 1967, s. 41;
offences under the CJPO 1994, s. 13(1);
offences under the Sexual Offences Act 1956, ss. 1, 17, 18, 20;
an offence under the CJA 1991, s. 90(1);
aiding or abetting the commission of any such offence;
attempting to commit any such offence.

OFFENCES INVOLVING CARRYING OF FIREARMS

Carrying Firearm or Imitation Firearm with Intent to commit Indictable Offence or to resist Arrest

Firearms Act 1968, s. 18   B12.63

(1)   It is an offence for a person to have with him a firearm or imitation firearm with
intent to commit an indictable offence, or to resist arrest or prevent the arrest of another,
in either case while he has a firearm or imitation firearm with him.

As to procedure and sentence, see ss. 51, 52, sch. 6, and **B12.2** and **B12.3**.

The Court of Appeal in *Stoddart* [1998] 2 Cr App R 25 has made clear that there are
three elements to this offence:

(a)   that the defendant had with him a firearm;
(b)   that he intended to have it with him; and
(c)   that at the same time he had the intention to commit an indictable offence or to resist
or prevent arrest.

The general definition of 'firearm' in s. 57(1) applies, see **B12.4**. Since there is an
express reference to 'imitation firearm', the definition in s. 57(4) applies, and the FA
1982 has no application, see **B12.13**.

It is not sufficient to establish that a person has a firearm in his possession for him to
have it 'with him', but he does not have to be 'carrying' it, despite the marginal note to
the section (*Kelt* [1977] 1 WLR 1365 and *Pawlicki* [1992] 1 WLR 827; for the meaning
of 'possession', see **B12.19**). The Court of Appeal in *Kelt* appeared to require a very
close physical link and that the firearm be immediately available. However, the Court
of Appeal in *Pawlicki* explained this decision on the basis that the court had been trying
to highlight the importance of propinquity as a necessary ingredient distinguishing this
offence from those relating to possession. Whilst rejecting the possibility of a statutory
definition, the court, taking into account a purposive approach, relied upon a concept
of 'ready accessibility' and decided that the defendants in an auction room had firearms
with them which were in a car some 50 yards away. See also **B12.92** which deals with
the meaning of the phrase 'has with him'.

The accused must also have intended to have the firearm with him. Section 18(2)
renders proof that the accused had the firearm with him and that he intended to commit

an indictable offence or to resist or prevent arrest probative of his intention to have the firearm with him (*Stoddart*). Section 18(2) provides:

Firearms Act 1968, s. 18

(2)   In proceedings for an offence under this section proof that the accused had a firearm or imitation firearm with him and intended to commit an offence, or to resist or prevent arrest, is evidence that he intended to have it with him while doing so.

The Court of Appeal in *Houghton* [1982] Crim LR 112 held that it is necessary to establish the intent only at the moment to which the charge relates, which in this case was when the imitation firearm was pulled out of a holster by the accused. The intent may be formed at the same time as the accused begins to have the gun with him. It need not be formed at any earlier stage. It is not necessary to show an intention to use the firearm in the furtherance of the indictable offence (*Stoddart*).

By virtue of the Interpretation Act 1978, s. 5 and sch. 1, 'indictable offence' means an offence which, if committed by an adult, is triable on indictment, whether it is exclusively so triable or triable either way.

Carrying Loaded Firearm in Public Place

B12.64   **Firearms Act 1968, s. 19**

A person commits an offence if, without lawful authority or reasonable excuse (the proof whereof lies on him), he has with him in a public place a loaded shotgun or loaded air weapon, or any other firearm (whether loaded or not) together with ammunition suitable for use in that firearm.

As to procedure and sentence, see ss. 51, 52, sch. 6, and **B12.1** and **B12.3**.

By s. 57(4) a 'public place' includes 'any highway and any other premises or place to which at the material time the public have or are permitted to have access whether on payment or otherwise' (*Anderson* v *Miller* (1976) 64 Cr App R 178, where it was held that the space behind a shop counter is a public place).

The meaning of 'shotgun' and 'air weapon' is considered at **B12.7** and **B12.8**. The term 'loaded' is defined as follows:

Firearms Act 1968, s. 57

(6)   For purposes of this Act—
. . .
(b)   a shotgun or an air weapon shall be deemed to be loaded if there is ammunition in the chamber or barrel or in any magazine or other device which is in such a position that the ammunition can be fed into the chamber or barrel by the manual or automatic operation of some part of the gun or weapon.

Imitation firearms do not fall within the provisions of this offence, because there is no express reference to imitation firearms and the FA 1982 does not apply. See the FA 1982, s. 2(2)(b), (3) and **B12.12** to **B12.14**.

The offence is, like that contrary to s. 1, an absolute offence, see **B12.21**. The same principles apply even though s. 1 requires possession and s. 19 that the accused has the firearm with him. In *Vann* [1996] Crim LR 52, V had a loaded weapon with her because 'she had the gun with her in the present case, physically in her possession, and . . . was aware that she had it, even if she was ignorant of the fact that it was a gun'. In *Jones* [1995] QB 235, the Court of Appeal held, following the Divisional Court in *Ross* v *Collins* [1982] Crim LR 368, that possession of a firearm or ammunition certificate was not in itself lawful authority to have a firearm and ammunition in a public place. Further, it was held that, whereas an honest, mistaken belief in facts, which if true would provide a lawful authority, is capable of being a reasonable excuse, there can be no reasonable excuse where the belief is in something which could not be lawful authority even if true, such as the accused's belief that he held a valid certificate when the certificate was, in fact, invalid (see also *Taylor* v *Mucklow* (1973) 117 SJ 792). Reasonable excuse is unlikely to include an argument that the defendant was unaware of the nature of the item that he had with him or that the firearm was in a container and he did not know its contents nor had a reasonable opportunity to inspect, but the point was left undecided in *Vann*.

PROHIBITION ON POSSESSION OR ACQUISITION OF FIREARMS BY CONVICTED PERSONS AND PERSONS UNDER SPECIFIED AGES

Contravention of Prohibition on Possession or Acquisition of Firearms by Convicted Persons

Section 21 of the FA 1968 imposes certain restrictions on the possession and acquisition **B12.65** of firearms by convicted persons. By s. 21(4), it is an offence for a person to contravene any of the 'foregoing provisions' of the section. The 'foregoing provisions' are the provisions of s. 21(1) to (3A), which provide as follows.

A person who has been sentenced to custody for life or to preventive detention, or to imprisonment, or to corrective training, youth custody or detention in a young offender institution (or Scottish equivalent) for three years or more, must not at any time have a firearm or ammunition in his possession (s. 21(1)). A person who has been sentenced to imprisonment, youth custody, detention in a young offender institution (or Scottish equivalent), a secure training order, or a detention and training order for three months or more, but less than three years, must not at any time before the expiration of the period of five years from the date of his release have a firearm or ammunition in his possession (s. 21(2)). (By virtue of s. 21(2A), 'date of release' means, for a sentence partly served and partly suspended, the date on which the offender completes the part to be served in prison and, in the case of a person subject to a secure training order or detention and training order, the date on which he is released from detention (under the order or under the CJPO 1994, s. 4 or under the CDA 1998, s. 77, as the case may be) or the date halfway through the total period specified by the court in making the order, whichever is the latest.) A person who holds a licence issued under the CYPA 1933, s. 53 (or Scottish equivalent), or is subject to a recognisance to keep the peace or be of good behaviour with a condition relating to the possession of firearms (or Scottish equivalent), must not, at any time during which he holds the licence, or is so subject, have a firearm or ammunition in his possession (s. 21(3)). As to procedure and sentence, see ss. 51, 52 and sch. 6 and **B12.2** and **B12.3**. If a person is prohibited in Northern Ireland from having a firearm or ammunition in his possession, he is also so prohibited in Great Britain (s. 21(3A)).

A person may apply to the Crown Court for the removal of such prohibitions, see the FA 1968, s. 21(6). For the procedure see s. 21(7) and sch. 3.

Section 21 does not extend to imitation firearms, because there is no express reference to such firearms and because the FA 1982 only extends to firearms to which section 1 of the FA 1968 applies, whereas this section applies to firearms generally.

Firearms Act 1968, s. 21

(5) It is an offence for a person to sell or transfer a firearm or ammunition to, or to repair, test or prove a firearm or ammunition for, a person whom he knows or has reasonable ground for believing to be prohibited by this section from having a firearm or ammunition in his possession.

The offence carries the same range of sentence as the offence contrary to s. 21(4) above (see sch. 6 at **B12.3**) and is triable either way.

Contravention of Prohibition on Possession or Acquisition of Firearms by Persons under Specified Ages

B12.66   A series of summary offences created by the FA 1968, ss. 22 to 24, deals with the acquiring, having in possession, use, sale or letting to, supply to and making a gift to a young person of a variety of firearms. The requisite age of the young person is not the same in each case; the various ages are 14, 15 and 17. As to procedure and sentence, see ss. 51, 52, sch. 6 at **B12.2** and **B12.3**. The following relevant definitions have been given above: 'firearm' (**B12.4**); 'shotgun' (**B12.7**); 'air weapon' (**B12.8**); 'ammunition' (**B12.10**); firearm to which the Firearm Act 1968, s. 1, applies (**B12.5**); ammunition to which the FA 1968, s. 1, applies (**B12.11**).

Person under 17 Acquiring Firearm   It is an offence, contrary to the FA 1968, s. 22(1), for a person under the age of 17 to purchase or hire any firearm or ammunition. This section does not extend to imitation firearms.

Person under 18 Possessing Firearm   A person under 18 may, as the holder of a certificate, have a firearm in his possession, but it is an offence to use that firearm for a purpose not authorised by the European weapons directive (s. 22(1A); see also **B12.44**).

Person under 14 Having Firearm in his Possession Without Lawful Authority It is an offence, contrary to the FA 1968, s. 22(2), for a person under the age of 14 to have in his possession any firearm or ammunition to which s. 1 of this Act or s. 15 of the F(A)A 1988 applies, except in circumstances where under s. 11(1), (3) or (4) of this Act or s. 15 of the F(A)A 1988 he is entitled to have possession of it without holding a firearm certificate (see **B12.26**). Since this offence refers to firearms to which s. 1 of the FA 1968 applies, the FA 1982 applies and so this section extends to imitation firearms within that Act, see **B12.13**.

Person under 15 Having with him a Shotgun without Adult Supervision   It is an offence, contrary to the FA 1968, s. 22(3), for a person under the age of 15 to have with him an assembled shotgun except while under the supervision of a person over the age of 21, or while the shotgun is so covered with a securely fastened gun cover that it cannot be fired. This section does not extend to imitation firearms because there is no express reference to such firearms and the FA 1982 does not apply. The offence consists in a person 'having with him' such a weapon, see **B12.63**.

Person under 14 Having with him an Air Weapon or Ammunition Therefor   It is an offence, contrary to the FA 1968, s. 22(4), and subject to s. 23, for a person under the age of 14 to have with him an air weapon or ammunition for an air weapon. This section does not extend to imitation firearms, because there is no express reference to such firearms and the FA 1982 does not apply. As with the previous offence, this offence is concerned with a person having such a weapon with him. As to this, see **B12.63**. The offence is subject to s. 23, which introduces certain defences and one further offence. No offence is committed, according to s. 23(1), while the person is under the supervision of a person of or over the age of 21, but, where a person has with him an air weapon on any premises in circumstances where he would be prohibited from having it with him but for s. 23, it is an offence for him to use it for firing any missile beyond those premises or for the person under whose supervision he is to allow him so to use it. The offence contrary to s. 23(1) carries the same penalty as the offence under s. 22(4) as well as the same forfeiture and disposal provisions (see sch. 6). 'Premises' is defined by s. 57(4) as including any land. Section 23 also provides that no offence is committed where a person has with him an air weapon or ammunition at a time when being a member of a rifle club or miniature rifle club for the time being approved by the Secretary of State for the purposes of s. 23, or of the F(A)A 1988, s. 15 (see **B12.26**), he is engaged as such a member or in connection with target practice or he is using the weapon or ammunition at a shooting gallery where the only firearms used are either air weapons or miniature rifles not exceeding 0.23 inch calibre.

Person under 17 Having with him an Air Weapon in a Public Place   It is an offence, contrary to the FA 1968, s. 22(5), and subject to the defence in s. 23 (see above), for a person under the age of 17 to have an air weapon with him in a public place, except an airgun or air rifle which is so covered with a securely fastened gun cover that it cannot be fired. This section does not apply to imitation firearms, because there is no express reference to such firearms and the FA 1982 does not apply. As with the offence contrary to s. 22(3), this offence is concerned with a person having such a weapon with him, see **B12.63**. The accused must have the weapon in a 'public place' and this phrase is defined by s. 57(4); see **B12.64**.

Selling or Letting on Hire a Firearm to Person under 17   It is an offence, contrary to the FA 1968, s. 24(1), to sell or let on hire any firearm or ammunition to a person under the age of 17. This section does not extend to imitation firearms, because there is no express reference to such firearms and the FA 1982 does not apply. It is a defence, according to s. 24(5), to prove that the person charged with the offence believed the other person to be of or over the age mentioned in that provision and had reasonable ground for that belief.

Supplying Certain Firearms or Ammunition to Person under 14   It is an offence, contrary to the FA 1968, s. 24(2):

(a)   to make a gift of or lend any firearm or ammunition to which s. 1 applies to a person under the age of 14; or
(b)   to part with the possession of any such firearm or ammunition to a person under that age, except in circumstances where that person is entitled under s. 11(1), (3) or (4), or under the F(A)A 1988, s. 15, to have possession thereof without holding a firearm certificate.

Since this offence refers to firearms to which s. 1 of the FA 1968, applies, the FA 1982 applies and so this section extends to imitation firearms within that Act; see **B12.13**. As with the previous offence it is a defence to make a reasonable mistake as to age; see the defence under the FA 1968, s. 24(1). It is also a defence if possession is permitted under s. 11(1), (3) or (4); or under the F(A)A 1988, s. 15 (sports, athletics and other approved activities; rifle and pistol clubs; see **B12.26**).

Making Gift of Shotgun to Person under 15   It is an offence, contrary to the FA 1968, s. 24(3), to make a gift of a shotgun or ammunition for a shotgun to a person under the age of 15. This section does not extend to imitation firearms because there is no express reference to such firearms and the FA 1982 does not apply. As with the offence contrary to the FA 1968, s. 24(1), it is a defence to make a reasonable mistake as to age; see the defence under s. 24(1).

Supplying Air Weapon to Person under 14   It is an offence, contrary to the FA 1968, s. 24(4):

(a)   to make a gift of an air weapon or ammunition for an air weapon to a person under the age of 14; or
(b)   to part with the possession of an air weapon or ammunition for an air weapon to a person under that age except where by virtue of s. 23 (see above) the person is not prohibited from having it with him.

Since this offence refers to firearms to which s. 1 applies, the FA 1982 applies and so this section extends to imitation firearms within that Act.

There are the following defences to this offence:

(i)   As with the offence contrary to the FA 1968, s. 24(1), it is a defence to make a reasonable mistake as to age; see the defence under s. 24(1).

(ii)   A person may be entitled to have the weapon or ammunition with him under s. 23, see the offence under s. 22(4).

SHORTENING AND CONVERSION OF FIREARMS

Definitions

B12.67   There are three offences concerned with the conversion of firearms. The first two are concerned with the shortening of guns and the third with conversion of firearms.

The first, contrary to the FA 1968, s. 4(1), makes it an offence to shorten the barrel of a shotgun to a length less than 24 inches.

The second, contrary to the F(A)A 1988, s. 6(1), makes it an offence to shorten to a length less than 24 inches the barrel of any smooth-bore gun to which the FA 1968, s. 1, applies, other than one which has a barrel with a bore exceeding two inches in diameter.

The third, contrary to the FA 1968, s. 4(3) makes it an offence for a person other than a registered firearms dealer to convert into a firearm anything which, though having the appearance of being a firearm, is so constructed as to be incapable of discharging any missile through its barrel.

Procedure and Sentence

B12.68   All three offences are triable either way.

The range of sentence for all three offences is the same, that is, the guilty person is liable, on summary conviction, to a term of imprisonment not exceeding six months, or a fine not exceeding the prescribed sum, or both, and, on conviction on indictment, to a term of imprisonment not exceeding five years or a fine or both.

As to the courts' power to order forfeiture or disposal of firearms and ammunition, see the FA 1968, ss. 51, 52 and sch. 6 at **B12.2** and **B12.3**.

Elements and Defences

B12.69   As to the meaning of: 'shotgun', see **B12.7** above; 'smooth-bore gun to which s. 1 of the FA 1968 applies', see **B12.5** above; 'registered firearms dealer', see **B12.23** above; 'firearm' see **B12.4** above.

The length to which the barrel may be shortened is crucial for the first two offences, and this is to be measured, by virtue of s. 57(6)(a), from the muzzle to the point at which the charge is exploded on firing.

By virtue of the FA 1968, s. 4(2), a registered firearms dealer does not commit the offence contrary to s. 4(1) if the barrel is shortened for the sole purpose of replacing a defective part of the barrel so as to produce a barrel not less than 24 inches in length. The F(A)A 1988, s. 6(2), provides the same defence to the offence under s. 6(1).

TRANSFER OF FIREARMS ETC. TO BE IN PERSON

B12.70   The F(A)A 1997 introduces a number of provisions concerned with the transfer etc. of firearms and ammunition. In all cases it is an offence to breach the provisions provided for in ss. 32 to 35.

Punishment and Mode of Trial

The punishment and mode of trial of the offences depends upon the weaponry involved **B12.71**
(F(A)A 1997, s. 36):

(a)   where the offence is committed 'in relation to a transfer or other event involving
a firearm or ammunition to which section 1 of the 1968 Act applies' it is punishable, on
summary conviction, with a term of imprisonment not exceeding six months, or a fine
not exceeding the statutory maximum or both and, on conviction on indictment, with
a term of imprisonment not exceeding five years, or a fine, or both (s. 36(a));

(b)   where the offence is committed 'in relation to a transfer or other event involving
a shot gun' it is punishable, on summary conviction only, with a term of imprisonment
not exceeding six months, or a fine not exceeding level 5 on the standard scale, or both
(s. 36(b)).

The Offences

The offences to which these sentence and mode of trial provisions apply are set out in **B12.72**
the detailed provisions of ss. 32 to 35 and are summarised below.

Failure to Comply with s. 32(2)   It is an offence for a transferor or transferee to fail **B12.73**
to comply with s. 32(2). There must be a transfer to which s. 32 applies. Under s. 32(1),
such a transfer is where, in Great Britain:

(a)   a firearm or ammunition to which section 1 of the 1968 Act applies is sold, let on
hire, lent or given by any person, or
(b)   a shot gun is sold, let on hire or given, or lent for a period of more than 72 hours by
any person,
to another person who is neither a registered firearms dealer nor a person who is entitled to
purchase or acquire the firearm or ammunition without holding a firearm or shot gun
certificate or a visitor's firearm or shot gun permit.

The obligations on the transferor or transferee are that 'the transferee must produce to
the transferor the certificate or permit entitling him to purchase or acquire the firearm
or ammunition being transferred' (s. 32(2)(a)); 'the transferor must comply with any
instructions contained in the certificate or permit produced by the transferee'
(s. 32(2)(b)), and 'the transferor must hand the firearm or ammunition to the transferee,
and the transferee must receive it, in person' (s. 32(2)(c)).

Failure to Give Notice under s. 33   The failure by a party to a transaction to which **B12.74**
the F(A)A 1997, s. 33 applies to give the notice required by that section is an offence
(s. 33(4)). The relevant transaction occurs where, in Great Britain any firearm to which
s. 1 of the 1968 Act applies is sold, let on hire, lent or given or any shot gun is sold, let
on hire or given, or lent for a period of more than 72 hours (s. 33(1)). Any party to a
transfer to which s. 33 applies who is the holder of a firearm or shot gun certificate or,
as the case may be, a visitor's firearm or shot gun permit which relates to the firearm in
question must within seven days of the transfer give notice to the chief officer of police
who granted his certificate or permit (s. 33(2)). The notice must contain a description
of the firearm in question (giving its identification number if any) and state the nature
of the transaction and the name and address of the other party; any such notice must be
sent by registered post or by recorded delivery (s. 33(3)).

Failure to Give Notice under s. 34   The failure, without reasonable excuse, to give **B12.75**
the notice required by s. 34 is an offence (s. 34(4)). There is an obligation to give a notice
in two sets of circumstances. First, the firearm or shot gun certificate holder who was
last in possession of the firearm before it was de-activated, destroyed or lost (whether
by theft or otherwise) must, within seven days of that event, give notice of it to the chief
officer of police who granted the certificate or permit (s. 34(1)). This requirement

applies to firearms to which a firearm or shot gun certificate relates, firearms to which a visitor's firearm or shot gun permit relates (s. 34(1)). Secondly, where there is ammunition to which s. 1 of the 1968 Act applies and to which a firearm certificate or a visitor's firearm permit relates and that ammunition has been lost (whether by theft or otherwise), the certificate or permit holder who was last in possession of the ammunition before the loss must, within seven days of that event, give notice of it to the chief officer of police who granted the certificate or permit (s. 34(2)). A notice must describe the firearm or ammunition in question (giving the identification number of the firearm if any), must state the nature of the event and must be sent by registered post or the recorded delivery service (s. 34(3)). A firearm is deactivated 'if it would, by virtue of section 8 of the 1988 Act be presumed to be rendered incapable of discharging any shot, bullet or other missile' (s. 34(5)).

B12.76   ***Breach of s. 35***   Section 35 creates two offences. First, failure to give a notice required by s. 35(1) (s. 35(2)) and, secondly, the failure, without reasonable excuse, to give a notice required by s. 35(3) (s. 35(4)). Under s. 35(1), a transferor must, within 14 days of any disposal, give notice of it to the chief officer of police who granted his certificate where, outside Great Britain, 'any firearm or shot gun is sold or otherwise disposed of by a transferor whose acquisition or purchase of the firearm or shot gun was authorised by a firearm certificate or shot gun certificate'. Under s. 35(3), a firearm or shot gun certificate holder 'who was last in possession of the firearm or ammunition before [the] event [must] within 14 days of the event give notice of it to the chief officer of police who granted the certificate'. The 'event' in question is where, outside Great Britain, a firearm to which a firearm or shot gun certificate relates is de-activated, destroyed or lost (whether by theft or otherwise) or any ammunition to which s. 1 of the 1968 Act applies, and a firearm certificate relates, is lost (whether by theft or otherwise) (s. 35(3)). To comply with s. 35, the notice must contain a description of the firearm or ammunition in question (including any identification number), state the nature of the event and, in the case of a disposal, the name and address of the other party (s. 35(5)). 'De-activated' is defined in the same way as for s. 34, see **B12.75**. Such a notice must be sent within 14 days of the disposal or other event if it is sent from a place in the United Kingdom, by registered post or by the recorded delivery service and, in any other case, in such manner as most closely corresponds to the use of registered post or the recorded delivery service (s. 35(6)).

BUSINESS, EXPORT AND OTHER TRANSACTIONS INVOLVING FIREARMS AND AMMUNITION

Scope of Offences

B12.77   There are 14 firearms offences concerned with business and other transactions. These can be considered in four separate groups reflecting the varying modes of trial and penalties.

Either-way offences:

    (a)   trading in firearms without being registered as a firearms dealer (FA 1968, s. 3(1));
    (b)   selling firearms to person without a certificate (s. 3(2));
    (c)   repairing, testing etc. firearms for person without a certificate (s. 3(3));
    (d)   falsifying a certificate etc. with a view to the acquisition of a firearm (s. 3(5));
    (e)   transactions with person not a registered firearms dealer (s. 42(2));
    (f)   supplying firearms to person denied them under s. 21(5) (this offence is dealt with at **B12.65**).

Summary offences with maximum penalty three months' imprisonment or level 5 fine:

    (a)   failure to report transaction authorised by visitor's shotgun permit (FA 1968, s. 42A(3));

(b)   failure by person who resides in Great Britain to report purchase or acquisition of firearms in other Member States (FA 1968, s. 18A(6));

(c)   failure of firearms dealer to include particulars of agreement as required by the European weapons directive and FA 1968, s. 18(1A) (s. 18(6)).

Summary offences with maximum penalty six months' imprisonment or level 5 fine:

(a)   failure of registered firearms dealer to notify police of export transaction (F(A)A 1988, s. 18(5));

(b)   transfer of shotguns (s. 4(5));

(c)   restriction on sale of ammunition for smooth-bore guns (s. 5(2)).

Summary offences with maximum penalty six months' imprisonment or level 3 fine:

(a)   pawnbroker taking firearm in pawn (FA 1968, s. 3(6));

(b)   supplying firearm to person drunk or insane (s. 25);

(c)   contravention of order prohibiting movement of arms and ammunition (s. 6(3)).

Either-Way Offences

Firearms Act 1968, s. 3   B12.78

(1)   A person commits an offence if, by way of trade or business, he—

(a)   manufactures, sells, transfers, repairs, tests or proves any firearm or ammunition to which section 1 of this Act applies, or a shotgun; or

(b)   exposes for sale or transfer, or has in his possession for sale, transfer, test or proof any such firearm or ammunition, or a shotgun,

without being registered under this Act as a firearms dealer.

(2)   It is an offence for a person to sell or transfer to any other person in the United Kingdom, other than a registered firearms dealer, any firearm or ammunition to which section 1 of this Act applies, or a shotgun, unless that other produces a firearm certificate authorising him to purchase or acquire it, or as the case may be, his shotgun certificate, or shows that he is by virtue of this Act entitled to purchase or acquire it without holding a certificate.

(3)   It is an offence for a person to undertake the repair, test or proof of a firearm or ammunition to which section 1 of this Act applies, or of a shotgun, for any other person in the United Kingdom other than a registered firearms dealer as such, unless that other produces or causes to be produced a firearm certificate authorising him to have possession of the firearm or ammunition or, as the case may be, his shotgun certificate, or shows that he is by virtue of this Act entitled to have possession of it without holding a certificate. . . .

(5)   A person commits an offence if, with a view to purchasing or acquiring, or procuring the repair, test or proof of, any firearm or ammunition to which section 1 of this Act applies, or a shotgun, he produces a false certificate or a certificate in which any false entry has been made or personates a person to whom a certificate has been granted or makes any false statement.

As to procedure and sentence, see ss. 51, 52 and sch. 6, and **B12.2** and **B12.3**.

The FA 1982, on imitation firearms, applies to these offences see **B12.13**.

For the meaning of: 'firearm or ammunition to which the FA 1968, s. 1, applies', see **B12.5**; 'shotgun', see **B12.7**; 'firearm certificate', see **B12.18**; 'shotgun certificate', see **B12.36**; 'registered firearms dealer', see **B12.23**. 'Transfer' is defined by the FA 1968, s. 57(4), as including let on hire, give, lend and part with possession, and 'transferee' and 'transferor' are construed accordingly.

The offence in s. 3(2) is an absolute one (*Paul* [1999] Crim LR 79). This must be true of the similar offences. The test is an objective one: 'whether the firearm in question corresponds with the description relied on in a certificate produced by the transferee'. The intentions of the transferee as to use are irrelevant (*Paul*).

In the offence contrary to s. 3(5) the offence requires consideration of what is a 'false certificate', a 'false entry' or a 'false statement'. The consideration of the analogous phrases in the Forgery and Counterfeiting Act 1981 (see **B6.23** to **B6.26**) may be of assistance in ascertaining the meaning of these terms.

With respect to s. 3(1), relevant exemptions include exemption where the accused is authorised to deal with firearms, for persons in the service of the Crown, for proof houses, and where the firearm is an antique firearm sold or purchased as a curiosity or ornament, although all of the exemptions in ss. 7 to 13, 15, 54 and 58(1) and (2) of the FA 1968, and ss. 15 to 19 of the F(A)A 1988 (see **B12.22** to **B12.35**) apply.

By s. 9(2) it is not an offence for an auctioneer to sell by auction, expose for sale by auction or have in his possession for sale by auction, a firearm or ammunition when he is not a registered firearms dealer, provided he has a permit from the chief officer of police and he complies with the terms of that permit. It is a summary offence for a person knowingly or recklessly to make a statement false in any material particular for the purpose of procuring for himself or another the grant of such a permit (s. 9(3)).

The same exemptions apply to offences under the FA 1968, s. 3(2), (3). In addition, by virtue of s. 8(2), a person does not commit an offence under s. 3(2) if he (a) parts with possession of any firearm or ammunition, otherwise than in pursuance of a contract of sale or hire by way of gift or loan, to a person who shows that he is by virtue of this Act entitled to have possession of the firearm or ammunition without holding a certificate, or (b) returns to another person a shotgun which he has lawfully undertaken to repair, test or prove for another. By virtue of s. 9(4) it is not an offence under s. 3(2) for a carrier or warehouseman, or a servant, to deliver any firearm or ammunition in the ordinary course of his business or employment as such.

Summary Offences with Maximum Penalty Six or Three Months' Imprisonment and/or Level 5 Fine

B12.79 Five offences which are only triable summarily are to be found in the F(A)A 1988.

The two offences introduced in compliance with the European weapons directive (breach of s. 18(6) or s. 18A(6) of the 1988 Act) are punishable with a maximum penalty of three months' imprisonment, or a fine not exceeding level 5 on the standard scale, or both.

The penalty in respect of the remaining three offences is that a guilty person is liable to a term of imprisonment not exceeding six months, or a fine not exceeding level 5 on the standard scale, or both. The provision extending the usual time within which proceedings must be instituted applies to these offences, see **B12.2**. The first offence, contrary to s. 18(5), is designed to ensure that a registered firearms dealer, who sells a firearm or shotgun to a person entitled to purchase the same under s. 18(1) without a certificate, sends a notice of the transaction within 48 hours to the chief officer of police. The required details of such a notice are laid down by s. 18(3). The second offence, contrary to s. 4(5), is designed to enable the police to be aware of who has possession of a shotgun when it is transferred without the intervention of a registered firearms dealer. Section 4 requires the police to be given notice of such a transfer and it is an offence to fail to comply with the provisions of s. 4. The third offence, contrary to s. 5(2), makes it an offence to sell certain ammunition to a person who is not a registered firearms dealer and is not permitted by a certificate or otherwise to have the gun for which certain ammunition is required. The ammunition covered is that to which the FA 1968, s. 1, does not apply and which can be used in a shotgun or smooth-bore gun to which that section applies.

Summary Offences with Maximum Penalty Six Months' Imprisonment and/or Level 3 Fine

B12.80 It is a summary offence, contrary to the FA 1968, s. 3(6), for a pawnbroker to take in pawn any firearm or ammunition to which s. 1 applies.

It is a summary offence, contrary to s. 25, for a person to sell or transfer any firearm or ammunition to, or to repair, prove or test any firearm or ammunition for, another person whom he knows to be, or has reasonable cause for believing to be, drunk or of unsound mind.

It is a summary offence, contrary to s. 6(3), to contravene any order prohibiting the movement of arms and ammunition made under s. 6, any earlier corresponding legislation or any corresponding Northern Ireland legislation. This offence is supported by the power of the police, under s. 49, to search for and seize any firearms or ammunition which they have reason to believe are being removed in contravention of such an order. A person having custody or control of the firearms or ammunition must allow the police reasonable facilities to examine and inspect such articles and any documentation. Failure to comply with this power is a summary offence punishable in the same way as the offence contrary to s. 6(3).

Failure to Comply with Instructions by Police Officers

It is an offence, contrary to the FA 1968, s. 47(2), for a person having a firearm or **B12.81** ammunition with him to fail to hand it over when required to do so by a constable acting under s. 47(1). This provision enables a constable to require a person whom he has reasonable cause to suspect of having a firearm, with or without ammunition, with him in a public place, or (b) to be committing, or about to commit, elsewhere than in a public place, an offence contrary to ss. 18(1), (2) and 20, to hand over the firearm or any ammunition for examination by the constable. Section 47 also provides a power of search of person and vehicle (s. 47(3) and (4)).

It is also an offence, contrary to s. 48(3), for a person to refuse to declare to a constable his name and address or to fail to give his true name and address when required to do so by a constable acting under s. 48. This enables a constable to require the production of a relevant certificate when he believes a person to be in possession of a firearm to which s. 1 applies, or a shotgun.

As to procedure and sentence, see ss. 51, 52 and sch. 6 at **B12.2** and **B12.3** above.

Miscellaneous Offences Relating to Permits, Certificates and Authorisations

Permits, certificates and authorisations perform an important function under the **B12.82** Firearms Acts 1968 to 1992 since, when relevant, they authorise what would otherwise be an offence. Since they are so important a number of offences are created which relate to their obtaining and use. Reference has already been made to some of these offences under specific offences in the preceding parts of this section.

In addition, the following offences have also been created:

(a)   It is a summary offence, contrary to the FA 1968, s. 26(5), to make a false statement in order to procure the grant or renewal of a firearm or shotgun certificate. It is punishable with a term of imprisonment not exceeding six months, or a fine not exceeding level 5 on the standard scale, or both.

(b)   It is a summary offence, contrary to s. 29(3), to make a false statement in order to procure the variation of a firearm certificate. It is punishable with a term of imprisonment not exceeding six months, or a fine not exceeding level 5 on the standard scale, or both.

(c)   It is a summary offence, contrary to s. 30(4), to fail to surrender a certificate on revocation. It is punishable with a fine not exceeding level 3 on the standard scale.

(d)   It is a summary offence, contrary to s. 38(8), on removal of a firearms dealer's name from the register, to fail to surrender a certificate of registration or register of transactions. It is punishable with a fine not exceeding level 3 on the standard scale.

(e)   It is a summary offence, contrary to s. 39(1), to make a false statement in order to secure firearms dealer registration or entry in the register of a place of business. It is punishable with a term of imprisonment not exceeding six months, or a fine not exceeding level 5 on the standard scale, or both.

(f)   It is a summary offence, contrary to s. 39(2), for a registered firearms dealer to have a place of business not entered on the register. It is punishable with a term of imprisonment not exceeding six months, or a fine not exceeding level 5 on the standard scale, or both.

(g)   It is a summary offence, contrary to s. 39(3), not to comply with a condition of firearms dealer registration. It is punishable with a term of imprisonment not exceeding six months, or a fine not exceeding level 5 on the standard scale, or both.

(h)   It is a summary offence, contrary to s. 40(5), for a firearms dealer not to comply with provisions as to the register of transactions and to make a false entry in the register. These offences are punishable with a term of imprisonment not exceeding six months, or a fine not exceeding level 5 on the standard scale, or both.

(i)   It is a summary offence, contrary to s. 52(2)(c), to fail to surrender a firearm or shotgun certificate cancelled by a court on conviction. It is punishable with a fine not exceeding level 3 on the standard scale.

(j)   It is a summary offence, contrary to the F(A)A 1988, s. 12(2), to fail to comply with a notice from a chief officer of police who has revoked a certificate requiring the holder of the certificate to surrender forthwith the certificate and any firearms and ammunition which are in the holder's possession by virtue of the certificate. The offence is punishable with imprisonment for a term not exceeding three months, or a fine not exceeding level 4 on the standard scale, or both.

Further summary offences (under the FA 1968, ss. 32B(5), 32C(6), 42A(3) and 48A(4)) have been created to ensure compliance with the European weapons directive.

SENTENCING GUIDELINES FOR FIREARMS OFFENCES

B12.83   There are several Court of Appeal decisions which provide guidance on the appropriate sentencing bracket for the most serious firearms offences. The Court of Appeal in *Avis* [1998] 1 Cr App R 420 reviewed sentencing levels for a number of such offences. It was noted that these offences were coming before the courts more frequently in recent years, and that on some occasions in the past sentencing levels had failed properly to reflect public concern. Lord Bingham CJ said that, given the clear public need to discourage unlawful possession and use of firearms (both real and imitation) and Parliament's intention expressed by the continuing increase in maximum penalties, the courts should treat offences under the FA 1968 as serious. Save for minor infringements which might be and were properly dealt with summarily, offences committed under ss. 1(1), 2(1), 3, 4, 5(1A), 16, 16A, 17(1) and (2), 18(1), 19 and 21(4) would generally merit custodial sentences, even on a plea of guilty and where the offender had no previous record. On breaches of ss. 4, 5, 16, 16A, 17(1) and (2), 18(1), 19 or 21, the custodial term was likely to be considerable and where the four questions suggested by the court (set out below) yielded answers adverse to the offender, terms at or approaching the maximum might in a contested case be appropriate. An indeterminate sentence should, however, be imposed only where the established criteria for imposing such a sentence were met.

His lordship said that the appropriate level of sentence for firearms offences would, as for any other offence, depend on all the particular facts relevant to the offence and the offender, and it would be wrong for the Court of Appeal to prescribe unduly restrictive sentencing guidelines. However, it would usually be appropriate for the sentencing court to ask itself four questions:

(a)   What sort of weapon was involved? Genuine weapons were more dangerous than imitation firearms, loaded firearms than unloaded, unloaded for which ammunition was available than where none was available. Possession of a firearm which had no lawful use, such as a sawn-off shotgun, would be viewed even more seriously than possession of a firearm capable of unlawful use.

(b) What, if any, use had been made of the firearm? The court had to take account of all the circumstances surrounding any use made of the firearm; the more prolonged and premeditated and violent, the more serious the offence was likely to be.

(c) With what intention, if any, did the defendant possess or use the firearm? Generally the more serious offences under the Act were those requiring proof of a specific criminal intent to endanger life, cause fear of violence, resist arrest, or commit an indictable offence. The more serious the act intended, the more serious the offence.

(d) What was the defendant's record? The seriousness of any firearm offence was inevitably increased if the offender had an established record of committing firearms offences or crimes of violence.

In *Ecclestone* (1995) 16 Cr App R (S) 9, the Court of Appeal reviewed a number of earlier decisions relating to the possession of a sawn-off shotgun without a certificate and noted that the normal sentencing bracket for the offence was imprisonment for a term of between 12 months and two years. In *Ashman* [1997] 1 Cr App R (S) 241, however, the Court of Appeal upheld a sentence of 30 months' imprisonment on an offender who pleaded guilty to possession of a shortened shotgun without a certificate. It was noted that the maximum sentence for this offence had been increased to seven years by the CJPO 1994 and that a general increase in sentencing levels for such offences was in accordance with the intention of Parliament, even where possession was by a 'caretaker or minder' of the weapon. In *Clarke* [1997] 1 Cr App R (S) 323, the Court of Appeal confirmed that it was no longer appropriate to follow sentencing levels prescribed in pre-1994 Act cases involving possession of firearms.

Eight years was the proper sentence in *Dickins* [1997] 2 Cr App R (S) 134, where the offender was found to have a loaded submachine gun in his car and two sawn-off shotguns with various other weapons and ammunition were found at his home. Possession of an imitation firearm with intent to cause fear of unlawful violence merited a sentence of 12 months' imprisonment in *Mercredi* [1997] 2 Cr App R (S) 204. The offender, a woman with a large number of previous convictions for minor offences and a history of drug and alcohol abuse, entered a probation office in an agitated and emotional state and pointed the imitation gun at the receptionist. See also *Thompson* [1997] 2 Cr App R (S) 188, where the offender pointed an air pistol at a relative of the person he believed to be responsible for a burglary at his house. The appropriate sentence was two years.

OFFENSIVE WEAPONS

Definition

<table>
<tr><td align="center">**Prevention of Crime Act 1953, s. 1**</td><td align="right">**B12.84**</td></tr>
</table>

(1) Any person who without lawful authority or reasonable excuse, the proof whereof shall lie on him, has with him in any public place any offensive weapon shall be guilty of an offence.

Procedure

<table>
<tr><td>This offence is triable either way (Prevention of Crime Act 1953, s. 1(1)).</td><td align="right">**B12.85**</td></tr>
</table>

Indictment

<table>
<tr><td align="center">Statement of Offence</td><td align="right">**B12.86**</td></tr>
</table>

Having an offensive weapon in a public place contrary to section 1 of the Prevention of Crime Act 1953

Particulars of Offence

A on the . . . day of . . . had with him in a public place, namely . . . an offensive weapon, namely . . . without lawful authority or reasonable excuse

'Time' and 'place' are material elements of the instant offence which must, therefore, be stated with accuracy in the particulars of the offence (*Allamby* [1974] 1 WLR 1494).

Where the weapon may be offensive under two of the categories of offensive weapons, the indictment need not contain two counts (*Flynn* (1985) 82 Cr App R 319).

Sentencing Guidelines

B12.87 The maximum penalty is: on conviction on indictment, imprisonment for a term not exceeding four years or a fine or both; on summary conviction, a term of imprisonment not exceeding six months, or a fine not exceeding £1,000 or both (Prevention of Crime Act 1953, s. 1(1), as amended by the Offensive Weapons Act 1996, s. 2(1)). The increase in penalty from two years to four years does not apply in respect of offences committed before 4 July 1996, when s. 2 of the 1996 Act came into force (1996 Act, s. 2(4)).

When dealt with summarily, the Magistrates' Association Guidelines (1997) indicate the following:

Aggravating Factors ⊕
For example location of offence; group action or joint possession; people put in fear/weapon brandished; planned use; offence committed on bail; previous convictions and failures to respond to previous sentences, if relevant.

Mitigating Factors ⊖
For example acting out of genuine fear; not premeditated.

Guideline: Is it so serious that only custody is appropriate?

In *Webster* (1985) 7 Cr App R (S) 359 the offender, aged 27, was found to be in possession of a Stanley knife, which he claimed to carry in case he was attacked. He had 11 previous convictions for violence and one previous conviction, two years earlier, for possession of an offensive weapon, for which he had received three months' imprisonment. The Court of Appeal noted that a Stanley knife was capable of inflicting a very serious injury, and in light of the fact that he had contested the case and had a poor record, no mitigation was available from either of those sources, and 12 months' imprisonment was upheld. In *Shorter* (1988) 10 Cr App R (S) 4, where the offender had two similar previous convictions, six months' imprisonment was upheld on an offender found in possession of a vegetable knife. Nine months' imprisonment was held to be proper in *Simpson* (1992) 13 Cr App R (S) 665 where the offender was convicted for possession of a flick-knife. In *Norman* (1995) 16 Cr App R (S) 848, 15 months' imprisonment was upheld in respect of an offender with a previous conviction for the offence who was found in possession of a broken pool cue and a nasal spray containing ammonia. See also *Hopkins* [1996] 1 Cr App R (S) 18.

Meaning of 'Offensive Weapon'

B12.88   **Prevention of Crime Act 1953, s. 1**

(4)   In this section 'offensive weapon' means any article made or adapted for use for causing injury to the person, or intended by the person having it with him for such use by him or by some other person.

It is not necessarily easy to establish whether a particular article is an offensive weapon. The definition provided above means, according to the Court of Appeal in *Simpson* [1983] 1 WLR 1494, that there are three possible categories of offensive weapon:

(a)   an article made for use for causing injury to the person, commonly known as weapons offensive *per se*;

(b) an article adapted for use for causing injury to the person;

(c) an article which the person carrying it intends to use for the purpose of causing injury to the person.

In many cases little or no distinction is drawn between the first two categories, but there is a very clear distinction between the first two and the third categories. It is the requirement that the prosecution must prove the intent to injure in cases involving weapons in the third category.

Weapons Offensive *per se*

It has been held that a flick-knife is an offensive weapon *per se* (*Lawrence* (1971) 57 Cr **B12.89** App R 64, *Allamby* [1974] 1 WLR 1494, and *Gibson* v *Wales* [1983] 1 WLR 393). The Court of Appeal held in *Simpson* [1983] 1 WLR 1494 that trial judges are entitled to take judicial notice of the fact that a flick-knife is an offensive weapon *per se*. Whilst, therefore, it is clear that a flick-knife is an offensive weapon, this will not be the case with all articles. Not even all knives are offensive weapons *per se* (*Simpson*, where it was held that not all sheath knives are offensive weapons; *Patterson* v *PC 108D PK* (1984) *The Times*, 21 June 1984, where it was held that a lock knife is not an offensive weapon *per se*). In a decision on the Aviation Security Act 1982, s. 4(2)(c), it was held that a butterfly knife is necessarily an article for use for causing injury to the person and judicial notice can be taken of that fact (*DPP* v *Hynde* [1998] 1 WLR 1222, where the court referred to both the definition in the CJA 1988 and the decision in *Simpson*).

The Court of Appeal in the following cases was satisfied that the articles in question were offensive weapons *per se*. It remains to be seen whether trial judges may now regard it as determined that the following cases have decided that the items are offensive weapons *per se*, either by regarding the matter as one of which they may take judicial notice or by being bound by previous decisions. The judgments in both cases indicate no hesitation in stating that the weapons were offensive *per se*. However, against this must be weighed the consideration, referred to in the following paragraph, that the decision as to whether a weapon is offensive *per se* is one for a jury to take (see, in particular, the decision of the Court of Appeal in *Williamson* (1977) 67 Cr App R 35). It was held in *Butler* [1988] Crim LR 695, that a sword stick is a weapon, offensive *per se*. The trial judge had left the matter to the jury, but the Court of Appeal regarded this as, if anything, over generous. In *Houghton* v *Chief Constable of Greater Manchester* (1986) 84 Cr App R 319, it was held that a truncheon is an offensive weapon *per se*, in part because it does not contain *per se* any innocent quality. Where an article has no readily apparent use except to cause injury to the person, it is submitted that judicial notice may well be appropriate.

Where there is doubt as to whether an article is an offensive weapon *per se*, the deciders of fact must have their attention drawn to the statutory definition, but determining whether any particular article is such a weapon is a matter of fact (*Williamson* (1977) 67 Cr App R 35, *Simpson* [1983] 1 WLR 1494, *Humphries* (1987) *Independent*, 13 April 1987). The conclusion by magistrates that a rice flail was an offensive weapon *per se* could not successfully be challenged, because it was legitimately reached in accordance with the evidence (*Copus* v *DPP* [1989] Crim LR 577).

If an article has an innocent purpose, which may have to be the main purpose for which it is produced, it will not be an offensive weapon *per se*. This follows from, for example, the cases on knives (see above), from *Houghton* v *Chief Constable of Greater Manchester* (1986) 84 Cr App R 319, from *Petrie* [1961] 1 WLR 358, where it was held that an ordinary razor is not an offensive weapon *per se*, and from *Humphreys* [1977] Crim LR 225, where it was held that an ordinary penknife is not an offensive weapon *per se*.

Where the article is a weapon, offensive *per se*, there is no requirement on the prosecution that it be proved that the possessor also had an intention to use it to cause injury (*Davis* v *Alexander* (1970) 54 Cr App R 398, and *Southwell* v *Chadwick* (1986) 85 Cr App R 235). While the prosecution must prove that the accused had possession of the offensive weapon, they need not prove a specific intent to injure (see **B12.91**).

Weapons Adapted to Cause Injury

B12.90   Whether an article falls into this category is a decision of fact to be answered by the jury or magistrates (*Williamson* (1977) 67 Cr App R 35). The need for determination by either the jury or the magistrates was reaffirmed in *Warne* v *DPP* (3 June 1997 unreported), where the Divisional Court also made clear that the fact that the item was later used for a violent purpose did not determine the question of its earlier adaptation. It was not possible, in this case, to sustain the conclusion that the pick-axe handle, when it had lost its head, had, on the evidence available, been adapted for use for causing injury to the person. Experimentation with the article may assist the jury in determining whether it is an offensive weapon. If such experimentation is permitted, the Court of Appeal decided in *Higgins* (1989) *The Times*, 16 February 1989, that the experiment must take place in open court, when, of course, it is possible for counsel to address the issue. Clear examples of articles falling within this category are a bottle which is deliberately broken so that the jagged end can be pushed into the victim's face (*Simpson* [1983] 1 WLR 1494) and a potato with a razor blade inserted into it (*Williamson*).

It may be that the 'injury to the person' includes injury to the possessor of the weapon, i.e. self-inflicted injury. The decision of the Crown Court to this effect was not challenged in the Divisional Court in *Bryan* v *Mott* (1975) 62 Cr App R 71. On the other hand, the Crown Court sitting at Beverley took the view in *Fleming* [1989] Crim LR 71 that an element in the offence was injury to a person other than the possessor of the weapon. In *Bryan* v *Mott*, the court held that, even though the expressed intention of the accused (to commit suicide) was not unlawful, he had no reasonable excuse for having the article in a public place for that purpose.

Weapons Intended to Be Used to Cause Injury

B12.91   In order for a weapon to satisfy this category, it is essential that an intention to cause injury to the person be proved. It is essential that the defendant have an intention to cause such injury at the time and place of the charge. It is not sufficient that he had the necessary intention at some earlier stage (*Allamby* [1974] 1 WLR 1494).

The intention to cause injury to the person may apparently be satisfied by the intention to inflict injury on one's self, but the authorities, weak as they are, conflict; see **B12.90**. It is essential that an intention to cause injury rather than an intention to frighten or to intimidate be established. If, however, what is established is that the defendant's intention was to cause injury by shock and hence injury to the person, that, although probably a rare situation, would be sufficient (*Rapier* (1979) 70 Cr App R 17, following *Edmonds* [1963] 2 QB 142, and explaining *Woodward* v *Koessler* [1958] 1 WLR 1255). It is, therefore, necessary for the judge to give a careful direction so that the jury is aware that, if it determines that the defendant's intention was to scare others away, that does not amount to an intention to use a weapon to cause injury (*Snooks* [1997] Crim LR 230).

When considering whether an article falls into this category of offensive weapon, it is for the prosecution to prove the element of specific intention (*Petrie* [1961] 1 WLR 358 (making the comparative point that, if the article is an offensive weapon *per se*, there is no need to prove such intention)). This is a matter of circumstantial evidence based on all the circumstances of the case. Some assistance is provided by the general approach taken to the concept of intention, see **A2.2**. In particular it is clear that the use to which the weapon is actually put can assist in determining what the intention of the possessor was. Indeed in some cases it may itself be sufficient to establish the necessary intent, but each case must depend upon its own facts (*Harrison* v *Thornton* (1966) 68 Cr App R 28, *Dayle* [1974] 1 WLR 181, *Ohlson* v *Hylton* [1975] 1 WLR 724).

The phrase 'has with him' (see **B12.92**) emphasises that the offence is concerned with the situation where a person carries a weapon with the intent to use it if the occasion arises. The offence is not concerned with the actual use of the weapon, or with the situation where a person arms himself with a weapon for an instant attack on the victim.

Actual use can, of course, be dealt with by charging appropriate offences against the person. This was made clear by the Court of Criminal Appeal in *Jura* [1954] 1 QB 503, where a conviction for this offence was quashed where the appellant had possession of an air rifle at a shooting gallery, which he then used to fire at a woman companion. It was his use of the rifle which was unlawful, not his carrying of it, for which he had a reasonable excuse. As Lord Goddard CJ put it: 'The Act of 1953 is meant to deal with a person who goes out with an offensive weapon, it may be a cosh or a knife, without any reasonable excuse'. The point is confirmed by the Court of Appeal in *Dayle* [1974] 1 WLR 181. The trial judge, following *Jura*, held that it was open to a jury to find that there was no possession of an offensive weapon when an inoffensive article lawfully carried was offensively used. The Court of Appeal agreed with this approach. Consequently, it appeared that the appellant would not have been in possession of an offensive weapon when he took the car jack and brace in the heat of the moment.

Both these Court of Appeal decisions were applied by the Divisional Court in *Ohlson* v *Hylton* [1975] 1 WLR 724, where a workman was held not to be guilty of the offence where he took a hammer from his work bag and struck a fellow traveller at an Underground station. The hammer was properly in his possession. Lord Widgery CJ delivering the judgment of the court, said at pp. 728–9:

> . . . I would hold that an offence under section 1 is not committed where a person arms himself with a weapon for *instant* attack on his victim. It seems to me that the section is concerned only with a man who, possessed of a weapon, forms the necessary intent before an occasion to use actual violence has arisen. In other words, it is not the actual use of the weapon with which the section is concerned, but the carrying of a weapon with intent to use it if occasion arises. . . .

> I accept that it is unnecessary for the prosecution to prove that the relevant intent was formed from the moment when the defendant set out on his expedition. An innocent carrying of say, a hammer can be converted into an unlawful carrying when the defendant forms the guilty intent, provided, in my view, that the intent is formed before the actual occasion to use violence has arisen.

In *Humphreys* [1977] Crim LR 225, the Court of Appeal, following *Ohlson* v *Hylton*, decided that no offence was committed where a person who happened to have a penknife on him then used it in desperation, because it had not been carried in a public place with the necessary intent. In *Bates* v *Bulman* [1979] 1 WLR 1190, the Divisional Court, applying *Ohlson* v *Hylton* held that the accused, who acquired an unopened clasp knife (which was not made or adapted for causing injury) with the immediate intention of using it as an offensive weapon, did not commit the instant offence, since 'the purport of the [1953] Act . . . is to cover the situation where an accused person . . . has with him and is carrying an offensive weapon intending that it shall be used, if necessary, for offensive purposes'. Again, it was indicated that if there was use of an offensive weapon, that was better dealt with by a substantive offence. Stocker J giving the judgment of the court, also said that it 'would be a rather academic and over-analytical approach [to make] a distinction between an innocent weapon subsequently used with the intention of an assault and which is being carried innocently . . ., and a similar article which is acquired either by borrowing from somebody else or fortuitously by being picked up in the street'. On the assumption that this is a correct interpretation of the cases, it casts doubts upon the accuracy of an earlier decision of the Divisional Court where it was held that an offence was committed when the accused, in the course of a fight between others, picked up a stone, thus arming himself, and threw it at one of the fighters, but missed him (*Harrison* v *Thornton* (1966) 68 Cr App R 28). See also **B12.63**.

The Court of Appeal returned to this issue in *Veasey* [1999] Crim LR 158. It confirmed that in cases where the real issue is the use of an offensive weapon a charge of assault is 'quite adequate'. The instant offence is concerned with carrying and not use, a distinction drawn by Professor Sir John Smith and approved by the Court (see now Smith and Hogan: *Criminal Law* (9th ed., 1999) at p. 448). The direction to the jury in *Veasey* did not sufficiently draw this distinction. It would not necessarily follow that the accused did have the requisite intent if, as the judge had directed, he left the car with a Krooklok, which he intended to use to cause injury.

In *Edmonds* [1963] 2 QB 142, the Court of Criminal Appeal held (at pp. 149–50) that in a case of joint possession, the direction which was appropriate and requisite was:

> . . . consider the nature of each article and the case of each man individually and separately, and have regard to the circumstances as a whole and the time of day. Are you sure that each man intended to use the article he carried to injure someone? Alternatively, are you satisfied that he was party to a common purpose, with one or more of the others, of using one or more of the articles for inflicting injury upon someone? And, when you consider this alternative, you must first be sure that he knew that one or both of the others had the article which each of them was shown to be carrying.

Meaning of 'Has with Him'

B12.92 In *Densu* [1998] 1 Cr App R 400, the Court of Appeal noted that counsel for the defendant had taken a point in skeleton argument which he had abandoned when shown two unreported cases by the Registrar of the Court of Appeal Criminal Division. Counsel had indicated that he wished to argue that the trial judge was wrong when he ruled that the phrase 'has with him' was satisfied 'if the prosecution proved that the appellant merely knew that he had the baton with him but did not know that it was a weapon'. The reliability of this as a statement of law is open to question. The Court of Appeal makes no comment on the abandonment of the argument. The decisions are not ones concerned with the Prevention of Crime Act 1953. *Vann* [1996] Crim LR 52 is concerned with a 'have with him' offence contrary to the FA 1968, s. 19 (and which followed *Hussain* [1981] 1 WLR 416, a possession offence under the FA 1968, s. 1: see **B12.64** and **B12.21**). *Matrix* [1997] Crim LR 901 is concerned with a possession offence contrary to the Protection of Children Act 1978. In both cases, the drugs decision, *Warner* v *Metropolitan Police Commissioner* [1969] 2 AC 256 (see **B20.13**), was significant. It may be that, nevertheless, the point, in principle, is correct. It is consistent with these, and other areas of law (e.g. drugs possession), and there is no good reason (as there is on some issues) why the approach should be different in this offence from the others. Further, the point is consistent with one view of the approach of the Court of Criminal Appeal in *Cugullere* [1961] 1 WLR 858. In that case, the court held that the phrase under consideration 'must mean "knowingly has with him in any public place"'. The court went on to make clear that it meant that the defendant must knowingly have possession of the article in question. This has been interpreted to mean that a person who forgets that he has the offensive weapon in his possession, nevertheless has it with him (*McCalla* (1988) 87 Cr App R 372). However, there is another view of *Cugullere*. This was expounded by the Court of Appeal in *Russell* (1984) 81 Cr App R 315. It stated that the court in *Cugullere* had been applying 'the general principle of criminal responsibility which makes it incumbent on the prosecution to prove full *mens rea*'. *Russell* is also a decision that is directly contradictory to *McCalla*. As Professor Sir John Smith has pointed out ([1998] Crim LR 347), the Court of Appeal in *Densu* made no reference to *Russell* (or indeed *Cugullere*) and he does not accept that *Russell* was decided *per incuriam*. It is submitted, therefore, that the point is open for conclusive consideration.

Meaning of 'Public Place'

Prevention of Crime Act 1953, s. 1   B12.93

(4)   In this section 'public place' includes any highway and any other premises or place to which at the material time the public have or are permitted to have access, whether on payment or otherwise. . .

'Public place' was considered in *Knox* v *Anderton* (1982) 76 Cr App R 156. The Divisional Court, in part relying on decisions on other pieces of legislation such as the Public Order Act 1936 (see **B11.15**), concluded that a reasonable bench of justices could decide that the upper landing of a block of flats which could be reached without hindrance was a 'public place', as there were no barriers or notices restricting access. In *Williams* v *DPP* (1992) 95 Cr App R 415, the landing of a block of flats, to which access could be gained only by way of key, security code, tenants' intercom or caretaker, was not a 'public place' for the purposes of the Criminal Law Act 1967, s. 91 (being drunk and disorderly, see **B11.74**), because only those admitted by or with the implied consent of the occupiers of the block of flats had access. People with access were not present as members of the public. The justices had misread *Knox* v *Anderton* believing that the mere absence of notices restricting access had been sufficient in that case to determine that the area was a public place.

Lawful Authority or Reasonable Excuse: the Burden of Proof

The Prevention of Crime Act 1953, s. 1(1) (see **B12.84**), clearly lays the burden of **B12.94** proving either lawful authority or reasonable excuse upon the defendant, but only once the possession of an offensive weapon has been established (*Petrie* [1961] 1 WLR 358). Thus, if the weapon is either made or adapted to be offensive, the prosecution has to prove no more than possession of the article, whereas with the third category of offensive weapons the prosecution has to prove the requisite intent before the burden passes to the defendant to prove either lawful authority or reasonable excuse.

It is for the defendant to satisfy the jury as to either a lawful authority or reasonable excuse on a balance of probability and not beyond a reasonable doubt (*Brown* (1971) 55 Cr App R 478). See generally **F3.4** and **F3.18**.

It follows from what has already been said about the purpose of the offence, that the reasonable excuse (or lawful authority) must be identified with the carrying of the weapon, and not with its use, as is made clear by Lord Goddard CJ giving the judgment of the Court of Criminal Appeal in *Jura* [1954] 1 QB 503 (see also *Dayle* [1974] 1 WLR 181 and *Bryan* v *Mott* (1975) 62 Cr App R 71).

Lawful Authority

The Divisional Court in *Bryan* v *Mott* (1975) 62 Cr App R 71 at p. 73 said: **B12.95**

The reference to lawful authority in the section is a reference to those people who from time to time carry an offensive weapon as a matter of duty - the soldier and his rifle and the police officer with his truncheon.

See also *Houghton* v *Chief Constable of Greater Manchester* (1986) 84 Cr App R 319.

Private security guards would not have lawful authority to carry, for example a truncheon, since they are exercising no duty in the sense that *Bryan* v *Mott* (1975) 62 Cr App R 71 perceives that word, i.e. any contractual duty would be irrelevant, see *Spanner* [1973] Crim LR 704. However, such a person may have a reasonable excuse, see *Malnik* v *DPP* [1989] Crim LR 451 (see **B12.96**).

Reasonable Excuse

B12.96   In *Densu* [1998] 1 Cr App R 400, the Court of Appeal held that the defence of reasonable excuse arises only once it is established that the accused was in possession of an offensive weapon. A reasonable excuse does not then arise if the argument is that the accused did not know that what he was carrying was an offensive weapon. Any other approach would defeat the statutory purpose. The court also held that 'the cases where the defence of reasonable excuse will be available are restricted'. A number of reasonable excuses have been recognised. The obvious form is where a person has an article properly in his possession for a legitimate purpose, such as the penknife in *Humphreys* [1977] Crim LR 225, and the workman's hammer in *Ohlson* v *Hylton* [1975] 1 WLR 724 (see **B12.91**).

A frequently recurring argument has been that it amounts to a reasonable excuse that the weapon is carried for the purposes of self-defence in case the carrier should be attacked. The problem with this argument is that the carrier is likely to be permanently or constantly carrying the weapon because of some constant or enduring (supposed or actual) threat of danger to the carrier. Carrying of a weapon simply as a general precaution was thought by the Divisional Court in *Evans* v *Hughes* [1972] 1 WLR 1452, following *Evans* v *Wright* [1964] Crim LR 466, and *Grieve* v *Macleod* [1967] Crim LR 424, to be insufficient to establish a reasonable excuse, and this approach has recently been confirmed by the Court of Appeal in *Densu*. What would be acceptable would be where the carrier was in anticipation of imminent attack and was carrying the weapon for his own personal defence against that specific danger. The decision in *Evans* v *Hughes* has consistently been followed; see *Peacock* [1973] Crim LR 639, *Bradley* v *Moss* [1974] Crim LR 430, *Bryan* v *Mott* (1975) 62 Cr App R 71. *Evans* v *Hughes* was followed by the Divisional Court in *Malnik* v *DPP* [1989] Crim LR 451. Bingham LJ giving the judgment of the court said that ordinarily one cannot legitimately arm oneself with an offensive weapon with which to repel unlawful violence when one has deliberately and knowingly brought about the situation in which such violence was liable to be inflicted. Bingham LJ went on to state that the position was quite different in the case of those to whom society has entrusted the responsibility for enforcing the law, and indeed there is a difference in the case of those such as security guards who are handling valuable property in the course of their ordinary occupation and have reason to fear attack.

It would seem that the courts strive to permit a person to have a reasonable excuse where there is 'good' reason for the possession of the offensive weapon. So in *Southwell* v *Chadwick* (1986) 85 Cr App R 235, the Court of Appeal accepted that it was a reasonable excuse for a person to have in his possession a machete knife in its scabbard and a catapult for use for killing grey squirrels, so that he could obtain food for his wild birds which he kept under licence. Also in *Callaghan* 30 October 1987 (unreported), the Court of Appeal was of the view that the jury should have been left to consider whether the defendant had a reasonable excuse for being in possession of a machete, which he used in a fight, when his claim was that he had bought it for domestic use and was taking it back to his home after having lent it to a friend. Even where a weapon offensive *per se* was carried, but merely as a theatrical property as part and parcel of fancy dress worn by a person going to or from a fancy dress party, the Court of Appeal accepted that the innocent motive could amount to a reasonable excuse (*Houghton* v *Chief Constable of Greater Manchester* (1987) 84 Cr App R 319). The defendant was dressed in a police uniform and was carrying a truncheon and was held, on the facts of the case, to have a reasonable excuse. In *Densu* the Court of Appeal thought that the following example provided by May LJ in *McCalla* (1988) 87 Cr App R 372 was an example where the excuse might be reasonable:

> if someone driving along a road where earlier there had been a demonstration were to see and pick up a police truncheon which had obviously been dropped there and were to put it

into the boot of his car, intending to take it to the nearest police station, and then were to be stopped within a few minutes, he would have a reasonable excuse for having the truncheon with him in the boot of the car.

In *Glidewell* (1999) 163 JP 557, the Court of Appeal held that 'depending on the circumstances of the particular case, forgetfulness may be relevant to whether or not a defendant has a reasonable excuse for possession of an offensive weapon'. Factors that might be relevant are (in relation to the facts of the instant case): the defendant did not introduce the weapons into his car; the weapons had been in the car for a relatively short period of time; the defendant was very busy on the night in question. As these all bore on the question of the defendant's forgetfulness, they were matters for the jury. As to forgetfulness in relation to having the item with him, see **B12.92**.

OTHER OFFENCES INVOLVING POSSESSION OF WEAPONS

Having Article with Blade or Point in a Public Place

It is an offence triable either way, contrary to the CJA 1988, s. 139(1), for a person to **B12.97** have with him in a public place an article to which the section applies. The section covers any article which has a blade or is sharply pointed except a folding pocket knife, but a folding pocket knife is covered if the cutting edge of its blade exceeds three inches. If a knife is secured in the open position by a locking device, it is not a folding pocket knife because it is not immediately foldable at all times by virtue of the folding process (*Harris* v *DPP* (1992) 96 Cr App R 235). *Harris* was followed in *Deegan* [1998] 2 Cr App R 121, where a challenge to the established meaning on the basis of what Ministers said in *Hansard* was rejected on the basis that what they said was not sufficiently clear. In *Davis* [1998] Crim LR 564, the Court of Appeal decided that determining whether an article fell within s. 139 is a matter of law for the judge to determine. There is no room for applying the decision in *Brutus* v *Cozens* [1973] AC 854, because the 'issue was not the simple etymological meaning of the word "blade"'. The test is not whether the article is capable of causing injury, because the offence is limited to articles which 'happen to have something that could be described as a blade', so a common-sense test is to be applied that the article must be 'within the same broad category as a knife or a sharply pointed instrument'. Thus the court allowed the appeal on the basis that a screwdriver does not fall within s. 139. It is submitted that this is an example of the sometime judicial desire not to use the approach in *Brutus* v *Cozens* (cf. the different approach in *Manning* [1998] Crim LR 198). 'Public place' includes any place to which, at the material time, the public have or are permitted access, whether on payment or otherwise.

Two defences are created by s. 139(4) and (5). First it is a defence for the defendant to prove (on a balance of probabilities, so merely providing an uncontradicted explanation is not necessarily sufficient: *Godwin* v *DPP* (1992) 96 Cr App R 244, where it was held that magistrates were entitled to disbelieve such a defence) that he had good reason or lawful authority for having the article with him in a public place. Forgetfulness does not constitute this defence (*DPP* v *Gregson* (1992) 96 Cr App R 240, confirmed in *Manning*). For assistance on the meaning of 'good reason', the Court of Appeal in *Emmanuel* [1998] Crim LR 347 looked to the concept of 'reasonable excuse' under the Prevention of Crime Act 1953 (see **B12.96**). However, as Professor Sir John Smith points out ([1998] Crim LR 347), the defence in the 1996 Act was intended to be a narrower one than that of reasonable excuse in the 1953 Act. In *Emmanuel* the Court of Appeal decided that 'good reason' includes self-defence. Secondly, and without prejudice to the generality of the first, it is a defence for the defendant to prove that he had the article with him for use at work, or for religious reasons, or as part of any national costume. Whether an article was for use for work (and therefore the other purposes also) is a matter to be determined in accordance with the approach in *Brutus* v *Cozens*, as the statute uses words of the ordinary English language. It is, therefore, a matter for the jury to determine having been so directed by the judge (*Manning*). It may well be that there is good reason for following the approach in *Brutus* v *Cozens* in this case on the basis that there is no special meaning required for the terms of the defence, whereas whether the article falls within the offence in the first place does not warrant application of that approach (see *Deegan*) but perhaps only because of a fear that juries might apply the offence too widely to such items as screwdrivers.

The offence is punishable, on summary conviction, with imprisonment for a term not exceeding six months or a fine not exceeding the statutory maximum or both and, on conviction on indictment, to a term of imprisonment not exceeding two years or a fine or both. These maxima are increases on the original summary offence, and do not apply to offences committed before 4 July 1996, the date on which s. 3 of the Offensive Weapons Act 1996 came into force (Offensive Weapons Act 1996, s. 3(2)). The original offence was a summary offence punishable with a fine not exceeding level 3 on the standard scale.

When dealt with summarily, the Magistrates' Association Guidelines (1997) are the same as those for possession of an offensive weapon (see **B12.87**).

Having Article with Blade or Point on School Premises

B12.98 It is an offence triable either way, contrary to the CJA 1988, s. 139A(1), for a person to have an article to which s. 139 applies (see **B12.97**) with him on school premises. 'Has with him' will be understood in the same way as under the Prevention of Crime Act 1953 (see **B12.91**). By virtue of the CJA 1988, s. 139A(6) 'school premises' means land used for the purposes of a school excluding any land occupied solely as a dwelling by a person employed at the school, and 'school' has the meaning given by the Education Act 1996, s. 4(1), i.e.:

> an educational institution which is outside the further education sector and the higher education sector and is an institution for providing any one or more of the following:
> (a) primary education;
> (b) education which is secondary education by virtue of section 2(2)(a) of the Education Act 1996; or
> (c) full-time education suitable to the requirements of persons who are over compulsory school age but under the age of 19, whether or not the institution also provides part-time education suitable to the requirements of junior pupils, further education or secondary education not within paragraph (b).

The offence is punishable, on summary conviction, with a term of imprisonment not exceeding six months or a fine not exceeding the statutory maximum or both and, on conviction on indictment, to a term of imprisonment not exceeding two years or a fine or both (CJA 1988, s. 139A(5)(a)).

It is a defence for a person charged with the offence to prove that he had good reason or lawful authority for having the article with him on the premises in question (s. 139A(3)); as to lawful authority, see **B12.94** and **B12.95**. It is also a defence for an accused to prove that he had the article with him for use at work, for educational purposes, for religious reasons, or as part of any national costume (s. 139A(4)).

Under the CJA 1988, s. 139B, a constable has a power of entry to school premises to search the premises and any person on them for any article to which s. 139 applies or for any offensive weapon within the meaning of the Prevention of Crime Act 1953, s. 1, if he has reasonable grounds for suspecting that an offence under the CJA 1988, s. 139A, is being or has been committed. If the constable finds any article which he has reasonable grounds for suspecting is such an article, he may seize and retain it. Reasonable force may be used, if necessary.

Having Offensive Weapon on School Premises

It is an offence triable either way, contrary to the CJA 1988, s. 139A(2), for a person to **B12.99** have an offensive weapon as defined in the Prevention of Crime Act 1953 (see **B12.88** to **B12.91**) with him on school premises. 'Has with him' will be understood in the same way as under the Prevention of Crime Act 1953 (see **B12.92**). As to the meaning of 'school premises' and 'school', see **B12.98**. The offence is punishable, on summary conviction, with a term of imprisonment not exceeding six months or a fine not exceeding the statutory maximum or both and, on conviction on indictment, to a term of imprisonment not exceeding four years or a fine or both (CJA 1988, s. 139A(5)(b)). The same defences as for the offence contrary to s. 139A(1) apply to this offence, see **B12.98**. For the power of entry and search, see **B12.98**.

Possession of Crossbow by Person under 17

It is a summary offence, contrary to the Crossbows Act 1987, s. 3, for a person under **B12.100** the age of 17 to have with him: (a) a crossbow which is capable of discharging a missile; or (b) parts of a crossbow which together (and without any other parts) can be assembled to form a crossbow capable of discharging a missile, unless he is under the supervision of a person who is 21 years of age or older. The offence does not apply to crossbows with a draw weight of less than 1.4 kilograms. A person guilty of the offence is liable to a fine not exceeding level 3 on the standard scale. The court may also make such order as it thinks fit as to the forfeiture or disposal of any crossbow or part of a crossbow in respect of which the offence was committed.

For offences by trespassers on premises carrying weapons, see **B13.62** and **B13.63**.

MANUFACTURE, SALE, HIRE AND PURCHASE OF WEAPONS

There are four summary offences concerned with the manufacture etc. of various types of weapons generally:

   (a)   manufacture, sale or hire etc. of dangerous weapons, contrary to the Restriction of Offensive Weapons Act 1959, s. 1(1);

   (b)   manufacture, sale and hire of offensive weapons, contrary to the CJA 1988, s. 141(1);

   (c)   sale and letting on hire of a crossbow to a person under 17, contrary to the Crossbows Act 1987, s. 1;

   (d)   purchase and hiring of a crossbow by a person under 17, contrary to the Crossbows Act 1987, s. 2.

In addition to these offences, there are certain offences of a similar nature which relate only to knives (see **B12.105** *et seq.*).

Manufacture, Sale or Hire etc. of Dangerous Weapons

Restriction of Offensive Weapons Act 1959, s. 1   B12.101

   (1)   Any person who manufactures, sells or hires or offers for sale or hire or exposes or has in his possession for the purposes of sale or hire, or lends or gives to any other person—
     (a)   any knife which has a blade which opens automatically by hand pressure applied to a button, spring or other device in or attached to the handle of the knife, sometimes known as a 'flick-knife' or 'flick gun'; or
     (b)   any knife which has a blade which is released from the handle or sheath thereof by the force of gravity or the application of centrifugal force and which, when released, is locked in place by means of a button, spring, lever, or other device, sometimes known as a 'gravity knife', shall be guilty of an offence and shall be liable on summary conviction to imprisonment for a term not exceeding six months or to a fine not exceeding level 5 on the standard scale or to both such imprisonment and fine.

In addition, the Restriction of Offensive Weapons Act 1959, s. 1(2), prohibits the importation of any such knife described in s. 1(1).

Manufacture, Sale and Hire of Offensive Weapons

B12.102   **Criminal Justice Act 1988, s. 141**

(1)   Any person who manufactures, sells or hires or offers for sale or hire, exposes or has in his possession for the purpose of sale or hire, or lends or gives to any other person, a weapon to which this section applies shall be guilty of an offence.

Subsection (4) also prohibits the importation of a weapon to which this section applies.

By virtue of the CJA 1988, s. 141(1), a person guilty of the offence is liable to imprisonment for a term not exceeding six months, or to a fine not exceeding level 5 on the standard scale, or both.

The weapons to which s. 141 applies are those listed by the Secretary of State in an order, and must not include any weapon subject to the FA 1968, or crossbows. The current relevant order is the CJA 1988 (Offensive Weapons) Order 1988 (SI 1988 No. 2019) which, by the schedule, makes the following offensive weapons for the purpose of the instant offence, other than weapons which are antiques:

Criminal Justice Act 1988 (Offensive Weapons) Order 1988 (SI 1988 No. 2019), Sch.

. . .

(a)   a knuckleduster, that is, a band of metal or other hard material worn on one or more fingers, and designed to cause injury, and any weapon incorporating a knuckleduster;

(b)   a swordstick, that is, a hollow walking-stick or cane containing a blade which may be used as a sword;

(c)   the weapon sometimes known as a 'handclaw', being a band of metal or other hard material from which a number of sharp spikes protrude, and worn around the hand;

(d)   the weapon sometimes known as a 'belt buckle knife', being a buckle which incorporates or conceals a knife;

(e)   the weapon sometimes known as a 'push dagger', being a knife the handle of which fits within a clenched fist and the blade of which protrudes from between two fingers;

(f)   the weapon sometimes known as a 'hollow kubotan', being a cylindrical container containing a number of sharp spikes;

(g)   the weapon sometimes known as a 'footclaw', being a bar of metal or other hard material from which a number of sharp spikes protrude, and worn strapped to the foot;

(h)   the weapon sometimes known as a 'shuriken', 'shaken' or 'death star', being a hard non-flexible plate having three or more sharp radiating points and designed to be thrown;

(i)   the weapon sometimes known as a 'balisong' or 'butterfly knife', being a blade enclosed by its handle, which is designed to split down the middle, without the operation of a spring or other mechanical means, to reveal the blade;

(j)   the weapon sometimes known as a 'telescopic truncheon', being a truncheon which extends automatically by hand pressure applied to a button, spring or other device in or attached to its handle;

(k)   the weapon sometimes known as a 'blowpipe' or 'blow gun' being a hollow tube out of which hard pellets or darts are shot by the use of breath;

(l)   the weapon sometimes known as a 'kusari gama', being a length of rope, cord, wire or chain fastened at one end to a sickle;

(m)   the weapon sometimes known as a 'kyoketsu shoge', being a length of rope, cord, wire or chain fastened at one end to a hooked knife;

(n)   the weapon sometimes known as a 'manrikigusari' or 'kusari', being a length of rope, cord, wire or chain fastened at each end to a hard weight or hand grip.

For the purposes of the schedule, a weapon is an antique if it was manufactured more than 100 years before the date of any offence alleged to have been committed in respect of the weapon.

It is a defence for the accused to prove that he is:

(i)   carrying out functions on behalf of the Crown or a visiting force; see the CJA 1988, s. 141 (5) to (7); or

(ii)   making a weapon available to a museum or gallery; see the CJA 1988, s. 141(8), (10), (11); or

(iii)   a person acting on behalf of a museum or gallery loaning or hiring a weapon for proper purposes, see the CJA 1988, s. 141(9).

Sale or Letting on Hire of a Crossbow to a Person under 17

Crossbows Act 1987, s. 1   B12.103

> A person who sells or lets on hire a crossbow or a part of a crossbow to a person under the age of 17 is guilty of an offence, unless he believes him to be 17 years of age or older and has reasonable ground for the belief.

A person guilty of the offence is liable to imprisonment for a term not exceeding six months, to a fine not exceeding level 5 on the standard scale, or to both. The court also has power to order the forfeiture or disposal of any crossbow or part of a crossbow in respect of which the offence was committed (s. 6(1) and (3)).

Purchase or Hiring of a Crossbow by a Person under 17

Crossbows Act 1987, s. 2   B12.104

> A person under the age of 17 who buys or hires a crossbow or part of a crossbow is guilty of an offence.

A person guilty of the offence is liable to a fine not exceeding level 3 on the standard scale. The court has power to order the forfeiture or disposal of any crossbow or part of a crossbow in respect of which the offence was committed (s. 6(2) and (3)).

MANUFACTURE, MARKETING, SALE, HIRE AND PURCHASE OF KNIVES

The Offensive Weapons Act 1996, s. 6, created an offence relating to the sale of knives   B12.105
to persons under 16. The Knives Act 1997 has created two either way offences (unlawful marketing of knives and publications in connection with the marketing of knives). All these offences, are in addition to the existing summary offences mentioned at **B12.100**.

Sale of Knives and Certain Articles with Blade or Point to Persons under 16

Criminal Justice Act 1988, s. 141A   B12.106

> (1)   Any person who sells to a person under the age of sixteen years an article to which this section applies shall be guilty of an offence and liable on summary conviction to imprisonment for a term not exceeding six months, or a fine not exceeding level 5 on the standard scale, or both.

By CJA 1988, s. 141A(2), the offence applies to:

(a)   any knife, knife blade or razor blade,

(b)   any axe, and

(c)   any other article which has a blade or which is sharply pointed and which is made or adapted for use for causing injury to the person.

Section 141A(1) does not apply to:

(a)   a folding knife if the cutting edge of its blade does not exceed 7.62 centimetres (3 inches);

(b)   razor blades permanently enclosed in a cartridge or housing where less than 2 millimetres of any blade is exposed beyond the place which intersects the highest point of the surfaces preceding and following such blades (Criminal Justice Act 1988 (Offensive Weapons) (Exemptions) Order 1996 (SI 1996 No. 3064), art. 2).

As to articles made or adapted to cause injury under the Prevention of Crime Act 1953, see **B12.89** and **B12.90**. Section 141A does not apply to any article described in the Restriction of Offensive Weapons Act 1959, s. 1 (see **B12.101**), an order made under the CJA 1988, s.141(2) (see **B12.102**), or any order made under s. 141A itself (s. 141A(3)). It is a defence for a person charged with the offence to prove that he took all reasonable precautions and exercised due diligence to avoid the commission of the offence (s. 141A(4)).

Unlawful Marketing of Knives

B12.107

Knives Act 1997, s. 1

(1)   A person is guilty of an offence if he markets a knife in a way which—
(a)   indicates, or suggests, that it is suitable for combat; or
(b)   is otherwise likely to stimulate or encourage violent behaviour involving the use of the knife as a weapon.

The offence is triable either way s. 1(5)). The maximum penalty is: on conviction on indictment, imprisonment for a term not exceeding two years or a fine, or both; on summary conviction, imprisonment for a term not exceeding six months or a fine not exceeding the statutory maximum, or both (s. 1(5)).

B12.108   ***Elements***   'Knife' means an instrument which has a blade or is sharply pointed (s. 10). A person markets a knife if he sells or hires it, he offers, or exposes, it for sale or hire or has it in his possession for the purpose of sale or hire (s. 1(4)). A knife is suitable for combat if it is suitable for use as a weapon for inflicting injury on a person or causing a person to fear injury (s. 10). 'Violent behaviour' means an unlawful act inflicting injury on a person or causing a person to fear injury (s. 10).

An indication or suggestion that a knife is suitable for combat may, in particular, be given or made by a name or description which is applied to the knife, which is on the knife or any packaging in which it is contained or which is included in any advertisement which, expressly or by implication, relates to the knife (s. 1(3)).

Defences

B12.109

Knives Act 1997, ss. 3 and 4

3.—(1)   It is a defence for a person charged with an offence under section 1 to prove that—
(a)   the knife was marketed—
(i)   for use by the armed forces of any country;
(ii)   as an antique or curio; or
(iii) as falling within such other category (if any) as may be prescribed;
(b)   it was reasonable for the knife to be marketed in that way; and
(c)   there were no reasonable grounds for suspecting that a person into whose possession the knife might come in consequence of the way in which it was marketed would use it for an unlawful purpose.

4.—(1)   It is a defence for a person charged with an offence under section 1 to prove that he did not know or suspect, and had no reasonable grounds for suspecting, that the way in which the knife was marketed—
(a)   amounted to an indication or suggestion that the knife was suitable for combat; or
(b)   was likely to stimulate or encourage violent behaviour involving the use of the knife as a weapon.
(2)   It is a defence for a person charged with an offence under section 2 to prove that he did not know or suspect, and had no reasonable grounds for suspecting, that the way in which the knife was marketed—
(a)   amounted to an indication or suggestion that the knife was suitable for combat; or

(b)   was likely to stimulate or encourage violent behaviour involving the use of the knife as a weapon.

(3)   It is a defence for a person charged with an offence under section 1 or 2 to prove that he took all reasonable precautions and exercised all due diligence to avoid committing the offence.

Publications relating to Knives

Knives Act 1997, s. 2

B12.110

(1)   A person is guilty of an offence if he publishes any written, pictorial or other material in connection with the marketing of any knife and that material—
(a)   indicates or suggests that the knife is suitable for combat; or
(b)   is otherwise likely to stimulate or encourage violent behaviour involving the use of the knife as a weapon.

The maximum penalty is: on conviction on indictment, imprisonment for a term not exceeding two years or a fine, or both; on summary conviction, imprisonment for a term not exceeding six months or a fine not exceeding the statutory maximum, or both.

For definition of the terms used in s. 2, see **B12.108**.

Specific defences are provided by s. 4(2) and (3) (see **B12.109**).

CAUSING EXPLOSION LIKELY TO ENDANGER LIFE OR PROPERTY

Definition

Explosive Substances Act 1883, s. 2

B12.111

A person who in the United Kingdom or (being a citizen of the United Kingdom and Colonies) in the Republic of Ireland unlawfully and maliciously causes by any explosive substance an explosion of a nature likely to endanger life or to cause serious injury to property shall, whether any injury to person or property has actually been caused or not, be guilty of an offence. . . .

Indictment

Statement of Offence

B12.112

Causing an explosion contrary to section 2 of the Explosive Substances Act 1883

Particulars of Offence

A on or about the . . . day of . . . maliciously caused by an explosive substance an explosion of a nature likely to endanger life or to cause serious injury to property, namely the explosion at . . . Town Hall on the . . . day of . . .

Procedure

The offence is triable on indictment only (Explosive Substances Act 1883, s. 2) and is a B12.113
class 3 offence.

Proceedings for a crime under this Act shall not be instituted except by or with the consent of the A-G (s. 7(1)); proceedings are not instituted until following remands in custody or bail since such remands are expressly excluded from the operation of s. 7(1) by the Prosecution of Offences Act 1979, s. 25(2) (*Wale* (1991) *The Times*, 9 May 1991, in which the proceedings for the offence contrary to s. 4 were held not to be effectively instituted until the committal proceedings). Further, in *Elliott* (1984) 81 Cr App R 115 at p. 121, the Court of Appeal concluded that the Explosive Substances Act 1883, s. 7 'should be interpreted as meaning that instituting proceedings relates to the time when a person comes to court to answer the charge' so the relevant time is 'when he attends at the magistrates' court to answer the charge'; it held that any other interpretation would 'overlook and ignore' the provisions of the Prosecution of Offences Act 1979, s. 6. As to the Prosecution of Offences Act 1979, ss. 25 and 6, see **D1.86** and **D2.34** respectively.

Sentence

B12.114 The maximum penalty is imprisonment for life (Explosive Substances Act 1883, s. 2). Powers of forfeiture and disposal of matter are provided by the Explosives Act 1875, ss. 89 and 96; these apply to this offence (1983 Act, s. 8(1)). See also **B12.122**.

Explosive Substance and Explosion

B12.115 'Explosive substance' is 'deemed to include any materials for making any explosive substance; also any apparatus, machine, implement or materials used, or intended to be used, or adapted for causing, or aiding in causing, any explosion in or with any explosive substance; also any part of any such apparatus, machine or implement' (Explosive Substances Act 1883, s. 9(1)).

The Court of Appeal decided in *Wheatley* [1979] 1 WLR 144 that the definition of 'explosive' in the Explosives Act 1875, s. 3, applies to the 1883 Act.

Explosives Act 1875, s. 3

The term 'explosive' in this Act — (1) Means gunpowder, nitroglycerine, dynamite, gun-cotton, blasting powders, fulminate of mercury or of other metals, coloured fires and every other substance, whether similar to those above mentioned or not, used or manufactured with a view to producing a practical effect by explosion or a pyrotechnic effect; and (2) includes fog-signals, fireworks, fuses, rockets, percussion caps, detonators, cartridges, ammunition of all description, and every adaptation or preparation of an explosive as above defined.

Thus, the fire-dampened sodium chlorate mixture used in a pipe bomb, in *Wheatley*, was an explosive substance even if it had only a pyrotechnic effect. In *Bouch* [1983] QB 246, the Court of Appeal decided that 'pyrotechnic effect' has a broad meaning and is not limited to, e.g., fireworks. A flare is a pyrotechnic device. There does not have to be an explosion. A fireball produced by a petrol bomb clearly has a pyrotechnic effect.

The meaning of 'explosion' was considered by the Court of Appeal in *Bouch*, where the definition used in the 1886 edition of the *Encyclopaedia Britannica* was approved:

'explosion' may for our purpose be defined as the sudden or extremely rapid conversion of a solid or liquid body of small bulk into gas or vapour, occupying very many times the volume of the original substance, and, in addition, highly expanded by the heat generated during the transformation. This sudden or very rapid expansion of volume is attained by an exhibition of force, more or less violent according to the constitution of the original substance and the circumstances of explosion. Any substance capable of undergoing such a change upon the application of heat, or other disturbing cause, is called 'explosive'.

Thus the inevitable concomitant of a successful petrol bomb is an explosion because it produces a fireball, though it does not always have a blast effect. In any case, a petrol bomb will produce a blast effect where it does not ignite immediately upon impact but ignites after a pause. See also *Elliott* (1984) 81 Cr App R 115 adopting this approach.

Explosive substances have included a shot gun (*Downey* [1971] NI 224), a firearm (*Fegan* (1971) 78 Cr App R 189), part of a vessel filled with an explosive substance (*Charles* (1892) 17 Cox CC 499) and electronic timers (*Berry (No. 3)* [1994] 2 All ER 913), as well as the more obvious substances, such as dynamite or gunpowder (*Hallam* [1957] 1 QB 569), plaster gelatine and detonators (*Stewart and Harris* (1959) 44 Cr App R 29), and a stick of gelignite, a length of fuse and a detonator (*McCarthy* [1964] 1 WLR 196). The petrol in a petrol bomb combines with the air to create an explosive substance, so the petrol, bottle and wick are materials for making that explosive substance (*Bouch*).

Who in the United Kingdom

B12.116 In *Ellis* (1991) 95 Cr App R 52, Swinton Thomas J held, on a motion to quash two counts in an indictment, that 'the words "who in the United Kingdom" do not govern the person but govern the acts'. In reaching this conclusion the judge had pointed out that 'to construe section 3 . . . so as to limit the offence to a person who is physically present in the United Kingdom when he causes explosions runs not only wholly contrary to common sense but wholly contrary to the whole tenor of the law as it has developed over the last century and particularly over the last two decades'.

Mens Rea

The *mens rea is* that the act must be done 'maliciously' (see **B2.34** and **A2.7**). There is **B12.117** no need for foresight by the defendant of endangerment of life or serious injury to property. The likelihood of either is assessed objectively by the jury.

Punishment of Accessories

See **B12.132**.   **B12.118**

Power of Search, etc.

Section 8(1) of the Explosive Substances Act 1883 extends certain powers in the **B12.119** Explosives Act 1875 to this offence. The powers are: to search for explosives (s. 73); to seize and detain explosives liable to forfeiture (s. 74); and to inspect wharves, carriages, boats, etc. with explosives in transit (s. 75).

ATTEMPT TO CAUSE EXPLOSION OR MAKING OR KEEPING EXPLOSIVE WITH INTENT TO ENDANGER LIFE OR PROPERTY

Definition

Explosive Substances Act 1883, s. 3   **B12.120**

(1)   A person who in the United Kingdom or a dependency or (being a citizen of the United Kingdom and Colonies) elsewhere unlawfully and maliciously—
(a)   does any act with intent to cause, or conspires to cause, by an explosive substance an explosion of a nature likely to endanger life, or cause serious injury to property, whether in the United Kingdom or the Republic of Ireland, or
(b)   makes or has in his possession or under his control an explosive substance with intent by means thereof to endanger life, or cause serious injury to property, whether in the United Kingdom or the Republic of Ireland, or to enable any other person so to do,
shall, whether any explosion does or does not take place, and whether any injury to person or property is actually caused or not, be guilty of an offence . . .

Procedure

The offence is triable on indictment only (Explosive Substances Act 1883, s. 3(1)) and **B12.121** is a class 3 offence. As to the need for the Attorney General's consent, see **B12.113**.

Sentence

The maximum penalty is imprisonment for life (Explosive Substances Act 1883, **B12.122** s. 3(1)). The explosive substance is forfeited. The related provisions of the Explosives Act 1875 (ss. 89 and 96) apply (s. 8(1)). In *Martin* [1999] 1 Cr App R (S) 477, the Court of Appeal issued guidelines for the sentencing of this offence. Lord Bingham CJ said that the appropriate sentence would depend upon a number of factors, including the nature, size and likely effect of the explosive device, the nature and extent of any death, injury or damage caused, together with the role and motivation of the individual offenders. Where conspiracy was involved, key factors would be the target of that conspiracy, and the likely result of any explosion. A conspiracy whose primary object was to endanger life should attract a higher sentence than one primarily directed to damaging property. On the facts of the case before the court, the offenders were members of the IRA who had planned to cause explosions, using 37 bombs at electricity substations. They had been arrested before the plan could be implemented. The political, economic and social threat in this case had been grave, and death or personal injury, though not the primary intention, had been an obvious risk. The sentence was reduced from 35 years' imprisonment to 28 years, a term designed to correlate with the period typically served by the perpetrator of a murder with severely aggravating features.

Elements

B12.123 For the meaning of 'in the United Kingdom', see **B12.116**; 'dependency' means the Channel Islands, the Isle of Man and any colony, other than a colony for whose external relations a country other than the United Kingdom is responsible (Explosive Substances Act 1883, s. 3(2)).

For the meaning of 'explosive substance' and 'explosive', see **B12.115**. For the meaning of 'making explosives', see **B12.129**.

Mens Rea

B12.124 The *mens rea* is that the act, whatever it might be, must be done 'maliciously' (see **B2.34** and **A2.7**). It would appear not to be possible to possess a substance maliciously if it is not known what the substance is. Thus the approach in the cases decided on the Explosive Substances Act 1883, s. 4, by the Court of Criminal Appeal in *Hallam* [1957] 1 QB 569 and *Stewart* (1959) 44 Cr App R 29 (see **B12.129**) may be applicable to this offence also, rather than the rules relating to possession developed in relation to controlled drugs (see **B20.10**).

Punishment of Accessories and Powers of Search

B12.125 See **B12.132** for punishment of accessories. See **B12.119** for powers of search.

MAKING OR POSSESSION OF EXPLOSIVE UNDER SUSPICIOUS CIRCUMSTANCES

Definition

B12.126   **Explosive Substances Act 1883, s. 4**

> (1)   Any person who makes or knowingly has in his possession or under his control any explosive substance, under such circumstances as to give rise to a reasonable suspicion that he is not making it or does not have it in his possession or under his control for a lawful object, shall, unless he can show that he made it or had it in his possession or under his control for a lawful object, be guilty of [an offence] . . .

Procedure

B12.127 The offence is triable on indictment only (Explosive Substances Act 1883, s. 4(1)) and is a class 3 offence. As to the need for the Attorney General's consent, see **B12.113**.

Sentence

B12.128 On conviction on indictment, the maximum penalty is 14 years' imprisonment, and the explosive substance must be forfeited (Explosive Substances Act 1883, s. 4(1)).

Possession, Control or Making and *Mens Rea*

B12.129 The defendant must know that he has the substance in his possession or control (*Berry (No. 3)* [1994] 2 All ER 913, at p. 918h). In *Hallam* [1957] 1 QB 569, the Court of Criminal Appeal decided the meaning of the section was clear and that 'the person must not only knowingly have in his possession the substance but must know that it is an explosive substance', but he does not have to have 'any particular chemical knowledge'.

This decision was followed by the Court of Criminal Appeal in *Stewart* (1959) 44 Cr App R 29. The word 'knowingly' prefaces 'possession' and 'control' and not 'making', but, nevertheless, 'all three categories of person must be shown to have known that the substance was an explosive substance' (*Berry (No. 3)* [1994] 2 All ER 913 at p. 918g). It was said in *Berry* that 'no person who makes a substance can be unaware that he had done so' although this must be read as being subject to the general defences (see **A3**).

The Court of Appeal in *Hallam* also said that 'if evidence is given that the person had the substance in his possession, and some evidence of circumstances which give rise to a reasonable suspicion that he had not got it for a lawful purpose is given, the jury are then entitled to infer that he knew it was an explosive substance'. However, there is nothing in this approach which should be interpreted as suggesting that the burden of proof is not on the prosecution to prove *mens rea*, and that is particularly so where the substance is not so obviously an explosive substance, e.g., a timer as opposed to gunpowder or gelignite. The jury must be sure that the maker intended the timer to be used to cause explosions (*Berry (No. 3)* [1994] 2 All ER 913 at p. 919).

Reasonable Suspicion

'Reasonable suspicion' is an objective requirement, which must be proved by the prosecution (see *Fegan* (1971) 78 Cr App R 189). **B12.130**

Lawful Object

In *Fegan* (1971) 78 Cr App R 189, the Court of Criminal Appeal, Northern Ireland, decided that 'the expression "lawful object" cannot be defined exhaustively or with precision'. The court decided that possession and purpose must not be confused, so, 'possession of a firearm for the purpose of protecting the possessor, his wife or family from acts of violence may be possession for a lawful object'. However, that purpose 'cannot be founded on a mere fancy, or some aggressive motive' and the 'threatened danger must be reasonably and genuinely anticipated, must appear reasonably imminent, and must be of a nature which could not reasonably be met by more pacific means' (*Fegan*). The Court of Appeal in *A-G's Ref (No. 2 of 1983)* [1984] QB 456 agreed with this approach. It would appear that the House of Lords also adopted the same approach in *Berry* [1985] AC 246. Further, the court in *Fegan* held that a person cannot possess an item for a lawful object if he also has it for an unlawful object. **B12.131**

As the statute makes clear, the burden of proof of this defence lies upon the defence (see *Berry (No. 3)* [1994] 2 All ER 913 at p. 920f and *Fegan*) and it must be proved on a balance of probabilities (*Fegan*).

Punishment of Accessories

Explosive Substances Act 1883, s. 5 **B12.132**

Any person who within or (being a subject of Her Majesty) without Her Majesty's dominions by the supply of or solicitation for money, the providing of premises, the supply of materials, or in any manner whatsoever, procures, counsels, aids, abets, or is accessory to, the commission of any crime under this Act, shall be guilty of [an offence], and shall be liable to be tried and punished for that crime, as if he had been guilty as a principal.

Notwithstanding s. 5, the commission of an offence contrary to s. 4 may be aided and abetted (*McCarthy* [1964] 1 WLR 196). For a general consideration of participation in crime, see **A5**, and, in particular, **A5.7**.

Powers of Search

See **B12.119** for powers of search. **B12.133**

CAUSING BODILY INJURY BY GUNPOWDER

Definition

B12.134   **Offences Against the Person Act 1861, s. 28**

Whosoever shall unlawfully and maliciously, by the explosion of gunpowder or other explosive substance, burn, maim, disfigure, disable, or do any grievous bodily harm to any person, shall be guilty of [an offence].

Procedure and Sentence

B12.135 The offence is triable on indictment (OAPA 1861, s. 28) and is a class 3 offence.

The maximum penalty is imprisonment for life (s. 28).

Elements

B12.136 In *Howard* [1993] Crim LR 213, the Court of Appeal decided that a petrol bomb is an explosive substance. The definition of 'explosive substance' under the Explosive Substances Act 1883 (see **B12.115**) was used by the trial judge and noted by the Court of Appeal. It clearly is of assistance, but may not be determinative of the concept as it appears in the OAPA 1861. It is submitted that the term should mean the same in both pieces of legislation. The Court of Appeal wondered if the trial judge should not have asked the jury to determine whether the petrol bomb was an explosive substance. This can be correct only if the jury were being asked to determine whether the facts about a petrol bomb satisfied the definition of explosive substance given to them by the judge.

It is to be assumed that the words 'burn, maim, disfigure, disable, or do any grievous bodily harm' will carry their ordinary meaning, unless a decision suggests otherwise. Indeed this was the approach of the Court of Appeal in interpreting the meaning of 'disable' in *James* (1979) 70 Cr App R 215. 'Maim' has a technical legal meaning which is injury of any part of a man's body which may make him less able to defend himself (12 *Halsbury's Statutes*, at p. 109), so there was no proof of an intent to maim or disable in *Sullivan* (1841) Car & M 209 where the blow was aimed at the head of the victim, but it would have been otherwise had it been aimed at his arm to prevent his being able to use it. 'Disfigure' means to do an external injury which may detract from the personal appearance (12 *Halsbury's Statutes*, at p. 109). 'Disable' covers both permanent and temporary disablement (*James*, a decision on s. 29, and not applying *Boyce* (1824) 1 Mood CC 29). As to 'grievous bodily harm', see **B2.34**.

Mens Rea

B12.137 The *mens rea* is 'maliciously', which, it is submitted, refers both to the consequence as well as the explosion. As to the meaning of 'maliciously', see **B2.34** and **A2.7**.

CAUSING GUNPOWDER TO EXPLODE, SENDING AN EXPLOSIVE SUBSTANCE OR THROWING CORROSIVE FLUID WITH INTENT

Definition

B12.138   **Offences Against the Person Act 1861, s. 29**

Whosoever shall unlawfully and maliciously cause any gunpowder or other explosive substance to explode, or send or deliver or to cause to be taken or received by any person any explosive substance or any other dangerous or noxious thing, or put or lay at any place, or cast or throw at or upon or otherwise apply to any person, any corrosive fluid or any destructive or explosive substance, with intent in any of the cases aforesaid to burn, maim, disfigure, or disable any person, or to do some grievous bodily harm to any person, shall, whether any bodily injury be effected or not, be guilty of [an offence].

Procedure and Sentence

This offence is triable on indictment (OAPA 1861, s. 29) and is a class 3 offence.   **B12.139**

On conviction on indictment, the maximum penalty is life imprisonment.

Elements

For the meaning of 'explosive substance' and 'burn, maim, disfigure, or disable', see   **B12.140**
B12.136. For 'grievous bodily harm', see **B2.34**.

In *Crawford* (1845) 2 Car & Kir 129, the Court for Crown Cases Reserved upheld a
conviction on the basis that boiling water was 'destructive matter'. For the meaning of
noxious thing, see **B2.54**.

Mens Rea

The *mens rea* of the offence consists of 'maliciously' doing one of the prohibited acts and   **B12.141**
with intent to produce one of the prohibited consequences. As to the meaning of
'maliciously', see **B2.34** and **A2.7**. As to 'intention', see **A2.2**.

PLACING GUNPOWDER NEAR A BUILDING, ETC., WITH INTENT TO DO BODILY INJURY TO ANY PERSON

Definition

Offences Against the Person Act 1861, s. 30   **B12.142**

Whosoever shall unlawfully and maliciously place or throw in, into, upon, against, or near
any building, ship or vessel any gunpowder or other explosive substance, with intent to do
any bodily injury to any person, shall, whether or not any explosion take place, and whether
or not any bodily injury be effected, be guilty of [an offence].

Procedure and Sentence

The offence is triable on indictment (OAPA 1861, s. 30) and is a class 3 offence.   **B12.143**

The maximum penalty is 14 years' imprisonment.

Elements

For the meaning of 'explosive substance', see **B12.136**. Although the substance need   **B12.144**
not explode, it must be capable of exploding, so to throw a bottle containing only
gunpowder and an unlit fuse would not constitute the offence, because the act would
merely be that of throwing a bottle (*Shephard* (1868) 19 LT 19 at p. 20).

Mens Rea

The placing or throwing must be done 'maliciously' (as to which see **B2.34** and **A2.7**),   **B12.145**
and it must be done with intent to do bodily injury (as to 'intent', see **A2.2**). It is to be
noted that the phrase is bodily injury and not grievous bodily harm. It appears to be a
wider term in the sense that it need not be serious, but it may be more limited if it applies
only to physical injury.

MAKING OR HAVING GUNPOWDER, ETC., WITH INTENT TO COMMIT OR ENABLE ANY PERSON TO COMMIT A FELONY

Definition

Offences Against the Person Act 1861, s. 64   **B12.146**

Whosoever shall knowingly have in his possession, or make or manufacture, any
gunpowder, explosive substance, or any dangerous or noxious thing, or any machine,

engine, instrument, or thing, with intent by means thereof to commit, or for the purpose of enabling any other person to commit, any of the felonies in this Act mentioned shall be guilty of an [offence].

Procedure and Sentence

B12.147   The offence is triable on indictment and is a class 3 offence.

The maximum penalty is two years' imprisonment.

Elements

B12.148   For the meaning of 'possession', see, by analogy, the drug possession cases at **B20.10**, but note that the possession in this offence must be 'knowingly', see **B12.147**.

For the meaning of 'explosive substance', see **B12.136**. For the meaning of 'noxious thing', see **B2.54**.

Mens Rea

B12.149   The *mens rea* requires that there be an act (possession, making or manufacturing) which is done 'knowingly'. As to the meaning of 'knowingly', see **A2.9**. There must also be an intent to commit a felony within the OAPA 1861. As to the meaning of 'intent', see **A2.2**. The reference to 'felonies' is to any offence within the 1861 Act for which a person (not previously convicted) may be tried on indictment otherwise than at his own instance (Criminal Law Act 1967, s. 10 and sch. 2, para. 8).

SECTION B13: OFFENCES AFFECTING ENJOYMENT OF PREMISES

UNLAWFUL EVICTION AND HARASSMENT OF OCCUPIER

Definition

The Protection from Eviction Act 1977, s. 1, creates three offences which may be **B13.1** considered together. The first offence, contrary to s. 1(2), is concerned with unlawful eviction (the statute using the words 'deprives'); the other two offences, contrary to s. 1(3) and (3A), are concerned with harassment of a residential occupier. The main differences between the two harassment offences is that the one contrary to s. 1(3) can be committed by any person and it is necessary to prove intention, whereas the offence contrary to s. 1(3A) can be committed only by the landlord or agent and no intention need be proved. Section 1(3) does not create two offences (*Schon v Camden London Borough Council* (1986) 84 LGR 830, per Glidewell LJ).

Protection from Eviction Act 1977, s. 1

(2)   If any person unlawfully deprives the residential occupier of any premises of his occupation of the premises or any part thereof, or attempts to do so, he is guilty of an offence unless he proves that he believed, and had reasonable cause to believe, that the residential occupier had ceased to reside in the premises.

(3)   If any person with intent to cause the residential occupier of any premises—

(a)   to give up the occupation of the premises or any part thereof; or

(b)   to refrain from exercising any right or pursuing any remedy in respect of the premises or part thereof;

does acts likely to interfere with the peace or comfort of the residential occupier or members of his household, or persistently withdraws or withholds services reasonably required for the occupation of the premises as a residence, he shall be guilty of an offence.

(3A)   Subject to subsection (3B) below the landlord of a residential occupier or an agent of the landlord shall be guilty of an offence if—

(a)   he does acts likely to interfere with the peace or comfort of the residential occupier or members of his household, or

(b)   he persistently withdraws or withholds services reasonably required for the occupation of the premises in question as a residence,

and (in either case) he knows, or has reasonable cause to believe, that that conduct is likely to cause the residential occupier to give up the occupation of the whole or part of the premises or to refrain from exercising any right or pursuing any remedy in respect of the whole or part of the premises.

Procedure

The Protection from Eviction Act 1977, s. 6, provides that proceedings may be **B13.2** instituted by councils of districts and London boroughs, the Common Council of the City of London, and the Council of the Scilly Isles.

The offence is triable either way. When tried on indictment it is a class 4 offence.

Indictment

First Count **B13.3**

Statement of Offence

Unlawful eviction contrary to section 1(2) of the Protection from Eviction Act 1977

Particulars of Offence

A on the . . . day of . . . unlawfully deprived V, the residential occupier, of his occupation of premises, namely . . . , by changing the locks of the said premises during the absence of V and the members of his household

Second Count

Statement of Offence

Unlawful harassment contrary to section 1(3) of the Protection from Eviction Act 1977

Particulars of Offence

A on divers dates between . . . and . . . did acts likely to interfere with the peace and comfort of [or: withdrew (or withheld) services reasonably required for occupation, namely . . . , from] V, the residential occupier of premises at . . . , namely . . . , with intent to cause V to give up his occupation of the said premises [or: to refrain from exercising the right to . . .] [or: to refrain from pursuing a remedy of . . .], without reasonable cause to believe that he had ceased to reside in the premises

Although strictly speaking in an indictment for the offence contrary to s. 1(3) there need be no reference to a 'persistent' withdrawing or withholding of services, as a matter of practice it is desirable that it should be included (*Abrol* [1972] Crim LR 318). It would not appear that s. 1(3) is a possible alternative offence to s. 1(2), although Glidewell LJ, giving the judgment of the Divisional Court in *Costelloe v London Borough of Camden* [1986] Crim LR 249, stated that charging the two offences in the alternative would not be objectionable.

Sentence

B13.4   The maximum penalty is: on summary conviction, a fine not exceeding the prescribed sum or imprisonment for a term not exceeding six months or both; on conviction on indictment, a fine or imprisonment for a term not exceeding two years or both (Protection from Eviction Act 1977, s. 1(4)).

In *Pittard* (1994) 15 Cr App R (S) 108, the offender was convicted of unlawful eviction and of interfering with the peace and comfort of a residential occupier. He had let a house to an old lady as sole occupier and, while she was away, he had broken in, changed the locks, and indicated his intention to remain in the house. He left after 12 hours. Fines imposed by the sentencing judge were reduced by the Court of Appeal to a fine of £100 on the first count, together with no separate penalty on the second. An order for costs in the sum of £2,000 was upheld.

Persons who can Commit Offence

B13.5   The offences contrary to the Protection from Eviction Act 1977, s. 1(2) and (3), may be committed by 'any person', whereas the offence contrary to s. 1(3A) may be committed only by 'the landlord of a residential occupier or an agent of the landlord'. It may be that if the eviction is 'unlawful' within s. 1(2) only by virtue of the provisions of s. 3(1), the offence can be committed only by a landlord or agent (see **B13.11**).

Liability of Corporate Officers

B13.6   The Protection from Eviction Act 1977, s. 1(6), makes provision for the liability of officers of a body corporate which is guilty of one of the two offences:

Protection from Eviction Act 1977, s. 1

(6)   Where an offence under this section committed by a body corporate is proved to have been committed with the consent or connivance of, or to be attributable to any neglect on the part of, any director, manager or secretary or other similar officer of the body

corporate or any person who was purporting to act in any such capacity, he as well as the body corporate shall be guilty of that offence and shall be liable to be proceeded against and punished accordingly.

Meaning of 'Residential Occupier'

Protection from Eviction Act 1977, s. 1   B13.7

(1) In this section 'residential occupier', in relation to any premises, means a person occupying the premises as a residence, whether under a contract or by virtue of any enactment or rule of law giving him the right to remain in occupation or restricting the right of any other person to recover possession of the premises.

Provided an occupier has a right to remain in occupation, or the right of any other person to recover possession of the premises is restricted, he is a 'residential occupier'. It has to be ascertained whether a given occupier has sufficient residential protection to qualify under this statute. In *Blankley* [1979] Crim LR 166, Judge Clover in the Knightsbridge Crown Court held, considering the earlier offence contrary to the Rent Act 1965, s. 30, that there was no case to answer since the occupier was not a tenant but merely a contractual licensee. With respect, this decision cannot be correct, since the Protection from Eviction Act 1977 is not concerned with whether the occupier is a tenant, but whether the occupation that he has, granted by whatever means, satisfies the statutory requirements. Those requirements may be satisfied under a contractual licence. Lord Widgery CJ, giving the judgment of the Divisional Court, accepted in *Thurrock Urban District Council* v *Shina* (1972) 70 LGR 301 that a licensee could be a residential occupier, whilst recognising that a licence may more easily be terminated than a tenancy. This case is also a decision on the Rent Act 1965, s. 30. Of course, once a licence is ended, the person is usually no longer a residential occupier and falls outside the protection provided by these offences (see *Portsmouth City Council, ex parte Knight* (1983) 82 LGR 184; *Surrey Heath Borough Council, ex parte Li* (1984) 16 HLR 79).

The wider approach being put forward also follows from the decision of the Divisional Court in *Norton* v *Knowles* [1969] 1 QB 572 (a decision on the Rent Act 1965, s. 30) that a person living in a caravan which was not attached to the land was a residential occupier. Although the caravan was connected to the drains, water pipes and electricity supply and had a telephone, it does not appear that these factors were necessarily essential to the decision. What was essential was the relationship between the landlord and the caravan dweller.

Belief that Person not Residential Occupier

In relation to the harassment offence contrary to the Protection from Eviction Act 1977,   **B13.8** s. 1(3), the Court of Appeal in *Phekoo* [1981] 1 WLR 1117 held, on the basis that conviction for the offence is conviction for a truly criminal offence and attaches serious social stigma to the offender, that, where the issue is raised that the accused believed that the person who was harassed was not a residential occupier, it is for the Crown to prove that that belief was not honest. Further there must be a reasonable basis for the asserted belief. Although this decision directly applies only to the offence contrary to s. 1(3), there appears to be no good reason why it does not also apply to the offence contrary to s. 1(2) and 1(3A).

Whether it is still good law that there must be a reasonable basis for the belief, or whether the belief has only to be an honest one, is a question which is open. See the discussion of 'mistake' at **A3.2** to **A3.6**.

Meaning of 'Premises'

Lord Widgery CJ, giving the judgment of the Divisional Court in *Thurrock Urban District*   **B13.9** *Council* v *Shina* (1972) 70 LGR 301, decided that the word 'premises' in the Rent Act

1965, s. 30, the precursor to the Protection from Eviction Act 1977, should be given its normal wide meaning. He had no doubt that a single room, together with shared use of a bathroom and kitchen, did fall within the meaning of 'premises'. 'Premises' may include a caravan, together with the land upon which it stands (see *Norton* v *Knowles* [1969] 1 QB 572).

Meaning of 'Occupying Premises as a Residence'

B13.10 'Occupying premises as a residence' has the same meaning as it had in the Rent Act 1977 (*Schon* v *Camden London Borough Council* (1986) 84 LGR 830). Thus, a person may occupy premises as his residence although he is physically absent from them, provided that the absence is not, and is not intended to be, permanent, and either his spouse or some other member of the family is physically in occupation or, at the very least, his furniture and belongings remain in the premises.

Elements Specific to s. 1(2)

B13.11 ***Unlawfully Depriving Occupier*** The Protection from Eviction Act 1977, s. 3(1), makes it unlawful for the owner to enforce against the occupier, otherwise than by court proceedings, his right to recover possession of the premises where those premises have been let as a dwelling under a tenancy (which is not a statutorily protected tenancy or an excluded tenancy) and the tenancy has come to an end but the occupier continues to reside in the premises.

The Court of Appeal in *Yuthiwattana* (1984) 80 Cr App R 55 was satisfied that s. 1(2) is concerned with eviction, and so an unlawful deprivation must have the character of an eviction. Kerr LJ, giving the judgment of the Court, held that it was going too far to require an eviction to be of a permanent character. He said (at p. 63):

> For instance, if the owner of the premises unlawfully tells the occupier that he must leave the premises from some period, it may be months or weeks, and then excludes him from the premises, or does anything else with the result that the occupier effectively has to leave the premises and find other accommodation, then it would in our view be open to a jury to convict the owner under subsection (2) on the ground that he had unlawfully deprived the occupier of his occupation. On the other hand, cases which are more properly described as 'locking out' or not admitting an occupier on one or even more isolated occasions, so that in effect he continues to be allowed to occupy the premises but is then unable to enter, seem to us to fall appropriately under subsection (3)(a) or (b), which deal with acts of harassment.

Consequently the conviction under a count charging the offence contrary to s. 1(2) had to be quashed because the occupier was excluded for only one night. This decision was followed by the Divisional Court in *Costelloe* v *London Borough of Camden* [1986] Crim LR 249, where Glidewell LJ held that there is an offence under s. 1(2) where the landlord intends to exclude the occupier permanently and the occupier thinks he has been excluded permanently, even if the landlord then changes his mind and the occupier is later admitted. What matters is whether the exclusion appears to be permanent. Woolf J put the point slightly differently saying:

> The proper test is: What was the nature of the exclusion? Was it, whether it be short or long, an exclusion designed to evict the tenant from the premises? If it was, then it falls within section 1(2). If on the other hand all that occurred was the deprivation of the occupation of the premises for a short period of time and that was the object of the exercise, then it would not fall within section 1(2).

B13.12 ***Belief that Occupier had Ceased to Reside in Premises*** No offence is committed if the accused believes, on reasonable grounds, that a residential occupier has ceased to reside in the premises. This is a matter for the jury to determine. Thus the trial judge erred in *Davidson-Acres* [1980] Crim LR 50, when he himself decided questions as to the time and existence of the accused's belief.

Elements Specific to s. 1(3)

Harassment with Intent   It is essential for this offence to establish the necessary   **B13.13**
intent. If it is not present, it may be that an offence contrary to the Protection from
Eviction Act 1977, s. 1(3A), has been committed. The meaning of the word 'intent'
must be approached in the same way as in the law of murder (see **B1.6** and **B1.11**, as
indicated in *AMK (Property Management) Ltd* [1985] Crim LR 600). On the other hand,
the House of Lords in *Burke* [1991] AC 135 held that 'intention' in this context means
with the purpose or motive of causing the occupier to give up occupation of the premises.
This would appear to be a more limited understanding of the word 'intent' than usually
applies in criminal law, and might not, therefore, be followed in a case to which the usual
understanding actually applied on the facts. See generally, **A2.2**. The intention must be
either to cause the occupier to give up the premises (s. 1(3)(a)), or to refrain from
exercising any right or pursuing any remedy in respect of the premises (s. 1(3)(b)).

With regard to s. 1(3)(a), the Court of Appeal in *AMK (Property Management) Ltd*
[1985] Crim LR 600 allowed the appeals in part because the trial judge had not made
clear to the jury that the consequences of the building work designed to refurbish a block
of flats were not simply to be equated with an intention to evict. An intention to evict
must be established and, whilst the works could have been carried out without an
intention to evict, the company's acts were reasonable and not of the kind covered by
s. 1(3)(a). Ormrod LJ, giving the judgment of the Court of Appeal in *McCall* v *Abelesz*
[1976] QB 585 (a decision on the Rent Act 1965, s. 30), held that it is not sufficient to
establish that the accused was completely indifferent as to the cutting off of the gas
supply to the occupier, nor would it be sufficient for the accused simply to allow things
to happen which might have the effect of causing the occupier to leave, since these could
not be equated with an intent to cause the occupier to give up the occupation of the
premises. If the accused realised that there was a real likelihood that these activities
would result in the occupier leaving, the general approach to the meaning of 'intent'
might result in a decision that the accused did intend to cause the occupier to give up
occupation of the premises (as to the general approach to 'intent', see **A2.2**).

With regard to s. 1(3)(b), the Divisional Court in *Schon* v *Camden London Borough
Council* (1986) 84 LGR 830 held that 'an intention to persuade [the occupier] to leave
for a limited period of time in order to enable work to be done and thereafter to allow
her to return, was not an intent to cause her to give up her occupation of the premises.
Notwithstanding that, it would be an intent which fell within the second intention within
s. 1(3) because it would be an intention to cause her to refrain from exercising her right
to live in the premises and to be physically present in the premises.' Since the charge was
specifically worded to refer to s. 1(3)(b), the necessary intent was not established and
the appeal against conviction was allowed.

Belief that Person Harassed not Residential Occupier   The decision of the Court   **B13.14**
of Appeal on this matter in *Phekoo* [1981] 1 WLR 1117 applies to this offence, and is
considered at **B13.8**.

Acts Likely to Interfere with Peace or Comfort   The Protection from Eviction Act   **B13.15**
1977, uses the phrase 'does acts', which requires that there be conduct on the part of
the accused, but that phrase does not require that there be more than one act (*Polycarpou*
(1978) 9 HLR 129). Consequently, removing the sole source of heat of a tenant would
satisfy this requirement of the offence.

It may be that the Court of Appeal in *McCall* v *Abelesz* [1976] 1 QB 585 had in mind
the need to establish conduct, rather than merely taking advantage of the acts of others
with the accused actually doing nothing. In *Ahmad* (1987) 84 Cr App R 64, the Court
of Appeal held that the phrase 'does acts' does not impose a responsibility to rectify

damage which the accused has already caused by an act done innocently. Thus, a later failure to take steps to rectify what he has caused, even if with the requisite intent, is not the doing of an act or acts for the purposes of s. 1(3). Clearly an act and not an omission is required, and the doctrine established by the House of Lords in *Miller* [1983] 2 AC 161 (see **A1.16**) does not apply. In *Yuthiwattana* (1984) 80 Cr App R 55, there was conduct in addition to the failure to provide a front door key, thereby satisfying the requirement that acts be done. The other acts included entering the occupier's room without permission, removing his record player and records, and shouting at him. The omission or failure to provide a front door key would not of itself have sufficed.

Kerr LJ, delivering the judgment of the Court of Appeal in *Yuthiwattana* (1984) 80 Cr App R 55, and explaining the *obiter dictum* of Ormrod LJ in *McCall* v *Abelesz* [1976] 1 QB 585, held that it is not necessary that the acts in question should constitute a breach of the civil law, but simply that the accused's act be one calculated to interfere with the occupier's peace and comfort which was intended to cause him to give up his occupation of the premises. The House of Lords has held that *Yuthiwattana* was correctly decided (*Burke* [1991] AC 135).

These acts must be 'likely to' interfere with peace or comfort. It should be noted that until the amendment introduced by the Housing Act 1988, s. 29(1), this phrase read 'calculated to', which caused uncertainty. The phrase 'likely to' is a matter of objective analysis, not of realisation or calculation on the part of the accused.

B13.16 ***Persistently Withdrawing or Withholding Services*** The Divisional Court in *Westminster City Council* v *Peart* (1968) 66 LGR 561, a decision on the Rent Act 1965, s. 30, held that 'persistently' in the identically worded precursor of the present provision, refers to the withholding of as well as the withdrawing of services. Withdrawal of a service on one day was not sufficient to satisfy the element of persistency. Lord Parker CJ, giving the judgment of the court, left open the question of whether failing to pay for a gas or electricity supply, as a result of which a gas or electricity company disconnects the service, can properly be described as the landlord withholding a service. Clearly, where the accused permanently cuts off the electricity supply, there is a persistent withholding (see *Boaks* (1967) 205 EG 103, a decision on the Rent Act 1965, s. 30).

Elements Specific to s. 1(3A)

B13.17 ***Landlord Harassing Residential Occupier*** The main differences between the offence contrary to s. 1(3A) and that contrary to s. 1(3) are that the former offence may be committed only by a landlord (or agent) and it is not necessary to establish intention, although knowledge or belief must be established. In consequence, the points made in relation to the offence contrary to s. 1(3) about the meaning of 'does acts likely to interfere with the peace or comfort of the residential occupier or members of his household' and 'persistently withdraws or withholds services reasonably required for the occupation of the premises in question as a residence', apply to the instant offence.

B13.18 ***Meaning of 'Landlord'***

Protection from Eviction Act 1977, s. 1

(3C) In subsection (3A) above 'landlord', in relation to a residential occupier of any premises, means the person who, but for—
(a) the residential occupier's right to remain in occupation of the premises, or
(b) a restriction on the person's right to recover possession of the premises,
would be entitled to occupation of the premises and any superior landlord under whom that person derives title.

If it is necessary to discover the identity of the landlord, a notice may be served on his agent or other person under s. 7 of the Act, requiring the disclosure of the landlord's full name and address. If such is not forthcoming, the person on whom the notice is served is guilty of a summary offence and liable to a fine not exceeding level 4 on the standard scale.

Knowledge or Belief The landlord, though not requiring an intention, must know **B13.19** or have reasonable cause to believe that the residential occupier is likely to be caused to give up occupation of the premises.

Specific Defences

The Protection from Eviction Act 1977, s. 1(2), provides that a person is not guilty of **B13.20** the eviction offence if 'he proves that he believed, and had reasonable cause to believe, that the residential occupier had ceased to reside in the premises'. The defendant must prove the belief and its reasonable foundation on a balance of probabilities (*Desai* (1992) *The Times*, 3 February 1992).

Protection from Eviction Act 1977, s. 1

(3B)   A person shall not be guilty of an offence under subsection (3A) above if he proves that he had reasonable grounds for doing the acts or withdrawing or withholding the services in question.

Related Offences

The offences contrary to the Criminal Law Act 1977, part I (see **B13.22** to **B13.32**), **B13.21** may be relevant. In particular, even if a person's activity does not fall within the Protection from Eviction Act 1977 offence because, for example, the 'victim' is not a residential occupier, the offence contrary to the Criminal Law Act 1977, s. 6, using or threatening violence to secure entry, may nevertheless cover the relevant activity.

USE OR THREAT OF VIOLENCE FOR PURPOSE OF SECURING ENTRY TO PREMISES

Definition

It is a summary offence, by virtue of the Criminal Law Act 1977, s. 6(1), for any person, **B13.22** without lawful authority, to use or threaten violence for the purpose of securing entry into any premises for himself or for any other person, provided that:

(a)   there is someone present on those premises at the time who is opposed to the entry which the violence is intended to secure; and
(b)   the person using or threatening the violence knows that that is the case.

Procedure and Sentence

The Criminal Law Act 1977, s. 12(8), provides that 'no rule of law ousting the **B13.23** jurisdiction of magistrates' courts to try offences where a dispute of title to property is involved shall preclude magistrates' courts from trying offences under this part of this Act'. By virtue of s. 6(5), a person found guilty of this offence is liable to imprisonment for a term not exceeding six months or to a fine not exceeding level 5 on the standard scale or to both.

Elements

Some of the elements of this offence are further defined by the Criminal Law Act 1977: **B13.24**

(a)   *Uses or threatens violence*: according to s. 6(4)(a), it is immaterial whether the violence in question is directed against the person or against property.
(b)   *Entry*: according to s. 6(4)(b), it is immaterial whether the entry which the violence is intended to secure is for the purpose of acquiring possession of the premises

in question or for any other purpose. As to the meaning of entry in the analogous offence of burglary, see **B4.61**.

(c) *Premises*: according to s. 12, this means any building, any part of a building under separate occupation, any land ancillary to a building, the site comprising any building or buildings together with any land ancillary thereto. By s. 12(2) the references to a building apply to any structure other than a movable one, and to any movable structure, vehicle or vessel designed or adapted for residential purposes; and further that (i) part of a building is under separate occupation if anyone is in occupation or entitled to occupation of that part as distinct from the whole, and (ii) land is ancillary to a building if it is adjacent to it and used (or intended for use) in connection with the occupation of that building or any part of it.

(d) *Lawful authority* is considered in s. 6(2), which provides that the fact that a person has any interest in or right to possession or occupation of any premises shall not constitute lawful authority for the use or threat of violence by him or anyone else for the purpose of securing his entry into those premises.

Specific Defence

B13.25 No offence is committed if the person is a displaced residential occupier or a protected intending occupier of the premises in question or is acting on behalf of such an occupier. If the accused adduces sufficient evidence that he was, or was acting on behalf of, such an occupier he is presumed to be, or to be acting on behalf of, such an occupier unless the contrary is proved by the prosecution (Criminal Law Act 1977, s. 6(1A)).

B13.26 ***Displaced Residential Occupier*** Section 6(7) of the Criminal Law Act 1977 makes clear that it is s. 12 which determines when a person is to be regarded as a 'displaced residential occupier' of any premises or of any access to any premises, which involves also considering the meaning of 'trespasser' (the meaning of 'premises' has been considered at **B13.24**).

Section 12(3) defines 'displaced residential occupier' by providing that any person who was occupying any premises as a residence immediately before being excluded from occupation by anyone who entered those premises, or any access to those premises, as a trespasser, is a displaced residential occupier of the premises for the purposes of this part of the Act, so long as he continues to be excluded from occupation of the premises by the original trespasser or any subsequent trespasser. Such a person is also regarded, by s. 12(5), as a displaced residential occupier of any access to those premises.

Section 12(4) provides that a person, who was himself occupying the premises in question as a trespasser immediately before being excluded from occupation, is not a displaced residential occupier of the premises. Section 12(6) provides an extended meaning of 'trespasser' so that anyone who enters or is on or in occupation of any premises by virtue of (a) any title derived from a trespasser, or (b) any licence or consent given by a trespasser or by a person deriving title from a trespasser, is himself treated as a trespasser for present purposes alone, and phrases involving a reference to a trespasser will be construed accordingly. Further s. 12(7) provides that anyone who is on any premises as a trespasser does not cease to be a trespasser by virtue of being allowed time to leave the premises, nor does anyone cease to be a displaced residential occupier of any premises by virtue of any such allowance of time to a trespasser.

It is also important to consider the meaning of 'access' which is provided by s. 12. It means, in relation to any premises, any part of any site or building within which those premises are situated which constitutes an ordinary means of access to those premises (whether or not that is its sole or primary use).

B13.27 ***Protected Intending Occupier*** Section 6(7) of the Criminal Law Act 1977 also indicates that s. 12A has effect for determining when any person is to be regarded as a protected intending occupier of any premises (or any access to those premises: s. 12A(11)).

Criminal Law Act 1977, s. 12A

(1)   For the purposes of this part of this Act [part II] an individual is a protected intending occupier of any premises at any time if at that time he falls within subsection (2), (4) or (6) below.

(2)   An individual is a protected intending occupier of any premises if—

(a)   he has in those premises a freehold interest or a leasehold interest with not less than two years still to run;

(b)   he requires the premises for his own occupation as a residence;

(c)   he is excluded from occupation of the premises by a person who entered them, or any access to them, as a trespasser; and

(d)   he or a person acting on his behalf holds a written statement—

(i)   which specifies his interest in the premises;

(ii)   which states that he requires the premises for occupation as a residence for himself; and

(iii)   with respect to which the requirements in subsection (3) below are fulfilled.

(3)   The requirements referred to in subsection (2)(d)(iii) above are—

(a)   that the statement is signed by the person whose interest is specified in it in the presence of a justice of the peace or commissioner for oaths; and

(b)   that the justice of the peace or commissioner for oaths has subscribed his name as a witness to the signature.

(4)   An individual is also a protected intending occupier of any premises if—

(a)   he has a tenancy of those premises (other than a tenancy falling within subsection (2)(a) above or (6)(a) below) or a licence to occupy those premises granted by a person with a freehold interest or a leasehold interest with not less than two years still to run in the premises;

(b)   he requires the premises for his own occupation as a residence;

(c)   he is excluded from occupation of the premises by a person who entered them, or any access to them, as a trespasser; and

(d)   he or a person acting on his behalf holds a written statement—

(i)   which states that he has been granted a tenancy of those premises or a licence to occupy those premises;

(ii)   which specifies the interest in the premises of the person who granted that tenancy or licence to occupy ('the landlord');

(iii)   which states that he requires the premises for occupation as a residence for himself; and

(iv)   with respect to which the requirements in subsection (5) below are fulfilled.

(5)   The requirements referred to in subsection (4)(d)(iv) above are—

(a)   that the statement is signed by the landlord and by the tenant or licensee in the presence of a justice of the peace or commissioner for oaths;

(b)   that the justice of the peace or commissioner for oaths has subscribed his name as a witness to the signatures.

(6)   An individual is also a protected intending occupier of any premises if—

(a)   he has a tenancy of those premises (other than a tenancy falling within subsection (2)(a) or (4)(a) above) or a licence to occupy those premises granted by an authority to which this subsection applies;

(b)   he requires the premises for his own occupation as a residence;

(c)   he is excluded from occupation of the premises by a person who entered the premises, or any access to them, as a trespasser; and

(d)   there has been issued to him by or on behalf of the authority referred to in paragraph (a) above a certificate stating that—

(i)   he has been granted a tenancy of those premises or a licence to occupy those premises as a residence by the authority; and

(ii)   the authority which granted that tenancy or licence to occupy is one to which this subsection applies, being of a description specified in the certificate.

(7)   Subsection (6) above applies to the following authorities—

(a) any body mentioned in section 14 of the Rent Act 1977 (landlord's interest belonging to local authority etc.);
(b) the Housing Corporation;
(c) Housing for Wales; and
(d) a registered social landlord within the meaning of the Housing Act 1985 . . .

If a person makes a statement for the purposes of s. 12A(2)(d) or (4) which he knows to be false in a material particular, or if he recklessly makes such a statement which is false in a material particular, he commits an offence (s. 12A(8)) and is liable on summary conviction to imprisonment for a term not exceeding six months or a fine not exceeding level 5 on the standard scale or both (s. 12A(10)).

Power of Arrest

B13.28 The Criminal Law Act 1977, s. 6(6), creates a power of arrest without warrant for a constable in uniform of anyone who is, or whom he with reasonable cause suspects to be, guilty of an offence under s. 6. This power of arrest was preserved by the PACE 1984, s. 26(2) and sch. 2.

ADVERSE OCCUPATION OF RESIDENTIAL PREMISES

Definition

B13.29   **Criminal Law Act 1977, s. 7**

(1) . . . any person who is on any premises as a trespasser after having entered as such is guilty of an offence if he fails to leave those premises on being required to do so by or on behalf of—
(a) a displaced residential occupier of the premises; or
(b) an individual who is a protected intending occupier of the premises.

Procedure and Sentence

B13.30 The offence is triable summarily (Criminal Law Act 1977, s. 7(5)). Where the offence relates to a protected intending occupier, a document purporting to be a certificate under the Criminal Law Act 1977, s. 12A(6)(d) (see **B13.27**) is to be received in evidence and, unless the contrary is proved, is deemed to have been issued by or on behalf of the authority stated in the certificate (s. 12A(9)(b)).

The maximum penalty is imprisonment for a term not exceeding six months or a fine not exceeding level 5 on the standard scale or both (s. 7(5)).

Elements

B13.31 Premises includes a reference to any access to them, whether or not such access itself constitutes premises within the meaning of the Criminal Law Act 1977, part II (s. 7(4)).

For the meaning of 'displaced residential occupier' and 'protected intending occupier', see **B13.26** and **B13.27**.

Specific Defences

B13.32 It is a defence for the accused to prove that:

(a) he believed that the person requiring him to leave the premises was not a displaced residential occupier or protected intending occupier of the premises or a person acting on behalf of a displaced residential occupier or protected intending occupier (Criminal Law Act 1977, s. 7(2));
(b) the premises in question are or form part of premises used mainly for non-residential purposes, and that he was not on any part of the premises used wholly or mainly for residential purposes (s. 7(3)).

Where the accused was requested to leave the premises by a person claiming to be or to act on behalf of a protected intending occupier of the premises, it is a defence for the accused to prove that, although asked to do so by the accused at the time the accused was requested to leave, that person failed at that time to produce to the accused a s. 12A statement or certificate (s. 12A(9)(a)) (see **B13.27**).

Power of Arrest

By virtue of the Criminal Law Act 1977, s. 7(6), a constable in uniform has a power of **B13.33** arrest without warrant of anyone who is, or whom he, with reasonable cause, suspects to be guilty of an offence under s. 7.

TRESPASSING DURING THE CURRENCY OF AN INTERIM POSSESSION ORDER

Definition

Criminal Justice and Public Order Act 1994, s. 76   **B13.34**

(2) . . . a person who is present on premises as a trespasser at any time during the currency of the order commits an offence.

. . .

(4) A person who was in occupation of the premises at the time of service of the order but leaves them commits an offence if he re-enters the premises as a trespasser or attempts to do so after the expiry of the order but within the period of one year beginning with the day on which it was served.

Procedure and Sentence

The offences are triable summarily only (CJPO 1994, s. 76(5)).   **B13.35**

The maximum penalty is a term of imprisonment not exceeding six months or a fine not exceeding level 5 on the standard scale or both (s. 76(5)).

Elements

References to 'the order' are to be construed as referring to an interim possession order **B13.36** which has been made in respect of any premises and served in accordance with rules of court (CJPO 1994, s. 76(1)); references to 'the premises' are to the premises covered by the order (s. 76(1)). For the meaning of 'premises', which has the same meaning as in the Criminal Law Act 1977, part II, see **B13.24**. An interim possession order means an interim possession order (so entitled) made under rules of court for the bringing of summary proceedings for possession of premises which are occupied by trespassers (CJPO 1994 (s. 75(4)).

A person who is in occupation of the premises at the time of service of the order is to be treated for the purposes of s. 76 as being present as a trespasser (s. 76(6)).

Specific Defence

Section 76(3) of the CJPO 1994 provides a specific defence to a charge under s. 76(2). **B13.37** No offence is committed by a person if he leaves the premises within 24 hours of the time of service of the order and does not return, or a copy of the order was not fixed to the premises in accordance with rules of court.

Power of Arrest and Entry to Arrest

A constable in uniform has a power to arrest without warrant anyone who is or whom **B13.38** he reasonably suspects to be guilty of one of the offences (CJPO 1994, s. 76(7)). The power to enter premises to arrest under the PACE 1984, s. 17, extends to this power of arrest (s. 17(1)(c)(iv)).

INTERIM POSSESSION ORDERS: FALSE OR MISLEADING STATEMENTS

Definition

B13.39   **Criminal Justice and Public Order Act 1994, s. 75**

(1)   A person commits an offence if, for the purpose of obtaining an interim possession order, he—

(a)   makes a statement which he knows to be false or misleading in a material particular; or

(b)   recklessly makes a statement which is false or misleading in a material particular.

(2)   A person commits an offence if, for the purpose of resisting the making of an interim possession order, he—

(a)   makes a statement which he knows to be false or misleading in a material particular; or

(b)   recklessly makes a statement which is false or misleading in a material particular.

Procedure and Sentence

B13.40   This offence is triable either way (CJPO 1994, s. 75(3)).

The maximum penalty is, on indictment, imprisonment for a term not exceeding two years or a fine or both, and, summarily, imprisonment for a term not exceeding six months or a fine not exceeding the statutory maximum or both (s. 75(3)).

Elements

B13.41   'Statement' in relation to an interim possession order, means any statement, in writing or oral and whether as to fact or belief, made in or for the purposes of the proceedings (CJPO 1994, s. 75(4)). For the meaning of 'interim possession order', see **B13.36**; for the meaning of 'premises', see **B13.24**.

AGGRAVATED TRESPASS

Definition

B13.42   **Criminal Justice and Public Order Act 1994, s. 68**

(1)   A person commits the offence of aggravated trespass if he trespasses on land in the open air and, in relation to any lawful activity which persons are engaging in or are about to engage in on that or adjoining land in the open air, does there anything which is intended by him to have the effect—

(a)   of intimidating those persons or any of them so as to deter them or any of them from engaging in that activity,

(b)   of obstructing that activity, or

(c)   of disrupting that activity.

Procedure and Sentence

B13.43   The offence is triable summarily (CJPO 1994, s. 68(3)). A charge is not void for duplicity where it states that the defendant intended to 'deter, disrupt or obstruct' a hunt because these elements overlap. Therefore, there is no need for each element to be the subject of a separate charge (*Nelder* v *DPP* (1998) *The Times*, 11 June 1998.

The maximum penalty is imprisonment for a term not exceeding three months or a fine not exceeding level 4 on the standard scale or both (s. 68(3)).

Elements

B13.44   Section 68(2) of the CJPO 1994 provides a definition of lawful activity.

There are three elements to the offence: trespass, an intention to disrupt a lawful activity and an act done towards that end (*Winder* v *DPP* (1996) 160 JP 713 and *Barnard* v *DPP* (1999) *The Times*, 9 November 1999).

Criminal Justice and Public Order Act 1994, s. 68

(2) Activity on any occasion on the part of a person or persons on land is 'lawful' for the purpose of this section if he or they may engage in the activity on the land on that occasion without committing an offence or trespassing on the land.

By s. 68(5), 'land' does not include those highways and roads excluded for the purposes of the CJPO 1994, s. 61(9) (see **B13.48**). Where the charge is under s. 68(1)(c), it is essential that an intention to disrupt be proved. In *Winder* v *DPP* (1996) 160 JP 713, the Divisional Court was satisfied that it was possible to decide that the intention was present since the trespassers on land in the open air were running towards a hunt which was an act more than merely preparatory to the act of disruption (such as blowing a horn).

Powers of Arrest and Removal of Persons

A constable in uniform has a power of arrest without warrant where he reasonably **B13.45** suspects a person of committing an offence under s. 68 (CJPO 1994, s. 68(4)). It follows that the actual commission of the offence is not a pre-requisite for the exercise of this power, what is required is the reasonable suspicion (*Capon* v *DPP* (1998) *Independent*, 23 March 1998). Under s. 69(1) the senior police officer present at the scene has the power to direct a person or persons to leave land if he reasonably believes:

(a) that a person is committing, has committed or intends to commit the offence of aggravated trespass on land in the open air; or

(b) that two or more persons are trespassing on land in the open air and are present there with the common purpose of intimidating persons so as to deter them from engaging in a lawful activity or of obstructing or disrupting a lawful activity.

If a person knowing that a direction under s. 69(1) has been given which applies to him fails to leave the land as soon as practicable or, having left, again enters the land as a trespasser within the period of three months beginning with the day on which the direction was given, he commits an offence and is liable on summary conviction to imprisonment for a term not exceeding three months or a fine not exceeding level 4 on the standard scale or both (s. 69(3)). If the police officer giving the direction does not communicate it, any constable at the scene may communicate it (s. 69(2)).

It is a defence for the accused to show (i) that he was not trespassing on land, or (ii) that he has a reasonable excuse for failing to leave the land as soon as practicable or, as the case may be, for again entering the land as a trespasser (s. 69(4)). A constable in uniform has a power of arrest without warrant if he reasonably suspects a person is committing an offence under s. 69(3) (s. 69(5)).

FAILURE TO LEAVE OR RE-ENTRY TO LAND AFTER POLICE DIRECTION TO LEAVE

Definition

Criminal Justice and Public Order Act 1994, s. 61   B13.46

(4) If a person knowing that a direction under subsection (1) above has been given which applies to him—

(a) fails to leave the land as soon as reasonably practicable, or

(b) having left again enters the land as a trespasser within the period of three months beginning with the day on which the direction was given,

he commits an offence . . .

Procedure and Sentence

B13.47 The offence is triable summarily (CJPO 1994, s. 61(4)).

The maximum penalty is imprisonment for a term not exceeding three months or a fine not exceeding level 4 on the standard scale or both (s. 61(4)).

Elements

B13.48 The offence is committed only where a direction to leave has been given.

Criminal Justice and Public Order Act 1994, s. 61

(1) If the senior police officer present at the scene reasonably believes that two or more persons are trespassing on land and are present there with the common purpose of residing there for any period, that reasonable steps have been taken by or on behalf of the occupier to ask them to leave and—

(a) that any of those persons has caused damage to the land or to property on the land or used threatening, abusive or insulting words or behaviour towards the occupier, a member of his family or an employee or agent of his, or

(b) that those persons have between them six or more vehicles on the land, he may direct those persons, or any of them, to leave the land and to remove any vehicles or other property they have with them on the land.

Where the senior police officer reasonably believes that the person was not originally a trespasser on the land, a direction may still be made if the person has become a trespasser and the senior police officer reasonably believes that the conditions in s. 61(1) are satisfied after the person became a trespasser (s. 61(2)).

Section 61(9) defines certain terms used in the section.

(a) 'Land' does not include:

(i) buildings other than agricultural buildings (within the meaning of the Local Government Finance Act 1988, sch. 5, paras 3 to 8) or scheduled monuments (within the meaning of the Ancient Monuments and Archaeological Areas Act 1979);

(ii) land forming part of a highway (unless it is a footpath, bridleway or byway open to all traffic or road used as a public path under the Wildlife and Countryside Act 1981, s. 54, or is a cycle track under the Highways Act 1980 or the Cycle Tracks Act 1984).

(b) 'Occupier' means the person entitled to possession of the land by virtue of an estate or interest held by him.

(c) Subject to the extension of its meaning with regard to common land (see below), 'trespass' means trespass as against the occupier of the land.

(d) In relation to damage to property on land, 'property' has the meaning in the Criminal Damage Act 1971, s. 10(1) (see **B8.6**), and 'damage' includes the deposit of any substance capable of polluting the land.

(e) 'Vehicle' includes:

(i) any vehicle, whether or not it is in a fit state for use on roads, and includes any chassis or body, with or without wheels, appearing to have formed part of such a vehicle, and any load carried by, and anything attached to, such a vehicle; and

(ii) a caravan as defined in the Caravan Sites and Control of Development Act 1960, s. 29(1).

(f) A person may be regarded as having a purpose of residing in a place notwithstanding that he has a home elsewhere.

Where the persons are on common land (as defined in the Commons Registration Act 1965, s. 22), the references to trespassing or trespassers are references to acts and persons doing acts which constitute either a trespass as against the occupier or an infringement of the commoners' rights; references to 'the occupier' include the commoners or any of them or, in the case of common land to which the public has access, the local authority as well as any commoner (s. 61(7)). Persons are not trespassers as against any commoner or the local authority if they are permitted to be there by the other occupier (s. 61(8)(b)).

The person must know of the direction and, it would appear, that it applies to him (s. 61(4)). If the police officer giving the direction does not communicate it to the persons to be removed, any constable may do so (s. 61(3)).

Specific Defence

It is a defence for the accused to show that he was not trespassing on the land, or that **B13.49** he had a reasonable excuse for failing to leave the land as soon as reasonably practicable or, as the case may be, for again entering the land as a trespasser (CJPO 1994, s. 61(6)).

Powers of Arrest and Seizure

A constable in uniform has a power to arrest without warrant anyone he reasonably **B13.50** suspects of the committing this offence (CJPO 1994, s. 61(5)). A constable may seize and remove vehicles after a s. 61 direction provided the criteria in s. 62 are satisfied.

FAILURE TO LEAVE LAND OR RE-ENTRY TO LAND: RAVES

Definition

Criminal Justice and Public Order Act 1994, s. 63   B13.51

(6) If a person knowing that a direction has been given which applies to him—
   (a) fails to leave the land as soon as reasonably practicable, or
   (b) having left again enters the land within the period of 7 days beginning with the day on which the direction was given,
he commits an offence . . .

Procedure and Sentence

The offence is triable summarily (CJPO 1994, s. 63(6)).   B13.52

The maximum penalty is imprisonment for a term not exceeding three months or a fine not exceeding level 4 on the standard scale or both (CJPO 1994, s. 63(6)). Where a person has been convicted of this offence and the court is satisfied that sound equipment which has been seized from him under s. 64(4), or which was in his possession or under his control at the relevant time, has been used at the gathering, it may make an order for forfeiture in respect of that property in compliance with the provisions of s. 66 (s. 66(1)).

Elements

The section applies only to gatherings of the kind specified in the CJPO 1994, s. 63(1); **B13.53** in the marginal note to s. 63, and in common parlance, such gatherings are called raves. The offence is committed only where a direction to leave has been given.

Criminal Justice and Public Order Act 1994, s. 63

(1) This section applies to a gathering on land in the open air of 100 or more persons (whether or not trespassers) at which amplified music is played during the night (with or without intermissions) and is such as, by reason of its loudness and duration and the time at which it is played, is likely to cause serious distress to the inhabitants of the locality; and for this purpose—
   (a) such a gathering continues during intermissions in the music and, where the gathering extends over several days, throughout the period during which the amplified music is played at night (with or without intermissions); and

 (b) 'music' includes sounds wholly or predominantly characterised by the emission of a succession of repetitive beats.

 (2) If, as respects any land in the open air, a police officer of at least the rank of superintendent reasonably believes that—

  (a) two or more persons are making preparations for the holding there of a gathering to which this section applies,

  (b) ten or more persons are waiting for such a gathering to begin there, or

  (c) ten or more persons are attending such a gathering which is in progress,

he may give a direction that those persons and any other persons who come to prepare or wait for or to attend the gathering are to leave the land and remove any vehicles or other property they have with them on the land.

The terms 'trespasser' and 'vehicle' have the same meaning as in s. 61 of the 1994 Act (see **B13.48**). 'Land in the open air' includes a place partly open to the air (s. 63(10)).

The person must know of the direction and, it would appear, that it applies to him (s. 63(6)). If the police officer giving the direction does not communicate it to the persons to be removed, any constable at the scene may do so (s. 63(3)). Persons shall be treated as having had a direction communicated to them if reasonable steps have been taken to bring it to their attention (s. 63(4)).

Exempt Persons and Gatherings

B13.54 Directions do not apply to 'exempt persons' (CJPO 1994, s. 63(5)). An 'exempt person', in relation to land (or any gathering on land), means the occupier, any member of his family and any employee or agent of his and any person whose home is situated on the land (s. 63(10)). As to the meaning of 'occupier', see **B13.48**.

Directions do not apply, in England and Wales, to a gathering licensed by an entertainment licence (s. 63(9)(a)).

Specific Defence

B13.55 It is a defence for the accused to show that he had a reasonable excuse for failing to leave the land as soon as reasonably practicable or, as the case may be, for again entering the land (CJPO 1994, s. 63(7)).

Power of Arrest and Other Police Powers

B13.56 Sections 63 to 65 and 67 of the CJPO 1994 provide certain additional police powers for the purpose of controlling or prohibiting gatherings of the kind specified in s. 63(1) (see **B13.52**).

 (a) A constable in uniform has a power to arrest without warrant anyone he reasonably suspects of committing an offence under s. 63 (s. 63(8)).

 (b) A constable authorised to enter land for any purpose in accordance with s. 64(1) and (2) by a police officer of at least the rank of superintendent may enter the land without a warrant (s. 64(3)).

 (c) A constable may seize and remove vehicles or sound equipment (as defined in s. 64(6)) after a s. 63 direction provided the criteria in s. 64(4) and (5) are satisfied. Any vehicles so seized and removed may be retained in accordance with regulations made by the Secretary of State (s. 67(1)). Any sound equipment so seized and removed may be retained until the conclusion of proceedings against the person from whom it was seized for an offence under s. 63 (s. 67(2)). Any authority is entitled to recover from a person from whom a vehicle has been seized such charges as may be prescribed in respect of the removal, retention, disposal and destruction of the vehicle by the authority (s. 67(4)).

 (d) A constable in uniform has power, at a place within five miles of the boundary of the site of the rave, to stop a person, except an exempt person, whom the constable reasonably believes to be on his way to a rave and direct him not to proceed in the direction of the rave (s. 65(1), (2) and (3)). It is a summary offence for a person, knowing that such a direction has been given to him, to fail to comply with that direction, and such a person is liable on conviction to a fine not exceeding level 3 on the standard scale (s. 65(4)). The constable has a power of arrest without warrant (s. 65(5)).

UNAUTHORISED CAMPERS: FAILURE TO LEAVE OR RETURNING TO THE LAND

Definition

Criminal Justice and Public Order Act 1994, s. 77 B13.57

(3) If a person knowing that a direction under subsection (1) has been given which applied to him—
(a) fails, as soon as practicable, to leave the land or remove from the land any vehicle or other property which is the subject of the direction, or
(b) having removed any such vehicle or property again enters the land with a vehicle within the period of three months beginning with the day on which the direction was given, he commits an offence . . .

Procedure and Sentence

The offence is triable summarily only (CJPO 1994, s. 77(3)). B13.58

The maximum penalty is a fine not exceeding level 3 on the standard scale (s. 77(3)).

Direction

Criminal Justice and Public Order Act 1994, s. 77 B13.59

(1) If it appears to a local authority that persons are for the time being residing in a vehicle or vehicles within that authority's area—
(a) on any land forming part of a highway;
(b) on any other unoccupied land; or
(c) on any occupied land without the consent of the occupier,
the authority may give a direction that those persons and any others with them are to leave the land and remove the vehicle or vehicles and any other property they have with them on the land.

Notice of a direction must be served on the persons to whom the direction applies, but it is sufficient for the direction to specify the land and (except where it applies to only one person) to be addressed to all occupants of the vehicles on the land, without naming them (s. 77(2)). Where it is impracticable to serve a direction on a person named in it, it is treated as duly served on him if a copy is fixed in a prominent place to the vehicle concerned; and where the direction is directed to unnamed occupants of vehicles, it is treated as duly served on those occupants if it is fixed in a prominent place to every vehicle on the land in question at the time when service is thus effected (s. 79(2)). The local authority must take such steps as are reasonably practicable to secure that a copy of the direction is displayed on the land in question (otherwise than by being fixed to a vehicle) in a manner designed to ensure that it is likely to be seen by any person camping on the land (s. 79(3)). Notice of a direction is to be given by the local authority to the owner of the land and to any occupier of that land unless, after reasonable inquiries, it is unable to ascertain their names and addresses (s. 79(4)).

A direction operates to require persons who re-enter the land within the period of three months with vehicles or other property to leave and remove the vehicles or other property as it operates in relation to the persons and vehicles or other property on the land when the direction was given (s. 77(4)).

Definitions

B13.60 Section 77(6) of the CJPO 1994 provides definitions for certain terms used in the section. A person may be regarded as residing on any land notwithstanding that he has a home elsewhere. 'Land' means land in the open air. 'Vehicle' and 'occupier' are defined in the same terms as in s. 61 (see **B13.48**).

Specific Defence

B13.61 It is a defence for the accused to show that his failure to leave or to remove the vehicle or other property as soon as practicable, or his re-entry with a vehicle, was due to illness, mechanical breakdown or other immediate emergency (CJPO 1994, s. 77(5)).

Magistrates' Removal Order

B13.62 On a complaint made by a local authority, a magistrates' court, if satisfied that persons and vehicles in which they are residing are present on land within that authority's area in contravention of such a direction, may make an order requiring the removal of any vehicle or other property and any person residing in it (CJPO 1994, s. 78(1)). Such an order may authorise the local authority to take such steps as are reasonably necessary to ensure that the order is complied with and, in particular, may authorise the authority, by its officers and servants, to enter upon the land specified in the order, and to take, in relation to any vehicle or property to be removed in pursuance of the order, such steps for securing entry and rendering it suitable for removal as may be specified in the order (s. 78(2)). The local authority must give to the owner and occupier at least 24 hours' notice of its intention to enter any occupied land unless after reasonable inquiries it is unable to ascertain their names and addresses (s. 78(3)). A person who wilfully obstructs any person in the exercise of any power conferred on him by an order under s. 78 commits an offence and is liable, on summary conviction, to a fine not exceeding level 3 on the standard scale (s. 78(4)). Where a complaint is made, a summons issued by the court requiring the person(s) to whom it is directed to appear before it to answer to the complaint may be directed either to the occupant of a particular vehicle on the land in question or to all occupants of vehicles on the land in question, without naming him or them (s. 78(5)). There is no power to issue a warrant for arrest upon failure to appear (s. 78(6)). The owner and occupier of the land are entitled to appear and be heard at any proceedings (s. 79(4)).

OTHER OFFENCES BY TRESPASSERS

Trespassing with Firearm in a Building or on Land

B13.63   **Firearms Act 1968, s. 20**

> (1) A person commits an offence if, while he has a firearm or imitation firearm with him, he enters or is in any building or part of a building as a trespasser and without reasonable excuse (the proof whereof lies on him).
>
> (2) A person commits an offence if, while he has a firearm or imitation firearm with him, he enters or is on any land as a trespasser and without reasonable excuse (the proof whereof lies on him).

The mode of trial for trespassing with firearm in a building is either way, although if the weapon is an air weapon or an imitation firearm, the offence is triable summarily only. The mode of trial for trespassing with a firearm on any land is summary only. As to the extension of the usual time-limit within which summary proceedings must be instituted, see **B12.2**.

The offence of trespassing with a firearm in a building is punishable, on summary conviction, with a term of imprisonment not exceeding six months or a fine not exceeding the prescribed sum or both; and, on conviction on indictment, with a term of imprisonment not exceeding five years or a fine or both. The offence of trespassing with a firearm on any land is punishable, on summary conviction, with a term of imprisonment not exceeding three months or a fine not exceeding level 4 on the standard scale or both. As to the courts' power to order forfeiture or disposal of firearms and ammunition, see **B12.3**.

The meaning of 'firearm' is considered at **B12.4**. Imitation firearms (see **B12.12**) fall within this section. The Firearms Act 1968, s. 20(3), defines 'land' as including land covered by water.

Trespassing with Weapon of Offence

It is a summary offence, contrary to the Criminal Law Act 1977, s. 8(1), for a person **B13.64** who is on any premises as a trespasser, after having entered as such, without lawful authority or reasonable excuse to have with him on the premises any weapon of offence. As to disputes as to title to property on summary trial, see **B13.23**.

By virtue of s. 8(3), a person guilty of this offence is liable to imprisonment for a term not exceeding six months or to a fine not exceeding level 5 on the standard scale or to both.

The meanings of the words 'premises' and 'trespasser' have been considered at **B13.24** and **B13.25**. The phrase, 'weapon of offence' is defined by s. 8(2) as meaning any article made or adapted for causing injury to or incapacitating a person, or intended by the person having it with him for such use. The same definition of 'weapon of offence' is used in the offence of aggravated burglary contrary to the Theft Act 1968, s. 10. For further discussion of this subject, see **B4.76**.

By virtue of s. 8(4), a constable in uniform may arrest without warrant anyone who is, or whom he with reasonable cause suspects to be, in the act of committing this offence. This power of arrest was preserved by the PACE 1984, s. 26(2) and sch. 2.

Trespassing on Premises of Foreign Missions, etc.

It is a summary offence, contrary to the Criminal Law Act 1977, s. 9(1), for a person to **B13.65** enter or be on any premises to which s. 9 applies as a trespasser. As to disputes as to title to property on summary trial, see **B13.23**.

By virtue of s. 9(6), proceedings for this offence may not be instituted against any person except by or with the consent of the A-G.

By virtue of s. 9(5), a person guilty of this offence is liable to imprisonment for a term not exceeding six months or to a fine not exceeding level 5 on the standard scale or to both.

The phrase 'enters as a trespasser', is partly defined by the 1977 Act, since meanings are given for 'entry' and 'trespasser' (see **B13.24** and **B13.25** respectively). Similar terms also appear in the offence of burglary (see **B4.61** and **B4.62**).

The premises to which s. 9 applies are listed in s. 9(2):

Criminal Law Act 1977, s. 9

> (2)   This section applies to any premises which are or form part of—
>   (a)   the premises of a diplomatic mission within the meaning of the definition in Article 1(i) of the Vienna Convention on Diplomatic Relations signed in 1961 as that Article has effect in the United Kingdom by virtue of section 2 of and schedule 1 to the Diplomatic Privileges Act 1964;
>   (aa)   the premises of a closed diplomatic mission;

> (b) consular premises within the meaning of the definition in paragraph 1(j) of Article 1 of the Vienna Convention on Consular Relations signed in 1963 as that Article has effect in the United Kingdom by virtue of section 1 of and schedule 1 to the Consular Relations Act 1968;
>
> (bb) the premises of a closed consular post;
>
> (c) any other premises in respect of which any organisation or body is entitled to inviolability by or under any enactment; and
>
> (d) any premises which are the private residence of a diplomatic agent (within the meaning of Article 1(e) of the Convention mentioned in paragraph (a) above) or of any other person who is entitled to inviolability of residence by or under any enactment.
>
> (2A) In subsection (2) above—
>
> > 'the premises of a closed diplomatic mission' means premises which fall within Article 45 of the Convention mentioned in subsection (2)(a) above (as that Article has effect in the United Kingdom by virtue of the section and schedule mentioned in that paragraph); and
> >
> > 'the premises of a closed consular post' means premises which fall within Article 27 of the Convention mentioned in subsection (2)(b) above (as that Article has effect in the United Kingdom by virtue of the section and schedule mentioned in that paragraph).

Insofar as the general meaning of 'premises' is relevant, see **B13.24**. Section 9(4) creates an important evidential provision in relation to establishing whether given premises are covered by s. 9 or not, since in any proceedings for this offence 'a certificate issued by or under the authority of the Secretary of State stating that any premises were or formed part of premises of any description mentioned in paragraphs (a) to (d) of subsection (2) above at the time of the alleged offence shall be conclusive evidence that the premises were or formed part of premises of that description at that time.'

By virtue of s. 9(3), it is a defence for the accused to prove that he believed that the premises in question were not premises to which s. 9 applies.

By virtue of s. 9(7), a constable in uniform may arrest without warrant anyone who is, or whom he with reasonable cause suspects to be, in the act of committing this offence. This power of arrest was preserved by the PACE 1984, s. 26(2) and sch. 2.

Obstruction of Court Officers Executing Process against Unauthorised Occupiers

B13.66 It is a summary offence, contrary to the Criminal Law Act 1977, s. 10(1), and without prejudice to the Sheriffs Act 1887, s. 8(2), if a person resists or intentionally obstructs any person who is in fact an officer of a court engaged in executing any process issued by the High Court or any county court for the purpose of enforcing any judgment or order for the recovery of any premises or for the delivery of possession of any premises. As to disputes as to title to property on summary trial, see **B13.23**.

By virtue of s. 6(5), a person guilty of this offence is liable to imprisonment for a term not exceeding six months or to a fine not exceeding level 5 on the standard scale or to both.

A similar phrase to 'resists or intentionally obstructs' appears in the offence involving the obstruction of a constable contrary to the Police Act 1996, s. 89(2) (see **B2.25** to **B2.28**).

'Officer of a court' according to s. 10(6) means any sheriff, under sheriff, deputy sheriff, bailiff or officer of a sheriff, and any bailiff or other person who is an officer of a county court within the meaning of the County Courts Act 1984, s. 147.

The offence does not apply unless the judgment or order in question was given or made in proceedings brought under any provisions of rules of court applicable only in circumstances where the person claiming possession of any premises alleges that the premises in question are occupied solely by a person or persons (not being a tenant or tenants holding over after the termination of the tenancy) who entered into or remained in occupation of the premises without the licence or consent of the person claiming possession or any predecessor in title of his.

'Premises' in this section has a slightly wider meaning than in the other offences in part II of the Criminal Law Act 1977. Section 12 states that 'premises' means any building, any part of a building under separate occupation, any land ancillary to a building, the site comprising any building or buildings together with any land ancillary thereto, and (for the purposes only of ss. 10 and 11) any other place. The references to a building apply also to any structure other than a movable one, and to any movable structure, vehicle or vessel designed or adapted for residential purposes; and:

    (a)   part of a building is under separate occupation if anyone is in occupation or entitled to occupation of that part as distinct from the whole; and

    (b)   land is ancillary to a building if it is adjacent to it and used (or intended for use) in connection with the occupation of that building or any part of it.

Note that the PACE 1984, s. 17(1)(c)(ii) provides the police with a power of entry to premises to arrest a person for this offence.

By virtue of s. 10(3), it is a defence for the accused to prove that he believed that the person he was resisting or obstructing was not an officer of a court.

By virtue of s. 10(5), a constable in uniform may arrest without warrant anyone who is, or whom he with reasonable cause suspects to be, guilty of this offence. This power of arrest was preserved by the PACE 1984, s. 26(2) and sch. 2.

Poaching Offences

There are four poaching offences, the primary focus of which is the protection of game **B13.67** rights, but which involve trespass to land, see Game Act 1831, s. 30 (poaching by day and poaching by day in company), and Night Poaching Act 1828, s. 1 (night poaching by unlawfully entering land and night poaching by unlawfully being on land).

SECTION B14: OFFENCES AGAINST THE ADMINISTRATION OF JUSTICE

PERJURY IN A JUDICIAL PROCEEDING

Definition

B14.1

Perjury Act 1911, s. 1

(1) If any person lawfully sworn as a witness or as an interpreter in a judicial proceeding wilfully makes a statement material in that proceeding, which he knows to be false or does not believe to be true, he shall be guilty of perjury, and shall, on conviction thereof on indictment, be liable to imprisonment for a term not exceeding seven years, or to a fine or to both imprisonment and fine.

(2) The expression 'judicial proceeding' includes a proceeding before any court, tribunal, or person having by law power to hear, receive, and examine evidence on oath.

(3) Where a statement made for the purposes of a judicial proceeding is not made before the tribunal itself, but is made on oath before a person authorised by law to administer an oath to the person who makes the statement, and to record or authenticate the statement, it shall, for the purposes of this section, be treated as having been made in a judicial proceeding.

(4) A statement made by a person lawfully sworn in England for the purposes of a judicial proceeding:

(a) in another part of His Majesty's dominions; or

(b) in a British tribunal lawfully constituted in any place by sea or land outside His Majesty's dominions; or

(c) in a tribunal of any foreign state,

shall, for the purposes of this section, be treated as a statement made in a judicial proceeding in England.

(5) Where, for the purposes of a judicial proceeding in England, a person is lawfully sworn under the authority of an Act of Parliament:

(a) in any other part of His Majesty's dominions; or

(b) before a British tribunal or a British officer in a foreign country, or within the jurisdiction of the Admiralty of England;

a statement made by such person so sworn as aforesaid (unless the Act of Parliament under which it was made otherwise specifically provides) shall be treated for the purposes of this section as having been made in the judicial proceeding in England for the purposes whereof it was made.

(6) The question whether a statement on which perjury is assigned was material is a question of law to be determined by the court of trial.

The Perjury Act 1911, s. 1, will apply to intermediaries appointed under the YJCEA 1999, s. 29, as it applies to interpreters (s. 29(7)). This includes intermediaries who assist in the examination of a witness otherwise than in the course of judicial proceedings: the examination shall be taken to be part of the judicial proceeding in which that witness's evidence is given.

Procedure

B14.2
Perjury in a judicial proceeding is triable only on indictment. It is a class 3 offence.

The Perjury Act 1911, provides:

Perjury Act 1911, s. 8

Where an offence against this Act or any offence punishable as perjury or as subornation of perjury under any other Act of Parliament is committed in any place either on sea or land

630

outside the United Kingdom, the offender may be proceeded against, indicted, tried, and punished . . . in England.

It is not altogether clear whether this provision was intended to extend the ambit of the Act in any way, or whether it was, as the marginal note ('venue') suggests, intended merely to provide for the trial of any extraterritorial offences created under the preceding sections. On balance, the latter interpretation is to be preferred. The extraterritorial scope of s. 1, for example, is precisely governed by subsections (4) and (5), and these provisions would not have been necessary if s. 8 had any wider meaning. As to territorial jurisdiction generally, see **D1.72** *et seq*.

Indictment

Statement of Offence

B14.3

Perjury contrary to section 1(1) of the Perjury Act 1911

Particulars of Offence

A on the . . . day of . . ., having been lawfully sworn as a witness in a judicial proceeding, namely the trial of a criminal cause at the Central Criminal Court entitled The Queen v B.C., wilfully made a statement material in that proceeding which he knew to be false, namely that the accused B.C. had been in the City of Leicester on the . . . day of . . .

As to the drafting of indictments for perjury and related offences under the Perjury Act 1911, s. 12 provides as follows:

Perjury Act 1911, s. 12

(1)   In an indictment—
    (a)   for making any false statement or false representation punishable under this Act; or
    (b)   for unlawfully, wilfully, falsely, fraudulently, deceitfully, maliciously, or corruptly taking, making, signing, or subscribing any oath, affirmation, solemn declaration, statutory declaration, affidavit, deposition, notice, certificate, or other writing,
it is sufficient to set forth the substance of the offence charged, and before which court or person (if any) the offence was committed without setting forth the proceedings or any part of the proceedings in the course of which the offence was committed, and without setting forth the authority of any court or person before whom the offence was committed.

(2)   In an indictment for aiding, abetting, counselling, suborning, or procuring any other person to commit any offence hereinbefore in this section mentioned, or for conspiring with any other person, or with attempting to suborn or procure any other person, to commit any such offence, it is sufficient—
    (a)   where such offence has been committed, to allege that offence, and then to allege that the defendant procured the commission of the offence; and
    (b)   where such offence has not been committed, to set forth the substance of the offence charged against the defendant without setting forth any matter or thing which it is unnecessary to aver in the case of an indictment for a false statement or false representation punishable under this Act.

Sentencing Guidelines

The maximum penalty for perjury in judicial proceedings is seven years (Perjury Act **B14.4** 1911, s. 1).

There are numerous Court of Appeal decisions dealing with sentencing for this offence. They indicate that a custodial sentence is almost always necessary since, as Roskill LJ said in *Davies* (1974) 59 Cr App R 311 at p. 313:

> It is often said there is too much perjury committed in courts, and it is regrettably true as everyone sitting in court knows. But it is one thing to suspect that perjury has been committed and another thing to prove it. Perjury is not always easy to prove. Perjurers are not easily brought to justice. When they are they must be punished.

In *Hall* (1982) 4 Cr App R (S) 153 Talbot J (at p. 155) said that '. . . it is almost inconceivable that a sentence of less than three months would be given for a deliberate perjury in the face of the court', since 'such false evidence strikes at the whole basis of the administration of the law'. In that case a three month sentence was upheld on a 62-year-old woman who had given false alibi evidence at a magistrates' court in respect of a man charged with asssault occasioning actual bodily harm.

In *Lewins* (1979) 1 Cr App R (S) 246, the offender, a police officer, was sentenced to four years for perjury and subornation. He had persuaded witnesses to testify that he had taken drink between the time of a road accident he had been involved in and the administration of a breath test. The sentence was reduced to two years to take account of personal mitigation including loss of his employment, the fact that the perjury was not committed in his capacity as a police officer and the fact that a custodial sentence 'for an ex-police officer is a great deal more unpleasant than it is for other members of the community.' It seems that where the original charge in relation to which the perjury was committed was one of very serious crime, the penalty for the perjury should be proportionately higher. In *Knight* (1984) 6 Cr App R (S) 31 the offender gave false evidence at the trial of a man charged with armed robbery in which £750,000 was stolen. A three-year sentence was held to be correct, bearing in mind the offender's antecedents and plea of guilty to the perjury charge.

A sentence of six months' imprisonment was upheld in *Healey* (1990) 12 Cr App R (S) 297, in respect of perjury committed in the course of a means inquiry in a magistrates' court. The offender appeared in court for failure to pay a fine of £200. He then gave evidence on oath that he was employed, and that the fine could be recovered by an attachment of earnings order. This evidence was untrue.

Meaning of 'Statements in Judicial Proceedings'

B14.5 The effect of the Perjury Act 1911, s. 1 (2) and (3), is that perjury need not take the form of false evidence in court. A false affidavit sworn in connection with a judicial proceeding may amount to perjury, as may false evidence given on oath before a tribunal.

The position is slightly different in the case of false written evidence tendered in criminal proceedings under the CJA 1967, s. 9, and of false written evidence admitted in committal proceedings under the MCA 1980, s. 5A. Wilful falsity in such cases attracts a maximum penalty of two years and/or a fine, as opposed to the seven year maximum for perjury itself, but in all other respects the principles contained within the Perjury Act 1911 are applicable. These offences are dealt with at **B14.18**.

The CJA 1988, s. 32, enables a person outside the United Kingdom to give evidence at a criminal trial in England or Wales through a live television link. As with evidence to which the Perjury Act 1911, s. 1(5), applies, any such evidence is treated for the purposes of the Perjury Act 1911, s. 1, as given in the trial concerned (CJA 1988, s. 32(3)).

By the European Communities Act 1972, s. 11(1)(a), all relevant provisions of the Perjury Act 1911 are applicable to statements made on oath before the European Court of Justice, or any court attached thereto, whether or not the person responsible is a British citizen. See also the Evidence (European Court) Order 1976 (SI 1976 No. 428).

Meaning of 'Lawfully Sworn'

B14.6 By the Evidence Act 1851, s. 16:

Evidence Act 1851, s. 16

Every court, judge, justice, officer, commissioner, arbitrator, or other person, now or hereafter having by law or by consent of parties authority to hear, receive, and examine evidence, is hereby empowered to administer an oath to all such witnesses as are legally called before them respectively.

A conviction for perjury is impossible if the accused was incompetent to testify in the proceedings in which his perjury is alleged to have been committed (*Clegg* (1868) 19 LT 47).

It is possible for a witness or interpreter to make a solemn affirmation in place of the oath, whether or not the taking of an oath would be contrary to his religious beliefs, and the Perjury Act 1911, s. 15(2), provides that references therein to 'oaths' and 'swearing' embrace affirmations. The affirming witness is thus equally subject to the Perjury Act 1911. Furthermore, s. 15(1) provides that:

Perjury Act 1911, s. 15

(1)   For the purposes of this Act, the forms and ceremonies used in administering an oath are immaterial, if the court or person before whom the oath is taken has power to administer an oath for the purpose of verifying the statement in question, and if the oath has been administered in a form and with ceremonies which the person taking the oath has accepted without objection, or has declared to be binding on him.

As to oaths and affirmations generally, see **F4.21** to **F4.26**.

Wilfulness

It might seem at first sight that the requirement of wilfulness in the Perjury Act 1911, **B14.7** s. 1, is otiose, since an offence under the section can be committed only by someone who does not believe it to be true; but conduct is wilful only if it is deliberate or intentional (*Senior* [1899] 1 QB 283), and it must therefore be proved that any alleged perjury was not the result of a misunderstanding or a slip of the tongue, whereby the accused might perhaps have said something he did not mean (*Millward* [1985] QB 519). As to wilfulness generally, see **A2.8**.

Materiality

'Material' means important or significant: something which matters. See *Mallett* [1978] **B14.8** 1 WLR 820, in which the Court of Appeal so construed the phrase 'false in a material particular', in a prosecution under the Theft Act 1968, s. 17(1). Under the Perjury Act 1911, s. 1(6), the question of what is material is one of law (i.e. for the judge to decide). Although A must know of the falsity of his statement (or not believe in its truth) he need not know or believe it to be material (*Millward* [1985] QB 519).

The truth or falsity of the accused's statement need not be crucial to the outcome of the case. It would suffice, for example, if the accused's lies prevented the other side from pursuing a certain line of questioning which might have been material to the question of his credibility (*Millward* [1985] QB 519; and see also *Baker* [1895] 1 QB 797). A statement may also be material even though it ought strictly to have been excluded by the court or judge before whom it was made (*Gibbon* (1862) Le & Ca 109; cf. *Philpotts* (1851) 2 Den CC 302).

Clear examples of immaterial statements are hard to find amongst the reported cases. It was held in *Tate* (1871) 12 Cox CC 7 that it was not perjury for the accused to swear at X's trial for assault that he had seen X's wife commit adultery, because that would have been irrelevant to the question whether X had indeed committed the assault; but this decision has been doubted (*Hewitt* (1913) 9 Cr App R 192) and it has since been held that evidence is material if it may affect the likely penalty in criminal proceedings, even if it is immaterial to the question of liability (*Wheeler* [1917] 1 KB 283). One modern example of false but immaterial evidence is provided by *Sweet-Escott* (1971) 55 Cr App R 316, where the accused denied in the course of committal proceedings that he had any previous convictions, but did in fact have some dating from over 20 years before. It was held that the convictions were so old and of such a kind that in the circumstances they could not possibly have influenced the decision of the magistrates to commit the accused person for trial, and the accused's false denial was therefore immaterial. Old convictions might, however, be considered material in other circumstances: it would depend on the facts in every case. (See also **E25** on rehabilitation of offenders.)

Truth or Falsity of the Statement

B14.9   On a literal interpretation of the Perjury Act 1911, s. 1, it would seem that a person could be convicted of perjury as a result of a statement which he did not believe to be true, but which was in fact true after all. Prosecutions are hardly likely to be brought in respect of manifestly true statements, but if this literal interpretation is correct, it would ease the prosecution's task in cases where the accused's state of mind is easier to prove than the truth or falsity of his evidence. If, for example, the accused had testified that event X took place on 5 July, and the prosecution can prove that the accused had no idea whether that event took place or not, this should suffice as proof of his perjury, even if there is no evidence that it did not take place on 5 July. See *Rider* (1986) 83 Cr App R 207.

This was indeed the position at common law (*Allen* v *Westley* (1629) Het 97) and although the Court of Appeal appears to have assumed in *Millward* [1985] QB 519 that proof of falsity is required under the Perjury Act 1911, this was unconsidered and strictly *obiter*. Most commentators support the literal interpretation, which also found some favour with the Court of Appeal in *Rider* (1986) Cr App R 207, although the point was ultimately left open in that case.

It may at first seem rather difficult to reconcile the 'literal' interpretation of the Perjury Act 1911, s. 1, with s. 13, which effectively requires corroboration of any allegation of falsity before a conviction for perjury can be obtained, but the wording of s. 13 is not in fact inconsistent with that interpretation, as the Court of Appeal noted in *Rider* (1986) 83 Cr App R 207. As to s. 13, see **B14.14**.

False Statements of Opinion

B14.10   An expression of opinion, not genuinely held by the witness making it, may amount to perjury (*Schlesinger* (1847) 10 QB 670).

Perjury Based on Inconsistent Statements

B14.11   Where A has on separate occasions made two or more inconsistent statements on oath, and must have been guilty of deliberate perjury on at least one of those occasions, a conviction will not be possible unless the prosecution can prove which of the statements were perjured.

Prosecution for Perjury where Accused's Evidence Secured his Acquittal in Previous Trial

B14.12   Difficult problems can arise where a person has been acquitted of a criminal charge after giving evidence of his own innocence, and further evidence has since come to light which tends to prove, not just that he lied in the course of his testimony, but that he must indeed have been guilty of the original offence. At his trial for perjury, can the prosecution adduce evidence which is flatly inconsistent with his acquittal at the earlier trial?

The decision of the House of Lords in *DPP* v *Humphrys* [1977] AC 1 establishes that the doctrine of issue estoppel has no place in criminal proceedings, and that verdicts obtained by false evidence could not in any event have supported an issue estoppel; but arguably *DPP* v *Humphrys* does not directly preclude a defence based on the similar but somewhat narrower doctrine established in *Sambasivam* v *Public Prosecutor of Malaya*

Federation [1950] AC 458 and applied more recently in *Hay* (1983) 77 Cr App R 70, under which the prosecution is bound to accept the accused's innocence of alleged crimes of which he has previously been acquitted. It would obviously be undesirable for the *Sambasivam* doctrine to apply where issue estoppel has been so firmly excluded, and it is submitted that any defence based upon it should be rejected. Any other response would involve granting a large measure of immunity to any defendant who has successfully employed perjury in his own defence.

On the other hand, it would clearly be oppressive and unfair for an accused to be prosecuted for perjury after successfully defending himself on some other charge, unless significant new prosecution evidence is available to contradict his original evidence. If the prosecution are merely hoping that a different jury might believe their original witnesses rather than the accused, the prosecution should be stopped as vexatious and an abuse of the process of the court (*DPP* v *Humphrys*).

As to the effect of previous verdicts in criminal cases generally, see **F11**.

Proof of Previous Judicial Proceeding

If the fact of the proceeding at which the perjury is alleged to have taken place is not **B14.13** admitted, this may be proved by production of the record of the trial (or a copy thereof: CJA 1988, s. 27) or, in the case of trials on indictment, in accordance with the Perjury Act 1911, s. 14, which provides:

Perjury Act 1911, s. 14

On a prosecution—
    (a) for perjury alleged to have been committed on the trial of an indictment . . .; or
    (b) for procuring or suborning the commission of perjury on any such trial,
the fact of the former trial shall be sufficiently proved by the production of a certificate containing the substance and effect (omitting the formal parts) of the indictment and trial purporting to be signed by the clerk of the court, or other person having the custody of the records of the court where the indictment was tried, or by the deputy of that clerk or other person, without proof of the signature or official character of the clerk or person appearing to have signed the certificate.

A's allegedly perjured statements, if not admitted, may be proved by the testimony of persons who were present at the trial. One such witness would suffice, since s. 13 (see **B14.14**) applies only to evidence of falsity. Alternatively, the shorthand writer's record may be admissible under the CJA 1988, s. 24.

Requirement of Corroboration as to Falsity

Perjury Act 1911, s. 13   **B14.14**

A person shall not be liable to be convicted of any offence against this Act, or of any offence declared by any other Act to be perjury or subornation of perjury, or to be punishable as perjury or subornation of perjury, solely upon the evidence of one witness as to the falsity of any statement alleged to be false.

This provision does not lay down any corroboration requirement as to the fact that the accused made the alleged statement, or as to his knowledge or belief at the time (*O'Connor* [1980] Crim LR 43). If it is not being alleged that the statement was false (e.g., where it is alleged that neither the accused nor anyone else could have known whether it was true or not), then s. 13 has no application.

Where s. 13 does apply, its interpretation is troublesome. It does not expressly refer to 'corroboration' at all, and it was accordingly argued in *Hamid* (1979) 69 Cr App R 324 that, provided the prosecution case does not depend on a single witness as to falsity, the technicalities of the law relating to corroboration do not apply; but the Court of Appeal disagreed. It follows that a jury will need to be directed as to what other evidence might be capable of providing that corroboration, and the absence of any such direction will amount to a material irregularity. See also *Rider* (1986) 83 Cr App R 207 and *Carroll* [1993] Crim LR 613.

Although a single witness to falsity must be corroborated, this corroboration may take the form of documentary evidence, and may originate from the accused himself, as in *Threlfall* (1914) 10 Cr App R 112, where the accused had written a letter, parts of which appeared to be self-incriminating.

Where the accused is alleged to have confessed prior to the trial, the evidence of two witnesses to the confession has been held to be sufficient for the purposes of s. 13. It is not necessary that they should have witnessed confessions on separate occasions (*Peach* [1990] 2 All ER 966).

Aiding and Abetting etc.

B14.15

Perjury Act 1911, s. 7

    (1) Every person who aids, abets, counsels, procures, or suborns another person to commit an offence against this Act shall be liable to be proceeded against, indicted, tried and punished as if he were a principal offender.
    (2) Every person who incites another person to commit an offence against this Act shall be guilty of an offence, and, on conviction thereof on indictment, shall be liable to imprisonment, or to a fine, or to both such imprisonment and fine.

'Suborning' is merely another term, in this context, for procuring, and s. 7(1) thus adds nothing of significance to the general law of secondary participation in crime, as governed by the Accessories and Abettors Act 1861 (see generally **A5.1** *et seq.*).

The Perjury Act 1911, s. 7(2), similarly adds nothing of substance to the common law rules governing incitement; but the maximum term of imprisonment for an offence under s. 7(2) is limited by the Powers of the Criminal Courts Act 1973, s. 18, to two years, a restriction which does not apply to the common-law offence.

The Perjury Act 1911, s. 13 (see **B14.14**), applies to offences under this provision. All complicity offences are triable either way except complicity in an offence under the Perjury Act 1911, s. 1 (perjury in judicial proceedings).

OFFENCES AKIN TO PERJURY

False Testimony of Unsworn Child Witnesses in Criminal Proceedings

B14.16 The Perjury Act 1911, s. 16(2), provides that nothing in that Act applies to the unsworn evidence of children (see **F4.17**) but the CYPA 1933, s. 38(2), creates an offence:

Children and Young Persons Act 1933, s. 38

    (2) If any child whose evidence is received unsworn in any proceedings for an offence by virtue of section 52 of the Criminal Justice Act 1991 wilfully gives false evidence in such circumstances that he would, if the evidence had been given on oath, have been guilty of perjury, he shall be liable on summary conviction to be dealt with as if he had been summarily convicted of an indictable offence punishable in the case of an adult with imprisonment.

Under the YJCEA 1999, s. 57, which is not yet in force, children or other persons who wilfully give false evidence in criminal proceedings when testifying unsworn (by virtue of s. 56 of that Act: see **F4.19**) and who would be guilty of perjury if testifying on oath will be guilty of a summary offence, which supplants that under the CYPA 1933, s. 38. The penalty for children (aged under 14) is a fine not exceeding £250; others may face a fine not exceeding £1,000 and/or imprisonment for a term not exceeding six months (YJCEA 1999, s. 57(2) and (3)).

False Unsworn Evidence under the Evidence (Proceedings in Other Jurisdictions) Act 1975

Perjury Act 1911, s. 1A

B14.17

If any person, in giving any testimony (either orally or in writing) otherwise than on oath, where required to do so by an order under section 2 of the Evidence (Proceedings in Other Jurisdictions) Act 1975, makes a statement:

    (a)   which he knows to be false in a material particular, or

    (b)   which is false in a material particular and which he does not believe to be true,

he shall be guilty of [an offence] and shall be liable on conviction on indictment to imprisonment for a term not exceeding two years or a fine or both.

This section serves a function similar to that served in respect of sworn evidence by the Perjury Act 1911, s. 1(4) (see **B14.1**). In contrast to the uncertainty concerning the need for proof of actual falsity in prosecutions under s. 1, it is clear in this case that such proof is indeed required. As to the meaning of the phrase 'false in a material particular', see the discussion at **B14.8**.

Section 13 applies (see **B14.14**); and offences under this provision are triable either way (MCA 1980, s. 17 and sch. 1, para. 14).

False Written Statements Tendered in Criminal Proceedings

Criminal Justice Act 1967, s. 89

B14.18

    (1)   If any person in a written statement tendered in evidence in criminal proceedings by virtue of section 9 of this Act, or in proceedings before a court-martial by virtue of the said section 9 as extended by section 12 . . . or by section 99A of the Army Act 1955 or section 99A of the Air Force Act 1955, wilfully makes a statement material in those proceedings which he knows to be false or does not believe to be true, he shall be liable on conviction on indictment to imprisonment for a term not exceeding two years or a fine or both.

    (2)   The Perjury Act 1911 shall have effect as if this section were contained in that Act.

Magistrates' Courts Act 1980, s. 106

    (1)   If any person in a written statement admitted in evidence in criminal proceedings by virtue of section 5B above wilfully makes a statement material in those proceedings which he knows to be false or does not believe to be true, he shall be liable on conviction on indictment to imprisonment for a term not exceeding two years or a fine or both.

    (2)   The Perjury Act 1911 shall have effect as if this section were contained in that Act.

The only obvious distinction between these offences and perjury itself lies in the maximum penalties, which stand at two years compared with the maximum of seven under the Perjury Act 1911, s. 1. Although there is no specific provision, it would seem that these offences are triable either way, since, in each of the two sections set out above, subsection (2) assimilates them into the Perjury Act 1911 and, by virtue of the MCA 1980, s. 17 and sch. 1, para. 14, all offences under the Perjury Act 1911, except those under ss. 1, 3 and 4, are so triable. (Sections 3 and 4 of the Perjury Act 1911 expressly made offences under those sections triable either way.)

Section 13 of the Perjury Act 1911 is applicable to both offences: see **B14.14**.

False Statements Made on Oath outside Judicial Proceedings

Perjury Act 1911, s. 2

B14.19

If any person:

    (1)   being required or authorised by law to make any statement on oath for any purpose, and being lawfully sworn (otherwise than in a judicial proceeding) wilfully makes a statement which is material for that purpose and which he knows to be false or does not believe to be true; or

(2)   wilfully uses any false affidavit for the purposes of the Bills of Sale Act 1878, as amended by any subsequent enactment,

he shall be guilty of [an offence], and, on conviction thereof on indictment, shall be liable to imprisonment for a term not exceeding seven years or to a fine or to both such imprisonment and fine.

The offence created by this section is of limited application. Affidavits sworn in connection with judicial proceedings must be dealt with under the Perjury Act 1911, s. 1(3). As to statutory declarations, see s. 5, discussed in **B14.22**.

Section 13 applies (see **B14.14**), and offences under this provision are triable either way (MCA 1980, sch. 1, para. 14).

False Statements with Reference to Marriage

B14.20   **Perjury Act 1911, s. 3**

(1)   If any person:
(a)   for the purpose of procuring a marriage, or a certificate or licence for marriage, knowingly and wilfully makes a false oath, or makes or signs a false declaration, notice or certificate required under any Act of Parliament for the time being in force relating to marriage; or
(b)   knowingly and wilfully makes, or knowingly and wilfully causes to be made, for the purpose of being inserted in any register of marriage, a false statement as to any particular required by law to be known and registered relating to any marriage; or
(c)   forbids the issue of any certificate or licence for marriage by falsely representing himself to be a person whose consent to the marriage is required by law knowing such representation to be false; or
(d)   with respect to a declaration made under section 16(1A) or 27B(2) of the Marriage Act 1949:
(i)   enters a caveat under subsection (2) of the said section 16, or
(ii)   makes a statement mentioned in subsection (4) of the said section 27B, which he knows to be false in a material particular,
he shall be guilty of [an offence,] and, on conviction thereof on indictment, shall be liable to imprisonment for a term not exceeding seven years or to a fine or to both imprisonment and fine [and on summary conviction thereof shall be liable to a penalty not exceeding the prescribed sum].
(2)   No prosecution for knowingly and wilfully making a false declaration for the purpose of procuring any marriage out of the district in which the parties or one of them dwell shall take place after the expiration of eighteen months from the solemnization of the marriage to which the declaration refers.

An offence under the Perjury Act 1911, s. 3, is committed only by a person who acts for the purpose of procuring a marriage or licence etc. but whether or not he succeeds in this purpose is irrelevant. A false statement cannot, however, give rise to liability under the Perjury Act 1911, s. 3(1)(a) or (b), unless it concerns something which must by law be stated correctly (*Frickey* [1956] Crim LR 421).

Section 13 applies; see **B14.14**.

False Statements about Births and Deaths

B14.21   **Perjury Act 1911, s. 4**

(1)   If any person:
(a)   wilfully makes any false answer to any question put to him by any registrar of births or deaths relating to the particulars required to be registered concerning any birth or death, or, wilfully gives to any such registrar any false information concerning any birth or death or the cause of any death; or
(b)   wilfully makes any false certificate or declaration under or for the purposes of any Act relating to the registration of births or deaths, or, knowing any such certificate or

declaration to be false, uses the same as true or gives or sends the same as true to any person; or

    (c)   wilfully makes, gives or uses any false statement or declaration as to a child born alive as having been still-born, or as to the body of a deceased person or still-born child in any coffin, or falsely pretends that any child born alive was still-born; or

    (d)   makes any false statement with intent to have the same inserted in any register of births or deaths:

he shall be guilty of [an offence] and shall be liable:

    (i)   on conviction thereof on indictment, to imprisonment for a term not exceeding seven years, or to a fine instead of the said punishments; and

    (ii)   on summary conviction thereof, to a penalty not exceeding [the prescribed sum].

    (2)   A prosecution on indictment for an offence against this section shall not be commenced more than three years after the commission of the offence.

As to the particulars requiring registration in relation to births or deaths, see the Births and Deaths Registration Act 1953, s. 39, and orders made thereunder. In contrast to the position under the Perjury Act 1911, s. 3, the wilful provision of any false information concerning a birth or death may involve liability, whether or not its provision was a strict legal requirement.

False statements as to the paternity of a child are obvious examples of the s. 4 offence, but cases of artificial insemination by donor (AID) can give rise to problems. The Family Law Reform Act 1987, s. 27, provides that, where a married couple agree to such a scheme, the child 'shall be treated as the child of the parties to the marriage', and this probably means that the husband can lawfully be registered as the father; but some doubts have been expressed as to this, especially since subsection (3) of that section precludes the inheritance of titles of honour by such children.

Section 13 of the Perjury Act 1911, applies: see **B14.14** above.

False Statutory Declarations etc.

Perjury Act 1911, s. 5   **B14.22**

If any person knowingly and wilfully makes (otherwise than on oath) a statement false in a material particular, and the statement is made:

    (a)   in a statutory declaration; or

    (b)   in an abstract, account, balance sheet, book, certificate, declaration, entry, estimate, inventory, notice, report, return, or other document which he is authorised or required to make, attest, or verify, by any public general Act of Parliament for the time being in force; or

    (c)   in any oral declaration or oral answer which he is required to make by, under, or in pursuance of any public general Act of Parliament for the time being in force,

he shall be guilty of [an offence] and shall be liable on conviction thereof on indictment to imprisonment for any term not exceeding two years, or to a fine or to both such imprisonment and fine.

Perjury Act 1911, s. 15(2)

. . . The expression 'statutory declaration' means a declaration made by virtue of the Statutory Declarations Act 1835, or of any Act, order in council, rule or regulation applying or extending the provisions thereof;

As to the meaning of the phrase 'knowingly and wilfully' in this context, see *Sood* [1998] 2 Cr App R 355. The principal limitation on the scope of s. 5 (b) and (c) is the need to prove that A was statutorily authorised or required to make the declaration etc. which is alleged to be false. It would not appear to suffice that the declaration was made in connection with, or for the purpose of procuring, some benefit which is the subject of legislative control; but false statements in such circumstances are frequently penalised under other legislation. See, for example, the CJA 1925, s. 36, which creates an offence of making a statement which one knows to be untrue for the purpose of procuring a passport.

Section 13 applies to offences under s. 5 (see **B14.14**), and offences under s. 5 are triable either way (MCA 1980, s. 17 and sch. 1, para. 14).

False Declarations etc. to Obtain Registration for Carrying on a Vocation

B14.23   Perjury Act 1911, s. 6

If any person:
    (a)   procures or attempts to procure himself to be registered on any register or roll kept under or in pursuance of any public general Act of Parliament for the time being in force of persons qualified by law to practise any vocation or calling; or
    (b)   procures or attempts to procure a certificate of the registration of any person on any such register or roll as aforesaid,
by wilfully making or producing or causing to be made or produced either verbally or in writing, any declaration, certificate, or representation which he knows to be false or fraudulent, he shall be guilty of [an offence] and shall be liable on conviction thereof on indictment to imprisonment for any term not exceeding 12 months, or to a fine, or to both such imprisonment and fine.

A person should be charged with 'procuring' only where he has succeeded in his purpose under s. 6 (a) or (b). Where he fails in this, the charge should be one of attempting to procure, and this would be construed in accordance with the Criminal Attempts Act 1981, s. 3: see generally **A6.31** *et seq*.

Section 13 applies (see **B14.14**); and offences under this section are triable either way (MCA 1980, s. 17 and sch. 1, para. 14).

Suppression of Documents or Facts etc. Punishable under the Land Registration Act 1925

B14.24   Land Registration Act 1925, ss. 115 to 117

115.   If in the course of any proceedings before the registrar or the court in pursuance of this Act any person concerned in such proceedings as principal or agent, with intent to conceal the title or claim of any person or to substantiate a false claim, suppresses, attempts to suppress, or is privy to the suppression of, any document or fact, the person so suppressing, attempting to suppress, or privy to suppression, shall be guilty of [an offence].

116.   (1)   If any person fraudulently procures, attempts fraudulently to procure, or is privy to the fraudulent procurement of, any entry on, erasure from or alteration of the register, or any land or charge certificate, he shall be guilty of [an offence].
    (2)   Any entry, erasure, or alteration, so made by fraud, shall be void as between all persons who are parties or privy to the fraud.

117.   A person guilty of [an offence] under this Act shall—
    (a)   on conviction on indictment, be liable to imprisonment for a term not exceeding two years or to a fine;
    (b)   on summary conviction, be liable to imprisonment for a term not exceeding three months or to a fine not exceeding [£5,000].

Relationship of Perjury Act 1911 to Other Enactments

B14.25   Perjury Act 1911, s. 16

    (1)   Where the making of a false statement is not only an offence under this Act, but also by virtue of some other Act is a corrupt practice or subjects the offender to any forfeiture or disqualification or to any penalty other than imprisonment, or fine, the liability of the offender under this Act shall be in addition to and not in substitution for his liability under such other Act.
    (2)   Nothing in this Act shall apply to a statement made without oath by a child under the provisions of the Children and Young Persons Act 1933.

(3)   Where the making of a false statement is by any other Act, whether passed before or after the commencement of this Act, made punishable on summary conviction, proceedings may be taken either under such other Act or under this Act:

Provided that where such an offence is by any Act passed before the commencement of this Act, as originally enacted, made punishable only on summary conviction, it shall remain only so punishable.

(Subsection (2) must now refer to unsworn evidence received by virtue of the CJA 1991, s. 52, or (once it is in force) the YJCEA 1999, s. 56.)

PERVERTING THE COURSE OF JUSTICE

Definition

It is an offence at common law to do an act tending and intended to pervert the course **B14.26** of public justice (including proceedings before tribunals).

Procedure

This offence is triable only on indictment. It is a class 3 offence.   **B14.27**

Indictment

Statement of Offence   **B14.28**

Perverting the course of justice

Particulars of Offence

A on or about the . . day of . . . did an act tending to pervert the course of justice, namely falsifying a number of documents, namely . . ., intended to be used as evidence in the prosecution of one X on indictment number . . . preferred against the said X according to law in the Central Criminal Court, intending that the course of justice should thereby be perverted

Sentencing Guidelines

The maximum penalty is life imprisonment and/or a fine.   **B14.29**

A number of Court of Appeal authorities have given guidance on the appropriate sentencing bracket for this offence. In *Hill* (1980) 2 Cr App R (S) 110, a sentence of 18 months' imprisonment was upheld, where the offender, awaiting trial on a charge of attempted theft of a battery, threatened to kill an intending prosecution witness. The attempt to pervert the course of justice was committed on the spur of the moment; according to the Court of Appeal, if there had been an element of premeditation the sentence should have been longer. The relative triviality of the attempted theft charge was, apparently, irrelevant. In *Bilby* (1987) 9 Cr App R (S) 185, a girl aged 17, of previous good character, pleaded guilty to doing an act tending to pervert the course of justice. Her father and brother were due to appear for trial at a magistrates' court, and the offender approached an intending prosecution witness and threatened to kill her if she gave evidence. A sentence of three months' youth custody was upheld, Ian Kennedy J saying that: 'In very few cases will threats to witnesses not be followed by immediate sentences of custody. A feeling of family loyalty will be of no avail. This is not one of the exceptional cases. The sentence passed by the learned judge was correct in principle and its length was not excessive.'

In *Johnson* [1998] 1 Cr App R (S) 169, the offender was seen by police officers indecently exposing himself and, when interviewed, he gave his brother's name and address. A summons was issued to the brother, at which point the deception was discovered. The Court of Appeal reduced a sentence of six months' imprisonment for doing an act tending to pervert the course of justice to two months on appeal. See also *Reid* (1991)

13 Cr App R (S) 513 and *Hurst* (1990) 12 Cr App R (S) 373. *Hurst* was a more serious case, where the offender gave another man's name, and presented that other man's driving licence, when he was stopped by the police and arrested for having excess blood alcohol. The offender was convicted and disqualified in the other man's name before the deception came to light. A sentence of three and a half years' imprisonment following a guilty plea was reduced to 18 months on appeal.

Comparable sentences would appear to be appropriate where the offence takes the form of a false allegation of crime. In *Goodwin* (1989) 11 Cr App R (S) 194 a 20-year-old woman made a false complaint of rape, naming a particular man. The man was arrested and held in custody for 14 days, released subsequently when the woman admitted what she had done. A sentence of three years' detention in a young offender institution was reduced on appeal to 18 months. Lord Lane CJ said that: 'It is necessary to make people understand that this sort of lie will be met by severe punishment. But we have to balance against that the age of this young woman and the circumstances in which she saw fit to tell these lies.' See also *Kyriakou* (1990) 12 Cr App (S) 603.

Substantive Offences, Conspiracy and Attempt

B14.30 Indictments tended to allege attempts or conspiracies to pervert the course of justice, because it was thought that actual perversion of the course of justice would often be difficult to prove. Indeed, this form of indictment was used even in some cases where the course of justice had been wholly frustrated: see *Britton* [1973] RTR 502. It is now recognised, however, that an act which is intended to have this effect, and is capable of succeeding, may constitute the substantive offence, and should be charged accordingly. The Criminal Attempts Act 1981 does not generally have any application in such cases (unless perhaps A has failed to perform the act he intended) and references to 'attempts' to pervert the course of justice are accordingly misleading (*Rowell* [1978] 1 WLR 132; *Machin* [1980] 1 WLR 763; *Williams* (1991) 92 Cr App R 158).

Where there appears to have been a conspiracy, there may sometimes be certain advantages in charging the statutory offence under the Criminal Law Act 1977, s. 1; but see the *Practice Direction (Crime: Conspiracy)* [1977] 1 WLR 537 on the use of conspiracy charges.

Acts which May Amount to Perverting the Course of Justice

B14.31 The following acts have been held capable of amounting to this offence. It will be noted that some of them are equally capable, in certain circumstances, of amounting to contempt of court, offences under the Criminal Law Act 1967, s. 4 or s. 5, or subornation etc. of perjury; but in many cases the present offence has a wider scope, and may be easier to establish. In every case, however, there must be some positive act; mere failure to point out an error, as where the wrong person is prosecuted, cannot suffice (*Headley* [1995] Crim LR 737).

(a) Deliberately assisting a person to evade lawful arrest (*Thomas* [1979] QB 326). In contrast to the offence under the Criminal Law Act 1967, s. 4, it does not matter whether the offence was arrestable, and it is not strictly necessary to prove the guilt of the person assisted. Cf. *Spinks* [1982] 1 All ER 587.

(b) Destroying, falsifying or concealing potential evidence, whether or not legal proceedings have already been instigated (*Vreones* [1891] 1 QB 360; *Murray* [1982] 2 All ER 225; *Firetto* [1991] Crim LR 208; *Rafique* [1993] 3 WLR 617; *Kiffin* [1994] Crim LR 449). It was said in *Selvage* [1982] QB 372 that, if proceedings have not been instigated at that time, an investigation must have been in progress; but this would fail to deal with measures designed to prevent an offence ever being discovered, and cannot be reconciled with *Vreones*. In *Selvage*, the accused attempted to falsify details on X's driving licence, so as to obscure the fact he had endorsements; but this was with a view to protecting him if he should ever commit, and be charged with, a future road traffic offence. Insofar as the dicta in that case seem to refer to evidence in actual but undiscovered crimes or potential civil disputes, it is submitted that they are *obiter* and wrong. See also *Sharpe* [1938] 1 All ER 48 and *Sinha* [1995] Crim LR 68.

(c)   Interfering with jurors (*Mickleburgh* [1995] 1 Cr App R 297) or interfering with potential witnesses, so as to prevent or dissuade them from testifying (*Kellett* [1976] QB 372; *Panayiotou* [1973] 1 WLR 1032), or so as to persuade them to change their evidence. There must be an intent to influence the course or outcome of the case in some way (*Lalani* [1999] 1 Cr App R 481). If the accused knowingly sought to prevent true evidence being given, or to procure false evidence, then his guilt is clear, even if no bribe, threat, undue pressure or other unlawful means were used (*Toney* [1993] 1 WLR 364). Problems may, however, arise where the accused claims that his object was to prevent a witness giving false evidence. Mere persuasion will not necessarily be an offence in such a case, even if the accused was wrong in believing that the witness's proposed evidence was false; but if the accused resorted to improper measures, he may be guilty. What is improper is generally a question of fact, but a jury should be directed that any threats, or any use of force, amounts to perversion of the course of justice, even where the threat is to take legal action for defamation or to exercise some other legal right, as long as the prosecution can prove necessary intent to influence the witness's evidence (*Toney*). One kind of threat should however be distinguished from the rest: a mere warning to a witness that he may be prosecuted for perjury if he gives false evidence should be insufficient to constitute an offence of perverting the course of justice. The new offences of witness or jury intimidation, which are created by the CJPO 1994, s. 51, operate in addition to, rather than in derogation of, the common law: see **B14.34**.

(d)   An offer or agreement by a potential witness to withhold (or, presumably, to change) his evidence in return for payment etc. (*Bassi* [1985] Crim LR 671). *Bassi* has been criticised as being inconsistent with *Murray* [1982] 2 All ER 225, where it was said that the offence would only be complete where a person has done something which might, without further action on his part, lead to potential injustice; but it could be argued that the course of justice is jeopardised as soon as any such offer or agreement is made, even if the witness could eventually decide to tell the truth after all, and if *Bassi* is inconsistent with *Murray*, it is to be preferred. See also the Criminal Law Act 1967, s. 5(1), discussed in **B14.49** to **B14.53**.

(e)   Confessing to, or pleading guilty to, another person's crime, in order to shield him (*Devito* [1975] Crim LR 175 but cf. *Headley* [1995] Crim LR 737).

(f)   Knowingly acting outside the limits of one's discretion as a police officer, so as to shield or excuse another person (e.g., a friend) from criminal charges (*Coxhead* [1986] RTR 411). It is for the jury to decide whether A had any discretion to act as he did, and, if not, whether he might mistakenly have believed he had (*Coxhead*). See also *Ward* [1995] Crim LR 398.

(g)   Making false allegations against X, intending that he should be prosecuted or knowing that he might be (*Rowell* [1978] 1 WLR 132). Where false stories merely waste police time (e.g., in looking for a non-existent offender), a charge under the Criminal Law Act 1967, s. 5(2), would be more appropriate; see **B14.58**.

Compensation of Victims and Settlement of Disputes

No offence is committed where one person merely offers to settle his civil dispute with **B14.32** another by offering (or asking for) payment, or where a third party offers such a settlement on behalf of one or other litigant (*Panayiotou* [1973] 1 WLR 1032 at p. 1038).

The position becomes more complicated and uncertain where the offer is made to the victim of a crime, who is a potential prosecution witness; but the Criminal Law Act 1967, s. 5(1) (see **B14.49**), appears to recognise that the victim would commit no offence merely by accepting an offer of 'reasonable compensation for loss or injury' in return for not disclosing the crime, and it may be inferred that the offeror would equally commit no offence. An agreement to accept more than such reasonable compensation (i.e. a bribe) would appear to be an offence under s. 5(1) (assuming the offence to have been arrestable) and the offeror would be a party to this, whether or not he is also guilty of perverting the course of justice (see *Ali* [1993] Crim LR 396). And see, with regard to advertisements offering rewards for the return of stolen goods, the Theft Act 1968, s. 23.

OFFENCES AKIN TO PERVERSION OF COURSE OF JUSTICE

B14.33 Certain other kinds of conduct might be regarded as amounting to the perversion of public justice, but are more commonly charged under other heads. In addition to those dealt with below, certain forms of advertisement offering rewards for the return of stolen goods contravene the Theft Act 1968, s. 23 (see **B4.150** and **B4.151**). Concealing or transferring the proceeds of criminal conduct for the purpose of avoiding prosecution may be punishable under the CJA 1988, s. 93C, and 'tipping off' another person as to a proposed money laundering investigation may be punishable under s. 93D of that Act (see **B22** for the offences); there are similar offences under the Drug Trafficking Act 1994 (see **B20.92**). As to offences relating to the investigation of terrorist activities, see **B10.55** *et seq*.

Intimidation of, or Retaliation against, Witnesses, Jurors and Others

B14.34 The intimidation of witnesses, jurors or other persons involved in legal proceedings or investigations may be punishable at common law, not only as tending to the perversion of the course of justice (see **B14.31**), but also as contempt of court. Retaliation against former witnesses etc. is also punishable as contempt (see **B14.72**). Indeed, any improper interference with or approach to a witness or juror (present past or future), whether based on intimidation, bribery or persuasion, will almost invariably be punishable under one or other of those heads. See, for example, *Mickleburgh* [1995] 1 Cr App R 297 and *A-G v Judd* [1995] COD 15 at **B14.72**.

Intimidation or retaliation may, alternatively, be punishable as one of two statutory offences created by the CJPO 1994, s. 51.

Criminal Justice and Public Order Act 1994, s. 51

(1)   A person who does to another person—
   (a)   an act which intimidates, and is intended to intimidate, that other person;
   (b)   knowing or believing that the other person is assisting in the investigation of an offence or is a witness or potential witness or a juror or potential juror in proceedings for an offence; and
   (c)   intending thereby to cause the investigation or the course of justice to be obstructed, perverted or interfered with,
commits an offence.
(2)   A person who does or threatens to do to another person—
   (a)   an act which harms or would harm, and is intended to harm, that other person;
   (b)   knowing or believing that the other person, or some other person, has assisted in an investigation into an offence or has given evidence or particular evidence in proceedings for an offence, or has acted as a juror or concurred in a particular verdict in proceedings for an offence; and
   (c)   does or threatens to do the act because of what (within paragraph (b)) he knows or believes,
commits an offence.
(3)   A person does an act 'to' another person with the intention of intimidating, or (as the case may be) harming, that other person not only where the act is done in the presence

of that other and directed at him directly but also where the act is done to a third person and is intended, in the circumstances, to intimidate or (as the case may be) harm the person at whom the act is directed.

(4) The harm that may be done or threatened may be financial as well as physical (whether to the person or a person's property) and similarly as respects an intimidatory act which consists of threats.

(5) The intention required by subsection (1)(c) and the motive required by subsection (2)(c) above need not be the only or the predominating intention or motive with which the act is done or, in the case of subsection (2), threatened.

(6) A person guilty of an offence under this section shall be liable—

(a) on conviction on indictment, to imprisonment for a term not exceeding five years or a fine or both;

(b) on summary conviction, to imprisonment for a term not exceeding six months or a fine not exceeding the statutory maximum or both.

(7) If, in proceedings against a person for an offence under subsection (1) above, it is proved that he did an act falling within paragraph (a) with the knowledge or belief required by paragraph (b), he shall be presumed, unless the contrary is proved, to have done the act with the intention required by paragraph (c) of that subsection.

(8) If, in proceedings against a person for an offence under subsection (2) above, it is proved that he did or threatened to do an act falling within paragraph (a) within the relevant period with the knowledge or belief required by paragraph (b), he shall be presumed, unless the contrary is proved, to have done the act with the motive required by paragraph (c) of that subsection.

(9) In this section—

'investigation into an offence' means such an investigation by the police or other person charged with the duty of investigating offences or charging offenders;

'offence' includes an alleged or suspected offence;

'potential', in relation to a juror, means a person who has been summoned for jury service at the court at which proceedings for the offence are pending; and

'the relevant period'—

(a) in relation to a witness or juror in any proceedings for an offence, means the period beginning with the institution of the proceedings and ending with the first anniversary of the conclusion of the trial or, if there is an appeal or reference under section 17 of the Criminal Appeal Act 1968, of the conclusion of the appeal;

(b) in relation to a person who has or is believed by the accused to have, assisted in an investigation into an offence, but was not also a witness in proceedings for an offence, means the period of one year beginning with any act of his, or any act believed by the accused to be an act of his, assisting in the investigation; and

(c) in relation to a person who both has or is believed by the accused to have, assisted in the investigation into an offence and was a witness in proceedings for the offence, means the period beginning with any act of his, or any act believed by the accused to be an act of his, assisting in the investigation and ending with the anniversary mentioned in paragraph (a) above.

The YJCEA 1999, sch. 4, para. 22, amends the CJPO 1994, s. 51, by substituting subsections (1) to (3) and amending subsection (8); these amendments are not in force. The new subsection and subsection (8) in its amended form are set out below. The amendments appear to make little difference in practice, as they largely confirm the effect of earlier judicial interpretation of s. 51.

(1) A person commits an offence if—

(a) he does an act which intimidates, and is intended to intimidate, another person ('the victim'),

(b) he does the act knowing or believing that the victim is assisting in the investigation of an offence or is a witness or potential witness or a juror or potential juror in proceedings for an offence, and

(c) he does it intending thereby to cause the investigation or the course of justice to be obstructed, perverted or interfered with.

(2) A person commits an offence if—

(a)   he does an act which harms, and is intended to harm, another person or, intending to cause another person to fear harm, he threatens to do an act which would harm that other person,

(b)   he does or threatens to do the act knowing or believing that the person harmed or threatened to be harmed ('the victim'), or some other person, has assisted in an investigation into an offence or has given evidence or particular evidence in proceedings for an offence, or has acted as a juror or concurred in a particular verdict in proceedings for an offence, and

(c)   he does or threatens to do it because of that knowledge or belief.

(3)   For the purposes of subsections (1) and (2) it is immaterial that the act is or would be done, or that the threat is made—

(a)   otherwise than in the presence of the victim, or

(b)   to a person other than the victim.

(8)   If, in proceedings against a person for an offence under subsection (2) above, it is proved that within the relevant period—

(a)   he did an act which harmed, and was intended to harm, another person, or

(b)   intending to cause another person fear of harm, he threatened to do an act which would harm that other person,

and that he did the act, or (as the case may be) threatened to do the act with the knowledge or belief required by paragraph (b), he shall be presumed, unless the contrary is proved, to have done the act or (as the case may be) threatened to do the act with the motive required by paragraph (c) of that subsection.

As to the meaning of 'knowing or believing' in this context, see *Singh* [1999] Crim LR 681.

Apart from being triable either way, the offence created by s. 51(1) appears to offer few advantages over the common law offence of perverting the course of justice (which is preserved under s. 51(11)). The latter would indeed be committed even if bribery or persuasion were used in place of intimidation. The new offence may, in some cases, be easier to prove, as a result of the presumption imported under s. 51(7), but it seems unlikely that this would make much difference in practice.

In contrast, the offence created by s. 51(2) covers conduct that would not ordinarily amount to perverting the course of justice, and carries heavier penalties than those available for contempt of court (as to which, see **B14.69**). Committal for contempt may not, in any case, be a wholly satisfactory method of dealing with conduct of this type, especially where it occurs after the original trial has ended.

In *Williams* [1997] 2 Cr App R (S) 221 the offender, after having been convicted of false imprisonment and unlawful wounding, wrote to the victim of those offences from prison, threatening her with violence. For this offence under s. 51(2), to which the offender pleaded guilty, a further sentence of two years' imprisonment, consecutive to the three-year term being served, was upheld by the Court of Appeal. Harrison J noted that the offence under s. 51(2) carried a maximum of five years, as compared with two years for contempt of court, and said that such intimidation must be viewed extremely seriously. The Court of Appeal in *Watmore* [1998] 2 Cr App R (S) 46 upheld a sentence of four years' imprisonment where the offender was convicted of an offence under s. 51. The offender had encountered a man who had earlier given evidence against him in a magistrates' court, and had punched and butted the victim, causing severe cuts and bruises. The court noted that incidents of witness intimidation were now endemic, and becoming worse.

Embracery and Bribery

B14.35   The bribery of a juror, or other attempts to influence him out of court, may be charged as embracery, or dealt with as contempt of court (*Owen* [1976] 1 WLR 840).

Improper payments to judges, magistrates, or other judicial officers may be punished as contempt or as bribery at common law (*Harrison* (1800) 1 East PC 382). Receipt of the bribe could also be charged as the common-law offence of misconduct in a public office (as to which see *Llewellyn-Jones* [1968] 1 QB 429).

As to contempt of court, see **B14.59** to **B14.98**.

Personating a Juror

It is an offence at common law, punishable with a fine and imprisonment at large, to impersonate someone summoned for jury service, so as to sit in his place. The motive is irrelevant (*Clark* (1918) 82 JP 295).   **B14.36**

Disposing of a Body with Intent to Prevent an Inquest

The concealment, disposal or destruction of a corpse is a common-law offence, punishable with a fine and imprisonment at large, if done to prevent the holding of a lawful inquest as to the death (*Stephenson* (1884) 13 QBD 331). There is a separate common law offence of preventing the decent and lawful burial of a body (see *Hunter* [1974] QB 95).   **B14.37**

In *Godward* [1998] 1 Cr App R (S) 385 the offender pleaded guilty to obstructing the coroner by concealing a body. The police found the decomposed body of a man in the offender's flat. Godward had failed to disclose the whereabouts of the body, despite being twice asked by the police to assist them in tracing him. Lord Bingham CJ, in the Court of Appeal, said that the most important factor in sentencing for this offence was the intention of the perpetrator. If the purpose was to obstruct the course of justice and to make it difficult to bring home a charge against the offender or another person, the offence would merit punishment towards the top of the appropriate bracket. If such intention was lacking, a lesser sentence was appropriate. On the present facts, a prison sentence of four years was reduced to three years. See also *Blakemore* [1997] 2 Cr App R (S) 255.

On sentencing for the latter offence, see *Swindell* (1981) 3 Cr App R (S) 255, *Parry* (1986) 8 Cr App R (S) 470 and *King* (1990) 12 Cr App R (S) 76. In the last of these cases the offender concealed the body of a drug addict friend who died in her flat. She did not report the matter to the police as she was in breach of a community service order and feared arrest if she did so. Pill J commented (at p. 77) that 'The gravity of the offence will vary enormously from case to case. The length of the term of imprisonment which is appropriate will depend upon the circumstances of the particular offence.' A prison sentence of 21 months was reduced on appeal to one of 12 months.

ASSISTING OFFENDERS

Definition

Criminal Law Act 1967, s. 4   **B14.38**

(1) Where a person has committed an arrestable offence, any other person who, knowing or believing him to be guilty of the offence or of some other arrestable offence, does without lawful authority or reasonable excuse any act with intent to impede his apprehension or prosecution shall be guilty of an offence.

(1A) In this section . . . 'arrestable offence' has the meaning assigned to it by section 24 of the Police and Criminal Evidence Act 1984.

At common law, a person knowingly rendering assistance to a person who had committed a felony became an accessory after the fact, and thus guilty of that felony. This provision created a specific offence to replace that principle.

Procedure

Criminal Law Act 1967, s. 4   **B14.39**

(4) No proceedings shall be instituted for an offence under subsection (1) . . . except by or with the consent of the Director of Public Prosecutions.

By virtue of the MCA 1980, s. 17 and sch. 1, para. 26, an offence under the Criminal Law Act 1967, s. 4, is triable either way where the offence to which the assisting relates is triable either way. *Quaere,* where the underlying offence is taking a conveyance without authority which, although an arrestable offence regardless of maximum punishment (see the PACE 1984, s. 24(2)(d)) is nonetheless triable only summarily (Theft Act 1968, s. 12). It is submitted that, technically, assisting an offender in this case remains triable only on indictment, in the absence of an express provision to the contrary – an obviously illogical and inconvenient result. The point has evidently been overlooked and should, it is submitted, be clarified by statute at an early date.

Indictment

B14.40

Statement of Offence

Assisting an offender contrary to section 4(1) of the Criminal Law Act 1967

Particulars of Offence

A on the . . . day of . . ., X having committed an arrestable offence, namely robbery, knowing or believing that X had committed the said offence or some other arrestable offence, without lawful authority or reasonable excuse harboured X in his house, with intent to impede the apprehension or prosecution of X

Alternative Verdicts

B14.41

Criminal Law Act 1967, s. 4

(2) If on the trial of an indictment for an arrestable offence the jury are satisfied that the offence charged (or some other offence of which the accused might on that charge be found guilty) was committed, but find the accused not guilty of it, they may find him guilty of any offence under subsection (1) . . . of which they are satisfied that he is guilty in relation to the offence charged (or that other offence).

If A is not initially charged with a s. 4 offence, but with a substantive arrestable offence, and the possibility of an alternative verdict under subsection (2) manifests itself in the course of the trial, the defence should be given sufficient opportunity to meet such a possibility. The possibility should not be raised after the court has finished hearing evidence (*Cross* [1971] 3 All ER 641; *Vincent* (1972) 56 Cr App R 281).

Sentencing Guidelines

B14.42 Where the principal offence is subject to a sentence fixed by law the maximum penalty is ten years, a fine, or both, on indictment (Criminal Law Act 1967, s. 4(3)); and six months, a fine not exceeding the statutory maximum, or both, summarily.

Where the principal offence is subject to a sentence of 14 years, the maximum penalty is seven years, a fine, or both, on indictment (Criminal Law Act 1967, s. 4(3)); and six months, a fine not exceeding the statutory maximum, or both, summarily.

Where the principal offence is subject to a sentence of 10 years, the maximum penalty is five years, a fine, or both, on indictment (Criminal Law Act 1967, s. 4(3)); and six months, a fine not exceeding the statutory maximum, or both, summarily.

In other cases: the maximum penalty is three years, a fine, or both, on indictment (Criminal Law Act 1967, s. 4(3)); and six months, a fine not exceeding the statutory maximum, or both, summarily.

In *Matthews* (1982) 4 Cr App R (S) 233 the offender had allowed another man, wanted by the police in connection with an armed robbery, to stay in his flat for 3 to 4 weeks; a sentence of 12 months' imprisonment was upheld. In *Hunter* (1984) 6 Cr App R (S) 54 the offender harboured a man wanted for the shooting of another man and, when the police came to his flat, told them he was not there; a sentence of 12 months' imprisonment was held to be appropriate. By contrast, in *Mosely* (1988) 10 Cr App R (S) 55 the offender hid two men away from the police without knowing what crimes they were wanted for. The men were subsequently sentenced to lengthy custodial terms for robbery and burglary. A sentence of eight months imposed on the offender was reduced on appeal to three months. See also *Urwin* [1996] 2 Cr App R (S) 281.

Offence Cannot be Committed by Omission

This offence is not capable of taking the form of an omission. Shielding another person **B14.43** by silence etc. is rarely a crime, but see the Criminal Law Act 1967, s. 5, and **B14.49**.

Requirement that Arrestable Offence has been Committed

An offence under the Criminal Law Act 1967, s. 4, can be committed only where an **B14.44** arrestable offence has previously been committed by the person assisted, and proof of that person's guilt is accordingly an essential element in proof of this offence.

It is not necessary for the person allegedly assisted to be convicted of his arrestable offence before someone can be convicted of assisting him (*Donald* (1986) Cr App R 49), nor is the person assisted's conviction conclusive proof of his guilt at the subsequent trial of a person accused of assisting; but the prior conviction of the person assisted will raise a presumption that he was guilty, and this will simplify the task of the prosecution at the alleged assister's trial. It would be for the defence to prove, on balance of probabilities, that the conviction of the person assisted was wrong. See the PACE 1984, s. 74 and **F11.3**.

Evidence of the acquittal of the person assisted at a previous trial is not admissible at the assister's trial, however; and even where the assister and the person assisted are tried together, confession evidence etc. admissible against one might not be admissible against the other. Thus an admission by the person assisted that he committed the arrestable offence would be inadmissible against the accused on a charge of assisting him (*Spinks* [1982] 1 All ER 587). There might even be cases in which the person assisted is acquitted of the original offence, even though someone is convicted of assisting him to evade apprehension. Such cases would be exceptional. If the jury have any real doubts of the person assisted, the assister should also be acquitted. See *Shannon* [1975] AC 717 (conviction of single conspirator). Only where the person assisted is acquitted on an unusual evidential basis which does not affect the case against the assister would the contrary result be satisfactory.

Many of the problems arising from use of s. 4 can be avoided by charging an assister with perverting the course of justice: see **B14.26** to **B14.32**, especially **B14.31**. In some cases there may be an overlap between s. 4 and the money laundering offences in the CJA 1988, ss. 93A to 93D (see **B22**).

Knowledge of or Belief in the Guilt of the Person Assisted

By analogy with decisions concerning the offence of handling stolen goods (where **B14.45** knowledge or belief is similarly a *mens rea* element), it is clear that the accused must either know or positively believe in the guilt of the person assisted. Mere suspicion, however strong and well founded, would not suffice. On the other hand, the Criminal Law Act 1967, s. 4(1), expressly provides that an accused may be guilty even if he is mistaken about what offence the person assisted has committed; and the language used is wide enought to embrace cases where the accused knew that the person assisted must have committed a serious offence, but had no idea what offence it may have been (*Morgan* [1972] 1 QB 436).

Intent to Impede Apprehension or Prosecution

The intent to impede the apprehension etc. of the person assisted is an ulterior intent. **B14.46** It is not necessary that the person assisted should have benefited from the accused's actions; indeed, they may be wholly unsuccessful and lead unwittingly to his immediate arrest.

Lawful Authority or Reasonable Excuse

B14.47 The legal burden of proving the accused's absence of lawful authority etc. appears to rest on the prosecution (*Brindley* [1971] 2 QB 300). In contrast to certain other offences in which lawful authority or reasonable excuse may be raised, the Criminal Law Act 1967, s. 4, does not impose the burden of proof on the accused; see, e.g., the Prevention of Crime Act 1953, s. 1 (**B12.94**). However, the accused must raise the issue by some admissible evidence, before this burden arises. As to evidential burdens on the defence, see generally **F3.6** to **F3.12**. It is difficult to imagine what might amount to lawful authority or reasonable excuse in any normal circumstances.

No Offence of Attempting to Assist

B14.48 There can be no offence of attempting to commit an offence under the Criminal Law Act 1967, s. 4 (Criminal Attempts Act 1981, s. 1(4)).

CONCEALING ARRESTABLE OFFENCES

Definition

B14.49   **Criminal Law Act 1967, s. 5**

(1) Where a person has committed an arrestable offence, any other person who, knowing or believing that the offence or some other arrestable offence has been commited, and that he has information which might be of material assistance in securing the prosecution or conviction of an offender for it, accepts or agrees to accept for not disclosing that information any consideration other than the making good of loss or injury caused by the offence, or the making of reasonable compensation for that loss or injury, shall be liable on conviction on indictment to imprisonment for not more than two years. . . .

(5)   The compounding of an offence other than treason shall not be an offence otherwise than under this section.

Procedure

B14.50 No proceeding shall be instituted for an offence under this section except by or with the consent of the DPP (s. 5(3)).

Concealing an arrestable offence is triable either way where the underlying arrestable offence is so triable (MCA 1980, s. 17 and sch. 1, para. 26). As in the case of assisting offenders, contrary to the Criminal Law Act 1967, s. 4, an anomalous position arises with respect to the purely summary arrestable offence of taking a conveyance without authority (see **B14.39**).

Indictment

B14.51   Statement of Offence

Concealing an arrestable offence contrary to section 5(1) of the Criminal Law Act 1967

Particulars of Offence

A on the . . . day of . . ., X having committed an arrestable offence, namely robbery, knowing or believing that the said or some other arrestable offence had been committed and that he had information which might be of material assistance in securing the prosecution or conviction of X for it, accepted (or agreed to accept) consideration, namely a payment of £1,000, which was neither a making good of loss or injury caused by the said offence nor the making of reasonable compensation therefor, for not disclosing the said information

Sentencing Guidelines

B14.52 The maximum penalty on indictment is two years (Criminal Law Act 1967, s. 5(1)). Summarily, the maximum penalty is six months and/or a fine not exceeding the statutory maximum. As to sentencing, see the cases considered in respect of assisting offenders in **B14.40**.

Elements

B14.53 The common-law offences of misprision of felony and compounding a felony were both abolished by the Criminal Law Act 1967. Misprision of treason remains an offence (see **B9.26** to **B9.30**) and there are now statutory offences of non-disclosure in relation to certain terrorist offences and the laundering of drug money (see **B10.60** and **B20.115**). With these exceptions, the non-disclosure of offences cannot ordinarily be punishable. Compounding an offence other than treason cannot now be an offence other than under the Criminal Law Act 1967, s. 5(1) (s. 5(5)).

The striking of a bargain, in which a promise of silence or non-disclosure is exchanged for consideration going beyond reasonable compensation to the victim, is another matter, and is punishable under s. 5(1). It is the agreement which constitutes the gist of the offence. The accused will remain guilty, even if he later breaks the agreement and informs the police.

As with the Criminal Law Act 1967, s. 4 (see **B14.38** to **B14.48**), the prosecution must prove that the other person did indeed commit an arrestable offence (see **B14.44**); and where this might be difficult there may similarly be advantages in charging a person who has agreed to conceal a crime with perverting the course of justice. A person who demands money for his silence might also be guilty of blackmail (see **B5.81** to **B5.89**).

As with assisting offenders there can be no offence of attempting to commit an offence under this section (Criminal Attempts Act 1981, s. 1(4)).

OTHER OFFENCES RELATING TO OFFENDERS

Escape

B14.54 It is a common-law offence, punishable on indictment by a fine and imprisonment at large, to escape from legal custody. The escape may be from police custody following arrest (*Timmis* [1976] Crim LR 129) or from custody or imprisonment etc. following remand or conviction (*Moss* (1985) 82 Cr App R 116).

The prosecution must prove that the custody was legal (*Dillon* v *The Queen* [1982] AC 484), but if it was, it is irrelevant whether the accused was guilty of the crime for which he was arrested or imprisoned (*Waters* (1873) 12 Cox CC 390).

A partial definition of 'legal custody' is provided by s. 13(2) of the Prison Act 1952:

Prison Act 1952, s. 13

(2) A prisoner shall be deemed to be in legal custody while he is confined in, or is being taken to or from, any prison and while he is working, or is for any other reason, outside the prison in the custody or under the control of an officer of the prison and while he is being taken to any place to which he is required or authorised by or under this Act or the CJA 1982 to be taken, or is kept in custody in pursuance of any such requirement or authorisation.

The references to 'prison' apply equally to remand centres and young offender institutions (Prison Act 1952, s. 43(5)). The reference to 'an officer of the prison' is to be construed as a reference to a prisoner custody officer performing custodial duties at the prison (CJA 1991, s. 87(6)).

In *Page* (1987) 9 Cr App R (S) 348 the offender pleaded guilty to escaping from lawful custody. There was no pre-planning involved. The offender took the opportunity to escape from custody in the cells of a magistrates' court by taking advantage of a disturbance in the cells, pushing the officer behind a gate and tying it with a belt. A sentence of 21 months' imprisonment was upheld on appeal. Eighteen months was said to be proper in respect of each count in *Williams* (1987) 9 Cr App R (S) 531, where the offender escaped twice, once from a police station and once from a remand centre. According to the Court of Appeal in *Clarke* (1994) 15 Cr App R (S) 825, in most cases of escape from custody it is necessary to impose a custodial sentence to run consecutively to the sentence being served. See also *Hammond* (1995) 16 Cr App R (S) 142.

Breach of Prison

B14.55 This offence is similar to escape, but must involve some breaking, cutting, or forcing in the course of the escape. It need not involve escape from an actual prison (forcing open a police station window would suffice) and need not involve any deliberate damage (see *Haswell* (1821) Russ & Ry 458, where accidental dislodging of loose bricks while scaling the prison wall was held to suffice).

The case of *Coughtrey* [1997] 2 Cr App R (S) 269 provides sentencing guidelines for this offence. The offender was serving a life sentence for murder and escaped after two years by burning through the perimeter fence with cutting equipment and then scaling the outer wall. He gave himself up a week later. A sentence of seven years' imprisonment for prison breach was reduced on appeal to four years. McCowan LJ in the Court of Appeal noted that breaking prison is a very serious offence for which a substantial sentence of imprisonment is always to be expected because of the fear and apprehension it generates, the disruption to prison life, the violence and disorder that it may lead to, and the need to deter the culprit and others. Factors to be taken into account in fixing the length of the sentence will include (i) the nature and circumstances of the original offence, (ii) the offender's conduct while in prison, (iii) the methods employed in effecting escape and, in particular, whether any violence was used and whether there was extensive planning and outside assistance, (iv) whether he surrendered himself and how soon, and (v) a plea of guilty. If the original sentence is a determinate one, the sentence for prison breach should almost always be ordered to run consecutively. If the original sentence is a life sentence, the sentence for prison breach should usually be the same as if he had been serving a determinate sentence, but it will have to be served concurrently.

Remaining at Large after Temporary Release

B14.56 Under the Prisoners (Return to Custody) Act 1995, s. 1(1), a person who has been temporarily released in pursuance of rules made under the Prison Act 1952, s. 47(5), will be guilty of a summary offence, punishable by imprisonment for a term not exceeding six months and/or a fine not exceeding level 5 on the standard scale if:

(a) without reasonable excuse he remains unlawfully at large at any time after the expiry of the period for which he was temporarily released; or

(b) knowing or believing an order recalling him to have been made, and while unlawfully at large by virtue of such an order, he fails, without reasonable excuse, to take all necessary steps for complying as soon as reasonably practicable with that order.

The offence does not apply to persons temporarily released from secure training centres (s. 1(2)).

Assisting Escape and Harbouring Escapees

B14.57 The following offences have been created by statute:

Prison Act 1952, s. 39

Any person who aids any prisoner in escaping or attempting to escape from a prison or who, with intent to facilitate the escape of any prisoner, conveys any thing into a prison or to a prisoner sends anything (by post or otherwise) into a prison or to a prisoner or places any thing anywhere outside a prison with a view to its coming into the possession of a prisoner, shall be guilty of [an offence] and liable to imprisonment for a term not exceeding ten years.

Criminal Justice Act 1961, s. 22

(2) If any person knowingly harbours a person who has escaped from a prison or other institution to which . . . section 39 [of this Act] applies, or who, having been sentenced in any part of the United Kingdom or in any of the Channel Islands or the Isle of Man to imprisonment or detention, is otherwise unlawfully at large, or who gives to any such person any assistance with intent to prevent, hinder or interfere with his being taken into custody, he shall be liable—

(a) on summary conviction, to imprisonment for a term not exceeding six months, or to a fine not exceeding [£5,000] or to both;

(b) on conviction on indictment, to imprisonment for a term not exceeding ten years, or to a fine, or to both.

These offences apply where the escape is from a prison, remand centre or young offender institution; but the Prison Act 1952, s. 13, does not apply to, and neither statutory offence can therefore be committed in respect of, a person who escapes from custody whilst in transit to or from prison, or from court etc. (*Nicoll* v *Catron* (1985) 81 Cr App R 339; *Moss* (1985) 82 Cr App R 116). In both *Nicoll* v *Catron*, and *Moss*, it was stated (*obiter*) that common-law offences had been committed, even though the statutory offences under the Prison Act 1952, s. 39, and the CJA 1961, s. 22, had not. These offences were not identified in *Moss*, and *Nicoll* v *Catron* contains only a reference to perverting the course of justice; but there is also a common-law offence of forcible rescue from lawful custody (see 2 Hawk PC, ch. 21).

The most serious reported sentencing case is *Bowman* [1997] 1 Cr App R (S) 282, where a sentence of seven years' imprisonment was upheld in respect of a conspiracy to assist prisoners to escape by smuggling a pistol into Durham Prison. The pistol was found after a search by prison officers. In *Walker* (1990) 12 Cr App R (S) 65, a sentence of nine months' imprisonment was upheld on an offender who pleaded guilty to aiding a prisoner to escape from an open prison by meeting him outside the prison and giving him a lift in his car. In *Williams* (1992) 13 Cr App R (S) 236, the appropriate sentence was said to be 15 months where the offender had changed places with a prisoner in an open prison for one night to allow the prisoner to spend a night at home. Twelve months' imprisonment was reduced to nine months in *Taylor* (1994) 15 Cr App R (S) 893 where the offender pleaded guilty to harbouring an escaped prisoner, his brother.

Mental Health Act 1983, s. 128

(1) Where any person induces or knowingly assists another person who is liable to be detained in a hospital within the meaning of part II of this Act or is subject to guardianship under this Act to absent himself without leave he shall be guilty of an offence.

(2) Where any person induces or knowingly assists another person who is in legal custody by virtue of section 137 [of this Act] to escape from such custody he shall be guilty of an offence.

(3) Where any person knowingly harbours a patient who is absent without leave or is otherwise at large and liable to be retaken under this Act or gives him any assistance with intent to prevent, hinder or interfere with his being taken into custody or returned to the hospital or other place where he ought to be he shall be guilty of an offence.

(4) Any person guilty of an offence under this section shall be liable—

(a) on summary conviction, to imprisonment for a term not exceeding six months or to a fine not exceeding the statutory maximum, or to both;

(b) on conviction on indictment, to imprisonment for a term not exceeding two years or to a fine of any amount, or to both.

Wasting Police Time

B14.58   **Criminal Law Act 1967, s. 5**

(2) Where a person causes any wasteful employment of the police by knowingly making to any person a false report tending to show that an offence has been committed, or to give rise to apprehension for the safety of any persons or property, or tending to show that he has information material to any police inquiry, he shall be liable on summary conviction to imprisonment for not more than six months or to a fine of not more than level 4 on the standard scale or to both.

No proceeding for this offence may be instituted except by or with the consent of the DPP (Criminal Law Act 1967, s. 5(3)).

This offence was created to deal with conduct which had previously been thought to be indictable at common law as effecting a public mischief (*Manley* [1933] 1 KB 529). The existence of any such offence at common law is, to say the least, unclear (see *DPP* v *Withers* [1975] AC 842), and such conduct should now always be charged under s. 5(2).

CONTEMPT OF COURT

The last part of this section is primarily concerned with criminal contempt of court, and more particularly with that offence in so far as it affects the criminal courts. Some reference is necessarily made to civil contempt and to the jurisdiction of the civil courts in respect of criminal contempt, but those topics are not covered in any detail.

Nature of Contempt

B14.59   Criminal contempt of court is a broadly based offence, and can take a number of different forms. At common law, it has been defined as behaviour 'involving an interference with the due administration of justice, either in a particular case or more generally as a continuing process' (*A-G* v *Leveller Magazine Ltd* [1979] AC 440, per Lord Diplock at p. 449). It is not possible to provide an exhaustive list of the ways in which the offence can be committed, although a substantial number of typical examples are given at **B14.71** to **B14.88**. As Donaldson MR said in *A-G* v *Newspaper Publishing plc* [1988] Ch 333 at p. 368:

> The law of contempt is based on the broadest of principles, namely that the courts cannot and will not permit interference with the due administration of justice. Its application is universal. The fact that it is applied in novel circumstances . . . is not a case of widening its application. It is merely a new example of its application.

Broadly based though it is, criminal contempt can nevertheless be categorised according to whether it is committed 'in the face of the court' or committed indirectly (i.e. a 'constructive' contempt, such as the publication of a book or article prejudicing a forthcoming trial in a way which may influence potential jurors or witnesses). Only the superior courts have jurisdiction to punish for constructive contempts (*Lefroy* (1873) LR 8 QB 134), whereas any court of record (including county courts and coroners' courts) may punish contempt in the face of the court. (As to the position of magistrates' courts, see **B14.63**.) It does not follow that constructive contempt of an inferior court must go unpunished; jurisdiction to commit for such contempt may be exercised by the Divisional Court of the Queen's Bench Division under Rules of the Supreme Court 1965, ord. 52 (see **B14.65**).

Criminal contempt of court has traditionally been distinguished from civil contempt, which takes the form of non-compliance with a court order (or an undertaking in lieu of an order) favouring another party. This distinction has always been problematic, particularly since quasi-criminal sanctions are applicable to both categories. It has also been held that the appropriate standard of proof is that beyond reasonable doubt, even in cases of civil contempt (see e.g., *Re Bramblevale Ltd* [1970] Ch 128), and even though the proceedings may remain civil proceedings to which the Civil Evidence Acts apply (see e.g., *Savings & Investment Bank Ltd v Gasco Investments (Netherlands) BV (No. 2)* [1988] Ch 422). The distinction has been criticised both by the Phillimore Committee (Cmnd 5794), which advocated its abolition, and by the Court of Appeal (Civil Division) in *A-G v Newspaper Publishing plc* [1988] Ch 333, which suggested a reclassification under which the misleading terms 'civil' and 'criminal' would no longer be used.

Few real points of distinction remain; but in cases of civil contempt it is usually up to the opposing party to instigate proceedings, and he generally retains the right to waive the contempt. In contrast, cases of criminal contempt are generally prosecuted by the A-G or by the court acting of its own motion, and opposing parties have no say in the matter (*Home Office v Harman* [1983] 1 AC 280 per Lord Scarman at p. 310); and see s. 7 (**B14.95**) and s. 10 (**B14.85**) of the Contempt of Court Act 1981, which limit the right to prosecute for some forms of criminal contempt. A minor point of distinction is that certain persons, notably peers and Members of Parliament, are generally immune from arrest for civil contempt (*Stourton v Stourton* [1963] P 302), but not for criminal contempt.

Parties

In *Balogh v St Albans Crown Court* [1975] QB 73, Lord Denning MR held that criminal **B14.60** contempt of court is governed by the ordinary principles of criminal liability. If this is correct, it follows that complicity in the offence, as a secondary party, would require *mens rea*, even where liability of the principal offender is strict under the Contempt of Court Act 1981 (see **B14.89** to **B14.95**). Where a corporation publishes material amounting to contempt, the corporation itself is the obvious principal offender, but a newspaper editor (or his counterpart in television etc.) would usually be regarded as a joint principal, because of his special responsibility for the content of the publication, and, where *mens rea* is required, his *mens rea* could arguably be imputed to the company on the basis that he manages that part at least of the company's business.

The dictum of Lord Goddard CJ in *Evening Standard Co. Ltd* [1954] 1 QB 578, that the liability of the editor and company is vicarious, is contrary to principle and has generally been doubted. Employees (e.g., reporters) are not publishers, but might be liable as secondary parties if they act with *mens rea*. See *Griffiths, ex parte A-G* [1957] 2 QB 192.

Courts and Tribunals Protected by the Law of Contempt

One must distinguish between the protection of the law of contempt, which is afforded **B14.61** to all courts and tribunals exercising the judicial power of the State, and the jurisdiction to punish for contempt, which is possessed at common law only by courts of record, and to differing extent according to whether the court is superior or inferior. (As to the position of magistrates' courts, which are not courts of record, but which have statutory powers to deal with some contempts, see **B14.63**).

There appears to be no definitive list of the bodies which qualify for protection. Some do not qualify, even though they are called 'courts', e.g., local valuation courts. Others do qualify, even though they lack that title, e.g., industrial tribunals (*Peach Grey & Co. v Sommers* [1995] 2 All ER 513) and mental health review tribunals (*P v Liverpool Daily Post and Echo Newspapers plc* [1991] 2 AC 370). The ones which lack protection are those which exercise administrative, rather than judicial functions. It is not enough that they act judicially in discharging such functions (*A-G* v *British Broadcasting Corporation* [1981] AC 303; *General Medical Council* v *British Broadcasting Corporation* [1998] 1 WLR 1573). Even magistrates lose the protection of the law of contempt when sitting as licensing justices, because this is an administrative function (*A-G* v *British Broadcasting Corporation* [1981] AC 303 at p. 348).

Mode of Trial

B14.62 Cases of alleged contempt are tried by procedures which are peculiar to that offence. It remains theoretically possible to prosecute criminal contempt on indictment, but this is hardly ever done, and in the last reported case in which it was, the Court of Appeal condemned the procedure as inappropriate, and quashed the convictions which had been imposed (*D* [1984] AC 778 at p. 792). In practice, therefore, criminal contempt is dealt with summarily, either by the court acting of its own motion (as it will usually do in respect of contempt in the face of the court) or by a more formal process in which an application for committal is made to the Divisional Court of the Queen's Bench Division under the Rules of the Supreme Court 1965, ord. 52 (**B14.65**).

Jurisdiction and Procedure: Magistrates' Courts

B14.63 Since magistrates' courts are generally assumed not to be courts of record, they have no inherent jurisdiction to deal with contempts. They do, however, have statutory powers. Apart from their powers to commit a person to prison for default in paying a fine or an order under the Legal Aid Act 1988, s. 63(3) of the MCA 1980 empowers them to fine or commit to custody for default in respect of other orders. This is a power primarily directed at civil defaults, and exercisable either of the court's own motion or by order on complaint (Contempt of Court Act 1981, s. 17). The maximum fine is £50 per day or £5,000; the maximum period of custody is two months.

Contempt in the face of the court is partly (but not entirely) dealt with in the Contempt of Court Act 1981, s. 12 and the MCA 1980, s. 97(4).

Magistrates' Courts Act 1980, s. 97

(4) If any person attending or brought before a magistrates' court refuses without just excuse to be sworn or give evidence, or to produce any document or thing, the court may commit him to custody until the expiration of such period not exceeding one month as may be specified in the warrant or until he sooner gives evidence or produces the document or thing or impose on him a fine not exceeding £2,500 or both.

Contempt of Court Act 1981, s. 12

(1) A magistrates' court has jurisdiction under this section to deal with any person who—
  (a) wilfully insults the justice or justices, any witness before or officer of the court or any solicitor or counsel having business in the court, during his or their sitting or attendance in court or in going to or returning from the court; or
  (b) wilfully interrupts the proceedings of the court or otherwise misbehaves in court.
(2) In any such case the court may order any officer of the court, or any constable, to take the offender into custody and detain him until the rising of the court; and the court may, if it thinks fit, commit the offender to custody for a specified period not exceeding one month or impose on him a fine not exceeding £2,500, or both.
(2A) A fine imposed under subsection (2) above shall be deemed, for the purposes of any enactment, to be a sum adjudged to be paid by a conviction.
(4) A magistrates' court may at any time revoke an order of committal made under subsection (2) and, if the offender is in custody, order his discharge.
(5) The following provisions of the Magistrates' Courts Act 1980 apply in relation to an order under this section as they apply in relation to a sentence on conviction or finding of guilty of an offence, namely: section 36 (restriction on fines in respect of young persons); sections 75 to 91 (enforcement); section 108 (appeal to Crown Court); section 136 (overnight detention in default of payment); and section 142(1) (power to rectify mistakes).

Section 12, must be strictly construed. Section 12(1)(a) is not applicable in cases where A has uttered threats rather than insults (*Havant Justices, ex parte Palmer* (1985) 149 JP 609, though it is submitted that threats might be charged as 'interruption of the proceedings' or 'misbehaviour' in court under s. 12(1)(b)) and magistrates similarly have no power to deal with indirect or constructive contempts. These may, however, be dealt with by a Divisional Court of the Queen's Bench Division under the Rules of the Supreme Court 1965, ord. 52 (see ord. 52, r. 1(2), discussed in **B14.68**).

Jurisdiction and Procedure: the Crown Court

Although the Crown Court is a superior court of record, the Rules of the Supreme Court **B14.64** 1965, ord. 52, r. 1(2), provides that the Divisional Court of the Queen's Bench Division has exclusive jurisdiction over contempts committed in the course of criminal proceedings, 'except where the contempt is committed in the face of the court, or where it consists of disobedience to an order of the court or a breach of an undertaking to the court'. This would appear at first sight to limit the Crown Court's inherent jurisdiction over contempt to those exceptions, but it does not, because the Supreme Court Act 1981, s. 45(4), provides that the Crown Court has, in relation to contempt, 'the like powers, rights, privileges and authority as the High Court'. The power of the High Court to make an order of its own initiative against a person guilty of contempt is expressly preserved intact by the Rules of the Supreme Court 1965, ord. 52, r. 5, and the Crown Court's power is preserved with it (see **B14.68**).

There is nevertheless some uncertainty as to the type of case in which it might be proper for the Crown Court (or for that matter the High Court) to act of its own motion, without the institution of formal committal proceedings under ord. 52. The question was considered *obiter*, but at length, by the Court of Appeal (Civil Division) in *Balogh* v *St Albans Crown Court* [1975] QB 73. Lord Denning MR and Stephenson LJ rejected suggestions that the Crown Court could properly so act only in respect of contempt committed *in* court, but at the same time stressed that judges should be slow to invoke their powers. As Stephenson LJ said (at pp. 89–90):

> Procedure for contempt by motion under the Rules of the Supreme Court 1965, ord. 52, rr. 1 and 2, might be described as summary, but when a judge of the High Court or Crown Court proceeds of his own motion, the procedure is more summary still. It must never be invoked unless the ends of justice really require such drastic means: it appears to be rough justice; it is contrary to natural justice; and it can only be justified if nothing else will do.

Further guidance has been provided by the Divisional Court in *DPP* v *Channel Four Television Co. Ltd* [1993] 2 All ER 517, in which it was stated that 'sensitive' contempt cases, involving such issues as the duty of a journalist to disclose the source of his information, should invariably be determined by the Divisional Court. Even in less sensitive cases, a trial judge should act of his own motion only where the contempt is clear and affects a trial already in progress or one just about to start. He should satisfy himself that no other procedure would suffice to prevent the obstruction of justice or the integrity of the trial, and he should avoid appearing to be the prosecutor in his own cause; the CPS may take over this role and may in some cases bring proceedings before another judge of the Crown Court. The suggestion that judges should where possible avoid determining contempts against themselves is supported by *Balogh* and by the House of Lords in *Re Lonrho plc* [1990] 2 AC 154.

An example of contempt calling for immediate action is conduct which deliberately disrupts the trial, whether committed inside the courtroom or outside it. In *Morris* v *Crown Office* [1970] 2 QB 114, Welsh language campaigners who physically disrupted a sitting of the High Court were summarily committed to prison for three months, and on appeal Salmon LJ warned that judges might consider sentences of up to six months to be appropriate in any future cases.

The intimidation of witnesses or jurors during the course of a trial, or other forms of interference with them, has also been held to warrant an immediate judicial response. In *Goult* (1982) 76 Cr App R 140, the offender was summarily committed to prison by a Crown Court judge for 18 months (reduced on appeal to nine months) for intimidating jurors, both in and out of court. Lord Lane CJ said (at p. 144):

> ... there is every reason ... for the judge to take the sort of steps which the judge took here ... not only for the question of the dignity of the court, but also for the reassurance of other jurors who would be awaiting their call to duty in the court.

See also *Giscombe* (1983) 79 Cr App R 79.

Various other contempts in the face of the court may require immediate action. These include contempts by witnesses who refuse to be sworn, or who refuse to answer questions, and contempts by jurors.

Where a judge considers summarily imprisoning the alleged contemnor, certain procedural safeguards should be adhered to. In *Moran* (1985) 81 Cr App R 51, Lawton LJ offered the following guidance (at p. 53):

> The following principles should be borne in mind. First, a decision to imprison the man for contempt of court should never be taken too quickly. The judge should give himself time for reflection as to what is the best course to take. Secondly, he should consider whether that time for reflection should not extend to a different day because overnight thoughts are sometimes better than thoughts on the spur of the moment. Thirdly, the judge should consider whether the seeming contemnor should have some advice. We do not accept the proposition which was tentatively put forward on this appeal that this contemnor had a right to legal advice. Sometimes situations arise in court when the judge has to act quickly and to pass such sentence as he thinks appropriate at once; so there cannot be any right to legal advice. Justice does not require a contemnor in the face of the court to have a right to legal advice. But if the circumstances are such that it is possible for the contemnor to have advice, he should be given an opportunity of having it. In practice what usually happens is that somebody gives the contemnor advice. He takes it, apologises to the court and that is the end of the matter. Giving a contemnor an opportunity to apologise is one of the most important aspects of this summary procedure, which in many ways is draconian. If there is a member of the Bar in court who could give advice, a wise judge would ask that member of the Bar if he would be willing to do so. The member of the Bar is entitled to say no, but in practice never does.

See also *Bromell* (1995) *The Times*, 9 February 1995.

Jurisdiction and Procedure: the Divisional Court of the Queen's Bench Division

B14.65   The Divisional Court inherently possesses all the powers of a superior court and may act of its own motion in respect of contempts committed against it; but its more important jurisdiction is under the Rules of the Supreme Court 1965, ord. 52, r. 1(2), in respect of contempts which are committed against lower courts, and which either cannot be dealt with by the court in question (e.g., constructive contempt of an inferior court) or are not suitable for summary punishment by a court acting of its own motion (see *Balogh* v *St Albans Crown Court* [1975] QB 73 and **B14.64**). In particular, contempts in the form of publications prejudicial to current or forthcoming Crown Court trials would ordinarily be dealt with by the Divisional Court: see for example *A-G* v *English* [1983] 1 AC 116. The Rules of the Supreme Court 1965, ord. 52, insofar as it is relevant to contempt of criminal courts, is set out at **B14.68**.

Jurisdiction and Procedure: The Court of Appeal and the House of Lords

B14.66   Contempt of the Court of Appeal may be dealt with either by the court acting of its own motion or by application for committal under the Rules of the Supreme Court 1965, ord. 52. Such an application may be made to the Court of Appeal itself. Order 52, r. 1(2), does not apply. An alleged contempt of the House of Lords is determinable by the House alone (see *Re Lonrho plc* [1990] 2 AC 154).

Jurisdiction and Procedure: Courts Martial

Courts martial are inferior courts, and jurisdiction over contempts in relation to their **B14.67** proceedings may be exercised by the Divisional Court under the Rules of the Supreme Court 1965, ord. 52, r. 1(2); but they themselves possess limited statutory powers to deal with contemptuous witnesses and certain other contempts committed in the face of the court. See the Army Act 1955, ss. 57 and 101, and corresponding provisions in the Air Force Act 1955 and the Naval Discipline Act 1957.

Rules of Court Governing Committal for Contempt

Rules of the Supreme Court 1965, ord. 52   B14.68

Committal for contempt of court
1.—(1)   The power of the High Court or Court of Appeal to punish for contempt of court may be exercised by an order of committal.
    (2)   Where contempt of court—
      (a)   is committed in connection with—
        (i)   any proceedings before a Divisional Court of the Queen's Bench Division, or
        (ii)   criminal proceedings, except where the contempt is committed in the face of the court or consists of disobedience to an order of the court or a breach of an undertaking to the court, or
        (iii)   proceedings in an inferior court,
      (b)   is committed otherwise than in connection with any proceedings,
then . . . an order of committal may be made only by a Divisional Court of the Queen's Bench Division.
    This paragraph shall not apply in relation to contempt of the Court of Appeal.
    (3) and (4)   [Omitted as they deal with the powers of the civil courts.]

Application to Divisional Court
2.—(1)   No application to a Divisional Court for an order of committal against any person may be made unless permission to make such an application has been granted in accordance with this rule.
    (2)   An application for such permission must be made without notice to a Divisional Court, except in vacation when it may be made to a judge in chambers, and must be supported by a statement setting out the name and description of the applicant, the name, description and address of the person sought to be committed and the grounds on which his committal is sought, and by an affidavit, to be filed before the application is made, verifying the facts relied on.
    (3)   The applicant must give notice of the application for permission not later than the preceding day to the Crown Office and must at the same time lodge in that office copies of the statement and affidavit.
    (4)   Where an application for permission under this rule is refused by a judge in chambers, the applicant may make a fresh application for such permission to a Divisional Court.
    (5)   An application made to a Divisional Court by virtue of paragraph (4) must be made within eight days after the judge's refusal to give permission or, if a Divisional Court does not sit within that period, on the first day on which it sits thereafter.

Application for order after leave to apply granted
3.—(1)   When permission has been granted under rule 2 to apply for an order of committal, the application for the order must be made by motion to a Divisional Court and, unless the court or judge granting permission has otherwise directed, there must be at least eight clear days between the service of the notice of motion and the day named therein for the hearing.

(2)   Unless within 14 days after such permission was granted the claim form is issued the permission shall lapse.

(3)   Subject to paragraph (4), the claim form, accompanied by a copy of the statement and affidavit in support of the application for permission, must be served personally on the person sought to be committed.

(4)   Without prejudice to the powers of the court or judge under part 6 of the CPR, the court or judge may dispense with service under this rule if it or he thinks it just to do so.

Application to court other than Divisional Court
4.—(1)   Where an application for an order of committal may be made to a court other than a Divisional Court, the application must be made by motion and be supported by an affidavit.

(2)   Subject to paragraph (3), the notice of motion, stating the grounds of the application and accompanied by a copy of the affidavit in support of the application, must be served personally on the person sought to be committed.

(3)   Without prejudice to its powers under part 6 of the CPR, the court may dispense with service under this rule if it thinks it just to do so.

(4)   This rules does not apply to committal applications which under rules 1(2) and 3(1) should be made to a Divisional Court but which, in vacation, have been properly made to a single judge in accordance with RSC Order 64, rule 4.

Saving for power to commit without application for purpose
5.   Nothing in the foregoing provisions of this order shall be taken as affecting the power of the High Court or Court of Appeal to make an order of committal of its own initiative against a person guilty of contempt of court.

Provisions as to hearing
6.—(1)   Subject to paragraph (2), the court hearing an application for an order of committal may sit in private in the following cases, that is to say—

(a)   where the application arises out of proceedings relating to the wardship or adoption of an infant or wholly or mainly to the guardianship, custody, maintenance or upbringing of an infant, or rights of access to an infant;

(b)   where the application arises out of proceedings relating to a person suffering or appearing to be suffering from mental discorder within the meaning of the Mental Health Act 1983;

(c)   where the application arises out of proceedings in which a secret process, discovery or invention was in issue;

(d)   where it appears to the court that in the interests of the administration of justice or for reasons of national security the application should be heard in private;
but, except as aforesaid, the application shall be heard in open court.

(2)   If the court hearing an application in private by virtue of paragraph (1) decides to make an order of committal against the person sought to be committed, it shall in open court state—

(a)   the name of that person,

(b)   in general terms the nature of the contempt of court in respect of which the order of committal is being made, and

(c)   the length of the period for which he is being committed.

(3)   Except with the leave of the court hearing an application for an order of committal, no grounds shall be relied upon at the hearing except the grounds set out in the statement under rule 2 or, as the case may be, in the claim form or application notice under rule 4.

(4)   If on the hearing of the application the person sought to be committed expresses a wish to give oral evidence on his own behalf, he shall be entitled to do so.

Power to suspend execution of committal order
7.—(1)   The court by whom an order of committal is made may by order direct that the execution of the order of committal shall be suspended for such period or on such terms or conditions as it may specify.

(2)   Where execution of an order of committal is suspended by an order under paragraph (1), the applicant for the order of committal must, unless the court otherwise directs, serve on the person against whom it was made a notice informing him of the making and terms of the order under that paragraph.

Discharge of person committed
8.—(1)   The court may, on the application of any person committed to prison for any contempt of court, discharge him.

(2)   [Deals with sequestration.]

Saving for other powers
9.   Nothing in the foregoing provisions of this order shall be taken as affecting the power of the court to make an order requiring a person guilty of contempt of court, or a person punishable by virtue of any enactment in like manner as if he had been guilty of contempt of the High Court, to pay a fine or to give security for his good behaviour, and those provisions, so far as applicable, and with the necessary modifications, shall apply in relation to an application for such an order as they apply in relation to an application for an order of committal.

Penalties for Contempt

The maximum penalties which may be imposed for contempt of court are now governed **B14.69** by the Contempt of Court Act 1981, s. 14.

Contempt of Court Act 1981, s. 14

(1)   In any case where a court has power to commit a person to prison for contempt of court and (apart from this provision) no limitation applies to the period of committal, the committal shall (without prejudice to the power of the court to order his earlier discharge) be for a fixed term, and that term shall not on any occasion exceed two years in the case of committal by a superior court, or one month in the case of committal by an inferior court.

(2)   In any case where an inferior court has power to fine a person for contempt of court and (apart from this provision) no limit applies to the amount of the fine, the fine shall not on any occasion exceed £2,500.

(2A)   In the exercise of jurisdiction to commit for contempt of court or any kindred offence the court shall not deal with the offender by making an order under section 17 of the Criminal Justice Act 1982 (an attendance centre order) if it appears to the court, after considering any available evidence, that he is under 17 years of age.

(2A)   A fine imposed under subsection (2) above shall be deemed, for the purposes of any enactment, to be a sum adjudged to be paid by a conviction.

(4)   Each of the superior courts shall have the like power to make a hospital order or guardianship order under section 37 of the Mental Health Act 1983 or an interim hospital order under section 38 of that Act in the case of a person suffering from mental illness or severe mental impairment who could otherwise be committed to prison for contempt of court as the Crown Court has under that section in the case of a person convicted of an offence.

(4A)   Each of the superior courts shall have the like power to make an order under section 35 of the said Act of 1983 (remand for report on accused's mental condition) where there is reason to suspect that a person who could be committed to prison for contempt of court is suffering from mental illness or severe mental impairment as the Crown Court has under that section in the case of an accused person within the meaning of the section.

(4A)   For the purposes of the preceding provisions of this section a county court shall be treated as a superior court and not as an inferior court.

(By oversight there are now *two* subsections numbered 2A and *two* numbered 4A.)

As to the maximum penalties which may be imposed by magistrates' courts, see **B14.63**.

There is no power to impose a custodial sentence on an offender under the age of 18 for contempt of court (CJA 1982, s. 1(1); *Byas* (1995) 16 Cr App R (S) 869). For offenders aged between 18 and 20 inclusive, detention may be ordered where appropriate under s. 9 of the 1982 Act (see further **E17.2**). Courts dealing with persons who are found guilty of criminal contempt have no power to make probation orders (*Palmer* [1992] 1 WLR 568).

Sentencing Guidelines: Contempts Amounting to Other Offences

B14.70 Where the same conduct can amount both to contempt of court and to a more specific statutory offence (as is the case with deliberate non-attendance by a person summoned as a witness), the courts must have some regard to the maximum penalty in respect of the statutory offence when considering a possible penalty for contempt, but they are not bound by any such maximum if there are aggravating features (*Montgomery* [1995] 2 Cr App R 23).

Imprisonment without Legal Representation

B14.71 The PCCA 1973, s. 21, which generally prohibits the imprisonment of legally unrepresented persons, does not apply in cases of committal for contempt (*Newbury Justices, ex parte Pont* (1984) 78 Cr App R 255); but see the observation of the court in *Moran* (1985) 81 Cr App R 51 as to the wisdom of making advice available (**B14.64**).

Forms of Contempt: Intimidation of or Interference with or Retaliation against Witnesses or Jurors

B14.72 Any attempt to interfere with jurors or witnesses, whether by way of intimidation, bribery or persuasion, may be punished as contempt at common law, and may also amount to perverting the course of justice. This principle extends not only to litigants and members of the public but also to court officials and jury bailiffs, who should avoid any discussion of cases with jurors (*Mickleburgh* [1995] 1 Cr App R 297). The offence of witness or jury intimidation, created by the CJPO 1994, s. 51, will operate in addition to, rather than in derogation of, the common law (see **B14.34**).

Intimidation or harassment of former witnesses or jurors, or retaliation against them, is an equally serious matter (*A-G v Judd* [1995] COD 15). Although the original trial may be over, it is essential that former witnesses or jurors are protected, so that they will not be afraid to do their duty (*A-G v Butterworth* [1963] 1 QB 696).

In *Connolly v Dale* [1996] QB 120, a police inspector was found to be in contempt for obstructing attempts by an accused person's enquiry agent to obtain alibi evidence on behalf of his client, and for threatening him with prosecution under what is now the Police Act 1996, s. 89(2). This was despite the fact that the officer had acted in good faith, for the purpose, as he saw it, of preventing the contamination of identification evidence.

Sentencing Guidelines

B14.73 In *Maloney* (1986) 8 Cr App R (S) 123 the offender's brother was on trial for burglary and the offender walked past a witness who was waiting to give evidence and said: 'You're in for a seeing to.' A sentence of six months' detention was upheld. Farquharson J said: 'It cannot be overemphasised how seriously this kind of interference or attempted interference with witnesses will be regarded by the courts'. Six months' imprisonment was upheld in *Bryan* [1998] 2 Cr App R (S) 109, where the offender, the brother of a man on trial for murder, mouthed threatening words from the public gallery at a witness giving evidence in the case. See also *Stredder* [1997] 1 Cr App R (S) 209, where 12 months' imprisonment was upheld in a case where the offender, who was about to stand trial for theft, approached the sole prosecution witness in the court building, referred to damage which had been done to the witness's car, and said 'that was just a warning'.

Comparable sentences have been upheld by the Court of Appeal in respect of attempts to influence jurors. A sentence of 18 months was reduced to nine months in *Goult* (1982) 4 Cr App R (S) 355 where the offender intimidated women jurors by staring at them in a threatening manner and driving past them slowly in his car so that they felt frightened.

Exceptionally, the maximum sentence of two years was upheld in *James* (1988) 10 Cr App R (S) 392 where the offender, a friend of the man on trial, threatened a witness with violence to persuade him to give false evidence. According to Kennedy J: 'This seems to us to have been a very serious contempt committed within the precincts of the court upon a man who was clearly susceptible to precisely the kind of threats which were made to him'.

Forms of Contempt: Disruption of Proceedings and Misbehaviour in Court

A deliberate disruption of proceedings in court, whether staged by persons involved in **B14.74** those proceedings, or by demonstrators etc. may be punished as contempt, and in most cases will be dealt with by the court acting of its own motion. The same is true of misconduct, such as wolfwhistling at female jurors or witnesses (see *Powell* (1993) 98 Cr App R 224), and of assaults on court officials whilst they are engaged in the administration of justice (*Re de Court* (1997) *The Times*, 27 November 1997). Whether noisy protests from the public gallery following conviction or sentence are so serious as to amount to contempt is a matter which the trial court or judge is usually best placed to decide, but in many cases the best way of dealing with it may be for the judge to rise, and let the disturbance subside (*Lewis* (1999) *The Times*, 4 November 1999).

Sentencing Guidelines

In *McDaniel* (1990) 12 Cr App R (S) 44, the offender was aged 31 and had minor **B14.75** previous convictions. He attended the trial of his brother at the Crown Court where he and others had been warned about noisy conversations during the proceedings. When his brother was convicted and sentenced there was a general commotion during which the offender called the judge 'a dog'. A sentence of three months' imprisonment for addressing such personal abuse to the judge was reduced on appeal to 14 days. See also *Lewis* (1999) *The Times*, 4 November 1999.

Forms of Contempt: Committed by Witnesses or Jurors

A witness who refuses to be sworn, or who refuses to produce documents or answer **B14.76** questions properly put to him, will ordinarily be in contempt of court. In *Wicks* (31 January 1995 unreported), the Court of Appeal emphasised that witnesses who have been threatened are not thereby excused from giving evidence. As to the position of journalists who wish to protect their sources of information, special provision is made by the Contempt of Court Act 1981, s. 10 (see **B14.85**).

Jurors may be punished for contempt if they refuse or fail to discharge their obligations in accordance with the jury oath (*Schot* [1997] 2 Cr App R 383).

Sentencing Guidelines

Detailed guidance on sentencing for contempt where a witness refuses to give evidence **B14.77** has been provided by the Court of Appeal in *Phillips* (1983) 5 Cr App R (S) 297 and in *Montgomery* [1995] 2 Cr App R 23. In the former case, a prosecution witness at a murder trial refused to give evidence, but his evidence was not crucial to the case. A committal to prison for four months was varied by the Court of Appeal to 14 days. In the latter case a sentence of 12 months' imprisonment for failure to attend court and persistent refusal to testify or explain the refusal was reduced to three months. It emerges from these decisions that, in the absence of wholly exceptional circumstances, an immediate custodial sentence is appropriate for a refusal to testify, but that the sentence will often be shorter than that imposed in a case of interference with a witness or juror. The principal matters affecting sentence are the gravity of the offence being tried, the extent to which the failure to testify affected the course of the trial, whether the refusal was aggravated by defiance or impertinence to the judge, the antecedents and personal circumstances of the contemnor, and whether a special deterrent is needed (such as where it becomes clear that there has been systematic intimidation of witnesses to prevent their giving evidence). The contemnor should normally be sentenced at the end of the trial, or at least at the end of the prosecution case, to allow him time to reconsider his position. See also *Cole* [1997] 1 Cr App R (S) 228.

Forms of Contempt: Contempt by Advocates

B14.78　An advocate who deliberately fails to attend a hearing with intent to hinder or delay the course of justice would be guilty of contempt (*Weston* v *Central Criminal Court Courts Administrator* [1977] QB 32). It could also be a contempt to persist in adducing inadmissible evidence, or in a forbidden line of questioning, or generally to disobey or disregard orders of the court or to treat the court with gross disrespect. It is not, however, contempt to do whatever is ethically and professionally appropriate to provide a client with zealous representation, even if this brings the advocate into conflict with the court for such is his duty.

Forms of Contempt: Conduct or Publication Scandalising the Court

B14.79　The courts must be slow to hold that criticism of judges or of the court system itself can amount to contempt, however outspoken or intemperate it may be (*Editor of the New Statesman, ex parte DPP* (1928) 44 TLR 301; *Metropolitan Police Commissioner, ex parte Blackburn (No. 2)* [1968] 2 QB 150); but it may be contempt if it uses scurrilous abuse to discredit the judge or the judicial system (*Gray* [1900] 2 QB 36).

Forms of Contempt: Publication Prejudicial to the Administration of Justice

B14.80　This is one of the most important and complex varieties of contempt. Prejudice may be caused, *inter alia*, by revealing matters which might be inadmissible in evidence, and which may influence jurors etc. (as in *Clarke, ex parte Crippen* (1910) 103 LT 636 and *Parke* [1903] 2 KB 432); by sensational and misleading coverage of a trial (see the comments of McCowan LJ in *Taylor* (1993) 98 Cr App R 361); by commenting on the merits of the case or prejudging it (see *Hutchison, ex parte McMahon* [1936] 2 All ER 1514); or by publicly disclosing sensitive material that was subject to a court order restricting such disclosure, even where the order was addressed to another (*A-G* v *Newspaper Publishing plc* [1997] 1 WLR 926). Newspapers and other publishers may also commit contempt where they make payments to witnesses on terms which may encourage perjured evidence, or seek to pressurise litigants into abandoning their actions (see *A-G* v *Hislop* [1991] 1 QB 514). Publication of material by one person, when another person has already been served with an injunction prohibiting disclosure of that material pending trial of the issue of its confidentiality, may be a criminal contempt by the publisher because it destroys the subject-matter of the dispute (*A-G* v *Times Newspapers Ltd* [1992] 1 AC 191).

Publication of material capable of prejudicing or impeding forthcoming legal proceedings does not necessarily amount to contempt. If the proceedings in question are not 'active' within the meaning of the Contempt of Court Act 1981 (see **B14.91**) or if there is no substantial risk of serious prejudice at the time of publication, then publication amounts to contempt only if there is proof of an intent to interfere with the course of justice in those proceedings. Recklessness or negligence will not suffice (*A-G* v *News Group Newspapers plc* [1989] QB 110; *A-G* v *Newspaper Publishing plc*). Where there is a substantial risk of serious prejudice to active proceedings, liability may be strict, but subject to certain defences (see generally **B14.90** to **B14.97**).

According to the Divisional Court in *A-G* v *News Group Newspapers plc*, publications which deliberately set out to prejudice possible future legal proceedings, and which do in fact create a real risk of such prejudice, may constitute contempt, even where those proceedings were not even imminent at the time of publication (e.g., where nothing had yet been done to instigate them). The case involved a highly prejudicial campaign run by the *Sun* newspaper with a view to ensuring that a doctor accused of raping a child would in due course be prosecuted. Watkins LJ acknowledged that this decision represented an extension of the law, but argued that the common law was 'a living body of law capable of adaption and expansion to meet fresh needs'. Doubts have subsequently been expressed as to the correctness of this view, which could be seen as a threat to investigative journalism. In *A-G v Sport Newspapers Ltd* [1991] 1 WLR 1194, a differently constituted Divisional Court held that material published by the *Sport* concerning a suspect in a murder inquiry did not amount to intentional interference in the course of justice, but Hodgson J went on to state (*obiter*) that *News Group Newspapers* was wrongly decided, and it seems that Bingham LJ would have been prepared to follow it only on the basis that he considered it wrong to depart from such a recent precedent.

Sentencing Guidelines

In *A-G v News Group Newspapers Ltd* (1984) 6 Cr App R (S) 418 the Divisional Court **B14.81** dealt with a case where a newspaper had published, during the course of a trial, a picture of one of two defendants on trial for causing injury to their baby, with the headline: 'Baby was blinded by dad'. This statement was wholly misleading. The newspaper subsequently apologised and the court accepted that the contempt was not deliberate. According to Stephen Brown LJ (at p. 420):

> We are bound to say that this newspaper headline and photograph greatly surprised us and gravely disturbed us. It is fortunate indeed that the trial was not interrupted but it has to be made plain that there is a strict duty of care placed upon those who publish news items relating to trials to see that they do not run the risk of interfering with the course of justice. There was a clear and grave risk of that in this case.

> Taking into account all the facts, bearing in mind the nature of the apology, and bearing in mind the fact that it was not intentional but nevertheless a serious contempt, the order of this court is that the respondents be fined the sum of £5,000.

Forms of Contempt: Disclosures Relating to Jury Deliberations

Contempt of Court Act 1981, s. 8   B14.82

(1) Subject to subsection (2) below, it is a contempt of court to obtain, disclose or solicit any particulars of statements made, opinions expressed, arguments advanced or votes cast by members of a jury in the course of their deliberations in any legal proceedings.

(2) This section does not apply to any disclosure of any particulars—

(a) in the proceedings in question for the purpose of enabling the jury to arrive at their verdict, or in connection with the delivery of that verdict, or

(b) in evidence in any subsequent proceedings for an offence alleged to have been committed in relation to the jury in the first mentioned proceedings,

or to the publication of any particulars so disclosed.

(3) Proceedings for a contempt of court under this section (other than Scottish proceedings) shall not be instituted except by or with the consent of the Attorney-General or on the motion of a court having jurisdiction to deal with it.

This provision was enacted following the failure of the prosecution in *A-G v New Statesman and Nation Publishing Co. Ltd* [1981] QB 1. The contempt may be committed both by jurors and by a person who further discloses or publishes the information he has been given (see *A-G v Associated Newspapers Ltd* [1994] 2 AC 238). In *Mickleburgh* [1995] 1 Cr App R 297, Lord Taylor CJ warned that defence solicitors who take statements from former jurors, or make enquiries of former jurors, run a grave risk of being in contempt of court under s. 8, unless they first obtain leave from the Court of Appeal. Similar advice was given by Henry J in *McGlusky* (1993) 98 Cr App R 223.

Forms of Contempt: Misuse of Tape Recorders In Court

Contempt of Court Act 1981, s. 9   B14.83

(1) Subject to subsection (4) below, it is a contempt of court—

(a)   to use in court, or bring into court for use, any tape recorder or other instrument for recording sound, except with the leave of the court;

(b)   to publish a recording of legal proceedings made by means of any such instrument, or any recording derived directly or indirectly from it, by playing it in the hearing of the public or any section of the public, or to dispose of it or any recording so derived, with a view to such publication;

(c)   to use any such recording in contravention of any conditions of leave granted under paragraph (a).

(2)   Leave under paragraph (a) of subsection (1) may be granted or refused at the discretion of the court, and if granted may be granted subject to such conditions as the court thinks proper with respect to the use of any recording made pursuant to the leave; and where leave has been granted the court may at the like discretion withdraw or amend it either generally or in relation to any particular part of the proceedings.

(3)   Without prejudice to any other power to deal with an act of contempt under paragraph (a) of subsection (1), the court may order the instrument, or any recording made with it, or both, to be forfeited; and any object so forfeited shall (unless the court otherwise determines on application by a person appearing to be the owner) be sold or otherwise disposed of in such manner as the court may direct.

(4)   This section does not apply to the making or use of sound recordings for purposes of official transcripts of proceedings.

In a *Practice Direction (Tape Recorders)* [1981] 1 WLR 1526, Lord Lane CJ noted the terms of s. 9 and issued the following guidance on the granting of leave to make recordings:

> The discretion given to the court to grant, withhold or withdraw leave to use tape recorders or to impose conditions as to the use of the recording is unlimited, but the following factors may be relevant to its exercise: (a) the existence of any reasonable need on the part of the Iapplicant for leave, whether a litigant or a person connected with the press or broadcasting, for the recording to be made; (b) in a criminal case, or a civil case in which a direction has been given excluding one or more witnesses from the court, the risk that the recording could be used for the purpose of briefing witnesses out of court; (c) any possibility that the use of a recorder would disturb the proceedings or distract or worry any witnesses or other participants.

> Consideration should always be given whether conditions as to the use of a recording made pursuant to leave should be imposed. The identity and role of the applicant for leave and the nature of the subject-matter of the proceedings may be relevant to this.

> The particular restriction imposed by section 9(1)(b) [of the Contempt of Court Act 1981] applies in every case, but may not be present to the mind of every applicant to whom leave is given. It may, therefore, be desirable on occasion for this provision to be drawn to the attention of those to whom leave is given.

> The transcript of a permitted re cording is intended for the use of the person given leave to make it and is not intended to be used as, or to compete with, the official transcript mentioned in section 9(4) [of the 1981 Act].

Forms of Contempt: Photography and Sketching etc. in Court

B14.84   The taking of photographs in court, or the publication of such photographs, is sometimes punished as contempt (see *The Times*, 15 July 1986), but may also be punished as a summary offence (carrying a level 3 fine) under the CJA 1925, s. 41, which also deals with sketches. It is an offence under s. 41(1) to:

(a)   take or attempt to take in any court any photograph, or with a view to publication make or attempt to make in any court any portrait or sketch of any person, being a judge of the court or a juror or a witness in or a party to any proceedings before the court, whether civil or criminal; or

(b)   publish any photograph, portrait or sketch taken or made in contravention of the foregoing provisions of this section or any reproduction thereof.

'Judge' includes a registrar, magistrate, justice and coroner (s. 41(2)(a)). Photography in the precincts of the court building is also covered (s. 41(2)(c)). The publication of sketches drawn from memory once outside the court is not prohibited.

Forms of Contempt: Refusal to Disclose Sources of Published Information

A journalist or other person who refuses to disclose the source of information he has **B14.85** published may be in contempt of court, but regard must be had to the Contempt of Court Act 1981, s. 10, which provides:

> No court may require a person to disclose, nor is any person guilty of contempt of court for refusing to disclose, the source of information contained in a publication for which he is responsible, unless it be established to the satisfaction of the court that disclosure is necessary in the interests of justice or national security or for the prevention of disorder or crime.

In order to satisfy the court of the necessity of disclosure, proof is required, on balance of probabilities; it is not enough merely to assert the need (see *Secretary of State for Defence* v *Guardian Newspapers Ltd* [1985] AC 339). Nor is convenience the same thing as necessity; but necessity is a relative concept, and may be something less than absolute indispensability (*Re an Inquiry under the Company Securities (Insider Dealing) Act 1985* [1988] AC 660). 'Prevention of crime' includes the general control of crime and not just the prevention of specific acts (*Re an Inquiry under the Company Securities (Insider Dealing) Act 1985*). See generally **F9.7**.

Forms of Contempt: Breaches of Reporting Restrictions on Cases Heard in Public

Deliberate (or perhaps reckless) breach of reporting restrictions imposed under the **B14.86** Contempt of Court Act 1981, s. 4 (see **D2.52**) would appear to be a form of statutory contempt, whether or not any real risk of prejudice is involved. See generally *Horsham Justices, ex parte Farquharson* [1982] QB 762.

In *Practice Direction (Contempt: Reporting Restrictions)* [1982] 1 WLR 1475, Lord Lane CJ said:

> It is necessary to keep a permanent record of such orders for later reference. For this purpose all orders made under s. 4(2) [of the Contempt of Court Act 1981] must be formulated in precise terms, having regard to the decision of *Horsham Justices, ex parte Farquharson* [1982] QB 762, and orders under both sections [i.e. s. 4(2) and s. 11 of the 1981 Act] must be committed to writing either by the judge personally or by the clerk of the court under the judge's directions. An order must state (a) its precise scope, (b) the time at which it shall cease to have effect, if appropriate, and (c) the specific purpose of making the order.

> Courts will normally give notice to the press in some form that an order has been made under either section of the [Contempt of Court Act 1981] and court staff should be prepared to answer any inquiry about a specific case, but it is and will remain, the responsibility of those reporting cases, and their editors, to ensure that no breach of any order occurs and the onus rests with them to make inquiry in any case of doubt.

As to reporting restrictions generally, see **D2.52**; as to restrictions on the reporting of committal proceedings, see **D7.16**.

Forms of Contempt: Publication of Matter Exempted from Disclosure in Court

Contempt of Court Act 1981, s. 11 **B14.87**

> In any case where a court (having power to do so) allows a name or other matter to be withheld from the public in proceedings before the court, the court may give such directions prohibiting the publication of that name or matter in connection with the proceedings as appear to the court to be necessary for the purpose for which it was so withheld.

See the *Practice Direction (Contempt: Reporting Restrictions)* [1982] 1 WLR 1475 (at **B14.86**). Breach of the order could (as with breaches of orders under the Contempt of Court Act 1981, s. 4), constitute a statutory contempt. As to the principles of 'open justice', see **D2.47 to D2.56**.

The power to make such an order must not be used merely 'for the benefit of the comfort and feelings of defendants' as by safeguarding them from unwanted publicity or molestation (*Evesham Justices, ex parte McDonagh* [1988] QB 553). It is properly employed to safeguard the identity of children and young persons, complainants in rape cases, witnesses who might later be exposed to violence or blackmail, or revelation of whose identity might prejudice national security.

It may be necessary for a court to sit in camera when hearing evidence in support of an application under the Contempt of Court Act 1981, s. 11 (*Tower Bridge Magistrates' Court, ex parte Osbourne* (1989) 88 Cr App R 28).

Forms of Contempt: Publications Relating to Proceedings in Camera

B14.88 **Administration of Justice Act 1960, s. 12**

(1)   The publication of information relating to proceedings before any court sitting in private shall not of itself be contempt of court except in the following cases, that is to say—
  (a)   where the proceedings—
    (i)   relate to the exercise of the inherent jurisdiction of the High Court with respect to minors;
    (ii)   are brought under the Children Act 1989; or
    (iii)   otherwise relate wholly or mainly to the maintenance or upbringing of a minor;
  (b)   where the proceedings are brought under part VIII of the Mental Health Act 1959, or under any provision of that Act authorising an application or reference to be made to a Mental Health Review Tribunal or to a county court;
  (c)   where the court sits in private for reasons of national security during that part of the proceedings about which the information in question is published;
  (d)   where the information relates to a secret process, discovery or invention which is in issue in the proceedings;
  (e)   where the court (having power to do so) expressly prohibits the publication of all information relating to the proceedings or of information of the description which is published.
(2)   Without prejudice to the foregoing subsection, the publication of the text or a summary of the whole or part of an order made by a court sitting in private shall not of itself be contempt of court except where the court (having power to do so) expressly prohibits the publication.
(3)   In this section references to a court include references to a judge and to a tribunal and to any person exercising the functions of a court, a judge or a tribunal; and references to a court sitting in private include references to a court sitting in camera or in chambers.
(4)   Nothing in this section shall be construed as implying that any publication is punishable as contempt of court which would not be so punishable apart from this section.

In *P* v *Liverpool Daily Post and Echo Newspapers plc* [1991] 2 AC 370, the House of Lords held that nothing in s. 12(1) prohibits publication of the fact that a court or tribunal is to sit etc., nor does it prohibit the naming of a person involved (but see **B14.87**).

Attempted Contempt

B14.89 Criminal contempt can take the form either of conduct which is intended to interfere with the course of justice, or of conduct which tends to have that effect. It is not therefore essential that any real harm is done. If the intent is proved, the measures adopted may be hopelessly ineffective (*Castro, Skipworth's and the Defendant's Case* (1873) LR 9 QB 230), and if the tendency is proved, there may sometimes be an element of strict liability, although this is now largely confined to certain publications (see **B14.91**).

This leaves little scope for offences of attempted contempt, but one could have a case in which a person fails, not only to interfere with the proceedings, but to perform the act by which he intends so to do. An example of such a case is *Balogh* v *St Albans Crown Court* [1975] QB 73, where Balogh intended to disrupt a trial by pumping laughing-gas into the court-room, but was arrested before he could do so. Doubts were expressed by Stephenson LJ about the very existence of any crime of attempted contempt, but Balogh had not in any case got beyond the stage of mere preparation, and the doubts were left unresolved. It is submitted that there are no compelling reasons for denying the existence of that offence (see the judgment of Lord Denning MR), but the problem will seldom arise in practice.

Mens Rea

It has been recognised that *mens rea* in criminal contempt cases is something of a **B14.90** minefield, owing to the piecemeal development of the common-law offence, and the lack of codification (see the observations of Lord Donaldson MR in *A-G* v *Newspaper Publishing plc* [1988] Ch 333 at p. 373).

At common law, some forms of contempt carried strict liability. Thus, in *Odhams Press Ltd, ex parte A-G* [1957] 1 QB 73, Odhams Press was held to be guilty of contempt for publishing an article which tended to prejudice the course of justice in a forthcoming trial, even though it was not informed that the trial was forthcoming, and was not even proved to have been reckless as to the possibility. This rule seems to have been confined in practice to publication cases (see *A-G* v *English* [1983] 1 AC 116 per Lord Diplock at p. 141), and insofar as interference with the course of justice in 'particular proceedings' is concerned, it is now expressly so confined by ss. 1 and 2 of the Contempt of Court Act 1981, which indeed limit its application more tightly still (see **B14.91**).

This leaves two further issues to be considered. First, whether strict liability can still apply in any areas not covered by the Contempt of Court Act 1981; and secondly, whether anything less than a specific intent may suffice where strict liability is excluded under the Act. These issues are considered at **B14.96** and **B14.97** respectively.

Strict Liability: the Contempt of Court Act 1981

Contempt of Court Act 1981, ss. 1 and 2 and sch. 1   **B14.91**

The strict liability rule
1. In this Act 'the strict liability rule' means the rule of law whereby conduct may be treated as a contempt of court as tending to interfere with the course of justice in particular legal proceedings regardless of intent to do so.

Limitation of scope of strict liability
2.—(1) The strict liability rule applies only in relation to publications, and for this purpose 'publication' includes any speech, writing, broadcast cable programme or other communication in whatever form, which is addressed to the public at large or any section of the public.
    (2) The strict liability rule applies only to a publication which creates a substantial risk that the course of justice in the proceedings in question will be seriously impeded or prejudiced.
    (3) The strict liability rule applies to a publication only if the proceedings in question are active within the meaning of this section at the time of the publication.
    (4) Schedule 1 applies for determining the times at which proceedings are to be treated as active within the meaning of this section.

SCHEDULE 1

TIMES WHEN PROCEEDINGS ARE ACTIVE FOR PURPOSES OF SECTION 2

Preliminary

    1. In this schedule 'criminal proceedings' means proceedings against a person in respect of an offence, not being appellate proceedings or proceedings commenced by motion for committal or attachment in England and Wales or Northern Ireland; and 'appellate

proceedings' means proceedings on appeal from or for the review of the decision of a court in any proceedings.

2. Criminal, appellate and other proceedings are active within the meaning of section 2 at the times respectively prescribed by the following paragraphs of this schedule; and in relation to proceedings in which more than one of the steps described in any of those paragraphs is taken, the reference in that paragraph is a reference to the first of those steps.

Criminal proceedings

3. Subject to the following provisions of this schedule, criminal proceedings are active from the relevant initial step specified in paragraph 4 until concluded as described in paragraph 5.

4. The initial steps of criminal proceedings are:—
   (a)   arrest without warrant;
   (b)   the issue, or in Scotland the grant, of a warrant for arrest;
   (c)   the issue of a summons to appear; [or in Scotland the grant of a warrant to cite;]
   (d)   the service of an indictment or other document specifying the charge;
   (e)   except in Scotland, oral charge.

5. Criminal proceedings are concluded—
   (a)   by acquittal or, as the case may be, by sentence;
   (b)   by any other verdict, finding, order or decision which puts an end to the proceedings;
   (c)   by discontinuance or by operation of law.

6. The reference in paragraph 5(a) to sentence includes any order or decision consequent on conviction or finding of guilt which disposes of the case, either absolutely or subject to future events, and a deferment of sentence under section 1 of the Powers of Criminal Courts Act 1973, section 202 of the Criminal Procedure (Scotland) Act 1995 or Article 14 of the Treatment of Offenders (Northern Ireland) Order 1976.

7. Proceedings are discontinued within the meaning of paragraph 5(c)—
   (a)   in England and Wales or Northern Ireland, if the charge or summons is withdrawn or a *nolle prosequi* entered;
   (aa)   in England and Wales, if they are discontinued by virtue of section 23 of the Prosecution of Offences Act 1985;
   (b)   in Scotland, if the proceedings are expressly abandoned by the prosecutor or are deserted *simpliciter*;
   (c)   in the case of proceedings in England and Wales or Northern Ireland commenced by arrest without warrant, if the person arrested is released, otherwise than on bail, without having been charged.

8. Criminal proceedings before a court-martial or standing civilian court are not concluded until the completion of any review of finding or sentence.

9. Criminal proceedings in England and Wales or Northern Ireland cease to be active if an order is made for the charge to lie on the file, but become active again if leave is later given for the proceedings to continue.

9A. Where proceedings in England and Wales have been discontinued by virtue of section 23 of the Prosecution of Offences Act 1985, but notice is given by the accused under subsection (7) of that section to the effect that he wants the proceedings to continue, they become active again with the giving of that notice.

10. Without prejudice to paragraph 5(b) above, criminal proceedings against a person cease to be active—
   (a)   if the accused is found to be under a disability such as to render him unfit to be tried or unfit to plead or, in Scotland, is found to be insane in bar of trial; or
   (b)   if a hospital order is made in his case under section 51(5) of the Mental Health Act 1983 or Article 57(5) of the Mental Health (Northern Ireland) Order 1986 or, in Scotland, where a transfer order ceases to have effect by virtue of section 73(1) of the Mental Health (Scotland) Act 1984,
but become active again if they are later resumed.

11.   Criminal proceedings against a person which become active on the issue or the grant of a warrant for his arrest cease to be active at the end of the period of 12 months beginning with the date of the warrant unless he has been arrested within that period, but become active again if he is subsequently arrested.

Other proceedings at first instance

12.   Proceedings other than criminal proceedings and appellate proceedings are active from the time when arrangements for the hearing are made or, if no such arrangements are previously made, from the time the hearing begins, until the proceedings are disposed of or discontinued or withdrawn; and for the purposes of this paragraph any motion or application made in or for the purposes of any proceedings, and any pre-trial review in the county court, is to be treated as a distinct proceeding.

13.   In England and Wales or Northern Ireland arrangements for the hearing of proceedings to which paragraph 12 applies are made within the meaning of that paragraph—
(a)   in the case of proceedings in the High Court for which provision is made by rules of court for setting down for trial, when the case is set down;
(b)   in the case of any proceedings, when a date for the trial or hearing is fixed.

14.   In Scotland arrangements for the hearing of proceedings to which paragraph 12 applies are made within the meaning of that paragraph—
(a)   in the case of an ordinary action in the Court of Session or in the sheriff court, when the record is closed;
(b)   in the case of a motion or application, when it is enrolled or made;
(c)   in any other case, when the date for a hearing is fixed or a hearing is allowed.

Appellate proceedings

15.   Appellate proceedings are active from the time when they are commenced—
(a)   by application for leave to appeal or apply for review, or by notice of such an application;
(b)   by notice of appeal or of application for review;
(c)   by other originating process,
until disposed of or abandoned, discontinued or withdrawn.

16.   Where, in appellate proceedings relating to criminal proceedings, the court—
(a)   remits the case to the court below; or
(b)   orders a new trial or a *venire de novo*, or in Scotland grants authority to bring a new prosecution,
any further or new proceedings which result shall be treated as active from the conclusion of the appellate proceedings.

Prior to the enactment of these provisions, it had been held that the prejudging of court proceedings was necessarily contempt (see e.g., *A-G* v *Times Newspapers Ltd* [1974] AC 273), and this is still true of publications which create a real risk of prejudicing a fair trial and which are intended to influence jurors, to dissuade one of the parties from contesting the case, or otherwise to interfere with the proceedings (*A-G* v *Hislop* [1991] 1 QB 514); but in the absence of proof of such intent, it would have to be proved that the prejudgment or other comment created a substantial risk of serious prejudice etc. in respect of active proceedings (as defined in sch. 1). Strict liability will then apply, subject to qualifications and defences contained or preserved within the Contempt of Court Act 1981, ss. 3 to 5 (**B14.92**).

The question whether a publication creates a substantial risk of serious prejudice etc. is ultimately one of fact (*Re Lonrho plc* [1990] 2 AC 154, per Lord Bridge at p. 208). The creation of such a risk must accordingly be proved beyond reasonable doubt (*A-G* v *Unger* [1998] 1 Cr App R 308). 'Substantial' in this context does not mean 'weighty', but rather 'not insubstantial' or 'not minimal' (*A-G* v *News Group Newspapers Ltd* [1987] QB 1). Account may be taken of the likely effect of the publication on the parties, witnesses or court. Whilst it may sometimes be material, in assessing the risk of prejudice to any proceedings, that the defendant has already confessed or has intimated an intention to plead guilty, it would be most dangerous for publishers to rely on such considerations, because pleas may be changed and confessions retracted or excluded from evidence (*A-G* v *Unger*). Still less should a publisher assume that the weight of evidence against a defendant would place the outcome of any contested trial beyond doubt (*ibid.*). The courts do however recognise that the proximity of the publication to any future trial may be an important consideration. The longer the interval between publication and trial, the less likely it is that any serious prejudice will be caused, especially if the publication contains nothing that could amount to inadmissible evidence (*A-G* v *News Group Newspapers Ltd*; *A-G* v *Independent Television News Ltd* [1995] 1 Cr App R 204; *A-G* v *Unger*). In contrast, the risk of prejudicing the court (and especially a jury) may be heightened by the vulnerability of the defendant, the high profile of the case or any inaccuracy in the reporting (*A-G* v *Unger*).

In recent cases (notably *A-G* v *Unger* (above), *A-G* v *Birmingham Post and Mail* [1999] 1 WLR 361 and *A-G* v *Guardian Newspapers Ltd* (1999) *Independent*, 30 July 1999) the courts have sought to ensure that the test applied in contempt cases is consistent with the test applied in appeals against conviction, where it is alleged that a jury may have been prejudiced by improper media coverage. The courts should not reason, on the one hand, that any jurors who read or viewed the publication would have ignored the offending publication when reaching their verdict, and yet reason, on the other hand, that the publication in question created a substantial risk of serious prejudice. How this consistency should be achieved is more problematic, given that the risk in contempt cases must be judged prospectively, and without regard to the actual outcome of the trial, but in *A-G* v *Guardian Newspapers* Sedley LJ argued that a publication should be found in contempt only if of such a nature that it would be asking too much of any juror to put it out of his mind when directed to do so by the trial judge. Sedley LJ was also influenced by considerations of human rights issues; in particular by the consideration that any restrictions on media freedom should be necessary and proportionate to any risk of prejudice that such publications might involve.

Innocent Publication or Distribution

B14.92 **Contempt of Court Act 1981, s. 3**

    (1) A person is not guilty of contempt of court under the strict liability rule as the publisher of any matter to which that rule applies if at the time of publication (having taken all reasonable care) he does not know and has no reason to suspect that relevant proceedings are active.

    (2) A person is not guilty of contempt of court under the strict liablity rule as the distributor of a publication containing any such matter if at the time of distribution (having taken all reasonable care) he does not know that it contains such matter and has no reason to suspect that it is likely to do so.

    (3) The burden of proof of any fact tending to establish a defence afforded by this section to any person lies upon that person.

    (4) Section 11 of the Administration of Justice Act 1960 is repealed.

This section (which replaces the provision repealed in s. 3(4)) falls short of providing a general 'no fault' defence. In particular it does not protect publishers who are aware of the proceedings, but blamelessly unaware of the prejudicial effect of the publication (see *Evening Standard Co. Ltd* [1954] 1 QB 578).

Fair and Accurate Reports of Proceedings

B14.93 **Contempt of Court Act 1981, s. 4**

    (1) Subject to this section a person is not guilty of contempt of court under the strict liability rule in respect of a fair and accurate report of legal proceedings held in public, published contemporaneously and in good faith.

(2)   [See **B14.86**.]

(3)   [If publication of a report is postponed as a result of an order under subsection (2), a report published as soon as practicable after the order expires is to be treated as contemporaneous and therefore entitled under subsection (1) to protection from contempt proceedings.]

Discussion of Public Affairs

B14.94

Contempt of Court Act 1981, s. 5

A publication made as or as part of a discussion in good faith of public affairs or other matters of general public interest is not to be treated as a contempt of court under the strict liability rule if the risk of impediment or prejudice to particular legal proceedings is merely incidental to the discussion

Whereas the Contempt of Court Act 1981, s. 3, creates defences to charges of contempt, s. 5 follows ss. 2 and 4(1) in restricting the scope of the strict liability rule itself, and the burden of proof does not lie on the alleged contemnor. If the publication is part of a wider discussion, the publisher is guilty of contempt under the strict liability rule only if it is proved that there is a substantial risk of prejudice to active proceedings (s. 2) and that this is not merely incidental to the wider discussion. See generally *A-G* v *English* [1983] 1 AC 116.

If, in the course of a wider discussion, the publisher intends to influence the outcome of proceedings, then (even apart from the good faith issue) he may be guilty of contempt independently of the Act (see s. 6(c) at **B14.95**).

Contempt of Court Act 1981: General Provisions

B14.95

Contempt of Court Act 1981, ss. 6 and 7

6.   Nothing in the foregoing provisions of this Act—

(a)   prejudices any defence available at common law to a charge of contempt of court under the strict liability rule;

(b)   implies that any publication is punishable as contempt of court under that rule which would not be so punishable apart from those provisions;

(c)   restricts liability for contempt of court in respect of conduct intended to impede or prejudice the administration of justice.

7.   Proceedings for a contempt of court under the strict liability rule (other than Scottish proceedings) shall not be instituted except by or with the consent of the A-G or on the motion of a court having jurisdiction to deal with it.

Strict Liability: Where the Act Does Not Apply

It is possible (but, it is submitted, unlikely) that strict liability may apply in certain **B14.96** circumstances not covered by the Contempt of Court Act 1981. This is because the Act only defines the scope of the strict liability rule insofar as it applies to conduct tending to interfere with particular proceedings. In *A-G* v *Newspaper Publishing plc* [1988] Ch 333, Sir John Donaldson MR suggested that examples of possible strict liability outside the scope of the Contempt of Court Act 1981 could include retaliation against a person who has given evidence in previous proceedings (which could themselves no longer be affected) and marrying a ward of court without the court's consent. The better view, however, would seem to be that such contempts do not carry strict liability. A person who punishes another for giving evidence or serving on a jury must at the very least be reckless as to the implications of his conduct on the due administration of justice, and this recklessness is the more probable basis of his liability. As for the wardship example (or other cases of interference with a court order), there is clear authority to the effect that recklessness as to the existence of the order is the minimum *mens rea* that will suffice (*Re F (A Minor) (Publication of Information)* [1977] Fam 58).

Cases in which Intent is Required by the Contempt of Court Act 1981

B14.97 Where the Contempt of Court Act 1981 expressly rules out any question of strict liability (e.g., in respect of publications tending to prejudice proceedings which may be forthcoming but which are not active), it is clear that a specific intent must be present. In *A-G v Newspaper Publishing plc* [1988] Ch 333, Lloyd LJ said:

> In cases covered by the Act to which the strict liability rule does not apply, there is no room for a state of mind which falls short of intention. There is no middle way.

> I would therefore hold that the *mens rea* required in the present case is an intent to interfere with the course of justice. As in other branches of the criminal law, that intent may exist, even though there is no desire to interfere with the course of justice. Nor need it be the sole intent. It may be inferred, even though there is no overt proof. The more obvious the interference with the course of justice, the more readily will the requisite intent be inferred.

See also *A-G v Newspaper Publishing plc* [1997] 1 WLR 926 per Lord Bingham CJ at p. 936.

Appeals

B14.98 Appeals in contempt cases are governed by the Administration of Justice Act 1960, s. 13.

Administration of Justice Act 1960, s. 13

(1)   Subject to the provisions of this section, an appeal shall lie under this section from any order or decision of a court in the exercise of jurisdiction to punish for contempt of court (including criminal contempt); and in relation to any such order or decision the provisions of this section shall have effect in substitution for any other enactment relating to appeals in civil or criminal proceedings.

(2)   An appeal under this section shall lie in any case at the instance of the defendant and, in the case of an application for committal or attachment, at the instance of the applicant; and the appeal shall lie—

(a)   from an order or decision of any inferior court not referred to in the next following paragraph, to a divisional court of the High Court;

(b)   from an order or decision of a county court or any other inferior court from which appeals generally lie to the Court of Appeal, and from an order or decision of a single judge of the High Court or of a judge of that court, to the Court of Appeal;

(bb)   from an order or decision of the Crown Court to the Court of Appeal;

(c)   from an order or decision of a divisional court or the Court of Appeal (including a decision of either of those courts on an appeal under this section), and from an order or decision of the . . . Courts-Martial Appeal Court, to the House of Lords.

(3)   The court to which an appeal is brought under this section may reverse or vary the order or decision of the court below and make such other order as may be just; and without prejudice to the inherent powers of any court referred to in subsection (2) of this section, provision may be made by rules of court for authorising the release on bail of an appellant under this section.

(4)   Subsections (2) to (4) of section 1 and section 2 of this Act shall apply to an appeal to the House of Lords under this section as they apply to an appeal to that House under the said section 1, except that so much of the said subsection (2) as restricts the grant of leave to appeal shall apply only where the decision of the court below is a decision on appeal to that court under this section.

(5)   In this section 'court' includes any tribunal or person having power to punish for contempt; and references in this section to an order or decision of a court in the exercise of jurisdiction to punish for contempt of court include references—

(a)   to an order or decision of the High Court, the Crown Court or a county court under any enactment enabling that court to deal with an offence as if it were contempt of court;

(b)   to an order or decision of a county court, or of any court having the powers of a county court, under section 14, 92 or 118 of the County Courts Act 1984;

(c)   to an order or decision of a magistrates' court under subsection (3) of section 63 of the Magistrates' Courts Act 1980, but do not include references to orders under section 5 of the Debtors Act 1869, or under any provision of the Magistrates' Courts Act 1980, or the County Courts Act 1984, except those referred to in paragraphs (b) and (c) of this subsection and except section 38 and 142 of the last mentioned Act so far as those sections confer jurisdiction in respect of contempt of court.

(6)   This section does not apply to a conviction or sentence in respect of which an appeal lies under part I of the Criminal Appeal Act 1968, or to a decision of the Criminal Division of the Court of Appeal under that part of that Act.

Section 13(2) was considered by the Court of Appeal in *A-G* v *Hislop* [1991] 1 QB 514. It was held that the words 'application for committal or attachment' refer to the original application, rather than to the appeal itself: in other words, it gives a right of appeal to an unsuccessful applicant for a committal or attachment order. It does not matter if the applicant is actually seeking to have the alleged contemnor fined rather than committed to prison (this in any case being a matter for the court), nor if the alleged contemnor is a corporation which could not be committed or attached.

Appeals from the Crown Court were originally heard by the Civil Division of the Court of Appeal, but are now, more appropriately, heard by the Criminal Division; see the Supreme Court Act 1981, s. 53(2)(b).

SECTION B15: CORRUPTION

SCOPE OF OFFENCES AT COMMON LAW AND BY STATUTE

B15.1 At common law, '[a] man accepting an office of trust concerning the public is answerable criminally to the King for misbehaviour in his office . . . by whomever and in whatever way the officer is appointed' (*Bembridge* (1783) 3 Doug 327, per Lord Mansfield). The penalty for this offence is imprisonment and a fine at large, or both. In *Bowden* [1996] 1 WLR 98, the Court of Appeal held that a local authority manager, who improperly arranged for his men to carry out work at his girlfriend's house, was guilty of that offence.

It is also an offence at common law, punishable in the same way, to bribe the holder of a public office, and it is similarly an offence for any such office holder to accept a bribe (*Whitaker* [1914] 3 KB 1283; *Lancaster* (1890) 16 Cox CC 737). If the offer of a bribe is not accepted, the offeror might be guilty of an attempt to commit the common-law offence. In practice, however, prosecutions for corruption are generally brought under one of the relevant statutory provisions, which are considered below.

The principal legislation dealing with corruption is to be found in the Public Bodies Corrupt Practices Act 1889 and the Prevention of Corruption Act 1906, which are supplemented by the Prevention of Corruption Act 1916. The 1889 Act deals with corruption in local government and in other public bodies; the 1906 Act deals with the corruption of agents, whether the agents of public bodies or not. There is a degree of overlap between the two principal Acts where the agents of public bodies are involved, but it should be noted that councillors in local government are not agents, and corruption of such councillors cannot therefore be dealt with under the 1906 Act.

CORRUPTION IN PUBLIC OFFICE

Definition

B15.2 **Public Bodies Corrupt Practices Act 1889, s. 1**

(1) Every person who shall by himself or by or in conjunction with any other person, corruptly solicit or receive, or agree to receive, for himself, or for any other person, any gift, loan, fee, reward, or advantage whatever as an inducement to, or reward for, or otherwise on account of any member, officer, or servant of a public body as in this Act defined, doing or forbearing to do anything in respect of any matter or transaction whatsoever, actual or proposed, in which the said public body is concerned, shall be guilty of [an offence].

(2) Every person who shall by himself or by or in conjunction with any other person corruptly give, promise, or offer any gift, loan, fee, reward, or advantage whatsoever to any person, whether for the benefit of that person or of another person, as an inducement to or reward for or otherwise on account of any member, officer, or servant of any public body as in this Act defined, doing or forbearing to do anything in respect of any matter or transaction whatsoever, actual or proposed, in which such public body as aforesaid is concerned, shall be guilty of [an offence].

Procedure

B15.3 No prosecution for this offence may be instituted except by or with the consent of the A-G (Public Bodies Corrupt Practices Act 1889, s. 4). The offence is triable either way (s. 2(a)). When tried on indictment it is a class 4 offence.

Indictment

B15.4 Statement of Offence

Corruption contrary to section 1(2) of the Public Bodies Corrupt Practices Act 1889

Particulars of Offence

A on or about the . . . day of . . . corruptly offered as a gift to X, a member of a public body, namely . . ., the sum of £5,000, as an inducement to the said X to cast his vote at a meeting of the said public body held on . . . in favour of the award to A & Co. Ltd of a contract with the said public body for the construction of new municipal swimming-baths

Penalties

Public Bodies Corrupt Practices Act 1889, s. 2 — B15.5

Any person on conviction for offending as aforesaid shall, at the discretion of the court before which he is convicted,—

(a) be liable—

(i)   on summary conviction, to imprisonment for a term not exceeding six months or to a fine not exceeding the statutory maximum, or to both; and

(ii)   on conviction on indictment, to imprisonment for a term not exceeding seven years or to a fine, or to both; and

(b)   in addition be liable to be ordered to pay to such body, and in such manner as the court directs, the amount or value of any gift, loan, fee, or reward received by him or any part thereof; and

(c)   be liable to be adjudged incapable of being elected or appointed to any public office for five years from the date of his conviction, and to forfeit any such office held by him at the time of his conviction; and

(d)   in the event of a second conviction for a like offence he shall, in addition to the foregoing penalties, be liable to be adjudged to be for ever incapable of holding any public office, and to be incapable for five years of being registered as an elector, or voting at an election either of members to serve in Parliament or of members of any public body, and the enactments for preventing the voting and registration of persons declared by reason of corrupt practices to be incapable of voting shall apply to a person adjudged in pursuance of this section to be incapable of voting; and

(e)   if such person is an officer or servant in the employ of any public body upon such conviction he shall, at the discretion of the court, be liable to forfeit his right and claim to any compensation or pension to which he would otherwise have been entitled.

For sentencing guidelines, see **B15.17**.

Definition of Relevant Terms

Public Bodies Corrupt Practices Act 1889, s. 7 — B15.6

The expression 'public body' means any council of a county or council of a city or town, any council of a municipal borough, also any board, commissioners, select vestry, or other body which has power to act under and for the purposes of any Act relating to local government, or the public health, or to poor law or otherwise to administer money raised by rates in pursuance of any public general Act, but does not include any public body as above defined existing elsewhere than in the United Kingdom:

The expression 'public office' means any office or employment of a person as a member, officer, or servant of such public body:

The expression 'person' includes a body of persons, corporate or unincorporate:

The expression 'advantage' includes any office or dignity, and any forbearance to demand any money or money's worth or valuable thing, and includes any aid, vote, consent, or influence, or pretended aid, vote, consent, or influence, and also includes any promise or procurement of or agreement or endeavour to procure, or the holding out of any expectation of any gift, loan, fee, reward, or advantage, as before defined.

The definition of a public body in s. 7 is supplemented by the Prevention of Corruption Act 1916, s. 4(2), which provides that it also includes 'local and public authorities of all descriptions'. The Public Bodies Corrupt Practices Act 1889 is not therefore confined to corruption in local government. Any body with public or statutory duties to perform, other than one run for private profit, comes within its scope (*DPP* v *Holly* [1978] AC 43). Some, such as the Civil Aviation Authority, are expressly described as such in the legislation creating them, but this is not essential. Parliament is probably such a body.

Meaning of 'Corruptly'

B15.7 'Corruptly' means purposefully doing an act which the law forbids as tending to corrupt (*Wellburn* (1979) 69 Cr App R 254). Any improper and unauthorised gift, payment or other inducement offered to a councillor or other such officer is likely to be considered corrupt. The accused need not be proved to have offered or received the gift etc. dishonestly, as long as he knew that the offer etc. was connected with the performance of public duties, whether by way of reward for past performance, or of inducement to secure future performance. It is not necessary that any bargain be struck between the offeror and the recipient (*Andrews-Weatherfoil Ltd* [1972] 1 WLR 118), nor is it any defence for the recipient to prove that his acceptance of a corrupt gift failed to influence him in the performance of his duties. See *Parker* (1985) 82 Cr App R 69.

In *Smith* [1960] 2 QB 423 the offer of a bribe to a mayor was held to amount to an offence under the Public Bodies Corrupt Practices Act 1889, s. 1, even though the accused's motive was supposedly to expose the mayor as corrupt. He intended that the mayor should accept the bribe and knew that in so doing the mayor would be acting improperly. His conduct was accordingly corrupt within the meaning of the Act. This must be contrasted with the position where the accused is offered a bribe and purports to accept it for the purpose of exposing the offeror or of procuring evidence against him; the Court of Appeal has said that this 'would plainly not be corrupt' (*Mills* (1978) 68 Cr App R 154 at p. 159). The distinction can hardly rest merely on the difference between offering and receiving. The only satisfactory distinction would be between instigation and cooperation, the latter being innocent if the motive is exposure of the instigator; but the former being corrupt in any event.

It is possible that a payment intended as a corrupt gift could be received innocently by the recipient, i.e. without him understanding it to be a reward or inducement. In such a case, only the giver would be guilty of corruption (*Millray Window Cleaning Co. Ltd* [1962] Crim LR 99).

Under the Local Government Act 1972, ss. 94 and 95, any member of a local authority who has a direct pecuniary interest in a contract or a proposed contract involving that authority must disclose it and refrain from taking part in consideration of the matter. Failure to comply with this requirement is punishable on summary conviction by a fine.

The Presumption of Corruption

B15.8 In certain cases, it will be for the defence to prove that any payment, gift or other consideration was not given or received corruptly.

Prevention of Corruption Act 1916, s. 2

> Where in any proceedings against a person for an offence under the Prevention of Corruption Act 1906, or the Public Bodies Corrupt Practices Act 1889, it is proved that any money, gift, or other consideration has been paid or given to or received by a person in the employment of His Majesty or any government department or a public body by or from a person, or agent of a person, holding or seeking to obtain a contract from His Majesty or any government department or public body, the money, gift, or consideration shall be deemed to have been paid or given and received corruptly as such inducement or reward as is mentioned in such Act unless the contrary is proved.

This presumption applies only to payments etc. given to or received by employees (thus excluding payments to councillors) and only to cases in which a contract is being sought or has been obtained. It would not apply where the accused seeks only the granting of planning permission (*Dickinson* (1948) 33 Cr App R 5). In relevant cases, it will remain necessary for the prosecution to prove that the payment etc. was made or offered, and that the person offering or giving it was holding or seeking a relevant contract. If (and only if) these points are proved or admitted, the burden switches to the defence, and a jury may be directed that they may convict unless they consider it more likely than not that an innocent explanation offered by the defence is true. See *Braithwaite* [1983] 1 WLR 385; *Evans-Jones* (1923) 17 Cr App R 121. The presumption is problematic in that it seems to infringe the European Convention on Human Rights, Art. 6(2) (see **appendix** 7) but it may be avoided where the charge is one of conspiracy (*A-G, ex parte Rockall* [1999] 4 All ER 312) or attempt.

Corrupt Intent and Companies

Corruption cases often involve improper gifts etc. made by directors on behalf of their **B15.9** companies. In such cases, the company may itself be liable on the basis that the *mens rea* of such directors is that of the company's own mind. See generally **A5.11**.

Invalid Appointment or Election

Public Bodies Corrupt Practices Act 1889, s. 3   B15.10

(2)   A person shall not be exempt from punishment under this Act by reason of the invalidity of the appointment or election of a person to a public office.

CORRUPTION OF AGENTS

Definition and Penalty

Prevention of Corruption Act 1906, s. 1   B15.11

(1)   If any agent corruptly accepts or obtains, or agrees to accept or attempts to obtain, from any person, for himself or for any other person, any gift or consideration as an inducement or reward for doing or forbearing to do, or for having after the passing of this Act done or forborne to do, any act in relation to his principal's affairs or business, or for showing or forbearing to show favour or disfavour to any person in relation to his principal's affairs or business; or

If any person corruptly gives or agrees to give or offers any gift or consideration to any agent as an inducement or reward for doing or forbearing to do, or for having after the passing of this Act done or forborne to do, any act in relation to his principal's affairs or business, or for showing or forbearing to show favour or disfavour to any person in relation to his principal's affairs or business; or

If any person knowingly gives to any agent, or if any agent knowingly uses with intent to deceive his principal, any receipt, account, or other document in respect of which the principal is interested, and which contains any statement which is false or erroneous or defective in any material particular, and which to his knowledge is intended to mislead the principal; he shall be guilty of [an offence] and shall be liable:

(a)   on summary conviction, to imprisonment for a term not exceeding 6 months or to a fine not exceeding the statutory maximum, or to both; and

(b)   on conviction on indictment, to imprisonment for a term not exceeding seven years or to a fine, or to both.

(2)   For the purposes of this Act the expression 'consideration' includes valuable consideration of any kind; the expression 'agent' includes any person employed by or acting for another; and the expression 'principal' includes an employer.

(3)   A person serving under the Crown or under any corporation or any . . . borough, county, or district council, or any board of guardians, is an agent within the meaning of this Act.

For sentencing guidelines, see **B15.17**.

Procedure

No prosecution for this offence may be instituted execpt by or with the consent of the A-G **B15.12** (Prevention of Corruption Act 1906, s. 2). The offence is triable either way (s. 1). When tried on indictment it is a class 4 offence.

Meaning of 'Agent'

B15.13 The definition of an agent in the Prevention of Corruption Act 1906, s. 1(2) and (3), is supplemented by the Prevention of Corruption Act 1916, s. 4(3), which provides that a person serving under any other public body within the meaning of that Act is an agent for the purposes of the 1906 Act. (As to the meaning of the term 'public body', see **B15.6**.) This does not appear to embrace local authority councillors, who should be dealt with under the Public Bodies Corrupt Practices Act 1889, but the definition is otherwise extremely wide, and applies to both the public and the private or commercial fields. An agent may be an employee, and any person serving under the Crown or under any public body comes within the Prevention of Corruption Act 1916, s. 4(3), whether or not an agent or employee within the ordinary meaning of the term. In *Barrett* [1976] 1 WLR 946 it was held that a superintendent registrar is accordingly an agent, serving under the Crown.

Outside the public domain, the term 'agent' must probably be more narrowly construed, so as to apply only to employees and agents in the strict sense (i.e. those who act on behalf of others). A retailer who is described as an 'agent' for particular manufacturers, but who is in fact an independent dealer or stockist, would not appear to be an agent for the purposes of this Act. A bribe offered direct to such a retailer, with a view to securing preferential allocation of products or services, would not therefore appear to be proscribed under the Prevention of Corruption Acts, or for that matter at common law. A bribe offered to his agent or employee would be another matter.

An agent need not be acting as an agent of his principal at the relevant time, as long as the Act in question is done 'in relation to his principal's affairs' (*Morgan* v *DPP* [1970] 3 All ER 1053).

Comparison with the Public Bodies Corrupt Practices Act 1889

B15.14 In most respects the offences created by the Prevention of Corruption Act 1906 correspond with those in the Public Bodies Corrupt Practices Act 1889. The concept of corruption is the same (see *Harvey* [1999] Crim LR 70), as is the scope of the 'presumption of corruption' in the Prevention of Corruption Act 1916, s. 2 (see **B15.8**); and although the 1906 Act uses the words, 'gift or consideration' instead of the 1889 formula, 'gift, loan, fee, reward or advantage', this would not seem to be of any real significance. The 1906 Act also refers to *attempts* to obtain gifts etc., whereas the 1889 Act refers to the *soliciting* of such gifts, and this may be more significant in that the solicitation of a gift may not necessarily be regarded by a jury as anything more than 'merely preparatory' to the obtaining of such a gift. It would be a question of fact in every case.

False Statements under the Prevention of Corruption Act 1906

B15.15 The Prevention of Corruption Act 1906, s. 1(1), does create one offence which has no equivalent in the 1889 legislation: that of knowingly giving to an agent, or knowing use by an agent, of documents etc. which are false, erroneous or defective, and which are intended to mislead the agent's principal. It was held in *Sage* v *Eicholz* [1919] 2 KB 171 that this offence does not require any bribery or corruption of the agent; the agent may himself be deceived by it. More recently, however, it was held in *Tweedie* [1984] QB 729 that such liability can arise only where the document in question originates from outside any business or organisation in which both principal and agent are involved. Were it otherwise, 'an employee who put a false entry on his timesheet would be guilty of an offence under the Act' (per Lawton LJ at p. 734).

'Knowingly' must here mean knowledge of the falsity etc. as well as of the giving, but proof of wilful blindness will suffice. See *Westminster City Council* v *Croyalgrange Ltd* [1986] 1 WLR 674.

ABUSES IN RESPECT OF HONOURS

Under the Honours (Prevention of Abuses) Act 1925, s. 1, a person who accepts, **B15.16** obtains, gives or offers gifts or other valuable consideration, or who agrees to do so, as an inducement or reward for procuring, assisting or endeavouring to procure the grant of a dignity or title of honour to any person, is liable on conviction on indictment to imprisonment for a term not exceeding two years, and/or to a fine, or on summary conviction to three months' imprisonment and/or a fine not exceeding £5,000.

SENTENCING GUIDELINES FOR CORRUPTION OFFENCES

At the top end of the scale of seriousness is *Donald* [1997] 2 Cr App R (S) 272, where **B15.17** sentences totalling 11 years were upheld in respect of a detective-constable in a regional crime squad who pleaded guilty, at a late stage of his trial, to four counts of corruption. He had accepted various sums of money from a man against whom criminal proceedings were being brought to disclose confidential information about the inquiry and to destroy surveillance logs. The officer had agreed to accept about £50,000 and actually received about £18,500. The sentencing judge commented that the case was 'almost unique' in its seriousness. The Court of Appeal said the sentence was severe, but not manifestly excessive. In *Foxley* (1995) 16 Cr App R (S) 879, the offender was convicted of 12 counts of corruption contrary to the Prevention of Corruption Act 1906. While employed by the Ministry of Defence he had received payments in excess of £2 million in relation to the placing of government contracts. Four years' imprisonment was upheld, the Court of Appeal observing that six years would have been appropriate for a younger man (the offender was aged 71).

In *Wilson* (1982) 4 Cr App R (S) 337 the offender, a man of previous good character, was convicted of conspiracy to commit corruption and three counts of corruption. He was a purchasing agent and chief buyer with a manufacturing concern, and he accepted gifts of £2,500 in return for showing favour to a company supplying parts to his employer. A sentence of three and a half years was reduced to 18 months, taking into account personal mitigation, including the break-up of his family, the loss of his home and his business. In *Jones* (1981) 3 Cr App R (S) 238 the offenders were employed at a council waste tip. They allowed contractors, who were not authorised by the council to deposit waste at the tip, to use it in return for payment. Custodial sentences of six months (on three offenders) and three months (on a fourth) were reduced to three months and nine weeks respectively to take account of their consequent loss of employment. See also *Allday* (1986) 8 Cr App R (S) 288 and *Wilcox* (1995) 16 Cr App R (S) 197.

The offenders in *Garner* (1988) 10 Cr App R (S) 445 pleaded guilty to conspiracy to corrupt. They were concerned in bribing a prison officer to take various items, including luxury foods, alcohol and cigars to one of the offenders who was serving a prison sentence: sentences of 18 months, 12 months, and 12 months suspended were upheld. Offering a bribe to a police officer was the nature of the corruption in *McGovern* (1980) 2 Cr App R (S) 389. The offender was arrested in connection with a burglary, and offered a bribe of £2,000 to the police involved in the case. Fifteen months was reduced to nine months' imprisonment for the corruption offence. In *Oxdemir* (1985) 7 Cr App R (S) 382 the offender tried to bribe a police officer with £50 or a free meal at the offender's restaurant if he did not report a driving offence by the offender's son. The appropriate sentence was said by the Court of Appeal to be three months' imprisonment.

SECTION B16: REVENUE AND SOCIAL SECURITY OFFENCES

Scope of Revenue Offences

B16.1 Frauds committed against the Public Revenue can often be charged most conveniently under provisions dealt with elsewhere in this work, notably one or more of the provisions of the Theft Acts (e.g., under s. 2 of the 1978 Act, which deals with the evasion of liability by deception (see **B5.58** to **B5.66**), or under s. 17 of the 1968 Act, which deals with false accounting (see **B6.3** to **B6.13**)). False statements knowingly made in tax returns may be punishable under the Perjury Act 1911, s. 5(b) (**B14.22**): see *Bradbury* [1921] 1 KB 562. Provisions of this kind will often provide the most appropriate charges in cases of tax evasion, but there are also several specific revenue offences, which are dealt with in this section.

Cheating the Public Revenue

B16.2 The common-law offence of cheating was abolished for most purposes by the Theft Act 1968, s. 32(1), but was preserved therein 'as regards offences relating to the public revenue'. It is punishable on indictment by a fine and/or imprisonment at large. It is a Group A offence for jurisdiction purposes under the CJA 1993, part I (see **D1.75**).

The offence can be committed by deliberately making false statements with intent to deceive or prejudice the Inland Revenue or the Customs and Excise authorities or the Department of Social Security, as in *Hudson* [1956] 2 QB 252; but dishonest failure to declare a tax or national insurance liability may equally suffice. In *Mavji* (1987) 84 Cr App R 34, it was held (per Michael Davies J, at p. 37) that: 'This appellant . . . had a statutory duty to make VAT returns and pay over to the Crown the VAT due. He dishonestly failed to do either. Accordingly, he was guilty of cheating . . . the public revenue. No further act or omission required to be alleged or proved.' See also *Redford* (1988) 89 Cr App R 1 and *Dimsey* (1999) *The Times*, 14 July 1999.

B16.3 ***Cheating and Statutory Offences*** As far as VAT frauds are concerned, there are now several wide-ranging indictable offences contained within the Valued Added Tax Act 1994, s. 72 (see **B16.6**). The maximum penalty for any offence under that section is seven years' imprisonment, making recourse to the common-law offence unnecessary (albeit still possible) in the vast majority of cases.

Frauds against the Inland Revenue are another matter, since there are no comparably broad offences contained within the relevant legislation. Certain specific frauds are subject to criminal sanctions under the Income and Corporation Taxes Act 1988 or the Taxes Management Act 1970, but maximum penalties of two years or less (plus fine) may compare unfavourably, from the prosecution viewpoint, with the unlimited penalties available at common law, and many tax frauds are not covered by statutory offences at all. The Inland Revenue is usually content to rely on the common-law offence or on offences under the Theft Acts in those relatively few cases in which criminal proceedings of any kind are considered necessary. In the majority of cases, statutory penalties are imposed (in particular under part X (ss. 93 to 107) of the Taxes Management Act 1970), and these are deemed to be civil in character (see s. 100D(3) of the Act).

Although the Inland Revenue does not ordinarily couple penalty proceedings with criminal prosecution, it has the option of so doing. The Taxes Management Act 1970, s. 104, provides that: 'The provisions of the Taxes Acts shall not, save as otherwise provided, affect any criminal proceedings for any offence'.

Falsification etc. of Documents Called for Inspection

The Taxes Management Act 1970, s. 20, empowers a tax inspector to require delivery **B16.4**
to him of documents which he believes may contain information relevant to a person's
tax liability. Further powers are granted to inspectors under s. 20A (power to call for
papers of tax accountant).

Falsification of such documents with a view to deceiving the inspector might be charged
under various general provisions (including false accounting under the Theft Act 1968,
s. 17 (see **B6.3** to **B6.13**)), or as cheating at common law, but s. 20BB deals specifically
with such behaviour.

Taxes Management Act 1970, s. 20BB

(1) Subject to subsections (2) to (4) below, a person shall be guilty of an offence if he
intentionally falsifies, conceals, destroys or otherwise disposes of, or causes or permits the
falsification, concealment, destruction or disposal of, a document which—
  (a) he has been required by a notice under section 20 or 20A above, or
  (b) he has been given an opportunity in accordance with section 20B(1) above,
to deliver, or to deliver or make available for inspection.
(2) A person does not commit an offence under subsection (1) above if he acts—
  (a) with the written permission of a General or Special Commissioner, the inspector
or an officer of the board,
  (b) after the document has been delivered or, in a case within section 20(3) or (8A)
above, inspected, or
  (c) after a copy has been delivered in accordance with section 20B(4) or (14) above
and the original has been inspected.
(3) A person does not commit an offence under subsection (1)(a) above if he acts after
the end of the period of two years beginning with the date on which the notice is given,
unless before the end of that period the inspector or an officer of the Board has notified the
person in writing that the notice has not been complied with to his satisfaction.
(4) A person does not commit an offence under subsection (1)(b) above if he acts—
  (a) after the end of the period of six months beginning with the date on which an
opportunity to deliver the document was given, or
  (b) after an application for consent to a notice being given in relation to the document
has been refused.
(5) A person guilty of an offence under subsection (1) above shall be liable—
  (a) on summary conviction, to a fine not exceeding the statutory maximum;
  (b) on conviction on indictment, to imprisonment for a term not exceeding two years
or to a fine or to both.

'Lump' Frauds in Construction Industry

Sections 559 to 567 of the Income and Corporation Taxes Act 1988 contain highly **B16.5**
complex provisions designed to ensure that subcontractors (often casual workers) in the
construction industry do not avoid payment of income tax. Such subcontractors must
ordinarily have a sum deducted from their payments at source, on account of tax.
Certificates and vouchers authorising companies, firms or individuals to receive
payments untaxed at source are issued only to those who satisfy stringent conditions,
designed to ensure that they are genuine subcontractors who can be relied upon to meet
their own tax liabilities.

Section 561 of the Act creates a number of summary offences involving the improper
acquisition, disposal or possession of such documents, which are punishable by fines not
exceeding £5,000; but 'lump' frauds may well merit more serious charges, notably
cheating the public revenue (**B16.2**), conspiracy (see *Mulligan* [1990] STC 220), or
theft or handling of the documents, which remain the property of the Inland Revenue,
and cannot therefore be disposed of as if they were the holder's own property. See
Downes (1983) 77 Cr App R 260.

VAT Frauds

B16.6   **Value Added Tax Act 1994, s. 72**

(1)   If any person is knowingly concerned in, or in the taking of steps with a view to, the fraudulent evasion of VAT by him or any other person, he shall be liable—

(a)   on summary conviction, to a penalty of the statutory maximum or of three times the amount of the VAT, whichever is the greater, or to imprisonment for a term not exceeding 6 months or to both; or

(b)   on conviction on indictment, to a penalty of any amount or to imprisonment for a term not exceeding 7 years or to both.

(2)   Any reference in subsection (1) above or subsection (8) below to the evasion of VAT includes a reference to the obtaining of—

(a)   the payment of a VAT credit; or

(b)   a refund under section 35, 36 or 40 of this Act or section 22 of the [Value Added Tax Act 1983]; or

(c)   a refund under any regulations made by virtue of section 13(5); or

(d)   a repayment under section 39;

and any reference in those subsections to the amount of the VAT shall be construed—

(i)   in relation to VAT itself or a VAT credit, as a reference to the aggregate of the amount (if any) falsely claimed by way of credit for input tax and the amount (if any) by which output was falsely understated, and

(ii)   in relation to a refund or repayment falling within paragraph (b), (c) or (d) above, as a reference to the amount falsely claimed by way of refund or repayment.

(3)   If any person—

(a)   with intent to deceive produces, furnishes or sends for the purposes of this Act or otherwise makes use for those purposes of any document which is false in a material particular; or

(b)   in furnishing any information for the purposes of this Act makes any statement which he knows to be false in a material particular or recklessly makes a statement which is false in a material particular,

he shall be liable—

(i)   on summary conviction, to a penalty of the statutory maximum or, where subsection (4) or (5) below applies, to the alternative penalty specified in that subsection if it is greater, or to imprisonment for a term not exceeding 6 months or to both; or

(ii)   on conviction on indictment, to a penalty of any amount or to imprisonment for a term not exceeding 7 years or to both.

(4)   In any case where—

(a)   the document referred to in subsection (3)(a) above is a return required under this Act, or

(b)   the information referred to in subsection (3)(b) above is contained in or otherwise relevant to such a return,

the alternative penalty referred to in subsection (3)(i) above is a penalty equal to three times the aggregate of the amount (if any) falsely claimed by way of credit for input tax and the amount (if any) by which output tax was falsely understated.

(5)   In any case where—

(a)   the document referred to in subsection (3)(a) above is a claim for a refund under section 35, 36 or 40 of this Act or section 22 of the [Value Added Tax Act 1983] for a refund under any regulations made by virtue of section 13(5) or for a repayment under section 39, or

(b)   the information referred to in subsection (3)(b) above is contained in or otherwise relevant to such a claim,

the alternative penalty referred to in subsection (3)(i) above is a penalty equal to three times the amount falsely claimed.

(6)   The reference in subsection (3)(a) above to furnishing, sending or otherwise making use of a document which is false in a material particular, with intent to deceive, includes a reference to furnishing, sending or otherwise making use of such a document, with intent to secure that a machine will respond to the document as if it were a true document.

(7)   Any reference in subsection (3)(a) or subsection (6) above to producing, furnishing or sending a document includes a reference to causing a document to be produced, furnished or sent.

(8) Where a person's conduct during any specified period must have involved the commission by him of one or more offences under the preceding provisions of this section, then, whether or not the particulars of that offence or those offences are known, he shall, by virtue of this subsection, be guilty of an offence and liable—

(a) on summary conviction, to a penalty of the statutory maximum or, if greater, three times the amount of any VAT that was or was intended to be evaded by his conduct, or to imprisonment for a term not exceeding 6 months or to both; or

(b) on conviction on indictment to a penalty of any amount or to imprisonment for a term not exceeding 7 years or to both.

(9) Where an authorised person has reasonable grounds for suspecting that an offence has been committed under the preceding provisions of this section, he may arrest anyone whom he has reasonable grounds for suspecting to be guilty of the offence.

(10) If any person acquires possession of or deals with any goods, or accepts the supply of any services, having reason to believe that VAT on the supply of the goods or services, on the acquisition of the goods from another member State or on the importation of the goods from a place outside the member States has been or will be evaded, he shall be liable on summary conviction to a penalty of level 5 on the standard scale or three times the amount of the VAT, whichever is the greater.

(11) If any person supplies goods or services in contravention of paragraph 4(2) of Schedule 11, he shall be liable on summary conviction to a penalty of level 5 on the standard scale.

(12) Subject to subsection (13) below, sections 145 to 155 of the [Customs and Excise Management Act 1979] (proceedings for offences, mitigation of penalties and certain other matters) shall apply in relation to offences under this Act (which include any act or omission in respect of which a penalty is imposed) and penalties imposed under this Act as they apply in relation to offences and penalties under the customs and excise Acts as defined in that Act; and accordingly in section 154(2) as it applies by virtue of this subsection the reference to duty shall be construed as a reference to VAT.

(13) In subsection (12) above the references to penalties do not include references to penalties under sections 60 to 70.

For the Customs and Excise Management Act 1979, ss. 145 to 155, see **B17.1** to **B17.6**.

Section 72(8) enables a charge to be brought on the basis of a general deficiency. As to the circumstances in which this should be resorted to, see *Rasool* [1997] 1 WLR 1092. As to the wording of indictments generally, see *Ike* [1996] Crim LR 515.

The Court of Appeal held in *McCarthy* [1981] STC 298 that a dishonest omission to register for VAT may constitute an offence of taking steps to evade that tax under what is now s. 72(1).

Taxation etc. in the European Community

The CJA 1993, s. 71, creates an offence of involvement, within the United Kingdom, in **B16.7** specified EC fraud offences committed against the laws of other Member States. Despite this international dimension, the offence is not, strictly speaking, an extraterritorial one. The courts of England and Wales will not be concerned with acts committed in other parts of the United Kingdom, nor does s. 71 penalise fraudulent conduct that takes place in other Member States.

Definition

Criminal Justice Act 1993, s. 71   B16.8

(1) A person who, in the United Kingdom, assists in or induces any conduct outside the United Kingdom which involves the commission of a serious offence against the law of another Member State is guilty of an offence under this section if—

(a) the offence involved is one consisting in or including the contravention of provisions of the law of that Member State which relate to any of the matters specified in subsection (2);

(b) the offence involved is one consisting in or including the contravention of other provisions of that law so far as they have effect in relation to any of those matters; or

(c)   the conduct is such as to be calculated to have an effect in that Member State in relation to any of those matters.

(2)   The matters mentioned in subsection (1) are—

(a)   the determination, discharge or enforcement of any liability for a Community duty or tax;

(b)   the operation of arrangements under which reliefs or exemptions from any such duty or tax are provided or sums in respect of any such duty or tax are repaid or refunded;

(c)   the making of payments in pursuance of Community arrangements made in connection with the regulation of the market for agricultural products and the enforcement of the conditions of any such payments;

(d)   the movement into or out of any Member State of anything in relation to the movement of which any Community instrument imposes, or requires the imposition of, any prohibition or restriction; and

(e)   such other matters in relation to which provision is made by any Community instrument as the Secretary of State may by order specify.

(3)   For the purposes of this section—

(a)   an offence against the law of a Member State is a serious offence if provision is in force in that Member State authorising the sentencing, in some or all cases, of a person convicted of that offence to imprisonment for a maximum term of twelve months or more; and

(b)   the question whether any conduct involves the commission of such an offence shall be determined according to the law in force in the Member State in question at the time of the assistance or inducement.

. . .

(9)   In this section—

'another Member State' means a Member State other than the United Kingdom;

'Community duty or tax' means any of the following, that is to say—

(a)   any Community customs duty;

(b)   an agricultural levy of the Economic Community;

(c)   value added tax under the law of another Member State;

(d)   any duty or tax on tobacco products, alcoholic liquors or hydrocarbon oils which, in another Member State, corresponds to any excise duty;

(e)   any duty, tax or other charge not falling within paragraphs (a) to (d) of this definition which is imposed by or in pursuance of any Community instrument on the movement of goods into or out of any Member State;

'conduct' includes acts, omissions and statements;

'contravention' includes a failure to comply; and

'the customs and excise Acts' has the same meaning as in the Customs and Excise Management Act 1979.

(10)   References in this section, in relation to a Community instrument, to the movement of anything into or out of a Member State include references to the movement of anything between Member States and to the doing of anything which falls to be treated for the purposes of that instrument as involving the entry into, or departure from, the territory of the Community of any goods (within the meaning of that Act of 1979).

Procedure and Sentence

B16.9   An offence under s. 71 is triable either way, and is punishable following conviction on indictment by imprisonment for up to seven years or by a fine or both; six months and/or a fine not exceeding the statutory maximum following summary conviction (CJA 1993, s. 71(6)). When tried on indictment, it is a class 4 offence.

Elements

B16.10   The term 'induce' in s. 71(1) must presumably be construed as an ordinary English word. Its dictionary meaning is 'to prevail upon, persuade, bring about or give rise to'; it implies a causal link that would not have been implied by alternatives such as 'counsel' or 'encourage'. It follows that a serious offence against the laws of another Member State must actually be committed by the person(s) assisted or induced before the assister can incur liability under s. 71. The conduct giving rise to that offence may involve or may merely be 'calculated' (i.e. objectively likely) to have an effect in relation to the matters listed in s. 71(2).

Evidence of Foreign Law

Criminal Justice Act 1993, s. 71   **B16.11**

 (5) For the purposes of any proceedings for an offence under this section, a certificate purporting to be issued by or on behalf of the government of another Member State which contains a statement, in relation to such times as may be specified in the certificate—
  (a) that a specified offence existed against the law of that Member State,
  (b) that an offence against the law of that Member State was a serious offence within the meaning of this section,
  (c) that such an offence consists in or includes the contravention of particular provisions of the law of that Member State,
  (d) that specified provisions of the law of that Member State relate to, or are capable of having an effect in relation to, particular matters,
  (e) that specified conduct involved the commission of a particular offence against the law of that Member State, or
  (f) that a particular effect in that Member State in relation to any matter would result from specified conduct,
shall, in the case of a statement falling within paragraphs (a) to (d), be conclusive of the matters stated and, in the other cases, be evidence, and in Scotland sufficient evidence, of the matters stated.

Section 71(5) facilitates proof of the relevant law in the state concerned (although other methods of proving foreign law may still be used, as to which see **F10.9**). If, however, there is any dispute as to what was done by the persons allegedly assisted by the accused, one cannot rely upon a certificate to prove that they were in fact guilty of the 'specified conduct' alleged. The use of the past tense in s. 71(5)(e), as in s. 71(5)(a) and (b), can be explained on the basis that it refers to the law of the Member State at the times specified in the certificate. In other words, s. 71(5)(e) deals with the question whether specified conduct, if proved, would amount to a specified offence; even on this, it is not conclusive.

Proof of the offences allegedly assisted or induced may not be easy. Convictions imposed by foreign courts are not admissible evidence of the commission of such offences. The PACE 1984, s. 74 (see **F11.2**) does not apply to the judgments of foreign courts, which remain inadmissible opinion under the rule in *Hollington* v *F. Hewthorn & Co. Ltd* [1943] KB 587. The obtaining of evidence may however be facilitated by procedures established in the Criminal Justice (International Co-operation) Act 1990.

Defences

Criminal Justice Act 1993, s. 71   **B16.12**

 (4) In any proceedings against any person for an offence under this section it shall be a defence for that person to show—
  (a) that the conduct in question would not have involved the commission of an offence against the law of the Member State in question but for circumstances of which he had no knowledge; and
  (b) that he did not suspect or anticipate the existence of those circumstances and did not have reasonable grounds for doing so.

The burden of proving any such defence clearly lies on the defendant, the standard being that of balance of probabilities.

Evasion of Duty

The principal offences under the Customs and Excise Management Act 1979 are dealt **B16.13** with at **B17**. The statutory offences are backed by the common-law offence of cheating the public revenue (**B16.2**), which used to be preferred in serious cases where the statutory penalties (typically two years' imprisonment following trial on indictment) were perceived to be inadequate. Since the maximum penalties for the main statutory offences have been raised to seven years (Finance Act 1988, s. 12), this may no longer be the case.

Sentencing Guidelines for Revenue Offences

B16.14 The maximum penalty for cheating or making false statements to the prejudice of the public revenue is at large (common-law offence). The maximum penalty for evasion of duty is seven years (Customs and Excise Management Act 1979, s. 170).

In respect of revenue offences, charges may be brought under a range of statutory provisions. The sentencing decisions listed below relate to cases where the offenders were found guilty of theft, conspiracy to defraud, false accounting, and VAT offences, as well as cheating or making a false statement to the Public Revenue. Sentencing principles appear to be similar, whichever offence is established.

In *Ford* (1981) 3 Cr App R (S) 15, the Court of Appeal offered the following general observations on sentencing for these offences. The offender, aged 53 and with a clean record, pleaded guilty to nine counts of making false statements to the Revenue, having concealed income over a period of years, resulting in a loss of £14,500 to the Revenue. According to Watkins LJ (at p. 17):

> Those who refrain from paying their taxes and who avoid doing so by telling lies in statements to the Inland Revenue when making returns of income and when called upon to explain discrepancies in certificates which are supposed to contain the truth, must be led to expect punishment when the truth is laid bare. Sending a person to prison therefore who behaves in that way is right in principle. The period of imprisonment imposed cannot be governed by any particular yardstick. It has to be determined according to the particular facts of the case and the power of the court to fine. We lay particular stress on that. Where a person has the means at his disposal and has behaved as wickedly as this appellant did over a long time, it is fair and just that he should be deprived as a form of punishment of some assets honestly come by as well as totally those dishonestly gained. So in sentencing for this kind of fraud, a balance should usually be sought by imposing a prison sentence to be served forthwith and imposing a swingeing fine in addition. In this manner the punishment is likely to fit the crime as well as acting as a deterrent to others.

The sentence of 18 months was reduced to six months on appeal, together with a fine of £9,000. The sum outstanding was also repaid, with interest.

In *Milbern Investments Ltd* (1981) 3 Cr App R (S) 107, it was suggested in argument that the majority of people in the offender's position would, in the discretion of the tax authorities, not have been prosecuted. Watkins LJ, however, said (at p. 110):

> Courts are not to be hamstrung by the practice of some other arbitrary body in coming to its conclusions within the different powers given to it by Parliament, in the way it should exercise those powers in respect of people who do not deal with the Revenue honestly. That is not to say that a court is not permitted to look at what the Revenue would or might have done in any given case. It might be helpful to do so at times. However, it would be wholly improper for the court to regard itself as in any way governed by the practice of the Revenue.

Several groups of cases may be identified under the general heading of Revenue offences. The first group concerns employers or business people who fail to deduct tax from wages. In *Thornhill* (1980) 2 Cr App R (S) 310, the loss to the Revenue was £3,278. Six months' imprisonment, for conspiracy to defraud, was reduced to two months, since, in this type of case 'it is the effect of imprisonment rather than perhaps its length which is of importance'. In *Hayes* (1981) 3 Cr App R (S) 205, a case referred to as a 'guideline' in several later cases, the loss was £19,424, the offender had a clean record and pleaded guilty to theft. The prison sentence of two and a half years was reduced to nine months.

In *Ball* (1987) 9 Cr App R (S) 94 the loss was between £60,000 and £70,000. The Court of Appeal noted that the loss was substantially greater than in the last cited case, and that the offender in this case had served custodial sentences in the past. Three and a half years' imprisonment was reduced to two years. The case of *Sivyer* (1987) 9 Cr App R (S) 428 was on a different scale, with losses of £400,000. Sentences varying from four years for conspiracy to defraud in respect of the main actors, with lesser terms for those playing minor roles or who pleaded guilty to the charges, were upheld on appeal.

A second group of cases concerns failure to disclose income to the Revenue and making false claims for allowances. In *Trevithick* (1986) 8 Cr App R (S) 31, a two-year prison sentence was upheld on an offender who pleaded guilty to seven counts of making a false statement with intent to defraud the Revenue, in the event evading payment of £48,000 in income tax. The offender had previous convictions for dishonesty. In *Rogers* (1995) 16 Cr App R (S) 720 the offender pleaded guilty to two counts of cheating the public revenue, by concealing £112,000 of income from his business. In the Court of Appeal, Hobhouse LJ observed that the normal sentencing bracket for such offences would be somewhere between six months and 18 months. Eighteen months was upheld in this case, because the dishonesty was systematic and persistent. In *James* [1997] 2 Cr App R (S) 294, however, a sentence of nine months' imprisonment was reduced to five months, where the sum involved was £35,000, the offender had co-operated with the tax authorities and had been 'unfortunate to find himself in the hands of a dishonest accountant'.

A third group of cases is VAT frauds. Examples are *Richardson* (1992) 13 Cr App R (S) 51, where the offender registered for VAT as a haulage business and made three fraudulent claims for repayment to a total sum of £7,900 and a custodial sentence of 18 months was reduced to 12 months on appeal, and *Lal* (1993) 15 Cr App R (S) 143, where the offender made a series of fraudulent claims in respect of VAT, with a total loss to the Revenue of £41,000 and a sentence of two and a half years' imprisonment was upheld. In *Aziz* [1996] 1 Cr App R (S) 265, where the offender misdescribed adult footwear as children's footwear, which was zero-rated, with an estimated loss to the Revenue of £400,000, a sentence of four and a half years' imprisonment was upheld. About £1.5 million was obtained by means of fraudulent claims for repayment in *Alibhai* (1992) 13 Cr App R (S) 682. A term of seven years, for the offence of conspiring to obtain by deception, was said by the Court of Appeal to be right in principle and not excessive.

Social Security Frauds

Although the dishonest obtaining and/or retention of social security benefits may well **B16.15** involve the commission of offences under the Theft Act 1968, s. 1, 15 or 17, the Social Security Administration Act 1992 contains specific offences concerning such conduct. Offences under the new s. 111A carry comparable penalties to Theft Act offences and similarly require proof of dishonesty. The summary offences created by s. 112 cover much of the same ground as s. 111A and require *mens rea* in the form of knowledge, but do not require proof of dishonesty.

Social Security Administration Act 1992, ss. 111A and 112

111A.—(1) If a person dishonestly—
  (a) makes a false statement or representation;
  (b) produces or furnishes, or causes or allows to be produced or furnished, any document or information which is false in a material particular;
  (c) fails to notify a change of circumstances which regulations under this Act require him to notify; or
  (d) causes or allows another person to fail to notify a change of circumstances which such regulations require the other person to notify,
with a view to obtaining any benefit or other payment or advantage under the social security legislation (whether for himself or for some other person), he shall be guilty of an offence.

(2)   In this section 'the social security legislation' means the Acts to which section 110 above applies and the Jobseekers Act 1995.

(3)   A person guilty of an offence under this section shall be liable—

(a)   on summary conviction, to imprisonment for a term not exceeding six months, or to a fine not exceeding the statutory maximum, or to both; or

(b)   on conviction on indictment, to imprisonment for a term not exceeding seven years, or to a fine, or to both.

112.—(1)   If a person for the purpose of obtaining any benefit or other payment under the social security legislation whether for himself or some other person, or for any other purpose connected with that legislation—

(a)   makes a statement or representation which he knows to be false; or

(b)   produces or furnishes, or knowingly causes or knowingly allows to be produced or furnished, any document or information which he knows to be false in a material particular, he shall be guilty of an offence.

(1A)   If a person without reasonable excuse—

(a)   fails to notify a change of circumstances which regulations under this Act require him to notify; or

(b)   knowingly causes or knowingly allows another person to fail to notify a change of circumstances which such regulations require the other person to notify, and he knows that he, or the other person, is required to notify the change of circumstances, he shall be guilty of an offence.

(2)   A person guilty of an offence under this section shall be liable on summary conviction to a fine not exceeding level 5 on the standard scale, or to imprisonment for a term not exceeding 3 months, or to both.

(3)   In this section 'the social security legislation' means the Acts to which section 110 above applies and the Jobseekers Act 1995.

The legislation to which s. 110 applies is defined in ss. 110(8) and 191 as the Social Security Act 1973, the Social Security Contributions and Benefits Act 1992, the Social Security Pensions Act 1975, the Pension Schemes Act 1993 and the Social Security Administration Act itself.

Procedural provisions relating to the prosecution of offences under the Social Security Administration Act 1992 are contained in s. 116.

Social Security Administration Act 1992, s. 116

(1)   Any person authorised by the Secretary of State in that behalf may conduct any proceedings under this Act before a magistrates' court although not a barrister or solicitor.

(2)   Notwithstanding anything in any Act—

(a)   proceedings for an offence under this Act other than an offence relating to housing benefit or community charge benefits may be begun at any time within the period of 3 months from the date on which evidence, sufficient in the opinion of the Secretary of State to justify a prosecution for the offence, comes to his knowledge or within a period of 12 months from the commission of the offence, whichever period last expires; and

(b)   proceedings for an offence under this Act relating to housing benefit or community charge benefits may be begun at any time within the period of 3 months from the date on which evidence, sufficient in the opinion of the appropriate authority to justify a prosecution for the offence, comes to the authority's knowledge or within a period of 12 months from the commission of the offence, whichever period last expires.

(2A)   Subsection 2 above shall not be taken to impose any restriction on the time when proceedings may be begun for an offence under section 111A above.

(3)   For the purposes of subsection (2) above—

(a)   a certificate purporting to be signed by or on behalf of the Secretary of State as to the date on which such evidence as is mentioned in paragraph (a) of that subsection came to his knowledge shall be conclusive evidence of that date; and

(b)   a certificate of the appropriate authority as to the date on which such evidence as is mentioned in paragraph (b) of that subsection came to the authority's knowledge shall be conclusive evidence of that date.

Amendments to s. 116 are contained in the Social Security Contributions (Transfer of Functions) Act 1999, s. 1 (which is not yet in force).

Sentencing Guidelines for Social Security Fraud B16.16

Sentencing guidelines for social security fraud cases which reach the Crown Court were laid down by the Court of Appeal in *Stewart* (1987) 9 Cr App R (S) 135 (see **B5.26**). For sentencing for the summary offence under the Social Security Administration Act 1992, s. 112, the Magistrates' Association Guidelines (1997) indicate the following:

Aggravating Factors ⊕
For example fraudulent claims over a long period; large amount; organised group offence; planned deception; offence committed on bail; previous convictions and failures to respond to previous sentences, if relevant.

Mitigating Factors ⊖
For example misunderstanding of regulations; pressurised by others; small amount.

Guideline: Is it serious enough for a community penalty?

SECTION B17: OFFENCES UNDER CUSTOMS AND EXCISE LEGISLATION

This section deals with the most important offences under the Customs and Excise Management Act 1979 (which will be referred to as 'the Act'). The Act is one of six pieces of legislation which it refers to collectively as 'the customs and excise Acts 1979' (see s. 1) and any reference to offences under those Acts therefore includes all offences under the Act.

There are a number of specific procedural provisions applicable to prosecutions for any offence under the Act, and it will be convenient to consider these before turning to the offences themselves.

Institution of Proceedings

B17.1 Section 145 of the Act provides that, with limited exceptions, prosecution under the Act may be commenced by order of the Commissioners and in the name of an officer of the Customs and Excise Service, or by order and in the name of a law officer of the Crown.

Customs and Excise Management Act 1979, s. 145

(1)   Subject to the following provisions of this section, no proceedings for an offence under the customs and excise Acts or for condemnation under schedule 3 to this Act shall be instituted except by order of the Commissioners.

(2)   Subject to the following provisions of this section, any proceedings under the customs and excise Acts instituted in a magistrates' court . . . shall be commenced in the name of an officer.

(3)   [Applies to Scotland only.]

(4)   In the case of the death, removal, discharge or absence of the officer in whose name any proceedings were commenced under subsection (2) above; those proceedings may be continued by any officer authorised in that behalf by the Commissioners.

(5)   Nothing in the foregoing provisions of this section, shall prevent the institution of proceedings for an offence under the customs and excise Acts by order and in any case in which he thinks it proper that proceedings should be so instituted.

(6)   Notwithstanding anything in the foregoing provisions of this section, where any person has been detained for any offence for which he is liable to be detained under the customs and excise Acts, any court before which he is brought may proceed to deal with the case although the proceedings have not been instituted by order of the Commissioners or have not been commenced in the name of an officer.

This provision applies also to conspiracy to commit an offence under the Act (*Whitehead* [1982] QB 1272).

Time-limits

B17.2 Section 146A of the Act provides the following time-limits for instituting proceedings, which override the general limitation provisions of the MCA 1980, s. 127.

Customs and Excise Management Act 1979, s. 146A

(1)   Except as otherwise provided in the customs and excise Acts, and notwithstanding anything in any other enactment, the following provisions shall apply in relation to proceedings for an offence under those Acts.

(2)   Proceedings for an indictable offence shall not be commenced after the end of the period of 20 years beginning with the day on which the offence was committed.

(3)   Proceedings for a summary offence shall not be commenced after the end of the period of three years beginning with that day but, subject to that, may be commenced at

any time within six months from that date on which sufficient evidence to warrant the proceedings came to the knowledge of the prosecuting authority.

(4)   For the purposes of subsection (3) above, a certificate of the prosecuting authority as to the date on which such evidence as is there mentioned came to that authority's knowledge shall be conclusive evidence of that fact.

(5)   [Applies to Scotland only.]

(6)   [Applies to Northern Ireland only.]

(7)   In this section, 'prosecuting authority' means the Commissioners.

Proceedings in Magistrates' Courts

Customs and Excise Management Act 1979, s. 147   B17.3

(2)   Where, in England or Wales, a magistrates' court has begun to inquire into an information charging a person with an offence under the customs and excise Acts as examining justices the court shall not proceed under section 25(3) of the Magistates' Courts Act 1980 to try the information summarily without the consent of—

(a)   the Attorney-General, in a case where the proceedings were instituted by his order and in his name; or

(b)   the Commissioners, in any other case.

(3)   In the case of proceedings in England or Wales, without prejudice to any right to require the statement of a case for the opinion of the High Court, the prosecutor may appeal to the Crown Court against any decision of a magistrates' court in proceedings for an offence under the customs and excise Acts.

Place of Trial

Customs and Excise Management Act 1979, s. 148   B17.4

(1)   Proceedings for an offence under the customs and excise Acts may be commenced—

(a)   in any court having jurisdiction in the place where the person charged with the offence resides or is found; or

(b)   if any thing was detained or seized in connection with the offence, in any court having jurisdiction in the place where that thing was so detained or seized or was found or condemned as forfeited; or

(c)   in any court having jurisdiction anywhere in that part of the United Kingdom, namely—

(i)   England and Wales,

(ii)   Scotland, or

(iii)   Northern Ireland,

in which the place where the offence was committed is situated.

(2)   Where any such offence was committed at some place outside the area of any commission of the peace, the place of the commission of the offence shall, for the purposes of the jurisdiction of any court, be deemed to be any place in the United Kingdom where the offender is found or to which he is first brought after the commission of the offence.

(3)   The jurisdiction under subsection (2) above shall be in addition to and not in derogation of any jurisdiction or power of any court under any other enactment.

Powers of Court and Commissioners in Relation to Penalties

Customs and Excise Management Act 1979, ss. 149 to 152   B17.5

149.—(1)   Where, in any proceedings for an offence under the customs and excise Acts, a magistrates' court in England or Wales or a court of summary jurisdiction in Scotland, in addition to ordering the person convicted to pay a penalty for the offence—

(a)   orders him to be imprisoned for a term in respect of the same offence; and

(b)   further (whether at the same time or subsequently) orders him to be imprisoned for a term in respect of non-payment of that penalty or default of a sufficient distress to satisfy the amount of that penalty,

the aggregate of the terms for which he is so ordered to be imprisoned shall not exceed 15 months.

(2)   [Applies to Scotland only.]

(3)   [Applies to Northern Ireland only.]

150.—(1)   Where liability for any offence under the customs and excise Acts is incurred by two or more persons jointly, those persons shall each be liable for the full amount of any pecuniary penalty and may be proceeded against jointly or severally as the Commissioners may see fit.

(2)   In any proceedings for an offence under the customs and excise Acts instituted in England, Wales or Northern Ireland, any court by whom the matter is considered may mitigate any pecuniary penalty as they see fit.

(3)   In any proceedings for an offence or for the condemnation of any thing as being forfeited under the customs and excise Acts, the fact that security has been given by bond or otherwise for the payment of any duty or for compliance with any condition in respect of the non-payment of which or non-compliance with which the proceedings are instituted shall not be a defence.

151.   The balance of any sum paid or recovered on account of any penalty imposed under the customs and excise Acts, after paying any such compensation or costs as are mentioned in section 139 of the Magistrates' Courts Act 1980 to persons other than the Commissioners, shall, notwithstanding any local or other special right or privilege of whatever origin, be accounted for and paid to the Commissioners or as they direct.

152.   The Commissioners may, as they see fit—

(a)   stay, sist or compound any proceedings for an offence or for the condemnation of any thing as being forfeited under the customs and excise Acts; or

(b)   restore, subject to such conditions (if any) as they think proper, any thing forfeited or seized under those Acts; or

(c)   after judgment, mitigate or remit any pecuniary penalty imposed under those Acts; or

(d)   order any person who has been imprisoned to be discharged before the expiration of his term of imprisonment, being a person imprisoned for any offence under those Acts or in respect of the non-payment of a penalty or other sum adjudged to be paid or awarded in relation to such an offence or in respect of the default of a sufficient distress to satisfy such a sum.

Evidential Provisions

B17.6   The Act makes the following important provisions regarding the burden of proof as to certain documents and certain frequently recurring facts.

Customs and Excise Management Act 1979, ss. 153 and 154

153.—(1)   Any document purporting to be signed either by one or more of the Commissioners, or by their order, or by any other person with their authority, shall, until the contrary is proved, be deemed to have been so signed and to be made and issued by the Commissioners, and may be proved by the production of a copy thereof purporting to be so signed.

(2)   Without prejudice to subsection (1) above, the Documentary Evidence Act 1868, shall apply in relation to—

(a)   any document issued by the Commissioners;

(b)   any document issued before 1st April 1909, by the Commissioners of Customs or the Commissioners of Customs and the Commissioners of Inland Revenue jointly;

(c)   any document issued before that date in relation to the revenue of excise by the Commissioners of Inland Revenue,

as it applies in relation to the documents mentioned in that Act.

(3)   That Act shall, as applied by subsection (2) above, have effect as if the persons mentioned in paragraphs (a) to (c) of that subsection were included in the first column of the schedule to that Act, and any of the Commissioners or any secretary or assistant secretary to the Commissioners were specified in the second column of that schedule in connection with those persons.

(4)   A photograph of any document delivered to the Commissioners for any customs or excise purpose and certified by them to be such a photograph shall be admissible in any proceedings, whether civil or criminal, to the same extent as the document itself.

154.—(1)   An averment in any process in proceedings under the customs and excise Acts—

(a)   that those proceedings were instituted by the order of the Commissioners; or

(b)   that any person is or was a Commissioner, officer or constable, or a member of Her Majesty's armed forces or coastguard; or

(c)   that any person is or was appointed or authorised by the Commissioners to discharge, or was engaged by the orders or with the concurrence of the Commissioners in the discharge of, any duty; or

(d)   that the Commissioners have or have not been satisfied as to any matter as to which they are required by any provision of those Acts to be satisfied; or

(e)   that any ship is a British ship; or

(f)   that any goods thrown overboard, staved or destroyed were so dealt with in order to prevent or avoid the seizure of those goods,

shall, until the contrary is proved, be sufficient evidence of the matter in question.

(2)   Where in any proceedings relating to customs or excise any question arises as to the place from which any goods have been brought or as to whether or not—

(a)   any duty has been paid or secured in respect of any goods; or

(b)   any goods or other things whatsoever are of the description or nature alleged in the information, writ or other process; or

(c)   any goods have been lawfully imported or lawfully unloaded from any ship or aircraft; or

(d)   any goods have been lawfully loaded into any ship or aircraft or lawfully exported or were lawfully water-borne; or

(e)   any goods were lawfully brought to any place for the purpose of being loaded into any ship or aircraft or exported; or

(f)   any goods are or were subject to any prohibition of or restriction on their importation or exportation,

then where those proceedings are brought by or against the Commissioners, a law officer of the Crown or an officer, or against any other person in respect of anything purporting to have been done in pursuance of any power or duty conferred or imposed on him by or under the custom and excise Acts, the burden of proof shall be upon the other party to the proceedings.

OFFENCES IN CONNECTION WITH COMMISSIONERS AND OFFICERS

Unlawful Assumption of Character of Commissioner or Officer

Customs and Excise Management Act 1979, s. 13   B17.7

> If, for the purpose of obtaining admission to any house or other place, or of doing or procuring to be done any act which he would not be entitled to do or procure to be done of his own authority, or for any other unlawful purpose, any person falsely assumes the name, designation or character of a Commissioner or officer or of a person appointed by the Commissioners he may be arrested and shall . . . be liable . . . .

The offence is triable either way.

The penalties, which are prescribed by s. 13 are, on indictment, a penalty of any amount, or imprisonment for a term not exceeding two years or both. The penalties on summary conviction are a penalty of the prescribed sum or imprisonment for a term not exceeding three months or both (Customs and Excise Management Act 1979, s. 171, and MCA 1980, s. 32).

There appear to be no reported cases on this provision. The words 'for any other unlawful purpose' are obviously wide and could apply to an entry the purported purpose of which is not in relation to duties under the Customs and Excise Management Act 1979.

Bribery and Collusion

Bribery and collusion, both asking for and accepting payment or reward or offering it, **B17.8** are made offences under s. 15.

Customs and Excise Management Act 1979, s. 15

(1) If any Commissioner or officer or any person appointed or authorised by the Commissioners to discharge any duty relating to an assigned matter—

(a) directly or indirectly asks for or takes in connection with any of his duties any payment or other reward whatsoever, whether pecuniary or other, or any promise or security for any such payment or reward, not being a payment or reward which he is lawfully entitled to claim or receive; or

(b) enters into or acquiesces in any agreement to do, abstain from doing, permit, conceal or connive at any act or thing whereby Her Majesty is or may be defrauded or which is otherwise unlawful, being an act or thing relating to an assigned matter,

he shall be guilty of an offence under this section.

(2) If any person—

(a) directly or indirectly offers or gives to any Commissioner or officer or to any person appointed or authorised by the Commissioners as aforesaid any payment or reward whatsoever, whether pecuniary or other, or any promise or security for any such payment or reward; or

(b) proposes or enters into any agreement with any Commissioner, officer or person appointed or authorised as aforesaid,

in order to induce him to do, abstain from doing, permit, conceal or connive at any act or thing whereby Her Majesty is or may be defrauded or which is otherwise unlawful, being an act or thing relating to an assigned matter, or otherwise to take any course contrary to his duty, he shall be guilty of an offence under this section.

This offence is triable summarily only and is punishable by a fine at level 5 on the standard scale (s. 15(3), which also provides a power of arrest).

This section strikes at corrupt conduct both by officers of the Customs and Excise and by persons dealing with the Customs and Excise. The bribes or rewards mentioned by the section need not be pecuniary in character.

Obstruction of Officers etc.

B17.9 ## Customs and Excise Management Act 1979, s. 16

(1) Any person who—

(a) obstructs, hinders, molests or assaults any person duly engaged in the performance of any duty or the exercise of any power imposed or conferred on him by or under any enactment relating to an assigned matter, or any person acting in his aid; or

(b) does anything which impedes or is calculated to impede the carrying out of any search for any thing liable to forfeiture under any such enactment or the detention, seizure or removal of any such thing; or

(c) rescues, damages or destroys any thing so liable to forfeiture or does anything calculated to prevent the procuring or giving of evidence as to whether or not any thing is so liable to forfeiture; or

(d) prevents the arrest of any person by a person duly engaged or acting as aforesaid or rescues any person so arrested,

or who attempts to do any of the aforementioned things, shall be guilty of an offence under this section.

This offence is triable either way.

The penalties, which are prescribed by s. 16(2) are, on indictment, a penalty in any amount or imprisonment for not more than two years, or both. The penalties on summary conviction are a penalty of the prescribed sum or imprisonment for a term not exceeding three months or both.

The general principles concerning obstruction of a police officer (see **B2.25** to **B2.28**) apply. A person who, for example, gives false information to officers of the Customs and Excise, so making it harder for officers to perform their duty, is guilty of obstruction (*George* [1981] Crim LR 185).

IMPROPER IMPORTATION AND EXPORTATION OF GOODS

Improper Importation of Goods

Section 50 of the Act makes it an offence improperly to import goods.   **B17.10**

Customs and Excise Management Act 1979, s. 50

(1)   Subsection (2) below applies to goods of the following descriptions, that is to say—
    (a)   goods chargeable with a duty which has not been paid; and
    (b)   goods the importation, landing or unloading of which is for the time being prohibited or restricted by or under any enactment.
(2)   If any person with intent to defraud Her Majesty of any such duty or to evade any such prohibition or restriction as is mentioned in subsection (1) above—
    (a)   unships or lands in any port or unloads from any aircraft in the United Kingdom or from any vehicle in Northern Ireland any goods to which this subsection applies, or assists or is otherwise concerned in such unshipping, landing or unloading; or
    (b)   removes from their place of importation or from any approved wharf, examination station, transit shed or customs and excise station any goods to which this subsection applies or assists or is otherwise concerned in such removal,
he shall be guilty of an offence under this subsection and may be arrested.
(3)   If any person imports or is concerned in importing any goods contrary to any prohibition or restriction for the time being in force under or by virtue of any enactment with respect to those goods, whether or not the goods are unloaded, and does so with intent to evade the prohibition or restriction, he shall be guilty of an offence under this subsection and may be arrested.

This offence is triable either way. As to the power of arrest, see *Smith* [1973] QB 924.

Section 50(4), (5) and (5A) of, and sch. 1 to, the Act provide penalties. The standard penalties, provided by s. 50(4), are, on indictment, a penalty of any amount, or imprisonment for a term not exceeding seven years or both. The standard penalties, on summary conviction, are a penalty of the prescribed sum or of three times the value of the goods, whichever is the greater, or imprisonment for a term not exceeding six months, or both. Enhanced penalties are provided for by s. 50(5) and sch. 1 and are imposed in the following types of cases.

Where the goods in respect of which the offence is committed are drugs, the importation of which is prohibited by the Misuse of Drugs Act 1971, s. 3 (see **B17.11**), the following penalties apply. If the drug is a Class A or Class B drug (as to the meaning of which, see **B20.5**), on summary conviction, the penalty is six months and/or a penalty not exceeding the prescribed amount, or three times the value of the goods, whichever is the greater. On indictment, there is a penalty of unlimited amount and, in the case of a Class A drug, life imprisonment, or, in the case of a Class B drug, 14 years' imprisonment. If the drug is a Class C drug (see **B20.5**), the penalty is, on summary conviction, three months and/or a penalty of £500, or three times the value of the goods, whichever is the greater. On indictment there is a penalty of unlimited amount and five years' imprisonment.

Where the importation is of a counterfeit of a currency note or of a protected coin without the Treasury's consent (Forgery and Counterfeiting Act 1981, s. 20), the maximum penalty on indictment is enhanced to 10 years by s. 50(5A) of, and sch. 1 to, the Act. As to this offence, see **B6.90**.

As to prohibition or restriction, see *Superheater Co. Ltd* v *Commissioners of Customs and Excise* [1969] 1 WLR 858.

Goods entering the country by air are imported before they are unloaded, and goods brought in by sea are imported before they are landed. By s. 5(2) of the Act, the time of importation of goods brought in by sea is the time when the ship comes within the limits of the port. Goods which are unloaded at an airport and held in a customs area pending trans-shipment to a foreign destination are nonetheless regarded as having been imported into the United Kingdom (*Smith* [1973] QB 924, applying dicta in *DPP* v *Doot* [1973] AC 807).

As to who may be an importer, a person who brings in items under a 'duty free' arrangement for others, for example a bus driver bringing in goods for his passengers, is an importer of the goods and if they are beneficially his he can be convicted of being knowingly concerned in the fraudulent evasion of duty payable on them (*Collins* [1987] Crim LR 256).

The Customs and Excise Management Act 1979, s. 50(7), in order to prevent duplication of proceedings and possible double jeopardy problems, provides:

Customs and Excise Management Act 1979, s. 50

(7)   In any case where a person would, apart from this subsection, be guilty of—
   (a)   an offence under this section in connection with the importation of goods contrary to a prohibition or restriction; and
   (b)   a corresponding offence under the enactment or other instrument imposing the prohibition or restriction, being an offence for which a fine or other penalty is expressly provided by that enactment or other instrument,
he shall not be guilty of the offence mentioned in paragraph (a) of this subsection.

Prohibition on Importation and Exportation of Controlled Drugs

B17.11   **Misuse of Drugs Act 1971, s. 3**

(1)   Subject to subsection (2) below—
   (a)   the importation of a controlled drug; and
   (b)   the exportation of a controlled drug,
are hereby prohibited.
(2)   Subsection (1) above does not apply—
   (a)   to the importation or exportation of a controlled drug which is for the time being excepted from paragraph (a) or, as the case may be, paragraph (b) of subsection (1) above by regulations under section 7 of this Act; or
   (b)   to the importation or exportation of a controlled drug under and in accordance with the terms of a licence issued by the Secretary of State and in compliance with any conditions attached thereto.

The reference in s. 3(2)(b) to licences issued by the Secretary of State includes those licences granted for the purpose of the Drugs (Prevention of Misuse) Act 1964, s. 5, or the Dangerous Drugs Act 1965, ss. 2, 3 or 10 (Misuse of Drugs Act 1971, sch. 5, para. 2). Section 18(2) of the Misuse of Drugs Act 1971 makes it an offence to contravene any conditions imposed on such a licence. As to controlled drugs generally, see **B20**.

Section 3 of the Misuse of Drugs Act 1971 creates a prohibition, but does not expressly create an offence. Consequently, evasion of this prohibition should be charged as an offence of fraudulent evasion of duty (Customs and Excise Management Act 1979, s. 170) or improper importation or exportation of goods (ss. 50 and 68). It is also possible, where appropriate, to charge a conspiracy to evade the prohibition imposed by the Misuse of Drugs Act 1971, s. 3.

Where an offence of improper importation or exportation of goods, or fraudulent evasion of duty, involves controlled drugs, enhanced penalties come into effect; see Customs and Excise Management Act 1979, ss. 50(4) and (5), 68(3) and (4), 170(3) and (4) and sch. 1 (**B17.10, B17.14, B17.18**). For sentencing guidelines relating to controlled drugs, including importation of drugs, see **B20.137** *et seq*.

Misdescription of Imported Goods

B17.12   **Customs and Excise Management Act 1979, s. 50**

(6)   If any person—

(a) imports or causes to be imported any goods concealed in a container holding goods of a different description; or

(b) directly or indirectly imports or causes to be imported or entered any goods found, whether before or after delivery, not to correspond with the entry made thereof,

he shall be liable on summary conviction to a penalty of three times the value of the goods or level 3 on the standard scale, whichever is the greater.

This offence appears clearly to be a strict liability offence. It meets the criteria for strict liability and in particular it emphasises the need to take care in the furnishing of information, packaging of imports, etc. (*Gammon (Hong Kong) Ltd* v *A-G of Hong Kong* [1985] AC 1; and see generally **A4**).

Improper Unloading of Goods Loaded etc. for Exportation

The Customs and Excise Management Act 1979, s. 67, deals with the unloading of **B17.13** goods which have been loaded or retained on board any ship or aircraft for the purposes of exportation from the United Kingdom. It provides:

Customs and Excise Management Act 1979, s. 67

(1) If any goods which have been loaded or retained on board any ship or aircraft for exportation are not exported to and discharged at a place outside the United Kingdom but are unloaded in the United Kingdom, then, unless—

(a) the unloading was authorised by the proper officer; and

(b) except where the officer otherwise permits, any duty chargeable and unpaid on the goods is paid and any drawback or allowance paid in respect thereof is repaid,

the master of the ship or the commander of the aircraft and any person concerned in the unshipping, relanding, landing, unloading or carrying of the goods from the ship or aircraft without such authority, payment or repayment shall each be guilty of an offence under this section.

(2) The Commissioners may impose such conditions as they see fit with respect to any goods loaded or retained as mentioned in subsection (1) above which are permitted to be unloaded in the United Kingdom.

(3) If any person contravenes or fails to comply with, or is concerned in any contravention of or failure to comply with, any condition imposed under subsection (2) above he shall be guilty of an offence under this section.

(4) Where any goods loaded or retained as mentioned in subsection (1) above or brought to a customs and excise station for exportation by land are—

(a) goods from a warehouse, other than goods which have been kept, without being warehoused, in a warehouse by virtue of section 92(4) . . .;

(b) transit goods;

(c) other goods chargeable with a duty which has not been paid; or

(d) drawback goods,

then if any container in which the goods are held is without the authority of the proper officer opened, or any mark, letter or device on any such container or on any lot of the goods is without that authority cancelled, obliterated or altered, every person concerned in the opening, cancellation, obliteration or alteration shall be guilty of an offence under this section.

The offence is triable only summarily. The penalty is forfeiture of goods and a penalty of three times the value of the goods or level 3 on the standard scale, whichever is the greater (s. 67(5)).

Offences in Relation to Exportation of Prohibited or Restricted Goods

Customs and Excise Management Act 1979, s. 68   B17.14

(1) If any goods are—

(a) exported or shipped as stores; or

(b) brought to any place in the United Kingdom for the purpose of being exported or shipped as stores, and the exportation or shipment is or would be contrary to any prohibition or restriction for the time being in force with respect to those goods under or by virtue of any enactment, the goods shall be liable to forfeiture and the exporter or intending exporter of the goods and any agent of his concerned in the exportation or shipment or intended exportation or shipment shall each be liable on summary conviction to a penalty of three times the value of the goods or level three on the standard scale, whichever is the greater.

(2)   Any person knowingly concerned in the exportation or shipment as stores, or in the attempted exportation or shipment as stores, of any goods with intent to evade any such prohibition or restriction as is mentioned in subsection (1) above shall be guilty of an offence under this subsection and may be arrested.

. . .

(5)   If by virtue of any such restriction as is mentioned in subsection (1) above any goods may be exported only when consigned to a particular place or person and any goods so consigned are delivered to some other place or person, the ship, aircraft or vehicle in which they were exported shall be liable to forfeiture unless it is proved to the satisfaction of the Commissioners that both the owner of the ship, aircraft or vehicle and the master of the ship, commander of the aircraft or person in charge of the vehicle—

(a)   took all reasonable steps to secure that the goods were delivered to the particular place to which or person to whom they were consigned; and

(b)   did not connive at or, except under duress, consent to the delivery of the goods to that other place or person.

(6)   In any case where a person would, apart from this subsection be guilty of—

(a)   an offence under subsection (1) or (2) above; and

(b)   a corresponding offence under the enactment or instrument imposing the prohibition or restriction in question, being an offence for which a fine or other penalty is expressly provided by that enactment or other instrument,

he shall not be guilty of the offence mentioned in paragraph (a) of this subsection.

The offence is triable either way. As to the power of arrest, see *Smith* [1973] QB 924.

Section 68(3), (4), (4A), and sch. 1 to the Act prescribe the penalties. On summary conviction there may be imposed a penalty of the prescribed sum or of three times the value of the goods whichever is the greater, or imprisonment for a term not exceeding six months or both. On conviction on indictment there may be imposed a penalty of any amount, or imprisonment for a term not exceeding two years, or both (s. 68(3)).

By sch. 1 to the Act, and by subsections (4) and (4A) of s. 68, dealing respectively with drugs and counterfeit notes and currency, provision is made for enhancement of penalties; the provisions are those discussed in relation to prohibited imports under s. 50 of the Act (see **B17.10**). The penalties are modified where a person is convicted of an offence contrary to s. 68 by virtue of the application of reg. 3 of the Controlled Drugs (Substances Useful for Manufacture) Regulations 1991 (SI 1991 No. 1285), which makes provision in relation to the breach of certain EC legislation designed to enable the authorities to obtain information on any orders for, or operations involving, substances used for the manufacture of controlled drugs. In these cases, the maximum penalty under s. 68(1)(b) is a fine not exceeding the statutory maximum, and, under s. 68(3)(a), the maximum penalty is a fine not exceeding the statutory maximum or imprisonment for a term not exceeding three months.

Provision for forfeiture is made, subject to defences, by s. 68(5) above.

It has been held, under similar defence legislation, that a person may be convicted of an offence of unlawful exportation even though he intends to bring the goods back to the United Kingdom (*Berner* (1953) 37 Cr App R 113).

A person can be concerned with the exportation of goods even if the acts which he performs take place at a time other than that which constitutes exportation. A person can be so concerned, for example, at a time prior to the departure of an aircraft (*Garrett v Arthur Churchill (Glass) Ltd* [1970] 1 QB 92).

The prosecution must show both that the export of the goods was prohibited (e.g., by the Export of Goods (Control) Order 1992 (SI 1992 No. 3092)), and that the accused knew that the goods fell into a prohibited category (*Daghir* [1994] Crim LR 945). Section 68(2) is cast in terms of evasion. This, by contrast with the interpretation given to evasion in the law of income tax, does not require an element of fraud or dishonesty, but is, rather, given its ordinary English meaning, i.e. 'to get around' or 'avoid' (*Hurford-Jones* (1977) 65 Cr App R 263).

Garrett v *Arthur Churchill (Glass) Ltd* [1970] 1 QB 92 is also of importance in holding that a person who hands over goods belonging to another, knowing that the other proposes to export them unlawfully, is knowingly concerned in the unlawful importation. The person's duty to hand over goods to their owner yields to the public interest in preventing such exportation.

Under the Export of Goods (Control) Order 1992, an export which would otherwise be forbidden may be licensed by the Department of Trade and Industry. Such a licence will not bar a prosecution under s. 68(2) where a shipment is in fact to a destination other than that specified in the licence. Even if it cannot be proved that a licence was obtained by misrepresentation, a prosecution may still be brought if the actor seeks to evade the prohibition by specifying a sham consignee (*Redfern and Dunlop Ltd (Aircraft Division)* [1993] Crim LR 43).

An order prohibiting exportation is no less valid where its substance falls within a matter governed by the common commercial policy of the EU; this is so even though the matter is also covered by an EEC Regulation provided that the order and the Regulation are not incompatible (*Searle and KCS Products* [1996] Crim LR 58).

FRAUDULENT EVASION OF DUTY ('SMUGGLING')

Definition

Customs and Excise Management Act 1979, s. 170   B17.15

(1)   Without prejudice to any other provision of the Customs and Excise Acts 1979, if any person—
(a)   knowingly acquires possession of any of the following goods, that is to say—
(i)   goods which have been unlawfully removed from a warehouse or Queen's warehouse;
(ii)   goods which are chargeable with a duty which has not been paid;
(iii)   goods with respect to the importation or exportation of which any prohibition or restriction is for the time being in force under or by virtue of any enactment; or
(b)   is in any way knowingly concerned in carrying, removing, depositing, harbouring, keeping or concealing or in any manner dealing with any such goods,
and does so with intent to defraud Her Majesty of any duty payable on the goods or to evade any such prohibition or restriction with respect to the goods he shall be guilty of an offence under this section and may be arrested.

(2)   Without prejudice to any other provision of the Customs and Excise Acts 1979, if any person is, in relation to any goods, in any way knowingly concerned in any fraudulent evasion or attempt at evasion—
(a)   of any duty chargeable on the goods;
(b)   of any prohibition or restriction for the time being in force with respect to the goods under or by virtue of any enactment; or
(c)   of any provision of the Customs and Excise Acts 1979 applicable to the goods,
he shall be guilty of an offence under this section and may be arrested.
. . .
(5)   In any case where a person would, apart from this subsection, be guilty of—
(a)   an offence under this section in connection with a prohibition or restriction; and
(b)   a corresponding offence under the enactment or other instrument imposing the prohibition or restriction, being an offence for which a fine or other penalty is expressly provided by that enactment or other instrument,

he shall not be guilty of the offence mentioned in paragraph (a) of this subsection.

Procedure

B17.16   The offence is triable either way. Subsection (5) operates to prevent duplication of proceedings and possible double jeopardy problems.

Indictment (for offences under s. 170(1)(b))

B17.17   Statement of Offence

Being knowingly concerned in concealing goods with intent to avoid prohibition on importation contrary to section 170(1)(b) of the Customs and Excise Management Act 1979

Particulars of Offence

A on the . . . day of . . . was knowingly concerned in concealing goods, that is to say a quantity of a controlled drug, namely . . . valued at £ . . ., with intent to evade the prohibition on importation of the said goods then in force pursuant to section 3 of the Misuse of Drugs Act 1971

As to the Misuse of Drugs Act 1971, s. 3, see **B17.11** and as to controlled drugs generally, see **B20**.

Sentencing Guidelines

B17.18   The maximum penalty on summary conviction is a penalty of the prescribed sum or of three times the value of the goods, whichever is the greater, and/or to imprisonment for a term not exceeding six months. The maximum penalty on indictment is a penalty of any amount and/or imprisonment for a term not exceeding seven years.

In cases involving drugs and counterfeiting, penalties may be enhanced (s. 170(4), (4A) and sch. 1). The enhancement is identical to that provided for in the case of s. 50 of the Act (see **B17.10**). For sentencing guidelines in such cases, see section **B20.137** *et seq*.

Apart from the cases on importation on drugs, there are relatively few cases on the appropriate sentencing bracket for 'smuggling'. Sentencing guidelines for this offence were issued by the Court of Appeal in *Dosanjh* [1998] 3 All ER 603, where a sentence of three years' imprisonment was upheld on an offender who was a passenger in a van which was stopped by the police and found to contain a large number of cans of beer. The offender had been involved in making trips across the Channel in hired vehicles at about twice weekly intervals to obtain drink and cigarettes from duty free shops. He had been stopped by Customs authorities on two previous occasions, when the goods had been confiscated. It was accepted that a total of £164,000 in duty had been evaded.

The Court of Appeal noted that the maximum penalty for the offence under s. 170 had been increased from two years to seven years in 1988, which made earlier sentencing cases, such as *Hart* (1986) 8 Cr App R (S) 337, unreliable as guides to the appropriate level of sentence. There were similarities between defrauding the customs and excise authorities by evading duty and the evasion of payment of VAT, for which offence the maximum penalty was also seven years. Some assistance in sentencing was to be derived from the authorities on VAT evasion, such as *Aziz* [1996] 1 Cr App R (S) 265 (see **B16.14**), as well as some of the authorities on duty evasion. As had been said in *Ollerenshaw* [1999] 1 Cr App R (S) 65, those who evaded significant amounts of duty should expect to receive prison sentences, the term of imprisonment being dependent upon a number of factors including the amount of duty evaded. Aggravating factors on sentence would include playing an organisational role in the importation, repeated importations over a period of time, continuing to make importations despite a warning, and importing more than one type of dutiable goods. Mitigation would lie in a prompt plea of guilty, previous good character and in the personal circumstances of the offender. A distinction should be drawn between offenders who imported comparatively small quantities on a few occasions, those who imported greater quantities, and those involved on a large, commercial scale.

Cases involving less than £10,000 would frequently, though not always, properly be dealt with by magistrates. In any event, where the amount evaded was in thousands of pounds, custody would generally be called for and, on a plea of guilty, sentences of up to six months would be appropriate. For amounts between £10,000 and £100,000, sentences between six months and two years would generally be appropriate on a guilty plea. For amounts between £100,000 and £500,000, two to three years on a guilty plea, and up to four years following a trial, would generally be appropriate. For amounts in excess of £500,000, sentences in the region of four years, increasing to the statutory maximum of seven years when £1 million or more in duty is evaded, would be appropriate following a trial, with a suitable discount for a plea of guilty. In exceptional cases, where very many millions of pounds in duty were evaded, it might be appropriate to charge conspiracy to cheat, which was capable of attracting higher sentences. In addition to ordering imprisonment, in an appropriate case the court might also consider making an order under the PCCA 1973, s. 43 (see **E20.1**), and disqualifying drivers under s. 44 of the same Act (see **E23.4**).

In *Sperr* (1992) 13 Cr App R (S) 8, a sentence of nine months' imprisonment was imposed on an offender who pleaded guilty to being knowingly involved in fraudulently evading the prohibition on the importation of a prohibited species of endangered falcon. He was stopped when entering the country and found to have four young birds concealed in his car. The material imported by the offender in *Payne* (1995) 16 Cr App R (S) 782 was 1,796 canisters of CS gas, found concealed within the bodywork of his car. The possession of CS gas is prohibited by the Firearms Act 1968. The Court of Appeal said that importation of CS gas in anything other than a modest quantity should be dealt with by a custodial sentence, notwithstanding that its possession for personal protection is lawful in other countries, although the offender's sentence was reduced from three years' to two years' imprisonment.

Scope of Offence

These are wide prohibitions. Section 170 of the Customs and Excise Management Act **B17.19** 1979 is in the nature of a clearing-up provision, which covers importing, exporting, those concerned in actual import and export, and even persons who cannot be proved to be implicated in an actual import or export; s. 170(1) is a sweeping provision and it is hard to think of anything in s. 170(2) which does not in fact come within s. 170(1) (*Neal* [1984] 3 All ER 156). One possibility may be, however, that a person could knowingly come into possession of unlawfully imported goods contrary to s. 170(1)(a)(iii) without himself being concerned in their importation contrary to s. 170(2)(b).

Mens Rea

Under s. 170(1) of the Act it must be shown that the accused knowingly performed **B17.20** certain acts with intent to defraud Her Majesty or with intent to evade a relevant prohibition or restriction. In relation to knowingly harbouring goods, it is usually enough to show that goods which were subject to duty were found in the possession of the accused. This will establish a prima facie case of knowingly harbouring subject to the accused's ability to rebut this by evidence casting doubt upon his knowledge. Once the Crown has adduced a case of knowing possession, the accused must prove that the goods were in fact customed (see the Customs and Excise Management Act 1979, s. 154 (**B17.6** above) and *Cohen* [1951] 1 KB 505).

Under s. 170(2) the words 'fraudulent evasion' refer not to behaviour before a customs officer, but to the evasion or attempted evasion of the prohibition. They include more than merely entering the United Kingdom with goods concealed and with no intention of declaring them; they extend to any conduct which was directed and intended to lead to the importation of goods covertly in breach of a prohibition on import (*Latif* [1995] 1 Cr App R 270). It was held in *Latif* that the guilty mind need not subsist at the time of the importation: thus one who is recruited to pick up a package which has already arrived has a sufficient *mens rea* because he is then concerned with bringing about the importation. The offence is thus not limited to acts of deceit perpetrated upon a customs officer in his presence (*A-G's Ref (No. 1 of 1981)* [1982] QB 848). A person who presents goods for an assessment of duty does not act fraudulently by not disclosing his assessment of their worth, or by failing to alert a customs officer that the officer's valuation is wrong. In the absence of a false statement or concealment, the payment of duty demanded by a customs officer discharges the person's liability (*Customs and Excise Commissioners* v *Tan* [1977] AC 650).

The prosecution must under s. 170(2) prove both an intent to evade a prohibition and knowledge on the part of the accused of the relevant circumstances, for example in a case of smuggling by sea that he had in fact entered territorial waters. Mere knowledge by the accused that he was at the relevant time running the risk of entering territorial waters is not enough (*Panayi (No. 2)* [1989] 1 WLR 187).

The accused may have formed a guilty intent outside the United Kingdom. As will be seen, the offence under s. 170(2) may be committed by a person abroad, and if the intent is formed abroad and acts constituting the offence are done there, liability will be complete. Subsequent repentance will not found a defence (*Jakeman* (1983) 76 Cr App R 223).

Actus Reus

B17.21 These are wide provisions and in procedural terms s. 170(2) is an 'activity' offence which could relate to a single incident or a series of incidents forming an activity, any of which could be charged in a single count (*Martin* [1998] 2 Cr App R 385). Section 170(2) of the Act does not require an actual fraudulent importation or the deceiving of anyone; an offence contrary to s. 170 can be committed by evasion or attempted evasion and it matters not that the accused's acts took place abroad (*Latif* [1996] 1 WLR 104). Neither s. 170(1) nor s. 170(2) is restricted to those who form part of an original smuggling team (*Neal* [1984] 3 All ER 156). A person may be liable for acts done abroad prior to the actual smuggling, as well as for participation in the act of entry itself, and for acts subsequent to entry relating for example to disposal of the goods (*Jakeman* (1983) 76 Cr App R 223; *Wall* [1974] 1 WLR 930 where the accused took part in Afghanistan in the loading of cannabis for the purpose of exporting it to the United Kingdom). In certain cases the courts have construed the section very widely. In *Green* [1976] QB 985 the accused and another arranged customs clearance for a crate which, at the moment of importation, contained cannabis. Customs officials substituted a harmless substance before the crate left the warehouse. The accused who assisted in the operation by renting a garage and unloading a crate was held liable on the footing that the evasion of the prohibition continues until the goods cease to be prohibited goods or, possibly, are exported. Renting a garage is an act concerned in the evasion of the prohibition. A narrower and, it is submitted, less difficult ground for decision might be that the making of such arrangements constituted being concerned in the evasion, at least if it was done before substitution of the contents, though such an approach could encounter difficulties of proof. Evasion of the relevant prohibition is a continuing process; thus a person who, even after goods have been innocently imported by a carrier, falsely declares that his possessions contain no prohibited material, commits the offence (*Coughlan* (12 May 1997 unreported)).

The same principles as to when the offence begins and ends appear in cases of conspiracy to evade a prohibition, etc. There can, it is said, be no abstract limit to the time when or place at which the crime is committed, provided always that the goods, the subject matter of the charge, are goods which are the subject of a prohibition on importation and the acquisition is done knowingly and with intent to evade that prohibition or restriction (*Ardalan* [1972] 1 WLR 463; *Caippara* (1987) 87 Cr App R 316). In *Caippara*, in the context of importation of drugs, the Court of Appeal held that a person may be guilty if it be proved that he was willing to participate in a chain of activities which would result in drugs being imported into the United Kingdom, notwithstanding that the Customs has substituted a harmless substance for them before delivery to the recipient. Acts done after importation can be done in furtherance of a conspiracy since the conspiracy is not to import but to evade a restriction (*Borro* [1973] Crim LR 513).

It need not be proved that the accused was aware of the exact nature of the articles to which a restriction applies. If a person believes himself to be engaged in the importation of goods which are not subject to a restriction or prohibition, he cannot be convicted (*Taaffe* [1984] AC 539). He is to be judged on the facts as he believed them to be. If he believes himself to be importing narcotics whereas the substance is snuff, he may be convicted of attempting to evade a prohibition or restriction (*Shivpuri* [1987] AC 1). If on the other hand he imports drugs believing them to be pornography, he will be liable for the offence (*Ellis* (1986) 84 Cr App R 235; *Hennessey* (1978) 68 Cr App R 419). In the context of importing an obscene article, a person who knows the nature of the material imported and who believes it to be obscene will be liable for the offence even though no jury trying a case under the Obscene Publications Act 1959 has determined the article to be so: knowledge and belief suffice for guilt (*Dunne* (1998) 162 JP 399).

Particular problems concern drugs where, as noted, importation and exportation offences vary in severity according to whether the drug is a class A, B, or C drug. Rejecting an argument based on *Courtie* [1984] AC 463, Lord Bridge intimated in *Shivpuri* [1987] AC 1 that the legislative history of the Misuse of Drugs Act 1971, from where the prohibition comes, makes it clear that while possession of class A, B, or C drugs are distinct offences, the offence of being concerned in importation requires proof only that the accused knew that he was engaged in evading restrictions on the importation of a prohibited article. Lord Bridge's dictum has been followed in *Siracusa* (1989) 90 Cr App R 340. The prosecution must prove that the accused knew that the goods in question were prohibited goods, but need not prove that the accused knew (precisely) what they were. The same case holds that, on a charge of conspiracy to contravene s. 170(2) of the Customs and Excise Management Act 1979, by the importation of heroin for example, the prosecution must prove that the agreed course of conduct was to import heroin, simply because the agreement is the essence of conspiracy and one cannot prove an agreement to import heroin by proving an agreement to import cannabis.

The fact of importation, where relevant, must be proved. It is then incumbent on the accused to prove factors in justification mentioned in the Customs and Excise Management Act 1979, s. 154 (see **B17.6**), such as that the goods were made here or that duty has been paid (*Watts* (1979) 70 Cr App R 187; *Mizel* v *Warren* [1973] 1 WLR 899).

Armed 'Smuggling'

Customs and Excise Management Act 1979, s. 86   B17.22

Any person concerned in the movement, carriage or concealment of goods—
(a)   contrary to or for the purpose of contravening any prohibition or restriction for the time being in force under or by virtue of any enactment with respect to the importation or exportation thereof; or

(b)   without payment having been made of or security given for any duty payable thereon,

who, while so concerned, is armed with any offensive weapon or disguised in any way, and any person so armed or disguised found in the United Kingdom in possession of any goods liable to forfeiture under any provision of the customs and excise Acts relating to imported goods or prohibited or restricted goods, shall be liable on conviction on indictment to imprisonment for a term not exceeding three years and may be arrested.

The expression 'armed' is an ordinary English word. Normally, it will involve either physically carrying arms or proof that, to the accused's knowledge, the arms concerned are immediately available. It is not necessary to prove an intent to use those arms if the situation should require it (*Jones* [1987] 1 WLR 692, in which the earlier authorities are extensively discussed). As to the meaning of 'offensive weapon' (which is not defined by the Act) see the meaning assigned by the Prevention of Crime Act 1953, s. 1(4) (see **B12.88** to **B12.91**), which may be applicable to the offence under s. 86.

Untrue Declarations

B17.23 **Customs and Excise Management Act 1979, s. 167**

(1)   If any person either knowingly or recklessly—

(a)   makes or signs, or causes to be made or signed, or delivers or causes to be delivered to the Commissioners or an officer, any declaration, notice, certificate or other document whatsoever; or

(b)   makes any statement in answer to any question put to him by an officer which he is required by or under any enactment to answer,

being a document or statement produced or made for any purpose or any assigned matter, which is untrue in any material particular, he shall be guilty of an offence under this subsection and may be arrested; and any goods in relation to which the document or statement was made shall be liable to forfeiture.

(2)   Without prejudice to subsection (4) below, a person who commits an offence under subsection (1) above shall be liable—

(a)   on summary conviction, to a penalty of the prescribed sum, or to imprisonment for a term not exceeding six months, or to both; or

(b)   on conviction on indictment, to a penalty of any amount, or to imprisonment for a term not exceeding two years, or to both.

(3)   If any person—

(a)   makes or signs, or causes to be made or signed, or delivers or causes to be delivered to the Commissioners or an officer, any declaration, notice, certificate or other document whatsoever; or

(b)   makes any statement in answer to any question put to him by an officer which he is required by or under any enactment to answer,

being a document or statement produced or made for any purpose of any assigned matter, which is untrue in any material particular, then, without prejudice to subsection (4) below, he shall be liable on summary conviction to a penalty of level 4 on the standard scale.

(4)   Where by reason of any such document or statement as is mentioned in subsection (1) or (3) above the full amount of any duty payable is not paid or any overpayment is made in respect of any drawback, allowance, rebate or repayment of duty, the amount of the duty unpaid or of the overpayment shall be recoverable as a debt due to the Crown or may be summarily recovered as a civil debt.

There is little case law interpreting this provision though in *Cross* [1987] Crim LR 43 it was, not surprisingly, held that the construction of documents is for the judge and not the jury.

It would seem that inadvertent *Caldwell* recklessness is applicable to the offence, under s. 167(1), because it does not require dishonesty. See generally **A2.5** *et seq*. The offence under subsection (3) would seem to be an offence of strict liability (*Patel* v *Comptroller of Customs* [1966] AC 356).

Counterfeiting Documents

Customs and Excise Management Act 1979, s. 168   B17.24

(1)   If any person—
    (a)   counterfeits or falsifies any document which is required by or under any enactment relating to an assigned matter or which is used in the transaction of any business relating to an assigned matter; or
    (b)   knowingly accepts, receives or uses any such document so counterfeited or falsified; or
    (c)   alters any such document after it is officially issued; or
    (d)   counterfeits any seal, signature, initials or other mark of, or used by, any office
for the verification of such a document or for the security of goods or for any other purpose relating to an assigned matter,
he shall be guilty of an offence under this section and may be arrested.

Offences under s. 168(1) are triable either way.

Under s. 168(2) of the Act the penalty, on indictment, is a penalty of any amount and/or imprisonment for a term not exceeding two years. The penalty on summary conviction, is a penalty of the prescribed sum and/or imprisonment for a term not exceeding six months.

There do not seem to be any cases interpreting this provision. In *Patel* v *Comptroller of Customs* [1966] AC 356, however, it was held that falsification and counterfeiting require *mens rea*. It may be helpful to refer to the law on these subjects under the Forgery and Counterfeiting Act 1981. See generally **B6.23** to **B6.26** and **B6.60**.

SECTION B18: OFFENCES INVOLVING MISUSE OF COMPUTERS

Unauthorised Access Offence ('Hacking')

B18.1   **Computer Misuse Act 1990, s. 1**

(1)   A person is guilty of an offence if—

(a)   he causes a computer to perform any function with intent to secure access to any program or data held in any computer;

(b)   the access he intends to secure is unauthorised; and

(c)   he knows at the time when he causes the computer to perform the function that that is the case.

(2)   The intent a person has to have to commit an offence under this section need not be directed at—

(a)   any particular program or data;

(b)   a program or data of any particular kind; or

(c)   a program or data held in any particular computer.

(3)   A person guilty of an offence under this section shall be liable on summary conviction to imprisonment for a term not exceeding six months or to a fine not exceeding level 5 on the standard scale or to both.

Section 1 creates a summary offence. The *actus reus* of the offence requires the defendant to 'cause a computer to perform any function'. This is meant to exclude mere physical contact with a computer and the scrutiny of data without any interaction with a computer (thus the reading of confidential computer output, the reading of data displayed on the screen, or 'computer eavesdropping', are not covered). On the other hand there is no requirement that the defendant should succeed in obtaining access to the program or data, or be successful in subverting computer security measures in place. A remote hacker would, thus, 'cause a computer to perform any function' if he accessed it remotely and the computer responded, e.g., by activating a computer security device or by offering a log-on menu. The substantive offence is thus drafted in such a way as to include conduct which might usually be thought to fall within the scope of the law of attempt. The words 'any computer' in s. 1(1)(a) entail that the offence is not restricted to a case where the accused uses one computer to gain unauthorised access to the target computer. Direct access to the target computer is also covered (see *A-G's Ref (No. 1 of 1991)* [1993] QB 94).

The access to the program or data which the defendant intends to secure must be 'unauthorised' access (s. 1(1)(b)). In *DPP* v *Bignell* [1998] 1 Cr App R 1, the Divisional Court held that an offence under s. 1 of the Act was not committed where police officers extracted details of two cars from a police computer for private purposes, since the officers were entitled to access the police computer, albeit only for legitimate police purposes. *Bignell* was, however, overruled by the House of Lords in *Bow Street Metropolitan Stipendiary Magistrate, ex parte Government of the USA* [1999] 3 WLR 620. There, the accused was authorised by her employer to access computer records of those who owed money to American Express. She accessed accounts on which she had not been instructed to work and supplied information to co-defendants, allowing them to forge credit cards and obtain large amounts of money. Lord Hobhouse explained that s. 1 and s. 17(5)(a) of the 1990 Act were concerned with whether the defendant was authorised to access the actual data involved, rather than data of that general kind.

There are two limbs to the *mens rea* of the offence. The first limb is the 'intent to secure access to any program or data held in any computer'. The word 'any' makes it clear that the intent need not relate to the computer which the defendant is at that time operating.

Subsection (2) explains that the defendant's intent need not be directed at any particular program or data, so as to include the hacker who accesses a computer without any clear idea of what he will find there. Recklessness is insufficient; still less would careless or inattentive accessing of the computer suffice for liability. The second limb is that the defendant must know at the time when he causes the computer to perform the function that the access which he intends to secure is unauthorised. The prosecution must prove both limbs.

Since this offence is summary only, there can be no charge of an attempt in respect of it. There is, however, the possibility of secondary liability arising under the MCA 1980, s. 44(1), where, for example, a person supplies a hacker with information which would assist him, such as a confidential computer password. The operator of a computer hacker 'bulletin board' might, therefore, come within the reach of the offence.

A number of terms are defined in the Computer Misuse Act 1990, s. 17.

Computer Misuse Act 1990, s. 17

(1)   The following provisions of this section apply for the interpretation of this Act.

(2)   A person secures access to any program or data held in a computer if by causing a computer to perform any function he—

(a)   alters or erases the program or data;

(b)   copies or moves it to any storage medium other than that in which it is held or to a different location in the storage medium in which it is held;

(c)   uses it; or

(d)   has it output from the computer in which it is held (whether by having it displayed or in any other manner);

and references to access to a program or data (and to an intent to secure such access) shall be read accordingly.

(3)   For the purposes of subsection (2)(c) above a person uses a program if the function he causes the computer to perform—

(a)   causes the program to be executed; or

(b)   is itself a function of the program.

(4)   For the purposes of subsection (2)(d) above—

(a)   program is output if the instructions of which it consists are output; and

(b)   the form in which any such instructions or any other data is output (and in particular whether or not it represents a form in which, in the case of instructions, they are capable of being executed or, in the case of data, it is capable of being processed by a computer) is immaterial.

(5)   Access of any kind by any person to any program or data held in a computer is unauthorised if—

(a)   he is not himself entitled to control access of the kind in question to the program or data; and

(b)   he does not have consent to access by him of the kind in question to the program or data from any person who is so entitled,

but this subsection is subject to section 10.

(6)   References to any program or data held in a computer include references to any program or data held in any removable storage medium which is for the time being in the computer; and a computer is to be regarded as containing any program or data held in any such medium.

(7)   A modification of the contents of any computer takes place if, by the operation of any function of the computer concerned or any other computer—

(a)   any program or data held in the computer concerned is altered or erased; or

(b)   any program or data is added to its contents;

and any act which contributes towards causing such a modification shall be regarded as causing it.

(8)   Such a modification is unauthorised if—

(a)   the person whose act causes it is not himself entitled to determine whether the modification should be made; and

(b) he does not have consent to the modification from any person who is so entitled.

(9) References to the home country concerned shall be read in accordance with section 4(6) above.

(10) References to a program include references to part of a program.

The terms 'computer', 'data' and 'program' are not defined in the Computer Misuse Act 1990 and should, therefore, be given their ordinary meaning by the courts. Section 10 of the Act deals with access to computer material for law enforcement purposes.

Unauthorised Access Offence with Intent to Commit Further Offences

B18.2   **Computer Misuse Act 1990, s. 2**

(1) A person is guilty of an offence under this section if he commits an offence under section 1 above ('the unauthorised access offence') with intent—

(a) to commit an offence to which this section applies; or

(b) to facilitate the commission of such an offence (whether by himself or by any other person);

and the offence he intends to commit or facilitate is referred to below in this section as the further offence.

(2) This section applies to offences—

(a) for which the sentence is fixed by law; or

(b) for which a person of 21 years of age or over (not previously convicted) may be sentenced to imprisonment for a term of five years (or, in England and Wales, might be so sentenced but for the restrictions imposed by section 33 of the Magistrates' Courts Act 1980).

(3) It is immaterial for the purposes of this section whether the further offence is to be committed on the same occasion as the unauthorised access offence or on any future occasion.

(4) A person may be guilty of an offence under this section even though the facts are such that the commission of the further offence is impossible.

(5) A person guilty of an offence under this section shall be liable—

(a) on summary conviction, to imprisonment for a term not exceeding six months or to a fine not exceeding the statutory maximum or to both; and

(b) on conviction on indictment, to imprisonment for a term not exceeding five years or to a fine or to both.

Section 2 creates an offence, triable either way, of committing the unauthorised access offence under s. 1 (see **B18.1**) with intent to commit or facilitate the commission of a more serious 'further' offence. It is not necessary to prove that the intended further offence has actually been committed. Where a charge is brought under s. 2, a conviction for the lesser offence under s. 1 is possible if the further intention is not proved (s. 12).

A person will be guilty of an offence under the Computer Misuse Act 1990, s. 2, in a range of situations. Obtaining the unauthorised access may, for example, be done with the intention of committing theft, such as by diverting funds, which are in the course of an electronic funds transfer, to the defendant's own bank account, or to the bank account of an accomplice. It would also cover the case where the defendant gained unauthorised access to sensitive information held on computer with a view to blackmailing the person to whom that information related.

Section 2(2) explains what qualifies as a further offence for the purposes of the s. 2 offence. Section 2(3) makes clear that the defendant may intend to commit the further offence on the same occasion as the unauthorised access offence (as in the theft example just given) or on a future occasion (as in the blackmail example). Section 2(4) makes it possible to convict a person who intended to commit the further offence even if, on the facts, that would be impossible (e.g., where the intended blackmail victim was, unknown to the defendant, dead). This rule is analogous to that in the Criminal Attempts Act 1981, s. 1(2), as applied in *Shivpuri* [1987] AC 1. See **A6.40**.

Unauthorised Modification of Computer Material

Computer Misuse Act 1990, s. 3   **B18.3**

(1) A person is guilty of an offence if—

(a) he does an act which causes an unauthorised modification of the contents of any computer; and

(b) at the time when he does the act he has the requisite intent and the requisite knowledge.

(2) For the purposes of subsection (1)(b) above the requisite intent is an intent to cause a modification of the contents of any computer and by so doing—

(a) to impair the operation of any computer;

(b) to prevent or hinder access to any program or data held in any computer; or

(c) to impair the operation of any such program or the reliability of any such data.

(3) The intent need not be directed at—

(a) any particular computer;

(b) any particular program or data or a program or data of any particular kind; or

(c) any particular modification or a modification of any particular kind.

(4) For the purposes of subsection (1)(b) above the requisite knowledge is knowledge that any modification he intends to cause is unauthorised.

(5) It is immaterial for the purposes of this section whether an unauthorised modification or any intended effect of it of a kind mentioned in subsection (2) above is, or is intended to be, permanent or merely temporary.

(6) For the purposes of the Criminal Damage Act 1971 a modification of the contents of a computer shall not be regarded as damaging any computer or computer storage medium unless its effect on that computer or computer storage medium impairs its physical condition.

(7) A person guilty of an offence under this section shall be liable—

(a) on summary conviction, to imprisonment for a term not exceeding six months or to a fine not exceeding the statutory maximum or to both; and

(b) on conviction on indictment, to imprisonment for a term not exceeding five years or to a fine or to both.

Section 3 creates an offence triable either way. When read in the context of s. 17 (see **B18.1**), it is clear that a wide range of different forms of conduct are included. It covers all cases involving deliberate (recklessness is insufficient) alteration or erasure of any program or data held on a computer (s. 17(7)(a)), where the defendant intended thereby to impair a computer's operation, hinder access to computer material by a legitimate user or impair the operation or reliability of computer held material, and where he knew that the intended modification was unauthorised. It does not have to be proved that the defendant had any specific target computer, program or data in mind.

The section would also extend to a case where the defendant intentionally introduced a computer 'worm' program into a computer system, where such a program uses up all the spare capacity on the computer by adding programs or data to the computer's contents (s. 17(7)(b)), thereby impairing its operation (s. 3(2)(a)). A likely effect of the introduction of a 'worm' is to prevent or hinder access to a legitimate user (s. 3(2)(b)).

Also within the section is the intentional inroduction of a computer 'virus' into a computer system. Where X deliberately introduces into circulation a floppy disk contaminated with a computer virus and Y, an innocent party, uses the disk on his computer, impairing its operation, it seems that X would be guilty of the offence at the time he introduced the disk into circulation, since s. 17(7) states that any act which contributes towards causing such a modification shall be regarded as causing it. The liability of X would be unaffected by Y passing the disk, unused, to another innocent party, Z, who uses the disk and impairs the operation of Z's computer since X's intent need not be directed at any particular computer, program or data (s. 3(3)).

The s. 3 offence would also cater for a case where the defendant intentionally causes an unauthorised modification of the contents of a computer, intending thereby to prevent or hinder access by legitimate users to any data or program held on the computer (see, e.g., *Turner* (1984) 13 CCC (3d) 430, where a hacker placed a 'locking device' on computer-held data, rendering the data inaccessible). By s. 3(5) it is immaterial whether this modification or its intended effect is, or is intended to be, permanent or temporary.

Section 3(6) deals with the relationship between this offence and the offence of criminal damage under the Criminal Damage Act 1971. In *Cox* v *Riley* (1986) 83 Cr App R 54 the defendant deliberately erased computer programs which were held on a physical storage medium, a 'printed circuit card', by pressing the 'delete' button repeatedly. His conviction for criminal damage was approved by the Divisional Court on the basis that the erasure of programs from the card damaged the *card* (the programs themselves, being intangible property, fall outside the scope of the 1971 Act, by virtue of s. 10(1) of that Act). See also *Whiteley* (1991) 93 Cr App R 25, decided prior to the coming into force of the Computer Misuse Act 1990. Section 3(6) of the 1990 Act states that the scope of the 1971 Act in computer cases is confined to circumstances where the physical condition of the computer, or computer storage medium, has been impaired. The intended effect of this is that were the facts of *Cox* v *Riley* to recur, the defendant would be guilty not of criminal damage, but of the offence under s. 3 of the 1990 Act. This result will follow so long as the card, or floppy disk, is at the relevant time in the computer, since it will then form part of the 'contents of any computer' (s. 3(1)(a) and 17(6)), but would not apply where the defendant removes the disk first and then wipes it with a magnet. In such a case, it would still seem to be necessary to rely upon the Criminal Damage Act 1971.

Where a charge is brought under s. 3, a conviction for an offence under s. 1 is possible (s. 12).

Offences under the Data Protection Act 1984

B18.4   Section 5(1) to (4) of the Data Protection Act 1984 creates offences relating to breach of the registration requirements of the Act.

Data Protection Act 1984, s. 5

(1)   A person shall not hold personal data unless an entry in respect of that person as a date user, or as a data user who also carries on a computer bureau, is for the time being contained in the register.

(2)   A person in respect of whom such an entry is contained in the register shall not—

(a)   hold personal data of any description other than that specified in the entry;

(b)   hold any such data, or use any such data held by him, for any purpose other than the purpose or purposes described in the entry;

(c)   obtain such data, or information to be contained in such data, to be held by him from any source which is not described in the entry;

(d)   disclose such data held by him on any person who is not described in the entry; or

(e)   directly or indirectly transfer such data held by him to any country or territory outside the United Kingdom other than one named or described in the entry.

By subsection (3) a servant or agent of a person to whom subsection (2) applies is made subject to the same restrictions. Subsection (4) requires that a person carrying on a computer bureau must register accordingly. Subsection (5) provides that a person contravening subsection (1) (which is an offence of strict liability) or knowingly or recklessly contravening any other foregoing provision of s. 5 shall be guilty of an offence. For the purposes of s. 5, 'recklessness' bears the meaning ascribed to that term in *Lawrence* [1982] AC 510 (see **A2.5**) (*Data Protection Registrar* v *Amnesty International* [1995] Crim LR 633). In *Brown* [1996] AC 543, the House of Lords held that a person could not be said to have 'used' personal data for a purpose other than described in the entry, within the meaning of s. 5(2)(b), where they had done no more than access the data and peruse that data when it was displayed on a computer screen. On these facts, a charge under s. 1 of the Computer Misuse Act 1990 might well succeed, although the prosecution would have to show that access by the defendant to the relevant material was in fact unauthorised and that the accused was aware that it was unauthorised (see **B18.1**).

Data Protection Act 1984, s. 5

(6)   A person who procures the disclosure to him of personal data the disclosure of which to him is in contravention of subsection (2) or (3) above, knowing or having reason to believe that the disclosure constitutes such a contravention, shall be guilty of an offence.

(7)   A person who sells personal data shall be guilty of an offence if (in contravention of subsection (6) above) he has procured the disclosure of the data to him.

(8)   A person who offers to sell personal data shall be guilty of an offence if (in contravention of subsection (6) above) he has procured or subsequently procures the disclosure of the data to him.

(9)   For the purposes of subsection (8) above, an advertisement indicating that personal data are or may be for sale is an offer to sell the data.

(10)   For the purposes of subsection (7) and (8) above, 'selling' or 'offering to sell', in relation to personal data, includes selling, or offering to sell, information ˴xtracted from the data.

(11)   In determining, for the purposes of subsection (6), (7) or (8) above, whether a disclosure is in contravention of subsection (2) or (3) above, section 34(6)(d) below shall be disregarded.

It should be noted that these provisions apply only to the disclosure etc. of 'personal data', within the meaning of the Data Protection Act 1984, s. 1(3): 'data consisting of information which relates to a living individual who can be identified from that information (or from that and other information in the possession of the data user)'. Thus, data relating to companies, or to persons who are now deceased, would be excluded. Further, the provisions are applicable only where the data is held on a computer, and where the data user is registered under the Act. It would also have to be shown that the 'person who procures the disclosure', referred to in s. 5(6), was not a person who comes within the description in the entry in the register, and that he knew that such was the case. The phrase 'procures the disclosure' indicates the need for a causal link. An unsolicited leak of data to, say, a journalist about the financial affairs of a prominent person would not be covered. The term 'procures' might be taken to extend to procurement by blackmail as well as to procurement by deception. Liability under s. 5(7) is restricted to 'selling': revealing the information for motives other than financial ones is not within its scope. Section 5(7) seems also to be limited to cases in which the seller was the same person who procured the disclosure. Finally, it seems that liability of a person who 'offers for sale' (under s. 5(8)) or who 'advertises' (under s. 5(9)) can arise only where that person has already procured the disclosure of the data under s. 5(6).

Proceedings for any criminal offence under the 1984 Act may be brought only by the Data Protection Registrar, or by or with the consent of the DPP (s. 19(1)).

The maximum penalties for the offences created by the 1984 Act are, on indictment, an unlimited fine and, in summary proceedings, a fine not exceeding the statutory maximum (s. 19(2)). Whenever a person is convicted of an offence under s. 5 of the Act, a court may additionally order that data material appearing to the court to be connected with the offence be forfeited or erased (s. 19(4)), but such an order shall not be made in any case before any person other than the offender claiming to be the owner or otherwise interested in it who has applied to the court is given an opportunity to show cause why the order should not be made. For liability of directors, see s. 20 of the Act.

Offences Under the Data Protection Act 1998

The Data Protection Act 1984 is repealed and replaced by the Data Protection Act **B18.5** 1998, with different provisions of the 1998 Act being brought into force at different times. For those provisions in force as from the date on which the Act was passed, see s. 75(2) of the 1998 Act. The offence-creating provisions which will replace the offences in s. 5 of the 1984 Act, are not yet in force. The maximum penalties for the offences under the 1998 Act are the same as those applicable under the 1984 Act, and the 1998 Act contains, in ss. 60(1), (2), (4) and 61, provisions equivalent to those in ss. 19(1), (2), (4) and 20 of the 1984 Act.

Section 17(1) requires that personal data within the meaning of the Act must not be processed unless an entry in respect of the data controller is included in the register maintained by the Commissioner (formerly the Data Protection Registrar) under s. 19, although by s. 17(3) regulations may provide that s. 17(1) does not apply in respect of processing of a particular description, where that processing is unlikely to prejudice the rights and freedoms of data subjects. Contravention of s. 17(1) by a data controller is an offence under s. 21(1). Section 20 imposes a duty on every data controller included in the register to notify the Commissioner, as and when required by regulations, of details of the registrable particulars and of measures taken by the data controller to ensure compliance with the seventh data protection principle (that appropriate technical and organisational measures shall be taken against unauthorised or unlawful processing of personal data and against accidental loss or destruction of, or damage to, personal data). Failure by a data controller to comply with this duty is an offence (s. 21(2)). This is an offence of strict liability, although s. 21(3) provides for a due diligence defence.

It is an offence for a person to fail to comply with an enforcement notice issued under s. 40 where the Commissioner is satisfied that a data controller has contravened or is contravening any of the data protection principles, or an information notice issued under s. 43 or a special information notice issued under s. 44 (s. 47(1)). This is an offence of strict liability, although s. 47(3) provides for a due diligence defence. It is also an offence under s. 47(2), for a person to make a statement in purported compliance with an information notice or a special information notice which he knows to be false in a material particular, or where he recklessly makes such a statement which is false.

The 1998 Act, by s. 55, recasts the offences set out in s. 5(6) to (11) of the 1984 Act (see **B18.4**).

Data Protection Act 1998, s. 55

(1)   A person must not knowingly or recklessly, without the consent of the data controller—

(a)   obtain or disclose personal data or the information contained in personal data, or

(b)   procure the disclosure to another person of the information contained in personal data.

(2)   Subsection (1) does not apply to a person who shows—

(a)   that the obtaining, disclosing or procuring—

(i)   was necessary for the purpose of preventing or detecting crime, or

(ii)   was required or authorised by or under any enactment, by any rule of law or by the order of a court.

(b)   that he acted in the reasonable belief that he had in law the right to obtain or disclose the data or information or, as the case may be, to procure the disclosure of the information to the other person,

(c)   that he acted in the reasonable belief that he would have had the consent of the data controller if the data controller had known of the obtaining, disclosing or procuring, and the circumstances of it, or

(d)   that in the particular circumstance the obtaining, disclosing or procuring was justified as being in the public interest.

(3)   A person who contravenes subsection (1) is guilty of an offence.

(4)   A person who sells personal data is guilty of an offence if he has obtained the data in contravention of subsection (1).

(5)   A person who offers to sell personal data is guilty of an offence if—

    (a)   he has obtained the data in contravention of subsection (1), or

    (b)   he subsequently obtains the data in contravention of that subsection.

    (6)   For the purposes of subsection (5) an advertisement indicating that personal data are or may be for sale is an offer to sell the data.

Further it is made an offence under s. 56 for a person, in connection with the recruitment of another person as an employee, or the continued employment of another person, or any contract for the provision of services to him by another person, to require that other person to supply or produce certain records which, by s. 56(6), includes records of that other person's previous convictions and cautions.

SECTION B19: OFFENCES INVOLVING WRITING, SPEECH OR PUBLICATION

CRIMINAL LIBEL

Definition

B19.1   It is an offence at common law to publish a defamatory libel whether false or not (*Boaler* v *The Queen* (1888) 21 QBD 284 per Field J at pp. 286–7). A defamatory libel is a libel which tends to vilify a person and bring that person into hatred, contempt and ridicule (see *Thorley* v *Lord Kerry* (1812) 4 Taunt 355 per Mansfield CJ at p. 364; *Goldsmith* v *Pressdram Ltd* [1977] QB 83 at p. 87; *Wells Street Stipendiary Magistrate, ex parte Deakin* [1980] AC 477 at p. 487).

By virtue of the Libel Act 1843 (Lord Campbell's Act), ss. 4 and 5, the maximum sentence for criminal libel depends on whether the offender knew the libel to be false. Arguments that either s. 4 or s. 5 or both created one or more statutory offences in addition to or substitution for the common-law offence were rejected in *Boaler* v *The Queen* (1888) 21 QBD 284 and *Munslow* [1895] 1 QB 758.

Procedure

B19.2   Criminal libel is triable only on indictment. It is a class 3 offence.

By the Law of Libel Amendment Act 1888, s. 8:

> No criminal prosecution shall be commenced against any proprietor, publisher, editor, or any person responsible for the publication of a newspaper for any libel published therein without the order of a judge at chambers being first had and obtained.
>   Such application shall be made on notice to the person accused, who shall have an opportunity of being heard against such application.

No appeal lies against the judge's decision (*Ex parte Pulbrook* [1892] 1 QB 86). As to the criteria to be considered, see *Goldsmith* v *Pressdram Ltd* [1977] QB 83 at **B19.6**.

Indictment and Subsequent Pleadings

B19.3   *Indictment*

Statement of Offence

Unlawfully publishing a defamatory libel [knowing the same to be false]

Particulars of Offence]

A on or about the . . . day of . . . published a defamatory libel concerning V in the form of an article published in the . . . newspaper entitled 'Crooked Politician Exposed', [knowing the same to be false], which article contained the following defamatory statements concerning V:
   1   'V has not exactly suffered financially from public office because of his power to influence the placing of contracts for municipal works' (meaning thereby that V had corruptly solicited or received money or other consideration for influencing the award of such contracts in his capacity as . . .)
   2   etc.

Additional explanation of meaning may have to be given where the statements consist of innuendo (*Yates* (1872) 12 Cox CC 233).

Plea of Justification and Public Benefit etc.   **B19.4**

> A says he is not guilty and for a further plea, says that all the defamatory matters alleged in the indictment are true.
>
> Particulars
>
> 1 In reply to the statement numbered 1 set out in the indictment, A says that the statement is true, in that V did on or about . . . corruptly solicit payment from X in return for voting to award a contract to X for the construction of . . . at a meeting of . . . to be held on . . .
> 2 etc.
>
> A further says that it was for the public benefit that the defamatory matters charged in the indictment should be published because V is an elected public official of . . . and because the said corruption should be exposed.

The prosecution may simply join issue with this plea by replication. These forms are based on those suggested in the now superseded Indictment Rules 1915 and 1916. Because of the terms of the Libel Act 1843, s. 6 (see **B19.6**), this is one of the rare cases in which the defence must submit a written plea if the plea of justification and public benefit is to be considered. This does not, of course, affect the right of the accused to plead not guilty.

Alternative Verdicts and Sentence

Libel Act 1843, ss. 4 and 5   **B19.5**

> **4.** If any person shall maliciously publish any defamatory libel, knowing the same to be false, every such person, being convicted thereof, shall be liable to be imprisoned . . . for any term not exceeding two years, and to pay such fine as the court shall award.
>
> **5.** If any person shall maliciously publish any defamatory libel, every such person being convicted thereof, shall be liable to fine or imprisonment, or both, as the court may award, such imprisonment not to exceed the term of one year.

Sections 4 and 5 of the Libel Act 1843 are not definitional, offence-creating provisions, they merely prescribe maximum penalties for the common-law offence (*Boaler* v *The Queen* (1888) 21 QBD 284; *Munslow* [1895] 1 QB 758). On a count alleging that the accused unlawfully published a defamatory libel knowing it to be false it is open to the jury to convict the accused of publishing a defamatory libel without knowing it to be false (*Boaler* v *The Queen*). A finding that the accused published a defamatory libel unlawfully is a finding that he published it maliciously (*Munslow*).

Elements and Defences

The *mens rea* of criminal libel is an intention to publish the statement actually found to   **B19.6** be a defamatory libel, and probably nothing more (*Munslow* [1895] 1 QB 758 at p. 765 – there is a similar rule for blasphemous libel: *Whitehouse* v *Lemon* [1979] AC 617, see **B19.11**). In order to render the accused liable to the heavier penalty provided for in the Libel Act 1843, s. 4, it is necessary to prove that the accused knew that the libel was false.

Publication to the person defamed is sufficient, at least if it is likely to result in a breach of the peace (*Adams* (1888) 22 QBD 66), even though civil liability for libel is not incurred without publication to a third party. The publication must be in permanent form in order to constitute a libel rather than a slander. Writing is the principal form of libel; the spoken word is the principal form of slander. Which other forms of publication are libel and which are slander is a question of some difficulty. The publication of words in the course of a public performance of a play is deemed by the Theatres Act 1968, ss. 4 and 7, to be publication in a permanent form, but a prosecution arising from such publication would require the consent of the A-G (Theatres Act 1968, s. 8). The publication of words in the course of any programme included in a programme service,

717

as defined in the Broadcasting Act 1990, is deemed by s. 166(1) of that Act to be publication in permanent form.

Where the prosecution is of a 'proprietor, publisher, editor or any person responsible for the publication of a newspaper for any libel published therein', the leave of a judge in chambers is required (Law of Libel Amendment Act 1888, s. 8). The proper criteria for exercising this discretion were discussed and found to be satisfied in *Goldsmith* v *Pressdram Ltd* [1977] QB 83 and include the showing of a clear prima facie case and that the public interest requires the institution of criminal proceedings. The likelihood of the libel provoking a serious breach of the peace would be a relevant but not necessary factor. See also *Desmond* v *Thorne* [1983] 1 WLR 163. Although it would appear that employers can be vicariously liable for criminal libels published by their employees in the course of their employment, it is a defence under the Libel Act 1843, s. 7, for any such defendant 'to prove that such publication was made without his authority, consent, or knowledge, and that the said publication did not arise from want of due care or caution on his part'.

The prosecution need not prove that the alleged libel was untrue, and it is not even a defence in itself for the defendant to show that his statement was true (though this would be sufficient to avoid civil liability) unless it was for the public benefit that the matters charged should be published (Libel Act 1843, s. 6).

Libel Act 1843, s. 6

On the trial of any indictment or information for a defamatory libel, the defendant having pleaded such plea as hereinafter mentioned, the truth of the matters charged may be inquired into, but shall not amount to a defence, unless it was for the public benefit that the said matters charged should be published; and to entitle the defendant to give evidence of the truth of such matters charged as a defence to such indictment or information it shall be necessary for the defendant, in pleading to the said indictment or information, to allege the truth of the said matters charged in the manner now required in pleading a justification to an action for defamation, and further to allege that it was for the public benefit that the said matters charged should be published, and the particular fact or facts by reason whereof it was for the public benefit that the said matters charged should be published, to which plea the prosecutor shall be at liberty to reply generally, denying the whole thereof; and if after such plea the defendant shall be convicted on such indictment or information it shall be competent to the court, in pronouncing sentence, to consider whether the guilt of the defendant is aggravated or mitigated by the said plea, and by the evidence given to prove or to disprove the same:

Provided always, that the truth of the matters charged in the alleged libel complained of by such indictment or information shall in no case be inquired into without such plea of justification: Provided also, that in addition to such plea it shall be competent to the defendant to plead a plea of not guilty: Provided also, that nothing in this Act contained shall take away or prejudice any defence under the plea of not guilty which it is now competent to the defendant to make under such plea to any action or indictment or information for defamatory words or libel.

The defence of privilege applies to criminal libel as it does in tort (*Rule* [1937] 2 KB 375) and the defence of fair comment on a matter of public interest probably also applies although the point was left open in *Goldsmith* v *Pressdram Ltd* [1977] QB 83 at p. 90.

BLASPHEMY AND BLASPHEMOUS LIBEL

Definition

B19.7   At common law, blasphemy is defined as the publication (orally or, for libel, in writing) of matter which vilifies or is contemptuous of or which denies the truth of the Christian religion or the Bible or the Book of Common Prayer and which is couched in indecent, scurrilous or offensive terms likely to shock and outrage the feelings of the general body of Christian believers.

Procedure

Blasphemy and blasphemous libel are triable only on indictment. They are class 3 **B19.8** offences. For the restriction provided by the Law of Libel Amendment Act 1888, s. 8, on prosecution for a libel contained in a newspaper, see **B19.2**.

Indictment

The following form of indictment is based on that used in *Whitehouse* v *Lemon* [1979] **B19.9** AC 671 (see at p. 620), which was a private prosecution.

Statement of Offence

Blasphemous libel contrary to common law

Particulars of Offence

A on or about the . . . day of . . . published or caused to be published in a newspaper called . . . a blasphemous libel concerning the Christian religion, namely . . ., vilifying Christ in his life and in his crucifixion, which libel was likely to shock and outrage the feelings of the general body of Christian believers

Sentence

The maximum penalty is imprisonment for life and/or a fine. **B19.10**

Elements

The two most significant cases are *Whitehouse* v *Lemon* [1979] AC 617 and *Chief* **B19.11** *Metropolitan Stipendiary Magistrate, ex parte Choudhury* [1991] 1 QB 429.

In *Whitehouse* v *Lemon*, it was held by the House of Lords that the *mens rea* of blasphemy requires only an intention to publish the words found to be blasphemous. There is no requirement that the accused should have recognised or intended that his words would be blasphemous or be taken by others to be blasphemous.

The defence under the Libel Act 1843, s. 7 (see **B19.6**), would appear to apply to blasphemous libel (*Bradlaugh* (1883) 15 Cox CC 217). Section 6 of the Libel Act 1843 (plea of justification), however, is clearly expressed to apply to defamatory libel and hence not to blasphemous libel.

In *Chief Metropolitan Stipendiary Magistrate, ex parte Choudhury*, it was decided that blasphemy is only concerned with the Christian religion and does not extend to attacks on other religions such as the Islamic religion. The Court of Appeal was not prepared to extend an offence for which there had only been two prosecutions in 70 years and which the Law Commission had recommended in 1985 should be abolished (Law Com. No. 145). There was also the danger that: 'Since the only mental element in the offence is the intention to publish the words complained of, there would be a serious risk that the words might, unknown to the author, scandalise and outrage some sect or religion' (p. 448). Even where the Christian religion is concerned, since the middle of the nineteenth century, it has been no longer blasphemous to make a sober reasoned attack; a libel is not blasphemous unless it is a scurrilous vilification (at p. 442). In *Wingrove* v *UK* (1996) 24 EHRR 1 the refusal of a classification certificate for a video recording on the grounds that it infringed the criminal law of blasphemy did not amount to a violation of the right to freedom of expression under the European Convention on Human Rights, Art. 10.

SEDITION AND SEDITIOUS LIBEL

Definition

B19.12 Sedition is any act done, or words spoken (or, for seditious libel, written and published), with a seditious intention and having a seditious tendency (Stephen's Digest, 9th ed, 1950). The meaning of 'seditious' is considered at **B19.16** and **B19.17**.

Procedure and Indictment

B19.13 Sedition and seditious libel are triable only on indictment. They are class 2 offences.

The words alleged to be seditious must be specified in the indictment (see *Bradlaugh* v *The Queen* (1878) 3 QBD 607 at p. 619).

Sentence

B19.14 The maximum penalty is imprisonment for life and/or a fine.

Seditious Tendency

B19.15 According to Stephen's Digest the tendency of an act or words is seditious if it is a tendency:

(a) to bring into hatred or contempt, or to excite disaffection against, the sovereign or the government and constitution of the United Kingdom or either House of Parliament or the administration of justice; or

(b) to excite the sovereign's subjects to attempt, otherwise than by lawful means, the alteration of any matter in Church or State by law established; or

(c) to incite persons to any crime in disturbance of the peace; or

(d) to raise discontent or disaffection amongst the sovereign's subjects; or

(e) to promote feelings of ill will and hostility between different classes of those subjects.

Seditious Intention

B19.16 Given the potentially broad scope of the categories of seditious tendency, the requirement of the *mens rea* of seditious intention is an important limitation on the scope of the offence. Although it is possible to find older cases belittling this requirement of intention (e.g., *Grant* (1848) 7 St Tr NS 507) later cases such as *Burns* (1886) 16 Cox CC 355 emphasise that the intention must be proved subjectively to exist and in the light of the CJA 1967, s. 8, this is surely right. In *Chief Metropolitan Stipendiary Magistrate, ex parte Choudhury* [1991] 1 QB 429, the seditious intention required was said (at p. 453) to be:

> an intention to incite to violence or to create public disturbance or disorder against [Her] Majesty or the institutions of government. Proof of an intention to promote feelings of ill will and hostility between different classes of subjects does not alone establish a seditious intention. Not only must there be proof of an incitement to violence in this connection, but it must be violence or resistance or defiance for the purpose of disturbing constituted authority.

As to intention generally, see **A2.2**.

OBSCENE LIBEL AND OUTRAGING PUBLIC DECENCY

B19.17 It is an offence at common law to publish an obscene libel, but the Obscene Publications Act 1959, s. 2(4), provides that:

> A person publishing an article shall not be proceeded against for an offence at common law consisting of the publication of any matter contained or embodied in the article where it is of the essence of the offence that the matter is obscene.

Subsection (4A) makes similar provision in respect of a film exhibition as defined in the Cinemas Act 1985.

The rationale for these provisions is to prevent evasion by the prosecution of the defences available under the 1959 Act by charging the common-law offence. Section 2(4) does not apply to the common-law offence of conspiracy to corrupt public morals since such a conspiracy does not consist of publication within s. 2(4) but rather of the *agreement* to corrupt public morals by publishing (*Shaw* v *DPP* [1962] AC 220). The law officers, however, gave undertakings to Parliament in 1964 (*Parliamentary Debates (Hansard), House of Commons*, 3 June 1964, col. 1212) that conspiracy to corrupt public morals would not be used so as to circumvent the defences available under s. 4 of the 1959 Act.

On the other hand, there is a separate offence at common law of outraging public decency (see **B3.120**), and conspiracy to do so, and this, it was held in *Gibson* [1990] 2 QB 619, is not barred by s. 2(4), even though in that case the offence involved the publication of an article (a human foetus earring) which was, in a loose sense, obscene. The article was not likely to deprave or corrupt and was therefore not obscene within the meaning of the Obscene Publications Act 1959 and was not therefore covered by s. 2(4). The Court of Appeal therefore upheld the convictions for outraging public decency, holding also that, by analogy with *Whitehouse* v *Lemon* [1979] AC 617 (see **B19.11**), the only intention required was an intention to do an act that in fact outraged public decency. An intention to outrage public decency or an appreciation of the risk of such outrage was not required; if it were otherwise, it was said, an accused might escape liability by the very baseness of his own standards. Conversely, in *Rowley* [1991] 1 WLR 1020, it was held that, if the accused's acts are not in themselves likely to outrage public decency, evidence of his lewd or disgusting intention or motive could not so render them and was irrelevant.

For conspiracy to outrage public decency and conspiracy to corrupt public morals, see **A6.10**.

PUBLISHING, OR HAVING FOR PUBLICATION FOR GAIN, AN OBSCENE ARTICLE

Definition

Obscene Publications Act 1959, s. 2   **B19.18**

(1) Subject as hereinafter provided, any person who, whether for gain or not, publishes an obscene article or who has an obscene article for publication for gain (whether gain to himself or gain to another) shall be liable . . .

Procedure

Offences under the Obscene Publications Act 1959, s. 2(1), are triable either way. When **B19.19** tried on indictment they are class 4 offences. A prosecution for an offence against s. 2 must not be commenced more than two years after the commission of the offence (s. 2(3)).

Where the article in question is a moving picture film of width 16 mm or more, and the publication in question is by a film exhibition as defined in the Cinemas Act 1985, then proceeding may not be instituted except by, or with the consent of, the DPP (Obscene Publications Act 1959, s. 2(3A)).

For restrictions on prosecuting for common-law offences in cases involving obscenity, see the Obscene Publications Act 1959, s. 2(4) and (4A), at **B19.17**.

Indictment (for Offence of Having for Gain)

B19.20

Statement of Offence

Having an obscene article for publication for gain, contrary to section 2(1) of the Obscene Publications Act 1959

Particulars of Offence

A on or about the . . . day of . . . had an obscene article, namely . . . for publication for gain to himself or another

Sentencing Guidelines

B19.21 The maximum penalty is three years' imprisonment, a fine, or both, on indictment (Obscene Publications Act 1959, s. 2(1)); six months' imprisonment, a fine not exceeding the statutory maximum, or both, summarily.

A number of Court of Appeal decisions deal with sentencing for offences in relation to obscene publications. In *Holloway* (1982) 4 Cr App R (S) 128, where the offender had been selling pornographic books, films and tapes on a commercial scale, Lawton LJ said:

> Experience has shown . . . that fining these pornographers does not discourage them. Fines merely become an expense of the trade and are passed on to purchasers of the pornographic matter, so that prices go up and sales go on.

> In the judgment of this court, the only way of stamping out this filthy trade is by imposing sentences of imprisonment on first offenders and all connected with the commercial exploitation of pornography: otherwise front men will be put up and the real villains will hide behind them. It follows, in our judgment, that the salesmen, projectionists, owners and suppliers behind the owners should on conviction lose their liberty. For first offenders sentences need only be comparatively short, but persistent offenders should get the full rigour of the law. In addition, the courts should take the profit out of this illegal filthy trade by imposing very substantial fines.

> . . . We wish to make it clear that the guidelines we have indicated apply to those who commercially exploit pornography. We do not suggest that sentences of imprisonment would be appropriate for a newsagent who is carrying on a legitimate trade in selling newspapers and magazines and who has the odd pornographic magazine in his possession, probably because he has been careless in not looking to see what he is selling. . . . he can be discouraged, and usually should be, by a substantial fine from repeating his carelessness. Nor do we suggest that a young man who comes into possession of a pornographic videotape and who takes it along to his rugby or cricket club to amuse his friends by showing it should be sentenced to imprisonment. On conviction he too can be dealt with by the imposition of a fine. The matter might be very different if owners or managers of clubs were to make a weekly practice of showing 'blue' films to attract custom. Like the pornographers of Soho they would be engaging in the commercial exploitation of pornography.

A case towards the top end of the scale is *Lamb* [1998] 1 Cr App R (S) 77, where a sentence of 30 months' imprisonment was appropriate for an offender who pleaded guilty to five offences of possessing an obscene article for publication for gain. The offender had three previous convictions for similar offences and earned his living by supplying pornographic videos by mail order. Sentences totalling 18 months were upheld in *Ibrahim* [1998] 1 Cr App R (S) 157, where the offender was employed in a shop which supplied obscene videos, the offences being aggravated by his continuing to do so after having been warned by the police. Custodial sentences of six months were approved in *Doorgashurn* (1988) 10 Cr App R (S) 195 and *Knight* (1990) 12 Cr App R (S) 319 where, in both cases, shopkeepers kept obscene books and video tapes for sale as part of their general trade. A fine of £2,000 was also imposed in the latter case; in the former case the shopkeeper was bankrupt by the time of sentence. In *Knight*, Wright J regarded it as a significant aggravating factor that children's comics were for sale in the shop and that children could and sometimes did see the obscene material which was on

722

display. In *Ibrahim*, Lord Bingham CJ referred to the comments of Maurice Kay J in *Mather* (10 June 1997 unreported) to the effect that there is now a greater awareness of the link between the supply of pornographic material and the commission of serious sexual offences, and that sentences in this area are likely to increase rather than remain at the level indicated in *Knight*. Three months' imprisonment was appropriate in *Pace* [1998] 1 Cr App R (S) 121 for an offender who worked as a 'front man' in a shop selling pornographic videos, who was convicted in respect of possession of one tape. The Court of Appeal indicated the continuing relevance of the guidelines in *Holloway*.

Meaning of 'Obscenity'

Obscene Publications Act 1959, s. 1 B19.22

(1) For the purposes of this Act an article shall be deemed to be obscene if its effect or (where the article comprises two or more distinct items) the effect of any one of its items is, if taken as a whole, such as to tend to deprave and corrupt persons who are likely, having regard to all relevant circumstances, to read, see or hear the matter contained or embodied in it.

Although this does not purport to be an exhaustive definition of obscenity it is the only definition which counts for the purposes of the Act and the judge must not leave the jury with the impression that it is sufficient if the article is obscene in the ordinary sense of being 'filthy', 'loathsome' or 'lewd' (*Anderson* [1972] 1 QB 304 [1971] 3 All ER 1152). It is the tendency to deprave and corrupt which is important. This can refer merely to the effect on the mind in terms of stimulating fantasies and it is not necessary that physical or overt sexual activity should result (*DPP v Whyte* [1972] AC 849). Indeed obscenity is not necessarily concerned with sexual depravity but also includes material advocating drug taking or violence (*John Calder (Publications) Ltd v Powell* [1965] 1 QB 509; *Calder and Boyars Ltd* [1969] 1 QB 151).

The persons likely to be depraved or corrupted need not be wholly innocent to begin with: the further corruption of the less innocent is also included. Nor is it necessary that all those likely to read, see or hear the article should be corrupted. It is sufficient that the article should tend to deprave or corrupt a significant proportion of them. This may be much less than 50 per cent but must not be numerically negligible (*DPP v Whyte* [1972] AC 849).

It is the effect of the publication by the accused that counts (that is, the effect on persons likely to read, see or hear the article as a result of *that* publication) rather than the effect of publication by anyone else, 'unless it could reasonably have been expected that the publication by the other person would follow from publication by the person charged' (Obscene Publications Act 1959, s. 2(6)).

The fact that there are other materials in circulation which are as obscene as, or which are not materially different from, the articles in question is not of itself relevant nor does it render the articles in question acceptable. The jury should apply the standards of 'ordinary, decent right-minded people' to the actual articles before them (*Elliott* [1996] 1 Cr App R 432).

Admittedly shocking, disgusting and outrageous material may not be obscene if 'instead of tending to encourage anyone to homosexuality, drug taking or senseless brutal violence, it would have precisely the opposite effect' (per Salmon LJ in *Calder and Boyars Ltd* [1969] 1 QB 151 at p. 169) – a limitation on the meaning of obscenity approved by the Court of Appeal in *Anderson* [1972] 1 QB 304 as the 'aversion argument'.

Meaning of 'Article'

The term 'article' is defined in the Obscene Publications Act 1959, s. 1(2), as 'any B19.23 description of article containing or embodying matter to be read or looked at or both, any sound record, and any film or other record of a picture or pictures'.

A video cassette is within s. 1(2) (*A-G's Ref (No. 5 of 1980)* [1981] 1 WLR 88).

Articles which are not themselves to be read or looked at or listened to are still treated as within s. 1(2) if they are 'intended to be used . . . for the reproduction or manufacture therefrom of articles containing or embodying matter to be read, looked at or listened to' (Obscene Publications Act 1964, s. 2(1), which thus now makes it clear that, e.g., a photographic negative would be an article within the Obscene Publications Act 1959, s. 1(2), even if it was not itself to be looked at but merely used for producing prints). See also *Fellows* [1997] 1 Cr App R 244 (images held on computer disk in digitised form).

An 'article' may be regarded as a single item (e.g., a novel as in *Penguin Books* [1961] Crim LR 176), in which case, in assessing whether it has a tendency to deprave and corrupt, the jury should look at the effect of the article as a whole rather than at the effect in isolation of specific passages within it. However, an article may comprise a number of items (as in the case of the magazine in *Anderson* [1972] 1 QB 304); each item must then be judged individually and it is sufficient if the effect of any one of the items, taken as a whole, is to tend to deprave and corrupt. In *Anderson* [1972] 1 QB 304, Lord Widgery CJ said (at p. 312):

> A novelist who writes a complete novel and who cannot cut out particular passages without destroying the theme of the novel is entitled to have his work judged as a whole, but a magazine publisher who has a far wider discretion as to what he will and will not insert by way of items is to be judged under the 1959 Act on what we call the item to item basis.

In *Goring* [1999] Crim LR 670, one film was treated as containing a number of distinct items, and whether a particular film is to be judged as a whole or on an item by item basis is a question of law for the judge.

Role of Expert Evidence

B19.24   Expert evidence is not admissible on the question whether an article is obscene since that is a matter for the jury. However, where the subject-matter of an article is beyond the experience of the ordinary person, such as the characteristics and effects of cocaine and the methods of ingesting it, expert evidence is admissible to inform the jury about that subject-matter. It then remains a matter entirely for the jury, armed with this information, whether an article advocating the taking of cocaine has a tendency to deprave or corrupt (*Skirving* [1985] QB 819). In contrast, where an article is concerned with sexual activity, the jury need no special information to assess that activity before proceeding to the question of whether the article itself is obscene.

Where the persons likely to be depraved or corrupted are members of a special class, such as primary schoolchildren, there may be a special rule allowing expert evidence on the likely effect of unusual material on them if a jury cannot be expected to understand the likely impact of the material without assistance (*DPP* v *A & BC Chewing Gum Ltd* [1968] 1 QB 159). However, it still remains, even in this 'highly exceptional' (*Anderson* [1972] 1 QB 304 at p. 313) type of case, for the jury to decide whether the factual effect should be classified as depraving or corrupting, and expert evidence would not be admissible on that issue.

As to expert evidence generally, see **F10.3** to **F10.14**, especially **F10.8**.

Meaning of 'Publication'

B19.25   **Obscene Publications Act 1959, s. 1**

(3)   For the purposes of this Act a person publishes an article who—
    (a)   distributes, circulates, sells, lets on hire, gives, or lends it, or who offers it for sale or for letting for hire; or
    (b)   in the case of an article containing or embodying matter to be looked at or a record, shows, plays or projects it, or, where the matter is data stored electronically, transmits that data.

(4)   For the purposes of this Act a person also publishes an article to the extent that any matter recorded on it is included by him in a programme included in a programme service.

(5)   Where the inclusion of any matter in a programme so included would, if that matter were recorded matter, constitute the publication of an obscene article for the purposes of this Act by virtue of subsection (4) above, this Act shall have effect in relation to the inclusion of that matter in that programme as if it were recorded matter.

(6)   In this section 'programme' and 'programme service' have the same meaning as in the Broadcasting Act 1990.

In *Taylor* [1995] 1 Cr App R 131, the Court of Appeal held that a photographic developer, who develops a film sent to him by customers depicting obscene acts and who makes prints as requested and sends the prints back to those customers, publishes the prints by way of selling or distributing them.

Having an Obscene Article for Publication for Gain

This form of the offence was added by the Obscene Publications Act 1964, s. 1(1), to **B19.26** deal with limitations on the publication form of the offence, notably that displaying an obscene article in a shop window does not amount to offering it for sale (*Mella* v *Monahan* [1961] Crim LR 175) and that supplying to a supposedly non-corruptible person (e.g., a police officer) may not be a publication tending to deprave or corrupt anyone (*Clayton* [1963] 1 QB 163).

By s. 1(2) of the 1964 Act '. . . a person shall be deemed to have an article for publication for gain if with a view to such publication he has the article in his ownership, possession or control'. Thus a person having obscene articles for sale in sex shops (cf. *O'Sullivan* [1995] 1 Cr App R 455) 'has' them *'for* publication for gain' even though he may not yet have technically offered them for sale and actually published them in that sense. Since the provision deals with prospective publication rather than actual publication, s. 1(3)(b) of the 1964 Act provides that:

> the question whether the article is obscene shall be determined by reference to such publication for gain of the article as in the circumstances it may reasonably be inferred he had in contemplation and to any further publication that could reasonably be expected to follow from it, but not to any other publication.

In a case such as *O'Sullivan*, the original prospective publication which it may reasonably be inferred D had in contemplation would be the sale in a sex shop, and the further publication that may reasonably be expected to follow from it (note the absence here of any reference to reasonably inferring *D's contemplation*) might (or might not, depending on the circumstances) include such matters as further circulation, lending, selling or showing the article by the original purchaser from the sex shop. The jury then has to consider the tendency to deprave and corrupt as a result of those prospective publications. The Court of Appeal in *O'Sullivan* thought that the complexity of the direction to the jury necessitated by this provision and its relationship with the provisions of the Obscene Publications Act 1959 was such that the judge would be best advised to follow the order of the statutory provisions without attempting to improve upon them or to redefine the wording of the Acts. If a judge had any doubts about his proposed direction, he ought to commit it to writing and invite comment from counsel before they made their final speeches.

Things (such as negatives) from which obscene articles are to be made for publication but which things are not themselves to be published are deemed by s. 2(2) of the 1964 Act to be had for publication.

Defence of Having No Reasonable Cause to Suspect

Under the Obscene Publications Act 1959, s. 2(5), it is a defence for the accused to **B19.27** prove that 'he had not examined the article in respect of which he is charged' and that he 'had no reasonable cause to suspect that it was such that his publication of it would make him liable to be convicted of an offence under this section'.

This defence applies where the form of the alleged offence is publishing. Where the alleged offence is having for publication for gain, the Obscene Publications Act 1964, s. 1(3)(a), provides a similar defence except that it refers to 'no reasonable cause to suspect that it was such that his having it would make him liable'.

Defence of Public Good

B19.28   Obscene Publications Act 1959, s. 4

> (1)   Subject to subsection (1A) of this section a person shall not be convicted of an offence against section 2 of this Act . . . if it is proved that publication of the article in question is justified as being for the public good on the ground that it is in the interests of science, literature, art or learning, or of other objects of general concern.

Under s. 4(1A) the defence of public good does not apply to moving picture films or soundtracks but in relation to such articles there is instead a defence of public good 'on the ground that it is in the interests of drama, opera, ballet or any other art, or of literature or learning'. Section 4(2) declares: 'that the opinion of experts as to the literary, artistic, scientific or other merits of an article may be admitted in any proceedings under this Act either to establish or to negative the said ground'.

The issue of public good arises only if the article is first shown to be obscene and the expert evidence authorised by s. 4(2) is only admissible in relation to whether the article is in the interests of science, literature, art etc. and not in relation to whether the article is obscene in the first place. This should be pointed out to the jury (*A-G's Ref (No. 3 of 1977)* [1978] 1 WLR 1123). In *DPP* v *Jordan* [1978] AC 699, Lord Wilberforce said (at p. 719):

> The judgment to be reached under section 4(1) and the evidence to be given under section 4(2) must be in order to show that publication should be permitted in spite of obscenity – not to negative obscenity.

The jury need some explanation of their task under s. 4, and should not be left, as was said in *Calder and Boyars Ltd* [1969] 1 QB 151 at p. 172, 'to sink or swim in its dark waters'. The Court of Appeal went on to say that the jury should consider:

> on the one hand, the number of readers they believe would tend to be depraved and corrupted by the book, the strength of the tendency to deprave and corrupt and the nature of the depravity or corruption. On the other hand they should assess the strength of the literary, sociological or ethical merit which they consider the book to possess. They should then weigh up all these factors and decide whether on balance the publication is proved to be justified as being for the public good.

It is for the jury to decide the issue of public good, the evidence of the experts going merely to the literary merits etc. which the jury then have to balance against the admitted obscenity of the article (see *Penguin Books* [1961] Crim LR 176).

The phrase 'other objects of general concern' in s. 4(1), refers to objects falling within the same area as those specifically mentioned there, namely science, literature, art or learning, and thus expert evidence that obscene material is psychologically beneficial to persons with certain sexual tendencies in that it would relieve their sexual tensions and might divert them from antisocial activities is inadmissible (*DPP* v *Jordan* [1977] AC 699). On the other hand, the ethical merits of a book do come within 'other merits' in s. 4(2) and expert evidence on that issue is admissible (*Penguin Books*).

The word 'learning' in s. 4(1) is a noun and means the product of scholarship, rather than being a verb encompassing teaching. Therefore, expert evidence that obscene articles have merit for the purposes of sex education, or value in teaching or providing information about sexual matters, is not admissible because such matters are not in the interests of 'learning' as that word is used in s. 4(1) (*A-G's Ref (No. 3 of 1977)* [1978] 1 WLR 1123).

Search, Seizure and Forfeiture

Section 3 of the Obscene Publications Act 1959 empowers a justice of the peace to issue **B19.29** a warrant for the search and seizure of obscene articles kept for publication for gain. A warrant which authorised a search for 'any other material of a sexually explicit nature' is on the face of it bad since such articles are not necessarily obscene (*Darbo* v *DPP* [1991] Crim LR 56).

The CJA 1967, s. 25, requires that the information must be laid by, or on behalf of, the DPP, or by a constable. The articles must then be brought before a justice of the peace who may issue a summons to the occupier of the premises from where the articles were seized to show cause why the articles should not be forfeited. See *Olympia Press Ltd* v *Hollis* [1973] 1 WLR 1520 and R.T.H. Stone, 'Obscene Publications: the problems persist' [1986] Crim LR 139 for discussion of the procedure. The defence of public good under s. 4(1) applies to the procedure under s. 3. So also does s. 2(2) of the Obscene Publications Act 1964 deeming negatives etc. to be had or kept for publication even though not themselves to be published. By virtue of the Prosecution of Offences Act 1985, s. 3(2)(d) it is the duty of the DPP to take over the conduct of any proceedings commenced by summons under the Obscene Publications Act 1959, s. 3. Section 3 (and, no doubt, the offence of having for publication for gain) applies equally to articles kept for publication abroad as it does to articles kept for publication in England and Wales (*Gold Star Publications Ltd* v *DPP* [1981] 1 WLR 732).

OBSCENE PERFORMANCES OF PLAYS

The obscene *performance* of a play, being unlike the written script of the play a transient **B19.30** thing, cannot amount to an article within the Obscene Publication Act 1959. Nor, it seems does the performance of an obscene play amount to the publication of its script. However, the Theatres Act 1968, s. 2(2), makes it an offence 'if an obscene performance of a play is given, whether in public or private'. The offence is committed by 'anyone who (whether for gain or not) presented or directed' the performance and the penalties are the same as under the Obscene Publications Act 1959 (see **B19.21**), which is also echoed in the definition of obscenity (Theatres Act 1968, s. 2(1); cf. **B19.22**), in the time-limit of two years for prosecution (s. 2(3); cf. **B19.19**), the exclusion of proceedings at common law in respect of the performance of a play (s. 2(4); cf. **B19.17**) and the defence of public good (s. 3, cf. **B19.28**). Section 7 of the Theatres Act 1968 contains a number of exceptions to the offence under s. 2 including the performance of a play given on a domestic occasion in a private dwelling, and s. 18 contains interpretation provisions explaining, *inter alia*, what is a play and who is, and who is not, to be treated as a presenter or director.

INDECENT DISPLAYS

Definition

Indecent Displays (Control) Act 1981, s. 1   **B19.31**

(1)   If any indecent matter is publicly displayed the person making the display and any person causing or permitting the display to be made shall be guilty of an offence.

Procedure

B19.32 Offences under the Indecent Displays (Control) Act 1981, s. 1(1), are, by s. 4(1) of the Act, triable either way. When tried on indictment they are class 4 offences.

Sentence

B19.33 The maximum penalty is two years or a fine or both, on indictment; a fine not exceeding the statutory maximum, summarily (Indecent Displays (Control) Act 1981, s. 4(1)).

Meaning of 'Indecent'

B19.34 It seems clear that something can be indecent for the purposes of the Indecent Displays (Control) Act 1981 without being obscene for the purposes of the Obscene Publications Act 1959 (see *Stanley* [1965] 2 QB 327, decided under the Post Office Act 1953, s. 11 – posting obscene or indecent matter). There is no defence of public good to a charge under the Indecent Displays (Control) Act 1981, s. 1(1). Section 1(5) provides that, in determining whether any displayed matter is indecent, '(a) there shall be disregarded any part of that matter which is not exposed to view'. This underlines the fact that the offence is only concerned with that which is publicly displayed, so this is one occasion where one can judge a book (or magazine or any other article) by its cover. On the other hand, in assessing indecency, 'account may be taken of the effect of juxtaposing one thing with another' (s. 1(5)(b)).

Meaning of 'Matter'

B19.35 'Matter' includes 'anything capable of being displayed, except that it does not include an actual human body or any part thereof' (Indecent Displays (Control) Act 1981, s. 1(5)). By s. 1(2), 'Any matter which is displayed in or so as to be visible from any public place shall, for the purposes of this section, be deemed to be publicly displayed'.

Meaning of 'Public Place'

B19.36   **Indecent Displays (Control) Act 1981, s. 1**

> (3)   In subsection (2) above, 'public place', in relation to the display of any matter, means any place to which the public have or are permitted to have access (whether on payment or otherwise) while that matter is displayed except—
> (a)   a place to which the public are permitted to have access only on payment which is or includes payment for that display; or
> (b)   a shop or any part of a shop to which the public can only gain access by passing beyond an adequate warning notice;
> but the exclusions contained in paragraphs (a) and (b) above shall only apply where persons under the age of 18 years are not permitted to enter while the display in question is continuing.

Section 1(6) sets out minimum requirements with which an adequate warning notice must comply.

Exclusions

B19.37 Section 1(4) of the Indecent Displays (Control) Act 1981 contains a number of exclusions for matter:

(a)   included in a television broadcasting service or other television programme service (as defined in the Broadcasting Act 1990), or
(b)   displayed in an art gallery or museum and only visible from within the gallery or museum, or
(c)   displayed by or with the authority of, and visible only from within a building occupied by, the Crown or a local authority, or
(d)   included in a performance of a play (as defined in the Theatres Act 1968) or a film exhibition (as defined in the Cinemas Act 1985).

OTHER OFFENCES

Sending Indecent etc. Articles through Post

Post Office Act 1953, s. 11(1)　　　　　　　　　　　　　　**B19.38**

A person shall not send or attempt to send or procure to be sent a postal packet which—

. . .

(b) encloses any indecent or obscene print, painting, photograph, lithograph, engraving, cinematograph film, book, card or written communication, or any indecent or obscene article whether similar to the above or not; or

(c) has on the packet, or on the cover thereof, any words, marks or designs which are grossly offensive or of an indecent or obscene character.

This offence is triable either way. The maximum penalty is 12 months, on indictment; a fine not exceeding the statutory maximum, summarily.

Whether something is 'obscene' under this section does not depend on the person or persons to whom the packet is addressed, but is to be determined using an objective test, regardless of the addressees (*Kosmos Publications Ltd* v *DPP* [1975] Crim LR 345; see also *Stanley* [1965] 2 QB 327; *Stamford* [1972] 2 QB 391).

Unsolicited Publications

Unsolicited Goods and Services Act 1971, s. 4　　　　　　　**B19.39**

(1) A person shall be guilty of an offence if he sends or causes to be sent to another person any book, magazine or leaflet (or advertising material for any such publication) which he knows or ought reasonably to know is unsolicited and which describes or illustrates human sexual techniques.

(2) A person found guilty of an offence under this section shall be liable on summary conviction to a fine not exceeding level 5 on the standard scale.

(3) A prosecution for an offence under this section shall not in England and Wales be instituted except by, or with the consent of, the DPP.

The sending of advertising material may be an offence even if that material does not itself describe or illustrate human sexual techniques (*DPP* v *Beate Uhse Ltd* [1974] QB 158).

Improper Use of Public Telecommunication Systems

Telecommunications Act 1984, s. 43　　　　　　　　　　　**B19.40**

(1) A person who—

(a) sends, by means of a public telecommunication system, a message or other matter that is grossly offensive or of an indecent, obscene or menacing character; or

(b) sends by those means, for the purpose of causing annoyance, inconvenience or needless anxiety to another, a message that he knows to be false or persistently makes use for that purpose of a public telecommunication system,

shall be guilty of an offence and liable on summary conviction to imprisonment for a term not exceeding six months or a fine not exceeding level 5 on the standard scale or both.

(2) Subsection (1) above does not apply to anything done in the course of providing a programme service (within the meaning of the Broadcasting Act 1990).

For the meaning of 'public telecommunication system', see **B9.85**. Programme services are covered by the Obscene Publications Act 1959 (see **B19.25**).

Threatening Letters etc.

Malicious Communications Act 1988, s. 1　　　　　　　　　**B19.41**

(1) Any person who sends to another person—

(a) a letter or other article which conveys—

(i) a message which is indecent or grossly offensive;

    (ii)   a threat; or

    (iii)   information which is false and known or believed to be false by the sender; or

  (b)   any other article which is, in whole or part, of an indecent or grossly offensive nature,

is guilty of an offence if his purpose, or one of his purposes, in sending it is that it should, so far as falling within paragraph (a) or (b) above, cause distress or anxiety to the recipient or to any other person to whom he intends that it or its contents or nature should be communicated.

(2)   A person is not guilty of an offence by virtue of subsection (1)(a)(ii) above if he shows—

  (a)   that the threat was used to reinforce a demand which he believed he had reasonable grounds for making; and

  (b)   that he believed that the use of the threat was a proper means of reinforcing the demand.

(3)   In this section references to sending include references to delivering and to causing to be sent or delivered and 'sender' shall be construed accordingly.

(4)   A person guilty of an offence under this section shall be liable on summary conviction to a fine not exceeding level 4 on the standard scale.

Publications Harmful to Children and Young Persons

B19.42   **Children and Young Persons (Harmful Publications) Act 1955, s. 2**

(1)   A person who prints, publishes, sells or lets on hire a work to which this Act applies, or has any such work in his possession for the purpose of selling it or letting it on hire, shall be guilty of an offence and liable, on summary conviction, to imprisonment for a term not exceeding four months or to a fine not exceeding level 3 on the standard scale or to both.

Provided that, in any proceedings taken under this subsection against a person in respect of selling or letting on hire a work or of having it in his possession for the purpose of selling it or letting it on hire, it shall be a defence for him to prove that he had not examined the contents of the work and had no reasonable cause to suspect that it was one to which this Act applies.

(2)   A prosecution for an offence under this section shall not, in England and Wales, be instituted except by, or with the consent of, the Attorney-General.

By s. 1, the works to which the Act applies are:

... any book, magazine or other like work which is of a kind likely to fall into the hands of children or young persons and consists wholly or mainly of stories told in pictures (with or without the addition of written matter) being stories portraying—

  (a)   the commission of crimes; or

  (b)   acts of violence or cruelty; or

  (c)   incidents of a repulsive or horrible nature;

in such a way that the work as a whole would tend to corrupt a child or young person into whose hands it might fall.

Section 3 provides powers of entry, search, seizure and, on conviction, forfeiture.

Indecent Photographs of Children

B19.43   The offences under the Protection of Children Act 1978 dealing with indecent photographs of children are dealt with at **B3.115** to **B3.119**.

Video Recordings Act 1984 Offences

B19.44   The Video Recordings Act 1984 established a system for the classification by the British Board of Film Classification of video recordings supplied to the public through video rental and other outlets. Sections 9 to 14 of the 1984 Act create various offences, all originally summary and punishable only by fines, relating to the supply, or possession for supply, of video recordings which have not been classified or with a false indication as to their classification etc. However, the CJPO 1994, s. 88, made the two most serious offences (under ss. 9 and 10 of the 1984 Act) indictable and punishable by a maximum of two years' imprisonment or six months on summary conviction. The other offences under the 1984 Act remain summary but the offences under ss. 11, 12 and 14 of the Act have been made imprisonable with a maximum sentence of six months.

In brief, the offences under the 1984 Act are as follows.

(a)   supplying a video recording of an unclassified work (s. 9);

(b)   possessing a video recording of an unclassified work for the purposes of supply (s. 10);

(c)   supplying a video recording of a classified work to a person who has not attained the age specified in the classification certificate (s. 11);

(d)   supplying a video recording with a restricted classification from a place other than a licensed sex shop (s. 12);

(e)   supplying a video recording which does not comply with the requirements as to labelling (s. 13);

(f)   supplying a video recording containing a false indication as to classification (s. 14).

Section 10 is set out below as an example of the provision made.

Video Recordings Act 1984, s. 10

(1)   Where a video recording contains a video work in respect of which no classification certificate has been issued, a person who has the recording in his possession for the purpose of supplying it is guilty of an offence unless—

(a)   he has it in his possession for the purpose only of a supply which, if it took place, would be an exempted supply, or

(b)   the video work is an exempted work.

(2)   It is a defence to a charge of committing an offence under this section to prove—

(a)   that the accused believed on reasonable grounds that the video work concerned or, if the video recording contained more than one work to which the charge relates, each of those works was either an exempted work or a work in respect of which a classification certificate had been issued,

(b)   that the accused had the video recording in his possession for the purpose only of a supply which he believed on reasonable grounds would, if it took place, be an exempted supply by virtue of section 3(4) or (5) of this Act, or

(c)   that the accused did not intend to supply the video recording until a classification certificate had been issued in respect of the video work concerned.

(3)   A person guilty of an offence under this section shall be liable—

(a)   on conviction on indictment to imprisonment for a term not exceeding two years or a fine or both,

(b)   on summary conviction, to imprisonment for a term not exceeding six months or a fine not exceeding £20,000 or both.

Certain video works are exempted from the provisions of the 1984 Act. The meaning of an exempted work is set out in s. 2 of the Act. Broadly, a work is exempted if it is designed to inform, educate or instruct, it is concerned with sport, religion or music or it is a video game. However, there are restrictions on these exemptions where, for example, the video work depicts, to any significant extent, human sexual activity, gross violence, human excretory functions or techniques likely to be useful in the commission of offences. For a minimalist view of what is required for such depictions, see *Kent County Council* v *Multi Media Marketing (Canterbury) Ltd* (1995) *The Times*, 9 May 1995. 'Human sexual activity' does not require material that would be regarded as hard pornography or as offensive. A video work is also not exempted if to any significant extent it depicts criminal activity which is likely to any significant extent to stimulate or encourage the commission of offences. Section 3 of the 1984 Act provides for the meaning of exempted supply, which includes a supply which is neither for reward nor in the course or furtherance of a business.

SECTION B20: OFFENCES RELATED TO DRUGS

POSSESSION OF CONTROLLED DRUGS

Definition

B20.1   **Misuse of Drugs Act 1971, s. 5**

> (1)   Subject to any regulations under section 7 of this Act for the time being in force, it shall not be lawful for a person to have a controlled drug in his possession.
> (2)   Subject to section 28 of this Act and to subsection (4) below, it is an offence for a person to have a controlled drug in his possession in contravention of subsection (1) above.

'Contravention' includes a failure to comply (MDA 1971, s. 37(1)).

Since the range of sentence for this offence depends upon the class of drug involved (see **B20.137**), the House of Lords decision in *Courtie* [1984] AC 463 establishes that s. 5(2) creates not one, but three offences. See also *Ellis* (1986) 84 Cr App R 235.

Procedure

B20.2   For powers of entry, search and seizure under the MDA 1971, see **B20.76**.

Offences under the MDA 1971, s. 5(2), are (by s. 25 of and sch. 4 to the Act) triable either way. When tried on indictment they are class 4 offences. According to *Practice Note (Mode of Trial: Guidelines)* (1995) (see **D3.7**), cases of possession of Class A drugs should be committed for trial unless the amount is small and consistent with only personal use; cases of possession of Class B drugs should be committed for trial when the quantity is substantial. No guidelines are given in relation to Class C drugs.

Summary trial may be instituted by an information laid 12, rather than the usual six, months from the date of commission of the offence (MDA 1971, s. 25(4)).

For the liability of corporate officers, see **B20.21**.

Indictment

B20.3   Statement of Offence

Possession of controlled drug contrary to section 5(1) of the Misuse of Drugs Act 1971

Particulars of Offence

A on the . . . day of . . . unlawfully had in his possession a controlled drug of Class B, namely
. . .

Since both cannabis and cannabis resin are Class B drugs, the Court of Appeal in *Best* (1979) 70 Cr App R 21 held that there was no duplicity where a count alleged possession of one or the other. If the count charges possession of only one, then the existence of that one must be established (see *Muir* v *Smith* [1978] Crim LR 293), but where possession of several drugs is alleged, it is sufficient to prove possession of one or more (*Peevey* (1973) 57 Cr App R 554).

It is not necessary to distinguish between a controlled drug and its stereoisomeric form, or a salt or ester in a count (see **B20.6**).

Sentencing Guidelines

B20.4   See **B20.137** to **B20.141**.

Meaning of 'Controlled Drug'

Misuse of Drugs Act 1971, s. 2   **B20.5**

(1) In this Act—

(a) the expression 'controlled drug' means any substance or product for the time being specified in part I, II, or III of schedule 2 to this Act; and

(b) the expressions 'Class A drug', 'Class B drug' and 'Class C drug' mean any of the substances and products for the time being specified respectively in part I, part II and part III of that schedule;

and the provisions of part IV of that schedule shall have effect with respect to the meanings of expressions used in that schedule.

The schedule may be, and has been, amended by regulations made in accordance with s. 2 of the 1971 Act.

Misuse of Drugs Act 1971, sch. 2

CONTROLLED DRUGS
PART I   CLASS A DRUGS

1. The following substances and products, namely:—

(a) Acetorphine.
Alfentanil.
Allylprodine.
Alphacetylmethadol.
Alphameprodine.
Alphamethadol.
Alphaprodine.
Anileridine.
Benzethidine.
Benzylmorphine (3-benzylmorphine).
Betacetylmethadol.
Betameprodine.
Betamethadol.
Betaprodine.
Bezitramide.
Bufotenine.
Cannabinol, except where contained in cannabis or cannabis resin.
Cannabinol derivatives.
Carfentanil.
Clonitazene.
Coca leaf.
Cocaine.
Desomorphine.
Dextromoramide.
Diamorphine.
Diampromide.
Diethylthiambutene.
Difenoxin (1-(3-cyano-3, 3-diphenylpropyl)-4-phenylpiperidine-4-carboxylic acid).
Dihydrocodeinone *O*-carboxymethyloxime.
Dihydromorphine.
Dimenoxadole.
Dimepheptanol.
Dimethylthiambutene.
Dioxaphetyl butyrate.
Diphenoxylate.

Dipipanone.
Drotebanol (3,4-dimethoxy-17-methylmorphinan-6β, 14-diol).
Ecgonine, and any derivative of ecgonine which is convertible to ecgonine or to cocaine.
Ethylmethylthiambutene.
Eticyclidine.
Etonitazene.
Etorphine.
Etoxeridine.
Etryptamine.
Fentanyl.
Furethidine.
Hydrocodone.
Hydromorphinol.
Hydromorphone.
Hydroxypethidine.
Isomethadone.
Ketobemidone.
Levomethorphan.
Levomoramide.
Levophenacylmorphan.
Levorphanol.
Lofentanil.
Lysergamide.
Lysergide and other *N*-alkyl derivatives of lysergamide.
Mescaline.
Metazocine.
Methadone.
Methadyl acetate.
Methyldesorphine.
Methyldihydromorphine (6-methyldihydromorphine).
Metopon.
Morpheridine.
Morphine.

Morphine methoromide, morphine
  N-oxide and other pentavalent nitrogen
  morphine derivatives.
Myrophine.
Nicomorphine (3,6-dinicotinoyl-
  morphine).
Noracymethadol.
Norlevorphanol.
Normethadone.
Normorphine.
Norpipanone.
Opium, whether raw, prepared or
  medicinal.
Oxycodone.
Oxymorphone.
Pethidine.
Phenadoxone.
Phenampromide.
Phenazocine.
Phencyclidine.
Phenomorphan.
Phenoperidine.
Piminodine.
Piritramide.
Poppy-straw and concentrate
  of poppy-straw.
Proheptazine.
Properidine (1-methyl-4-phenyl-
  piperidine-4-carboxylic acid
  isopropyl ester).

Psilocin.
Racemethorphan.
Racemoramide.
Racemorphan.
Rolicyclidine.
Sufentanil.
Tenocylidine.
Thebacon.
Thebaine.
Tilidate.
Trimeperidine.
4-Bromo-2,5-dimethoxy-α-
  methylphenethylamine.
4-Cyano-2-dimethylamino-4,
  4-diphenylbutane.
4-Cyano-1-methyl-4-phenyl-piperidine.
N,N-Diethyltryptamine.
N,N-Dimethyltryptamine.
2,5-Dimethoxy-α,
  4-dimethylphenethylamine.
N-Hydroxy-tenamphetamine
1-Methyl-4-phenylpiperidine-
  4-carboxylic acid.
2-Methyl-3-morpholino-1,
  1-diphenylpropanecarboxylic acid.
4-Methyl-aminorex
4-Phenylpiperidine-4-carboxylic acid
  ethyl ester.

(b) any compound (not being a compound for the time being specified in subparagraph (a) above) structurally derived from tryptamine or from a ring-hydroxy tryptamine by substitution at the nitrogen atom of the sidechain with one or more alkyl substituents but no other substituent;

(c) any compound (not being methoxyphenamine or a compound for the time being specified in subparagraph (a) above) structurally derived from phenethylamine, an N-alkylphenethylamine, α-methylphenethylamine, an N-alkyl-α-methylphenethylamine, α-ethylphenethylamine, or an N-alkyl-α-ethylphenethylamine by substitution in the ring to any extent with alkyl, alkoxy, alkylenedioxy or halide substituents, whether or not further substituted in the ring by one or more other univalent substituents.

(d) any compound (not being a compound for the time being specified in subparagraph (a) above) structurally derived from fentanyl by modification in any of the following ways, that is to say,

(i) by replacement of the phenyl portion of the phenethyl group by any heteromonocycle whether or not further substituted in the heterocycle;

(ii) by substitution in the phenethyl group with alkyl, alkenyl, alkoxy, hydoxy, halogeno, haloalkyl, amino or nitro groups;

(iii) by substitution in the piperidine ring with alkyl or alkenyl groups;

(iv) by substitution in the aniline ring with alkyl, alkoxy, alkylenedioxy, halogeno or haloalkyl groups;

(v) by substitution at the 4-position of the piperidine ring with any alkoxycarbonyl or alkoxyalkyl or acyloxy group;

(vi) by replacement of the N-propionyl group by another acyl group;

(e) any compound (not being a compound for the time being specified in subparagraph (a) above) structurally derived from pethidine by modification in any of the following ways, that is to say,

(i) by replacement of the 1-methyl group by an acyl, alkyl whether or not unsaturated, benzyl or phenethyl group, whether or not further substituted;

(ii)   by substitution in the piperidine ring with alkyl or alkenyl groups or with a propano bridge, whether or not further substituted;

(iii)   by substitution in the 4-phenyl ring with alkyl, alkoxy, aryloxy, halogeno or haloalkyl groups;

(iv)   by replacement of the 4-ethoxycarbonyl by any other alkoxycarbonyl or any alkoxyalkyl or acyloxy group;

(v)   by formation of an *N*-oxide or of a quaternary base.

2.   Any stereoisomeric form of a substance for the time being specified in paragraph 1 above not being dextromethorphan or dextrorphan.

3.   Any ester or ether of a substance for the time being specified in paragraph 1 or 2 above not being a substance for the time being specified in part II of this schedule.

4.   Any salt of a substance for the time being specified in any of paragraphs 1 to 3 above.

5.   Any preparation or other product containing a substance or product for the time being specified in any of paragraphs 1 to 4 above.

6.   Any preparation designed for administration by injection which includes a substance or product for the time being specified in any of paragraphs 1 to 3 of part II of this schedule.

PART II   CLASS B DRUGS

1.   The following substances and products, namely:—

(a) Acetyldihydrocodeine.	Methylamphetamine.
Amphetamine.	Methylphenidate.
Cannabis and cannabis resin.	Methylphenobarbitone.
Codeine.	Nicodine.
Dihydrocodeine.	Nicodicodine
Ethylmorphine (3-ethylmorphine).	(6-nicotinoyldihydrocodeine).
Glutethimide.	Norcodeine.
Lefetamine.	Pentazocine.
Mecloqualone.	Phenmetrazine.
Methaqualone.	Pholcodine.
Methcathinone.	Propiram.
	Zipeprol.

(b)   Any 5,5 disubstituted barbituric
acid.

2.   Any stereoisomeric form of a substance for the time being specified in paragraph 1 of this part of this schedule.

3.   Any salt of a substance for the time being specified in paragraph 1 or 2 of this part of this schedule.

4.   Any preparation or other product containing a substance or product for the time being specified in any of paragraphs 1 to 3 of this part of this schedule, not being a preparation falling within paragraph 6 of part I of this schedule.

PART III   CLASS C DRUGS

1.   The following substances, namely:—

(a) Alprazolam.	Clotiazepam.
Aminorex.	Cloxazolam.
Benzphetamine.	Delorazepam.
Bromazepam.	Dextropropoxyphene.
Brotizolam.	Diazepam.
Buprenorphine.	Diethylpropion.
Camazepam.	Estazolam.
Cathine.	Ethchlorvynol.
Cathinone.	Ethinamate.
Chlordiazepoxide.	Ethyl loflazepate.
Chlorphentermine.	Fencamfamin.
Clobazam.	Fenethylline.
Clonazepam.	Fenproporex.
Clorazepic acid.	Fludiazepam.

Flunitrazepam.	Nimetazepam.
Flurazepam.	Nitrazepam.
Halazepam.	Nordazepam.
Haloxazolam.	Oxazepam.Oxazolam.
Ketazolam.	Pemoline.
Loprazolam.	Phendimetrazine.
Lorazepam.	Phentermine.
Lormetazepam.	Pinazepam.
Mazindol.	Pipradrol.
Medazepam.	Prazepam.
Mefenorex.	Pyrovalerone.
Mephentermine.	Temazepam.
Meprobamate.	Tetrazepam.
Mesocarb.	Triazolam.
Methyprylone.	N-Ethylamphetamine.
Midazolam.	

(b)

Atamestane.	Methenolone.
Bolandiol.	Methyltestosterone.
Bolasterone.	Metribolone.
Bolazine.	Mibolerone.
Boldenone.	Nandrolone.
Bolenol.	Norboletone.
Bolmantalate.	Norclostebol.
Calusterone.	Norethandrolone.
4-Chloromethandienone.	Ovandrotone.
Clostebol.	Oxabolone.
Drostanolone.	Oxandrolone.
Enestebol.	Oxymesterone.
Epitiostanol.	Oxymetholone.
Ethyloestrenol.	Prasterone.
Fluoxymesterone.	Propetandrol.
Formebolone.	Quinbolone.
Furazabol.	Roxibolone.
Mebolazine.	Silandrone.
Mepitiostane.	Stanolone.
Mesabolone.	Stanozolol.
Mestanolone.	Stenbolone.
Mesterolone.	Testosterone.
Methandienone.	Thiomesterone.
Methandriol.	Trenbolone.

(c) any compound (not being Trilostane or a compound for the time being specified in sub-paragraph (b) above) structurally derived from 17-hydroxyandrostan-3-one or from 17-hydroxyestran-3-one by modification in any of the following ways, that is to say,

(i) by further substitution at position 17 by a methyl or ethyl group;

(ii) by substitution to any extent at one or more of positions 1, 2, 4, 6, 7, 9, 11 or 16, but at no other position;

(iii) by unsaturation in the carbocyclic ring system to any extent, provided that there are no more than two ethylenic bonds in any one carbocyclic ring;

(iv) by fusion of ring A with a heterocyclic system;

(d) any substance which is an ester or ether (or, where more than one hydroxyl function is available, both an ester and an ether) of a substance specified in sub-paragraph (b) or described in sub-paragraph (c) above;

(e)

Chorionic Gonadotrophin (HCG).	Somatotropin.
Clenbuterol.	Somatrem.
Non-human chorionic gonadotrophin.	Somatropin.

2. Any stereoisomeric form of a substance for the time being specified in paragraph 1 of this part of this schedule not being phenylpropanolamine.

3.   Any salt of a substance for the time being specified in paragraph 1 or 2 of this part of this schedule.

4.   Any preparation or other product containing a substance for the time being specified in any of paragraphs 1 to 3 of this part of this schedule.

PART IV   MEANING OF CERTAIN EXPRESSIONS USED IN THIS SCHEDULE

For the purposes of this schedule the following expressions (which are not among those defined in section 37(1) of this Act) have the meanings hereby assigned to them respectively, that is to say—

'cannabinol derivatives' means the following substances, except where contained in cannabis or cannabis resin, namely tetrahydro derivatives of cannabinol and 3-alkyl homologues of cannabinol or of its tetrahydro derivatives;

'coca leaf' means the leaf of any plant of the genus *Erythroxylon* from whose leaves cocaine can be extracted either directly or by chemical transformation;

'concentrate of poppy-straw' means the material produced when poppy-straw has entered into a process for the concentration of its alkaloids;

'medicinal opium' means raw opium which has undergone the process necessary to adapt it for medicinal use in accordance with the requirements of the British Pharmacopoeia, whether it is in the form of powder or is granulated or is in any other form, and whether it is or is not mixed with neutral substances;

'opium poppy' means the plant of the species *Papaver somniferum* L;

'poppy straw' means all parts, except the seeds, of the opium poppy after mowing;

'raw opium' includes powdered or granulated opium but does not include medicinal opium.

Unnecessary to Distinguish between Drugs in Usual Form as Opposed to **B20.6** ***Stereoisomeric Form, Salts or Esters***   The MDA 1971, sch. 2, lists drugs in their basic form, and by paragraphs included after such lists makes clear that stereoisomeric forms of the drugs and esters or salts of them are also included. The Court of Appeal in *Greensmith* [1983] 1 WLR 1124 held that it is not necessary to distinguish between the natural substance or a substance resulting from chemical transformation, and that both substances, in that case cocaine, are the controlled drug.

The word 'cocaine' in para. 1 of sch. 2, part I (Class A drugs), is the generic word, including not only the direct extracts of the coca leaf, the natural form, but also whatever results from a chemical transformation, listed in paras 2 to 5. The Court of Appeal in *Watts* [1984] 1 WLR 757, without referring to *Greensmith*, arrived at the same conclusion. The court decided that 'amphetamine' in sch. 2, part II, para. 1 (Class B drugs), is a generic word including all of its stereoisomers. Consequently, pure dexamphetamine (even though this was also mentioned in para. 1) and pure levoamphetamine were included in the word 'amphetamine'. Thus possession of amphetamine could be established by the possession of a substance which contained a racemic mixture of dexamphetamine and levoamphetamine.

The significance of these decisions is that heroin (diamorphine) is usually available in the form of a salt. Prosecutions would have failed if possession of heroin were charged and not its salt (diamorphine hydrochloride). These Court of Appeal decisions mean that prosecutions will succeed where the charge is of possession of heroin but what is in fact possessed is its salt.

Material Occurring Naturally   Controlled drugs are defined by their scientific **B20.7** name (for example, heroin is not referred to in Class A by that name, but by its scientific name, diamorphine). But it is important to be aware that, as Lord Diplock stated in delivering a speech in *DPP* v *Goodchild* [1978] 1 WLR 578, at p. 583, with which the other members of the House of Lords agreed, 'the offence of unlawful possession of any controlled drug described in schedule 2 by its scientific name is not established by proof of possession of naturally occurring material of which the described drug is one of the constituents unseparated from the others. This is so whether or not the naturally occurring material is also included as another item in the list of controlled drugs.' In the latter possibility, therefore, the offence would be possession of that naturally occurring material, and not its constituent elements. This decision caused particular trouble with regard to cannabis, which has since been resolved by the introduction of a new definition by the Criminal Law Act 1977, s. 52 (see **B20.8**). This decision does not affect the decisions referred to in **B20.6**, because they are concerned with specified chemical transformations of a substance and not the extraction of a drug from a naturally occurring material, as considered in this case.

The Divisional Court in *Hodder v DPP* [1989] Crim LR 261, decided that magic mushrooms which had been picked, packed and frozen were not 'a preparation' within the MDA 1971, sch. 2, part I, para. 5, because 'prepare' means 'to make ready or fit; to bring into a suitable state; to subject to a process of bringing it to a required state'. Freezing, therefore, was not an act of preparation but of preservation. In order to prepare something it is not necessary to undertake a chemical or technical process (see *Stevens* [1981] Crim LR 568, where the drying and then powdering of mushrooms was a preparation of them). What is required for preparation is that they be altered in some way so as to make them usable, as in *Cunliffe* [1986] Crim LR 547, where mushrooms were merely dried. In *Walker* [1987] Crim LR 565, the Court of Appeal declined to express any view as to whether merely picking mushrooms amounted to a preparation. However, magic mushrooms did fall within para. 5 because they were a 'product'. Consequently, magic mushrooms were a controlled drug which could be unlawfully possessed.

The court went on to point out that the decision of the House of Lords in *DPP v Goodchild* [1978] 1 WLR 578 did not necessarily prevent the use of sch. 2, part I, para. 3, since that case was dealing with cannabis products where separation of the hallucinatory part was essential, rather than magic mushrooms where it was not.

B20.8 *Meaning of 'Cannabis' and 'Cannabis Resin'*

Misuse of Drugs Act 1971, s. 37

'cannabis' (except in the expression 'cannabis resin') means any plant of the genus *Cannabis* or any part of any such plant (by whatever name designated) except that it does not include cannabis resin or any of the following products after separation from the rest of the plant, namely—

(a) mature stalk of any such plant,
(b) fibre produced from mature stalk of any such plant, and
(c) seed of any such plant,

'cannabis resin' means the separated resin, whether crude or purified, obtained from any plant of the genus *Cannabis*.

The definition covers both the plant and any part of it (*Harris* [1996] 1 Cr App R 369). In *Thomas* [1981] Crim LR 496, the Court of Appeal held that the substance was cannabis resin, even though on microscopic examination it was shown to contain elements of the natural form from which the resin had not been extracted. There was sufficient separated material. Thus *DPP v Goodchild* [1978] 1 WLR 578 did not lead to the conclusion that the wrong charge had been laid. In *Hill* (1993) 96 Cr App R 456 the Court of Appeal held that, where an accused is charged with supplying cannabis resin, it is not enough to prove that he supplied either cannabis or cannabis resin. The court distinguished *Best* (1979) 70 Cr App R 21 (see **B20.3**) where the Court of Appeal held that the difference does not matter since both are Class B drugs.

Proof of Substance as Controlled Drug

Although expert evidence (such as an analyst's certificate) is not required in all cases, **B20.9** the prosecution must establish the identity of the drug referred to in the charge with sufficient certainty (*Hill* (1993) 96 Cr App R 456). However, it may be possible to rely on the Court of Appeal decision in *Chatwood* [1980] 1 WLR 874 and use the admissions of the accused as to their knowledge of the substance. The court approved the statement of the law made by Lord Widgery CJ in *Bird* v *Adams* [1972] Crim LR 174:

> If a man admits possession of a substance which he says is a dangerous drug, if he admits it in circumstances like the present where he also admits that he has been peddling the drug, it is of course possible that the item in question was not a specified drug at all but the admission in those circumstances is not an admission of some fact about which the admitter knows nothing. This is the kind of case in which the appellant had certainly sufficient knowledge of the circumstances of his conduct to make his admission at least prima facie evidence of its truth and that was all that was required at the stage of the proceedings at which the submission to the justices was made.

The statements of the accused in *Chatwood*, either orally to the police officer or when reduced to writing, were sufficient to provide prima facie evidence of the nature of the substance in their possession. Only one of the accused gave evidence claiming that the substance was flour; the jury disbelieved him and convicted. The appeal against conviction was dismissed.

Whilst this approach is available, it would only arise in those cases where the knowledge and experience of the accused was such that his statements were reliable. Further, it is unlikely that reliance on such evidence will satisfy the jury beyond a reasonable doubt in most cases. Consequently, the usefulness of such statements by the accused may be limited to committal proceedings. As to admissions by the accused generally, see **F17**.

Meaning of 'Possession'

The central concept in the offence under the MDA 1971, s. 5(2), is that the accused **B20.10** must be in possession of a controlled drug. The starting-point in a consideration of possession, according to the Court of Appeal in *McNamara* (1988) 87 Cr App R 246, is that the prosecution must prove 'basic possession'. Unfortunately, what amounts to possession is, as the Court of Appeal stated in *Lewis* (1988) 87 Cr App R 270, 'an illusive concept at common law'. It is, according to Lord Scarman in *Boyesen* [1982] AC 768, a concept which is 'deceptively simple'. The problem is created in essence by a proposition which has been put forward by the House of Lords, not only when considering the 1971 Act in *Boyesen* [1982] AC 768, but also when considering its predecessor, the Drugs (Prevention of Misuse) Act 1964, in *Warner* v *Metropolitan Police Commissioner* [1969] 2 AC 256. The same proposition is to be found put forward by the Court of Appeal, for example, in *Lewis* (1988) 87 Cr App R 270. The proposition is that it is not sufficient merely physically to be in possession of the drug, which may in itself be a difficult matter to resolve, but that it is necessary for a person who has possession to know that he has the drug. This proposition does not, however, require that the person in possession knows the nature of the drug; he may be in possession of it even if he does not know its nature. Indeed, the offence in s. 5(2) is an absolute offence (see **B20.17**). Thus consideration of the concept demands consideration of two main issues:

   (a)   What is physical possession?
   (b)   When does a person know he has possession of a controlled drug?

Physical Possession The only assistance which the MDA 1971 itself provides in **B20.11** determining what is possession is to be found in s. 37(3): 'For the purposes of this Act the things which a person has in his possession shall be taken to include any thing subject to his control which is in the custody of another'.

The meaning of 'possession' is inextricably linked with the requirement of knowledge of possession. However, it is worth noting that Lord Scarman, in a speech with which the other four Law Lords agreed, in *Boyesen* [1982] AC 768, indicated that possession 'denotes a physical control or custody of a thing'. Lord Scarman also adopted the following description of possession given by Lord Wilberforce in *Warner* v *Metropolitan Police Commissioner* [1969] 2 AC 256, at pp. 310–311:

> The question, to which an answer is required, and in the end a jury must answer it, is whether in the circumstances the accused should be held to have possession of the substance, rather than mere control. In order to decide between these two, the jury should, in my opinion, be invited to consider all the circumstances – to use again the words of *Pollock and Wright* [*Possession in the Common Law*, p. 119] – the 'modes or events' by which the custody commences and the legal incident in which it is held. By these I mean, relating them to typical situations, that they must consider the manner and circumstances in which the substance, or something which contains it, has been received, what knowledge or means of knowledge or guilty knowledge as to the presence of the substance, or as to the nature of what has been received, the accused had at the time of receipt or thereafter up to the moment when he is found with it; his legal relation to the substance or package (including his right of access to it).

The aspect of knowledge of possession raised here is dealt with at **B20.13**.

The Court of Appeal in *Peaston* (1978) 69 Cr App R 203 held that if a person orders a controlled drug, directing that it be sent by post to his address, he is in possession of that drug from the time it arrives through the letter box. In *Chief Constable of Cheshire Constabulary* v *Hunt* (1983) 147 JP 567, the Divisional Court held that a person smoking cannabis resin, has cannabis resin in his possession at the time of the smoking otherwise he would not be able to smoke it.

B20.12 *Joint Possession*   One or more co-accused may be jointly charged with possession, in which case 'joint possession' must be established. The Court of Appeal in *Searle* [1971] Crim LR 592 held that mere knowledge of the presence of a drug in the hands of a confederate is not enough: joint possession must be established. Lord Widgery CJ, giving the judgment of the court, said, 'The sort of direction to which the deputy recorder should have opened the jury's mind was to ask them to consider whether these drugs formed a common pool from which all had the right to draw.' See also *Wright* (1975) 119 SJ 825. In *Strong* (1989) *The Times*, 26 January 1990, the prosecution put the case on the basis that there was joint possession, that is, that each of the co-accused jointly had control of one or more of the packages of cannabis. The Court of Appeal followed *Searle* in indicating that what was being looked for was whether each person had the right to say what should be done with the cannabis. Clearly, knowledge was required for possession (see **B20.13**), but was not sufficient in itself. Consequently, mere presence in the same vehicle as the drugs and knowing they were there was not sufficient, and so Strong's conviction was quashed. Alternatively, aiding and abetting possession by another may be considered (see *Bland* [1988] Crim LR 41, *Conway* [1994] Crim LR 826 and *McNamara* [1998] Crim LR 278).

B20.13 *Knowledge of Possession*   It is clear that the basic proposition is that a person must know that he is in possession of something which is, in fact, a controlled drug.

This is abundantly clear from the decisions of the House of Lords in both *Warner* v *Metropolitan Police Commissioner* [1969] 2 AC 256 and *Boyesen* [1982] AC 768. Any contrary indications in *Lewis* (1988) 87 Cr App R 270 are to be regarded as wrong (see, by implication, *Conway* [1994] Crim LR 826). Lord Scarman, as was indicated at **B20.11**, adopted the description of possession given by Lord Wilberforce in *Warner* v *Metropolitan Police Commissioner* [1969] 2 AC 256 at pp. 310–11. He continued by considering the issue of knowledge of possession:

On such matters as these . . . [that is those mentioned in the passage quoted in **B20.11**] [the jury] must make the decison whether, in addition to physical control, he has, or ought to have imputed to him the intention to possess, or knowledge that he does possess, what is in fact a prohibited substance. If he has this intention or knowledge, it is not additionally necessary that he should know the nature of the substance.

The general consequences that flow from the decisions of the House of Lords are, first, that a person does not possess something of which he is completely unaware. Thus, if a drug is put into a person's pocket without his knowledge, he is not in possession of that drug (see *Warner* v *Metropolitan Police Commissioner* and *McNamara* (1988) 87 Cr App R 246). In *Marriott* [1971] 1 All ER 595, the accused was held not to be in possession of cannabis resin detected on the blade of a knife in his possession by forensic scientists, unless he knew of the existence of a substance on the knife. The courts, bearing in mind this approach, have held that a person who has forgotten that he has possession of a controlled drug is in possession of it (see *Martindale* [1986] 1 WLR 1042 following *Buswell* [1972] 1 WLR 64; compare *Russell* (1984) 81 Cr App R 315).

Secondly, it is quite clear that ignorance of, or mistake as to the quality of, the substance in question does not prevent the accused being in possession of it, provided that the substance turns out to be a controlled drug. Thus, the accused was in possession of the amphetamine tablets in a bottle in her holdall, even if she was mistaken as to their quality (see *Lockyer* v *Gibb* [1967] 2 QB 243). In *Searle* v *Randolph* [1972] Crim LR 779, the accused knew that he had cigarettes; he simply made a mistake about the quality of the tobacco, and so was in possession of a controlled drug since one of the cigarettes contained cannabis. If in *Marriott* [1971] 1 All ER 595 (see above) the accused had known that there was a substance on the knife, but had thought it was toffee, his mistake about the nature of the matter would not have availed him: he would have been in possession of a controlled drug. In all these cases the accused might have the defence provided by the MDA 1971, s. 28 (see **B20.23**).

Cases Involving Small Quantities of Controlled Drug

Where the amount of the drug is small, two important issues arise. The first is whether **B20.14** there is a sufficient amount of the drug for the court to be satisfied that it is possible to find as a matter of fact that there is something which is capable of being possessed. The second is whether the quantity of drug is relevant to knowledge of possession.

With regard to the first issue, Lord Widgery CJ, giving the majority judgment of the Divisional Court in *Bocking* v *Roberts* [1974] QB 307, said (at pp. 309–10):

> . . . it is quite clear that the prosecution have to prove that there was some of the drug in the possession of the defendant to justify the charge, and the distinction which has to be drawn in cases of this kind is whether the quantity of the drug was enough to justify the conclusion that he was possessed of a quantity of the drug or whether, on the other hand, the traces were so slight that they really indicated no more than that at some previous time he had been in possession of the drug. It seems to me that that is the distinction that has to be drawn, although its application to individual cases is by no means easy.

This test was approved by the House of Lords in *Boyesen* [1982] AC 768. Their lordships provided a formulation which will assist in determining whether there is a sufficient quantity to amount to something: 'if it is visible, tangible, and measurable, it is certainly something'. This approach is consistent with that taken by the Court of Appeal in cases concerned with the 1965 Act, such as *Worsell* [1970] 1 WLR 111, *Graham* [1970] 1 WLR 113, and *Searle* v *Randolph* [1972] Crim LR 779. The House of Lords categorically rejected a 'usability' test, i.e. a test requiring that there be an amount of a drug sufficient to be used (or misused) for there to be something present. *Carver* [1978] QB 472 was overruled.

With regard to the second issue, i.e. that quantity may be relevant to knowledge of possession, Lord Scarman, in his speech in *Boyesen*, first drew attention to the statement of Lord Diplock delivering the judgment of the Privy Council in *DPP* v *Brooks* [1974] AC 862, where he said: 'In the ordinary use of the word "possession", one has in one's possession whatever is, to one's own knowledge, physically in one's custody or under one's physical control'. Lord Scarman went on to say: 'If the quantity in custody or control is so minute, the question arises: was it so minute that it cannot be proved that the accused knew he had it?'

A good illustration, according to Lord Scarman, is the New Zealand case of *Police* v *Emirali* [1976] 1 NZLR 286. The only problem with referring to this case is that in it Mahon J adopted a 'usability' test which the House of Lords has categorically rejected (see above). However, if we assume that it is the facts that are important, the case may be of some assistance. Small quantities of drug were found, for example, in a vacuum cleaner which others had used, and as a burned deposit on a metal clip of the type used for smoking marijuana cigarettes. The quantities in both cases were very small, indeed in the case of the clip were so small that it was only just measurable. These may well be examples of circumstances where it would be possible for an accused to argue that he was not in possession of the substance at all.

That the quantity was so minute that the accused did not know that he possessed something was one of the approaches taken by Stinson J in *Colyer* [1974] Crim LR 243.

Drugs in Containers

B20.15 In these cases the person in question clearly knows that he is in possession of the container. What causes the problem is whether he is in possession of the contents, even if he is not aware of what they actually are. The House of Lords in *Warner* v *Metropolitan Police Commissioner* [1969] 2 AC 256 was reluctant to conclude that it followed automatically that if a person possesses the container he possesses whatever is in it. However, it must be assumed that if a person does possess a container, and knows that he possesses that container, then he also possesses anything in it. Indeed, the Court of Appeal in *McNamara* (1988) 87 Cr App R 270 has indicated that there is a strong inference that if a person is in possession of a container he is also in possession of the contents.

It is not entirely clear what the House of Lords did decide in *Warner* v *Metropolitan Police Commissioner*. It is submitted that what the House of Lords did was to establish that there are some circumstances where the possessor of a container will not be in possession of the contents, and thus not guilty of an offence under the MDA 1971, s. 5(2), even if they turn out to be controlled drugs. It would seem that the House of Lords decided that the possessor of the container would not be in possession of the contents in the following circumstances:

(a)   Where he is completely mistaken as to the nature of the contents of the container. See, e.g., Lord Reid at p. 281, Lord Morris at pp. 285, 290, and 296, Lord Guest at p. 302, Lord Pearce at p. 305, Lord Wilberforce at p. 311. That such a mistake means that a person is not in possession of the contents of the container was confirmed by the Court of Appeal in *McNamara* (1988) 87 Cr App R 246. If the person claiming to have made such a mistake had an opportunity to open the package and discover its contents (see (b) below), he is likely to have the requisite knowledge of possession imputed to him. A house is not likely to be regarded as a container (consider *Conway* [1994] Crim LR 826 and *Lewis* (1988) 87 Cr App R 270).

(b)   Where he has no opportunity or right to open the container and ascertain the nature of such contents. See, e.g., Lord Morris at pp. 287 and 296, Lord Pearce at p. 306, Lord Wilberforce at p. 312. That such a mistake means that a person is not in possession of the contents of the container was confirmed by the Court of Appeal in *McNamara* (1988) 87 Cr App R 246. In *Wright* (1975) 62 Cr App R 169 a person was held not to be in possession of a drug in a tin which was handed to him, without his knowing or suspecting what it contained, and which he was told to throw away, which he did immediately.

A particular problem which has arisen is as to where the burden of proof of these various matters lies. On the basis of an examination of *Warner* v *Metropolitan Police Commissioner* and other related cases, this would be a particularly difficult matter to resolve. However, since that time, Parliament has introduced the MDA 1971, s. 28, which provides a statutory defence ensuring that apparent possessors are not necessarily liable for possession in certain circumstances (see **B20.23**). This provision clearly overlaps with the exceptions to liability for the possession of drugs in containers established in *Warner* v *Metropolitan Police Commissioner*. In order to achieve consistency, the Court of Appeal in *McNamara* established that the same approach to the burden of proof must apply to both the *Warner* issues and the statutory defence in s. 28. Consequently, the prosecution have the initial burden of proving that the accused had, and knew that he had, a container in his control, and also that it contained something. They must also prove that the box in fact contained the drug alleged. The burden then passes to the accused to bring himself within either the provisions of *Warner* or s. 28, as relevant.

Evidence Establishing Earlier Possession

A further way of approaching the problem of small quantities of drug (see **B20.14**) is **B20.16** that if the quantity of the drug is too small to amount to something, it might be possible to establish earlier possession, as was indicated by the Court of Appeal in both *Worsell* [1970] 1 WLR 111 and *Graham* [1970] 1 WLR 113. However, it is important that care is taken in bringing charges on this basis, since the Court of Appeal in *Pragliola* [1977] Crim LR 612 held that the charge of unlawful possession was oppressive and not justifiable where the accused was charged solely on the basis that a pipe, which contained a drug trace, was returned to him.

A related situation is that in which a trace of a controlled drug, e.g., amphetamine powder, was found in a urine sample. The character of the substance had changed. However, Lord Parker CJ in *Hambleton* v *Callinan* [1968] 2 QB 427 indicated that he thought that it might be possible to use the urine sample to prove that that person was in possession of the drug at an earlier time.

Mens Rea

The House of Lords in *Warner* v *Metropolitan Police Commissioner* [1969] 2 AC 256 **B20.17** clearly established that the offence of unlawful possession of a controlled drug under the Drugs (Prevention of Misuse) Act 1964, s. 1(1), was an absolute offence. The decision means that, provided the accused is proved to have the appropriate knowledge of possession (see **B20.13**), he is guilty of the offence whether he had a guilty or an innocent mind. That decision also applies to the MDA 1971, s. 5(2), as, for example, the Court of Appeal in *Lewis* (1988) 87 Cr App R 270 accepted. That court went on to explain what it means to describe the offence as an absolute offence: 'in order to be satisfied of guilt, there is no need for the jury to be satisfied of any mental element in the ingredients of the offence, such as we used to describe as *mens rea*.'

Regulations Authorising Possession of Controlled Drugs

The MDA 1971, s. 5(2), is concerned only with 'unlawful' possession of controlled **B20.18** drugs. Possession is not lawful unless regulations made under s. 7 permit it (s. 5(1)). Section 7(1) provides a general power for the Secretary of State to make regulations to except from s. 5(1) (and ss. 3(1)(a) or (b) and 4(1)(a)) such controlled drugs as are specified in the regulations and to make such other provision as he thinks fit to make lawful activity which under ss. 4(1), 5(1), and 6(1) would otherwise be unlawful, see the Misuse of Drugs Regulations 1985 (SI 1985 No. 2066), **B20.20**. The Secretary of State is required to exercise this power to secure that it is not unlawful under s. 5(1) for a doctor, dentist, veterinary practitioner, veterinary surgeon, pharmacist or person lawfully conducting a retail pharmacy business to have a controlled drug in his possession for the purpose of his acting in such a capacity; similar provision is made with regard to the offence in s. 4(1) (s. 7(3)). However, that power is subject to s. 7(4), whereby the production, supply and possession of a drug may be made wholly unlawful or unlawful except for research or other special purposes or whereby the activities of practitioners, pharmacists and person lawfully conducting retail pharmacy businesses may be made unlawful except where they act under a licence or other authority from the Secretary of State. The relevant regulations are the Misuse of Drugs (Designation) Order 1986 (SI 1986 No. 2331), as amended by SI 1990 No. 2631, SI 1995 No. 2047 and SI 1998 No. 881.

B20.19 ***Burden of Proof of Exceptions under Regulations*** The House of Lords in *Hunt* [1987] AC 352 decided where the burden of proof lies in establishing whether or not possession is lawful within the regulations. First, it was established that a statute may place a burden of proof on the accused by implication, although it does not do so expressly (as to the significance of *Hunt* on issues of burden of proof generally, see **F3.5**). Secondly, it was held that what is now reg. 4(1) of the Misuse of Drugs Regulations 1985 was concerned with the definition of the essential ingredients of an offence. Thus, the burden was on the prosecution to prove possession of morphine in a prohibited form. Further, Lord Griffiths held that the MDA 1971, s. 7(1), gives the Secretary of State power to make two kinds of exceptions:

(a) those under s. 7(1)(a), within which reg. 4 falls, whereby the power is given to provide that it is not an offence to possess certain drugs;

(b) those under s. 7(1)(b), where the power is given to clothe certain persons with immunity from what would otherwise be unlawful acts, which is achieved by the remainder of the regulations.

Lord Griffiths went on to say (at pp. 376–7) that 'These latter regulations provide special defences to what would otherwise be unlawful acts and would, I accept, place a burden upon defendants to bring themselves within the exceptions if it were necessary to do so. I say "if it were necessary to do so" because of the extreme improbability that an exempted person would be charged with an offence.' This *obiter dictum* appears to mean that establishing the protection of any of regs 5 to 13 places a burden of proof on the accused. Where, however, reg. 4 defines the essential ingredient of an offence, the prosecution must prove possession of the drug alleged beyond reasonable doubt. Thus, in *Hunt* where preparations of morphine containing not more than 0.2 per cent of morphine were exempted from the offence under s. 5(2), and the prosecution adduced no evidence of the composition of the preparation in question, it was held that the prosecution had failed to prove their case, and that the accused was entitled to an acquittal.

Despite this decision, all the regulations are treated together here, but it must be recognised that the burden of proof may vary, depending upon whether the claim is under reg. 4, when the burden of proof is on the prosecution, or under any other regulation, when the burden of proof is on the accused.

B20.20 ***The Misuse of Drugs Regulations 1985*** The regulations contain seven schedules; the first five indicate the drugs and preparations to which the regulations apply (reg. 3). Regulation 4 exempts drugs in schs. 4 and 5 and poppy-straw from the general prohibition, and therefore requires the prosecution to prove that the material in question is not exempted. This regulation has been extended to 'exempt products' by the Misuse of Drugs (Amendment) Regulations 1999 (SI 1999 No. 1404).

Misuse of Drugs Regulations 1985, reg. 4

(1) Section 3(1) of the Act (which prohibits the importation and exportation of controlled drugs) shall not have effect in relation to the drugs specified in part II of schedule 4 and schedule 5.

(1A)   The application of section 3(1) of the Act in so far as it creates an offence and of sections 50(1) to (4), 68(2) and (3) or 170 of the Customs and Excise Management Act 1979 in so far as they apply in relation to a prohibition or restriction on importation or exportation having effect by virtue of section 3 of the Act, are hereby excluded in the case of importation or exportation by any person for administration to himself of any drug specified in part I of schedule 4 which is contained in a medicinal product.

(2)   Section 5(1) of the Act (which prohibits the possession of controlled drugs) shall not have effect in relation to—

(a)   any drug specified in schedule 4 which is contained in a medicinal product;

(b)   the drugs specified in schedule 5.

(3)   Section 4(1) (which prohibits the production and supply of controlled drugs) and 5(1) of the Act shall not have effect in relation to poppy-straw.

(4)   Sections 3(1), 4(1) and 5(1) of the Act shall not have effect in relation to any exempt product.

'Exempt product' is defined in reg. 2:

'exempt product' means a preparation or other product consisting of one or more component parts, any of which contains a controlled drug, where—

(a)   the preparation of other product is not designed for administration of the controlled drug to a human being or animal;

(b)   the controlled drug in any component part is packaged in such a form, or in combination with other active or inert substances in such a manner, that it cannot be recovered by readily applicable means or in a yield which constitutes a risk to health; and

(c)   no one component part of the product or preparation contains more than one milligram of the controlled drug or one microgram in the case of lysergide or any other N-alkyl derivative of lysergamide;

Regulations 5 and 6 create exemptions which must be proved by the accused.

Misuse of Drugs Regulations 1985, regs 5 and 6

5.   Where any person is authorised by a licence of the Secretary of State issued under this regulation and for the time being in force to produce, supply, offer to supply or have in his possession any controlled drug, it shall not by virtue of section 4(1) or 5(1) of the Act be unlawful for that person to produce, supply, offer to supply or have in his possession that drug in accordance with the terms of the licence and in compliance with any conditions attached to the licence.

6.—(1)   Notwithstanding the provisions of section 4(1)(b) of the Act, any person who is lawfully in possession of a controlled drug may supply that drug to the person from whom he obtained it.

(2)   Notwithstanding the provisions of section 4(1)(b) of the Act, any person who has in his possession a drug specified in schedule 2, 3, 4 or 5 which has been supplied by or on the prescription of a practitioner for the treatment of that person, or of a person whom he represents, may supply that drug to any doctor, dentist or pharmacist for the purpose of destruction.

(3)   Notwithstanding the provisions of section 4(1)(b) of the Act, any person who is lawfully in possession of a drug specified in schedule 2, 3, 4 or 5 which has been supplied by or on the prescription of a veterinary practitioner or veterinary surgeon for the treatment of animals may supply that drug to any veterinary practitioner, veterinary surgeon or pharmacist for the purpose of destruction.

(4)   It shall not by virtue of section 4(1)(b) or 5(1) of the Act be unlawful for any person in respect of whom a licence has been granted and is in force under section 16(1) of the Wildlife and Countryside Act 1981 to supply, offer to supply or have in his possession any drug specified in schedule 2 or 3 for the purposes for which that licence was granted.

(5)   Notwithstanding the provisions of section 4(1)(b) of the Act, any of the persons specified in paragraph (7) may supply any controlled drug to any person who may lawfully have that drug in his possession.

(6)   Notwithstanding the provisions of section 5(1) of the Act, any of the persons so specified may have any controlled drug in his possession.

(7)   The persons referred to in paragraphs (5) and (6) are—

(a)   a constable when acting in the course of his duty as such;

(b)   a person engaged in the business of a carrier when acting in the course of that business;

(c)   a person engaged in the business of the Post Office when acting in the course of that business;

(d)   an officer of customs and excise when acting in the course of his duty as such;

(e)   a person engaged in the work of any laboratory to which the drug has been sent for forensic examination when acting in the course of his duty as a person so engaged;

(f)   a person engaged in conveying the drug to a person who may lawfully have that drug in his possession.

Regulations 7 to 11 deal with exemptions from the prohibitions on possession, supply and production of controlled drugs, as to which the accused has the burden of proof, for, in general, medical personnel, pharmacists and midwives. Regulations 12 and 13 deal with the cultivation and smoking of cannabis for research purposes.

Misuse of Drugs Regulations 1985, schs 1 to 6

SCHEDULE 1   CONTROLLED DRUGS SUBJECT TO THE REQUIREMENTS OF REGULATIONS 14, 15, 16, 18, 19, 20, 23, 25 and 26

1.   The following substances and products, namely:—

(a)   Bufotenine

Cannabinol

Cannabinol derivatives not being dronabinol or its stereoismers

Cannabis and cannabis resin

Cathinone

Coca leaf

Concentrate of poppy-straw

Eticyclidine

Etryptamine

Lysergamide

Lysergide and other *N*-alkyl derivatives of lysergamide

Mescaline

Methcathinone

Psilocin

Raw opium

Rolicyclidine

Tenocyclidine

4-Bromo-2,5-dimethoxy-α-methylphenethylamine

N,*N*-Diethyltryptamine

N,*N*-Dimethyltryptamine

2,5-Dimethoxy-α,4-dimethylphenethylamine

N-Hydroxytenamphetamine

4-Methyl-aminorex

(b)   any compound (not being a compound for the time being specified in subparagraph (a) above) structurally derived from tryptamine or from a ring-hydroxy tryptamine by substitution at the nitrogen atom of the sidechain with one or more alkyl substituents but no other substituent;

(c)   any compound (not being methoxyphenamine or a compound for the time being specified in subparagraph (a) above) structurally derived from phenthylamine, an *N*-alkylphenethylamine, α-methylphenethylamine, an *N*-alkyl-α-methylphenethylamine, α-ethylpenethylamine; *N*-alkyl-α-ethylphenethylamine by substitution in the ring to any extent with alkyl, alkoxy, alkylenedioxy or halide substituents, whether or not further substituted in the ring by one or more other univalent substituents.

(d)   any compound (not being a compound for the time being specified in schedule 2) structurally derived from fentanyl by modification in any of the following ways, that is to say:

(i)   by replacement of the phenyl portion of the phenethyl group by any heteromonocycle whether or not further substituted in the heterocycle:

(ii)   by substitution in the phenethyl group with alkyl, alkenyl, alkoxy, hydroxy, halogeno, haloalkyl, amino or nitro groups:

(iii)   by substitution in the piperidine ring with alkyl or alkenyl groups:

(iv)   by substitution in the aniline ring with alkyl, alkoxy, alkylenedioxy, halogeno or haloalkyl groups:

(v)   by substitution at the 4-position of the piperidine ring with any alkoxycarbonyl or alkoxyalkyl or acyloxy group:

(vi)   by replacement of the N-propionyl group by another acyl group:

(e)   any compound (not being a compound for the time being specified in schedule 2) structurally derived from pethidine by modification in any of the following ways, that is to say:

(i)   by replacement of the 1-methyl group by an acyl, alkyl whether or not unsaturated, benzyl or phenethyl group, whether or not further substituted:

(ii)   by substitution in the piperidine ring with alkyl or alkenyl groups or with a propano bridge, whether or not further substituted:

(iii)   by substitution in the 4-phenyl ring with alkyl, alkoxy, aryloxy, halogeno or haloalkyl groups:

(iv)   by replacement of the 4-ethoxycarbonyl by any other alkoxycarbonyl or any alkoxyalkyl or acyloxy group:

(v)   by formation of an N-oxide or of a quarternary base.

2.   Any stereoisomeric form of a substance specified in paragraph 1.

3.   Any ester or ether of a substance specified in paragraph 1 or 2.

4.   Any salt of a substance specified in any of paragraphs 1 to 3.

5.   Any preparation or other product containing a substance or product specified in any of paragraphs 1 to 4, not being a preparation specified in schedule 5.

SCHEDULE 2   CONTROLLED DRUGS SUBJECT TO THE REQUIREMENTS OF REGULATIONS 14, 15, 16, 18, 19, 20, 21, 23, 25 and 26

1.   The following substances and products, namely:

Acetorphine
Alfentanil
Allylprodine
Alphacetylmethadol
Alphameprodine
Alphamethadol
Alphaprodine
Anileridine
Benzethidine
Benzylmorphine (3-benzylmorphine)
Betacetylmethadol
Betameprodine
Betamethadol
Betaprodine
Bezitramide
Corfentanil
Clonitazene
Cocaine
Desomorphine
Dextromoramide
Diamorphine
Diampromide
Diethylthiambutene
Difenoxin
Dihydrocodeinone
     O-carboxymethyloxime
Dihydromorphine
Dimenoxadole
Dimepheptanol
Dimethylthiambutene

Dioxaphetyl butyrate
Diphenoxylate
Dipipanone
Dronabinol
Drotebanol
Ecgonine, and any derivative of ecgonine
     which is convertible to ecgonine or to
     cocaine
Ethylmethylthiambutene
Etonitazene
Etorphine
Etoxeridine
Fentanyl
Furethidine
Hydrocodone
Hydromorphinol
Hydromorphone
Hydroxypethidine
Isomethadone
Ketobemidone
Levomethorphan
Levomoramide
Levophenacylmorphan
Levorphanol
Lofentanil
Medicinal opium
Metazocine
Methadone
Methadyl acetate
Methyldesorphine

Methyldihydromorphine
  (6-methyldihydromorphine)
Metopon
Morpheridine
Morphine
Morphine methobromide, morphine
  N-oxide and other pentavalent
  nitrogen morphine derivatives
Myrophine
Nicomorphine
Noracymethadol
Norlevorphanol
Normethadone
Normorphine
Norpipanone
Oxycodone
Oxymorphone
Pethidine
Phenadoxone
Phenampromide
Phenazocine
Phencyclidine
Phenomorphan

Phenoperidine
Piminodine
Piritramide
Proheptazine
Properidine
Racemethorphan
Racemoramide
Racemorphan
Sufentanil
Thebacon
Thebaine
Tilidate
Trimeperidine
Zipeprol
4-Cyano-2-dimethylamino-4,
  4-diphenylbutane
4-Cyano-1-methyl-4-phenylpiperidine
1-Methyl-4-phenylpiperidine-4-
  carboxylic acid
2-Methyl-3-morpholino-1,
  1-diphenylpropanecarboxylic acid
4-Phenylpiperidine-4-carboxylic acid
  ethyl ester

2. Any stereoisomeric form of a substance specified in paragraph 1 not being dextromethorphan or dextrorphan.

3. Any ester or ether of a substance specified in paragraph 1 or 2, not being a substance specified in paragraph 6.

4. Any salt of a substance specified in any of paragraphs 1 to 3.

5. Any preparation or other product containing a substance or product specified in any of paragraphs 1 to 4, not being a preparation specified in schedule 5.

6. The following substances and products, namely:—

Acetyldihydrocodeine
Amphetamine
Codeine
Dextropropoxyphene
Dihydrocodeine
Ethylmorphine (3-ethylmorphine)
Fenethylline
Glutethimide
Lefetamine
Mecloqualone
Methaqualone

Methylamphetamine
Methylphenidate
Nicocodine
Nicodicodine
  (6-nicotinoyldihydrocodeine)
Norcodeine
Phenmetrazine
Pholocodine
Propiram
Quinalbarbitone

7. Any stereoisomeric form of a substance specified in paragraph 6.

8. Any salt of a substance specified in paragraph 6 or 7.

9. Any preparation or other product containing a substance or product specified in any of paragraphs 6 to 8, not being a preparation specified in schedule 5.

SCHEDULE 3 CONTROLLED DRUGS SUBJECT TO THE REQUIREMENTS OF REGULATIONS 14, 15 (EXCEPT TEMAZEPAM), 16, 18, 22, 23, 24, 25 and 26

1. The following substances, namely:—
    (a) Benzphetamine
Buprenorphine
Cathine
Chlorphentermine
Diethylpropion
Ethchlorvynol

Ethinamate
Flunitrazepam
Mazindol
Mephentermine
Meprobamate
Methylphenobarbitone

Methyprylone	Phentermine
Pentazocine	Pipradrol
Phendimetrazine	Temazepam

(b)   any 5,5 disubstituted barbituric acid not being quinalbarbitone.

2.   Any stereoisomeric form of a substance specified in paragraph 1 not being phenylpropanolamine.

3.   Any salt of a substance specified in paragraph 1 or 2.

4.   Any preparation or other product containing a substance specified in any of paragraphs 1 to 3, not being a preparation specified in schedule 5.

SCHEDULE 4

PART I

CONTROLLED DRUGS EXCEPTED FROM THE PROHIBITION ON POSSESSION WHEN IN THE FORM OF A MEDICINAL PRODUCT; EXCLUDED FROM THE APPLICATION OF OFFENCES ARISING FROM THE PROHIBITION ON IMPORTATION AND EXPORTATION WHEN IMPORTED OR EXPORTED IN THE FORM OF A MEDICINAL PRODUCT BY ANY PERSON FOR ADMINISTRATION TO HIMSELF; AND SUBJECT TO THE REQUIREMENTS OF REGULATIONS 22, 23, 25 AND 26

1.   The following substances, namely—

Atamestane	Methenolone
Bolandiol	Methyltestosterone
Bolasterone	Metribolone
Bolazine	Mibolerone
Boldenone	Nandrolone
Bolenol	Norboletone
Bolmantalate	Norclostebol
Calusterone	Norethandrolone
4-Chloromethandienone	Ovandrotone
Clostebol	Oxabolone
Drostanolone	Oxandrolone
Enestebol	Oxymesterone
Epitiostanol	Oxymetholone
Ethyloestrenol	Prasterone
Fluoxymesterone	Propetandrol
Formebolone	Quinbolone
Furazabol	Roxibolone
Mebolazine	Silandrone
Mepitiostane	Stanolone
Mesabolone	Stanozolol
Mestanolone	Stenbolone
Mesterolone	Testosterone
Methandienone	Thiomesterone
Methandriol	Trenbolone

2.   Any compound (not being Trilostane or a compound for the time being specified in paragraph 1 of this part of this schedule) structurally derived from 17-hydroxyandrostan-3-one or from 17-hydroxyestran-3-one by modification in any of the following ways, that is to say,

(a)   by further substitution at position 17 by a methyl or ethyl group;

(b)   by substitution to any extent at one or more of positions 1, 2, 4, 6, 7, 9, 11 or 16, but at no other position;

(c)   by unsaturation in the carbocyclic ring system to any extent, provided that there are no more than two ethylenic bonds in any one carbocyclic ring;

(d)   by fusion of ring A with a heterocyclic system.

3.   Any substance which is an ester or ether (or, where more than one hydroxyl function is available, both an ester and ether) of a substance specified in paragraph 1 or described in paragraph 2 of this part of this schedule.

4.   The following substances, namely—
Chorionic Gonadotrophin (HCG)
Clenbuterol
Non-human chorionic gonadotrophin
Somatotropin
Somatrem
Somatropin

5.   Any stereoisomeric form of a substance specified or described in any of paragraphs 1 to 4 of this part of this schedule.

6.   Any salt of a substance specified or described in any of paragraphs 1 to 5 of this part of this schedule.

7.   Any preparation of other product containing a substance or product specified or described in any of paragraphs 1 to 6 of this part of this schedule, not being a preparation specified in schedule 5.

PART II

CONTROLLED DRUGS EXCEPTED FROM THE PROHIBITION ON IMPORTATION, EXPORTATION AND, WHEN IN THE FORM OF A MEDICINAL PRODUCT, POSSESSION AND SUBJECT TO THE REQUIREMENTS OF REGULATIONS 22, 23, 25 AND 26

1.   The following substances and products, namely:—

Alprazolam	Ketazolam
Aminorex	Loprazolam
Bromazepam	Lorazepam
Brotizolam	Lormetazepam
Camazepam	Medazepam
Chlordiazepoxide	Mefenorex
Clobazam	Mesocarb
Clonazepam	Midazolam
Clorazepic acid	Nimetazepam
Clotiazepam	Nitrazepam
Cloxazolam	Nordazepam
Delorazepam	Oxazepam
Diazepam	Oxazolam
Estazolam	Pemoline
Ethyl loflazepate	Pinazepam
Femcamfin	Prazepam
Fenproporex	Pyrovalerone
Fludiazepam	Tetrazepam
Flurazepam	Triazolam
Halazepam	N-Ethylamphetamine
Haloxazolam	

2.   Any stereoisomeric form of a substance specified in paragraph 1.
3.   Any salt of a substance specified in paragraph 1 or 2.
4.   Any preparation or other product containing a substance or product specified in any of paragraphs 1 to 3, not being a preparation specified in schedule 5.

SCHEDULE 5   CONTROLLED DRUGS EXCEPTED FROM THE PROHIBITION ON IMPORTATION, EXPORTATION AND POSSESSION AND SUBJECT TO THE REQUIREMENTS OF REGULATIONS 24 and 25

1.   (1)   Any preparation of one or more of the substances to which this paragraph applies, not being a preparation designed for administration by injection, when compounded with one or more other active or inert ingredients and containing a total of not more than 100 milligrammes of the substance or substances (calculated as base) per dosage unit or with a total concentration of not more than 2.5 per cent (calculated as base) in undivided preparations.

(2)   The substances to which this paragraph applies are acetyldihydrocodeine, codeine, dihydrocodeine, ethylmorphine, nicocodine, nicodicodine (6-nicotinoyldihydrocodeine), norcodeine, pholcodine and their respective salts.

2.   Any preparation of cocaine containing not more than 0.1 per cent of cocaine calculated as cocaine base, being a preparation compounded with one or more other active or inert ingredients in such a way that the cocaine cannot be recovered by readily applicable means or in a yield which would constitute a risk to health.

3.   Any preparation of medicinal opium or of morphine containing (in either case) not more than 0.2 per cent of morphine calculated as anydrous morphine base, being a preparation compounded with one or more other active or inert ingredients in such a way that the opium, or as the case may be, the morphine, cannot be recovered by readily applicable means or in a yield which would constitute a risk to health.

4.   Any preparation of dextropropoxyphene, being a preparation designed for oral administration, containing not more than 135 milligrammes of dextropropoxyphene (calculated as base) per dosage unit or with a total concentration of not more than 2.5 per cent (calculated as base) in undivided preparations.

5.   Any preparation of difenoxin containing, per dosage unit, not more than 0.5 milligrammes of difenoxin and a quantity of atropine sulphate equivalent to at least 5 per cent of the dose of difenoxin.

6.   Any preparation of diphenoxylate containing, per dosage unit, not more than 2.5 milligrammes of diphenoxylate calculated as base, and a quantity of atropine sulphate equivalent to at least 1 per cent of the dose of diphenoxylate.

7.   Any preparation of propiram containing, per dosage unit, not more than 100 milligrammes of propiram calculated as base and compounded with at least the same amount (by weight) of methylcellulose.

8.   Any powder of ipecacuanha and opium comprising—

10 per cent opium, in powder,

10 per cent ipecacuanha root, in powder, well mixed with

80 per cent of any other powdered ingredient containing no controlled drug.

9.   Any mixture containing one or more of the preparations specified in paragraphs 1 to 8, being a mixture of which none of the other ingredients is a controlled drug.

SCHEDULE 6   FORM OF REGISTER

PART I
Entries to be made in case of obtaining
. . .

PART II
Entries to be made in case of supply
. . .

The MDA 1971, s. 30, provides that a licence or other authority issued by the Secretary of State may be, to any degree, general or specific, may be issued on such terms and subject to such conditions (including, the case of a licence, the payment of a prescribed fee) as the Secretary of State thinks proper, and may be modified or revoked by him at any time.

The Court of Appeal in *Dunbar* [1981] 1 WLR 1536 had to consider the meaning of the Misuse of Drugs Regulations 1973, reg. 10(2), in determining whether or not a doctor was unlawfully in possession of drugs. This case is applicable to reg. 10(2) of the 1985 Regulations and probably states a principle applicable to licences and authorisations generally. It was held that, for the purposes of reg. 10(2), it is not necessary for the doctor to have patients, since self-administration may well be appropriate. However, what matters is whether the doctor was acting bona fide in his capacity as a medical practitioner. This is a matter for the jury to decide. The jury in this case had not been given the opportunity to consider whether the doctor wanted the drugs for self-treatment or to commit suicide, and his conviction of unlawful possession was quashed. The mere fact that a person holds a licence or authorisation will not afford a defence where the possession of the drug is clearly outside the terms or conditions of the licence or authorisation, or is for an improper purpose. The issue must, however, be left to the tribunal of fact to determine.

Liability of Corporate Officers

B20.21   **Misuse of Drugs Act 1971, s. 21**

Where any offence under this Act or part II of the Criminal Justice (International Co-operation) Act 1990 or section 49 of the Drug Trafficking Act 1994 committed by a body corporate is proved to have been committed with the consent or connivance of, or to be attributable to any neglect on the part of, any director, manager, secretary or other similar officer of the body corporate, or any person purporting to act in such capacity, he as well as the body corporate shall be guilty of that offence and liable to be proceeded against accordingly.

As to corporate liability generally, see **A5.11**.

Defence under s. 5(4)

B20.22 The MDA 1971, s. 5(4), provides a defence specifically to the possession offence in s. 5(2), but the existence of that defence does not preclude any other defences, either specific ones under the MDA 1971, or relevant general defences.

                                    Misuse of Drugs Act 1971, s. 5

(4)   In any proceedings for an offence under subsection (2) above in which it is proved that the accused had a controlled drug in his possession, it shall be a defence for him to prove—
(a)   that, knowing or suspecting it to be a controlled drug, he took possession of it for the purpose of preventing another from committing or continuing to commit an offence in connection with that drug and that as soon as possible after taking possession of it he took all such steps as were reasonably open to him to destroy the drug or to deliver it into the custody of a person lawfully entitled to take custody of it; or
(b)   that, knowing or suspecting it to be a controlled drug, he took possession of it for the purpose of delivering it into the custody of a person lawfully entitled to take custody of it and that as soon as possible after taking possession of it he took all such steps as were reasonably open to him to deliver it into the custody of such a person.
. . .
(6)   Nothing in subsection (4) above shall prejudice any defence which it is open to a person charged with an offence under this section to raise apart from that subsection.

The Court of Appeal in *Dempsey* (1985) 82 Cr App R 291 made clear that the defence in s. 5(4)(b) is available only if the accused's purpose is to act in accordance with that subsection. The accused bears the burden of proving this defence (see generally, **F3.4** and **F3.18**).

Defence under s. 28

B20.23   **Misuse of Drugs Act 1971, s. 28**

(1)   This section applies to offences under any of the following provisions of this Act, that is to say section 4(2) and (3), section 5(2) and (3), section 6(2) and section 9.
(2)   Subject to subsection (3) below, in any proceedings for an offence to which this section applies it shall be a defence for the accused to prove that he neither knew of nor suspected nor had reason to suspect the existence of some fact alleged by the prosecution which it is necessary for the prosecution to prove if he is to be convicted of the offence charged.
(3)   Where in any proceedings for an offence to which this section applies it is necessary, if the accused is to be convicted of the offence charged, for the prosecution to prove that some substance or product involved in the alleged offence was the controlled drug which the prosecution alleges it to have been, and it is proved that the substance or product in question was that controlled drug, the accused—

(a)   shall not be acquitted of the offence charged by reason only of proving that he neither knew nor suspected nor had reason to suspect that the substance or product in question was the particular controlled drug alleged; but

(b)   shall be acquitted thereof—

(i)   if he proves that he neither believed nor suspected nor had reason to suspect that the substance or product in question was a controlled drug; or

(ii)   if he proves that he believed the substance or product in question to be a controlled drug, or a controlled drug of a description, such that, if it had in fact been that controlled drug or a controlled drug of that description, he would not at the material time have been committing any offence to which this section applies.

(4)   Nothing in this section shall prejudice any defence which it is open to a person charged with an offence to which this section applies to raise apart from this section.

The Courts-Martial Appeal Court in *Young* [1984] 2 All ER 164 held that the test of whether the accused had no 'reason to suspect' that the substance was a controlled drug is an objective and not a subjective one. In consequence it is irrelevant if the accused claims that he was suffering from self-induced intoxication which meant that he did not hold a belief or register a suspicion.

The burden of proof requirement with relation to s. 28 means that it is for the prosecution to prove knowledge of the article (see **B20.10 *et seq*.** and *Warner* v *Metropolitan Police Commissioner* [1969] 2 AC 256). See also *McNamara* (1988) 87 Cr App R 246 and *Champ* (1982) 73 Cr App R 367. In *Ashton-Rickard* [1978] 1 WLR 37 the Court of Appeal made clear that the burden imposed upon the accused under s. 28(2) does not affect the burden on the prosecution to prove possession of the drug by the accused, including the necessary knowledge.

It was held in *McGowan* [1990] Crim LR 399 that conspiracies are not offences under the MDA 1971, and therefore the defence under s. 28 is not available in such cases.

SUPPLYING OR OFFERING TO SUPPLY ETC. CONTROLLED DRUG

Definition

Misuse of Drugs Act 1971, s. 4   B20.24

(1)   Subject to any regulations under section 7 of this Act for the time being in force, it shall not be lawful for a person—

(a)   to produce a controlled drug; or

(b)   to supply or offer to supply a controlled drug to another.

(2)   . . .

(3)   Subject to section 28 of this Act, it is an offence for a person—

(a)   to supply or offer to supply, a controlled drug to another in contravention of subsection 1 above; or

(b)   to be concerned in the supplying of such a drug to another in contravention of that subsection; or

(c)   to be concerned in the making to another in contravention of that subsection of an offer to supply such a drug.

Each of paragraphs (a), (b) and (c) in s. 4(3) appears to create at least one separate offence. However, despite the fact that there is more than one offence created, there are a number of elements common to each of these offences. The common elements are: that there must be a 'controlled drug'; that the activity with regard to that drug must involve a 'supply' in some form; and that the activity must be in contravention of s. 4(1). The question of what substances are controlled drugs is dealt with at **B20.5** and **B20.8**.

Since the range of sentence for this offence varies dependent upon the class of drug involved (see **B20.137**), the House of Lords decision in *Courtie* [1984] AC 463 establishes that each paragraph of s. 4(3) creates not one, but three offences.

Procedure

B20.25   Offences under the MDA 1971, s. 4(3), are (by s. 25 of and sch. 4 of the Act) triable either way. When tried on indictment they are class 4 offences. According to *Practice Note (Mode of Trial: Guidelines)* (1995) (see **D3.7**), cases of supplying Class A drugs should be committed for trial; cases of supplying Class B drugs should be committed for trial unless there is only small-scale supply for no payment. No guidelines are given in relation to Class C drugs.

Summary trial may be instituted by an information laid 12, rather than the usual six, months from the date of commission of the offence (MDA 1971, s. 25(4)).

For the liability of corporate officers, see **B20.21**. For possible problems which may arise with identifying the person to whom the supply is made, see **B20.30**.

Sentencing Guidelines

B20.26   See **B20.137** to **B20.141**. This is a drug trafficking offence (DTA 1994, s. 1(3)(a)), and so, additionally, a forfeiture order (see **E20.4**) or a confiscation order (see **E21.1**) may be imposed.

Meaning of 'Supply'

B20.27   This word appears as an element in the offences contrary to both the MDA 1971, s. 4(3) and s. 5(3) (see **B20.32**), and means the same in each context (see *Maginnis* [1987] AC 303). Section 37(1) states that 'supplying' includes distributing. It follows, therefore, that there can be no argument that the accused has not supplied where the accused has purchased drugs for two (or more) people by arrangement and then handed out the appropriate proportion of the whole on the basis that both were in possession from the outset because of their agreement. Clearly the accused is distributing and, therefore, supplying the drug to the other (*Buckley* (1979) 69 Cr App R 371 and *Denslow* [1998] Crim LR 566).

The courts have endeavoured to supplement the statutory guidance. Lord Keith, giving a speech with which three other members of the House of Lords fully agreed in *Maginnis* [1987] AC 303, held that the word 'supply' is to be ascertained 'by reference to the ordinary natural meaning of the word together with any assistance which may be afforded by the context'. (See also *Holmes* v *Chief Constable Merseyside Police* [1976] Crim LR 125.) Lord Keith went further (at p. 309):

> The word 'supply', in its ordinary natural meaning, conveys the idea of furnishing or providing to another something which is wanted or required in order to meet the wants or requirements of that other. It connotes more than there mere transfer of physical control of some chattel or object from one person to another. No one would ordinarily say that to hand over something to a mere custodier was to supply him with it. The additional concept is that of enabling the recipient to apply the thing handed over to purposes for which he desires or has a duty to apply it.

Clearly there is no problem in the usual case where a person transfers both the custody and control of a controlled drug to another (see *Mills* [1963] 1 QB 522).

Lord Keith in *Maginnis* [1987] AC 303 stated that it is not a necessary element in the concept of supply that the provision should be made out of the personal resources of the person who does the supplying, which is of particular relevance when considering the return of drugs from a custodier to the original holder. This decision needs to be examined carefully, since it provides an approach of general value to the meaning of the word 'supply' and also deals with a particular problem case.

The particular problem case is where a person places the drugs in the custody of another person, the custodier. In *Dempsey* (1985) 82 Cr App R 291, the Court of Appeal held that there was no supply by the possessor of the drug to the custodier on the facts of that particular case. Michael, who was a registered drug addict and in lawful possession of a controlled drug, asked Maureen to hold some of the drug for him while he went to the toilet to inject himself with the rest of it. The police then arrested both of them. The Court of Appeal held that whether or not Michael had supplied the drug to Maureen was a question of fact, and since the matter was not left to the jury to decide, his conviction for an offence contrary to the MDA 1971, s. 4(3)(a), had to be quashed. The court took the view that Michael had transferred the drug to Maureen either for her own use or to hand on to someone else, in which case there would have been a supply, or he may simply have given them to her for safekeeping and return to him in which case there was no supply. The reason for this distinction is that the court took the view that a supply only occurs where there is a transfer for the benefit of the transferee (Maureen) rather than the transferor (Michael).

This case appeared to be inconsistent with the earlier Court of Appeal decision in *Delgado* [1984] 1 WLR 89. Delgado appealed against conviction for an offence contrary to s. 5(3) of the 1971 Act. The trial judge had directed that Delgado's intention to return the cannabis, having been given it for a couple of hours by two people who told him that they had stolen the cannabis and had nowhere to keep it, was an intention to supply. The Court of Appeal dismissed the appeal, saying that while 'supply' covers a wide range of transactions, a 'feature common to all those transactions is a transfer of physical control of a drug from one person to another'.

Both these cases exercised the minds of the members of the House of Lords in *Maginnis* [1987] AC 303. Maginnis was found guilty of an offence contrary to the MDA 1971, s. 5(3). A package containing cannabis resin was found in his car. He claimed that the drug had been left by a friend who was to pick it up later. Lord Keith, in a speech with which three of the other Law Lords agreed, had no difficulty in concluding that a return of the drugs to the trafficker would be a supply, thus satisfying s. 4(3), and that possession by the custodier would be with intent to supply, thus satisfying s. 5(3). Lord Keith pointed out that the trafficker has no legal right to require the drugs to be given back to him. 'Indeed, it is the duty of the custodier not to hand them back to him but to destroy them or deliver them to a police officer so that they may be destroyed [see the terms of the defence in s. 5(4), for example]. The custodier in choosing to return the drugs to the depositor does something which he is not only not obliged to do, but which he has a duty not to do.' Lord Keith, however, held that the position is different where the custodier is merely holding the drugs temporarily and not for any purpose of his own. Consequently, Lord Keith decided that there was no conflict between the Court of Appeal decisions in *Delgado* and in *Dempsey*.

Thus, a transfer of drugs from one person to another is a supply only if it is for the purposes of the transferee (see *Maginnis*, per Lord Keith). It should be noted that Lord Goff dissented in *Maginnis* because he regarded *Dempsey* and *Delgado* as inconsistent. Lord Goff took the view that *Delgado* was wrongly decided, on the basis that it relied on the passing of physical control to establish that drugs had been supplied. It is important not to confuse purpose or intention with motive, which is irrelevant (*X* [1994] Crim LR 827, where X was a registered police informer; his motive of causing a drugs dealer to be caught did not affect whether there was a supply).

The following cases may be of assistance in determining in other circumstances whether there is a supply:

(a)   In *Harris* [1968] 1 WLR 769, it was held that injecting another with a drug in the recipient's possession is not 'supplying' that drug to the recipient, particularly since physical control was not transferred to the recipient.

(b)   Bearing in mind that the 1971 Act makes clear that supplying includes distributing, the Divisional Court in *Holmes* v *Chief Constable Merseyside Police* [1976] Crim LR 125, held that the division of drugs in joint possession was a supply. This decision was approved in *Buckley* (1979) 69 Cr App R 371 (CA), where it was held that the distribution of drugs purchased after money had been pooled by the co-accused amounted to the supply of those drugs.

    (c) In *Moore* [1979] Crim LR 789, it was held that there was an offer to supply when the accused offered two girls a reefer cigarette to smoke. On the other hand, in *King* [1978] Crim LR 228, it was held that the offence of possessing a controlled drug with intent to supply was not committed when the accused made reefer cigarettes which were then passed round a group of people. The reason for this decision was that taking a puff and passing on a cigarette does not amount to a supply of the drug.

There is, therefore, a conflict between these decisions which remains to be resolved, although they can be reconciled, in one sense, by relying on the fact that whether or not there has been a supply will depend upon the circumstances of each individual case.

When Supply etc. Lawful

B20.28   Conduct otherwise proscribed by the MDA 1971, s. 4(1), may be licensed or authorised by the Misuse of Drugs Regulations 1985 (see generally, **B20.20**). Regulation 4(3) provides in effect that it shall not be unlawful to supply or offer to supply poppy-straw. Subsequent regulations provide various exemptions for medical personnel, pharmacists and midwives, and for research activities.

Section 4(3)(a): Offering to Supply

B20.29   An offer may be by words or conduct. If it is by words, it must be ascertained whether an offer to supply a controlled drug was made. It does not matter whether or not the accused had a controlled drug in his possession or had easy access to one, or whether or not the substance in his possession was a controlled drug. It might be different where the offer is made by conduct (*Mitchell* [1992] Crim LR 723; *Haggard* v *Mason* [1976] 1 WLR 187). Whether the accused intends to carry the offer into effect is irrelevant; the offence is complete upon the making of an offer to supply (*Goodard* [1992] Crim LR 588, see also *Gill* (1993) 97 Cr App R 215 and *Showers* [1995] Crim LR 400).

Section 4(3)(b): Being Concerned in Supply to Another

B20.30   The Court of Appeal in *Hughes* (1985) Cr App R 344, p. 348, established that there are three ingredients of this offence:

    (a)   the supply of a drug to another, or, as the case may be, the making of an offer to supply the drug to another in contravention of s. 4(1) of the Act;
    (b)   participation by the accused in an enterprise involving such supply or, as the case may be, such an offer to supply; and
    (c)   knowledge by the accused of the nature of the enterprise, i.e. that it involved supply of a drug or, as the case may be, offering to supply a drug.

The Court also made clear that it is the duty of the judge to assist the jury as to the meaning of the phrase 'concerned in'. So the attention of the jury might have to be drawn to the principle expressed in the decision of the Court of Appeal in *Blake* (1978) 68 Cr App R 1, that a person may be concerned by being involved at a distance in making an offer to supply a controlled drug.

Recently attention has been paid to who can be 'another' for the purposes of this section. It cannot be someone charged in the same count, but it can be someone charged in other counts in the same indictment (*Smith* (14 February 1983 unreported), *Ferrera* (1984 unreported), *Adepoju* [1988] Crim LR 378, *Connelly* (1991) 156 JP 406).

Defence under s. 28

B20.31   The defence under the MDA 1971, s. 28, is dealt with at **B20.23**; it does not apply to an offer by words to supply a controlled drug (*Mitchell* [1992] Crim LR 723).

POSSESSION OF CONTROLLED DRUG WITH INTENT TO SUPPLY

Definition

Misuse of Drugs Act 1971, s. 5

B20.32

(3)   Subject to section 28 of this Act, it is an offence for a person to have a controlled drug in his possession, whether lawfully or not, with intent to supply it to another in contravention of section 4(1) of this Act.

Since the range of sentence for this offence varies dependent upon the class of drug involved (see **B20.137**), the House of Lords decision in *Courtie* [1984] AC 463 establishes that s. 5(3) creates not one, but three offences.

For the meaning of 'controlled drug', see **B20.5**; as to the meaning of 'possession', see **B20.10** *et seq*. For circumstances in which possession may be lawful by virtue of the Misuse of Drugs Regulations 1985, see **B20.20**.

Procedure

Offences under the MDA 1971, s. 5(3), are (by s. 25 of and sch. 4 to the Act) triable **B20.33** either way. When tried on indictment they are class 4 offences. According to *Practice Note* (*Mode of Trial: Guidelines*) (1995) (see **D3.7**), cases of possessing Class A drugs with intent to supply should be committed for trial; cases of possessing Class B drugs with intent to supply should be committed for trial unless there is only small-scale supply for no payment. No guidelines are given in relation to Class C drugs.

Summary trial may be instituted by an information laid 12, rather than the usual six, months from the date of commission of the offence (MDA 1971, s. 25(4)).

For the liability of corporate officers, see **B20.21**.

Indictment

The form of indictment provided at **B20.3** may be adapted by addition of the specific **B20.34** intent to the particulars of the offence.

Alternative Verdicts

In *Blackford* (1989) 89 Cr App R 239, the Court of Appeal, exercising its general power **B20.35** under the Criminal Law Act 1967, substituted a conviction of possession under the MDA 1971, s. 5(2), for that under s. 5(3).

Sentencing Guidelines

See **B20.137** to **B20.141**. This is a drug trafficking offence (DTA 1994, s. 1(3)(a)), and **B20.36** so, additionally, a forfeiture order (see **E20.4**) or a confiscation order (see **E21.1**) may be imposed.

Intent to Supply

All that the prosecution has to establish is that the defendant had the drug in his **B20.37** possession with intent to supply the substance which was in his possession to another. A mistake as to the drug in question is irrelevant (*Leeson* (1999) *The Times*, 2 November 1999).

The Court of Appeal in *Greenfield* (1983) 78 Cr App R 179 made clear that 'intent to supply' means an intent on the part of the possessor of the drugs to supply and not an intention that the drug should be supplied by another person. As to proving an intent to supply, and the admissibility of evidence of large amounts of money, an extravagant life-style or drug equipment, see **F1.9**.

In *Downes* [1984] Crim LR 552, the Court of Appeal decided that where two people were in joint possession (for the meaning of this phrase, see **B20.12**) they were not both involved in a joint venture to supply unless both had an intention to supply. Mere knowledge on the part of one that the other intended to supply is not sufficient.

'Supply' appears as an element in the offences contrary to both the MDA 1971, s. 4(3) and s. 5(3), and means the same in each context (see *Maginnis* [1987] AC 303). Its meaning is dealt with at **B20.27**.

Defence under s. 28

B20.38   This defence is dealt with at **B20.23**.

PRODUCTION OF CONTROLLED DRUG

Definition

B20.39   **Misuse of Drugs Act 1971, s. 4**

> (2)   Subject to section 28 of this Act, it is an offence for a person—
> > (a)   to produce a controlled drug in contravention of subsection (1) [of section 4]; or
> > (b)   to be concerned in the production of such a drug in contravention of that subsection by another.

For the meaning of 'controlled drug', see **B20.5**. As to the circumstances in which production may be lawful pursuant to the Misuse of Drugs Regulations 1985, see **B20.20**.

Each of paras (a) and (b) creates a separate offence.

Since the range of sentence for this offence varies dependent upon the class of drug involved (see **B20.137**), the House of Lords decision in *Courtie* [1984] AC 463 establishes that each paragraph to s. 4(2) creates not one but three offences.

Procedure

B20.40   Offences under the MDA 1971, s. 4(2), are (by s. 25 of and sch. 4 to the Act) triable either way. When tried on indictment they are class 4 offences.

Summary trial may be instituted by an information laid 12, rather than the usual six, months from the date of commission of the offence (MDA 1971, s. 25(4)).

For the liability of corporate officers, see **B20.21**.

Sentencing Guidelines

B20.41   See **B20.119** to **B20.123**. This is a drug trafficking offence (DTA 1994, s. 1(3)(a)), and so, additionally, a forfeiture order (see **E20.4**) or a confiscation order (see **E21.1**) may be imposed.

Meaning of 'Produce', 'Concerned in Production'

B20.42   **Misuse of Drugs Act 1971, s. 37**

> (1)   . . . 'produce', where the reference is to producing a controlled drug, means producing it by manufacture, cultivation or any other method, and 'production' has a corresponding meaning; . . .

The Court of Appeal in *Russell* (1991) 94 Cr App R 351 held that the conversion of one form of Class A drug into another form of the same genus may be production and that the conversion of the salt cocaine hydrochloride to free base cocaine, i.e. from a substance described in the MDA 1971, sch. 2, para. 4 to a substance described in para. 5 of that schedule, was a production. This was because it was 'the production of a substance (not by manufacture or cultivation but by "other means" [referring to the definition in s. 37(1)]) with physical and chemical features different from the cocaine hydrochloride from which it springs, albeit sharing the same generic term, cocaine'.

Stripping a cannabis plant, which had been cut and harvested, is producing a controlled drug because the action, by 'other means', produces a part of the plant which is a controlled drug (*Harris* [1996] 1 Cr App R 369).

Being concerned in production requires that the accused take an identifiable role in the production. This was not satisfied where the accused simply permitted two others who were producing drugs to use his kitchen (*Farr* [1982] Crim LR 745).

Defence under s. 28

As to the defence under the MDA 1971, s. 28, see **B20.23**. B20.43

PROHIBITION ON IMPORTATION AND EXPORTATION OF CONTROLLED DRUGS

Misuse of Drugs Act 1971, s. 3 B20.44

(1) Subject to subsection (2) below—
(a) the importation of a controlled drug: and
(b) the exportation of a controlled drug,
are hereby prohibited.
(2) Subsection (1) above does not apply—
(a) to the importation or exportation of a controlled drug which is for the time being excepted from paragraph (a) or, as the case may be, paragraph (b) of subsection (1) above by regulations under section 7 of this Act; or
(b) to the importation or exportation of a controlled drug under and in accordance with the terms of a licence issued by the Secretary of State and in compliance with any conditions attached thereto.

This section, which is of considerable importance, imposes a prohibition, but does not create an offence. It is generally enforced by the use of charges of improper importation or exportation of goods, fraudulent evasion of duty or, where appropriate, conspiracy to evade the prohibition contained in the section. As to these offences, see **B17.10**.

The meaning of the term 'controlled drug' and the circumstances in which exemptions may be permitted by regulation are discussed in **B20.5** to **B20.9** and **B20.18** to **B20.20**.

CULTIVATING PLANT OF THE GENUS CANNABIS

Definition

Misuse of Drugs Act 1971, s. 6 B20.45

(1) Subject to any regulations under section 7 of this Act for the time being in force, it shall not be lawful for a person to cultivate any plant of the genus *Cannabis*.
(2) Subject to section 28 of this Act, it is an offence to cultivate any such plant in contravention of subsection (1) above.

Procedure

Offences under the MDA 1971, s. 6, are (by s. 25 of and sch. 4 to the Act) triable either B20.46
way. When tried on indictment they are class 4 offences.

Summary trial may be instituted by an information laid 12, rather than the usual six, months from the date of commission of the offence (MDA 1971, s. 25(4)).

For the liability of corporate officers, see **B20.21**.

Sentencing Guidelines

B20.47   See **B20.119** to **B20.122**.

Meaning of 'Cannabis'

B20.48   The definition of 'cannabis' provided in the MDA 1971, s. 37(1) (see **B20.8**), does not apply to the use of the word 'cannabis' in s. 6 of the Act, since the context of the instant offence clearly requires that the plant itself be cultivated.

Meaning of 'Cultivate'

B20.49   This term is not defined in the Act. *Quaere*, whether it would be sufficient for a person who did not introduce it passively to permit a plant of the genus *Cannabis* to continue in a place over which he has control without tending it, or whether some active steps to keep the plant alive or to cause it to grow must be taken. It may be more appropriate to charge possession in such a case.

Mens Rea

B20.50   The accused does not have to know that the plant he cultivated was in fact cannabis (*Champ* (1981) 73 Cr App R 367).

The defence under the MDA 1971, s. 28, applies (see **B20.23**).

When Cultivation may be Lawful

B20.51   As set forth at **B20.45**, the MDA 1971, s. 6(1), provides that, subject to any regulations under s. 7 for the time being in force, it shall not be lawful for a person to cultivate any plant of the genus *Cannabis*.

The Misuse of Drugs Regulations 1985 (**B20.20**) contain various exemptions from this prohibition. See, in particular, reg. 12, by virtue of which a person licensed by the Secretary of State may cultivate a plant of the genus *Cannabis* in accordance with the terms of the licence and in compliance with any conditions attached to it.

OFFENCES RELATING TO OPIUM

Definition

B20.52
                      Misuse of Drugs Act 1971, s. 9

Subject to section 28 of this Act, it is an offence for a person—
  (a)   to smoke or otherwise use prepared opium; or
  (b)   to frequent a place used for the purpose of opium smoking; or
  (c)   to have in his possession
    (i)   any pipes or other utensils made or adapted for use in connection with the smoking of opium, being pipes or utensils which have been used by him or with his knowledge and permission in that connection or which he intends to use or permit others to use in that connection; or
    (ii)   any utensils which have been used by him or with his knowledge and permission in connection with the preparation of opium for smoking.

Section 9 appears to establish three difference offences, rather than three methods of committing the same offence, in paragraphs (a), (b), and (c).

Procedure

B20.53   Offences under the MDA 1971, s. 9, are (by s. 25 of and sch. 4 to the Act) triable either way. When tried on indictment they are class 4 offences.

Summary trial may be instituted by an information laid 12, rather than the usual six, months from the date of commission of the offence (MDA 1971, s. 25(4)).

For the liability of corporate officers, see **B20.21**.

Sentence

See **B20.137** *et seq*.   B20.54

Elements and Defence

By the MDA 1971, s. 37(1), 'prepared opium' means opium prepared for smoking and B20.55
includes dross and any other residues remaining after opium has been smoked.

For the meaning of 'possession' in relation to the offence of the unlawful possession of
a controlled drug, see **B20.10** to **B20.17**.

The defence under s. 28 of the Act also applies to these offences (see **B20.23**).

PROHIBITION OF SUPPLY ETC. OF ARTICLES FOR ADMINISTERING OR PREPARING CONTROLLED DRUGS

Definition

Misuse of Drugs Act 1971, s. 9A   B20.56

> (1)   A person who supplies or offers to supply any article which may be used or adapted
> to be used (whether by itself or in combination with another article or other articles) in the
> administration by any person of a controlled drug to himself or another, believing that the
> article (or the article as adapted) is to be so used in circumstances where the administration
> is unlawful, is guilty of an offence.
>
> . . .
>
> (3)   A person who supplies or offers to supply any article which may be used to prepare
> a controlled drug for administration by any person to himself or another believing that the
> article is to be so used in circumstances where the administration is unlawful is guilty of an
> offence.

There are only two offences, one under s. 9A(1), and the other under s. 9A(3), since the
penalty does not vary with the controlled drug in question.

Procedure

Offences under the MDA 1971, s. 9A, are (by s. 25 of and sch. 4 to the Act) triable only B20.57
summarily. Summary trial may be instituted by an information laid 12, rather than the
usual six, months from the date of commission of the offence (MDA 1971, s. 25(4)).

For the liability of corporate officers, see **B20.21**.

Sentence

See **B20.137** and **B20.141**.   B20.58

Elements

This offence deals with articles which enable people to administer controlled drugs to B20.59
themselves or others. Some of these articles will be known as drug kits.

As to the meaning of 'controlled drug' see **B20.5**.

While in this offence what is being supplied or offered for supply is an article rather than
a controlled drug, it may be that the same approach as in, for example, the MDA 1971,
s. 4(3), applies to the interpretation of the phrase 'supplies or offers to supply' (see
B20.27).

The articles must be for the unlawful administration of a controlled drug.

Misuse of Drugs Act 1971, s. 9A

> (4)   For the purposes of this section, any administration of a controlled drug is unlawful
> except—

(a)   the administration by any person of a controlled drug to another in circumstances where the administration of the drug is not unlawful under section 4(1) of this Act, or

(b)   the administration by any person of a controlled drug to himself in circumstances where having the controlled drug in his possession is not unlawful under section 5(1) of this Act.

As to the circumstances in which such administration or possession would not be unlawful, see the Misuse of Drugs Regulations 1985, at **B20.20**.

Misuse of Drugs Act 1971, s. 9A

(5)   In this section, references to administration by any person of a controlled drug to himself include a reference to his administering it to himself with the assistance of another.

Defence under s. 9A(2)

B20.60   **Misuse of Drugs Act 1971, s. 9A**

(2)   It is not an offence under subsection (1) above to supply or offer to supply a hypodermic syringe, or any part of one.

OCCUPIERS AND THOSE CONCERNED IN MANAGEMENT OF PREMISES KNOWINGLY PERMITTING OR SUFFERING DRUG-RELATED ACTIVITIES

Definition

B20.61   **Misuse of Drugs Act 1971, s. 8**

A person commits an offence if, being the occupier or concerned in the management of any premises, he knowingly permits or suffers any of the following activities to take place on those premises, that is to say—

(a)   producing or attempting to produce a controlled drug in contravention of section 4(1) of this Act;

(b)   supplying or attempting to supply a controlled drug to another in contravention of section 4(1) of this Act, or offering to supply a controlled drug to another in contravention of section 4(1);

(c)   preparing opium for smoking;

(d)   smoking cannabis, cannabis resin or prepared opium.

As to the meaning of 'controlled drug', see **B20.5**; 'producing', see **B20.42**; 'supplying', see **B20.27**.

Since the range of sentence for this offence varies dependent upon the class of drug involved (see **B20.137**), the House of Lords decision in *Courtie* [1984] AC 463, establishes that s. 8 creates not one, but three offences.

Procedure

B20.62   Offences under the MDA 1971, s. 9, are (by s. 25 of and sch. 4 to the Act) triable either way. When tried on indictment they are class 4 offences.

Summary trial may be instituted by an information laid 12, rather than the usual six, months from the date of commission of the offence (MDA 1971, s. 25(4)).

For the liability of corporate officers, see **B20.21**.

Indictment

B20.63   Statement of Offence

Being the occupier [or: concerned in the management] of premises knowingly permitting or suffering production of a controlled drug, contrary to section 8 of the Misuse of Drugs Act 1971.

Particulars of Offence

A on or about the . . . day of . ., being the occupier [or: being concerned in the management] of certain premises situated at and known as . . . , knowingly permitted or suffered on the said premises the production of a controlled drug of Class B, namely . . ., such production being contrary to section 4(1) of the Misuse of Drugs Act 1971.

Sentence

See **B20.137** and **B20.141**.   **B20.64**

Meaning of 'Occupier'

The term 'occupier' should be given a commonsense interpretation (*Tao* [1977] QB 141).   **B20.65** What should not be involved is an overly narrow or legalistic definition. A person 'in occupation', whatever his legal status, may be covered by the MDA 1971, s. 8, provided he has the requisite degree of control over the premises which enables him to exclude people who would, for example, smoke cannabis. Thus the Court of Appeal was able to dismiss an appeal against conviction by an undergraduate who had an exclusive contractual licence from college of a room, which gave him not merely a right to use the room, but also sufficient exclusivity of possession to ensure that he was an occupier. The Court of Appeal in *Read* v *DPP* (1997 unreported), confirmed the rejection of legalistic submissions in relation to who is an occupier. It rejected the argument that an occupier had to have a legal right to exclude others. The appellant was the cohabitee of a woman who was the tenant of a house. If the questions posited in *Tao* were asked, i.e. 'who, on the facts of the particular case, could fairly be said to be in occupation of the premises in question so as to have the requisite degree of control over those premises to exclude from them those who might otherwise intend to carry on those forbidden activities' and 'who can fairly be said to be "the occupier" for the purpose of' s. 8, then the appellant was the occupier (as much as his cohabitee). A similar approach was adopted in summary rejection of the appellant's appeal in *Coid* [1998] Crim LR 199. Here the appellant lived, for most of the time, with his girlfriend who was the tenant of the house, though he did sometimes live with his sister when his relationship with his girlfriend demanded it. When with his girlfriend he exercised sufficient control over the premises to be an occupier, which is the tenor in which the trial judge had directed the jury.

The Court of Appeal in *Tao* approved the decision on the 1964 Act in *Mogford* (1970) 63 Cr App R 168, but not the reasoning, since there the court had indicated that it was important to consider whether the accused was in legal possession. The result, of which approval was signified, was that two sisters were not occupiers when they allowed cannabis to be smoked in their parent's house when their parents were away. Presumably, the Court of Appeal in *Tao* assumed that the sisters in *Mogford* did not have sufficient control. It must be correct that whether or not a person is an 'occupier' depends upon the facts of each case. The reasoning in *Mogford* was, therefore, of no assistance to the Court of Appeal in *Coid*. It must follow that the decision in *Campbell* [1981] Crim LR 595 is open to reconsideration as that involved a simple following of *Mogford*. The decision, that C who lived at his mother's address was not an occupier when he held a party there when she was away, is strange. There is no requirement that the accused be the sole or exclusive occupier; the question should focus on the degree of control, and this would appear to have been satisfied in *Campbell*.

A limited ability to control the use of the premises will suffice. A co-tenant who permits another co-tenant to smoke cannabis commits the offence (see *Ashdown* (1974) Cr App R 193).

Meaning of 'Concerned in the Management of Premises'

A person satisfies the requirement of a manager even if he has no lawful right or title to be on   **B20.66** the premises. To be a manager he must run, organise and plan the use of the premises (see

Josephs (1977) 65 Cr App R 253), and so must be involved in more than menial or routine duties (see *Abbott* v *Smith* [1964] 2 QB 662).

It should be noted that there is no definition of 'premises' in the MDA 1971, although it appears in other legislation where it is provided with a wide definition, e.g, under the Protection from Eviction Act 1977 (see **B13.9**).

'Knowingly Permits or Suffers'

B20.67 The Court of Appeal in *Thomas* (1976) 63 Cr App R 65 held that 'knowingly' adds nothing to the words 'permits or suffers', because they require knowledge. The word was there probably to make doubly sure that there must be knowledge. The House of Lords had decided that, considering the precursor of the instant offence, 'permits' requires *mens rea*, i.e. knowledge (see *Sweet* v *Parsley* [1970] AC 132). The Court of Appeal in *Thomas* also expressed views as to the meaning of knowledge, indicating that wilful blindness may be sufficient, but not mere suspicion (cf. consideration of the phrase 'knowing or believing' in the Theft Act 1968, s. 22, at **B4.141**). What the accused must know, e.g. for the offence under s. 8(b), is that there is supplying of a controlled drug; he need not know which class of drug is being supplied (*Bett* [1999] 1 All ER 600).

As to the meaning of 'permits' and 'suffers', the Court of Appeal in *Thomas* pointed out that these two words mean the same thing, and thus the trial judge was not wrong to refer only to 'permits'. Whether in any given case a person has permitted or suffered a certain activity to take place will be a matter of fact for the jury to decide. In *Thomas* the Court upheld a conviction where the occupier knew that cannabis smoking was taking place and was unwilling to do anything about it, exemplified by his failure to take reasonable steps readily available to prevent the prohibited activity. In *Souter* [1971] 1 WLR 1187 (a decision on the Rent Act 1965), the occupier let rooms to drug addicts, because, so he claimed, he wanted to help them, which involved allowing free access to his living room. However, he claimed, he did not want anyone to smoke cannabis and he had taken reasonable steps to prevent it by putting up a notice in such terms. When he discovered that his hospitality was abused, he would turn people away. Since this might have satisfied the sort of approach now stated in *Thomas*, it was held that the evidence should have been left to the jury, and since it had not been left to them, the conviction had to be quashed. It would seem that mere acquiescence in what is going on is unlikely to amount to permitting that activity (see *Bradbury* [1996] Crim LR 808).

The Divisional Court has made clear in *Taylor* v *Chief Constable of Kent* [1981] 1 WLR 606 that an occupier who permits another to cultivate cannabis plants permits or suffers their production (i.e. there is an overlap between the offences contrary to the MDA 1971, ss. 4 and 6, see **B20.39** and **B20.45**), and so commits an offence contrary to s. 8.

ASSISTING IN OR INDUCING COMMISSION OUTSIDE UNITED KINGDOM OF OFFENCE PUNISHABLE UNDER CORRESPONDING LAW

Definition

B20.68 **Misuse of Drugs Act 1971, s. 20**

> A person commits an offence if in the United Kingdom he assists in or induces the commission in any place outside the United Kingdom of an offence punishable under the provisions of a corresponding law in force in that place.

Procedure

B20.69 The offence under the MDA 1971, s. 20, is (by s. 25 of and sch. 4 to the Act) triable either way. When tried on indictment it is a class 4 offence.

Summary trial may be instituted by an information laid 12, rather than the usual six, months from the date of commission of the offence (MDA 1971, s. 25(4)).

For the liability of corporate officers, see **B20.21**.

Sentence

See **B20.137** and **B20.138**. This is a drug trafficking offence (DTA 1994, s. 1(3)(b)), **B20.70** and so, additionally, a forfeiture order (see **E20.4**) or a confiscation order (see **E21.1**) may be imposed.

Meaning of 'Assisting'

Assisting is not to be narrowly construed but must be construed as an ordinary English **B20.71** word (*Vickers* [1975] 1 WLR 811; *Evans* (1977) 64 Cr App R 237; and *Panayi* (1987) 86 Cr App R 261). Indeed, 'assisting' is, in practice, interpreted widely. In *Vickers* the defendant was guilty when, as he had agreed, he took speaker cabinets to Italy, knowing that cannabis would then be loaded into them and shipped to the United States. In *Evans* the defendant had assisted in the United Kingdom in the importation of cannabis into Canada from Brussels by the making of arrangements to provide for a human carrier and by carrying those arrangements through.

Commission of Offence outside United Kingdom

The offence outside the United Kingdom must actually be committed (*Panayi* (1987) **B20.72** 86 Cr App R 261). It is only if such an offence is committed that there is something which can be assisted, so the convictions of the accused in *Panayi* were quashed when they had been arrested in British territorial waters having sailed from Spain in a yacht with a quantity of cannabis destined for Holland. If an offence is committed and the defendant did an act of assistance, the s. 20 offence is committed even if it is not possible to identify the principal offender and the final act of importation was effected by an innocent third party (*Ahmed* [1990] Crim LR 648).

Meaning of 'Corresponding Law'

Misuse of Drugs Act 1971, s. 36　　　　　　　　　　　　　　**B20.73**

(1)   In this Act the expression 'corresponding law' means a law stated in a certificate purporting to be issued by or on behalf of the government of a country outside the United Kingdom to be a law providing for the control and regulation in that country of the production, supply, use, export and import of drugs and other substances in accordance with the provisions of the Single Convention on Narcotic Drugs signed at New York on 30 March 1961 or a law providing for the control and regulation in that country of the production, supply, use, export and import of dangerous or otherwise harmful drugs in pursuance of any treaty, convention or other agreement or arrangement to which the government of that country and Her Majesty's Government in the United Kingdom are for the time being parties.

(2)   A statement in any such certificate as aforesaid to the effect that any facts constitute an offence against the law mentioned in the certificate shall be evidence . . . of the matters stated.

Mens Rea

The offence is not one of strict liability (*Vickers* [1975] 1 WLR 811), but it is required **B20.74** that (a) the defendant intend to assist, i.e. he must know what he is doing and the purpose with which it is done (*Vickers*, at p. 818), and (b) the defendant was aware that the person he was assisting was involved in drug smuggling (*Ahmed* [1990] Crim LR 648). It is not necessary to establish that the defendant intended that the goods be imported into a particular country (*Ahmed*).

INCITEMENT

B20.75   **Misuse of Drugs Act 1971, s. 19**

It is an offence for a person to incite another to commit [an offence under the Act].

The offence of incitement is triable and punishable in the same way as the substantive offence incited (MDA 1971, s. 25(3) and sch. 4). It applies to all offences in the 1971 Act (*Marlow* [1997] 10 CL 119). For the meaning of incitement, see **A6.1** and **A6.5** to **A6.8**.

ENFORCEMENT PROVISIONS

Powers of Entry, Search and Seizure

B20.76   **Misuse of Drugs Act 1971, s. 23**

(1)   A constable or other person authorised in that behalf by a general or special order of the Secretary of State (or in Northern Ireland either of the Secretary of State or the Ministry of Home Affairs for Northern Ireland) shall, for the purposes of the execution of this Act, have power to enter the premises of a person carrying on business as a producer or supplier of any controlled drugs and to demand the production of, and to inspect, any books or documents relating to dealings in any such drugs and to inspect any stocks of any such drugs.

(2)   If a constable has reasonable grounds to suspect that any person is in possession of a controlled drug in contravention of this Act or of any regulations made thereunder, the constable may—

(a)   search that person, and detain him for the purpose of searching him;

(b)   search any vehicle or vessel in which the constable suspects that the drug may be found, and for that purpose require the person in control of the vehicle or vessel to stop it;

(c)   seize and detain, for the purposes of proceedings under this Act, anything found in the course of the search which appears to the constable to be evidence of an offence under this Act.

In this subsection 'vessel' includes a hovercraft within the meaning of the Hovercraft Act 1968; and nothing in this subsection shall prejudice any power of search or any power to seize or detain property which is exercisable by a constable apart from this subsection.

(3)   If a justice of the peace (or in Scotland a justice of the peace, a magistrate or a sheriff) is satisfied by information on oath that there is reasonable ground for suspecting—

(a)   that any controlled drugs are, in contravention of this Act or of any regulations made thereunder, in the possession of a person on any premises; or

(b)   that a document directly or indirectly relating to, or connected with, a transaction or dealing which was, or an intended transaction or dealing which would if carried out be, an offence under this Act, or in the case of a transaction or dealing carried out or intended to be carried out in a place outside the United Kingdom, an offence against the provisions of a corresponding law in force in that place, is in the possession of a person on any premises, he may grant a warrant authorising any constable acting for the police area in which the premises are situated at any time or times within one month from the date of the warrant, to enter, if need be by force, the premises named in the warrant, and to search the premises and any persons found therein and, if there is reasonable ground for suspecting that an offence under this Act has been committed in relation to any controlled drugs found on the premises or in the possession of any such persons, or that a document so found is such a document as is mentioned in paragraph (b) above, to seize and detain those drugs or that document, as the case may be.

(3A)   The powers conferred by subsection (1) above shall be exercisable also for the purposes of the execution of part II of the Criminal Justice (International Co-operation) Act 1990 or section 49 of the Drug Trafficking Act 1994 and subsection (3) above (excluding paragraph (a)) shall apply also to offences under section 12 or 13 of that Act of 1990, taking references in those provisions to controlled drugs as references to scheduled substances within the meaning of that part.

Offences of Obstruction, Concealment etc.

The powers of enforcement are supported by offences created by the MDA 1971, **B20.77**
s. 23(4).

Misuse of Drugs Act 1971, s. 23

(4)   A person commits an offence if he—

(a)   intentionally obstructs a person in the exercise of his powers under this section; or

(b)   conceals from a person acting in the exercise of his powers under subsection (1)
above any such books, documents, stocks or drugs as are mentioned in that subsection; or

(c)   without reasonable excuse (proof of which shall lie on him) fails to produce any
such books or documents as are so mentioned where their production is demanded by a
person in the exercise of his powers under that subsection.

These offences are triable either way (MDA 1971, s. 25 and sch. 4).

As to the time for commencement of proceedings, see **B20.2**. As to sentence, see
B20.137 and **B20.138**.

In *Forde* (1985) 81 Cr App R 19, the Court of Appeal held that a person only committed
an offence under s. 23(4)(a) if, on the facts of that case, the accused knew that he was
being detained for the purposes of a search under s. 23(2)(a) and if the obstruction was
intentional, that is to say the act viewed objectively, through the eyes of a bystander, did
obstruct the constable's detention or search, and viewed subjectively, that is to say
through the eyes of the accused himself, was intended so to obstruct.

For consideration of the similar phrasing in the offence of the wilful obstruction of a
police officer in the execution of his duty contrary to the Police Act 1996, s. 89(2), see
B2.25 to **B2.28**.

OTHER OFFENCES RELATED TO MISUSE OF DRUGS

Contravention of Directions relating to Safe Custody of Controlled Drugs

It is an offence, contrary to the MDA 1971, s. 11(2), to contravene any directions given **B20.78**
under s. 11(1). The offence is punishable, on summary conviction, with imprisonment
for a term not exceeding six months or a fine not exceeding the prescribed sum or both,
and, on conviction on indictment, with imprisonment for a term not exceeding two years
or a fine or both. Section 11(1) enables the Secretary of State, by notice in writing to be
served on the occupier of any premises on which controlled drugs are or are proposed
to be kept, to give directions as to the taking of precautions or further precautions for
the safe custody of any controlled drugs of a description specified in the notice which
are kept on those premises.

Contravention of Direction Prohibiting Practitioner etc. from Possessing, Supplying etc. Controlled Drugs

It is an offence, contrary to the MDA 1971, s. 12(6), to contravene a direction given **B20.79**
under s. 12(2). The range of sentence for the offence depends upon whether the drug is
a Class A, Class B or Class C drug. It should first be noted that the different penalties
mean, in accordance with *Courtie* [1984] AC 463, that s. 12(6) creates two offences,
since the punishment where the drug is Class A or Class B is the same. For the penalties
available on conviction, see sch. 4 to the 1971 Act (set out at **B20.137**).

Directions under s. 12(2) can be made by the Secretary of State with regard to people
who fall within s. 12(1), that is, a practitioner or pharmacist who has been convicted of:

(a)   an offence under the 1971 Act, or the Dangerous Drugs Act 1965 or any
enactment repealed by that Act; or

(b)   an offence under the Customs and Excise Act 1952, s. 45, 56, or 304, or under the Customs and Excise Management Act 1979, s. 50, 68, or 170, in connection with a prohibition of or restriction on importation or exportation of a controlled drug having effect by virtue of s. 3 of the 1971 Act or which had effect by virtue of any provision contained in or repealed by the Dangerous Drugs Act 1965;

(c)   an offence under the Criminal Justice (International Co-operation) Act 1990, s. 12 or 13.

The directions which the Secretary of State imposes shall:

(a)   if that person is a practitioner, be a direction prohibiting him from having in his possession, prescribing, administering, manufacturing, compounding and supplying and from authorising the administration and supply of such controlled drugs as may be specified in the direction;

(b)   if that person is a pharmacist, be a direction prohibiting him from having in his possession, manufacturing, compounding and supplying and from supervising and controlling the manufacture, compounding and supply of such controlled drugs as may be specified in that direction.

Such directions may at any time be cancelled or suspended by the Secretary of State by direction under s. 12(3). Any direction must be served on the person in question and be published in the London, Edinburgh and Belfast Gazettes in accordance with s. 12(4). The direction takes effect when a copy is served on the person to whom it applies (s. 12(5)). Section 37(1) of the Act defines 'practitioner' as meaning a doctor, dentist, veterinary practitioner or veterinary surgeon, and 'pharmicist' as having the same meaning as in the Medicines Act 1968.

Contravention of Direction Prohibiting Practitioner etc. from Prescribing etc. Controlled Drugs

B20.80   It is an offence, contrary to the MDA 1971, s. 13(3), to contravene a direction given under s. 13(1) or (2). The range of sentence for the offence depends upon whether the drug is a Class A, Class B or Class C drug. It should first be noted that the different penalties mean, in accordance with *Courtie* [1984] AC 463, that s. 13(3) creates two offences, since the punishment where the drug is Class A or Class B is the same. For the penalties available on conviction, see sch. 4 to the 1971 Act (set out at **B20.137**).

The Secretary of State's power to give directions under s. 13(1) and (2) are as follows:

(a)   Where there has been a contravention of the Misuse of Drugs (Supply to Addicts) Regulations 1997 (SI 1997 No. 1001) (or other regulations concerned with doctors prescribing controlled drugs for addicts made under s. 10(2)(h) or (i)), or contravention of the terms of a licence issued to a doctor in pursuance of those regulations, the Secretary of State may, subject to and in accordance with s. 14, give a direction in respect of the doctor concerning prohibiting him from prescribing, administering and supplying and authorising the administration and supply of such controlled drugs as may be specified in the direction. (Note that s. 12(3) makes clear that contravention of the regulations is not in itself an offence.)

(b)   Where the Secretary of State is of the opinion that a practitioner is, or has, after the coming into operation of s. 13(2), been prescribing, administering or supplying or authorising the administration or supply of any controlled drugs in an irresponsible manner, the Secretary of State may, subject to and in accordance with ss. 14 and 15, give a direction in respect of the practitioner concerned prohibiting him from prescribing, administering and supplying and authorising the administration and supply of such controlled drugs as may be specified in the direction.

The supplementary provisions to s. 13 are to be found in the MDA 1971, ss. 14, 15, and 16 and sch. 3.

Failure to Comply with Notice Requiring Information Relating to Prescribing Supply etc. of Drugs

It is an offence, contrary to the MDA 1971, s. 17(3), if a person without reasonable **B20.81** excuse (proof of which shall lie on him) fails to comply with any requirement to which he is subject by virtue of s. 17(1). The offence is punishable, on summary conviction, with a fine not exceeding level 3 on the standard scale.

Giving False Information in Purported Compliance with Notice Requiring Information Relating to Prescribing, Supply etc. of Drugs

It is an offence, contrary to the MDA 1971, s. 17(4), if a person, in purported compliance **B20.82** with a requirement imposed under s. 17, gives any information which he knows to be false in a material particular or recklessly gives any information which is false. The offence is punishable, on summary conviction, with a term of imprisonment not exceeding six months or a fine not exceeding the prescribed sum or both, and, on conviction on indictment, with a term of imprisonment not exceeding two years or a fine or both.

Both this and the offence in **B20.81** rely on the provisions of s. 17(1) and (2):

Misuse of Drugs Act 1971, ss. 17 and 37

17.—(1)   If it appears to the Secretary of State that there exists in any area in Great Britain a social problem caused by the extensive misuse of dangerous or otherwise harmful drugs in that area, he may by notice in writing served on any doctor or pharmacist practising in or in the vicinity of that area, or on any person carrying on a retail pharmacy business within the meaning of the Medicines Act 1968 at any premises situated in or in the vicinity of that area, require him to furnish to the Secretary of State, with respect to any such drugs specified in the notice and as regards any period so specified, such particulars as may be so specified relating to the quantities in which and the number and frequency of the occasions on which those drugs—
> (a)   in the case of a doctor, were prescribed, administered or supplied by him;
> (b)   in the case of a pharmacist, were supplied by him; or
> (c)   in the case of a person carrying on a retail pharmacy business, were supplied in
the course of that business at any premises so situated which may be specified in the notice.
   (2)   A notice under this section may require any such particulars to be furnished in such manner and within such time as may be specified in the notice and, if served on a pharmacist or person carrying on a retail pharmacy business, may require him to furnish the names and addresses of doctors on whose prescriptions any dangerous or otherwise harmful drugs to which the notice relates were supplied, but shall not require any person to furnish any particulars relating to the identity of any person for or to whom any such drug has been prescribed, administered or supplied.

37.—(2)   References in this Act to misusing a drug are references to misusing it by taking it; . . .

Contravention of Regulations (other than Regulations Relating to Addicts)

It is an offence, contrary to the MDA 1971, s. 18(1), for a person to contravene any **B20.83** regulations made under the 1971 Act other than regulations relating to addicts. The offence is punishable, on summary conviction, with a term of imprisonment not exceeding six months or a fine not exceeding the prescribed sum or both, and, on conviction on indictment, with a term of imprisonment not exceeding two years or a fine or both. The significance of this offence, in particular, is that it means any breach of the Misuse of Drugs (Safe Custody) Regulations 1973 (SI 1973 No. 798) is an offence.

Contravention of Terms of Licence or other Authority (other than Licence Issued under Regulations Relating to Addicts)

It is an offence, contrary to the MDA 1971, s. 18(2), for a person to contravene a **B20.84** condition or other term of a licence issued under s. 3 of the 1971 Act or of a licence or other authority under regulations made under the 1971 Act, not being a licence issued under regulations relating to addicts. The offence is punishable, on summary conviction, with a term of imprisonment not exceeding six months or a fine not exceeding the prescribed sum or both, and, on conviction on indictment, with a term of imprisonment not exceeding two years or a fine or both.

Giving False Information in Purported Compliance with Obligation to give Information Imposed under Regulations

B20.85 It is an offence, contrary to the MDA 1971, s. 18(3), if a person, in purported compliance with any obligation to give information to which he is subject under or by virtue of regulations made under the 1971 Act, gives any information which he knows to be false in a material particular or recklessly gives any information which is so false. It may be that 'recklessly' has the same meaning as laid down by the House of Lords in *Metropolitan Police Commissioner* v *Caldwell* [1982] AC 341 (see **A2.5** and **A2.6**). The offence is punishable, on summary conviction, with a term of imprisonment not exceeding six months or a fine not exceeding the prescribed sum or both, and, on conviction on indictment, with a term of imprisonment not exceeding two years or a fine or both. Information has to be supplied under the Misuse of Drugs (Supply to Addicts) Regulations 1997 (SI 1997 No. 1001).

Giving False Information, or Producing Document Containing False Statement etc. for Purpose of Obtaining Issue of Licence

B20.86 It is an offence, contrary to the MDA 1971, s. 18(4), if a person for the purpose of obtaining, whether for himself or another, the issue or renewal of a licence or other authority under the 1971 Act or any regulations made under it:

(a) makes any statement or gives any information which he knows to be false in a material particular or recklessly gives any information which is so false; or

(b) produces or otherwise makes use of any book, record or other document which to his knowledge contains any statement or information which he knows to be false in a material particular.

The offence is punishable, on summary conviction, with a term of imprisonment not exceeding six months or a fine not exceeding the prescribed sum or both, and, on conviction on indictment, with a term of imprisonment not exceeding two years or a fine or both.

SUPPLY OF INTOXICATING SUBSTANCE

Definition

B20.87   **Intoxicating Substances (Supply) Act 1985, s. 1**

(1) It is an offence for a person to supply or offer to supply a substance other than a controlled drug—

(a) to a person under the age of 18 whom he knows, or has reasonable cause to believe, to be under that age; or

(b) to a person—

(i) who is acting on behalf of a person under that age; and

(ii) whom he knows, or has reasonable cause to believe, to be so acting,

if he knows or has reasonable cause to believe that the substance is, or its fumes are, likely to be inhaled by the person under the age of 18 for the purpose of causing intoxication.

Procedure

B20.88 The offence is triable summarily only.

Sentence

The maximum penalty is imprisonment for a term not exceeding six months or a fine **B20.89** not exceeding level 5 or both (Intoxicating Substances (Supply) Act 1985, s. 1(3)).

Elements and Defence

Since similar concepts apply in the MDA 1971, s. 4(3) (see **B20.27**), it may be that the **B20.90** same meaning of 'supply or offer to supply' appertains in the 1985 Act, but the statute does not make that clear and the point remains open.

The Intoxicating Substances (Supply) Act 1985, s. 1(4), makes clear that 'controlled drug' has the same meaning as in the MDA 1971 (see **B20.5**).

Intoxicating Substances (Supply) Act 1985, s. 1

(2) In proceedings against any person for an offence under subsection (1) above it is a defence for him to show that at the time he made the supply or offer he was under the age of 18 and was acting otherwise than in the course or furtherance of a business.

DRUG TRAFFICKING GENERALLY

Definition of Drug Trafficking Offences

The DTA 1994, s. 1(3), defines drug trafficking offences not only as including the **B20.91** following offences, but also as including offences contrary to the MDA 1971, s. 4(2), 4(3), 5(3) or 20 (see **B20.39, B20.32, B20.24** and **B20.68**) and the Customs and Excise Management Act 1979, s. 50(2), 50(3), 68(2) or 170 (see **B17.10, B17.14** and **B17.15**). Also included are conspiracy, attempt, and incitement (either at common law or contrary to the MDA 1971, s. 19 (see **B20.74**)) and participation in any of those offences.

Commision of Offence on a Ship

Anything which would constitute a drug trafficking offence if done on land in any **B20.92** part of the United Kingdom constitutes that offence if done on a British ship (Criminal Justice (International Co-operation) Act 1990, ss. 18 and 24). Proceedings for such an offence committed on a ship may be taken, and the offence may for all incidental purposes be treated as having been committed, in any place in the United Kingdom (Criminal Justice (International Co-operation) Act 1990, s. 21(1)). No such proceedings may be instituted in England and Wales except by or with the consent of the DPP or the Commissioners of Customs and Excise (s. 21(2)(a)). As to the definition of 'ship' and 'British ship', see **B20.135**.

Prejudicing Drug Trafficking Investigation

The DTA 1994, s. 58, makes it an offence for a person, in certain circumstances and **B20.93** subject to defences of lack of knowledge or suspicion of an investigation and of lawful authority or reasonable excuse, to prejudice an investigation into drug trafficking by the making of a disclosure. The offence is triable either way; it carries a maximum penalty, on conviction on indictment, of a term of imprisonment not exceeding five years or a fine or both, or, on summary conviction, of a term of imprisonment not exceeding six months or a fine not exceeding the statutory maximum or both. Section 58(3) provides a specific defence for professional legal advisers.

Proceedings Instituted by the Commissioners of Customs and Excise

Proceedings for any offence contrary to the DTA 1994, part III (ss. 49 to 54) and s. 58 **B20.94** or any attempt, conspiracy or incitement to commit such an offence or any prescribed offence may be instituted by the Commissioners of Customs and Excise in accordance with the provisions of the DTA 1994, s. 60.

Extension of Drug Trafficking Offences to Crown servants

B20.95 By virtue of the Drug Trafficking Offences Act 1986 (Crown Servants and Regulators etc.) Regulations 1994 (SI 1994 No. 1757), regs. 3 and 4:

(a)   the DTA 1994, ss. 50 to 53, apply to the Director of Savings and any person employed by or otherwise engaged in his service in circumstances where the Director or any such person is carrying on relevant financial business, as defined in the Money Laundering Regulations 1993 (SI 1993 No. 1933), reg. 4;

(b)   s. 52 does not apply, as regards England and Wales, to the following organisations or persons employed by or otherwise engaged in their service: the Bank of England; the Building Societies Commission; a designated agency or self-regulating organisation for friendly societies within the meaning of the Financial Services Act 1986; the Council of Lloyd's; the Friendly Societies Commission; and the Central Office of the Registry of Friendly Societies.

CONCEALING OR TRANSFERRING PROCEEDS OF DRUG TRAFFICKING

Definition

B20.96   **Drug Trafficking Act 1994, s. 49**

(1)   A person is guilty of an offence if he—
(a)   conceals or disguises any property which is, or in whole or in part directly or indirectly represents, his proceeds of drug trafficking; or
(b)   converts or transfers that property or removes it from the jurisdiction,
for the purpose of avoiding prosecution for a drug trafficking offence or the making or enforcement in his case of a confiscation order.
(2)   A person is guilty of an offence if, knowing or having reasonable grounds to suspect that any property is, or in whole or in part directly or indirectly represents, another person's proceeds of drug trafficking, he—
(a)   conceals or disguises that property, or
(b)   converts or transfers that property or removes it from the jurisdiction,
for the purpose of assisting any person to avoid prosecution for a drug trafficking offence or the making or enforcement of a confiscation order.

Procedure

B20.97 The offence is triable either way (DTA 1994, s. 54(1)). When tried on indictment it is a class 4 offence.

As to the position where the offence is committed on a British ship, see **B20.92**. As to proceedings instituted by Customs and Excise, see **B20.94**.

For the liability of corporate officers, see **B20.21**.

Sentence

B20.98 The maximum penalty on conviction on indictment is imprisonment for a term not exceeding 14 years or a fine or both; on summary conviction, the maximum sentence is imprisonment for a term not exceeding six months or a fine not exceeding the statutory maximum or both (DTA 1994, s. 54(1)).

Offences under s. 49 are drug trafficking offences (DTA 1994, s. 1(3)(f)), so a confiscation order (**E21.1**) or forfeiture order (**E20.4**) may be imposed.

Meaning of 'Drug Trafficking Offence', 'Drug Trafficking' and 'Proceeds of Drug Trafficking'

B20.99 As to the meaning of 'drug trafficking offence', see **B20.91**. 'Drug trafficking' and 'proceeds of drug trafficking are defined as follows.

Drug Trafficking Act 1994, s. 1

(1)   In this Act 'drug trafficking' means, subject to subsection (2) below, doing or being concerned in any of the following, whether in England and Wales or elsewhere—

(a)   producing or supplying a controlled drug where the production or supply contravenes section 4(1) of the Misuse of Drugs Act 1971 or a corresponding law;

(b)   transporting or storing a controlled drug where possession of the drug contravenes section 5(1) of that Act or a corresponding law;

(c)   importing or exporting a controlled drug where the importation or exportation is prohibited by section 3(1) of that Act or a corresponding law;

(d)   manufacturing or supplying a scheduled substance within the meaning of section 12 of the Criminal Justice (International Co-operation) Act 1990 where the manufacture or supply is an offence under that section or would be such an offence if it took place in England and Wales;

(e)   using any ship for illicit traffic in controlled drugs in circumstances which amount to the commission of an offence under section 19 of that Act;

(f)   conduct which is an offence under section 49 of this Act or which would be such an offence if it took place in England and Wales;

(g)   acquiring, having possession of or using property in circumstances which amount to the commission of an offence under section 51 of this Act or which would amount to such an offence if it took place in England and Wales.

(2)   'Drug trafficking' also includes a person doing the following, whether in England and Wales or elsewhere, that is to say, entering into or being otherwise concerned in an arrangement whereby—

(a)   the retention or control by or on behalf of another person of the other person's proceeds of drug trafficking is facilitated, or

(b)   the proceeds of drug trafficking by another person are used to secure that funds are placed at the other person's disposal or are used for the other person's benefit to acquire property by way of investment.

As to the MDA 1971, ss. 4(1) and 5(1) see **B20.24** and **B20.39**. Section 3(1) of that Act is dealt with at **B17.11**. 'Corresponding law', according to the DTA 1994, s. 1(4), has the same meaning as in the 1971 Act (see **B20.73**).

The phrase 'proceeds of drug trafficking' is defined by the DTA 1994, s. 4(1)(a). For a full consideration of its meaning, see **E21.4**.

Drug Trafficking Act 1994, s. 4

(1)   For the purposes of this Act—

(a)   any payments or other rewards received by a person at any time (whether before or after the commencement of section 1 of this Act) in connection with drug trafficking carried on by him or another are his proceeds of drug trafficking . . .

Property and Related Concepts

For the meaning of property and how it may be treated as representing the proceeds of drug trafficking, see **E21.4**.   **B20.100**

References to concealing or disguising property in s. 49(1)(a) and (2)(a) include references to concealing or disguising its nature, source, location, disposition, movement or ownership or any rights with respect to it (s. 49(3)).

The offence contrary to s. 49(2) applies to the Director of Savings and any person employed by or otherwise engaged in his service in circumstances where the Director or any such person is carrying on relevant financial business, as defined in the Money Laundering Regulations 1993 (SI 1993 No. 1933), reg. 4 (Criminal Justice (International Co-operation) Act 1990 (Crown Servants) Regulations 1994 (SI 1994 No. 1756), reg. 3).

ASSISTING DRUG TRAFFICKERS

Definition

B20.101
Drug Trafficking Act 1994, s. 50

(1) Subject to subsection (3) below, a person is guilty of an offence if he enters into or is otherwise concerned in an arrangement whereby—

(a) the retention or control by or on behalf of another (call him 'A') of A's proceeds of drug trafficking is facilitated (whether by concealment, removal from the jurisdiction, transfer to nominees or otherwise), or

(b) A's proceeds of drug trafficking—

(i) are used to secure that funds are placed at A's disposal, or

(ii) are used for A's benefit to acquire property by way of investment,

and he knows or suspects that A is a person who carries on or has carried on drug trafficking or has benefited from drug trafficking.

Procedure

B20.102 The offence is triable either way (DTA 1994, s. 54(1)). When tried on indictment it is a class 4 offence. As to the position where the offence is committed on a British ship, see **B20.92**. As to proceedings instituted by Customs and Excise, see **B20.94**.

Sentence

B20.103 The maximum penalty is: on conviction on indictment, imprisonment for a term not exceeding 14 years or a fine or both; on summary conviction, imprisonment for a term not exceeding six months or a fine not exceeding the statutory maximum or both (DTA 1994, s. 54(1)). This offence is a drug trafficking offence (s. 1(3)(f)), and so a forfeiture order (see **E20.4**) or a confiscation order (see **E21.1**) may be imposed. In *Hanna* (1994) 15 Cr App R (S) 44, a sentence of 12 months' imprisonment was upheld for this offence. The female offender had passed £16,000 through a building society account at the request of a woman friend, who had been arrested for a drug trafficking offence and released on bail. In *O'Meally* (1994) 15 Cr App R (S) 831, sentences of 18 months and nine months were upheld. The offender who attracted the longer sentence had travelled to Jamaica to deposit nearly £30,000, most of which sum was subsequently recovered. The Court of Appeal declined to lay down sentencing guidelines for this offence, commenting that the facts were 'infinitely variable'. See also *Greenwood* (1995) 16 Cr App R (S) 614.

Elements

B20.104 What is 'facilitated' for the purposes of the DTA 1994, s. 50(1)(a) is the retention or control of the proceeds of drug trafficking. It is not necessary that this be achieved by way of concealment. Thus the conversion of sterling into guilders satisfied s. 50. The purpose for which the facilitation takes place is not relevant. There would seem to be a degree of overlap between ss. 49, 50 and 51, but that does not mean that s. 50(1)(a) should be interpreted in a narrow way contrary to the clear words of the section (*MacMaster* [1999] 1 Cr App R 402). As to the meaning of 'drug trafficking', see **B20.99**; as to property and related concepts, see **B20.100**.

Proceeds of Drug Trafficking

B20.105
Drug Trafficking Act 1994, s. 50

(2) In this section, references to any person's proceeds of drug trafficking include a reference to any property which in whole or in part directly or indirectly represented in his hands his proceeds of drug trafficking.

A further definition of the phrase 'proceeds of drug trafficking' is to be found at s. 4(1)(a) (see **E21.4**).

Mens Rea   The *mens rea*, as stated in s. 50(1), requires the defendant to know or **B20.106** suspect that A is a person who carries on or has carried on drug trafficking or had benefited from it (*Colle* (1991) 95 Cr App R 67).

Defences

Section 50(3) of the DTA 1994 provides a defence where a person makes proper **B20.107** disclosure of any suspicion or belief that funds are derived from or used in connection with drug trafficking; the defence is in identical terms to that under s. 51(5) (see **B20.113**). Section 50(4) provides a defence of lack of knowledge and suspicion.

Drug Trafficking Act 1994, s. 50

(4)   In proceedings against a person for an offence under this section, it is a defence to prove—
(a)   that he did not know or suspect that the arrangement related to any person's proceeds of drug trafficking, or
(b)   that he did not know or suspect that by the arrangement the retention or control by or on behalf of A of any property was facilitated or, as the case may be, that by the arrangement any property was used as mentioned in subsection (1) above, or
(c)   that—
(i)   he intended to disclose to a constable such a suspicion, belief or matter as is mentioned in subsection (3) above in relation to the arrangement, but
(ii)   there is reasonable excuse for his failure to make any such disclosure in the manner mentioned in paragraph (b)(i) or (ii) of that subsection.
(5)   In the case of a person who was in employment at the time in question, subsections (3) and (4) above shall have effect in relation to disclosures, and intended disclosures, to the appropriate person in accordance with the procedure established by his employer for the making of such disclosures as they have effect in relation to disclosures, and intended disclosures, to a constable.

The burden of proving this defence on a balance of probabilities lies on the accused (*Colle* (1991) 95 Cr App R 67) and see **F3.4** and **F3.18**.

ACQUISITION, POSSESSION OR USE OF PROCEEDS OF DRUG TRAFFICKING

Definition

Drug Trafficking Act 1994, s. 51   **B20.108**

(1)   A person is guilty of an offence if, knowing that any property is, or in whole or in part directly or indirectly represents, another person's proceeds of drug trafficking, he acquires or uses that property or has possession of it.

Procedure

The offence is triable either way (DTA 1994, s. 54(1)). When tried on indictment it is **B20.109** a class 4 offence. As to the position where the offence is committed on a British ship, see **B20.92**. As to proceedings instituted by Customs and Excise, see **B20.94**.

Sentence

The maximum penalty is: on conviction on indictment, imprisonment for a term not **B20.110** exceeding 14 years or a fine or both; on summary conviction, imprisonment for a term not exceeding six months or a fine not exceeding the statutory maximum or both (DTA 1994, s. 54(1)). This offence is a drug trafficking offence (s. 1(3)(f)) and so a forfeiture order (see **E20.4**) or a confiscation order (see **E21.1**) may be imposed.

Elements

B20.111 As to 'drug trafficking offence', 'drug trafficking' and 'proceeds of drug trafficking', see **B20.91** and **B20.99**. For the meaning of 'property', see **B20.100**.

Defence of Acquisition, Use or Possession for Adequate Consideration

B20.112   **Drug Trafficking Act 1994, s. 51**

>   (2)   It is a defence to a charge of committing an offence under this section that the person charged acquired or used the property or had possession of it for adequate consideration.
>   (3)   For the purposes of subsection (2) above—
>   (a)   a person acquires property for inadequate consideration if the value of the consideration is significantly less than the value of the property; and
>   (b)   a person uses or has possession of property for inadequate consideration if the value of the consideration is significantly less than the value of his use or possession of the property.
>   (4)   The provision for any person of services or goods which are of assistance to him in drug trafficking shall not be treated as consideration for the purposes of subsection (2) above.

Effect of Making Proper Disclosure

B20.113   **Drug Trafficking Act 1994, s. 51**

>   (5)   Where a person discloses to a constable a suspicion or belief that any property is, or in whole or in part directly or indirectly represents, another person's proceeds of drug trafficking, or discloses to a constable any matter on which such a suspicion or belief is based—
>   (a)   the disclosure shall not be treated as a breach of any restriction upon the disclosure of information imposed by statute or otherwise; and
>   (b)   if he does any act in relation to the property in contravention of subsection (1) above, he does not commit an offence under this section if—
>   (i)   the disclosure is made before he does the act concerned and the act is done with the consent of the constable, or
>   (ii)   the disclosure is made after he does the act, but on his initiative and as soon as it is reasonable for him to make it.
>   (6)   For the purposes of this section, having possession of any property shall be taken as doing an act in relation to it.
>   (7)   In proceedings against a person for an offence under this section, it is a defence to prove that—
>   (a)   he intended to disclose to a constable such a suspicion, belief or matter as is mentioned in subsection (5) above, but
>   (b)   there is reasonable excuse for his failure to make any such disclosure in the manner mentioned in paragraph (b)(i) or (ii) of that subsection.
>   (8)   In the case of a person who was in employment at the time in question, subsections (5) and (7) above shall have effect in relation to disclosures, and intended disclosures, to the appropriate person in accordance with the procedure established by his employer for the making of such disclosures as they have effect in relation to disclosures, and intended disclosures, to a constable.

'Constable' includes a person commissioned by the Commissioners of Customs and Excise (s. 63(1)).

Defence for People Enforcing Enactments in relation to Drug Trafficking

B20.114   **Drug Trafficking Act 1994, s. 51**

>   (9)   No constable or other person shall be guilty of an offence under this section in respect of anything done by him in the course of acting in connection with the enforcement, or intended enforcement, of any provision of this Act or of any other enactment relating to drug trafficking or the proceeds of such trafficking.

For the meaning of 'constable', see **B20.113**.

LAUNDERING MONEY FROM DRUG TRAFFICKING

Failure to Disclose Knowledge or Suspicion of Money Laundering

Definition

Drug Trafficking Act 1994, s. 52   B20.115

(1)   A person is guilty of an offence if—
    (a)   he knows or suspects that another person is engaged in drug money laundering,
    (b)   the information, or other matter, on which that knowledge or suspicion is based
came to his attention in the course of his trade, profession, business or employment, and
    (c)   he does not disclose the information or other matter to a constable as soon as is
reasonably practicable after it comes to his attention.

Procedure   The offence is triable either way (DTA 1994, s. 54(1)). When tried on   B20.116
indictment it is a class 4 offence. As to proceedings instituted by Customs and Excise,
see **B20.94**.

Sentence   The maximum penalty is: on conviction on indictment, imprisonment for   B20.117
a term not exceeding five years or a fine or both; on summary conviction, imprisonment
for a term not exceeding six months or a fine not exceeding the statutory maximum or
both (DTA 1994, s. 54(1)).

Elements   'Drug money laundering' means doing any act which constitutes an offence   B20.118
under the DTA 1994, s. 49, 50 or 51, or, in the case of an act done otherwise than in
England and Wales, which would constitute such an offence if done in England and
Wales. Having possession of any property is taken as doing an act in relation to it.

Defences   It is a defence that a person had a reasonable excuse for not disclosing the   B20.119
information or other matter in question (DTA 1994, s. 52(3)).

It is a defence for an employee that he disclosed the information or other matter in
question to the appropriate person in accordance with the procedure established by his
employer for the making of such disclosures (s. 52(5)). Such a disclosure is not treated
as a breach of any restriction imposed by statute or otherwise (s. 52(6)).

Section 52(1) does not make it an offence for a professional legal adviser to fail to
disclose any information or other matter which has come to him in privileged
circumstances (s. 52(2)). Information or other matter comes to a professional legal
adviser in privileged circumstances if it is communicated or given to him (s. 52(8)):

    (a)   by, or by a representative of, his client in connection with him giving legal advice
to the client,
    (b)   by, or by a representative of, a person seeking legal advice from him, or
    (c)   by any person in contemplation of, or in connection with, legal proceedings, and
for the purpose of those proceedings.

No privileged circumstances arise if the information or other matter is communicated
or given with a view to furthering any criminal purpose (s. 52(9)).

Where a person discloses to a constable his suspicion or belief that another person is
engaged in drug money laundering, or any information or other matter on which that
suspicion or belief is based, the disclosure is not treated as a breach of any restriction
imposed by statute or otherwise (s. 52(4)).

Tipping-off

Definition

Drug Trafficking Act 1994, s. 53   B20.120

(1)   A person is guilty of an offence if—

(a) he knows or suspects that a constable is acting, or is proposing to act, in connection with an investigation which is being, or is about to be, conducted into drug money laundering, and

(b) he discloses to any other person information or any other matter which is likely to prejudice that investigation, or proposed investigation.

(2) A person is guilty of an offence if—

(a) he knows or suspects that a disclosure has been made to a constable under section 50, 51 or 52 of this Act ('the disclosure'), and

(b) he discloses to any other person information or any other matter which is likely to prejudice any investigation which might be conducted following the disclosure.

(3) A person is guilty of an offence if—

(a) he knows or suspects that a disclosure of a kind mentioned in section 50(5), 51(8) or 52(5) of this Act ('the disclosure') has been made, and

(b) he discloses to any person information or any other matter which is likely to prejudice any investigation which might be conducted following the disclosure.

For the meaning of 'drug money laundering', see **B20.118**.

B20.121 **Procedure** An offence under s. 53 is triable either way (DTA 1994, s. 54(1)). When tried on indictment such an offence is a class 4 offence. As to the institution of proceedings by Customs and Excise, see **B20.94**.

B20.122 **Sentence** The maximum penalty is: on conviction on indictment, imprisment for a term not exceeding five years or a fine or both; on summary conviction, imprisonment for a term not exceeding six months or a fine not exceeding the statutory maximum or both (DTA 1994, s. 54(1)).

B20.123 **Defences** In relation to any offence under the DTA 1994, s. 53(1), (2) or (3), it is a defence for an accused to prove that he did not know or suspect that the disclosure was likely to be prejudicial in the way mentioned in the offences (s. 53(6)).

Nothing in s. 53(1), (2) or (3) makes it an offence for a professional legal adviser to disclose any information or other matter:

(a) to, or to a representative of, his client in connection with the giving of legal advice to him, or

(b) to any person in contemplation of, or in connection with, legal proceedings, and for the purpose of those proceedings (s. 53(4)).

The defence under s. 53(4) does not apply in relation to any information or other matter which is disclosed with a view to furthering any criminal purpose (s. 53(5)).

No constable or other person is guilty of an offence under s. 53(1), (2) or (3) in respect of anything done by him in the course of acting in connection with the enforcement, or intended enforcement, of any provision of the Act or of any other enactment relating to drug trafficking or the proceeds of such trafficking (s. 53(7)).

'Constable' includes a person commissioned by the Commissioners of Customs and Excise (s. 63(1)).

MANUFACTURE AND SUPPLY OF SCHEDULED SUBSTANCES

Definition

B20.124 **Criminal Justice (International Co-operation) Act 1990, s. 12**

(1) It is an offence for a person—

(a) to manufacture a scheduled substance; or

(b) to supply such a substance to another person,

knowing or suspecting that the substance is to be used in or for the unlawful production of a controlled drug.

Procedure

No proceedings may be instituted in England and Wales except by or with the consent **B20.125** of the DPP or the Commissioners of Customs and Excise (Criminal Justice (International Co-operation) Act 1990, s. 21(2)(a)). The offence is triable either way (s. 12(2)). When tried on indictment it is a class 4 offence.

As to the position where the offence is committed on a British ship, see **B20.92**. Section 21 of the MDA 1971 (liability of corporate officers – see **B20.21**) applies to this offence.

Sentence

The maximum penalty on conviction on indictment is imprisonment for a term not **B20.126** exceeding 14 years or a fine or both; on summary conviction, the maximum penalty is imprisonment for a term not exceeding six months or a fine not exceeding the statutory maximum or both (Criminal Justice (International Co-operation) Act 1990, s. 12(2)).

This is a drug trafficking offence (DTA 1994, s. 1(3)(d)), so a confiscation order (**E21.1**) or forfeiture order (**E20.4**) may be imposed.

Scheduled Substance

A scheduled substance is a substance specified in the Criminal Justice (International Co- **B20.127** operation) Act 1990, sch. 2. Schedule 2 may be amended by Her Majesty by Order in Council, except that no substance may be added unless it appears to Her Majesty to be frequently used in or for the unlawful production of a controlled drug, or it has been added to the Annex to the 1988 Vienna Convention against Illicit Traffic in Narcotic Drugs and Psychotic Substances (s. 12(5)).

Criminal Justice (International Co-operation) Act 1990, sch. 2

TABLE I

N-Acetylanthranilic acid	3,4-Methylene-dioxyphenyl-2-
Ephedrine	propanone
Ergometrine	1-Phenyl-2-propanone
Ergotamine	Piperonal
Isosafrole	Pseudoephedrine
Lysergic acid	SaFrole

The salts of the substances listed in this table whenever the existence of such salts is possible.

TABLE II

Acetic anhydride	Phenylacetic acid
Acetone	Piperidine
Anthranilic acid	Potassium permanganate
Ethyl ether	Sulphuric acid
Hydrochloric acid	Toluene
Methyl ethyl ketone (also referred to as 2-Butanone or M.E.K.)	

The salts of the substances listed in this table except hydrochloric acid and sulphuric acid whenever the existence of such salts is possible.

Unlawful Production of a Controlled Drug

The phrase 'controlled drug' has the same meaning as in the MDA 1971 (Criminal **B20.128** Justice (International Co-operation) Act 1990, s. 12(3)). For that definition see **B20.5**. 'Unlawful production of a controlled drug' means production of such a drug which is unlawful by virtue of the MDA 1971, s. 4(1)(a) (Criminal Justice (International Co-operation) Act 1990, s. 12(3)). See **B20.39** *et seq.*

A person does not commit this offence if 'he manufactures or, as the case may be, supplies the scheduled substance with the express consent of a constable' (s. 12(1A), inserted by the Criminal Justice (International Co-operation) (Amendment) Act 1998).

Supply

B20.129 Supply is not defined in the Criminal Justice (International Co-operation) Act 1990, but it is presumed that it has the same meaning as in the MDA 1971 (see **B20.27**), as is explicitly the case in the regulations made under the Criminal Justice (International Co-operation) Act 1990, s. 13 (see **B20.130**).

CONTROLLED DRUGS (SUBSTANCES USEFUL FOR MANUFACTURE) REGULATIONS 1991

Making and Preserving Records of Production and Supply of Certain Scheduled Substances

B20.130 It is an offence for a person to fail to comply with any requirement imposed by regulations made under the Criminal Justice (International Co-operation) Act 1990, s. 13, or, in purported compliance with any such requirement, to furnish information which he knows to be false in a material particular or recklessly furnishes information which is false in a material particular. The offence is triable either way and is punishable, on indictment, with imprisonment for a term not exceeding two years or a fine or both and, on summary conviction, with imprisonment for a term not exceeding six months or a fine not exceeding the statutory maximum or both (s. 13(5)). The Controlled Drugs (Substances Useful for Manufacture) Regulations 1991 (SI 1991 No. 1285) have been made in accordance with s. 13. Regulation 7 requires a person who produces or supplies a scheduled substance specified in the Criminal Justice (International Co-operation) Act 1990, sch. 2, table I (see **B20.127**) to make a record of each quantity of such scheduled substance produced or supplied by him, and preserve all such records for a period of not less than two years from the end of the calendar year in which the production or supply took place. Regulation 7 provides that 'produce' and 'supply' have the same meaning as in the MDA 1971 (see **B20.42** and **B20.27** respectively).

Enforcement of European Community Obligations

B20.131 The Controlled Drugs (Substances Useful for Manufacture) Regulations 1991 enforce the obligations imposed on operators and the requirement of notification under Council Regulation (EEC) No. 3677/90 laying down measures to be taken to discourage the diversion of certain substances to the illicit manufacture of narcotic drugs and psychotropic substances (reg. 3). If a person fails to satisfy these obligations, an offence is committed contrary to the Criminal Justice (International Co-operation) Act 1990, s. 13(5) (see **B20.130**). However, on summary conviction, the maximum prison sentence is three and not six months (reg. 6(d)).

SHIPS USED FOR ILLICIT TRAFFIC

Definition

B20.132 **Criminal Justice (International Co-operation) Act 1990, s. 19**

(2) A person is guilty of an offence if on a ship to which this section applies, wherever it may be, he—
(a) has a controlled drug in his possession; or
(b) is in any way knowingly concerned in the carrying or concealing of a controlled drug on the ship,
knowing or having reasonable grounds to suspect that the drug is intended to be imported or has been exported contrary to section 3(1) of the Misuse of Drugs Act 1971 or the law of any state other than the United Kingdom.

Procedure

No proceedings shall be instituted except by or with the consent of the DPP or the **B20.133** Commissioners of Customs and Excise (Criminal Justice (International Co-operation) Act 1990, s. 21(2)(a)). Further, no proceedings for the offence which is alleged to have been committed outside the landward limits of the territorial sea of the United Kingdom on a ship registered in a state which is a party to the Vienna Convention may be instituted except in pursuance of the exercise with the authority of the Secretary of State of the powers conferred by sch. 3, and the Territorial Waters Jurisdiction Act 1878, s. 3, does not apply to these proceedings (Criminal Justice (International Co-operation) Act 1990, s. 21(3)).

As sentences for the offence vary according to the class of drug involved, there are three offences created by s. 19(2) (see *Courtie* [1984] AC 463). The offences are all triable either way (s. 19(4)). When tried on indictment they are class 4 offences.

Proceedings for these offences in respect of an offence on a ship may be taken, and the offence may for all incidental purposes by treated as having been committed, in any place in the United Kingdom (s. 21(1)).

Section 21 of the MDA 1971 (liability of corporate officers – see **B20.21**) applies to this offence.

Sentence

Where a class A drug is involved, the maximum penalty on indictment is imprisonment **B20.134** for life or a fine or both; on summary conviction, the maximum penalty is imprisonment for a term not exceeding six months or a fine not exceeding the statutory maximum or both (Criminal Justice (International Co-operation) Act 1990, s. 15(4)(a)).

Where a Class B drug is involved, the maximum penalty on indictment is imprisonment for a term not exceeding 14 years or a fine or both; on summary conviction, the maximum penalty is imprisonment for a term not exceeding six months or a fine not exceeding the statutory maximum or both (s. 15(4)(b)).

Where a Class C drug is involved, the maximum penalty on indictment is imprisonment for a term not exceeding five years or a fine or both; on summary conviction, the maximum penalty is imprisonment for a term not exceeding three months or a fine not exceeding the statutory maximum or both (s. 15(4)(c)).

It is clearly established that where drugs have been intercepted on the high seas and those drugs were destined for a country other than England and Wales, the maximum available sentence for such offences in that other country is not a relevant sentencing consideration (*Maguire* [1997] 1 Cr App R (S) 130; *Wagenaar* [1997] 1 Cr App R (S) 178). The sentencing guidelines laid down by the Court of Appeal should be followed (see **B20.137** *et seq.*).

These are drug trafficking offences (DTA 1994, s. 1(3)(e)), so a confiscation order (**E20.1**) or forfeiture order (**E21.4**) may be imposed.

Elements

The Criminal Justice (International Co-operation) Act 1990, s. 19(2), applies to a **B20.135** British ship, a ship registered in a state other than the United Kingdom which is a party to the Vienna Convention (a Convention state) and a ship not registered in any country or territory (s. 19(1)). Ship includes any vessel used in navigation; British ship means a ship registered in the United Kingdom or a colony (s. 24(1)).

'Controlled drug', and the classes of controlled drugs, have the same meaning as in the MDA 1971, see **B20.5** (s. 19(5)). Since the defence in the MDA 1971, s. 28, applies, the meaning of possession in that Act should apply to the present offence. See **B20.10** *et seq*.

As to the MDA 1971, s. 3(1), see **B17.11**. A certificate purporting to be issued by or on behalf of the government of any state to the effect that the importation or export of a controlled drugs is prohibited by the law of that state shall be evidence of the matters stated (s. 19(3)).

Defence

B20.136   The defence in the MDA 1971, s. 28, applies (Criminal Justice (International Co-operation) Act 1990, s. 19(5)). See **B20.23** for full details of the defence.

SENTENCING GUIDELINES FOR OFFENCES UNDER THE MISUSE OF DRUGS ACT 1971

Maximum Sentences: MDA 1971, s. 25 and sch. 4

B20.137   For sentencing purposes it is necessary to draw a distinction between three different types of drugs:

(a)   Class A drugs (especially heroin, morphine, cocaine, LSD, opium and Ecstasy);
(b)   Class B drugs (especially amphetamine, cannabis, cannabis resin and codeine); and
(c)   Class C drugs (especially benzphetamine and pemoline).

For powers of forfeiture of drugs and drug-related equipment from offenders, see the MDA 1971, s. 27, at **E20.4**, and for powers to deprive drug traffickers of the proceeds of their offending under the DTA 1994, see **E21.1**.

Section 25 of the 1971 Act provides that the range of punishment for offences under the Act shall be as set out in sch. 4.

Misuse of Drugs Act 1971, sch. 4

SCHEDULE 4   PROSECUTION AND PUNISHMENT OF OFFENCES

Section 25

Section Creating Offence	General Nature of Offence	Mode of Prosecution	Punishment			
			Class A drug involved	Class B drug involved	Class C drug involved	General
Section 4(2)	Production, or being concerned in the production, of a controlled drug	(a) Summary	6 months or the prescribed sum, or both	6 months or the prescribed sum, or both	3 months or £2,500, or both	
		(b) On indictment	Life or a fine, or both	14 years or a fine, or both	5 years or a fine, or both	
Section 4(3)	Supplying or offering to supply a controlled drug or being concerned in the doing of either activity by another	(a) Summary	6 months or the prescribed sum, or both	6 months or the prescribed sum, or both	3 months or £2,500 or both	
		(b) On indictment	Life or a fine, or both	14 years or a fine, or both	5 years or a fine, or both	
Section 5(2)	Having possession of a controlled drug	(a) Summary	6 months or the prescribed sum, or both	3 months or £2,500 or both	3 months or £1,000 or both	
		(b) On indictment	7 years or a fine, or both	5 years or a fine, or both	2 years or a fine, or both	
Section 5(3)	Having possession of a controlled drug with intent to supply it to another	(a) Summary	6 months or the prescribed sum, or both	6 months or the prescribed sum, or both	3 months or £2,500 or both	
		(b) On indictment	Life or a fine, or both	14 years or a fine, or both	5 years or a fine, or both	
Section 6(2)	Cultivation of cannabis plant	(a) Summary	—	—	—	6 months or the prescribed sum, or both
		(b) On indictment	—	—	—	14 years or a fine, or both
Section 8	Being the occupier, or concerned in the management, of premises and permitting or suffering certain activities to take place there	(a) Summary	6 months or the prescribed sum, or both	6 months or the prescribed sum, or both	3 months or £2,500 or both	
		(b) On indictment	14 years or a fine, or both	14 years or a fine, or both	5 years or a fine, or both	

Misuse of Drugs Act 1971, sch. 4

SCHEDULE 4   PROSECUTION AND PUNISHMENT OF OFFENCES

Section 25

Section Creating Offence	General Nature of Offence	Mode of Prosecution	Punishment			
			Class A drug involved	Class B drug involved	Class C drug involved	General
Section 9	Offences relating to opium	(a) Summary	—	—	—	6 months or the prescribed sum or both
		(b) On indictment	—	—	—	14 years or a fine, or both
Section 9A	Prohibition of supply etc of articles for administering or preparing controlled drugs	Summary	—	—	—	6 months or level 5 on the standard scale, or both
Section 11(2)	Contravention of direction relating to safe custody of controlled drugs	(a) Summary	—	—	—	6 months or the prescribed sum, or both
		(b) On indictment	—	—	—	2 years or a fine, or both
Section 12(6)	Contravention of direction prohibiting practitioner etc from possessing, supply etc controlled drugs	(a) Summary	6 months or the prescribed sum, or both	6 months or the prescribed sum, or both	3 months or £2,500 or both	
		(b) On indictment	14 years or a fine, or both	14 years or a fine, or both	5 years or a fine, or both	
Section 13(3)	Contravention of direction prohibiting practitioner etc from prescribing, supplying etc controlled drugs	(a) Summary	6 months or the precribed sum, or both	6 months or the prescribed sum, or both	3 months or £2,500 or both	
		(b) On indictment	14 years or a fine, or both	14 years or a fine, or both	5 years or a fine, or both	
Section 17(3)	Failure to comply with notice requiring information relating to prescribing, supply etc of drugs	Summary	—	—	—	level 3 on the standard scale
Section 17(4)	Giving false information in purported compliance with notice requiring information relating to prescribing, supply etc of drugs	(a) Summary	—	—	—	6 months or the prescribed sum, or both
		(b) On indictment	—	—	—	2 years or a fine, or both

		Mode of trial	Punishment
Section 18(1)	Contravention of regulations (other than regulations relating to addicts)	(a) Summary	6 months or prescribed sum, or both
		(b) On indictment	2 years or a fine, or both
Section 18(2)	Contravention of terms of licence or other authority (other than licence issued under regulations relating to addicts)	(a) Summary	6 months or the prescribed sum, or both
		(b) On indictment	2 years or a fine, or both
Section 18(3)	Giving false information in purported compliance with obligation to give information imposed under or by virtue of regulations	(a) Summary	6 months or the prescribed sum, or both
		(b) On indictment	2 years or a fine, or both
Section 18(4)	Giving false information, or producing documents etc containing false statement etc, for purposes of obtaining issue or renewal of a licence or other authority	(a) Summary	6 months or the prescribed sum, or both
		(b) On indictment	2 years or a fine, or both
Section 20	Assisting in or inducing commission outside United Kingdom of an offence punishable under a corresponding law	(a) Summary	6 months or the prescribed sum, or both
		(b) On indictment	14 years or a fine, or both
Section 23(4)	Obstructing exercise of powers of search etc or concealing books, drugs, etc	(a) Summary	6 months or the prescribed sum, or both
		(b) On indictment	2 years or a fine, or both

Forfeiture and Confiscation

B20.138 For the court's powers of forfeiture under the MDA 1971, s. 27, see **E20.4**. For powers of confiscation under the DTA 1994, see **E21.1**.

Class A Drug Offences

B20.139 The starting-point for sentencing for these offences is the guideline case of *Aramah* (1982) 4 Cr App R (S) 407, modified in certain respects by *Bilinski* (1987) 9 Cr App R (S) 360, *Singh* (1988) 10 Cr App R (S) 402, *Aroyewumi* (1994) 99 Cr App R 347, *Warren* [1996] 1 Cr App R (S) 233 and *Hurley* [1998] 1 Cr App R (S) 299. The following guidelines from *Aramah* per Lord Lane CJ at pp. 408–9 have, therefore, been amended where appropriate to incorporate those modifications:

> Class A Drugs and particularly heroin and morphine: It is common knowledge that these are the most dangerous of all the addictive drugs . . . Consequently anything which the courts of this country can do by way of deterrent sentences on those found guilty of crimes involving these Class A drugs should be done.
>
> I turn to the importation of heroin, morphine and so on: Large scale importation, that is where [the weight of the drugs at 100 per cent purity is of the order of 500 grammes] or more, sentences of [10 years] and upwards are appropriate. There will be cases where [the weight at 100 per cent purity is of the order of 5 kilogrammes] or more, in which case the offence should be visited by sentences of [14 years and upwards]. It will be seldom that an importer of any appreciable amount of the drug will deserve less than four years.
>
> This, however, is one area in which it is particularly important that offenders should be encouraged to give information to the police, and a confession of guilt, coupled with considerable assistance to the police can properly be marked by a substantial reduction in what would otherwise be the proper sentence.
>
> Next, supplying heroin, morphine etc.: It goes without saying that the sentence will largely depend on the degree of involvement, the amount of trafficking and the value of the drug handled. It is seldom that a sentence of less than [five] years will be justified and the nearer the source of supply the defendant is shown to be, the heavier will be the sentence. There may well be cases where sentences similar to those appropriate to large scale importers may be necessary. It is however unhappily all too seldom that those big fish amongst the suppliers get caught.
>
> Possession of heroin, morphine etc. (simple possession): It is at this level that the circumstances of the individual offender become of much greater importance. Indeed the possible variety of considerations is so wide, including often those of a medical nature, that we feel it impossible to lay down any practical guidelines. On the other hand the maximum penalty for simple possession of Class A drugs is seven years' imprisonment and/or a fine, and there will be very many cases where deprivation of liberty is both proper and expedient.

In *Martinez* (1984) 6 Cr App R (S) 364, at p. 365, Lord Lane CJ confirmed that the *Aramah* guidelines on Class A drugs were not confined to heroin and that 'any idea that those who import or deal in cocaine or LSD, as it is known, should be treated more leniently is entirely wrong'. Further, in *Allery* (1993) 14 Cr App R (S) 699, the Court of Appeal rejected an argument that Ecstasy was to be treated as a drug less dangerous than other Class A drugs, such as heroin or cocaine. In *Warren* [1996] 1 Cr App R (S) 233, the Court of Appeal said that in cases involving importation of 5,000 or more Ecstasy tablets the appropriate sentence would be in the order of 10 years and upwards; for 50,000 tablets or more, it would be 14 years and upwards. These figures were based on the assumption that the tablets were of average, or near average, quality. If analysis showed a substantially different content, then the weight of the constituent would be the determinative factor. The Court of Appeal stressed that other matters were also of importance, such as the role of the offender in the offence, his plea, and whether he had provided assistance to the authorities. In *Hurley* [1998] 1 Cr App R (S) 299, the Court of Appeal issued guidance on sentencing levels for importation of LSD. In the case of 25,000 or more quarter-inch squares or dosage units the sentence should in the ordinary case be 10 years plus. For 250,000 or more dosage units the sentence should ordinarily be 14 years plus. In each case their lordships were assuming that the dosage unit was of approximately 50 micrograms content pure LSD. Adjustment might be needed when it was shown to vary significantly from that figure. Where the seizure was of tablets or of crystals in a form which enabled a precise weight to be ascertained readily there should be no problem in calculating the number of 50 microgram doses. The Court of Appeal appreciated that cases might arise where, to do justice in individual cases, the sentence level could vary accordingly from the guidelines indicated. It should be noted that the case report in *The Times* of 3 October 1997 contains an error and gives a figure of 500,000, rather than 250,000 units.

The *Aramah* guidelines show that most offences relating to Class A drugs are not suitable for summary trial. When cases of simple possession of Class A drugs are dealt with summarily, the Magistrates' Association Guidelines (1997) indicate the following:

Aggravating Factors ⊕
For example an amount other than a very small quantity; offence committed on bail; previous convictions and failures to respond to previous sentences, if relevant.

Mitigating Factors ⊖
For example very small quantity.

Guideline: Is it serious enough for a community penalty?

When cases of production and supply of Class A drugs are dealt with summarily, the Guidelines indicate the following:

Aggravating Factors ⊕
For example commercial production; large amount; deliberate adulteration; venue, e.g. prisons, educational establishments; sophisticated operation; offence committed on bail; previous convictions and failures to respond to previous sentences, if relevant.

Mitigating Factors ⊖
For example small amount.

Guideline: Is it so serious that only custody is appropriate?

In all cases, whether of possession or supply, the Guidelines indicate that forfeiture of all drugs and equipment should be considered.

There are numerous Court of Appeal decisions which apply the *Aramah* guidelines in respect of Class A drug offences. The first group is concerned with *importation*. A sentence of 20 years was upheld in *Latif* [1995] 1 Cr App R 270 where 20 kg of heroin had been imported by a 'principal organiser', and 24 years' imprisonment was upheld in *Main* [1997] 2 Cr App R (S) 63, where the offenders were concerned in an attempt to import 1.2 million tablets of Ecstasy in a furniture van. Following interception of the van, a further 111,275 Ecstasy tablets were discovered at their premises. See also *Tattenhove* [1996] 2 Cr App R (S) 91. In *Bayley* (1995) 16 Cr App R (S) 605, 15 years' imprisonment was upheld for the importation of 58 kg of Ecstasy. In *Bilinski* (1987) 9 Cr App R (S) 360, the offender pleaded guilty to importing 3.036 kg of heroin. The Court of Appeal said that a sentence of eight years was appropriate, bearing in mind the guilty plea and the assistance the offender gave to the authorities. The case also establishes that an offender's belief that the drugs were in fact Class B and not Class A drugs is relevant to sentence. If this matter is in dispute, a *Newton* hearing may be appropriate to determine it. In *Bilinski*, it seems, a cursory inquiry would have revealed the true nature of the drug and, accordingly, the appropriate reduction was small. Other relevant cases are *Daniel* (1995) 16 Cr App R (S) 892 (offender stopped at Gatwick

Airport and found to be in possession of 1.43 kg of heroin at 45 per cent purity; nine years' imprisonment upheld); and *Mouzulukwe* [1996] 2 Cr App R (S) 48 (offender concealed within his body 31 packets containing 231 grammes of powder, including 38 grammes of pure heroin; six years' imprisonment upheld).

As far as *distribution* of Class A drugs is concerned, in *France* (1984) 6 Cr App R (S) 283 the offender had been dealing in heroin and other Class A drugs for a few weeks, on a small scale, in order to finance his own consumption of heroin: four years' imprisonment was upheld. See also *Eliot* (1988) 10 Cr App R (S) 454, where the offender was a heroin addict who also supplied heroin to others to service his own addiction. It was argued that the offender was on the bottom rung of suppliers, that he supplied only addicts and hence had corrupted no one, had been frank with the police and had pleaded guilty. The Court of Appeal approved a custodial sentence of 30 months, commenting that the sentencer had given a proper discount for the mitigation. Four years' detention in a young offender institution was appropriate in *Thompson* [1997] 2 Cr App R (S) 223, where the 20-year-old offender, who had one previous conviction for possession of drugs, pleaded guilty to supplying Ecstasy tablets at a nightclub. In *Chesterton* [1997] 2 Cr App R (S) 297 a sentence of three years' detention under the CYPA 1933, s. 53(2) was upheld where two 17-year-old offenders pleaded guilty to supplying LSD tabs to pupils at a school. In *Bowman-Powell* (1985) 7 Cr App R (S) 85, the offender pleaded guilty to possession of 92 doses of LSD and admitted that he intended to sell about half of the LSD to a regular set of friends and customers. He had a number of drug-related convictions over the previous nine years, including two previous convictions for possession of LSD. A sentence of four years' imprisonment was upheld. The same sentence was upheld in *Jones* (1994) 15 Cr App R (S) 856, where the offender was in possession of 27 Ecstasy tablets (worth about £400) with intent to supply. The Court of Appeal observed that, having regard to the *Aramah* guidelines, the sentence was lenient. In *Harvey* [1997] 2 Cr App R (S) 306 the offender was acting as a warehouseman for drugs, and pleaded guilty to possessing 900 Ecstasy tablets with intent to supply. A sentence of five years' imprisonment was reduced to three and a half years on appeal. See also *McLaughlin* (1995) 16 Cr App R (S) 357. Supplying a single tablet of Ecstasy merited a sentence of two years in *McLellan* (1994) 15 Cr App R (S) 351. See also *Foggarty* [1997] 1 Cr App R (S) 238.

As far as sentencing for *possession* of Class A drugs is concerned, the *Aramah* guidelines indicate that sentence may differ widely according to the circumstances, but that 'there will be very many cases where deprivation of liberty is both proper and expedient'. In *Layton* (1988) 10 Cr App R (S) 109, the offender, who had a bad criminal record but no previous drug-related convictions, pleaded guilty to possession of 5.6 grammes of cocaine. A sentence of three months' imprisonment was substituted for the 30 months imposed by the sentencer. Three-month sentences were also held to be appropriate in *Long* (1984) 6 Cr App R (S) 115, where the offenders pleaded guilty to possession of heroin for personal use and each had a previous conviction for possession of cannabis and in *Cox* (1994) 15 Cr App R (S) 216, where the offender was in possession of 16 Ecstasy tablets and 1.5 grammes of crack cocaine. In *Roberts* [1997] 2 Cr App R (S) 187, a prisoner serving a four-year sentence for possession of heroin with intent to supply was found to be in possession of a small quantity of heroin when searched by prison officers. The Court of Appeal stated that possession of drugs by a prisoner was more serious than possession of drugs outside prison, and upheld a consecutive sentence of 15 months' imprisonment.

Examples of cases of permitting premises to be used for supplying Class A drugs are *Gregory* (1993) 14 Cr App R (S) 403, where a custodial sentence of 15 months' imprisonment, imposed consecutively to terms of imprisonment for other drug offences, was reduced to six months on appeal, and *Bradley* [1997] 1 Cr App R (S) 59, where the offender's premises were used a brothel at which cocaine was supplied. The appropriate sentence for the offence was two years' imprisonment.

Class B Drug Offences

The Court of Appeal guideline case for these offences is *Aramah* (1982) 4 Cr App R (S) **B20.140**
407, where Lord Lane CJ (at pp. 409–10) distinguished importation, supply and possession of cannabis. The guidelines are set out here as amended by the Court of Appeal in *Ronchetti* [1998] 2 Cr App R (S) 100, on importation of large quantities of cannabis.

> Class B Drugs, particularly cannabis: We select this from among the Class B drugs as being the drug most likely to be exercising the minds of the courts.
>
> Importation of cannabis: Importation of very small amounts for personal use can be dealt with as if it were simple possession, with which we will deal later. Otherwise importations of amounts up to about 20 kg of herbal cannabis or cannabis resin, or the equivalent in cannabis oil, will, save in the most exceptional circumstances, attract sentences of between 18 months and three years, with the lowest ranges reserved for pleas of guilty where there has been small profit to the offender. The good character of the courier (as he usually is) is of less importance than the good character of the defendant in other cases. The reason for this is, it is well known that the large scale operator looks for couriers of good character and for people of a sort which are likely to exercise the sympathy of the court if they are detected and arrested. Consequently one will frequently find that students and sick and elderly people are used as couriers for two reasons: first of all they are vulnerable to suggestion and vulnerable to the offer of quick profit, and secondly it is felt that the courts may be moved to misplaced sympathy in their case. There are few, if any, occasions when anything other than an immediate custodial sentence is proper in this type of importation.
>
> Medium quantities over 20 kg will attract sentences of three to six years' imprisonment, depending upon the amount involved, and all the other circumstances of the case.
>
> The importation of 100 kg by persons playing more than a subordinate role should attract a sentence of seven to eight years. Ten years was the appropriate starting point following a trial for importation by such persons of 500 kg or more. Larger importations would attract a higher starting point, which should rise according to the roles played, the weight involved and all the other circumstances of the case, up to the statutory maximum of 14 years. A discount from all the figures indicated would, of course, be called for according to the roles played and where there was a plea of guilty.
>
> Supply of cannabis: Here again the supply of massive quantities will justify sentences in the region of 10 years for those playing anything more than a subordinate role. Otherwise the bracket should be between one to four years' imprisonment, depending on the scale of the operation. Supplying a number of small sellers – wholesaling if you like – comes at the top of the bracket. At the lower end will be the retailer of a small amount to a consumer. Where there is no commercial motive (for example, where cannabis is supplied at a party) the offence may well be serious enough to justify a custodial sentence.
>
> Possession of cannabis: When only small amounts are involved being for personal use, the offence can often be met by a fine. If the history shows however a persisting flouting of the law, imprisonment may become necessary.

In *Wijs* [1998] 2 Cr App R 436, the Court of Appeal issued sentencing guidelines in respect of the unlawful importation of amphetamine and the possession of amphetamine with intent to supply. Lord Bingham CJ referred to the guidelines in *Aramah* and stated that no distinction should be drawn between different drugs included within Class B on the basis that one such drug is more pernicious than another. His lordship noted, however, that weight for weight amphetamine has always been vastly more valuable than cannabis, and that amphetamine was retailed to customers in a highly adulterated form. Goods seized at point of importation may contain a high percentage of the drug, but at a retail level the purity may be 10 per cent to 12 per cent or less. It followed that a trafficker in possession of a given quantity of amphetamine stood to earn very much larger sums than a trafficker in possession of the same weight of cannabis. For amphetamine-related offences, sentencing should not depend on market value but, subject to other considerations, on the quantity of the amphetamine in question calculated on the basis of 100 per cent pure amphetamine base (i.e. the maximum theoretical purity of 73 per cent amphetamine base in amphetamine sulphate, the remaining 27 per cent being the sulphate. On conviction of importing amphetamine following a contested trial, a custodial sentence will almost invariably be called for save in exceptional circumstances or where the quantity of the drug is so small as to be compatible with personal consumption by the importer. The ordinary level of sentence on conviction following a contested trial (subject to all other considerations, and on quantities calculated on the basis of 100 per cent pure amphetamine base) should be:

(a) up to 500 grammes: up to two years' imprisonment;
(b) more than 500 grammes but less than 2.5 kg: two to four years;
(c) more than 2.5 kg but less than 10 kg: four to seven years;
(d) more than 10 kg but less than 15 kg: seven to ten years;
(e) more than 15 kg: upwards of ten years, subject to the statutory maximum of 14 years.

The penalty for importing a controlled drug would in many cases be higher, and would rarely be lower, than for possession with intent to supply.

When cases of possession of Class B drugs with intent to supply are dealt with summarily the Magistrates' Association Guidelines (1997) indicate the following:

Aggravating Factors ⊕
For example commercial production; large amount; venue, e.g. prisons, educational establishments; deliberate adulteration; offence committed on bail; previous convictions and failures to respond to previous sentences, if relevant.

Mitigating Factors ⊖
For example not commercial; small amount.

Guideline: Is it so serious that only custody is appropriate?

In all cases forfeiture of all drugs and equipment should be considered.

When cases of simple possession of Class B drugs are dealt with summarily the Magistrates' Association Guidelines (1997) indicate the following:

Aggravating Factors ⊕
For example large amount; offence committed on bail; previous convictions and failures to respond to previous sentences, if relevant.

Mitigating Factors ⊖
For example small amount.

Guideline: Is compensation, discharge or fine appropriate?

The guideline fine is £90 (low income), £225 (average income) and £540 (high income). In all cases forfeiture of all drugs and equipment should be considered.

There are several Court of Appeal decisions following and applying the guidelines in *Aramah*, dealing with the appropriate sentences for offences in connection with Class B drug offences, mainly cannabis. The first group is concerned with *importation*. At the top end of the scale, the offenders in *Royle* [1997] 1 Cr App R (S) 184 received sentences of 13 years and 7 years respectively for their roles in the importation by boat of 1,609 kg of cannabis resin, estimated to be worth in excess of £5.5 million. The sentences were upheld, the Court of Appeal noting that only a modest reduction was appropriate for their guilty pleas since the offenders had been caught red-handed by the customs authorities. The prime mover in a conspiracy to import and supply by sea 320 kg of cannabis was sentenced to nine years' imprisonment, together with a confiscation order of £21,000, in *Rescorl* (1992) 14 Cr App R (S) 522. The female offender pleaded guilty, and the Court of Appeal accepted that an appropriate sentence had the case been contested would have been 11 or 12 years. In *Frazer* [1998] 1 Cr App R (S) 287, a sentence of six years was upheld in respect of an offender who was found to have 36 kg of cannabis in his suitcase at Gatwick Airport. The sentence, at the top end of the bracket in *Aramah*, was justified since this was the offender's third such conviction. See also *King* (1987) 9 Cr App R (S) 173. Towards the lower end of the importation scale, in *Watson* (1988) 10 Cr App R (S) 256, the offender and another woman imported 12 kg of cannabis, the offender's suitcase containing 7.4 kg. She was convicted after a trial and sentenced to four years' imprisonment. This was reduced to two years, in line with the *Aramah* guidelines. The offender in *Blyth* [1996] 1 Cr App R (S) 388 arrived in Dover by coach and was found to be in possession of 16 kg of cannabis resin. He admitted having made several previous trips for the purposes of importing cannabis from Spain. A sentence of two years' imprisonment was upheld. In *Astbury* [1997] 2 Cr App R (S) 93, three months' imprisonment was said to be appropriate for importing 1,100 grammes of cannabis, to the value of about £1,500, for personal use. The Court of Appeal in *Elder* (1993) 15 Cr App R (S) 514 found, with some hesitation, that importation by two defendants of 200 grammes of cannabis resin and 700 grammes of herbal cannabis for personal use was an offence which did not cross the custody threshold and could properly be dealt with by way of a community service order.

The second group of cases involves *distribution* of Class B drugs, mainly cannabis. Again, a scale of sentences may be ascertained, following the *Aramah* guidelines. At the top end of the range, the offender in *Netts* [1997] 2 Cr App R (S) 117 was convicted of possessing cannabis with intent to supply. He was stopped while driving his car, which was found to contain 90 kg of cannabis resin in 24 packages. It was accepted that the offender was acting as a courier within the UK. A sentence of seven years' imprisonment was reduced to five years on appeal, the Court of Appeal noting that the very large quantity of cannabis involved took the case above the four year level referred to in *Aramah* but also took account of the fact that the offender had no previous involvement with drugs and no convictions of any kind. In *Chatfield* (1983) 5 Cr App R (S) 289, the offenders pleaded guilty to possession of 2 kg of cannabis, with intent to supply. Sentences of 30 months were upheld by the Court of Appeal, Watkins LJ commenting that: 'They came somewhere between about half-way towards and the end of the bracket, allowance being made for the fact that they pleaded guilty and for their characters.' Thirty months was said to be 'at the top end of the appropriate scale' but was upheld in *Daley* (1989) 11 Cr App R (S) 242, where the offender, shortly after release from prison for burglary, was seen by a police officer selling cannabis. He sold the officer a small quantity and agreed to supply more; when arrested he was in possession of 450.5 grammes of cannabis resin. He pleaded guilty. In *Hill* (1988) 10 Cr App R (S) 150 the offender had been dealing in cannabis from his home on a regular basis for some time, earning £100 per week from this activity. A 30-month sentence, described by the Court of Appeal as 'near the top end of the bracket for offences of this sort', was reduced to 21 months, since 'although the supply was on a regular basis to a large number of people the amounts involved were comparatively small' and greater recognition should have been given to the offender's guilty plea. Fifteen months' imprisonment was appropriate in *Freeman* [1997] 2 Cr App R (S) 224, where the offender, a man with previous convictions though not related to drugs, pleaded guilty to possession of cannabis resin with intent to supply. The offence was aggravated by the fact that he took the drug into prison to supply a serving prisoner. See also *Doyle* [1998] 1 Cr App R (S) 79.

For cases of simple *possession* of small amounts of cannabis for personal use, the *Aramah* guidelines indicate that a fine will often be an appropriate penalty, unless there is repetition involving 'flouting of the law'. In *Jones* (1981) 3 Cr App R (S) 51 the offender was convicted of possession of 3.2 grammes of cannabis. Five years earlier he had been convicted of cultivating and possessing cannabis, and fined £30. This time he was sentenced to three months' imprisonment, suspended, plus a £50 fine. The Court of Appeal said that the prison sentence was inappropriate, and quashed it, leaving the fine in place. Immediate and suspended custodial sentences were also quashed in *Robertson-Coupar* (1982) 4 Cr App R (S) 150, in spite of this being a second offence. By contrast, in *Osborne* (1982) 4 Cr App R (S) 262, a 40-year-old offender, who had six previous cannabis-related convictions, was convicted of possessing 3.83 grammes of cannabis. A three-month custodial sentence was upheld.

In cases involving the cultivation of cannabis, a crucial matter is whether the cannabis was for personal use, or for supply. For production of cannabis on a serious commercial scale, imprisonment for four years was upheld in *Booth* [1997] 2 Cr App R (S) 67. It was estimated that the operation would produce between eight and ten kilogrammes of cannabis each year. See also *Lyall* (1994) 16 Cr App R (S) 600. In *Blackham* [1997] 2 Cr App R (S) 275, 12 months' imprisonment was appropriate in a case where the offender cultivated 75 cannabis plants at home. The offender was intending to supply the cannabis, though not on a commercial basis, and he had a previous conviction for possession of cannabis with intent to supply. See also *Marsland* (1994) 15 Cr App R (S) 665. A financial penalty will often be appropriate for cultivation of a small amount of cannabis for personal use, but three months' imprisonment was upheld on those facts in *Case* (1992) 13 Cr App R (S) 20.

Where tried summarily, the Magistrates' Association Guidelines (1997) indicate the following in respect of cultivation of cannabis:

Aggravating Factors ⊕
For example commercial cultivation; large quantity; offence committed on bail; previous convictions and failures to respond to previous sentences, if relevant.

Mitigating Factors ⊖
For example for personal use; not commercial; not responsible for planting; small scale cultivation.

Guideline: Is compensation, discharge or fine appropriate?

The guideline fine is £90 (low income), £225 (average income) or £540 (high income). In all cases forfeiture of all drugs and equipment should be considered.

Few cases are reported on the appropriate sentencing pattern for the offence of permitting premises to be used for smoking cannabis. In *Pusser* (1983) 5 Cr App R (S) 225, however, the offender was the licensee of a public house at which cannabis was smoked, though there was no evidence that he used cannabis himself. After a warning, the police searched the premises and found cannabis in several forms. The Court of Appeal described this as 'a bad case' and upheld the sentence of six months' imprisonment. Twelve months' imprisonment was upheld in *Morrison* [1996] 1 Cr App R (S) 263, where the offender allowed young people aged 14 or 15 to visit his house and smoke cannabis; there was no evidence that the offender supplied cannabis to them.

Class C Drug Offences

B20.141 Class C drugs include benzphetamine and pemoline. There is no guideline judgment in respect of these offences.

SECTION B21: OFFENCES RELATING TO DANGEROUS DOGS

OFFENCES UNDER THE DANGEROUS DOGS ACT 1991

Control and Possession of Dogs Bred for Fighting

The Dangerous Dogs Act 1991, s. 1, controls the possession, disposal and breeding of **B21.1** dogs of the type known as pit bull terriers. 'Type' is a wider term than 'breed', and in *Knightsbridge Crown Court, ex parte Dunne* [1994] 1 WLR 296, the Divisional Court held that it can apply to dogs possessing a substantial number of breed characteristics, even if some other breed characteristics are missing. In other words, pit bull/staffordshire crosses and similar cross breeds will often be deemed subject to the controls. As to the burden of proof in disputed cases, see s. 5 of the Act at **B21.4**.

These controls also apply to the Japanese tosa and have been extended by SI 1981 No. 1743 to the dogo Argentino and fila Braziliero. Other types of fighting dog may be included by further orders made under s. 1(1)(c) of the Act. The rottweiler is not a fighting dog, but it would be possible for the Secretary of State to impose limited controls (e.g., muzzling requirements under s. 1(2)(d)) to this or other dangerous types, under powers conferred by s. 2 of the Act.

Offences

It is an offence to possess or have custody of any type of dog to which the Dangerous **B21.2** Dogs Act 1991, s. 1, applies (except in pursuance of a power of seizure or an order for its destruction made under the Act) unless a certificate of exemption has been obtained (Dangerous Dogs Compensation and Exemption Schemes Order 1991 (SI 1991 No. 1744, as amended by SI 1991 Nos. 2297 and 2636 and the Dangerous Dogs (Amendment) Act 1997, s. 4(1)) and its terms complied with (s. 1(3) and (5)). Section 1(2) creates certain offences which apply to any person (including a holder of an exemption certificate relating to possession or custody of a dog).

Dangerous Dogs Act 1991, s. 1

(2) No person shall—
(a) breed, or breed from, a dog to which this section applies;
(b) sell or exchange such a dog or offer, advertise or expose such a dog for sale or exchange;
(c) make or offer to make a gift of such a dog or advertise or expose such a dog as a gift;
(d) allow such a dog of which he is the owner or of which he is for the time being in charge to be in a public place without being muzzled and kept on a lead; or
(e) abandon such a dog of which he is the owner or, being the owner or for the time being in charge of such a dog, allow it to stray.

Penalties and Defences in relation to Offences under s. 1

Dangerous Dogs Act 1991, s. 1

B21.3

(7) Any person who contravenes this section is guilty of an offence and liable on summary conviction to imprisonment for a term not exceeding six months or a fine not exceeding level 5 on the standard scale or both except that a person who publishes an advertisement in contravention of subsection 2(b) or (c)—
(a) shall not on being convicted be liable to imprisonment if he shows that he published the advertisement to the order of someone else and did not himself devise it; and

(b)   shall not be convicted if, in addition, he shows that he did not know and had no reasonable cause to suspect that it related to a dog to which this section applies.

Voluntary intoxication is no defence to a charge under s. 1(7) (*DPP* v *Kellett* [1994] Crim LR 916). Indeed it seems clear from s. 1(7)(b) that the offence is one of strict liability, as are those created by s. 3 (see **B21.5**). As to disqualification and destruction orders, see **B21.6**.

Definitions and Evidence Provisions

B21.4   The term 'advertisement' is defined in the Dangerous Dogs Act 1991, s. 10(2), as including any means of bringing a matter to the attention of the public; 'public place' is defined in s. 10(2) as meaning any street, road or other place to which the public have or are permitted access, whether for payment or otherwise (see *Cummings* v *DPP* (1999) *The Times*, 26 March 1999), and includes the common parts of a building containing two or more separate dwellings. A pit bull terrier sitting in a car parked in a public place is itself in a public place and must be muzzled in accordance with s. 1(2)(d) (*Bates* v *DPP* (1993) 157 JP 1004). Muzzling remains necessary even if the dog is ill and would be distressed by muzzling; no defence of necessity applies in such circumstances (*Cichon* v *DPP* [1994] Crim LR 918). However, a private path or driveway is not a public place merely because visitors or postmen may use it when calling on the owner (*Fellowes* v *DPP* (1993) 157 JP 936).

Dangerous Dogs Act 1991, ss. 5, 6 and 7

5.—(5)   If in any proceedings it is alleged by the prosecution that a dog is one to which section 1 or an order under section 2 above applies it shall be presumed that it is such a dog unless the contrary is shown by the accused by such evidence as the court considers sufficient; and the accused shall not be permitted to adduce such evidence unless he has given the prosecution notice of his intention to do so not later than the fourteenth day before that on which the evidence is to be adduced.

6.   Where a dog is owned by a person who is less than sixteen years old any reference to its owner in section 1(2)(d) or (e) or 3 above shall include a reference to the head of the household, if any, of which that person is a member or, in Scotland, to the person who has his actual care and control.

7.—(1)   In this Act—
(a)   references to a dog being muzzled are to its being securely fitted with a muzzle sufficient to prevent it biting any person; and
(b)   references to its being kept on a lead are to its being securely held on a lead by a person who is not less than sixteen years old.
(2)   [Power of Secretary of State to prescribe the type of muzzle or lead to be used.]

Section 5(5) applies only in respect of criminal proceedings and not, for example, in cases where a destruction order is sought in respect of a dog which has been seized under s. 5(1) or (2) but in respect of which no prosecution has been brought (*Walton Street Magistrates' Court, ex parte Crothers* (1996) 160 JP 427).

Failing to Keep Dogs under Proper Control

B21.5   ### Dangerous Dogs Act 1991, s. 3

(1)   If a dog is dangerously out of control in a public place—
(a)   the owner; and
(b)   if different, the person for the time being in charge of the dog,
is guilty of an offence, or, if the dog while so out of control injures any person, an aggravated offence, under this subsection.
(2)   In proceedings for an offence under subsection (1) above against a person who is the owner of a dog but was not at the material time in charge of it, it shall be a defence for the accused to prove that the dog was at the material time in the charge of a person whom he reasonably believed to be a fit and proper person to be in charge of it.

(3)   If the owner or, if different, the person for the time being in charge of a dog allows it to enter a place which is not a public place but where it is not permitted to be and while it is there—

(a)   it injures any person; or

(b)   there are grounds for reasonable apprehension that it will do so,

he is guilty of an offence, or, if the dog injures any person, an aggravated offence, under this subsection.

(4)   A person guilty of an offence under subsection (1) or (3) above other than an aggravated offence is liable on summary conviction to imprisonment for a term not exceeding six months or a fine not exceeding level 5 on the standard scale or both; and a person guilty of an aggravated offence under either of those subsections is liable—

(a)   on summary conviction, to imprisonment for a term not exceeding six months or a fine not exceeding the statutory maximum or both;

(b)   on conviction on indictment, to imprisonment for a term not exceeding two years or a fine or both.

As to the meaning of 'public place', see **B21.4**. The question whether someone other than the owner is 'in charge' of the dog is one of fact and degree and should ordinarily be left to the jury (*Rawlings* [1994] Crim LR 433). As to the scope of the defence under s. 3(2), see *Huddart* [1999] Crim LR 568.

Whereas the offences created by s. 3(1) may be committed by both the owner (subject to the s. 3(2) defence) *and* the person in charge of the dog, the s. 3(3) offences can be committed only by an owner *or* person in charge who 'allows' the dog to enter the place in question. This suggests that, if someone else is in charge, the owner cannot ordinarily be liable under s. 3(3), but liability may still arise where, for example, the owner knows that a friend or member of his family regularly exercises the dog in such a place. Failure to take adequate precautions to prevent a dog from escaping and entering such a place may also give rise to liability for 'allowing' entry under s. 3(3). Proof of negligence is not required, as liability is strict (*Greener* v *DPP* (1996) 160 JP 265).

Under s. 3, the type of dog concerned is irrelevant; it is enough to show that the dog is dangerously out of control. Section 10(3) provides that:

> . . . a dog shall be regarded as dangerously out of control on any occasion on which there are grounds for reasonable apprehension that it will injure any person, whether or not it actually does so, but references to a dog injuring a person or there being grounds for reasonable apprehension that it will do so do not include references to any case in which the dog is being used for a lawful purpose by a constable or a person in the service of the Crown.

It is submitted that references to dogs injuring persons must, in this context, be confined to bites, etc., directly inflicted by dogs and should not include traffic injuries indirectly caused by dogs running loose on a road.

No *mens rea* is specified under s. 3, and the offence would appear to be one of strict liability (see **A4.1** *et seq.*). This legislation was enacted for reasons of public safety, and would become very much harder to enforce if some fault element, such as negligence, had to be proved against the owner of a dog which becomes dangerously out of control. (See *Bezzina* [1994] 1 WLR 1057.) On the other hand, the effect of s. 10(3) is that liability can arise only where the dog behaves in such a way that there are 'reasonable grounds for apprehension that it will injure any person'. This might seem to exclude cases in which a dog suddenly and unexpectedly bites or snaps at some person, assuming it is immediately restrained thereafter, but in *Rafiq* v *DPP* (1997) 161 JP 412 it was held that, even if a dog bites without warning, it may still be open to a court to infer that there were grounds for reasonable apprehension under s. 10(3) that the dog would renew the attack immediately afterwards.

Even where it seems likely that a dog may injure someone, the words 'dangerously out of control' must be given their natural meaning. If, for example, X teases Y's Doberman in a cruel and stupid way, it may be apparent to any onlooker that X is likely to be bitten unless he desists, but it does not follow that the dog is out of control.

Where the dog is owned by a person under the age of 16, s. 6 (see **B21.4**) applies.

Destruction and Disqualification Orders

B21.6   As originally drafted, the Dangerous Dogs Act 1991, s. 4(1), demanded the mandatory destruction of the dogs involved wherever offences were committed under s. 1 or aggravated offences committed under s. 3. Trivial incidents, such as the temporary removal of a pit bull's muzzle so that it could drink, could lead to innocent dogs being destroyed, and this rule caused widespread outrage, not least amongst the magistrates and judges who were required to enforce the law (see the attack on the legislation by Rougier J in *Ealing Magistrates' Court, ex parte Fanneran* (1996) 160 JP 409). The severity of the law is now tempered by the Dangerous Dogs (Amendment) Act 1997, which (*inter alia*) adds s. 4(1A) and s. 4A to the original statute.

Dangerous Dogs Act 1991, ss. 4 and 4A

4.—(1)   Where a person is convicted of an offence under section 1 or 3(1) or (3) above or of an offence under an order made under section 2 above the court—

(a)   may order the destruction of any dog in respect of which the offence was committed and, subject to subsection (1A) below, shall do so in the case of an offence under section 1 or an aggravated offence under section 3(1) or (3) above; and

(b)   may order the offender to be disqualified, for such period as the court thinks fit, for having custody of a dog.

(1A)   Nothing in subsection (1)(a) above shall require the court to order the destruction of a dog if the court is satisfied—

(a)   that the dog would not constitute a danger to public safety; and

(b)   where the dog was born before 30th November 1991 and is subject to the prohibition in section 1(3) above, that there is a good reason why the dog has not been exempted from that prohibition.

(2)   Where a court makes an order under subsection (1)(a) above for the destruction of a dog owned by a person other than the offender, the owner may appeal to the Crown Court against the order.

(3)   A dog shall not be destroyed pursuant to an order under subsection (1)(a) above—

(a)   until the end of the period for giving notice of appeal against the conviction, or against the order; and

(b)   if notice of appeal is given within that period, until the appeal is determined or withdrawn,

unless the offender and, in a case to which subsection (2) above applies, the owner of the dog give notice to the court that made the order that there is to be no appeal.

(4)   Where a court makes an order under subsection (1)(a) above it may—

(a)   appoint a person to undertake the destruction of the dog and require any person having custody of it to deliver it up for that purpose; and

(b)   order the offender to pay such sum as the court may determine to be the reasonable expenses of destroying the dog and of keeping it pending its destruction.

(5)   Any sum ordered to be paid under subsection (4)(b) above shall be treated for the purposes of enforcement as if it were a fine imposed on conviction.

4A.—(1)   Where—

(a)   a person is convicted of an offence under section 1 above or an aggravated offence under section 3(1) or (3) above;

(b)   the court does not order the destruction of the dog under section 4(1)(a) above; and

(c)   in the case of an offence under section 1 above, the dog is subject to the prohibition in section 1(3) above,

the court shall order that, unless the dog is exempted from that prohibition within the requisite period, the dog shall be destroyed.

(2)   Where an order is made under subsection (1) above in respect of a dog, and the dog is not exempted from the prohibition in section 1(3) above within the requisite period, the court may extend that period.

(3)   Subject to subsection (2) above, the requisite period for the purposes of such an order is the period of two months beginning with the date of the order.

(4)   Where a person is convicted of an offence under section 3(1) or (3) above, the court may order that, unless the owner of the dog keeps it under proper control, the dog shall be destroyed.

(5)   An order under subsection (4) above—

(a)   may specify the measures to be taken for keeping the dog under proper control, whether by muzzling, keeping on a lead, excluding it from specified places or otherwise; and

(b)   if it appears to the court that the dog is a male and would be less dangerous if neutered, may require it to be neutered.

(6)   Subsections (2) to (4) of section 4 above shall apply in relation to an order under subsection (1) or (4) above as they apply in relation to an order under subsection (1)(a) of that section.

As to the making of destruction orders otherwise than on conviction (i.e. where the proceedings are not strictly criminal), see *Walton Street Magistrates' Court, ex parte Crothers* (1996) 160 JP 427 and s. 4B.

Any person who has custody of a dog in contravention of s. 4(1)(b), or who fails to comply with a requirement imposed on him under s. 4(4)(a) commits a summary offence and is liable to a fine not exceeding level 5 on the standard scale (s. 4(8)).

OTHER OFFENCES RELATING TO DANGEROUS DOGS

The Dangerous Dogs Act 1991 does not reduce the powers of courts under the Dogs **B21.7** Act 1871, s. 2. Orders requiring the destruction or proper control of dangerous dogs may still be made under that provision, whether or not any person has been injured, and may require a dog to be muzzled and/or castrated (Dangerous Dogs Act 1991, s. 3(5) and (6)). Under the Dangerous Dogs Act 1989, s. 1(3), it is an offence, punishable on summary conviction by a fine not exceeding level 3 on the standard scale, not to comply with a control or destruction order; and where under that Act an owner has been disqualified from having custody of a dog, contravention of that order is punishable by a fine not exceeding level 5 on the standard scale (Dangerous Dogs Act 1989, s. 1(6)).

Control of Guard Dogs

Guard Dogs Act 1975, s. 1   **B21.8**

(1)   A person shall not use or permit the use of a guard dog at any premises unless a person ('the handler') who is capable of controlling the dog is present on the premises and the dog is under the control of the handler at all times while it is being so used except while it is secured so that it is not at liberty to go freely about the premises.

(2)   The handler of a guard dog shall keep the dog under his control at all times while it is being used as a guard dog at any premises except—

(a)   while another handler has control over the dog; or

(b)   while the dog is secured so that it is not at liberty to go freely about the premises.

(3)   A person shall not use or permit the use of a guard dog at any premises unless a notice containing a warning that a guard dog is present is clearly exhibited at each entrance to the premises.

Under the Guard Dogs Act 1975, s. 5, non-compliance with s. 1 is an offence punishable on summary conviction by a fine not exceeding level 5 on the standard scale.

SECTION B22: OFFENCES RELATING TO THE PROCEEDS OF CRIMINAL CONDUCT

INTRODUCTION

B22.1 The CJA 1993, ss. 29 to 32, amended the CJA 1988 by inserting into that Act a number of new provisions (ss. 93A to 93D) dealing with money laundering and related offences involving the proceeds of criminal conduct. These are largely based on comparable provisions concerning the proceeds of drug trafficking (see **B20.91 *et seq.***) but overlap is avoided by defining 'criminal conduct' for the purposes of ss. 93A to 93D in such a way as to exclude drug trafficking offences. There are, however, significant overlaps between the new offences and a number of existing ones, including handling stolen goods, assisting offenders, concealing arrestable offences and perverting the course of justice.

Under the Money Laundering Regulations 1993 (SI 1993 No. 1933), persons carrying on a relevant financial business within the United Kingdom are required to maintain specified procedures and take appropriate measures to avoid involvement in money laundering operations. This requires, *inter alia*, procedures for employee training and the adoption of a system of internal reporting, under which employees can disclose knowledge or suspicions of money laundering to an appropriate person within the firm. Detailed consideration of the regulations falls beyond the scope of this work but, under reg. 5(2), contraventions are punishable on indictment by a fine and/or imprisonment for a maximum of two years; or on summary conviction by a fine not exceeding the statutory maximum.

Commencement

B22.2 The CJA 1988, ss. 93A to 93C came into force on 15 February 1994; s. 93D and the Money Laundering Regulations came into force on 1 April 1994. The new provisions apply only to things done after their respective commencement dates, but the laundering etc. may itself involve the proceeds of criminal conduct dating from long before.

The Proceeds of Criminal Conduct

B22.3 The concept of property that represents the proceeds of criminal conduct is central to each of the offences under the CJA 1988, ss. 93A to 93C. It is defined in such a way as to include the proceeds of any conduct (other than drug trafficking) which amounts to an indictable offence, or which would do so if it occurred within the jurisdiction (CJA 1988, ss. 71(9)(c) and 93A(7)). This includes 'either way' offences, but the proceeds of summary offences are covered only if the offence in question is listed in sch. 4 to the Act (as to which, see **E17.8**).

All forms of tangible or intangible property are covered (not merely money), and, in relation to anyone who has benefited from criminal conduct, the 'proceeds of criminal conduct' means that benefit (s. 102(1)).

Sections 93A to 93C each, in different ways, widen the concept of proceeds of criminal conduct so as to include property which represents such proceeds, whether partly, directly or indirectly. Property purchased wholly or partly with the proceeds of criminal conduct may itself become tainted. The definition of stolen goods under the Theft Act 1968, s. 24, is broadly similar in this respect. See **B4.130 *et seq***.

The prosecution must prove that the property concerned represents the proceeds of criminal conduct, but, as with handling stolen goods, the conviction of another person in respect of such conduct is neither essential nor conclusive on that issue. A conviction may raise a limited presumption in favour of the prosecution (see **B4.143** and **F11.3**); but see *Causey* [1999] All ER (D) 1121, unreported in printed form.

ASSISTING ANOTHER TO RETAIN THE BENEFIT OF CRIMINAL CONDUCT

Definition

Criminal Justice Act 1988, s. 93A

B22.4

    (1)   Subject to subsection (3) below, if a person enters into or is otherwise concerned in an arrangement whereby—

    (a)   the retention or control by or on behalf of another ('A') of A's proceeds of criminal conduct is facilitated (whether by concealment, removal from the jurisdiction, transfer to nominees or otherwise); or

    (b)   A's proceeds of criminal conduct—

    (i)   are used to secure that funds are placed at A's disposal; or

    (ii)   are used for A's benefit to acquire property by way of investment,

knowing or suspecting that A is a person who is or has been engaged in criminal conduct or has benefited from criminal conduct, he is guilty of an offence.

    (2)   In this section, references to any person's proceeds of criminal conduct include a reference to any property which in whole or in part directly or indirectly represented in his hands his proceeds of criminal conduct.

Procedure

The offence is triable either way (CJA 1988, s. 93A(9)). When tried on indictment, it is a class 4 offence. Proceedings may be instituted by order of the Commissioners for Customs and Excise under s. 93F of the Act.

B22.5

Indictment

Statement of Offence

B22.6

Assisting another to retain the benefit of criminal conduct, contrary to section 93A of the Criminal Justice Act 1988.

Particulars of Offence

B on or about the day of . . . entered into an arrangement whereby A's retention of the proceeds of his criminal conduct was facilitated, namely by arranging for A to transfer to nominees the sum of £50,000 representing in A's hands the proceeds of the supply by A of unclassified video recordings, knowing or suspecting A to be a person who was engaged in criminal conduct.

Sentence

The penalty on conviction on indictment is imprisonment for a term not exceeding 14 years or a fine or both; six months and/or a fine not exceeding the statutory maximum on summary conviction (CJA 1988, s. 93A(9)).

B22.7

Elements

The meaning of the term 'arrangement' has often been considered in taxation cases but is not defined in the CJA 1988. It would seem to be applicable, in this context, both to contractual agreements and to informal schemes or understandings, which may or may not involve agreements. As to the definition of 'proceeds of criminal conduct', see **B22.3**. Under the CJA 1988, s. 93A(2), any property which is the subject of a charge under s. 93A must either be the original proceeds of another person's criminal conduct or property which has directly or indirectly represented that original property in that other person's hands. This concept is similar to that adopted in relation to stolen goods by the Theft Act 1968, s. 24(2), as to which see **B4.132** and **B4.133**.

B22.8

The prosecution do not need to prove that the defendant knew or believed that the property in question represented such proceeds. In this respect, the prosecution's task is considerably easier than it would be on a comparable charge of handling stolen goods. The minimum *mens rea* which must be proved under the CJA 1988, s. 93A, is suspicion that the other person has been engaged in or has benefited from some form of criminal conduct, as defined in s. 71(9)(c) of the Act (see **B22.3** and *Butt* [1999] Crim LR 414). The defendant may have suspected that the other person was involved in theft, when he was in reality engaged in counterfeiting, but such a mistake would not in itself be a defence. If, however, the accused did not suspect that the arrangement in question was related to the proceeds of criminal conduct at all, he may be able to prove a defence under s. 93A(4) (see **B22.9**).

Defences

B22.9   **Criminal Justice Act 1988, s. 93A**

(3)   Where a person discloses to a constable a suspicion or belief that any funds or investments are derived from or used in connection with criminal conduct or discloses to a constable any matter on which such a suspicion or belief is based—

(a)   the disclosure shall not be treated as a breach of any restriction upon the disclosure of information imposed by statute or otherwise; and

(b)   if he does any act in contravention of subsection (1) above and the disclosure relates to the arrangement concerned, he does not commit an offence under this section if—

(i)   the disclosure is made before he does the act concerned and the act is done with the consent of the constable; or

(ii)   the disclosure is made after he does the act, but is made on his initiative and as soon as it is reasonable for him to make it.

(4)   In proceedings against a person for an offence under this section, it is a defence to prove—

(a)   that he did not know or suspect that the arrangement related to any person's proceeds of criminal conduct; or

(b)   that he did not know or suspect that by the arrangement the retention or control by or on behalf of A of any property was facilitated or, as the case may be, that by the arrangement any property was used, as mentioned in subsection (1) above; or

(c)   that—

(i)   he intended to disclose to a constable such a suspicion, belief or matter as is mentioned in subsection (3) above in relation to the arrangement; but

(ii)   there is reasonable excuse for his failure to make disclosure in accordance with subsection (3)(b) above.

(5)   In the case of a person who was in employment at the relevant time, subsections (3) and (4) above shall have effect in relation to disclosures, and intended disclosures, to the appropriate person in accordance with the procedure established by his employer for the making of such disclosures as they have effect in relation to disclosures, and intended disclosures, to a constable.

The defence under s. 93A(3)(b) differs from that under s. 93A(4) in respect of the burden of proof. The defence expressly bears the legal burden of proof under s. 93A(4), but it would be for the prosecution to disprove any defence raised under s. 93A(3) (cf. *Colle* (1991) 95 Cr App R 67).

References in the 1988 Act to a constable include any person commissioned by the Commissioners of Customs and Excise (s. 102(1)).

ACQUISITION, POSSESSION OR USE OF PROCEEDS OF CRIMINAL CONDUCT

Definition

B22.10   **Criminal Justice Act 1988, s. 93B**

(1)   A person is guilty of an offence if, knowing that any property is, or in whole or in part directly or indirectly represents, another person's proceeds of criminal conduct, he acquires or uses that property or has possession of it.

Procedure

The offence is triable either way (CJA 1988, s. 93B(9)). When tried on indictment it is **B22.11** a class 4 offence. Proceedings may be instituted by order of the Commissioners of Customs and Excise under s. 93F of the Act.

Sentence

The penalty on conviction on indictment is imprisonment for a term not exceeding 14 **B22.12** years or a fine or both; six months and/or a fine not exceeding the statutory maximum on summary conviction (CJA 1988, s. 93B(9)).

Elements

In contrast to the offences contained within the CJA 1988, ss. 93A and 93C, s. 93B **B22.13** requires proof that the defendant knew the property in question to be the direct or indirect proceeds of criminal conduct (as to the meaning of which, see **B22.3**). Suspicion will not suffice. Nor will belief, even though, if coupled with dishonesty, such belief would suffice for liability in cases of handling stolen goods. As to the distinction between knowledge, belief and suspicion, see **B4.141**.

On the other hand, the *actus reus* of the s. 93B offence is wider than that of handling by receiving. It is not confined to cases involving stolen goods, or to cases where the accused had *mens rea* at the time of receiving the property in question. Innocent receipt or acquisition may be followed by realisation that the property represents the proceeds of (say) a burglary committed by X. If the defendant continues to use or possess the property, he may incur liability under s. 93B, but cannot be guilty of receiving under the Theft Act 1968, s. 22 (see **B4.140** and **B4.141**). As to the possible application of s. 93B to cases involving the receipt of retention of wrongful credits, see **B4.149**.

Defences

Criminal Justice Act 1988, s. 93B

B22.14

(2) It is a defence to a charge of committing an offence under this section that the person charged acquired or used the property or had possession of it for adequate consideration.

(3) For the purposes of subsection (2) above—

(a) a person acquires property for inadequate consideration if the value of the consideration is significantly less than the value of the property; and

(b) a person uses or has possession of property for inadequate consideration if the value of the consideration is significantly less than the value of his use or possession of the property.

(4) The provision for any person of services or goods which are of assistance to him in criminal conduct shall not be treated as consideration for the purposes of subsection (2) above.

(5) Where a person discloses to a constable a suspicion or belief that any property is, or in whole or in part directly or indirectly represents, another person's proceeds of criminal conduct or discloses to a constable any matter on which such a suspicion or belief is based—

(a) the disclosure shall not be treated as a breach of any restriction upon the disclosure of information imposed by statute or otherwise; and

(b) if he does any act in relation to that property in contravention of subsection (1) above, he does not commit an offence under this section if—

(i) the disclosure is made before he does the act concerned and the act is done with the consent of the constable; or

(ii) the disclosure is made after he does the act, but on his initiative and as soon as it is reasonable for him to make it.

(6) For the purposes of this section, having possession of any property shall be taken to be doing an act in relation to it.

(7) In proceedings against a person for an offence under this section, it is a defence to prove that—

(a)   he intended to disclose to a constable such a suspicion, belief or matter as is mentioned in subsection (5) above; but

(b)   there is reasonable excuse for his failure to make the disclosure in accordance with paragraph (b) of that subsection.

(8)   In the case of a person who was in employment at the relevant time, subsections (5) and (7) above shall have effect in relation to disclosures, and intended disclosures, to the appropriate person in accordance with the procedure established by his employer for the making of such disclosures as they have effect in relation to disclosures, and intended disclosures, to a constable.

(10)   No constable or other person shall be guilty of an offence under this section in respect of anything done by him in the course of acting in connection with the enforcement, or intended enforcement, of any provision of this Act or of any other enactment relating to criminal conduct or the proceeds of such conduct.

References in the 1988 Act to a constable include any person commissioned by the Commissioners of Customs and Excise (s. 102(1)).

The location of the burden of proof in respect of the above defences is not always entirely clear. Section 93B(7) expressly places the legal burden on the defendant; s. 93B(2) also appears to do so, but only by implication. By contrast, s. 93B(5) and (10) are worded as limitations on the scope of the offence, and the prosecution would have to disprove any defence raised under either of these subsections (cf. *Colle* (1991) 95 Cr App R 67).

It is surprising that both s. 93B(5) and s. 93B(7) refer to disclosure of suspicion or belief when the requisite *mens rea* for the offence is knowledge; but more surprising still is the rule that a defence of 'adequate consideration' under s. 93B(2) may succeed even where the accused was well aware that he was using or acquiring proceeds of criminal conduct.

CONCEALING OR TRANSFERRING PROCEEDS OF CRIMINAL CONDUCT

Definition

B22.15   **Criminal Justice Act 1988, s. 93C**

(1)   A person is guilty of an offence if he—

(a)   conceals or disguises any property which is, or in whole or in part directly or indirectly represents, his proceeds of criminal conduct; or

(b)   converts or transfers that property or removes it from the jurisdiction,

for the purpose of avoiding prosecution for an offence to which this part of this Act applies or the making or enforcement in his case of a confiscation order.

(2)   A person is guilty of an offence if, knowing or having reasonable grounds to suspect that any property is, or in whole or in part directly or indirectly represents, another person's proceeds of criminal conduct, he—

(a)   conceals or disguises that property; or

(b)   converts or transfers that property or removes it from the jurisdiction,

for the purpose of assisting any person to avoid prosecution for an offence to which this part of this Act applies or the making or enforcement in his case of a confiscation order.

(3)   In subsections (1) and (2) above, the references to concealing or disguising any property include references to concealing or disguising its nature, source, location, disposition, movement or ownership or any rights with respect to it.

Procedure

B22.16   The offences are triable either way (CJA 1988, s. 93C(4)). When tried on indictment, they are class 4 offences. Proceedings may be instituted by order of the Commissioners for Customs and Excise under s. 93F of the Act.

Indictment

B22.17   Statement of Offence

Removing proceeds of criminal conduct from the jurisdiction, contrary to section 93(2) of the Criminal Justice Act 1988.

Particulars of Offence

A on the . . . day of . . . removed the sum of £250,000 from the jurisdiction, namely from
. . . to . . ., knowing or having reasonable grounds to suspect it to represent B's proceeds of
criminal conduct, namely insider dealing in the securities of X plc, for the purpose of
assisting B to avoid prosecution for that offence.

Sentence

The penalty on conviction on indictment is imprisonment for a term not exceeding 14 **B22.18**
years or a fine or both; six months and/or a fine not exceeding the statutory maximum
on summary conviction (CJA 1988, s. 93C(4)).

Elements

The offences created by the CJA 1988, s. 93C, cover much of the ground already **B22.19**
covered by the common law offence of perverting the course of justice (as to which, see
B14.26 *et seq.*).

An offence under s. 93C(2) may also involve an offence under s. 93A (see **B22.4**) insofar
as either may involve concealment, transfer etc. of the proceeds of another person's
crimes, but s. 93C makes no mention of entering into arrangements and the requisite
mens rea is quite different. The defendant must act for the purpose of assisting another
person to avoid prosecution etc. He need not, however, intend to facilitate anyone's
retention of the proceeds and need not believe in or even suspect the other person's guilt.
If, objectively, he has grounds to suspect that person's guilt and intends to help him (or
anyone else) to avoid prosecution etc., then his sincere belief in that other person's
innocence will be no defence.

As with perverting the course of justice, there seems to be no requirement that any
proceedings or investigation need have begun at the time of the offence (see **B14.31**).

TIPPING-OFF

Definition

Criminal Justice Act 1988, s. 93D   B22.20

(1)　A person is guilty of an offence if—

(a)　he knows or suspects that a constable is acting, or is proposing to act, in
connection with an investigation which is being, or is about to be, conducted into money
laundering; and

(b)　he discloses to any other person information or any other matter which is likely
to prejudice that investigation, or proposed investigation.

(2)　A person is guilty of an offence if—

(a)　he knows, or suspects that a disclosure ('the disclosure') has been made to a
constable under section 93A or 93B above; and

(b)　he discloses to any other person information or any other matter which is likely
to prejudice any investigation which might be conducted following the disclosure.

(3)　A person is guilty of an offence if—

(a)　he knows or suspects that a disclosure of a kind mentioned in section 93A(5) or
93B(8) above ('the disclosure') has been made; and

(b)　he discloses to any person information or any other matter which is likely to
prejudice any investigation which might be conducted following the disclosure.

. . .

(7)　In this section 'money laundering' means doing any act which constitutes an offence
under section 93A, 93B or 93C above or, in the case of an act done otherwise than in
England and Wales or Scotland, would constitute such an offence if done in England and
Wales or (as the case may be) Scotland.

(8)　For the purposes of subsection (7) above, having possession of any property shall
be taken to be doing an act in relation to it.

References in the 1988 Act to a constable include any person commissioned by the Commissioners of Customs and Excise (s. 102(1)).

Procedure

B22.21 The offences are triable either way (CJA 1988, s. 93D(9)). When tried on indictment, they are class 4 offences. Proceedings may be instituted by order of the Commissioners of Customs and Excise under s. 93F of the Act.

Sentence

B22.22 The penalty on conviction on indictment is imprisonment for a term not exceeding 14 years or a fine or both; six months and/or a fine not exceeding the statutory maximum on summary conviction (CJA 1988, s. 93D(9)).

Elements

B22.23 In contrast to the offences of perverting the course of justice or assisting offenders (as to which, see **B14.26** *et seq*.), the offences created by the CJA 1988, s. 93D, do not require proof of any intent to prejudice inquiries or prevent the detection or prosecution of offenders. Nor do they require the wilful obstruction of any constable etc. Where the disclosure was merely thoughtless or unguarded it will be for the accused to establish a defence under s. 93D(6).

Defences

B22.24   **Criminal Justice Act 1988, s. 93D**

(4)   Nothing in subsections (1) to (3) above makes it an offence for a professional legal adviser to disclose any information or other matter—

   (a)   to, or to a representative of, a client of his in connection with the giving by the adviser of legal advice to the client, or

   (b)   to any person—

      (i)   in contemplation of, or in connection with, legal proceedings; and

      (ii)   for the purpose of those proceedings.

(5)   Subsection (4) above does not apply in relation to any information or other matter which is disclosed with a view to furthering any criminal purpose.

(6)   In proceedings against a person for an offence under subsection (1), (2) or (3) above, it is a defence to prove that he did not know or suspect that the disclosure was likely to be prejudicial in the way mentioned in that subsection.

. . .

(10)   No constable or other person shall be guilty of an offence under this section in respect of anything done by him in the course of acting in connection with the enforcement, or intended enforcement, of any provision of this Act or of any other enactment relating to an offence to which this part of this Act applies.

A defence under s. 93D(6) differs from those in s. 93D(4) and (10) in respect of the burden of proof. The defence expressly bears the legal burden of proof under s. 93A(6), but it would be for the prosecution to disprove a defence raised under either of the other provisions (cf. *Colle* (1991) 95 Cr App R 67).

PART C

ROAD TRAFFIC OFFENCES

Peter Fortune, MA, Barrister

Richard McMahon, LLB, LLM, Barrister

Legislative Draftsman, States of Guernsey
Advocate of the Royal Court of Guernsey
Formerly Lecturer in Law, The University of Reading

SECTION C1: DEFINITIONS AND BASIC PRINCIPLES IN ROAD TRAFFIC CASES

Accident

The word 'accident' has been given a number of different meanings depending upon the **C1.1** context in which it is used. In *Chief Constable of West Midlands Police* v *Billingham* [1979] 1 WLR 747, the Divisional Court expressed a preference for an 'ordinary man' test, stating that the definition of the word by the Court of Appeal in *Morris* [1972] 1 WLR 228 as 'some unintended occurrence which has an adverse physical result' should be understood in relation to the facts of that case. Nonetheless, the Court did state (per Bridge LJ) that the word 'accident' was 'capable of applying to an untoward occurrence which has adverse physical results' even if one event in the chain was deliberate. The main doubt was at one time whether an accident could result from one or more intentional or deliberate acts.

In *Chief Constable of Staffordshire* v *Lees* [1981] RTR 506, the argument that a 'deliberate act' does not constitute an 'accident', at least for the purposes of the Road Traffic Acts, appears to have been finally laid to rest. In that case the defendant deliberately drove his car at a locked gate. The Divisional Court held that an 'accident' could be said to have occurred within the meaning of the RTA 1972, s. 8(2), when arising through a deliberate and intended act, provided that any ordinary person would say that there had been an accident owing to the presence of a motor vehicle on a road. Bingham J stated (at p. 510):

> It would be an insult to common sense if a collision involving a motor car arising from some careless and inadvertent act entitled a constable to exercise his powers under the [Road Traffic] Act but a similar result caused by a deliberate antisocial act did not. Previous cases have made it clear that one should look at the ordinary meaning of the word 'accident'.

It should also be noted that in *Morris* [1972] 1 WLR 228 Lord Widgery CJ acknowledged the possibility of a *de minimis* argument where the physical consequences were so trivial that an ordinary person would not regard the occurrence as an accident.

Aiding, Abetting, Counselling, Procuring

For the meaning of these terms, see generally the Accessories and Abettors Act 1861, **C1.2** s. 8; the MCA 1980, s. 44(1); and **A5.1** *et seq*.

By the MCA 1980, s. 44, a person convicted of aiding, abetting, counselling or procuring a summary offence is guilty of the like offence, and if the substantive offence carries endorsement the defendant must have his licence endorsed and may be disqualified.

Where disqualification is mandatory for the principal offence (e.g., driving with excess alcohol in the breath), a person convicted of aiding and abetting etc. is liable to discretionary disqualification by virtue of the RTOA 1988, s. 34(5), and his licence must be endorsed with 10 penalty points (RTOA 1988, s. 28(1)(b)).

Attempts

As to attempts generally, see **A6.31** *et seq*. **C1.3**

By virtue of the Criminal Attempts Act 1981, s. 1(4), it is not possible to attempt the commission of an offence which is purely summary, unless such an offence is created by statute (e.g., the RTA 1988, s. 5(1)(a), attempting to drive a motor vehicle on a road after consuming so much alcohol that the proportion of it in the breath etc. exceeds the prescribed limit). The Criminal Attempts Act 1981, s. 3, enacts similar provisions in relation to statutory attempts as are contained in ss. 1(2), (3) and (4) of the Act.

Automatism and Insanity

C1.4   As to insanity generally, see **A3.12** to **A3.18**. As to automatism generally, see **A3.7**.

Questions of fitness to plead and insanity are triable by a jury under the Criminal Procedure (Insanity) Act 1964 (see **D10.6** and **D10.10**). In indictable offences, where these issues are raised, the magistrates' court is obliged to commit to the Crown Court in pursuance of that statute.

In the magistrates' court questions relating to automatism usually arise in the form of defences of involuntary behaviour on the part of the driver. (See also mechanical defect at **C1.10**, and duress or necessity at **A3.20** to **A3.28**.)

In *Hill* v *Baxter* [1958] 1 QB 277, a case on the *mens rea* required under certain sections of the RTA 1930 (now repealed), Lord Goddard CJ (at p. 282) quoted the dictum of Humphreys J in *Kay* v *Butterworth* (1945) 61 TLR 452:

> I do not mean to say that a person should be made liable at criminal law who, through no fault of his own becomes unconscious while driving, as for example, a person who has been struck by a stone or overcome by a sudden illness, or when the car has been put temporarily out of his control owing to his being attacked by a swarm of bees . . .

Lord Goddard CJ then went on to say (at p. 283):

> I agree that there may be cases where the circumstances are such that the accused could not really be said to be driving at all. Suppose he had a stroke or an epileptic fit, both instances of what may properly be called acts of God; he might well be in the driver's seat even with his hands on the wheel, but in such a state of unconsciousness that he could not be said to be driving. A blow from a stone or an attack by a swarm of bees I think introduces some conception akin to *novus actus interveniens*.

In such circumstances, the defendant is not 'driving' but has been rendered incapable of physical control of the vehicle. This is not automatism of the type considered in *Bailey* [1983] 1 WLR 760 and *Hardie* [1985] 1 WLR 64, but nonetheless arises without fault and should not therefore be the subject of any criminal sanction. There must, however, be 'a total destruction of voluntary control'; impaired or reduced control is not enough (per Lord Taylor CJ in *A-G's Ref (No. 2 of 1992)* [1994] QB 91). Sneezing may produce a state of automatism (*Whoolley* (13 November 1997 unreported)). The lack of control must arise from causes which do not bring the defendant within the M'Naghten rules. Thus driving with 'a reduced or imperfect awareness', which is brought on by the repetitive stimuli experienced on a long journey and which reduces a driver's capacity to avoid collisions, cannot, as a matter of law, found a defence of automatism. Similarly, in *Watmore* v *Jenkins* [1962] 2 QB 572, Winn J pointed out that a finding by the justices that the defendant 'continued to perform the functions of driving, after a fashion' for five miles on a road which was not straight, was inconsistent with a finding of automatism 'extending throughout the whole of the distance . . . to which it related'.

It would seem from the authorities that in cases involving the use of a motor vehicle, a failure to take precautions would be sufficient to establish criminal liability, where the state of automatism could or should have been reasonably foreseen as a likely result of such a failure. In short, such a failure is tantamount to a self-induced incapacity which will not excuse the defendant from criminal liability in any cases involving a basic or lesser intent.

Causing

C1.5   A number of offences in the Road Traffic Acts may be committed by causing or permitting the use of, as well as using, a vehicle in a prohibited manner. Each of these gives rise to a separate offence.

'Causing' demands a positive act on the part of the defendant (*Price* v *Cromack* [1975] 1 WLR 988). It also requires prior knowledge. In *Milstead* v *Sexton* [1964] Crim LR 474, the defendant was convicted of causing a car to be used on a road where the car was being towed and he was driving the towing vehicle. In *Ross Hillman Ltd* v *Bond* [1974] QB 435, the *mens rea* involved in 'causing' was considered. The defendant was a limited company which owned a number of vehicles and employed a number of drivers, all of whom had been warned against driving their vehicles whilst overloaded. One of the employees drove his vehicle while it was overloaded, and the company was convicted of 'causing' that use. Having reviewed the authorities, May J stated (at p. 446):

> Unassisted by any authority I would as a matter of ordinary English construe both the word 'causes' and the word 'permits' in section 40(5)(b) of the Act of 1972 as requiring prior knowledge of the facts constituting the unlawful user. . . . if, as I think and as is supported by authority, actual user of a vehicle in contravention of the regulations is an absolute offence, and if, as I also think, a master 'uses' the vehicle which his servant is driving on that master's business, then I think that the mischief against which the regulations are directed, that of having unsafe vehicles on the roads is adequately dealt with. Having regard to the ordinary meaning of 'causes' I do not find it surprising that, whereas on given facts a master charged with using will be convicted, on the same facts a master charged with causing that use will be acquitted.

The appeal was allowed as there was no evidence of prior knowledge.

In *Mounsey* v *Campbell* [1983] RTR 36, the defendant caused an obstruction by parking his van immediately in front of another motor vehicle so that vehicle was unable to move. The defence had argued that it was only when the defendant refused to move the van that the vehicle became an obstruction, and therefore the proper charge should have been one of 'permitting'. This argument was described as 'nebulous' by the court, who found that the initial act of parking and subsequent refusal to move the vehicle could both constitute 'causing'.

A company which shut its eyes to the failure of its employee to fill in tachograph records could not be said to have 'caused' that failure. Such wilful ignorance may amount to 'permitting' but falls short of the 'positive mandate or . . . other sufficient act required for the offence' (*Redhead Freight Ltd* v *Shulman* [1989] RTR 1).

Permitting

In *Vehicle Inspectorate* v *Nuttall* [1999] 1 WLR 629, the House of Lords drew a distinction **C1.6** between positive acts where a person 'allows' or 'authorises' the use of the vehicle by another and omissions which amount to 'failure to take reasonable steps to prevent' such use. When the second, wider meaning applies to the context of the offence charged, it is not an offence of strict liability and, therefore, requires proof of nothing less than wilfulness or recklessness. This may be demonstrated by adducing actual evidence or by raising a rebuttable presumption. For example, in respect of regulatory tachograph requirements, if the employer fails to take reasonable steps to prevent employee drivers from contravening the statutory provisions, it raises a rebuttable presumption that the necessary mental element has been established (per Lord Steyn at p. 637C)

For 'permission' involving a positive act, proof of prior knowledge remains necessary (*Ross Hillman Ltd* v *Bond* [1974] QB 435). This connotes express or implied permission or acquiescence as much as direct participation.

'Knowledge' includes actual and constructive knowledge, such as 'the state of mind of a man who shuts his eyes to the obvious or allows his servant to do something in the circumstances where a contravention is likely, not caring whether a contravention takes place or not' (*James & Son Ltd* v *Smee* [1955] 1 QB 78, per Parker J at p. 91). Where justices had found that an employer did not know and had no reasonable cause to suspect that one of his vehicles had a defective braking system, it was not open to them to convict of an offence of permitting the vehicle's use, notwithstanding that he would have had no answer to a charge of 'using' the vehicle in a defective condition (*Robinson v DPP* [1991] RTR 315).

Negligence not amounting to recklessness did not justify an inference that a managing director, someone who might be said to be 'the "brains" of the company rather than its hands', was wilfully closing his eyes to the obvious, and therefore that a company was guilty of permitting the use of a vehicle on a road with defective brakes (*Hill & Sons (Botley and Denmead) Ltd* v *Hampshire Chief Constable* [1972] RTR 29).

That decision closely follows *Magna Plant Ltd* v *Mitchell* [1966] Crim LR 394, where a plant hire company was charged with unlawfully permitting the use of a vehicle in a dangerous condition. Lord Parker CJ, in giving the judgment of the court, said:

> A company was not criminally liable in the absence of knowledge of the facts constituting the offence for the failure of a servant to whom it had delegated a task. The servant was not in the position of the brains of the company and his knowledge could not be imputed to a director. . .

However, an employer's failure to operate an adequate, or any, system of checking tachograph charts was regarded as sufficiently reckless 'shutting of the eyes' so as to amount to implied knowledge in *Vehicle Inspectorate* v *Shane Raymond Nuttall t/a Redline Coaches* (1997) 161 JP 701. The test is one of fact and degree.

In cases of no insurance, permitting has a stricter interpretation. Where an owner allows the use of a vehicle, believing that use to be insured, such a belief is no defence to a charge of permitting the uninsured use of the vehicle (*Lyons* v *May* [1948] 2 All ER 1062; *Baugh* v *Crago* [1975] RTR 453). In exceptional circumstances a conditional permission to use a vehicle only with insurance does not constitute an offence (*Sheldon Deliveries Ltd* v *Willis* [1972] RTR 217; *Newbury* v *Davis* [1974] RTR 367), but such a defence must be regarded with extreme caution before it is capable of application (see *DPP* v *Fisher* [1991] RTR 93, where it was held that the permission must be given direct to the would-be driver).

Using

C1.7 'Using' has a restricted meaning when found in the same section as 'causing' and 'permitting'. In such cases it is only the driver, or his employer, when the driver is driving on his employer's business, who can be said to be 'using' the vehicle (*Mickleborough* v *BRS (Contracts) Ltd* [1977] RTR 389; *Robinson* v *DPP* [1991] RTR 315; *West Yorkshire Trading Standards Service* v *Lex Vehicle Leasing Ltd* [1996] RTR 170; *Jones* v *DPP* [1999] RTR 1). 'User' must involve an element of controlling, managing or operating the vehicle by the person concerned (*Hatton* v *Hall* [1997] RTR 212). For a non-driver of the vehicle, this element could exist as a result of a joint venture to use it for a particular purpose or where the passenger procures the making of the journey (*O'Mahoney* v *Joliffe* [1999] RTR 245); whether it does is a question of fact and degree.

These propositions extend to cases where the word 'use' is found, either alone, or in conjunction with another word such as 'keeps' (*James & Son Ltd* v *Smee* [1955] 1 QB 78; *Richardson* v *Baker* [1976] RTR 56). Use, however, by a person other than a servant, even a business partner, does not constitute use by the owner, albeit that the vehicle is being driven at his request and with his full knowledge (*Crawford* v *Haughton* [1972] 1 WLR 572; *Garrett* v *Hooper* [1973] RTR 1). That sort of use may, of course, amount to 'permitting' or even 'causing'. However, *Hallett Silberman* v *Cheshire County Council* [1993] RTR 32 shows that a vehicle which exceeds its permitted weight may be being used by the owner even if its driver is self-employed and provides the tractor unit. The ratio of that decision rests heavily on the degree of control exercised by the defendants, who supplied the trailer and chose the route; as such their position was analogous to that of an employer. It was considered to be contrary to the intention of Parliament that the driver be held primarily responsible in such circumstances and the defendant owners were properly held to be using the combination of tractor and trailer for the purposes of the RTA 1988, s. 42(1)(b). By contrast, in *DPP* v *Seawheel Ltd* (1994) 158 JP 444, mere ownership of a part of the assembly on which a load was carried and which was secured to the trailer was insufficient to establish use for the purposes of s. 42(1); the tractor and trailer unit were owned by a person who had contracted to transport the load and there was no finding that the defendants were in possession of any of the relevant parts. It was suggested *obiter*, however, that a wider meaning should be given to 'use' when applied to a trailer rather than when applied to a lorry.

Vehicles left unattended on a road can still be regarded as being used, as 'use' has been held to mean 'having the use of' for these purposes (*Eden* v *Mitchell* [1975] RTR 425). Accordingly, the mere fact of having two defective tyres did not preclude the vehicle's use and the owner's intention in respect of using the vehicle was held to be irrelevant. Similarly, in *Elliott* v *Grey* [1960] 1 QB 367, despite having an engine that did not work, no battery and no petrol, the vehicle in question was being 'used' without insurance, as it could be moved, albeit not driven. The distinction drawn in *Hewer* v *Cutler* [1974] RTR 155, that immobile vehicles whose wheels would not rotate were outside the definition 'use', was found to be unjustified by Mitchell J in *Pumbien* v *Vines* [1996] RTR 37. In that case the vehicle's tyres were deflated, the handbrake was on, the rear brakes were seized and the gearbox contained no oil because there was a leak in the transmission pipe. It was held that, provided that vehicle was a 'motor vehicle' within the definition of the RTA 1988, s. 185 (see generally **C1.11**), and was on a road, the owner had the use of it on a road, whether at the material time it could move on its wheels or not. This decision has also apparently removed the requirement of an 'element of controlling, managing or operating the vehicle as a vehicle' (*Nichol* v *Leach* [1972] RTR 476), in the sense of the vehicle being capable of movement 'as a vehicle'. Consequently, for the purposes of the RTA 1988, ss. 47 and 143, 'use' should be accorded the same meaning and mobility of the vehicle is irrelevant.

Driver and Driving

The definition of 'driver' is set out in the RTA 1988, s. 192. It includes, except in cases   **C1.8** of causing death by dangerous driving, a person who is steering, as well as any other person engaged in driving. As respects establishing the identity of the driver of a vehicle concerned in an offence, there is no general presumption that the owner of a vehicle is the driver of it at a particular time, notwithstanding the various statutory provisions which establish owner liability in certain specific circumstances; the question of the driver's identity is one of fact on which the tribunal must be sure (see *Clarke* v *DPP* (1992) 156 JP 605 and *Powell* v *DPP* [1992] RTR 270; for directions on car identification, see *Browning* (1991) 94 Cr App R 109). Evidence of ownership is merely one strand in the evidential rope which may go to establish the identity of the driver.

The act of driving is a physical one which can only be performed by a natural person, and the words 'drive' and 'driver' should be construed accordingly. Consequently, the Divisional Court declined to make the respondent, a limited company, vicariously liable for an offence under the RTRA 1984, s. 8(1) (*Richmond London Borough Council* v *Pinn and Wheeler Ltd* [1989] RTR 354).

In *MacDonagh* [1974] QB 448 (a five-judge Court of Appeal), the essence of driving was said to be the use of 'the driver's controls for the purpose of directing the movement of the vehicle'. The defendant, who was disqualified from driving, had been asked to move his car by a police officer and, on the defendant's version of events, he had pushed it with his two feet on the road and one hand on the steering wheel. The recorder directed the jury that this could properly be described as driving. Lord Widgery CJ, in giving the judgment of the court allowing the appeal, stated (at p. 451):

> There are an infinite number of ways in which a person may control the movement of a motor vehicle, apart from the orthodox one of sitting in the driving seat and using the engine for propulsion. He may be coasting down a hill with the gears in neutral and the engine switched off; he may be steering a vehicle which is being towed by another. As has already been pointed out, he may be sitting in the driving seat while others push, or half sitting in the driving seat but keeping one foot on the road in order to induce the car to move. Finally, as in the present case, he may be standing in the road and himself pushing the car with or without using the steering wheel to direct it. Although the word 'drive' must be given a wide meaning, the courts must be alert to see that the net is not thrown so widely that it includes activities which cannot be said to be driving a motor vehicle in any ordinary use of that word in the English language.

MacDonagh was followed in *McQuaid* v *Anderton* [1981] 1 WLR 154, in which the court expressed the hope that the ghost of *Wallace* v *Major* [1946] KB 473, where Lord Goddard stated that the person in the driving seat of a towed vehicle could not be described as a driver, had been finally exorcised. In *McQuaid* v *Anderton* the appellant, who was disqualified, was steering a towed vehicle which had an operational braking system. The court held that the method of propulsion was irrelevant and dismissed his appeal. See also *Whitfield* v *DPP* [1998] Crim LR 349.

In *Saycell* v *Bool* [1948] 2 All ER 83, steering a lorry for 100 yards downhill, without the engine running, was held to be driving, but in *Roberts* [1965] 1 QB 85, it was held that releasing the handbrake of a lorry which then ran downhill under its own momentum and caused damage, was not 'driving' for the purpose of what is now the Theft Act 1968, s. 12, as the appellant was not in the driving seat or steering.

In *Blayney* v *Knight* (1974) 60 Cr App R 269, a case under the Theft Act 1968, s. 12, accidentally depressing the accelerator of a car with automatic transmission whilst in the course of a struggle with the driver, but without any intention to drive, or, indeed, permission to be in the driver's seat, could not amount to driving.

In *Evans* v *Walkden* [1956] 1 WLR 1019, occupying the front passenger seat and supervising the driver, thereby being in a position to assume control if necessary, was held not to be equivalent to being in control, with the result that the supervisor was not a 'driver'. *Langman* v *Valentine* [1952] 2 All ER 803 was distinguished because there the degree of control exercised throughout by the supervisor was considerably greater.

A person steering a vehicle from the passenger seat, over an appreciable period of time, was driving, as was the person sitting in the driver's seat (*Tyler* v *Whatmore* [1976] RTR 83), but a momentary seizure of the steering wheel causing the vehicle to leave the road, whilst borderline, could not properly be described as 'driving' (*Jones* v *Pratt* [1983] RTR 54). In neither case did the court consider the interpretation provisions and any possible definition of 'steersman'. *Jones* v *Pratt* was followed in *DPP* v *Hastings* [1993] RTR 205, where there was a similar momentary seizure of the wheel. Although the seizure in *Hastings* was intended to cause danger there was no finding that the driver relinquished control and the seizure was regarded as 'an act of interfering with the driving of the car rather than an act of driving in itself'.

In *Burgoyne* v *Phillips* [1983] RTR 49, releasing the handbrake and sitting in the car with the steering locked and the engine off whilst the vehicle moved by reason of gravity was held to be driving, although the defendant had left the keys to the car elsewhere. In *Leach* v *DPP* [1993] RTR 161, however, sitting in the driving seat of a stationary motor vehicle with hands on the steering wheel and the engine off was held not to be, *per se*, driving within the meaning of the RTA 1988, s. 163(1), so as to make it an offence to fail to stop for a constable. However, in *Whelehan* v *DPP* [1995] RTR 177, quite apart from the defendant's admission to driving to the location where he was found by a constable, the Divisional Court concluded that being discovered in the driving seat of a stationary motor vehicle on a road at 1.20 a.m. with the keys in the ignition switch afforded sufficient evidence from which to infer that the defendant had driven to that location.

Kneeling on the driving seat, releasing the handbrake and attempting to re-apply the handbrake was material upon which justices might find a defendant was driving (*Rowan* v *Chief Constable of Merseyside* (1985) *The Times*, 10 December 1985).

Controlling the movement and direction of a motor cycle by pushing and steering with the ignition and lights on constituted 'driving', as long as the defendant was wearing motor cyclist's clothing and a crash helmet (*McKoen* v *Ellis* [1987] RTR 26).

In *Selby* v *DPP* [1994] RTR 157n, Taylor LJ stated (at p. 162) that 'riding' is carried out 'if a person is being carried on a motor cycle as it moves on its wheels, whether propelled by the engine or by his feet or by gravity', which would seem to be equally applicable as the test for 'driving' a motor cycle (*Gunnell* v *DPP* [1994] RTR 151).

Once the act of driving has commenced, ascertained by applying the *MacDonagh* test, it continues until it terminates, and a person may still be 'driving' although the vehicle is stationary (*Pinner* v *Everett* [1969] 1 WLR 1266; *Skelton* [1995] Crim LR 635). In *Edkins* v *Knowles* [1973] QB 748, it was emphasised that the reason for stopping is relevant, as it may be part of the journey, e.g., traffic lights or a junction, or may mark a break in the journey, in which case the length of break and whether the driver leaves the vehicle becomes important. The issue is one of fact and degree, just as it is at the end of a journey, when various activities connected with driving must be completed before the driving is terminated, e.g., switching off the ignition and securing the vehicle.

Duress and Necessity

As to duress generally, see **A3.20** to **A3.28**. As to necessity generally, see **A3.27**.   **C1.9**

Mechanical Defect

Where a driver is deprived of control of a motor vehicle as a result of a mechanical defect **C1.10** of which he has no knowledge, real or constructive, then such a defect is a defence to a charge of careless driving and a charge of contravening the regulations relating to pedestrian crossings.

This defence of mechanical or latent defect stems from *Kay* v *Butterworth* (1945) 61 TLR 452, *Simpson* v *Peat* [1952] 2 QB 24, *Hill* v *Baxter* [1958] 1 QB 227, and the general proposition that in cases not involving fault the law should seek to avoid the imposition of any criminal sanction.

The defence was first considered in *Spurge* [1961] 2 QB 205, where the appellant had recently purchased a car with a tendency to move to the right when the brakes were applied. His appeal against conviction and sentence for dangerous driving was dismissed on the basis that he was, or should have been, aware of the mechanical defect. The court, stressing that successful reliance on the defence would be rare and that it did not apply where the defect was known, or would have been discovered by the exercise of reasonable prudence, stated (per Salmon J, at p. 212): 'The essence of the defence is that the danger has been created by a sudden total loss of control in no way due to any fault on the part of the driver'. It is for the defence to raise the issue, but the onus of disproving it remains with the prosecution.

In *Burns* v *Bidder* [1967] 2 QB 227, the defence was recognised as applying to offences under the Pedestrian Crossings Regulations. The defendant's appeal was allowed, as the convicting magistrate, thinking the offence an absolute one and not being satisfied that the brakes had not failed, should have taken the defence of mechanical defect into account in considering whether the prosecution had discharged the onus of proof. In giving the judgment of the court, James J reviewed the authorities, and stated (at pp. 240–41):

> The cases of the driver suddenly stung by a swarm of bees or suffering a sudden epileptic form of disabling attack, or a vehicle being propelled forward by reason of another vehicle hitting it from behind, are illustrations of where no offence may be shown, because control over the vehicle is taken completely out of the hands of the driver, and his failure to accord precedence on that account would be no offence.

> Likewise in my view a sudden removal of control over the vehicle occasioned by a latent defect of which the driver did not know and could not reasonably be expected to know would render the resulting failure to accord precedence no offence, provided he is in no way at fault himself.

The court again stated that it was for the defence to raise the issue, and it should then be considered with all the other evidence; if a reasonable doubt remained, the prosecution would not have proved the offence. The defence at that time extended to offences of driving in a dangerous manner, and there seems little or no reason why it should not be of general application.

In *Beckford* [1996] 1 Cr App R 96, the Court of Appeal hoped that procedures have been put in place to ensure that vehicles are not scrapped before express permission is given by the police and that such permission will not be forthcoming if serious criminal charges which may involve the possibility of some mechanical defect in the vehicle have been brought.

Motor Vehicle and Mechanically Propelled Vehicle

C1.11 The term 'motor vehicle' is defined in the RTA 1988, s. 185, as a mechanically propelled vehicle intended or adapted for use on roads. A mechanically propelled vehicle does not need to be intended or adapted for such use; whether a vehicle is mechanically propelled remains a question of fact.

A vehicle which has more than one source of power does not cease to be 'mechanically propelled', even though it is propelled by means other than an engine at the relevant time (*Floyd* v *Bush* [1953] 1 WLR 242). This extends to a vehicle which is being towed, even though that vehicle may be in such a poor condition that it could not be propelled under its own power, and even though it was at the same time a 'trailer', a 'vehicle' drawn by a 'motor vehicle' (*Cobb* v *Whorton* [1971] RTR 392).

A suitably adapted vehicle, even though originally constructed for use on the roads, may, as a question of fact, cease to be a 'motor vehicle' within the meaning of s. 185, as in *Lawrence* v *Howlett* [1952] 2 All ER 74, where the auxiliary engine had been removed from a moped making it into a 'pedal cycle'. Normally, however, only when it is clear that a vehicle will not become mobile again can it be said that it ceases to be a 'motor vehicle', and in each case that is a question of fact for the court.

In *Burns* v *Currell* [1963] 2 QB 433, Lord Parker CJ, adopting a 'reasonable person' test as to the use of the vehicle, stated (at p. 440):

> ... in the ordinary case ... there will be little difficulty in saying whether a particular vehicle is a motor vehicle or not. But to define exactly the meaning of the words 'intended or adapted' is by no means easy. I think that the expression 'intended' ... does not mean 'intended by the user of the vehicle either at the moment of the alleged offence or for the future'.

This case was followed in *Chief Constable of Avon and Somerset Constabulary* v *F (A Juvenile)* [1987] RTR 378, where justices dismissed seven informations laid against a juvenile on the basis that they could not be sure the vehicle in question came within the definition. The Divisional Court dismissed the prosecution's appeal. Glidewell LJ said (at pp. 382–3):

> I emphasise that that test is what would be the view of the reasonable man as to the general user of this particular vehicle; not what was the particular user to which this particular defendant put it. . . . if a reasonable man were to say 'Yes, this vehicle might well be used on the road', then, applying the test, the vehicle is intended or adapted for such use. If that be the case, it is nothing to the point if the individual defendant says: 'I normally use it for scrambling and I am only pushing it along the road on this occasion because I have no other means of getting it home', or something of that sort.

For a motor vehicle to change its character from that intended by the manufacturer a very substantial or dramatic alteration would be required for it to cease to be a motor vehicle; the addition of something that may make the vehicle unusable on a road might suffice, but the absence of registration plates, reflectors, lights or the speedometer would, it is submitted, be insufficient (see *DPP* v *Ryan* [1992] RTR 13).

In *Maddox* v *Storer* [1962] 1 All ER 831, the court stated that it was necessary to look to the context in which the word 'adapted' was used, and when used alone it was held to have the adjectival meaning of 'being fit and apt for the purpose'. If used disjunctively, as an alternative to 'constructed', its meaning was 'being altered so as to make it fit'.

In *Millard* v *Turvey* [1968] 2 QB 390, a chassis without a cab, doors, roof, windscreen or seats for the accommodation of passengers was held to be a motor vehicle, albeit under construction, but was not a 'motor tractor'. In *Tahsin* [1970] RTR 88, it was held that a moped did not cease to be a 'motor vehicle' merely because its engine would not work. A moped, however, does not become a motor cycle merely because one pedal is missing (*G (A Minor)* v *Jarrett* [1981] RTR 186). For a vehicle to change in such a manner requires an alteration in its design or construction.

Owner

See the RTA 1988, s. 192, at **C1.15**.   **C1.12**

In relation to a vehicle which is subject to a hiring or hire-purchase agreement, 'owner' includes the person in possession of the vehicle under that agreement. It is submitted that even if the person lawfully in possession of the vehicle under a hiring agreement parts with it to a third party, who may then drive the vehicle without documents, insurance etc., unless the agreement provides for instant termination of the hire, so that property in the vehicle immediately reverts to the person who has legal title to the vehicle, the third party is not guilty of an offence under the Theft Act 1968, s. 12, although both he and the person in possession of the vehicle under the hiring agreement may be guilty of other offences relating to the absence of insurance, etc.

Road or Other Public Place

The word 'road' is defined by the RTA 1988, s. 192. It includes any highway and any **C1.13** other road to which the public has access, including bridges over which a road passes. The Concise Oxford Dictionary defines 'road' as 'a line of communication between places for use of pedestrians, riders, and vehicles'. Section 34(1)(b) of the 1988 Act includes footpaths and bridleways as being within the definition of a road.

In *Randall* v *Motor Insurers' Bureau* [1968] 1 WLR 1900, a pedestrian pavement was accepted as forming part of the road, so that a lorry, the greater part of which was on the road, could properly be said to be using the road, even though the plaintiff and that part of the lorry which caused injury to him were at the relevant time on private property. Similarly, in *Price* v *DPP* [1990] RTR 413, where the defendant drove across a pavement (part of which was maintained at public expense and part of which was privately owned) thereby causing a pedestrian to jump out of the way, it was held that the justices were fully entitled to conclude that the pavement as a whole constituted a road and the defendant was, therefore, properly convicted of driving without reasonable consideration for another road user. In *Clarke v Kato* [1998] 1 WLR 1647, the House of Lords confirmed that whether a place which is not a highway is a 'road' within the meaning of the RTA 1988, s. 192, is a question of fact to be determined after consideration of its physical character and the function it exists to serve. Lord Clyde gave the following guidance (at p. 1652):

> One obvious feature of a road as commonly understood is that its physical limits are defined or at least definable. It should always be possible to ascertain the sides of a road or to have them ascertained. Its location should be identifiable as a route or way. It will often have a prepared surface and have been manufactured or constructed. But it may simply have developed by the repeated passage of traffic over the same area of land. It may be continuous, like a circular route, or it may come to a termination, as in the case of a cul-de-sac. A road may run on a single line without diversion or it may have branches.
>
> . . . it is also necessary to consider the function of the place in order to see if it qualifies as a road. Essentially a road serves as a means of access. It leads from one place to another and constitutes a route whereby travellers may move conveniently between the places to which and from which it leads. It is thus a defined or at least a definable way intended to enable those who pass over it to reach a destination. Its precise extent will require to be a matter of detailed decision as matter of fact in the particular circumstances. Lines may require to be drawn to determine the point at which the road ends and the destination has been reached. Where there is a door or a gate the problem may be readily resolved. Where there is no physical point which can be readily identified, then by an exercise of reasonable judgment an imaginary line will have to be drawn to mark the point where it should be held that the road has ended. Whether or not a particular area is or is not a road eventually comes to be a matter of fact.

Accordingly, a place that can reasonably be described as a car park does not, save in exceptional circumstances, qualify as a road, and in the event of a carriageway being found to exist within its bounds which does so qualify, the remaining area will retain its integrity as a car park.

In *Holliday v Henry* [1974] RTR 101, a case under the Vehicles (Excise) Act 1971, the respondent kept his car on a road, with a roller skate under each wheel, contending that by this device the car was not 'on' the road. This ingenious defence failed to find favour with the Divisional Court who allowed the prosecutor's appeal, stating that it was perfectly clear that, for the purposes of the 1971 Act, the vehicle was on the road.

In *Hawkins v Phillips* [1980] RTR 197, a filter lane or slip road was held to be part of the main carriageway for the purposes of the RTRA 1967. 'Highway' is defined as a 'public road, main route by land or water'. In *Lang v Hindhaugh* [1986] RTR 271, a footpath which was not designed for motor vehicles or passable by motor cars was held to be a highway. In giving the judgment of the court, Croom-Johnson LJ said (at p. 275):

> Highways are anywhere that the public has a right to pass and repass, either on foot or with animals or in vehicles, as the case may be. If they are only fit for travelling on foot, they are footpaths, but they will still be highways if the public has the right to use them for that purpose. This clearly was a footpath. It also was that kind of a footpath which was a highway.

In *Worth v Brooks* [1959] Crim LR 855, the grass verge by the side of a carriageway was held to form part of the highway which itself constituted a road.

The question of whether or not a particular road is one to which the public has access is one of fact and degree (*Waterfield* [1964] 1 QB 164). In *Oxford v Austin* [1981] RTR 416, consideration was given as to whether or not a car park was a road. In giving the judgment of the court, Kilner Brown J said (at p. 418):

... in all these cases there is a well established process which is founded on findings of fact. The first question which has to be asked is whether there is in fact in the ordinary understanding of the word a road, that is to say, whether or not there is a definable way between two points over which vehicles could pass. The second question is whether or not the public, or a section of the public, has access to that which has the appearance of a definable way.

The primary intention of the place does not appear to be of relevance, as in all cases it remains a question of fact whether or not the area is a road to which the public has access, irrespective of whether it is publicly or privately owned (*Price* v *DPP* [1990] RTR 413). A road which is not maintainable and manageable at public expense does not preclude it from being 'a road open to the public' as that expression refers to a road to which the public has access (*DPP* v *Cargo Handling Ltd* [1992] RTR 318).

It is a truism to state that a public place is one to which the public has access. It is not, however, definitive. Whether or not such access is sufficient for a finding that the place is a 'public place' for the purposes of the Road Traffic Acts is a question of fact and degree to be arrived at after consideration of the evidence. Justices are entitled to use their 'local knowledge' in arriving at their conclusion on this point, but it is good practice to inform the prosecution and defence so that they can comment (*Bowman* v *DPP* [1991] RTR 263).

In *Rodger* v *Normand* 1995 SLT 411, the High Court of Justiciary decided that, as members of the public chose to go to the school grounds in question, either because they were open to the public or because they were permitted to have access to them, the grounds were a 'public place' within the meaning of the RTA 1988.

In *Montgomery* v *Loney* [1959] NILR 171, which concerned a petrol station forecourt, Lord MacDermott drew the distinction between members of the general public and persons who belong to a special class of members of the public and who have 'some reason personal to them for their admittance', such as postmen, meter readers and employees going to work along a factory road.

In *DPP* v *Vivier* [1991] RTR 205, a case under the RTA 1988, s. 5(1)(a), the Divisional Court gave wide consideration to the meaning of 'public place'. V had been driving a car in a caravan park which covered 80 acres and contained between three and four miles of road. The number of people present in the caravan park, whether admitted as caravanners, campers, or their guests, varied between 800 and 3,500, depending on the time of year. The Divisional Court referred to *Montgomery* v *Loney* (which in turn had considered *Harrison* v *Hill* 1932 JC 13, a case concerning access to a farm road adjacent to the public highway) and applied the test adopted there, concluding that:

> the decision whether a place was a place to which the public had access ... was a matter of fact and degree but whether the material for consideration sufficed to support one view or the other was a matter of law.

Whether a place is a public place or not can be identified by looking at the people who use it and their reasons for doing so. In giving the judgment of the court in *DPP* v *Vivier*, Simon Brown J separated such persons into two categories, those who seek entry for the purposes of the occupier and those who seek entry for their own purposes (at p. 212):

> How then, in cases where some particular road or place is used by an identifiable category of people, should justices decide whether that category is 'special' or 'restricted' or 'particular' such as to distinguish it from the public at large? What, in short, is the touchstone by which to recognise a special class of people from members of the general public? ... one asks whether there is about those who obtain permission to enter 'some reason personal to them for their admittance'. If people come to a private house as guests, postmen or meter readers, they come for reasons personal to themselves, to serve the purposes of the occupier.

But what of the rather different type of case such as the present where those seeking entry are doing so for their own, rather than the occupier's purposes and yet are screened in the sense of having to satisfy certain conditions for admission. Does the screening process operate or endow those passing through with some special characteristic whereby they lose their identity as members of the general public and become instead a special class?

Our approach would be as follows. By the same token that one asks in the earlier type of case whether permission is being granted for a reason personal to the user, in these screening cases one must ask: do those admitted pass through the screening process for a reason, or on account of some characteristic, personal to themselves? Or are they in truth merely members of the public who are being admitted as such and processed simply so as to make them subject to payment and whatever other conditions the landowner chooses to impose.

In *DPP* v *Coulman* [1993] RTR 230, the respondent's presence in the Freight Immigration Lanes at Dover Eastern Docks after disembarkation, whilst personal to himself, was not material as it was incapable of removing him from being a member of the public and consequently the Lanes constituted a public place for the purposes of the RTA 1988, s. 5. In *Havell* v *Director of Public Prosecutions* (1994) 158 JP 680, however, use of a car park, which was readily accessible from the road, without restricted access and not marked as being private, as a member of a bona fide club whose membership was not of such a size 'that it was indistinguishable from the public at large in the locality' did not constitute use as a member of the general public; therefore the defendant's appeal against a conviction for being 'in charge' of a motor vehicle on a road or other public place whilst unfit through drink or drugs was allowed. A company car park for the use of staff, customers and other visitors is not a public place unless there is proof of actual use of that car park by members of the public (*Spence* [1999] RTR 353).

Vehicle

C1.14 The word 'vehicle' does not appear to have been given any statutory meaning, and may therefore include things as diverse as a bicycle or a poultry shed on wheels (see *Garner* v *Burr* [1951] 1 KB 31). The Concise Oxford Dictionary defines 'vehicle' as a 'carriage or conveyance of any kind used on land'.

Interpretation Provisions of Road Traffic Act 1988

C1.15   **Road Traffic Act 1988, ss. 185, 186, 189, 192**

185.—(1) In this Act—
'heavy locomotive' means a mechanically propelled vehicle which is not constructed itself to carry a load other than any of the excepted articles and the weight of which unladen exceeds 11690 kilograms,
'heavy motor car' means a mechanically propelled vehicle, not being a motor car, which is constructed itself to carry a load or passengers and the weight of which unladen exceeds 2540 kilograms,
'invalid carriage' means a mechanically propelled vehicle the weight of which unladen does not exceed 254 kilograms and which is specially designed and constructed, and not merely adapted, for the use of a person suffering from some physical defect or disability and is used solely by such a person,
'light locomotive' means a mechanically propelled vehicle which is not constructed itself to carry a load other than any of the excepted articles and the weight of which unladen does not exceed 11690 kilograms but does exceed 7370 kilograms,
'motor car' means a mechanically propelled vehicle, not being a motor cycle or an invalid carriage, which is constructed itself to carry a load or passengers and the weight of which unladen—
　　(a)　if it is constructed solely for the carriage of passengers and their effects, is adapted to carry not more than seven passengers exclusive of the driver and is fitted with tyres of such type as may be specified in regulations made by the Secretary of State, does not exceed 3050 kilograms,
　　(b)　if it is constructed or adapted for use for the conveyance of goods or burden of any description, does not exceed 3050 kilograms, or 3500 kilograms if the vehicle carries a

container or containers for holding for the purposes of its propulsion any fuel which is wholly gaseous at 17.5 degrees Celsius under a pressure of 1.013 bar or plant and material for producing such fuel,

(c)   does not exceed 2540 kilograms in a case not falling within subparagraph (a) or (b) above,

'motor cycle' means a mechanically propelled vehicle, not being an invalid carriage, with less than four wheels and the weight of which unladen does not exceed 410 kilograms,

'motor tractor' means a mechanically propelled vehicle which is not constructed itself to carry a load, other than the excepted articles, and the weight of which unladen does not exceed 7370 kilograms,

'motor vehicle' means, subject to section 20 of the Chronically Sick and Disabled Persons Act 1970 (which makes special provision about invalid carriages, within the meaning of that Act), a mechanically propelled vehicle intended or adapted for use on roads, and

'trailer' means a vehicle drawn by a motor vehicle.

(2)   In subsection (1) above 'excepted articles' means any of the following: water, fuel, accumulators and other equipment used for the purpose of propulsion, loose tools and loose equipment.

186.—(1)   For the purposes of section 185 of this Act, a side car attached to a motor vehicle, if it complies with such conditions as may be specified in regulations made by the Secretary of State, is to be regarded as forming part of the vehicle to which it is attached and as not being a trailer.

(2)   For the purposes of section 185 of this Act, in a case where a motor vehicle is so constructed that a trailer may by partial superimposition be attached to the vehicle in such a manner as to cause a substantial part of the weight of the trailer to be borne by the vehicle, that vehicle is to be deemed to be a vehicle itself constructed to carry a load.

(3)   For the purposes of section 185 of this Act, in the case of a motor vehicle fitted with a crane, dynamo, welding plant or other special appliance or apparatus which is a permanent or essentially permanent fixture, the appliance or apparatus is not to be deemed to constitute a load or goods or burden of any description, but is to be deemed to form part of the vehicle.

189.—(1)   For the purposes of the Road Traffic Acts—

(a)   a mechanically propelled vehicle being an implement for cutting grass which is controlled by a pedestrian and is not capable of being used or adapted for any other purpose,

(b)   any other mechanically propelled vehicle controlled by a pedestrian which may be specified by regulations made by the Secretary of State for the purposes of this section and section 140 of the Road Traffic Regulation Act 1984, and

(c)   an electrically assisted pedal cycle of such a class as may be prescribed by regulations so made,

is to be treated as not being a motor vehicle.

(2)   In subsection (1) above 'controlled by a pedestrian' means that the vehicle either—

(a)   is constructed or adapted for use only under such control, or

(b)   is constructed or adapted for use either under such control or under the control of a person carried on it, but is not for the time being in use under, or proceeding under, the control of a person carried on it.

192.—(1)   In this Act—

'approved testing authority' means a person authorised by the Secretary of State under section 8 of the Transport Act 1982 to carry on a vehicle testing business within the meaning of Part II of that Act,

'bridleway' means a way over which the public have the following, but no other, rights of way: a right of way on foot and a right of way on horseback or leading a horse, with or without a right to drive animals of any description along the way,

'carriage of goods' includes the haulage of goods,

'cycle' means a bicycle, a tricycle, or a cycle having four or more wheels, not being in any case a motor vehicle,

'driver', where a separate person acts as a steersman of a motor vehicle, includes (except for the purposes of section 1 of this Act) that person as well as any other person engaged in the driving of the vehicle, and 'drive' is to be interpreted accordingly, 'footpath', in relation to England and Wales, means a way over which the public have a right of way on foot only,

'goods' includes goods or burden of any description,

'goods vehicle' means a motor vehicle constructed or adapted for use for the carriage of goods, or a trailer so constructed or adapted,

'highway authority', in England and Wales, means—

(a)   in relation to a road for which he is the highway authority within the meaning of the Highways Act 1980, the Secretary of State, and

(b)   in relation to any other road, the council of the county, metropolitan district or London borough, or the Common Council of the City of London, as the case may be;

'international road haulage permit' means a licence, permit, authorisation or other document issued in pursuance of a Community instrument relating to the carriage of goods by road between member States or an international agreement to which the United Kingdom is a party and which relates to the international carriage of goods by road,

'owner', in relation to a vehicle which is the subject of a hiring agreement or hire-purchase agreement, means the person in possession of the vehicle under that agreement,

'petty sessions area' has the same meaning as in the Magistrates' Courts Act 1980,

'prescribed' means prescribed by regulations made by the Secretary of State,

'road'—

(a)   in relation to England and Wales, means any highway and any other road to which the public has access, and includes bridges over which a road passes, and

(b)   [Applies only to Scotland.],

'the Road Traffic Acts' means the Road Traffic Offenders Act 1988, the Road Traffic (Consequential Provisions) Act 1988 (so far as it reproduces the effect of provisions repealed by that Act) and this Act,

'statutory', in relation to any prohibition, restriction, requirement or provision, means contained in, or having effect under, any enactment (including any enactment contained in this Act),

'the Traffic Acts' means the Road Traffic Acts and the Road Traffic Regulation Act 1984,

'traffic sign' has the meaning given by section 64(1) of the Road Traffic Regulation Act 1984,

'tramcar' includes any carriage used on any road by virtue of an order under the Light Railways Act 1896, and

'trolley vehicle' means a mechanically propelled vehicle adapted for use on roads without rails under power transmitted to it from some external source (whether or not there is in addition a source of power on board the vehicle).

(1A)   In this Act—

(a)   any reference to a county shall be construed in relation to Wales as including a reference to a county borough; and

(b)   section 17(4) and (5) of the Local Government (Wales) Act 1994 (references to counties and districts to be construed generally in relation to Wales as references to counties and county boroughs) shall not apply.

(2)   [Applies only to Scotland.]

(3)   References in this Act to a class of vehicles are to be interpreted as references to a class defined or described by reference to any characteristics of the vehicles or to any other circumstances whatsoever and accordingly as authorising the use of 'category' to indicate a class of vehicles, however defined or described.

SECTION C2: EVIDENCE AND PROCEDURE IN ROAD TRAFFIC CASES

Notice of Intended Prosecution

Road Traffic Offenders Act 1988, ss. 1 and 2

C2.1

1.—(1) Subject to section 2 of this Act, a person shall not be convicted of an offence to which this section applies unless—

(a) he was warned at the time the offence was committed that the question of prosecuting him for some one or other of the offences to which this section applies would be taken into consideration, or

(b) within 14 days of the commission of the offence a summons (or, in Scotland, a complaint) for the offence was served on him, or

(c) within 14 days of the commission of the offence a notice of the intended prosecution specifying the nature of the alleged offence and the time and place where it is alleged to have been committed, was—

(i) in the case of an offence under section 28 or 29 of the Road Traffic Act 1988 (cycling offences), served on him,

(ii) in the case of any other offence, served on him or on the person, if any, registered as the keeper of the vehicle at the time of the commission of the offence.

(1A) A notice required by this section to be served on any person may be served on that person—

(a) by delivering it to him;

(b) by addressing it to him and leaving it at his last known address;

(c) by sending it by registered post, recorded delivery service or first class post addressed to him at his last known address.

(2) A notice shall be deemed for the purposes of subsection (1)(c) above to have been served on a person if it was sent by registered post or recorded delivery service addressed to him at his last known address, notwithstanding that the notice was returned as undelivered or was for any other reason not received by him.

(3) The requirement of subsection (1) above shall in every case be deemed to have been complied with unless and until the contrary is proved.

(4) Schedule 1 to this Act shows the offences to which this section applies.

2.—(1) The requirement of section 1(1) of this Act does not apply in relation to an offence if, at the time of the offence or immediately after it, an accident occurs owing to the presence on a road of the vehicle in respect of which the offence was committed.

(2) [Exception for fixed penalty notices.]

(3) Failure to comply with the requirement of section 1(1) of this Act is not a bar to the conviction of the accused in a case where the court is satisfied—

(a) that neither the name and address of the accused nor the name and address of the registered keeper, if any, could with reasonable diligence have been ascertained in time for a summons or, as the case may be, a complaint to be served or for a notice to be served or sent in compliance with the requirement, or

(b) that the accused by his own conduct contributed to the failure.

(4) Failure to comply with the requirement of section 1(1) of this Act in relation to an offence is not a bar to the conviction of a person of that offence by virtue of the provisions of—

(a) section 24 of this Act, or

(b) any of the enactments mentioned in section 24(6);

but a person is not to be convicted of an offence by virtue of any of those provisions if section 1 applies to the offence with which he was charged and the requirement of section 1(1) was not satisfied in relation to the offence charged.

The oral warning must have been understood by the defendant. The test was set out in *Gibson* v *Dalton* [1980] RTR 410, by Donaldson LJ (at pp. 413–14):

The obligation on the prosecutor is to warn the accused, not merely to address a warning to him or to give a warning. The mischief to which this section is directed is clear. It is that motorists are entitled to have it brought to their attention at a relatively early stage that there is likely to be a prosecution in order that they may recall and, it may be, record the facts as they occurred at the time. . . . But a warning which does not get through to the accused person is of no value at all, and prima facie, therefore, the words might be expected to mean that the warning must get through. . . .

If, viewing the matter objectively, one would expect that the words addressed to the accused person would have been heard and understood by him, then prima facie he was warned within the meaning of the statute. But it is only a prima facie case. It is open to the defendant to prove, if he can, that he did not understand or hear or appreciate the warning and therefore that he was not warned.

The warning must have been given 'at the time' the offence was committed. The latter was held to be a matter of fact and degree, and that the test was what was reasonable (*Okike* [1978] RTR 489). This test was repeated in *Stacey* [1982] RTR 20, where it was added that whether or not the chain of circumstances was unbroken and whether or not all that took place was connected with the incident were relevant factors. In addition, the court held that the issue was to be decided by the judge.

The warning must relate to one or other of the offences to which s. 1 applies (see **C8.1**). It need not specify the particular offence or offences but rather their nature. Alternative verdicts may be entered in accordance with the provisions of the Criminal Law Act 1967, s. 6(3), or the RTOA 1988, s. 24 (see **C2.15**), if the requirements of s. 1(1) have been complied with in relation to the original offence charged.

If the warning was not given at the time, then a summons must be served within 14 days. See the MCA 1980, s. 47, for a saving provision where service by post has not been proved, enabling a second summons to be issued on the same information. In other cases a notice of intended prosecution must be served within 14 days on the driver or registered keeper of the vehicle. Service is deemed under s. 1(2) if sent by registered post or recorded delivery service, as long as it was sent so as to be delivered, in the ordinary course of post, within the 14 days (*Groome* v *Driscoll* [1969] 3 All ER 1638).

Section 1(3) places the burden of proving failure to comply with the section on the defence on a balance of probabilities.

The requirement in s. 1 does not apply if there has been an accident of which the defendant was aware or to the occurrence of which he has shut his eyes but if the incident was so trivial that the driver was unaware of it a notice of intended prosecution is necessary (*Bentley* v *Dickinson* [1983] RTR 356, approving *Metropolitan Police* v *Scarlett* [1978] Crim LR 234, and distinguishing *Harding* v *Price* [1948] 1 KB 695). For these purposes, 'accident' should be given a commonsense meaning and not be restricted to untoward or unintended consequences having an adverse physical effect (*Bremner* v *Westwater* 1994 SLT 707). The principle applied in *Bentley* v *Dickinson*, however, does not extend to cases where the driver's injuries are so severe that he has no recollection of the accident (*DPP* v *Pidhajeckyj* [1991] RTR 136).

Section 2(3) contains a saving where the prosecution have acted with reasonable diligence or the accused has by his own conduct contributed to a failure to comply with s. 1.

Time-limits

C2.2   The MCA 1980, s. 127, lays down a general time-limit of six months for the laying of an information for a summary offence, subject to any enactment which expressly permits a longer period.

The RTOA 1988, s. 6, provides for an extended time-limit in relation to certain offences specified in sch. 1 to the Act (see **C8.1**). In those cases proceedings may be commenced within a period of six months from the date on which sufficient evidence came to the prosecutor's knowledge. That date is proved by a signed certificate. No proceedings are to be brought more than three years after the offence.

A traffic examiner employed by the vehicle inspectorate to investigate traffic offences, but not authorised to decide whether to prosecute, is not a prosecutor for the purposes of the 1988 Act (*Swan* v *Vehicle Inspectorate* [1997] RTR 187).

Duty to Produce Licence to Court

Road Traffic Offenders Act 1988, s. 7   C2.3

A person who is prosecuted for an offence involving obligatory or discretionary disqualification and who is the holder of a licence must—
    (a)   cause it to be delivered to the clerk of the court not later than the day before the date appointed for the hearing, or
    (b)   post it, at such a time that in the ordinary course of post it would be delivered not later than that day, in a letter duly addressed to the clerk and either registered or sent by the recorded delivery service, or
    (c)   have it with him at the hearing,
and the foregoing obligations imposed on him as respects the licence also apply as respects the counterpart.

'Licence' includes a Community licence (RTOA 1988, s. 91A(1)).

Admissibility of Highway Code

The RTA 1988, s. 38(8), defines 'the Highway Code' as the Code comprising directions   C2.4 for the guidance of persons using roads issued under the RTA 1930, s. 45, and subsequently revised.

Section 38(7) provides that a failure to observe a provision of the Code shall not of itself render a person liable to criminal proceedings, but any such failure may be relied upon by any party to civil or criminal proceedings as tending to establish or negative any liability in question in those proceedings. The subsection does not provide for the admissibility of evidence of due observance of the Code. But a defendant may rely on the failure of any other person to observe a relevant provision of the Code (*Baker* v *E. Longhurst & Sons Ltd* [1933] 2 KB 461; *Croston* v *Vaughan* [1938] 1 KB 540).

The Code itself is issued by the Secretary of State under authority of Parliament, pursuant to the RTA 1988, s. 38, and is Crown Copyright. The latest edition was published in 1999. Any copy of it purporting to be printed under the superintendence or authority of Her Majesty's Stationery Office is conclusive evidence of the contents of the Code (Documentary Evidence Act 1882, s. 2).

Evidence by Certificate as to Driver, Owner or User

Road Traffic Offenders Act 1988, s. 11   C2.5

(1)   In any proceedings in England and Wales for an offence to which this section applies, a certificate in the prescribed form, purporting to be signed by a constable and certifying that a person specified in the certificate stated to the constable—
    (a)   that a particular mechanically propelled vehicle was being driven or used by, or belonged to, that person on a particular occasion, or
    (b)   that a particular mechanically propelled vehicle on a particular occasion was used by, or belonged to, a firm and that he was, at the time of the statement, a partner in that firm, or
    (c)   that a particular mechanically propelled vehicle on a particular occasion was used by, or belonged to, a corporation and that he was, at the time of the statement, a director, officer or employee of that corporation,

shall be admissible as evidence for the purpose of determining by whom the vehicle was being driven or used, or to whom it belonged, as the case may be, on that occasion.

(2) Nothing in subsection (1) above makes a certificate admissible as evidence in proceedings for an offence except in a case where and to the like extent to which oral evidence to the like effect would have been admissible in those proceedings.

(3) Nothing in subsection (1) above makes a certificate admissible as evidence in proceedings for an offence—

(a) unless a copy of it has, not less than seven days before the hearing or trial, been served in the prescribed manner on the person charged with the offence, or

(b) if that person, not later than three days before the hearing or trial or within such further time as the court may in special circumstances allow, serves a notice in the prescribed form and manner on the prosecutor requiring attendance at the trial of the person who signed the certificate.

The form of the certificate and rules for service are prescribed by the Evidence by Certificate Rules 1961 (SI 1961 No. 248). The functions of a constable have been extended to traffic wardens by the Functions of Traffic Wardens Order 1970 (SI 1970 No. 1958).

Section 11 provides an exception to the 'hearsay' rule. The offences to which the section applies are set out in sch. 1 to the RTOA 1988 (see **C8.1**).

Proof of Identity of Driver in Summary Proceedings

C2.6   Road Traffic Offenders Act 1988, s. 12

(1) Where on the summary trial in England and Wales of an information for an offence to which this subsection applies—

(a) it is proved to the satisfaction of the court, on oath or in manner prescribed by rules made under section 144 of the Magistrates' Courts Act 1980, that a requirement under section 172(2) of the Road Traffic Act 1988 to give information as to the identity of the driver of a particular vehicle on the particular occasion to which the information relates has been served on the accused by post, and

(b) a statement in writing is produced to the court purporting to be signed by the accused that the accused was the driver of that vehicle on that occasion,

the court may accept that statement as evidence that the accused was the driver of that vehicle on that occasion,

(2) Schedule 1 to this Act shows the offences to which subsection (1) above applies.

(3) [Enacts a similar provision to subsection (1) above in relation to offences under the RTRA 1984.]

The relevant rule for proving service is the Magistrates' Courts Rules 1981, r. 67(2).

Admissibility of Records of Secretary of State

C2.7   **Road Traffic Offenders Act 1988, s. 13**

(1) This section applies to a statement contained in a document purporting to be—

(a) a part of the records maintained by the Secretary of State in connection with any functions exercisable by him by virtue of part III of the Road Traffic Act 1988 or a part of any other records maintained by the Secretary of State with respect to vehicles, or

(b) a copy of a document forming part of those records, or

(c) a note of any information contained in those records,

and to be authenticated by a person authorised in that behalf by the Secretary of State.

(2) A statement to which this section applies shall be admissible in any proceedings as evidence (in Scotland, sufficient evidence) of any fact stated in it to the same extent as oral evidence of that fact is admissible in those proceedings.

(3) In the preceding subsections, except in Scotland—

'copy', in relation to a document, means anything onto which information recorded in the document has been copied, by whatever means and whether directly or indirectly;

'document' means anything in which information of any description is recorded; and

'statement' means any representation of fact, however made.

(3A)   In any case where—

(a)   a person is convicted by a magistrates' court of a summary offence under the Traffic Acts or the Road Traffic (Driver Licensing and Information Systems) Act 1989,

(b)   a statement to which this section applies is produced to the court in the proceedings,

(c)   the statement specifies an alleged previous conviction of the accused of an offence involving obligatory endorsement or an order made on the conviction, and

(d)   the accused is not present in person before the court when the statement is so produced,

the court may take account of the previous conviction or order as if the accused had appeared and admitted it.

(3B)   Section 104 of the Magistrates' Courts Act 1980 (under which the previous convictions may be adduced in the absence of the accused after giving him seven days' notice of them) does not limit the effect of subsection (3A) above.

(4)   In any case where—

(a)   a statement to which this section applies is produced to a magistrates' court in any proceedings for an offence involving obligatory or discretionary disqualification other than a summary offence under any of the enactments mentioned in subsection (3A)(a) above,

(b)   the statement specifies an alleged previous conviction of an accused person of any such offence or any order made on the conviction,

(c)   it is proved to the satisfaction of the court, on oath or in such manner as may be prescribed by rules under section 144 of the Magistrates' Courts Act 1980, that not less than seven days before the statement is so produced a notice was served on the accused, in such form and manner as may be so prescribed, specifying the previous conviction or order and stating that it is proposed to bring it to the notice of the court in the event of or, as the case may be, in view of his conviction, and

(d)   the accused is not present in person before the court when the statement is so produced,

the court may take account of the previous conviction or order as if the accused had appeared and admitted it.

(5)   Nothing in the preceding provisions of this section enables evidence to be given in respect of any matter other than a matter of a description prescribed by regulations made by the Secretary of State.

(6)   [Power to make regulations.]

The records to be maintained and which are admissible (see s. 13(5)) are set out in the Vehicle and Driving Licences Records (Evidence) Regulations 1970 (SI 1970 No. 1997). They usually take the form of a computer printout from DVLA at Swansea. For the prescribed manner of proving previous convictions, see the Magistrates' Courts Rules 1981, r. 72. The form of the document is a computer printout appropriately endorsed.

Records Kept by Operators of Goods Vehicles

Road Traffic Offenders Act 1988, s. 14   C2.8

In any proceedings for an offence under section 40A of the Road Traffic Act 1988 or for a contravention of or failure to comply with construction and use requirements (within the meaning of part II of the Road Traffic Act 1988) or regulations under section 74 of that Act, any record purporting to be made and authenticated in accordance with regulations under that section shall be evidence . . . of the matters stated in the record and of its due authentication.

Admissibility of Vehicle Markings as Evidence of Weight or Date

Road Traffic Offenders Act 1988, s. 17   C2.9

(1)   If in any proceedings for an offence under section 40A, 41A, 41B or 42 of the Road Traffic Act 1988 (using vehicle in dangerous condition or contravention of construction and use regulations)—

(a)   any question arises as to a weight of any description specified in the plating certificate for a goods vehicle, and

    (b)   a weight of that description is marked on the vehicle,
it shall be assumed, unless the contrary is proved, that the weight marked on the vehicle is the weight so specified.

    (2)   If, in any proceedings for an offence—

    (a)   under part II of the Road Traffic Act 1988, except sections 47 and 75, or

    (b)   under section 174(2) or (5) (false statements and deception) of that Act,

any question arises as to the date of manufacture of a vehicle, a date purporting to be such a date and marked on the vehicle in pursuance of regulations under that part of that Act shall be evidence . . . that the vehicle was manufactured on the date so marked.

    (3)   If in any proceedings for the offence of driving a vehicle on a road, or causing or permitting a vehicle to be so driven, in contravention of a prohibition under section 70(2) of the Road Traffic Act 1988 any question arises whether a weight of any description has been reduced to a limit imposed by construction and use requirements, or so that it has ceased to be excessive, the burden of proof shall lie on the accused.

Admissibility of Evidence from Prescribed Devices

C2.10

Road Traffic Offenders Act 1988, s. 20

    (1)   Evidence (which in Scotland shall be sufficient evidence) of a fact relevant to proceedings for an offence to which this section applies may be given by the production of—

    (a)   a record produced by a prescribed device, and

    (b)   (in the same or another document) a certificate as to the circumstances in which the record was produced signed by a constable or by a person authorised by or on behalf of the chief officer of police for the police area in which the offence is alleged to have been committed;

but subject to the following provisions of this section.

    (2)   [Offences to which section applies.]

    (3)   [Power to add offences.]

    (4)   [Requirement of approval of devices.]

    (5)   [Approval may be subject to conditions concerning the purposes and use of the device.]

    (6)   In proceedings for an offence to which this section applies, evidence (which in Scotland shall be sufficient evidence)—

    (a)   of a measurement made by a device, or of the circumstances in which it was made, or

    (b)   that a device was of a type approved for the purposes of this section, or that any conditions subject to which an approval was given were satisfied,

may be given by the production of a document which is signed as mentioned in subsection (1) above and which, as the case may be, gives particulars of the measurement or of the circumstances in which it was made, or states that the device was of such a type or that, to the best of the knowledge and belief of the person making the statement, all such conditions were satisfied.

    (7)   For the purposes of this section a document purporting to be a record of the kind mentioned in subsection (1) above, or to be a certificate or other document signed as mentioned in that subsection or in subsection (6) above, shall be deemed to be such a record, or to be so signed, unless the contrary is proved.

    (8)   Nothing in subsection (1) or (6) above makes a document admissible as evidence in proceedings for an offence unless a copy of it has, not less than seven days before the hearing or trial, been served on the person charged with the offence; and nothing in those subsections makes a document admissible as evidence of anything other than the matters shown on a record produced by a prescribed device if that person, not less than three days before the hearing or trial or within such further time as the court may in special circumstances allow, serves a notice on the prosecutor requiring attendance at the hearing or trial of the person who signed the document.

As to the requirement for corroboration of the opinion evidence of a witness concerning speed in such cases, and the use of measurements as corroboration, see the RTRA 1984, s. 89; *Nicholas* v *Penny* [1950] 2 KB 466; and *Swain* v *Gillet* [1974] RTR 446. This section applies to offences under the RTRA 1984, ss. 16, 17(4), 88(7) and 89(1) (speeding offences), offences under that Act in respect of bus lanes or routes for use by buses only, and offences under the RTA 1988, s. 36(1) (failure to comply with automatic traffic light signal).

In the case of any offence to which s. 20 applies, the prosecution will be able to rely on evidence produced by automatic devices of a specified and approved type, without the need for corroboration. To date such evidence is photographic although s. 20(6) envisages the recording of, amongst other things, distance travelled and time taken. The evidence must be accompanied by the appropriate certificate signed by a constable or other authorised person, and, where there is such a certificate, s. 20(7) imposes the burden on the defence of disproving that the document is a record. In addition a copy of the document, or documents, must be served on the person charged, at least seven days before the hearing or trial. The defence may serve a counter-notice requiring the presence of the signatory to the certificate, presumably so that the validity or accuracy of the document may be challenged. See also **C5.81**.

A device designed or adapted for measuring by radar the speed of motor vehicles is a prescribed device for the purposes of s. 20 (Road Traffic Offenders (Prescribed Devices) Order 1992 (SI 1992 No. 1209)); a device designed or adapted for recording, by photographic or other image recording means, the position of vehicles in relation to light signals is also a prescribed device (Road Traffic Offenders (Prescribed Devices) (No. 2) Order 1992 (SI 1992 No. 2843)). A camera designed or adapted to record the presence of a vehicle on an area of road which is a bus lane or a route for use by buses only is a prescribed device (Road Traffic Offenders (Additional Offences and Prescribed Devices) Order 1997 (SI 1997 No. 384)); as is a device designed or adapted for recording the measurement of a motor vehicle's speed by capturing two images at predetermined positions on a road, digitally recording each image and the time at which it was captured and calculating the average speed of the vehicle over the distance between those two positions (Road Traffic Offenders (Prescribed Devices) Order 1999 (SI 1999 No. 162)).

In *Roberts* v *DPP* [1994] RTR 31, the Divisional Court held that the prosecution were required to prove that the Home Secretary had approved the use of the device (in this case a Falcon radar gun) before the measurement of speed could be admitted in evidence. Similarly, in *Pickard* v *Carmichael* 1995 SLT 675, the High Court of Justiciary observed that it could not be said that it was within judicial knowledge that the Gatso mini radar device was an approved one, so that no inference of approval was possible in the absence of explicit evidence.

If the device in question is a computer, the requirements of the PACE 1984, s. 69, must be complied with (see **F8.31** *et seq.*, particularly *Shephard* [1993] AC 380). See also *Darby* v *DPP* [1995] RTR 294, *East West Transport Ltd* v *DPP* [1996] RTR 184, and **C5.28**.

Use of Specimens

Road Traffic Offenders Act 1988, s. 15   **C2.11**

(1)   This section and section 16 of this Act apply in respect of proceedings for an offence under section 3A, 4 or 5 of the Road Traffic Act 1988 (driving offences connected with drink or drugs); and expressions used in this section and section 16 of this Act have the same meaning as in sections 3A to 10 of that Act.

(2)   Evidence of the proportion of alcohol or any drug in a specimen of breath, blood or urine provided by the accused shall, in all cases (including cases where the specimen was not provided in connection with the alleged offence), be taken into account and, subject to subsection (3) below, it shall be assumed that the proportion of alcohol in the accused's breath, blood or urine at the time of the alleged offence was not less than in the specimen.

(3)   That assumption shall not be made if the accused proves—

(a)　that he consumed alcohol before he provided the specimen and—

(i)　in relation to an offence under section 3A, after the time of the alleged offence, and

(ii)　otherwise, after he had ceased to drive, attempt to drive or be in charge of a vehicle on a road or other public place, and

(b)　that had he not done so the proportion of alcohol in his breath, blood or urine would not have exceeded the prescribed limit and, if it is alleged that he was unfit to drive through drink, would not have been such as to impair his ability to drive properly.

(4)　A specimen of blood shall be disregarded unless it was taken from the accused with his consent by a medical practitioner.

(5)　Where, at the time a specimen of blood or urine was provided by the accused, he asked to be provided with such a specimen, evidence of the proportion of alcohol or any drug found in the specimen is not admissible on behalf of the prosecution unless—

(a)　the specimen in which the alcohol or drug was found is one of two parts into which the specimen provided by the accused was divided at the time it was provided, and

(b)　the other part was supplied to the accused.

Only the first two specimens of breath are admissible (*Howard v Hallett* [1984] RTR 353). This, it is submitted, extends to make only the first specimen of blood or urine admissible. Where blood has been taken on two occasions and then divided the resulting analysis is inadmissible (*Dear v DPP* [1988] RTR 148). In *DPP v Elstob* [1992] RTR 45, it was held that the expression 'divided at the time' in s. 15(5)(a) meant that the taking and division of the specimen had to be closely linked in time and performed as part of the same event, even though it is inevitable that some time will pass between the two acts. It is important to maintain the integrity of what occurs, and therefore it is desirable (albeit not strictly necessary for compliance with the statute) for the defendant to be present. Incorrect labelling by a police doctor of the part specimen handed to the defendant, in pursuance of s. 15(5)(b), is not fatal to the admissibility of evidence relating to the proportion of alcohol or drug found in the specimen, unless it is supplied in such a way as to deter or prevent the defendant from having it analysed (*Butler v DPP* [1990] RTR 377). Where the laboratory analysing the sample sub-divides it for the purpose of analysis, it is lawful to use the average result and not necessary to use only the lowest result (*DPP v Welsh* (1997) 161 JP 57). However, for evidence of a specimen requested under the RTA 1988, s. 7(1), to be admissible under the RTOA 1988, s. 15(2), the procedural requirements of the RTA 1988, ss. 7 and 8 (see **C5.25** *et seq*. and **C5.35**), including the mandatory warning under s. 7(7), must be fully complied with, even where no prejudice results from a breach of those requirements (*Murray v DPP* [1993] RTR 209).

The assumption in s. 15(2) relates to the proportion of alcohol in the defendant's breath. On a plea of guilty there is no need to produce the original printout. If there is a genuine change of plea, reasonable adjournments must be given to the prosecution if there is a problem about production of the printout (*Tower Bridge Magistrates' Court, ex parte DPP* (1988) 86 Cr App R 257).

As a breath-testing machine is a computer (*Castle v Cross* [1984] 1 WLR 1372), affirmative evidence in the form of a signed certificate (whether produced by the device or in a separate document) or by means of oral evidence called by or on behalf of the prosecution is needed to satisfy s. 69 of the PACE 1984 (*Medway Magistrates' Court, ex parte Goddard* [1995] RTR 206). For the PACE 1984, s. 69 and sch. 3, see **F8.31**.

A failure to produce the printout in evidence in a case where the officer does not give evidence of the reading, his familiarity with the instrument, its working or calibration means that the prosecution have failed to establish a case against the defendant (*Hasler v DPP* [1989] RTR 148). Evidence of the breath alcohol reading, in the absence of the statement automatically produced by the machine, is not, in itself, sufficient (*Owen v Chesters* [1985] RTR 191). The prosecution should establish that the machine is working correctly by evidence relating to the calibration. An officer giving such evidence has to be trained in the use and manner of performance of the machine so as to understand the calibration process and to recognise that, unless the result of the process lies within accepted limits, the device may be unreliable (*Denneny* v *Harding* [1986] RTR 350). It is now clear that the operator of the Intoximeter is entitled to give oral evidence, without production of the printout being a pre-condition, so as to support a conviction, provided that the evidence demonstrates the actual reading on which the charge is founded and demonstrates that the device was working properly and reliable, i.e. by the operator looking at the figures on the device's display (*Thom* v *DPP* [1994] RTR 11; *Greenaway* v *DPP* [1994] RTR 17).

Challenging the reliability of the device is notoriously difficult. In *Tower Bridge Magistrates' Court, ex parte DPP* [1989] RTR 118, the Divisional Court quashed a witness summons issued by the magistrates' court for a police officer to produce the service record and machine log in respect of the device used, castigating the defence for engaging in a fishing expedition. Evidence of the amount of alcohol allegedly taken prior to providing the breath-test may be used (*Cracknell* v *Willis* [1988] AC 450), although this will often depend on the evidence of the defendant alone and, in the absence of the right to provide a sample of blood or urine, the defendant is unlikely to prevail. For example, in *Lafferty* v *DPP* [1995] Crim LR 429, the defendant adduced evidence as to the amount of alcohol consumed supported by expert evidence indicating that, on such a level of consumption, the Intoximeter reading should not have been as high as it was; if the defendant's evidence to that effect was accepted, it followed that the device was unreliable. The Divisional Court decided that the justices had properly admitted evidence of the results of the roadside breath test, as this went to the veracity of the defendant when attacking the reliability of the device, which attack the prosecution was entitled to rebut by any relevant evidence. It is not strictly necessary to adduce expert evidence establishing the reading which should have been produced on the basis of what the defendant claims to have consumed (*DPP* v *Spurrier* (1999) *The Times*, 12 August 1999) but, except in exceptional circumstances, to do so is always likely to make the defendant's evidence more credible.

Where a defendant has been offered the blood/urine option and he initially refuses but then consents, the prosecution are still entitled to rely on the breath specimens. The statutory procedure ends when the defendant rejects the option (*Smith* v *DPP* [1989] RTR 159). Where the blood/urine option is taken, the breath samples become simply a step leading to the procuring of the evidence to be used in the case against the defendant, therefore there is no requirement to prove the reliability of the device (*Prince* v *DPP* [1996] Crim LR 343).

Where there are two specimens of blood or urine which differ in the amount of alcohol contained in them, it is for the justices to evaluate the evidence before them. If in any reasonable doubt, they should choose that most favourable to the defendant (*Froggatt* v *Allcock* [1975] RTR 372n).

The Statutory Defence

Section 15(3) of the RTOA 1988 (see **C2.11**) affords a defence to a person charged with **C2.12** an offence under s. 3A, 4 or 5 of the RTA 1988, see **C3.14**, **C5.9** and **C5.16**. In the case of an offence under s. 3A, evidence of post-accident consumption of alcohol is admissible even if the accused drove after the accident because s. 3A looks at the state of intoxication of the accused at the time that the cause of death arose. This defence was considered in *Dawson* v *Lunn* [1986] RTR 234, where Robert Goff LJ said (at p. 238):

> . . . there are circumstances in which, as a matter of common sense, laymen can reach a
> perfectly sensible conclusion unaided by scientific evidence. We need only to take the simple

case of somebody who satisfies the justices on the evidence that he had drunk only a small amount before driving, and that after ceasing to drive he had drunk a substantial quantity of alcohol. The justices can then conclude as laymen, reliably and confidently ... that the defendant has satisfied them, on the balance of probabilities, that he has consumed alcohol after ceasing to drive and that had he not done so the proportion of alcohol in his breath, or blood, or urine would not have exceeded the prescribed limit. But there must be cases where the justices cannot sensibly draw that conclusion themselves unaided by expert evidence.

The court then went on to adopt the passage in *Pugsley* v *Hunter* [1973] 1 WLR 578 (a case on 'special reasons'), where Lord Widgery CJ observed that 'unless the case really is an obvious one . . . the only way in which a defendant can discharge the onus is by calling medical evidence'. The court also discouraged reliance upon extracts from scientific journals. This case was distinguished in *DPP* v *Lowden* [1993] RTR 349, where, despite apparent discrepancies, the justices were said to be entitled to find that the defendant had discharged the onus as they had had the benefit of expert evidence.

In *Rynsard* v *Spalding* [1986] RTR 303, the defendant, who was charged with an offence of driving with excess alcohol, successfully made out the statutory defence. The justices convicted the defendant of being 'in charge'. The court held that the use of the word 'or' in the RTA 1972, s. 6, was disjunctive and set aside the conviction. Whilst it may be open to amend a charge of driving with excess alcohol (as long as the time-limits are complied with) to one of attempting to drive or being in charge, once the prosecution have 'nailed their colours to the mast' and closed their case the magistrates should not substitute an alternative charge.

In *Beauchamp-Thompson* v *DPP* [1988] RTR 54 (a case also dealing with 'special reasons'), the appellant contended that, although he was above the limit at the time that the specimen was provided, expert evidence could be called to show that he was or may have been below the limit at the time he was driving. The Divisional Court held, however, that the existence of the statutory exception meant that the assumption contained in s. 15(2) was irrebuttable. This case has been followed in *Millard* v *DPP* (1990) 91 Cr App R 108. On the face of it both cases appear to be in conflict with s. 15(3) but their effect is limited to a challenge of the specimen on the basis that drink taken before driving may not have entered the defendant's system at the time he was driving although it had at the time of providing the specimen.

A specimen of blood must be taken by a medical practitioner and may only be taken with the consent of the defendant.

A failure to notify the accused of the procedure set out in s. 15(5) was held to be fatal in *Anderton* v *Lythgoe* [1985] RTR 395. See also *Dear* v *DPP* [1988] RTR 148. Where a point is taken on the procedure, in what is now s. 15(5), it must be taken before evidence of the analysis is adduced (*Hudson* v *Hornby* [1973] RTR 4).

Documentary Evidence as to Specimens

C2.13

Road Traffic Offenders Act 1988, s. 16

(1) Evidence of the proportion of alcohol or a drug in a specimen of breath, blood or urine may, subject to subsections (3) and (4) below and to section 15(5) of this Act, be given by the production of a document or documents purporting to be whichever of the following is appropriate, that is to say—

(a) a statement automatically produced by the device by which the proportion of alcohol in a specimen of breath was measured and a certificate signed by a constable (which may but need not be contained in the same document as the statement) that the statement relates to a specimen provided by the accused at the date and time shown in the statement, and

(b) a certificate signed by an authorised analyst as to the proportion of alcohol or any drug found in a specimen of blood or urine identified in the certificate.

(2)   Subject to subsections (3) and (4) below, evidence that a specimen of blood was taken from the accused with his consent by a medical practitioner may be given by the production of a document purporting to certify that fact and to be signed by a medical practitioner.

(3)   Subject to subsection (4) below—

(a)   a document purporting to be such a statement or such a certificate (or both such a statement and such a certificate) as is mentioned in subsection (1)(a) above is admissible in evidence on behalf of the prosecution in pursuance of this section only if a copy of it either has been handed to the accused when the document was produced or has been served on him not later than seven days before the hearing, and

(b)   any other document is so admissible only if a copy of it has been served on the accused not later than seven days before the hearing.

(4)   A document purporting to be a certificate (or so much of a document as purports to be a certificate) is not so admissible if the accused, not later than three days before the hearing or within such further time as the court may in special circumstances allow, has served notice on the prosecutor requiring the attendance at the hearing of the person by whom the document purports to be signed.

(5)   [Applies only to Scotland.]

(6)   A copy of a certificate required by this section to be served on the accused or a notice required by this section to be served on the prosecutor may be served personally or sent by registered post or recorded delivery service.

(6A)   [Applies only to alleged offences into which no criminal investigation began before 1 April 1997.]

(7)   [Defines 'authorised analyst'.]

In *Garner* v *DPP* (1990) 90 Cr App R 179 (following *Castle* v *Cross* [1984] 1 WLR 1372), the Court of Appeal held that the admissibility of the 'statement automatically produced' did not just arise through the RTOA 1988, s. 16(1), but the statement is in itself an admissible document and represented real evidence as long as it is properly produced. The purpose and effect of s. 16 is to enable the 'statement automatically produced' together with an appropriate certificate to be tendered at the hearing and to 'be capable of establishing the facts stated in it without the necessity of anybody being called' (per Stocker LJ at p. 184). In other words, s. 16 is permissive and provides one method for proving the proportion of alcohol in a specimen of breath (*Thom* v *DPP* [1994] RTR 11).

The printout or 'statement automatically produced by the device' and the operator's certificate may be separate or contained in the same document. Section 16(4) relates to the operator's, medical practitioner's and analyst's certificates, and not to the 'statement automatically produced' (*Temple* v *Botha* [1985] Crim LR 517). In the absence of the printout, the prosecution may call evidence as to the proper working of the machine (see **C2.11**). A printout which is timed according to Greenwich Mean Time is admissible even though British Summer Time was operating at the time of the incident (*Parker* v *DPP* [1993] RTR 283). Indeed, in *DPP* v *McKeown* [1997] 1 WLR 295, a printout recording a wholly inaccurate time due to a malfunctioning clock was still held admissible because the malfunction did not affect the way in which the computer processed, stored or retrieved the information used to generate the statement in evidence. This reasoning has been applied to typographical abnormalities on the face of printouts which clearly do not affect the proper functioning of the device (*Reid* v *DPP* [1999] RTR 357; *DPP* v *Barber* (1999) 163 JP 457).

If the defendant wishes to challenge the lack of service of any of the certificates, it must be done before the contents are put in evidence (*Banks* [1972] 1 WLR 346).

The certificate under s. 16(2) is termed an HORT/5. Section 16(3) imposes a duty to serve the analyst's certificate which cannot be waived (*Tobi* v *Nicholas* [1988] RTR 343). However, where only the lack of a signature on the certificate is in issue, and not service itself, strict proof of service can be waived (*Louis* v *DPP* [1998] RTR 354). Section 16(6) provides for service of the various notices, and s. 16(4) for the service of a counter-notice. This procedure is distinct from that contained in the CJA 1967, s. 9.

Notification as to Disabilities

C2.14   **Road Traffic Offenders Act 1988, s. 22**

(1)   If in any proceedings for an offence committed in respect of a motor vehicle it appears to the court that the accused may be suffering from any relevant disability or prospective disability (within the meaning of part III of the Road Traffic Act 1988) the court must notify the Secretary of State.

(2)   A notice sent by a court to the Secretary of State in pursuance of this section must be sent in such manner and to such address and contain such particulars as the Secretary of State may determine.

'Relevant disability' means the disabilities set out in the Motor Vehicles (Driving Licences) Regulations 1996, part VI. There must be some evidence of such a disability before the court may notify the Secretary of State.

Alternative Verdicts

C2.15   **Road Traffic Offenders Act 1988, s. 24**

(1)   Where—

(a)   a person charged with an offence under a provision of the Road Traffic Act 1988 specified in the first column of the table below (where the general nature of the offences is also indicated) is found not guilty of that offence, but

(b)   the allegations in the indictment or information (or in Scotland complaint) amount to or include an allegation of an offence under one or more of the provisions specified in the corresponding entry in the second column,

he may be convicted of that offence or of one or more of those offences.

Offence charged	Alternative
Section 1 (causing death by dangerous driving)	Section 2 (dangerous driving) Section 3 (careless, and inconsiderate, driving)
Section 2 (dangerous driving)	Section 3 (careless, and inconsiderate, driving)
Section 3A (causing death by careless driving when under influence of drink or drugs)	Section 3 (careless, and inconsiderate, driving) Section 4(1) (driving when unfit to drive through drink or drugs) Section 5(1)(a) (driving with excess alcohol in breath, blood or urine) Section 7(6) (failing to provide specimen)
Section 4(1) (driving or attempting to drive when unfit to drive through drink or drugs)	Section 4(2) (being in charge of a vehicle when unfit to drive through drink or drugs)
Section 5(1)(a) (driving or attempting to drive with excess alcohol in breath, blood or urine)	Section 5(1)(b) (being in charge of a vehicle with excess alcohol in breath, blood or urine)
Section 28 (dangerous cycling)	Section 29 (careless, and inconsiderate, cycling)

(2)   Where the offence with which a person is charged is an offence under section 3A of the Road Traffic Act 1988, subsection (1) above shall not authorise his conviction of any offence of attempting to drive.

(3)   Where a person is charged with having committed an offence under section 4(1) or 5(1)(a) of the Road Traffic Act 1988 by driving a vehicle, he may be convicted of having committed an offence under the provision in question by attempting to drive.

(4)   Where by virtue of this section a person is convicted before the Crown Court of an offence triable only summarily, the court shall have the same powers and duties as a magistrates' court would have had on convicting him of that offence.

(5)   [Applies only to Scotland.]

(6)   This section has effect without prejudice to section 6(3) of the Criminal Law Act 1967 (alternative verdicts on trial on indictment) . . . and section 23 of this Act.

Where the offence charged is one under the RTA 1988, s. 4(1) (driving, or attempting to drive, when unfit through drink or drugs) or s. 5(1)(a) (driving, or attempting to drive, with excess alcohol in breath, blood or urine), it is open to the magistrates to convict of the alternative offence of 'being in charge of' or, if the allegation is of driving, to convict of the alternative of attempting to drive (s. 24(3)). However, s. 24(2) states that where the offence charged is that under the RTA 1988, s. 3A, no alternative verdict involving attempting to drive is authorised. If the conviction is in the Crown Court and the offence is one that is triable only summarily, for example, where the conviction is under s. 3 of the 1988 Act (careless driving) as an alternative to a count alleging causing death by dangerous driving under s. 1, the powers of the Crown Court will be the same as those of the magistrates (s. 24(4)).

The six-month time-limit imposed by the MCA 1980, s. 127, does not apply (*Coventry Justices, ex parte Sayers* [1979] RTR 22).

In *Jeavons* [1990] RTR 263, a case of reckless driving, the prosecution alleged that the accused and another were racing, although this was denied in interview. The co-accused pleaded guilty and the appellant did not give evidence. The judge did not leave an alternative verdict of careless driving to the jury. His decision was upheld on the basis that it is for the judge to exclude irrelevant charges and allegations as well as to ensure that the indictment covers offences which the facts might disclose. In the instant case, if the prosecution's case of 'racing' was rejected by the jury there was, in the circumstances, no ground for an allegation of careless driving. In *Griffiths* [1998] Crim LR 348, the Court of Appeal held that, in the absence of a verdict of not guilty on the count of dangerous driving, there was no power under s. 24(1) for the jury to return a verdict of guilty of careless driving. Where the defendant has already been acquitted of the 'lesser' charge (by the prosecution offering no evidence or otherwise), the alternative verdict is not available on the trial of the 'greater' charge and that should be made clear to the arbiters of fact (*DPP* v *Khan* [1997] RTR 82). For a full discussion of alternative verdicts and the relevant procedure, see **D16.18** *et seq.*, particularly **D16.30**.

Information as to Date of Birth and Sex

Road Traffic Offenders Act 1988, s. 25   C2.16

(1)   If on convicting a person of an offence involving obligatory or discretionary disqualification or of such other offence as may be prescribed by regulations under section 105 of the Road Traffic Act 1988 the court does not know his date of birth, the court must order him to give that date to the court in writing.

(2)   If a court convicting a person of such an offence in a case where—

(a)   notification has been given to the clerk of a court in pursuance of section 12(4) of the Magistrates' Courts Act 1980 (written pleas of guilty) . . . and

(b)   the notification . . . did not include a statement of the person's sex,

does not know the person's sex, the court must order the person to give that information to the court in writing.

(3)   A person who knowingly fails to comply with an order under subsection (1) or (2) above is guilty of an offence.

(4)   Nothing in section 56(5) of the Criminal Justice Act 1967 (where magistrates' court commits a person to the Crown Court to be dealt with, certain powers and duties transferred to that court) applies to any duty imposed upon a magistrates' court by subsection (1) or (2) above.

(5)   Where a person has given his date of birth in accordance with this section or section 8 of this Act, the Secretary of State may serve on that person a notice in writing requiring him to provide the Secretary of State—

(a)   with such evidence in that person's possession or obtainable by him as the Secretary of State may specify for the purpose of verifying that date, and

(b)   if his name differs from his name at the time of his birth, with a statement in writing specifying his name at that time.

(6)   A person who knowingly fails to comply with a notice under subsection (5) above is guilty of an offence.

(7)   A notice to be served on any person under subsection (5) above may be served on him by delivering it to him or by leaving it at his proper address or by sending it to him by post; and for the purposes of this subsection and section 7 of the Interpretation Act 1978 in its application to this subsection the proper address of any person shall be his latest address as known to the person serving the notice.

Failure to comply with s. 25 is punishable by a fine up to level 3.

C2.17   Interim Disqualification

Road Traffic Offenders Act 1988, s. 26

(1)   Where a magistrates' court—

(a)   commits an offender to the Crown Court under subsection (1) of section 56 of the Criminal Justice Act 1967, or any enactment to which that section applies, or

(b)   remits an offender to another magistrates' court under section 39 of the Magistrates' Courts Act 1980,

to be dealt with for an offence involving obligatory or discretionary disqualification, it may order him to be disqualified until he has been dealt with in respect of the offence.

(2)   Where a court in England and Wales—

(a)   defers passing sentence on an offender under section 1 of the Powers of Criminal Courts Act 1973 in respect of an offence involving obligatory or discretionary disqualification, or

(b)   adjourns after convicting an offender of such an offence but before dealing with him for the offence,

it may order the offender to be disqualified until he has been dealt with in respect of the offence.

(3)   [Applies only to Scotland.]

(4)   Subject to subsection (5) below, an order under this section shall cease to have effect at the end of the period of six months beginning with the day on which it is made, if it has not ceased to have effect before that time.

(5)   [Applies only to Scotland.]

(6)   Where a court orders a person to be disqualified under this section ('the first order'), no court shall make a further order under this section in respect of the same offence or any offence in respect of which an order could have been made under this section at the time the first order was made.

(7) to (9)   [Production of licences and consequences of failure to produce.]

(10) and (11)   [Duty to send notice of order to Secretary of State and contents of notice.]

(12)   Where on any occasion a court deals with an offender—

(a)   for an offence in respect of which an order was made under this section, or

(b)   for two or more offences in respect of any of which such an order was made,

any period of disqualification which is on that occasion imposed under section 34 or 35 of this Act shall be treated as reduced by any period during which he was disqualified by reason only of an order made under this section in respect of any of those offences.

(13)   Any reference in this or any other Act (including any Act passed after this Act) to the length of a period of disqualification shall, unless the context otherwise requires, be construed as a reference to its length before any reduction under this section.

(14)   [References to counterparts to be disregarded for pre-June 1990 licences.]

Section 26 enables magistrates, when committing an offender to the Crown Court under the CJA 1967, s. 56 (see **D20.20**), remitting him to another court, deferring sentence or adjourning, to disqualify him from driving until he has been finally dealt with. Any period of disqualification finally imposed is reduced accordingly. Such an order is termed a 'first order' and only one such order may be made under s. 26. The order may only be made for a maximum of six months inclusive of the day on which the order is made. The defendant must produce his licence and, where appropriate, its counterpart, which the court must retain. Failure to do so is an offence unless the licence and its counterpart have been posted in accordance with s. 7 of the Act (see **C2.3**), a new licence and counterpart have been applied for but not received, or the defendant tenders a valid receipt under s. 56 of the Act and immediately produces the licence and counterpart to the court on their return.

Duty to Provide Information

Road Traffic Act 1988, s. 172   **C2.18**

(1)   This section applies—
  (a)   to any offence under the preceding provisions of this Act except—
    (i)   an offence under part V, or
    (ii)   an offence under section 13, 16, 51(2), 61(4), 67(9), 68(4), 96 or 120,
and to an offence under section 178 of this Act,
  (b)   to any offence under sections 25, 26 and 27 of the Road Traffic Offenders Act 1988,
  (c)   to any offence against any other enactment relating to the use of vehicles on roads, except an offence under paragraph 8 of schedule 1 to the Road Traffic (Driver Licensing and Information Systems) Act 1989, and
  (d)   to manslaughter, or in Scotland culpable homicide, by the driver of a motor vehicle.
(2)   Where the driver of a vehicle is alleged to be guilty of an offence to which this section applies—
  (a)   the person keeping the vehicle shall give such information as to the identity of the driver as he may be required to give by or on behalf of a chief officer of police, and
  (b)   any other person shall if required as stated above give any information which it is in his power to give and may lead to identification of the driver.
(3)   Subject to the following provisions, a person who fails to comply with a requirement under subsection (2) above shall be guilty of an offence.
(4)   A person shall not be guilty of an offence by virtue of paragraph (a) of subsection (2) above if he shows that he did not know and could not with reasonable diligence have ascertained who the driver of the vehicle was.
(5)   Where a body corporate is guilty of an offence under this section and the offence is proved to have been committed with the consent or connivance of, or to be attributable to neglect on the part of, a director, manager, secretary or other similar officer of the body corporate, or a person who was purporting to act in any such capacity, he, as well as the body corporate, is guilty of that offence and liable to be proceeded against and punished accordingly.
(6)   Where the alleged offender is a body corporate, . . . or the proceedings are brought against him by virtue of subsection (5) above or subsection (11) below, subsection (4) above shall not apply unless, in addition to the matters there mentioned, the alleged offender shows that no record was kept of the persons who drove the vehicle and that the failure to keep a record was reasonable.
(7)   A requirement under subsection (2) may be made by written notice served by post; and where it is so made—
  (a)   it shall have effect as a requirement to give the information within the period of 28 days beginning with the day on which the notice is served, and
  (b)   the person on whom the notice is served shall not be guilty of an offence under this section if he shows either that he gave the information as soon as reasonably practicable after the end of that period or that it has not been reasonably practicable for him to give it.
(8)   Where the person on whom a notice under subsection (7) above is to be served is a body corporate, the notice is duly served if it is served on the secretary or clerk of that body.
(9)   For the purposes of section 7 of the Interpretation Act 1978 as it applies for the purposes of this section the proper address of any person in relation to the service on him of a notice under subsection (7) above is—

(a) in the case of the secretary or clerk of a body corporate, that of the registered or principal office of that body or (if the body corporate is the registered keeper of the vehicle concerned) the registered address, and

(b) in any other case, his last known address at the time of service.

(10) In this section—

'registered address', in relation to the registered keeper of a vehicle, means the address recorded in the record kept under the Vehicle Excise and Registration Act 1994 with respect to that vehicle as being that person's address, and

'registered keeper', in relation to a vehicle, means the person in whose name the vehicle is registered under that Act;

and references to the driver of a vehicle include references to the rider of a cycle.

The justices must be satisfied that the document requiring information as to the identity of the driver was sent on behalf of a chief officer of police, but there is no need for that document to be signed, provided the document's authenticity can clearly be established by the prosecution (*Arnold* v *DPP* [1999] RTR 99).

The obligation to provide information is mandatory. If the keeper of the vehicle pleads ignorance as to who was the driver, the onus is on him to show that he did not know, and could not with reasonable diligence have ascertained, the identity of the driver. In the case of any person other than the keeper, the onus is on the prosecution to establish that the person had information which may have led to the identification of the driver and which it was in his power to give.

Contravention of the section constitutes an offence for which the defendant can be disqualified or have his licence endorsed with three penalty points. It also attracts a fine up to level 3 on the standard scale.

SECTION C3: OFFENCES RELATING TO DRIVING TRIABLE ON INDICTMENT

Manslaughter

Manslaughter is considered here only in relation to so-called 'motor' or 'vehicular' **C3.1** manslaughter. As to manslaughter generally, see **B1.25** to **B1.40**.

Indictment For the form of indictment for manslaughter, see **B1.28**. **C3.2**

Elements In general see **B1.37** to **B1.39**. **C3.3**

The RTA 1988, s. 38, is applicable; see **C2.4**.

Where the prosecution can satisfy the terms of the direction in *Adomako* [1995] 1 AC 171 (see **B1.38**), charging 'motor manslaughter' may still be appropriate, albeit rare, even if the test for dangerous driving in the RTA 1988, s. 2A (see **C3.9**), is also satisfied.

In 'motor manslaughter', however, the risk of death involved in an offence must be very high (*Pimm* [1994] RTR 391), thereby reflecting the greater degree of turpitude that Parliament must be taken to have intended by restricting the maximum penalty for the statutory offence under s. 1 to 10 years' imprisonment.

Defences Automatism, mechanical defect, and duress. See **C1.4**, **C1.10** and **A3.20** **C3.4** to **A3.28**. See also *Renouf* [1986] 1 WLR 522 at **C3.24**.

Punishment See generally, **B1.40**. **C3.5**

Life imprisonment and/or a fine. See *Pimm* [1994] RTR 391.

By the RTOA 1988, s. 34 and sch. 2, part II, disqualification for at least two years and endorsement are obligatory, unless the court finds 'special reasons'. Manslaughter by the use of a motor vehicle carries between 3 and 11 penalty points for the purposes of the RTOA 1988, s. 35. The offence also carries mandatory retesting by way of an extended driving test (see **C6.11**). Forfeiture of a motor vehicle used in connection with the crime may be ordered (see **C6.22** and **E20.1**).

Sentencing See generally, **B1.40**. **C3.6**

In *Mitchell* (1988) *The Times*, 21 December 1988, the Court of Appeal, upholding a sentence of four years' imprisonment, stated that the hostility of a driver directed towards the group of men that he drove into should be taken into account. The guidelines applicable to causing death by reckless driving laid down in *Boswell* [1984] 1 WLR 1047 (and see **C3.13**) were 'of relevance but did not cover the whole picture'. Manslaughter is a more serious charge, and as the risk of death is higher, it seems logical that the offence would usually merit a proportionately greater sentence. In *Pimm* [1994] RTR 391, when holding a sentence of nine years' detention in a young offender institution to be wholly justified, Lord Taylor CJ described the appellant's conduct (at p. 395) as 'appalling, combining repeated theft, excess alcohol, attempts to escape lawful apprehension and gross disregard for human life and limb'. See also *Gault* [1996] RTR 348. In *Ripley* [1997] 1 Cr App R (S) 19, where a van had been driven at the deceased with the intention of frightening him, the Court of Appeal upheld six years' imprisonment, commenting that those who use motor vehicles in this way when grossly over the prescribed alcohol limit can expect heavy sentences when life is lost.

Causing Death by Dangerous Driving

C3.7   **Road Traffic Act 1988, s. 1**

A person who causes the death of another person by driving a mechanically propelled vehicle dangerously on a road or other public place is guilty of an offence.

This offence is triable only on indictment.

C3.8   *Indictment*

Statement of Offence

Causing death by dangerous driving, contrary to section 1 of the Road Traffic Act 1988.

Particulars of Offence

D, on the . . . day of . . ., drove a mechanically propelled vehicle dangerously on a road [or public place], namely . . ., and thereby caused the death of V.

C3.9   *Elements*   The RTA 1988, s. 38, and the RTOA 1988, s. 11, are applicable; see **C2.4** and **C2.5**. For the meaning of 'public place', see **C1.13**.

For the purposes of the RTA 1988, s. 1, the definition of 'driver' does not include a separate person acting as a steersman.

Section 2A sets out to define what constitutes dangerous driving.

Road Traffic Act 1988, s. 2A

(1)   For the purposes of sections 1 and 2 above a person is to be regarded as driving dangerously if (and, subject to subsection (2) below, only if)—
(a)   the way he drives falls far below what would be expected of a competent and careful driver, and
(b)   it would be obvious to a competent and careful driver that driving in that way would be dangerous.
(2)   A person is also to be regarded as driving dangerously for the purposes of sections 1 and 2 above if it would be obvious to a competent and careful driver that driving the vehicle in its current state would be dangerous.
(3)   In subsections (1) and (2) above 'dangerous' refers to danger either of injury to any person or of serious damage to property; and in determining for the purposes of those subsections what would be expected of, or obvious to, a competent and careful driver in a particular case, regard shall be had not only to the circumstances of which he could be expected to be aware but also to any circumstances shown to have been within the knowledge of the accused.
(4)   In determining for the purposes of subsection (2) above the state of a vehicle, regard may be had to anything attached to or carried on or in it and to the manner in which it is attached or carried.

Section 2A relies on an objective test. Danger refers to the danger of injury to a person or serious damage to property. The prosecution need to establish that death resulted from the accused's dangerous driving. It should be noted that danger to the person is not qualified by any adjective and therefore, as long as it is not *de minimis*, any danger to any person, even though slight, if obvious to the 'competent and careful' driver, would suffice. In *Hennigan* [1971] 3 All ER 133, a case of causing death by reckless driving under the RTA 1960, the recklessness consisted mainly of the speed at which the defendant was driving; the driver of the other car, which contained the two persons who were killed, may well have been substantially to blame for the accident. The court held that there was nothing in the legislation which required the manner of the accused's driving to be a substantial or major cause of the accident, as long as it was 'a cause and something more than *de minimis*'. Similarly, it was said in *Skelton* [1995] Crim LR 635 that no particular degree of contribution to the death, beyond a negligible one, is required. An acceptable direction to the jury is that they do not have to be sure that the defendant's driving 'was the principal, or a substantial, cause of the death, as long as [they] are sure that it was a cause and that there was something more than a slight or a trifling link' (*Kimsey* [1996] Crim LR 35).

The standard of driving must fall 'far below' that expected of a 'competent and careful' driver and it must be obvious to a 'competent and careful' driver that the manner of driving is dangerous. The prosecution must demonstrate both elements before s. 2A(1) is satisfied (*Aitken* v *Lees* 1993 JC 228). The introduction of the concept of a careful driver as an objective observer places the question of what constitutes dangerous driving within the province of the tribunal of fact. The matter is one of fact and degree (*Trippick* v *Orr* 1995 SLT 272), so that where the tribunal of fact concluded that driving at 114 mph along a dual carriageway subject to a 70 mph speed limit constituted dangerous driving, even though the potential hazards were minimal, the High Court of Justiciary was not prepared to interfere and, where the speed is grossly excessive (114 mph along a single carriageway road subject to a 60 mph limit), there might be no need to conduct a minute examination of the layout of the road and the presence or otherwise of other traffic (*McQueen* v *Buchanan* 1997 SLT 765). No guidance exists as to what is meant by the term 'far below', and such a test introduces an unwelcome degree of imprecision in an area already overburdened with difficulty. It is inevitable that many courts will be asked to rule at the close of the prosecution case on whether or not the way an accused has driven falls 'far below' the standard of the competent and careful driver.

The police and the CPS have issued an agreed 'Driving Offences Charging Standard' (January 1996), in which the following are given as examples which may support an allegation of dangerous driving: racing or competitive driving; prolonged, persistent or deliberate bad driving; speed which is highly inappropriate for the prevailing or traffic conditions; aggressive or intimidatory driving, such as sudden lane changes, cutting into a line of vehicles or driving much too close to the vehicle in front, especially when the purpose is to cause the other vehicle to pull to one side to allow the accused to overtake; disregard of traffic lights and other road signs, which, on an objective analysis, would appear to be deliberate; failure to pay proper attention, amounting to something significantly more than a momentary lapse; overtaking which could not have been carried out with safety; and driving a vehicle with a load which presents a danger to other road users. These are indicative only and not conclusive as to the type of behaviour which might constitute dangerous driving.

Mens rea plays no part in the offence. In *Loukes* [1996] 1 Cr App R 444, the Court of Appeal decided that (at p. 450):

> Proof of guilt depends on an objective standard of driving, namely, what would have been obvious to a competent and careful driver. The accused driver's state of mind is relevant only if and to the extent that it attributes additional knowledge to the notional competent and careful driver . . . It should be noted too that the threshold of proof is high. It must be shown that the defect was 'obvious' to a 'competent and careful driver'. It is not enough to show in the case of such a driver that, say, if he had examined the vehicle by going underneath it, he would have seen the defect.

See also *Collins* [1997] RTR 439.

The offence may also be committed if the state of a vehicle, including any attachment or load and the way in which it is attached or carried, would make driving it dangerous in the eyes of a 'competent and careful' driver. This too may cause great difficulties; it could be argued that some loads and vehicles (e.g., certain tractor units and their attachments or a go-kart (*Carstairs* v *Hamilton* 1997 SCCR 311)) are inherently dangerous. In *Crossman* (1986) 82 Cr App R 333, a case of causing death by reckless driving, the defendant was driving an articulated lorry loaded, *inter alia*, with a large piece of machinery weighing between three and five tons. He was advised by the loader that the load was unsafe, but disregarding that advice, drove the vehicle without having chained or sheeted the load. Whilst driving, the machinery, which was top heavy, fell off the vehicle and killed a pedestrian on the footpath. Lord Lane CJ stated (at p. 336):

> The jury could, and no doubt would, have found that the appellant foresaw the high degree of risk that the load would fall off and if it did might injure someone, but nevertheless decided to run that risk. He caused that risk, or put it into operation by driving the vehicle on to the road. He was driving with the knowledge that by doing so, however slowly, however gingerly, however carefully he drove, he was putting other road users at risk of serious injury or death.

In such circumstances it would appear that, by the mere act of driving the vehicle on the road, there would be dangerous driving within the meaning of s. 2A(2) and also s. 2A(1)(a) and (b). To that extent s. 2A(2) is superfluous, but it underlines the point that driving a vehicle in a dangerous condition may well constitute an offence under s. 1 or 2 (depending on the consequences of the dangerous driving) as well as under the construction and use regulations (see also *Spurge* [1961] 2 QB 205 and *Robert Millar Contractors Ltd* [1970] 2 QB 54). The danger presented by the current state of the vehicle must, however, be capable of being seen or realised at first glance, in the sense of being 'evident to' the competent and careful driver, before it can be regarded as 'obvious'; it should not be discoverable only by taking some additional steps to ascertain the vehicle's defective state (*Strong* [1995] Crim LR 428). Moreover, where the driver is an employee driving the employer's vehicle, it will be important to consider the instructions given to him about checking the vehicle's condition. Unless those instructions appear inadequate, the driver cannot be expected to do more than comply with them (*Roberts* [1997] RTR 462); such compliance satisfies the 'competent and careful driver' test.

The purpose of this provision appears to be to widen the ambit of the law to punish offences of bad driving where death results. As the offence is one of negligence, although it purports to be a species of gross negligence, its scope is considerably wider than that previously covered by the offence of causing death by reckless driving. In *Evans* [1963] 1 QB 412, the test for dangerous driving was stated to be objective. Atkinson J in giving the judgment of the Court of Appeal stated (at p. 418):

> ... if a driver in fact adopts a manner of driving which the jury think was dangerous to other road users in all the circumstances, then on the issue of guilt it matters not whether he was deliberately reckless, careless, momentarily inattentive or even doing his incompetent best. Such considerations are highly relevant if it ever comes to sentence and equally relevant for any person who has to consider whether a prosecution is justified or not.

This is a harsh test but essentially the same as contained in the statute. If a person's driving is, as a result of any of those factors mentioned, 'far below' what would be expected of a competent and careful driver (and obviously dangerous to such a driver), then the offence would be established and the test in *Evans* resurrected (see also the absolute prohibition mentioned in *Hill* v *Baxter* [1958] 1 QB 277).

The fact that a driver was adversely affected by alcohol is a circumstance relevant to the issue of dangerous driving. In *Woodward* [1995] 1 WLR 375, the Court of Appeal distinguished the line of cases which had developed in relation to reckless driving and re-affirmed the earlier principle from *McBride* [1962] 2 QB 167 (a five-judge Court of Appeal), where Ashworth J stated (at p. 172):

> ... if a driver is adversely affected by drink, this fact is a circumstance relevant to the issue whether he was driving dangerously. Evidence to this effect is of probative value and is admissible in law. In the application of this principle two further points should be noticed. In the first place, the mere fact that the driver has had drink is not of itself relevant: in order

to render evidence as to the drink taken by the driver admissible, such evidence must tend to show that the amount of drink taken was such as would adversely affect a driver or, alternatively, that the driver was in fact adversely affected. Secondly, there remains in the court an overriding discretion to exclude such evidence if in the opinion of the court its prejudicial effect outweighs its probative value.

The provisions of the RTOA 1988, s. 15 (see **C2.11**), are applicable only to the alcohol-related offences specified therein. Accordingly, where only a single specimen has been taken from which to assess the level of the defendant's alcohol consumption, such evidence is still admissible on the issue of whether the defendant drove dangerously (*Ash* [1999] RTR 347).

In *Marison* [1997] RTR 457, driving in a dangerously defective state owing to diabetes was considered no different to driving in a dangerously defective state owing to alcohol, constituting circumstances of which the defendant could be expected to be aware and of which he had knowledge, within the meaning of s. 2A(3).

Defences Automatism, mechanical defect, and duress. See **C1.4**, **C1.10** and **A3.20** **C3.10** to **A3.28**. See also *Renouf* [1986] 1 WLR 522 at **C3.24**. No offence is committed under s. 1 where the driving was in a public place other than a road in the course of an authorised motoring event (RTA 1988, s. 13A).

Alternative Verdicts The RTOA 1988, s. 24, provides alternative verdicts of **C3.11** dangerous driving and careless, and inconsiderate, driving under the RTA 1988, ss. 2 and 3 (see **C2.15**). See also *Fairbanks* [1986] 1 WLR 1202 (discussed at **D16.30**) and *Jeavons* [1990] RTR 263. Section 24 operates without prejudice to the Criminal Law Act 1967, s. 6(3). Accordingly, no separate count for such an offence is required. Indeed, as careless driving has not been specified under the CJA 1988, s. 40, a separate count for that offence would be invalid, thereby rendering ineffective a guilty plea entered in respect of it (*Davis* (19 April 1996 unreported)). By the RTOA 1988, s. 2, a failure to warn a suspect of an intended prosecution or to serve such a warning notice does not act as a bar to conviction of the alternative offences.

Punishment Ten years' imprisonment and/or a fine. Obligatory disqualification for **C3.12** two years and endorsement, unless the court finds 'special reasons' (RTOA 1988, s. 34(4) and sch. 2). The offence carries between 3 and 11 penalty points and mandatory retesting by way of an extended driving test (see **C6.11**). Forfeiture of the motor vehicle used for the purpose of the crime may be ordered (see **C6.22** and **E20.1**).

Sentencing The Court of Appeal has consistently referred to the guidelines in *Boswell* **C3.13** [1984] 1 WLR 1047, where it had examined at some length the approach to sentencing in cases of reckless driving and causing death by reckless driving, setting out features which amongst others aggravated and mitigated the offences. Consequently, these features have clearly been adopted for cases of dangerous driving and causing death by dangerous driving, always bearing in mind the increased maximum penalty which applies to the latter offence (see **C3.12**). The features were set out in *Boswell* at pp. 1051–52:

> The following, amongst others, may be regarded as aggravating features: first of all, the consumption of alcohol or drugs, and that may range from a couple of drinks to . . . a 'motorised pub crawl'. Secondly, the driver who races: competitive driving against another vehicle on the public highway; grossly excessive speed; showing off. Thirdly, the driver who disregards warnings from his passengers, a feature which occurs quite frequently in this type of offence. Fourthly, prolonged, persistent and deliberate course of very bad driving . . . , a person who over a lengthy stretch of road ignores traffic signals, jumps red lights, passing other vehicles on the wrong side, driving with excessive speed, driving on the pavement and so on. Next, other offences committed at the same time and related offences, that is to say, driving without ever having had any licence, driving whilst disqualified, driving whilst a

learner driver without a supervising driver and so on. Next, previous convictions for motoring offences, particularly offences which involve bad driving or offences involving the consumption of excessive alcohol before driving. In other words the man who demonstrates that he is determined to continue driving badly despite past experience. Next, where several people have been killed as a result of the particular incident of reckless driving. Then, behaviour at the time of the offence, for example, failure to stop, or, even more reprehensible, the driver who tries to throw off the victim from the bonnet of the car by swerving in order that he may escape. Finally causing death in the course of reckless driving carried out in an attempt to avoid detection or apprehension.

. . . the mitigating features may be numbered as follows amongst others. First of all the piece of reckless driving which might be described in the vernacular as a 'one-off', a momentary reckless error of judgment: briefly dozing off at the wheel (see *Beeby* (1983) 5 Cr App R (S) 56 . . .); sometimes failing to notice a pedestrian on a crossing. Next, a good driving record will serve the defendant in good stead. Good character generally will also serve him in good stead. A plea of guilty will always be taken into account by the sentencing court in favour of the defendant. Sometimes the effect on the defendant, if he is genuinely remorseful, if he is genuinely shocked. That is sometimes coupled with . . . a possible mitigating factor, namely, where the victim was either a close relative of the defendant or a close friend and the consequent emotional shock was likely to be great.

The absence of aggravating features may make a non-custodial penalty appropriate, but the presence of such a feature or features would generally necessitate a custodial sentence. While emphasising that it was not possible to generalise about what a proper sentence should be, the court indicated that in bad cases, particularly those involving 'racing' or alcohol, a period of imprisonment for two years or more accompanied by a disqualification of between seven and 10 years would be appropriate. In *Barber* [1997] 1 Cr App R (S) 65, the Court of Appeal suggested that the reference to 'two years or more' should now be replaced by 'upwards of five years' and that 'in the very worst cases, if contested, sentences would be in the higher range of those now permitted'. In serious cases, a community service order or suspended or partly suspended sentence would seldom be appropriate. It is not, however, possible to categorise every case in accordance with *Boswell*.

In general, where the aggravating features clearly outweigh any mitigating features, particularly where the defendant is several times over the prescribed alcohol limit, a substantial custodial sentence can be expected, the discount allowed for good character being somewhat limited. In *A-G's Ref (No. 24 of 1994)* [1995] RTR 119, a sentence of four years' imprisonment was imposed where the offender had been three times over the limit. In *A-G's Ref (No. 22 of 1994)* (1995) 16 Cr App R (S) 670 and *A-G's Ref (No. 42 of 1994)* (1995) 16 Cr App R (S) 742, involving slightly higher alcohol readings, sentences of five years' imprisonment were imposed, although there were also additional aggravating features in both cases. In the former, the offender had driven at excessive speed, there was a prolonged period of uncontrolled driving, he had a previous excess alcohol conviction and had killed two people; in the latter, the offender had gone on a pub crawl, got into a car, driven off without even putting on the lights, drove all over the road, mounted a pavement and mowed down an innocent member of the public. Allowing for the element of double jeopardy involved in such references, the tariff being set appears to be in the range of six years (following a guilty plea) to eight years (after trial).

Where the amount of alcohol consumed is more towards the borderline of the prescribed limit, sentences of four years' imprisonment following guilty pleas were considered appropriate in *Groves* (1995) 16 Cr App R (S) 768 and *Burns* (1995) 16 Cr App R (S) 821. In both cases an additional aggravating feature was the excessive speed at which the appellant had been driving. See also *A-G's Ref (No. 16 of 1998)* [1999] 1 Cr App R (S) 149. Where there is no conclusive evidence of the amount of alcohol consumed, that factor should not be taken into account (*Mallone* [1996] 1 Cr App R (S) 221, which also decided that severe injuries sustained by the defendant were relevant to mitigate the sentence). See also *Wood* [1998] 2 Cr App R (S) 234.

Even without alcohol playing a part, the presence of aggravating features will still normally lead to a lengthy custodial sentence. In *Lucas* [1998] 1 Cr App R (S) 195, a sentence of seven years' imprisonment was considered too high because it did not take sufficient account of the guilty plea, so it was reduced to five and a half years. In *A-G's Ref (No. 38 of 1994)* (1995) 16 Cr App R (S) 714, which involved racing or competitive driving on the public highway, a sentence of four years' detention in a young offender institution was imposed. In *A-G's Ref (No. 37 of 1994)* (1995) 16 Cr App R (S) 760, the Court of Appeal indicated that a sentence of more than four years' imprisonment could be expected where the driving involved was prolonged and very bad. In that case the defendant was also disqualified from driving at the time and had taken the vehicle without authority. In *Robbins* [1996] 1 Cr App R (S) 312, where the defendant was disqualified from driving and drove at twice the speed limit, a sentence of five years' imprisonment was reduced to three and a half. In *Duncan* [1994] RTR 93, the court pointed out that an important aggravating factor was that the appellant should not have been driving at all in the circumstances, particularly when putting four passengers at risk by his inexperience and the grossly excessive speed. Additionally, the fact of showing off and engaging in sustained conduct plus causing two deaths and injuring others aggravated the offence. These matters had to be viewed in a changing climate in which levels of sentencing had risen and a sentence of three years' detention in a young offender institution and disqualification for four years and, thereafter, until a driving test was passed was upheld. In similar cases, the consequences of imposing a 'threshold' four-year sentence (see **E1.20**) may also be considered relevant (*Howell* [1999] 1 Cr App R (S) 449).

Where the impact of the aggravating features is less or the mitigating features present rise, the period of imprisonment will be reduced accordingly. Thirty months' imprisonment was upheld in *Kang* [1997] 1 Cr App R (S) 306, where the fatal accident was caused by driving a heavy goods vehicle with defective brakes. The Court of Appeal commented that those who operate such vehicles frequently allow commercial considerations to keep vehicles on the road at the expense of regular maintenance, and the risk of potentially catastrophic consequences is thereby enhanced, so sentences in cases of these kinds must contain an element of deterrence. See also *Lightfoot* [1999] 2 Cr App R (S) 55. Sentences of some 21 months' imprisonment are likely for grossly excessive speed which does not constitute racing (*A-G's Ref (Nos. 17 and 18 of 1996)* [1997] 1 Cr App R (S) 247; *A-G's Ref (No. 6 of 1996)* [1997] 1 Cr App R (S) 79, where the defendant also left the scene and only went to the police the following day).

Overtaking in a dangerous and aggressive manner attracted sentences of 18 months in *Bevan* [1996] 1 Cr App R (S) 14 and 12 months in *A-G's Ref (No. 30 of 1995)* [1996] 1 Cr App R (S) 364. In *Le Mouel* [1996] 1 Cr App R (S) 42, where a French lorry driver had driven on the wrong side of the road for about 20 to 30 seconds over a distance of some 500 metres and collided with and killed a motorcyclist, but had a good driving record and pleaded guilty, such mitigating factors justified substituting four months' imprisonment for the two years originally imposed. Disqualification for four years was unaffected.

The views of the close family of the deceased, whether they seek a lenient or more severe sentence, are not relevant considerations for sentencing (*Nunn* [1996] 2 Cr App R (S) 136; *Hird* [1998] 2 Cr App R (S) 241). Where, however, it is shown that the sentence passed on the defendant is actually aggravating the family's anguish and suffering over their bereavement, it may be a relevant factor in reducing the sentence, in mercy to them

(*Roche* [1999] 2 Cr App R (S) 105, where the defendant's and deceased's families were particularly closely related), so far as that is consistent with the court's duty to impose appropriate sentences for serious offences. See also *Richards* [1998] 2 Cr App R (S) 346 and *A-G's Ref (No. 16 of 1998)* [1999] 1 Cr App R (S) 149.

At the lower end of the spectrum, a custodial sentence may still prove necessary, even where none of the *Boswell* aggravating features are present (*Merryweather* (1999) *The Times*, 7 September 1999), though each case will depend on the degree of criminality involved. In *A-G's Ref (No. 34 of 1994)* (1995) 16 Cr App R (S) 785, the offender had pulled out to pass two cars ahead of him, which were indicating an intention to turn left. These vehicles, and others approaching from the opposite direction, had actually stopped at a pedestrian crossing to allow two young girls to cross from the offender's offside. Without slowing down, the offender collided with one of the girls, causing her death. The judge sentenced the offender to 28 days' imprisonment and disqualified for three years. The Court of Appeal indicated that a sentence of six months' imprisonment would have been appropriate on a contested case, but exercised its discretion not to return the offender to prison. In *A-G's Ref (No. 1 of 1994)* (1995) 16 Cr App R (S) 193, the Court of Appeal regarded an order of community service for 240 hours as lenient, but not unduly so. In this case, the offender had driven at excessive speed in wet conditions on a road with which he was familiar, lost control of his car, which mounted a pavement and struck a schoolgirl who was thrown over a wall and fell 27 feet into a garden, later dying from her injuries. In both cases, the old maximum sentence of five years' imprisonment applied. As the increased maximum sentence appears to have been reflected in the more serious cases, there is no reason to doubt that some increase is appropriate in the less serious ones, a factor alluded to in the latter case, so that a non-custodial penalty might now rarely be considered to be appropriate.

For a decision on the question of concurrent or consecutive sentencing in relation to matters which arise out of the same incident, see *Lawrence* [1990] RTR 45, where the Court of Appeal stated that it was immaterial if the sentence was made to run consecutively or concurrently as long as the overall sentence was appropriate to the whole of the criminal activity of the accused.

Causing Death by Careless Driving when under the Influence of Drink or Drugs

C3.14   **Road Traffic Act 1988, s. 3A**

> (1)   If a person causes the death of another person by driving a mechanically propelled vehicle on a road or other public place without due care and attention, or without reasonable consideration for other persons using the road or place, and—
>   (a)   he is, at the time when he is driving, unfit to drive through drink or drugs, or
>   (b)   he has consumed so much alcohol that the proportion of it in his breath, blood or urine at that time exceeds the prescribed limit, or
>   (c)   he is, within 18 hours after that time, required to provide a specimen in pursuance of section 7 of this Act, but without reasonable excuse fails to provide it,
> he is guilty of an offence.
> (2)   For the purposes of this section a person shall be taken to be unfit to drive at any time when his ability to drive properly is impaired.
> (3)   Subsection (1)(b) and (c) above shall not apply in relation to a person driving a mechanically propelled vehicle other than a motor vehicle.

This offence is triable only on indictment.

C3.15   *Indictment*

Statement of Offence

Causing death by careless driving when under the influence of drink or drugs, contrary to s. 3A(1) of the Road Traffic Act 1988.

Particulars of Offence

D, on the . . . day of . . ., caused the death of V by driving a motor [or mechanically propelled] vehicle on a road [or public place], namely . . ., without due care and attention and after having consumed so much alcohol that the proportion of it in his breath [or blood or urine] at the time exceeded the prescribed limit [or when unfit to drive through drink or drugs].

Elements For the meaning of 'careless' and 'without reasonable consideration', see **C5.3** and **C5.4**. For the meaning of 'public place', see **C1.13**.   **C3.16**

The RTA 1988, s. 38, and the RTOA 1988, s. 11, are applicable; see **C2.4** and **C2.5**.

The offence can be committed in six separate ways. The prosecution need to establish either that the accused was driving without due care and attention or without reasonable consideration for other persons using the road, that the death of another person was caused by the manner of his driving and that at the time he came within s. 3A(1)(a) or (b), or that within 18 hours he was required to provide a specimen of breath, blood or urine and failed without reasonable excuse to provide it. The prosecution would therefore have to prove careless driving, the requisite causal link and the related 'drink-driving' offence in exactly the same way as if both offences had been charged (see **C5.1** *et seq*. and **C2.11** and **C2.13**). The offence does not require any causal connection between the alcohol or drugs and the death (*Shepherd* [1994] 1 WLR 530).

In applying the appropriate test to determine whether a defendant has driven without due care and attention, the jury is entitled to look at all the circumstances of the case, including evidence that the defendant had been affected by alcohol or had taken such an amount of alcohol as would be likely to affect a driver (*Millington* [1996] RTR 80). Thus, the principle stated in *McBride* [1962] 2 QB 167 (see **C3.9**) in relation to causing death by dangerous driving applies equally to the offence in s. 3A(1).

In practice it is submitted that it will be rare to charge this offence in the form of driving without reasonable consideration. It may be that the actions of a driver, for instance, pulling out suddenly and causing another driver to swerve and collide with a person who then dies, could be interpreted as driving without reasonable consideration, but it would also encompass an offence of driving without due care and would normally be charged as such.

Evidence of impairment would normally be provided by a doctor who examines the accused, but evidence may also be provided by non-expert witnesses. It may take the form of a description of the actions of the accused, including the manner of driving, as long as the witness does not express an opinion as to the condition of the accused.

If the offence relates to s. 3A(1)(c), the request to provide a specimen must be made within 18 hours, presumably from the time of driving rather than the time of death.

Section 3A(1)(b) and (c) apply only where the driving is of a 'motor vehicle', but the offence under s. 3A(1)(a) may be committed whilst driving any 'mechanically propelled vehicle'.

Defences Duress and mechanical defect (see **A3.20** to **A3.28** and **C1.10**). Auto-   **C3.17** matism may be a defence (see **C1.4**), but in practice will be very difficult to establish given the nature of this offence and the possibility of interpreting such a situation as arising from self-induced intoxication. See also **C5.18**.

Alternative Verdicts The RTOA 1988, s. 24, provides alternative verdicts under the   **C3.18** RTA 1988, ss. 3, 4(1), 5(1)(a) and 7(6). It would therefore seem that, if someone is accused of an offence based on s. 3A(1)(c), he could theoretically be convicted, for example, of driving whilst unfit even though the indictment contains an allegation that he refused to provide a specimen.

C3.19   ***Punishment***   Ten years' imprisonment and/or a fine. In the absence of 'special reasons', obligatory disqualification for not less than two years and endorsement with between 3 and 11 penalty points. Retesting by way of an extended driving test is mandatory (see **C6.11**). Forfeiture of the motor vehicle used for the purpose of the crime may be ordered (see **C6.22** and **E20.1**).

C3.20   ***Sentencing***   The Court of Appeal provided some guidance as to the relevant factors to be taken into consideration when sentencing for this offence in *Shepherd* [1994] 1 WLR 530. The cases considered were references under the CJA 1988, s. 36, against unduly lenient sentences. Lord Taylor of Gosforth CJ suggested that a prison sentence will ordinarily be appropriate, its length being determined by the aggravating factors present and, in particular, depending on the extent of carelessness and the amount the driver was above the prescribed limit. Where the level of alcohol at the time is borderline and the carelessness of the driving momentary, a non-custodial penalty may suffice if the mitigation is strong. Generally, however, the Lord Chief Justice stated (at p. 536) that 'a prison sentence is required to punish the offender, to deter others from drinking and driving, and to reflect the public's abhorrence of deaths being caused by drivers with excess alcohol'.

As with cases of causing death by dangerous driving (see **C3.13**), the doubling of the maximum sentence has led to an overall increase in penalties. In many respects, the sentencing principles to be applied to both offences are akin where alcohol is concerned, the principal factor being the amount by which the defendant is above the prescribed limit (*A-G's Ref (No. 49 of 1994)* (1995) 16 Cr App R (S) 837) and a substantial sentence will normally be imposed. The starting point for drivers consuming large quantities of alcohol before driving carelessly and causing death is around five years' imprisonment (*A-G's Ref (No. 49 of 1994)*, where four years' imprisonment was actually imposed due to the 'double jeopardy' associated with such references). Where other aggravating features are also present a longer sentence can be expected. In *Jackson* [1997] 1 Cr App R (S) 34, the defendant demanded his car keys back from friends, ignored requests to slow down and left the scene of the accident, surrendering the following day. Six years' imprisonment and disqualification for 10 years was upheld. Four years' imprisonment was substituted for the original five-year term in *Corcoran* [1996] 1 Cr App R (S) 416, where the defendant had pleaded guilty, having provided a specimen of 93 microgrammes in 100 millilitres of breath. In *A-G's Ref (No. 11 of 1998)* [1999] 1 Cr App R (S) 145, in respect of an identical reading, 30 months' imprisonment and a five-year disqualification were substituted for the original suspended sentence and two-year disqualification; the Court of Appeal commented that the sentencer must judge the case dispassionately and not be unduly influenced by the feelings of the relatives of victims of the defendant's driving.

In *A-G's Ref (No. 13 of 1995)* [1996] 1 Cr App R (S) 120 (which related to an offence committed prior to the doubling of the maximum penalty), the Court of Appeal decided that it was impossible to avoid a custodial sentence in a case where the defendant's driving had been more than minimally careless and involved excessive speed on a road known well to him. In this case, the defendant had provided a specimen of 111 milligrammes in 100 millilitres of blood. A sentence of nine months' imprisonment was substituted for the suspended sentence imposed by the trial judge.

Where the alcohol level is only a little above the prescribed limit, a custodial sentence may well still be appropriate, if other aggravating features are present. In *Tame* [1996] 1 Cr App R (S) 205, the defendant exceeded the speed limit and collided with a pedestrian crossing the road, taking no evasive action. He did not stop at the scene of the accident but was traced shortly afterwards and found to have an alcohol level of 112 milligrammes in 100 millilitres of urine. A sentence of 12 months' imprisonment and disqualification for four years was upheld.

In *Jordan* (1995) 16 Cr App R (S) 663, the Court of Appeal suggested that the guidelines on sentencing for driving offences with fatal consequences in cases where alcohol had been consumed were not helpful when considering a case where amphetamines had been consumed. The difference was that the taking of such drugs in itself was unlawful and so aggravated the offence. In that case a sentence of two years' imprisonment and disqualification from driving for five years was deemed appropriate.

Dangerous Driving

Road Traffic Act 1988, s. 2   C3.21

A person who drives a mechanically propelled vehicle dangerously on a road or other public place is guilty of an offence.

This offence is triable either way.

Indictment   C3.22

Statement of Offence

Dangerous driving, contrary to section 2 of the Road Traffic Act 1988.

Particulars of Offence

D, on the . . . day of . . ., drove a mechanically propelled vehicle dangerously on a road [or public place], namely . . .

Elements   For the meaning of 'dangerous' and 'dangerous driving', see **C3.9**. For the   C3.23
meaning of 'public place', see **C1.13**.

The RTA 1988, s. 38, and the RTOA 1988, ss. 1, 11 and 12(1), are applicable; see **C2.1**, **C2.4**, **C2.5** and **C2.6**.

Where the evidence permits, charging aggravated vehicle-taking as well as dangerous driving does not result in double jeopardy nor amount to an abuse of process (*Harding* [1995] Crim LR 733).

Defences   Automatism, mechanical defect and duress. See **C1.4**, **C1.10** and **A3.20** to   C3.24
A3.28. No offence is committed under this section where the driving took place in a public place other than a road in the course of an authorised motoring event (RTA 1988, s. 13A).

In *Renouf* [1986] 1 WLR 522, the appellant pursued a Volvo containing persons who had thrown a barrage of objects which struck the appellant, occasioning actual bodily harm, and damaged the windscreen of his car. The appellant caught up with the Volvo and edged it off the road and on to the grass verge. The only risk caused was that of damage to the Volvo and, in response to a charge of reckless driving, the defence submitted that, in creating that risk, the appellant was using only such force as was reasonable to assist in the lawful arrest of the offenders in accordance with the Criminal Law Act 1967, s. 3(1). The trial judge directed that s. 3(1) of the 1967 Act was incapable of affording a defence to reckless driving. The Court of Appeal, however, held that the jury might, on the unusual evidence in the case, have accepted such a defence, which should therefore have been left to them. If this, albeit unusual, defence could extend to offences of reckless driving, it is submitted that it could also, in appropriate circumstances, be extended to excuse or provide a defence to a charge of dangerous driving, causing death by dangerous driving or manslaughter.

Alternative Verdicts   The RTOA 1988, s. 24, provides an alternative verdict under the   C3.25
RTA 1988, s. 3 (see **C2.15**). Where the defendant has already been acquitted of the s. 3 charge (by the prosecution offering no evidence), the alternative verdict is no longer available and that should be made clear to the arbiters of fact (*DPP v Khan* [1997] RTR 82).

C3.26 **_Punishment_** On indictment, two years' imprisonment and/or a fine. On summary trial, six months' imprisonment and/or the statutory maximum. Disqualification is obligatory. The offence carries obligatory endorsement with between 3 and 11 penalty points. Retesting by way of an extended driving test is mandatory (see **C6.11**). Forfeiture of the vehicle used may also be ordered (see **C6.22** and **E20.1**).

C3.27 **_Sentencing_** A plea of guilty will not always attract a discount from the statutory maximum sentence. In *Hastings* [1995] 1 Cr App R (S) 167, the Court of Appeal upheld a sentence of two years' imprisonment, commenting that the appellant had had no realistic option but to plead guilty. The appellant, who had never held a driving licence, drove at 70–90 mph in the early hours of the morning in a densely populated 30 mph area, with the vehicle's lights switched off, caused another moving vehicle to take evasive action, travelled on the wrong side of the road, went through red lights, collided with a moving vehicle and ended up on the pavement. He had also consumed excessive alcohol.

In *Moore* (1995) 16 Cr App R (S) 536, the Court of Appeal upheld a sentence of nine months' imprisonment, following a guilty plea, referring to the guidelines in *Boswell* [1984] 1 WLR 1047 (see **C3.13**). The appellant had driven a heavy goods vehicle on a main road in patchy thick fog. On approaching road works, he had been unable to stop in time and collided with a stationary van, injuring the driver and damaging the vehicle. The aggravating features were the speed in those conditions, the nature of vehicle being driven and the appellant's failure to observe the roadside. The period of disqualification, however, was reduced from five years to three. In *Templeton* [1996] 1 Cr App R (S) 380, the defendant drove for nearly four minutes at speeds of up to 70 mph in a built up area, travelling about three miles and crossing seven red lights. Nine months' imprisonment and disqualification for two years was upheld. See also *Nicholls* [1998] 2 Cr App R (S) 296 and *Hicks* [1999] 1 Cr App R (S) 228.

In *Kennion* [1997] RTR 421, the Court of Appeal commented that 'where otherwise perfectly respectable people of impeccable character lose control when sitting behind the wheel of a motor car because they imagine in some way that they have been provoked', i.e. road rage, they 'can expect immediate custodial sentences'.

Wanton or Furious Driving

C3.28   Offences Against the Person Act 1861, s. 35

> Whosoever, having the charge of any carriage or vehicle, shall by wanton or furious driving or racing, or other wilful misconduct, or by wilful neglect, do or cause to be done any bodily harm to any person whatsoever, shall be guilty of an offence . . .

This offence is triable only on indictment.

C3.29 **_Indictment_**

                    Statement of Offence

                    Causing bodily harm, contrary to section 35 of the Offences Against the Person Act 1861.

                    Particulars of Offence

> D, on the . . . day of . . ., having the charge of a taxi cab [or carriage etc.], by wanton [or furious] driving [or racing etc.] caused bodily harm to V.

C3.30 **_Elements_** The RTA 1988, s. 38, is applicable if the offence is committed on a 'road'. See **C1.13** and **C2.4**.

In *Mohan* [1976] QB 1, it was held that the prosecution had to prove an intention to cause bodily harm. This was a case of attempting to cause bodily harm by wanton driving, and the court held that the full *mens rea* of the offence was necessary, namely (at p. 11):

> . . . proof of specific intent, a decision to bring about, insofar as it lies within the accused's power, the commission of the offence which it is alleged the accused attempted to commit, no matter whether the accused desired that consequence of his act or not.

The full offence, it is submitted, would appear to require a specific intention to cause bodily harm or *Cunningham* recklessness (see generally, **A2.4**), an approach which the Court of Appeal assumed to be correct, but without deciding the issue, in *Okosi* [1997] RTR 450. Although s. 35 of the OAPA 1861 is not specifically mentioned in s. 38 of the RTA 1988, a failure to observe a provision of the Highway Code may be relied upon to establish or negative liability where the conduct takes place on the highway. However, s. 35 applies whether or not the conduct takes place on a road (*Cooke* [1971] Crim LR 44). It also covers any kind of vehicle or carriage, including bicycles (*Parker* (1895) 59 JP 793).

The definition of 'driving' in this context is generally thought to be the older definition, which would include bicycles and even box carts, although such 'vehicles' or 'carriages' would often be propelled manually or by means of pedals and could rarely be said to be 'driven' in the modern sense of that term. 'Wanton' has no technical meaning, and may be construed in the light of its ordinary dictionary definition of irresponsible, capricious, unrestrained or random.

Alternative Verdicts Assault occasioning actual bodily harm, contrary to the OAPA **C3.31** 1861, s. 47. Common assault, contrary to the CJA 1988, s. 39, but only if specifically included as a separate count on the indictment (*Mearns* [1991] QB 82).

Punishment The offence carries two years' imprisonment and/or a fine. The offence **C3.32** is not endorsable but disqualification may be ordered under the PCCA 1973, s. 44 (see **C7.6**), if an assault is involved and the accused was driving a motor vehicle. Forfeiture of the vehicle used for the purposes of the crime may be ordered (see **C6.22** and **E20.1**).

Causing Danger to Road-Users

Road Traffic Act 1988, s. 22A C3.33

(1) A person is guilty of an offence if he intentionally and without lawful authority or reasonable cause—

(a) causes anything to be on or over a road, or

(b) interferes with a motor vehicle, trailer or cycle, or

(c) interferes (directly or indirectly) with traffic equipment,

in such circumstances that it would be obvious to a reasonable person that to do so would be dangerous.

(2) In subsection (1) above 'dangerous' refers to danger either of injury to any person while on or near a road, or of serious damage to property on or near a road; and in determining for the purposes of that subsection what would be obvious to a reasonable person in a particular case, regard shall be had not only to the circumstances of which he could be expected to be aware but also to any circumstances shown to have been within the knowledge of the accused.

(3) In subsection (1) above 'traffic equipment' means—

(a) anything lawfully placed on or near a road by a highway authority;

(b) a traffic sign lawfully placed on or near a road by a person other than a highway authority;

(c) any fence, barrier or light lawfully placed on or near a road—

(i) in pursuance of section 174 of the Highways Act 1980, or section 65 of the New Roads and Street Works Act 1991 (which provide for guarding, lighting and signing in streets where works are undertaken), or

(ii) by a constable or a person acting under the instructions (whether general or specific) of a chief officer of police.

(4)   For the purposes of subsection (3) above anything placed on or near a road shall unless the contrary is proved be deemed to have been lawfully placed there.

(5)   In this section 'road' does not include a footpath or bridleway.

This offence is triable either way.

C3.34   *Indictment*

Statement of Offence

Causing danger to road users, contrary to section 22A(1) of the Road Traffic Act 1988.

Particulars of Offence

D, on the . . . day of . . ., intentionally and without lawful authority or reasonable cause interfered with a motor vehicle [or trailer, cycle or traffic equipment], namely . . ., [or caused . . . to be on [or over] a road, namely . . .,] in such circumstances that to do so was dangerous.

C3.35   *Elements*   The prosecution must establish that the accused intentionally performed the act. The question must arise as to who bears the burden of proof in relation to a defence of acting with lawful authority or reasonable cause (see **F3.2** *et seq.*).

Following the decision in *Hunt* [1987] AC 352, it will be for the courts to determine the intention of Parliament as to where the burden of proof should lie. It is submitted, however, that, because questions of lawful authority and reasonable excuse are peculiarly within the competence of the accused and the defence is in the nature of an exception, the decision in *Edwards* [1975] QB 27 and the principle contained in the MCA 1980, s. 101, make it likely that the burden of proving the defence should lie on the accused, to be discharged on the balance of probabilities. It may be argued, however, that Parliament's failure to provide expressly for the incidence of the burden of proof (as it has in other cases, see, for example, the Prevention of Crime Act 1953, s. 1, and generally **F3.4**) should dictate that, once the accused raises the issue of lawful authority or reasonable excuse, the burden must lie on the prosecution to disprove the defence beyond reasonable doubt. For more detailed treatment of the burden of proof in such cases generally, see **F3.5**.

The danger which arises must be of serious damage to property or of injury to any person while on or near a road. The test is an objective one but the danger must exist and must be obvious to a reasonable person. In other words there has to be a serious likelihood that injury or serious damage may be the result of the actions of the accused. It is not necessary, however, for injury or damage to result and it seems that any injury, however slight and as long as it could be termed an injury, would qualify. The extent of the potential damage or injury must, of course, have relevance to any sentence.

C3.36   *Punishment*   On indictment, seven years' imprisonment and/or a fine. On summary trial, six months' imprisonment and/or the statutory maximum fine. The offence is not endorsable.

Driving while Disqualified

C3.37   **Road Traffic Act 1988, s. 103**

(1)   A person is guilty of an offence if, while disqualified for holding or obtaining a licence, he—

(a)   obtains a licence, or

(b)   drives a motor vehicle on a road.

(2)   A licence obtained by a person who is disqualified is of no effect (or, where the disqualification relates only to vehicles of a particular class, is of no effect in relation to vehicles of that class).

(3)   A constable in uniform may arrest without warrant any person driving a motor vehicle on a road whom he has reasonable cause to suspect of being disqualified.

(4) Subsections (1) and (3) above do not apply in relation to disqualification by virtue of section 101 of this Act.

(5) Subsections (1)(b) and (3) above do not apply in relation to disqualification by virtue of section 102 of this Act.

(6) In the application of subsections (1) and (3) above to a person whose disqualification is limited to the driving of motor vehicles of a particular class by virtue of—

(a) section 102, 117 or 117A of this Act, or

(b) subsection (9) of section 36 of the Road Traffic Offenders Act 1988 (disqualification until test is passed),

the references to disqualification for holding or obtaining a licence and driving motor vehicles are references to disqualification for holding or obtaining a licence to drive and driving motor vehicles of that class.

Indictment   C3.38

Statement of Offence

Driving while disqualified, contrary to section 103(1) of the Road Traffic Act 1988.

Particulars of Offence

D, on the . . . day of . . ., drove a motor vehicle on a road, namely . . ., while disqualified for holding or obtaining a driving licence.

A count charging a person with this offence may be included in an indictment in the circumstances specified in the CJA 1988, s. 40 (see generally, **D3.1**). Sections 6, 11, and 12(1) of the RTOA 1988 apply (see **C2.2**, **C2.5**, and **C2.6**).

Elements   In the absence of duress, the RTA 1988, s. 103(1)(b), creates an absolute   C3.39 offence. It is usual to produce either the register of the magistrates' court where the defendant was disqualified, or a properly certified extract. These are admissible as evidence of the proceedings of the court by virtue of the Magistrates' Courts Rules 1981, r. 68. If the conviction was in the Crown Court (or, indeed, the magistrates' court), it may be proved under the PACE 1984, s. 73, by the production of a certificate signed by the clerk of the court. (As to the proof of convictions generally, see **F11.1 *et seq*.**) Other authorised methods of proving the conviction are equally admissible, but it is not necessary to prove that the defendant knew of the disqualification (*Taylor v Kenyon* [1952] 2 All ER 726).

In *Derwentside Justices, ex parte Heaviside* [1996] RTR 384, the Divisional Court held that strict proof linking the defendant to the person named in the certificate of conviction is required. In doing so, it identified three methods by which this requirement could be satisfied: an admission under the CJA 1967, s. 10; comparison of fingerprints; or evidence from a person who was present in court when the disqualification was imposed. The fear that this list was exhaustive has been allayed by subsequent decisions of the Divisional Court (*Derwentside Justices, ex parte Swift* [1997] RTR 89; *DPP v Mansfield* [1997] RTR 96; *DPP v Mooney* [1997] RTR 434). Consequently, whilst strict proof is necessary, the prosecution can rely on any admissible evidence from which it could properly be concluded that the defendant and the individual named in the certificate are one and the same person, and the issue is one for the court to determine on the basis of the evidence placed before it. Where the defendant has an unusual name, proof that it is identical to that of a person previously disqualified raises a prima facie case that the defendant is that disqualified person (*Olakunori v DPP* [1998] COD 443), especially if he has also lied about his identity.

If a defendant drives on a 'road', his mistaken belief that it was not a road is incapable of amounting to a defence (*Miller* [1975] 1 WLR 1222).

In *Thames Magistrates' Court, ex parte Levy* (1997) *The Times*, 17 July 1997, it was confirmed that the offence of driving while disqualified can be committed during a period of disqualification which is not suspended pending an appeal (see RTOA 1988, s. 39 and **C6.13**), even where the conviction which led to the disqualification is subsequently quashed. Similarly, the offence can be committed in the period between disqualification following conviction and the swearing of a statutory declaration under the MCA 1980, s. 14, as the earlier proceedings become void from the time of the declaration and not *ab initio* (*Singh* v *DPP* [1999] Crim LR 914).

Where a person has been disqualified until he passes a test, under the RTOA 1988, s. 36, a failure to comply with the conditions of a provisional driving licence is an offence under s. 103(1)(b). This would seem to be the case whether or not the defendant has actually obtained such a licence (*Scott* v *Jelf* [1974] RTR 256).

Aiding and abetting the offence of driving while disqualified requires knowledge of the disqualification; this may be actual or constructive, in the sense that the defendant failed to make inquiries which a reasonable man should have made, or deliberately closed his eyes to the possibility of the driver being disqualified (*Pope* v *Minton* [1954] Crim LR 711; *Bateman* v *Evans* [1964] Crim LR 601).

The CJA 1988 made the offence summary only, but provides for certain circumstances where it may be included in an indictment and that thereafter it 'shall be tried in the same manner as if it were an indictable offence'. It is submitted that the offence is therefore no longer an 'indictable offence' within the meaning of the Criminal Attempts Act 1981 (see **A6.31**), and the offence of attempting to drive while disqualified has ceased to exist.

The RTA 1988, s. 103(3), allows a constable in uniform to arrest any person whom he reasonably suspects to be driving while disqualified. In *James* v *DPP* [1997] Crim LR 831 it was held that this power does not extend to a person whom the constable reasonably suspects to have driven, being confined to circumstances where the person concerned was driving. Thus, once the matters associated with driving (see **C1.8**) have concluded the power to arrest lapses.

C3.40   *Defences*   Duress or necessity may provide a defence in the proper circumstances. See **C1.9**.

C3.41   *Punishment*   Six months' imprisonment and/or a fine up to level 5 on the standard scale. Disqualification is discretionary but endorsement is obligatory. The offence carries six penalty points. Forfeiture of the vehicle used may also be ordered (see **C6.22** and **E20.1**). In *Morris* (1988) 10 Cr App R (S) 216, where a defendant with five previous convictions for driving while disqualified had elected trial before pleading guilty, the Court of Appeal upheld the imposition of the maximum period of imprisonment of (at that time) one year. Given the nature of the offence, there is often a strong argument against imposing a long period of disqualification (*Mew* (24 January 1997 unreported)).

Other Offences

C3.42   Other indictable offences that may be related to driving include criminal damage (dealt with at **B8.1** to **B8.18**) and taking a motor vehicle without authority (dealt with at **B4.90** *et seq.*) in both the simple and aggravated form.

SECTION C4: OFFENCES RELATING TO DOCUMENTS TRIABLE ON INDICTMENT

Forgery, Alteration etc. of Documents etc.

Goods Vehicles (Licensing of Operators) Act 1995, s. 38   C4.1

(1) A person is guilty of an offence if, with intent to deceive, he—

  (a) forges, alters or uses a document or other thing to which this section applies;

  (b) lends to, or allows to be used by, any other person a document or other thing to which this section applies; or

  (c) makes or has in his possession any document or other thing so closely resembling a document or other thing to which this section applies as to be calculated to deceive.

(2) This section applies to the following documents and other things, namely—

  (a) any operator's licence;

  (b) any document, plate, mark or other thing by which, in pursuance of regulations, a vehicle is to be identified as being authorised to be used, or as being used, under an operator's licence;

  (c) any document evidencing the authorisation of any person for the purposes of sections 40 and 41;

  (d) any certificate of qualification under section 49; and

  (e) any certificate or diploma such as is mentioned in paragraph 13(1) of Schedule 3.

Indictment   C4.2

Statement of Offence

Forgery [or Use etc.] of a document [or licence etc.] with intent to deceive, contrary to section 38(1) of the Goods Vehicles (Licensing of Operators) Act 1995.

Particulars of Offence

D, on the . . . day of . . ., with intent to deceive, forged [or used etc.] a document [or licence etc.], namely . . .

Statement of Offence

Making [or Possessing] a document [or licence etc.] with intent to deceive, contrary to section 38(1) of the Goods Vehicles (Licensing of Operators) Act 1995.

Particulars of Offence

D, on the . . . day of . . ., with intent to deceive, made [or had in his possession] a document [or thing] so closely resembling an operator's licence [or document etc.] as to be calculated to deceive.

This offence is triable either way.

Elements The RTOA 1988, s. 6 (see **C2.2**), applies by virtue of the Goods Vehicles **C4.3** (Licensing of Operators) Act 1995, s. 51.

For the meaning of 'intent to deceive' and 'calculated to deceive' see **B5.2** and **B6.1**. As to forgery, see s. 38(4) of the 1995 Act and, generally, **B6.1** *et seq.* The term 'operator's licence' is defined in s. 2(1) of the 1995 Act and the vehicles authorised to be used under such a licence are set out in s. 5(1). Power to seize documents or articles is contained in s. 41.

Punishment The offence under s. 38 is punishable on summary conviction by a fine **C4.4** up to the statutory maximum, or on indictment by a term of imprisonment not exceeding two years and/or a fine (s. 38(3)).

C4.5   *Sentencing*   See *Raven* (1988) 10 Cr App R (S) 354 and **C4.9**.

False Records or Entries Relating to Drivers' Hours

C4.6   **Transport Act 1968, s. 99**

> (5)   Any person who makes, or causes to be made, any record or entry on a record sheet kept or carried for the purposes of the Community Recording Equipment Regulation or section 97 of this Act or any entry in a book, register or document kept or carried for the purposes of regulations under section 98 thereof or the applicable Community rules which he knows to be false or, with intent to deceive, alters or causes to be altered any such record or entry shall be liable—
>
>   (a)   on summary conviction, to a fine not exceeding the statutory maximum;
>
>   (b)   on conviction on indictment, to imprisonment for a term not exceeding two years.

C4.7   *Indictment*

Statement of Offence

Making [or Causing] a false record [or entry] [to be made], contrary to section 99(5) of the Transport Act 1968.

Particulars of Offence

D, on the . . . day of . . ., made [or caused] a record [or entry on a record sheet etc.] kept [or carried] for the purposes of the Community Recording Equipment Regulation [or section 97 of the Transport Act 1968 etc.] [to be made], namely . . ., which he knew to be false.

This offence is triable either way.

C4.8   *Elements*   For 'intent to deceive', see **B5.2**.

The 'applicable Community rules' means any directly applicable Community provision which, in this case, is Council Regulation (EEC) No. 3820/85 which sets the hours and conditions of work of drivers and their mates whilst on national or international journeys.

The 'Community Recording Equipment Regulation' is Council Regulation (EEC) No. 3821/85 of 20 December 1985 on recording equipment in road transport, as read with the Community Drivers' Hours and Recording Equipment (Exemptions and Supplementary Provisions) Regulations 1986 (SI 1986 No. 1456). The Regulation, which is of direct effect, requires that drivers of passenger and goods vehicles (see the Transport Act 1968, s. 95(2)) be subject to the 'tachograph' provisions which govern the keeping of records in relation to the hours of work of drivers and their mates whilst on national or international journeys. It is given statutory effect by ss. 97, 97A and 97B of the Act, the Passenger and Goods Vehicles (Recording Equipment) Regulations 1979 (SI 1979 No. 1746) and the Community Drivers' Hours and Recording Equipment Regulations 1986 (SI 1986 No. 1457). Regulations made under s. 98 are the Drivers' Hours (Goods Vehicles) (Keeping of Records) Regulations 1987 (SI 1987 No. 1421) which provide for the making of entries in the driver's record book according to the instructions contained therein. These regulations apply where the 'Community rules' do not (i.e. to certain domestic journeys) and impose obligations upon employers, where relevant, as well as drivers. In any proceedings under s. 99(5), it is necessary for the prosecution to establish that the record or book etc. is being 'carried for the purpose' of the relevant regulation or rule, and as certain vehicles are exempt, a thorough examination of the various provisions is essential. In *J. F. Alford Transport Ltd* [1997] 2 Cr App R 326, the Court of Appeal held that knowledge of and passive acquiescence in a principal's offence under s. 99(5) is insufficient to amount to aiding and abetting its commission, but indicated that such knowledge and an ability to control the action of an offender coupled with a deliberate decision to refrain from doing so might suffice.

Sentencing In *Raven* (1988) 10 Cr App R (S) 354, a sentence of nine months' **C4.9** imprisonment was upheld in a case where the appellant had pleaded guilty to six counts of making a false entry on a driver's record sheet and one of using a document with intent to deceive under the RTA 1960, s. 233 (which s. 38 of the 1995 Act replaced). The appellant was involved in the running of a haulage business, a number of whose vehicles had their tachograph wiring interfered with. He had entered into an agreement with another man to operate using that man's operator's licence and discs. Two drivers said that they were instructed by the appellant, from time to time, to drive with the tachograph switched off. He had been convicted in 1985 and fined for six offences of failing to secure the return of record sheets and one offence of permitting a driver to exceed his permitted hours.

The judge who sentenced stressed the importance of safety provisions, the unfairness of competition to 'fair traders', the level of sophistication shown, the public danger which must have arisen, and the fraudulent nature of the appellant's activities. His remarks were quoted and approved by the Court of Appeal.

Forgery, Alteration etc. of Licences, Marks, Trade Plates etc.

Vehicle Excise and Registration Act 1994, ss. 44 and 45   C4.10

44.—(1) A person is guilty of an offence if he forges, fraudulently alters, fraudulently uses, fraudulently lends or fraudulently allows to be used by another person anything to which subsection (2) applies.

    (2) This subsection applies to—
      (a) a vehicle licence,
      (b) a trade licence,
      (c) a document in the form of a licence which is issued in pursuance of regulations under this Act in respect of a vehicle which is an exempt vehicle under paragraph 19 of schedule 2,
      (d) a registration mark,
      (e) a registration document, and
      (f) a trade plate (including a replacement trade plate).

45.—(1) A person who in connection with—
      (a) an application for a vehicle licence or a trade licence,
      (b) a claim for a rebate under section 20, or
      (c) an application for an allocation of registration marks,
makes a declaration which to his knowledge is either false or in any material respect misleading is guilty of an offence.

    (2) A person who makes a declaration which—
      (a) is required by regulations under this Act to be made in respect of a vehicle which is an exempt vehicle under paragraph 19 of schedule 2, and
      (b) to his knowledge is either false or in any material respect misleading,
is guilty of an offence.

    (3) A person who—
      (a) is required by this Act to furnish particulars relating to, or to the keeper of, a vehicle, and
      (b) furnishes particulars which to his knowledge are either false or in any material respect misleading,
is guilty of an offence.

Indictment

Statement of Offence   C4.11

Forgery [or Fraudulent use etc.] of a vehicle licence [or trade licence etc.], contrary to section 44(1) of the Vehicle Excise and Registration Act 1994.

Particulars of Offence

D, on the . . . day of . . ., forged [or fraudulently used etc.] a vehicle licence [or trade licence etc.], namely . . .

Statement of Offence

Making a false or misleading declaration, contrary to section 45(1) of the Vehicle Excise and Registration Act 1994.

Particulars of Offence

D, on the . . . day of . . ., in connection with an application for a vehicle licence [or trade licence etc.] knowingly made a declaration, which he knew to be false or in a material respect misleading, namely . . .

C4.12   ***Procedure and Evidence***   The admissibility of records maintained by the Secretary of State is governed by the Vehicle Excise and Registration Act 1994, s. 52.

C4.13   ***Elements***   Section 53 of the Vehicle Excise and Registration Act 1994 provides that for certain specified matters, relevant to declarations which may be prosecuted under s. 45, the burden of proof shall lie on the defendant.

For the purposes of s. 44, 'fraudulently' means dishonestly deceiving a police officer or other person responsible for a public duty. There is no requirement to prove an intention to cause any economic loss (*Terry* [1984] AC 374). In *Johnson* [1995] RTR 15, it was held that an offence under the Vehicles (Excise) Act 1971, s. 26 (which s. 44 of the 1994 Act replaced), relating to fraudulent use of a licence could be committed only where there was evidence that the vehicle was being or had been used on a public road while displaying the offending licence.

Forgery does not necessarily connote an intention to defraud but may be taken to include an intention to deceive for the purposes of the Vehicle Excise and Registration Act 1994 (*Clifford* v *Bloom* [1977] RTR 351; *Clayton* (1980) 72 Cr App R 135).

In *Macrae* (1995) 159 JP 359, the offence of forging a licence was said to involve the defendant making a false licence, with the intent that he or another should use it to induce a third party to accept it as genuine and by reason of so accepting it to do or not to do some act to his own or another's prejudice as a result of such acceptance of the false licence as genuine in connection with the performance of any duty, i.e. akin to the ulterior intent found in the Forgery and Counterfeiting Act 1981, see **B6.23** *et seq.*

Section 44 applies to any application for a licence in respect of a duty exempt vehicle.

C4.14   ***Punishment***   On indictment, the maximum sentence for an offence under the Vehicle Excise and Registration Act 1994, s. 44 or 45, is two years' imprisonment and/or a fine; on summary conviction, a fine not exceeding the statutory maximum.

Forgery and Misuse of Documents Relating to Public Service Vehicles

C4.15   **Public Passenger Vehicles Act 1981, s. 65**

(1)   This section applies to the following documents and other things, namely—
     (a)   a licence under part II of this Act;
     (b)   a certificate of initial fitness under section 6 of this Act;
     (c)   a certificate under section 10 of this Act that a vehicle conforms to a type vehicle;
     (d)   an operator's disc under section 18 of this Act;
     (e)   a certificate under section 21 of this Act as to the repute, financial standing or professional competence of any person.
(2)   A person who, with intent to deceive—
     (a)   forges or alters, or uses or lends to, or allows to be used by, any other person, a document or other thing to which this section applies, or
     (b)   makes or has in his possession any document or other thing so closely resembling a document or other thing to which this section applies as to be calculated to deceive, shall be liable—
         (i)   on conviction on indictment, to imprisonment for a term not exceeding two years;

(ii)   on summary conviction, to a fine not exceeding the statutory maximum.

(3)   In the application of this section to England and Wales—

'forges' means makes a false document or other thing in order that it may be used as genuine.

Indictment   The forms provided in **C4.2** may be adapted for use in relation to this **C4.16** offence.

Elements   As to the meaning of 'forgery' and 'calculated to deceive', see **C4.3**. By **C4.17** virtue of the Public Passenger Vehicles Act 1981, s. 73, a time-limit of six months from the date on which evidence, sufficient to warrant proceedings, comes to the attention of the prosecutor is imposed, and a correctly signed certificate to that effect is conclusive evidence of that date unless the contrary is proved, but no proceedings may be commenced more than three years after the commission of the offence.

Mishandling of Parking Documents and Related Offences

Road Traffic Regulation Act 1984, s. 115   C4.18

(1)   A person shall be guilty of an offence who, with intent to deceive,—

(a)   uses, or lends to, or allows to be used by, any other person,—

(i)   any parking device or apparatus designed to be used in connection with parking devices;

(ii)   any ticket issued by a parking meter, parking device or apparatus designed to be used in connection with parking devices;

(iii)   any authorisation by way of such a certificate, other means of identification or device as is referred to in any of sections 4(2), 4(3), 7(2), and 7(3) of this Act; or

(iv)   any such permit or token as is referred to in section 46(2)(i) of this Act;

(b)   makes or has in his possession anything so closely resembling any such thing as is mentioned in paragraph (a) above as to be calculated to deceive; . . .

Indictment   The forms provided in **C4.2** may be adapted for use in relation to **C4.19** offences under this section.

Elements   As to 'intent to deceive' and 'calculated to deceive', see **C4.3**.   **C4.20**

Punishment   See the RTOA 1988, sch. 2 at **C8.2**. On indictment, the maximum **C4.21** sentence is two years' imprisonment and/or a fine; on summary conviction, a fine not exceeding the statutory maximum.

Forgery of Documents etc.: Road Traffic Act 1988, s. 173

Road Traffic Act 1988, s. 173   C4.22

(1)   A person who, with intent to deceive—

(a)   forges, alters or uses a document or other thing to which this section applies, or

(b)   lends to, or allows to be used by, any other person a document or other thing to which this section applies, or

(c)   makes or has in his possession any document or other thing so closely resembling a document or other thing to which this section applies as to be calculated to deceive,

is guilty of an offence.

(2)   This section applies to the following documents and other things—

(a)   any licence under any part of this Act or, in the case of a licence to drive, any counterpart of such a licence,

(aa)   any counterpart of a Community licence,

(b)   any test certificate, goods vehicle test certificate, plating certificate, certificate of conformity or Minister's approval certificate (within the meaning of part II of this Act),

(c)   any certificate required as a condition of any exception prescribed under section 14 of this Act,

(cc)   any seal required by regulations made under section 41 of this Act with respect to speed limiters,

  (d) any plate containing particulars required to be marked on a vehicle by regulations under section 41 of this Act or containing other particulars required to be marked on a goods vehicle by sections 54 to 58 of this Act or regulations under those sections,

  (dd) any document evidencing the appointment of an examiner under section 66A of this Act,

  (e) any records required to be kept by virtue of section 74 of this Act,

  (f) any document which, in pursuance of section 89(3) of this Act, is issued as evidence of the result of a test of competence to drive,

  (ff) any certificate provided for by regulations under section 97(3A) of this Act relating to the completion of a training course for motor cyclists,

  (g) any certificate under section 133A or any badge or certificate prescribed by regulations made by virtue of section 135 of this Act,

  (h) any certificate of insurance or certificate of security under part VI of this Act,

  (j) any document produced as evidence of insurance in pursuance of Regulation 6 of the Motor Vehicles (Compulsory Insurance) (No. 2) Regulations 1973 (SI 1973 No. 2143),

  (k) any document issued under regulations made by the Secretary of State in pursuance of his power under section 165(2)(a) of this Act to prescribe evidence which may be produced in lieu of a certificate of insurance or a certificate of security,

  (l) any international road haulage permit, and

  (m) a certificate of the kind referred to in section 34B(1) of the Road Traffic Offenders Act 1988.

  (3) In the application of this section to England and Wales 'forges' means makes a false document or other thing in order that it may be used as genuine.

  (4) In this section 'counterpart' and 'Community licence' have the same meanings as in part III of this Act.

C4.23 ***Indictment*** The forms provided in **C4.2** may be adapted for use in relation to offences under this section.

C4.24 ***Elements*** 'Use' extends to use by an employer, see **C1.7**.

Particular words must be read 'against the mischief which that particular section seeks to avoid or prevent'; the production of a driving licence unconnected with any driving on the road is not 'using' it for the purposes of the RTA 1988, s. 173 (*Howe* [1982] RTR 45).

A document which has been completed by someone other than the proper person does not cease to be a document to which the section applies for the purposes of 'using' (*Pilditch* [1981] RTR 303).

A forged document which is not specified within the section, but which closely resembles a document specified within the section, is not 'used' but may fall within paragraph (c) of s. 173(1) (*Holloway* v *Brown* [1978] RTR 537).

Where an 'intent to deceive' has been established, it is not necessary for the prosecution to prove that the defendant knew the documents were false; if that was the case, the statute would include the word 'knowingly'. Such an intent may be shown by evidence that 'they were irregular documents either by way of irregular acquisition or by the irregular disposing of them' (*Greenberg* [1942] 2 All ER 344, per Birkett J at p. 347). The court in *Greenberg* also stated that it is unnecessary to allege or prove an intent to deceive any particular person. Knowledge that the documents are false may, however, be relevant to the issue of whether the defendant had an 'intent to deceive'.

In *Cleghorn* [1938] 3 All ER 398, a certificate of insurance which had been cancelled was held to be properly described as one resembling a certificate of insurance. Similarly, in *Aworinde* [1996] RTR 66, bogus blank insurance certificates were held to be documents so closely resembling certificates as to be calculated to deceive.

'Calculated to deceive' means 'likely to deceive' (*Davison* [1972] 3 All ER 1121; *Turner* v *Shearer* [1972] 1 WLR 1387; *Anon.* (1918) 82 JP 447).

Punishment   On conviction on indictment, the maximum sentence is two years' **C4.25** imprisonment and/or a fine; on summary conviction, a fine not exceeding the statutory maximum.

Forgery of Documents etc.: Motor Vehicles (EC Type Approval) Regulations 1992, reg. 11(1) and Motor Cycle (EC Type Approval) Regulations 1995, reg. 10(1)

The Motor Vehicles (EC Type Approval) Regulations 1992 (SI 1992 No. 3107) and **C4.26** the Motor Cycle (EC Type Approval) Regulations 1995 (SI 1995 No. 1513) contain identical provisions (in reg. 11 and reg. 10 respectively) relating to the forgery and other misuse of type approval documents:

> (1)   A person who, with intent to deceive—
>   (a)   forges, alters or uses a document to which this paragraph applies, or
>   (b)   lends to, or allows to be used by, any other person a document to which this paragraph applies, or
>   (c)   makes or has in his possession any document so closely resembling a document to which this paragraph applies as to be calculated to deceive,
> shall be guilty of an offence

Indictment   The forms provided in **C4.2** may be adapted for use in relation to **C4.27** offences under these regulations.

Elements   As to 'intent to deceive' and 'calculated to deceive', see **C4.3**.   **C4.28**

Regulation 11 of the 1992 Regulations concerns the approval and conformity of 'light passenger vehicles' to European standards in accordance with Council Directive 70/156/EEC, as amended. It applies to an EC certificate of conformity issued by a manufacturer under reg. 4 or under any provision of the law of a Member State other than the United Kingdom which gives direct effect to Article 6 of the Directive or an EC type approval certificate issued under reg. 3(5) or under any provision of the law of a Member State other than the United Kingdom which gives direct effect to Article 4 of the Directive (reg. 2(1)).

Regulation 10 of the 1995 Regulations concerns the approval and conformity of 'motor cycles' to European standards in accordance with Council Directive 92/61/EEC.

Punishment   On indictment, the maximum sentence is two years' imprisonment **C4.29** and/or a fine; on summary conviction, a fine not exceeding the statutory maximum (reg. 11(2) of the 1992 Regulations; reg. 10(2) of the 1995 Regulations).

SECTION C5: SUMMARY OFFENCES WHICH MAY BE COMMITTED TO CROWN COURT BY VIRTUE OF CRIMINAL JUSTICE ACT 1988, S. 41

Careless and Inconsiderate Driving

C5.1
Road Traffic Act 1988, s. 3

> If a person drives a mechanically propelled vehicle on a road or other public place without due care and attention, or without reasonable consideration for other persons using the road or place, he is guilty of an offence.

C5.2 **Elements** The RTOA 1988, ss. 1, 11, and 12(1), apply; see **C2.1**, **C2.5**, and **C2.6**.

For the meaning of the terms 'drive', 'road or other public place' and 'mechanically propelled vehicle', see **C1.8**, **C1.13**, and **C1.11**. Section 3 creates two separate offences, commonly called 'careless driving' and 'driving without reasonable consideration'.

The term 'other persons using the road' includes persons who are pedestrians or passengers in vehicles, including that driven by the defendant, as well as other motorists (*Pawley* v *Wharldall* [1966] 1 QB 373).

C5.3 **Careless Driving** In *Simpson* v *Peat* [1952] 2 QB 24, Lord Goddard CJ stated that if a driver was 'exercising the degree of care and attention which a reasonable prudent driver would exercise, he ought not to be convicted' of careless driving.

Following the amendment of the RTA 1972 by the Criminal Law Act 1977, Lord Diplock in *Lawrence* [1982] AC 510 considered, albeit *obiter*, the position of offences of careless driving after the offence of dangerous driving (in its former existence) had been abolished (at p. 525):

> Section 3 creates an absolute offence in the sense in which that term is commonly used to denote an offence for which the only *mens rea* needed is simply that the prohibited physical act (*actus reus*) done by the accused was directed by a mind that was conscious of what his body was doing, it being unnecessary to show that his mind was also conscious of the possible consequences of his doing it. So section 3 takes care of the kind of inattention or misjudgment to which the ordinarily careful motorist is occasionally subject without its necessarily involving any moral turpitude, although it causes inconvenience and annoyance to other users of the road.

In *DPP* v *Cox* (1993) 157 JP 1044, Clarke J explained the underlying principles of the offence, and that in certain circumstances there is effectively a presumption of carelessness, stating (at p. 1047):

> The appellant advances the following propositions of law. First, for justices to convict a defendant of driving without due care and attention contrary to section 3 of the Road Traffic Act 1988, the prosecution must prove beyond reasonable doubt that the defendant was not exercising that degree of care and attention that a reasonable and prudent driver would exercise in the circumstances. Secondly, that standard is an objective one, impersonal and universal, fixed in relation to the safety of other users of the highway. Thirdly, if the facts are such that in the absence of an explanation put forward by the defendant, or that explanation is objectively inadequate, and the only possible conclusion is that he was careless, he should be convicted. In my judgment, all those propositions of law are correct.

Departure from the standard of driving required by the Highway Code, whilst not in itself an offence, may well establish liability under the RTA 1988, s. 3, but adherence to the Highway Code may, equally, negative such a liability. For the admissibility of the provisions of the Highway Code, see the RTA 1988, s. 38, and **C2.4**. Each case must be objectively decided on its own facts in the surrounding circumstances. Only if the court considers that the driver has or must have failed to exercise the degree of care and attention which the reasonable, prudent and competent driver would have exercised, should a conviction result. It follows that a particular manner of driving may be careless in one situation but not in another.

On occasions, for example where a driver veers off in the course of overtaking and collides with an oncoming vehicle, the only inference that can be drawn is that the defendant drove carelessly. To draw another inference, such as mechanical defect, without any evidence to support that inference means that the justices have misdirected themselves (*DPP* v *Tipton* (1992) 156 JP 172).

In *DPP* v *Parker* [1989] RTR 413, the respondent, who did not appear in either court, at any stage of the proceedings, had been driving in a line of traffic which came to a halt, and he ran into the back of the car in front which then ran into another car in front. He was not driving fast immediately before the accident and because of the rain, road conditions were wet and slippery. There was evidence that other cars were involved in similar accidents at the same time and that neither the respondent's car nor the car in front were badly damaged. The justices concluded that a reasonable and prudent driver could have been involved in such an accident, that the case was therefore not proved beyond reasonable doubt, and that they should acquit the respondent. The Divisional Court held that while such driving might in other circumstances be sufficient to constitute an offence, whether it was sufficient in this case had been a question of fact. There was insufficient material to justify a finding that the justices' decision on the facts was perverse, and the appeal accordingly failed.

In *Wilson* v *MacPhail* 1991 SCCR 170, it was decided that overtaking a long line of stationary cars at temporary traffic lights and causing obstruction to oncoming traffic after the lights had changed in their favour was a failure to exercise the degree of care to be expected of a reasonable, competent and prudent driver.

The police and the CPS have issued an agreed 'Driving Offences Charging Standard' (January 1996), in which the following are given as examples which may support an allegation of careless driving: acts of driving caused by more than momentary inattention and where the safety of road users is affected, such as overtaking on the inside, driving inappropriately close to another vehicle, driving through a red light, emerging from a side road into the path of another vehicle, or turning into a minor road and colliding with a pedestrian; conduct which clearly caused the driver not to be in a position to respond in the event of an emergency on the road, for example using a hand-held mobile telephone while the vehicle is moving (especially at speed), tuning a car radio, reading a newspaper or map, selecting and lighting a cigarette, talking to and looking at a passenger which causes the driver more than momentary inattention, having a leg and/or arm in plaster, or fatigue or nodding off. These are indicative only and not conclusive as to the type of behaviour which might constitute careless driving.

Although there is no rule of law which requires justices to adjourn any trial involving a fatal road traffic accident until the inquest has been concluded, as a matter of practice it is desirable for them to do so (*Smith* v *DPP* (1999) *The Times*, 28 July 1999).

Driving without Reasonable Consideration   The essence of this limb of the RTA **C5.4** 1988, s. 3, is that other road users are inconvenienced by the driving of the defendant. Evidence of such inconvenience may be provided either by the direct testimony of another road user, or by inference to be drawn from evidence of the reactions or behaviour of other road users.

The examples of conduct appropriate for a charge of driving without reasonable consideration given in the 'Driving Offences Charging Standard' (January 1996) are:

flashing of lights to *force* other drivers in front to give way; misuse of any lane to avoid queuing or gain some advantage over other drivers; unnecessarily remaining in an overtaking lane; unnecessarily slow driving or braking without good cause; driving with undipped headlights which dazzle oncoming drivers; and driving through a puddle causing pedestrians to be splashed.

C5.5   ***Defences***   Mechanical defect, automatism, and necessity (*Backshall* [1998] 1 WLR 1506); see **C1.10, C1.4** and **A3.27**. No offence is committed under s. 3 where the driving took place in a public place other than a road in the course of an authorised motoring event (RTA 1988, s. 13A).

C5.6   ***Alternative Verdicts***   See the RTOA 1988, s. 24, set out at **C2.15**.

On a trial on indictment for an offence under the RTA 1988, s. 1, 2 or 3A, the jury may find the defendant guilty of an offence under s. 3, (unless he has already been acquitted of it (*DPP* v *Khan* [1997] RTR 82)), and the Crown Court has the same sentencing powers as a magistrates' court when that occurs. Where the prosecution have not accepted a guilty plea to careless driving and the defendant has been found not guilty of dangerous driving, without an alternative verdict having been entered, the previous guilty plea is a nullity and the court cannot proceed to sentence in respect of it (*McGregor-Read* [1999] Crim LR 860). The requirement for a notice under s. 1(1) of the RTOA 1988 is waived by s. 2(4) of that Act as long as the original requirement for a warning notice, if any, has been complied with.

It is not open to the prosecution to accept a plea of guilty to a charge of careless driving which has been committed for trial under the CJA 1988, s. 41, and offer no evidence on the indictable offence of reckless (now dangerous) driving (*Foote* [1993] RTR 171). Offences committed for trial under s. 41 can be dealt with only following a conviction for an indictable offence arising out of circumstances which are the same as or connected with the summary offence. The question whether the alternative finding of careless driving can be accepted as a guilty plea was left open in *Foote*, and now seems to have been answered in the affirmative in *Davis* (19 April 1996 unreported), which decided that a separate count for careless driving on an indictment containing a fatal driving count was invalid, the inference being that a plea to the latter count is available, despite the wording of s. 24 militating against any alternative finding of guilt other than by the jury.

If a defendant is acquitted, by magistrates, of an offence under s. 2, the court may direct or allow a charge for an offence under s. 3 to be preferred (RTOA 1988, s. 24(3)). This power extends to the Crown Court on an appeal against conviction for dangerous driving (see *Killington* v *Butcher* [1979] Crim LR 458; Supreme Court Act 1981, s. 79(3)). The requirement for a notice of intended prosecution is waived by the RTOA 1988, s. 2(6), as long as the original requirement for a warning notice, if any, has been complied with.

In *Coventry Justices, ex parte Sayers* [1979] RTR 22, the court held that the six-month time limit did not apply to a charge preferred under s. 24(3).

C5.7   ***Punishment***   The penalty for the offence is a fine up to level 4 on the standard scale. Disqualification is discretionary but endorsement, in the absence of 'special reasons', with between three and nine penalty points is obligatory. In appropriate cases, the court may disqualify the defendant until an extended driving test is passed under the RTOA 1988, s. 36 (see *Miller* (1994) 15 Cr App R (S) 505 at **C6.11**).

C5.8   ***Sentencing***   In *Simpson* (1981) 3 Cr App R (S) 148, a young man of 18 was driving a loaded lorry on a wet road. The lorry had a tendency to pull to the left when the brakes were applied, and on the relevant occasion it did so causing a fatal accident. The court felt the sentence should be in excess of the recommended fine suggested by the

Magistrates' Association but, given the otherwise blameless record of the appellant, a disqualification for 12 months should be reduced to three months. In *Farenden* (1984) 6 Cr App R (S) 42, the appellant was indicted for reckless driving, but convicted of careless driving which occurred whilst he was being pursued by the police. He was disqualified for three months. In the magistrates' court he was convicted of driving with excess alcohol in his blood (120 milligrammes). The court reduced the period of disqualification to one month, which it considered sufficient on a first conviction for careless driving. In *Palmer* (1995) 16 Cr App R (S) 85, the appellant, who was driving a fire engine which was responding to an emergency call, pleaded guilty after colliding with a car in a bank of fog and causing injury to two of the car's occupants. The Court of Appeal, noting that disqualification could not be avoided, considered that three months would have been an adequate period.

Sanders (1987) 9 Cr App R (S) 390 was a case where a 44-year-old managing director earning a very considerable salary was fined £750 and disqualified for 12 months. He had driven his car at an excessive speed, lost control on a bridge, and collided with an oncoming car. Russell LJ said (at p. 391):

> Our attention has been drawn by counsel to certain guidelines which are applied in the magistrates' courts, where of course offences of driving without due care and attention have to be dealt with from day to day. Just as on previous occasions this court has taken account of those guidelines, so we do, but we remind ourselves that they are no more than guidelines and that each individual case has to be considered upon its individual merits.

The court, nonetheless, reduced the disqualification from 12 to six months, but felt that the fine (the maximum at that time being £1,000) was entirely appropriate.

In *Soutar* (1994) 15 Cr App R (S) 432, where the appellant had driven at an excessive speed and caused grave injury to a pedestrian in a collision, the fine imposed was halved to £750 and the period of disqualification reduced from two years to 18 months.

Where one or more deaths result from the careless driving, the sentencer is entitled to bear that fact in mind when sentencing, although the defendant's culpability or criminality remains the primary consideration (*Simmonds* [1999] 2 Cr App R 18). This is a departure from the previous line of authority established by *Krawec* [1985] RTR 1 (see Lord Lane CJ at p. 3) and subsequent cases. Henry LJ found 'the concept of a road traffic offence in which the sentencing court is obliged to disregard the fact that a death has been caused as wholly anomalous'. In the years since *Krawec* there has been a general toughening of sentencing policy reflecting public opinion in respect of fatal road traffic incidents which has finally filtered down to offences under the RTA 1988, s. 3. Equally, however, the distinction between careless driving and those other more serious offences is that the latter require a death to have been caused as one of their elements. Two identical pieces of careless driving may now attract disparate sentences simply because one instance results in death. If such a consequence is to lead to different considerations in respect of the appropriate penalty for the offence, it would be preferable for Parliament to create an aggravated careless driving offence to meet the public's perceived concerns.

As to compensation orders, see **E14**, particularly **E14.1**.

Driving, or Being in Charge, when under Influence of Drink or Drugs

Road Traffic Act 1988, s. 4

C5.9

(1) A person who, when driving or attempting to drive a mechanically propelled vehicle on a road or other public place, is unfit to drive through drink or drugs is guilty of an offence.

(2) Without prejudice to subsection (1) above, a person who, when in charge of a mechanically propelled vehicle which is on a road or other public place, is unfit to drive through drink or drugs is guilty of an offence.

(3)   For the purposes of subsection (2) above, a person shall be deemed not to have been in charge of a mechanically propelled vehicle if he proves that at the material time the circumstances were such that there was no likelihood of his driving it so long as he remained unfit to drive through drink or drugs.

(4)   The court may, in determining whether there was such a likelihood as is mentioned in subsection (3) above, disregard any injury to him and any damage to the vehicle.

(5)   For the purposes of this section, a person shall be taken to be unfit to drive if his ability to drive properly is for the time being impaired.

(6)   A constable may arrest a person without warrant if he has reasonable cause to suspect that that person is or has been committing an offence under this section.

(7)   For the purpose of arresting a person under the power conferred by subsection (6) above, a constable may enter (if need be by force) any place where that person is or where the constable, with reasonable cause, suspects him to be.

C5.10   **_Elements_**   The RTOA 1988, ss. 11 and 12(1), apply; see **C2.5** and **C2.6**. The RTA 1988, s. 11, defines 'drugs' as including any intoxicant other than alcohol. For the meaning of the terms 'attempting', 'driving', 'motor vehicle' and 'road or other public place', see **C1.3**, **C1.8**, **C1.11**, and **C1.13**.

Section 4 creates three separate offences. The section contains a power of arrest and entry in addition to any other powers under the PACE 1984.

If a defendant is acquitted of being 'in charge', a further summons for driving with excess alcohol relating to an earlier time does not raise an issue estoppel analagous to _autrefois acquit_.

The prosecution must establish that the defendant was driving or attempting to drive, or was in charge of a motor vehicle on a road or other public place, and that at the time his ability to drive properly was impaired through drink or drugs. The charge may read 'drink or drugs' without either being duplicitous or bad for uncertainty.

C5.11   **_In Charge_**   It was confirmed in _Drake_ v _DPP_ [1994] RTR 411 that a person can be in charge of a motor vehicle when the vehicle is immobile. In _Leach_ v _Evans_ [1952] 2 All ER 264, a motorist emerging from a public house considerably under the influence of alcohol told a police officer that he was looking for his van, walked towards it and was then arrested within three yards of it. Lord Goddard CJ posed the question that if the motorist was not in charge of the van 'who was?' and the court remitted the case back to the justices with a direction to continue the hearing. This case was then followed in _Haines_ v _Roberts_ [1953] 1 WLR 309, where Lord Goddard CJ said (at p. 311):

> It may be that, if a man goes to a public house and leaves his car outside or in the car park and, getting drunk, asks a friend to look after the car for him or to take it home, he has put it in charge of somebody else; but if he has not put it in charge of somebody else he is in charge until he does. His car is out on the road or in the car park – it matters not which – and he is in charge.

In _DPP_ v _Watkins_ [1989] QB 821, it was held that a person was in charge of a vehicle if he acted in a manner which showed that he had assumed control or intended to assume control of the vehicle preparatory to driving it. Thereafter the burden of proving the statutory defence shifts to the defence. Amongst factors which merited consideration were:

(a)   whether and where he was in the vehicle or how far he was from it;

(b)   what he was doing at the relevant time;

(c)   whether he was in possession of a key that fitted the ignition;

(d)   whether there was evidence of an intention to take or assert control of the car by driving or otherwise;

(e)   whether any other person was in, at or near the vehicle and, if so, the like particulars in respect of that person.

Evidence of Impairment   This may be provided by the opinion evidence of an expert **C5.12**
witness, normally a doctor, who has examined the defendant, even if he has refused to
be examined, and his testimony should be treated as that of any 'independent expert
witness giving evidence to assist the court', whether he be a police surgeon or anyone
else (*Lanfear* [1968] 2 QB 77). Opinion evidence of the defendant's state or of the
amount he has drunk may be given even by a lay witness, but the opinion of such a lay
witness as to whether or not the defendant was fit to drive is not admissible. Nor could
a lay witness give evidence as to the amount of alcohol in the defendant's blood. As to
opinion evidence by lay witnesses generally, see **F10.2**.

The prosecution are not obliged to adduce opinion evidence of an expert witness in
order to establish the defendant's impairment to drive, provided that the totality of the
evidence actually adduced suffices to satisfy the justices of this element (*Leetham* v *DPP*
[1999] RTR 29). Such evidence may include the manner of the driving, the defendant's
apparent physical state and any admission made relating to the consumption of drugs
and, presumably, alcohol.

The prosecution may adduce evidence of the amount of alcohol in the defendant's
breath, blood or urine from any specimen provided under the RTA 1988, s. 7. This
evidence is admissible by virtue of the RTOA 1988, ss. 15 and 16. In such circumstances
it is a rebuttable presumption that the proportion of alcohol at the time of the alleged
offence was not less than the proportion contained in the specimen. See the RTOA
1988, s. 15(3), at **C2.11**.

Drugs   Medicines are drugs for the purposes of the RTA 1988, s. 4, and include, for **C5.13**
instance, insulin and toluene (*Armstrong* v *Clark* [1957] 2 QB 391; *Bradford* v *Wilson*
(1983) 78 Cr App R 77). In *Watmore* v *Jenkins* [1962] 2 QB 572, the appellant had been
overtaken by a hypoglycaemic episode and coma through a fall in his cortisone level and
a consequent increase in his insulin level, brought about by a combination of injected
insulin and an improvement in his liver function following recovery from an attack of
jaundice. In those unusual circumstances, the Divisional Court upheld an acquittal of
driving whilst unfit through drugs as the justices were entitled to 'entertain a reasonable
doubt whether the injected insulin was more than a predisposing or historical cause' of
the appellant's state.

In *Ealing Magistrates' Court, ex parte Woodman* [1994] RTR 181, the conviction of a
diabetic suffering a hypoglycaemic attack was quashed because there was no evidence
entitling the stipendiary magistrate to conclude that the presence of insulin in the
applicant's blood was the real effective cause of the attack. The Divisional Court decided
that it would only be appropriate to rely on s. 4 for cases of this type where there is
evidence of a clear overdose of insulin having been taken by the accused.

Evidence of impairment must be adduced by the prosecution, and any specimen, while
admissible under the RTOA 1988, ss. 15 and 16, may only be taken in accordance with
the RTA 1988, s. 7 (see **C5.25**).

Defences   Section 4(3) of the RTA 1988 provides a defence to an allegation of 'in **C5.14**
charge', based on the likelihood of the defendant driving while unfit. The onus is on the
defendant, on a balance of probabilities, to prove that at the time there was no likelihood
of his driving while unfit.

The defence may also adduce evidence of post-incident consumption to rebut the
assumption that he was unfit at the time of the alleged offence or that the proportion of
any alcohol or drug in a specimen was the same as at the time of the alleged offence (see
the RTOA 1988, s. 15(3), at **C2.11**).

Punishment   For offences of driving or attempting to drive when unfit, the penalty is **C5.15**
a maximum of six months' imprisonment and/or a fine up to level 5. Endorsement and

disqualification for one year is obligatory unless there are 'special reasons'. The offence carries between 3 and 11 penalty points. Forfeiture of the vehicle may be ordered (see **C6.22** and **E20.1**).

The offence of being 'in charge' carries three months' imprisonment and/or a fine up to level 4. Disqualification is discretionary but endorsement with 10 penalty points is obligatory.

Driving, or Being in Charge, with Alcohol Concentration above Prescribed Limit

C5.16   **Road Traffic Act 1988, s. 5**

(1)   If a person—
(a)   drives or attempts to drive a motor vehicle on a road or other public place, or
(b)   is in charge of a motor vehicle on a road or other public place,
after consuming so much alcohol that the proportion of it in his breath, blood or urine exceeds the prescribed limit he is guilty of an offence.
(2)   It is a defence for a person charged with an offence under subsection (1)(b) above to prove that at the time he is alleged to have committed the offence the circumstances were such that there was no likelihood of his driving the vehicle whilst the proportion of alcohol in his breath, blood or urine remained likely to exceed the prescribed limit.
(3)   The court may, in determining whether there was such a likelihood as is mentioned in subsection (2) above, disregard any injury to him and any damage to the vehicle.

C5.17   *Elements*   For the meaning of the terms 'road or other public place', 'driving' and 'attempting', see **C1.13**, **C1.8**, and **C1.3**. For 'in charge', see **C5.11**.

The RTA 1988, s. 11, sets out the 'prescribed limit'. If the lower reading in breath is 39 microgrammes in 100 millilitres or less, proceedings are not usually instituted. The RTOA 1988, ss. 11 and 12(1), apply (see **C2.5** and **C2.6**). For the provisions relating to specimens, see **C2.11** and **C2.13**.

Section 5 creates nine separate offences of driving, or attempting to drive or of being in charge of a vehicle, each with an alcohol concentration above the prescribed limit in relation to breath, blood or urine (*Bolton Justices, ex parte Khan* [1999] Crim LR 912). The charge must state which specimen is to be relied upon by the prosecution. Referring to more than one type of specimen renders the charge bad for duplicity. However, a late amendment to the charge to refer to the correct specimen is likely to be permitted as it should not prejudice the defendant, who knows that driving with excess alcohol in his body is what is being alleged (*Fenwick* v *Valentine* 1994 SLT 485).

In *DPP* v *Johnson* [1995] 1 WLR 728, the Divisional Court was asked to consider whether 'consuming' was confined solely to drinking, as the stipendiary magistrate had found as a reasonable possibility that the level of alcohol in the respondent's blood had been affected by an injection of Kenalog a month before the alleged offence. It was held that the meaning of 'consuming' was sufficiently wide to cover ingestion otherwise than by mouth and the important element of the offence was the concentration of alcohol in the accused's body at the relevant time.

In *Carter* v *Richardson* [1974] RTR 314, a supervising driver who was aware that the learner driver had drunk so much that the alcohol level in his blood must have exceeded the prescribed limit, was held to have been properly convicted of aiding and abetting an offence under what is now s. 5, even though the driver had not been tested. That the defendant knew his pupil had too much to drink and that his blood alcohol content was over the limit was a proper inference to be drawn from the behaviour of the defendant when the police arrived, as he had lied about who was the driver.

The prosecution are entitled to produce evidence by way of a back-calculation to show that at the time of driving, attempting to drive or of being in charge, the amount of alcohol in the defendant's breath, blood or urine was in excess of the prescribed amount. In *Gumbley* v *Cunningham* [1988] QB 170, the appellant was driving his motor vehicle at 11.15 p.m. when it was involved in a fatal accident. At 3.35 a.m. on the following morning he gave a specimen of blood with a reading of 59 milligrammes. The prosecution adduced evidence that a person of the height, age, weight and physical condition of the appellant would eliminate blood alcohol at the rate of 10 to 25 milligrammes per hour (the most likely rate being 15), and therefore his blood alcohol level at the time of driving would have been between 120 to 130 milligrammes of alcohol per 100 millilitres of blood. He was convicted and his appeal to the Crown Court was dismissed. In giving the judgment of the Divisional Court, Mann J stated (at p. 181):

> Evidence which is material to the question of what was the proportion of alcohol at the moment of driving must be admissible. The provisions of [the RTOA 1988, s. 15(2) and (3)] do not preclude evidence other than that revealed by a specimen to show a greater level of alcohol although, subject to the 'hip-flask' defence, the specimen will always provide a 'not less' or base figure. If that figure is above the prescribed limit, other evidence is unnecessary to establish the offence.

> Our conclusion means that those who drive whilst above the prescribed limits cannot necessarily escape punishment because of the lapse of time. However, our conclusion also means that in cases where a sample provided a substantial period of time after driving has ceased shows a level below the prescribed limit justices may find themselves confronted with evidence of a complicated and scientific nature. . . . We think it needs to be said, therefore, that in our view the prosecution should not seek to rely on evidence of back-calculation save where that evidence is easily understood and clearly persuasive of the presence of excess alcohol at the time when a defendant was driving. Moreover, justices must be very careful especially where there is conflicting evidence not to convict unless, upon the scientific and other evidence which they find it safe to rely on, they are sure an excess of alcohol was in the defendant's body when he was actually driving as charged.

In *A-G's Ref (No. 1 of 1975)* [1975] QB 773, the court held that a person who laces the drink of another driver may be convicted of procuring an offence under what is now s. 5, if it is proved beyond reasonable doubt that he knew that the person whose drink was laced was going to drive and that the ordinary result of his activity was to bring the driver's blood alcohol level above the limit.

In *Blakely* v *DPP* [1991] RTR 405, which also involved a charge of procuring a person to commit an offence under s. 5, the appellants had laced a driver's drinks with the intention that he should stay with one of the appellants rather than drive. Before they could tell him that his drink had been laced, he left the public house where they had been and was subsequently arrested. In giving the judgment of the court, McCullough J stated (at p. 415):

> It must, at the least, be shown that the accused contemplated that his act would or might bring about or assist the commission of the principal offence: . . . The requirements match those needed to convict principals in the second degree. And they fit well with the liability of the parties to a joint enterprise.

The Divisional Court may grant certiorari to quash a conviction where a defendant pleads guilty to an offence under s. 5 on the basis of a blood sample which shows excess alcohol but the reliability of which is subsequently impugned because it had been taken using a cleaning swab impregnated with alcohol (*Bolton Magistrates' Court, ex parte Scally* [1991] 1 QB 537).

Defences The RTA 1988, s. 5(2), provides a defence to an allegation that the **C5.18** defendant was 'in charge' of the vehicle which is similar to that contained in s. 4(3) (see **C5.14**). In *Drake* v *DPP* [1994] RTR 411, the Divisional Court held that the presence of a wheel clamp on a motor vehicle could not be disregarded when considering the likelihood of the person in charge of the vehicle being able to drive it while over the prescribed limit. As to duress see **A3.20** to **A3.28**.

It is also a defence for the defendant to prove that he had consumed alcohol after the time he was driving and that his subsequent consumption took him over the prescribed limit (RTOA 1988, s. 15(3), see **C2.12**). This defence, commonly known as a 'hip-flask' defence, was considered in *Patterson* v *Charlton* [1986] RTR 18. In that case the defendant was arrested on suspicion of theft of a motor car. He was questioned at the police station, and stated that he owned the car, that he had earlier driven it and then parked it on a double yellow line. He was then arrested for driving a motor vehicle with alcohol in excess of the prescribed limit. He provided two specimens of breath, the lower reading being 71 microgrammes. The magistrates accepted a defence submission that the prosecution had not raised a prima facie case that the defendant had driven his car on the day. Allowing the prosecutor's appeal, the Divisional Court held that the defendant's admission, coupled with the provision of specimens of breath which exceeded the limit, meant that it had to be assumed, in accordance with the RTA 1972, s. 10(2) (now the RTOA 1988, s. 15(2)), that the proportion of alcohol at the time of the alleged offence was not less than in the specimen. The onus therefore shifted to the defence in accordance with s. 10(2)(a) (now s. 15(3) of the 1988 Act). If expert evidence is to be called in relation to the statutory defence or the 'hip flask' defence, it should be disclosed to the prosecution to avoid unnecessary adjournments (*DPP* v *O'Connor* [1992] RTR 66).

In *DPP* v *Frost* [1989] RTR 11, the respondent was at a party where he had arranged to spend the night. He went outside for some fresh air and then, rather than returning to the noise of the party sat in his car and fell asleep. He was arrested at 3 a.m. and provided a lower breath specimen of 97 microgrammes in 100 millilitres of breath at 3.51 a.m. He was acquitted of charges under ss. 4 and 5 of being 'in charge', on the basis that he was not going to drive until around 9 a.m. The Divisional Court upheld his acquittal under s. 4 but allowed the prosecutor's appeal on the charge under s. 5 as there had been no evidence on which the justices, as laymen, could conclude without medical or expert evidence that the defendant would not have been in excess of the breath alcohol limit when he intended to drive at around 9 a.m. the following morning. It seems clear from this decision that in order to discharge the burden of proof placed upon him, the defendant must, except in the clearest cases, call scientific evidence (*DPP* v *Singh* [1988] RTR 209). The standard of proof is that on a balance of probabilities.

Insanity cannot be raised as a defence as there is no *mens rea* element to which it can relate (*DPP* v *H* [1997] 1 WLR 1406).

C5.19 ***Punishment*** For offences of driving or attempting to drive, the penalty is six months' imprisonment and/or a fine up to level 5. Disqualification and endorsement are obligatory unless there are 'special reasons', and the offence carries between 3 and 11 penalty points. An order for forfeiture may be made under either offence (see **C6.22** and **E20.1**).

The offence of being 'in charge' is punishable by imprisonment for up to three months and/or a fine up to level 4. Disqualification is discretionary; endorsement with 10 penalty points is obligatory.

C5.20 ***Sentencing*** The Magistrates' Association's Sentencing Guidelines indicate that as a starting point a custodial sentence might properly be considered for readings of 100 microgrammes in 100 millilitres of breath (equating to 230 milligrammes in 100 millilitres of blood or 307 milligrammes in 100 millilitres of urine). In *Nokes* [1978] RTR 101, it was accepted that there is no rule that a first offence should not attract a custodial sentence if the facts show it to be appropriate. However, in *Cook* [1996] 1 Cr App R (S) 350, where the lower reading was 140 microgrammes in breath, the Court of Appeal quashed a sentence of two months' imprisonment, substituting a fine of £500; Sachs J said that it 'can never be appropriate to send a man for this criminality, at the lower end of the scale as it is, to prison'. The inference was that, in the absence of some aggravating feature, an immediate custodial sentence would not be imposed for this offence. The consternation caused was quickly met by a differently constituted Court of Appeal in *Shoult* [1996] RTR 298, in which Lord Taylor CJ explained that the decision had been based on a misunderstanding of the effect of the reading and that any general observations on sentencing were *obiter* and not to be followed. The Magistrates' Association's guidelines were expressly approved as the basic starting point, from which increases or reductions could be made depending on the individual facts of each case.

Failure to Provide Specimen of Breath

Road Traffic Act 1988, s. 6   C5.21

(1) Where a constable in uniform has reasonable cause to suspect—

(a)   that a person driving or attempting to drive or in charge of a motor vehicle on a road or other public place has alcohol in his body or has committed a traffic offence whilst the vehicle was in motion, or

(b)   that a person has been driving or attempting to drive or been in charge of a motor vehicle on a road or other public place with alcohol in his body and that that person still has alcohol in his body, or

(c)   that a person has been driving or attempting to drive or been in charge of a motor vehicle on a road or other public place and has committed a traffic offence whilst the vehicle was in motion,

he may, subject to section 9 of this Act, require him to provide a specimen of breath for a breath test.

(2)   If an accident occurs owing to the presence of a motor vehicle on a road or other public place, a constable may, subject to section 9 of this Act, require any person who he has reasonable cause to believe was driving or attempting to drive or in charge of the vehicle at the time of the accident to provide a specimen of breath for a breath test.

(3)   A person may be required under subsection (1) or subsection (2) above to provide a specimen either at or near the place where the requirement is made or, if the requirement is made under subsection (2) above and the constable making the requirement thinks fit, at a police station specified by the constable.

(4)   A person who, without reasonable excuse, fails to provide a specimen of breath when required to do so in pursuance of this section is guilty of an offence.

(5)   A constable may arrest a person without warrant if—

(a)   as a result of a breath test he has reasonable cause to suspect that the proportion of alcohol in that person's breath or blood exceeds the prescribed limit, or

(b)   that person has failed to provide a specimen of breath for a breath test when required to do so in pursuance of this section and the constable has reasonable cause to suspect that he has alcohol in his body,

but a person shall not be arrested by virtue of this subsection when he is at a hospital as a patient.

(6)   A constable may, for the purpose of requiring a person to provide a specimen of breath under subsection (2) above in a case where he has reasonable cause to suspect that the accident involved injury to another person or of arresting him in such a case under subsection (5) above, enter (if need be by force) any place where that person is or where the constable, with reasonable cause, suspects him to be.

(7)   [Applies only to Scotland.]

(8)   In this section 'traffic offence' means an offence under—

(a)   any provision of part II of the Public Passenger Vehicles Act 1981,

(b)   any provision of the Road Traffic Regulation Act 1984,

(c)   any provision of the Road Traffic Offenders Act 1988 except part III, or

(d)   any provisions of this Act except part V.

Elements   The RTOA 1988, ss. 11 and 12(1), apply; see **C2.5** and **C2.6**.   C5.22

For the meaning of the terms 'accident', 'driving', 'attempting to drive', 'motor vehicle' and 'road or other public place', see **C1.1**, **C1.8**, **C1.3**, **C1.11**, and **C1.13**. For the meaning of 'in charge', see **C5.11**.

The term 'fail' includes a refusal (RTA 1988, s. 11). Section 6(4) creates one offence of failing, without a reasonable excuse, to provide a specimen of breath (often called the 'roadside breath test'). It sets out the circumstances in which a constable may require a specimen before the procedure under s. 7 is commenced. In the absence of evidence of unfitness through drink or drugs, if a defendant passes the test, there is no power to arrest or to compel him to attend at the police station to provide a further specimen.

A constable is still in uniform even though he is without his helmet or wearing a mackintosh. The point of the requirement is that the person who requests the breath test should be easily identifiable as a constable, and in the absence of evidence to the contrary, justices are entitled to infer or assume from the surrounding circumstances that a constable is in uniform (*Gage* v *Jones* [1983] RTR 508).

The power of the police to stop a vehicle is now contained in the RTA 1988, s. 163. There is nothing to prevent random stopping, but the law requires one of the conditions in s. 6(1) or (2) to be complied with before a breath test is administered. The suspicion that a motorist has alcohol in his body does not, therefore, have to arise before the vehicle has been stopped by the police but can be formed at any stage (*Patterson* v *Charlton* [1986] RTR 18). In *Chief Constable of Gwent* v *Dash* [1986] RTR 41, police were stopping vehicles at random in order to apprehend drivers who might be suspected of having excess alcohol in their bodies. Macpherson J, giving the judgment of the Divisional Court, said (at pp. 46–7, emphasis added):

> . . . there is no restriction upon the stopping of motorists by a policeman *in the execution of his duty* and the subsequent requirement for a breath test should the policeman then and there genuinely suspect the ingestion of alcohol. It may be said by some to be bad luck that such a situation arises but it is not unlawful provided the officer is in uniform and acts without oppression, or caprice, or some false pretence or proved 'malpractice'.

> . . . these police officers were making genuine inquiries as to crime, and thus acting in the execution of their duty, in the sense that they were stopping vehicles in order to detect whether or not the drivers smelt of alcohol or showed other signs of having alcohol in their bodies, and provided there was nothing oppressive or capricious in what the police officers were doing, then there was not the material available on which malpractice should have been found to be present in their conduct. . . .

> Even if there was malpractice it would then probably, in my judgment, remain a matter for the exercise of the discretion of the court in order to decide whether or not to exclude the evidence of what followed depending on the court's view of the malpractice found to exist: see *Sang* [1980] AC 402.

The court did, however, distinguish cases where a person is arrested in his own house in a situation similar to that in *Morris* v *Beardmore* [1981] AC 446. See **C5.31**.

There must be reasonable cause to suspect that a person has alcohol in his body before a breath test may be required. This can be provided by information supplied by other persons and may arise after a motorist has ceased to drive, so long as it relates to the period when he was actually driving (*Moss* v *Jenkins* [1975] RTR 25; *Blake* v *Pope* [1986] 1 WLR 1152). Evidence of what the officer has been told is admissible if it goes to his state of mind at the time that he required the specimen of breath. Whilst the absence of 'reasonable cause' may invalidate an arrest under s. 6(5), it will now no longer invalidate the subsequent procedure unless the court exercises its discretion to exclude evidence under the PACE 1984, s. 78 (see *Griffiths* v *Willett* [1979] RTR 195). In *DPP* v *Wilson* [1991] RTR 284, it was held that the power to exclude evidence could arise from *Fox* [1986] AC 281 or *Dash*, and co-existed with a wide discretion under s. 78, but, distinguishing *Monaghan* v *Corbett* (1983) 147 JP 545, there was no duty on the police to warn a driver of a potential offence and failure to do so was not oppressive.

In *DPP* v *Godwin* [1991] RTR 303, the absence of a reasonable cause to suspect alcohol in the defendant's body, following a routine traffic stop check, which made an arrest unlawful did not automatically lead to the exclusion of evidence arising from the police station procedure, but justices had a discretion to exclude the breath analysis evidence under s. 78 without any finding of bad faith or oppression on the part of the police. The defendant had been denied the protection of the RTA 1988, s. 6, and the prosecution had obtained evidence which they would not otherwise have had. In those circumstances, the justices' decision to exclude the evidence was upheld.

Failing to follow the manufacturer's instructions about allowing a 20-minute gap to elapse after the consumption of alcohol before commencing the roadside test does not of itself render the result of the Intoximeter test and arrest unlawful (*DPP* v *Kay* [1999] RTR 109).

A person may be required to provide a specimen either at or near the place where the requirement is made (usually the roadside) or at a police station (see, e.g., *Moore* [1994] RTR 360). There must be a request but no particular form of words is necessary provided the constable is not acting *mala fides* and spoke 'the words in the honest and reasonable belief that they would be, and were being, heard and understood'; it is not necessary to prove that the person required to provide the specimen heard or understood (*Nicholls* [1972] 1 WLR 502).

Reasonable Excuse If a defendant has a 'reasonable excuse' for not taking the C5.23 roadside breath test, it is a defence to a charge under the RTA 1988, s. 6(4), but a subsequent arrest under s. 6(5)(b) may be lawful, and even if unlawful will not, in the absence of 'malpractice' etc., invalidate the procedure at the police station (*Hirst* v *Wilson* [1969] 3 All ER 1566; *Matto* v *Wolverhampton Crown Court* [1987] RTR 337; *Thomas* [1990] Crim LR 269). This, however, must be subject to the discretion to exclude evidence under the PACE 1984, s. 78. In such circumstances, the discretion is much wider than that envisaged in earlier authorities and, although the common-law discretion remains, it will, no doubt, be effectively superseded by further decisions under s. 78. It should be noted, however, that the statutory procedure under the RTA 1988, ss. 7 and 8, does not constitute an 'interview' for the purposes of Code C of the codes of practice under the PACE 1984 (*DPP* v *Rous* [1992] RTR 246).

A request made while a person is at a hospital as a patient is subject to the RTA 1988, s. 9, which is set out at **C5.36**.

Once the defence have raised a 'reasonable excuse', it is for the prosecution to negative it. A medical condition, such as a chest complaint, may constitute a reasonable excuse, or where the person required to provide the specimen is 'physically or mentally unable to provide it or its provision would entail a substantial risk to health' (*Lennard* [1973] 1 WLR 483). See also **C5.32**.

Punishment The penalty is a fine up to level 3 on the standard scale. Disqualification C5.24 is discretionary, but in the absence of 'special reasons' endorsement with four penalty points is obligatory.

Provision of Specimens

Road Traffic Act 1988, s. 7   C5.25

    (1) In the course of an investigation into whether a person has committed an offence under section 3A, 4 or 5 of this Act a constable may, subject to the following provisions of this section and section 9 of this Act, require him—
        (a) to provide two specimens of breath for analysis by means of a device of a type approved by the Secretary of State, or
        (b) to provide a specimen of blood or urine for a laboratory test.

(2)   A requirement under this section to provide specimens of breath can only be made at a police station.

(3)   A requirement under this section to provide a specimen of blood or urine can only be made at a police station or at a hospital; and it cannot be made at a police station unless—

(a)   the constable making the requirement has reasonable cause to believe that for medical reasons a specimen of breath cannot be provided or should not be required, or

(b)   at the time the requirement is made a device or a reliable device of the type mentioned in subsection (1)(a) above is not available at the police station or it is then for any other reason not practicable to use such a device there,

(bb)   a device of the type mentioned in subsection (1)(a) above has been used at the police station but the constable who required the specimens of breath has reasonable cause to believe that the device has not produced a reliable indication of the proportion of alcohol in the breath of the person concerned, or

(c)   the suspected offence is one under section 3A or 4 of this Act and the constable making the requirement has been advised by a medical practitioner that the condition of the person required to provide the specimen might be due to some drug;

but may then be made notwithstanding that the person required to provide the specimen has already provided or been required to provide two specimens of breath.

(4)   If the provision of a specimen other than a specimen of breath may be required in pursuance of this section the question whether it is to be a specimen of blood or a specimen of urine shall be decided by the constable making the requirement, but if a medical practitioner is of the opinion that for medical reasons a specimen of blood cannot or should not be taken the specimen shall be a specimen of urine.

(5)   A specimen of urine shall be provided within one hour of the requirement for its provision being made and after the provision of a previous specimen of urine.

(6)   A person who, without reasonable excuse, fails to provide a specimen when required to do so in pursuance of this section is guilty of an offence.

(7)   A constable must, on requiring any person to provide a specimen in pursuance of this section, warn him that a failure to provide it may render him liable to prosecution.

C5.26   ***Elements***   The RTOA 1988, ss. 11 and 12(1), apply; see **C2.5** and **C2.6**. 'Fail' includes a refusal (RTA 1988, s. 11). Whether there is a refusal is a matter of fact and degree for the tribunal of fact (*Smyth* v *DPP* [1996] RTR 59). The only conclusion where a motorist initially declined to provide the requested specimens of breath but indicated a desire to change his mind within some five seconds was that there had not been a refusal.

The RTA 1988, s. 11(4) and the RTOA 1988, s. 15(4), provide that a blood specimen may be taken only with the consent of the person who provides it and must be taken by a medical practitioner, otherwise it is to be disregarded.

In *DPP* v *Radford* [1995] RTR 86, the Divisional Court recommended that when prosecuting under the RTA 1988, s. 7(6), the prosecutor should draw the attention of the justices to the relevant authorities set out in the appropriate paragraph of *Stone's Justices' Manual* and to the criteria for consideration set out in *DPP* v *Curtis* [1993] RTR 72.

Section 7 creates one offence of failing to provide a specimen, but its provisions govern the procedure for obtaining evidence in relation to charges under ss. 3A, 4 and 5 of the RTA 1988. Failure without reasonable excuse to provide any specimen requested during the course of such an investigation is not cured by the subsequent provision of a different specimen as a result of a separate request, even if that specimen is below the prescribed limit (*Lorimer* v *Russell* 1996 SLT 501).

In *DPP* v *Butterworth* [1995] 1 AC 381, the House of Lords confirmed that s. 7(6) creates only one offence, overruling *DPP* v *Corcoran* [1993] 1 All ER 912 and approving *Shaw* v *DPP* [1993] 1 All ER 918 in the process. The essence of the offence is that the police are investigating whether the accused committed any of the offences in ss. 3A, 4 and 5 of the 1988 Act and so there is no need to identify in the charge a specific offence to which the mind of the investigating officer was directed.

Although s. 7(6) creates a single offence, two charges can be brought against the same defendant where two separate failures are alleged (*Chichester Justices, ex parte DPP* [1994] RTR 175). In that case the defendant was required to provide two specimens of breath for analysis. When a potential medical reason was raised, the investigating officer then required an alternative specimen, to which the defendant did not respond. Both failures were charged but the justices refused to hear them together and directed that they should be tried by differently constituted benches. The Divisional Court disagreed, finding that there was no rational basis for concluding that separate trials were needed.

As only one offence is created by s. 7(6), a charge stating that 'having been required to provide a specimen of breath/blood/urine for analysis, [the defendant] failed without reasonable excuse to do so' was found not to be duplicitous (*Worsley* v *DPP* [1995] Crim LR 572). Where, as in that case, the prosecution adduce evidence of failure to provide only one type of specimen, the additional words may appear immaterial but, on its face, the information looks capable of relating to three separate demands for three separate specimens, a refusal of any of which would be capable of providing the foundation for a separate charge, and therefore objectionable on the ground of duplicity. Tighter drafting of s. 7(6) charges would appear to be preferable.

The requirement to provide a specimen must arise 'in the course of an investigation', but the word 'investigation' does not imply any greater formality than is normally involved in the plain and ordinary meaning of the word (*Graham* v *Albert* [1985] RTR 352). Nor does the 'requirement' have to be in any formalised language, as long as it can be said to amount to a requirement, made at the correct place.

Where there is some doubt as to who was driving the motor vehicle at the relevant time, a constable may request all the persons suspected of driving to provide a specimen (*Pearson* v *Metropolitan Police Commissioner* [1988] RTR 276). Indeed, the defendant need not have been driving the motor vehicle on a road or other public place provided the request for a specimen is made in the course of an investigation and is made bona fide (*Hawkes* v *DPP* [1993] RTR 116).

A constable may only take two specimens under the RTA 1988, s. 7(1)(a), and one specimen under s. 7(1)(b), although in the face of a refusal or in order to make himself understood he may make as many requirements as he feels appropriate. If more than two specimens of breath are provided, the third and any subsequent specimens are inadmissible. In *Howard* v *Hallett* [1984] RTR 353, the constable operating the evidential breath test machine did not ask the appellant to provide a second specimen of breath after the first one had been obtained. He realised his mistake and then recommenced the procedure so that three specimens were taken. The prosecution sought to rely on the second specimen, the third having to be disregarded in accordance with what is now s. 8(1) of the 1988 Act. The Divisional Court rejected this approach on the ground that the second specimen provided was the one to be disregarded, and held that what is now the RTOA 1988, s. 15(2), refers to specimens taken in accordance with the statutory procedure which is now contained in the RTA 1988, s. 7.

Denny v *DPP* [1990] RTR 417 appears to run contrary to the decision in *Howard* v *Hallett*. In that case the Lion Intoximeter malfunctioned after the second breath sample had been provided. The police then took the appellant to another station where he agreed to provide two further specimens. Watkins LJ expressed the opinion that in a situation where the device is not working properly the motorist does not provide two valid specimens unless and until he blows properly into a device which is working properly 'so as to receive and properly analyse those specimens'. The question whether a refusal to provide further specimens amounts to a defence, in a situation where the machine malfunctions after two specimens have been provided, must therefore remain doubtful, despite Robert Goff LJ's assertion in *Sparrow* v *Bradley* [1985] RTR 122 at p. 127 that a motorist faced with such a situation might decline to provide further specimens into a second device. It was not mandatory for the police to require a specimen of blood or urine but at no stage does the Court of Appeal appear to have been referred to what is now s. 8(1) of the RTA 1988 nor the decision in *Howard* v *Hallett*. If the machine malfunctions it would therefore appear that there is no 'provision of specimens' in accordance with s. 7 of the Act and s. 8(1) would not be called into operation as both it and the decision in *Howard* v *Hallett* would only be of effect if a number of 'valid' specimens had been provided.

Howard v *Hallett* was followed in *Wakeley* v *Hyams* [1987] RTR 49, where it was held that failure to notify and allow the voluntary exercise of rights, in that case the blood/urine option available where a specimen does not exceed 50 microgrammes in 100 millilitres of breath (now in s. 7(4)), rendered both the breath and blood specimens inadmissible.

C5.27 **Blood or Urine** In *DPP* v *Warren* [1993] AC 319, the House of Lords held that, where a specimen of blood is required under the RTA 1988, s. 7(4), or because one of the circumstances in s. 7(3) applies, the driver need not be invited to express a preference for giving blood or urine, provided that if a specimen of blood is required he has the opportunity to raise objection to giving blood on medical grounds, to be determined by a medical practitioner, or for any other reason which might afford a reasonable excuse. The standard wording which appears to have been approved in that case (at p. 327) is as follows:

> I require you to provide an alternative specimen, which will be submitted for laboratory analysis. The specimen may be of blood or urine, but it is for me to decide which. If you provide a specimen you will be offered part of it in a suitable container. If you fail to provide a specimen you may be liable to prosecution. Are there any reasons why a specimen of blood cannot or should not be taken by a doctor?

In *Baldwin* v *DPP* [1996] RTR 238, the Divisional Court pointed out that these were guidelines as to interpretation rather than the statute itself (see **C5.35**).

The requirements stated by Lord Bridge in *Warren* were reviewed in *DPP* v *Jackson* [1998] 3 WLR 514. The House of Lords decided that, with three exceptions, those requirements were not to be treated as mandatory but as indicating the matters of which a driver should be aware so that he could know the role of the doctor in the taking of a specimen and in determining any medical objection which he might raise to the giving of such a specimen. The three mandatory exceptions are:

(a) in a s. 7(3) case, the warning as to the risk of prosecution required by s. 7(7) (see **C5.30**);

(b) in a s. 7(3) case, the statement of the reason under that subsection why breath could not be used; and

(c) in a s. 8(2) case (see **C5.35**), the statement that the specimen of breath which the driver had given containing the lower proportion of alcohol did not exceed 50 microgrammes in 100 millilitres of breath.

As well as complying with those three mandatory requirements, police officers, in order to seek to ensure that a driver would be aware of the role of the doctor, should continue to use the formula set out in *Warren* or words to the same effect.

Thus, the first issue for the justices to decide is whether the matters set out in the *Warren* formula were brought to the driver's attention by the police officer. If the answer is 'no', the second issue is whether, in relation to the non-mandatory requirements, the police officer's failure to give the full formula deprived the driver of the opportunity to express his position or caused him to express it in a way which he would not have done had everything been said. If the answer to the second issue is 'yes', the driver should be acquitted. But if the answer to the second issue is 'no', the police officer's failure to use the full formula should not be a reason for an acquittal. Both issues are questions of fact, so that if the justices, having heard the defendant's evidence, are not satisfied beyond a reasonable doubt that he was not prejudiced, they should acquit.

There is no requirement for a police officer to ask a driver if there is any non-medical reason why a specimen of blood should not be taken (*DPP* v *Jackson*).

A failure to allow the defendant the right to object to the giving of blood for medical reasons will lead to a conviction being quashed (*Meade* v *DPP* [1993] RTR 151; *Edge* v *DPP* [1993] RTR 146).

Section 7(3) may entitle a constable to require a specimen of blood or urine, even though specimens of breath have been required and provided. This requirement may be made only at a police station or at a hospital, and may be made at a police station only where the person's condition is due to drugs, or a breath testing device is not available or the constable has reasonable cause to believe either that the device has malfunctioned and not produced a reliable analysis of the specimen provided or that for medical reasons a specimen of breath cannot or should not be provided. See **C5.35**.

A failure to turn on the evidential breath testing machine 'modem' switch, as a result of which the device did not produce a printout, did not render a request under s. 7(3)(b), and a sample of urine thereby provided, inadmissible for the purposes of s. 8(2) of the Act (*Jones* v *DPP* [1991] RTR 41). Likewise, an invalid but unproductive request for a specimen of blood did not render evidence of a subsequent correctly-taken specimen of urine inadmissible (*DPP* v *Garrett* [1995] RTR 302). The investigating officer is entitled to change his mind as to the type of specimen being required until the defendant has complied with the requirement in s. 7(1).

Reliability of Device Whether or not a device is reliable depends upon how it **C5.28** functions. If it does not produce the correct date (*Slender* v *Boothby* [1986] RTR 385n) or if it operates outside its range of tolerance, it may not be regarded as reliable. In *DPP* v *McKeown* [1997] 1 WLR 295, however, the House of Lords held that the PACE 1984, s. 69, is concerned solely with the proper operation and functioning of a computer and that all the section requires for a computer-generated statement to be admissible is positive evidence that the computer had properly processed, stored and reproduced whatever information was received. So where the malfunctioning of the device's clock did not affect the way in which the device operated in these respects, the statement produced was admissible evidence upon which the justices were entitled to convict. On the other hand, where the challenge to the admissibility of the printout from the Intoximeter is more general, e.g., relating to the compensatory element where the device detects a substance believed to be acetone, reducing the alcohol reading accordingly, the Divisional Court has held that using s. 78 rather than s. 69 of the 1984 Act would be more appropriate (*Ashton* v *DPP* [1998] RTR 45).

The question of reliability was formerly subjective and depended upon the officer's reasonable belief (*Thompson* v *Thynne* [1986] RTR 293). With the introduction of s. 7(3)(bb), a replacement specimen can now be required where the investigating officer is presented objectively with reasonable cause to believe in the unreliability of the analysis produced. This might occur where the reading which is produced is wholly inconsistent with the defendant's admitted alcohol consumption and perceived physical state, although this course of action was not taken in the circumstances considered in *DPP* v *Spurrier* (1999) *The Times*, 12 August 1999.

A number of cases have called the reliability of the Intoximeter into question. Few seem to have met with success. In *Anderton v Waring* [1986] RTR 74, on a charge of failing to provide a specimen, the defendant had blown into the Intoximeter. The printout had then registered 'no sample'. The officer gave evidence that the respondent had appeared to be blowing round, and not into, the mouthpiece. The justices found that the defendant had made a full and proper attempt and, without any evidence about the visual display on the machine, further found that it should have shown the word 'aborted' if the officer's evidence was correct. They dismissed the charge. Allowing the prosecutor's appeal, May J, giving the judgment of the Divisional Court, said (at p. 80):

> ... the Intoximeter ought to have been assumed by the justices to have been in good working order unless the contrary was proved. In my judgment, they were not entitled to make use of their experience of these machines nor to draw any inference from the absence of evidence that the visual display on the Lion Intoximeter 3000 showed the word 'Aborted', at least without raising the point in the course of the trial, hearing whatever evidence either side wished to call in consequence and then deciding the point on that evidence, rather than on what they have learned during, for instance, demonstrations of the machine or previous prosecutions of a similar nature.

In addition the court criticised the justices for failing to take sufficient account of what is now the RTA 1988, s. 11(3) (see **C5.38**), and found, therefore, that in all the circumstances there was no material on which the justices could find a 'reasonable excuse'.

C5.29 ***Medical Reason***   The question of what constitutes a 'medical reason' for the purposes of the RTA 1988, s. 7(3)(a), is a question for the constable. What is important is the state of knowledge of the constable and his reasonable state of belief, bearing in mind that he is a layman. As long as he has 'reasonable cause to believe' that a specimen of breath cannot be provided for medical reasons, then that is sufficient, whether or not the medical reason advanced appears, 'in the cold light of day', to be an unsatisfactory one for declining to provide a specimen of breath (*Davies v DPP* [1989] RTR 391, per Neill LJ).

Incapacity due to a defendant being upset, shaken, intoxicated, distressed and of slight build can amount to a medical reason where the defendant was doing her best to provide a specimen and there was no other reason why she could not comply (*Webb v DPP* [1992] RTR 299, applying *Davies v DPP*). Intoxication alone may constitute such a medical reason (*Young v DPP* [1992] RTR 328). Reasonable cause may, it would appear (following *Andrews v DPP* [1992] RTR 1), arise as a result of a medical opinion no matter how wrong that opinion was. Fear of needles may constitute a medical reason in relation to the provision of a blood specimen (*Epping Justices, ex parte Quy* [1998] RTR 158n; see also *Johnson v West Yorkshire Metropolitan Police* [1986] RTR 167). The taking of tablets is also capable of being a medical reason (*Wade v DPP* [1996] RTR 177).

C5.30 ***Warning***   The warning in the RTA 1988, s. 7(7), is mandatory and must be understood by the person requested to provide the specimen. If he does not understand it, the warning is invalid; the subsequent procedure is then ineffectual and a defence becomes available to a charge under s. 7(6) (*Simpson v Spalding* [1987] RTR 221; *Chief Constable of Avon and Somerset Constabulary v Singh* [1988] RTR 107). A finding that the defendant understood the request for a specimen being made and the penal warning attached thereto is not affected by the fact that the defendant was being detained under s. 136 of the Mental Health Act 1983 (*Francis v DPP* [1997] RTR 113). A failure to give the warning in s. 7(7) or to comply with any of the appropriate statutory procedures will render evidence of the specimen inadmissible under the RTOA 1988, s. 15(2), even if there is no prejudice to the defendant (*Murray v DPP* [1993] RTR 209). However, self-induced intoxication rendering a person incapable of understanding what was being said could not provide a reasonable excuse for failing to provide as requested (*DPP v Beech* [1992] RTR 239).

Excluding Improperly Obtained Specimens Since the decision in *Fox* [1986] AC **C5.31**
281, a lawful arrest is not an essential prerequisite of a breath test under the RTA 1988,
s. 7. In that case, police officers had entered the appellant's home following an accident.
On his refusal to provide a specimen of breath, he was arrested, taken to the police
station, and provided a specimen containing 57 microgrammes of alcohol in 100
millilitres of breath. It was accepted that the powers of entry contained in what is now
s. 6(6) of the 1988 Act were not applicable and, since the arrest was unlawful, a
conviction under what is now s. 6(4) could not stand. The specimen provided at the
station was, however, admissible on the main charge of driving with excess alcohol in
the breath. Lord Fraser of Tullybelton said (at p. 292) 'the Divisional Court in the
present case was in my view right in treating the fact that the appellant was in the police
station because he had been unlawfully arrested merely as a historical fact, with which
the court was not concerned'. Indeed, it is arguable that no irregularity in the procedure
under s. 6 can have any effect on the subsequent procedure under s. 7 (*Carmichael* v
Wilson 1993 JC 83). See also *DPP* v *Heywood* [1998] RTR 1. As to the admissibility of
evidence illegally or unlawfully obtained, see generally **F2.6 *et seq***.

The judgment of the Divisional Court in *Fox* was applied in *Anderton* v *Royle* [1985]
RTR 91, a case where the defendant accompanied police officers to the station without
being arrested. The court found that there was no impropriety on the part of the police.
Consequently, the justices had been wrong to find that the legality of the procedure at
the police station was dependent on the presence or absence of an arrest, lawful or
otherwise. In *Bunyard* v *Hayes* [1985] RTR 348n and *Hartland* v *Alden* [1987] RTR 253,
the decision in *Fox* was extended to cover cases where the defendant refused to provide
a specimen.

The decision in *Fox* did, however, recognise a discretion to exclude admissible evidence
obtained by some trick, deception or other impropriety as envisaged in *Sang* [1980] AC
402. In *Matto* v *Wolverhampton Crown Court* [1987] RTR 337, officers followed the
appellant on to private property, continued to administer a breath test to him and
thereafter arrested him after their implied licence to remain had been terminated. The
Crown Court was of the opinion that in order to exercise the discretion under the PACE
1984, s. 78, it must find that the police officers were knowingly acting in excess of their
powers, and therefore acting *mala fide*, and that evidence had been obtained other than
voluntarily. In allowing the appeal, Woolf LJ stated that the approach of the Crown
Court was wrong (at p. 347):

> . . . it was at least open to the Crown Court, if the matter had been properly left before them,
> for them to have come to a conclusion that what happened at the house was still affecting
> the fairness of what happened in the police station and, because it affected the fairness of
> what happened at the police station, that would in turn give rise to an argument as to the
> admissibility of the evidence under section 78 of the Police and Criminal Evidence Act
> 1984.

In *Thomas* [1991] RTR 292, Tudor-Evans J stated (at p. 294):

> . . . in principle and upon authority, it is open to a defendant to argue that the procedures
> at the police station were so tainted by the previous conduct of the police at the roadside
> that there was a discretion to exclude the evidence of what happened at the police station.

It must now be regarded as established law that in road traffic cases a court has power
to exclude evidence under the PACE 1984, s. 78, even where there is no evidence of
mala fides. It is not normally permissible, however, to raise this issue before the
Divisional Court if it was not raised initially before the justices themselves (*Braham* v
DPP [1996] RTR 30).

Reasonable Excuse A person who fails without reasonable excuse to provide a **C5.32**
specimen is guilty of an offence. 'Fail' includes a refusal. In *Campbell* v *DPP* [1989] RTR

256, the appellant, having been cautioned, thereafter exercised his right of silence, so that when asked if he agreed to provide a specimen of breath he made no reply. The breath testing machine was in another room but it was not shown to him. Dismissing his appeal against a conviction for failing to provide a specimen of breath, the court was of the view that it was unnecessary to show the device to the appellant, and that his exercise of the right of silence had no bearing on his failure to provide a specimen. Self-induced intoxication which renders a defendant incapable of understanding the procedure cannot amount to a reasonable excuse (*DPP* v *Beech* [1992] RTR 239).

Once the defendant has agreed to provide breath specimens, the existence of a reasonable excuse has been negatived, so that, in the absence of any suggestion as to why there was subsequently a failure to provide, the court is entitled to regard the prosecution as having discharged the onus of proving the absence of a reasonable excuse (*Duncan* v *Normand* 1995 SLT 629).

Under the RTA 1988, s. 7(4), a specimen of urine is mandatory if a medical practitioner is of the opinion that for medical reasons blood cannot or should not be taken. If however the officer decides on the basis of a medical opinion that the specimen should be blood and a defendant refuses to provide a specimen it is open to him to raise a defence of 'reasonable excuse' or, indeed, if the opinion is wrong to rely on the PACE 1984, s. 78, to exclude evidence of the refusal (see *Andrews* v *DPP* [1992] RTR 1). Given the various authorities it would appear that a reasonable excuse for a failure to provide blood would have to be a medical one but if s. 78 were applicable the evidential onus to raise a 'reasonable excuse' might not have to arise.

Once a defence of reasonable excuse is raised it is for the prosecution to negative it. What constitutes a 'reasonable excuse' must always remain a matter of fact for the court. But in *Lennard* [1973] 1 WLR 483, Lawton LJ said (at p. 487):

> In our judgment no excuse can be adjudged a reasonable one unless the person from whom the specimen is required is physically or mentally unable to provide it or the provision of the specimen would entail a substantial risk to his health.

Normally, expert medical evidence of the physical or mental incapacity to provide the specimen is required to support the defence and demonstrate the existence of the necessary causative link between the incapacity and the failure to provide (*DPP* v *Crofton* [1994] RTR 279; *DPP* v *Brodzky* [1997] RTR 425n).

Lennard was applied in *DPP* v *Eddowes* [1991] RTR 35, when the Divisional Court stated that post-accident stress could not, without evidence showing mental or physical disability, constitute a reasonable excuse for failing to provide a specimen. In that case the justices had been persuaded by *Cotgrove* v *Cooney* [1987] RTR 124, that, where a defendant had tried as hard as he could to provide a specimen and been unable to do so, their decision that there was a reasonable excuse was a matter of fact for them and could not be assailed. The Divisional Court (per Watkins LJ) specifically disapproved *Cotgrove* v *Cooney*, stating that *Lennard* should be followed (see also *Spalding* v *Payne* [1985] Crim LR 673), and stated that post-accident stress could not, without evidence showing mental or physical disability, constitute a reasonable excuse for failing to provide a specimen. *Eddowes* was followed in *DPP* v *Ambrose* [1992] RTR 285. If a medical reason is claimed as a reason for not providing a specimen of blood, a medical practitioner's opinion that such a reason is not a medical one is conclusive.

Omitting to warn the defendant that there is a time limit for completing the breathalyser process, after which the Intoximeter stops functioning, will not amount to a reasonable excuse (*DPP* v *Coyle* [1996] RTR 287). Indeed *Cosgrove* v *DPP* [1997] RTR 153 confirmed that the investigating officer is not obliged to permit the driver the test's full three minutes in which to provide the required specimens.

Where a medical reason is advanced as a reasonable excuse, the justices should still give proper weight to the other evidence relating to the defendant's failure to provide, e.g., where the defendant put the device's tube to his mouth and no breath was registered, after having satisfactorily provided a first specimen and a roadside test (*DPP* v *Radford* [1995] RTR 86). Only if the Divisional Court decides that the justices' decision in this respect is perverse will it interfere.

Even without medical evidence justices are entitled, if they have the test in *Lennard* well in mind, to find that shock combined with inebriation which renders a defendant physically incapable may amount to a reasonable excuse for failing to provide a specimen (*DPP* v *Pearman* [1992] RTR 407; *DPP* v *Crofton* [1994] RTR 279). In *De Freitas* v *DPP* [1993] RTR 98, a phobia of catching AIDS, established by medical evidence, amounted to a reasonable excuse. Justices should however be wary of using their own knowledge of a medical condition which is not supported by or is beyond the evidence before them (*DPP* v *Curtis* [1993] RTR 72).

In *Chief Constable of Avon and Somerset Constabulary* v *Singh* [1988] RTR 107, it was held that a failure to provide a roadside breath test merely because the respondent claimed that he had not been driving at the time did not constitute a 'reasonable excuse'. His understanding of what was being required of him was held to be irrelevant, because he was putting forward a false story as to the driving of the vehicle. The court did accept that in certain circumstances a failure to understand the nature of that obligation might constitute a reasonable excuse, but added that before something could amount to an excuse 'it has to be causative in this sense, that it was the reason why the thing was not done'. However, failure to understand the mandatory warning which must accompany any request for a specimen, under what is now the RTA 1988, s. 7, was held to be fatal to the prosecutor's appeal. See also *Murray* v *DPP* [1993] RTR 209.

Insisting upon reading the PACE 1984 codes of practice before providing a specimen of breath is not a 'reasonable excuse' for failing to provide a specimen (*DPP* v *Cornell* [1990] RTR 254). In *Dickinson* v *DPP* [1989] Crim LR 741, legal advice given to the defendant by a solicitor who accompanied him to the police station to the effect that he should refuse a specimen was held not to constitute a reasonable excuse. Failure to provide a specimen because the defendant was waiting for the arrival of, or telephone advice from, a solicitor did not amount to a reasonable excuse (*DPP* v *Skinner* [1990] RTR 231 and *DPP* v *Varley* (1999) 163 JP 443, following *DPP* v *Billington* [1988] 1 WLR 535). The decision in *Smith* v *Hand* [1986] RTR 265 was explained as applying only to cases where the defendant has been told positively that he can wait for his solicitor although *Billington* clearly makes the distinction between imposing a condition and merely making a request in relation to the provision of legal advice.

In *DPP* v *Whalley* [1991] RTR 161, a finding that the notice given to detained persons misled the respondent to think that he had a right to consult the codes before further procedures was not enough to constitute a reasonable excuse for failing to provide a specimen. It was reiterated that an excuse would not be reasonable unless it followed *Lennard*, or was as a result of failing to understand the obligation to provide a specimen. In *Hudson* v *DPP* [1992] RTR 27, a differently constituted Divisional Court decided, however, that where a defendant had been provided with forms at the police station, which stated that he had a right to see a solicitor 'at any time', there was a discretion, under the PACE 1984, s. 78, to exclude evidence of a defendant's refusal to provide two specimens of breath until after he had seen a solicitor. Given the forms and the timescale of events at the station, it was not possible to say that there was no material upon which the court could exercise its discretion, and the case was remitted to the Crown Court for reconsideration. However, in *DPP* v *Rous* [1992] RTR 246, it was held that the procedure as to the provision of specimens, whether relating to a request under s. 7(4) or 8(2), does not constitute an interview and therefore there is no discretion under the PACE 1984, s. 78, to exclude evidence relating to the procedure. Indeed note 6C to Code C of the codes of practice issued under the 1984 Act specifically states that procedures under s. 7 do not constitute interviewing. It is submitted, however, that, whilst the procedure may not be an interview, the PACE 1984, s. 78, is of general application and, if material arises in the course of the procedure which comes within s. 78, the court has a discretion under s. 78, which must be exercised judicially, to exclude evidence which is unfairly obtained.

C5.33 ***Punishment*** Where the defendant was driving or attempting to drive, the penalty is six months' imprisonment and/or a fine up to level 5. Disqualification and endorsement are, in the absence of 'special reasons', obligatory. The offence carries between 3 and 11 penalty points.

In any other case, the penalty is three months' imprisonment and/or a fine up to level 4. Disqualification is discretionary, but endorsement with 10 penalty points, in the absence of 'special reasons', is obligatory.

Forfeiture of the vehicle may be ordered under either offence (see **C6.22** and **E20.1**).

C5.34 ***Sentencing*** In *George* v *DPP* [1989] RTR 217, it was held that justices erred in considering disqualification to be obligatory where a defendant had pleaded guilty to an information alleging he had failed to provide two (*sic*) specimens of breath on the basis that he was 'in charge' rather than driving. The justices had based their conclusion on the fact that he had made an admission that he had driven the vehicle to the point where police officers found him asleep. However, the prosecution case having been put on the 'in charge' basis, sentence could be passed only on the basis that he was 'in charge' and not driving. In *Waltham Forest Justices, ex parte Barton* [1990] RTR 49, the Divisional Court indicated that where a defendant is charged with failing to provide a specimen at the police station the charge itself should indicate that 'the specimen was required to ascertain the ability of the defendant at the time he was driving or attempting to drive'. The decision in *DPP* v *Butterworth* [1995] 1 AC 381, however, makes it clear that there is no need to specify in the charge whether the allegation is that the defendant was only 'in charge' or driving or attempting to drive. Lord Slynn stated (at p. 394) that 'the question whether the person was driving or in charge of the motor vehicle is not part of the inquiry into whether there has been a refusal for the purposes of section 7(6). That question only becomes relevant after conviction and goes to the appropriate penalty'. Accordingly, the charge itself does not need to indicate whether the defendant faces a mandatory or discretionary disqualification, although the prosecution might be asked informally on what basis the case is being put.

C5.35 ***Replacement Specimens***

Road Traffic Act 1988, s. 8

(1) Subject to subsection (2) below, of any two specimens of breath provided by any person in pursuance of section 7 of this Act that with the lower proportion of alcohol in the breath shall be used and the other shall be disregarded.

(2) If the specimen with the lower proportion of alcohol contains no more than 50 microgrammes of alcohol in 100 millilitres of breath, the person who provided it may claim that it should be replaced by such specimen as may be required under section 7(4) of this Act and, if he then provides such a specimen, neither specimen of breath shall be used.

(3) The Secretary of State may by regulations substitute another proportion of alcohol in the breath for that specified in subsection (2) above.

When specimens have been provided, the lower of the two specimens is the relevant one for the purposes of proceedings. If both are the same, then both are admissible. The failure to offer the statutory option is fatal (*Clwyd Justices, ex parte Charles* (1990) 154 JP 486).

If the specimen provided is 50 microgrammes or less, the person providing the specimen must be offered the option of giving another specimen, either of blood or urine, under the RTA 1988, s. 7(4). There is however no requirement to give the warning in s. 7(7) where the driver is asked if he wishes to give a replacement specimen (*Hayes* v *DPP* [1994] RTR 163). The driver is not entitled to legal advice before deciding whether to exercise the option (*DPP* v *Ward* [1999] RTR 11, following *DPP* v *Billington* [1988] RTR 231: see **C5.32**). If the driver gives a medical reason as to why he should not provide a particular replacement specimen, a failure to investigate the validity of that reason or to give the option of providing the other type of replacement specimen may preclude the prosecution from relying on the breath specimen (*Epping Justices, ex parte Quy* [1998] RTR 158n).

The decision of the House of Lords in *DPP* v *Warren* [1993] AC 319 (see **C5.27**), which relates to the choice of specimen (blood or urine), is applicable where the defendant claims to have the breath specimen replaced by one of blood or urine in accordance with s. 7(4). As long as the driver has an opportunity to raise objection to giving blood on medical grounds and the option is given, the requirements of the procedure will be satisfied. The explanation of the matters that the driver has to be told in order to exercise his proper right in this respect must be sufficiently detailed (*Turner* v *DPP* [1996] RTR 274n). *DPP* v *Hill-Brookes* [1996] RTR 279 decided that the procedure outlined in *DPP* v *Warren* should be followed but that slavish adherence to precise wording was unnecessary as long as the meaning was retained, and a differently constituted Divisional Court (relying generally on the analysis of *DPP* v *Warren* provided in *DPP* v *Charles* [1996] RTR 247, especially at p. 265) pointed out in *Baldwin* v *DPP* [1996] RTR 238 that Lord Bridge's words provided guidelines as to interpretation only and did not constitute the statute itself. Curtis J suggested that so long as the option provided for in s. 8(2) was given fairly and properly so that the driver could make an informed choice, the requirements of justice would be satisfied. Indeed, in *Fraser* v *DPP* [1997] RTR 373, Lord Bingham CJ explained that, when offered the option, there were plainly several things which a driver had to be told at some stage, but it did not follow that he had necessarily to be told all of them at the outset. In that case, it was held that there is no statutory requirement to tell the driver in terms that a blood sample would be taken by a doctor. Similarly, applying *Fraser*, a differently constituted Divisional Court held in *Cheshire Stipendiary Magistrate, ex parte DPP* (1997) *The Times*, 13 March 1997 that an investigating officer is not required to ask the driver in advance of his refusal to provide a specimen of blood or urine whether there are any reasons why a specimen of blood could not or should not be taken from him by a doctor. These decisions and *Beaufont* v *DPP* [1998] RTR 175 must now be regarded in the light of the decision of the House of Lords in *DPP* v *Jackson* [1998] 3 WLR 514 (see **C5.27**). In addition to telling the driver that a specimen of blood 'will be taken by a doctor unless the doctor considers that there are medical reasons for not taking the blood', the officer should ask the driver if there are any medical reasons why a specimen could not or should not be taken by a doctor. The driver should be told of the doctor's role at the outset before he has to make the decision to give blood. It is a question of fact whether the driver's statement that he does not like needles raises a potential medical reason for not providing a blood specimen and the justices may be entitled to find on the facts that the officer was not obliged to investigate the issue further.

As there is no statutory requirement to tell a driver that his breath specimen was above the prescribed limit, failing to do so does not render any replacement specimen provided inadmissible (*DPP* v *Ormsby* [1997] RTR 394n).

One consequence of *DPP* v *Warren* was a spate of applications for judicial review of earlier convictions where the police had not followed the procedure laid down by Lord Bridge (*Cheshire Justices, ex parte Sinnott* [1995] RTR 281; *Cheshire Justices, ex parte*

Cunningham [1995] RTR 287n). Initially, any departure from the *Warren* procedure led to the convictions being quashed. Since then, however, the Divisional Court has doubted that there is jurisdiction to grant judicial review where there has been an unequivocal plea of guilty, in the absence of conduct on the part of the prosecutor which is either fraudulent or analogous to fraud (*Burton upon Trent Justices, ex parte Woolley* [1995] RTR 139; *Dolgellau Justices, ex parte Cartledge* [1996] RTR 207). Consequently, the scope for re-opening such convictions has been drastically reduced, unless there are other means of demonstrating injustice to the applicant.

A failure by the driver to provide an alternative specimen does not render the specimen of breath unavailable for use; a condition precedent to the exclusion of the breath test is the provision of an alternative specimen (*DPP* v *Winstanley* [1993] RTR 222; *Hague* v *DPP* [1997] RTR 146). In *Winstanley* the defendant asked to provide a specimen in accordance with s. 8(2). He did not object to that specimen being of blood. A doctor was called but did not arrive and after an hour the officer required two specimens of urine which the defendant was unable, through no fault of his own, to provide. In the circumstances, it was held that the officer was entitled to change the request from blood to urine, and that, unless the defendant did in fact provide such a specimen or specimens, the breath test specimen remained admissible.

If the blood specimen is inadmissible as a result of any irregularity, or if the prosecution do not, for any reason, rely upon it, the effect of s. 8(2) is mandatory in precluding the use of the breath specimens (*Archbold* v *Jones* [1986] RTR 178; *Wakeley* v *Hyams* [1987] RTR 49). This extends to cases in which the defendant advances 'special reasons' (*Smith* v *Geraghty* [1986] RTR 222). Where the justices find that an unrecorded conversation may have taken place between the police and the defendant, which may have had the effect of dissuading the accused from exercising the right to claim a replacement specimen, they should acquit, as the prosecutor would have failed to have proved beyond reasonable doubt that the correct statutory procedure had been followed (*Rush* v *DPP* [1994] RTR 268). However, where a driver frustrates the efforts of a police officer to explain the blood/urine option, the prosecution are entitled to rely on the result of the breath test (*DPP* v *Poole* [1992] RTR 177). Where the defendant's consumption of alcohol results, at least partly, in an inability to comprehend the offer being made, the breath specimen is not rendered inadmissible (*DPP* v *Berry* (1996) 160 JP 707).

In *Yhnell* v *DPP* [1989] RTR 250, the prosecution were entitled to adduce evidence of the breath specimen when the defendant had provided a sample of blood. His deliberate falsification of his part of the blood specimen, by the injection of blood unaffected by alcohol, called the procedure into question. It was held that the justices were entitled to admit evidence of the Intoximeter specimen but so that they might be satisfied the procedure had been strictly gone through in order to ascertain that the prosecution had established their right to rely on the blood sample. Where a defendant has provided a blood sample and the kit used by the doctor contains ethanol (the alcohol contained in alcoholic drinks), that may produce an artificially high blood/alcohol reading. The Divisional Court may in such circumstances exercise their supervisory role (even though the defendant has pleaded guilty) and quash a conviction (*Bolton Justices, ex parte Scally* [1991] 1 QB 537).

C5.36 **Protection for Hospital Patients**

Road Traffic Act 1988, s. 9

(1) While a person is at a hospital as a patient he shall not be required to provide a specimen of breath for a breath test or to provide a specimen for a laboratory test unless the medical practitioner in immediate charge of his case has been notified of the proposal to make the requirement; and—

(a) if the requirement is then made, it shall be for the provision of a specimen at the hospital, but

(b) if the medical practitioner objects on the ground specified in subsection (2) below, the requirement shall not be made.

(2) The ground on which the medical practitioner may object is that the requirement or the provision of a specimen or, in the case of a specimen of blood or urine, the warning required under section 7(7) of this Act, would be prejudicial to the proper care and treatment of the patient.

A person is at a hospital as a patient when he is within the hospital's curtilage and he is there for treatment, even as an out-patient. Once the treatment has been performed it would seem that the person is no longer a patient within the meaning of s. 9 (*A-G's Ref (No. 1 of 1976)* [1977] 1 WLR 646). The doctor who is directly responsible for the patient is the medical practitioner in immediate charge of his case.

In *Burton upon Trent Justices, ex parte Woolley* [1995] RTR 139, the Divisional Court did not follow the guidance previously given in *DPP* v *Duffy* [1994] RTR 241 and concluded that, in a case involving a patient in a hospital, there is no obligation for the constable to inform the driver why a specimen of breath cannot be taken but, at some stage during the process at the hospital, the constable has to ask the driver whether there is any reason why a specimen of blood should not be taken. Thereafter, the details of the procedure laid down in *DPP* v *Warren* [1993] AC 319 (see **C5.27**) should be followed. A requirement lawfully made under s. 9 remains valid after the patient's discharge from hospital and must therefore be complied with unless it is abundantly plain that, following discharge, the investigating officer is setting in train the s. 7 procedure (*Webber* v *DPP* [1998] RTR 111).

Detention of Persons Affected by Alcohol or a Drug By virtue of the RTA 1988,   **C5.37** s. 10, following a request for a specimen of breath, blood or urine, a person may be detained at a police station until it appears to a constable that if he were driving or attempting to drive he would not be committing an offence under s. 4 or 5 of the Act. If, however, it appears to the constable that there is no likelihood of that person driving or attempting to drive whilst his ability is impaired or he is over the limit, then he may not be detained under s. 10. If a question arises in relation to detention as to whether or not a person's ability to drive is, or might be, impaired through drugs, the constable must consult a medical practitioner and act on his advice.

Interpretation of the Road Traffic Act 1988, ss. 3A to 10

Road Traffic Act 1988, s. 11   **C5.38**

(1) The following provisions apply for the interpretation of sections 3A to 10 of this Act.

(2) In those sections—

'breath test' means a preliminary test for the purpose of obtaining, by means of a device of a type approved by the Secretary of State, an indication whether the proportion of alcohol in a person's breath or blood is likely to exceed the prescribed limit,

'drug' includes any intoxicant other than alcohol,

'fail' includes refuse,

'hospital' means an institution which provides medical or surgical treatment for in-patients or out-patients,

'the prescribed limit' means, as the case may require—

(a) 35 microgrammes of alcohol in 100 millilitres of breath,

(b) 80 milligrammes of alcohol in 100 millilitres of blood, or

(c) 107 milligrammes of alcohol in 100 millilitres of urine,

or such other proportion as may be prescribed by regulations made by the Secretary of State.

(3) A person does not provide a specimen of breath for a breath test or for analysis unless the specimen—

(a) is sufficient to enable the test or the analysis to be carried out, and

(b)   is provided in such a way as to enable the objective of the test or analysis to be satisfactorily achieved.

(4)   A person provides a specimen of blood if and only if he consents to its being taken by a medical practitioner and it is so taken.

Motor Racing on Highways

C5.39   **Road Traffic Act 1988, s. 12**

(1)   A person who promotes or takes part in a race or trial of speed between motor vehicles on a public way is guilty of an offence.

C5.40   *Elements*   The RTOA 1988, ss. 11 and 12(1), apply; see **C2.5** and **C2.6**.

This offence seems intended to prohibit organised motor racing on a highway, but might equally apply where two or more drivers are engaged in an unofficial race or speed trial. Such conduct may, of course, be an offence under the RTRA 1984, s. 88(7), or the RTA 1988, s. 2 or 3, but its ambit appears to be wider as persons who 'promote' or 'take part' may be convicted, and there is thus no requirement to prove an act of driving but merely of participation.

C5.41   *Punishment*   The offence carries a fine of up to level 4 on the standard scale. Unless 'special reasons' are established, there is a minimum disqualification from driving for a period of 12 months. Persons who 'promote' or 'take part' must be disqualified even though they are not drivers. The offence is endorsable with between 3 and 11 penalty points.

Leaving Vehicle in Dangerous Position

C5.42   **Road Traffic Act 1988, s. 22**

If a person in charge of a vehicle causes or permits the vehicle or a trailer drawn by it to remain at rest on a road in such a position or in such condition or in such circumstances as to involve a danger of injury to other persons using the road, he is guilty of an offence.

C5.43   *Elements*   For the meaning of the terms 'causing', 'permitting' and 'using', see **C1.5**, **C1.6**, and **C1.7**. The RTOA 1988, ss. 1, 11, and 12(1), apply; see **C2.1**, **C2.5**, and **C2.6**.

Section 22 applies to any vehicle, not just a motor vehicle. The offence may be established either where the vehicle itself involves a danger of injury (e.g., if it is on fire or parked on a hill without brakes and secured only by stones or bricks placed under the wheels), or where, because of its position on the road, it creates a danger. For example, parking a car or other vehicle on the corner of a busy intersection, obstructing the view of other motorists emerging from a side road, involves a danger of injury, because motorists would be forced to emerge 'blind' and, however cautiously this was done, the likelihood of a collision and consequent injury would remain.

C5.44   *Punishment*   A fine up to level 3 on the standard scale. If committed in respect of a motor vehicle, disqualification is discretionary and endorsement with three penalty points is obligatory.

Restriction of Carriage of Persons on Motor Cycles

C5.45   **Road Traffic Act 1988, s. 23**

(1)   Not more than one person in addition to the driver may be carried on a motor bicycle.

(2)   No person in addition to the driver may be carried on a motor bicycle otherwise than sitting astride the motor cycle and on a proper seat securely fixed to the motor cycle behind the driver's seat.

(3)   If a person is carried on a motor cycle in contravention of this section, the driver of the motor cycle is guilty of an offence.

Elements The RTOA 1988, ss. 11 and 12(1), apply; see **C2.5** and **C2.6**.   **C5.46**

Punishment The offence carries a fine up to level 3. Disqualification is discretionary   **C5.47**
and endorsement with three penalty points obligatory.

Neglect or Refusal to Comply with Traffic Directions Given by Constable

Road Traffic Act 1988, s. 35   C5.48

(1)   Where a constable is for the time being engaged in the regulation of traffic in a road,
a person driving or propelling a vehicle who neglects or refuses—
    (a)   to stop the vehicle, or
    (b)   to make it proceed in, or keep to, a particular line of traffic,
when directed to do so by the constable in the execution of his duty is guilty of an offence.
    (2)   Where—
    (a)   a traffic survey of any description is being carried out on or in the vicinity of a
road, and
    (b)   a constable gives to a person driving or propelling a vehicle a direction—
        (i)   to stop the vehicle,
        (ii)   to make it proceed in, or keep to, a particular line of traffic, or
        (iii)   to proceed to a particular point on or near the road on which the vehicle is
being driven or propelled,
being a direction given for the purposes of the survey (but not a direction requiring any
person to provide any information for the purposes of a traffic survey),
the person is guilty of an offence if he neglects or refuses to comply with the direction.
    (3)   The power to give such a direction as is referred to in subsection (2) above for the
purposes of a traffic survey shall be so exercised as not to cause any unreasonable delay to
a person who indicates that he is unwilling to provide any information for the purposes of
the survey.

Elements The RTOA 1988, ss. 1, 11 and 12(1) apply; see **C2.1, C2.5**, and **C2.6**.   **C5.49**

This section extends to any vehicle as long as it is being driven or propelled. The
reference to a constable includes a traffic warden if he is engaged in accordance with
s. 35 in the regulation of traffic in the road.

There are two offences created. For an offence under s. 35(2), the constable must be
giving a direction for the purposes of a traffic survey. Under s. 35(1), the constable must
be acting in the execution of his duty, which in this case means a duty to protect life and
property arising from the dangers created by unregulated traffic (*Hoffman* v *Thomas*
[1974] 1 WLR 374; *Johnson* v *Phillips* [1976] 1 WLR 65). It is arguable, therefore, that
for s. 35 to operate, the constable must have been engaged upon traffic duties and not
exercising his powers either under the PACE 1984 or the RTA 1988, s. 163.

Punishment The offence carries a fine up to level 3. If the offence is committed in   **C5.50**
respect of a motor vehicle, disqualification is discretionary, but endorsement with three
penalty points is obligatory.

Failure to Comply with Indication Given by Traffic Sign

Road Traffic Act 1988, s. 36   C5.51

(1)   Where a traffic sign, being a sign—
    (a)   of the prescribed size, colour and type, or
    (b)   of another character authorised by the Secretary of State under the provisions in
that behalf of the Road Traffic Regulation Act 1984,
has been lawfully placed on or near a road, a person driving or propelling a vehicle who fails
to comply with the indication given by the sign is guilty of an offence.
    (2)   A traffic sign shall not be treated for the purposes of this section as having been
lawfully placed unless either—
    (a)   the indication given by the sign is an indication of a statutory prohibition,
restriction or requirement, or

(b) it is expressly provided by or under any provision of the Traffic Acts that this section shall apply to the sign or to signs of a type of which the sign is one;

and, where the indication mentioned in paragraph (a) of this subsection is of the general nature only of the prohibition, restriction or requirement to which the sign relates, a person shall not be convicted of failure to comply with the indication unless he has failed to comply with the prohibition, restriction or requirement to which the sign relates.

C5.52   ***Elements***   The RTOA 1988, ss. 1, 11, 12(1) and 20, apply; see **C2.1**, **C2.5**, **C2.6** and **C2.10**.

Traffic signs are prescribed by regulations made under the RTRA 1984, s. 64. If a sign indicates a statutory prohibition, restriction or requirement, or if it is expressly provided under any provision of the Traffic Acts that the section applies to the sign, a failure to comply with it is an offence.

The main relevant statutory instrument is the Traffic Signs Regulations and General Directions 1994 (SI 1994 No. 1519). Failure to comply with any traffic sign may constitute an offence but only failure by a person driving a motor vehicle to comply with a sign of a kind specified in reg. 10(2) of the regulations carries endorsement and disqualification. The signs so specified are 'Stop' signs at the junction of minor and major roads; 'double white lines'; 'Drivers of Large or Slow Vehicles Must Phone' signs at automatic half-barrier level crossings or automatic open crossings; and the red signal when shown by light signals prescribed by the regulations.

Emergency traffic signs are included, and all signs are deemed to conform unless the contrary is proved.

Save for possible defences of mechanical defect or automatism (as to which, see **C1.10** and **C1.4**), the section creates an absolute offence.

For contravention of the 'Stop' sign, it is necessary to prove either that the vehicle did not stop before crossing the line or, if the line is unclear, before entering the major road, or that the vehicle when proceeding past the line or entering the major road, if that line is not clearly visible, did so in a manner likely to cause danger to the driver of another vehicle on the major road, or so as to cause that driver to change his speed or course so as to avoid an accident.

For contravention of a red light, it is necessary to prove that the vehicle proceeded beyond the stop line or, if that is not visible or there is no stop line, beyond the mounting of the primary signal.

Regulation 33(1)(b) contains a waiver of the prohibition conveyed by the red light for vehicles being used for fire brigade, ambulance or police purposes, and substitutes instead a requirement that the vehicle will not proceed so as to cause danger to the driver of another vehicle, or to necessitate the driver of any such vehicle to change his speed or course in order to avoid an accident or so as to cause danger to non-vehicular traffic. See also *DPP* v *Harris* [1995] 1 Cr App R 170.

The prohibition contained by 'double white lines' operates not only to prevent the vehicle crossing those lines, but also to forbid vehicles stopping on any length of road along which the marking has been placed. Regulation 26 does, however, contain certain exemptions for vehicles which have to cross the line for the purposes of obtaining access or to pass a stationary vehicle, to enable passengers to board and alight, and so forth. Stopping within double white lines to pick up a taxi fare is not an offence (*McKenzie* v *DPP* [1997] RTR 175).

Where there was a failure to place a white arrow before solid double white lines in the centre of the road the lines were not a sign 'lawfully placed' for the purposes of regs. 10,

26 and direction 43 of the Traffic Signs Regulations and General Directions 1994 and failure to comply with the double white lines was, therefore, not an offence contrary to s. 36 of the RTA 1988 (*O'Halloran* v *DPP* [1990] RTR 62).

Punishment The offence carries a fine up to level 3. If committed in respect of a **C5.53** motor vehicle by a failure to comply with a specified sign (see **C5.52**), disqualification is discretionary, but endorsement with three penalty points is obligatory.

Using Vehicle in Dangerous Condition

Road Traffic Act 1988, s. 40A   C5.54

A person is guilty of an offence if he uses, or causes or permits another to use, a motor vehicle or trailer on a road when—
   (a)   the condition of the motor vehicle or trailer, or of its accessories or equipment, or
   (b)   the purpose for which it is used, or
   (c)   the number of passengers carried by it, or the manner in which they are carried, or
   (d)   the weight, position or distribution of its load, or the manner in which it is secured,
is such that the use of the motor vehicle or trailer involves a danger of injury to any person.

Elements The RTOA 1988, ss. 11 and 12(1) apply; see **C2.5** and **C2.6**. For the **C5.55** meaning of the terms 'using', 'causing' and 'permitting' see **C1.7**, **C1.5**, and **C1.6**.

Section 40A puts into statute the more important construction and use requirements and widens the scope of their operation. For example, if the circumstances applying in *Young and C. F. Abraham (Transport) Ltd* v *CPS* [1992] RTR 194 (see **C5.58**) were to be repeated, s. 40A(d) would apply. Where a passenger is carried in the rear of a van and there are no seats or restraints of any kind there, the speed at which the van is driven will be a material consideration in relation to whether the manner of carriage is such as to involve a danger of injury under s. 40A(c) (*Akelis* v *Normand* 1997 SLT 136). Section 40A(c) involves considering objectively whether there was a danger inherent in the circumstances in which the vehicle was being driven at the material time (*Gray* v *DPP* [1999] RTR 339).

Punishment The offence is endorsable with three penalty points; disqualification is **C5.56** discretionary. Where the offence is committed in respect of a goods vehicle or a vehicle adapted to carry more than eight passengers, a fine of up to level 5 may be imposed; in other cases, a fine up to level 4 may be imposed.

Contravention of Construction and Use Regulations

Road Traffic Act 1988, s. 41A   C5.57

A person who—
   (a)   contravenes or fails to comply with a construction and use requirement as to brakes, steering-gear or tyres, or
   (b)   uses on a road a motor vehicle or trailer which does not comply with such a requirement, or causes or permits a motor vehicle or trailer to be so used,
is guilty of an offence.

Section 41B makes contravention of a requirement in relation to the weight of a goods vehicle or a passenger vehicle adapted to carry more than eight passengers an offence. It is a defence if the vehicle is proceeding to or from the nearest weighbridge. In addition a 5 per cent excess may be excluded in certain circumstances.

Section 42 makes contravention of the other construction and use requirements an offence and extends this to cover 'using', 'causing' or 'permitting'.

Elements The RTOA 1988, ss. 11 and 12(1) apply to all three sections; see **C2.5** and **C5.58** **C2.6**. For the meaning of the terms 'using', 'causing' and 'permitting', see **C1.7**, **C1.5**, and **C1.6**. The relevant requirements are those contained in the Road Vehicles (Construction and Use) Regulations 1986 (SI 1986 No. 1078).

In order to show that a vehicle does not fall within any of the definitions contained either in the regulations or the Act, the burden of proof is on the defendant (*Wakeman* v *Catlow* [1977] RTR 174).

Regulations 13 to 18 and sch. 3 deal with brakes. Even if a trailer is not required to have brakes under reg. 18, any brakes fitted must be maintained in efficient working order (*DPP* v *Young* [1991] RTR 56). Regulation 27 deals with tyres.

Regulation 100 deals with vehicles which are in a dangerous condition and loads which cause a danger. See the RTA 1988, s. 42(2), for a statutory defence to a summons alleging a failure to comply with a requirement relating to any description of weight applicable to a goods vehicle. In *Young and C. F. Abraham (Transport) Ltd* v *CPS* [1992] RTR 194, a trailer loaded with an excavator collided with a footbridge because the excavator arms and bucket had not been lowered. The driver and the company were prosecuted for using a trailer for an unsuitable purpose 'as to cause or be likely to cause danger or nuisance to any person . . . on a road'. The Divisional Court decided that the risk came from the incorrect loading rather than the use of the trailer and that, in such circumstances, the offence was not made out.

An examination of a vehicle, for the purposes of a prosecution, which involves a permanent alteration to its condition does not render the evidence thereby obtained inadmissible under the PACE 1984, s. 78, merely because the defence are unable to examine the vehicle in its original condition. It would be prudent for the prosecution to inform the defence of their examination and to afford them an opportunity to be present, but justices should hear such evidence and the fact that the defence are denied an opportunity to examine the vehicle goes to weight rather than admissibility (*DPP* v *British Telecommunications plc* [1991] Crim LR 532).

If the weight of a vehicle is measured by computer, the PACE 1984, s. 69(1) (see **F8.31** *et seq.*), places the burden of proving its correct operation at the time on the prosecution. In the absence of the normal certificate to that effect, direct evidence would be required from the weighbridge operator and it would be wrong for the justices to infer a proper functioning of the computer where there is a substantial lapse of time from the last test of the machinery in question (*Connolly* v *Lancashire County Council* [1994] RTR 79; *East West Transport Ltd* v *DPP* [1996] RTR 184).

C5.59   *Punishment*   A breach of s. 41A is endorsable with three penalty points; disqualification is discretionary. Where an offence is committed in respect of a goods vehicle or a vehicle adapted to carry more than eight passengers, a fine of up to level 5 may be imposed; in other cases, a fine up to level 4.

Breaches of s. 41B or 42 are not endorsable. Section 41B carries a fine up to level 5 and s. 42 carries a fine up to level 4 if committed in respect of a goods vehicle or a vehicle adapted to carry more than eight passengers; in other cases, a fine of up to level 3.

Driving Otherwise than in Accordance with a Licence

C5.60   **Road Traffic Act 1988, s. 87**

> (1)   It is an offence for a person to drive on a road a motor vehicle of any class otherwise than in accordance with a licence authorising him to drive a motor vehicle of that class.
> (2)   It is an offence for a person to cause or permit another person to drive on a road a motor vehicle of any class otherwise than in accordance with a licence authorising that other person to drive a motor vehicle of that class.

This offence encompasses driving without 'L' plates or (an alternative applicable only within Wales) 'D' plates, without supervision, driving under age and driving without a licence.

Elements   The RTOA 1988, ss. 11 and 12(1), apply; see **C2.5** and **C2.6**. For the   **C5.61**
meaning of 'cause' and 'permit', see **C1.5** and **C1.6**.

Section 88 of the Act creates certain exceptions.

Foreign drivers are subject to the Motor Vehicles (International Circulation) Order 1975 (SI 1975 No. 1208). If a person resident abroad and temporarily resident in Great Britain holds a Convention driving permit, a foreign driving permit or a British Forces (BFG) driving licence, it shall be lawful for him to drive during a period of 12 months from his last entry into the United Kingdom (unless he is under the minimum age or disqualified by court order). Community licence holders normally resident in Great Britain are no longer obliged to exchange their licences for ones issued under the 1988 Act so as to obtain continuing authorisation to drive (s. 99A of the Act), the only requirement being to deliver their Community licences within the prescribed period to the Secretary of State to enable counterparts to be issued (s. 99B of the Act).

Punishment   The offence carries a fine up to level 3. If the offender's driving would   **C5.62**
not have been in accordance with a licence that could have been granted, then, in the absence of 'special reasons', disqualification is discretionary and endorsement with between three and six penalty points is obligatory.

An offence of causing or permitting a person to drive without an appropriate licence contrary to s. 87(2) is punishable only by a fine up to level 3 on the standard scale.

False Declaration as to Physical Fitness

Road Traffic Act 1988, s. 92   **C5.63**

> (10)   A person who holds a licence authorising him to drive a motor vehicle of any class and who drives a motor vehicle of that class on a road is guilty of an offence if the declaration included in accordance with subsection (1) above in the application on which the licence was granted was one which he knew to be false.

The RTOA 1988, ss. 6, 11 and 12(1) apply; see **C2.2**, **C2.5** and **C2.6**. The offence carries a fine up to level 4 and in the absence of 'special reasons' carries disqualification and endorsement with between three and six penalty points.

Failure to Notify Disability

Road Traffic Act 1988, s. 94   **C5.64**

> (3A)   A person who holds a licence authorising him to drive a motor vehicle of any class and who drives a motor vehicle of that class on a road is guilty of an offence if at any earlier time while the licence was in force he was required by subsection (1) above to notify the Secretary of State but has failed without reasonable excuse to do so.

The RTOA 1988, ss. 6, 11, and 12(1), apply; see **C2.2**, **C2.5** and **C2.6**. By virtue of the RTA 1988, s. 99D(b), a modified version of s. 94(3A) applies to holders of Community licences normally resident in Great Britain. The offence carries a fine up to level 3 on the standard scale. In the absence of 'special reasons', disqualification is discretionary and the offence is endorsable with between three and six penalty points.

Driving after Refusal or Revocation of Licence

Road Traffic Act 1988, s. 94A   **C5.65**

> (1)   A person who drives a motor vehicle of any class on a road otherwise than in accordance with a licence authorising him to drive a motor vehicle of that class is guilty of an offence if—

    (a)   at any earlier time the Secretary of State—
       (i)   has in accordance with section 92(3) of this Act refused to grant such a licence,
      (ii)   has under section 93(1) or (2) of this Act revoked such a licence, or
     (iii)   has served notice on that person in pursuance of section 99C(1) or (2) of this
Act requiring him to deliver to the Secretary of State a Community licence authorising him
to drive a motor vehicle of that or a corresponding class, and
    (b)   since that earlier time he has not been granted—
       (i)   a licence under this part of this Act, or
      (ii)   a Community licence,
authorising him to drive a motor vehicle of that or a corresponding class.
    (2)   Section 88 of this Act shall apply in relation to subsection (1) above as it applies in
relation to section 87.

The RTOA 1988, ss. 6, 11 and 12(1), apply; see **C2.2, C2.5** and **C2.6**. The offence is
punishable by six months' imprisonment and/or a fine up to level 5. In the absence of
'special reasons' disqualification is discretionary and the offence is endorsable with
between three and six penalty points. Forfeiture of the vehicle involved may also be
ordered (see **C6.22** and **E20.1**).

Driving with Uncorrected Defective Eyesight

C5.66   **Road Traffic Act 1988, s. 96**

    (1)   If a person drives a motor vehicle on a road while his eyesight is such (whether
through a defect which cannot be or one which is not for the time being sufficiently
corrected) that he cannot comply with any requirement as to eyesight prescribed under this
part of this Act for the purposes of tests of competence to drive, he is guilty of an offence.
    (2)   A constable having reason to suspect that a person driving a motor vehicle may be
guilty of an offence under subsection (1) above may require him to submit to a test for the
purpose of ascertaining whether, using no other means of correction than he used at the
time of driving, he can comply with the requirement concerned.
    (3)   If that person refuses to submit to the test he is guilty of an offence.

The test is set out in the Motor Vehicles (Driving Licences) Regulations 1996 (SI 1996
No. 2824).

C5.67   ***Punishment***   The offence carries a fine up to level 3 on the standard scale.
Disqualification is discretionary, but the offence is endorsable with three penalty points.

Using etc. Motor Vehicle without Insurance

C5.68   **Road Traffic Act 1988, s. 143**

    (1)   Subject to the provisions of this part of this Act—
    (a)   a person must not use a motor vehicle on a road unless there is in force in relation
to the use of the vehicle by that person such a policy of insurance or such a security in respect
of third party risks as complies with the requirements of this part of this Act, and
    (b)   a person must not cause or permit any other person to use a motor vehicle on a
road unless there is in force in relation to the use of the vehicle by that other person such a
policy of insurance or such a security in respect of third party risks as complies with the
requirements of this part of this Act.
    (2)   If a person acts in contravention of subsection (1) above he is guilty of an offence.
    (3)   A person charged with using a motor vehicle in contravention of this section shall
not be convicted if he proves—
    (a)   that the vehicle did not belong to him and was not in his possession under a
contract of hiring or of loan,
    (b)   that he was using the vehicle in the course of his employment, and
    (c)   that he neither knew nor had reason to believe that there was not in force in
relation to the vehicle such a policy of insurance or security as is mentioned in subsection
(1) above.
    (4)   This part of this Act does not apply to invalid carriages.

Elements   The RTOA 1988, ss. 6, 11, and 12(1), apply; see **C2.2**, **C2.5**, and **C2.6**.   **C5.69**
For the meaning of the terms 'use', 'cause', and 'permit', see **C1.7**, **C1.5**, and **C1.6**.

The burden of proof rests on the defendant, i.e. he is required to produce evidence of a valid insurance policy (*DPP* v *Kavaz* [1999] RTR 40).

For the owner of a vehicle to be convicted of using without insurance when it was being driven by someone else, it has to be proved that the defendant owned the vehicle and that the driver at the time was employed by the owner and was, at the material time, acting in the course of his employment (*Jones* v *DPP* [1999] RTR 1).

The section imposes an absolute liability irrespective of knowledge, even if the charge is for 'causing' or 'permitting' (*Lyons* v *May* [1948] 2 All ER 1062; *Tapsell* v *Maslen* [1967] Crim LR 53). However, if the person who allows the use of a vehicle does so on the express condition that the user insures it, he is not 'permitting' the uninsured use of the vehicle within the meaning of s. 143 (*Newbury* v *Davis* [1974] RTR 367). That case, however, appears to be confined to its own facts. In *DPP* v *Fisher* [1992] RTR 93, the Divisional Court declined to follow *Newbury* where the driver of the vehicle was not in communication directly with the owner even though the owner only authorised the use of the vehicle by a suitably insured person. Lack of knowledge of unauthorised use of a vehicle does not constitute 'permitting'.

Section 144 of the RTA 1988 contains certain exceptions. The requirements of a policy of insurance are set out in the RTA 1988, s. 145.

By s. 161, 'policy of insurance' includes a covering note. By s. 147(1), a policy of insurance is of no effect under s. 143 until delivered to the party by whom the policy is effected. The burden is on the defendant to prove the facts necessary to establish the statutory defence for employees in s. 143(3).

A policy of insurance obtained by misrepresentation or non-disclosure of material facts is not a 'policy of insurance' for the purposes of the RTA 1930, s. 36(4) (*Guardian Assurance Co. Ltd* v *Sutherland* [1939] 2 All ER 246, per Branson J). A voidable policy does, however, satisfy the requirements of s. 143 until it is avoided (*Durrant* v *MacLaren* [1956] 2 Lloyd's Rep 70; *Adams* v *Dunne* [1978] RTR 281).

Payment of petrol money on a regular 'school run' which went beyond the bounds of mere social kindness may bring the vehicle (if it is adapted to carry more than eight passengers) within the meaning of the term 'public service vehicle' (*DPP* v *Sikondar* [1993] RTR 90). This may in turn vitiate a policy of insurance so as to bring the driver within the ambit of s. 143.

Punishment   Disqualification is discretionary, but endorsement with between six and   **C5.70**
eight penalty points is obligatory. A fine up to level 5 may be imposed.

Failing to Stop and Failing to Report Accident

Road Traffic Act 1988, s. 170   C5.71

    (1)   This section applies in a case where, owing to the presence of a mechanically propelled vehicle on a road, an accident occurs by which—
      (a)   personal injury is caused to a person other than the driver of that mechanically propelled vehicle, or
      (b)   damage is caused—
        (i)   to a vehicle other than that mechanically propelled vehicle or a trailer drawn by that mechanically propelled vehicle, or
        (ii)   to an animal other than an animal in or on that mechanically propelled vehicle or a trailer drawn by that mechanically propelled vehicle, or
        (iii)   to any other property constructed on, fixed to, growing in or otherwise forming part of the land on which the road in question is situated or land adjacent to such land.

(2)   The driver of the mechanically propelled vehicle must stop and, if required to do so by any person having reasonable grounds for so requiring, give his name and address and also the name and address of the owner and the identification marks of the vehicle.

(3)   If for any reason the driver of the mechanically propelled vehicle does not give his name and address under subsection (2) above, he must report the accident.

(4)   A person who fails to comply with subsection (2) or (3) above is guilty of an offence.

(5)   If, in a case where this section applies by virtue of subsection (1)(a) above, the driver of a motor vehicle does not at the time of the accident produce such a certificate of insurance or security, or other evidence, as is mentioned in section 165(2)(a) of this Act—

(a)   to a constable, or

(b)   to some person who, having reasonable grounds for so doing, has required him to produce it,

the driver must report the accident and produce such a certificate or other evidence.

This subsection does not apply to the driver of an invalid carriage.

(6)   To comply with a duty under this section to report an accident or to produce such a certificate of insurance or security, or other evidence, as is mentioned in section 165(2)(a) of this Act, the driver—

(a)   must do so at a police station or to a constable, and

(b)   must do so as soon as is reasonably practicable and, in any case, within 24 hours of the occurrence of the accident.

(7)   A person who fails to comply with a duty under subsection (5) above is guilty of an offence, but he shall not be convicted by reason only of a failure to produce a certificate or other evidence if, within seven days after the occurrence of the accident, the certificate or other evidence is produced at a police station that was specified by him at the time when the accident was reported.

(8)   In this section 'animal' means horse, cattle, ass, mule, sheep, pig, goat or dog.

C5.72   ***Elements***   For the meaning of the terms 'accident', 'driver' and 'vehicle', see **C1.1**, **C1.8** and **C1.14**.

The RTOA 1988, ss. 11 and 12(1), apply; see **C2.5** and **C2.6**.

Section 170(2) creates one offence which may be committed in a number of different ways. Section 170(3) creates a separate offence, as does s. 170(7) (*DPP* v *Bennett* [1993] RTR 175).

The object of s. 170, it is submitted, is to identify the parties involved for the purposes of both civil and criminal proceedings. To that end, it is a question of fact whether providing the name and address of a third party satisfies the requirements of the section (*DPP* v *McCarthy* [1999] RTR 323); in that case, the driver gave his name and the address of his solicitors, which was found to be sufficient. It is not necessary for the motor vehicle to be directly involved with the accident, but the prosecution must establish causation because of the presence of the defendant's motor vehicle on the road (*Quelch* v *Phipps* [1955] 2 QB 107). Nor is it necessary for the driver to be physically present in the vehicle at the time of the accident (provided his absence does not terminate the act of 'driving': (see **C1.8**) (*Cawthorn* v *DPP* (1999) *The Times*, 31 August 1999). In *Harding* v *Price* [1948] 1 KB 695, it was established that where a driver is unaware of an accident, he cannot be aware of a duty to stop or report and is entitled to be acquitted. When it is sought to establish this, the onus of proof rests on the defendant (see also *Hampson* v *Powell* [1970] 1 All ER 929).

Following such an accident as is mentioned in s. 170(1), the driver is obliged to remain at the scene for a reasonable time so that he can fulfil his obligations under s. 170(2) (*Lee* v *Knapp* [1967] 2 QB 442; *Ward* v *Rawson* [1978] RTR 498). The obligation does not extend to searching out persons who might be entitled to the information required under s. 170(2) (*Mutton* v *Bates* [1984] RTR 256).

Whether or not the vehicle is stopped at the appropriate point is a question of fact; where a driver chose to drive on for 80 yards before stopping and returning to the scene of the accident, the Divisional Court was not prepared to interfere with a decision finding that this constituted a failure to stop as required, because it could not be said to be one which no court, properly directing itself upon the law, could rationally have arrived at (*McDermott* v *DPP* [1997] RTR 474). Under s. 170(2), a driver is required to stop immediately so that witnesses might make themselves known and any person wishing to request the driver's particulars might do so (*Hallinan* v *DPP* [1998] Crim LR 754).

Partial compliance with the requirements will not suffice, but if he has stopped and has not been required to provide any or all of the details mentioned in s. 170(2), the driver will fulfil his obligation, subject, however, to a duty to report the accident in the manner prescribed by s. 170(6) if he has not given his name and address. The obligation to report an accident under s. 170(3) therefore exists whenever a driver has not provided his name and address.

In *DPP* v *Drury* [1989] RTR 165, it was held that a driver who is not aware of an accident but who subsequently becomes aware of it, must report the accident to a police station personally if he becomes aware within 24 hours of the accident occurring. Reporting an accident by telephone is insufficient, and the obligation appears to be one that must, in the absence of physical impossibility, be performed personally (*Wisdom* v *Macdonald* [1983] RTR 186).

In an accident involving more than one other person or vehicle, the driver may be required to provide details to a number of people, and failure to provide those details to any one who has reasonable grounds for requiring them is an offence. If, however, the driver has furnished particulars, including his name and address, to at least one person and has satisfied all other requests made, then it is submitted he is not obliged to report the accident in the manner prescribed by s. 170(6), unless personal injury has been caused to someone other than the driver.

Where personal injury is caused to anyone other than the driver of the vehicle, the driver must produce his insurance certificate (or such other documentation as would satisfy s. 165(2)(a) of the Act) at the time of the accident either to a constable or any other person who has reasonable grounds for requesting him to produce it. If he does not produce insurance (or such other documentation as would satisfy s. 165(2)(a) of the Act), either because he was not able to or because he was not so required, he must report the accident in the manner prescribed by s. 170(6).

Punishment An offence under s. 170(4) is punishable with up to six months' **C5.73** imprisonment and/or a fine up to level 5 on the standard scale. Disqualification is discretionary but endorsement, with between five and ten penalty points, is obligatory. Forfeiture of the vehicle concerned may also be ordered (see **C6.22** and **E20.1**).

Traffic Regulation in Special Cases

Under ss. 14 and 15 of the RTRA 1984 where works are being or are proposed to be **C5.74** executed on or near a road, the highway authority may make temporary orders restricting or prohibiting the use of that road by vehicles. A person who contravenes or uses or permits the use of a vehicle in contravention of the restriction or prohibition commits an offence under s. 16 of the Act, punishable by a fine up to level 3 and, where the offence is committed in respect of a speed restriction, discretionary disqualification and endorsement with between three and six penalty points (or three points in the case of a fixed penalty). The RTOA 1988, ss. 1, 11 and 12(1) apply; see **C2.1**, **C2.5** and **C2.6**.

The RTRA 1984, s. 17 allows the Secretary of State to make regulations concerning the class of vehicles authorised to use special roads and the manner in which they can be used. A special road has the same meaning as in the Highways Act 1980. The section does not apply to Crown servants and vehicles. Contravention of the section or regulations made thereunder is an offence punishable by a fine up to level 4. Disqualification is discretionary if the offence is committed in accordance with the RTOA 1988, sch. 2, part 1, col. 5 but, if committed in that manner, endorsement (in the absence of 'special reasons') with three penalty points is obligatory, except where the offence is committed in respect of a speed restriction when endorsement with between three and six penalty points (or three points in the case of a fixed penalty) is obligatory. The RTOA 1988, ss. 1, 11 and 12(1) apply; see **C2.1**, **C2.5** and **C2.6**.

Pedestrian Crossing Regulations

C5.75   The RTRA 1984, s. 25, enables the Secretary of State to make regulations in respect of vehicles and pedestrians at and in the vicinity of crossings. The current regulations are the Zebra, Pelican and Puffin Pedestrian Crossings Regulations and General Directions 1997 (SI 1997 No. 2400). Contravention of the regulations is an offence punishable by a fine up to level 3 on the standard scale. Disqualification when a motor vehicle is involved is discretionary, but endorsement with three penalty points is obligatory. The regulations apply to all vehicles.

Street Playgrounds

C5.76   Section 29 of the RTRA 1984 makes provision for orders for certain streets to be designated street playgrounds. Contravention of any order is an offence punishable with a fine up to level 3 on the standard scale. Disqualification when a motor vehicle is involved is discretionary, but endorsement with two penalty points is obligatory.

Failing to Stop at School Crossing

C5.77   **Road Traffic Regulation Act 1984, s. 28**

(1)   When between the hours of eight in the morning and half-past five in the afternoon a vehicle is approaching a place in a road where children on their way to or from school, or from one part of a school to another, are crossing or seeking to cross the road, a school crossing patrol wearing a uniform approved by the Secretary of State shall have power, by exhibiting a prescribed sign, to require the person driving or propelling the vehicle to stop it.
(2)   When a person has been required under subsection (1) above to stop a vehicle—
(a)   he shall cause the vehicle to stop before reaching the place where the children are crossing or seeking to cross and so as not to stop or impede their crossing, and
(b)   the vehicle shall not be put in motion again so as to reach the place in question so long as the sign continues to be exhibited.
(3)   A person who fails to comply with paragraph (a) of subsection (2) above, or who causes a vehicle to be put in motion in contravention of paragraph (b) of that subsection, shall be guilty of an offence.

C5.78   *Elements*   The driver of a motor vehicle must stop unless the sign has been removed by the time he arrives at the crossing (*Franklin* v *Langdown* [1971] 3 All ER 662).

C5.79   *Punishment*   A fine up to level 3 may be imposed. Discretionary disqualification if the offence is committed by using a motor vehicle, but obligatory endorsement with three penalty points.

Speeding

C5.80   **Road Traffic Regulation Act 1984, s. 89**

(1)   A person who drives a motor vehicle on a road at a speed exceeding a limit imposed by or under any enactment to which this section applies shall be guilty of an offence.
(2)   A person prosecuted for such an offence shall not be liable to be convicted solely on the evidence of one witness to the effect that, in the opinion of the witness, the person prosecuted was driving the vehicle at a speed exceeding a specified limit.
(3)   The enactments to which this section applies are—
(a)   any enactment contained in this Act except section 17(2);

(b)   section 2 of the Parks Regulation (Amendment) Act 1926; and

(c)   any enactment not contained in this Act, but passed after 1 September 1960, whether before or after the passing of this Act.

(4)   If a person who employs other persons to drive motor vehicles on roads publishes or issues any timetable or schedule, or gives any directions, under which any journey, or any stage or part of any journey, is to be completed within some specified time, and it is not practicable in the circumstances of the case for that journey (or that stage or part of it) to be completed in the specified time without the commission of such an offence as is mentioned in subsection (1) above, the publication or issue of the timetable or schedule, or the giving of the directions, may be produced as prima facie evidence that the employer procured or (as the case may be) incited the persons employed by him to drive the vehicle to commit such an offence.

Elements   The section applies only to 'motor vehicles', see **C1.11**. The RTOA 1988,   **C5.81**
ss. 1, 11 and 12(1) apply; see **C2.1**, **C2.5** and **C2.6**.

Driving at grossly excessive speed might, in itself, constitute dangerous driving (see *McQueen* v *Buchanan* 1997 SLT 765 at **C3.9**).

Section 87 of the 1984 Act exempts motor vehicles being used for fire brigade, ambulance or police purposes, if observance of the speed limit would be likely to hinder the purpose for which they are being used.

Evidence from an approved device is admissible to prove speeding offences under s. 89 (see RTOA 1988, s. 20 at **C2.10**). In *Darby* v *DPP* [1995] RTR 294, the Divisional Court held that a speed trap device was a computer and its reading was, therefore, admissible in evidence without a certificate under the PACE 1984, s. 69, as it was corroborating the evidence of the constable.

Section 89(2) provides a statutory requirement of corroboration. Opinion evidence as to speed is admissible, but because of the danger of inaccuracy inherent in such evidence, it was felt necessary to require corroboration. See generally, *Nicholas* v *Penny* [1950] 2 KB 466 and *Swain* v *Gillet* [1974] RTR 446. The reading of a police car's speedometer is capable of supplying the necessary corroboration, even if there is no evidence of testing, though the weight of such evidence is open to question (see *Swain* v *Gillet* [1974] RTR 446). It would satisfy the statutory requirement to have the opinion evidence of two or more witnesses, provided that their observations occurred at the same time (*Brighty* v *Pearson* [1938] 4 All ER 127).

Factual evidence, however, does not require corroboration, and evidence of the speed recorded on the speedometer of a police car, driven at an even distance behind the appellant's car, was held to be sufficient to sustain a conviction (*Nicholas* v *Penny* [1950] 2 KB 466). The speedometer does not need to be tested, and in the absence of evidence to the contrary can be presumed, as can radar guns, radar speed meters and other mechanical instruments, to be in order at the material time (*Castle* v *Cross* [1984] 1 WLR 1372; *Burton* v *Gilbert* [1984] RTR 162). Where the prosecution has been given notice that a serious issue is being raised in relation to evidence based on the radar gun, it is quite simple either for the approval of the device to be established by production of the necessary schedule or for the constable to give evidence that the device used was an approved one; if this line of defence is taken at the last minute, the justices can be invited to take judicial notice on the point or allow the constable to be recalled (*Roberts* v *DPP* [1994] RTR 31). Where an adjournment is occasioned in these circumstances, the defendant is highly likely to be at risk of having to pay the costs occasioned by it.

The expert evidence of an 'Accident Examiner' which entails the reconstruction of events from various tests, skid marks and damage, is considered to be based on more than mere opinion where he describes the facts on which his opinion is based (*Crossland* v *DPP* [1988] 3 All ER 712).

It is not open to the prosecution to accept a plea of guilty to a charge of speeding which had been committed for trial under the CJA 1988, s. 41, and offer no evidence on the indictable offence (*Avey* [1994] RTR 419). Offences committed for trial under s. 41 can be dealt with only following a conviction for an indictable offence arising out of circumstances which are the same as or connected with the summary offence. In such circumstances, the proper course for the Crown Court is to remit the s. 41 offence to be dealt with by the justices.

C5.82   ***Punishment***   A fine up to level 3 on the standard scale may be imposed. Disqualification is discretionary. Endorsement, with three penalty points when a fixed penalty is imposed and with between three and six penalty points in any other case, is obligatory.

SECTION C6: SENTENCING GENERALLY

Production of Licence

Road Traffic Offenders Act 1988, s. 27

(1)   Where a person who is the holder of a licence is convicted of an offence involving obligatory or discretionary disqualification, and a court proposes to make an order disqualifying him or an order under section 44 of this Act, the court must, unless it has already received them, require the licence and its counterpart to be produced to it.

(2)   [Repealed.]

(3)   If the holder of the licence has not caused it and its counterpart to be delivered, or posted it and its counterpart, in accordance with section 7 of this Act and does not produce it and its counterpart as required under this section or section 44 of the Powers of Criminal Courts Act 1973, ... then, unless he satisfies the court that he has applied for a new licence and has not received it—

(a)   he is guilty of an offence, and

(b)   the licence shall be suspended from the time when its production was required until it and its counterpart are produced to the court and shall, while suspended, be of no effect.

(4)   Subsection (3) above does not apply where the holder of the licence—

(a)   has caused a current receipt for the licence and its counterpart issued under section 56 of this Act to be delivered to the clerk of the court not later than the day before the date appointed for the hearing, or

(b)   has posted such a receipt, at such time that in the ordinary course of post it would be delivered not later than that day, in a letter duly addressed to the clerk and either registered or sent by the recorded delivery service, or

(c)   surrenders such a receipt to the court at the hearing,

and produces the licence and its counterpart to the court immediately on their return.

'Licence' includes a Community licence and 'new licence' includes a counterpart of a Community licence (RTOA 1988, s. 91A(1) and (2)). The reference in s. 27(3) to the PCCA 1973, s. 44, has effect as if it also included a reference to the C(S)A 1997, s. 39 (C(S)A 1997, s. 39(5)).

When an offender has been requested to produce his driving licence, a failure to produce it is, unless he has applied for a new licence which he has not received or s. 27(4) applies, an offence punishable by a fine up to level 3 on the standard scale. The licence is also suspended until it is produced, and if the offender drives during that suspension, he is guilty of an offence under the RTA 1988, s. 87(1).

Penalty Points

Road Traffic Offenders Act 1988, s. 28

(1)   Where a person is convicted of an offence involving obligatory endorsement, then, subject to the following provisions of this section, the number of penalty points to be attributed to the offence is—

(a)   the number shown in relation to the offence in the last column of part I or part II of schedule 2 to this Act, or

(b)   where a range of numbers is shown, a number within that range.

(2)   Where a person is convicted of an offence committed by aiding, abetting, counselling or procuring, or inciting to the commission of, an offence involving obligatory disqualification, then, subject to the following provisions of this section, the number of penalty points to be attributed to the offence is 10.

(3)   Where both a range of numbers and a number followed by the words '(fixed penalty)' is shown in the last column of part I of schedule 2 to this Act in relation to an offence, that number is the number of penalty points to be attributed to the offence for the

purposes of sections 57(5) and 77(5) of this Act; and, where only a range of numbers is shown there, the lowest number in the range is the number of penalty points to be attributed to the offence for those purposes.

(4)   Where a person is convicted (whether on the same occasion or not) of two or more offences committed on the same occasion and involving obligatory endorsement, the total number of penalty points to be attributed to them is the number or highest number that would be attributed on a conviction of one of them (so that if the convictions are on different occasions the number of penalty points to be attributed to the offences on the later occasion or occasions shall be restricted accordingly).

(5)   In a case where (apart from this subsection) subsection (4) above would apply to two or more offences, the court may if it thinks fit determine that that subsection shall not apply to the offences (or, where three or more offences are concerned, to any one or more of them).

(6)   Where a court makes such a determination it shall state its reasons in open court and, if it is a magistrates' court . . . shall cause them to be entered in the register . . . of its proceedings.

(7) to (9)   [Powers of Secretary of State to alter penalty points and matters consequent.]

The effect of s. 28 is to give the court a discretion to impose penalty points in respect of two or more offences committed on the same occasion and thereby aggregate the penalty points imposed in order to disqualify under the 'penalty points' system (s. 28(5)). Reasons must be given in open court and magistrates have to enter them in the register. The power can be used where none of the offences is so serious as to merit disqualification in its own right but the totality of the offending merits disqualification, possibly because of the number of offences or because the offences are of different types.

It should be noted that aiding and abetting etc. an offence involving obligatory disqualification, such as driving with excess alcohol, carries 10 penalty points but does not entail mandatory disqualification. In offences not involving obligatory disqualification, secondary participation entails the same punishment as for the principal.

The expression 'same occasion' was considered in *Johnson* v *Finbow* [1983] 1 WLR 879, where the appellant was charged with offences of failing to stop after an accident and failing to report the accident to the police. The Divisional Court accepted that there was an argument that the offences were not committed on the same occasion, but Robert Goff LJ, giving the judgment of the court, went on to say (at pp. 882–3):

> . . . looking at the matter more broadly (and, for my part, I think more sensibly), it can be said that the lapse of time, although significant, is not sufficiently great to be able to say, as a matter of common sense, that those offences were committed on different occasions. It is true that they were committed at different moments of time; indeed, they might even have been committed on different days. On the other hand, they certainly arose out of the same accident. And when one sees how closely they are connected with the accident, and how very similar, in fact, the two offences are in their nature, then I think the proper conclusion is that when arising out of the same accident these two offences are committed on the same occasion.

In *Johnston* v *Over* (1984) 6 Cr App R (S) 420, the defendant had parked two vehicles outside his home. He was charged with two offences of 'using' a vehicle without insurance. The Divisional Court stated that whether or not an offence was 'committed on the same or on different occasions' depended upon the facts of each case, and that in this case, as a matter of common sense, both offences were committed on the same occasion. However, in *McKeever* v *Walkinshaw* 1996 SLT 1228, the High Court of Justiciary upheld a finding that offences of speeding and crossing a double white line committed at separate points on the same stretch of road during a single course of driving had not occurred on the same occasion. Given the temporal link and the possibility of invoking s. 28(5) to justify imposing separate sets of penalty points, this appears to be an unduly harsh interpretation of s. 28(4).

Offences which are committed on separate occasions have the number or highest number of penalty points awarded separately, and, if committed within three years of each other, those points are added up for the purposes of the RTOA 1988, s. 35.

For further details, see **C7.1** *et seq*. and **C8.2**.

Points to be Taken into Account on Conviction

Road Traffic Offenders Act 1988, s. 29   **C6.3**

    (1)   Where a person is convicted of an offence involving obligatory endorsement, the penalty points to be taken into account on that occasion are (subject to subsection (2) below)—

    (a)   any that are to be attributed to the offence or offences of which he is convicted, disregarding any offence in respect of which an order under section 34 of this Act is made, and

    (b)   any that were on a previous occasion ordered to be endorsed on the counterpart of any licence held by him, unless the offender has since that occasion and before the conviction been disqualified under section 35 of this Act.

    (2)   If any of the offences was committed more than three years before another, the penalty points in respect of that offence shall not be added to those in respect of the other.

The effect of s. 29 is that penalty points remain on the licence; it is not 'wiped clean' by a disqualification under the RTOA 1988, s. 34. If a disqualification is imposed under s. 34, any points attributable to that offence are to be disregarded for the purposes of penalty points to be taken into account on conviction. Thus if a defendant is convicted of two offences committed on the same occasion, one of which carries mandatory disqualification, points on the other offence will be taken into account for the purposes of s. 35. Under the previous legislation, points taken into account were the highest number attributable to one of them. Where there is a disqualification under s. 34, the licence is not endorsed with penalty points.

Even if the offender is disqualified for an offence before the court, the relevant number of penalty points (denoted in sch. 2, part I, col. 7 of the Act) must still be 'taken into account' for the purposes of s. 35.

A previous disqualification under the penalty points system has the effect of wiping the licence clean. Points ordered since the disqualification have to be taken into account even if they are imposed in respect of an offence committed before the disqualification, unless, of course, the offence was committed more than three years before another.

For further details, see **C7.1** *et seq*. and **C8.2**.

For the purposes of this section, the date of conviction means the date on which sentence is imposed (*Brentwood Justices, ex parte Richardson* (1992) 95 Cr App R 187).

Modification where Fixed Penalty Points also in Question

Road Traffic Offenders Act 1988, s. 30   **C6.4**

    (1)   Sections 28 and 29 of this Act shall have effect subject to this section in any case where—

    (a)   a person is convicted of an offence involving obligatory endorsement, and

    (b)   the court is satisfied that the counterpart of his licence has been or is liable to be endorsed under section 57 or 77 of this Act in respect of an offence (referred to in this section as the 'connected offence') committed on the same occasion as the offence of which he is convicted.

    (2)   The number of penalty points to be attributed to the offence of which he is convicted is—

    (a)   the number of penalty points to be attributed to that offence under section 28 of this Act apart from this section, less

899

(b)   the number of penalty points required to be endorsed on the counterpart of his licence under section 57 or 77 of this Act in respect of the connected offence (except so far as they have already been deducted by virtue of this paragraph).

The offences to which the procedure applies are set out in sch. 3 to the 1988 Act (see **C8.3**). Where the 'fixed penalty' procedure is appropriate, a notice giving reasonable information must either be served on the offender or given to him by a constable in uniform. If the offence is endorsable, the offender must produce his licence to the constable or, within seven days, to an authorised person at a specified police station. If the constable or authorised person is satisfied that the offender is not liable to disqualification under the RTOA 1988, s. 35, the licence is retained and then sent to the 'fixed penalty clerk' (the justices' clerk of the relevant area) so that it can be endorsed.

Every notice must contain a suspended enforcement period during which no proceedings may be brought. That period must be of a minimum duration of 21 days.

If the offender is later convicted of an offence which arose on the 'same occasion' as the offence for which his licence has already been endorsed, the number of penalty points to be imposed in respect of that offence is the highest number of points attributable less the number of points already endorsed under the fixed penalty procedure.

For further details, see **C7.1** *et seq.*, **C8.2** and **C8.3**.

Taking Previously Endorsed Particulars into Consideration

C6.5
           Road Traffic Offenders Act 1988, s. 31

(1)   Where a person is convicted of an offence involving obligatory or discretionary disqualification and his licence and its counterpart are produced to the court—
(a)   any existing endorsement on his licence is prima facie evidence of the matters endorsed, and
(b)   the court may, in determining what order to make in pursuance of the conviction, take those matters into consideration.
(2)   [Applies only to Scotland.]

This is one of a number of ways that previous convictions may be proved. In addition, an extract from the Criminal Records Office may be produced by the prosecution and is admissible if agreed by the defendant. On a number of occasions the only evidence relating to the defendant's driving record will be contained in a computer printout from the DVLA, which may be admitted under the RTOA 1988, s. 13 (see **C2.7**). In other circumstances previous convictions may be proved under the PACE 1984, ss. 73 to 75 (see generally, **F11.1** *et seq.*).

Fines and Imprisonment

C6.6   The RTOA 1988, s. 33, provides that the maximum punishments for offences against the Traffic Acts should be those set out in sch. 2, part I, col. 4. References to years or months are references to terms of imprisonment. Schedule 2 is set out at **C8.2**.

Probationary Period for Newly Qualified Drivers

C6.7   The Road Traffic (New Drivers) Act 1995, s. 1, introduced, with effect from 1 June 1997, a probationary period of two years commencing from the day on which a person becomes a qualified driver, during which time a driver who acquires six or more penalty points will have his licence revoked and be required to present himself for retesting before qualifying for a full driving licence.

A person becomes a 'qualified driver' on the first occasion of passing a United Kingdom driving test or a driving test conducted in any EEA State, the Isle of Man, any of the Channel Islands or Gibraltar (s. 1(2)). Any person who became a qualified driver before the Act entered into force is not affected by its provisions (s. 10(3)). By virtue of s. 7, the period may be terminated early if the person is disqualified until a driving test is passed under the RTOA 1988, s. 36 (see **C6.11**), or if he has already had to surrender his licence under the terms of the 1995 Act and has since been granted a full driving licence after re-taking and passing a driving test.

During the probationary period, if the driver commits an offence or offences involving obligatory endorsement where the penalty points to be taken into account under the RTOA 1988, s. 29 (see **C6.3**), are six or more, the sentencing court or fixed penalty clerk must send a notice, together with the driver's licence and its counterpart, to the Secretary of State (s. 2), who must then serve a notice on the driver revoking the licence (s. 3). (Schedule 1 to the 1995 Act makes similar provisions for the surrender and revocation of test certificates and provisional driving licences, where the driver has not yet applied for his full driving licence.) There is no discretion involved although 'special reasons' (see **C7.8**) may, if appropriate, be raised against endorsement to prevent such an eventuality.

Where a licence is revoked the holder has to re-take and pass an 'ordinary' driving test for each class of vehicle affected by the revocation before being able to drive unsupervised and being eligible to apply once again for a full driving licence (s. 4). After passing the retest, the person has the normal two-year period in which to apply for a full driving licence, otherwise the test certificate obtained ceases to have effect. On this occasion, however, no probationary period attaches, otherwise persistent offenders could find themselves in a vicious circle of retesting.

By s. 5, if the driver appeals against the conviction or penalty points that led to his licence being revoked under s. 3 and the Secretary of State receives due notification, his licence will be temporarily restored to him pending determination of the appeal. If the appeal is successful, a new full licence will be granted and, if appropriate, the probationary period will continue to run. If the appeal fails to reduce the relevant penalty points below six, the temporary licence will be treated as revoked. These provisions are supplemented by the New Drivers (Appeals Procedure) Regulations 1997 (SI 1997 No. 1098).

Any penalty points which lead to the revocation of a licence, remain effective for the normal three-year period from the date of commission of the offence (RTOA 1988, s. 29(2); see **C6.3**). Revocation of the driving licence does not 'wipe clean' the person's driving record for the purposes of disqualification for repeated offences under the RTOA 1988, s. 35 (see **C6.10**). A short discretionary disqualification under the RTOA 1988, s. 34(2), would, however, lead to there being no penalty points to be taken into account. As this would result in the retesting requirement and therefore Parliament's clear intention being circumvented, it is suggested that an appropriate approach in a case where the offence might merit a short period of disqualification would be to consider the effect of the 1995 Act first, before turning to the possibility of a discretionary disqualification under the 1988 Act.

Disqualification for Certain Offences

Road Traffic Offenders Act 1988, s. 34   **C6.8**

(1) Where a person is convicted of an offence involving obligatory disqualification, the court must order him to be disqualified for such period not less than 12 months as the court thinks fit unless the court for special reasons thinks fit to order him to be disqualified for a shorter period or not to order him to be disqualified.

(1A) Where a person is convicted of an offence under section 12A of the Theft Act 1968 (aggravated vehicle-taking), the fact that he did not drive the vehicle in question at any particular time or at all shall not be regarded as a special reason for the purposes of subsection (1) above.

(2) Where a person is convicted of an offence involving discretionary disqualification, and either—

    (a)   the penalty points to be taken into account on that occasion number fewer than 12, or

    (b)   the offence is not one involving obligatory endorsement,

the court may order him to be disqualified for such period as the court thinks fit.

    (3)   Where a person convicted of an offence under any of the following provisions of the Road Traffic Act 1988, that is—

    (aa)   section 3A (causing death by careless driving when under the influence of drink or drugs),

    (a)   section 4(1) (driving or attempting to drive while unfit),

    (b)   section 5(1)(a) (driving or attempting to drive with excess alcohol), and

    (c)   section 7(6) (failing to provide a specimen) where that is an offence involving obligatory disqualification,

has within the 10 years immediately preceding the commission of the offence been convicted of any such offence, subsection (1) above shall apply in relation to him as if the reference to 12 months were a reference to three years.

    (4)   Subject to subsection (3) above, subsection (1) above shall apply as if the reference to 12 months were a reference to two years—

    (a)   in relation to a person convicted of—

       (i)   manslaughter, . . . or

       (ii)   an offence under section 1 of the Road Traffic Act 1988 (causing death by dangerous driving), or

       (iii)   an offence under section 3A of that Act (causing death by careless driving while under the influence of drink or drugs), and

    (b)   in relation to a person on whom more than one disqualification for a fixed period of 56 days or more has been imposed within the three years immediately preceding the commission of the offence.

    (4A)   For the purposes of subsection (4)(b) above there shall be disregarded any disqualification imposed under section 26 of this Act or section 44 of the Powers of Criminal Courts Act 1973 or section 248 of the Criminal Procedure (Scotland) Act 1995 (offences committed by using vehicles) and any disqualification imposed in respect of an offence of stealing a motor vehicle, an offence under section 12 or 25 of the Theft Act 1968, an offence under section 178 of the Road Traffic Act 1988, or an attempt to commit such an offence.

    (5)   The preceding provisions of this section shall apply in relation to a conviction of an offence committed by aiding, abetting, counselling or procuring, or inciting to the commission of, an offence involving obligatory disqualification as if the offence were an offence involving discretionary disqualification.

    (6)   This section is subject to section 48 of this Act.

For a more detailed consideration of disqualification, see **C7.2 *et seq***.

Where disqualification is mandatory, the minimum period is 12 months, unless the offence is manslaughter or an offence under the RTA 1988, s. 1 or 3A, or the defendant has had more than one disqualification of at least 56 days within the three years preceding the commission of the offence. In those cases the minimum period is two years. If s. 34(3) applies, the minimum period is three years.

In *Learmont* v *DPP* [1994] RTR 286, the appellant had previously been sentenced to an 18-month disqualification and the four notional penalty points imposed for that offence led to a concurrent disqualification for six months under the penalty points regime then in force. Consequently, the justices had taken the view that two disqualifications of 56 days or more had been imposed within the relevant three-year period when sentencing the appellant for the instant offence of dangerous driving. The Divisional Court held this approach to be wrong as the double disqualification was effectively for a single offence, thereby rendering the increased minimum period for disqualification inapplicable.

Section 48 of the Act deals with exemptions from disqualification and endorsement in construction and use offences (see **C6.18**).

The penalty points to be taken into account are set out in s. 29 (see **C6.3**) and include any attributable to the offence or offences for which the defendant is before the court and any points previously endorsed, unless the defendant has been disqualified under

s. 35 since their imposition. It is submitted that the effect of s. 29 is that, where an offender has 12 or more points to be taken into account, the court may not disqualify for the substantive offence unless the offence is one which carries discretionary disqualification without obligatory endorsement; in such circumstances, it would seem that Parliament intended the penalty points procedure to take priority.

The effect of s. 34(4A) is that disqualifications under the RTOA 1988, s. 26, the PCCA 1973, s. 44, and any disqualification imposed in respect of an offence of stealing a motor vehicle, or an offence under s. 12 or 25 of the Theft Act 1968, are to be disregarded for the purposes of s. 34(4)(b).

Reduced Disqualification for Attendance on Courses

Sections 34A to 34C of the RTOA 1988 set up a procedure for driver retraining for **C6.9** offenders convicted of drink-driving offences and provide an incentive to drivers to attend such courses by reducing the period of disqualification for those who do. After an extended experimental period, the scheme now operates permanently in all areas.

Road Traffic Offenders Act 1988, s. 34A

(1)   This section applies where—
(a)   a person is convicted of an offence under section 3A (causing death by careless driving when under influence of drink or drugs), 4 (driving or being in charge when under influence of drink or drugs), 5 (driving or being in charge with excess alcohol) or 7 (failing to provide a specimen) of the Road Traffic Act 1988, and
(b)   the court makes an order under section 34 of this Act disqualifying him for a period of not less than twelve months.
(2)   Where this section applies, the court may make an order that the period of disqualification imposed under section 34 shall be reduced if, by a date specified in the order under this section, the offender satisfactorily completes a course approved by the Secretary of State for the purposes of this section and specified in the order.
(3)   The reduction made by an order under this section in a period of disqualification imposed under section 34 shall be a period specified in the order of not less than three months and not more than one quarter of the unreduced period (and accordingly where the period imposed under section 34 is 12 months, the reduced period shall be nine months).
(4)   The court shall not make an order under this section unless—
(a)   it is satisfied that a place on the course specified in the order will be available for the offender,
(b)   the offender appears to the court to be of or over the age of 17,
(c)   the court has explained the effect of the order to the offender in ordinary language, and has informed him of the amount of the fees for the course and of the requirement that he must pay them before beginning the course, and
(d)   the offender has agreed that the order should be made.
(5)   The date specified in an order under this section as the latest date for completion of a course must be at least two months before the last day of the period of disqualification as reduced by the order.
(6)   An order under this section shall name the petty sessions area (. . . or, where an order has been made under this section by a stipendiary magistrate, the commission area) in which the offender resides or will reside.

For an order to be made, the period of disqualification must be at least 12 months and the 'reduced period' of disqualification cannot be less than three months or more than a quarter of the entire period of disqualification. The retraining course should be completed at least two months before the expiry of the period of disqualification as reduced by the order. The offender has to be aged at least 17. Before making such an order under s. 34A, the court must be satisfied that a place is available, that the offender agrees to the order and that it is explained to him that he must pay the fees for the course in advance and how much those fees are. This provision has certain disadvantages for the impecunious offender, particularly if that offender has relied on driving for previous employment.

Section 34B deals with certificates in relation to completion of the course. The order reducing the period of disqualification does not come into effect until the certificate has been received by the clerk of the supervising court. If the certificate is received by the clerk before the end of the 'reduced period', the order reducing the period of disqualification comes into effect on the day that the certificate is received. The organiser of the retraining course has a power to refuse to give a certificate (s. 34B(4)). If a certificate is not given to the offender in accordance with s. 34B, an application may be made to the supervising court which, if successful, has the effect of a certificate duly received by the clerk. Section 41A of the RTOA 1988 enables the court to suspend a disqualification pending determination of such an application.

Section 34C deals with the powers of the Secretary of State to give guidance to course organisers and other supplementary matters. See the Road Traffic (Courses for Drink-Drive Offenders) Regulations 1992 (SI 1992 No. 3013) and Courses for Drink-Drive Offenders (Designation of Areas) Order 1997 (SI 1997 No. 2913) for further details.

Disqualification for Repeated Offences

C6.10   **Road Traffic Offenders Act 1988, s. 35**

(1)   Where—
(a)   a person is convicted of an offence to which this subsection applies, and
(b)   the penalty points to be taken into account on that occasion number 12 or more,
the court must order him to be disqualified for not less than the minimum period unless the court is satisfied, having regard to all the circumstances, that there are grounds for mitigating the normal consequences of the conviction and thinks fit to order him to be disqualified for a shorter period or not to order him to be disqualified.
(1A)   Subsection (1) above applies to—
(a)   an offence involving discretionary disqualification and obligatory endorsement, and
(b)   an offence involving obligatory disqualification in respect of which no order is made under section 34 of this Act.
(2)   The minimum period referred to in subsection (1) above is—
(a)   six months if no previous disqualification imposed on the offender is to be taken into account, and
(b)   one year if one, and two years if more than one, such disqualification is to be taken into account;
and a previous disqualification imposed on an offender is to be taken into account if it was for a fixed period of 56 days or more and was imposed within the three years immediately preceding the commission of the latest offence in respect of which penalty points are taken into account under section 29 of this Act.
(3)   Where an offender is convicted on the same occasion of more than one offence to which subsection (1) above applies—
(a)   not more than one disqualification shall be imposed on him under subsection (1) above,
(b)   in determining the period of the disqualification the court must take into account all the offences, and
(c)   for the purposes of any appeal any disqualification imposed under subsection (1) above shall be treated as an order made on the conviction of each of the offences.
(4)   No account is to be taken under subsection (1) above of any of the following circumstances—
(a)   any circumstances that are alleged to make the offence or any of the offences not a serious one,
(b)   hardship, other than exceptional hardship, or
(c)   any circumstances which, within the three years immediately preceding the conviction, have been taken into account under that subsection in ordering the offender to be disqualified for a shorter period or not ordering him to be disqualified.

(5)   References in this section to disqualification do not include a disqualification imposed under section 26 of this Act or section 44 of the Powers of Criminal Courts Act 1973 . . . or a disqualification imposed in respect of an offence of stealing a motor vehicle, an offence under section 12 or 25 of the Theft Act 1968, an offence under section 178 of the Road Traffic Act 1988, or an attempt to commit such an offence.

(5A)   The preceding provisions of this section shall apply in relation to a conviction of an offence committed by aiding, abetting, counselling, procuring, or inciting to the commission of, an offence involving obligatory disqualification as if the offence were an offence involving discretionary disqualification.

(6)   [Applies only to Scotland.]

(7)   This section is subject to section 48 of this Act.

For further details, see **C7.2** *et seq*.

Disqualification Pending Passing of Driving Test

Road Traffic Offenders Act 1988, s. 36   C6.11

(1)   Where this subsection applies to a person the court must order him to be disqualified until he passes the appropriate driving test.

(2)   Subsection (1) above applies to a person who is disqualified under section 34 of this Act on conviction of—

(a)   manslaughter . . . by the driver of a motor vehicle, or

(b)   an offence under section 1 (causing death by dangerous driving) or section 2 (dangerous driving) of the Road Traffic Act 1988.

(3)   Subsection (1) above also applies—

(a)   to a person who is disqualified under section 34 or 35 of this Act in such circumstances or for such period as the Secretary of State may by order prescribe, or

(b)   to such other persons convicted of such offences involving obligatory endorsement as may be so prescribed.

(4)   Where a person to whom subsection (1) above does not apply is convicted of an offence involving obligatory endorsement, the court may order him to be disqualified until he passes the appropriate driving test (whether or not he has previously passed any test).

(5)   In this section—

'appropriate driving test' means—

(a)   an extended driving test, where a person is convicted of an offence involving obligatory disqualification or is disqualified under section 35 of this Act,

(b)   a test of competence to drive, other than an extended driving test, in any other case,

'extended driving test' means a test of competence to drive prescribed for the purposes of this section, and

'test of competence to drive' means a test prescribed by virtue of section 89(3) of the Road Traffic Act 1988.

(6)   In determining whether to make an order under subsection (4) above, the court shall have regard to the safety of road users.

(7)   Where a person is disqualified until he passes the extended driving test—

(a)   any earlier order under this section shall cease to have effect, and

(b)   a court shall not make a further order under this section while he is so disqualified.

(8)   Subject to subsection (9) below, a disqualification by virtue of an order under this section shall be deemed to have expired on production to the Secretary of State of evidence, in such form as may be prescribed by regulations under section 105 of the RTA 1988, that the person disqualified has passed the test in question since the order was made.

(9)   A disqualification shall be deemed to have expired only in relation to vehicles of such classes as may be prescribed in relation to the test passed by regulations under that section.

(10)   Where there is issued to a person a licence on the counterpart of which are endorsed particulars of a disqualification under this section, there shall also be endorsed the particulars of any test of competence to drive that he has passed since the order of disqualification was made.

(11) and (11A)   [Extensions to tests taken in Northern Ireland, the Isle of Man, the Channel Islands, an EEA State, Gibraltar, or a designated country or territory or for the

purposes of a British Forces licence, if passing such a test would give entitlement to an exchangeable licence.]

The effect of this section is to make disqualification until a test is passed mandatory for those offenders convicted of offences specified in subsection (2). This obligation to disqualify under s. 36 also extends to such persons disqualified under ss. 34 and 35 as may be prescribed and to such other persons convicted of offences involving obligatory endorsement as may be prescribed.

The test to be passed by the offender will be an 'extended driving test' in any case where he has been convicted of an offence involving obligatory disqualification or has been disqualified under s. 35. The matters to be tested are broadly similar to those prescribed for the 'ordinary' driving test, but the minimum length of the extended test is 60 minutes, considerably longer than the normal test of competence to drive (Motor Vehicles (Driving Licences) Regulations 1996 (SI 1996 No. 2824), reg. 37).

The power to order a person to take a driving test where he has been convicted of an offence involving obligatory endorsement which has not been prescribed under s. 36(3)(b) may be exercised only after the court has had regard to the safety of road users in accordance with s. 36(6). The insertion of s. 36(6) seems to indicate that such a regard is paramount in deciding whether to exercise the discretion to disqualify. The fact of its insertion, it is submitted, means that all courts should consider using s. 36 when it is not mandatory to order a retest. None the less, on the previous authorities an order was to be made only on evidence that the ability of the defendant to drive is in some way in question. It should not be used as an additional punishment but only where because of 'age or infirmity or the circumstances of the offence a person may not be a competent driver' (*Buckley* (1988) 10 Cr App R (S) 477).

In *Miller* (1994) 15 Cr App R (S) 505, the Court of Appeal upheld the sentencing judge's order that the appellant be disqualified until passing a driving test on the ground that it was clear his driving was grossly incompetent. The appellant had pleaded guilty to careless driving on an indictment alleging dangerous driving. He had never passed a driving test and had numerous previous convictions, including 10 for driving while disqualified. In *Bannister* [1991] RTR 1, where the appellant was imprisoned for three months and disqualified for two years under s. 36, the court took the view that competence to drive included proper regard for other road users as well as control of the vehicle.

For s. 48, see **C6.18**.

For further details, see **C7.2 *et seq.***

Effect of Order of Disqualification

C6.12   **Road Traffic Offenders Act 1988, s. 37**

(1)   Where the holder of a licence is disqualified by an order of a court, the licence shall be treated as being revoked with effect from the beginning of the period of disqualification.
(1A)   Where—
(a)   the disqualification is for a fixed period shorter than 56 days in respect of an offence involving obligatory endorsement, or
(b)   the order is made under section 26 of this Act,
subsection (1) above shall not prevent the licence from again having effect at the end of the period of disqualification.
(2)   Where the holder of the licence appeals against the order and the disqualification is suspended under section 39 of this Act, the period of disqualification shall be treated for the purpose of subsection (1) above as beginning on the day on which the disqualification ceases to be suspended.
(3)   Notwithstanding anything in part III of the Road Traffic Act 1988, a person disqualified by an order of a court under section 36 of this Act is (unless he is also

disqualified otherwise than by virtue of such an order) entitled to obtain and to hold a provisional licence and to drive a motor vehicle in accordance with the conditions subject to which the provisional licence is granted.

For further details, see **C7.2** *et seq.*

Appeal against and Suspension of Disqualification

Road Traffic Offenders Act 1988, s. 38   C6.13

(1) A person disqualified by an order of a magistrates' court under section 34 or 35 of this Act may appeal against the order in the same manner as against a conviction.

Road Traffic Offenders Act 1988, s. 39

(1) Any court in England and Wales (whether a magistrates' court or another) which makes an order disqualifying a person may, if it thinks fit, suspend the disqualification pending an appeal against the order.

(2) [Applies only to Scotland.]

(3) [Notice to the Secretary of State.]

(4) [Manner of sending notice.]

Removal of Disqualification

Road Traffic Offenders Act 1988, s. 42   C6.14

(1) Subject to the provisions of this section, a person who by an order of a court is disqualified may apply to the court by which the order was made to remove the disqualification.

(2) On any such application the court may, as it thinks proper having regard to—

    (a) the character of the person disqualified and his conduct subsequent to the order,

    (b) the nature of the offence, and

    (c) any other circumstances of the case,

either by order remove the disqualification as from such date as may be specified in the order or refuse the application.

(3) No application shall be made under subsection (1) above for the removal of a disqualification before the expiration of whichever is relevant of the following periods from the date of the order by which the disqualification was imposed, that is—

    (a) two years, if the disqualification is for less than four years,

    (b) one half of the period of disqualification, if it is for less than 10 years but not less than four years,

    (c) five years in any other case;

and in determining the expiration of the period after which under this subsection a person may apply for the removal of a disqualification, any time after the conviction during which the disqualification was suspended or he was not disqualified shall be disregarded.

(4) Where an application under subsection (1) above is refused, a further application under that subsection shall not be entertained if made within three months after the date of the refusal.

(5) If under this section a court orders a disqualification to be removed, the court—

    (a) must cause particulars of the order to be endorsed on the counterpart of the licence, if any, previously held by the applicant, and

    (b) may in any case order the applicant to pay the whole or any part of the costs of the application.

(5A) Subsection (5)(b) above shall apply only where the disqualification was imposed in respect of an offence involving obligatory endorsement; and in any other case the court must send notice of the order made under this section to the Secretary of State.

(5B) [Manner of sending notice to the Secretary of State.]

(6) The preceding provisions of this section shall not apply where the disqualification was imposed by order under section 36(1) of this Act.

By the RTOA 1988, s. 43, any period of suspension shall be disregarded in determining the expiration of a period of disqualification. Thus, if a defendant is disqualified for three years and during that period the disqualification is suspended for three months, then the expiry of the disqualification is three years and three months after the date of disqualification.

An applicant under s. 42 is eligible to apply for representation under part V of the Legal Aid Act 1988 (*Liverpool Crown Court, ex parte McCann* [1995] RTR 23). The chances of such an application being successful, however, are slim.

The procedure on an application to remove a disqualification is not fixed and is, therefore, a matter for the court. It is usual for the police to respond to the application and they may be represented. One procedure which is often adopted is that the police outline the facts of the offence and give the details of the applicant's record, calling such evidence as they deem appropriate and the court allows. The applicant then gives evidence and may be cross-examined with the permission of the court. Thereafter the applicant or his representative is allowed to address the court. There is no power to award the applicant costs but even if successful he may be ordered to pay the costs of the application. There appears to be nothing to prevent the court from fixing the hearing date at any stage as long as the application is actually heard after the expiry of the 'relevant time'.

Endorsement

C6.15 **Road Traffic Offenders Act 1988, ss. 44 and 45**

44.—(1) Where a person is convicted of an offence involving obligatory endorsement, the court must order there to be endorsed on the counterpart of any licence held by him particulars of the conviction and also—

   (a)   if the court orders him to be disqualified, particulars of the disqualification, or

   (b)   if the court does not order him to be disqualified—

      (i)   particulars of the offence, including the date when it was committed, and

      (ii)   the penalty points to be attributed to the offence.

   (2)   Where the court does not order the person convicted to be disqualified, it need not make an order under subsection (1) above if for special reasons it thinks fit not to do so.

   (3)   [Applies only to Scotland.]

   (4)   This section is subject to section 48 of this Act.

45.—(1) An order that any particulars or penalty points are to be endorsed on the counterpart of any licence held by the person convicted shall, whether he is at the time the holder of a licence or not, operate as an order that the counterpart of any licence he may then hold or may subsequently obtain is to be so endorsed until he becomes entitled under subsection (4) below to have a licence issued to him with its counterpart free from the particulars or penalty points.

   (2)   On the issue of a new licence to a person, any particulars or penalty points ordered to be endorsed on the counterpart of any licence held by him shall be entered on the counterpart of the licence unless he has become entitled under subsection (4) below to have a licence issued to him with its counterpart free from those particulars or penalty points.

   (3)   [Repealed.]

   (4)   A person the counterpart of whose licence has been ordered to be endorsed is entitled to have issued to him with effect from the end of the period for which the endorsement remains effective a new licence with a counterpart free from the endorsement if he applies for a new licence in pursuance of section 97(1) of the Road Traffic Act 1988, surrenders any subsisting licence and its counterpart, pays the fee prescribed by regulations under part III of that Act and satisfies the other requirements of section 97(1).

   (5)   An endorsement ordered on a person's conviction of an offence remains effective (subject to subsections (6) and (7) below)—

   (a)   if an order is made for the disqualification of the offender, until four years have elapsed since the conviction, and

   (b)   if no such order is made, until either—

      (i)   four years have elapsed since the commission of the offence, or

(ii)   an order is made for the disqualification of the offender under section 35 of this Act.

(6)   Where the offence was one under section 1 or 2 of that Act (causing death by dangerous driving and dangerous driving), the endorsement remains in any case effective until four years have elapsed since the conviction.

(7)   Where the offence was one—

(a)   under section 3A, 4(1) or 5(1)(a) of that Act (driving offences connected with drink or drugs), or

(b)   under section 7(6) of that Act (failing to provide specimen) involving obligatory disqualification,

the endorsement remains effective until 11 years have elapsed since the conviction.

For further details, see **C7.1 *et seq***.

Combination of Disqualification and Endorsement with Orders for Discharge

The RTOA 1988, s. 46, makes provision as to the combination of orders for **C6.16** disqualification and endorsement with the provisions in the PCCA 1973, s. 1C, which have the effect of treating a conviction in respect of which a discharge is imposed as if it were not a conviction at all (see **E14.6**). Section 46(1) provides that the PCCA 1973, s. 1C(3), does not operate to prevent the court from endorsing an offender's licence or disqualifying him from driving. Section 46(2) provides that the PCCA 1973, s. 1C(1), does not operate to prevent a court from taking into account previous orders of disqualification or endorsement imposed on an occasion when the offender was discharged.

Supplementary Provisions: Decision Not to Disqualify or Endorse or to Shorten Period of Disqualification

Road Traffic Offenders Act 1988, s. 47   **C6.17**

(1)   In any case where a court exercises its power under section 34, 35 or 44 of this Act not to order any disqualification or endorsement or to order disqualification for a shorter period than would otherwise be required, it must state the grounds for doing so in open court and, if it is a magistrates' court . . ., must cause them to be entered in the register . . . of its proceedings.

(2)   [Notification to the Secretary of State.]

(2A)   [Approach under the Road Traffic (New Drivers) Act 1995.]

(3)   [Notification when appeal is allowed.]

(4)   [Manner of notification.]

Any court must state, in open court, the grounds on which it has found 'special reasons' or 'mitigating circumstances', but despite the use of the word 'must', the Divisional Court in *Barnes* v *Gevaux* [1981] RTR 236 held that this requirement was discretionary in cases where the power to disqualify is discretionary.

Exemption from Disqualification and Endorsement for Offences against Construction and Use Regulations

Road Traffic Offenders Act 1988, s. 48   **C6.18**

(1)   Where a person is convicted of an offence under section 40A of the Road Traffic Act 1988 (using vehicle in dangerous condition etc) the court must not—

(a)   order him to be disqualified, or

(b)   order any particulars or penalty points to be endorsed on the counterpart of any licence held by him,

if he proves that he did not know, and had no reasonable cause to suspect, that the use of the vehicle involved a danger of injury to any person.

(2)   Where a person is convicted of an offence under section 41A of the Road Traffic Act 1988 (breach of requirement as to brakes, steering-gear or tyres) the court must not—

(a)   order him to be disqualified, or

(b)   order any particulars or penalty points to be endorsed on the counterpart of any licence held by him,

if he proves that he did not know, and had no reasonable cause to suspect, that the facts of the case were such that the offence would be committed.

This provision is, in effect, the equivalent of statutory 'special reasons' in relation to construction and use offences. The onus is on the defendant, on a balance of probabilities, to prove lack of knowledge or reasonable cause for suspicion.

Offender Escaping Consequences of Endorsable Offence by Deception

C6.19   **Road Traffic Offenders Act 1988, s. 49**

(1)   This section applies where in dealing with a person convicted of an offence involving obligatory endorsement a court was deceived regarding any circumstances that were or might have been taken into account in deciding whether or for how long to disqualify him.

(2)   If—

(a)   the deception constituted or was due to an offence committed by that person, and

(b)   he is convicted of that offence,

the court by or before which he is convicted shall have the same powers and duties regarding an order for disqualification as had the court which dealt with him for the offence involving obligatory endorsement but must, in dealing with him, take into account any order made on his conviction of the offence involving obligatory endorsement.

Meaning of 'Offence Involving Obligatory Endorsement'

C6.20   **Road Traffic Offenders Act 1988, s. 96**

For the purposes of this Act, an offence involves obligatory endorsement if it is an offence under a provision of the Traffic Acts specified in column 1 of part I of schedule 2 to this Act or an offence specified in column 1 of part II of that schedule and either—

(a)   the word 'obligatory' (without qualification) appears in column 6 (in the case of part I) or column 3 (in the case of part II) against the offence, or

(b)   that word appears there qualified by conditions relating to the offence which are satisfied.

Meaning of 'Offence Involving Obligatory Disqualification' and 'Offence Involving Discretionary Disqualification'

C6.21   **Road Traffic Offenders Act 1988, s. 97**

(1)   For the purposes of this Act, an offence involves obligatory disqualification if it is an offence under a provision of the Traffic Acts specified in column 1 of part I of schedule 2 to this Act or an offence specified in column 1 of part II of that schedule and either—

(a)   the word 'obligatory' (without qualification) appears in column 5 (in the case of part I) or column 2 (in the case of part II) against the offence, or

(b)   that word appears there qualified by conditions or circumstances relating to the offence which are satisfied or obtain.

(2)   For the purposes of this Act, an offence involves discretionary disqualification if it is an offence under a provision of the Traffic Acts specified in column 1 of part I of schedule 2 to this Act or an offence specified in column 1 of part II of that schedule and either—

(a)   the word 'discretionary' (without qualification) appears in column 5 (in the case of part I) or column 2 (in the case of part II) against the offence, or

(b)   that word appears there qualified by conditions or circumstances relating to the offence which are satisfied or obtain.

Forfeiture of Motor Vehicle

C6.22   Section 43 of the PCCA 1973 (see **E20.1 *et seq*.**) makes it possible, in some circumstances, for a court to order the forfeiture of a motor vehicle where it has been used in committing or facilitating the commission of an offence.

General Interpretation Provisions

Road Traffic Offenders Act 1988, s. 98   **C6.23**

(1)   In this Act—

'disqualified' means disqualified for holding or obtaining a licence and 'disqualification' is to be construed accordingly,

'drive' has the same meaning as in the Road Traffic Act 1988,

'licence' means a licence to drive a motor vehicle granted under part III of that Act,

'provisional licence' means a licence granted by virtue of section 97(2) of that Act,

'the provisions connected with the licensing of drivers' means sections 7, 8, 22, 25 to 29, 31, 32, 34 to 48, 91A, 91B, 96 and 97 of this Act,

'road'—

(a)   in relation to England and Wales, means any highway and any other road to which the public has access, and includes bridges over which a road passes, and

(b)   [Applies only to Scotland.],

'the Road Traffic Acts' means the Road Traffic Act 1988, the Road Traffic (Consequential Provisions) Act 1988 (so far as it reproduces the effect of provisions repealed by that Act) and this Act, and

'the Traffic Acts' means the Road Traffic Acts and the Road Traffic Regulation Act 1984,

and 'Community licence', 'counterpart' and 'EEA State' have the same meanings as in part III of the Road Traffic Act 1988.

(2)   Sections 185 and 186 of the Road Traffic Act 1988 (meaning of 'motor vehicle' and other expressions relating to vehicles) apply for the purposes of this Act as they apply for the purposes of that Act.

(3)   In the schedules to this Act—

'RTRA' is used as an abbreviation for the Road Traffic Regulation Act 1984, and

'RTA' is used as an abbreviation for the Road Traffic Act 1988 or, if followed by '1989', the Road Traffic (Driver Licensing and Information Systems) Act 1989.

(4)   Subject to any express exception, references in this Act to any part of this Act include a reference to any schedule to this Act so far as relating to that part.

SECTION C7: ENDORSEMENT, PENALTY POINTS AND DISQUALIFICATION

Endorsement Generally

C7.1   In all cases involving obligatory or discretionary disqualification, the court, in the absence of 'special reasons' (see **C7.8**) or the operation of the RTOA 1988, s. 48 (see **C6.18**), or the Mental Health Act 1986, s. 37, is obliged to order particulars of the offence to be endorsed on the counterpart of the offender's licence or any licence that might be held by the defendant in the future. Each offence is denoted by a particular code, and the DVLA is notified. Where the offender is not disqualified, penalty points must also be endorsed (RTOA 1988, s. 44).

The number of points applicable to an offence is set out in the RTOA 1988, sch. 2, part II, col. 5 (see **C8.2**). Certain offences carry a variable number of points (see **C8.2**).

The points to be endorsed should reflect the seriousness of the offence. Therefore, an offence of driving without due care and attention consisting of momentary inattention might be suitably endorsed with three or four penalty points, whereas an offence consisting of prolonged, blatantly bad driving should carry a higher number of points to reflect the greater degree of culpability. In cases involving variable penalty points, the court should allow mitigation before arriving at any decision as to the number of points that might be imposed.

If there are a number of offences committed on the 'same occasion', then, subject to the RTOA 1988, s. 28 (see **C6.2**), the points to be endorsed are those relating to the offence which carries the highest number. Thus, if a defendant is convicted of careless driving and contravention of a street playground order, the highest number of penalty points relates to the careless driving. For the meaning of 'same occasion' see **C6.2**. If the penalty points are the same for both offences, then it is normal practice to endorse the more serious offence with the points. Where penalty points for a fixed penalty have already been endorsed, the maximum number of points available to the court in respect of an offence committed on the same occasion must be reduced accordingly (*Green* v *O'Donnell* 1997 SCCR 315). By virtue of the RTOA 1988, s. 28, the court may, following a determination under s. 28(5), order the endorsement of the counterpart to the licence with penalty points in relation to more than one offence committed on the same occasion. Points would then be aggregated for the purposes of the RTOA 1988, s. 35 (disqualification for repeated offences: see **C6.10**) and the Road Traffic (New Drivers) Act 1995 (surrender of licences: see **C6.7**).

It is not unusual for a defendant to face a number of charges relating to different occasions. In those circumstances the court must establish the total number of points for each occasion, and is then obliged to aggregate those points for the purposes of the penalty points procedure.

If the court disqualifies for any of the substantive offences under the RTOA 1988, s. 34, it does not order endorsement of the counterpart with any penalty points relating to that offence; the counterpart is merely endorsed with particulars of the offence. The points relating to that offence are disregarded for the purposes of s. 35 (see *Martin* v *DPP* (1999) *The Times*, 30 November 1999).

The effect of a disqualification under the penalty points procedure is to wipe the licence and its counterpart clean. If the defendant is subsequently convicted of an offence, previously endorsed points are not taken into consideration, but the fact of a penalty points disqualification is relevant to any future points disqualification.

With the exception of offences involving mandatory disqualification, aiders and abettors etc. are punished as principals and the same procedure applies.

As to attempts, see generally **C1.3**. If the offence attempted is summary only, then it must be statutory (e.g., attempting to drive while unfit through drink or drugs), and the penalty is set out in the RTOA 1988, sch. 2, part II, col. 5 (see **C8.2**). If it is triable either way then, by virtue of the Criminal Attempts Act 1981, s. 4(1)(b), the same liability to penalties exists as for the complete offence.

Disqualification under Penalty Points Procedure

The penalty points procedure was introduced by the Transport Act 1981 to replace the **C7.2** previous system of 'totting up'. The purpose of the procedure is to punish repeated offences which in themselves are not sufficiently grave to warrant disqualification, but which taken together indicate repeated offences of bad driving or disregard for the law.

Once points have been imposed they are added to any other points imposed in respect of offences committed within three years of the latest offence or offences (points to be taken into consideration). If the total is 12 or more, the court is obliged to disqualify under the RTOA 1988, s. 35. This disqualification is mandatory unless the court finds mitigating circumstances and is in addition to, but not consecutive to, any disqualification which the court may order for the offences before it on that day.

Even if the court disqualifies for a substantive offence, it is obliged to take into account other offences which were committed and to take into account and attribute points in accordance with the RTOA 1988, ss. 28 and 29, with a view to disqualification under s. 35. Points are not endorsed on the counterpart under s. 44 if there is a penalty points disqualification.

Period of Disqualification under Road Traffic Offenders Act 1988, s. 35 The **C7.3** disqualification must be for a minimum period, unless there are grounds for mitigating the normal consequences and the court thinks fit to order a shorter period or no disqualification at all.

If the offender has no previous disqualification of 56 days or more imposed within three years of the commission of the latest offence for which penalty points are to be taken into account, then the period is six months. If there is one such disqualification in the three years, the period is a minimum of one year. If there are two or more such disqualifications imposed within three years of the commission of the latest offence, then the minimum period is two years.

Disqualifications under the RTOA 1988, s. 26, and PCCA 1973, s. 44, are not to be taken into account.

Mitigating Circumstances Mitigating circumstances may be circumstances which **C7.4** relate to the offender and the offence, and may include the offender's record and good works.

The RTOA 1988, s. 35(4), specifically excludes circumstances which are alleged to make the offence not serious, hardship, other than exceptional hardship, and any 'mitigating circumstances' which have been advanced as such during the three years preceding the conviction for the latest offence. For those reasons s. 47 of the 1988 Act requires grounds for mitigating the normal consequences of the conviction to be stated in open court, and entered in the register if the case is heard by a magistrates' court. It is necessary to demonstrate not only that the defendant will lose his employment but also that there are other circumstances associated with that loss which might involve reflected hardship of a serious kind on the defendant's business, family or long-term prospects (*Brennan* v *McKay* 1997 SLT 603).

It is for the offender to establish that grounds which are advanced are different from any so previously put before the court (*Sandbach Justices, ex parte Pescud* (1983) 5 Cr App R (S) 177). In practice, most of the mitigating circumstances advanced relate to 'exceptional hardship'. In *Owen* v *Jones* (1987) 9 Cr App R (S) 34, the court expressed the view that in the vast majority of cases justices would need to have evidence to satisfy themselves of the existence of exceptional hardship, but that on occasions they might rely upon their own knowledge. In that case a police officer had acquired a total of 13 points and, if disqualified, would have, by the usual practice of his Chief Constable, been forced to resign, thereby losing his job and his home. This practice was known to the bench, who did not require the defendant to provide evidence, as they found that the facts amounted to exceptional hardship.

'Exceptional hardship' is often advanced in relation to the offender's employment. In those circumstances the court might consider whether or not a licence to drive is necessary for the offender either to go to work or because his occupation is, or entails, driving. Such matters as his hours and pattern of work, together with the distances he must travel in order to reach his work and the availability of public transport, are relevant, as are details of his age and health and any other means of transport available to him. If loss of his licence may mean loss of his job or reduced wages, the court may consider any unusual hardship that may result to the family of the defendant and any unusual hardship that may be occasioned to them if he were to lose his licence. The fact that he is a businessman, with employees dependent upon him and his ability to drive, may be considered, but the court should be careful to inquire as to other means of transport or available methods of effecting his necessary business.

The court must have regard to all the circumstances. This has been held to include, in the case of a young offender with a bad record who was disqualified for two years under the penalty points procedure, the counter-productive nature of long periods of disqualification. In *Thomas* [1983] 1 WLR 1490, Lord Lane CJ said (at p. 1491):

> . . . with persons like the present appellant, who seem to be incapable of leaving motor vehicles alone, to impose a period of disqualification which will extend for a substantial period after their release from prison may well, and in many cases certainly will, invite the offender to commit further offences in relation to motor vehicles. In other words a long period of disqualification may well be counter-productive and so contrary to the public interest. So well established has this sentencing policy become in recent years that it is not necessary to refer to a line of cases.

The disqualification of two years was consequently reduced to one.

Disqualification Generally

C7.5 Disqualification for an offence may be either obligatory or discretionary (see RTOA 1988, sch. 2, at **C8.2**).

Where a person is convicted of an offence involving obligatory disqualification, the court must order him to be disqualified for a minimum period of 12 months in the absence of special reasons (see **C7.8**). Where the offence is one of manslaughter by the driver of a motor vehicle or is an offence under s. 1 or 3A of the RTA 1988, the minimum period of disqualification is two years; the minimum period is also two years where the offender has had two or more periods of disqualification of 56 days or more within the period of three years preceding the commission of the offence. A second or subsequent conviction for an offence relating to 'drink driving' (i.e. under s. 3A, 4(1), 5(1)(a) or 7(6)) carries a minimum period of disqualification of three years, if it is committed within 10 years of another such conviction.

A person convicted of aiding and abetting etc. an offence mentioned in the RTOA 1988, s. 34(3), must be disqualified for three years if he is subsequently convicted of an offence mentioned in s. 34(3) (*Makeham* v *Donaldson* [1981] RTR 511).

In any case where a magistrates' court is considering imposing a period of disqualification and the person to be disqualified is not present in court, the court must, by virtue of the MCA 1980, s. 11(4), adjourn in order to warn the defendant that they have disqualification in mind. If the defendant fails to attend, they may disqualify in his absence or, more usually, issue a warrant under the MCA 1980, s. 13, to compel his attendance. Before a court imposes disqualification in a case where it is discretionary, either the defendant or his representative should be warned and then given the opportunity to address the court (*Ireland* (1988) 10 Cr App R (S) 474 and *Money* (1988) 10 Cr App R (S) 237).

In general, when considering the length of disqualification courts should attempt to avoid long periods, particularly when the disqualification is imposed at the same time as a sentence of imprisonment as it may have an adverse effect on 'the defendant's prospects of effective rehabilitation upon his release from custody' (per Ognall J in *Russell* [1993] RTR 249n). In addition lengthy disqualifications tend to be counterproductive and often hamper the offender in the job market, sometimes leading to further crime, in particular, driving while disqualified. See *Thomas* (1983) 5 Cr App R (S) 354, *Matthews* (1987) 9 Cr App R (S) 1, *West* (1986) 8 Cr App R (S) 266 and *Callum* [1995] RTR 248. Against those considerations the court must also consider its duty to protect the public, and a lengthy period of disqualification to enable the defendant to mature may be justified (*Gibbons* (1987) 9 Cr App R (S) 21).

Where the length of sentence alone is being challenged on appeal (which is preferable to instituting proceedings for judicial review), the appropriate test to apply is whether the sentence is 'truly astonishing' (*Ealing Justices, ex parte Scrafield* [1994] RTR 195). In cases involving additional factors, the 'harsh and oppressive' test might be more appropriate.

Disqualification for life may be imposed (*Tunde-Olarinde* [1967] 1 WLR 911), but such a disqualification is inappropriate and wrong in principle in the absence of either psychiatric evidence or evidence of many previous convictions which indicates that the defendant would indefinitely be a danger to the public if he is allowed to drive (per Morland J in *King* (1992) 13 Cr App R (S) 668). In *King*, although the appellant had used his car as a weapon, he had no previous convictions which related to dangerous or careless driving. The Court of Appeal reduced the period of disqualification from life to five years on the basis that the judge had failed to give weight to the rehabilitative principle set out in *Russell*. Similarly, in *Rivano* (1994) 158 JP 288, the Court of Appeal decided that there were no very exceptional circumstances requiring disqualification for life or leading to the conclusion that, as a man of only 30, the appellant would be a danger to the public indefinitely. See also *Fazal* [1999] 1 Cr App R (S) 152. In *Buckley* (1994) 15 Cr App R (S) 695, however, the fact that the appellant had such an appalling driving record, including six convictions for reckless driving, demonstrated an astonishing readiness to imperil the public and clearly satisfied the second limb in *King*; in those circumstances disqualification for life was justified.

Harrington-Griffin [1989] RTR 138 was a case of causing death by reckless driving, where a number of the aggravating features in *Boswell* [1984] 1 WLR 1047 (see **C3.13**), particularly alcohol, were present. The appellant was sentenced to 30 months' imprisonment and disqualified for seven years after a trial in which the only issue was the location of the point of impact in the collision which caused the fatality. Upholding the sentence, the Court of Appeal said (at p. 141):

> . . . it must be remembered that the discount which attaches to a plea of guilty is not the converse of a penalty for the manner in which a defendant has conducted his defence, but is rather a discount which acknowledges the defendant's contrition. . . . In no class of case is a plea of guilty of more significance than in the present type, for acknowledgement of

blame in driving gives some assurance that the driver will remember what has happened and take heed of that lesson.

In arriving at the length of disqualification which is appropriate, the court should not have regard to the application of the RTOA 1988, s. 42, and the power of the court to remove a disqualification, but merely to the length of time that is appropriate for the offence before it. In *Bannister* [1991] RTR 1, the Court of Appeal upheld a disqualification of two years. (See also **C6.11**.)

Where a disqualification is discretionary, courts may not consider, except in the more serious cases, that disqualification is appropriate, particularly where it is a first offence. It 'should generally be restricted to cases involving bad driving, persistent motoring offences or the use of vehicles for the purposes of crime' (per Morland J in *Callister* [1993] RTR 70). In that case, theft of a vehicle by sale while it was subject to a credit agreement did not fall into any of those categories. Each case must be taken on its own merits, bearing in mind that certain types of offence will be viewed with greater seriousness. The appropriate test appears to be whether the sentence imposed is 'truly astonishing' (*Tucker* v *DPP* [1994] RTR 203n); if it is not, an appeal is unlikely to succeed. Offences of using a vehicle without insurance and failing to stop after an accident or to report an accident are always viewed seriously and often attract disqualification, even as a first offence. Also viewed seriously is driving while disqualified. In *Pegrum* (1986) 8 Cr App R (S) 27, an appellant, who had numerous previous disqualifications and several convictions for driving while disqualified, was sentenced to the then maximum period of imprisonment of one year. This sentence was upheld by the Court of Appeal.

C7.6 **_Disqualification under Powers of Criminal Courts Act 1973, s. 44 and Crime (Sentences) Act 1997, s. 39_** Under the PCCA 1973, s. 44, the Crown Court has power to disqualify where a motor vehicle was used for the purpose of committing or facilitating the commission of an offence. In *Fazal* [1999] 1 Cr App R (S) 152, this power was exercised upon conviction for affray. The section also covers offences of assault, including secondary participation, when committed by driving a motor vehicle (s. 44(1A)).

Under the C(S)A 1997, s. 39, a court has power to disqualify where a person is convicted of any offence in addition to or instead of dealing with the offender in any other way.

For further details of these provisions, see **E23**.

C7.7 **_Disqualification until Test Passed_** For the provisions of the RTOA 1988, s. 36, see **C6.11**. If a defendant is disqualified under the RTOA 1988, s. 36, he must obtain a provisional driving licence before driving and comply with its conditions of use, or else he may run the risk of being convicted under the RTA 1988, s. 103 (*Hunter* v *Coombs* [1962] 1 WLR 573).

Special Reasons

C7.8 A 'special reason' was defined in *Whittal* v *Kirby* [1947] KB 194 as being special to the facts of the offence and not the offender. In doing so the Divisional Court adopted the definition in *Crossan* [1939] NI 106 (at pp. 112–13):

> A 'special reason' within the exception is one which is special to the facts of the particular case, that is, special to the facts which constitute the offence. It is, in other words, a mitigating or extenuating circumstance, not amounting in law to a defence to the charge, yet directly connected with the commission of the offence, and one which the court ought properly to take into consideration when imposing punishment. A circumstance peculiar to the offender as distinguished from the offence is not a 'special reason' within the exception.

Those four requirements were confirmed in *Wickins* (1958) 42 Cr App R 236 and a large number of authorities thereafter.

The effect of a finding of 'special reasons' is to allow the court a discretion as to whether or not it:

(a)   disqualifies under the RTOA 1988, s. 34(1); or

(b)   endorses under the RTOA 1988, s. 44.

Even though 'special reasons' have been established, there is no obligation to exercise the discretion and the court may still disqualify and endorse as it considers appropriate. In cases involving obligatory disqualification the court may therefore find 'special reasons' and not disqualify but still endorse. In cases where disqualification is discretionary the court may still endorse. In *Agnew v DPP* [1991] RTR 147, a case of careless driving, the Divisional Court found that the conditions were satisfied but refused to exercise their discretion. The applicant was a police officer on a training exercise who had gone through a red light, failing to follow instructions in treating the light in the same way as a 'give way' sign. Morland J, in giving the judgment of the Court, quoted Lord Widgery CJ in *Taylor v Rajan* [1974] QB 424, that 'justices should only exercise the discretion in favour of the driver in clear and compelling circumstances'. He then went on to say (at p. 150):

> There are two competing considerations: the need for realistic police driver training in actual road conditions and the safety of lawful users of the highway, motorists and pedestrians. The second must always be paramount.

Whether or not to exercise the discretion 'is peculiarly a question for [the justices], seeing and hearing the witnesses and making their assessment of the answers which are given to them, to determine whether in the circumstances it is a case in which they, in the exercise of that discretion, feel justified in imposing penalties other than disqualification' (per Beldam J in *Donahue v DPP* [1993] RTR 156). In *DPP v Bristow* [1998] RTR 100, the Divisional Court held that the key question justices should ask themselves when assessing if special reasons exist and whether their discretion should be exercised is what a sober, reasonable and responsible friend of the defendant, who was present at the time but who was a non-driver and thus unable to help, would have advised in the circumstances: drive or not drive. Unless the justices thought it was a real possibility rather than just an off-chance that such a friend would have advised the defendant to drive, they should not find special reasons and exercise their discretion.

In *Cambridge Magistrates' Court and the CPS, ex parte Wong* (1991) 155 JP 554, the applicant had taken cough linctus on medical advice. Unbeknown to him it contained alcohol, although nothing on the container or wrapping indicated that. When breathalysed the reading was 40 microgrammes of alcohol. Evidence from the analyst showed that the amount of linctus taken would have increased the amount of the reading by 1.7 microgrammes. Where the reading is below 40 microgrammes, it is policy not to prosecute but the justices were unaware of this. The Divisional Court held that this amounted to a special reason but, applying *Newton* [1974] RTR 451, 'as there were two stages, the case would be remitted to the magistrates for them to determine whether the discretion not to disqualify (the second stage) should be exercised having regard to all the circumstances and, in particular, to the driver's own conduct'.

Endorsement under s. 44 includes endorsement with penalty points. If the court does exercise the discretion not to endorse with particulars of the conviction, there is no power to endorse penalty points separately. Nor is there any power to endorse either without penalty points or with a lesser number than the amount set out in sch. 2 of the Act.

The onus of establishing that there are 'special reasons' lies with the defence on a balance of probabilities. Where there has been a trial resulting in a conviction and the defendant then advances special reasons, justices should readily accede to an application that a defendant be recalled when the earlier evidence has not fully dealt with the relevant facts (see *DPP v Kinnersley* [1993] RTR 105). In most cases (save for obvious ones) the justices might expect to hear expert evidence, particularly where the defence seek to establish that drinks were laced, although where corroboration does not exist or is unavailable for some good reason it is still open to the court to find special reasons where the defendant's evidence is believed (*Watson* v *Adam* 1996 SLT 459). Notice of the defence's intention to produce evidence of such special reasons should be given to the prosecution so that unnecessary adjournments are avoided. Failure to notify the prosecution could reflect on the *bona fides* of the defendant (*DPP* v *O'Connor* [1992] RTR 66; see also *Pugsley* v *Hunter* [1973] 1 WLR 578). The defendant's failure to give an appropriate explanation or account at the time of arrest or commission of the offence does not, as a matter of law, exclude the possibility of a finding that special reasons exist, but it would usually form an important factor for the court in considering all the relevant circumstances of a case (*Kinnersley*).

'Special reasons' may be advanced on appeal to the Crown Court as part of an appeal against sentence, or, if an appeal against conviction includes an appeal against sentence, where the Crown Court have upheld the conviction. The appeal is by way of rehearing of the evidence relevant to the issue of whether or not there are special reasons and, if so, as to how the discretion is to be exercised. Where special reasons have not been found an appeal by way of case stated is a more convenient procedure than an application for judicial review (see *DPP* v *O'Connor*).

There are probably more examples of what do not constitute 'special reasons'. The offender's physical disability or occupation, or the effects of disqualification upon him have all been held not to be 'special reasons'. Many of the cases relate to drink-related offences where the defendant may be anxious to avoid a mandatory disqualification. The courts have consistently sought to limit the application of 'special reasons' to cases which are plainly meritorious. For example, in *Beauchamp-Thompson* v *DPP* [1988] RTR 54, a part of the appellant's case, and that part which related to 'special reasons', rested upon his inability to distinguish Chardonnay from Riesling and therefore their respective alcoholic strengths. The court rejected this argument, which, if accepted, would be tantamount to a licence to 'lace' one's own drink. See also *DPP* v *Doyle* [1993] RTR 369. In *DPP* v *Jowle* (1997) *The Times*, 13 December 1997, the Divisional Court decided that justices should not have found special reasons where the defendant had not knowingly consumed alcohol for many years but was addicted to the mouthwash 'Listerine' which contains alcohol and the consumption of which he knew gave him a lift.

Examples of successful cases of 'special reasons' include driving after alcoholic and non-alcoholic drinks have been 'doctored' or 'laced' by a third party without the defendant's knowledge; driving with excess alcohol in cases of emergency (*DPP* v *Upchurch* [1994] RTR 366; *DPP* v *Knight* [1994] RTR 374n) or where the driver has been asked to move the vehicle by a police officer or where the vehicle has been driven from the public highway or from a place which would be subject to parking restrictions when the vehicle is only driven for a short distance; driving at excess speed in cases of emergency, in one particular case so as not to hold up the business of the Crown Court.

When considering the plea in relation to emergency situations, the court can divide the driving into separate chapters to ascertain whether there was any interruption after which a fresh explanation would be required as to why the defendant had chosen to drive again (*Hamilton* v *Neizer* 1993 JC 63; *DPP* v *Goddard* [1998] RTR 463).

In *Aichroth* v *Cottee* [1954] 1 WLR 1124, Lord Goddard CJ stated (at p. 1127) that the 'mere fact that there is a sudden emergency will not be enough if it is shown that there are other reasonable methods of meeting it'. In *DPP* v *Cox* [1996] RTR 123, the defendant was a key-holder at a golf club and was contacted in the night when the burglar alarm was activated. Despite the short distance involved and having consumed a considerable amount of alcohol, he drove to the club premises without considering alternative methods of responding to the alarm. The Divisional Court confirmed that the issue of whether an emergency exists must be viewed objectively and held that the justices were justified in concluding that this was an emergency within the guidelines of *Aichroth* v *Cottee*. Similarly, in *DPP* v *Tucker* (6 November 1996 unreported), the Divisional Court upheld the justices' view that the defendant, responding to a burglar alarm at a jewellery business he ran, had considered all alternatives to driving himself, none of which were feasible, thereby justifying their finding of special reasons.

A private crisis, such as being blackmailed by a threat of crying rape, can justify a finding of special reasons as long as the justices guard against being taken in by hard luck stories and approach the issue in the proper objective fashion (*DPP* v *Enston* [1996] RTR 324). Provided justices have considered all the relevant facts, have reached a conclusion on those facts that could not be said to be perverse and have directed themselves properly on the law, the Divisional Court should be very slow to overturn the decision of the justices, even if it does not agree with the conclusions of the justices as to the facts (*Chapman* v *O'Hagan* [1949] 2 All ER 690).

In *DPP* v *Whittle* [1996] RTR 154, however, the Divisional Court overturned a finding of special reasons on grounds of a medical emergency, re-affirming the objective approach required, because the reasonable man would not have regarded the situation as one in which no other course of action was possible. The defendant had taken over the driving from his wife, who had complained of dizziness and blurred vision, but was driving fellow passengers home when stopped by the police. In passing, Simon Brown LJ wondered whether a genuine medical emergency might more properly fall within the complete defence of duress of circumstances (see **A3.28**) rather than being raised only as a special reason. In cases involving the risk of death or serious injury, such a course would certainly be advisable.

Recent cases involving 'special reasons' include the following: *DPP* v *Barker* [1990] RTR 1, *Smith* v *DPP* [1990] RTR 17, *DPP* v *Younas* [1990] RTR 22, concerning 'laced drinks'; *DPP* v *Feeney* (1988) 89 Cr App R 173, emergency; *DPP* v *White* [1988] RTR 267, continuing to drive after a negative roadside breath test.

'Laced drinks' as a special reason received a comprehensive review in *DPP* v *O'Connor*. The Divisional Court took the view that some justices required guidance as to how they should evaluate evidence in such cases. The court reiterated the view that it was for the defence to establish special reasons on the balance of probabilities by admissible and relevant evidence. The defence must show:

(a)   that the defendant's drink or drinks had been laced;
(b)   that the defendant did not know or suspect that his drink had been laced;
(c)   that, if the defendant had not taken the laced drink, his level of alcohol would not have exceeded the prescribed limit.

Evidence needs to be examined with some care and expert evidence, which justices should normally expect to receive, is usually highly relevant as it goes to both credibility and whether or not the driver's admitted, voluntary consumption of alcohol would have taken him above the prescribed limit (per Woolf LJ at p. 79).

The need for a two-stage process was stressed, and Woolf LJ stated (at p. 81E):

> . . . in cases where there is erratic driving, or there is a substantial amount of alcohol in the defendant's bloodstream, justices will want to consider carefully whether, even if special reasons are established, this is a case where the defendant should have appreciated that he was not in a condition in which he should have driven.

In appropriate cases, legal aid should be made available to enable a defendant to adduce expert evidence to support a plea of special reasons in 'laced drinks' cases (*Gravesham Magistrates' Court, ex parte Baker* [1998] RTR 451).

In *Chatters* v *Burke* [1986] 1 WLR 1321, following an accident the defendant drove his motor vehicle a very short distance from a field onto the side of the highway, where he stopped, got out, and waited for the arrival of the police. He was charged with driving with excess alcohol in his breath and no insurance. After a plea of guilty was entered, justices were advised by their clerk that the facts might amount to 'special reasons'. The defendant gave evidence and the justices found 'special reasons' and did not disqualify. Upholding that finding, the court referred to a number of authorities, including *James* v *Hall* [1972] 2 All ER 59, *Coombs* v *Kehoe* [1972] 1 WLR 797 and *McIntyre* [1976] RTR 330. It also enumerated seven matters which ought to be taken into account in such cases (at p. 1327):

> First of all they should consider how far the vehicle was in fact driven; secondly, in what manner it was driven; thirdly, what was the state of the vehicle; fourthly, whether it was the intention of the driver to drive any further; fifthly, the prevailing conditions with regard to the road and the traffic upon it; sixthly, whether there was any possibility of danger by contact with other road users; and finally, what was the reason for the vehicle being driven at all.

In *DPP* v *Corcoran* [1991] RTR 329, the respondent, having parked in the street because he was late for the theatre, drove some 40 yards to a car park from which a colleague was to collect the car on the following day. The car was travelling without lights, albeit slowly, and there were pedestrians in the vicinity but no other vehicles were visible and no danger was caused to other road users. The lack of danger by contact with other road users and the distance travelled were central to the decision to uphold the justices' finding of special reasons.

In *Daniels* v *DPP* [1992] RTR 140, the appellant, in the course of attempting to start his motor cycle, travelled 35 yards and was then arrested on suspicion of theft. At the police station he was asked to provide a breath test but was not told that he was no longer arrested on suspicion of theft or that he was under arrest in relation to an allegation of 'drink driving'. He refused to provide a specimen and was charged with an offence contrary to what is now the RTA 1988, s. 7(6). Unsuccessful applications were made to exclude the evidence of the breath test procedure (under s. 78 of the PACE 1984) in both the magistrates' court and the Crown Court, on the basis that the appellant was distracted by the charge of theft which he thought he was facing. On that basis the Divisional Court, whilst stating that it would not amount to a 'reasonable excuse' (and therefore a defence), found the particular facts of the matter might amount to a 'special reason'. Although fear of AIDS is potentially a defence to a charge of refusing to provide a specimen if it is medically established as a phobia (see *De Freitas* v *DPP* [1993] RTR 98 at **C5.31**) it was also held, in *DPP* v *Kinnersley* [1993] RTR 105, to be capable of being a 'special reason' for not disqualifying after a refusal to give a breath specimen.

In cases concerning no insurance, a mistaken, albeit honest, belief that there was insurance has been held to be insufficient to amount to 'special reasons' in the absence of reasonable grounds for the belief (*Knowles* v *Rennison* [1947] KB 488); where a defendant has enquired as to whether he is insured and has been assured that he is, this may amount to reasonable grounds, and special reasons (*Marshall* v *McLeod* 1998 SCCR 317). The mere fact that a vehicle is parked and unlikely to be driven while uninsured will not amount to 'special reasons' (*Heywood* v *O'Connor* 1994 SLT 254). In *DPP* v *Powell* [1993] RTR 266, the defendant's view that he did not require insurance to road test a motorised children's bike, which he regarded as a toy, was held to come within the test set out in *Whittal* v *Kirby* [1947] KB 194.

The question of what constitutes 'special reasons' therefore depends upon the facts of any particular case within the overall test as expressed in *Whittal* v *Kirby*. As long as the justices or Crown Court have properly directed themselves in accordance with that test, the appellate courts will not interfere with their finding.

SECTION C8: THE SCHEDULES TO THE ROAD TRAFFIC OFFENDERS ACT 1988

Road Traffic Offenders Act 1988, sch. 1

SCHEDULE 1   C8.1
OFFENCES TO WHICH SECTIONS 1, 6, 11 AND 12(1) APPLY

1. (1) Where section 1, 6, 11 and 12(1) of this Act is shown in column 3 of this Schedule against a provision of the Road Traffic Act 1988 specified in column 1, the section in question applies to an offence under that provision.

(2) The general nature of the offence is indicated in column 2.

1A. Section 1 also applies to—

(a) an offence under section 16 of the Road Traffic Regulation Act 1984 consisting in the contravention of a restriction on the speed of vehicles imposed under section 14 of that Act,

(b) an offence under subsection (4) of section 17 of that Act consisting in the contravention of a restriction on the speed of vehicles imposed under that section, and

(c) an offence under section 88(7) or 89(1) of that Act (speeding offences).

2. Section 6 also applies—

(a) to an offence under section 67 of this Act,

(b) [Applies only to Scotland.]

(c) to an offence under section 1(5) of the Road Traffic (Driver Licensing and Information Systems) Act 1989, and

(d) to an offence under paragraph 3(5) of schedule 1 to the Road Traffic (New Drivers) Act 1995.

3. Section 11 also applies to—

(a) any offence to which section 112 of the Road Traffic Regulation Act 1984 (information as to identity of driver or rider) applies except an offence under section 61(5) of that Act,

(b) any offence which is punishable under section 91 of this Act,

(bb) an offence under paragraph 3 of schedule 1 to the Road Traffic (Driver Licensing and Information Systems) Act 1989, and

(c) any offence against any other enactment relating to the use of vehicles on roads.

4. Section 12(1) also applies to—

(a) any offence which is punishable under section 91 of this Act,

(aa) an offence under paragraph 3(1) of schedule 1 to the Road Traffic (Driver Licensing and Information Systems) Act 1989, and

(b) any offence against any other enactment relating to the use of vehicles on roads.

(1) Provision creating offence	(2) General nature of offence	(3) Applicable provisions of this Act
RTA section 1	Causing death by dangerous driving.	Section 11 of this Act.
RTA section 2	Dangerous driving.	Sections 1, 11 and 12(1) of this Act.
RTA section 3	Careless, and inconsiderate, driving.	Sections 1, 11 and 12(1) of this Act.
RTA section 3A	Causing death by careless driving when under influence of drink or drugs.	Section 11 of this Act.
RTA section 4	Driving or attempting to drive, or being in charge of a mechanically propelled vehicle, when unfit to drive through drink or drugs.	Sections 11 and 12(1) of this Act.

(1) Provision creating offence	(2) General nature of offence	(3) Applicable provisions of this Act
RTA section 5	Driving or attempting to drive, or being in charge of a motor vehicle, with excess alcohol in breath, blood or urine.	Sections 11 and 12(1) of this Act.
RTA section 6	Failing to provide a specimen of breath for a breath test.	Sections 11 and 12(1) of this Act.
RTA section 7	Failing to provide specimen for analysis or laboratory test.	Sections 11 and 12(1) of this Act.
RTA section 12	Motor racing and speed trials.	Sections 11 and 12(1) of this Act.
RTA section 14	Driving or riding in a motor vehicle in contravention of regulations requiring wearing of seat belts.	Sections 11 and 12(1) of this Act.
RTA section 15	Driving motor vehicle with child not wearing seat belt.	Sections 11 and 12(1) of this Act.
RTA section 19	Prohibition of parking of heavy commercial vehicles on verges and footways.	Sections 11 and 12(1) of this Act.
RTA section 22	Leaving vehicles in dangerous positions.	Sections 1, 11 and 12(1) of this Act.
RTA section 23	Carrying passenger on motor-cycle contrary to section 23.	Sections 11 and 12(1) of this Act.
RTA section 24	Carrying passenger on bicycle contrary to section 24.	Sections 11 and 12(1) of this Act.
RTA section 25	Tampering with motor vehicles.	Section 11 of this Act.
RTA section 26(1)	Holding or getting onto vehicle in order to be carried.	Section 11 of this Act.
RTA section 26(2)	Holding on to vehicle in order to be towed.	Sections 11 and 12(1) of this Act.
RTA section 28	Dangerous cycling.	Sections 1, 11 and 12(1) of this Act.
RTA section 29	Careless, and inconsiderate, cycling.	Sections 1, 11 and 12(1) of this Act.
RTA section 30	Cycling when unfit through drink or drugs.	Sections 11 and 12(1) of this Act.
RTA section 31	Unauthorised or irregular cycle racing, or trials of speed.	Sections 11 and 12(1) of this Act.
RTA section 33	Unauthorised motor vehicle trial on footpaths or bridleways.	Sections 11 and 12(1) of this Act.
RTA section 34	Driving motor vehicles elsewhere than on roads.	Sections 11 and 12(1) of this Act.
RTA section 35	Failing to comply with traffic directions.	Sections 1, 11 and 12(1) of this Act.
RTA section 36	Failing to comply with traffic signs.	Sections 1, 11 and 12(1) of this Act.
RTA section 40A	Using vehicle in dangerous condition etc.	Sections 11 and 12(1) of this Act.
RTA section 41A	Breach of requirement as to brakes, steering-gear or tyres.	Sections 11 and 12(1) of this Act.
RTA section 41B	Breach of requirement as to weight: goods and passenger vehicles.	Sections 11 and 12(1) of this Act.
RTA section 42	Breach of other construction and use requirements.	Sections 11 and 12(1) of this Act.
RTA section 47	Using, etc., vehicle without required test certificate being in force.	Sections 11 and 12(1) of this Act.

(1) Provision creating offence	(2) General nature of offence	(3) Applicable provisions of this Act
RTA section 53	Using, etc., goods vehicle without required plating certificate or goods vehicle test certificate being in force, or where Secretary of State is required by regulations under section 49 to be notified of an alteration to the vehicle or its equipment but has not been notified.	Sections 11 and 12(1) of this Act.
RTA section 63	Using, etc., vehicle without required certificate being in force showing that it, or a part fitted to it, complies with type approval requirements applicable to it, or using, etc., certain goods vehicles for drawing trailer when plating certificate does not specify maximum laden weight for vehicle and trailer, or using, etc., goods vehicle where Secretary of State has not been but is required to be notified under section 48 of alteration to it or its equipment.	Sections 11 and 12(1) of this Act.
RTA section 71	Driving, etc., vehicle in contravention of prohibition on driving it as being unfit for service or overloaded, or refusing, neglecting or otherwise failing to comply with a direction to remove a vehicle found overloaded.	Sections 11 and 12(1) of this Act.
RTA section 78	Failing to comply with requirement about weighing motor vehicle or obstructing authorised person.	Sections 11 and 12(1) of this Act.
RTA section 87(1)	Driving otherwise than in accordance with a licence.	Sections 11 and 12(1) of this Act.
RTA section 87(2)	Causing or permitting a person to drive otherwise than in accordance with a licence.	Section 11 of this Act.
RTA section 92(10)	Driving after making false declaration as to physical fitness.	Sections 6, 11 and 12(1) of this Act.
RTA section 94(3) and that subsection as applied by RTA section 99D	Failure to notify the Secretary of State of onset of, or deterioration in, relevant or prospective disability.	Section 6 of this Act.
RTA section 94(3A) and that subsection as applied by RTA section 99D(b)	Driving after such a failure.	Sections 6, 11 and 12(1) of this Act.
RTA section 94A	Driving after refusal of licence under section 92(3), revocation under section 93 or service of a notice under section 99C.	Sections 6, 11 and 12(1) of this Act.
RTA section 99(5)	Driving licence holder failing to surrender licence and counterpart.	Section 6 of this Act.

(1) Provision creating offence	(2) General nature of offence	(3) Applicable provisions of this Act
RTA section 99B(11)	Driving after failure to comply with a requirement under section 99B(6), (7) or (10).	Section 6 of this Act.
RTA section 103(1)(a)	Obtaining driving licence while disqualified.	Section 6 of this Act.
RTA section 103(1)(b)	Driving while disqualified.	Sections 6, 11 and 12(1) of this Act.
RTA section 114(1)	Failing to comply with conditions of LGV, PCV licence or LGV Community licence.	Sections 11 and 12(1) of this Act.
RTA section 114(2)	Causing or permitting a person under 21 to drive LGV or PCV in contravention of conditions of that person's licence.	Section 11 of this Act.
RTA section 143	Using motor vehicle, or causing or permitting it to be used, while uninsured or unsecured against third party risks.	Sections 6, 11 and 12(1) of this Act.
RTA section 163	Failing to stop vehicle when required by constable.	Sections 11 and 12(1) of this Act.
RTA section 164(6)	Failing to produce driving licence and counterpart to constable or to state date of birth.	Sections 11 and 12(1) of this Act.
RTA section 165(3)	Failing to give constable certain names and addresses or to produce certificate of insurance or certain test and other like certificates.	Sections 11 and 12(1) of this Act.
RTA section 165(6)	Supervisor of learner driver failing to give constable certain names and addresses.	Section 11 of this Act.
RTA section 168	Refusing to give, or giving false, name and address in case of reckless, careless or inconsiderate driving or cycling.	Sections 11 and 12(1) of this Act.
RTA section 170	Failure by driver to stop, report accident or give information or documents.	Sections 11 and 12(1) of this Act.
RTA section 171	Failure by owner of motor vehicle to give police information for verifying compliance with requirement of compulsory insurance or security.	Sections 11 and 12(1) of this Act.
RTA section 174(1) or (5)	Making false statements in connection with licences under this Act and with registration as an approved driving instructor; or making false statement or withholding material information in order to obtain the issue of insurance certificates, etc.	Section 6 of this Act.
RTA section 175	Issuing false documents.	Section 6 of this Act.

Road Traffic Offenders Act 1988, sch. 2

SCHEDULE 2
PROSECUTION AND PUNISHMENT OF OFFENCES

PART I
OFFENCES UNDER THE TRAFFIC ACTS

(1) Provision creating offence	(2) General nature of offence	(3) Mode of prosecution	(4) Punishment	(5) Disqualification	(6) Endorsement	(7) Penalty points
Offences under the Road Traffic Regulation Act 1984						
RTRA section 5	Contravention of traffic regulation order.	Summarily.	Level 3 on the standard scale.			
RTRA section 8	Contravention of order regulating traffic in Greater London.	Summarily.	Level 3 on the standard scale.			
RTRA section 11	Contravention of experimental traffic order.	Summarily.	Level 3 on the standard scale.			
RTRA section 13	Contravention of experimental traffic scheme in Greater London.	Summarily.	Level 3 on the standard scale.			
RTRA section 16(1)	Contravention of temporary prohibition or restriction.	Summarily.	Level 3 on the standard scale.	Discretionary if committed in respect of a speed restriction.	Obligatory if committed in respect of a a speed restriction.	3–6 or 3 (fixed penalty).
RTRA section 16C(1)	Contravention of prohibition or restriction relating to relevant event.	Summarily.	Level 3 on the standard scale.			
RTRA section 17(4)	Use of special road contrary to scheme or regulations.	Summarily.	Level 4 on the standard scale.	Discretionary if committed in respect of a motor vehicle otherwise than by unlawfully stopping or allowing the vehicle to remain at rest on a part of a special road on which vehicles are in certain circumstances permitted to remain at rest.	Obligatory if committed as mentioned in the entry in column 5.	3–6 or 3 (fixed penalty) if committed in respect of a speed restriction, 3 in any other case.
RTRA section 18(3)	One-way traffic on trunk road.	Summarily.	Level 3 on the standard scale.			
RTRA section 20(5)	Contravention of prohibition or restriction for roads of certain classes.	Summarily.	Level 3 on the standard scale.			
RTRA section 25(5)	Contravention of pedestrian crossing regulations.	Summarily.	Level 3 on the standard scale.	Discretionary if committed in respect of a motor vehicle.	Obligatory if committed in respect of a motor vehicle.	3
RTRA section 28(3)	Not stopping at school crossing.	Summarily.	Level 3 on the standard scale.	Discretionary if committed in respect of a motor vehicle.	Obligatory if committed in respect of a motor vehicle.	3
RTRA section 29(3)	Contravention of order relating to street playground.	Summarily.	Level 3 on the standard scale.	Discretionary if committed in respect of a motor vehicle.	Obligatory if committed in respect of a motor vehicle.	2

(1) Provision creating offence	(2) General nature of offence	(3) Mode of prosecution	(4) Punishment	(5) Disqualification	(6) Endorsement	(7) Penalty points
			Offences under the Road Traffic Regulation Act 1984 — continued			
RTRA section 35A(1)	Contravention of order as to use of parking place.	Summarily.	(a) Level 3 on the standard scale in the case of an offence committed by a person in a street parking place reserved for disabled persons' vehicles or in an off-street parking place reserved for such vehicles, where that person would not have been guilty of that offence if the motor vehicle in respect of which it was committed had been a disabled person's vehicle. (b) Level 2 on the standard scale in any other case.			
RTRA section 35A(2)	Misuse of apparatus for collecting charges or of parking device or connected apparatus.	Summarily.	Level 3 on the standard scale.			
RTRA section 35A(5)	Plying for hire in parking place.	Summarily.	Level 2 on the standard scale.			
RTRA section 43(5)	Unauthorised disclosure of information in respect of licensed parking place.	Summarily.	Level 3 on the standard scale.			
RTRA section 43(10)	Failure to comply with term or conditions of licence to operate parking place.	Summarily.	Level 3 on the standard scale.			
RTRA section 43(12)	Operation of public off-street parking place without licence.	Summarily.	Level 5 on the standard scale.			
RTRA section 47(1)	Contraventions relating to designated parking places.	Summarily.	(a) Level 3 on the standard scale in the case of an offence committed by a person in a street parking place reserved for disabled persons' vehicles where that person would not have been guilty of the offence if the motor vehicle in respect of which it was committed had been a disabled person's vehicle. (b) Level 2 in any other case.			
RTRA section 47(3)	Tampering with parking meter.	Summarily.	Level 3 on the standard scale.			
RTRA section 52(1)	Misuse of parking device.	Summarily.	Level 2 on the standard scale.			

(1) Provision creating offence	(2) General nature of offence	(3) Mode of prosecution	(4) Punishment	(5) Disqualification	(6) Endorsement	(7) Penalty points
			Offences under the Road Traffic Regulation Act 1984 — continued			
RTRA section 53(5)	Contravention of certain provisions of designation orders.	Summarily.	Level 3 on the standard scale.			
RTRA section 53(6)	Other contraventions of designation orders.	Summarily.	Level 2 on the standard scale.			
RTRA section 61(5)	Unauthorised use of loading area.	Summarily.	Level 3 on the standard scale.			
RTRA section 88(7)	Contravention of minimum speed limit.	Summarily.	Level 3 on the standard scale.			
RTRA section 89(1)	Exceeding speed limit.	Summarily.	Level 3 on the standard scale.	Discretionary.	Obligatory.	3–6 or 3 (fixed penalty).
RTRA section 104(5)	Interference with notice as to immobilisation device.	Summarily.	Level 2 on the standard scale.			
RTRA section 104(6)	Interference with immobilisation device.	Summarily.	Level 3 on the standard scale.			
RTRA section 105(5)	Misuse of disabled person's badge (immobilisation devices).	Summarily.	Level 3 on the standard scale.			
RTRA section 108(2) (or that subsection as modified by section 109(2) and (3)).	Non-compliance with notice (excess charge).	Summarily.	Level 3 on the standard scale.			
RTRA section 108(3) (or that subsection as modified by section 109(2) and (3)).	False response to notice (excess charge).	Summarily.	Level 5 on the standard scale.			
RTRA section 112(4)	Failure to give information as to identity of driver.	Summarily.	Level 3 on the standard scale.			
RTRA section 115(1)	Mishandling or faking parking documents.	(a) Summarily. (b) On indictment.	(a) The statutory maximum. (b) 2 years.			
RTRA section 115(2)	False statement for procuring authorisation.	Summarily.	Level 4 on the standard scale.			
RTRA section 116(1)	Non-delivery of suspect document or article.	Summarily.	Level 3 on the standard scale.			
RTRA section 117	Wrongful use of disabled person's badge.	Summarily.	Level 3 on the standard scale.			
RTRA section 129(3)	Failure to give evidence at inquiry.	Summarily.	Level 3 on the standard scale.			
			Offences under the Road Traffic Act 1988			
RTA section 1	Causing death by dangerous driving.	On indictment.	10 years.	Obligatory.	Obligatory.	3–11
RTA section 2	Dangerous Driving.	(a) Summarily. (b) On indictment.	(a) 6 months or the statutory maximum or both. (b) 2 years or a fine or both.	Obligatory.	Obligatory.	3–11
RTA section 3	Careless, and inconsiderate, driving.	Summarily.	Level 4 on the standard scale.	Discretionary.	Obligatory.	3–9
RTA section 3A	Causing death by careless driving when under influence of drink or drugs.	On indictment.	10 years or a fine or both.	Obligatory.	Obligatory.	3–11
RTA section 4(1)	Driving or attempting to drive when unfit to drive through drink or drugs.	Summarily.	6 months or level 5 on the standard scale or both.	Obligatory.	Obligatory.	3–11
RTA section 4(2)	Being in charge of a mechanically propelled vehicle when unfit to drive through drink or drugs.	Summarily.	3 months or level 4 on the standard scale or both.	Discretionary.	Obligatory.	10

(1) Provision creating offence	(2) General nature of offence	(3) Mode of prosecution	(4) Punishment	(5) Disqualification	(6) Endorsement	(7) Penalty points
		Offences under the Road Traffic Act 1988 — continued				
RTA section 5(1)(a)	Driving or attempting to drive with excess alcohol in breath, blood or urine.	Summarily.	6 months or level 5 on the standard scale or both.	Obligatory.	Obligatory.	3–11
RTA section 5(1)(b)	Being in charge of a motor vehicle with excess alcohol in breath, blood or urine.	Summarily.	3 months or level 4 on the standard scale or both.	Discretionary.	Obligatory.	10
RTA section 6	Failing to provide a specimen of breath for a breath test.	Summarily.	Level 3 on the standard scale.	Discretionary.	Obligatory.	4
RTA section 7	Failing to provide specimen for analysis or laboratory test.	Summarily.	(a) Where the specimen was required to ascertain ability to drive or proportion of alcohol at the time offender was driving or attempting to drive, 6 months or level 5 on the standard scale or both. (b) In any other case, 3 months or level 4 on the standard scale or both.	(a) Obligatory in case mentioned in column 4(a). (b) Discretionary in any other case.	Obligatory.	(a) 3–11 in case mentioned in column 4(a). (b) 10 in any other case.
RTA section 12	Motor racing and speed trials on public ways.	Summarily.	Level 4 on the standard scale.	Obligatory.	Obligatory.	3–11
RTA section 13	Other unauthorised or irregular competitions or trials on public ways.	Summarily.	Level 3 on the standard scale.			
RTA section 14	Driving or riding in a motor vehicle in contravention of regulations requiring wearing of seat belts.	Summarily.	Level 2 on the standard scale.			
RTA section 15(2)	Driving motor vehicle with child not wearing seat belt.	Summarily.	Level 2 on the standard scale.			
RTA section 15A(3) or (4)	Selling etc. in certain circumstances equipment as conducive to the safety of children in motor vehicles.	Summarily.	Level 3 on the standard scale.			
RTA section 16	Driving or riding motor cycles in contravention of regulations requiring wearing of protective headgear.	Summarily.	Level 2 on the standard scale.			
RTA section 17	Selling, etc., helmet not of the prescribed type as helmet for affording protection for motor cyclists.	Summarily.	Level 3 on the standard scale.			
RTA section 18(3)	Contravention of regulations with respect to use of head-worn appliances on motor cycles.	Summarily.	Level 2 on the standard scale.			
RTA section 18(4)	Selling, etc., appliance not of prescribed type as approved for use on motor cycles.	Summarily.	Level 3 on the standard scale.			
RTA section 19	Prohibition of parking of heavy commercial vehicles on verges, etc.	Summarily.	Level 3 on the standard scale.			
RTA section 21	Driving or parking on cycle track.	Summarily.	Level 3 on the standard scale.			

(1) Provision creating offence	(2) General nature of offence	(3) Mode of prosecution	(4) Punishment	(5) Disqualification	(6) Endorsement	(7) Penalty points
			Offences under the Road Traffic Act 1988 — continued			
RTA section 22	Leaving vehicles in dangerous positions.	Summarily.	Level 3 on the standard scale.	Discretionary if committed in respect of a motor vehicle.	Obligatory if committed in respect of a motor vehicle.	3
RTA section 22A	Causing danger to road users.	(a) Summarily. (b) On indictment.	(a) 6 months or the statutory maximum or both. (b) 7 years or a fine or both.			
RTA section 23	Carrying passenger on motor-cycle contrary to section 23.	Summarily.	Level 3 on the standard scale.	Discretionary.	Obligatory.	3
RTA section 24	Carrying passenger on bicycle contrary to section 24.	Summarily.	Level 1 on the standard scale.			
RTA section 25	Tampering with motor vehicles.	Summarily.	Level 3 on the standard scale.			
RTA section 26	Holding or getting on to vehicle, etc., in order to be towed or carried.	Summarily.	Level 1 on the standard scale.			
RTA section 27	Dogs on designated roads without being held on lead.	Summarily.	Level 1 on the standard scale.			
RTA section 28	Dangerous cycling.	Summarily.	Level 4 on the standard scale.			
RTA section 29	Careless, and inconsiderate, cycling.	Summarily.	Level 3 on the standard scale.			
RTA section 30	Cycling when unfit through drink or drugs.	Summarily.	Level 3 on the standard scale.			
RTA section 31	Unauthorised or irregular cycle racing or trials of speed on public ways.	Summarily.	Level 1 on the standard scale.			
RTA section 32	Contravening prohibition on persons under 14 driving electrically assisted pedal cycles.	Summarily.	Level 2 on the standard scale.			
RTA section 33	Unauthorised motor vehicle trial on footpaths or bridleways.	Summarily.	Level 3 on the standard scale.			
RTA section 34	Driving motor vehicles elsewhere than on roads.	Summarily.	Level 3 on the standard scale.			
RTA section 35	Failing to comply with traffic directions.	Summarily.	Level 3 on the standard scale.	Discretionary, if committed in respect of a motor vehicle by failure to comply with a direction of a constable or traffic warden.	Obligatory if committed as described in column 5.	3
RTA section 36	Failing to comply with traffic signs.	Summarily.	Level 3 on the standard scale.	Discretionary, if committed in respect of a motor vehicle by failure to comply with an indication given by a sign specified for the purposes of this paragraph in regulations under RTA section 36.	Obligatory if committted as described in column 5.	3
RTA section 37	Pedestrian failing to stop when directed by constable regulating traffic.	Summarily.	Level 3 on the standard scale.			

(1) Provision creating offence	(2) General nature of offence	(3) Mode of prosecution	(4) Punishment	(5) Disqualification	(6) Endorsement	(7) Penalty points
			Offences under the Road Traffic Act 1988 — continued			
RTA section 40A	Using vehicle in dangerous condition etc.	Summarily.	(a) Level 5 on the standard scale if committed in respect of a goods vehicle or a vehicle adapted to carry more than eight passengers. (b) Level 4 on the standard scale in any other case.	Discretionary.	Obligatory.	3
RTA section 41A	Breach of requirement as to brakes, steering-gear or tyres.	Summarily.	(a) Level 5 on the standard scale if committed in respect of a goods vehicle or a vehicle adapted to carry more than eight passengers. (b) Level 4 on the standard scale in any other case.	Discretionary.	Obligatory.	3
RTA section 41B	Breach of requirement as to weight: goods and passenger vehicles.	Summarily.	Level 5 on the standard scale.			
RTA section 42	Breach of other construction and use requirements.	Summarily.	(a) Level 4 on the standard scale if committed in respect of a goods vehicle or a vehicle adapted to carry more than eight passengers. (b) Level 3 on the standard scale in any other case.			
RTA section 47	Using, etc., vehicle without required test certificate being in force.	Summarily.	(a) Level 4 on the standard scale in the case of a vehicle adapted to carry more than eight passengers. (b) Level 3 on the standard scale in any other case.			
Regulations under RTA section 49 made by virtue of section 51(2)	Contravention of requirement of regulations (which is declared by regulations to be an offence) that driver of goods vehicle being tested be present throughout test or drive, etc., vehicle as and when directed.	Summarily.	Level 3 on the standard scale.			
RTA section 53(1)	Using, etc., goods vehicle without required plating certificate being in force.	Summarily.	Level 3 on the standard scale.			
RTA section 53(2)	Using, etc., goods vehicle without required goods vehicle test certificate being in force.	Summarily.	Level 4 on the standard scale.			

(1) Provision creating offence	(2) General nature of offence	(3) Mode of prosecution	(4) Punishment	(5) Disqualification	(6) Endorsement	(7) Penalty points
			Offences under the Road Traffic Act 1988 — continued			
RTA section 53(3)	Using, etc., goods vehicle where Secretary of State is required by regulations under section 49 to be notified of an alteration to the vehicle or its equipment but has not been notified.	Summarily.	Level 3 on the standard scale.			
Regulations under RTA section 61 made by virtue of subsection (4)	Contravention of requirement of regulations (which is declared by regulations to be an offence) that driver of goods vehicle being tested after notifiable alteration be present throughout test and drive, etc., vehicle as and when directed.	Summarily.	Level 3 on the standard scale.			
RTA section 63(1)	Using, etc., goods vehicle without required certificate being in force showing that it complies with type approval requirements applicable to it.	Summarily.	Level 4 on the standard scale.			
RTA section 63(2)	Using, etc., certain goods vehicles for drawing trailer when plating certificate does not specify maximum laden weight for vehicle and trailer.	Summarily.	Level 3 on the standard scale.			
RTA section 63(3)	Using, etc., goods vehicle where Secretary of State is required to be notified under section 59 of alteration to it or its equipment but has not been notified.	Summarily.	Level 3 on the standard scale.			
RTA section 64	Using goods vehicle with unauthorised weights as well as authorised weights marked on it.	Summarily.	Level 3 on the standard scale.			
RTA section 64A	Failure to hold EC certificate of conformity for unregistered light passenger vehicle.	Summarily.	Level 3 on the standard scale.			
RTA section 65	Supplying vehicle or vehicle part without required certificate being in force showing that it complies with type approval requirements applicable to it.	Summarily.	Level 5 on the standard scale.			
RTA section 65A	Light passenger vehicles not to be sold without EC certificate of conformity.	Summarily.	Level 5 on the standard scale.			
RTA section 67	Obstructing testing of vehicle by examiner on road or failing to comply with requirements of RTA section 67 or Schedule 2.	Summarily.	Level 3 on the standard scale.			

(1) Provision creating offence	(2) General nature of offence	(3) Mode of prosecution	(4) Punishment	(5) Disqualification	(6) Endorsement	(7) Penalty points

Offences under the Road Traffic Act 1988 — continued

(1)	(2)	(3)	(4)	(5)	(6)	(7)
RTA section 67A (including application by section 67B(4))	Failure of owner of apparently defective vehicle to give required certificate or declaration or failure of person in charge of vehicle being tested to give information.	Summarily.	Level 3 on the standard scale.			
RTA section 67B	Obstructing further testing of vehicle of Secretary of State's officer or failing to comply with requirements of RTA section 67B or paragraph 3 or 4 of Schedule 2.	Summarily.	Level 3 on the standard scale.			
RTA section 68	Obstructing inspection, etc., of vehicle by examiner or failing to comply with requirement to take vehicle for inspection.	Summarily.	Level 3 on the standard scale.			
RTA section 71	Driving, etc., vehicle in contravention of prohibition on driving it as being unfit for service, or refusing, neglecting or otherwise failing to comply with direction to remove a vehicle found overloaded.	Summarily.	Level 5 on the standard scale.			
RTA section 74	Contravention of regulations requiring goods vehicle operator to inspect, and keep records of inspection of, goods vehicles.	Summarily.	Level 3 on the standard scale.			
RTA section 75	Selling, etc., unroadworthy vehicle or trailer or altering vehicle or trailer so as to make it unroadworthy.	Summarily.	Level 5 on the standard scale.			
RTA section 76(1)	Fitting of defective or unsuitable vehicle parts.	Summarily.	Level 5 on the standard scale.			
RTA section 76(3)	Supplying defective or unsuitable vehicle parts.	Summarily.	Level 4 on the standard scale.			
RTA section 76(8)	Obstructing examiner testing vehicles to ascertain whether defective or unsuitable part has been fitted, etc.	Summarily.	Level 3 on the standard scale.			
RTA section 77	Obstructing examiner testing condition of used vehicle at sale rooms, etc.	Summarily.	Level 3 on the standard scale.			
RTA section 78	Failing to comply with requirement about weighing motor vehicle or obstructing authorised person.	Summarily.	Level 5 on the standard scale.			
RTA section 81	Selling, etc., pedal cycle in contravention of regulations as to brakes, bells, etc.	Summarily.	Level 3 on the standard scale.			
RTA section 83	Selling, etc., wrongly made tail lamps or reflectors.	Summarily.	Level 5 on the standard scale.			

(1) Provision creating offence	(2) General nature of offence	(3) Mode of prosecution	(4) Punishment	(5) Disqualification	(6) Endorsement	(7) Penalty points
		Offences under the Road Traffic Act 1988 — continued				
RTA section 87(1)	Driving otherwise than in accordance with a licence.	Summarily.	Level 3 on the standard scale.	Discretionary in a case where the offender's driving would not have been in accordance with any licence that could have been granted to him.	Obligatory in the case mentioned in column 5.	3–6
RTA section 87(2)	Causing or permitting a person to drive otherwise than in accordance with a licence.	Summarily.	Level 3 on the standard scale.			
RTA section 92(7C)	Failure to deliver licence revoked by virtue of section 92(7A) and counterpart to Secretary of State.	Summarily.	Level 3 on the standard scale.			
RTA section 92(10)	Driving after making false declaration as to physical fitness.	Summarily.	Level 4 on the standard scale.	Discretionary.	Obligatory.	3–6
RTA section 93(3)	Failure to deliver revoked licence and counterpart to Secretary of State.	Summarily.	Level 3 on the standard scale.			
RTA section 94(3) and that subsection as applied by RTA section 99D	Failure to notify Secretary of State of onset of, or deterioration in, relevant or prospective disability.	Summarily.	Level 3 on the standard scale.			
RTA section 94(3A) and that subsection as applied by RTA section 99D(b)	Driving after such a failure.	Summarily.	Level 3 on the standard scale.	Discretionary.	Obligatory.	3–6
RTA section 94A	Driving after refusal of licence under section 92(3), revocation under section 93 or service of a notice under section 99C.	Summarily.	6 months or level 5 on the standard scale or both.	Discretionary.	Obligatory.	3–6
RTA section 96	Driving with uncorrected defective eyesight, or refusing to submit to test of eyesight.	Summarily.	Level 3 on the standard scale.	Discretionary.	Obligatory.	3
RTA section 99(5)	Driving licence holder failing to surrender licence and counterpart.	Summarily.	Level 3 on the standard scale.			
RTA section 99B(11)	Driving after failure to comply with a requirement under section 99B(6), (7) or (10).	Summarily.	Level 3 on the standard scale.			
RTA section 99C(4)	Failure to deliver Community licence to Secretary of State when required by notice under section 99C.	Summarily.	Level 3 on the standard scale.			
RTA section 103(1)(a)	Obtaining driving licence while disqualified.	Summarily.	Level 3 on the standard scale.			

(1) Provision creating offence	(2) General nature of offence	(3) Mode of prosecution	(4) Punishment	(5) Disqualification	(6) Endorsement	(7) Penalty points
		Offences under the Road Traffic Act 1988 — continued				
RTA section 103(1)(b)	Driving while disqualified.	(a) Summarily, in England and Wales. (b) Summarily, in Scotland. (c) On indictment, in Scotland.	(a) 6 months or level 5 on the standard scale or both. (b) 6 months or the statutory maximum or both. (c) 12 months or a fine or both.	Discretionary.	Obligatory.	6
RTA section 109	Failing to produce to court Northern Ireland driving licence and its counterpart.	Summarily.	Level 3 on the standard scale.			
RTA section 114	Failing to comply with conditions of LGV, PCV licence or LGV Community licence, or causing or permitting person under 21 to drive LGV or PCV in contravention of such conditions.	Summarily.	Level 3 on the standard scale.			
RTA section 115A(4)	Failure to deliver LGV or PCV Community licence when required by notice under section 115A.	Summarily.	Level 3 on the standard scale.			
RTA section 118	Failing to surrender revoked or suspended LGV or PCV licence and counterpart.	Summarily.	Level 3 on the standard scale.			
Regulations made by virtue of RTA section 120(5)	Contravention of provision of regulations (which is declared by regulations to be an offence) about LGV or PCV drivers' licences or LGV or PCV Community licence.	Summarily.	Level 3 on the standard scale.			
RTA section 123(4)	Giving of paid driving instruction by unregistered and unlicensed persons or their employers.	Summarily.	Level 4 on the standard scale.			
RTA section 123(6)	Giving of paid instruction without there being exhibited on the motor car a certificate of registration or a licence under RTA part V.	Summarily.	Level 3 on the standard scale.			
RTA section 125A(4)	Failure, on application for registration as disabled driving instructor, to notify Registrar of onset of, or deterioration in, relevant or prospective disability.	Summarily.	Level 3 on the standard scale.			
RTA section 133C(4)	Failure by registered or licensed disabled driving instructor to notify Registrar of onset of, or deterioration in, relevant or prospective disability.	Summarily.	Level 3 on the standard scale.			

(1) Provision creating offence	(2) General nature of offence	(3) Mode of prosecution	(4) Punishment	(5) Disqualification	(6) Endorsement	(7) Penalty points
			Offences under the Road Traffic Act 1988 — continued			
RTA section 133D	Giving of paid driving instruction by disabled persons or their employers without emergency control certificate or in unauthorised motor car.	Summarily.	Level 3 on the standard scale.			
RTA section 135	Unregistered instructor using title or displaying badge, etc., prescribed for registered instructor, or employer using such title, etc., in relation to his unregistered instructor or issuing misleading advertisement, etc.	Summarily.	Level 4 on the standard scale.			
RTA section 136	Failure of instructor to surrender to Registrar certificate or licence.	Summarily.	Level 3 on the standard scale.			
RTA section 137	Failing to produce certificate of registration or licence as driving instructor.	Summarily.	Level 3 on the standard scale.			
RTA section 143	Using motor vehicle while uninsured or unsecured against third-party risks.	Summarily.	Level 5 on the standard scale.	Discretionary.	Obligatory.	6–8
RTA section 147	Failing to surrender certificate of insurance or security to insurer on cancellation or to make statutory declaration of loss or destruction.	Summarily.	Level 3 on the standard scale.			
RTA section 154	Failing to give information, or wilfully making a false statement, as to insurance or security when claim made.	Summarily.	Level 4 on the standard scale.			
RTA section 163	Failing to stop motor vehicle or cycle when required by constable.	Summarily	Level 3 on the standard scale.			
RTA section 164	Failing to produce driving licence and its counterpart or to state date of birth, or failing to provide the Secretary of State with evidence of date of birth, etc.	Summarily.	Level 3 on the standard scale.			
RTA section 165	Failing to give certain names and addresses or to produce certain documents.	Summarily.	Level 3 on the standard scale.			
RTA section 168	Refusing to give, or giving false, name and address in case of reckless, careless or inconsiderate driving or cycling.	Summarily.	Level 3 on the standard scale.			
RTA section 169	Pedestrian failing to give constable his name and address after failing to stop when directed by constable controlling traffic.	Summarily.	Level 1 on the standard scale.			
RTA section 170(4)	Failing to stop after accident and give particulars or report accident.	Summarily.	Six months or level 5 on the standard scale or both.	Discretionary.	Obligatory.	5–10

(1) Provision creating offence	(2) General nature of offence	(3) Mode of prosecution	(4) Punishment	(5) Disqualification	(6) Endorsement	(7) Penalty points
			Offences under the Road Traffic Act 1988 — continued			
RTA section 170(7)	Failure by driver, in case of accident involving injury to another, to produce evidence of insurance or security or to report accident.	Summarily.	Level 3 on the standard scale.			
RTA section 171	Failure by owner of motor vehicle to give police information for verifying compliance with requirement of compulsory insurance or security.	Summarily.	Level 4 on the standard scale.			
RTA section 172	Failure of person keeping vehicle and others to give police information as to identity of driver, etc., in the case of certain offences.	Summarily.	Level 3 on the standard scale.	Discretionary if committed otherwise than than by virtue of subsection (5) or (11).	Obligatory if committed otherwise than than by virtue of subsection (5) or (11).	3
RTA section 173	Forgery, etc., of licences, counterparts of Community licences, certificates of insurance and other documents and things.	(a) Summarily. (b) On indictment.	(a) The statutory maximum. (b) 2 years.			
RTA section 174	Making certain false statements, etc., and withholding certain material information.	Summarily.	Level 4 on the standard scale.			
RTA section 175(1)	Issuing false documents.	Summarily.	Level 4 on the standard scale.			
RTA section 175(2)	Falsely amending certificate of conformity.	Summarily.	Level 4 on the standard scale.			
RTA section 177	Impersonation of, or of person employed by, authorised examiner.	Summarily.	Level 3 on the standard scale.			
RTA section 178	[Scotland.]					
RTA section 180	Failing to attend, give evidence or produce documents to, inquiry held by Secretary of State, etc.	Summarily.	Level 3 on the standard scale.			
RTA section 181	Obstructing inspection of vehicles after accident.	Summarily.	Level 3 on the standard scale.			
RTA schedule 1 paragraph 6	Applying warranty to equipment, protective helmet, appliance or information in defending proceedings under RTA section 15A, 17 or 18(4) where no warranty given, or applying false warranty.	Summarily.	Level 3 on the standard scale.			

(1) Provision creating offence	(2) General nature of offence	(3) Mode of prosecution	(4) Punishment	(5) Disqualification	(6) Endorsement	(7) Penalty points
			Offences under this Act			
Section 25 of this Act.	Failing to give information as to date of birth or sex to court or to provide Secretary of State with evidence of date of birth, etc.	Summarily.	Level 3 on the standard scale.			
Section 26 of this Act.	Failing to produce driving licence and its counterpart to court making order for interim disqualification	Summarily.	Level 3 on the standard scale.			
Section 27 of this Act.	Failing to produce licence and its counterpart to court for endorsement on conviction of offence involving obligatory endorsement or on committal for sentence, etc., for offence involving obligatory or discretionary disqualification when no interim disqualification ordered.	Summarily.	Level 3 on the standard scale.			
Section 62 of this Act.	Removing fixed penalty notice fixed to vehicle.	Summarily.	Level 2 on the standard scale.			
Section 67 of this Act.	False statement in response to notice to owner.	Summarily.	Level 5 on the standard scale.			
		Offences under the Road Traffic (Driver Licensing and Information Systems) Act 1989				
RTA 1989 section 1(5)	Failure of holder of existing HGV or PSV driver's licence to surrender it upon revocation or surrender of his existing licence under part III of RTA.	Summarily.	Level 3 on the standard scale.			
RTA 1989 schedule 1, para. 3	Failing to comply with conditions of existing HGV driver's licence, or causing or permitting a person under 21 to drive HGV in contravention of such conditions.	Summarily.	Level 3 on the standard scale.			
RTA 1989 schedule 1, para. 8(2)	Contravention of provision of regulations (which is declared by regulations to be an offence) about existing HGV or PSV drivers' licences.	Summarily.	Level 3 on the standard scale.			
RTA 1989 schedule 1, para. 10(4)	Taking PSV test before applying for licence or within prescribed period afterwards.	Summarily.	Level 3 on the standard scale.			
RTA 1989 schedule 1, para. 10(5)	Taking PSV test after refusal of a licence.	Summarily.	Level 3 on the standard scale.			

PART II
OTHER OFFENCES

(1) Offence	(2) Disqualification	(3) Endorsement	(4) Penalty points
Manslaughter or, in Scotland, culpable homicide by the driver of a motor vehicle.	Obligatory.	Obligatory.	3–11
An offence under section 12A of the Theft Act 1968 (aggravated vehicle-taking).	Obligatory.	Obligatory.	3–11
Stealing or attempting to steal a motor vehicle.	Discretionary.		
An offence or attempt to commit an offence in respect of a motor vehicle under section 12 of the Theft Act 1968 (taking conveyance without consent of owner etc. or, knowing it has been so taken, driving it or allowing oneself to be carried in it).	Discretionary.		
An offence under section 25 of the Theft Act 1968 (going equipped for stealing, etc.) committed with reference to the theft or taking of motor vehicles.	Discretionary.		

Road Traffic Offenders Act 1988, sch. 3

C8.3

SCHEDULE 3
FIXED PENALTY OFFENCES

(1) Provision creating offence	(2) General nature of offence
Offence under the Greater London Council (General Powers) Act 1974	
Section 15 of the Greater London Council (General Powers) Act 1974.	Parking vehicles on footways, verges, etc.
Offence under the Highways Act 1980	
Section 137 of the Highways Act 1980.	Obstructing a highway, but only where the offence is committed in respect of a vehicle.
Offences under the Road Traffic Regulation Act 1984	
RTRA section 5(1)	Using a vehicle in contravention of a traffic regulation order outside Greater London.
RTRA section 8(1)	Breach of traffic regulation order in Greater London.
RTRA section 11	Breach of experimental traffic order.
RTRA section 13	Breach of experimental traffic scheme regulations in Greater London.
RTRA section 16(1)	Using a vehicle in contravention of temporary prohibition or restriction of traffic in case of execution of works, etc.
RTRA section 17(4)	Wrongful use of special road.
RTRA section 18(3)	Using a vehicle in contravention of provision for one-way traffic on trunk road.
RTRA section 20(5)	Driving a vehicle in contravention of order prohibiting or restricting driving vehicles on certain classes of roads.
RTRA section 25(5)	Breach of pedestrian crossing regulations, except an offence in respect of a moving motor vehicle other than a contravention of regulation 8 of the 'Zebra' Pedestrian Crossings Regulations 1971 or of regulations 16 or 17 of the 'Pelican' Crossings Regulations and General Directions 1987. [These regulations have been revoked and replaced by the Zebra, Pelican and Puffin Pedestrian Crossings Regulations and General Directions 1997 (see **C5.75**) but no specific amendment to sch. 3 has been made.]
RTRA section 29(3)	Using a vehicle in contravention of a street playground order.

(1) Provision creating offence	(2) General nature of offence
Offences under the Road Traffic Regulation Act 1984 — continued	
RTRA section 35A(1)	Breach of an order regulating the use, etc., of a parking place provided by a local authority, but only where the offence is committed in relation to a parking place provided on a road.
RTRA section 47(1)	Breach of a provision of a parking place designation order and other offences committed in relation to a parking place designated by such an order, except any offence of failing to pay an excess charge within the meaning of section 46.
RTRA section 53(5)	Using vehicle in contravention of any provision of a parking place designation order having effect by virtue of section 53(1)(a) (inclusion of certain traffic regulation provisions).
RTRA section 53(6)	Breach of a provision of a parking place designation order having effect by virtue of section 53(1)(b) (use of any part of a road for parking without charge).
RTRA section 88(7)	Driving a motor vehicle in contravention of an order imposing a minimum speed limit under section 88(1)(b).
RTRA section 89(1)	Speeding offences under RTRA and other Acts.
Offences under the Road Traffic Act 1988	
RTA section 14	Breach of regulations requiring wearing of seat belts.
RTA section 15(2)	Breach of restriction on carrying children in the front of vehicles.
RTA section 15(4)	Breach of restriction on carrying children in the rear of vehicles.
RTA section 16	Breach of regulations relating to protective headgear for motor cycle drivers and passengers.
RTA section 19	Parking a heavy commercial vehicle on verge or footway.
RTA section 22	Leaving vehicle in dangerous position.
RTA section 23	Unlawful carrying of passengers on motor cycles.
RTA section 34	Driving motor vehicle elsewhere than on a road.
RTA section 35	Failure to comply with traffic directions.
RTA section 36	Failure to comply with traffic signs.
RTA section 40A	Using vehicle in dangerous condition etc.
RTA section 41A	Breach of requirement as to brakes, steering-gear or tyres.
RTA scction 41B	Breach of requirement as to weight: goods and passenger vehicles.
RTA section 42	Breach of other construction and use requirements.
RTA section 87(1)	Driving vehicle otherwise than in accordance with requisite licence.
RTA section 163	Failure to stop vehicle on being so required by constable in uniform.
Offences under the Vehicle Excise and Registration Act 1994	
Section 33 of the Vehicle Excise and Registration Act 1994.	Using or keeping a vehicle on a public road without vehicle licence, trade licence or nil licence being exhibited in manner prescribed by regulations.
Section 42 of that Act.	Driving or keeping a vehicle without required registration mark.
Section 43 of that Act.	Driving or keeping a vehicle with registration mark obscured etc.

PART D
PROCEDURE

Christopher J. Emmins, MA, Barrister

John Sprack, BA, LLB, Barrister

Reader, Inns of Court School of Law

Leonard Leigh, PhD, Barrister

Commission Member, Criminal Cases Review Commission
Formerly Professor of Criminal Law in the University of London,
London School of Economics and Political Science

SECTION D1: POLICE POWERS: ARREST, SEARCH, DETENTION, INTERROGATION, DECISION TO PROSECUTE

POLICE POWERS IN INVESTIGATION OF CRIME

The police enjoy considerable powers in the investigation of crime. These include **D1.1** powers to stop and search individuals and vehicles, to arrest and to search premises. Some of these operations may be conducted on their own authority; others require the authorisation of a court, or in the case of electronic surveillance, of a Secretary of State, usually the Home Secretary. Despite efforts at simplification in recent years, the structure of police powers remains complex.

POWER TO STOP AND SEARCH

Police powers to stop and search people and vehicles are conferred by the PACE 1984 **D1.2** and some earlier and later legislation. A constable, whether in uniform or plain clothes, may search any person or vehicle for stolen or prohibited articles, the latter term including all offensive weapons, and articles made or adapted for use in respect of such offences as burglary, theft or taking and driving away a motor vehicle, and obtaining property by deception (PACE 1984, s. 1(2), (7), (8) and (9)). A constable who discovers such an article may seize it.

Police and Criminal Evidence Act 1984, s. 1

1.—(1)   A constable may exercise any power conferred by this section—
    (a)   in any place to which at the time when he proposes to exercise the power the public or any section of the public has access, on payment or otherwise, as of right or by virtue of express or implied permission; or
    (b)   in any other place to which people have ready access at the time when he proposes to exercise the power but which is not a dwelling.
    (2)   Subject to subsection (3) to (5) below, a constable—
        (a)   may search—
            (i)   any person or vehicle;
            (ii)   anything which is in or on a vehicle,
for stolen or prohibited articles or any article to which subsection (8A) below applies; and
        (b)   may detain a person or vehicle for the purpose of such a search.
    (3)   This section does not give a constable power to search a person or vehicle or anything in or on a vehicle unless he has reasonable grounds for suspecting that he will find stolen or prohibited articles or any article to which subsection (8A) below applies.
    (4)   If a person is in a garden or yard occupied with and used for the purposes of a dwelling or on other land so occupied and used, a constable may not search him in the exercise of the power conferred by this section unless the constable has reasonable grounds for believing—
        (a)   that he does not reside in the dwelling; and
        (b)   that he is not in the place in question with the express or implied permission of a person who resides in the dwelling.
    (5)   If a vehicle is in a garden or yard occupied with and used for the purposes of a dwelling or on other land so occupied and used, a constable may not search the vehicle or anything in or on it in the exercise of the power conferred by this section unless he has reasonable grounds for believing—
        (a)   that the person in charge of the vehicle does not reside in the dwelling; and
        (b)   that the vehicle is not in the place in question with the express or implied permission of a person who resides in the dwelling.

(6)   If in the course of such a search a constable discovers an article which he has reasonable grounds for suspecting to be a stolen or prohibited article, he may seize it.

(7)   An article is prohibited for the purposes of this part of this Act if it is—

(a)   an offensive weapon; or

(b)   an article—

(i)   made or adapted for use in the course of or in connection with an offence to which this subparagraph applies; or

(ii)   intended by the person having it with him for such use by him or by some other person.

(8)   The offences to which subsection (7)(b)(i) above applies are—

(a)   burglary;

(b)   theft;

(c)   offences under section 12 of the Theft Act 1968 (taking motor vehicle or other conveyance without authority); and

(d)   offences under section 15 of that Act (obtaining property by deception).

(8A)   This subsection applies to any article in relation to which a person has committed, or is committing or is going to commit an offence under section 139 of the Criminal Justice Act 1988.

(9)   In this part of this Act 'offensive weapon' means any article—

(a)   made or adapted for use for causing injury to persons; or

(b)   intended by the person having it with him for such use by him or by some other person.

Sections 2 and 3 of the PACE 1984 contain provisions relating to the powers conferred by s. 1. Failure to respect these provisions may turn an otherwise lawful search into a trespass and so deprive police officers who face resistance of the protection afforded by the offence of assaulting a constable acting in the execution of his duty. Section 2(3), for example, requires a constable conducting a search to inform the person to be searched before the search commences of his name and police station; failure to do so renders the search unlawful, and the illegality is not cured either by the fact that the search was reasonable or that the person concerned consented to it (*Osman* v *DPP* (1999) *The Times*, 28 September 1999).

Under specific legislation, the police are empowered to search for drugs (Misuse of Drugs Act 1971, s. 23(2)), flora and fauna of various descriptions (Wildlife and Countryside Act 1981, s. 19; Deer Act 1991, s. 12; Poaching Prevention Act 1862), in relation to terrorism (Prevention of Terrorism (Temporary Provisions) Act 1989, s. 15), and in relation to the security of aircraft and airports (Aviation Security Act 1982, s. 27(1); Aviation and Maritime Security Act 1990, ss. 2 and 22).

Powers to stop, search and seize are essentially intended for use in public places, meaning places to which the public, or any section of the public has access, on payment or otherwise, as of right or by virtue of express or implied permission, or any other place to which people have ready access at the time when it is proposed to exercise the powers but which is not a dwelling (PACE 1984, s. 1(1)(b)). For example, although powers to stop and search may not be exercised in a dwelling-house, they may be exercised in a garden or yard of a house (PACE 1984, s. 1(4) and (5)).

The foregoing powers concern situations in which either the suspect is thought to have weapons in his possession or is thought to possess evidence relating to one of the specific offences noted above. Section 60 of the CJPO 1994, bestows powers on police to stop and search in anticipation of violence.

Criminal Justice and Public Order Act 1994, s. 60

(1)   If a police officer of or above the rank of inspector reasonably believes—

(a)   that incidents involving serious violence may take place in any locality in his police area, and that it is expedient to give an authorisation under this section to prevent their occurrence, or

(b)   that persons are carrying dangerous instruments or offensive weapons in any locality in his police area without good reason,

he may give an authorisation that the powers conferred by this section are to be exercisable at any place within that locality for a specified period not exceeding 24 hours.

These powers may also be exercised in relation to ships, aircraft and hovercraft (s. 60(7)). They may, in circumstances of emergency, be exercised by a chief inspector or inspector provided that such officer reasonably believes that incidents involving serious violence are imminent and no superintendent is available (s. 60(2)). Any such authorisation must be in writing, but it may be given orally and recorded in writing as soon as is practicable thereafter where it is given in anticipation of imminent violence (s. 60(9)).

An officer of or above the rank of superintendent may, where he deems it expedient to do so (having regard to offences which have, or are reasonably suspected to have, been committed in relation to any activity falling within the authorisation), direct that the authorisation shall be continued for a further 24 hours. It will be noted that an extension cannot be ordered on the ground that offences or further offences may be committed. It follows that whereas the original order may be regarded as in some measure preventive, extensions are granted only in aid of the detection of offences which have been or are believed to have been committed (s. 60(3)).

Section 60 confers the following powers on police (s. 60(4)):

(a)   to stop any pedestrian and search him or anything carried by him for offensive weapons or dangerous instruments;

(b)   to stop and search any vehicle, its driver and any passenger for offensive weapons or dangerous instruments.

The powers of stop and search under s. 60(4) may be exercised by a constable notwithstanding that he has no grounds for suspecting that the person or vehicle is carrying offensive weapons or dangerous instruments (s. 60(5)). It is thus enough that the person or vehicle is within the geographical areas in which the powers have been invoked. A constable may seize any dangerous instrument or any article which he has reasonable grounds for suspecting to be an offensive weapon (s. 60(6)).

Under s. 60(4A), a power is conferred to require any person to remove any item which a constable reasonably believes the person is wearing wholly or mainly for the purpose of concealing his identity, and to seize any item which he reasonably believes any person intends to wear wholly or mainly for that purpose.

A person searched or the driver of a stopped vehicle is entitled to obtain, within 12 months from the date of the stop, a written statement that he or the vehicle was stopped under such powers (s. 60(10) and (10A)). This provides some safeguard against unauthorised stops and searches. By 'dangerous instrument' is meant an instrument which has a blade or is sharply pointed; 'offensive weapon' bears the same meaning as under the PACE 1984, s. 1(9); 'vehicle' includes a caravan as defined in the Caravan Sites and Control of Development Act 1960, s. 29(1) (s. 60(11)).

Exceptional powers to stop and search vehicles and persons are contained in the Prevention of Terrorism (Temporary Provisions) Act 1989, s. 13A. In respect of the Metropolitan Police or the City of London Police a commander and in other forces an assistant chief constable may, where it appears to him expedient to do so in order to prevent acts of terrorism, give an authorisation that powers to stop and search vehicles (including ships and aircraft) shall be exercisable at any place in his area or in a specified locality within his area for a specified period not exceeding 28 days. Such an authorisation may be extended for a further period of 28 days (s. 13A(8)).

The terrorism referred to must be connected with the affairs of Northern Ireland or be acts of terrorism of any other description provided that they are not solely connected with the affairs of the United Kingdom apart from Northern Ireland (s. 13A(2)). It would follow that the powers could not, for example, be exercised with respect to Welsh nationalism. The powers conferred on a constable are set out in s. 13A(3).

Prevention of Terrorism (Temporary Provisions) Act 1989, s. 13A

   (3)   This section confers on any constable in uniform power—
      (a)   to stop any vehicle;
      (b)   to search any vehicle, its driver or any passenger for articles of a kind which could be used for a purpose connected with the commission, preparation or instigation of acts of terrorism to which this section applies.

A constable may stop any person or vehicle and make any search he thinks fit whether or not he has any grounds for suspecting the presence of articles of a kind to which s. 13A refers (s. 13A(4)). A constable's power to require the removal of clothing under s. 13A is restricted to headgear, footwear, outer coat, jacket or gloves (s. 13(4A)). As with the preceding, more general powers to stop and seize under the CJPO 1994, power is given to a stopped person to obtain a written statement that the stop was under these powers (s. 13A(9)); this serves as a safeguard against unauthorised stops.

The powers of stop and search were further expanded by the Prevention of Terrorism (Additional Powers) Act 1996. Section 1 inserted s. 13B (powers to stop and search pedestrians) into the Prevention of Terrorism (Temporary Provisions) Act 1989, which confers a power on an officer of the like rank as s. 13A to authorise the employment of stop and search powers in his area or in any specified locality within his area. These are powers to stop and search any pedestrian or any thing carried by such a pedestrian for articles which could be used for a purpose connected with the commission, preparation or instigation of an act of terrorism. There is no requirement that there be reasonable grounds for suspicion. Consistent with other like provisions the power to require a person to remove clothing in public is limited to outer clothes.

Section 4 of the 1996 Act added s. 16C to the 1989 Act, which enables a police officer of the rank of superintendent or above to impose a police cordon on a specified area. It further added sch. 6A, which grants additional powers to require persons to leave the area including premises partly within or abutting onto it, and to remove vehicles. Furthermore, a superintendent is given powers to authorise the search of premises in the area and persons found therein where he has reasonable cause for believing that to do so will uncover material which is likely to be of substantial value to a terrorist investigation. It also enables him to impose parking restrictions.

As to the conduct of searches, see Code of Practice A, sect. 3. The annexe to Code of Practice A summarises powers to stop and search. The codes of practice and annexes are reproduced in full in **appendix 2**. Failure to record a search does not render the search illegal (*Basher* v *DPP* [1993] COD 372).

The police may, if necessary, use reasonable force in stopping and searching (PACE 1984, s. 117). Powers to stop and search may be used on the basis of 'reasonable cause', a formula which, given the diverse circumstances in which such powers are exercised, does not lend itself to easy definition. An officer who searches a person for drugs must himself have objective reasons for doing so: he may not rely on the unparticularised assertion of other officers (*French* v *DPP* [1997] COD 174). Reasonable cause involves reasonable grounds for suspecting that an offence has been committed or that evidence of the commission of an offence may exist, which in turn is usually the result of a person's actions together with all relevant circumstances. Among the former may be flight when approached by a police officer, or an attempt to conceal articles. Among the latter may be whether there have been burglaries or thefts recently in the area, or the fact that young drug users have been seen to congregate at a particular place. All these are somewhat nebulous criteria. Guidance issued to the police states that powers to stop and search must be used with restraint. A decision to stop and search must be based, not on the stereotyping of particular groups, but on substantial factual information, which would give rise to reasonable cause in the mind of a careful officer, and which can be considered and evaluated by a reasonable third person (Code of Practice A, paras 1.6 to 1.7A reproduced in **appendix 2**).

ARREST: GENERAL PRINCIPLES

Legal Characteristics of Arrest

Arrest is the beginning of imprisonment (per Lord Simonds in *Christie* v *Leachinsky* **D1.3** [1947] AC 573 at p. 600). Its purposes may be classified as: preventative (for example, in order to terminate a breach of the peace), punitive (for example, to take a person before a magistrate to answer for an offence or to be bound over) and protective (as where inebriated or mentally ill persons are arrested for their own protection). There is no necessary assumption that arrest will be followed by a charge; a constable who reasonably suspects a person of involvement in an offence may arrest that person with a view to interrogating him in the more formal atmosphere of a police station (*Holgate-Mohammed* v *Duke* [1984] AC 437). The power to arrest must however be exercised for a proper purpose. In *Chalkley* [1998] QB 848, the Court of Appeal affirmed that it is proper for police to arrest on a holding charge provided that they have reasonable grounds for suspecting the person arrested to have committed that offence. The fact that such an arrest is motivated by a desire to investigate another, more serious, offence does not render it invalid. An arrest will, however, be unlawful, even though made on the basis of reasonable suspicion, where the arrester knows at the time of arrest that there is no possibility of a charge being made; this is consistent with general principles of administrative law as expounded in *Holgate-Mohammed* v *Duke*. It is clear however that even though, for example, a complainant withdraws his complaint a constable may still arrest a suspect where he hopes by so doing to obtain a confession (*Plange* v *Chief Constable of South Humberside Police* (1992) *The Times*, 23 March 1992).

Arrest must be justified by some rule of positive law. A constable who cannot justify his actions by reference to lawful authority is said not to act in the execution of his duty. In determining whether conduct is an unlawful interference with a person's liberty or property the court must consider whether such conduct falls within the general scope of any duty imposed by statute or recognised at common law, and whether such conduct, albeit within the general scope of such a duty, involved an unjustifiable use of powers associated with the duty (*Waterfield* [1964] 1 QB 164). *Waterfield* involved detention of a car to provide evidence of dangerous driving which was beyond the powers of the police: compare detention by a constable of a vehicle which he believes to be stolen (*Sanders* v *DPP* [1988] Crim LR 605). In *Rice* v *Connolly* [1966] 2 QB 414, it was held that police may not restrain a person from going about his business unless they act under powers of stop and search or arrest. On the other hand, simply to take a man's arm, not intending to detain or arrest him, but simply to draw his attention to what is being said to him is neither an arrest nor an actionable trespass to the person, unless it goes beyond what is acceptable by the ordinary standards of everyday life (*Mepstead* v *DPP* (1996) 160 JP 475).

In *Murray* v *Ministry of Defence* [1988] 1 WLR 692, the House of Lords stated categorically that any restraint within defined bounds which is a restraint in fact amounts to an imprisonment. Arrest, it has been said, is an ordinary English word, and whether or not a person has been arrested depends not on the legality of the arrest but on whether he has been deprived of his liberty to go where he pleases (*Lewis* v *Chief Constable of the South Wales Constabulary* [1991] 1 All ER 206). These expansive statements must be read restrictively in context, that of a civil action for false imprisonment; in both cases the circumstances were that the plaintiff was restrained by persons purporting to act pursuant to lawful powers to arrest. Taken literally, they would require every compulsory stop on the street to be treated as an arrest. The true view, it is submitted, is that, while every arrest involves a deprivation of liberty, not every deprivation of liberty involves an arrest (*Brown* (1976) 64 Cr App R 231). A deprivation of liberty may amount to false imprisonment if it is unlawful, and it will be unlawful if it is not based on the proper exercise of a specific legal power. Any unlawful detention (whether or not an unlawful arrest) may amount to false imprisonment (see *Spicer* v *Holt* [1977] AC 987 at p. 1005 per Lord Edmund-Davies). A person who is arrested unlawfully by a police officer is thus falsely imprisoned.

Elements of Lawful Arrest

D1.4   An arrest occurs when a police officer states in terms that a person is arrested, when he uses force to restrain the individual concerned, or when by words or conduct he makes it clear that he will, if necessary, use force to prevent the individual from going where he wants to go (*Murray* v *Ministry of Defence* [1988] 1 WLR 692). If sufficiently clear words are not used, and they are particularly important where the arrestee is inebriated or his hearing is impaired, the person concerned will not be regarded as arrested (*Alderson* v *Booth* [1969] 2 QB 216). This may have implications in cases where a procedure must commence with arrest. It could also affect a claim for false imprisonment. In every case, however, it is essential that it be made clear to the person arrested that he has been arrested and is not free to leave, and (even if it is obvious from the circumstances) why he has been arrested. This must be done at the time of arrest or (if, for example, it cannot be done because the person arrested offers violent resistance) as soon as practicable afterwards (PACE 1984, s. 28).

There is no room for distinguishing between 'symbolic' and 'custodial' arrest. There is either a complete arrest or there is not, and an arrest is complete only when the person arrested is in fact prevented from leaving the custody of the officer. This may be achieved by physical restraint or by words alone provided that he submits to the restraint (*Whitfield* [1970] SCR 46; cf. *Sandon* v *Jervis* (1859) E B & E 942 per Bramwell B). A person is arrested where he is detained by automatic operation of a door which prevents him from leaving a room or a vehicle. The arrest is not, however, lawful until he is informed of the facts and grounds of arrest (*Dawes* v *DPP* [1994] Crim LR 604).

Reasonable Cause for Arrest

D1.5   Many, albeit not all, powers of arrest, are premised upon the constable having reasonable cause to believe that the suspect has committed, is committing or is about to commit an offence. The term 'reasonable cause' relates to the existence of facts and not to the state of the law. An officer who reasonably but mistakenly, proceeds on a particular view of the law, and thus exercises his power of arrest, does not have reasonable suspicion (*Todd* v *DPP* [1996] Crim LR 344).

Reasonable cause imports an objective standard. It must be determined according to what the constable knew and perceived at the time; reasonableness is to be evaluated without reference to hindsight (*Redmond-Bate* v *DPP* (1999) *The Times*, 28 July 1999). It is a lower standard than information sufficient to prove a prima facie case. Prima facie proof must rest on admissible evidence. Reasonable suspicion may take into account matters which are not admissible in evidence or matters which, while admissible, could not form part of a prima facie case (*Hussien* v *Chong Fook Kam* [1970] AC 942). The circumstances should be such that a reasonable man, acting without passion or prejudice, would fairly have suspected the person of committing the offence (*Allen* v *Wright* (1838) 8 C & P 522 per Tindal CJ). A constable may rely on hearsay provided that it is reasonable and that the constable believes in it (*McArdle* v *Egan* (1933) 150 LT 412; *Glinski* v *McIver* [1962] AC 726 at p. 758 per Lord Denning). Thus a constable may arrest a person as a result of radio information or even an anonymous telephone call, provided that the person arrested corresponds to the description in the message (*King* v *Gardner* (1979) 71 Cr App R 13; *DPP* v *Wilson* [1991] RTR 284); he may act on the word of an informer, but such a source should be treated with considerable reserve (*James* v *Chief Constable of South Wales* [1991] 6 CL 80). The mere fact that an arresting officer has been instructed by his superior to effect an arrest cannot amount to reasonable grounds for suspecting that the arrested person committed the offence (*O'Hara* v *Chief Constable of the Royal Ulster Constabulary* [1997] AC 286).

The constable's reasonable suspicion must relate to the offence for which he arrests the suspect. A constable who suspects a person of committing an offence to which only a limited power of arrest applies cannot later defend himself on the footing that the facts might have fallen into a more serious offence category; he must reasonably suspect the person at the time of arrest of involvement in an offence to which an appropriate power of arrest applies (*Chapman* v *DPP* (1988) 89 Cr App R 190).

Despite statements by Scott LJ in *Dumbell* v *Roberts* [1944] 1 All ER 326 (at p. 329) that officers should approach the arrest function in an objective spirit and should, before arresting, make all such inquiries as are immediately practicable, courts have consistently held that a constable who has formed reasonable grounds to suspect that an offence has been committed is not obliged to discount all possible defences or seek complete proof before carrying out an arrest (*Ward* v *Chief Constable of Avon and Somerset Constabulary* (1986) *The Times*, 26 June 1986; *McCarrick* v *Oxford* [1983] RTR 117). Failure to follow an obvious course of inquiry or verification in exceptional circumstances may, however, be grounds for attacking the exercise of the power to arrest as a wrongful exercise of discretion (*Castorina* v *Chief Constable of Surrey* (1988) 138 NLJ 180).

Communication of Reasons for Arrest

Every person arresting another must inform the person arrested of the reason for the **D1.6** arrest, either at the time or as soon as practicable thereafter. In the case of a constable, this applies even though the reason for the arrest is obvious (PACE 1984, s. 28). Unless this information is given, the arrest is not lawful (*Edwards* v *DPP* (1993) 97 Cr App R 301). The duty to give information 'at the time of the arrest' is not a duty which must be fulfilled at the precise moment of arrest but may be fulfilled during a reasonable period before and after that moment (*Nicholas* v *Parsonage* [1987] RTR 199). Where no reasons are given at the time of arrest because it is impracticable to inform the suspect in terms of the statute, acts done at the time of arrest do not become retrospectively invalid because of a later failure to inform him (*DPP* v *Hawkins* [1988] 1 WLR 1166; *Lewis* v *Chief Constable of the South Wales Constabulary* [1991] 1 All ER 206).

The grounds for arrest may be given in colloquial language which the officer thinks the person being arrested is likely to understand, for example, 'You're nicked' (*Christie* v *Leachinsky* [1947] AC 573). They must sufficiently indicate the basis for the arrest (*Telfer* [1976] Crim LR 562). The words used will suffice even though they are apt to describe more than one offence, provided that they aptly describe the offence for which the arrest is made (*Abbassy* v *Metropolitan Police Commissioner* [1990] 1 WLR 385). An arresting officer may not, however, properly give reasons on which he does not rely; that is, he may not lead a person to think that he is arresting him for one offence when in truth he wishes to arrest him for another (*Christie* v *Leachinsky*; *Abbassy* v *Metropolitan Police Commissioner* [1990] 1 WLR 385; *Waters* v *Bigmore* [1981] RTR 356). An arrest will be invalid where the reasons given point to an offence for which no power of arrest is given (or for which there is only a qualified power of arrest) and it is clear that no other reasons were present to the mind of the constable (*Edwards* v *DPP*).

Use of Force in Making Arrests

D1.7   Apart from the general provision in the PACE 1984, s. 117, specifying that all police powers not exercisable only with the consent of a person must be exercised with reasonable force, the Criminal Law Act 1967, s. 3, which applies to all arrests and to action in the prevention of crime, specifies that only such force as is reasonable in the circumstances may be used. The court, in determining what force is reasonable, will take into account all the circumstances including the nature and degree of the force used, the gravity of the offence for which arrest is to be made, the harm that would flow from the use of force against the suspect, and the possibility of effecting the arrest or preventing the harm by other means. The use of excessive force will not, however, render the arrest unlawful (*Simpson* v *Chief Constable of South Yorkshire Police* (1991) *The Times*, 7 March 1991).

Force cannot be used where the suspect does not resist arrest or attempt to escape (*Truscott* v *Carpenter* (1697) 1 Ld Raym 229). If he does, force may then be used but it must be proportionate to the gravity of the offence or the harm to be averted. Only that force may be used which is necessary to secure and subdue the fugitive (*Allen* v *Metropolitan Police Commissioner* [1980] Crim LR 441; *O'Connor* v *Hewitson* [1979] Crim LR 46; *Marshall* v *Osmond* QB 857 [1982] at p. 862 per Milmo J, point not taken on appeal). Similar principles apply to the use of force in maintaining the peace (*Lynch* v *Fitzgerald* [1938] IR 382). In respect of the use of lethal force, the court must take account of the time available to the actor (in all probability a constable or, in Northern Ireland, a soldier) for reflection and whether he could be of opinion that the risk of harm to others from not arresting or taking preventive action outweighs the harm, including the possibility of death, that might be caused to the person concerned (*A-G for Northern Ireland's Reference (No. 1 of 1975)* [1977] AC 105 per Lord Diplock at p. 137). It follows that gross or lethal force cannot be used, whatever the other circumstances, simply because this is the only way to prevent a suspect from escaping.

Handcuffs should be used only where they are reasonably necessary to prevent an escape, or to prevent a violent breach of the peace by a prisoner (*Lockley* (1864) 4 F & F 155). The same rule applies to the handcuffing of prisoners in court (*Cambridge Justices, ex parte Peacock* (1992) 156 JP 895). It would seem that where handcuffs are unjustifiably resorted to, their use will constitute a trespass even though the arrest itself be lawful (*Taylor* (1895) 59 JP 393; and see *Hamilton* v *Massie* (1889) 18 OR 585; *Gordon* v *Denison* (1895) 22 OAR 315 and the discussion of force generally in *Allen* v *Metropolitan Police Commissioner* [1980] Crim LR 441). Guidelines on the use of handcuffs were issued in 1999 by the Association of Chief Police Officers and are obtainable from the relevant chief officer of police.

Resisting Arrest

D1.8   A person has an unqualified right at common law to resist an unlawful arrest (*Christie* v *Leachinsky* [1947] AC 573). But while the right to resist arrest is unqualified, the degree of force which may be used in so doing is qualified. A person wrongly arrested may not use grossly excessive force in resisting arrest. Certainly, he may not use lethal force to do so (*Palmer* v *The Queen* [1971] AC 814 at p. 825). Where no death ensues a person who uses excessive force in resisting arrest may well be guilty of common assault or some other offence of assault or wounding (*Wilson* [1955] 1 WLR 493; *Long* (1836) 7 C & P 314). He will not, however, be guilty of assaulting a constable in the execution of his duty (*Kenlin* v *Gardiner* [1967] 2 QB 510). It is submitted that a person who appreciates both that the person seeking to arrest him is a constable and that he has at most to fear a short period of unlawful imprisonment may not use a high degree of force, even where the use of such force is the only way to maintain his liberty; he ought to submit to the arrest, vindicating his rights by later civil action if appropriate.

Search on Arrest

A constable who arrests a person elsewhere than at a police station may search that **D1.9** person if he has reason to believe that he may present a danger to himself or others, and he may seize and retain any object which that person may use to injure himself or another (PACE 1984, s. 32(3)). He may also search the person for, and seize and retain, anything which that person might use to escape from lawful custody or which might be evidence in relation to an offence, provided that he has reasonable cause to believe that the arrested person has such material on his person (s. 32(2) and (5)). The power in respect of evidence is based on objective considerations. Search is only authorised to the extent that is reasonably required for the purpose of discovering any such thing or evidence (s. 32(3)). Where the search takes place in public, the constable may only require the arrested person to remove an outer coat, jacket or gloves, but he is authorised to search a person's mouth (s. 32(4)). Hats, including turbans, are exempt from this requirement.

A constable may enter and search any premises where the person was at the time of or immediately before the arrest (s. 32(2)(b)). The power extends to the search of vehicles and, in the case of ticket touting (see **B11.133**), extends to the search of any vehicle which the constable has reasonable grounds for believing was being used for any purpose connected with the offence. However, where the premises consist of two or more dwellings, the power is confined to a dwelling where the arrest took place, or where the person arrested was immediately before arrest, and to common areas (s. 32(7)). This power is to search for material of evidentiary value in relation to the offence for which the person was arrested, and the constable must have reasonable grounds for believing that there is material of evidentiary value on the premises which relates to it. Search is only permitted to the extent necessary for discovering any injurious thing or item of evidentiary value (s. 32(3), (6) and (10)). Whether police entered for that purpose is a question of fact (*Beckford* (1991) 94 Cr App R 43). For an example of a search which would clearly be unlawful today, see *Jeffrey* v *Black* [1978] QB 490.

Retention of Seized Property

Police who seize property lawfully may keep it in their possession against the will of the **D1.10** person from whom it was seized until trial, provided that they consider in good faith that it will be required as evidence (*Uxbridge Justices, ex parte Metropolitan Police Commissioner* [1981] QB 829). Police also have power to retain goods allegedly stolen with a view to restoring them to their owner (*Malone* v *Metropolitan Police Commissioner* [1980] QB 49).

More contentious is the action of the courts in allowing the police to freeze bank accounts and to trace property into bank accounts. There appears to be a conflict implicit in the cases. In *Malone* v *Metropolitan Police Commissioner*, a second ground advanced by the police for retaining the money was that it might be needed to satisfy a compensation order or an order for costs against the accused. This argument was rejected. The goods were not stolen, and so could not form the subject of a restitution order. All that the statutory provision relating to compensation orders does is to provide for such orders without specifying the source of funds. Roskill LJ concluded that the section did not intend to permit any police authority to constitute itself a stakeholder, or perhaps a trustee, for a class of possible future beneficiaries who would or might thereby become almost potentially secured creditors at the expense of others less fortunate. Nor did any other provision produce that result.

The premise in *Malone* v *Metropolitan Police Commissioner*, apart from cases where the goods are stolen, is that police retention of seized property can be justified on evidentiary grounds. But the right of the police to seize goods, at least on arrest and where no warrant has been issued, is that the goods are arguably stolen and as such have evidentiary value. The right to detain is consequent upon lawful seizure. It is submitted, with respect, that the evidentiary ground also governs the warrant cases. Where the dispute concerns entitlement to possession, the remedy has always, restitution orders apart, been by way of a civil action.

Recent cases, however, permit the police to go farther on the theory that they may detain goods with a view to returning them ultimately to their rightful owner. It is this ground which is dominant because, in the case of moneys paid by the thief into a bank account, it could hardly be said that freezing the account was required for evidentiary purposes. On the other hand, if the moneys in the account represent stolen goods, they may be the subject of a restitution order under the Theft Act 1968, s. 28(1)(b).

In *West Mercia Constabulary* v *Wagener* [1982] 1 WLR 127, the court granted an application to restrain the accused from operating certain bank accounts, but only as to amounts arguably obtained by crime. While the police cannot obtain a warrant to seize moneys in a bank account, there is, the court held, no lacuna in police powers because the court under the civil rules can make an order to preserve the proceeds of allegedly criminal activities in the bank account. The nature of the chief constable's cause of action was hardly discussed. In *Chief Constable of Kent* v *V* [1983] QB 34, an application for an interlocutory injunction to restrain the accused from operating two named bank accounts in which funds obtained by crime had allegedly been deposited, Lord Denning MR held that, as a result of the Supreme Court Act 1981, s. 37, an injunction need no longer be ancillary to an action claiming legal or equitable relief; application for an injunction may be brought independently. Furthermore the chief constable has *locus standi*; his interest is on behalf of the public to detain goods pending trial, and to restore them to their rightful owner. Otherwise, the accused could evade a restitution order by disposing of the moneys before trial. Donaldson LJ was also prepared to make such an order provided first that there was a subsisting matter between the police and the suspect; and provided that the moneys in the account could be shown to have been obtained by crime, so that the situation was parallel to one in which police could seize under warrant articles actually stolen. In *Chief Constable of Hampshire* v *A Ltd* [1985] QB 132, a police claim to detain moneys allegedly obtained by fraudulent trading failed for two reasons, first because the relevant fraud was not easily identifiable and secondly and precisely because of the tracing problem. But, in the light of *Malone* v *Metropolitan Police Commissioner*, the police could not claim a right to freeze intangible property not in their possession for the purpose of satisfying a possible compensation or forfeiture order.

In *Chief Constable of Kent* v *V*, Slade J dissented. In his lordship's opinion, neither by statute nor by common law is the chief constable invested with any special rights or *locus standi* to seek relief from the courts by way of injunction as protector of the public interest. He therefore has no legal or equitable right which can be enforced by injunction. He cannot assert the victim's right of action, and an injunction can only be brought to vindicate an existing legal right. This in turn seems to accept the premise in *Malone* v *Metropolitan Police Commissioner* that the right of the police to seize is to preserve for use matter having evidentiary value.

It is submitted, with respect, that the dissenting judgment of Slade J is better founded in precedent than that of the majority. The right to retain property physically seized is ancillary; the police are obliged to return it to the owner if it is stolen, or to the accused if it is not. But that obligation was not intended to found a right of action to trace and freeze intangibles. This indeed is the basis of Orr LJ's judgment in *Chief Constable of Hampshire* v *A Ltd*. On the other hand, the courts have steadily extended the ancillary powers of the police, and elaborated their duties as well. It is not inconceivable that a duty in the police to secure and restore stolen property should be held to found a novel right of action. Nor should one overlook that today the historic strict separation between criminal and civil matters is being eroded somewhat. On the other hand, to go beyond cases which may justify restitution into the wider grounds unsuccessfully urged by the police in *Malone* v *Metropolitan Police Commissioner* would in some cases be to risk the distortion of the system of priorities in insolvency and prejudice the claims of creditors of the accused other than the victim.

Disposition after Arrest

A person making an arrest is obliged to ensure that the person arrested is properly taken **D1.11** into custody. Where a person is arrested at any place other than a police station, or is taken into custody by a constable following an arrest made by a civilian, the constable is obliged to take him to a designated police station as soon as is practicable thereafter (PACE 1984, s. 30(1) and (2)). In exceptional circumstances the person may be taken to a non-designated station (s. 30(5) and (6)). Consistently with the position at common law, a constable who comes to believe that there are no grounds for further detaining a person whom he has arrested may release him before reaching a police station (s. 30(7)) but the facts must be recorded (s. 30(8) and (9)).

In determining whether a constable or private person has brought the arrested person to a police station as soon as practicable, the court looks to all the circumstances of the case. In particular, it may sometimes be appropriate to detain the person arrested for a short time at the scene if to do so is reasonable in the interests of deciding whether or not to proceed further. It is, however, wrong to arrest a person without reasonable cause in the hope that making an arrest will bolster the case against him (*John Lewis & Co. Ltd* v *Tims* [1952] AC 676). It may be, however, that constables have a wider power than civilians in the sense that the former may, where reasonable cause is present, be justified in arresting a suspect with a view to facilitating inquiries (*Holgate-Mohammed* v *Duke* [1984] AC 437).

A constable (but, it would seem, not a civilian) may delay taking an arrested person to a police station if the presence of the arrested person is required elsewhere in order to carry out such investigations as it is reasonable to carry out immediately (PACE 1984, s. 30(10) and (11)). Delay can be justified, however, only where the matter requires immediate investigation (*Kerawalla* [1991] Crim LR 451). This could include taking the suspect from one place to another to check his alibi (*Dallison* v *Caffery* [1965] 1 QB 348) or to his lodgings with a view to searching them (PACE 1984, s. 18). Questioning in such circumstances should not go beyond what is necessary for the search and investigation; full interrogation should await arrival at a police station (*Khan* [1993] Crim LR 54).

ARREST WITHOUT WARRANT

Powers of Arrest without Warrant

Powers of arrest without warrant are conferred under the PACE 1984, sundry other **D1.12** statutes the operation of which has been continued in effect by the 1984 Act, common law powers of arrest for breach of the peace, powers under the Public Order Act 1986 and other powers contained in legislation passed after 1984. Section 26(1) of the PACE 1984 rendered ineffective statutory powers enabling a constable to arrest without warrant (unless the powers were specially preserved). It has now been held, however, that s. 26 does not affect general powers of arrest contained in the Vagrancy Act 1824, s. 6 (*Gapper* v *Chief Constable of Avon and Somerset Constabulary* [1999] 2 WLR 928).

The PACE 1984 creates three categories of powers of arrest together with a power to bring in a person for fingerprinting (PACE 1984, ss. 24, 25, 26 and 27). The first such category is that of the arrestable offence. The second, which confers general powers of arrest, applies to lesser offences. The third preserves certain pre-existing statutory powers of arrest.

Arrestable Offences

D1.13 The category of 'arrestable offences' comprises (a) offences bearing a fixed penalty, in particular, murder, (b) offences for which a previously unconvicted offender aged 21 years or over could be sentenced to imprisonment for five years or more, and (c) offences specially listed (PACE 1984, s. 24). In group (b) are to be found the most commonly committed offences with the exception of vehicle offences. Examples are theft, obtaining by deception, handling, criminal damage, forgery, counterfeiting, commercial frauds of various descriptions, and all the serious offences against the person. In the third group are found certain customs offences, certain offences against the Official Secrets Acts 1911 to 1989, which would not otherwise be arrestable because the maximum penalty is too low, certain sexual offences, and taking a motor vehice without authority. This list is frequently added to. For example, the CJPO 1994 adds the following offences to the list of arrestable offences: publication of obscene matter contrary to the Obscene Publications Act 1959; offences under the Protection of Children Act 1978, s. 1 (indecent photographs and pseudo-photographs of children); publishing material intended or likely to stir up racial hatred (contrary to the Public Order Act 1986, s. 19); sale of football tickets by touts (contrary to the CJPO 1994, s. 166); and touting for car hire services (contrary to s. 167 of the same Act).

Police and Criminal Evidence Act 1984, s. 24

(4)   Any person may arrest without a warrant—

(a)   anyone who is in the act of committing an arrestable offence;

(b)   anyone whom he has reasonable grounds for suspecting to be committing such an offence.

(5)   Where an arrestable offence has been committed, any person may arrest without a warrant—

(a)   anyone who is guilty of the offence;

(b)   anyone whom he has reasonable grounds for suspecting to be guilty of it.

(6)   Where a constable has reasonable grounds for suspecting that an arrestable offence has been committed, he may arrest without a warrant anyone whom he has reasonable grounds for suspecting to be guilty of the offence.

(7)   A constable may arrest without a warrant—

(a)   anyone who is about to commit an arrestable offence;

(b)   anyone whom he has reasonable grounds for suspecting to be about to commit an arrestable offence.

These powers of arrest also apply to conspiracy and attempts to commit and to inciting, aiding and abetting, counselling or procuring the commission of an arrestable offence. Moreover, the PACE 1984, s. 17, confers a power of entry on a constable to enter premises to arrest any person for an arrestable offence.

Certain powers of arrest in respect of such offences may be exercised by any person; others only by constables. Any person may arrest without warrant anyone who is, or whom he has reasonable grounds to believe to be in the act of committing, an arrestable offence (PACE 1984, s. 24(4)(a) and (b)). Equally, where an arrestable offence has been committed, any person may arrest anyone who is guilty of the offence, and anyone whom he has reasonable grounds for suspecting to be guilty of it (s. 24(5)). Both of these headings enable and are meant to enable an arrester to take advantage of what has been described as 'second sight', that is, arrest is justified if the accused has committed a crime in fact, even though the arrester may have had no reasonable grounds for suspecting him of having done so.

Only a constable may arrest without warrant a person whom he reasonably suspects to be guilty of having committed an arrestable offence, regardless of whether or not such an offence has in fact been committed (*Self* [1992] 1 WLR 657). Only a constable may arrest a person who is, or whom he reasonably expects to be, about to commit an arrestable offence (s. 24(6) and (7)). These powers of arrest extend also to conspiracies to commit the offences in question, and to attempts to commit them, and incitement of and complicity in them other than an offence of taking a motor vehicle without consent contrary to the Theft Act, 1968, s. 12(1).

Other Powers of Arrest under, or preserved by, the Police and Criminal Evidence Act 1984

A narrower power of arrest applies to offences which fall outside the category of **D1.14** arrestable offences. Where a constable has reasonable grounds for suspecting that any such offence has been committed or attempted, he may arrest any person whom he suspects of doing so provided that any one of a list of general arrest conditions is made out (PACE 1984, s. 25). Even in such a case he is not obliged to arrest: his power is a discretionary one; but he may not arrest a person unless at least one of the conditions is made out. The powers of arrest conferred by s. 25 do not extend to persons who are, or who are suspected of being, about to commit an offence nor to those whose involvement takes the form of conspiracy to commit the offence or inciting, aiding, abetting or procuring another to do so.

These general arrest conditions indicate circumstances in which service of a summons is impracticable or inappropriate. They include inability to verify name and address, possible injury to person or property, possible offences against public decency, obstruction of the highway, and for protective purposes in respect of a child or other vulnerable person. The use of summons rather than arrest as a means of bringing an offender before the courts is to be preferred. This preference is, however, weak simply because the general arrest conditions are numerous and wide. Furthermore, there are situations where recourse to arrest simplifies later proceedings for the prosecution, for example, where questions of identification are in issue (*Allen* v *Ireland* [1984] 1 WLR 903). The arrest conditions do not appear to permit an arrest where, for example, the offence, perhaps one of obstructing a statutory undertaker, seems likely to be continued or repeated see, e.g., the legislation considered in *Chief Constable of Devon and Cornwall, ex parte Central Electricity Generating Board* [1982] QB 458). This situation is likeliest to arise where a breach of the peace is in issue. The PACE 1984, s. 26, does save common-law powers of arrest in that context (*DPP* v *Orum* [1989] 1 WLR 88).

The first two general arrest conditions (relating to identity) permit arrest either where the name of the person is unknown to and cannot readily be ascertained by the constable, or where he has reasonable grounds for doubting whether the name furnished by the suspect is his real name (PACE 1984, s. 25(3)(a) and (b)). A constable cannot be said reasonably to doubt that a suspected person has given his correct name and address simply because in the past other persons suspected of the like offence have not given correct particulars (*G* v *DPP* [1989] Crim LR 150). A constable, in asking for an address, need not inform a suspect why he wants it – for example, to facilitate service of a summons (*Nicholas* v *Parsonage* [1987] RTR 199). He must, however, first indicate to the suspect the nature of the offence of which he is suspected. Failure to give a name and address is not, of itself, a ground for arrest.

The third set of arrest conditions permit arrest where the person has failed to furnish a satisfactory address for service or the constable has reasonable grounds for doubting whether an address so furnished is a satisfactory address for service (PACE 1984, s. 25(3)(c)(i) and (ii)). An address is satisfactory for this purpose if it appears to the constable either that the person will be there for a sufficiently long time for it to be possible to serve him with a summons, or that some other person specified by the offender will accept service of a summons there (s. 25(4)(a) and (b)). The address need not, therefore, be a permanent or long-term residence, nor need the person identified as being willing to accept service be related to the offender or the owner or a lessor of the premises. Something more than a mere transient stopping place is doubtless required.

The fourth set of arrest conditions refers to personal injury or damage to property. A constable may arrest an offender where he has reasonable grounds for believing that this step is necessary to prevent him from causing physical injury to another person or to himself, or suffering physical injury (s. 25(3)(d)(i) and (ii)). Such a situation can arise where the constable believes that a suspected person is likely to commit suicide or is so intoxicated that he is likely to suffer injury. An offender may also be arrested where it is reasonably thought necessary to do so to prevent him from causing loss or damage to property (s. 25(3)(d)(iii)). This in some circumstances can include his own property. An example could well be where a violent husband, having assaulted his wife, is thought likely to damage the matrimonial home or objects in it.

A constable may arrest a person where he reasonably thinks it to be necessary to prevent the person from committing an offence against public decency (s. 25(3)(d)(iv)). The arrest condition is not satisfied under this head unless members of the public going about their business cannot reasonably be expected to avoid the person to be arrested (s. 25(5)). The test of whether members of the public can avoid the offender is, it is submitted, one of reasonableness, not impossibility.

A person may be arrested where a constable thinks it necessary to prevent the person from causing an obstruction to the highway (s. 25(3)(d)(v)); it is irrelevant that the police have previously permitted an act of obstruction to take place there (*Arrowsmith* v *Jenkins* [1963] 2 QB 561).

By virtue of the final general arrest condition, a constable may arrest an offender where he believes that it is necessary to protect a child or other vulnerable person (perhaps a mentally ill person) from him (s. 25(3)(e)). Vulnerability is not defined. The arrest condition is not premised upon there being any family or other continuing relationship with the arrested person, though this is to be anticipated in most cases.

A constable who relies upon an arrest condition to justify an arrest bears the burden of proving that his action was lawful. Any other constable, coming to his assistance, is only protected to the extent that the original arrest was lawful or that new facts have intervened which give him an autonomous power of arrest (*Riley* v *DPP* (1989) 91 Cr App R 14).

Section 25 does not prejudice any power of arrest conferred apart from it. This preserves common-law powers of arrest for breach of the peace. Certain statutory powers are saved by the PACE 1984, sch. 2. Presumably, the word 'prejudice' in s. 25 is apt both to preserve such powers and to ensure that they are not made subject to the necessity conditions. The power of arrest conferred in cases of drunkenness under the CJA 1967, s. 91, survives (*DPP* v *Kitching* (1989) 154 JP 293).

A person who has been convicted of a recordable offence, and who has not at any time been in police detention for the offence and who has not had his fingerprints taken either in the course of police investigation of the offence or thereafter, may be required by a constable to attend at a police station to have his fingerprints taken. Such a requirement may be made within one month of conviction (PACE 1984, s. 27(1)). A person who fails to attend in accordance with competent directions may be arrested without warrant (s. 27(2) and (3)).

Schedule 2 to the PACE 1984 preserves various diverse powers of arrest.

Police and Criminal Evidence Act 1984, sch. 2

PRESERVED POWERS OF ARREST

1892 c. 43	Section 17(2) of the Military Lands Act 1892.
1911 c. 27	Section 12(1) of the Protection of Animals Act 1911.
1920 c. 55	Section 2 of the Emergency Powers Act 1920.
1936 c. 6	Section 7(3) of the Public Order Act 1936.
1952 c. 52	Section 49 of the Prison Act 1952.
1952 c. 67	Section 13 of the Visiting Forces Act 1952.
1955 c. 18	Sections 186 and 190B of the Army Act 1955.
1955 c. 19	Sections 186 and 190B of the Air Force Act 1955.
1957 c. 53	Sections 104 and 105 of the Naval Discipline Act 1957.
1959 c. 37	Section 1(3) of the Street Offences Act 1959.
1969 c. 54	Section 32 of the Children and Young Persons Act 1969.
1971 c. 77	Section 24(2) of the Immigration Act 1971 and paragraphs 17, 24 and 33 of schedule 2 and paragraph 7 of schedule 3 to that Act.
1976 c. 63	Section 7 of the Bail Act 1976.
1977 c. 45	Sections 6(6), 7(11), 8(4), 9(7) and 10(5) of the Criminal Law Act 1977.
1980 c. 9	Schedule 5 to the Reserve Forces Act 1980.
1981 c. 22	Sections 60(5) and 61(1) of the Animal Health Act 1981.
1983 c. 2	Rule 36 in schedule 1 to the Representation of the People Act 1983.
1983 c. 20	Sections 18, 35(10), 36(8), 38(7), 136(1) and 138 of the Mental Health Act 1983.
1984 c. 47	Section 5(5) of the Repatriation of Prisoners Act 1984.

A constable has powers to arrest a bailed person whom he has reasonable grounds to believe is not likely to surrender to custody or who has broken the conditions of his bail (Bail Act 1976, s. 7(3)). A similar power has now been conferred on an officer of HM Customs and Excise to arrest a suspect who has been released on bail in respect of possession of controlled drugs or drug trafficking, and who it is believed is not likely to surrender to custody (CJA 1988, s. 151).

Powers of Arrest under Public Order Act 1986

The Public Order Act 1986 contains specific powers of arrest in connection with the offences of fear or provocation of violence (s. 4(3)), and harassment, alarm or distress (s. 5(4)). In the former case a constable may arrest anyone whom he reasonably suspects of committing the offence. In the latter the constable must first warn the offender to stop his offensive conduct and may then arrest if the offender engages in further offensive conduct immediately or shortly after the warning. The offensive conduct must be such as the constable reasonably believes to constitute an offence under the section and the conduct and further conduct need not be of the same nature. **D1.15**

These powers will cover almost all the cases which are arrestable under the common-law power pertaining to breach of the peace, but the latter is wider in that it permits the arrest of a person engaged in an incident occurring inside a dwelling between persons who are in adjoining dwellings (*McConnell* v *Chief Constable of Greater Manchester Police* [1990] 1 WLR 364 at p. 381G per Glidewell LJ).

A constable in uniform may arrest without warrant any person whom he reasonably suspects of committing an offence under the Public Order Act 1986, s. 12(4), (5) or (6). These provisions essentially refer to failing to comply with conditions imposed in respect of public processions or inciting others to fail to do so. Powers of arrest similarly apply to organising, taking part in, or inciting others to take part in a prohibited procession (s. 13(10), and to failure to comply etc. with conditions imposed in respect of public assemblies (s. 14(7)). Again, the constable must be in uniform.

A constable, who need not be in uniform, may arrest without warrant any person whom he reasonably suspects of using threatening etc. words with intent to stir up racial hatred (s. 18(3)). A constable who reasonably suspects that a person has entered premises in defiance of an exclusion order (made in connection with football) may arrest that person without warrant (s. 32(3)). A constable may both search and arrest a person whom he has reasonable grounds to suspect is committing or has committed an offence under the Sporting Events (Control of Alcohol etc.) Act 1985 (by s. 7(2) of that Act).

Powers of Arrest under Criminal Justice and Public Order Act 1994

D1.16   The CJPO 1994, part V, created new powers of arrest. Section 61 gives powers to remove trespassers from land (for circumstances, see **B13.46 *et seq*.**). A constable in uniform who reasonably suspects that a person is committing an offence under the section (e.g., by failing to leave land or by re-entering it within three months) may arrest him without warrant (s. 61(5)). It would seem that the general arrest conditions under s. 25 of the PACE 1984 cannot operate so as to limit this power of arrest where the offence is a continuing one. To hold otherwise would be to render the power largely nugatory.

Furthermore, under the CJPO 1994, s. 62, a constable may seize and remove any vehicle which a person failed to remove after being required to do so. A similar power of seizure and removal applies to a vehicle with which a person has wrongfully sought to re-enter land.

Under s. 63(8), a similar power of arrest in favour of a constable in uniform applies in the case of raves (see **B13.51 *et seq*.**). It is submitted that this power of arrest is also unaffected by the limiting provisions of s. 25 of the PACE 1984. Furthermore, by virtue of the CJPO 1994, s. 64(1) and (3), a superintendent who reasonably believes that circumstances exist which would justify giving a direction that those present leave the land may authorise any constable (whether or not in uniform) to enter land and to seize and remove any vehicle or sound equipment which that person failed to remove or with which he entered the land within seven days of being directed to leave it.

A constable in uniform may stop a person who he believes to be proceeding to a rave and direct him not to do so. A person who refuses to comply commits an offence and a constable in uniform who reasonably suspects that such a person is committing that offence may arrest him without a warrant (s. 65(5)). These powers are, it is submitted, also unaffected by the necessity conditions under s. 25 of the PACE 1984.

The court has power to order the forfeiture of sound equipment seized in connection with a rave (s. 66). Vehicles may be retained and a charge levied against the person from whom the vehicle was seized in respect of its removal, retention, disposal and destruction (s. 67).

Similar powers of arrest in connection with a person committing an offence, and again not, it is submitted, limited by the necessity conditions of s. 25 of the PACE 1984 since the overriding purpose of the power of arrest is to terminate a continuing offence, are conferred in respect of continuing trespass (s. 69(4)), trespassory assemblies (Public Order Act 1986, s. 14B(4)) and proceeding to a trespassory assembly (Public Order Act 1986, s. 14C(4)). For the offences themselves, see **B13.45 and B11.120**.

Cross-border Powers of Arrest

D1.17   The CJPO 1994, part X (ss. 136 to 140), makes extensive provision for cross border powers of arrest. Briefly, the scheme enables a constable from one part of the United Kingdom who has reasonable grounds for suspecting that an offence has been committed or attempted in his jurisdiction to arrest a suspected person in another part of the United Kingdom (s. 137). Apart from the provisions of the Act itself, a certain amount of cross-referencing to Scottish law in particular will be necessary should questions arise under the scheme and in particular in relation to habeas corpus.

In respect of an arrest made by a constable of a police force in England and Wales the offence must either be an arrestable offence or it must be impracticable to serve a summons on the same necessity conditions as would justify arrest in England and Wales for a non-arrestable offence (ss. 137(4) and 138(3)). The like conditions apply to an arrest by an officer from Northern Ireland in England and Wales or Scotland (s. 137(3) and (6)). An officer of a police force in Scotland may arrest outside Scotland provided that it would have been lawful to arrest the person had he been found in Scotland (s. 137(2) and (5)). It is apparent that the scheme allows an officer to arrest where the conditions are made out which would enable him to arrest without warrant in his own jurisdiction.

Where a person is arrested in England and Wales, the arresting officer must take the arrested person to such a police station in Scotland or Northern Ireland as is specified in the legislation (s. 137(7)(b)). If a constable from Scotland detains a person in England and Wales, he may either take him to a designated police station in Scotland or to the nearest designated convenient police station in England and Wales (s. 137(7)(c)).

A constable may use reasonable force in effecting an arrest in the other jurisdiction (s. 137(8)(a)). A constable from Scotland arresting or detaining a suspect in England and Wales has the same powers and duties and the arrested person the same rights as if the arrest had taken place in Scotland (s. 137(8)(b) and (c) and s. 138(2)). Scottish procedure is modified in certain respects to take account of the exigencies of this scheme.

Search powers are available under these cross-border schemes in respect of arrests under warrant or without warrant. A constable from England and Wales arresting under warrant in Scotland or Northern Ireland, or a constable from Scotland or Northern Ireland arresting under warrant in England and Wales, is given extensive powers under s. 139. The same powers apply to arrests without warrant by a constable from England and Wales making an arrest without warrant in Scotland or Northern Ireland or a constable from Northern Ireland making an arrest in England and Wales (s. 139(1)). Under these powers a constable may search the person if he has reasonable grounds for believing that the person may present a danger to himself or to others (s. 139(2)). The powers are virtually the same as those which apply under s. 32 of the PACE 1984 to a search of the person or premises on arrest (see **D1.9**).

The scheme further provides for reciprocal powers of arrest. Where a police constable in England and Wales would have powers to arrest in respect of arrestable offences or non-arrestable offences (where the necessity conditions are made out), a constable from Scotland or Northern Ireland who is in England and Wales has the same powers of arrest (s. 140(1)). Reciprocal powers apply in favour of a constable from England and Wales in Scotland or Northern Ireland (s. 140(3), (4) and (5)). The scheme is premised upon the arresting officer having the same powers and coming under the same obligations as he would were he a local constable operating under local law.

The powers of a constable in England and Wales are extended to include adjacent United Kingdom waters.

ARREST UNDER WARRANT

Warrants Issued by Magistrates' Courts

The most important of the statutes which authorise arrest under warrant is the MCA **D1.18** 1980. Section 1 of that Act empowers a justice to issue a warrant on the basis of a written information substantiated on oath. (Among other statutes bestowing such powers are the Army Act 1955, the Air Force Act 1955, the Naval Discipline Act 1957 and the Armed Forces Act 1980.) Such a warrant may or may not be endorsed for bail. If endorsed for bail, the warrant will specify the amounts in which any sureties are to be bound. If bail is to be granted with sureties, then the police must release the offender if the sureties approved by the officer enter into recognisances in accordance with the endorsement. The person bailed is then obliged to appear before a magistrates' court at the time and place named in the recognisance (MCA 1980, s. 117).

Power is given under the MCA 1980, s. 13, to issue a warrant for the arrest of a suspect who has failed to appear to answer a summons.

The power of a magistrates' court to issue a warrant for the arrest of any person who has attained the age of 17 years is limited by the MCA 1980, s. 1(4). The offence concerned must be indictable, or punishable with imprisonment, or the person's address must be not sufficiently established for a summons to be served on him. A warrant to arrest any person for non-appearance before a magistrates' court is not to issue unless the offence to which the warrant relates is also punishable with imprisonment or where the court, having convicted the defendant, proposes to impose a disqualification upon him.

The Children Act 1989, s. 46, provides that a constable who has reasonable cause to believe that a child would otherwise be likely to suffer significant harm may remove the child to suitable accommodation and keep him there. The power is not in essence criminal and we do no more than note its existence.

In connection with proceedings where a court is hearing an application for an order under part IV (care and supervision) or part V (protection of children) of the Children Act 1989, where a court has ordered a child to attend the proceedings but the child has not done so, the court may authorise a constable or other person to take charge of the child and bring him to the court, and to search premises where he believes that child may be found (Children Act 1989, s. 95).

A court may issue a summons or warrant to secure the attendance of a witness.

Warrants Issued by the Crown Court

D1.19   Section 80(2) of the Supreme Court Act 1981 provides that where an indictment has been signed but the person charged has not been committed for trial, the Crown Court may issue a summons requiring that person to appear before the Crown Court, or may issue a warrant for his arrest. A similar power applies where a person charged with or convicted of an offence has entered into a recognisance to appear at the Crown Court and fails to do so. A warrant for arrest may be endorsed for bail in which case the officer in charge of the police station to which the accused is taken has the same powers and duties as in the parallel case where the warrant is issued by magistrates (Supreme Court Act 1981, s. 81). Orders for arrest in criminal matters may also be issued by the Court of Appeal (Criminal Appeal Rules 1968, rr. 5 and 23). Warrants may also issue to ensure the attendance of a witness (MCA 1980, s. 97; Criminal Procedure (Attendance of Witnesses) Act 1965, s. 4).

Extradition Cases

D1.20   Warrants for arrest may be issued under the Extradition Act 1989. A warrant may be definitive or provisional (s. 8). A warrant issued under the Extradition Act 1989, s. 8(5), may be executed anywhere within the United Kingdom by the person to whom it is addressed or by any constable, without being backed.

Irish and Other Warrants

D1.21   A warrant issued in the Republic of Ireland may be endorsed for execution by a magistrate provided that the offence is not a military offence or a summary offence, or one relating to taxes or exchange control, and provided that the offender is not sought for an offence of a political character (Backing of Warrants (Republic of Ireland) Act 1965, ss. 1 and 4; the warrant is endorsed for execution in the area for which the magistrate acts). Such a warrant may be executed anywhere in England and Wales (MCA 1980, s. 125).

There is provision for the execution of warrants emanating from one part of the United Kingdom in another part of the United Kingdom. In brief, the scheme provides for the execution of such a warrant either by a constable of the police force of the country of issue or the country of execution. This regime applies to warrants issued in England and Wales, Scotland, or Northern Ireland (CJPO 1994, s. 136). A constable arresting a person under warrant pursuant to these provisions has the same powers of search as apply to a cross-border arrest without warrant (s. 139 and see further **D1.17**).

Warrants emanating from the Isle of Man and the Channel Islands may be enforced in England and Wales provided that they have been endorsed by a justice of the peace (Indictable Offences Act 1848, s. 13). A person may not lawfully be taken into custody on such a warrant unless it is properly endorsed and if so taken into custody must be discharged (*Metropolitan Police Commissioner, ex parte Melia* [1957] 1 WLR 1065).

Execution of Warrants

The principal provision dealing with the execution of warrants is the MCA 1980, s. 125. **D1.22** This provides, first, that a warrant of arrest issued by a justice of the peace remains in force until it is executed or withdrawn. Such a warrant may be executed anywhere in England by any person to whom it is directed or by any constable acting within his police area. The effect of this taken together with the Police Act 1996, s. 30, is to enable such a warrant to be executed by a constable anywhere in England and Wales. Furthermore, any constable may execute the warrant in his own police area even though it is addressed to a constable in another police area. Provision is made by the Police (Scotland) Act 1967, s. 18, to enable constables appointed for any one of the border regions of Scotland to execute a lawful warrant of a justice or sheriff for the arrest of a person accused or convicted of a criminal offence, or for the recovery of stolen goods.

A warrant to which the MCA 1980, s. 125(3), applies, that is a warrant to arrest a person in connection with an offence or for certain offences pertaining to the armed forces, or under the Domestic Proceedings and MCA 1978, s. 18(4) (protection of parties to the marriage and children of the family), and under ss. 55, 76, 93 or 97 of the MCA 1980 itself, may be executed by a constable even though it is not in his possession at the time. It must be shown to the person arrested, if he demands it, as soon as practicable. These provisions do not, however, apply to a search warrant or other warrant which must be in the constable's possession at the time (*Purdy* [1975] QB 288).

An issue which not infrequently arises concerns the meaning of 'offence' in the MCA 1980, s. 125(3). This imports an act or omission punishable under criminal law. The wording is apt to include a warrant to arrest a person charged with breach of a community service order since the offence is regarded as a vital and relevant factor in the operation of arrest (*Jones* v *Kelsey* (1986) 85 Cr App R 226). It does not include arrest for a civil proceeding such as the non-payment of maintenance (*Horsfield* v *Brown* [1932] 1 KB 355) or for non-payment of a fine (*Peacock* (1989) 153 JP 199). The purpose of requiring that the constable have the warrant in his possession in the latter case is so that the person concerned can pay the fine and buy his freedom.

A constable who arrests a person under warrant must inform the person of the reason for his arrest and that he is acting under warrant (PACE 1984, s. 28).

DETENTION AND TREATMENT OF SUSPECTS

Introduction

D1.23   The PACE 1984 and its associated codes of practice provide for the questioning and treatment of detained suspects. The Act and recent decisions validate the use of detention of arrested persons as an aid to interrogation (*Holgate-Mohammed* v *Duke* [1984] AC 437). Code C, para. 1.1, states as the leading principle that all persons in custody must be dealt with expeditiously and released as soon as the need for detention has ceased to apply.

Voluntary Attendance at a Police Station

D1.24   A person who attends voluntarily at a police station or at any other place where a constable is present, or who accompanies a constable to a police station or such other place without having been arrested, is entitled to leave at will unless he is arrested. The word 'attends' would presumably extend to interviews held at a person's place of work, but not, it is submitted, at his home. If a constable decides that a suspect is to be prevented from leaving at will, he is to inform the suspect at once that he is under arrest and bring him before the custody officer. If he is not placed under arrest but is cautioned as a prelude to putting questions to him for the purpose of obtaining evidence which may be put before a court concerning the offence under investigation, the officer administering the caution must immediately inform him that he is not under arrest, and that he is free to leave if he wishes, and that he may obtain free and independent legal advice if he wishes (PACE 1984, s. 29 and Code C, para. 3.15).

The Custody Officer

D1.25   The PACE 1984, s. 34(1), provides that only an arrested person may be kept in police detention and then only in accordance with the provisions of part IV of the Act. The supervision of detention and the conditions which apply to it is the responsibility of a custody officer who must hold at least the rank of sergeant and who, in principle, should come from the uniform branch unless there is no officer of that or superior rank at the station to perform his functions (PACE 1984, s. 36(3)).

A police officer who has been involved in the matter under investigation will not act as custody officer save that, in cases of necessity (for example, where the only officer available has had some prior acquaintance with the case), this rule may be departed from. Save in the case where a custody officer, in accordance with any code of practice transfers or permits the transfer of a person in police detention to an investigating officer (for example, where detectives take a suspect from cells in order to visit the scene of a crime to search for evidence), none of the functions of a custody officer are to be performed by an officer engaged in the investigation of the particular offence (PACE 1984, ss. 34(3) and 39).

Detention, Charge and Release

D1.26   Where a person is arrested for an offence, whether without a warrant or under a warrant not endorsed for bail, the custody officer at the station where he is detained is to determine whether he has sufficient evidence to charge the suspect with the offence for which he is arrested. He must perform this task as soon as is practicable after the arrested person arrives at the station or, if the arrest occurs there, as soon as possible after the arrest. He may detain the person at the police station for so long as is necessary to enable him to discharge this function (PACE 1984, s. 37(1)). A custody officer who becomes aware at any time that the grounds for detaining a suspect in police custody have ceased to apply and who is not aware of any other grounds which would justify his continued detention must release him, immediately (s. 39). He is not, however, to release a suspect who appears to him to have been unlawfully at large when arrested (s. 34(4)).

Code of Practice C outlines the procedure. Before reaching a decision concerning release, detention and charge, the custody officer must open a custody record in respect of the arrested person (Code C, para. 2.1) which may later be inspected by the person detained, the appropriate adult or legal representative (Code C, para. 2.5). The custody officer must also inform the arrested person of his rights to have someone informed of his arrest, to consult privately with a solicitor and the fact that independent legal advice is available free of charge, and to consult the appropriate codes of practice (Code C, para. 3.1). The custody officer must also give the arrested person a written notice of his rights (which include a right to a copy of the custody record) and a caution that he is not obliged to say anything but that what he says may be given in evidence. The note must also explain the arrangements for obtaining legal advice. The custody officer must also give the person an additional written notice briefly setting out his entitlements while in custody (Code C, para. 3.2). This letter includes entitlements to minimum conditions of comfort while in custody. The person is to be asked to sign the custody record to acknowledge receipt of the notices (Code C, para. 3.2).

A custody officer does not have to satisfy himself that the arrest of a person was lawful before holding that person in custody; he is entitled to assume that it was lawful (*DPP v L* [1999] Crim LR 752).

Treatment of Special Categories of Persons

If an arrested person does not understand English or appears to be deaf and the custody **D1.27** officer cannot communicate with him, he must call an interpreter as soon as practicable and ask him to provide the information noted in **D1.26** (Code C, para. 3.6). If the arrested person is a juvenile, the custody officer must, if it is practicable, ascertain the identity of a person responsible for his welfare and inform that person that the juvenile has been arrested, the reason why and where he is detained (Code C, para. 3.7). If the juvenile is known to be subject to a supervision order, reasonable steps must be taken to notify the person supervising him (Code C, para. 3.8).

If a person is a juvenile or is suffering from mental illness or mental handicap, then the custody officer must, as soon as practicable, inform the appropriate adult of the grounds for his detention and his whereabouts and ask the adult to come to the police station to see the person (Code C, para. 3.9). A solicitor attending a police station on a suspect's behalf is not an 'appropriate adult' for these purposes (*Lewis* [1996] Crim LR 260). What counts is the fact that the person questioned is suffering from mental disorder or mental handicap and not whether he exhibits acute systems and is able to understand procedures and answer questions (*Ali (Haroon)* (24 November 1998 unreported)). If the interview of such a person is admitted in evidence without any intimation of the presence of an appropriate adult, this might lead the jury to believe that the person concerned was normal (*Aspinall* [1999] 2 Cr App R 115).

It would seem, as a matter of practice at any rate, that an appropriate adult should also be called where a person, although not suffering from mental illness or handicap, is illiterate. The Code is ambiguous on the point but the above represents best practice and is so regarded by Crown Court judges.

If the appropriate adult is already at the station when information is given to the arrested person then that information must be given in the presence of the adult. If that adult is not then present, the information must be given on his arrival (Code C, para. 3.11). By 'appropriate adult' is meant a parent or guardian, or if a juvenile is in care the care authority or a voluntary organisation, or a social worker, or another responsible adult who is not a police officer or police employee (Code C, para. 1.7). The appropriate adult has an important part to play in advising, observing for fairness, and to help in communication (in the case of juveniles and handicapped persons). An estranged parent whom an arrested juvenile does not wish to attend is not an appropriate adult because that parent cannot perform the functions of such an adult. For the same reason, a mentally subnormal and illiterate parent who cannot appreciate the gravity of the situation in which his child is placed is not an appropriate adult (*Morse* [1991] Crim LR 195). Where the juvenile is in care, the relevant social worker or his representative should be prepared to attend as soon as practicable (*DPP* v *Blake* [1989] 1 WLR 432).

The detainee should be advised that the appropriate adult is there to assist him and that he can consult privately with him at any time (Code C, para. 3.12). If the appropriate adult or the person detained wishes legal advice to be taken, the provisions of sect. 6 of Code C apply (Code C, para. 3.13). This provision is to protect the rights of a juvenile, or mentally disordered or handicapped person. If such a person asks for legal assistance, the full panoply of protections come into play (Code C, note for guidance 3G).

A custody officer who authorises an arrested juvenile to be kept in police custody must secure that the arrested juvenile is moved to local authority accommodation unless he certifies that, by reason of such circumstances as are specified in the certificate, it is impracticable to do so or that, in the case of a juvenile who has attained the age of 12, that no secure accommodation is available and that keeping in other local authority accommodation would not be adequate to protect the public from serious harm from him (PACE 1984, s. 38(6)).

If the person is blind or seriously visually handicapped or is unable to read, the custody officer should ensure that his solicitor, relative, the appropriate adult or some other person likely to take an interest in him is available to help him in checking any documentation. Where Code C requires written consent or signification then the person who is assisting may be asked to sign instead if the detained person so wishes (Code C, para. 3.14).

The Decision to Detain or Release

D1.28 If the custody officer determines under the PACE 1984, s. 34(5), to release a person, then that person is to be released without bail unless it appears to the custody officer either that there is need for further investigation of any matter for which he was detained, or that proceedings may be taken against him in respect of any such matter. If neither of these appears, he is to be released on bail (s. 34(9)). An arrest in respect of a breath test is considered, for the purposes of the detention provisions, to be an arrest under part IV of the PACE 1984. The effect of this is that a person so arrested may be held for his own protection and not released until he is fit to leave the police station (s. 34(6)).

The custody officer is authorised to detain an arrested person at a police station for such period as is necessary to enable him to decide what action to take (s. 37(1)). It is submitted that a period of not more than six hours will generally be considered acceptable by the courts, given that most instances of police detention last in practice no longer than this. In many instances the time involved will be much less.

A custody officer who considers that there are grounds for holding the suspect, but who determines that he does not have sufficient evidence to charge him, is to release him with or without bail unless he reasonably believes that detention of the suspect is necessary to secure or preserve evidence relating to an offence for which he is under arrest or to obtain evidence by questioning him (s. 37(2)). This is inconsistent with the use of a holding charge (as to which see *Hussien* v *Chong Fook Kam* [1970] AC 942), even one in respect of which there is reasonable cause not only to arrest the suspect but also to charge him, as a means of detaining a person in custody in order to facilitate the investigation of a more serious offence in which he is thought to be involved. If, however, the custody officer becomes aware that there are grounds for arresting or detaining him in respect of another, perhaps more serious offence, he may be arrested at the police station for that other offence and the question would then arise whether to detain him, *inter alia*, for questioning (PACE 1984, ss. 31 and 34(1)). Limits to the use of holding charges would seemingly operate only where the police lack reasonable grounds to arrest the suspect in respect of another offence, and if such reasonable cause appears during the course of interrogation concerning the lesser offence, as it well might where the offences are related, arrest for the greater will then be appropriate.

A custody officer who believes that it is necessary to detain a suspect without charge in order to secure or preserve evidence relating to an offence for which he is under arrest or to obtain such evidence by questioning him may authorise his detention in police custody (PACE 1984, s. 37(2) and (3)). Apart from interrogation, the steps envisaged may relate to locating physical evidence, where the presence of the suspect at the scene may be important, and identification parades. The custody officer is obliged to make a written record of the grounds for detention as soon as is practicable (s. 37(5)). That record is to be made in the presence of the person arrested (Code C, para. 2.1)). He must at that time be informed of the grounds for detention and in any event before he is then questioned about any offence (Code C, para. 3.4). The written record need not, however, be made in the presence of the person arrested where that person is, at the time, incapable of understanding what is said to him, is violent, or is likely to become violent, or is in need of urgent medical attention (PACE 1984, s. 37(6)).

If the custody officer determines that he has sufficient evidence to charge the suspect with the offence for which he was arrested, then he must either charge the person, or release him without charge, either on bail or without bail. If such a person is released and at that time a decision whether he is to be prosecuted for the offence for which he was arrested has not been taken, the custody officer must inform him of the fact. A person who is not in a fit state to be charged or released may be kept in police custody until he is (s. 37(7) to (9)).

The custody officer is to inform a juvenile against whom there are grounds which would justify laying of an information that a decision concerning whether he is to be charged is to be taken (s. 37(12)). He is also to specify the offence concerned. The custody officer is also under a duty to take such steps as are practicable to ascertain the identity of a person responsible for the arrested juvenile's welfare. Such a person may be the juvenile's parent or guardian or any other person who has for the time being assumed responsibility for his welfare (s. 37(13) and Code C, para. 3.7). This is a wide phrase, apt to comprehend anyone who in fact has assumed such responsibility, even under an informal arrangement.

A duty officer who ascertains the identity of a person responsible for the juvenile's welfare is to give to that person, if practicable, the information which he is obliged to give to the arrested juvenile as soon as it is practicable to do so (s. 37(11)). A similar requirement exists in respect of a person responsible for the supervision of an arrested juvenile in respect of whom a supervision order has been made (s. 37(14)).

Calculating Time of Detention

Save in the case where prolonged detention has been authorised, that is, in the case of **D1.29** a serious arrestable offence, a suspect may not be held in detention without charge for more than 24 hours. If, at the expiry of that time, he has not been charged, he must be released either on bail or without bail (PACE 1984, s. 41(1) and (7)). He may then not be rearrested without warrant for the offence for which he was previously arrested unless new evidence justifying a further arrest has come to light since his arrest (s. 41(9)); it is submitted that 'evidence' is used in a broad sense to mean any indicia which might justify a further arrest, which could include credible hearsay. Section 41(9) is plainly intended to prevent the police from playing cat and mouse with a suspect.

Complicated rules relate to the calculation of the detention period. In the case of a suspect who is arrested in a particular police area and who is to be dealt with there, time begins to run from the moment when he is brought to a station in that police area (s. 41(2)(d)). Where the arrest of a person is sought in one police area in England and Wales and he is arrested in another area, but is not questioned there, time runs either from the moment when the suspect arrives at the station where he is to be detained in the police area where he is sought or from the time 24 hours after the time of his arrest, whichever is the earlier (s. 41(2)(a) and (3)). Where a person is already in custody in a police area in England and Wales, and is wanted in some other such police area and is taken there for the purposes of investigating the offence, then time runs from the expiration of a period of 24 hours after he leaves the place where he is detained in the first force area, or from the time when he arrives at the first police station to which he is taken in the second area, whichever is the earlier. This is, however, premised upon the suspect not having been questioned about the matter in the force area where he already was in detention. In such case, the normal period of detention applies, that is, time runs from the moment of his arrival at the first police station (s. 41(5)).

When a person is arrested outside England and Wales, time runs either from the time at which he arrives at the first police station in the police area in England and Wales in which the offence for which he was arrested is being investigated, or the time 24 hours after his entry into England and Wales, whichever is the earlier (s. 41(2)(b)). Where a person who has been arrested before for an offence is rearrested at a station, time runs from the moment at which he arrived at the station in respect of the first arrest (s. 41(4)). Where a detained person is removed to hospital for medical treatment, only those periods during which he is questioned, either in transit or at the hospital, count as periods of detention (s. 41(6)).

It is noteworthy that in all these cases the period of detention runs not from the time when a decision to hold a person in detention was made but generally from his time of arrival at the relevant police station. This is an important protection for the suspect.

Responsibilities during Detention

D1.30   The custody officer is the guarantor of the integrity of the system of detention. He must ensure that detainees are treated in accordance with the requirements of the PACE 1984 and the codes of practice issued under it, and that proper custody records are kept (PACE 1984, s. 39). In certain circumstances these duties can be transferred.

Review of Detention

D1.31   The PACE 1984 requires that the detention of persons in police detention be reviewed. In the case of persons who have been arrested and charged, this is done by the custody officer; for persons who have not been charged, it is done by an officer of at least the rank of inspector who has not been directly involved in the investigation (PACE 1984, s. 40(1)). In either case the officer concerned is referred to as a 'review officer' (s. 40(2)).

Failure to carry out a timely review of a person's detention in custody before charge renders previously lawful detention unlawful and amounts to the tort of false imprisonment (*Roberts* v *Chief Constable of the Cheshire Constabulary* [1999] 1 WLR 662).

The provisions concerning review are dealt with in s. 40. In all cases, the first review must be not later than six hours after the detention was first authorised; the second review must be not later than nine hours after the first; and subsequent reviews must be at intervals of not more than nine hours. A review may, however, be postponed if, in general, it is impracticable to carry it out at the latest time specified for it. The statute gives two examples. The first is where the review officer is satisfied that a review would interrupt questioning then in progress and would prejudice the investigation. The second is where no review officer is readily available at that time. This avoids an entirely rigid regime. On the other hand, it is not clear what other matters might be thought to render review impracticable. Periods spent in hospital are in general excluded from the effluxion of time. If a station is very busy or a riot of prisoners is in progress, a review officer might not be available. The phrase remains obscure. A postponed review must be carried out as soon after the latest period specified as is practicable, and the review officer is required to record the reasons for any postponement in the custody record.

The fact that a review is carried out after postponement does not operate to extend the time in which any later review is to be carried out.

In the case of a person not yet charged at the time of the review, the review officer must determine whether to charge him, release him on bail or otherwise, or detain him further. This procedure is subject to the same principles as apply to the custody officer in making his initial decision whether to charge or not, and whether to hold a person in custody or not. If a person is held because he was not in a fit state to be dealt with, the review officer must determine on review whether or not he is now in a fit state.

If a person has already been charged at the time of review, the review officer is to consider whether to order his release on bail, applying the same principles as those which the custody officer is obliged to employ. Thus both the emphasis on bail and the restrictive conditions already discussed in connection with bail are applicable (PACE 1984, s. 40(10)).

If directions relating to a person in police detention given by a higher-ranking officer are at variance with an actual or proposed decision or action of the review officer, the matter is to be referred to an officer of the rank of superintendent or above who is in charge of the station (s. 40(11)).

Before determining whether to authorise continued detention of a person, whether under the PACE 1984 or under sch. 3 to the Prevention of Terrorism (Temporary Provisions) Act 1989, the review officer is to give either the detained person (unless he is asleep) or any solicitor (including a duty solicitor) representing him, who is available at the time of the review, an opportunity to make representations to him about the detention (PACE 1984, s. 40(12)). Before conducting a review, the review officer must ensure that the detained person is reminded of his entitlement to free legal advice (Code C, para. 15.3). The review officer may also, in his discretion, allow other persons having an interest in the person's welfare to make representations to him (Code C, para. 15.1). The detainee or his solicitor may make representations either orally or in writing, but the review officer need not hear oral representations from a detainee whom he considers unfit to make such representations by reason of his condition or behaviour (PACE 1984, s. 40(13) and (14); Code C, para. 15.1). A violent, hostile or abusive detainee may risk going unheard. In case of necessity, a review may be conducted over the telephone provided that the requirements of the PACE 1984, s. 40, or the Prevention of Terrorism (Temporary Provisions) Act 1989, sch. 3, are adhered to.

Detention for More than 24 Hours, up to 36 Hours

Normally, a person may not be detained at a police station without charge for more than **D1.32** 24 hours from the commencement of detention. Detention may, however, be extended to 36 hours provided that three conditions are met (PACE 1984, s. 42(1)). These are:

(a)   that a police officer of the rank of superintendent or above who is responsible for the police station at which the person is detained has reasonable grounds for believing that such detention is necessary to secure or preserve evidence relating to an offence for which the person is under arrest or to obtain such evidence by questioning him;

(b)   that the offence for which he is under arrest is a serious arrestable offence;

(c)   that the investigation is being conducted diligently and expeditiously.

The first of the three criteria noted above is common to all cases of detention before charge, and the third requires little explanation. The review officer must decide whether an investigation is being conducted diligently and expeditiously in the light of such matters as the complexity of the case, the nature of the inquiries to be made, and the ease or otherwise of obtaining information from those approached to give it. A suspect who puts obstacles in the way of the police, for example, by exercising his right to remain silent, may well not be able to complain that police inquiries were unduly protracted.

'Serious arrestable offence' is defined in the PACE 1984. The term applies first to certain listed offences which are always serious (s. 116 and sch. 5, parts I and II). Three groups are involved. The first (sch. 5, part I), which contains both statutory and common-law offences, comprehends treason, murder, manslaughter, rape, kidnapping, incest with a girl under 13, buggery with a person under 16, and indecent assault which constitutes an act of gross indecency. The second group (sch. 5, part II) contains a list of statutory offences and includes causing an explosion likely to endanger life or property, intercourse with a girl under the age of 13, possession, use and carrying of firearms with certain specified intents, causing death by dangerous driving, hostage taking, and hijacking of aircraft. This list in part II is varied from time to time, for example, the CJPO 1994, s. 85, adds the taking and distribution of indecent photographs or pseudo-photographs of children and the publication of obscene matter to the list. The third group consists of the drug trafficking offences referred to in the Drug Trafficking Act 1994, s. 1(3)(a) to (f) (s. 116(2)(aa)).

Any other arrestable offence may be regarded as serious if its commission has led to certain specified consequences or is intended to or is likely to lead to any of those consequences. An arrestable offence which consists of a threat, for example, blackmail, or attempting to pervert the course of justice, will also be regarded as a serious arrestable offence if carrying out the threat would be likely to lead to any of the specified consequences. The consequences referred to are: serious harm to the security of the State or to public order; serious interference with the administration of justice or the investigation of an offence or offences; the death of any person; serious injury to any person; substantial financial gain to any person; and substantial financial loss to any person. Injury includes any disease and any impairment of a person's physical or mental condition (s. 116(3) to (7)). The notion of substantial financial loss is of course relative; but it may be thought to apply to a person suspected of a chain of petty thefts and burglaries from old people, or to a person or persons who obtain successive small amounts of money by deception, for example, from gullible immigrants.

Certain terrorism offences are regarded as serious arrestable offences for the purpose of delaying contact by suspects with their families and legal advisers. This point is discussed further in that context.

If the above conditions are met, the review officer may authorise holding a suspect in detention for 36 hours from the commencement of detention. If he authorises keeping a suspect in detention for less than 36 hours, he may authorise further detention up to the maximum 36 hours provided that the above conditions still apply (PACE 1984, s. 42(2)).

If it is proposed to transfer a person to police detention in another police area, the officer, in determining whether or not to keep the accused in detention, is to have regard to the distance and the time the journey would take (s. 42(3)). Presumably, if the time involved is likely to take detention beyond the 36 hours permitted, the review officer will have either to refuse the transfer or seek an extension to detention from a magistrates' court, a procedure dealt with in **D1.33**.

Strict time-limits apply in respect of an authorisation extending detention up to 36 hours from its inception. No authorisation may be made more than 24 hours after the inception of detention; there is thus no room for any practice of holding a person beyond the normal maximum of 24 hours subject to retrospective validation. Where an extension has been ordered within the 24-hour period, a further extension may be applied for and granted provided that the total period does not extend beyond 36 hours (*Taylor* [1991] Crim LR 541). In order to prevent over-hasty decisions, no order may be made before the second review of detention, that is, review by the review officer 15 hours after the inception of detention (s. 42(4)).

When an officer first authorises the keeping of a suspect in extended detention, he is obliged to inform the suspect of the grounds for continuing detention, and to record the grounds in the suspect's custody record (s. 42(5)). As with the case of normal detention, the suspect and his solicitor, if any, must be, and a person interested in his welfare may be, given the opportunity to make oral and written representations (s. 42(7) and Code C, para. 15.2). As with normal detention, the officer may decline to hear oral representations from the suspect himself if he considers that the suspect's condition or behaviour is such as to render him unfit to do so (s. 42(8)).

Every person in detention has the right, subject to exceptions, to contact his family, or a friend, and his solicitor (ss. 56 and 58). If an officer authorises keeping a suspect in extended detention, and the suspect has not at that time availed himself of his rights, the officer must (a) inform the suspect of his right, (b) decide whether the suspect shall be permitted to exercise it, (c) record his decision in the custody record and (d) if he decides to refuse to allow the suspect to contact the outside world, must also record the grounds for the decision in the suspect's custody record (s. 42(9)).

A person whose extended detention has been ordered under the foregoing procedure must be released from detention either with or without bail at the expiration of 36 hours unless either he has been charged with an offence or his further detention has been ordered by a magistrates' court (s. 42(10)). A person who has been released may not be rearrested for the same offence unless new evidence justifying such a course has come to light (s. 42(11)).

Detention for More than 36 Hours, up to 96 Hours

Detention beyond 36 hours and extending to a maximum of 96 hours from the inception **D1.33** of detention may be ordered by a magistrates' court, defined for the purpose as a court consisting of two or more justices sitting otherwise than in open court (PACE 1984, s. 45(1)).

A magistrates' court may, on an application made on oath by a constable and supported by an information, issue a warrant of further detention to keep a person whose further detention is believed to be reasonably justified in police detention. The hearing is *inter partes*. The detainee must be given a copy of the information and be brought before the court for the hearing. He is entitled to be legally represented at the hearing. If he is not so represented, a situation which could arise either because he has not wished to see a solicitor or because access to a solicitor has been denied, the court must adjourn the hearing to enable him to be represented. He may be held in detention during the adjournment. No limit is placed on the time for which an adjournment may be granted (s. 43(1) to (3)).

An application for a warrant of further detention must, as a general rule, be made before the expiry of 36 hours from the commencement of detention (s. 43(4)(a)). This period may be extended where it is not practicable for the magistrates' court to which the application will be made to sit at the expiry of that period but where it will sit within six hours following the 36-hour period (s. 43(4)(c)). If the application cannot be heard before the expiry of the 36-hour period, the custody officer is to note in the detainee's custody record the fact that he was detained for the extra period and the reason why he was so kept (s. 43(5)). If, however, the application is made out of time and the magistrates consider that the police in all the circumstances acted unreasonably in not bringing the matter before the court in time, they must dismiss the application (*Slough Justices, ex parte Stirling* (1987) 151 JP 603). Where an extension beyond the 24-hour period granted by a police officer is involved, the court has no jurisdiction to extend it (*Re an Application for a Warrant of Further Detention* [1988] Crim LR 296).

The notes for guidance in Code of Practice C specify that an application for a warrant of further detention or its extension should be made between 10.00 a.m. and 9.00 p.m. and if possible during normal court business. If it appears possible that a special sitting will be needed (either at a weekend or on a weekday outside normal court hours but between 10.00 a.m. and 9.00 p.m.) then the clerk to the justices should be notified of this possibility, while the court is sitting if possible (Code C, note 15B).

The PACE 1984 in no way restricts the police concerning the justices they may use. The police may make use of justices and their staffs who are available, wherever they come from. There should therefore be no difficulty in working the review machinery (s. 43(5)).

The police must prove to the court that a warrant of further detention is justified. Furthermore, the detainee must be given the reasons why further detention is sought. Any information submitted in support of an application must state the nature of the offence involved, the general nature of the evidence upon which his arrest was based, what inquiries have been made by the police, what further inquiries they propose to make, and the reasons for believing the continued detention of the suspect to be necessary for the purpose of such further inquiries (s. 43(14)). If a magistrates' court is not satisfied that a case for further detention has been made out, it may either dismiss the application or adjourn the hearing of it to a time not later than 36 hours from the inception of the detention (s. 43(8)). If, therefore, the court sits at a time close to the 36-hour limit, it may well not be possible for the police to obtain an adjournment in order to improve their case. Furthermore, where an application for a warrant of further detention has been refused, no further application may be made under the section unless fresh evidence has come to light since the refusal (s. 43(17)). This of course assumes that the hearing took place before the expiry of the 36-hour period and that it is possible for the suspect still to be in lawful custody.

A warrant of further detention may be made for a maximum period of 36 hours. Within that global limit, a court is to have regard, where it is intended to transfer a suspect to another police area, to the distance and time involved in a journey. At the expiry of a warrant of further detention, where no extension of it has been made, the suspect must be charged or released either on bail (which would be police bail) or without bail. In that case he may not be rearrested without a warrant for the offence for which he was previously arrested unless new evidence justifying a further arrest has come to light since his release (s. 43(12) to (19)). As with the provisions in s. 41 discussed in **D1.29**, this is meant to prevent resort to cat-and-mouse tactics.

As a general rule, where an application for a warrant is refused, the police must either charge the detainee or release him either on bail or without bail (s. 43(15)). The police may, however, under s. 43(16), be able to detain him notwithstanding a refusal, provided that refusal was made before the expiry of a period of 24 hours after the commencement of custody, or before the expiry of any longer period for which his custody has been authorised under s. 40.

A magistrates' court may, on application and information, extend a warrant of further detention. Such extension may be made for any period which the court thinks fit, having regard to the evidence before it, but it may not be for longer than 36 hours, and the total period for which the person is to be held in detention may not exceed 96 hours from the commencement of detention. There is no formal limit to the number of occasions on which such a further extension may be granted, but the total period of 96 hours cannot be exceeded (s. 44(1) to (14)).

The police must prove that an extension of a warrant of further detention is necessary. The court must be furnished with the same particulars as are required in the original application. The detainee has the same rights of representation (s. 44(6)). If the extension is refused, the detainee must either be released with or without bail or charged, save that, if the application for extension is made before the expiry of the period specified in the warrant itself, the detainee may be held until the expiry of that period (s. 44(7) to (18)). Once released, the detainee may not be arrested again for the offence without warrant unless new evidence justifying rearrest has emerged (s. 43(19)).

Treatment of Children

The Children Act 1989, sch. 15, repealed the PACE 1984, s. 52, and the CYPA 1969, **D1.34** s. 28. The provisions of the PACE 1984 therefore now have effect in relation to any child arrested without a warrant. Where a child is taken into police protection under the Children Act 1989, s. 46 (see **D1.18**), different provisions apply.

Remands to Police Custody

A suspect may be remanded in detention at a police station for a period not exceeding **D1.35** three clear days. A suspect so detained is not to be kept in police detention unless it is necessary so to detain him for the purpose of inquiring into other offences. As soon as that necessity ceases, he is to be brought back before the court which committed him (MCA 1980, s. 128(7) and (8)(a)). The duties of the custody officer apply in the case of such a suspect as to other detainees, and his detention is subject to the same rules concerning periodic review as apply to other charged prisoners (MCA 1980, s. 128(8)(b) and (c)).

Detention after Charge

Once a person in police custody, or a juvenile detained by a local authority, is charged, **D1.36** the police must bring him before a magistrates' court (PACE 1984, s. 46(1)). If he is to be brought before a magistrates' court for the petty-sessions area in which the police station is situated, that must be done as soon as is practicable. He must in any event be brought there not later than the first sitting after he is charged with the offence (s. 46(2)). This will result in the accused person being brought before the court on the day on which he is charged or on the next day. If no magistrates' court for the area is due to sit in either period, the custody officer must inform the clerk to the justices for that area that there is a charged and detained person who must be brought before the court (s. 46(3)). The clerk must then arrange for a magistrates' court to sit not later than the day after the day when the accused was charged (ss. 46(6)(a) and 46(7)(a)).

Provisions, identical in effect, apply to a person who is to be brought before a court in a petty-sessions area other than that in which the police station where he was charged is located. He is to be moved to that area as soon as is practicable, and is to be brought before a magistrates' court there as soon as is practicable (s. 46(4)). Identical provisions apply to a case in which no magistrates' court for the area will sit on the day of the person's arrival in the area or the next day; the clerk, on notification by the custody officer, arranges a sitting of the court (ss. 46(6)(b) and 46(7)(b)).

Notification of Arrest

A person who has been arrested and who is being held in custody at a police station has **D1.37** a right, at his request, to have one friend, or relative or other person who is known to him or who is likely to take an interest in his welfare, told of his arrest and the place where he is being detained. This is to be done as soon as is practicable (PACE 1984, s. 56(1)). His right to have another person notified is exercisable whenever he is transferred from one police station to another (s. 56(8)). Code of Practice C, para. 3.1(i), requires the police to inform the suspect of this right.

The person chosen by the detainee is to be informed of the detainee's whereabouts at public expense, and, if the detainee requests, on each occasion that he is taken to another police station (Code C, para. 5.2). If that person cannot be contacted, the detainee may choose up to two alternatives. If they too cannot be contacted, the custody officer has discretion to allow further attempts until the information has been conveyed (Code C, para. 5.1). If the detainee does not know of anyone to contact for advice, the custody officer should bear in mind local voluntary bodies who may be able to help (Code C, notes 5C and 5D).

A detainee may receive visits at the custody officer's discretion (Code C, para. 5.4).

A detainee is entitled to writing materials and to speak on the telephone for a reasonable time to one person, though in certain circumstances this may be delayed (Code C, para. 5.6). All letters, save those to his solicitor, may be read and the detainee must be warned of this (Code C, para. 5.7). Unless a telephone call is to the detainee's solicitor, a police officer may listen in to it and may terminate the call if the facility is being abused. The detainee is to be cautioned that what he says in any communication, other than one to his solicitor, may be given in evidence (Code C, para. 5.7).

If a friend or relative of a detainee, or a person with an interest in a detainee's welfare, asks where the detainee is then this information must be given provided that the detainee agrees and provided that the case is not one, involving a serious arrestable offence, where the detainee is being held incommunicado (Code C, para. 5.5). This latter qualification can have the effect both of isolating the detainee and of depriving his family of any information concerning his whereabouts.

An officer of the rank of superintendent or above may authorise delay in giving notification of a suspect's detention. This may be done either orally or in writing, but if done orally the authorisation is to be confirmed in writing as soon as practicable (PACE 1984, s. 56(4)). Delay is permitted only where the suspect is in police detention for a serious arrestable offence (s. 56(2)) and where he is being held in a police station and not elsewhere (*Kerawalla* [1991] Crim LR 451). It is subject to a maximum period of 36 hours from the commencement of detention, save in the case of terrorism where a 48-hour maximum applies (s. 56(3) and (11)). In the latter case detention may be in connection with the terrorism provisions rather than for a serious arrestable offence (s. 56(10)). The importance of this is that arrest under the Prevention of Terrorism (Temporary Provisions) Act 1989 need not be for a criminal offence as such. If delay is authorised, the detained person must be told the reason for it, and that reason must be noted on his custody record (PACE 1984, s. 56(6)).

Delay in notifying the person chosen by a detainee is only permitted in the case of a serious arrestable offence where the officer has reasonable grounds for believing that telling that person will lead to interference with, or harm to, evidence connected with a serious arrestable offence or interference with, or physical injury to, other persons; or will lead to the alerting of other persons suspected of having committed such an offence but not yet arrested for it; or will hinder the recovery of property obtained as the result of such offence (s. 56(6)). Notification may also be delayed where the serious arrestable offence is either (a) a drug-trafficking offence and the officer has reasonable grounds for believing that the detained person has benefited from drug trafficking and that the recovery of the value of that person's proceeds of drug trafficking will be hindered by notifying the chosen person, or (b) an offence to which part VI of the CJA 1988 (offences in respect of which confiscation orders may be made) applies and the officer has reasonable grounds for believing that the detained person has benefited from the offence, and that the recovery of the property obtained by that person from or in connection with the offence or of the pecuniary advantage derived by him from or in connection with it will be hindered by notifying the chosen person the exercise of the right (PACE 1984, s. 56(5A)). In the case of terrorism, the criteria are that there are reasonable grounds for believing that telling the chosen person will lead to inferference with the gathering of information about the commission, preparation or instigation of acts of terrorism, or will make it more difficult to secure the apprehension, prosecution or conviction of any person in connection with the commission, preparation or instigation of an act of terrorism (s. 56(11)).

Additional rights are conferred in respect of children and young persons. Where a child or young person is in police detention, which includes detention under the terrorism provisions, the police are to take such steps as are practicable to ascertain the identity of a person responsible for his welfare (CYPA 1933, s. 34). The persons who may be responsible for the welfare of a child or young person are his parent or guardian, or any other person who has for the time being assumed responsibility for his welfare. This includes, in the case of a child or young person in the care of a local authority, a reference to that authority, and, in the case of such a person in the care of a voluntary organisation having statutorily conferred parental rights and duties, a reference to that organisation. Additionally, if the person arrested is subject to a supervision order, the person responsible for his supervision is included as a person to be notified.

Unless it is not practicable to do so, the person who is responsible for the welfare of the child or young person is to be informed that he has been arrested, and of the reason why, and where he is being detained. That information is to be given as soon as it is practicable to do so. The rights thus conferred upon the child or young person are in addition to his rights under the PACE 1984, s. 56, to have a person of his choice notified of his detention.

The codes of practice give a citizen of an independent Commonwealth country or a national of a foreign country (including the Republic of Ireland) an unqualified right to communicate at any time with the diplomatic representatives of his country (Code C, para. 7.1). If the person detained is a national of a Commonwealth or foreign country with which a bilateral consular convention or agreement requiring notification of arrest is in force, the police must inform the appropriate high commission, embassy or consulate of his detention as soon as practicable, unless the detained person is a political refugee or is seeking political asylum when such information is only to be given at the detainee's express request (Code C, paras 7.2 to 7.4). Any other foreign national must be informed as soon as practicable of his right to communicate with his consul if he so wishes and that the police will, on request, notify his consul for him. The right of consuls to visit their nationals is unqualified.

Right of Access to Solicitor

A person who is arrested and held in custody at a police station has a right, at his request, **D1.38** to consult and communicate privately with a solicitor at any time (PACE 1984, s. 58; Code C, para. 6.1). While the statutory right does not apply in respect of a prisoner on remand in custody at a magistrates' court, there is a common-law right to consult a solicitor as soon as is reasonably practicable and police cannot refuse access to a prisoner in custody simply because the request falls outside customary hours (*Chief Constable of South Wales, ex parte Merrick* [1994] 1 WLR 663). If he does not know of a solicitor but a duty solicitor scheme is in force, he must be told of the availability of a duty solicitor. If a person, whether under arrest or voluntarily at a police station, requests to see a solicitor he must be permitted to do so as soon as practicable. No attempt should be made to dissuade a suspect from obtaining legal advice (Code C, para. 6.4). Wrongful denial of access to a solicitor may lead to the exclusion of evidence (see **F2.12** and **F17.17**). A suspect may not be refused access to a solicitor simply because the police fear that the solicitor will advise the suspect not to answer questions (Code C, annexe B, para. 3; *Alladice* (1988) 87 Cr App R 380).

Reminders of the right to legal advice are to be given before interviews are commenced or recommenced (Code C, paras 6.5 and 11.2). For the circumstances in which an interview may be held notwithstanding that a solicitor is unavailable, see **D1.54**.

The right of access to a solicitor is a right to legal advice; the legislation does not give the detainee the right to have a solicitor present during his questioning by the police. However, Code of Practice C, para. 6.8, specifies that if a detainee has asked to see a solicitor, and the solicitor is available at the time the interview begins or is in progress, the detainee must be allowed to have his solicitor present while he is interviewed. A solicitor's clerk may also be admitted to a police station subject to a discretion to exclude him. Code of Practice C, para. 6.13, reproducing the effect of *Chief Constable of Avon and Somerset, ex parte Robinson* [1989] 1 WLR 793, provides that the officer should take into account whether the identity and status of the clerk or legal executive have been satisfactorily established, whether he is of suitable character to provide legal advice, and any other matters in any written letter or authorisation provided by the solicitor concerned. In particular, a person with a criminal record, unless for a minor and not recent offence, is likely to be unsuitable (Code C, para. 6.13). As the Divisional Court said in *Ex parte Robinson*, where a person is ostensibly capable of giving advice, he cannot be excluded simply because the police believe that he will give poor advice. The solicitor may only be required to leave if an officer of the rank of superintendent or above considers that by his misconduct he has prevented the proper putting of questions to his client. In particular, a solicitor is not guilty of misconduct if he seeks to challenge an improper question to his client or the manner in which it is put or if he advises his client not to reply to particular questions or if he wishes to give his client further legal advice. A solicitor may only be excluded from an interview for misconduct which, Code C, note 6D, suggests, could include answering questions on the client's behalf or providing written replies for the client to quote.

As with the right to have someone notified of detention, exercise of the right of a person not yet charged to see a solicitor may be delayed. The criteria are identical (PACE 1984, s. 58; Code C, annexe B and see *Kerawalla* [1991] Crim LR 451). In any event, the detainee must be allowed to see a solicitor within 36 hours of the commencement of custody if he is being held for a serious arrestable offence and within 48 hours if he is being held under terrorism legislation. These are, however, maximum periods; if the reason for denying access ceases to subsist sooner, the suspect must then be allowed access to a solicitor. The result is that a person may well be held incommunicado for 36 or 48 hours. Where the effect of delays of this magnitude which are permitted by English law is to cause irretrievable prejudice to the defence, this may result in a denial of the fair trial guaranteed under Art. 6 of the European Convention on Human Rights (*Murray* v *United Kingdom* (1996) 22 EHRR 29). It is perhaps not fanciful to suggest that such a delay, unless stringently justified by operational necessities, might result in an exercise of judicial discretion to exclude evidence or stop a prosecution.

A principal reason for delaying access to a solicitor is the fear that the solicitor may be an innocent dupe, conveying information to other suspects still at liberty. In *Samuel* [1988] QB 615, the Court of Appeal held that (a) the police officer must believe that one of the statutory grounds for exclusion applies and (b) that belief must be reasonable. He must believe that the consequence will very probably happen. It will rarely happen that a police officer will be entitled to believe that a solicitor will knowingly pass on information in breach of the statute, and any grounds put forward would have to be specific to the solicitor concerned. Solicitors are also unlikely to be unwitting dupes, and suspicion that the suspect will try to use the solicitor thus must be specific to him, for example, where he is known or suspected to be a member of a criminal gang. In *Alladice* (1988) 87 Cr App R 380, the Court of Appeal seems to have considered the risks of innocent transmission to be greater than it contemplated in *Samuel*, but considered itself to be bound by *Samuel*. In *Davison* [1988] Crim LR 442, the effect of *Samuel* was said to be that if the police seek to deny access to a solicitor they must show more than a substantial risk of their fears being realised.

If delay is authorised, the detained person must be told the reason for it, and the reason must be noted on his custody record. These duties must be performed as soon as is practicable (PACE 1984, s. 58(9) and (10)). When it is decided that it is no longer necessary to keep a suspect incommunicado, the suspect should be informed in specific and easily understandable terms that this means he can notify someone and have access to a solicitor (*Sat-Bhambra* (1988) 88 Cr App R 55; *Cochrane* [1988] Crim LR 449; *Quayson* [1989] Crim LR 218).

An officer of at least the rank of commander or assistant chief constable may, in terrorism cases and in those cases only, direct that a suspect may consult a solicitor only in the sight and hearing of a police officer (PACE 1984, s. 58(14)). The criteria are that there must be reason to think that otherwise there will be interference with investigations into terrorism, or in securing the apprehension, prosecution or conviction of a person in connection with the commission, preparation or instigation of an act of terrorism. The officer in whose sight and hearing the interview must take place must be from the uniformed branch, at least of the rank of inspector, and he must have no connection with the case. The intention is to enable the police officer to prevent the suspect from conveying to a solicitor a message which could have dangerous consequences.

SEARCH OF THE PERSON

With the exception of searches after arrest for terrorism, searches by a constable of **D1.39** persons in detention at a police station and intimate searches can only take place under the authority of the PACE 1984 (s. 53(1) and (2)).

The custody officer at a police station is obliged to ascertain and ensure the recording of everything which a person has with him when he is brought to the station after having been arrested (PACE 1984, s. 54(1); Code C, para. 4.1). He must ascertain what property the suspect may have acquired for an unlawful or harmful purpose while in custody, and is responsible for the safe keeping of property taken from the detainee and kept at the police station (Code C, para. 4.1). The custody officer may seize and retain anything in the possession of the prisoner, save for clothes and personal effects. These may be seized only if the custody officer believes that the person from whom they are seized may use them to cause physical injury to himself or another, or to damage property, or to interfere with evidence, or to escape, or if the custody officer has reasonable grounds for believing that they may be evidence relating to an offence (PACE 1984, s. 54(3) and (4); Code C, para. 4.2). In respect of most of these criteria, the custody officer need only have a subjective belief that seizure is necessary, but in respect of matters of supposed evidentiary value, his belief must be reasonable.

Paragraphs 4.2 and 4.3 of Code of Practice C expressly state that a detained person may retain clothing and personal effects other than cash and other items of value at his own risk, unless the custody officer considers that the detainee might use them in the manner noted above.

A person from whom an article is seized is to be told the reason for the seizure unless he is either violent or likely to become so, or is incapable of understanding what is said to him (PACE 1984, s. 54(5); Code C, paras. 1.8 and 4.2).

A custody officer may, if he considers it necessary in order that he may perform his duties of securing and recording articles, order that the prisoner be searched (PACE 1984, s. 54(6); Code C, para. 4.1). It is for the custody officer to determine, in his discretion, how extensive the search ought to be.

Strip and Intimate Searches

D1.40 A strip search (that is, a search involving the removal of more than outer clothing) may only take place where the custody officer thinks it necessary in order to remove an article which the detained person would not be allowed to keep (Code C, annexe A, para. 10). A strip search may only be carried out by a constable of the same sex as the person being searched.

A person who has been arrested and is in police detention may, under certain circumstances, be subjected to an intimate search, that is, a search into the bodily orifices other than the mouth (PACE 1984, ss. 54(8) and (9) and 65). An intimate search cannot be ordered for the purpose of securing evidence relating to an offence. In order for such a search to be authorised, an officer of at least the rank of superintendent must have reasonable grounds for believing that the detained person has concealed on him an article which he could use to cause physical injury to himself or others, and which he might so use while he is in police detention or in the custody of a court (s. 55(1)(a)). An additional ground is a suspicion that such a person may have concealed on him a class A drug and have been in possession of it before his arrest with the intent either to supply it to another, or to export it with intent to evade a prohibition or restriction (s. 55(1)(b)). The officer must further have reasonable grounds for believing that the article in question cannot be found unless the detainee is intimately searched (s. 55(2)). The reasons why an intimate search is considered necessary must be explained to the person before the search takes place (Code C, annexe A, para. 2).

The legislation thus makes provision for two different cases. The first, and rarest, is where the person has concealed in a bodily orifice an article which may be used to cause physical injury. The second case relates to drugs; these are the likeliest articles to be secreted. The structure of powers provided by the section differentiates between the two cases; in the former case emergency searches may be conducted by the police; in the latter only a suitably qualified person, that is a registered medical practitioner or a registered nurse, may conduct the search (PACE 1984, s. 55(5) and (6); Code C, annexe A, para. 3).

An officer may authorise an intimate search either orally, subject to confirmation in writing, or in writing (PACE 1984, s. 55(4)). The general rule is that an intimate search should be carried out by a suitably qualified person. Searches in respect of drugs offences must always be so carried out (s. 55(5) and (6)). In other cases, searches may be conducted by a constable where to wait for a medically qualified person would not be practicable (s. 55(7)). An example might be where a suspect is believed to have concealed a poisonous drug in his anus. No intimate search of an arrested juvenile or a mentally ill or mentally handicapped person may be carried out unless the appropriate adult of the same sex is present unless the suspect requests the presence of a particular adult of the opposite sex who is readily available. In the case of a juvenile, the search may take place in the absence of the appropriate adult only if the juvenile approves this in the adult's presence (Code C, annexe A, para. 5). A constable may not carry out an intimate search of a person of the opposite sex, but this restriction does not apply to a search carried out by a medically qualified person (Code C, annexe A, para. 6). Before an intimate search takes place, the person to be searched may request legal advice (Code C, annexe A, para. 6).

Intimate searches may be carried out only at a police station, a hospital, surgery or other medical premises (PACE 1984, s. 55(a); Code C, annexe A, para. 4). This latter term is undefined; presumably it could, for example, include a factory first-aid post or an industrial health centre. An intimate search which is only a drug offence search may not be carried out at a police station (PACE 1984, s. 55(10)). The person's custody record is to state what parts of his body were searched, and why, and this information is to be recorded as soon as practicable after the search (s. 55(11)).

A person from whom anything is seized is to be told the reason why, unless, as with superficial searches, he is incapable of understanding or violent or likely to become so (s. 55(14)). Articles seized as the result of an intimate search may be retained by the police for the same reasons as justify detention in the case of a non-intimate search (s. 55(13)). No privilege attaches to any matter so seized.

ENTRY UNDER WARRANT

Warrant Issued by Justice of the Peace

On an application by a constable, a justice of the peace may issue a warrant to a constable **D1.41** to enter and search premises if the justice has reasonable grounds for believing (a) that a serious arrestable offence has been committed and (b) that there is material on the specified premises which is likely to be of substantial value (whether by itself or together with other material) to the investigation of the offence (PACE 1984, s. 8(1)) and is likely to be admissible in evidence at a trial for the offence (s. 8(4)). Such material must not consist of or include items subject to legal privilege, excluded material or special procedure material (s. 8(1)(d)). Such a warrant is in respect of premises; warrants are not granted to search for evidence against individuals or companies wherever such evidence may be found. Furthermore, a magistrate is not barred from issuing a search warrant because there may be special procedure or excluded material on the premises; the issue of a warrant is only barred if the material falls into these categories and is or forms part of the subject matter of such an application (*Chief Constable of Warwickshire Constabulary, ex parte Fitzpatrick* [1999] 1 WLR 564).

In determining whether an offence is a serious arrestable offence, the court must focus on the position which obtained at the time the warrant was issued. The fact that no serious charge resulted is immaterial (*Billericay Justices and Dobbyn, ex parte Frank Harris (Coaches) Ltd* [1991] Crim LR 472).

An application for a search warrant should be made on the authority of an officer of at least the rank of inspector, but where no such officer is on duty, the senior officer on duty may authorise an application (Code of Practice B, para. 2.4).

No such warrant may be issued unless any one of the conditions in s. 8(3) is satisfied:

    (a)   that it is not practicable to communicate with any person entitled to grant entry to the premises; or

    (b)   if it is, that it is not practicable to communicate with any person entitled to grant access to the evidence; or

    (c)   that entry to the premises will not be granted unless a warrant is produced; or

    (d)   that the purpose of a search may be frustrated or seriously prejudiced unless a constable arriving at the premises can secure immediate entry to them.

It is not a condition precedent to the issue of a magistrates' court warrant that other methods have been tried and failed or would be bound to fail, nor that no other statutory procedure for securing the material exists (*Ex parte Frank Harris (Coaches) Ltd*). Where there are grounds for seeking search warrants, the police are entitled to choose when to apply for them and when, within the time permitted by law, to execute them (*Ex parte Fitzpatrick*).

A constable may seize and retain anything for which a search has been authorised under such a warrant (s. 8(2)).

By s. 23 of the PACE 1984, in all provisions of the Act, 'premises' includes any place, not only buildings, and in particular includes:

(a)   Any vehicle, vessel, aircraft or hovercraft.
(b)   Any offshore installation within the Mineral Workings (Offshore Installations) Act 1971, s. 1.
(c)   Any tent or movable structure.

The 1984 Act power is in addition to powers provided in other statutes, e.g., Betting, Gaming and Lotteries Act 1963, s. 51; Children Act 1989, s. 48; Criminal Damage Act 1971, s. 6(1); Firearms Act 1968, s. 46; Misuse of Drugs Act 1971, s. 23(3); Obscene Publications Act 1959, s. 3; Theft Act 1968, s. 26(1) and (3). Also preserved are powers of the police to enter and search premises on the written authority of a police officer, normally of the rank of at least superintendent. However, all statutory powers of search enacted before the PACE 1984 have ceased to have effect in relation to items subject to legal professional privilege, excluded material and special procedure material consisting of documents or other records (PACE 1984, s. 9(2)).

Under the Prevention of Terrorism (Temporary Provisions) Act 1989, sch. 7, para. 2A, a justice of the peace may issue a warrant to search non-residential premises if he is satisfied that a terrorism investigation is being carried out and that there are reasonable grounds for believing that there is material on the premises which is likely to be of substantial value to the investigation. He must further be satisfied that the material does not consist of or include items subject to legal privilege, excluded material, or special procedure material.

Items Subject to Legal Privilege

D1.42   The term 'items subject to legal privilege' is defined in the PACE 1984, s. 10(1). It includes, of course, lawyer-client communications when giving legal advice. But it goes beyond this and includes communications between either of these or a representative and another person if it was in connection with or in contemplation of and for the purpose of legal proceedings. It also includes items enclosed with or referred to in any of these communications when such items are in the possession of a person entitled to possession of them. If such items are in the possession of a person not so entitled it would appear that the protection afforded by the PACE 1984 is lost. Material in the hands of a solicitor which is not subject to legal privilege is special procedure material (*Norwich Crown Court, ex parte Chethams* [1991] COD 271).

However, in accordance with the common-law rule governing privilege (see **F9.17**), if any items are held with the intention of furthering a criminal purpose they are not to be regarded as items subject to legal privilege (s. 10(2)).

Excluded Material

D1.43   'Excluded material' means certain material *if it is held in confidence*. That material is (PACE 1984, s. 11(1)):

(a)   Personal records acquired or created in a trade, business, profession or other occupation or for the purpose of any office, paid or unpaid.

(b)   Human tissue or tissue fluid taken for purposes of diagnosis or medical treatment.
(c)   Journalistic material consisting of documents or records.

Material of types (a) and (b) is held in confidence if there is an express or implied undertaking to that effect, or a statutory requirement to restrict disclosure or maintain secrecy (s. 11(2)). Material of type (c) will be held in confidence if it is held subject to such an undertaking, restriction or obligation and has been so held since it was first acquired or created for the purpose of journalism (s. 11(3)). It cannot acquire the status of excluded material at a later time just to avoid a search and seizure.

'Personal records' means records concerning an individual (living or dead) who can be identified from them, and relating to that person's physical or mental health, spiritual counselling, or counselling for his personal welfare by a voluntary organisation, or a person with responsibility for so doing, either by virtue of his office or occupation or on authority from a court to supervise that person (e.g., probation officers, clergymen) (s. 12). Hospital records of patients' admissions and discharges are excluded material because they relate to the physical or mental health of persons who could be identified from them (*Cardiff Crown Court, ex parte Kellam* (1993) *The Times*, 3 May 1993).

'Journalistic material' means material acquired or created for the purposes of journalism, but only if it is in the possession of a person who acquired it or created it for that purpose. That person will be deemed to have acquired it for that purpose if it was given to him with the intention that it be used for that purpose (s. 13).

Special Procedure Material

'Special procedure material' means (PACE 1984, s. 14(1) and (2)):   **D1.44**

(a)   'journalistic material' other than that already falling within the meaning of excluded material; and
(b)   material, other than items subject to legal privilege and excluded material, acquired or created in a trade, business, profession or occupation, or for the purpose of any office paid or unpaid, *where it is held in confidence* subject to an express or implied undertaking to that effect or a statutory requirement to restrict disclosure or maintain secrecy.

Material acquired by an employee in the course of his employment, or by a company from an associated company, will be special procedure material only if it was so immediately before it was acquired (s. 14(3)); it cannot later be redesignated as confidential. Material created by an employee in the course of his employment, or by a company on behalf of an associated company, will be special procedure material only if it would have been had the employer or associated company created it (s. 14(4) and (5)).

Holding material in confidence is an essential ingredient of both excluded material and special procedure material.

Order for Access Made by Circuit Judge

The PACE 1984, s. 9(1), enables access to be obtained to excluded material and special **D1.45**
procedure material for the purposes of a criminal investigation if the procedures set out in sch. 1 to the Act are followed.

An application must be made to a circuit judge who may make an order requiring the person in possession of the material to produce it to a constable for him to take away, or to give a constable access to it, within a specified period, normally seven days (sch. 1, para. 4). Once such an order has been made it cannot be rescinded; the only recourse is judicial review (*Liverpool Crown Court, ex parte Wimpey plc* [1991] Crim LR 635).

Before an order to produce or a search warrant is applied for, careful consideration must be given to what material it is hoped a search might reveal, and the application must also make it clear that the material sought relates to the crime under investigation (*Central Criminal Court, ex parte AJD Holdings* [1992] Crim LR 669). An order to produce special procedure material may be made even though some of the material is not of that description. This avoids making separate but necessarily sequential applications (*Preston Crown Court, ex parte McGrath* [1993] COD 103).

The person against whom the order is to be made is not entitled to be given notice of the application. He may be heard where the judge thinks it helpful to hear him, but this will not be appropriate where notice to the person might impede the progress of the investigation; conversely, it may be appropriate where documents are held by a bank (*Leeds Crown Court, ex parte Hill* [1991] COD 197).

The approach which a circuit judge should take towards applications is set out in *Crown Court at Lewes, ex parte Hill* (1991) 93 Cr App R 60. The court stated that the Act provides a careful balance between the public interest in the effective investigation and prosecution of crime and the interests of citizens in protecting their personal and property rights. The circuit judge is entrusted with the primary duty of giving effect to that scheme. He must exercise his powers with great care and caution. He must be shown such material as is necessary to enable him to be satisfied before making the order, and he should be told anything which, to the knowledge of the applicant, might weigh against his making such an order (*Leeds Crown Court, ex parte Hill*; *Acton Crown Court, ex parte Layton* [1993] Crim LR 458). He should not allow the police to engage in a fishing expedition. Any order which he makes must be specific as to the material sought.

A judge may make an access order only if he is satisfied on a balance of probabilities that one of the sets of access conditions is fulfilled. If the conditions are made out, the judge cannot refuse an order (*Northamptonshire Magistrates' Court, ex parte DPP* (1991) 93 Cr App R 376).

The first set of access conditions (sch. 1, para. 2) requires that:

    (a)   There are reasonable grounds for believing that a serious arrestable offence has been committed and that on the premises there is special procedure material which is likely to be of substantial value to the investigation and is likely to be relevant evidence. Material is not relevant evidence simply because it could be used as the basis for cross-examination (*Norwich Crown Court, ex parte Chethams* [1991] COD 271).

    (b)   Other methods of obtaining the special procedure material have failed or have not been tried because it appeared they would be bound to fail. Thus if, for example, a motion under the Bankers' Books Evidence Act 1879 (see **F8.27**) would be possible, it must be shown that such a motion was brought and failed or that the material could not have been secured by such a motion (*Crown Court at Lewes, ex parte Hill*). An application cannot however be impugned simply because some further and remote step to uncover evidence might possibly have been taken.

    (c)   It is in the public interest to produce or allow access to the material, having regard to the benefit to the investigation and the circumstances under which the person holds the material.

The second set of access conditions (sch. 1, para. 3) requires that there are reasonable grounds for believing that there is excluded material on the premises, in respect of which the issue of a warrant by a magistrate would have been appropriate and available but for the repeal by s. 9(2) of all the provisions allowing a magistrate to issue warrants to search for this type of material.

Notice of an application to make an order must be served on the person in possession of the material (sch. 1, para. 8). That person may not conceal, destroy, alter or dispose of the material without leave of a judge or written permission of a constable until the application is dismissed or abandoned, or he has complied with the order (para. 11). Failure to comply with an order is to be treated as a contempt of court (para. 15).

Bodies such as banks in respect of which such applications are made often let them go by default. It is thus particularly important the the judge be given adequate material to enable him to form a reliable judgment. This will include details of the charges, the dates covered by them, whether previous steps to secure the evidence have been tried and failed, and what the nature of the material is.

A suspect has no statutory right to be heard on an application for access, but the judge may in his discretion hear him where this appears likely to be helpful (*Crown Court at Lewes, ex parte Hill*).

Search Warrant Issued by Circuit Judge

There are circumstances in which, on an application by a constable, a judge may issue **D1.46** a warrant authorising a constable to enter and search premises (PACE 1984, sch. 1, para. 12). The approach which a circuit judge must take towards an application for a search warrant is set out in *Crown Court at Lewes, ex parte Hill* (1991) 93 Cr App R 60 (see **D1.45**).

In the case of excluded material the judge must be satisfied that the second set of access conditions (see **D1.45**) is fulfilled and that there has been a failure to comply with an order. He may also issue a warrant to enter and search premises if he is satisfied that either set of access conditions is fulfilled and that any of the following are also fulfilled (sch. 1, para. 14):

    (a)   that it is not practicable to communicate with a person entitled to grant entry; or
    (b)   if it is, that it is not practicable to communicate with a person entitled to grant access; or
    (c)   that there is a statutory restriction on disclosure or obligation of secrecy and disclosure would be in breach of the statute unless a warrant is issued; or
    (d)   that service of notice of an application for an order would seriously prejudice the investigation.

The term 'practicable' bears a wider meaning than feasible or phyically possible. The court may consider not only the available means of communication, but also all the circumstances, including the nature of the inquiries and the persons against whom they are directed. For example, the usual procedure where a solicitor's office is to be searched would be by order to produce, but a search warrant may be proper where the firm is under investigation (*Leeds Crown Court, ex parte Switalski* [1991] Crim LR 559; *Maidstone Crown Court, ex parte Waitt* [1988] Crim LR 384; *Central Criminal Court, ex parte Hutchinson* [1996] COD 14).

A constable may seize and retain anything for which such a search has been authorised (sch. 1, para. 13).

An application for a search warrant under this provision should be made on the authority of an officer of at least the rank of inspector, but where no such officer is on duty, the senior officer on duty may authorise an application (Code of Practice B, para. 2.4).

Safeguards

Courts have consistently held that the issue of a search warrant is very severe interference **D1.47** with individual liberty. It is a step which should be taken only after mature consideration of the facts and in some, doubtless exceptional instances, the judge should give reasons for his decision (*Southwark Crown Court and HM Customs and Excise, ex parte Sorsky Defries* [1996] Crim LR 195).

All entries on and searches of premises under a warrant issued *under any enactment* are unlawful unless they comply with ss. 15 and 16 of the PACE 1984. Thus failure by a constable to produce a warrant and provide the occupier with a copy will render the resulting search unlawful and the police will be obliged to return any seized articles (*Chief Constable of Lancashire, ex parte Parker* [1993] QB 577). Assuming the warrant to be valid, the question, in respect of any seizure made thereunder is whether the acts performed fell within the acts authorised by the warrant. A trivial excess of power in taking an object not authorised by the warrant will not vitiate the legality of a search (*IRC, ex parte Rossminster* [1980] AC 952; *A-G of Jamaica* v *Williams* [1998] AC 351; *Chief Constable of the Warwickshire Constabulary, ex parte Fitzpatrick* [1999] 1 WLR 564). The ideal remains that of a principled search (*Reynolds* v *Commissioner of Police of the Metropolis* [1985] QB 881. Thus, where constables are executing a warrant under s. 8 of the PACE 1984, they should ensure both that the material to be seized falls within the terms of the warrant and, because such a warrant is granted to search for material of evidential value, that there are reasonable grounds for believing it to be so and to be likely to be of substantial value in the investigation. While it may not be possible to specify with great precision the nature of the articles to be searched for, the police may not seize items found in the premises to be searched unless they fall within the stated offence or there are reasonable grounds for believing that they are likely to be of value in the investigation or to be evidence of the stated offence. A police officer executing a warrant is not entitled to remove items from premises in order to sift through them to determine whether they fall within the scope of the warrant. There is no absolute prohibition on seizing an item which is in fact subject to legal professional privilege provided that the police officer seizing the item did not have reasonable grounds for believing the item to be privileged (*Chesterfield Justices, ex parte Bramley* (1999) *The Times*, 10 November 1999). If the warrant in question is a magistrates' warrant, the police must, in addition, satisfy themselves as far as possible that the material seized does not fall within the categories of special procedure, excluded, or legally privileged material. It may be that a constable may rely in assessing material for seizure upon information not before the magistrate when a search warrant was issued (*Ex parte Fitzpatrick*). On what may be seized by a constable lawfully in premises, see **D1.50**.

On application for a warrant, a constable has a duty to state the ground on which the application is made, the enactment under which the warrant would issue, the premises concerned, and, so far as is practicable, the articles or persons sought (s. 15(2)). A constable who wishes to search only a part of premises divided into separate dwellings and the common parts of those premises must make this clear in the information when applying for the warrant (*South Western Magistrates' Court, ex parte Cofie* [1996] 1 WLR 885). The application will be made *ex parte* but must be supported by an information in writing (s. 15(3)). The constable must answer on oath any questions put to him by the justice of the peace or the judge at a hearing of an application (s. 15(4)).

A warrant can only authorise entry on one occasion (s.15(5)). It must specify the name of the person applying for it, the date of issue, the Act under which it is issued, the premises to be searched, and, so far as is practicable, the identity of the articles or persons sought (s. 15(6)). Two copies, clearly certified as such, must be made of the warrant (s. 15(7) and (8)).

Code of Practice B applies to all applications for a search warrant, not just those made under the 1984 Act.

It requires, *inter alia*, that an officer check the accuracy of his information, and where possible the motive behind the giving of the information. It also prohibits any application being made on the basis of information provided anonymously. The officer must also try to ascertain as much information as possible about the premises to be searched, the likely occupier and the articles concerned. Where any adverse effect on community relations might occur the community liaison officer of the force must be consulted, unless the search is needed urgently. Furthermore, a constable must not, when applying for a warrant, state that the purposes of the search will be frustrated or prejudiced unless immediate access is granted where he does not believe this to be so. In particular no such statement can properly be made where the subject of the search has already demonstrated that he is prepared to cooperate in producing material. Police acting in conjunction with another agency must form their own opinion whether it is necessary to apply for a warrant (*Reading Justices, ex parte South West Meat Ltd* [1992] Crim LR 672).

No application for a search warrant may be made without the authority of an officer of at least the rank of inspector, except in the case of urgency when it must be authorised by the senior officer on duty. In the case of an application for a production order under sch. 1, authorisation must be given by an officer of at least the rank of superintendent (Code B, para. 2.4).

If an application is refused, no further application may be made unless supported by additional grounds.

Subsections (1) to (4) of s. 16 of the Act provide that a warrant may be executed by any constable and may authorise persons to accompany him. 'Such other person' does not refer to one who might assist in a purely ancillary capacity such as those skilled in opening cabinets. It permits the police, when executing a warrant to search under the Taxes Management Act 1970, s. 20C, to take with them a lawyer for the purpose of determining whether any of the documents found during the search are subject to legal professional privilege (*Commissioners of Inland Revenue, ex parte Tamosius & Partners* (1999) *The Times*, 10 November 1999). The police when acting with another body are responsible for the execution of the warrant. The number of other persons who accompany the police should be limited. The fundamental principle is that the police must not delegate their powers in such a way as to occupy a role ancillary to that of the other agency (*Ex parte South West Meat Ltd*). It must be executed within one month of its issue, but only at a reasonable hour unless the purpose of the search would be frustrated. The search must be limited to the purpose for which the warrant was issued.

Where the occupier of premises is present the constable must identify himself and, if not in uniform, produce his identity (warrant) card, produce the search warrant and supply a copy to the occupier (s. 16(5)). If the occupier is not present then the constable must do these things for the person who appears to be in charge of the premises (s. 16(7)). If there is no person present who appears to be in charge then a copy of the warrant must be left in a prominent place on the premises (s. 16(7)).

An executed warrant must be endorsed with information about whether the articles or persons sought were found, and whether any other articles were seized (s. 16(9)).

After a warrant has been executed, or if it has not been executed within the prescribed time, it must be returned either to the clerk to the justices or, if it was issued by a judge, to the appropriate court officer (s. 16(10)). Returned warrants are to be retained by those persons for 12 months (s. 16(11)). This is so that the occupier of the premises to which the warrant related may exercise his right under s. 16(12) to inspect the warrant.

ENTRY WITHOUT WARRANT

Entry to Arrest

The PACE 1984, s. 17(1), empowers a constable to enter and search any premises: **D1.48**

(a)   To execute a warrant of arrest or commitment.

(b)   To arrest a person for an arrestable offence.

(c)   To arrest a person for any offence under the Public Order Act 1936, s. 1 (prohibition of uniforms in connection with political objects) or the Public Order Act 1986, s. 4 (fear or provocation of violence).

(d)   To arrest a child or young person who has been remanded or committed to local authority accommodation under s. 23(1) of the CYPA 1969.

(e)   To recapture a person unlawfully at large while liable to be detained in a prison, remand centre, young offender institution, or secure training centre, or in pursuance of s. 53 of the CYPA 1969 in any other place.

(f)   If he is in uniform, to arrest for any offence under ss. 6, 7, 8 and 10 of the Criminal Law Act 1977 (offences relating to entering and remaining on property) or s. 76 of the CJPO 1994 (failure to comply with interim possession order).

(g)   To recapture a person who is unlawfully at large and whom he is pursuing.

(h)   To save life or limb or prevent serious damage to property.

When entering premises, including dwellings, to search for a person (except for the purpose of saving life or preventing property damage), the constable must have reasonable grounds for believing that the person he is seeking is on the premises (s. 17(2)(a)). A constable may enter any dwelling in which he has reasonable grounds for believing the suspect to be, and, where the premises consist of two or more dwellings, he may enter any parts of the premises used in common by the occupiers (s. 17(2)(b)).

A constable may enter premises by force where it is necessary to do so. Where the occupier of the premises is present and can be spoken to, forcible entry will not be justified unless the constable explains by what right and for what purpose he seeks to enter. That reason must be lawful: a wish to talk to a suspect cannot, for example, be elided into a wish to arrest a suspect. There is an exception to the duty above where the circumstances are such as to make it impossible, impracticable or unnecessary to make such an explanation to the occupier (*O'Loughlin* v *Chief Constable of Essex* [1998] 1 WLR 374).

Any search made must be restricted to that which is reasonably required to achieve the object of the search (s. 17(4)).

The provisions of the 1984 Act are quite comprehensive and were intended to replace most of the powers which constables previously had to enter premises. The power under the Criminal Law Act 1967, s. 2(6), to enter and arrest a person for an arrestable offence was repealed and re-enacted in s. 17(1)(b) of the 1984 Act. Also repealed are those common-law powers to enter which a constable had, except for any power of entry to deal with or prevent a breach of the peace (s. 17(5) and (6)). These common-law powers of entry were defined by Donaldson LJ in *Swales* v *Cox* [1981] QB 849 to be: entry by a constable or a citizen in order to prevent murder, entry by a constable or a citizen if a felony had been or was about to be committed, and entry by a constable only following an affray. These situations are now covered by the 1984 Act.

Swales v *Cox* did not deal with the question of entry when there is a breach of the peace. A power of entry in such circumstances has been recognised at least since it was held in *Thomas* v *Sawkins* [1935] 2 KB 249 that the police are entitled to enter and remain on premises to prevent a breach of the peace, i.e., to prevent it from starting or prevent it from continuing. The power to enter to deal with a breach of the peace is of greater antiquity.

The power under s. 17(1)(d) extends to entry to retake a mental patient unlawfully at large provided that such a patient is liable to be retaken and returned to a hospital and provided that the pursuit of such person is almost contemporaneous with the entry to the premises, a term which is somewhat wider than 'hot pursuit'. Where the element of contemporaneity cannot be satisfied, but the situation is one of real emergency, the police could enter the premises in reliance on s. 17(6) (*D'Souza* v *DPP* (1993) 96 Cr App R 278).

Entry and Search after Arrest

A constable may enter and search any premises occupied or controlled by a person who **D1.49** is under arrest for an arrestable offence if the constable has reasonable grounds for suspecting that there is on the premises evidence (other than items subject to legal privilege) relating to that offence or to some other arrestable offence which is connected with or similar to that offence (PACE 1984, s. 18(1)). The premises must as a fact, or perhaps as a matter of mixed fact and law, be occupied or controlled by the person under arrest if the search is to be lawful. A senior officer cannot make lawful that which is unlawful simply by granting his authority (*Krohn* v *DPP* [1997] COD 345). As with entry to arrest, it is submitted that a constable must first demand entry (where this is practicable) before resorting to force (see **D1.48**).

The constable may seize and retain anything for which he may search (s. 18(2)). The scope of the search must be restricted to that which is reasonably required for the purpose of discovering such evidence (s. 18(3)).

There are limitations on this power to enter and search after arrest. Generally it must be authorised in writing by an officer of at least the rank of inspector (s. 18(4)). However, a constable may search without this authorisation, and without first taking the arrested person to the police station, if that person's presence is necessary at some other place for the effective investigation of the offence (s. 18(5)). If a constable does search then he must inform an officer of at least the rank of inspector as soon as practicable (s. 18(6)).

An officer who authorises or is informed under s. 18(6) of such a search must make a written record of the grounds for the search and the nature of the evidence sought (s. 18(7)). If the person in occupation or control of the premises at the time of the search is in police detention at the time the record is to be made then it must be made a part of his custody record (s. 18(8)).

While the authorisation requirements of s. 18 are mandatory, a failure to comply with them fully (as by not specifying precisely the grounds of the search and the property to be searched for) will not necessarily render the search unlawful. While the section is to be obeyed, the court will, in determining the consequences of any breach, have regard to whether the failure to record prejudiced the person arrested (*Krohn*).

SEIZURE OF, ACCESS TO AND RETENTION OF MATERIALS

A constable who is lawfully on any premises has power: **D1.50**

    (a)   To seize anything which is on the premises if he has reasonable grounds to believe that it has been obtained in consequence of the commission of an offence, or that it is evidence in relation to an offence, and that it is necessary to seize it in order to prevent it being concealed, lost, altered or destroyed (PACE 1984, s. 19(2) and (3)).

    (b)   Where he has similar reasonable grounds, to require that information which is contained in a computer and is accessible from the premises be produced in a visible and legible form which can be taken away (s. 19(4)).

This power is in addition to any power otherwise conferred (s. 19(5)). However, no power to seize given under any statute applies to items which the constable has reasonable grounds to suspect are subject to legal privilege (s. 19(6)).

Section 19 gives statutory authority to seize that which the courts had previously decided could be seized, i.e., material evidence of a crime (*Chic Fashions* (*West Wales*) *Ltd* v *Jones*

[1968] 2 QB 299; *Garfinkel* v *Metropolitan Police Commissioner* [1972] Crim LR 44) or the fruit of the crime (*Ghani* v *Jones* [1970] 1 QB 693). The power applies whenever the constable is lawfully on any premises either by virtue of a warrant or at common law, or with the consent of a person. Where a constable is on premises with consent and begins to look around, but before he finds anything is asked to leave, he becomes a trespasser if he refuses to leave, and any search or seizure would not be within the statute and would be unlawful.

Where a constable has statutory power to enter and search, and seize material, he can require that any computerised information accessible from the premises be produced in a visible and legible form that can be taken away (s. 20).

On the request of either the occupier of premises or the person in control of the item immediately before seizure, the constable must provide a record for what was seized within a reasonable time of the request (s. 21(1) and (2)). If requested by the person who had custody or control of the item immediately before it was seized, the officer in charge of the investigation must allow that person access to the item under the supervision of a constable (s. 21(3)). Similarly he must allow access for photographing or copying, or get it photographed or copied himself and supply it to the person requesting within a reasonable time (s. 21(4), (6) and (7)). A constable may also photograph or copy anything he has power to seize without such a request (s. 21(5)). The requests do not need to be acceded to if there are reasonable grounds to believe that it would prejudice any investigation, or any criminal proceedings resulting therefrom (s. 21(8)).

Anything seized by a constable under his statutory power may be retained as long as is necessary in all the circumstances (s. 22(1)). In particular, anything seized for the purposes of a criminal investigation may be retained for use as evidence at a trial, or forensic examination or further investigation, unless a photograph or copy would suffice, and where there are reasonable grounds for believing it has been obtained in consequence of the commission of an offence, anything may be retained in order to establish its lawful owner (s. 22(2) and (4)). The police cannot retain items seized because they may be used to cause physical injury, or to damage property, or to interfere with evidence, or to assist in escape from lawful custody, when the person from whom they were seized is no longer in police detention or the custody of the court, or has been released on bail (s. 22(3)).

It follows from these provisions that the only permitted use of seized articles is for the purpose of investigating and prosecuting crime, after which they must be returned to their true owner. Documents and information may be communicated to others for the purpose of investigation and prosecution, and may perhaps be disclosed to other public authorities. They may not be made available to private individuals for private purposes (*Marcel* v *Commissioner of Police for the Metropolis* [1992] Ch 225).

Section 22(5) declares that the provisions of s. 22 do not affect the power of a court to make an order in respect of property under the Police (Property) Act 1897, s. 1. Anyone claiming property seized by the police should be advised of this procedure where appropriate.

Code of Practice B, para. 7.1, requires that records be kept of all searches of premises and that the records must include the address of the premises searched, the date and time of the search, the authority under which the search was made, e.g., statutory power to search without warrant, the power, or a copy of the warrant or a copy of the written consent, the names of the officers who searched, the names of any persons on the premises if known, list of articles seized, whether force used, and any damage caused.

At each subdivisional police station a search register must be kept in which all records of searches must be noted (Code B, para. 8.1).

INTERCEPTION OF COMMUNICATIONS AND SURVEILLANCE OF PREMISES

This is dealt with under the Interception of Communications Act 1985 which applies **D1.51** to the post and to messages sent by a public telecommunications system (Interception of Communications Act 1985, ss. 2 and 10). The Act applies to all public telecommunications systems including links between British systems and those linking this country with other countries. All forms of telecommunications, whatever their nature, are covered, but the statute does not apply to messages across a system which is not 'comprised in' a public telecommunications system. It thus does not apply to cordless telephones since such an apparatus, though connected to such a system, is not comprised in it (*Effik* [1995] 1 AC 309).

Interception of such communications may only lawfully be conducted under warrant granted by the Secretary of State (Interception of Communications Act 1985, s. 2). The grounds for issue of such a warrant are: national security, for the purpose of preventing or detecting serious crime (in practice crime for which a sentence of three years' imprisonment on first conviction would be justified), or for the purpose of safeguarding the economic well-being of the United Kingdom (s. 2(2)(a) to (c)). It must be shown that other methods are likely to fail.

The warrant permits the interception of such communications as are sent from addresses specified in the warrant. The warrant is specific as to the person to or from whom or the premises to or from which messages are to be intercepted. The examination of communications selected by reference to particular addresses in the United Kingdom is authorised only for the purpose of preventing acts of terrorism (s. 3). The warrant power does not, however, extend to the amassing of *evidence* with a view to prosecution; all material must be destroyed as soon as its retention is no longer necessary for the prevention or detection of serious crime (*Preston* [1994] 2 AC 130).

A warrant must be issued by the Secretary of State personally, save that in case of urgency it may be issued by his delegate (s. 4). A warrant issued personally by the Secretary of State is valid, unless renewed or further renewed, for a period of six months. If issued under the emergency procedure, it is valid until the end of the second working day following the day of issue. The Secretary of State may personally renew a warrant at any time before its expiry, and may, conversely, cancel the warrant before it would otherwise expire. He may modify a warrant by inserting any address which he considers likely to be used for the transmission of messages to or from a particular person or set of premises (s. 5). He may modify the certificate so as to include other material, he may delete an address, and he may exclude material from the category of certified material (s. 5(2) and (3)).

A person who considers that communications to or from him have been unlawfully intercepted may apply to a tribunal established under the Act for an investigation. The tribunal may, if it considers that the statutory requirements have been breached, *inter alia*, order the payment of compensation to the person aggrieved (s. 7). Unfortunately, the Secretary of State is not obliged to inform a person that he is the object of surveillance, and it is unlikely, therefore, that the machinery will be much used.

The provisions of the Interception of Communications Act 1985 do not apply to cases where a line is tapped with the subscriber's consent. In such a case, evidence obtained by means of such a tap is admissible (*Rasool* [1997] 1 WLR 1092).

Interception of communications is lawful where it takes place under warrant of the Secretary of State, or is done for the provision of telecommunication services, their operation or engineering. However, it is an offence for a person engaged in the running of a public telecommunications system intentionally to disclose to any person the contents of an intercepted message or any information concerning the use made of telecommunications services provided for any other person by means of that system (Telecommunications Act 1984, s. 45(1)).

Electronic surveillance other than that which is provided for above is now regulated by statute. The Police Act 1997 provides for the use of surveillance devices. Part III of the Act allows for the authorisation of entry upon and interference with property by the police, Customs and Excise, National Criminal Intelligence Service and the National Crime Squad. Authority may be given for such an activity where the authorising officer believes that it is necessary to give authorisation on the ground that it is likely to be of substantial value in the prevention or detection of serious crime and that what that action seeks to achieve cannot be achieved by other means (s. 93(2)). By serious crime is meant conduct which involves the use of violence, results in substantial financial gain, or is conduct by a large number of persons in pursuit of a common purpose, where the offence is one for which an offender aged 21 or more with no prior criminal record could expect to be sentenced to a term of three years' imprisonment or more, or where it relates to an assigned matter within the meaning of the Customs and Excise Management Act 1979 (s. 93(4)).

Where the property concerned is used wholly or mainly as a dwelling or a room in a hotel, or constitutes office premises, and the action to be authorised is likely to result in any person acquiring knowledge of matters covered by legal professional privilege, confidential personal information, or confidential journalistic material, authority may be given only by a Commissioner (s. 97). Each of these terms are extensively defined (s. 98). Commissioners are designated serving or former High Court judges.

The exercise of powers by persons other than Commissioners is regulated by a Code of Practice.

Evidence obtained by the use of such surveillance practices is admissible in evidence subject to the normal rules of evidence.

It may, parenthetically, be noted that the Security Service may obtain warrants authorising intrusive acts upon property in cases of serious crime. It would seem that such warrants may be obtained from the Secretary of State (Security Services Act 1996, s. 2). In this instance it is assumed that the Security Service will be concerned in the investigation of crime and not in relation to intelligence activities as such.

A Home Office circular to the police details arrangements in which postmasters and telephone managers have authority to assist the police when the latter are engaged in the investigation of crime, or in assisting a government department in relation to a document which it has issued. Home Office circulars also regulate the use of listening devices and aural and visual surveillance procedures. The criteria are virtually the same as those which apply under the Interception of Communications Act 1985, but the procedure is wholly extra-statutory.

As to offences concerned with the interception of telecommunication messages, see generally **B9.96** *et seq*.

TERRORIST INVESTIGATIONS

D1.52   Schedule 7 to the Prevention of Terrorism (Temporary Provisions) Act 1989 makes provision for orders to produce and to seize material which is akin to that made under the PACE 1984 concerning criminal investigations. As to offences involving terrorism generally, see **B10**. As to special powers of stop and search, see **D1.2**.

A justice of the peace may issue a warrant to search for and seize material which it is reasonably believed is on particular premises and is likely to be of substantial value to the investigation. It need not, however, have evidential value (sch. 7, para. 2). No such warrant may be issued in respect of items subject to legal privilege, or excluded or special procedure material, these latter terms bearing the same definition as in the PACE 1984 (see **D1.42** to **D1.44**).

Any of the following conditions must be made out: that it is not practicable to communicate with any person entitled to grant access to the premises; that it is not practicable to communicate with a person entitled to give access to the material; that a warrant is necessary to secure entry to the premises; or that immediate entry is required to avoid frustration or serious prejudice to the enquiry. A constable may enter and seize anything (other than legally privileged material) found on the premises or on any person found on the premises if he has reasonable grounds for thinking that it is likely to be of substantial value to the investigation, and that it is necessary to seize it in order to prevent it being concealed, lost, damaged or destroyed. It is clear from the foregoing that the right to seize extends beyond matter actually specified in the warrant.

The 1989 Act also provides for orders for the production of excluded or special procedure material (para. 3). Application must be made to a circuit judge. Unlike the procedure under the PACE 1984, no special restriction applies to excluded material. There must be a reasonable belief that the material is of substantial value to the investigation and that its production is justified in the public interest. A warrant may issue where an order for production has not been complied with or where it is not practicable to communicate with a person entitled to grant access to the premises or the material, or immediate access is necessary in order to avoid prejudice to the investigation. Powers of seizure as wide as those discussed above in connection with magistrates' warrants apply (sch. 7, paras 4 and 5).

A circuit judge may require any person to provide an explanation of any material the production of which has been obtained by order or which has been obtained by warrant under these procedures, including a search warrant issued by a magistrate. Legally privileged information is exempt from disclosure, save that a lawyer may be required to disclose the name of his client. Such a statement may be used in evidence on a prosecution for giving a false statement in purported compliance with the paragraph, or on a prosecution for some other offence where he makes a statement inconsistent with it (para. 6).

If a police officer of at least the rank of superintendent has reasonable grounds for believing that the case is one of great urgency and that the interests of the State so require, he may authorise a search and call for explanations, subject to an obligation to notify the Secretary of State (para. 7).

A superintendent may on application to the Chief Land Registrar obtain access to information held in the Land Register (para. 9).

The powers of seizure conferred by sch. 7 are (by para. 10 of the schedule) without prejudice to powers conferred by the PACE 1984, s. 19.

INTERROGATION OF SUSPECTS

The Codes

The interrogation of suspects is governed partly by common law, partly by the PACE **D1.53** 1984, but primarily by Code of Practice C made under s. 66 of the 1984 Act. Code C contains rules regulating the treatment of persons who are being questioned, and the questioning itself. Code C must be followed not only by constables but by others, such as store detectives, who are charged with the investigation of crime (s. 67(9)). Whether a person is so charged is a question of fact in each case; one test is whether a prosecution might be commenced as a result of the investigation concerned (*Bayliss* (1994) 98 Cr App R 235). It would seem that this is not an exclusive test: pragmatic considerations concerning the capacity of the interviewer to follow the Code may apply depending on the context and the status of the person concerned. Code C does not, for example, apply where a head teacher interviews a teacher who is alleged to have assaulted a pupil. Unfairness can be dealt with by the exclusion of evidence (*DPP* v *Goodfellow* [1998] COD 94). In respect of a public body, it is irrelevant whether the body is required to investigate offences (*Smith* [1994] 1 WLR 1396).

Breach of Code C may cause evidence to be excluded. For detailed treatment of this subject, see **F17.12** *et seq*.

The conditions which apply to the actual interview are set out in some detail in the code. The custody officer must determine whether to deliver a person whom a police officer wishes to interview or to have with him while conducting an inquiry into the custody of that officer (Code C, para. 12.1). Investigating officers may require to take the suspect into their custody, for example, where they desire to visit a place, whether the suspect's premises or elsewhere, to search for evidence.

Code C deals with two aspects of interviews. The first (Code C, sects 8 and 9) concerns the conditions in which interviews are to take place, the physical treatment of the suspect, and the like and is not dealt with in detail here. The full text of the code is given in **appendix 2**. The second concerns what practices may not be engaged in by the police and is directed towards ensuring against oppressive practices at the interrogation itself. Some matters are common to both aspects.

Interviews Generally

D1.54 'Interview' is widely defined by Code C, para. 11.1A, in purposive terms. An interview is the questioning of a person regarding his involvement or suspected involvement in a criminal offence or offences which, by virtue of para. 10.1, is required to be carried out under caution. The giving of an opportunity to a suspected person to say anything more where an officer decides that the point has come where he has enough evidence to charge is an interview within the definition of para. 11.1A (*Pointer* [1997] Crim LR 676). Code C, consistently with the common law, specifies that questioning a person only to establish his identity or the ownership of a vehicle or to obtain information in accordance with any relevant statutory requirements (for example under the Road Traffic Act 1988) does not constitute an interview (see *Marsh* [1991] Crim LR 455), nor does questioning which is confined to the proper and effective conduct of a search (*Gilbert* (1977) 66 Cr App R 237; *Knight* (1905) 20 Cox CC 711). Thus an informal conversation which does not relate to the circumstances of an offence which the police are investigating is not an interview (*Pullen* [1991] Crim LR 457). Questions asked of a person not to verify his identity but to secure admissions do constitute an interview (*Cox* (1993) 96 Cr App R 464). So too do questions intended to elicit an explanation of circumstances which appear to amount to the commission of a criminal offence such as blatant after-hours drinking in a public house (*Batley* v *DPP* (1998) *The Times*, 5 March 1998). An extensive conversation elsewhere than in a police station, for example, a police car, is an interview (see *Parchment* [1989] Crim LR 290). An informal discussion can be an interview (see *Keenan* [1990] 2 QB 54). The critical question for determining whether questioning at the time of arrest is an interview is whether questions are directed towards obtaining admissions on a vital part of the case against the arrested person (*Cox*).

The general rules for the conduct of interviews are contained in Code C, sect. 11. A suspect should only be interviewed about an offence at a police station or other authorised place of detention, but with the following exceptions based upon necessity:

(a)   where delay would lead to interference with or harm to evidence connected with an offence or interference with or physical harm to other persons; or

(b)   where delay would lead to the alerting of other persons suspected of having committed an offence but not yet arrested for it; or

(c)   where delay would hinder the recovery of property obtained in consequence of the commission of an offence.

Interviewing in any of these circumstances should cease once the relevant risk has been averted or the necessary questions have been put (Code C, para. 11.1 and see *Cox*).

It is legitimate for police officers to pursue their interrogation of a suspect with a view to eliciting admissions even where the suspect denies involvement in the offence or declines to answer specific questions. Police questioning which is carried on after repeated denials or refusals may become oppressive. In these circumstances a solicitor present at interview should not remain passive. In the face of oppressive questioning he should intervene since otherwise police officers may fail to appreciate that their conduct has become oppressive (*Paris* (1993) 97 Cr App R 99).

The suspect is entitled to legal advice, and this may be delayed only in the specific circumstances specified in the PACE 1984, ss. 56 and 58 (see **D1.38**). In particular, the suspect has a right to have a solicitor present at any interview. Violations of a suspect's entitlement to legal advice not uncommonly lead to the exclusion of evidence (see **F2.12** and **F17.16**).

The interviewing officer should remind the suspect of his entitlement to free legal advice immediately prior to the commencement or recommencement of any interview (Code C, para. 11.2). A person who requests legal advice may not be interviewed or continue to be interviewed without advice being provided to him unless he is properly being held incommunicado in accordance with the PACE 1984, s. 58, or an officer of the rank of superintendent or above has reasonable grounds for believing that delay will involve an immediate risk of harm to persons or serious loss of, or damage to, property; or where a solicitor, including a duty solicitor, has been contacted and agreed to attend but awaiting his arrival would cause unreasonable delay to the process of investigation; or where attendance by the solicitor nominated by the suspect cannot be secured and the suspect does not want to avail himself of the services of a duty solicitor. In this latter case or where the person has indicated that he does not want legal advice, the interview may be started without further delay. An interview conducted without the presence of a solicitor (where the suspect desires to see a solicitor) on the basis of danger to person or property must cease once sufficient information to avert the risk has been obtained, unless the suspect is properly being held incommunicado or to await the arrival of a solicitor would unduly delay matters (Code C, para. 6.7). A suspect may have his solicitor present during an interview (see **D1.38**). Procedures under the Road Traffic Act 1988, s. 7, do not constitute an interview to which the code applies (*DPP* v *Billington* [1988] 1 WLR 535; Code C, para. 11.1A; *DPP* v *Whalley* [1991] RTR 161).

At the beginning of an interview carried out at a police station, the interviewing officer must put to the suspect any significant statement or silence which occurred prior to his arrival at the police station. Such statement or silence is one which may be used in evidence against the suspect.

No police officer may try to obtain answers to questions or to elicit a statement by the use of oppression, nor shall he indicate, except in answer to a direct question, what action the police will take if the suspect answers or refuses to answer questions or make a statement. If the suspect asks the officer directly what action will be taken in any of those events then the officer may inform the suspect of his proposed action, which could be, for example, retaining the person in detention if further action is to be taken. The proposed action must, however, be proper and warranted (Code C, para. 11.3).

As soon as a police officer believes that a prosecution should be brought against a person and that there is sufficient evidence for it to succeed, he should ask the person whether he has anything more to say. If the person replies in the negative, the officer must cease to question him about that offence (Code C, para. 11.4; and see *Osbourne* [1973] QB 678; *Dodd* (1981) 74 Cr App R 50). Code C, however, permits officers in Revenue cases or acting under the confiscation provisions of the CJA 1988 or the Drug Trafficking Act 1994 to invite suspects to complete a formal question-and-answer record after the interview is completed.

Caution

D1.55   A person whom there are grounds to suspect of an offence must be cautioned before any questions about it (or further questions if it is his answers to previous questions that provide grounds for suspicion) are put to him for the purpose of obtaining evidence which may be given to a court in a prosecution. This rule applies to customs officers as well as police officers (*Okafor* [1994] 3 All ER 741). He need not be cautioned if questions are put for other purposes (Code C, para. 10.1). Where the interviewing officer already suspects the person to be questioned, a caution should be given before any questions are asked (*Cox* (1993) 96 Cr App R 464). Whenever a person who is not under arrest is initially cautioned before or during an interview, he must at the same time be told that he is not under arrest and is not obliged to remain with the officer (Code C, para. 10.2).

A person must be cautioned upon arrest for an offence unless his condition or behaviour makes it impracticable to do so, or he has already been cautioned immediately prior to arrest (Code C, para. 10.3). When there is a break in questioning under caution, the interviewing officer must ensure that the suspect is aware that he remains under caution, and in case of doubt, the caution should be given again (Code C, para. 10.5). If a juvenile or mentally disordered or handicapped person is cautioned in the absence of an appropriate adult, the caution must be repeated in the adult's presence (Code C, para. 10.6). The caution is in terms that the suspect need not say anything but that it may harm his defence if he does not mention something which he later relies on in court and that anything he says may be given in evidence (Code C, para. 10.4: see **F19.6** for the full text of the caution). Code C, paras. 10.5A and 10.5B, provide for special warnings where a suspect is found on arrest with compromising objects, marks or substances and fails to account for these.

It is of fundamental importance that the person cautioned should be clear about the significance of the caution. The officer should, if necessary, explain it in his own words (Code C, note 10C). The suspect may furthermore have to pay a price for his silence in the form of continued detention for the purposes of interrogation. Code C, para. 10.5C provides that a suspect should not be left with the false impression that his continued silence will have no effect on his immediate treatment. It is but a short step from this to inducements of a sort which might provoke a statement. It is submitted that a police officer may, in good faith, assure a suspect that cooperation in the investigation will or may lead to a release on bail if that is what the officer has in mind anyway.

Treatment of Special Categories of Persons

D1.56   A juvenile or a mentally disordered or handicapped person, whether suspected or not, must not be interviewed or asked to provide or sign a written record in the absence of the appropriate adult unless the circumstances are such as to pose an immediate danger to persons or serious harm to property (Code C, para. 11.14 and annexe C). A juvenile should only be interviewed at his place of education in exceptional circumstances and then only if the principal or his nominee agrees. Efforts should be made to notify parents and the appropriate adult. In cases of necessity, and provided that the school was not the victim of the alleged offence, the principal may act as the appropriate adult (Code C, para. 11.15). The appropriate adult is to be reminded of his functions as adviser and observer as well as that of facilitating communication with the person being interviewed (Code C, para. 11.16). As to the special rules applying where a child who is to be interviewed is a ward of court, see **F4.4**.

Deaf persons, as well as those who do not understand or who have difficulty in understanding English may require interpreters. The procedure is outlined in Code C, para. 13. A person who has difficulty in understanding English must be provided with an interpreter, though he may waive this right. If he does wish an interpreter, no interview can proceed without one unless the necessity provisions of annexe C apply. This applies also to deaf persons and in the case of juveniles if the parent or guardian present as the appropriate adult is deaf. A police officer may not interpret where interpretation is needed for the purpose of giving legal advice. Interpretation may be necessary when a suspect is charged.

Intoxicated Persons

Code C, para. 12.3, precludes the questioning of any person who is unfit through drink **D1.57** or drugs to the extent that he is unable to appreciate the significance of questions put to him and his answers unless the necessity provisions of annexe C apply.

Effect of Charge

The decision to charge the suspect may be viewed as the third of three stages in the **D1.58** investigation of a crime which leads to someone being brought before a court for a criminal offence. These stages are:

   (a)   the gathering of information;
   (b)   an intermediate stage where the police officer has the beginnings of suspicion;
   (c)   the final stage where the police officer has enough evidence to lay a charge.

After a charge has been laid, the accused person must be brought speedily before a court (PACE 1984, s. 46). In general, questioning of him must stop (Code C, para. 16.5).

Code C provides that as soon as a police officer believes that a prosecution should be brought against a suspect and there is sufficient evidence for it to succeed and that the person has said all that he wishes to say about the offence, he shall without delay bring him before the custody officer who is then responsible for considering whether or not he should be charged. Where a detained person is suspected of more than one offence it is permissible to delay bringing him before the custody officer until the above conditions are satisfied in respect of all the offences. If the person is a juvenile or suffering from mental disease or handicap, this step is to be performed in the presence of the responsible adult (Code C, para. 16.1). By evidence is meant information which can be put before a court (*Osbourne* [1973] QB 678). The police are not always obliged to charge a suspect where they have some evidence implicating him; they are entitled to take into account the cogency and weight of the evidence (*Dodd* (1982) 74 Cr App R 50).

A person who is charged or informed that he may be prosecuted must be cautioned. He must be given a written notice showing particulars of the offence, and certain information relating to the police officer and station responsible. Particulars of the charge are to be stated in simple terms, but must show the precise offence in law with which he is charged. The notice must also contain the new form of caution. If the person is a juvenile or mentally ill or mentally handicapped, the notice must be given to the appropriate adult (Code C, para. 16.3).

To the rule that questioning must cease after the charge there are three exceptions. The first is where a police officer wishes to bring to the notice of the accused any written statement made by another person or the content of an interview with another person.

In such a case, the officer must hand to the accused a true copy of any such statement or interview record, but he must not do or say anything to invite any reply or comment, except to caution him. A police officer may read the statement or record to an illiterate person. If the person is a juvenile or mentally ill or mentally handicapped, the copy or interview record must be given or shown to the appropriate adult (Code C, para. 16.4). The second exception is that questions may not be put to a person concerning an offence for which he stands charged or in respect of which he has been informed that he may be prosecuted unless questions are necessary for the purpose of preventing or minimising harm or loss to some other person or to the public, or where it is in the interests of justice that the person should have put to him and should have an opportunity to comment on information concerning the offence which has come to light since the charging stage. He must first be cautioned before any such questions are put (Code C, para. 16.5). The third exception relates to the power of the Director of the Serious Fraud Office under the CJA 1987, s. 2 (see **D1.59**).

Code C, para. 16.4, prohibits the confrontation of one accused with the evidence of another. This has long been considered objectionable on the two grounds that it amounts to cross-examination after arrest, and also that such questions and answers may relate to the complicity of a prisoner who may not in the event be called as a witness (*Gardner* (1915) 11 Cr App R 265; *Mills* [1947] KB 297). However, Code C provides against this practice only in respect of a suspect who has been charged.

A custody officer who authorises the continued detention of a juvenile charged with an offence must try to make arrangements for the juvenile to be taken into the care of a local authority to be detained pending his appearance in court (Code C, para. 16.6). Neither a juvenile's unruliness nor the nature of the offence with which he is charged justify retaining him in police custody rather than seeking to arrange his transfer to a local authority, nor does the lack of secure local authority accommodation make it impracticable to transfer him (Code C, note 16B).

Commercial Fraud

D1.59   Different rules apply in relation to investigation of certain serious commercial frauds. While the police are obliged to follow the normal procedure when questioning suspects, including the administration of a caution, the Director of the Serious Fraud Office has power under the CJA 1987, s. 2, to require a person under investigation or any other person whom he has reason to believe has relevant information to produce documents and to provide an explanation of them. This includes the right to re-interview witnesses even following the delivery of a case statement by the defence (*Turner* (1993) *The Times*, 2 July 1993). The Director is not obliged to provide the interviewee with advance information of the subject matter of the interview but he may do so should he deem it helpful and not likely to prejudice the investigation (*Serious Fraud Office, ex parte Maxwell* (1992) *The Independent*, 7 October 1992). Such powers may be used only to provide the Serious Fraud Office with information; they may not be used to produce material useful for the defence (*Re Barlow Clowes Gilt Managers Ltd* [1992] Ch 208). The court has no power to direct liquidators of an insolvent company not to comply with a notice served by the Serious Fraud Office requesting production of transcripts of examinations under the Insolvency Act 1986, s. 236. It is for the judge at the criminal trial to determine whether to admit such a transcript at the criminal trial. The privilege against self-incrimination has been overridden by statute and the admissibility of the transcript is not, of itself, unfair (*Re Arrows Ltd (No. 4)* [1995] 2 AC 75). Legal professional privilege affords a ground for refusing to produce, and it will enure to the benefit of liquidators (*Re Barlow Clowes Gilt Managers Ltd*).

A person who without reasonable excuse fails to comply with a requirement under s. 2 commits an offence punishable on summary conviction with up to six months' imprisonment and/or a fine not exceeding level 5.

It would seem that the fact that a person who is required to answer questions in the course of an enquiry by the Serious Fraud Office is the spouse of a party charged with fraud is not a reasonable excuse for declining to answer questions (*Director of the Serious Fraud Office, ex parte Johnson* [1993] COD 58). This seemingly follows from the consideration that such enquiries are administrative and must represent something of a triumph of form over function.

A statement obtained in response to a requirement under s. 2 may be used in evidence against its maker only on a prosecution for an offence of supplying false information or on a prosecution for another offence where he gives evidence inconsistent with it (s. 2(8)). The fact that such a statement may incriminate its maker is not a reasonable excuse for failing to comply with the Director's order (*Director of Serious Fraud Office, ex parte Smith* [1993] AC 1).

THE DECISION TO PROSECUTE

The Role of the Police

In the case of offences investigated by the police, deciding whether to prosecute is a two-stage process. First, the police themselves, having gathered the evidence and, if appropriate, interviewed the suspect, must decide whether to initiate proceedings. This is a matter within the discretion of the chief officer of the force in question, acting through the officers to whom he delegates his authority. Neither the police authority, nor the government, nor even, subject to one exception, the courts can dictate to the chief officer how he exercises his discretion. In *Metropolitan Police Commissioner, ex parte Blackburn* [1968] 2 QB 118, Lord Denning MR said (at p. 136): **D1.60**

> I hold it to be the duty of the Commissioner of Police of the Metropolis, as it is of every chief constable, to enforce the law of the land. . . . He must decide whether or no suspected persons are to be prosecuted. . . . But [in this] he is not the servant of anyone, save of the law itself. No Minister of the Crown can tell him . . . that he must, or must not, prosecute this man or that one. Nor can any police authority tell him so. The responsibility for law enforcement lies on him. He is answerable to the law and to the law alone.

The one restraint on the chief officer's otherwise unfettered discretion is inherent in Lord Denning's statement that he is answerable to the law. It follows that, if he should operate a policy which amounts to a dereliction of his duty to uphold the law, mandamus could issue requiring him to alter the policy. An example might be a policy of *never* prosecuting persons for simple possession of cannabis on the basis that use of the drug is now socially acceptable even though it remains a criminal offence. Such a policy would, it is submitted, be open to judicial review.

The level within the police at which the decisions on whether to prosecute are actually taken is a matter of administrative organisation, and is beyond the scope of this work. Essentially, if a prosecution is commenced by way of charge, the charging is the culmination of the investigation process at the police station. The charge has to be accepted by the custody officer on duty at the time. It is the duty and prerogative of the arresting officer and others involved in the investigation to bring the suspect before the custody officer with a view to his being charged once they have sufficient evidence to warrant that course, unless they decide that, for the discretionary reasons described below, criminal proceedings are not required even though the evidence is there to secure a conviction (see especially Code C, paras 16.1 to 16.3). If more time is needed to gather evidence or decide whether a prosecution would be in the public interest, the suspect can be bailed under the PACE 1984, s. 47(3)(b), to return to the police station on a later day. Alternatively, he can be released unconditionally from the police station but warned that consideration will be given to the question of whether to prosecute him.

Proceedings may then be commenced by way of information and summons. As to prosecutions for road traffic and other minor offences, the vast majority of these do not even result in an arrest or questioning at the station, and the decision whether to lay an information is taken some time after the event in the police process department, probably without the involvement of the reporting officers. There is nothing to prevent the officers responsible for deciding whether to initiate a prosecution delaying their decision until after legal advice has been obtained from the CPS. However, this rarely happens in practice, save in particularly important or complicated cases. Thus, the initial police decision on whether to commence proceedings is usually taken without any input from a trained lawyer.

The Role of the Crown Prosecution Service

D1.61 Subject to limited exceptions, it is the duty of the CPS to take over the conduct of all prosecutions initiated by the police (Prosecution of Offences Act 1985, s. 3(2)(a)). (For the sake of convenience, the duty of taking over the conduct of prosecutions and thereafter deciding whether the proceedings shall be continued is attributed here to the CPS. In fact, the Prosecution of Offences Act 1985 formally places the duty and confers the powers of discontinuance on the DPP, but he, of course, acts through the CPS of which he is the head.)

By the Prosecution of Offences Act 1985, s. 23, the CPS have an unfettered discretion to discontinue at a preliminary stage any proceedings of which they have the conduct. Alternatively, they may, like any other prosecutor and without resorting to the machinery provided in s. 23, simply offer no evidence or (if no plea has yet been entered) withdraw the summons. Before a case is accepted for continued prosecution by the CPS it must be reviewed by a lawyer. If he considers that proceedings should not have been brought, he will serve notice of discontinuance (or, if it seems more appropriate in the circumstances, simply offer no evidence in court). In deciding whether to allow a prosecution to continue, the CPS lawyer must apply the guidance given by the DPP and set out by him in his annual report (see Prosecution of Offences Act 1985, s. 10). The guidance is set out in full at **appendix 4**. The broad effect of the arrangements described above is that a police prosecution will go ahead only if both the responsible officers and the CPS lawyer to whom the case is sent agree that proceedings are appropriate.

Formal Caution

D1.62 The obvious alternative to prosecuting a suspect for an offence is to take no action, i.e. release him without charge if he was arrested or, if he was not arrested but warned that he might be prosecuted, send him notice that no summons will be issued. There can be no objection in such cases to the police giving the suspect an informal warning about his future behaviour. However, quite apart from informal warnings, the police have a discretion to issue a formal caution. This is a procedure which was developed with special reference to the cases of juveniles but is now used quite extensively for adults also. Sections 65 and 66 of the CDA 1998 make provision for reprimands and warnings for children and young persons. They came into force in specified pilot areas on 30 September 1998; it is proposed that they will be brought fully into force in April 2000 (see **D1.70**). Guidance on when to caution is contained in Home Office Circulars of 1990 and 1994 (1990/59 and 1994/18). The main points that emerge from the circular are as follows:

(a) *Status of cautions.* Although records are kept of the administering of cautions, they do not rank as convictions. The Home Secretary has power to direct for what period of time cautions are to be kept but he has not done so. In practice cautions are kept for a minimum of five years. Should a cautioned person subsequently be convicted of an offence, the caution may be cited at the sentencing stage, although it should be shown on a sheet separate from the form listing previous convictions. This preserves the distinction between convictions and cautions. In practice, previous cautions are rarely cited in the cases of adult offenders, but it is normal to refer to them where juveniles are concerned. However, formal cautions should be cited in court if they are relevant to the crime under consideration.

(b) *Administering cautions.* A caution for a juvenile is administered in formal circumstances at a police station by an officer of at least the rank of inspector. The juvenile's parents or guardians should be present. Where the person is elderly, infirm or vulnerable, the caution may, at the discretion of the police, be given less formally (e.g., at the person's home). The adult should sign a form acknowledging that he agrees to the caution and admits the offence in respect of which it is given.

(c) *Preconditions for a caution.* There are three conditions which must always be satisfied if a matter is to be dealt with by way of caution. They are that:

(i) the evidence is sufficient to have warranted a prosecution (see below for the guidelines of the A-G and DPP on when evidence justifies prosecution);
(ii) the offender admits his guilt, and
(iii) the parents (in the case of a juvenile) or the person being cautioned (in the case of an adult) agrees to such a disposal, having been made aware, *inter alia*, that the caution may be cited in court in the event of future offending.

The fact that the person concerned does not admit his guilt (and therefore cannot be cautioned) should not automatically lead to a prosecution. The police must consider whether, in all the circumstances, the appropriate course is to take no action at all.

An admission of guilt is a precondition to a caution and a court may strike down a caution where no admission has been obtained (*Metropolitan Police Commissioner, ex parte P* [1995] TLR 305). An admission maybe considered sufficient for the purposes of a caution even though it is obtained in circumstances which do not satisfy Code C. The fundamental question is whether the person has admitted the offence. The police may, however, be well advised to take precautions to ensure that the requirements of the Code are satisfied (*Chief Constable of the Lancashire Constabulary, ex parte Atkinson* (1998) 162 JP 275).

While a confession is a precondition to cautioning, a confession should not be sought as part of the cautionary process; a confession obtained by an inducement in the context of cautioning cannot be regarded as reliable so as to be admissible in any later proceedings (*Commissioner of Police of the Metropolis, ex parte Thompson* [1997] 1 WLR 1519).

(d) *Discretionary factors affecting cautioning.* There are strong policy reasons for delaying a juvenile's entry into the criminal justice system for as long as possible, in the hope that he will grow out of his delinquent behaviour and never enter the system at all. In the case of first-time juvenile offenders where the offence is not serious, it is unlikely that prosecution will be a justifiable course'. The choice will then lie between an informal word of warning and no further action or, if the matter is too serious for that, a formal caution. An immediate decision on whether to caution can be taken either where the offence and the offender's record are not serious, so that a prosecution is clearly unnecessary, or, at the opposite extreme where the offence is so serious (e.g., homicide or rape) that a caution would be inappropriate whatever the offender's previous character. The fact that a person has previously been cautioned (or even convicted) should as a general principle (from which departures may sometimes be desirable) preclude the administering of a second or subsequent caution. Much will depend on the time lapse since the last caution (or conviction) and whether the offences are of a similar type. Cautioning may be indicated where the later offence is trivial. Where it is not possible to decide quickly on the propriety of a caution, further consideration must be given to the matter, with agencies other than the police (e.g., social services and the education authority) being consulted. Most police forces formalise consultation with the other interested agencies through juvenile bureaux. At this secondary stage, factors such as the views of the victim, the previous character and family circumstances of the juvenile, and, in the case of joint offences, the way in which it is proposed to deal with other members of the group, should all be taken into account.

(e)   *Factors relevant to the cautioning of adults.* In the case of adults, there is no general presumption in favour of cautioning such as exists in respect of juveniles. However, membership of certain vulnerable groups may point to 'sympathetic consideration' of the case. The groups mentioned in the circular are those also mentioned in the A-G's guidelines on when to prosecute (see below). The groups are the elderly or infirm and those suffering from mental illness or impairment (especially where the strain of criminal proceedings would lead to a worsening of the condition), those suffering from severe physical illness and also those showing signs of severe emotional distress. The use of multiple cautioning is discouraged.

The issue of a caution is not a guarantee against future prosecution. The statutory regime permits a prosecution by the CPS even after a formal discontinuance has been issued. While the DPP should take account of a discontinuance letter he is not bound by it (*DPP, ex parte Burke* [1997] COD 169). Nor does a caution preclude a private prosecution since to permit it to do so would be to impose a constraint on the statutorily recognised right to bring such a prosecution. Circumstances pertinent to the individual case may, however, permit the defendant to move successfully for an order that the prosecution be stayed (*Hayter* v *L* [1998] 1 WLR 854).

General Factors Governing the Decision to Prosecute

D1.63   In addition to the principles applying to children and young persons by virtue of the CDA 1998, ss. 65 and 66, where those sections are in force (see **D1.70**), three overlapping sets of guidelines have been issued relevant to the decision to commence or continue with a prosecution. The first is the Home Office circular on cautioning discussed in **D1.62**. Obviously, the corollary of a decision to administer a caution is a decision not to prosecute. The second is the A-G's guidelines, entitled 'Criteria for Prosecution'. These were issued in 1984 (before the creation of the CPS). Although formally a statement of the criteria used by the A-G and DPP in determining whether to prosecute in the minority of cases for which (prior to 1986) they had direct responsibility, they were intended more broadly as a guide to the police on how they should reach similar decisions. The third guideline is the Code for Crown Prosecutors, issued by the DPP under the Prosecution of Offences Act 1985, s. 10. The main provisions of the code are summarised below, comparisons being drawn with the A-G's criteria where appropriate. The Code is reproduced in full at **appendix 4**.

The Code commences with a statement of general principles. Among these are the duty of Crown Prosecutors to be fair, independent and objective, not to be affected by improper pressure, and not to let their view of a case be coloured by considerations of ethnic or national origin, sex, religious or political beliefs or sexuality of the offender.

D1.64   *Evidential Sufficiency*   A prosecution must not go ahead, no matter how serious it may be, if it does not pass the evidential test (Code for Crown Prosecutors, para. 4.1). The Crown Prosecutor must be satisfied that there is enough evidence to provide a 'realistic prospect of conviction' against each defendant on each charge. This assessment is made also in the light of what the Crown Prosecutor considers the defence case may be (para. 5.1). The test for realistic prospect of conviction is objective and means that a trier of fact, properly directed, is more likely than not to convict the person of the offence charged (para. 5.2).

In assessing evidential sufficiency, Crown Prosecutors must decide whether the evidence can be used and is reliable. This involves considering the following matters: (a) whether the evidence must be or may well be excluded on general evidential grounds (for example, hearsay) or on grounds of breach of the PACE 1984 or the Codes made thereunder; (b) whether a confession is unreliable, owing to the defendant's age, intelligence or apparent lack of understanding; (c) whether a witness's background is likely to weaken the prosecution case (for example, does the witness have any dubious motive for lying or have a relevant previous conviction); and (d) in cases of questioned identity, is the evidence about this strong enough (para. 5.3(a) to (d)). Crown Prosecutors should not ignore evidence because they are not sure that it can be used or is reliable, but they should look closely at it when deciding whether there is a realistic prospect of conviction (para. 5.4).

Public Interest Criteria Assuming there is sufficient evidence to justify proceedings, **D1.65** the Crown Prosecutor must then consider whether a prosecution will be in the public interest. In cases of any seriousness there is an assumption that prosecution will take place unless there are public interest factors tending against prosecution which clearly outweigh those tending in favour. In some cases, which the Code for Crown Prosecutors does not specify, public interest factors which militate against prosecution should not bar prosecution but should rather be raised in mitigation of sentence. It may be surmised that error of law would in some cases be so treated.

Subject to these points, the fact that the case falls within any of the categories mentioned in para. 6.4 which reflect certain matters of public concern such as repeated burglaries or racially motivated attacks) is an indication that proceedings may be required:

(a) a conviction for the offence is likely to result in a significant sentence;

(b) the offence involved the use of a weapon or a threat of violence favours prosecution;

(c) the offence was committed against a person serving the public (e.g., a police or prison officer or a nurse): in practice, in the case of violence against police officers, there is a virtually irrefragable rule that prosecution will follow;

(d) the defendant was in a position of authority or trust;

(e) the evidence shows that the defendant was a ringleader or an organiser of the offence;

(f) there is evidence that the offence was premeditated;

(g) there is evidence that the offence was carried out by a group;

(h) the victim of the offence was vulnerable, has been put in considerable fear, or suffered personal attack, damage or disturbance;

(i) the attack was motivated by any form of discrimination against the victim's ethnic or national origin, sex, religious beliefs, political view or sexual preference (which should give some reassurance for example to victims of racially motivated attacks);

(j) there is a marked difference between the actual or mental ages of the defendant and the victim or if there is any element of corruption;

(k) the defendant's previous convictions or cautions are relevant to the present offence;

(l) the defendant is alleged to have committed the offence whilst under an order of the court;

(m) there are grounds for believing that the offence is likely to be continued or repeated (e.g., there is a history of recurring conduct); or

(n) the offence, though not serious in itself, is widespread in the area where it was committed.

The following factors militate against prosecution (para. 6.5):

(a) the likelihood that the court will impose a very small or nominal penalty;

(b)   the offence was committed as a result of a genuine mistake or misunderstanding (but this is to be weighed against the gravity of the offence and, it is submitted, it may be thought that the more serious the offence, particularly where the traditional crimes are concerned, the less likely it is that the defendant laboured under a genuine mistake, at any rate where mistake of law is concerned);

(c)   the loss or harm can be described as minor and was the result of a single incident, particularly if it was caused by a misjudgment;

(d)   there has been a long delay between the commission of the offence and the date of trial unless the offence is serious, the delay has been caused in part by the defendant, the offence has only recently come to light, or the complexity of the case has entailed a very long investigation;

(e)   a prosecution is likely to have a very bad effect on the victim's physical or mental health, always bearing in mind the seriousness of the offence;

(f)   the defendant has put right the loss or harm caused (but defendants must not avoid prosecution simply because they can pay compensation);

(g)   details may be made public that could harm sources of information, international relations, or national security; or

(h)   the defendant is elderly or is, or was at the time of the offence, suffering from significant mental or physical ill health, unless the offence is serious or there is a real possibility that it may be repeated.

The Code specifies that the CPS applies Home Office Guidelines concerning how to deal with mentally disordered offenders. The need to divert a mentally ill or physically ill defendant must be balanced with the need to safeguard the general public. Presumably, individual factors such as the possibility of re-offending take priority over such matters as general deterrence, although the Code does not say so.

The Code further points out that Crown Prosecutors do not simply add up the number of factors on each side; theirs is an evaluative exercise and requires an overall view of the case (para. 6.6).

(a)   *Interests of victim*   The CPS, while acting generally in the public interest, has regard to the interests of the victim since these are an important factor in determining where the public interest lies (para. 6.7). It follows that the mere fact that a victim wants a prosecution stopped is not decisive against prosecution. The fact that a victim will lose an opportunity to obtain compensation is again, it is submitted, relevant.

(b)   *Youth offenders*   Crown Prosecutors must consider the interests of a youth when deciding whether it is in the public interest to prosecute. The Code notes the harm which the stigma of conviction can cause to the prospects of a youth offender or a young adult. It specifies, however, that the defendant's youth notwithstanding, the seriousness of the offence or the offender's past behaviour may make prosecution necessary (para. 6.8).

(c)   *Police cautions*   The Code notes that the police, operating under Home Office Guidelines, make the decision to caution an offender. Crown Prosecutors should, where necessary, apply the same principles when they are considering alternatives to prosecution in the public interest and should tell the police if they consider that a caution would be more suitable than a prosecution (para. 6.9).

D1.66   ***Charges***   Crown Prosecutors should select charges which reflect the gravity of the offending, give the court adequate sentencing powers and enable the case to be presented in a clear and simple way. The Crown Prosecutor need not necessarily continue with the most serious charge available where there is a choice and should not continue with more charges than is necessary (Code for Crown Prosecutors, para. 7.1). Crown Prosecutors should not proceed with more, or more serious charges than are necessary, in order to provoke a guilty plea (para. 7.2). They should not change the charge simply because of a decision made by the court or the defendant about where the case will be heard (para. 7.3). Parenthetically, it may be noted that this should militate against reducing charges simply in order to bring the offence within the exclusive jurisdiction of magistrates, though there are perfectly legitimate reasons sometimes for doing so.

Mode of Trial Crown Prosecutors should recommend Crown Court trial when they **D1.67** are satisfied that the *Practice Note (Mode of Trial Guidelines)* (1995) (see **D3.7**) requires them to do so. Speed is not, of itself, a sufficient reason for asking that a case stay in the magistrates' court, but the effect of any likely delay if the case is sent to Crown Court and the effect of such delay on victims and witnesses are relevant considerations (Code for Crown Prosecutors, para. 8).

Accepting Guilty Pleas Crown Prosecutors should accept a plea arrangement **D1.68** suggested by the defendant only if they think that the court would be able to pass a sentence commensurate with the gravity of the offending and should never accept such an arrangement as a matter of convenience (Code for Crown Prosecutors para. 9.1).

Re-starting a Prosecution Normally a case will not re-start if the Crown Prosecutor **D1.69** has told the defendant that there will not be a prosecution or the prosecution has been stopped (para. 10.1). In some instances the CPS will re-start the prosecution, especially if the case is serious. The special circumstances which may justify re-starting a prosecution are (para. 10.2):

(a)   where a new look at the original decision shows that it was clearly wrong;

(b)   where the case has been stopped so that the prosecution can obtain further evidence in which case the Crown Prosecutor will tell the defendant that the case may well start again; and

(c)   where a case has stopped for want of evidence but more significant evidence is discovered later.

Reprimands and Warnings

Sections 65 and 66 of the CDA 1998 introduce a new procedure for the reprimand and **D1.70** warning of children and young persons who have committed offences and prohibit the use of the caution for such offenders. The sections were brought into force on 30 September in specified pilot areas and are expected to be brought fully into force in April 2000. Essentially they apply where:

(a)   a constable has sufficient evidence for there to be a reasonable prospect of the child or young person being convicted of an offence;

(b)   the offender admits the offence and has not previously been convicted of any offence;

(c)   the constable is satisfied that it would not be in the public interest for the offender to be prosecuted.

The constable may in these circumstances reprimand an offender who has not previously been reprimanded or warned. Alternatively the constable may take the more serious step of warning an offender who has not previously been warned or, if the offence is not so serious as to require a charge to be brought, who has committed the offence more than two years after his previous warning. Reprimands and warnings must be given at a police station and, where the offender is aged under 17, in the presence of an appropriate adult.

A person who receives a warning will be referred to a youth offending team and, unless it is considered inappropriate, arrangements will be made for him to participate in a rehabilitation programme (s. 66(1)). A reprimand, a warning and a failure to participate in a rehabilitation scheme may be cited in criminal proceedings in the same circumstances as a conviction (s. 66(5)).

Judicial Review of Decision to Prosecute

D1.71 A decision not to prosecute is susceptible to judicial review because no other remedy is available. A decision to prosecute stands on a different footing: arguments relating to abuse of process may, for example, be raised in the course of the criminal trial itself. It thus appears that in the absence of dishonesty, *mala fides* or some exceptional circumstance, a decision to prosecute cannot be raised by way of judicial review (*DPP, ex parte Kebilene* [1999] 3 WLR 972). Their lordships have not, however, pronounced in respect of decisions to prosecute based on cautioning policy. It may be possible to secure an order for judicial review of a decision as to whether to prosecute, but it would have to be shown that the decision was clearly contrary to settled policy concerning juveniles. Where adults are concerned, the heavy burden on the applicant may be insurmountable (*Chief Constable of Kent and CPS, ex parte GL* (1991) 93 Cr App R 416).

TERRITORIAL JURISDICTION OF ENGLISH COURTS

Introduction

D1.72 Apart from the general considerations of evidential sufficiency and public interest criteria which apply in all cases and have been discussed above, there are a number of special considerations which may absolutely preclude a prosecution in the sense that the court would not have jurisdiction to deal with the putative offender even if proceedings were commenced. Chief among these is the issue of territorial jurisdiction of the courts.

General Rule

D1.73 The general rule is that the English courts do not accept jurisdiction over offences committed outside England and Wales, even if the accused is a British subject (see *Harden* [1963] 1 QB 8). The same point may be put another way by stating that, in the absence of express provision to the contrary, Parliament is presumed to have intended that the conduct prohibited by any offence-creating provision shall be an offence under English law only if it took place within the jurisdiction. In *Treacy* v *DPP* [1971] AC 537, Lord Morris of Borth-y-Gest summarised the position thus (at pp. 552–3):

> In general, . . . acts committed out of England, even though they are committed by British subjects, are not punishable under the criminal law of this country. But, as Parliament is supreme, it is open to Parliament to pass an enactment in relation to such acts. It is, however, a general rule of construction that unless there is something which points to a contrary intention a statute will be taken to apply only to the United Kingdom. It would be open to Parliament to enact that if a British subject committed anywhere an act designated as blackmail he would commit an offence punishable in England. Such an enactment would, however, have to be in clear and express terms: specific provision would have to be made with regard to acts committed abroad.

> The general rule as expressed by Lord Halsbury LC in *Macleod* v *A-G for New South Wales* [1891] AC 455 at p. 458 is that 'All crime is local' and that jurisdiction over a crime belongs to the country where it is committed. Unless, therefore, there is some provision pointing to a different conclusion, a statute which makes some act (or omission) an offence will relate to some act (or omission) in the United Kingdom. Even where a statute creating a criminal offence is clearly expressed so as to cover acts committed outside the jurisdiction, it will, in the absence of further clear provision only be regarded as covering such acts when committed by British subjects.

Whether an offence was committed abroad or within the jurisdiction would seem to depend on where the *actus reus* was completed (i.e., if it was completed abroad, the offence is treated as having been committed abroad even if earlier parts of the offence took place in England).

In *Harden* [1963] 1 QB 8, jurisdiction over an alleged offence of obtaining property by deception was declined because, although the false representation was made in England

and the property obtained (a cheque) was physically received by H in England, nonetheless the victim had posted it to H from Jersey and, on the facts of that particular case, there was an express or implied agreement between H and the victim that delivery of the letter containing the cheque to the postman would be equivalent to personal delivery to H. It followed that the offence was completed in Jersey.

Problems such as that which fell for decision in *Harden* will arise only in respect of that minority of offences the definitions of which may be divided into an 'initiatory element' (i.e., the physical acts of the accused) and a 'terminatory' element to describe its subsequent consequences. As regards most offences (special rules apply to offences of dishonesty), the initiatory and terminatory elements coincide, and there is no difficulty, other than the purely factual, in determining where it occurred. Lord Diplock in his speech in *Treacy* v *DPP*, while apparently accepting that the English courts do indeed approach the question of jurisdiction on the terminatory basis, stated that the restrictions on jurisdiction are founded on the comity of nations (i.e. the English courts do not wish to offend foreign courts by usurping their authority over what has happened in their countries). Where an offence is rightly to be construed as containing both initiatory and terminatory elements, no friction with foreign jurisdictions would be created by the offence being tried here provided either element occurred here.

Despite the attractive nature of Lord Diplock's approach, the terminatory theory of jurisdiction has been reasserted in the Court of Appeal (*Manning* [1998] 2 Cr App R 461, disapproving *Smith (W.D.)* [1996] 2 Cr App R 1).

Determination of where the offence occurred is especially problematic where inchoate offences (other than offences of fraud and dishonesty) are concerned. The rules emerging from the cases are that:

(a) An attempt to commit an offence is triable in England, even though none of the physical acts constituting the attempt took place here, provided the completed offence would have been triable here had the attempt succeeded (*DPP* v *Stonehouse* [1978] AC 55 and see also *Baxter* [1972] 1 QB 1). It follows that the presence of the accused in England at the time of the alleged attempt is unnecessary to jurisdiction.

(b) A conspiracy formed abroad to commit an offence in England or Wales is triable here provided the conspirators come within the jurisdiction while the conspiracy is still in existence and act in furtherance thereof (*DPP* v *Doot* [1973] AC 807, in which it was held that the appellants were rightly indicted for conspiracy to import dangerous drugs because, even though the plan was worked out in Belgium and Morocco, the appellants had later come within the jurisdiction and had shipped vehicles containing the drugs from Morocco to Southampton and Liverpool). The predominant reasoning in *DPP* v *Doot* is that conspiracy is a continuing offence and should not be regarded as being wholly committed abroad just because it was entered into abroad (see especially the speeches of Lords Dilhorne and Pearson). Since the significance of the accused's acts in England in furtherance of the conspiracy is merely to show that the conspiracy had not been abandoned prior to their arrival here, jurisdiction arises whether or not their acts were in themselves unlawful (*Sansom* [1991] 2 QB 130; indeed, no act need be done within the United Kingdom at all (*Liangsiriprasert* v *United States* [1991] 1 AC 225). The entry of one conspirator into the country is sufficient to found jurisdiction against them all. English courts will try a case where there had been entry by one or more conspirators but no overt acts here (lawful or otherwise) in furtherance of the conspiracy (*Liangsiriprasert* v *United States* per Lord Griffith at p. 250). In the converse situation of an agreement being entered into in England to commit a crime abroad, the English courts refuse jurisdiction, even if the conduct contemplated by the agreement would be an offence under English law were it to be carried out here (*Board of Trade* v *Owen* [1957] AC 602, but cf. *Hornett* [1975] RTR 256 and *El-Hakkaoui* [1975] 1 WLR 396 where jurisdiction was accepted because, although the ultimate effect of the conspiracies would have been felt abroad, they incidentally entailed offences here, namely, in *Hornett,* the forgery of road haulage permits which were to be used to deceive authorities on the Continent, and, in *El-Hakkaoui,* the possession of a firearm with intent to endanger the life of a person abroad).

Conspiracy to Commit Offences Abroad

D1.74   Sections 5 to 8 of the Criminal Justice (Terrorism and Conspiracy) Act 1998 give English courts jurisdiction to try conspiracies to commit offences abroad provided that the appropriate qualifying conditions are met. The Act came into force on 4 September 1998. The statutory provisions do not extend to incitement.

It is an offence to conspire to pursue a course of conduct that would amount to an offence in the foreign state provided that the conduct in question would also amount to an offence within England and Wales (Criminal Law Act 1977, s. 1A(1) to (4), as substituted by the 1998 Act). The party to be tried or his agent must have done some act in relation to agreement before it was formed in England and Wales, or have joined the agreement in England and Wales, or have done or omitted to do something in England and Wales in pursuance of the agreement (s. 1A(5)). Any act done by means of a message, however communicated, is to be treated for the purposes of the fourth condition, (i.e. whether anything was done in England and Wales in relation to the agreement etc. for the purposes of s. 1A(5)), as done in England and Wales if the message is either sent or received in England and Wales (s. 1A(11)).

The defence must, if it wishes to challenge the proposition that the conduct sought to be engaged in abroad does not amount to a crime in the foreign state, raise the issue by notice, informing the prosecution of the grounds for their opinion and requiring the prosecution to show that the condition is satisfied (s. 1A(8)). The question is treated as a question of law (s. 1A(9)).

These provisions do not impose liability on persons holding office under the Crown (s. 1A(14)). The purpose of this exemption is to ensure that for example, customs officers engaged in undercover work abroad will not be subject to prosecution in respect of it.

No prosecution may be brought under this provision without the consent of the A-G (s. 1A(15)).

Offences of Fraud and Dishonesty: Criminal Justice Act 1993, Part I

D1.75   Jurisdiction in respect of offences of fraud and dishonesty and inchoate offences associated with them are dealt with by the CJA 1993, part I, brought into force on 1 June 1999. They do not apply to offences committed before that date.

The jurisdictional provisions of these sections apply to offences designated as Group A and Group B offences. The Group A offences are as follows:

(a)   an offence under any of the following provisions of the TA 1968: theft (s. 1), obtaining property by deception (s. 15), obtaining a money transfer by deception (s. 15A), false accounting (s. 17), false statements by company directors (s. 19), procuring execution of a valuable security by deception (s. 20(2)), blackmail (s. 21), handling stolen goods (s. 22), retaining credits from dishonest sources (s. 24A);

(b)   an offence under either the TA 1978, s. 1 (obtaining services by deception) or s. 2 (avoiding liability by deception);

(c)   an offence under any of the following provisions of the Forgery and Counterfeiting Act 1981: forgery (s. 1), copying a false instrument (s. 2), using a false instrument (s. 3), using a copy of a false instrument (s. 4), and certain offences relating to money orders, share certificates, passports, etc. (s. 5);

(d)   the common-law offence of cheating the public revenue.

The Group B offences are conspiracy to commit a Group A offence, conspiracy to defraud, attempting to commit a Group A offence and incitement to commit a Group A offence.

Jurisdiction over Group A Offences   The jurisdictional scheme is closely tied to the **D1.76** definitional elements of the offence by way of what is termed a relevant event. For the purposes of a Group A offence, 'relevant event' means any act or omission or other event (including the result of one or more acts or omissions) proof of which is required for conviction of the offence (CJA 1993, s. 2(1)).

The jurisdictional requirement is fulfilled provided that any of the relevant events occurred in England and Wales (s. 2(2)). It is immaterial whether all the other relevant events occur abroad. Thus it matters not whether the offence was initiated in England and completed abroad, or even whether it was initiated and completed abroad provided that some relevant event (such as the transmission of money obtained by fraud) occurred in England and Wales.

A person may be guilty of a Group A offence whether or not he was a British citizen at any material time and whether or not he was in England and Wales at any such time (s. 3(1)), except where the jurisdiction is given to try the offence by reference to the nationality of the person charged (s. 3(4)).

Jurisdiction over Group B Offences   On a charge of conspiracy to commit a Group **D1.77** A offence, or on a charge of conspiracy to defraud in England and Wales, the accused may be guilty of the offence whether or not he became party to the conspiracy in England and Wales and whether or not any act or omission or other event in relation to the conspiracy occurred in England and Wales (CJA 1993, s. 3(2)). Section 3(2) does not apply in relation to any charge brought under the Criminal Law Act 1977 by virtue of s. 1A of that Act.

On a charge of attempting to commit a Group A offence, the accused may be guilty of an offence whether or not the attempt was made in England and Wales or had an effect in England and Wales (s. 3(3)(a) and (b)). This subsection does not apply in relation to any charge brought under the Criminal Attempts Act 1981 by virtue of s. 1A of that Act.

A person may be guilty of conspiracy to defraud if a party to the agreement constituting the conspiracy or his agent did anything in England and Wales in relation to the agreement before its formation, a party to it became a party to it in England and Wales by joining it in person or through an agent, or either himself or through an agent did or omitted anything in England and Wales in pursuance of it (CJA 1993, s. 5(3)). Similarly, a person may be guilty of incitement to commit a Group A offence if the incitement takes place in England and Wales and would be triable in England and Wales but for the fact that what the person charged had in view would not be an offence in England and Wales, e.g. because the offence was intended to occur abroad (s. 5(4)).

In relation to inchoate offences having as a purpose the commission of a crime abroad, it must be proved that the act or omission would constitute an offence under the law in force where the act, omission or other event was intended to take place (CJA 1993, s. 6(1) and (2)). This comprehends both common-law conspiracy to cheat and defraud and statutory conspiracies. The description of the conduct in the foreign law is immaterial; it is enough if the conduct in question is punishable under the foreign law (s. 6(3)). Generally, a condition specified in s. 6(1) or (2) is taken to be satisfied but the prosecution can be put to proof of this requirement where the defence, within the permitted time, serve a notice on the prosecution stating that in their opinion this requirement is not satisfied in respect of the relevant conduct, showing grounds for their opinion, and requiring the prosecution to show that it is satisfied; the need to serve notice may be dispensed with by the court (s. 6(4)). In the case of conspiracy the relevant conduct means the agreed course of conduct and, where attempt under the Criminal Attempts Act 1981, s. 1A, is concerned, the relevant event is what the defendant had in view (s. 6(5)). In the Crown Court the question whether the condition is satisfied is to be decided by the judge alone (s. 6(7)).

D1.78 ***Determining the Location of Events*** Section 4 of the CJA 1993 contains rules for determining jurisdictional questions relating to the location of events. In relation to both Group A and Group B offences there is an obtaining of property in England and Wales if the property is either despatched from or received at a place within the jurisdiction. Again, in relation to both groups there is a communication in England and Wales of any information, instruction, request, demand or other matter if it is sent by any means from a place within England and Wales to a place elsewhere, or vice versa.

Exceptions to the General Rule

D1.79 In addition to the exceptions created by part I of the CJA 1993, there are several further exceptions to the rule that the English courts only accept jurisdiction over offences committed here. In summary, the exceptions are as follows.

D1.80 ***Offences of Incitement to Commit Sexual Acts Involving Children*** The Sexual Offences (Conspiracy and Incitement) Act 1996 confers jurisdiction on British courts in respect of certain offences of incitement to commit sexual acts against infants, abroad. The offences concerned are:

(a) rape, contrary to s. 1 of the Sexual Offences Act 1956 (where the victim is under 16 years of age);

(b) intercourse with a girl under the age of 13 contrary to s. 5 of the 1956 Act;

(c) intercourse with a girl under the age of 16 contrary to s. 6 of the 1956 Act;

(d) buggery contrary to s. 12 of the 1956 Act (provided that the victim is under 16 years of age);

(e) indecent assault upon a boy contrary to s. 14 of the 1956 Act (provided that the victim is under 16 years of age);

(f) indecent assault upon a boy contrary to s. 15 of the 1956 Act (provided that the victim is under 16 years of age);

(g) an offence under s. 1 of the Indecency with Children Act 1960.

Section 2 confers jurisdiction in respect of offences of incitement to commit one of the offences listed above. The incitement must be to do an act which, if committed in England and Wales, would amount to such an offence therein. The whole or part of what the accused had in view must be intended to take place outside the United Kingdom. What he had in view must amount to an offence in the foreign jurisdiction. Any act of incitement by means of a message, however communicated, is treated as done in England and Wales if the message is sent or received in England and Wales.

Section 3 contains supplementary provisions. For the purposes of s. 2 it matters not what the offence is called in the foreign jurisdiction. The condition in respect of both conspiracy and incitement that the conduct would involve the commission an offence within the foreign jurisdiction is taken to be satisfied unless the defence serve a notice stating that in their opinion the condition is not satisfied and their reason for holding this opinion, although the Court may, if it thinks fit, allow the defence to challenge the condition notwithstanding that it has failed to give proper notice.

By s. 3(5) it is irrelevant whether or not the accused was a British citizen at the time of the act or event which must be proved to constitute the offence; the fundamental requirement is one of territorial nexus as specified above, and any person may be tried whose conduct satisfies that nexus.

Sexual Offences   The Sex Offenders Act 1997, part II, which came into force on 1   **D1.81**
September 1997, confers jurisdiction on British courts over certain sexual offences
committed abroad. The offences to which the provisions apply are listed in sch. 2 to the
Act. For England and Wales these offences are the same as those specified for the purposes
of the Sexual Offences (Conspiracy and Incitement Act 1996 (see **D1.80**) and in addition
offences under the Sexual Offences Act 1956, s. 16 (assault with intent to commit buggery)
and the Protection of Children Act 1978, s. 1 (indecent photographs of children).

Sex Offenders Act 1997, s. 7

(1)   Subject to subsection (2) below, any act done by a person in a country or territory
outside the United Kingdom which—
(a)   constituted an offence under the law in force in that country or territory; and
(b)   would constitute a sexual offence to which this section applies if it had been done
in England and Wales, or in Northern Ireland,
shall constitute that sexual offence under the law of that part of the United Kingdom.
(2)   No proceedings shall by virtue of this section be brought against any person unless
he was at the commencement of this section, or has subsequently become, a British citizen
or resident in the United Kingdom.
(3)   An act punishable under the law in force in any country or territory constitutes an
offence under that law for the purposes of this section, however it is described in that law.

Certain 'Foreign' Offences Triable Here if the Accused is a British Subject or   **D1.82**
Resident   Murder and manslaughter committed on land (OAPA 1861, s. 9), bigamy
(ibid., s. 57) and offences under the Official Secrets Act 1911 (by s. 10 of that Act) are
all triable by the English courts, even if committed abroad, provided the accused is a
British subject. Also, if a victim is injured in England but dies abroad or vice versa, any
offence of murder or manslaughter arising from the matter may be tried here (OAPA
1861, s. 10). Although s. 10 of the 1861 Act (unlike s. 9) does not expressly limit its
application to British subjects, such a limitation has been implied in decided cases (see
Lewis (1857) Dears & B 82, where the offence was committed on an American vessel
and *Jameson* [1896] 2 QB 425 per Lord Russell of Killowen CJ at p. 430; see also **B1.9**).
Perjury committed abroad is also punishable in England and Wales provided that it
consists of evidence given in 'English' proceedings (Perjury Act 1911, s. 8 and see
s. 1(5)). The section is not restricted in application to British subjects but applies to
anyone sworn as a witness in such proceedings.

By virtue of the War Crimes Act 1991, s. 1, proceedings for murder may be brought in
the United Kingdom against a person who on 8 March 1990 or later was a British citizen
or resident if that offence was committed between 1 September 1939 and 5 June 1945
in a place which was then part of Germany or under German occupation. The offence
must have constituted a violation of the laws and customs of war. The nationality of the
offender at the time the alleged offence was carried out is immaterial. The consent of
the A-G is required for prosecution (see **D1.89**).

Offences Committed at Sea   British territorial waters are, in effect, treated as an   **D1.83**
extension of the land off which they lie. Therefore, offences committed by or on vessels
within territorial waters are triable here (Territorial Waters Jurisdiction Act 1878, s. 2).
This applies whatever the nationality of the accused and regardless of whether the ship
in question is British or foreign (ibid.). In addition, offences committed on board any
British ship on the high seas (whether by a British subject or foreign national) are triable
here, as are offences committed by a British subject in a foreign port or harbour or on
board any foreign ship to which he does not belong (Merchant Shipping Act 1995,
s. 281). 'High seas' in s. 281 has the same meaning as when used with reference to the
Admiralty jurisdiction, namely, all oceans, seas, bays, channels, rivers, creeks and waters
below low-water mark where 'great ships could go' unless they are within the body of a
county (see *Liverpool Justices, ex parte Molyneux* [1972] 2 QB 384 — theft committed in

the port of Nassau by a British seaman on board a British ship triable in England because, although the offence could be regarded as having occurred within the internal waters of the Bahamas, it could equally well be said to have occurred on the high seas in the extended sense of the phrase given above). It has been held that British passengers on a Danish ferry who committed acts of criminal damage while the vessel was on the high seas did not belong to the vessel and therefore were amenable to English jurisdiction by virtue of what is now s. 281 (*Kelly* [1982] AC 665). It has also been held that offences committed by British subjects on a French vessel while it was in the port of Dieppe but still had its ramp down were committed on the vessel, rather than being committed in Dieppe itself (*Cumberworth* (1989) 89 Cr App R 187). The decision might have been otherwise if the vessel had been dry-docked or been a museum piece, in which case it might have been regarded as permanently annexed to the land. Section 281 of the Merchant Shipping Act 1995 should be read in conjunction with s. 279, which provides that, for purposes of conferring jurisdiction, every offence shall be deemed to have been committed '*in any place in the United Kingdom where the offender may for the time being be*'. The purpose of the italicised words would seem to be to give a magistrates' court for any area where the offender happens to be found jurisdiction to issue process against him and (if the offence is summary) to try him for matters brought within English jurisdiction by the 1995 Act, thus overriding for those purposes the territorial restrictions that normally limit the magistrates' powers.

Prior to the enactment of the Merchant Shipping Act 1894, the jurisdiction of the Admiralty of England had included jurisdiction over offences committed on the high seas. Indeed, the definition of 'high seas' adopted in *Liverpool Justices, ex parte Molyneux* was developed in cases decided under the Admiralty jurisdiction (see especially *Anderson* (1868) LR 1 CCR 161 where a foreigner's conviction for manslaughter committed on board a British ship in the river Garonne was upheld, even though the ship was 35 miles from the open sea and only 300 yards from the nearest shore, on the basis that the ship was nonetheless on the high seas). The Admiralty jurisdiction was originally exercised by King's Commission, but was later transferred to the ordinary criminal courts (see now the Supreme Court Act 1981, s. 46(2): 'The jurisdiction of the Crown Court with respect to proceedings on indictment shall include jurisdiction in proceedings . . . on indictment for offences within the jurisdiction of the Admiralty of England'). The Admiralty jurisdiction thus coexists with the jurisdiction given to the courts by s. 281 of the 1995 Act. Until the decision in *Kelly*, it was arguable that the survival of the Admiralty jurisdiction was of significance because, on one view of what is now s. 281, it did not confer jurisdiction over offences which would otherwise be outside the English courts' competence, but merely provided for the particular place and mode of trial on the assumption that the offence alleged was triable here. But, in *Kelly*, the House of Lords took a broad view of the effect of the section, holding that 'any offence' as used in the section meant simply an offence against English law. It would therefore seem that any offence which, in former times, would have been triable here as being within the Admiralty jurisdiction, will now be triable here by virtue of s. 281 as being an offence committed on a British ship on the high seas.

Offences Committed by Crew-Members of British Ships

D1.84 Any offence against property or person committed at any place, ashore or afloat, by a person who, at the time of the offence or within the three months preceding it, was employed as a master, seaman or apprentice in any British ship is triable here regardless of where it was committed (Merchant Shipping Act 1995, s. 282). The legislative history of s. 281 is different from that of s. 282, and the interpretation of the one section will not necessarily cast light on the interpretation of the other (per Lord Roskill in *Kelly* [1982] AC 665 at p. 678B, in discussing the sections which then applied). Although the section is wide enough on its face to cover offences committed by foreigners abroad if they were crew-members of British ships at the relevant time, it is more probable that its application should be restricted to British subjects (see *Dudley* (1884) 14 QBD 273, decided on an earlier equivalent provision, and Lord Morris's statement in *Treacy* v *DPP* [1971] AC 537 that, even where a statute confers extraterritorial criminal jurisdiction, it should be construed as relating only to British subjects abroad unless there is clear indication to the contrary).

Government Employees British subjects employed by the government in the **D1.85** service of the Crown are triable here for any offence committed in a foreign country when acting (or purporting to act) in the course of their employment (CJA 1948, s. 31(1).

Offences on British Aircraft Offences committed on British-controlled aircraft **D1.86** while in flight elsewhere than over the United Kingdom are nevertheless triable here (Civil Aviation Act 1982, s. 92(1)). The section does not extend to military aircraft (s. 92(5)). 'In flight' includes any point from the moment when power is applied in order to take off to the conclusion of the plane's landing run (s. 92(4)). The consent of the DPP is required for the initiation of proceedings (s. 92(2)). Offences committed by or in planes over the UK are triable here without the Director's consent on the basis that UK air space is equivalent for jurisdictional purposes to the ground.

Terrorist Offences By the Suppression of Terrorism Act 1978, s. 4, certain offences **D1.87** listed in sch. 1 to the Act are triable here if they were committed in a 'convention country' (i.e. a country for the time being designated in an order made by the Secretary of State as a party to the European Convention on the Suppression of Terrorism signed on 27 January 1977). The convention countries at present are Austria, Denmark, Germany, Sweden, Norway, Iceland, Luxembourg, Belgium, the Netherlands, Portugal, Switzerland, Italy, Spain, France and the Republic of Ireland. Jurisdiction arises regardless of the nationality of the accused (i.e. he need not be either a British subject or a national of the convention country in question). The principal offences covered by s. 4 are murder, manslaughter, kidnapping, abduction and false imprisonment (all common-law offences); offences under the Taking of Hostages Act 1982; offences under the Explosive Substances Act 1883, ss. 2 and 3 (causing an explosion likely to endanger life or property, doing any act with intent to cause such an explosion, conspiring to cause such explosion and possessing explosives with intent to endanger life or property), offences under the Nuclear Material (Offences) Act 1983 and offences under the Firearms Act 1968, ss. 16 and 17 (possessing firearm with intent to injure and use of firearm with intent to resist arrest). As to murder, manslaughter and offences under the Explosive Substances Act 1883, jurisdiction is even wider, extending to offences committed by a national of a convention country anywhere outside the UK and his own country (s. 4(3)). Section 4 does not specifically state that the jurisdiction conferred by subsections (1) and (3) is limited to cases where the offenders were allegedly engaged in terrorist activities. However, s. 4(4) provides that, unless the offence would be triable here apart from the section, proceedings require the consent of the A-G. It is submitted that, having regard to the title and overall purpose of the 1978 Act, the Attorney would not give his consent to proceedings here for an offence not otherwise triable here unless it had a terrorist background. See generally **B10.1** *et seq.*

Piracy and Aircraft Hijacking The offence of piracy is regarded as an offence **D1.88** against the law of nations, and is triable here wherever it occurred and whatever the nationality of the ship or defendants involved. The same applies to aircraft hijacking (Aviation Security Act 1982, s. 1). See generally **B10.75** *et seq.*

CASES IN WHICH CONSENT IS REQUIRED FOR PROSECUTION

As regards certain offences, the obtaining of consent from either the A-G or the DPP is **D1.89** a precondition of the bringing of a prosecution. The most striking example is the statutory requirement under the Law Reform (Year and a Day) Act 1996 for the A-G's consent to a prosecution for an offence of homicide if the victim dies after three years from the event causing death or if the accused has already received a custodial sentence of two years' imprisonment or more in respect of the event which caused the death. Such consent need not necessarily be in writing. It may be inferred from the material supplied to the prosecutor (*Jackson* [1997] Crim LR 293).

In general, the A-G's consent is required where issues of public policy, national security or relations with other countries may affect the decision whether to prosecute. An example is the Suppression of Terrorism Act 1978, s. 4(4) (see **D1.87**), by which he must sanction any proceedings here for terrorist offences allegedly committed in a convention country. Other examples are offences of bribery under the Public Bodies Corrupt Practices Act 1889 or Prevention of Corruption Act 1906 (s. 4 of the 1889 Act; s. 2 of the 1906 Act); offences under the Official Secrets Act 1911 (s. 8); offences of stirring up racial hatred etc. contrary to part III of the Public Order Act 1986 (s. 27); offences of belonging to a proscribed organisation, contributing money to proscribed organisations, acting in contravention of an exclusion order and other offences under the Prevention of Terrorism (Temporary Provisions) Act 1989 (s. 19); and offences contrary to the Explosive Substances Act 1883 (s. 7).

It is necessary to obtain the consent of the DPP to prosecute, for example: (a) offences of theft or criminal damage where the property in question belongs to the accused's spouse (Theft Act 1968, s. 30(4)); (b) offences of assisting offenders and wasting police time (Criminal Law Act 1967, ss. 4(4) and 5(3)); (c) homosexual offences where either party was under the age of 21 (Sexual Offences Act 1967, s. 8); (d) incest (Sexual Offences Act 1956, sch. 2); (e) aiding and abetting suicide (Suicide Act 1961, s. 2); (f) riot (Public Order Act 1986, s. 7); (g) under the War Crimes Act 1991; (h) offences under the Prevention of Terrorism (Temporary Provisions) Act 1989, ss. 13A, 13B, 16A, 16B and 16 and sch. 6A (of which the most serious is having an article in possession for terrorist purposes). The linking factor between the above disparate offences may be that, in each instance, although sometimes for different reasons, the weighing of the discretionary factors relevant to the decision to prosecute is likely to be a particularly sensitive and difficult exercise, thus making it desirable for the police or CPS to obtain prior approval for a prosecution.

The A-G's consent to a prosecution is normally signified in writing, although there would appear to be no bar to its being given orally (per Lord Widgery CJ in *Cain* [1976] QB 496 at p. 502C). The consent need not specify the precise form of charges to which approval is given. Thus, in *Cain*, the Court of Appeal held that the Crown Court had had jurisdiction to try C for possessing explosives under suspicious circumstances contrary to the Explosive Substances Act 1883, s. 4, even though the A-G's consent did not relate specifically to s. 4 but merely stated in general terms that he consented to the prosecution of C 'for an offence or offences contrary to the provisions of the [1883 Act]'. Although it is theoretically open to an accused to challenge the validity of an apparent consent on the basis that the A-G did not genuinely consider the propriety or otherwise of a prosecution, the initial presumption in the case of a written consent is that it would not have been issued unless the A-G had applied himself to his duty, considered the relevant facts, and reached a conclusion upon them' (ibid. at p. 502F). Lord Widgery in *Cain* summarised the A-G's role in respect of consents to prosecutions as follows (at pp. 502G–503A):

> First, the purpose of requiring the Attorney-General's consent to prosecutions under the Act of 1883 is to protect potential defendants from prosecutions under an Act whose language is necessarily vague and general. Hence it is not necessary that the Attorney-General should have considered and approved every detail of the charge as it ultimately

appears in the indictment. His duty is to consider the general circumstances of the case, and to decide whether any, and, if he thinks fit, which, of the provisions of the Act can properly be pursued against the defendant. . . . If the Attorney-General considers that the prosecutor should be at liberty to pursue any charge under the Act which is justified by the evidence, there is no constitutional objection to his giving consent in the wide terms adopted in the present case. Furthermore, when consent is given in any terms it should be presumed that the Attorney-General has made the necessary and proper inquiries before giving that consent.

By the Prosecution of Offences Act 1985, s. 1(7), the consent of the DPP to a prosecution may be given on his behalf by a Crown Prosecutor. The level of the CPS at which the granting of a consent to prosecution is considered is a matter for administrative arrangement within the Service. It is understood that, as regards some offences requiring consent, the papers are automatically sent to the headquarters office, whereas in other categories of case the application is considered at branch office level. In view of the creation of the CPS and the requirement that all prosecutions commenced by the police must be taken over by the Service, reviewed by a Crown Prosecutor and, if need be, discontinued, it may be thought that the provisions requiring the DPP's consent have lost some of their original importance, at least as regards police prosecutions. However, they still have the effect that, where consent is required, the propriety or otherwise of a prosecution must (subject to the Prosecution of Offences Act 1985, s. 25) be considered *before* proceedings are commenced, whereas in the normal case the CPS merely exercise a retrospective control, approving or disapproving a basic decision which has already been taken by the police. Such proceedings are regarded as instituted when an accused appears before a court for the purposes of committal and not earlier (*Whale* [1991] Crim LR 692).

Sections 25 and 26 of the Prosecution of Offences Act 1985 contain supplementary provisions relating to consents to prosecution. Section 25 provides that a requirement for consent shall not prevent the arrest of a suspect for the offence in question nor his initial remand (whether in custody or on bail). Section 26 provides that a document duly signed and purporting to be a consent to prosecution shall be admissible as prima facie evidence that consent has in fact been given.

Prosecution of Offences Act 1985, ss. 1(7), 25 and 26

1.—(7)   Where any enactment (whenever passed)—
 (a)   prevents any step from being taken without the consent of the Director or without his consent or the consent of another; . . .
any consent given by . . . a Crown Prosecutor shall be treated, for the purposes of that enactment, as given by . . . the Director.

25.—(1)   This section applies to any enactment which prohibits the institution or carrying on of proceedings for any offence except—
 (a)   with the consent (however expressed) of a Law Officer of the Crown or the Director; or
 (b)   where the proceedings are instituted or carried on by or on behalf of a Law Officer of the Crown or the Director;
and so applies whether or not there are other exceptions to the prohibition (and in particular whether or not the consent is an alternative to the consent of any other authority or person).
 (2)   An enactment to which this section applies—
 (a)   shall not prevent the arrest without warrant, or the issue or execution of a warrant for the arrest, of a person for any offence, or the remand in custody or on bail of a person charged with any offence; and
 (b)   shall be subject to any enactment concerning the apprehension or detention of children or young persons.

26.   Any document purporting to be the consent of a Law Officer of the Crown, the Director or a Crown Prosecutor for, or to—

(a)   the institution of any criminal proceedings; or

(b)   the institution of criminal proceedings in any particular form;

and to be signed by a Law Officer of the Crown, the Director or, as the case may be, a Crown Prosecutor shall be admissible as prima facie evidence without further proof.

TIME-LIMITS

D1.90   English law starts from the proposition that there is no restriction on the time which may elapse between the commission of an offence and the commencement of a prosecution for it. This applies even if the prosecutor has available to him evidence prima facie establishing the guilt of the accused for a lengthy period before he chooses to initiate proceedings. However, the staleness of the alleged offence is one discretionary factor which the police and the CPS ought to take into account when deciding whether a prosecution is justified (see **D1.65**). In addition, there are a number of specific statutory provisions prohibiting proceedings once a certain time has elapsed. These include:

(a)   MCA 1980, s. 127, which provides that a magistrates' court shall not try an information for a summary offence unless it was laid within six months of the offence.

(b)   Sexual Offences Act 1956, sch. 2, para. 10, which provides that prosecutions for unlawful sexual intercourse with a girl under 16 contrary to s. 6 of the Act must be commenced within 12 months.

(c)   Sexual Offences Act 1967, s. 7, which provides that prosecutions for gross indecency between men and buggery where no assault is involved and the 'victim' is 16 or over must be commenced within 12 months.

(d)   Trade Descriptions Act 1968, s. 19(1), which provides that prosecutions for any indictable offence under the Act must be commenced within three years of the offence or one year from its discovery whichever is the earlier.

If no time-limit is mentioned for an indictable offence, then the general rule applies, and prosecutions may be commenced for it however long ago the relevant events occurred. It should be noted that the restriction in the MCA 1980, s. 127, applies only to trials of *summary* offences. There is no time-limit on the summary trial of either-way offences save in those exceptional cases where a trial on indictment would equally be time-barred (in which event the same limitation applies in the magistrates' court as would apply in the Crown Court: MCA 1980, s. 127(4)).

The commencement of a prosecution is normally regarded as the charging of the accused at the police station or, where proceedings are not taken by way of charge, the laying of an information for the offence. A written information is treated as laid once it is delivered to the clerk's office of a magistrates' court with jurisdiction to issue process for the offence (see **D18.7**). Consequently, if that is done within any applicable time-limit, proceedings will be held to have been commenced timeously even if the information is not put before a justice or justices' clerk until a later date or, indeed, is never considered by him but is improperly dealt with by an assistant in the clerk's office acting in excess of his powers (see *Manchester Stipendiary Magistrate, ex parte Hill* [1983] 1 AC 328).

PERSONAL IMMUNITY FROM PROSECUTION

D1.91   The final special consideration relevant to commencement of proceedings is whether the offender is entitled to a personal immunity. The main categories of immunity are:

(a)   Age: children under 10 are irrebuttably presumed to be incapable of crime. Prosecutors should also consider, in the cases of children aged 10 to 13 inclusive, whether there is evidence to rebut the initial presumption that such a child is *doli incapax* (i.e. incapable of forming any necessary criminal intent).

(b)   Sovereign and diplomatic immunity: the Queen, foreign sovereigns or heads of State, their families and their private servants are all immune from criminal jurisdiction (State Immunity Act 1978, s. 20). In addition, the Diplomatic Privileges Act 1964 gives immunity to diplomatic agents, members of the staff of a diplomatic mission and their families.

SECTION D2: COURTS, JUDGES AND PARTIES

D2.1 The criminal trial of an adult takes place either in the Crown Court or in a magistrates' court. The criminal trial of a juvenile usually takes place in a special form of magistrates' court, known as the youth court, but sometimes takes place in either the Crown Court or an ordinary magistrates' court. The first part of this section describes the status, structure, judges and main heads of jurisdiction of the Crown Court and ordinary magistrates' courts. Youth courts are described in **D21.13** to **D21.20**.

THE CROWN COURT

Creation and Status

The Crown Court was created by the Courts Act 1971, and came into being on 1 January 1972. It replaced the former courts of assize and quarter sessions and a number of other criminal courts. The legislation governing it is largely contained in the Supreme Court Act 1981. Its practice and procedure are prescribed, *inter alia*, by the Crown Court Rules 1982 (SI 1982 No. 1109: see **appendix 1**), made by the Crown Court Rule Committee under s. 84 of the 1981 Act.

The Crown Court is part of the Supreme Court, and derives its jurisdiction from the provisions of the Supreme Court Act 1981 and any other jurisdiction-conferring enactments (see s. 1(1) of the 1981 Act, which provides that: 'The Supreme Court of England and Wales shall consist of the Court of Appeal, the High Court of Justice and the Crown Court, each having such jurisdiction as is conferred on it by or under this or any other Act'). As is apparent from the use of the singular in s. 1, the Crown Court is a *single* court. It follows that, although the Crown Court sits in many different locations and a case will normally be tried at a location near where the offence allegedly occurred, there are no territorial restrictions on the offences which may be tried at a certain location other than the general restriction by which the criminal courts of England and Wales do not (subject to certain exceptions) accept jurisdiction over offences committed abroad. Provided the Crown Court has jurisdiction to try the offence charged, the trial may take place at any location of the Crown Court. The choice of location will depend on the convenience of the parties, the nature of the offence charged and any directions given by the presiding judge of the relevant circuit as to the locations to which the magistrates' courts in the area of the circuit should normally commit for trial. (See MCA 1980, s. 7, and *Practice Direction (Crown Court: Allocation of Business)* [1995] 1 WLR 1083, para. 3 under the heading 'Classification'.)

In status, the Crown Court occupies a somewhat ambiguous position. Like the High Court, it is part of the Supreme Court and a superior court of record (Supreme Court Act 1981, s. 45(1)), with the same powers in relation to, for example, contempt and enforcement of its orders as are possessed by the High Court (s. 45(4)). Furthermore, when it exercises its jurisdiction in relation to trials on indictment, appeals from its decisions lie only to the Court of Appeal (Criminal Division), just as appeals from the High Court go to the Court of Appeal (Civil Division). On the other hand, decisions of the Crown Court which do not relate to trial on indictment (e.g., a decision taken in respect of an appeal from a magistrates' court) may be challenged in the High Court either by an appeal by way of case stated or by application for judicial review (see ss. 28(2) and 29(3) of the 1981 Act). Thus, for some purposes the Crown Court is treated as on a par with the High Court while for other purposes it is subject to the same supervisory jurisdiction as the High Court exercises in relation to magistrates' courts.

Structure

The many different locations in which the Crown Court sits are classified according to **D2.2** (a) geographical position and (b) status. As to (a), every location belongs to one of six 'circuits': (i) Midland and Oxford, (ii) North-Eastern, (iii) Northern, (iv) Wales and Chester, (v) Western, and (vi) South-Eastern. Each circuit is presided over by a High Court judge called the 'presiding judge' who has responsibility for taking certain decisions about the administration and distribution of work on the circuit. If considered desirable, a circuit may have both a senior presiding judge and one or more other presiding judges to assist him. As to (b), locations are either first, second or third tier. At first-tier locations, High Court judges regularly sit; at third-tier locations, High Court judges do not normally sit. Each circuit contains locations of each of the three tiers. The most serious cases will normally be committed to either a first or second-tier location, so that there will be at least the possibility of the trial being conducted by a High Court judge. At each location there is a senior judge (known as the 'resident judge') who is responsible, *inter alia*, for the allocation of business amongst the judges sitting at the location. There may also be 'responsible judges', to whom the resident judge may delegate some of his functions, and 'liaison judges' responsible for liaising between the Crown Court and the local magistrates' courts.

Judges

Supreme Court Act 1981, s. 8

(1)   The jurisdiction of the Crown Court shall be exercisable by–   **D2.3**
    (a)   any judge of the High Court; or
    (b)   any circuit judge or recorder; or
    (c)   subject to and in accordance with the provisions of sections 74 and 75(2), a judge of the High Court, circuit judge or recorder sitting with not more than four justices of the peace, and any such persons when exercising the jurisdiction of the Crown Court shall be judges of the Crown Court.

For ss. 74 and 75(2) (justices sitting in Crown Court), see **D2.8**. Section 8(1) must be read in conjunction with s. 24 (deputy circuit judges and assistant recorders) – see **D2.7**.

There are thus three principal categories of Crown Court judge, namely High Court judges, circuit judges and recorders. Justices of the peace also have the status of a judge of the Crown Court when they sit therein, but they are not empowered to exercise the Crown Court's jurisdiction save in association with one of the other categories of Crown Court judge. It is convenient to use the term 'professional judges' to refer to the judges of the Crown Court other than the justices of the peace referred to in s. 8(1)(c). All proceedings in the Crown Court must be heard and disposed of before a single professional judge of the court except where there is provision for justices to sit with such a judge (s. 73(1)).

High Court Judges   About 20 High Court judges may, at any one time, be asked by **D2.4** the Lord Chancellor to sit in the Crown Court. The Lord Chief Justice's *Practice Direction (Crown Court: Allocation of Business)* [1995] 1 WLR 1083 requires that certain categories of case either must or normally will be tried by a High Court judge (see **D12.1** and paras 1 and 2 of the direction under the heading 'Allocation of business within the Crown Court').

Circuit Judges   The office of circuit judge was created by the Courts Act 1971 at the **D2.5** same time as the Crown Court. Circuit judges are appointed by the Crown on the recommendation of the Lord Chancellor 'to serve in the Crown Court and county courts and to carry out such other judicial functions as may be conferred on them under this or any other enactment' (Courts Act 1971, s. 16(1)). The maximum number of circuit judges is to be 'determined from time to time by the Lord Chancellor with the concurrence of the [Treasury]' (s. 16(2)). The minimum qualification for a circuit judge is to be the holder of a ten-year Crown Court or ten-year county court qualification within the meaning of the Courts and Legal Services Act 1990, s. 71, or a recorder, or a person who has held as a full-time appointment for at least three years one of the offices listed in the Courts Act 1971, sch. 2, para. 1A (s. 16(3)). The appointment is a full-time one (s. 17(6)), with retirement normally at the end of the completed year of service in which the judge attains the age of 72 (s. 17(1)), though the Lord Chancellor has a discretion to allow him to continue in office until his 75th birthday (s. 17(2)). Conversely, the Lord Chancellor may remove a circuit judge from office before retirement age on the ground of 'incapacity or misbehaviour' (s. 17(4)). The salaries and pensions of circuit judges are determined by the Lord Chancellor with the consent of the Treasury (ss. 18 and 19).

D2.6   ***Recorders***   Recorders are appointed by the Crown on the recommendation of the Lord Chancellor 'to act as part-time judges of the Crown Court and to carry out such other judicial functions as may be conferred on them under this or any other enactment' (Courts Act 1971, s. 21(1) and (2)). The minimum qualification for a recorder is to have a ten-year Crown Court or ten-year county court qualification within the meaning of the Courts and Legal Services Act 1990, s. 71 (s. 21(2)). The appointment must specify the term for which the recorder is appointed and the frequency and duration of the occasions during that term on which he must be available to undertake his duties (s. 21(3)). The original term of appointment may subsequently be extended at the Lord Chancellor's discretion (s. 21(4)). When not sitting, the recorder may and normally does revert to private practice. Neither the initial term of appointment nor any extension thereof may be such as to last beyond the end of the completed year of service in which the recorder attains the age of 72 (s. 21(5)). A recorder's appointment may be terminated by the Lord Chancellor on grounds of incapacity, misbehaviour or failure to comply with the terms of his appointment (s. 21(6)). Remuneration and allowances are determined by the Lord Chancellor with the consent of the Treasury (s. 21(7)). Thus, the major difference between a circuit judge and a recorder is that the former is a full-time and the latter a part-time appointment.

D2.7   ***Deputy Circuit Judges and Assistant Recorders***   Section 8(1) of the Supreme Court Act 1981 (see **D2.3**) must be read in conjunction with the Courts Act 1971, s. 24:

Courts Act 1971, s. 24

(1)   If it appears to the Lord Chancellor that it is expedient as a temporary measure to make an appointment under this section in order to facilitate the disposal of business in the Crown Court . . . he may—

(a)   appoint to be a deputy circuit judge, during such period or on such occasions as he thinks fit, any person who has held office as a judge of the Court of Appeal or of the High Court or as a circuit judge; or

(b)   appoint to be an assistant recorder, during such period or on such occasions as he thinks fit, any barrister or solicitor of at least 10 years' standing.

(2)   . . . during the period or on the occasions for which a deputy circuit judge or assistant recorder is appointed under this section he shall be treated for all purposes as, and accordingly may perform any of the functions of, a circuit judge or a recorder as the case may be.

The combined effect of s. 8 of the 1981 Act and s. 24 of the 1971 Act is that there are five categories of paid, legally qualified judges sitting as judges of the Crown Court, namely, High Court judges, circuit judges, recorders, deputy circuit judges and assistant recorders.

D2.8   Justices   The circumstances in which the Crown Court either may or must comprise a professional judge sitting with justices are prescribed by: the Supreme Court Act 1981, ss. 74 and 75(2); the Crown Court Rules 1982, rr. 3 and 4; and para. 8 under the heading 'Allocation of business within the Crown Court' of the *Practice Direction (Crown Court: Allocation of Business)* [1995] 1 WLR 1083). In summary, their effect is that any proceedings which are listed for hearing by a circuit judge or recorder, other than cases listed for a plea of not guilty, *may* be allocated to a court including one or more justices, up to a maximum of four (s. 75(2); *Practice Direction*). For the hearing of appeals from a magistrates' court and for proceedings on a committal for sentence by a magistrates' court, the Crown Court *must* normally include not less than two and not more than four justices (s. 74(1)). The exceptions are that:

(a)　If the professional judge is of the opinion that arranging for two justices to sit would cause unreasonable delay, the court may consist of the judge and one justice (r. 4(1)).

(b)　If one or more of the justices who initially comprised the court subsequently withdraws or is absent for any reason, the proceedings may continue even if the professional judge is left by himself (r. 4(3)).

(c)　If, immediately after the conclusion of a person's trial on indictment (or the dismissal of his appeal against conviction), it is desired to deal with him for another offence in respect of which he has been committed for sentence, the court for sentence on the latter offence may consist of a professional judge sitting by himself or with only one justice (r. 4(2)).

Rule 5 prevents a justice from sitting in the Crown Court if he adjudicated in the relevant proceedings in the magistrates' court. Rule 3(4) provides that, where the appeal or committal for sentence is in respect of a juvenile, the justices sitting in the Crown Court must be members of a juvenile court panel (see **D21.15**) and the court must include both a man and a woman.

Supreme Court Act 1981, ss. 74 and 75

74.—(1)　On any hearing by the Crown Court—
　　(a)　of any appeal; or
　　(b)　of proceedings on committal to the Crown Court for sentence,
the Crown Court shall consist of a judge of the High Court or a circuit judge or a recorder who, subject to the following provisions of this section, shall sit with not less than two nor more than four justices of the peace.

　　(2)　[Within the limits prescribed in subsection (1), Crown Court Rules may prescribe the number of justices to constitute the court and the qualifications they must possess in order to sit.]

　　(3)　[Crown Court Rules may authorise a professional judge to enter upon the hearing of an appeal or committal for sentence even though the court is not constituted as required by subsection (1) or rules made under subsection (2).]

　　(4) and (5)　[The Lord Chancellor, having regard to the number of justices available for service in the Crown Court, may give directions that the requirements for justices to sit be relaxed.]

　　(6)　No decision of the Crown Court shall be questioned on the ground that the court was not constituted as required by or under subsections (1) and (2) unless objection was taken by or on behalf of a party to the proceedings not later than the time when the proceedings were entered on, or when the alleged irregularity began.

75.—(2)　Subject to section 74(1), the cases or classes of cases in the Crown Court suitable for allocation to a court comprising justices of the peace (including those by way of trial on indictment which are suitable for allocation to such a court) shall be determined in accordance with directions given by or on behalf of the Lord Chief Justice with the concurrence of the Lord Chancellor.

Crown Court Rules 1982

3.—(4)　On the hearing of an appeal from a youth court or of proceedings on committal by a youth court to the Crown Court under section 37 of the Magistrates' Courts Act 1980 or [section 43 of the Mental Health Act 1983], the Crown Court shall consist of a judge sitting with two justices each of whom is a member of a youth court panel and who are chosen so that the court shall include a man and a woman.

4.—(1)   The Crown Court may enter on any appeal or any proceedings on committal to the court for sentence notwithstanding that the court is not constituted as required by section 74(1) of the Supreme Court Act 1981 or rule 3 if it appears to the judge that the court could not be so constituted without unreasonable delay and the court includes—
    [(a) and (b)   concern, respectively, appeals under the Licensing Act 1964 and the Betting, Gaming and Lotteries Act 1963;]
    (c)   in a case to which paragraph (4) of [rule 3] applies, one justice who is a member of a youth court panel;
    [(d)   concerns affiliation proceedings (which have now been abolished)]
    (e)   in any other case, one justice . . .
    (2)   Without prejudice to paragraph (1), immediately after the conclusion of a person's trial on indictment for an offence or the determination of a person's appeal to the Crown Court in respect of his conviction by a magistrates' court for an offence, the Crown Court may enter on proceedings on his committal to the Crown Court for sentence in respect of any other offence notwithstanding that the Crown Court is not constituted as required by section 74(1) of the Supreme Court Act 1981 or paragraph 1(e).
    (3)   The Crown Court may at any stage continue with any proceedings with a court from which any one or more of the justices initially comprising the court has withdrawn, or is absent for any reason.

5.   A justice of the peace shall not sit in the Crown Court on the hearing of an appeal in a matter on which he adjudicated or of proceedings on committal of a person to the court for sentence under section 37 or 38 of the Magistrates' Courts Act 1980 by a court of which he was a member.

Practice Direction (Crown Court: Allocation of Business) [1995] 1 WLR 1083

Allocation of proceedings to a court comprising lay justices
8.   In addition to the classes of case specified in section 74 of the Supreme Court Act 1981 (appeals and proceedings on committal for sentence) any other proceedings apart from cases listed for pleas of not guilty which in accordance with these directions are listed for hearing by a circuit judge or recorder are suitable for allocation to a court comprising justices of the peace.

When the Crown Court comprises a professional judge sitting with a justice or justices, the decision of the court may be by a majority (Supreme Court Act 1981, s. 73(3)). It follows that the justices may out-vote the professional judge, although if an even-numbered court is equally divided the professional judge has a casting vote (ibid.). The principle that the justices participate equally with the judge in the decisions of the court applies not only to a final decision, such as the sentence to be passed in proceedings on a committal for sentence or the determination of an appeal, but also to interlocutory decisions (e.g., about the admissibility of evidence). Thus, in *Orpin* [1975] QB 283 the Court of Appeal held that a circuit judge and the justices with whom he was sitting acted correctly in retiring to consider together whether a confession which the defence had claimed to be involuntary was admissible or not. In matters of law, however, 'the lay justices must take a ruling from the presiding judge in precisely the same way as the jury is required to take his ruling when the jury considers its verdict' (per Lord Widgery CJ in *Orpin* at p. 287F).

The precise facts of *Orpin* would not occur today because justices are not allowed to sit with a professional judge if a case is listed for a plea of not guilty. The principles on the role of the justices stated in the case do, however, remain valid.

The role of the justices was further considered in *Newby* (1984) 6 Cr App R (S) 148, an appeal against sentence passed by a court consisting of a recorder and two justices following N's plea of guilty. Criticising the recorder for announcing sentence immediately after defence counsel's plea in mitigation and without any apparent consultation with the justices (although there had been consultation before coming into court and the passing of notes during counsel's speech), Caulfield J said (at p. 150):

> One would hardly need *Orpin* to recognise that where a recorder or any other judge is sitting with justices, the court consists of the presiding judge and the justices who sit with the judge, and of course on matters of fact the majority decision decides. So obviously there has to be consultation between the presiding judge and the justices who sit with him. [In the present case there had, as a matter of fact, been consultation but there had been no appearance of consultation.] . . .
>
> This court would like to emphasise that where a learned judge is sitting with magistrates, not only should he consult his fellow magistrates by law but he should make sure that the court appreciates that he has consulted. It is not necessary for the court to retire after each particular case. There is nothing wrong in notes being passed between members of the court. But when it comes to the point of sentence having to be given, it is far wiser for the court to show the public that the court is a composite court and that each member has a view which is expressed eventually through the president or chairman of the court.

It is submitted that his lordship's remarks are applicable not only to the passing of sentence but to all decisions (whether interlocutory or final) taken by a court which includes justices. It is also noteworthy that in both *Orpin* and *Newby* the court need not have included justices, since in neither case were the proceedings on appeal or committal for sentence. Nonetheless, since the justices had been chosen to sit, they were entitled to play as full a role in the court's decisions as if their presence were obligatory.

Modes of Address

Circuit judges, recorders, deputy circuit judges and assistant recorders should all be **D2.9** addressed when sitting in court as 'Your Honour', save that any judge sitting at the Central Criminal Court and any circuit judge who holds the office of honorary Recorder of Cardiff, honorary Recorder of Liverpool or honorary Recorder of Manchester should be addressed as 'My Lord' or 'My Lady' (*Practice Direction (Judges: Modes of Address)* [1982] 1 WLR 101 and *Practice Direction (Judges: Recorder of Cardiff)* [1999] 1 WLR 597).

High Court judges sitting in the Crown Court should be addressed as 'My Lord' or 'My Lady' as they would in the High Court.

In cause lists, forms and orders, the following descriptions are appropriate:

Circuit judges	His (or Her) Honour Judge A
Recorders	Mr (or Mrs) Recorder B
Deputy circuit judges	His (or Her) Honour CD, sitting as a deputy circuit judge
Assistant recorders	Mr (or Mrs, Miss or other title) EF, sitting as an assistant recorder

Jurisdiction

By the Supreme Court Act 1981, s. 1(1), the Crown Court has 'such jurisdiction as is **D2.10** conferred on it by or under this or any other Act'. By s. 45(2):

> there shall be exercisable by the Crown Court—
> (a)   all such appellate and other jurisdiction as is conferred on it by or under this or any other Act; and
> (b)   all such other jurisdiction as was exercisable by it immediately before the commencement of this Act.

Immediately before the commencement of the 1981 Act, the Crown Court exercised the jurisdiction which had been given to it by the Courts Act 1971, which jurisdiction included 'all appellate and other jurisdiction conferred on any court of quarter sessions . . . by or under any Act' (Courts Act 1971, s. 8 and sch. 1, para. 1). The Crown Court has thus inherited the jurisdiction of the older quarter sessions. Furthermore, s. 79(1) of the 1981 Act provides that 'All enactments and rules of law relating to proceedings in connection with indictable offences shall continue to have effect in relation to proceedings in the Crown Court'. It follows that, although the great bulk of the Crown Court's jurisdiction is statute-based, there may still be occasions when — before, during or after a trial on indictment — it is able to exercise a power derived from a rule of common law. An example is the power to release an offender and bind him over to come up for judgment, which is occasionally used in circumstances where the statutory powers to bind a person over to keep the peace or to defer sentence would be inappropriate.

Trial on Indictment

D2.11   The Crown Court has exclusive jurisdiction over trials on indictment (Supreme Court Act 1981, s. 46(1)). The jurisdiction is not geographically restricted: 'The jurisdiction of the Crown Court . . . shall include jurisdiction in proceedings on indictment for offences *wherever committed*, and in particular proceedings on indictment for offences within the jurisdiction of the Admiralty of England' (s. 46(2) emphasis added). This should not, however, be construed to mean that the Crown Court will in general accept jurisdiction over offences committed abroad. The basic rule is that the English criminal courts only inquire into offences allegedly committed in England or Wales or within the jurisdiction of the Admiralty, by which phrase is meant essentially offences committed on British ships on the high seas or on British or foreign ships in British territorial waters (see **D1.65** *et seq.* both for the general rule and the exceptions to it). Thus, the effect of s. 46(2) is that, assuming the alleged offence is indictable and is an offence in respect of which the English criminal courts accept jurisdiction, the Crown Court will have jurisdiction to try the accused for it.

Appeal

D2.12   A person convicted by a magistrates' court may, if he pleaded not guilty, appeal to the Crown Court against conviction and/or sentence; if he pleaded guilty, he may appeal against sentence (MCA 1980, s. 108, and see **D25.3**).

Committal for Sentence

D2.13   The numerous statutory provisions enabling magistrates' courts to commit an offender to the Crown Court to be sentenced are described fully elsewhere in this work (see **D20.13** *et seq.*).

Summary Offences

D2.14   In certain limited circumstances the Crown Court may have jurisdiction to deal with certain summary offences, pursuant to the CJA 1988, ss. 40 and 41. These sections are dealt with in detail in **D7.23** and **D9.6**.

Bail

D2.15   As well as being able to grant bail during the course of a trial on indictment or other proceedings before it, the Crown Court has jurisdiction, *inter alia*, to grant bail to a person: (a) who has been committed to it in custody for trial or sentence; (b) who is in custody and against whom proceedings have been transferred for trial; (c) who is appealing to it from a magistrates' court following the imposition of a custodial sentence by the justices; (d) who is appealing from it to the Court of Appeal and has been granted a certificate that the case is fit for appeal; (e) or who has been remanded in custody by a magistrates' court following an argued bail application (see Supreme Court Act 1981, s. 81 and **D5.6**).

These powers are subject to the restrictions on bail in the case of certain persons charged with homicide or rape (see **D5.10**).

Contempt etc.

The Supreme Court Act 1981, s. 45(4), provides that 'the Crown Court shall, in relation **D2.16** to the attendance and examination of witnesses, any contempt of court, the enforcement of its orders and all other matters incidental to its jurisdiction, have the like powers, rights, privileges and authority as the High Court'. In particular, the Crown Court is able to deal summarily (i.e. without the empanelling of a jury) with any contempt committed in the face of the court (see generally **B14.59** *et seq*.). The generality of s. 45(4) is subject to the saving that, for purposes of securing the attendance of witnesses, the Crown Court must use the powers given to it by the Criminal Procedure (Attendance of Witnesses) Act 1965, s. 8, and not proceed by way of subpoena.

Supreme Court Act 1981, ss. 45 and 46

45.—(1)   The Crown Court shall be a superior court of record.

(2)   Subject to the provisions of this Act, there shall be exercisable by the Crown Court—

(a)   all such appellate and other jurisdiction as is conferred on it by or under this or any other Act; and

(b)   all such other jurisdiction as was exercisable by it immediately before the commencement of this Act.

(3)   Without prejudice to subsection (2), the jurisdiction of the Crown Court shall include all such powers and duties as were exercisable or fell to be performed by it immediately before the commencement of this Act.

(4)   Subject to section 8 of the Criminal Procedure (Attendance of Witnesses) Act 1965 (substitution in criminal cases of procedure in that Act for procedure by way of subpoena) and to any provision contained in or having effect under this Act, the Crown Court shall, in relation to the attendance and examination of witnesses, any contempt of court, the enforcement of its orders and all other matters incidental to its jurisdiction, have the like powers, rights, privileges and authority as the High Court.

(5)   The specific mention elsewhere in this Act of any jurisdiction covered by subsections (2) and (3) shall not derogate from the generality of those subsections.

46.—(1)   All proceedings on indictment shall be brought before the Crown Court.

(2)   The jurisdiction of the Crown Court with respect to proceedings on indictment shall include jurisdiction of the Crown Court with respect to proceedings on indictment for offences wherever committed, and in particular proceedings on indictment for offences within the jurisdiction of the Admiralty of England.

MAGISTRATES' COURTS

Magistrates' courts consist of justices of the peace. The great majority of justices are **D2.17** unpaid lay men or women; a minority are salaried stipendiaries, with the minimum qualification of being barristers or solicitors of at least seven years' standing. A justice is appointed to act as such for a particular county, and is then assigned to the bench for one of the petty sessions areas into which the county is divided. Normally, he sits only in the magistrates' court for his petty sessions area. The bulk of the criminal jurisdiction of magistrates' courts has to be exercised by a court consisting of at least two lay justices sitting in open court in the area's petty-sessional court-house. Stipendiaries may sit alone. The law on justices and magistrates' courts is contained principally in: (a) the Justices of the Peace Act 1997 (appointment, removal etc. of justices and organisation of magistrates' courts); (b) the MCA 1980 (jurisdiction and powers of the courts); and (c) the Magistrates' Courts Rules 1981 (SI 1981 No. 552) (detailed practice and procedure).

By the Interpretation Act 1978, sch. 1, 'magistrates' courts', when used in any enactment, has the meaning assigned to it by the MCA 1980, s. 148. Section 148(1) provides that: 'the expression "magistrates' court" means any justice or justices of the peace acting under any enactment or by virtue of his or their commission or under the common law'. Thus, whenever a justice or justices sit for the purpose of exercising their jurisdiction as justices they constitute a magistrates' court. Moreover, the expression 'magistrates' court' has been held to include examining justices holding committal proceedings (*Atkinson* v *United States of America Government* [1971] AC 197, per Lord Reid at p. 234) and clearly also includes magistrates proceeding with a view to transfer for trial. Where proceedings, whether authorised or required by the 1980 Act or the CPIA 1996, in respect of a person fall into a number of distinct stages (as when a magistrates' court, after convicting an offender and imposing a fine, subsequently takes steps to enforce payment of the fine), the court for the later stage need not be constituted by the same justices as constituted the court on the first occasion (s. 148(2) and s. 76 of the 1996 Act). The obligation of a magistrates' court to sit in either a petty-sessional court-house or an occasional court-house for purposes of exercising the bulk of their jurisdiction is dealt with in **D2.22**.

Magistrates' Courts Act 1980, s. 148

(1)   In this Act the expression 'magistrates' court' means any justice or justices of the peace acting under any enactment or by virtue of his or their commission or under the common law.

(2)   Except where the contrary is expressed, anything authorised or required by this Act to be done by, to or before the magistrates' court by, to or before which any other thing was done, or is to be done, may be done by, to or before any magistrates' court acting for the same petty sessions area as that court.

Justices of the Peace (Magistrates)

D2.18   The titles 'justice' or 'justice of the peace' and 'magistrate' are interchangeable, although enactments normally use the former terminology. Justices are appointed by the Lord Chancellor 'on behalf and in the name of Her Majesty' (Justices of the Peace Act 1997, s. 5(1)). The Lord Chancellor normally acts on the recommendation of local advisory committees, of which there is at least one for each county. (There are different arrangements in the Duchy of Lancaster.)

Save in the special case of stipendiary magistrates (see below), justices are not required to possess any particular qualifications, whether legal or otherwise. There is, however, an obligation on new justices to complete, within a year of appointment, a course of basic instruction in the duties which they will be carrying out. Also a minority of justices are academic lawyers, and there is no objection to the holders or past holders of high judicial office serving as justices. For the special restrictions on the practice of solicitors who are justices, see the Solicitors Act 1974, s. 38. The only significant category of persons actually to be excluded from appointment are undischarged bankrupts (Justices of the Peace Act 1997, s. 65).

A justice may be removed from office by the Lord Chancellor (Justices of the Peace Act 1997, s. 5(1)). Assuming that does not occur, he retains his status as a justice for life. However, upon his attaining the age of 70 (75 in the case of those who hold or have held high judicial office), a justice's name is put on the 'supplemental list', which means that the only functions of a justice which he may perform are insignificant administrative ones, such as authenticating a person's signature. In addition, the Lord Chancellor may direct entry of a name on the supplemental list if either that is expedient because of the justice's age, infirmity or other like cause, or the justice declines or neglects to take a proper part in the work of the bench. A justice may also take the initiative and ask for his name to go on the supplemental list. For the provisions about the supplemental list, see s. 7 of the 1997 Act.

Justices, other than stipendiary magistrates, are not paid a salary for their work. They are, however, entitled to a travelling and/or subsistence allowance, and to compensation for loss of earnings etc. (Justices of the Peace Act 1997, s. 10).

Stipendiary Magistrates

Although the great majority of justices are lay, a minority are both paid and legally **D2.19** qualified. The latter are stipendiary magistrates, and the provisions regarding their appointment, removal, remuneration etc. are contained in the Justices of the Peace Act 1997, ss. 11 to 20.

Acting on the Lord Chancellor's recommendation, Her Majesty may appoint a barrister or solicitor of not less than seven years' standing to be a whole-time stipendiary magistrate in any commission area outside the Inner London area and City of London, and a person so appointed is, by virtue of his office, a justice of the peace for the area concerned (Justices of the Peace Act 1997, s. 11(1) to (3)). The total number of these non-metropolitan stipendiary magistrates shall not, at any one time, exceed 50 (s. 11(4)), but more than one stipendiary magistrate may be appointed for a single commission area. Section 16 of the 1997 Act contains analogous provisions for the appointment of metropolitan stipendiary magistrates. The maximum number of metropolitan stipendiaries shall not at any one time exceed 60 (s. 16(1)), and one of their number is to be designated by the Lord Chancellor as the chief metropolitan stipendiary magistrate (s. 16(3)). By virtue of his office, a metropolitan stipendiary magistrate is a justice of the peace for each of the London commission areas and for the counties of Essex, Hertfordshire, Kent and Surrey (s. 16(4)). Stipendiaries (both metropolitan and non-metropolitan) vacate their office – and thus cease to be justices – when they attain the age of 70, unless the Lord Chancellor authorises them to continue until the age of 75 (s. 12). The Lord Chancellor may remove a metropolitan stipendiary from office for inability or misbehaviour (s. 16(4)(b)), and recommend Her Majesty to remove a non-metropolitan stipendiary (s. 11(3)(b)). When it is expedient to do so to avoid delays in the administration of justice, the Lord Chancellor may appoint a barrister or solicitor of at least seven years' standing to act as a stipendiary magistrate for a period not exceeding three months (ss. 13 and 19).

Structure of the Magistrates' Courts System

By contrast with the Crown Court, which is a single court, there are a great number of **D2.20** separate benches of justices who form magistrates' courts as and when required to dispose of the business arising in the areas for which they act. The courts and justices are organised on the basis of commission areas, petty sessions areas and petty sessional divisions, which are defined as follows:

(a) *Commission areas* comprise the following geographical units: every county (both the six metropolitan ones and the non-metropolitan ones); every London commission area; and the City of London (Justices of the Peace Act 1997, s. 1(1)). Greater London is divided into five commission areas, namely the Inner, North-East, South-East and South-West London areas and the Middlesex area (s. 2). The rules concerning the jurisdiction of magistrates' courts in criminal matters are based on the commission areas. Since the great majority of commission areas are counties, it will be convenient to refer to them henceforth by that name. This also helps to avoid confusion with the petty sessions areas.

(b) *Petty sessional divisions.* Any non-metropolitan county, district of a metropolitan county or outer London borough may be split into petty sessional divisions by the magistrates' courts committee for the county, district or borough, acting in conjunction with the Lord Chancellor (Justices of the Peace Act 1997, s. 33). Analogous provisions apply to petty sessional divisions in the Inner London area.

(c) *Petty sessions areas.* These comprise all the petty sessional divisions, plus any non-metropolitan county, metropolitan district or outer London borough which is not split into divisions, plus the City of London (Justices of the Peace Act 1997, s. 4).

Jurisdiction

D2.21 The main heads of jurisdiction of magistrates' courts in criminal matters are as follows.

A court may try summary offences allegedly committed within the county for which the court acts (MCA 1980, s. 2(1)). If the accused is convicted, the court may sentence him to anything up to the maximum penalty provided for by the statute creating the offence.

A court may try offences triable either way allegedly committed by an adult if (a) the offence is not so serious that the court's powers of punishment in the event of conviction would be inadequate, and (b) the accused agrees (ss. 18 to 21). In the event of conviction, the court may impose a penalty of anything up to six months' imprisonment and a fine of £5,000 (s. 32(1)).

Where a court has convicted an adult of an offence triable either way it may commit him to the Crown Court for sentence if the court considers its powers of punishment to be inadequate (s. 38). Magistrates' courts have numerous other powers to commit for sentence (see **D20.13** *et seq.*).

A youth court has jurisdiction to try juveniles (persons who have not attained the age of 18) for any offence, whether indictable or summary, other than one of homicide, although in certain circumstances the court may choose instead to send the juvenile to the Crown Court for trial (s. 24).

A magistrates' court sitting as examining justices may inquire into an indictable offence allegedly committed by a person who appears or is brought before the court and, if there is a case to answer, commit him to the Crown Court to be tried. Both in respect of committal and in respect of summary trial of indictable offences, a magistrates' court's jurisdiction is not limited by the county in which the offence allegedly occurred but is dependent merely on the accused appearing or being brought before the court.

Before or during summary trial or proceedings for committal, a magistrates' court may adjourn the proceedings and remand the accused either on bail or in custody (ss. 5(1), 10(1) and 128). There is also power to bail: (a) an offender whose case has been adjourned for inquiries to be made about him prior to the passing of sentence (s. 10(3)); (b) a person who is being committed to the Crown Court for trial or sentence (ss. 6(3) and 38); and (c) a person who is appealing to the Crown Court or the High Court against conviction or sentence by the magistrates (s. 113).

Magistrates' courts are responsible for enforcing the payment of fines, both those fines imposed by a magistrates' court and those imposed by the Crown Court (see PCCA 1973, s. 32(1), and MCA 1980, ss. 75 to 91). Magistrates' courts act as supervising courts for community orders and, if an offender is brought before the court for allegedly failing to comply with the requirements of the order, the court may either fine him or impose a community service order on him or deal with him for the original offence or (if the probation order was made by the Crown Court) commit him to the Crown Court (see CJA 1991, sch. 2). A magistrates' court may deal with a person for misbehaviour etc. in court by imposing imprisonment for up to a month and a fine of £2,500 (Contempt of Court Act 1981, s. 12).

Several enactments give to metropolitan stipendiary magistrates and Inner London area lay justices a jurisdiction somewhat greater than that possessed by non-metropolitan stipendiaries and justices. In particular, extradition proceedings must be brought before a metropolitan court (see Extradition Act 1870 and Fugitive Offenders Act 1967).

Constitution and Place of Sitting

D2.22 Unless an enactment specifically provides to the contrary, a magistrates' court may not try an information summarily unless it is composed of at least two justices (MCA 1980,

s. 121(1)). This applies whether the offence charged is summary or indictable. Similarly, a court holding a means inquiry under s. 82 of the 1980 Act in respect of a fine defaulter must comprise at least two justices (s. 121(2)). The maximum number of justices who may sit is three (Justices of the Peace (Size and Chairmanship of Bench) Rules 1995 (SI 1995 No. 971), r. 3). In modern practice, the court practically always consists of two or three justices. If they include the chairman or one of the deputy chairmen elected by the justices for the petty sessions area at their annual meeting, then he presides unless he asks one of the others to do so (Justices of the Peace Act 1997, s. 22(2)). Where neither the chairman nor a deputy chairman is present, precedence will be determined either by any established rule or custom of the bench or, failing that, the order of names on the commission of the peace (see Home Office circular dated 16 October 1907). The justices composing the court before which any proceedings take place must remain present throughout the proceedings, save that (a) if one or more absent themselves but the court nonetheless is still validly constituted having regard to the nature of the proceedings and the provisions of the MCA 1980, s. 121, then the proceedings may continue before the remaining justices, and (b) where the court has convicted an accused and adjourned before sentencing him, the court which passes sentence need not be composed of the same justices who formed the 'convicting' court (s. 121(6) and (7)). Any decision of the bench may be arrived at by a majority (*Barnsley* v *Marsh* [1947] KB 672). In the event of an even-numbered court being equally divided the court must adjourn for re-hearing before a differently constituted bench (see **D19.10**). The above rules do not apply to stipendiary magistrates who may, and normally do, sit alone unless there is an express provision to the contrary (Justices of the Peace Act 1997, ss. 14(2) and 18(6)). For the special rules governing the constitution of youth courts, see **D21.13** *et seq*.

A magistrates' court may not try summarily an information for an indictable offence except when sitting in a petty-sessional court-house (MCA 1980, s. 121(3)(a)). It may not (a) try an information for a summary offence, or (b) hold an inquiry into the means of a fine defaulter under s. 82 of the 1980 Act, or (c) impose imprisonment, except when sitting in either a petty-sessional court-house or an occasional court-house (s. 121(3)(b)). Moreover, a magistrates' court composed of a single justice or sitting in an occasional court-house may not impose imprisonment for a period exceeding 14 days, and may not order a person to pay more than £1, whether by way of fine, costs, compensation or otherwise (s. 121(5)). A petty-sessional court-house is one at which 'justices are accustomed to assemble for holding special or petty sessions', and there may be more than one such court-house in a single petty sessions area (see the definition in the 1980 Act, s. 150). The magistrates' courts committee for the county of which the petty sessions area is a part determines, after consultation with the appropriate local authority what shall be provided in the way of petty-sessional court-houses and other accommodation. An occasional court-house is any place which the justices acting for a petty sessions area, after giving public notice, appoint to be used as such (s. 147). Thus, a justice's house or the justices' clerk's office may be used as occasional court-houses. Stipendiary magistrates sit at court-houses determined in accordance with directions given by the Lord Chancellor (Justices of the Peace Act 1997, ss. 14(1) and 17(2)). Unless there is a statutory provision to the contrary, when a magistrates' court is required to sit in a petty-sessional or occasional court-house, it shall sit in open court (MCA 1980, s. 121(4) and see **D2.47** *et seq*.).

Normal practice is for committal proceedings to take place in the petty-sessional court-house before a bench of two or three lay justices (or a single stipendiary).

Magistrates' Courts Act 1980, ss. 121, 147 and 150

121.—(1)   A magistrates' court shall not try an information summarily . . . except when composed of at least two justices unless the trial . . . is one that by virtue of any enactment may take place before a single justice.

(2)   A magistrates' court shall not hear an inquiry into the means of an offender for the purposes of section 82 above [court must normally have held a means inquiry before issuing a warrant for the imprisonment of a fine defaulter] except when composed of at least two justices.

(3)   A magistrates' court shall not—

(a)   try summarily an information for an indictable offence . . . except when sitting in a petty-sessional court-house;

(b)   try an information for a summary offence or hold an inquiry into the means of an offender for the purposes of section 82 above, or impose imprisonment, except when sitting in a petty-sessional court-house or an occasional court-house.

(4)   Subject to the provisions of any enactment to the contrary, where a magistrates' court is required by this section to sit in a petty-sessional or occasional court-house, it shall sit in open court.

(5)   A magistrates' court composed of a single justice, or sitting in an occasional court-house, shall not impose imprisonment for a period exceeding 14 days or order a person to pay more than £1.

(6)   Subject to the provisions of subsection (7) below, the justices composing the court before which any proceedings take place shall be present during the whole of the proceedings; but, if during the course of the proceedings any justice absents himself, he shall cease to act further therein and, if the remaining justices are enough to satisfy the requirements of the preceding provisions of this section, the proceedings may continue before a court composed of those justices.

(7)   Where the trial of an information is adjourned after the accused has been convicted and before he is sentenced or otherwise dealt with, the court which sentences or deals with him need not be composed of the same justices as that which convicted him [but in that event the 'new' justices must be made fully acquainted with the facts and circumstances of the case].

147.—(1)   The justices acting for a petty sessions area may appoint as an occasional court-house any place that is not a petty-sessional court-house.

(2)   A place appointed as an occasional court-house after 31st May 1953 shall not be used as such unless public notice has been given that it has been appointed.

[(3)   There may be more than one occasional court-house per petty sessions area, and the court-house need not be within the area for which it is appointed.]

150.—(1)   . . . 'petty-sessional court-house' means any of the following, that is to say—

(a)   a court-house or place at which justices are accustomed to assemble for holding special or petty sessions or for the time being appointed as a substitute for such a court-house or place (including, where justices are accustomed to assemble for either special or petty sessions at more than one court-house or place in a petty sessional division, any such court-house or place);

(b)   a court-house or place at which a stipendiary magistrate is authorised by law to do alone any act authorised to be done by more than one justice of the peace.

Justices of the Peace (Size and Chairmanship of Bench) Rules 1995 (SI 1995 No. 971), r. 3

3.   The number of justices sitting to deal with a case as a magistrates' court, other than such a court sitting as a youth court . . . shall not be greater than three.

Justices' Clerks

D2.23   A justices' clerk must be a barrister or solicitor of at least five years' standing, or a barrister or solicitor who has served for not less than five years as assistant to a justices' clerk (Justices of the Peace Act 1997, s. 43). There is normally one clerk for each petty sessional division, although more than one may be appointed (s. 42(1)). Clerks are appointed by the magistrates' courts committee for the county. An appointment requires the Lord Chancellor's approval. The clerk may be removed from office by the committee, but this requires the Lord Chancellor's approval if the magistrates for the division do not consent (s. 42(5)).

The duties of the justices' clerk, most of which he can delegate to his staff, include: sitting in court with the justices during the conduct of proceedings; advising the justices (whether in court or out) on matters of law, practice and procedure; organising the administration of the petty sessional division's work; processing legal aid applications; collecting fines; and preparing summonses for issue by the justices (or issuing summonses himself).

As to sitting in court, it is not necessary for the clerk himself to be there – he can delegate the task to an assistant who, if need be, can ask him to come into court and advise should any particularly difficult point arise. However, an assistant clerk in court must have certain minimum qualifications (see Justices' Clerks (Qualification of Assistants) Rules 1979 (SI 1979 No. 570).

DISQUALIFICATION OF JUSTICES AND JUDGES FROM HEARING PARTICULAR CASES

A justice may be disqualified from adjudicating in certain proceedings either by reason **D2.24** of the rule of natural justice that a member of a tribunal must not be biased, or by reason of a specific statutory provision. Where a justice sits when he ought not to have done, the decision of the court is liable to be quashed through the High Court issuing an order of certiorari upon an application for judicial review. However, the issue of a certiorari is discretionary, so, if a party knew of an objection to a justice before the commencement of the proceedings but failed to ask him to withdraw, certiorari may be refused (per Lord Alverstone CJ in *Byles, ex parte Hollidge* (1912) 108 LT 270). The same rules apply to judges sitting in the Crown Court, though the problem occurs less frequently, and is mitigated by the role of the jury in deciding the facts of the case.

One of the two commonly stated rules of natural justice is *nemo iudex in causa sua* (no one shall be a judge in his own cause). A justice may not sit if he has any direct pecuniary or proprietary interest, however slight, in the outcome of the proceedings (*Rand* (1866) LR 1 QB 230: 'There is no doubt that any direct pecuniary interest, however small, in the subject of inquiry, does disqualify a person from acting as a judge in the matter', per Blackburn J at p. 232). Thus, in *Hammond* (1863) 9 LT 423, certiorari issued to quash H's conviction for travelling on the railway without a valid ticket, because members of the convicting court were shareholders in the relevant railway company. The applicant for certiorari need not show that the magistrate was actually biased by reason of his pecuniary interest, or even that there was a real danger of bias (see *Dimes v Grand Junction Canal Proprietors* (1852) 3 HL Cas 759 where a ruling by Lord Cottenham, the then Lord Chancellor, in equity proceedings was set aside by the House of Lords because he owned shares in the canal company which benefited from the ruling, even though Lord Campbell said that: 'No one can suppose that Lord Cottenham could be, in the remotest degree, influenced by the interest that he had in this concern').

However, an indirect (as opposed to direct) pecuniary interest will not automatically disqualify a justice, although it may be sufficient to disqualify him under the principles described in *Gough* [1993] AC 646 (which is discussed in **D2.25**). The distinction between direct and indirect interests was drawn by Lord Denning MR in *Metropolitan Properties Co. (FGC) Ltd v Lannon* [1969] 1 QB 577, where the Court of Appeal rejected the argument that the chairman of a rent assessment committee had a disqualifying pecuniary interest in the outcome of an application to reduce the rent payable for a flat in one property owned by a large property company merely because he lived with his father in a flat in a different property owned by the same company, and any reduction of rents at the property the subject of the application might have been used as an argument for reducing the rents at the property where he lived. Such pecuniary interest as the chairman had was merely indirect. Nonetheless, the Court of Appeal held that he ought not to have adjudicated.

In *Bow Street Metropolitan Stipendiary Magistrate, ex parte Pinochet Ugarte (No. 2)* [1999] 2 WLR 272, the House of Lords examined the circumstances in which a judge ought to be disqualified from hearing a case by reason of an interest in the outcome of the hearing. The context was that Senator Pinochet, former Chilean head of state, faced extradition for crimes against humanity. The appellate committee of the House of Lords had decided that he did not have immunity from arrest and extradition. Before the main hearing of that appeal began, the organisation Amnesty International was granted leave to intervene in the appeal. One of the members of the committee which heard the appeal was Lord Hoffmann, who was an unpaid director and chairman of the Amnesty International Charity Ltd. This organisation was closely associated with Amnesty International, and shared many of its goals, including an interest in establishing that there was no immunity for ex-heads of state in relation to crimes against humanity. Lord Hoffman's position became known to Pinochet's solicitors after the judgment in the appeal, whereupon they petitioned the House of Lords to set aside their earlier decision. At the hearing of this application, Lord Browne-Wilkinson (with whom the other law lords concurred) stressed that the fundamental principle was that a man could not be a judge in his own cause. Although the cases had all dealt with automatic disqualification on the ground of pecuniary interest, there was no good reason in principle for so limiting automatic disqualification. If a judge was a party to the cause, or had a relevant interest in the subject matter, he was disqualified without any investigation into whether there was a likelihood or suspicion of bias. Unless he had made adequate disclosure, the mere fact of his interest was sufficient to disqualify him, even in a case such as this where actual bias was not alleged. In this case, Amnesty was a party to the appeal, joined to argue for a particular result (that Pinochet was not immune). The judge was a director of a charity closely allied to Amnesty and sharing its objects in respect of that result. Their lordships set aside the earlier order, and directed a rehearing of the appeal before a differently constituted committee.

Actual or Apparent Bias

D2.25   If a justice has an interest other than a direct pecuniary or proprietary one in the outcome of a case, he is disqualified from sitting if there is a real possibility of bias on his part. Although a non-pecuniary interest does not automatically disqualify a justice, it is not essential to show that he actually was biased. It is sufficient that there was a real danger of bias on his part. This is the test laid down by the House of Lords in *Gough* [1993] AC 646, which their lordships stated to be applicable with equal force to proceedings before the justices and to trial upon indictment. For fuller discussion of *Gough*, see **D11.11**. See also *Altrincham Justices, ex parte Pennington* [1975] QB 549; *Allinson v General Council of Medical Education and Registration* [1894] 1 QB 750; *Hannam v Bradford Corporation* [1970] 1 WLR 937; *Bradford v McLeod* 1986 SLT 244; *Hereford Magistrates' Court, ex parte Rowlands* [1997] 2 Cr App R 340 at p. 359; *Bow Street Metropolitan Stipendiary Magistrate, ex parte Pinochet Ugarte (No. 2)* [1999] 2 WLR 272.

Bench's Knowledge of Accused's Record or Pending Matters

D2.26   The same principles are to be applied where facts about the accused which might cause prejudice against him are known to the justice. In *Liverpool City Justices, ex parte Topping* [1983] 1 WLR 119, T was to be tried by the justices on a charge of criminal damage to which he had pleaded not guilty. He was also charged with six offences of failing to answer bail and one of being drunk in a public place, on all of which no plea had been taken. The court sheets placed before the justices showed all eight charges (i.e. the one the justices were to try and the seven outstanding). T's solicitor submitted that the bench as constituted should not continue with the hearing since they would or might be prejudiced by their knowledge of the other outstanding matters. The justices rejected the submission, proceeded to trial and convicted T. The Divisional Court quashed the conviction.

However, contrary to dicta in *Ex parte Topping*, there is no blanket rule that the court sheets placed before justices must not reveal that there are other charges outstanding against the accused in the same court or that there are offences for which he is awaiting sentence. Where a submission is made that such knowledge disqualifies the justices from acting, they have a discretion to order that the case be tried by a differently constituted bench, but if, having applied the correct test, they conclude that it is proper for them to continue with the case, the Divisional Court will not interfere with their decision (*Weston-super-Mare Justices, ex parte Shaw* [1987] QB 640, in which a conviction for wasting police time was upheld even though the convicting justices knew from the court sheets that S faced six unrelated charges relating to 'an escapade with a motor scooter').

Similar considerations apply where a justice knows from previous dealings with the accused that he is of bad character. The question is whether, having regard to the circumstances of the particular case, there is a real danger of bias on the part of the justice were he to sit (see *Downham Market Magistrates' Court, ex parte Nudd* [1989] RTR 169, in which N's conviction for failing to provide a specimen of breath to ascertain whether the proportion of alcohol therein was over the prescribed limit was quashed because the chairman of the convicting bench had a month earlier passed a suspended sentence on N for threatening behaviour towards his wife and had, on that occasion, been shown N's criminal record, which included a conviction for driving while unfit through drink).

Nonetheless, there is no proposition of law that a justice who knows of the accused's previous convictions must never adjudicate (*McElligott, ex parte Gallagher* [1972] Crim LR 332 – conviction upheld even though the stipendiary magistrate had an intimate knowledge of G's record). Where a petty sessional bench is small in number it may be difficult to arrange for justices who have not had previous dealings with a local recidivist offender to form a court to try him. For example, the Downham Market bench, at the time *Ex parte Nudd* was decided, consisted of only 11 justices. Nudd's solicitor had written in advance of trial to the clerk requesting that a different chairman sit, but the clerk made no attempt to comply with the request, and it may be that this arbitrary rejection of an apparently reasonable defence request was a crucial factor in persuading the Divisional Court that the conviction should be quashed.

For the special statutory rule applying where a justice has previously ruled on a bail application by the accused and thereby learned his previous convictions, see **D2.27**. See also **D18.27** for the trial of successive informations by the same bench. For the practical application of the test for bias, see *Romsey Justices, ex parte Gale* (1991) 156 JP 567 (preparation by a justice during the trial of a note of the comments he might make upon conviction); *Marylebone Magistrates' Court, ex parte Perry* (1992) 156 JP 696 (stipendiary dealing with paperwork in other cases while evidence was being given), *Ely Justices, ex parte Burgess* [1992] Crim LR 888 (prosecutor travelling in the same car as the justices to an inspection of the scene of the alleged offence), and *Hereford Magistrates' Court, ex parte Rowlands* [1997] 2 Cr App R 340 at p. 361g (disclosure that accused awaiting trial on a more serious charge). For further useful dicta on the test for bias, see *Allinson* v *General Council of Medical Education & Registration* [1894] 1 QB 750 at p. 758; *Metropolitan Properties Co. (FGC) Ltd* v *Lannon* [1969] 1 QB 577 at p. 599; *Hannam* v *Bradford Corporation* [1970] 1 WLR 937 at p. 949. For pre-trial expressions of opinion by justices see *Bradford* v *McLeod* 1986 SLT 244.

Specific Statutory Provisions Disqualifying Justices from Hearing Particular Cases

Specific statutory provisions on the appropriateness or otherwise of justices being **D2.27** members of a court include the following:

(a) A justice who is a member of a local authority (i.e. a county council, district council, London borough council, parish or community council, joint authority, housing action trust or police authority) may not be a member of the Crown Court or of a magistrates' court in any proceedings brought by or against (or by way of appeal from the decision of) the authority or any committee or officer of the authority (Justices of the Peace Act 1997, s. 66(1)). The disqualification does not extend to justices' clerks (see *Camborne Justices, ex parte Pearce* [1955] 1 QB 41). Nor does anything in s. 66 prevent a justice acting in proceedings solely because they are brought by a police officer (s. 66(5)). If it were not for that express saving, it might be argued that s. 66(1) disqualifies a justice from hearing any prosecution brought by the police simply because the local authority of which he is a member is represented on the police authority and contributes towards the cost of maintaining the force. The position of justices who actually serve on the police authority was considered *obiter* by Lord Widgery CJ in *Altrincham Justices, ex parte Pennington* [1975] QB 549. Rejecting the argument that holding the justice in that case to have been disqualified by reason of her membership of the education committee would lead, by analogy, to holding a member of a police authority disqualified for purposes of any police prosecution, his lordship said (at p. 555B): 'In my judgment the situation there is wholly different. The police authority are concerned with the administration of the police force. They are not concerned with the rights and wrongs of individual prosecutions. They are not given an interest in the rights and wrongs of individual prosecutions merely because the prosecutor is, as he must normally be, a police officer. That seems to me to be a wholly different situation and not susceptible to the same test at all.'

(b)   A justice may not be a member of a court trying an accused summarily on a not guilty plea if, in the course of the same proceedings, he has been informed, for the purpose of determining whether to grant bail, that the accused has one or more previous convictions (MCA 1980, s. 42(1)). (Contrast the position in the Crown Court, where no such restraints are imposed on a judge or recorder.)

Disqualification of Judges of the Crown Court from Hearing Particular Cases

D2.28   The rule that nobody may be a judge in his own cause applies generally, and is certainly not restricted to magistrates' courts or other inferior tribunals (for the most striking illustration, see *Bow Street Stipendiary Magistrate, ex parte Pinochet Ugarte (No. 2)* [1999] 2 WLR 272 at **D2.24**). What, then, is the position as far as Crown Court judges are concerned? The issue arose, apparently for the first time in *Mulvihill* [1990] 1 WLR 438. M was charged with conspiracy to rob persons at premises belonging to banks and building societies, including at least one branch of the National Westminster Bank. The presiding judge was at the time of the trial the owner of 1,650 shares in National Westminster Bank plc. M was convicted and appealed, *inter alia*, on the ground that the judge should have disclosed his ownership of the shares. The Court of Appeal held that the rules relating to automatic disqualification (based upon *Dimes v Grand Junctions Canal Proprietors* (1852) 3 HL Cas 759 – see **D2.24**) had no direct application. Their lordships held, on the basis that the summing-up was impeccable and the conduct of the trial was not open to criticism, that there could be no reasonable suspicion of bias. The function of a judge conducting a trial on indictment is, they said, 'different from that of a lay justice who is one of the primary decision makers in . . . the magistrates' court'. This was so despite the fact that the judge had to make direct decisions on the admissibility of evidence during the course of trials within the trial. (For the contrasting position relating to jurors, see **D11.11** *et seq.*)

As far as the Crown Court's jurisdiction on appeal from magistrates is concerned, see *Bristol Crown Court, ex parte Cooper* [1989] 1 WLR 878. In that case, it was said that if there was any doubt about whether it was appropriate for a particular justice to sit in on an appeal when he has been involved in any way in the matter below, that fact should be mentioned at the outset, so that the parties could make submissions to the appellate court, and the question could be considered in the light of the submissions. It is submitted that the considerations which should apply to a judge sitting with justices on an appeal from a magistrates' court are similar to those which were relevant in *Ex parte Cooper*. The judge in this situation is part of the tribunal of fact (contrast his position in a trial by jury in the Crown Court) and the same test should be applied as would be to one of the justices.

PARTIES TO CRIMINAL PROCEEDINGS

The parties to criminal proceedings are the prosecutor and the accused. **D2.29**

Prosecutor

The prosecutor is the person who commences the prosecution process, even if he plays little or no direct part in the subsequent court proceedings. Therefore, identifying the prosecutor involves appreciation of the methods by which prosecutions may be commenced. Hence, these paragraphs should be read in conjunction with **D4.2** *et seq*.

(a) Where a prosecution is commenced by the laying of an information before a magistrate (or a magistrates' clerk), the prosecutor is he who lays the information. In the case of a written information, the prosecutor is the person who signs it or who authorises another to lay the information on his behalf (see Magistrates' Courts Rules 1981, r. 4(1)). In the case of an oral information, the prosecutor is the person who goes before the magistrate (or clerk) to make the allegation against the accused.

(b) Where a prosecution is commenced by the accused being charged at the police station, the prosecutor (subject to one possible qualification discussed below) is the police officer who signs the charge sheet, charge sheets being by practice equated with informations laid before magistrates.

It follows from the above that, in legal theory, all prosecutions are commenced by private individuals, not by the State or State organisations. However, should the accused be tried on indictment for the alleged offence, the prosecutor is at that stage regarded as acting on behalf of the Crown, and the case will be entitled 'The Queen and [name of accused]'. But even this does not of itself mean that the State has any direct influence or control over the trial – it is a matter of form and nomenclature rather than substance.

Despite the theory that that prosecutor is an individual, the practical reality is normally very different, since the great majority of prosecutions are commenced either by police officers as part of their duties or by the officers of governmental or quasi-governmental organisations such as local authorities, the Inland Revenue, Customs and Excise or the Department of Social Security. It is then more realistic to describe the proceedings as being brought by the organisation concerned, not by an individual. Thus, in the case of a police officer's prosecution, the costs, insofar as they are not met by the Crown Prosecution Service (see **D2.33**), will be met by the force of which the officer is a member. Moreover, in any civil proceedings against the officer for malicious prosecution, the plaintiff may join the chief officer of the force as a co-defendant, and any damages awarded will be paid out of the police fund (Police Act 1996, s. 88). The fact that virtually no significance attaches to which officer commences a prosecution is reflected in the differing practices of police forces concerning the signature of a written information. Some forces have a practice of always laying the information in the name of the chief constable or other senior officer; other forces prefer the officer who reported the offence to sign the information. In *Hawkins* v *Bepey* [1980] 1 WLR 419 the Divisional Court implicitly confirmed that prosecutions begun by police officers are in effect brought by the relevant police force, by holding that the death of the nominal informant shortly after magistrates had dismissed the case against the accused did not prevent the bringing of an appeal by case stated against the acquittal.

Can an Association Commence a Prosecution?

D2.30   By r. 4(1) of the Magistrates' Courts Rules 1981, 'An information may be laid . . . by the prosecutor . . . or by his counsel or solicitor or other person authorised in that behalf'. It might be thought that, by permitting informations to be laid by an agent acting on behalf of the actual prosecutor, r. 4(1) is impliedly recognising that associations may bring prosecutions through the agency of a legal representative or duly authorised member. Such an interpretation of the rule was, however, rejected by the Divisional Court in *Rubin* v *DPP* [1990] 2 QB 80. The facts were that an information against R for speeding purported to have been preferred by 'The Thames Valley Police'. It was conceded that a police force is an unincorporated association but reliance was placed on sch. 1 to the Interpretation Act 1978 which states that, unless the contrary intention appears, the word 'person' in a statute or statutory instrument 'includes a body of persons corporate or unincorporate'. Nevertheless, Watkins LJ (giving the court's judgment) rejected any suggestion that the Thames Valley Constabulary could be regarded as the prosecutor. He said (at pp. 89G–90A):

> . . . when the police bring a prosecution it has to be commenced by an information which has been laid by a member of the force; that is to say, by that member who reported the offence and the person accused of committing it or by the chief constable himself or some other member of the force authorised by him to lay an information.

> I cannot accept that Parliament intended the definition of 'person' in schedule 1 to the Interpretation Act 1978 to apply to the laying of informations. . . . In any event, I do not see from where a chief constable could derive the power to, so to speak, delegate his authority to commence a prosecution by laying an information to an inanimate body, corporate or unincorporate.

The last sentence quoted, especially, suggests that no distinction is to be drawn for these purposes between incorporated and unincorporated associations – neither is capable of laying an information or having an information laid on its behalf, hence neither is capable of bringing prosecutions. This proposition was, however, doubted by Woolf LJ in *Ealing Justices, ex parte Dixon* [1990] 2 QB 91, where his lordship said that 'passages in the judgment of Watkins LJ could be regarded as indicating that a prosecution has to be by an individual rather than a corporate person' but that he (Woolf LJ) had 'reservations as to the reasoning which would lead to this conclusion' (at p. 101D). Even so, his lordship thought it preferable for an individual to be the informant, albeit that he was acting on behalf of a body corporate. The importance of the point at issue in *Rubin* and *Ex parte Dixon* should not be exaggerated. It goes only to the form of an information and who should nominally be regarded as the prosecutor. Where an actual individual lays an information in the course of his duties as an officer or employee of an association, the association will almost certainly lend its resources and authority to the conduct of the prosecution and, in that sense, will be the prosecutor. That is so whether the association is a company with legal personality or an unincorporated association such as a police force.

Can Persons Who Are Not Police Officers Commence Prosecutions by Way of Charge?

D2.31   The procedure of charging a suspect at a police station is described at **D1.56**. It is a procedure which, by its very nature, must take place at a police station. Moreover, the PACE 1984, s. 37, places the responsibility for deciding whether or not a person should be charged on the custody officer on duty at the station where the suspect is being detained at the relevant time (see s. 37(7) especially). Prior to the enactment of the 1984 Act, it sometimes happened that non-police officers who had effected a 'citizen's arrest' would accompany the person arrested to a police station and there ask for a charge to be preferred. The private individual might then be asked to sign the charge sheet, and it would be understood that, from then on, he – not the police – would be responsible for the conduct of the prosecution. The legality of such a procedure was called into question by *Ealing Justices, ex parte Dixon* [1990] 2 QB 91. In that case, an incorporated association known as 'FACT' (the Federation against Copyright Theft Ltd) investigated possible infringements of the Copyright Act 1956 by a number of persons (the defendants). The investigations were conducted in cooperation with the police, who eventually arrested the defendants at FACT's request. Ultimately they were charged at the police station. The charge sheet was signed both by the custody officer and by D, a senior investigating officer of FACT, who was present at the police station and who had been principally involved in the inquiries. It was the understanding of the custody officer that the prosecution would henceforward be conducted by D and/or FACT (which has special expertise in the area of copyright infringements). On the defendants appearing before the magistrates' court, a solicitor present to represent FACT sought to conduct the prosecution. The defendants successfully argued that he had no *locus standi* and, since the representative of the CPS had no file or instructions in the matter, the proceedings had to be dismissed for want of prosecution.

FACT applied for judicial review of the justices' decision. The Divisional Court held that, where proceedings are commenced by way of charge, the prosecutor is the custody sergeant who accepts the charge, and the prosecution is therefore brought on behalf of the police. By the Prosecution of Offences Act 1985, s. 3(2), the DPP (acting through the CPS) is obliged to take over the conduct of all police prosecutions, and the police cannot themselves choose to delegate the responsibility for prosecuting to another person or organisation such as D or FACT. Although the DPP can authorise an agent to prosecute a case on his behalf (see s. 5 of the 1985 Act), no such authorisation had been given in the instant case. It followed that the solicitor for FACT indeed had no *locus standi* and, the CPS not being in a position to proceed in the matter, the justices correctly dismissed the charge. The logic of *Ex parte Dixon* is that a custody sergeant who is invited to prefer a charge on behalf of a person or organisation other than a police officer should decline to do so, unless he (the custody officer) is prepared for the prosecution to be henceforward the responsibility of the police and the CPS. If he is not willing for that to be so, he should release the suspect without charge and inform the putative prosecutor that he should lay an information before a magistrate.

Ex parte Dixon was, however, expressly disapproved in *Stafford Justices, ex parte Customs and Excise Commissioners* [1991] 2 QB 339. In that case, L was arrested without warrant. She was subsequently charged under the Drug Trafficking Offences Act 1986, s. 24(1)(a). The charge was drafted by a customs officer, who took her to a police station where the custody officer formally charged her. At the subsequent old-style committal, it was submitted that the justices had no jurisdiction to commit, since Customs and Excise had no standing to prosecute under that provision as it then stood (relying on *Ex parte Dixon*). The justices dismissed the case. They based their decision on the Prosecution of Offences Act 1985, s. 3(2)(a), which states that it is the duty of the DPP to take over the conduct of all criminal proceedings (other than proceedings specified by order of the A-G) which have been 'instituted on behalf of a police force'. The justices ruled that this prosecution had been instituted on behalf of a police force, so that only the CPS (on behalf of the DPP) could conduct the case. The Commissioners of Customs and Excise sought orders of certiorari and mandamus and a declaration that they could prosecute under the Drug Trafficking Offences Act 1986, notwithstanding that a police officer had charged the accused.

The Divisional Court granted the applications. A person such as a customs officer, who has investigated an offence, and arrested a suspect, does not, by taking him to a police station to be charged by the custody officer, surrender prosecution of the proceedings to the DPP. The court held that *Ex parte Dixon* had been wrongly decided.

The reasoning in *Stafford Justices, ex parte Customs and Excise Commissioners* was followed in *Croydon Justices, ex parte Holmberg* (1993) 157 JP 277, where it was held that seeking police assistance did not turn proceedings brought by a local authority into proceedings brought on behalf of a police force.

The Director of Public Prosecutions

D2.32 Insofar as the State plays a direct role in the prosecution system, it does so through the DPP and the law officers of the Crown (the A-G and Solicitor-General).

The office of DPP was created in 1879, although the present legislation concerning him is contained in the Prosecution of Offences Act 1985. He is a barrister or solicitor of at least ten years' standing, appointed by the A-G and paid such remuneration as is agreed between the A-G and the Treasury (Prosecution of Offences Act 1985, s. 2). He discharges his functions under the superintendence of the A-G (s. 3(1)). The DPP's duties are listed in s. 3(2)(a) to (g) and are as follows:

(a) To take over the conduct of all criminal proceedings instituted on behalf of a police force, whether by a member of that force or any other person. An exception is made in the case of 'specified proceedings', that is, those falling within any category specified by the A-G by order made by statutory instrument. The Prosecution of Offences Act 1985 (Specified Proceedings) Order 1999 (SI 1999 No. 904) exempts from compulsory taking over by the DPP various minor road traffic offences dealt with on a plea of guilty or under the fixed penalty procedure. 'Police force', in this context, means any of the forces maintained by police authorities under the Police Act 1996, plus any other body of constables specified by an order made by the Secretary of State. The City of London Police, Metropolitan Police, British Transport Police, Ministry of Defence Police, the Royal Parks Constabulary and numerous harbour police forces have been so specified (see Prosecution of Offences Act 1985 (Specified Police Forces) Order 1985 (SI 1985 No. 1956)).

(b) To institute and conduct criminal proceedings in any case where it appears to him appropriate to do so either on account of the importance or difficulty of the case or for any other reason.

(c) To take over the conduct of all binding-over proceedings instituted on behalf of a police force.

(d) To take over the conduct of all proceedings begun by a summons issued under the Obscene Publications Act 1959, s. 3 (forfeiture of obscene articles).

(e) To advise police forces, to the extent he considers appropriate, on all matters relating to criminal offences.

(f) To appear for the prosecution when directed by the court to do so on:

(i) appeals from the High Court to the House of Lords in criminal cases;
(ii) appeals from the Crown Court to the Court of Appeal (Criminal Division) and from thence to the House of Lords; and
(iii) appeals to the Crown Court against the exercise by a magistrates' court of its powers under s. 12 of the Contempt of Court Act 1981 to deal with offences of contempt of the court.

The court with authority to give a direction under this paragraph is, in the case of (i), the Divisional Court; in the case of (ii), the Court of Appeal; and in the case of (iii), the Crown Court.

(g) To discharge such other functions as may from time to time be assigned to him by the A-G.

Where the DPP has the conduct of proceedings in consequence of the duties imposed upon him under (a), (b), (c) or (d) above, he may discontinue the proceedings or take any other step in relation to them, including the bringing of an appeal and the making of representations at defence applications for bail (Prosecution of Offences Act 1985, s. 15(3)).

Further duties imposed on the DPP by the 1985 Act are: (a) to make an annual report to the A-G, which the latter is required to lay before Parliament (s. 9); and (b) to issue a code for the guidance of Crown Prosecutors in the performance of various aspects of their duties (s. 10). A final duty resting on the DPP is to give or refuse his consent to a prosecution in those cases where statute provides that the prosecutor may not proceed without it (see **D1.88** for prosecutions requiring the DPP's consent).

By s. 8(1) of the 1985 Act, the A-G may make regulations requiring the chief officer of any police force to give to the DPP information with respect to every offence of a kind prescribed by the regulations which is alleged to have been committed in the area for which the officer's force has responsibility and in respect of which it appears to him that there is a prima facie case for proceedings. The regulations may also require chief officers to give the DPP such information with respect to cases as he (the DPP) may from time to time specify (s. 8(2)). The apparent purpose of s. 8 is to ensure that the DPP is given sufficient advance warning about important, difficult or sensitive cases so as to be able, if necessary, to advise the police force concerned at an early stage. The relevant regulation is reg. 6 of the Prosecution of Offences Regulations 1978 (SI 1978 No. 1357), made under the earlier equivalent of s. 8 of the 1985 Act. The 1978 Regulations, which are set out below, also repeat and amplify some of the duties now imposed on the DPP by s. 3 of the 1985 Act.

Prosecution of Offences Regulations 1978 (SI 1978 No. 1357), regs. 3, 4, 6, 7 and 9

[**1. and 2.**   Citation and revocation of earlier regulations.]

3.   It shall be the duty of the Director of Public Prosecutions to institute, undertake or carry on criminal proceedings in any case which appears to him to be of importance or difficulty or which for any other reason requires his intervention.

4.   The Director of Public Prosecutions shall give advice whether on application by or on his own initiative to Government Departments, clerks to justices, chief officers of police and such other persons as he may think right in any criminal matter which appears to him to be of importance or difficulty or which for any other reason appears to him to require his intervention by way of advice and any such advice may be given at his discretion either orally or in writing.

[**5.**   Employment of solicitor to act as the DPP's agent.]

6.—(1)   The chief officer of police of every police area within the meaning of the Police Act 1996, shall give to the Director of Public Prosecutions information with respect to any of the following offences where it appears to him that there is a prima facie case for proceedings—
    (a)   offences in which the prosecution has by statute to be undertaken by or requires the consent of the Attorney-General, the Solicitor–General or the Director of Public Prosecutions;
    (b)   offences where it appears to the chief officer of police that the advice or assistance of the DPP is desirable;
    (c)   offences punishable with death;
    (d)   offences of homicide except offences of causing death by reckless driving;
    (e)   offences of abortion;
    (f)   offences of treason felony, misprision of treason, sedition, seditious libel or libel on holders of public offices;
    [(g)   has been deleted];
    [(h)   offences under ss. 21, 23, 28, 29, 32 and 33 of the OAPA 1861];
    (i)   conspiracies, attempts or incitements to commit any of the above offences;
    (j)   offences which may be the subject of an application under the Extradition Acts 1870 to 1935 or the Fugitive Offenders Act 1967.

(2)   The chief officer of every such police area shall give to the Director of Public Prosecutions such information as he may require with respect to such other cases as the Director of Public Prosecutions may from time to time specify as appearing to him to be of importance or difficulty or for any other reason requiring his intervention.

7.   Where a chief officer of police is required under regulation 6(1) to give information to the Director of Public Prosecutions he shall provide to the Director of Public Prosecutions a report of the circumstances together with such further information and material as the Director of Public Prosecutions, having regard to arrangements available locally for the prosecution of criminal offences, may require of him.

[8.   Concerns justices delivering documents etc. to the DPP.]

9.   In any case in which the prosecution for any offence instituted before examining justices or a court of summary jurisdiction is wholly withdrawn or is not proceeded with within a reasonable time and there is some ground for suspecting that there is no satisfactory reason for the withdrawal or failure to proceed, it shall be the duty of the clerk of the court to send to the Director of Public Prosecutions a report of the case and to supply him with such information or documents in relation to the case as he may specify.

The list of offences which the DPP, acting on the power given to him by reg. 6(2) of the Prosecution of Offences Regulations 1978, has required to be reported is as follows:

(a) Conspiracy to manufacture controlled drugs; large-scale conspiracy to supply controlled drugs in large amounts.

(b)   Large-scale conspiracy to contravene immigration laws.

(c)   Criminal libel.

(d)   Offences in relation to the Backing of Warrants (Republic of Ireland) Act 1965, where the order is resisted under s. 2(2) of the Act.

(e)   Cases which involve obscene exhibitions or publications in respect of which:

(i)   a criminal charge including conspiracy is contemplated;

(ii)   the issue of obscenity or the defence of public good may be raised in forfeiture proceedings by a reputable seller, keeper or publisher;

(iii)   an application for forfeiture under s. 3 of the Obscene Publications Act 1959 has been made against a seller or keeper but the publisher wishes to intervene and seek a jury trial.

(f)   All cases in which questions of European Union law have been or are likely to be raised and all cases which have been referred by the Crown Court or magistrates' courts in England and Wales to the European Court of Justice.

The Crown Prosecution Service

D2.33   Section 3(2)(a) of the Prosecution of Offences Act 1985 requires the DPP to 'take over the conduct of all criminal proceedings . . . instituted on behalf of a police force'. To enable him to perform this task, the Act also provided for the creation of a CPS, of which the DPP is the head.

Prior to the Act, the DPP had been directly responsible for the conduct of prosecutions only in the minority of cases which he considered important or difficult enough for his intervention. The conduct of the great majority of police prosecutions remained solely the responsibility of the force which (through one of its officers) had initiated the proceedings. Most police authorities financed an 'in-house' solicitors' department to give legal advice, appear in the magistrates' courts, brief counsel for the Crown Court and perform any other legal duties associated with a prosecution. A minority instructed firms in private practice. The relationship between the police and their salaried legal staff or, as the case might be, the firms they instructed, was (at least in theory) the ordinary client-solicitor relationship. Thus, in the last resort, the police rather than the lawyers decided questions such as whether it was right to proceed with a certain charge having regard to the available evidence. Conceptually speaking, the establishment of the CPS effected a fundamental change in the relationship between the police and their lawyers. The Service is not instructed by the police – acting on behalf of the DPP it *takes over* prosecutions begun by the police, and should therefore exercise an independent judgment in deciding any legal questions which arise.

The DPP is the head of the Service (Prosecution of Offences Act 1985, s. 1(1)(a)). He is responsible for dividing the country into areas and appointing a Chief Crown Prosecutor for each area (s. 1(4)). The DPP appoints such staff as 'he considers necessary for the discharge of his functions', subject to obtaining Treasury approval as to both numbers and remuneration (s. 1(2)). He may designate any member of the Service who is a barrister or solicitor to be a Crown Prosecutor (s. 1(3)). Crown Prosecutors have the same rights of audience as practising solicitors, which means essentially that they may appear for the Service in magistrates' courts but not in the Crown Court (s. 4 and see **D2.43** for rights of audience in general). Furthermore, without prejudice to any other functions assigned to him as a member of the Service, a Crown Prosecutor has 'all the powers of the Director as to the institution and conduct of proceedings but shall exercise those powers under the direction of the Director' (s. 1(6)). Where an enactment prevents any step being taken without the DPP's consent or requires any step to be taken by or in relation to him, the consent or step may be taken by or in relation to a Crown Prosecutor (s. 1(7)). Thus, the DPP may delegate to Crown Prosecutors his power to sanction a prosecution in cases where proceedings require his consent.

The relationship between Crown Prosecutors and the DPP, and the extent to which they are entitled to act without specific authority from him, was considered in *Liverpool Crown Court, ex parte Bray* [1987] Crim LR 51. A Crown Prosecutor applied successfully to a High Court judge for a voluntary bill of indictment against B. No affidavit verifying the truth of the statements made in the application was filed. By the Indictments (Procedure) Rules 1971 (SI 1971 No. 2084), such an affidavit is required unless the application for the bill is made by or on behalf of the DPP. It was argued before the Divisional Court that, in the absence of an affidavit, the indictment was preferred without lawful authority because the DPP had given no express instructions to the Crown Prosecutor to make the application, and it was therefore not made by the DPP or on his behalf. Watkins LJ, giving the judgment of the court, said that the Prosecution of Offences Act 1985, s. 1(6), conferred on Crown Prosecutors 'all the powers of the Director as to the institution and conduct of the proceedings'. To construe the subsection so as to mean that a Crown Prosecutor enjoyed the DPP's powers only when acting on the latter's express instructions would produce 'absurd results'. It followed that, since the DPP could have obtained a voluntary bill of indictment without filing an affidavit in support, the Crown Prosecutor could do the same, despite his lack of any express authority from the DPP.

The principle in *Ex parte Bray* – namely that the DPP's powers may be exercised by Crown Prosecutors acting within the general authority delegated to them but without express instructions from the DPP – appears to be of general application, and not limited to a decision to apply for a voluntary bill of indictment or otherwise commence proceedings. Thus, the DPP's powers to take over the conduct of privately commenced prosecutions and to serve a notice discontinuing a prosecution in its preparatory stages are, in practice, exercised by Crown Prosecutors rather than the DPP himself. The risk of individual Crown Prosecutors coming to widely divergent decisions in similar factual situations is reduced by s. 10 of the 1985 Act, which requires the DPP to issue a code for Crown Prosecutors giving guidance on the general principles to be applied by them in: (a) determining whether proceedings for an offence should be instituted or (if already instituted) discontinued; (b) determining what charges should be preferred; and (c) considering what representations should be made by them to a magistrates' court about the mode of trial suitable for a particular case. The code, which may be altered from time to time, is annexed to the annual report which the DPP is required to make to the A-G, and is reproduced in **appendix 4**.

In addition to establishing the CPS, the Prosecution of Offences Act 1985 empowers the DPP to appoint persons who are not members of the Service to institute or take over the conduct of such criminal proceedings as he may assign to them (s. 5(1)). The appointed person must be either (a) a solicitor or (b) a barrister who is a member of the staff of a public authority (ibid.). A person appointed under s. 5(1) shall have, in conducting the proceedings assigned to him, all the powers of a Crown Prosecutor, but he is to exercise those powers subject to any instructions given to him by a Crown Prosecutor (s. 5(2)). Section 5 places no fetter on the circumstances in which the DPP may exercise the power to assign cases to non-Service personnel. In practice, the volume of CPS work in the magistrates' courts is such that a large proportion of it cannot be covered by internal staff and so has to be delegated to agents under s. 5. Moreover, although s. 5 only specifically provides for delegation to solicitors or barristers working for public authorities, it has never been doubted that the Service may also, if it chooses, use counsel or solicitors in private practice as agents. An agent is, however, expected to obtain authority from a CPS lawyer before taking steps in relation to a case such as offering no evidence on a charge or accepting a bind-over (contrast the independence that prosecuting counsel in the Crown Court enjoys: see **D12.5**). It is important to realise, however, that only the DPP or CPS can lawfully authorise an agent to conduct a prosecution which would otherwise be its responsibility.

Section 7A of the Prosecution of Offences Act 1985 gives the DPP an additional power of appointment. A member of the Crown Prosecution staff (other than a Crown Prosecutor) can be designated as having all the powers of a Crown Prosecutor in relation to bail applications and the conduct of criminal proceedings in magistrates' courts, other than trials. Trials are therefore excluded from the remit of such designated lay staff, as are indictable only cases and cases where the magistrates have declined jurisdiction or the accused has elected trial by jury.

The legal and administrative framework described above means that, once a police officer has laid an information against a suspect or caused him to be charged, the papers in the case are sent to the local branch office of the CPS. A Crown Prosecutor then reviews the papers to check that the charges are the correct ones and that the prosecution ought to proceed. If additional evidence is needed, appropriate advice can be given to the police. If the Crown Prosecutor is against continuing the proceedings, he is empowered to serve notice of discontinuance). Assuming the prosecution is approved, the case is listed for hearing in a magistrates' court. Normally a Crown Prosecutor or agent appointed by the CPS appears to handle all the Service cases in the court list for a certain session, although there is nothing to prevent counsel being briefed for an individual case of particular importance or difficulty, with the remainder of the list covered by another representative. Should a case be sent for trial at the Crown Court, the papers are transferred internally to the Service staff handling Crown Court prosecutions. A brief is then prepared and counsel instructed for the trial.

Prosecution of Offences Act 1985, ss. 5, 7A and 15

5.—(1) The Director may at any time appoint a person who is not a Crown Prosecutor but who is—
    (a)   a solicitor; or
    (b)   a barrister who is a member of the staff of a public authority;
to institute or take over the conduct of such criminal proceedings as the Director may assign to him.

(2)   Any person conducting proceedings assigned to him under this section shall have all the powers of a Crown Prosecutor but shall exercise those powers subject to any instructions given to him by a Crown Prosecutor.

7A.—(1)   The Director may designate, for the purposes of this section, members of the staff of the Crown Prosecution Service who are not Crown Prosecutors.

(2)   Subject to such exceptions (if any) as may be specified in the designation, a person so designated shall have such of the following as may be so specified, namely—

(a)   the powers and rights of audience of a Crown Prosecutor in relation to—

(i)   applications for, or relating to, bail in criminal proceedings;

(ii)   the conduct of criminal proceedings in magistrates' courts other than trials;

(b)   the powers of such a Prosecutor in relation to the conduct of criminal proceedings not falling within paragraph (a)(ii) above.

(3)   A person so designated shall exercise any such powers subject to instructions given to him by the Director.

(4)   Any such instructions may be given so as to apply generally.

(5)   For the purposes of this section—

(a)   'bail in criminal proceedings' has the same meaning as it would have in the Bail Act 1976 by virtue of the definition in section 1 of that Act if in that section 'offence' did not include an offence to which subsection (6) below applies;

(b)   'criminal proceedings' does not include proceedings for an offence to which subsection (6) below applies; and

(c)   a trial begins with the opening of the prosecution case after the entry of a plea of not guilty and ends with the conviction or acquittal of the accused.

(6)   This subsection applies to an offence if it is triable only on indictment, or is an offence—

(a)   for which the accused has elected to be tried by a jury;

(b)   which a magistrates' court has decided is more suitable to be so tried; or

(c)   in respect of which a notice of transfer has been given under section 4 of the Criminal Justice Act 1987 or section 53 of the Criminal Justice Act 1991.

(7)   Details of the following for any year, namely—

(a)   the criteria applied by the Director in determining whether to designate persons under this section;

(b)   the training undergone by persons so designated; and

(c)   any general instructions given by the Director under subsection (4) above, shall be set out in the Director's report under section 9 of this Act for that year.

15.—(2)   For the purpose of [ss. 1 to 15 of the Act] proceedings in relation to an offence are instituted—

(a)   where a justice of the peace issues a summons under section 1 of the Magistrates' Courts Act 1980, when the information for the offence is laid before him;

(b)   where a justice of the peace issues a warrant for the arrest of any person under that section, when the information for the offence is laid before him;

(c)   where a person is charged with the offence after being taken into custody without a warrant, when he is informed of the particulars of the charge;

(d)   where a bill of indictment is preferred under section 2 of the Administration of Justice (Miscellaneous Provisions) Act 1933 in a case falling within paragraph (b) of subsection (2) of that section, when the bill of indictment is preferred before the court;

and where the application of this section would result in there being more than one time for the institution of the proceedings, they shall be taken to have been instituted at the earliest of those times.

(3)   For the purposes of [ss. 1 to 15 of the Act], references to the conduct of any proceedings include references to the proceedings being discontinued and to the taking of any steps (including the bringing of appeals and making of representations in respect of applications for bail) which may be taken in relation to them.

Prosecutions by Other Persons

Section 6(1) of the Prosecution of Offences Act 1985 provides that: 'Nothing in this Part **D2.34** [of the Act] shall preclude any person from instituting any criminal proceedings to which the Director's duty to take over the conduct of proceedings does not apply'. Since the DPP is only required to take over prosecutions begun by the police, it follows that, save in those limited categories of cases where a statute other than the 1985 Act requires a prosecution to have the prior consent of either the DPP or the A-G, there is no restriction on the right of any individual to bring criminal proceedings. This applies whether the individual acts in a purely personal capacity or in the course of his duties for a local authority, government department, business enterprise or other organisation. In these respects the 1985 Act preserves what was formerly the position at common law. However, the 1985 Act also follows the pre-existing law in providing that the DPP shall have a discretion to take over the conduct of proceedings begun by somebody other than himself (s. 6(2)). Since the DPP also has power to discontinue at a preliminary stage proceedings of which he has the conduct, it follows that he can in effect bar the continuance of a privately commenced prosecution by taking over its conduct and then serving notice of discontinuance. Alternatively, he can take over a prosecution to ensure its more efficient conduct in the public interest. Where a non-Service prosecution is withdrawn or not proceeded with within a reasonable time, the clerk of the magistrates' court concerned is under a duty to send copies of the documents in the case to the DPP (s. 7(4)). The DPP may then consider whether it is appropriate for him to take over the proceedings.

In *DPP, ex parte Duckenfield* [1999] 2 All ER 873, the Divisional Court considered the basis upon which the DPP ought to take over private prosecutions in order to stop them. It was held that the DPP acted quite properly in not adopting the same test for stopping a prosecution as for starting one. The policy of the DPP was that he would only intervene to stop a private prosecution on evidential grounds where there was clearly no case to answer, and the Divisional Court made it clear that such a policy was in accordance with s. 6(1) of the 1985 Act. It follows that, provided there is evidence to support a private prosecution, the DPP will not intervene to stop it, even though he would not have commenced proceedings himself.

In *Bow Street Metropolitan Stipendiary Magistrate, ex parte South Coast Shipping Co.* [1993] QB 645, the Divisional Court held that the fact that the public prosecuting authorities had instituted proceedings for a minor offence arising out of an incident did not preclude a private prosecution for a more serious offence, where there was evidence suggesting culpability. The case arose from the sinking of the Thames pleasure cruiser, the *Marchioness*, by the *Bowbelle*, a disaster in which 51 people died. The master of the *Bowbelle* had been charged under the Merchant Shipping Act 1979, s. 32, and was tried twice, the jury failing to reach a verdict on each occasion. A private prosecution for manslaughter was then instituted against the owners of the *Bowbelle* and others. The stipendiary magistrate's decision to commit them was upheld by the Divisional Court.

Where an accused has been committed for trial in proceedings being conducted by a private prosecutor the police can be compelled through an application for a witness summons under the Criminal Procedure (Attendance of Witnesses) Act 1965 to produce all statements and exhibits in their possession relevant to the case (*Pawsey* [1989] Crim LR 152). The position is different where proceedings have not yet begun but a person is merely considering whether it is a suitable case for a prosecution – at that stage neither the police, the CPS nor anybody else is obliged to disclose relevant material in their possession (*DPP, ex parte Hallas* (1987) 87 Cr App R 340).

The Serious Fraud Office

D2.35 Several departments of government and quasi-governmental organisations initiate and conduct prosecutions as one aspect of performing the major function for which they exist (e.g., the Department of Trade and Industry prosecutes for some business frauds and violations of the Companies Acts; the Department of Social Security for fraudulent benefit claims; the Inland Revenue for tax evasion; Customs and Excise for evading import duties, unlawful importation of drugs, and VAT frauds; and local authorities for violations of food and hygiene and other health regulations). However, apart from the CPS there is only one governmental organisation that exists principally to prosecute crime – the Serious Fraud Office.

The Serious Fraud Office was set up by the CJA 1987. It is headed by a Director, who is appointed and superintended by the A-G (s. 1(2)). The Director may appoint such staff as the Director considers necessary for the discharge of the Director's functions (sch. 1, para. 2). Those functions are to 'investigate any suspected offence which appears to [the Director] on reasonable grounds to involve serious or complex fraud', and to initiate and conduct (or take over and then conduct) any criminal proceedings relating to such fraud (s. 1(3) and (5)). The Director may designate any barrister or solicitor who is a member of the Office to have the same powers as the Director in relation to the institution and conduct of proceedings (s. 1(7) and (8)). A designated lawyer has the same rights of audience as a solicitor holding a practising certificate (s. 1(9)). The Director of Public Prosecution's duties in relation to the initiation and/or conduct of proceedings where a case appears to be of difficulty or importance do not extend to serious frauds under investigation by the Serious Fraud Office (Prosecution of Offences Act 1985, s. 3(2)).

The Serious Fraud Office bears many resemblances to the CPS, but the two organisations differ in that:

(a)   The Serious Fraud Office involves itself only with very serious fraud. Which cases to investigate and prosecute is in the Office's discretion.

(b)   The Office's role is to investigate possible serious fraud and then, if the evidence justifies it, to initiate proceedings. To that end, the CJA 1987, s. 2, gives the Director of the Serious Fraud Office wide investigatory powers (see **D1.59**). The CPS by contrast, is not involved in the primary investigation of crime but merely initiates or takes over the conduct of proceedings after the evidence has been gathered by the police (or other prosecutor).

(c)   Reflecting its investigatory function, the Serious Fraud Office comprises not only lawyers but also accountants and fraud investigators seconded to it by other branches of government such as the Department of Trade and Industry. In investigating a possible serious fraud, the Office works in conjunction with other interested parties (e.g., police fraud squads), its role being to oversee and give direction to the investigation and assess the evidence as it emerges.

Prosecution of Offences Act 1985, ss. 6 and 7

6.—(1)   Subject to subsection (2) below, nothing in this Part shall preclude any person from instituting any criminal proceedings or conducting any criminal proceedings to which the Director's duty to take over the conduct of proceedings does not apply.

(2)   Where criminal proceedings are instituted in circumstances in which the Director is not under a duty to take over their conduct, he may nevertheless do so at any stage.

7.—[(1) to (3) Documents to be sent to the Director or any Crown Prosecutor who gives notice to a justice of the peace that he has instituted or is conducting any criminal proceedings.]

(4)   It shall be the duty of every justices' clerk to send to the Director, in accordance with the regulations, a copy of the information and of any depositions and other documents relating to any case in which—

(a)   a prosecution for an offence before the magistrates' court to which he is clerk is withdrawn or is not proceeded with within a reasonable time;

(b)   the Director does not have the conduct of the proceedings; and

(c)   there is some ground for suspecting that there is no satisfactory reason for the withdrawal or failure to proceed.

The Attorney-General

D2.36 The main functions of the A-G in respect of criminal proceedings are as follows:

(a)   He appoints the DPP, who discharges his functions 'under the superintendence of the Attorney-General' (Prosecution of Offences Act 1985, ss. 2 and 3(1)).

(b)   Through his office, he may institute and conduct the prosecution of offences of exceptional gravity or complexity, especially those which impinge upon the security of the State and/or this country's relationships with other countries. He may also take over the conduct of a privately commenced prosecution (or direct the DPP to do so). Very occasionally, the A-G appears in court to represent the prosecution.

(c)   Certain offences may only be prosecuted by or with the consent of the A-G (see **D1.88**).

(d)   From time to time he issues guidelines on aspects of prosecution practice (e.g., in relation to the decision to institute proceedings or the prosecution material which should be made available to the defence). Strictly speaking, such guidelines merely state what practice the DPP intends to follow, but they are clearly meant to be observed by prosecutors in general and not merely the DPP or the CPS.

(e)   At any stage after the bill of indictment against an accused has been signed and before judgment, the A-G may enter a *nolle prosequi*, which terminates the prosecution.

It would appear that, notwithstanding the earlier entry of a *nolle prosequi*, the accused may be re-indicted for the same matter (*Ridpath* (1713) 10 Mod 152), but this is most unlikely to occur in practice. Whether or not to enter a *nolle prosequi* is entirely within the A-G's discretion, and is not subject to control by the courts (*Comptroller-General of Patents, Designs, & Trade Marks* [1899] 1 QB 909, and see also dicta by Mars-Jones J in *Turner v DPP* (1978) 68 Cr App R 70 at p. 76: 'The Attorney-General could always enter a *nolle prosequi* in criminal proceedings before courts of record, and the courts have never sought to interfere with the exercise of that power', and Viscount Dilhorne, a former A-G, in *Gouriet v Union of Post Office Workers* [1978] AC 435 at p. 487: 'The Attorney-General has many powers and duties. He may stop any prosecution on indictment by entering a *nolle prosequi*. . . . He need not give any reasons.').

Either the prosecution or defence may apply informally to the A-G for entry of a *nolle prosequi*. The commonest reason for the power being exercised is that the accused is physically or mentally unfit to be produced in court and his incapacity is likely to be permanent, but there are occasionally other exceptional situations in which a *nolle prosequi* is the best means of halting proceedings which the prosecution agree ought not to be continued. In *Re Beresford* (1952) 36 Cr App R 1, a coroner's jury found the cause of a cyclist's death in a collision with B's car to have been manslaughter by B, and B was accordingly committed for trial for that offence by the coroner's court (using a power since abrogated). However, B had already been convicted of and fined for dangerous driving arising out of the same incident. The trial judge directed that the matter be referred to the A-G and he entered a *nolle prosequi*.

The power of the A-G to enter a *nolle prosequi* is not shared by the DPP (*Rowlands* (1851) 17 QB 671), but it may be viewed as complementing the latter's powers under the Prosecution of Offences Act 1985, s. 23. By virtue of that section, the Director may serve a notice discontinuing proceedings of which he has the conduct only if they have not gone beyond the preparatory stages. Once an accused has been committed for trial, a s. 23 notice is impossible and, although it would be open to counsel instructed by the Director to offer no evidence when the case comes on for trial, subject to the need either to seek approval of the judge or to explain the decision in open court (see **D10.44**). The only way this can be avoided is by asking the A-G to enter a *nolle prosequi*. As it was put by A.L. Smith LJ in *Comptroller-General of Patents, Designs, & Trade Marks*: 'Another case in which the Attorney-General is pre-eminent is the power to enter a *nolle prosequi* in a criminal case. I do not say that when a case is before a judge a prosecutor may not ask the judge to allow the case to be withdrawn, and the judge may do so if he is satisfied that there is no case; but the Attorney-General alone has power to enter a *nolle prosequi*, and that power is not subject to any control.'

Although the A-G is a member of the government, he is by constitutional convention obliged to exercise an independent discretion when performing his non-political functions, including the exercise of his powers in respect of criminal proceedings. He is responsible to Parliament for the discharge of his duties but is only asked to account for his decisions after the event when, for example, a prosecution which he chose to institute (or instructed the DPP to institute) has reached its conclusion.

By the Law Officers Act 1997, s. 1, the functions of the A-G may be discharged by the Solicitor-General.

The Accused

Little need be said here about the second party to criminal proceedings, namely the **D2.37** accused. More than one accused may be charged jointly with committing a single offence. Furthermore, several accused may be tried together for separate offences if those offences are so linked together that a single trial is in the interests of justice (see **D9.29** *et seq*. and **D18.27** *et seq*. for the rules governing joinder of defendants in one indictment and summary trial of more than one information). As to special categories of defendants, the liability of companies for criminal offences is considered in **A5.11** *et seq*.; the categories of potential defendants who may avoid prosecution by claiming sovereign or diplomatic immunity are described in **D1.88**. For the rule that the accused must be present for a trial on indictment and the circumstances in which a summary trial may proceed despite his absence, see **D12.23** and **D18.11** *et seq*.

The manner of referring to the person charged with the offence has varied over the decades. In the 19th and early 20th centuries, it was common to refer to him as 'the prisoner', probably a derivation from the Commission of Jail Delivery. This would be inappropriate today if only because most accused persons are granted bail and thus are only prisoners during their trial, in the technical sense that they surrender to the custody of the court at the commencement of the day's hearing. The modern terminology is either 'accused' or 'defendant'.

DISCONTINUANCE OF AND JUDICIAL RESTRAINT ON CRIMINAL PROSECUTION

Discontinuance of Prosecutions Conducted by the Director of Public Prosecutions

Where the DPP is conducting a prosecution, he may, at any time during the 'preliminary **D2.38** stages' of the proceedings, give notice to the clerk of the court that he does not want the proceedings to continue (Prosecution of Offences Act 1985, s. 23(3)). 'Preliminary stage' does *not* include: (a) in the case of a summary offence, any stage after the court has begun to hear the evidence for the prosecution at the trial; (b) in the case of an indictable offence, any stage after *either* the accused has been committed for trial *or* (where the offence is to be tried summarily) the court has begun to hear evidence for the prosecution (s. 23(2)). The effect of the DPP giving notice of discontinuance is that the proceedings are discontinued from the giving of notice. However, they may be revived by the accused himself giving notice within the 'prescribed time' (at present, 35 days from the date of discontinuance) that he wishes them to continue (s. 23(3) and (7)). The apparent purpose of allowing the accused to insist on the case continuing is, first, that a full hearing may establish innocence and vindicate him in a way which the mere withdrawal of proceedings could not, and, secondly, if there is an acquittal following trial he may rely on the plea of autrefois acquit if further proceedings are commenced. Conversely, notice of discontinuance does not guarantee that the proceedings will not be revived should additional evidence later be discovered (see s. 23(9), which provides that discontinuance shall not prevent the subsequent institution of fresh proceedings in respect of the same offence). When giving notice to the clerk under s. 23(3) the DPP must give his reasons for not wanting the proceedings to continue (s. 23(5)). He must also inform the accused that notice has been given and that he (the accused) has the right to require the proceedings to be continued, but he is not obliged to indicate to the accused his reasons for desiring discontinuance (s. 23(6)). The 1985 Act does not state expressly to which clerk of the court notice of discontinuance must be given but, since the reference to 'the clerk of the court' in s. 23(3) comes immediately after references in s. 23(2)(a) and (b) to 'the court' hearing evidence for purposes of a summary trial, it is submitted that 'clerk of the court' must mean the clerk of the magistrates' court in which the case is proceeding. If the accused has been charged at the police station and the DPP wishes to discontinue before there has even been a court appearance, it is merely necessary to serve notice to that effect on the accused himself, and he does not then have the right to require the proceedings to continue (s. 23(4)). Further detailed regulations relating to the giving of notice of discontinuance and 'counter-notices' by the accused are contained in the Magistrates' Courts (Discontinuance of Proceedings) Rules 1986 (SI 1986 No. 367), excerpts from which are set out below.

The power to serve a formal notice discontinuing proceedings had no equivalent in pre-1985 legislation or practice. However, the DPP was able to achieve the same effect by simply offering no evidence before the magistrates' court seised of the case, thus compelling the accused's acquittal or, in the case of committal proceedings, his discharge. Unlike a Crown Court judge at a trial on indictment, magistrates have no power to prevent the offering of no evidence (see Lord Lane CJ in *Canterbury and St Augustine Justices, ex parte Klisiak* [1982] QB 398 at p. 411C–D and *Horseferry Road Magistrates' Court, ex parte O'Regan* (1986) 150 JP 535). Whether it was legitimate for the Director to take over a prosecution with the sole purpose of offering no evidence was considered by the Court of Appeal in *Raymond* v *A-G* [1982] QB 839. In March 1979, R was committed for trial on charges of conspiring to pervert the course of justice for which, in February 1980, he was sentenced to imprisonment. A witness at the committal proceedings was one C, an accomplice in the offence who was to give evidence for the Crown. In May 1979 (i.e. while the Crown Court trial was pending), R laid informations alleging that C had committed perjury at the committal proceedings. The justices thereupon issued summonses against C. After initially intimating that he would take no action, the Director intervened in July to take over the conduct of the proceedings and, through his representative, offered no evidence, with the result that C was discharged. The reasons given in court for adopting this course were that: (a) the allegations which R was making against C had already been canvassed at R's own committal; and (b) the Director was satisfied for a number of reasons that R's prosecution of C was 'vexatious and designed to discredit C as a witness and not to bring him to justice in regard to the allegations on which the summonses were founded'. Thus, continuing with the summonses would be contrary to the public interest and the interests of justice. R sought a declaration that the DPP had acted unlawfully in not allowing C to be prosecuted. Refusing the declaration, the Court of Appeal held that the DPP's decision was not open to attack unless it was so manifestly wrong that it could not have been honestly and reasonable arrived at. Giving the judgment of the court, Sir Sebag Shaw said (at pp. 846H–847D).

> Section 4 of the [Prosecution of Offences Act 1979] has already been cited. It may be observed that while any person may institute or 'carry on' any criminal proceedings the Director may undertake, at any stage, the 'conduct' of those proceedings. The word

'conduct' appears to us to be wider than the phrase 'carry on' and suggests to our minds that when the Director intervenes in a prosecution which has been privately instituted he may do so not exclusively for the purpose of pursuing it by carrying it on, but also with the object of aborting it; that is to say, he may 'conduct' the proceedings in whatever manner may appear expedient in the public interest. The Director will thus intervene in a private prosecution where the issues in the public interest are so grave that the expertise and the resources of the Director's office should be brought to bear in order to ensure that the proceedings are properly conducted from the point of view of the prosecution.

On the other hand, there may be what appear to the Director substantial reasons in the public interest for not pursuing a prosecution privately commenced. What may emerge from those proceedings might have an adverse effect upon a pending prosecution involving far more serious issues. The Director, in such a case, is called upon to make a value judgment. Unless his decision is manifestly such that it could not be honestly and reasonably arrived at it cannot, in our opinion, be impugned. The safeguard against an unnecessary or gratuitous exercise of this power is that . . . the Director's duties are exercised 'under the superintendence of the Attorney-General' [Prosecution of Offences Act 1979, s. 2(1)]. That officer of the Crown is, in his turn, answerable to Parliament if it should appear that his or the Director's powers under the statute have in any case been abused.

Although the above judgment was based on the terms of s. 4 of the Prosecution of Offences Act 1979 and concerned the offering of no evidence rather than the service of a notice of discontinuance, it is submitted that the principles enunciated by Sir Sebag Shaw apply equally under the new legislation. Thus, the service of a notice of discontinuance is in the unfettered discretion of the Director, subject only to his decision not being manifestly unreasonable or arrived at in bad faith. This applies both where the Director has intervened in a private prosecution and where he has taken over the conduct of a police prosecution in pursuance of the duty imposed on him by the Prosecution of Offences Act 1985, s. 3 (2)(a). In the latter case, the effect of s. 23 of the 1985 Act is that, while the initial decision whether to commence proceedings and what charges to prefer is for the police, the Director and through him the CPS may review the correctness of the police decision after the event and, if appropriate, discontinue the proceedings on some or all of the charges.

A question not expressly dealt with in the 1985 Act is whether the power to serve a notice of discontinuance under s. 23 was to replace or to be in addition to the option of offering no evidence in the magistrates' court. *Cooke v DPP* (1992) 156 JP 497 makes it clear, however, that the statutory power to discontinue a prosecution is additional to the common-law power to offer no evidence. This confirms the regular practice of Crown Prosecutors in offering no evidence in appropriate cases.

Prosecution of Offences Act 1985, s. 23

23.—(1) Where the Director of Public Prosecutions has the conduct of proceedings for an offence, this section applies in relation to the preliminary stages of those proceedings.

(2) In this section, 'preliminary stage' in relation to proceedings for an offence does not include—

(a) in the case of a summary offence, any stage of the proceedings after the court has begun to hear evidence for the prosecution at the trial;

(b) in the case of an indictable offence, any stage of the proceedings after—

(i) the accused has been committed for trial; or

(ii) the court has begun to hear evidence for the prosecution at a summary trial of the offence.

(3) Where, at any time during the preliminary stages of the proceedings, the Director gives notice under this section to the clerk of the court that he does not want the proceedings to continue, they shall be discontinued with effect from the giving of that notice but may be revived by notice given by the accused under subsection (7) below.

(4) Where, in the case of a person charged with an offence after being taken into custody without a warrant, the Director gives him notice, at a time when no magistrates' court has

been informed of the charge, that the proceedings against him are discontinued, they shall be discontinued with effect from the giving of that notice.

(5)   The Director shall, in any notice given under subsection (3) above, give reasons for not wanting the proceedings to continue.

(6)   On giving any notice under subsection (3) above the Director shall inform the accused of the notice and of the accused's right to require the proceedings to be continued; but the Director shall not be obliged to give the accused any indication of his reasons for not wanting the proceedings to continue.

(7)   Where the Director has given notice under subsection (3) above, the accused shall, if he wants the proceedings to continue, give notice to that effect to the clerk of the court within the prescribed period; and where notice is so given the proceedings shall continue as if no notice had been given by the Director under subsection (3) above.

(8)   Where the clerk has been so notified by the accused he shall inform the Director.

(9)   The discontinuance of any proceedings by virtue of this section shall not prevent the institution of fresh proceedings in respect of the same offence.

[(10)   Meaning of 'prescribed'.]

The CDA 1998, sch. 8, paras 63 and 64, amend s. 23 and insert a new s. 23A into the 1985 Act. The amendments apply from 4 January 1999 but initially only in those pilot areas in which the CDA 1998, s. 51 (no committal proceedings for indictable-only and related offences: see **D8.21**), is in force.

Magistrates' Courts (Discontinuance of Proceedings)
Rules 1986 (SI 1986 No. 367), rr. 2 to 5

2.   In these rules 'section 23' means section 23 of the Prosecution of Offences Act 1985.

3.   The period within which an accused person may give notice under subsection (7) of section 23 that he wants proceedings against him to continue is 35 days from the date when the proceedings were discontinued under that section.

4.   Notice under subsection (3), (4) or (7) of section 23 shall be given in writing and shall contain sufficient particulars to identify the particular offence to which it relates; and, without prejudice to any other lawful method of giving notice, may be given by post in a registered letter or by the recorded delivery service, in which case it shall be treated as having been given on the date on which it is received for dispatch by the Post Office.

5.   On giving notice under subsection (3) or (4) of section 23 the DPP shall inform any person who is detaining the accused person for the offence in relation to which the notice is given that he has given such notice and of the effect of the notice.

6.   [Where notice has been given under subsection (3) and the accused has been bailed, the magistrates' court's clerk is to inform (a) any sureties and (b) any persons responsible for securing the accused's compliance with any conditions of bail of the giving of the notice.]

Court Order Restricting the Commencement of a Prosecution

D2.39   By s. 42 of the Supreme Court Act 1981, the A-G may apply to the High Court for a 'criminal proceedings order'. Such an order prevents the person against whom it is made laying an information or applying for a voluntary bill of indictment unless the High Court gives him leave. Before making the order, the High Court must, after giving the proposed subject the opportunity of making representations, be satisfied that he has 'habitually and persistently and without any reasonable ground . . . instituted vexatious prosecutions (whether against the same person or different persons)'. Where an order has been made, leave to lay an information or apply for a voluntary bill may not be given unless the High Court is satisfied that: (a) the institution of the prosecution would not be an abuse of the criminal process; and (b) the applicant has reasonable grounds for instituting it. There is no appeal against refusal of leave. Thus, instead of being forced to take over the conduct of each prosecution commenced by a vexatious prosecutor and then either offer no evidence or serve a notice of discontinuance, the DPP may request the A-G to obtain a criminal proceedings order, which will prevent further prosecutions by its subject unless he satisfies the High Court that he has good grounds.

Judge's Power to Stay Proceedings

A trial judge has a discretion to stay a prosecution, ordering that the indictment remain **D2.40** on the file marked 'Not to be proceeded with without leave of the court or of the Court of Appeal'. The existence of this discretion was long disputed. For example, in *Connelly* v *DPP* [1964] AC 1254 Lord Devlin justified his restrictive view of the ambit of the plea of autrefois acquit by relying on the trial judge's discretion to stay proceedings in cases where autrefois could not be relied upon but the prosecution appeared oppressive in the light of previous linked proceedings against the accused. Lord Hodson, on the other hand, denied the existence of any such discretion, implying that an order that an indictment or counts lie on the file had no legal validity or effect whatsoever.

The conflict was finally resolved by the House of Lords in *DPP* v *Humphrys* [1977] AC 1. According to the majority (Lord Hailsham of St Marylebone, Lord Salmon and Lord Edmund-Davies) the discretion does exist, although circumstances justifying its exercise will occur but rarely. Viscount Dilhorne dissented on the point while Lord Fraser of Tullybelton declined to express an opinion. The facts were that H had been convicted of perjury, the prosecution arising out of evidence he had given at an earlier trial when he was acquitted of driving while disqualified. At that trial he testified that he had not driven on 18 July 1972 (the date alleged in the indictment) nor at any time during 1972. The only prosecution evidence against him came from a police officer (W) whose evidence related solely to 18 July. At the perjury trial the prosecution called three neighbours of H who spoke to his driving on other dates in 1972. The prosecution were also allowed, despite defence objections, to call W to repeat his evidence about H driving on 18 July. H appealed principally on the basis that the prosecution were estopped by the finding of the first jury from again raising the issue that H drove on the day mentioned in the indictment for driving while disqualified (i.e. 18 July). The main holding of the House of Lords was that the doctrine of issue estoppel does not apply in criminal cases (see **F11.5**). However, it was further argued that, as a matter of discretion, the trial judge should not have allowed the perjury trial to proceed as H was effectively being retried for a matter (driving while disqualified) of which he had already been acquitted.

On this question, Lord Salmon referred with approval to passages in the speeches of Lords Devlin and Pearce in *Connelly* v *DPP* [1964] AC 1254 in which they affirmed the existence of a discretion to stay proceedings. He also approved a dictum of Lord Parker CJ in *Mills* v *Cooper* [1967] 2 QB 459 at p. 467E that 'every court has undoubtedly a right in its discretion to decline to hear proceedings on the ground that they are oppressive and an abuse of the process of the court'. He then said ([1977] AC 1 at p. 46C–E):

> I respectfully agree with [Viscount Dilhorne] that a judge has not and should not appear to have any responsibility for the institution of prosecutions; nor has he any power to refuse to allow a prosecution to proceed merely because he considers that, as a matter of policy, it ought not to have been brought. It is only if the prosecution amounts to an abuse of the process of the court and is oppressive and vexatious that the judge has the power to intervene. Fortunately, such prosecutions are hardly ever brought but the power of the court to prevent them is, in my view, of great constitutional importance and should be jealously preserved. For a man to be harassed and put to the expense of perhaps a long trial and then given an absolute discharge is hardly from any point of view an effective substitute for the exercise by the court of the power to which I have referred.

Similarly, Lord Edmund-Davies approved the statement of Lord Parker CJ in *Mills* v *Cooper* already quoted and referred to the case of *Riebold* [1967] 1 WLR 674 where a judge had stayed proceedings. He then said (at p. 55E–F):

> While judges should pause long before staying proceedings which on their face are perfectly regular, it would indeed by bad for justice if in such fortunately rare cases as *R* v *Riebold*

their hands were tied and they were obliged to allow the further trial to proceed. In my judgment, *Connelly* v *DPP* established that they are vested with the power to do what the justice of the case clearly demands.

In view of the above dicta, the existence of a discretion on the part of the trial judge to stay proceedings must now be regarded as incontrovertibly established. However, it is equally clear that the circumstances in which the discretion may properly be exercised are extremely limited. The judge must be satisfied that the prosecution is oppressive and vexatious (per Lord Salmon) or an abuse of the process of the court (per Lord Parker CJ). If he merely thinks that, as a matter of policy, the proceedings should not have been brought or that the evidence disclosed by the committal statements is insufficient to support a conviction, he should allow the evidence to be called. To do otherwise would be an 'assertion of judicial omnipotence . . . unacceptable in any country acknowledging the supremacy of the rule of law' (per Lord Edmund-Davies). Both Lord Edmund-Davies and Lord Salmon emphatically approved the decision in *Chairman, County of London Quarter Sessions, ex parte Downes* [1954] 1 QB 1 where the Divisional Court held that the chairman had had no power to quash an indictment simply on the ground that the evidence on the depositions did not in his view disclose a prima facie case. Moreover, on the facts of *DPP* v *Humphrys* itself, even those of their lordships who affirmed the existence of the discretion to stay nonetheless held that, in the particular circumstances, the appeal should fail. If the prosecution evidence at the appellant's perjury trial had been identical to that which they called at the driving while disqualified trial (or if the only additional evidence had been available for the earlier proceedings but not led) then there would have been a breach of the rule against double jeopardy and the judge ought to have intervened. But in fact the prosecution were able to call extra witnesses at the second trial who testified to the accused driving on occasions that were not in issue at the first trial. Consequently, there was no oppression or abuse of the court's procedure. See also *Birch* [1983] Crim LR 193; *Noe* [1985] Crim LR 97; *Smyth* [1983] Crim LR 46; *Moxon-Tritsch* [1988] Crim LR 46 and the discussion in **D9.41**).

LEGAL REPRESENTATION AND RIGHTS OF AUDIENCE

The Prosecution in the Crown Court

D2.41   At a trial on indictment, the position at common law was that the prosecution had to be legally represented. The only clear modern ruling to that effect was by Judge David QC in *George Maxwell (Developments) Ltd* [1980] 2 All ER 99, where one C (a private prosecutor) obtained summonses against the company for various offences arising out of its sale to him of a house. The company was committed for trial and an indictment signed against it. At a pre-trial review, C indicated that he intended to prosecute in person. The learned judge ruled that C 'could take no part in the forthcoming trial unless called as a witness in the proceedings'. Moreover, the judge would not adopt the course sometimes resorted to in 'bygone days' of inviting a counsel present in court to call the witnesses. It followed that the case would fail for want of prosecution unless C instructed solicitors and counsel. Judge David ultimately adopted the statement of the law to be found in *Halsbury's Laws of England*, 4th ed. reissue, vol. 3(1), para. 402:

> In criminal proceedings in the High Court and in the Crown Court prosecutors are not allowed to appear in person to conduct proceedings, but prosecutions must be conducted by barristers, who, when acting in this capacity, are said to be in the nature of public officers.

In fact, the authorities supporting that clear statement are, as Judge David observed, scanty. Nineteenth-century cases prayed in aid, such as *Brice* (1819) 2 B & Ald 606, usually went no further than holding that a prosecutor could not open his own case to the jury and give evidence as well. In *Lancashire Justices, ex parte Hunt* (1819) 1 Chit 602, however, there occurs the general proposition that no private individual may be heard in any proceedings in the name of the King, and trials on indictment, unlike proceedings in the magistrates' courts, are in the sovereign's name. However, the main thrust of Judge David's judgment is that, notwithstanding the dubious quality of the old authorities, modern practice and common sense require that a prosecutor on indictment be legally represented. Prosecuting counsel owes a duty to the public and the court to present his case fairly and impartially, and it would be difficult for a prosecutor in person to maintain the necessary objectivity. While acknowledging that the practice is otherwise in magistrates' courts, the learned judge justified the difference on the basis that: (a) a prosecution in the Crown Court is a 'very serious matter' and should not be used to 'ventilate a private grievance or to pursue a personal vendetta', and (b) once the indictment has been signed, the prosecutor ceases to be a litigant in person since the proceedings are thereafter conducted in the name of the sovereign.

According to *Southwark Crown Court, ex parte Tawfick* [1995] Crim LR 658, the position has now been altered by s. 27(2)(c) of the Courts and Legal Services Act 1990, which provides that a person shall have a right of audience before a court in relation to any proceedings only where he has a right of audience granted by that court in relation to those proceedings. The Divisional Court observed that this gave the Crown Court power in its discretion to allow a private individual to conduct a private prosecution before it. Glidewell LJ added, however, that it was a discretion which would be exercised only occasionally. It is respectfully submitted that this is correct, but that, where there is an appeal against conviction or sentence from a magistrates' court it is arguably anomalous to require the prosecutor to be represented, since (a) he was entitled to conduct the summary proceedings in person, and (b) the appeal is not resisted in the name of the sovereign but in the name of the prosecutor.

The Accused in the Crown Court

The accused is entitled to decline legal representation and present his case in person. If **D2.42** he is represented during the initial stages of a trial on indictment and then wishes to dispense with counsel's services, application to that effect must be made to the trial judge, who has a discretion to refuse to release counsel (*Woodward* [1944] KB 118). It is, however, rare for the accused's application to be refused. The modern practice was considered by Waller LJ in *Lyons* (1978) 68 Cr App R 104. L's trial for perjury lasted over five working days. At the end of the prosecution evidence, he applied to the judge to be allowed to conduct the remainder of the case personally. Having ascertained from counsel that he would not be 'forensically embarrassed' in continuing to act, the judge first refused to allow L to state his reasons for not wanting counsel (since that might have led to 'extremely embarrassing' matters coming out) and then ruled against the application. In giving the Court of Appeal's reasons for dismissing the appeal, Waller LJ said (at p. 108):

> It may well be that in the vast majority of cases a judge, faced with an application to dispense with counsel, in the circumstances of this case would allow the application. . . . It may well be that in most cases the appellant would be allowed to state his reasons.

> But at the end of the day it is a matter for the discretion of the learned judge, and we have come to the conclusion that he was perfectly entitled to make his decision in the way that he did in this case, namely, to refuse the appellant's application.

In the reverse situation of counsel who has been instructed for the defence not being present in court when the trial comes on, the judge's insistence on the case proceeding immediately coupled with his refusal to allow alternative counsel to act for the accused may lead to any conviction being quashed (*Kingston* (1948) 32 Cr App R 183). If an accused who has not arranged for legal representation intimates to the judge before the trial commences that he now wishes counsel to act for him, the judge clearly has a discretion to adjourn so that an application for legal aid may be made, with solicitors and counsel thereafter being instructed. Furthermore, it was often said in cases in the 19th century and in the first half of the 20th century, that a judge might properly request any barrister present in court to provide his services for an accused desirous of representation (see *Yscuado* (1854) 6 Cox CC 386). Whether this practice has survived the abolition of 'dock briefs' is doubtful.

Rights of Audience in the Crown Court

D2.43 Until recently, only practising barristers had a right of audience in the Crown Court. As with all work undertaken by a barrister in a professional capacity, it is necessary for counsel appearing in the Crown Court to have been instructed by a solicitor (para. 210 of the Code of Conduct of the Bar: 'A barrister in independent practice . . . may supply legal services only if he is briefed or instructed by a professional client').

The Courts and Legal Services Act 1990 enacted a statutory scheme for the definition and regulation of rights of audience before the courts. It preserves all existing rights of audience (ss. 31 and 32), and sets up a framework for the granting of new rights (s. 27). Machinery has been introduced for advocates who are not barristers to obtain rights of audience formerly held only by barristers. In particular, the right of audience in the Crown Court was extended to solicitors in private practice, subject to arrangements drawn up by the Law Society and approved by the Lord Chancellor. A number of solicitors who have complied with these arrangements have been granted full rights of audience in the Crown Court.

Even without the machinery introduced by the Courts and Legal Services Act, however, the Bar's right of audience in the Crown Court is not completely exclusive. By the Supreme Court Act 1981, s. 83, the Lord Chancellor is empowered to direct that solicitors may 'appear in, conduct, defend and address the court in any proceedings in the Crown Court, or proceedings in the Crown Court of any description specified in the direction' (s. 83(1)). A direction may apply to all or only some Crown Court locations (s. 83(2)). In considering whether to make a direction, the Lord Chancellor must have regard to: (a) any shortage of counsel in the area to be affected by the direction; (b) any rights of audience which, before the establishment of the Crown Court, had been exercised by solicitors at quarter sessions in the locality in question; and (c) any other circumstances affecting the public interest (s. 83(3)). *Practice Directions* by the Lord Chancellor [1972] 1 WLR 307 and [1988] 1 WLR 1427 set out below entitle solicitors to appear in the Crown Court for the hearing of appeals and proceedings on committal for sentence when they (or a member of their firm) represented the defendant in the magistrates' court. In five specified Crown Court locations, they have wider rights of audience, including that of representing a client at trial on indictment for a class 4 offence.

Practice Direction (Solicitors: Audience in Crown Court) [1988] 1 WLR 1427

1.   Solicitors may appear in, conduct, defend and address the court in proceedings mentioned in paragraph 2 of this direction at any sitting of the Crown Court at Caernarvon, Barnstaple, Truro, Doncaster or (subject to paragraph 3 hereof), Lincoln.
2.   The proceedings in which solicitors may exercise the right of audience conferred by paragraph 1 of this direction are: (a) appeals from magistrates' courts; (b) proceedings on committal of a person for sentence or to be dealt with; (c) proceedings in respect of the offences included in class 4 in the directions given by the Lord Chief Justice with the concurrence of the Lord Chancellor under section 75 of the Supreme Court Act 1981 ([*Practice Direction (Crown Court: Allocation of Business)* [1995] 1 WLR 1083]); and (d) proceedings under the original or appellate civil jurisdiction of the Crown Court.
[3. The right of audience at Lincoln Crown Court in criminal matters is restricted to trials etc. where the proceedings were initially in a magistrates' court in the County of the Parts of Holland.]

Practice Direction (Solicitors: Right of Audience) (No. 2) [1972] 1 WLR 307

1. A solicitor may appear in, conduct, defend and address the court in:
    (a)   criminal proceedings in the Crown Court on appeal from a magistrates' court or on committal of a person for sentence or to be dealt with, if he, or any partner of his, or any solicitor in his employment or by whom he is employed, appeared on behalf of the defendant in the magistrates' court;
    [(b)   relates to civil proceedings].
2.   The rights of audience conferred by this direction are in addition to and not in derogation from the rights of audience conferred by the direction dated 7 December 1971 [which has been superseded by the direction of 1988 reproduced above].

Magistrates' Courts

In the magistrates' court, neither the prosecutor nor the accused need be legally **D2.44** represented. This applies both at summary trial and for purposes of committal proceedings. A private prosecutor (meaning here one who institutes proceedings solely in a personal capacity and not on behalf of a body to which he belongs) will often appear in person, as when the victim of an alleged assault takes out a summons against his assailant and then both argues the case himself and gives the principal evidence for the prosecution. In the case of police prosecutions, it used to be common for one of the investigating officers to 'double up' as the prosecution advocate. However, the requirement in the Prosecution of Offences Act 1985, s. 3(2)(a), that the DPP through the CPS must take over the conduct of all police prosecutions (see **D2.32** and **D2.33**) has brought the practice to an end, save in respect of those 'specified proceedings' where the Secretary of State has ordered that the general rule need not apply.

Representation in a magistrates' court may be either by counsel or by solicitor, since both have the right of audience. Furthermore, magistrates have an inherent power to regulate procedure in their courts in the interests of justice, and that would appear to include a limited discretion to allow someone other than counsel, a solicitor or the party himself to present a case. Thus, in the days prior to the creation of the CPS, it was never essential that a police officer representing the prosecution be the prosecutor in the technical sense of having laid the information. In certain circumstances the clerk of the court may question prosecution witnesses if no other appropriate person is available to do so (see *O'Toole* v *Scott* [1965] AC 939; *Simms* v *Moore* [1970] 2 QB 327; and **D18.35**).

Arranging for Legal Representation for the Prosecution

It is the responsibility of the CPS to arrange for the prosecution to be legally represented **D2.45** in cases where the DPP has the conduct of the proceedings. As the DPP is obliged to take over the conduct of virtually all police prosecutions (see Prosecution of Offences Act 1985, s. 3(2)(a)), police forces no longer need to employ large solicitors' departments to appear for them in the magistrates' courts and brief advocates for the Crown Court. By virtue of s. 4 of the 1985 Act, barristers or solicitors who are members of the Service and have been designated Crown Prosecutors by the DPP enjoy the same rights of audience as solicitors holding practising certificates. It follows that Crown Prosecutors may and commonly do represent the Service at proceedings in magistrates' courts. For trials on indictment (and, in practice, for appeals to the Crown Court and committals for sentence), the Service are obliged to brief an advocate with the right of audience in the Crown Court. There is nothing to stop the Service briefing an advocate for a specific case in a magistrates' court, although the usual practice is to employ counsel or solicitor as agent to handle the entire CPS list for a court session (s. 5).

Major prosecuting authorities other than the CPS (such as the Inland Revenue, Customs and Excise, Department of Social Security and local authorities) have salaried legal departments to prepare cases. Otherwise, a non-police prosecutor who wishes to be legally represented must instruct solicitors privately, and they will, if necessary, brief counsel. Various enactments also permit certain types of prosecution in the magistrates' courts to be presented by officials who are not practising solicitors and may not even be lawyers (e.g., Local Government Act 1972, s. 233, Customs and Excise Management Act 1979, s. 155, and Social Security Administration Act 1992, s. 116, which all allow authorised persons to prosecute).

Arranging for Legal Representation for the Accused

D2.46 An accused secures legal representation by instructing solicitors. It is always open to him to apply for legal aid to cover the costs. The great majority of defendants in the Crown Court are legally aided, as are most tried summarily for indictable offences, but only a small minority of those charged with summary offences are granted aid. For legal aid, see **D27**.

OPEN JUSTICE

The General Rule that Proceedings Should be in Open Court

D2.47 It is not only the parties who have an interest in criminal proceedings. The public at large are concerned that justice should be properly administered, with the return of true verdicts and the proper sentencing of those found guilty. For this and other reasons, it has long been established that criminal trials should take place in open court and be freely reported. The general principles to be applied have been stated frequently and at the highest levels. A useful starting-point is Lord Diplock's speech in *A-G* v *Leveller Magazine Ltd* [1979] AC 440 at pp. 449H–450D:

> As a general rule the English system of administering justice does require that it be done in public: *Scott* v *Scott* [1913] AC 417. If the way that the courts behave cannot be hidden from the public ear and eye this provides a safeguard against judicial arbitrariness or idiosyncrasy and maintains the public confidence in the administration of justice. The application of this principle of open justice has two aspects: as respects proceedings in the court itself it requires that they should be held in open court to which the press and public are admitted and that, in criminal cases at any rate, all evidence communicated to the court is communicated publicly. As respects the publication to a wider public of fair and accurate reports of proceedings that have taken place in court the principle requires that nothing should be done to discourage this.
>
> However, since the purpose of the general rule is to serve the ends of justice it may be necessary to depart from it where the nature or circumstances of the particular proceeding are such that the application of the general rule in its entirety would frustrate or render impracticable the administration of justice or would damage some other public interest for whose protection Parliament has made some statutory derogation from the rule. Apart from statutory exceptions, however, where a court in the exercise of its inherent power to control the conduct of proceedings before it departs in any way from the general rule, the departure is justified to the extent and to no more than the extent that the court reasonably believes it to be necessary in order to serve the ends of justice.

On the basis of dicta in *A-G* v *Leveller Magazine Ltd* and *Scott* v *Scott* [1913] AC 417, it is submitted that:

    (a)   The normal rule is that criminal proceedings (like other litigation) should be conducted publicly.

    (b)   Nonetheless, courts do have power, by virtue of their general right to control their own procedure, to order that the public be excluded and the doors of the court-room closed.

    (c)   However, the exercise of the power, in common with any other derogation from the principles of open justice, should be strictly confined to cases where the public's presence would genuinely frustrate the administration of justice, and should not be used merely to save parties, witnesses or others from embarrassment or to conceal facts which it might, on more general grounds, be desirable to keep secret.

(d)   Therefore, insofar as it is correct to speak of a judge or magistrate having a discretion to sit in camera, that discretion may only be exercised in narrowly circumscribed circumstances and consistently with the general spirit of English jurisprudence, which is overwhelmingly in favour of open justice.

Lord Diplock's words in *A-G* v *Leveller Magazine Ltd*, quoted above, adverted to three aspects of the principle of open justice, namely: that the courts should be open to the public; that evidence communicated to the court should be communicated publicly; and that the media should not be impeded from reporting what has taken place publicly in court. The following discussion looks at each aspect of the principle in its bearing upon criminal proceedings.

Sitting in Camera

The gravest interference with open justice is to order that all or some of the evidence be **D2.48** given in camera. It is necessary to consider (a) when in camera hearings are allowed at common law, and (b) certain statutory provisions on the subject.

The Common Law   There is a dearth of case law expressly upholding a decision at **D2.49** first instance to sit in camera, but examples of when it may be appropriate to do so can be culled from dicta in authorities where the actual decision was that the hearing should have been public. Excluding the public by virtue of the court's inherent common-law power is justifiable on the following grounds:

(a)   *Possibility of disorder*   In *Scott* v *Scott* [1913] AC 417, Earl Loreburn said (at pp. 445–6): 'Again, the court may be closed or cleared if such a precaution is necessary for the administration of justice. Tumult or disorder, or the just apprehension of it, would certainly justify the exclusion of all from whom such interruption is expected, and, if discrimination is impracticable, the exclusion of the public in general.'

(b)   *Witness would refuse to testify publicly*   According to Viscount Haldane LC, again in *Scott* v *Scott* (at p. 439): 'If the evidence to be given is of such a character that it would be impracticable to force an unwilling witness to give it in public, the case may come within the exception to the principle that . . . a public hearing must be insisted on in accordance with the rules which govern the general procedure in English courts of justice.' It is submitted, however, that this dictum must be treated with some caution. First, although there is nothing to indicate that the Lord Chancellor did not regard his words as of general application, they in fact occur within a paragraph which specifically deals with proceedings in the divorce court. Secondly, a witness's fears may be overcome by action stopping short of allowing him to testify in camera – e.g., he may be allowed to write down his name and address for the eyes of the court only. Thirdly, it may be more appropriate to deal with a reluctant witness by the threat of contempt proceedings than by depriving the public of their access to the courts.

(c)   *Effect of public hearing on possible future prosecutions*   Lord Scarman in *A-G* v *Leveller Magazine Ltd* [1979] AC 440, a case concerning the right to publish the name of a witness whom examining justices (sitting in open court) had allowed to be referred to by the pseudonym of 'Colonel B', held that the decision turned upon whether the justices could, had they so wished, have heard Colonel B's evidence in camera. His lordship stated (at p. 471C–D) that, at common law, even prejudice to national safety would not *per se* justify excluding the public but a court might sit in private, 'if the factor of national safety appears to endanger the due administration of justice, e.g., *by deterring the Crown from prosecuting in cases where it should do so*' (emphasis added). Arguably, there may be extrapolated from this dictum a general proposition that if refusal to sit in camera would prejudice future prosecutions (e.g., because the Crown would consider that the harm done by publicity would outweigh the good done by securing an offender's conviction, or because potential witnesses would not come forward in future unless they could reasonably anticipate being allowed to testify in private) then the court may exclude the public in the instant case. However, examples of this actually being done are lacking, and (as with (b) above) such problems can usually be dealt with by action short of sitting in camera.

A decision to sit in camera is *not* justified merely on the ground that, having regard to the nature of the witness's proposed evidence, he would find it embarrassing to testify publicly (*Malvern Justices, ex parte Evans* [1988] QB 540, in which the Divisional Court held that it was an inappropriate (though not unlawful) exercise of discretion for justices to sit in camera in a case involving special reasons for not disqualifying, for the sole purpose of sparing the defendant the ordeal of giving evidence of 'embarrassing and intimate details' of her personal life). Even when it is claimed that the safety of a witness or party will be endangered by an open hearing, the court should consider carefully whether he can be adequately protected by means less drastic than totally excluding the public (e.g., by handing the court an agreed statement of sensitive facts – in this case, an offender's history as a supergrass – which the court could consider privately (see (b) above): *Reigate Justices, ex parte Argus Newspapers* (1983) 5 Cr App R (S) 181). Furthermore, the protection of public decency is an insufficient basis for proceeding in private (per Viscount Haldane LC in *Scott* v *Scott* at p. 439: 'A mere desire to consider feelings of delicacy or to exclude from publicity details which it would be desirable not to publish is not . . . enough'). Moreover, according to Lord Scarman in the passage from *A-G* v *Leveller Magazine Ltd* referred to above, at common law even considerations of national safety are also insufficient (but see **D2.50** and the Official Secrets Act 1920, s. 8, for the statutory power to sit in camera in secrets cases).

D2.50   ***Statutory Provisions***   The extremely limited power at common law to sit in camera is supplemented by certain statutory provisions. First, in proceedings for offences under the Official Secrets Act 1911 or 1920, the court may, on application being made by the prosecution that the publication of any evidence to be given or of any statement to be made in the course of the proceedings would be prejudicial to national safety, order that the public be excluded for some or all of the hearing, though the passing of sentence must take place in public (Official Secrets Act 1920, s. 8(4)). Secondly, no child (i.e. a person under the age of 14) is permitted to be in court while criminal proceedings are in progress against a person other than himself save insofar as his presence is required as a witness or 'otherwise for the purposes of justice' (CYPA 1933, s. 36). Thirdly, where a juvenile (i.e. any person under 18) is called as a witness in proceedings in relation to an offence against or any conduct contrary to decency or morality, the court may direct that any persons not directly involved in the case be excluded from the court during the taking of the juvenile's evidence, save that bona fide representatives of the press may not be so excluded (s. 37). Lastly, some interlocutory matters connected with criminal proceedings may be determined in chambers (e.g., bail applications to the Crown Court and applications to a judge in chambers for a voluntary bill of indictment), and special rules govern public access to youth courts.

The procedure where a prosecutor or a defendant intends to apply for an order that all or part of a Crown Court trial be held in camera is set out in the Crown Court Rules 1982, r. 24A. The prospective applicant must serve notice of application, seven days before the trial is due to begin, upon the Crown Court and upon his opponent. The appropriate officer of the Crown Court will then ensure that a copy of the notice is prominently displayed within the precincts of the court. The application is then heard, unless the court orders otherwise, in camera, after the accused has been arraigned but before the jury is sworn. The trial is then adjourned for 24 hours or until the appeal is determined or leave to appeal refused.

Re Godwin [1991] Crim LR 302 held that a trial judge had no inherent power to override the rules and order evidence to be heard in camera. But should some matter arise suddenly so as to preclude compliance with r. 24A, the court might have inherent powers to order that evidence be heard in camera, despite that lack of compliance.

Official Secrets Act 1920, s. 8

(4)   In addition and without prejudice to any powers which a court may possess to order the exclusion of the public from any proceedings if, in the course of proceedings before a court against any person for an offence under [the Official Secrets Act 1911] or this Act or the proceedings on appeal, or in the course of the trial of a person for [any offence under the Official Secrets Act 1911] or this Act, application is made by the prosecution, on the ground that the publication of any evidence to be given or of any statement to be made in the course of the proceedings would be prejudicial to the national safety, that all or any portion of the public shall be excluded during any part of the hearing, the court may make an order to that effect, but the passing of sentence shall in any case take place in public.

Children and Young Persons Act 1933, ss. 36 and 37

36.   No child (other than an infant in arms) shall be permitted to be present in court during the trial of any other person charged with an offence, or during any proceedings preliminary thereto, except during such time as his presence is required as a witness or otherwise for the purposes of justice; and any child present in court when under this section he is not permitted to be so shall be ordered to be removed.

37.—(1)   Where, in any proceedings in relation to an offence against, or any conduct contrary to, decency or morality, a person who, in the opinion of the court is a child or young person, is called as a witness, the court may direct that all or any persons, not being members or officers of the court or parties to the case, their counsel or solicitors, or persons otherwise directly concerned with the case, be excluded from the court during the taking of the evidence of that witness:

Provided that nothing in this section shall authorise the exclusion of bona fide representatives of a newspaper or news agency.

(2)   The powers conferred on a court by this section shall be in addition and without prejudice to any other powers of the court to hear proceedings in camera.

Evidence Communicated Confidentially

The second aspect of the principle of open justice to which Lord Diplock drew attention **D2.51** in the passage quoted at **D2.47** is that 'in criminal cases at any rate, all evidence communicated to the court is communicated publicly'. Obviously this applies only when the court is in open session. Moreover, like the more fundamental requirement that criminal courts shall sit in public, the requirement that evidence be communicated publicly may be waived if not to do so would frustrate or render impracticable the administration of justice. Since allowing a particular piece of evidence or other material to be communicated privately to the tribunal is a less drastic interference with open justice than conducting the whole proceedings in camera, it is correspondingly more likely to occur in practice and less likely to be disapproved by the appellate courts in the event of a subsequent challenge to its propriety.

Probably the commonest example of evidence being communicated privately during the course of the trial of a not guilty plea is where the victim of an offence of blackmail called as a witness for the prosecution is allowed to write down his name and address for the court's eyes only and thereafter is referred to by a pseudonym. Not to adopt this practice would frustrate the administration of justice in that future victims of blackmail would be reluctant to report the matter to the police if they thought there was a risk of their identities eventually being revealed in court. However, mere sympathy with the embarrassment a person will suffer through being publicly identified is not a sufficient ground for keeping the evidence of his name and/or address confidential. Thus, in *Evesham Justices, ex parte McDonagh* [1988] QB 553, Watkins LJ in the Divisional Court disapproved the decision of the justices to allow the address of a defendant (charged with using a motor vehicle without an MOT test certificate) to be given on a piece of paper seen only by them, solely because he feared harassment by his former wife if she discovered where he was now living. In *Watford Magistrates' Court, ex parte Lenman* [1993] Crim LR 388, however, the Divisional Court upheld the decision of the magistrate to allow witnesses to a series of violent attacks to retain their anonymity while giving evidence at committal proceedings. The Court said that a magistrate who was satisfied that there was a real risk to the administration of justice because a witness reasonably feared for his safety if his identity were disclosed was entitled to take reasonable steps to protect and reassure the witness. If, on the other hand, the defendant's ability to prepare and conduct his defence was prejudiced by the witness' anonymity, then justice might require the witness' identity to be disclosed.

By contrast with the strictly limited derogations from the requirement that information be communciated publicly allowed at the pre-conviction stages of procedure, it is standard practice at the sentencing stage for reports on the offender (e.g. social inquiry report or medical and psychiatric reports) to be read privately by the court. The defence are entitled to copies of the reports, and may refer to particular portions thereof in mitigation, but they are not read out in full; nor are the public or press entitled to see them (see *Beckett* (1967) 51 Cr App R 180 for approval of the practice, and see also *Reigate Justices, ex parte Argus Newspapers* (1983) 5 Cr App R (S) 181).

Freedom of the Media to Report Court Proceedings

D2.52   The liability of the media of mass communication to proceedings for contempt if they publish anything which creates a substantial risk that the course of justice will be seriously impeded or prejudiced is discussed in detail in **B14.80** and **B 14.84** to **B14.88**. This is known as the 'strict liability rule' (see Contempt of Court Act 1981, s. 1) since the media may be held in contempt notwithstanding that there was no intent to interfere with justice. There has, however, always been a major exception to the rule in respect of the contemporaneous reporting of actual court proceedings, as opposed to comment on matters which are *sub iudice*. This exception was recognised by Lord Diplock in *A-G v Leveller Magazine Ltd* [1979] AC 440 when he said that open justice required that nothing should be done to discourage the publication to a wider public of fair and accurate reports of proceedings that have taken place in open court.

Section 4 of the Contempt of Court Act 1981 now governs liability for the reporting of court proceedings.

Contempt of Court Act 1981, s. 4

(1)   Subject to this section a person is not guilty of contempt of court under the strict liability rule in respect of a fair and accurate report of legal proceedings held in public, published contemporaneously and in good faith.

(2)   In any such proceedings the court may, where it appears to be necessary for avoiding a substantial risk of prejudice to the administration of justice in those proceedings, or in any other proceedings pending or imminent, order that the publication of any report of the proceedings, or any part of the proceedings, be postponed for such period as the court thinks necessary for that purpose.

[(3)   If publication of a report is postponed as a result of an order under subsection (2), a report published as soon as practicable after the order expires is to be treated as contemporaneous and therefore entitled under subsection (1) to protection from contempt proceedings.]

For consideration of the effect of s. 4 of the Contempt of Court Act 1981, see *Horsham Justices, ex parte Farquharson* [1982] QB 762.

The *Practice Direction (Contempt: Reporting Restrictions)* [1982] 1 WLR 1475 states that all orders under s. 4(2) must be 'formulated in precise terms', and must include: (a) the order's precise scope; (b) the time at which it shall cease to have effect; and (c) the specific purpose for which it was made. The order must be put into writing, and the press should be informed.

There are two situations in which the power given to the courts by s. 4(2) may often be of value. They are: (a) when an accused is to be tried successively on separate indictments (or several accused are to be tried separately for connected offences) and reports of the evidence given at the trial held first are likely to prejudice jurors for the later trials; and (b) when evidence and/or argument is put before the judge at a trial on indictment in the absence of the jury, the purpose of sending the jury out being to prevent their being prejudiced by, for example, evidence which the judge ultimately rules to be inadmissible. In both these situations, premature publication of reports, especially if the court had expressly asked that there should not be any reporting until the risk of prejudice was past, could amount to contempt at common law (see *Clement* (1821) 4 B & Ald 218 on successive trials, and Lord Diplock in *A-G v Leveller Magazine Ltd* [1979] AC 440 at p. 450D–F on reporting a trial within a trial). The correct analysis of the basis of liability was not that the court had directed that reporting should be postponed (it probably did not have power so to do), but that the premature reporting had in fact prejudiced the administration of justice (see especially Lords Diplock, Edmund-Davies and Russell of Killowen in *A-G v Leveller Magazine Ltd* at pp. 451F–452B, 463H–464B and 468H–469A respectively). A warning in court that anybody who published reports prematurely might be at risk of contempt proceedings was no doubt desirable, but it was not essential to liability. By contrast, the possibly inconvenient effect of s. 4 is that, should the court inadvertently fail to make an order under s. 4(2), the general protection given to the publication of fair and accurate contemporaneous reports by s. 4(1) means that those who publish such reports cannot be guilty of contempt, even though it was obvious that their reporting would gravely prejudice criminal proceedings (e.g., by informing jurors of what took place in court when they had been sent out). Whatever the legal position, however, responsible journalists would no doubt refrain from publishing in such situations, whether or not the court formally made a s. 4(2) order.

The court must avoid making an order under s. 4(2) unless no other course is available for avoiding a substantial risk of prejudice (*Re Section 4(2) of the Contempt of Court Act 1981* (1990) *Guardian*, 8 November 1990). In this case, the trial judge made an order under s. 4(2) prohibiting radio or television reporting of the trial of two defendants on charges of fraud and corruption. The order was made when the jury had retired to consider their verdict, and were to spend a night at a hotel. The order applied that night. The Court of Appeal held that the judge should not have made the order. There were cases when it was necessary so to do, for example, where there was a *voir dire*, but that was not the case here. In any event, where a jury is confined to a hotel, it is possible to deprive them of television, radio or newspapers. When such an alternative was reasonably available it should be used rather than action under s. 4(2). See also *Ex parte The Telegraph plc* (1993) 98 Cr App R 91.

The Contempt of Court Act 1981 has subsumed pre-existing common law powers to prohibit or postpone publication of the court's proceedings. The reason for an order under s. 4(2) is 'a substantial risk of prejudice to the administration of justice'. It follows that the court is not able to impose an embargo on publication to protect the welfare of the defendant (*Newtonabbey Magistrates' Court, ex parte Belfast Telegraph Newspapers Ltd* (1997) *The Times*, 27 August 1997).

In *A-G v Guardian Newspapers Ltd* [1992] 1 WLR 874, one of the issues considered by the Divisional Court was whether the making of an order under s. 4(2), and its terms, could themselves be reported. Mann LJ thought it very doubtful whether such a report could be published. If it could, then that might cause the very mischief which the order was intended to prevent. It might therefore be appropriate in some cases for the judge to make plain whether the making of the order and its terms could be published. Brooke J added that, if the judge needed help in determining whether to make an order, he could adjourn until the press was represented, or he had the help of an *amicus curiae*. In *Clerkenwell Stipendiary Magistrate, ex parte The Telegraph Plc* (1992) *The Times*, 22 October 1992, the Divisional Court made it clear that the magistrates' court had the power to hear representations from the press regarding a s. 4(2) order. Although the power was discretionary, it would generally be right to exercise it by hearing from the press, who were best qualified to represent that public interest in publicity which the court had to take into account in performing the necessary balancing exercise.

In addition to their power to postpone publication of court reports by virtue of a s. 4(2) order, the courts are empowered by a number of statutory provisions to impose a *permanent* ban on the reporting of certain matters.

Contempt of Court Act 1981, s. 11

> In any case where a court (having power to do so) allows a name or other matter to be withheld from the public in proceedings before the court, the court may give such directions prohibiting the publication of that name or matter in connection with the proceedings as appear to the court to be necessary for the purpose for which it was so withheld.

Section 11 complements the common law power of a court, sitting in public, to receive a small part of the evidence (such as the name and address of a witness) in a form which is not communicated to the public. The terms of the s. 11 show that an order under it may be without limitation of time but may only be made where the court has legitimately exercised its common law power to receive evidence or other information without allowing it to be disclosed to the public (see *Arundel Justices, ex parte Westminster Press Ltd* [1985] 1 WLR 708, *Evesham Justices, ex parte McDonagh* [1988] QB 553 and *Dover Justices, ex parte Dover District Council* (1992) 156 JP 433). The *Practice Direction (Contempt: Reporting Restrictions)* [1982] 1 WLR 1475 requires that orders made under the Contempt of Court Act 1981 be precisely framed and put into writing, and applies to orders under s. 11 as well as to orders under s. 4(2).

Under the CYPA 1933, s. 39, the onus is on the Crown Court or magistrates' court to make an order protecting the child or young person's anonymity. The opposite applies in the youth court (see CYPA 1933, s. 49, and **D21.17**).

In *Leicester Crown Court, ex parte S* [1993] 1 WLR 111, S, a boy of 12 was sentenced to five years' detention after pleading guilty to arson. On his first appearance in the Crown Court, the judge had made an order under the CYPA 1933, s. 39, prohibiting publication of particulars which might help to identify him. A different judge sentenced him, and discharged the restriction order, allowing identifying details to be published. The order discharging the restriction order was suspended pending application for judicial review. The Divisional Court quashed the decision of the second judge, and restored the restriction order, holding:

(a)   the Supreme Court Act 1981, s. 29(3), did not apply so as to exclude judicial review (see **D25.30**);

(b)   the decision of the second judge was unreasonable within the meaning of *Associated Provincial Picture Houses* v *Wednesbury Corporation* [1948] 1 KB 223, since the publicity would have potentially disastrous effects upon S, without apparent benefit to anyone. Where a child or young person was before the court, it would only be in 'rare and exceptional cases' that directions under s. 39 would not be given or, having been given, would be discharged.

In *Lee* [1993] Crim LR 65, the Court of Appeal summarised the position in relation to appeals against a decision under s. 39 as follows:

(a)   a member of the press who is aggrieved by an order under s. 39 should go back to the Crown Court in the event of a change of circumstances, or should appeal to the Court of Appeal under the CJA 1988, s. 159;

(b)   a defendant aggrieved by the withholding or discharging of an order under s. 39 should go back to the Crown Court in the event of a change of circumstances or apply for relief to the Divisional Court;

(c)   if a defendant indicated that he was intending to apply to the Divisional Court, the Crown Court could grant a stay under s. 39 pending a decision of the Divisional Court.

Their lordships went on to comment on the approach which the court ought to adopt in considering applications under s. 39. Whereas in *Leicester Crown Court, ex parte S* the Divisional Court had said that a direction prohibiting publication should only be refused in 'rare and exceptional cases', the Court of Appeal in *Lee* said that, for its part, it would not wish to see the discretion fettered so strictly. This approach was confirmed by the Divisional Court in *Central Criminal Court, ex parte S* [1999] 1 FLR 480. Their lordships said that to say that a direction could be discharged only in rare and exceptional circumstances would place an unwarranted gloss upon the broad discretion conferred by statute. The age of the defendant was an important factor, but not the only one. The weight to be attributed to the different factors might shift at different stages of proceedings, and particularly after the defendant had been found or pleaded guilty and sentenced. It might then be appropriate to place greater weight on the public interest in knowing the identity of those who had committed crimes, particularly serious ones. The fact that the defendant was lodging an appeal might be a material consideration in deciding whether to lift a reporting restriction, but would not always be a weighty factor.

The courts also have powers under the Sexual Offences (Amendment) Acts 1976 and 1992. The broad effect of these Acts is that the victim in a case of rape (the 1976 Act, s. 4) or one of the sexual offences listed in the 1992 Act is entitled to anonymity. Once an allegation of one of the offences in question has been made, nothing may be published which is likely to lead members of the public to identify the alleged victim. The offences listed in the 1992 Act include unlawful sexual intercourse, incest, buggery, indecent conduct with a young child, indecent assault and conspiracy or incitement to commit any of these offences (s. 2). It follows that, in reporting the proceedings at and prior to a trial for rape or one of the offences covered by the 1992 Act, the media are obliged to omit anything likely to disclose the complainant's identity, even if that information was given in open court. The section does not in terms require that the complainant be referred to in court as 'Miss X', but the court might often choose to make an order to that effect. The prohibition on publicity may be lifted by order of the court if either: (a) publicity is required by the accused so that witnesses will come forward and the conduct of the defence is likely to be seriously prejudiced if the direction is not given; or (b) the judge at trial is satisfied that imposition of the prohibition in full would unreasonably and substantially restrict reporting of the proceedings.

All the provisions described above relate to the reporting of court proceedings held in public. The Administration of Justice Act 1960, s. 12 (see **B14.88**), deals with the reporting of proceedings which were held in camera. Strangely, there was at common law no automatic rule that the reporting of in camera proceedings amounted to contempt – just as when public proceedings were reported, it had to be shown that the reporting involved a substantial risk of prejudice to the administration of justice. This would appear to be still the case under s. 12 which, according to Lord Scarman, is merely declaratory of the common-law powers (see *A-G v Leveller Magazine Ltd* [1979] AC 440 at p. 472F–G).

The Principle of Open Justice and Magistrates' Courts

D2.53 Several of the cases on open justice discussed above have concerned decisions by magistrates' courts either to sit in private or to receive a piece of evidence privately. Prima facie, it is surprising that magistrates are ever entitled to exclude the public from summary trials since s. 121 of the MCA 1980 basically requires them to sit in a petty-sessional court-house or occasional court-house whenever they try an information, and s. 121(4) states that: 'Subject to the provisions of any enactment to the contrary, where a magistrates' court is required by this section to sit in a petty-sessional or occasional court-house, it shall sit in open court.' However, despite its apparently mandatory terms, s. 121(4) has been construed so as not to deprive magistrates of 'that inherent jurisdiction [which] exists in *any* court which enables it to exclude the public where it becomes necessary in order to administer justice' (per Viscount Reading CJ in *Governor of Lewes Prison, ex parte Doyle* [1917] 2 KB 254 at p. 271, emphasis added; applied to magistrates' courts by Watkins LJ in his judgment in *Malvern Justices, ex parte Evans* [1988] QB 540). Thus, in determining whether to exclude the public, magistrates' courts are in the same position as other courts and are not subject to any special statutory rule requiring them always to sit in open court.

Disclosure of the Names of Judges and Magistrates

D2.54 A further aspect of the principle of open justice is that the names of those administering it shall not be concealed. It has never been suggested that the name of a Crown Court judge should or could be kept secret. In recent years, however, certain benches of justices – in order to avoid invasions of their privacy, abuse from disgruntled members of the public or unwelcome approaches from the media – have adopted the practice of refusing to reveal the identities of those adjudicating on any particular occasion, or of only revealing that information as a matter of discretion. The legality of this procedure was tested in *Felixstowe Justices, ex parte Leigh* [1987] QB 582, where the applicant (a journalist) had asked for and been refused the name of the chairman of the bench which heard a case concerning gross indecency with children. During the course of the hearing, an order was made under the CYPA 1933, s. 39, that nothing which might lead to the identification of the children should be published. The applicant wanted the chairman's name for purposes of a planned article about the differing practices of courts in respect of s. 39 orders. Granting a declaration that the policy of the Felixstowe Bench to withhold from the public and the press the identity of justices was unlawful, Watkins LJ said (at p. 594):

> I would regard and I believe the general public likewise would regard a policy such as that maintained by the Felixstowe justices and their clerk to be inimical to the proper administration of justice and an unwarranted and an unlawful obstruction to the right to know who sits in judgment. There is, in my view, no such person known to law as the anonymous JP.

The decision in *Ex parte Leigh* does not, however, require that the names of the justices be given on the court lists posted outside court. Assuming the names are not so given, the clerk would have to be asked for them, either during or after the hearing. If the clerk reasonably believes that the information is wanted for a purely mischievous purpose, he would be justified in refusing to give it (per Watkins LJ at p. 595D–E). Furthermore, the principle of open justice merely requires that the *names* of judicial persons be supplied – there is certainly no obligation to give addresses as well. Watkins LJ's judgment appears broadly in line with a resolution passed by the Council of the Magistrates' Association in July 1985, which is set out below.

Resolution of the Magistrates' Association Council Relating to Publication of Names of Justices

> It does not appear necessary and will frequently be impracticable for the names of adjudicating magistrates to be publicly listed before courts sit. The names of adjudicating

magistrates should normally be available on request by persons having a bona fide interest (e.g., prosecutor or defendant or their legal representatives or press representatives) during or after proceedings in court but there will be a small number of occasions when it will be in the interests of justice for the names to be withheld. Names should be withheld where there are substantial grounds for belief that the magistrates concerned, or members of their families, or other associates might in consequence of the proceedings be subject to violence or harassment. Examples are where defendants are believed to be members of terrorist groups, or of other organisations using violence or harassment to achieve or publicise their objectives.

Meaning of 'Open Court'

The obligation of the criminal courts to sit in open court and the very limited **D2.55** circumstances in which they may choose to sit in camera have been discussed without explanation of the phrase 'open court'. To a large extent, the term is self-explanatory. However, in *Denbigh Justices, ex parte Williams* [1974] QB 759 the question arose of whether justices, trying members of the Welsh Language Society on charges of using television sets without licences, had conducted the proceedings in open court as they were undoubtedly obliged to do. The defendants had refused to buy licences as a political protest, and about 20–30 of their supporters and friends were present in the court building, hoping to observe the proceedings. However, the court-room to which the case was allocated had accommodation only for the press, plus five members of the public. On the direction of the chairman of the magistrates, the defendants selected five of their supporters to fill the public seats. Following conviction, the defendants applied for certiorari on the ground that the hearing had not been in open court. Lord Widgery CJ adopted a statement of principle made by Garoutte J in the Californian case of *People v Hartman* (1894) 37 P 153:

> The trial should be 'public' in the ordinary common-sense acceptation of that term. The doors of the court-room are expected to be kept open, the public are entitled to be admitted, and the trial is to be public in all respects, . . . with due regard to the size of the courtroom, the conveniences of the court, the right to exclude objectionable characters and youth of tender years, and to do other things which may facilitate the proper conduct of the trial.

Lord Widgery's gloss on those words was ([1974] QB 759 at p. 765A): '. . . the injunction to the presiding judge or magistrate is: do your best to enable the public to come in and see what is happening, having a proper common-sense regard for the facilities available and the facility for keeping order, security and the like'.

Thus, even though the majority of those members of the public who had wanted to be present at the defendants' trial had in fact been prevented from being there, the action of the presiding magistrate in ensuring that all the public seats available were filled with the defendants' supporters meant that the court had done what it reasonably could to let the public in. *Obiter*, Lord Widgery observed that, since most people obtained their news of how justice was administered through the mass media, exclusion of the press from a hearing would almost certainly entail the conclusion that it was not in open court. Admission of the press was a powerful argument for saying that a hearing was open, but it was not conclusive – there should always be facilities for at least some individual members of the public to be present (at p. 765B–C).

As to the use of tape recorders in court, the Contempt of Court Act 1981, s. 9, provides that it is a contempt of court to use in court (or bring into court for use) a tape recorder, unless the court gives leave. For the factors to be considered, see *Practice Direction (Tape Recorders)* [1981] 1 WLR 1526, discussed at **B14.83**. Where leave is granted, conditions may be attached to the use that may be made of the recording. It is also contempt to play in public a recording of legal proceedings.

Appeals against Derogations from Open Justice

D2.56   **Criminal Justice Act 1988, s. 159**

(1)   A person aggrieved may appeal to the Court of Appeal, if that court grants leave, against—

(a)   an order under section 4 or 11 of the Contempt of Court Act 1981 made in relation to a trial on indictment;

(b)   any order restricting the access of the public to the whole or any part of a trial on indictment or to any proceedings ancillary to such a trial; and

(c)   any order restricting the publication of any report of the whole or any part of a trial on indictment or any such ancillary proceedings;

and the decision of the Court of Appeal shall be final.

. . .

(5)   On the hearing of an appeal under this section the Court of Appeal shall have power—

(a)   to stay any proceedings in any other court until after the appeal is disposed of;

(b)   to confirm, reverse or vary the order complained of; and

(c)   to make such order as to costs as it thinks fit.

The creation of a specific right to appeal against orders of the Crown Court derogating from the principle of open justice was necessary because the ordinary system of appeals to the Court of Appeal (Criminal Division) gives a right of appeal only to the accused following his conviction and/or sentence. It is most unlikely that a decision, for example, to order that media reporting of a trial be postponed would provide a ground of appeal against conviction or sentence, and, even if it did, the Court of Appeal would have no power directly to quash or amend the order – its power would be to quash the conviction or reduce the sentence. Section 159(5), which deals with the Court of Appeal's powers upon disposing of an appeal under the section, contemplates the trial on indictment being stayed while the appeal is determined (see s. 159(5)(a)) as does r. 24A of the Crown Court Rules 1982. The power to stay the trial is necessary because quashing an order derogating from open justice after the relevant proceedings have been completed will often serve no practical purpose, since by that time any harm resulting from the order has already been done.

Section 159 does not extend to decisions of magistrates' courts in relation to open justice or to such decisions made by the Crown Court otherwise than in connection with trials on indictment (e.g., on an appeal from magistrates). In respect of such decisions, the remedy of an aggrieved person remains what it was prior to the enactment of s. 159, namely to apply to the Divisional Court for judicial review of the inferior tribunal's decision. This has the disadvantage that, even if the remedy sought is granted, it may come too late to be of practical value. Also, an application to quash an order of the lower court or have it declared unlawful is liable to be refused on the basis that, although the order was almost certainly misguided, it was within the court's jurisdiction (see, e.g., *Malvern Justices, ex parte Evans* [1988] QB 540).

SECTION D3: CLASSIFICATION OF OFFENCES AND DETERMINING MODE OF TRIAL

Criminal trials in England and Wales are either trials on indictment or summary trials. **D3.1** The former take place in the Crown Court before a judge and (if the accused pleads not guilty) jury; the latter take place in a magistrates' court before at least two lay justices (or a single stipendiary magistrate). Summary trials are also referred to as 'trials on information'. This section deals with: (a) the classification of offences according to whether they: (i) must be tried on indictment, or (ii) can be tried either on indictment or summarily, or (iii) must be tried summarily; and (b) the procedure for determining the appropriate mode of trial in those cases where there is a choice.

CLASSIFICATION OF OFFENCES

Definition of the Classes of Offences

Since the coming into effect of the Criminal Law Act 1977, there have been, as regards mode of trial, three classes of offence – namely, (a) those triable only on indictment, (b) those triable only summarily and (c) those triable either way. Section 14 of the 1977 Act, which expressly provided for this threefold classification, was repealed by the MCA 1980, but ss. 17 to 25 of the 1980 Act re-enacted the simplified system for classifying offences and determining mode of trial which had been introduced three years earlier. Sections 40 and 41 of the CJA 1988 have qualified, but not fundamentally altered, the system by providing that certain offences which would otherwise be triable only summarily may be disposed of on indictment if (a) they are linked with an offence in one of the other two categories, and (b) that other offence is going to be tried on indictment (see **D7.23** and **D9.6**).

Sections 17 to 25 of the MCA 1980 must be read in conjunction with sch. 1 to the Interpretation Act 1978, which gives the following definitions:

Interpretation Act 1978, sch. 1

(a) 'indictable offence' means an offence which, if committed by an adult, is triable on indictment, whether it is exclusively so triable or triable either way;

(b) 'summary offence' means an offence which, if committed by an adult, is triable only summarily;

(c) 'offence triable either way' means an offence, other than an offence triable on indictment only by virtue of [s. 40 or s. 41] of the Criminal Justice Act 1988 which, if committed by an adult, is triable either on indictment or summarily;

and the terms 'indictable', 'summary' and 'triable either way', in their application to offences, are to be construed accordingly.

The Interpretation Act 1978 qualifies the above definitions with the rider that: 'references [in the definitions] to the way or ways in which an offence is triable are to be construed without regard to the effect, if any, of section 22 of the MCA 1980 on the mode of trial in a particular case'. The broad effect of s. 22 of the MCA 1980 is that offences under s. 1 of the Criminal Damage Act 1971 involving damage worth less than the relevant sum must be dealt with as if they were triable only summarily (see **D3.12**). However, such an offence retains the status of an offence triable either way, even though the magistrates are barred from sending it to the Crown Court for trial (*Considine* (1980) 70 Cr App R 239; *Bristol Magistrates' Court, ex parte E* [1998] 3 All ER 798).

By s. 5 of the Interpretation Act 1978, the definitions set out in sch. 1 are to apply whenever the terms defined are used statutorily unless a contrary intention appears. Consequently, when an Act contains the phrase 'indictable offence' without any further qualification, it must be understood to mean both those offences which, in the case of an adult, *must* be tried on indictment and those which (again in the case of an adult) carry the right to trial on indictment although they can be tried summarily if the conditions in the MCA 1980, ss. 19 and 20, are satisfied. In other words, offences triable either way are a subdivision of indictable offences. Summary offences, on the other hand, are entirely distinct from indictable offences and must always be tried summarily, unless s. 40 or s. 41 of the CJA 1988 applies. The reason for the Interpretation Act 1978 definitions referring each time to the possible mode of trial in the case of an adult is that special rules apply to the trial of juveniles, greatly restricting their right to trial on indictment (see s. 24 of the MCA 1980 and **D21**). However, the fact that a juvenile charged with a certain offence would have to be tried for it summarily does not render the offence summary – the question is whether an adult would have to be so tried.

Determining Which Class an Offence Is In

D3.2   The definitions in the Interpretation Act 1978 do not help to determine whether any particular offence is indictable or summary, or whether, in the former case, it is triable only on indictment or either way. Those questions are answered as follows:

(a) *Statutory offences.*   The enactment creating the offence will prescribe the maximum penalty. If the statute provides for a maximum penalty imposable on summary conviction and does not provide for a penalty on conviction on indictment, then the offence is summary. If the statute provides for one penalty on summary conviction and a different (greater) penalty on conviction on indictment, then the offence is triable either way. If the statute provides only for a penalty on conviction on indictment, then the offence is triable only on indictment, unless the offence is listed in the MCA 1980, sch. 1 (see below).

(b) *Common-law offences.*   These are all indictable offences. They will be triable only on indictment unless listed in the MCA 1980, sch. 1.

It will be apparent from the above that some statutory offences are triable either way, even though there is no indication in the statute itself that that is so. Similarly, some common-law offences are triable either way even though common-law offences are prima facie triable only on indictment. This is because the MCA 1980, s. 17, provides that, without prejudice to any other enactment by virtue of which an offence is triable either way, the offences listed in sch. 1 shall be so triable. As regards determining the mode of trial, it makes no difference whether an offence is listed in sch. 1 or is made triable either way by virtue of the offence-creating statute specifically providing for differing penalties on summary conviction and on conviction on indictment. The significance of the distinction is that, on summary conviction for a sch. 1 offence, the maximum penalty that a magistrates' court may impose is six months' imprisonment and/or a fine not exceeding the 'prescribed sum', presently £5,000, whereas, on summary conviction for an offence made triable either way by the statute creating it, the maximum is basically whatever is prescribed in the statute, save that the maximum prison term imposable may not exceed six months (ss. 31 and 32). The modern tendency when creating new either-way offences is to provide in the statute for the penalties, rather than adding the new offence to the list in sch. 1.

The most important offence-creating statutes covered by sch. 1 are the OAPA 1861, the Perjury Act 1911, the Sexual Offences Act 1956, the Theft Act 1968 and the Criminal Damage Act 1971. Schedule 1 also deals with the trial of secondary parties and offences of incitement. Attempts are now covered by the Criminal Attempts Act 1981, s. 4(1)(c), the rule being – as it is for allegations of aiding and abetting or inciting – that the offence is triable either way only if the substantive offence is so triable.

Magistrates' Courts Act 1980, s. 17 and sch. 1

17.— (1)   The offences listed in Schedule 1 to this Act shall be triable either way.

(2)   Subsection (1) above is without prejudice to any other enactment by virtue of which any offence is triable either way.

SCHEDULE 1
OFFENCES TRIABLE EITHER WAY BY VIRTUE OF SECTION 17

1.   Offences at common law of public nuisance.

. . .

5.   Offences under the following provisions of the Offences against the Person Act 1861—
  (a)   section 16 (threats to kill);
  (b)   section 20 (inflicting bodily injury, with or without a weapon);
  (c)   section 26 (not providing apprentices or servants with food etc.);
  (d)   section 27 (abandoning or exposing a child);
  (e)   section 34 (doing or omitting to do anything so as to endanger railway passengers);
  (f)   section 36 (assaulting a clergyman at a place of worship etc.);
  (g)   section 38 (assault with intent to resist apprehension);
  (h)   section 47 (assault occasioning bodily harm);
  (i)   section 57 (bigamy);
  (j)   section 60 (concealing the birth of a child).

. . .

7.   Offences under section 13 of the Debtors Act 1869 (transactions intended to defraud creditors).

. . .

14.   All offences under the Perjury Act 1911 except offences under—
  (a)   section 1 (perjury in judicial proceedings);
  (b)   section 3 (false statements etc. with reference to marriage).
  (c)   section 4 (false statements etc. as to births or deaths).

. . .

16.   Offences under section 17 of the Deeds of Arrangement Act 1914 (trustee making preferential payments).
[17.   Repealed.]
18.   Offences under section 8(2) of the Census Act 1920 (disclosing census information).
19.   Offences under section 36 of the Criminal Justice Act 1925 (forgery of passports etc.).

. . .

22.   Offences under the following provisions of the Post Office Act 1953—
  (a)   section 53 (unlawfully taking away or opening mail bag);
  (b)   section 55 (fraudulent retention of mail bag or postal packet);
  (c)   section 57 (stealing, embezzlement, destruction etc. by officer of Post Office of postal packet);
  (d)   section 58 (opening or delaying of postal packets by officers of the Post Office).
23.   Offences under the following provisions of the Sexual Offences Act 1956—
  (a)   section 6 (unlawful intercourse with a girl under 16);
  (b)   section 13 (indecency between men);
  (c)   section 26 (permitting a girl under 16 to use premises for sexual intercourse).

. . .

26.   The following offences under the Criminal Law Act 1967—
  (a)   offences under section 4(1) (assisting offenders); and
  (b)   offences under section 5(1) (concealing arrestable offences and giving false information),
where the offence to which they relate is triable either way.
27.   Offences under section 4(1) of the Sexual Offences Act 1967 (procuring others to commit homosexual acts).
28.   All indictable offences under the Theft Act 1986 except—
  (a)   robbery, aggravated burglary, blackmail and assault with intent to rob;
  (b)   burglary comprising the commission of, or an intention to commit, an offence which is triable only on indictment;
  (c)   burglary in a dwelling if any person in the dwelling was subjected to violence or the threat of violence.

29.   Offences under the following provisions of the Criminal Damage Act 1971—
section 1(1) (destroying or damaging property);
section 1(1) and (3) (arson);
section 2 (threats to destroy or damage property);
section 3 (possessing anything with intent to destroy or damage property).
. . .

32.   Committing an indecent assault upon a person whether male or female.
33.   Aiding, abetting, counselling or procuring the commission of any offence listed in
the preceding paragraphs of this schedule except paragraph 26.
[34. and 35.   Repealed.]

DETERMINATION OF MODE OF TRIAL

Introduction

D3.3   Sections 17A to 21 of the MCA 1980 set out the standard method of determining the
mode of trial when an adult is charged with an offence triable either way. Section 22
provides for a special procedure where the charge is one of criminal damage, and s. 23
allows for proceedings under ss. 19 to 22 to be carried out in the absence of the accused
provided certain conditions are satisfied. Sections 24 (see **D21.3** *et seq.*) and 25 relate
respectively to determining where juveniles are to be tried, and to changing the decision
about mode of trial originally taken.

The Standard Procedure

D3.4   The standard procedure applies whenever a person who has attained the age of 18 (i.e.
an adult) appears or is brought before a magistrates' court charged with an offence
triable either way (MCA 1980, s. 17A(1)).

The precise wording of s. 17A(1) (with emphasis added) is: 'This section shall have effect
where a person who has attained the age of 18 appears or is brought before a magistrates'
court *on an information* charging him with an offence triable either way.' An information
alleging that a person has committed an offence is laid before (i.e. made to) a magistrate in
order to obtain from him either a summons or warrant for arrest. In addition, a charge
preferred against a suspect at a police station is conventionally treated as an information
for purposes of subsequent proceedings against that person in a magistrates' court.
Section 17A and the following sections plainly use 'information' in this extended sense.
The standard procedure must be complied with before any evidence is called for purposes
of a summary trial or committal proceedings, and should normally take place in the
presence of the accused (s. 17A(2)). The steps in the standard procedure are as follows:

(a)   The charge is written down (if that has not already been done) and read to the
accused (s. 17A(3)).

(b)   The court explains to the accused that he may indicate whether he would plead
guilty or not guilty if the offence proceeded to trial. The court should explain that, if the
accused pleads guilty, the proceedings will be treated as a summary trial at which a guilty
plea has been tendered. It must also explain that he may be committed for sentence
under the MCA 1980, s. 38, if it is of the opinion that its powers of punishment are
inadequate (s. 17A(4)). A form of words which may be used is suggested in Home Office
Circular 45/1997 (see below).

(c)   The court asks the accused whether (if the offence went to trial) he would plead
guilty or not guilty (s. 17A(5)).

(d)   If the accused indicates a guilty plea, the court proceeds as if he had pleaded
guilty at summary trial (s. 17A(6)).

(e)   If the accused indicates a not guilty plea, the court affords the prosecution and
defence the opportunity to make representations about whether the offence is more
suitable for summary trial or trial on indictment (s. 19(2)(b)). A form of words such

as – 'This can be tried either at the Crown Court or at this court. Where do you think it ought to be tried?' – is adequate for the purpose of asking an unrepresented accused for his representations (*Horseferry Road Magistrates' Court, ex parte Constable* [1981] Crim LR 504).

(f)   The court then considers which method of trial appears more suitable, having regard to:

(i)   the representations made at stage (e);

(ii)   the nature of the case;

(iii) whether the circumstances make the offence one of a serious character;

(iv) whether the punishment which a magistrate's court would have power to inflict for the offence would be adequate; and

(v)   any other circumstances which appear to the court to make the offence more suitable for it to be tried in one way rather than the other (s. 19(1) and (3)).

(g)   If it appears to the court that summary trial is more appropriate, the court (almost certainly through the clerk) explains to the accused:

(i)   that such is the court's view, and he can either consent to be tried summarily or, if he wishes, be tried by a jury; and

(ii)   if he is tried summarily and convicted, he may be committed for sentence to the Crown Court under s. 38 if the magistrates are of the opinion that greater punishment should be inflicted than they have power to inflict (s. 20(1) and (2)).

After so explaining, the court asks the accused whether he consents to be tried summarily or wishes to be tried by a jury. Depending on his answer, the court proceeds either to summary trial or to committal proceedings (s. 20(3)). The invariable practice is to ask the accused personally for his consent to summary trial, and even though in *Kent Justices, ex parte Machin* [1952] 2 QB 355 the Divisional Court made no express adverse comment on the fact that M's solicitor had told the justices, in M's presence, that his client wished them to deal with a charge of larceny, it is submitted that the practice of asking the accused personally should be adhered to.

(h)   If it appears to the court that trial on indictment is more appropriate, it tells the accused so and proceeds to committal proceedings (s. 21).

(i)   There are equivalent procedures to be followed where the court decides that the accused's unruly conduct makes it impracticable for proceedings to be conducted in his presence (ss. 17B and 18(3)).

Magistrates' Courts Act 1980, ss. 17A to 21

17A.—(1)   This section shall have effect where a person who has attained the age of 18 years appears or is brought before a magistrates' court on an information charging him with an offence triable either way.

(2)   Everything that the court is required to do under the following provisions of this section must be done with the accused present in court.

(3)   The court shall cause the charge to be written down, if this has not already been done, and to be read to the accused.

(4)   The court shall then explain to the accused in ordinary language that he may indicate whether (if the offence were to proceed to trial) he would plead guilty or not guilty, and that if he indicates that he would plead guilty—

(a)   the court must proceed as mentioned in subsection (6) below; and

(b)   he may be committed for sentence to the Crown Court under section 38 below if the court is of such opinion as is mentioned in subsection (2) of that section.

(5)   The court shall then ask the accused whether (if the offence were to proceed to trial) he would plead guilty or not guilty.

(6)   If the accused indicates that he would plead guilty the court shall proceed as if—

(a)   the proceedings constituted from the beginning the summary trial of the information; and

(b)   section 9(1) above was complied with and he pleaded guilty under it.

(7)   If the accused indicates that he would plead not guilty section 18(1) below shall apply.

(8)   If the accused in fact fails to indicate how he would plead, for the purposes of this section and section 18(1) below he shall be taken to indicate that he would plead not guilty.

(9)   Subject to subsection (6) above, the following shall not for any purpose be taken to constitute the taking of a plea—

(a)   asking the accused under this section whether (if the offence were to proceed to trial) he would plead guilty or not guilty;

(b)   an indication by the accused under this section of how he would plead.

17B.—(1)   This section shall have effect where—

(a)   a person who has attained the age of 18 years appears or is brought before a magistrates' court on an information charging him with an offence triable either way,

(b)   the accused is represented by a legal representative,

(c)   the court considers that by reason of the accused's disorderly conduct before the court it is not practicable for proceedings under section 17A above to be conducted in his presence, and

(d)   the court considers that it should proceed in the absence of the accused.

(2)   In such a case—

(a)   the court shall cause the charge to be written down, if this has not already been done, and to be read to the representative;

(b)   the court shall ask the representative whether (if the offence were to proceed to trial) the accused would plead guilty or not guilty;

(c)   if the representative indicates that the accused would plead guilty the court shall proceed as if the proceedings constituted from the beginning the summary trial of the information, and as if section 9(1) above was complied with and the accused pleaded guilty under it;

(d)   if the representative indicates that the accused would plead not guilty section 18(1) below shall apply.

(3)   If the representative in fact fails to indicate how the accused would plead, for the purposes of this section and section 18(1) below he shall be taken to indicate that the accused would plead not guilty.

(4)   Subject to subsection (2)(c) above, the following shall not for any purpose be taken to constitute the taking of a plea—

(a)   asking the representative under this section whether (if the offence were to proceed to trial) the accused would plead guilty or not guilty;

(b)   an indication by the representative under this section of how the accused would plead.

17C.   A magistrates' court proceeding under section 17A or 17B above may adjourn the proceedings at any time, and on doing so on any occasion when the accused is present may remand the accused, and shall remand him if—

(a)   on the occasion on which he first appeared, or was brought, before the court to answer to the information he was in custody or, having been released on bail, surrendered to the custody of the court; or

(b)   he has been remanded at any time in the course of proceedings on the information;

and where the court remands the accused, the time fixed for the resumption of proceedings shall be that at which he is required to appear or be brought before the court in pursuance of the remand or would be required to be brought before the court but for section 128(3A) below.

18.—(1)   Sections 19 to 23 below shall have effect where a person who has attained the age of 18 years appears or is brought before a magistrates' court on an information charging him with an offence triable either way and—

(a)   he indicates under section 17A above that (if the offence were to proceed to trial) he would plead not guilty, or

(b)   his representative indicates under section 17B above that (if the offence were to proceed to trial) he would plead not guilty.

(2)   Without prejudice to section 11(1) above [proceeding to summary trial of an information in the absence of the accused if he does not appear], everything that the court is required to do under sections 19 to 22 below must be done before any evidence is called and, subject to subsection (3) below and section 23 below, with the accused present in court.

[(3)   Proceeding in the accused's absence if his disorderly conduct makes it impracticable for him to be present: see **D3.6**.]

(4)   A magistrates' court proceeding under sections 19 to 23 below may adjourn the proceedings at any time, and on doing so on any occasion when the accused is present may remand the accused, and shall remand him if—

(a)   on the occasion on which he first appeared, or was brought, before the court to answer to the information he was in custody or, having been released on bail, surrendered to the custody of the court; or

(b)   if he has been remanded at any time in the course of proceedings on the information;

and where the court remands the accused, the time fixed for the resumption of the proceedings shall be that at which he is required to appear or be brought before the court in pursuance of the remand or would be required to be brought before the court but for section 128(3A) below [accused being remanded in custody agreeing to future remands in custody taking place in his absence].

(5)   The functions of a magistrates' court under sections 19 to 23 below may be discharged by a single justice, but the foregoing provision shall not be taken to authorise the summary trial of an information by a magistrates' court composed of less than two justices.

19.—(1)   The court shall consider whether, having regard to the matters mentioned in subsection (3) below and any representations made by the prosecutor or the accused, the offence appears to the court more suitable for summary trial or for trial on indictment.

(2)   Before so considering, the court—

(a)   [repealed]

(b)   shall afford the prosecutor and then the accused an opportunity to make representations as to which mode of trial would be more suitable.

(3)   The matters to which the court is to have regard under subsection (1) above are the nature of the case; whether the circumstances make the offence one of serious character; whether the punishment which a magistrates' court would have power to inflict for it would be adequate; and any other circumstances which appear to the court to make it more suitable for the offence to be tried in one way rather than the other.

(4)   If the prosecution is being carried on by the Attorney-General, the Solicitor-General or the Director of Public Prosecutions and he applies for the offence to be tried on indictment, the preceding provisions of this section and sections 20 and 21 below shall not apply, and the court shall proceed to inquire into the information as examining justices.

(5)   The power of the Director of Public Prosecutions under subsection (4) above to apply for an offence to be tried on indictment shall not be exercised except with the consent of the Attorney-General.

20.—(1)   If, where the court has considered as required by section 19(1) above, it appears to the court that the offence is more suitable for summary trial, the following provisions of this section shall apply (unless excluded by section 23 below).

(2)   The court shall explain to the accused in ordinary language—

(a)   that it appears to the court more suitable for him to be tried summarily for the offence, and that he can either consent to be so tried or, if he wishes, be tried by a jury; and

(b)   that if he is tried summarily and is convicted by the court, he may be committed for sentence to the Crown Court under section 38 below if the convicting court is of such opinion as is mentioned in subsection (2) of that section.

(3)   After explaining to the accused as provided by subsection (2) above the court shall ask him whether he consents to be tried summarily or wishes to be tried by a jury, and—

(a)   if he consents to be tried summarily, shall proceed to the summary trial of the information;

(b)   if he does not so consent, shall proceed to inquire into the information as examining justices.

21. If, where the court has considered as required by section 19(1) above, it appears to the court that the offence is more suitable for trial on indictment, the court shall tell the accused that the court has decided that it is more suitable for him to be tried for the offence by a jury, and shall proceed to inquire into the information as examining justices.

Annex to Home Office Circular 45/1997 (excerpt)

PLEA BEFORE VENUE PROCEDURE: INDICATION OF PLEA

Suggested form of wording for the use of the magistrates' court when inviting the defendant to indicate his plea.

This offence(s) may be tried either by this court or by the Crown Court before a judge and jury.

Whether or not this court can deal with your case today will depend upon your answers to the questions which I am going to put to you. Do you understand?

You will shortly be asked to tell the court whether you intend to plead guilty or not guilty to (certain of) the offence(s) with which you are charged. Do you understand?

If you tell us that you intend to plead guilty, you will be convicted of the offence. We may then be able to deal with (part of) your case at this hearing. The prosecutor will tell us about the facts of the case, you (your representative) will have the opportunity to respond (on your behalf), and we shall then go on to consider how to sentence you. Do you understand?

We may be able to sentence you today, or we may need to adjourn the proceedings until a later date for the preparation of a pre-sentence report by the Probation Service. If we believe that you deserve a greater sentence than we have the power to give you in this court, we may decide to send you to the Crown Court, either on bail or in custody, and you will be sentenced by that court which has greater sentencing powers. Do you understand?

[In cases where s. 38A of the Magistrates' Courts Act 1980 applies:

If you indicate a guilty plea for this/these offence(s), even if we believe that our own sentencing powers are great enough to deal with you here, we may still send you to the Crown Court to be sentenced there for this/these offence(s) because you have also been charged with a related offence(s) [for which you have already been committed for trial in that court.] [for which you will be committed for trial in that court.] Do you understand?]

If, on the other hand, you tell us that you intend to plead not guilty, or if you do not tell us what you intend to do, we shall go on to consider whether you should be tried by this court or by the Crown Court on some future date. If we decide that it would be appropriate to deal with your case in this court, we shall ask whether you are content for us to do so or whether you wish your case to be tried in the Crown Court.

Before I ask you how you intend to plead, do you understand everything I have said or is there any part of what I have said which you would like me to repeat or explain?

Jurisdiction to Conduct Mode-of-Trial Hearing

D3.5   The power to conduct a mode-of-trial hearing arises whenever an adult appears or is brought before a magistrates' court charged with an offence triable either way (MCA 1980, s. 18(1)). It does not arise where he indicates a plea of guilty (see **D3.4**). The court's jurisdiction is thus not limited to either-way offences allegedly occurring within the county for which it acts. Even if the accused's appearance before the court was secured unlawfully (e.g., in answer to a summons which had been issued *ultra vires*), the court will have jurisdiction, at least if no objection is raised to the illegality at the time (see *Hughes* (1879) 4 QBD 614). The proceedings may take place before one magistrate, whether lay or stipendiary (s. 18(5)), but in practice it is almost invariably the case that any lay bench will consist of at least two justices.

The determination of mode of trial need not necessarily take place on the first occasion when an accused charged with an either-way offence appears before magistrates. Section

18(4) allows the court to adjourn at any time before or during proceedings under ss. 19 to 23. If it does so, it must remand the accused (either in custody or on bail) to the date fixed for the resumption of the proceedings, unless he first appeared in answer to a summons and has not subsequently been remanded, in which case the court has a discretion simply to adjourn. One small administrative advantage of adjourning without remanding the accused is that the court need not at that stage fix the date for the next hearing, although it is, of course, under an obligation to give the accused adequate notice thereof once it has been fixed (ss. 18(4) and 10(2)).

The power of magistrates' courts to adjourn proceedings and the circumstances in which, on adjourning, they are obliged to remand the accused are considered in detail at **D4.7** *et seq*. It is submitted that magistrates are to be regarded as proceeding under the MCA 1980, ss. 19 to 23, from when an accused first appears charged with an either-way offence to when mode of trial is finally determined. Therefore, any adjournment during that period will be by virtue of s. 18(4), not by virtue of s. 5(1) of the 1980 Act (which empowers the court to adjourn before or during committal proceedings). This has one minor practical consequence, namely that until there has been a determination in favour of trial on indictment the magistrates can, in the circumstances specified in s. 18(4), adjourn without remanding the accused, whereas once s. 5(1) applies they are obliged to remand whenever they adjourn.

Where an accused who is a juvenile is charged with an offence triable either way, ss. 18 to 23 of the 1980 Act do not apply. Mode of trial is determined according to quite different criteria, set out in s. 24 of the Act. As to the point in time at which the age of the accused is to be taken for purposes of deciding whether ss. 18 to 23 or s. 24 are to apply, that point is 'the date of his appearance before the court on the occasion when the court makes its decision as to the mode of trial' (per Lord Diplock in *Islington North Juvenile Court, ex parte Daley* [1983] 1 AC 347 at p. 364E–F). If he is 18 or over at that date, the fact that he was under 18 when he made his first court appearance in connection with the charge is irrelevant. The procedural problems raised by the accused who celebrates his 18th birthday during the course of the proceedings against him are further discussed at **D21.30**.

Presence of the Accused

The accused must be present while the mode of his trial is determined (MCA 1980, **D3.6** s. 18(2)), unless:

    (a)   the court considers that, by reason of his disorderly conduct before the court, it is not practicable for the proceedings to be conducted in his presence (s. 18(3)); or

    (b)   the accused is represented by counsel or a solicitor who signifies to the court that the accused consents to the mode-of-trial proceedings being conducted in his absence, and the court is satisfied that there is good reason for the proceedings being so conducted (s. 23(1));

    (c)   the court has decided to use a live television link, in a case where the accused is held in custody and facilities are available at the institution where he is held (CDA 1998, s. 57: see **D4.11**).

There is no authority on what may or may not be 'good reason' for the accused's absence. Sickness is the obvious example, but it is submitted that 'good reason' extends beyond that. Assuming the court does proceed in the accused's absence and considers that the offence is more suitable for summary trial, his consent to such a trial may be signified by his legal representative, in which event 'the court shall proceed to the summary trial of the information' (s. 23(4)(a)). Clearly, this does not require the magistrates to commence the trial forthwith – they are entitled to adjourn under the general power given them by s. 10(1) of the 1980 Act if an immediate hearing is impracticable or undesirable (e.g., because of the accused's absence). If the court considers that trial on indictment is more appropriate or if the necessary signification of consent to summary trial is not forthcoming from the accused's legal representative, then the court must proceed with a view to committal (s. 23(4)(b) and (5)). It is expressly provided that the justices may adjourn the hearing without remanding the accused. This power appears to apply notwithstanding s. 5(1) of the Act which normally requires the accused to be remanded whenever there is an adjournment during committal proceedings. The provisions under which counsel or a solicitor may consent to summary trial on behalf of his client apply both when the accused's presence is dispensed with by virtue of s. 23(1) and when his disorderly conduct makes it impracticable for him to remain in court (see s. 18(3)).

Magistrates' Courts Act 1980, ss. 18(2) and (3) and 23

18.

. . .

(2) Without prejudice to section 11(1) above [proceeding to summary trial of an information in the absence of the accused if he does not appear], everything that the court is required to do under sections 19 to 22 below must be done before any evidence is called and, subject to subsection (3) below and section 23 below, with the accused present in court.

(3) The court may proceed in the absence of the accused in accordance with such of the provisions of sections 19 to 22 below as are applicable in the circumstances if the court considers that by reason of his disorderly conduct before the court it is not practicable for the proceedings to be conducted in his presence; and the subsections (3) to (5) of section 23 below, so far as applicable, shall have effect in relation to proceedings conducted in the absence of the accused by virtue of this subsection (references in those subsections to the person representing the accused being for this purpose read as references to the person, if any, representing him).

. . .

23.—(1) Where—

(a) the accused is represented by counsel or a solicitor who in his absence signifies to the court the accused's consent to the proceedings for determining how he is to be tried for the offence being conducted in his absence; and

(b) the court is satisfied that there is good reason for proceeding in the absence of the accused,

the following provisions of this section shall apply.

(2) Subject to the following provisions of this section, the court may proceed in the absence of the accused in accordance with such of the provisions of sections 19 to 22 above as are applicable in the circumstances.

(3) If, in a case where subsection (1) of section 22 above applies, it appears to the court as mentioned in subsection (4) of that section, subsections (5) and (6) of that section shall not apply and the court—

(a) if the accused's consent to be tried summarily has been or is signified by the person representing him, shall proceed in accordance with subsection (2) of that section as if that subsection applied; or

(b) if that consent has not been and is not so signified, shall proceed in accordance with subsection (3) of that section as if that subsection applied.

(4) If, where the court has considered as required by section 19(1) above, it appears to the court that the offence is more suitable for summary trial then—

(a) if the accused's consent to be tried summarily has been or is signified by the person representing him, section 20 above shall not apply, and the court shall proceed to the summary trial of the information; or

(b) if that consent has not been and is not so signified, section 20 above shall not apply and the court shall proceed to inquire into the information as examining justices and may adjourn the proceedings without remanding the accused.

(5) If, where the court has considered as required by section 19(1) above, it appears to the court that the offence is more suitable for trial on indictment, section 21 above shall not apply, and the court shall proceed to inquire into the information as examining justices and may adjourn the hearing without remanding the accused.

[26. Powers ancillary to s. 23 to issue a summons or warrant for arrest in respect of the accused if either the court considers that he should be present while the mode of trial is determined or, having proceeded in his absence and adjourned without remanding him prior to committal or transfer proceedings, he does not appear for the resumption of the hearing.]

The Magistrates' Decision

Section 19(3) of the MCA 1980 lists three specific matters to which the magistrates must **D3.7** have regard in considering whether summary trial or trial on indictment is more appropriate. The first two ('the nature of the case' and 'whether the circumstances make the offence one of serious character') are not so much independent considerations as factors of great relevance to the third and vital consideration, which is 'whether the punishment which a magistrates' court would have power to inflict for [the offence] would be adequate'. The maximum penalty which magistrates can impose on summary conviction for an offence triable either way is usually six months' imprisonment and/or a fine of £5,000 (an aggregate of one year and/or £5,000 per offence on conviction for two or more such offences). In cases decided under the MCA 1952, s. 19 (broadly similar in effect to the present legislation), the appellate courts repeatedly emphasised that it was wrong for magistrates to agree to summary trial if the offences charged were so serious that the court's powers would be insufficient to deal properly with the defendant should he be convicted (see *Coe* [1968] 1 WLR 195, *King's Lynn Justices, ex parte Carter* [1969] 1 QB 488 and *Bodmin Justices, ex parte McEwen* [1947] KB 321).

The *Practice Note (Mode of Trial: Guidelines)* [1990] 1 WLR 1439 (see the end of **D3.7** for the full text in the revised form issued with the endorsement of the Lord Chief Justice in 1995) showed a radical change of emphasis. The guidelines provide that '[in] general, except where otherwise stated, either-way offences should be tried summarily unless the court considers that the particular case has one or more of the features set out in the following pages *and* that its sentencing powers are insufficient'. It is stated that the object of the guidelines is to provide guidance and not direction. Nevertheless, the guidance is clearly to the effect that there is a presumption that offences triable either way should be tried summarily unless one of the given features is present *and* the magistrates regard their sentencing powers as inadequate.

It is difficult for the prosecution to mount a challenge against a decision in favour of summary trial, since it is essentially a matter within the magistrates' court's discretion. Thus, in *McLean, ex parte Metropolitan Police Commissioner* [1975] Crim LR 289, where a stipendiary magistrate accepted jurisdiction in respect of charges of obtaining £8,800 by deception, an application for certiorari failed because the magistrate's decision was not so obviously wrong that no reasonable magistrate could have arrived at it. Nevertheless, in an appropriately clearcut case, the Divisional Court will grant judicial review. Thus, in *Northampton Magistrates' Court, ex parte the Commissioners of Customs and Excise* [1994] Crim LR 598, the defendant was charged with a VAT fraud which on the prosecution case had caused a loss of £193,000. The magistrates decided to try him summarily and the prosecution sought judicial review. The Divisional Court said that the correct approach was to ask whether the acceptance of jurisdiction was 'truly astonishing'. Here they must have concluded that it was, as they allowed the application and remitted the matter with a direction to the magistrates to inquire into it as examining justices. In *Flax Bourton Magistrates' Court, ex parte Commissioners of Customs and Excise* (1996) 160 JP 481, the Divisional Court emphasised that the justices were bound by the statutory obligation set out in s. 19(3) to apply their minds to the question whether or not their powers of punishment would be adequate if they dealt with the case summarily. If they were in doubt as to what the level of sentence should be, they should seek advice from their clerk.

In *Derby Justices, ex parte DPP* (1999) *The Times*, 17 August 1999, the Divisional Court stressed that the National Mode of Trial Guidelines provided guidance not direction.

There was a duty upon justices to consider each case individually and on its own facts. The instant case was in fact an appeal by the CPS against the decision of the justices to accept jurisdiction in a case of unlawful wounding contrary to the OAPA 1861, s. 20. In rejecting the appeal, their lordships looked at the provisions in the Guidelines under '*Violence*', and said that it would be an abuse of language to describe bringing a victim's head against part of the structure of a building as using a weapon.

Section 19(3) of the 1980 Act concludes with a 'catch-all' phrase that the magistrates may take into account 'any other circumstances which appear to the court to make it more suitable for the offence to be tried in one way rather than the other'. The guidelines as to mode of trial give some guidance on what these circumstances might be. Clearly, however, no such guidance can be exhaustive and the fact that, for example, the proceedings are likely to attract a great deal of public attention (because they involve well-known persons) might constitute such a circumstance. In *Horseferry Road Magistrates' Court, ex parte K* [1997] QB 23, the Divisional Court made it clear that the possible defence of insanity was a matter embraced by the words 'any other circumstances' in s. 19(3). Also, notwithstanding that s. 19 refers throughout to 'the offence' in the singular, it is plain that, in the common situation of an accused appearing before the court charged with several offences, the magistrates can and should look at the totality of the allegations and not at each offence in isolation – the fact that a year's imprisonment would be inadequate should the accused by convicted of *all* the charges is a circumstance, within the meaning of s. 19(3), which makes summary trial inappropriate even though each offence taken by itself would not merit more than six months.

What happens in a case where two or more defendants are jointly charged with an offence and one (or more) co-defendant(s) wishes to elect summary trial, while another or others want to go to the Crown Court? In deciding whether summary trial is more suitable for one defendant, may the magistrates take into account that his co-accused has elected trial on indictment? In *Brentwood Justices, ex parte Nicholls* [1992] 1 AC 1, A, B, and C were jointly charged with affray. Representations were made on behalf of A and B and the prosecution that the case was more suitable for summary trial and no representations were made on C's behalf. The bench accepted jurisdiction. When C was put to his election, he elected trial in the Crown Court, while A and B elected summary trial. The magistrates committed all three for trial, saying that they would abide by age-old custom and practice, whatever the words of the 1980 Act might say. B sought judicial review of their decision. The Divisional Court held that the justices were right, albeit for the wrong reasons. If a number of defendants before the justices are jointly charged with one offence and one of them elects to be tried on indictment, although the others consent to summary trial, they must all be committed for trial. The House of Lords, reversing the decision, held that the right of election as to mode of trial given to the accused by s. 20(3) of the MCA 1980 is given to each accused individually, and not to all accused collectively. Hence, the election of one defendant is not affected by a different election made by his co-accused. In these circumstances, provided that the court believes summary trial to be appropriate on other grounds, the court should proceed to try summarily the accused who elected summary trial, and should proceed with a view to deciding whether those who elected trial on indictment should be sent to the Crown Court. (See also *Wigan Magistrates' Court, ex parte Layland* [1995] Crim LR 892 and *Ipswich Magistrates' Court, ex parte Callaghan* (1995) 159 JP 748.)

In any event, an accused who wished to have the matter dealt with in the magistrates' court but who is committed for trial ought to be able to rely on that willingness when he comes to be sentenced. Willingness to have a matter dealt with in the lower court is often advanced with success by way of mitigation in the Crown Court.

The question arises whether the court should be able to take into account the character of the accused at the stage of determining the mode of trial. In *Colchester Justices, ex parte North East Essex Building Co. Ltd* [1977] 1 WLR 1109, the company's committal for trial on a charge under the Town and Country Planning Act 1971, s. 55 (now the Planning (Listed Buildings and Conservation Areas) Act 1990, s. 9), was quashed because, prior to rejecting the defence application for summary trial, the bench were told by the prosecution of a previous conviction for a similar offence. Eveleigh J said: 'It is the policy in cases before magistrates' courts that the bench shall not be given in any form information which discloses previous convictions of the accused before them. That is a policy that has been established and followed over the years.' The result was that the magistrates had to form their view of whether their powers of punishment would be adequate in the event of a summary conviction on the assumption that the accused is of good character. It may be argued, however, that *Colchester Justices* was based upon a version of what is now s. 38 of the MCA 1980 which laid emphasis on the accused's previous convictions in the decision whether to commit for sentence. The current version of s. 38 contains no such emphasis (see **D20.14** for its terms). It has therefore been suggested that the *Colchester Justices* case no longer represents the law (see A. Edwards (1995) 92 (19) *Law Society's Gazette* 32). The suggestion seems to be based in part on the fact that the revised version of the *Mode of Trial Guidelines* issued in 1995 does not contain the statement that 'the defendant's antecedents and personal mitigating circumstances are irrelevant for the purpose of deciding mode of trial', although that statement did appear in the previous version. Their omission may, however, be due to a judgment that it is unnecessary to mention the defendant's antecedents and personal mitigating circumstances, since they should not be taken into account in determining mode of trial (see S. White 'The Antecedents of the Mode of Trial Guidelines' [1996] Crim LR 471 at p. 476). It is submitted that the law as laid down in *Colchester Justices* remains unchanged insofar as the prohibition on revealing the defendant's character is concerned, and that the practice adopted generally in the magistrates' courts is correct in reflecting this (see *Warley Justices, ex parte DPP* [1999] 1 WLR 216).

The *Mode of Trial Guidelines*, which are set out below, were revised and reissued in 1995 with the endorsement of the Lord Chief Justice. The guidelines broadly follow, but include some significant changes to, the guidelines published in *Practice Note (Mode of Trial: Guidelines)* [1990] 1 WLR 1439; the revised guidelines remain unreported.

National Mode of Trial Guidelines

The purpose of these guidelines is to help magistrates decide whether or not to commit 'either way' offences for trial in the Crown Court. Their object is to provide guidance not direction. They are not intended to impinge upon a magistrate's duty to consider each case individually and on its own particular facts.

These guidelines apply to all defendants aged 18 and above.

General mode of trial considerations

Section 19 of the Magistrates' Courts Act 1980 requires magistrates to have regard to the following matters in deciding whether an offence is more suitable for summary trial or trial on indictment: (1) the nature of the case; (2) whether the circumstances make the offence one of a serious character; (3) whether the punishment which a magistrates' court would have power to inflict for it would be adequate; (4) any other circumstances which appear to the court to make it more suitable for the offence to be tried in one way rather than the other; (5) any representations made by the prosecution or the defence.

Certain general observations can be made: (a) the court should never make its decision on the grounds of convenience or expedition; (b) the court should assume for the purpose of deciding mode of trial that the prosecution version of the facts is correct; (c) the fact that the offences are alleged to be specimens is a relevant consideration; the fact that the defendant will be asking for other offences to be taken into consideration, if convicted, is not; (d) where cases involve complex questions of fact or difficult questions of law, the court should consider [transfer] for trial; (e) where two or more defendants are jointly charged with an offence each has an individual right to elect his mode of trial; (f) in general, except where otherwise stated, either-way offences should be tried summarily unless the court considers that the particular case has one or more of the features set out in the following pages *and* that its sentencing powers are insufficient; (g) the court should also consider its powers to commit an offender for sentence, under section 38 of the Magistrates' Courts Act 1980, as amended by section 25 of the Criminal Justice Act 1991, if information emerges during the course of the hearing which leads them to conclude that the offence is so serious, or the offender such a risk to the public, that their powers to sentence him are inadequate. This amendment means that committal for sentence is no longer determined by reference to the character or antecedents of the defendant.

Features relevant to the individual offences

Note: Where reference is made in these guidelines to property or damage of 'high value' it means a figure equal to at least twice the amount of the limit (currently £5,000) imposed by statute on a magistrates' court when making a compensation order.

[*Note*: Each of the guidelines in respect of the individual offences set out below (except those relating to drugs offences) are prefaced by a reminder in the following terms 'Cases should be tried summarily unless the court considers that one or more of the following features is present in the case *and* that its sentencing powers are insufficient. Magistrates should take account of their powers under s. 25 of the Criminal Justice Act 1991 to commit for *sentence*'].

Burglary
1. *Dwelling-house*
    (1)   Entry in the daytime when the occupier (or another) is present.
    (2)   Entry at night of a house which is normally occupied, whether or not the occupier (or another) is present.
    (3)   The offence is alleged to be one of a series of similar offences.
    (4)   When soiling, ransacking, damage or vandalism occurs.
    (5)   The offence has professional hallmarks.
    (6)   The unrecovered property is of high value [see above for definition of 'high value'].

Note: Attention is drawn to para. 28(c) of schedule 1 to the Magistrates' Courts Act 1980, by which offences of burglary in a dwelling *cannot* be tried summarily if any person in the dwelling was subjected to violence or the threat of violence.

2. *Non-dwellings*
    (1)   Entry of a pharmacy or doctor's surgery.
    (2)   Fear is caused or violence is done to anyone lawfully on the premises (e.g. nightwatchman; security guard).
    (3)   The offence has professional hallmarks.
    (4)   Vandalism on a substantial scale.
    (5)   The unrecovered property is of high value [see above for definition of 'high value'].

Theft and fraud
    (1)   Breach of trust by a person in a position of substantial authority, or in whom a high degree of trust is placed.
    (2)   Theft or fraud which has been committed or disguised in a sophisticated manner.
    (3)   Theft or fraud committed by an organised gang.
    (4)   The victim is particularly vulnerable to theft or fraud (e.g. the elderly or infirm).
    (5)   The unrecovered property is of high value [see above for definition of 'high value'].

Handling
    (1)   Dishonest handling of stolen property by a receiver who has commissioned the theft.
    (2)   The offence has professional hallmarks.

    (3)   The property is of high value [see above for definition of 'high value'].

Social security frauds
    (1)   Organised fraud on a large scale.
    (2)   The frauds are substantial and carried out over a long period of time.

Violence (sections 20 and 47 of the Offences against the Person Act 1861)
    (1)   The use of a weapon of a kind likely to cause serious injury.
    (2)   A weapon is used and serious injury is caused.
    (3)   More than minor injury is caused by kicking, head-butting or similar forms of assault.
    (4)   Serious violence is caused to those whose work has to be done in contact with the public or who are likely to face violence in the course of their work.
    (5)   Violence to vulnerable people (e.g. the elderly and infirm).
    (6)   The offence has clear racial motivation.

Note: The same considerations apply to cases of domestic violence.

Public Order Act offences
1.   Cases of violent disorder should generally be committed for trial.
2.   Affray.
    (1)   Organised violence or use of weapons.
    (2)   Significant injury or substantial damage.
    (3)   The offence has clear racial motiviation.
    (4)   An attack upon police officers, prison officers, ambulancemen, firemen and the like.

Violence to and neglect of children
    (1)   Substantial injury.
    (2)   Repeated violence or serious neglect, even if the physical harm is slight.
    (3)   Sadistic violence (e.g. deliberate burning or scalding).

Indecent assault
    (1)   Substantial disparity in age between victim and defendant, and the assault is more than trivial.
    (2)   Violence or threats of violence.
    (3)   Relationship of trust or responsibility between defendant and victim.
    (4)   Several similar offences, and the assaults are more than trivial.
    (5)   The victim is particularly vulnerable.
    (6)   Serious nature of the assault.

Unlawful sexual intercourse
    (1)   Wide disparity of age.
    (2)   Breach of position of trust.
    (3)   The victim is particularly vulnerable.

Note: Unlawful sexual intercourse with a girl under 13 is triable only on indictment.

Drugs
1.   Class A
    (a)   Supply; possession with intent to supply: these cases should be committed for trial.
    (b)   Possession: should be committed for trial unless the amount is consistent only with personal use.

2.   Class B
    (a)   Supply; possession with intent to supply: should be committed for trial unless there is only small scale supply for no payment.
    (b)   Possession: should be committed for trial when the quantity is substantial and not consistent only with personal use.

Dangerous driving
    (1)   Alcohol or drugs contributing to dangerousness.
    (2)   Grossly excessive speed.
    (3)   Racing.

(4) Prolonged course of dangerous driving.
(5) Degree of injury or damage sustained.
(6) Other related offences.

Criminal damage
(1) Deliberate fire-raising.
(2) Committed by a group.
(3) Damage of a high value [see above for definition of 'high value'].
(4) The offence has clear racial motivation.

Note: Offences set out in schedule 2 to the Magistrates' Courts Act 1980 (which includes offences of criminal damage which do not amount to arson) *must* be tried summarily if the value of the property damaged or destroyed is £5,000 or less.

The Accused's Decision

D3.8   If the magistrates decide that the accused should be given the option of summary trial, it is essential that – at the time he makes his election – he should understand the 'nature and significance of the choice' put to him (*Birmingham Justices, ex parte Hodgson* [1985] QB 1131 per McCullough J at p. 1144E). Since one of the most important factors in the mind of an accused deciding which court he would like to deal with his case is whether or not he believes he has any defence, an election for summary trial made when unrepresented and intending to plead guilty through a misunderstanding of the law is invalid because, even if the accused understands the nature of the choice put to him in the sense of knowing the difference between trial on indictment and summary trial, he does not truly appreciate the *significance* of the choice for him (*Ex parte Hodgson*, see especially p. 1146D–H). Where the accused, at the time of election, intends to plead not guilty but is taken by surprise by the election being put, has not had the opportunity to consult either a lawyer or anybody else able to explain his rights to him and does not properly understand what a Crown Court is, then again his election will be invalid, this time on the ground that he does not understand the *nature* of the choice (*Highbury Corner Metropolitan Stipendiary Magistrate, ex parte Weekes* [1985] QB 1147).

Should an accused claim to have made an invalid election at a time when he was unrepresented, the remedy for the defence is, in the first place, to apply to the magistrates' court to allow him to withdraw his election (see **D3.18**). If that application is refused, application may be made to the Divisional Court for certiorari to reverse the refusal. It will, however, be necessary to show either that the magistrates took into account irrelevant factors or ignored relevant ones when deciding to hold the accused to his original election, or that their decision was so unreasonable that no bench properly directing itself could have reached it. In *Ex parte Weekes*, W's assertion that he had not understood what a Crown Court was when he elected went uncontradicted by the prosecution. In those circumstances, it was plainly unreasonable for the magistrate to have rejected the defence application that the election be withdrawn. The case may be contrasted with *Metropolitan Stipendiary Magistrate, ex parte Zardin* (14 May 1971 unreported), where, on the affidavits placed before the Divisional Court, the extent of Z's appreciation at the time of her election of the difference between trial on indictment and summary trial was in doubt, and a reasonable bench of magistrates could, on the available evidence, have concluded that she had sufficient knowledge to make a valid choice. Consequently, the application for certiorari succeeded in *Ex parte Weekes* but failed in *Ex parte Zardin*.

It will be difficult, if not impossible, for the defence to claim that the accused did not appreciate the nature and significance of his choice if he was legally represented at the time. The assumption is that counsel or a solicitor will provide whatever advice and explanation are necessary. However, McCullough J in *Ex parte Weekes* held that there is no rule of law that a magistrates' court *must* adjourn before putting an unrepresented accused to his election so as to allow him to apply for legal aid. Thus, although the action of the stipendiary magistrate in causing the election to be put to W on his first court appearance was open to criticism in that (a) W was only 17, and (b), given the relative gravity of the charge (assault occasioning actual bodily harm and unlawful wounding), he would almost certainly ultimately receive legal aid, the Divisional Court was only prepared to quash and remit for reconsideration the refusal to allow withdrawal of the election – it would not quash the original election itself. McCullough J said (at pp. 1152F–1153A):

> . . . bearing in mind the applicant's age and the serious nature of the charges, it should have been clear to anyone who had thought about it that the applicant would be granted legal representation and that his election would therefore be a more informed one if he were only asked to elect after he had obtained legal advice. The magistrate had power under section 18(4) of the Magistrates' Courts Act 1980 to adjourn the proceedings at any time prior to putting the accused to his election. However, I am loath to say anything here which would appear to lay down as a principle that an unrepresented defendant of any particular age should, in relation to 'serious charges' (whatever they may be), never be put to his election when he first appears before justices, and I find it very difficult to isolate any feature or features here which would make this a special case. It is one thing to say that justices should take account of the fact that a defendant did not understand what was being put to him when this is pointed out to them on an application to re-elect. It is another to say that this is something which they should presume for themselves when the election is put. I am not in the end persuaded that the decision of 23 January 1984 [to put the election to W] can be attacked successfully on the principles enunciated in *Associated Provincial Picture Houses Ltd v Wednesbury Corporation* [1948] 1 KB 223.

The Prosecution Influence on the Decision

The overall effect of ss. 19 to 21 of the MCA 1980 is that summary trial may be vetoed **D3.9** either by the court or by the accused but not by the prosecution. The most the prosecution can do, generally speaking, is to make representations that trial on indictment would be more appropriate having regard to the gravity of the offence. However, if the prosecution is being carried on by the A-G or Solicitor-General and he applies for the offence to be tried on indictment, that application is binding on the magistrates, who are thereupon obliged to hold committal or transfer proceedings (s. 19(4)). The same applies if the prosecution is being carried on by the DPP but s. 19(5) contains the important qualification that the DPP must obtain the consent of the A-G before making an application under subsection (4). Prior to the Prosecution of Offences Act 1985, when the Director was conducting a prosecution, he had – like the A-G and Solicitor-General – an unfettered discretion to insist on trial on indictment. Had the 1985 Act allowed him to retain that discretion, the vast increase in the number of prosecutions nominally carried on by the Director as a result of his new duty to take over the conduct of all police prosecutions would have made summary trial subject to a prosecution veto in a large majority of cases. As it is, the obligation on him to obtain the A-G's consent before applying for trial on indictment under s. 19(4) means that, in practice, the prosecution influence over mode of trial is almost always limited to the making of representations.

Failure to Comply with the Procedure

Since the jurisdiction of magistrates' courts to try offences triable either way derives **D3.10** solely from statute, any failure to comply with the statutory procedure laid down for determining mode of trial will have the consequence that, if the magistrates do proceed to trial, the hearing together with its result will be *ultra vires*, a nullity and liable to be quashed by certiorari even where the magistrates have purported to obtain the consent of the accused, and even where the accused is legally represented (*Kent Justices, ex parte Machin* [1952] 2 QB 355).

Because failure to comply with the procedure for determining mode of trial goes to the question of the lower court's jurisdiction, the Divisional Court has considered itself bound to quash the *ultra vires* proceedings however trivial the departure from the requirements of ss. 18 to 23 of the MCA 1980 and regardless of whether there has been any real injustice to the party applying for review. This is illustrated not only by the facts of *Ex parte Machin* but also by *Horseferry Road Magistrates' Court, ex parte Constable* [1981] Crim LR 504 and *Cardiff Magistrates' Court, ex parte Cardiff City Council* (1987) *The Times*, 24 February 1987. The last-mentioned case shows that the prosecution may obtain certiorari to quash an acquittal following infraction of the mode of trial procedure in just the same way that the defence may have a conviction quashed.

Mode-of-Trial Procedure and Advance Information

D3.11   In order that the accused may make an informed choice between summary trial and trial on indictment, the Magistrates' Courts (Advance Information) Rules 1985 (SI No. 601) require the prosecution, on request, to supply the defence with a summary of the prosecution case and/or copies of the statements of the proposed prosecution witnesses. The defence request for advance information should be made before the court considers mode of trial (r. 4), and, in a case where no request has been made, the court must satisfy itself, before proceeding further, that the accused is aware of his rights (r. 6). If information has been requested but not yet supplied, the court must adjourn (r. 7). The defence may always waive their right to advance information. In the normal case, the defence request advance information on the first represented appearance of the accused, and the magistrates then adjourn for perhaps a fortnight to enable the information to be served and considered, after which mode of trial is determined. For details of the Magistrates' Courts (Advance Information) Rules 1985, see **D4.14**.

THE SPECIAL PROCEDURE FOR CRIMINAL DAMAGE CHARGES

Procedure on Criminal Damage Charges

D3.12   Whenever the accused is charged with a 'scheduled offence', the procedure prescribed by ss. 18 to 21 of the MCA 1980 must be preceded by consideration of the value involved in the offence (s. 22(1)). Depending on what that value is, the accused may be deprived of his right to elect trial on indictment, notwithstanding that the scheduled offences are otherwise triable either way.

Scheduled offences comprise: (a) offences of damaging or destroying property contrary to s. 1 of the Criminal Damage Act 1971, excluding those committed by fire; and (b) offences of aiding, abetting, counselling or procuring the aforementioned and attempting or inciting them (see MCA 1980, sch. 2). Here, they will be referred to as 'criminal damage offences', although it will be appreciated that a minority of offences under the Criminal Damage Act 1971 are not, in fact, scheduled offences and so are not subject to the special procedure now under consideration. Conspiracy to commit criminal damage is not a scheduled offence (*Ward* (1997) 161 JP 297).

The minority of criminal damage offences which are *not* scheduled offences comprise (a) those committed by damaging or destroying property by fire; and (b) those committed with intent to endanger life or being reckless as to the endangering of life contrary to the Criminal Damage Act 1971, s. 1(2). The former are expressly excluded from scheduled offences by the terms of the MCA 1980, sch. 2; the latter, although not expressly dealt with in sch. 2, cannot be scheduled offences because they are not even triable either way (see MCA 1980, sch. 1, para. 29, which makes them triable only on indictment).

If the accused is charged with criminal damage, then the court must give the accused the opportunity to indicate his plea. It must then consider, having regard to any representations made by the prosecution or defence, whether the value involved in the offence exceeds the relevant sum (MCA 1980, s. 22(1)). If the property was allegedly destroyed or damaged beyond repair, the value involved is what it would probably have cost to purchase a replacement in the open market at the time of the offence; if the property was repairable, the value involved is the cost of repairs or the replacement cost whichever is the less (sch. 2). The 'relevant sum' is £5,000 (s. 22(1)). If it appears to the magistrates that the value involved clearly does *not* exceed the relevant sum, they must proceed as if the offence charged were triable only summarily. Consequently, ss. 19 to 21 of the 1980 Act do not apply and the accused has no right to elect trial on indictment. Nonetheless, the offence is an offence triable either way (see the final paragraph of the note on construction of certain expressions relating to offences in the Interpretation Act 1978, sch. 1, and **D3.1**).

If it appears to the court clear that the value involved exceeds the relevant sum, it is then obliged to determine the mode of trial in accordance with the MCA 1980, ss. 19 to 21, just as it would for any other offence triable either way (s. 22(3)). Where, for any reason, it is not clear to the court whether the value involved does or does not exceed the relevant sum, it must explain to the accused that he can, if he wishes, consent to summary trial and that, if he does, he will definitely be so tried and his liability to imprisonment or a fine will be limited in accordance with the provisions of s. 33 of the 1980 Act (see below). The accused is then asked if he consents. Depending on his response, the court either proceeds to summary trial or embarks on the ordinary procedure for determining mode of trial, which will presumably result in the accused electing trial on indictment (s. 22(5) and (6)). If the accused is tried summarily for a criminal damage offence as a result *either* of the court deciding that the value involved was clearly less than the relevant sum, *or* of the accused consenting to summary trial in a case where the court was in doubt, then the maximum penalty that may be imposed in the event of conviction is three months' imprisonment or a fine of £2,500, and the offender may not be committed for sentence under s. 38 of the 1980 Act (s. 33). If the accused is tried summarily in a case where the value involved clearly exceeded the relevant sum but he was nevertheless offered and accepted summary trial, the penalties available are as for any offence listed in sch. 1 to the 1980 Act (i.e. six months' imprisonment and/or a fine of £5,000). Moreover, there may be a committal for sentence under s. 38.

When s. 17A of the MCA 1980 was inserted by the CPIA 1996, s. 49 (see **D3.4**), there was no consequential amendment of s. 22. As a result, it is unclear whether a court sentencing a defendant who has indicated a plea of guilty to a charge of criminal damage where the value is below £5,000 is limited in its powers to a custodial sentence of three months and/or a fine of £2,500. It would clearly be more logical if the limit did apply. If it were not so, a defendant pleading guilty would be at risk of heavier penalties than one found guilty after trial.

The court's duty under the MCA 1980, s. 22(1), to have regard to the 'representations' of the parties when considering the value involved in a criminal damage offence does not entail an obligation to hear evidence (per Lord Lane CJ in *Canterbury & St Augustine Justices, ex parte Klisiak* [1982] QB 398 at p. 413D–E: 'The word "representations" implies something less than evidence. It comprises submissions, coupled with assertions of fact and sometimes production of documents. . . . The nearest analogy is, perhaps, the speech in mitigation.'). However, there is nothing to stop the court hearing evidence if it so wishes (ibid.). In a case where there is real difficulty in arriving at an appropriate basis for calculating the value involved, the prosecution are entitled to say that they will not seek to prove that the accused caused any more damage than can be established with clarity. Acting on that assurance, the court may conclude that the value was clearly less than the relevant sum even though, in the absence of such an assurance and adopting an alternative method of calculation, the question would have remained doubtful and the accused could therefore have elected trial on indictment (see *Salisbury Magistrates' Court, ex parte Mastin* (1986) 84 Cr App R 248, where the prosecution informed the court that, as regards numerous defendants charged with criminal damage to a field by driving their vehicles thereon, they would allege against each individual only that he had caused such damage as was referable to his driving from the gate to the point where his vehicle was eventually parked and would ignore the possibility that he had driven around the field so as to cause damage in excess of the relevant sum – the Divisional Court held that, given the difficulty of establishing precisely what damage each defendant had caused, the prosecution were entitled to limit themselves to proving *vis-à-vis* each individual only that which could be established against him 'with clarity', and, on that basis, the value involved in each offence was clearly under the then relevant sum of £400, so the defendants had to be tried summarily).

Two or More Criminal Damage Charges

D3.13   The above provisions are subject to the qualification that, if the accused is 'charged on the same occasion with two or more scheduled offences and it appears to the court that they constitute or form part of a series of two or more offences of the same or a similar character', then the relevant consideration is the *aggregate* value involved in the offences (MCA 1980, s. 22(11)). In other words, the accused will retain his right to trial on indictment if the value of the offences added together exceeds the relevant sum (£5,000), even if the value of each offence taken individually was under the relevant sum.

The reference in s. 22(11) to a 'series of two or more offences of the same or similar character' is taken from r. 9 of the Indictment Rules 1971 (SI 1971 No. 1253), governing joinder of counts in an indictment (see **D9.24 *et seq.***). That rule has been interpreted to mean that, in order for offences to come within its ambit, they must be linked by a legal and factual nexus (see *Ludlow* v *Metropolitan Police Commissioner* [1971] AC 29). However, the factual similarity need not be great (ibid.), and it is certainly not essential to show a 'striking similarity' between the offences such as would make evidence that the accused committed one offence admissible to prove that he committed the others. On the assumption that s. 22(11) will be interpreted in the same liberal way as r. 9, it is submitted that, when an accused is charged on one occasion with two or more scheduled offences, they will very probably form a series within the meaning of the subsection. Legally, they will be identical (or nearly identical), and factually they will almost certainly be linked by closeness in time and geographical location, otherwise they would not have been charged together. If there is, in addition, even a slight similarity in the *modus operandi* employed on the various occasions, then s. 22(11) will be satisfied.

One point on which s. 22(11) is ambiguous is the meaning of being 'charged on one occasion'. The phrase could be construed to mean either being charged at the police station or appearing before a magistrates' court to answer charges. It is submitted that the latter interpretation is preferable since otherwise the subsection would not apply to prosecutions for criminal damage offences begun by the laying of an information, and there can be no reason of policy why mode of trial should depend on the method of commencing proceedings. A further question arises of whether s. 22(11) is limited to cases where an accused is charged with a series of criminal damage offences on the occasion of his first court appearance or extends also to cases where he originally appears charged with only one offence but further charges are added prior to the determination of mode of trial. Again the latter interpretation seems preferable for otherwise the prosecution might artificially deprive an accused of the right to trial on indictment by initially bringing him before the court on only one charge even though they already have the evidence to found further charges.

Magistrates' Courts Act 1980, ss. 22 and 33 and sch. 2

22.—(1) If the offence charged by the information is one of those mentioned in the first column of schedule 2 to this Act (in this section referred to as 'scheduled offences') then the court shall, before proceeding in accordance with section 19 above, consider whether, having regard to any representations made by the prosecutor or the accused, the value involved (as defined in subsection (10) below) appears to exceed the relevant sum.

For the purposes of this section the relevant sum is £5,000.

(2) If, where subsection (1) above applies, it appears to the court clear that, for the offence charged, the value involved does not exceed the relevant sum, the court shall proceed as if the offence were triable only summarily, and sections 19 to 21 above shall not apply.

(3) If, where subsection (1) above applies, it appears to the court clear that, for the offence charged, the value involved exceeds that relevant sum, the court shall thereupon proceed in accordance with section 19 above in the ordinary way without further regard to the provisions of this section.

(4) If, where subsection (1) above applies, it appears to the court for any reason not clear whether, for the offence charged, the value involved does or does not exceed the relevant sum, the provisions of subsections (5) and (6) below shall apply.

(5) The court shall cause the charge to be written down, if this has not already been done, and read to the accused, and shall explain to him in ordinary language—

(a) that he can, if he wishes, consent to be tried summarily for the offence and that if he consents to be so tried, he will definitely be tried in that way; and

(b) that if he is tried summarily and is convicted by the court, his liability to imprisonment or a fine will be limited as provided in section 33 below.

(6) After explaining to the accused as provided by subsection (5) above, the court shall ask him whether he consents to be tried summarily and—

(a) if he so consents, shall proceed in accordance with subsection (2) above as if that subsection applied;

(b) if he does not so consent, shall proceed in accordance with subsection (3) above as if that subsection applied.

[(7) Repealed by CJA 1988.]

[(8) No appeal to the Crown Court against conviction for a scheduled offence on the ground that the decision as to the value involved was mistaken.]

[(9) Where a juvenile and an adult are jointly charged with a scheduled offence, the juvenile as well as the adult may make representations as to the value involved.]

[(10) 'The value involved' to be given the meaning set out in sch. 2, and 'material time', when used in sch. 2, means the time of the alleged offence.]

(11) Where—

(a) the accused is charged on the same occasion with two or more scheduled offences and it appears to the court that they constitute or form part of a series of two or more offences of the same or a similar character; or

(b) the offence charged consists in incitement to commit two or more scheduled offences,

this section shall have effect as if any reference in it to the value involved were a reference to the aggregate of the values involved.

(12) Subsection (8) of section 12A of the Theft Act 1968 (which determines when a vehicle is recovered) shall apply for the purposes of paragraph 3 of schedule 2 to this Act as it applies for the purposes of that section.

33.—(1) Where in pursuance of subsection (2) of section 22 above a magistrates' court proceeds to the summary trial of an information, then, if the accused is summarily convicted of the offence—

(a) subject to subsection (3) below the court shall not have power to impose on him in respect of that offence imprisonment for more than 3 months or a fine greater than £2,500; and

(b) section 38 below [committal for sentence if the magistrates' powers of punishment inadequate] shall not apply as regards that offence.

(2) In subsection (1) above 'fine' includes a pecuniary penalty but does not include a pecuniary forfeiture or pecuniary compensation.

(3)   Paragraph (a) of subsection (1) above does not apply to an offence under section 12A of the Theft Act 1968 (aggravated vehicle-taking).

SCHEDULE 2

OFFENCES FOR WHICH THE VALUE INVOLVED IS RELEVANT TO THE MODE OF TRIAL

[Column 1 shows the offences subject to the special procedure; column 2 defines the value involved, and column 3 indicates how the value involved is calculated.]

Offence	*Value involved*	*How measured*

1. Offences under section 1 of the Criminal Damage Act 1971 (destroying or damaging property), excluding any offence committed by destroying or damaging property by fire.	As regards property alleged to have been destroyed, its value.
	
	As regards property alleged to have been damaged, the value of the alleged damage.
		What the property would probably have cost to buy in the open market at the material time.
		    (a) If immediately after the material time the damage was capable of repair—
		        (i) what would probably then have been the market price for the repair of the damage, or
		        (ii) what the property alleged to have been damaged would probably have cost to buy in the open market at the material time,
		whichever is the less; or
		        (b) if immediately after the material time the damage was beyond repair, what the said property would probably have cost to buy in the open market at the material time.

2.   The following offences, namely
    (a)   aiding, abetting, counselling or procuring the commission of any offence mentioned in paragraph 1 above;
    (b)   attempting to commit any offence so mentioned; and
    (c)   inciting another to commit any offence so mentioned.
	The value indicated in paragraph 1 above for the offence alleged to have been aided, abetted, counselled or procured, or attempted or incited.	As for the corresponding entry in paragraph 1 above.

3. Offences under section 12A of the Theft Act 1968 (aggravated vehicle-taking) where no allegation is made under subsection (1)(b) other than of damage, whether to the vehicle or other property or both.	The total value of the damage alleged to have been caused.	(1) In the case of damage to any property other than the vehicle involved in the offence, as for the corresponding entry in paragraph 1 above, substituting a reference to the time of the accident

Offence	Value involved	How measured
		concerned for any reference to the material time.
		(2) In the case of damage to the vehicle involved in the offence—
		(a) if immediately after the vehicle was recovered the damage was capable of repair—
		(i) what would probably then have been the market price for the repair of the damage, or
		(ii) what the vehicle would probably have cost to buy in the open market immediately before it was unlawfully taken, whichever is the less; or
		(b) if immediately after the vehicle was recovered the damage was beyond repair, what the vehicle would probably have cost to buy in the open market immediately before it was unlawfully taken.

VARIATION OF ORIGINAL DECISION AS TO MODE OF TRIAL

Introduction

D3.14 The decision in respect of mode of trial taken after proceedings under the MCA 1980, ss. 18 to 22, may be varied as a result either of the magistrates' court exercising the powers given to it by s. 25 of the 1980 Act or of it acceding to an application by the accused that his original election be withdrawn.

Statutory Powers under the Magistrates' Courts Act 1980, s. 25

D3.15 Subsections (1) and (2) of the MCA 1980, s. 25, govern switching from summary trial to committal for trial; subsections (3) and (4) govern switching from committal for trial to summary trial. Section 28 contains an ancillary provision about the use, for purposes of the summary trial, of evidence already considered during the discontinued committal proceedings.

Converting Summary Trial into Committal Proceedings   **D3.16** Where a magistrates' court has begun to try summarily an information against an adult for an offence triable either way, it may, at any time before the conclusion of the evidence for the prosecution, discontinue the trial and hold committal proceedings instead (MCA 1980, s. 25(1) and (2)). This is subject to the qualification that, if the summary trial is in respect of a scheduled offence of criminal damage and the court is proceeding under s. 22(2) of the 1980 Act because the value involved in the offence clearly did not exceed £5,000, then the court may not alter the mode of trial (see parenthesis in s. 25(2)).

In the context of subsection (2) 'evidence for the prosecution' means evidence adduced in order to establish the guilt of the accused following a not guilty plea (*Dudley Justices*, *ex parte Gillard* [1986] AC 442). Consequently, if the accused pleads guilty, there is no evidence in the sense intended by s. 25(2), and no power to switch to committal proceedings. The House of Lords in *Ex parte Gillard* rejected the argument that, where there is a guilty plea, 'evidence' in s. 25(2) might mean the prosecuting lawyer's summary of the facts, or antecedents evidence from a police officer, or even evidence adduced at a *Newton* hearing to resolve a dispute about how the offence was committed. Thus, the apparent intention of s. 25(2) is to allow the magistrates to withdraw their initial agreement to summary trial if the full facts of the offence, as they emerge during the course of the prosecution evidence following a not guilty plea, make their powers of punishment inadequate.

Usually, the magistrates will have to hear at least some prosecution evidence before announcing their decision to change the mode of trial (*Birmingham Stipendiary Magistrate, ex parte Webb* (1992) 95 Cr App R 75), even in a case where the bench has already effectively decided to send the case to the Crown Court for trial, for example, because additional charges have been preferred (see *St Helens Magistrates' Court, ex parte Critchley* (1987) 152 JP 102). The court may be said to have 'begun to try the information summarily', however, after taking a not guilty plea but before hearing evidence (e.g., where it has heard submissions on a preliminary point of law which has a direct and immediate bearing on the process of determining the accused's guilt or innocence: see *Horseferry Road Magistrates' Court, ex parte K* [1997] QB 23, where the submissions related to the availability or otherwise of the defence of insanity in the magistrates' court). However, once the prosecution case is finished, the power to switch to committal proceedings is lost. If there is no prosecution case in the sense intended by the subsection because the accused pleads guilty, the decision for summary trial is irreversible. In *West Norfolk Justices, ex parte McMullen* (1993) 157 JP 61 and in *Bradford Magistrates' Court, ex parte Grant* (1999) 163 JP 717, the Divisional Court held that the procedure under s. 25(2) may not be used as a device to circumvent the decision in *Brentwood Justices, ex parte Nicholls* [1992] 1 AC 1 (see **D3.7**). Justices must respect the right of each defendant to elect to be tried summarily, regardless of the election of his co-defendants; they must not attempt to negate that right by later converting the summary proceedings into committal proceedings.

D3.17 ***Converting Committal Proceedings into Summary Trial*** A magistrates' court which has commenced committal proceedings in respect of an offence triable either way may switch to summary trial if, having regard to any repesentations made by the prosecution and/or defence and to the nature of the case, it considers that the offence is after all more suitable for summary trial (MCA 1980, s. 25(3)). The switch may take place at any stage during committal proceedings, but is subject to the accused giving his consent (ibid.). Before he is asked for his consent, he must be warned of the possibility of being committed for sentence, unless such a warning has already been given (s. 25(4)(b)). Where the prosecution is being carried on by the A-G or Solicitor-General, exercise of the powers given to the court by subsection (3) is dependent on the law officer's consent; where it is being carried on by the DPP, the A-G (but not the DPP himself) may direct that the powers shall not be exercised (s. 25(3A)). By s. 28 of the MCA 1980, oral evidence given in the committal proceedings is, following a switch to summary trial, deemed to have been given in and for purposes of the trial.

Somewhat inconveniently, the power to switch to summary trial contained in s. 25(3) does not arise unless the accused 'appears or is brought before a magistrates' court on an information charging him with an offence triable either way' (see s. 25(1)). Therefore, if the only charge against him is for an offence triable only on indictment (e.g., wounding with intent contrary to s. 18 of the OAPA 1861) but the justices decide that there is a case to answer only for an either-way offence (e.g., unlawful wounding contrary to s. 20 of the 1861 Act), there is no jurisdiction to try the latter offence summarily since the accused did not appear before the bench charged with it as required by s. 25(1) (*Cambridgeshire Justices, ex parte Fraser* [1984] 1 WLR 1391).

The magistrates' court can only change its decision from trial on indictment to summary trial *after* it has begun the committal proceedings. In *Liverpool Justices, ex parte CPS, Liverpool* (1990) 90 Cr App R 261, D was charged with reckless driving and a number of other offences. The justices decided on trial on indictment. At a later hearing, a differently constituted bench heard an application from D's solicitor for summary trial. The application was made before committal proceedings began. The justices acceded to the request and accepted pleas of guilty to all matters charged. The prosecution applied for judicial review of their decision, on the ground that they had no jurisdiction to change the mode of trial. The Divisional Court held that there was no power to vary the decision for trial on indictment except that contained in the MCA 1980, s. 25. Since D's submissions had been made before the justices began committal proceedings, the provisions of s. 25(3) had not been complied with. Thus the decision to change to summary trial was a nullity. The case was remitted to the magistrates to continue the committal proceedings, bearing in mind that D's admission of guilt in open court was a compelling reason for changing to summary trial. They could make the desired change in the mode of trial, provided that they had complied with s. 25(3) by hearing some evidence.

Magistrates' Courts Act 1980, s. 25

25.—(1) Subsections (2) to (4) below shall have effect where a person who has attained the age of 18 appears or is brought before a magistrates' court on an information charging him with an offence triable either way.

(2) Where the court has (otherwise than in pursuance of section 22(2) above) begun to try the information summarily, the court may, at any time before the conclusion of the evidence for the prosecution, discontinue the summary trial and proceed to inquire into the information as examining justices and, on doing so, shall adjourn the hearing.

(3) Where the court has begun to inquire into the information as examining justices, then, if at any time during the inquiry it appears to the court, having regard to any representations made in the presence of the accused by the prosecutor, or made by the accused, and to the nature of the case, that the offence is after all more suitable for summary trial, the court may, after doing as provided in subsection (4) below, ask the accused whether he consents to be tried summarily and, if he so consents, may subject to subsection below proceed to try the information summarily.

(3A) Where the prosecution is being carried on by the Attorney-General or the Solicitor-General, the court shall not exercise the power conferred by subsection (3) above without his consent and, where the prosecution is being carried on by the Director of Public Prosecutions, shall not exercise that power if the Attorney-General directs that it should not be exercised.

(4) Before asking the accused under subsection (3) above whether he consents to be tried summarily, the court shall in ordinary language—

(a) explain to him that it appears to the court more suitable for him to be tried summarily for the offence, but that this can only be done if he consents to be so tried; and

(b) unless it has already done so, explain to him, as provided in section 20(2)(b) above, about the court's power to commit to the Crown Court for sentence.

[(5) to (7) relate to changing the mode of trial in the case of a juvenile: see **D21.8**.]

(8) If the court adjourns the hearing under subsection (2) or (6) above it may (if it thinks fit) do so without remanding the accused.

Withdrawal by Accused of Original Election

The approach a magistrates' court should adopt when an accused who has already **D3.18** chosen between summary trial and trial on indictment asks to withdraw his original election was fully considered by McCullough J in *Birmingham Justices, ex parte Hodgson* [1985] QB 1131. The earlier authorities are helpfully summarised at pp. 1138–44 of his lordship's judgment. The case itself has already been discussed at **D3.8** when considering the closely connected topic of the necessity for the accused to understand the nature and significance of his choice as to mode of trial. The following propositions emerge from *Ex parte Hodgson* and the cases mentioned therein:

(a)   The magistrates have a discretion to permit the accused to withdraw an election for summary trial, notwithstanding that the MCA 1980, s. 20(3)(a), provides that if an accused consents to be tried summarily, the court *shall* proceed to the summary trial of the information. The existence of the discretion was affirmed by *Craske, ex parte Metropolitan Police Commissioner* [1957] 2 QB 591, which was decided under the analogous provisions of s. 19(3) and (5) of the MCA 1952. In that case, the prosecution sought an order of mandamus to compel C (a stipendiary magistrate) to continue with the summary trial of an information for receiving, the accused having agreed to summary trial and pleaded not guilty when unrepresented, after which the case had been adjourned for him to instruct solicitors who, at the resumed hearing, successfully applied for the election to be withdrawn. Devlin J said (at pp. 599–600):

> I do not think that [the use of the word 'shall' in s. 19] means that once the procedure is set in motion, the court has ineluctably to allow the wheels to revolve without any power to stop them if the accused wants to change his mind. I think it means no more than this, that if the summary trial is to be proceeded with in the way in which section 19 provides, [the steps set out in the section] are the steps that must be taken, but I can find nothing . . . which would deprive a magistrate or any court of the ordinary right which they must have in the interests of justice of allowing an accused who has given his consent ill-advisedly to abandoning his right to trial by jury, to be given the opportunity of reconsidering it.

Lord Goddard CJ and Byrne J similarly affirmed the existence of the court's discretionary power, although, on their interpretation of s. 19(5) of the 1952 Act, any withdrawal of election had to take place before the magistrates had started to hear evidence for purposes of summary trial. Devlin J differed on that point but, in any event, s. 19(5) does not have an equivalent in the present legislation, so it would seem that the accused can in theory be allowed to re-elect even after his trial on a not guilty plea has begun. However, it is submitted that, once a significant portion of the prosecution evidence has been given, a change of election should be allowed only in very exceptional circumstances, since otherwise the defence would be tempted to ask to re-elect as a tactical ploy whenever the trial seems to be going badly.

(b)   In exercising their discretion whether or not to accede to an application to re-elect, magistrates must have regard to the 'broad justice' of the situation (per Lord Widgery CJ in *Southampton Justices, ex parte Briggs* [1972] 1 WLR 277). They are entitled to take into account: (i) that the defendant had his rights as to mode of trial fully explained to him; (ii) that he understood those rights; (iii) that he voluntarily consented to be tried summarily; and (iv) that there were no unusual, difficult or grave features in the case (*Lambeth Metropolitan Stipendiary Magistrate, ex parte Wright* [1974] Crim LR 444, as explained by McCullough J in *Ex parte Hodgson* [1985] QB 1131 at p. 1140A–C). The fact that the accused was unrepresented when he elected summary trial is not sufficient by itself to compel the court to allow a withdrawal of election, even if he is subsequently advised that trial on indictment would be preferable (see, e.g., *Metropolitan Stipendiary Magistrate, ex parte Zardin* (14 May 1971 unreported)). Conversely, although his having had legal advice before electing would obviously be a very powerful argument against an application to re-elect, there is no reason to suppose that it must inevitably be decisive.

(c)   Where the material before the magistrates shows that the accused, when he elected summary trial, did not properly understand the nature and significance of the choice put to him, the broad justice of the situation demands that he be allowed to re-elect. Although it is still a matter for the court's discretion, in such a case the discretion may be properly exercised in only one way, that is, in favour of the accused. Therefore, refusal of the accused's application will be quashed by certiorari (see *Ex parte Hodgson*; *Highbury Corner Metropolitan Stipendiary Magistrates, ex parte Weekes* [1985] QB 1147 and **D3.8**).

(d)   The accused's election as to mode of trial is likely, in practice, to be closely connected to whether he is pleading guilty or not. If, therefore, having elected summary trial, he pleads guilty but is then allowed to change his plea after legal advice, he should be allowed to withdraw his consent to summary trial and be put to his election again (*Bow Street Magistrates' Court, ex parte Welcombe* (1992) 156 JP 609).

(e)   At least in cases such as *Ex parte Hodgson* and *Ex parte Weekes*, where it is said that the accused did not understand the nature and significance of his choice, the court's view that the case is more suitable for summary trial is *not* a factor which should tell against an application to withdraw the election (see per McCullough J in *Ex parte Hodgson* [1985] QB 1131 at p. 1145A–B and *Ex parte Weekes* [1985] QB 1147 at p. 1152C–E where he criticised the magistrate for making the irrelevant comment that 'this court can grapple with the difficulties in the case').

(f)   Most of the authorities concern cases where the accused wishes to withdraw his election for summary trial. However, the same general principles apply where he wishes to elect summary trial having originally insisted on trial on indictment. Usually, the court is more willing to accede to such an application because of the saving in time and money which will result. But, if the first election appears to have been nothing more than a tactical ploy (e.g., to obtain a sight of the statements made by the prosecution witnesses), the court is justified in refusing the application to withdraw it (*Warrington Justices, ex parte McDonagh* (5 June 1981 unreported)).

Concerning the procedure that justices should follow at an application to re-elect, the Divisional Court has stated that they should inform themselves of what happened on the occasion of the original election. If they themselves were then sitting, their unaided recollection may be sufficient. If not the clerk should provide the information (e.g., through consulting the court files). If the accused is arguing that he did not understand the consequences of his original election, it is for him to establish that, whether by his own evidence or other means (see *Forest Magistrates' Court, ex parte Spicer* [1988] Crim LR 619, a case in which the justices' decision was set aside because they made it without the necessary evidence).

ADJUSTMENT OF CHARGES TO DICTATE MODE OF TRIAL

If the offence charged is triable either way, the prosecution can neither insist on nor, **D3.19** generally speaking, veto a summary trial. On the other hand, whether or not to commence a prosecution for an either-way offence is essentially within the unfettered discretion of the police or other prosecuting authority (*Metropolitan Police Commissioner, ex parte Blackburn (No. 1)* [1968] 2 QB 118). A potential prosecutor cannot be compelled to prosecute if he does not wish to do so. *Ex hypothesi*, if he chooses to prefer a charge which does not fully reflect the gravity of the alleged criminal conduct, nobody (including the accused) may force him to add a graver charge. The possibility therefore arises of the prosecution depriving the accused of the right he would otherwise have had to trial on indictment by alleging an offence which is triable only summarily when the evidence would equally have justified charging an offence triable either way. The propriety of such a practice was considered in *Canterbury & St Augustine Justices, ex parte Klisiak* [1982] QB 398.

The question raised in *Ex parte Klisiak* was: if the accused first appears before a magistrates' court charged with an offence triable either way, can or should the court prevent the prosecutor offering no evidence on the original charge and replacing it with a summary charge if his reason for so doing is to prevent the accused electing trial on indictment? The Divisional Court's answer was that, even on the assumption that magistrates do have an inherent power to act so as to prevent any flagrant abuse of the process of their court, that power may only be exercised 'in the most obvious circumstances which disclose blatant injustice' (per Lord Lane CJ at p. 411F). In the instant case there was certainly no such blatant injustice. If the prosecution had originally charged the offences triable only summarily which they eventually charged, there could have been no possible complaint by the defendants that they had been deprived of their right to elect trial on indictment. Achieving the same result by the procedural course of offering no evidence on the either-way charge and replacing it with a lesser charge was therefore unobjectionable. Indeed, it was 'Gilbertian' for the defence to complain that the eventual allegations were less serious than the original ones.

Nonetheless, it is wrong for the prosecution to reduce a charge to one which the magistrates may or must deal with if the offence was patently too serious for summary disposition (see *Bodmin Justices, ex parte McEwen* [1947] KB 321 where Lord Goddard CJ strongly criticised the substitution of a charge of unlawful wounding for one of wounding with intent, the facts being that the accused had stabbed the victim in the back during the course of a brawl and almost killed him; and see the comments on *Nottingham Crown Court, ex parte DPP* [1995] Crim LR 902 in **D17.15**).

In *Cooke* v *DPP* (1992) 156 JP 497, it was held that the prosecution could rely upon its common-law powers to withdraw a charge which is triable either way and then proceed with an offence triable only summarily. It was under no obligation to abide by the procedure under the Prosecution of Offences Act 1985, s. 23, which would give the accused a right to insist that the charge triable either way continue so that he could be tried by a jury (see also **D2.38**).

The cases discussed above deal with the situation where the prosecution avoids trial on indictment by reducing the charge. What about the converse situation, where the prosecution increases the charge to avoid the possibility of summary trial?

In *Brooks* [1985] Crim LR 385, B was originally charged with unlawful wounding contrary to the OAPA 1861, s. 20. It was alleged that he had struck his lover's husband over the head with a hammer. Contrary to the prosecution's representations, the magistrates decided that summary trial would be more suitable and B agreed. During an adjournment, the prosecution solicitor, who was dissatisfied with the magistrates' decision, advised the preferment of a charge of wounding with intent contrary to s. 18 of the 1861 Act, that being triable only on indictment. At the resumed hearing, the magistrates were obliged to hold committal proceedings, the ultimate result being that B was tried on indictment and sentenced to 15 months' imprisonment. In the course of reducing the sentence, the Court of Appeal criticised the course adopted by the prosecution solicitor as 'unjust and wrong'. Given the timing of the preferment of the s. 18 charge, it smacked of some sort of informal appellate control by the solicitor over the magistrates' decision to accept jurisdiction.

In *Redbridge Justices, ex parte Whitehouse* (1992) 94 Cr App R 332, F, a private prosecutor, issued a summons against W, a police officer, alleging an offence under the OAPA 1861, s. 20. When W elected summary trial, F applied for a further summons under s. 18 of the 1861 Act. The justices granted it and, in view of the fact that s. 18 offences must be tried on indictment, committal proceedings followed. W applied to the Divisional Court to quash his committal. It was held that the justices were, in these circumstances, obliged to scrutinise the prosecution's addition of a charge with particular care. The prosecutor must not be allowed improperly to frustrate the bench's earlier decision, but, provided that the justices exercised their discretion properly, the Divisional Court was unlikely to interfere unless the decision was unreasonable in the sense described in *Associated Provincial Picture Houses Ltd* v *Wednesbury Corporation* [1948] 1 KB 223).

The Code for Crown Prosecutors (see **appendix 4**) addresses the fundamental issue raised by the above cases in its revised 1994 edition. Paragraph 7.3 states 'Crown Prosecutors should not change the charge simply because of the decision made by the court or the defendant about where the case will be heard'.

MODE OF TRIAL FOR SUMMARY OFFENCES

It follows from the basic definition of a summary offence as one which is triable *only* **D3.20** summarily that the question of mode of trial for such an offence does not normally arise. However, the provisions of ss. 40 and 41 of the CJA 1988 allow for summary offences to be tried at the Crown Court in two situations. The first is when certain summary offences (namely, common assault, driving while disqualified and taking a motor vehicle without the owner's consent) are disclosed by the evidence on the basis of which an accused has been committed for trial in respect of an indictable offence, and the summary offence is either founded on the same facts as the indictable offence or forms with it a series of offences of the same or similar character (s. 40). In such cases, the prosecution may at their discretion include a count for the summary offence in the indictment and, if the accused pleads not guilty, the issue will be determined by a jury. The second situation is when the accused is being committed for trial for an offence triable either way and the magistrates take the view that a summary offence punishable with imprisonment or disqualification with which the accused is also charged arose out of circumstances the same as or connected with the circumstances of the either-way offence (s. 41). In such cases, the magistrates may also commit the accused for 'trial' in respect of the summary offence, although that charge will not be put to the accused unless and until he has been convicted of the either-way matter and, if he denies the summary offence, the Crown Court's powers over it cease. Both ss. 40 and 41 thus involve decisions being taken about the mode of trial for a summary offence. However, as the need to take the decision is dependent on the accused having been committed for trial on an indictable charge it will be more convenient to deal with the sections in detail in the context of committal proceedings (see **D7.23** and **D9.6**).

SECTION D4: PROCEDURE BETWEEN FIRST COURT APPEARANCE AND COMMENCEMENT OF COMMITTAL PROCEEDINGS OR SUMMARY TRIAL

This section describes the preliminary proceedings in the magistrates' court which precede either the summary trial of an accused or his committal for trial.

PROCEDURE FOR SECURING PRESENCE OF ACCUSED

Introduction

D4.1 The first appearance of an accused before a magistrates' court is secured by either:

(a) his arrest without warrant, followed by his being charged with an offence at a police station, followed by his being bailed to attend at court on a specified day to answer the charge; or

(b) as in (a), save that instead of being bailed from the police station, he is held there until he is brought before the court in police custody; or

(c) the laying of an information by the prosecutor before a magistrate (or a magistrates' clerk) resulting in the issue of a summons requiring the accused to attend at court on a specified day to answer the allegation in the information; or

(d) as in (c), save that instead of issuing a summons the magistrate issues a warrant for the accused to be arrested and brought before the court (or, alternatively, a warrant backed for bail by virtue of which the accused is arrested and then released on bail under a duty to attend court on a specified day).

The powers and procedures for arresting an accused without warrant, questioning him in detention at a police station and then charging him are dealt with in **D1** which also deals with the circumstances in which the police may refuse to bail a person once he has been charged and the period within which they must bring such a person before the magistrates' court. This section describes the issue of summonses or warrants for arrest (collectively referred to as 'issue of process').

Laying an Information

D4.2 On an information being laid before him, a magistrate may issue either:

(a) a summons requiring the person named in the information to appear before a magistrates' court to answer thereto; or

(b) a warrant to arrest that person and bring him before a magistrates' court (MCA 1980, s. 1(1)).

An information (i.e., an allegation that a person has committed an offence) may be laid orally or in writing (Magistrates' Courts Rules 1981 (SI 1981 No. 552), r. 4(2)). It may be laid either by the prosecutor in person, or by counsel or a solicitor on his behalf, or by any other authorised person (r. 4(1)). However, an information may not be laid on behalf of an unincorporated association, such as a police force, since the definition of 'person' in the Interpretation Act 1978 as including a 'body of persons corporate or unincorporate' was not intended to apply to the laying of informations (*Rubin* v *DPP* [1990] 2 QB 80 and see **D2.30**). It follows that an information must be laid by a named, actual person and must disclose the identity of that person. However, the appeal in *Rubin* against a conviction for speeding was dismissed because, although the information was defective in that the informant purported to be 'Thames Valley Police', the appellant could easily have ascertained who the real prosecutor was by asking the police force concerned which individual constable had laid the information. In other words, the defect in the information did not nullify the proceedings or cause injustice. As an alternative to laying an information in the name of the officer reporting the offence, some police forces have a policy of laying all informations in the name of the chief constable or other senior officer.

The decision in *Rubin* should be contrasted with *Norwich Justices, ex parte Texas Homecare* [1991] Crim LR 555. That was a case under the Shops Act 1950, in which the informations were signed by the senior environmental health officer, who had no authority to do so under that Act. The informations were later amended to substitute the signature of the deputy director of administration who did have the necessary authority, but the amendment took place after the six month deadline for the laying of an information had elapsed (see **D18.7**). At the hearing, the justices decided that there had been no prejudice to the defendants, and allowed the amended informations to stand. On conviction, the defendants applied for judicial review. The Divisional Court granted certiorari, and quashed the convictions. The person laying the informations had no authority to lay them. Since the informations as laid were invalid, they could not found any jurisdiction, and were not curable by amendment.

An information should give the name of the informant and his address (the police station will suffice in the case of a police officer); the name and address of the accused; brief particulars of the offence suspected, and the statutory provision contravened if the offence is statutory (see the form for an information set out in the Magistrates' Courts (Forms) Rules 1981 (SI 1981 No. 533) and see also Watkins LJ in *Rubin* v *DPP* at p. 87). A written information is laid when it is received in the office of the clerk to the justices (*Manchester Stipendiary Magistrate, ex parte Hill* [1983] 1 AC 328). It follows that, if an information is duly delivered to the court, it may be treated as having been laid for purposes of any rule that an information has to be laid within a certain period, notwithstanding that it has not thereafter been considered by a magistrate or clerk (ibid. and see **D18.7**). An oral information is laid by the informant going before a magistrate or clerk to make his allegation. He may, but need not, give his information on oath (Magistrates' Courts Rules 1981, r. 4(2)). In order to obtain the issue of a warrant for arrest, an information must be (a) in writing, and (b) substantiated on oath (MCA 1980, s. 1(3)). The information should, in such cases, be taken down in the form of a deposition, the deponent confirming on oath that the contents of the deposition are true to the best of his belief (see also the Magistrates' Courts (Forms) Rules 1981, which give a suggested form by which a magistrate might record a sworn information).

Issuing a Summons

By s. 1(2) of the MCA 1980, a justice before whom an information has been laid has **D4.3** jurisdiction to issue a summons requiring the person named in the information to attend court to answer the charge if either:

    (a)   the offence was committed or is suspected to have been committed within the justice's area; or

    (b)   it appears to the justice that it is necessary or expedient for the better administration of justice that the accused should be tried jointly with or in the same place as another person who is charged with an offence and is either in custody in the area (e.g., following arrest by the police without a warrant), or is being (or is to be) proceeded against within the area; or

    (c)   the accused resides or is (or is believed to reside or be) within the area; or

    (d)   a magistrates' court for the area, by virtue of a statutory provision, has jurisdiction to try the offence alleged; or

    (e)   the offence was committed outside England and Wales and (if the offence is summary) a magistrates' court for the area would have jurisdiction to try the offence were the accused before it.

Although subsections (1) and (2) of s. 1 of the MCA 1980 expressly empower only justices to issue summonses, the power is in fact extended to justices' clerks by virtue of the Justices' Clerks Rules 1999 (SI 1999 No. 2784). The power does not, however, extend to assistants employed in the clerk's office, even if they are legally qualified (see *Gateshead Justices, ex parte Tesco Stores Ltd* [1981] QB 470, where the applicant's summary convictions were quashed because the informations by which the prosecution had been commenced were processed in the clerk's office by assistants who themselves issued the summonses without reference to a justice or a justices' clerk.

The following comments are offered on subparagraphs (a) to (e) of s. 1(2).

Subparagraph (a). References to 'area' in s. 1(2) are references to the *county* or (in the case of London) the commission area for which the justice acts. It follows that a magistrate may issue a summons in respect of an offence committed anywhere within his county even if it was not committed within the petty sessional division for which he normally sits. Offences committed within 500 yards of the boundary between two counties, or begun in one county and completed in another, or committed while on a journey through several counties may be treated as having been wholly committed within any one of the counties concerned (MCA 1980, s. 3).

Subparagraph (b). It has been held that only the justice issuing the summons need take the view that the accused should be tried in the same place as another accused being proceeded against within the county – there is no further requirement that the court which ultimately tries the case should be of the same view as the justice who issued the summons (*Turf Publishers Ltd* v *Davies* [1927] WN 190). An example of the exercise of the power given by the paragraph is *Blandford* [1955] 1 WLR 331, where a justice for the county in which the thief of certain goods was to be tried was held to have acted properly in issuing a summons against an alleged receiver of the goods, albeit that the latter neither committed the offence within the county nor lived there.

Subparagraph (c). The operation of this subparagraph is subject to the important limitation that the power to issue a summons under it (as opposed to issuing a warrant for arrest) only arises if the offence alleged in the information is indictable (see s. 1(5)(a)). Thus, if the offence is summary and was committed outside the county, there is in general no power to issue a summons (although on occasions it will be possible to do so under subparagraphs (b), (d) or (e)).

Subparagraph (d). This should be read in conjunction with s. 2(6) of the 1980 Act, which gives to a magistrates' court trying an accused for one offence jurisdiction to try him also for any summary offence for which he could be tried by a magistrates' court for a different county. The significance of the subsection is that it provides an exception to the general rule that magistrates may try summary offences only if they were committed within their county. It follows that, if a justice for county A is told that the person named in an information for a summary offence is already being proceeded against within county A for any offence (whether summary or indictable), then the justice may issue a summons for the offence in the information even if it was allegedly committed within county B, and both matters may be heard by the same magistrates' court.

Subparagraph (e). The possibility of issuing a summons against a person for an offence committed abroad will not normally arise since the jurisdiction of the criminal courts is limited to offences occurring within England and Wales. In the exceptional cases where a person may be tried here for a 'foreign' offence, any magistrate may issue a summons if the offence alleged is indictable. If a summary offence is alleged, jurisdiction to issue a summons is limited to magistrates for the county in which the accused could be tried were he before a magistrates' court for that county. In fact, there are hardly any circumstances in which the English courts exercise jurisdiction over summary offences committed outside England or Wales, but one example is found in s. 280 of the Merchant Shipping Act 1995 (offences, whether summary or indictable, committed on ships lying off the coast of a county are triable by a court for that county, and hence any magistrate for the county is able to issue a summons in respect of the offence).

The decision to issue a summons is judicial, not merely administrative (*Gateshead Justices, ex parte Tesco Stores Ltd* [1981] QB 470). Therefore, a justice or clerk must actually apply his mind to the information on the basis of which a summons is sought ('no summons can be issued . . . without a prior judicial consideration by [the justice or clerk] of the information upon which the summons is based': ibid. at p. 478A). The minimum matters of which the issuer of a summons should be satisfied are that:

(a)   the information alleges an offence known to the law;
(b)   it was laid within any time-limit applicable to commencing a prosecution for the offence in question;
(c)   any consent necessary for the bringing of the prosecution has been obtained; and
(d)   there is jurisdiction to issue a summons having regard to the provisions of the MCA 1980, s. 1(2) (see per Donaldson LJ in *Ex parte Tesco Stores Ltd* and Lord Widgery CJ in *West London Metropolitan Stipendiary Magistrate, ex parte Klahn* [1979] 1 WLR 933 at p. 935H expanding on his comments in *Brentford Justices, ex parte Catlin* [1975] QB 455).

Where the above criteria are satisfied, a summons will be issued almost automatically, at least where the informant is a police officer or is acting on behalf of some other recognised prosecuting agency. There is, however, a residual discretion to refuse a summons if the application appears frivolous or vexatious or to be an abuse of the process of the court (*Bros* (1901) 66 JP 54, in which the Divisional Court refused mandamus to compel a magistrate to summons a Jewish baker for Sunday trading in a predominantly Jewish area, the information having been laid under a local Act which (unlike the public general Act then in force) did not require the prosecutor to have the consent of a chief officer of police or two magistrates in order to commence proceedings). Failure by the prosecutor to lay his information within a reasonable time may also be a ground for refusing a summons (*Clerk to the Medway Justices, ex parte DHSS* (1986) 150 JP 401, in which the Divisional Court upheld the clerk's decision not to issue a summons against X for defrauding the DHSS because almost four months had been allowed to elapse between an official interviewing X and the laying of the information: the Department were within a statutory time-limit of 12 months but offered no explanation for not having acted promptly after the interview). It was held in *Clerk to the Bradford Justices, ex parte Sykes* (1999) 163 JP 224 that the magistrate or clerk has no obligation to make inquiries before issuing a summons. However, if there was material which persuaded him that it would be wrong to issue a summons, he was entitled to act on that information, and should not shut his eyes to it. If he was aware that the individual informant was one who had plagued the court with vexatious informations, for example, he could and probably should act upon that knowledge. There was, however, no obligation to investigate before the summons was issued. The protection for the individual summonsed was to apply to the magistrates' court to dismiss it, or stay it on the grounds of abuse of process. For a discussion of the approach which the court should take when considering whether to issue a summons which would have the effect of depriving the accused of Crown Court trial (or summary trial, as the case may be) see **D3.19**.

It is not the practice for the justice or clerk to consider the evidence before issuing a summons, but, very exceptionally, process might be refused because of the apparent inadequacy of the prosecutor's case (see Ridley J's judgment in *Mead, ex parte National Insurance Commissioners* (1916) 80 JP 332 for a statement of the principle, although on the facts mandamus was granted against a magistrate who had refused a summons for the extraneous reason that he believed others ought also to have been prosecuted, not because evidence was lacking against the proposed defendant.) Neither is it the practice for the person named in the information to attend and oppose the issue of a summons, but again the justice or clerk has a discretion to let him do so (*West London Stipendiary Magistrate, ex parte Klahn* [1979] 1 WLR 933).

Where the application for a summons appears to have been frivolous, vexatious or otherwise an abuse of process, the Divisional Court may quash any summons issued, notwithstanding that the person summoned has the alternative remedy of asking the magistrates' court before which he is required to appear to strike out the proceedings (*Bury Magistrates, ex parte Anderton* (1987) 137 NLJ 410, in which the Divisional Court quashed a summons obtained by T against the Chief Constable of the Greater Manchester Police for conspiring to pervert the course of justice in that he had caused police officers to lay false informations for the obtaining of a warrant to search T's home and an order allowing inspection of T's company's bank accounts).

Service etc. of the Summons

D4.4 A summons must be signed by the justice or clerk issuing it or (in the case of a summons issued by a justice) must state his name and be authenticated by the clerk's signature (Magistrates' Courts Rules 1981, r. 98(1)). It is standard practice for the necessary signature to be affixed by means of a rubber stamp, and, provided the information has been considered and issue of a summons approved by a justice or clerk, even the manual task of rubber-stamping the signature on the document may be performed by an assistant in the clerk's office (see *Brentford Justices, ex parte Catlin* [1975] QB 455 at p. 462E–G for approval of the practice). As to its contents, a summons should state (a) the substance of the information which has been laid against the person summoned, and (b) the time and place at which he is required to appear to answer the charge (r. 98(2)). Although r. 98(3) permits one summons to be issued in respect of several informations against a person, it is more common for a separate summons to be issued for each information.

A summons may be served on a person by:

    (a)   personally delivering it to him; or
    (b)   leaving it for him with another person at his last known or usual place of abode; or
    (c)   posting it to the aforementioned place of abode (Magistrates' Courts Rules 1981, r. 99(1)).

This is qualified by r. 99(2), which states that service by either of the methods set out in (b) and (c) above shall not be 'treated as proved' (e.g., for purposes of proceedings in an accused's absence) unless it is further established that the summons came to the person's knowledge. A communication to the court from him may be sufficient to establish the necessary knowledge. The qualification to r. 99(1) made by r. 99(2) is itself qualified by the proviso that, where the offence alleged is summary and the summons was either left as required by (b) above or sent by registered letter or recorded delivery to the person's last known or usual place of abode, it is not then necessary to prove that it came to his knowledge. Service of a summons on a corporation may be effected by delivering it at or sending it by post to its registered office (unless there is no registered office in the UK in which case it should be sent to the corporation's place of trade or business) (r. 99(3)). References to a person's 'last known or usual place of abode' are construed as including any address which he gives for the purposes of service (r. 99(8)).

In providing that a justice may issue a summons 'upon' an information being laid before him, the MCA 1980, s. 1, does not imply that the issue of a summons must follow immediately upon the consideration of the information by the justice or clerk (*Fairford Justices, ex parte Brewster* [1976] QB 600). It is open to the prosecutor to lay his information and then suggest that a summons should not immediately be issued (e.g., because the accused is out of the country and service could not be effected for a considerable time). However, if the delay between the laying of the information and issue of the summons is so great as to be unreasonable and to cause prejudice, then the High Court has a discretion to intervene and quash the summons (ibid. at p. 604F–H). Moreover, an information should be laid with the intention of having the consequent summons served as soon as reasonably possible. Therefore, if the prosecutor has not in fact made his mind up whether to proceed at the time of laying his information but is concerned merely that any possible prosecution should not be out of time, then his conduct amounts to an abuse of the process of the court and the magistrates should stay the proceedings if ultimately he does decide to proceed (*Brentford Justices, ex parte Wong* [1981] QB 445).

Issue of Warrant for Arrest

The MCA 1980, s.1(1)(b), provides that, whenever a justice before whom an **D4.5** information is laid has power to issue a summons, he may alternatively issue a warrant for the arrest of the person named in the information, save that:

(a)   the information must be in writing and substantiated on oath (s. 1(3)); and

(b)   either the offence alleged must be indictable or punishable with imprisonment, or the accused's address must be insufficiently established for a summons to be served (s. 1(4)).

The restriction in (b) does not apply if the accused is a juvenile. The restriction in (a) means that a clerk may not issue a warrant for arrest since, under the Justices' Clerks Rules, clerks may not take informations on oath. As a matter of discretion, a magistrate should not issue a warrant if a summons would appear to be an equally effectual means of securing the accused's attendance before the court (*O'Brien* v *Brabner* (1885) 49 JPN 227). In most cases where the allegations are serious enough to cast doubt on whether the accused would appear in answer to a summons, the offence will in any event carry a power of arrest without warrant, making an application for a warrant superfluous. It follows that warrants for arrest issued under s. 1 of the 1980 Act are the least common means of commencing proceedings. Whenever magistrates issue a warrant for arrest they have a discretion to 'back it for bail', that is, they may direct that, having been arrested, the person arrested shall thereafter be bailed by the police to attend court on a named day (see s. 117 of the 1980 Act). The backing for bail may be unconditional or conditional on the arrestee providing sureties.

The MCA 1980, s. 1(6), specifically provides that if the offence alleged is indictable, a warrant for arrest may be issued under s. 1 notwithstanding that a summons has already been issued on the basis of the information. If the offence is summary and process initially takes the form of a summons, it would seem that there is then no power to issue a warrant under s. 1, although circumstances may subsequently arise which justify a warrant under other provisions of the Act (e.g., s. 13, issue of a warrant where the accused fails to appear in answer to a summons).

The effect of a warrant for arrest is to order and empower the constables of the police force for the area in which it is issued to arrest the person named in the warrant and bring him before the magistrates' court specified therein. That court will normally be the court for the petty-sessional division to which the magistrate issuing the warrant is assigned. However, the warrant may specify any convenient court in the magistrates' county (MCA 1980, s. 1(1)(b)). If the warrant is issued by virtue only of s. 1(1)(c) of the 1980 Act (i.e. the accused is believed to be in the county although the offence was not committed within the county) and the offence is summary, the court specified must be one having jurisdiction to try the offence, that is, a court for the county where the offence was committed (s. 1(5)(b)).

Effect of Defect in Process on Jurisdiction of Court

D4.6 The jurisdiction of a magistrates' court to determine mode of trial for an offence triable either way, to try such an offence summarily or to hold committal proceedings for an offence to be tried on indictment is dependent, *inter alia*, on the accused appearing or being brought before the court (see MCA 1980, ss. 2(3) to (4) and 18). However, there is no express requirement in those provisions that the accused's presence shall have been obtained by lawful means. Therefore, if he in fact appears before the court (e.g., in answer to a summons) or is brought before the court following arrest, the magistrates will have jurisdiction to deal with his case even if the process by which his attendance was secured was faulty, provided, of course, that any other preconditions of jurisdiction are satisfied (see *Hughes* (1879) 4 QBD 614). As to jurisdiction to try summary offences, that depends on the venue of the offence, not on the accused's attendance (see s. 2(1) of the 1980 Act), so it inevitably follows that defects in process cannot be fatal to jurisdiction.

In *Hughes*, H was convicted of perjury committed at the summary trial of S. The conviction was upheld on appeal even though S's attendance before the magistrates' court was as a result of an invalidly issued warrant for arrest. Despite the defect in process, S's trial was a valid one, and therefore constituted proceedings in which perjury could be committed. *Hughes* was approved by the House of Lords in *Manchester Stipendiary Magistrate, ex parte Hill* [1983] 1 AC 328, a case in which H sought an order of prohibition to prevent the magistrates' court trying him on an information alleging a drink-driving offence. His argument was that the summons had been improperly issued in that the information had never been considered by a justice or a justices' clerk. But, although that was undoubtedly an irregularity and contravened the guidance given by Donaldson LJ in *Gateshead Justices, ex parte Tesco Stores Ltd* [1981] QB 470 (see **D4.3**), it did not affect the validity of the information itself. That had been laid within the statutory six months when it was received in the clerk's office. The subsequent defect in the issue of process, H having in fact appeared in answer to the summons, could not deprive the court of its jurisdiction to try a summary offence committed within its county. Insofar as it held that an information is not laid until it has actually been considered by a justice or clerk, *Ex parte Tesco Stores Ltd* was wrongly decided, although it is good authority for the proposition stated earlier, that issue of a summons is a non-delegable judicial act.

In *Horseferry Road Magistrates' Court, ex parte Bennett* [1994] 1 AC 42, however, the House of Lords dealt with a situation where the accused had been forcibly brought back to the United Kingdom in disregard of the extradition procedures which were available. Their lordships held that, where the police, prosecution or other executive authorities in this country had been a knowing party to such irregularity, the courts should stay the prosecution as an abuse of process. This decision was in effect an extension of the concept of abuse of process as there was no suggestion that a fair trial was impossible. As to the proper procedure in such cases, it was stated that, if a serious question as to the deliberate abuse of extradition procedures arose before justices, they should adjourn to allow an application to the Divisional Court, which was the proper forum to consider such matters.

Magistrates' Courts Act, s. 1

1.—(1) Upon an information being laid before a justice of the peace for an area to which this section applies that any person has, or is suspected of having, committed an offence, the justice may, in any of the events mentioned in subsection (2) below, but subject to subsections (3) to (5) below—

(a) issue a summons directed to that person requiring him to appear before a magistrates' court for the area to answer to the information, or

(b) issue a warrant to arrest that person and bring him before a magistrates' court for the area or such magistrates' court as is provided in subsection (5) below.

(2) A justice of the peace for an area to which this section applies may issue a summons or warrant under this section—

(a) if the offence was committed or is suspected of having been committed within the area, or

(b) if it appears to the justice necessary or expedient, with a view to the better administration of justice, that the person charged should be tried jointly with, or in the same place as, some other person who is charged with an offence, and who is in custody, or is being or is to be proceeded against, within the area, or

(c) if the person charged resides or is, or is believed to reside or be, within the area, or

(d) if under any enactment a magistrates' court for the area has jurisdiction to try the offence, or

(e) if the offence was committed outside England and Wales and, where it is an offence exclusively punishable on summary conviction, if a magistrates' court for the area would have jurisdiction to try the offence if the offender were before it.

(3) No warrant shall be issued under this section unless the information is in writing and substantiated on oath.

(4) No warrant shall be issued under this section for the arrest of any person who has attained the age of 18 years unless—

(a) the offence to which the warrant relates is an indictable offence or is punishable with imprisonment, or

(b) the person's address is not sufficiently established for a summons to be served on him.

(5) Where the offence charged is not an indictable offence—

(a) no summons shall be issued by virtue only of paragraph (c) of subsection (2) above, and

(b) any warrant issued by virtue only of that paragraph shall require the person charged to be brought before a magistrates' court having jurisdiction to try the offence.

(6) Where the offence charged is an indictable offence, a warrant under this section may be issued at any time notwithstanding that a summons has previously been issued.

(7) A justice of the peace may issue a summons or warrant under this section upon an information being laid before him notwithstanding any enactment requiring the information to be laid before two or more justices.

(8) The areas to which this section applies are any county, any London commission area and the City of London.

Magistrates' Courts Rules 1981 (SI 1981 No. 552), rr. 4, 98 and 99

4.—(1) An information may be laid or complaint made by the prosecutor or complainant in person or by his counsel or solicitor or other person authorised in that behalf.

(2) Subject to any provision [of the MCA 1980] and any other enactment an information or complaint need not be in writing or on oath.

[(3) Concerns the contents of an information where there is an exception etc. to liability contained in the statute creating the offence.]

98.—(1) A summons shall be signed by the justice issuing it or state his name and be authenticated by the signature of the clerk of a magistrates' court.

(2) A summons requiring a person to appear before a magistrates' court to answer to an information or complaint shall state shortly the matter of the information or complaint and shall state the time and place at which the defendant is required by the summons to appear.

(3) A single summons may be issued against a person in respect of several informations or complaints. . . .

99.—(1) Service of a summons issued by a justice of the peace on a person other than a corporation may be effected—

(a)   by delivering it to the person to whom it is directed; or

(b)   by leaving it for him with some person at his last known or usual place of abode; or

(c)   by sending it by post in a letter addressed to him at his last known or usual place of abode.

(2)   If the person summoned fails to appear, service of a summons in manner authorised by subparagraph (b) or (c) of paragraph (1) shall not be treated as proved unless it is proved that the summons came to his knowledge; and for that purpose any letter or other communication purporting to be written by him or on his behalf in such terms as reasonably to justify the inference that the summons came to his knowledge shall be admissible as evidence of that fact;

Provided that this paragraph shall not apply to any summons in respect of a summary offence served in manner authorised by—

(a)   the said subparagraph (b); or

(b)   the said subparagraph (c) in a registered letter or by recorded delivery service.

[(3) and (4)   Service of summons on corporations.]

[(5)   Requirements of enactments other than the MCA 1980 that a summons or document be served in a particular way to be deemed complied with if the summons or document is served as required by this rule.]

[(6) and (7)   Not relevant to service of summonses on an accused.]

(8)   Where this rule or any other of these rules provides that a summons or other document may be sent by post to a person's last known or usual place of abode that rule shall have effect as if it provided also for the summons or other document to be sent in the manner specified in the rule to an address given by that person for that purpose.

ADJOURNMENTS AND REMANDS

Power to Adjourn

D4.7   At any stage before or during committal proceedings, during proceedings to determine mode of trial or during a summary trial, a magistrates' court may adjourn the proceedings. Unless the accused is pleading guilty to a minor offence, it is rare for a case to be disposed of on the occasion of his first appearance. An adjournment is likely to be necessitated by factors such as the accused wishing to instruct solicitors, the prosecution needing to prepare advance information for the defence and/or statements for committal, or the court not having time for the immediate hearing of a not guilty plea. Whether to grant an adjournment is always a matter for the court's discretion but it must be exercised judicially. In *Sunderland Justices, ex parte Dryden* (1994) *The Times*, 18 May 1994, the defendant sought an adjournment to obtain expert evidence. The justices refused on the basis that the prosecution had supplied an independent expert report. The Divisional Court stated that this was not a ground in law for refusing the application. An accused cannot require an adjournment as of right so as to instruct solicitors (*Lipscombe, ex parte Biggins* (1862) 26 JP 244). However, an accused is entitled to a reasonable opportunity to prepare his case which, depending on the nature and complexity of the charge, will almost certainly necessitate allowing him to take legal advice if he wishes (*Thames Magistrates' Court, ex parte Polemis* [1974] 1 WLR 1371 – P, the captain of a foreign ship, appeared before the magistrates at 2 p.m. to answer a summons for discharging oil which had been served on him at 10.30 that morning; an application by a hastily instructed solicitor for an adjournment was refused because of fears that P would sail and not return; P's conviction was quashed by the Divisional Court because the refusal of an adjournment had made it impossible for the defence case to be properly prepared and presented, which was effectively a breach of the rule of natural justice that a tribunal must hear both sides of a case). The same principles apply on a prosecution application for an adjournment, which must not be unreasonably refused (*Barnet Magistrates' Court, ex parte the DPP* (1994) *The Times*, 8 April 1994; see also **D18.14**).

The power to adjourn is contained in the MCA 1980, ss. 5, 10(1) and 18(4).

Magistrates' Courts Act 1980, ss. 5, 10 and 18

5.—(1) A magistrates' court may, before beginning to inquire into an offence as examining justices, or at any time during the inquiry, adjourn the hearing, and if it does so shall remand the accused.

(2) The court shall when adjourning fix the time and place at which the hearing is to be resumed; and the time fixed shall be that at which the accused is required to appear or be brought before the court in pursuance of the remand [or would be brought before the court were it not for his agreeing to further remands being in his absence].

10.—(1) A magistrates' court may at any time, whether before or after beginning to try an information, adjourn the trial, and may do so, notwithstanding anything in this Act, when composed of a single justice.

(2) The court may when adjourning either fix the time and place at which the trial is to be resumed, or, unless it remands the accused, leave the time and place to be determined later by the court. . . .

[(3) Adjournments after summary conviction.]

(4) On adjourning the trial of an information the court may remand the accused and, where the accused has attained the age of 18 years, shall do so if the offence is triable either way and—

(a) on the occasion on which the accused first appeared, or was brought, before the court to answer to the information he was in custody or, having been released on bail, surrendered to the custody of the court; or

(b) the accused has been remanded at any time in the course of proceedings on the information;

and, where the court remands the accused, the time fixed for the resumption of the trial shall be that at which he is required to appear or be brought before the court in pursuance of the remand [or would be brought before the court were it not for his agreeing to further remands being in his absence].

18.—(1) Sections 19 to 23 below shall have effect where a person who has attained the age of 18 years appears or is brought before a magistrates' court on an information charging him with an offence triable either way and—

(a) he indicates under section 17A above that (if the offence were to proceed to trial) he would plead not guilty, or

(b) his representative indicates under section 17B above that (if the offence were to proceed to trial) he would plead not guilty.

. . .

(4) A magistrates' court proceeding under sections 19 to 23 below may adjourn the proceedings at any time, and on doing so on any occasion when the accused is present may remand the accused, and shall remand him if—

(a) on the occasion on which he first appeared, or was brought, before the court to answer to the information he was in custody or, having been released on bail, surrendered to the custody of the court; or

(b) he has been remanded at any time in the course of proceedings on the information;

and where the court remands the accused, the time fixed for the resumption of the proceedings shall be that at which he is required to appear or be brought before the court in pursuance of the remand [or would be brought before the court were it not for his agreeing to further remands being in his absence].

References in the above sections to 'remanding' an accused mean either remanding him in custody (i.e. committing him to custody to be brought before the court at the end of the period of remand or at such earlier time as the court may require), or remanding him on bail in accordance with the provisions of the Bail Act 1976 (i.e. directing him to appear before the court at the end of the period of the remand or, if bail is made continuous, directing him to appear at every time to which the proceedings may be adjourned) (see MCA 1980, s. 128(1) and (4)). References in ss. 10 and 18 to the trial of an 'information' or an accused appearing in answer to an information extend to cases where the proceedings commenced by way of a charge being preferred by the police, since the charge sheet prepared at the police station is conventionally treated as equivalent to an information laid before a magistrate. Sections 19 to 23 of the 1980 Act, which are referred to in s. 18(1) and (4), are the sections that govern procedure to determine the mode of trial (see **D7.4**).

Sections 5(2), 10(4) and 18(4) each deal with a different situation. Section 5(1) gives the context in which s. 5(2) applies, i.e. when either (a) the accused is charged with an offence triable only on indictment, or (b) he is charged with an offence triable either way and proceedings to determine the mode of trial have already resulted in a decision for trial on indictment. Section 18(4) is the governing provision for all appearances in respect of an either-way offence until mode of trial has been determined. Section 10(1) applies (a) to appearances for summary offences up until conviction, and (b) to appearances for either-way offences from after mode of trial has been determined in favour of summary trial to conviction.

Sections 10(4) and 18(4) provide in almost identical terms that, on adjourning proceedings for an offence triable either way, the court must remand the accused unless: (a) he first appeared in answer to a summons (as opposed to being brought before the court in custody or appearing in answer to police bail); and (b) he has not been remanded at an earlier hearing. On adjourning under s. 5(1) the court is always obliged to remand the accused. In all other cases, the court has power to remand but may simply adjourn without also remanding. Thus, magistrates may, at their discretion, adjourn without remanding the accused: (a) at all appearances for summary offences up to conviction; and (b) at appearances for either-way offences up to either a determination for trial on indictment or summary conviction, provided the accused initially appeared in answer to a summons and has not subsequently been remanded. Where a case is simply adjourned, there is no need to fix the date for the next hearing at the time of adjourning, whereas if there is a remand the adjournment date must be fixed forthwith and is the date to which the accused is remanded. An accused who is not remanded and who then fails to appear on the date to which his case is adjourned commits no offence, but it may be possible either for a warrant to be issued for his arrest or for the proceedings to be conducted in his absence. An accused who has been remanded on bail commits an offence under the Bail Act 1976, s. 6, if he fails without reasonable cause to answer to his bail.

Period of Remand in Custody

D4.8   The maximum period for which a magistrates' court may remand an accused in custody is eight clear days (MCA 1980, s. 128(6)). This is subject to the following exceptions:

(a)   following summary conviction, there may be a remand of up to three weeks for inquiries (e.g., a social inquiry report) to be made into the most suitable method of dealing with the accused's case (s. 10(3) of the 1980 Act);

(b)   following the court being satisfied that the accused 'did the act or made the omission charged', there may be a remand of up to three weeks for a medical examination and reports if the court considers that an inquiry should be made into his physical or mental condition before deciding how to deal with him (s. 30(1) of the 1980 Act);

(c)   where mode of trial is determined in favour of summary trial but the court is not constituted so as to proceed immediately to trial (e.g., because it consists of a single lay justice), there may be a remand in custody to a date on which the court will be properly constituted (s. 128(6)(c) of the 1980 Act);

(d)   where s. 128A of the 1980 Act applies, a second or subsequent remand in custody may be for up to 28 days; and

(e) if the accused is already being detained under a custodial sentence he may be remanded in custody for up to 28 days or his anticipated release date whichever is the shorter (s. 131 of the 1980 Act).

A remand on bail prior to the conclusion of committal proceedings or summary trial may exceed eight clear days provided the parties consent (s. 128(6)(a)). In practice, there is virtually never an objection to whatever period of remand on bail appears necessary for the parties to be ready for the next effective stage in dealing with the case.

Where a person is brought before the court after an earlier remand, the court may remand him again (s. 128(3)). Thus, there may be several remand hearings before the commencement of committal proceedings or summary trial. The only limitation on the number of remands is the general discretion of magistrates to refuse an adjournment if it would be against the interests of justice (e.g., because they consider that the party requesting the adjournment should have been ready to proceed on the present occasion). By s. 130, a court remanding an accused in custody may order that, for subsequent remands, he be brought up before a different magistrates' court nearer to the prison where he is to be confined while on remand. That alternate court then enjoys those powers in relation to remand (and the granting of legal aid) that the original court would otherwise have. Furthermore, quite apart from the specific powers given by s. 130 to remand to an alternate magistrates' court, there is power, whenever an accused is brought before a magistrates' court for a certain petty-sessional division on a charge that he committed an offence in a different petty-sessional division of the same county, to remand him in custody or on bail to the court for the division where the offence occurred (see *Avon Magistrates' Court Committee, ex parte Bath Law Society* [1988] QB 409, which approved the Avon justices' practice of centralising Saturday morning sittings in the county by requiring that all overnight arrestees not granted bail should be brought before the Bristol Magistrates' Court and thereafter remanded by that court to the court for the division where the offence occurred).

The MCA 1980, s. 128, is without prejudice to the provisions of s. 129 governing further remands where the accused is sick etc. and the enlargement of bail. By s. 129(1), if the accused is unable to appear or be brought before the court at the end of the remand period because of 'illness or accident', the magistrates may remand him in his absence to a convenient date, and any restrictions on the period of the remand which would otherwise be imposed by s. 128(6) shall not apply. By s. 129(3), where an accused has been remanded on bail, the court may enlarge his bail in his absence by appointing a later time for him to appear. It will be noted that s. 129(1) applies whether the remand is in custody or on bail, but is restricted to cases where non-attendance on the day originally fixed is due to accident or illness. Section 129(3) applies only to remands on bail but places no restrictions on the reasons for which the court may choose to exercise its powers under the subsection. Thus, bail may be enlarged where it becomes apparent during the remand period that the court will not have time to deal with the case on the day originally fixed, or where the accused fails to attend but some acceptable reason is advanced for his non-appearance (not necessarily sickness or accident). Where bail is enlarged, the court may also enlarge the recognisances of any sureties (i.e. they will be under an obligation to secure the accused's attendance on the new hearing date).

Remands in Custody in the Absence of Accused

To avoid the necessity for an accused to be brought before the court in custody when it **D4.9** is apparent that no effective progress in his case will be possible at the hearing to which he is brought, he may be remanded in custody in his absence under the MCA 1980, s. 128(3A) to (3E). The conditions that must be satisfied for there to be a custodial remand in absence are that:

(a)   the accused has consented (almost certainly at an earlier hearing) to not being present at future remands;

(b)   he has a solicitor acting for him in the case (although the solicitor need not be present in court);

(c)   he has not been remanded in absence on more than two consecutive occasions prior to the present application for remand in absence; and

(d)   he has not withdrawn his original consent.

To facilitate the giving of consent to remands in absence, it is provided in s. 128(1A) to (1C) that, where magistrates are proposing to remand in custody an accused who is present in court, they shall (if he is legally represented in court) explain to him the possibility of further remands being in his absence and ask him whether he consents to that procedure being adopted. It is thus a pre-condition of the accused being asked in court for his consent to remands *in absentia* that he has solicitor or counsel actually present representing him, whereas (assuming consent has been given) the remands in absence themselves can and normally would take place without the attendance of a lawyer, provided the accused still has a solicitor acting for him in the case. The restriction of the number of consecutive remands in absence to three means that the accused cannot be remanded for more than approximately a month without being brought before the court. He could, on attending after three remands in his absence, again agree to the next three remands being in his absence. If a case is listed for a formal remand in absence, but it appears to the magistrates that the conditions for such a remand are not in fact satisfied (e.g., because the accused has withdrawn his consent or no longer has solicitors acting for him), they must remand the accused for the shortest period possible that will enable him to be brought before them (s. 128(3C) to (3D)). It should be noted that, although remands in absence are pure formalities, the rule that remands in custody shall not exceed eight clear days must still be complied with in the sense that the accused's case must be listed within each eight-day period so that the magistrates can formally say that he is remanded to the next appropriate date, he having consented not to be produced.

Remands in absence are limited to cases where the court is adjourning under s. 5, 10(1) or 18(4) of the 1980 Act (i.e. adjournments prior to or during summary trial or committal proceedings). If the adjournment is under s. 10(3) or 30 (adjournments for reports after conviction or after being satisfied that the accused committed the *actus reus* of the offence), the period of a custodial remand may extend to three weeks but there is no power to remand in absence.

Remands in Custody for up to 28 days

D4.10   By s. 128A of the MCA 1980, a magistrates' court may remand an accused in custody for a period exceeding eight clear days if (s. 128A(2)):

(a)   he has previously been remanded in custody for the same offence;

(b)   he is now before the court; and

(c)   the court (after allowing the parties to make representations) has fixed a date on which it expects the next effective hearing to take place.

The words 'effective hearing' used in (c) above are intended to denote a hearing other than one solely for the purpose of a further remand — the phrase itself does not appear in the section. In the generality of cases, the next effective hearing after the accused becomes eligible for an extended remand will be the hearing to determine mode of trial. The maximum period of a remand under s. 128A is 28 days or to the date of the next effective hearing whichever is the shorter. Section 128A now has effect in all petty sessions areas. It does not, however, apply on the occasion of a first remand in custody (see the express terms of s. 128A(2)(a)), although the accused may at that stage be invited to consent to the next three remands being in his absence. The making of a remand under s. 128A does not affect the right of the accused to apply for bail during the period thereof (s. 128A(3)). It is unclear whether, in preserving the right to make a bail application even though there has been a 28-day remand in custody, s. 128A(3) entitles the defence to put before the magistrates forthwith a change in circumstances arising during the period of the remand, or whether it merely confirms that an application for bail may be made to a tribunal other than the magistrates' court (i.e. the Crown Court or a High Court judge in chambers).

Pre-Trial Hearings by Television Link

The CDA 1998, s. 57, provides for pre-trial hearings involving a defendant in custody **D4.11** to be conducted over a live television link between the court and the prison. If facilities approved by the Home Secretary are available at the prison in question, the court has discretion whether to conduct the hearing using the link. Both prosecution and defence may make representations to the court on the issue. If the option is available to the court, but it decides not to make use of it, then it must state its reasons. Television links, having been piloted in certain magistrates' courts, will be extended to the remaining magistrates' courts and to the Crown Court in due course.

STATUTORY PROVISIONS ON DURATION OF REMANDS

Magistrates' Courts Act 1980, ss. 128, 128A and 129 to 131   D4.12

128.—(1) Where a magistrates' court has power to remand any person, then, subject to section 4 of the Bail Act 1976 and to any other enactment modifying that power, the court may—

(a) remand him in custody, that is to say, commit him to custody to be brought before the court, subject to subsection (3A) below, at the end of the period of remand or at such earlier time as the court may require; or

(b) where it is inquiring into or is trying an offence alleged to have been committed by that person or has convicted him of an offence, remand him on bail in accordance with the Bail Act 1976, that is to say, by directing him to appear as provided in subsection (4) below; or

[(c) relates to bail in non-criminal proceedings.]

(1A) Where—

(a) on adjourning a case under section 5, 10(1), 17C or 18(4) above the court proposes to remand or further remand a person in custody; and

(b) he is before the court; and

(c) [repealed]; and

(d) he is legally represented in that court,

it shall be the duty of the court—

(i) to explain the effect of subsections (3A) and (3B) below to him in ordinary language; and

(ii) to inform him in ordinary language that, notwithstanding the procedure for a remand without his being brought before a court, he would be brought before a court for the hearing and determination of at least every fourth application for his remand, and of every application for his remand heard at a time when it appeared to the court that he had no solicitor acting for him in the case.

(1B) For the purposes of subsection (1A) above a person is to be treated as legally represented in a court if, but only if, he has the assistance of counsel or a solicitor to represent him in the proceedings in that court.

(1C) After explaining to an accused as provided by subsection (1A) above the court shall ask him whether he consents to hearing and determination of such applications in his absence.

[(2) If bail is granted subject to the provision of sureties but they are not immediately available, the accused must be remanded in custody until such time as they enter into their recognisances.]

(3) Where a person is brought before the court after remand, the court may further remand him.

(3A) Subject to subsection (3B) below, where a person has been remanded in custody and the remand was not a remand under section 128A below for a period exceeding eight clear days, the court may further remand him (otherwise than in the exercise of the power conferred by that section) on an adjournment under section 5, 10(1), 17C or 18(4) above without his being brought before it if it is satisfied—

(a)   that he gave his consent, either in response to a question under subsection (1C) above or otherwise, to the hearing and determination in his absence of any application for his remand on an adjournment of the case under any of those provisions; and

(b)   that he has not by virtue of this subsection been remanded without being brought before the court on more than two such applications immediately preceding the application which the court is hearing; and

(c)   [repealed]; and

(d)   that he has not withdrawn his consent. . . .

(3B)   The court may not exercise the power conferred by subsection (3A) above if it appears to the court, on an application for a further remand being made to it, that the person to whom the application relates has no solicitor acting for him in the case (whether present in court or not).

(3C)   Where—

(a)   a person has been remanded in custody on an adjournment of a case under section 4(4), 10(1), 17C or 18(4) above; and

(b)   an application is subsequently made for his further remand on such an adjournment; and

(c)   he is not brought before the court which hears and determines the application; and

(d)   that court is not satisfied as mentioned in subsection (3A) above,

the court shall adjourn the case and remand him in custody for the period for which it stands adjourned.

(3D)   An adjournment under subsection (3C) above shall be for the shortest period that appears to the court to make it possible for the accused to be brought before it.

[(3E)   Procedure to be adopted if it appears to the court at some stage after a remand in absence that the accused ought not have been so remanded.]

(4)   Where a person is remanded on bail under subsection (1) above the court may . . . direct him to appear . . .—

(a)   before that court at the end of the period of remand; or

(b)   at every time and place to which during the course of the proceedings the hearing may be from time to time adjourned;

and, where it remands him on bail conditionally on his providing a surety when it is proceeding with a view to transfer for trial, may direct that the recognisance of the surety be conditioned to secure that the person so bailed appears—

(c)   at every time and place to which during the course of the proceedings the hearing may be from time to time adjourned and also before the Crown Court in the event of the person so bailed being committed for trial there.

(5)   Where a person is directed to appear or a recognisance is conditioned for a person's appearance in accordance with paragraph (b) or (c) of subsection (4) above, the fixing at any time of the time for him next to appear shall be deemed to be a remand; but nothing in this subsection or subsection (4) above shall deprive the court of power at any subsequent hearing to remand him afresh.

(6)   Subject to the provisions of sections 128A and 129 below, a magistrates' court shall not remand a person for a period exceeding eight clear days, except that—

(a)   if the court remands him on bail, it may remand him for a longer period if he and the other party consent;

(b)   where the court adjourns a trial under section 10(3) or 30 above, the court may remand him for the period of the adjournment;

(c)   where a person is charged with an offence triable either way, then, if it falls to the court to try the case summarily but the court is not at the time so constituted, and sitting in such a place, as will enable it to proceed with the trial, the court may remand him until the next occasion on which it will be practicable for the court to be so constituted, and to sit in such a place, as aforesaid, notwithstanding that the remand is for a period exceeding eight clear days.

[(7) and (8)   Concern committing an accused to police detention for a period not exceeding three clear days where there is a need to question him about other offences — see **D1.35**.]

128A.—(1)   The Secretary of State may by order made by statutory instrument provide that this section shall have effect—

    (a)   in an area specified in the order; or

    (b)   in proceedings of a description so specified,

in relation to any person ('the accused').

    (2)   A magistrates' court may remand the accused in custody for a period exceeding eight clear days if—

    (a)   it has previously remanded him in custody for the same offence; and

    (b)   he is before the court,

but only if, after affording the parties an opportunity to make representations, it has set a date on which it expects that it will be possible for the next stage in the proceedings, other than a hearing relating to a further remand in custody or on bail, to take place, and only—

    (i)   for a period ending not later than that date; or

    (ii)   for a period of 28 clear days,

whichever is the less.

    (3)   Nothing in this section affects the right of the accused to apply for bail during the period of remand.

    [(4)   Making of statutory instruments under the section.]

129.—(1)   If a magistrates' court is satisfied that any person who has been remanded is unable by reason of illness or accident to appear or be brought before the court at the expiration of the period for which he was remanded, the court may, in his absence, remand him for a further time; and section 128(6) above shall not apply.

    (2)   Notwithstanding anything in section 128(1) above, the power of a court under subsection (1) above to remand a person on bail for a further time—

    (a)   where he was granted bail in criminal proceedings, includes power to enlarge the recognisance of any surety for him to a later time;

    [(b)   concerns bail in non-criminal proceedings.]

    (3)   Where a person remanded on bail is bound to appear before a magistrates' court at any time and the court has no power to remand him under subsection (1) above, the court may in his absence—

    (a)   where he was granted bail in criminal proceedings, appoint a later time as the time at which he is to appear and enlarge the recognisances of any sureties for him to that time;

    [(b)   concerns bail in non-criminal proceedings];

and the appointment of the time . . . shall be deemed to be a further remand.

    [(4)   Concerns enlargement of a surety's recognisance upon committal for trial.]

130.—(1)   A magistrates' court adjourning a case under section 5, 10(1), 17C or 18(4) above, and remanding the accused in custody, may, if he has attained the age of 17, order that he be brought up for any subsequent remands before an alternate magistrates' court nearer to the prison where he is to be confined while on remand.

    [(2)–(5)   and sch. 5 contain detailed provisions governing remands to alternate magistrates' courts.]

131.—(1)   When a magistrates' court remands an accused person in custody and he is already detained under a custodial sentence, the period for which he is remanded may be up to 28 clear days.

    (2)   But the court shall inquire as to the expected date of his release from that detention; and if it appears that it will be before 28 clear days have expired, he shall not be remanded in custody for more than eight clear days or (if longer) a period ending with that date.

OPTIONS WHEN THE ACCUSED FAILS TO APPEAR

If an accused who has been bailed to appear at a magistrates' court fails to do so, the **D4.13** court may:

    (a)   issue a warrant for his arrest under the Bail Act 1976, s. 7; or

    (b)   enlarge his bail in accordance with the MCA 1980, s. 129(3); or

    (c)   proceed in his absence under MCA 1980, s. 11(1) (see below).

If a warrant for arrest is issued the court may, at its discretion, back it for bail (MCA 1980, s. 117).

If the accused fails to appear for the trial or adjourned trial of an information, the case may proceed in his absence provided, where the prosecution commenced by issue of a summons, that it is proved to the satisfaction of the court that either the summons was served a reasonable time before the hearing or the accused appeared on a previous occasion to answer the information (MCA 1980, s. 11(1) and (2)). Proof of service of the summons will entail proving that it came to the accused's knowledge, unless the offence alleged is summary, in which case it is sufficient to prove that it was sent by registered letter or recorded delivery to his last known or usual address (Magistrates' Courts Rules 1981, r. 99(2)). Where the accused fails to appear for an adjourned trial, it is also necessary to prove that he had adequate notice of the adjournment date (MCA 1980, s. 10(4)).

The Magistrates' Courts Rules 1981, r. 99, applies only to service of summonses. Therefore, where an adjournment notice is sent to the accused, there is no requirement in the rules to show that it came to his knowledge or, alternatively, that it was sent by recorded delivery or registered letter to his last known address. It is merely necessary to satisfy the court that he had 'adequate notice' of the adjournment date (MCA 1980, s. 10(2)). Arguably, this gives the magistrates greater discretion as to what amounts to adequate notice. Most courts in fact require service of an adjournment notice to be proved as strictly as service of a summons, but some are willing to proceed on less satisfactory evidence.

It should be noted that the provisions of s. 11 of the MCA 1980 apply only to the trial or adjourned trial of an information. The conditions attached to proving an offence in the absence of the accused, the remedies open to him if he is so convicted but did not in fact know of the proceedings and the limitations on the sentences which may be passed in his absence are further discussed at **D18.11** and **D20.2**.

Should the court decide to adjourn the trial of an information rather than proceeding in the accused's absence, it may issue a warrant for his arrest provided: (a) the information has been substantiated on oath; (b) the offence is punishable with imprisonment; and (c) service of the summons, in a case where proceedings so commenced, is proved or the accused was present when the court adjourned the case on the last occasion (MCA 1980, s. 13(1) to (3)). Assuming the summons was not issued on the basis of a sworn information, substantiating the information on oath will require the attendance of a police officer or other suitable person to confirm on oath that the allegations in the information are true to the best of his knowledge. The requirement that the offence alleged be punishable with imprisonment does not apply if the accused is a juvenile (s. 13(3A)). Although warrants under s. 13 are not expressly limited to prosecutions commenced by way of summons, reliance on the section in cases where the accused has been bailed to appear will be unnecessary because non-attendance in answer to bail may always be dealt with by issue of a warrant under the Bail Act 1976, s. 7. If a prosecution for an indictable offence is commenced by way of summons and the accused does not appear, a warrant will not be issuable under s. 13 of the 1980 Act unless and until it is determined to try the information summarily, but the prosecutor is entitled to apply for the issue of a first-instance warrant for arrest under the MCA 1980, s. 1 (see s. 1(6) which provides that, where the offence charged is indictable, a warrant may be issued under s. 1 notwithstanding that a summons has previously been granted).

Magistrates' Courts Act 1980, ss. 10, 11 and 13

10.

. . .

    (2)   The court may when adjourning either fix the time and place at which the trial is to be resumed, or, unless it remands the accused, leave the time and place to be determined

later by the court; but the trial shall not be resumed at that time and place unless the court is satisfied that the parties have had adequate notice thereof.

11.—(1)   Subject to the provisions of this Act, where at the time and place appointed for the trial or adjourned trial of an information the prosecutor appears but the accused does not, the court may proceed in his absence.

(2)   Where a summons has been issued, the court shall not begin to try the information in the absence of the accused unless either it is proved to the satisfaction of the court, on oath or in such other manner as may be prescribed, that the summons was served on the accused within what appears to the court to be a reasonable time before the trial or adjourned trial or the accused has appeared on a previous occasion to answer to the information.

[(3) and (4)   Limitations on sentences which may be passed in the accused's absence.]

13.—(1)   Subject to the provisions of this section, where the court, instead of proceeding in the absence of the accused, adjourns or further adjourns the trial, the court may issue a warrant for his arrest.

(2)   Where a summons has been issued, the court shall not issue a warrant under this section unless the condition in subsection (2A) below or that in subsection (2B) below is fulfilled.

(2A)   The condition in this subsection is that it is proved to the satisfaction of the court, on oath or in such other manner as may be prescribed, that the summons was served on the accused within what appears to the court to be a reasonable time before the trial or adjourned trial.

(2B)   The condition in this subsection is that—

(a)   the adjournment now being made is a second or subsequent adjournment of the trial,

(b)   the accused was present on the last (or only) occasion when the trial was adjourned, and

(c)   on that occasion the court determined the time for the hearing at which the adjournment is now being made.

(3)   A warrant for the arrest of any person who has attained the age of 18 years shall not be issued under this section unless—

(a)   the information has been substantiated on oath and the offence to which the warrant relates is punishable with imprisonment; or

(b)   the court, having convicted the accused, proposes to impose a disqualification on him.

(3A)   A warrant for the arrest of any person who has not attained the age of 18 shall not be issued under this section unless—

(a)   the information has been substantiated on oath, or

(b)   the court having convicted the accused, proposes to impose a disqualification on him.

[(4)   Warrant not to be issued under s. 13 where the accused has pleaded guilty by post under the provisions of s. 12 of the MCA 1980 but the court either does not accept the plea or wishes to have the accused attend for purposes of sentencing.]

[(5)   Further restriction on the issue of a warrant under s. 13 in cases where the court adjourns after having already heard evidence either on the present or a previous occasion.]

ADVANCE INFORMATION

If the offence charged is triable either way, the court may not proceed to determine mode **D4.14** of trial unless either the defence have been given advance information about the prosecution case or they have waived their right to it. Although advance information is sometimes both requested and served prior to the accused's first appearance (in which case the court may proceed immediately to determine mode of trial), it is more usual for the provision of the information to necessitate at least one adjournment. Thus, one incidental function of remand hearings is to facilitate the service of advance information.

The right to advance information is given by the Magistrates' Courts (Advance Information) Rules 1985 (SI 1985 No. 601). The rules are set out in full below. In essence, they provide as follows:

(a)   They apply only when the accused is charged with an offence triable either way (r. 2). Since sch. 1 to the Interpretation Act 1978 defines 'offence triable either way' so as to include criminal damage, the rules would seem to apply to any charge of criminal damage, even if it is clear that the value involved is less than the relevant sum and that the matter will therefore have to be dealt with summarily (see **D3.12** and *Considine* (1980) 70 Cr App R 239).

(b)   As soon as possible after the accused has been charged with or summoned for an either-way offence, the prosecutor must give him a written notice, explaining his right to advance information and stating the address at which a request for it may be made (r. 3). The request may but need not be in writing. Often it is made orally at court.

(c)   If, prior to determination of mode of trial, the accused (or his legal representative) asks for advance information, the prosecutor must serve either copies of the statements of the proposed prosecution witnesses or a summary of his case (r. 4(1)). This is subject to the prosecutor's discretion to withhold disclosure of some or all of his case if he considers that full compliance with r. 4(1) might lead to a witness being intimidated or some other interference with the course of justice (r. 4(2)).

(d)   Before proceeding to determination of mode of trial, the court must satisfy itself that the accused is aware of his right to advance information (r. 6(1)). It is open to the defence to waive their rights (e.g., if the accused has already decided to elect trial on indictment and an adjournment for advance information would be pointless because the prosecution case will in any event be fully disclosed by committal proceedings).

(e)   Should the defence fail to request advance information before mode of trial is determined and the determination is then for summary trial, there is then no obligation under the rules for the prosecution to make disclosure, even though lack of it may hamper the defence at trial. However, the CPS usually provide advance information for either-way offences even if the request is made after the time contemplated by the Rules. In *Stratford Justices, ex parte Imbert* [1999] 2 Cr App R 276, the Divisional Court considered whether this gap in the prosecution duty is a violation of Art. 6(3)(a) of the European Convention on Human Rights 'to be informed promptly . . . and in detail, of the nature and cause of the accusation against him'. The Divisional Court held that it was not, although their lordships recognised that their decision was clearly *obiter* (doubly so when it came to their view that it would still not be after the implementation of the Human Rights Act 1998, now expected to take place in October 2000). It is submitted that the absence of advance information might in certain circumstances be a violation of Art. 6(3)(b), which lays down the accused's right 'to have adequate time and facilities for his defence', as well as a violation of Art. 6(3)(a). In order that the trial should be fair, it is necessary that the defence should be able to consider the prosecution evidence, and prepare upon the basis of knowledge rather than guesswork. Sometimes the nature of that evidence will be predictable, and the defence advocate will be able to respond with the necessary agility of thought. But in other instances, the defence may be ambushed by an unexpected line of evidence. A request for an adjournment is likely to meet with a stony reception in the magistrates' court, where justice is after all supposed to be summary. Overall, it may be that what is generally recognised as good practice (the provision of the statements of prosecution witnesses in summary trials) should also be regarded as part of the rights provided by the Convention.

(f)   If a request for advance information has been made but not complied with at the time when the court would otherwise be ready to commence determining mode of trial, the case must be adjourned, unless the court is satisfied that the defence will not be substantially prejudiced by the non-compliance (r. 7(1)).

(g)   The above rules apply with modifications in the cases of juveniles charged with offences triable either way.

Magistrates' Courts (Advance Information) Rules 1985 (SI 1985 No. 601)

[**1.**   Citation and commencement.]

2. These rules apply in respect of proceedings against any person ('the accused') for an offence triable either way. . . .

3. As soon as practicable after a person has been charged with an offence in proceedings in respect of which these rules apply or a summons has been served on a person in connection with such an offence, the prosecutor shall provide him with a notice in writing explaining the effect of rule 4 below and setting out the address at which a request under that rule may be made.

4.—(1) If, in any proceedings in respect of which these rules apply, either before the magistrates' court considers whether the offence appears to be more suitable for summary trial or trial on indictment or, where the accused has not attained the age of 18 years when he appears or is brought before a magistrates' court, before he is asked whether he pleads guilty or not guilty, the accused or a person representing the accused requests the prosecutor to furnish him with advance information, the prosecutor shall, subject to rule 5 below, furnish him as soon as practicable with either—

    (a)   a copy of those parts of every written statement which contain information as to the facts and matters of which the prosecutor proposes to adduce evidence in the proceedings, or

    (b)   a summary of the facts and matters of which the prosecutor proposes to adduce evidence in the proceedings.

    [(2)   'Written statements' within the rules comprise any statement by a person on whose evidence the prosecutor proposes to rely, save that, where such a person has made several statements but all the matters on which the prosecutor proposes to rely are contained in one of those statements, it is only that one which need be disclosed.]

    [(3)   Where the advance disclosure refers to a document on which the prosecutor proposes to rely, the prosecutor must either furnish a copy of the document or allow the defence to inspect it (or a copy of it).]

5.—(1) If the prosecutor is of the opinion that the disclosure of any particular fact or matter in compliance with the requirements imposed by rule 4 above might lead to any person on whose evidence he proposes to rely in the proceedings being intimidated, to an attempt to intimidate him being made or otherwise to the course of justice being interfered with, he shall not be obliged to comply with those requirements in relation to that fact or matter.

    (2)   Where, in accordance with paragraph (1) above, the prosecutor considers that he is not obliged to comply with the requirements imposed by rule 4 in relation to any particular fact or matter, he shall give notice in writing [to that effect to the defence].

6. (1) Subject to paragraph (2) below, where an accused appears or is brought before a magistrates' court in proceedings in respect of which these rules apply, the court shall, before it considers whether the offence appears to be more suitable for summary trial or trial on indictment, satisfy itself that the accused is aware of the requirements which may be imposed on the prosecutor under rule 4 above.

    (2)   Where the accused has not attained the age of 18 years when he appears or is brought before a magistrates' court in proceedings in respect of which these rules apply, the court shall, before the accused is asked whether he pleads guilty or not guilty, satisfy itself that the accused is aware of the requirements which may be imposed on the prosecutor under rule 4 above.

7.—(1) If, in any proceedings in respect of which these rules apply, the court is satisfied that, a request under rule 4 of these rules having been made to the prosecutor by or on behalf of the accused, a requirement imposed on the prosecutor by that rule has not been complied with, the court shall adjourn the proceedings pending compliance with the requirement unless the court is satisfied that the conduct of the case for the accused will not be substantially prejudiced by non-compliance with the requirement.

    [(2)   A record of any decision not to adjourn under (1) above and of the reasons for it must be entered in the court register.]

SECTION D5: BAIL

Introduction

D5.1   Bail in criminal proceedings is governed by the BA 1976 (see s. 1(6) of the Act). The Act is set out at **D5.56**. 'Bail in criminal proceedings' is defined in s. 1(1) of the Act as: '(a) bail grantable in or in connection with proceedings for an offence to a person who is accused or convicted of the offence, or (b) bail grantable in connection with an offence to a person who is under arrest for the offence or for whose arrest for the offence a warrant (endorsed for bail) is being issued'. This section is chiefly concerned with bail from magistrates' courts and the Crown Court. For bail from the police station and bail on appeal to the Court of Appeal, see **D1.28** to **D1.31** and **D23.11** respectively.

PERSONS AND COURTS HAVING JURISDICTION TO GRANT BAIL

D5.2   **Bail from the Police Station without Charge**

If a person has been arrested without warrant or under a warrant not backed for bail (or, having on an earlier occasion been bailed from a police station pending further inquiries, returns to the police station in answer to his bail) but the custody officer at the police station where he is detained is neither satisfied that there is sufficient evidence to charge him nor is willing to authorise his detention for questioning etc., then the custody officer must release him, and may so release him either unconditionally or on bail (PACE 1984, s. 37(1) and (2)). If bailed, the condition of bail will be to return to the station on a specified future date. Similarly, if the officer conducting a review of detention as required by s. 40 of the 1984 Act concludes that detention without charge can no longer be justified, then he must release the detainee with or without bail (s. 40(8)). A similar decision must be taken at the end of 24 hours' detention without charge unless the detainee is suspected of a serious arrestable offence and a senior officer authorises his continued detention for up to 36 hours (s. 41(7)). If continued detention is so authorised, release with or without bail must be allowed at the expiry of the 36 hours, unless application is successfully made to a magistrates' court for a warrant of further detention (s. 42(10)). In short, whenever it is determined that an arrested detainee who has not been charged can no longer properly be held at the police station, the officer making that decision must also take the secondary decision of whether to release the detainee unconditionally or bail him to reattend at the station.

Bail Following Charge

D5.3   Where a person has been arrested (otherwise than on a warrant backed for bail) and is then charged at the police station, the custody officer must decide: (a) whether to keep him in custody at the police station until he can be brought before a magistrates' court or to release him; and (b) if the decision is to release him, whether to do so unconditionally or on bail (PACE 1984, s. 38(1)). Almost invariably a person who has been charged will, if released, be released on bail with a requirement to attend at the magistrates' court on a specified day, that is, he will not be released unconditionally. The specified day must be that of the next available court sitting (CDA 1998, s. 46, inserting s. 47(3A) into the 1984 Act: s. 46 is in force throughout England and Wales from 1 November 1999).

Warrants Backed for Bail

D5.4   In all cases where a magistrate or a court determines to issue a warrant for arrest, the warrant may be endorsed with a direction that the person named in it – having been arrested – shall be released on bail. This is known as 'backing the warrant for bail'. As regards the power of magistrates to back a warrant for bail, see MCA 1980, s. 117; as regards the power of the Crown Court to do so, see Supreme Court Act 1981, s. 81(4). The principal situations in which it falls to magistrates or courts to issue warrants for arrest (and hence to decide whether or not to back them for bail) are:

(a)   when an information is laid before a magistrate and he decides to issue a warrant for the arrest of the person named in the information rather than issuing a summons;

(b)   when a person fails to attend a magistrates' court in answer to a summons, the court determines not to proceed in his absence, and the conditions in the MCA 1980, s. 13, for the issue of a warrant are satisfied; and

(c)   when a person granted bail to attend at either the Crown Court or a magistrates' court fails to appear, in which case a 'bench warrant' may be issued under the BA 1976, s. 7.

Bail by Magistrates' Court

A magistrates' court, on adjourning a case and determining to remand the accused, may   **D5.5** remand him in custody or on bail (see MCA 1980, ss. 5(1), 10(1) and 18(4) for the jurisdiction to adjourn and remand when, respectively, the court is inquiring into an offence as examining justices, trying an information summarily or determining mode of trial for an offence triable either way; and see also s. 128(1), which states that, whenever a magistrates' court has power to remand a person, it may either remand him in custody or remand him on bail in accordance with the BA 1976). For the time restrictions on remands in custody and the possibility of remanding an accused in his absence, see **D4.8** *et seq*. Magistrates also nave power to grant bail for the period of any remand for reports etc. after summary conviction (see MCA 1980, s. 10(3), and also s. 30(1) for remands on bail for medical examination). Where a magistrates' court determines to commit an accused to the Crown Court for trial, it may either order that he be kept in custody or release him on bail (s. 6(8) of the 1980 Act). Similarly, committals for sentence under either s. 37 or s. 38 of the 1980 Act may be in custody or on bail. Where a magistrates' court has summarily convicted an accused and passed a custodial sentence, it may grant him bail pending the determination of an appeal (s. 113 of the 1980 Act, which applies both when the accused has given notice of appeal to the Crown Court and when he has asked the magistrates to state a case for the opinion of the Divisional Court). Finally, where the magistrates are sending a defendant to the Crown Court for trial under the CDA 1998, s. 51, which relates to indictable-only offences (see **D8.21**), they may do so in custody or on bail.

Bail by the Crown Court

The persons to whom the Crown Court may grant bail are listed in the Supreme Court   **D5.6** Act 1981, s. 81(1)(a) to (g). They are as follows:

(a)   any person committed to the Crown Court in custody by a magistrates' court (or in respect of whom a notice of transfer has been given under the CJA 1987, s. 4, or under the CJA 1991, s. 53);

(b)   any person summarily convicted and given a custodial sentence who is appealing to the Crown Court against his conviction and/or sentence;

(c)   any person who is in the custody of the Crown Court pending disposal of his case;

(d) and (e)   any person whose case has been decided by the Crown Court but who has applied to the court to state a case for the Divisional Court's opinion or is seeking certiorari to quash the decision;

(f)   any person to whom the Crown Court has granted a certificate that his case is fit for appeal to the Court of Appeal whether against conviction or against sentence, and whether on a question of law or fact; and

(g)   any person who has been remanded in custody by a magistrates' court on adjourning a case under the MCA 1980, s. 5, 10, 18 or 30, provided the magistrates' court has granted a certificate that, before refusing bail, it heard full argument.

The power in s. 81(1)(c) means that, whenever the Crown Court adjourns a trial or adjourns between conviction and sentence, it has a discretion to grant the accused bail for the period of the adjournment.

All the above powers are subject to the CJPO 1994, s. 25 (see **D5.10**).

Bail by the High Court

D5.7 The High Court has jurisdiction to grant bail to:

(a) any person who has been refused bail by a magistrates' court (CJA 1967, s. 22(1));
(b) any person who has applied to the Crown Court to state a case for the Divisional Court's opinion or who is seeking certiorari to quash the Crown Court's decision (CJA 1948, s. 37(1)(b)); and
(c) any person who has been convicted or sentenced by a magistrates' court and is seeking certiorari (s. 37(1)(d)).

All the above powers are subject to the CJPO 1994, s. 25 (see **D5.10**).

There is also jurisdiction to vary the terms on which bail was granted by a magistrates' court (CJA 1967, s. 22(1)). The High Court's jurisdiction to grant bail is customarily exercised by a single judge in chambers.

Bail by Court of Appeal

D5.8 The Court of Appeal has jurisdiction to grant bail to a person who has served notice of appeal or notice of application for leave to appeal against his conviction and/or sentence in the Crown Court (Criminal Appeal Act 1968, s. 19). The Court of Appeal also has power to bail a person who is appealing from it to the House of Lords (s. 36).

The above powers are subject to the CJPO 1994, s. 25 (see **D5.10**).

PRINCIPLES GOVERNING BAIL

Presumption in Favour of Bail

D5.9 Section 4(1) of the BA 1976, in combination with sch. 1 thereto, creates what may loosely be described as a presumption in favour of bail. It provides that: 'A person to whom this section applies shall be granted bail except as provided in schedule 1 to this Act'. Subsections (2) to (4) of s. 4 then define the persons to whom subsection (1) applies. They are:

(a) any person who appears before the Crown Court or a magistrates' court in the course of or in connection with proceedings for an offence, or applies to a court for bail in connection with the proceedings (s. 4(2));
(b) any person who has been convicted of an offence and whose case is adjourned for reports before sentencing (s. 4(4)); and
(c) any person subject to a probation, community service, combination or curfew order who is brought before a court to be dealt with for alleged breach of a requirement in the order (s. 4(3)).

Except as mentioned in (b) above, s. 4(1) does *not* apply once a person has been convicted of an offence (proviso to s. 4(2)). Therefore, an appellant seeking bail pending determination of his appeal has no 'right' to bail under s. 4. Neither does an offender who is committed to the Crown Court for sentence following conviction in a magistrates' court. In both those situations, there is power to grant bail, but its granting or refusal is entirely at the discretion of the court to which application is made and there is no initial presumption either way. It will also be noted that s. 4(1) does not apply to bail from the police station, although, once a detainee has been charged, the PACE 1984, s. 38(1), imposes on the custody officer a duty to grant him bail unless its refusal can be justified on grounds similar to those which would justify refusing bail to a person prima facie entitled to bail under s. 4(1). Despite the fact that there is no presumption in favour of bail in the situations mentioned above, it nevertheless remains the case that, if bail should be granted, it would be 'bail in criminal proceedings' within the definition in the BA 1976, s. 1(1). Therefore, the general provisions of the Act concerning bail in criminal proceedings apply (e.g., if the person bailed fails without reasonable cause to surrender he commits an offence under s. 6).

In *Rafferty* [1998] 2 Cr App R (S) 449, the Court of Appeal dealt with the position where an accused gives an indication, as part of the plea before venue procedure (see **D3.4**), that he will plead guilty, and is then committed for sentence to the Crown Court. Their lordships stated that, in most such cases, it would not be usual to alter the position as regards bail or custody. When a person who had been on bail pleaded guilty at the plea before venue, the usual practice should be to continue bail, even if it was anticipated that a custodial sentence would be imposed by the Crown Court, unless there were good reasons for remanding the accused in custody. If the defendant was in custody, then it would be unusual, if the reasons for remanding him in custody remained unchanged, to alter the position.

Part I of sch. 1 to the 1976 Act sets out the circumstances in which any accused may be refused bail if at least one offence with which he is charged (or for which he awaits sentence) is punishable with imprisonment. Part II applies when none of the offences are imprisonable.

No Bail for Homicide or Rape if Previous Conviction

The effect of the CJPO 1994, s. 25, is that the court may not grant bail to a defendant **D5.10** who is charged with (or has been convicted of) murder, attempted murder, manslaughter, rape or attempted rape, if he has been convicted of any of these offences (or culpable homicide) in the past unless it is satisfied that there are exceptional circumstances which justify it. In a case where the previous conviction was for manslaughter, the restriction applies only if the defendant received a custodial sentence for that offence. 'Conviction' is widely defined to include a finding that the defendant was not guilty by reason of insanity, or was found to have done the act or made the omission charged in a case where he was unfit to plead.

Criminal Justice and Public Order Act 1994, s. 25

(1) A person who in any proceedings has been charged with or convicted of an offence to which this section applies in circumstances to which it applies shall be granted bail in those proceedings only if the court or, as the case may be, the constable considering the grant of bail is satisfied that there are exceptional circumstances which justify it.

(2) This section applies, subject to subsection (3) below, to the following offences, that is to say—

    (a) murder;
    (b) attempted murder;
    (c) manslaughter;
    (d) rape; or
    (e) attempted rape.

(3) This section applies to a person charged with or convicted of any such offence only if he has been previously convicted by or before a court in any part of the United Kingdom of any such offence or of culpable homicide and, in the case of a previous conviction of manslaughter or of culpable homicide, if he was then sentenced to imprisonment or, if he was then a child or young person, to long-term detention under any of the relevant enactments.

(4) This section applies whether or not an appeal is pending against conviction or sentence.

(5) In this section—

'conviction' includes—

(a) a finding that a person is not guilty by reason of insanity;

(b) a finding under section 4A(3) of the Criminal Procedure (Insanity) Act 1964 (cases of unfitness to plead) that a person did the act or made the omission charged against him; and

(c) a conviction of an offence for which an order is made placing the offender on probation or discharging him absolutely or conditionally;

and 'convicted' shall be construed accordingly; and

'the relevant enactments' means—

(a) as respects England and Wales, section 53(2) of the Children and Young Persons Act 1933;

(b) as respects Scotland, sections 205(1) to (3) and 208 of the Criminal Procedure (Scotland) Act 1995;

(c) as respects Northern Ireland, section 73(2) of the Children and Young Persons Act (Northern Ireland) 1968.

(6) This section does not apply in relation to proceedings instituted before its commencement.

Refusing Bail to an Accused Charged with an Imprisonable Offence

D5.11 An unconvicted accused charged with an imprisonable offence need not be granted bail if one or more of five grounds for a remand in custody applies. These are listed in the BA 1976, sch. 1, part I, paras 2 to 7. The first – and most commonly relied on – ground subdivides into three. As regards offenders convicted but remanded for reports, there is a sixth ground on which reliance may also be placed. The grounds for refusing bail are as follows.

D5.12 *Risk of Absconding, Further Offences or Interference with Witnesses*

Bail Act 1976, sch. 1

2. The defendant need not be granted bail if the court is satisfied that there are substantial grounds for believing that the defendant, if released on bail (whether subject to conditions or not) would—

(a) fail to surrender to custody, or

(b) commit an offence while on bail, or

(c) interfere with witnesses or otherwise obstruct the course of justice, whether in relation to himself or any other person.

The opening part of the paragraph is carefully phrased. It does *not* require the court to be satisfied that the consequences specified in subparagraphs (a) to (c) actually would occur in the event of bail being granted, or even to be satisfied that they would be more likely than not to occur. The court merely has to be satisfied that there are substantial grounds for believing that they would occur. In other words, it is the grounds rather than the putative event itself about which the court must be satisfied. On the other hand, it is not enough for the justices simply to have a subjective perception of a risk of failure to surrender to custody etc. (per Lord Lane CJ in *Mansfield Justices, ex parte Sharkey* [1985] QB 613 at p. 625C–E, where he contrasts the less rigorous requirements which attach when the question is whether a man who is being granted bail should be granted it subject to conditions with the stricter requirements applying when the question is whether bail should be refused altogether – in the former situation the court need only perceive a real rather than fanciful risk of absconding etc., whereas in the latter situation the perception must be based on substantial grounds).

A decision that there are substantial grounds for believing that the accused would abscond, commit offences or interfere with witnesses amounts to a finding of the court, and therefore sets up something akin to a *res iudicata*. Accordingly, in *Nottingham Justices, ex parte Davies* [1981] QB 38, it was held that an accused who had earlier been remanded in custody by a magistrates' court and was appearing before another bench at the end of the remand period, could not reopen the question of whether grounds for belief under para. 2 existed unless fresh considerations had arisen in the interim which were not before the bench originally refusing bail. The decision in *Ex parte Davies* has now been subsumed in part IIA of sch. 1 to the Act, but it would still seem to be good law as to the status of findings that there are grounds for refusing bail.

Although the question posed by para. 2 is whether substantial grounds exist for believing that a future event would occur and to that extent is a question of fact, it is not a question which can be answered according to the usual rules of evidence. Thus in *Re Moles* [1981] Crim LR 170 it was held that a police officer explaining the objections to bail was entitled to recount what he had been told by a potential witness about the threats the latter had received, with a view to showing that the granting of bail would lead to further interference with witnesses. In *Ex parte Sharkey* Lord Lane referred to *Re Moles* and said (at p. 626A): ' . . . there is no requirement for formal evidence to be given [at an application for bail] . . . It was for example sufficient for the facts to be related to the justices at second hand by a police officer.' Current practice when presenting objections to bail in a magistrates' court is not even to have a police officer present, but for the CPS representative to argue that bail is inappropriate on the basis of a police pro forma included in the file.

Certain factors to which the court should have regard when taking a decision under para. 2 are listed in para. 9. These factors are:

    (a)   the nature and seriousness of the offence and the probable method of dealing with the offender for it;
    (b)   the character, antecedents, associations and community ties of the accused;
    (c)   his 'record' for having answered bail in the past; and
    (d)   the strength of the evidence against him.

These factors are largely self-explanatory. As to (a), the gravity of the charge is not an automatic reason for refusing bail (although, by virtue of the CJPO 1994, s. 25, a defendant must normally be refused bail where the charge is, for example, homicide or rape and he has previously been convicted of such an offence (see **D5.10**)). However, the relevance of the offence alleged being serious is that the accused will know that, if convicted, he is likely to receive a severe sentence and will therefore be tempted to abscond rather than run the risk of such a sentence. A similar argument applies where the offence in itself is less serious but, having regard to the accused's previous record (in particular the fact that a conviction would put him in breach of a suspended sentence or other court order), a severe sentence is likely in his case notwithstanding that an offender of good character might expect to be dealt with by non-custodial means. This is one way in which the accused's 'character and antecedents' (see subparagraph (b)) are relevant to bail decisions. The other, obviously, is that a man of previous good character is more likely to be trusted by the courts than one with a record. Previous convictions under the BA 1976, s. 6, for failing to surrender to custody in answer to bail are especially relevant (see subparagraph (c)). (For the effect of the CJPO 1994, s. 26, which restricts the 'right to bail' where a defendant is charged with an offence which is indictable or triable either way and which appears to have been committed while he was on bail, see **D5.18**.) 'Community ties' (referred to in subparagraph (b)) encompass matters such as how long the accused has lived at his present address, whether he is married or single, in employment or not, and whether he is buying or renting his house or merely 'squatting'. An accused of 'no fixed abode' or living in short-term accommodation is not automatically debarred from bail, but the ease with which he could disappear to another address is a factor to be considered. The consideration mentioned in (d) – the strength of the prosecution evidence – is relevant to whether an accused would answer bail in the sense that one who knows there is a good chance of being acquitted is less likely to abscond than one who anticipates almost certain conviction. Perhaps, though, the primary relevance of this factor to a court's thinking is that a remand in custody followed by acquittal creates a manifest, if sometimes unavoidable, injustice. In borderline cases, where the arguments against bail are strong but not overwhelming, the court may prefer to run the risk of the accused absconding etc. rather than run the risk of his being acquitted after a long period in custody on remand.

The considerations mentioned in para. 9(a) to (d) are *not* exhaustive; the court is also to have regard to 'any other things which appear relevant'. Amongst those 'other things' might be the fact that the accused has previously committed offences while on bail; his having allegedly committed the present offence while on bail for something else (but see **D5.18**); his having failed to answer to his bail after previous adjournments during the current proceedings; and the suggestion that potential prosecution witnesses have already received threats and/or are known to the accused and could easily be contacted by him if he were at liberty.

D5.13 ***Own Protection*** By the BA 1976, sch. 1, part I, para. 3, an accused need not be granted bail if the court is satisfied that he should be kept in custody for his own protection. This will cover cases where the offence alleged has caused anger in the area where it was committed and there is a risk of members of the public exacting instant revenge on the person believed to be responsible. Where the accused is a juvenile, bail may also be refused if he should be kept in custody 'for his own welfare' (ibid.).

D5.14 ***Already in Custody*** By the BA 1976, sch. 1, part I, para. 4, an accused need not be granted bail if he is already serving a custodial sentence (whether imposed by a civilian court or by a court-martial). The paragraph applies only if the accused is in custody pursuant to a sentence, not when he is in custody as a result of a remand in other proceedings currently outstanding against him, although in the latter situation bail could almost cerainly be refused under para. 2 if the court so wished. In fact, courts often find it more convenient to remand an accused certain to be in custody for the foreseeable future as a result of other matters on technical bail. This avoids the restrictions on the periods for which remands in custody may be ordered and the consequent need to bring the accused back to court for a further remand hearing. A frequently occurring practical problem where an accused is in custody to another court or is a serving prisoner is that the prison staff are unwilling to bring him to court when required. The onus is on the CPS to obtain a Home Office production order (HOPO) obliging the prison service to arrange for the accused's attendance, but even Home Office production orders by no means always have the desired result.

D5.15 ***Insufficient Time*** By the BA 1976, sch. 1, part I, para. 5, the accused need not be granted bail if the court is satisfied that, owing to lack of time since the commencement of the proceedings, it has not been practicable to obtain sufficient information for the purposes of taking the decisions required to be taken by the other paragraphs. In such cases, the court might remand in custody for seven days (or even for a shorter period) to enable the necessary information to be discovered. Examples where para. 5 might apply are if the police are not satisfied that the accused has given them his correct particulars and think he may have previous convictions under another name, or if time is needed to check an address given by the accused, or if inquiries are still in hand which may reveal the offence to be more serious than originally supposed and/or that the accused has committed additional offences. It is submitted that para. 5 should be relied on sparingly, and should not be used to justify dilatoriness in marshalling the objections to bail.

A remand in custody under para. 5 does not amount to a decision not to grant bail for the purposes of para. 2 of part IIA. In other words, it does not restrict further applications for bail (see **D5.36**).

Absconded in the Present Proceedings By the BA 1976, sch. 1, part I, para. 6, bail **D5.16** need not be granted if the accused has already been released on bail in the present proceedings and then has been arrested under the BA 1976, s. 7. Section 7 sanctions the arrest of a person bailed if: either he fails to surrender to custody as required and the court issues a bench warrant for his arrest; or a police officer has reasonable grounds for believing that he will fail to surrender to custody and/or break a condition of bail; or he has in fact broken a condition of bail; or he was bailed subject to a requirement for sureties and a surety has withdrawn.

Reports By the BA 1976, sch. 1, part I, para. 7, if the case of a convicted offender is **D5.17** adjourned for inquiries or reports, he need not be granted bail if it appears to the court that it would be impracticable to complete the inquiries or make the report without keeping him in custody (e.g., because he would not voluntarily attend for purposes such as seeing a probation officer or being medically examined). Leaving aside the special circumstances posited by para. 7, it has been held that, where a court needs a social inquiry report or community service assessment before it will be in a position to decide the appropriate sentence, the normal practice should be to grant bail unless there are exceptional reasons for keeping the offender in custody. This is especially so where the court, in order to impose a custodial sentence, has to be satisfied after considering reports that such a sentence is the only appropriate disposition (*McGoldrick* v *Normand* 1988 SLT 273). Although this was a Scottish case, in which the judgment was delivered by Lord Grieve in the High Court of Justiciary, the statement of principle would seem to be equally applicable to English courts. The reason why bail is normally appropriate is that a remand in custody might appear to be prejudging the question of whether the ultimate sentence should be custodial.

No 'Right to Bail' for Certain Offences Committed on Bail

The CJPO 1994, s. 26, states that the court need not grant bail to a defendant who **D5.18** appears to have committed an offence which is triable on indictment only, or triable either way, if he was on bail at the time when he allegedly committed it.

The fact that an offence was allegedly committed while the defendant was on bail may in any case be a relevant matter for consideration under sch. 1, para. 9 (see **D5.12**).

Refusing Bail to an Accused Charged with a Non-imprisonable Offence

Part II of sch. 1 to the BA 1976 sets out the reasons justifying refusal of bail to an accused **D5.19** charged solely with non-imprisonable offences. Three of those reasons are identical to reasons for refusing bail to an accused charged with an imprisonable offence, namely, that he should be kept in custody for his own protection (or welfare in the case of a juvenile), that he is serving a sentence, or that he has been arrested in pursuance of s. 7 of the 1976 Act. The grounds of 'risk of absconding etc.,' and 'insufficient time' for refusing bail to accused charged with imprisonable offences do *not* apply where the offences are non-imprisonable. However, one reason applies only in such cases, namely, that the accused has absconded on a previous occasion after being granted bail in criminal proceedings and, in view of that, the court believes that he would fail to surrender to custody if granted bail on the present occasion.

Bail and Custody Time-limits

Grafted on to the general system of a 'right to bail' which is lost if one of the exceptions **D5.20** defined in sch. 1 to the BA 1976 applies, are special rules applying where the prosecution fail to comply with a custody time-limit. Such limits have been introduced by the

Prosecution of Offences (Custody Time Limits) Regulations 1987 (SI 1987 No. 299) made by the Secretary of State in exercise of the powers given to him by the Prosecution of Offences Act 1985, s. 22 (see **D10.4** for full discussion). Regulation 8 modifies the BA 1976 in that, where a custody time-limit has expired, the words 'except as provided in Schedule 1 to this Act' are treated as omitted from s. 4(1) of the Act. The effect of that is to give the accused an absolute right to bail. Moreover, s. 3 of the 1976 Act (which deals with the conditions which may be imposed when granting bail) is also modified so as to prevent a court, when bailing an accused entitled to bail by reason of the expiry of a custody time-limit, from imposing requirements of a surety or deposit of security or any other condition which has to be complied with *before* release on bail (although it can impose conditions such as residence, curfew or reporting to a police station which have to be complied with after release).

Further, reg. 6(6) expressly states that, where the Crown Court is notified that an accused in custody pending his trial on indictment has the benefit of a custody time-limit and that it is about to expire, then it must grant him bail as from the expiry of the time-limit. By reg. 6(1) to (5), the prosecution are obliged to notify the Crown Court at least five days before the limit's expiry of whether they intend to ask the Crown Court to impose conditions on the grant of bail. They must also arrange for the accused to be brought before the court within the two days preceding expiry. The above is without prejudice to the prosecution's right to apply for an extension of the time-limit under the Prosecution of Offences Act 1985, s. 22(3). The 1987 Regulations make no express provision as to the procedure to be adopted in a magistrates' court when a custody time-limit is about to expire – the fact that an accused not granted bail has to appear before the magistrates at regular intervals, by reason of the restrictions on the period for which he may be remanded in custody at that stage of the proceedings, perhaps makes it unnecessary to provide expressly for bringing him before the court in anticipation of the expiry of a custody time-limit.

INCIDENTS OF BAIL

Introduction

D5.21 The BA 1976, s. 3, governs the duties resting on a person granted bail in criminal proceedings and the various requirements which may be attached to a grant of bail.

Duty to Surrender to Custody

D5.22 A person granted bail in criminal proceedings is under a duty to surrender to custody (BA 1976, s. 3(1)). 'Surrender to custody' is defined in s. 2(2) as surrendering into the custody of the court the accused has been bailed to attend, or – if he was bailed to reattend at a police station – surrendering to the custody of a constable at the station. For the problem of what precisely is meant by surrendering to the custody of a court, whether it merely entails reporting to an usher at the court building or extends to being in the dock when the case is called on, see **D5.44**. The date and place at which the accused should surrender is fixed when bail is granted, save that when he is committed to the Crown Court for trial or sentence the obligation is to surrender on the day his case comes up for hearing, it never being possible to notify him of the hearing date at the time of transfer. The date originally fixed for surrender to custody may be varied to a later date (see MCA 1980, ss. 43 and 129, for a magistrates' court's powers in this respect). Failure without reasonable cause to surrender to custody is an offence under the BA 1976, s. 6. The introduction of the s. 6 offence coincided with the abolition of the former system whereby the person bailed entered into a recognisance to secure his own attendance and might be ordered to forfeit the amount of the recognisance if he absconded. By s. 3(2) of the 1976 Act an accused granted bail in criminal proceedings may no longer be bailed on his own recognisance (cf. the position where bail is granted otherwise than in criminal proceedings). The accused may, however, be required to provide other people to stand surety for him (see **D5.23**; or he may be required to give security for his surrender to custody (see **D5.24**).

A person granted bail subject to no conditions or requirements other than the requirement of surrendering to custody at the end of the period of bail is said to be granted 'unconditional bail'. A person granted bail subject to any of the requirements described below is said to be on 'conditional bail'.

Sureties

A person granted bail in criminal proceedings may be required before release on bail to **D5.23** provide one or more sureties to secure his surrender to custody (BA 1976, s. 3(4)). Unlike s. 3(6) (which deals with requirements other than sureties), s. 3(4) does not state that the requirement must be imposed by a court. It follows that a custody officer bailing a detainee from a police station is as much entitled to ask for sureties as is a court. Neither does s. 3(4) of itself place any fetter on the court or officer's discretion to demand a surety (cf. s. 3(6)). However, sch. 1, part I, para. 8 provides that no conditions shall be imposed under any of subsections (4) to (7) of s. 3 unless that appears to the court necessary to prevent the occurrence of any of the events mentioned in sch. 1, part I (i.e. the absconding of the defendant, the commission of further offences by him or his interfering with witnesses etc). A surety's only obligation is to ensure the accused's attendance at court – he is not expected to prevent further offences or interference with witnesses. It follows that sureties should be required only in cases where there appears to be a risk of absconding. For discussion of the kind of material entitling the court to apprehend the occurrence of a para. 2 event and hence to be entitled to impose a requirement (whether for a surety or otherwise), see **D5.12**.

The BA 1976, s. 8, contains detailed provisions about the taking of sureties. In considering whether a proposed surety is suitable, regard may be had, *inter alia*, to (a) his financial resources, (b) his character and previous convictions and (c) his relationship to the person for whom he stands surety (s. 8(2)). When a surety is taken in court, it is the invariable practice to ask him how he would pay the sum in which he is to stand surety were the accused to abscond. It is also standard practice for the police to check whether the surety has previous convictions; if he has, and depending on their age and nature, objection may be made to him as surety. If no satisfactory surety is forthcoming at court, the court simply fixes the amount in which the surety is to be bound and the accused remains in custody until the court's requirement can be fulfilled (s. 8(3)). To facilitate early release where the sureties are not at court, they may enter into their recognisances outside court (s. 8(4)). Paragraphs (a) to (d) of s. 8(4), in conjunction with the Magistrates' Courts Rules 1981, r. 86(1), and the Crown Court Rules 1982, r. 20, list the persons who may accept a surety's recognisance. They are: a justice of the peace; a justices' clerk; a police officer who is either of or above the rank of inspector or is in charge of a police station; the governor of the prison or remand centre where the accused is being held; or, if bail has been granted by the Crown Court, an officer of that court. The court granting bail may, however, specify the person (or class of person) before whom the surety is to be taken or require that the surety be taken in court (opening words of s. 8(4)). If a person asked to accept a surety outside court refuses to do so because he is not satisfied about the surety's suitability, the surety may apply either to the court which granted bail or to a magistrates' court for the area where he resides to take his recognisance (s. 8(5)).

The normal consequence for the surety if the person for whom he stands surety fails to answer to his bail is that the surety is ordered to forfeit the entire sum in which he stood surety (see **D5.48** *et seq*. for further detail).

Deposit of Security

A person granted bail may be required to give security for his surrender to custody, i.e. **D5.24** deposit with the court money or some other valuable item which will be liable to forfeiture in the event of non-attendance in answer to bail (BA 1976, s. 3(5)). The security may be given either by the accused himself or by somebody on his behalf (ibid.). The comments made at **D5.23** about when sureties may be required apply equally to a requirement for security (i.e. the requirement may be imposed either on bail from the police station or on bail by a court, but only if it is considered necessary to prevent absconding). Where security has been given in pursuance of s. 3(5) and the person bailed absconds, the court may, unless there appears to have been reasonable cause for the failure to surrender to custody, order forfeiture of the security (see s. 5(7) to (9)).

General Discretionary Requirements Imposable

D5.25 By the BA 1976, s. 3(6), a person bailed may be required by a court to comply with such requirements as appear to the court necessary to secure that he (a) surrenders to custody, (b) does not commit an offence on bail, (c) does not interfere with witnesses or otherwise obstruct the course of justice, and (d) makes himself available for the making of inquiries or a report to assist in sentencing. Section 3(6) is largely duplicated by para. 8(1) of part I of sch. 1 insofar as imprisonable offences are concerned.

Bail Act 1976, sch. 1, part I

8.—(1) . . . where the defendant is granted bail, no conditions shall be imposed under subsections (4) to (7) (except subsection (6)(d) or (e)) of section 3 of this Act unless it appears to the court that it is necessary to do so for the purpose of preventing the occurrence of any of the events mentioned in paragraph 2 of this part of this schedule.

The events mentioned in para. 2 of part I of sch. 1 are precisely the same as those mentioned in paras (a) to (c) of s. 3(6): failure to surrender to custody, further offences and interference with witnesses. There is thus an almost complete overlap between s. 3(6) itself and sch. 1, part I, para. 8. This was attributed by Lord Lane CJ in *Mansfield Justices, ex parte Sharkey* [1985] QB 613 to 'indifferent drafting' (at p. 625C). The contention advanced by counsel for the applicants in that case – namely that, by incorporating in itself a reference to para. 2, para. 8 impliedly restricted the imposition of requirements to cases where the court was satisfied that there were substantial grounds for believing that one of the adverse consequences would occur unless bail was made conditional – was rejected by the Divisional Court. There is thus a distinction to be drawn between that which the court must be satisfied about in order to refuse bail to an accused prima facie entitled to it under s. 4(1) and that which it must be satisfied about in order to impose conditions on a grant of bail. Having quoted s. 3(6) and para. 8, Lord Lane in *Ex parte Sharkey* explained their effect in the context of a condition imposed to prevent further offences. His lordship said (at p. 625E):

In the present circumstances the question the justices should ask themselves is a simple one: 'Is this condition necessary for the prevention of the commission of an offence when on bail?' They are not obliged to have substantial grounds. *It is enough if they perceive a real and not a fanciful risk of the offence being committed.* Thus, section 3(6) and paragraph 8 give the court a wide discretion to inquire whether the condition is necessary. [Emphasis added.]

On the facts of *Ex parte Sharkey*, the justices were entitled to impose in respect of accused arrested on suspicion of public order offences allegedly committed by them while on duty as flying pickets during the miners' strike of 1984–85, conditions of bail that they should not in future picket otherwise than peacefully at their own pits. The justices were *not* obliged to have substantial grounds for believing that a repetition of the accused's conduct would occur. It was enough that they perceived a real risk of that happening. Moreover, they were entitled to base that perception on their local knowledge of what had been happening during the picketing of pits in the area. The fact that the accused were of previous good character and, having regard to the relatively trivial nature of the offences alleged, would normally have been granted unconditional bail was irrelevant in the particular circumstances of the case. The justices were, however, under a duty to exercise their discretion to impose conditions judicially in each individual case – a blanket policy of imposing conditions in all cases where a flying picket was charged with an offence under the Public Order Act 1936 would have been wrong. Although given in the context of determining the legality of conditions imposed to prevent offences while on bail, the Lord Chief Justice's judgment is obviously applicable, *mutatis mutandis*, to conditions designed to prevent absconding or interference with witnesses.

In *Bournemouth Magistrates' Court, ex parte Cross* [1989] Crim LR 207, the point at issue was whether conditions could be imposed on bail for non-imprisonable offences. C was a hunt protester who was arrested for an offence under the Public Order Act 1986, s. 5 (which is not an imprisonable offence). He was bailed on condition he did not attend another hunt meeting before his next court appearance. He was arrested for alleged breach of this condition, and remanded in custody. On application for judicial review, the Divisional Court held that the condition had been validly imposed. The magistrates had been of the view that it was necessary to prevent the commission of further offences, and they were entitled to impose it by the BA 1976, s. 3(6).

Conditions frequently imposed in reliance on paras (a) to (c) of s. 3(6) include:

(a) a condition of residence, frequently expressed as a condition that the accused is to live and sleep at a specified address;

(b) a condition that the accused is to notify any changes of address to the police;

(c) a condition of reporting (whether daily, weekly or at other intervals) to a local police station;

(d) a curfew (i.e. the accused must be indoors between certain hours);

(e) a condition that the accused is not to enter a certain area or building or go within a specified distance of a certain address;

(f) a condition that he is not to contact (whether directly or indirectly) the victim of the alleged offence and/or any other probable prosecution witness; and

(g) a condition that he is to surrender his passport to the police.

Conditions (a) to (c) and (g) are particularly relevant to reducing the risk of absconding. A special form of residential condition, which is not available to a constable granting police bail, is that the accused is to reside at a bail hostel or probation hostel. When imposing such a condition the court may, and no doubt normally will, impose an additional requirement that the accused is to comply with the rules of the hostel (s. 3(6ZA)). In the case of a convicted offender being remanded for reports, a requirement of residence at a hostel may be imposed not simply to reduce the risk of absconding but, additionally or alternatively, to assess his suitability for being ultimately dealt with by a means which would involve residence at a probation hostel (see the last words of sch. 1, part I, para. 8). Conditions (d) and (e) are designed to prevent further offences when on bail. A curfew may be appropriate where the offence with which the accused is charged was allegedly committed at night; a geographical restriction is useful if the offence was one of violence committed at a certain address (in effect the accused is ordered to stay well away from the address). Condition (f) minimises the risk of interference with witnesses.

Breach of conditions imposed under s. 3(6) may result in the accused being arrested without warrant and his bail being withdrawn. It should be noted that, unlike requirements for a surety or deposit of security, conditions under s. 3(6) may be imposed only by a court.

Condition of Cooperation in the Making of Reports or Taking of Legal Advice

One of the purposes for which the court may impose a requirement under the BA 1976, **D5.26** s. 3(6), is to ensure that the accused will make himself 'available for the purpose of enabling inquiries or a report to be made to assist the court in dealing with him for the offence' (see s. 3(6)(d)). For obvious reasons, such a requirement will not generally be considered until the stage of an adjournment between conviction and sentence. However, there are two situations in which the court is obliged – not merely empowered – to make a requirement under s. 3(6)(d), and both can arise even before conviction. The situations are:

(a)   *When a magistrates' court adjourns under the Magistrates' Courts Act 1980, s. 30(1), for a medical examination of the accused.* Such an adjournment is conditional on the court being satisfied that the accused committed the *actus reus* of the offence, but there is no need for a conviction to have been recorded. The underlying purpose of ordering the examination will be to discover whether the accused's mental condition is such that he might be dealt with by means such as a hospital order (whether with or without a prior conviction for the offence charged) or a probation order with a condition for medical treatment. By s. 30(2), where there is an adjournment under s. 30(1) and the magistrates determine to remand the accused on bail, the court *shall* impose conditions under s. 3(6)(d). Those conditions must include requirements that he: (i) submits to examination by a duly qualified medical practitioner (or, if the inquiry is into his mental condition and the court so directs, by two practitioners); and (ii) for the purpose of the examination, attends at such place or on such practitioner as the court directs and complies with any directions given by the practitioner.

(b)   *Bail on murder charges.* Where a court grants bail to an accused charged with murder, it must, unless satisfied that satisfactory reports on his mental condition have already been obtained, impose as conditions of bail requirements that he undergo examination by two medical practitioners (including one Home Office approved psychiatrist) and attend hospital etc. as directed for the purpose of the examination (BA 1976, s. 3(6A) and (6B)). The importance in such cases of obtaining full medical and, in particular, psychiatric reports on the accused while he is still on remand prior to trial or even committal is that the reports may lay the foundation for a defence of diminished responsibility or, alternatively, assist the prosecution in rebutting such a defence. Subsections (6A) and (6B) ensure that the reports will be forthcoming, even though the granting of bail precludes the necessary examinations being conducted while the accused is detained in prison or remand centre. Prior to the insertion of subsections (6A) and (6B) it had been stated by the Court of Appeal in *Vernege* [1982] 1 WLR 293 that, when considering the granting of bail to an accused being committed for trial for murder, the court was entitled to take into account the fact that the accused's own best interests might be served by a remand in custody, during which he could be examined by the prison doctor. In *Central Criminal Court, ex parte Porter* [1992] Crim LR 121, the Divisional Court said that the power to impose a condition requiring a medical report arose at the time of granting bail. Further, if no such condition was imposed, then the decision to grant bail would be a nullity. As far as the disclosure of a medical report obtained pursuant to subsection (6A) was concerned, that was within the discretion of the trial judge when he had seen the report (or, exceptionally, the discretion of such other judge as had to conduct any pre-trial review).

The court has power to require a defendant, as a condition of bail, to attend an interview with a legal adviser before his next appearance in court (BA 1976, s. 3(6)(e)). The aim is to save the time of the court by ensuring that he receives legal advice, in advance of the hearing, to decide on how to respond to the charge. Clearly, if the defendant indicates that he does not wish to be legally represented, such a condition should not be imposed. If the condition is attached, then the defendant should be told of the consequences of failing to comply. Guidance issued to judges and magistrates has made it clear that, if the defendant fails to attend an interview, his solicitor should not be expected to report the breach of the condition (Home Office Circular 34/1998).

Requirement that a Parent Standing Surety for a Juvenile Secures Compliance with Conditions of Bail

The general rule is that the obligations of a surety extend only to securing the accused's **D5.27** attendance at court. A surety is *not* responsible for preventing any other possible defaults of the accused while on bail (e.g., his intimidating witnesses or breaching a condition of bail). The last proposition is subject to the BA 1976, s. 3(7), which provides that, where the accused is a juvenile and his parent or guardian stands surety for him, the court may require the parent or guardian to secure that the juvenile complies with any condition of bail imposed by virtue of s. 3(6). A requirement under s. 3(7) can be imposed only with the consent of the parent or guardian, and the sum in which he binds himself may not exceed £50.

It will be appreciated that s. 3(7) is of very limited application. However, in cases where the prosecution object to bail on the basis that the accused (be he adult or juvenile) is likely to commit further offences, some magistrates' courts avoid the limitations on s. 3(7) by asking both for a surety under the BA 1976 to secure the accused's attendance at court and also for a surety to secure his good behaviour. The latter demand is not made under the BA 1976 but under the general powers given to magistrates by the Justices of the Peace Act 1361 and the Justices of the Peace Act 1968, s. 1(7) (see **E15** for the power to bind persons over to keep the peace and be of good behaviour). One problem with using the powers in the Justices of the Peace Acts 1361 and 1968 in the context of a grant of bail is that binding over to keep the peace is only appropriate where the court has reason to fear a future breaking of the peace, for example, the repetition of an offence of violence or the like. It is therefore difficult to see how a surety for the good behaviour of a person bailed can properly be demanded if the offence charged is not one which in itself involved a breach of the peace. Also, a court requiring a surety for good behaviour as a condition for granting bail would seem to be contravening the BA 1976, s. 3(3)(c), which provides that, 'Except as provided *by this section* . . . no other requirement shall be imposed [on the accused] as a condition of bail' (emphasis added).

Applications to Vary the Conditions of Bail

Where bail has been granted in criminal proceedings subject to conditions, the **D5.28** defendant may apply for the conditions to be varied (BA 1976, s. 3(8)(a)). The application should be made to the court which granted bail (or, in the case of a committal for trial or sentence, the Crown Court). Furthermore, the prosecution may make a similar application either for existing conditions to be varied or, in a case where the court originally granted unconditional bail, for conditions to be imposed (s. 3(8)(b)). It should also be noted that the CJA 1967, s. 22, gives the High Court jurisdiction to vary the terms of bail whenever a magistrates' court has granted it subject to conditions.

SUPPLEMENTARY PROVISIONS RELATING TO DECISIONS ABOUT BAIL

Introduction

Section 5 of the BA 1976 imposes on courts and persons taking decisions in respect of **D5.29** bail a number of supplementary duties.

Duty to Make a Record of the Decision

A court or police officer granting bail in criminal proceedings, a court refusing bail to an **D5.30** accused prima facie entitled to bail under s. 4(1) of the 1976 Act, a court appointing a different time or place for a person already granted bail to surrender to custody, and a court imposing or varying conditions of bail are all under a duty to make a record of the decision (BA 1976, s. 5(1)). The record should be 'in the prescribed form', that is, in the form prescribed by the Magistrates' Courts Rules 1981 (SI 1981 No. 552) or the

Crown Court Rules 1982 (SI 1982 No. 1109) if the decision in question was taken by a court and in the form prescribed by the Secretary of State if the decision was by a police officer (s. 5(1) and (10)). The person in respect of whom the decision was made is entitled to a copy of the record on request (ibid.). By the Magistrates' Courts Rules 1981, r. 90, any record relating to bail that a magistrates' court is required to make must be entered in the court register and must contain the particulars set out in the appropriate forms (i.e. forms 149 to 153 of the Magistrates' Courts (Forms) Rules 1981 (SI 1981 No. 553)). As to Crown Court decisions on bail, the Crown Court Rules 1982, r. 19(8), requires the record to be entered into the court file for the case and to include: (a) the effect of the decision; (b) a statement of any condition imposed in respect of bail or, in a case where the conditions of bail have been varied, a statement of the conditions as varied; and (c) where bail is withheld, a statement of the paragraph of sch. 1 to the BA 1976 on which the decision was based.

Reasons for Withholding Bail or Imposing Conditions

D5.31 Where a magistrates' court or Crown Court: (a) withholds bail from an accused prima facie entitled to bail under the BA 1976, s. 4(1), or (b) imposes conditions on the grant of bail to such a person (or varies conditions already imposed upon him), it must give reasons for withholding bail or, as the case may be, imposing or varying conditions of bail (BA 1976, s. 5(3)). The purpose of giving the reasons is to enable the accused to consider making an application for bail (or for the variation or removal of conditions of bail) to another court. A note of the reasons must be included in the record of the court's decision (s. 5(4)). Also, the accused must be given a copy of the note (ibid.), unless he is legally represented, in which case a copy need be provided only if his counsel or solicitor so requests (s. 5(5)). It should be noted that the obligation to give reasons under s. 5(4) only arises if the accused has the benefit of s. 4(1). If, for example, bail pending appeal is refused to a person summarily convicted and given a custodial sentence, the court is under no duty to explain the refusal, since the case falls outside s. 4(1).

Reasons for Granting Bail in Serious Cases

D5.32 By para. 9A of part I of sch. 1 to the BA 1976, a court granting bail to an accused charged with murder, manslaughter, rape, attempted murder or attempted rape must, in any case where the prosecution has made representations as to any of the matters mentioned in para. 2 of part I of sch. 1, state its reasons and include them in the record of proceedings. Even in cases where the accused is charged with one of the offences listed in para. 9A, it is clear that the presumption in favour of bail contained in s. 4(1) of the 1976 Act still applies. The effect of para. 9A is that, if the prosecution raises one of the statutory exceptions to that presumption, but the court nonetheless decides to grant bail, it must state its reasons for doing so.

Informing Unrepresented Accused of his Right to Apply to Other Courts

D5.33 A magistrates' court which withholds bail from an unrepresented accused must inform him of the other courts to which he may make further application for bail (BA 1976, s. 5(6)). The duty under s. 5(6) arises even in respect of persons not entitled to bail under s. 4(1). If the accused is being committed for trial or if a certificate of full argument (see **D5.34**) has been issued, he must be told that he may apply either to the High Court or to the Crown Court; in all other cases, he is told that he may apply to the High Court (s. 5(6)). Where the accused is represented the court is under no duty to state the above, no doubt because Parliament anticipated that counsel or solicitor would in any event discuss the matter with his client.

Certificates of Full Argument

D5.34 Subsections (6A) to (6C) of s. 5 of the BA 1976 deal with certificates of full argument. Where a magistrates' court adjourns prior to or during committal, summary trial or proceedings to determine the mode of trial and remands the accused in custody after hearing a fully argued bail application, it must, subject to what follows, issue a certificate confirming that full argument was heard (s. 5(6A)). An adjournment during summary trial should be understood as including an adjournment for reports after conviction, so the obligation to issue a certificate may arise if the accused is remanded in custody at that stage. Moreover, the obligation to issue a certificate also applies where bail is refused on an adjournment under the MCA 1980, s. 30, for medical reports.

This only applies if either the court has not previously heard argument on a bail application made by the accused in the proceedings in question, or it has previously heard such argument but is satisfied that there has since then been a change in circumstances or that new considerations have been placed before it (s. 5(6A)(b)). Form 151A in the Magistrates' Courts (Forms) Rules 1981 (SI 1981 No. 553) sets out a precedent for a certificate. In a case where the court heard a second or subsequent fully argued application on the basis of a change in circumstances or new considerations, the certificate must state what the change etc. was (s. 5(6B)). The accused must be given a copy of the certificate (s. 5(6C)). The significance of the issue of a certificate of full argument is that the right to apply to the Crown Court for bail is dependent on it (Supreme Court Act 1981, s. 81(1)(g) and (1J)).

PROCEDURE FOR BAIL APPLICATIONS IN MAGISTRATES' COURTS

Application Procedure

D5.35 The Magistrates' Courts Rules 1981 (SI 1981 No. 552) do not specifically deal with the procedure to be followed when a person wishes to apply to a magistrates' court for bail in criminal proceedings. Assuming he is an accused with a prima facie right to bail by virtue of the BA 1976, s. 4(1), the onus is on the court to justify any refusal of bail in accordance with sch. 1 to the Act. This applies both when the accused first appears and at all subsequent appearances while he remains within the scope of s. 4(1) (see para. 1 of part IIA of sch. 1). However, where the accused has already been remanded in custody twice and on at least one of those occasions a fully argued application for bail was made, the magistrates may treat the finding of the previous bench that there were grounds for refusing bail as a form of *res iudicata*. They may therefore refuse to hear argument in favour of bail, and need consider the question only to the limited extent of satisfying themselves that the accused has exhausted the argued bail applications to which he is entitled as of right and that there has been no change of circumstances since the last argued application to entitle him to reopen the matter (see part IIA of sch. 1, which is discussed in detail at **D5.36**).

The question of bail is always for the court. However, when adjourning the case of an unconvicted accused who both has a right to bail under s. 4(1) and is also entitled to make an argued bail application under sch. 1, part IIA, normal practice is to ask the prosecution if they have any objections to bail. The prosecution representative then summarises the objections (or, as the case may be, states that there are no objections). Usually, there is included in the CPS file a standard form on which the police officer in the case outlines his objections to bail, if any. Counsel or solicitor has little alternative but to base his remarks on the police form, although he may have little means of assessing the validity or otherwise of the objections. Where the accused has a criminal record, a copy thereof may be handed in to the court, but as far as possible detailed oral reference to it should be avoided (*Dyson* (1943) 29 Cr App R 104). Following the prosecution objections, the defence representative (or the accused in person if unrepresented) may present the arguments for bail. Even where the defence choose not to make a bail application, it is submitted that the prosecution should still be prepared to present at least cursory objections to bail so that the court will be able to base a refusal on one of the reasons contained in sch. 1. Either party may adduce evidence in support of their respective arguments, for example, a police officer to substantiate the objections to bail or proposed sureties to further the application. Such witnesses give their evidence on the *voir dire* form of oath. Following the above, the court announces its decision. If it refuses bail to an accused entitled to it under s. 4(1) or imposes conditions on the grant of bail to such an accused, it must give its reasons (see s. 5(3)). The reasons are usually stated very briefly by reference to the paragraph of part I of sch. 1 on which reliance is placed. For the court's further duty to inform an unrepresented accused of his right to make further applications to other courts and to supply him with a copy of the reasons why bail was refused, see s. 5(6). Where bail is granted subject to sureties, the sureties may either be taken in court or outside court before certain specified categories of person (see s. 8). A bailed accused must be given on request a copy of the bail record which the court is required to make by s. 5(1).

Where a case is adjourned for reports following conviction, the prosecution are *not* usually asked if they object to bail. At this stage the question is conventionally regarded as one for the court, subject to representations from the defence. This may reflect the general rule that, in matters of sentencing, the prosecution stay neutral rather than trying to influence the court one way or the other.

Right to Make Repeated Argued Bail Applications

D5.36   On his first appearance before a magistrates' court, the accused is plainly entitled to present any arguments of fact or law he considers appropriate in support of an application for bail. Should the accused be remanded in custody, he may make an argued application at the next hearing. This is his right, regardless of whether he is repeating arguments already placed before the previous bench (BA 1976, sch. 1, part IIA, para. 2). Unless he consents to being remanded in his absence, the next hearing will be within eight clear days (MCA 1980, s. 128(6)). (Section 128A of the MCA 1980, which permits remands in custody of up to 28 days, applies only if the defendant has already been remanded in custody for the offence on at least one previous occasion.) Therefore, the wait between being refused bail on a first appearance and being able to argue again for bail on a second appearance is relatively short. However, should that second argued application fail, the defendant may not in general present argument on the subsequent occasions he appears before the court for remand hearings (sch. 1, part IIA, para. 3), although each time the court should nominally consider whether he ought to remain in custody (sch. 1, part IIA, para. 1).

It is, of course, possible for the court to grant bail without an application by the accused. Further, once bail has been refused, it is the court's duty to consider the grant of bail at each hearing thereafter. The only real point at issue is whether, on a particular occasion, the court is obliged to hear a bail *application* from the accused or his representative.

The above is a summary of the position arrived at by virtue of part IIA of sch. 1 to the BA 1976 (see **D5.56**). Essentially, part IIA was intended to give statutory effect to the Divisional Court's decision in *Nottingham Justices, ex parte Davies* [1981] QB 38. The present status of that decision in the light of the subsequent statutory development is unclear. However, reference to it may be useful if only to clarify the meaning of part IIA. In *Ex parte Davies*, the court was asked to rule on the lawfulness of the policy of the Nottingham Bench when there were several successive remand hearings in respect of an accused refused bail on the occasion of his first appearance. That policy was always to allow him (or his representative) to make a full bail application at the first and second hearings. At all subsequent hearings, the bench would refuse to consider matters previously before the court. In other words, from the third remand hearing onwards, they would not entertain an argued bail application unless there had been a change in circumstances since the last such application. Donaldson LJ (with whose judgment Bristow J concurred) upheld the policy. He said (at pp. 43G–44G; emphasis added):

I fully accept the submission that, in accordance with section 4 of the Bail Act 1976, every accused person who appears or is brought before a magistrates' court in the course of or in connection with proceedings for the offence or who applies to a court for bail in connection with the proceedings is entitled to be granted bail except as provided by schedule 1 to the Act. I also fully accept that on each occasion the exceptions specified [in the paragraphs of the schedule] only apply if the justices then sitting are satisfied in terms of those paragraphs. Finally, I accept that the fact that a bench of the same or a different constitution has decided on a previous occasion or occasions that one or more of the schedule 1 exceptions applies and has accordingly remanded the accused in custody, does not absolve the bench on each subsequent occasion from considering whether the accused is entitled to bail, whether or not an application is made.

However, this does not mean that the justices should ignore their own previous decision or a previous decision of their colleagues. Far from it. On those previous occasions, the court will have been under an obligation to grant bail unless it was satisfied that a schedule 1 exception was made out. If it was so satisfied, it will have recorded the exceptions which in its judgment were applicable. This . . . is a finding by the court that schedule 1 circumstances then existed and it is to be treated like every other finding of the court. *It is* res iudicata *or analogous thereto.* It stands as a finding unless and until it is overturned on appeal. . . . It follows that on the next occasion when bail is considered [by the magistrates] the court should treat, as an essential fact, that at the time when the matter of bail was last considered, schedule 1 circumstances did indeed exist. *Strictly speaking, they can and should only investigate whether that situation has changed since then.* . . .

I would inject only one qualification to the general rule that justices can and should only investigate whether the situation has changed since the last remand in custody. The finding on that occasion that schedule 1 circumstances existed will have been based upon matters known to the court at that time. The court considering afresh the question of bail is both entitled and bound to take account not only of a change in circumstances which has occurred since that last occasion, but also of circumstances which, although they then existed, were not brought to the attention of the court. . . . The question is a little wider than 'Has there been a change?' It is 'Are there any new considerations which were not before the court when the accused was last remanded in custody?'

Applying the above principles, Donaldson LJ held that the practice of always allowing two (rather than one) argued applications was justified because, although the finding that there were sch. 1 circumstances for refusing bail on the occasion of the first remand in custody was in theory as much a finding of the court as the similar finding on the second occasion and so ought to have precluded the making of the second application, in practice the experience of the justices showed that first bail applications were almost invariably underprepared, so that there would in fact be new considerations before the second bench which were not before the first. Therefore, 'Where this is the experience of any particular bench of justices, the Nottingham practice is not only convenient, but right' (p. 45B).

It will be apparent that part IIA uses different terminology from that used by Donaldson LJ in *Ex parte Davies*. In particular, paras 2 and 3 refer to 'any argument as to fact or law' which has not been advanced previously, whereas Donaldson LJ referred to 'new considerations'. It is submitted that the change in terminology is not significant, and that both the case and the statutory schedule oblige a later bench deciding on bail to consider any relevant arguments, whether of fact or law, which were not before their colleagues who previously refused bail. This is so whether the argument arises out of a change in circumstances since the last unsuccessful application, or is an argument that could have been put on the previous occasion but, for whatever reason, was not. Particular points arising from part IIA are:

(a) *Does the accused have to make his argued application on his first and second appearances?* Paragraph 2 does not state, as it might have done, that the accused is entitled to two fully argued bail applications. It merely provides that, *at the first hearing* after he was refused bail, he may support his application with any argument of fact or law, regardless of whether it was previously advanced. Thus, on a literal interpretation of para. 2, if an accused chooses not to make a bail application on the occasion of his first appearance and is accordingly remanded in custody, he may make an argued application at any one of his subsequent appearances, but if that application fails he is debarred from a further argued application unless he can rely on matters which were not earlier placed before the court. In other words, an accused arguing for bail who wants two bites at the cherry should have those bites on the first and second remand appearances, otherwise a court interpreting part IIA strictly would be justified in saying that he had turned down one of his bites by not making an argued application on his first appearance.

(b) *What is the situation where the justices conclude (using their powers under para. 5 of part I of sch. 1) that it has not been practicable to obtain sufficient information to decide to grant bail?* In *Calder Justices, ex parte Kennedy* (1992) 156 JP 716, the Divisional Court held that a decision under para. 5 was not a decision not to grant bail. It merely expressed the justices' satisfaction that they were not in a position to decide about bail. It did not therefore count for the purposes of para. 2 of part IIA of sch. 1.

(c) *What is the position if the accused consents to being remanded in his absence?* In *Dover and East Kent Justices, ex parte Dean* (1991) 156 JP 357, D made no bail application on his first appearance and consented to be remanded in his absence for three weeks. He appeared before the justices at the end of that period and wished to make a bail application. The justices decided that the hearing at which he had the right to do so was the first date on which he was remanded in his absence. Not surprisingly, the Divisional Court held that the occasions when he was remanded in his absence were not 'hearings' for the purpose of para. 2, and D had a right to make a bail application when he came before the justices at the end of the period of remand by consent.

(d) *Is the court obliged to consider only the new arguments?* Where the accused has exhausted his automatic entitlement of fully argued applications but claims that a new consideration has arisen which was not placed before the earlier benches, para. 3 could be construed merely as obliging the later bench to hear the argument of fact or law not previously advanced, rather than obliging it to reopen the entire question of bail. It is submitted, however, that to consider only the new consideration in isolation from the other arguments for bail would be an artificial exercise, and that the identifying of a new consideration relevant to bail should entitle the accused to make a further full bail application in which both the fresh and the old arguments may be relied on.

(e) *Does the court have a discretion to allow as many argued applications as it wishes?* Paragraph 3 merely states that, at the third and subsequent remand hearings, the court 'need not' hear arguments which it has heard previously. Prima facie the paragraph is not debarring the court from entertaining yet another argued application, but merely giving it a discretion in the matter. On the other hand, Donaldson LJ in *Ex parte Davies* based his approval of the practice of the Nottingham Justices on the principle of *res iudicata*, which he considered to apply as a matter of law. It is unclear whether para. 3 is meant to override *Ex parte Davies* (in which case magistrates always have a discretion to hear as many argued applications for bail as they wish), or is merely giving statutory force to the main thrust of the decision (in which case a scrupulous bench might say that, much as they would like to reopen the question of bail, they are bound by their colleagues' earlier decisions and can do nothing in the absence of fresh arguments or considerations).

(f) *Is the accused always entitled to an argued application on committal for trial?* A question which arose when applying the decision in *Ex parte Davies* and remains relevant under the provisions of part IIA of sch. 1 is whether the mere passage of time since the accused was first remanded in custody can be regarded as a new argument or consideration justifying a further full bail application. This is linked with the important practical question of whether an accused should always be allowed an argued application at the stage of committal for trial, on the basis that he will by then almost certainly have spent a minimum of four weeks in custody and, if not granted bail, will face at least a further month of the same before his trial comes on. In giving the judgment of the Divisional Court in *Reading Crown Court, ex parte Malik* [1981] QB 451, Donaldson LJ said at p. 454C–F:

> The justices declined to hear an application for bail on [the occasion of committal for trial]. In passing, we would have thought that there had been a very clear change of circumstances, namely, that the prosecution had by then completed its investigations and that the applicants had been committed for trial. Although there may be exceptional cases, as a general rule the moment of committal for trial must, in our judgment, be an occasion upon which an accused person is entitled to have his right to bail fully reviewed. In any particular case, the eligibility of the accused for bail may or may not have improved, but it is almost inevitable that there will have been a change in circumstances. For example, the court will be in a much better position to assess 'the nature and seriousness of the offence' (Bail Act 1976, sch. 1, part I, para. 9(a)). In addition, the strength of the prosecution case can for the first time be fully assessed, both by the committing court and by the accused himself. This can be very material in considering the likelihood that the accused may fail to surrender to custody (sch. 1, part I, para. 2(a)).

The above passage was *obiter*, the matter for decision in the case being whether a Crown Court judge was debarred from hearing an application for bail where the accused had already made an unsuccessful application to a High Court judge in chambers.

However, the point touched on *obiter* by Donaldson LJ was directly in issue in *Slough Justices, ex parte Duncan* (1982) 75 Cr App R 384. The justices declined to reopen the question of bail at D's committal, he having previously been remanded in custody on four occasions, on at least one of which full argument was heard. Asked whether there was anything contained in the evidence presented at committal which would affect the reasons why bail had been refused on the previous occasions, D's legal representative answered that there had been no material change in circumstances except, 'the committal proceedings and the changes which flow from those proceedings'. The Divisional Court held that, on those facts, the justices were correct not to hear a bail application. It follows that a committal for trial cannot of itself be treated as a fresh matter justifying the reopening of the question of bail; and, although the clarifying of the evidence and issues which is associated with committal may often amount to a change in circumstances, there will (*pace* Donaldson LJ in *Ex parte Malik*) also be many occasions when that is not so.

(g) *How should the justices express a decision not to allow an argued application?* Since in theory the court is obliged to consider bail each time an accused entitled to the benefit of the BA 1976, s. 4(1), appears before it in custody, it is unwise for the magistrates simply to say that they 'will not allow a fresh application for bail', or words to that effect. The more accurate terminology is: 'As there is no new material before us relevant to bail, bail will be refused'. This avoids giving the impression that they have simply refused to consider the question (per Ormrod LJ in *Ex parte Duncan* at p. 389).

Options Open to an Accused Remanded in Custody by Magistrates

The restrictions described above on the right of an accused to make repeated bail **D5.37** applications to the magistrates' court in which his case is proceeding are offset by the possibility of his applying to the Crown Court for bail. The right to apply is contained in the Supreme Court Act 1981, s. 81(1)(g), as qualified by s. 81(1J). Paragraph (g) provides that the Crown Court may grant bail to 'any person . . . who has been remanded in custody by a magistrates' court on adjourning a case under' ss. 5, 10, 18 or 30 of the MCA 1980. Section 81(1J) provides that the Crown Court may grant bail under

s. 81(1)(g) only if 'the magistrates' court which remanded [the accused] in custody has certified under section 5(6A) of the Bail Act 1976 that it heard full argument on his application for bail before it refused the application'. The BA 1976, s. 5(6A), imposes a duty on a magistrates' court which refuses bail following full argument to issue a certificate to that effect if either it was the first occasion of such argument or there has been a change in circumstances or new considerations since the previous argued application. Thus, the combined effect of s. 81(1)(g) and (1J) of the Supreme Court Act 1981 and s. 5(6A) of the BA 1976 is that, on an argued bail application being refused by magistrates at the remand stage, the defence should obtain a certificate of full argument from the court which they may then use to found a further application to the Crown Court. The right to apply to the Crown Court is thus dependent on an argued application having been made before the magistrates. In addition or as an alternative to applying to the Crown Court, an application may be made to a High Court judge in chambers (see CJA 1967, s. 22, which gives the High Court jurisdiction to grant bail whenever it has been refused by a magistrates' court). However, it is generally simpler and cheaper to go to the Crown Court.

Once the accused has been committed for trial, he may apply to the Crown Court for bail by virtue of s. 81(1)(a) of the 1981 Act ('The Crown Court may grant bail to any person who has been committed in custody for appearance before the Crown Court'). At this stage, there is no need to rely on a certificate of full argument.

D5.38 Prosecution Right of Appeal against Decision to Grant Bail

The Bail (Amendment) Act 1993 confers upon the prosecution the right to appeal to the Crown Court against a decision by magistrates to grant bail (for text, see **D5.57**). The right is limited to cases where:

(a) the defendant is charged with or convicted of an offence which is (or would be in the case of an adult) punishable by a term of imprisonment of five years or more or an offence of taking a conveyance without authority or aggravated vehicle-taking; and

(b) the prosecution is conducted by the CPS, or by a person falling within a class prescribed by statutory instrument (the Bail (Amendment) Act 1993 (Prescription of Prosecuting Authorities) Order 1994 (SI 1994 No. 1438) gives the right to the Serious Fraud Office, the Department of Trade and Industry, Customs and Excise, the Department of Social Security, the Post Office and the Inland Revenue); and

(c) the prosecution made representations against bail before it was granted.

The 1993 Act lays down procedural requirements with which the prosecution must comply in order to exercise its right. It must give oral notice of appeal at the conclusion of the proceedings in which bail was granted, and before the defendant is released from custody. In *Isleworth Crown Court, ex parte Clarke* [1998] 1 Cr App R 257, this requirement was held to be satisfied where notice was given to the justices' clerk about five minutes after the court rose and before the defendant had been released from custody. This notice must be confirmed in writing and served on the defendant within two hours after proceedings end; otherwise the appeal is deemed to be disposed of. Pending appeal, the magistrates must remand the defendant in custody. The Crown Court, for its part, must hear the appeal within 48 hours (excluding weekends and public holidays). The appeal takes place by way of rehearing (see **D5.42**), and the judge may then remand the defendant in custody or grant bail with or without conditions.

Where the defendant has not yet been committed to the Crown Court, and the judge decides to remand him in custody, the prosecution should invite the judge to stipulate a date which is within the limits imposed by ss. 128 and 129 of the MCA 1980 (*Governor of Pentonville Prison, ex parte Bone* (1994) *The Times*, 15 November 1994; for the operation of ss. 128 and 129, see **D4.8** to **D4.12**).

Guidance issued by the CPS states that 'the power of appeal against a grant of bail must be used judiciously and responsibly, and the CPS expects the number of appeals to be small. It is not to be used merely because the Crown Prosecutor disagrees with the decision of the magistrates . . . [I]t should only be used in cases of grave concern'. Wherever possible, approval for use of the power has to be sought in advance of the hearing from a Crown Prosecutor of at least four years' standing.

Prosecution Application for Reconsideration of Bail

Under the BA 1976, s. 5B, the prosecution can, in certain circumstances, apply for the **D5.39** grant of bail to be reconsidered. The power to make such an application is limited to offences which are triable either way or on indictment only. Any application must be based on information not available to the court or the police officer granting bail (s. 5B(3)). When considering the application, the court may impose or vary bail conditions, or withhold bail (s. 5B(1)). In so deciding, it must act in accordance with the presumptive 'right to bail' and the exceptions to it (s. 5B(4)). If the decision is to withhold bail then, if the defendant is before the court, he will be remanded in custody. If absent, he must surrender to custody and is liable to arrest without warrant (s. 5(5) and (7)). It is clear, therefore, that an application can be made in respect of an absent defendant.

Making Sureties Continuous

Where an accused is granted bail at a remand hearing and it is anticipated that there **D5.40** may be several further appearances in the magistrates' court before his case is finally disposed of or sent to the Crown Court for trial, the court may, instead of simply directing him to appear at the end of the period of the remand, direct that he appear 'at every time and place to which during the course of the proceedings the hearing may be from time to time adjourned' (MCA 1980, s. 128(4)). Similarly, where bail is granted subject to a requirement for sureties, the surety's recognisance may be conditioned to secure that the accused 'appears at every time and place to which during the course of the proceedings the hearing may be from time to time adjourned and also before the Crown Court in the event of [the accused] being committed for trial there' (ibid.). Making the sureties continuous in this way is a useful device to avoid their having to come to court for each remand hearing. If they have not been made continuous and are not at court, the accused, even if granted bail on precisely the same terms as previously, cannot be released until they have renewed their undertakings (e.g., by going to a local police station). Section 128(4) even empowers magistrates to make the sureties' recognisances extend beyond committal (i.e. at a remand hearing they undertake to secure the accused's attendance before the Crown Court if he is committed). Where the accused's bail is conditional both on sureties and other conditions, there is no obligation to inform the surety should the other conditions be relaxed or varied, but it might be good practice to warn him of this possibility at the time he enters into his recognisance (*Wells Street Magistrates' Court, ex parte Albanese* [1982] QB 333).

Enlarging Bail

The MCA 1980, s. 129, empowers a magistrates' court which has already remanded an **D5.41** accused to make further remands in his absence. This power should be distinguished from the power in s. 128(3A) to remand an accused in custody on up to three consecutive occasions without his being brought before the court if he has consented not to be produced. Section 129(1) applies if the court is satisfied that, on the day to which the accused was remanded, he is unable to attend 'by reason of illness or accident'. It may then remand him again in his absence. The subsection applies regardless of whether the remand is in custody or on bail. Moreover, notwithstanding s. 128(6), a remand in custody under s. 129(1) may exceed eight clear days. Thus, if an accused remanded in custody on an earlier occasion is ill in prison and will not be well enough to attend court for several weeks, the magistrates may extend the period of the remand until such time as he is likely to have recovered.

By contrast with s. 129(1), s. 129(3) applies only if the accused has been remanded on bail. The subsection permits the court to appoint in his absence a later time as the time at which he is to appear. The appointment of the new time is deemed to be a further remand (ibid.). This power is useful when unforeseen developments mean that the case will not be able to proceed on the date to which it was originally adjourned. By agreement between the court and the parties, a new date can be fixed without the necessity for the accused appearing. The power is also useful when the accused fails to appear on the date to which he was bailed but an acceptable explanation for his non-appearance is put before the court. Instead of issuing a warrant for his arrest, the magistrates may simply adjourn and enlarge bail in his absence. Whenever bail is enlarged under either s. 129(1) or s. 129(3), the recognisances of the sureties may be correspondingly enlarged to secure the accused's appearance on the new date (s. 129(2) and (3)(a)).

The MCA 1980, s. 129, is supplemented by s. 43(1), which relates to first appearances before a magistrates' court. Section 43(1) provides that, where an accused has been bailed from the police station following charge subject to a duty to surrender at court on a certain date, the court may 'appoint a later time as the time at which he is to appear and may enlarge the recognisances of any sureties'.

PROCEDURE FOR BAIL APPLICATIONS IN THE CROWN COURT

D5.42 The procedure for bail applications in the Crown Court is governed by r. 19 of the Crown Court Rules 1982 (SI 1982 No. 1109). The rule applies only when the application is made otherwise than during the actual hearing of the proceedings (r. 19(1)). By r. 19(2) written notice of intention to make the application must be given to the prosecutor and, if the prosecution is being carried on by the Crown Prosecution Services, to the appropriate Crown Prosecutor; this must be done at least 24 hours before the hearing of the application. Schedule 4 to the Rules sets out a form for giving notice which, *inter alia*, requires the applicant to give details of the previous applications for bail, to state the nature and grounds of the present application, to mention any proposed sureties and to disclose the previous convictions of the accused. The options open to the prosecutor on receiving notice are:

(a)   to notify the court and the applicant that he wishes to be represented at the hearing; or

(b)   to notify them that he does not oppose the application; or

(c)   to send the court a written statement of his reasons for opposing the application, at the same time sending a copy of the statement to the applicant (r. 19(3)).

Usually, the CPS instruct counsel to oppose the application. The accused has no right to be present at the hearing of the application, but may be given leave to attend by the court (r. 19(5)). An accused who has been unable to instruct a solicitor to act on his behalf may request the court to assign the Official Solicitor to act for him (r. 19(6)). Where that is done, the court may dispense with the requirements of notice etc. and deal with the application in a summary manner (r. 19(7)). Since legal aid in criminal proceedings covers bail applications to the Crown Court, it is unlikely that an applicant would be forced to ask for the Official Solicitor's aid.

The hearing of the application is normally in chambers (see r. 27(2)(a)). Where possible it should be listed before the judge by whom the case is expected to be tried (see the Lord Chief Justice's *Practice Direction (Crown Court Business: Classification)* [1987] 1 WLR 1671, para. 6 under the heading 'Allocation of business within the Crown Court'). In practice, it is unlikely that any particular judge will have been allocated to the case at such an early stage, and the application will therefore be heard by any circuit judge or recorder sitting at the location of the Crown Court to which the accused has been or is expected to be committed. The hearing follows the pattern of a bail application in the magistrates' court, with counsel for the prosecution summarising the objections and counsel for the applicant replying. If bail is granted to an accused who was refused it by magistrates at a remand hearing, the Crown Court may direct him to appear 'at a time and place which the magistrates' court could have directed' (Supreme Court Act 1981, s. 81(1H)). If bail is granted to an accused committed for trial in custody, his obligation is simply to appear on the day the case is listed for trial. Any sureties required by the Crown Court may enter into their recognisances before, *inter alia*, an officer of the Crown Court, a police officer who is either in charge of a police station or of the rank of inspector or above, or the governor of the prison or remand centre where the accused is presently detained (Crown Court Rules 1982, r. 20(2)).

Part IIA of sch. 1 to the BA 1976 applies to bail applications in the Crown Court just as it applies to applications before the magistrates. Therefore, if one application for bail has already been made to the Crown Court, a further argued application may not be presented unless there are fresh arguments or considerations to put before the court (see **D5.36**). However, the fact that the accused has already applied unsuccessfully for bail to a High Court judge in chambers does not preclude him from making an application to the Crown Court (*Reading Crown Court, ex parte Malik* [1981] QB 451).

Applications for bail during the actual course of the proceedings (e.g., for the period of a midday or overnight adjournment) are not governed by the Crown Court Rules 1982. Where the accused has been on bail until the commencement of his trial, it may be convenient to ask immediately before the jury in waiting come into court that bail be allowed for all adjournments until further order of the court. Whether to continue bail is in the discretion of the trial judge. It is not uncommon, where a custodial sentence is anticipated in the event of conviction and the trial is nearing completion, for the judge at that stage to withdraw bail (e.g., for the last overnight adjournment).

FAILURE TO COMPLY WITH BAIL

Introduction

Where an accused who has been granted bail in criminal proceedings fails to comply **D5.43** with the obligations thereby imposed upon him, two main questions arise. The first is how the court should ensure that he will attend court for the remaining stages of the proceedings; the second is how he (and any sureties) will be dealt with in consequence of his breach of bail.

Powers of the Court when a Bailed Accused Fails to Appear

Whenever a person bailed to attend court fails to surrender to custody in answer to his **D5.44** bail, the court may issue a warrant for his arrest (BA 1976, s. 7(1)). This applies whatever court he was bailed to attend and regardless of whether bail was granted by the custody officer at the police station or by the court itself at an earlier hearing. At the court's discretion, the warrant may be backed for bail, either with or without a requirement for sureties as the court sees fit (see MCA 1980, s. 117, and Supreme Court Act 1981, s. 81(4), respectively for the power of magistrates and the Crown Court to back warrants for bail). As an alternative to issuing a warrant, a magistrates' court may adjourn and enlarge the accused's bail under the MCA 1980, s. 129 (see **D5.41**). It would only do so if satisfied that there is a good reason for the accused's non-attendance (e.g., a doctor's certificate has been sent to the court indicating that he is unfit to attend). Similarly, the Crown Court, in appropriate cases, may simply order that the case be stood out of the list and take no further action in respect of the accused. He will remain under an obligation to attend whenever the case is next listed.

The power to issue a warrant under the BA 1976, s. 7(1), arises only if the accused fails to surrender to custody at the time appointed. In this context, 'surrendering to custody' merely connotes complying with whatever procedure is prescribed by the court for those answering to their bail (*DPP* v *Richards* [1988] QB 701 per Glidewell LJ at p. 711). Thus, if a court operates a system whereby persons bailed are required to report to an usher and are then allowed to wait in the court precincts until their case is called, a person who so reports has surrendered to custody, even though he is under no physical restraint and is not in the cell area. It follows that, if he subsequently goes away before the court is ready to deal with his case, he has not absconded within the meaning of s. 6, and a warrant may *not* be issued under s. 7(1). However, the situation is covered by s. 7(2), which provides that, where a person who has been released on bail in criminal proceedings absents himself from the court at any time after he has surrendered to custody but before the court is ready to begin or resume the hearing of the proceedings, the court may issue a warrant for his arrest. In *Central Criminal Court, ex parte Guney* [1996] AC 616, the House of Lords held that, where a defendant was formally arraigned, the arraignment amounted to a surrender to the custody of the court. Since the defendant's further detention was solely within the judge's power, the obligations of the surety were also extinguished at that point. The judge could not deprive the effect of arraignment as a surrender to custody. A fortiori, the agreement of the parties could not divest an arraignment of its effect on bail. In *Kent Crown Court, ex parte Jodka* (1997) 161 JP 638, the Divisional Court held that bail granted by magistrates ceases when the defendant surrenders to the custody of the Crown Court, whether or not the defendant is arraigned at that hearing.

Options Open to the Police when Breach of Bail is Anticipated

D5.45 Where a suspect bailed from the police station under the PACE 1984, s. 37(2), on condition that he reattend at the police station on a later date fails to do so, he may be arrested without warrant (PACE 1984, s. 46A).

Under s. 7(3) of the BA 1976, where a person has been bailed to attend a court, a police officer may arrest him without warrant prior to the bail date if either:

(a) the officer has reasonable grounds for believing that he is not likely to surrender to custody; or
(b) the officer has reasonable grounds for believing that he either has broken or is likely to break any condition of his bail; or
(c) a surety has given written notice to the police that the person bailed is unlikely to surrender to custody and for that reason the surety wishes to be relieved of his obligations.

Following arrest under s. 7(3), the person arrested must be brought before a magistrate as soon as practicable and, in any event, within 24 hours, save that, in reckoning the 24-hour period, no account is to be taken of Sundays (s. 7(4)). Thus, a person arrested on a Saturday under s. 7(3) need not be brought before a magistrate until the following Monday. The wording of s. 7(4) makes it clear that the person arrested may be brought before a single justice, who need not be sitting in court. However, it is usually more convenient to take him before a bench. The magistrate or bench must be one for the petty sessions area in which the person was arrested.

The question for a magistrate before whom a person is brought in furtherance of s. 7(3) and (4) is whether the person either is not likely to surrender to custody, or has broken or is likely to break a condition of his bail. If of the opinion that either of those two matters is established, the magistrate may remand him in custody (s. 7(5)). Alternatively, he may readmit him to bail subject to different conditions (or even readmit him to bail on the same conditions if he considers that new conditions would not assist but it is nevertheless not a case where a remand in custody would be justified). Where the magistrate is *not* of the opinion mentioned above (i.e. he neither thinks that the person arrested is unlikely to surrender to custody nor thinks that he has broken or will break a condition of bail), then he *must* readmit him to bail on the same terms as previously. A difficulty arises if the person arrested contests the allegation that he is unlikely to surrender to custody etc. but, owing to the shortness of time since arrest, it is not possible to resolve the issue forthwith. In *Liverpool Justices, ex parte DPP* [1993] QB 233, the Divisional Court set out the following guidance for magistrates' courts in carrying out the procedure under s. 7(5). First, the matter is one which can be heard by a single justice (unlike the hearing of an information). Second, s. 7 does not create an offence; it provides a procedure for dealing with the situation where the police believe that the person arrested is unlikely to surrender to custody, or has broken or is likely to break a condition of bail. Third, the magistrate is not required to hear evidence on oath. What is envisaged is that the police officer will state the grounds for his belief, which might involve hearsay evidence. The magistrate would, in fairness, no doubt then give the person arrested a chance to respond, and thereafter make a decision on the basis of what he had heard. Fourth, the magistrate has no power to adjourn. Unless he is of the opinion that the person arrested is not likely to surrender to custody, or has broken or is likely to break a condition of his bail, bail must be granted, subject to the same conditions, if any, as were originally imposed.

Consequences for Accused who Absconds

The BA 1976, s. 6, creates the offence of absconding. By s. 6(1), if a person released on **D5.46** bail fails without reasonable cause to surrender to custody, he is guilty of an offence. The burden of showing reasonable cause is on the accused (s. 6(3)). Moreover, a person who had reasonable cause for failing to surrender on the appointed day nevertheless commits an offence if he fails to surrender as soon after the appointed time as is reasonably practicable (s. 6(2)). Being mistaken about the day on which one should have appeared was held in *Laidlaw* v *Atkinson* (1986) *The Times*, 2 August 1986 not to amount to a reasonable cause. The question whether a mistake by the defendant's lawyer might be a reasonable excuse for failure to surrender is one to be determined in all the circumstances (*DPP* v *Speede* [1998] 2 Cr App R 108).

An offence under s. 6(1) or (2) is 'punishable either on summary conviction or as if it were a criminal contempt of court' (s. 6(5)). An offender summarily convicted of a s. 6 offence is liable to imprisonment for up to three months and/or a fine of £5,000 (s. 6(7)). One dealt with in the Crown Court as if he had been guilty of a criminal contempt is liable to 12 months' imprisonment and/or an unlimited fine (ibid.). Furthermore, a magistrates' court which has convicted of an s. 6 offence may commit the offender to the Crown Court for sentence if: either it considers that the offence merits greater punishment than it has power to inflict; or it is committing the offender for trial to the Crown Court for another offence and it considers that the Crown Court should deal with him for the absconding as well (s. 6(6)). The meaning of 'surrendering to custody' in s. 6(1) and (2) was considered by the Divisional Court in *DPP* v *Richards* [1988] QB 701 (see **D5.44**).

Procedure for Prosecuting Offences under the Bail Act 1976, s. 6

The BA 1976, s. 6(5), provides that an offence under s. 6(1) or (2) shall be punishable **D5.47** 'either on summary conviction or as if it were a criminal contempt of court'. This cryptic phraseology has created confusion both about the nature of the offence and about the correct procedure for dealing with it. The leading authority is *Schiavo* v *Anderton* [1987]

QB 20, the effect of which has been clarified by *Practice Direction (Bail: Failure to Surrender)* [1987] 1 WLR 79.

In *Schiavo* v *Anderton*, S, having been bailed to appear before a magistrates' court on 9 June 1983, absconded to Spain. On his return to the UK in May 1985, he was arrested and brought before the court charged with failing to surrender to custody. It was argued on his behalf that the s. 6(1) offence is summary and that, since no information had been laid until almost two years after the alleged date of commission, the court had no jurisdiction to try the matter (see MCA 1980, s. 127, which requires an information for a summary offence to be laid within six months). The stipendiary magistrate ruled that the offence was not summary but indictable, and that therefore no time-limit applied. On appeal to the Divisional Court, Watkins LJ, having reviewed the statutory provisions and earlier authorities, set out six propositions. The essence of these propositions is that s. 6 creates a unique offence which is not a contempt of court but is analogous thereto. It does not fit into the normal classifications of triable only on indictment, triable either way and triable only summarily, but is invariably to be tried by the court disposing of the offence for which the accused was bailed. The offence is also unique in that proceedings for it are not to be initiated by information or charge, but of the court's own motion. Therefore no time-limit applies. His lordship said (at p. 34B–D):

> . . . upon a proper construction of section 6 in its setting, Parliament intended effects of the provisions of the section other than those which are plainly obvious from the text of them. They are (1) the magistrates' court and the Crown Court each require separately a power to punish for the offence of absconding. (2) The offence is not subject to the general rule that trial be commenced by information. (3) The initiation of the simple procedure for trial by the court's own motion and not by formal charge, as seems to have happened here, is the only proper way to proceed. (4) It is not one of those offences triable on indictment or either way. (5) It is an offence only triable in the court at which proceedings are to be heard in respect of which bail has been granted. (6) It is expected that the trial of the offence will take place immediately following the disposal of the offence in respect of which bail was granted.

Applying the above to the circumstances of S's case, the appeal failed because, although S had come before the court by the wrong procedure (i.e. on a charge under s. 6(1) preferred by the police when the prosecution should have been initiated by the court's own motion), nonetheless he did appear to answer for his conduct in absconding, and the time which had elapsed since the offence did not deprive the court of jurisdiction, as it would have done had it been simply a summary matter.

In *Lubega* (1999) *The Times*, 10 February 1999, the Court of Appeal held that s. 6(5) did not have the effect of converting an offence under the Act to a contempt of court. It followed that the judge was not entitled to deal with the matter in the same way as a contempt of court.

The absconding which gave rise to the proceedings in *Schiavo* v *Anderton* was a failure to answer to bail which had been granted *by the court*. The status of the offence and the procedure which should be adopted where a person fails to appear at court in compliance with bail granted by the police following charge was not directly considered by Watkins LJ. However, such a failure cannot be equated with contempt of court in the way that failure to answer to court bail can. The *Practice Direction (Bail: Failure to Surrender)* [1987] 1 WLR 79 issued to clarify the decision in *Schiavo* v *Anderton* draws the distinction between the two types of absconding.

Practice Direction (Bail: Failure to Surrender) [1987] 1 WLR 79

1. [Purpose of the direction.]
2. *Bail granted by a magistrates' court*
Where a person has been granted bail by a court and subsequently fails to surrender to custody as contemplated by section 6(1) or 6(2) of the Bail Act 1976, on arrest that person

should be brought before the court at which the proceedings in respect of which bail was granted are to be heard. It is neither necessary nor desirable to lay an information in order to commence proceedings for the failure to surrender. Having regard to the nature of the offence which is tantamount to the defiance of a court order, it is more appropriate that the court itself should initiate the proceedings by its own motion, following an express invitation by the prosecutor. The court will only be invited so to move if, having considered all the circumstances, the prosecutor considers proceedings are appropriate. Where a court complies with such an invitation, the prosecutor will naturally conduct the proceedings and, where the matter is contested, call the evidence. Any trial should normally take place immediately following the disposal of the proceedings in respect of which bail was granted.

3. *Bail granted by a police officer*

Where a person has been bailed from a police station subject to a duty to appear before a magistrates' court or to attend a police station on an appointed date and/or time, a failure so to appear or attend cannot be said to be tantamount to the defiance of a court order. There does not exist the same compelling justification for a court to act by its own motion. Where bail has been granted by a police officer, any proceedings for a failure to surrender to custody, whether at a court or a police station, should accordingly be initiated by charging the accused or by the laying of an information.

The direction is largely self-explanatory. However, some comments on it may assist. First, the absconder should *always* be brought before the court at which the proceedings in respect of which bail was granted are to be heard. This will usually be the court which granted bail but, where bail was granted by a magistrates' court on committal for trial or sentence, it will be the Crown Court. A suggestion by Roskill LJ in *Harbax Singh* [1979] QB 319 that the Crown Court might, exceptionally and in its discretion, remit a contested BA 1976 offence to the magistrates for summary trial, was rejected by Watkins LJ in *Schiavo* v *Anderton* [1987] QB 20 (see p. 33D). Secondly, although criminal contempts can in theory be dealt with by being tried on indictment and the s. 6(1) and (2) offences are analogous to contempts, trial on indictment should *never* in practice be adopted for them (*Schiavo* v *Anderton* at p. 34A). Thirdly, the indication in the *Practice Direction* that there should be a two-stage consideration of whether proceedings should be initiated (i.e., the prosecutor decides whether to invite the court to proceed and the court then decides whether to act on his invitation) may not always coincide with practice. Many magistrates' courts informally ask the absconder or his legal representative what the reason for his non-appearance was. If the explanation seems prima facie satisfactory, the bench indicates that no further action is necessary; otherwise the clerk is instructed to put the charge. The prosecution's views are not necessarily canvassed. Where a bench, on the occasion of an absconder's first appearance after his absconding, indicates, albeit informally, that no charge need be preferred, that decision is binding on subsequent benches (*France* v *Dewsbury Magistrates' Court* [1988] Crim LR 295, where the Divisional Court did, however, reiterate *obiter* the necessity to ask the CPS for their wishes in the matter). Fourthly, a certified copy of the record made under the BA 1976, s. 5(1), of the granting of bail is evidence of the time and place at which the accused should have surrendered. The court file will show whether he did in fact surrender. Thus, although it is in theory for the prosecution to call the evidence of absconding, the basic facts will usually be established from court documents which prove themselves. The prosecution's role will be simply one of testing in cross-examination any reason put forward by the accused to explain his non-appearance. Lastly, the distinction between failing to answer to court bail and failing to answer police bail means that, as regards the latter, the prosecution should be careful to lay an information within six months of the alleged offence. Since the offence in that form is to be treated as an ordinary summary offence and not tantamount to defiance of a court order, the usual rules apply and failure to commence proceedings within six months will render them void (*Murphy* v *DPP* [1990] 1 WLR 601; see also *Teesside Magistrates' Court, ex parte Bujnowski* (1997) 161 JP 302).

What procedure should the court adopt once it comes to deal with an offence of absconding? In *Davis* (1986) 8 Cr App R (S) 64 it was indicated that the sentencer should give the accused an opportunity to explain himself, and invite submissions from counsel. If the accused was unrepresented he should be afforded legal representation to explain why he absented himself (see also *Boyle* [1993] Crim LR 40 and *How* [1993] Crim LR 201). In *Woods* (1989) 11 Cr App R (S) 551, W was sentenced to 18 months' imprisonment on charges of theft and handling, with three months consecutive for failing to surrender to bail. The Court of Appeal quashed the sentence for the bail offence because the simple procedure laid down in *Davis* had not been followed. In particular, the sentencer had given no indication that he intended to impose a separate consecutive sentence for the bail offence (on this latter point, see **D17.28**).

In *Maguire* (1992) *The Times*, 1 July 1992, the Court of Appeal held that an appeal lay as of right against a Crown Court sentence which had been imposed for a breach of bail treated as a criminal contempt of court.

When sentencing for failure to surrender to bail, under the BA 1976, s. 6, the Magistrates' Association Guidelines (1997) indicate the following as relevant considerations:

Aggravating factors ⊕
For example leaves jurisdiction; wilful evasion; appears after arrest; offence committed on bail; previous convictions and failure to respond to previous sentences, if relevant.

Mitigating factors ⊖
For example appears late on day of hearing; genuine misunderstanding; voluntary surrender.

Guideline: Is compensation, discharge or fine appropriate?

The guideline fine is £60 (low income), £150 (average income) or £350 (high income).

Consequences for Sureties when Accused Absconds

D5.48 If an accused bailed with sureties fails to surrender at the appointed time, the court must forfeit their recognisances (i.e. order them to pay the amounts in which they respectively stood surety). This is the normal consequence of the accused's absconding, although the court has a discretion in exceptional circumstances to order that the surety pay less than the full sum or even to order that none of the sum it previously declared forfeited should in fact be forfeited. The power to forfeit recognisances is contained in the MCA 1980, s. 120(1) and (3), and the Crown Court Rules 1982, rr. 21 and 21A. After declaring the automatic forfeiture of any recognizance entered into by a surety, the court is required to issue a summons to the surety to appear before it (unless, of course, he is present) to explain why he should not pay the sum. If the surety fails to answer the summons, the court has the discretion to proceed in his absence provided that it is satisfied that the summons has been correctly served. In any event, the court may decide whether to order all, part or none of the sum to be paid.

The principles governing forfeiture of a surety's recognisance were stated by Lord Denning MR in *Southampton Justices, ex parte Green* [1976] QB 11 and also by Lord Widgery CJ in *Horseferry Road Stipendiary Magistrate, ex parte Pearson* [1976] 1 WLR 511. Before making an order the court should consider both the surety's means and the extent of his responsibility for the accused's non-appearance, including any steps he took to ensure that he would surrender (*Ex parte Green*, where an order by the justices that the wife of an absconding accused should forfeit the full sum of £3,000 in which she had stood surety was remitted to the court for reconsideration because they had (a) failed to inquire into the extent of her culpability, and (b) taken into account, when determining her means, a boat valued at £3,000, which in fact belonged to the accused himself). However, there is a strong presumption that the surety should forfeit the full recognisance. As it was put in *Ex parte Pearson* at p. 514C:

> . . . the surety has seriously entered into a serious obligation and ought to pay the amount which he or she has promised unless there are circumstances in the case, relating either to . . . means or . . . culpability, which make it fair and just to pay a smaller sum.

(See also *Maidstone Crown Court, ex parte Lever* [1995] 1 WLR 928.)

The authorities were extensively reviewed by McCullough J in *Uxbridge Justices, ex parte Heward-Mills* [1983] 1 WLR 56. His lordship then summarised their effect thus (at p. 62A–B):

> . . . the more important principles to be derived from the authorities [are] as follows. (1) When a defendant for whose attendance a person has stood surety fails to appear, the full recognisance should be forfeited, unless it appears fair and just that a lesser sum should be forfeited or none at all. (2) The burden of satisfying the court that the full sum should not be forfeited rests on the surety and is a heavy one. It is for him to lay before the court the evidence of want of culpability and of means on which he relies. (3) Where a surety is unrepresented the court should assist him by explaining these principles in ordinary language, and giving him the opportunity to call evidence and advance argument in relation to them.

Want of Means In both *Southampton Justices, ex parte Green* [1976] QB 11 and **D5.49** *Uxbridge Justices, ex parte Heward-Mills* [1983] 1 WLR 56, the orders for forfeiture were quashed because the magistrates had failed properly to take into account the surety's want of means. Nevertheless, the cases emphasise that the burden is on the surety to show impecuniosity. If he wishes to put forward evidence on the matter, the court is under a duty to consider it, even if he had earlier claimed when being accepted as surety that he was worth the sum which he now states he cannot pay (*Ex parte Heward-Mills*). However, there is no obligation on the court to initiate the inquiry (ibid.). Moreover, it is submitted that, if a proper inquiry was conducted into the surety's means at the time he stood, he should be relieved from his obligations on financial grounds only if something unforeseen has arisen between then and the consideration of forfeiture which prevents him meeting his obligation. Otherwise he benefits from having misled the court which accepted him as surety. The magistrates' error in *Ex parte Heward-Mills* lay in refusing to consider the evidence as to means which the surety wished to advance, rather than in the conclusion they reached.

In *Kaur v DPP* (1999) *The Times*, 5 October 1999, the Divisional Court dealt with the power of the magistrates to deal with a surety after the recognisance had been forfeited, and a term of imprisonment has been imposed in default. The appellant had stood surety in the sum of £150,000 when her son was charged with VAT fraud. She put up her matrimonial home, valued at £200,000, which was owned jointly with her husband and which had been purchased with the help of personal loans from friends and relatives in the sum of £58,000. The son absconded, and the Crown Court ordered forfeiture of the full sum or three years' imprisonment in default. The appellant failed to pay and was committed to prison for three years by the stipendiary magistrate, who found that she had been fully aware that the house would have to be used to raise funds. The Divisional Court held that the magistrate, in deciding whether to remit the recognisance in whole or in part, ought to have taken into account the impact on others if the matrimonial home had to be sold in order to provide the sum in question. In exercising their wide discretion whether to remit the whole or part of the recognisance, the bench could plainly have regard only to the assets of the surety herself. The assets of other persons could not properly be called on to satisfy the surety's liabilities. The matter was remitted for the stipendiary magistrate to take into account the fact that the appellant's share in the equity of the matrimonial home had never been worth anything approaching the amount of the recognisance.

D5.50 ***Culpability*** Although r. 21 of the Crown Court Rules 1982 empowers the court to forfeit a surety's recognisance only if there has been *default* in performing the obligations thereby imposed, the word 'default' merely connotes non-appearance by the accused. If the surety is not positively to blame for the absconding, is he thereby absolved from liability? According to *Warwick Crown Court, ex parte Smalley* [1987] 1 WLR 237, there is no requirement of proof that any blame attached to the surety. Further, in *Ipswich Crown Court, ex parte Reddington* [1981] Crim LR 618, it was held that the surety was not absolved from liability despite the fact that he had notified the police that he wished to withdraw as surety, and had done so immediately he became aware that the accused might not attend. The authorities were reviewed in *Reading Crown Court, ex parte Bello* [1992] 3 All ER 353. Parker LJ summarised the position as follows:

> The failure of the accused to surrender when required triggered the power to forfeit but the court before deciding what should be done had to enquire into the question of fault. If it was satisfied that the surety was blameless throughout it would then be proper to remit the whole of the amount of the recognisance and in exceptional circumstances that would be the only proper course.

One issue in *Ex parte Bello* was the failure of the court to notify the surety of the date on which the accused had to surrender. Parker LJ said that justice should require that the surety was notified by the court of the date. However, it was impossible to say that ignorance of the date was always an answer to proceedings for forfeiture: each case must depend on its facts.

If the surety has taken all reasonable steps to ensure attendance but the accused has nevertheless let him down, the recognisance ought not to be forfeited (*York Crown Court, ex parte Coleman* (1987) 86 Cr App R 151).

In the case of a surety made continuous (e.g., to committal or trial), who is not informed by the court of variations in other conditions of bail imposed on the accused, the failure to inform is relevant to culpability, although the primary obligation is on the surety to keep in touch with the accused and thus learn of any such variations (*Wells Street Magistrates' Court, ex parte Albanese* [1982] QB 333 – case remitted to the lower court by the Divisional Court since the stipendiary magistrate had estreated A's recognisance in full in the mistaken belief that a condition to deposit valuable security had not been altered, whereas in fact the condition had been relaxed by return of part of the security to the accused without A being aware of what had happened).

Forfeiture of Security

D5.51 Where the accused (or somebody on his behalf) has given security for his surrender to custody in pursuance of a requirement imposed under the BA 1976, s. 3(5), and the court is satisfied that he has absconded, then the court may, unless satisfied that he had reasonable cause for his failure, order forfeiture of part or all of the security (s. 5(7) and (8)). Section 5(8A) to (8C) sets out a procedure by which the accused may apply to have an order under s. 5(7) remitted on the grounds that, contrary to the court's original view, he did in fact have reasonable cause for not surrendering. The principles to be applied in deciding whether or not to order forfeiture of a security are no doubt analogous to those which apply when forfeiture of a surety's recognisance is under consideration.

JURISDICTION OF HIGH COURT IN RESPECT OF BAIL

D5.52   **Criminal Justice Act 1967, s. 22(1)**

> Where a magistrates' court withholds bail in criminal proceedings or imposes conditions in granting bail in criminal proceedings the High Court may grant bail or vary the conditions.

In addition to the above provision, under the CJA 1948, s. 37(1), the High Court may grant bail to:

(a)   a person who has applied to the Crown Court to state a case for the High Court's opinion;

(b)   a person who has applied (or applied for leave to apply) for certiorari in respect of a Crown Court decision; or

(c)   a person who, following conviction and sentence in a magistrates' court, has applied for certiorari (or applied for leave to apply).

All the above powers are subject to the restrictions contained in the CJPO 1994, s. 25 (see **D5.10**).

It will be seen from the above that there is a large overlap between the jurisdiction of the High Court to grant bail following its refusal by magistrates and the jurisdiction of the Crown Court to do the same. In particular, both where bail is refused at the remand stage following an argued application and where it is refused at the stage of committal for trial or sentence or appeal to the Crown Court, application can be made either to the Crown Court or to the High Court (or both) for a reversal of the lower court's decision. The High Court's jurisdiction is *wider* than that of the Crown Court in that: (a) it can vary the terms of bail which magistrates have made conditional, whereas the Crown Court's power to intervene is limited to cases where bail has been refused; and (b) it can grant bail when an accused summarily convicted and given a custodial sentence is appealing to itself rather than to the Crown Court. The procedure for applying to the High Court for bail is contained in the Rules of the Supreme Court 1965, ord. 79, r. 9. It is this procedure which should be used where a defendant seeks to remove or vary a condition imposed by the Crown Court; an application by way of judicial review is not appropriate (*Croydon Crown Court, ex parte Cox* [1997] 1 Cr App R 20).

(a)   An application must be made by way of claim form served on the prosecutor at least 24 hours before the return date (paras 1 and 2). The claim form calls on the respondents to show cause why bail should not be granted or, as the case may be, to show cause why the conditions of bail should not be varied.

(b)   The application must be supported by witness statement or affidavit (para. 3).

(c)   If an accused in custody wishes to apply to the High Court for bail but is unable to instruct solicitors through lack of means, he may make a written request to a judge asking that the Official Solicitor be assigned to act for him (para. 4). If the judge accedes to the request, he may also dispense with the requirement for service of a claim form and witness statement or affidavit, and deal with the application in a summary manner (para. 5).

(d)   Applications to the High Court concerning bail are heard by a single judge sitting in private. If an application to one judge fails, the applicant is not allowed to make further applications to other judges or to a Divisional Court (para. 12). He is not, however, prevented from applying to the Crown Court (*Reading Crown Court, ex parte Malik*) [1981] QB 451). Nor does an earlier refusal by the Crown Court preclude an application to the High Court.

(e)   Where the High Court grants bail subject to sureties, the surety may enter into his recognisance before a magistrate, magistrates' clerk, police inspector (or other officer in charge of a police station), or the governor of the custodial institution where the applicant is for the time being detained (para. 6A). Unless the court orders otherwise, the surety must give notice to the prosecution at least 24 hours before he stands, so that they may check his suitability (para. 7). The person taking the surety then sends the recognisance to an officer of the relevant court (i.e. an officer of the Crown Court where the applicant has been committed to that court and, in all other cases, to the justices' clerk) (para. 8).

(f)   Where a recognisance is 'acknowledged in or removed to' the Queen's Bench Division it may be estreated only by order of a judge sitting in private on an application by claim form served at least two clear days before the hearing date (RSC ord. 79, r. 8). If, however, a surety taken on bail being granted by a magistrates' court at committal thereafter agrees to continue to stand notwithstanding a High Court variation of other conditions of bail, the recognisance is not thereby removed to the High Court and jurisdiction to forfeit the recognisance remains vested in the Crown Court (*Warwick Crown Court, ex parte Smalley* [1987] 1 WLR 237).

The advantage of applying to the High Court for bail rather than going to the Crown Court is that hearings before the judge sitting in private can be arranged very speedily, whereas the Crown Court generally takes longer. The disadvantage is that legal aid for applications to a High Court judge is not available under the criminal legal aid scheme and, although theoretically available under the civil scheme, cannot in practice be granted in time to assist in what are necessarily urgent applications.

Rules of the Supreme Court 1965, ord. 79, r. 9

(1)   Subject to the provisions of this rule, every application to the High Court in respect of bail in any criminal proceeding—
    (a)   where the defendant is in custody, must be made by claim form to a judge sitting in private to show cause why the defendant should not be granted bail;
    (b)   where the defendant has been admitted to bail, must be made by claim form to a judge sitting in private to show cause why the variation in the arrangements for bail proposed by the applicant should not be made.
(2)   Subject to paragraph (5), the claim form . . . must, at least 24 hours before the day named therein for the hearing, be served—
    (a)   where the application was made by the defendant, on the prosecutor and on the Director of Public Prosecutions, if the prosecution is being carried on by him;
    (b)   where the application was made by the prosecutor or a constable under section 3(8) of the Bail Act 1976, on the defendant.
(3)   Subject to paragraph (5), every application must be supported by witness statement or affidavit.
(4)   Where a defendant in custody who desires to apply for bail is unable through lack of means to instruct a solicitor, he may give notice in writing to the judge sitting in private stating his desire to apply for bail and requesting that the Official Solicitor shall act for him in the application, and the judge may, if he thinks fit, assign the Official Solicitor to act for the applicant accordingly.
(5)   Where the Official Solicitor has been so assigned the judge may, if he thinks fit, dispense with the requirements of paragraphs (1) to (3) and deal with the application in a summary manner.
[(6) to (10)   Detailed rules concerning the recording of the judge's decision, the taking of sureties where he has granted conditional bail and the transmission of his decision to the lower court and other interested parties.]
(11)   Where in pursuance of an order of a judge sitting in private or of a Crown Court a person is released on bail in any criminal proceeding pending the determination of an appeal to the High Court or House of Lords or an application for an order of certiorari, then, upon the abandonment of the appeal or application, or upon the decision of the High Court or House of Lords being given, any justice (being a justice acting for the same petty sessions area as the magistrates' court by which that person was convicted or sentenced) may issue process for enforcing the decision in respect of which such appeal or application was brought or, as the case may be, the decision of the High Court or House of Lords.
(12)   If an applicant to the High Court in any criminal proceedings is refused bail by a judge sitting in private, the applicant shall not be entitled to make a fresh application for bail to any other judge or to a Divisional Court.
[(13) and (14)   Detailed rules as to court records and a modification in respect of extradition cases.]

DETENTION WHEN BAIL IS REFUSED

Detention of Adults

D5.53   Where a court refuses bail to an accused aged 21 or over he is detained in prison (or other remand centre) until the next hearing. As regards remands in custody by magistrates' courts, the MCA 1980 defines such a remand as a committal 'to custody to be brought before the court . . . at the end of the period of remand or at such earlier time as the court may require' (s. 128(1)(b)). 'Commit to custody' is in turn defined as 'commit to prison or, where any enactment authorises or requires committal to some other place of detention instead of committal to prison, to that other place' (s. 150(1)). As regards accused aged 17 to 20 inclusive who are remanded or committed for trial or sentence in custody, the court – if it has been notified that a remand centre is available for the reception from that court of persons of the accused's class or description – must commit him to the remand centre (CJA 1948, s. 27(1)). Otherwise it commits him to prison.

Juveniles Refused Bail

As regards a court's decision whether or not to grant bail to a person aged under 17, the **D5.54** only special rules applying are that (a) bail can be refused if that is necessary for his own welfare (not just if it is necessary for his protection), and (b) his parent or guardian may be asked to stand surety for his compliance with such conditions of bail as may have been imposed, as well as standing surety for his appearance at court. Where, however, bail is refused, the consequences are significantly different from the consequences in the case of a person aged over 17.

By the CYPA 1969, s. 23, if a child or young person under the age of 17 is remanded or committed for trial or sentence and is not bailed, then he must be remanded to local authority accommodation unless the criteria laid down in s. 23(5) of the CYPA 1969 are satisfied (s. 23(1)). If they are satisfied, then the court shall remand to a remand centre, or to prison (s. 23(4)). Section 23(5) lays down the criteria for the remand of a young person to a remand centre or prison, as follows:

Children and Young Persons Act 1969, s. 23

(5)   This subsection applies to a child who has attained the age of twelve, or a young person, who (in either case) is of a prescribed description, but only if—
(a)   he is charged with or has been convicted of a violent or sexual offence, or an offence punishable in the case of an adult with imprisonment for a term of fourteen years or more; or
(b)   he has a recent history of absconding while remanded to local authority accommodation, and is charged with or has been convicted of an imprisonable offence alleged or found to have been committed while he was so remanded,
and (in either case) the court is of opinion that only remanding him to a remand centre or prison would be adequate to protect the public from serious harm from him.

The 'prescribed description' referred to in s. 23(5) is supplied by the Secure Remands and Committals (Prescribed Description of Children and Young Persons) Order (SI 1999 No. 1265). It applies the provision to girls and boys aged 12, 13 or 14 and to girls aged 15 or 16.

In *Croydon Crown Court, ex parte G* (1995) *The Times*, 3 May 1995, the Divisional Court held that it was necessary for a court to assess the risk of 'serious harm' to the public by reference to the nature of the offences in respect of which the young person had been convicted or charged and the manner in which these had been carried out. It was not enough to consider only the risk that such offences might be repeated.

In addition to the powers mentioned above, a youth court can remand a young person aged 15 to 18 years in secure accommodation, by virtue of the CJA 1991, s. 60(3). The period of such remand is restricted by the Children (Secure Accommodation) Regulations 1991, reg. 13, to a period of 28 days at a time. The jurisdiction to make such an order is reserved to the youth court. Once the matter has been committed to the Crown Court, application must thereafter be made to a family proceedings court, under the Children Act 1989, s. 25, on the basis of the criteria therein.

By virtue of the CYPA 1969, s. 23A, the police can arrest a juvenile on reasonable suspicion that he has broken any condition of bail.

Children and Young Persons Act 1969, s. 23A

(1) A person who has been remanded or committed to local authority accommodation and in respect of whom conditions under subsection (7) or (10) of section 23 of this Act have been imposed may be arrested without warrant by a constable if the constable has reasonable grounds for suspecting that that person has broken any of those conditions.

(2) A person arrested under subsection (1) above—

(a) shall, except where he was arrested within 24 hours of the time appointed for him to appear before the court in pursuance of the remand or committal, be brought as soon as practicable and in any event within 24 hours after his arrest before a justice of the peace for the petty sessions area in which he was arrested; and

(b) in the said excepted case shall be brought before the court before which he was to have appeared.

Remands to Police Custody

D5.55 A remand in custody essentially involves the accused being detained either in prison (if over 21) or in a remand centre (if aged 17–20). There is, however, a limited alternative to that, namely, that a magistrates' court may, instead of remanding in custody, commit the accused to police detention for a period not exceeding three clear days; in the case of a person aged under 17, the period may not exceed 24 hours (MCA 1980, s. 128(7)). This may be done only if it is necessary for the purposes of inquiries into offences other than the one for which he appears before the court (s. 128(8)(a)). He must be brought back before the magistrates as soon as that need ceases (s. 128(8)(b)), and, while detained at the station, he is entitled to the same protection as regards conditions of detention and periodic review of the continuing need for detention as would be the case had he simply been arrested without warrant on suspicion of having committed an offence (s. 128(8)(c) and (d)).

TEXT OF THE BAIL ACT 1976

Bail Act 1976

D5.56 *Preliminary*

Meaning of 'bail in criminal proceedings'

1.—(1) In this Act 'bail in criminal proceedings' means—

(a) bail grantable in or in connection with proceedings for an offence to a person who is accused or convicted of the offence, or

(b) bail grantable in connection with an offence to a person who is under arrest for the offence or for whose arrest for the offence a warrant (endorsed for bail) is being issued.

(2) In this Act 'bail' means bail grantable under the law (including common law) for the time being in force.

(3) Except as provided by section 13(3) of this Act, this section does not apply to bail in or in connection with proceedings outside England and Wales.

. . .

(5) This section applies—

(a) whether the offence was committed in England or Wales or elsewhere, and

(b) whether it is an offence under the law of England and Wales, or of any other country or territory.

(6) Bail in criminal proceedings shall be granted (and in particular shall be granted unconditionally or conditionally), in accordance with this Act.

Other definitions

2.—(1) In this Act, unless the context otherwise requires, 'conviction' includes—

(a) a finding of guilt,

(b) a finding that a person is not guilty by reason of insanity,

(c)   a finding under section 30(1) of the Magistrates' Courts Act 1980 (remand for medical examination) that the person in question did the act or made the omission charged, and

(d)   a conviction of an offence for which an order is made placing the offender on probation or discharging him absolutely or conditionally,

and 'convicted' shall be construed accordingly.

(2)   In this Act, unless the context otherwise requires—

'bail hostel' and 'probation hostel' have the same meanings as in the Powers of Criminal Courts Act 1973,

'child' means a person under the age of fourteen,

'court' includes a judge of a court or a justice of the peace and, in the case of a specified court, includes a judge or (as the case may be) justice having powers to act in connection with proceedings before that court,

'Courts-Martial Appeal rules' means rules made under section 49 of the Courts-Martial (Appeals) Act 1968,

'Crown Court rules' means rules made under section 15 of the Courts Act 1971,

'magistrates' courts rules' means rules made under section 15 of the Justices of the Peace Act 1949,

'offence' includes an alleged offence,

'proceedings against a fugitive offender' means proceedings under section 9 of the Extradition Act 1870, section 7 of the Fugitive Offenders Act 1967 or section 2(1) or 4(3) of the Backing of Warrants (Republic of Ireland) Act 1965,

'Supreme Court rules' means rules made under section 99 of the Supreme Court of Judicature (Consolidation) Act 1925,

'surrender to custody' means, in relation to a person released on bail, surrendering himself into the custody of the court or of the constable (according to the requirements of the grant of bail) at the time and place for the time being appointed for him to do so,

'vary', in relation to bail, means imposing further conditions after bail is granted, or varying or rescinding conditions,

'young person' means a person who has attained the age of 14 and is under the age of 17.

(3)   Where an enactment (whenever passed) which relates to bail in criminal proceedings refers to the person bailed appearing before a court it is to be construed unless the context otherwise requires as referring to his surrendering himself into the custody of the court.

(4)   Any reference in this Act to any other enactment is a reference thereto as amended, and includes a reference thereto as extended or applied, by or under any other enactment, including this Act.

Incidents of bail in criminal proceedings

General provisions

3.—(1)   A person granted bail in criminal proceedings shall be under a duty to surrender to custody, and that duty is enforceable in accordance with section 6 of this Act.

(2)   No recognisance for his surrender to custody shall be taken from him.

(3)   Except as provided by this section—

(a)   no security for his surrender to custody shall be taken from him,

(b)   he shall not be required to provide a surety or sureties for his surrender to custody, and

(c)   no other requirement shall be imposed on him as a condition of bail.

(4)   He may be required, before release on bail, to provide a surety or sureties to secure his surrender to custody.

(5)   He may be required, before release on bail, to give security for his surrender to custody.

The security may be given by him or on his behalf.

(6)   He may be required to comply, before release on bail or later, with such requirements as appear to the court to be necessary to secure that—

(a)   he surrenders to custody,

(b)   he does not commit an offence while on bail,

(c)   he does not interfere with witnesses or otherwise obstruct the course of justice whether in relation to himself or any other person,

(d)   he makes himself available for the purpose of enabling inquiries or a report to be made to assist the court in dealing with him for the offence,

(e)   before the time appointed for him to surrender to custody, he attends an interview with an authorised advocate or authorised litigator, as defined by section 119(1) of the Courts and Legal Services Act 1990;

and, in any Act, 'the normal powers to impose conditions of bail' means the powers to impose conditions under paragraph (a), (b) or (c) above.

(6ZA)   Where he is required under subsection (6) above to reside in a bail hostel or probation hostel, he may also be required to comply with the rules of the hostel.

(6A)   In the case of a person accused of murder the court granting bail shall, unless it considers that satisfactory reports on his mental condition have already been obtained, impose as conditions of bail—

(a)   a requirement that the accused shall undergo examination by two medical practitioners for the purpose of enabling such reports to be prepared; and

(b)   a requirement that he shall for that purpose attend such an institution or place as the court directs and comply with any other directions which may be given to him for that purpose by either of those practitioners.

(6B)   Of the medical practitioners referred to in subsection (6A) above at least one shall be a practitioner approved for the purposes of section 12 of the Mental Health Act 1983.

(7)   If a parent or guardian of a child or young person consents to be surety for the child or young person for the purposes of this subsection, the parent or guardian may be required to secure that the child or young person complies with any requirement imposed on him by virtue of subsection (6) or (6A) above but—

(a)   no requirement shall be imposed on the parent or the guardian of a young person by virtue of this subsection where it appears that the young person will attain the age of 17 before the time to be appointed for him to surrender to custody; and

(b)   the parent or guardian shall not be required to secure compliance with any requirement to which his consent does not extend and shall not, in respect of those requirements to which his consent does extend, be bound in a sum greater than £50.

(8)   Where a court has granted bail in criminal proceedings that court or, where that court has committed a person on bail to the Crown Court for trial or to be sentenced or otherwise dealt with, that court or the Crown Court may on application—

(a)   by or on behalf of the person to whom bail was granted, or

(b)   by the prosecutor or a constable,

vary the conditions of bail or impose conditions in respect of bail which has been granted unconditionally.

(8A)   Where a notice of transfer is given under a relevant transfer provision, subsection (8) above shall have effect in relation to a person in relation to whose case the notice is given as if he had been committed on bail to the Crown Court for trial.

(8B)   Subsection (8) above applies where a court has sent a person on bail to the Crown Court for trial under section 51 of the Crime and Disorder Act 1998 as it applies where a court has committed a person on bail to the Crown Court for trial. [This subsection is inserted by the CDA 1998, sch. 8 and is in force from 4 January 1999 only in certain pilot areas where s. 51 of the CDA 1998 is in force: see **D8.21**.]

(9)   This section is subject to subsection (2) of section 30 of the Magistrates' Courts Act 1980 (conditions of bail on remand for medical examination).

(10)   This section is subject, in its application to bail granted by a constable, to section 3A of this Act.

(10)   In subsection (8A) above 'relevant transfer provision' means—

(a)   section 4 of the Criminal Justice Act 1987, or

(b)   section 53 of the Criminal Justice Act 1991.

Conditions of bail in case of police bail

3A.—(1)   Section 3 of this Act applies, in relation to bail granted by a custody officer under part IV of the Police and Criminal Evidence Act 1984 in cases where the normal powers to impose conditions of bail are available to him, subject to the following modifications.

(2)   Subsection (6) does not authorise the imposition of a requirement to reside in a bail hostel or any requirement under paragraph (d) or (e).

(3)   Subsection (6ZA), (6A) and (6B) shall be omitted.

(4)   For subsection (8), substitute the following—

'(8)   Where a custody officer has granted bail in criminal proceedings he or another custody officer serving at the same police station may, at the request of the person to whom it was granted, vary the conditions of bail; and in doing so he may impose conditions or more onerous conditions.'.

(5)   Where a constable grants bail to a person no conditions shall be imposed under subsections (4), (5), (6) or (7) of section 3 of this Act unless it appears to the constable that it is necessary to do so for the purpose of preventing that person from—

(a)   failing to surrender to custody, or

(b)   committing an offence while on bail, or

(c)   interfering with witnesses or otherwise obstructing the course of justice, whether in relation to himself or any other person.

(6)   Subsection (5) above also applies on any request to a custody officer under subsection (8) of section 3 of this Act to vary the conditions of bail.

Bail for accused persons and others

General right to bail of accused persons and others

4.—(1)   A person to whom this section applies shall be granted bail except as provided in schedule 1 to this Act.

(2)   This section applies to a person who is accused of an offence when—

(a)   he appears or is brought before a magistrates' court or the Crown Court in the course of or in connection with proceedings for the offence, or

(b)   he applies to a court for bail or for a variation of the conditions of bail in connection with the proceedings.

This subsection does not apply as respects proceedings on or after a person's conviction of the offence or proceedings against a fugitive offender for the offence.

(3)   This section also applies to a person who, having been convicted of an offence, appears or is brought before a magistrates' court to be dealt with under part II of schedule 2 to the Criminal Justice Act 1991 (breach of requirement of probation, community service, combination or curfew order).

(4)   This section also applies to a person who has been convicted of an offence and whose case is adjourned by the court for the purpose of enabling inquiries or a report to be made to assist the court in dealing with him for the offence.

(5)   Schedule 1 to this Act also has effect as respects conditions of bail for a person to whom this section applies.

(6)   In schedule 1 to this Act 'the defendant' means a person to whom this section applies and any reference to a defendant whose case is adjourned for inquiries or a report is a reference to a person to whom this section applies by virtue of subsection (4) above.

(7)   This section is subject to section 41 of the Magistrates' Courts Act 1980 (restriction of bail by magistrates' court in cases of treason).

(8)   This section is subject to section 25 of the Criminal Justice and Public Order Act 1994 (exclusion of bail in cases of homicide and rape).

Supplementary

Supplementary provisions about decisions on bail

5.—(1)   Subject to subsection (2) below, where—

(a)   a court or constable grants bail in criminal proceedings, or

(b)   a court withholds bail in criminal proceedings from a person to whom section 4 of this Act applies, or

(c)   a court, officer of a court or constable appoints a time or place or a court or officer of a court appoints a different time or place for a person granted bail in criminal proceedings to surrender to custody, or

(d)   a court or constable varies any conditions of bail or imposes conditions in respect of bail in criminal proceedings,

that court, officer or constable shall make a record of the decision in the prescribed manner and containing the prescribed particulars and, if requested to do so by the person in relation to whom the decision was taken, shall cause him to be given a copy of the record of the decision as soon as practicable after the record is made.

(2) Where bail in criminal proceedings is granted by endorsing a warrant of arrest for bail the constable who releases on bail the person arrested shall make the record required by subsection (1) above instead of the judge or justice who issued the warrant.

(3) Where a magistrates' court or the Crown Court—

(a) withholds bail in criminal proceedings, or

(b) imposes conditions in granting bail in criminal proceedings, or

(c) varies any conditions of bail or imposes conditions in respect of bail in criminal proceedings,

and does so in relation to a person to whom section 4 of this Act applies, then the court shall, with a view to enabling him to consider making an application in the matter to another court, give reasons for withholding bail or for imposing or varying the conditions.

(4) A court which is by virtue of subsection (3) above required to give reasons for its decision shall include a note of those reasons in the record of its decision and shall (except in a case where, by virtue of subsection (5) below, this need not be done) give a copy of that note to the person in relation to whom the decision was taken.

(5) The Crown Court need not give a copy of the note of the reasons for its decision to the person in relation to whom the decision was taken where that person is represented by counsel or a solicitor unless his counsel or solicitor requests the court to do so.

(6) Where a magistrates' court withholds bail in criminal proceedings from a person who is not represented by counsel or a solicitor, the court shall—

(a) if it is committing him for trial to the Crown Court, or if it issues a certificate under subsection (6A) below inform him that he may apply to the High Court or to the Crown Court to be granted bail;

(b) in any other case, inform him that he may apply to the High Court for that purpose.

(6A) Where in criminal proceedings—

(a) a magistrates' court remands a person in custody under any of the following provisions of the Magistrates' Courts Act 1980—

(i) section 5 (adjournment of inquiry into offence);

(ii) section 10 (adjournment of trial);

(iii) section 18 (initial procedure on information against adult for offence triable either way); or

(iv) section 30 (remand for medical examination),

after hearing full argument on an application for bail from him; and

(b) either—

(i) it has not previously heard such argument on an application for bail from him in those proceedings; or

(ii) it has previously heard full argument from him on such an application but it is satisfied that there has been a change in his circumstances or that new considerations have been placed before it,

it shall be the duty of the court to issue a certificate in the prescribed form that they heard full argument on his application for bail before they refused the application.

(6B) Where the court issues a certificate under subsection (6A) above in a case to which paragraph (b)(ii) of that subsection applies, it shall state in the certificate the nature of the change of circumstances or the new considerations which caused it to hear a further fully argued bail application.

(6C) Where a court issues a certificate under subsection (6A) above it shall cause the person to whom it refuses bail to be given a copy of the certificate.

(7) Where a person has given security in pursuance of section 3(5) above, and a court is satisfied that he failed to surrender to custody then, unless it appears that he had reasonable cause for his failure, the court may order the forfeiture of the security.

(8) If a court orders the forfeiture of a security under subsection (7) above, the court may declare that the forfeiture extends to such amount less than the full value of the security as it thinks fit to order.

[Subsections (8A) to (9A) detail procedure for taking and forfeiting a security.]

(10) In this section 'prescribed' means, in relation to the decision of a court or an officer of a court, prescribed by Supreme Court rules, Courts-Martial Appeal rules, Crown Court

rules or magistrates' courts rules, as the case requires or, in relation to a decision of a constable, prescribed by direction of the Secretary of State.

(11)   This section is subject, in its appliation to bail granted by a constable, to section 5A of this Act.

Supplementary provisions in cases of police bail

5A.—Section 5 of this Act applies, in relation to bail granted by a custody officer under part IV of the Police and Criminal Evidence Act 1984 in cases where the normal powers to impose conditions of bail are available to him, subject to the following modifications.

(2)   For subsection (3) substitute the following—

'(3)   Where a custody officer, in relation to any person,—

(a)   imposes conditions in granting bail in criminal proceedings, or

(b)   varies any conditions of bail or imposes conditions in respect of bail, in criminal proceedings,

the custody officer shall, with a view to enabling that person to consider requesting him or another custody officer, or making an application to a magistrates' court, to vary the conditions, give reasons for imposing or varying the conditions.'.

(3)   For subsection (4) substitute the following—

'(4)   A custody officer who is by virtue of subsection (3) above required to give reasons for his decision shall include a note of those reasons in the custody record and shall give a copy of that note to the person in relation to whom the decision was taken.'.

(4)   Subsections (5) and (6) shall be omitted.

Reconsideration of decisions granting bail

5B.—(1)   Where a magistrates' court has granted bail in criminal proceedings in connection with an offence, or proceedings for an offence, to which this section applies or a constable has granted bail in criminal proceedings in connection with proceedings for an offence, that court or the appropriate court in relation to the constable may, on application by the prosecutor for the decision to be reconsidered,—

(a)   vary the conditions of bail,

(b)   impose conditions in respect of bail which has been granted unconditionally, or

(c)   withhold bail.

(2)   The offences to which this section applies are offences triable on indictment and offences triable either way.

(3)   No application for the reconsideration of a decision under this section shall be made unless it is based on information which was not available to the court or constable when the decision was taken.

(4)   Whether or not the person to whom the application relates appears before it, the magistrates' court shall take the decision in accordance with section 4(1) (and schedule 1) of this Act.

(5)   Where the decision of the court on a reconsideration under this section is to withhold bail from the person to whom it was originally granted the court shall—

(a)   if that person is before the court, remand him in custody, and

(b)   if that person is not before the court, order him to surrender himself forthwith into the custody of the court.

(6)   Where a person surrenders himself into the custody of the court in compliance with an order under subsection (5) above, the court shall remand him in custody.

(7)   A person who has been ordered to surrender to custody under subsection (5) above may be arrested without warrant by a constable if he fails without reasonable cause to surrender to custody in accordance with the order.

(8)   A person arrested in pursuance of subsection (7) above shall be brought as soon as practicable, and in any event within 24 hours after his arrest, before a justice of the peace for the petty sessions area in which he was arrested and the justice shall remand him in custody.

In reckoning for the purposes of this subsection any period of 24 hours, no account shall be taken of Christmas Day, Good Friday or any Sunday.

(9)   Magistrates' court rules shall include provision—

(a)   requiring notice of an application under this section and of the grounds for it to be given to the person affected, including notice of the powers available to the court under it;

(b)   for securing that any representations made by the person affected (whether in writing or orally) are considered by the court before making its decision; and

(c)   designating the court which is the appropriate court in relation to the decision of any constable to grant bail.

Offence of absconding by person released on bail

6.—(1)   If a person who has been released on bail in criminal proceedings fails without reasonable cause to surrender to custody he shall be guilty of an offence.

(2)   If a person who—

(a)   has been released on bail in criminal proceedings, and

(b)   having reasonable cause therefor, has failed to surrender to custody,

fails to surrender to custody at the appointed place as soon after the appointed time as is reasonably practicable he shall be guilty of an offence.

(3)   It shall be for the accused to prove that he had reasonable cause for his failure to surrender to custody.

(4)   A failure to give to a person granted bail in criminal proceedings a copy of the record of the decision shall not constitute a reasonable cause for that person's failure to surrender to custody.

(5)   An offence under subsection (1) or (2) above shall be punishable either on summary conviction or as if it were a criminal contempt of court.

(6)   Where a magistrates' court convicts a person of an offence under subsection (1) or (2) above the court may, if it thinks—

(a)   that the circumstances of the offence are such that greater punishment should be inflicted for that offence than the court has power to inflict, or

(b)   in a case where it commits that person for trial to the Crown Court for another offence, that it would be appropriate for him to be dealt with for the offence under subsection (1) or (2) above by the court before which he is tried for the other offence, commit him in custody or on bail to the Crown Court for sentence.

(7)   A person who is convicted summarily of an offence under subsection (1) or (2) above and is not committed to the Crown Court for sentence shall be liable to imprisonment for a term not exceeding three months or to a fine not exceeding level 5 on the standard scale or to both and a person who is so committed for sentence or is dealt with as for such a contempt shall be liable to imprisonment for a term not exceeding 12 months or to a fine or to both.

(8)   In any proceedings for an offence under subsection (1) or (2) above a document purporting to be a copy of the part of the prescribed record which relates to the time and place appointed for the person specified in the record to surrender to custody and to be duly certified to be a true copy of that part of the record shall be evidence of the time and place appointed for that person to surrender to custody.

(9)   For the purposes of subsection (8) above—

(a)   'the prescribed record' means the record of the decision of the court, officer or constable made in pursuance of section 5(1) of this Act;

(b)   the copy of the prescribed record is duly certified if it is certified by the appropriate officer of the court or, as the case may be, by the constable who took the decision or a constable designated for the purpose by the officer in charge of the police station from which the person to whom the record relates was released;

(c)   'the appropriate officer' of the court is—

(i)   in the case of a magistrates' court, the justices' clerk or such other officer as may be authorised by him to act for the purpose;

(ii)   in the case of the Crown Court, such officer as may be designated for the purpose in accordance with arrangements made by the Lord Chancellor;

(iii)   in the case of the High Court, such officer as may be designated for the purpose in accordance with arrangements made by the Lord Chancellor;

(iv)   in the case of the Court of Appeal, the registrar of criminal appeals or such other officer as may be authorised by him to act for the purpose;

(v)   in the case of the Courts-Martial Appeal Court, the registrar or such other officer as may be authorised by him to act for the purpose.

Liability to arrest for absconding or breaking conditions of bail

7.—(1)   If a person who has been released on bail in criminal proceedings and is under a duty to surrender into the custody of a court fails to surrender to custody at the time appointed for him to do so the court may issue a warrant for his arrest.

(2)   If a person who has been released on bail in criminal proceedings absents himself from the court at any time after he has surrendered into the custody of the court and before the court is ready to begin or to resume the hearing of the proceedings, the court may issue a warrant for his arrest; but no warrant shall be issued under this subsection where that person is absent in accordance with leave given to him by or on behalf of the court.

(3)   A person who has been released on bail in criminal proceedings and is under a duty to surrender into the custody of a court may be arrested without warrant by a constable—

(a)   if the constable has reasonable grounds for believing that that person is not likely to surrender to custody;

(b)   if the constable has reasonable grounds for believing that that person is likely to break any of the conditions of his bail or has reasonable grounds for suspecting that that person has broken any of those conditions; or

(c)   in a case where that person was released on bail with one or more surety or sureties, if a surety notifies a constable in writing that that person is unlikely to surrender to custody and that for that reason the surety wishes to be relieved of his obligations as a surety.

(4)   A person arrested in pursuance of subsection (3) above—

(a)   shall, except where he was arrested within 24 hours of the time appointed for him to surrender to custody, be brought as soon as practicable and in any event within 24 hours after his arrest before a justice of the peace for the petty sessions area in which he was arrested; and

(b)   in the said excepted case shall be brought before the court at which he was to have surrendered to custody.

In reckoning for the purposes of this subsection any period of 24 hours, no account shall be taken of Christmas Day, Good Friday or any Sunday.

(5)   A justice of the peace before whom a person is brought under subsection (4) above may, subject to subsection (6) below, if of the opinion that that person—

(a)   is not likely to surrender to custody, or

(b)   has broken or is likely to break any condition of his bail,

remand him in custody or commit him to custody, as the case may require, or alternatively, grant him bail subject to the same or to different conditions, but if not of that opinion shall grant him bail subject to the same conditions (if any) as were originally imposed.

(6)   Where the person so brought before the justice is a child or young person and the justice does not grant him bail, subsection (5) above shall have effect subject to the provisions of section 23 of the Children and Young Persons Act 1969 (remands to the care of local authorities).

Bail with sureties

8.—(1)   This section applies where a person is granted bail in criminal proceedings on condition that he provides one or more surety or sureties for the purpose of securing that he surrenders to custody.

(2)   In considering the suitability for that purpose of a proposed surety, regard may be had (amongst other things) to—

(a)   the surety's financial resources;

(b)   his character and any previous convictions of his; and

(c)   his proximity (whether in point of kinship, place of residence or otherwise) to the person for whom he is to be surety.

(3)   Where a court grants a person bail in criminal proceedings on such a condition but is unable to release him because no surety or no suitable surety is available, the court shall fix the amount in which the surety is to be found and subsections (4) and (5) below, or in a case where the proposed surety resides in Scotland subsection (6) below, shall apply for the purpose of enabling the recognisance of the surety to be entered into subsequently.

(4)   Where this subsection applies the recognisance of the surety may be entered into before such of the following persons or descriptions of persons as the court may by order specify or, if it makes no such order, before any of the following persons, that is to say—

(a)   where the decision is taken by a magistrates' court, before a justice of the peace, a justices' clerk or a police officer who either is of the rank of inspector or above or is in charge of a police station or, if magistrates' courts rules so provide, by a person of such other description as is specified in the rules;

(b)   where the decision is taken by the Crown Court, before any of the persons specified in paragraph (a) above or, if Crown Court rules so provide, by a person of such other description as is specified in the rules;

(c)   where the decision is taken by the High Court or the Court of Appeal, before any of the persons specified in paragraph (a) above or, if Supreme Court rules so provide, by a person of such other description as is specified in the rules;

(d)   where the decision is taken by the Courts-Martial Appeal Court, before any of the persons specified in paragraph (a) above or, if Courts-Martial Appeal rules so provide, by a person of such other description as is specified in the rules;

and Supreme Court rules, Crown Court rules, Courts-Martial Appeal rules or magistrates' courts rules may also prescribe the manner in which a recognisance which is to be entered into before such a person is to be entered into and the persons by whom and the manner in which the recognisance may be enforced.

(5)   Where a surety seeks to enter into his recognisance before any person in accordance with subsection (4) above but that person declines to take his recognisance because he is not satisfied of the surety's suitability, the surety may apply to—

(a)   the court which fixed the amount of the recognisance in which the surety was to be bound, or

(b)   a magistrates' court for the petty sessions area in which he resides,

for that court to take his recognisance and that court shall, if satisfied of his suitability, take his recognisance.

(6)   Where this subsection applies, the court, if satisfied of the suitability of the proposed surety, may direct that arrangements be made for the recognisance of the surety to be entered into in Scotland before any constable, within the meaning of the Police (Scotland) Act 1967, having charge at any police office or station in like manner as the recognisance would be entered into in England or Wales.

(7)   Where, in pursuance of subsection (4) or (6) above, a recognisance is entered into otherwise than before the court that fixed the amount of the recognisance, the same consequences shall follow as if it had been entered into before that court.

Miscellaneous

Offence of agreeing to indemnify sureties in criminal proceedings

9.—(1)   If a person agrees with another to indemnify that other against any liability which that other may incur as a surety to secure the surrender to custody of a person accused or convicted of or under arrest for an offence, he and that other person shall be guilty of an offence.

(2)   An offence under subsection (1) above is committed whether the agreement is made before or after the person to be indemnified becomes a surety and whether or not he becomes a surety and whether the agreement contemplates compensation in money or in money's worth.

(3)   Where a magistrates' court convicts a person of an offence under subsection (1) above the court may, if it thinks—

(a)   that the circumstances of the offence are such that greater punishment should be inflicted for that offence than the court has power to inflict, or

(b)   in a case where it commits that person for trial to the Crown Court for another offence, that it would be appropriate for him to be dealt with for the offence under subsection (1) above by the court before which he is tried for the other offence,

commit him in custody or on bail to the Crown Court for sentence.

(4)   A person guilty of an offence under subsection (1) above shall be liable—

(a)   on summary conviction, to imprisonment for a term not exceeding 3 months or to a fine not exceeding the prescribed sum or to both; or

(b)   on conviction on indictment or if sentenced by the Crown Court on committal for sentence under subsection (3) above, to imprisonment for a term not exceeding 12 months or to a fine or to both.

(5)   No proceedings for an offence under subsection (1) above shall be instituted except by or with the consent of the Director of Public Prosecutions.

[**10.** and **11.**   Repealed.]

[**12.**   Amendments, repeals and transitional provisions.]

[**13.**   Short title, commencement, application and extent.]

SCHEDULE 1 PERSONS ENTITLED TO BAIL:
SUPPLEMENTARY PROVISIONS

PART I DEFENDANTS ACCUSED OR CONVICTED OF IMPRISONABLE OFFENCES

Defendants to whom part I applies

1. Where the offence or one of the offences of which the defendant is accused or convicted in the proceedings is punishable with imprisonment the following provisions of this part of this schedule apply.

Exceptions to right to bail

2. The defendant need not be granted bail if the court is satisfied that there are substantial grounds for believing that the defendant, if released on bail (whether subject to conditions or not) would—

    (a)   fail to surrender to custody, or

    (b)   commit an offence while on bail, or

    (c)   interfere with witnesses or otherwise obstruct the course of justice, whether in relation to himself or any other person.

2A. The defendant need not be granted bail if—

    (a)   the offence is an indictable offence or an offence triable either way; and

    (b)   it appears to the court that he was on bail in criminal proceedings on the date of the offence.

3. The defendant need not be granted bail if the court is satisfied that the defendant should be kept in custody for his own protection or, if he is a child or young person, for his own welfare.

4. The defendant need not be granted bail if he is in custody in pursuance of the sentence of a court or of any authority acting under any of the Services Acts.

5. The defendant need not be granted bail where the court is satisfied that it has not been practicable to obtain sufficient information for the purpose of taking the decisions required by this part of this schedule for want of time since the institution of the proceedings against him.

6. The defendant need not be granted bail if, having been released on bail in or in connection with the proceedings for the offence, he has been arrested in pursuance of section 7 of this Act.

Exception applicable only to defendant whose case is adjourned for inquiries or a report

7. Where his case is adjourned for inquiries or a report, the defendant need not be granted bail if it appears to the court that it would be impracticable to complete the inquiries or make the report without keeping the defendant in custody.

Restriction of conditions of bail

8.—(1) Subject to subparagraph (3) below, where the defendant is granted bail, no conditions shall be imposed under subsections (4) to (7) (except subsection (6)(d) or (e)) of section 3 of this Act unless it appears to the court that it is necessary to do so for the purpose of preventing the occurrence of any of the events mentioned in paragraph 2 of this part of this schedule.

(2) Subparagraph (1) above also applies on any application to the court to vary the conditions of bail or to impose conditions in respect of bail which has been granted unconditionally.

(3) The restriction imposed by subparagraph (1) above shall not apply to the conditions required to be imposed under section 3(6A) of this Act or operate to override the direction in section 30(2) of the Magistrates' Courts Act 1980 to a magistrates' court to impose conditions of bail under section 3(6)(d) of this Act of the description specified in the said section 30(2) in the circumstances so specified.

Decisions under paragraph 2

9. In taking the decisions required by paragraph 2 or 2A of this part of this schedule, the court shall have regard to such of the following considerations as appear to it to be relevant, that is to say—

(a) the nature and seriousness of the offence or default (and the probable method of dealing with the defendant for it),

(b) the character, antecedents, associations and community ties of the defendant,

(c) the defendant's record as respects the fulfilment of his obligations under previous grants of bail in criminal proceedings,

(d) except in the case of a defendant whose case is adjourned for inquiries or a report, the strength of the evidence of his having committed the offence or having defaulted,

as well as to any others which appear to be relevant.

9A.—(1) If—

(a) the defendant is charged with an offence to which this paragraph applies; and

(b) representations are made as to any of the matters mentioned in paragraph 2 of this part of this schedule; and

(c) the court decides to grant him bail,

the court shall state the reasons for its decision and shall cause those reasons to be included in the record of the proceedings.

(2) The offences to which this paragraph applies are—

(a) murder;

(b) manslaughter;

(c) rape;

(d) attempted murder; and

(e) attempted rape.

Cases under section 128A of Magistrates' Courts Act 1980

9B. Where the court is considering exercising the power conferred by section 128A of the Magistrates' Courts Act 1980 (power to remand in custody for more than 8 clear days), it shall have regard to the total length of time which the accused would spend in custody if it were to exercise the power.

PART II DEFENDANTS ACCUSED OR CONVICTED OF NON-IMPRISONABLE OFFENCES

Defendants to whom part II applies

1. Where the offence or every offence of which the defendant is accused or convicted in the proceedings is one which is not punishable with imprisonment the following provisions of this part of this schedule apply.

Exceptions to right to bail

2. The defendant need not be granted bail if—

(a) it appears to the court that, having been previously granted bail in criminal proceedings, he has failed to surrender to custody in accordance with his obligations under the grant of bail; and

(b) the court believes, in view of that failure, that the defendant, if released on bail (whether subject to conditions or not) would fail to surrender to custody.

3. The defendant need not be granted bail if the court is satisfied that the defendant should be kept in custody for his own protection or, if he is a child or young person, for his own welfare.

4. The defendant need not be granted bail if he is in custody in pursuance of the sentence of a court or of any authority acting under any of the Services Acts.

5. The defendant need not be granted bail if, having been released on bail in or in connection with the proceedings for the offence, he has been arrested in pursuance of section 7 of this Act.

PART IIA DECISIONS WHERE BAIL REFUSED ON PREVIOUS HEARING

1. If the court decides not to grant the defendant bail, it is the court's duty to consider, at each subsequent hearing while the defendant is a person to whom section 4 above applies and remains in custody, whether he ought to be granted bail.

2. At the first hearing after that at which the court decided not to grant the defendant bail he may support an application for bail with any argument as to fact or law that he desires (whether or not he has advanced that argument previously).

3. At subsequent hearings the court need not hear arguments as to fact or law which it has heard previously.

PART III   INTERPRETATION

1. For the purposes of this schedule the question whether an offence is one which is punishable with imprisonment shall be determined without regard to any enactment prohibiting or restricting the imprisonment of young offenders or first offenders.

2. References in this schedule to previous grants of bail in criminal proceedings include references to bail granted before the coming into force of this Act; and so as respects the reference to an offence committed by a person on bail in relation to any period before the coming into force of paragraph 2A of part I of this schedule.

3. References in this schedule to a defendant's being kept in custody or being in custody include (where the defendant is a child or young person) references to his being kept or being in the care of a local authority in pursuance of a warrant of commitment under section 23(1) of the Children and Young Persons Act 1969.

4. In this schedule—
'court', in the expression 'sentence of a court', includes a service court as defined in section 12(1) of the Visiting Forces Act 1952 and 'sentence', in that expression, shall be construed in accordance with that definition;
'default', in relation to the defendant, means the default for which he is to be dealt with under section 6 or section 16 of the Powers of Criminal Courts Act 1973;
'the Services Acts' means the Army Act 1955, the Air Force Act 1955 and the Naval Discipline Act 1957.

TEXT OF THE BAIL (AMENDMENT) ACT 1993

Bail (Amendment) Act 1993, s. 1   D5.57

(1)   Where a magistrates' court grants bail to a person who is charged with or convicted of—
  (a)   an offence punishable by a term of imprisonment of 5 years or more, or
  (b)   an offence under section 12 (taking a conveyance without authority) or 12A (aggravated vehicle taking) of the Theft Act 1968,
the prosecution may appeal to a judge of the Crown Court against the granting of bail.
(2)   Subsection (1) above applies only where the prosecution is conducted
  (a)   by or on behalf of the Director of Public Prosecutions; or
  (b)   by a person who falls within such class or description of person as may be prescribed for the purposes of this section by order made by the Secretary of State.
(3)   Such an appeal may be made only if—
  (a)   the prosecution made representations that bail should not be granted; and
  (b)   the representations were made before it was granted.
(4)   In the event of the prosecution wishing to exercise the right of appeal set out in subsection (1) above, oral notice of appeal shall be given to the magistrates' court at the conclusion of the proceedings in which such bail has been granted and before the release from custody of the person concerned.
(5)   Written notice of appeal shall thereafter be served on the magistrates' court and the person concerned within two hours of the conclusion of such proceedings.
(6)   Upon receipt from the prosecution of oral notice of appeal from its decision to grant bail the magistrates' court shall remand in custody the person concerned, until the appeal is determined or otherwise disposed of.
(7)   Where the prosecution fails, within the period of two hours mentioned in subsection (5) above, to serve one or both of the notices required by that subsection, the appeal shall be deemed to have been disposed of.

(8)   The hearing of an appeal under subsection (1) above against a decision of the magistrates' court to grant bail shall be commenced within forty-eight hours, excluding weekends and any public holiday (that is to say, Christmas Day, Good Friday or a bank holiday), from the date on which oral notice of appeal is given.

(9)   At the hearing of any appeal by the prosecution under this section, such appeal shall be by way of re-hearing, and the judge hearing any such appeal may remand the person concerned in custody or may grant bail subject to such conditions (if any) as he thinks fit.

(10   In relation to a child or young person (within the meaning of the Children and Young Persons Act 1969)—

(a)   the reference in subsection (1) above to an offence punishable by a term of imprisonment is to be read as a reference to an offence which would be so punishable in the case of an adult; and

(b)   the reference in subsection (5) above to remand in custody is to be read subject to the provisions of section 23 of the Act of 1969 (remands to local authority accommodation).

SECTION D6: DISCLOSURE

D6.1

An important issue in criminal procedure is the extent to which the prosecution and the **D6.1**
defence must before trial disclose to each other the information pertaining to the case.
Concentrating for the moment upon the prosecution, there is a central distinction
between:

(a) the disclosure by the prosecution of its case, i.e. the evidence upon which it will
rely at trial; and
(b) the disclosure of other material pertaining to the case, which it does not intend
to use — 'unused material'.

As far as (a) is concerned, the position differs according to whether trial is taking place
summarily or in the Crown Court. The extent to which the prosecution are under a duty
to reveal their case is dealt with in **D12.16** *et seq*. (so far as trial on indictment is
concerned), and in **D19.2** (for the much more limited obligations relating to summary
trial).

This section is concerned with the disclosure by the prosecution of unused material. It
also covers the duty of the defence to make disclosure, not of unused material, but of
the case upon which they will rely at trial.

Disclosure in this sense is now subject to the statutory regime set out in the CPIA 1996,
part I (ss. 1 to 21), as supplemented by the Code of Practice issued under part II of that
Act (ss. 22 to 27). The full text of the Code is set out at **appendix 6**.

The scheme of the legislation is as follows:

(a) there is a statutory duty upon the police officer investigating an offence to record
and retain information and material gathered or generated during the investigation (see
D6.2);
(b) the prosecution should, in what the Act terms 'primary disclosure', inform the
defence of certain categories of that material which they *do not* intend to use at trial (see
D6.3) — as mentioned above, there are separate obligations to inform the defence of
material which they *do* intend to use;
(c) the defence then have a duty to inform the prosecution of the case which they
intend to present at trial (**D6.4**);
(d) the defence disclosure triggers off a duty on the part of the prosecution to present
further material to the defence, 'secondary disclosure' (see **D6.5**).

The legislation makes provision for applications to be made to the court in certain
circumstances where there is a dispute about whether the prosecution should disclose
certain material (see **D6.6**); and there are sanctions laid down for defence failure to
disclose or disclosure which is late, false or inconsistent (**D6.9**).

The categories of case to which this legislative scheme applies are laid down in s. 1. In
summary, it is compulsory in relation to cases sent to the Crown Court to be tried on
indictment. It may also apply on a voluntary basis to any summary trial, including those
in the youth court (see **D6.10**).

The disclosure provisions of part I of the Act were brought into effect on 1 April 1997
(the appointed day). They apply to any alleged offence for which no criminal
investigation had begun before the appointed day. In order to pinpoint when the
investigation began, it is necessary to look at the definition of criminal investigation

contained in s. 1(4). (The scope of the definition in s. 1(4) is potentially broad: see the Code of Practice, para. 1.4, which is set out at **D6. 2**.) If the investigation began before 1 April 1997, then the disclosure regime under part I cannot apply.

Criminal Procedure and Investigations Act 1996, s. 1

(1) This part applies where—

(a) a person is charged with a summary offence in respect of which a court proceeds to summary trial and in respect of which he pleads not guilty,

(b) a person who has attained the age of 18 is charged with an offence which is triable either way, in respect of which a court proceeds to summary trial and in respect of which he pleads not guilty, or

(c) a person under the age of 18 is charged with an indictable offence in respect of which a court proceeds to summary trial and in respect of which he pleads not guilty.

(2) This part also applies where—

(a) a person is charged with an indictable offence and he is committed for trial for the offence concerned,

(b) a person is charged with an indictable offence and proceedings for the trial of the person on the charge concerned are transferred to the Crown Court by virtue of a notice of transfer given under section 4 of the Criminal Justice Act 1987 (serious or complex fraud),

(c) a person is charged with an indictable offence and proceedings for the trial of the person on the charge concerned are transferred to the Crown Court by virtue of a notice of transfer served on a magistrates' court under section 53 of the Criminal Justice Act 1991 (certain cases involving children),

(d) a count charging a person with a summary offence is included in an indictment under the authority of section 40 of the Criminal Justice Act 1988 (common assault etc.),

(e) a bill of indictment charging a person with an indictable offence is preferred under the authority of section 2(2)(b) of the Administration of Justice (Miscellaneous Provisions) Act 1933 (bill preferred by direction of Court of Appeal, or by direction or with consent of a judge), or

(f) a bill of indictment charging a person with an indictable offence is referred under section 22B(3)(a) of the Prosecution of Offences Act 1985.

(3) This part applies in relation to alleged offences into which no criminal investigation has begun before the appointed day.

(4) For the purposes of this section a criminal investigation is an investigation which police officers or other persons have a duty to conduct with a view to it being ascertained—

(a) whether a person should be charged with an offence, or

(b) whether a person charged with an offence is guilty of it.

(5) . . .

(6) In this Part—

(a) subsections (3) to (5) of section 3 (in their application for the purposes of section 3, 7 or 9), and

(b) sections 17 and 18,

have effect subject to subsections (2) and (3) of section 9 of the Sexual Offences (Protected Material) Act 1997 (by virtue of which those provisions of this Act do not apply in relation to disclosures regulated by that Act).

The CDA 1998, sch. 8, para. 125(a), adds a new s. 1(2)(cc), which provides that part I of the CPIA 1996 applies where a person is charged with an offence for which he is sent for trial under the CDA 1998, s. 51 (no committal proceedings for indictable-only offences): see **D8.21**). The amendment is in force from 4 January 1999 but in certain pilot areas only.

The Investigator's Duty

D6.2   Under s. 23 of the CPIA 1996, a Code of Practice (set out in full at **appendix 6**) has been issued. The Code applies to criminal investigations carried out by police officers. By s. 26, those other than police officers charged with the duty of conducting criminal investigations must have regard to the code's provisions.

The Code of Practice, para. 2.1 defines a criminal investigation as:

> an investigation conducted by police officers with a view to it being ascertained whether a person should be charged with an offence, or whether a person charged with an offence is guilty of it. This will include:
>
> — investigations into crimes that have been committed;
> — investigations whose purpose is to ascertain whether a crime has been committed, with a view to the possible institution of criminal proceedings; and
> — investigations which begin in the belief that a crime may be committed, for example when the police keep premises or individuals under observation for a period of time, with a view to the possible institution of criminal proceedings;

Paragraph 5.1 makes the investigator responsible for ensuring that any information relevant to the investigation is recorded and retained, whether it is gathered in the course of the investigation (e.g., documents seized in the course of searching premises) or generated by the investigation (e.g., interview records). Where there is any doubt about the relevance of material, the investigator should retain it. The duty to retain material includes for example the following categories: crime reports, including crime report forms, relevant parts of incident report books and police officers' notebooks; final versions of witness statements; draft versions of witness statements where their content differs from the final version; interview records (written or taped); expert reports and schedules; any material casting doubt upon the reliability of a confession; and any material casting doubt on the reliability of a witness (see the list in para. 5.4). However, the duty to retain material does not extend to items purely ancillary to that in the above categories which possess no independent significance, such as duplicate copies of documents. The material must be retained at least until criminal proceedings are concluded. In the event of a conviction, material must be retained until the convicted person is released from custody or discharged from hospital (where the court imposes a custodial sentence or a hospital order) and, in any event, for at least six months from the date of conviction. Where an appeal against conviction is in progress when the release or discharge occurs, or at the end of the six months, the material must be retained until the appeal is determined. A similar rule applies where an application is being considered by the Criminal Cases Review Commission (paras 5.8 and 5.9).

Where the investigator believes that the person charged with an offence is likely to plead not guilty at a summary trial, or that the offence will be tried in the Crown Court, he must prepare a schedule listing material which has been retained and which does not form part of the case against the accused. If the investigator has obtained any 'sensitive material', this should be listed in a separate schedule or, in exceptional circumstances, disclosed to the prosecutor separately; 'sensitive material' is material which the investigator believes it is not in the public interest to disclose. The Code, para. 6.12, gives a number of examples of such material, which range from material relating to national security to material given in confidence, and includes material relating to informants, undercover police officers, premises used for police surveillance, techniques used in the detection of crime, and material relating to a child witness (e.g., material generated by a local authority social services department).

The investigator should draw the prosecutor's attention to any material which might undermine the prosecution case including certain specified categories detailed in para. 7.3. The disclosure officer (defined as the person responsible for examining the records created during the investigation and criminal proceedings and disclosing material as required to the prosecutor or the accused) must certify that to the best of his knowledge and belief the duties imposed under the Code have been complied with. After the defence have complied with their duty of disclosure (see **D6.4**), the investigator must look again at the material retained, and draw the prosecutor's attention to any material which might reasonably be expected to assist the defence if it were to be disclosed. Again the disclosure officer must certify compliance with the duties imposed by the Code. If the investigator comes into possession of any new material after complying with the duties described above, then this must be treated in the same way (para. 9.1).

If the prosecutor so requests, the investigator must disclose to the accused (para. 10.17):

    (a)   material which might undermine the prosecution case;

    (b)   where the accused has given the prosecutor a defence statement (see **D6.4**), material which might reasonably be expected to assist the defence which the accused has disclosed;

    (c)   any material which the court orders be disclosed.

Criminal Procedure and Investigations Act 1996, ss. 22, 26 and 27

22.—(1) For the purposes of [part II] a criminal investigation is an investigation conducted by police officers with a view to it being ascertained—

    (a)   whether a person should be charged with an offence, or

    (b)   whether a person charged with an offence is guilty of it.

    (2) In [part II] references to material are to material of all kinds, and in particular include references to—

    (a)   information and

    (b)   objects of all descriptions.

    (3) In [part II] references to recording information are to putting it in a durable or retrievable form (such as writing or tape).

26.—(1) A person other than a police officer who is charged with the duty of conducting an investigation with a view to it being ascertained—

    (a)   whether a person should be charged with an offence, or

    (b)   whether a person charged with an offence is guilty of it,

shall in discharging that duty have regard to any relevant provision of a code which would apply if the investigation were conducted by police officers.

    (2) A failure—

    (a)   by a police officer to comply with any provision of a code for the time being in operation by virtue of an order under section 25, or

    (b)   by a person to comply with subsection (1),

shall not in itself render him liable to any criminal or civil proceedings.

    (3) In all criminal and civil proceedings a code in operation at any time by virtue of an order under section 25 shall be admissible in evidence.

    (4) If it appears to a court or tribunal conducting criminal or civil proceedings that—

    (a)   any provision of a code in operation at any time by virtue of an order under section 25, or

    (b)   any failure mentioned in subsection (2)(a) or (b),

is relevant to any question arising in the proceedings, the provision or failure shall be taken into account in deciding the question.

27.—(1) Where a code prepared under section 23 and brought into operation under section 25 applies in relation to a suspected or alleged offence, the rules of common law which—

    (a)   were effective immediately before the appointed day, and

    (b)   relate to the matter mentioned in subsection (2),

shall not apply in relation to the suspected or alleged offence.

    (2) The matter is the revealing of material—

    (a)   by a police officer or other person charged with the duty of conducting an investigation with a view to it being ascertained whether a person should be charged with an offence or whether a person charged with an offence is guilty of it;

    (b)   to a person involved in the prosecution of criminal proceedings.

    (3) In subsection (1) 'the appointed day' means the day appointed under section 25 with regard to the code as first prepared.

Primary Prosecution Disclosure

Section 3 of the CPIA 1996 requires the prosecutor to disclose previously undisclosed **D6.3** material to the accused if, in the prosecutor's opinion, it might undermine the case for the prosecution. The test is a subjective one, in that it is based on the opinion of the prosecutor (compare the objective test for secondary prosecution disclosure laid down in s. 7(2): see **D6.5**). If there is no such material, then the accused must be given a written statement to that effect. Prosecution material includes material which the prosecutor possesses or has been allowed to inspect under the provisions of the Code of Practice (see **D6.2** and **appendix 6**). It may be disclosed either by giving it to the defence, or allowing them to inspect it at a reasonable time and place. This step is called 'primary prosecution disclosure', and it must be carried out within a time-limit which is to be laid down by statutory instrument, or (until such a limit is set) as soon as reasonably practicable after the happening of a particular event, such as the accused being committed for trial (s. 13(1)). Material must not, however, be disclosed under this provision if a court has concluded that it is not in the public interest that it be disclosed (s. 3(6) and see **D6.5**). Material obtained under s. 2 of the Interception of Communications Act 1985 is exempted from disclosure (s. 3(7)).

Where material is 'protected' by virtue of the Sexual Offences (Protected Material) Act 1997, it is not subject to the usual procedure for prosecution disclosure under the CPIA 1996 (see s. 1(6) of the 1996 Act, reproduced in **D6.2**). Material is protected where it is a statement, photograph or medical report of the physical condition of the victim of a sexual offence (defined so as to include rape, indecent assault, unlawful sexual intercourse, incest, buggery or possession of indecent photographs of children, *inter alia*: see the schedule to the 1997 Act). Where material is protected, the prosecutor should disclose it not to the defendant but to his legal representative. Where he is not legally represented, disclosure should be made to the governor of the prison where he is detained, or (if he is not detained in prison) to the officer in charge of a suitable police station (ss. 3 and 5). The 1997 Act lays down duties on the recipients of the protected material to ensure that the defendant cannot retain possession of it or pass it on to any person except in connection with the proceedings for which it has been disclosed (ss. 4 and 5). Section 8 creates a series of offences where the material is held or revealed in circumstances other than those authorised in the 1997 Act.

In determining whether unused material should be revealed to the defence as part of the process of primary disclosure, the statutory test for the prosecution is whether it 'might undermine' their case. Prior to judicial interpretation, it is difficult to predict how the crucial test will be implemented in practice. One pointer is provided by the intention of the legislature, as revealed by the Parliamentary debates on the Criminal Procedure and Investigations Bill, prior to its enactment in 1996, under the rules in *Pepper* v *Hart* [1993] AC 593. During the passage of the Bill through Parliament, the government made it clear that material which might undermine the prosecution case would include more than evidence which was *fatal* to the prosecution case. The test was, for example, described as follows by the Home Office Minister, Mr David McLean:

> The test for primary disclosure is designed to ensure that the prosecutor discloses at the first stage material that, generally speaking, has an adverse effect on the strength of the prosecution case. It is not confined to material raising a fundamental question about the prosecution . . . The disclosure scheme is aimed at undisclosed material that might help the accused, notwithstanding the fact that there is enough evidence to provide a realistic prospect of conviction . . . (*Hansard,* House of Commons Standing Committee B, 14 May 1996, col. 34).

It is submitted that the formulae used by the Minister ('has an adverse effect on the prosecution case' and 'might help the accused') are in any event in line with the wording of the statute. Something can be said to be undermined if it becomes more likely to fall (or fail) as a result. The prosecution case will be more likely to fail as a result of evidence which shows a defect, discrepancy or inconsistency in that case. Such evidence ought to be revealed as part of primary disclosure. But it *might* be undermined as a result of a particular defence, which the defendant may or may not run. Clearly it is not possible to say at the stage of primary disclosure with certainty whether the defence will take a particular course. That will become clearer after defence disclosure, although it will actually only be entirely certain once the trial itself takes place. But the mere fact that material in the possession of the prosecution raises a new issue in the case which may assist the defence is sufficient, it is submitted, to fulfil the test contained in the phrase 'might undermine', since all that is required is a tendency to undermine.

It should also be noted that prosecutors (at any rate those acting on behalf of the CPS) will be governed in their decisions on disclosure by the Code for Crown Prosecutors (see **appendix 4**), para 2.2 of which states that the 'duty of the CPS is to make sure . . . that all relevant facts are given to the court'. In the adversarial framework within which the criminal justice process operates in this country, ensuring that the court receives the relevant facts will often mean that they are revealed to the defence for it to present to the court.

In *DPP, ex parte Lee* [1999] 1 WLR 1950, the Divisional Court considered whether the prosecution had a duty to disclose unused material in indictable-only offences prior to committal. The statutory framework for disclosure set out in the CPIA 1996 is silent as to any such duty until after committal. But there may well be reasons why it would be helpful to the defence to know of unused material at an earlier stage. For example, the following circumstances were considered by the court:

   (a)   the previous convictions of the alleged victim when they might be expected to help the defence in a bail application;
   (b)   material to help an application to stay proceedings as an abuse of process;
   (c)   material to help the defendant's arguments at committal;
   (d)   material to help the defendant prepare for trial, e.g. eye witnesses whom the prosecution did not intend to use.

Kennedy LJ said that a responsible prosecutor might recognise that fairness required that some of this material might be disclosed. The question was: what immediate disclosure (if any) did justice and fairness require in the circumstances of the case? It is submitted that this approach is consistent with the objective of ensuring that the legitimate rights of the defendant are preserved. It is likely that the appellate courts will continue to back the discretion of the prosecutor to disclose unused material in circumstances where such a course of action is in accordance with fairness, even if it is not strictly required by the statute. There has always been an ethical dimension to the duty to disclose, and the decision in *Ex parte Lee* is an indication that it survives the introduction of the CPIA 1996.

In *Mills* [1998] AC 382, the House of Lords considered the question of whether the prosecution had a duty to disclose to the defence only the name and address of a witness who had given a statement as to material aspects of the case but whom the prosecution regarded as unreliable and did not therefore intend to call at trial (the rule in *Bryant* (1946) 31 Cr App R 146). Their lordships, in considering the common-law position as it applied to the instant case, held that the prosecution duty was wider than this, and now required them to supply to the defence copies of such witness statements. It is submitted that a similar result would be reached under the statutory scheme contained in the CPIA 1996, which requires the disclosure of 'any prosecution material which has not previously been disclosed' (s. 3(1)), and defines 'prosecution material' so as include material possessed or inspected by the prosecutor in connection with the case against the accused (s. 3(2)).

By s. 4, if the prosecutor has been given a document indicating any non-sensitive material which has not been given to the accused, that document must be given to the accused at the same time as primary prosecution disclosure takes place.

Criminal Procedure and Investigations Act 1996, ss. 3 and 4

3.—(1) The prosecutor must—

(a) disclose to the accused any prosecution material which has not previously been disclosed to the accused and which in the prosecutor's opinion might undermine the case for the prosecution against the accused, or

(b) give to the accused a written statement that there is no material of a description mentioned in paragraph (a).

(2) For the purposes of this section prosecution material is material—

(a) which is in the prosecutor's possession, and came into his possession in connection with the case for the prosecution against the accused, or

(b) which, in pursuance of a code operative under part II, he has inspected in connection with the case for the prosecution against the accused.

(3) Where material consists of information which has been recorded in any form the prosecutor discloses it for the purposes of this section—

(a) by securing that a copy is made of it and that the copy is given to the accused, or

(b) if in the prosecutor's opinion that is not practicable or not desirable, by allowing the accused to inspect it at a reasonable time and a reasonable place or by taking steps to secure that he is allowed to do so;

and a copy may be in such form as the prosecutor thinks fit and need not be in the same form as that in which the information has already been recorded.

(4) Where material consists of information which has not been recorded the prosecutor discloses it for the purposes of this section by securing that it is recorded in such form as he thinks fit and—

(a) by securing that a copy is made of it and that the copy is given to the accused, or

(b) if in the prosecutor's opinion that is not practicable or not desirable, by allowing the accused to inspect it at a reasonable time and a reasonable place or by taking steps to secure that he is allowed to do so.

(5) Where material does not consist of information the prosecutor discloses it for the purposes of this section by allowing the accused to inspect it at a reasonable time and a reasonable place or by taking steps to secure that he is allowed to do so.

(6) Material must not be disclosed under this section to the extent that the court, on an application by the prosecutor, concludes it is not in the public interest to disclose it and orders accordingly.

(7) Material must not be disclosed under this section to the extent that—

(a) it has been intercepted in obedience to a warrant issued under section 2 of the Interception of Communications Act 1985, or

(b) it indicates that such a warrant has been issued or that material has been intercepted in obedience to such a warrant.

(8) The prosecutor must act under this section during the period which, by virtue of section 12, is the relevant period for this section.

4.—(1) This section applies where—

(a) the prosecutor acts under section 3, and

(b) before so doing he was given a document in pursuance of provision included, by virtue of section 24(3), in a code operative under part II.

(2) In such a case the prosecutor must give the document to the accused at the same time as the prosecutor acts under section 3.

Defence Disclosure

By the CPIA 1996, s. 5, once primary prosecution disclosure has taken place and the **D6.4**
case is committed to the Crown Court, the accused must give a defence statement to the prosecutor. The defence statement is a written statement setting out in general terms the nature of the defence and the matters on which the accused takes issue with the prosecution, with reasons. By the CPIA 1996 (Defence Disclosure Time Limits)

Regulations 1997 (SI 1997 No. 684), reg. 2, the defence statement must be served within 14 days of the prosecution's compliance (or purported compliance) with the duty of primary disclosure. Whilst the defence may apply for an extension, specifying their belief on reasonable grounds that it is not possible to meet the deadline, the application must be made before the deadline expires (reg. 3). The court may grant an extension 'entirely at [its] discretion', and may order further extensions on the same basis. (For voluntary disclosure by the accused in cases involving summary trial (under s. 6), see **D6.10**.)

If the defence statement discloses an alibi, particulars of alibi must be given, including the name and address of any alibi witness, or information which might be of use in finding the witness if his or her name or address is not known. This provision replaces s. 11 of the CJA 1967 (see **D14.14**), which ceases to have effect except in certain limited circumstances by virtue of the CPIA 1996, s. 74, although a similar definition of alibi evidence is adopted, namely 'evidence tending to show that by reason of the presence of the accused at a particular place or in a particular area at a particular time he was not, or was unlikely to have been, at the place where the offence is alleged to have been committed at the time of its alleged commission' (for interpretation of this definition, see **D14.14**).

It should be stressed that the duty of disclosure imposed on the defence is of a different kind from what is normally meant when one talks about 'the prosecution duty of disclosure'. The prosecution duty is to disclose *unused material*, i.e. material which they do not intend to introduce at trial. As far as defence disclosure is concerned, the duty is to reveal the case which *will* be presented at trial. There is no obligation on the *defence*, either at common law or under the new statutory scheme, to reveal material which is *not* to be used at trial.

In interpreting the intended scope of the defence statement, the remarks of the Solicitor-General in the Parliamentary debate on what is now s. 5(6) are apposite. He said: 'There is no suggestion that in giving the reason [why it takes issue with the prosecution], detail of the evidence to support that reason should be given'. In particular, he stated that 'the fear that this might require the defence to set out its oral cross-examination is not well founded. That is not intended at all' (*Hansard*, House of Commons Committee, 16 May 1996, cols 66–69). This statement of intent by the government may prove of relevance to the courts when they come to interpret the wording of s. 5(6), in accordance with the approach outlined in *Pepper* v *Hart* [1993] AC 593. It should in any event be viewed in the context of what might reasonably be required of the defence at a stage when they may not be clear about the way in which the prosecution are to put their case.

As has been described, the duty to provide a defence statement has subsumed the narrower obligation to serve notice of alibi, so that the CJA 1967, s. 11, has been repealed. One of the issues which the courts were called upon to resolve in relation to the now extinct notice of alibi was whether the prosecution were permitted to put it in evidence as part of their case. It is submitted that to allow the prosecution to put the defence statement in evidence would be a serious derogation from the privilege against self-incrimination, and the principle that the burden of proof should rest upon the prosecution throughout. There is no specific authority in the statute for such a course of action, and the prosecution would have to clear two hurdles in order to be able to use the defence statement:

(a) they would have to show that the statement was the defendant's; and
(b) they would have to establish an evidential route for its admission.

In the normal course of events, where the defence statement is prepared and issued by the defendant's solicitors, the prosecution would need to show that it was issued with the defendant's authority so as to be, in effect, his statement. The position at common law, however, is that in criminal cases a client is not bound by statements written by his solicitor in the absence of proof of specific instructions. In the absence of statutory authority, evidence would be required to establish that the defence statement under s. 5 was issued with the accused's authority, before it could properly be said to be the *defendant's* statement. The Act contains no such authority. The issue was dealt with differently in the provisions relating to alibi evidence contained in the CJA 1967, which are repealed by the 1996 Act. In s. 11(5) of the 1967 Act, there was a deeming provision: 'Any notice purporting to be given under this section on behalf of the defendant by his solicitor shall, unless the contrary is proved, be deemed to be given with the authority of the defendant'. In *Rossborough* (1985) 81 Cr App R 141, it was held that a notice of alibi could be proved by the prosecution as part of their case. The case may be distinguished, however, because of the deeming provision contained in the 1967 Act, which has no counterpart in the disclosure provisions of the 1996 Act.

On the other hand, it should be noted that s. 5 of the 1996 Act requires the accused, rather than his legal representative, to give a defence statement to the court and the prosecutor. If the statement is drawn up and served by the accused's legal representative then it might be argued that it should be treated as a statement of the accused. This interpretation is lent some credence by a statement by the government during the debates on the Bill:

> It is implicit that things that may be done by the accused may also be done through his legal representative or an expert acting on their instructions. Where the legislation mentions the accused, both the accused and his legal representative are automatically included in the term. (David Maclean, Home Office Minister in *Hansard*, House of Commons Committee, 14 May 1996, col. 30.)

It is submitted, however, that in the absence of a specific deeming provision, this is not enough to overcome the caution with which the criminal law has treated statements made by agents on behalf of a defendant, especially given the breadth and looseness of the phrase used ('his legal representative or an expert acting on their instructions').

Assuming that the prosecution are able to clear the hurdle of establishing the accused's authority for the s. 5 statement so that it is treated as the defendant's statement, it is still an out-of-court statement, and they must then establish its admissibility notwithstanding its hearsay nature, for example by showing that it was a confession or that it is original evidence of the defendant's state of mind (e.g. a lie) (see **F16.36**, **F16.51** and **F17.3**). Once the s. 5 statement is established as the defendant's statement, it is clear that there are several potential evidential routes to admissibility. It is doubtful whether this was an intended (or an expected) consequence of defence disclosure. If the prosecution attempt to adduce the defence statement in evidence as part of their case, then in appropriate cases the judge may be asked to exercise a discretion under the PACE 1984, s. 78, to exclude it on the basis that 'it would have such an adverse effect on the fairness of proceedings that the court ought not to admit it' (see **F17.16** *et seq.*).

Criminal Procedure and Investigations Act 1996, s. 5

(1)   Subject to subsections (2) to (4), this section applies where—
   (a)   [part I] applies by virtue of section 1(2), and
   (b)   the prosecutor complies with section 3 or purports to comply with it.
(2)   Where [part I] applies by virtue of section 1(2)(b), this section does not apply unless—
   (a)   a copy of the notice of transfer, and
   (b)   copies of the documents containing the evidence, have been given to the accused under regulations made under section 5(9) of the Criminal Justice Act 1987.
(3)   Where [part I] applies by virtue of section 1(2)(c), this section does not apply unless—

(a)   a copy of the notice of transfer, and

(b)   copies of the documents containing the evidence,

have been given to the accused under regulations made under paragraph 4 of Schedule 6 to the Criminal Justice Act 1991.

(4)   Where [part I] applies by virtue of section 1(2)(e), this section does not apply unless the prosecutor has served on the accused a copy of the indictment and a copy of the set of documents containing the evidence which is the basis of the charge.

(5)   Where this section applies, the accused must give a defence statement to the court and the prosecutor.

(6)   For the purposes of this section a defence statement is a written statement—

(a)   setting out in general terms the nature of the accused's defence,

(b)   indicating the matters on which he takes issue with the prosecution, and

(c)   setting out, in the case of each such matter, the reason why he takes issue with the prosecution.

(7)   If the defence statement discloses an alibi the accused must give particulars of the alibi in the statement, including—

(a)   the name and address of any witness the accused believes is able to give evidence in support of the alibi, if the name and address are known to the accused when the statement is given;

(b)   any information in the accused's possession which might be of material assistance in finding any such witness, if his name or address is not known to the accused when the statement is given.

(8)   For the purposes of this section evidence in support of an alibi is evidence tending to show that by reason of the presence of the accused at a particular place or in a particular area at a particular time he was not, or was unlikely to have been, at the place where the offence is alleged to have been committed at the time of its alleged commission.

(9)   The accused must give a defence statement under this section during the period which, by virtue of section 12, is the relevant period for this section.

The CDA 1998, sch. 8, para. 126, amends s. 5 by introducing a new s. 5(3A) which takes account of the introduction of the new procedure under the CDA 1998, s. 51 (no committal proceedings for indictable offences: see **D8.21**). The amendment and the new procedure are in force from 4 January 1998 in certain pilot areas only.

Criminal Procedure and Investigations Act 1996 (Defence Disclosure Time Limits) Regulations 1997 (SI 1997 No. 684), regs 2 to 5

2.   Subject to regulations 3, 4 and 5, the relevant period for sections 5 and 6 of the Act (disclosure by the accused) is a period beginning with the day on which the prosecutor complies, or purports to comply, with section 3 of that Act and ending with the expiration of 14 days from that day.

3.—(1)   The period referred to in regulation 2 shall, if the court so orders, be extended by so many days as the court specifies.

(2)   The court may only make such an order if an application which complies with paragraph (3) below is made by the accused before the expiration of the period referred to in regulation 2.

(3)   An application under paragraph (2) above shall—

(a)   state that the accused believes, on reasonable grounds, that it is not possible for him to give a defence statement under section 5 or, as the case may be, 6 of the Act during the period referred to in regulation 2;

(b)   specify the grounds for so believing; and

(c)   specify the number of days by which the accused wishes that period to be extended.

(4)   The court shall not make an order under paragraph (1) above unless it is satisfied that the accused cannot reasonably give or, as the case may be, could not reasonably have given a defence statement under section 5 or, as the case may be, 6 of the Act during the period referred to in regulation 2.

(5)   The number of days by which the period referred to in regulation 2 may be extended shall be entirely at the court's discretion.

4.—(1)   Where the court has made an order under regulation 3(1), the period referred to in regulation 2 as extended in accordance with that order shall, if the court so orders, be further extended by so many days as the court specifies.

(2)   Paragraphs (2) to (5) of regulation 3 shall, subject to paragraph (4) below, apply for the purposes of an order under paragraph (1) above as they apply for the purposes of an order under regulation 3(1).

(3)   There shall be no limit on the number of applications that may be made under regulation 3(2) as applied by paragraph (2) above; and on a second or subsequent such application the court shall have the like powers under paragraph (1) above as on the first such application.

(4)   In the application of regulation 3(2) to (5) in accordance with paragraph (2) above, any reference to the period referred to in regulation 2 shall be construed as a reference to that period as extended or, as the case may be, further extended by an order of the court under regulation 3(1) or paragraph (1) or (3) above.

5.—(1)   Where the period referred to in regulation 2 or that period as extended or, as the case may be, further extended by an order of the court under regulation 3(1) or 4(1) or (3) would, apart from this regulation, expire on any of the days specified in paragraph (2) below, that period shall be treated as expiring on the next following day which is not one of those days.

(2)   The days referred to in paragraph (1) above are Saturday, Sunday, Christmas Day, Good Friday and any day which . . . is a bank holiday in England and Wales.

Secondary Prosecution Disclosure

Once the accused has served a statement under the CPIA 1996, s. 5 or s. 6, the **D6.5** prosecutor must disclose to the accused any previously undisclosed prosecution material 'which might be reasonably expected to assist the accused's defence as disclosed by the defence statement' (s. 7). If there is no such material, the prosecutor must give to the accused a statement to that effect. This obligation on the part of the prosecutor is complemented by the duty which the Code (para. 8.2) places on the investigator, who is required to look again at the material retained, and draw the prosecutor's attention to any material which might reasonably be expected to assist the defence disclosed in the defence statement. This process is termed 'secondary prosecution disclosure', and must be carried out within a time-limit to be laid down by statutory instrument or (until such a limit is set) as soon as reasonably practicable (s. 13(2)). The methods of disclosure are identical to those set out in respect of primary prosecution disclosure, and the process is subject to the same exception in respect of material which the court orders should not be disclosed because it would not be in the public interest to do so (s. 7(5)). The test for secondary disclosure is an objective one ('any prosecution material which might be reasonably expected . . .') and is subject to challenge by the accused and review by the court (see **D6.6**). Material obtained under s. 2 of the Interception of Communications Act 1985 is exempted from secondary prosecution disclosure (s. 7(6)).

Criminal Procedure and Investigations Act 1996, s. 7

(1)   This section applies where the accused gives a defence statement under section 5 or 6.

(2)   The prosecutor must—

(a)   disclose to the accused any prosecution material which has not previously been disclosed to the accused and which might be reasonably expected to assist the accused's defence as disclosed by the defence statement given under section 5 or 6, or

(b)   give to the accused a written statement that there is no material of a description mentioned in paragraph (a).

(3)   For the purposes of this section prosecution material is material—

(a)   which is in the prosecutor's possession and came into his possession in connection with the case for the prosecution against the accused, or

(b)   which, in pursuance of a code operative under part II, he has inspected in connection with the case for the prosecution against the accused.

(4)   Subsections (3) to (5) of section 3 (method by which prosecutor discloses) apply for the purposes of this section as they apply for the purposes of that.

(5)   Material must not be disclosed under this section to the extent that the court on an application by the prosecutor, concludes it is not in the public interest to disclose it and orders accordingly.

(6)   Material must not be disclosed under this section to the extent that—

(a)   it has been intercepted in obedience to a warrant issued under section 2 of the Interception of Communications Act 1985, or

(b)   it indicates that such a warrant has been issued or that material has been intercepted in obedience to such a warrant.

(7)   The prosecutor must act under this section during the period which, by virtue of section 12, is the relevant period for this section.

Review by the Court

D6.6   The prosecutor may make application to the court that material should not be disclosed, either at the primary or the secondary stage, on the basis that it is not in the public interest to disclose it (CPIA 1996, s. 7(5): see **D6.5** for the text and **D6.8** for commentary). Although the legislation does not specifically so state, such application is likely to be on the basis that the material in question falls within one of the categories of 'sensitive' material outlined in the Code of Practice (see **D6.2**). For its part, the defence can, under s. 8, apply to the court for an order that the prosecutor should disclose any material which might be reasonably expected to assist the accused's defence. This applies to material held or inspected by the prosecutor (s. 8(3)), but also to any material which the disclosure officer must either supply to the prosecutor, or allow the prosecutor to inspect if requested (s. 8(4)). Such an application may only be made, however, after the defence have served a defence statement (s. 8(1)).

Criminal Procedure and Investigations Act 1996, s. 8

(1)   This section applies where the accused gives a defence statement under section 5 or 6 and the prosecutor complies with section 7 or purports to comply with it or fails to comply with it.

(2)   If the accused has at any time reasonable cause to believe that—

(a)   there is prosecution material which might be reasonably expected to assist the accused's defence as disclosed by the defence statement given under section 5 or 6, and

(b)   the material has not been disclosed to the accused,

the accused may apply to the court for an order requiring the prosecutor to disclose such material to the accused.

(3)   For the purposes of this section prosecution material is material—

(a)   which is in the prosecutor's possession and came into his possession in connection with the case for the prosecution against the accused,

(b)   which, in pursuance of a code operative under part II, he has inspected in connection with the case for the prosecution against the accused, or

(c)   which falls within subsection (4).

(4)   Material falls within this subsection if in pursuance of a code operative under part II the prosecutor must, if he asks for the material, be given a copy of it or be allowed to inspect it in connection with the case for the prosecution against the accused.

(5)   Material must not be disclosed under this section to the extent that the court, on an application by the prosecutor, concludes it is not in the public interest to disclose it and orders accordingly.

(6)   Material must not be disclosed under this section to the extent that—

(a)   it has been intercepted in obedience to a warrant issued under section 2 of the Interception of Communications Act 1985, or

(b)   it indicates that such a warrant has been issued or that material has been intercepted in obedience to such a warrant.

Continuing Duty to Review

D6.7   Under the CPIA 1996, s. 9, the prosecutor remains under a continuing duty to review questions of disclosure. If, at any time before the accused is acquitted or convicted, the prosecutor forms the opinion that there is material which might undermine the prosecution case, or be reasonably expected to assist the accused's defence, then it must be disclosed to the accused as soon as reasonably practicable (provided that the court has not ruled against disclosure in respect of that material). Material obtained under s. 2 of the Interception of Communications Act 1985 is exempt from such disclosure (s. 9).

This duty of continuous review would come into play, for example, where a prosecution witness gives evidence which is materially inconsistent with a statement made earlier to the police. If the defence are unaware of the statement, prosecuting counsel should disclose it to his opposite number so that he can use it in cross-examination to discredit the testimony of the witness (*Clarke* (1931) 22 Cr App R 58 — although the case was many years before the 1996 Act, it is submitted that the principle still holds).

Where the court has ruled against disclosure in relation to a matter which is being tried on indictment, it must keep under review the question whether it is still in the public interest not to disclose the material affected by its order. The position so far as summary trial is concerned is dealt with in **D6.10**.

Criminal Procedure and Investigations Act 1996, s. 9

(1) Subsection (2) applies at all times—
    (a) after the prosecutor complies with section 3 or purports to comply with it, and
    (b) before the accused is acquitted or convicted or the prosecutor decides not to proceed with the case concerned.
(2) The prosecutor must keep under review the question whether at any given time there is prosecution material which—
    (a) in his opinion might undermine the case for the prosecution against the accused, and
    (b) has not been disclosed to the accused;
and if there is such material at any time the prosecutor must disclose it to the accused as soon as is reasonably practicable.
(3) In applying subsection (2) by reference to any given time the state of affairs at that time (including the case for the prosecution as it stands at that time) must be taken into account.
(4) Subsection (5) applies at all times—
    (a) after the prosecutor complies with section 7 or purports to comply with it, and
    (b) before the accused is acquitted or convicted or the prosecutor decides not to proceed with the case concerned.
(5) The prosecutor must keep under review the question whether at any given time there is prosecution material which—
    (a) might be reasonably expected to assist the accused's defence as disclosed by the defence statement given under section 5 or 6, and
    (b) has not been disclosed to the accused;
and if there is such material at any time the prosecutor must disclose it to the accused as soon as is reasonably practicable.
(6) For the purposes of this section prosecution material is material—
    (a) which is in the prosecutor's possession and came into his possession in connection with the case for the prosecution against the accused, or
    (b) which, in pursuance of a code operative under part II, he has inspected in connection with the case for the prosecution against the accused.
(7) Subsections (3) to (5) of section 3 (method by which prosecutor discloses) apply for the purposes of this section as they apply for the purposes of that.
(8) Material must not be disclosed under this section to the extent that the court, on an application by the prosecutor, concludes it is not in the public interest to disclose it and orders accordingly.
(9) Material must not be disclosed under this section to the extent that—
    (a) it has been intercepted in obedience to a warrant issued under section 2 of the Interception of Communications Act 1985, or
    (b) it indicates that such a warrant has been issued or that material has been intercepted in obedience to such a warrant.

Public Interest Immunity

D6.8   Where the prosecution are subject to a duty of disclosure, they may seek to establish that the duty does not apply to certain information, on the basis that they can claim public interest immunity. Although the 1996 Act generally disapplies the rules of common law in relation to the prosecution duty of disclosure (s. 21(1)), it preserves 'the rules of common law as to whether disclosure is in the public interest' (s. 21(2)). The provisions of the CPIA 1996 which provide for disclosure to the defendant allow relevant material to be withheld on public interest grounds only if the court so decides (ss. 3(6), 7(5), 8(5) and 9(8)). In this respect, the 1996 Act reflects the rule established in *Ward* [1993] 1 WLR 619. In that case Judith Ward had been convicted of multiple murder and explosives offences. The prosecution had failed to disclose material relevant to her alleged confessions and certain scientific evidence. The Court of Appeal made it clear that the court, rather than the prosecution, had to be the final arbiter as to whether the prosecution was entitled to avoid disclosure on the basis of public interest immunity. It would be wrong to allow the prosecution to withhold material documents without giving notice of that fact to the defence. The court could then, if necessary, be asked to rule on the legitimacy of the prosecution's asserted claim. If the prosecution was not prepared to have the issue of public interest immunity determined by a court, they would inevitably have to abandon the case.

Inclusion of material upon a 'sensitive' schedule is of course in no way conclusive of the question of whether its disclosure is in the public interest. That question is quite clearly one to be answered by the court, both in terms of the statutory provisions referred to above, and the common-law rules which the statute preserves. The principle in *Ward* remains intact and is reinforced by the terms of the 1996 Act: the court, rather than the prosecutor (let alone the investigator) is the final arbiter as to whether disclosure can be avoided on the basis of public interest immunity. Further, it is clear that the categories of 'sensitive material' spelt out in the Code of Practice on Disclosure (see **appendix 6**) are wider than the types of material which the courts have been prepared to shield behind public interest immunity. The Code gives as an example of sensitive material, 'material given in confidence'; but the fact that material has been given in confidence is not sufficient of itself to ensure that it attracts public interest immunity, so as to enable the prosecution to avoid disclosing it (see **F9.1**).

In *Menga* [1998] Crim LR 58, the Court of Appeal emphasised that prosecution counsel should ensure, as far as he can, that he has sight of all material in respect of which public interest immunity is to be claimed before the trial commences so that the applications can be made at the most convenient time. The CPS, said their lordships, had an obvious obligation to ensure that all such material was in their possession, and the police had a duty to pass the material on.

Where the court has been given the role of final arbiter as to whether the refusal to disclose is justified, as it is under the 1996 Act in respect of questions relating to public interest immunity, it is submitted that the judge must himself examine or view the evidence, so that he can have the facts of what it contained in mind. Only then can he be in a position to balance the competing interests of public interest immunity and fairness to the party claiming disclosure (*K (T.D.)* (1993) 97 Cr App R 342). In *Law* (1996) *The Times*, 15 August 1996, the Court of Appeal held that, in deciding whether to order the prosecution to disclose information, the judge was not restricted to considering only evidence admissible in a court of law. He was entitled to see additional material, even if it amounted to hearsay evidence. For examples of circumstances in which the prosecution can successfully claim immunity from disclosure, see **F9.5**.

In *Davis* [1993] 1 WLR 613, the Court of Appeal set out further guidance as to the procedure which should be adopted where the prosecution claim immunity from disclosure. After reiterating that it is for the court, not the prosecution, to decide whether disclosure must be made, Lord Taylor CJ put forward certain principles as to the proper approach to disclosure.

(a)   In general it is the prosecution's duty to make disclosure voluntarily, and in accordance with para. 2 of the A-G's guidelines.

(b)   If the prosecution wish to rely on public interest immunity or sensitivity to justify non-disclosure, then, whenever possible, which will be in most cases, they must notify the defence that they are applying for a ruling by the court, and indicate to the defence at least the category of the material which they hold. The defence must then have the opportunity of making representations to the court.

(c)   Where, however, the disclosure of the category of material would be to reveal that which the prosecution contend it would not be in the public interest to reveal, a different procedure will apply. The prosecution should still notify the defence of the application, but need not specify the category of material, and the application will be *ex parte*. If the court, on hearing the application, considers that the normal procedure under (b) ought to have been followed, it will so order. If not, it will rule on the *ex parte* application.

(d)   In a highly exceptional case, the prosecution might take the view that to reveal even the fact that an *ex parte* application is to be made could 'let the cat out of the bag' so as to stultify the application. Such a case would be rare indeed, but if it did occur then the prosecution should apply to the court *ex parte* without notice. Again, if the court on hearing the application considered that notice should have been given to the defence, or even that the normal *inter partes* hearing should have been adopted, it will so order.

After setting out these principles, Lord Taylor went on to say:

> We should add that where the court, on application by the Crown, rules in favour of non-disclosure before the hearing of a case begins, that ruling is not necessarily final. In the course of the hearing, the situation may change. Issues may emerge so that the public interest in non-disclosure may be eclipsed by the need to disclose in the interests of securing fairness to the defendant. If that were to occur, the court would have to indicate to the Crown its change of view. The Crown would then have to decide whether to disclose or offer no further evidence.

> It will therefore be necessary for the court to continue to monitor the issue. For that reason, it is desirable that the same judge or constitution of the court which decides the application should conduct the hearing. If that is not possible, the judge or constitution which does conduct the hearing should be apprised at the outset of the material upon which non-disclosure was upheld on the Crown's earlier application.

The Crown Court (Criminal Procedure and Investigations Act 1996) (Disclosure) Rules 1997 (SI 1997 No. 698) in effect reproduce the procedure laid down in *Davis*, although they contain no explicit provision about the judge's responsibility, if he thinks fit, to ensure that the defence should have appropriate information about an *ex parte* application by the prosecution. It is clear, however, that the dicta of Lord Taylor CJ continue to apply. If the judge takes the view, therefore, that the defence should have had notice of the application, or of the nature of the material, or that the application should be made *inter partes*, then he should direct accordingly.

In due course, the appellants in *Davis* petitioned the Court in Strasbourg under the European Convention on Human Rights (reported as *Davis and Rowe* [1999] Crim LR 410), alleging that the *ex parte* procedure for hearing public interest immunity arguments adopted and endorsed by the Court of Appeal violated their rights under Art. 6. In October 1998, the Commission held that the application was admissible, and should be heard by the Court. This decision was based in part upon the nature of the *ex parte* procedure given statutory force in the 1997 Rules. The problem perceived by the

Commission was that none of the judges who heard the case had the benefit of arguments from both sides on the balance to be struck between the need for secrecy and the defendants' right to a fair trial. It is not altogether surprising that the Commission saw this as potentially infringing the right to a fair trial entrenched in Art. 6(1) (see **D26.4** and **appendix** 7). The decision of the full Court in due course as to whether there was a violation is awaited, and is likely to be a most important one for the practice adopted in relation to disclosure in public interest immunity cases.

In *Smith* [1998] 2 Cr App R 1, the Court of Appeal stressed that no *ex parte* application should be made in circumstances where there was nothing to be said which could not be said in the presence of defence counsel. In any event, said their lordships, such proceedings must be conducted in the presence of a shorthand writer to ensure that a permanent record is made.

Section 16 of the 1996 Act provides for interventions by interested third-parties when the court is considering the issue of public interest immunity.

Criminal Procedure and Investigations Act 1996, ss. 14 to 16

14.—(1)   This section applies where [part I] applies by virtue of section 1(1).
   (2)   At any time—
      (a)   after a court makes an order under section 3(6), 7(5), 8(5) or 9(8), and
      (b)   before the accused is acquitted or convicted or the prosecutor decides not to proceed with the case concerned,
the accused may apply to the court for a review of the question whether it is still not in the public interest to disclose material affected by its order.
   (3)   In such a case the court must review that question, and if it concludes that it is in the public interest to disclose material to any extent—
      (a)   it shall so order, and
      (b)   it shall take such steps as are reasonable to inform the prosecutor of its order.
   (4)   Where the prosecutor is informed of an order made under subsection (3) he must act accordingly having regard to the provisions of [part I] (unless he decides not to proceed with the case concerned).

15.—(1)   This section applies where [part I] applies by virtue of section 1(2).
   (2)   This section applies at all times—
      (a)   after a court makes an order under section 3(6), 7(5), 8(5) or 9(8), and
      (b)   before the accused is acquitted or convicted or the prosecutor decides not to proceed with the case concerned.
   (3)   The court must keep under review the question whether at any given time it is still not in the public interest to disclose material affected by its order.
   (4)   The court must keep the question mentioned in subsection (3) under review without the need for an application; but the accused may apply to the court for a review of that question.
   (5)   If the court at any time concludes that it is in the public interest to disclose material to any extent—
      (a)   it shall so order, and
      (b)   it shall take such steps as are reasonable to inform the prosecutor of its order.
   (6)   Where the prosecutor is informed of an order made under subsection (5) he must act accordingly having regard to the provisions of [part I] (unless he decides not to proceed with the case concerned).

16.   Where—
      (a)   an application is made under section 3(6), 7(5), 8(5), 9(8), 14(2) or 15(4),
      (b)   a person claiming to have an interest in the material applies to be heard by the court, and
      (c)   he shows that he was involved (whether alone or with others and whether directly or indirectly) in the prosecutor's attention being brought to the material,
the court must not make an order under section 3(6), 7(5), 8(5), 9(8), 14(3) or 15(5) (as the case may be) unless the person applying under paragraph (b) has been given an opportunity to be heard.

**Crown Court (Criminal Procedure and Investigation Act 1996)
(Disclosure) Rules 1997 (SI 1997 No. 698)**

[**1.** Commencement, citation and interpretation.]

2.—(1)   This rule applies to the making of an application by the prosecutor under section 3(6), 7(5), 8(5) or 9(8) where part I applies by virtue of section 1(2) (trial on indictment).

(2)   Subject to paragraphs (3) to (5) below, notice of an application to which this rule applies shall be served on the appropriate officer of the Crown Court and on the accused and shall specify the nature of the material to which the application relates.

(3)   Where the prosecutor has reason to believe that to reveal to the accused the nature of the material to which the application relates would have the effect of disclosing that which the prosecutor contends should not in the public interest be disclosed, paragraph (2) above shall have effect as if the words from 'and shall specify' to the end were omitted.

(4)   Where the prosecutor has reason to believe that to reveal to the accused the fact that an application is being made would have the effect of disclosing that which the prosecutor contends should not in the public interest be disclosed, paragraph (2) above shall have effect as if the words from 'and on the accused' to the end were omitted.

(5)   Where an application to which this rule applies is made under paragraph (2) above as it has effect in accordance with paragraph (4) above, notice of the application may be served on the trial judge or, if the application is made before the start of the trial, on the judge, if any, who has been designated to conduct the trial instead of on the appropriate officer of the court.

3.—(1)   This rule applies to the hearing of an application by the prosecutor under section 3(6), 7(5), 8(5) or 9(8) where part I applies by virtue of section 1(2).

(2)   On receipt of an application to which this rule applies the appropriate officer of the Crown Court shall refer it—

(a)   if the trial has started, to the trial judge, or

(b)   if the application is received before the start of the trial either—

(i)   to the judge who has been designated to conduct the trial, or

(ii)   if no judge has been designated for that purpose, to such judge as may be designated for the purposes of hearing the application.

(3)   Subject to paragraphs (4) and (5) below and to rule 6(4), where the application is made in accordance with rule 2(2)—

(a)   the appropriate officer of the Crown Court shall give notice to—

(i)   the prosecutor;

(ii)   the accused; and

(iii)   any person claiming to have an interest in the material to which the application relates who has applied under section 16(b) to be heard by the court,

of the date and time when and the place where the hearing will take place and, unless the court orders otherwise, such notice shall be given in writing;

(b)   the hearing shall be *inter partes;* and

(c)   the prosecutor and the accused shall be entitled to make representations to the court.

(4)   Where the prosecutor applies to the court for leave to make representations in the absence of the accused, the court may for that purpose sit in the absence of the accused and any legal representative of his.

(5)   Subject to rule 6(4), where the application is made under rule 2(2) as it has effect in accordance with rule 2(3) or (4)—

(a)   the hearing shall be *ex parte*;

(b)   only the prosecutor shall be entitled to make representations to the court; and

(c)   the accused shall not be given notice as specified in paragraph (3) above;

and, where notice of the application has been served in pursuance of rule 2(5), the judge on whom it is served shall take such steps as he considers appropriate to ensure that notice is given as required by paragraph (3)(a)(i) and (iii) above.

4.—(1)   This rule applies to an order under section 3(6), 7(5), 8(5) or 9(8).

(2)   On making an order to which this rule applies, the court shall state its reasons for doing so and a record shall be made of that statement.

(3)   In a case where such an order is made following—

(a)   an application which has been made under rule 2(2) as it has effect in accordance with rule 2(3), or

(b)   an application which has been made in accordance with rule 2(2) but the accused has not appeared or been represented at the hearing of that application,

the appropriate officer of the Crown Court shall notify the accused that an order has been made:

Provided that no notification shall be given under this paragraph in a case where an order is made following an application which has been made under rule 2(2) as it has effect in accordance with rule 2(4).

5.—(1)   This rule applies to an application by the accused under section 15(4).

(2)   An application to which this rule applies shall be made by notice in writing to the appropriate officer of the Crown Court and shall specify the reason why the accused believes the court should review the question mentioned in section 15(3).

(3)   A copy of the notice referred to in paragraph (2) above shall be served on the prosecutor at the same time as it is sent to the appropriate officer of the court.

(4)   On receipt of an application to which this rule applies the appropriate officer of the Crown Court shall refer it—

(a)   if the trial has started, to the trial judge, or

(b)   if the application is received before the start of the trial either—

(i)   to the judge who has been designated to conduct the trial, or

(ii)   if no judge has been designated for that purpose, to the judge who made the order to which the application relates.

(5)   The judge to whom an application to which this rule applies has been referred under paragraph (4) above shall consider whether the application may be determined without a hearing and, subject to paragraph (6) below, may so determine it if he thinks fit.

(6)   No application to which this rule applies shall be determined without a hearing if it appears to the judge that there are grounds on which the court might conclude that it is in the public interest to disclose material to any extent.

(7)   Subject to paragraphs (8) and (9) below and to rule 6(4), the hearing of an application to which this rule applies shall be *inter partes* and the accused and the prosecutor shall be entitled to make representations to the court.

(8)   Where after hearing the accused's representations the prosecutor applies to the court for leave to make representations in the absence of the accused, the court may for that purpose sit in the absence of the accused and any legal representative of his.

(9)   Subject to rule 6(4), where the order to which the application relates was made following an application which was made under rule 2(2) as it has effect in accordance with rule 2(4), the hearing shall be *ex parte* and only the prosecutor shall be entitled to make representations to the court.

(10)   The appropriate officer of the court shall give notice in writing to—

(a)   the prosecutor;

(b)   except where a hearing takes place in accordance with paragraph (9) above, the accused; and

(c)   any person claiming to have an interest in the material to which the application relates who has applied under section 16(b) to be heard by the court,

of the date and time when and the place where the hearing of an application to which this rule applies will take place and of any order which is made by the court following its determination of the application.

(11)   Where an application to which this rule applies is determined without a hearing in pursuance of paragraph (5) above, the appropriate officer of the court shall give notice in writing in accordance with paragraph (10) above of any order which is made by the judge following his determination of the application.

6.—(1)   Where the prosecutor has reason to believe that a person who was involved (whether alone or with others and whether directly or indirectly) in the prosecutor's attention being brought to any material to which an application under section 3(6), 7(5), 8(5), 9(8) or 15(4) relates may claim to have an interest in that material, the prosecutor shall—

(a)   in the case of an application under section 3(6), 7(5), 8(5) or 9(8), at the same time as notice of the application is served under rule 2(2) or (5),

(b)   in the case of an application under section 15(4), when he receives a copy of the notice referred to in rule 5(2),
give notice in writing to—
    (i)   the person concerned of the application, and
    (ii)   the appropriate officer of the Crown Court or, as the case may require, the judge of his belief and the grounds for it.

(2)   An application under section 16(b) shall be made by notice in writing to the appropriate officer of the Crown Court or, as the case may require, the judge as soon as is reasonably practicable after receipt of notice under paragraph (1)(i) above or, if no such notice is received, after the person concerned becomes aware of the application referred to in that sub-paragraph and shall specify the nature of the applicant's interest in the material and his involvement in bringing the material to the prosecutor's attention.

(3)   A copy of the notice referred to in paragraph (2) above shall be served on the prosecutor at the same time as it is sent to the appropriate officer of the court or the judge.

(4)   At the hearing of an application under section 3(6), 7(5), 8(5), 9(8) or 15(4) a person who has made an application under section 16(b) in accordance with paragraph (2) above shall be entitled to make representations to the court.

7.—(1)   This rule applies to an application by the accused under section 8(2).

(2)   An application to which this rule applies shall be made by notice in writing to the appropriate officer of the Crown Court and shall specify—
    (a)   the material to which the application relates;
    (b)   that the material has not been disclosed to the accused;
    (c)   the reason why the material might be expected to assist the applicant's defence as disclosed by the defence statement given under section 5; and
    (d)   the date of service of a copy of the notice on the prosecutor in accordance with paragraph (3) below.

(3)   A copy of the notice referred to in paragraph (2) above shall be served on the prosecutor at the same time as it is sent to the appropriate officer of the court.

(4)   On receipt of an application to which this rule applies, the appropriate officer of the Crown Court shall refer it—
    (a)   if the trial has started, to the trial judge, or
    (b)   if the application is received before the start of the trial—
        (i)   to the judge who has been designated to conduct the trial, or
        (ii)   if no judge has been designated for that purpose, to such judge as may be designated for the purposes of determining the application.

(5)   The judge to whom an application to which this rule applies has been referred under paragraph (4) above shall consider whether the application may be determined without a hearing and, subject to paragraph (7) below, may so determine it if he thinks fit.

(6)   The prosecutor shall give notice in writing to the appropriate officer of the court within 14 days of service of a notice under paragraph (3) above that—
    (a)   he wishes to make representations to the court concerning the material to which the application relates; or
    (b)   if he does not so wish, that he is willing to disclose that material;
and a notice under sub-paragraph (a) above shall specify the substance of the representations he wishes to make.

(7)   No application to which this rule applies shall be determined without a hearing if—
    (a)   the prosecutor has given notice under paragraph (6)(a) above and the judge to whom the application has been referred considers that the representations should be made at a hearing; or
    (b)   that judge considers a hearing to be necessary in the interests of justice for the purposes of determining the application.

(8)   Subject to paragraph (9) below, where a hearing is held in pursuance of this rule—
    (a)   the appropriate officer of the court shall give notice in writing to the prosecutor and the applicant of the date and time when and the place where the hearing will take place;
    (b)   the hearing shall be *inter partes;* and
    (c)   the prosecutor and the applicant shall be entitled to make representations to the court.

(9)   Where the prosecutor applies to the court for leave to make representations in the

absence of the accused, the court may for that purpose sit in the absence of the accused and any legal representative of his.

(10)   A copy of any order under section 8(2) shall be served on the prosecutor and the applicant.

8.—(1)   This rule applies to an application under paragraph (2) of regulation 3 of the Criminal Procedure and Investigations Act 1996 (Defence Disclosure Time Limits) Regulations 1997 ('the 1997 Regulations'), including that paragraph as applied by regulation 4(2) of the 1997 Regulations.

(2)   An application to which this rule applies shall be made by notice in writing to the appropriate officer of the Crown Court and shall, in addition to the matters referred to in paragraphs (a) to (c) of regulation 3(3) of the 1997 Regulations, specify the date of service of a copy of the notice on the prosecutor in accordance with paragraph (3) below.

(3)   A copy of the notice referred to in paragraph (2) above shall be served on the prosecutor at the same time as it is sent to the appropriate officer of the court.

(4)   The prosecutor may make representations to the court concerning the application and if he wishes to do so he shall do so in writing within 14 days of service of a notice under paragraph (3) above.

(5)   On receipt of representations under paragraph (4) above, or on the expiration of the period specified in that paragraph if no such representations are received within that period, the court shall consider the application and may, if it wishes, do so at a hearing.

(6)   Where a hearing is held in pursuance of this rule—

(a)   the appropriate officer of the court shall give notice in writing to the prosecutor and the applicant of the date and time when and the place where the hearing will take place;

(b)   the hearing shall be *inter partes;* and

(c)   the prosecutor and the applicant shall be entitled to make representations to the court.

(7)   A copy of any order under regulation 3(1) or 4(1) of the 1997 Regulations shall be served on the prosecutor and the applicant.

9.—(1)   Any hearing held in pursuance of or in accordance with these Rules may be adjourned from time to time.

(2)   Any hearing referred to in paragraph (1) above other than one held in pursuance of rule 8 may be held in private.

(3)   Where a hearing or any part thereof, is held in private in pursuance of paragraph (2) above, the court may specify conditions subject to which the record of its statement of reasons made in pursuance of rule 4(2) is to be kept.

(4)   Where an application or order to which any provision of these rules applies is made after the start of the trial, the trial judge may direct that any provision of these rules requiring notice of the application or order to be given to any person shall not have effect and may give such direction as to the giving of notice in relation to that application or order as he thinks fit.

Sanctions for Failure in Defence Disclosure

D6.9   Integral to the scheme of the disclosure provisions is the notion that, if the defence fail to make disclosure, it will not trigger off the prosecution's obligation to make secondary disclosure (which is of material which may reasonably be expected to assist the defence advanced in the defence statement). Section 11 of the CPIA 1996 lays down additional sanctions to which the defence will be liable if they are deficient in their duty of disclosure which apply if the defence:

(a)   fail to make disclosure;

(b)   make disclosure after the deadline laid down by statutory instrument;

(c)   set out inconsistent defences in its statement;

(d)   put forward a defence at trial which is different from the defence statement;

(e)   at trial adduce evidence of alibi without having given particulars of alibi in the statement;

(f)   at trial call an alibi witness without having given details of that witness in the statement.

If any of these conditions apply then deficiencies in the defence's disclosure may be commented on by the court (or by a party with the court's leave), and the court or the jury may draw inferences from the accused's failure to disclose properly.

In deciding what to do where the accused has put forward different defences, however, the court is to have regard to the extent of the difference and whether there is any justification for it. Further, an accused may not be convicted solely on the basis of an inference drawn under s. 11.

It would seem that the wording of s. 11(3)(b) would preclude the use of an inference from defective disclosure to bolster the prosecution case against a submission of no case to answer, since the phrase 'whether the accused is guilty of the offence concerned' is not apt to describe the decision which the court has to make on such a submission. The context in which such an inference can be drawn is therefore narrower than that applicable to inferences from silence under the CJPO 1994, s. 34 (see **F19.4**), which explicitly allows an inference to be drawn when the court determines whether there is a case to answer, reserving the wording replicated in s. 11(3)(b) of the 1996 Act to apply to the verdict.

Where the judge decides to allow the jury to draw an inference, it may trigger off the need for a direction in accordance with *Lucas* [1981] QB 720 (see *Burge* [1996] 1 Cr App R 163 as to the circumstances in which a *Lucas* direction ought to be given). The judge would need to direct the jury to consider whether the defence statement constituted a deliberate lie on a material issue, which was due to the realisation of guilt and the fear of the truth (see **F1.12** and **F18.19**).

Criminal Procedure and Investigations Act 1996, s. 11

(1)   This section applies where section 5 applies and the accused—
(a)   fails to give a defence statement under that section,
(b)   gives a defence statement under that section but does so after the end of the period which, by virtue of section 12, is the relevant period for section 5,
(c)   sets out inconsistent defences in a defence statement given under section 5,
(d)   at his trial puts forward a defence which is different from any defence set out in a defence statement given under section 5,
(e)   at his trial adduces evidence in support of an alibi without having given particulars of the alibi in a defence statement given under section 5, or
(f)   at his trial calls a witness to give evidence in support of an alibi without having complied with subsection (7)(a) or (b) of section 5 as regards the witness in giving a defence statement under that section.
(2)   This section also applies where section 6 applies, the accused gives a defence statement under that section, and the accused—
(a)   gives the statement after the end of the period which, by virtue of section 12, is the relevant period for section 6,
(b)   sets out inconsistent defences in the statement,
(c)   at his trial puts forward a defence which is different from any defence set out in the statement,
(d)   at his trial adduces evidence in support of an alibi without having given particulars of the alibi in the statement, or
(e)   at his trial calls a witness to give evidence in support of an alibi without having complied with subsection (7)(a) or (b) of section 5 (as applied by section 6) as regards the witness in giving the statement.
(3)   Where this section applies—
(a)   the court or, with the leave of the court, any other party may make such comment as appears appropriate;
(b)   the court or jury may draw such inferences as appear proper in deciding whether the accused is guilty of the offence concerned.
(4)   Where the accused puts forward a defence which is different from any defence set out in a defence statement given under section 5 or 6, in doing anything under subsection (3) or in deciding whether to do anything under it the court shall have regard—

(a)   to the extent of the difference in the defences, and

(b)   to whether there is any justification for it.

(5)   A person shall not be convicted of an offence solely on an inference drawn under subsection (3).

(6)   Any reference in this section to evidence in support of an alibi shall be construed in accordance with section 5.

Summary Trial

D6.10   As far as summary trial is concerned, the CPIA 1996 partially incorporates proceedings into the statutory disclosure scheme, by virtue of s. 1(1) (see **D6.1**). The prosecution's duty of primary disclosure applies whenever the accused pleads not guilty and the court proceeds to summary trial. Once the prosecutor has complied (or purported to comply) with that duty, the accused *may* give the prosecutor and the court a defence statement (s. 6). If he does so, that triggers off secondary disclosure. It also means that the court may allow comment or draw inferences from disclosure which is late, defective or inconsistent, in much the same circumstances as it may in a jury trial (s. 11(2)) (see **D6.9**). These sanctions for the defence apply also to the notification of alibi evidence (which until the 1996 Act had no formal role in summary proceedings). The voluntary regime applies to summary trial, whether it is of a summary or a triable-either-way offence or even (in the case of a juvenile) of an indictable-only offence (s. 1(1)).

The question of public interest immunity in summary trial is dealt with in s. 14. Where the court has made an order that material should not be disclosed because it is not in the public interest, the accused may apply at any time for the ruling to be reviewed. Section 14 does not impose upon the court an obligation to review non-disclosure on public interest grounds in summary trial, even though s. 15 does impose such an obligation upon the Crown Court in respect of trial on indictment. The difference would appear to stem from the dual role of the magistrates as triers of both fact and law, which was encountered in *South Worcester Justices, ex parte Lilley* [1995] 1 WLR 1595 (see **D19.3**). The problem is that, when the magistrates (in their role as triers of law) conduct a review of documents for which immunity is claimed, it may appear to prejudice them in their role as triers of fact. The problem is compounded when the review is conducted *ex parte*, in the absence of the defendant and the defence lawyer. As a result, a new bench may be needed to try the case, after the old bench rules against disclosure. If that new bench were under a duty of continuous review, it would mean that it would be impossible ever to recruit a bench which was proof against the contamination which results from looking at the material. Hence the onus is put on the defendant to make the application (see also *Stipendiary Magistrate for Norfolk, ex parte Taylor* (1997) 161 JP 773).

Applications to the magistrates under ss. 3, 7, 8, 9, 14 and 16 of the 1996 Act are to be made in accordance with the Magistrates' Courts (Criminal Procedure and Investigations Act 1996) (Disclosure) Rules 1997 (SI 1997 No. 703). These rules are similar to those in respect of the Crown Court (see **D6.8**), the main points of difference being that:

(a)   there is a different procedure for making an application under r. 2 (reproduced below);

(b)   there is no requirement under r. 4 to keep a record of reasons for a non-disclosure order;

(c)   there is a requirement on the clerk under r. 5 to make papers available to the court reviewing a non-disclosure order;

(d)   there is no power under r. 9 to waive the requirements relating to the giving of notice.

Criminal Procedure and Investigations Act 1996, s. 6

(1)   This section applies where—
    (a)   [part I] applies by virtue of section 1(1), and
    (b)   the prosecutor complies with section 3 or purports to comply with it.
(2)   The accused—
    (a)   may give a defence statement to the prosecutor, and
    (b)   if he does so, must also give such a statement to the court.
(3)   Subsections (6) to (8) of section 5 apply for the purposes of this section as they apply for the purposes of that.
(4)   If the accused gives a defence statement under this section he must give it during the period which, by virtue of section 12, is the relevant period for this section.

Magistrates' Courts (Criminal Procedure and Investigations Act 1996) (Disclosure) Rules 1997, r. 2

2.—(1)   This rule applies to the making of an application by the prosecutor under section 3(6), 7(5), 8(5) or 9(8) where Part I applies by virtue of section 1(1) (summary trial).
(2)   Notice of an application to which this rule applies shall be served on the clerk of the magistrates' court trying the offence referred to in section 1(1) and shall specify the nature of the material to which the application relates.
(3)   Subject to paragraphs (4) and (5) below, a copy of the notice of application shall be served on the accused by the prosecutor.
(4)   Where the prosecutor has reason to believe that to reveal to the accused the nature of the material to which the application relates would have the effect of disclosing that which the prosecutor contends should not in the public interest be disclosed, paragraph (3) above shall not apply but the prosecutor shall notify the accused that an application to which this rule applies has been made.
(5)   Where the prosecutor has reason to believe that to reveal to the accused the fact that an application is being made would have the effect of disclosing that which the prosecutor contends should not in the public interest be disclosed, paragraph (3) above shall not apply.

Third Party Disclosure

Sometimes the information which the accused needs for his defence will be in the hands **D6.11** of someone other than the prosecution — a 'third party' as far as the criminal case is concerned. In some cases, the material in question may have come into the possession of the police and/or the prosecution in the course of the investigation. If so, it should generally be retained by the police, and will fall within the disclosure regime (Code, paras 5.1 to 5.3).

If the material remains in the hands of the third party, then the accused is obviously entitled to request it. If the third party is not prepared to hand it over, then the course of action available to the accused (or anyone else seeking disclosure from a third party, but it is usually the accused who is in this position) is to seek a witness summons. The procedure is laid down by the Criminal Procedure (Attendance of Witnesses) Act 1965, s. 2(1) (for the text, see **D12.29**), as far as Crown Court trial is concerned. In the magistrates' court, it is governed by the MCA 1980, s. 97 (see **D19.4**). The procedure involves issuing a witness summons to compel the third party to attend with the document(s) to give evidence, and/or to produce the document(s) in advance. The person seeking the witness summons must satisfy the court that the third party:

    (a)   is likely to be able to give or produce material evidence in the case; and
    (b)   will not voluntarily attend or produce the evidence.

The application should, in the case of Crown Court trial, be made 'as soon as reasonably practicable after the committal' or the equivalent where an alternative to committal has been used, e.g., a notice of transfer. It will usually be heard on notice to the person to whom the summons is directed (the third party), who may appear or be represented at the hearing. The application should be supported by an affidavit, setting out the charges, identifying the evidence or document sought, stating the grounds for believing that the third party is able to give or produce it, and the grounds for believing that it is material. At the hearing, the third party would be able to argue, for example, that there is no evidence held, or that it is not material, or that it should not be disclosed on grounds of public interest immunity.

SECTION D7: COMMITTAL PROCEEDINGS

Introduction

Committal proceedings have traditionally been the means by which a magistrates' court **D7.1** determines whether there is sufficient evidence against an accused in respect of an indictable offence to justify sending him to the Crown Court to stand trial on indictment. They are held when an adult accused either (a) comes before a magistrates' court charged with an offence triable only on indictment, or (b) comes before the court charged with an offence triable either way, mode of trial having been determined in favour of trial on indictment. For the limited occasions on which committal proceedings will be necessary in the cases of juveniles, see **D21**. Magistrates sitting for purposes of committal proceedings are usually referred to as 'examining justices'.

When s. 51 of the CDA 1998 comes fully into effect, cases triable on indictment only, and certain related offences, will be sent immediately to the Crown Court without committal proceedings being held (see **D8.21**). This provision is the subject of a pilot scheme with a view to national implementation in Spring 2000.

The necessity for the holding of committal proceedings arises from s. 2(2) of the Administration of Justice (Miscellaneous Provisions) Act 1933.

Administration of Justice (Miscellaneous Provisions) Act 1933, s. 2

(2)   Subject as hereinafter provided no bill of indictment charging any person with an indictable offence shall be preferred unless either—

(a)   the person charged has been committed for trial for the offence; or

(aa)   the offence is specified in a notice of transfer under section 4 of the Criminal Justice Act 1987 (serious or complex fraud); or

(ab)   the offence is specified in a notice of transfer under section 53 of the Criminal Justice Act 1991 (violent or sexual offences against children); or

(ac)   the person charged has been sent for trial for the offence under section 51 (no committal proceedings for indictable-only offences) of the Crime and Disorder Act 1998 ('the 1998 Act'); or

(b)   the bill is preferred by the direction of the Criminal Division of the Court of Appeal or by the direction or with the consent of a judge of the High Court; or

(c)   the bill is preferred under section 22B(3)(a) of the Prosecution of Offences Act 1985. Provided that—

(i)   where the person charged has been committed for trial, the bill of indictment against him may include, either in substitution for or in addition to counts charging the offence for which he was committed, any counts founded on facts or evidence disclosed to the magistrates' court inquiring into that offence as examining justices, being counts which may lawfully be joined in the same indictment;

(iA)   in a case to which paragraph (aa) or (ab) above applies, the bill of indictment may include, either in substitution for or in addition to any count charging an offence specified in the notice of transfer, any counts founded on material that accompanied the copy of that notice which, in pursuance of regulations under the relevant provision, was given to the person charged, being counts which may lawfully be joined in the same indictment;

(iB)   in a case to which paragraph (ac) above applies, the bill of indictment may include, either in substitution for or in addition to any count charging an offence specified in the notice under section 51(7) of the 1998 Act, any counts founded on material which, in pursuance of regulations made under paragraph 1 of schedule 3 to that Act, was served on the person charged, being counts which may be lawfully joined in the same indictment; and in paragraph (iA) above 'the relevant provision' means section 5(9) of the Criminal Justice Act 1987 in a case to which paragraph (aa) above applies, and paragraph 4 of schedule 6 to the Criminal Justice Act 1991 in a case to which paragraph (ab) above applies.

Section 2 is shown as amended by the CDA 1998, sch. 8, para. 5. The amendments inserting s. 2(2)(ac) and 2(2)(iB) are in force in the pilot areas in which s. 51 of the 1998 Act applies from 4 January 1999. The amendment inserting s. 2(2)(c) is not yet in force.

A 'bill of indictment' is a draft indictment, prepared by or on behalf of the prosecution, which is thereafter preferred, that is, put before an appropriate officer of the Crown Court for his signature. Once signed, it becomes the indictment on which the accused will be tried. If a bill of indictment is preferred without authority, the resulting indictment is liable to be quashed on application to the trial judge, and the accused will be discharged without pleading to the charges against him (1933 Act, s. 2(3)). Therefore, the combined effect of s. 2(2) and (3) is that a trial on indictment may not validly take place unless either:

(a)   the accused has been committed for trial (s. 2(2)(a)); or
(b)   a notice of transfer has been given by a designated prosecuting authority transferring a case direct to the Crown Court (s. 2(2)(aa) or (ab)); or
(c)   the accused has been sent to the Crown Court by the magistrates under the CDA 1998, s. 51 (provisions relating to indictable-only offences); or
(d)   the Court of Appeal has directed the preferment of a bill of indictment; or
(e)   the bill is preferred by the direction or with the consent of a High Court judge (s. 2(2)(b)).

As to (b), notices of transfer are a procedure introduced by the CJA 1987, and built upon by the CJA 1991. As to (d), the Court of Appeal's power to direct preferment of a bill is an adjunct of the discretion given to it by s. 7 of the Criminal Appeal Act 1968 to quash a conviction on indictment but order that the successful appellant be retried. As to (e), preferment of a bill by the direction or with the consent of a High Court judge (also known as the 'voluntary bill' procedure) could in theory occur in any type of case but is in practice considered appropriate only for a few fairly exceptional situations. Consequently, the normal preliminary to a trial on indictment is the holding of committal proceedings as a result of which the magistrates commit the accused to the Crown Court for trial. The effect of the proviso to s. 2(2) is that, provided the accused was validly committed for trial on a charge of an indictable offence, the indictment against him may include counts for other indictable offences (in respect of which he was not committed) if those offences are disclosed by the evidence adduced at the committal proceedings.

The use of notices of transfer in serious fraud and child witness cases, the procedure in respect of indictable-only offences and voluntary bills of indictment are considered in **D8**. This section deals with committal proceedings. As already stated, their basic purpose is to determine whether there is sufficient evidence against an accused to justify his being tried on indictment. This is variously referred to as a 'prima facie' case or 'a case to answer'.

Major changes to the nature of committal were brought about by the CPIA 1996, which limited the evidence which could be considered to documentary evidence tendered by the prosecution, together with any exhibits. It abolished the right of the defence to call evidence of its own or to require prosecution witnesses to attend to give evidence orally. It introduced a new procedure for taking depositions from reluctant witnesses in advance of committal proceedings. These provisions came into effect on 1 April 1997, and, by virtue of the Criminal Procedure and Investigations Act 1996 (Commencement) (Section 65 and Schedules 1 and 2) Order 1997 (SI 1997 No. 683), they apply to any alleged offence in respect of which part I of the 1996 Act (which deals with disclosure) applies. They therefore govern offences into which no criminal investigation began prior to that day (see **D6.1** for interpretation). Where the investigation began before that day, the unmodified system of committals applies (i.e. that in existence prior to the 1996 Act). If charges are changed or substituted during the course of the investigation, and that investigation began before 1 April 1997, then the unmodified system applies. Where there are co-accused or more than one offence, and the investigation began at different times, before and after 1 April 1997, then two different systems of committal proceedings will apply. Details of the law applicable to the unmodified system of committals can be found in **D7** of the 1997 edition of this work.

JURISDICTION TO HOLD COMMITTAL PROCEEDINGS

Basis for Committal Proceedings

Magistrates' Courts Act 1980, s. 2   **D7.2**

> (3)   A magistrates' court for a county, a London commission area or the City of London shall have jurisdiction as examining justices over any offence committed by a person who appears or is brought before the court, whether or not the offence was committed within the county, the London commission area or the City (as the case may be).

Thus, by s. 2(3), a magistrates' court is empowered to conduct committal proceedings whenever an accused is before it charged with an indictable offence, regardless of where the offence was committed, provided only that the English courts accept jurisdiction in respect of the allegation. If, however, the offence is triable either way, committal proceedings may not take place unless and until the court has complied with the procedure to determine the mode of trial laid down by the MCA 1980, ss. 19 to 23 (see **D3.3** to **D3.19**) and either it is of the opinion that trial on indictment would be more suitable or the accused, having been offered summary trial, has elected trial on indictment. In those pilot areas where the CDA 1998, s. 51, is in force (or when it is fully implemented), the magistrates will no longer hold committal proceedings in relation to indictable-only offences, but will send them immediately to the Crown Court (see **D8.21**).

The reference in s. 2(3) to a person 'appearing' before the court is apt to cover cases where the accused comes to court voluntarily either in answer to a summons or in compliance with the terms of his bail (whether he was bailed from the police station after being charged there, or bailed after being arrested on a warrant 'backed for bail', or bailed by the court following an earlier appearance in connection with the charge). The reference to a person being 'brought before' the court covers both those cases where the accused, having been charged at the police station, was kept there until brought to court in custody by the police, and those cases where he was remanded in custody by the court at a previous hearing. The rules governing jurisdiction to issue process (see the MCA 1980, s. 1, and **D4.1** *et seq.*) mean that, if the accused first appears in answer to a summons or is brought before the court following arrest with warrant, then he will normally appear or be brought before either a court acting for the county in which the offence allegedly occurred or a court acting for the county in which he lived or was (or was believed to live or to be) at the time the summons or warrant was issued. Where the accused is charged at a police station following arrest without warrant the police usually choose to bring him before (or bail him to appear at) the court for the petty-sessional division in which the offence allegedly occurred. However, this is a matter within the discretion of the police. The relevant statutory provisions (PACE 1984, ss. 46 and 47) merely fix time-limits within which a charged person must be brought before a magistrates' court or released – they are silent about which court he should be brought or bailed to appear before. Defect or illegality in the process by which the accused appears or is brought before the court will not deprive the magistrates of jurisdiction (see **D4.6**).

Manner and Place of Committal Proceedings

A single lay justice may conduct committal proceedings (MCA 1980, s. 4(1)). The court **D7.3**
need not sit in a petty-sessional court-house or occasional court-house (s. 121(3)), but in practice will do so unless there are exceptional reasons for not doing so.

Magistrates' Courts Act 1980, s. 4

(1)   The functions of examining justices may be discharged by a single justice.

(2)   Examining justices shall sit in open court except where any enactment contains an express provision to the contrary and except where it appears to them as respects the whole of any part of committal proceedings that the ends of justice would not be served by their sitting in open court.

Adjournments

D7.4   The court may adjourn before or at any time during committal proceedings (MCA 1980, s. 5(1)). If it does so, it must fix the time and place at which the hearing is to be resumed and remand the accused (either on bail or in custody) to appear or be brought before the court on that date (s. 5(2)). It is submitted that s. 5 must be read in conjunction with s. 18(4) (which empowers the court to adjourn proceedings to determine the mode of trial and, in certain circumstances, permits adjournments without an associated remand), so that, if the accused is charged with an offence triable either way, the court's power to adjourn is to be found in the latter subsection until the moment when it is determined that the offence shall be tried on indictment. If a decision in favour of trial on indictment is taken in the absence of the accused under the provisions of s. 23 of the 1980 Act and the court decides to adjourn before embarking on the committal proceedings, it may adjourn without remanding the accused (s. 23(4)(b) and (5)). Adjournments prior to the commencement of committal proceedings are considered more fully at **D4.7 *et seq*.**

Abuse of Process: the Discretion to Discharge Accused

D7.5   Examining justices have a discretion to discharge the accused without hearing the prosecution evidence if there has been delay in bringing the proceedings of such magnitude as to render them vexatious and an abuse of the court's process (*Grays Justices, ex parte Graham* [1982] QB 1239). Usually it will be necessary for the defence either to demonstrate *mala fides* on the prosecution's part or to show genuine prejudice and unfairness to the accused.

In *Bow Street Stipendiary Magistrate, ex parte DPP* (1989) 91 Cr App R 283, the Divisional Court made it clear that mere delay which gave rise to prejudice and unfairness might by itself amount to an abuse of process. It had to be shown that the delay had produced genuine prejudice and unfairness. In some cases, prejudice would be presumed from substantial delay which the Crown would have to rebut. The DPP had applied for judicial review of the magistrate's decision to refuse to commit police officers for trial. It was alleged that the officers concerned had conspired to pervert the course of justice. The prosecutions arose from the Wapping demonstrations on 24 January 1987. Notices of disciplinary proceedings were not served on the officers until 17 December 1987. At the committal on 3 May 1989, magistrate A declined jurisdiction on the ground that it would be an abuse of process to hear the charges. In addition, C, another police officer, applied for judicial review of the decision by magistrate B that his prosecution for assault was not an abuse of process. Again, the allegation arose from events on 24 January 1987. C was said to have assaulted W in the course of arrest. C was not served with a disciplinary notice until 16 February 1988 and the summons was not issued until January 1989. Magistrate B held that the delay was not an abuse of process and that C should be committed for trial. The Divisional Court refused the application of the DPP but granted C's, thus holding in effect that both prosecutions involved delays which were an abuse of process. It was perfectly proper, in the circumstances, to infer prejudice from the mere passage of time. With regard to the allegation of assault against C, such an inference was more easily drawn in the case of a single, brief, but confused event which must depend on the recollections of those involved.

In *Ex parte Graham*, G was summoned for a total of 29 offences relating to the theft of a cheque-book and the obtaining by deception of property worth £1,600 by forging the loser's signature on cheques from the book. The offences occurred in mid January 1980. In late January, G was interviewed by the police, her fingerprints were taken, and she was then bailed to return to the station in April. Through pressure of work, the officer dealing with the case had not decided by April whether or not to prefer charges. G was accordingly notified that her presence back at the police station was not required. In June 1981 (i.e. over 16 months after G had originally been interviewed), summonses were issued. The prosecution were not, however, ready to proceed on either of the first two dates originally set for committal, with the result that, on the second occasion, the justices refused an adjournment and discharged G. The prosecution then laid 29 fresh informations, identical to the first. That was done in December 1981. In February 1982 (when the court would have been ready for committal proceedings), the defence were granted an adjournment to apply to the High Court for an order of prohibition to prevent the justices proceeding further. The defence grounds for an order were that:

> . . . because of the delay of two years since the alleged original offences, the continued prosecution of the applicant for them was in the circumstances vexatious, an abuse of the process of the court, the delay being in no way due to any fault on the part of the applicant herself, and that in all the circumstances of the case such continued prosecution was contrary to natural justice. ([1982] QB at p. 1243E–F.)

The prosecution responded that the type of case (cheque fraud) involved 'a substantial amount of detailed travelling and expenditure of time on the part of the police' which partially explained the delay, but, in any event, mere delay in the absence of *mala fides* could never entitle the court to make an order of prohibition. There was 'unfortunately, nothing very extraordinary in a Crown Court having to try a "stale" case' (p. 1243G). Having reviewed the authorities, May LJ (giving the court's judgment) said (at pp. 1247F–1248B):

> In our opinion, although delay of itself, with nothing more, if sufficiently prolonged, could in some cases be such as to render criminal proceedings brought long after the events said to constitute the offence both vexatious and an abuse, we do not think that delay of the order that there has been in and in the circumstances of this case can be so described.

> Clearly, as a matter of policy, prosecutions should be brought and heard as quickly as practicable. . . . We are well aware that there is today a substantial amount of delay and inefficiency in criminal proceedings, both before and at trial. This is to be deplored. . . . But we do not think that this court should create any form of artificial limitation period for criminal proceedings where it cannot truly be said that the due process of the criminal courts is being used improperly to harass a defendant. Although we appreciate that it will not be easy for the Crown to present its case, or for the applicant to meet it, in these proceedings because of the delay that there has been, there has been no instance of *mala fides* on the prosecution's part.

> In all the circumstances . . . we do not think that it can be said to be vexatious to require this applicant to stand her trial later this year on the allegations of theft and obtaining property by deception which have been made against her.

In *Derby Crown Court, ex parte Brooks* (1984) 80 Cr App R 164, Lord Lane CJ propounded a somewhat more liberal test. He held that there would be an abuse of the process of the court (and hence the need to halt committal proceedings) if either the prosecution have deliberately manipulated the normal criminal process so as to take unfair advantage of the accused (e.g., delayed matters in the hope that a potential defence witness would become unavailable), or it is likely that the accused will be prejudiced in the conduct of his defence by delay on the prosecution's part which, although not deliberate, was nevertheless unjustifiable. On the facts of that case, however, a delay of five years between the offence and committal proceedings was held not to amount to an abuse of process. But contrast *Sunderland Magistrates' Court, ex parte Z* [1989] Crim LR 56, where Z, a doctor, was charged in 1987 with having raped a patient (X) in 1979. X was blind, epileptic, alcoholic and depressive. Following the original investigation it had been decided not to prefer charges because of insufficient evidence but the inquiry was reopened because, in 1987, a different patient (Y) complained that she too had been raped by Z. The defence did not allege bad faith on the prosecution's part in charging Z with X's rape so long after the event, but the delay had caused prejudice in that relevant documents had been destroyed, as had clothing and vaginal swabs which might have established Z's innocence. The Divisional Court therefore granted prohibition to prevent the justices proceeding with the committal.

In *Telford Justices, ex parte Badhan* [1991] 2 QB 78, a complaint was made against the applicant in 1988 that he had committed an offence of rape in 1973 or 1974. He appeared before the examining justices in May 1989. It was submitted that the committal should not proceed, since it would be an abuse of process. The justices rejected the submission, and the applicant sought judicial review. In the Divisional Court, the prosecution launched a full frontal assault on the doctrine of abuse of process, arguing that it had no application to committal proceedings, and that *Ex parte Brooks* and subsequent decisions were *per incuriam* and contrary to the House of Lords decision in *Atkinson* v *United States Government* [1971] AC 197. The Divisional Court allowed the application and granted prohibition. *Atkinson* was distinguished on the ground that it was an extradition case, where the final decision was in the hands of the Secretary of State, who could consider matters of natural justice. Examining justices had the power to decide that the initiation of the process of committal was an abuse of that process. If their decision was disputed, the complainant could seek judicial review. In the present case, it was for the accused to show on a balance of probabilities that he was prejudiced in his defence. Where the period of delay was long, it was legitimate for the court to infer prejudice. The period in question here was that between the date of the alleged offence and the opening of committal — some 15 or 16 years. The court could infer prejudice and conclude that a fair trial was impossible.

In determining whether the defendant is prejudiced, the justices ought not to take into account breaches of the PACE 1984, or the codes issued pursuant to that Act (*Bow Street Metropolitan Stipendiary Magistrate, ex parte DPP* [1992] Crim LR 790, where the alleged breach was a failure to caution). The reasoning seems to be that such points can be argued at trial, and are within the powers of the judge to regulate the admissibility of evidence, and give directions to the jury (*A-G's Ref (No. 1 of 1990)* [1992] QB 630).

In *Croydon Justices, ex parte Dean* [1993] QB 769, the Divisional Court held that, where the police gave to a person an undertaking, promise or representation that he would not be charged, in exchange for his co-operation, it could amount to an abuse of process if he was subsequently prosecuted. In such circumstances, it was not necessary for the defendant to show that there was bad faith. (See also *Thomas* [1995] Crim LR 938 and *Liverpool Magistrates' Court, ex parte Slade* [1998] 1 WLR 531.)

In *Sheffield Stipendiary Magistrate, ex parte Stephens* (1992) 156 JP 555, the Divisional Court warned against the excessive citing of cases in determining abuse of process applications. Their lordships stressed that each case depended on its own facts, and that the suggestion that there were separate rules for any particular category of cases, such as sexual offences, was wrong.

The application of the doctrine of abuse of process to trial on indictment (see **D9.41**) and to summary trial (see **D18.8 *et seq*.**) is also relevant.

As to the procedure which the examining justices ought to adopt, it is submitted that they should deal with the question prior to the committal proceedings proper. They should consider evidence on the course of proceedings thus far, particularly as to the extent of the delay, the reasons for it, and any prejudice which the defence may suffer as a result. They should hear from both the prosecution and the defence. Thus, in *Clerkenwell Stipendiary Magistrate, ex parte Bell* [1991] Crim LR 468, the magistrate heard evidence from a police officer explaining that the delay of two and a half years between commission of the offence and committal proceedings was due to B's change of address. He declined to hear evidence from B, and then committed him for trial. The Divisional Court held that this was a breach of natural justice and quashed the committal. Conversely, in *Crawley Justices, ex parte DPP* (1991) 155 JP 841, the Divisional Court quashed the decision of the justices to dismiss informations because of delay. The bench had not heard from the prosecution nor enquired fully of the accused as to the facts.

The fact that the magistrates have heard, and adjudicated upon, argument as to abuse of process does not mean that they have commenced committal proceedings for the purposes of the MCA 1980, s. 6(1) (*Worcester Magistrates' Court, ex parte Bell* [1994] Crim LR 133). In that case, the applicants appeared before the justices for committal. The prosecution had no witnesses at court and could not proceed. The applicants submitted that the proceedings should be stayed as an abuse of process. The justices rejected that submission and adjourned. Subsequently, the applicants were told that a stipendiary magistrate had been appointed to hear their committal and they applied for a writ of certiorari to quash his decision that he had power to conduct the committal hearing. The Divisional Court held that he did have such power, as the justices had not embarked on an enquiry into the offence until the prosecution had opened the case, witnesses were called or some step was taken pertinent to committal. It was stated that it was desirable that the same bench consider the question of abuse of process and the committal itself, but in wholly exceptional cases there might be good reasons why different justices should adjudicate upon the two questions.

THE CHARGE

Putting a Charge in Writing

The Magistrates' Courts Rules 1981 imply that the charge against the accused need not be **D7.6** put into writing before the commencement of the committal proceedings, and that the ultimate responsibility for producing a written charge rests with the court and not the prosecutor (see r. 7(7) which states that 'After hearing any submission [of no case to answer] the court shall [if there is a case to answer] cause the charge to be written down, if this has not already been done'). In practice, however, a written charge is normally formulated by the prosecutor at the very outset of the prosecution process, either through the accused being charged at the police station and the charge sheet being sent to the magistrates' court or through an information being laid before a magistrate. Thus, both the court and the accused will know from an early stage on what charges the prosecution seek committal, although there is nothing to prevent the preferment of alternative or additional charges between the commencement of the prosecution and the committal proceedings.

Multiple Charges and Accused

Committal proceedings may be held in respect of more than one charge and/or more **D7.7** than one accused. Where two or more accused are jointly charged with a single offence, it is clearly appropriate to conduct a single committal inquiry in respect of them all unless there are special reasons for not doing so (e.g., on the date fixed for the proceedings, one of the accused fails to appear, and the court considers it in the interests of justice to hold a committal forthwith for those who are present, adjourning the absent accused's committal until such time as his attendance is secured). Where accused are charged with separate offences, the question of whether the charges – and hence the accused – may properly be the subject of a single committal proceeding is one for the practice of the court (*Camberwell Green Stipendiary Magistrate, ex parte Christie* [1978] QB 602). The normal and correct practice is to deal with the accused together if, and only if, their alleged offences are so related by time or other factors that, in the event of their being committed for trial, it would be appropriate to draft a single indictment against them all within the principles established by *Assim* [1966] 2 QB 249 (see **D9.31**). In *Ex parte Christie,* C was charged with wilfully ill-treating her child contrary to s. 1 of the CYPA 1933. The father of the child (F) was charged with its murder, and the prosecution case was that, at the material time, C and F had been living together. Refusing C's application for judicial review to prevent the magistrate proceeding with joint committal proceedings against herself and F, the Divisional Court (Lord Widgery CJ) stated the law as follows (at p. 606E–H):

> [The] principle that joinder is a matter of practice, if established, goes a very long way to solving all the problems which have arisen in this case. I think that it is proper for us to accept the decision in *Assim* as laying down a principle that these are matters of practice, and I think that from there we can inquire into whether there is an established practice of joinder in committal proceedings which will by virtue of the *Assim* doctrine become authoritative properly to be followed by individual courts.

> There seems to me to be no answer to the contention that the experience of practice is overwhelming that where two offences, which can properly be tried together on indictment, are the subject of committal proceedings, they can be the subject of concurrent committal proceedings without the necessity of obtaining the consent of the parties concerned. . . .

> Since it cannot be challenged that both the defendants in these two informations could be tried together, it seems to me that we can properly adopt the principle that where two offences could be tried together then they could be the subject of concurrent committal proceedings as well.

PRESENCE OF THE ACCUSED

D7.8 Evidence tendered at committal proceedings must be tendered in the presence of the accused (MCA 1980, s. 4(3)). This is subject to the qualification that the examining justices may allow evidence to be tendered in his absence if either they consider that, by reason of his disorderly conduct before them, it is not practicable for the evidence to be tendered in his presence, or he cannot be present for health reasons but he is represented by counsel or solicitor and has consented to proceedings *in absentia* (s. 4(4)). Where the necessary conditions are fulfilled, the accused can be committed in his absence, whether the committal is under s. 6(1) or s. 6(2) (*Liverpool City Magistrates' Court, ex parte Quantrell* [1999] 2 Cr App R 24). If the accused does not appear for committal proceedings, the court may issue a warrant for his arrest (see MCA 1980, s. 1(6), and Bail Act 1976, s. 7(1), which are respectively applicable where the accused fails to answer to a summons or fails to answer to his bail). For the analogous, but slightly less restrictive, rules on the accused needing to be present for proceedings to determine the mode of trial, see **D3.6**.

Magistrates' Courts Act 1980, s. 4

. . .

(3) Subject to subsection (4) below, evidence tendered before examining justices shall be tendered in the presence of the accused.

(4) Examining justices may allow evidence to be tendered before them in the absence of the accused if—

(a) they consider that by reason of his disorderly conduct before them it is not practicable for the evidence to be tendered in his presence, or

(b) he cannot be present for reasons of health but is represented by counsel or a solicitor and has consented to the evidence being tendered in his absence.

COMMITTALS WITH CONSIDERATION OF THE EVIDENCE

Stages in Outline

D7.9 The procedure for committals with consideration of the evidence is to be found chiefly in r. 7 of the Magistrates' Courts Rules 1981. The major stages are listed below, and are then considered in detail at **D7.10** to **D7.14**.

The prosecutor is entitled to outline the case and explain any relevant points of law, before tendering the evidence (all of which is written: see **D7.10**). The evidence may be read through or, with the leave of the court, summarised. The magistrates' court may view any original exhibits and may retain them. No witnesses are called and no evidence can be tendered by the defence. The accused may then make a submission of no case to answer and, if he does so or the court is minded not to commit for trial, the prosecutor is entitled to respond (r. 7(5) and (6)). The court then reaches its decision as to whether to commit the accused for trial in the Crown Court, on the basis of the test laid down in the MCA 1980, s. 6(1).

Magistrates' Courts Act 1980, s. 6

(1)   A magistrates' court inquiring into an offence as examining justices shall on consideration of the evidence—
(a)   commit the accused for trial if it is of opinion that there is sufficient evidence to put him on trial by jury for any indictable offence;
(b)   discharge him if it is not of that opinion and he is in custody for no other cause than the offence under inquiry;
but the preceding provisions of this subsection have effect subject to the provisions of this and any other Act relating to the summary trial of indictable offences.

Magistrates' Courts Rules 1981, r. 7

(1)   This rule does not apply to committal proceedings where under section 6(2) of the [MCA 1980] a magistrates' court commits a person for trial without consideration of the evidence.
(2)   A magistrates' court inquiring into an offence as examining justices, having ascertained—
(a)   that the accused has no legal representative acting for him in the case; or
(b)   that the accused's legal representative has requested the court to consider a submission that there is insufficient evidence to put the accused on trial by jury for the offence with which he is charged, as the case may be,
shall permit the prosecutor to make an opening address to the court, if he so wishes, before any evidence is tendered.
(3)   After such opening address, if any, the court shall cause evidence to be tendered in accordance with sections 5B(4), 5C(4), 5D(5) and 5E(3) of the Act of 1980, that is to say by being read out aloud, except where the court otherwise directs or to the extent that it directs that an oral account be given of any of the evidence.
(4)   The court may view any exhibits produced before the court and may take possession of them.
(5)   After the evidence has been tendered the court shall hear any submission which the accused may wish to make as to whether there is sufficient evidence to put him on trial by jury for any indictable offence.
(6)   The court shall permit the prosecutor to make a submission—
(a)   in reply to any submission made by the accused in pursuance of paragraph (5); or
(b)   where the accused has not made any such submission but the court is nevertheless minded not to commit him for trial.
(7)   After hearing any submission made in pursuance of paragraph (5) and (6) the court shall, unless it decides not to commit the accused for trial, cause the charge to be written down, if this has not already been done, and, if the accused is not represented by counsel or a solicitor, shall read the charge to him and explain it in ordinary language.

Evidence at Committal Proceedings

Section 5A of the MCA 1980 stipulates that, for evidence to be admissible at committal: **D7.10**

(a)   it must be tendered by the prosecutor; and
(b)   it must fall within one of the categories of evidence defined in ss. 5B, 5C, 5D and 5E of the Act.

In most cases, the evidence will be in the form of witness statements under s. 5B. Any such statement may be admitted if it is adduced by the prosecutor, has been served on each of the other parties to the committal, and complies with the other formalities set out in s. 5B(2) and (3).

Although the usual route for a statement to be admitted in committal proceedings is by s. 5B, there are other possibilities. Section 5C is an innovation introduced by the CPIA 1996. It allows for evidence by way of deposition taken in advance of the committal where a prosecution witness is reluctant to provide a written statement. Such a deposition may be taken under the MCA 1980, s. 97A where a person 'is likely to be able to make on behalf of the prosecutor a written statement containing material evidence' and 'the person will not voluntarily make the statement'. If a magistrate is satisfied of these conditions, then a summons and, if necessary, a warrant, can be issued to secure that person's attendance, using the procedure set out in s. 97A. The procedure does not require a court to be convened for the deposition to be taken, and neither the accused nor his legal advisers need be present, nor need they even be notified that the deposition is being taken. The taking of the evidence of the witness is governed by r. 4A of the Magistrates' Courts Rules 1981, which envisages that the prosecutor will be present to examine the witness and that the evidence will be reduced to a signed deposition. The deposition once taken is admissible by virtue of s. 5C in a subsequent committal. It is submitted that the absence of the accused and, even more crucially, his legal representative will mean that the prosecutor, the justice conducting proceedings and the clerk to the justices in attendance will bear the responsibility for ensuring that evidence is not elicited by means of leading questions.

A further route of admissibility is provided by s. 5D, which allows in first-hand hearsay which might be admissible by virtue of the CJA 1988, s. 23 or 24. This covers statements made by persons now dead, unfit to attend trial, abroad and not reasonably expected to attend or who will be kept away from a trial by fear or threat to their safety, as well as evidence contained in business or trade documents. The prosecutor need not prove that the conditions laid down in s. 23 or 24 are satisfied, but must notify the court of his belief that the statement will be admissible. Such belief must be based on reasonable grounds.

Documents which 'prove themselves' or are made admissible by other legislation, such as certificates of conviction or DVLA certificates in road traffic proceedings, are made admissible in committal proceedings by s. 5E.

Section 5F lays down that any of the documents admissible by virtue of ss. 5B to 5E may be proved by the original or a copy (even if the original is still in existence).

Magistrates' Courts Act 1980, ss. 5A to 5F and 97A

5A.—(1) Evidence falling within subsection (2) below, and only that evidence, shall be admissible by a magistrates' court inquiring into an offence as examining justices.
   (2)   Evidence falls within this subsection if it—
      (a)   is tendered by or on behalf of the prosecutor, and
      (b)   falls within subsection (3) below.
   (3)   The following evidence falls within this subsection—
      (a)   written statements complying with section 5B below;
      (b)   the documents or other exhibits (if any) referred to in such statements;
      (c)   depositions complying with section 5C below;
      (d)   the documents or other exhibits (if any) referred to in such depositions;
      (e)   statements complying with section 5D below;
      (f)   documents falling within section 5E below.
   (4)   In this section 'document' means anything in which information of any description is recorded.

5B.—(1) For the purposes of section 5A above a written statement complies with this section if—

    (a)   the conditions falling within subsection (2) below are met, and

    (b)   such of the conditions falling within subsection (3) below as apply are met.

  (2)   The conditions falling within this subsection are that—

    (a)   the statement purports to be signed by the person who made it;

    (b)   the statement contains a declaration by that person to the effect that it is true to the best of his knowledge and belief and that he made the statement knowing that, if it were tendered in evidence, he would be liable to prosecution if he wilfully stated in it anything which he knew to be false or did not believe to be true;

    (c)   before the statement is tendered in evidence a copy of the statement is given, by or on behalf of the prosecutor, to each of the other parties to the proceedings.

  (3)   The conditions falling within this subsection are that—

    (a)   if the statement is made by a person under 18 years old, it gives his age;

    (b)   if it is made by a person who cannot read it, it is read to him before he signs it and is accompanied by a declaration by the person who so read the statement to the effect that it was so read;

    (c)   if it refers to any other document as an exhibit, the copy given to any other party to the proceedings under subsection (2)(c) above is accompanied by a copy of that document or by such information as may be necessary to enable the party to whom it is given to inspect that document or a copy of it.

  (4)   So much of any statement as is admitted in evidence by virtue of this section shall, unless the court commits the accused for trial by virtue of section 6(2) below or the court otherwise directs, be read aloud at the hearing; and where the court so directs an account shall be given orally of so much of any statement as is not read aloud.

  (5)   Any document or other object referred to as an exhibit and identified in a statement admitted in evidence by virtue of this section shall be treated as if it had been produced as an exhibit and identified in court by the maker of the statement.

  (6)   In this section 'document' means anything in which information of any description is recorded.

5C.—(1)   For the purposes of section 5A above a deposition complies with this section if—

    (a)   a copy of it is sent to the prosecutor under section 97A(9) below,

    (b)   the condition falling within subsection (2) below is met, and

    (c)   the condition falling within subsection (3) below is met, in a case where it applies.

  (2)   The condition falling within this subsection is that before the magistrates' court begins to inquire into the offence concerned as examining justices a copy of the deposition is given, by or on behalf of the prosecutor, to each of the other parties to the proceedings.

  (3)   The condition falling within this subsection is that, if the deposition refers to any other document as an exhibit, the copy given to any other party to the proceedings under subsection (2) above is accompanied by a copy of that document or by such information as may be necessary to enable the party to whom it is given to inspect that document or a copy of it.

  (4)   So much of any deposition as is admitted in evidence by virtue of this section shall, unless the court commits the accused for trial by virtue of section 6(2) below or the court otherwise directs, be read aloud at the hearing; and where the court so directs an account shall be given orally of so much of any deposition as is not read aloud.

  (5)   Any document or other object referred to as an exhibit and identified in a deposition admitted in evidence by virtue of this section shall be treated as if it had been produced as an exhibit and identified in court by the person whose evidence is taken as the deposition.

  (6)   In this section 'document' means anything in which information of any description is recorded.

5D.—(1)   For the purposes of section 5A above a statement complies with this section if the conditions falling within subsections (2) to (4) below are met.

  (2)   The condition falling within this subsection is that, before the committal proceedings begin, the prosecutor notifies the magistrates' court and each of the other parties to the proceedings that he believes—

    (a)   that the statement might by virtue of section 23 or 24 of the Criminal Justice Act 1988 (statements in certain documents) be admissible as evidence if the case came to trial, and

(b)   that the statement would not be admissible as evidence otherwise than by virtue of section 23 or 24 of that Act if the case came to trial.

(3)   The condition falling within this subsection is that—

(a)   the prosecutor's belief is based on information available to him at the time he makes the notification,

(b)   he has reasonable grounds for his belief, and

(c)   he gives the reasons for his belief when he makes the notification.

(4)   The condition falling within this subsection is that when the court or a party is notified as mentioned in subsection (2) above a copy of the statement is given, by or on behalf of the prosecutor, to the court or the party concerned.

(5)   So much of any statement as is in writing and is admitted in evidence by virtue of this section shall, unless the court commits the accused for trial by virtue of section 6(2) below or the court otherwise directs, be read aloud at the hearing; and where the court so directs an account shall be given orally of so much of any statement as is not read aloud.

5E.—(1)   The following documents fall within this section—

(a)   any document which by virtue of any enactment is evidence in proceedings before a magistrates' court inquiring into an offence as examining justices;

(b)   any document which by virtue of any enactment is admissible, or may be used, or is to be admitted or received, in or as evidence in such proceedings;

(c)   any document which by virtue of any enactment may be considered in such proceedings;

(d)   any document whose production constitutes proof in such proceedings by virtue of any enactment;

(e)   any document by the production of which evidence may be given in such proceedings by virtue of any enactment.

(2)   In subsection (1) above—

(a)   references to evidence include references to prima facie evidence;

(b)   references to any enactment include references to any provision of this Act.

(3)   So much of any document as is admitted in evidence by virtue of this section shall, unless the court commits the accused for trial by virtue of section 6(2) below or the court otherwise directs, be read aloud at the hearing; and where the court so directs an account shall be given orally of so much of any document as is not read aloud.

(4)   In this section 'document' means anything in which information of any description is recorded.

5F.—(1)   Where a statement, deposition or document is admissible in evidence by virtue of section 5B, 5C, 5D or 5E above it may be proved by the production of—

(a)   the statement, deposition or document, or

(b)   a copy of it or the material part of it.

(2)   Subsection (1)(b) above applies whether or not the statement, deposition or document is still in existence.

(3)   It is immaterial for the purposes of this section how many removes there are between a copy and the original.

(4)   In this section 'copy', in relation to a statement, deposition or document, means anything onto which information recorded in the statement, deposition or document has been copied, by whatever means and whether directly or indirectly.

97A.—(1)   Subsection (2) below applies where a justice of the peace for any commission area is satisfied that—

(a)   any person in England or Wales is likely to be able to make on behalf of the prosecutor a written statement containing material evidence, or produce on behalf of the prosecutor a document or other exhibit likely to be material evidence, for the purposes of proceedings before a magistrates' court inquiring into an offence as examining justices,

(b)   the person will not voluntarily make the statement or produce the document or other exhibit, and

(c)   the magistrates' court mentioned in paragraph (a) above is a court for the commission area concerned.

(2)   In such a case the justice shall issue a summons directed to that person requiring him to attend before a justice at the time and place appointed in the summons to have his

evidence taken as a deposition or to produce the document or other exhibit.

(3)   If a justice of the peace is satisfied by evidence on oath of the matters mentioned in subsection (1) above, and also that it is probable that a summons under subsection (2) above would not procure the result required by it, the justice may instead of issuing a summons issue a warrant to arrest the person concerned and bring him before a justice at the time and place specified in the warrant.

(4)   A summons may also be issued under subsection (2) above if the justice is satisfied that the person concerned is outside the British Islands, but no warrant may be issued under subsection (3) above unless the justice is satisfied by evidence on oath that the person concerned is in England or Wales.

(5)   If—
   (a)   a person fails to attend before a justice in answer to a summons under this section,
   (b)   the justice is satisfied by evidence on oath that he is likely to be able to make a statement or produce a document or other exhibit as mentioned in subsection (1)(a) above,
   (c)   it is proved on oath, or in such other manner as may be prescribed, that he has been duly served with the summons and that a reasonable sum has been paid or tendered to him for costs and expenses, and
   (d)   it appears to the justice that there is no just excuse for the failure,
the justice may issue a warrant to arrest him and bring him before a justice at a time and place specified in the warrant.

(6)   Where—
   (a)   a summons is issued under subsection (2) above or a warrant is issued under subsection (3) or (5) above, and
   (b)   the summons or warrant is issued with a view to securing that a person has his evidence taken as a deposition,
the time appointed in the summons or specified in the warrant shall be such as to enable the evidence to be taken as a deposition before a magistrates' court begins to inquire into the offence concerned as examining justices.

(7)   If any person attending or brought before a justice in pursuance of this section refuses without just excuse to have his evidence taken as a deposition, or to produce the document or other exhibit, the justice may do one or both of the following—
   (a)   commit him to custody until the expiration of such period not exceeding one month as may be specified in the summons or warrant or until he sooner has his evidence taken as a deposition or produces the document or other exhibit;
   (b)   impose on him a fine not exceeding £2,500.

(8)   A fine imposed under subsection (7) above shall be deemed, for the purposes of any enactment to be a sum adjudged to be paid by a conviction.

(9)   If in pursuance of this section a person has his evidence taken as a deposition, the clerk of the justice concerned shall as soon as is reasonably practicable send a copy of the deposition to the prosecutor.

(10)   If in pursuance of this section a person produces an exhibit which is a document, the clerk of the justice concerned shall as soon as is reasonably practicable send a copy of the document to the prosecutor.

(11)   If in pursuance of this section a person produces an exhibit which is not a document, the clerk of the justice concerned shall as soon as is reasonably practicable inform the prosecutor of the fact and of the nature of the exhibit.

Magistrates' Courts Rules 1981, rr. 4A and 70

4A.—(1)   Where a person attends before a justice of the peace in pursuance of section 97A of the Act of 1980 [or paragraph 4 of schedule 3 to the Act of 1998] the justice shall—
   (a)   where that person attends for the purpose of giving evidence, cause his evidence to be put in writing;
   (b)   where that person attends for the purpose of producing a document or other exhibit, cause the document or exhibit to be handed over for examination and any evidence given by that person in respect of it to be put in writing;
   (c)   where that person refuses to have his evidence taken or to produce the document or other exhibit, as the case may be, explain to him the consequences of so refusing without just excuse, and ask him to explain why he has so refused; and

(d)   cause a record of any such refusal to be made in writing.

(2)   As soon as practicable after the examination by the prosecutor of a witness whose evidence is put in writing the justice shall cause his deposition to be read to him and shall require the witness to sign the deposition.

(3)   Any such deposition shall be authenticated by a certificate signed by the justice.

(4)   Subject to rule 11 the clerk of the justice concerned, on sending a copy of any deposition or documentary exhibit to the prosecutor under section 97A(9) or (10) of the Act of 1980, as the case may be—

(a)   shall retain the original deposition or exhibit; and

(b)   may retain any other exhibit produced in pursuance of that section.

70.—(1)   Written statements to be tendered in evidence in accordance with section 5B of the Act of 1980 or section 9 of the Criminal Justice Act 1967 shall be in the prescribed form.

(2)   When a copy of any of the following evidence, namely—

(a)   evidence tendered in accordance with section 5A of the Act of 1980, or

(b)   a written statement tendered in evidence under section 9 of the Criminal Justice Act 1967,

is given to or served on any party to the proceedings a copy of the evidence in question shall be given to the clerk of the magistrates' court as soon as practicable thereafter, and where a copy of any such statement as is referred to in sub-paragraph (b) is given or served by or on behalf of the prosecutor, the accused shall be given notice by or on behalf of the prosecutor of his right to object to the statement being tendered in evidence.

(3)   [Revoked.]

(4)   Where—

(a)   a statement or deposition to be tendered in evidence in accordance with section 5A of the Act of 1980; or

(b)   a written statement to be tendered in evidence under section 9 of the Criminal Justice Act 1967,

refers to any document or object as an exhibit, that document or object shall wherever possible be identified by means of a label or other mark of identification signed by the maker of the statement or deposition, and before the magistrates' court treats any document or object referred to as an exhibit in such a statement or deposition as an exhibit produced and identified in court by the maker of the statement or deposition, the court shall be satisfied that the document or object is sufficiently described in the statement or deposition for it to be identified.

(5)   If it appears to a magistrates' court that any part of any evidence tendered in accordance with the said section 5A or a written statement tendered in evidence under section 9 of the Criminal Justice Act 1967 is inadmissible there shall be written against that part—

(a)   in the case of any evidence tendered in accordance with the said section 5A, but subject to paragraph (5A), the words 'Treated as inadmissible' together with the signature and name of the examining justice or, where there is more than one examining justice, the signature and name of one of the examining justices by whom the evidence is so treated;

(b)   in the case of a written statement tendered in evidence under the said section 9 the words 'Ruled inadmissible' together with the signature and name of the justice or, where there is more than one justice, the signature and name of one of the justices who ruled the statement to be inadmissible.

(5A)   Where the nature of the evidence referred to in paragraph (5)(a) is such that it is not possible to write on it, the words set out in that sub-paragraph shall instead be written on a label or other mark of identification which clearly identifies the part of the evidence to which the words relate and contains the signature and name of an examining justice in accordance with that sub-paragraph.

(6)   Where, before a magistrates' court,—

(a)   a statement or deposition is tendered in evidence in accordance with the said section 5A, or

(b)   a written statement is tendered in accordance with the said section 9,

the name of the maker of the statement or deposition shall be read aloud unless the court otherwise directs.

(7)   Where—

    (a)   under section 5B(4), 5C(4), 5D(5) or 5E(3) of the Act of 1980; or

    (b)   under sub-section (6) of the said section 9,

in any proceedings before a magistrates' court any part of the evidence has to be read aloud, or an account has to be given orally of so much of any evidence as is not read aloud, the evidence shall be read or the account given by or on behalf of the party which has tendered the evidence.

    (8)   Statements and depositions tendered in evidence in accordance with the said section 5A before a magistrates' court acting as examining justices shall be authenticated by a certificate signed by one of the examining justices.

    (9)   Where, before a magistrates' court—

    (a)   evidence is tendered as indicated in paragraph (2)(a), retained by the court, and not sent to the Crown Court under rule 11, or

    (b)   a written statement is tendered in evidence as indicated in paragraph (2)(b) and not sent to the Crown Court under rule 17 or 18;

all such evidence shall, subject to any direction of the court in respect of non-documentary exhibits falling within sub-paragraph (a), be preserved for a period of three years by the clerk of the magistrates' court.

The words in square brackets in r. 4A(1) apply only where the pilot scheme under the CDA 1998, s. 51, applies (see **D8.21**).

Composite Statements and Edited Statements

A *Practice Direction (Crime: Evidence by Written Statements)* [1986] 1 WLR 805 deals with **D7.11** the procedure to be followed by the prosecution when either a witness has made two or more statements to the police and it is desired to combine them into a single statement potentially admissible at committal, or a witness has included in his statement material on which the prosecution do not after all wish to rely because it is inadmissible, prejudicial or irrelevant. The main points of the direction are that:

    (a)   A composite statement giving the effect of several earlier statements must comply with the statutory requirements and be signed by the witness (para. 3).

    (b)   Any editing of a statement should be done by a Crown Prosecutor (or legal representative of the prosecutor if it is not a CPS case) (para. 2). It should not be done by a police officer (ibid.).

    (c)   There are two acceptable methods of editing a single witness statement, namely, to indicate on the copy statements served on the defence those parts of the original on which the prosecution do not seek to rely, or to prepare and have signed by the witness a fresh statement omitting all mention of the superfluous material (para. 4). If the former method is adopted, the original signed statement tendered to the court must be left unmarked, and the deleting of the defence and court copies must be done in such a way (e.g., by bracketing or light striking out) as to permit what is deleted still to be read. It is not permissible to serve a photocopy with the deleted material completely obliterated. The index to the bundle of statements served by the prosecution should contain words to the effect that: 'The prosecution does not propose to adduce evidence of those passages of the attached copy statements which have been struck out and/or bracketed'.

    (d)   Usually the first course of action described in (c) above will be more appropriate, but the second (i.e., preparing a fresh statement) should be used, for example, when a police officer's original statement refers to interviews with suspects who were not eventually charged and/or to the officer's questioning of the accused about other matters (para. 5). The new statement should omit the superfluous material, save that, for the sake of continuity, it might contain a phrase such as, 'After referring to other matters, I then said . . .'.

    (e)   The direction applies both to statements which the prosecution wish to tender in committal proceedings and to statements which are to be tendered under the CJA 1967, s. 9 (written statements admissible in criminal proceedings other than committal proceedings). Documents exhibited to committal statements (including statements by a suspect under caution and signed contemporaneous notes) should, however, be left in their original state in the committal bundles, any editing being left for counsel at the Crown Court (para. 7). Similarly, oral answers of the accused recorded in police officers' written statements should not be edited at the committal stage save to the extent mentioned in (d) above (i.e., questions about matters not the subject of the committal charges to be omitted from a second statement prepared by the officer).

(f)   Where two or more statements by a witness are coalesced into a composite statement or when a fresh 'edited' statement is prepared, a copy of the earlier unedited statements should normally be served on the defence in accordance with the A-G's guidelines on disclosure of information to the defence in cases to be tried on indictment (see **appendix 3**) (para. 8).

The *Practice Direction*, and in particular the guidance which it gives in relation to disclosure, must now be read in the light of the CPIA 1996 (see **D6**) and the Code of Practice issued under it (see **appendix 6**).

Objections to Evidence

D7.12   Committal proceedings are generally an inappropriate forum in which to raise objections to the admissibility of prosecution evidence. This is because (a) the standard of proof which the prosecution are at that stage required to satisfy is a low one (see **D7.13**) and (b) assuming there is a committal for trial, the admissibility of evidence at the trial on indictment is a matter entirely for the Crown Court judge. The Divisional Court has consistently discouraged the making of such objections both by refusing to issue mandamus or prohibition requiring examining justices to receive or, as the case may be, not to receive proposed evidence, and by holding that the reception of inadmissible evidence is not a ground for granting certiorari to quash a committal.

Nonetheless, reluctance to interfere with examining justices' decisions in respect of evidence cannot mean that they are obliged to receive evidence even though it is plainly inadmissible. On the contrary, Lord Hewart CJ in *Phillips* [1939] 1 KB 63 implied that one reason for the statutory requirement that the accused be present at the taking of depositions is that he 'should be able to object to any question put improperly'. Furthermore, the Magistrates' Courts Rules 1981, r. 70(5), makes specific provision for a part of a written statement tendered under the MCA 1980, s. 102, being inadmissible (the provision being that the words 'treated as inadmissible' should be written against the offending part: for the text, see **D7.10**). The correct approach therefore appears to be that examining justices should exclude and ignore proposed evidence which no reasonable tribunal could hold to be admissible, but, where the admissibility of evidence is doubtful and especially where its exclusion depends on the exercise of discretion by the court, the evidence should be received by the justices and any challenge to it reserved for the trial (see, e.g., *Highbury Magistrates' Court, ex parte Boyce* (1984) 79 Cr App R 132 where one ground on which the Divisional Court refused judicial review of B's committal for trial was that the examining justices had correctly ruled that they had no discretion to refuse to allow a 'dock identification' of B – the evidence was legally admissible, and the discretion to exclude on the basis that its prejudicial effect exceeded its probative value was to be exercised by the Crown Court, not the justices). In any event, the examining justices are not permitted to delegate the decision on admissibility to another bench (*Ormskirk Justices, ex parte Davies* [1994] Crim LR 850). As to the effect of a committal based upon inadmissible evidence, see **D7.22**.

In any event, by virtue of the amendments made to the PACE 1984 by the CPIA 1996, sch. 1, paras 25 and 26, examining justices may not consider whether confessions are inadmissible under the PACE 1984, s. 76, or should be excluded under s. 78 of that Act. This is in accordance with the concept of committal proceedings as a means of assessing whether the prosecution has assembled, in the proper documentary form, a case for the defendant to answer at trial in the Crown Court. The magistrates will be unable to go behind what appears on the face of the prosecution documents.

The Test to be Applied in Deciding Whether to Commit

The MCA 1980, s. 6(1) (see **D7.9**) sets out the nature of the decision which the **D7.13** examining justices must make, on the basis of the evidence tendered to them. They must commit for trial if they are of the opinion that there is sufficient evidence to put the accused on trial for any indictable offence; and they must discharge if they are not of that opinion. The Magistrates' Courts Rules 1981, r. 7 (see **D7.9**), makes it clear that the defence is entitled to make a submission of no case to answer after the evidence has been tendered, and the prosecution has the right to reply to such a submission (giving statutory effect, as far as the latter point is concerned, to *Barking and Dagenham Justices, ex parte DPP* (1995) 159 JP 353). Both the Act and the rules are silent, however as to precisely what test the examining justices are to apply when such a submission is made – s. 6(1) merely refers to 'sufficient evidence to put the accused on trial by jury' but gives no indication of what it means by 'sufficient'. By contrast, Sir John Jervis's Act of 1848 (which laid the foundations for the modern magistrates' courts system) provided that magistrates should commit for trial only if the proceedings raised 'a strong or probable presumption of guilt'. This was interpreted as something akin to the civil standard of proof, that is, evidence making it more likely than not that the accused was guilty but not necessarily proof beyond reasonable doubt. But, by the time of the MCA 1952, the phrase 'strong or probable presumption of guilt' had been dropped from the legislation, and the accepted practice was that examining justices would commit if there was evidence on which a reasonable jury could properly convict. Thus, the standard of proof the prosecution are now required to satisfy at committal proceedings is very low, lower than that resting on a plaintiff in civil proceedings. It is commonly expressed as establishing a 'prima facie case' or a 'case to answer'.

One attempt to set out the test for a 'case to answer' is that put forward by Lord Parker CJ in *Practice Direction (Submission of No Case)* [1962] 1 WLR 227:

> A submission that there is no case to answer may properly be made and upheld: (a) when there has been no evidence to prove an essential element in the alleged offence; (b) when the evidence adduced by the prosecution has been so discredited as a result of cross-examination or is so manifestly unreliable that no reasonable tribunal could safely convict upon it.

The direction was handed down in relation to summary trials rather than committal proceedings, and has never been binding upon examining justices. Nevertheless, a practice developed in a number of courts of clerks advising examining justices in accordance with Lord Parker's direction.

The terms of the *Practice Direction* relate to a committal where witnesses give oral evidence, a feature which was abolished by the CPIA 1996. Clearly, limb (a) of the test still retains its force; the magistrates should uphold a submission of no case to answer where 'there has been no evidence to prove an essential element in the alleged offence'. On the other hand, that part of the formulation which refers to cross-examination is now irrelevant, since there are no witnesses, and hence no cross-examination. What about evidence which 'is so manifestly unreliable that no reasonable tribunal could safely convict on it'? Frequently in the criminal process, the issue of reliability or credibility of evidence arises in the context of oral testimony. It is quite possible, however, that written evidence, whether in the form of statements under the MCA 1980, s. 5B, or depositions under s. 5C, could be judged 'manifestly unreliable' if it is hopelessly contradictory or inherently unlikely. In *Governor of Pentonville Prison, ex parte Osman (No. 4)* [1989] 3 All ER 701, for example, the Divisional Court accepted (in the context of oral evidence) that an examining justice could reject any evidence considered 'worthless' (per Lloyd LJ at p. 721). (See also *Brooks* v *DPP* [1994] 1 AC 568 at p. 581, and Brownless and Furniss 'Committed to Committals?' [1997] Crim LR 3.) In general, however, it is likely that the bench will be concerned only with evidential sufficiency and will leave questions of credibility to the Crown Court, where the jury will have a chance to assess the witnesses at first-hand. It would therefore seem that the test as set out by the Court of Appeal in *Galbraith* [1981] 1 WLR 1039, in respect of trial on indictment, is likely to gain increasing currency in committals. The nub of the decision in *Galbraith* is that the defence submission of no case to answer should be upheld (and the jury consequently directed to acquit) if, and only if, the prosecution evidence *taken at its highest* is such that a jury properly directed could not properly convict (see **D13.32** and **D19.8** on submissions of no case to answer in trials on indictment and summary trials respectively).

Section 6(1) of the MCA 1980 obliges the examining justices to commit if there is sufficient evidence to put the accused on trial for *any* indictable offence. Where he is charged with several offences, they may commit on one or more but not necessarily on all the charges. They are also entitled to commit for an offence which has not been charged by the prosecutor, but in that event, the court must ensure that the charge is written down (Magistrates' Courts Rules 1981, r. 7(6) and (12)). If examining justices are considering committing for an offence other than that charged by the prosecutor, they should give the defence the opportunity of addressing the court upon that possibility, as well as upon the original charge, before deciding on the submissions as a whole (*Gloucester Magistrates' Court, ex parte Chung* (1989) 153 JP 75).

Effect of Discharge

D7.14 If there is insufficient evidence to put the accused on trial by jury for an indictable offence, then the examining justices must discharge him, unless he is in custody for some other matter (MCA 1980, s. 6(1)). Discharge at committal proceedings does not amount to an acquittal and so cannot found a plea of autrefois acquit to bar proceedings should the accused be prosecuted again on the same charges (*Manchester City Stipendiary Magistrate, ex parte Snelson* [1977] 1 WLR 911). Consequently, if one magistrates' court sitting as examining justices finds that there is insufficient evidence and discharges the accused, the prosecution may, as a matter of law, have the case reconsidered by a second court; if that court is of the same opinion as the first, the matter may go before a third court, and so on *ad infinitum*. The Divisional Court may, however, grant an order of prohibition to prevent successive benches of examining justices repeatedly holding committal proceedings in respect of the same charge if that would be vexatious or an abuse of the process of the court (per Lord Widgery CJ in *Ex parte Snelson* at p. 913G). In fact, the almost invariable practice, where justices refuse to commit after full consideration of the evidence and the prosecution are unwilling to accept their decision, is to apply to a High Court judge for his consent to the preferment of a voluntary bill of indictment (see **D8.2** to **D8.5** for discussion of voluntary bills of indictment, and see also *Horsham Justices, ex parte Reeves* (1980) 75 Cr App R 236 for an example of the Divisional Court prohibiting a second attempted committal on the basis that the prosecution ought to have applied for a voluntary bill).

COMMITTALS WITHOUT CONSIDERATION OF THE EVIDENCE

D7.15 Committals without consideration of the evidence were introduced by the CJA 1967, s. 1. The present legislation is contained in the MCA 1980, s. 6(2). The conditions on which such committals may take place are:

(a) all the evidence before the court must consist of written statements tendered under s. 5A(3) of the 1980 Act (see **D7.10**);

(b)   the accused must have a solicitor acting for him in the case, though he need not necessarily be present in court; and

(c)   counsel or solicitor for the accused must not have requested the justices to consider a submission that the statements disclose insufficient evidence to put the accused on trial by jury for the offence into which the court is inquiring.

If there are two or more accused, *each* must have a solicitor acting for him and a request by counsel or solicitor for *any* of them to make a submission of insufficient evidence will preclude a committal under the subsection.

The greater convenience and speed of the procedure make it appropriate for the defence to agree to use it unless there is a specific reason for having the evidence considered. The obvious case for an 'old-style' committal, with consideration of the evidence, is when the defence consider that there is a realistic chance of a submission of no case succeeding.

The procedure to be followed for a committal without consideration of the evidence is set out in the Magistrates' Courts Rules 1981, r. 6.

At a committal without consideration of the evidence, the court does not even read or have read to it the written evidence tendered under the MCA 1980, s. 5A(2). The documents are simply handed in by the prosecution (together with a copy bundle for transmission to the Crown Court). It may, however, be necessary for the magistrates subsequently to be referred to passages in the statements (e.g., to assist in deciding an application for bail or legal aid). Even though it is not strictly necessary for a solicitor or barrister to be present in court for the accused when an s. 6(2) committal takes place, defence solicitors usually arrange for representation since ancillary questions such as bail, witness orders or legal aid may require legal expertise even if the committal itself is a pure formality. The court's satisfying itself as to the matters mentioned in (b) above usually involves nothing more than the clerk asking defence counsel or solicitor whether he agrees to an s. 6(2) committal.

Magistrates' Courts Act 1980, s. 6

(2)   If a magistrates' court inquiring into an offence as examining justices is satisfied that all the evidence tendered by or on behalf of the prosecutor falls within section 5A(3) above, it may commit the accused for trial for the offence without consideration of the contents of any statements, depositions or other documents, and without consideration of any exhibits which are not documents, unless—

(a)   the accused or one of the accused has no legal representative acting for him in the case, or

(b)   a legal representative for the accused or one of the accused, as the case may be, has requested the court to consider a submission that there is insufficient evidence to put that accused on trial by jury for the offence;

and subsection (1) above shall not apply to a committal for trial under this subsection.

Magistrates' Courts Rules 1981, r. 6

(1)   This rule applies to committal proceedings where the accused has a solicitor acting for him in the case (whether present in court or not) and where the court has been informed that all the evidence falls within section 5A(2) of the [MCA 1980].

(2)   A magistrates' court inquiring into an offence in committal proceedings to which this rule applies shall cause the charge to be written down, if this has not already been done, and read to the accused and shall then ascertain whether he wishes to submit that there is insufficient evidence to put him on trial by jury for the offence with which he is charged.

(3)   If the court is satisfied that the accused or, as the case may be, each of the accused does not wish to make such a submission as is referred to in paragraph (2) it shall, after receiving any written evidence falling within section 5A(3) of the Act of 1980, determine whether or not to commit the accused for trial without consideration of the evidence, and where it determines not to so commit the accused it shall proceed in accordance with rule 7.

The topics dealt with in **D7.16** to **D7.23** are all equally relevant both to committals with and to committals without consideration of the evidence.

PUBLICITY

D7.16   The MCA 1980, s. 8(1), provides that, subject to the exceptions hereafter mentioned, it is unlawful to publish a report (written or broadcast) of committal proceedings which contains anything not listed in s. 8(4). The latter subsection allows publication of the following:

(a)   the identity of the court and the names of the examining justices;
(b)   the names, addresses and occupations of the parties and witnesses and the ages of the accused and witnesses;
(c)   the offence with which the accused is charged (or a summary thereof);
(d)   the names of counsel and solicitors engaged in the proceedings;
(e)   any decision of the court to commit the accused (or any of them) for trial, and any decision of the court on the disposal of the case of any accused not committed;
(f)   where the court commits the accused (or any of them) for trial, the court to which and the charge on which he is committed (or a summary thereof);
(g)   in the event of an adjournment, the date and place to which the proceedings are adjourned;
(h)   any arrangements as to bail on committal or adjournment; and
(i)   whether legal aid was granted to the accused (or any of them).

Full reporting of committal proceedings (i.e., including the evidence, argument and any other matters not falling within s. 8(4)) is allowed if either:

(a)   the court determined not to commit the accused for trial, or, if there were several accused, it determined not to commit any of them (s. 8(3)(a)); or
(b)   the court did commit one or more of the accused but the trials consequent on the committal have all been concluded (s. 8(3)(b)); or
(c)   the court has made an order under s. 8(2) (see below) that the reporting restrictions contained in s. 8(1) shall not apply.

By s. 8(2) and subject to s. 8(2A), the court *shall*, on application being made by the accused or any of them, order that s. 8(1) is not to apply to the proceedings, thus allowing the media to report the proceedings in full. By s. 8(2A), where there are two or more accused and one applies for reporting restrictions to be lifted but another objects (as opposed to merely refraining from making an application himself), then the court is to make an order 'if, and only if, it is satisfied, after hearing the representations of the accused, that it is in the interests of justice to do so'. Subsection (2A) was inserted into s. 8 by the Criminal Justice (Amendment) Act 1981 because the section as originally enacted was perceived to be unfair in that, where there were several accused, any one of them was entitled to have the restrictions on reporting lifted, and his application was binding on the others whatever their wishes. Moreover, the terms of s. 8(2) make it plain that, even if it were practicable to report only those parts of the proceedings relating to defendant X and omit everything relating to defendant Y, the court has no power under the subsection to make an order to that effect. The latter point was incidentally confirmed by the Divisional Court in *Leeds Justices, ex parte Sykes* [1983] 1 WLR 132, where Griffiths LJ said (at p. 136A): 'If the reporting restrictions are to be lifted, then they are to be lifted in respect of the committal proceedings in their entirety. They cannot be lifted piecemeal.'

The justices could, however, achieve an effect akin to that by first lifting reporting restrictions through an order under the MCA 1980, s. 8(2), and then making a further order under the Contempt of Court Act 1981, s. 4, postponing reporting of some of the evidence until after the trial on indictment.

The main question at issue in *Ex parte Sykes* was whether, in the circumstances of that particular case, the magistrates were entitled to hold that it was in the interests of justice to make an order under s. 8(2) of the 1980 Act on the application of S's co-defendant (P), the order being opposed by S. P's argument for an order was that, three weeks earlier, a police officer had indicated to his solicitor that the charges against him would be dropped, but the police had gone back on that indication, and P wished to make a public protest about their behaviour. Having summarised the broad effect of s. 8(2) and (2A) and said that (in the event of disagreement between the defendants) the burden was on the accused who wanted reporting to show that it was in the interests of justice for the normal restrictions to be lifted, Griffiths LJ continued (at p. 134H–135B):

> Without attempting any comprehensive definition, the interests of justice incorporate as a paramount consideration that the defendants should have a fair trial. When the justices have to balance the request for the committal proceedings to be reported, they must bear in mind that the prima facie rule is that committal proceedings should not be reported, and only if a powerful case is made out for their reporting, should they be prepared to make an order when one of the defendants objects, particularly, if the ground of the objection is that very reason that led Parliament to provide that, as a general rule, proceedings should not be reported, namely that there is a risk that if the proceedings are widely reported, the reports may colour the views of the jury which ultimately has to try the case.

On the facts of *Ex parte Sykes*, giving immediate publicity to P's grievance against the police could be of little or no assistance to either his case or the case of his co-defendants. Indeed, strictly speaking, the question of whether the police had at one stage contemplated dropping the proceedings against P was irrelevant to his guilt or innocence (ibid., p. 137D). Therefore, the interests of justice (in the sense of ensuring that P had a fair trial) would not be advanced by publicity. On the other hand, S believed that 'his trial [would be] prejudiced if there [was] wide publicity of the evidence upon which the prosecution [would] ultimately ask the jury to try the case' (p. 137E). Set against that argument, P's argument could be 'of no weight', and the justices' order raising reporting restrictions was accordingly quashed. *Obiter*, Griffiths LJ suggested that an application for restrictions to be lifted on the ground that publicity might induce potential witnesses for the defendant making the application to come forward would 'merit really serious consideration by the justices' (ibid., p. 137B).

Under the MCA 1980, s. 8(2A), the court should lift reporting restrictions only if it is satisfied, after hearing the representations of the accused, that it is in the interests of justice to do so. The court must therefore give all the co-accused a chance to make representations. In *Wirral District Magistrates' Court, ex parte Meikle* (1990) 154 JP 1035, M was charged with murder and conspiracy to blackmail. She was one of four co-accused. On 22 December 1989, the solicitor for a co-accused A applied to lift reporting restrictions. The clerk to the justices advised them of the need to afford all the co-accused an opportunity to make representations. Only the solicitor for co-accused C was in court; he said he had no objection. The justices made an order under s. 8. On 12 January 1990, M's solicitor applied for the reimposition of reporting restrictions. The justices held that they were powerless to do that. On M's application, the Divisional Court quashed the decision to lift reporting restrictions. Any such lifting without hearing from a defendant was a breach of natural justice, procedurally invalid and *ultra vires*. Lifting of reporting restrictions could be highly prejudicial. A failure to ensure that all accused were given the opportunity to make representations was a serious breach of s. 8(2A).

Section 8(7) of the 1980 Act provides that the restrictions on publicity in s. 8(1) are 'in addition to, and not in derogation from, the provisions of any other enactment with respect to the publication of reports and proceedings of magistrates' and other courts'. It follows that, even where reporting restrictions have been lifted as a result of an order under s. 8(2), the court may order, under the Contempt of Court Act 1981, s. 4(2), that publication of reports of part or all of the proceedings be postponed (see *Horsham Justices, ex parte Farquharson* [1982] QB 762 and, generally, **D2.47** *et seq.*).

Magistrates' Courts Act 1980, s. 8

(1)   Except as provided by subsections (2), (3) and (8) below, it shall not be lawful to publish in Great Britain a written report, or to broadcast or include in a cable programme in Great Britain a report, of any committal proceedings in England and Wales containing any matter other than that permitted by subsection (4) below.

(2)   Subject to subsection (2A) below a magistrates' court shall, on an application for the purpose made with reference to any committal proceedings by the accused or one of the accused, as the case may be, order that subsection (1) above shall not apply to reports of those proceedings.

(2A)   Where in the case of two or more accused one of them objects to the making of an order under subsection (2) above, the court shall make the order if, and only if, it is satisfied, after hearing the representations of the accused, that it is in the interests of justice to do so.

(2B)   An order under subsection (2) above shall not apply to reports of proceedings under subsection (2A) above, but any decision of the court to make or not to make such an order may be [reported].

(3)   It shall not be unlawful under this section to publish, broadcast or include in a cable programme a report of committal proceedings containing any matter other than that permitted by subsection (4) below—

(a)   where the magistrates' court determines not to commit the accused, or determines to commit none of the accused, for trial, after it so determines;

(b)   where the court commits the accused or any of the accused for trial, after the conclusion of his trial or, as the case may be, the trial of the last to be tried;

and where at any time during the inquiry the court proceeds to try summarily the case of one or more of the accused under section 25(3) or (7) below [switching to summary trial from committal proceedings], while committing the other accused or one or more of the other accused for trial, it shall not be unlawful under this section to publish, broadcast or include in a cable programme as part of a report of the summary trial, after the court determines to proceed as aforesaid, a report of so much of the committal proceedings containing any such matter as takes place before the determination.

(4)   The following matters may be contained in a report of committal proceedings published, broadcast or included in a cable programme without an order under subsection (2) above before the time authorised by subsection (3) above, that is to say—

(a)   the identity of the court and the names of the examining justices;

(b)   the names, addresses and occupations of the parties and witnesses and the ages of the accused and witnesses;

(c)   the offence or offences, or a summary of them, with which the accused is or are charged;

(d)   the names of counsel and solicitors engaged in the proceedings;

(e)   any decision of the court to commit the accused or any of the accused for trial, and any decision of the court on the disposal of the case of any accused not committed;

(f)   where the court commits the accused or any of the accused for trial, the charge or charges, or a summary of them, on which he is committed and the court to which he is committed;

(g)   where the committal proceedings are adjourned, the date and place to which they are adjourned;

(h)   any arrangements as to bail on committal or adjournment;

(i)   whether legal aid was granted to the accused or any of the accused.

[(5)   Persons involved in the publication etc. of reports in contravention of s. 8 to be liable on summary conviction to a fine not exceeding level 5 on the standard scale.]

(6)   Proceedings for an offence under this section shall not, in England and Wales, be instituted otherwise than by or with the consent of the Attorney-General.

(7)   Subsection (1) above shall be in addition to, and not in derogation from, the provisions of any other enactment with respect to the publication of reports and proceedings of magistrates' and other courts.

(8)   For the purposes of this section committal proceedings shall, in relation to an information charging an indictable offence, be deemed to include any proceedings in the magistrates' court before the court proceeds to inquire into the information as examining justices; but where a magistrates' court which has begun to try an information summarily discontinues the summary trial in pursuance of section 25(2) or (6) below [reverting from summary trial to committal proceedings] and proceeds to inquire into the information as examining justices, that circumstance shall not make it unlawful under this section for a report of any proceedings on the information which was published, broadcast or included in a cable programme before the court determined to proceed as aforesaid to have been so published, broadcast or included in a cable programme.

Magistrates' Courts Rules 1981, r. 5

(1)   Except in a case where evidence is, with the consent of the accused, to be tendered in his absence under section 4(4)(b) of the [MCA 1980] (absence caused by ill health), a magistrates' court acting as examining justices shall before admitting any evidence explain to the accused the restrictions on reports of committal proceedings imposed by section 8 of the Act of 1980 and inform him of his right to apply to the court for an order removing those restrictions.

[(2)   Any order under s. 8(2) of the 1980 Act removing reporting restrictions to be entered in the court register.]

(3)   Where the court adjourns any such proceedings to another day, the court shall, at the beginning of any adjourned hearing, state that the order has been made.

WITNESSES AT TRIAL

The CPIA 1996, sch. 2, para. 1(2), states that a statement under the MCA 1980, s. 5B, **D7.17** tendered at committal 'may without further proof be read as evidence on the trial of the accused'. By para. 1(3)(c), if the accused (or one of them) objects to the statement then it cannot be read. The objection must be given in writing to the prosecutor and the Crown Court within 14 days of committal (Magistrates' Courts Rules 1981, r. 8). However, by para. 1(4), even where there has been an objection, the court 'may order that the objection shall have no effect if the court considers it to be in the interests of justice so to order', thus allowing the statement to be read. Identical provisions apply to a deposition taken under s. 97A of the 1980 Act (para. 2(2), (3)(c) and (4)). For details on the evidential consequences at trial, see **D13.13**.

Criminal Procedure and Investigations Act 1996, sch. 2

1.—(1)   Sub-paragraph (2) applies if—

(a)   a written statement has been admitted in evidence in proceedings before a magistrates' court inquiring into an offence as examining justices,

(b)   in those proceedings a person has been committed for trial,

(c)   for the purposes of section 5A of the Magistrates' Courts Act 1980 the statement complied with section 5B of that Act prior to the committal for trial,

(d)   the statement purports to be signed by a justice of the peace, and

(e)   sub-paragraph (3) does not prevent sub-paragraph (2) applying.

(2)   Where this sub-paragraph applies the statement may without further proof be read as evidence on the trial of the accused, whether for the offence for which he was committed for trial or for any other offence arising out of the same transaction or set of circumstances.

(3)   Sub-paragraph (2) does not apply if—

(a)   it is proved that the statement was not signed by the justice by whom it purports to have been signed,

(b)   the court of trial at its discretion orders that sub-paragraph (2) shall not apply, or

(c)   a party to the proceedings objects to sub-paragraph (2) applying.

(4)   If a party to the proceedings objects to sub-paragraph (2) applying the court of trial may order that the objection shall have no effect if the court considers it to be in the interests of justice so to order.

2.—(1)   Sub-paragraph (2) applies if—

(a)   in pursuance of section 97A of the Magistrates' Courts Act 1980 (summons or warrant to have evidence taken as a deposition etc.) a person has had his evidence taken as a deposition for the purposes of proceedings before a magistrates' court inquiring into an offence as examining justices,

(b)   the deposition has been admitted in evidence in those proceedings,

(c)   in those proceedings a person has been committed for trial,

(d)   for the purposes of section 5A of the Magistrates' Courts Act 1980 the deposition complied with section 5C of that Act prior to the committal for trial,

(e)   the deposition purports to be signed by the justice before whom it purports to have been taken, and

(f)   sub-paragraph (3) does not prevent sub-paragraph (2) applying.

(2)   Where this sub-paragraph applies the deposition may without further proof be read as evidence on the trial of the accused, whether for the offence for which he was committed for trial or for any other offence arising out of the same transaction or set of circumstances.

(3)   Sub-paragraph (2) does not apply if—

(a)   it is proved that the deposition was not signed by the justice by whom it purports to have been signed,

(b)   the court of trial at its discretion orders that sub-paragraph (2) shall not apply, or

(c)   a party to the proceedings objects to sub-paragraph (2) applying.

(4)   If a party to the proceedings objects to sub-paragraph (2) applying the court of trial may order that the objection shall have no effect if the court considers it to be in the interests of justice so to order.

Magistrates' Courts Rules 1981, rr. 4B and 8

4B.—(1)   The prosecutor shall, when he serves on any other party a copy of the evidence to be tendered in committal proceedings, notify that party that if he is committed for trial he has the right to object, by written notification to the prosecutor and the Crown Court within 14 days of being so committed unless the court in its discretion permits such an objection to be made outside that period, to a statement or deposition being read as evidence at the trial without oral evidence being given by the person who made the statement or deposition and without the opportunity to cross-examine that person.

(2)   The prosecutor shall, on notifying a party as indicated in paragraph (1) above, send a copy of such notification to the clerk of the magistrates' court.

8.   A magistrates' court which commits a person for trial shall forthwith remind him of his right to object, by written notification to the prosecutor and the Crown Court within 14 days of being committed unless that court in its discretion permits such an objection to be made outside that period, to a statement or deposition being read as evidence at the trial without oral evidence being given by the person who made the statement or deposition, and without the opportunity to cross-examine that person.

DECISIONS INCIDENTAL TO COMMITTAL FOR TRIAL

The Venue of the Trial

D7.18   By the MCA 1980, s. 7, a magistrates' court committing for trial must specify the Crown Court location at which the trial is to take place, having regard to: (a) the convenience of the defence, prosecution and witnesses; (b) the expediting of the trial; and (c) directions given by the Lord Chief Justice as to the distribution of work in the Crown Court. The division of indictable offences into four categories effected by the Lord Chief Justice's directions, and the relationship of that division to the venue to which examining justices should normally commit, is explained at **D2.2**; **D12.1** *et seq*. However, the justices are rarely asked by the parties to make a reasoned choice between rival locations of the Crown Court. Each magistrates' court is informed by the presiding judge of the relevant Crown Court circuit of the location to which it should normally commit for trial, and (in the absence of any representations to the contrary by either party) it will automatically commit to that location. In other words, the location specified by the presiding judge will be presumed to be the most convenient, and the parties hardly ever seek to persuade the magistrates to commit elsewhere. If the location specified by the magistrates subsequently appears unsatisfactory to a party, he may apply to the Crown Court for a change of venue.

Bail or Custody

A committal for trial may be on bail or in custody (MCA 1980, s. 6(3)). This is subject **D7.19** to the provisions of the Bail Act 1976, s. 4 and sch. 1, which require defendants to criminal proceedings to be granted bail unless the court is satisfied of certain matters (e.g., that there are substantial grounds for believing that the defendant would abscond). There are conflicting authorities as to whether a defendant remanded in custody at several previous remand hearings is entitled to present a fully argued bail application on committal, even though he has already used up the right to make two full applications given to him by part IIA of sch. 1 to the Bail Act 1976 (see *Reading Crown Court, ex parte Malik* [1981] QB 451 and *Slough Justices, ex parte Duncan* (1982) 75 Cr App R 384 discussed at **D5.35** *et seq.*).

Legal Aid

A magistrates' court committing a person for trial may grant him legal aid for purposes **D7.20** of the Crown Court proceedings (Legal Aid Act 1988, s. 20). In the majority of cases, the accused will have enjoyed legal aid for the committal proceedings, and, on application being made, the court will almost automatically extend his aid to the Crown Court, assuming there has been no significant change in his means. The grant of aid is, however, discretionary, and examining justices might refuse aid if, for example, they consider the charge too trivial or simple to necessitate legal representation at the State's expense. Even if the magistrates refuse (or are not asked) to grant legal aid, application may be made to the Crown Court itself. In a minority of cases, the original grant of legal aid by the magistrates' court takes the form of a 'through order', by which the accused is granted aid for the proceedings in the magistrates' court and, if committed, the trial on indictment also. If such an order has been made, it is unnecessary to make any further application at committal.

Transmission of Evidence etc. to the Crown Court

The various documents which it is the duty of the magistrates' court to send to the **D7.21** Crown Court are listed in r. 11 of the Magistrates' Courts Rules 1981 (or, where the pilot scheme under the CDA 1998, s. 51, applies (see **D8.21**), r. 11A).

Magistrates' Courts Act 1980, s. 7

A magistrates' court on committing a person for trial shall specify the place at which he is to be tried, and in selecting that place shall have regard to—
(a) the convenience of the defence, the prosecution and the witnesses,
(b) the expediting of the trial, and
(c) any direction given by or on behalf of the Lord Chief Justice with the concurrence of the Lord Chancellor under section 4(5) of the Courts Act 1971.

Magistrates' Courts Rules 1981, rr. 11 and 11A

11.—(1) [Revoked.]
(2) As soon as practicable after the committal of any person for trial, and in any case within four days . . . the clerk of the magistrates' court that committed him shall, subject to the provisions of section 7 of the Prosecution of Offences Act 1985 (which relates to the sending of documents and things to the Director of Public Prosecutions), send to the appropriate officer of the Crown Court—
(a) the information if it is in writing;
(b)(i) the evidence tendered in accordance with section 5A of the Act of 1980 and, where any of that evidence consists of a copy of a deposition or documentary exhibit which is in the possession of the court, any such deposition or documentary exhibit; and

(ii) a certificate to the effect that that evidence was so tendered;

(c) any notification by the prosecutor under section 5D(2) regarding the admissibility of a statement under section 23 or 24 of the Criminal Justice Act 1988;

(d) [revoked];

(e) a copy of the record [made under s. 5 of the Bail Act 1976] relating to the grant or withholding of bail in respect of the accused on the occasion of the committal;

(f) any recognisance entered into by any person as surety for the accused together with a statement of any enlargement thereof under section 129(4) of the Act of 1980;

(g) a list of the exhibits produced in evidence before the justices or treated as so produced;

(h) such of the exhibits referred to in [subparagraph (g)] as have been retained by the justices;

(i) the names and addresses of any interpreters engaged for the defendant for the purposes of the committal proceedings, together with any telephone numbers at which they can readily be contacted, and details of the languages or dialects in connection with which they have been so engaged;

(j) if the committal was under section 6(2) of the Act of 1980 (committal for trial without consideration of the evidence), a statement to that effect;

(k) if the magistrates' court has made an order under section 8(2) of the Act of 1980 (removal of restrictions on reports of committal proceedings), a statement to that effect;

(l) the certificate of the examining justices as to costs of prosecution . . . ;

(m) if any person under the age of 18 is concerned in the committal proceedings, a statement whether the magistrates' court has given a direction under section 39 of the Children and Young Persons Act 1933 (prohibition of publication of certain matter in newspapers);

(n) a copy of any legal aid order previously made in the case;

(o) a copy of any contribution order previously made in the case under section 23 of the Legal Aid Act 1988;

(p) a copy of any legal aid application previously made in the case which has been refused;

(q) any statement of means already submitted.

(3) [Revoked.]

(4) The period of four days specified in paragraph (2) may be extended in relation to any committal for so long as the appropriate officer of the Crown Court directs, having regard to the length of any documents mentioned in that paragraph or any other relevant circumstances.

11A.—(1) As soon as practicable after any person is sent for trial (pursuant to section 51 of the [CDA 1998], and in any event within 4 days . . . the clerk of the magistrates' court that sent him shall, subject to section 7 of the Prosecution of Offences Act 1985 (which relates to the sending of documents and things to the Director of Public Prosecutions), send to the appropriate officer of the Crown Court—

(a) the information, if it is in writing;

(b) the notice required by section 51(7) of the [CDA 1998];

(c) a copy of the record made in pursuance of section 5 of the Bail Act 1976 relating to the grant or withholding of bail in respect of the accused on the occasion of the sending;

(d) any recognisance entered into by any person as surety for the accused together with any enlargement thereof under section 129(4) of the Act of 1980;

(e) the names and addresses of any interpreters engaged for the defendant for the purposes of the appearance in the magistrates' court, together with any telephone numbers at which they can be readily contacted, and details of the languages or dialects in connection with which they have been so engaged;

(f) if any person under the age of 18 is concerned in the proceedings, a statement whether the magistrates' court has given a direction under section 39 of the Children and Young Persons Act 1933 (prohibition of publication of certain matter in newspapers);

(g) a copy of any legal aid order previously made in the case;

(h) a copy of any contribution order previously made in the case under section 23 of the Legal Aid Act 1988;

(i) a copy of any legal aid application previously made in the case which has been refused;

(j) any statement of means already submitted; and

(k)   any documents relating to an appeal by the prosecution against the granting of bail.

(2)   The period of 4 days specified in paragraph (5) may be extended in relation to any sending for trial for so long as the appropriate officer of the Crown Court directs, having regard to any relevant circumstances.

CHALLENGING THE DECISIONS OF EXAMINING JUSTICES

The prosecution may, in effect, challenge the decision of examining justices not to **D7.22** commit for trial by applying to a High Court judge for a voluntary bill of indictment (see **D8.2** to **D8.5**).

The extent to which the defence may challenge either an ultimate decision to commit for trial or decisions taken during the course of the proceedings (e.g., as to the admissibility of evidence) is very limited. The following are the main principles established by the authorities:

(a)   A decision to commit for trial cannot be appealed to the High Court by way of case stated. This is because appeal under the MCA 1980, s. 111, which allows any party aggrieved by a proceeding of a magistrates' court to state a case for the opinion of the High Court on a question of law or jurisdiction arising in the proceeding, applies only if the court has reached a final determination in the case, and a decision to commit for trial is not classified as a final determination (see *Cragg* v *Lewes District Council* [1986] Crim LR 800).

(b)   It is not open to the Crown Court to quash an indictment or otherwise stay a prosecution on the ground that the evidence of an incompetent witness was tendered at committal proceedings or a competent witness gave evidence that was inadmissible (*Norfolk Quarter Sessions, ex parte Brunson* [1953] 1 QB 503). This is, of course, without prejudice to the judge's power at the end of the prosecution case to uphold a submission of no case to answer and direct the jury to acquit.

(c)   The High Court's powers of judicial review may be exercised in respect of committal proceedings. However, it has been established that where examining justices take a decision during committal proceedings which a party considers to be wrong, his correct course is to wait until the proceedings have concluded before applying for judicial review. The justices should not adjourn simply for the purpose of allowing an application for judicial review to be made (*Wells Street Stipendiary Magistrate, ex parte Seillon* [1978] 1 WLR 1002).

The High Court has consistently been reluctant to grant certiorari on the basis that the examining justices admitted inadmissible evidence (see *Highbury Magistrates' Court, ex parte Boyce* (1984) 79 Cr App R 132 and **D7.12**). In *Neill* v *North Antrim Magistrates' Court* [1992] 1 WLR 1221 however, the House of Lords made it clear that certiorari does lie to quash a committal where inadmissible evidence was relied upon. Lord Mustill said that statements in the authorities that the admissibility of evidence was for the trial judge, and not the justices, no longer reflected the law in England and Wales, or in Northern Ireland (where the instant case originated). It was, however, only in the case of a really substantial error leading to demonstrable injustice that the Divisional Court should contemplate granting the remedy (see also *Bedwellty Justices, ex parte Williams* [1997] AC 225). These cases must now be read subject to the statutory prohibition upon consideration by the examining justices of admissibility in terms of the PACE 1984, ss. 76 and 78 (see **D7.12**).

Judicial review of committal proceedings is also appropriate either where the examining justices are proposing to act in excess of jurisdiction (in which case prohibition may be ordered to prevent the excess), or where the decision etc. complained of amounted to a total refusal of jurisdiction (in which case certiorari and/or mandamus may issue to compel the court to exercise the jurisdiction which rightfully belongs to it). See *Hatfield*

Justices, ex parte Castle [1981] 1 WLR 217 for an example of prohibition to prevent a magistrates' court commencing committal proceedings where the effect of the MCA 1980, s. 22, was that they were required to proceed as if an offence of criminal damage were triable only summarily, and *Carden* (1879) 5 QBD 1, *Ex parte Seillon*, and *Oxford City Justices, ex parte Berry* [1988] QB 507 for discussion of the distinction between refusal of jurisdiction and mistakes in exercising jurisdiction.

(d)   If an error occurring at committal proceedings was of such a fundamental nature that the committal must be regarded as null, the consequent trial on indictment is also a nullity, and any conviction resulting therefrom is liable to be quashed by the Court of Appeal (*Gee* [1936] 2 KB 442 and *Phillips* [1939] 1 KB 63). Similarly, if a fundamental error vitiates committals on certain charges while leaving unaffected the committals on other charges, convictions on the counts based on the former are liable to be quashed although the remainder may stand (*Phillips*). On quashing a conviction in the circumstances here described, the Court of Appeal has power to issue a writ of *venire de novo*, the effect of which would be that the prosecution could reinstitute proceedings in the magistrates' court.

COMMITTAL FOR 'TRIAL' IN RESPECT OF A SUMMARY OFFENCE

D7.23   The power of examining justices to commit for trial in respect of an indictable offence given by the MCA 1980, s. 6, is supplemented by a limited power to commit in respect of summary offences. The power is contained in the CJA 1988, s. 41, and arises if (s. 41(1)):

(a)   the court is committing an accused for trial for one or more offences triable either way; and
(b)   he is also charged with a summary offence punishable with imprisonment and/or disqualification from driving; and
(c)   the summary offence arises out of circumstances which appear to the court to be the same as or connected with the circumstances of the (or one of the) offences triable either way.

On exercising the power in s. 41(1), the court must give both the accused and the Crown Court a notice stating which of the either-way offences is the one which appears to it to be linked with the summary offence (s. 41(2)). A decision to commit under s. 41 is unchallengeable whether by appeal or by application for judicial review (s. 41(3)), but, before proceeding to deal with the accused in pursuance of the powers given to it by s. 41, the Crown Court must be satisfied that the conditions for a committal were in fact satisfied. Where there is no legal basis for the magistrates' decision, however, it is a nullity, and an application can be made to the Divisional Court for it to be quashed. This is the case, for example, where the primary offence for which the accused is committed is triable only on indictment, rather than triable either way (*Miall* [1992] QB 836).

In the areas where the CDA 1998, s. 51, is in force (or when it is fully implemented), summary offences which are related to an indictable-only offence and are punishable with imprisonment or disqualification from driving *must* be sent immediately to the Crown Court for trial if the accused appears for them at the same time as for the indictable-only offence. If he appears for them after being sent to the Crown Court for trial on an indictable-only offence, the magistrates *may* send the summary offences for trial to the Crown Court (see **D8.21**).

Following committal, the proceedings in the magistrates' court for the summary offence are treated as if they had been adjourned *sine die* (s. 41(1)). Although the section itself refers to the accused being committed for trial, in fact the charge for the summary offence is not put to him unless and until he is convicted of one or more of the either-way offences. Should he deny the allegation, the Crown Court has no power to proceed further in the matter, but simply informs the magistrates' court of what has occurred. Thus, it would be more accurate to describe committals under s. 41 as 'committals with a view to sentence on a guilty plea', rather than 'committals for trial' in the sense that that term is normally understood. (Contrast the use of the CJA 1988, s. 40, discussed at **D9.6**.) In the event that the defendant does deny the allegation, so that the Crown Court is unable to deal with it, the matter can be revived in the magistrates' court. Although this does mean that the defendant is accused of the same offence in two courts at the same time, it does not constitute double jeopardy, since, if he did plead guilty in the Crown Court, he could enter a plea of autrefois convict to any further proceedings before the magistrates (*King* [1992] Crim LR 47).

In *Foote* (1991) 94 Cr App R 82, F was committed for trial on a charge of reckless driving (triable either way). At the same time he was committed under the CJA 1988, s. 41, on a charge of careless driving. In effect, the latter was an alternative count, since both alleged offences related to the same driving. At the Crown Court, he pleaded not guilty to reckless driving. The offence of careless driving was then put to him, and he pleaded guilty. The Crown indicated that the plea was acceptable. The judge directed a verdict of not guilty to be entered on the charge of reckless driving and proceeded to sentence on the careless driving. On appeal, the Court of Appeal quashed F's conviction for careless driving, reasoning that, once F had been found not guilty of the offence which was triable either way, the powers of the Crown Court ceased in respect of the offence which was triable only summarily.

Provided that the defendant has been validly convicted on a count which has been properly included within the indictment, however, the Crown Court may deal with the offence sent to them by virtue of s. 41. In *Bird* [1995] Crim LR 745, there were two counts in the indictment, one of possessing an offensive weapon and one of driving whilst disqualified. The latter offence had been included in the indictment by virtue of the CJA 1988, s. 40 (see **D9.6**). In addition, the magistrates sent up to the Crown Court under s. 41 an offence of having no insurance. B was acquitted of the offensive weapon count after the prosecution offered no evidence, but he was convicted of driving whilst disqualified. The question then arose whether the Crown Court had power to deal with the no insurance offence or should have remitted it to the magistrates. The Court of Appeal held that the conviction on the driving whilst disqualified count (which had been properly included within the indictment) triggered off the power to deal with the no insurance offence under s. 41, and the judge had acted within his jurisdiction in sentencing B for the latter offence.

Section 41 of the 1988 Act does not specify how examining justices should satisfy themselves that a summary charge before them is appropriate for committal. It is, however, expressly stated that the evidence of the summary offence need not be disclosed in the statements and/or depositions relied on by the prosecution to secure the committal of the either-way matters (see last words of s. 41(1)). It is submitted, therefore, that the prosecution need do no more than make representations to the court explaining how the summary and either-way charges are linked so as to fall within the terms of the section.

Criminal Justice Act 1988, s. 41

(1) Where a magistrates' court commits a person to the Crown Court for trial on indictment for an offence triable either way or a number of such offences, it may also commit him for trial for any summary offence with which he is charged and which—

    (a) is punishable with imprisonment or involves obligatory or discretionary disqualification from driving; and

   (b)   arises out of circumstances which appear to the court to be the same as or connected with those giving rise to the offence, or one of the offences, triable either way, whether or not evidence relating to that summary offence appears on the depositions or written statements in the case; and the trial of the information for the summary offence shall then be treated as if the magistrates' court had adjourned it under section 10 of the Magistrates' Courts Act 1980 and had not fixed the time and place for its resumption.

   (2)   Where a magistrates' court commits a person to the Crown Court for trial on indictment for a number of offences triable either way and exercises the power conferred by subsection (1) above in respect of a summary offence, the magistrates' court shall give the Crown Court and the [accused] a notice stating which of the offences triable either way appears to the court to arise out of circumstances which are the same as or connected with those giving rise to the summary offence.

   (3)   A magistrates' court's decision to exercise the power conferred by subsection (1) above shall not be subject to appeal or liable to be questioned in any court.

   [(4) to (13)   Relate to the procedure and powers of the Crown Court following a committal under subsection (1).]

SECTION D8: ALTERNATIVES TO COMMITTAL PROCEEDINGS

Introduction

This section deals with the methods (other than a retrial ordered by the Court of Appeal) **D8.1** by which a person may lawfully be required to stand trial on indictment without having first been committed for trial by a magistrates' court. There are three main sets of circumstances in which this may happen:

(a)   the preferment of a bill of indictment by the direction or with the consent of a High Court judge (also known as the 'voluntary bill' procedure);

(b)   a notice of transfer given by the prosecution under the CJA 1987, s. 4; or

(c)   a notice of transfer given by the prosecution under the CJA 1991, s. 53;

(d)   an order by the magistrates that the accused be sent for trial for an indictable-only offence under the CDA 1998, s. 51.

VOLUNTARY BILLS OF INDICTMENT

Statutory Provision

The Administration of Justice (Miscellaneous Provisions) Act 1933, s. 2(2)(b), provides **D8.2** that a bill of indictment may be preferred 'by the direction or with the consent of a judge of the High Court'.

Procedure for Obtaining a Voluntary Bill

The procedure for obtaining a High Court judge's consent to the preferment of a bill of **D8.3** indictment is prescribed by the Indictments (Procedure) Rules 1971, rr. 6 to 10. It is also dealt with in *Practice Direction (Crime: Voluntary Bills)* [1999] 1 WLR 1613. In summary, the procedure is as follows:

(a)   An application must be made in writing, signed by the applicant (i.e. the prosecutor) or his solicitor (Indictments (Procedure) Rules 1971, r. 7).

(b)   The application must state:

(i)   whether there has been any previous application for a voluntary bill;

(ii)   whether there have been any committal proceedings;

(iii)   the result of any previous application and/or committal proceedings; and

(iv)   the reason, if there have not been committal proceedings or if the committal proceedings resulted in committal, why it is desired to prefer a bill rather than seeking committal or, as the case may be, relying on the committal as sufficient authority for preferring a bill (rr. 8(b), 9(1) and (3)).

(c)   The application must be accompanied by the bill of indictment which it is proposed to prefer (r. 8(1)(a)). It has been held that this requirement is sufficiently complied with if the application is marked to the effect that the indictment will follow later, and the proposed bill is in fact delivered in time to be placed before the judge when he is making his decision (*Rothfield* (1937) 26 Cr App R 103). The application must also be accompanied by a copy of any existing indictment which has been preferred in consequence of the committal (*Practice Direction (Crime: Voluntary Bills)*, para. 2(c)).

(d)   Where there have already been committal proceedings, the application must also be accompanied by a copy of the documents received in evidence at the committal, including any documentary exhibits (Indictments (Procedure) Rules 1971, r. 9(2) and (3)). A copy of any charges on which the accused has been committed for trial should also accompany the application, as should a copy of any charges on which committal was refused by the examining justices (*Practice Direction (Crime: Voluntary Bills)*, para. 2(a) and (b)).

If there is any additional evidence the prosecutor intends to rely on which does not appear on the depositions or statements, proofs of that evidence must also be sent. Where there have not been committal proceedings, the applicant simply sends the proofs of evidence of his proposed witnesses (Indictments (Procedure) Rules 1971, r. 9(1)(a)). In each case, the application must contain a statement that the evidence contained in the depositions, statements and proofs of evidence will be available at trial and that the case thereby disclosed is – to the best of the applicant's knowledge, information and belief – substantially a true case (ibid.).

Further, the application must be accompanied by a summary of the evidence or other document which (i) identifies the counts in the proposed indictment on which the accused has been committed for trial (or their equivalent) and (ii) in relation to each count in the proposed indictment, identifies the pages in the accompanying statements and exhibits where the essential relevant evidence can be found (*Practice Direction (Crime: Voluntary Bills)*, para. 2(d) and (e)).

(e) Except where the application is made by or on behalf of the DPP, it must further be accompanied by an affidavit verifying that the statements contained in the application are true to the best of the applicant's knowledge and belief (r. 8(a)). Where a Crown Prosecutor applies for a voluntary bill in exercise of the powers delegated to him by the DPP, the application is made by or on behalf of the DPP and therefore does not have to be supported by an affidavit (see the Prosecution of Offences Act 1985, s. 1(6), and *Ex parte Bray* (1986) *The Times*, 7 October 1986). This is so even if the application was not expressly authorised by the DPP, but merely made by the Crown Prosecutor carrying out his general duties (ibid.).

(f) Subject to a contrary direction by the judge, the application is determined without the attendance of the applicant or his witnesses (r. 10). Should they be required to attend, their attendance is not in open court (ibid.). The judge's decision is signified in writing.

(g) The proposed defendant has no right to attend, to be represented before or even submit written representations to the judge. In exceptional cases, the judge in his discretion may consider written representations, but it seems likely that he does not even have a discretion to allow the defendant to be present in person (*Raymond* [1981] QB 910). Dicta in *Raymond* suggest that, should the defendant be allowed to make representations, they must be limited to the question of whether it is appropriate to proceed by way of voluntary bill rather than by the ordinary method of committal proceedings, and should not extend to the question of whether the statements disclose a prima facie case.

Indictments (Procedure) Rules 1971 (SI 1971 No. 2084), rr. 2 and 6 to 11

2. . . . 'committal documents' means evidence falling within section 5A(3) of the Magistrates' Courts Act 1980 and tendered at any committal proceedings:
Provided that any requirement of these Rules that an application should be accompanied by a copy of any committal documents shall, as respects documents mentioned in paragraphs (b) and (d) of section 5A(3) of the Magistrates' Courts Act 1980, be satisfied if a copy of such parts only of those documents as are, in the opinion of the applicant, material, accompanies the application, and the application contains an express statement to that effect.

6. An application under section 2(2)(b) of [the Administration of Justice (Miscellaneous Provisions) Act 1933] for the preferment of a bill of indictment may be made to a judge of the High Court.

7. Every such application shall be in writing and shall be signed by the applicant or his solicitor.

8. Every such application—
(a) shall be accompanied by the bill of indictment which it is proposed to prefer and, unless the application is made by or on behalf of the DPP, shall also be accompanied by an affidavit by the applicant, or, if the applicant is a corporation, by an affidavit by some director or officer of the corporation, that the statements contained in the application are, to the best of the deponent's knowledge, information and belief, true; and
(b) shall state whether or not any application has previously been made under these rules . . . and whether there have been any committal proceedings, and the result of any such application or proceedings.

9.—(1) Where there have been no committal proceedings, the application shall state why it is desired to prefer a bill without such proceedings and—
(a) there shall accompany the application proofs of the evidence of the witnesses whom it is proposed to call in support of the charges; and
(b) the application shall embody a statement that the evidence shown by the proofs will be available at the trial and that the case disclosed by the proofs is, to the best of the knowledge, information and belief of the applicant, substantially a true case.
(2) Where there have been committal proceedings, and the justice or justices have refused to commit the accused for trial, the application shall be accompanied by—
(a) a copy of the committal documents; and
(b) proofs of any evidence which it is proposed to call in support of the charges so far as that evidence is not contained in the committal documents;
and the application shall embody a statement that the evidence shown by the proofs and (except so far as may be expressly stated to the contrary in the application) the evidence shown by the committal documents, will be available at the trial and that the case disclosed by the committal documents and proofs is, to the best of the knowledge, information and belief of the applicant, substantially a true case.
(3) Where the accused has been committed for trial the application shall state why the application is being made and shall be accompanied by proofs of any evidence which it is proposed to call in support of the charges, so far as that evidence is not contained in the committal documents, and, unless the committal documents have already been transmitted to the judge to whom the application is made, shall also be accompanied by a copy of the committal documents; and the application shall embody a statement that the evidence shown by the proofs will be available at the trial, and that the case disclosed by the committal documents and proofs is, to the best of the knowledge, information and belief of the applicant, substantially a true case.

10. Unless the judge otherwise directs in any particular case, his decision on the application shall be signified in writing on the application without requiring the attendance before him of the applicant or of any of the witnesses, and if the judge thinks fit to require the attendance of the applicant or of any of the witnesses, their attendance shall not be in open court.

Unless the judge gives a direction to the contrary, where an applicant is required to attend as aforesaid, he may attend by a solicitor or by counsel.

As far as cases sent for trial under the CDA 1998, s. 51, are concerned, in the pilot areas where that procedure is in operation (see **D8.21**), there are certain minor consequential amendments to the Indictments (Procedure) Rules 1971, which are not reproduced here.

Practice Direction (Crime: Voluntary Bills) **[1999] 1 WLR 1613**

1. Section 2(2)(b) of the Administration of Justice (Miscellaneous Provisions) Act 1933 allows the preferment of a bill of indictment by the direction or with the consent of a judge of the High Court. Bills so preferred are known as voluntary bills.

2. Applications for such consent must not only comply with each paragraph of the Indictments (Procedure) Rules 1971 but must also be accompanied by (a) a copy of any

charges on which the defendant has been committed for trial; (b) a copy of any charges on which his committal for trial was refused by the magistrates' court; (c) a copy of any existing indictment which has been preferred in consequence of his committal; (d) a summary of the evidence or other document which (i) identifies the counts in the proposed indictment on which he has been committed for trial (or which are substantially the same as charges on which he has been so committed), and (ii) in relation to each other count in the proposed indictment, identifies the pages in the accompanying statements and exhibits where the essential evidence said to support that count is to be found; (e) marginal markings of the relevant passages on the pages of the statements and exhibits identified under 2(d)(ii) above. These requirements should be complied with in relation to each defendant named in the indictment for which consent is sought, whether or not it is proposed to prefer any new count against him.

3.   The preferment of a voluntary bill is an exceptional procedure. Consent should only be granted where good reason to depart from the normal procedure is clearly shown and only where the interests of justice, rather than considerations of administrative convenience, require it.

4.   Neither the 1933 Act nor the 1971 Rules expressly require a prosecuting authority applying for consent to the preferment of a voluntary bill to give notice of the application to the prospective defendant or to serve on him a copy of documents delivered to the judge; nor is it expressly required that the prospective defendant have any opportunity to make any submissions to the judge, whether in writing or orally.

5.   The prosecuting authorities for England and Wales [issued on 29 July 1999] revised guidance to prosecutors on the procedures to be adopted in seeking judicial consent to the preferment of voluntary bills. These procedures will direct prosecutors—

(1)   on the making of application for consent to preferment of a voluntary bill, forthwith to give notice to the prospective defendant that such application has been made;
(2)   at about the same time, to serve on the prospective defendant a copy of all the documents delivered to the judge (save to the extent that these have already been served on him);
(3)   to inform the prospective defendant that he may make submissions in writing to the judge provided that he does so within 9 working days of the giving of notice under (1) above.

Prosecutors will be directed that these procedures should be followed unless there are good grounds for not doing so, in which case prosecutors will inform the judge that the procedures have not been followed and seek his leave to dispense with all or any of them. Judges should not give leave to dispense unless good grounds are shown.

6.   A judge to whom application for consent to the preferment of a voluntary bill is made will of course wish to consider carefully the documents submitted by the prosecutor and any written submissions timeously made by the prospective defendant, and may properly seek any necessary amplification. The judge may invite oral submissions from either party, or accede to a request for an opportunity to make such oral submissions, if the judge considers it necessary or desirable to receive such oral submissions in order to make a sound and fair decision on the application. Any such oral submissions should be made on notice to the other party, who should be allowed to attend.

Finality of High Court Judge's Decision

D8.4   Where a High Court judge directs the preferment of a voluntary bill of indictment under the Administration of Justice (Miscellaneous Provisions) Act 1933, s. 2(2)(b), the Court of Appeal will not inquire into the correctness or otherwise of his decision, providing only that he was acting within his jurisdiction (*Rothfield* (1937) 26 Cr App R 103). The issuing of a voluntary bill of indictment is not subject to judicial review (*Manchester Crown Court, ex parte Williams* (1990) 154 JP 589). In *Rothfield*, R, having been convicted on an indictment preferred under s. 2(2)(b), argued on appeal that the trial judge should have quashed the indictment and discharged him without trial as the High Court judge had erred in directing preferment. Dismissing the appeal, Humphreys J held that a High Court judge's authorisation for the preferring of a bill is binding on a trial judge, and the latter has no jurisdiction to quash the indictment simply on the basis that the former, according to the defence, made a mistake. His lordship continued (at p. 106): '. . . it cannot be made too plain, or stated too definitely, that this court will not inquire into the exercise of the discretion of a judge who is sitting and dealing with an application under the Administration of Justice (Miscellaneous Provisions) Act 1933, so long as it is clear that he had jurisdiction to entertain the application.' Accordingly, the Court of Criminal Appeal declined to consider arguments advanced by the appellant which went to whether it had been, in all the circumstances, an appropriate case for a voluntary bill, but their lordships did consider, although ultimately rejecting, an argument that the High Court judge had had no power to direct preferment because of an irregularity in the way the prosecutor made his application (failing to accompany the application with a copy of the proposed bill of indictment in breach of what is now the Indictment (Procedure) Rules 1971 – see **D8.3** for the decision on that point). Since only High Court judges have jurisdiction to direct preferment of a voluntary bill, a conviction on an indictment purportedly preferred on the direction of a circuit judge will plainly have to be quashed (see *Thompson* [1975] 1 WLR 1425).

Circumstances in which It Is Appropriate to Apply for a Voluntary Bill

Neither the Administration of Justice (Miscellaneous Provisions) Act nor the Indict- **D8.5** ments (Procedure) Rules 1971 expressly indicate when it is appropriate to proceed by way of voluntary bill rather than by committal proceedings. The implication of r. 9(1) and (3) is that the normal way to secure authority to prefer a bill of indictment is to bring the accused before a magistrates' court for the holding of committal proceedings, since, if there have not been committal proceedings or if there have been such proceedings resulting in a committal, the applicant is required to state in his application why it is being made. Conversely, if there have been committal proceedings but the examining justices refused to commit, the application need not state the reason for its making, presumably because the voluntary bill procedure is accepted as always being appropriate in such cases. This is confirmed by *Horsham Justices, ex parte Reeves* (1980) 75 Cr App R 236, where it was held that the prosecution, having failed after a hearing on the merits to satisfy the examining justices that there was a case to answer, ought to have applied for a voluntary bill rather than initiating a second committal before a different bench of justices. In *Brooks v DPP for Jamaica* [1994] 1 AC 568, however, the Privy Council stressed that the decision to prefer a voluntary bill in these circumstances is one to be exercised with the greatest circumspection, treating the magistrates' decision with the utmost respect.

Decided cases indicate a variety of circumstances in which the prosecution may properly apply for a voluntary bill even though committal proceedings never reached the stage of the examining justices actually refusing to commit for trial. Thus, in *Rothfield* (1937) 26 Cr App R 103, the prosecution were granted a voluntary bill where the chairman of the examining justices fell ill during an adjournment with the result that, had a bill not been applied for, it would have been necessary to retake the depositions of some 30 witnesses before a fresh bench. In *Raymond* [1981] QB 910, the reason for the voluntary bill was that R, during the early part of committal proceedings, 'gave such unmistakable indications of an intention seriously to disrupt the committal proceedings as to make a mockery of them that counsel for the Crown decided to abandon them' (pp. 913H–914A). Similarly, a voluntary bill was obtained in *Paling* (1978) 67 Cr App R 299, where the committal proceedings for an alleged assault were discontinued after P became abusive to the bench and, during a short adjournment, allegedly committed further assaults on officers concerned in the case. The greater speed of the voluntary bill procedure as compared with committal may lead to its being used where a second suspect is arrested shortly before the date fixed for the trial of an alleged co-offender who was arrested earlier and has already been committed, and it is desired to join them both in a fresh indictment rather than having them tried separately. Indeed, whenever the indictment or indictments originally preferred as a result of a committal later appear unsatisfactory, it may be preferable to regularise the position by applying for a voluntary bill to replace them, rather than simply preferring an additional indictment on the authority of the committal. One advantage of so doing is that the High Court judge can also direct what is to happen to the existing indictment or indictments, rather than leaving them in limbo. However, there is no objection in law to several indictments being in existence as a result of one committal (see *Groom* [1977] QB 6), although, if an indictment has actually been quashed, the effect of the committal is then exhausted and the prosecution will be forced either to have a second committal or, more probably, apply for a voluntary bill (see *Thompson* [1975] 1 WLR 1425 and **D9.7** where the complex law on the power to prefer more than one indictment on the basis of a single committal is fully discussed).

NOTICES OF TRANSFER

The Notice of Transfer System

D8.6 The CJA 1987, s. 4, enables certain specified prosecuting authorities, when conducting proceedings for a serious or complex fraud, to avoid the necessity of having the accused committed for trial by giving a *notice of transfer*. The effect of a notice is that the magistrates' court which would otherwise be seised of the case ceases to have jurisdiction save in respect of ancillary matters such as legal aid and bail (s. 4(1)), and the prosecution are entitled, simply by virtue of their own notice, to prefer a bill of indictment for the offences concerned (Administration of Justice (Miscellaneous Provisions) Act 1933, s. 2(2)(aa)). The accused is provided with some protection against being put on trial for offences of which there is no satisfactory evidence through a procedure allowing him to apply to a Crown Court judge at a preparatory hearing for the charges specified in the notice of transfer to be dismissed and the indictment quashed (CJA 1987, s. 6). The basic provisions of the 1987 Act are supplemented by the Criminal Justice Act 1987 (Notice of Transfer) Regulations 1988 (SI 1988 No. 1691) and the Criminal Justice Act 1987 (Dismissal of Transferred Charges) Rules 1988 (SI 1988 No. 1695).

As to the use of the notice of transfer system in cases where a child will be a witness at the trial of an offence to which the CJA 1988, s. 32(2) applies (sexual offences and offences of violence or cruelty), see **D8.20**.

Conditions for Giving a Notice of Transfer in Serious Fraud Cases

D8.7 A notice may be given whenever, in the opinion of a 'designated authority' (or one of its officers acting on its behalf), the evidence against an accused charged with an indictable offence is (a) sufficient for him to be committed for trial, and (b) 'reveals a case of fraud of such seriousness or complexity that it is appropriate that the management of the case should without delay be taken over by the Crown Court' (CJA 1987, s. 4(1)(a) and (b)). 'Designated authorities' comprise the DPP, the Director of the Serious Fraud Office, the Commissioners of Inland Revenue, the Commissioners of Customs and Excise and the Secretary of State (s. 4(2)). Although the Serious Fraud Office was set up specifically to coordinate and conduct the investigation and prosecution of serious fraud, the power to give a notice of transfer is not restricted to the Serious Fraud Office, but extends, *inter alia*, to the CPS by virtue of the DPP being head of the CPS and able to delegate his powers to Crown Prosecutors.

Time for Giving Notice

D8.8 Notice of transfer may be given at any time between the accused being charged and the commencement of committal proceedings (CJA 1987, s. 4(1)(a) and (c)). It must be given to the 'magistrates' court in whose jurisdiction the offence has been charged' (s. 4(1)(c)). To avoid unnecessary hearings in that court, it would seem preferable to serve the notice on the clerk to the justices as soon as possible after the accused has been charged.

Contents of Notice

The notice must specify the location of the Crown Court at which it is proposed the trial **D8.9** shall take place and the charges to which it relates (CJA 1987, s. 5(1) and (2)). In choosing the place of trial the designated authority must have regard to the matters set out in the MCA 1980, s. 7 (i.e. the convenience of the parties and witnesses, the expediting of the trial and any directions given by the Lord Chief Justice). A form of notice is set out in the schedule to SI 1988 No. 1691. In addition to giving the notice to the magistrates' court, the prosecuting authority must give a copy to the accused (or his solicitor) and to the Crown Court (SI 1988 No. 1691, regs 4 and 5 respectively). The copy notices must be accompanied by a 'statement of the evidence on which any charge to which the notice of transfer relates is based' (ibid.). Save insofar as it may be implied in the requirement to provide a statement of evidence, the regulations do not make specific provision for service on the defence or the Crown Court of copies of the statements of the proposed prosecution witnesses. However, it is submitted that such copies should always be served, for otherwise the defence in a notice of transfer case would be at a disadvantage in respect of disclosure of evidence as compared with the defence in an ordinary committal for trial case.

Effect of Notice

The effect of a notice is that the magistrates' court's functions in relation to the case **D8.10** cease save in respect of bail, witness orders and legal aid (last clause of CJA 1987, s. 4(1)). Further, the decision of a designated authority to give notice of transfer cannot be appealed or questioned in any court (s. 4(3)), other than by an application to the Crown Court for dismissal (see **D8.16** *et seq.*).

Bail or Custody If the magistrates have already remanded in custody, they may, on **D8.11** the next occasion the accused appears before them (or in his absence if he consents), either order that he be kept in custody 'until delivered in due course of law', or bail him to appear before the Crown Court for trial (s. 5(3)). Where, on the other hand, he was bailed prior to the giving of notice, the requirement that he appear before the magistrates on the day to which he was bailed ceases unless the notice states to the contrary (s. 5(6)). Should there be such a contrary statement, the accused remains under a duty to surrender to the magistrates' court as required by his bail, and the magistrates may then remand in custody or bail him again as they see fit (s. 5(7A)). Where the notice cancels the requirement to appear before the magistrates, the accused is simply under a duty to appear for his trial at the Crown Court location specified in the notice (s. 5(7)).

Legal Aid Where there has been a notice of transfer, legal aid for the proceedings in **D8.12** the Crown Court may be granted either by the magistrates' court which was given the notice or by the Crown Court itself (see Legal Aid Act 1988, s. 20(2) and (4)(b)).

Witness Orders The CPIA 1996, s. 65, abolished witness orders in respect of cases **D8.13** where no investigation had commenced prior to 1 April 1997. For the powers of the magistrates in respect of offences not covered by the 1996 Act, reference should be made to **D8.13** in the 1997 edition of this work.

Preferring the Bill of Indictment

Within 28 days of the giving of notice or such longer time as is permitted by the rules, **D8.14** the prosecution must prefer a bill of indictment (Indictments (Procedure) Rules 1971

(SI 1971 No. 2084, r. 5(1)). For r. 5 of the 1971 Rules and general discussion of the time restrictions on preferring indictments, see **D9.4**.

Applications for Dismissal of Transferred Charges

D8.15   At any time after the giving of notice but before arraignment (and irrespective of whether a bill of indictment has yet been preferred), the accused may apply to the Crown Court for the charges specified in the notice of transfer to be dismissed (CJA 1987, s. 6(1)). The application itself may be made (i.e., presented and determined) either orally or in writing according, initially, to the wishes of the defence (ibid. and see SI 1988 No. 1695), but even an oral application must be preceded by a written notice (SI 1988 No. 1695, r. 2(1)).

D8.16   *Notice of Application for Dismissal*   Notice of an application for dismissal must be given in the prescribed form within 28 days of the notice of transfer unless the Crown Court gives leave for late notice (SI 1988 No. 1695, rr. 2(2) to (5) and 3(4)). The notice: (a) indicates whether the defence wish to make the application orally or are content for it to be determined without a hearing on the documents; (b) must be accompanied by a copy of any material on which the applicant proposes to rely (r. 2(6)); and (c) must state whether the judge's leave to call oral evidence is being sought (r. 2(6)(b)).

D8.17   *Oral Evidence*   By s. 6(3) of the CJA 1987, oral evidence may be given at an application for dismissal only with the judge's leave (or by his order) such leave not to be given (or order made) unless the interests of justice require it. The recommendation of the Roskill Committee (whose report of January 1986 led to the CJA 1987) was that delays in the prosecution of major fraud should be reduced, *inter alia*, by prohibiting oral evidence at the preliminary stages. In practice the Crown Court hears witnesses at an application for dismissal only if there are exceptional circumstances warranting such a course.

D8.18   *Prosecution Response*   Within seven days of the service of notice of intention to apply for dismissal the prosecution may apply for leave to call oral evidence (SI 1988 No. 1695, r. 4(1)). If the defence in their notice of application chose not to require an oral hearing of the application, the prosecution may ask for one (r. 4(2)). Regardless of whether they desire to call oral evidence, the prosecution must serve on the court and defence copies of any comments, documents or statements they intend to adduce in reply to the defence application (r. 4(5)).

D8.19   *Determination of the Application*   A judge determining an application for dismissal must dismiss any of the charges specified in the notice of transfer in respect of which 'it appears to him that the evidence against the applicant would not be sufficient for a jury properly to convict him' (CJA 1987, s. 6(1)). The corresponding counts in any indictment that has been preferred against the accused must be quashed (ibid.). The effect of a successful application for dismissal is basically the same as a refusal by examining justices to commit for trial, that is, the accused is not acquitted but may be re-prosecuted for the same matters; but it is provided that any further proceedings on the dismissed charge must be brought by way of an application to a High Court judge for preferment of a voluntary bill of indictment (s. 6(5)). The rules do not prescribe the procedure to be followed by the Crown Court judge at determination of an application for dismissal, save to provide that – where the application is written – all parties must be informed of the result as soon as practicable (SI 1988 No. 1695, r. 5(2)). In practice, the application for dismissal is made at an oral hearing, and the judge announces the decision in court.

The Divisional Court does have jurisdiction to review the decision to dismiss under s. 6, but it should be exercised only in extremely limited circumstances (*Central Criminal Court and Nadir, ex parte Director of the Serious Fraud Office* [1993] 1 WLR 949).

Criminal Justice Act 1987, ss. 4 to 6

4.—(1) If—

(a) a person has been charged with an indictable offence; and

(b) in the opinion of an authority designated by subsection (2) below or of one of such an authority's officers acting on the authority's behalf the evidence of the offence charged—

(i) would be sufficient for the person charged to be committed for trial; and

(ii) reveals a case of fraud of such seriousness or complexity that it is appropriate that the management of the case should without delay be taken over by the Crown Court; and

(c) before the magistrates' court in whose jurisdiction the offence has been charged begins to inquire into the case as examining justices the authority or one of the authority's officers acting on the authority's behalf gives the court a notice (in this Act referred to as a 'notice of transfer') certifying that opinion,

the functions of the magistrates' court shall cease in relation to the case except as provided by section 5(3), (7A) and (8) below and by section 20(4) of the Legal Aid Act 1988.

(2) The authorities mentioned in subsection (1) above (in this Act referred to as 'designated authorities') are—

(a) the DPP;

(b) the Director of the Serious Fraud Office;

(c) the Commissioners of Inland Revenue;

(d) the Commissioners of Customs and Excise; and

(e) the Secretary of State.

(3) A designated authority's decision to give notice of transfer shall not be subject to appeal or liable to be questioned in any court.

5.—(1) A notice of transfer shall specify the proposed place of trial and in selecting that place the designated authority shall have regard to the considerations to which section 7 of the Magistrates' Courts Act 1980 requires a magistrates' court committing a person for trial to have regard when selecting the place at which he is to be tried.

(2) A notice of transfer shall specify the charge or charges to which it relates and include or be accompanied by such additional matter as regulations under subsection (9) below may require.

(3) If a magistrates' court has remanded a person to whom a notice of transfer relates in custody, it shall have power, subject to section 4 of the Bail Act 1976 and regulations under section 22 of the Prosecution of Offences Act 1985—

(a) to order that he shall be safely kept in custody until delivered in due course of law;

(b) to release him on bail in accordance with the Bail Act 1976, that is to say, by directing him to appear before the Crown Court for trial;

and [may direct that he be kept in custody until any sureties required have entered into their recognisances.]

[(4) and (5) Deal with remanding a person to whom a notice of transfer relates in his absence provided he consents.]

(6) Where notice of transfer is given after a person to whom it relates has been remanded on bail to appear before a magistrates' court on an appointed day, the requirement that he shall so appear shall cease on the giving of the notice, unless the notice states that it is to continue.

(7) Where the requirement that a person to whom the notice of transfer relates shall appear before a magistrates' court ceases by virtue of subsection (6) above, it shall be his duty to appear before the Crown Court at the place specified by the notice of transfer as the proposed place of trial or at any place substituted for it by a direction under section 76 of the Supreme Court Act 1981.

(7A) If the notice states that the requirement is to continue, when a person to whom the notice relates appears before the magistrates' court, the court shall have—

(a) the powers and duty conferred on a magistrates' court by subsection (3) above, but subject as there provided;

[(b) power to enlarge a surety's recognisance in his absence.]

(8) For the purposes of the Criminal Procedure (Attendance of Witnesses) Act 1965—

(a)   any magistrates' court for the petty sessions area for which the court from which a case was transferred sits shall be treated as examining magistrates;

(b)   a person indicated in the notice of transfer as a proposed witness shall be treated as a person who has been examined by the court.

[(9) to (11)   Empower the A–G to make regulations concerning the giving of notice of transfer.]

6.—(1)   Where notice of transfer has been given, any person to whom the notice relates, at any time before he is arraigned (and whether or not an indictment has been preferred against him), may apply orally or in writing to the Crown Court sitting at the place specified by the notice of transfer as the proposed place of trial for the charge, or any of the charges, in the case to be dismissed; and the judge shall dismiss a charge (and accordingly quash a count relating to it in any indictment preferred against the applicant) if it appears to him that the evidence against the applicant would not be sufficient for a jury properly to convict him.

(2)   No oral application may be made under subsection (1) above unless the applicant has given the Crown Court sitting at the place specified by the notice of transfer as the proposed place of trial written notice of his intention to make the application.

(3)   Oral evidence may be given on such an application only with the leave of the judge or by his order, and the judge shall give leave or make an order only if it appears to him, having regard to any matters stated in the application for leave, that the interests of justice require him to do so.

(4)   If the judge gives leave permitting, or makes an order requiring, a person to give oral evidence, but he does not do so, the judge may disregard any document indicating the evidence that he might have given.

(5)   Dismissal of the charge, or all the charges, against the applicant shall have the same effect as a refusal by examining magistrates to commit for trial, except that no further proceedings may be brought on a dismissed charge except by means of the preferment of a voluntary bill of indictment.

[(6)   Makes provision for Crown Court Rules to govern the procedure on applications for dismissal.]

Criminal Justice Act 1987 (Dismissal of Transferred Charges) Rules 1988 (SI 1988 No. 1695)

[**1.**   Citation and commencement.]

2.—(1)   Where notice of transfer has been given by the prosecution under section 4 of the [CJA 1987] and a person to whom it relates proposes to apply orally under section 6(1) thereof for any charge in the case to be dismissed, he shall give notice in writing in form 5301 of his intention to the appropriate officer of the Crown Court at the place specified by the notice of transfer as the proposed place of trial.

(2)   A notice of intention to make such an application shall be given not later than 28 days after the day on which notice of transfer was given, and a copy thereof shall be given at the same time to the authority by or on behalf of whom notice of transfer was given and to any other person to whom the notice of transfer relates.

(3)   The time for giving notice may be extended, either before or after it expires, by the Crown Court, on an application made in accordance with paragraph (4) below.

[(4)   Application for extension of time be made in the appropriate form and to specify the grounds of the application – copies to be served on the prosecution and co-accused.]

[(5)   Judge's decision on an application for extension of time to be given in writing to the applicant, the prosecution and any co-accused.]

(6)   A notice of intention to make an application under section 6(1) of the [CJA 1987] shall be accompanied by a copy of any material on which the applicant relies and shall—

(a)   specify the charge or charges to which it relates; and

(b)   state whether the leave of the judge is sought under section 6(3) of the Act to adduce oral evidence on the application, indicating what witnesses it is proposed to call at the hearing.

[(7)   Notice of the judge's decision on an application to call oral evidence at an application for dismissal to be given to the applicant, the prosecution and any co-accused.]

[(8)   Oral applications for dismissal to be listed for hearing before a judge of the Crown Court.]

3.—(1)   A written application for dismissal under section 6(1) of the [CJA 1987] shall be made in form 5301.

(2)   The application shall be sent to the appropriate officer of the Crown Court and shall be accompanied by a copy of any statement or other document, and identify any article, on which the applicant relies.

[(3)   Copies of the application and any accompanying documents to be given to the prosecution and any co-accused.]

(4)   A written application for dismissal shall be made not later than 28 days after the day on which notice of transfer was given unless the time for making the application is extended, either before or after it expires, by the Crown Court; and paragraphs (4) and (5) of rule 2 above shall apply for the purposes of this paragraph as if references therein to giving notice of intention to make an oral application were references to making a written application under this rule.

4.—(1)   Not later than seven days from the date of service of notice of intention to apply orally for the dismissal of any charge contained in a notice of transfer, the authority by or on behalf of whom notice of transfer was given may apply to the Crown Court for leave under section 6(3) of the Act to adduce oral evidence at the hearing of the application, indicating what witnesses it is proposed to call.

(2)   Not later than seven days from the date of receiving a copy of an application for dismissal under rule 3(2) above, the authority by or on behalf of whom notice of transfer was given may apply to the Crown Court for an oral hearing of the application.

[(3)   Applications under paras (1) or (2) to be made in the appropriate form, and to specify the grounds on which they are made.]

[(4)   Notice of the judge's decision re an application under para (1) or (2) to be given to the prosecution and all accused.]

[(5)   Service of copies of documents on the court and parties.]

[(6) and (7)   The time for complying with paras (1), (2) and (5) above may be extended by the Crown Court upon written application being made in the appropriate form.]

5.—(1)   A judge may grant leave for a witness to give oral evidence on an application for dismissal notwithstanding that notice of intention to call the witness has not been given in accordance with the foregoing provisions of these rules.

(2)   Where an application for dismissal is determined otherwise than at an oral application, the appropriate officer of the Crown Court shall, as soon as practicable, send to all the parties to the case a notice, in form 5304, of the outcome of the application.

[**6.**   Method of service of documents.]

Notice of Transfer in Child Witness Cases

The CJA 1991, s. 53, brought into effect a major extension of the notice of transfer **D8.20** system, so that it covers offences of a violent or sexual nature where there is a child witness. The offences to which s. 53 applies are:

(a)   an offence which involved an assault on, or injury or a threat of injury to, a person;
(b)   an offence under s. 1 of the CYPA 1933 (cruelty to persons under 16);
(c)   an offence under the Sexual Offences Act 1956, the Indecency with Children Act 1960, the Sexual Offences Act 1967, s. 54 of the Criminal Law Act 1977 or the Protection of Children Act 1978; and
(d)   attempting or conspiring to commit, or aiding, abetting, counselling, procuring or inciting the commission of, an offence within (a), (b) or (c) above.

According to s. 53(6), the meaning of 'child' for the purposes of the section varies according to which of the above categories the offence charged belongs. For an offence under (a) or (b) above (i.e. an offence of violence or cruelty) it means a person aged under 14. For an offence under (c) above (i.e. a sexual offence), it means a person under

17). Offences of attempt, conspiracy etc. attract the age limit appropriate to the substantive offence. In each case, if a video recording was made in accordance with the CJA 1988, s. 32A(2) (see **F16.24**), by the child witness when he was below the relevant age, then the age limit is increased from 14 to 15 or from 17 to 18, as the case may be. The relevant date for determining the child's age is not laid down in s. 53, but the context suggests that it is the date of the notice of transfer.

The conditions for the issue of a notice of transfer are laid down in s. 53(1). The DPP must be of the opinion that:

(a)   the evidence of the offence would be sufficient for the accused to be committed for trial;

(b)   a child who is alleged to be the victim, or to have witnessed the commission of the offence, will be called as a witness at trial; and

(c)   for the purpose of avoiding any prejudice to the welfare of the child, the case should be taken over and proceeded with without delay by the Crown Court.

If the Director is of that opinion, then he may serve a notice of transfer on the magistrates' court in whose jurisdiction the offence has been charged. In accordance with the principle in *Liverpool Crown Court, ex parte Bray* [1987] Crim LR 51 (see **D2.33**), the Director's powers may be exercised by Crown Prosecutors acting within the general authority delegated to them, even if they have no express instructions from the Director. Further, s. 53(4) states that the Director's decision shall not be subject to appeal or liable to question in any court. The notice must specify the proposed place of trial and the charge(s) to which it relates (CJA 1991, sch. 6, para. 1). It must be issued before committal proceedings have started (s. 53(1)).

In the case of a juvenile, where the youth court has determined under the MCA 1980, s. 24(1), that the defendant should be tried summarily, the prosecution cannot reverse that decision by issue of a notice of transfer (*Fareham Youth Court, ex parte M* [1999] Crim LR 325).

The functions of the magistrates' court cease once the notice is served (s. 53(3)), except in relation to bail, legal aid and witness orders (sch. 6, paras. 2, 3 and 9).

The procedure for challenging a notice of transfer is laid down in sch. 6, para. 5. The accused may, at any time before he is arraigned, apply to the Crown Court specified in the notice of transfer for the charges, or any of them, to be dismissed. The application can be made orally (with notice) or in writing. The judge must dismiss the disputed charge if it appears to him that there is insufficient evidence for a jury properly to convict thereon. The judge's leave is required for oral evidence to be given, and this is only to be granted if the interests of justice so require. There is, moreover, an absolute prohibition upon the hearing of evidence from a child witness within the definition outlined above.

Rule 5(1)(c) of the Indictment Rules 1971 specifies that the indictment must be preferred within 28 days commencing with the date on which the notice of transfer is served.

Criminal Justice Act 1991, s. 53 and sch. 6

53.—(1)   If a person has been charged with an offence to which section 32(2) of the 1988 Act applies (sexual offences and offences involving violence or cruelty) and the Director of Public Prosecutions is of the opinion—

(a)   that the evidence of the offence would be sufficient for the person charged to be committed for trial;

(b)   that a child who is alleged—

(i)   to be a person against whom the offence was committed; or

(ii)   to have witnessed the commission of the offence,
will be called as a witness at the trial; and

(c)   that, for the purpose of avoiding any prejudice to the welfare of the child, the case should be taken over and proceeded with without delay by the Crown Court,
a notice ('notice of transfer') certifying that opinion may be given by or on behalf of the Director to the magistrates' court in whose jurisdiction the offence has been charged.

(2)   A notice of transfer shall be given before the magistrates' court begins to inquire into the case as examining justices.

(3)   On the giving of a notice of transfer the functions of the magistrates' court shall cease in relation to the case except as provided by paragraphs 2 and 3 of schedule 6 to this Act or by section 20(4) of the Legal Aid Act 1988.

(4)   The decision to give a notice of transfer shall not be subject to appeal or liable to be questioned in any court.

(5)   Schedule 6 to this Act (which makes further provision in relation to notices of transfer) shall have effect.

(6)   In this section 'child' means a person who—

(a)   in the case of an offence falling within section 32(2)(a) or (b) of the 1988 Act , is under fourteen years of age or, if he was under that age when any such video recording as is mentioned in section 32A(2) of that Act was made in respect of him, is under fifteen years of age; or

(b)   in the case of an offence falling within section 32(2)(c) of that Act, is under seventeen years of age or, if he was under that age when any such video recording was made in respect of him, is under eighteen years of age.

(7)   Any reference in subsection (6) above to an offence falling within paragraph (a), (b) or (c) of section 32(2) of that Act includes a reference to an offence which consists of attempting or conspiring to commit, or of aiding, abetting, counselling, procuring or inciting the commission of, an offence falling within the paragraph.

SCHEDULE 6   NOTICES OF TRANSFER: PROCEDURE IN LIEU OF COMMITTAL

1.—(1)   A notice of transfer shall specify the proposed place of trial; and in selecting that place the Director of Public Prosecutions shall have regard to the considerations to which a magistrates' court committing a person for trial is required by section 7 of the 1980 Act to have regard when selecting the place at which he is to be tried.

(2)   A notice of transfer shall specify the charge or charges to which it relates and include or be accompanied by such additional material as regulations under paragraph 4 below may require.

2.—(1)   If a magistrates' court has remanded in custody a person to whom a notice of transfer relates, it shall have power, subject to section 4 of the Bail Act 1976 and regulations under section 22 of the Prosecution of Offences Act 1985—

(a)   to order that he shall be safely kept in custody until delivered in due course of law; or

(b)   to release him on bail in accordance with the Bail Act 1976, that is to say, by directing him to appear before the Crown Court for trial.

(2)   Where—

(a)   a person's release on bail under paragraph (b) of sub-paragraph (1) above is conditional on his providing one or more sureties; and

(b)   in accordance with subsection (3) of section 8 of the Bail Act 1976, the court fixes the amount in which a surety is to be bound with a view to his entering into his recognisance subsequently in accordance with subsections (4) and (5) or (6) of that section,
the court shall in the meantime make an order such as is mentioned in paragraph (a) of that sub-paragraph.

(3)   If the conditions specified in sub-paragraph (4) below are satisfied, a court may exercise the powers conferred by sub-paragraph (1) above in relation to a person charged without his being brought before it in any case in which by virtue of subsection (3A) of section 128 of the 1980 Act it would have the power further to remand him on an adjournment such as is mentioned in that subsection.

(4)   The conditions referred to in sub-paragraph (3) above are—

(a)   that the person in question has given his written consent to the powers conferred by sub-paragraph (1) above being exercised without his being brought before the court; and

(b)   that the court is satisfied that, when he gave his consent, he knew that the notice of transfer had been issued.

(5)   Where a notice of transfer is given after a person to whom it relates has been remanded on bail to appear before a magistrates' court on an appointed day, the requirement that he shall so appear shall cease on the giving of the notice unless the notice states that it is to continue.

(6)   Where that requirement ceases by virtue of sub-paragraph (5) above, it shall be the duty of the person in question to appear before the Crown Court at the place specified by the notice of transfer as the proposed place of trial or at any place substituted for it by a direction under section 76 of the Supreme Court Act 1981.

(7)   If, in a case where the notice states that the requirement mentioned in sub-paragraph (5) above is to continue, a person to whom the notice relates appears before the magistrates' court, the court shall have—

(a)   the powers and duties conferred on a magistrates' court by sub-paragraph (1) above but subject as there provided; and

(b)   power to enlarge, in the surety's absence, a recognisance conditioned in accordance with section 128(4)(a) of the 1980 Act so that the surety is bound to secure that the person charged appears also before the Crown Court.

3.   For the purposes of the Criminal Procedure (Attendance of Witnesses) Act 1965—

(a)   any magistrates' court for the petty sessions area for which the court from which a case was transferred sits shall be treated as examining magistrates; and

(b)   a person indicated in the notice of transfer as a proposed witness shall be treated as a person who has been examined by the court.

4.   [Power to make further provision by regulations.]

5.—(1)   Where a notice of transfer has been given, any person to whom the notice relates may, at any time before he is arraigned (and whether or not an indictment has been preferred against him), apply orally or in writing to the Crown Court sitting at the place specified by the notice of transfer as the proposed place of trial for the charge, or any of the charges, in the case to be dismissed.

(2)   The judge shall dismiss a charge (and accordingly quash a count relating to it in any indictment preferred against the applicant) which is the subject of any such application if it appears to him that the evidence against the applicant would not be sufficient for a jury properly to convict him.

(3)   No oral application may be made under sub-paragraph (1) above unless the applicant has given the Crown Court mentioned in that sub-paragraph written notice of his intention to make the application.

(4)   Oral evidence may be given on such an application only with the leave of the judge or by his order; and the judge shall give leave or make an order only if it appears to him, having regard to any matters stated in the application for leave, that the interests of justice require him to do so.

(5)   No leave or order under sub-paragraph (4) above shall be given or made in relation to oral evidence from a child (within the meaning of section 53 of this Act) who is alleged—

(a)   to be a person against whom an offence to which the notice of transfer relates was committed; or

(b)   to have witnessed the commission of such an offence.

(6)   If the judge gives leave permitting, or makes an order requiring, a person to give oral evidence, but that person does not do so, the judge may disregard any document indicating the evidence that he might have given.

(7)   Dismissal of the charge, or all the charges, against the applicant shall have the same effect as a refusal by examining magistrates to commit for trial, except that no further proceedings may be brought on a dismissed charge except by means of the preferment of a voluntary bill of indictment.

(8)   [Provision authorising the making of Crown Court rules.]

6.—(1)   Except as provided by this paragraph, it shall not be lawful—

(a)   to publish in Great Britain a written report of an application under paragraph 5(1) above; or

(b)   to include in a relevant programme for reception in Great Britain a report of such an application,

if (in either case) the report contains any matter other than that permitted by this paragraph.

(2)   An order that sub-paragraph (1) above shall not apply to reports of an application under paragraph 5(1) above may be made by the judge dealing with the application.

(3)   Where in the case of two or more accused one of them objects to the making of an order under sub-paragraph (2) above, the judge shall make the order if, and only if, he is satisfied, after hearing the representations of the accused, that it is in the interests of justice to do so.

(4)   An order under sub-paragraph (2) above shall not apply to reports of proceedings under sub-paragraph (3) above, but any decision of the court to make or not to make such an order may be contained in reports published or included in a relevant programme before the time authorised by sub-paragraph (5) below.

(5)   It shall not be unlawful under this paragraph to publish or include in a relevant programme a report of an application under paragraph 5(1) above containing any matter other than that permitted by sub-paragraph (8) below where the application is successful.

(6)   Where—

(a)   two or more persons were jointly charged; and

(b)   applications under paragraph 5(1) above are made by more than one of them,

sub-paragraph (5) above shall have effect as if for the words 'the application is' there were substituted the words 'all the applications are'.

(7)   It shall not be unlawful under this paragraph to publish or include in a relevant programme a report of an unsuccessful application at the conclusion of the trial of the person charged, or of the last of the persons charged to be tried.

(8)   The following matters may be contained in a report published or included in a relevant programme without an order under sub-paragraph (2) above before the time authorised by sub-paragraphs (5) and (7) above, that is to say—

(a)   the identity of the court and the name of the judge;

(b)   the names, ages, home addresses and occupations of the accused and witnesses;

(c)   the offence or offences, or a summary of them, with which the accused is or are charged;

(d)   the names of counsel and solicitors engaged in the proceedings;

(e)   where the proceedings are adjourned, the date and place to which they are adjourned;

(f)   the arrangements as to bail;

(g)   whether legal aid was granted to the accused or any of the accused.

(9)   The addresses that may be published or included in a relevant programme under sub-paragraph (8) above are addresses—

(a)   at any relevant time; and

(b)   at the time of their publication or inclusion in a relevant programme.

(10)   If a report is published or included in a relevant programme in contravention of this paragraph, the following persons, that is to say—

(a)   in the case of a publication of a written report as part of a newspaper or periodical, any proprietor, editor or publisher of the newspaper or periodical;

(b)   in the case of a publication of a written report otherwise than as part of a newspaper or periodical, the person who publishes it;

(c)   in the case of the inclusion of a report in a relevant programme, any body corporate which is engaged in providing the service in which the programme is included and any person having functions in relation to the programme corresponding to those of the editor of a newspaper;

shall be liable on summary conviction to a fine not exceeding level 5 on the standard scale.

(11)   Proceedings for an offence under this paragraph shall not, in England and Wales, be instituted otherwise than by or with the consent of the Attorney General.

(12)   Sub-paragraph (1) above shall be in addition to, and not in derogation from, the provisions of any other enactment with respect to the publication of reports of court proceedings.

(13)   In this paragraph—

'publish', in relation to a report, means publish the report, either by itself or as part of a newspaper or periodical, for distribution to the public;

'relevant programme' means a programme included in a programme service (within the meaning of the Broadcasting Act 1990);

'relevant time' means a time when events giving rise to the charges to which the proceedings relate occurred.

7.—(1) Where a notice of transfer has been given in relation to any case—

(a) the Crown Court before which the case is to be tried; and

(b) any magistrates' court which exercises any functions under paragraph 2 or 3 above or section 20(4) of the Legal Aid Act 1988 in relation to the case,

shall, in exercising any of its powers in relation to the case, have regard to the desirability of avoiding prejudice to the welfare of any relevant child witness that may be occasioned by unnecessary delay in bringing the case to trial.

(2) In this paragraph 'child' has the same meaning as in section 53 of this Act and 'relevant child witness' means a child who will be called as a witness at the trial and who is alleged—

(a) to be a person against whom an offence to which the notice of transfer relates was committed; or

(b) to have witnessed the commission of such an offence.

Procedure relating to Indictable-only Offences

D8.21 When s. 51 of the CDA 1998 comes fully into effect, offences triable only on indictment will no longer be subject to committal proceedings, but will have to be sent immediately to the Crown Court from a preliminary hearing in the magistrates' court. These provisions and are expected to be implemented nationally in Spring 2000.

The new measures provide that the magistrates *must* send for trial in the Crown Court, without holding committal proceedings:

(a) an adult defendant charged with an indictable-only offence, to be tried for that offence (s. 51(1)(a));

(b) an adult defendant sent for trial for an indictable-only offence, to be tried also for any related offence which is triable either way for which he appears at the same time (s. 51(1)(b));

(c) an adult defendant sent for trial for an indictable-only offence, to be tried also for any related summary offence which is imprisonable or carries disqualification (s. 51(1)(b)); and

(d) an adult co-defendant appearing on the same occasion charged with a related offence which is triable either way (s. 51(3)).

In addition, the magistrates *may* send immediately to the Crown Court for trial:

(a) an adult defendant already sent to the Crown Court for trial for an indictable-only offence, to be tried for a related offence which is triable either way (or summary and imprisonable or carrying disqualification) and which has been charged subsequently (s. 51(2));

(b) an adult co-defendant charged with a related triable either-way offence, who appears subsequently to a defendant sent to the Crown Court for an indictable-only offence (s. 51(3)); and

(c) a juvenile jointly charged with an adult defendant with an indictable-only offence, where the magistrates consider that it is in the interests of justice for the juvenile to be tried jointly with the adult (s. 51(5));

(d) a juvenile sent to the Crown Court by virtue of (c), in respect of any related either-way or summary offence (provided it is imprisonable or carries disqualification).

An offence triable either way is related to an indictable-only offence if they could be joined in the same indictment (s. 51(12)(c)). A summary offence is related to an indictable-only offence if it arises out of circumstances which are the same as or connected with those giving rise to it (s. 51(12)(d)).

The procedure to be followed in respect of those offences sent directly to the Crown Court in this way is set out in sch. 3 to the Act. The schedule provides that the defendant may apply to a Crown Court judge for the charge(s) to be dismissed. The judge shall dismiss the charge and quash any related count in the indictment if it appears to him that the evidence against the applicant would not be sufficient for a jury properly to convict him (para. 2). The schedule also sets out provisions which are broadly equivalent to those applicable to committal proceedings in respect of reporting restrictions (para. 3), and depositions (para. 4). It sets out the power of the Crown Court to deal with any summary offence sent up to it under these provisions (para. 5), and with the procedure to be followed where the indictable-only offence which triggered off the process has disappeared for whatever reason (para. 6).

The procedure to be followed when there is an application for dismissal of charges sent under the CDA 1998, s. 51, is set out in the Crime and Disorder Act 1998 (Dismissal of Charges Sent) Rules 1998 (SI 1998 No. 3048). Such applications may be made orally (r. 2) or in writing (r. 3). With the leave of the judge, the prosecution may call oral evidence at the hearing of the application for dismissal (r. 4). Other aspects of the s. 51 procedure are dealt with in the Indictments (Procedure) (Modification) Rules 1998 (SI 1998 No. 3045), the Magistrates' Courts (Modification) Rules 1998 (SI 1998 No. 3046), the Crown Court (Modification) Rules 1998 (SI 1998 No. 3047) and the Crime and Disorder Act 1998 (Service of Prosecution Evidence) Regulations 1998 (SI 1998 No. 3115).

Crime and Disorder Act 1998, s. 51, and sch. 3

51.—(1) Where an adult appears or is brought before a magistrates' court ('the court') charged with an offence triable only on indictment ('the indictable-only offence'), the court shall send him forthwith to the Crown Court for trial—
    (a) for that offence, and
    (b) for any either-way or summary offence with which he is charged which fulfils the requisite conditions (as set out in subsection (11) below).
    (2) Where an adult who has been sent for trial under subsection (1) above subsequently appears or is brought before a magistrates' court charged with an either-way or summary offence which fulfils the requisite conditions, the court may send him forthwith to the Crown Court for trial for the either-way or summary offence.
    (3) Where—
    (a) the court sends an adult for trial under subsection (1) above;
    (b) another adult appears or is brought before the court on the same or a subsequent occasion charged jointly with him with an either-way offence; and
    (c) that offence appears to the court to be related to the indictable-only offence,
the court shall where it is the same occasion, and may where it is a subsequent occasion, send the other adult forthwith to the Crown Court for trial for the either-way offence.
    (4) Where a court sends an adult for trial under subsection (3) above, it shall at the same time send him to the Crown Court for trial for any either-way or summary offence with which he is charged which fulfils the requisite conditions.
    (5) Where—
    (a) the court sends an adult for trial under subsection (1) or (3) above; and
    (b) a child or young person appears or is brought before the court on the same or a subsequent occasion charged jointly with the adult with an indictable offence for which the adult is sent for trial,
the court shall, if it considers it necessary in the interests of justice to do so, send the child or young person forthwith to the Crown Court for trial for the indictable offence.
    (6) Where a court sends a child or young person for trial under subsection (5) above, it may at the same time send him to the Crown Court for trial for any either-way or summary offence with which he is charged which fulfils the requisite conditions.

(7)   The court shall specify in a notice the offence or offences for which a person is sent for trial under this section and the place at which he is to be tried; and a copy of the notice shall be served on the accused and given to the Crown Court sitting at that place.

(8)   In a case where there is more than one indictable-only offence and the court includes an either-way or a summary offence in the notice under subsection (7) above, the court shall specify in that notice the indictable-only offence to which the either-way offence or, as the case may be, the summary offence appears to the court to be related.

(9)   The trial of the information charging any summary offence for which a person is sent for trial under this section shall be treated as if the court had adjourned it under section 10 of the 1980 Act and had not fixed the time and place for its resumption.

(10)   In selecting the place of trial for the purpose of subsection (7) above, the court shall have regard to—

(a)   the convenience of the defence, the prosecution and the witnesses;

(b)   the desirability of expediting the trial; and

(c)   any direction given by or on behalf of the Lord Chief Justice with the concurrence of the Lord Chancellor under section 75(1) of the Supreme Court Act 1981.

(11)   An offence fulfils the requisite conditions if—

(a)   it appears to the court to be related to the indictable-only offence; and

(b)   in the case of a summary offence, it is punishable with imprisonment or involves obligatory or discretionary disqualification from driving.

(12)   For the purposes of this section—

(a)   'adult' means a person aged 18 or over, and references to an adult include references to a corporation;

(b)   'either-way offence' means an offence which, if committed by an adult, is triable either on indictment or summarily;

(c)   an either-way offence is related to an indictable-only offence if the charge for the either-way offence could be joined in the same indictment as the charge for the indictable-only offence;

(d)   a summary offence is related to an indictable-only offence if it arises out of circumstances which are the same as or connected with those giving rise to the indictable-only offence.

SCHEDULE 3
PROCEDURE WHERE PERSONS ARE SENT FOR TRIAL UNDER SECTION 51

Regulations

1.—(1)   The Attorney General shall by regulations provide that, where a person is sent for trial under section 51 of this Act on any charge or charges, copies of the documents containing the evidence on which the charge or charges are based shall, on or before the relevant date—

(a)   be served on that person; and

(b)   be given to the Crown Court sitting at the place specified in the notice under subsection (7) of that section.

(2)   In sub-paragraph (1) above 'the relevant date' means the date prescribed by the regulations.

Applications for dismissal

2.—(1)   A person who is sent for trial under section 51 of this Act on any charge or charges may, at any time—

(a)   after he is served with copies of the documents containing the evidence on which the charge or charges are based; and

(b)   before he is arraigned (and whether or not an indictment has been preferred against him),

apply orally or in writing to the Crown Court sitting at the place specified in the notice under subsection (7) of that section for the charge, or any of the charges, in the case to be dismissed.

(2)   The judge shall dismiss a charge (and accordingly quash any count relating to it in any indictment preferred against the applicant) which is the subject of any such application if it appears to him that the evidence against the applicant would not be sufficient for a jury properly to convict him.

(3)   No oral application may be made under sub-paragraph (1) above unless the applicant has given to the Crown Court sitting at the place in question written notice of his intention to make the application.

(4)   Oral evidence may be given on such an application only with the leave of the judge or by his order; and the judge shall give leave or make an order only if it appears to him, having regard to any matters stated in the application for leave, that the interests of justice require him to do so.

(5)   If the judge gives leave permitting, or makes an order requiring, a person to give oral evidence, but that person does not do so, the judge may disregard any document indicating the evidence that he might have given.

(6)   If the charge, or any of the charges, against the applicant is dismissed—

(a)   no further proceedings may be brought on the dismissed charge or charges except by means of the preferment of a voluntary bill of indictment; and

(b)   unless the applicant is in custody otherwise than on the dismissed charge or charges, he shall be discharged.

(7)   Crown Court Rules may make provision for the purposes of this paragraph and, without prejudice to the generality of this sub-paragraph, may make provision—

(a)   as to the time or stage in the proceedings at which anything required to be done is to be done (unless the court grants leave to do it at some other time or stage);

(b)   as to the contents and form of notices or other documents;

(c)   as to the manner in which evidence is to be submitted; and

(d)   as to persons to be served with notices or other material.

Reporting restrictions

3.—(1)   Except as provided by this paragraph, it shall not be lawful—

(a)   to publish in Great Britain a written report of an application under paragraph 2(1) above; or

(b)   to include in a relevant programme for reception in Great Britain a report of such an application,

if (in either case) the report contains any matter other than that permitted by this paragraph.

(2)   An order that sub-paragraph (1) above shall not apply to reports of an application under paragraph 2(1) above may be made by the judge dealing with the application.

(3)   Where in the case of two or more accused one of them objects to the making of an order under sub-paragraph (2) above, the judge shall make the order if, and only if, he is satisfied, after hearing the representations of the accused, that it is in the interests of justice to do so.

(4)   An order under sub-paragraph (2) above shall not apply to reports of proceedings under sub-paragraph (3) above, but any decision of the court to make or not to make such an order may be contained in reports published or included in a relevant programme before the time authorised by sub-paragraph (5) below.

(5)   It shall not be unlawful under this paragraph to publish or include in a relevant programme a report of an application under paragraph 2(1) above containing any matter other than that permitted by sub-paragraph (8) below where the application is successful.

(6)   Where—

(a)   two or more persons were jointly charged; and

(b)   applications under paragraph 2(1) above are made by more than one of them,

sub-paragraph (5) above shall have effect as if for the words 'the application is' there were substituted the words 'all the applications are'.

(7)   It shall not be unlawful under this paragraph to publish or include in a relevant programme a report of an unsuccessful application at the conclusion of the trial of the person charged, or of the last of the persons charged to be tried.

(8)   The following matters may be contained in a report published or included in a relevant programme without an order under sub-paragraph (2) above before the time authorised by sub-paragraphs (5) and (6) above, that is to say—

(a)   the identity of the court and the name of the judge;

(b)   the names, ages, home addresses and occupations of the accused and witnesses;

(c)   the offence or offences, or a summary of them, with which the accused is or are charged;

  (d) the names of counsel and solicitors engaged in the proceedings;

  (e) where the proceedings are adjourned, the date and place to which they are adjourned;

  (f) the arrangements as to bail;

  (g) whether legal aid was granted to the accused or any of the accused.

 (9) The addresses that may be published or included in a relevant programme under sub-paragraph (8) above are addresses—

  (a) at any relevant time; and

  (b) at the time of their publication or inclusion in a relevant programme.

 (10) If a report is published or included in a relevant programme in contravention of this paragraph, the following persons, that is to say—

  (a) in the case of a publication of a written report as part of a newspaper or periodical, any proprietor, editor or publisher of the newspaper or periodical;

  (b) in the case of a publication of a written report otherwise than as part of a newspaper or periodical, the person who publishes it;

  (c) in the case of the inclusion of a report in a relevant programme, any body corporate which is engaged in providing the service in which the programme is included and any person having functions in relation to the programme corresponding to those of the editor of a newspaper;

shall be liable on summary conviction to a fine not exceeding level 5 on the standard scale.

 (11) Proceedings for an offence under this paragraph shall not, in England and Wales, be instituted otherwise than by or with the consent of the Attorney General.

 (12) Sub-paragraph (1) above shall be in addition to, and not in derogation from, the provisions of any other enactment with respect to the publication of reports of court proceedings.

 (13) In this paragraph—

'publish', in relation to a report, means publish the report, either by itself or as part of a newspaper or periodical, for distribution to the public;

'relevant programme' means a programme included in a programme service (within the meaning of the Broadcasting Act 1990);

'relevant time' means a time when events giving rise to the charges to which the proceedings relate occurred.

Power of justice to take depositions etc.

 4.—(1) Sub-paragraph (2) below applies where a justice of the peace for any commission area is satisfied that—

  (a) any person in England and Wales ('the witness') is likely to be able to make on behalf of the prosecutor a written statement containing material evidence, or produce on behalf of the prosecutor a document or other exhibit likely to be material evidence, for the purposes of proceedings for an offence for which a person has been sent for trial under section 51 of this Act by a magistrates' court for that area; and

  (b) the witness will not voluntarily make the statement or produce the document or other exhibit.

 (2) In such a case the justice shall issue a summons directed to the witness requiring him to attend before a justice at the time and place appointed in the summons, and to have his evidence taken as a deposition or to produce the document or other exhibit.

 (3) If a justice of the peace is satisfied by evidence on oath of the matters mentioned in sub-paragraph (1) above, and also that it is probable that a summons under sub-paragraph (2) above would not procure the result required by it, the justice may instead of issuing a summons issue a warrant to arrest the witness and to bring him before a justice at the time and place specified in the warrant.

 (4) A summons may also be issued under sub-paragraph (2) above if the justice is satisfied that the witness is outside the British Islands, but no warrant may be issued under sub-paragraph (3) above unless the justice is satisfied by evidence on oath that the witness is in England and Wales.

 (5) If—

  (a) the witness fails to attend before a justice in answer to a summons under this paragraph;

    (b)   the justice is satisfied by evidence on oath that the witness is likely to be able to make a statement or produce a document or other exhibit as mentioned in sub-paragraph (1)(a) above;

    (c)   it is proved on oath, or in such other manner as may be prescribed, that he has been duly served with the summons and that a reasonable sum has been paid or tendered to him for costs and expenses; and

    (d)   it appears to the justice that there is no just excuse for the failure,

the justice may issue a warrant to arrest the witness and to bring him before a justice at the time and place specified in the warrant.

    (6)   Where—

    (a)   a summons is issued under sub-paragraph (2) above or a warrant is issued under sub-paragraph (3) or (5) above; and

    (b)   the summons or warrant is issued with a view to securing that the witness has his evidence taken as a deposition,

the time appointed in the summons or specified in the warrant shall be such as to enable the evidence to be taken as a deposition before the relevant date.

    (7)   If any person attending or brought before a justice in pursuance of this paragraph refuses without just excuse to have his evidence taken as a deposition, or to produce the document or other exhibit, the justice may do one or both of the following—

    (a)   commit him to custody until the expiration of such period not exceeding one month as may be specified in the summons or warrant or until he sooner has his evidence taken as a deposition or produces the document or other exhibit;

    (b)   impose on him a fine not exceeding £2,500.

    (8)   A fine imposed under sub-paragraph (7) above shall be deemed, for the purposes of any enactment, to be a sum adjudged to be paid by a conviction.

    (9)   If in pursuance of this paragraph a person has his evidence taken as a deposition, the clerk of the justice concerned shall as soon as is reasonably practicable send a copy of the deposition to the prosecutor and the Crown Court.

    (10)   If in pursuance of this paragraph a person produces an exhibit which is a document, the clerk of the justice concerned shall as soon as is reasonably practicable send a copy of the document to the prosecutor and the Crown Court.

    (11)   If in pursuance of this paragraph a person produces an exhibit which is not a document, the clerk of the justice concerned shall as soon as is reasonably practicable inform the prosecutor and the Crown Court of that fact and of the nature of the exhibit.

    (12)   In this paragraph—

'prescribed' means prescribed by rules made under section 144 of the 1980 Act;

'the relevant date' has the meaning given by paragraph 1(2) above.

Use of depositions as evidence

5.—(1)   Subject to sub-paragraph (3) below, sub-paragraph (2) below applies where in pursuance of paragraph 4 above a person has his evidence taken as a deposition.

    (2)   Where this sub-paragraph applies the deposition may without further proof be read as evidence on the trial of the accused, whether for an offence for which he was sent for trial under section 51 of this Act or for any other offence arising out of the same transaction or set of circumstances.

    (3)   Sub-paragraph (2) above does not apply if—

    (a)   it is proved that the deposition was not signed by the justice by whom it purports to have been signed;

    (b)   the court of trial at its discretion orders that sub-paragraph (2) above shall not apply; or

    (c)   a party to the proceedings objects to sub-paragraph (2) above applying.

    (4)   If a party to the proceedings objects to sub-paragraph (2) applying the court of trial may order that the objection shall have no effect if the court considers it to be in the interests of justice so to order.

Power of Crown Court to deal with summary offence

6.—(1)   This paragraph applies where a magistrates' court has sent a person for trial under section 51 of this Act for offences which include a summary offence.

(2)   If the person is convicted on the indictment, the Crown Court shall consider whether the summary offence is related to the offence that is triable only on indictment or, as the case may be, any of the offences that are so triable.

(3)   If it considers that the summary offence is so related, the court shall state to the person the substance of the offence and ask him whether he pleads guilty or not guilty.

(4)   If the person pleads guilty, the Crown Court shall convict him, but may deal with him in respect of the summary offence only in a manner in which a magistrates' court could have dealt with him.

(5)   If he does not plead guilty, the powers of the Crown Court shall cease in respect of the summary offence except as provided by sub-paragraph (6) below.

(6)   If the prosecution inform the court that they would not desire to submit evidence on the charge relating to the summary offence, the court shall dismiss it.

(7)   The Crown Court shall inform the clerk of the magistrates' court of the outcome of any proceedings under this paragraph.

(8)   If the summary offence is one to which section 40 of the Criminal Justice Act 1988 applies, the Crown Court may exercise in relation to the offence the power conferred by that section; but where the person is tried on indictment for such an offence, the functions of the Crown Court under this paragraph in relation to the offence shall cease.

(9)   Where the Court of Appeal allows an appeal against conviction of an indictable-only offence which is related to a summary offence of which the appellant was convicted under this paragraph—

(a)   it shall set aside his conviction of the summary offence and give the clerk of the magistrates' court notice that it has done so; and

(b)   it may direct that no further proceedings in relation to the offence are to be undertaken;

and the proceedings before the Crown Court in relation to the offence shall thereafter be disregarded for all purposes.

(10)   A notice under sub-paragraph (9) above shall include particulars of any direction given under paragraph (b) of that sub-paragraph in relation to the offence.

(11)   The references to the clerk of the magistrates' court in this paragraph shall be construed in accordance with section 141 of the 1980 Act.

(12)   An offence is related to another offence for the purposes of this paragraph if it arises out of circumstances which are the same as or connected with those giving rise to the other offence.

Procedure where no indictable-only offence remains

7.—(1)   Subject to paragraph 13 below, this paragraph applies where—

(a)   a person has been sent for trial under section 51 of this Act but has not been arraigned; and

(b)   the person is charged on an indictment which (following amendment of the indictment, or as a result of an application under paragraph 2 above, or for any other reason) includes no offence that is triable only on indictment.

(2)   Everything that the Crown Court is required to do under the following provisions of this paragraph must be done with the accused present in court.

(3)   The court shall cause to be read to the accused each count of the indictment that charges an offence triable either way.

(4)   The court shall then explain to the accused in ordinary language that, in relation to each of those offences, he may indicate whether (if it were to proceed to trial) he would plead guilty or not guilty, and that if he indicates that he would plead guilty the court must proceed as mentioned in sub-paragraph (6) below.

(5)   The court shall then ask the accused whether (if the offence in question were to proceed to trial) he would plead guilty or not guilty.

(6)   If the accused indicates that he would plead guilty the court shall proceed as if he had been arraigned on the count in question and had pleaded guilty.

(7)   If the accused indicates that he would plead not guilty, or fails to indicate how he would plead, the court shall consider whether the offence is more suitable for summary trial or for trial on indictment.

(8)   Subject to sub-paragraph (6) above, the following shall not for any purpose be taken to constitute the taking of a plea—

(a)   asking the accused under this paragraph whether (if the offence were to proceed to trial) he would plead guilty or not guilty; ,

(b)   an indication by the accused under this paragraph of how he would plead.

8.   [Deals with the procedure where the court considers it necessary to proceed in the accused's absence due to his disorderly conduct.]

9.—(1)   This paragraph applies where the Crown Court is required by paragraph 7(7) or 8(2)(d) above to consider the question whether an offence is more suitable for summary trial or for trial on indictment.

(2)   Before considering the question, the court shall afford first the prosecutor and then the accused an opportunity to make representations as to which mode of trial would be more suitable.

(3)   In considering the question, the court shall have regard to—

(a)   any representations made by the prosecutor or the accused;

(b)   the nature of the case;

(c)   whether the circumstances make the offence one of a serious character;

(d)   whether the punishment which a magistrates' court would have power to impose for it would be adequate; and

(e)   any other circumstances which appear to the court to make it more suitable for the offence to be dealt tried in one way rather than the other.

10.—(1)   This paragraph applies (unless excluded by paragraph 15 below) where the Crown Court considers that an offence is more suitable for summary trial.

(2)   The court shall explain to the accused in ordinary language—

(a)   that it appears to the court more suitable for him to be tried summarily for the offence, and that he can either consent to be so tried or, if he wishes, be tried by a jury; and

(b)   that if he is tried summarily and is convicted by the magistrates' court, he may be committed for sentence to the Crown Court under section 38 of the 1980 Act if the convicting court is of such opinion as is mentioned in subsection (2) of that section.

(3)   After explaining to the accused as provided by sub-paragraph (2) above the court shall ask him whether he wishes to be tried summarily or by a jury, and—

(a)   if he indicates that he wishes to be tried summarily, shall remit him for trial to a magistrates' court acting for the place where he was sent to the Crown Court for trial;

(b)   if he does not give such an indication, shall retain its functions in relation to the offence and proceed accordingly.

11.   If the Crown Court considers that an offence is more suitable for trial on indictment, the court—

(a)   shall tell the accused that it has decided that it is more suitable for him to be tried for the offence by a jury; and

(b)   shall retain its functions in relation to the offence and proceed accordingly.

12.   [Deals with the position where the A-G, Solicitor-General or DPP applies for an offence to be tried on indictment.]

13.—(1)   This paragraph applies, in place of paragraphs 7 to 12 above, in the case of a child or young person who—

(a)   has been sent for trial under section 51 of this Act but has not been arraigned; and

(b)   is charged on an indictment which (following amendment of the indictment, or as a result of an application under paragraph 2 above, or for any other reason) includes no offence that is triable only on indictment.

(2)   The Crown Court shall remit the child or young person for trial to a magistrates' court acting for the place where he was sent to the Crown Court for trial unless—

(a)   he is charged with such an offence as is mentioned in subsection (2) of section 53 of the 1933 Act (punishment of certain grave crimes) and the Crown Court considers that if he is found guilty of the offence it ought to be possible to sentence him in pursuance of subsection (3) of that section; or

(b)   he is charged jointly with an adult with an offence triable eitherway and the Crown Court considers it necessary in the interests of justice that they both be tried for the offence in the Crown Court.

(3)   In sub-paragraph (2) above 'adult' has the same meaning as in section 51 of this Act.

14.   [Describes the procedure for determining whether offences of criminal damage etc. are summary offences.]

15.   [Deals with the power of the Crown Court, with consent of legally-represented accused, to proceed in his absence.]

SECTION D9: THE INDICTMENT

The indictment is the document containing the charges against the accused on which **D9.1** he is arraigned at the commencement of a trial on indictment. The law on indictments is contained principally in the Indictments Act 1915 and the Indictment Rules 1971 (SI 1971 No. 1253). Detailed procedural provisions concerning the preferring of bills of indictment are in the Indictments (Procedure) Rules 1971 (SI 1971 No. 2084).

REQUIREMENT THAT AN INDICTMENT BE SIGNED

An indictment must be signed by a proper officer of the Crown Court (Administration **D9.2** of Justice (Miscellaneous Provisions) Act 1933, s. 2(1)). Until it has been so signed, it is a 'bill of indictment', not an indictment. The officer of the Crown Court before whom a bill of indictment is preferred for signing *shall* sign it, provided only that he is satisfied that the requirements of s. 2(2) of the 1933 Act have been complied with. Section 2(2) provides that no bill of indictment may be preferred unless the accused has been committed for trial, or a notice of transfer has been given to the relevant magistrates' court, or a High Court judge has directed or consented to the preferment of a voluntary bill of indictment, or the Court of Appeal has ordered a retrial. Should the officer of the Crown Court wrongly decline to sign a bill of indictment, a judge of the Crown Court may, on the application of the prosecutor or of his own motion, direct him to sign. If an accused is tried on an 'indictment' which has not been signed, the trial and any consequent conviction will be null (see *Morais* (1988) 87 Cr App R 9, in which the Court of Appeal, quashing M's sentence of four years' imprisonment for supplying drugs, and ordering a retrial, stated that the proper officer's signature was not 'a comparatively meaningless formality' but a 'necessary condition precedent to the existence of a proper indictment'). In *Jackson* [1997] 2 Cr App R 497, the Court of Appeal held that two fresh indictments were valid, notwithstanding the fact that they had not been signed by an officer of the court. The judge had directed in open court that the proper officer should sign the indictments, but she had failed to comply with the judge's direction. Distinguishing *Morais*, their lordships said that in these circumstances, the officer's signature *was* a meaningless formality, and she was deemed to have appended her signature. In *Laming* (1989) 90 Cr App R 450, the appropriate officer of the court signed the indictment on the front page thereof. Schedule 1 to the Indictment Rules 1971 and section 13.9.1 of the Crown Court Manual both indicate that it should be signed after the last count. The Court of Appeal held that it was nonetheless valid. The important fact was that the appropriate officer of the court had signed the indictment, intending thereby to validate it. The court added, however, that any departure from the normal practice of signing indictments at the end was to be strongly discouraged. In *Stewart* (1990) 91 Cr App R 301, the Court of Appeal said that, when the bill of indictment is signed (thus converting it into an indictment), the date should be added.

For the sake of convenience, in the remainder of this section, reference will be made to the drafting of 'an indictment' rather than the drafting of 'a bill of indictment', except where the context requires a distinction to be drawn between the unsigned bill and the signed document.

Administration of Justice (Miscellaneous Provisions) Act 1933, s. 2

(1) Subject to the provisions of this section, a bill of indictment charging any person with an indictable offence may be preferred by any person before [the Crown Court], and where a bill of indictment has been so preferred the proper officer of the court shall, if he is

satisfied that the requirements of the next following subsection have been complied with, sign the bill, and it shall thereupon become an indictment and be proceeded with accordingly: Provided that if the judge of the court is satisfied that the said requirements have been complied with, he may, on the application of the prosecutor or of his own motion, direct the proper officer to sign the bill and the bill shall be signed accordingly.

RESPONSIBILITY FOR DRAFTING AN INDICTMENT

D9.3   Ultimate responsibility for the indictment rests with counsel for the prosecution, who must ensure that it is in proper form before arraignment. This principle was affirmed by Watkins LJ, giving the judgment of the Court of Appeal in *Newland* [1988] QB 402. The appeal arose out of a misjoinder of counts in the indictment against N, which necessitated the quashing of his convictions, even though he had in fact pleaded guilty. His lordship said (at p. 409):

> Before parting with this case we think the time has come – it may be overdue – when it is necessary to say something about the responsibility for drafting of indictments. It is undertaken by and large by staff of the Crown Courts in this country. The unfortunate fact is, so we are informed and as we from some experience in this court know, that the defective manner in which indictments are drafted is giving cause for concern, having regard to the number of occasions when this occurs.
>
> It is we think necessary for a restatement to be made upon the question of responsibility for the ultimate presentation of an indictment to the court. It was the responsibility of counsel to ensure that the indictment was in proper form before arraignment. A return to that practice – it seems not to be followed generally – may in our view be a salutary thing for everyone concerned, and moreover relieve the staff of the Crown Court of any responsibility it may be felt they have in that respect, and also to have the result of there being fewer appeals to this court based on defective indictments.

The reference in the above passage to Crown Court staff drafting the bulk of indictments reflects the practice at the time Watkins LJ gave his judgment, which was that, once the depositions and statements relied on by the prosecution at committal had been transmitted to the Crown Court, an appropriate officer would consider them and settle an indictment as he saw fit. In serious and/or complex cases the prosecution might give notice that they wanted the indictment to be drawn by counsel; conversely, the Crown Court officer might refuse to draft on the ground that the case was too difficult for him. But, in the great majority of cases, the drafting was done by Crown Court staff. Perhaps as a result of the dicta in *Newland*, the practice has since changed, at least for CPS prosecutions. The usual system now is for the CPS to prepare a schedule of charges for committal drafted in the form of counts suitable for inclusion in an indictment – indeed, the schedule is sometimes simply headed 'draft indictment'. The schedule – in effect a draft indictment – is sent to the Crown Court with the committal papers, and all the Crown Court officer has to do is to check that there has been no contravention of the Administration of Justice (Miscellaneous Provisions) Act 1933, s. 2(2), and then to sign. Responsibility for the wording of the indictment and the choice of counts has thus been transferred to the CPS. It is still open to the CPS to instruct counsel to draft the indictment in any case whose difficulty seems to justify it. In any event, once counsel is instructed, it becomes his responsibility to ensure that the indictment is in proper form (*Moss* [1995] Crim LR 828).

TIME-LIMIT FOR PREFERRING A BILL OF INDICTMENT

D9.4   A bill of indictment should be preferred (i.e. delivered to an appropriate officer of the Crown Court) within 28 days of the date on which the accused is committed (or transferred) for trial, or the date on which a notice of transfer is given (Indictments (Procedure) Rules 1971, r. 5(1)). If the bill is drafted by the appropriate officer, it is deemed to be preferred as soon as it is settled to his satisfaction (proviso to r. 4). The 28-day time-limit prescribed by r. 5(1) may be extended for up to 28 days by an appropriate officer (r. 5(3)). A judge of the Crown Court may extend the limit for any period, and may further extend an already extended period (r. 5(2)). Should the appropriate officer refuse to make a first extension, he must refer the application to a judge (r. 5(3)). Applications for extension of time should be in writing (unless a judge otherwise directs), and should state why the extension is necessary (r. 5(4)). Where an application is made after the period it is sought to extend has expired, it must state why it was not made within that period (r. 5(5)).

Rule 5 of the Indictments (Procedure) Rules 1971 has been held to be directory, not mandatory. Consequently, breach of the rule is not in itself a good ground of appeal, although it is submitted that inordinate delay of a magnitude sufficient to prejudice the accused in the preparation of his defence might render a conviction unsafe. The effect of breach of r. 5 was considered in *Sheerin* (1976) 64 Cr App R 68, *Soffe* (1982) 75 Cr App R 133 and *Farooki* (1983) 77 Cr App R 257. At the time all three cases were decided, r. 5 simply provided that 'the bill of indictment must be preferred within 28 days of . . . committal or within such longer period as a judge of the Crown Court may allow'. In *Sheerin*, defence counsel moved to quash an indictment preferred 21 days out of time, no application for an extension of time having been made before trial because prosecuting counsel simply did not know of the existence of r. 5. The trial judge, finding that S had not suffered any prejudice by reason of the delay, gave leave for preferment of a late bill and rejected the motion to quash. On appeal, Lawton LJ held, first, that the judge had had jurisdiction to grant the extension of time even though the application therefor was not made until after the 28 days had elapsed. This is now expressly confirmed by r. 5(3). Secondly, as to the status of r. 5, his lordship said (at p. 70): 'It is to be noted that the very title of the rules is 'Procedure Rules' – that is rules for the guidance of courts in the administration of justice. They are not rules setting boundaries beyond which the courts cannot go'. Thirdly, the judge had properly exercised his discretion in allowing late preferment since, even though the only express reason given by the prosecution for their delay was ignorance of the rule, it was obvious from the complexity of the case (17 defendants and 200 pages of depositions) that preparation of the indictment would have taken longer than the usual period. In *Soffe*, the argument on appeal was that authorisation for an extension of time for preferment had been given by the chief clerk of the Crown Court concerned, not by a judge, and that r. 5 (as it then stood) had therefore been breached. Donaldson LJ, giving the Court of Appeal's judgment, said (at p. 136):

> There must be some doubt in this case whether the chief clerk in fact purported to extend the time limited by rule 5 or whether the bill was preferred out of time. So far as this application is concerned, it matters not which occurred. A breach of the Indictments (Procedure) Rules 1971 does not constitute a material irregularity in the course of the trial or in any way invalidate the proceedings, and the applicant accordingly has no valid grounds of appeal.

Similarly, when dismissing the appeal in *Farooki*, the Court relied on the dicta in *Sheerin* and *Soffe*, and could find no valid distinction between the circumstances of the case before them (where an appropriate officer had apparently signed a late-preferred bill without consultation with or authorisation from a judge) and the circumstances of *Sheerin* and *Soffe*.

The lack of effective sanction for breach of r. 5 should not, however, be treated by prosecutors as a licence to take as long as they like to draft the indictment. In *Sheerin*, Lawton LJ gave this warning (at p. 71):

> In coming to the conclusion we have about this matter we would not wish any prosecuting authority to think that they are being given a licence by this court to delay in preparing bills of indictment. As [counsel for the appellant] said in the course of his argument: 'It may well

be that in many cases . . . it is from a practical point of view virtually impossible to get the indictment preferred within the period of 28 days, but it is probable that if the prosecution are alive to the existence of rule 5 they could make an application to the court before the expiration of 28 days.' They are encouraged by this court so to do. If there is inordinate delay in preferring a bill of indictment, which clearly has caused, or clearly is likely to cause prejudice to accused persons, then the judge may very well not exercise his discretion and leave the prosecution to take such course as they think fit. Prosecutors should not assume that they will always be granted leave to prefer a voluntary bill of indictment.

Similarly, in *Soffe* (1982) 75 Cr App R 133, Donaldson LJ (at pp. 136–7), 'first and foremost', emphasised 'that it is the duty of all concerned to take all reasonable steps to ensure that bills of indictment are preferred within the 28-day period mentioned in rule 5'. He also recommended that Crown Court centres should keep a diary to assist the judges in monitoring the extent to which the 28-day period is being exceeded and 'to instigate remedial action' if that is necessary. A Crown Court officer should draw to the attention of a judge any case in which there has been improper delay, and the judge can then decide whether to allow an extension of time. At his discretion, the judge may allow the accused to make representations about any prejudice the delay may have caused him. As to points of detail, his lordship's recommendations have been largely overtaken by the subsequent amendments to r. 5.

Indictments (Procedure) Rules 1971 (SI 1971 No. 2084), rr. 4 and 5

4. Subject as hereinafter provided, a bill of indictment shall be preferred before the Crown Court by delivering the bill to the appropriate officer of the Crown Court:
   Provided that where with the assent of the prosecutor the bill is preferred by, or under the supervision of, the appropriate officer it shall not be necessary for the bill to be delivered to the appropriate officer but as soon as it has been settled to his satisfaction it shall be deemed to have been duly preferred.

5.—(1) Subject to the provisions of this rule, a bill of indictment shall be preferred—
   (a)   where a defendant has been committed for trial, within a period of 28 days commencing with the date of committal, or
   (b)   where a notice of transfer has been given under section 4 of the Criminal Justice Act 1987, within a period of 28 days commencing with the date on which notice is given.
   (2)   The period referred to in paragraph (1) may, on the application of the person preferring the bill of indictment or otherwise, be extended by a judge of the Crown Court before or after it has expired; and any period so extended may be further extended in like manner.
   (3)   Notwithstanding paragraph (2), the first extension of the period may be granted by the appropriate officer of the Crown Court provided that the period of the extension does not exceed 28 days; but if the appropriate officer is of the opinion that the first extension of the period should not be granted, he shall refer the application to a judge of the Crown Court who shall determine the application himself.
   (4)   An application under paragraph (2) shall—
   (a)   be in writing unless a judge of the Crown Court otherwise directs, and
   (b)   include a statement of the reasons why an extension of the period referred to in paragraph (1) is necessary.
   (5)   Where an application under paragraph (2) is made after the expiry of the period referred to in paragraph (1) or, as the case may be, the expiry of that period as extended under paragraph (2), the application shall in addition include a statement of the reasons why the application was not made before the expiry of the period or, as the case may be, the extended period.

COUNTS WHICH MAY BE INCLUDED IN AN INDICTMENT

D9.5   Subject to the rules on when counts and/or defendants are sufficiently closely linked to be properly joined in a single indictment (see **D9.24** *et seq*. and **D9.29** *et seq*.), the drafter of an indictment may include in it counts (i.e. charges) for *any* indictable offence that he considers to be disclosed by the evidence from the committal proceedings. This follows from the Administration of Justice (Miscellaneous Provisions) Act 1933, s. 2(2)(a), which allows a bill of indictment charging an offence to be preferred if 'the person charged has been committed for trial for the offence', read in conjunction with proviso (i) to the subsection. The proviso is: 'where the person charged has been committed for trial, the bill of indictment against him may include, either in substitution for or in addition to counts charging the offence for which he was committed, any counts founded on facts or evidence disclosed to the magistrates' court inquiring into that offence as examining justices, being counts which may lawfully be joined in the same indictment'. There are similar provisions in relation to the procedures governing notices of transfer, voluntary bills and indictable-only offences (see (iA) and (iB) of the proviso to s. 2(2) at **D7.1**).

Usually the counts in the indictment simply follow the committal charges. Where the drafter chooses to include a count for an offence in respect of which the examining justices did not commit, he must be careful to ensure that the offence is in fact disclosed by the statements for, if it is not, the defence will be entitled to move before arraignment to quash the count on the basis that it was preferred without authority in contravention of s. 2 of the 1933 Act. Further points as to the effect of proviso (i) are that:

(a)   The power to depart from the committal charges extends even to including a count for an offence in respect of which the justices were expressly asked to commit but took a considered decision not to do so (*Dawson* [1960] 1 WLR 163). However, the power should be used sparingly in such cases (*Dawson* and *Kempster* [1989] 1 WLR 1125). The potential dangers of reinstating a count after the examining justices have said that there is no case to answer for that offence are graphically illustrated by *Moloney* [1985] AC 905, in which the justices committed M in respect of manslaughter but would not commit for murder; the prosecution nonetheless indicted for murder, and M's conviction had to be quashed because of errors in the judge's summing up as to the *mens rea* for murder. Lord Hailsham of St Marylebone LC, commenting that justice had been done 'at the end of an unduly long and circuitous route', regretted that the prosecution had not 'followed the very sensible course taken by the committing justices' (p. 913D).

(b)   The prosecution may not rely on the proviso to s. 2(2) of the 1933 Act to prefer an indictment consisting *entirely* of counts for charges in respect of which there has been no committal for trial, even where the accused has been committed on other charges and the offences charged in the indictment are disclosed by the evidence that was before the justices (*Lombardi* [1989] 1 WLR 73). The reasoning in *Lombardi* was that, in the absence of at least one count on the indictment for a 'committal' offence, the 'non-committal' counts cannot properly be said to be in addition to or in substitution for counts charging the offence in respect of which the accused was committed, as required by the terms of the proviso. That reasoning would seem to apply even when the additional or substituted counts could properly have been joined in the same indictment with counts for the committal charges, had the prosecution so wished. However, it may be that the decision in *Lombardi* should be confined to its own facts, which were that joinder of the committal charges and non-committal charges in one indictment would have contravened the Indictment Rules 1971, r. 9, on the joinder of counts. Lord Lane CJ said (at p. 77):

> Section 2(2) is clearly restrictive. Its primary purpose is to prevent indictments being preferred save after committal or alternative judicial leave. The proviso allows some relaxation, which is itself restricted by the final words 'being counts which may lawfully be joined in the same indictment'.
>
> It would, in our judgment, be contrary to the whole tenor of the section to allow the prosecution to prefer indictments in the way they here suggest without any reference to justices, judge or appellate court. . . .

It is true that the words 'bill of indictment' are apt to include more than one bill of indictment. Thus, . . . where the justices have committed on more than one charge, the prosecution are at liberty, in the appropriate case, to prefer a separate indictment in respect of each. However, charges in respect of which there has been no committal, even though based on evidence which was before the justices, can only be the proper subject of indictment where two conditions are satisfied. First, they must be in 'substitution' for or in addition to the counts in respect of which [the] defendant was committed. The contentions advanced by the prosecution involve the necessity . . . of treating this provision as otiose, or, even worse, of allowing the prosecution to prefer two indictments to create a notional 'substitution'.

The second condition which has to be satisfied is that the new counts 'may lawfully be joined in the same indictment'. That must . . . mean the same indictment as that containing the charges on which the appellant was committed. That is clear from the whole context and also from the use of the word 'include'. The prosecution contentions require that those words should mean simply that no indictment must contain counts which cannot lawfully be joined, which scarcely needs stating. If Parliament had intended the law to be as the prosecution claims it to be, it would have been easy in plain terms to say so.

In short, in the judgment of this court, the words of section 2(2) and its proviso are not apt to entitle the prosecution to prefer the second indictment.

(c)   Insofar as an indictment consists of separate counts against several accused who are individually charged (i.e. there is no joint count), the counts against each accused should be treated for purposes of proviso (i) as a separate indictment. Therefore, if two accused, A1 and A2, were separately committed for trial (e.g., because, although their offences are linked, one was not arrested until after the committal of the other) and the prosecution – wishing to have a joint trial – then prefer a single indictment against them both, neither can successfully argue that the counts were preferred without authority simply because the offence alleged against his co-accused happened not to be disclosed by the evidence at the committal proceedings in respect of himself (*Groom* [1977] QB 6). Shortly after the decision in *Groom*, the then Lord Chief Justice issued *Practice Direction (Crime: Indictment)* [1976] 1 WLR 409 (see **D9.7**) confirming that separately committed accused may be joined in one indictment, and making the additional point that the existence of one or more indictments drawn against the accused individually as a result of the separate committals is no bar to a later joint indictment, although the prosecution will have to elect on which indictment (the joint or the individual) they wish to proceed.

(d)   The proviso requires that any offence, other than one on which the accused was committed, must be founded on the committal statements, but it does not require that the evidence which those statements contain must be conclusive (*Biddis* [1993] Crim LR 392). In *Biddis*, a count of possessing a firearm was added to the charge of robbery upon which the accused had been committed. It was argued on appeal that the committal bundle did not include any evidence to show that the gun was a firearm within the meaning of the Firearms Act 1968, s. 57(1), as there was no evidence before the justices that the gun could be fired. The Court of Appeal held that there was evidence that the gun had been loaded and that this was, in the circumstances of the case, sufficient evidence from which the jury could reasonably have inferred that it was an effective weapon.

(e)   Section 2(2) and its proviso do not apply to the amendment of an indictment, being concerned with the question of what offences can be included in the bill of indictment when it is *preferred*. The power to amend derives from the Indictment Act 1915, s. 5 (*Wells* (1995) 159 JP 243 and *Osieh* [1996] 1 WLR 1260; and see **D9.35**).

Counts for Summary Offences

D9.6   In addition to being able to indict the accused for those offences for which he has been committed for trial plus any other indictable offences disclosed by the evidence on which the committal was founded, the drafter of an indictment has a limited power to include counts for certain summary offences. The power is contained in the CJA 1988, s. 40, and arises when (s. 40(1)):

(a) the accused has been sent for trial for an indictable offence; and

(b) a summary offence to which s. 40 applies is either (i) 'founded on the same facts or evidence as a count charging an indictable offence', or (ii) 'is part of a series of offences of the same or similar character as an indictable offence which is also charged'; and

(c) the facts or evidence relating to the summary offence were disclosed 'to a magistrates' court inquiring into the offence as examining justices', or are disclosed by material served on the accused as part of the procedure for sending indictable-only offences to the Crown Court under the CDA 1998, s. 51 and sch. 3 (see **D8.21**).

The summary offences to which s. 40 applies are common assault, assaulting a prison custody officer or a secure training centre custody officer, taking a motor vehicle without the owner's consent, driving while disqualified and criminal damage where the value involved is the relevant sum or less (s. 40(3)). Although included within the scope of s. 40, criminal damage is not, strictly speaking, a summary offence, even when the value involved is less than the relevant sum. The MCA 1980, s. 22, merely provides that, where it is clear that the value does not exceed the relevant sum, the court 'shall proceed *as if* the offence were triable only summarily'. (See also *Considine* (1980) 70 Cr App R 239, although *Burt* [1996] Crim LR 660 appears to support a contrary interpretation.) The relevant sum for the purposes of s. 22 is £5,000. There is also power for the Secretary of State by order made by statutory instrument to extend s. 40 of the 1988 Act so as to apply to any other summary offence punishable with imprisonment or disqualification from driving (s. 40(4) and (5)).

Where a count for a summary offence is included in an indictment by virtue of s. 40(1), it is tried exactly as if it were an indictable offence, but, if the accused is convicted, the maximum penalty that may be imposed is that which could have been imposed for the offence by a magistrates' court (s. 40(2)). As to the preconditions for including a count for a summary offence, s. 40(1) does *not* require the magistrates actually to have committed the accused for trial for the summary matter, although in practice the prosecution usually ask them so to do. What is essential is that the facts relating to the summary offence shall have been disclosed 'to a magistrates' court inquiring into the offence as examining justices'. The phrases 'founded on the same facts *or evidence* as a count charging an indictable offence' and 'part of a series of offences of the same or similar character as an indictable offence', are taken almost verbatim from the Indictment Rules 1971, r. 9, which governs joinder of counts in an indictment. The only significant difference between s. 40(1) and r. 9 is that the latter does not contain the words 'or evidence', and so to that extent the rule is narrower in ambit than the section. As to interpretation of the phrase, in *Bird* [1995] Crim LR 745, B was stopped by the police and found to be a disqualified driver. A search of his car revealed a wooden pole, which was two feet in length and which he said he kept for personal protection. He was charged on an indictment containing two counts: (1) possession of an offensive weapon (triable either way) and (2) driving while disqualified (summary only). On appeal, it was argued that count (2) was improperly joined to the indictment. Dismissing the appeal, the Court of Appeal held that the two offences were committed at the same time as he drove along and were 'founded on the same facts or evidence'.

In *Smith* [1997] QB 837, the Court of Appeal held that offences of driving a conveyance taken without authority and driving whilst disqualified were not offences of a similar character to dangerous driving (which was the only indictable offence in the indictment on which the defendant was tried). Since the first two offences were not founded on the same facts as the third offence, they were improperly joined to the indictment, and the convictions in respect of them were quashed. Their lordships went on to hold, however, that the trial as a whole was not a nullity, since there was no possible prejudice to the accused (see **D9.24** for details of this latter aspect).

Section 40 of the CJA 1988 should be read in conjunction with s. 41 of the same Act (see **D7.23**), which allows a magistrates' court to commit for *any* summary offence punishable with imprisonment or disqualification which arose out of circumstances the same as or connected with the circumstances of an either-way offence in respect of which they are also committing. Unlike s. 40, s. 41 does not entitle the prosecution to include in the indictment a count for the summary offence, nor does it allow the accused to be tried by judge and jury for it – it merely enables the Crown Court to sentence him for the offence if, having been convicted on the indictable charge, he then admits the summary matter also. Should a magistrates' court commit under s. 41 in respect of a summary offence to which s. 40 also applies, the prosecution may in effect elect to proceed under the latter section simply by indicting for the summary offence (s. 41(4)).

Criminal Justice Act 1988, s. 40

(1)   A count charging a person with a summary offence to which this section applies may be included in an indictment if the charge—

(a)   is founded on the same facts or evidence as a count charging an indictable offence; or

(b)   is part of a series of offences of the same or similar character as an indictable offence which is also charged,

but only if (in either case) the facts or evidence relating to the offence were disclosed to a magistrates' court inquiring into the offence as examining justices.

(2)   Where a count charging an offence to which this section applies is included in an indictment, the offence shall be tried in the same manner as if it were an indictable offence; but the Crown Court may only deal with the offender in respect of it in a manner in which a magistrates' court could have dealt with him.

(3)   The offences to which this section applies are—

(a)   common assault;

(aa)   an offence under section 90(1) of the Criminal Justice Act 1991 (assaulting a prisoner custody officer);

(ab)   an offence under section 13(1) of the Criminal Justice and Public Order Act 1994 (assaulting a secure training centre custody officer);

(b)   an offence under section 12(1) of the Theft Act 1968 (taking motor vehicle or other conveyance without authority etc.);

(c)   an offence under section 103(1)(b) of the Road Traffic Act 1988 (driving a motor vehicle while disqualified);

(d)   an offence [of criminal damage etc.] which would otherwise be triable only summarily by virtue of section 22(2) of [MCA 1980]; and

(e)   any summary offence specified under subsection (4) below.

(4)   The Secretary of State may by order made by statutory instrument specify for the purposes of this section any summary offence which is punishable with imprisonment or involves obligatory or discretionary disqualification from driving.

The CDA 1998, sch. 8, para. 66, amends s. 40(1) so as to insert at the end of that subsection 'or are disclosed by material which, in pursuance of regulations made under the CDA 1998, sch. 3, para. 1 (procedure where person sent for trial under section 51), has been served on the person charged'. The amendment has effect from 4 January 1999 only in those pilot areas where the CDA 1998, s. 51, is in force.

DUPLICATION OF INDICTMENTS

D9.7   Closely linked with the questions of authority to prefer an indictment and counts that may be included in an indictment (see **D9.5**) is the question of whether there may be more than one indictment outstanding against an accused for the same offence. The effect of the somewhat intricate case law is as follows:

(a)   Subject to the qualification mentioned at (c) below, a single committal may be used as authority to prefer several indictments (see, e.g., *Follett* [1989] QB 338 per Lord Lane CJ at p. 344H). Thus, in *Lombardi* [1989] 1 WLR 73 it was common ground that, had the magistrates committed L for trial both for the forgery offences and for the bankruptcy offences, there would have been no possible objection to the preferment of two indictments against him, one for each set of offences, albeit that there had been only one committal. Similarly, if several accused are all committed for trial on one occasion, the prosecution may choose to indict them separately if, for example, the offences are not sufficiently linked for a single trial to be in the interests of justice or they wish to use the evidence of one accused against the others.

(b)   An accused may have two or more indictments outstanding against him for the same offence (*Poole* [1961] AC 223). Thus, if X has been committed for trial for offence A and an indictment is signed against him for that offence, the prosecution may subsequently commence separate committal proceedings against X for offence B (e.g., because evidence of that only becomes available after the first committal) and may then, if offences A and B are connected as required by the rules on joinder of counts, prefer a joint indictment for both offences. The existence of the prior indictment for offence A by itself is no bar to the later joint indictment but the prosecution will be required to elect before trial on which of the two they wish to proceed. Similarly, where two accused are separately committed for trial and it is then wished to have them tried together, the prosecution may prefer a joint indictment regardless of whether separate indictments have already been preferred against the two accused individually (*Groom* [1977] QB 6 and *Practice Direction (Crime: Indictment)* [1976] 1 WLR 409 issued as a result of that decision. Similarly, the prosecution may, where counts in an indictment are improperly joined, ask the judge for leave to prefer two or more fresh indictments out of time and then elect to proceed on those instead of on the original. The consequent duplication of counts between the original and fresh indictments is irrelevant (see *Follett* [1989] QB 338 at p. 345C–D). The prosecution must, however, ensure that the fresh indictments are preferred before the original one is quashed.

Practice Direction (Crime: Indictment) [1976] 1 WLR 409

There is no rule of law or practice which prohibits two indictments being in existence at the same time for the same offence against the same person on the same facts. But the court will not allow the prosecution to proceed on both such indictments. They cannot in law be tried together and the court will insist that the prosecution elect the one on which the trial shall proceed. Where different persons have been separately committed for trial for offences which can lawfully be charged in the same indictment it is permissible to join in one indictment the counts founded upon the separate committals despite the fact that an indictment in respect of any one of those committals has already been signed.

(c)   There is one qualification to the rule that a single committal may be used to found several indictments, namely that, if the indictment originally preferred as a result of the committal has been quashed, its effect is exhausted and authority to prefer a replacement indictment must be sought either through fresh proceedings or application to a High Court judge for a voluntary bill of indictment (*Thompson* [1975] 1 WLR 1425). In that case James LJ said (at p. 1429G):

. . . the Crown is not entitled to prefer indictment after indictment if one indictment, then another and then another fails on a motion to quash. [So] having elected the form of indictment to be put before the trial court on the authority of the committal, if it is found that the election results in the quashing of that indictment the only course open to the Crown is to obtain leave to prefer a new bill and that leave can only be obtained from a High Court judge.

There are dicta in *Thompson* to the effect that it is never permissible to prefer more than one indictment on the basis of one committal. That proposition, however, runs counter to the decision in *Groom*, to *Practice Direction (Crime: Indictment)* and to the judgment of Lord Lane CJ in *Follett*, where he concluded (at p. 345E) that the narrower *ratio* of *Thompson* (i.e. the one just quoted) was undoubtedly the correct one.

GENERAL FORM OF AN INDICTMENT

D9.8   By r. 4(1) of the Indictment Rules 1971, the layout of an indictment should substantially follow the form given in sch. 1 to the Rules. Each offence charged should be set out in a separate paragraph or *count*, and each count should be divided into a statement of offence and particulars of offence. If there is more than one count, they should be numbered (r. 4(3)). The statement of offence describes the offence shortly, and, if the offence is statutory, should specify by section and subsection the provision contravened (Indictments Act 1915, s. 3(1), and Indictment Rules 1971, r. 6). The particulars of offence should give 'such particulars as may be necessary for giving reasonable information as to the nature of the charge' (Indictments Act 1915, s. 3(1) and Indictment Rules 1971, r. 5(2)). All the essential elements of the offence should be disclosed (r. 6(b)), save that (a) it is not necessary to allege that the accused falls outside any 'exception, proviso, excuse or qualification' to liability, and (b) failure to disclose an essential element may be disregarded if the accused is not thereby 'prejudiced or embarrassed in his defence' (proviso to r. 6(b) and r. 6(c)). Modern practice is to keep even the particulars of offence very short (cf. the drafting of a count for a complicated conspiracy to defraud where it is established practice to give extended particulars). Generally speaking, brevity in a count does not prejudice the defence since the way the prosecution put their case and the evidence they intend to call will sufficiently emerge from the committal documents. It is, however, open to the defence to ask for additional particulars.

In *Teong Sun Chuah* [1991] Crim LR 463, for example, the appellants were convicted of false accounting and obtaining by deception. One of the grounds of appeal was that no particulars were given of the false representations relied on in support of the counts of deception. The Court of Appeal said that, although it was advantageous for particulars to be given of the false representations in such cases, it was plain in the present case what the particulars were. No injustice was done by failing to spell them out in advance. By contrast, in *Warburton-Pitt* (1991) 92 Cr App R 136, the prosecution's failure to particularise the facts upon which they relied in support of allegations of recklessness formed the basis of a successful appeal. W was convicted of offences of recklessness, flowing from the crash of a microlight aircraft in which a by-stander was killed. He appealed *inter alia* on the basis that the defence had not had particulars of the case which they had to meet. The Court of Appeal said that particulars of the allegations of recklessness should have been included in the particulars of offence in the indictment, or provided in writing by way of voluntary particulars. These were needed because the case was a complicated one; there were a number of possible explanations for the crash. The court stated that there would be no need for such particulars in a simple case of reckless driving, since it would be obvious what facts the prosecution were relying on. It appears from a comparison of *Teong Sun Chuah* and *Warburton-Pitt* that the test is: do the particulars provided, whether in the indictment or elsewhere, make clear to the defence the nature of the case which it must meet?

What if the particulars of offence are incorrect? In *Moses* [1991] Crim LR 617, the appellants were charged with a conspiracy to defraud by facilitating applications by immigrants to obtain work permits. The particulars of the counts stated that M and A conspired to defraud the DSS by 'submitting application forms which were false in that . . .' The Court of Appeal held that these words were not apt to describe what M and A had done but that the defect was not fatal to the conviction and it was not believed that the words had misled anyone. Particulars of offence were not like the words of a statute, such that failure of the facts proved to fall precisely within them was fatal. It seems that the test to apply in relation to incorrect particulars is whether the defence were prejudiced by the erroneous description of the offence. (See also *Hancock* [1996] 2 Cr App R 554.)

Rule 5(2) of the Indictment Rules 1971 makes provision for the rules to include specimen forms of count approved by the Lord Chief Justice, but the present rules do not include any such specimens. Such authority as there is on drafting counts for specific offences must therefore be derived from decided cases. A suggested form of count for the major offences will be found in the section of this work dealing with the offence in question. The standard components of particulars are:

(a)   the names of the defendants charged in the count;
(b)   the date of the offence (or the dates within which it occurred if the precise date is not known);
(c)   the act constituting the offence (e.g., 'stole' such and such an item of property, or 'inflicted grievous bodily harm' on such and such a person);
(d)   the name of the victim of the offence (e.g., the owner of the property stolen or the person wounded or assaulted); and
(e)   the state of mind on the part of the accused which the prosecution must establish in order to secure a conviction.

Points of drafting procedure which apply generally, whatever the specific offence alleged, are considered below.

Indictments Act 1915, s. 3

(1)   Every indictment shall contain, and shall be sufficient if it contains, a statement of the specific offence or offences with which the accused person is charged, together with such particulars as may be necessary for giving reasonable information as to the nature of the charge.

(2)   Notwithstanding any rule of law or practice, an indictment shall, subject to the provisions of this Act, not be open to objection in respect of its form or contents if it is framed in accordance with the rules under this Act.

Indictment Rules 1971 (SI 1971 No. 1253) rr. 4 to 6

4.—(1)   An indictment shall be in the form in schedule 1 to these rules or in a form substantially to the like effect.

(2)   Where more than one offence is charged in an indictment, the statement and particulars of each offence shall be set out in a separate paragraph called a count, and rules 5 and 6 of these rules shall apply to each count in the indictment as they apply to an indictment where one offence is charged.

(3)   The counts shall be numbered consecutively.

5.—(1)   Subject only to the provisions of rule 6 of these rules, every indictment shall contain, and shall be sufficient if it contains, a statement of the specific offence with which the accused person is charged describing the offence shortly, together with such particulars as may be necessary for giving reasonable information as to the nature of the charge.

(2)   An indictment for a specific offence shall not be open to objection in respect of its form if it is framed in accordance with a form of indictment for that offence for the time being approved by the Lord Chief Justice.

6.   Where the specific offence with which an accused person is charged in an indictment is one created by or under an enactment, then (without prejudice to the generality of rule 5 of these rules)—

(a)   the statement of offence shall contain a reference to—

(i)   the section of, or the paragraph of the schedule to, the Act creating the offence in the case of an offence created by a provision of an Act;

(ii)   the provision creating the offence in the case of a subordinate instrument;

(b)   the particulars shall disclose the essential elements of the offence.

Provided that an essential element need not be disclosed if the accused person is not prejudiced or embarrassed in his defence by the failure to disclose it;

(c)   It shall not be necessary to specify or negative an exception, proviso, excuse or qualification.

Date of the Offence

D9.9   In order to provide reasonable particulars of the offence charged, the count should state the date on which it occurred insofar as it is known. Normal practice is to give the day of the month, followed by the month, followed by the year (e.g., 'on 1 January 1999'). If the precise date is unknown, it is sufficient to allege that the offence occurred 'on or about' a specified date, or 'on a day unknown' before a specified date, or 'on a date other than the date in count one', or 'on a day unknown between' two specified dates. If the last-mentioned formula is adopted, the days specified should be those immediately before the earliest and immediately after the latest days on which the offence could have been committed. Thus, if the accused is found in possession of stolen goods on 31 December 1998 and the prosecution case is that the goods were stolen on 1 January 1997, a count for handling would allege that he received the goods 'on a day unknown between 31 December 1997 and 1 January 1999'.

If the evidence at trial as to time differs from the date laid in the count, that is not, as a rule, fatal to a conviction (*Dossi* (1918) 13 Cr App R 158). There may, however, be cases in which the allegation as to date is not merely procedural, but may determine the outcome of the case, for example where the age of a victim is important.

In *Radcliffe* [1990] Crim LR 524, R faced counts of indecency with a child, contrary to the Indecency with Children Act 1960, s. 1(1). One count alleged that between 14 March 1984 and 13 March 1985 he behaved indecently towards his stepdaughter aged 12, and the other count alleged similar conduct between 14 March 1985 and 13 March 1986, when she was 13. The judge in summing up said 'The dates which are set out in the indictment . . . are immaterial. The prosecution do not have to prove that any particular act happened between those dates. What you have to prove is that it happened.' The jury convicted, and R appealed, alleging that the judge had misdirected them. The Court of Appeal allowed the appeal. The judge's direction was open to the interpretation that it did not matter when the events took place, provided the jury were sure that they happened. Although they had copies of the indictment in front of them and the Crown had emphasised that the girl must have been under 14, they may have been left with the belief that her age was immaterial and that they could convict even if she was over 14 at the time.

It has, however, been stated that, where the formula 'on or about' a date is used, the evidence must show the offence to have been committed 'within some period that has a reasonable approximation to the date mentioned in the indictment' (per Sachs LJ in *Hartley* [1972] 2 QB 1 at p. 7). Where the defence may have been prejudiced in the preparation of their case by a divergence between the evidence as to time and the date specified in the count, it is submitted that the trial should be adjourned to allow them to respond to the altered situation. Alternatively, it might be necessary to discharge the jury and have a second trial on an amended indictment. Failure to allow an adjournment could result in the quashing of any resultant conviction as being unsafe or unsatisfactory. The above propositions are derived from *Wright* v *Nicholson* [1970] 1 WLR 142, although some caution is necessary in applying that decision in the present context because (a) the appeal was not against conviction on indictment but against the dismissal by the Crown Court of an appeal against summary conviction, and (b) the Divisional Court's reasoning was partly based on the faulty premise that the Crown Court had power to amend the information on which the magistrates had convicted the appellant. Since divergence between a count and the evidence as to date is not in itself fatal to conviction, there is, strictly speaking, no need for the prosecution even to apply for the indictment to be amended on the divergence becoming apparent (*Dossi*; but see *Bonner* [1974] Crim LR 479, where the Court of Appeal apparently overlooked the point). However, as a matter of practice, it may be preferable to eliminate the divergence by an appropriate amendment, thus avoiding confusing the jury.

Continuous Offences

The rule against duplicity (i.e. each count may allege only one offence – see **D9.16** *et* **D9.10** *seq*.) means that, subject to what follows, a count must allege that the offence occurred on *one* day, not on several days. Particulars stating, for example, that the accused stole items of property on '1 and 2 January 1999' or 'on a day or days unknown in January 1999' would be invalid because the only sensible interpretation of such an allegation is that the accused, according to the prosecution, committed several distinct thefts, each theft being on a different day. The convenient rule of practice allowing the prosecution to have one count for what are technically distinct criminal acts provided those acts formed a single activity or transaction cannot apply to such a count because the mention of more than one day (whether conjunctively or disjunctively) is inconsistent with there having been a single activity on the accused's part. However, by way of exception to the general principle just stated, if an offence, on its true construction, is to be regarded as a continuing offence which may take place continuously or intermittently over a period of time, then a count may properly allege that it occurred on more than one day.

The leading authority on drafting charges for continuous offences is *Hodgetts* v *Chiltern District Council* [1983] 2 AC 120, in which the House of Lords ruled on the validity of an information under the Town and Country Planning Act 1971, s. 89(5), alleging that H had '*on and since* May 27, 1980' permitted certain lands and buildings to be used for the purpose of storing building materials in contravention of an enforcement notice served on him under s. 87 of the Act. Section 89(5) has since been redrafted and re-enacted as the Town and Country Planning Act 1990, s. 179(6), (7) and (8), and the penalties have been increased. At the time of this case, the provision was: 'Where, by virtue of an enforcement notice, a use of land is required to be discontinued . . . then if any person uses the land . . . in contravention of the notice, he shall be guilty of an offence and liable on summary conviction to a fine not exceeding £400; . . . and if the use is continued after the conviction, he shall be guilty of a further offence and liable on summary conviction to a fine not exceeding £50 for each day on which the use is so continued.' Interpreting the subsection, Lord Roskill held that it created two offences, an initial one committed immediately there was non-compliance with an enforcement notice requiring the subject of the notice to desist from a certain use of land, and a further offence committed by a person who had already been convicted of the initial offence and who still failed to desist from the prohibited use. Since the information against H did not allege a prior conviction, it was plainly for an 'initial' offence, not a 'further offence'. The argument for H was that, whether the prosecution alleged an initial offence or a further offence, a separate infraction of s. 89(5) occurred on each day of the period during which an enforcement notice was ignored, and the prosecution should therefore have had a separate information for each day, rather than alleging that the failure to comply was 'on and since May 27'. Rejecting the argument, Lord Roskill said (at p. 128, emphasis added):

> It is not an essential characteristic of a criminal offence that any prohibited act or omission, in order to constitute a single offence, should take place once and for all on a single day. It may take place, whether continuously or intermittently, over a period of time.

> . . . as respects non-compliance with a 'desist' notice, it is in my view clear that the initial offence (as well as the further offence) though it too may take place over a period, whether continuously or intermittently (e.g., holding a Sunday market), is a single offence and not

a series of separate offences committed each day that the non-compliance prior to the first conviction for non-compliance continues. If it were otherwise it would have the bizarre consequence that upon summary conviction a fine of £400 per diem could be imposed for each such separate offence committed before the offender received his first conviction, whereas for any further offence committed after the offender against a 'desist notice' had been convicted, a daily fine of only £50 could be inflicted. Uniquely a previous conviction would be a positive advantage to the offender. This can hardly have been Parliament's intention.

. . . in the instant case each information . . . charged the offence 'on and since' a specified date. . . . I see no objection to [that wording], but it might be preferable if hereafter offences under the first limb of section 89(5) were charged as having been committed between two specified dates, the termini usually being on the one hand the date when compliance with the enforcement notice first became due and on the other hand a date not later than the date when the information was laid, or of course some earlier date if meanwhile the enforcement notice has been complied with. *Indictments frequently charge offences as having been committed between certain dates.* I see no reason in principle why the same practice should not be followed with these informations.

Points on drafting counts for continuous offences emerging from the above are as follows:

(a)   Although *Hodgetts v Chiltern District Council* concerned an information for a summary offence, the same principles apply to counts in an indictment – indeed, Lord Roskill supported his opinion by reference to the practice in drafting indictments (see the italicised words).

(b)   Determining whether an offence is properly to be treated as continuous will require detailed analysis of the offence-creating provision. In the absence of specific authority, the drafter of an indictment may have no means of knowing with certainty whether the offence for which he is indicting the accused is continuous or not. In such cases, it may be preferable to avoid potential complications by stating that the offence occurred on one day (not on several), unless the continuation of the misconduct significantly adds to the gravity of the case.

(c)   One clear example of a continuous indictable offence is conspiracy. The offence begins when any two or more parties enter into the unlawful agreement and continues until it comes to an end. Thus, in *Greenfield* [1973] 1 WLR 1151 (and see **D9.16**) a count for conspiring to cause explosions between 1 January 1968 and July 1971 was held not to be bad for duplicity, while in *Landy* [1981] 1 WLR 355 the Court of Appeal, in indicating how the prosecution should have drafted a count for conspiracy to defraud a bank, suggested that the particulars could have begun, '[The defendants] *on divers days* between . . . and . . . conspired together and with . . . '.

(d)   Theft is clearly not a continuous offence. However, the prosecution may have difficulty in drafting an indictment for theft where the evidence is that the accused, on numerous separate occasions over a lengthy period, stole small sums or items of property, but it is not possible to particularise the exact days on which the appropriations occurred since none of them came to light until the end of the period by which time even the accused may not remember when he did what. To overcome the difficulty it is possible to have a single count alleging that, on a day within the overall period, the accused stole all the relevant money or property. The cases on this point (known as the general deficiency cases) are considered at **B4.3** (see also the discussion of sample counts at **D9.15**).

Place of the Offence

D9.11   Provided the conduct alleged against the accused constitutes an offence regardless of where it occurred, it is unnecessary for the particulars to specify venue. In *Wallwork* (1958) 42 Cr App R 153, the particulars for incest stated that: '[W], being a man, on a day unknown between the 7th and the 12th June, 1957, *in the county of Sussex or elsewhere,* had sexual intercourse with [A], a girl of the age of five years, who is, and whom he then knew to be, his daughter.' On appeal, it was argued that the indictment was bad on its face because it alleged more than one venue (Sussex or elsewhere). In laying particulars of venue, the drafter no doubt followed what was then conventional practice, but the Court of Criminal Appeal held that the indictment was not bad for duplicity as the venue need not have been mentioned at all. Lord Goddard CJ said (at pp. 156–7):

> So far as place is concerned, I think [counsel for the prosecution's] point is a perfectly good one, that incest is an offence wherever it is committed, and it matters not whether it is committed in one place or another, provided the prisoner knows the substance of the charge against him. It makes no difference whether the incest in this case was committed in Sussex or Surrey or any other place. It is not intended by this single count to charge him with more than one offence of incest, and the words 'County of Sussex or elsewhere' in the opinion of the court are surplusage. It would have been a perfectly good indictment to charge him with the offence if the words 'in the County of Sussex or elsewhere' had been omitted, and there is no pretence for saying that he did not know the nature of the offence with which he was being charged. . . . There are cases . . . in which it is necessary to indicate a particular place in the indictment, and an illustration [is] the offence of larceny on a ship which was at the time of the larceny in a harbour or in a creek or other place of anchorage . . . where it would be necessary to show that the theft took place while the ship was in a harbour or some particular creek, and then it would be necessary to mention the name of the harbour or creek. But . . . it is not necessary to refer to any place in the indictment in an offence of this description.

The example given in the above passage of a count in which, contrary to the general rule, particulars of place should be included is now anachronistic, but current examples of the same requirement are burglary and dangerous driving. Counts for the former should state the building entered as a trespasser, and counts for the latter the road, roads or other public places where the driving took place. The reason, in both cases, is that, having regard to the definition of the offences, the place where the prohibited conduct occurred is an essential ingredient of the crime (i.e. if the accused entered premises other than a building with intent to steal he would not be guilty of burglary and, similarly, if he drove dangerously on private land he would not be guilty of dangerous driving). Where the general rule applies and the count accordingly does not specify venue, the defence will almost certainly be able to ascertain where the offence was allegedly committed from the committal documents. Should there be any real doubt such as might prejudice the preparation of the defence, further particulars could no doubt be requested.

Indicting Secondary Parties

When indicting a secondary party to an offence (i.e. an aider, abettor, counsellor or **D9.12** procurer), there is no need to indicate, either in the statement of offence or particulars, that such was his role. This convenient rule flows from the Accessories and Abettors Act 1861, s. 8, which provides that: 'Whosoever shall aid, abet, counsel, or procure the commission of any indictable offence, whether the same be an offence at common law or by virtue of any Act passed or to be passed, shall be liable to be tried, *indicted,* and punished as a principal offender' (emphasis added). The usual practice is to take advantage of the 1861 Act and employ the same form of words in indicting a secondary party as would be used against a principal offender. There is, however, no objection to an express allegation of aiding and abetting, and it may be preferable so to draft if the circumstances are such that the accused could not possibly have been guilty as a principal offender (e.g., when the allegation is that a woman aided and abetted a man to commit rape; or that one entitled to drive aided and abetted another to drive while disqualified). In such cases, the precedent for a count against a principal offender may be adapted by prefixing the statement of offence with the words 'Aiding and abetting', and by inserting in the particulars 'aided and abetted [name of principal offender] to . . . '. Where the prosecution are unsure of the precise role played by the accused, it is permissible to allege aiding, abetting, counselling or procuring in the alternative in one count (*Ferguson* v *Weaving* [1951] 1 KB 814).

The normal practice of indicting secondary parties as if they were principals in the first degree was criticised in *Maxwell* [1978] 1 WLR 1350 where the particulars for an offence of doing an act with intent, contrary to the Explosive Substances Act 1883, s. 3(a), alleged that M had placed a pipe bomb in an inn. The prosecution did not attempt to prove that M had personally placed the bomb, or even that he had been present when others placed it. Their case was that M, in his car, had guided the principal offenders, in their car, to the inn, and had then driven off at high speed. The House of Lords dismissed M's appeal against conviction, but Viscount Dilhorne said, *obiter*, at p. 1352G: 'It is desirable that the particulars of the offence should bear some relation to the realities and where, as here, it is clear that the appellant was alleged to have aided and abetted the placing of the bomb and its possession or control, it would . . . have been better if the particulars of offence had made that clear'. Lords Hailsham of St Marylebone, Fraser and Edmund-Davies all commented to like effect. Nevertheless, it was accepted that, even if less than ideal, the particulars were perfectly lawful ('However surprising and unreal such allegations might have sounded to a jury, . . . it has to be said that such wording [of the count] was strictly in accordance with section 8 of the Accessories and Abettors Act 1861': per Lord Edmund-Davies at p. 1359G). In fact, the strictures of the House of Lords have not noticeably altered drafting practice, and it is submitted that indicting secondary parties as if they were principals does not cause undue confusion either to the defence (who know from the committal documents the role each accused is alleged to have played) or to the jury (whose confusion, if any, should be dispelled by prosecuting counsel's opening speech).

Names; Allegations as to Money and Property

D9.13 **Names**   A person named in an indictment (whether as accused, victim or otherwise) should be described by his or her forenames and surname. Errors in stating names will not, however, affect the validity of the proceedings, provided that the misnamed person is identified with reasonable precision and the parties are not misled. By r. 8 of the Indictment Rules 1971: 'It shall be sufficient in an indictment to describe a person whose name is not known as a person unknown'.

D9.14 **Allegations as to Money and Property**   The Criminal Procedure Act 1851, s. 18, provides that: 'In every indictment in which it shall be necessary to make any averment as to any money or any note of the Bank of England or any other bank, it shall be sufficient to describe such money or bank note simply as money, without specifying any particular coin or bank note; and such allegation, so far as regards the description of the property, shall be sustained by proof of any amount of coin or of any bank note, although the particular nature of the bank note shall not be proved.' Thus, a count for robbery might read: 'AB, on 1 January 1998, robbed CD of a wallet, a cheque card and £50.35 in money.' There is no need to specify what coins and notes made up the sum.

Where the offence alleged is one against property, the count must give reasonable particulars of the property concerned. This is normally done by stating what the property was (e.g., a car, a window, a bag, a joint of meat), and then stating the owner's name. If that is not known, the count may read 'belonging to a person unknown'. The value of the property need not be stated.

Specimen or Sample Counts

D9.15 Where a person is accused of adopting a systematic course of criminal conduct, the prosecution sometimes proceeds by way of specimen or sample counts. This is frequently the case, for example, where dishonesty over a period of time is alleged. In order to avoid too lengthy an indictment, a limited number of sample counts are included. The practice which the prosecution ought to adopt in these circumstances is to provide the defence with a list of all the similar offences of which it is alleged that those selected in the indictment are samples. Evidence of some or all of these additional offences may in appropriate cases be led as evidence of system. In other cases, the additional offences need not be referred to until after a verdict of guilty upon the sample offence is returned (*DPP* v *Anderson* [1978] AC 964). Clearly, if this course is adopted, care must be taken to ensure that the accused is not deprived of his right to trial by jury upon those offences which do not appear in the indictment. Further, it is crucial that the defendant should know the case he has to meet (*Evans* [1995] Crim LR 245). Where sample or specimen counts are used there are difficulties for the sentencer (discussed at **D17.33**). In *Rackham* [1997] 2 Cr App R 222, the Court of Appeal emphasised that the indictment had to be drafted in such a way as to enable the defendant to know with as much particularity as the circumstances would admit what case he had to meet. Also relevant is the position with regard to the general deficiency cases, where the prosecution's case is that there were acts of dishonesty over a period of time, amounting to a certain value, but they are unable to be specific about the dates of individual acts of dishonesty (see **D9.10** and **B4.3**).

THE RULE AGAINST DUPLICITY

Duplicity Generally

Each count in an indictment must allege only one offence (see Indictment Rules 1971, **D9.16** r. 4(2), which requires that, where more than one offence is alleged in an indictment, each offence 'shall be set out in a separate paragraph called a count'). If a count alleges more than one offence, it is said to be bad for duplicity, and should be quashed before arraignment. Rejection of a defence motion to quash a count bad for duplicity is a good ground of appeal, although it may be open to the Court of Appeal to apply the proviso and dismiss the appeal if there has been no miscarriage of justice.

Whether or not a count is bad for duplicity is decided by looking at its wording without reference to the prosecution evidence as disclosed by the committal documents (*Greenfield* [1973] 1 WLR 1151). In *Greenfield* the appellants and others were charged in a count which alleged that between 1 January 1968 and 21 August 1971 they had conspired together to cause by explosive substances explosions in the United Kingdom of a nature to endanger life or to cause serious injury to property. There were a further 10 counts alleging substantive offences committed in furtherance of the conspiracy. The prosecution called evidence of about 25 explosions or attempted explosions occurring in different parts of England during the relevant period. On the basis of common features in the explosions, the jury were invited to conclude that they had all been the work of the same group. The appellants lived at a flat in which were found explosives similar to the explosives used in many of the 25 incidents, plus firearms, ammunition and documents linking them to a group called the 'Angry Brigade' which had claimed responsibility for the majority of the explosions. However, others of the explosions had no obvious connection with the Angry Brigade (e.g., six explosions aimed at Spanish targets in England and three at Italian). Shortly before the trial started defence counsel asked prosecuting counsel to deliver particulars of the conspiracy count, but was told that the prosecution opening would give the defence all the particulars they needed. In the opening speech, it was made clear that the prosecution alleged only one conspiracy in which all the accused named in the count had joined. On appeal, the defence argued that the conspiracy count was bad for duplicity because, as the trial progressed, the evidence was consistent with the existence of more than one conspiracy (i.e. the 'Angry Brigade conspiracy', the anti-Spanish conspiracy and the anti-Italian conspiracy). The

Court of Appeal held that, even if that were so, it did not affect the validity of the count, although it was essential that the jury should be directed (as they in fact were) to convict only if they found the offence charged proved, not if they found the defendants to have participated in conspiracies other than the one alleged. Lawton LJ said (at pp. 1155F–1156B):

> [Counsel for the appellants] submitted that count 1 [the conspiracy count] was bad in law because as the trial progressed the evidence was consistent with the existence of more than one conspiracy. In our judgment that did not make the count bad in law. A conspiracy count is bad in law if it *charges* the defendants with having been members of two or more conspiracies. This is elementary law. . . . [Count 1] referred to one conspiracy only. . . . judges may be in doubt as to what they should consider before deciding whether a conspiracy count is bad for duplicity. They should look first at the count itself. In most cases it will be unnecessary to look at any other material. If particulars of the count have been requested and given, those too should be considered. . . . If the prosecution has been requested to give particulars and has refused to do so, the judge may have to look at the depositions to discover the nature of the charge.

> Duplicity in a count is a matter of form; it is not a matter relating to the evidence called in support of the count.

Although the above passage was delivered in the context of an appeal against conviction on a count for conspiracy and refers specifically to the drafting of conspiracy counts, it is submitted that the principles stated are of general application. Thus, leaving aside the exceptional case of the defence having asked for and been refused additional particulars of a count, the only matters to be considered by a judge determining whether a count is bad for duplicity are the form (i.e. wording) of the count and any additional particulars supplied by the prosecution. The evidence as disclosed on the committal documents is irrelevant. If the evidence called at trial in fact establishes more than one offence, then, subject to amendment of the indictment, if possible, the accused will be entitled to an acquittal, not because the count was bad, but because the prosecution have failed to prove him guilty of the precise offence charged in the count, even though they may have proved him guilty of some other offence (see *Griffiths* [1966] 1 QB 589).

The proposition that a count must charge one and only one offence is, however, deceptively simple, for it begs the question, What is an offence? The issue came before the House of Lords in *DPP v Merriman* [1973] AC 584, where FM and his brother (JM) were charged in a joint count with wounding P with intent to do him grievous bodily harm. FM pleaded guilty; JM pleaded not guilty, was convicted and appealed. The prosecution case against JM was that, following a dispute in a public house, he stabbed P in the back, after which both he and FM joined in stabbing P about seven times. The judge directed the jury that they should ignore any possibility that JM was acting in concert with his brother, and should concentrate solely on whether he had personally stabbed P. This was, if anything, a direction unduly favourable to JM since it ruled out the possibility of the jury convicting on the basis that, even though he had not personally wounded P, he had been present encouraging and assisting FM when the latter did so. Unfortunately, the direction was contrary to a line of authority (see especially *Scaramanga* [1963] 2 QB 807) which established that, if one of two defendants charged in a single count was found or pleaded guilty, the other could be convicted only if the jury were satisfied that he had taken part in the *joint* offence. In other words, it was not open to the jury to find both defendants guilty on the basis that each had acted independently in committing the offence charged, since, it was said, that would be to find two offences proved when only one had been charged. The decision of the House of Lords in *Merriman* was to overrule the *Scaramanga* line of authority and reinstate JM's conviction, which had been quashed by the Court of Appeal, reluctantly applying *Scaramanga*. In reaching their ultimate decision, the House of Lords considered the true import of the rule against duplicity. Lord Morris of Borth-y-Gest said (at p. 593A-E):

It is . . . a general rule that not more than one offence is to be charged in a count in an indictment. . . . The question arises – what is an offence? If A attacks B and, in doing so, stabs B five times with a knife, has A committed one offence or five? If A in the dwelling-house of B steals 10 different chattels, some perhaps from one room and some from others, has he committed one offence or several? In many different situations comparable questions could be asked. In my view, such questions when they arise are best answered by applying common sense and by deciding what is fair in the circumstances. No precise formula can usefully be laid down but I consider that clear and helpful guidance was given by Lord Widgery CJ in . . . *Jemmison* v *Priddle* [1972] 1 QB 489 at p. 495. I agree . . . that it will often be legitimate to bring a single charge in respect of what might be called one activity even though that activity may involve more than one act. It must, of course, depend upon the circumstances. In the present case, it was not at any time suggested, and in my view could not reasonably have been suggested, that count 1 was open to objection because evidence was to be tendered that the respondent stabbed [P] more than once.

In similar vein, Lord Diplock said (at p. 607C):

The rule against duplicity, viz. that only one offence should be charged in any count of an indictment . . . has always been applied in a practical, rather than in a strictly analytical, way for the purpose of determining what constituted one offence. Where a number of acts of a similar nature committed by one or more defendants were connected with one another, in the time and place of their commission or by their common purpose, in such a way that they could fairly be regarded as forming part of the same transaction or criminal enterprise, it was the practice, as early as the 18th century, to charge them in a single count of an indictment. Where such a count was laid against more than one defendant, the jury could find each of them guilty of one offence only: but a failure by the prosecution to prove the allegation, formerly expressly stated in the indictment but now only implicit in their joinder in the same count, that the unlawful acts of each were done jointly in aid of one another, did not render the indictment *ex post facto* bad or invalidate the jury's verdict against those found guilty.

Although both Lord Morris and Lord Diplock were concerned with the verdicts which may lawfully be returned on a joint count, the thrust of their remarks – that a count is not to be held bad on its face for duplicity merely because its words are logically capable of being construed as alleging more than one criminal act – applies whether a count is against one accused or several. The test of whether it is proper to have a single count is: Can the separate acts attributed to the accused fairly be said to form a single activity or transaction? (see **D9.20**). It follows from that test that, if the particulars of a count can sensibly be interpreted as alleging a single activity, it will not be bad for duplicity, even if a number of distinct criminal acts are implied. Thus, the rule against duplicity rests ultimately on common sense and pragmatic considerations of what is fair in all the circumstances. That being so, the rule is best understood in terms of past decisions on what is acceptable drafting practice, rather than by applying an artificial concept of what is a single offence. The following guidelines emerge from the cases.

Several Dates   Unless the offence charged is properly to be construed as a continuing **D9.17** offence, a count alleging that the accused committed criminal acts on more than one day is bad for duplicity. (See *Thompson* [1914] 2 KB 99, in which T was charged with having committed incest with his daughter 'on divers days between the month of January, 1909, and the 4th day of October, 1910' – the Court of Criminal Appeal dismissed the appeal because the appellant had had ample notice of the precise dates on which the acts of incest were said to have occurred and had therefore not been prejudiced in his defence, but it was common ground that the count was 'irregular' because it patently alleged more than one offence. Although the count in *Thompson* alleged the acts of incest cumulatively, it has never been doubted that the result would have been the same had they been alleged in the alternative.)

In *DPP* v *McCabe* [1992] Crim LR 885, a charge alleging that M stole 76 library books from South Glamorgan Library between two specified dates was held not to be bad for duplicity. The Divisional Court held that where there is appropriation of a number of articles, but no evidence as to when the individual appropriations took place, the prosecution is entitled to charge the appropriation of the aggregate number within a specified period.

D9.18 **Several Items of Property** A count for an offence against property may allege that several items were stolen, damaged, obtained by deception, unlawfully possessed or otherwise subjected to the accused's criminal behaviour (per Lord Morris of Borth-y-Gest in the passage from *DPP* v *Merriman* [1973] AC 584, quoted in **D9.16** and see *Wilson* (1979) 69 Cr App R 83 for an example of a conviction on such a count being upheld). Provided there is nothing on the face of the count to indicate to the contrary, it will be presumed that, even if a separate criminal act is being alleged in respect of each item, those acts were so closely related as to form part of a single activity and are therefore properly charged in a single count. *Ex hypothesi*, if only one act is being alleged, albeit that the act was in respect of several items, a single count is prima facie appropriate (e.g., *Thomas* (1800) 2 East PC 934, in which a count for uttering a number of forged receipts in one bundle was upheld). But the special circumstances of a case may make separate counts for each item necessary or desirable even if what is alleged against the accused is a single act or activity (see *Bristol Crown Court, ex parte Willets* (1985) 149 JP 416, in which the Divisional Court upheld W's conviction on an information that he, on a certain day, had in his possession for publication for gain a number of obscene articles, namely, five video tapes, but said that in an indictment it would have been better to have had five separate counts – that would have allowed the jury to find, for example, that one article was obscene but the remainder not, without the necessity for bringing in a special verdict; see also *Malhi* [1994] Crim LR 755).

D9.19 **Several Victims** Old cases provide examples of a single count naming more than one person as the victim of the offence. Thus, in *Giddins* (1842) Car & M 634, a count for robbing A of one shilling and B of two shillings was held valid, since the prosecution case was that the two acts of robbery had been virtually simultaneous. Modern practice, however, is in general to have a separate count per victim (see, e.g., *Mansfield* [1977] 1 WLR 1102, in which M was charged, *inter alia*, with seven counts of murder, a different victim being named in each count, even though all seven deaths resulted from a single fire allegedly started by M). Even so, what is appropriate must depend ultimately on the facts of each case. In *Shillingford* [1968] 1 WLR 566 the Court of Appeal quashed S's conviction under s. 4(1) of the Sexual Offences Act 1956 for administering a drug to Miss X with intent to stupefy her so as to enable V to have unlawful sexual intercourse with her because he had also been convicted on the same indictment for administering the drug so that he himself could have intercourse with Miss X. According to Salmon LJ: ' . . . the essence of this offence consists in administering the drug, and . . . accordingly in this particular case there was only one offence under the section. . . . In the view of this court, if there is only one administration there is only one offence, whether the administration was for the purpose of enabling one man or half a dozen men to have intercourse with the woman in question.' Similarly, in *Jemmison* v *Priddle* [1972] 1 QB 489, an information for taking and killing two red deer was held not to be bad for duplicity because the deer were shot within seconds of each other. In that case, however, there certainly could not have been any objection to two informations (cf. *Shillingford*), and it is submitted that the prosecution are, in general, wise to avoid possible complications by always having separate counts or informations if there is any doubt as to the validity of a single one.

'Quasi-duplicity'

D9.20 The foregoing discussion of the rule against duplicity has distinguished between a prosecution case to the effect that the accused committed a number of distinct offences, which must always be put in separate counts, and an allegation merely that he committed a number of distinct criminal acts which, since they formed part of one activity or transaction, can properly go into a single count. The distinction was mentioned by both Lord Morris of Borth-y-Gest and Lord Diplock in their opinions in *DPP* v *Merriman* [1973] AC 584 (quoted at **D9.16**), but the leading authority is the Court of Appeal decision in *Wilson* (1979) 69 Cr App R 83, which incorporates the essential parts of Lord Widgery CJ's judgment in *Jemmison* v *Priddle* [1972] 1 QB 489.

In *Wilson* the indictment against W contained counts for (a) theft, on 10 August 1977, from Debenhams of three jumpers, a pair of shorts, two pairs of trousers, four dimmer switches and a casette tape, and (b) theft, on the same day, from Boots of eight records and a bottle of after-shave. At the close of the prosecution case, the defence submitted that the evidence called (if accepted) proved that the items stolen had come from different departments of the stores in question. Therefore the counts were bad for duplicity and should be split so as to have a separate count for the items allegedly stolen from each department (or, possibly, a separate count for each item). The submission was rejected by the trial judge. On appeal, Browne LJ (giving the judgment of the court) distinguished between duplicity in the full sense of the term and what he described as quasi-duplicity or divergence. He said (at p. 85):

> The word duplicity is used in a rather ambiguous sense. . . . First there is a case where it appears on the face of the indictment, or particulars of the indictment, that a count is charging more than one offence. It may sometimes be legitimate to look at the depositions in this context (see *Greenfield* [1973] 1 WLR 1151). That has been referred to in the course of the argument as true duplicity. Secondly, there is a case where, although the indictment is good on its face, it appears at the close of the prosecution case that the evidence establishes that more than one offence was committed on the occasion to which a particular count relates. Perhaps that is best described as divergence or departure, but it often seems to be called duplicity. . . . in whatever sense one uses the word duplicity, it is confined to those two situations. But even if a case is not within either the first or the second of those situations, there may be cases where, in the interests of justice, it may be right to make the prosecution split a count or elect on what particular charge they are going to proceed.

In *Wilson* it was argued that the appellant's case fell within the second of Browne LJ's two situations (i.e. it was a case of divergence or departure rather than true duplicity). Having reviewed the authorities (especially *Jemmison* v *Priddle* [1972] 1 QB 489), Browne LJ adopted what Lord Widgery CJ had said in *Jemmison* v *Priddle* as correctly stating the law ((1979) 69 Cr App R 83 at pp. 86–7):

> Lord Widgery CJ said this . . . 'What is the principle which distinguishes between [cases where one count is appropriate and cases where there should be several counts]? . . . one finds that the explanation is given in somewhat inappropriate language, namely, that the test is whether the acts were all one transaction. That is a phrase hallowed by time, but not, in my judgment, of particular assistance in dealing with a particular problem. I find more assistance from somewhat different language used by Lord Parker CJ in *Ware* v *Fox* [1967] 1 WLR 379.' Then Lord Widgery CJ quotes from what Lord Parker CJ had said at p. 381 . . . and went on: 'I think perhaps that the phraseology of Lord Parker is more helpful to me than the phraseology often found in the text books, and I think that what it means is this, that it is legitimate to charge in a single information one activity even though the activity may involve more than one act. One looks at this case [i.e., *Jemmison* v *Priddle*] and asks oneself what was the activity with which the appellant was being charged. It was the activity of shooting red deer without a game licence, and although as a nice debating point it might well be contended that each shot was a separate act, indeed that each killing was a separate offence, I find that all these matters, occurring as they must have done within a very few seconds of time and all in the same geographical location are fairly to be described as components of a single activity, and that made it proper for the prosecution in this instance to join them in a single charge.'

Browne LJ concluded that: 'Whether there is one or more offence disclosed is really a question of fact and degree' ((1979) 69 Cr App R 83 at p. 88). On the facts of *Wilson*, the appellant 'entirely failed to satisfy' the court that the counts complained of disclosed more than one offence.

Thus, the principle emerging from *Wilson* and the earlier cases is simply that more than one criminal act may properly be alleged in one count if the acts formed a single activity. Whether there was one activity or several depends on the facts of each individual case, which means that any further quoting of authority would be of limited value.

Count Alleging Acts or Omissions in the Alternative

D9.21   **Indictment Rules 1971, r. 7**

> Where an offence created by or under an enactment states the offence to be the doing or the omission to do any one of any different acts in the alternative, or the doing or the omission to do any act in any one of any different capacities, or with any one of any different intentions, or states any part of the offence in the alternative, the acts, omissions, capacities or intentions, or other matters stated in the alternative in the enactment or subordinate instrument may be stated in the alternative in an indictment charging the offence.

It follows from r. 7 that a count containing particulars framed in the alternative is not necessarily bad for duplicity. However, the rule only applies in the circumstances delimited by its opening phrase. The use of the singular ('Where *an* offence . . . ') shows that if, on its true construction, an enactment creates several offences and it is desired to charge two or more of those offences in the alternative, the indictment must contain a separate count for each. Furthermore, it is plain that a single section, subsection or paragraph of a statute may be construed as creating more than one offence (see, e.g., *Naismith* [1961] 1 WLR 952 where it was held that s. 18 of the OAPA 1861, as it then stood (it has since been amended), created three separate offences of wounding, shooting or causing grievous bodily harm to a person, each of which could be committed with any of the intents specified in the section, namely, to do grievous bodily harm, to maim, disfigure or disable, or to prevent or resist arrest). The application of r. 7 therefore depends on a correct assessment of whether a statutory provision is creating one offence that may be committed in a number of alternative ways, or is creating several separate offences. If the former, r. 7 authorises the alleging of the statutory alternatives as alternatives in one count; if the latter, the rule against duplicity applies and each alternative the prosecution wish to put before the jury must go into a separate count.

Notwithstanding that r. 7 expressly contemplates a single count alleging acts or omissions in the alternative, the decisions on whether an enactment creates one or several offences have consistently turned on whether, in defining the conduct prohibited, the enactment refers to a single act (or omission) or to several. If one act is referred to, the enactment will almost certainly be construed as creating one offence, even if the *mens rea* or other elements thereof are defined in the alternative; if more than one, it will be held that the enactment creates a separate offence for each separate act. Thus, in *Naismith*, Ashworth J, giving the judgment of the Courts-Martial Appeal Court on whether an allegation under military law that N had 'caused grievous bodily harm to H with intent to do him grievous bodily harm or to maim, disfigure or disable him' was bad for duplicity, said (at p. 954):

> It seems to this court that the proposition with which [counsel for the Crown] started his argument is the right approach. That approach is to keep in mind the distinction between a section creating two or more offences and a section creating one offence but providing that that offence may be committed in more than one way. . . . so far as the intents specified in section 18 are concerned, they are variations of method rather than creations of separate offences in themselves. It is probably true to say that the species of assault mentioned in that section, of which there are three, are each in themselves different offences, that is to say, wounding, causing grievous bodily harm and shooting, but that difference does not affect the result of this case in the least because the only act or species of assault alleged was causing grievous bodily harm.

His lordship then held that a count in the same terms as the charge preferred against N under military law would have been valid by reason of the then equivalent of r. 7 of the Indictment Rules 1971.

Similarly, it was held in *Thomson* v *Knights* [1947] KB 336 that a count for being in charge of a motor vehicle when unfit through drink or drugs contrary to what is now s. 4 of the Road Traffic Act 1988 was valid because the section (as then drafted) was to be construed as prohibiting three acts (driving, attempting to drive or being in charge of a motor vehicle when incapable of having proper control of it), each prohibited course of conduct being criminal if committed in either of two ways (namely, when under the influence of drink or when under the influence of drugs). In other words, the section created three offences (one per act), not six, and the count complained of was accordingly not bad for duplicity. By contrast, in *Mallon* v *Allon* [1964] 1 QB 385 an information for admitting and allowing to remain in a licensed betting office a person apparently under 18 contrary to s. 5 of the Betting and Gaming Act 1960 (now Betting, Gaming and Lotteries Act 1963, sch. 4, para. 2) was held bad because the enactment referred to two separate acts, first of all admitting a person on to licensed premises, and secondly allowing him to remain after he had got on to the premises. The prosecution construction of the section (that there was only one offence, namely, failing to prevent an apparently under-age person being on the premises) was rejected.

Comparison of *Mallon* v *Allon* with *Thomson* v *Knights* indicates that the number of offences an enactment is held to create, whether one or several, turns on fine analysis of the enactment in question and also, no doubt, on pragmatic considerations ofn whether one or several counts or informations would make for a fairer disposal of alleged contraventions of the enactment. Further discussion of the cases is not given here, but decisions relevant to particular offences will be found in the sections dealing with them (see, for example, **B4.128** and **B4.136**, and *Nicklin* [1977] 1 WLR 403, on the number of counts appropriate when the accused is charged with handling stolen goods.

Charging Offences Conjunctively in an Effort to Avoid the Rule against Duplicity

It has so far been assumed that the rule against duplicity will apply whether separate **D9.22** offences are alleged in one count as alternatives or conjunctively. That assumption is in line with the overwhelming weight of authority. However, there is one decision apparently to the contrary, namely *Clow* [1965] 1 QB 598. In that case, the particulars of the count against C alleged that he had caused the death of the victim by 'driving at a speed *and* in a manner dangerous to the public' contrary to s. 1(1) of the Road Traffic Act 1960. Previous authority had held that the subsection created three separate offences of (a) causing death by reckless driving, (b) causing death by driving at a speed dangerous to the public, and (c) causing death by driving dangerously. To allege any combination of those offences in the alternative in a single count would have contravened the rule against duplicity. But the Court of Criminal Appeal, perhaps constrained by earlier authority, held that, 'it is permissible to charge them [i.e. the separate offences under s. 1(1)] conjunctively as in the present case if the matter relates to one single incident, as of course it does in the present case'.

The decision in *Clow* is, however, open to the gravest question since, if applied generally, it would allow the prosecution to circumvent the rule against duplicity simply by using the word 'and' in a count rather than 'or'. It would, for example, allow an accused to be charged with murder and arson in a single count if the prosecution case were that he had caused a death through lighting a fire. In practice, however, that course is simply not followed (see *Mansfield* [1977] 1 WLR 1102 where the prosecution, in just such a case, had separate counts for murder and arson). *Clow* was distinguished in *Mallon* v *Allon* [1964] 1 QB 385 (see **D9.21**) – information under s. 5 of the Betting and Gaming Act

1960 for allowing an under-age person to 'enter *and* remain upon licensed premises' held invalid, despite the use of the conjunctive rather than the disjunctive). Furthermore, the replacement of the offences in s. 1(1) of the Road Traffic Act 1960 with a single offence under s. 1 of the Road Traffic Act 1988 means that, as regards the actual point it decided, *Clow* is no longer significant. That being so, it is submitted that the case should no longer be regarded as authority for its suggestion that a count alleging offences cumulatively may be valid even though a count alleging the same offences in the alternative would be bad for duplicity. The same rule should apply whether a count is framed conjunctively or disjunctively.

Effect of Breaching of the Rule against Duplicity

D9.23 Where a count is bad on its face for duplicity, the defence should move to quash it before the accused is arraigned. Although the objection can be taken at a later stage (*Johnson* [1945] KB 419), the Court of Appeal has disapproved of the defence postponing the application to quash for purely tactical reasons (see *Asif* (1982) 82 Cr App R 123). It is open to the prosecution to defeat a motion to quash by asking the judge to allow a suitable amendment of the indictment (e.g., splitting a single count into two – see Indictments Act 1915, s. 5(1), for the power to amend indictments).

The procedure of applying to quash a count will be available only if it is a case of 'true' duplicity, that is, the wording of the count, without reference to the evidence, shows that two or more offences are being alleged. In a case of quasi-duplicity or divergence (see *Wilson* (1979) 69 Cr App R 83 and **D9.20** for the distinction between true and quasi-duplicity), a motion to quash is inappropriate, since the motion has to be determined solely by considering the wording of the indictment and, by its nature, quasi-duplicity becomes apparent only after the evidence has been called. Therefore, it is submitted that, in cases of quasi-duplicity, the defence should wait until the close of the prosecution case and then ask the judge to split the count on the basis that, in the light of the evidence, the criminal conduct alleged against the accused comprises separate activities which should have been charged in separate counts.

Rejection by the trial judge of a motion to quash a count bad on its face for duplicity and/or rejection of an application to split a count open to objection for quasi-duplicity are plainly valid grounds of appeal. However, even in a case of uncorrected true duplicity, the Court of Appeal may uphold the conviction if it is safe (see *Thompson* [1914] 2 KB 99). In *Donnelly* [1998] Crim LR 131, the Court of Appeal made it clear that cases of true duplicity and quasi-duplicity would be differently treated upon appeal. In a case where the count was plainly duplicitous in form, even if the point had not been taken at trial, the appeal must be allowed. Where the count was not duplicitous in form, and any duplicity could only be discovered by examining the evidence or by requiring particulars before trial, a motion to quash the indictment should be moved before the trial judge. If it was not, the appeal would fail unless it was accompanied by an allegation of incompetence by counsel.

JOINDER OF COUNTS IN INDICTMENT

D9.24 The circumstances in which the prosecution may lawfully join two or more counts against one accused in a single indictment are prescribed by r. 9 of the Indictment Rules 1971.

Indictment Rules 1971, r. 9

> Charges for any offences may be joined in the same indictment if those charges are founded on the same facts, or form or are a part of a series of offences of the same or a similar character.

An indictment containing counts which are not linked in either of the ways mentioned in r. 9 is invalid (although not a nullity), and any convictions returned on such an indictment are liable to be quashed on appeal. In *Newland* [1988] QB 402, N was charged in an indictment containing counts for (a) possessing a Class B drug with intent to supply, and (b) three assaults occasioning actual bodily harm. The prosecution case on the drugs matter was that, when police searched N's home on 28 November 1986, they found enough cannabis to make 600 reefers plus pipes, scales and other items usually found at the premises of drugs dealers. As to the assaults, they had occurred on 18 December 1986 when N involved himself in a disturbance to which the police had been called, was arrested for obstructing the police, and inflicted minor injuries on officers while being arrested. It will be apparent that the drugs offence and the assault offences were entirely unconnected. In including them all in one indictment, the drafter had overlooked the provisions of r. 9. At trial, counsel for N submitted and counsel for the prosecution conceded that the indictment was invalid. However, contrary to N's counsel's arguments, the judge held that he had power under s. 5(3) of the Indictments Act 1915 (see **D9.27**) to sever the indictment. Thereupon, N entered pleas of guilty to all counts on what had become two indictments, and was sentenced to a total of 21 months' imprisonment.

On appeal, the Court of Appeal held that:

(a)   The power to sever under s. 5(3) applies only to a valid indictment. Watkins LJ, giving the court's judgment, said (at p. 406C–D):

> It was contended by counsel for the prosecution that the [trial judge] rightly derived the power he used from [Indictments Act 1915, s. 5(3)]. But we are in no doubt, in accepting the contrary submission of counsel for the appellant, that that subsection can only apply to a valid indictment. It states what the court may do by way of ordering separate trials of counts in a valid indictment in the interests of a fair trial for a defendant or defendants. The [trial judge] was wrong in his interpretation of that subsection.

(b)   The trial judge could have amended the indictment so as to delete either the drugs count or the assault counts. That having been done, the trial could validly have proceeded on what remained (p. 406F). (See also *Follett* [1989] QB 338.)

(c)   Given that no amendment had in fact been made, the court had to decide the status of the unamended indictment. It was invalid by reason of the contravention of r. 9. Because it was capable of being rendered valid by an appropriate amendment, it was not a nullity (p. 408C–D applying *Bell* (1984) 78 Cr App R 305). But, even though the indictment itself was not a nullity, the fact of its being invalid was sufficient to render null the proceedings flowing from it – i.e. the pleas of guilty, convictions and sentence were nullities (p. 408E). In the circumstances, no valid trial ever commenced and the court's powers under the Criminal Appeal Act 1968, s. 2(1), to quash a conviction and sentence therefore did not come into play. The only power by which the court could quash the convictions was its inherent power at common law. Having concluded that the proceedings against N were null, the court had no option but to exercise that power. The court did consider whether to exercise its power to order a retrial but decided in its discretion not to do so (p. 408G–H).

In *Smith* [1997] QB 837, the Court of Appeal disapproved of *Newland* insofar as it related to the effect of misjoinder, as outlined in (c) above. Their lordships held that it was wrong to suggest that all proceedings flowing from an indictment containing a count improperly joined were a nullity (as opposed to the proceedings on the improperly joined count). *Smith* was approved and followed in *Lockley* [1997] Crim LR 455.

Charges Founded on the Same Facts

The first limb of r. 9 of the Indictment Rules 1971 is clearly satisfied if the offences alleged   **D9.25** in counts joined in one indictment arose out of a single incident or an uninterrupted course of conduct (see, e.g., *Mansfield* [1977] 1 WLR 1102 where the indictment against M contained counts for, *inter alia*, arson and seven murders, the deaths being caused by a fire at a hotel which M had allegedly started – on appeal it was unsuccessfully contended that the judge had erred in refusing to grant an application for separate trials in relation to two further counts for arson at a different hotel, but there was no dispute about the propriety of joining the murder counts with the first-mentioned arson count since all eight offences were clearly founded on the same facts).

Rule 9 is not, however, restricted to offences that were committed contemporaneously or substantially contemporaneously with each other, as in *Mansfield*, but extends to situations where later offences would not have been committed but for the prior commission of an earlier offence. The leading authority is *Barrell* (1979) 69 Cr App R 250, where the appellants were charged jointly in counts 1 and 2 with affray and assault occasioning actual bodily harm, and W alone was charged in count 3 with attempting to pervert the course of justice. The prosecution case on the first two counts was that the appellants, on being refused entry to a discotheque, had attacked the manager and an attendant. As to the third count, it was alleged that, about two months later, W visited the discotheque and offered the manager money to 'modify' his evidence. Following the conviction of both appellants, it was argued on appeal that count 3, 'far from being founded on the same facts as count 1, derived from a new and different set of facts which was not only different in its nature but separated by a substantial interval of time from the set of facts which gave rise to counts 1 and 2. [Counsel] contended that to justify a joinder within the terms of section 4 and rule 9 the subsidiary offence must (to use counsel's terminology) be an integral part of the primary offences and must not be separated from them by any distance in time.' The argument was rejected by the Court of Appeal. Shaw LJ, giving the judgment of the court, said (at pp. 252–3):

> The phrase 'founded on the same facts' does not mean that for charges to be properly joined in the same indictment, the facts in relation to the respective charges must be identical in substance or virtually contemporaneous. The test is whether the charges have a common factual origin. If the charge described by counsel as the subsidiary charge is one that could not have been alleged but for the facts which give rise to what he called the primary charge, then it is true to say for the purposes of rule 9 that those charges are founded, that is to say have their origin, in the same facts and can legitimately be joined in the same indictment.

If W had not been involved in the violence at the discotheque which gave rise to the charges of assault and affray, he would have had no motive for offering the manager of the discotheque a bribe. It followed that all three counts had a common factual origin and were properly joined in one indictment.

Difficulty has arisen over whether the principle in *Barrell* can properly be extended to counts that are mutually destructive, that is, the prosecution evidence is such that, if their case on one count is accepted, the accused cannot have committed the offence alleged in the other count and vice versa. The House of Lords settled the point in *Bellman* [1989] AC 836, in which it was alleged that B and another had obtained sums of money from various individuals by representing that the money was to be used to import controlled drugs into the UK, thus making large profits for all concerned. The primary case for the prosecution was that the representations were false (i.e. B never intended to import drugs) and he had therefore obtained the money by deception. Alternatively, it was alleged that, if the representations were true, he was guilty of conspiracy to evade the prohibition on the importation of controlled drugs. The indictment contained counts both for conspiracy and for obtaining by deception. The trial judge directed the jury to consider, first, whether the plan to import drugs had been genuine (in which case they would convict of conspiracy). They should go on to consider the deception counts only if they had first decided to acquit of conspiracy. In the event, the jury found B guilty of obtaining by deception. The Court of Appeal quashed the convictions on the ground that, at the end of their case, the prosecution should have been required to elect between the conspiracy counts and the deception counts. In the

House of Lords, it was conceded that that ground of appeal was incorrect since, if the prosecution have put before the jury evidence which is capable of sustaining a conviction on any one of alternative counts, it is for the jury (not the judge and still less the prosecution) to evaluate the evidence and determine which, if any, of the alternatives are in fact proved (see p. 846F–G). Counsel for B therefore relied 'upon the more fundamental proposition that under our adversarial procedure of trial in which the burden of establishing the guilt of the accused is placed on the prosecution, it can never be right for mutually contradictory counts to be contained in one indictment. He submitted that to do so would be contrary to the prosecution's duty of proving the case, unfair to the accused and an embarrassment for the jury' (pp. 846H–847A).

Lord Griffiths rejected the argument. There was nothing in the Indictments Act 1915 to support it; r. 9 of the Indictment Rules 1971 prima facie contradicted it, and counsel for B could cite no authority in which joinder had been refused on the ground that the facts of two counts were mutually destructive (p. 849B–D). On the other hand, it had long been the practice to include in one indictment counts for stealing and handling the same property even though a conviction for theft would necessarily preclude a conviction for handling and vice versa (see *Shelton* (1986) 83 Cr App R 379 for recent approval of the practice).

Moreover, there will be occasions when justice can be done only by drafting mutually contradictory counts. An example is provided by the facts of *Barnes* (1985) 83 Cr App R 38 where the indictment contained counts for perjury and wounding with intent, the case being that Barnes – who had given evidence at his brother's earlier trial for the same wounding that he (Barnes) had committed the offence, not the brother – was either telling the truth at the brother's trial and so was guilty of wounding, or he was telling lies, in which case he was guilty of perjury. The Court of Appeal dismissed the appeal on the ground that, whether or not the joinder of the mutually destructive counts was lawful, there had on the facts been no miscarriage of justice. In *Bellman*, Lord Griffiths, *obiter*, confirmed the legality of the joinder because the factual origin of both counts was the attack on the victim (see p. 850F–G). Furthermore, the joinder was necessary in the interests of justice since, had Barnes been tried separately for the two offences, he might have 'played the system' by obtaining an acquittal for perjury through testifying that he had indeed wounded the victim and then, at his later trial for wounding, he could have reversed his evidence, secure in the knowledge that he could not be reprosecuted for perjury.

Although the decision in *Bellman* puts beyond doubt the propriety of joining mutually destructive counts in one indictment, it is submitted that, as a matter of practice, the prosecution will rarely wish to prefer such an indictment, since it leaves them open to the obvious defence argument that, if the prosecution cannot decide which offence the accused has committed, the jury cannot be sure either and must therefore acquit of both. As a matter of evidence, it is clear that if, at the end of the prosecution case, it is established that the accused has committed a crime but it is impossible to say which, the judge must direct the jury to acquit. Similarly, if, as in *Bellman* itself, there is evidence on which the jury could properly convict of either count, they must nonetheless be directed in the summing up that, should they be left in doubt about which of the two offences the accused has committed, they are under a duty to acquit of both, even though they are sure he committed one or other. The various evidential problems that may arise from mutually destructive counts are discussed by Lord Griffiths in *Bellman* at p. 847. See further **D13.29**.

Series of Offences of the Same or a Similar Character

The circumstances in which two or more offences may be said to amount to a series of **D9.26** offences of the same or similar character within the meaning of the second limb of r. 9 of the Indictment Rules 1971 were considered by the House of Lords in *Ludlow* v

Metropolitan Police Commissioner [1971] AC 29. The indictment against L contained counts for (a) attempted theft on 20 August 1968 and (b) robbery on 5 September 1968. The prosecution case on count 1 was that L was seen emerging from the window of the staff room of a public house in Acton, and there was evidence that he had been attempting to steal. On count 2, it was alleged that, at a different public house in Acton, L had had an altercation with the barman about payment for drinks and, after initially handing over a note in payment, he punched the barman and snatched back the money. The trial judge refused an application that the two charges should be tried separately, and L was convicted on both counts.

The defence appealed unsuccessfully to the Court of Appeal and thence to the House of Lords, where Lord Pearson delivered the leading opinion with which the other Law Lords agreed. The main points emerging from this opinion are that:

(a)   Two offences are capable of constituting a 'series' for purposes of r. 9 (see p. 38E–G confirming the Court of Appeal decision in *Kray* [1970] 1 QB 125).

(b)   In deciding whether offences exhibit the similarity demanded by the rule, the court should take into account both their legal and their factual characteristics (p. 39B). The prosecution submission (that the phrase 'a similar character' means exclusively of a similar legal character) and the defence submission (that the phrase means exclusively of a similar factual character) were each rejected.

(c)   To show the existence of a series of offences, the prosecution must be able to point to some nexus between them. 'Nexus' is defined somewhat circularly as 'a feature of similarity which in all the circumstances of the case enables the offences to be described as a series' (p. 39D). If the offences are so connected that the evidence of one would be admissible to prove the commission of the other in accordance with the rules on similar-fact evidence, a nexus is clearly established, but r. 9 is not confined to such cases (p. 39D–F, quoting with approval from *Kray* and *Clayton-Wright* [1948] 2 All ER 763).

(d)   On the facts of *Ludlow*, the offences were similar in law in that they each had the ingredient of actual or attempted theft. They were also similar in fact because they involved stealing or attempting to steal in neighbouring public houses at a time interval of only 16 days. A sufficient nexus was therefore present to make the offences a series of a similar character within the meaning of r. 9, even though the similarity was not nearly striking enough to bring them within the similar-fact evidence rule (p. 39H).

Court of Appeal decisions on whether the degree of similarity between offences justified joinder under r. 9 of the Indictment Rules 1971 include:

Mansfield [1977] 1 WLR 1102 – three counts for arson properly included in one indictment since the offences were committed within a short space of time (on 12, 19 and 28 December 1974), and occurred at hotels in the West End of London with which the accused had a connection either because he worked at the hotel in question or because he stayed there in hotel accommodation.

Harward (1981) 73 Cr App R 168 – a count against H and co-defendants for conspiring to defraud banks by the use of stolen cheques and cheque cards wrongly joined with a second count against H alone for handling stolen goods. The goods (stereo equipment) were found at H's home when it was searched during the investigation of the bank fraud. The only possible nexus between the charges was the elements of dishonesty, but the dishonesty in the conspiracy count related to H's involvement in fraudulent practices, whereas that in the handling count related to his state of mind when he received the goods. In the absence of any factual similarity between the offences, the dishonesty element was insufficient to justify joinder. H's conviction for handling was quashed (the jury had already acquitted him of conspiracy).

McGlinchey (1983) 78 Cr App R 282 – two counts for handling stolen goods properly joined, the first being for receiving photographic equipment on 19 July 1982 and the second for receiving a credit card on or before 2 September of the same year. The only factual similarity between the offences seems to have been their closeness in time. (*McGlinchey* was applied in *Mariou* [1992] Crim LR 511.)

Marsh (1985) 83 Cr App R 165 – the indictment against M contained five counts, two pairs for criminal damage and reckless driving and a fifth for assault occasioning actual bodily harm. The allegation on the first four counts was that M had, on two separate occasions, deliberately or recklessly driven his car into his neighbour's car. The assault charge arose out of an argument with C following C's retraction of an alibi that he was originally prepared to provide for M in connection with a totally separate matter. The joinder was improper because (a) there was no legal similarity between criminal damage and reckless driving on the one hand and assault on the other, and (b) the common factual element of violence was insufficient by itself to provide a nexus. M's convictions were all quashed, but not solely on grounds of the misjoinder.

Baird [1993] Crim LR 778 – the indictment alleged two counts of indecent assault against boy A, and a count of indecent assault against boy B, which was alleged to have been committed nine years later. Although there was no coincidence in time or place, there were similarities in the offences against A and that against B which, their lordships said, 'were truly remarkable'. They concluded that the judge was entitled to hold that the various counts could properly be joined under r. 9, and was justified in refusing to exercise his discretion to sever under the Indictments Act 1915, s. 5(3) (see **D9.28**).

C (1993) *The Times*, 4 February 1993 – the accused was charged with rape and attempted rape. Although the counts were separated in time by 11 years, the victim in each case was the defendant's daughter. It was held that the counts were properly joined.

Williams [1993] Crim LR 533 – it was alleged that W had falsely imprisoned a girl of 13, and that he had indecently assaulted her five days earlier. He was convicted of false imprisonment and acquitted of indecent assault. He appealed against conviction, submitting that the counts had been wrongly joined. The Court of Appeal quashed the conviction on the basis that there were two separate incidents and the two offences were not of a similar character, despite an evidential nexus.

Discretion to Order Separate Trials

Indictments Act 1915, s. 5   **D9.27**

> (3)   Where, before trial, or at any stage of a trial, the court is of opinion that a person accused may be prejudiced or embarrassed in his defence by reason of being charged with more than one offence in the same indictment, or that for any other reason it is desirable to direct that the person should be tried separately for any one or more offences charged in an indictment, the court may order a separate trial of any count or counts of such indictment.

Section 5(3) is supplemented by:

(a)   s. 5(4), which requires the court, following an order for severance under s. 5(3), to make such order for postponement of the trial as appears necessary and expedient; and

(b)   s. 5(5), which provides that the procedure on the separate trial of a count following an order under s. 5(3) shall be the same in all respects as if the count had been preferred in a separate indictment.

The power to sever an indictment contained in s. 5(3) was held to apply only to valid indictments (*Newland* [1988] QB 402). However, the decisions of the Court of Appeal in *Smith* [1997] QB 837 and *Lockley* [1997] Crim LR 455 have altered the effect upon the indictment where a count has been improperly joined (see **D9.24**).

The proper exercise of the power had earlier been considered by Lord Pearson in his speech in *Ludlow* v *Metropolitan Police Commissioner* [1971] AC 29 (see also **D9.26**).

Having held that the joinder of the counts against L for attempted theft and robbery was lawful and within the terms of the Indictment Rules 1971, r. 9, his lordship dealt with the appellant's further argument that a single trial of the two offences inevitably prejudiced or embarrassed the accused in his defence since the jury heard evidence on count 1 that was inadmissible on count 2 and vice versa. Therefore, the trial judge should have ordered separate trials in exercise of the discretion given him by s. 5(3). In rejecting this argument Lord Pearson said (at pp. 40–2 emphasis added):

> Before the Indictments Act 1915, it was a tenable theory . . . to say that any joinder of counts relating to distinct alleged offences was necessarily so prejudicial to the accused that such joinder ought not to be permitted. [His lordship then reviewed pre-1915 cases lending support to the theory.]
>
> In my opinion, this theory – that a joinder of counts relating to different transactions is in itself so prejudicial to the accused that such a joinder should never be made – cannot be held to have survived the passing of the Indictments Act 1915. No doubt the juries of that time were much more literate and intelligent than the juries of the late 18th and 19th centuries, and could be relied upon in any ordinary case not to infer that, because the accused is proved to have committed one of the offences charged against him, therefore he must have committed the others as well. I think the experience of judges in modern times is that the verdicts of juries show them to have been careful and conscientious in considering each count separately. Also in most cases it would be oppressive to the accused, as well as expensive and inconvenient for the prosecution, to have two or more trials when one would suffice. *At any rate, . . . the manifest intention of the Act is that charges which either are founded on the same facts or relate to a series of offences of the same or a similar character properly can and normally should be joined in one indictment, and a joint trial of the charges will normally follow, although the judge has a discretionary power to direct separate trials under section 5(3).* If the theory were still correct, it would be the duty of the judge in the proper exercise of his discretion under section 5(3) to direct separate trials in every case where the accused was charged with a series of offences of the same or a similar character, and the manifest intention appearing from section 4 and [r. 9] would be defeated. *The judge has no duty to direct separate trials under section 5(3) unless in his opinion there is some special feature of the case which would make a joint trial of the several counts prejudicial or embarrassing to the accused and separate trials are required in the interests of justice.* In some cases the offences charged may be too numerous and complicated, . . . or too difficult to disentangle, . . . so that a joint trial of all the counts is likely to cause confusion and the defence may be embarrassed or prejudiced. In other cases objection may be taken to the inclusion of a count on the ground that it is of a scandalous nature and likely to arouse in the minds of the jury hostile feelings against the accused. . . . In the present case there was no multiplicity or complexity in the offences charged, and no difficulty for the learned commissioner in dealing separately with the two charges in his summing-up.

Thus, if counts for separate offences have validly been joined in one indictment, the normal consequence is that they will be tried together. The trial judge should exercise his discretion to order separate trials only if there is a special feature in the case which would make a single trial prejudicial or embarrassing. Two examples of such special features (number and/or complexity of the counts and scandalous nature of the evidence as to one of the counts) are given in the judgment, although the examples are no doubt not intended to be exhaustive.

An application to sever the indictment might be renewed on a later occasion. Sometimes the second application will be before the same judge. It might, however, be before a different judge on the second occasion – for example, where the first application was made at a pre-trial review (see **D12.14**). In *Wright* (1989) 90 Cr App R 325, Judge G at the pre-trial review refused to sever a conspiracy count from an indictment which also contained a series of counts relating to substantive offences of buggery and gross indecency. Before the trial itself began, defence counsel applied again to sever, this time before Judge C. Judge C rejected the submission on the ground that the matter had been concluded by Judge G. The Court of Appeal held that this was a material irregularity. The original ruling by Judge G was unassailable. Judge C, however, should have considered whether there had been a sufficient change to justify reopening the question. If there had not, he was not obliged to hear the same point argued again. Here he had simply regarded the matter as concluded by the previous ruling of Judge G. That was a material irregularity which, taken with others which occurred during the trial, led to the convictions being quashed.

As to the overloading of indictments with too many counts and hence undue complexity, see **D9.33**. As to the difficulty a jury might have in disentangling evidence on one count from that on the other count or counts, special considerations govern the trial of counts for sexual offences (see **D9.28**). The fact that the accused wishes to give evidence in his own defence on one of the counts but not on the others is not, in the normal case, a sufficient reason for severance, even though non-severance will oblige him to choose between not testifying at all and exposing himself to cross-examination about all the charges (*Phillips* (1987) 86 Cr App R 18). See also *Lanford* v *General Medical Council* [1990] 1 AC 13.

Severance of Multi-count Indictments for Sexual Offences In *DPP* v *Boardman* **D9.28** [1975] AC 421, the indictment contained counts that B, the headmaster of a boarding-school, had (a) committed buggery on S, a 16-year-old pupil, and (b) had incited H, a 17-year-old pupil, to commit buggery on him. The primary question for the House of Lords was whether the trial judge correctly directed the jury that the evidence of S on the count concerning him was admissible as corroborative evidence in relation to the count concerning H and vice versa. *Obiter*, Lord Cross of Chelsea stated that questions of the admissibility of similar-fact evidence in such cases ought to be decided in the absence of the jury as a preliminary issue, and, 'if it is decided that the evidence is inadmissible and the accused is being charged in the same indictment with offences against the other men the charges relating to the different persons ought to be tried separately' (p. 459D). That was because, however scrupulously the judge might direct the jury to ignore the allegations made by B and C when considering whether the accused committed a roughly similar offence against A, '. . . it is asking too much of any jury to tell them to perform mental gymnastics of this sort. If the charges are tried together it is inevitable that the jurors will be influenced, consciously or unconsciously, by the fact that the accused is being charged not with a single offence against one person but with three separate offences against three persons.' Further, even where the respective offences bear such a striking similarity to each other that the evidence as to each would be mutually corroborative, the judge should consider – again as a preliminary issue – whether there is material in the committal statements suggesting that the 'victims' colluded together to tell false stories. If there is a real danger that that happened, separate trials should be ordered, but the judge should not use his imagination to invent a conspiracy to make false allegations where there is no evidence in the statements that such a conspiracy existed (see especially *Johannsen* (1977) 65 Cr App R 101 – the mere fact that four out of the five boys named as victims of homosexual offences by J knew each other gave rise to no more than a speculative possibility that they had put their heads together to tell lies, and there was accordingly no need to direct severance of the counts).

In deciding to refuse or, as the case may be, order severance, the judge is not taking a final decision on the admissibility of each incident alleged in the indictment as similar-fact evidence to prove the others. Should he refuse severance, it will still fall to him, during the course of the trial, to rule whether the evidence of one victim corroborates that of the other victims. If the judge decides, contrary to the provisional view he took at the application for severance, that each victim's evidence is relevant only to the offence against him, then he could allow the trial to continue and direct the jury accordingly in his summing-up, but it is submitted that the better course of action would be to discharge the jury and direct severance at that stage. Conversely, if the judge initially ordered severance, the prosecution could still ask to be allowed to lead evidence of the other incidents in support of whichever incident the jury is trying, although it is most improbable that the judge, in such a case, would be converted from his provisional view that the offences should be considered quite independently. Detailed guidance from Scarman LJ on how trial judges should approach applications for severance and problems of similar-fact evidence in multi-count sexual cases will be found in *Scarrott* [1978] 1 QB 1016 at pp. 1027–8.

The arguments that Lord Cross used in *DPP* v *Boardman* to justify his dictum that, in cases involving sexual offences, the indictment should be severed if the evidence of one victim could not be used as corroboration of the evidence of the other victims, might be thought to apply with equal force whatever the nature of the offence charged. However, the Court of Appeal in subsequent cases has refused to extend the principles stated in *Boardman* and *Scarrott* beyond multi-count indictments for sexual offences. Where there is a multi-count indictment for some other type of offence, the principles in *Ludlow* v *Metropolitan Police Commissioner* [1971] AC 29 apply (see **D9.26**), and the judge should order separate trials only if there is a special feature in the case likely to cause the defence prejudice or embarrassment (see especially *McGlinchey* (1984) 74 Cr App R 282 where, having held that two counts for handling stolen goods on dates approximately six weeks apart were properly joined in one indictment even though there was manifestly no striking similarity between the offences, the Court of Appeal went on approve the judge's exercise of discretion against severance – *Ludlow* applied and *Boardman* distinguished).

More recently, in *Cannan* (1991) 92 Cr App R 16, the Court of Appeal made it clear that, even where an indictment charged a series of sexual offences, the judge had a discretion whether to sever. This was so even though there was no striking similarity between the evidence on the various counts. C was charged, *inter alia*, with the abduction, rape and buggery of H, the attempted kidnapping of J and the abduction and murder of S. The trial judge found that the three sets of offences were evidentially separate, but declined to sever the indictment. C was convicted on all six counts. On appeal, it was argued on his behalf that the judge should have followed 'the general modern practice in sexual cases', and severed the counts in the absence of striking similarity. The Court of Appeal dismissed the appeal and held that the discretion had been properly exercised. Lord Lane CJ said (at p. 23):

> It may well be that often the judge in sexual cases will order severance . . . But the fact remains that the Indictments Act 1915 gives the judge a discretion, and . . . that is not a matter with which this Court will interfere, unless it is shown that the judge has failed to exercise his discretion upon the usual and proper principles . . .'

In the case of *DPP* v *P* [1991] 2 AC 447, the central issue dealt with by the House of Lords was that of similar fact evidence, and particularly whether the evidence of one victim of a sexual offence was admissible to support the allegation of another in the absence of 'striking similarity' between them (see **F12.6** and **F12.12** for the facts and a discussion of the case). In Lord Mackay's speech, however, he does make the following comment about a second issue, which was whether, in the absence of striking similarity, there should have been joinder:

> I would answer the first question posed by the Court of Appeal by saying that the evidence referred to is admissible if the similarity is sufficiently strong, or there is other sufficient relationship between the events described in the evidence of the other young children of the family and the abuse charged that the evidence if accepted, would so strongly support the truth of that charge that it is fair to admit it notwithstanding its prejudicial effect. It follows that the answer to the second question is no, provided there is a relationship between the offences of a kind which I have just described.

On one interpretation, this could be taken to mean that the rule on joinder in cases of multiple sexual offences is the same as for admissibility (i.e. that they should constitute similar fact evidence). In *Christou* [1997] AC 117, however, the House of Lords considered the words used by Lord Mackay, and stated that they were *obiter*. The approach to the question of severance in *Cannan* was endorsed. The trial judge had a discretion, with which the appellate courts should not interfere except on grounds of *Wednesbury* unreasonableness. In exercising his discretion, the essential task of the trial judge was to achieve a fair resolution of the issues. That required fairness to the accused but also to the prosecution and those involved in it. Among the factors which he might consider were: how discrete or inter-related were the facts giving rise to the counts; the impact of ordering two or more trials on the defendant and his family, on the victims and their families and on press publicity; and, importantly, whether directions the judge could give to the jury would suffice to secure a fair trial if the counts were tried together. (See also *Dixon* (1991) 92 Cr App R 43 and *F* [1996] Crim LR 257.)

Indictments Act 1915, s. 5

(4)   Where, before trial, or at any stage of a trial, the court is of opinion that the postponement of the trial of a person accused is expedient as a consequence of the exercise of any power of the court under this Act to amend an indictment or to order a separate trial of a count, the court shall make such order as to the postponement of the trial as appears necessary.

(5)   Where an order of the court is made under this section for the postponement of a trial—

(a)   if such an order is made during a trial the court may order that the jury are to be discharged from giving a verdict on the count or counts the trial of which is postponed or on the indictment, as the case may be; and

(b)   the procedure on the separate trial of a count shall be the same in all respects as if the count had been found in a separate indictment, and the procedure on the postponed trial shall be the same in all respects (if the jury has been discharged) as if the trial had not commenced; and

(c)   the court may make such order as to granting the accused person bail and as to the enlargement of recognisances and otherwise as the court thinks fit.

JOINDER OF ACCUSED

Introduction

Two or more accused may be joined in one indictment either as a result of being named **D9.29** together in one or more counts on the indictment, or as a result of being named individually in separate counts, albeit that there is no single count against them all.

Joint Counts

All parties to a joint offence may be indicted for it in a single count. In drafting the count **D9.30** there is no need to distinguish between principal offenders and secondary parties (Accessories and Abettors Act 1861, s. 8; see **D9.12**). Nor need the count expressly allege that the unlawful acts of each accused were done in aid of the others – that allegation is implicit in the drafting of a single count (see *DPP* v *Merriman* [1973] AC 584 per Lord Diplock at p. 607C). However, notwithstanding that the accused have been charged in a single count, the jury may convict all or any of them on the basis that they committed the offence charged independently of the others (see *DPP* v *Merriman*, in which two brothers were charged in a joint count with wounding with intent and one pleaded guilty and the other not guilty – the latter's conviction was upheld even though the judge directed the jury to ignore any possibility that he had acted in concert with his brother). Lord Diplock said (at p. 607F):

. . . whenever two or more defendants are charged in the same count of an indictment with any offence which men can help one another to commit it is sufficient to support a conviction against any and each of them to prove *either* that he himself did a physical act which is an essential ingredient of the offence charged *or* that he helped another to do such an act, *and,* that in doing the act or in helping the other defendant to do it, he himself had the necessary criminal intent.

In short, if two accused, A1 and A2, are charged in a joint count the jury may (a) acquit both, or (b) convict both, or (c) acquit one and convict the other. Should they convict both it will usually be on the basis implicit in the joint count that they helped each other to commit the crime, but, if the evidence suggests that the two acted independently of each other and there was no joint enterprise, the jury ought still to convict provided they are satisfied that each accused committed the full *actus reus* with the necessary mental element. Similarly, if there is a split verdict, the verdict against the convicted accused is not open to challenge on the ground that the jury must have found that he acted alone without assistance either from his acquitted co-accused or anybody else. The argument that to uphold convictions on a single count in the absence of proof of joint enterprise contravenes the rule against duplicity was rejected in *Merriman.* However, it is submitted that, despite the convenient decision in *Merriman,* the prosecution ought not to draft a joint count unless their evidence indeed points towards a joint enterprise on the part of the accused – if the case is that A1 and A2 were acting without reference to each other separate counts against them are preferable, albeit that the counts will be identically worded but for the names of the accused.

Separate Counts

D9.31 The joining of two or more accused in one indictment notwithstanding the absence of a joint count against them is governed by the decision in *Assim* [1966] 2 QB 249. In that case, the indictment against A and his co-accused (C) contained two counts, the first alleging that A, on 29 October 1965, had maliciously wounded W contrary to s. 20 of the OAPA 1861, and the second alleging that C, on the same day, had assaulted L occasioning him actual bodily harm contrary to s. 47 of the 1861 Act. The prosecution case was that A and C were employed at the same night-club as, respectively, receptionist and doorman. The victims were customers of the club who, on the night in question, had an argument about the bill and attempted to leave without paying the full amount. According to W, both A and C approached him and threatened violence if he did not pay. Shortly after, A slashed his face with a knife. L then came to the assistance of W and a struggle ensued in the course of which C's assault on L occurred. At the trial, defence counsel said that they had no objection to a joint hearing. Both accused were convicted. On appeal, A argued that it was bad in law to charge two different people in one indictment with two different offences. Offenders could properly be joined in one indictment only as principals said to have jointly committed one offence, or as principals and accessories (see p. 251F–G for counsel's argument). A five-judge Court of Appeal extensively reviewed the authorities, and (in a judgment given by Sachs J) reached the following conclusions:

(a) Questions of joinder, whether of offences or offenders, are 'matters of practice on which the court has, unless restrained by statute, inherent power both to formulate its own rules and to vary them in the light of current experience and the needs of justice' (p. 258F). On the assumption that what is now r. 9 of the Indictment Rules 1971 covered only joinder of offences, the propriety of the joinder of A and C in one indictment (being a case of joinder of offenders) was unaffected either by the Indictments Act 1915 or by any other legislation, whether subordinate or primary, passed since then (p. 258E). In assuming, without expressly deciding, that the Indictment Rules 1971 do not govern joinder of offenders, the court favoured the appellant, since the offences alleged against A and C were clearly founded on the same facts within the terms of r. 9 and would therefore properly have been joined in one indictment had that rule applied. Subsequently, Lord Widgery CJ in *Camberwell Green*

Stipendiary Magistrate, ex parte Christie [1978] QB 602 said that *Assim* should be accepted as laying down a principle that joinder of offenders is a matter of the practice of the courts.

(b)   Since joinder of offenders is merely a matter of practice, errors in the application of the relevant rules, though amounting to an irregularity in the proceedings, will not deprive the trial court of jurisdiction. Consequently, if such an irregularity is made the ground of an appeal against conviction, the Court of Appeal will be able to dismiss the appeal if there has been no miscarriage of justice (p. 259D–E). Failure by the defence to object to the joint trial is a strong argument in favour of dismissing the appeal.

(c)   Following an extensive review of the authorities, Sachs J 'came to some general conclusions as to what would nowadays be an appropriate rule of practice on the basis that none of the rules of 1915 deal with the joinder of offenders'. The gist of his observations is that joinder is appropriate if the offences separately alleged against the accused are, on the evidence, so closely related by time or other factors that the interests of justice are best served by a single trial. His lordship said (at p. 261B–F):

> As a general rule it is, of course, no more proper to have tried by the same jury several offenders on charges of committing individual offences that have nothing to do with each other than it is to try before the same jury offences committed by the same person that have nothing to do with each other. Where, however, the matters which constitute the individual offences of the several offenders are upon the available evidence so related, whether in time or by other factors, that the interests of justice are best served by their being tried together, then they can properly be the subject of counts in one indictment and can, subject always to the discretion of the court, be tried together. Such a rule, of course, includes cases where there is evidence that several offenders acted in concert but is not limited to such cases.

> Again, while the court has in mind the classes of case that have been particularly the subject of discussion before it, such as incidents which, irrespective of there appearing a joint charge in the indictment, are contemporaneous (as where there has been something in the nature of an affray), or successive (as in protection racket cases), or linked in a similar manner, as where two persons individually in the course of the same trial commit perjury as regards the same or a closely connected fact, the court does not intend the operation of the rule to be restricted so as to apply only to such cases as have been discussed before it.

(d)   It was conceded by the appellant and accepted by the court that, where there is a joint count against two defendants, that count may be followed by a separate count or counts against one or more of the accused even in relation to a distinct matter, provided that there is no breach of the Indictment Rules 1971, r. 9 (p. 257D, quoting *Cox* [1898] 1 QB 179). See also *Barrell* (1979) 69 Cr App R 250 for a subsequent instance of such a joinder being upheld on appeal.

(e)   On the facts of *Assim*, the joinder of A and C in one indictment was clearly proper, however narrowly any rule as to joinder of offenders might have been formulated (p. 260G). The offence of malicious wounding alleged against A was preceded by conduct on C's part which would have justified the prosecution, had they so wished, in having a joint count against both on the basis that C encouraged and was a party to A's subsequent conduct. If there had been a joint count, there could have been no possible objection to the indictment containing a further separate count against C alone for assault, that offence being founded on the same facts as the wounding (see proposition (d) above). As it was, there were simply the separate counts against the two accused, but, having regard to the rule of practice Sachs J had stated, those counts were so closely related by time and other factors that indicting the accused jointly was the correct course.

Discretion to Order Separate Trials

The court has a discretion to order separate trials of accused who have properly been **D9.32** joined in one indictment in accordance with the principles stated in **D9.27**. The existence of the discretion was acknowledged by Sachs J in *Assim* [1966] 2 QB 249. His lordship said at p. 261B–C): 'Where . . . the matters which constitute the individual offences of the several offenders are upon the available evidence so related . . . that the interests of justice are best served by their being tried together, then they can properly be the subject of counts in one indictment and can, *subject always to the discretion of the court*, be tried together' (emphasis added). Although that was said in the context of an indictment which did not contain a joint count, it has never been doubted that the discretion may be exercised as much in respect of accused charged in a joint count as in respect of those charged in separate counts on one indictment. The discretion may be attributed either to the court's inherent power to control its own proceedings or to the power to sever contained in the Indictments Act 1915, s. 5(3) (see **D9.27**).

Severance of the trial of jointly indicted accused being a matter of discretion, the way in which the discretion is exercised – whether for or against severance – is unlikely to provide a successful ground of appeal, since, in general, the Court of Appeal interferes with the exercise of a discretion only if it can be shown that the trial judge took into account irrelevant considerations, or ignored relevant ones, or arrived at a manifestly unreasonable decision (see especially *Moghal* (1977) 65 Cr App R 56, where the appeal failed even though the members of the court indicated strongly that, had they been trying the case, they would not have acted as the trial judge had done). In fact, in the present context, the test of whether to intervene is usually stated simply as: Did the trial judge's decision cause unacceptable prejudice to the appellant such as might have led to a miscarriage of justice? (*Grondkowski* [1946] KB 369, and *Moghal* (1977) 65 Cr App R 56). Guidance on ordering separate trials does, however, emerge from the decided cases, even if the ultimate decision is that the trial judge's exercise of discretion ought not to be disturbed. The following propositions summarise that guidance:

(a)   Where the accused are charged in a joint count, the arguments in favour of a joint trial are very strong. Severance will necessitate much or all of the prosecution evidence being given twice before different juries and increase the risk of inconsistent verdicts. Even if the accused are expected to blame each other for the offence (i.e. will run 'cut-throat' defences), the interests of the prosecution and the public in a single trial will generally outweigh the interests of the defence in not having to call each accused before the same jury to give evidence for himself which will incriminate the other (see *Grondkowski* [1946] KB 369, *Moghal* (1977) 65 Cr App R 56, *Edwards* [1998] Crim LR 756 and *Crawford* [1997] 1 WLR 1329).

(b)   Where the prosecution case against one accused (A1) includes evidence that is admissible against him but not against his co-accused (A2) – a very common occurrence – the judge is certainly not obliged to order severance simply because the evidence in question might prejudice the jury against A2. However, the judge should balance the advantages of a single trial against the possible prejudice to A2, and should consider especially how far an appropriate direction to the jury is really likely to ensure that they take into account the evidence only for its proper purpose of proving the case against A1 (see *Lake* (1976) 64 Cr App R 172). A common example of the problem is where A1 has made a confession in the absence of A2 which implicates them both.

(c)   Where a joint trial of numerous accused would lead to a very long and complicated trial, the judge should consider whether a number of shorter trials, each involving only some of the accused, might make for a fairer and more efficient disposition of the issues. This reason for severance is tied up with the rule against overloading indictments, which is considered in **D9.33**.

(d)   Although the point has not specifically been made by the Court of Appeal, it is submitted that some distinction should be drawn between cases where the accused are jointly charged in a single count and those where they allegedly committed separate offences which were nonetheless sufficiently linked to be put in one indictment. In the latter situation, the cases against the accused are unlikely to be as closely intertwined as when a joint offence is alleged, and the public interest argument in favour of a single trial is correspondingly less strong. There should, therefore, be a greater willingness to order separate trials.

The authorities cited above indicate that the decision whether or not to grant severance is one within the discretion of the trial judge, and that the decision should be in favour of joint trial unless the risk of prejudice is unusually great. Thus in *Josephs* (1977) 65 Cr App R 253, where the same issue arose as had in *Lake*, Lord Widgery CJ said (at p. 255, emphasis added):

> . . . it is a very rare thing for this court to interfere with the trial judge's decision about separate trials. Nothing is more peculiarly left to the trial judge as his concern with that particular point. *Of course we have jurisdiction to interfere where something has clearly gone wrong*, but it is very rare, and members of the court today cannot remember a case in which such an interference with the trial judge's decision was made.

> . . . the fact that some of [a co-accused's] statements may rub off on the other accused . . . is just one of those things that happens in the course of a multiple criminal trial. The advantages of having co-defendants tried together is so great that the right to order a separate trial will not be granted unless there is good reason for it.

In a suitable case, however, the Court of Appeal has shown that it is willing to exercise its power to intervene 'where something has clearly gone wrong'. In *O'Boyle* (1991) 92 Cr App R 202, O was charged with conspiracy to supply cocaine. His co-defendant R alleged that he had acted under duress from O. R said that O had links with the Mafia. Following a *voir dire* the judge ruled that O's confession to agents of the United States Drugs Enforcement Agency should be excluded because O had not been cautioned or informed about his rights, and had been treated as an informer, giving his account 'in confidence'. Counsel for R then stated that he wished to cross-examine O on the contents of the interview, in accordance with the Criminal Procedure Act 1865. O applied for separate trials, but the judge refused. On appeal, the Court of Appeal held that the trial judge had a discretion and that generally, conspirators should be tried together. However, this was an exceptional case, where separate trials would have done little or no harm to the co-defendant or prosecution, while joint trial prejudiced the appellant. Accordingly, the judge had erred in the exercise of his discretion. (See also *Randle* [1995] Crim LR 331.)

Another example of intervention by the Court of Appeal where joint trial resulted in injustice is provided by the case of *Smith* (1966) 51 Cr App R 22 where the prosecution alleged that S and his two co-accused had carefully planned and carried out a large-scale theft. The evidence against the co-accused consisted largely of their admissions to the police in which they also implicated S, but the evidence directly admissible against S was scanty. The co-accused were acquitted and S alone convicted. The Court of Criminal Appeal quashed the conviction, not because the trial judge had been wrong to reject an application for separate trials, but because the acquittals of the co-accused showed that the jury could not have accepted the prosecution case that there had been an elaborate plot to steal involving all the accused, and the only explanation for S alone being convicted was that the jury must have been prejudiced against him by the material in the co-accused's statements, notwithstanding the judge's direction that those statements were evidence only against the co-accused. Therefore, the conviction was unsafe, even though the original decision in favour of a joint trial was correct (see the discussion of *Smith* in *Lake* (1976) 64 Cr App R 172 at p. 177).

Perhaps the key to understanding the attitude of the court in *Lake* and in *Josephs* is to appreciate that there is a distinction between what might be considered as ordinary prejudice and what Lord Widgery referred to as 'dangerous prejudice'. The former is almost bound to arise when co-accused run inconsistent defences and does not in general justify severing the indictment. The latter, exemplified by *Smith*, should be dealt with by severance.

Overloading Indictments

D9.33 In drafting indictments and in ruling on applications to sever indictments, the drafter and judge respectively should have regard not only to what is permitted by the rules on joinder (discussed in **D9.24** to **D9.32**) but also to whether one long trial or several shorter ones is more likely to be in the interests of justice. If a single indictment, containing numerous counts and/or accused, would result in an unduly long or complicated trial, such as to place an unfair burden on the jury, then the prosecution should opt for however many shorter indictments are necessary to cover the same ground, notwithstanding that a single indictment would be within the rules. Similarly, if, in the circumstances just described, the prosecution do prefer a single indictment, then the judge should intervene to order separate trials, whether of counts or accused. Put briefly, no jury ought to be required to try an overloaded indictment.

Dicta on overloaded indictments are contained especially in *Novac* (1976) 65 Cr App R 107 and *Thorne* (1977) 66 Cr App R 6. In *Novac*, there were some 19 counts against four accused (N, R, A-C and A), all of whom pleaded not guilty but were convicted on all but three charges. The major count was against N, R and A-C. It was for conspiracy between May and July 1974 to procure males under 21 to commit acts of gross indecency, the prosecution evidence being that the accused had frequented the Playland amusement arcade in Piccadilly, picked up young male prostitutes, and brought them back to a flat in Wandsworth where acts of indecency occurred. Linked with the conspiracy count were counts for a number of specific offences committed during the currency of the conspiracy, such as living on the earnings of male prostitution, importuning in a public place and buggery or gross indecency with named persons. The indictment also contained counts against the alleged conspirators for roughly similar offences committed outside the period of the conspiracy. The fourth accused (A) was not said to have been a member of the conspiracy, but he was charged with eight specific offences of indecency with different males. The evidence of these offences was gathered while the police were keeping watch on the activities of the other accused. The trial lasted 47 working days. Ultimately, many of the convictions had to be quashed because of errors in the summing-up as to similar-fact evidence and corroboration. After dealing with those errors, Bridge LJ, giving the judgment of the court, said (at p. 188):

> We cannot conclude this judgment without pointing out that . . . most of the difficulties which have bedevilled this trial, which have led in the end to the quashing of all convictions except on the conspiracy and related counts, arose directly out of the overloading of the indictment. . . . the indictment of 19 counts against four defendants resulted . . . in a trial of quite unnecessary length and complexity. If the specific offence counts against [N, R and A-C] and all the counts against [A] had been tried separately, the main trial of the conspiracy and related counts would have been reasonably manageable and the four separate trials would have been short and straightforward. Quite apart from the question whether the prosecution could find legal justification for joining all these counts in one indictment and resisting severance, the wider and more important question has to be asked whether in such a case the interests of justice were likely to be better served by one very long trial, or by one moderately long and four short separate trials.

> We answer unhesitatingly that whatever advantages were expected to accrue from one long trial, . . . they were heavily outweighed by the disadvantages. A trial of such dimensions puts an immense burden on both judge and jury. In the course of a four or five-day summing-up the most careful and conscientious judge may so easily overlook some essential matter. Even if the summing-up is faultless, it is by no means cynical to doubt whether the average juror can be expected to take it all in and apply all the directions given. Some criminal prosecutions involve consideration of matters so plainly inextricable and indivisible that a

long and complex trial is an ineluctable necessity. But we are convinced that nothing short of the criterion of absolute necessity can justify the imposition of the burdens of a very long trial on the court.

Much the same sentiments were expressed in *Thorne*, where the trial was even longer. The indictment related essentially to three separate armed robberies, evidence as to which came mainly from one O'M, who had 'turned Queen's evidence'. As well as counts for robbery, there were counts for related conspiracies to rob, handling some of the proceeds, and conspiracy to pervert the course of justice by making threats against a potential prosecution witness. In all, there were 10 counts and 14 accused. The trial lasted nearly seven months, the summing-up alone took 12 days. Although declining to quash any conviction solely on the basis of the inordinately long trial, the Court of Appeal (Lawton LJ) said that the indictment was undoubtedly overloaded, and the trial placed 'a burden on the judge which he should never be asked to bear' (p. 14). Presumably the Court of Appeal would have preferred a separate indictment for each robbery, and also separate indictments for peripheral offenders such as the handlers.

A further aspect of not overloading indictments is that when, as not infrequently happens, the criminal conduct alleged against an accused may be said in law to amount to a number of distinct offences but the gist of what he did can conveniently be brought under one charge, then the prosecution should have just one count for the obviously appropriate offence – nothing is gained and much is lost in terms of simplicity of presentation to the jury if the indictment contains counts for all the offences of which the accused might possibly be guilty (see *Staton* [1983] Crim LR 190). This is without prejudice to cases where the prosecution evidence is such that the drafter is genuinely unsure about which of a number of possible alternative offences the jury might choose to convict on. In that situation it is proper to put all the alternatives in the indictment.

Both *Novac* and *Thorne* were cases in which the complexity of the indictment was in part attributable to the combination of conspiracy and substantive charges. In an effort to meet this particular problem, the following practice direction was issued.

Practice Direction (Crime: Conspiracy) [1977] 1 WLR 537

1. In any case where an indictment contains substantive counts and a related conspiracy count, the judge should require the prosecution to justify the joinder, or, failing justification, to elect whether to proceed on the substantive or on the conspiracy counts.
2. A joinder is justified for this purpose if the judge considers that the interests of justice demand it.

Generally, then, if a substantive count and a related conspiracy count are joined in the indictment, the prosecution will have to justify their inclusion. If they are not justified, then they will have to decide on which they wish to proceed. It follows that a conspiracy count which adds nothing to the charge of a substantive offence has no place in the indictment (*Jones* (1974) 59 Cr App R 120; see *Watts* (1995) *The Times*, 14 April 1995).

If the prosecution elects to proceed upon the substantive charge, then the election is not necessarily irreversible. In *Findlay* [1992] Crim LR 372, for example, the prosecution elected at the outset to proceed on substantive robbery counts. Evidence necessary to sustain a conviction on those counts was later ruled inadmissible. They then applied to re-elect, adding a new count alleging conspiracy to rob, and proceeding no further on the substantive robbery counts. The trial judge permitted the amendment. F was convicted and appealed. The Court of Appeal dismissed the appeal, in view of the fact that there was no demonstrable prejudice to F.

In recent years, the most striking instances of overloaded indictments have emerged in serious fraud cases. In *Cohen* (1992) *The Independent*, 29 July 1992 (the 'Blue Arrow' case), the jury did not retire until the 184th day of the trial. The indictment was long and complex, and the judge's summing-up was limited to just one of the issues in it. Four appellants appealed successfully against their convictions for conspiracy to defraud. The Court of Appeal said that the basic assumption that the jury determined guilt or innocence on evidence which it was able to comprehend and remember had been destroyed in this case; the summing-up showed that the appellants could have been tried manageably and fairly. The prosecution had a heavy responsibility not to overload the indictment, but the ultimate responsibility lay with the trial judge, whose powers of severance should have been used at an early stage to overcome the problems of an overloaded indictment. The confinement of the summing-up to only one of the issues in the indictment was a material irregularity. In *Wright* [1995] Crim LR 251, however, it was made clear that the mere length of a trial is not sufficient in itself to characterise convictions as unsafe. (See also *Kellard* [1995] 2 Cr App R 134.)

AMENDING THE INDICTMENT

Statutory Provision

D9.34   **Indictments Act 1915, s. 5**

(1) Where, before trial, or at any stage of a trial, it appears to the court that the indictment is defective, the court shall make such order for the amendment of the indictment as the court thinks necessary to meet the circumstances of the case, unless, having regard to the merits of the case, the required amendments cannot be made without injustice.

Extent of the Power to Amend

D9.35   The power to amend may be exercised both in respect of formal defects in the wording of a count (as when the statement of offence fails to specify the statute contravened or when the particulars do not disclose an essential element of the offence), and in respect of substantial defects such as divergences between the allegations in the count and the evidence foreshadowed in the committal statements or called at trial. This was confirmed by the Court of Criminal Appeal in *Pople* [1951] 1 KB 53 at p. 54:

The argument for the appellants appeared to involve the proposition that an indictment, in order to be defective, must be one which in law did not charge any offence at all and therefore was bad on the face of it. We do not take that view. In our opinion, any alteration in matters of description, and probably in many other respects, may be made in order to meet the evidence in the case so long as the amendment causes no injustice to the accused person.

It followed that the trial judge in *Pople*, in allowing an amendment at the close of the prosecution case to make the property allegedly obtained by deception from a building society a cheque itself rather than the sum of money for which the cheque was drawn, acted within the powers given to him by the Indictments Act 1915, s. 5(1). Furthermore, there was no injustice to the accused because the matter in which the indictment was defective was 'the mere description of the thing obtained', while 'in substance, the charge was the same'. Similarly, in *Radley* (1973) 58 Cr App R 394, Lord Widgery CJ quoted with approval the passage from *Pople* quoted above, and held that an indictment may be defective if it merely fails to allege an offence disclosed by the committal statements. 'Defective', in the context of s. 5(1), is not restricted to defects in form, but 'has got a very much wider meaning' (p. 401). Moreover, this wide meaning is acceptable because the power to amend is subject to the overriding limitation that it must not cause injustice (p. 402).

If the indictment is so defective as to be a nullity, then it is not capable of amendment and there is a mistrial. An indictment is invalid from the outset in this way where, for example, it alleges an offence unknown to law. Where a count describes a known offence inaccurately, however, then it is capable of amendment (subject to the usual considerations of prejudice to the defendant) (*McVitie* [1960] 2 QB 483, applied in *Tyler* (1992) 96 Cr App R 332).

As well as enabling amendments to be made to existing counts, s. 5(1) of the Indictments Act 1915 permits the insertion of an entirely new count into an indictment, whether in addition to or in substitution for the original counts (*Johal* [1973] QB 475). In that case an indictment originally containing counts for wounding with intent and unlawful wounding against both accused jointly was amended by the addition of four counts alleging that each accused had committed the same offences individually. The amendment, which was made after arraignment but before the empanelling of a jury, was approved by the Court of Appeal, saying (per Ashworth J at p. 481A): 'In the judgment of this court there is no rule of law which precludes amendment of an indictment after arraignment, either by addition of a new count or otherwise'. The words 'after arraignment' appear in the sentence quoted because the main point at issue was whether the amendment was made too late, but obviously the addition of a count before arraignment is even less open to objection than a subsequent addition. Where the addition is made after arraignment it will be necessary to put the new counts to the accused for him to plead to them.

The amendment to an indictment can be so extensive that the question arises whether it amounts to the substitution of a fresh indictment. This was the issue in *Fyffe* [1992] Crim LR 442, where the Crown amended an 11-count indictment so that it contained 27 counts. On appeal, the appellants argued that the 27-count indictment was a fresh indictment and therefore the judge should have gone through the procedural steps of staying the 11-count indictment and granting the prosecution leave to prefer the 27-count indictment out of time, whereupon the defendants should have been arraigned once more. The appeal was dismissed since for all material purposes, the 27 counts reproduced what had appeared in the 11 counts. No new allegations had been added; the amendments were of form rather than substance and it was not necessary to go through the process of re-arraignment. A further question arises as to whether it is necessary for the amendment to be founded on facts or evidence disclosed to the examining justices at committal. According to the Court of Appeal in *Osieh* [1996] 1 WLR 1260, it is not necessary (although their lordships held that the amendment in that particular case *had* been founded on evidence disclosed at committal). The dicta in *Osieh* to this effect, however, seem to run counter to dicta in *Dixon* (1991) 92 Cr App R 43, and *Hall* [1968] 2 QB 788. In discussing the amendment of indictments in *Hall*, Lord Parker CJ said (at p. 792) that, granted that there was power to amend, the question is really 'whether the amendment asked for and granted was supported by evidence given at the committal proceedings'. As Professor J. C. Smith comments in 'Adding Counts to an Indictment' [1996] Crim LR 889, 'Plainly the court thought that an amendment not so supported was invalid'. In any event, the fact that an amendment raises for the first time something not foreshadowed in the committal documents may be a ground for not permitting the amendment, or permitting it only on terms as to an adjournment (per Schiemann LJ in *Osieh*).

The power to amend may be exercised in respect of voluntary bills of indictment preferred on the direction of a High Court judge just as it may be exercised in respect of 'ordinary' indictments preferred on the authority of a committal for trial (*Allcock* [1999] 1 Cr App R 227; *Wells* [1995] 2 Cr App R 417 at p. 422; *Walters* (1979) 69 Cr App R 115).

Timing of Amendment

An amendment may be made at any stage of a trial, whether before or after arraignment. **D9.36** That is the plain wording of the Indictments Act 1915, s. 5(1), and is confirmed by the decision in *Johal* [1973] QB 475, where the insertion of the new counts was after arraignment but before the empanelling of the jury. Similarly, in *Pople* [1951] 1 KB 53, where the amendment took the form of an alteration in the description of the property obtained by deception as opposed to adding a count, the Court of Criminal Appeal took no point on the amendment not being granted until after the close of the prosecution case. In *Collison* (1980) 71 Cr App R 249 the amendment was later still, being made after the jury had been out considering their verdict for over three hours. On appeal, counsel for C accepted 'that the words in section 5(1) of the Indictments Act 1915 "at any stage of a trial" do permit amendment even after the jury have gone into retirement if the circumstances otherwise justify it and no injustice is caused to the defendant' (p. 253). However, the later the amendment, the greater the risk of its causing injustice and therefore the less likely it is to be allowed.

Risk of Injustice

D9.37   The main consideration for a judge deciding whether to allow an amendment is the risk of injustice. If the amendment cannot be made without injustice, then it must not be made (last clause of s. 5(1) of the Indictments Act 1915). The timing of the amendment is a major factor in determining whether there will be injustice. Thus, in *Johal* [1973] QB 475, the Court of Appeal, while rejecting the view in *Harden* [1963] 1 QB 8 that an amendment that substantially substitutes another offence for that originally charged can *never* be made after arraignment, agreed that such amendments would usually cause injustice. Ashworth J said (at pp. 480G–481C):

> As a statement of principle, to be applied generally, this [i.e., the decision in *Harden*] is . . . too wide. No doubt in many cases in which, after arraignment, an amendment is sought for the purpose of substituting another offence for that originally charged, or for the purpose of adding a further charge, injustice would be caused by granting the amendment. But in some cases (of which the present is an example) no such injustice would be caused and the amendment may properly be allowed. . . .
>
> In the judgment of this court there is no rule of law which precludes amendment of an indictment after arraignment, either by addition of a new count or otherwise. . . .
>
> On the other hand this court shares the view expressed in some of the earlier cases that amendment of an indictment during the course of a trial is likely to prejudice an accused person. The longer the interval between arraignment and amendment, the more likely it is that injustice will be caused, and in every case in which amendment is sought, it is essential to consider with great care whether the accused person will be prejudiced thereby.

On the facts of *Johal*, there was no injustice because the amendment was made immediately after arraignment, and 'the situation was to all intents and purposes the same as if application to amend had been made before arraignment'. In *Collison* (1980) 71 Cr App R 249, where the amendment was as late as it could possibly be, there was still no injustice because the addition of a count for unlawful wounding to the original count for wounding with intent merely removed a technical impediment to the jury convicting of the lesser offence. Such a verdict had been dealt with at length by the judge in his summing-up but the failure of the jury to agree that the accused was not guilty as charged meant that, having regard to the wording of the Criminal Law Act 1967, s. 6(3), they could not lawfully bring in a verdict of guilty of unlawful wounding on the original one-count indictment, even though they were all satisfied that C was at least guilty of that offence. (See also *Teong Sun Chuah* [1991] Crim LR 463 for an example of amendment at a relatively late stage which was held to be acceptable since it caused no injustice.) On the other hand, in *Gregory* [1972] 1 WLR 991 the Court of Appeal quashed G's conviction on a count which originally charged him with handling a stolen starter motor 'the property of William Alan Wilkes', because the judge, at the close of the evidence, amended the particulars by deleting the allegation as to ownership. In the circumstances of that particular case, where much of the evidence from both parties had related to the true ownership of a starter motor admittedly found in the appellant's possession, it could not be said that the allegation that the motor belonged to a named person was 'mere surplusage'. In fact, the amendment altered the whole basis of the prosecution case, requiring G to answer a charge which was substantially different from that which he had come prepared to meet. Given the late stage at which it was made, the amendment caused injustice.

In *O'Connor* [1997] Crim LR 516, the managing agent of a company whose fishing vessel foundered at sea, with the loss of all six crew members, was tried for manslaughter. The prosecution applied to amend the indictment on the 27th day of the trial, after a submission of no case to answer by the defence. The effect of the amendment was to allow the prosecution to shift its ground from alleging that the defendant was criminally responsible for the sinking, to relying upon his alleged responsibility for inadequacies in the ship's safety equipment. The judge allowed the amendment, and the defendant was convicted and appealed. The Court of Appeal, in allowing the appeal, held that the amendment was unfair. The Crown's case had changed very significantly, and the appellant had been confronted with a different and more difficult case. He had been deprived of the opportunity to mount the defence which he would have mounted if the Crown case had been put in that way from the beginning. It was for the prosecution to decide how to put their case, and they could not rely on the court granting leave to change it as the trial progressed. The defence were entitled to confine their attention to the case against the appellant as charged, and were not entitled (let alone obliged) to fashion their defence to meet allegations which the Crown might later choose to pursue.

Procedure on Amendment

In *Moss* [1995] Crim LR 828, it was stated that, where counsel seeks an amendment, **D9.38** he ought to ensure that there is a properly amended form of indictment before the judge, and that any order of the court is clear and is complied with.

When amendment is allowed, a note of the order must be endorsed on the indictment (Indictments Act 1915, s. 5(2)). If necessary, an adjournment may be granted to allow the parties (in particular the defence) to deal with the altered position (s. 5(4)). Where the amendment comes during the course of a trial, there is power to discharge the jury from giving a verdict and order a retrial on the amended indictment (s. 5(5)(a)).

MOTION TO QUASH AN INDICTMENT

Either party may move the judge to quash the indictment or a count thereof. The **D9.39** obvious time for doing so is before the accused is arraigned, although it would seem that the defence (but perhaps not the prosecution) may make the application at any stage of the trial. The effect of a successful application is that the accused may not be tried on the indictment (or particular count thereof if the motion does not relate to the whole), but he is not thereby acquitted and further proceedings may be brought for the same offence. However, the quashing of the indictment exhausts the effect of the committal proceedings on which it was founded (see *Thompson* [1975] 1 WLR 1425). It follows that, in order to have the accused tried, the prosecution will either have to institute fresh committal proceedings or apply for a voluntary bill of indictment.

A motion to quash may be brought in any of three circumstances:

(a) Where the indictment is bad on its face (e.g., for duplicity or because the particulars of a count do not disclose an offence known to law). Thus, in *Yates* (1872) 12 Cox CC 233 an indictment for criminal libel was quashed because the words attributed to the accused were not prima facie libellous and the particulars contained no allegation of an innuendo.

(b)   Where the indictment (or a count thereof) has been preferred otherwise than in accordance with the provisions of the Administration of Justice (Miscellaneous Provisions) Act 1933, s. 2. In such a case, the indictment is preferred without authority and must be quashed (see *Lombardi* [1989] 1 WLR 73 where the trial judge refused defence applications to quash on grounds of breach of s. 2 and the accused thereafter appealed against conviction).

(c)   Where the indictment contains a count for an offence in respect of which the accused was not committed for trial and the committal documents do not disclose a case to answer for that offence (*Jones* (1974) 59 Cr App R 120).

Save for the situation in (c), the judge on a motion to quash is *not* entitled to consider the prosecution evidence as foreshadowed in the documents (see *Jones* (1974) 59 Cr App R 120). Therefore, if the indictment follows the committal charges and is properly drafted on its face, it is not open to the defence to invite the judge to quash on the basis that the evidence before the justices did not in fact disclose a case to answer and the accused was wrongly committed for trial (*Chairman, County of London Quarter Sessions, ex parte Downes* [1954] 1 QB 1). Where, however, the indictment contains a count on which the accused was not committed the normal rule has to be relaxed in respect of that count, because otherwise the accused would be put on trial for the offence without any prior opportunity of arguing that the evidence is insufficient.

Motions to quash are of little practical importance for the defence both because of the limited grounds on which they may be brought and because the prosecution are often able to prevent a motion succeeding by making a suitable amendment to the indictment (e.g., splitting into two a count that the defence say should be quashed on grounds of duplicity). In any event, a successful motion does not result in acquittal, merely in the accused being discharged. Failure to apply to quash may, however, prejudice the chances of a successful appeal by making it possible for the Court of Appeal to find that the conviction was safe, since it may be argued that, if the defence at trial had felt themselves to be prejudiced by a defect in the indictment rendering it liable to be quashed, they would surely have made the appropriate application. The lack of a motion to quash may show that there was no miscarriage of justice (see, e.g., *Thompson* [1914] 2 KB 99 and *Donnelly* [1998] Crim LR 131).

Although motions to quash are most obviously a remedy available to the defence, the prosecution may wish to quash if they realise that an indictment they have preferred is invalid. However, inviting the judge to quash is dangerous from the prosecution viewpoint because, once that has been done, the committal on which the quashed indictment was founded may not be used as authority to prefer another indictment for the same offence (*Thompson* [1975] 1 WLR 1425 and dicta in *Newland* [1988] QB 402). The better course will usually be to ask the judge to stay (but not quash) the defective indictment and at the same time prefer a fresh indictment correcting the error in the original bill (see *Follett* [1989] QB 338 and **D9.27**).

DEFECTS IN THE INDICTMENT AS A GROUND OF APPEAL

D9.40   Where a trial proceeds on a defective indictment that is not amended, there is an irregularity in the course of the trial which may result in the Court of Appeal finding that the conviction is unsafe (see, for example, *Ayres* [1984] AC 447).

Decided cases do, however, show a marked reluctance on the part of the Court of Appeal to allow appeals on grounds of errors in the indictment. The precise reasoning varies. Sometimes it is said that the defect concerned a matter which was 'mere surplusage' (see *Dossi* (1918) 13 Cr App R 158). Sometimes a distinction is drawn between an indictment which is a nullity and one which is merely defective (see *McVitie* [1960] 2

QB 483 and *Nelson* (1977) Cr App R 119). It is submitted, however, that the most helpful approach is that adumbrated by Lord Bridge in *Ayres*. He said (at pp. 460G–461B):

> In a number of cases where an irregularity in the form of the indictment has been discussed in relation to the application of the proviso a distinction, treated as of crucial importance, has been drawn between an indictment which is 'a nullity' and one which is merely 'defective'. For my part, I doubt if this classification provides much assistance in answering the question which the proviso poses. If the statement and particulars of the offence in an indictment disclose no criminal offence whatever or charge some offence which has been abolished, in which case the indictment could fairly be described as a nullity, it is obvious that a conviction under that indictment cannot stand. But if the statement and particulars of offence can be seen fairly to relate to and to be intended to charge a known and subsisting criminal offence but plead it in terms which are inaccurate, incomplete or otherwise imperfect, then the question whether a conviction on that indictment can properly be affirmed under the proviso must depend on whether, in all the circumstances, it can be said with confidence that the particular error in the pleading cannot in any way have prejudiced or embarrassed the defendant.

Thus, save in the almost unimaginable event of the accused being convicted on an indictment which charged an offence totally unknown to the criminal law, the crucial question is whether the defect has caused prejudice or embarrassment to the defence. On the facts of *Ayres*, the House of Lords held that there had been no such prejudice. The appellant had been convicted on a count for 'conspiracy to defraud', the particulars alleging that he and others had conspired to make fraudulent insurance claims in respect of a lorry and its load that was falsely said to have been stolen. The main point of the judgment is that, on the law as it then stood (the point would not now arise because of the CJA 1987, s. 12), he should have been charged with and convicted of conspiracy to obtain by deception contrary to s. 1 of the Criminal Law Act 1977, not with common law conspiracy to defraud. It followed that the indictment 'did not charge him accurately with the only offence for which he could properly be convicted' (p. 460C). Nonetheless, the conviction was upheld because (at p. 462):

> The particulars of offence in this indictment left no one in doubt that the substance of the crime alleged was a conspiracy to obtain money by deception. The judge in summing up gave all the appropriate directions in relation to that offence. . . . the evidence amply proved that offence against the present appellant. The jury in returning a verdict of guilty must have been sure of his guilt of that offence. The judge passed a modest sentence comfortably below the maximum for that offence. The misdescription of the offence in the statement of offence as a common-law conspiracy to defraud had in the circumstances not the slightest practical significance. . . . there [cannot] possibly have been any actual miscarriage of justice.

Ayres is an extreme and somewhat questionable example of a defect in the indictment not resulting in a successful appeal as the conviction for the offence apparently indicated by the statement of offence (common-law conspiracy) was upheld even though the evidence showed the appellant to be guilty of what in law was a quite different offence (statutory conspiracy). Appeals have also failed in the following cases notwithstanding the defects indicated below:

(a) *Thompson* [1914] 2 KB 99 – count for incest bad for duplicity because it alleged offences 'on divers days' in a 21-month period;

(b) *McVitie* [1960] 2 QB 483 – particulars for an offence of possessing explosives for an unlawful purpose contrary to s. 4(1) of the Explosive Substances Act 1883 breached the Indictment Rules 1971, r. 5(1), by omitting the essential allegation that McV 'knowingly' had the explosives;

(c) *Nelson* (1977) 65 Cr App R 119 – statement of offence for possessing an offensive weapon breached r. 6(a)(i) of the 1971 Rules by failing to specify the statute contravened;

(d) *Power* (1977) 66 Cr App R 159 – statement of offence for an offence contrary to s. 5 of the Perjury Act 1911 breached r. 5(1) of the 1971 Rules by wrongly describing the offence as 'perjury' when it should have been making a false declaration not on oath.

In each of the above, the reasoning of the court was essentially that the indictment, although defective, was not null as it described an offence known to the law albeit in inaccurate terms, and the accused, on the facts, had not been misled or prejudiced in the conduct of his defence by the error.

Court's Discretion to Prevent Abuse of Process

D9.41 It is generally agreed that the Crown Court has inherent power to protect its process from abuse (for details on the position in the magistrates' courts, see **D4.6, D7.5** and **D18.10**). In *Connelly* v *DPP* [1964] AC 1254, for example, Lord Devlin stated that, where particular criminal proceedings constitute an abuse of process, the court is empowered to refuse to allow the indictment to proceed to trial. The remarks of Lord Salmon in *DPP* v *Humphrys* [1977] AC 1 stress the importance of this discretion:

> . . . a judge has not and should not appear to have any responsibility for the institution of prosecutions; nor has he any power to refuse to allow a prosecution to proceed merely because he considers that, as a matter of policy, it ought not to have been brought. It is only if the prosecution amounts to an abuse of the process of the court and is oppressive and vexatious that the judge has the power to intervene. Fortunately, such prosecutions are hardly ever brought but the power of the court to prevent them is, in my view, of great constitutional importance and should be jealously preserved. For a man to be harassed and put to the expense of perhaps a long trial and then given an absolute discharge is hardly from any point of view an effective substitute for the exercise by the court of the power to which I have referred.

Several cases have dealt with the issue of whether undue delay can constitute an abuse of process. There is, of course, no general time-limit upon the issue of proceedings for indictable offences (compare the six month time-limit in respect of summary offences discussed at **D18.7**). Nevertheless, in *Bell* v *DPP of Jamaica* [1985] AC 937, the Privy Council accepted that courts have an inherent jurisdiction to prevent a trial which would be oppressive because of unreasonable delay (see also **D7.5** and **D18.8** *et seq.*). In *Central Criminal Court, ex parte Randle* [1991] 1 WLR 1087, the applicants were charged with offences arising out of the escape from custody of George Blake while he was serving a 42-year sentence for spying. They appeared before the Central Criminal Court in 1990, some 23 years after the alleged offences. They applied for the proceedings to be stayed on the grounds of unreasonable delay, but were refused, and they sought judicial review of that decision. Whilst the Divisional Court refused their application, it was accepted that delay itself could, in appropriate circumstances, be such as to render criminal proceedings an abuse of process. In this case, however, the applicants had published a book in 1989, which had provided much of the material upon which the prosecution relied. In the light of its contents, the plea of failing memory could not be advanced, and the Divisional Court refused to interfere with the judge's discretion.

In *Bell*, the Privy Council laid down guidelines for determining whether the delay would deprive the accused of a fair trial. The relevant factors were said to be:

(a) the length of delay;
(b) the prosecution's reasons to justify the delay;
(c) the accused's efforts to assert his rights; and
(d) the prejudice caused to the accused.

It seems that, where the defendant's allegation of abuse of process is based on delay, he must show that as a result of the delay he will suffer serious prejudice to the extent that no fair trial can be held (see *R* [1994] Crim LR 948, *Dutton* [1994] Crim LR 910 and see the discussion at **D2.40** and **D7.5**). Further, 'delay due merely to the complexity of the case or contributed to by the actions of the defendant himself' cannot be the foundation for a stay (*A-G's Ref (No. 1 of 1990)* [1992] QB 630).

Clearly, in *Ex parte Randle*, the lack of prejudice to the defendants was held to be fatal to their argument, despite a delay of 23 years. In *Buzalek* [1991] Crim LR 115, the appellants were convicted of fraudulent trading over six years after they had been suspended from their jobs. The alleged fraud was exceptionally complicated and required the inspection of a great number of documents, many of which had to be translated from German. The trial judge had held that there was no reason why they should not receive a fair trial despite the passage of time involved and the Court of Appeal dismissed their appeal. The case turned largely on documents, and it was possible for the memories of witnesses to be refreshed by referring to them; the passage of time would be much more prejudicial where a case turned, for example, on what witnesses saw in an affray, an assault or a road accident.

If there has been a lengthy delay between the alleged offences and the trial, even if the trial judge does not stay the indictment on the ground of abuse of process, he may well comment on any difficulties which the defence may have faced because of the age of the complaints (*Birchall* (1995) *The Times*, 23 March 1995, *E* [1996] 1 Cr App R 88 , *B* [1996] Crim LR 406 and *King* [1997] Crim LR 298). In *H* [1998] 2 Cr App R 161, the Court of Appeal stated that such a direction was not inevitable, but was required only when some significant difficulty for the defence was raised or became apparent to the judge (see also *M* [1999] Crim LR 922).

Delay is not the only basis upon which an abuse of process may be founded. Where the prosecution have deliberately manipulated the criminal process so as to take unfair advantage of the accused, that may also constitute an abuse of process (*Derby Crown Court, ex parte Brooks* (1984) 80 Cr App R 164; *Croydon Justices, ex parte Dean* [1993] QB 769; *Schlesinger* [1995] Crim LR 137; and *Townsend* [1997] 2 Cr App R 540: see also **D10.29**, particularly in relation to *Beedie* [1998] QB 356). Even if no complaint can be made as to the fairness of the trial itself, unconscionable conduct on the part of the authorities in bringing the defendant before the court may amount to an abuse of process (*Mullen* [1999] 3 WLR 777, where the security services and police had procured the defendant's unlawful deportation from Zimbabwe). *Mullen* is also authority for the proposition that a conviction may be regarded as unsafe on the basis that the trial on which it was founded was an abuse of process (see **D22.15**). It appears, in any event, that questions which may be argued at trial, such as the admissibility of evidence or the existence of reliable identification, may not, in themselves, form part of an abuse application, whether that application is on the basis of delay (see *A-G's Ref (No. 1 of 1990)* [1992] QB 630) or unfair manipulation (*Bow Street Stipendiary Magistrate, ex parte DPP* (1992) 95 Cr App R 9).

In *Munro* (1993) 97 Cr App R 183, Steyn LJ stated that the power to stay criminal proceedings under an indictment extended to a stay of part of an indictment.

SECTION D10: ARRAIGNMENT AND PLEAS

THE ARRAIGNMENT

Procedure on Arraignment

D10.1 The arraignment consists of the clerk of the court reading the indictment to the accused and asking him whether he pleads guilty or not guilty to the counts contained therein. If there are several counts, a plea must be taken on each one separately immediately after it is read out (see *Boyle* [1954] 2 QB 292, where it was stated that the practice of reading the whole of a multi-count indictment to an accused and then asking him for a single, global plea should no longer be followed). If, however, two counts are in the alternative and the accused pleads guilty to the count first put to him, it is unnecessary to take a plea on the second (ibid.). Therefore, when it is known that the accused wishes to plead guilty to one of two alternative counts, it is advisable to put that count to him first whether or not it appears first on the indictment. If there is a joint indictment against several accused, normal practice is to arraign them together. Separate pleas must be taken from each of those named in any joint count.

It is now standard practice to exclude the jurors in waiting from court until after the arraignment has been completed. This avoids the possibility of potential jurors being prejudiced by hearing the accused plead guilty to some but not all the counts on the indictment. After the jury have been sworn, they are told by the clerk the counts to which the accused has pleaded not guilty, no mention being made of any matters to which he has pleaded guilty nor of any co-accused who may have pleaded guilty.

Effect of Lack of Arraignment on the Validity of the Proceedings

D10.2 Failure by the court to have the accused arraigned does not necessarily render invalid subsequent proceedings on the indictment (*Williams* [1978] QB 373). Thus, the defence may waive the accused's right to be arraigned, either expressly or by simply remaining silent while the trial proceeds without arraignment (see the passage from the 1961 edition of vol. 22 of *Corpus Juris Secundum* (stating the law of the USA), which the Court of Appeal quoted in *Williams* [1978] QB 373 at pp. 381H–382D and said was consonant with the law of England – in the 1989 edition of vol. 22, at para. 359, the passage was extensively revised). A dictum of Edmund Davies LJ in *Ellis* (1973) 57 Cr App R 571 at p. 575 that the 'only safe and proper course . . . is to say . . . that (apart from a few very special cases) it is an invariable requirement that the initial arraignment must be conducted between the clerk of the court and the accused person himself' should be understood in the context of the facts of that case, namely, the entry of a guilty plea. On the facts of *Williams*, where W had always intended to plead not guilty and the trial proceeded in all respects as if he had so pleaded but in fact (through an administrative muddle) the indictment was never put, the pre-trial irregularity did not invalidate the proceedings and W's conviction was upheld despite lack of arraignment. The appellant, who was the only person in court who knew he had not been arraigned, raised no objection at the time. Had he objected but the court nonetheless refused to arraign him, it is submitted that any conviction would have had to have been quashed. Further, the decision in *Williams* is without prejudice to the principle that a plea of guilty must be entered by the accused personally, the corollary of which is that a conviction on a guilty plea will be valid only if the accused has been properly arraigned.

Time for Arraignment

The Supreme Court Act 1981, s. 77(1), provides that rules of court are to prescribe the **D10.3** minimum and maximum periods which may elapse between a person's committal for trial and the beginning of the trial (i.e. the arraignment). By s. 77(2), the trial of a person committed for trial (or in respect of whom a notice of transfer has been given) shall not begin within the minimum period prescribed by the rules unless the defence and the prosecution consent, and shall not begin after the maximum period unless a Crown Court judge orders otherwise. Rule 24 of the Crown Court Rules 1982, made in pursuance of s. 77, provides that the minimum and maximum periods shall be 14 days and eight weeks respectively. Leave for late arraignment is left entirely at the Crown Court judge's discretion, and is in practice readily granted. No specific provisions are made as to how or when an application for such leave should be made (cf. the detailed terms of r. 5 of the Indictments (Procedure) Rules 1971, which deals with the time in which a bill of indictment must be preferred). Failure by the prosecution to comply with r. 24 of the Crown Court Rules 1982 is, in any case, of little or no consequence since the rule has been held to be directory not mandatory (*Urbanowski* [1976] 1 WLR 455). It follows that a conviction will be upheld even though the arraignment took place more than eight weeks after committal and no leave for late arraignment was sought or obtained until after the expiry of that period (ibid.). Further, it is submitted that, by analogy with the cases on failure to obtain leave for preferment of a late bill of indictment (see **D9.4**), a trial will not be invalidated by late arraignment even if no leave was given at any time for the period prescribed by r. 24 to be exceeded.

Section 77(3) of the Supreme Court Act 1981 defines the beginning of the trial as the time when the accused is arraigned. It should be noted, however, that the Crown Court has an unfettered discretion to adjourn proceedings, and there is thus no objection to the accused being arraigned within the eight weeks prescribed by r. 24 and then the case being immediately adjourned to a later date if the parties are still not ready for trial.

Crown Court Rules 1982 (SI 1982 No. 1109), r. 24

The periods prescribed for the purposes of paragraphs (a) and (b) of section 77(2) of the Supreme Court Act 1981 [minimum and maximum periods between committal or the giving of a notice of transfer and arraignment] shall be 14 days and eight weeks respectively and accordingly the trial of a person committed by a magistrates' court—

(a) shall not begin until the expiration of 14 days beginning with the date of his committal, except with his consent and the consent of the prosecution, and

(b) shall, unless the Crown Court has otherwise ordered, begin not later than the expiration of eight weeks beginning with the date of his committal.

Prosecution of Offences Act 1985, s. 22, and Regulations Made Thereunder

The manifest inadequacy of r. 24 of the Crown Court Rules 1982 to ensure that trials **D10.4** on indictment begin within a reasonable time of the accused having been sent for trial led to the passing of s. 22 of the Prosecution of Offences Act 1985, by virtue of which the Secretary of State is empowered to make regulations fixing (a) the maximum period available to the prosecution to complete any preliminary stage of proceedings for an offence and/or (b) the maximum period for which an accused may be kept in custody while awaiting completion of such a stage. In the discussion which follows, references to 'committal' should be taken to include the giving of a notice of transfer under the CJA 1987, s. 4, or under the CJA 1991, s. 53.

Regulations under s. 22 may apply not just to the time between committal and arraignment, but also to the time between the accused being charged and committal or (if the offence charged is triable either way or summarily) to the time between charge and the commencement of summary trial. The section is thus relevant to the timing both of committal and summary trial, as well as to the timing of arraignment. For the sake of convenience, however, the section and the regulations so far made under it are discussed in their entirety at this point.

The general effect of s. 22 of the Prosecution of Offences Act 1985 is as follows:

(a)   The Secretary of State may by regulation impose time-limits in respect of any specified 'preliminary stage' of proceedings for an offence (s. 22(1)). The regulations may relate to any type of offence, whether triable only on indictment, triable either way or summarily. 'Preliminary stage' is defined as *not* including anything after the start of trial. As far as trial on indictment is concerned, the 'start of trial' is defined as the point when a jury is sworn, or the court accepts a plea of guilty (s. 22(11A)). There is an exception, however, where a preparatory hearing is held, whether for a serious or complex fraud (by the CJA 1987, s. 8: see **D12.15**), or for a long or complex case (by the CPIA 1996, s. 30: see **D12.14**). As far as summary trial is concerned, the start of trial is 'when the court begins to hear evidence for the prosecution at trial' or accepts a plea of guilty (s. 22(11B)). There is an exception where the court begins to consider whether to exercise its power, under the Mental Health Act 1983, s. 37(3), to make a hospital order without convicting the accused. The regulations may prescribe an *overall time-limit* within which the prosecution must complete the stage of the proceedings in question (s. 22(1)(a)). Alternatively or additionally, they may prescribe a *custody time-limit*, that being the maximum period for which the accused may be remanded in custody while the stage is being completed (s. 22(1)(b)). To date, regulations have related only to indictable offences and have imposed only custody time-limits.

(b)   At any time before the expiry of a time-limit, the appropriate court (i.e. the Crown Court if the accused has already been committed for trial, otherwise the magistrates' court) may extend the limit if satisfied (i) that there is 'good and sufficient cause for doing so' and (ii) that 'the prosecution has acted with all due diligence and expedition' (s. 22(3): instances of 'good and sufficient cause' are given in s. 22(3)(a)(i) and (ii), but they are clearly meant to be no more than examples). An already extended limit may be further extended (ibid.). By reg. 7 of the Prosecution of Offences (Custody Time-Limits) Regulations 1987 (SI 1987 No. 299) an application for extension may be made orally or in writing, notice of intention to make the application to be given to the defence and the court not less than five days before an application to the Crown Court and not less than two days before an application to a magistrates' court. Notice may, however, be dispensed with if the court is satisfied that it is not practicable for the prosecution to give it in the time specified (reg. 7(4)). The terms 'overall time-limit' and 'custody time-limit' are defined so as to include any extensions granted under s. 22(3) (s. 22(11)). The effect of a failure by the prosecution to give proper notice was considered in *Governor of Canterbury Prison, ex parte Craig* [1991] 2 QB 195. It was held in that case that the justices still had a discretion under s. 22(3) of the 1985 Act to extend a time-limit 'at any time before . . . expiry'. Hence they could extend the time-limit of the period that C was remanded in custody despite the prosecution's failure to show that it had been impracticable to give him two days' notice of an application for extension.

(c)   In *Governor of Winchester Prison, ex parte Roddie* [1991] 1 WLR 303, the Divisional Court considered the criteria for extension as set out in s. 22(3): the court must be satisfied (i) that there was good and sufficient cause and (ii) that the Crown had acted with all due expedition (the need for 'diligence' was added by the CDA 1998). In the instant case, the applicants were charged with conspiracy to rob. The justices had granted an extension, and the Crown Court had dismissed an appeal against that extension on the grounds that there was good and sufficient cause because of the seriousness of the charge, the fact that committal papers were only a few days late, and the fact that a refusal would have led to automatic bail. The Divisional Court held that these grounds were not good and sufficient cause. As to the seriousness of the offence,

Parliament had provided the same time-limit for all offences except treason. The more serious the charge, the more important it was for the police to get on with preparing the case. Further, the fact that the police were understaffed and suffered delays in the receipt of typing and forensic evidence did not mean there was due expedition as was required by the second criterion. Due expedition must be measured against some objective yardstick, or it would defeat the Act's objects. The applicants were, accordingly, unlawfully detained until committal took place whereupon a new custody time-limit would take effect.

In *Manchester Crown Court, ex parte McDonald* [1999] 1 WLR 841, Lord Bingham CJ set out the principles underlying the custody time limit provisions in the Prosecution of Offences Act 1985, s. 23, and gave guidance upon the practicalities of interpreting the tests laid down by the statute. Although the judgment pre-dated the new wording of s. 22(3)(a) of the 1985 Act, as inserted by the CDA 1998, s. 43, both the statement of principle and the practical guidance retain their full validity.

As far as the fundamental principles of the provisions are concerned, the Lord Chief Justice emphasised the presumption of liberty set out in Art. 5(3) of the European Convention on Human Rights: 'Everyone arrested or detained [for trial] . . . shall be entitled to trial within a reasonable time or to release pending trial'. With that provision in mind, the overriding purposes of the statutory provisions were said to be:

(a) to ensure that the periods for which unconvicted defendants are held in custody are as short as is reasonably and practically possible;

(b) to oblige the prosecution to prepare cases for trial with due diligence and expedition; and

(c) to give the court power to control any extension of the maximum period for which any defendant may be held awaiting trial.

The main points of practical guidance which emerge from *Ex parte McDonald* are:

(1) It is for the prosecution to satisfy the court on the balance of probabilities that the statutory conditions are met.

(2) The necessary standard is that of a competent prosecutor conscious of his duty to bring the case to trial as quickly as is reasonably and fairly possible.

(3) In judging whether the standard was met, the court should consider the nature and complexity of the case, the preparation necessary, the conduct of the defence, and the extent to which the prosecutor was dependent on others outside his control, and other relevant factors.

(4) What amounts to good and sufficient cause is a matter for the court on the facts of the case.

(5) Staff shortages and sickness will be inadequate reasons for extension. The unavailability of a judge or a courtroom may be good and sufficient cause, but such cases should be approached with 'great caution'.

(6) The court should state the reasons for its decision.

(7) Once the court had heard full argument and decided, the Divisional Court would be most reluctant to disturb its decision, and would only do so on the familiar grounds which supported an application for judicial review.

In *Central Criminal Court, ex parte Abu-Wardeh* [1997] 1 WLR 1083, the Divisional Court held that the protection of the public was, in itself, an insufficient ground for the extension of a custody time limit, disagreeing with *Luton Crown Court, ex parte Neaves* (1993) 157 JP 80. In *Birmingham Crown Court, ex parte Bell* [1997] 2 Cr App R 363, the Divisional Court accepted that, although protection of the public might not be enough in itself to constitute good and sufficient cause, where protection of prosecution witnesses was an issue, that might be capable in conjunction with other factors of giving rise to good and sufficient cause.

Several cases have turned upon the question of whether the fact that there is no judge or courtroom in which a case may be tried can constitute good and sufficient cause so as to satisfy the first condition for the grant of an extension. In *Norwich Crown Court, ex parte Stiller* (1992) 156 JP 624, the Crown Court granted an extension of 56 days on the ground that there was no judge or courtroom available for the case to be tried. The Divisional Court quashed the order, and remitted the matter to the Crown Court for bail to be granted. The applicants were unlikely to be tried until a date eight months after their committal and might not be tried until 14 months after committal. In *Norwich Crown Court, ex parte Cox* (1993) 97 Cr App R 145, however, the Divisional Court made it plain that, in appropriate circumstances, the lack of a judge and courtroom is capable of constituting the 'good and sufficient cause' which the Act requires. The decision of the Crown Court judge to grant an extension of 20 days, to a date upon which the case could be listed for trial, was upheld. Mann LJ stated that whether the lack of a court and judge should be regarded as being a good and sufficient cause 'must depend upon the facts of that instant case including, in particular, whether a trial date has been specified'. In *Maidstone Crown Court, ex parte Schulz* (1993) 157 JP 601, it was held that a decision by the Crown Court judge to grant an extension of 14 days to enable an earlier trial date to be sought, when the court had been informed that the earliest possible date was in 93 days, was not for good and sufficient cause.

As to the phrase 'all due expedition', in *Norwich Crown Court, ex parte Parker* (1992) 96 Cr App R 68, the Divisional Court said that all concerned with the prosecution were not required to act as though this were their only task at hand; 'all due expedition' meant the expedition appropriate in the circumstances, one of those circumstances being the custody time-limit. In *Central Criminal Court, ex parte Behbehari* [1994] Crim LR 352, the Divisional Court held that, in determining whether the prosecution had acted with 'all due expedition', the court should take into account whether papers were served on the defence in time to allow adequate consideration of the type of committal. In considering whether the prosecution had acted with all due expedition, the judge ought to consider the matter by reference to the presence or absence of all due expedition at the stage to which the custody time limit relates (*Ex parte Bell*). In *Leeds Crown Court, ex parte Briggs (No. 2)* [1998] 2 Cr App R 424, the Divisional Court held that 'due expedition' on the part of the prosecution was not confined to achieving the possibility of a s. 6(2) committal within the custody time-limit. All due expedition had to be directed towards achieving a contested committal within that period.

In *Leeds Crown Court, ex parte Bagoutie* (1999) *The Times*, 31 May 1999, Lord Bingham CJ emphasised that the requirement of due expedition was not disciplinary in intention. It aimed to protect defendants from being kept in prison awaiting trial longer than was justifiable. Parliament had intended to insist that prosecutors could not seek extensions where the need for the extension was attributable to their own failure to act with due expedition. Hence, if the court was satisfied that there was good and sufficient cause for the extension, but was not satisfied that the prosecution had acted with all due expedition, it was not obliged to refuse the application if it concluded that the prosecution's failure had neither caused nor contributed to the need for the extension.

In *Chelmsford Crown Court, ex parte Mills* (1999) *The Times*, 31 May 1999, Lord Bingham CJ said that when a contested application was made for an extension, turning wholly or partly on whether the prosecution had acted with all due expedition, the judge should be given a detailed chronology (preferably agreed), showing the dates of all material events and orders. When the judge ruled on such an application, he should give reasons for his decision, which need not be long or elaborate.

(d)   Each offence with which the accused is charged attracts its own time-limit (*Wirral District Magistrates' Court, ex parte Meikle* (1990) 154 JP 1035). In this case, M was charged with five different offences at different dates, being held in custody from the date of the first charge, which was one of murder. It was unsuccessfully contended on her behalf that the charges should be regarded as one for the purposes of custody time-limits. In effect, this would have led to her release on bail 70 days after the murder charge. Not surprisingly, in view of the fact that the 1987 Regulations repeatedly refer to 'offence' in the singular, the Divisional Court held that each offence attracts its own custody time-limit. (See also *Great Yarmouth Magistrates, ex parte Thomas* [1992] Crim LR 116, *Waltham Forest Magistrates' Court, ex parte Lee* (1993) 157 JP 811, *Leeds Crown Court, ex parte Stubley* [1999] Crim LR 822 and *Wolverhampton Justices and Stafford Crown Court, ex parte Uppal* (1995) 159 JP 86.)

(e) In *White* v *DPP* [1989] Crim LR 375, the Divisional Court upheld the Crown Court's dismissal of an appeal against the magistrates' extension of the custody time-limit (70 days) applicable to the period between W's first court appearance and committal, the reason for the extension being that the defence had successfully applied for an adjournment to consider the prosecution statements that had only just been served on them and the adjournment would have entailed breach of the limit had it not been extended. The Divisional Court stated that the reasonable requirement of the defence to consider the papers was capable of being a good and sufficient cause for extension of time, although each case must turn on its own facts. Their lordships did not necessarily agree with the Crown Court judge's approach, namely, that he had to be satisfied beyond reasonable doubt of the existence of good cause before granting an extension. In *Governor of Canterbury Prison, ex parte Craig* [1990] 3 WLR 126, Watkins LJ (giving the judgment of the Divisional Court) referred (at p. 132) to the doubt expressed in *White* v *DPP* and stated:

> In our view, the standard to be applied is that of the balance of probabilities. That is the standard for determining bail applications. It should apply equally, we think, to related interlocutory questions of the sort here in question.

(f) If an overall time-limit expires, the proceedings in the case are stayed (s. 22(4), as amended by the CDA 1998, s. 43(3)). The effects of such a stay are set out in s. 22B. The proceedings for the offence can be reinstituted only if the DPP, a Chief Crown Prosecutor or one of the other senior figures named in s. 22B(2) so directs. Fresh proceedings may be instituted within three months of the original stay of proceedings, or longer with the leave of the court. No overall time limits have yet been fixed.

(g) If a custody time-limit expires before completion of the stage of proceedings in question, the accused must be granted bail, but the expiry of the limit otherwise has no effect on the proceedings. In *Sheffield Magistrates' Court, ex parte Turner* [1991] 2 QB 472, T was held to have been unlawfully detained, contrary to s. 22 of the 1985 Act and the regulations thereunder, between 23 August and 20 September. The Divisional Court accordingly granted a declaration to that effect. He had been committed for trial on 20 September, however, and that committal was held to be valid. A fresh custody time-limit was therefore laid down by reg. 5(3) and so he was at the date of the application, in lawful custody; the application for a writ of habeas corpus failed. The regulations may make provision for the Bail Act 1976 and the MCA 1980 to apply in cases where the accused is bailed as a result of a custody time-limit's expiry with such modifications as the Secretary of State considers necessary (s. 22(2)(d) and see (i) below for details of how the regulations so far made deal with bail on expiry of a custody time-limit).

(h) Where the accused acquires the right to bail as a result of the expiry of a custody time limit, that right, it is submitted, continues until the start of the trial. *Croydon Crown Court, ex parte Lewis* (1994) 158 JP 886 no longer represents the law since it was decided before the CPIA 1996, s. 71, came into effect, when the Prosecution of Offences Act 1985, s. 22, referred to 'arraignment' rather than 'start of the trial' as the boundary of preliminary proceedings.

(i) Escape from custody during the running of a custody time-limit automatically leads to the regulation imposing the time-limit being disregarded (s. 22(5)). Similarly, if an accused has been released in consequence of the expiry of a custody time-limit and then fails to attend court in answer to his bail, the earlier expiry of the limit is disregarded and the question, once he has been arrested, of whether to bail him again or remand in custody is therefore entirely in the discretion of the court (ibid.). As to overall time-limits, both escape from custody and failure to surrender to bail mean that the period during which the accused is at large, together with any additional period directed by the court, shall be disregarded for the purposes of computing the overall time limit (s. 22(6) and (6A)).

(j) Following an application to a magistrates' court for extension of a time-limit, the party against whom the magistrates' decision goes may appeal to the Crown Court (s. 22(7) and (8)). An appeal by the prosecution against refusal to extend must be commenced before the actual expiry of the limit, but, provided that is done, the limit is deemed not to have expired until after the determination of the appeal (s. 22(9)). Rule 27A of the Crown Court Rules 1982 sets out the procedure to be followed on such appeals, in particular, the requirement for notice to the court and the other party and the contents of the notice. Both applications to the Crown Court for extension of a time-limit and appeals against magistrates' decisions on applications to extend are matters that may and normally would be determined by a Crown Court judge in chambers (r. 27(2)). In *Leeds Crown Court, ex parte Briggs (No. 1)* [1998] 2 Cr App R 413, the Divisional Court stated that the Crown Court judge dealing with an application should give reasons for granting an extension.

(k) A challenge to the decision of the Crown Court to grant an extension of time limits on the basis that there was insufficient evidence to justify that decision should be made by way of appeal by case stated to the Divisional Court. In that way, the Crown Court judge will be able to set out clearly the facts found and the material on which the findings were based (*Central Criminal Court, ex parte Behbehari* [1994] Crim LR 352).

(l) The exercise of the power to extend a time-limit cannot be used as a ground of appeal should the accused ultimately be convicted (s. 22(10)).

(m) As far as custody time-limits are concerned, 'custody' includes local authority accommodation to which a juvenile is committed by virtue of the CYPA 1969, s. 23 (s. 22(11) of the 1985 Act). In *Stratford Youth Court, ex parte S* (1998) 162 JP 552, the point at issue was whether the 56-day custody time-limit imposed by reg. 4(3) for completion of preliminary stages in indictable offences applied to a young person charged with robbery. The Divisional Court held that it did, robbery being, in the case of a young person, an offence triable either way, so that the 56-day limit in reg. 4(3) applied. In *Re Ofili* [1995] Crim LR 880, the Divisional Court held that a defendant who remained in custody because of inability to provide a surety met the definition in s. 22(11), since he fell within the terms of the MCA 1980, s. 128. He was therefore entitled to the benefit of custody time limits.

(n) The Secretary of State has used his powers under s. 22 to issue the Prosecution of Offences (Custody Time-Limits) Regulations 1987 (SI 1987 No. 299). As their name suggests, the regulations do *not* fix any overall time-limits.

By reg. 4(2) and (4), the maximum period for which an accused charged with an indictable offence may be held in the custody of the magistrates' court between his first appearance and committal proceedings is 70 days. If the offence is triable either way and the court determines to try the case summarily, the maximum period in custody between first appearance and the court beginning to hear evidence for the prosecution is again 70 days, unless the decision for summary trial is taken within 56 days, in which case the limit is reduced to 56 days (reg. 4(2) and (3)).

By reg. 5(3)(a), the maximum period for which an accused committed for trial to the Crown Court may be held in custody between committal and the start of trial is 112 days.

Paragraphs (4) to (6) of reg. 5 contain detailed rules covering atypical situations, such as the bill of indictment against the accused being preferred by the direction of a High Court judge but nonetheless consisting entirely of counts for offences in respect of which the accused was in fact committed for trial. The effect of these detailed rules is beyond the scope of this work, save to say that, if a single indictment is preferred containing counts in respect of which the accused was committed for trial on two or more different occasions, the 112-day limit applies separately in relation to each offence (reg. 6(4)).

Where proceedings are by way of a voluntary bill of indictment (not committal) the 112-day period runs from the date of preferment of the bill (reg. 5(3)(b)).

The Bail Act 1976 is modified in its application to accused persons in respect of whom custody time-limits have expired in that:

(a)   they are automatically entitled to bail;
(b)   on granting bail, the court may not require sureties or the deposit of security; and
(c)   following the grant of bail, they may not be arrested without warrant merely on the ground that a police officer believes they are unlikely to surrender to custody (reg. 8).

It is, however, open to the court granting bail to impose conditions such as curfew, residence or reporting to a police station, and the rule that actual or feared breach of such conditions is a ground for arrest without warrant (Bail Act 1976, ss. 3(6) and 7(3)(b)) applies to accused bailed on expiry of a time-limit just as it applies to accused granted bail in any other circumstances (see also **D5.20**). Regulation 6 requires the prosecution to give notice to the Crown Court and the accused stating whether they intend to ask the court to impose conditions on the bail of an accused in respect of whom a custody time-limit is about to expire. In response to an indication that the prosecution are asking for conditions, the defence must give either:

(a)   written notice of a wish to be represented at the hearing of the application;
(b)   written notice that the accused does not object to the proposed conditions; or
(c)   a written statement of the accused's reasons for objecting.

It is the prosecution's duty to arrange for the accused to be brought before the Crown Court within the two days preceding expiry of a custody time-limit (reg. 6(1)(b)). Regulation 6(6) states what would in any event appear obvious, namely that, where the Crown Court is notified that the 112-day time-limit between committal and the start of the trial is about to expire in a certain case, it must bail the accused as from the expiry of the limit, subject to a duty to attend for trial. The regulations do not expressly deal with the procedure for bailing an accused who has the benefit of the 70-day charge-committal/summary trial time-limit.

Prosecution of Offences Act 1985, ss. 22, 22A and 22B

22.—(1)   The Secretary of State may by regulations make provision, with respect to any specified preliminary stage of proceedings for an offence, as to the maximum period—
(a)   to be allowed to the prosecution to complete that stage;
(b)   during which the accused may, while awaiting completion of that stage, be—
(i)   in the custody of a magistrates' court; or
(ii)   in the custody of the Crown Court;
in relation to that offence.
(2)   The regulations may, in particular—
(a)   be made so as to apply only in relation to proceedings instituted in specified areas or proceedings of, or against persons of, specified classes or descriptions;
(b)   make different provision with respect to proceedings instituted in different areas, or different provision with respect to proceedings of, or against persons of, different classes or descriptions;
(c)   make such provision with respect to the procedure to be followed in criminal proceedings as the Secretary of State considers appropriate in consequence of any other provision of the regulations;

(d)   provide for the Magistrates' Courts Act 1980 and the Bail Act 1976 to apply in relation to cases to which custody or overall time-limits apply subject to such modifications as may be specified (being modifications which the Secretary of State considers necessary in consequence of any provision made by the regulations); and

(e)   make such transitional provision in relation to proceedings instituted before the commencement of any provision of the regulations as the Secretary of State considers appropriate.

(3)   The appropriate court may, at any time before the expiry of a time-limit imposed by the regulations, extend, or further extend that limit; but the court shall not do so unless it is satisfied—

(a)   that the need for the extension is due to—

(i)   the illness or absence of the accused, a necessary witness, a judge or a magistrate;

(ii)   a postponement which is occasioned by the ordering by the court of separate trials in the case of two or more accused or two or more offences; or

(iii)   some other good and sufficient cause; and

(b)   that the prosecution has acted with all due diligence and expedition.

(4)   Where, in relation to any proceedings for an offence, an overall time-limit has expired before the completion of the stage of the proceedings to which the limit applies, the appropriate court shall try the proceedings.

(5)   Where—

(a)   a person escapes from the custody of a magistrates' court or the Crown Court before the expiry of a custody time-limit which applies in his case; or

(b)   a person who has been released on bail in consequence of the expiry of a custody time-limit—

(i)   fails to surrender himself into the custody of the court at the appointed time; or

(ii)   is arrested by a constable on a ground mentioned in section 7(3)(b) of the Bail Act 1976 (breach, or likely breach, of conditions of bail);

the regulations shall, so far as they provide for any custody time-limit in relation to the preliminary stage in question, be disregarded.

(6)   Subsection (6A) below applies where—

(a)   a person escapes from the custody of a magistrates' court or the Crown Court; or

(b)   a person who has been released on bail fails to surrender himself into the custody of the court at the appointed time;

and is accordingly unlawfully at large for any period.

(6A)   The following, namely—

(a)   the period for which the person is unlawfully at large; and

(b)   such additional period (if any) as the appropriate court may direct, having regard to the disruption of the prosecution occasioned by—

(i)   the person's escape or failure to surrender; and

(ii)   the length of the period mentioned in paragraph (a) above,

shall be disregarded, so far as the offence in question is concerned, for the purposes of the overall time limit which applies in his case in relation to the stage which the proceedings have reached at the time of the escape or, as the case may be, at the appointed time.

(7)   Where a magistrates' court decides to extend, or further extend, a custody or overall time-limit, or to give a direction under subsection (6A) above, the accused may appeal against the decision to the Crown Court.

(8)   Where a magistrates' court refuses to extend, or further extend, a custody or overall time-limit, or to give a direction under subsection (6A) above, the prosecution may appeal against the refusal to the Crown Court.

(9)   An appeal under subsection (8) above may not be commenced after the expiry of the limit in question; but where such an appeal is commenced before the expiry of the limit the limit shall be deemed not to have expired before the determination or abandonment of the appeal.

(10)   Where a person is convicted of an offence in any proceedings, the exercise, in relation to any preliminary stage of those proceedings, of the power conferred by subsection (3) above shall not be called into question in any appeal against that conviction.

(11)   In this section—

'appropriate court' means—

(a)   where the accused has been committed for trial or indicted for the offence, the Crown Court; and

(b)   in any other case, the magistrates' court specified in the summons or warrant in question or, where the accused has already appeared or been brought before a magistrates' court, a magistrates' court for the same area;

'custody' includes local authority accommodation to which a person is remanded or committed by virtue of section 23 of the Children and Young Persons Act 1969, and references to a person being committed to custody shall be construed accordingly;

'custody of the Crown Court' includes custody to which a person is committed in pursuance of—

(a)   section 6 of the Magistrates' Courts Act 1980 (magistrates' court committing accused for trial); or

(b)   section 43A of that Act (magistrates' court dealing with a person brought before it following his arrest in pursuance of a warrant issued by the Crown Court); or

(c)   section 5(2)(a) of the Criminal Justice Act 1987 (custody after transfer order in fraud case); or

(d)   paragraph 2(1)(a) of Schedule 6 to the Criminal Justice Act 1991 (custody after transfer order in certain cases involving children).

'custody of a magistrates' court' means custody to which a person is committed in pursuance of section 128 of the Magistrates' Courts Act 1980 (remand);

'custody time-limit' means a time-limit imposed by regulations made under subsection (1)(b) above or, where any such limit has been extended by a court under subsection (3) above, the limit as so extended;

'preliminary stage', in relation to any proceedings, does not include any stage after the start of the trial (within the meaning given by subsections (11A) and (11B) below);

'overall time-limit' means a time-limit imposed by regulations made under subsection (1)(a) above or, where any such limit has been extended by a court under subsection (3) above, the limit as so extended; and

'specified' means specified in the regulations.

(11ZA)   For the purposes of this section, proceedings for an offence shall be taken to begin when the accused is charged with the offence or, as the case may be, an information is laid charging him with the offence.

(11A)   For the purposes of this section, the start of a trial on indictment shall be taken to occur when a jury is sworn to consider the issue of guilt or fitness to plead or, if the court accepts a plea of guilty before a jury is sworn, when that plea is accepted; but this is subject to section 8 of the Criminal Justice Act 1987 and section 30 of the Criminal Procedure and Investigations Act 1996 (preparatory hearings).

(11B)   For the purposes of this section, the start of a summary trial shall be taken to occur—

(a)   when the court begins to hear evidence for the prosecution at the trial or to consider whether to exercise its power under section 37(3) of the Mental Health Act 1983 (power to make hospital order without convicting the accused), or

(b)   if the court accepts a plea of guilty without proceeding as mentioned above, when that plea is accepted.

(12)   For the purposes of the application of any custody time-limit in relation to a person who is in the custody of a magistrates' court or the Crown Court—

(a)   all periods during which he is in the custody of a magistrates' court in respect of the same offence shall be aggregated and treated as a single continuous period; and

(b)   all periods during which he is in the custody of the Crown Court in respect of the same offence shall be aggregated and treated similarly.

(13)   For the purposes of section 29(3) of the Supreme Court Act 1981 (High Court to have power to make prerogative orders in relation to jurisdiction of Crown Court in matters which do not relate to trial on indictment) the jurisdiction conferred on the Crown Court by this section shall be taken to be part of its jurisdiction in matters other than those relating to trial on indictment.

22A.—(1)   The Secretary of State may by regulations make provision—

(a)   with respect to a person under the age of 18 at the time of his arrest in connection with an offence, as to the maximum period to be allowed for the completion of the stage beginning with his arrest and ending with the date fixed for his first appearance in court in connection with the offence ('the initial stage');

(b)   with respect to a person convicted of an offence who was under that age at the time of his arrest for the offence or (where he was not arrested for it) the laying of the information charging him with it, as to the period within which the stage between his conviction and his being sentenced for the offence should be completed.

(2)   Subsection (2) of section 22 above applies for the purposes of regulations under subsection (1) above as if—

(a)   the reference in paragraph (d) to custody or overall time limits were a reference to time limits imposed by the regulations; and

(b)   the reference in paragraph (e) to proceedings instituted before the commencement of any provisions of the regulations were a reference to a stage begun before that commencement.

(3)   A magistrates' court may, at any time before the expiry of the time limit imposed by the regulations under subsection (1)(a) above ('the initial stage time limit'), extend, or further extend, that limit; but the court shall not do so unless it is satisfied—

(a)   that the need for the extension is due to some good and sufficient cause; and

(b)   that the investigation has been conducted, and (where applicable) the prosecution has acted, with all due diligence and expedition.

(4)   Where the initial stage time limit (whether as originally imposed or as extended or further extended under subsection (3) above) expires before the person arrested is charged with the offence, he shall not be charged with it unless further evidence relating to it is obtained, and—

(a)   if he is then under arrest, he shall be released;

(b)   if he is then on bail under part IV of the Police and Criminal Evidence Act 1984, his bail (and any duty or conditions to which it is subject) shall be discharged.

22B.—(1)   This section applies where proceedings for an offence ('the original proceedings') are stayed by a court under section 22(4) or 22A(5) of this Act.

(2)   If—

(a)   in the case of proceedings conducted by the Director, the Director or a Chief Crown Prosecutor so directs;

(b)   in the case of proceedings conducted by the Director of the Serious Fraud Office, the Commissioners of Inland Revenue or the Commissioners of Customs and Excise, that Director or those Commissioners so direct; or

(c)   in the case of proceedings not conducted as mentioned in paragraph (a) or (b) above, a person designated for the purpose by the Secretary of State so directs,

fresh proceedings for the offence may be instituted within a period of three months (or such longer period as the court may allow) after the date on which the original proceedings were stayed by the court.

(3)   Fresh proceedings shall be instituted as follows—

(a)   where the original proceedings were stayed by the Crown Court, by preferring a bill of indictment;

(b)   where the original proceedings were stayed by a magistrates' court, by laying an information.

(4)   Fresh proceedings may be instituted in accordance with subsections (2) and (3)(b) above notwithstanding anything in section 127(1) of the Magistrates' Courts Act 1980 (limitation of time).

(5)   Where fresh proceedings are instituted, anything done in relation to the original proceedings shall be treated as done in relation to the fresh proceedings if the court so directs or it was done—

(a)   by the prosecutor in compliance or purported compliance with section 3, 4, 7 or 9 of the Criminal Procedure and Investigations Act 1996; or

(b)   by the accused in compliance or purported compliance with section 5 or 6 of that Act.

(6)   Where a person is convicted of an offence in fresh proceedings under this section, the institution of those proceedings shall not be called into question in any appeal against that conviction.

FAILURE TO PLEAD

Introduction

An accused may fail to plead to the indictment when arraigned either because he is **D10.5** mentally incapable of doing so, or because he is physically incapable (i.e. deaf and/or speech handicapped), or because he wilfully chooses to stay silent. In the first event, he is said to be unfit to plead; in the second, he is mute by visitation of God; and in the third he is mute of malice.

Unfitness to Plead

Whether or not an accused is fit to plead is determined in accordance with tests laid **D10.6** down by common law. The procedure to be followed when an accused might be unfit and the consequences of a finding of unfitness are contained in the Criminal Procedure (Insanity) Act 1964, ss. 4, 4A and 5. As is suggested by the title of the relevant statutes, unfitness to plead in modern times is virtually invariably associated with mental illness or disability. There is, however, at least a theoretical possibility that a person who is mentally normal could be found unfit to plead (see **D10.7**).

The Test of Unfitness to Plead The leading case of *Pritchard* (1836) 7 C & P 303 **D10.7** concerned a deaf mute who was otherwise of sound mind. Alderson B directed the jury empanelled to determine whether P was fit to plead in terms which Lord Parker CJ was later to say had become 'firmly embodied in our law' (see *Podola* [1960] 1 QB 325 at p. 353). Alderson B said (7 C & P 303 at pp. 304–5):

> There are three points to be inquired into: First, whether the prisoner is mute of malice or not; secondly, whether he can plead to the indictment or not; thirdly, whether he is of sufficient intellect to comprehend the course of proceedings on the trial, so as to make a proper defence – to know that he might challenge [any jurors] to whom he may object – and to comprehend the details of the evidence. . . . if you think that there is no certain mode of communicating the details of the trial to the prisoner, so that he can clearly understand them, and be able properly to make his defence to the charge; you ought to find that he is not of sane mind. It is not enough, that he may have a general capacity of communicating on ordinary matters.

It will be apparent from the above that the issue of unfitness to plead may sometimes be linked with and almost indistinguishable from the issue of whether an accused is mute of malice or mute by visitation of God. Indeed, the result of Pritchard's case was that he was found unfit to plead, even though his disability (being deaf and speech handicapped) also constitutes the classic example of muteness by visitation of God. Similarly, in *Governor of Stafford Prison, ex parte Emery* [1909] 2 KB 81 a finding of unfitness in respect of a deaf accused who could neither read nor write nor communicate by sign language was upheld by the High Court. Factually, however, *Pritchard* and *Ex parte Emery* are atypical cases. One would not today expect the issue of unfitness to be raised unless the accused is thought to be suffering from some degree of mental illness or deficiency, even if this may be exacerbated by physical problems. Nonetheless, Alderson B's direction in *Pritchard* remains the basis of the modern law, and the following points emerge from it:

(a)   As intimated above, an accused may be unfit to plead even though he is not insane within the meaning of the M'Naghten rules. The point was expressly decided in *Governor of Stafford Prison, ex parte Emery*, a particularly strong decision since the statutory provision then governing unfitness to plead (Lunatics Act 1800, s. 2) actually referred to the jury finding that the person indicted was insane (and see also Lord Parker CJ's judgment in *Podola* [1960] 1 QB 325 at p. 353). Similarly, it is submitted that an accused may be unfit even though he is not suffering from any of the forms of mental disorder defined in s. 37(1) of the Mental Health Act 1983, the existence of one of which is a precondition for the making of a hospital order in the case of a convicted offender.

(b)   The test of unfitness to plead is whether the accused will be able to comprehend the course of the proceedings so as to make a proper defence (*Pritchard*). Whether he can understand and reply rationally to the indictment is obviously a relevant factor, but the jury must also consider whether he would be able to exercise his right to challenge jurors, understand details of the evidence as it is given, instruct his legal advisers and give evidence himself if he so desires.

(c)   Assuming the accused can understand the course of the proceedings, he will be fit to plead even though the jury take the view that he may act against his own best interests as a consequence of his mental condition (*Robertson* [1968] 1 WLR 1767 – paranoiac who might, for example, have made irrational objections to potential jurors, held fit to plead). Similarly, a high degree of abnormality does not *ipso facto* render the accused unfit to plead (*Berry* (1977) 66 Cr App R 156 – finding of unfitness quashed because, although B was suffering from paranoid schizophrenia, was in a 'grossly abnormal mental state' and unable to 'view his actions in any sort of sensible manner', the judge failed to direct the jury on the crucial issue of whether those abnormalities made him incapable of following the trial etc.).

(d)   Loss of memory through hysterical amnesia does not amount to unfitness to plead if the accused is otherwise normal at the time of trial (*Podola*). Such an accused will be able to comprehend the proceedings and communicate with his legal advisers, although it is submitted that he can hardly make a proper defence if his instructions as to the prosecution evidence are necessarily limited to, 'It might or might not be true, but I cannot remember'.

D10.8   ***Procedure for Determining Unfitness to Plead***   The issue of whether the accused is fit to plead may be raised by either the prosecution or defence. The prosecution might wish to assert that the accused is unfit to plead (even though that will at least delay a conviction) either because of the general principle that prosecuting counsel should act as a 'minister of justice' assisting the court and not strive for a conviction at all costs, or because in certain circumstances (e.g., where the offence charged requires proof of a specific or ulterior intent on the part of the accused) it may in practice be difficult to establish guilt if, at the time of trial, the accused is manifestly suffering from mental illness.

Subject to a special procedure contained in the Criminal Procedure (Insanity) Act 1964, s. 4(2), the issue must be determined as soon as it arises (s. 4(4)). Assuming the possibility of the accused being unfit is known to the parties before trial, it is submitted that the court should be informed of the situation before arraignment so that, if he is unfit, the accused will not be called on to plead. A jury must be empanelled to determine the issue, the form of oath being: 'I swear by almighty God that I will faithfully try whether the prisoner at the bar is under disability so that he cannot be tried and give a true verdict according to the evidence'. There is no right of challenge in respect of jurors empanelled to try the issue of whether the accused is mute of malice (see *Paling* (1978) 67 Cr App R 299) but there seems to be no direct authority on whether the same applies where the issue is unfitness.

Following the evidence, the jury are directed to consider whether the defendant is capable of understanding the proceedings so that he can:

(a)   put forward his defence;
(b)   challenge any juror to whom he has cause to object;
(c)   give proper instructions to his legal representatives; and
(d)   follow the evidence.

They should then return their verdict. A majority verdict is permissible in the circumstances laid down by the Juries Act 1974, s. 17. If the issue was raised by the defence, the burden of proof is on them to establish on a balance of probabilities that the accused is unfit (*Robertson*) [1968] 1 WLR 1767); if raised by the prosecution, they bear the burden of proof beyond reasonable doubt (*Podola* [1960] 1 QB 325).

Section 4(2) of the 1964 Act permits the court to postpone consideration of unfitness until any time up to the opening of the defence case. The court must be of the opinion that, having regard to 'the nature of the supposed disability', postponement is 'expedient' and 'in the interests of the accused'.

Section 4A of the 1964 Act applies where the jury has determined that the accused is unfit to plead. It must then be determined by a jury whether the accused 'did the act or made the omission charged against him as the offence' (s. 4A(2)). If they are satisfied that he did, they must find accordingly (s. 4A(3)). If they are not satisfied, they must acquit. If the question of fitness to plead was determined on arraignment, then a fresh jury must be empanelled to try the issue of whether the accused did the act or made the omission. If it was postponed under s. 4(2), the jury by whom the accused was being tried should also determine whether he did the act or made the omission (s. 4A(5)). The purpose of this 'trial of the facts' is to ensure that the case against a defendant who has been found unfit to plead is tested. It aims in this way to avoid the detention of innocent persons in hospital, merely because they are mentally unfit. Although the statute is silent on the standard of proof, it is submitted that the test is 'beyond reasonable doubt', in accordance with general principle.

In addition, s. 4(6) lays down that a jury may not determine the question of fitness to plead except on the evidence (written or oral) of two or more registered medical practitioners, at least one of whom must have been approved by the Secretary of State as having special experience in the diagnosis or treatment of mental disorder. (See **D17.21** for the power of the court to remand an accused for the preparation of reports on his mental condition under the Mental Health Act 1983, s. 35.)

Consequences of a Finding of Unfitness

Under the Criminal Procedure (Insanity) Act 1964, s. 5, if the accused is found unfit to plead, and the jury determines that he did the act or made the omission as charged, then the court may make one of the following orders: **D10.9**

(a) an admission order to such hospital as the Secretary of State specifies;
(b) a guardianship order under the Mental Health Act 1983;
(c) a supervision and treatment order; or
(d) an order for the accused's absolute discharge.

The court's power of disposal is confined to cases where the accused has been found to have committed the act charged as the offence. Once there has been such a finding, there is a range of options open to the court.

The first such option is an admission order, for compulsory hospital treatment. Such an order may be made the subject of a restriction order without limit of time or for a specified period. Where the offence to which the findings relate is murder, then the court must make an admission order without limit of time (see **E24.3**). Second, the court may make a guardianship order under the provisions of the Mental Health Act 1983, s. 37. The purpose of such an order is to ensure that the accused receives care and protection, rather than medical treatment (see **E24.4** and Home Office Circular 66/90, paragraph 8(iv)(c)). Third, the court may make a supervision and treatment order. These orders are similar to those in the PCCA 1973, sch. 1A, which provide for probation orders with a requirement as to psychiatric treatment (see **E24.1**). Finally, the court may decide to discharge the accused absolutely.

Where there has been a finding of unfitness to plead, and a jury has to consider whether the accused did the act charged against him as murder, then he cannot rely on the defence of diminished responsibility under the Homicide Act 1957, s. 2 (*Antoine* [1999] 2 Cr App R 225).

D10.10 ***Procedure where Accused is Found Fit to Plead***   If the accused is found fit to plead before the calling of any prosecution evidence, he will thereafter be arraigned in the usual way and plead to the indictment. Should he plead not guilty, a fresh jury must be empanelled to try the case (Criminal Procedure (Insanity) Act 1964, s. 4(5)(a)). If consideration of fitness to plead is postponed under s. 4(2), the jury already trying the substantive issue may also determine fitness to plead or the judge may, at his discretion, direct that it be determined by a separate jury (s. 4(5)(b)).

Criminal Procedure (Insanity) Act 1964, ss. 4, 4A and 5

4.—(1)   This section applies where on the trial of a person the question arises (at the instance of the defence or otherwise) whether the accused is under a disability, that is to say, under any disability such that apart from this Act it would constitute a bar to his being tried.

(2)   If, having regard to the nature of the supposed disability, the court are of opinion that it is expedient to do so and in the interests of the accused, they may postpone consideration of the question of fitness to be tried until any time up to the opening of the case for the defence.

(3)   If, before the question of fitness to be tried falls to be determined, the jury return a verdict of acquittal on the count or each of the counts on which the accused is being tried, that question shall not be determined.

(4)   Subject to subsections (2) and (3) above, the question of fitness to be tried shall be determined as soon as it arises.

(5)   The question of fitness to be tried shall be determined by a jury and—

(a)   where it falls to be determined on the arraignment of the accused and the trial proceeds, the accused shall be tried by a jury other than that which determined that question;

(b)   where it falls to be determined at any later time, it shall be determined by a separate jury or by the jury by whom the accused is being tried, as the court may direct.

(6)   A jury shall not make a determination under subsection (5) above except on the written or oral evidence of two or more registered medical practitioners at least one of whom is duly approved.

4A.—(1)   This section applies where in accordance with section 4(5) above it is determined by a jury that the accused is under a disability.

(2)   The trial shall not proceed or further proceed but it shall be determined by a jury—

(a)   on the evidence (if any) already given in the trial; and

(b)   on such evidence as may be adduced or further adduced by the prosecution, or adduced by a person appointed by the court under this section to put the case for the defence,

whether they are satisfied, as respects the count or each of the counts on which the accused was to be or was being tried, that he did the act or made the omission charged against him as the offence.

(3)   If as respects that count or any of those counts the jury are satisfied as mentioned in subsection (2) above, they shall make a finding that the accused did the act or made the omission charged against him.

(4)   If as respects that count or any of those counts the jury are not so satisfied, they shall return a verdict of acquittal as if on the count in question the trial had proceeded to a conclusion.

(5)   A determination under subsection (2) above shall be made—

(a)   where the question of disability was determined on the arraignment of the accused, by a jury other than that which determined that question; and

(b)   where that question was determined at any later time, by the jury by whom the accused was being tried.

5.—(1)   This section applies where—

(a)   a special verdict is returned that the accused is not guilty by reason of insanity; or

(b) findings are recorded that the accused is under a disability and that he did the act or made the omission charged against him.

(2) Subject to subsection (3) below, the court shall either—

(a) make an order that the accused be admitted, in accordance with the provisions of schedule 1 to the Criminal Procedure (Insanity and Unfitness to Plead) Act 1991, to such hospital as may be specified by the Secretary of State; or

(b) where they have the power to do so by virtue of section 5 of that Act, make in respect of the accused such one of the following orders as they think most suitable in all the circumstances of the case, namely—

(i) a guardianship order within the meaning of the Mental Health Act 1983;

(ii) a supervision and treatment order within the meaning of schedule 2 to the said Act of 1991; and

(iii) an order for his absolute discharge.

(3) Paragraph (b) of subsection (2) above shall not apply where the offence to which the special verdict or findings relate is an offence the sentence for which is fixed by law.

Muteness

If an accused stays silent when arraigned the issue arises whether he is silent by deliberate **D10.11** choice or for reasons beyond his control. In the former case, he is said to be mute of malice; in the latter case, he is mute by visitation of God. Section 6(1)(c) of the Criminal Law Act 1967 provides that: 'Where a person is arraigned on an indictment . . . if he stands mute of malice or will not answer directly to the indictment, the court may order a plea of not guilty to be entered on his behalf, and he shall then be treated as having pleaded not guilty.' The court may not itself conclude that a silent accused is mute of malice but must empanel a jury to determine the issue (*Schleter* (1866) 10 Cox CC 409), the burden of proof being on the prosecution to establish malice beyond reasonable doubt (*Sharp* [1960] 1 QB 357). The accused has no right of challenge in respect of the jurors so empanelled (*Paling* (1978) 67 Cr App R 299).

If the finding of the jury is that the accused is mute by visitation of God, the court has the option of adjourning for a short period in order that means of communicating with him may be found (e.g., through bringing an expert in sign language or lip-reading to court, and see also *Harris* (1897) 61 JP 792 where the jury found that a wound in H's throat which prevented him speaking was due to an attempt at suicide and the case was simply adjourned for the wound to heal). Alternatively, if it seems that the muteness will be permanent and cannot be overcome, the jury should be asked to go on to consider whether the accused is unfit to plead. An accused who is deaf and/or speech handicapped and for that reason cannot comprehend the proceedings so as to make a proper defence is treated as being unfit to plead, even though he is mentally normal (see **D10.**7; see also *Pritchard* (1836) 7 C & P 303, and *Governor of Stafford Prison, ex parte Emery* [1909] 2 KB 81). Therefore, a finding that the accused is mute by visitation of God is likely to be merely a stage *en route* to a finding of unfitness to plead – indeed, the classic direction of Alderson B in *Pritchard* required the jury to consider in turn whether P was (a) mute of malice; (b) able to plead, and (c) able to comprehend the course of the proceedings. If the accused is found mute of malice, there is no objection to the jury that has so found him going on to try the case, subject only to the general rule that a jury empanelled to try one issue may not try a second issue unless the trial of the latter commences within 24 hours of their empanelment to try the first (Juries Act 1974, s. 11).

In modern times, a silent accused will almost certainly be mute of malice. Should there be reasons beyond his control rendering him unable to answer to the indictment, that will have been realised long before arraignment and steps will have been taken to overcome the problem (e.g., by the provision of an interpreter). Alternatively, if he is or may be unfit to plead, either the prosecution or defence will raise that issue with the judge before the indictment is put, thus avoiding the question of muteness arising as a separate issue unless the accused should be found fit to plead and then stay silent when arraigned.

PLEAS THAT MAY BE ENTERED ON ARRAIGNMENT

D10.12 In the great majority of cases, the plea entered by the accused will be simply one of guilty or not guilty. It is sometimes open to him to plead not guilty as charged but guilty of an alternative (lesser) offence. Very occasionally the issue arises of whether he has previously been acquitted or convicted of the offence now charged, in which case he enters a plea of autrefois acquit or, as the case may be, autrefois convict. Should the defence wish to argue that the Crown Court does not have jurisdiction to deal with the case (e.g., because the offence was committed abroad), there may be a plea to the jurisdiction. Finally, there are one or two obsolete pleas such as demurrer which are theoretically open to an accused but which are now rarely if ever used in practice.

PLEA OF NOT GUILTY

Effect of Plea of Not Guilty

D10.13 A plea of not guilty puts the prosecution to proof of their entire case. The burden is therefore on them to satisfy the jury beyond reasonable doubt that the accused committed the *actus reus* of the offence (or aided, abetted, counselled or procured its commission), and that in doing so he had the necessary *mens rea*. Should the prosecution fail to adduce sufficient evidence as to *any* element of the offence, the accused is entitled to be acquitted on the judge's direction following a submission of no case to answer made at the close of the prosecution case. The defence statement should have indicated in advance of trial those parts of the prosecution case which are disputed (see **D6.4**). Nevertheless defence counsel is still entitled to take advantage of any deficiency in the prosecution evidence (e.g., a witness not coming up to proof) and submit that there is no case to answer, whether or not the element of the offence of which evidence is lacking would otherwise have been contested. The only method by which the prosecution may be released from their obligation to prove each essential element of the offence is if the defence have made formal admissions under s. 10 of the CJA 1967, or where a fact is presumed or judicially noticed (see **F1.3** *et seq.*; **F3.19** *et seq.*).

Entry of Plea of Not Guilty

D10.14 Normal practice is for the accused to enter a plea of not guilty personally when arraigned by the clerk in the absence of any potential jurors (see **D10.1**). It is not, however, essential to the validity of a trial that he formally says the words 'not guilty' (see *Williams* [1978] QB 373 where W's conviction was upheld even though, through an administrative muddle, he had never been arraigned – he intended to plead not guilty; the trial proceeded exactly as if he had done so, and he did not draw the court's attention to the lack of arraignment). If an accused wilfully stays silent when arraigned, or fails to give a direct answer to the charge, or enters a plea which purports to be one of guilty but is in fact ambiguous, the court may and should enter a plea of not guilty on his behalf (see Criminal Law Act 1967, s. 6(1)(c)).

Options Available to the Prosecution on Plea of Not Guilty Being Entered

D10.15 Apart from the obvious course of proceeding to a contested trial, there are two options available to the prosecution on the accused pleading not guilty, namely, to offer no evidence or to ask that the indictment remain on the court file. Both courses may be taken either in respect of the entire indictment or in respect of certain counts only.

D10.16 *Offering No Evidence*

Criminal Justice Act 1967, s. 17

> Where a defendant arraigned on an indictment or inquisition pleads not guilty and the prosecutor proposes to offer no evidence against him, the court before which the defendant

is arraigned may, if it thinks fit, order that a verdict of not guilty shall be recorded without the defendant being given in charge to a jury, and the verdict shall have the same effect as if the defendant had been tried and acquitted on the verdict of a jury.

The obvious situation for reliance on s. 17 is if the prosecution have reviewed their evidence since committal, or have become aware of additional evidence favourable to the defence, and have concluded that they cannot properly ask a jury to convict. Alternatively, offering no evidence on some counts in an indictment may be part of an agreement with the defence under which the accused pleads guilty to other counts. The plain wording of s. 17 gives the court a discretion to decline to order a verdict of not guilty to be entered even though the prosecution intimate that they do not wish to proceed. If prosecuting counsel adheres to his decision not to call evidence, the jury will obviously be obliged to acquit. It is submitted that, in the last resort, the prosecution cannot be forced by the court to call evidence, although in practice prosecuting counsel are naturally very reluctant to go against a judge's wishes (see **D10.44**).

In *Renshaw* [1989] Crim LR 811, the Court of Appeal stressed the importance of the judge listening to the reasons given by the prosecution for proposing to offer no evidence. The judge should keep in mind that the prosecution will have information which he does not. If he fails to heed what the prosecution say, he will deprive himself of a proper basis for approving or disapproving of their proposed course of action.

Letting Counts Lie on the File As an alternative to offering no evidence, the **D10.17** prosecution may ask the judge to order that an indictment (or counts thereof) shall lie on the file, marked not to be proceeded with without leave of the court or of the Court of Appeal. Such a course is particularly appropriate where the accused pleads guilty to the bulk of the charges against him (whether contained in one indictment or several) but not guilty to some subsidiary charges. Leaving the latter on the file avoids the necessity of a trial (which would be a waste of time and money in view of the sentence likely to be imposed on the guilty pleas), but also avoids the accused actually being acquitted on the 'not guilty' counts, which might seem inappropriate if the evidence against him is in fact strong. Contrary to what was previously understood to be the position, there is no objection to an entire indictment remaining on the file, as opposed to merely dealing with some counts of a multi-count indictment in that way (see *Central Criminal Court, ex parte Raymond* [1986] 1 WLR 710 for a case where, as a result of R's conviction on one count of a severed 14-count indictment, the trial judge ordered that both the remaining counts of the original indictment and all counts of a completely separate indictment should lie on the file).

Whether to order that counts lie on the file is a matter totally within the judge's discretion since there is no method by which either party can challenge his decision. There is no appeal to the Court of Appeal as that only arises once there has been a conviction and, if counts remain on the file, there will not be a trial, let alone a conviction. Neither can there be an application to the High Court for judicial review since a decision to leave counts on the file has been held to relate to a trial on indictment and so, by virtue of s. 29(3) of the Supreme Court Act 1981, is unreviewable (*Ex parte Raymond*). The reasoning in *Ex parte Raymond* was that, although an order to leave counts on the file is effectively an order that a trial shall not take place unless something out of the ordinary subsequently happens to alter the court's mind, it 'starts off by having the same effect as an order for an adjournment' (per Woolf LJ at p. 714H). As to decisions to adjourn, even Lord Denning MR's judgment in *Sheffield Crown Court, ex parte Brownlow* [1980] QB 530 – which has since been held to give too narrow a meaning to the phrase 'relating to trial on indictment' – instanced such decisions as something on which 'the trial judge should have the final word'. Therefore, orders that counts or indictments should lie on the file, like decisions to adjourn with which they are for these purposes equated, relate to trial on indictment and are beyond the scope of the High Court's supervisory jurisdiction.

Had the decision on jurisdiction gone the other way, the applicant in *Ex parte Raymond* would have argued that a Crown Court judge should not order that counts lie on the file unless the defence agree to that course, and, in the absence of such agreement, he ought to require the prosecution to elect between proceeding to trial and offering no evidence. Although the court in *Ex parte Raymond* heard full argument on the point, it ultimately refused to state its view or give any guidance on when orders to lie on the file are appropriate. This reticence was because of its primary decision that it did not in any event have jurisdiction to review the decision of the court below. It is thus still arguable in theory that orders to lie on the file should be dependent on the defence's consent but, whether that be right or wrong, there is nothing *in practice* to prevent a judge doing what the judge in *Raymond's* case did, that is, making the order in the face of defence objections. (See also *Mackell* (1981) 74 Cr App R 27 on the Court of Appeal's lack of jurisdiction to reverse an order that counts lie on the file, and Dunn LJ's dictum, quoted with approval in *Ex parte Raymond*, that, '. . . there are certain matters upon which the trial judge should have the final say. It seems to us this is one of them.')

The only situation in which the Crown Court or Court of Appeal is likely to give leave for a count or indictment ordered to lie on the file to be tried is if the accused's convictions on the other matters (i.e. the charges on the same or separate indictments to which he pleaded guilty or of which he was found guilty at the same time as the order to lie on the file was made) are quashed on appeal. The use and practical effect of the order is helpfully summarised by Woolf LJ in *Ex parte Raymond* (at pp. 714H–715B):

> [It is important] to analyse the nature of the order that an indictment should lie on the file.
>
> It starts off by having the same effect as an order for an adjournment but an adjournment which it is accepted may never result in a trial. Frequently the order is made to safeguard the position of the prosecution and the defence in case a defendant, who has been convicted, should appeal, it being the intention of the court if there is no appeal or if the appeal is unsuccessful the defendant should never stand trial. That the defendant can still stand trial is indicated by the limits on the discretion of the court (laid down by the House of Lords in *Connelly* v *DPP* [1964] AC 1254) to prevent the Crown proceeding with a prosecution if it wishes to do so. However, in the majority of cases where such an order is made, there will be no trial and there will certainly come a stage when either the prosecution would not seek a trial or if it did seek a trial, the court would regard it as so oppressive to have a trial that leave to proceed would inevitably be refused.

PLEA OF GUILTY

Requirement that Accused Plead Personally

D10.18 A plea of guilty must be entered by the accused personally. If counsel purports to plead guilty on behalf of an accused, the purported plea has no validity and the proceedings constitute a mistrial (*Ellis* (1973) 57 Cr App R 571). On appeal, the Court of Appeal will be obliged either to quash the conviction or to grant a writ of *venire de novo* (i.e. set the conviction aside but order that the accused be retried) (ibid.). In *Ellis*, defence counsel intervened during the arraignment and before his client had actually pleaded to say that the intended plea to an indictment for burglary involving entry as a trespasser and theft of £1,687 plus some cheques contrary to s. 9(1)(b) of the Theft Act 1968 was guilty but only in respect of £380 cash and no cheques. Having been told that the prosecution were prepared to accept that plea, the judge proceeded to sentence. At no stage did the accused himself say he was guilty, although that was undoubtedly what he would have said had he been allowed to. On appeal, Edmund Davies LJ reviewed the authorities and then said (at pp. 574–5):

. . . great mischief would ensue if a legal representative was generally regarded as entitled to plead on an accused's behalf. It would open the door to dispute as to whether, for example, counsel had correctly understood and acted upon the instructions which the accused had given him, and, if a dispute of that kind arose, the consequential embarrassment and difficulty could be difficult in the extreme.

We think that the only safe and proper course accordingly is to say . . . that (apart from a few very special cases) it is an invariable requirement that the initial arraignment must be conducted between the clerk of the court and the accused person himself or herself directly.

Accordingly, the court set aside the conviction and sentence but ordered a retrial.

Edmund-Davies LJ's dicta quoted above do not expressly distinguish between cases where the accused intends to plead guilty and those where he intends to plead not guilty or refuses to plead. As regards the latter, it is possible for a valid trial to take place despite the absence of a personal plea from the accused (see **D10.14**). As regards guilty pleas, however, there can be no derogation whatsoever from the rule that the plea must come from the mouth of the accused. This is confirmed by *Williams* [1978] QB 373 where Shaw LJ, giving the judgment of the Court of Appeal, said (at p. 378G): 'No qualification of or deviation from the rule that a plea of guilty must come from him who acknowledges guilt is . . . permissible. A departure from the rule in a criminal trial would therefore necessarily be a vitiating factor rendering the whole procedure void and ineffectual'.

Effect of Plea of Guilty

If the accused pleads guilty, the prosecution are released from their obligation to prove **D10.19** the case. There is no need to empanel a jury, and the accused stands convicted simply by virtue of the word that has come from his own mouth. The only evidence the prosecution then need call in the ordinary case is that of the accused's antecedents and criminal record (see **D17.17** to **D17.21**). Exceptionally, there may be a dispute between the parties about the precise facts of the offence, in which event – if the dispute is serious enough to have a significant effect on sentence – the prosecution will either have to call evidence in support of their own version at a so-called '*Newton* hearing' or allow sentence to be passed on the basis of the defence version (for *Newton* hearings, see **D17.2** to **D17.13**). However, even in such cases, the prosecution evidence goes to *how* the offence was committed, not whether it was committed, and the accused remains convicted by his own plea whatever the outcome of the *Newton* hearing.

Adjournments Following Plea of Guilty

Once a plea of guilty has been entered the court may forthwith commence the procedure **D10.20** leading up to the passing of sentence. It may, on the other hand, take the plea and then adjourn. Whether or not to adjourn is entirely at the discretion of the court. Common reasons for an adjournment are to obtain reports on the accused or to await the outcome of other proceedings outstanding against him with a view to his being sentenced on one occasion for all matters (see *Bennett* (1980) 2 Cr App R (S) 96 for the desirability of linking up outstanding charges). *Ex hypothesi*, if an accused enters mixed pleas on a multi-count indictment and the prosecution are not prepared to accept those pleas, sentencing for the counts to which he has pleaded guilty should be postponed until after he has been tried on the not guilty counts. By virtue of the Supreme Court Act 1981, s. 81(1)(c), on adjourning, the court may either commit the accused to custody or grant him bail (subject to the restrictions which will apply in the case of certain persons charged with homicide or rape described at **D5.10**). Despite having been convicted, an accused who is remanded for inquiries or report at this stage still has a prima facie right to bail under the Bail Act 1976, s. 4, although in practice bail is usually withdrawn if the accused has pleaded guilty to a serious offence.

Practice where There Are Mixed Pleas by Co-accused

D10.21   Where there are co-accused, one of whom pleads guilty and the other not guilty, normal practice is to adjourn sentencing the former until after the trial of the latter. In the event of a conviction, they can then both be sentenced together. The desirability of co-accused being sentenced on one occasion by the same judge has frequently been stressed. Separate sentencing may lead to unacceptable disparity in the ways they are respectively treated. Also, the judge will hear, during the course of the trial of the accused pleading not guilty, evidence indicating the gravity of the offence charged and the extent of each accused's role in it, which information may ultimately assist him in sentencing the one pleading guilty.

The above principles were stated by Lord Goddard CJ in *Payne* [1950] 1 All ER 102 where P successfully appealed against a sentence of two years' imprisonment for housebreaking on the basis that his co-offenders received only 15 months. P had pleaded guilty and had been sentenced forthwith by one judge; the co-offenders had pleaded not guilty but had been convicted and sentenced by a different judge. Lord Goddard CJ said:

> [Where several persons are indicted together, and one pleads guilty and the other or others not guilty] the proper course is to postpone sentence on the man who has pleaded guilty until the others have been tried and then to bring up all the prisoners to be dealt with together because by that time the court will be in possession of the facts relating to all of them and will be able to assess properly the degree of guilt of each.

A still stronger statement of the same principle occurs in the judgment of Boreham J in *Weekes* (1980) 74 Cr App R 161. His lordship said:

> Here are made manifest the difficulties that arise when persons involved with others are sentenced before the full facts have been heard, particularly where a trial is to take place, as it was to take place here . . . . There may be exceptions but generally it is clearly right, it is clearly fairer and it is better for both the public and all the defendants concerned, that all are sentenced at the same time by the same court whenever that is possible.

D10.22   *Practice where Accused Pleads Guilty and Gives Evidence for Prosecution against Co-accused*   The 'difficulties' arising in *Weekes's* case to which Boreham J referred in the passage quoted in **D10.21** were that W, one of four co-accused charged with armed robbery, was sentenced to seven years' imprisonment while a co-accused (S) was given only 12 months, a term described by the Court of Appeal as 'ludicrously light'. Part of the explanation for the leniency shown to S was that, having intimated an intention to testify for the Crown against his co-accused, he pleaded guilty and was separately sentenced prior to the trial of the others. They were then tried, convicted partly on S's evidence and sentenced by a different judge. W appealed against his sentence mainly on the ground of its disparity with that given to S. The appeal was dismissed (disparity is not always recognised as a sufficient reason for reducing a sentence) but Boreham J criticised the decision to sentence S separately (at p. 166):

> It may be . . . that [S] was sentenced at that early stage by a different court because it had been made known that he was to give evidence on behalf of the Crown against the other three. If that was the reason . . . it is not sufficient reason. . . . it should be left to the judge who may sentence those who have pleaded not guilty, to sentence all.

His lordship then continued with the dictum already quoted that it is fairer and better to sentence co-accused together whenever that is possible.

The clear statement in *Weekes* that an accused turning Queen's evidence should not be sentenced until after the co-accused's trial is in direct conflict with the practice obtaining until the late 1970s. Lord Goddard CJ in *Payne* [1950] 1 All ER 102 qualified his general exhortation to sentence co-accused together with this: 'What I have said does not apply in the exceptional case where a man who pleads guilty is going to be called as a witness.

In those circumstances it is right that he be sentenced there and then so that there can be no suspicion that his evidence is coloured by the fact that he hopes to get a lighter sentence.' For the same reason, it has been held that, if an accused turning Queen's evidence is sentenced forthwith and then fails to give the evidence expected against his co-accused, the sentence passed on him may *not* be increased, even if he received a discount on sentence in anticipation of the help he would give the prosecution (*Stone* [1970] 1 WLR 1112). It may be thought that the reason given by Lord Goddard for sentencing forthwith in the exceptional case applies with as much force now as it did when *Payne* was decided. However, a reversal of practice was signalled by two unreported cases in 1977 (*Potter* (15 September 1977 unreported) and *Woods* (25 October 1977 unreported)), and that reversal has been confirmed by *Weekes* and *Chan Wai-keung* [1995] 1 WLR 251. In *Coffey* (1976) 74 Cr App R 168, the principle was held to apply when the accused who has pleaded guilty is going to testify for the co-accused, just as it applies when he is to testify for the prosecution.

Even so, whether to sentence a co-accused pleading guilty forthwith or adjourn until after the co-accused's trial must, in the last resort, remain a question for the individual judge (see *Palmer* (1994) 158 JP 138). A possible issue is whether the accused might attempt to resile from the agreement to give evidence for the prosecution or do so in an unsatisfactory manner. As Lord Denning MR said in *Sheffield Crown Court, ex parte Brownlow* [1980] QB 530, a decision to adjourn is 'a matter in relation to which the trial judge should have the final word', and circumstances may arise in which – notwithstanding the normally strong arguments in favour of joint sentencing – the interests of justice are better served by disposing of the accused pleading guilty (A1) before the trial of his co-accused (A2). Thus, if A2 absconds before his trial so that A1 is likely to have a long wait for sentence if the usual practice is followed, or if A1's offence is self-contained and trivial by comparison with A2's, as when A1 pleads to handling a small part of the proceeds of an armed robbery with which A2 is charged, or if A1 is turning Queen's evidence and there are more than usually strong reasons for suspecting that he might perjure himself in hopes of obtaining a lenient sentence – in all these, and no doubt in other, cases there are, it is submitted, good reasons for departing from the usual practice by sentencing A1 at the first opportunity.

Ambiguous Pleas

If an accused purports to enter a plea of guilty but, either at the time he pleads or **D10.23** subsequently in mitigation, qualifies it with words that suggest he may have a defence (e.g., 'Guilty, but it was an accident' or 'Guilty, but I was going to give it back'), then the court must not proceed to sentence on the basis of the plea but should explain the relevant law and seek to ascertain whether he genuinely intends to plead guilty. If the plea cannot be clarified, the court should order a not guilty plea to be entered on the accused's behalf (Criminal Law Act 1967, s. 6(1)(c): 'if [the accused] stands mute of malice *or will not answer directly to the indictment*, the court may order a plea of not guilty to be entered'). Should the court proceed to sentence on a plea which is imperfect, unfinished or otherwise ambiguous, the accused will have a good ground of appeal. Since the defect in the plea will have rendered the original proceedings a mistrial, the Court of Appeal will have the options either of setting the conviction and sentence aside and ordering a retrial (see, e.g., *Ingleson* [1915] 1 KB 512) or of simply quashing the conviction (e.g., *Field* (1943) 29 Cr App R 151). If the former course is chosen (i.e. there is to be a retrial), the court may either then and there direct that a not guilty plea be entered or order that the accused be re-arraigned in the court below (e.g., *Baker* (1912) 7 Cr App R 217).

Involuntary Pleas

A plea of guilty must be entered voluntarily. If, at the time he pleaded, the accused was **D10.24** subject to such pressure that he did not genuinely have a free choice between 'guilty' and 'not guilty', then his plea is a nullity (*Turner* [1970] 2 QB 321). On appeal, the Court of Appeal will have the same options as it has when a plea is adjudged ambiguous (i.e., it must quash the conviction and sentence but will be able, in its discretion, to issue a writ of *venire de novo* for a retrial as the original proceedings constitute a mistrial). In *Turner* the accused was given the impression by his counsel that the judge had privately told counsel that, in the event of a change of plea to guilty, the sentence would be non-custodial whereas, if the plea remained not guilty, there was 'a very real possibility' of a sentence of imprisonment. T decided to plead guilty. Lord Parker CJ, giving the Court of Appeal's judgment, said (at p. 326B):

> . . . once [T] felt that this [i.e. counsel's advice on sentence] was an intimation emanating from the judge, it is really idle in the opinion of this court to think that he really had a free choice in the matter.

> Accordingly, . . . the court feels that this appeal must succeed. . . . the court feels that the proper course will be to treat the plea that was given as a nullity, with the result that the trial that had taken place is a mistrial, and that there should be an order for a *venire de novo*.

A further example of the same principle is provided by *Barnes* (1970) 55 Cr App R 100, where the judge, during a submission of no case to answer made in the absence of the jury but in the presence of the accused, said that, having regard to the prosecution evidence, B was plainly guilty and was wasting the court's time by pleading not guilty. Despite this pressure, B did not change his plea. Allowing his appeal against conviction on other grounds, the court indicated that the judge's remarks were 'wholly improper', and, if B had pleaded guilty in consequence of them, the plea would have been null.

Pressure on the accused to plead guilty may come not only from the judge but from defence counsel. It is the duty of counsel to advise his client on the strength of the evidence and the advantages of a guilty plea as regards sentencing (see *Cain* [1976] QB 496 and *Herbert* (1991) 94 Cr App R 233, where Taylor LJ stated that defence counsel was under a duty to advise his client on the strength of his case and, if appropriate, the possible advantages in terms of sentence which might be gained from pleading guilty). Such advice may, if necessary, be given in forceful terms (*Peace* [1976] Crim LR 119). Where an accused is so advised and thereafter pleads guilty reluctantly, his plea is not *ipso facto* to be treated as involuntary (ibid.). It will be involuntary only if the advice was so very forceful as to take away his free choice. Thus, in *Inns* (1974) 60 Cr App R 231, defence counsel, as he was then professionally required to do, relayed to the accused the judge's warning in chambers that, in the event of conviction on a not guilty plea, the accused would definitely be given a sentence of detention whereas if he pleaded guilty a more lenient course might be possible. This rendered the eventual guilty plea a nullity. On appeal, there was a dispute about whether the judge had really been threatening a custodial sentence to induce a plea or merely indicating to counsel how his mind was working, but, whether counsel's or the judge's recollection was correct mattered not, because what the judge had said was sufficient to deprive the accused of his free choice.

However, in the absence of a suggestion that counsel was acting as a conduit to pass on a threat or promise from the judge, it will be extremely difficult for an appellant to satisfy the court that he was deprived by counsel's advice of a voluntary choice when pleading. Thus, in *Hall* [1968] 2 QB 788, H was charged with participation in a major burglary from an art gallery, alternatively with handling some of the stolen pictures. The prosecution were willing to accept a plea to the latter. Counsel advised H that, if he pleaded not guilty to both counts, he ran the risk of being convicted of the burglary itself since, although the evidence on that count was not strong, the defence would involve attacks on the prosecution witnesses' characters and the appellant's own bad character would therefore go before the jury. If so convicted, he could expect to receive up to 12 years' imprisonment, whereas if he pleaded guilty to handling the maximum sentence would be five years. Dismissing H's appeal, Lord Parker CJ said (at pp. 534–7):

What the court is looking to see is whether a prisoner in these circumstances has a free choice; the election must be his, the responsibility his, to plead guilty or not guilty. At the same time, it is the clear duty of any counsel representing a client to assist the client to make up his mind by putting forward the pros and cons, if need be in strong language, to impress upon the client what the likely results are of certain courses of conduct.

[His lordship then paraphrased the advice given by counsel.]

[Defence counsel], in the opinion of this court, was only doing his duty in setting forth the dangers, even, as [he] said, in strong language.

. . . anybody who has heard the evidence in this case and has understood the workings of the law and our procedure, could not fail to realise that the appellant has no grievance at all . . . and that his counsel performed his duty to the best of his ability. This court has no hesitation in those circumstances in dismissing the appeal.

The Code of Conduct of the Bar, annexe F, standards applicable to criminal cases, para. 12.3, confirms that defence counsel should explain to the accused the advantages and disadvantages of a guilty plea. It goes on to say that he must make it clear that the client has complete freedom of choice and that the responsibility for the plea is the accused's. It is common practice, endorsed by para. 12.5.1 of annexe F to the code, to tell an accused that he should plead guilty only if he is guilty (see Lord Parker CJ's observation in *Turner* [1970] 2 QB 321 at p. 326F that: 'Counsel of course will emphasise that the accused must not plead guilty unless he has committed the acts constituting the offence charged'). However, it may be felt that, on occasions, realistic advice about the strength of the prosecution case and the sentencing discount for a guilty plea will effectively force an accused into a guilty plea however punctilious defence counsel may be in saying that he should plead guilty only if he is guilty.

Where an accused persists in pleading guilty notwithstanding telling counsel that he is in fact innocent, counsel may continue to act for him but must say nothing in mitigation that is inconsistent with the guilty plea (Code of Conduct of the Bar, annexe F, standards applicable to criminal cases, para. 12.5.2 and 12.5.3). Counsel may thus be forced to confine his mitigation to the circumstances and background of the offender and any matters minimising the gravity of the offence which are apparent on the face of the prosecution statements – since his only instructions about the offence itself are that the accused is not guilty of it, counsel cannot explain (as he might otherwise do) the immediate temptations etc. that led to its commission.

Apart from cases where pressure has been brought to bear on the accused to plead guilty, there may be other situations where his mind did not go with his plea and he is therefore entitled to have his conviction set aside. An example is *Swain* [1986] Crim LR 480, in which S changed his plea to guilty half-way through the prosecution case. He gave no coherent explanation to counsel at the time, but it was afterwards discovered that he had been under the influence of the drug LSD. Psychiatric evidence called before the Court of Appeal established that LSD can put the user into a state akin to schizophrenia where he drifts in and out of a delusional world and makes irrational decisions. The court held the change of plea to have been a nullity.

PLEA OF GUILTY TO A LESSER OFFENCE

Introduction

Where the indictment contains a count on which, if the accused were to plead not guilty, **D10.25** the jury could find him not guilty as charged but guilty of an alternative (hereafter referred to as 'lesser') offence, he may enter a plea to the same effect (i.e. guilty only of the lesser offence) (Criminal Law Act 1967, s. 6(1)(b)). If the plea is accepted, he is treated as having been acquitted of the offence actually charged and the court proceeds to sentence him for the lesser offence (Criminal Law Act 1967, s. 6(5)). The circumstances in which a jury have the power to return a verdict of guilty of a lesser offence are defined by legislation, chiefly subsections (2) to (4) of s. 6 of the 1967 Act, which are considered in detail at **D16.18** to **D16.30**.

Accepting or Rejecting a Plea to a Lesser Offence

D10.26 The prosecution may refuse to accept a plea of guilty to a lesser offence. If so, the plea is deemed to be withdrawn and the case proceeds as if the accused had simply pleaded not guilty (*Hazeltine* [1967] 2 QB 857). In *Hazeltine* the accused, on being arraigned for wounding with intent contrary to s. 18 of the OAPA 1861, replied, 'Not guilty, but guilty to unlawful wounding'. The prosecution would not accept the plea, and H was put in charge of a jury who were simply told that he had pleaded not guilty. For reasons explained below, there was an appeal to the Court of Appeal. In the course of his speech Salmon LJ explained the purpose and effect of the then equivalent of s. 6(1) of the Criminal Law Act 1967 (s. 39(1) of the Criminal Justice Administration Act 1914). His lordship said (at p. 861A–F):

> Prior to that statutory provision, it was not possible for an accused to plead guilty to unlawful wounding when charged with wounding with intent but it was and always has been possible for a jury, when a man is charged with wounding with intent, to return a verdict of unlawful wounding; so before the Act of 1914 the position was that an accused man might be saying, 'Of course, I am guilty of unlawful wounding but I had no intention of doing grievous bodily harm', the prosecution might be satisfied that a plea of that kind ought to be accepted, and the judge might be so satisfied, yet a great deal of unnecessary time and money had to be wasted by holding a full-dress trial in order to obtain a verdict from a jury which the prosecution, the defence and the judge were satisfied was the only proper verdict in the circumstances.

> This court has no doubt but that section 39(1) of the Act of 1914 was introduced so as to remove this anomaly which resulted in the great waste of time and money to which I have referred. In the view of this court, however, that statutory provision did not get rid of the rule that there can be but one plea to one count should the trial proceed on that count. Accordingly if an accused pleads not guilty to wounding with intent but guilty to unlawful wounding and counsel for the prosecution or the judge takes the view that that plea ought not to be accepted and the trial proceeds, the plea of guilty to unlawful wounding is deemed to be withdrawn and the only plea is the plea of not guilty to wounding with intent. It is then for the jury to consider the evidence and at the end of the case to say either quite simply that the man is not guilty or that he is guilty of wounding with intent or that he is not guilty of wounding with intent but guilty to unlawful wounding.

Although couched in terms of wounding with intent and unlawful wounding, the above passage is obviously applicable whenever a plea of guilty to a lesser offence is rejected.

Salmon LJ referred to the prosecution *or the judge* taking the view that a plea to unlawful wounding should not be accepted and the trial therefore proceeding. However, the extent of the judge's control over the acceptance of a plea to a lesser offence is open to argument. In *Soanes* (1948) 32 Cr App R 136, Lord Goddard CJ said, '. . . it must always be in the discretion of the judge whether he will allow [a plea of guilty to a lesser offence] to be accepted'. Thus, even where the prosecution wish to accept the plea, the judge, according to Lord Goddard, *always* has the last word and can insist that the accused be tried for the offence charged. But it is doubtful whether, in an adversarial system of justice, the court can in fact (or at any rate, whether it should attempt to) insist on one of the parties calling evidence. Neither is there any precedent for the court calling all the witnesses itself. Therefore, if the prosecution absolutely refuse to call evidence to prove the accused guilty as charged, the court would have no real alternative but to accept the situation, subject to any proper question of professional misconduct.

Moreover, in the analogous situation of the accused pleading to some counts on the indictment in exchange for the prosecution offering no evidence on others, the rule seems to be that the prosecution are bound by the judge's views of the bargain if, and only if, they have expressly asked him to approve it in advance. If they choose not to seek his prior approval, they may accept the pleas even though the judge indicates in court that they ought to proceed on all counts (see *Coward* (1979) 70 Cr App R 70 and *Broad* (1978) 68 Cr App R 281). The report of the Farquharson Committee on the role of prosecuting counsel (*Counsel*, Trinity 1986) suggested that the same rule should apply in cases of a plea of guilty to a lesser offence. If that is correct, Lord Goddard's statement in *Soanes* over-simplifies the true position (see **D10.44**).

As to the circumstances in which it is appropriate to accept a plea to a lesser offence, Lord Goddard in *Soanes* could not lay down a 'hard and fast rule' but expressed the view that, 'where nothing appears on the depositions which can be said to reduce the crime from the more serious offence charged to some lesser offence for which a verdict may be returned, the duty of counsel for the Crown would be to present the offence charged in the indictment'. The possible effect on the prosecution witnesses of testifying at a contested trial (e.g., where the offence charged is of a sexual nature) and/or the reaction of the victim to the charge being reduced may also have a bearing on counsel's ultimate decision (see, for example, *Coward* (1979) 70 Cr App R 70 and the reasons that led counsel in that case to accept a plea to the least serious count on an indictment).

Status of Original Plea in Event of Verdict of Not Guilty

In *Hazeltine* [1967] 2 QB 857, H's plea of guilty to unlawful wounding was rejected and **D10.27** the trial proceeded. He offered a defence of acting in reasonable self-defence which was inconsistent with his original plea. No evidence was adduced as to that plea, nor was he cross-examined about it. The judge did refer to it in his summing-up but in a manner that almost certainly left the jury confused. In the event they simply acquitted H, although a question they asked after they retired strongly indicated that they were satisfied of guilt in respect of the lesser offence. The judge then sentenced H to nine months' imprisonment. That sentence had to be quashed on appeal as H had not been convicted of any offence. His original plea to unlawful wounding was impliedly withdrawn on the prosecution saying that it was not acceptable, and the jury (however perversely) had simply found him not guilty. That verdict implied an acquittal both in respect of the offence charged and in respect of the lesser included offence.

To avoid a repetition of the manifestly unsatisfactory result in *Hazeltine*, the Court of Appeal suggested that, in cases where the accused offers a defence that is inconsistent with his earlier plea to a lesser offence, the prosecution ought to do what they had failed to do in *Hazeltine*, namely, call evidence of the plea and, if the accused testifies, cross-examine him about it (ibid. at p. 862F–G). There was no need to adopt a policy of always having separate counts for the greater and lesser offences. However, should the prosecution fail to adduce evidence of the plea, it is not open to the judge to repair the omission in his summing-up by informing the jury of what occurred (*Lee* [1985] Crim LR 798). Nor may the judge direct the jury to convict of the lesser offence as opposed to informing them that such a verdict is open to them (ibid., and see *Notman* [1994] Crim LR 518).

AUTREFOIS ACQUIT AND AUTREFOIS CONVICT

Introduction

The pleas of autrefois acquit and autrefois convict, together with the plea of pardon (see **D10.28** **D10.41**), are known as pleas in bar, because, if upheld, they bar any further proceedings on the indictment. The basic purpose of the two pleas of autrefois acquit and autrefois convict is to protect the subject against repeated prosecutions for the same offence. A large body of case law has developed defining the precise circumstances in which the pleas may be relied on, although it is rarely necessary to raise them in practice as prosecutions are simply not commenced if it is known that the proposed accused has already been acquitted or convicted of the offence that would be charged. Consideration of the pleas will involve asking: (a) precisely what is meant by being prosecuted twice for the same offence? (b) what amounts to an acquittal or a conviction in this context? and (c) what is the procedure to be followed on the pleas being raised? If one or other of the pleas does apply it is a total bar to any further proceedings on the indictment. Hence, they are sometimes referred to as special pleas in bar. The leading authority on the subject is *Connelly* v *DPP* [1964] AC 1254.

Scope of the Pleas

D10.29   ***At Common Law***   In *Connelly* v *DPP* [1964] AC 1254, C and three others were jointly charged in two indictments, the first for murder and the second for armed robbery. The prosecution case was that the four accused had all participated in a robbery of the premises of the Royal Arsenal Co-operative Society during the course of which an employee of the society (one H) was shot and killed. The employee named in the second indictment as the victim of the robbery was one D (i.e. *not* the murder victim). The preferring of two indictments was necessitated by the then rule of practice that, if there was a count for murder on an indictment, no counts for other offences could be joined with it. The murder indictment was tried first and all the accused were convicted. C offered a defence of alibi. His counsel also argued that, even if the jury found that C had been present when the murder was committed, there was insufficient evidence to show that he was a knowing participant in it. C successfully appealed against conviction, the Court of Criminal Appeal finding that there had been errors in the judge's summing-up on the issue of alibi. The quashing of C's conviction meant that he had to be treated as if he had been acquitted of murder, and he could not therefore be reprosecuted either for that offence or for manslaughter. However, the prosecution obtained leave from the Court of Criminal Appeal to proceed on the indictment for robbery. C pleaded autrefois acquit. A jury was empanelled (such an issue would now be determined by the judge – see CJA 1988, s. 122) to determine the following question: '. . . has this man Connelly proved that he has already been tried and acquitted of the same felony or offence, or of substantially the same offence, or has he already been tried and acquitted on an indictment on which he could have been convicted of the same or substantially the same offence?' The judge pointed out that the murder alleged in the first indictment took place in the course of the robbery alleged in the second indictment, but he nonetheless directed the jury that murder of H could not be regarded as 'substantially or practically the same' as robbery with aggravation of a sum of money from D. The jury accordingly found that autrefois acquit did not apply. C then pleaded not guilty to robbery; essentially the same evidence was advanced by the prosecution at that trial as had been advanced by them at the trial for murder, and C was again convicted. He appealed against conviction, this time on the ground that his plea of autrefois acquit should have been upheld. The House of Lords dismissed the appeal. The speech of Lord Morris of Borth-y-Gest reviewed at length the old authorities and summarised their effect in nine propositions ([1964] AC 1254 at pp. 1305–6), which may be further summarised as follows:

    (a)   *A man may not be tried for a crime in respect of which he has previously been acquitted or convicted.* This is the straightforward and obvious application of autrefois, and covers cases where the offence charged in a count is identical in law and on the facts to a crime of which the accused has previously been acquitted or convicted. For example, had the prosecution in *Connelly* v *DPP* included in their second indictment a count for H's murder, autrefois acquit would plainly have succeeded in respect of that.

    (b)   *A man cannot be tried for a crime in respect of which he could on some previous indictment have been convicted.* This is the corollary of the power of a jury to return a verdict of not guilty as charged but guilty of a lesser offence. The reasoning is that, where

the jury on a certain count could have convicted of a lesser offence but chose simply to find the accused not guilty, they have impliedly acquitted him both of the offence charged and of the lesser offence. Consequently, their verdict can be relied on to bar a later indictment for either or both offences. Lord Morris traced the principle back to Hale's *Pleas of the Crown* (1778), giving the example of an acquittal for murder barring any later indictment for manslaughter ([1964] AC 1254 at p. 1311); but see *Old Street Magistrates' Court, ex parte Davies* [1995] Crim LR 629, which is perhaps best regarded as confined to its own unusual facts. Indeed, on the facts of *Connelly* itself, it was common ground that the appellant's notional acquittal for murder deriving from his earlier successful appeal prevented the prosecution indicting him for the manslaughter of H, the victim of the shooting. It is submitted that the above rule applies whether or not the jury were expressly invited by the judge to consider an alternative verdict, the question being whether the verdict was open to them as a matter of law not whether the judge, as a matter of discretion, drew their attention to the possibility in his summing-up.

(c) *A man cannot be tried for a crime which is in effect the same, or is substantially the same, as a crime of which he has previously been acquitted or convicted (or could have been convicted by way of alternative verdict).* The bulk of Lord Morris's speech (see pp. 1310–28) consists of a survey of the decided cases (principally from the 19th century) which directly or indirectly indicate when a count is to be regarded as alleging a crime that is substantially (though not exactly) the same as one of which the accused has previously been acquitted or convicted. One clear example of the test being satisfied is provided by an accused being indicted for murder after he has been acquitted of the alleged victim's manslaughter. Having regard to the definitions of murder and manslaughter, the evidence necessary to prove the victim's murder would have been sufficient to procure a conviction for manslaughter on the earlier indictment, and the accused can therefore rely on autrefois acquit (see *Wrote* v *Wigges* (1591) 4 Co Rep 45b and *Tancock* (1876) 34 LT 455). The same will apply whenever proof of an offence of which the accused has already been acquitted is a necessary step towards proving the offence now charged. The strictness of the test is, however, illustrated by *Salvi* (1857) 10 Cox CC 481 n where S, after being acquitted on a charge of wounding with intent to murder, was – after his victim's death – indicted for murder. His plea of autrefois failed because murder could be committed without there being an intention to murder. Therefore, the evidence on the second indictment would not necessarily have to be such as to support a conviction on the first (it could show merely an intention to do the victim grievous bodily harm).

(d) *What has to be considered is whether the crime or offence charged in the later indictment is the same, or is in effect or is substantially the same, as the crime charged in the former indictment and it is immaterial that the facts under examination or the witnesses being called in the later proceedings are the same as those in some earlier proceedings.* The actual decision in *Connelly* v *DPP* provides the best illustration. The evidence called and facts relied on by the prosecution against C at the trial for robbery were precisely the same as they had called and relied on at the earlier trial for murder. The jury were even informed that a person had been killed in the course of the robbery, although proof of the death was not, of course, a necessary element of the robbery charge. But, despite the coincidence of prosecution facts and evidence at the two trials, the House of Lords were unanimous in holding that autrefois acquit did not avail.

The above analysis should now be considered in the light of the decision of the Court of Appeal in *Beedie* [1998] QB 356. B was the landlord of a bedsit whose occupant died of carbon monoxide poisoning caused by a defective gas fire. He was prosecuted by the Health and Safety Executive for failing to maintain the fire and flue properly, pleaded guilty and was fined. He was later required by the coroner to give evidence at the deceased's inquest on the basis that, as he had already been convicted, there was no realistic prospect of a prosecution for manslaughter. B was later charged with manslaughter. At trial, his counsel applied to stay the indictment, relying upon *Connelly*, but the judge refused. B pleaded guilty and appealed. It was argued on his behalf that the judge had wrongly rejected his plea of autrefois convict. The Court of Appeal held that the House of Lords in *Connelly* had identified a narrow principle of autrefois. It was applicable only where the *same* offence was alleged in the second indictment. Rose LJ, delivering the judgment of the Court of Appeal in *Beedie*, quoted with approval Lord Devlin in *Connelly* (at p. 1340): 'For the doctrine to apply it must be the same offence both in fact and in law'. Rose LJ went on to say that Lord Morris' speech did not represent the *ratio* of the House of Lords' decision. The majority in *Connelly* had defined autrefois in a narrow way, i.e. it applies when the second indictment charges the same offence as the first. Importantly, however, judicial discretion should be exercised where the second offence arises out of the same or substantially the same set of facts as the first. In addition, there should be no sequential trials for offences on an ascending scale of gravity (relying on the principle in *Elrington* (1861) 1 B & S 688). As it was put in *Forest of Dean Justices, ex parte Farley* [1990] RTR 228 at p. 239, there is an 'almost invariable rule that when a person is tried on a lesser offence he is not to be tried again on the same facts for a more serious offence'. As to the way in which the trial judge ought to exercise his discretion, Rose LJ emphasised that it was for the prosecution to show that there were special circumstances before the judge should allow the trial to proceed. In the instant case, a stay should have been ordered because the manslaughter allegation was based on substantially the same facts as the earlier summary prosecutions and it was a prosecution for an offence of greater gravity (no new facts having emerged) — and thus was in breach of the *Elrington* principle. There were no special circumstances such as to allow the prosecution to proceed, and the appeal was allowed (see also *South East Hampshire Magistrates' Court, ex parte CPS* [1998] Crim LR 422).

D10.30 **Statutory Provisions** The common law on the ambit of autrefois is supplemented by two sets of statutory provisions and a procedure to deal with tainted acquittals.

First, ss. 44 and 45 of the OAPA 1861 provide that, if justices, 'upon the hearing of any case of assault or battery upon the merits, *where the complaint was preferred by or on behalf of the party aggrieved,* shall deem the offence not to be proved, or shall find the assault or battery to have been justified, or so trifling as not to merit any punishment, and shall accordingly dismiss the complaint, they shall forthwith make out a certificate under their hands stating the fact of such dismissal and shall deliver such certificate to the party against whom the complaint was preferred' (s. 44, emphasis added). The obtaining of an s. 44 certificate of dismissal releases the party 'from all further or other proceedings, civil or criminal, *for the same cause*' (s. 45). The italicised words indicate the main limitations on the scope of ss. 44 and 45. First, a certificate of dismissal may be granted only where the complainant (i.e., prosecutor) in the summary assault proceedings is the victim of the alleged offence. Therefore, if the victim reported the offence to the police and the police commenced proceedings either by charging the accused or laying an information, s. 44 cannot apply since the police, in commencing proceedings, do not act on behalf of the aggrieved. Secondly, a certificate only frees the recipient from further proceedings 'for the same cause'.

The second relevant statutory provision is s. 18 of the Interpretation Act 1978, which states that: 'Where an act or omission constitutes an offence under two or more Acts, or both under an Act and at common law, the offender shall, unless the contrary intention appears, be liable to be prosecuted and punished under either or any of those Acts or at common law, but shall not be liable to be punished more than once for the same offence'. According to Humphreys J in *Thomas* [1950] 1 KB 26, the predecessor of s. 18 of the 1978 Act (s. 33 of the Interpretation Act 1889) 'added nothing and detracted nothing from the common law'. In particular, the prohibition in the section on being punished more than once for the same offence did not protect an accused from being convicted and sentenced on successive occasions for different offences arising out of the same criminal act (conviction for wounding with intent no bar to later indictment for murder).

Tainted Acquittals The provisions of the CPIA 1996, ss. 54 to 57, which relate to **D10.31** 'tainted acquittals', constitute a major exception to the availability of autrefois acquit. They enable the prosecution of an accused for a second time for a crime of which he has already been acquitted at trial, provided certain conditions are met. Sections 54 and 55 are set out below; they lay down a procedure relating to tainted acquittals where the following conditions are met:

(a)   an accused has been acquitted of an offence (s. 54(1)(a)); and

(b)   a person has been convicted of an administration of justice offence involving interference with or intimidation of a juror or a witness or potential witness (s. 54(1)(b)); and

(c)   the court convicting of the administration of justice offence certifies that there is a real possibility that, but for the interference or intimidation, the acquitted person would not have been acquitted, and that it would not be contrary to the interests of justice to proceed against the acquitted person (s. 54(2) and (5)); and

(d)   the High Court grants an order quashing the acquittal after deciding that the four conditions set out in s. 55 are satisfied.

The provisions of ss. 54 to 57 apply in relation to acquittals in respect of offences alleged to have been committed on or after 15 April 1997. It should be emphasised that it is the *original* offence of which the defendant was acquitted which must be alleged to have been committed on or after that date (s. 54(7)).

The formalities relating to the tainted acquittal procedure are set out in the Crown Court (Criminal Procedure and Investigations Act 1996) (Tainted Acquittals) Rules 1997 (SI 1997 No. 1054) and the Magistrates' Courts (Criminal Procedure and Investigations Act 1996) (Tainted Acquittals) Rules 1997 (SI 1997 No. 1055). These rules make it clear that the certification referred to in s. 54(2) must take place, at the latest, immediately after sentence (or committal for sentence, or remittal of a juvenile to the youth court to be dealt with for an offence).

Criminal Procedure and Investigations Act 1996, ss. 54 and 55

54.—(1)   This section applies where—

(a)   a person has been acquitted of an offence, and

(b)   a person has been convicted of an administration of justice offence involving interference with or intimidation of a juror or a witness (or potential witness) in any proceedings which led to the acquittal.

(2)   Where it appears to the court before which the person was convicted that—

(a)   there is a real possibility that, but for the interference or intimidation, the acquitted person would not have been acquitted, and

(b)   subsection (5) does not apply,

the court shall certify that it so appears.

(3)   Where a court certifies under subsection (2) an application may be made to the High Court for an order quashing the acquittal, and the Court shall make the order if (but shall not do so unless) the four conditions in section 55 are satisfied.

(4)   Where an order is made under subsection (3) proceedings may be taken against the acquitted person for the offence of which he was acquitted.

(5)   This subsection applies if, because of lapse of time or for any other reason, it would be contrary to the interests of justice to take proceedings against the acquitted person for the offence of which he was acquitted.

(6)   For the purposes of this section the following offences are administration of justice offences—

(a)   the offence of perverting the course of justice;

(b) the offence under section 51(1) of the Criminal Justice and Public Order Act 1994 (intimidation etc. of witnesses, jurors and others);

(c) an offence of aiding, abetting, counselling, procuring, suborning or inciting another person to commit an offence under section 1 of the Perjury Act 1911.

(7) This section applies in relation to acquittals in respect of offences alleged to be committed on or after the appointed day.

55.—(1) The first condition is that it appears to the High Court likely that, but for the interference or intimidation, the acquitted person would not have been acquitted.

(2) The second condition is that it does not appear to the Court that, because of lapse of time or for any other reason it would be contrary to the interests of justice to take proceedings against the acquitted person for the offence of which he was acquitted.

(3) The third condition is that it appears to the Court that the acquitted person has been given a reasonable opportunity to make written representations to the Court.

(4) The fourth condition is that it appears to the Court that the conviction for the administration of justice offence will stand.

(5) In applying subsection (4) the Court shall—

(a) take into account all the information before it, but

(b) ignore the possibility of new factors coming to light.

(6) Accordingly, the fourth condition has the effect that the Court shall not make an order under section 54(3) if (for instance) it appears to the Court that any time allowed for giving notice of appeal has not expired or that an appeal is pending.

Meaning of 'Acquittal' and 'Conviction' in Context of Autrefois Pleas

D10.32 For autrefois to succeed, the earlier conviction or acquittal relied on by the accused must have been by a court of competent jurisdiction and the proceedings must not have been ultra vires. This is illustrated in respect of autrefois convict by *Kent Justices, ex parte Machin* [1952] 2 QB 355, in which the Divisional Court quashed by certiorari M's conviction and committal for sentence for the offences of larceny and obtaining credit by fraud on the ground that the correct procedure for determining mode of trial had not been complied with and the magistrates therefore acted *ultra vires*. Lord Goddard CJ – while hoping that, in the particular circumstances, there would be no further proceedings – stated that the prosecution were entitled to recharge the accused as he 'has never been technically in peril and he could be tried again'. The same applies to *ultra vires* acquittals. Thus, where magistrates purport to acquit an accused of an offence triable only on indictment, he cannot rely on the 'acquittal' either to resist committal or to bar a trial on indictment (*West* [1964] 1 QB 15 and see also *Cardiff Magistrates' Court, ex parte Cardiff City Council* (1987) *The Times*, 24 February 1987).

D10.33 *Findings that Cannot Form Basis for Plea of Autrefois Acquit* The following findings do *not* amount to acquittals and therefore cannot found a plea of autrefois acquit:

(a) Discharge of the accused at committal proceedings (*Manchester City Stipendiary Magistrate, ex parte Snelson* [1977] 1 WLR 911).

(b) Quashing of an indictment following a motion to quash. This point would not seem to be covered by specific authority but follows inevitably from the nature of the remedy, which is to prevent any proceedings on the indictment in question and, *ex hypothesi*, prevent the returning of a verdict (see *Newland* [1988] QB 402).

(c) The withdrawal of a summons by the prosecution in the magistrates' court prior to the accused having pleaded to it – see *Bedford and Sharnbrook Justices, ex parte Ward* [1974] Crim LR 109 and *Grays Justices, ex parte Low* [1990] QB 54. In the latter case, Nolan J reviewed the earlier authorities and concluded: ' . . . it must now be regarded as settled law that . . . the withdrawal of a summons with the consent of the justices will not of itself operate as a bar to the issue of a further summons in respect of the same charge where there has been no adjudication upon the merits of the charge in the original summons, and the defendant has not been put in peril of conviction upon it' (at p. 59A–B). See also *Brookes* [1995] Crim LR 630, where B pleaded not guilty to a charge under the Offences against the Person Act 1861, s. 20, and the prosecution offered no evidence and laid a charge under s. 18. In the Crown Court, B entered a plea of autrefois acquit which the judge refused to uphold. The Court of Appeal held that the judge's decision was entirely correct.

(d)   The dismissal of an information under s. 15 of the MCA 1980 on account of the non-appearance of the prosecutor (*Bennett and Bond, ex parte Bennet* (1908) 72 JP 362) or where the information is so faulty in form and content that the accused could never have been in jeopardy on it (see *DPP* v *Porthouse* (1988) 89 Cr App R 21 and *Dabhade* [1993] QB 329).

(e)   The prosecution serving notice of discontinuance under s. 23 of the Prosecution of Offences Act 1985.

(f)   The jury being discharged from giving a verdict.

(g)   Where the provisions relating to tainted acquittals in the CPIA 1996, ss. 54 to 57 apply (see **D10.31**).

Findings that Can Form Basis for Plea of Autrefois Acquit   The following   **D10.34** findings *do* amount to acquittals and therefore can found a plea of autrefois acquit:

(a)   The quashing of a conviction by the Court of Appeal, provided it does not at the same time order a retrial (see Criminal Appeal Act 1968, s. 2(3)).

(b)   An acquittal by a foreign court of competent jurisdiction (*Aughet* (1919) 13 Cr App R 101). This was confirmed, *obiter*, by Lord Diplock in *Treacy* v *DPP* [1971] AC 537, when he said (at p. 562D) that the common-law doctrine of autrefois acquit and convict was 'a doctrine which has always applied whether the previous conviction or acquittal based on the same facts was by an English court or by a foreign court'.

Findings that Cannot Form Basis for Plea of Autrefois Convict   The following   **D10.35** findings do *not* amount to convictions and therefore cannot found a plea of autrefois convict:

(a)   The taking of an offence into consideration when passing sentence for other offences of which the offender has been convicted (*Nicholson* [1947] 2 All ER 535).

(b)   A finding of guilt in disciplinary proceedings, albeit that the finding is followed by the imposition of a penalty (*Hogan* [1960] 2 QB 513 – escapees from prison who had been found guilty by the visiting magistrates of the appropriate offence under the Prison Rules and punished by loss of remission could not rely on autrefois convict to defeat a subsequent indictment for the common-law offence of escaping by force).

(c)   A finding of contempt of court in civil proceedings, e.g., breach of a non-molestation injunction (*Green* [1993] Crim LR 46).

Findings that Can Form Basis for Plea of Autrefois Convict   As with acquittals,   **D10.36** a conviction by a foreign court will found autrefois convict, subject to the qualification that if he who now relies on the foreign conviction was found guilty and sentenced in his absence and there is no likelihood of his ever returning to the country concerned to serve his sentence, then the plea will fail (*Thomas* [1985] QB 604).

Can a plea of autrefois convict be founded simply upon a conviction, or is it necessary for the accused to have been sentenced? In *Sheridan* [1937] 1 KB 223, magistrates tried S for an offence triable either way and, after hearing the evidence, announced that they found him guilty. Having then been informed that S was of bad character, they decided not to proceed to sentence but to commit S to quarter sessions for trial (at the time there was no power to commit for sentence). At quarter sessions, S unsuccessfully pleaded autrefois convict. On appeal, the Court of Criminal Appeal held that it was a plain case of autrefois, and the prosecution argument that 'there can be no conviction such as will support a plea of autrefois convict unless there is also a sentence' was simply wrong. The case of *Grant* [1936] 2 All ER 1156 was on all fours with *Sheridan* save that there the accused pleaded guilty in the magistrates' court prior to being committed for trial whereas Sheridan had pleaded not guilty. It was held that the difference in plea made no difference to the decision (i.e. the appellant was entitled to rely on autrefois convict). In *Richards* v *The Queen* [1993] AC 217, the Privy Council concluded that *Sheridan* and *Grant* were wrongly decided. The underlying rationale was to prevent double punishment. But, if a finding of guilt was all that was necessary to support the plea in bar, an accused might escape punishment altogether. A plea of autrefois convict could only be based upon a complete adjudication against the accused, including the final disposal of the case by passing sentence or some other order such as an absolute discharge.

Procedure on Autrefois Pleas

D10.37 Under the Criminal Procedure Act 1851, s. 28, an accused may raise a plea of autrefois simply by stating that he has already been lawfully acquitted or convicted of the offence now charged. Where, however, he is legally represented, the correct procedure is for the plea to be entered in writing signed by counsel. A suggested form of words is, '[The accused] says that the Queen ought not further to prosecute the indictment against him because he has been lawfully acquitted/convicted of the offence charged therein'. The prosecution either admit that the plea is good (in which case the accused is discharged) or join issue in writing. The obvious time for pleading autrefois is before the indictment is put to the accused, but failure to do so then will not prevent the defence raising the issue at a later stage ('. . . the plea may be raised at any time either as a plea in bar to the second indictment or at any stage in the proceedings': per Lord Hodson in *Connelly* v *DPP* [1964] AC 1254 at p. 1331). Similarly, failure to observe the correct formalities in entering the plea does not prevent reliance on it (*Flatman* v *Light* [1946] KB 414).

In *Cooper* v *New Forest District Council* [1992] Crim LR 877, the Divisional Court held that the Crown Court (acting in its appellate capacity) had power to consider a plea of autrefois, even though the accused had pleaded guilty to the instant offence in the magistrates' court below. Although C had unequivocally pleaded guilty before the justices, the Crown Court was entitled to consider her application to appeal against conviction and withdraw her plea on the ground of her special plea in bar.

Once the plea has been entered and issue joined by the prosecution, the burden of proof is on the accused to make good the plea on a balance of probabilities (*Coughlan* (1976) 63 Cr App R 33). The issue is determined by the judge without empanelling a jury (CJA 1988, s. 122). The parties are not restricted to the formal record of the earlier proceedings (which will establish only the date and place of conviction or acquittal, the wording of the charges and the name of the accused), but may call relevant evidence. Such evidence might relate to the identity of the person named in the court record (was it the accused or some other person?). It is rare for there to be a significant dispute between prosecution and defence about the facts underlying a plea of autrefois. In the absence of such a dispute, counsel should shorten the proceedings by reading to the court a brief statement of the relevant facts from (a) the previous trial, and (b) the statements in the present case on which they respectively intend to rely in argument (see *Coughlan* (1976) 63 Cr App R 33).

If a plea of autrefois convict or acquit succeeds, it is a bar to any further proceedings on the indictment. If the plea fails, the indictment is put and the accused is entitled to plead not guilty to the general issue notwithstanding his earlier unsuccessful reliance on autrefois (Criminal Law Act 1967, s. 6(1): 'Where a person is arraigned on indictment . . . he shall in all cases be entitled to make a plea of not guilty in addition to any demurrer or special plea.').

A Note on Issue Estoppel

D10.38 A further question raised by the appeal in *Connelly* v *DPP* [1964] AC 1254 was whether the doctrine of issue estoppel applies in criminal cases, i.e. can either the prosecution or the defence prevent the other side reopening a question of fact if that question has already been decided in previous proceedings between the same parties? Lord Morris, for example, explained some decisions which seemed to go beyond the strict limits he was imposing on autrefois as cases either of issue estoppel or *res iudicata*. However, in *DPP* v *Humphrys* [1977] AC 1 it was held that issue estoppel has no place in criminal proceedings. (There is a limited exception in the case of an application for habeas corpus: *Governor of Brixton Prison, ex parte Osman* [1991] 1 WLR 281.) Thus, H – who had been acquitted of driving while disqualified following a trial at which the only live issue before the jury was whether he had been driving on the day specified in the indictment – was unable to prevent the prosecution at a later trial for perjury calling evidence that he had been driving on that day as part of their case that the evidence he gave at the first trial had been perjured. For full discussion of issue estoppel, see **F11.5**.

OTHER PLEAS

Demurrer

This is 'an objection to the form or substance of the indictment, apparent on the face of **D10.39** the indictment' (per Cantley J in *Inner London Quarter Sessions, ex parte Metropolitan Police Commissioner* [1970] 2 QB 80 at p. 83G).

The plea must be entered in writing, filed in the Crown Office, and a copy served on the opposite party, preferably prior to the accused being arraigned (ibid.). On demurring, the defence are *not* entitled to refer the judge to the contents of the depositions and/or statements tendered at committal proceedings (see *Ex parte Metropolitan Police Commissioner*, where mandamus issued requiring quarter sessions to hear and determine an indictment which the trial judge had quashed following demurrer by the defence, the grounds of demurrer being that the committal documents did not disclose the offence charged). It follows that the scope of the remedy by demurrer is no wider than the scope of motions to quash, and Lord Parker CJ, noting that there had been a revival in the use of demurrers after a period during which they had been regarded as totally obsolete, said that he hoped they would now 'be allowed to die naturally' (ibid. at p. 85G). Similarly, Cantley J said that demurrers had been 'supplanted in practice by the safe and convenient procedures of motion to quash the indictment or motion in arrest of judgment' (at p. 83C). However, in *Cumberworth* (1989) 89 Cr App R 187, where the defence submitted at the end of the prosecution evidence that the Crown Court lacked jurisdiction in respect of offences allegedly committed on a French ship in Dieppe harbour, the Court of Appeal stated, *obiter*, that it would have been more convenient procedurally to raise the point by way of demurrer at the outset of the trial, thus avoiding the necessity of hearing the evidence if the point were good. The court's suggestion appears to conflict with the clear statement in *Ex parte Metropolitan Police Commissioner* that a defect founding demurrer must be apparent on the face of the indictment, since the venue of the offence is not normally specified in a count.

The entry of a demurrer does not affect the accused's right to plead not guilty to the indictment should the demurrer fail (Criminal Law Act 1967, s. 6(1)(a)).

Plea to the Jurisdiction

The purpose of this plea is apparent from its name. It is a plea that the Crown Court has **D10.40** no jurisdiction to try the offence charged (e.g., because it is a summary offence or because it was committed abroad and does not come within the exceptional categories of 'foreign' offences that may be tried in England and Wales). Like a demurrer, the plea should be entered in writing prior to arraignment, although it is always open to the defence to take any jurisdictional point simply under a general not guilty plea (see, e.g., *Treacy* v *DPP* [1971] AC 537 where that was done). However, in *Cumberworth* (1989)

89 Cr App R 187 (see **D10.39**) the defence were criticised for waiting until the close of the prosecution case to submit that the court had no jurisdiction, since, had the point been good, the court and jury would have heard much evidence on the general issue unnecessarily. Somewhat strangely, the Court of Appeal suggested that a demurrer, rather than a plea to the jurisdiction, would have been the appropriate course.

Pardon

D10.41 This is the third special plea in bar (the other two being autrefois acquit and autrefois convict). It may be relied on where a pardon has been granted by the Crown on the advice of the Home Secretary in exercise of the royal prerogative of mercy. It must be pleaded at the first opportunity (i.e. before arraignment if the pardon has by then been granted). In modern times, the granting of a pardon is restricted to cases where, *after* conviction, it becomes apparent that the accused ought never to have been convicted but the normal avenues of appeal have already been exhausted or are otherwise inappropriate. Since pardons now follow rather than precede conviction, the plea has become obsolete.

PLEA BARGAINING

Introduction

D10.42 Under this heading are discussed: (a) the extent to which the judge may properly influence the accused's decision as to plea by indicating the probable sentence, and (b) the propriety of bargains between the prosecution and defence involving the offering of no evidence in respect of certain charges in return for the accused pleading guilty to others.

Judicial Indications of Sentence

D10.43 A plea of guilty must be entered voluntarily. If the accused is deprived of a genuine choice as to plea and in consequence purports to plead guilty, the plea is a nullity and the conviction will be quashed on appeal (see *Turner* [1970] 2 QB 321 and **D10.24**). In *Turner* the reason for holding the appellant's plea to be a nullity was that his counsel, during discussions about whether there should be a change of plea to guilty, went to see the judge, and, on returning to his client, stated that a conviction on a not guilty plea would entail a 'very real possibility' of a prison sentence whereas if T pleaded guilty it would be a 'fine or some other sentence not involving imprisonment'. Although counsel was merely passing on his own views, it was accepted by the Court of Appeal that T might well have got the impression from the overall circumstances that counsel was repeating what the judge had told him. In those circumstances, the promise of a non-custodial sentence in the event of a guilty plea, coupled with an implied threat of a custodial sentence should the not guilty plea be unsuccessfully maintained, took away T's free choice. Having decided that the conviction must therefore be quashed, the Court of Appeal made the following observations designed to assist counsel and judges over what was referred to as 'the vexed question of plea bargaining' (at pp. 326E–327D emphasis added):

> 1.   Counsel must be completely free to do what is his duty, namely to give the accused the best advice he can and if need be advice in strong terms. This will often include advice that a plea of guilty, showing an element of remorse, is a mitigating factor which may well enable the court to give a lesser sentence than would otherwise be the case. Counsel of course will emphasise that the accused must not plead guilty unless he has committed the acts constituting the offence charged.
> 2.   The accused, having considered counsel's advice, must have a complete freedom of choice whether to plead guilty or not guilty.
> 3.   There must be freedom of access between counsel and judge. Any discussion, however, which takes place must be between the judge and both counsel for the defence

and counsel for the prosecution. If a solicitor representing the accused is in the court he should be allowed to attend the discussion if he so desires. This freedom of access is important because there may be matters calling for communication or discussion, which are of such a nature that counsel cannot in the interests of his client mention them in open court. . . . It is of course imperative that so far as possible justice must be administered in open court. Counsel should, therefore, only ask to see the judge when it is felt to be really necessary, and the judge must be careful only to treat such communications as private where, in fairness to the accused person, this is necessary.

4. The judge should, subject to the one exception referred to hereafter, never indicate the sentence which he is minded to impose. A statement that on a plea of guilty he would impose one sentence but that on a conviction following a plea of not guilty he would impose a severer sentence is one which should never be made. This could be taken to be undue pressure on the accused, thus depriving him of that complete freedom of choice which is essential. Such cases, however, are in the experience of the court happily rare. What on occasions does appear to happen however is that a judge will tell counsel that, having read the depositions and the antecedents, he can safely say that on a plea of guilty he will for instance, make a probation order, something which may be helpful to counsel in advising the accused. The judge in such a case is no doubt careful not to mention what he would do if the accused were convicted following a plea of not guilty. Even so, the accused may well get the impression that the judge is intimating that in that event a severer sentence, maybe a custodial sentence would result, so that again he may feel under pressure. This accordingly must also not be done.

The only exception to this rule is that it should be permissible for a judge to say, if it be the case, that whatever happens, whether the accused pleads guilty or not guilty, the sentence will or will not take a particular form, e.g., a probation order or a fine, or a custodial sentence.

Finally, where any such discussion on sentence has taken place between judge and counsel, counsel for the defence should disclose this to the accused and inform him of what took place.

Certain qualifications to the observations in *Turner's* case were advanced by the Court of Appeal in *Cain* [1976] Crim LR 464. However, following the reporting of *Cain*, the Court of Appeal issued a *Practice Direction* [1976] Crim LR 561 stating that if *Cain* is inconsistent with the observations in *Turner* the latter should prevail.

The principles in Turner's case have since been consistently applied by the Court of Appeal (which is not, of course, the same as saying that they are always observed at first instance). In *Coward* (1979) 70 Cr App R 70, for example, Lawton LJ (giving the court's judgment on an appeal against sentence) strongly deprecated an attempt made in that case by defence counsel to persuade the trial judge to give an indication of sentence. In the course of the appeal, counsel for the appellant argued: (a) that 'it was common practice for members of the Bar defending in criminal cases to ask to see the judge for the purpose of finding out what sort of sentence the judge would pass if there were a plea of guilty'; and (b) that to forbid such approaches would be 'to the detriment of the administration of justice'. Lawton LJ responded by saying that he did not believe the practice counsel referred to was in fact common; to the extent that it did exist it should cease, and, if persisted in, it would only lead to misunderstandings such as had occurred in the instant case (counsel misinterpreted the judge's remark that counsel 'would have to trust him' as the promise of a non-custodial sentence in the event of a guilty plea). Thus, it was for counsel to make up his own mind about the likely sentence and advise his client accordingly. The only guidance he could expect from the judge was that sanctioned by Lord Parker in paragraph (4) in the passage from *Turner* [1970] 2 QB 321 quoted above. Although the case was not expressly referred to, Lawton LJ's views are plainly inconsistent with the first qualification to *Turner* contained in *Cain* (see above). Further cases applying *Turner* include:

Ryan (1977) 67 Cr App R 177 – conviction on a guilty plea quashed and *venire de novo* issued because R clearly pleaded guilty out of fear of a custodial sentence and as a result of the judge telling counsel that, as then advised and on the basis of a guilty plea, the sentence would be non-custodial, probably a probation order with a requirement for medical treatment attached.

Grice (1977) 66 Cr App R 167 – sentence for incest varied so as to be suspended rather than immediate for reasons not directly connected with the plea, but the Court of Appeal also strongly criticised the trial judge for offering the accused, via counsel, a 'plea bargain', namely, a non-custodial sentence in exchange for a guilty plea. The judge's reason for so doing was his concern at the potential effect on the victim of having to testify (she had already attempted suicide). Nonetheless, the Court of Appeal were 'astonished' at the blatant breach of the *Turner* guidelines. Had there been an appeal against conviction, it would have been allowed.

Bird (1977) 67 Cr App R 203 – repeated attempts by the judge to extract from B a guilty plea by the promise to counsel in private of a suspended sentence if there were such a plea did not have the effect the judge desired. B was, however, found guilty and the judge passed a sentence of immediate imprisonment. Having regard to the qualifications to *Turner* contained in *Cain*, defence counsel had not directly told B of the judge's offer, although it was accepted that B must have realised that counsel's advice on sentence reflected what the judge was saying privately. At the stage of mitigation, however, counsel did say in open court that the judge had earlier professed himself willing to deal with the offence by way of a suspended sentence, and he should not now resile from that indication. The judge imposed an immediate sentence of 21 months. The Court of Appeal commended counsel's making public what the judge had said; criticised the breach of the *Turner* observations; and suspended the sentence, not because it was in itself excessive (the offence was one of theft of £2,000 from employers), but because justice had not been seen to be done.

Llewellyn (1978) 67 Cr App R 149 – judge before the trial asked to see counsel and told them that he considered L (one of three co-accused charged with conspiracy to steal) to be the ringleader. He probably (though not certainly) indicated that a guilty plea would be looked on very favourably and the sentence, in the event of such a plea, would be around four years' imprisonment. L pleaded not guilty and was convicted. The Court of Appeal quashed the conviction because, although there was no error in the trial itself, the judge's view that the appellant was the ringleader, which had inevitably been passed on to him by counsel, left him with a burning sense of grievance. Justice was not seen to be done if the accused was understandably left with the impression that he was being tried by a judge who had made his mind up against him even before the trial had started.

Atkinson [1978] 1 WLR 425 – judge at a pre-trial review said that he could see no reason 'at the present time' why the accused should go to prison for an alleged offence of handling a bicycle. He suggested that counsel should have a word with his client and explain the position, emphasising that the accused should plead guilty only if he was guilty. In the event, A pleaded not guilty, was convicted and sentenced to six months' immediate imprisonment. The Court of Appeal commended the judge for giving his indication about sentence in open court, but nonetheless held that what occurred 'could very well give the impression' of a plea bargain. That was 'damaging to the face of justice' and resulted in the sentence being varied so as to allow for the appellant's immediate release.

Smith [1990] 1 WLR 1311 – counsel for defence and prosecution saw the judge and discussed likely sentence on a count of affray and consequent breach of probation. As a result, defence counsel saw his client and indicated to him that, provided the probation report was not unfavourable, the judge would deal with him by way of suspended sentence. S then pleaded guilty. The case was put back for reports. When the reports were received, the judge imposed sentences of 10 months' imprisonment in total and, according to the Court of Appeal, what ensued was 'an unseemly dispute between the judge and counsel in open court'. In the event, the Court of Appeal accepted that S had in any event been misled by his own counsel into believing that the judge had given an undertaking that he would pass a suspended sentence. Reluctantly, therefore, they quashed the sentence imposed and substituted a suspended sentence.

James [1990] Crim LR 815 – J was charged with rape. At the end of the first day of the trial, the judge sent for both counsel. He made it clear that he thought the prosecution case was a strong one, that J was entitled to the jury's verdict, that a plea of guilty would allow for a reduction in sentence, and that he did not feel J had been carefully and competently advised as to his position. J's counsel repeated to his client what the judge had said, mentioning the credit for a plea of guilty but adding that it was J's decision. The next day, J changed his plea to guilty. He appealed against conviction in due course. The Court of Appeal ordered a *venire de novo*. Although the judge was acting from the best of motives, the effect of what had been said vitiated J's plea. Their lordships felt that this was not a case in which the judge should have seen counsel in his room. Further he should not have expressed his personal view about the prospect of the defence succeeding. Nor, when a change of plea is under consideration, should he give an assurance that a plea of guilty will result in a lesser sentence.

It will be apparent from the above that, depending on the precise circumstances, the result of a breach of the *Turner* observations may be as in *Turner* itself, a quashing of a conviction on a guilty plea and issue of *venire de novo*; or the quashing of a guilty verdict where the appellant maintained a not guilty plea despite improper pressure; or a reduction in the appellant's sentence to avoid the appearance of a miscarriage of justice.

If the judge does give a sentencing indication of the sort allowed by *Turner* he is clearly bound thereby even if he later regrets it (*Cullen* (1984) 81 Cr App R 17 – suspended sentence of imprisonment quashed because it seemed that the judge had promised counsel a non-custodial sentence whatever the plea, and a suspended sentence ranks as custodial, albeit that the term may never be served). Where the judge's indication breaches *Turner* it is submitted that counsel is nonetheless justified – indeed under a duty – to communicate the indication to his client. That is the implication of the last of Lord Parker's observations in *Turner*. Moreover, in none of the cases summarised immediately above was counsel criticised for his conduct, although their precise response to a difficult situation appears to have varied. In *Grice* and *Ryan*, for example, they seem simply to have told their clients what the judge had said, whereas counsel in *Bird* took the view that the judge's remarks were confidential and therefore discussed the matter with B without in terms revealing the source of the advice that was being given. However, counsel in *Coward* was held at fault for trying to extract from the judge an indication about sentence which, if given, would have been improper. Whether he intended it or not, counsel was trying to involve the judge in plea bargaining. See also *Bigley* (1993) 14 Cr App R (S) 201 (at p. 205).

The fact that a judge has given an indication of sentence before plea will not bind the Court of Appeal if the A-G appeals on the basis that the sentence is unduly lenient (*A-G's Ref (No. 40 of 1996)* [1997] 1 Cr App R (S) 357: see **D24.4**).

Arrangements between Prosecution and Defence

It is common practice for the prosecution and defence to agree through counsel prior to **D10.44** arraignment that, in the event of the accused pleading guilty to parts of the indictment, the Crown will not seek to prove him guilty as charged. The precise nature of the arraignment will vary according to circumstances. It may take the form of accepting a plea of guilty to a lesser offence, or of offering no evidence on counts to which the accused pleads not guilty, or of asking the judge to allow some counts to remain on the file marked not to be proceeded with. The chief point of contention is the extent to which the trial judge can control such bargains. As to this, see **D10.26**.

In 1986, Farquharson J chaired a committee on the role of prosecuting counsel, with special reference to the then imminent introduction of the CPS. The committee reported in May 1986, and its report may be found in the Trinity 1986 issue of *Counsel*. Dealing with counsel's control over the acceptance of pleas, the committee discussed the authorities, and also made the point that, in the reverse situation of the judge thinking that the evidence on the depositions does not warrant a conviction or that further proceedings would be unfair, he has no power to prevent the prosecution calling their evidence save in the very exceptional case of the proceedings amounting to an abuse of the process of the court. The following is a summary of the Farquharson Committee's views.

In accepting a plea of guilty to a lesser offence or guilty to some counts only on the indictment, prosecuting counsel is in reality making a decision to offer no evidence on a particular charge. Since the committee were of the opinion that counsel was undoubtedly entitled to offer no evidence on the indictment as a whole and could not be forced to call evidence against his will, it followed that he must also be entitled to decide to accept pleas to part only of the indictment. This general rule is, however, subject to three qualifications:

(a)   If prosecuting counsel expressly asks for the judge's approval of his proposed acceptance of certain pleas, he must abide by the judge's decision (*Broad* (1978) 68 Cr App R 281). There is no obligation on him to seek such approval, but he might feel it right to do so where either it is desirable to reassure the public at large that the course proposed is being properly taken, or he has been unable to reach agreement with his instructing solicitor about what ought to be done.

(b)   In a case where the judge's approval is not sought beforehand, it is nonetheless usual for counsel to explain in open court his reasons for accepting the plea. It is then open to the judge to express his views. If he disapproves of the course proposed by counsel, he will no doubt say so. Should the judge, on the information available to him (depositions, exhibits, antecedents, perhaps reports on the accused) feel such strong disapproval of the proposal that 'he cannot consistently with his duty, as he sees it, proceed to sentence on that basis' (i.e., on the basis of a plea to part only of the indictment), then, although he cannot insist on prosecuting counsel proceeding on the major or other charge, he 'may decline to proceed with the case without counsel first consulting with the DPP on whether he should proceed in the light of the comments the judge will have made'. In extreme cases, he may even think it right to invite counsel to take the advice of the A-G. However, in the final analysis and once the steps just referred to have been taken, the judge has no power to prevent counsel taking the course he thinks fit – 'any attempt by him to do so would give the impression that he was stepping into the arena and pressing the prosecution case'. However, the committee expressed the opinion that 'the occasions when counsel felt it right to resist the judge's views would be rare'. The above reflects and amplifies the Bar Committee's Guidelines to Prosecution Counsel, dated 9 May 1984, which were approved by the Court of Appeal in *Jenkins* (1986) 83 Cr App R 152).

The report of the Farquharson Committee was referred to with approval in *Grafton* [1993] QB 101. In that case, there was a conflict of evidence between two witnesses called for the Crown. Prosecution counsel consulted those instructing him, and said he would call no further evidence. Apparently, the judge disagreed profoundly with this decision and had an animated argument with prosecuting counsel, who held his ground and took no part in the proceedings thereafter. The judge then himself called a police officer, who was the Crown's remaining witness. G was convicted, and appealed. The appeal was allowed on the basis that the decision whether to continue with the case or not had to be that of the prosecution. By proceeding as he did, the judge was no longer holding the ring between adversaries but took over the prosecution, and the reaction of any neutral bystander could only be that he had become the adversary of the defence.

(c)   Should the decision to accept proposed pleas fall to be taken during the course of the trial, prosecuting counsel's position remains as in (b) above until the close of his case. Once, however, he has called his evidence and the judge has either found there is a case to answer or no submission to the contrary has been made, then the position is different. At that stage there is, *ex hypothesi*, a case for the accused to answer, and therefore 'it would be an abuse of process for the prosecution to discontinue without leave'. But, even though the judge can rule that the case shall proceed, 'it would not be the duty of counsel to cross-examine the defence witnesses or address the jury if he was of the view that it would not be proper to convict'. In *Grafton*, their lordships stated that the Farquharson Report was correct. They added, however, that where the prosecution's case is complete, but the judge refuses leave to the Crown to discontinue, it was prosecution counsel's duty to remain in the case. If the prosecution's view later changed (perhaps as a result of hearing the defendant testify) he would then be free to cross-examine witnesses or address the jury.

Although the committee's report obviously does not have the force of law, it is extremely persuasive, by reason of its intrinsic merit and the composition of the committee.

CHANGE OF PLEA

From Not Guilty to Guilty

The judge may allow the accused to change his plea from not guilty to guilty at any stage **D10.45** prior to the jury returning their verdict. The procedure is that the defence ask for the indictment to be put again; the accused then pleads guilty, and the jury empanelled as a result of the original not guilty plea formally return a verdict. Assuming the change of plea comes after the accused has been put in the charge of a jury, it is essential that they find him guilty. A conviction recorded simply on the accused's change of plea without the jury's verdict is a nullity and will be quashed on appeal, the Court having a discretion to order a retrial (*Heyes* [1951] 1 KB 29). In *Heyes*, H pleaded not guilty to charges of stealing and receiving certain property. During the opening of the prosecution case and after advice from counsel who had at that stage been allotted to him, he changed his plea to guilty of receiving. This was done in the jury's presence but they were not asked to return a verdict, and the judge proceeded forthwith to sentence. On appeal, Lord Goddard CJ said:

> Once the jury had heard the appellant say that he wished to withdraw his plea and admit his guilt, the proper proceeding was for the court to ask them to return a verdict. It appears that counsel did suggest to the learned recorder that this was the proper course; but the recorder thought that it did not matter. It does matter because, once a prisoner is in charge of a jury, he can only be either convicted or discharged by the verdict of the jury.

> As there was no verdict of the jury here, the trial was a nullity to such an extent that the court could set aside the proceedings and order a retrial or *venire de novo* [but, in the circumstances of this case we] will merely quash the conviction.

Although having the indictment put again with a view to a change of plea to guilty is a matter for the judge's discretion, it is difficult to envisage circumstances in which he would be unwilling to allow it to be done. Depending on the stage of the trial at which it comes, the change of plea will provide some mitigation for the accused when sentence is passed. As to the effect of such a change of plea upon the trial of a co-accused, see **D11.21** and the case of *Fedrick* [1990] Crim LR 403 dealt with there.

From Guilty to Not Guilty

The judge has a discretion to allow the accused to withdraw a plea of guilty at any stage **D10.46** before sentence is passed. This was confirmed in *Plummer* [1902] 2 KB 339 where the major question for the court was whether P's conviction on a guilty plea for conspiracy to steal could be sustained in view of his five co-accused (who were the only others named in the conspiracy count) having been acquitted. P was not sentenced until after the acquittal of the others, and, prior to sentence, asked to withdraw his plea. Wright J said (at p. 347):

> Another point is raised in this case, namely, whether the court had power to allow the appellant to withdraw his plea of guilty. There cannot be any doubt that the court had such power at any time before, though not after, judgment [i.e., sentence] and, as we infer that but for the erroneous opinion that there was no such power the withdrawal would have been allowed, this might of itself be a ground for a *venire de novo*.

Similarly, Bruce J held that the first-instance court clearly had a discretion to allow the change of plea; that, if it had exercised its discretion against the appellant, the appellate court might have had no power to interfere; but, in fact, the discretion was never exercised one way or the other and that had deprived the appellant of a chance of an acquittal, with the consequence that the conviction could not stand (at p. 349). The existence of the discretion was indirectly confirmed by the House of Lords in *S* v *Recorder of Manchester* [1971] AC 481, holding that, in the context of change of plea, there is no conviction until sentence has been passed, and therefore magistrates (like the Crown Court) can allow a change to not guilty provided they have not yet passed sentence. Finally, in *Dodd* (1981) 74 Cr App R 50, the Court of Appeal unhesitatingly accepted the three following propositions from counsel for D, namely that: (a) the court has a discretion to allow a defendant to change a plea of guilty to one of not guilty at any time before sentence; (b) the discretion exists even where the plea of not guilty is unequivocal; and (c) the discretion must be exercised judicially (see p. 57).

While confirming the existence of the discretion now under consideration, the cases tend to show that it should be sparingly exercised in favour of the accused. Thus, in *McNally* [1954] 1 WLR 933, where the accused had indicated even in the magistrates' court an intention to plead guilty, could not possibly have misunderstood the nature of a straightforward charge of burglary and had unequivocally admitted guilt when the indictment was put to him, the Court of Criminal Appeal approved the trial judge's decision to refuse a change of plea. Even if the accused was unrepresented when he pleaded but instructs solicitors during an adjournment prior to sentencing and is advised by them that he has a defence, the court is not obliged to accede to a change of plea (*South Tameside Magistrates' Court, ex parte Rowland* [1983] 3 All ER 689). In *Ex parte Rowland*, R unequivocally pleaded guilty to theft of a handbag and asked for a further similar offence to be taken into consideration. Having heard the facts and considered R's record, the magistrates indicated that they were considering a custodial sentence and offered R an adjournment to obtain legal aid. She accepted and gave instructions to her solicitor indicating a possible defence along the lines that her co-accused actually took the bag and she neither abetted her co-accused nor knew what she was going to do. On an application for a change of plea, the magistrates 'rightly, balanced the instructions which the applicant had given to her solicitor after [the original plea] against the prospect that she was changing her story because of the possibility that she might be sentenced to a custodial sentence' (per Glidewell J at p. 692J). Furthermore, the magistrates 'were perfectly entitled to come to the conclusion to which they did come' (i.e. that fear of a custodial sentence was the real motivation for the change of plea), and thus were justified in exercising their discretion against R. Glidewell J approved the advice given to the magistrates by their clerk that, 'to allow a change of plea was a matter for [the magistrates'] absolute discretion and that once an unequivocal plea had been entered the discretionary power should be exercised judicially, very sparingly and only in clear cases' (at p. 692A). However, the implication is that, had the magistrates thought the plea to have been entered under a misapprehension of law as to the nature of the offence, then their only proper course would have been to allow the application. Although *Ex parte Rowland* was a case concerning change of plea in the magistrates' court, it is submitted that the same principles must apply in the Crown Court. If the accused was represented when he entered his plea of guilty, there would seem to be no absolute bar to his applying to withdraw the plea, but it will obviously be very difficult to convince the court that the plea was entered by a genuine mistake. (See also *Drew* [1985] 1 WLR 914 where Lord Lane CJ said (at p. 923C): ' . . . only rarely would it be appropriate for the trial judge to exercise his undoubted discretion in favour of an accused person wishing to change an unequivocal plea of guilty to one of not guilty. Particularly this is so in cases where, as here, the accused has throughout been advised by experienced counsel.')

Provided the court at first instance recognised that it had a discretion to allow a change of plea and applied the correct principles in determining the application, the Court of Appeal will not interfere with the trial judge's exercise of discretion – see *Dodd* (1981) 74 Cr App R 50 (above) and *Cantor* [1991] Crim LR 481.

Double Change of Plea

Where the accused has changed his plea from not guilty to guilty, the judge still has a **D10.47** discretion to allow him to change back to not guilty (*Drew* [1985] 1 WLR 914). The fact that the jury empanelled to try him as a result of the original not guilty plea formally found him guilty on hearing the change to guilty does not affect the existence of the judge's discretion. In *Drew*, Lord Lane CJ said (at p. 922C): 'There appears to this court no greater difficulty in altering the record following a jury's verdict than doing so upon a change of plea in any other situation. The jury's verdict where, as here, it is entered upon the direction of the judge, is essentially a formality. In our judgment, logic and good sense dictate that the trial judge should have the same power to allow a change of plea even where the verdict of guilty has been returned formally by the jury.' On the facts of the case, the Court of Appeal held that, had the trial judge exercised his discretion judicially (he had ruled that he did not have a discretion), he would have been bound to disallow the change, and therefore the appeal was dismissed by application of the proviso.

SECTION D11: JURIES

This section deals with eligibility for jury service, the summoning of jurors, the selection and empanelling of jurors for a particular case, the conduct of jurors during a trial, the judge's power to discharge the jury or individual jurors and the extent to which errors in the formation of the jury may ground an appeal. The rules governing retirement of the jury while they consider their verdict and the verdicts they may return are considered in **D16**. The main source of the law on jurors is the Juries Act 1974.

ELIGIBILITY FOR JURY SERVICE

Introduction

D11.1   The basic rule is that all persons aged 18 to 70 who:

(a)   are registered either as parliamentary or local government electors; and
(b)   have been ordinarily resident in the UK for any period of at least five years since attaining the age of 13,

are eligible for jury service and are therefore under a duty to attend for service if summoned (Juries Act 1974, s. 1). Parts I and II of sch. 1 to the Juries Act 1974 set out respectively four categories of persons who are *ineligible* for jury service and those persons who are *disqualified* by reason of their previous convictions. If a person serves on a jury knowing that he is ineligible for or disqualified from so doing he commits a summary offence punishable with a fine of up to £1,000 if he was ineligible, £5,000 if he was disqualified (Juries Act 1974, s. 20(5)).

In summary, the main ineligible groups are:

(a)   *The judiciary*, including circuit judges, recorders and magistrates as well as all holders of high judicial office.
(b)   *Members of the legal profession and others concerned with the administration of justice*, including barristers and solicitors (whether practising or not), articled clerks and barristers' clerks, legal executives in the employment of solicitors, court staff, justices' chief executives, justices' clerks and their assistants, police officers, civilian staff employed by police forces, prison officers, court security officers and probation officers.
(c)   *The clergy*, meaning a man in holy orders of any religious denomination and members of religious orders living in a monastery, convent etc.
(d)   *The mentally disordered*, meaning those who suffer from mental illness, psychopathic disorder, mental handicap or severe mental handicap and who are consequently either resident in hospital or regularly attending for treatment by a doctor.

Past members of group (a) and persons who within the last 10 years have fallen within group (b) are also ineligible.

Persons disqualified from jury service comprise the following:

(a)   Those who have *at any time* been sentenced to life imprisonment, custody for life or detention during Her Majesty's pleasure, or who have been sentenced to a term of five years' or more imprisonment, detention in a young offender institution or youth custody.
(b)   Those who *in the past 10 years* have served *any part* of a sentence of imprisonment, youth custody, detention under s. 53(3) of the CYPA 1933, detention in a detention centre or detention in a young offender institution.

(c)   Those who *in the past 10 years* have had passed on them a suspended sentence of imprisonment (whether or not the term was later activated).

(d)   Those who *in the past 10 years* have been ordered to perform community service.

(e)   Those who *in the past five years* have been put on probation.

(f)   Those who are on bail in criminal proceedings.

The above summary sets out what, it is submitted, must surely have been Parliament's intention when it introduced the sentence of detention in a young offender institution to replace youth custody and detention centre orders, namely that offenders sentenced to a term of five years or more in a young offender institution would be disqualified from jury service for life, just as were those sentenced to a similar term of youth custody under the old system. However, CJA 1988, sch. 8 (which makes minor amendments consequential on the introduction of the new sentence) is not happily drafted, and it may be that Parliament has inadvertently equated the position of those given less than five years in a young offender institution with the position of those given more than that, that is, they are all disqualified for 10 years, but not for life. Also, (b) above is based on the assumption that, when the schedule as amended disqualifies for 10 years persons who have served any part of a sentence 'of detention', it is referring to offenders sentenced to any of: (a) a detention centre order made under the CJA 1982, s. 4 (now repealed); (b) a sentence of detention in a young offender institution passed under s. 1A of the 1982 Act; or (c) detention in accordance with the Home Secretary's directions passed under the CYPA 1933, s. 53(2). Again, with respect, the amended paragraph is not as clearly expressed as it might have been.

Juries Act 1974, s. 1

Subject to the provisions of this Act, every person shall be qualified to serve as a juror in the Crown Court, the High Court and county courts and be liable accordingly to attend for jury service when summoned under this Act, if—

(a)   he is for the time being registered as a parliamentary or local government elector and is not less than 18 or more than 70 years of age; and

(b)   he has been ordinarily resident in the United Kingdom . . . for any period of at least five years since attaining the age of 13, but not if he is for the time being ineligible or disqualified for jury service; and the persons who are ineligible, and those who are disqualified, are those respectively listed in parts I and II of schedule 1 to this Act.

Excusal as of Right

Certain narrowly defined groups are entitled to be excused from jury service even though **D11.2** they are eligible to serve and have been duly summoned to attend for service under the Juries Act 1974, s. 2. Section 8 of the Juries Act 1974 deals with those excusable by virtue of having served in the recent past; s. 9 and part III of sch. 1 list those groups excusable by virtue of age or profession. If a member of an excusable group is summoned, the onus is on him to apply for excusal and satisfy an appropriate officer of the Crown Court that he does indeed belong to the group in question. Should he not ask to be excused, he (like anybody else who has been summoned) commits an offence by not attending for service. In summary, the groups excusable as of right are as follows:

(a)   those who have served on a jury (or attended for service without actually being on a jury) within the two years ending with the service of the summons (s. 8(1)(a));

(b)   those who have been excused from jury service by the Crown Court (or any other court) for a period which has not yet terminated (s. 8(1)(b));

(c)   members and officers of either House of Parliament or of the European Parliament;

(d)   members of the medical and other similar professions, including doctors, dentists, nurses, chemists and vets;

(e)   full-time serving members of the armed forces; and

(f)   those aged 65 or over; and

(g)   those who are practising members of a religious society or order, the tenets or beliefs of which are incompatible with jury service.

Groups (c) to (g) above are all excused by s. 9(1) and (2) and part III of sch. 1.

Although ss. 8 and 9 of the Juries Act 1974 plainly contemplate that applications for excusal should be made initially to an officer of the Crown Court, there is also provision for the court itself to excuse the juror without the application first going through an officer (see ss. 8(1) and 9(4)). In addition, s. 9(3) provides that Crown Court rules shall enable a juror refused excusal by an officer to appeal to the court against the refusal. The relevant rule is r. 25 of the Crown Court Rules 1982, which requires the juror to give written notice of appeal to the appropriate officer, specifying the matters on which he relies as grounds for excusal. The juror must also be given an opportunity to make representations to the court. The appeal would normally be determined in chambers (see r. 27(2)(d)).

Juries Act 1974, ss. 8 and 9 and sch. 1, part III

8.—(1)   If a person summoned under this Act shows to the satisfaction of the appropriate officer, or of the court (or any of the courts) to which he is summoned —
    (a)   that he has served on a jury, or duly attended to serve on a jury, in the prescribed period ending with the service of the summons on him, or
    (b)   that the Crown Court or any other court has excused him from jury service for a period which has not terminated, the officer or court shall excuse him from attending, or further attending, in pursuance of the summons.
    (2)   In subsection (1) above 'the prescribed period' means two years or such longer period as the Lord Chancellor may prescribe . . . .

9.—(1)   A person summoned under this Act shall be entitled, if he so wishes, to be excused from jury service if he is among the persons listed in part III of schedule 1 to this Act but, except as provided by that part of that schedule in the case of members of the forces, a person shall not by this section be exempt from his obligation to attend if summoned unless he is excused from attending under subsection (2) below.
    (2)   If any person summoned under this Act shows to the satisfaction of the appropriate officer that there is good reason why he should be excused from attending in pursuance of the summons, the appropriate officer may excuse him from so attending and shall do so if the reason shown is that the person is entitled under subsection (1) above to excusal.
    (3)   Crown Court rules shall provide a right of appeal to the court (or one of the courts) before which the person is summoned to attend against any refusal of the appropriate officer to excuse him under subsection (2) above.
    (4)   Without prejudice to the preceding provisions of this section, the court (or any of the courts) before which a person is summoned to attend under this Act may excuse that person from so attending.

SCHEDULE 1 INELIGIBILITY AND DISQUALIFICATION FOR AND EXCUSAL FROM JURY SERVICE
PART III PERSONS EXCUSABLE AS OF RIGHT

General
Persons more than 65 years of age.

Parliament
Peers and peeresses entitled to receive writs of summons to attend the House of Lords.
Members of the House of Commons.
Officers of the House of Lords.
Officers of the House of Commons.

European Assembly
Representatives to the Assembly of the European Communities.

The Forces

Full-time serving members of—

> any of Her Majesty's naval, military or air forces,
> the Women's Royal Naval Service,
> Queen Alexandra's Royal Naval Nursing Service.

(A person excusable under this head shall be under no obligation to attend in pursuance of a summons for jury service if his commanding officer certifies to the officer issuing the summons that it would be prejudicial to the efficiency of the service if the person were required to be absent from duty.)

Medical and other similar professions

The following, if actually practising their profession and registered . . . under the enactments relating to that profession — medical practitioners, dentists, nurses, midwives, veterinary surgeons and veterinary practitioners, pharmaceutical chemists.

Members of certain religious bodies

A practising member of a religious society or order the tenets or beliefs of which are incompatible with jury service.

Discretionary Excusal

Section 9(2) of the Juries Act 1974 does not restrict the power to order excusal to cases **D11.3** where the juror has a right of excusal by virtue of falling within one of the groups set out in part III of sch. 1, but also permits discretionary excusal wherever he can show to the satisfaction of the appropriate officer that 'there is good reason why he should be excused from attending'. There is again a right of appeal against the appropriate officer's refusal to excuse. *Practice Direction (Jury Service: Excusal)* [1988] 1 WLR 1162 gives guidance on how applications for discretionary excusal should be approached. It reads:

> Jury service is an important public duty which individual members of the public are chosen at random to undertake. The normal presumption is that, unless a person is excusable as of right from jury service under part III of schedule 1 to the Juries Act 1974, he or she will be required to serve when summoned to do so. There will however be circumstances where a juror should be excused, for instance where he or she is personally concerned in the facts of the particular case or is closely connected with a party or prospective witness.

> He or she may also be excused on grounds of personal hardship or conscientious objection to jury service. Each such application should be dealt with sensitively and sympathetically.

> Any person who appeals to the court against a refusal by the appropriate officer to excuse him or her from jury service must be given an opportunity to make representations in support of his or her appeal.

The second paragraph of the direction appears to represent a slight relaxation of the strict approach to applications for excusal recommended by a direction of 1973 (*Practice Direction (Jurors)* [1973] 1 WLR 134), revoked by the 1988 direction. The 1973 direction had said that it was 'contrary to established practice for jurors to be excused on more general grounds such as race, religion or political beliefs or occupation'. Nothing equivalent to that sentence appears in the present direction, which merely requires each application on grounds of hardship or conscientious objection to be dealt with 'sensitively and sympathetically'.

Both the proper procedures for determining applications for discretionary excusal and the extent to which a religious objection to serving on a jury may be a sufficient ground for excusal were considered by Watkins LJ in the course of his judgment in *Guildford Crown Court, ex parte Siderfin* [1990] 2 QB 683. S was a member of the Plymouth Brethren (a Christian denomination). In common with at least some members of the denomination she took the view that serving on a jury would be contrary to her religious beliefs and would create a serious crisis of conscience for her. It was accepted that her beliefs were genuinely and sincerely held, but nonetheless both the appropriate officer of the Crown Court and Judge Lewisohn on appeal from the appropriate officer refused her application for excusal. S applied to the Divisional Court for judicial review. On the broad question of whether and, if so, in what circumstances conscientious and/or religious objection to serving on a jury should entitle a juror to be excused, Watkins LJ stated that the practice direction of 1988 must be read subject to s. 9(2) of the Juries Act 1974. In other words, the ultimate question for the court is whether the applicant has established a good reason for excusal. A conscientious objection arising out of religious belief is unlikely *on its own* to amount to a good reason, since it will not outweigh the necessity to insist on the observance of the public duty or obligation to perform jury service. 'Adherence to some kind of religious belief cannot be regarded as an unchallengeable right to excusal from jury service' (p. 159F). But, where the applicant's belief would stand in the way of her fulfilling her duty as a juror 'properly, responsibly and honestly', then she should be excused. An affidavit from S indicated that, if forced to serve, she would have reached her verdict without reference to the other members of the jury and would even have insisted on announcing her decision separately. Such an attitude would be incompatible with the notion of the jury pooling their ideas and experience in order to reach an agreement. Partly because Judge Lewisohn appeared not to have appreciated the significance of S's difficulties in cooperating with colleagues on the jury, his refusal to excuse was quashed and the matter remitted to the Crown Court for reconsideration by a different judge.

As to procedure, Watkins LJ held that Judge Lewisohn had further erred in refusing S an adjournment to enable her to be legally represented at the hearing of her appeal. Although there is no right to be represented, the judge hearing the appeal has a discretion to allow it and, in the instant case, there was no reason why an adjournment should not have been allowed for solicitors to be instructed (see p. 158G–H). His lordship also held that any application for excusal from jury service must first be independently considered by an appropriate officer – it is unacceptable for certain types of application to be automatically transferred to a judge.

Deferral of Jury Service

D11.4 The Juries Act 1974, s. 9, empowers the appropriate officer or the court to excuse attendance in pursuance of a summons for jury service but does not give power merely to defer to a later date the days on which the juror should attend at court (*St Albans Crown Court, ex parte Perkins* (1981) *The Times*, 12 December 1981). A power to defer attendance has, however, been introduced by s. 9A, which provides that, if a juror shows to the satisfaction of the appropriate officer that there is good reason why his attendance should be deferred, the officer shall vary the summons accordingly (s. 9A(1)). Obvious reasons for deferral are if the dates in the summons clash with the juror's holiday arrangements or business commitments. Attendance may be deferred only once in respect of one summons (s. 9A(2)). An application for deferral may be made direct to the court (s. 9A(4)), and, in any event, there is a right of appeal against the appropriate officer's refusal to defer (s. 9A(3) and r. 25 of the Crown Court Rules 1982).

Reference to the Judge for Discharge of a Summons

D11.5 Should it appear to the appropriate officer of the court that a person attending for jury service in pursuance of a summons may be unable to act effectively as a juror on account of 'physical disability or insufficient understanding of English', that person may be brought before a judge who 'shall determine whether or not he should act as a juror and, if not, shall discharge the summons' (Juries Act 1974, s. 10). Furthermore, by s. 2(5), an officer may 'at any time put or cause to be put to [a person summoned for jury service] such questions as the officer thinks fit in order to establish whether or not the person is qualified for jury service'. Knowingly or recklessly to give false answers to such questions is a summary offence punishable with a fine of up to £1,000.

The procedure in relation to those who may be unable to act as jurors because of physical disability is governed by the Juries Act 1974, s. 9B. This states that the judge 'shall affirm the summons unless he is of the opinion that the person will not, on account of his disability, be capable of acting effectively as a juror, in which case he shall discharge the summons'.

In *Re Osman* [1996] 1 Cr App R 126, the Recorder of London, Sir Lawrence Verney, held at first instance that a person summonsed to be a juror who was profoundly deaf should be discharged from jury service pursuant to s. 9B. The prospective juror could not follow the proceedings in court or the deliberations in the jury room without the assistance of an interpreter in sign language, and it would be an incurable irregularity in the proceedings for the interpreter to retire with the jury when they considered their verdict.

SUMMONING FOR JURY SERVICE

Responsibility for summoning jurors for service rests with the Lord Chancellor (Juries **D11.6** Act 1974, s. 2(1)). In making arrangements for the discharge of that duty, the Lord Chancellor is to have regard to the convenience of the persons summoned and the desirability of selecting jurors who live within reasonable daily travelling distance of the Crown Court location they are summoned to attend (s. 2(2)). Subject to that, a person may be required to attend for service anywhere in England and Wales (s. 2(3)). The summons may be served by ordinary post (s. 2(4)).

To enable the Lord Chancellor to perform his duties in relation to the summoning of jurors, he must be provided with as many copies of published electoral registers as he requires (s. 3). The copies must indicate those persons on the register who are either under 18 or over 70 (i.e. ineligible for jury service by reason of age). The choice of those to be summoned is made on a random basis from amongst those who are (a) on the register and (b) of an eligible age. It follows that a summons may be sent to a person who is ineligible on a ground other than age or who is disqualified by reason of his convictions. Therefore, s. 2(5) provides that the summons for service shall be accompanied by a notice informing the person summoned of the categories of persons who may not sit on a jury and the possibility of being prosecuted for serving when ineligible or disqualified. The notice must also inform him of his right to apply for excusal from or deferral of jury service.

Unless the person summoned has been excused from jury service under the provisions described he commits an offence if he either fails to attend on a day covered by the summons, or, having attended, is then either not available when called on to serve or is unfit by reason of drink or drugs (Juries Act 1974, s. 20(1)). The offence is punishable either on summary conviction or as if it were a criminal contempt committed in the face of the court, that is, the Crown Court judge may and normally would determine whether an offence has been committed rather than causing a summary prosecution to be brought (s. 20(2)). The offence is punishable with a fine of up to £1,000 (ibid.). If the juror can show reasonable cause for his failure to attend etc., he is not liable to any penalty (s. 20(4)).

As well as summoning jurors, the Lord Chancellor is required to prepare panels (i.e. lists) of those persons who have been summoned (Juries Act 1974, s. 5(1)). The arrangement of and the information contained in the panels is a matter for his discretion (ibid.). At present the only information given is the names and addresses of those summoned and the dates and place of attendance. The former practice of giving their occupation was discontinued in 1973. Despite a suggestion that that practice might be revived on the abolition of peremptory challenges to jurors, nothing has yet been done to that effect. Parties to a case which will or may be tried by jury are entitled to reasonable facilities for inspecting the panel from which their jurors will be drawn (s. 5(2)). The right must be exercised before the close of the trial (s. 5(3)).

In the unlikely event of it appearing to the court that there will be insufficient jurors on the panel to form a complete jury to try an issue, the court may require any persons who are in the vicinity to be summoned without written notice for service (s. 6(1)). This practice is known as *'praying a tales'*. The names of persons so summoned are added to the panel, and the court then proceeds as if they had been on the panel in the first instance (s. 6(2)). It would seem from the wording of the Juries Act 1974, s. 6, that the jury must always include at least one person who was on the original panel, since the section refers to 'making up' a full jury by means of additional panellists. Such an interpretation is consistent with the decision in *Solomon* [1958] 1 QB 203 (jury consisting entirely of 'talesmen' – i.e. jurors not on the original panel – held to be no jury at all).

Juries Act 1974, ss. 2, 5 and 6

2.—(1)   Subject to the provisions of this Act, the Lord Chancellor shall be responsible for the summoning of jurors to attend for service in the Crown Court, the High Court and county courts and for determining the occasions on which they are to attend when so summoned, and the number to be summoned.

(2)   In making arrangements to discharge his duty under subsection (1) above the Lord Chancellor shall have regard to the convenience of the persons summoned and to their respective places of residence, and in particular to the desirability of selecting jurors within reasonable daily travelling distance of the place where they are to attend.

(3)   Subject to subsection (2) above, there shall be no restriction on the places in England and Wales at which a person may be required to attend or serve on a jury under this Act.

[(4)   Summons can be served either by post or by hand.]

(5)   A written summons sent or delivered to any person under subsection (4) above shall be accompanied by a notice informing him—

(a)   of the effect of sections 1 [eligibility for jury service], 9(1) [excusal from jury service], 10 [reference of juror to judge with a view to discharge] and 20(5) [penalties for serving on a jury when disqualified etc.] of this Act; and

(b)   that he may make representations to the appropriate officer with a view to obtaining the withdrawal of the summons, if for any reason he is not qualified for jury service, or wishes or is entitled to be excused;

and where a person is summoned under subsection (4) above . . . the appropriate officer may at any time put or cause to be put to him such questions as the officer thinks fit in order to establish whether or not the person is qualified for jury service.

[(6)   Proof of service by post may be given by certificate.]

5.—(1)   The arrangements to be made by the Lord Chancellor under this Act shall include the preparation of lists (called panels) of persons summoned as jurors, and the information to be included in panels, the court sittings for which they are prepared, their divisions into parts or sets, . . . their enlargement or amendment, and all other matters relating to the contents and form of the panels shall be such as the Lord Chancellor may from time to time direct.

(2)   A party to proceedings in which jurors are or may be called on to try an issue, and any person acting on behalf of a party to such proceedings, shall be entitled to reasonable facilities for inspecting the panel from which the jurors are or will be drawn.

(3)   The right conferred by subsection (2) above shall not be exercisable after the close of the trial by jury (or after the time when it is no longer possible for there to be a trial by jury).

(4)   The court may, if it thinks fit, at any time afford to any person facilities for inspecting the panel, although not given the right by subsection (2) above.

6.—(1)   If it appears to the court that a jury to try any issue before the court will be, or probably will be, incomplete, the court may, if the court thinks fit, require any persons who are in, or in the vicinity of, the court, to be summoned (without any written notice) for jury service up to the number needed (after allowing for any who may not be qualified under section 1 of this Act, and for excusals and challenges) to make up a full jury.

(2)   The names of the persons so summoned shall be added to the panel and the court shall proceed as if those summoned had been included in the panel in the first instance.

SELECTION OF JURY FOR A PARTICULAR CASE

Juries Act 1974, s. 11

D11.7 (1)   The jury to try an issue before a court shall be selected by ballot in open court from the panel, or part of the panel, of jurors summoned to attend at the place and time in question.

The issue most likely to be put before a jury in the Crown Court for them to try is the issue of the accused's guilt or innocence on an indictment to which he has pleaded not guilty. They might alternatively be asked to try the issues of fitness or unfitness to plead, or mute by visitation of God or of malice.

The 'ballot in open court' referred to in s. 11(1) is conventionally conducted by the clerk of the court. Following a plea of not guilty, part of the jury panel (sufficient to provide a full jury of 12 allowing for the possibility that some may be successfully challenged) is brought into the back of the court by an usher. These jurors are usually referred to as the 'jury in waiting'. The clerk is given the juror cards for each of the jurors in waiting (i.e., a card on which is printed the juror's name and address). He selects at random 12 of the cards, and reads out the names on them, inviting the jurors in waiting to step into the jury-box should their names be called (see *Salt* [1996] Crim LR 517 and *Tarrant* [1998] Crim LR 342, on the need for selection to be random so far as practicable). Once 12 jurors are in the box, the clerk informs the accused of his right to challenge jurors. He then reads out the names again, pausing after each name so that the juror may take the juror's oath (or affirm). The form of oath is: 'I swear by almighty God that I will faithfully try the defendant[s] and give [a] true verdict[s] according to the evidence' (see *Practice Direction (Crime: Jury Oath)* [1984] 1 WLR 1217 for the sanctioning of that oath). Each juror must take the oath separately (s. 11(3)) – the practice sometimes adopted before 1974 of all 12 jurors reciting the oath together is now unlawful.

In *Comerford* [1998] 1 WLR 191, the Court of Appeal considered whether the decision of the trial judge that jurors should be identified, not by name, but by number when they came into the box to be sworn, in order to reduce the risk that the jury might be 'nobbled'. Their lordships took the view that such a departure from the normal procedure did not render the trial a nullity, unless it violated the appellant's legal rights, or made the proceedings unfair to him. There was no mandatory requirement that names should be called. It was made clear, however, that the appellant could have exercised his right to ascertain the names of all the jurors forming the panel if he had so desired and it was said that it is 'highly desirable that in normal circumstances the usual procedure for empanelling a jury should be followed'.

CHALLENGING JURORS

Introduction

D11.8 The methods of replacing one or more of the prospective jurors called into the box as a result of the clerk's ballot with others from the jury in waiting are:

(a)   for either the prosecution or defence to challenge for cause;
(b)   for the prosecution to ask a juror to stand by;
(c)   for the judge to exercise his discretionary power to remove a juror.

Prior to 5 January 1989, the defence were entitled to remove three jurors per accused by means of peremptory challenges, that is, challenges for which no cause had to be shown and which automatically succeeded provided they were made in the correct form before the challenged juror began to take the oath. The number of peremptory challenges permitted had been progressively reduced from the 35 allowed at common law to seven (in 1948) and thence to three by the Criminal Law Act 1977. Section 118(1) of the CJA 1988 simply provides that: 'The right to challenge jurors without cause in proceedings for the trial of a person on indictment is abolished'. However, the former existence of the power to remove jurors without providing reasons is indirectly relevant to the present law since it helps explain the paucity of modern practice and authority on challenges for cause, it having been much easier to use peremptory challenges as a means of excluding possibly unfavourable jurors rather than resorting to reasoned challenges.

Challenges for Cause

D11.9 A challenge for cause may be made by either the prosecution or defence. It is either a challenge to the whole panel of jurors or to an individual juror. The former is known as a challenge 'to the array' and the latter as a challenge 'to the polls'.

D11.10 *Challenges to the Array*   At common law either party could challenge the whole panel summoned for their case on the ground that the person responsible for the summoning acted improperly or was biased. This right is preserved by the Juries Act 1974, s. 12(6).

Juries Act 1974, s. 12

> (6)   Without prejudice to subsection (4) above [right to challenge individual jurors], the right of challenge to the array, that is to say the right of challenge on the ground that the person responsible for summoning the jurors in question is biased or has acted improperly, shall continue to be unaffected by the fact that, since the coming into operation of section 31 of the Courts Act 1971 (which is replaced by this Act), the responsibility for summoning jurors for service in the Crown Court . . . has lain with the Lord Chancellor.

Nineteenth-century cases indicate that the array was open to challenge when the sheriff had any apparent interest in the outcome of the trial, arising, for example, from his actually being the prosecutor or victim of the offence; or from his being related to a party; or from his being the counsel, solicitor or servant of a party; or from his having a pecuniary interest in the result. In *Dolby* (1823) 2 B & C 104 the array was successfully challenged because the sheriff was a subscriber to the society which was the prosecutor. Specific malfeasance in the summoning was also a ground of challenge, as when jurors were summoned at the express request of prosecution or defence, or had been selected on grounds of their religion (see *O'Doherty* (1848) 6 St Tr NS 831, part of the headnote to which reads: 'it is good ground of challenge to the array that the sheriff has selected the jurors on account of their religion, and rejected other persons because they belonged to a different religion').

In the absence of evidence of bias or improper conduct by the person responsible for summoning, the jury panel's being imbalanced racially or not reflecting the overall racial composition of the catchment area from which jurors are summoned is *not* sufficient ground for challenge (*Danvers* [1982] Crim LR 680 – West Indian accused at Nottingham Crown Court objected to the jury panel because it was entirely white and he was anxious that there should be a substantial representation of black people on the jury; challenge failed, even though the black population in Nottingham apparently represented about 10 per cent of the total). Similarly, in *Broderick* [1970] Crim LR 155, where the accused desired an all-black jury, the Court of Appeal held that the judge, in asking for enquiries to be made as to whether there was one black person on the panel, had 'gone quite as far as law and consideration required'. *Danvers* and *Broderick* have been approved by the Court of Appeal in *Ford* [1989] QB 868 (see **D11.15**). The principle of these decisions will apply equally to other apparent imbalances in the jury panel (e.g., as to the proportion of men to women).

The lack of modern authority on challenges to the array indicates that, from about the middle of the 19th century onwards, bias or impropriety on the part of the summoning officer ceased to be a live problem. The vesting of responsibility for the summoning of jurors in the Lord Chancellor (i.e. in Crown Court officers) has made even more remote the possibility of challenges to the array being resorted to in practice.

Challenges to the Polls   D11.11

Juries Act 1974, s. 12

> (4)   The fact that a person summoned to serve on a jury is not qualified to serve shall be a ground of challenge for cause; but subject to that, and to the foregoing provisions of this section, nothing in this Act affects the law relating to challenge of jurors.

Thus, jurors who are too old or too young to be on a jury, or who have not been resident in the UK for a five-year period since attaining the age of 13, or who are not on the electoral roll, or who come within one of the ineligible groups (judges, lawyers, clerics etc.), or who are disqualified by convictions may all be successfully challenged for cause. The qualifications for jury service are set out in the Juries Act 1974, s. 1 and parts I and II of sch. 1 (see **D11.1**). In the absence of any challenge from the parties, a juror may in effect challenge himself by stating, if it be the case, that he is not qualified (*Cook* (1696) 13 St Tr 311). The summons sent to each juror is accompanied by a notice which sets out the ineligible and disqualified groups and warns him of his duty to inform the court if he comes within any of them.

At common law a qualified juror could be challenged *propter affectum*, i.e. on the ground of some presumed or actual bias which would make him unsuitable to try the case. This ground of challenge is preserved by the last clause of s. 12(4) of the Juries Act 1974. Most authorities on challenges to the polls *propter affectum* are old, and reflect the very different social and legal conditions of their time. The broad thrust of the decisions is that a juror is challengeable if he has expressed hostility to one side or the other (*O'Coigley* (1798) 26 St Tr 1191), has expressed a wish as to the outcome of the case, is related to a party, or has some other connection with a party (e.g., was his servant or agent).

One modern decision of substantial relevance is *Kray* (1969) 53 Cr App R 412. In that case, the defence wished to object to any jurors who had read newspaper articles published immediately after two of the accused before the court had been convicted at an earlier trial for murder. One of the charges on the present indictment was murder. The articles complained of had not only reported the earlier verdict and commented on the evidence, but had also 'set out a number of facts which were not in evidence at the trial and which were discreditable of those to whom they referred'. Lawton J, giving a preliminary ruling on the validity of the proposed challenges, criticised the newspapers for publishing the additional facts about the accused not disclosed in evidence at the first trial and then said (at p. 415 emphasis added):

> This does, in my judgment, lead to a prima facie presumption that anybody who may have read that kind of information might find it difficult to reach a verdict in a fair-minded way. It is, however, a matter of human experience . . . first, that the public's recollection is short, and, secondly, that the drama . . . of a trial almost always has the effect of excluding from recollection that which went before. A person summoned for this case would not . . . disqualify himself merely because he had read any of the newspapers containing allegations of the kind I have referred to; but the position would be different if, as a result of reading

what he had, *his mind had become so clogged with prejudice that he was unable to try the case impartially.*

Insofar as a general principle may be extracted from the above passage, it seems to be that a juror may be challenged for cause if his mind is so prejudiced that he is unable to try the case impartially, but merely having once been informed of matters discreditable to the accused will not necessarily occasion such prejudice.

D11.12 ***Procedure for Challenging for Cause*** The Juries Act 1974, s. 12(1)(b), provides that 'any challenge for cause shall be tried by the judge before whom [the accused] is to be tried'. The challenge must be entered after the juror's name has been drawn by ballot and before he is sworn (s. 12(3)). Should the challenge not be made until after the juror has begun to take the oath the judge has a discretion to allow it but is not obliged to do so (*Harrington* (1976) 64 Cr App R 1, but note that the late challenge in that case was a peremptory one rather than a challenge for cause). Conventionally, a challenge is indicated simply by counsel for the challenging party saying the word 'Challenge' as the juror is about to take the oath. The burden of proof is on the challenging party, and the judge may order that the hearing be in camera or in chambers (CJA 1988, s. 118(2)).

If the challenge is of any substance, it will be proper for it to be heard in the absence of the jurors. The challenged juror should be kept outside the court except in so far as it is necessary to question him. The remaining jurors should leave the court, retiring to the jury room in the charge of the jury bailiff if they have already been sworn. A shorthand note of proceedings should in any event be taken, and the court's decision should be entered on the court record. The judge can hear evidence and question the juror concerned. Counsel may be allowed to ask questions directed to the ground on which the juror is challenged. After hearing the evidence and any submissions, the judge will decide whether to allow the challenge. If he does so, the juror is discharged and a fresh juror called to replace him. If the challenge is rejected, the judge should tell the juror not to disclose any of the matters dealt with during the challenge to other jurors, and not to allow the fact that the challenge was made to influence him.

It is clear from *Morris* (1991) 93 Cr App R 102 that the right to challenge for cause is limited to the time when the jury is sworn, and cannot be exercised during the course of the trial. M was accused of stealing from a Marks and Spencer store. After the store detective had given evidence, one of the jurors said that she was a personnel assistant with a different branch of the company. The judge refused to discharge the juror saying that the right way to deal with the matter was by a challenge for cause. The trial proceeded and M was convicted. The Court of Appeal allowed his appeal. By the time the facts about the juror had emerged, it was too late for the defence to challenge for cause – that could only be done when the jury were sworn.

The main difficulty in challenging for cause is that, having indicated a challenge, the challenging party must provide prima facie evidence of his grounds. *After* he has done so, the juror may be asked questions on the *voir dire* to determine whether the challenge is well founded. It is, however, the almost invariable practice to refuse any request to parade the jury panel before the challenging party so that he may ask preliminary questions with a view to establishing a prima facie ground of challenge (a practice which is regarded as an important right of the parties in the USA). The initial requirement of prima facie evidence from the challenger was stated in, for example, *Dowling* (1848) 7 St Tr NS 382, and was confirmed by Lord Parker CJ in *Chandler (No. 2)* [1964] 2 QB 322, in which his lordship said (at p. 338):

> . . . before any right to cross-examine the juror arose, the defendant would have had to lay a foundation of fact in support of his ground of challenge. It is no good his saying, "I think this man is antagonistic". . . . There must be a foundation of fact creating a prima facie case before the juror can be cross-examined.

Similarly, in *Broderick* [1970] Crim LR 155, where the accused desired an all-black jury and defence counsel unsuccessfully sought to cross-examine each member of the panel to determine whether he or she might be biased against B on racial grounds, the Court of Appeal held that it had never been the practice to allow potential jurors to be paraded for cross-examination in a fishing way to ascertain whether there might possibly be some grounds on which a challenge might subsequently be made. Very occasionally, however, there is a departure from the normal practice. Thus, in *Kray* (1969) 53 Cr App R 412 (see **D11.11**) defence counsel was permitted to examine each juror who came into the box to be sworn on whether he had read certain newspaper articles discreditable to the accused. The only initial evidence of bias adduced was that of a clerk from the accused's solicitors who produced the offending articles. Although Lawton J stated that that evidence was in itself sufficient to raise a prima facie ground of challenge, it is, with respect, difficult to see how that can be right since the defence were unable to show of any individual juror that he had read the articles, let alone that he might have been prejudiced by them. It is submitted that the case of *Kray* was simply one in which, because of a wholly exceptional combination of circumstances, the court departed from the usual practice of preventing the preliminary questioning of jurors.

Standing Jurors By

This is a right possessed by the prosecution but not the defence (see *Chandler (No. 2)* **D11.13** [1964] 2 QB 322 at p. 337, where Lord Parker CJ held that the accused, having exhausted the seven peremptory challenges to which he was then entitled, might challenge subsequent jurors for cause but could not require them to stand by, although 'in an exceptional case the judge [could] in his discretion stand by a juror or allow the defendant to do so'). Standing a juror by differs from challenging him for cause in that counsel need not give a reason for the stand-by; it differs from the peremptory challenges formerly available to the defence in that the juror is not conclusively removed from the jury but will be recalled to the jury-box should the entire jury panel be exhausted without a full jury being obtained, at which stage the prosecution must either accept him or show cause why he should not serve. In the leading case of *Mason* [1981] QB 881, Lawton LJ, giving the Court of Appeal's judgment, summarised the position thus (at pp. 890H–891A):

> In our judgment, *Mansell* v *The Queen* (1857) 8 E & B 54 established beyond argument that prosecuting counsel have a right to request that a member of the jury panel shall stand by, and that this right can be exercised without there being a provable valid objection, until such time as the panel is exhausted; and when it is, if the Crown still wants to exclude a member of the jury from the panel, a valid objection must be shown.

In practice, the size of the panels summoned to Crown Court locations and the number of 'spare' jurors who can be called on to complete a jury if some of those initially selected by ballot are stood by means that the right of stand-by is virtually equivalent to a prosecution right of peremptory challenge. Moreover, as a matter of law, prosecuting counsel may stand a juror by for any or no reason. Certainly, he does not need a reason which would stand up as ground for a challenge for cause (see the passage from *Mason* quoted above), although Lawton LJ added the rider that he expected that prosecuting counsel would act responsibly and would not request a stand-by unnecessarily (p. 891c).

Since *Mason* was decided the defence right of peremptory challenge, which was perceived as a counterbalance to the prosecution right of stand-by, has been abolished. The A-G's guidelines on the exercise by the Crown of its right of stand-by (see **appendix 3**) affirm the general principles that: (a) members of a jury should be selected at random from the panel subject to any rule of law as to right of challenge by the defence; and (b) the Juries Act 1974 as amended identifies those classes of persons who *alone* are disqualified from or ineligible for service on a jury, and no other class of person may be so treated (para. 2). Primary responsibility for ensuring that an individual does not serve on a jury if he is not competent to discharge his duties properly rests, first, with the appropriate court officer and, ultimately, with the trial judge. In the context of that legislative background, para. 5 of the guidelines defines the two situations in which it is appropriate for prosecuting counsel to use his right of stand-by as follows:

> The circumstances in which it would be proper for the Crown to exercise its right to stand by a member of a jury panel are:
>
> (a)   where a jury check authorised in accordance with the Attorney-General's guidelines on jury checks [see **D11.16** and **appendix 3**] reveals information justifying exercise of the right to stand by in accordance with para. 9 of the guidelines and the Attorney-General personally authorises the exercise of the right to stand by; or
> (b)   where a person is about to be sworn as a juror who is manifestly unsuitable and the defence agree that, accordingly, the exercise by the prosecution of the right to stand by would be appropriate. An example of the sort of *exceptional* circumstances which might justify stand-by is where it becomes apparent that . . . a juror selected for service to try a complex case is in fact illiterate.

On the assumption that the guidelines are loyally followed, the importance of the right of stand-by has been vastly reduced. Counsel will exercise the right only in (a) the tiny minority of cases which involve national security or terrorism (para. 5(a)), or (b) 'ordinary' cases where a juror is obviously unsuitable *and the defence agree* (para. 5(b)). Thus, the chief function of the right now seems to be to avoid the clumsy mechanics of a challenge for cause where the parties concur that a juror should not serve. In addition to the example given in para. 5(b) itself, it is submitted that, subject to defence consent, jurors could properly be stood by if, for example, counsel has been informed that they are in fact disqualified by previous convictions, or if they know the accused or any witnesses in the case. The manner in which the right was exercised in *Mason* [1981] QB 881 – namely, to stand by jurors who, although not disqualified, had previous convictions for dishonesty – is impermissible in the light of the guidelines. However, the guidelines are presumably not meant to inhibit prosecuting counsel from challenging for cause on grounds of bias if he considers that a juror's previous convictions or other involvement with the police might make him so prejudiced against the Crown as to be unable to try the case fairly. Whether such a challenge would succeed is open to question.

Judge's Power to Exclude Juror

D11.14   Even in the absence of a formal challenge from either party, the trial judge has a residual discretion to exclude from the jury a juror selected by the initial ballot. Existence of the discretion can be traced back to Lord Campbell CJ's judgment in *Mansell* v *The Queen* (1857) 8 E & B 54, and has since been confirmed by Lord Parker CJ (see *Chandler (No. 2)* [1964] 2 QB 322 at p. 327), by Lawton LJ (see *Mason* [1981] QB 881 at p. 887G–H) and, most recently, by Lord Lane CJ in *Ford* [1989] QB 868. The discretion may and should be exercised where an individual juror is obviously incompetent to act but, for whatever reason, counsel do not challenge or exercise the right of stand-by. It is then the judge's duty to prevent the 'scandal and perversion of justice which would arise from compelling or permitting such a juryman to be sworn' (per Lord Campbell CJ in *Mansell*, who then gave as specific examples for the judge's intervention cases where the juror was mentally or physically infirm, or insane or drunk, or preoccupied with the dangerous illness of a relative). Lawton LJ in *Mason* [1981] QB 881 succinctly described modern practice by saying (at p. 887G–H):

> . . . trial judges, as an aspect of their duty to see that there is a fair trial, have had a right to intervene to ensure that a competent jury is empanelled. The most common form of judicial intervention is when a judge notices that a member of the panel is infirm or has difficulty in

reading or hearing; and nowadays jurors for whom taking part in a long trial would be unusually burdensome are often excluded from the jury by the judge.

However, judicial intervention should not be extended beyond the kinds of situation mentioned above. The judge must not intervene in a systematic way so as to undermine the random nature of jury selection or influence the overall composition of the jury (per Lord Lane CJ in *Ford*). In particular, he has no power to discharge jurors on account of their race or ethnic group in hopes that eventually a racially balanced jury will be obtained. Lord Lane said (at p. 872A) that the discretion to exclude a juror 'is to be exercised to prevent individual jurors who are not competent from serving. It has never been held to include a discretion to discharge a competent juror or jurors in an attempt to secure a jury drawn from particular sections of the community, or otherwise to influence the overall composition of the jury.' By parity of reasoning, a judge ought not to exclude jurors merely on account of their political opinions, sex or social background (see also the discussion of racially balanced juries at **D11.15**).

Racial Balance of Jury From time to time defence counsel have sought judicial **D11.15** intervention to ensure that at least some members of the jury are black or come from the same ethnic group as the accused. Examples are *Binns* [1982] Crim LR 522 (trial of West Indian accused of public order offences committed during racial riot in Bristol); *Bansal* [1985] Crim LR 151 (trial of Asians for offences of violence committed when protesting against a National Front march); *McCalla* [1986] Crim LR 335 (black accused alleging that his admissions to robbery were extracted from him by racially prejudiced white police officers); and *Broderick* [1970] Crim LR 155 (black accused simply wished to be tried by an all-black jury). The precise form of judicial aid sought has varied from case to case. In *Binns*, counsel asked the judge to exercise his right to stand jurors by until a jury representing 'the corporate good sense of the community' had been obtained; in *Bansal* the application was to move the venue of trial to a racially mixed area, while in *Broderick* the defence wished to have the jury panel paraded and asked 'fishing' questions about their possible racial prejudice. Judicial response to the applications has been equally varied. The judges in *Binns* and *Bansal* were basically sympathetic to the defence request (although in doubt about how far they could go in ordering a certain racial mix on the jury or jury panel). By contrast, Judge Mander in *McCalla* ruled that he had no power to order that a jury be racially balanced and, even if he had such power, he would not have chosen to exercise it because a jury should be selected at random subject only to the law on disqualified jurors and challenges for cause. Moreover, to allow interference with jury selection on racial grounds would open the way to further manipulation, for example, on grounds of political view, sex, or religion, or for some similar reason.

It is the latter view which has found favour with the Court of Appeal. In *Ford* [1989] QB 868, F appealed against his convictions for reckless driving and taking a motor vehicle without authority on the ground that the trial judge had refused an application for a racially balanced jury. The main points established by Lord Lane CJ's judgment are as follows:

(a) A challenge to the array of jurors summoned must be on the ground of bias or other irregularity on the part of the summoning officer. Therefore, the fact that the jury panel contains few if any jurors of the same racial group as the accused cannot of itself found a challenge or justify the judge in discharging the panel and ordering the summoning of a new one (see *Danvers* [1982] Crim LR 680 and **D11.10**). It follows that if, for example, an accused of West Indian parentage is tried at a Crown Court located in a predominantly white area the jury panel (being drawn from the locality of the court) is unlikely to include many members of the accused's race, and there is nothing the defence can do about it.

(b)   Summoning of jurors is the responsibility of the Lord Chancellor. It is not the judge's function to alter the composition of the jury panel or give directions about the area from which it should be drawn. Woolf J's direction in *Bansal* [1985] Crim LR 151 – namely that the panel should be drawn from a part of the court's catchment area in which a high proportion of Asians lived – was made without benefit of full argument and was wrong.

(c)   Nor should the judge consider a complaint that the jury panel is not truly random because it contains a lower proportion of persons of a certain race or ethnic group than live in the court's catchment area for jurors, unless, of course, the disproportion can be attributed to bias or impropriety on the part of the summoning officer. If the disproportion may be due to maladministration in the procedures for summoning jurors, that must be corrected by *administrative*, not judicial intervention.

(d)   The mere fact that a juror is of a particular race or holds a particular religious belief cannot found a challenge for cause by a party on the ground of bias.

(e)   The judge may not use his power to stand by or discharge individual jurors selected in the ballot from the jury panel for the purpose of securing a jury of a certain racial mix. To do so would conflict with the principle of random jury selection. In effect, the judge would be altering the composition of the jury panel by his own fiat when no irregularity on the part of the summoning officer had been shown and upholding a challenge when there was no ground in law for it. The judge's intervention should be restricted to the exceptional circumstances indicated in *Mansell* v *The Queen* (1857) 8 E&B 54 (see **D11.14**). Insofar as the judge in *Binns* [1982] Crim LR 522 had been prepared to stand jurors by until a balanced jury had been obtained, he was in error.

(f)   In short, there is not (as had been suggested in *Frazer* [1987] Crim LR 418 and *Bansal*) any principle that a jury should be racially balanced, and it is impermissible for the judge to use his residual discretionary powers over the composition of the jury as a device for obtaining such a balance.

INVESTIGATION OF THE JURY PANEL

D11.16   Effective challenging of jurors depends on the amount of information about the jury panel available to the parties. Section 5(2) and (3) of the Juries Act 1974 entitles the parties to inspect the jury panel before or during trial but such inspection will inform them only of the names and addresses of the panel members. It will not of itself yield material capable of founding a challenge for cause. However, there would seem to be no objection in theory to a party identifying the panellists summoned to the location of the Crown Court for the time when his case is listed to be heard and then making such inquiries as he sees fit into their employment, background, attitudes etc., on the off-chance that grounds for a challenge for cause may emerge. He must, of course, take care not to infringe the general law on privacy or interfere with the jurors in a way which might amount to contempt of court or interference with the course of justice.

In practice, the defence do not have the resources to conduct the kind of inquiries mentioned above. The one inquiry that the prosecution are likely to make is into the criminal records of the panellists, a practice which was approved by the Court of Appeal in *Mason* [1981] QB 881. In that case, the police checked whether the panellists summoned to Northampton Crown Court for the time of the appellant's trial had convictions. They passed on the results of their inquiries to prosecuting counsel who in consequence stood by certain jurors without informing defence counsel of the reason. Some but not all the jurors stood by were disqualified by their convictions. Lawton LJ, giving the judgment of the Court of Appeal, justified the police action as being part of their usual function of preventing crime, it being an offence to serve on a jury when disqualified by convictions (see p. 891D–F). Further, their lordships could see no reason why the information obtained should not be communicated to prosecuting counsel who could then make such use of it as he considered fit. 'The practice of supplying prosecuting counsel with information about potential jurors' convictions has been followed during the whole of our professional lives . . . . It is not unlawful, and has not until recently been thought to be unsatisfactory' (p. 891G). Prosecuting counsel is under no duty to transmit the information to the defence, although he may do so if he so wishes (p. 891B–D). On the narrow point of whether counsel ought to stand a juror by if he has convictions but they are not such as to disqualify him, the decision in *Mason* (that there is no objection to that being done) has been effectively reversed by the A-G's guidelines on the matter (see below). On the broader question of 'vetting' jurors by running a preliminary check on their criminal records, the case remains good authority to justify the practice.

Following the decision in *Mason*, the Association of Chief Police Officers issued recommendations on when the police 'should undertake a check of the names of potential jurors against records of previous convictions'. The recommendations are annexed to the A-G's guidelines on jury checks (see **appendix 3**). They identify three circumstances in which a check may be carried out.

   (a)   when 'there is reason to believe that attempts are being made to circumvent the statutory provisions excluding disqualified persons from service on a jury, including any case when there is reason to believe that a particular juror may be disqualified';
   (b)   when it is 'believed that in a previous related abortive trial an attempt was made to interfere with a juror or jurors'; and
   (c)   when, 'in the opinion of the DPP or the chief constable it is particularly important to ensure that no disqualified person serves on the jury'.

Save when authorised by the A-G's guidelines (see below), no further checks on jurors should be carried out. Nor will the police check jurors on behalf of the defence unless requested to do so by the DPP. Should a jury check reveal that a juror, although not disqualified by his criminal record, may be unsuitable to sit as a member of the jury in a particular case, that information will be communicated to prosecuting counsel who will decide what use to make of it (recommendations (2) to (4)).

In addition to the recommendations of the chief constables, jury vetting by the police or prosecution is controlled by guidelines issued by the A-G (see **appendix 3**). In brief, they affirm that the provisions of the Juries Act 1974 on disqualified and ineligible jurors, combined with majority verdicts (which prevent one perverse juror stopping his colleagues from reaching a verdict) will, in all normal cases, be sufficient to ensure the proper administration of justice without recourse to any investigation of the jury panel going beyond that sanctioned by the Association of Chief Police Officers' recommendations on checking criminal records. In two classes of case, however, the public interest may demand additional checks (para. 3). Those classes are (a) cases in which national security is involved and part of the evidence is likely to be heard in camera, and (b) terrorist cases (para. 4). In both types of case there is a risk that a juror's political views might be so extreme as to interfere with his fair assessment of the case or lead him to exert improper pressure on his fellow jurors, while in security cases there is the additional risk of the juror either voluntarily or under pressure making improper use of evidence given in camera (para. 5). To ascertain whether a juror might be unsuitable for the above reasons, it may be necessary to investigate the panel by checking the records of Police Special Branches. In security (but not in terrorist) cases the investigation may additionally involve the security services (para. 6). Such checks may be made *only* on the personal authority of the A-G, and are therefore known as 'authorised checks' (para. 7). If a chief officer of police considers that an authorised check is likely to be desirable, he should refer the matter to the DPP, who will make the appropriate application to the A-G (ibid.). The result of any authorised check will be sent to the DPP, who in turn will decide how much of the information should be passed on to prosecuting counsel (para. 8). In any event, no right of stand-by should be exercised by counsel on the basis of information derived from an authorised check unless he has the personal authority of the A-G and unless the information affords 'strong reason for believing that a particular juror might be a security risk, be susceptible to improper approaches or be influenced in arriving at a verdict for the reasons given [in the guidelines]' (para. 9). Where a juror is stood by, prosecuting counsel may, in his discretion, disclose to the defence the information on which the stand-by was based, but he is under no duty to do so (para. 10). If an authorised check suggests that a juror might be biased against the accused, the defence should be informed of that in general terms although it may not be possible to give them precise details of the information revealed by the check (para. 11). It will be apparent that authorised checks are a possibility in only a tiny proportion of trials. In the general run of criminal cases, there will either be no check at all on the jury panel or there will be a check only of their criminal records.

COMPOSITION OF THE JURY AS A GROUND OF APPEAL

D11.17 The Juries Act 1974, s. 18, governs the extent to which the defence may use as a ground of appeal against conviction errors in the way the jury panel was summoned or the particular jury for their case was selected or empanelled. The overall effect is to prevent the verdict being challenged unless the irregularity complained of was objected to at trial and not corrected. Section 18 also prevents lack of qualification or unfitness on the part of an individual juror being a ground of appeal.

Juries Act 1974, s. 18

(1)   No judgment after verdict in any trial by jury in any court shall be stayed or reversed by reason—
   (a)   that the provisions of this Act about the summoning or empanelling of jurors, or the selection of jurors by ballot, have not been complied with, or
   (b)   that a juror was not qualified in accordance with section 1 of this Act, or
   (c)   that any juror was misnamed or misdescribed, or
   (d)   that any juror was unfit to serve.
(2)   Subsection (1)(a) above shall not apply to any irregularity if objection is taken at, or as soon as practicable after, the time it occurs, and the irregularity is not corrected.
(3)   Nothing in subsection (1) above shall apply to any objection to a verdict on the ground of personation.

The section is largely self-explanatory. It should be noted that the saving in subsection (2) applies only to appeals based on contraventions of the Act's provisions as to the summoning or empanelling of jurors or their selection by ballot. If objection to such an irregularity was taken when or as soon as practicable after it occurred and the court did not correct it, it may be relied on as a material irregularity in the course of the trial justifying the quashing of a conviction by virtue of s. 2(1) of the Criminal Appeal Act 1968. However, it is submitted that s. 18(2) will not assist in a case where the defence did not know of the irregularity in summoning etc. until after conviction, since it will not have been possible to object until a stage at which the Crown Court was *functus officio*.

Save in the special case of impersonation of a juror, a juror's having been disqualified from or ineligible for jury service (s. 18(1)(b)) or more generally unfit to serve (s. 18(1)(d)) cannot be a ground of appeal. The statutory provision follows the common law (see *Kelly* [1950] 2 KB 164, in which it was held that the only instances of convictions being quashed on account of a defect in a juror, that defect not having been raised at trial by means of a challenge for cause, were cases in which the juror actually summoned had been impersonated by another – e.g., *Tremearne* (1826) 5 B & C 254). In *Tremearne*, on one J. Williams being called into the jury-box, his son, who was not on the panel and was under age, answered for his father and served. The fact that the defence did not discover the defect in the juror until after conviction (and therefore could not have challenged for cause) is irrelevant to the application of s. 18 (see *Chapman* (1976) 63 Cr App 75 and especially *Pennington* (1985) 81 Cr App R 217). On a literal reading of the section it is even possible to argue that, where a challenge was made at trial and wrongly rejected, the defence still cannot rely on the error on appeal, but it is submitted that in such a case the ground of appeal would not be the lack of qualification or unfitness of the juror *per se* but the judge's error of law in ruling against the challenge. Therefore, the appellant would not be caught by s. 18. See also *Tomar* [1997] Crim LR 682.

The broad and somewhat Draconian effect of s. 18 of the Juries Act 1974 is illustrated by the leading case of *Chapman* (1976) 63 Cr App R 75. After C and L had been convicted, the defence learnt that one of the jurors who tried the case was deaf and had heard only half the evidence. The appeal against conviction failed because the express terms of s. 18(1)(d) prevent any unfitness in a juror being used to reverse a verdict, and to argue that a juror was too deaf to hear the evidence with the consequence that there was a material irregularity in the course of the trial is simply to argue that the juror was unfit. Therefore, the defence could not use as their basis of appeal s. 2(1)(c) of the Criminal Appeal Act 1968 (material irregularity in the course of the trial one of the grounds on which a conviction may normally be quashed). Plainly there had been no wrong decision on a question of law as required by s. 2(1)(b) of the 1968 Act, since the juror (albeit for reasons beyond the defence's control) had never been challenged in the lower court. That left as a possible ground of appeal only the contention that the verdict was unsafe or unsatisfactory (s. 2(1)(a)). On the facts of *Chapman*, their lordships held without difficulty that the verdict was safe. The convictions were unanimous. Therefore, even on the assumption that, had he heard all the evidence, the deaf juror would have been for acquittal, the jury could and no doubt would have convicted by an 11–1 majority. Moreover, if the juror's incapacity had come to light during the course of the trial, the judge could simply have discharged him from the jury (see **D11.19**), allowing his colleagues to complete the trial and convict. But, even though the argument failed on the facts, the Court of Appeal did indicate, *obiter*, that a juror's unfitness or lack of qualification was in principle a factor capable of rendering a conviction unsafe in conjunction with other circumstances.

It is unclear whether, when the Juries Act 1974, s. 18(1)(d), prevents a juror's unfitness to serve being used as the ground for reversing a verdict, the prohibition is intended to apply only to an argument that the juror was unfit to serve on *any* jury or extends to an argument that, although in general a qualified and competent juror, he was unfit to serve on the jury trying the appellant because of bias arising out of his knowledge of or previous dealings with him. Whichever is the correct interpretation of the section matters little, since common law, even before the passing of the 1974 Act, had made it virtually impossible to use subsequently discovered bias in a juror as a ground of appeal. In *Box* [1964] 1 QB 430 the foreman of the jury which convicted the appellants of office-breaking and use of explosives gave evidence before the Court of Appeal that, at the time he served on the jury, he knew the appellants to be ex-burglars and associates of prostitutes. He said he had formed a low opinion of them, and also knew that one of them had recently been released from prison. Neither the court nor the parties were aware of the juror's knowledge of the accused when the jury was empanelled; nor did the juror ask to be excused as he plainly should have done. In addition to the evidence of the foreman himself, the Court of Appeal read affidavits from two members of the public, apparently to the effect that they had spoken to the foreman during an adjournment of the trial after the evidence had been completed, and he had said that he did not need to hear the evidence and would see that they (the appellants) got 10 years. However, the court refused to hear testimony from those two witnesses because it would not have been evidence about the foreman's state of mind at the relevant time (i.e. *before* entering on the hearing). As to whether the foreman's own evidence justified quashing the conviction, Lord Parker CJ adopted a dictum of Bankes J in *Syme* (1914) 10 Cr App R 284 to the effect that, unless the evidence shows the juror to have been determined *before* trial to come to a certain verdict regardless of the evidence, the court would not interfere. In the instant case, the foreman deposed that, when the trial commenced, he had had no views on the appellant's guilt or innocence but he formed very definite views as the case went along. Such evidence fell far short of that required by Bankes J, and the appeal failed. Similarly, the foreman's knowledge of the appellants' bad character was not an automatic disqualification from serving on the jury, nor did it mean that he was unable to listen to the evidence and give the accused a fair trial in accordance with his oath. See also *Pennington* (1985) 81 Cr App R 217 and *Bliss* (1986) 84 Cr App R 1. In practice it will be difficult if not impossible to satisfy the Court of Appeal that a juror was so biased against the accused before the case started that he was determined to convict whatever the evidence might turn out to be.

DISCHARGE OF JURORS OR ENTIRE JURY

Introduction

D11.18 The judge has a discretion to discharge up to three jurors from the jury and allow the trial to continue to verdict with the remainder. He also has a discretion to discharge the entire jury from giving a verdict, in which case the accused is not acquitted but may be retried before a fresh jury. Once a jury has been discharged the general rule is that it is *functus officio* and cannot be reconvened to return a verdict, even if it is realised almost immediately after the order for discharge that the order was made in error (see *Russell* (1984) 148 JP 765). In *Follen* [1994] Crim LR 225, it was stated that there was no fixed rule of law that once the judge had discharged the jury he could not set aside that order, but it would be only in very rare circumstances that this should be done. In *Aylott* [1996] 2 Cr App R 169, the Court of Appeal adopted a more flexible approach, and stated that the underlying principle was to ensure that proceedings were fair and to do justice in the particular case (see **D16.9** for more detail).

Discharge of Individual Jurors

Juries Act 1974, s. 16

D11.19 (1) Where in the course of a trial of any person for an offence on indictment any member of the jury dies or is discharged by the court whether as being through illness incapable of continuing to act or for any other reason, but the number of its members is not reduced below nine, the jury shall nevertheless . . . be considered as remaining for all the purposes of that trial properly constituted, and the trial shall proceed and a verdict may be given accordingly.

Section 16(1) is without prejudice to the judge's power to discharge the entire jury if he considers it preferable to do that, rather than continuing with reduced numbers (s. 16(3)). Discharge of jurors is *not* dependent on the consent of the parties, save in one instance (trials for offences punishable with death) which may for all practical purposes be disregarded.

In a case where the jury has to consider more than one verdict, the judge retains the power to discharge a juror even after one or more of the verdicts has been given. The reasoning is that the trial (and the accompanying power to discharge) continues in respect of those counts on which the verdict has not been delivered (*Wood* [1997] Crim LR 229).

Section 16(1) does not define the circumstances in which the judge may or should discharge a juror beyond implying that it may be on account of illness making the juror incapable of continuing to act or 'any other reason'. In *Hambery* [1977] QB 924, H's trial for theft and false accounting commenced on Monday 16 July 1976. It was originally expected that the hearing would last three or four days, but in fact the judge did not commence summing up until the morning of the following Friday when it became obvious that the case would not finish until after the weekend. The judge explained the position to the jury and then asked if any of them were going on holiday. One juror replied that she was planning to go to Somerset the next day, and she made no offer to postpone that arrangement. After a short discussion with counsel, the judge discharged the juror in reliance on s. 16. Defence counsel does not seem to have expressly objected to the course taken, but neither did he give his consent to it. On the next Monday, the judge concluded his summing up, and the 11 remaining jurors unanimously convicted.

On appeal it was argued: (a) that the judge had had no jurisdiction to discharge the juror; (b) that, even if he had, he exercised the discretion wrongly, and (c) the Court of Appeal had power to review his exercise of discretion. As to (a), Lawton LJ held (p. 927D–H) that the extent of the jurisdiction to discharge a juror is a matter of common law, since s. 16 does not confer the power but merely sets out the consequences of exercising it. At common law a jury could be discharged 'in cases of evident necessity' (*Blackstone's Commentaries*, 1857 ed. and see also Erle CJ's judgment in *Winsor* v *R* (1866) LR 1 QB 39 where he refers (at p. 394) to 'a high degree of need . . . such as . . . might be denoted by the word necessity'). At that time and until 1925, if one juror had to be discharged then so had the whole jury (i.e. there was no power to continue with a reduced jury). Therefore, the present test for jurisdiction to discharge a juror must be the same as the old test for discharging the whole jury, namely, has an evident necessity for it arisen? Neither the old authorities nor Lawton LJ's judgment in *Hambery* give specific guidance on what may constitute an evident necessity. However, it would seem to be a fairly elastic concept and is certainly not limited to illness or other cause making it literally impossible for the juror to continue to act. On the facts of *Hambery*, the judge was entitled to take the juror's statement that she was going on holiday on Saturday as indicating a 'high degree of need' for discharging her. It might have been better to have enquired more closely whether the holiday could be postponed for a short period, but the judge had had the benefit of seeing her demeanour in court and it was noticeable that she (unlike a second juror who had also planned to go away) made no offer to alter her arrangements. Trial by jury depends on the willing cooperation of the public, and 'If the administration of justice can be carried on without inconveniencing jurors unduly it should be' (see p. 930C–G). Therefore, in the circumstances that had arisen, the judge both had jurisdiction to discharge the juror and could not be criticised for the way he exercised his discretion.

On the third point raised by the appellant (namely, whether the judge's decision to discharge was in principle open to review by the Court of Appeal), Lawton LJ considered the earlier authorities, in particular *Winsor* v *R*, and held that dicta therein indicating that discharge was solely a matter for the trial judge should be understood as referring only to discharge of the entire jury (pp. 928F–929E). A decision to discharge one juror and continue with the remainder is a matter that may be raised on appeal. If the judge acted capriciously (e.g., by discharging for no good or discernible reason three black jurors when a black accused was being tried), that would be a material irregularity in the course of the trial which, subject to application of the proviso, would lead to the quashing of any conviction (p. 929F). Alternatively, there may be misconduct on the juror's part. Since misconduct by a juror often necessitates discharge of the whole jury, the approach to be adopted by the judge in such cases is considered under discharge of the entire jury (see **D11.20**). However, it should be borne in mind that, depending on the precise circumstances, the judge might be able to deal with the problem by discharging only the juror guilty of the misconduct.

Prior to deciding on the course of action which he will adopt, the judge will usually need to question one or more individual jurors, or the entire jury. In *Blackwell* [1995] 2 Cr App R 625, the Court of Appeal emphasised that the judge has a duty to investigate if there is any realistic suspicion that any juror has been approached or pressurised or otherwise tampered with. Such investigation will probably include questioning of individual jurors or even the jury as a whole. Questioning must be directed to the possibility that the jury's independence has been compromised, rather than to their deliberations on the issues in the case (see also *Oke* [1997] Crim LR 898 and *Appiah* [1998] Crim LR 134, and **D16.7** on the need to preserve the privacy of the jury room).

In *Orgles* [1994] 1 WLR 108, the point at issue was whether the recorder at trial had acted correctly in questioning individual jurors. The defendants were charged with threatening to destroy or damage property. The alleged threats were of a racist nature, the defendants being white, and the property belonging to a black family. Part way through the trial, two jurors complained to the recorder that, due to the nature of the case, there was dissension among the jury which was affecting concentration. The complainant jurors were each brought separately into open court and questioned by the recorder as to their ability to consider the evidence properly. Thereafter, the entire jury were brought back and asked whether they could continue their duties. The defendants were in due course convicted, and appealed. The Court of Appeal held that the procedure adopted by the recorder of initially questioning the two jurors separately was wrong and amounted to an irregularity. The circumstances giving rise to an inference that an individual juror or jurors could not fulfil his duties normally arose externally (e.g., an improper approach made to a juror). It was usual in that situation to question the individual juror in open court so that the trial judge might make enquiries without jeopardising the continued participation of the whole jury. Occasionally, however, the circumstances were internal to the jury, whether through individual characteristics or through interaction with fellow jury members. In the latter circumstances, such separation of a juror could not be justified. The problem was not the capacity of one or more individuals to carry out their duties, but the capacity of the jury as a whole. When the jury as a whole had been asked in open court as to their capacity to continue with the trial, it would then be a matter for the judge's exercise of discretion as to whether he made no order, discharged the whole jury or discharged individual jurors up to three in number. See also *Farooq* [1995] Crim LR 169.

After making such enquiries as are appropriate, it is submitted that the judge should, as a matter of good practice, ask the parties for their views before discharging a juror. However, discharge is not dependent on their consent (see above) and it is not absolutely essential even to consult them (see *Richardson* [1979] 1 WLR 1316, where the court received a telephone message from a juror that her husband had died during an overnight adjournment and the judge caused her to be told by the court staff not to attend court for the resumption of the trial – the first the parties knew of the discharge was when they saw only 11 jurors in the box, but the conviction was nonetheless upheld).

Discharge of the Entire Jury

D11.20 The judge has a discretion to discharge the whole jury from giving a verdict. If he does so, the accused is not acquitted but may be retried on the same indictment before a fresh jury (see e.g., *Winsor v R* (1866) LR 1 QB 390, although the point hardly needs authority since it inevitably follows from the jury not having returned a verdict that the accused has been neither acquitted nor convicted, and therefore cannot rely on a plea of autrefois). According to *Blackstone's Commentaries* (1857 ed.), a jury should not be discharged unless an 'evident necessity' for it has arisen. In *Winsor v R* Erle CJ gave some further limited guidance on the subject, which may be summarised as follows: (a) a jury should not be discharged unless a high degree of need for it arises; (b) whether to discharge is purely a matter for the judge's discretion; and (c) if he exercises his discretion wrongly by discharging the jury when he ought not to have done so, the appellate courts are powerless to correct the error.

The latter point was confirmed in *Gorman* [1987] 1 WLR 545 where G, who was convicted at a retrial following the jury at his first trial being discharged, appealed on the ground that a note from the first jury to the judge had revealed them to be split 9–3 in favour of acquittal. The note was sent some 25 minutes after they had received the majority verdict direction, and further indicated that they were deadlocked. The judge simply told counsel that the jury were split and would be incapable of reaching a verdict, but he did not reveal the provisional voting figures. Thereupon, both counsel agreed with the judge that the jury would have to be discharged. After G's conviction at the retrial, the defence discovered by chance the proportions in which the first jury had been split and argued on appeal that the judge at the first trial (a) had erred in not revealing the full contents of the jury's note to counsel, and (b) had exercised his discretion to discharge the jury improperly. If defence counsel had known that the jury were so near to a majority acquittal he would presumably have been less ready to agree to their discharge. The Court of Appeal reviewed the authorities (*Winsor* v *R*, *Lewis* (1909) 2 Cr App R 180, *Beadell* (1933) 24 Cr App R 39 and *Randall* [1960] Crim LR 435) and concluded that the law remained as stated in *Winsor* v *R*, namely that, if the first jury had as a matter of fact been discharged, a court hearing an appeal against the second jury's verdict had no power to review the propriety or otherwise of the discharge. The appeal therefore had to be dismissed regardless of the merits of the appellant's arguments.

The position is different should the judge be invited to discharge the jury and refuse to do so. If the accused is then convicted, he may appeal on the basis that continuing with the original jury casts doubt on the safety of his conviction. Such cases have given rise to a considerable amount of authority on when judges ought to discharge juries, although its being a matter for discretion means that the appellate court is unlikely to interfere save in extreme cases. The test to be applied by the trial judge was laid down in *Sawyer* (1980) 71 Cr App R 283. The facts were that, when a trial for importing cannabis had been in progress for a week, three members of the jury were seen in the court canteen speaking to two customs officers, who were prosecution witnesses. This was reported to the judge, who heard evidence from the customs officers, independent witnesses of the conversation and the jurors themselves about what precisely took place. From that evidence it appeared that the conversation had lasted for at most five minutes, and had been on subjects unconnected with the trial, save that one of the customs officers had given an estimate of when it would finish. The judge declined to discharge the jury and S was convicted. On appeal, Lord Widgery CJ said (at pp. 285–6 emphasis added):

> Upon those facts the learned judge had to decide whether or not there was a real danger that the appellant's position had been compromised by what had happened. *Was there a real danger that she was or might have been prejudiced by what had gone on?* The discretion which he undoubtedly had to stop the trial had of course to be exercised judicially and had to be exercised upon the facts as he knew them.
>
> It seems to us that what he principally had to decide was whether there was any danger from anything done or said that the jury might have been prejudiced against the appellant.

In short, the jury must be discharged only if, in the circumstances that have arisen, there is 'real danger' of prejudice to the accused in their continuing to try the case. On the facts of *Sawyer* such danger of prejudice was not demonstrated because there was no conversation about the case itself other than about its probable duration, and to think that the jurors might have been influenced to believe the customs officers simply because, in general conversation, the latter had presumably presented themselves as reasonable men was 'not to credit the jury with any wisdom at all.' The '*Sawyer* test' was approved by the House of Lords in *Spencer* [1987] AC 128 (see Lord Ackner's opinion at p. 144C: 'The correct test is the one stated in *Sawyer* namely, whether there was a "real danger" that the appellants' position had been prejudiced'). Contrary to what prosecution counsel had submitted at first instance, it is not necessary for the defence to demonstrate 'a very high risk' of prejudice in order to be entitled to the jury's discharge (ibid.).

In *Gough* [1993] AC 646, the House of Lords held that the 'real danger' test applied in all cases of apparent bias, whether concerned with justices, members of other inferior tribunals, jurors or abitrators'. Lord Goff of Chievely emphasised (at p. 904) that he would 'prefer to state the test in terms of real danger rather than real likelihood, to ensure that the court is thinking in terms of possibility rather than probability'. In considering whether to discharge the jury, the judge should have regard only to the 'real danger' test, he ought to exclude from his mind any matters which he ought not to take into account, such as the inconvenience of a re-trial or the fact that there has been an earlier abortive trial (*Walker* [1996] Crim LR 752).

The decided cases deal with four main situations in which the question of discharge arises, namely, when the jury cannot agree on their verdict; when they may have been inadvertently prejudiced against the accused; when some of their number have misconducted themselves; and when they acquire personal knowledge of the accused or his bad character. Failure to agree is discussed at **D16.31** and **D16.32**. The other three reasons for discharge are considered in the following paragraphs.

D11.21 **Accidental Prejudice** The way in which this most commonly arises is if a witness refers to the accused's bad character during a trial where character has not been put in issue. The leading authority is *Weaver* [1968] 1 QB 353 which held that, even in such cases, whether or not to discharge the jury is for the judge's discretion. Although it had been said in *Palmer* (1935) 25 Cr App R 97 that, once a jury was wrongly allowed to hear evidence of a previous conviction, it was very difficult for them to dismiss that evidence from their minds, that case should not now be treated as establishing a general rule that they must inevitably be discharged. How the judge should act will depend on the facts of the particular case, and the court 'will not lightly interfere with' what he does (see Sachs LJ's judgment in *Weaver* [1968] 1 QB 353 at p. 359G).

In *Weaver*, a police officer who had interviewed the accused was asked in chief by prosecuting counsel whether he said anything to him 'by way of introduction', to which the officer replied 'I cautioned him'. This was a form of words which had obviously been agreed beforehand in what was thought to be the best interests of the accused. However, when defence counsel in cross-examination asked further questions on the matter, the officer revealed that he had not himself said the words of the caution, but the accused had recited them to him in a light-hearted fashion, to which the officer had replied 'That is the caution'. Later in his cross-examination, defence counsel incautiously asked whether the accused's address had been given to the police by a prosecution witness. The officer hinted that it might be inappropriate for him to answer the question but defence counsel persisted and the officer finally said, 'It is an address known to the police and has been circulated.' Defence counsel then asked for the jury to be discharged as the cumulative effect of the answers in cross-examination was to reveal to the jury that the accused had previous convictions or, at the very least, was known to the police and was himself familiar with the words of the caution. Approving the judge's refusal to discharge and dismissing W's appeal against conviction, Sachs LJ said that every decision turned on its own facts and depended especially on 'the nature of what has been admitted into evidence, the circumstances in which it has been admitted and what, in the light of the circumstances of the case as a whole, is the correct course' (p. 360B). The factors which particularly weighed against discharge were (a) that defence counsel had himself been responsible for inviting the answers which he then complained of, and (b) the degree of prejudice had been minimised by the judge's wise summing-up. *Weaver* may be contrasted with *Blackford* (1989) 89 Cr App R 239, in which the appellant was convicted of possessing cannabis with intent to supply after a police officer in cross-examination had gratuitously revealed that he had a previous conviction for a similar offence. Defence counsel's question was 'not of outstanding simplicity or clarity', but nonetheless the officer was not entitled to answer it in the way he did – it was 'a deliberate attempt by the police to queer the appellant's pitch'. In those circumstances, the trial judge should have discharged the jury and ordered a retrial. The Court of Appeal substituted a conviction for simple possession which had always been admitted by the appellant.

Should an improper indication that one accused may be of bad character come from his co-accused, the Court of Appeal will be particularly loth to interfere with the trial judge's exercise of discretion against discharging the jury (*Sutton* (1969) 53 Cr App R 504). In that case, one of three accused, during cross-examination by prosecution counsel, gratuitously suggested that his co-accused had at one stage been on the run from prison and that they all had previous convictions. The judge refused to discharge the jury, and Fenton Atkinson LJ (giving the Court of Appeal's judgment) said (at pp. 512-13):

> We have considered this matter with some anxiety, but . . . in all the circumstances of this case the judge was justified in exercising his discretion in the manner in which he did, and we would certainly be slow to lay down as a general rule that where one co-defendant says something of this nature about his co-accused, a judge must automatically allow a fresh trial, because it would simply make it too easy if a trial is not going well for one co-accused to say something which would secure his co-accused the advantages, if they are advantages, of a new trial. . . . there was an exercise of discretion by the trial judge, and the court is always slow to interfere with such an exercise of discretion.

Where the accused is represented by counsel and prejudicial matters are accidentally disclosed it would seem that counsel must take the initiative and apply at trial for the jury to be discharged. If he fails to do so, any appeal is liable to be dismissed, even if the circumstances were such that, had an application for discharge been made, it would probably have been granted (see *Wattam* [1942] 1 All ER 178, in which a police officer gave evidence that he had first seen the accused's face when looking through an album of photographs and the Court of Criminal Appeal held that, even if the reference to the album could be regarded as an irregularity in that the jury might have thought that it was a rogues' gallery of convicted criminals, the appeal must fail because defence counsel had omitted to apply for a retrial). It is different if the accused is unrepresented. Should circumstances then arise in which an application for discharge might succeed, the judge is under a duty so to inform the accused. Failure to do so will be a material irregularity in the course of the trial necessitating the quashing of any conviction unless the proviso can be applied (*Featherstone* [1942] 2 All ER 672). However, provided the accused is invited to consider applying for discharge, no complaint may be made if the judge, in the proper exercise of his discretion, then decides to rule against the application (ibid.).

Dubarry (1976) 64 Cr App R 7 is a further illustration of how accidental prejudice may arise necessitating discharge of the jury: while a jury trying D on one charge were considering their verdict, at least one member of the jury probably saw D being tried on another charge – the Court of Appeal held that the jury should have been discharged.

In *Fedrick* [1990] Crim LR 403, F's co-accused S changed his plea to guilty during the course of the trial. The prosecution had opened the case on the basis that F and S were 'in cahoots' (although no conspiracy charge was laid). The judge emphasised to the jury that S's plea of guilty made no difference to F's position. In his summing-up, he again warned the jury that S's plea of guilty was irrelevant to F's case. F was convicted and appealed on the grounds, *inter alia*, that the plea of guilty by S was prejudicial to his case, and the judge should have discharged the jury. The Court of Appeal held that the jury could not properly consider F's case in isolation from S's. They should therefore have been discharged and a fresh trial held.

In *Hutton* [1990] Crim LR 875, H was tried on charges of deception and obtaining credit whilst an undischarged bankrupt. Further trials were pending, so an order was made under the Contempt of Court Act 1981, s. 4(2), banning publication of the proceedings. Instead of a notice being pinned to the door, a copy of the order was attached. This published the fact that H faced further trials. A juror was seen to read the order, but the judge was not informed of this until the jury had retired. The defence applied to discharge the jury, but the judge refused. The Court of Appeal quashed the ensuing conviction. The juror who read the order might well have discussed it with his fellow jurors. Potential prejudice resulted directly from the irregularity.

In *Boyes* [1991] Crim LR 717, as the judge concluded his summing-up on charges of rape and indecent assault, the complainant's mother shouted from the public gallery, 'When is it going to come out about the other five girls he has attacked?' The judge told the jury not to pay any attention to the outburst. The jury convicted. The Court of Appeal allowed the appeal. One of the bases for the decision was the judge's failure to enquire of the jury whether they had heard the outburst. If they had, one could hardly think of more damaging and prejudicial evidence being taken to the jury room. It was only after such enquiry, with the help of counsel and a very careful contemplation by the judge, that he could decide what to do. He should have considered a fresh trial. His failure to do so was a serious irregularity which could not be overcome by use of the proviso.

In *McCann* (1991) 92 Cr App R 239, M and others were tried for conspiracy to murder Mr. King, who was then Secretary of State for Northern Ireland, and others. They elected not to give evidence. During the closing stages of the trial, the Home Secretary announced in the House of Commons the government's intention of changing the law on the right to silence. That night, interviews with Mr. King and Lord Denning were televised, expressing in strong terms their view that in terrorist cases a failure to answer questions or give evidence was tantamount to guilt. The trial judge refused to dismiss the jury, and the defendants were convicted. The Court of Appeal allowed the appeal. Although the court had to give great weight to the trial judge's exercise of discretion, its powers to review was not confined to cases or error of principle or lack of material upon which the judge could properly have arrived at his decision. If necessary, it must examine anew the relevant facts and circumstances, and exercise a discretion by way of review if it considered the failure to discharge the jury might have resulted in injustice. In this case there was a real risk that the jury had been influenced by the statements and the only way in which justice could be done and be seen to be done was by discharging the jury and ordering a retrial.

In *Ricketts* [1991] Crim LR 915, the trial judge gave leave for the statement of S to be read, on the basis that S's absence was caused by fear. After the jury had retired, S arrived, and the judge saw him in chambers, without informing counsel. Apparently S denied that he had failed to appear because he was frightened. The judge told S that his evidence had been read and was not in dispute and that he was free to go. The judge gave no indication to counsel that S had denied staying away through fear. R was convicted and appealed. The Court of Appeal held that S's evidence had been given prominence on a false basis, i.e. that it was so damning that R or someone on his behalf would seek violent revenge if he testified. In those circumstances, an application to discharge the jury could not properly have been resisted.

In *Robson* [1992] Crim LR 655, the Crown's case at trial was that the deceased was murdered on a specific date. Defence witnesses testified that they had seen her alive after that date. The trial judge, after hearing representations from counsel, decided to direct the jury on the basis that it was for them to consider to what extent the date of death mattered; and that if they were not sure that it occurred on the date in question they could still find R guilty. The judge offered the defence the opportunity to recall witnesses, or re-open their case, or ask for more time, but the defence refused. R was convicted and appealed. The Court of Appeal quashed the conviction and ordered a re-trial. The fresh issue raised by the judge did not merely introduce a new interpretation of the evidence. It opened up the possibility of conviction on a different factual basis from that put forward by the Crown, and one which had not been fully explored. That resulted in unfairness to the defence, and was a material irregularity. The best course would have been to discharge the jury.

In *Wilson* (1995) *The Times*, 24 February 1995, the Court of Appeal held that there was a real danger of bias where one of the jurors was the wife of a prison officer at the prison where the defendants were held on remand.

In *Maguire* [1997] 1 Cr App R 61, the judge told a defence witness who had refused to answer certain questions that he was to be arrested for contempt of court and would be dealt with at the end of the day. Defence counsel made an application to the judge to discharge the jury on the basis that M had been severely prejudiced. The judge refused, and directed the jury in due course that the arrest of the witness was not to affect their approach to the evidence, had nothing to do with M, and was to be ignored. M was convicted and appealed. The appeal was allowed. The judge should have dealt with the witness in the absence of the jury. The direction given to the jury was not an adequate remedy as it could not have dispelled the inevitable prejudice which had been created.

Misconduct by a Juror The judge in his discretion may allow the jury to separate   **D11.22**
(Juries Act 1974, s. 13). Contrary to the practice of earlier years (when juries were kept rigorously secluded from the moment of their empanelling until the trial had concluded), it is now standard practice to allow them to separate both for luncheon and overnight adjournments. It inevitably follows that they will have the opportunity to speak about the case with those who are not of their number. However, they should be warned on the first occasion they separate that that is something they must not do. In *Prime* (1973) 57 Cr App R 632, Lord Widgery CJ said (at p. 637): 'It is important in all criminal cases that the judge should on the first occasion when the jury separate warn them not to talk about the case to anybody who is not one of their number. If he does that and brings that home to them, then it is to be assumed that they will follow the warning and only if it can be shown that they have misbehaved themselves does the opportunity of an application [for discharge] arise.' Most cases coming before the Court of Appeal on discharge of the jury due to misconduct concern allegations that, in defiance of the warning, one or more jurors spoke to prosecution witnesses or members of the public about the case.

The discretion of the judge to allow the jury to separate was extended by CJPO 1994, s. 43. That section allows the judge to permit separation even after the jury have retired to consider their verdict.

Juror's Personal Knowledge of Accused or of Accused's Bad Character A   **D11.23**
further situation in which the judge will have to consider discharge either of the whole jury or of an individual juror is when it comes to light that a juror knows the accused or knows a witness in the case. The problem is particularly acute where the juror may know

the accused to be of bad character. The following propositions summarise the Court of Appeal's decisions relating to a juror's possible bias on account of his knowledge of the accused's character, both in cases where the facts were discovered during trial and an application for discharge was accordingly made, and in cases where the defence did not learn of it until after conviction.

(a) A juror who knows the accused or who knows from hearsay of the accused's bad character ought not to sit on the jury. He should inform the clerk beforehand and ask to be excused from service. Even if he does not do that and is called into the jury-box as a result of the ballot, he can still write a note for the judge indicating the reason why he should not serve. Failure to disqualify himself on account of his knowledge of the accused is 'quite improper' (per Lord Parker CJ in *Box* [1964] 1 QB 430 at p. 435). In practice, it is not uncommon for a juror to realise when the accused comes into the dock (or when a witness is called into the witness-box) that he knows the person, and to write a note to that effect for the judge. Depending on the facts of the particular case, previous contact with a witness may not disqualify the juror, but it is submitted that, if the juror has any previous acquaintance with the accused, however slight, it is safer for him to be removed.

(b) If the defence are aware at the time the jury is empanelled that a juror is open to objection for the reasons stated in (a) they should obviously challenge for cause or (more simply) ask prosecuting counsel to stand the juror by. Although the Court of Appeal has stated that a juror is not automatically disqualified by knowledge of the accused's previous convictions (see per Lord Parker CJ in *Box*), those statements are in the context of cases where the relevant facts were not known to the defence until after the time for challenging had passed. They do not, it is submitted, cast doubt on the fundamental proposition that a person who knows facts detrimental to the accused should not be on the jury.

(c) Where a juror's possible knowledge of the accused is not brought to the court's attention until after the trial has commenced, the judge will have to consider discharging the individual juror and/or the entire jury. In *Hood* [1968] 1 WLR 773, defence counsel informed the judge that H's wife, who had just given evidence for the defence, had recognised a jury member as a person who lived in the same road as her mother and she (the wife) believed that the juror would consequently know about her husband's previous convictions. The judge heard arguments on both sides and eventually ruled against discharge because there was no concrete evidence that the juryman recognised the witness, much less recognised H. The Court of Appeal had the benefit of an affidavit from the juror which disclosed that he had in fact suspected from the outset of the trial that the accused was the man who had married his neighbours' daughter and who had subsequently been to prison. When Mrs Hood entered the witness-box his uncertainty was dispelled because he recognised her immediately. It followed that the trial judge had made his decision not to discharge on an inaccurate factual basis. The Court of Appeal confirmed that (a) a juror is not automatically disqualified by knowledge of the accused's previous convictions, and (b) that the Court of Appeal will not enquire into what occurred in the jury room. Moreover, the judge was right not to address questions to the juror himself about the allegations the defence had made, for that course would have presented very grave problems. Where the judge could be criticised was in not hearing evidence from Mrs Hood herself concerning her suspicions about the juror, but that irregularity did not justify quashing the conviction in the light of the very strong evidence there had been against the appellant. The implication of his lordship's judgment is that, if the judge had enquired more closely at the time and discovered the true situation regarding the juror, he would have been obliged to discharge the jury.

(d) If a juror's knowledge of or bias against the accused does not come to the defence's attention until after conviction, an appeal is most unlikely to succeed since the appellant will have to show that the juror had made up his mind before the trial started to convict the accused regardless of the evidence (see *Box* [1964] 1 QB 430).

ISSUES THAT MAY BE TRIED BY ONE JURY

Subject to the exceptions mentioned below, a jury may try only one issue, that is, once **D11.24**
it has brought in a verdict on the issue for which it was empanelled, it must be split up
with the individual jurors going back into the pool of jurors in waiting with a view to
being selected by ballot for further juries. The exceptional cases in which a jury may be
kept together to try a second issue are: (a) where the trial of the second issue begins
within 24 hours from the time when the jury was constituted, and (b) where the trial of
an issue of unfitness to plead has been postponed until the end of the prosecution
evidence and the judge directs that the jury empanelled to try the general issue shall also
try unfitness (see Juries Act 1974, s. 11(5)). Even where it is decided that a jury shall try
a second issue, the court may order individual members of it to be replaced by others
selected by ballot from the jury panel (s. 11(6)).

Juries Act 1974, s. 11

(4)   Subject to subsection (5) below, the jury selected by any one ballot shall try only
one issue (but any juror shall be liable to be selected on more than one ballot).
(5)   Subsection (4) above shall not prevent—
(a)   the trial of two or more issues by the same jury if the trial of the second or last
issue begins within 24 hours from the time when the jury is constituted, or
(b)   in a criminal case, the trial of fitness to plead by the same jury as that by whom
the accused is being tried, if that is so directed by the court under section 4(4)(b) of the
Criminal Procedure (Insanity) Act 1964, or
(c)   in a criminal case beginning with a special plea, the trial of the accused on the
general issue by the jury trying the special plea.
(6)   In the cases within subsection (5)(a) and (b) above the court may, on the trial of the
second or any subsequent issue, instead of proceeding with the same jury in its entirety,
order any juror to withdraw, if the court considers that he could be justly challenged or
excused, or if the parties to the proceedings consent, and the juror to replace him shall . . .
be selected by ballot in open court.

An important corollary of the rule that a jury may try only one issue is that, if an accused
is charged in two or more separate indictments, there must be a separate trial for each
indictment (see *Crane* v *DPP* [1921] 2 AC 299), and, subject to the Juries Act 1974,
s. 11(5)(a), a fresh jury must be empanelled for each trial. A purported trial by one jury
of two indictments is a nullity (*Crane*). That is so even if the parties consented to the
course adopted (*Dennis* [1924] 1 KB 867).

SECTION D12: TRIAL ON INDICTMENT:
GENERAL MATTERS AND PRE-TRIAL PROCEDURE

The purpose of this chapter is to describe the order of proceedings at a trial on indictment and to consider other topics of a predominantly procedural nature associated with the trial.

PLACE OF TRIAL

Venue of Trial

D12.1   **Supreme Court Act 1981, s. 75**

(1) The cases or classes of cases in the Crown Court suitable for allocation respectively to a judge of the High Court and to a circuit judge or recorder, and all other matters relating to the distribution of Crown Court business, shall be determined in accordance with directions given by or on behalf of the Lord Chief Justice with the concurrence of the Lord Chancellor.

(2) Subject to section 74(1) [which requires that when hearing an appeal the Crown Court shall normally consist of a professional judge together with at least two justices of the peace], the cases or classes of cases in the Crown Court suitable for allocation to a court comprising justices of the peace (including those by way of trial on indictment which are suitable for allocation to such a court) shall be determined in accordance with directions given by or on behalf of the Lord Chief Justice with the concurrence of the Lord Chancellor.

In addition, s. 7 of the MCA 1980 (see **D7**) provides that, when specifying the particular location of the Crown Court to which an accused should be committed or transferred for trial, a magistrates' court must have regard, *inter alia*, to the directions given by the Lord Chief Justice under s. 75(1) of the Supreme Court Act 1981. Thus, both the location of the Crown Court to which an accused is initially committed and the nature of the tribunal before which he is ultimately tried (i.e. High Court judge, circuit judge or recorder) are governed by the Lord Chief Justice's directions.

The s. 75 directions currently in force were issued in May 1995 and are reported as *Practice Direction (Crown Court: Allocation of Business)* [1995] 1 WLR 1083; an amendment was made by the *Practice Direction (Crown Court: Allocation of Business) (No. 2)* [1998] 1 WLR 1244. The direction is divided into two main headings, namely 'Classification' and 'Allocation of business within the Crown Court' (which will be referred to for convenience as 'part 1' and 'part 2' respectively). Paragraph 1 of part 1 divides indictable offences into four classes in roughly descending order of gravity. Class 1 consists principally of murder and offences contrary to s. 1 of the Official Secrets Act 1911; class 2 includes manslaughter, rape and sexual intercourse or incest with a girl under 13; class 4 comprises robbery, offences contrary to s. 18 of the OAPA 1861 and all offences triable either way, and class 3 is simply all offences triable only on indictment other than those in class 1, 2 or 4. When committing for trial in respect of an offence in classes 1 to 3, magistrates must commit to the most convenient location of the Crown Court where a High Court judge regularly sits; when committing for trial in respect of an offence in class 4, they must commit to the most convenient location of the Crown Court regardless of whether a High Court judge sits there (part 1, para. 2). Further, in deciding what is the most convenient location for committal, the magistrates must have regard not only to the matters mentioned in the MCA 1980, s. 7, but also to 'the location or locations of the Crown Court designated by a presiding judge as the location to which cases should normally be committed from their petty sessions area' (part 1, para. 3).

Thus, the combined effect of the Lord Chief Justice's direction and the indications from the presiding judges of the circuits as to the normal place of committal is to remove from the committing justices the discretion as to venue which is prima facie given them by s. 7 of the MCA 1980. In any event, the place of trial specified by the magistrates' court may be varied by the Crown Court itself under the provisions of s. 76 of the Supreme Court Act 1981.

Cases in class 1 must be tried by a High Court judge, save that murder may be released by or on the authority of a presiding judge to be tried by an approved circuit judge (i.e. one who has been approved by the Lord Chief Justice for the purpose of trying murder cases) (part 2, para. 1). Cases in class 2 are to be tried by a High Court judge unless a particular case is released by or on the authority of a presiding judge for trial by a circuit judge (part 2, para. 2). This is subject to the qualification that a case of rape or any serious sexual offence against a child (whatever its class) may be released only to a circuit judge approved by the Lord Chief Justice (ibid.). Cases in class 3 may be tried either by a High Court judge or, in accordance with general or particular directions given by the presiding judge, by a circuit judge or recorder (part 2, para. 3). Cases in class 4 may be tried by a High Court judge, circuit judge, recorder or assistant recorder, but must not be listed for trial by a High Court judge except with the consent of the judge himself or the presiding judge. To facilitate the disposal of business on a circuit, the presiding judges of the circuits (with the approval of the senior presiding judge) have the responsibility of issuing directions as to the types of cases to be reserved for trial by High Court judges and as to the general allocation of work between circuit judges, recorders and assistant recorders (part 2, para. 11). Where necessary the directions may devolve responsibility for such allocation to the resident or designated judges of a Crown Court location. The directions are required to make specific provision for the allocation of certain defined types of case, they being (broadly speaking) cases of special gravity, cases where the accused holds a responsible position in society and cases where the trial is likely to be long or complex. Any case listed for hearing by a circuit judge or recorder, other than those in which there is expected to be a not guilty plea, may be allocated to a court which includes justices of the peace (part 2, para. 8).

Practice Direction (Crown Court: Allocation of Business)
[1995] 1 WLR 1083

CLASSIFICATION

1.   For the purposes of trial in the Crown Court, offences are to be classified as follows:

Class 1:
   (1)   Any offences for which a person may be sentenced to death.
   (2)   Misprision of treason and treason felony.
   (3)   Murder.
   (4)   Genocide.
   (5)   An offence under section 1 of the Official Secrets Act 1911.
   (6)   Incitement, attempt or conspiracy to commit any of the above offences.

Class 2:
   (1)   Manslaughter.
   (2)   Infanticide.
   (3)   Child destruction.
   (4)   Abortion (section 58 of the Offences against the Person Act 1861).
   (5)   Rape.
   (6)   Sexual intercourse with a girl under 13.
   (7)   Incest with a girl under 13.
   (8)   Sedition.
   (9)   An offence under section 1 of the Geneva Conventions Act 1957.
   (10)   Mutiny.

(11)   Piracy.

(12)   Incitement, attempt or conspiracy to commit any of the above.

Class 3:

All offences triable only on indictment other than those in Classes 1, 2 and 4.

Class 4:

(1)   Wounding or causing grievous bodily harm with intent (section 18 of the Offences against the Person Act 1861).

(2)   Robbery or assault with intent to rob (section 8 of the Theft Act 1968).

(3)   Incitement or attempt to commit any of the above offences.

(4)   Conspiracy at common law, or conspiracy to commit any offence other than those included in Classes 1 and 2.

(5)   All offences which are triable either way.

Committals for trial

2(a)   Save as provided in paragraph 2(b) below for certain offences in class 2, a magistrates' court on committing a person for trial under section 6 of the Magistrates' Courts Act 1980 shall, if the offence or any of the offences is included in classes 1 to 3, specify the most convenient location of the Crown Court where a High Court judge regularly sits, and if the offence is in class 4 shall specify the most convenient location of the Crown Court.

2(b)   Where a presiding judge has directed that class 2 offences within the categories below may be committed from a specified magistrates' court or courts to a specified location of the Crown Court at which a High Court Judge does not regularly sit, the magistrates' court shall specify that location

• Rape

• Sexual intercourse with a girl under 13

• Incest with a girl under 13

• Incitement, attempt or conspiracy to commit any of the above offences.

3.   In selecting the most convenient location of the Crown Court, the justices shall have regard to the considerations referred to in section 7 of the Magistrates' Courts Act 1980, and to the location or locations of the Crown Court designated by a presiding judge as the location to which cases should normally be committed from their petty sessions area.

4.   Where on one occasion a person is committed in respect of a number of offences, all the committals shall be to the same location of the Crown Court and that location shall be the one where a High Court judge regularly sits if such a location is appropriate for any of the offences.

. . .

ALLOCATION OF BUSINESS WITHIN THE CROWN COURT

General

1.   Cases in class 1 are to be tried by a High Court judge. A case of murder, or incitement, attempt or conspiracy to commit murder may be released, by or on the authority of a presiding judge, for trial by a circuit judge approved for the purpose by the Lord Chief Justice.

2.   Cases in class 2 are to be tried by a High Court judge unless a particular case is released by or on the authority of a presiding judge for trial by a circuit judge. A case of rape, or of a serious sexual offence against a child of any class, may be released by a presiding judge for trial only by a circuit judge or recorder approved for the purpose by the senior presiding judge with the concurrence of the Lord Chief Justice.

3.   Cases in class 3 may be tried by a High Court judge or, in accordance with general or particular directions given by a presiding judge, by a circuit judge or a recorder.

4.   Cases in class 4 may be tried by a High Court judge, a circuit judge, a recorder or an assistant recorder. A case in class 4 shall not be listed for trial by a High Court judge except with the consent of that judge or of a presiding judge.

. . .

6.   With the exception of courts operating the plea and directions scheme established under practice rules issued by the Lord Chief Justice, the following arrangements for

pre-trial proceedings shall apply. (i) Applications or matters arising before trial (including those relating to bail) should be listed where possible before the judge by whom the case is expected to be tried. Where a case is to be tried by a High Court judge who is not available, the application or matter should be listed before any other High Court judge then sitting at the Crown Court centre at which the matter has arisen; before a presiding judge; before the resident or designated judge for the centre; or, with the consent of the presiding judge, before a circuit judge nominated for the purpose. (ii) In other cases, if the circuit judge, recorder or assistant recorder who is expected to try the case is not available, the matter shall be referred to the resident or designated judge or, if he is not available, to any judge or recorder then sitting at the centre.

. . .

Presiding judges' directions
11.   For the just, speedy and economical disposal of the business of a circuit, presiding judges shall, with the approval of the senior presiding judge, issue directions as to the need where appropriate to reserve a case for trial by a High Court judge and as to the allocation of work between circuit judges, recorders and assistant recorders and where necessary the devolved responsibility of resident or designated judges for such allocation. In such directions specific provision should be made for cases in the following categories.

(a)   Cases where death or serious risk to life, or the infliction of grave injury are involved, including motoring cases of this category arising from [dangerous] driving and/or excess alcohol.

(b)   Cases where loaded firearms are alleged to have been used.

(c)   Cases of arson or criminal damage with intent to endanger life.

(d)   Cases of defrauding government departments or local authorities or other public bodies of amounts in excess of £25,000.

(e)   Offences under the Forgery and Counterfeiting Act 1981 where the amount of money or the value of goods exceeds £10,000.

(f)   Offences involving violence to a police officer which result in the officer being unfit for duty for more than 28 days.

(g)   Any offence involving loss to any person or body of a sum in excess of £100,000.

(h)   Cases where there is a risk of substantial political or racial feeling being excited by the offence or the trial.

(i)   Cases which have given rise to widespread public concern.

(j)   Cases of robbery or assault with intent to rob where gross violence was used, or serious injury was caused, or where the accused was armed with a dangerous weapon for the purpose of the robbery, or where the theft was intended to be from a bank, a building society or a post office.

(k)   Cases involving the manufacture or distribution of substantial quantities of drugs.

(l)   Cases the trial of which is likely to last more than 10 days.

(m)   Cases involving the trial of more than five defendants.

(n)   Cases in which the accused holds a senior public office, or is a member of a profession or other person carrying a special duty or responsibility to the public, including a police officer when acting as such.

(o)   Cases where a difficult issue of law is likely to be involved, or a prosecution for the offence is rare or novel.

12.   With the approval of the senior presiding judge, general directions may be given by the presiding judges of the South Eastern Circuit concerning the distribution and allocation of business of all classes at the Central Criminal Court.

Transfer of Cases between Locations of the Crown Court

Section 76(1) of the Supreme Court Act 1981 provides that the Crown Court may give **D12.2** directions altering the place of any trial on indictment. The alteration may be either to the committing magistrates' original decision as to venue or to an earlier decision of the Crown Court itself (ibid.). An officer of the Crown Court may give such directions on behalf of the court (s. 76(2)). Either party, if dissatisfied with the place of trial that has been fixed, may apply to the Crown Court for a variation (s. 76(3)), such application to be heard in open court by a High Court judge (s. 76(4)). The place of trial specified in notices of transfer under s. 4 of the 1987 Act to be varied in the same way that the place specified on committal may be varied (s. 76(2A)).

Section 76 is of no assistance on how the powers it gives are to be exercised, save that s. 76(1) contains the qualification that it is 'Without prejudice to the provisions of this Act about the distribution of Crown Court business'. It is submitted that, on an application by a party under s. 76(3) for variation of the venue specified by the magistrates (or by the prosecution in a notice of transfer), the High Court judge determining the application is entitled to consider factors additional to those listed in the MCA 1980, s. 7, as governing the decision of the lower court. In other words, whereas the committing magistrates are to consider only the convenience of the parties and witnesses, the expediting of the trial and the Lord Chief Justice's directions, the High Court judge may give weight to, for example, the possible prejudice to the accused of being tried in the area where the offence was allegedly committed if the nature of the charge has provoked exceptional public hostility. However, in the light of the Court of Appeal's decision in *Ford* [1989] QB 868 (see **D11.15**), it would be inappropriate to vary the location to one where a higher proportion of black people live simply with a view to obtaining a multiracial jury panel (see also *Bansal* [1985] Crim LR 151 where Woolf J declined to order that the trial of Asians accused of public order offences arising out of an anti-National Front demonstration be switched from Maidstone to a London Crown Court, although he did give the indication, later criticised in *Ford*, that the jury panel should be drawn from Gravesend rather than from Maidstone itself).

The power given to listing officers of the Crown Court to switch a trial from one court centre to another (see s. 76(2)) is used principally to even out the workload between neighbouring courts. Such decisions to switch are made on administrative rather than judicial grounds.

Supreme Court Act 1981, s. 76

(1)   Without prejudice to the provisions of this Act about the distribution of Crown Court business, the Crown Court may give directions, or further directions, altering the place of any trial on indictment, whether by varying the decision of the magistrates' court under section 7 of the Magistrates' Courts Act 1980 or by substituting some other place for the place specified in a notice under a relevant transfer provision (notices of transfer from magistrates' court to Crown Court) or by varying a previous decision of the Crown Court.

(2)   Directions under subsection (1) may be given on behalf of the Crown Court by an officer of the court.

(2A)   Where a preparatory hearing has been ordered under section 7 of the Criminal Justice Act 1987, directions altering the place of trial may be given under subsection (1) at any time before the jury are sworn.

(3)   The defendant or the prosecutor, if dissatisfied with the place of trial as fixed by the magistrates' court, as specified in a notice under a relevant transfer provision or as fixed by the Crown Court, may apply to the Crown Court for a direction, or further direction, varying the place of trial; and the court shall take the matter into consideration and may comply with or refuse the application, or give a direction not in compliance with the application, as the court thinks fit.

(4)   An application under subsection (3) shall be heard in open court by a judge of the High Court.

(5)   In this section 'relevant transfer provision' means—
   (a)   section 4 of the Criminal Justice Act 1987, or
   (b)   section 53 of the Criminal Justice Act 1991.

DUTIES AND ROLE OF COUNSEL

Introduction

D12.3   The manner in which counsel should conduct themselves in a criminal trial (in particular a trial on indictment) and the duties resting upon them emerge partly from dicta in Court of Appeal decisions but chiefly from the Code of Conduct of the Bar and from the recommendations of the Farquharson Committee on the role of prosecuting counsel, published in *Counsel*, Trinity 1986.

Prosecuting Counsel

The *locus classicus* on the role and approach of the prosecuting counsel is *Puddick* (1865) **D12.4** 4 F & F 497, in which Crompton J said (at p. 499) that they 'are to regard themselves as ministers of justice, and not to struggle for a conviction'. See also per Avory J in *Banks* [1916] 2 KB 621 at p. 623. Some of the implications of this lofty role are identified in the introductory paragraphs of the Farquharson Report:

> There is no doubt that the obligations of prosecution counsel are different from those of counsel instructed for the defence in a criminal case or of counsel instructed in civil matters. His duties are wider both to the court and to the public at large. Furthermore, having regard to his duty to present the case for the prosecution fairly to the jury he has a greater independence of those instructing him than that enjoyed by other counsel. It is well known to every practitioner that counsel for the prosecution must conduct his case moderately, albeit firmly. He must not strive unfairly to obtain a conviction; he must not press his case beyond the limits which the evidence permits; he must not invite the jury to convict on evidence which in his own judgment no longer sustains the charge laid in the indictment. If the evidence of a witness is undermined or severely blemished in the course of cross-examination, prosecution counsel must not present him to the jury as worthy of a credibility he no longer enjoys. . . . Great responsibility is placed upon prosecution counsel and although his description as a 'minister of justice' may sound pompous to modern ears it accurately describes the way in which he should discharge his function.

In *Gonez* [1999] All ER (D) 674 (unreported in printed form), the Court of Appeal endorsed the description of prosecuting counsel as a minister of justice, stating that it was incumbent on him not to be betrayed by personal feelings, not to excite emotions or to inflame the minds of the jury and not to make comments which could reasonably be construed as racist and bigoted. He was to be clinical and dispassionate.

For discussion of the role of prosecuting counsel in relation to the judge, see **D10.44** and **D13.8**.

Relationship of Prosecution Counsel with those Instructing Him As the **D12.5** Farquharson Committee stated in the passage quoted in **D12.4**, prosecution counsel is recognised as enjoying greater independence from those instructing him, whether it be the CPS or other prosecuting agency or private prosecutor, than does defence counsel from his solicitor or lay client. The report considers in detail the limits of this greater independence with special reference to the creation of the CPS. The report's conclusions may be summarised as follows:

(a)   A prosecuting solicitor is in the same position as any other instructing solicitor in the sense that he will not brief counsel unless he has confidence in his ability and judgment. Moreover, if dissatisfied with the way a particular case has been conducted, he has – again like any other solicitor – the ultimate sanction of not briefing that counsel in the future.

(b)   Occasionally, however, there will be differences of opinion between a prosecuting solicitor and counsel whom he has briefed for a case and on whose judgment he would normally rely. Most such differences will be of relatively little importance and will be resolved in the normal give and take of discussion between members of the professions. But, sometimes the disagreement will be on a fundamental matter (e.g., the acceptance of a plea to a lesser offence). If such a disagreement cannot be resolved and assuming it is still practicable to do so, the prosecuting solicitor is not bound by counsel's view but may seek a second opinion either by taking in a leader or by instructing fresh counsel.

(c)   Difficult problems arise if a significant disagreement becomes apparent at too late a stage for other counsel to be instructed. In such cases, counsel's view must prevail. His total control of the case thus runs from the moment when it becomes impracticable for his instructions to be withdrawn. From then on, it is for him 'to make the necessary decisions on all matters relating to the general conduct of the trial . . . including, for example: what evidence should be called; which witnesses are to be relied upon and which are to be abandoned; what submissions are appropriate to be made to the judge on matters of law and/or to the judge and jury on the existence and strength of the evidence required and available to prove the count(s) in the indictment.'

(d)   While the general position remains as stated in (c), a distinction must be drawn between 'evidential' decisions and 'policy' decisions. By the latter the committee meant decisions on (i) the acceptance of pleas of guilty to lesser counts or groups of counts or available alternatives; (ii) offering no evidence on particular counts; and (iii) the withdrawal of the prosecution as a whole. All other decisions, including those instanced in (c), are classified by the committee as evidential decisions.

(e)   The committee's experience was that disagreements between prosecuting solicitor and counsel, whether on evidential or policy matters, were almost always resolved by discussion. They did not expect that to change. However, in the very unlikely event of there being an unresolved conflict (and an adjournment being undesirable or refused by the judge), then 'the exigencies of trial' would usually require a decision to be taken by someone, and *that person has to be counsel:* 'in our view, there is no alternative to the practical position that prosecution counsel must take those decisions and do what he conscientiously believes to be right.'

(f)   Although the ultimate authority for any prosecution is the A-G, it will almost certainly not be possible to refer a dispute to him during a trial. But, if counsel has taken a course with which the prosecuting solicitor has not agreed it would be appropriate for the A-G, *ex post facto*, to require counsel to submit to him a written report of all the circumstances, including his reason for disagreeing with those who instructed him. If the disagreement was on a policy (as opposed to merely evidential) matter, the committee would positively expect the A-G to require a report. There ought to be a practice and rule to that effect.

(g)   To minimise the chance of disagreements at trial, prosecution counsel should 'read the instructions delivered to him expeditiously' so that either potential disagreements can be resolved in advance by discussion or the prosecuting solicitor has time to withdraw instructions (or take in a leader) well before the hearing. Where counsel is at fault by not advising until the last moment that, for example, the prosecution should be dropped or a plea to a lesser charge accepted, and the solicitor disagrees with the advice, then counsel (if so instructed) should apply for an adjournment so that the DPP can be consulted before any decision is made about the future conduct of the case.

(h)   The above principles were stated in the light of the then imminent introduction of the CPS and the need to define the relationship between Crown Prosecutors and prosecution counsel. The committee recommended that the same thinking and practices should apply to prosecutions conducted independently of the CPS, hence the references above to 'prosecuting solicitor' rather than Crown Prosecutor.

The committee themselves helpfully summarised their views in the following propositions:

(a)   It is the duty of prosecution counsel to read the instructions delivered to him expeditiously and to advise or confer with those instructing him on all aspects of the case well before its commencement.

(b)   A solicitor who has briefed counsel to prosecute may withdraw his instructions before the commencement of the trial up to the point when it becomes impracticable to do so, if he disagrees with the advice given by counsel or for any other proper professional reason.

(c)   While he remains instructed it is for counsel to take all necessary decisions in the presentation and general conduct of the prosecution.

(d)   Where matters of policy fall to be decided after the point indicated in (b) above (including offering no evidence on the indictment or on a particular count, or the acceptance of pleas to lesser counts) it is the duty of counsel to consult those instructing him whose views at this stage are of crucial importance.

(e)   In the rare case where counsel and his instructing solicitor are unable to agree on a matter of policy, it is (subject to (g) below) for prosecution counsel to make the necessary decisions.

(f)   Where counsel has taken a decision on a matter of policy with which his instructing solicitor has not agreed, then it would be appropriate for the A-G to require counsel to submit to him a written report of all the circumstances, including his reasons for disagreeing with those who instructed him.

(g)   When counsel has had the opportunity to prepare his brief and to confer with those instructing him, but at the last moment before trial unexpectedly advises that the case should not proceed or that pleas to lesser offences should be accepted, and his instructing solicitor does not accept such advice, counsel should apply for an adjournment if instructed so to do.

(h)   Subject to the above, it is for prosecution counsel to decide whether to offer no evidence on a particular count or on the indictment as a whole and whether to accept pleas to a lesser count or counts.

Appropriate points from the above list have been incorporated in annexe F to the Code of Conduct of the Bar.

Provisions of the Code of Conduct of the Bar Relating to Prosecuting D12.6
Counsel   The status of the Code of Conduct of the Bar was explained as follows in
McFadden (1975) 62 Cr App R 187 by James LJ (at p. 190):

> The Bar Council issues statements from time to time to give guidance to the profession in matters of etiquette and procedure. A barrister who conforms to the Council's rulings knows that he cannot be committing an offence against professional discipline. But such statements, although they have strong persuasive force, do not bind the courts. If therefore a judge requires a barrister to do, or refrain from doing, something in the course of a case, the barrister may protest and may cite any relevant ruling of the Bar Council, but since the judge is the final authority in his own court, if counsel's protest is unavailing, he must either withdraw or comply with the ruling or look for redress in a higher court.

Paragraph 11 of the standards applicable to criminal cases in annexe F to the Code of Conduct deals especially with the duties of prosecuting counsel (for provisions relevant to both prosecution and defence counsel see **D12.8 et seq.**). Paragraph 11.1 describes the general role and approach of prosecuting counsel in terms similar to those used by Avory J in *Banks* [1916] 2 KB 621 and the Farquharson Committee (see **D12.4**). Paragraph 16.1 requires counsel to be present throughout the trial (including the summing-up and return of the jury), unless given leave by the court to be absent. If two or more counsel have been instructed, the attendance of one is sufficient (ibid.). At the conclusion of the summing-up, it is counsel's duty to draw to the judge's attention any apparent omissions or errors of fact or law (para. 11.7). Paragraph 11.8 concerns counsel's role at the sentencing stage. Paragraph 11.6 reflects what is contained in the report of the Farquharson Committee.

Duties and Role of Defence Counsel

Defence counsel is not subject to the constraints that apply to prosecuting counsel in   D12.7
the sense of regarding himself as a minister of justice. Subject to the duty resting on any barrister not deliberately to mislead the court, and to the rules of professional conduct generally, he may use all proper means to secure the acquittal or lenient sentencing of

his lay client. In presenting the accused's defence, counsel should not be influenced by his personal opinion of its truth. This cardinal principle was restated by the Professional Conduct Committee of the Bar following the decision of the Court of Appeal in *McFadden* (1975) 62 Cr App R 187, in which the trial judge had heavily criticised defence counsel for the prolixity of their cross-examination and for allegations that fingerprint evidence had been 'planted'. The committee said:

> It is the duty of counsel when defending an accused on a criminal charge to present to the court, fearlessly and without regard to his personal interests, the defence of that accused. It is not his function to determine the truth or falsity of that defence, nor should he permit his personal opinion of that defence to influence his conduct of it. No counsel may refuse to defend because of his opinion of the character of the accused nor of the crime charged. That is a cardinal rule of the Bar, and it would be a grave matter in any free society were it not. Counsel also has a duty to the court and to the public. This duty includes the clear presentation of the issues and the avoidance of waste of time, repetition and prolixity. In the conduct of every case counsel must be mindful of this public responsibility.

Applying the above principles to the particular circumstances of *McFadden's* case, the committee stated that, if the accused's defence is that a fingerprint on an article – although his – was not put there by him, then counsel is under a duty to present that defence to the jury. If the circumstances indicate that one or more witnesses called by the prosecution were responsible for planting the prints, that should be put to the individuals concerned in cross-examination; otherwise the evidence should be probed in a general way to establish that planting is a possibility albeit that the individual responsible cannot be identified.

Very occasionally, the question will arise as to whether it is proper for defence counsel to be called as a witness on behalf of his client. In *Jaquith* [1989] Crim LR 563, counsel for B gave evidence on his behalf. The evidence was aimed at rebutting an allegation of recent fabrication put on behalf of B's co-defendant, J. B was in due course acquitted on the judge's direction, and J and E were convicted. The Court of Appeal commented that it was 'unfortunate' that B's junior counsel had given evidence, and made certain suggestions for the guidance of the Bar Council and the Law Society. These include the following:

(a) No advocate should give evidence in a criminal trial if doing so can possibly be avoided.

(b) If an advocate does give evidence, he should thereafter take no further part in the trial. It follows that, unless he has a leader, there must be a retrial.

(c) Counsel should be able to anticipate before the trial whether it will be necessary for him to give evidence. If it will be, he should withdraw as advocate.

(d) If the giving of evidence by an advocate causes real embarrassment or prevents proper cross-examination by other counsel, a retrial should be ordered.

In *Wood* [1996] 1 Cr App R 207, the Court of Appeal said that the rule should be enforced that a member of the Bar giving evidence could no longer act as counsel in the same case. The comment was made in response to a ground of appeal which concerned the tone of voice used by the trial judge and the physical expression of views by sighing, shrugging his shoulders and raising his eyebrows in a way that was said to be hostile to the defence. Their lordships' view was that they could not act on such information unless it was either agreed between counsel or supported by evidence.

In *Batt* [1996] Crim LR 910, the Court of Appeal stated that it was generally undesirable for husband and wife, or other partners living together, to appear as advocates against each other in a contested criminal matter.

In *Dann* [1997] Crim LR 46, the Court of Appeal considered a case where junior counsel for the Crown had appeared for D previously on an unrelated matter. Their lordships examined para. 501(f) of the Code of Conduct, which refers to the risk that a barrister may have confidential information or special knowledge disadvantageous to a former client, and said that it was the *risk* which was material. It was contrary to the spirit of the Code that a barrister should put himself in the position that such a risk might be perceived. In the circumstances of the instant case, however, D had provided no evidence for arguing that any injustice had been done to him and the appeal was dismissed.

Matters of relevance to defence counsel in the Code of Conduct of the Bar can be summarised as follows:

(a) He 'must endeavour to protect his client from conviction except by a competent tribunal and upon legally admissible evidence sufficient to support a conviction for the offence charged' (annexe F, standards applicable to criminal cases, para. 12.1).

(b) He should satisfy himself, if he is briefed to represent more than one defendant, that no conflict of interest is likely to arise (para. 12.2(a)).

(c) He should arrange a conference and if necessary a series of conferences with the accused and the solicitor (para. 12.2(b)).

(d) He should consider whether any enquiries are necessary, and, if so, advise in writing as soon as possible (para. 12.2(c)).

(e) He should consider whether defence witnesses are required (para. 12.2(d)).

(f) He should consider whether notice of alibi is required and, if so, draft it (para. 12.2(e)).

(g) He should consider whether to call expert evidence and notify the prosecution in accordance with the rules of the Crown Court if appropriate (para. 12.2(f)).

(h) He should 'ensure that he has sufficient instructions for the purpose of deciding which prosecution witnesses should be cross-examined, and should then ensure that no other witnesses remain fully bound at the request of the defendant' (para. 12.2(g)). Clearly, the laudable aim of this provision is to avoid the expense and inconvenience caused by compelling the attendance of witnesses fully bound at committal who are no longer required because of a defence change of course. The problem, however, is that the provision does not appear to permit the perfectly proper decision of defence counsel to insist that a witness give evidence to see whether he is 'up to proof', even if there is no intention of cross-examining. It is submitted that such a decision would clearly be within the spirit of the code (see point (a) above).

(i) He should consider what admissions can be made, and what admissions and/or exhibits can be requested from the prosecution (para. 12.2(h), (i) and (j)).

(j) The fact that the accused confesses to counsel that he did commit the offence charged does not bar counsel from appearing or continuing to appear for the defence on a not guilty plea, nor is counsel released 'from his imperative duty to do all that he honourably can for his client' (para. 13.2). Counsel should bear in mind that, in a criminal trial, the issue is always whether the accused is guilty of the offence charged (never whether he is innocent), and the burden of proof is on the prosecution. However, receiving a confession places very strict limitations on counsel's conduct of the defence since 'he may not assert that which he knows to be a lie' or 'connive at, much less attempt to substantiate, a fraud'. It follows that counsel may properly take objections to the competency of the court, the form of the indictment and the admissibility of any evidence but he may not himself call evidence (e.g., of alibi) which he must, having regard to the confession made to him, know to be false. Nor may he in any way set up an affirmative defence inconsistent with the confession. On the other hand, he is entitled in cross-examination to test the evidence given by each individual prosecution witness and then argue that, taken as a whole, the evidence is insufficient to prove the offence charged – 'further than this he ought not to go'. Where the accused makes a series of inconsistent statements to counsel, or his statements point almost irresistibly to guilt without amounting to an express confession, counsel is faced with very difficult problems on which the code declines to give any general advice.

(k) Counsel's duty to advise on pleas and his position if the accused says he is not guilty but for reasons of his own insists on pleading guilty are dealt with (paras 12.3 and 12.5).

(l) Defence counsel must ensure that the accused is not left unrepresented at any stage of the trial (paras 16.2.1 to 16.2.4). If two counsel represent the accused, neither may absent himself unless he has good reason and obtains the consent of both his professional and lay client. Where only one counsel is instructed, he may absent himself only if (i) exceptional circumstances have arisen which he could not have been expected to foresee; (ii) he obtains the consent of his professional and lay clients, and (iii) he arranges for a competent deputy to take his place. The above is all subject to the qualification that, in lengthy trials involving numerous accused, counsel may absent himself for any part of the trial during which he considers that there is no serious possibility of events occurring that will affect his client. He needs the consent of professional and lay clients, must arrange for 'other defending counsel to guard the interests of his client', must keep himself informed of the progress of the trial (in particular of developments affecting his client), and must not accept other commitments which would prevent his making himself available at reasonable notice should the interests of his client require it. Also, the client's consent to counsel's absence may be dispensed with in legally aided cases if counsel considers that, by being present, he would involve the fund in unnecessary expenditure (see para. 16.2.3)

(m) The position of counsel should the accused abscond during the trial is considered in paras 16.3.1 and 16.3.2.

(n) Advice on whether the accused should testify in his own defence is dealt with in para. 12.4.

(o) Allegations that may properly be made during a speech in mitigation are dealt with in para. 5.10.

(p) After conviction and sentence, it is counsel's duty to see his client and advise (if necessary in writing) on whether there are grounds of appeal (para. 17.2). The professional client should also be present.

Provisions of the Code of Conduct of the Bar Relevant to Both Prosecution and Defence Counsel

D12.8 The Code of Conduct of the Bar contains numerous provisions relevant to the conduct of both prosecution and defence counsel. They include the following.

D12.9 *Limits of Proper Cross-examination* The legal limitations on cross-examination imposed by the rules of evidence and the concept of relevancy are considered at **F7.5 *et seq***. However, counsel is required to consider not only whether a proposed question is legally allowable but whether it is ethically justified. He must, therefore, 'not make statements or ask questions which are merely scandalous or intended or calculated only to vilify, insult or annoy either a witness or some other person' (Code of Conduct of the Bar, para. 610(e) and annexe F, general standards, para. 5.10(e)). Moreover, it is for the barrister to 'exercise personal judgment upon the substance and purpose of questions asked and statements made', since he is 'personally responsible for the conduct and presentation of his case' (Code of Conduct of the Bar, para. 610(a) and (annexe F, general standards, para. 5.10(a)).

Counsel must not suggest that a witness or other person is guilty of crime, fraud or misconduct or attribute to another person the crime or conduct of which his lay client is accused unless such allegations go to a matter in issue (including the credibility of the witness) which is material to his lay client's age, and which appear to him to be supported by reasonable grounds (Code of Conduct of the Bar, para. 610(h) and annexe F, general standards, para. 5.10(h)). A witness should never be impugned in a speech by counsel unless counsel has first given him an opportunity in cross-examination to answer the allegation (annexe F, general standards, para. 5.10(g)).

A limitation on defence counsel's unfettered discretion to cross-examine about the issues and impugn the witness's character in the process was suggested by Lord Goddard CJ in *O'Neill* (1950) 34 Cr App R 108. The appellant was convicted of attempted robbery partly on the evidence of a confession made to the police. It was suggested to the officers concerned that they had 'dragged' the statement out of the accused by threats and violence, but the accused, who was of bad character, chose not to testify. Lord Goddard criticised defence counsel for his cross-examination, saying that it was 'quite wrong and improper conduct on the part of counsel' to make charges against the police (or any other prosecution witnesses) if he did not intend to call evidence in support of those charges. A distinction had to be drawn between proper and temperate cross-examination as to credit (where one was bound by the witness's answer) and the kind of allegations made by counsel. It is submitted, however, that Lord Goddard's dicta are at variance with the Code of Conduct of the Bar, para. 610(h) and annexe F, general standards, para. 5.10(h). Those paragraphs permit suggestions of misconduct provided they go to a material issue and appear to be supported by reasonable grounds. They do not contain a caveat that counsel must intend to call positive evidence in support of the allegations. The judge can deal adequately with the situation in his summing-up by drawing attention to the gap in the defence evidence.

Assisting the Court   In criminal cases, just as in civil, a barrister is under a duty to   **D12.10**
bring all relevant authorities to the court's attention even if some are unfavourable to his own argument. Further, he must bring any procedural irregularity to the attention of the court during the hearing and not reserve such matter to be raised on appeal (e.g., where a juror is seen speaking to a witness). The duties outlined so far apply equally to prosecution and defence counsel (see Code of Conduct of the Bar, para. 610(c) and annexe F, general standards, para. 5.10(c)). In *Smith* [1994] Crim LR 458, one of the grounds of appeal was the fact that contact with a child witness during her evidence was alleged to be irregular. The Court of Appeal said that counsel should have raised the matter at the time with the judge, in the absence of the jury. Failure to do so was reprehensible.

A specific obligation is placed upon prosecuting counsel to assist the court at the conclusion of the judge's summing-up by drawing attention to any apparent errors or omissions of fact or law. No corresponding duty is placed upon defence counsel, but if he ignores a misdirection in the hope of using it as a ground of appeal, he runs a considerable risk. The Court of Appeal may dismiss the appeal on the basis that, if the error had been likely to make a difference to the verdict, counsel would have wanted to correct it at the time (but see *Holden* [1991] Crim LR 478 at **D22.20**, for a case in which the appeal was allowed).

Documents Coming into Counsel's Possession   Paragraphs 7.2, 7.3.1 and 7.3.2   **D12.11**
of the general standards in annexe F to the Code of Conduct of the Bar deal with problems which may arise from counsel coming into possession of documents to which neither he nor his lay or professional clients are entitled. The provisions of the code are in part the consequence of what occurred in *Tompkins* (1977) 67 Cr App R 181. In that case, a representative of the prosecuting solicitor, having picked up a note from the accused to defence counsel which had apparently been dropped on the floor, handed the note to prosecuting counsel. After receiving answers in cross-examination which were at variance with the contents of the note, prosecuting counsel handed it to the accused and asked him whether he still maintained his original evidence. The defence objected to this course, but the judge ruled that the cross-examination might continue,

although with no direct reference to what was in the note. The accused thereupon reversed his evidence. The Court of Appeal upheld the conviction since, although the note was privileged as a communication between client and legal adviser, the doctrine of privilege merely protects a party from the obligation of producing a document and does not determine its admissibility or the use which may be made of it should it come into the hands of the other side. Moreover, even if the note had been inadmissible in itself, that would not have prevented counsel asking questions based upon it and, on the facts of *Tompkins*, counsel had been able to achieve his purpose merely by handing the note to the accused without directly revealing its contents to the jury. The practice adopted in *Tompkins* is not, however, approved by the code which states that: (a) a barrister must not try to obtain a document belonging to the other side (or knowledge of its contents) except through the normal and proper channels (annexe F, general standards, para. 7.1); (b) if he should accidentally come into possession of such a document he should at once return it unread (para. 7.2), and (c) if he reads a document before realising that he ought not to have done so and would be embarrassed in conducting the case by the knowledge thus inadvertently obtained, then he should return his instructions, provided he can do so without prejudice to his lay client (paras 7.3.1 and 7.3.2).

D12.12   *Conferences, Speaking to Witnesses etc.*   The interlocking matters of conferences, counsel being attended at court by his professional client, and the seeing of witnesses are dealt with in various provisions of the Code of Conduct of the Bar, which may be summarised as follows:

(a)   It is counsel's duty to make himself available for a conference with his client before or on the day of the trial (annexe F, general standards, para. 5.9).

(b)   Provided that the interests of justice and of the lay client will not be prejudiced, counsel may agree with his professional client that attendance by the latter's representative may be dispensed with for any hearing at the magistrates' court. The same rule applies in the Crown Court, with the proviso that counsel must have been supplied with any necessary proofs of evidence (para. 608).

(c)   Where counsel ought to be attended under (b) above, but the solicitor's representative unexpectedly fails to attend and it is not practicable to ask for an adjournment, counsel may continue with the case unattended (para. 609(b)).

(d)   There is no longer a general rule preventing a barrister from having contact with any witness. A barrister may exchange common courtesies with the other side's witnesses, provided he does not discuss the substance of the case with them. More crucially, he may have contact with a witness whom he expects to call and examine in chief, with a view to introducing himself, explaining the court's procedure, and answering any questions about it which the witness might have. The barrister does in fact have a positive responsibility to ensure that a witness facing unfamiliar court procedures is put as much at ease as possible, particularly when that witness is nervous, vulnerable or apparently the victim of criminal conduct (annexe F, paras 6.1.2, 6.1.3, 6.1.4 and 6.2.7).

(e)   In a contested case in the Crown Court, however, it is wholly inappropriate for a barrister to *interview* any potential witness. Interviewing includes discussing the substance of the witness' evidence, or the evidence of other witnesses. The lay client, and character and expert witnesses are excluded from this prohibition (annexe F, para. 6.3.1).

(f)   Prosecuting counsel should not confer with any investigator witness unless he has also had a supervisory responsibility in the investigation, and should not confer with or receive factual instructions directly from investigators on matters which may be in dispute (annexe F, para. 6.3.2).

(g)   There may be extraordinary circumstances in which departure from the principles set out in (e) and (f) is unavoidable. The Code of Conduct (annexe F, para.

6.3.3) quotes as an example the circumstances in *Fergus* (1994) 98 Cr App R 313. In that case, Steyn LJ stated (at p. 323) that since defence solicitors had failed to see the alibi witnesses in order to ask why they had remembered the events of the day in question, counsel should have seen them himself.

(h)   Where a barrister has interviewed a potential witness, that fact should be disclosed to all the other parties in the case before the witness is called. The substance of the interview should be recorded, together with the reason for it (annexe F, para. 6.3.4).

(i)   Counsel must not rehearse, practise or coach any witness, in relation either to the evidence itself or to the way in which to give it (para. 607). (In *Dye* [1992] Crim LR 449, the Court of Appeal seems to have thought that the interviewing of the most important prosecution witnesses for a documentary film about drug trafficking, which was to be screened after the trial was over, was irregular — presumably because it involved an element of rehearsal before the television cameras.)

(j)   The above rules are all subject to the overriding principle that a barrister must not 'devise facts which will assist in advancing his lay client's case' (annexe F, general standards, para. 5.8). In particular, when defence counsel sees the accused, he must be careful not to suggest a defence that would be more plausible than the one actually being advanced by the lay client.

PRE-TRIAL AND PREPARATORY HEARINGS

Pre-trial Hearings

The CPIA 1996, ss. 39 to 43, provide reinforcement in statutory form for the various **D12.13** pre-trial procedures developed in the Crown Court in order to promote the efficient conduct of trials on indictment. The central provisions are those contained in ss. 39 and 40. They consolidate and bolster the rules for plea and directions hearings, which were set out in the *Practice Direction* reproduced below (see also the judge's questionnaire, reproduced as **appendix 5**).

Criminal Procedure and Investigations Act 1996, ss. 39 and 40

39.—(1)   For the purposes of this part a hearing is a pre-trial hearing if it relates to a trial on indictment and it takes place—

(a)   after the accused has been committed for trial for the offence concerned or after the proceedings for the trial have been transferred to the Crown Court, and

(b)   before the start of the trial.

(2)   For the purposes of this part a hearing is also a pre-trial hearing if—

(a)   it relates to a trial on indictment to be held in pursuance of a bill of indictment preferred under the authority of section 2(2)(b) of the Administration of Justice (Miscellaneous Provisions) Act 1933 (bill preferred by direction of Court of Appeal or by direction or with consent of a judge), and

(b)   it takes place after the bill of indictment has been preferred and before the start of the trial.

(3)   For the purposes of this section the start of a trial on indictment occurs when a jury is sworn to consider the issue of guilt or fitness to plead or, if the court accepts a plea of guilty before a jury is sworn, when that plea is accepted; but this is subject to section 8 of the Criminal Justice Act 1987 and section 30 of this Act (preparatory hearings).

40.—(1)   A judge may make at a pre-trial hearing a ruling as to—

(a)   any question as to the admissibility of evidence;

(b)   any other question of law relating to the case concerned.

(2)   A ruling may be made under this section—

(a)   on an application by a party to the case, or

(b)   of the judge's own motion.

(3)   Subject to subsection (4), a ruling made under this section has binding effect from the time it is made until the case against the accused or, if there is more than one, against each of them is disposed of; and the case against an accused is disposed of if—

(a)   he is acquitted or convicted, or

(b)   the prosecutor decides not to proceed with the case against him.

(4)   A judge may discharge or vary (or further vary) a ruling made under this section if it appears to him that it is in the interests of justice to do so; and a judge may act under this subsection—

(a)   on an application by a party to the case, or

(b)   of the judge's own motion.

(5)   No application may be made under subsection (4)(a) unless there has been a material change of circumstances since the ruling was made or, if a previous application has been made, since the application (or last application) was made.

(6)   The judge referred to in subsection (4) need not be the judge who made the ruling or, if it has been varied, the judge (or any of the judges) who varied it.

(7)   For the purposes of this section the prosecutor is any person acting as prosecutor, whether an individual or a body.

The hearings covered in ss. 39 to 43 are pre-trial hearings, and they can therefore be conducted by a judge who will not be the eventual trial judge. They differ from preparatory hearings in long or complex cases (see **D12.14**) in this respect. Restrictions on the reporting of pre-trial rulings are contained in ss. 41 and 42. There are no exemptions in respect of the publication of formal details, such as the name, address and occupation (again, in contrast with the position in relation to preparatory hearings).

Practice Direction: Crown Court (Plea and Directions Hearings)
[1995] 1 WLR 1318

These rules establish plea and directions hearings (PDHs) in the Crown Court and will apply to all cases (other than serious fraud) in Crown Court centres which have notified the magistrates' courts that PDHs have been introduced.

At the PDH, pleas will be taken and, in contested cases, prosecution and defence will be expected to assist the judge in identifying the key issues, and to provide any additional information required for the proper listing of the case.

The detailed operation of the rules will be a matter for the judiciary at each Crown Court Centre, taking the views of other agencies, and the legal profession, into account.

1.   In every case, other than serious fraud cases in relation to which a notice of transfer to the Crown Court is given under section 4 of the Criminal Justice Act 1987, the magistrates' court should commit the defendant to appear in the Crown Court on a specific date fixed in liaison with the Crown Court listing officer for an initial plea and directions hearing (PDH).

2.   The purpose of the PDH will be to ensure that all necessary steps have been taken in preparation for trial and to provide sufficient information for a trial date to be arranged. It is expected that the advocate briefed in the case will appear in the PDH wherever practicable.

3.   At least 14 days' notice of the PDH shall be given unless the parties agree to shorter notice. The PDH should be within six weeks of committal in cases where the defendant is on bail, and four weeks where the defendant is in custody.

Preparation for the PDH

4.   Where the defendant intends to plead guilty to all or part of the indictment, the defence must notify the probation service, the prosecution and the court, as soon as this is known.

5.   The defence must supply the court and the prosecution with a full list of the prosecution witnesses they require to attend at the trial. This must be provided at least 14 days prior to the PDH or within three working days of the notice of the hearing where the PDH is fixed less than 17 days ahead.

6.   For all class 1 offences, and for lengthy and complex cases, a case summary should be prepared by the prosecution for use by the judge at the PDH. All class 2 cases should be scrutinised by the prosecution to determine whether the provision of a summary is appropriate in any particular case. The summary will assist the judge by indicating the nature of the case, and focusing on the issues of fact and/or law likely to be involved. The summary should also assist the judge in estimating the trial length.

Form of hearing

7.   The PDH should normally be held, and orders made, in open court and all defendants should be present (except with the leave of the court). It shall be conducted:

(a)   in all cases other than those in class 1 or class 2 and serious sexual offences of any class against a child, by the trial judge or such judge as the presiding judge or resident judge shall appoint;

(b)   in cases in class 1 or class 2 and serious sexual offences of any class against a child, by a High Court judge, or by a circuit judge to whom the case has been specifically released in accordance with *Practice Direction (Crown Court: Allocation of Business)* [1995] 1 WLR 1083, or by a directions judge authorised by the presiding judges to conduct such hearings, but

(i)   pleas of guilty when entered before a directions judge in such cases will be adjourned for sentencing by a High Court judge or circuit judge to whom the case has been specifically released; and

(ii)   a directions judge will deal only with those matters necessary to see that such cases are prepared conveniently for trial, including identifying any issues suitable for a preliminary hearing before the trial judge, and making such necessary directions as may facilitate the conduct of such a preliminary hearing.

Conduct of the hearing

8.   At the PDH arraignment will normally take place.

9.   If the defendant pleads guilty, the judge should proceed to sentencing whenever possible.

10.   Following a not guilty plea, and where part or alternative pleas have not been accepted, the prosecution and defence will be expected to inform the court of:

(a)   the issues in the case;

(b)   issues, if any, as to the mental or medical condition of any defendant or witness;

(c)   the number of witnesses whose evidence will be placed before the court either orally or in writing;

(d)   the defence witnesses in (c) above whose statements have been served and whose evidence the prosecution will agree and accept in writing;

(e)   any additional witnesses who may be called by the prosecution and the evidence that they are expected to give;

(f)   facts which are to be admitted and which can be reduced into writing in accordance with section 10(2)(b) of the Criminal Justice Act 1967, within such time as may be directed at the hearing, and of the witnesses whose attendance will not be required at trial;

(g)   exhibits and schedules which are to be admitted;

(h)   the order and pagination of the papers to be used by the prosecution at the trial and the order in which the prosecution witnesses are likely to be called;

(i)   any alibi which should already have been disclosed in accordance with the Criminal Justice Act 1967;

(j)   any point of law which it is anticipated will arise at trial, any questions as to the admissibility of evidence which appear on the face of the papers, and of any authority on which the party intends to rely;

(k)   any applications to be made for evidence to be given through live television links by child witnesses, as defined by section 32 of the Criminal Justice Act 1988 amended by section 54 of the Criminal Justice Act 1991, in cases involving violent or sexual offences, particulars of which should already have been lodged with the court in writing on the form at schedule 5 to the Crown Court Rules 1982 . . . (within 28 days after the date of committal of the defendant, or the referral of a bill of indictment in relation to the case);

(l)   any applications to submit pre-recorded interviews with a child witness as evidence in chief;

(m)   any applications for screens, for use by witnesses seeking a visual break between themselves and any relevant parties; whether any video, tape recorder or other technical equipment will be required during a trial; where tape recorded interviews have taken place, of any dispute or agreement as to the accuracy of any transcript or summary;

(n)   any other significant matter which might affect the proper and convenient trial of the case, and whether any additional work needs to be done by the parties;

(o)   the estimated length of the trial, to be agreed more precisely taking account of any views expressed by the judge and the other parties;

(p)   witness availability and the approximate length of witness evidence so that attendance can be staggered during lengthy trials, agreeing likely dates and times of attendance, taking into consideration real hardship and inconvenience to a witness where applicable;

(q)   availability of advocate;

(r)   whether there is a need for any further directions.

11.   Subject to the provisions of sections 9 and 10 of the Criminal Justice Act 1967, admissions under paragraph 10(f), above, may be used at the trial.

12.   The judge may make such order or orders as lie within his powers as appear to be necessary to secure the proper and efficient trial of the case. Each party shall, at least 14 days before the date of trial, confirm to the court that all such orders have been fully complied with.

13.   The questionnaire annexed to these rules provides a recommended structure for use by the judiciary in conducting a PDH. A single copy of the questionnaire, completed as far as possible with the agreement of both advocates, is to be handed in to the court prior to the commencement of the PDH.

14.   The defence shall apply to the court for the case to be listed for mention if they are unable to obtain instructions from the defendant. If the defendant fails to attend court, the judge will wish to consider whether a warrant of arrest should be issued.

In *Diedrick* [1997] 1 Cr App R 361, the appeal concerned the actions of the trial judge in questioning the defendant about what he thought was a lie which the defendant had told in the questionnaire. The Court of Appeal observed that what was said at the plea and directions hearing was not expected to form part of the material for trial, and it would rarely be appropriate to refer to it. Where the trial judge was considering the use of such material, counsel should be allowed to address the judge first.

Preparatory Hearings under the Criminal Procedure and Investigations Act 1996, ss. 28 to 38

D12.14   Sections 28 to 38 of the CPIA 1996 contain provisions for preparatory hearings in long or complex cases. They originate from the procedure established for serious fraud cases, which came into force by virtue of the CJA 1987 (see **D12.15**). The Criminal Procedure and Investigations Act 1996 (Preparatory Hearings) Rules 1997 (SI 1997 No. 1052) lay down deadlines for the defence or prosecution to apply for a preparatory hearing and set out the procedure for determining any such application. The rules state that any application for a preparatory hearing must be made within 28 days of committal or preferment of a voluntary bill of indictment. In the case of transfer for trial, the application for a preparatory hearing must be made within 28 days of the transfer or no later than seven days after an application for dismissal is determined or withdrawn, whichever is the later.

The decision to hold a preparatory hearing may be made by a Crown Court judge at any time before a jury is sworn, on the application of any of the parties or by the court of its own motion. In practice, the decision is likely to be made at the plea and directions hearing (see **D12.13**). The preparatory hearing is in fact a stage of the trial itself, which may be used in order to settle various issues without requiring the jury to attend (s. 30). Since the trial begins with the preparatory hearing, the same judge must preside throughout, save for exceptional circumstances such as death or serious illness (see *Southwark Crown Court, ex parte Commissioners for Customs and Excise* [1993] 1 WLR 764 and **D12.15**; cf. the position as far as the plea and directions hearing is concerned).

Among the powers available to the judge at a preparatory hearing is the power to order the prosecutor and the defence to make disclosure in advance of the hearing (s. 31(4) to (6)), in addition to any disclosure already made as a result of the general duties on the parties (see **D6** and rr. 7 and 8 of the 1997 Rules). He may also make rulings as to any question of law relating to the case, including questions as to the admissibility of evidence (s. 31(2)), but his powers in this respect may be circumscribed by the principle in *Re Gunawardena* [1990] 1 WLR 703. In that case, it was held that the power to make binding rulings in a preparatory hearing in a serious fraud case was limited by implication to the purposes for which preparatory hearings may be ordered (see **D12.15**). In relation to the set of provisions presently under discussion, these are set out in s. 29(2), and may be summarised as:

    (a)   identifying material issues for the jury;
    (b)   assisting them to understand those issues;
    (c)   expediting proceedings before them; and
    (d)   helping the judge to manage the trial.

There are provisions for appealing from rulings made by the judge at a preparatory hearing to the Court of Appeal and, ultimately, the House of Lords (see ss. 35 and 36 and the Criminal Procedure and Investigations Act 1996 (Preparatory Hearings) (Interlocutory Appeals) Rules 1997 (SI 1997 No. 1053)). Where leave to appeal has been granted, the preparatory hearing may continue, but the jury trial cannot begin until the appeal has been determined or abandoned.

Restrictions on reporting preparatory hearings are contained in s. 37, although certain formal details (e.g., the names, ages, home addresses and occupations of the accused and witnesses, and the offence(s) charged) may be published by virtue of s. 37(9). The court has power to lift the restrictions (s. 37(3)).

Criminal Procedure and Investigations Act 1996, ss. 29 to 32 and 34

29.—(1)   Where it appears to a judge of the Crown Court that an indictment reveals a case of such complexity, or a case whose trial is likely to be of such length, that substantial benefits are likely to accrue from a hearing—
    (a)   before the jury are sworn, and
    (b)   for any of the purposes mentioned in subsection (2),
he may order that such a hearing (in this part referred to as a preparatory hearing) shall be held.
    (2)   The purposes are those of—
    (a)   identifying issues which are likely to be material to the verdict of the jury;
    (b)   assisting their comprehension of any such issues;
    (c)   expediting the proceedings before the jury;
    (d)   assisting the judge's management of the trial.
    (3)   No order may be made under subsection (1) where it appears to a judge of the Crown Court that the evidence on an indictment reveals a case of fraud of such seriousness or complexity as is mentioned in section 7(1) of the Criminal Justice Act 1987 (preparatory hearings in cases of serious or complex fraud).
    (4)   A judge may make an order under subsection (1)—
    (a)   on the application of the prosecutor,
    (b)   on the application of the accused or, if there is more than one, any of them, or
    (c)   of the judge's own motion.

30.   If a judge orders a preparatory hearing—
    (a)   the trial shall start with that hearing, and
    (b)   arraignment shall take place at the start of that hearing, unless it has taken place before then.

31.—(1)   At the preparatory hearing the judge may exercise any of the powers specified in this section.
    (2)   The judge may adjourn a preparatory hearing from time to time.
    (3)   He may make a ruling as to—
    (a)   any question as to the admissibility of evidence;
    (b)   any other question of law relating to the case.

(4) He may order the prosecutor—

(a) to give the court and the accused or, if there is more than one, each of them a written statement (a case statement) of the matters falling within subsection (5);

(b) to prepare the prosecution evidence and any explanatory material in such a form as appears to the judge to be likely to aid comprehension by the jury and to give it in that form to the court and to the accused or, if there is more than one, to each of them;

(c) to give the court and the accused or, if there is more than one, each of them written notice of documents the truth of the contents of which ought in the prosecutor's view to be admitted and of any other matters which in his view ought to be agreed;

(d) to make any amendments of any case statement given in pursuance of an order under paragraph (a) that appear to the judge to be appropriate, having regard to objections made by the accused or, if there is more than one, by any of them.

(5) The matters referred to in subsection (4)(a) are—

(a) the principal facts of the case for the prosecution;

(b) the witnesses who will speak to those facts;

(c) any exhibits relevant to those facts;

(d) any proposition of law on which the prosecutor proposes to rely;

(e) the consequences in relation to any of the counts in the indictment that appear to the prosecutor to flow from the matters falling within paragraphs (a) to (d).

(6) Where a judge has ordered the prosecutor to give a case statement and the prosecutor has complied with the order, the judge may order the accused or, if there is more than one, each of them—

(a) to give the court and the prosecutor a written statement setting out in general terms the nature of his defence and indicating the principal matters on which he takes issue with the prosecution;

(b) to give the court and the prosecutor written notice of any objections that he has to the case statement;

(c) to give the court and the prosecutor written notice of any point of law (including any point as to the admissibility of evidence) which he wishes to take, and any authority on which he intends to rely for that purpose.

(7) Where a judge has ordered the prosecutor to give notice under subsection (4)(c) and the prosecutor has complied with the order, the judge may order the accused or, if there is more than one, each of them to give the court and the prosecutor a written notice stating—

(a) the extent to which he agrees with the prosecutor as to documents and other matters to which the notice under subsection (4)(c) relates, and

(b) the reason for any disagreement.

(8) A judge making an order under subsection (6) or (7) shall warn the accused or, if there is more than one, each of them of the possible consequence under section 34 of not complying with it.

(9) If it appears to a judge that reasons given in pursuance of subsection (7) are inadequate, he shall so inform the person giving them and may require him to give further or better reasons.

(10) An order under this section may specify the time within which any specified requirement contained in it is to be complied with.

(11) An order or ruling made under this section shall have effect throughout the trial, unless it appears to the judge on application made to him that the interests of justice require him to vary or discharge it.

32.—(1) This section applies where—

(a) a judge orders a preparatory hearing, and

(b) he decides that any order which could be made under section 31(4) to (7) at the hearing should be made before the hearing.

(2) In such a case—

(a) he may make any such order before the hearing (or at the hearing), and

(b) section 31(4) to (11) shall apply accordingly.

34.—(1) Any party may depart from the case he disclosed in pursuance of a requirement imposed under section 31.

(2) Where—

(a)   a party departs from the case he disclosed in pursuance of a requirement imposed under section 31, or

(b)   a party fails to comply with such a requirement,

the judge or, with the leave of the judge, any other party may make such comment as appears to the judge or the other party (as the case may be) to be appropriate and the jury may draw such inference as appears proper.

(3)   In deciding whether to give leave the judge shall have regard—

(a)   to the extent of the departure or failure, and

(b)   to whether there is any justification for it.

(4)   Except as provided by this section no part—

(a)   of a statement given under section 31(6)(a), or

(b)   of any other information relating to the case for the accused or, if there is more than one, the case for any of them, which was given in pursuance of a requirement imposed under section 31,

may be disclosed at a stage in the trial after the jury have been sworn without the consent of the accused concerned.

Preparatory Hearings under the Criminal Justice Act 1987

The CJA 1987, enacted as a result of the 1986 report of the Fraud Trials Committee **D12.15** (Roskill Committee), provides for special 'preparatory hearings' in serious cases of fraud. The relevant provisions are contained in ss. 7 to 11 of the Act, supplemented by the CJA 1987 (Preparatory Hearings) Rules 1997 (SI 1997 No. 1051). The provisions are similar to those in the CPIA 1996, ss. 29 to 38 (see **D12.14**), and are therefore described in outline only.

By s. 7(1) of the CJA 1987, if it appears to a Crown Court judge that the evidence on an indictment 'reveals a case of fraud of such seriousness or complexity that substantial benefits are likely to accrue from a [preparatory] hearing', then he may order such a hearing. The purposes of the hearing are: (a) to identify the issues which are likely to be material to the verdict of the jury; (b) to assist their comprehension of those issues; (c) to expedite the proceedings before the jury; and (d) to assist the judge's management of the trial (s. 7(1)(a) to (d)). An order for a preparatory hearing may be made on the application of a party or of the judge's own motion (s. 7(2)). Preparatory hearings are not restricted to cases that have been transferred to the Crown Court by notice under s. 4 of the Act but may be ordered where committal proceedings have been held in the usual way, provided the statements or depositions reveal a fraud case of the requisite gravity. The trial is deemed to begin with the preparatory hearing, the accused being arraigned at the start thereof (s. 8). Any question as to the admissibility of evidence and any other question of law relating to the case may be determined at the preparatory hearing (s. 9(3).

Either before or at the preparatory hearing the judge may, under s. 9(4) of the CJA 1987, order the prosecution to do any or all of the following:

(a)   Supply the court and the accused with a 'case statement' specifying (i) the principal facts of the prosecution case; (ii) the witnesses who will speak to those facts; (iii) any exhibits relevant thereto; (iv) any proposition of law on which the prosecution propose to rely, and (v) the relevance of the aforementioned to any of the counts in the indictment.

(b)   Prepare their evidence and other explanatory material in a form that appears to the judge to be likely to aid comprehension by the jury (and to supply it in that form to the court and the accused).

(c)   Give the court and the accused notice of matters which, in their view, ought to be agreed (including, where appropriate, the truth of the contents of relevant documents).

(d)   Amend the case statement in the light of objections from the defence.

Once an order to the prosecution to supply a case statement has been complied with, the judge may, under s. 9(5), order the defence to do any or all of the following:

(a)   Give the court and the prosecution a written statement setting out in general terms the nature of the defence and indicating the principal matters on which they take issue with the prosecution.

(b)   Give the court and the prosecution notice of any objection they have to the prosecution case statement.

(c)   Inform the court and the prosecution of any point of law (including one of admissibility of evidence) which they wish to take and the authorities on which they will be relying.

(d)   Give the court and the prosecution a notice stating the extent to which they are prepared to agree the documents and other matters which the prosecution have asked to have admitted, together with the reason for any refusal to agree.

Once the prosecution has received the defence case statement, it is entitled to make use of it by re-interviewing its own witnesses and asking them questions which arise from that statement. The judge has no power to forbid the prosecution from doing so or to prescribe the way in which they may carry out such re-interviews (*Nadir* [1993] 1 WLR 1322).

As already stated, the judge at the preparatory hearing may decide any question of law or admissibility of evidence relating to the case (CJA 1987, s. 9(3)). According to *Re Gunawardena* [1990] 1 WLR 703, however, that power is in fact confined to questions related to the purposes of the preparatory hearing, as outlined in s. 7(1)(a) to (d) (see also *Hedworth* [1997] 1 Cr App R 421). Subject to the possibility of being varied on appeal to the Court of Appeal, an order or ruling made at the preparatory hearing will have effect at the trial unless it then appears to the judge, on application by a party, that the interests of justice require him to vary or discharge it (s. 9(10)). The sanction for a party departing at trial from his case as disclosed at the preparatory hearing and/or failing to comply with an order made at the hearing is that the judge may comment on the departure or failure and the jury may draw such inferences as appear to them proper (s. 10(1)). The judge may also give leave to comment to any of the other parties, but, in deciding whether such leave is appropriate, must have regard to the extent of the departure from the case as earlier disclosed and the justification for it (s. 10(2)). Save as allowed under s. 10(1) and (2), no mention may be made to the jury of any information about the defence case disclosed at the preparatory hearing (s. 10(3)). In *Southwark Crown Court, ex parte Commissioners for Customs and Excise* [1993] 1 WLR 764, the point at issue was whether the judge who held the preparatory hearing must then preside at the trial. The Divisional Court held that a change of judge between preparatory hearing and proceedings in front of the jury could only be accepted in exceptional circumstances, e.g., the death or serious illness of the original judge.

An order or ruling made by the judge at a preparatory hearing may be appealed to the Criminal Division of the Court of Appeal (s. 9(10)). Leave to appeal is required from either the judge or the court (ibid.). The judge may continue with the preparatory hearing notwithstanding that leave to appeal has been granted, but no jury may be sworn until the appeal has been determined or abandoned (s. 9(13)). The Court of Appeal may confirm, reverse or vary the decision appealed against (s. 9(14)).

PRE-TRIAL DISCLOSURE OF INFORMATION: PROSECUTION OBLIGATIONS

D12.16   Regardless of whether the trial is preceded by a review or preparatory hearing, certain obligations rest upon the parties to disclose information about the evidence they intend to call or other material which is in their possession but which they do not intend to use at trial.

Disclosure of Evidence to Be Called   The defence at trial on indictment are entitled **D12.17**
to know in advance of trial the evidence the prosecution intend to call. Most if not all
the evidence will in fact have been disclosed by the statements or depositions relied on
by the prosecution at the committal proceedings (or served with a notice of transfer). If
the prosecution wish to call evidence they did not use at committal, they are under a
duty to serve notice of additional evidence on the defence (see **D13.19**).

Disclosure of Information Not Intended to Be Used as Evidence   The prosecu- **D12.18**
tion's duty to be fair to the defence extends to disclosing information which will not be
part of their case and might even contradict their case, and of which the defence might
otherwise be unaware. This obligation is now set out in the CPIA 1996, part I (see **D6**
for details). The common law relating to disclosure continues to govern alleged offences
for which no criminal investigation began before 1 April 1997 (see **D6.2**). For details of
the common-law rules applicable before that date, reference should be made to the 1997
edition of this work.

Custody Record etc.   By para. 2.4 of Code C of the codes of practice issued under **D12.19**
the PACE 1984, s. 66, the defence are entitled to a copy of the custody record which the
custody officer is required to keep in respect of each person detained at a police station
(see **appendix 2**). Although the obligation to supply a copy of the record rests primarily
upon the police, the defence will in practice channel any request through the CPS.
Failure to supply a copy would be a breach of the Code of Practice which might lead to
the exclusion of evidence through exercise of the court's discretion under the PACE
1984, s. 78 (see **F2.4**). Similarly, if the accused was stopped in the street and searched
under the powers given to the police by the PACE 1984, s. 1, the defence are entitled
to a copy of the record of search (see s. 2(9)).

PRE-TRIAL DISCLOSURE OF INFORMATION: DEFENCE OBLIGATIONS

Historically, there was no general obligation on the defence to disclose the nature of their
case, or the evidence they proposed to call before trial. The position altered radically
with the implementation of the CPIA 1996, part I (see **D6** for details), which applies to
alleged offences for which no criminal investigation began before 1 April 1997 (see
D6.2). For alleged offences not falling within this category, reference should be made
to the 1997 edition of this work.

Defence Statement of Case for a Preparatory Hearing   Where a preparatory hearing **D12.20**
is held in a case of serious fraud, the defence may be ordered to supply a written statement
setting out *in general terms* the nature of the defence and indicating the principal matters on
which they take issue with the prosecution (CJA 1987, s. 9(5)). There is no obligation,
however, to disclose the names of the witnesses they propose calling. See **D12.15** for details.

Expert Evidence   By the PACE 1984, s. 81, Crown Court rules may require any party **D12.21**
to proceedings before the court to disclose to the other parties any expert evidence which
he proposes to adduce. The Crown Court (Advance Notice of Expert Evidence) Rules
1987 (SI 1987 No. 716) have been made under this power. Originally the rules applied
following committal but they were extended in 1997 to cover cases transferred to the
Crown Court under the CJA 1987, s. 4 (serious or complex fraud), or the CJA 1991, s. 53
(child witnesses), or in respect of which a voluntary bill of indictment has been preferred.

The rules provide that, as soon as practicable after committal for trial (or transfer), any
party intending to rely on expert evidence (whether of fact or opinion) must, unless he
has already done so, provide the other parties with a written statement of any finding or
opinion which he proposes to adduce by way of such evidence (r. 3(1)(a)). On request,
he must also supply a copy of the record of any 'observation, test, calculation or other

procedure' on which the finding or opinion is based or, if it is more practicable, he must allow reasonable opportunity to examine such a record (r. 3(1)(b)). Entitlement to the information referred to above may be waived by the other party (r. 3(2)). Where there are reasonable grounds for believing that compliance with the rules would lead to intimidation of witnesses or interference with the course of justice, disclosure need not be made but notice must be served on the other parties both that the evidence is being withheld and of the grounds for withholding it (r. 4(1) and (2)). Otherwise failure to comply with the rules means that the expert evidence will be admissible at trial only with leave of the court (r. 5).

Nominally, the rules apply both to the prosecution and defence but they have little relevance to the prosecution because prosecution expert evidence (like the ordinary prosecution evidence) will normally be disclosed as a result of committal proceedings, and there is no need under the rules to repeat disclosure which has already been made (see r. 3(1)). Also, r. 3(1) makes a saving for expert evidence to be adduced in relation to sentencing (e.g., medical or psychiatric reports). Thus, expert medical evidence to be adduced on the question of guilt or innocence must (like any other expert evidence) be disclosed, but such evidence need not be disclosed if it goes only to sentencing.

PRIVATE MEETING BETWEEN JUDGE AND COUNSEL

D12.22 Before or during the trial, counsel may, with the judge's agreement, see him privately about the case. The usual purpose of counsel seeing the judge is to obtain guidance about appropriate pleas and the likely sentence (see **D10.43** for consideration of communications between judge and counsel in the context of so-called 'plea bargaining'). However, there may be matters other than plea and sentence which counsel wish to discuss with the judge privately, and it is therefore necessary to consider from a general viewpoint the rules governing such discussions.

The basic principles are contained in the third of Lord Parker CJ's observations about plea bargaining given in the course of his judgment in *Turner* [1970] 2 QB 321 at p. 324. The observations are set out in full at **D10.43**. First, they affirm that freedom of access between counsel and judge is essential. This is because there may be matters calling for communication or discussion which cannot, in the interests of the client, be mentioned in open court. Two examples are given, namely, (a) where defence counsel wishes to tell the judge that the accused (unbeknown to himself) is suffering from a terminal illness, and (b) where both counsel wish to discuss whether it would be proper for the prosecution to accept a plea of guilty to a lesser offence. But, secondly, it is imperative that so far as possible justice be administered in open court. Counsel should therefore ask to see the judge only when it is felt to be really necessary. Equally, the judge should be careful to treat communications made to him out of court as private only when fairness to the accused so requires. Thirdly, any private discussion that does take place should be between the judge and both prosecuting and defence counsel, regardless of who asked for the meeting. If the defence solicitor is in court he should also be allowed to attend if he wishes.

In *Llewellyn* (1978) 67 Cr App R 149 the trial judge reported that he had asked counsel to come to see him so that they could discuss whether the trial should proceed on a single count for conspiracy or on two conspiracy counts as in the indictment or on charges of substantive offences. Roskill LJ stated that there was 'nothing which justified the judge in sending for counsel'. If it were desired to discuss what counts should be tried, that could have been done either at a pre-trial review or in open court immediately before empanelment of the jury. The issues would then have been aired publicly and a full shorthand note taken which, *inter alia*, might assist the Court of Appeal should the judge's decison later be challenged on appeal. Lawton LJ, in *Coward* (1979) 70 Cr App R 70, went still further in his disapproval of private discussions, implying that, at least in the normal case, they are inappropriate even for guidance about whether certain proffered pleas ought to be accepted by the prosecution. However, his lordship's dictum contradicts one of the examples given by Lord Parker CJ in *Turner* of when access to the judge is essential, and it is submitted that counsel ought to be able (if they wish) to sound the judge privately before reaching an arrangement about what pleas are acceptable to both sides. Such private discussion may avoid the embarrassment of the judge in open court disapproving what counsel have thought to be right.

As to the mechanics of counsel seeing the judge, first, the initiative for the meeting should normally come from counsel, at least where the subject-matter of the discussion is to be the likely sentence (per Watkins LJ in *Cullen* (1984) 81 Cr App R 17 at p. 19). Secondly, a shorthand writer should be present so as to avoid the Court of Appeal later having to resolve conflicts of recollection as to what occurred (ibid.). The importance of having a note is illustrated by the facts of *Cullen*, which were that the judge thought he had promised counsel that the sentence would not take the form of *immediate* custody whereas counsel thought that he had simply been promised a non-custodial sentence. The Court of Appeal could not be sure who was right. Accordingly, they had to give the benefit of the doubt to the appellant and quash his suspended prison sentence because it was inconsistent with the assumed promise to deal with him non-custodially.

The need for a record of the meeting between judge and counsel has been stressed by the Court of Appeal in a number of cases. In *Smith* [1990] 1 WLR 1311, Russell LJ put it this way (at p. 1314B–C):

> Of course, on the authority of the well known case of *Turner* [1970] 2 QB 321, in some circumstances it is permissible for counsel to see the judge in his room to ascertain his reaction to possible sentencing options open to him. But that should never occur, as has been said on almost innumerable occasions in this court, in the absence of a shorthand note-taker or, alternatively, in the absence of some recording device. In this case there was neither a shorthand writer present nor a recording device.

His lordship went on to quote with approval the words of Mustill LJ in *Harper-Taylor* (1988) 138 NLJ 80 at pp. 80–1, which encapsulate the problems posed by 'unnecessary visits to the judge's room':

> Since we regard the discussion in the judge's room as the source of all the subsequent entanglements, some general observations on the practice of meeting the judge in his private room may be appropriate. A first principle of criminal law is that justice is done in public, for all to see and hear. By this standard a meeting in the judge's room is anomalous: the essence, and indeed the purpose, being that neither the defendant nor the jury nor the public are there to hear what is going on. Undeniably, there are circumstances where the public must be excluded. Equally, the jury cannot always be kept in court throughout. The withdrawal of the proceedings into private, without even the defendant being there, is another matter. It is true, as this court stated in *Turner* [1970] 2 QB 321 at p. 326, that there must be freedom of access between counsel and the judge when there are matters calling for communications or discussions of such a nature that counsel cannot in the interests of his client mention them in open court. Criminal trials are so various that a list of situations where an approach to the judge is permissible would only mislead; but it must be clear that communications should never take place unless there is no alternative.
>
> Apart from the question of principle, seeing the judge in private creates risks of more than one kind, as the present case has shown. The need to solve an immediate practical problem may combine with the more relaxed atmosphere of the private room to blur the formal outlines of the trial. Again, if the object of withdrawing the case from open court is to maintain a degree of confidence, as it plainly must be, there is room for misunderstanding about how far the confidence is to extend; and, in particular, there is a risk that counsel and solicitors for the other parties may hear something said to the judge which they would rather not hear, putting them into a state of conflict between their duties to their clients, and their obligation to maintain the confidentiality of the private room.

The absence of the defendant is also a potential source of trouble. He has to learn what the judge has said at second hand, and may afterwards complain (rightly or not) that he was not given an accurate account. Equally, he cannot hear what his counsel has said to the judge, and hence cannot intervene to correct a misstatement or an excess of authority: a factor which may not only be a source of unfairness to the defendant, but which may also deprive the prosecution of the opportunity to contend that admissions made in open court in the presence of the client and not repudiated by him may be taken to have been made with his authority.

The last of the problems mentioned in that passage (the absence of the accused from the private meeting) figured prominently in *Agar* [1990] 2 All ER 442. A was charged with possession of amphetamines with intent to supply. His defence was that the police had planted the drugs on him. It was part of his case that X (a police informer) had telephoned him so that he would arrive while the police were at X's house. On the initiative of prosecution counsel, both counsel went to see the judge in his private room. The judge, on being told that X was a police informer, ruled that defence counsel was not to put questions which might reveal X's status as an informer. He also forbade counsel to reveal to anyone, including his client and his instructing solicitor, the matters which had been discussed in the judge's private room. The Court of Appeal upheld A's appeal on the ground that his counsel should not have been restricted in cross-examination in the way that he was. As far as the prohibition on communication with the accused was concerned, Mustill LJ said this (at pp. 324–5):

> This makes it unnecessary to express a conclusion on the second ground of appeal which rests on the fact that there were proceedings in the private room which counsel was forbidden to disclose to his client. We are very much inclined to think, however, that this would in itself have been a ground upon which we would have been compelled to intervene. We recognise very well the problems which face a judge who is called upon without notice to rule upon a problem brought before him by counsel who have thought it appropriate to act in private; the risk of hindsight for an appellate court, looking at the case at leisure on paper, is obvious; the fact that counsel for the defence may already have been fatally compromised in his professional relationship with the appellant by the well-intentioned volunteering of confidential information by prosecuting counsel needs no emphasis.

> All this being said, we believe that the course adopted was mistaken. As this court has repeatedly emphasised, discussions in the judge's room, with the defendant absent, are an expedient of last resort. This appeal demonstrates once again how things can go wrong, and how a real sensation of injustice may be engendered in the absent client. This is not to say that a solution was easy to find, but we are sure that with some resource it would have been possible to deal with the matter in open court, if necessary at the price of successive objections and applications in the absence of the jury, whilst honouring the spirit of the two conflicting grounds of public policy emphasised in the cases which we have cited.

> Whether, if this objection had stood alone, we should have felt impelled to quash the conviction in the interest of underlining the principle of open justice is a difficult question. As we have already said, we are inclined to think that we would have been so impelled, but in the circumstances it is not a question which we need answer, given our conclusion on the first point.

PRESENCE OF THE ACCUSED AT TRIAL

D12.23 The attendance of the accused at the Crown Court is secured by the magistrates remanding him in custody or on bail when they commit him for trial. If, having been bailed, he fails to attend on the day notified to him as the day of trial, a bench warrant may be issued forthwith for his arrest under the Bail Act 1976, s. 7.

The accused must be present at the commencement of a trial on indictment in order to plead. It is then the almost invariable practice for him to be present throughout his trial.

The implication of this rule is that the defendant must not only be physically present, but must have the proceedings interpreted to him if that is necessary (*Kunnath* v *The State* [1993] 1 WLR 1315). It also means that the judge ought not to deal with matters which in reality constitute part of the trial proceedings in the absence of counsel for the defence. For example, in *Coolledge* [1996] Crim LR 748, an appeal was allowed because the judge inquired of a witness in chambers and in the absence of defence counsel as to the reason why he had failed to attend court to give evidence. The witness told the judge that he had been threatened by the defendant, and the judge then counselled the witness as to how he should give his evidence at trial. The Court of Appeal held that counsel should not have been excluded since the procedure went beyond a mere inquiry, and affected the conduct of the trial itself, which was therefore tainted.

Notwithstanding the general rule, the accused's presence may, however, be dispensed with in exceptional circumstances (per Lord Reading CJ in *Lee Kun* [1916] 1 KB 337 at p. 341). The situations in which the court may be justified in proceeding without the accused are as follows.

Misbehaviour by the Accused If the accused behaves in an unruly fashion in the **D12.24** dock by shouting out etc. and thus makes it impracticable for the hearing to continue in his presence, the judge may order that he be removed from court and that the trial proceed without him (*Lee Kun* [1916] 1 KB 337). It is submitted that the accused may similarly be removed if he is apparently trying to intimidate jurors or witnesses by his conduct. In practice, the judge would warn the accused before taking the extreme step of barring him from court. Also, it may be appropriate to allow him to return to the dock at a later stage if he undertakes not to repeat his unruly behaviour. Unruly behaviour may also be deterred by holding the accused to be guilty of a contempt in the face of the court and sentencing him for that (or warning him that proceedings for contempt are a possibility).

In *Brown* [1998] 2 Cr App R 364, the Court of Appeal dealt with the situation where a defendant on trial for sexual offences appeared to abuse his right to represent himself and cross-examine the complainant. Their lordships emphasised that if the defendant sought by his dress, bearing, manner or questions to dominate, intimidate or humiliate the complainant, or if it were reasonably apprehended that he would seek to do so, the judge should order that a screen be erected, in addition to exercising control over the way in which he cross-examined the complainant.

Voluntary Absence of the Accused If the accused, having been present for the **D12.25** commencement of his trial, later voluntarily absents himself (i.e. by escaping from custody or by failing to surrender having been bailed by the court for the period of an adjournment), then the judge has a discretion to complete the trial in his absence (*Jones (No. 2)* [1972] 1 WLR 887). Should he be convicted, sentence may also be passed in his absence (ibid.). Whether to proceed in the accused's absence must, however, be a matter for the judge's discretion. The alternative is to discharge the jury from giving a verdict, thus allowing a retrial to take place before a different jury once the accused's presence has been secured. Whether or not the court proceeds in the accused's absence, the judge may and almost certainly will issue a warrant for his arrest under the Bail Act 1976, s. 7.

The longer a trial has lasted, the more likely it is that the judge will exercise his discretion against discharging the jury. For example, in *Jones (No. 2)* [1972] 1 WLR 887, J and seven co-accused had been charged with conspiracy to defraud and fraudulent conversion. The trial began on 26 June 1970; on 22 July, the prosecution closed their case, and on 27 July the judge ruled against submissions of no case to answer made on J's behalf. On the next day, J failed to appear. On 5 August, at the time when, in the normal course of events, counsel would have begun to present J's defence, an application was made to discharge the jury from returning verdicts in his case. It was conceded by the prosecution that the trial should proceed in J's absence only if his absence was voluntary. Judge Gillis ruled: (a) that the ordinary inference to be drawn from an accused's non-appearance is that he has voluntarily absented himself and therefore the burden is on the defence to show involuntary absence not vice versa; (b) that, in any event, on the facts the prosecution had shown beyond reasonable doubt that the absence was voluntary, and (c) in all the circumstances the trial ought to proceed. The judge's decision is unreported as such but was considered by the Court of Appeal in the course of an application by J for leave to appeal against conviction out of time. Roskill LJ, quoting para. 61 of the Seventh Report of the Criminal Law Revision Committee, held (pp. 890-1) that a judge undoubtedly has power to continue a case in the absence of the accused, but the power should be used sparingly and only when this would not prejudice the defence. His lordship also referred with approval to the Australian case of *Abrahams* (1895) 21 VLR 343 where Williams J stated that any application to proceed in the accused's absence would in all probability be refused unless the accused elects to be absent and absents himself through caprice or malice or for the purpose of embarrassing the trial. Material was put before the Court of Appeal to indicate that J had been threatened on the night before he absented himself, but the evidence as to that was 'unparticularised' and did not cast doubt on the trial judge's decision that J's absence was not induced by duress. Thus, the only question was whether the judge had properly exercised his discretion to continue the trial in the voluntary absence of the accused, and the court held that he plainly had done so.

In *O'Nione* [1986] Crim LR 342, O'N absconded on the third day of his trial for theft by pickpocketing at a stage when prosecution witnesses from abroad – who might not have returned for retrial - had already testified. The Court of Appeal upheld the trial judge's decision to allow the trial to continue. Their lordships said that they would have made the same decision as the trial judge had they been sitting at first instance.

The position of defence legal representatives when a trial continues in the absence of an accused who has absconded was considered in *Shaw* [1980] 1 WLR 1526. The judge may *not* deem the accused's instructions to have been withdrawn and require counsel and solicitor to withdraw from the case. Whether counsel should continue to act and what part he may legitimately play in the proceedings are essentially matters for him having regard to the guidance given in the Code of Conduct of the Bar and the circumstances of the particular case (per Kilner Brown J in *Shaw* at p. 1529G). The most the judge may do is invite counsel to assist the court in the manner suggested by what is now para 16.3 of standards applicable to criminal cases in annexe F to the code.

Where an accused absconds and is convicted in his absence, the further question arises of whether his legal representatives (assuming they have chosen not to withdraw) may give notice of appeal on his behalf. A negative answer to the question was given in *Jones (No. 1)* [1971] 2 QB 456. The circumstances of the first instance trial have been set out above. Prior to absconding, J had told his solicitors that he intended to appeal against the judge's ruling that there was a case to answer. After conviction and sentence, J's solicitors, purporting to act upon the instructions they had been given, served notice of appeal. The Court of Appeal held that, save in the most exceptional circumstances, the proper time to take instructions on a possible appeal is *after* conviction. Therefore, what J said before absconding did not authorise the solicitors to prosecute an appeal; the notice they had served and purportedly signed on J's behalf was therefore invalid, and no proceedings could be taken upon it. Some 10 months after the above events J was located in Denmark and extradited back to England. Application was made to appeal out of time against conviction and sentence. In *Jones (No. 2)* [1972] 1 WLR 887, the Court of Appeal, having considered whether Judge Gillis's decision to continue the trial in the accused's absence was a proper one (see above for Roskill LJ's comments on that), further held that the leave sought should be refused. If an accused who has absconded, been convicted in absence and is eventually arrested were able to reopen his case before the Court of Appeal, perhaps seeking to adduce before that court the evidence that would have been before the jury had he not absconded, then a premium would be placed upon absconding and others would be tempted to do the same. Thus, the net effect of the two *Jones* decisions is that an absconder convicted in his absence is virtually precluded from appealing against his conviction or sentence since (a) his solicitors will not be authorised to serve notice of appeal within time, and (b) the Court of Appeal, in its discretion, will almost certainly refuse leave to appeal out of time.

Sickness of the Accused   If the accused's absence from court is for reasons beyond   **D12.26**
his control, the trial may *not* continue in his absence unless he consents (see, for example, the dicta of Williams J in *Abrahams* (1895) 21 VLR 343, adopted by Roskill LJ in *Jones* (*No. 2*) [1972] 1 WLR 887). The obvious and common example of involuntary absence is sickness. Thus, should the accused become ill during the course of his trial, the judge must either adjourn the case until he recovers or – if that is impractical having regard to the likely period of the illness – discharge the jury (*Howson* (1981) 74 Cr App R 172). The above proposition is, however, subject to one possible though limited exception mentioned in *Howson*. The exception is that, if there are several accused and one falls sick, the trial may continue in that accused's absence provided that the evidence and proceedings in his absence relate entirely to the cases against his co-accused and have no possible bearing on his case. The facts of *Howson* were that H and 28 co-accused were charged with riot and other offences of violence. H was present for the arraignment and the prosecution opening speech but then had to go into hospital and was absent from court throughout all the prosecution evidence. He was present for the defence cases but even then seemed in too much pain to concentrate properly. His counsel applied unsuccessfully for the jury to be discharged from giving a verdict on him, and he was convicted. The Court of Appeal quashed the conviction since H's absence had been involuntary and the proceedings in his absence had related to the case against him, not just to his co-accused. The decision also indicates that it is not enough for an accused to be physically present if he is too unwell to pay proper attention to the proceedings and give instructions to his legal representatives.

Death of the Accused   Where the accused dies before the trial is completed, formal   **D12.27**
evidence of death should be given, and endorsed upon the indictment. This may, for example, be the evidence of the officer in the case that he has seen and identified the remains of the man named in the indictment. If such evidence is not available, then other evidence such as a certified copy of the entry in the register of deaths will suffice.

ATTENDANCE OF WITNESSES

The police normally undertake the task of informing the prosecution witnesses when   **D12.28**
they are needed; it is for defence solicitors and/or the accused to ensure that their witnesses know. Since most cases are not given a fixed trial date but merely take their turn to come into the list, the notice given to witnesses is often unacceptably short. The accused himself, if he is on bail, should keep in touch with his solicitors who will inform him as soon as they know the date of trial. Once the case is in the warned list (i.e. it could come up at any time), it is advisable for him to telephone his solicitors daily. Most solicitors will in any event send a lexigram to reach the accused's address by at least the night before the hearing.

Where the prosecution or defence wish to secure the attendance of a witness, but are not satisfied that he will attend voluntarily, they can apply for a witness summons. The procedure is set out in the Criminal Procedure (Attendance of Witnesses) Act 1965, ss. 2 to 4, which are set out at **D12.29** (as amended by the CPIA 1996). These provisions apply in respect of alleged offences where an investigation did not commence before 1 April 1997. For the position in respect of offences which do not fall within this category, reference should be made to the 1997 edition of this work.

D12.29 ***Punishment for Failure to Attend*** A person who 'without just excuse' disobeys a witness order or summons requiring him to attend court is guilty of contempt of the court he fails to attend (Criminal Procedure (Attendance of Witnesses) Act 1965, s. 3(1)). He may be summarily punished as if he had committed a contempt in the court's face (ibid.). The maximum penalty is three months' imprisonment (s. 3(2)). The existence of a 'just excuse' will not be lightly inferred. Witnesses are required to submit even to very substantial inconvenience in their business and private lives. Culpable forgetfulness can certainly never amount to a 'just excuse' (*Lennock* (1993) 97 Cr App R 228). However, the prosecution must prove beyond reasonable doubt that proper notification of the trial date was given (*Abdulaziz* [1989] Crim LR 717).

Criminal Procedure (Attendance of Witnesses) Act 1965, ss. 2 to 4

2.—(1) This section applies where the Crown Court is satisfied that—
    (a) a person is likely to be able to give evidence likely to be material evidence, or produce any document or thing likely to be material evidence, for the purpose of any criminal proceedings before the Crown Court, and
    (b) the person will not voluntarily attend as a witness or will not voluntarily produce the document or thing.
    (2) In such a case the Crown Court shall, subject to the following provisions of this section, issue a summons (a witness summons) directed to the person concerned and requiring him to—
    (a) attend before the Crown Court at the time and place stated in the summons, and
    (b) give the evidence or produce the document or thing.
    (3) A witness summons may only be issued under this section on an application; and the Crown Court may refuse to issue the summons if any requirement relating to the application is not fulfilled.
    (4) Where a person has been committed for trial for any offence to which the proceedings concerned relate, an application must be made as soon as is reasonably practicable after the committal.
    (5) Where the proceedings concerned have been transferred to the Crown Court, an application must be made as soon as is reasonably practicable after the transfer.
    (6) Where the proceedings concerned relate to an offence in relation to which a bill of indictment has been preferred under the authority of section 2(2)(b) of the Administration of Justice (Miscellaneous Provisions) Act 1933 (bill preferred by direction of Court of Appeal, or by direction or with consent of judge) an application must be made as soon as is reasonably practicable after the bill was preferred.
    (7) An application must be made in accordance with Crown Court rules; and different provision may be made for different cases or descriptions of case.
    (8) Crown Court rules—
    (a) may, in such cases as the rules may specify, require an application to be made by a party to the case;
    (b) may, in such cases as the rules may specify, require the service of notice of an application on the person to whom the witness summons is proposed to be directed;
    (c) may, in such cases as the rules may specify, require an application to be supported by an affidavit containing such matters as the rules may stipulate;
    (d) may, in such cases as the rules may specify, make provision for enabling the person to whom the witness summons is proposed to be directed to be present or represented at the hearing of the application for the witness summons.
    (9) Provision contained in Crown Court rules by virtue of subsection (8)(c) above may in particular require an affidavit to—
    (a) set out any charge on which the proceedings concerned are based;
    (b) specify any stipulated evidence, document or thing in such a way as to enable the directed person to identify it;

(c)   specify grounds for believing that the directed person is likely to be able to give any stipulated evidence or produce any stipulated document or thing;

(d)   specify grounds for believing that any stipulated evidence is likely to be material evidence;

(e)   specify grounds for believing that any stipulated document or thing is likely to be material evidence.

(10)   In subsection (9) above—

(a)   references to any stipulated evidence, document or thing are to any evidence, document or thing whose giving or production is proposed to be required by the witness summons;

(b)   references to the directed person are to the person to whom the witness summons is proposed to be directed.

2A.   A witness summons which is issued under section 2 above and which requires a person to produce a document or thing as mentioned in section 2(2) above may also require him to produce the document or thing—

(a)   at a place stated in the summons, and

(b)   at a time which is so stated and precedes that stated under section 2(2) above, for inspection by the person applying for the summons.

2B.—(1)   If—

(a)   a document or thing is produced in pursuance of a requirement imposed by a witness summons under section 2A above,

(b)   the person applying for the summons concludes that a requirement imposed by the summons under section 2(2) above is no longer needed, and

(c)   he accordingly applies to the Crown Court for a direction that the summons shall be of no further effect,

the court may direct accordingly.

(2)   An application under this section must be made in accordance with Crown Court rules; and different provision may be made for different cases or descriptions of case.

(3)   Crown Court rules may, in such cases as the rules may specify, require the effect of a direction under this section to be notified to the person to whom the summons is directed.

2C.—(1)   If a witness summons issued under section 2 above is directed to a person who—

(a)   applies to the Crown Court,

(b)   satisfies the court that he was not served with notice of the application to issue the summons and that he was neither present nor represented at the hearing of the application, and

(c)   satisfies the court that he cannot give any evidence likely to be material evidence or, as the case may be, produce any document or thing likely to be material evidence, the court may direct that the summons shall be of no effect.

(2)   For the purposes of subsection (1) above it is immaterial—

(a)   whether or not Crown Court rules require the person to be served with notice of the application to issue the summons;

(b)   whether or not Crown Court rules enable the person to be present or represented at the hearing of the application.

(3)   In subsection (1)(b) above 'served' means—

(a)   served in accordance with Crown Court rules, in a case where such rules require the person to be served with notice of the application to issue the summons;

(b)   served in such way as appears reasonable to the court to which the application is made under this section, in any other case.

(4)   The Crown Court may refuse to make a direction under this section if any requirement relating to the application under this section is not fulfilled.

(5)   An application under this section must be made in accordance with Crown Court rules; and different provision may be made for different cases or descriptions of case.

(6)   Crown Court rules may, in such cases as the rules may specify, require the service of notice of an application under this section on the person on whose application the witness summons was issued.

(7)   Crown Court rules may, in such cases as the rules may specify, require that where—

(a)   a person applying under this section can produce a particular document or thing,
but
(b)   he seeks to satisfy the court that the document or thing is not likely to be material evidence,
he must arrange for the document or thing to be available at the hearing of the application.

(8)   Where a direction is made under this section that a witness summons shall be of no effect, the person on whose application the summons was issued may be ordered to pay the whole or any part of the costs of the application under this section.

(9)   Any costs payable under an order made under subsection (8) above shall be taxed by the proper officer of the court, and payment of those costs shall be enforceable in the same manner as an order for payment of costs made by the High Court in a civil case or as a sum adjudged summarily to be paid as a civil debt.

2D.   For the purpose of any criminal proceedings before it, the Crown Court may of its own motion issue a summons (a witness summons) directed to a person and requiring him to—
(a)   attend before the court at the time and place stated in the summons, and
(b)   give evidence, or produce any document or thing specified in the summons.

2E.—(1)   If a witness summons issued under section 2D above is directed to a person who—
(a)   applies to the Crown Court, and
(b)   satisfies the court that he cannot give any evidence likely to be material evidence or, as the case may be, produce any document or thing likely to be material evidence,
the court may direct that the summons shall be of no effect.

(2)   The Crown Court may refuse to make a direction under this section if any requirement relating to the application under this section is not fulfilled.

(3)   An application under this section must be made in accordance with Crown Court rules; and different provision may be made for different cases or descriptions of case.

(4)   Crown Court rules may, in such cases as the rules may specify, require that where—
(a)   a person applying under this section can produce a particular document or thing,
but
(b)   he seeks to satisfy the court that the document or thing is not likely to be material evidence,
he must arrange for the document or thing to be available at the hearing of the application.

3.—(1)   Any person who without just excuse disobeys a witness summons requiring him to attend before any court shall be guilty of contempt of that court and may be punished summarily by that court as if his contempt had been committed in the face of the court.

(1A)   Any person who without just excuse disobeys a requirement made by any court under section 2A above shall be guilty of contempt of that court and may be punished summarily by that court as if his contempt had been committed in the face of the court.

(2)   No person shall by reason of any disobedience mentioned in subsection (1) or (1A) above be liable to imprisonment for a period exceeding three months.

4.   [Describes the powers available to ensure compliance with a witness summons.]

The above sections are reproduced as amended *inter alia* by the CPIA 1996, ss. 66 and 67, and apply in that form in relation to any proceedings for the purpose of which no witness summons had been issued under s. 2 before 1 April 1999 (Criminal Procedure and Investigations Act 1996 (Appointed Day No. 9) Order (SI 1999 No. 718)). For proceedings to which the previous version of the statute applies, reference should be made to the 1998 edition of this work.

EVIDENCE THROUGH TELEVISION LINK

D12.30   The CJA 1988, s. 32, makes provision for the attendance of witnesses to be dispensed with in certain cases and for evidence to be given by way of a television link.

Criminal Justice Act 1988, s. 32

(1)   A person other than the accused may give evidence through a live television link in proceedings to which subsection (1A) below applies if—

    (a)   the witness is outside the United Kingdom; or

    (b)   the witness is a child, or is to be cross-examined following the admission under section 32A below of a video recording of testimony from him, and the offence is one to which subsection (2) below applies,

but evidence may not be so given without the leave of the court.

    (1A)   This subsection applies—

    (a)   to trials on indictment, appeals to the Criminal Division of the Court of Appeal and hearings of references under section 9 of the Criminal Appeal Act 1995; and

    (b)   to proceedings in youth courts and appeals to the Crown Court arising out of such proceedings and hearings of references under section 11 of the Criminal Appeal Act 1995 so arising.

    (2)   This subsection applies—

    (a)   to an offence which involves an assault on, or injury or a threat of injury to, a person;

    (b)   to an offence under section 1 of the Children and Young Persons Act 1933 (cruelty to persons under 16);

    (c)   to an offence under the Sexual Offences Act 1956, the Indecency with Children Act 1960, the Sexual Offences Act 1967, section 54 of the Criminal Law Act 1977 or the Protection of Children Act 1978; and

    (d)   to an offence which consists of attempting or conspiring to commit, or of aiding, abetting, counselling, procuring or inciting the commission of, an offence falling within paragraph (a), (b) or (c) above.

    (3)   A statement made on oath by a witness outside the United Kingdom and given in evidence through a link by virtue of this section shall be treated for the purposes of section 1 of the Perjury Act 1911 as having been made in the proceedings in which it is given in evidence.

    (3A) and (3B)   [Provision, in the case of proceedings before a youth court, for justices to sit outside the court-house where no suitable facilities exist there.]

    (3C)   Where—

    (a)   the court gives leave for a person to give evidence through a live television link, and

    (b)   the leave is given by virtue of subsection (1)(b) above,

then, subject to subsection (3D) below, the person concerned may not give evidence otherwise than through a live television link.

    (3D)   In a case falling within subsection (3C) above the court may give permission for the person to give evidence otherwise than through a live television link if it appears to the court to be in the interests of justice to give such permission.

    (3E)   Permission may be given under subsection (3D) above—

    (a)   on an application by a party to the case, or

    (b)   of the court's own motion;

but no application may be made under paragraph (a) above unless there has been a material change of circumstances since the leave was given by virtue of subsection (1)(b) above.

For the provision made in respect of such evidence under the Crown Court Rules 1982 (rr. 23A and 23B), see **appendix 1**; modification apply to those rules where a person is sent for trial under the CDA 1998, s. 51 (see the Crown Court (Modification) Rules 1998 (SI 1998 No. 3047)). The provisions of s. 32 insofar as they concern witnesses outside the United Kingdom (s. 32(1)(a) and (3)) are in force only for the following proceedings:

(a)   proceedings for murder, manslaughter or any other offence consisting of the killing of any person; and

(b)   proceedings being conducted by the Director of the Serious Fraud Office under the CJA 1987, s. 1(5), or any other proceedings in which a notice of transfer has been given under s. 4 of that Act (see **D8.6**).

As far as child witnesses are concerned (s. 32(1)(b)), the provisions apply to the offences specified in s. 32(2). In *McAndrew-Bingham* [1999] 1 WLR 1897, it was held that the offence of attempted child abduction came within the scope of s. 32(2)(a), as it was an offence 'which involves an assault on, or injury or threat of injury to a person'. Their lordships took the view that the section ought to be construed purposively. They agreed with the comment of Professor Birch on *Lee* [1996] Crim LR 412 that there were sound policy reasons for giving the definition a broad rather than a narrow and literal interpretation and extending the use of video and live-link facilities 'wherever the child is likely to be traumatised by confrontation with the accused'.

For the extension of the use of video recordings of children's evidence effected by the CJA 1988, s. 32A, see **F16.21**.

SECTION D13: TRIAL ON INDICTMENT: THE PROSECUTION CASE

Following a not guilty plea and the empanelling of a jury, the trial proper commences **D13.1** with the prosecution case. That falls into two parts, namely (a) counsel's opening speech and (b) the evidence.

OPENING SPEECH

There is little direct authority on what should or should not be said by prosecuting counsel in his opening address to the jury. By convention, he explains the legal elements of the offence charged and outlines the evidence he proposes to call. He also explains to the jury the burden and standard of proof. The extent to which counsel deals in detail with points of law that may arise during the trial or possible defences open to the accused is a matter for his discretion, depending on the circumstances of the particular case. For example, if the accused in a statement to the police has raised a particular defence (e.g., self-defence on a charge of assault), it may be advisable in the prosecution opening to indicate to the jury when the defence is available and whether the burden of proof in relation to the issue rests on the defence or on the prosecution. If counsel deals with a matter of law it is usual to remind the jury that matters of law are ultimately for the judge, and that counsel's remarks should therefore be disregarded insofar as they differ from the judge's directions.

Omission of Evidence Objected to by Defence If defence counsel has intimated **D13.2** that there is an objection to some of the prosecution evidence disclosed on the committal statements, no reference should be made to that evidence in opening. If the opening speech cannot be made coherently without reference to the disputed evidence then the judge should be invited to determine whether or not the evidence is admissible as a preliminary issue. See also **D13.18**.

References to Inadmissible Evidence Should counsel refer in opening to evidence **D13.3** which turns out to be inadmissible or which for any other reason is not called, that is not in itself a ground for quashing an accused's conviction (*Jackson* [1953] 1 WLR 591). However, depending on the extent to which the accused may have been prejudiced by counsel's remarks, the defence could argue that the conviction is rendered unsafe or unsatisfactory. A relevant consideration is how the irregularity was dealt with in the summing-up. If the judge compounded counsel's original error by treating what counsel said as if it had been evidence, then the chances of an appeal succeeding are enhanced (see dicta of Lord Goddard CJ in *Jackson*). In fact, both defence counsel and the judge are likely to point out to the jury that what prosecuting counsel has said is simply not evidence. If the defence – as a result of prosecuting counsel's improper remarks – applied unsuccessfully for the jury to be discharged, the refusal to discharge may be used as a ground of appeal. However, the Court of Appeal is generally reluctant to interfere with a trial judge's exercise of discretion in respect of discharging a jury (see **D11.18** *et seq.*).

References to Plea of Guilty by Co-accused How counsel in opening (and later **D13.4** the judge in summing-up) should deal with pleas of guilty entered by a co-accused may on occasion cause difficulty. Almost certainly, presentation of the evidence against the accused on trial will involve reference to the actions of the person who is in fact his co-accused, whether or not he is described as such to the jury. Since the co-accused will *ex hypothesi* not be before the court, and since the jury will inevitably speculate about why he is not, it is generally desirable to inform them as soon as possible of the reason.

This avoids unnecessary mystification of the jury. Therefore, if the defence consent, the jury may be told in opening of the co-accused's plea. It has been implied that they may be told of it even if the defence do not consent. In *Moore* (1956) 40 Cr App R 50 Lord Goddard CJ said (at pp. 53–4): 'When two people are indicted together for a criminal offence and one pleads guilty and the other does not, it is the commonest thing in the world to tell the jury, as was done in this case, "You must not pay any attention to the fact that the other man has pleaded guilty". Even if the plea has not been taken in the presence of the jury, it is very difficult to avoid telling the jury in some way that the other person has pleaded guilty.' However, the admissibility of convictions of persons other than the accused on trial (including guilty pleas by co-accused) is now governed by s. 74(1) of the PACE 1984 subject to s. 78 of the same Act (exclusion of evidence on grounds of unfairness). Therefore, it seems that, if the defence object to the jury knowing of the co-accused's plea, prosecuting counsel should deal with the objection in the same way as he would any other objection to proposed evidence (i.e., not mention it in opening). Whether or not the evidence later becomes admissible as part of the prosecution case will depend on whether it is relevant to an issue in the proceedings and, if it is so relevant, whether its admission would nonetheless have such an unfair effect on the trial that it ought to be excluded (see cases such as *Robertson* [1987] QB 920, *Kempster* [1989] 1 WLR 1125 and *Marlow* [1997] Crim LR 457). Unless and until the judge rules the evidence of the co-accused's guilty plea to be admissible, his absence from the dock should be dealt with by a formula such as: 'X, of whom you may hear mention in the course of this case, is not before you and is none of your concern'.

D13.5 ***Emotive Language***   In making his speeches to the jury, prosecuting counsel must remember his role as a minister of justice who ought not to strive over-zealously for a conviction (see **D12.4**). He should therefore avoid using emotive language liable to prejudice the jury against the accused. Avory J's oft-quoted description of prosecuting counsel as a minister of justice was given in the course of an appeal against a conviction for unlawful sexual intercourse with a girl under 16, one of the grounds of which was counsel's address to the jury (see *Banks* [1916] 2 KB 621). According to Avory J, counsel made a number of observations 'calculated to prejudice the jury'. In particular, he appealed to them to: 'protect young girls from men like the prisoner'. Although the appeal failed, the use of such language was criticised by his lordship as being 'not in good taste or strictly in accordance with the character which prosecuting counsel should always bear in mind'. It is not clear from the judgment whether the remarks objected to were made in the course of an opening or closing speech, but the same principle clearly applies to both speeches.

WITNESSES THE PROSECUTION SHOULD CALL OR TENDER

General Rule: Witnesses on Back of Indictment

D13.6   Having opened his case, prosecuting counsel calls his witnesses and reads out any written statements admissible under exceptions to the rule against hearsay. As a matter of practice, he should call (or, if appropriate, read the statements of) all witnesses whose names are on the back of the indictment. The phrase 'witnesses whose names are on the back of the indictment' (which derives from the former practice of writing the names in that place) now signifies all those persons whose evidence was tendered at committal. Although counsel has a discretion not to call a witness on the back of the indictment, he must exercise his discretion in a proper manner and not for what Lord Thankerton in *Adel Muhammed El Dabbah* v *A-G for Palestine* [1944] AC 156 described as 'some oblique motive' (e.g., unfairly so as to surprise or prejudice the defence).

The rationale for the above rule is that, by using a person's evidence at committal proceedings, the prosecution indicate that he is an intended prosecution witness for the trial. In those circumstances the defence may hesitate to approach the witness or take a further statement from him. Moreover, since it is assumed that the prosecution will ensure that the witness attends at the Crown Court, the defence will take no steps in that regard, even if the witness is one who on balance may assist their case rather than the prosecution's. Thus, to avoid the defence being taken by surprise and prejudiced by the loss of evidence of potential value to their case, the prosecution – having in effect laid claim to a witness by using his evidence at committal proceedings – are in general obliged to call him at the trial. It follows that the rule has no application to witnesses whose statements have never formed part of the prosecution case, but were served upon the defence as unused material. The prosecution is under no duty to call such witnesses to give evidence (*Richardson* (1994) 98 Cr App R 174). The general rule is subject to the following exceptions:

(a)   A witness on the back of the indictment need not be called or even brought to court if the prosecution anticipate being able to read his statement, for example by virtue of the CJA 1967, s. 9, or CJA 1988, ss. 23 and 24.

(b)   Prosecuting counsel has a discretion not to call a witness whose name is on the back of the indictment if the witness no longer appears to counsel to be a credible witness worthy of belief (*Oliva* [1965] 1 WLR 1028). This exception presupposes that something has occurred between committal and trial to cast doubt on the witness's veracity – if the witness was known not to be credible at the time of the committal proceedings the prosecution ought not to have used his evidence. In *Oliva*, the victim of an alleged offence of causing grievous bodily harm made a statement to the police naming O as the culprit. On the first day of committal proceedings, he was called by the prosecution and gave evidence consistent with his statement. However, following an overnight adjournment, he reversed his earlier evidence and exonerated O. Even so, O was committed for trial. At trial, prosecution counsel refused to call the victim. O was convicted and appealed on the ground that the prosecution's not calling a witness whose name was on the back of the indictment was a material irregularity in the course of the trial. The Court of Criminal Appeal dismissed the appeal, holding the prosecution's duty extended only to calling witnesses who appeared capable of belief. In view of his volte-face at committal proceedings, the victim could no longer be regarded as creditworthy and, in the circumstances, prosecuting counsel had a discretion not to call him which he exercised properly.

Does prosecuting counsel have a discretion not to call a witness on the back of the indictment whom he does regard as capable of belief? The ruling of Park J in *Nugent* [1977] 1 WLR 789 and the Privy Council cases of *Seneviratne v R* [1936] 3 All ER 36 and *Adel Muhammed El Dabbah v A-G for Palestine* [1944] AC 156 have lent some support to the proposition that the prosecution need not call a witness on the back of the indictment, even though they regard him as capable of belief, if his anticipated evidence would be likely to confuse the jury about the nature of the prosecution case. In *Balmforth* [1992] Crim LR 882, however, the Court of Appeal held that, once the prosecution had decided that a witness on the back of the indictment was capable of belief, they must call him. The witness in question was one Stanley, whose statement favoured the prosecution in part and the defence in part, and was included in the committal bundle. Counsel for the Crown took the view that Stanley was capable of belief. Before trial, prosecution and defence agreed that he would be called by the Crown and tendered to the defence for cross-examination. The judge told prosecuting counsel that he had a discretion whether to call the witness, referring him to *Nugent*. B was convicted and appealed, submitting that the judge had wrongly ruled that the Crown had a discretion whether to call a witness in such circumstances. The appeal was allowed. The Court of Appeal held that, where a witness upon whom a committal was founded remained capable of belief, the prosecution was under a duty to call him. *Oliva* and *Nugent* were examples of witnesses who were wholly unreliable, and whom the prosecution were entitled not to call, but in the instant case counsel for the Crown had properly exercised his discretion in deciding that Stanley was capable of belief and it was wrong to suggest that the prosecution had any remaining discretion after coming to that conclusion. The defence had been under a disadvantage in having to call Stanley, and thus being unable to cross-examine him as to that part of his evidence which assisted the prosecution.

It is submitted that the problems which arose in *Nugent* and earlier similar cases over which side should call witnesses were the result of a misguided view that the prosecution at committal proceedings were under a duty to tender the evidence of *all* witnesses who appeared to be (a) credible and (b) capable of giving evidence relevant to the case. In fact there is no obligation on the prosecution even to use all the evidence favouring their own case at committal (see *Epping and Harlow Justices, ex parte Massaro* [1973] QB 433). *A fortiori*, there can be no obligation to call evidence or tender statements helpful to the defence. The prosecution's duty is rather to inform the defence of all unused material, which will include statements taken from witnesses who are omitted from the committal bundle because their anticipated evidence contradicts the broad thrust of the prosecution case and/or lays the foundation for a defence (see **D12.18**.) Provided that is done, the defence will be able to interview the witnesses and arrange for them to be at the Crown Court to testify as *defence* witnesses if necessary. The absurdity of the prosecution being requested (as happened in *Nugent*) to call eight witnesses who would have provided the accused with an alibi is thus avoided (see also *Russell-Jones* [1995] 3 All ER 239 and *Brown* [1997] 1 Cr App R 112). A grey area still remains where the prosecution have a number of statements broadly agreeing with each other but differing on points of detail, some being more helpful to the defence than others. In such cases, the better practice may be to include all the statements in the committal bundle, and, subject to any later doubts as to credibility, all the statement-makers should then be called by the prosecution at trial (see also *Witts* [1991] Crim LR 562). Where there is a duty on the prosecution to call or tender a witness, then reading the statement of the witness may be an acceptable alternative (*Armstrong* [1995] Crim LR 831).

Similar principles apply in the magistrates' court, see *Haringey Justices, ex parte DPP* [1996] QB 351 and **D19.4**.

Duty to Have the Witnesses at Court

D13.7 Where the prosecution intend not to call a witness whose name appears on the back of the indictment they nonetheless have a duty to ensure that he is present at court for the trial so that the defence may call him if they wish (per Lord Parker CJ in *Oliva* [1965] 1 WLR 1028 at p. 1035: 'The prosecution must of course have in court the witnesses whose names are on the back of the indictment, but there is a wide discretion in the prosecution as to whether they should call them'). The disadvantage to the defence of calling the witness is that he may then be cross-examined and discredited by the prosecution, whereas if he had testified as a prosecution witness his evidence in chief could not have been attacked by prosecuting counsel unless and until he was declared hostile (see **F6.19 *et seq.***).

The above-stated rule as to attendance of witnesses does not apply if they are absent for reasons beyond the prosecution's control. In such cases, whether to proceed without the witness or adjourn is a matter for the trial judge's discretion (*Cavanagh* [1972] 1 WLR 676). The considerations relevant to the exercise of the judge's discretion were summarised by Geoffrey Lane J in giving the judgment of the Court of Appeal in *Cavanagh*. His lordship said (at p. 679B–F):

> The prosecution must take all reasonable steps to secure the attendance of any of their witnesses who are not the subject of a conditional witness order or whom the defence might

reasonably expect to be present. The reason for that is obvious and was expressed [by Alderson B] in *Woodhead* (1847) 2 Car & Kir 520. . . .

If, however, it proves impossible, despite such steps, to have the witnesses present, the court may in its discretion permit the trial to proceed provided that no injustice will be done thereby. What considerations will affect the exercise of the court's discretion will vary infinitely from case to case. Would the defence wish to call the witness if the prosecution did not? What are the chances of securing the witness's attendance within a reasonable time? Are the prosecution prepared to proceed in his absence? If so, to what extent would the evidence of the absent witness have been likely to assist the defendant? If the absent witness can be procured, will other witnesses by then have become unavailable? There will be many other matters which may have to be considered.

On the facts of *Cavanagh*, the Court of Appeal held that the judge was right to let the trial proceed in the absence of a witness (B) who was named on the back of the indictment. Although the prosecution still regarded B as a witness of truth who would assist their case, they opposed adjourning as (a) they had other evidence capable of proving the case, and (b) B was an Indian seaman whose attendance on any future occasion to which the case might be adjourned could not be guaranteed. The defence, perhaps paradoxically, wanted to have B called as a prosecution witness and therefore applied for an adjournment. Counsel saw advantage in cross-examining B about alleged homosexual advances he had made to the accused. He also hoped to bring out discrepancies between B's evidence and the evidence of a police officer so as to discredit the evidence of both. The Court of Appeal took the view that, on balance, the defence benefited rather than suffered from B's evidence not being before the jury. Therefore, there was no injustice in refusing the adjournment and C's conviction was upheld.

Does the Judge Have Power to Require the Prosecution to Call a Witness?

The authorities on the prosecution's duty to call witnesses are inconclusive as to **D13.8** whether, in the last resort, the judge may force counsel to call a witness against his will. In *Oliva* [1965] 1 WLR 1028 at p. 1036, Lord Parker CJ stated the position thus: 'If the prosecution appear to be exercising that discretion [not to call a witness] improperly, it is open to the judge of trial to interfere and in his discretion in turn to invite the prosecution to call a particular witness, and if they refuse there is the ultimate sanction in the judge himself calling that witness'. The implication of the dictum is that the judge can 'invite' rather than compel the calling of a witness by prosecution counsel. Counsel has the right to refuse the invitation, but must be aware that, if he does so, the judge could call the witness of his own motion. A contrary view was taken in *Sterk* [1972] Crim LR 391 where the Court of Appeal held that the trial judge should have *ordered* the prosecution at least to tender a witness on the back of the indictment for cross-examination by the defence, the position being that counsel had referred to the witness's evidence in opening but had later formed the view that he was unreliable and so declined to call him. The conflict between the two cases is, perhaps, of little practical importance as most counsel would treat an 'invitation' from the judge to call a witness as being virtually equivalent to a command, even if it is not expressed as such. See **D19.4** for the corresponding position in a summary trial.

Tendering a Witness

As an alternative to calling a witness and examining him in the normal way, it is open to **D13.9** prosecuting counsel to tender a witness for cross-examination. Counsel merely calls the witness, establishes his name and address, and then invites the defence to ask any questions they wish. This device is commonly adopted where there are numerous witnesses named on the back of the indictment, some of whom do not carry the prosecution case significantly forward. Rather than bore or confuse the jury with testimony that is of only marginal relevance (or has been amply established from other sources), counsel may choose to tender the witnesses for cross-examination.

SUPPLYING INCONSISTENT STATEMENTS TO THE DEFENCE

D13.10 The prosecution duty of disclosure may cover (a) potential witnesses whom they do not intend to call and (b) statements made by intended prosecution witnesses additional to their main statements included in the committal bundle.

In *Clarke* (1930) 22 Cr App R 58, the issue was whether a police officer was correct in his identification of the accused as the person he had seen in the vicinity of burgled premises. Defence counsel wished to cross-examine the officer about the description he gave to a senior officer of the person he saw, and to bring out discrepancies between that description and the descriptions given by the witness in his deposition to the examining justices and in his evidence in chief before the jury. To that end, prosecuting counsel was asked for a copy of the first-mentioned description (which had been taken down in writing), but counsel declined on the ground that it was confidential material. The Court of Criminal Appeal stated that counsel's attitude was unfortunate. If there had been any serious discrepancy between the description and the officer's testimony, the court 'would have had seriously to consider whether any miscarriage of justice had been caused by this attitude which was unfortunately assumed by the learned counsel for the prosecution'. In fact the description was produced on appeal, and counsel for C conceded that, if anything, it confirmed the officer's evidence on oath. *Clarke* was confirmed in *Liverpool Juvenile Court, ex parte R* [1988] QB 1, where the prosecution failed to inform the defence that a police officer who testified that he had been the victim of a head-butt from the accused had told his sergeant that he 'did not know what had happened but there must have been a clash of heads'. The Divisional Court held that the failure amounted to a breach of the rules of natural justice and quashed the Crown Court's dismissal of the accused's appeal against his summary conviction for assault.

It is submitted that the principle in *Clarke*, although articulated prior to the enactment of the statutory framework for disclosure contained in the CPIA 1996, is still valid. The prosecution must disclose material which 'might undermine the case for the prosecution against the accused' (s. 3(1)(a)). Even if the statement in question did not fall into the potentially undermining category at the time when primary disclosure was made, the prosecution has a continuing duty to keep disclosure under review (s. 9). If material moves into the category where it 'might undermine the case for the prosecution against the accused', it must be disclosed 'as soon as reasonably practicable' (s. 9(2)). Similar considerations apply to material which 'might be reasonably expected to assist the accused's defence as disclosed by the defence statement given under section 5' (s. 9(5)). Even if earlier non-disclosure was justified on the grounds that it fell outside the test in s. 3(1)(a) therefore, if a witness testifies in a manner inconsistent with a statement in the prosecution's possession, it should be disclosed if it might undermine the prosecution case or might reasonably be expected to assist the defence as reflected in the defence statement.

The defence are *not*, however, entitled to a witness summons under s. 2 of the Criminal Procedure (Attendance of Witnesses) Act 1965 ordering its subject to attend court and produce statements in his possession made by anticipated prosecution witnesses, which statements might then be used in cross-examination of the witnesses at the accused's trial (*Cheltenham Justices, ex parte Secretary of State for Trade* [1977] 1 WLR 95). See **D12.29** for the text of s. 2 of the 1965 Act.

READING STATEMENTS AS EVIDENCE AT THE TRIAL ON INDICTMENT

D13.11 The subject-matter of this heading might equally well be regarded as one of the exceptions to the rule against hearsay evidence and therefore allocated to the evidence part of this work. However, it is considered here as it also has crucial implications for the procedural question of which witnesses should attend at trial.

Statements Tendered at Committal

The CPIA 1996, sch. 2, provides for the statements tendered at committal (see **D7.17**) **D13.12** by the prosecution to be read in evidence at the subsequent Crown Court trial. Identical provisions apply to a deposition taken under the MCA 1980, s. 97A, and tendered in evidence at committal. If the defence wishes to prevent the statement or deposition in question being read at trial, then it must give written notification to the prosecutor and the Crown Court within 14 days of committal, stating that there is objection to the statement or deposition. That does not, however, conclude the matter. The objection of the defence can be overruled by the trial judge. According to sch. 2, para. 1(4), 'the court of trial may order that the objection shall have no effect if the court considers it to be in the interests of justice so to order'. This power is potentially most important, since if the trial judge overrules the objection, then the accused will have no opportunity to cross-examine the witness in question. In the Parliamentary debate on the subject, it was stated by the government that it was anticipated that the courts, in applying the 'interests of justice' test, would turn for guidance to the CJA 1988, s. 26 (see Baroness Blatch, *Hansard*, Lords, 26 June 1996, col. 951). That section refers to the admissibility of certain hearsay statements under the CJA 1988, ss. 23 and 24 (see **F16.14**). In considering whether the admission of such a statement under the 1988 Act would be in the interests of justice, the court must have regard to its contents, the risk of unfairness to the accused resulting from the inability to controvert the statement, and any other circumstances which may appear to be relevant. It would appear to have been the intention of Parliament, in the light of the statement of Baroness Blatch quoted above, that the courts should consider the same factors in deciding whether to overrule a defence objection by virtue of the power contained in sch. 2, para. 1(4) of the 1996 Act. In any event, a trial judge will no doubt be extremely wary about overruling the objections of the defence, and thus denying the accused the right to see those who are giving evidence against him, let alone the right to cross-examine them. Any suspicion that objections were overruled for reasons which were less than compelling would be contrary to well-established principle and, in addition to the normal channels for challenge, would be likely to lead to the prospect of a challenge based upon Article 6(3)(d) of the European Convention on Human Rights (see **D26.4**).

Written Statements in Criminal Proceedings other than Committals

The CJA 1967, s. 9, provides for the admissibility of written statements in criminal **D13.13** proceedings other than committal proceedings. Since it is used more frequently in summary trials than in trials on indictment, its terms are set out at **D19.5**. It is also used in trials on indictment, however, chiefly where the prosecution wish to adduce evidence additional to that which they used at committal proceedings. The party proposing to tender the statement in evidence must serve a copy of it on each of the other parties. If one of those parties, during the period of seven days from the date of service of the copy on him, serves notice on the party wishing to use the statement that he objects to it going into evidence, the statement cannot be read at the trial. In effect, s. 9 statements are admissible only if all the parties agree. Even if a statement is admissible under s. 9, the court may require that the maker attend to give evidence, e.g., where the defence dispute the contents of the statement but failed to object through an oversight.

Depositions of Children or Young Persons

Where a justice has taken a deposition out of court from a juvenile under the provisions **D13.14** of the CYPA 1933, s. 42, the deposition (subject to certain conditions) is admissible in any proceedings in respect of any of the offences mentioned in sch. 1 to the Act (s. 43).

Schedule 1 lists numerous specific sexual offences, and also refers to 'any other offence involving bodily injury to a child or young person' (see **F16.22**). The juvenile may but need not have been the victim of the offence. The conditions of admissibility are: (a) that attendance at court would involve serious danger o the juvenile's life or health; (b) that the deposition is signed by the justice by or before whom it purports to have been taken, and (c) that, if the deposition is to be admitted against the accused, he was given reasonable notice of the intention to take it and he (or his legal representative) had the opportunity of cross-examining the deponent. Evidence as to the effect of attending court on the juvenile's health must be provided by a duly qualified medical practitioner.

Address of Witness

D13.15 In its Statement of National Standards of Witness Care in the Criminal Justice System (1996) 161 JP 353, the Criminal Justice Consultative Council's Trial Issues Group proposed that, unless it was necessary for evidential purposes, witnesses should not be required to disclose their addresses in open court. The statement was approved by Lord Bingham CJ in July 1996, but has not been published as a practice direction in any of the law reports. The usual practice followed in the courts is for counsel to ask for the address of the witness at the beginning of evidence-in-chief. If there is a matter of sensitivity, however, the witness does not need to disclose the address in open court, and can write it down for the record. Witnesses are informed by means of a 'Witness Pack' of their right to use this latter method if appropriate.

OBJECTIONS TO PROSECUTION EVIDENCE

Standard Procedure

D13.16 Where the defence intend to object to the admissibility of prosecution evidence disclosed on the committal statements (hereafter referred to as 'disputed evidence'), the standard procedure is that:

(a)   Defence counsel informs prosecution counsel of the objection before the latter opens his case to the jury.

(b)   In his opening, counsel makes no mention of the disputed evidence.

(c)   The prosecution evidence is called in its natural order until the point at which the disputed evidence would otherwise be adduced. The jury are then sent out of court, a formula being used such as 'A matter of law has arisen which does not concern them'.

(d)   If the admissibility of the disputed evidence raises collateral factual issues as to how it was obtained, it may be necessary to adduce evidence about those facts before the judge in the absence of the jury. This is known as a trial 'on the *voir dire*' because the witnesses testify on a special form of oath (see **F4.23**). By way of exception to the general rule that issues of fact are for the jury, the judge must decide what facts have been established by evidence on the *voir dire*. Both prosecution and defence are entitled to call witnesses at this stage. However, their evidence (whether in chief or in cross-examination) should be limited to matters relevant to the admissibility of the disputed evidence. For the application of this rule to the admissibility of confessions, see PACE 1984, s. 76(2); *Brophy* [1982] AC 476.

(e)   Whether or not there has been evidence on the *voir dire*, the parties make their representations to the judge about the admissibility of the disputed evidence.

(f)   The judge then announces his findings on any factual issues arising on the *voir dire* and – in the light of those findings, the relevant law on admissibility of evidence and any discretionary power to exclude material which is legally admissible – rules on whether the disputed evidence should be admitted or not.

(g)   The jury return to court. If the judge ruled against the disputed evidence, the jury will know nothing about it since it was not mentioned in prosecution counsel's opening speech. If it is ruled admissible, the defence are still entitled to cross-examine on matters they raised on the *voir dire*, although at this stage the cross-examination goes to the weight, if any, that the jury should attach to the disputed evidence not to its admissibility.

The extent to which either the judge or the parties are entitled to depart from the procedure for excluding evidence described above has been considered by the appellate courts on several occasions, usually in the context of objections to the admissibility of confessions. The following points can be made.

Presence of Jury in Court during Determination of Question of Admissibility   D13.17

Dicta in *Anderson* (1929) 21 Cr App R 178 suggest that the jury should be sent out for the *voir dire* hearing only if the defence agree. Similarly, in *Ajodha* v *The State* [1982] AC 204 Lord Bridge of Harwich (giving the Privy Council's opinion) stated that 'at the appropriate time the judge will conduct a trial on the *voir dire* to decide on the admissibility of the statement; this will normally be in the absence of the jury, *but only at the request or with the consent of the defence*' (p. 223C – D emphasis added). However, in *Hendry* (1988) 88 Cr App R 187, the Court of Appeal refused to follow *Anderson* and *Ajodha* on this point, and dismissed an appeal brought on the ground that the jury – against the wishes of the defence – had been sent to their room while submissions on evidence were made. It was held that, in the last resort, requiring the jury to leave court was a matter for the judge's discretion. It is submitted, however, that the judge's discretion would not extend to requiring the jury to stay if the defence want them to go, since that would defeat one of the fundamental objectives of the *voir dire* procedure, namely, to prevent the jury knowing of potentially inadmissible evidence.

In *Mitchell* [1998] AC 695, the Privy Council considered whether it was proper for the judge to inform the jury of his ruling after a *voir dire*. Their lordships stressed that the judge should give no explanation of the outcome of the *voir dire* to the jury, as to do so would risk unfair prejudice to the accused.

Determination of Question of Admissibility as a Preliminary Issue   Where the   D13.18

evidence to which the defence indicate an objection is vital to the prosecution case, so that counsel cannot sensibly open his case without reference to it, the question of admissibility may – at the judge's discretion – be determined as a preliminary issue. If the judge excludes the evidence, the prosecution may have to consider whether, in the light of that ruling, they wish to proceed; if the evidence is admitted, the difficulty counsel would otherwise have had in opening his case is removed. In *Hammond* [1941] 3 All ER 318, the Court of Criminal Appeal, while stating that the appropriate time for determining admissibility of evidence is normally immediately prior to the evidence being called, also indicated that that practice should not be regarded as invariable. The facts were that prosecution counsel in opening a case of murder told the jury that H had confessed to the crime. Defence counsel then intervened to say that he intended to object to the confession, and the judge forthwith sent the jury out and heard the objection. On appeal, Humphreys J (giving the judgment of the Court of Criminal Appeal) said (at p. 320 emphasis added):

> The ordinary practice in such a case, if there is any objection on the part of the counsel for the defence to the admissibility of a piece of evidence, is that he should inform the prosecution of that fact beforehand, and that that piece of evidence should not be opened to the jury. This court desires to reiterate that what was said by this court in *Cole* (1941) 28 Cr App R 43 is a good practice which should be adhered to, certainly in most cases. *The court cannot lay down as a rule of practice that in no case should the judge decide to hear in advance arguments as to the admissibility of evidence.* There may be cases in which it is convenient, and in which it cannot possibly result in any harm in its being done.

It is unclear whether, if the exceptional course of determining admissibility of evidence as a preliminary issue is adopted, a jury has to be sworn in and then immediately sent out, or whether their empanelment can be delayed until after the preliminary point has been decided. The argument for first empanelling the jury is that – although for some purposes a trial begins with the arraignment of the accused (see, for example, the Supreme Court Act 1981, s. 77, which deals with time-limits for commencement of trial) – it is arguable that, in general, there is no trial in being until a jury has been sworn and therefore no question connected with the trial (such as whether evidence is admissible) can validly be determined. In deference to this argument, it seems to be the practice to empanel a jury *before* considering objections to evidence (or any other question of law).

D13.19 ***Objecting to Evidence without a* Voir Dire**   The *voir dire* procedure is designed to assist the defence by preventing the jury hearing possibly inadmissible evidence unless and until the judge rules it admissible. It therefore seems logical that the defence should not be forced to adopt the procedure if they consider that the accused's interests will best be served by having all the evidence (including the possibly inadmissible evidence and any evidence of how it was obtained) adduced before both judge and jury as part of the general case. The tactical reason sometimes advanced for not wanting a hearing on the *voir dire* is that, if the judge in fact rules the disputed evidence admissible, the prosecution witnesses may have to be asked the same questions before the jury as they were asked before the judge, albeit that the cross-examination before the jury goes to the weight of the evidence not its admissibility. Having had a 'dry run' before the judge, the witnesses are likely to give a better account of themselves before the jury than they would have done had the questions come as a surprise.

In *Ajodha* v *The State* [1982] AC 204, the Privy Council affirmed the defence's right to have evidence ruled inadmissible even though they do not seek to exclude it by means of the standard *voir dire* procedure. See **F17.24** to **F17.26** for details.

Some aspects of Lord Bridge's guidance in *Ajodha* have since been considered by the Court of Appeal. First, in *Jackson* [1985] Crim LR 442, the question was whether the defence, having elected not to have a *voir dire*, were entitled to a ruling from the judge on the admissibility of J's confession at the end of the prosecution case or were obliged to wait until the close of all the evidence. It was held that the judge ought *not* to exclude a confession of his own motion unless it is a totally exceptional case where the prosecution's own evidence makes it quite clear that the confession was improperly obtained. In all others cases in which there is no *voir dire*, the judge should not rule or be asked to rule on the confession's admissibility until the close of *all* the evidence, both prosecution and defence. This considerably reduces the attractiveness to the defence of forgoing the normal procedure, since – in the absence of a *voir dire* – their decision on whether or not to call evidence will have to be taken at a time when they still do not know whether the jury will ultimately be directed to ignore the accused's confession.

Secondly, in *Cunningham* [1985] Crim LR 374 the Court of Appeal took a liberal attitude to the prosecution being allowed to reopen their case when the defence evidence has raised matters relevant to the admissibility of a confession where there has not been a hearing on the *voir dire*. It was put to the police officers who had taken a confession statement from C that, prior to confessing, C had been visited by other officers who offered him an inducement to confess. The prosecution closed their case without calling those other officers, after which C gave evidence repeating what had been put in cross-examination. The trial judge allowed the prosecution to reopen their case so as to call the officers named by C. The Court of Appeal held that it would have been an affront to the course of justice to have done otherwise. The decision is noteworthy in that normally the prosecution may not call evidence after formally closing their case unless something has arisen *ex improviso* which they could not possibly have anticipated (see **D15.2**), and, on the facts of *Cunningham*, the defence cross-examination should surely have alerted the prosecution to the need for the evidence of the additional officers. Even so, they were allowed to call them after the defence evidence. Both *Jackson* and *Cunningham* perhaps indicate a wish by the Court of Appeal to encourage the defence to adopt the ordinary *voir dire* procedure.

The above discussion has proceeded on the assumption that the enactment of ss. 76 and 78 of the PACE 1984 (admissibility of confessions and unfairly obtained evidence) has not affected the procedure for excluding confessions. However, it has been stated (apparently *obiter*) by Lord Lane CJ in *Sat-Bhambra* (1988) 88 Cr App 55 at p. 62 that the wording of those two sections shows that – if it is sought to exclude evidence in reliance on them – the objection must always be made *before* the disputed evidence is adduced. Lord Lane's dictum in *Sat-Bhambra* was given in the context of deciding whether a judge could be obliged to reopen the question of admissibility of a confession after he had already ruled it admissible in a *voir dire* hearing. It is submitted that the dictum was not strictly necessary to the decision. Moreover, Lord Lane drew attention to the PACE 1984, s. 82(3), under which the trial judge's general common-law powers to exclude evidence are preserved. Thus, if the defence do not ask for a *voir dire*, but nonetheless evidence is adduced in the course of either the prosecution or defence cases which suggests that a confession was obtained in a manner prohibited by s. 76 or otherwise unfairly, then the judge can be invited to exercise his residual common-law powers and either direct the jury to ignore the confession or discharge them from giving a verdict. In the present uncertain state of the authorities, it is submitted that the guidance given in *Ajodha* should still be followed.

Asking for a Second Ruling Prior to the enactment of the PACE 1984 it was held **D13.20** that, where a judge ruled a confession admissible after a hearing on the *voir dire*, but fresh evidence later emerged before the jury which cast doubt on the correctness of the judge's ruling, then the judge could be invited to reconsider the question of admissibility (*Watson* [1980] 1 WLR 991). In *Watson*, Cumming-Bruce LJ adopted the following passage from *Cross on Evidence*, 5th ed., p. 72, as correctly stating the law:

> The judge retains his control over the evidence ultimately to be submitted to the jury throughout the trial. Accordingly, if, having admitted a confession as voluntary on evidence given in the absence of the jury, the judge concludes, in the light of subsequent evidence, that the confession was not voluntary, he may either direct the jury to disregard it, or, where there is no other sufficient evidence against the accused, direct an acquittal or, presumably, direct a new trial.

However, his lordship went on to say that 'the occasions on which a judge should allow counsel to invite him to reconsider a ruling already made are likely to be extremely rare' (p. 995D). On the facts of *Watson* (police officer who took a confession statement from W gave answers in the course of cross-examination before the jury by counsel for a co-accused which were slightly at variance with the answers he had earlier given to W's counsel on the *voir dire*), the trial judge was held to have erred in ruling that he had no power to reconsider his decision to admit the confession. Nonetheless, the appeal was dismissed as the additional evidence revealed before the jury was insufficient to cast doubt on the voluntary nature of the confession.

The general principle stated in *Watson* (i.e. that a trial judge may in exceptional circumstances be invited to reconsider his decision to admit disputed evidence) was no doubt intended to apply to any disputed evidence, whatever its nature, and not just to possibly inadmissible confessions. However, the position in respect of confession evidence has again been complicated by the wording of the PACE 1984, ss. 76 and 78. In *Sat-Bhambra* (1988) 88 Cr App R 55, the judge decided as a preliminary issue in the absence of the jury that answers given by the accused in the course of a tape-recorded interview with police officers were admissible. The defence had contended that the interview should be excluded under s. 76(2)(b) of the 1984 Act because, at the time, lack of food combined with drugs which the accused was taking for diabetes could have produced hypoglycaemia, which would have affected his ability to reason and comprehend. When a doctor who had given evidence on the *voir dire* was questioned before the jury, his evidence about the possibility of hypoglycaemia was more favourable to the defence than it had been at the earlier stage. The defence therefore asked the judge to reconsider the admissibility of the interview, to conclude that it should have been excluded, and – since it was now too late to exclude it – discharge the jury. The Court of Appeal held that s. 76 (mandatory exclusion of a confession on grounds of oppression or unreliability) only applies *before* the confession has gone into evidence. There was consequently no statutory obligation on the judge to reconsider his earlier ruling. However, under s. 82(3) of the 1984 Act (preservation of discretionary powers to exclude evidence) the judge could still take whatever steps were necessary to prevent injustice, whether by directing the jury to disregard the evidence they had heard, commenting on its weight in the light of the changed medical evidence, or even discharging them. But he was not, as the appellant contended, *obliged* to discharge them. The relevant paragraphs from the Court of Appeal's judgment (88 Cr App R 55 at p. 62) are set out below:

> In *Watson* [1980] 1 WLR 991, decided before the 1984 Act, it was held that a judge who has second thoughts about the voluntariness of a statement which he has earlier ruled admissible upon the *voir dire* may, where it is appropriate so to do, change his opinion as to its admissibility, and may take such steps as are necessary to put matters right, by, for example, directing the jury to disregard it or discharging the jury.

> The words of section 76 are crucial: 'proposes to give in evidence' and 'shall not allow the confession to be given' are not . . . appropriate to describe something which has happened in the past. They are directed solely to the situation before the statement goes before the jury. Once the judge has ruled that it should do so, section 76 (and section 78, for the same reasons) ceases to have effect. The judge, whatever his change of mind may be, is no longer acting under section 76 as the appellant contends. To that extent the decision in *Watson* does not survive the wording of the 1984 Act.

> That does not mean that the judge is powerless to act. He has the power, if only under section 82(3), to take such steps as are necessary, depending on the circumstances, to prevent injustice. He may, if he thinks that the matter is not capable of remedy by a direction, discharge the jury; he may direct the jury to disregard the statement; he may by way of direction point out to the jury matters which affect the weight of the confession and leave the matter in their hands. He is not, as is the submission here, obliged to discharge the jury and to order a new trial.

> If a defendant wishes under section 76 to exclude a confession, the time to make his submission to that effect is before the confession is put in evidence and not afterwards.

D13.21 *Circumstances in which* **Voir Dire** *Hearing is Necessary* Most authorities on the procedure for objecting to evidence concern disputed confessions and the holding of a trial on the *voir dire* to determine their admissibility. The Court of Appeal in *Flemming* (1987) 86 Cr App R 32 warned against resorting to the procedure unnecessarily. F appealed against his conviction for robbery on the grounds that (a) the identification evidence against him was unsatisfactory and should have been excluded, and (b) the judge was wrong to conclude that he had signed notes of his interview with the police on those pages which contained admissions. As regards both objections, the judge had heard evidence on the *voir dire* before deciding to admit the evidence. The Court of Appeal upheld his rulings but stated that he should have made them without himself hearing evidence. The issue of whether the accused had signed the relevant pages of the interview notes was one solely for the jury, the question being whether a confession had been made at all, not whether (assuming it had been made) it had been improperly obtained. As to the identification evidence, although the judge had a residual discretion to exclude it on the grounds that its prejudicial effect exceeded its probative value, that was something he could and should have decided simply by reading the depositions and inviting argument from counsel – there was no need to call the witnesses before the judge. In *Minors* [1989] 1 WLR 441, however, Steyn J stated that the trial within a trial procedure ought to be adopted where there is a disputed issue as to the admissibility of a computer printout (for further instances, see **F1.25**).

Guidance on* Voir Dire *Procedure where Objection to Evidence Taken under **D13.22** ***Police and Criminal Evidence Act 1984, s. 78*** Guidance has been given in *Keenan* [1990] 2 QB 54 on the appropriate procedure for asking the judge to rule under the PACE 1984, s. 78, that a confession obtained in breach of the codes of practice should be excluded because its reception would have such an adverse effect on the fairness of the proceedings that it ought not to be admitted. The Court of Appeal distinguished between (a) cases where a breach of the code is apparent from the custody record or statements of the prosecution witnesses; (b) cases where there may be a prima facie breach which, assuming objection is taken would have to be justified by the prosecution, and (c) alleged breaches which can only be established by evidence from the accused himself. An example of (a) is where (as in *Keenan* itself) there has been a breach of sects 11 and 12 of PACE Code C relating to the contemporaneous noting of interviews with a suspect and/or showing him the officer's note; an example of (b) is if access to a solicitor has been refused but the prosecution might be able to justify that refusal on grounds such as the risk of interference with evidence if access had been allowed, and examples of (c) are cases of alleged oppression or where the accused claims that he was a person at risk not given the extra protection provided for in paras 11.14 to 11.16 of PACE Code C. In situation (a), it ought only to be necessary for prosecution counsel to make an admission as to the breach, after which there may be legal argument about the consequences for admissibility; in (b), it will clearly be necessary for the prosecution to call evidence on the *voir dire* to explain away the prima facie breach, after which the accused may choose to testify in rebuttal; in (c), the accused will have to take the initiative by himself giving evidence on the *voir dire* to establish the breach. Hodgson J (who gave the Court of Appeal's judgment) thought that cases under (c) would be rare, and that in situations (a) and (b) it would be unlikely that the accused would want to testify in rebuttal. His lordship also said that the trial judge was obliged to give his ruling on whether admission of the evidence would be unfair in ignorance of what the defence's response to the evidence would be if it were admitted. That might seem unsatisfactory but was simply a consequence of the overall structure of a criminal trial. The judgment helpfully summarises many of the earlier cases dealing with similar issues.

Editing of Prosecution Evidence

Where the prosecution evidence as foreshadowed in the committal statements contains **D13.23** material which may be relevant and admissible according to the strict rules of evidence but which is of such prejudicial effect that the jury clearly ought not to hear it, the practice is for the parties to 'edit' the evidence by agreement before it is called. This practice was recognised by the Court of Appeal in *Weaver* [1968] 1 QB 353. Sachs LJ indicated as pp. 357G – 358A that the best way for such editing to take place is for the evidence to appear 'unvarnished' in the committal statements. Counsel can then confer at trial to ensure that 'the editing is done in the right way and to the right degree'. If necessary the judge can also play a part in the process. Editing of evidence is commonly required in respect of statements made by the accused to the police (e.g., if they imply that he is of bad character or refer to an offence other than that charged), and of police evidence suggesting that the accused was previously known to them.

In the *Practice Direction (Crime: Evidence by Written Statements)* [1986] 1 WLR 805, Lord Lane CJ gave detailed instructions on the treatment of committal statements where some of the material contained therein may be inadmissible or unduly prejudicial. The direction deals partly with the preparation of composite statements to replace several earlier statements made by a witness. It also deals with when it is preferable to prepare a completely fresh statement for a witness to sign, omitting those parts of the first statement which are inadmissible or prejudicial. Where, however, the prosecution decide that it is unnecessary to have a new statement, the procedure to be adopted is that the *original* of the witness's statement should be tendered to the court unmarked in any way, but, on the *copies* served on the defence and provided to the court, the passages on which the prosecution do not propose to rely should either be bracketed or lightly struck out. The striking out should not be done in such a way as to obscure what is being deleted. Paragraph 4 of the direction states that the following note should be attached to the committal bundle: 'The prosecution does not propose to adduce evidence of those passages of the attached copy statements which have been struck out and/or bracketed. (Nor will it seek to do so at the trial unless a Notice of Further Evidence is served.)' The advantage of this procedure is that the defence and court are aware both of the full text of the witness's original statement and of those portions which the prosecution provisionally consider should not be used against the accused. At trial, counsel can then discuss any further editing that may be necessary (or, conversely, the defence may indicate that they in fact have no objection to the jury hearing something that the prosecution had thought they should not). As regards (a) documentary exhibits (including statements under caution or interview notes signed by the accused) and (b) police officers' statements referring to oral answers by the accused, the above procedure should *not* be adopted but editing should be left entirely to prosecuting counsel at the Crown Court after discussion with defence counsel and, if appropriate, the trial judge (para. 7). A difficulty may arise where the jury ask to see the original of an edited document. They may be told that there are technical reasons why this cannot be permitted. Although this is not altogether satisfactory, it may be the only way of dealing with an inherent problem.

Calling of Additional Evidence

D13.24   The prosecution at trial on indictment are not confined to using solely the evidence they relied upon at the committal proceedings. Nor are they obliged to use at committal all the evidence then available to them (*Epping and Harlow Justices, ex parte Massaro* [1973] QB 433). If, however, they intend to call evidence at trial additional to the evidence used for committal, whether that be evidence which was not then available or evidence which they simply chose not to adduce, they are required to give the defence notice of their intention. They must also supply a copy of the statement of the additional witness or, as the case may be, a copy of the further statement made by a witness whose first statement was used at committal.

The above represents the invariable modern practice. However, a number of 19th century cases suggest not only that additional evidence is admissible at trial but also that the prosecution may take the defence by surprise with it (see, e.g., *Connor* (1845) 1 Cox CC 233 where the trial judge said that he could not force the prosecution to disclose to the defence a large amount of additional evidence which had been accumulated since committal). The present position was indicated in *Wright* (1934) 25 Cr App R 35, where W appealed, *inter alia*, on the ground that the prosecution, in order to prove that the handwriting on a certain envelope was his, called a witness to produce two specimens of his writing and then invited the jury to compare the writing on the envelope with the specimens. Apart from objecting to the lack of evidence from a handwriting expert, the defence contended that they had not been notified of the intention to put the specimens into evidence. Avory J said (at p. 40):

> At most that is a grievance and cannot affect the admissibility of the evidence put before the jury, and, if the appellant or his counsel thought that he was being prejudiced by having had

no notice and really desired to call expert evidence to deal with the question of handwriting, he could have applied for an adjournment, but he did not do so.

Although the appeal was dismissed and the lack of notice treated as a mere 'grievance' not fatal to the admissibility of the handwriting specimens, there is nonetheless an implication that the defence could have asked for an adjournment which – were there any real possibility of their being prejudiced by the lack of notice – should have been granted. Thus, the sanction requiring the prosecution to give timely notice of additional evidence is the knowledge that, in the absence of such notice, the trial may have to be adjourned until it has been served and the defence have had time to consider their response to it. Alternatively, if an adjournment is undesirable in the circumstances, the judge could exercise his discretion and exclude the evidence under the PACE 1984, s. 78, on the ground that to admit it would be unfair in view of the lack of notice.

Assuming notice of intention to call additional evidence is given, it is normal to serve with it a copy of a statement from the witness complying with the formal requirements of the CJA 1967, s. 9. If the defence do not object within seven days, it will then be possible to read the statement as evidence at the trial without calling the witness.

Formal Admissions

In order to avoid adducing evidence of matters which are not in reality in dispute, parties **D13.25** to criminal proceedings may make formal admissions as to any facts of which oral evidence could be given in those proceedings. The procedure for so doing is contained in the CJA 1967, s. 10, which is dealt with at **F1.2**.

SUBMISSION OF NO CASE TO ANSWER

Introduction

After the prosecution have closed their case, the defence may submit that the evidence **D13.26** does not disclose a case to answer in respect of any or all the counts on the indictment. If the submission succeeds on all counts, the judge directs the jury to acquit the accused. If the submission succeeds on only some of the counts, no verdict is taken forthwith on those counts but normal practice is to tell the jury that they will ultimately be directed to acquit the accused of them and they should therefore, for the remainder of the trial, concern themselves only with the counts on which there is a case. If the submission fails on all counts, the jury know nothing about the submission since they are sent out of court while it is made and no mention is made of what occurred in their absence.

The Test to Be Applied

The leading authority on the test a trial judge should apply in determining whether there **D13.27** is a case to answer is *Galbraith* [1981] 1 WLR 1039. In the course of his judgment in that case, Lord Lane CJ said (at p. 1042B–D):

> How then should the judge approach a submission of 'no case'? (1) If there is no evidence that the crime alleged has been committed by the defendant, there is no difficulty. The judge will of course stop the case. (2) The difficulty arises where there is some evidence but it is of a tenuous character, for example because of inherent weakness or vagueness or because it is inconsistent with other evidence. (a) Where the judge comes to the conclusion that the prosecution evidence, taken at its highest, is such that a jury properly directed could not properly convict upon it, it is his duty, upon a submission being made, to stop the case. (b) Where however the prosecution evidence is such that its strength or weakness depends on the view to be taken of a witness's reliability, or other matters which are generally speaking within the province of the jury and where on one possible view of the facts there *is* evidence upon which a jury could properly come to the conclusion that the defendant is guilty, then the judge should allow the matter to be tried by the jury. . . .

There will of course, as always in this branch of the law, be borderline cases. They can safely be left to the discretion of the judge.

The first limb of the *Galbraith* test does not, as Lord Lane remarked, cause any conceptual problems. His lordship refers to there being 'no evidence that the crime alleged has been committed by the defendant'. That phrase is, no doubt, intended to convey the same meaning as the words of Lord Parker CJ in his *Practice Direction (Submission of No Case)* [1962] 1 WLR 227 when he told magistrates that submissions of no case to answer at summary trial should be upheld, *inter alia*, if 'there has been no evidence to prove an essential element in the alleged offence'. Such cases may arise, for example, where an essential prosecution witness has failed to come up to proof, or where there is no direct evidence as to an element of the offence and the inferences which the prosecution ask the court to draw from the circumstantial evidence are inferences which, in the judge's view, no reasonable jury could properly draw. (See further **D7.13** and **D19.8**.)

The second limb of Lord Lane's test in *Galbraith* is far less straightforward, and has to be understood in the context of a practice that developed after the passing of the Criminal Appeal Act 1966, s. 4(1)(a) (now Criminal Appeal Act 1968, s. 2(1)), of inviting the judge to hold that there was no case to answer because a conviction on the prosecution evidence would be 'unsafe'. That form of submission reflected the power given to the Court of Appeal by first the 1966 and then the 1968 Act to quash a conviction on the basis that it was, in the court's opinion, 'unsafe or unsatisfactory' (but, since the Criminal Appeal Act 1995, part I, came into force, simply 'unsafe'). The argument at trial went as follows: since the Court of Appeal can ultimately quash a verdict of guilty if it appears to them unsafe, then you (the trial judge) ought to prevent the jury returning such a verdict in the first place if the evidence seems unsafe to you. However, once counsel were permitted to argue on a submission of no case that a conviction would be unsafe, the door was open to their asking the judge to consider the *quality* and *reliability* of the evidence, rather than its legal sufficiency. Traditionally, questions such as whether a crucial prosecution witness should be believed in the light of his performance in cross-examination or whether inconsistencies between a number of prosecution witnesses meant that none of them could be relied upon were regarded as matters for the jury, not the judge.

It is clear from Lord Lane's judgment that it is no longer appropriate to argue on a submission of no case that it would be unsafe for the jury to convict, if only because that tempts the judge to impose his own views of the witnesses' veracity (see especially p. 1041B–C). But it is submitted that the second limb of the *Galbraith* test still leaves a residual role for the judge as assessor of the reliability of the evidence. If that is so, the judge is not obliged to accept everything a prosecution witness has said, however implausible, but may at least ask whether it is too inherently weak or vague for any sensible person to rely on it. In other words, he should give the witness's evidence the greatest weight that any reasonable jury could give to it but need not pretend to believe arrant nonsense. Thus, if the witness undermines his own testimony by conceding that he is uncertain about vital points, or if what he says is manifestly contrary to reason, the judge may be entitled to hold that no reasonable jury properly directed could rely on the witness's evidence and therefore (in the absence of any other evidence), there is no case to answer.

The correct interpretation of the *Galbraith* test was considered by Turner J when ruling on a submission at the trial of *Shippey* [1988] Crim LR 767 for rape. The prosecution relied upon the virtually uncorroborated evidence of the complainant, and the defence conceded that there was some evidence which supported on 'a minimum basis' the allegation that the accused had committed the offence. However, the judge agreed with the defence that parts of the complainant's evidence were totally at variance with other parts supportive of the prosecution case. In particular she admitted to having returned voluntarily to the accused after he had (according to her) already told her that he wanted sexual intercourse with her and would use violence to get it. His lordship found that part of her evidence to be 'strikingly and wholly inconsistent with the allegation of rape'. Her evidence as a whole contained 'really significant inherent inconsistencies' and was 'frankly incredible'. Nevertheless, she never retracted her claim that she had been raped. On a literal view of *Galbraith* and *Barker* (1975) 65 Cr App R 287, the case should therefore have gone to the jury for them to weigh the inconsistencies and implausibilities and decide if she was telling the truth. Turner J took a more robust view. He said that 'taking the prosecution case at its highest' did not mean 'taking out the plums and leaving the duff behind'. It was for him to assess the evidence and, if it was 'self-contradictory and out of reason and all common sense', then he could properly conclude that it was 'inherently weak and tenuous' within the meaning of the second limb of Lord Lane's test. Moreover, in forming his judgment, he could take into account both internal inconsistencies in a witness's testimony and inconsistencies between one prosecution witness and another. Turner J therefore ruled that there was no case to answer. Although he does not in terms appear to have said that he thought the complainant was lying, it is difficult to explain his decision on any other basis.

With some hesitancy, the following propositions are advanced as representing the position that has now been reached on determining submissions of no case to answer:

(a) If there is no evidence to prove an essential element of the offence a submission must obviously succeed.

(b) If there is some evidence which – taken at face value – establishes each essential element, then the case should normally be left to the jury. The judge does, however, have a residual duty to consider whether the evidence is inherently weak or tenuous. If it is so weak that no reasonable jury properly directed could convict on it, then a submission should be upheld. Weakness may arise from the sheer improbability of what the witness is saying, from internal inconsistencies in the evidence or from its being of a type which the accumulated experience of the courts has shown to be of doubtful value (especially in identification evidence cases, which are considered in **D13.28**).

(c) The question of whether a witness is lying is nearly always one for the jury, but there may be exceptional cases (such as *Shippey*) where the inconsistencies (whether in the witness's evidence viewed by itself or between him and other prosecution witnesses) are so great that any reasonable tribunal would be forced to the conclusion that the witness is untruthful. In such a case (and in the absence of other evidence capable of founding a case) the judge should withdraw the case from the jury.

Identification and Confession Cases The correct approach to submissions of no **D13.28** case to answer in prosecutions turning upon identification evidence was laid down by the Court of Appeal in *Turnbull* [1977] QB 224 (see **F18.2** and **F18.22**). As one of several safeguards against erroneous convictions based on witnesses mistakenly identifying the accused, the Court of Appeal stated that, if the quality of the identification evidence on which the prosecution case depends is poor and there is no other evidence to support it, then the judge should direct the jury to acquit (pp. 229H–230A). However, supporting evidence capable of justifying leaving a case to the jury even if identifying evidence is poor need not be corroboration in the strict sense (p. 230B–D). Although *Turnbull* predates *Galbraith* [1981] 1 WLR 1039, there is no suggestion that the principles in it have been affected by the later decision. In fact, the obligation on the trial judge to uphold a submission if the identifying evidence is poor and there is no supporting evidence may be regarded as the clearest example of the application of the second limb of the *Galbraith* test. This is because the identifying witness undoubtedly provides *some* evidence of the accused's guilt (therefore a submission on the first limb would be bound to fail) but it is so weak or tenuous that no jury properly directed could properly convict on it (see *Daley* v *The Queen* [1994] 1 AC 117).

In *MacKenzie* (1992) 96 Cr App R 98, the Court of Appeal laid down special guidance for trial judges considering a submission of no case to answer in confession cases. Their lordships pointed out that cases depending solely or mainly on confessions, like cases depending upon identification evidence, had given rise to miscarriages of justice. Where certain conditions applied, therefore, the judge should, in the interests of justice, take the initiative and withdraw the case from the jury. The conditions requiring such action by the judge were:

    (a)   the prosecution case depended wholly upon confessions;
    (b)   the defendant suffered from a significant degree of mental handicap; and
    (c)   the confessions were unconvincing to a point where a jury properly directed could not properly convict upon them.

Confessions might be unconvincing, for example, because they lacked the incriminating details to be expected of a guilty and willing confessor, because they were inconsistent with other evidence, or because they were otherwise inherently improbable. See also *Wood* [1994] Crim LR 222.

D13.29 ***Mutually Destructive Counts***   Where two counts in an indictment are mutually destructive (e.g., alternative counts for theft and handling of the same goods) it may be possible for the defence to submit that, even though the prosecution evidence prima facie shows that the accused must have committed one or other of the offences, no reasonable jury properly directed could be sure which of the two he is guilty of and therefore they must be directed to acquit of both. The problem arose in *Bellman* [1989] AC 836, a case chiefly important for the House of Lords' decision that mutually destructive counts may be joined in one indictment. In the course of reaching that conclusion, the House also considered whether – given the state of the evidence at the close of the prosecution case – the judge ought to have upheld a submission of no case in respect of all counts. The prosecution evidence in *Bellman* was that B had told the two victims that, if they gave him approximately £18,000, he would use the money to buy drugs in the United States which would subsequently be smuggled back into the UK, making a large profit for all concerned. One of the victims went to the US with B. While he was there, he discovered that the bag containing the money had disappeared from the boot of the car they were using. No drugs were ever bought. The primary prosecution case was that the whole agreement between B and the victims was a charade and B had simply used the money for his own purposes. Alternatively, if the agreement was genuine and the money had been stolen from the car by some third person, then B was guilty of conspiracy to import controlled drugs. B did not make a statement to the police. Lord Griffiths said (at pp. 847G–848G):

> There are, of course, rare situations in which it is clear that the accused has committed a crime but the state of the evidence is such that it is impossible to say which crime he has committed. In such circumstances no prima facie case can be established to support either crime and neither crime can be left to the jury. The classic example arises where a man has given contradictory evidence on oath on two occasions. It is obvious that one statement must be false but in the absence of any evidence to indicate which statement was false it cannot be proved on which occasion the perjury was committed: see *Harris* (1822) 5 B & Ald 926. . . .

> An accused is always entitled to have the counts in the indictment considered separately by the judge at the end of the prosecution's evidence and if there is insufficient evidence to provide a prima facie case on any count to have that count withdrawn from the jury.

The situation in *Bellman* was different from that in the perjury example cited. Far from it being impossible to say which of the offences (conspiracy to import drugs or obtaining by deception) had been committed by B, the evidence was, as the defence eventually conceded, prima facie sufficient in relation to both alternatives. It was therefore a matter for the jury to decide at the end of all the evidence which of the two possible hypotheses based upon the prosecution evidence (i.e. that B never intended to buy drugs or that that was his original intention but the money was stolen) was the correct one. Of course, if they had then been left in doubt about the correct count on which to convict they ought – at least in theory – to have acquitted of both. See also *Tsang Ping-nam* v *The Queen* [1981] 1 WLR 1462.

Prima Facie Case against Two Accused Analogous problems to those discussed in **D13.30** D13.29 arise where there are co-accused and the evidence establishes that one or other committed the offence charged but it is impossible to say which. In such cases and assuming there is no evidence of joint enterprise, both are clearly entitled to be acquitted on a submission of no case. Lord Griffiths stated the principle succinctly in his judgment in *Bellman* [1989] AC 836 (at p. 849A): 'It, of course, goes without saying that if the evidence shows that one of two accused must have committed a crime but it is impossible to go further and say which of them committed it, both must be acquitted: see *Lane* (1985) 82 Cr App R 5.' The same point had earlier been made by Lord Goddard CJ in *Abbott* [1955] 2 QB 497 at p. 503. Whether the evidence really does leave the question of which accused committed the offence in total doubt or whether there is evidence just capable of pointing to one or the other as the person responsible will depend on close analysis of the evidence in the particular case (compare *Gibson* (1984) 80 Cr App R 24, *Lane* (1986) 82 Cr App R 5, *Aston* [1991] Crim LR 701 and *S* [1996] Crim LR 346, all of which involved injuries to young children where it was difficult to determine which of the two parents was responsible).

Procedure on a Submission of No Case

The jury should be out of court while a submission of no case is made. If the submission **D13.31** fails, no reference should be made to what occurred in their absence. Both points emerge from the Court of Appeal's decision in *Smith* (1986) 85 Cr App R 197. The prosecution case depended entirely upon a disputed identification of the accused. The defence submitted in the absence of the jury that the quality of the identifying evidence was poor and the case should therefore be withdrawn from the jury in accordance with *Turnbull* [1977] QB 224. The judge rejected the submission. No defence evidence was called. In summing up the case, the judge told the jury that, if he had not thought there was sufficient evidence of identification, he would have withdrawn the case from them. Watkins LJ said (at p. 200 emphasis added):

> That is an improper observation for a judge to make to a jury. Submissions [of no case to answer] are made in the absence of the jury. There is very good reason for that as all who take part in trials know. The question as to whether or not there is a sufficiency of evidence is one which is exclusively for the judge following submissions made to him *in the absence of the jury*. His decision *should not be revealed* to the jury lest it wrongly influences them. There is a risk that they might convict because they think the judge's view is a sufficient indication that the evidence is strong enough for that purpose.

In *Crosdale* v *The Queen* [1995] 1 WLR 864, it was emphasised that a trial judge should ask a jury to withdraw during a submission of no case to answer since it was a matter for him alone whether there was sufficient evidence to go before the jury.

Almost invariably, the proper time for making a submission of no case is after the prosecution have called their evidence (*Leadbeater* [1988] Crim LR 463). There may be exceptions to this rule, but they will be very rare, probably limited to cases where either (a) there is an objection to the jurisdiction of the court (see, for example, *DPP* v *Doot* [1973] AC 807 in which the question was whether an offence of conspiracy had been committed inside or outside the jurisdiction), or (b) where there is an agreed statement of facts and the judge is effectively being asked whether what undoubtedly happened amounts to the offence charged. In *Leadbeater*, counsel asked the judge before the case was opened to rule on whether there was a case to answer in respect of conspiracy to obtain property by deception. The judge held there was; L thereupon pleaded guilty, and he then appealed against conviction on the basis that the judge's ruling was wrong. The prosecution case was chiefly based on replies the accused had made to the police, indicating that he and others had made false reports of fires in order to boost their wages as retained firemen. Dismissing the appeal, the Court of Appeal criticised the judge for dealing with the submission as a preliminary issue. There was other evidence the prosecution proposed to call as well as the accused's answers in interview, and the case could not therefore be said to fall within either of the exceptional situations just mentioned.

As already indicated, the procedure upon the judge upholding a submission on all counts of the indictment is for the jury to return to court, whereupon what has occurred is briefly explained to them. One of their number is then asked to stand as foreman and he, on the judge's direction, formally returns a verdict of not guilty. If the submission has succeeded on some counts but failed on others, the defendant should be regarded during the rest of the trial as no longer being charged on the former (*Plain* [1967] 1 WLR 565). However, no verdict is taken until the end of the trial when the jury both announce their decision on the counts for which there was a case and, on the judge's direction, find the accused not guilty on the remainder of the indictment. Where the submission fails on all counts, the trial simply proceeds with no mention to the jury of the submission having been made (see *Smith* (1986) 85 Cr App R 197).

It is defence counsel's responsibility to make a submission of no case to answer should the circumstances warrant it (*Juett* [1981] Crim LR 113). In general, if experienced counsel fails so to submit in a case where the prosecution evidence is arguably insufficient, it is presumed that he has his own reasons for staying silent, and the trial judge is neither required nor even entitled to intervene. Exceptionally, however, the interests of justice may demand that the judge take the initiative and suggest that there may not be a case to answer. In such exceptional cases and assuming there was not in fact enough evidence to go to the jury at the end of the prosecution case, the Court of Appeal will quash the conviction, notwithstanding that defence counsel did not make a submission (see *Juett*).

Stopping the Case before the End of the Trial

D13.32 At common law a jury are entitled to decide at any stage after the prosecution have closed their case that they do not need to hear any further evidence or argument but wish to acquit forthwith. They may not, of course, convict without the trial running its full course. It is doubtful whether a modern jury will be aware of its power to acquit before all the normal stages of a trial have been gone through. However, the judge may 'remind' them that this course is open to them. The kind of case where such a reminder might be appropriate is if the prosecution evidence – although just satisfying the *Galbraith* test – is nonetheless very weak and the judge's experience leads him to think that the jury will almost certainly acquit at the end of the day. Whilst the judge may remind the jury of their right to stop the case, he should not go further and issue an invitation to them to acquit (*Kemp* [1995] 1 Cr App R 151, approving the observations of Roskill LJ in *Falconer-Atlee* (1973) 58 Cr App R 348 at p. 357). The judge must make it absolutely clear to the jury that, although they may acquit at this stage, they may not convict.

What if the judge has become convinced, during the course of the defence evidence that he ought to withdraw the case from the jury, rather than merely reminding them of their right to stop it? In *Boakye* (12 March 1992 unreported), Steyn LJ pointed out that, as a matter of principle, the judge was entitled to hold that there was no case to answer even at the end of the defence case:

> [Counsel for the Crown] has made a submission to us that it was not appropriate to make a submission of no case to answer at the end of the defence case. In our judgment a judge is

entitled, even at that late stage, if no evidence is available on a count or if there is no evidence of that count upon which a reasonable jury could convict, to rule that there is no case to go before the jury. The contrary proposition would be a startling one. It would contemplate that the judge might be powerless to prevent a real miscarriage of justice in a case where there was a sudden change in the strength of the prosecution case as a result of cogent evidence emerging in the defence case. We rule without any doubt that it was within the power of the judge to make the ruling that was requested of him.

In *Anderson* (1998) *The Independent*, 13 July 1998, the Court of Appeal stated that, although it was more usual for defence counsel to make a submission of no case to answer at the close of the prosecution case, a trial judge is not precluded from entertaining and ruling on such a submission at the close of the defence case. The reasoning of the Court of Appeal in *Brown* [1998] Crim LR 196 reinforces this approach. Their lordships stated that throughout the trial the judge has a duty not to allow a jury to consider evidence on which they could not safely convict. He should not invite them to acquit since, if they convicted, the accused would be left with a sense of grievance. But if, at the conclusion of the evidence, the trial judge is of the opinion that no reasonable jury properly directed could safely convict, he should raise the matter for discussion with counsel even if no submission of no case to answer is made. If, having heard submissions, he is of the same opinion, he should withdraw the case from the jury.

SECTION D14: TRIAL ON INDICTMENT: THE DEFENCE CASE

Defence Opening Speech

D14.1 If the defence intend to call evidence as to the facts of the case other than or in addition to the evidence of the accused, defence counsel has the right to an opening speech (*Hill* (1911) 7 Cr App R 1). If, however, the only defence evidence is to come from the accused (or from the accused and character witnesses), then counsel does not have an opening speech. That is the implication of s. 2 of the Criminal Evidence Act 1898 which provides that, where the accused is the only defence witness to the facts, he shall be called immediately after the close of the prosecution evidence.

In an opening speech, defence counsel may both outline the anticipated defence case and criticise the evidence already given for the prosecution (*Randall* (1973) *The Times*, 11 July 1973).

Defence Evidence Generally

D14.2 The burden of proof is always on the prosecution. Therefore, the defence are never obliged to call evidence. Should they choose to do so, they still have a choice as to whether to call the accused since he is a competent but not compellable witness (see Criminal Evidence Act 1898, s. 1(a)). The special evidential rules relating to the accused as a witness – in particular the application in his case of the rule against self-incrimination, the protection he generally enjoys from questions tending to show that he is of bad character and the circumstances in which he 'throws away his shield' against such questioning – are fully discussed in **part F**. Mentioned below are some further points of a specifically procedural nature concerning evidence from the accused.

D14.3 *The Accused as a Witness* Subject to a contrary direction from the court, an accused who chooses to testify should give his evidence from the witness-box, not the dock (Criminal Evidence Act 1898, s. 1(g) and see **F4.9**). The obvious situation for the court to exercise its discretion against allowing the accused physically to enter the witness-box is when there is a perceived risk of violence from him that can be controlled more easily if he remains in the dock while testifying (*Symonds* (1924) 18 Cr App R 100).

The accused should normally be called before any other defence witnesses (PACE 1984, s. 79; Criminal Evidence Act 1898, s. 2). The rationale for this rule is that, subject to limited exceptions, witnesses at criminal trials are kept out of court until they testify. That cannot apply to the accused as he has the right to be present throughout his trial and therefore has the opportunity of adjusting his evidence so as to counteract more effectively the prosecution evidence that he has heard. This potential advantage is, however, kept to a minimum by ensuring that the witnesses called on the accused's behalf will not testify until after he himself has. Where such defence witnesses are called as to the facts, the court has a discretion to depart from the usual rule and allow them to be called first (PACE 1984, s. 79). The section reflects the common law which was to the effect that, whilst the established practice was to call the accused first, there was no objection to a witness whose evidence was not substantially disputed testifying out of the normal order if circumstances made that convenient (see *Morrison* (1911) 6 Cr App R 159 and *Smith* [1968] 1 WLR 636). Oddly, it would seem that a character witness must *always* be called after the accused unless there are other witnesses as to the facts, in which case the time of his calling would again be discretionary (see Criminal Evidence Act 1898, s. 2).

The decision whether to testify or not is for the accused himself. This is emphasised in the Code of Conduct of the Bar, annexe F, standards applicable to criminal cases, para. 12.4:

A barrister acting for a defendant should advise his client as to whether or not to give evidence in his own defence but the decision must be taken by the client himself.

The Court of Appeal has stated that, when the defendant decides not to go into the witness box, it should be the invariable practice of counsel to have that decision recorded and to cause the defendant to sign the record giving a clear indication of (i) the fact of his having, of his own accord, decided not to give evidence and (ii) that he has done that bearing in mind the advice, regardless of what it was, given to him by counsel (*Bevan* (1994) 98 Cr App R 354). The usual practice is, in fact, for such a record to be made by way of an endorsement upon counsel's brief.

Since the CJPO 1994, s. 35, became law, it is particularly important that the accused should be advised whether to give evidence, since an inference may be drawn from his failure to do so. The procedure which the court should adopt is laid down in a *Practice Direction (Crown Court: Defendant's Evidence)* [1995] 1 WLR 657 (for details, see **F19.12**).

Failure to advise the defendant properly about the advisability of testifying may, in appropriate circumstances, constitute grounds for the Court of Appeal to decide that a conviction is unsafe and unsatisfactory (*Clinton* [1993] 1 WLR 1181: for further detail see **D22.23**). In the analogous case of *Irwin* [1987] 1 WLR 902 (decision without prior consultation by defence counsel not to call alibi witnesses whom his client wanted called) an appeal succeeded, the Court of Appeal referring with apparent approval to a statement in the then current Code of Conduct similar to para. 12.4 quoted above.

Police and Criminal Evidence Act 1984, s. 79

If at the trial of any person for an offence —
    (a)   the defence intends to call two or more witnesses to the facts of the case; and
    (b)   those witnesses include the accused, the accused shall be called before the other witness or witnesses unless the court in its discretion otherwise directs.

Criminal Evidence Act 1898, s. 2

Where the only witness to the facts of the case called by the defence is the person charged, he shall be called as a witness immediately after the close of the evidence for the prosecution.

ALIBI EVIDENCE

Introduction

Prior to the commencement of the CPIA 1996, part I, alibi evidence and expert opinion **D14.4** evidence were the only types of evidence of which the defence were required to warn the prosecution in advance. For offences governed by the law prior to the 1996 Act (i.e. those for which the investigation commenced before 1 April 1997), reference should be made to the 1997 edition of this work. For offences where the investigation commenced on or after that date, the CJA 1967, s. 11, has been repealed, and the duty to give notice of alibi thereunder has been replaced by the wider duty to provide a defence statement under s. 5 of the 1996 Act (see **D6.4**). The consequences flowing from a defence failure to comply with its duty to notify an alibi are different. Whereas under the 1967 Act, leave had to be sought from the trial judge to adduce evidence of alibi where the notice was late, under the 1996 Act there is no impediment to the calling of alibi evidence in such circumstances, but comment may be made or permitted or inferences drawn.

Giving Particulars and Definition of 'Alibi'

D14.5   The duty of defence disclosure under the CPIA 1996, s. 5, is wider in respect of a defence of alibi than it is for other defences. The accused must, by s. 5(7), give the name and address of any witness who is believed able to give evidence in support of the alibi. If the name or address is not known, the accused must give any information which might assist in finding such a witness. 'Evidence in support of an alibi' is defined in s. 5(8) in the same terms as were used in its predecessor (the CJA 1967, s. 11(8)). As a result, although the consequences of a failure to notify alibi are now different from those attached to s. 11 of the 1967 Act, the case law under that provision remains of relevance to s. 5(7) of the 1996 Act, and is dealt with at **D14.6**.

Criminal Procedure and Investigations Act 1996, s. 5

> (7)   If the defence statement discloses an alibi the accused must give particulars of the alibi in the statement, including—
>   (a)   the name and address of any witness the accused believes is able to give evidence in support of the alibi, if the name and address are known to the accused when the statement is given;
>   (b)   any information in the accused's possession which might be of material assistance in finding any such witness, if his name or address is not known to the accused when the statement is given.
> (8)   For the purposes of this section evidence in support of an alibi is evidence tending to show that by reason of the presence of the accused at a particular place or in a particular area at a particular time he was not, or was unlikely to have been, at the place where the offence is alleged to have been committed at the time of its alleged commission.

Further Guidance on the Meaning of 'Alibi'

D14.6   It would appear to follow from the definition of 'alibi' in the CPIA 1996, s. 5(8) (see **D14.5**) that, where the prosecution case includes circumstantial evidence putting the accused at a certain place on an occasion other than the commission of the offence and he claims that he was elsewhere, there is no obligation on the defence to give particulars of alibi (*Lewis* [1969] 2 QB 1).

In *Fields* [1991] Crim LR 38, F was charged, together with A, with robbery. They were identified by S, who lived near the scene of the crime. On the afternoon of the robbery, she waited for 10 minutes between 2.45 and 3.30 p.m. outside a telephone kiosk, which was occupied by a man whom she later identified in a parade as F. S returned to the kiosk at about 6 p.m. and, whilst waiting to use the kiosk again, witnessed the robbery by two men, now masked, whom she later identified in parades as A and F. In a letter from F's solicitor, it was claimed that he was in Durham (25 miles away from the scene of the crime) at around 3 p.m. and hence could not have been observed by S in the telephone kiosk. The Crown successfully sought to admit this letter at trial as a notice of alibi. On appeal F claimed that admitting the letter in evidence for the prosecution prejudiced him by forcing him to testify so as to support his alibi. He argued that the letter should not have been admitted because it was not a notice of alibi. The Court of Appeal dismissed the appeal. S's evidence on the committal papers was that the man whom she saw in the kiosk at about 3 p.m. was the same man whom she later saw taking part in the robbery. The alibi evidence would tend to show that F could not have been at the scene of the robbery when it took place. Hence the letter was a notice of alibi.

It has been held by the Court of Appeal that 'alibi' presupposes that the offence alleged was committed at a particular place and time, as opposed to being committed in an unspecified geographical area over a lengthy period (*Hassan* [1970] 1 QB 423). Therefore, failure by the defence to notify the prosecution that the accused was not where they claimed him to be on one day during the period of three weeks over which the offence allegedly occurred did not give the judge a discretion to exclude defence evidence of the accused's true whereabouts on that day (ibid.). On the other hand, evidence may amount to an alibi even though it comes from the accused only and is to the effect that, at the relevant time, he was by himself at a location other than the scene of the crime (*Jackson* [1973] Crim LR 356).

In *Johnson* [1995] 2 Cr App R 1, it was held that 'evidence in support of an alibi' must be evidence that the defendant was at some place or in a particular area other than the place where the offence was allegedly committed. J's instructions to his legal representatives were that he had not been present at the club where the offence was committed on the night in question. He was unable to say where he had been, since his arrest took place almost three months later. The Court of Appeal held that the trial judge was wrong to rule that an alibi notice was necessary in those circumstances.

Obligation to Consult Accused about Calling Alibi Evidence

Defence counsel is under a duty to consult the accused before deciding not to call alibi **D14.7** evidence (*Irwin* [1987] 1 WLR 902). In *Irwin*, the accused's defence to a charge of criminal damage was that he was at home with his family when the offence occurred. At a first trial which resulted in a 'hung' jury, the defence called his wife and daughter in support of the alibi. At the retrial, counsel decided for tactical reasons not to call those witnesses. He had not communicated his intention to his client – indeed, the decision was probably taken while the accused was in the course of testifying. The jury convicted. On appeal, it was held that failure to consult the accused about the non-calling of the alibi witnesses was a material irregularity, and the conviction was quashed. According to Michael Davies J at p. 906, it is not necessarily vital to consult the client immediately before the alibi witnesses are or, as the case may be, are not called, but it is essential to have discussed the matter thoroughly at some stage. If the client declines to accept counsel's advice that the witnesses should not be called, then counsel should either act on his client's instructions or ask the judge to discharge him from the case (p. 905C–D). If the client accepts counsel's advice, it is preferable to have that confirmed by him in writing (p. 906C).

Irwin is an exception to the rule that, if an accused chooses to be represented, decisions appertaining to the conduct of his case are ultimately a matter for counsel not for him. Moreover, alleged mistakes by counsel rarely amount to valid grounds of appeal (see the discussion of this issue at **D22.18**).

EXPERT EVIDENCE

By the PACE 1984, s. 81, Crown Court rules may make provision requiring any party **D14.8** to proceedings in the court to disclose to the other party (or parties) any expert evidence which he proposes to adduce. Furthermore, the rules may provide for such evidence to be excluded if notice has not been given. The rules in question are the Crown Court (Advance Notice of Expert Evidence) Rules 1987 (SI 1987 No. 716), the text of which is reprinted at **F10.14**. Where the accused is sent to the Crown Court for trial (whether by committal, transfer or preferment of a voluntary bill of indictment), or his retrial is ordered, any party to the proceedings who has not already done so shall, as soon as practicable, furnish the other parties with a written statement of any finding or opinion he proposes to adduce by way of expert evidence (r. 3(1)(a)). Upon request from any of the other parties, he must also provide a copy of the record of any 'observation, test, calculation or other procedure on which the expert finding or opinion is based' (r. 3(1)(b)). Alternatively, if it appears to him more practicable, he must give the other party the opportunity of examining the record (ibid.). The other parties may by notice in writing waive their rights under r. 3(1) or consent to the disclosure being made orally

(r. 3(2)). Conversely, the party proposing to adduce the expert evidence may, if he has reasonable grounds for believing that compliance with the requirements of r. 3 would lead to the intimidation or attempted intimidation of his witness, give notice that disclosure is being withheld on those grounds (r. 4). One trusts that the prosecution would never in practice give the defence reasonable grounds for believing that a proposed defence expert witness would be intimidated. In the event of failure to comply with the requirements of r. 3, the expert evidence may not be adduced without leave of the court (r. 5).

TREATMENT BY COURT OF UNREPRESENTED ACCUSED

D14.9 If an accused is not legally represented, the court will, as a matter of practice, seek to give him such assistance in conducting his defence as may seem appropriate (e.g., explaining to him his right to cross-examine witnesses and the purpose of cross-examination as an opportunity to put questions rather than to make speeches). In particular, the accused should always be told at the end of the prosecution case of his right to give evidence himself, to call witnesses in his defence (whether or not he himself goes into the witness-box), or to stay silent and call no evidence. Failure to give the accused this information may lead to any conviction being quashed (*Carter* (1960) 44 Cr App R 225).

There are certain restrictions upon the right of an unrepresented accused to cross-examine a child witness. By virtue of the CJA 1988, s. 34A, an accused charged with an offence falling within s. 32(2) of that Act may not cross-examine in person any child witness (see also **F7.1**). The term 'child' is defined by s. 32(6). (For the text of s. 32, see **D12.30**).

When the YJCEA 1999, ss. 34 to 39 (see **F7.1**), are brought into force (expected to be in Spring 2000), there will be further restrictions. Unrepresented defendants will be prohibited from cross-examining adult complainants and child witnesses in trials for certain offences. The courts will also have the power to prohibit cross-examination of witnesses by unrepresented defendants if satisfied that the circumstances of the witness and the case merit it, and that a prohibition would not be contrary to the interests of justice. There are provisions for the appointment of representatives to conduct cross-examinations on behalf of unrepresented defendants.

It is particularly important that an unrepresented accused should be informed of the inferences which may be drawn from a failure to give evidence. This matter is dealt with in the *Practice Direction (Defendant's Evidence)* [1995] 1 WLR 657 (for details, see **F19.12**).

For the position as to cross-examination by an unrepresented accused and related matters, see *Brown* [1998] 2 Cr App R 364, which is dealt with in detail at **F7.1**.

Where the accused dismisses his counsel and/or solicitors during the course of the trial (or they withdraw during trial) and the accused's legal aid certificate remains in force, the judge should grant an adjournment for the accused to be represented (see *Chambers* [1989] Crim LR 367 and *Sansom* [1991] 2 QB 130).

SECTION D15: TRIAL ON INDICTMENT: PROCEDURE BETWEEN CLOSE OF DEFENCE EVIDENCE AND RETIREMENT OF JURY

REOPENING OF PROSECUTION CASE

Introduction

The general principle is that once prosecuting counsel has stated his case to be closed **D15.1** he may not adduce any further evidence (see Tindal CJ in *Frost* (1839) 4 St Tr NS 85 at col. 386). The exceptions are described in **D15.2** to **D15.5**. It is clear from the Court of Appeal's reasoning in *Munnery* (1991) 94 Cr App R 164 that the list of exceptions is not exhaustive; but that the judge's discretion to admit fresh evidence after the close of the prosecution case must be exercised with great caution.

Matters which Arise *ex Improviso*

Where a matter arises *ex improviso* in the course of the defence case which no human **D15.2** ingenuity could have foreseen, the judge may allow the prosecution to adduce evidence on the point to rebut that which has been led by the defence. For further discussion, see **F6.2** *et seq.*

Evidence Becoming Available to the Prosecution Only after Close of Case

If evidence unexpectedly becomes available to the prosecution between the close of their **D15.3** case and the judge's summing-up, they may exceptionally be given leave to call it even though the issue to which it relates does not arise *ex improviso* (*Doran* (1972) 56 Cr App R 429). For further discussion, see **F6.2**.

Evidence of a Purely Formal Nature Inadvertently Omitted

It has been held in at least one case that an omission to call evidence of a purely formal **D15.4** nature, the lack of which leaves a technical gap in the prosecution case, may be repaired by allowing them to reopen (*McKenna* (1956) 40 Cr App R 65). In *McKenna*, on a charge of exporting 'manufactured goods wholly or mainly of iron or steel' contrary to legislation then in force, the prosecution failed to call evidence that a steamroller (the subject of the charge) was made of iron or steel. They were rightly allowed to reopen so as to call the necessary formal evidence about the composition of steamrollers. It is submitted, however, that the decision in *McKenna* should be narrowly confined and should not be used as a device for rescuing the prosecution when they have failed to prepare their case properly and have not brought the necessary evidence to court.

McKenna should be contrasted with *Central Criminal Court, ex parte Garnier* [1988] RTR 42. G was found guilty by the magistrates of parking his motorcycle with one or more of its wheels resting on the footway. To prove its case, the prosecution had to show that the site on which G parked in the City of London was a footway on an urban road. He was found guilty by the magistrates and appealed to the Crown Court. At the close of the prosecution case, counsel for G submitted that there was no case to answer since the prosecution had not attempted to prove that the site of the alleged offence was a footway on an urban road. Of his own motion, the judge adjourned the case to enable the prosecutor to produce evidence to prove that the spot on which the motor cycle had been left was one which came within the statutory provisions prohibiting parking. G sought judicial review of the decision. The Divisional Court granted the application.

The missing evidence was not purely concerned with formalities – there were many places within the City of London, the precise nature of which was doubtful, e.g., as to whether they were part of a footway. Nor could the matter be said to have arisen *ex improviso*. The prosecution knew the nature of the case both from the magistrates' court and from the cross-examination of their witness in the Crown Court. The Crown Court was ordered to deal with the matter only upon the evidence which had been adduced by the prosecution prior to the submission of no case to answer. (See further **F6.3**.)

Evidence to Rebut Answers in Cross-examination as to Credit

D15.5 Although a witness's answers to questions going only to his credit are generally final, there are important exceptions to the rule, notably where the question related to a previous conviction, a previous inconsistent statement, possible bias or a reputation for untruthfulness (see **F7.19** *et seq*.). It follows that where the accused or other defence witness is asked in cross-examination a question going to his credit and the question is such that the witness's answer is *not* final, then the prosecution must be allowed to reopen their case to adduce evidence to rebut a denial given in cross-examination.

Time for Reopening Prosecution Case

D15.6 As to the latest stage at which the prosecution may be permitted to reopen their case assuming one of the above exceptional situations applies, the majority of the decided cases contemplate the additional evidence being called either during or, more probably, at the end of the defence case. However, in *Flynn* (1957) 42 Cr App R 15, the judge – after counsel's closing speeches but before he began his summing-up – gave the prosecution leave to call a witness to rebut an alibi raised *ex improviso* by the defence. The Court of Criminal Appeal approved the course taken by the judge, notwithstanding the advanced stage the trial had reached. In *Sanderson* [1953] 1 WLR 392, the defence were allowed to call a witness even after the end of the summing-up. However, there is no reported instance of the prosecution being allowed to reopen at that stage.

The rule that the prosecution must adduce all the material on which they intend to rely as part of their case extends to the use they may make in cross-examination of statements or admissions not earlier proved in evidence (*Kane* (1977) 65 Cr App R 270, in which the conviction was quashed because prosecuting counsel cross-examined K about 'off the record' answers he had given to police officers, those answers not having been proved as part of the prosecution case). In *Kane*, the evidence was available to the prosecution before the trial commenced, although counsel was not told about it until after he had closed his case. The decision might have been different had the material come to light *ex improviso*, but even so counsel should have asked leave of the judge before using it in cross-examination. A distinction has been drawn between cases such as *Kane* where the cross-examination on fresh material goes to the issues in the case and cases where the cross-examination goes only to the credit of the defence witness (*Halford* (1978) 67 Cr App R 318, in which the accused was cross-examined on two statements he had made during the early stages of a police investigation into an affray, those statements not having been part of the prosecution case; conviction upheld because (a) there was no suggestion that the statements had been made involuntarily and (b) the cross-examination based on the statements went only to credit). However, it is submitted that, where the witness being cross-examined about a previous statement not proved as part of the prosecution case is the accused himself, the borderline between cross-examination as to credit and cross-examination on the issues is difficult if not impossible to fix. Unfortunately, the court in *Halford* apparently accepted without challenge the assertion of counsel for the Crown that his questioning about H's statements was intended only to cast doubt on the accused's credibility. It may be that, in analogous cases, the decision in *Kane* should be followed in preference to that in *Halford*.

REOPENING OF DEFENCE CASE

D15.7 The judge may in his discretion allow the defence to reopen their case at any stage before the jury retire to consider their verdict. In *Sanderson* [1953] 1 WLR 392, a potential defence witness arrived so late that the judge had almost concluded his summing-up. On application to the judge, counsel was allowed to call his witness after which the judge delivered a short supplementary summing-up. The Court of Criminal Appeal said that 'it was not a course one would wish to be taken often but, on the particular facts of this case, we think that there is no objection to what was done here. The learned recorder was fully justified in the course he took.' In the earlier case of *Morrison* (1911) 6 Cr App R 159 defence evidence was similarly allowed after counsel's closing speeches, the evidence having only just then come to light. However, once the jury have been enclosed to consider their verdict, evidence must never be received, whether it be favourable to the defence or the prosecution (*Owen* [1952] 2 QB 362).

JUDGE CALLING OR RECALLING A WITNESS

D15.8 The judge has a discretion to call a witness whom neither the prosecution nor defence have chosen to call (*Wallwork* (1958) 42 Cr App R 153). The power should be sparingly exercised (*Roberts* (1984) 80 Cr App R 89), and only where it is necessary in the interests of justice. One appropriate situation for the judge taking such a course is where the prosecution have wrongly refused to call a witness whose name is on the back of the indictment (see dicta to that effect in *Oliva* [1965] 1 WLR 1028). If the witness is likely to be adverse to the defence and the prosecution have already closed their case, the judge should not use his power so as to circumvent the restrictions on the prosecution reopening their case (*Cleghorn* [1967] 2 QB 584). (The situation where the prosecution decides to offer no further evidence, but the judge disagrees with their decision and wishes to call a further prosecution witness, is dealt with in **D10.44**.) If the defence want the judge to call a witness, he has greater latitude in the exercise of his discretionary powers and any conviction is unlikely to be quashed even if the evidence turns out to be in some respects adverse to the defence (*Tregear* [1967] 2 QB 574). The parties require leave to cross-examine a witness called by the judge, but such leave should be given if the witness's evidence has been adverse to the party wishing to put questions (*Cliburn* (1898) 62 JP 232). Moreover, an adjournment may then be necessary to enable a cross-examining party to call his own evidence in rebuttal (*Coleman* (1987) *The Times*, 21 November 1987).

CLOSING SPEECHES

D15.9 Subject to one exception, both the prosecution and defence have the right to a closing speech in which they may sum up their respective cases, criticise the opposition's case and comment upon the evidence. The prosecution speech is made immediately after the close of the defence evidence, and is in turn followed by the defence speech. Thus, the defence always have the last word. The exception is that if the accused is unrepresented and either called no evidence at all or was himself the only witness (apart from character witnesses), then the prosecution lose their right to a closing speech.

The above position was reached as a result of extensive case law and statutory provisions stretching from the early 19th century to modern times. Those authorities are summarised by Watkins J in the course of his judgment in *Bryant* [1979] QB 108 at pp. 113–18. The particular point in issue in *Bryant* was whether prosecuting counsel erred by commenting in his closing speech on the case against the appellants when the only defence evidence had come from a witness called by a co-accused (who was convicted but did not appeal). That witness's evidence did, however, assist the cases of all three accused. The appeal failed because (a) B and O were legally represented, and therefore there could have been no objection *in law* to the prosecution making a closing speech against them even if no defence evidence at all had been called, and (b) in any event, where the prosecution prima facie have the right to a closing speech against one accused but not the other, if the former has called evidence which does in fact assist the latter, then counsel can comment generally on the case against both (see *Trevelli* (1882) 15 Cox CC 289, approved by *Bryant*). However, the fact that prosecuting counsel is entitled to make a closing speech does not mean that he should as a matter of course exercise the right. In particular, if the accused is legally represented but does not give or call any evidence, the normal practice is for prosecuting counsel *not* to sum up his case. This was confirmed by Watkins J in *Bryant* at p. 117D:

> Prosecuting counsel in the case of a defendant who is himself represented by counsel and gives no evidence and calls none has the right to sum up the prosecution's evidence, or in modern parlance, to make a closing speech at the close of that evidence. It is, however, a right which . . . should only rarely be necessary to use save possibly in long and complex cases and whenever used should bear, as should the majority of speeches by prosecuting and defence counsel, the becoming hallmark of brevity.

In *Hoggard* [1995] Crim LR 747, it was emphasised that the prosecution had the statutory right, by virtue of the Criminal Procedure Act 1865, s. 2, to make a closing speech where the defendant was represented. The length of the speech should, however, be commensurate with the number and complexity of the issues. In a case where the defence relied on self-serving statements made in interviews, or allegations put in cross-examination to witnesses, it would generally be in order for the prosecution to make a closing speech in order to deal with them.

In *Tahir* [1997] Crim LR 837, the Court of Appeal held that prosecuting counsel should not be deprived of the right to make a closing speech in relation to a represented defendant where the co-defendant was unrepresented. In such circumstances, however, the speech must focus on the evidence relating to the represented defendant.

Neither counsel in a closing speech should allude to alleged facts or other matters which have not been the subject of evidence (see a resolution of the judges dated 26 November 1881, adopted in *Shimmin* (1882) 15 Cox CC 122 – the resolution in fact refers only to the impropriety of defence counsel stating in a speech matters which they have merely been told in their instructions and about which they do not intend to call evidence, but it is submitted that the resolution is, by analogy, good authority for the rather broader principle stated above). In delivering his closing speech, however, defence counsel is not confined to putting forward his client's version of events. He may advance hypotheses which go beyond his client's version of events, always provided that other evidence has been called which supports such hypotheses (*Bateson* (1991) *The Times*, 10 April 1991). For the position as to comment by counsel on the defendant's failure to give evidence, see **F19.12**. Defence counsel is obviously entitled to comment upon his own client's not testifying. He is also, in a case where a co-accused runs a defence which conflicts with that of the accused he represents, entitled to comment (no doubt adversely) upon the co–accused's not having entered the witness-box (*Wickham* (1971) 55 Cr App R 199). The judge has no power to prevent or restrict such comment, but may comment upon it himself if he considers it to have been unfair (ibid.).

Prosecuting counsel should not comment to the jury on the potentially serious consequences to police officers of their evidence being disbelieved, even where a police officer has raised the matter in evidence (*Gale* [1994] Crim LR 208). Defence counsel should not refer to the likely consequences of a conviction in terms of punishment since sentencing is no concern of the jury (*A-G for South Australia* v *Brown* [1960] AC 432). Neither should the jury be invited to add a recommendation of mercy to their verdict should it be one of guilty (*Black* [1963] 1 WLR 1311).

In *Gonez* [1999] All ER (D) 674 (unreported in printed form), G appealed, *inter alia*, on the ground that the terms in which prosecution counsel had addressed the jury in his closing speech was so prejudicial that it rendered the whole trial unfair. The Court of Appeal concluded that there was criticism to be made of the closing speech, and emphasised the role of prosecution counsel as a minister of justice (see **D12.4**). They dismissed the appeal, however, on the basis that the judge had remedied the objectionable aspects of the closing speech in his summing up, and that the evidence was in any event very powerful.

Final speeches are not normally recorded. Where it is apparent that exchanges of importance are likely to take place during final speeches, however, counsel should make this clear to the judge so that the presence of the shorthand writer can be ensured (*Osborne-Odelli* [1998] Crim LR 902).

JUDGE'S SUMMING-UP

Preliminary and General Matters

The trial concludes with the judge summing up the case for the jury. It is customary for **D15.10** there to be a discussion between counsel and the judge at the end of evidence and in any event before the judge begins his summing-up. Such a discussion is important so as to reach an understanding as to how points of law and evidence which have arisen during the course of the case should be dealt with (*N* [1998] Crim LR 886).

The summing-up itself conventionally falls into two parts, namely, a *direction* on the law and a summary of the evidence. At its beginning, the judge ought to remind the jury of their respective roles and hence the different status of the summing-up's two parts. As regards the law, the judge is the final arbiter (subject to correction in the Court of Appeal) and the jury must therefore accept what he says on the law and apply it to the facts as found by them; as regards the facts, they are the judges (see *Wootton* [1990] Crim LR 201). Therefore, if, in the course of his summing-up, the judge expresses a certain view as to the facts or as to the significance of a piece of evidence but they disagree; or he has omitted to mention certain evidence which they consider important; or, conversely, he has stressed something which they consider unimportant – in all such eventualities, it is the *jury's* view which matters. In other words, they should ignore the judge's apparent views or comments on the facts except insofar as they think them sensible and helpful.

Occasionally, in a complex case, the judge may provide the jury with a written list of questions or directions to assist them in their task. If he does so, he should submit them to counsel well in advance, so that they can comment upon any errors and can base their closing speeches upon the issues raised in the proposed directions. The jury should then be given the written list at the start of the summing-up, so that the judge can take them through the directions one by one, as he deals with each point. See *McKechnie* (1991) 94 Cr App R 51. The judge is, however, fully entitled to decline to provide the jury with written directions, even where they have been requested (*Lawson* [1998] Crim LR 883).

Where the judge discovers an error in his summing up, whether as a result of representations by counsel (see **D15.18**) or otherwise, he should expressly acknowledge and refer to the error, tell the jury to disregard it, and then go on to give the correct direction (*Cole* [1993] Crim LR 300).

Burden and Standard of Proof

According to *McVey* [1988] Crim LR 127, every summing-up must contain at least a **D15.11** direction to the jury as to the burden and standard of proof, and as to the ingredients of the offence or offences which the jury are called upon to consider. Thus, if the judge fails properly to direct the jury as to the prosecution (a) having the burden of proof and (b) having to discharge that burden beyond reasonable doubt or so that the jury are sure, then a conviction is liable to be quashed (see *Donoghue* (1987) 86 Cr App R 267 on the burden of proof and *Edwards* (1983) 77 Cr App R 5 on the standard of proof, in both of which cases the convictions were, however, upheld because there had been no miscarriage of justice). In *Bowditch* [1991] Crim LR 831, the Court of Appeal stressed that in cases involving injuries to a small child it was essential that a very clear direction should be given as to the burden of proof. This was to counteract any tendency on the part of the jury, albeit subconsciously, to succumb to their emotions.

Ingredients of Offence

D15.12 The facts of *McVey* [1988] Crim LR 127 illustrate the need for a direction as to the ingredients of the offence. McV, a British Rail ticket clerk, was charged with stealing £20 from his employers. The railway police had laid a trap by one night putting identifying marks on all bank notes at the station where McV worked. Two marked £10 notes were next day found in McV's possession. His defence was that he had changed a 'tatty' £20 note of his own for the two BR notes. The judge told the jury that there was only one issue for them to consider, namely, whether the accused might have changed his own money rather than simply taking British Rail's. The conviction was quashed because the jury had not been directed as to the ingredients of the offence – i.e. the judge had not said words to the effect that a person is guilty of theft if he dishonestly appropriates property belonging to another with the intention of permanently depriving the other of it. The implication of *McVey* is that a judge must almost ritualistically recite the entire definition of the offence charged, rather than informally directing the jury's minds to the live issues in the case. It may be thought that there was only one real issue in *McVey* (namely, whether the accused was dishonest when he appropriated the two £10 notes), and the judge fairly presented that issue to the jury. Even so, the lack of a full direction on the ingredients of the offence led to the conviction being quashed.

In other cases, the need for the judge to give a direction on the elements of an offence is much clearer. For example, in *James* [1997] Crim LR 598, a conviction for robbery was quashed because the jury had not been directed as to the ingredients of the offence, in particular that the use of force had to be with the intention of stealing.

The decision in *McVey* runs counter to older pronouncements on how judges should approach their direction on the law. In *Mowatt* [1968] 1 QB 421 Diplock LJ stated that the function of a summing-up was not to give a jury a general dissertation on some aspect of the criminal law, but to isolate the issues for the jury's consideration. Similarly, in *Lawrence* [1982] AC 510, a case where the accused was charged with causing death by reckless driving and the issue between the prosecution and defence was whether L had been riding his motor-bike at some 70 m.p.h. or merely at 30–40 m.p.h. when he struck the pedestrian victim, Lord Hailsham of St Marylebone LC remarked (at pp. 519F–520A):

> The purpose of a direction to a jury is not best achieved by a disquisition on jurisprudence or philosophy or a universally applicable circular tour round the area of law affected by the case. The search for universally applicable definitions is often productive of more obscurity than light . . . . A direction to a jury should be custom built to make the jury understand their task in relation to a particular case. Of course it must include references to the burden of proof and the respective roles of jury and judge. But it should also include a succinct but accurate summary of the issues of fact as to which a decision is required, a correct but concise summary of the evidence and arguments on both sides, and a correct statement of the inferences which the jury are entitled to draw from their particular conclusions about the primary facts. In the present instance . . . I doubt whether a direction could have been faulted if the jury had simply been told that if they were satisfied that the prosecution had proved that the accused had been travelling at a grossly excessive speed they were entitled

to infer that he had been driving recklessly and as a result had caused [the victim's] death, that if so they should convict, and that if they were not so satisfied they should acquit.

The jury should not generally be directed on matters which are not issues in the case. Nonetheless, there are occasions when a defence which has not been raised by the evidence nor by counsel should be referred to by the judge in summing up, so that the jury can consider it in their deliberations. In *Watson* [1992] Crim LR 434, for example, W was charged with rape (his defence being consent) and with buggery (which he denied). He was acquitted of rape and convicted of buggery. He appealed on the basis that the judge should have said that accidental penetration did not amount to buggery. The Court of Appeal upheld the appeal. Although the defence of accident had not been raised, there was a duty on the judge to spell out that penetration must have been deliberate. In the apparently similar case of *Johnson* [1994] Crim LR 376, the Court of Appeal reached the conclusion on the facts that the judge was under no obligation to give a direction as to the non-accidental nature of the offence of buggery. For a summary of the arguments and authorities, see Sean Doran, 'Alternative Defences: the invisible burden on the trial judge' [1991] Crim LR 878, cited in *Watson*.

Other Issues of Law

Directing the jury on the law will also involve directing them on any rules of evidence **D15.13** applicable in the particular circumstances of the case (e.g., the need for corroboration whether as a matter of law or practice; the right of the accused not to give or call evidence and the significance (if any) of his having stayed silent when questioned by the police; the relevance of the accused's previous convictions if that has been revealed either as part of the prosecution case or in cross-examination, or, conversely, the relevance of his good character). Beyond what has been stated in general terms above, how the judge ought to direct the jury about the ingredients of the offence and applicable rules of evidence is a function of the substantive law, for which reference should be made to the appropriate passages in this work.

Recently judges have tended to use a standard form for summing up on the law, and this has been encouraged by the Court of Appeal's policy of recommending model or specimen directions – that is, standard forms of words by which directions on frequently recurring matters of law may or ought to be given. It is understood that these specimen directions have been collected in a document issued by the Judicial Studies Board, with the approval of the Lord Chief Justice, to all Crown Court judges. The document is not for general publication. In *Jackson* [1992] Crim LR 214, the Court of Appeal quoted the specimen direction on the respective functions of judge and jury. Whilst their lordships made it clear that the specimen directions are suggested guidelines only and must be adapted to the circumstances of particular cases, they also indicated that their use would 'help to reduce the flow of appeals against conviction'. The Court of Appeal stressed in *Taylor* (1994) 98 Cr App R 361, however, that, where the circumstances or issues in the case required some adaptation of the specimen direction, care should be taken to adapt it appropriately. Specimen directions drafted for one purpose were not to be used for a different purpose. Hence it was wrong to take part of a specimen direction relating to consideration of a *defendant's* bad character and use it in directing the jury as to the way in which they should consider the *complainant's* bad character.

The Facts

In addition to directing the jury on the law, the judge may remind them of and comment **D15.14** upon the evidence. According to *Attfield* [1961] 1 WLR 1135, if it is a short and simple case, lack of any summing-up on the facts is not necessarily fatal to a conviction, although a discussion of the salient points of the evidence is always essential in more complicated proceedings. In modern practice, judges invariably sum up the facts however simple the case may have been. In *Brower* [1995] Crim LR 746, the judge summed up for no more than two minutes. The prosecution's case was that drugs were found on B during a search at the police station; the defence was that they had been planted. There were clear inconsistencies and discrepancies in the police evidence. It was argued on the appellant's behalf that the judge had not defined the constituents of the offence properly and that the defence had never been put properly to the jury. In upholding the appeal, their lordships commented that matters may have moved on since *Attfield* was decided. In the majority of cases, it was necessary for the judge to sum up on the facts in order to assist the jury and ensure a fair trial. This was such a case because of the nature of the police evidence. It was incumbent on the judge to define the issues and remind the jury of the evidence they had heard, albeit very recently.

Many judges sum up the facts simply by reading out an abbreviated version of the note of evidence which they have kept. This is satisfactory (although arguably of little value) in straightforward cases. If the trial has been more complex, judges are exhorted to assist the jury by analysing the evidence and relating it to the various issues raised (see *Gregory* [1993] Crim LR 623). Merely reading a note of evidence in such cases has been criticised, not least because it 'must bore the jury to sleep' (see pp. 339–41 of Lawton LJ's judgment in *Charles* (1976) 68 Cr App R 334). Similarly, in the passage from Lord Hailsham's speech in *Lawrence* [1982] AC 510 quoted at **D15.12**, reference is made to the desirability of the summing-up including a '*succinct* but accurate summary of the issues of fact as to which a decision is required, a correct but *concise* summary of the evidence and arguments on both sides, and a correct statement of the inferences which the jury are entitled to draw from their particular conclusions about the primary facts' (emphasis added). In other words, marshalling and arrangement of the evidence and arguments is preferable to recapitulation with running comments. However, the approach the judge adopts must ultimately be a matter for him having regard to the nature of the particular case.

Crucially, the judge must adequately put the defence before the jury. In *Curtin* [1996] Crim LR 831, the Court of Appeal stated that as part of his duty the judge must identify the defence. The way in which he does so will depend on the circumstances of the case. Where the defendant has given evidence, it will be desirable to summarise that evidence. Where he has given evidence and answered questions in interview, it may be appropriate to draw attention to consistencies and inconsistencies between the two. When he has done neither, it will usually be appropriate to remind the jury of counsel's speech. When a defendant is interviewed at length but does not give evidence, the judge has to decide how, fairly and conveniently, to place the interview before the jury. In *Curtin*, the appeal was allowed because the judge did not refer to the defendant' s answers in interview to issues of critical importance. (On the question whether defence counsel has a duty to draw the judge's attention to a failure to deal adequately with the defence, see **D15.18**.)

Provided he emphasises that the jury are entitled to ignore his opinions, the judge may comment on the evidence in a way which indicates his own views. Convictions have been upheld notwithstanding robust comments to the detriment of the defence case (e.g., *O'Donnell* (1917) 12 Cr App R 219, in which it was held that the judge was within his rights to tell the jury that the accused's story was a 'remarkable one' and contrary to previous statements that he had made). However, the judge must not be so critical as to effectively withdraw the issue of guilt or innocence from the jury (*Canny* (1945) 30 Cr App R 143, in which a conviction was quashed because the judge repeatedly told the jury that the defence case was absurd and that there was no foundation for defence allegations against the prosecution witnesses). It is the judge's duty to state matters 'clearly, impartially and logically', and not to indulge in inappropriate sarcasm or extravagant comment (*Berrada* (1989) 91 Cr App R 131). Similarly, in *Marr* (1989) 90 Cr App R 154, the Court of Appeal stressed the accused's right to have his case presented fairly by both counsel and judge. Observance of that right is never more important that when 'the cards seem to be stacked most heavily against the defendant' (p. 156). On the facts, M's conviction for indecent assault had to be quashed because his defence – that he had stumbled and accidentally put his hand between a woman's thighs – was in effect ridiculed by the trial judge. Lord Lane CJ said: 'however distasteful the offence, however repulsive the defendant, however laughable his defence, he is nevertheless entitled to have his case fairly presented to the jury both by counsel and by the judge' (p. 156).

The question sometimes arises whether the judge is confined, when summarising the case against the defendant, to the same basis as that on which the prosecution has put its case. In *Falconer-Atlee* (1973) 58 Cr App R 348, the judge left it open to the jury to convict on a basis which had never been put forward by the prosecution. This was one of the reasons given by the Court of Appeal for quashing the conviction. But in *Japes* [1994] Crim LR 605, the Court of Appeal said that a judge was not bound by the way in which the Crown opened its case. As the evidence developed, it might become apparent that the offence may have been committed on a somewhat different factual basis, e.g. the appropriation necessary for theft may have taken place at a later stage than the prosecution originally thought. If so, the judge was not debarred from putting that basis before the jury to consider, so long as the defendant was not disadvantaged or prejudiced by this course of action. Where the judge intends to direct the jury on a new legal basis, however, then it is important that he should give the parties an opportunity to consider and if necessary to argue the point (*Ramzan* [1998] 2 Cr App R 328; see also *Taylor* [1998] Crim LR 582).

Unanimity

At the end of the summing-up, the judge should advise the jury to appoint one of their **D15.15** number to be their foreman. The foreman will act as their spokesman and, in due course, announce their verdict. Finally, the judge will tell them to retire, consider their verdict and seek to reach a unanimous decision. The *Practice Direction (Crime: Majority Verdicts)* [1967] 1 WLR 1198 (see **D16.8 et seq.**) instructs judges that they 'should' direct the jury on unanimous verdicts, and the Specimen Direction from the Judicial Studies Board makes it clear that it is desirable that this should always be done. However, a failure on the part of the judge to give the jury the direction that their verdicts must be unanimous will not necessarily render a conviction unsafe (*Georgiou* (1969) 53 Cr App R 428). It is clear that it is crucial that the jury should be alert to the need for unanimity, although in exceptional circumstances the Court of Appeal may be prepared to assume such knowledge from the previous experience of a jury, and the clarity of the language when they are asked for their verdict after deliberation (*Daly* [1999] Crim LR 88).

Unanimity as to the Basis of a Guilty Verdict

Where the prosecution have put their case on more than one basis it may be necessary **D15.16** to tell the jury that, in order to convict, they must be unanimous not only as to the accused being guilty but also as to the basis on which he is guilty (*Brown* (1983) 79 Cr App R 115). In that case, the prosecution alleged the obtaining of property by the use by B of two deceptions. The Court of Appeal held that the jury should have been directed that, if they were unanimous that B used both deceptions, they should at least all agree as to which one he used. If, say, six thought he used one deception and the remainder thought he used the other deception, they must not convict. In *Mitchell* [1994] Crim LR 66, M was convicted of unlawful harassment of an occupier contrary to the Protection from Eviction Act 1977, s. 1(3)(a). A number of separate and different acts relevant to the count on which M was convicted were alleged by the prosecution, each amounting to unlawful harassment. M's evidence was to the effect either that the incidents had not occurred or, if they had, that there was a lawful explanation for them. M appealed on the basis that the trial judge had not directed the jury that all of them must be satisfied so that they were sure in respect of the same act. The Court of Appeal quashed the conviction, stating that the following principles were to be derived from the cases.

(a)   Where several matters were set out in a single count, the judge must consider whether to give the jury a direction that they must all be agreed on the particular ingredient which they rely on to find the accused guilty (*Brown*).

(b)   Such a direction will be necessary only comparatively rarely. In the great majority of cases (particularly where dishonesty is alleged and where the allegations stand or fall together), it will not be needed. Directions to the jury should not be overburdened with unnecessary warnings which serve only to confuse them (*Price* [1991] Crim LR 465 and *More* (1988) 86 Cr App R 234).

(c)   In the appropriate case, where there was a realistic danger that the jury might return a verdict of guilty on the basis that some of them found one ingredient proved and others found another ingredient proved, a direction should be given that they must be unanimous as to the proof of the ingredient which proved that offence. The instant case was one where the trial judge should have directed the jury in this way and, no such direction having been given, the conviction was quashed.

In *Jones* (1999) *The Times*, 17 February 1999, the Court of Appeal held that the considerations in *Brown* did not have any application to the circumstances where a verdict of manslaughter was returned as an alternative to murder. Provided a jury were agreed that a defendant was guilty of manslaughter in the sense that they were sure that he perpetrated an unlawful act which caused the death of the deceased, there was no need for unanimity as to the basis of that verdict (see **B1.25**).

In *Giannetto* [1997] 1 Cr App R 1, the Court of Appeal stated that the proposition that a jury must find each essential element in an offence proved was not contentious. There were two cardinal principles involved. First, the jury must be agreed upon the basis on which they found a defendant guilty. Second, a defendant must know what case he had to meet. Where the Crown alleged that on the evidence the defendant must have committed the offence either as principal or as secondary offender, and made it equally clear that they could not say which, the basis on which the jury had to be unanimous was that the defendant, having the necessary *mens rea*, by whatever means caused the result which was criminalised by the law. Their lordships added that their judgment should give no encouragement to prosecutors casting round for alternative possibilities where the essential evidence did not show a clear case against a defendant (see *Smith* [1997] 1 Cr App R 14 about the application of these principles to an offence of affray).

Summing-up Amounting to Direction

D15.17   Application of the principle that the judge should not dictate the jury's verdict by an over-robust summing-up becomes difficult where the defence case amounts – on the judge's view of the law – to an admission of guilt, and therefore *all* the evidence points to a conviction. May the judge, in such a case, tell the jury that the elements of the offence *have* been proved, thus indicating (if not in so many words) that the only correct verdict is one of guilty? In *DPP* v *Stonehouse* [1978] AC 55 one of the issues was whether the facts proved (and admitted by the defence) established an attempt to obtain property by deception or merely established acts which were preparatory to an attempt but not (on the then law) sufficiently proximate to the completed offence to amount to an actual attempt. Having ruled as a matter of law that the facts proved did constitute an attempt, the judge so directed the jury. The majority of the House of Lords held that, even where any reasonable jury properly directed on the law must upon the facts reach a verdict of guilty, the trial judge should nevertheless leave the issues of fact to them. That aspect of *Stonehouse* was followed in *Thompson* [1984] 1 WLR 962, a case which turned upon the jurisdiction of the English courts to try an offence of obtaining by deception where the defence argued that the property (credits falsely entered in T's bank accounts in Kuwait and then telexed to savings accounts he had opened in England) had been obtained abroad. Having ruled against the defence submissions, the judge in effect directed the jury to convict by telling them that there 'could not be room for any doubt at all' about the elements of the offence being made out, and that he (the judge) had already ruled that the offence was within the jurisdiction of the court. The Court of Appeal held that the judge's direction amounted to an irregularity in the course of the trial.

In both *Stonehouse* and *Thompson*, the respective appellate courts applied the proviso and upheld the convictions on the basis that any reasonable jury properly directed would have been certain to convict. Nevertheless, just how the judge should address the jury in such cases remains, it is submitted, problematic because he is obliged to direct them as to the law and expected to remind them of the evidence. If literally all the evidence points to the necessary facts having been proved, it is not easy to see how the judge can avoid giving the jury the impression that he is directing them to convict. It is perhaps fortunate that cases such as *Stonehouse* and *Thompson* are of very infrequent occurrence (but see also *Gent* (1989) 89 Cr App R 247 and *Mitchell* [1992] Crim LR 594).

Duty of Counsel in Relation to Summing-up

Prior to summing-up, the judge may, at his discretion, ask counsel in the absence of the **D15.18** jury for their representations on how certain aspects of the case should be dealt with. However, he should never seek counsel's help after the jury have retired, and only in very exceptional circumstances would it be appropriate to discuss the law with counsel after concluding his summing-up and before the jury's retirement (*Cocks* (1976) 63 Cr App R 79). The course adopted by the judge in *Charles* [1976] 1 WLR 248 of asking counsel to intervene in the course of the summing-up and correct any errors as they arose was criticised by the Court of Appeal as it detracted from the authority of what the judge was saying (especially as counsel had had to intervene no less than 33 times!).

According to *Donoghue* (1987) 86 Cr App R 267, prosecuting counsel is under a duty to attend carefully to the summing-up and draw any possible errors (whether of fact or law) to the judge's attention at its close. This is confirmed by the Code of Conduct of the Bar, annexe F, standards applicable to criminal cases, para. 11.7. Defence counsel is under no such duty but may, if he considers it in the best interests of his client, remain silent and take the point on appeal (*Curtin* [1996] Crim LR 831, relying upon *Cocks* (1976) 63 Cr App R 79 and see also *Edwards* (1983) 77 Cr App R 5). According to *Cox* [1995] 2 Cr App R 513, however, there *is* such a duty in the case of provocation in a murder trial. Their lordships stated that both prosecution and defence counsel should regard it as their duty to point out to the judge, before he sums up, where there is evidence on which the jury could find provocation, invite him to consider whether he agrees that the evidence would justify such a finding and, if so, remind him that he is required by statute to leave the remaining issues to the jury.

In *Holden* [1991] Crim LR 478, the Court of Appeal made it clear that the dismissal of the appeal would not be automatic where defence counsel failed to correct an error. H was charged with the theft of scrap tyres. He claimed he had seen others take tyres and that he had been granted permission to do so by a supervisor. The judge said to the jury that the test was whether he had a reasonable belief that he had a right to take them. Defence counsel did not indicate to the judge that there was anything wrong with this formulation. On appeal following conviction, the Court of Appeal held that the judge had misdirected the jury in saying that a reasonable belief was required; the question was whether he had an honest belief. Counsel for the Crown argued that the proviso ought to be applied, relying upon *obiter dicta* in *Edwards*. The argument was put forward that, since defence counsel had not drawn the error to the judge's attention, he must by inference have regarded the case against his client as so strong that any correction would have made no difference. The Court of Appeal held that this line of reasoning was fallacious. It was for the court, not counsel, to decide upon the weight of the evidence when measured against the importance of the irregularity.

Both counsel should take as full a longhand note of the summing-up as is possible. This is especially important where any sentence is likely to be short. A good note may avoid delay caused by waiting for a transcript and thus expedite an appeal (*Campbell* [1976] Crim LR 508).

SECTION D16: TRIAL ON INDICTMENT: PROCEDURE RELATING TO RETIREMENT OF THE JURY AND VERDICT

At the conclusion of the judge's summing-up, the jury retire to their room to consider their verdict.

RETIREMENT OF THE JURY

Basic Rules

If the summing-up concludes late in the day, the jury should not begin to consider their **D16.1** verdict until the following day. For example, in *Birch* (1992) *The Times*, 27 March 1992, the Court of Appeal said that, in a serious case, especially one involving more than one defendant and a number of verdicts, it was undesirable that a jury should be sent out after 3 p.m. unless there were exceptional circumstances. The decision as to whether the jury should retire late in the afternoon, or wait until the next morning, is one which the judge should take, and he should not leave it up to the jury to decide (*Hawkins* (1994) 98 Cr App R 228). See also *Akano* (1992) *The Times*, 3 April 1992, where retirements continuing until late in the evening were disapproved.

In *Rankine* [1997] Crim LR 757, the Court of Appeal considered whether the judge was permitted to ask a jury if they wished to consider their verdict without retiring. Their lordships held that there was nothing in the decided cases to render such an invitation wrong as a matter of course, but stressed the danger that the jury might feel under pressure, and said that such a course would be appropriate only in rare circumstances.

Three interlocking rules govern the keeping of the jury during the period between the close of the judge's summing-up and their returning to court to announce their verdict. Those rules are that (a) they must remain in the custody of a jury bailiff; (b) they must not separate except in cases of necessity, and (c) they must not leave the precincts of the court without permission of the trial judge. The purpose of the rules is to ensure that nobody interferes with the jury while they are considering their verdict. The principle was succinctly stated by James LJ in *Alexander* [1974] 1 WLR 422 at p. 426H: '. . . once the jury retires to consider their verdict it should not separate, one from another and from the jury bailiffs. They must remain in the charge of the court through the bailiffs throughout.'

Custody of the Jury Bailiff Immediately before the jury retire one or more court **D16.2** ushers takes an oath to escort the jurors to some 'private and convenient place' where [he] will not 'suffer anybody to speak to them about the trial this day, nor will he speak to them [himself] without leave of the court, except it be to ask them if they are agreed upon their verdict'. An usher who has so sworn is thereafter referred to as a 'jury bailiff'.

At all times during their retirement the jury must be in the custody of a jury bailiff in the sense that the bailiff must be near enough to the room where they are to ensure that no non-juror enters the room or otherwise communicates with them. If the jury leave the custody of the jury bailiff, it constitutes a material irregularity in the course of the trial which will almost certainly necessitate the quashing of any conviction (*Neal* [1949] 2 KB 590). In *Neal*, the jury (with the judge's permission) left the court building in order to buy lunch at a restaurant. No jury bailiff went with them. (By s. 15 of the Juries Act 1974, the jury may now purchase reasonable refreshment at their own expense during the course of their retirement. It is standard practice for the jury bailiff to enter their room at an appropriate time and ask for their orders for sandwiches.) In *Neal*, the conviction was quashed because – even assuming the circumstances justified the judge in allowing the jury to leave the court precincts – it was essential that the bailiff went with them. In his absence, there was no way of knowing who might have spoken to them about the case. Similarly, in *Ketteridge* [1915] 1 KB 467 K's appeal succeeded on the ground that one of the jurors by mistake did not go to the jury room on retirement but left the court and was on his own for some 15 minutes before rejoining his colleagues. In the circumstances there was a breach both of the rule that the jury must not separate (see **D16.3**) and of the rule that the jurors must remain in a bailiff's custody.

Once the bailiff has escorted the jury to their room, he must not enter it 'unless he is expressly ordered by the court to make a communication to, or inquiry of, the jury, and except in special circumstances and at the express order of the court no other persons should have any communication with the jury' (see para. 4(29)(i) of the Court Manual issued by the Lord Chancellor's office on the creation of the Crown Court, the terms of which were adopted by James LJ in his judgment in *Lamb* (1974) 59 Cr App R 196). In *Lamb*, the clerk of court – on the judge's authority – went into the jury room with the jury bailiff to tell the jury that they should continue to seek unanimity, they having sent a message via the bailiff asking if they could return a majority verdict. Although the appeal would have been dismissed had that been the only ground of appeal, the Court of Appeal held that the clerk's entry into the jury room was a material irregularity, there being no special circumstances such as might have justified it. It was further stated that: 'If it be the practice in any Crown Court for directions of this kind between judge and jury to be communicated through the medium of court officers, that practice should cease'. (See also *Davis (No. 2)* (1960) 44 Cr App R 235, introduction of shorthand writer into the jury room necessitated the quashing of the conviction, and *Rose* [1982] 1 WLR 614, conviction quashed partly because the clerk delivered a message from the judge indicating how much longer the latter was prepared to give them to reach a verdict.) It should be noted that in *Lamb* and *Rose* the mischief consisted not only in the clerk going into the jury room when no adequate justification for that had arisen but also in the judge communicating with the jury without the substance of that communication being stated in open court. The correct procedure for answering jury questions has been laid down by the Court of Appeal in, *inter alia*, *Lamb*, and is considered at **D16.6**.

The jury bailiffs are themselves strictly limited in the communication which they can make with the jury. In *Brown* (1989) *The Times*, 25 October 1989, it was stressed that their fundamental duty was to prevent approaches by outsiders and preserve the integrity of the deliberative process. On the facts of that case, however, it was held that nothing improper had been done. A juror had indicated to the bailiff that he and his fellow jurors were intimidated by the atmosphere in court. The bailiff asked why, and reported the answer to the trial judge, who then addressed the jury as to their duty. The Court of Appeal held that none of this constituted a material irregularity.

D16.3 ***Separation of Jury after Retirement*** By the Juries Act 1974, s. 13, the judge may permit the jury to separate. Since the CJPO 1994, s. 43, came into force, the judge has this power even after the jury have retired to consider their verdict. There is still a clear rule, however, that the jury must not separate other than with the permission of the judge. Lord Goddard CJ in *Neal* [1949] 2 KB 590 stated that, by way of exception to the rule, a juror could separate himself from the rest in a case of 'evident necessity'. The examples he gave of 'evident necessity' were if the juror required medical attention or wished to relieve himself. It is submitted that the juror must remain in the custody of a jury bailiff throughout the period that he is absent from the jury room.

The consequences of improper separation of the jury depend upon the extent to which the rule is breached. In *Alexander* [1974] 1 WLR 422 the jury retired, having been told that they were entitled to take with them any of the exhibits they wished. A very short time afterwards one of them returned by himself to court in order (it was later established) to collect the exhibits. Although the judge had by then risen, defence counsel was still in court, and he told the juror to return to the jury room. Upon the judge being informed what had occurred, the jury were brought back to court; the facts of the incident were confirmed, and they were simply given the exhibits they wanted. No application was made for discharge of the jury. After conviction, A appealed on the ground that the juror had separated himself from the rest of the jury and, for that very short period, had not been in the custody of a jury bailiff. James LJ acknowledged that this constituted a procedural irregularity. However, it was so trivial that it did not even amount to a *material* irregularity so as to be a ground for allowing an appeal. Moreover, even had it been classifiable as a material irregularity, the appeal would still have failed through application of the proviso since there was no possible prejudice to the accused (see also *Farooq* [1995] Crim LR 169).

The facts of *Alexander* may be compared with those of *Ketteridge* [1915] 1 KB 467 where the separation was for a much more substantial period, the separated juror had been out of the control of the court, and the conviction was quashed. *Alexander* may also be compared with *Goodson* [1975] 1 WLR 549, in which a juror was allowed by the bailiff to leave the jury room and speak to unidentified persons on the telephone. He was spotted by prosecuting counsel who took steps to prevent his returning to the jury room. On being told of the situation, the judge discharged the juror and the remaining 11 jurors convicted G. On appeal, it was held that what occurred was a material irregularity and – although the action of prosecuting counsel had prevented the juror at fault from returning to the jury room and prejudicing his colleagues by passing on anything that may have been said to him on the telephone – nonetheless, the irregularity had deprived the appellant of a potential voice in the jury room. The conviction was accordingly quashed. The Court of Appeal did not rule on whether what is now s. 17 of the Juries Act 1974 empowers a judge to discharge a juror even after the jury have retired to consider their verdict. (See also *Chandler* [1993] Crim LR 394.)

In *Oliver* [1996] 2 Cr App R 514, the Court of Appeal considered the directions which the judge ought to give the jury when allowing them to separate during consideration of their verdict, and stated that the jury ought to be told:

    (a)   to decide the case on the evidence and the arguments seen and heard in court, and not on anything seen or heard outside the court;

    (b)   that the evidence had been completed and it would be wrong for any juror to seek or receive further evidence or information of any sort about the case;

    (c)   not to talk to anyone about the case save to the other members of the jury and then only when they were deliberating in the jury room;

    (d)   not to allow anyone to talk to them about the case unless that person was a juror and he or she was in the jury room deliberating about the case; and

    (e)   on leaving the court, to set the case on one side until they retired to the jury room to continue the process of deliberating about their verdict.

Their lordships added that it was not necessary for the judge to use any precise form of words provided the above points were properly covered. It would be desirable for the direction to be given in full on the first dispersal by the jury, and a brief reminder to be given at each subsequent dispersal. Further directions might be necessary in particular circumstances.

Jury Leaving their Room after Retirement   The jury must not leave their room **D16.4** without the express permission of the trial judge, which should only be granted in cases of evident necessity (see *Neal* [1949] 2 KB 590). In that case, however, the Court of Criminal Appeal found it unnecessary to rule on whether the need for the jury to buy themselves lunch at an outside restaurant, having retired shortly before what would have been the midday adjournment, could amount to an evident necessity. The commonest reason for the jury being permitted to leave their room – and, indeed, the court precincts – is when they need to consider their verdict over a period of more than a day, and arrangements are therefore made to keep them at a hotel overnight. When this happens, the judge should direct the jury, before they leave court, that their deliberations should not continue at the hotel, but should await their return to court the next day (*Tharakan* [1995] 2 Cr App R 368).

Prohibition of Further Evidence Once Jury Enclosed

D16.5   It is an absolute rule, subject to no exceptions, that once the jury have retired to consider their verdict no further evidence may be adduced before them (*Owen* [1952] 2 QB 362). In *Owen*, the jury, having retired for some time, sent a note to the judge asking for evidence as to whether the clinic in a room of which the accused had allegedly had intercourse with a girl of 14 would have been empty or occupied at the material times. The judge, acting in what he considered to be the interests of justice, allowed a doctor who had already given evidence in the case about the victim's physical condition to be recalled to answer the question raised by the jury. His evidence was that the clinic was likely to have been empty. After a short further retirement, the jury convicted.

Having reviewed the earlier authorities (which were chiefly on the analogous question of whether the prosecution may reopen their case after the defence evidence or counsel's speeches), Lord Goddard CJ stated the law thus (at p. 369):

> ... we think it right to lay down that once the summing-up is concluded, no further evidence ought to be given. The jury can be instructed in reply to any question they may put on any matter on which evidence has been given, but no further evidence should be allowed.

Although the jury's question was most pertinent, they 'ought to have been told that the prosecution had laid before them such evidence as they had thought fit and the evidence could not now be reopened' (p. 369).

It is submitted that, although Lord Goddard's words, read literally, would prohibit evidence between the judge concluding his summing-up and the jury retiring, that cannot be the true position, having regard to the decision in *Sanderson* [1953] 1 WLR 392, in which the defence were allowed to call a witness who arrived while the judge was addressing the jury. In *Owen*, the jury retired immediately on the judge concluding his summing-up, and it was therefore unnecessary for the Lord Chief Justice to distinguish between the two occurrences. In a case such as *Sanderson*, however, where evidence is available at the moment the judge finishes his remarks and before the jury have actually retired, there would seem to be no rule of law preventing further evidence, provided it is adduced before the jury retire, and subject to the judge's discretion.

Although the prohibition on the receipt of fresh evidence after the jury has retired is absolute, its breach will not invariably lead to the discharge of the jury. In *Kaul* [1998] Crim LR 135, the jury found certain items of relevance in a rucksack, which was one of the exhibits which they took with them into the jury room after it had been in police custody overnight. The defence asked that the jury should not be discharged, but that the judge should give them a direction that the rucksack had been in police custody overnight. The judge refused, but told the jury that the rucksack had been empty at the start of the trial and that they should ignore the items in it. The jury convicted and the appellants appealed. The Court of Appeal allowed the appeal. Although the introduction of fresh evidence after a jury had retired should almost invariably lead to the discharge of that jury, in certain circumstances the defence might properly invite the judge to continue with the trial. Where defence counsel took that risk, that did not necessarily bar the way to an appeal on the basis of the irregularity.

The prohibition on evidence after retirement applies to documents as it does to oral evidence. Thus, in *Davis* (1975) 62 Cr App R 194, where the jury were inadvertently supplied with a copy of a witness's police statement which had not been exhibited although it had been used by defence counsel in cross-examination, the Court of Appeal held that there had been a material irregularity but were able, in the particular circumstances, to apply the proviso. Similarly, in *Thomas* (3 February 1987 unreported) it was held to have been quite wrong to have provided the jury with a map during their retirement, no map having been exhibited in evidence. Furthermore, if the jury asks to be supplied with tools or measuring equipment, great care must be taken to ensure that their intention is not to conduct a private experiment germane to the issues in the case. Thus in *Stewart* (1989) 89 Cr App R 273, the Court of Appeal held that the trial judge had erred in permitting the jury, at their request but without asking them why, to have a pair of scales. The case was one in which the weight of a quantity of drugs allegedly concealed in a holdall was highly relevant. In *Stewart*, McKinnon J, giving the Court of Appeal judgment, went on to warn against providing the jury with a ruler or magnifying glass should they request one after retirement. In *Maggs* (1990) 91 Cr App R 243, however, the Lord Lane CJ said that the observations in *Stewart* about the supply of a ruler or magnifying glass were plainly *obiter*, and too wide. Equipment that was required or designed to enable a jury to carry out unsupervised scientific experiments, such as the scales in *Stewart*, were not permissible. On the other hand, a magnifying glass or a ruler or a tape-measure did not normally raise even the possibility of any such experiment. They were the kind of objects which any person might normally have in his pocket when called to serve on a jury. There could be no objection to his using them in the jury room (see also *Crees* [1996] Crim LR 830).

In *Wallace* [1990] Crim LR 433, the usher supplied the jury in retirement with a dictionary, at their request, but without informing the judge. The jury had not understood what the judge had said about 'grievous' in 'grievous bodily harm'. After seeing the dictionary, they requested further guidance from the judge. The Court of Appeal held that it was an irregularity but not, in the circumstances, a material irregularity such as to lead to the quashing of the convictions.

In *McNamara* [1996] Crim LR 750, the Court of Appeal held that a request from the jury that the defendant stand up in the dock and turn around (presumably so that they could perform a dock identification by comparison with video films seen during the trial) should have been treated as a request for further evidence, and impermissible. The appeal was allowed, in part for this reason.

It is, of course, only new evidence which the jury may not have after retirement. In *Emmerson* (1991) 92 Cr App R 284, E's interviews with police were tape-recorded. At the end of the judge's summing-up, defence counsel asked that the jury be supplied with the tape of E's second interview, which had been played at trial. The judge refused, referring to the rule that evidence cannot be given after the jury retires. The Court of Appeal held that the tape was evidence, becoming an exhibit on production by the officer, regardless of whether it was played during the trial. The appeal was dismissed, however, since any irregularity was not material. In *Riaz* (1991) 94 Cr App R 339, it was suggested that, if the jury ask to hear an exhibited tape, the better practice would be for the judge to order the court to reassemble, so that the jury could hear it in open court. The dictum to the contrary in *Emmerson* was disapproved. (For further detail on jury requests for tapes, see **F6.3** and **F8.35**.)

If the jury, after retirement, asks for exhibits additional to those already in the jury room, the matter should be dealt with in open court. Counsel should be given an opportunity to ensure that the exhibits can properly go before the jury (*Ellis* (1991) 95 Cr App R 52; and see also *Devichand* [1991] Crim LR 446).

In *Fricker* (1999) *The Times*, 13 July 1999, the prohibition on new evidence after the jury's retirement was applied to specialist knowledge in the possession of one of the jurors. F was convicted of attempting to handle stolen goods. He had been found in possession of tyres and could provide no reasonable explanation as to why he had them. After the jury had retired, they sent the judge a note, which stated that one of their number was a tyre specialist, who knew by the number on the tyres when they had been manufactured, and that there was very little time for them to have gone through the normal purchase procedure before being acquired by the defendant. The jury asked whether they could take that into consideration. Shortly thereafter, the judge was informed that the jury had reached a verdict. He ruled that the jury had been entitled to take the specialist knowledge of the juror in question into account in their deliberations. The Court of Appeal allowed the appeal. It was wrong for a juror to be allowed to introduce entirely new evidence, particularly in circumstances where neither party had had an opportunity to test it. In these circumstances, it would have been appropriate to discharge the jury.

Questions from the Jury

D16.6   The jury are permitted to ask questions of the judge during their retirement. The normal method of so doing is to pass a note to the jury bailiff who takes it to the judge. Several cases have dealt with the procedures to be adopted in answering such questions. The object of the procedures is: (a) to remove any suspicion of private or secret communication between the court and jury, and (b) to enable the judge to assist the jury properly on any matter of law or fact which appears to be troubling them (per Lord Lane CJ in *Gorman* [1987] 1 WLR 545 at p. 546C; for the facts, see **D11.20**). Having reviewed the earlier authorities, Lord Lane set out a number of propositions to assist judges who receive a note from a jury who have retired to consider their verdict. He said (at pp. 550H–551B):

> First of all, if the communication raises something unconnected with the trial, for example a request that some message be sent to a relative of one of the jurors, it can simply be dealt with without any reference to counsel and without bringing the jury back to court. [See *Connor* (1985) *The Times*, 26 June 1985 where that very situation seems to have arisen].

> Secondly, in almost every other case a judge should state in open court the nature and content of the communication which he has received from the jury and, if he considers it helpful so to do, seek the assistance of counsel. This assistance will normally be sought before the jury is asked to return to court, and then, when the jury returns, the judge will deal with their communication.

> Exceptionally if, as in the present case, the communication from the jury contains information which the jury need not, and indeed should not, have imparted, such as details of voting figures . . . then, so far as possible the communication should be dealt with in the normal way, save that the judge should not disclose the detailed information which the jury ought not to have revealed.

As to the first proposition, the implication is that, since the jury's note does not concern the trial itself, it need not even be read in open court. Presumably any answer which needs to be given may be conveyed by the jury bailiff going into the jury room with an appropriate message. However, to avoid any possible complaint, it is as well to inform defence counsel of what has occurred (see *Connor* (1985) *The Times*, 26 June 1985 and *Brown* [1998] Crim LR 505).

Requiring notes connected with the trial to be read in open court, reflects a consistent line of authority going back to *Green* [1950] 1 All ER 38, in which Lord Goddard CJ said: '. . . any communication between a jury and the presiding judge must be read out in court, so that both parties, the prosecution and the defence, may know what the jury are asking and what is the judge's answer' (see also *Furlong* [1950] 1 All ER 636,

Townsend [1982] 1 All ER 509 and *Rose* [1982] 1 WLR 614). In *Kachikwu* (1968) 52 Cr App R 538 at p. 541 it was further said by Winn LJ that, whenever a jury note is received, immediate steps should be taken to show it to counsel before it is put in the court archives. Whether to ask counsel for assistance about how the note should be answered is within the judge's discretion. In *Gorman*, Lord Lane appears to contemplate that, however simple the answer might be (e.g., no to the question 'Can we return a majority verdict after deliberating for only one hour?'), the jury should return to court to be given the answer. Earlier authorities indicate that whether to have the jury back is in the judge's discretion – provided he reads out in open court the answer he is giving, it can be communicated by a note taken in by the jury bailiff. Thus, in *Lamb* (1974) 59 Cr App R 196, James LJ said (at p. 199): 'The practice should be that, on the court being informed by the jury bailiff of the jury's wish to make a request of the court or to communicate something to the court, the request or communication should either be delivered in writing to the court and the contents and any reply to be delivered through the bailiff, made known in public in court before delivery, or, the jury should be brought back into court to make the request themselves and the judge should answer their request in court'. What is always essential (subject to the minor qualification in Lord Lane's third proposition) is that – whether or not the jury return to court – both their question and the judge's answer be read aloud in open court at the first opportunity.

Lord Lane's third proposition arose directly out of the ground of appeal in *Gorman*. The jury at G's first trial were discharged from giving a verdict after sending a note to the judge indicating that they were 'voting' 9–3 for an acquittal but that the minority were 'adamant and would not change'. By this time the jury had been considering their verdict for over three hours and had already received the majority direction. The judge simply told counsel that he had received a note that the jury were split and there was no prospect of them reaching a verdict – he did not reveal the proportion in which they were split. Counsel agreed that, in the circumstances, there was no alternative to discharging the jury, and that was accordingly done. After a retrial ending in conviction, G learnt how near he had been to an acquittal at the first trial. On appeal, it was argued that failing to read out the jury's note in full was a material irregularity which had caused injustice in that, if defence counsel had known all the facts, he would not so readily have agreed to the jury being discharged. The appeal failed because, in any event, a judge's decision to discharge a jury from giving a verdict is not open to review. However, there had been no irregularity since the proportions in which the jury are split should not be revealed in open court, and the general rule that a jury note should be read out must therefore be qualified. In such circumstances, a judge should do as the judge did in *Gorman*, namely, give the gist of the note (i.e. the jury are split and unlikely to agree even if given more time) but keep secret that which the jury ought not to have communicated.

The consequences of failing to observe the procedures described above depend upon the gravity of the breach. If it 'goes to the root of the case', it will be treated as a material irregularity, leading to the quashing of any conviction. If it is less serious, the conviction may be upheld either by treating the irregularity as an immaterial one or by applying the proviso (compare *Green* [1950] 1 All ER 38 and *Furlong* [1950] 1 All ER 636). In *Green*, the jury's question and the judge's answer were never read in court at any stage and the judge could not even remember what the question had been about. In *Furlong* the respective communications were publicly read, albeit after verdict, and the answer the judge had given was clearly correct. Green's conviction was quashed, Furlong's was not.

The jury's usual aim in asking a question of the judge will be to seek assistance on a matter which is troubling them. As *Gascoigne* [1988] Crim LR 317 shows, the judge's response should be within strict limits, particularly as far as any new issue is concerned. The appellants were charged with theft from a shop. After retirement, the jury returned with a question about the evidence. The judge gave a direction upon that evidence. He then proceeded spontaneously to give a direction as to recent possession – an issue which the prosecution had never raised. The appellants were convicted, and duly appealed. The Court of Appeal quashed their convictions. It would seldom be proper for a trial judge to open up spontaneously with a jury, after they had deliberated for some time, an issue which had not been referred to in the trial or the summing-up. It might be proper to give a supplementary direction, where a matter canvassed at trial had accidentally been omitted from the summing-up. If this were done, it must be carried out with the utmost caution. It was very much more difficult to envisage any occasion where an entirely new basis for conviction should be volunteered at such a late stage. If, in a very exceptional case, such a direction were to be volunteered, counsel must be given an opportunity to make submissions.

Where the jury's question reveals that they have forgotten or failed to understand a crucial point, then it is incumbent on the judge to remind them of it. In *Wickramaratne* [1998] Crim LR 565, it was apparent from the jury's question that they had failed to take the standard direction on the burden of proof on board. In upholding the appeal, the Court of Appeal said that the trial judge should have reminded the jury in forcible terms that they should convict the accused only if they were sure of his guilt; failure to do so in the present circumstances rendered the conviction unsafe.

Where the jury ask the judge if they are allowed to recommend leniency, the Court of Appeal has held that the judge must tell them that they must try the case on the evidence according to their oath and leave questions of penalty to the judge (*Sahota* [1979] Crim LR 678). In *Langham* [1996] Crim LR 430, an appeal against conviction was allowed where the judge had indicated to the jury, in response to a question from them and after consulting counsel, that they could recommend leniency if they so wished. The Court of Appeal held that the case was indistinguishable from *Sahota*, and that members of the jury might have been influenced by the fact that they could add a rider recommending leniency to come to a verdict which they might not otherwise have done.

In *Thanki* (1991) 93 Cr App R 12, T was convicted at retrial of offences of indecent assault upon a boy at the school at which he taught. He relied on a diary, which was said to record the times at which he gave private lessons to the alleged victim and which was inconsistent with evidence given by the boy and his mother. The prosecution did not suggest that the diary was concocted. After retirement, the jury asked whether it had been produced before the magistrates or at the earlier trial. The judge directed them that there was no evidence on that point. T's appeal was upheld on the grounds that he should have been given an opportunity to meet the line of reasoning that the diary was a concoction (presumably by means other than the production of evidence, in view of the prohibition on new evidence after the jury retires: see **D16.5**).

In *Obellim* [1997] 1 Cr App R 355, a question from the jury caused the judge to suspect that the author of the note knew a good deal about police interviews, and might have previous convictions. The judge, without seeking the views of defence counsel, instigated enquiries into the identity of the juror in question, with a view to ascertaining whether he should have been disqualified from jury service. After the jury returned with their verdicts, they handed the judge another note, which expressed concern that a security check had been made on a juror on the basis of his having asked questions of the court. The Court of Appeal, in allowing the appeals, said that it was questionable whether the judge should have made any enquiry into the juror's eligibility, other than to check that the proper enquiries had been made before the juror was called to jury service. In any event, he should have informed defence counsel. Jury notes were from the whole of the jury, and it was not appropriate to make enquiries as to which juror had written a particular note. It was an irregularity that the jury had become aware that a security check was being made on one of their members.

Privacy of the Jury Room

What occurs in the jury room is absolutely privileged. It follows that alleged irregularities **D16.7** in the way the jury reached their verdict cannot be a ground of appeal. The leading authority is *Thompson* [1962] 1 All ER 65 where the proposed ground of appeal was that the jury had been going to acquit until the foreman read to his colleagues a list of T's previous convictions which, in some unexplained way, had come into the foreman's possession. T's character had not been revealed to the jury during the course of the trial. Upon learning that he was of bad character, they decided to convict. The Court of Criminal Appeal simply refused leave for the evidence of the irregularity to be adduced before them. To have allowed it would have breached the privacy of the jury room. It may be thought that, if the allegation made by the appellant was true, it was monstrous that his conviction should have been upheld. The case thus demonstrates the absolute nature of the rule that the Court of Appeal will not, metaphorically speaking, enter the jury room. (See also *Scholfield* [1993] Crim LR 217.) The prohibition does not, however, extend to events outside the jury room, for example, in the hotel at which a jury is accommodated overnight (*Young* [1995] QB 324). In *Young*, some of the jurors met in a group and sought the assistance of a ouija board as to the guilt of the accused. The Court of Appeal held that it could inquire into the incident, as it was not in the course of the jury's deliberation. Having done so, their lordships allowed the appeal.

Thompson should be distinguished from cases such as *Box* [1964] 1 QB 430 where the complaint is that a juror was biased because of his prior knowledge of the accused's character. If the bias can be established without calling evidence of the juror's conduct in the jury room (e.g., by remarks he made out of court to non-jurors), the appeal is not invalid *ab initio*, although it is in practice most unlikely to succeed. (See also **F9.6**.)

The confidentiality of jury deliberations is reinforced by the Contempt of Court Act 1981, s. 8, which makes it an offence to disclose, obtain, publish etc. information about what took place in the jury room (see **B14.82**). The prohibition applies to attempts to obtain information about proceedings in the jury room by the defence (*Mickleburgh* [1995] 1 Cr App R 297), the prosecution (*McCluskey* (1994) 98 Cr App R 216), or the court (*Schot* [1997] 2 Cr App R 383). Such enquiries may be embarked upon only with the consent of the court. After verdict and sentence, as the trial judge is *functus officio*, the consent of the Court of Appeal should be sought (*McCluskey*). In *Miah* [1997] 2 Cr App R 12, it was emphasised that the barrier to the Court of Appeal receiving material relating to the jury's deliberations was to be found in the common law authorities (including *Ellis* v *Deheer* [1922] 2 KB 113 at p. 121) rather than in the Contempt of Court Act 1981.

RETURNING THE VERDICT

General Procedure

The jury's verdict is delivered in open court, in the presence of the accused. The **D16.8** invariable practice is for the person the jury have selected to be their foreman to state in response to questions from the clerk of court whether they find the accused guilty or not guilty. Unless a juror indicates dissent at the time, it is conclusively presumed that they all agree with the verdicts announced on their behalf, and the Court of Appeal will not breach the privacy of the jury room by hearing evidence that the necessary unanimity was lacking (*Roads* [1967] 2 QB 108, and see also *Lalchan Nanan* v *The State* [1986] AC 860, in which, on appeal from the Court of Appeal of Trinidad and Tobago in a capital case, the Privy Council held that the court below had rightly refused to read affidavits from four jurors to the effect that they had not realised the need for unanimity and had wished to acquit the appellant).

If the jury return to court apparently with a verdict prior to their having been given the majority verdict direction, the first question the foreman is asked is whether they have reached a verdict (or verdicts) on which they are all agreed (see *Practice Direction (Crime: Majority Verdicts)* [1967] 1 WLR 1198, para. 1). If the foreman indicates that they have reached unanimous verdicts, he is then asked in respect of each count on the indictment and each accused charged in a count what the jury's verdict is. The jury are entitled to return a partial verdict in the sense of finding an accused guilty on one count but not on others, or finding one accused guilty but another not. They are also entitled to find an accused guilty in respect of some only of the allegations set out in the particulars of a count, as when a count for theft specifies several items as the subject-matter of the charge and the jury are satisfied that the accused stole some of them but are left in doubt as to others (see *Furlong* [1950] 1 All ER 636 where the jury sent a note asking the judge if they could return such a verdict and the Court of Criminal Appeal held that the judge's affirmative answer was undoubtedly correct, even though the method by which he had communicated the answer was at fault).

The general rule that there should be verdicts on each count is subject to the qualification that, where a jury wishes to convict on one of two counts which are in the alternative, it is preferable to take a verdict only on that count and discharge them from giving a verdict on the other. This is because the Court of Appeal will then, in appropriate circumstances, be able on appeal to substitute for the jury's verdict a verdict of guilty of the alternative count, whereas if the jury are allowed formally to acquit the accused of the alternative their verdict on that must stand, even though the conviction on the other count has to be quashed (see *Seymour* [1954] 1 WLR 678, *Melvin* [1953] 1 QB 481 and *Roma* [1956] Crim LR 46, and also the Criminal Appeal Act 1968, s. 3, for the Court of Appeal's power to substitute for the actual verdict a conviction for another offence of which the jury could lawfully have convicted the appellant on the indictment). Having regard to the above considerations, the procedure normally adopted where counts are in the alternative is for the clerk to ask the foreman whether the jury find the accused guilty on *either* of the counts. If the answer is yes, the foreman is asked on which count they wish to convict; a verdict is taken on that count, and the judge discharges them from giving a verdict on the other. If the answer is no, not guilty verdicts are taken on each count.

A rather different problem arises where counts are not strict alternatives, in the sense that a conviction for both would be unlawful, but they arise out of the same facts and are of differing degrees of gravity (e.g., counts for wounding with intent to cause grievous bodily harm and malicious wounding contrary to ss. 18 and 20 respectively of the OAPA 1861). It is usual in such cases for the judge in summing-up to tell the jury to consider first the more serious count and only to go on to consider the lesser one if they are not satisfied as to the former. Similarly, when verdicts are taken, the foreman will be asked first for the verdict on the graver count. If it is guilty, the jury will be discharged from giving a verdict on the other; if it is not guilty, a verdict is also taken on the lesser count. It would not be proper in such cases to allow the jury to convict on both counts because the lesser count really merges into the greater. In *Harris* [1969] 1 WLR 745, H was indicted for buggery and indecent assault on a boy of 14, the latter offence consisting in playing with the victim's private parts immediately prior to the act of buggery. He was convicted on both counts and sentenced to concurrent terms of imprisonment, the longer one being for the buggery offence. His appeal was dismissed save that the Court of Appeal quashed the secondary conviction for indecent assault. Edmund Davies LJ (giving the Court of Appeal's judgment) said:

> There is no suggestion of any indecent assault upon [the victim] except that which formed the preliminary to and was followed very shortly thereafter by the commission of the full act of buggery. It does not seem to this court right or desirable that one and the same incident should be made the subject-matter of distinct charges, so that hereafter it may appear to those not familiar with the circumstances that two entirely separate offences were

committed. Were this permitted generally, a single offence could frequently give rise to a multiplicity of charges and great unfairness could ensue. We accordingly allow the application for leave to appeal against the conviction of indecent assault, which really merges into the conviction for the graver charge.

Although his lordship appears to criticise even the formulating of distinct charges based on one incident, it is submitted that the mischief was not in having two counts on the indictment (which was necessary to cover the possibility of the jury being satisfied that indecency had occurred but not that there had been an act of buggery) but in allowing the jury, once they had convicted of buggery, to go on to convict of the lesser charge also. They should simply have been discharged from giving a verdict in respect of indecent assault.

In *Fernandez* [1997] 1 Cr App R 123, F was charged in an indictment containing, *inter alia*, counts of robbery and handling the proceeds of the robbery. In his summing-up, the judge failed to direct the jury that they were alternatives. The jury returned a verdict of guilty of handling, the court mistakenly taking that verdict before the verdict on the robbery count, contrary to the proper practice as described in the preceding paragraph. The judge then directed the jury that he could not accept their verdict on the handling charge until he had received their verdict on the robbery. The jury later returned a verdict of guilty of robbery, and were discharged from giving a verdict on the handling charge. F's appeal was dismissed. The verdict in respect of the handling charge was irregular. The judge was under a duty to take the verdict on the more serious alternative, robbery, first. Once he had appreciated his error, the course which he took was appropriate and did not render the verdict on the robbery count unsafe.

Correcting the Verdict

It occasionally happens that a jury return a verdict and then realise that it has been **D16.9** misunderstood. In such cases, there is a discretion in the trial judge to allow them to correct their verdict (unless they have been discharged and have dispersed) (*Andrews* (1985) 82 Cr App R 148). In *Andrews*, A and his wife (W) were charged with cruelty to a child contrary to the CYPA 1933, s. 1, in that 'having the charge or care of a child they wilfully assaulted, ill-treated or neglected him in a manner likely to cause him unnecessary suffering or injury'. The judge directed the jury that, if they decided A was guilty on the basis that he had personally assaulted the child, they should simply find him guilty, but if they favoured an alternative basis on which the prosecution presented their case – namely, that he had done nothing to stop W assaulting the child – then they should specify that they merely found him guilty of wilful neglect. They jury convicted W. When further asked for their verdict on A, the foreman simply said 'Not guilty' and A was accordingly discharged. The jury remained in court to hear the sentencing of W and, whilst that was in progress, handed a note to the judge saying, 'We thought we found A guilty of wilful neglect. What happens now?'. The judge then allowed the foreman to be asked whether they found A guilty of cruelty by neglect; he answered affirmatively, and A was dealt with for the offence. The Court of Appeal affirmed the conviction. They held that a jury does have power to alter a verdict from not guilty to guilty provided it acts promptly (see *Parkin* (1824) 1 Mood CC 45 and *Vodden* (1853) Dears CC 229). Whether such an alteration should be allowed is in the discretion of the trial judge, taking into account especially (a) the length of time which has elapsed between the original verdict and the moment when the jury express a wish to change; (b) the apparent reason for the mistake (in the instant case it was probably that the jury had been waiting to be asked for a separate verdict on cruelty by neglect and had not realised that the judge expected them to take the initiative by saying that that was their verdict), and (c) the necessity to ensure that justice was done both to the prosecution and to the defence. In *Andrews*, the accused's having been discharged was *not* fatal to allowing a change of verdict. However, if the jury had been discharged – certainly if they had been allowed to disperse – it would then have been too late to rectify the mistake.

Equally, if the jury had heard anything since returning the original verdict that might have affected their earlier thinking, that would preclude any alteration. On the facts of *Andrews*, however, such problems did not arise.

An alteration to the verdict may also be allowed where the original one was not so much incorrect as incomplete (*Carter* [1964] 2 QB 1 – conviction upheld where a jury which had not been directed by the judge about the possibility of finding the accused guilty of a lesser offence, although prosecuting counsel had referred to it, initially found the accused simply not guilty; after the accused had been discharged, the foreman explained to the judge that they had wished to convict of the lesser offence and the accused were then recalled for the verdict to be completed and sentence passed).

Although the general rule is that, once the jury has been discharged, it is *functus officio* (see **D11.18**), there are circumstances in which it can be reconvened in order to rectify its verdict. In *Aylott* [1996] 2 Cr App R 169, the judge discharged the jury because of a mistaken belief that they were unable to reach a verdict. When he received a further note from the jury which made it clear that they had already reached verdicts, he took the verdicts, as a result of which the appellant was convicted of murder. The appeal on the ground that the discharge of a jury was final was dismissed. The judge was entitled in the circumstances to set aside the discharge which he had ordered. The discharge had been based on a fundamental mistake. It was plain that the jury had remained together and had not spoken to anyone outside their number. The underlying principle was to ensure that proceedings were fair and to do justice in the particular case. In *Maloney* [1996] 2 Cr App R 303, a guilty verdict was taken by the court on Friday afternoon, without asking how many jurors had agreed with the verdict and how many dissented. The mistake was realised later that day, and the jury was reconvened the following Monday. They were then asked about the figures and the foreman replied that 11 agreed and one dissented. The Court of Appeal held that the discharge of the jury did not prevent the court carrying out the rectifying procedure. Nor were the lapse of time and the fact that the jury had dispersed fatal, in view of the CJPO 1994, s. 43, which permitted the jury to separate after retirement. There was no suggestion that they had deliberated further after the dispersal, nor that the numbers given as to the size of the majority were incorrect. The position would have been different if the jury had had to deliberate further, or, perhaps, if the verdict was being altered from not guilty to guilty.

Power of Judge to Refuse to Accept Verdict

D16.10 In general, a judge is obliged to accept the jury's verdict however much he may disagree with it (*Robinson* [1975] QB 508, following *Lester* (1938) 27 Cr App R 8). In the latter case, it was held that the judge should have allowed the jury's first verdict of guilty of receiving to stand even though his view was that the evidence pointed to guilt (if at all) only on an alternative count of larceny, and he had directed the jury solely in relation to that offence.

The exceptions to the general rule were succinctly stated by Lord Parker CJ in *Harris* [1964] Crim LR 54. The *Criminal Law Review's* paraphrase of his lordship's judgment reads:

> Where a single verdict is ambiguous, or two verdicts are inconsistent, or the verdict is one which cannot on the indictment or in the circumstances be lawfully returned, the judge is entitled, unless the jury insist, to refuse to accept the first verdict and ask the jury to reconsider the matter and if they change their verdict to record only the second verdict.

Similarly, in *Robinson* [1975] QB 508, James LJ said (at p. 512F):

> . . . once the jury has returned a verdict, then the judge cannot say 'I will not have it', provided, of course, it is a verdict that is not ambiguous and provided it is a verdict that can properly be returned upon the indictment they have been considering.

Thus, there are three categories of case in which the first verdict need not be accepted.

(a) *The original verdict is one which the jury cannot lawfully return on the indictment.* An example would be a verdict of guilty of a lesser offence when such a verdict does not, in the circumstances of the case, come within any of the statutory provisions allowing a jury to convict the accused of something other than that with which he is expressly charged in the indictment.

(b) *The original verdict is ambiguous.* In such cases the judge should ask whatever questions are necessary to resolve the ambiguity (*Hawkes* (1931) 22 Cr App R 172) and may, if necessary, give a supplementary direction on the law before taking a final verdict (*Sweetland* (1957) 42 Cr App R 62). If the judge proceeds to sentence on a purported verdict of guilty which remains ambiguous, both conviction and sentence will have to be quashed (*Hawkes*). Presumably, if a jury will not or cannot pronounce an unambiguous verdict, they should be discharged and the case retried by a different jury.

(c) *Inconsistency in the verdict.* If the individual verdicts on a number of counts or in respect of several accused are – having regard to the nature of the evidence that has been adduced – inconsistent with each other, then the judge may ask the jury to reconsider their decision. He should only do so, however, if the verdicts are *necessarily* inconsistent. If there is a possible, albeit unlikely, view of the evidence on which the verdicts can be justified, the judge should accept them without further query.

In *Burrows* [1970] Crim LR 419, for example, three co-accused (including B) were jointly charged with theft of a purse and one of them (P) was charged in the alternative with handling it. The jury initially acquitted all three of theft but convicted P of handling. The judge declined to accept the verdict, asking the jury how they could find P guilty of handling when their acquittal of all three accused on the theft count implied that they were not satisfied that the goods in question had ever been stolen. Further discussion then revealed a misunderstanding on the jury's part which the judge was able to correct. They then found B guilty of theft. On appeal, it was held that the judge should have accepted the original verdicts. They were not necessarily inconsistent *inter se* since the jury might have been sure that *either* B or the third co-accused had stolen the purse but have been unable to attribute responsibility to one or the other. If so, their conviction of P would have been logical since, in order to convict of handling, a jury merely has to be satisfied that the goods were stolen by somebody. On the facts, the proviso was applied because the judge's error had fortuitously led to the jury's mistake being corrected and hence to their returning what was plainly a proper verdict.

If the judge legitimately refuses to accept the jury's first verdict and in consequence they return a proper second verdict, it is the latter which is the operative decision. If the jury, notwithstanding the judge's intervention, persist in returning inconsistent verdicts, the inconsistency may be a good ground of appeal.

Supplementary Questions about the Verdict

It is not in general good practice to ask the jury questions about the basis on which they **D16.11** have returned a verdict of guilty (per Humphreys J in *Larkin* [1943] KB 174). Where the prosecution evidence is such that two or more views of the facts consistent with guilt are tenable but on one view the accused's culpability is greater than on the other, it is the judge's responsibility, following a guilty verdict, to decide what the circumstances of the offence were for purposes of sentencing (*Solomon* (1984) 6 Cr App R (S) 120 and *Stosiek* (1982) 4 Cr App R (S) 205). Asking the jury to refine their verdict may merely lead to confusion.

The one recognised exception to this principle is in cases where the accused is charged with murder and the jury have been left two or more alternative bases on which they might find the accused guilty of manslaughter and not guilty of murder. Exactly why the accused was found guilty of manslaughter (whether it was on grounds of provocation or diminished responsibility and, if the latter, whether the abnormality of mind was caused by medication or inherent causes) is then of crucial importance to sentence. Perhaps for that reason, it is common to ask the jury the basis of their verdict (see *Matheson* [1958] 1 WLR 474, *Frankum* (1983) 5 Cr App R (S) 259, *Solomon* (1984) 6 Cr App R (S) 120 per Beldam J at p. 126). In *Cawthorne* [1996] Crim LR 526, a verdict of guilty of manslaughter was returned on a count of murder. The issue was whether the verdict had been returned on the basis of unlawful killing without intent to kill or cause really serious injury, provocation or gross negligence. The judge asked the jury whether they were prepared to indicate the basis for the verdict, but the foreman declined. The Court of Appeal stressed that whether or not the judge asked the jury to indicate the basis of the verdict was a matter for his discretion; following the verdict, he was entitled to sentence on the basis of the facts which he had heard in evidence.

Having returned the general verdict, the jury are, however, entitled to decline to answer any supplementary question, in which event the responsibility for deciding the issue is thrown back on the judge. As a matter of procedure, a judge who intends to ask a jury the basis of a guilty verdict should warn them of his intention before they retire (*Heckstall-Smith* [1989] Crim LR 742). If they convict, they should then be asked the supplementary question immediately after returning the main verdict and before they separate (ibid.). In complicated cases, it may be a 'sensible precaution' to write the questions down for the jury. In *Frankum*, Dunn LJ approved the course adopted by the trial judge in the case who gave the jury a list of questions as follows: 'First, do you think it more probable than not that the accused was suffering from diminished responsibility? If so, you should find him guilty of manslaughter. If you find him guilty of manslaughter, you will be asked (1) Is that on the ground of diminished responsibility, and (2) If so, do you think the abnormality arose (a) as a result of inherent causes, (b) was induced by injury from the toxic effects of [a drug F was taking for a peptic ulcer] or (c) was both?'

In general, if the judge has summed up the case to the jury on one factual basis, he is entitled to assume that they will acquit or convict on that basis and not on some alternative view of the facts which may theoretically have been open on the evidence but was not a live issue during the trial (*Heckstall-Smith*). Where the jury do attempt to indicate while the judge is passing sentence that the factual basis on which he is doing so is different from that which they found proved, the judge may refuse to hear what they wish to say (*Ekwuyasi* [1981] Crim LR 574).

MAJORITY VERDICTS

Introduction

D16.12 At common law, the verdict of a jury had to be unanimous. The unanimity rule was qualified by provisions of the CJA 1967, now re-enacted as s. 17 of the Juries Act 1974. By s. 17(1) some majority verdicts are permissible, subject to certain conditions being satisfied. The procedure for taking majority verdicts is set out in *Practice Direction (Crime: Majority Verdicts)* [1967] 1 WLR 1198, supplemented by *Practice Direction (Crime: Majority Verdict)* [1970] 1 WLR 916.

Time Requirement

D16.13 A majority verdict may not be accepted unless the jury have been considering their verdict for such period as the court considers reasonable having regard to the nature and complexity of the case, being in any event a period of not less than two hours (Juries Act 1974, s. 17(4)). Any period during which the jury return to court to ask a question of or receive a communication from the judge should be included when computing the two hours (*Adams* [1969] 1 WLR 106). Time spent making their way to the jury room, settling themselves down in the room and electing a foreman is catered for by *Practice Direction (Crime: Majority Verdict)* [1970] 1 WLR 916, which states that, although s. 17(4) permits the receiving of a majority verdict after a bare two hours, the jury should in fact be allowed at least two hours and 10 minutes for deliberation before being told that they need not be unanimous.

How long over the minimum of two hours and 10 minutes should elapse before the majority verdict procedure is set in motion is a matter for the trial judge's discretion. It will depend largely on the complexity of the case. In *Wright* (1974) 58 Cr App R 444, following a five-day trial for murder, the judge had the jury back after a bare two hours; told them he could now accept a majority verdict, and asked them to retire for a short time to consider the matter. This was clearly a breach of the practice directions, but they are directory only, not mandatory (see **D16.16**). It was held on appeal that the majority conviction was lawful because (a) there had been no breach of the Juries Act 1974, s. 17, itself, and (b) the judge had not, in the circumstances of the case, unjustifiably rushed the jury into a majority verdict. Although the case had been relatively long and was not easy to decide, the issue was a very simple one – namely, were the jury satisfied that W's confession to the police had been genuine and not, as he claimed, designed to protect the wife of the deceased? In the circumstances, allowing the jury a longer time to reach unanimity would not have helped – either the individual jurors did accept the accused's explanation for his confession or they did not, and arguing about it for a long time was unlikely to change minds. It is unusual, however, for judges to invite a majority verdict at the earliest moment permitted by the statute and practice direction. In *Rose* [1982] 1 WLR 614, for example, the Court of Appeal indicated that a period of two hours and 40 minutes was 'a little soon' for the majority verdict direction in a murder trial which had lasted for 15 days.

Minimum Number for Acceptable Majority

By the Juries Act 1974, s. 17(1), the minimum majorities permissible are 11–1 or 10–2, **D16.14** or (in the case of a jury from which one or more of the original jurors have been discharged) 10–1 or 9–1. A jury reduced to nine must be unanimous.

Statement of Size of Majority and Minority in Open Court

If (and only if) the verdict is guilty, the foreman of the jury must state in open court the **D16.15** number of jurors who respectively agreed to and dissented from the verdict (Juries Act 1974, s. 17(3)). Since stating the size of a majority for conviction is expressed as a precondition of the court accepting the verdict, failure to comply with s. 17(3) will result in any purported conviction being quashed (*Barry* [1975] 1 WLR 1190, a case where the judge accepted a majority verdict of guilty without the foreman even being asked what the majority was). However, compliance with the subsection does not necessarily entail the foreman stating that (a) 10 or, as the case may be, 11 agreed with the verdict, *and* (b) 2 (or 1) dissented. It is sufficient if, as happened in *Pigg* [1983] 1 WLR 6, he states the number in the majority leaving the size of the minority to be inferred by the simplest of arithmetic. In *Pigg*, Lord Brandon of Oakbrook (with whose speech all the other Law Lords concurred) stated the position thus (at p. 13G–H, emphasis added):

> ... compliance with the requirement of section 17(3) of the Act of 1974 is mandatory before a judge can accept a majority verdict of guilty; but the precise form of words used by the clerk of the court when asking questions of the foreman of the jury, and the precise form of words used by the latter in answer to such questions, *as long as they make it clear to an ordinary person how the jury was divided*, do not constitute any essential part of that requirement.

It should be noted that the requirement to reveal the size of the majority only applies if the verdict is guilty. If the verdict is not guilty, the verdict is taken in such a way as not to reveal with certainty whether it was unanimous or by a majority.

Procedure for Taking Majority Verdicts

D16.16 The procedure for taking majority verdicts is set out in *Practice Direction (Crime: Majority Verdicts)* [1967] 1 WLR 1198. The main features of the procedure are that:

(a)   If the jury return to court in less than two hours and 10 minutes (or such longer period as the judge considers they should reasonably be given for trying to reach a unanimous verdict), the clerk of court asks the foreman if they have reached a verdict on which they are all agreed. If the answer is yes, the verdict is taken; if the answer is no, they are sent back to their room with a direction to continue to try to achieve unanimity.

(b)   If the jury return or are sent for after the period referred to in (a) has elapsed, the clerk similarly asks the foreman if they have reached a verdict on which they are all agreed. If the answer at this stage is no, the judge directs the jury that he can now accept a majority verdict, and tells them the size of the permissible majorities. However, he must also tell them that, when they again retire, they should make a further attempt to reach a unanimous verdict, and only if that last attempt at unanimity fails should they come back with a majority decision.

(c)   Upon the jury returning to court after the majority verdict direction has been given, the clerk asks the foreman whether they have reached a verdict on which at least 10 of them are agreed. If the answer is yes, they are asked for the verdict. A verdict of not guilty should be accepted without more ado. If the verdict is guilty, the foreman should be further asked whether it was unanimous or by a majority and, if the latter, how many agreed and how many dissented.

At the close of his summing-up, it is conventional for the judge to anticipate jury questions about the possibility of a majority verdict by telling them that, at this stage, they should try to reach a unanimous verdict. If the time should come when he can accept a verdict which is not the verdict of them all, he will give them a further direction. The judge should not, however, indicate the precise period which must elapse before a majority verdict becomes a possibility (*Thomas* [1983] Crim LR 745). If he does so, it will not necessarily be improper, e.g., where the effect is to alleviate anxiety or uncertainty which the jury may be feeling (*Guthrie* (1994) *The Times*, 23 February 1994 and *Porter* [1996] Crim LR 126).

Effect of Failure to Comply

D16.17 The effect of non-compliance with the procedures described above varies depending on whether the non-compliance amounts to a breach of the Juries Act 1974, s. 17, or is merely a breach of the relevant practice directions (*Practice Direction (Crime: Majority Verdicts)* [1967] 1 WLR 1198 and *Practice Direction (Crime: Majority Verdict)* [1970] 1 WLR 916). In the former case, since the court's power to accept a majority verdict depends entirely upon the statutory provision, any conviction must be quashed (see *Barry* [1975] 1 WLR 1190, and also *Pigg* [1983] 1 WLR 6 where, although the House of Lords held that in the circumstances s. 17(3) had been complied with, they accepted the premise that – had it not been – there would have been no alternative but to allow a completely unmeritorious appeal). If, on the other hand, there has been failure to comply with the practice directions and nothing more, the conviction may stand since the directions are (as the name implies) directory not mandatory (see *Wright* (1974) 58 Cr App R 444 and *Shields* [1997] Crim LR 758 for examples of an appeal being dismissed notwithstanding acknowledged breaches of the directions). The Court of Appeal has, however, stressed the importance of following the directions closely (see *Georgiou* (1969) 53 Cr App R 428).

Juries Act 1974, s. 17

(1)   Subject to subsections (3) and (4) below, the verdict of a jury in proceedings in the Crown Court . . . need not be unanimous if—

    (a)   in a case where there are not less than 11 jurors, 10 of them agree on the verdict; and

    (b)   in a case where there are 10 jurors, nine of them agree on the verdict.

. . .

    (3)   The Crown Court shall not accept a verdict of guilty by virtue of subsection (1) above unless the foreman of the jury has stated in open court the number of jurors who respectively agreed to and dissented from the verdict.

    (4)   No court shall accept a verdict by virtue of subsection (1) . . . above unless it appears to the court that the jury have had such period of time for deliberation as the court thinks reasonable having regard to the nature and complexity of the case; and the Crown Court shall in any event not accept such a verdict unless it appears to the court that the jury have had at least two hours for deliberation.

Practice Direction (Crime: Majority Verdicts) **[1967] 1 WLR 1198**

It is important that all those trying indictable offences should so far as possible adopt a uniform practice both in directing a jury in summing-up and also in receiving the verdict or giving further direction after retirement.

So far as the summing-up is concerned, it is inadvisable for the judge and indeed for counsel to attempt an explanation of the section for fear that the jury will be confused. Before the jury retire however the judge should direct the jury in some suh words as the following:

> As you may know, the law permits me in certain circumstances to accept a verdict which is not the verdict of you all. Those circumstances have not as yet arisen so that when you retire I must ask you to reach a verdict upon which each one of you is agreed. Should, however, the time come when it is possible for me to accept a majority verdict, I will give you a further direction.

Thereafter the practice should be as follows:

1.   Should the jury return *before* the two hours (or such longer time as the judge thinks reasonable) has elapsed (see subsection (3)), they should be asked
    (i)   Have you reached a verdict upon which you are all agreed? Please answer yes or no.
    (ii) (a) *If unanimous* – What is your verdict?
         (b) *If not unanimous* – the jury should be sent out again for further deliberation with a further direction to arrive if possible at a unanimous verdict.

2.   Should the jury return (whether for the first or second time) or be sent for *after* the two hours (or the longer period) has elapsed, questions (i) and (ii)(a) in the preceding paragraph should be put to them and if it appears that they are not unanimous they should be asked to retire once more and told that they should continue to endeavour to reach a unanimous verdict but that if they cannot the judge will accept a majority verdict as in subsection (1).

3.   When the jury finally return they should be asked
    (i)   Have at least 10 (or nine as the case may be) of you agreed upon your verdict? If yes,
    (ii)   What is your verdict? Please only answer 'Guilty' or 'Not guilty'.
    (iii) (a) If 'Not guilty' – accept the verdict without more ado.
         (b) If 'Guilty' – Is it the verdict of you all or by a majority?
    (iv) If 'Guilty' by a majority – How many of you agreed to the verdict and how many dissented?

Where there are several counts (or alternative verdicts) left to the jury the above practice will of course need to be adapted to the circumstances. The procedure will have to be repeated in respect of each count (or alternative verdict) the verdict being accepted in those cases where the jury are unanimous and the further direction in paragraph 2 being given in cases in which they are not unanimous.

Should the jury in the end be unable to agree on a verdict by the required majority (i.e., if the answer to the question in paragraph 3(i) be in the negative) the judge in his discretion will either ask them to deliberate further or discharge them.

VERDICT OF GUILTY OF AN ALTERNATIVE OFFENCE

Introduction

D16.18 It is sometimes open to a jury to find the accused not guilty of the offence alleged in a count but guilty of some other alternative offence. This is commonly referred to as a verdict of guilty of a lesser offence (although the word 'lesser' is not used in any of the relevant legislation). At common law, a jury could find an accused guilty of a lesser offence if the definition of the greater offence charged necessarily included the definition of the lesser. The common law is now largely irrelevant because of the enactment of a number of statutory provisions which permit alternative verdicts not only in all the situations covered by common law but also in some not so covered. Until the House of Lords decision in *Saunders* [1988] AC 148 it had been widely assumed that the common law had been abrogated and that all questions of the availability of alternative verdicts therefore had to be decided according to statute. However, it would seem from *Saunders* that that assumption was ill-founded and that, at least in the unusual circumstances of that case, there is still a residual role for the common law to play. Nevertheless, save when discussing the particular problem raised by *Saunders*, this discussion of alternative verdicts proceeds on the basis that the law is now to be found in statute.

The General Rule

D16.19 The general provision on the availability of alternative verdicts is contained in the Criminal Law Act 1967, s. 6(3), which provides as follows:

> Where, on a person's trial on indictment for any offence except treason or murder, the jury find him not guilty of the offence specifically charged in the indictment, but the allegations in the indictment amount to or include (expressly or by implication) an allegation of another offence falling within the jurisdiction of the court of trial, the jury may find him guilty of that other offence or of an offence of which he could be found guilty on an indictment specifically charging that other offence.

There are thus two principal situations covered by s. 6(3). One is where the offence charged *expressly* includes an allegation of another indictable offence; the other is where it *impliedly* includes such an allegation.

Express Allegation of Another Offence

D16.20 To determine whether a count expressly includes an allegation of another offence it is necessary to apply a 'blue-pencil test'. This involves striking from the particulars of the count in the indictment the allegations that the prosecution evidence cannot or may not be able to sustain and, if what remains is a valid count for another offence, that alternative may be left for the jury's consideration (*Lillis* [1972] 2 QB 236). In *Lillis*, the particulars of a count for burglary contrary to the Theft Act 1968, s. 9(1)(b), alleged that L, on a certain date, entered part of a building, namely the conservatory of a house situated at —— and stole therein a lawn-mower. The prosecution evidence in fact established that, on the day in question, L had been given permission to enter the conservatory and borrow the mower. The complaint of the owners was not that he had taken it in the first place but that he had failed to return it when he should have done. A submission of no case to answer on the charge of burglary inevitably succeeded. However, the judge held that there was a case to answer for theft by keeping, and he left that alternative verdict to the jury, who convicted. On appeal, it was argued that an offence of stealing on a day unknown subsequent to the date mentioned in the count at a place other than that mentioned in the count could not properly be said to be included in the offence alleged in the count. The Court of Appeal dismissed the appeal. Applying the test described above, they notionally struck from the count those allegations the prosecution could not prove. What remained were the following particulars: 'L stole a lawn-mower'. Although such wording was highly unsatisfactory, it would have been just sufficient to satisfy the Indictment Rules 1971 for a count of theft since an error in the date of offence alleged does not invalidate a conviction. Accordingly, the alternative verdict had been open to the jury.

The application of the *Lillis* test does not seem to have caused any difficulties. It was approved by the House of Lords in their decision in *Metropolitan Police Commissioner* v *Wilson* [1984] AC 242, and there has been little or no other authority on it.

Implied Allegation of Another Offence

There have been two distinct tests promulgated by the appellate courts for determining **D16.21** when a count impliedly includes an allegation of another offence. The first test was laid down by Sachs LJ in *Springfield* (1969) 53 Cr App R 608. It was that a count for offence A impliedly contains an allegation of offence B if, and only if, the commission of offence B is a necessary step towards committing offence A. Moreover, in applying the test, the court was entitled to look only at the wording of the count and the legal definitions of (a) the offence in the count and (b) the suggested alternative. Therefore, if there was any possibility in law – however remote – that the accused could have committed the 'count' offence without committing the alternative, then the latter could not be left to the jury. Moreover, it was irrelevant that the prosecution case was that the accused had in fact committed both offences.

However, this test was disapproved by Lord Roskill in *Metropolitan Police Commissioner* v *Wilson* [1984] AC 242. The question raised in that case was, in essence, whether a count for inflicting grievous bodily harm impliedly includes an allegation of assault occasioning actual bodily harm. An allegation that grievous bodily harm occurred obviously and probably expressly includes an allegation that there was actual bodily harm (p. 259C). But do the words 'inflicting harm' impliedly include assault? Lord Roskill assumed in the appellant's favour that, in exceptional circumstances, harm can be inflicted within the meaning of the relevant statutory provisions without an assault by the accused (e.g., by his deliberately creating panic which results in force being applied to the body of the victim by persons other than himself). Then follows the crucial passage from his lordship's speech (pp. 260H–261B):

> The critical question is, therefore, whether it being accepted that a charge of inflicting grievous bodily harm contrary to section 20 [of the Offences against the Person Act 1861] may not necessarily involve an allegation of assault, but may nonetheless do so, and in very many cases will involve such an allegation, the allegations in a section 20 charge 'include either expressly or by implication' allegations of assault occasioning actual bodily harm. If 'inflicting' can, as the cases show, include 'inflicting by assault', then even though such a charge may not necessarily do so, I do not for myself see why on a fair reading of section 6(3) these allegations do not at least impliedly *include* 'inflicting by assault'. That is sufficient for present purposes though I also regard it as also a possible view that those former allegations *expressly* include the other allegations.

Lord Roskill then held that the reasoning in *Springfield* should no longer be followed. Although the 'necessary step' test laid down in *Springfield* is thus no longer operative, it is not easy to discern precisely what, if anything, has been put in its place. However, it is submitted that the thrust of Lord Roskill's reasoning is that, where commission of the offence alleged in a count may and – in the great majority of cases – will involve commission of another offence, an allegation of the latter offence is impliedly included in the count, even if it is possible in law for the one offence to be committed without commission of the other. Listed below are a number of authorities on the availability of alternative verdicts. It should be borne in mind that, where a case decided under the *Springfield* test held that a certain alternative verdict was *not* open to the jury, it would not necessarily be decided the same way today under the less restrictive *Wilson* test.

(a)   *Springfield* cases:

(i)   In *Springfield* itself it was held that, on a count for robbery, the jury could not convict of common assault. The case was decided under the law as it was prior to the Theft Act 1968, and the question of whether the verdict might be available to the jury under the present law was left open. It is submitted that, whether or not common assault is a necessary step towards robbery within the meaning of the *Springfield* test, robbery may and usually does involve common assault, at least in the sense of putting the victim in fear of immediate unlawful violence. Therefore, a verdict of common assault should now be available applying Lord Roskill's test in *Metropolitan Police Commissioner* v *Wilson*. It has never been doubted that, on a count for robbery, the jury may convict of theft.

(ii)   *Mochan* [1969] 1 WLR 1331. On a count for rape the jury may not convict of unlawful sexual intercourse with a girl under 16 since it is obviously not an essential ingredient of rape that the victim be of any particular age. That the alleged victim, according to the prosecution, was in fact under 16 is irrelevant. The same reasoning applies even if the count for rape includes the unnecessary allegation that the girl was under age, since the reference in the Criminal Law Act 1967, s. 6(3), to an indictment impliedly including an allegation of another offence must refer to a correctly drawn indictment (*Fisher* [1969] 2 QB 114).

(iii)   *Hodgson* [1973] QB 565. On a count for rape the jury may convict of indecent assault contrary to the Sexual Offences Act 1956, s. 14. This is because the allegation of rape impliedly includes both an allegation of an assault and an allegation of indecency. Where the accused successfully raises a defence of consent, that will normally entitle him to an absolute acquittal since the woman's consent is as much a defence to the assault as it is to the rape. However, should the victim be under 16, s. 14(2) of the 1956 Act prevents the accused relying on such consent and the alternative verdict may therefore be left to the jury.

(iv)   *McCormack* [1969] 2 QB 442. On a count for unlawful sexual intercourse with a girl under 16 the jury may convict of indecent assault. The reasoning is similar to that in *Hodgson* (see above).

(v)   *McCready* [1978] 1 WLR 1376. On a count for causing grievous bodily harm with intent contrary to the OAPA 1861, s. 18, the jury may not convict either of malicious wounding contrary to s. 20 of the Act or of any form of assault. This is because harm can be caused within the meaning of s. 18 by, for example, poisoning the victim, without there having been either an application of force or a wounding. On the other hand, if the count under s. 18 is for wounding, the alternatives mentioned above would, it is submitted, be open to the jury even on the *Springfield* test since an assault is a necessary step towards a wounding, while an allegation of wounding with intent to do grievous bodily harm expressly includes an allegation of malicious wounding. It is unlikely that *McCready* would be followed if the same point arose today for determination in the light of *Metropolitan Police Commissioner* v *Wilson*.

(b)   *Wilson* cases:

(i)   In *Metropolitan Police Commissioner* v *Wilson* itself, the House of Lords restored W's conviction for assault occasioning actual bodily harm on a count alleging inflicting grievous bodily harm contrary to the OAPA 1861, s. 20 (the Court of Appeal, applying the *Springfield* test, had quashed the conviction). Similarly, in *Jenkins* (which was heard with *Wilson*), a conviction for actual bodily harm was restored on a count alleging burglary contrary to the Theft Act 1968, s. 9(1)(b), in that J, having entered a building as a trespasser, inflicted grievous bodily harm on a person therein.

(ii)   In *Savage* [1992] 1 AC 699, the House of Lords held that a verdict of assault occasioning actual bodily harm is a permissible alternative verdict on a count alleging unlawful wounding contrary to the Offences against the Person Act 1861, s. 20.

(iii)   In *Whiting* (1987) 85 Cr App R 78, the Court of Appeal held that on a count for burglary contrary to the Theft Act 1968, s. 9(1)(b), where the allegation is that the accused, having entered as a trespasser, stole certain property, the jury may convict of entry as a trespasser with intent to steal contrary to s. 9(1)(a). This case shows the importance of the decision in *Metropolitan Police Commissioner* v *Wilson* since it had earlier been held in *Hollis* [1971] Crim LR 525 that, applying the *Springfield* test, such an alternative verdict was not available.

(iv)   In *Mandair* [1995] 1 AC 208, the House of Lords held that 'causing' grievous bodily harm contrary to the OAPA 1861, s. 18, was wide enough to include any action that could amount to inflicting grievous bodily harm under s. 20. *Metropolitan Police Commissioner* v *Wilson* was applied, and *Field* (1993) 97 Cr App R 357 overruled.

Specific Statutory Provisions Relating to Alternative Verdicts

The Criminal Law Act 1967, s. 6(3), is supplemented by a number of other provisions prescribing the alternative verdicts which may be returned on counts for certain specific offences. **D16.22**

Murder   Section 6(2) of the Criminal Law Act 1967 provides that: **D16.23**

> On an indictment for murder a person found not guilty of murder may be found guilty—
> (a)   of manslaughter, or of causing grievous bodily harm with intent to do so; or
> (b)   of any offence of which he may be found guilty under an enactment specifically so providing, or under section 14(2) of this Act; or
> (c)   of an attempt to commit murder, or of an attempt to commit any other offence of which he might be found guilty;
> but may not be found guilty of any offence not included above.

Paragraph (b) of the subsection preserves the effect of the Infanticide Act 1938, s. 1(2) (upon the trial of a woman for murder of her newly born child the jury may convict of infanticide), and of the Infant Life (Preservation) Act 1929, s. 2(2) (upon a trial for, *inter alia*, murder of a child the jury may convict of child destruction). For s. 4(2) of the Criminal Law Act 1967, see **D16.24**.

The one problem raised by s. 6(2) is its requirement that the accused actually be found not guilty of murder. It is submitted that it would be a welcome simplification if the statute were amended to provide for a case in which the jury are unable to agree on a verdict on the murder charge.

Assisting Offenders   By the Criminal Law Act 1967, s. 4(2), if the jury are satisfied that the offence with which the accused is charged (or some other offence of which he might be found guilty on that charge) has been committed by someone, but they find the accused himself not guilty of it, they may, by way of alternative verdict, find him guilty of assisting whoever the offender was contrary to s. 4(1) of the Act. It has been held that, where it can be foreseen that a charge under s. 4(1) might be a proper way of dealing with the accused's case, the prosecution should not invoke s. 4(2) to put the matter before the jury but should have a separate count for assisting an offender (*Cross* [1971] 3 All ER 641). If, however, the possibility of a conviction under s. 4(1) only arises during the course of the case (e.g., as a result of the accused's own evidence), then the prosecution are entitled to rely on s. 4(2), although they should still raise the question or apply to amend the indictment to add an appropriate count before the evidence has been completed so that the defence have a fair opportunity of dealing with the new allegation (*Cross* and see also *Vincent* (1972) 56 Cr App R 281). **D16.24**

Attempts   By the Criminal Law Act 1967, s. 6(4), 'any allegation of an offence shall be taken as including an allegation of attempting to commit that offence'. It follows that, whenever a count charges the accused with a completed indictable offence, he may be convicted of an attempt to commit the same or of an attempt to commit any other **D16.25** completed offence of which he could be found guilty on the count (s. 6(3) read in conjunction with s. 6(4)). Conversely, if the accused is charged merely with an attempt (or with any assault or other act preliminary to an offence – e.g., assault with intent to rob) but the evidence in fact establishes the completed offence, he may nonetheless be convicted as charged (second limb of s. 6(4)). Alternatively, the judge may discharge the jury with a view to the preferment of an indictment for the completed offence (ibid.).

D16.26 ***Driving Offences***   The Road Traffic Offenders Act 1988, s. 24, makes provision for the alternative verdicts which may be returned where a person is tried for certain offences contrary to the Road Traffic Act 1981 (see **C2.15**).

D16.27 ***Offences under the Public Order Act 1986***   By the Public Order Act 1986, s. 7, if a jury find the accused not guilty on a count for either violent disorder (contrary to s. 2 of the Act) or affray (contrary to s. 3), they may (without prejudice to the Criminal Law Act 1967, s. 6(3)) find him guilty of the summary offence of threatening behaviour contrary to s. 4 of the 1986 Act. Although there is no authority on the point, it would seem that the offences under ss. 1, 2 and 3 of the 1986 Act (riot, violent disorder and affray) are in descending order of gravity, and a count under s. 1 will expressly or impliedly include an allegation of offences under the other two sections. Similarly, a count under s. 2 will include an allegation under s. 3. Therefore, alternative verdicts ought to be available under the general provision in the Criminal Law Act 1967, s. 6(3).

D16.28 ***Taking a Motor Vehicle without the Owner's Consent***   If, on a count for theft, the jury are not satisfied that the accused committed the offence charged, but it is proved that he committed an offence under the Theft Act 1968, s. 12(1) (taking a motor vehicle without the owner's consent etc.), they may convict him of the latter offence (Theft Act 1968, s. 12(4)).

D16.29 ***Common Assault***   Until the CJA 1988, s. 40, came into force, a person charged under the OAPA 1861, s. 47, with assault occasioning actual bodily harm could be convicted, as an alternative, of common assault. This followed from the Criminal Law Act 1967, s. 6(3), and was the case whether or not there was a specific allegation of common assault as an alternative in the indictment. By the CJA 1988, s. 40 (see **D9.6**), however, the position is that common assault is a summary offence. It is not within the jurisdiction of the Crown Court, unless a specific count alleging common assault is added to the indictment (*Mearns* [1991] 1 QB 82). Glidewell LJ, delivering the judgment in *Mearns*, went further, suggesting that all offences listed in s. 40 of the 1988 Act are excluded as alternative offences, unless specific counts are added. It is submitted that this is not accurate, at any rate with respect to an offence of taking a motor vehicle without the owner's consent etc. As indicated in **D16.28**, the jury can, by the Theft Act 1968, s. 12(4), convict an accused charged with theft of an offence under s. 12(1) (taking a motor vehicle without the owner's consent etc.). No specific count in the indictment is needed for such an alternative verdict to be available (see also the CJA 1988, s. 37).

Judge's Discretion in Directing Jury as to Alternative Offences

D16.30 The judge in summing up is not obliged to direct the jury about the option of finding the accused guilty of an alternative offence, even if that option is available to them as a matter of law. If, however, the possibility that the accused is guilty only of a lesser offence has fairly arisen on the evidence and if directing the jury about it will not unnecessarily complicate the case, then the judge should – in the interests of justice – leave the alternative to them (*Fairbanks* [1986] 1 WLR 1202, see below).

The judge's discretion in relation to alternative verdicts is usually invoked to protect the accused against being prejudiced by the unexpected introduction at a late stage of his trial of a suggestion that he is guilty on a charge that has never been expressly preferred against him and which he has not had a fair opportunity of countering in the course of his defence. Thus in *Metropolitan Police Commissioner* v *Wilson* [1984] AC 242, Lord Roskill rejected the defence argument that the extension of the availability of alternative verdicts implied in the abandonment of the *Springfield* test (see **D16.21**) might work injustice by referring to the judge's discretion. His lordship said (at p. 261F):

> If it be said that [our conclusion in this case] exposes the defendant to the risk of conviction on a charge which would not have been fully investigated at the trial on the count in the indictment, the answer is that a trial judge must always ensure, before deciding to leave the possibility of conviction of another offence to the jury under section 6(3) [of the Criminal Law Act 1967], that that course will involve no risk of injustice to the defendant and that he has had the opportunity of fully meeting that alternative in the course of his defence.

At the very least, a judge intending to leave an alternative verdict to the jury should warn counsel beforehand and should give them the opportunity of making representations about the propriety or otherwise of the proposed course (*Hazell* [1985] RTR 369). Counsel should also have an opportunity to address the jury about the alternative verdict, assuming it is to be left (ibid.). In *Hazell*, the accused was charged with reckless driving. The judge directed the jury that they could acquit H as charged but find him guilty of careless driving, which they did. The conviction was quashed because the possibility of an alternative verdict for careless driving had not apparently been canvassed by either side prior to the summing-up. It is submitted that giving the defence a fair opportunity to deal with an alternative verdict will, at least in most cases, involve drawing counsel's attention to the possibility of such a verdict before the close of defence evidence. In *Harris* (1993) *The Times*, 22 March 1993, Steyn LJ in the Court of Appeal expressly endorsed the preceding passage of this work and stated that it was appropriate to leave an alternative offence to the jury only if the defendant had a full opportunity to meet the revised case against him so as to ensure that he was not prejudiced.

The exercise of the judge's discretion in relation to alternative verdicts was further considered by the Court of Appeal in *Fairbanks* [1986] 1 WLR 1202 in the context of the defence wanting the alternative to be left. F was indicted for causing death by reckless driving, the prosecution case being that he had caused the death of a passenger in his car by driving at recklessly high speeds. Defence counsel in his closing speech conceded that F's driving had been careless but argued that it was a case of simple misjudgment rather than recklessness. However, the prosecution did not want the jury to be given the easy option of finding the accused guilty merely of driving without due care and attention. Following legal argument, the judge accepted the prosecution's submissions and told the jury to put out of their minds categories of bad driving other than recklessness. The jury, after a four-hour retirement during which a question they asked indicated that they might have wanted to convict of careless driving, found H guilty as charged. On appeal, the conviction was quashed. Reviewing the earlier authorities (*Vaughan* (1908) 1 Cr App R 25; *Naylor* (1910) 5 Cr App R 19 and *Parrott* (1913) 8 Cr App R 186), Mustill LJ said that an alternative offence should be left to the jury 'only if that is in the interests of justice' (p. 1205H). Since justice serves the interests of the public as well as those of the accused, there will be cases where, on the evidence, the accused *ought* to be convicted of at least the lesser offence and it would be wrong for the jury to acquit him entirely merely because they cannot be sure that he is guilty as charged (p. 1206D). In such cases the alternative should be left. Where, on the other hand, the lesser verdict simply did not arise on the way the case had been presented to the court (e.g., the defence was one of alibi), or where it might have arisen had a certain line of questioning been pursued but that had not in fact happened and the possible alternative had therefore ceased to be a live issue, then it will be wrong to direct the jury about the alternative. Similarly, if the possible alternative is very trivial by comparison with the offence charged, introducing it will be an unnecessary and undesirable complication. Applying those principles to the facts of *Fairbanks*, the judge erred by failing to direct the jury that they could return a verdict of careless driving. The subject-matter of the trial was, broadly speaking, the criminality of F's driving and, although the principal issue had always been whether he was reckless, that had never been the only issue. A verdict of careless driving would not have been fanciful. Neither would a direction on it have confused the jury. In short, not guilty of causing death by reckless driving but guilty of driving without due care and attention was a verdict at which a 'conscientious jury could properly arrive on the evidence', and it should have been available to them notwithstanding that they might use it as a bolt-hole to avoid facing up to the hard decision of whether the accused had been reckless.

The decision in *Fairbanks* was approved by the House of Lords in *Maxwell* [1990] 1 WLR 401. M was charged with robbery. He admitted that he would have pleaded guilty to burglary, but denied that he had intended any violence to the victims. The prosecution declined to apply to amend the indictment to include a count of burglary. A verdict of guilty of burglary was not, in law, open to the jury on the robbery count. About an hour after the jury had retired, they returned with the question: 'We would like to know if there is a lesser charge that we can bring against M . . . other than robbery?' The judge took the question as being directed to whether the jury were entitled to bring in a verdict of burglary. He directed that they could not. The jury could, of course, have been directed that they were entitled to bring in a verdict of guilty to the even lesser charge of theft. The judge did not deal with that possibility. After retiring for a further three and a half hours, the jury found M guilty of robbery. M appealed and his appeal was dismissed by the Court of Appeal. On appeal to the House of Lords, it was held that (a) the prosecution were entitled, on the evidence, to take the view that the jury should not be distracted by an inappropriate alternative count of burglary; (b) the judge had been entitled to accept that view; (c) the judge had been entitled to decline to leave the alternative of theft to the jury since it was relatively trifling, and the essential issue was: Did M intend violence to be used? Although coming to a conclusion which was different on the facts from *Fairbanks*, their lordships approved the reasoning in the latter case (see especially point (c) above). Lord Ackner, with whose reasons the other Law Lords agreed, stated the test, in cases where the judge has failed to leave an alternative offence to the jury as follows (at p. 408F):

> . . . the court, before interfering with the verdict, must be satisfied that the jury may have convicted out of a reluctance to see the defendant get clean away with what, on any view, was disgraceful conduct. If they are so satisfied then the conviction cannot be safe or satisfactory.

The need for the judge to exercise his discretion in such a way as to ensure that the accused is not prejudiced by the unexpected introduction of an alternative offence has been underlined by the European Court of Human Rights in *Pelissier and Sassi v France* (1999) 25 March 1999, App. No. 25444/94. In that case, the defendants were tried and acquitted of the substantive offence of criminal bankruptcy. The prosecution appealed to the regional court of appeal from the acquittal, and that court convicted them of aiding and abetting the substantive offence. It was not contested that the French court had the power so to do, but it had violated Art. 6 of the European Convention on Human Rights (see **D26.4**) by doing so without the possibility having been properly raised in advance of the judgment.

It is generally assumed that, if the judge does not direct the jury about an alternative verdict or even (as in *Fairbanks*) expressly tells them to ignore the possibility, they will be guided by him and either find the accused guilty as charged or acquit. However, in *Carter* [1964] 2 QB 1 a conviction for a lesser offence was upheld where prosecuting counsel had told the jury that the verdict was available but the judge made no reference to it in summing up. The possibility therefore seems to arise of counsel nullifying the judge's decision not to leave an alternative verdict simply by telling the jury in a closing speech that the verdict is open to them. In order to avoid criticism for flouting the judge's authority, it would seem advisable for counsel first to raise the issue in the absence of the jury after the close of the evidence.

Procedure where the Jury are Unable to Agree that the Accused is Not Guilty as Charged

In the Criminal Law Act 1967, ss. 4(2) and 6(2) and (3), make it a precondition of the **D16.31** jury convicting of an alternative offence that they should first find the accused not guilty of the offence specifically charged in the indictment. A difficulty arises when the jury cannot agree whether or not the accused is guilty as charged but are agreed that he is guilty of a lesser offence. On the clear wording of the legislation they are not entitled to return a verdict of guilty of the lesser offence, but it seems absurd for them to have to be discharged from giving any verdict whatsoever when they are agreed that the accused is guilty of something. It may be that, in practice, the great majority of juries will resolve the problem in the privacy of their room by the simple expedient of those who really want to convict as charged deferring to the views of their colleagues on the basis that half a loaf (i.e. a conviction for a lesser offence) is better than none. But, if the jurors who want to convict as charged adhere to their view, what should the court do?

The position reached by the cases is, it is submitted, by no means satisfactory. If the possibility of an alternative verdict arises under the Criminal Law Act 1967, s. 6(3) (the general provision), it would seem that, upon being informed that the jury cannot agree as to the greater offence but are agreed on the lesser, the judge may and should amend the indictment by adding a separate count for the lesser offence. A verdict (no doubt one of guilty) may then be taken on the added count and the jury will be discharged from giving a verdict on the other (see *Collison* (1980) 71 Cr App R 249 where that course was adopted by the trial judge and approved by the Court of Appeal). Whether the prosecution elect to have a retrial on the original charge is presumably a matter for their discretion, although – having secured at least a partial success – they may well think it right not to proceed further.

In *Collison*, the offence charged in the original count (on which the jury were split) was wounding with intent and the verdict on which the jury were agreed was guilty of unlawful wounding. Therefore, it was s. 6(3) which would have given them power to return an alternative verdict had they been able to agree that C was not guilty as charged. In *Saunders* [1988] AC 148 it was the effect of s. 6(2) that was in issue. The indictment charged murder only, but there was a possibility on one view of the facts that S had been too drunk at the time to form the necessary intent and was therefore guilty only of manslaughter. It became apparent towards the end of a five-hour retirement that that was the outstanding issue troubling the jury – a majority of 10 had concluded that S was at least guilty of manslaughter. The prosecution then indicated in the jury's absence that, were S to be found guilty of manslaughter, they would not wish to have him retried for murder. The judge accordingly took a verdict of guilty of manslaughter and discharged the jury from giving a verdict in respect of murder. However, no separate count for manslaughter was added. The defence appealed on the basis that the alternative verdict was unlawful bcause there was no finding of not guilty of murder as required by s. 6(2). They relied on *Collison*. The House of Lords distinguished *Collison* because Thompson J (giving the Court of Appeal's judgment in that case) had said that there was nothing 'wrong or improper' in what the trial judge did, but had added that the 'difficulty which had arisen might have been otherwise overcome'. As to the facts of the instant case, the House of Lords held that an additional count of manslaughter was unnecessary. Prior to the enactment of the Criminal Law Act 1967, alternative verdicts of manslaughter on a charge of murder had always been allowed by common law. The provisions of the Act did not abrogate the common law but were merely intended to deal with a procedural problem highlighted in *DPP* v *Nasralla* [1967] 2 AC 238, namely, whether the judge could ask for a verdict as to manslaughter if the jury had initially announced a verdict of not guilty *simpliciter*. Section 6(2) confirmed that he could. However, in situations not covered by s. 6(2), the common law continued to apply. In particular, if the jury could not agree on a verdict as regards murder, the 1967 Act by its very terms had no application, but the judge could do exactly what judges had always been able to do at common law, i.e. discharge the jury from giving a verdict on the express charge in the indictment and take a verdict as to the lesser offence.

Although the interpretation of s. 6(2) adopted in *Saunders* avoided the necessity of quashing S's conviction for manslaughter and ordering a retrial, it does seem surprising that the common law on alternative verdicts should have survived legislation which was apparently intended to define with some precision when such verdicts are, and when they are not, available. The further question arises of whether the Criminal Law Act 1967, s. 6(3) (the general provision), was also intended to supplement rather than abrogate the common law. If so, instead of simply asking whether a count expressly or impliedly includes an allegation of another offence, one would also be forced to ask whether, at common law, an alternative verdict would have been available. It is submitted that such an approach would introduce totally undesirable complications into an area of law which is already far from straightforward. With respect, the decision in *Saunders* was convenient but ought to be confined to its special facts. If problems similar to those in *Collison* arise in the future it would be safer to deal with them by means of adding a count rather than invoking the court's purported residual powers at common law. As indicated in **D16.23**, amendment of s. 6(2) to provide for this situation would seem desirable.

JURY UNABLE TO AGREE ON A VERDICT

If the jury cannot agree, the judge discharges them from giving a verdict. As always when the jury are discharged, the accused is not acquitted but may be retried by a different jury. Whether to ask for a retrial is in the discretion of the prosecution. In the absence of exceptional reasons to the contrary, it is the practice to have a retrial following failure by one jury to agree. If a second jury also fail to agree, the prosecution do not seek a third trial but instead offer no evidence.

Jury Must Not Be Pressurised

D16.32 The jury should be given as much time as they reasonably need to reach a verdict, and must not be pressurised into agreeing against their better judgment. As Cassels J said in *McKenna* [1960] 1 QB 411 at p. 422: 'It is a cardinal principle of our criminal law that in considering their verdict . . . a jury shall deliberate in complete freedom, uninfluenced by any promise, unintimidated by any threat'. In *McKenna*, McK's conviction was quashed because, after the jury had been deliberating for over two hours, they were told by the judge that, if they did not reach a verdict within the next 10 minutes, they would have to be 'kept all night'. That was at least capable of conveying the impression that they would be kept in their jury room. Thus warned, they took a mere five minutes more to convict, but the pressure to which they had been subjected meant that the verdict could not stand. Even a much gentler indication of a time-limit may result in unacceptable pressure on the jury. In *Duggan* [1992] Crim LR 513, the jury made it known at 3.52 p.m. that, as some of them had child care commitments, they wished to sit until they had reached a verdict. The judge said that he was prepared to wait until 5 p.m. if it would help. The jury said that it would, and convicted by a majority at 4.55 p.m. The Court of Appeal held that the judge's intimation of a time-limit was likely to put some of the jury under pressure, in view of their earlier indication of commitments and the fact that it was clear that they would have to spend the night in an hotel if they could not agree.

Provided the principle in *McKenna* is not breached, there is no objection to the jury being asked if there is any reasonable prospect of their reaching agreement and being told that if there is not the judge will discharge them, while if there is they may have as much time as they want (*Modeste* [1983] Crim LR 746 – conviction upheld where the judge, after $2\frac{1}{2}$ hours, spoke to the jury along the lines indicated above and they then returned with the verdict after only five more minutes in retirement). Any communication between the judge and jury about the chances of a verdict being reached etc. should take place in open court and should not be conducted by, for example, the clerk going into the jury room with a message (*Rose* [1982] 1 WLR 614). Where the jury request more time to deliberate, the judge may be obliged to allow more time; in any event, he is fully justified in permitting it (*Turner* [1994] Crim LR 287).

Wharton [1990] Crim LR 877 emphasises the importance of the judge enquiring of the jury in open court as to the prospect of a verdict being reached. W was tried for rape. The jury retired to consider their verdict at 3 p.m. At 5.34 p.m. they were given the majority verdict direction. At 6.10 p.m. they sent a note saying that they had reached a verdict 9 to 3. The judge, with counsel's concurrence, sent the jury a message asking them to continue their deliberations. At 6.25 p.m. they returned a 10 to 2 majority verdict of guilty. W appealed. The Court of Appeal quashed the conviction. Where the jury are unable to reach a verdict, the judge should reassemble them in court and ascertain from the foreman in open court at first hand what prospect there is of reaching a verdict. The failure to do so was a material irregularity and it seems that their lordships regarded the circumstances as constituting pressure upon the jury to reach a verdict.

When giving a majority direction, the judge should not refer to the possibility of another trial taking place if the jury cannot agree as to do so might put undue pressure on them to reach agreement (*Boyes* [1991] Crim LR 717).

Encouraging the Jury to Reach a Verdict

Watson [1988] QB 690 raised the vexed question of whether a judge is entitled to use a **D16.33** form of words encouraging the jury to listen to each other's views and thus, if possible, reach agreement. In particular, the Court of Appeal considering the appropriateness in modern circumstances of a direction approved in *Walhein* (1952) 36 Cr App R 167, which drew attention to the cost and inconvenience caused by a jury not being able to agree. Lord Lane CJ's judgment in *Watson* starts from the proposition that (at p. 700A–B):

> . . . a jury must be free to deliberate without any form of pressure being imposed upon them, whether by way of promise or of threat or otherwise. They must not be made to feel that it is incumbent upon them to express agreement with a view they do not truly hold simply because it might be inconvenient or tiresome or expensive for the prosecution, the defendant, the victim or the public in general if they do not do so.

Experience showed that the *Walhein* direction, with its reference to the unfortunate consequences of disagreement, was putting too much pressure on jurors who happened to be in the minority to concur with the majority. There was, however, no reason why a jury should not be directed as follows (at p. 700F–G):

> Each of you has taken an oath to return a true verdict according to the evidence. No one must be false to that oath, but you have a duty not only as individuals but collectively. That is the strength of the jury system. Each of you takes into the jury-box with you your individual experience and wisdom. Your task is to pool that experience and wisdom. You do that by giving your views and listening to the views of the others. There must necessarily be discussion, argument and give and take within the scope of your oath. That is the way

in which agreement is reached. If, unhappily, [10 of] you cannot reach agreement you must say so.

Whether or not to give the above direction at all is in the discretion of the trial judge – he may well feel that the jury will know how to go about reaching agreement without any guidance from him. If he does decide to give the direction, the time at which he does so is again a matter for his discretion. Probably it is best given as part of the summing-up or as a last resort should the jury have had the majority verdict direction but still be unable to reach the mimimum majority required (pp. 700H–701A). The Court of Appeal has indicated, in any event, that a *Watson* direction should never be given at the same time as a majority direction (*Buono* (1992) 95 Cr App R 338). If the direction is given, individual variations in its wording may prove dangerous and should if possible be avoided (*Watson*). Numerous earlier decisions on the *Walhein* direction and the appropriate time for it are reviewed in the course of Lord Lane's judgment. See also *Morgan* [1997] Crim LR 593.

SECTION D17: TRIAL ON INDICTMENT: SENTENCING PROCEDURE

The subject-matter of this section is the procedures that are gone through between the **D17.1**
moment an accused pleads guilty or is found guilty by a jury's verdict and the moment
the judge pronounces sentence. Sentencing procedure is essentially the same in both
Crown Court and magistrates' courts. It is the former that is here under consideration.
For ways in which the summary procedure differs, see **D20**.

ASCERTAINING THE FACTS OF THE OFFENCE

Where the accused pleads guilty, the first stage of the sentencing process is for prosecuting
counsel to summarise the facts of the offence. As well as assisting the court, this informs the
accused and the public of how the prosecution put their case. If the accused pleaded not
guilty, the facts will have emerged during the course of the evidence and there is no need for
them to be reiterated unless, for example, there has been an adjournment between verdict
and sentencing and the judge who presided at trial cannot be present to sentence. In the
event of split pleas by co-accused and the accused who pleaded not guilty being convicted,
the facts will have to be summarised for the benefit of the one who pleaded guilty.

By convention, the prosecution adopt a neutral attitude at the sentencing stage, not
seeking to influence the court in favour of a heavy sentence. This is reflected in the Code
of Conduct of the Bar, annexe F, para 11.8, which should be read in conjunction with
the Farquharson Committee's report on the general duties of prosecuting counsel (see
D12.5 et seq.). Paragraph 11.8(a) states:

> [Prosecuting counsel] should not attempt by advocacy to influence the court with regard
> to sentence: if, however, a defendant is unrepresented it is proper to inform the court of any
> mitigating circumstances about which counsel is instructed.

In addition to the general statements of principle just given, the following points may
be made about the rule of prosecuting counsel at the sentencing stage.

(a)   Where the possibility arises of the court making an ancillary order in conjunction
with the main sentence (e.g., compensation under the PCCA 1973, s. 35, deprivation
of property under s. 43 of the same Act, confiscation of the proceeds of crime, or
forfeiture of prohibited articles such as drugs or offensive weapons), counsel has a duty
to deal with the matter (see Code of Conduct of the Bar, annexe F, standards applicable
to criminal cases, para. 11.8(d)). For example, if personal injury, loss or damage has
resulted from the offence, counsel should be ready to apply for compensation on behalf
of the victim, quantifying the loss as far as possible and producing evidence to
substantiate what is alleged (e.g., receipts showing the cost to the victim of repairing or
replacing property lost or damaged).

(b)   Counsel must make himself aware of any legal limitations on the court's
sentencing powers so as to be in a position to assist the judge if necessary (para. 11.8(b)).
This statement in the code reflects dicta of the Court of Appeal (e.g., Lawton LJ in
Clarke (1974) 59 Cr App R 298: '. . . counsel as a matter of professional duty to the court
. . . should always before starting a criminal case satisfy themselves as to what the
maximum sentence is', and *Kennedy* [1976] Crim LR 508: 'It is the duty of counsel to
inform themselves what are the permissible sentences for the offences with which a
defendant is charged, so as to be in a position to assist the judge if he makes a mistake').
In *Komsta* (1990) 12 Cr App R (S) 63, it was emphasised that there was a positive
obligation on counsel, both for the prosecution and the defence, to ensure that no order

is made which the court has no power to make. See also *Brown* [1996] Crim LR 134 and *Johnstone* (1996) *The Times*, 18 June 1996.

(c)   Arising out of (b), the standards applicable to criminal cases state (para. 11.8(b) and (c)) that prosecuting counsel is under a more general duty to assist the court to avoid appealable error. According to the standards applicable to criminal cases, this goes beyond ensuring that the judge does not exceed his maximum powers and extends to reminding him of (i) statutory provisions guiding him in his sentencing task, and (ii) any relevant guidelines laid down by the Court of Appeal. The effect of para. 11.8(b) and (c) is that such assistance should be given either if requested by the court, or on counsel's own initiative if he considers that the judge has erred as a matter of sentencing law. In *Panayioutou* (1989) 11 Cr App R (S) 535, Hodgson J said that the time had come when judges were entitled to have guideline cases drawn to their attention by counsel for the prosecution, though he should not ask for any particular penalty. It is submitted that great care must be exercised in referring the court to an authority which suggests that the sentence initially announced is wrong in law as being too low, for such an intervention is difficult to reconcile with the prosecution's neutral stance on the level of sentence.

(d)   In *Virgo* (1988) 10 Cr App R (S) 427, the trial judge heard submissions from both counsel before imposing a life sentence. On hearing the appeal against sentence, the Court of Appeal made no specific comment on the merits of this procedure. The Court of Appeal will soon have to decide whether it is possible for prosecuting counsel to make submissions on whether a life sentence is appropriate and yet retain his neutrality on matters of sentence.

(e)   In *Hobstaff* (1993) 14 Cr App R (S) 632, the Court of Appeal stressed that allegations made by prosecuting counsel as to the effect of the offence upon the victim must be backed by potentially admissible evidence. After the accused had pleaded guilty to three counts of indecent assault, counsel for the Crown stated in opening the facts that the effect of the assaults had been horrific; he claimed that one of the children was now sleep-walking and suffered from nightmares from which she would awake screaming, both children had been seen by a child psychologist and that they were frightened of meeting the accused and would avoid going outside to play. Defence counsel was taken aback as he had received no prior information about these allegations. The Court of Appeal said that what prosecution counsel had said was wholly improper, especially when couched in colourful or emotive language. Evidence of such allegations had to be made in a proper form such as a witness statement, which should be served in advance on the defence and had to form part of the judge's papers. Defence counsel could then deal with it in such a manner as he thought fit and the judge's judgment would not be influenced by prosecution information alone (see also *A-G's Ref (No. 2 of 1995)* [1996] 1 Cr App R (S) 274). In *H (Indecent Assault)* (1999) *The Times*, 18 March 1999, the Court of Appeal emphasised that where the prosecution does provide a statement from the victim, then the sentencer should approach it with some care. Since it would ill-behove a defendant to attempt to investigate such a statement, it would necessarily reflect one side of the case only.

The great majority of summaries of the facts raise no procedural problems whatsoever. However, a considerable body of law has developed dealing with the proper approach to that minority of cases in which there is a dispute about the facts of the offence, in the sense that the prosecution version of how the offence was committed differs from that advanced by the defence in mitigation, albeit the accused is clearly guilty on either version. The principles to be applied are discussed below.

DISPUTES ABOUT THE FACTS FOLLOWING A PLEA OF GUILTY

Newton Hearings

D17.2   In *Newton* (1982) 77 Cr App R 13, N pleaded guilty to buggery of his wife. The prosecution in summarising the facts alleged that he had buggered her against her will and inflicted various other sexual indignities on her (the allegation of buggery without consent could now, of course, be charged as rape: see **B3.1 *et seq*.**). He claimed that she had consented both to the buggery and to the other sexual acts. In reducing the sentence of eight years to one which allowed for N's immediate release (he having by then served 10 months), the Court of Appeal indicated three ways in which the judge, in a case where there is a sharp divergence on the facts of the offence, 'can approach his difficult task of sentencing'. Lord Lane CJ said (at p. 15):

> It is in certain circumstances possible to obtain the answer to the problem from a jury. For example, when it is a question of whether the conviction should be under section 18 or section 20 of the Offences against the Person Act 1861, the jury can determine the issue on a trial under section 18 by deciding whether or not the necessary intent has been proved by the prosecution. . . .

> The second method which could be adopted by the judge in these circumstances is himself to hear the evidence on one side and another, and come to his own conclusion, acting so to speak as his own jury on the issue which is the root of the problem.

> The third possibility in these circumstances is for him to hear no evidence but to listen to the submissions of counsel and then come to a conclusion. But if he does that, . . . where there is a substantial conflict between the two sides, he must come down on the side of the defendant. In other words where there has been a substantial conflict, the version of the defendant must so far as possible be accepted.

On the facts of *Newton*, the judge had failed to adopt any of the three permissible courses since he had sentenced on the basis that the sexual acts were non-consensual without hearing any evidence.

The basic propositions set out in *Newton* have since been analysed and refined.

Duty of Legal Representatives

The Court of Appeal has held that counsel are under a duty to make it clear when a **D17.3** *Newton* hearing is appropriate. In *Gardener* [1994] Crim LR 301, their lordships said that, where there was a dispute about relevant facts which might affect sentence, defence counsel should make that clear to the prosecution. The court should be informed at the outset of the hearing, if not by the prosecution then by the defence. If for any reason this did not happen, defence counsel should ensure during mitigation that the judge was aware, not merely that there was a dispute, but that the defence wished it resolved in a *Newton* hearing. The Court of Appeal would not normally consider an argument that the sentencer had failed to order a hearing unless the possibility of such a hearing was raised unequivocally and expressly in the Crown Court. (See also *A-G's Refs (Nos. 3 and 4 of 1996)* [1997] 1 Cr App R (S) 29.) In *Tolera* [1998] Crim LR 425, the Court of Appeal emphasised that the initiative rested with the defence where it was asking the court to sentence on a basis other than that disclosed by the prosecution case. If the accused wished to rely on the account which he gave to the probation officer and which conflicted with the prosecution case, he should draw the relevant paragraphs to the attention of the court and ask that it be treated as the basis of sentence. The prosecution should be alerted to the fact that such a request would be made. A *Newton* hearing could then follow. This decision would appear to run counter to that in *Oakley* [1998] 1 Cr App R (S) 100, where there was a conflict over whether the version of facts presented by the prosecution, or that in the pre-sentence report ought to be adopted. The Court of Appeal held that the sentencer should have heard evidence to resolve the conflict, whether or not the prosecution or defence asked for a *Newton* hearing.

It is the responsibility of defence solicitors and counsel to notify the prosecution that a plea of guilty will be put forward on the basis that the accused disputes the prosecution version of the facts. The prosecution can then take steps to ensure that the necessary

SECTION D17: TRIAL ON INDICTMENT: SENTENCING PROCEDURE

witnesses are at court to enable a *Newton* hearing to proceed (*Mohun* (1993) 14 Cr App R (S) 5).

Change of Plea

D17.4 Some difficulty arises where the accused changes his plea to guilty after some evidence has been given by prosecution witnesses. In *Mottram* (1981) 3 Cr App R (S) 123, it was held that the judge should then hear evidence from the accused (and, presumably from any witnesses whom he wished to call), before deciding on the version of the facts which would form the basis for sentence. The totality of the evidence received on the point relevant to sentence can then be treated as a *Newton* hearing (see also *Archer* [1994] Crim LR 80).

Power of Court to Direct a Hearing

D17.5 A *Newton* hearing may arise by decision of the court, even where prosecution and defence are agreed on the facts on which the plea is based. In *McNulty* [1994] Crim LR 385, the judge was engaged in an inquiry as to whether a confiscation order should be made in respect of the proceeds of drug trafficking. M had tendered his plea on the basis of non-commercial supply of cannabis resin. Having found in the course of the inquiry that M held proceeds of drug trafficking to the value of £3,600, the judge raised the question whether he had supplied for gain. M applied to withdraw his plea, but was refused leave to do so, and the judge embarked on a *Newton* hearing, in which he found that M had been dealing commercially in cannabis during the period before his arrest. The Court of Appeal held that it was proper to hold a *Newton* hearing in these circumstances, and upheld the sentence and the confiscation order. It is submitted that particular care must be taken in such a situation, however, to ensure that the *Newton* hearing is governed by the criminal rules of evidence and procedure, regardless of the assumptions and standard of proof which may govern an inquiry under the Drug Trafficking Act 1994.

If an application of the principle stated in **D17.2** leads to the conclusion that there should be a *Newton* hearing, the judge is under a duty to hold one even if the defence are against that course. In *Smith* (1986) 8 Cr App R (S) 169, the issue was whether an offence of using a firearm with intent to resist arrest to which S pleaded guilty had been committed by his deliberately aiming an air pistol at a police officer or by its going off accidentally when he slipped and fell. The judge offered defence counsel a *Newton* hearing to resolve the issue, but counsel declined (partly, it seems, because he was misled into thinking that the judge would not allow the issue to affect his sentence greatly in any event). Sentence of three years was passed on the basis that the offender had taken deliberate aim at the police officer. The Court of Appeal, following *Williams* v *Another* (1983) 5 Cr App R (S) 134, reduced the term to that appropriate for non-deliberate use of the weapon. Peter Pain J quoted from Goff LJ in *Williams*: '. . . the question whether an issue should be tried does not depend upon the consent of counsel for the appellant or the accused person as the case may be. It is entirely a matter for the decision of the court in any particular case, although the court may of course hear submissions from counsel on the propriety of ordering such an issue to be tried. The question whether counsel for a party agrees or does not agree to the trial of the issue is a matter of no materiality, the decision being entirely within the control of the court.' (See also *Myers* [1996] 1 Cr App R (S) 187.)

In *Beswick* [1996] 1 Cr App R (S) 343, the Court of Appeal dealt with the situation where agreement had been reached between prosecution and defence counsel as to the facts upon which a plea of guilty was to be based, and the judge declined to give effect to that agreement. Their lordships set out five principles for the guidance of the court in such cases:

(1)   Whenever the court has to sentence an offender it should seek to do so on a basis which is true. The prosecution should not, therefore, lend itself to any agreement with the defence which was founded on an unreal and untrue set of facts.

(2)   When that had happened, the judge was entitled to direct the trial of an issue (i.e. a *Newton* hearing) in order to determine the true factual basis for sentence.

(3)   Such a decision did not create a ground upon which a defendant should be allowed to vacate his plea of guilty, provided he does admit his guilt of the offence to which he has pleaded guilty.

(4)   The decision that there should be a trial of an issue meant that the judge was entitled to expect the assistance of prosecuting counsel in presenting evidence, and in testing any evidence called by the defence. The agreement which the prosecution has previously entered into with the defence must be viewed as conditional on the approval of the judge. If the judge's approval is not forthcoming, the defence cannot seek to hold the prosecution to the agreement.

(5)   Before the trial of an issue was embarked on, the judge might consider whether there is any part of the agreement by which the prosecution should be bound. Counsel should also consider which issues are to be tried, and which of the prosecution statements are relevant to them.

Longer than Normal Sentence

In *Oudkerk* [1994] Crim LR 700, it was held that, where the imposition of a longer than **D17.6** normal sentence under the CJA 1991, s. 2(2)(b) (see **E1.15**), was contemplated, the sentencing court must resolve by a *Newton* hearing any important issue going to the application of that provision. In the case in question, the plea had been tendered throughout on the basis that the assaults in the indictment were the result of a lover's tiff, rather than a random attack on a woman whom the appellant did not know. That was an issue relevant to the application of s. 2(2)(b), and should have been resolved by a *Newton* hearing.

Burden and Standard of Proof

In 'true' *Newton* situations the burden of proof is on the prosecution to satisfy the judge **D17.7** beyond reasonable doubt that their version of events is the correct one (*Ahmed* (1984) 80 Cr App R 295). In *Ahmed*, the issue between prosecution and defence was whether A – who pleaded guilty to being concerned in the unlawful importation of diamorphine – had been a mere courier for a 'Mr Khan' who was not before the court, or had gone to Pakistan for the express purpose of buying the drug and would himself have sold it in this country for a large sum had he succeeded in smuggling it through customs. The trial judge, after hearing evidence from the appellant, decided against his account and sentenced accordingly. On appeal, the defence argument that the judge had misdirected himself as to the standard of proof failed, Parker LJ saying:

> It is apparent . . . that the judge had directed himself and the other members of the court that even if the 'Mr Khan' story might be true, the appellant must be sentenced on the basis that it was true. That direction was in the view of this court entirely proper and follows from *Newton* (1982) 77 Cr App R 13. If it be right that in the absence of evidence the submissions of the defence should be accepted and that the other two possible courses are to have the matter (where circumstances permit) determined by a jury or the judge, then it must in our view follow that the defence version of the facts must be accepted, unless a jury or the judge, as the case may be, is sure that it is wrong.

In *Kerrigan* (1993) 14 Cr App R (S) 179, it was said that it was better for the judge to direct himself openly as to the relevant standard and onus of proof, although the failure to do so was not fatal in every case.

Insignificant Disputes

The principles in *Newton* (1982) 77 Cr App R 13 apply only where the dispute between **D17.8** prosecution and defence is 'substantial' (see the words of Lord Lane's judgment quoted at **D17.2**). It follows that, where the judge's sentence would be the same whichever version of the facts he were to accept, there is no obligation on him to hear evidence but he can make up his mind one way or the other simply on the basis of counsel's representations (see *Bent* (1986) 8 Cr App R (S) 19). In *Bent*, a sentence of six months' youth custody for assault on a store detective in the course of resisting arrest was upheld because – although the judge in passing sentence clearly accepted without evidence the prosecution version that B had used a stick to hit the victim whereas the defence claimed that the victim had merely been threatened with it – the gravamen of the charge lay in the offender's having resisted arrest and it mattered little in that context whether the stick lightly came into contact with the victim's person. It is submitted that, in cases such as *Bent*, a judge should sentence on the assumption that the defence version is correct, and state that he is doing so (see dicta to that effect by Lincoln J in *Hall* (1984) 6 Cr App R (S) 321 at p. 324).

Defence Version Manifestly Absurd

D17.9 The guidance in *Newton* (1982) 77 Cr App R 13 requires a sentencer who chooses not to hear evidence about a significant dispute as to the facts of the offence to accept the defence version '*so far as possible*'. The implication is that the defence story may be so implausible that a judge ought not to be obliged to waste his time by hearing evidence before rejecting it. That interpretation of *Newton* has been confirmed by subsequent decisions, in particular *Hawkins* (1985) 7 Cr App R (S) 351. In that case, H's account of his involvement as the get-away driver in a joint offence of burglary committed by himself and two co-accused was that he was unaware until the very end of the episode that the reason the others had asked him to drive them to certain premises and collect them an hour later was so that they could break in and later be assisted to escape with the proceeds. The judge declined to hear evidence about the facts but sentenced on the prosecution version that H had been a knowing participant throughout. The Court of Appeal dismissed H's appeal because the suggestion that 'he was driving the car around to keep the engine warm or to look for a lavatory for himself, whilst unknown to him his colleagues were burgling a house was an incredible assertion'. The judge did not have to trouble himself with evidence. See also *Bilinski* (1987) 86 Cr App R 146, and *Walton* (1987) 9 Cr App R (S) 107 at p. 109 where Kennedy J said, '. . . the words used by this court in *Newton* (1982) 77 Cr App R 13 do not mean that in every case a judge must hear evidence before he rejects a version of the facts put forward in mitigation, but which for good reason he regards as untenable. . . . The judge was fully entitled [in the circumstances of this case] to reject the submission that was put forward [in mitigation] out of hand during the course of argument.'

Similar reasoning applies to the case where the accused gives an account on oath. The fact that the burden of proof is upon the prosecution does not inevitably lead to the conclusion that the accused's testimony must automatically be accepted in the absence of direct evidence to the contrary. If the accused's account on oath is incredible, the judge is entitled to reject it whether or not the prosecution call evidence. Thus, in *Kerr* (1980) 2 Cr App R (S) 54, K, who pleaded guilty to importing cannabis through Heathrow, gave evidence that, until almost the moment of leaving the plane, he had thought the packets in his luggage to be samples of marble, not drugs. It was held that the judge was entitled to reject that explanation even though the prosecution called no evidence, and did not even cross-examine K.

The judge's view that the defence version is manifestly absurd must, however, be in accordance with the facts. In *Costley* (1989) 11 Cr App R (S) 357, C pleaded guilty to inflicting grievous bodily harm. The prosecution alleged that C hit V about the head and body with a piece of wood, causing a fractured rib, a broken arm and extensive bruises. C claimed he struck V with his fists only, after V had made a homosexual approach and dripped blood on him, claiming that he was suffering from AIDS and would pass the condition on to C. The judge sentenced C solely on the basis of the prosecution opening and the defence speech in mitigation. He said: 'I find as a fact that the attack was totally unprovoked by anything [V] said or did. . . . I reject your explanation for the use of violence as being wholly incredible'. The Court of Appeal held that it was not open to the judge to come to these conclusions, and upheld the appeal against sentence. In a case where the sentencer is faced with a substantial conflict on issues such as this, a *Newton* hearing should be held. Where the court feels unable to accept the defence account, it should make that clear, and indicate why (*Tolera* [1998] Crim LR 425). It is submitted that this is important, so that the defendant can attempt to persuade the judge to accept his version. On the other hand, if the judge decides to hold a *Newton* hearing he should avoid giving the impression that he has made up his mind in advance that the defence version is implausible (*Satchell* [1997] 2 Cr App R (S) 258).

For discussion of the position where the defence relies on extraneous mitigation which is outside the prosecution's knowledge (the 'reverse *Newton*' situation), see **D17.28**.

Procedure on a *Newton* Hearing

Once the judge has decreed that there should be a *Newton* hearing, the hearing itself **D17.10** follows normal adversarial lines (per May LJ in *McGrath* (1983) 5 Cr App R (S) 460 at p. 463). The parties are given the opportunity to call such evidence as they wish and to cross-examine the witnesses called by the other side. The judge ought not to conduct his own cross-examination (ibid.). In order to avoid giving the impression that he has made up his mind in advance, the judge should usually wait until the defendant has been examined by his own counsel, and cross-examined by counsel for the prosecution, before questioning him (*Myers* [1996] 1 Cr App R (S) 187). In *Tolera* [1998] Crim LR 425, the Court of Appeal suggested that, in questioning the defendant, the prosecutor should adopt the role of *amicus curiae*, exploring matters which the court wished to be explored. It was not generally desirable that the prosecutor, on the ground that he had no evidence to contradict that of the defendant, should simply fold his hands and leave the questioning to the judge.

On the other hand, the defence cannot be forced to call evidence or otherwise participate, but may simply observe while the prosecution seek to establish their version to the judge's satisfaction. A defendant cannot, however, by declining to give evidence, frustrate the exercise which the judge has undertaken so as to enable him subsequently to complain that there has been no *Newton* hearing (*Mirza* (1993) 14 Cr App R (S) 64). Where the basic facts are not in dispute, the prosecution is not obliged to call any evidence, and the judge is then entitled to draw any appropriate inferences, provided that he directs himself properly as to the burden and standard of proof (ibid.).

It is clear from the Court of Appeal's decision in *Gandy* (1989) 11 Cr App R (S) 564 that a *Newton* hearing is analogous to a jury trial in other ways. In particular, the judge must himself, as trier of fact, observe the directions which he would have given the jury for their guidance. G pleaded guilty to violent disorder. The trial of his co-accused who pleaded not guilty proceeded. When it was complete, the judge held a *Newton* hearing to determine what part G played. The main point in issue was whether G was responsible for throwing a glass which caused serious injury to V. After the *Newton* hearing, the judge found as facts that G threw the glass, which caused the loss of V's eye; and that he threw other glasses. G was sentenced to three years' imprisonment, and appealed. The Court of Appeal observed that where there was a *Newton* hearing, it was important that the judge should approach the matter and direct himself as if he were a jury. The Court of Appeal was concerned that the judge in setting out his findings of fact had not gone through the steps which *Turnbull* [1977] QB 224 required the judge to set out when directing a jury. In addition, the court considered it was incorrect to admit the evidence of a witness who identified G as the glass thrower, after being shown photographs in a manner which breached the PACE 1984 codes of practice. There were other aspects of the evidence which gave the court concern, e.g., discrepancies between the contemporaneous descriptions of the glass thrower, and G's appearance. G's sentence was reduced to 21 months to conform to the pattern of sentences imposed on his co-accused. Hence it appears that, in the context of a *Newton* hearing: (a) the rules of evidence should be strictly followed and (b) the judge should direct himself appropriately as the trier of fact, in accordance with the guidelines in *Turnbull*, for example.

Loss of Mitigation for a Guilty Plea

D17.11 If the judge decides the issue of fact against the defence, the accused may lose some of the mitigation he would otherwise have received for a guilty plea (*Stevens* (1986) 8 Cr App R (S) 291; *Jauncey* (1986) 8 Cr App R (S) 401), but he is nonetheless entitled to some credit for his plea (*Williams* [1991] Crim LR 150). If the judge mentions the prospect of loss of mitigation prior to holding a *Newton* hearing, he should be careful to avoid giving the impression that he has decided against the defendant's version in advance (*Satchell* [1997] 2 Cr App R (S) 258).

Ascertaining Facts by Verdict of Jury

D17.12 In *Newton* (1982) 77 Cr App R 13, the third alternative to which Lord Lane referred (in addition to a *Newton* hearing and accepting the defence version insofar as that is possible) was to obtain the answer from a jury. This depends on there being a count which can be included in (or added to) the indictment which will indicate how, in the jury's view, the primary offence to which the accused pleads guilty was committed. An example is adding to an indictment for robbery a count for having a firearm with intent to commit an indictable offence, to resolve the issue of whether the robbery was armed or unarmed. On the facts of *Newton* itself, it was suggested *inter alia*, that the trial of a count for assault occasioning actual bodily harm would have indirectly resolved the issue of whether the buggery was consensual, since N's wife claimed that she had been bruised on the leg and head in an attempt to escape from N's attentions. Lord Lane rejected the suggestion since proving that N had assaulted his wife 'would not by any means necessarily have decided the vital question, did she consent to the act of buggery?'

In *Gandy* (1989) 11 Cr App R (S) 564 (see **D17.10** for the facts), the Court of Appeal felt 'some regret that the Crown had not seen fit in the circumstances of this case to include a specific count against [the appellant] for either wounding with intent under section 18 of the Offences against the Person Act [1861] or alternatively under section 20 of that Act for unlawful wounding'. G having pleaded guilty to violent disorder, this would then have left the question of fact, whether he was the glass thrower who caused the loss of V's eye, for a verdict from the jury (see also *Efionayi* (1995) 16 Cr App R (S) 380 and **D17.14**).

In *Dowdall* (1992) 13 Cr App R (S) 441, however, the Court of Appeal held that the jury should be used to decide the issue only where the difference in the versions of the facts alleged by the prosecution and the defence reflects different offences. D was charged with stealing a pension book from a bag carried by the victim. He was willing to plead guilty on the basis that he had found the book but denied that he had stolen it from the bag. On the application of the prosecution, the indictment was amended to include an additional count, so that D was charged with (1) stealing the book from the bag and (2) stealing the book by finding it. He pleaded not guilty to (1) and guilty to (2). He was then tried on count (1) and found guilty. On appeal, the Court of Appeal held that the trial judge should not have allowed the count to be split in two as the alternative averments added in each case were immaterial to guilt. The right course where sentence turned on which version was right was for the judge either to adopt D's version, or to try the issue himself. D's conviction for stealing from the bag was quashed, and he was sentenced on the count to which he had pleaded guilty.

Appeals in *Newton* Hearing Cases

The Court of Appeal does have power to interfere with the decision of the sentencing **D17.13** judge as to the facts of the offence, arrived at following a *Newton* hearing (*A-G's Refs (Nos. 3 and 4 of 1996)* [1997] 1 Cr App R (S) 29). However, provided the judge has properly directed himself as to the burden and standard of proof, the Court of Appeal will exercise its power only in 'exceptional cases' where 'no reasonable jury [properly] directed could have reached the judge's conclusion' (per Parker LJ in *Ahmed* (1984) 80 Cr App R 295). If the accused himself gave evidence at the *Newton* hearing, the occasions on which interference is justified will be 'rare indeed', bearing in mind the trial judge's advantage in having seen the demeanour etc. of the accused when testifying (ibid.). In an appropriate case, however, the Court of Appeal will depart from findings of fact made by a judge in a *Newton* hearing (see *Gandy* (1989) 11 Cr App R (S) 564, discussed in **D17.10**, for a case in which such findings of fact were successfully challenged). In appropriate cases, the Court of Appeal can itself hold a *Newton* hearing (*Guppy* [1994] Crim LR 614).

DISPUTES ABOUT THE FACTS FOLLOWING A VERDICT OF GUILTY

It is in general bad practice to ask the jury to supplement a verdict of guilty by stating **D17.14** the factual basis on which they reached their decision (see *Stosiek* (1982) 4 Cr App R (S) 205, and *Solomon* (1984) 6 Cr App R (S) 120). Although *Cranston* (1993) 14 Cr App R (S) 103 appears to give some encouragement to the practice, it is respectfully submitted that Dr Thomas's commentary on that case at [1992] Crim LR 831 is right in pointing out the inevitable problems. Therefore, in cases where the accused is convicted following a trial, it is for the judge to form his own view as to the facts of the offence established by the evidence, and to sentence accordingly. The following propositions emerge from the cases:

(a) The judge is not obliged to accept the version of events most favourable to the defence consistent with the jury's verdict (*Solomon* – judge entitled, in a case where the appellant T was found not guilty of attempted murder but guilty of causing grievous bodily harm with intent, to reject the defence contention that (i) injuries to the victim's leg were caused when a shotgun T was carrying went off accidentally, and (ii) a stab the victim also received in the same incident was inflicted by a co-accused without T's prior knowledge, albeit in circumstances which made T part of a joint enterprise to cause really serious injury: the judge rightly sentenced on the basis that T had deliberately caused grievous bodily harm with the shotgun, even though he had not intended to kill – see also *McGlade* (1990) 12 Cr App R (S) 105).

(b) Notwithstanding the rule in (a) above, the judge should be 'extremely astute' to give to the offender the benefit of any doubt about the facts of the offence (per Watkins LJ in *Stosiek*). In that case, S was found guilty of assaulting a plain-clothes police officer occasioning him actual bodily harm. The judge passed a prison sentence which would have been appropriate had S realised at the time of the assault that his victim was an officer. The Court of Appeal substituted a fine because sentence should have been passed on the basis that the appellant – not realising until too late that he had been touched on the arm by a policeman – over-reacted to what he took to be a minor assault by an ordinary member of the public. That explanation was a 'reasonable possibility' on the evidence, and should therefore have been accepted in preference to the unfavourable alternative hypothesis that S had known the true status of his victim all along.

In *Efionayi* (1995) 16 Cr App R (S) 380, the defendants were convicted of wilful neglect of a child 'on a day between 1st and 14th day of September 1993'. Before the trial started, their counsel expressed concern that the jury could convict of neglect over the whole period of 14 days, or the last two days of that period. The prosecution declined to add an alternative count alleging neglect on specific days within the 14-day period. The jury were directed that they could convict if satisfied that any neglect had occurred within the period specified in the count. After they convicted, the judge sentenced on the basis that the neglect covered the whole 14 days. The Court of Appeal allowed the appeal against sentence, stating that the approach in *Stosiek* was preferable in these circumstances. There was a clearly defined issue, the existence of which was well known to the prosecution. The indictment could easily have been amended to secure the jury's finding on the point. The judge should have taken the jury's verdict to relate to the shorter period and sentenced accordingly.

(c)   The judge must not adopt a view of the facts which is adverse to the offender and inconsistent with the jury's verdict, even if that verdict is difficult to understand. Thus, in *Hazelwood* (1984) 6 Cr App R (S) 52, a sentence of nine months' imprisonment for common assault (of which H was found guilty by way of alternative verdict) was reduced to allow for his immediate release because the jury had acquitted him of assaulting police officers with intent to resist arrest, and a sentence as severe as that passed was explicable only on the basis that the judge really thought H to be guilty as charged. H's defence was that he had not assaulted the officers at all, and that made the jury's verdict difficult to understand except as an illogical compromise. Nonetheless, 'the court has had to have respect for the jury's verdict and must avoid concluding or indeed suspecting that the appellant was in fact resisting arrest' (per Stephen Brown LJ). The above is really an aspect of the broader principle (see **D17.15**) that an offender must be sentenced only for those offences of which he has been found guilty or which he has admitted to the court whether by way of a guilty plea or by asking for them to be taken into consideration, or by otherwise agreeing that the indictment does not represent the full extent of his criminal conduct.

The judge can hold a *Newton* hearing after the jury has returned a verdict of guilty (*Finch* (1993) 14 Cr App R (S) 226). This would be appropriate where an issue material to sentence was not properly canvassed during the trial because it was not relevant to guilt. In *Finch*, the issue was whether the police had aided or encouraged F to commit the offence. Whilst this could not in law constitute a defence, it could, if true, amount to substantial mitigation. The failure of the judge to hold a *Newton* hearing on this issue (after the jury had convicted) led the Court of Appeal to reduce F's sentence from five years to three.

DUTY TO MAKE SENTENCE CONFORM TO FACTS CONSISTENT WITH VERDICT

D17.15   The above heading may seem a statement of the obvious. It is, however, a cardinal principle of sentencing, confirmed by *Ralf* (1989) 11 Cr App R (S) 121. It has a number of implications for determining the facts of the offence.

First, as explained immediately above, the sentencer must respect the jury's verdict when determining the facts of the offence and not pass a sentence appropriate to a more serious charge of which the offender has been acquitted (*Gillespie* [1998] 2 Cr App R (S) 61). Similarly, if the prosecution accept a plea to a lesser offence or to one of several counts, the judge must be careful to sentence for that only and not for the more serious matters left on the file (*Booker* (1982) 4 Cr App R (S) 53, and see also *Stubbs* (1988) 89 Cr App R 53 where a sentence of 30 months on a plea of guilty to unlawful wounding by stabbing was reduced by a year because the prosecution had not proceeded on the original charge of wounding with intent and the original term was only justifiable if the use of the knife had been 'purposeful' – 'the court must abide loyally by the plea which had been tendered'). The decision of the Divisional Court in *Nottingham Crown Court, ex parte DPP* [1995] Crim LR 902 would appear to run counter to this well-established principle. It is perhaps best viewed as confined to allowing the sentencer to take into account injuries sustained by the victim of assault by beating.

Secondly, the judge must not sentence on the basis that the offender has committed other similar offences on other occasions, even if the circumstances of the offence charged or admissions made by the offender when being questioned by the police strongly indicate that it was not a 'one-off' occurrence (*Reeves* (1983) 5 Cr App R (S) 292 and *Ayensu* (1982) 4 Cr App R (S) 248). This is subject to the major exception that the defence may concede that the counts in the indictment are merely samples of a continuing course of conduct or ask for other offences to be taken into consideration.

Thirdly, the judge must not, under the pretence of determining the facts of the offence at a *Newton* hearing, in effect find the accused guilty of an offence more serious than that with which he is charged (*Courtie* [1984] AC 463; *Druce* (1993) 14 Cr App R (S) 691).

Fourthly, difficult problems arise where the prosecution version of the facts of the offence on the indictment (the primary offence) implies that the accused is guilty of an additional offence (the secondary offence) with which he is not charged. There are some cases which seem to suggest that, provided the secondary offence is of no greater gravity than the primary offence, the judge may (subject to the need for a *Newton* hearing) sentence on the basis that the latter did indeed involve commission of the former as alleged by the prosecution (see especially *Ribas* (1976) 63 Cr App R 147 and *Rubinstein* (1982) 4 Cr App R (S) 202, which concerned, respectively, counts for importing controlled drugs and conspiracy to cultivate controlled drugs, and in which the question arose whether the sentencers were right to reject the defence mitigation that the drugs were intended only for personal consumption, given that there was no count on either indictment for possession with intent to supply or conspiracy to supply – the Court of Appeal in both cases upheld the judges' approach). These cases may be contrasted with *Lawrence* (1981) 3 Cr App R (S) 49, where L pleaded guilty to cultivating cannabis and the prosecution did not proceed on a count for possession with intent to supply. The Court of Appeal varied a short prison sentence to a fine because the sentencer had failed to 'banish from his mind' the possibility that L was growing the cannabis in order to sell it. *Lawrence* was considered and applied in *O'Prey* [1999] 2 Cr App R (S) 83, where the Court of Appeal stressed that it was not permissible for the sentencer to sentence for criminality not reflected in the indictment. It is submitted that, in the light of *Newton* (1982) 77 Cr App R 13 and especially Lord Lane's exhortation to obtain the answer about the facts of the offence from a jury if that is possible, the better course in the situation now under discussion is to add a count for the secondary offence if it is not already on the indictment and proceed to trial on that if the prosecution wish. This avoids the judge in effect finding the accused guilty of an offence with which he has never been charged. Should the secondary offence be summary, however, then the prosecution should give consideration to making use of the provisions of the CJA 1988, s. 40 or 41 (see **D9.6** and **D7.32** respectively).

ASCERTAINING THE FACTS OF THE OFFENCE WHERE ONE ACCUSED PLEADS GUILTY AND THE OTHER NOT GUILTY

The rule that, if there has been a not guilty plea followed by a verdict of guilty, it is for **D17.16** the judge to decide for sentencing purposes how the offence was committed on the basis of the evidence he has heard during the course of the trial, and the rule that, if the accused pleads guilty, the judge must accept the defence version of the facts unless he is satisfied at a *Newton* hearing that the prosecution version is correct, come into conflict with each other when one accused pleads guilty and the co-accused not guilty. The Court of Appeal has wavered in its approach to the problem. In *Taggart* (1979) 1 Cr App

R (S) 144 and *Depledge* (1979) 1 Cr App R (S) 183, it was held that, when sentencing the accused who pleaded guilty, the judge could take into account the evidence he had heard at the co-accused's trial, whereas in *Michaels* (1981) 3 Cr App R (S) 188 the sentence was reduced because the judge had sentenced on a view of the facts adverse to the appellants without having all the witnesses who had testified at the trial of their co-accused recalled for cross-examination.

The case of *Smith* (1988) 87 Cr App R 393 afforded the Court of Appeal the opportunity of resolving the conflict between the earlier authorities. S pleaded guilty to conspiracy to obtain property by deception, the case being that he had supplied stolen credit cards to three co-accused who worked as cashiers at a petrol filling-station. The co-accused then used the cards to create receipts in respect of non-existent transactions, and took an equivalent amount from the till. One co-accused pleaded guilty; the other two were found guilty by a jury, having offered the defence that they acted under duress stemming from S. When the time came to sentence, the judge indicated that he had taken a preliminary view that S was the ringleader in the enterprise, albeit that the jury had rejected the co-accused's claim that they had been subjected to duress by him. The judge was influenced by the records of the offenders (S had previous convictions for robbery and dishonesty whereas the others were of good character) and by the evidence that the accused who pleaded not guilty gave in their own defence. None of the evidence called at the trial was recalled at the sentencing stage. The judge did, however, offer S the opportunity to testify in his own defence that he was not the ringleader. The invitation was declined, and S was sentenced to 21 months' imprisonment (the co-accused were given community service). The Court of Appeal upheld the sentence and said that the judge had handled the procedural problem 'impeccably'. His primary task when sentencing was to decide what had been the facts of the conspiracy and, in doing that, he *was* entitled to take into account evidence he had heard at the trial of the co-accused and even witness statements. There was no need to have the witnesses recalled for cross-examination by the accused pleading guilty. To hold otherwise might have led to a situation where the judge felt constrained to sentence one conspirator on a view of the facts which he had rejected when sentencing a co-conspirator. It was, however, necessary for S himself to be offered the opportunity of giving evidence about the extent of his involvement. The judge had done that more than once, and the appeal was accordingly dismissed. *Taggart* and *Depledge* were preferred to *Michaels*.

The decision in *Smith*, while understandable as a pragmatic solution to a difficult problem, may lead to a sense of unfairness being felt by an offender who is sentenced on a view of the facts which he disputes and which his counsel has not been able to test in the usual way by cross-examination of the witnesses who support the prosecution case. In *Smith*, counsel was present in court during the trial of the co-accused, holding a noting brief. Thus, the defence at least knew what had been said against S. However, counsel had no standing to cross-examine the witnesses who impugned his client, and S himself never heard the evidence on the basis of which he was sentenced, let alone having a chance to challenge it except by giving contradictory evidence himself.

In *Mahoney* (1993) 14 Cr App R (S) 291, the Court of Appeal favoured the approach suggested in *Michaels*, although neither that case nor *Taggart* nor *Depledge* was referred to. Twenty-one prisoners were indicted for riot as a result of an outbreak of violence at Cardiff Prison. There were two trials, M being one of the defendants in the second trial. In the event, he pleaded guilty to the lesser offence of violent disorder and was sentenced at the end of the second trial. He appealed, in effect, on three grounds: first, disparity between his sentence and that of other participants; second, that the judge had sentenced him for riot rather than violent disorder; and third, that he was sentenced on the basis of evidence heard at the two trials at which he was not represented. The Court of Appeal reduced M's sentence, stating (Leonard J at p. 293):

A further submission is made that in this case what happened was that the learned judge heard the evidence in the first trial and in the second trial which led to acquittal, and that in large part he passed sentence upon the appellant on the basis of that material. The problem about that was that the appellant was neither present at, nor represented at, either of those two trials. It was, in our view, wrong therefore, for the learned judge to pay regard to what he had heard in those trials when he was passing sentence upon the appellant.

It is quite clear that the judge formed the view that the prosecution had been somewhat supine in accepting the pleas to violent disorder at the threshold of the second trial. That seems to be the point of his observation about his sentencing on the basis of the facts rather than the title of the offence. If there were matters which were in dispute, the learned judge should either have adopted the course which he indicated at the earlier stage and have sentenced on the basis of what the appellant through his counsel was accepting to be the appropriate facts of the case, or alternatively, if there was a need to resolve the dispute, it should have been resolved by means of a *Newton* hearing.

A further anomaly appears when one compares the approach outlined in *Smith* with that adopted in a case such as *Gandy* (1989) 11 Cr App R (S) 564 (see **D17.10**). In *Gandy*, G pleaded guilty to violent disorder. His co-accused were then tried. Once their trial was completed, the judge held a *Newton* hearing to determine whether G had thrown a glass, causing the loss of V's eye. The Court of Appeal held that the judge should, in the *Newton* hearing, have followed the rules which would govern the use of evidence in a jury trial. Clearly, there is no equivalent protection for the accused where the *Smith* procedure is concerned. The resultant distinction seems arbitrary and exacerbates the sense of unfairness already referred to. (See also *Winter* [1997] Crim LR 66.)

EVIDENCE OF CHARACTER AND ANTECEDENTS

Requirement for Evidence of Character and Antecedents

After the prosecution summary of the facts (or immediately after the jury's verdict of guilty if it was a not guilty plea), it is the responsibility of the prosecution to adduce evidence about the offender's character and antecedents. The evidence is based upon a copy of written antecedents prepared in advance by the police according to a basic pattern prescribed in *Practice Direction (Crime: Antecedents) (No. 2)* [1997] 1 WLR 1482. **D17.17**

Practice Direction (Crime: Antecedents) (No. 2) [1997] 1 WLR 1482

Standard for the Provision of Antecedent Information in the Crown Court and magistrates' courts

ANNEX

1   These procedures have been agreed by the Senior Judiciary, Lord Chancellor's Department, Magistrates' Association, Justices' Clerks, the CPS (CPS), and the Association of Chief Police Officers, and will assist the prosecution in presenting antecedents to both the Crown Court and the magistrates' courts. They replace those attached to *Practice Direction (Crime: Antecedents)* [1993] 1 WLR 1459 issued on 25 October 1993. They allow for the provision of information of antecedents in respect of previous convictions and cautions to be provided by the police directly from the Police National Computer (PNC). The procedures set the standard as to the level of information to be provided.

2   In the Crown Court the police will provide brief details of the circumstances of the last three similar convictions, and/or of convictions likely to be of interest to the court, the latter being judged on a case by case basis. This information should be provided separately and attached to the antecedents as set out below.

3   Where the current alleged offence is within the term of an existing community order, e.g. probation order, and it is known that that order is still in force then, so far as the Crown Court is concerned, to enable the court to consider the possibility of revoking that order, details of the circumstances of the offence leading to the community order should be included in the antecedents as set out below.

4   *Preparation of antecedents and standard formats to be used*

Magistrates' courts and Crown Court

• Personal details and summary of convictions and cautions	— PNC Court/Defence/Probation Summary Sheet.
• Previous convictions	— PNC Court/Defence/Probation printout, supplemented by Form MG16 if the police force holds convictions not shown on PNC.
• Recorded cautions	— PNC Court/Defence/Probation printout, supplemented by Form MG17 if the police force holds cautions not shown on PNC.

and in addition in the Crown Court

• Circumstances of last three similar convictions	— Form MG(c). The detail should be brief and include the date of the offence.
• Circumstances of offence leading to community order still in force	— Form MG(c). The detail should be brief and include the date of the offence.

5   *Provision of antecedents to the court and parties*

Crown Court

- The Crown Court antecedents will be prepared by the police immediately following committal proceedings, including committals for sentence, transfers under section 4 of the Criminal Justice Act 1987 or section 53 of the Criminal Justice Act 1991, or upon receipt of a notice of appeal, excluding non-imprisonable motoring offences.
- Seven copies of the antecedents will be prepared in respect of each defendant. Two copies are to be provided to the CPS direct, the remaining five to be sent to the Crown Court. The court will send one copy to the defence and one to the Probation Service. The remaining copies are for the court's use. Where following conviction a custodial order is made one copy is to be attached to the order sent to the prison.
- The antecedents must be provided as above, within 21 days of committal or transfer in each case. Any points arising from them are to be raised with the police by the defence solicitor as soon as possible and, where there is time, at least seven days before the hearing date so that the matter can be resolved prior to that hearing.
- Seven days before the hearing date, the police will check the record of convictions. Details of any additional convictions will be provided using the standard format above. These will be provided as above and attached to the documents already supplied. Details of any additional outstanding cases will also be provided at this stage.

Magistrates' courts

- The magistrates' court antecedents will be prepared by the police and submitted to the CPS with the case file.
- Five copies of the antecedents will be prepared in respect of each defendant and provided to the CPS who will be responsible for distributing them to others at the sentencing hearing. Normally two copies will be provided to the court, one to the defence and one to the Probation Service when appropriate. Where following conviction a custodial order is made, one of the court's copies is to be attached to the order sent to the prison.
- In instances where antecedents have been provided to the court some time before the hearing the police will, if requested to do so by the CPS, check the record of convictions. Details of any additional convictions will be provided using the standard format above. These will be provided as above and attached to the documents already supplied. Details of any additional outstanding cases will also be provided at this stage.

6   The above arrangements whereby the police provide the antecedents to the CPS for passing on to others will apply unless there is a local agreement between the CPS and the court that alters that arrangement.

Procedure for Giving Antecedents

Formerly, the usual practice was for the prosecution to call a police officer to give evidence **D17.18** of the defendant's antecedents on oath. Now, this information is normally given by prosecuting counsel, provided that the defence has agreed that the antecedents are not in dispute. Where, exceptionally, the evidence is given by an officer, he takes the *voir dire* oath (see **F4.23**) and, in effect, reads from the antecedents and previous convictions forms. The normal rules of evidence are relaxed in that counsel may ask leading questions. Moreover, the antecedents will not necessarily have been prepared by the officer giving the evidence or contain matters within his personal knowledge. In fact, most of the information will have come from the accused himself, either on the occasion of his present arrest or in the course of his previous dealings with the police. Once the officer has completed his evidence in chief, he may be asked further questions by counsel for the defence.

Improper Allegations in Antecedents

However the evidence relating to antecedents is given, it must not contain allegations of **D17.19** a generalised nature which are prejudicial to the offender and, by their very nature, incapable of proof (*Van Pelz* [1943] KB 157). It does not follow that, on every occasion, the prosecution are restricted to the basic and essentially uncontroversial form of antecedents specifically sanctioned by the *Practice Direction (Crime: Antecedents) (No. 2)* [1997] 1 WLR 1482. In exceptional cases, it may be proper to adduce additional information about the offender's involvement in gangland crime and organised prostitution (*Wilkins* (1977) 66 Cr App R 49) or his position in a chain of criminals supplying drugs (*Robinson* (1969) 53 Cr App R 314). Such allegations are, however, likely to be challenged by the defence, and, in the event of challenge, it is essential that the prosecution prove what they allege in accordance with the ordinary rules of criminal evidence. Thus, 'evidence' from the antecedents officer based on hearsay (even if it takes the form of recounting information supplied to him by colleagues) is inadmissible (*Wilkins*). This reflects a principle first stated in *Campbell* (1911) 6 Cr App R 131 that, whenever antecedents evidence is challenged by the defence, the onus is on the prosecution to prove their case by strict evidence. If they fail to do so, the judge should ignore the challenged allegation and state that he is ignoring it (ibid. and also *Sargeant* (1974) 60 Cr App R 74, where S disputed the antecedents officer's suggestion that he had been dismissed from his previous employment for drunkenness and Lawton LJ said that, if the prosecution really took the view that such information would assist the judge in his sentencing task, they ought – on discovering that the matter was disputed – to have brought their evidence to court). As to evidence of the offender's criminal associates, this appears to be sanctioned by the practice direction but in *Bibby* [1972] Crim LR 513 the Court of Appeal ruled that it was unfair of the antecedents officer to have told the judge that B mixed with criminals. Lord Goddard CJ in *Crabtree* [1952] 2 All ER 974, on the other hand, could see nothing wrong with such evidence provided that the officer could give it from first-hand knowledge.

If the prosecution anticipate that the antecedents will be disputed by the defence, it is good practice to give the defence notice of the proposed evidence (see dicta in both *Robinson* and *Wilkins*).

Evidence of the Offender's Convictions

If the offender disputes a previous conviction alleged against him at the antecedents **D17.20** stage, it must – like any other disputed part of the antecedents – either be proved in accordance with the strict rules of evidence or ignored. For the methods of proving a previous conviction, see **F11**.

If the offender has a long record, it is rare for it to be given in full. The judge will indicate which of the convictions he considers it necessary to read. In addition, the Rehabilitation of Offenders Act 1974, as applied to criminal proceedings by *Practice Direction (Crime: Spent Convictions)* [1975] 1 WLR 1065, restricts the circumstances in which it is proper to refer to 'spent convictions'. The scheme of the 1974 Act is that, where an offender is sentenced to 30 months' imprisonment or less for an offence, his conviction becomes spent upon the expiry of the 'rehabilitation period'. That period runs from the date of conviction and varies in length depending upon the sentence imposed (e.g., 10 years for a prison sentence exceeding six months but not exceeding 30 months; six months for an absolute discharge). Commission of a further offence during the rehabilitation period for an earlier one usually means that neither conviction becomes spent until the rehabilitation date for the later one. Thus, recidivist offenders rarely enjoy the advantages of their convictions becoming spent. For further details of periods of rehabilitation, see **E25.3**; for evidential considerations, see **F14.9**.

The main function of the 1974 Act is to protect a person with spent convictions from having to reveal his record in civil proceedings or when applying for a job. Indeed, s. 7(2) provides that the protection against questions relating to spent convictions afforded by s. 4(1) of the Act does *not* apply to evidence given in criminal proceedings. However, Lord Widgery CJ, in the practice direction referred to above, gave guidance on how the criminal courts should deal with spent convictions. The main points emerge from the following quotations from the direction:

(a) '. . . it is recommended that both court and counsel should give effect to the general intention of Parliament [in passing the 1974 Act] by never referring to a spent conviction when such reference can be reasonably avoided' (para. 4).

(b) 'After a verdict of guilty the court must be provided with a statement of the defendant's record for the purposes of sentence. The record supplied should contain all previous convictions, but those which are spent should, so far as practicable, be marked as such' (para. 5).

(c) 'No one should refer in open court to a spent conviction without the authority of the judge, which authority should not be given unless the interests of justice so require' (para. 6).

(d) 'When passing sentence the judge should make no reference to a spent conviction unless it is necessary to do so for the purpose of explaining the sentence to be passed' (para. 7).

Breach of Court Orders

D17.21 If the offender's present conviction apparently puts him in breach of an existing court order (e.g., a suspended sentence or conditional discharge), it will be necessary to put the breach to him. If he denies it, the matter must be proved by strict evidence. Upon the breach being admitted or proved, prosecuting counsel should, if possible, be able to give the court details of the offence in respect of which the order breached was made.

REPORTS ON THE ACCUSED

D17.22 After the prosecution summary of the facts and antecedents evidence, the court considers any reports that have been prepared on the offender. These may include pre-sentence reports, medical and psychiatric reports and assessments for suitability for community service.

Pre-sentence Report

Preparation of the Report Pre-sentence reports on adults are compiled by probation officers. In the cases of children under 13, reports are prepared by local authority social workers. In the cases of those aged 13 to 16 inclusive, responsibility is shared between the probation service and social services, precise arrangements varying from area to area (see CYPA 1969, ss. 9 and 34(3)).

It is the duty of the probation service or, as the case may be, social services to prepare a report if one is requested by the court. Alternatively, the service may take the initiative and prepare a report without being asked to do so. The practice as to this varies somewhat, but, in general, pre-trial reports are considered appropriate if it is anticipated that the accused will plead guilty and he is either aged 30 or less, or the conviction will put him in breach of a suspended sentence or other court order, or he has recently been in contact with the probation service, or medical reports are also being prepared. If the accused is female and pleading guilty, there will usually be a pre-trial report even if she does not fall within any of the aforementioned categories. The probation service is reluctant to prepare a report if the accused indicates a not guilty plea, both because it will be wasted effort in the event of an acquittal and also because one of the main purposes of a report is to assess the offender's attitude to his offence and that cannot be done if he denies having committed it. Where the court desires a report and one has not already been prepared, it will be necessary to adjourn. The usual periods are three weeks if the offender is to be remanded in custody and four weeks if he is granted bail. It may be made a condition of bail that he cooperates in the preparation of the report (Bail Act 1976, s. 3(6)).

Obligation to Obtain a Report   Section 3 of the CJA 1991 states that the court 'shall   **D17.23** obtain and consider a pre-sentence report' in determining whether a custodial sentence should be imposed. This is not obligatory, however, where the court is of the opinion that it is unnecessary and the defendant is over 18. In the case of a juvenile, a pre-sentence report is obligatory unless 'the offence or any other offence associated with it is triable only on indictment'. Even then, the court need not order a new pre-sentence report, but may have regard to an existing one (see **E1.8.**) In addition, s. 7 of the 1991 Act requires a court to obtain and consider a pre-sentence report before forming an opinion as to the suitability of an offender for various types of community sentence (for further details, see **E4.2**).

Procedure on Receiving Pre-sentence Report   A copy of the pre-sentence report   **D17.24** must be given either to the offender or to his legal representative (PCCA 1973, s. 46(1)). The above is qualified in the case of an unrepresented juvenile in that the report need not be given to him personally but must be given to his parent or guardian if present (s. 46(2)). The probation officer who prepared the report is not usually present in court when the report is submitted, but the defence may require his attendance if they wish in order to challenge what has been written. The report is not read out in full in open court, but counsel may refer to passages of it in mitigation if he so desires.

In *Cunnah* [1996] 1 Cr App R (S) 393, the accused's pleas of guilty of indecent assault were entered on a limited basis which was accepted by the prosecution. The pre-sentence report disclosed that the appellant now admitted the truth of most of the account given by the victims, which constituted a more serious version of the offences. There was no discussion of the implications of this new information before a sentence of 30 months' imprisonment was passed. The Court of Appeal stressed that when fresh and highly relevant material appeared in a pre-sentence report it must be discussed with counsel, particularly where pleas had been entered on a limited basis. In the light of the failure to canvass the report, the sentence was reduced to 18 months, which was thought to be appropriate on the basis of the pleas as tendered.

Medical and Psychiatric Reports

It is a precondition of the making of a hospital order under the Mental Health Act 1983,   **D17.25** s. 37(1) (or an interim hospital order under s. 38), that the court be satisfied on the written or oral evidence of two medical practitioners that the offender is suffering from mental disorder within the meaning of the Act such as to warrant the making of an order. One of the doctors making a report must be a psychiatrist approved by the Home Office

(s. 54(1) of the 1983 Act). Also, a report from at least one medical practitioner is required before a probation order with a requirement for medical treatment may be made (PCCA 1973, s. 3). Where a medical report is to be tendered in evidence under the provisions of the Mental Health Act 1983, a copy must be given to defence solicitors (Mental Health Act 1983, s. 54(3)(a)). If the accused is unrepresented, the gist of the report should be disclosed to him although he is not entitled to a copy (s. 54(3)(b)). The medical practitioner who made the report may be required to attend for cross-examination (s. 54(3)(c)).

Obtaining satisfactory medical and psychiatric reports is often difficult. A magistrates' court remanding an accused in custody may, in appropriate cases, request the prison medical service to prepare a report. There is also power for a magistrates' court which is satisfied that the accused 'did the act or made the omission charged' to remand him for up to three weeks in custody or four weeks on bail for a medical examination to be made and report prepared (MCA 1980, s. 30(1)). A remand under s. 30(1) may be ordered notwithstanding that the accused is unconvicted. If the accused is granted bail, it *must* be made a condition of his bail that he cooperate in the preparation of the reports (s. 30(2)). No specific provisions govern the obtaining of medical reports by the Crown Court. If none have been prepared as a result of proceedings in the court below, the court may exercise its inherent power to adjourn so as to give the opportunity for a report to be made.

Further, the courts have been given the power, under the Mental Health Act 1983, s. 35, to remand an accused (or convicted) person to hospital, for the preparation of reports on his mental condition. It is nevertheless sometimes necessary for defence solicitors to take the initiative and ensure that appropriate reports are before the court.

Mental Health Act 1983, s. 35

(1) Subject to the provisions of this section, the Crown Court or a magistrates' court may remand an accused person to a hospital specified by the court for a report on his mental condition.

(2) For the purposes of this section an accused person is—

(a) in relation to the Crown Court, any person who is awaiting trial before the court for an offence punishable with imprisonment or who has been arraigned before the court for such an offence and has not yet been sentenced or otherwise dealt with for the offence on which he has been arraigned;

(b) in relation to a magistrates' court, any person who has been convicted by the court of an offence punishable on summary conviction with imprisonment and any person charged with such an offence if the court is satisfied that he did the act or made the omission charged or he has consented to the exercise by the court of the powers conferred by this section.

(3) Subject to subsection (4) below, the powers conferred by this section may be exercised if—

(a) the court is satisfied, on the written or oral evidence of a registered medical practitioner that there is reason to suspect that the accused person is suffering from mental illness, psychopathic disorder, severe mental impairment or mental impairment; and

(b) the court is of the opinion that it would be impracticable for a report on his mental condition to be made if he were remanded on bail;

but those powers shall not be exercised by the Crown Court in respect of a person who has been convicted before the court if the sentence for the offence of which he has been convicted is fixed by law.

(4) The court shall not remand an accused person to a hospital under this section unless satisfied, on the written or oral evidence of the registered medical practitioner who would be responsible for making the report or of some other person representing the managers of the hospital, that arrangements have been made for his admission to that hospital and for his admission to it within the period of seven days beginning with the date of the remand; and if the court is so satisfied it may, pending his admission, give directions for his conveyance to and detention in a place of safety.

Other Reports

Before making a community service order, the court must be satisfied, on the basis of a **D17.26** report from a probation officer (or social worker of a local authority social services department) that the offender is a suitable person to perform work under an order (PCCA 1973, s. 14(2)). It must also be satisfied that arrangements can be made for him to work in the petty sessions area where he resides (s. 14(2A)). An assessment for suitability for community service is usually ordered in conjunction with a pre-sentence report.

Various other types of report may also be before the court. In particular, in the cases of juveniles, detailed reports by social workers may be prepared during the period of a remand in care prior to sentence. There may also be a report from the juvenile's school, dealing with his attendance, behaviour, performance etc.

Judicial Promise of Non-custodial Sentence on Adjournment for Reports

Where the court adjourns for reports in circumstances which justifiably lead the offender **D17.27** to expect that – assuming the report turns out to be favourable – the sentence will be non-custodial, then the court is bound by the implied promise it has given. Consequently, if the report is indeed favourable, a custodial sentence should not be passed, and will be quashed on appeal however deserved it would otherwise have been.

The principle was first stated in *Gillam* (1980) 2 Cr App R (S) 267. G (while still a serving prisoner) appeared to be sentenced for two burglaries and reckless driving. The indications were that he would receive a further prison term. However, the judge adjourned so that G's suitability for community service could be assessed. He also ordered that, upon the expiry of his present sentence, G should be released on bail. According to Watkins LJ (giving the Court of Appeal's judgment), the main (if not the sole) purpose of the adjournment was 'to ascertain whether community service was available for such a person as [G] and whether he was a fit subject to perform that service'. In the event, G was assessed suitable for community service. Moreover, an additional social inquiry report which had also been prepared was more favourable to him than the one originally before the judge. Nonetheless, the judge passed a sentence of six months' imprisonment. Having indicated that the proper sentence, given G's record, would have been in the region of 15 months, Watkins LJ allowed the appeal for the following reasons (at p. 269 emphasis added):

> . . . an important principle of sentencing is involved in this case. All the signs, when the appellant first appeared before the deputy circuit judge, . . . pointed to the imposition of an immediate prison sentence. For reasons best known to himself he decided against that course but to request the production of a report with a view to considering whether or not this man should perform community service. There was, therefore, created in the appellant's mind an expectation, not unnaturally, of performing that service if the probation officer and others who were called upon to assist in the production of the report were disposed to recommend such a course to the court. It was recommended. *When a judge in these circumstances purposely postpones sentence so that an alternative to prison can be examined and that alternative is found to be a satisfactory one in all respects the court ought to adopt the alternative.* A feeling of injustice is otherwise aroused.

Gillam has been followed in, for example, *Ward* (1982) 4 Cr App R (S) 103 (three-week adjournment so that W could stay at a probation hostel with a view to the making of a probation order with a condition of residence at the hostel), and *McMurray* (1987) 9 Cr App R (S) 101 (four-week adjournment so that McM could attend a day assessment centre). In both cases, the reports prepared on the offenders during the adjournments were favourable, and the custodial sentences ultimately imposed had to be quashed. In *Wilkinson* (1988) 9 Cr App R (S) 468, the facts of which were similar to *Ward*, the sentencing judge conceded that the judge who adjourned for social inquiry reports had, by so doing, more or less promised a non-custodial disposition, but said that the offence was so serious that he (the sentencing judge) was not prepared to incur public wrath by such a lenient course. The Court of Appeal held that, in the circumstances, he had no option but to honour the first judge's implied promise, whatever the public reaction.

However, there is no rule that adjourning for reports *inevitably* carries the implication that the sentence will be non-custodial if the report so recommends. The application of the *Gillam* principle depends upon 'there having been something in the nature of a promise, express or implied, that if a particular proposal is recommended, it will be adopted' (per Croom-Johnson J in *Moss* (1983) 5 Cr App R (S) 209). Thus, if the judge makes it clear when adjourning that he is *not* committing himself to a non-custodial disposition even if the report is generally favourable and recommends such a course, then the offender can have no complaints about the recommendation being rejected (*Horton* (1985) 7 Cr App R (S) 299 – appellants found guilty of a handbag snatching; judge adjourned for three weeks for a social inquiry report and community service assessment but said that he 'regarded any form of street robbery as extremely serious' and thought that an immediate custodial sentence would be the likely conclusion; detention centre orders upheld by the Court of Appeal even though community service was recommended). In *Horton*, one reason for the judge adjourning was the fact that the offender was under 21, and there was then a statutory requirement for a report in respect of such offenders (now subsumed within the wider ambit of the CJA 1991, s. 3: see **E3.2**). The combination of such a statutory requirement and the principle in *Gillam's* case creates a difficulty for the judge. He may well feel it necessary to obtain a report to comply with the statutory provisions. If he says nothing about his ultimate intentions, there is at least the risk that his silence will be construed as an implied promise to pass a non-custodial sentence in the event of a favourable recommendation. On the other hand, he ought not to give the impression that – no matter what is in the report – the sentence is bound to be one of immediate custody. It may be thought that the judge in *Horton* steered a judicious middle course, indicating that custody was probable but leaving open the possibility that something truly exceptional in the reports might persuade him to change his mind. See also *Norton* (1989) 11 Cr App R (S) 143. In *Renan* (1994) 15 Cr App R (S) 722, the Court of Appeal said that the silence of the judge when adjourning for a pre-sentence report should never be taken as an indication that a non-custodial sentence would be passed, even when the accused was granted bail. It was the duty of counsel in these circumstances to warn the defendant that the grant of bail did not mean that custody would be avoided.

The *Gillam* principle applies not only when the Crown Court is passing sentence following a conviction on indictment, but also when it is dealing with a committal for sentence or appeal from a magistrates' court. In both cases, if the ordering of reports by the court below created a reasonable expectation of a non-custodial sentence, the Crown Court is bound by the lower court's implied promise (see *Rennes* (1985) 7 Cr App R (S) 343 and *Gutteridge* v *DPP* (1987) 9 Cr App R (S) 279).

It need not be an adjournment for reports which creates the expectation of a non-custodial sentence. In *McMillan* (1988) 10 Cr App R (S) 205, counsel addressed the Crown Court judge on the basis that sentence might be deferred in view of the fact that employment was available to M. The judge asked counsel to obtain confirmation that employment was still open, and put the case back one hour. M's solicitor telephoned the potential employer and confirmed that the job offer was still open, but the judge passed a sentence of nine months' immediate custody. The Court of Appeal held that M's hopes had been raised by the judge's actions, resulting in a sense of grievance. It suspended three months of the sentence, leaving six months to serve. See also *Jackson* [1996] Crim LR 355.

Another situation in which the accused might have a legitimate expectation of a non-custodial sentence is where the judge has indicated to counsel privately that he will impose such a sentence.

Turner [1970] 2 QB 321 (see **D10.42**) establishes that any judicial indication of sentence must be given on the basis that it is irrespective of plea. If an indication is given on the basis that it applies only if the accused pleads guilty, the judge will be bound by the indication if the accused pleads not guilty and is convicted (see *Bird* (1978) 67 Cr App R 203 and *Atkinson* [1978] 1 WLR 425).

The case of *Keily* [1990] Crim LR 204 saw the combined operation of two of the principles dealt with above. K's counsel was told by a judge at a pre-trial review in chambers that if K pleaded guilty he would not receive a sentence of immediate imprisonment. K was told this, but pleaded not guilty, and was convicted following trial before a different judge. The second judge was told of the first judge's indication but sentenced K to immediate imprisonment. On appeal, the immediate custodial sentence was quashed and a suspended sentence substituted. Hence K was the beneficiary of the combined effect of two rules:

(a) the indication given by the first judge bound the second judge (*Wilkinson* (1988) 9 Cr App R (S) 468); and

(b) an indication given on the basis of a guilty plea binds the sentencer on conviction after a not guilty plea (*Turner*; *Bird*; *Atkinson*).

The fact that a judge gave an indication of sentence before plea will not bind the Court of Appeal if the A-G appeals against the sentence as unduly lenient (*A-G's Ref (No. 40 of 1996)* [1997] 1 Cr App R (S) 357: see **D24.4**).

MITIGATION OF SENTENCE

The final stage in the sentencing process is the presentation of defence mitigation. **D17.28** According to Comyn J in *Gross v O'Toole* (1982) 4 Cr App R (S) 283, this is 'purported to be the province of the most junior of counsel' but 'is in fact amongst the most difficult tasks any barrister can ever face'.

The plea in mitigation usually consists solely of a speech by defence counsel. In his discretion, counsel may additionally call witnesses to speak to the offender's generally good character or to explain why, in their view, he acted as he did on the occasion in question. Counsel may also, exceptionally, decide to call evidence in order to establish the facts he is advancing in mitigation. Whether to call evidence and, if so, whether to call it before, in the middle or at the end of his speech is a matter for counsel (per Comyn J in *Gross v O'Toole*). Having made his choice, he 'cannot easily go back on it' (ibid.).

The possibility of the defence having to prove the mitigation may seem to conflict with the principle in *Newton* (1982) 77 Cr App R 13 that, in the event of a significant conflict between the prosecution and defence as to the facts of the offence, the judge must either accept the defence version or hear evidence, and, if he does the latter, it is for the prosecution to prove their version beyond reasonable doubt (see **D17.2 *et seq.***). However, the cases appear to draw (at least implicitly) a distinction between 'true *Newton*' situations, where the dispute is about the immediate circumstances of the offence, and what have been described by Dr Thomas in his case commentaries in the *Criminal Law Review* as 'reverse *Newton*' situations. In the latter, the dispute is about extraneous matters about which the prosecution witnesses are unlikely to have any knowledge. Since the prosecution can hardly be expected to disprove – or even challenge by cross-examination – matters which would have formed no part of their case had there been a trial and which may well be within the peculiar knowledge of the accused, the rule is that the onus of satisfying the judge rests on the defence.

The general principles as to proving mitigation were stated by the Divisional Court in *Gross* v *O'Toole* (1982) 4 Cr App R (S) 283. G was convicted of offering his services as a driver at Heathrow Airport contrary to a by-law. He had many previous convictions for the same offence. In mitigation, it was contended that he had offered his services gratuitously, but no evidence was called to that effect – it was merely asserted as a fact in the course of his solicitor's speech in mitigation. Immediately before announcing their sentence, the magistrates stated that they did not accept the mitigation. They had given no earlier indication of their scepticism. On appeal it was argued that the court ought not to have rejected a substantial part of the mitigation without first warning the defence of its provisional view and giving an opportunity for affirmative evidence to be called. Although the appeal was allowed on other grounds, the Divisional Court rejected the argument, holding that whether to call evidence or rely solely on his own submissions was a decision for the defence advocate. As a matter of good practice, it might have been wise to warn G's solicitor of the risk he was running by not calling evidence. However, there was no duty to do so, especially as the other material placed before the magistrates (e.g., the appellant's previous convictions for the same offence) should have made it abundantly clear to the solicitor that his assertions might not be believed. Ormrod LJ said:

> The main point of the mitigation is a rather interesting one. It involves the question as to what should magistrates do when they do not accept statements made by defending advocates in mitigation which are essentially statements of fact. Are they entitled to look at such propositions as mitigation in general terms? Are they entitled to relate what has been said to them to the other facts of the case, and perhaps, find themselves in difficulty in accepting the statement made by the advocate, as often happens, of course, in mitigation? I think, for my part, that if an advocate is going to put forward in mitigation something which is, on the face of it, quite inconsistent with the other information that the magistrates have so far as sentence is concerned, e.g. the list of previous convictions, it really is for the defending advocate to indicate that he wishes to make good the submission. . . . he takes the chance himself if he does not offer to call evidence. . . .
>
> I do not think [the magistrates] were obliged to tell the defending advocate that they did not accept his mitigation, because I do not think anyone in court, least of all the defending advocate, could have supposed for a moment that they would accept his mitigation.

Comyn J, in a supplementary judgment, slightly qualified Ormrod LJ's remarks by stating that if, on a significant point on which there is room for some doubt, the magistrates do in fact doubt what the advocate is saying, they ought to tell him before he concludes his mitigation so he can try to remedy it. However, both their lordships clearly accepted the basic premise that it is for the defence to establish its own mitigation to the court's satisfaction, and whether they do that by a speech or evidence or both is essentially a matter for them, not the court. Everything said in the case no doubt applies *mutatis mutandis* to mitigation by counsel in the Crown Court.

It follows from the principles stated in *Gross* v *O'Toole* that the court may reject matters advanced in mitigation even if the offender or other defence witnesses testify in support of those facts and no contradictory evidence is adduced by the prosecution (see *Kerr* (1980) 2 Cr App R (S) 54). Similarly, in *Ogunti* (1987) 9 Cr App R (S) 325 the court was entitled to disbelieve counsel's mitigation to the effect that O – who pleaded guilty to possessing heroin with intent to supply – had been given the drugs by a stranger who threatened him with violence if he did not take them to Brighton where they would be collected by a third person. In that case, the defence were granted an adjournment in order to call evidence but failed to do so. The prosecution did not accept the mitigation but could call no evidence of their own to show how O in fact came by the drugs. On the contrary, O's statements to the police were consistent with the mitigation advanced. The Court of Appeal held that it was a 'reverse *Newton*' situation and the onus of proving the facts rested on the defence. The judge was entitled to draw reasonable inferences from the statements of the witnesses (e.g., as to the value of the drugs and the skilful way they were hidden in O's car), and therefore reject the defence account of the nature of O's involvement. In *Guppy* [1994] Crim LR 614, the Court of Appeal held that, where the defendant raised extraneous matters of mitigation, a burden of proof rested upon him to the civil standard. Their lordships did state, however, that in the general run of cases the sentencer would readily accept the accuracy of defence counsel's statements. (See also *Broderick* (1993) 15 Cr App R (S) 476, in which it was held that the mitigation alleging duress went to matters outside the prosecution's knowledge, so that *Newton* principles did not apply.) In *Tolera* [1998] Crim LR 425, however, the Court of Appeal held that there was an onus on the prosecution to rebut the appellant's explanation that he had been under a degree of compulsion, falling short of duress, to carry the heroin which was the subject of the charge.

Where counsel delivers a plea in mitigation after a trial and a verdict of guilty, it is generally unrealistic for him to reiterate in strong terms his client's innocence and at the same time ask for leniency. It should not therefore be taken as an admission of guilt on his client's behalf so as to undermine a subsequent appeal, if he accepts the jury's verdict and mitigates on that basis (*Wu Chun-piu v The Queen* [1996] 1 WLR 1113).

The Court of Appeal has encouraged the practice of counsel citing its previous decisions when mitigating at first instance (see *Ozair Ahmed* (1993) 15 Cr App R (S) 286, and *Johnson* [1994] Crim LR 537 and the commentary thereon).

For the role of prosecuting counsel when inaccurate mitigation is advanced, see **D17.29**.

Where the judge is contemplating imposing a sentence which defence counsel might not be anticipating, he is under a duty in fairness to the accused to give notice of what is in his mind so that defence counsel can then make submissions on that issue. See, for example, *Scott* (1989) 11 Cr App R (S) 249, where the judge disqualified S for life without giving his counsel the opportunity to make submissions on that aspect of the sentence, disqualification was reduced by the Court of Appeal to five years. Similarly, in *Woods* (1989) 11 Cr App R (S) 551, the Court of Appeal said that, if the judge intended to impose a separate custodial sentence for an offence under the Bail Act 1976 he should invite submissions from counsel. The consecutive prison sentence imposed for failure to surrender was therefore quashed, although it was said to be correct in principle.

In *O'Brien* (1995) 16 Cr App R (S) 556, the Court of Appeal said that, if a judge was considering imposing a longer than normal sentence by virtue of the CJA 1991, s. 2(2)(b), he should give a prior indication to counsel. The matter could then be properly dealt with in mitigation.

Derogatory Assertions in Mitigation

Defence counsel is under the same duty, in delivering a plea in mitigation, as is any **D17.29** barrister in the conduct of court proceedings. He 'must not make statements or ask questions which are merely scandalous or intended or calculated only to vilify, insult or annoy' any person (Code of Conduct of the Bar, para. 610(e)). Further he must, if possible, avoid the naming in open court of a third party whose character would be impugned thereby (para. 610(f)).

The Code of Conduct of the Bar, annexe F, para. 11.8(e), gives guidance to prosecution counsel on what to do if the defence in mitigation assert facts which the prosecution believe to be untrue. Counsel's duty is first to draw the attention of defence counsel to the assertion in question. If the defence persist, prosecution should invite the court to hold a *Newton* hearing on the issue (see **D17.2** to **D17.13**).

The CPIA 1996, ss. 58 to 61, allow the judge to impose reporting restrictions on false or irrelevant assertions made during a speech in mitigation. There is power to make a full order where there are substantial grounds for believing that the assertion is derogatory to a person's character, and either false or irrelevant to the proceedings. Whilst considering the matter, the court is empowered to make an interim order, provided that there is a real possibility that a full order will be made. The powers do not apply if the assertion has been made earlier in proceedings, e.g., at trial. Full orders may be revoked at any time by the court, and if not revoked will cease to have effect after one year. It is an offence to publish or broadcast in breach of a full or interim order, rendering the offender liable to a fine on summary conviction not exceeding level 5 on the standard scale.

Criminal Procedure and Investigations Act 1996, s. 58

(1)   This section applies where a person has been convicted of an offence and a speech in mitigation is made by him or on his behalf before—

(a)   a court determining what sentence should be passed on him in respect of the offence, or

(b)   a magistrates' court determining whether he should be committed to the Crown Court for sentence.

(2)   This section also applies where a sentence has been passed on a person in respect of an offence and a submission relating to the sentence is made by him or on his behalf before—

(a)   a court hearing an appeal against or reviewing the sentence, or

(b)   a court determining whether to grant leave to appeal against the sentence.

(3)   Where it appears to the court that there is a real possibility that an order under subsection (8) will be made in relation to the assertion, the court may make an order under subsection (7) in relation to the assertion.

(4)   Where there are substantial grounds for believing—

(a)   that an assertion forming part of the speech or submission is derogatory to a person's character (for instance, because it suggests that his conduct is or has been criminal, immoral or improper), and

(b)   that the assertion is false or that the facts asserted are irrelevant to the sentence, the court may make an order under subsection (8) in relation to the assertion.

(5)   An order under subsection (7) or (8) must not be made in relation to an assertion if it appears to the court that the assertion was previously made—

(a)   at the trial at which the person was convicted of the offence, or

(b)   during any other proceedings relating to the offence.

(6)   Section 59 has effect where a court makes an order under subsection (7) or (8).

(7)   An order under this subsection—

(a)   may be made at any time before the court has made a determination with regard to sentencing;

(b)   may be revoked at any time by the court;

(c)   subject to paragraph (b), shall cease to have effect when the court makes a determination with regard to sentencing.

(8)   An order under this subsection—

(a)   may be made after the court has made a determination with regard to sentencing, but only if it is made as soon as is reasonably practicable after the making of the determination;

(b)   may be revoked at any time by the court;

(c)   subject to paragraph (b), shall cease to have effect at the end of the period of 12 months beginning with the day on which it is made;

(d)   may be made whether or not an order has been made under subsection (7) with regard to the case concerned.

(9)   For the purposes of subsections (7) and (8) the court makes a determination with regard to sentencing—

(a)   when it determines what sentence should be passed (where this section applies by virtue of subsection (1)(a));

(b)   when it determines whether the person should be committed to the Crown Court for sentence (where this section applies by virtue of subsection (1)(b));

(c)   when it determines what the sentence should be (where this section applies by virtue of subsection (2)(a));

(d)   when it determines whether to grant leave to appeal (where this section applies by virtue of subsection (2)(b)).

LEGAL AID AT THE SENTENCING STAGE

An unrepresented offender may, of course, put forward mitigation on his own behalf. **D17.30** However, if the court is considering a custodial disposition it is generally desirable that the mitigation should be professionally presented. This is especially so if the offender is either young or has not previously been given a custodial sentence. To encourage such offenders to be legally represented, the PCCA 1973, s. 21, and the CJA 1982, s. 3, provide respectively that (a) adult offenders who have not previously been sentenced to imprisonment and (b) offenders under 21 whether or not they have previously lost their liberty shall not be sentenced to imprisonment or, as the case may be, one of the custodial sentences available for the under-21s unless either they are legally represented, or they have had the opportunity to apply for legal aid and either failed to apply or were refused on account of their means. Section 21 of the 1973 Act extends to the passing of suspended sentences of imprisonment, but a suspended sentence which has not taken effect is ignored for purposes of deciding if an offender has previously had a prison sentence (s. 21(3)). In *Wilson* [1995] Crim LR 510, the Court of Appeal suggested that s. 21 would be satisfied if at some time after conviction the defendant received advice from his lawyers, even if he rejected that advice and dismissed them.

The sections apply to both the Crown Court and magistrates' courts. Failure to comply with them has been held to have differing consequences depending upon the court in error. If a magistrates' court was at fault and the offender appeals to the Crown Court, the Crown Court must pass a sentence which the lower court could *lawfully* have passed, and therefore it must replace the custodial sentence with a non-custodial one (*Birmingham Justices, ex parte Wyatt* [1976] 1 WLR 260). If, on the other hand, the Crown Court was the sentencing court and the appeal is to the Court of Appeal, the latter may uphold the sentence below if they consider that it was the right one in all the circumstances (*McGinlay* (1975) 62 Cr App R 156; *Hollywood* (1990) 154 JP 705; *Wilson* [1995] Crim LR 510).

Powers of Criminal Courts Act 1973, s. 21

(1)   A magistrates' court on summary conviction or the Crown Court on committal for sentence or on conviction on indictment shall not pass a sentence of imprisonment on a person who is not legally represented in that court and has not been previously sentenced to that punishment by a court in any part of the United Kingdom, unless either—

(a)   he applied for legal aid and the application was refused on the ground that it did not appear his means were such that he required assistance; or

(b)   having been informed of his right to apply for legal aid and had the opportunity to do so, he refused or failed to apply.

(2)   For the purposes of this section a person is to be treated as legally represented in a court if, but only if, he has the assistance of counsel or a solicitor to represent him in the proceedings in that court at some time after he is found guilty and before he is sentenced, and in subsection 1(a) and (b) above 'legal aid' means legal aid for the purposes of proceedings in that court, whether the whole proceedings or the proceedings on or in relation to sentence; but in the case of a person committed to the Crown Court for sentence or trial, it is immaterial whether he applied for legal aid in the Crown Court to, or was informed of his right to apply by, that court or the court which committed him.

(3)   For the purposes of this section—

(a)   a previous sentence of imprisonment which has been suspended and which has not taken effect . . . shall be disregarded.

Criminal Justice Act 1982, s. 3

(1)   A magistrates' court on summary conviction or the Crown Court on committal for sentence or on conviction on indictment shall not—

(a)   pass a sentence of detention in a young offender institution under section 1A above;

(b)   [repealed]

(c)   pass a sentence of custody for life under section 8(2) below;

(d)   make an order for detention under section 53(2) of the Children and Young Persons Act 1933; or

(e)   make a secure training order,

in respect of or on a person who is not legally represented in that court, unless [the remainder of the section is in the same terms as the Powers of Criminal Courts Act 1973, s. 21].

SENTENCING THE OFFENDER FOR MATTERS OF WHICH HE HAS NOT BEEN CONVICTED

Introduction

D17.31   It is a basic principle of sentencing that the offender should be sentenced only for those crimes of which he has been convicted and not for anything else which the court may consider him to have done (see **D17.15**). There are three identifiable exceptions (or apparent exceptions) to this principle. The first has already been considered in the context of the judge determining the facts of the offence. It is that, if the facts as alleged by the prosecution involve the aggravating feature that the offender – in the process of committing the primary offence of which he has been convicted – also committed a secondary offence which is not on the indictment, and the judge is satisfied that the prosecution version of facts is correct, then he may take into account the secondary offence when passing sentence (see *Rubinstein* (1982) 4 Cr App R (S) 202). This only applies if the secondary offence is no more serious than the offence on the indictment. An example of the Court of Appeal positively exhorting sentencers to take into account other offences in this way is Lord Lane CJ's judgment in *Boswell* [1984] 1 WLR 1047 where, in the course of giving guidelines on sentencing for causing death by reckless driving, his lordship said that an aggravating feature conclusive towards a custodial sentence was if the offender's driving had involved other offences such as driving while disqualified or under the influence of drink.

The other two situations in which a sentencer may properly be influenced by other offences not officially before the court are (a) if the offender expressly asks for the other offences to be taken into consideration, and (b) if the prosecution case is that the offences on the indictment are merely samples of a continuing course of conduct and the defence accept that to be so.

Taking Other Offences into Consideration

D17.32   This is a common practice, resting entirely upon convention and not based upon statute or common law. It requires the cooperation of the police, the court and, most importantly, the offender himself. Since the practice is indeed a matter of pure practice, no set rules govern its operation. What normally happens, however, is that the police – having arrested a suspect for a certain offence and obtained admissions from him – then invite him to tell them about other crimes they think he may have committed. Depending on how the suspect responds, a list is drawn up of the other offences. The suspect is charged with only a limited number of offences (probably the most serious he has admitted or the ones for which he was actually arrested). Those offences are prosecuted in the normal way, and the accused pleads guilty. At some time before his court appearance he is served with the list of the other offences and asked to sign it if he agrees that he committed them. He may, of course, accept some but not all of the offences. Copies of the list (the 't.i.c.s') are given to the defence and included in prosecuting counsel's brief. At a convenient moment during the counsel's summary of the facts of the offence, the court is told that the offender wishes to have other offences taken into consideration. The judge is given the original of the list, signed by the offender. He confirms with him that he does admit the offences and wants them taken into consideration. The judge then decides whether to comply with the offender's request. Assuming he does, prosecuting counsel gives brief details of the offences, and the sentencing process thereafter continues in the normal way. When passing sentence, the judge should state that he has taken so many other offences into consideration. Although the t.i.c. procedure is geared for offenders expected to plead guilty, there is no objection to adapting it for an accused pleading not guilty. Thus, in anticipation of a guilty verdict, the police might prepare a t.i.c. list and then use an adjournment between conviction and sentence to invite the accused to sign the list.

Points to note about the t.i.c. procedure are:

(a) Since the offender is never charged with or convicted of the t.i.c.s, the court's powers of sentence are limited to the maximum for the offences on the indictment of which the offender has been convicted, whether by way of guilty plea or jury verdict (hereafter referred to as 'the conviction offences'). This is not a significant restriction on sentencing options since maximum penalties generally exceed by a considerable margin the penalty which a court is likely to want to impose in any but the most serious of cases. (This limitation is subject to the minor qualification that the Crown Court may order the offender to pay compensation for a matter taken into consideration, and to that extent may sentence directly for the offence – see PCCA 1973, s. 35(1).) However, a court should not take into consideration an offence which carries endorsement of the licence and discretionary or obligatory disqualification if the conviction offences are non-endorsable (*Collins* [1947] KB 560). Were it to do so, the offender would escape even endorsement whereas had the t.i.c. offence been prosecuted in the normal way the court would have been obliged to endorse in the absence of special reasons and might have chosen also to disqualify.

(b) Offences should not be taken into consideration unless the offender clearly requests the sentencer to do so and admits commission of the offences (*Griffiths* (1932) 23 Cr App R 153 and see also dicta by Scarman LJ in *Walsh* (8 March 1973 unreported), in which his lordship stressed the importance of the accused understanding what is being done, admitting the offences and genuinely wanting them taken into consideration). However, it is not the practice to read the list out in full. It is sufficient if the judge confirms with the offender that he has signed the list, that it contains so many offences, that he agrees he committed those offences, and he now wants them borne in mind when sentence is passed for the offences on the indictment. The request to take offences into consideration should come from the offender himself, not counsel (*Mortimer* (10 March 1970 unreported)).

(c) The judge always has a discretion whether or not to comply with a request to take an offence into consideration. It is submitted that it would be bad practice to take offences into consideration which are either more serious than or of a completely different type from the conviction offences.

(d) The fact that an offence has been taken into consideration does not entitle the offender to rely on autrefois convict should he subsequently be prosecuted for it (*Nicholson* [1947] 2 All ER 535). However, in the absence of quite exceptional circumstances, the prosecution would not consider instituting proceedings for a matter that they know to have been taken into consideration by a court on a previous occasion.

(e) In passing sentence, the judge may – and usually will – increase the penalty somewhat because of the t.i.c.s. However, the amount of the increase will almost certainly be considerably less than what would have been the sentence had the offences been separately prosecuted.

Despite its lack of any statutory or strictly legal basis, the t.i.c. system works well because it suits both the police and the accused. The police are enabled to clear up numerous offences which might otherwise remain unsolved, or could only be brought to trial through considerable expenditure of resources. As for the accused, he may well be resigned to being convicted of the offences for which he was actually arrested and in respect of which there is a strong case. By asking for other offences that he knows he has committed to be taken into consideration, he is able to 'wipe the slate completely clean' at a minimal cost in terms of increased sentence.

Sample Offences

D17.33 As an alternative to following strictly the procedure for taking other offences into consideration, the prosecution may invite the judge to treat the offences on the indictment of which the accused has been found, or to which he has pleaded, guilty as samples of a continuing course of conduct. (See **D9.15** for detail on the implications of sample counts when considering the indictment.) This is an attractive course where the offender appears to have committed a large number of similar offences over a protracted period, as when he has obtained money by deception from the Department of Social Security by signing on when he was working. It may be simplest to have counts for the first and last dates on which he made fraudulent claims and then inform the sentencer that between those dates he obtained so much per fortnight in similar fashion, making a total loss to the Department of £x. Although there is no reason, in such a case, why a list of t.i.c.s should not be prepared as described in **D17.32**, the list can become inordinately long (see, for example, *Sequeira* (1982) 4 Cr App R (S) 65 where the prosecution adopted the t.i.c. procedure in respect of an offender who had claimed social security benefit for four years when ineligible and the result was no less than 150 offences on the list).

It is generally accepted – although express authority is limited – that, where the accused pleads guilty and the defence agree with the prosecution that the offences on the indictment are merely samples, the judge may sentence on that basis even though the offender does not formally ask for other offences to be taken into consideration (see *Huchison* [1972] 1 WLR 398 per Phillimore LJ at p. 400C: 'Of course, there are cases where the prosecution puts forward a count as a sample count, and in those cases it is well understood that if that course is taken and the defence are notified, a judge is entitled to deal with the whole matter on the basis that the offence in fact was repeated more than once, or that there were other similar incidents'). If, however, the defence dispute the other occasions on which similar offences were allegedly committed, then the judge should sentence the offender only for those occasions which he does admit (whether by way of guilty plea or by asking for a limited number of other occasions to be taken into consideration). The leading authority is *Huchison*. H pleaded guilty to one count of incest with his daughter. According to the daughter's statement to the police, intercourse had occurred regularly over a period of years; the defence claimed that it was limited to the occasion alleged in the indictment. The judge heard evidence from both the accused and his daughter, and concluded that, although the latter's evidence might have been somewhat exaggerated, 'it was perfectly obvious that [H] had made a habit of having intercourse with his daughter'. On that basis, he sentenced him to four years' imprisonment. The Court of Appeal halved the sentence because the judge had adopted the wrong procedure. Upon it becoming obvious that the defence denied the suggestion that the offence on the indictment was a sample one, the judge's options were either to sentence H strictly for the one act of intercourse he had admitted, or to adjourn so that counts for the other occasions could be added to the indictment (or a fresh voluntary bill of indictment preferred). What the judge did effectively deprived H of his right to trial by jury in respect of the instances of intercourse which he did not admit. *Huchison* has been followed in *McKenzie* (1984) 6 Cr App R (S) 99 (sentence reduced for seven cheque card offences involving loss to the victims of £640 because the judge had apparently sentenced on the basis denied by the defence that the counts on the indictment were samples of continuing conduct in which £11,000 had been obtained), and *Ralf* (1989) 11 Cr App R (S) 121 (sentence for assault on a child reduced because the judge referred to the appellant having caused various injuries to the child over and above those she actually admitted).

Difficult problems arise where the accused pleads not guilty to the offences on the indictment but is found guilty. Is the judge then entitled to conclude, on the basis of evidence heard during the course of the trial, that the indictment offences are merely samples of continuing conduct?

The more recent authorities support the proposition that the accused should not be sentenced for offences which he has not admitted to the court, whether by plea, by asking the court to take them into consideration or in some other clear fashion (*Perkins* (1994) 15 Cr App R (S) 402). Hence, the fact that the charges upon which the accused was found guilty were described by the prosecution as 'specimens' does not entitle the judge to sentence him as if he had been found guilty of other offences, not included in the indictment. This is the view adopted in *Burfoot* (1990) Cr App R (S) 252, and it is respectfully submitted that it is in accordance with principle. The accused ought not to be deprived of his right to jury trial merely because offences are omitted from the indictment. In *Clark* [1996] 2 Cr App R (S) 351, the Court of Appeal followed the reasoning in *Burfoot* and in *McKenzie* (1984) 6 Cr App R 99. Their lordships said that the weight of authority supported the proposition that, where an offender was convicted on a single count, the sentencer must not sentence him on the basis that he was guilty of further offences of a similar nature unless the offender admitted that this was so. Such authority as had been cited to the contrary (*Mills* (1979) 68 Cr App R 154 and *Singh* (1981) 3 Cr App R (S) 90) was rejected. The Court suggested that prosecutors should charge sufficient offences fairly to reflect the criminality of the offending. In any event the CJA 1991, ss. 2(2)(a) and 31(2), prevent the court from taking into account offences other than those of which the defendant has been convicted or has had taken into consideration (see **E1.9** and **E1.14** for discussion of these provisions). A different conclusion was reached by the Court of Appeal in *Bradshaw* [1997] 2 Cr App R (S) 128. However, in *Canavan* [1998] 1 Cr App R 79, the Court of Appeal considered the conflict of authority and said that *Clark* was to be preferred to *Bradshaw*. Bingham LCJ stated in *Canavan* that the court could not base its decision as to sentence on the commission of offences not forming part of the offence for which the offender was to be sentenced. It is respectfully submitted that the decision in *Canavan* upholding that in *Clark* has resolved the question both authoritatively and in accordance with principle.

PRONOUNCEMENT OF SENTENCE

After the defence mitigation, the judge pronounces sentence. Normally he does so **D17.34** immediately upon the close of defence counsel's address, but there is no objection to his adjourning briefly to consider his decision.

Save where the statutory provisions mentioned below apply, there is no obligation on the judge to explain the reasons for his sentence. However, the Court of Appeal has encouraged the giving of reasons, and has indicated that that should certainly be done if the sentence might seem unduly severe in the absence of explanation (*Newton* (1979) 1 Cr App R (S) 252). A statutory obligation to give reasons is imposed by the following:

(a) CJA 1991, s. 1(4) – essentially this provides that any court passing a custodial sentence must explain in open court that either s. 1(2)(a) or (b) of the Act applies to the case, and why it has come to that conclusion. Further, the court must explain to the offender 'in open court and in ordinary language' why it is passing a custodial sentence. The court has a similar duty where it passes a custodial sentence which is longer than is merited by the seriousness of the offence, on the ground that it is necessary to protect the public (s. 2(3) of the 1991 Act).

(b)   PCCA 1973, s. 23(1) – a court dealing with an offender in breach of a suspended sentence which chooses not to activate the sentence in full must give reasons for its leniency.

(c)   PCCA 1973, s. 35 – a court with power to make a compensation order in an offender's case must explain its reasons for not doing so.

(d)   CJPO 1994, s. 48 – a court reducing the sentence passed on an offender because of his guilty plea must state in open court that it has done so.

It has been held that failure by the sentencing court to give reasons when required to do so does not invalidate the sentence (*McQueen* (1989) 11 Cr App R (S) 305), although the failure may no doubt be taken into account by the appellate court should the offender appeal. Where the sentencer does give reasons and what he says indicates an error of principle in the way he approached his task, the Court of Appeal sometimes reduces the sentence even though the penalty was not in itself excessive.

Whenever a custodial sentence is imposed, the court should explain the practical effect of the sentence, in addition to complying with any other statutory requirements (*Practice Direction (Custodial Sentences: Explanations)* [1998] 1 WLR 278: see **E1.20**). The *Practice Direction* includes a series of short statements which can be adapted by the sentencer, but prescribes no form of words, and makes it clear that what is to be given is merely an explanation — the sentence will be that which is pronounced by the court.

Criminal Justice Act 1982, s. 2(4)

Where—
(a)   the Crown Court passes a sentence of detention in a young offender institution or a sentence of custody for life under section 8(2) below, or
(b)   a magistrates' court passes a sentence of detention in a young offender institution, it shall be its duty—
(i)   to state in open court that it is satisfied that he qualifies for a custodial sentence under one or more of the paragraphs of section 4(1A) above, the paragraph or paragraphs in question and why it is so satisfied; and
(ii)   to explain to the offender in open court and in ordinary language why it is passing a custodial sentence on him.

Powers of Criminal Courts Act 1973, s. 20(2)

Where a magistrates' court passes a sentence of imprisonment on any such person as is mentioned in subsection (1) above, the court shall state the reason for its opinion that no other method of dealing with him is appropriate, and cause that reason to be specified in the warrant of commitment and to be entered in the register.

VARIATION OF SENTENCE

Introduction

D17.35   By the Supreme Court Act 1981, s. 47(2), a sentence imposed or other order made by the Crown Court when dealing with an offender may be varied or rescinded within 28 days of being passed or made. The judge who makes the variation must be the judge who originally passed sentence (s. 47(4)). If, however, he was accompanied by justices on the first occasion, they need not be present for the variation (ibid.). The 28-day limitation on exercising the power to vary is qualified in the case of accused who are jointly tried inasmuch as the period is 28 days from the conclusion of the joint trial or 56 days from the date of the sentence or order to be varied, whichever is the shorter (s. 47(3)). Conclusion of the trial, in this context, means the latest of any of the dates on which one of the accused was sentenced or acquitted (ibid.).

Extent of the Power to Vary

The power in the Supreme Court Act 1981, s. 47, may be used to replace one form of **D17.36** sentence with a quite different form – see, for example, *Sodhi* (1978) 66 Cr App R 260 and *Iqbal* (1985) 7 Cr App R (S) 35. In *Sodhi* the Crown Court, upon learning that S had been diagnosed by psychiatrists as suffering from paranoid psychosis and was dangerous, substituted for a six-month prison sentence a hospital order plus restriction order without time-limit. In *Iqbal* an unlawful sentence of 30 months' youth custody passed on a juvenile was replaced by an equivalent term of detention under the CYPA 1933, s. 53(2). The Court of Appeal upheld both variations, saying in *Sodhi* that the word 'varied' in the Supreme Court Act 1981, s. 47(2), has a wide meaning and the court's power is therefore not restricted to changing the length of a sentence. The section may also be used to add an extra order to the sentence already passed (*Reilly* [1982] QB 1208).

Increasing the Sentence by Variation

The obvious use of the power in the Supreme Court Act 1981, s. 47, is to correct minor **D17.37** errors made by the court when passing sentence. It is also clear that the power may be used to benefit the offender by reducing his sentence if, on reflection, the judge considers that he was originally too harsh. Whether the power should be used substantially to increase sentence has been a matter of some controversy but recent decisions indicate that, in appropriate circumstances, it may be so used.

(a) *Newsome* [1970] 2 QB 711. Under legislation then in force, the court was obliged to suspend any sentence of imprisonment it passed on the appellants unless the term thereof exceeded six months. The trial judge overlooked the relevant provisions, and imposed six months' immediate imprisonment. Upon realising his mistake, he increased the term to seven months. The Court of Appeal held that he had jurisdiction so to do since he had always intended to pass a short, immediate custodial sentence, and the increase he ordered was virtually the minimum necessary to achieve his original object.

(b) *Grice* (1977) 66 Cr App R 167. This is the decision most restrictive of the court's power to vary sentence. G was given a suspended sentence for unlawful sexual intercourse with his adopted daughter upon his giving an undertaking to the court that he would have no more contact with her. During the 28-day period for variation, it was reported to the court that G had broken his promise. In consequence, the judge varied the sentence by making the term of imprisonment immediate. The Court of Appeal restored the original sentence, holding that only in exceptional circumstances (such as in *Newsome*) should s. 47 be used to make a substantial increase in penalty.

(c) *Reilly* [1982] QB 1208. R pleaded guilty of offences of conspiracy to defraud the Revenue. At the outset, prosecution counsel informed the judge that he would be asking for the making of a criminal bankruptcy order. The judge passed a sentence of three years' imprisonment and made an order for prosecution costs but stated that he was not making a criminal bankruptcy order. Prosecution counsel asked to be heard on the latter matter. Despite defence objections, there was a short adjournment after which further material and argument were placed before the judge who in consequence varied his original sentence by adding the order sought. Relying on *Grice*, R argued on appeal that, once a sentence has been pronounced, there should be no 'fundamental change of mind' by the sentencer by adding to or varying the sentence so as to make it more severe. Kerr LJ, giving the Court of Appeal's judgment, held that *Grice* had to be considered in the light of *Sodhi* (1978) 66 Cr App R 260 and dicta of the House of Lords in *Menocal* [1980] AC 598. The latter concerned whether an order for forfeiture of money found on the appellant when she was arrested could be added to the original sentence outside the 28-day period for variation. The answer was no (see below), but Lords Salmon and Edmund-Davies especially indicated that had the addition of the forfeiture order been made within 28 days it would have been upheld. Lord Edmund-Davies said that, contrary to *Grice*, the Supreme Court Act 1981, s. 47(2), is not 'restricted to mere slips of the tongue or slips of the memory'. It was therefore clear 'almost beyond argument' that the judge in *Reilly* had jurisdiction to change his mind and add the criminal bankruptcy order.

(d) *Hart* (1983) 5 Cr App R (S) 25. H was sentenced to six months' imprisonment suspended for 18 months. In suspending the term, the judge was influenced by the offender's story that he was going to Italy with his girlfriend to start a new life there. Shortly afterwards, a newspaper reported that H had boasted that his story in court had been a false one, invented to trick the judge into passing a lenient sentence. The judge had H back before the court and replaced the suspended term with an immediate one. He did so outside the 28-day period, and therefore the variation had to be quashed. But Lord Lane CJ said: '. . . the learned judge was absolutely correct . . . to take this opportunity to review the sentence, had he done it within the stipulated time. Where someone makes it known after the event that he, as this appellant put it, has "conned the court", in other words told lies to the court and has thereby escaped his just punishment, is one of the plain cases for which section 47(2) is designed.'

(e) *McLean* (1988) 10 Cr App R (S) 18. M pleaded guilty to robbery and wounding. He had a large number of previous convictions. He claimed in mitigation that he was about to turn over a new leaf, and wrote to the judge expressing the intention of changing his ways. The judge accepted his remorse, and sentenced him to three years. Almost immediately after being sentenced, M escaped from custody through a door left open in error. When the judge became aware of this, he arranged for the case to be relisted. Some 26 days after the original sentence had been imposed, he varied it to four years. In due course, M was apprehended and sentenced to a further six months, consecutive, for the escape from custody. He appealed against the variation of his sentence for robbery from three years to four. The Court of Appeal took the view that the reasoning in *Hart* should be applied. Further, the variation in sentence here (unlike *Hart*) was within the 28-day period and hence the judge did have the power to increase the sentence. In the course of argument, McCullough J put to counsel that the proper approach of the court was to ask: (i) Did M's conduct create an exceptional situation? (ii) If it did, was the judge reasonably entitled to take the view that the exceptional situation undermined the whole basis upon which he passed sentence? If the answer to both questions was yes, then the judge could properly exercise the wide discretion given by the Supreme Court Act 1981, s. 47(2), to increase the sentence. In delivering the court's judgment, Woolf LJ confirmed that this was the correct approach (at p. 22). On the factual issue, the Court of Appeal decided that the judge was entitled to exercise his discretion and had done so properly. The appeal was dismissed.

The upshot of the above cases seems to be that the Crown Court may increase sentence by a variation under the Supreme Court Act 1981, s. 47(2), even to the extent of substituting an immediate custodial sentence for a suspended one, where additional argument put before the court (as in *Reilly*) or information that the original sentence was passed on an incorrect factual basis (as in *Hart* and *McLean*) justifies such variation. It is clear from *McLean* that the principle advanced in *Grice* remains good law: namely, that variations to the detriment of the offender are justified only in exceptional circumstances.

Procedure for Variation of Sentence

D17.38 In both *May* (1981) 3 Cr App R (S) 165 and *Cleere* (1983) 5 Cr App R (S) 465 it was held that the offender has a right to be present when his sentence is varied, and variations made in the absence of the respective appellants and without their having the benefit of legal representation were quashed. This was slightly qualified in *Shacklady* (1987) 9 Cr App R (S) 258 where Rose J, quoting a sentence from Watkins LJ's judgment in *Cleere*, stated the principle to be that 'the defendant or his counsel must have an opportunity to address the court' (p. 261). Accordingly, a variation made in the absence of the offender but with counsel in attendance on his behalf was upheld. The variation in *Shacklady* was made to correct an error the judge made when first passing sentence, and the appellant's sentence was not increased by the variation.

In *McLean* (1988) 10 Cr App R (S) 18 (see **D17.37**), M's sentence was increased from three to four years after his escape from custody and hence in his absence (voluntary on his part, unavoidable from the court's point of view). The judge heard representations from M's counsel on the occasion when he varied sentence. With the obvious exception of such circumstances, it is submitted that a genuine increase by variation should not be made unless both the offender and counsel are present.

In *Dowling* (1988) 88 Cr App R 88, it was stressed that any variation of sentence should take place in open court. D was sentenced to three years' imprisonment, to be served consecutively to a sentence of 15 months which he was already serving. Apparently, the judge was approached in his retiring room by a court clerk, who relayed doubts about the consecutive aspect of the sentence. The judge immediately reviewed that feature of the sentence and varied it so that the three years would run concurrently with the 15 months. He did not reconvene the court to state the variation. As a result, D, his counsel and the prison authorities all believed the sentence to be as originally pronounced. The Court of Appeal 'whether by way of clarification or by way of varying' ordered that the sentences be served concurrently. In so doing, their lordships emphasised that where the 'judge is minded to vary a sentence he has passed or even to clarify a doubt or ambiguity as to the effect of it, he should do so in open court'. Only in this manner would all those concerned hear the final decision from the judge directly, and in such a way that a shorthand note would be available. The court may rescind a sentence on one occasion, and then re-sentence at a later date, provided that the whole process is completed within the 28-day period (*Dunham* [1996] 1 Cr App R (S) 438).

Variations outside the 28-day Period

A sentence may not be varied outside the period specified in the Supreme Court Act **D17.39** 1981, s. 47(2) (*Menocal* [1980] AC 598, where the House of Lords quashed an order depriving the offender of £4,000 found in her possession when arrested on importation of controlled drugs charges because the order was not added to the original sentence until after the expiry of the time for variation). *Menocal* was followed in *Hart* (1983) 5 Cr App R (S) 25. The 28-day limit cannot be extended by rescinding the original sentence within the time-limit, and then not sentencing until after the time limit has expired (*Stillwell* (1991) 94 Cr App R 65).

A distinction is drawn, however, between varying the sentence by changing its length, adding an order to it or replacing it with a different type of disposition and merely correcting a technical defect in the sentence as originally announced (*Saville* [1981] QB 12 – criminal bankruptcy order corrected three months after it was made by specifying, as required by the relevant legislation, the amount of loss appearing to the court to have arisen from each of the seven offences to which the offender had pleaded guilty instead of merely specifying a lump sum: correction upheld by the Court of Appeal because the Crown Court has an inherent jurisdiction, apart from the Supreme Court Act 1981, s. 47(2), to remedy mistakes in its record and the correction or variation was of such a minor nature that it was appropriate to exercise the inherent jurisdiction).

DEFERRING SENTENCE

Power to Defer Sentence

The power to defer passing sentence is contained in the PCCA 1973, s. 1. The purpose **D17.40** for which sentence may be deferred is to enable the court, when it does deal with the offender, to have regard to (a) his conduct after conviction (including, where appropriate, the making by him of reparation for his offence), or (b) any change in his circumstances (s. 1(1)). The court must fix the date to which sentence is deferred, the maximum period allowed being six months (s. 1(2)). Subject to an exception mentioned below, sentence may be deferred only once (ibid.). Deferment requires the offender's consent (s. 1(3)). Moreover, the court must be satisfied that exercise of the power would be in the interests of justice (ibid.). The court dealing with the offender after the period of deferment may deal with him in any way the deferring court could have done (s. 1(8)(a)). By s. 1(8)(b), that includes, where sentence was deferred by a magistrates' court, committing the offender for sentence under the MCA 1980, s. 38. Where a magistrates' court defers sentence and then commits under s. 38, the Crown Court may also defer sentence, that being the exception to the rule that sentence may be deferred only once (PCCA 1973, s. 1(8A)). Upon deferring sentence, the court does not bail the offender (s. 1(6A)) but, if he should fail to appear on the deferment date, a warrant may be issued for his arrest (s. 1(5)).

A deferred sentence may, in appropriate circumstances, be referred by the A-G to the Court of Appeal for review, where he considers that it constitutes an unduly lenient sentence (*A-G's Ref (No. 27 of 1992)* [1993] Crim LR 630: see **D24.4**).

Recommended Procedure when Deferring Sentence

D17.41   Lord Lane CJ in his judgment in *George* [1984] 1 WLR 1082 gave guidance on the procedure which should be adopted when deferring sentence. The chief points to be noted are:

(a)   When deferring sentence the court must make it clear to the offender the particular purposes under the PCCA 1973, s. 1(1), that it has in mind, and the conduct that is expected of him during deferment. The court should also make it clear that it is deferring sentence as opposed to merely adjourning (*Fairhead* [1975] 2 All ER 737).

(b)   A careful note should be made by the court of what the offender is told. Ideally, the offender himself should also be given a written note of the conduct expected of him.

(c)   The court eventually passing sentence should, first, ascertain the purpose of the deferment and any requirement as to conduct then imposed. It must then determine whether the offender has substantially conformed (or attempted to conform) with the proper expectations of the deferring court. If he has, he may expect a non-custodial sentence; if he has not, the sentencing court should state with precision in what respects he has failed. Failure to do so may lead to any custodial sentence being quashed because of the appearance given that the sentencing court merely disagrees with the original decision to defer as opposed to being genuinely disappointed in the offender's conduct (*Glossop* (1981) 3 Cr App R (S) 347). In order to decide whether the offender has lived up to expectations, the sentencing court will almost certainly require an up-to-date social inquiry report. To avoid unnecessary delay, it may be appropriate to order the report when sentence is deferred.

(d)   The above procedure is recommended in part because the judge who passes sentence need not necessarily be the judge who deferred sentence, and it is therefore necessary to ensure as far as possible that the former knows how the latter was thinking. However, whenever possible, both the judge who deferred sentence and counsel who then represented the offender should make themselves available for the eventual sentencing (see *Gurney* [1974] Crim LR 472 and *Ryan* [1976] Crim LR 508).

(e)   Every effort should be made to sentence the offender on the date to which sentence was deferred (per Lord Lane CJ in *Anderson* (1983) 78 Cr App R 251). In exceptional circumstances, however, the court may adjourn to a later date, even if that is more than six months after the original deferment (see *Ingle* [1974] 3 All ER 811 and *Anderson* – in the latter case, sentence was originally deferred for five months but, through a chapter of accidents, A was not sentenced until seven months had elapsed:

the Court of Appeal held that the Crown Court had not been deprived of its jurisdiction to sentence by reason of the delay, but the sentence eventually passed should reflect how stale the offence had become).

Appropriate Circumstances for Deferring

In *George* [1984] 1 WLR 1082, Lord Lane CJ gave some indication of when it may be **D17.42** appropriate to defer sentence. He referred especially to cases where the improvement in the offender's conduct or steps which the court wants him to take are not sufficiently specific to be made the subject of a requirement in a probation order, but nonetheless the court wishes to see what progress he makes before sentencing (p. 1085G–H). His lordship cautioned against adopting deferment as an easy option when the sentencer's intentions could in fact be achieved by other means (e.g., a short probation order) (p. 1086A). In *Skelton* [1983] Crim LR 686 the Court of Appeal held that the judge deferring sentence on S erred by indicating that, during the deferment period, he expected S to go into hospital for treatment for a mental condition – such a restriction on the offender's freedom of action should have been imposed, if at all, by means of a hospital order or probation order with a requirement for medical treatment, not as a side wind of deferring sentence.

Custodial Sentence after Deferment

As indicated by Lord Lane CJ in *George* [1984] 1 WLR 1082, the tacit understanding **D17.43** between the court and the offender when sentence is deferred is that, if he substantially conforms (or, at least, tries to conform) with the deferring court's proper expectations, then the sentencing court will pass a non-custodial sentence. It follows that, although conviction for further offences during a deferment period will almost certainly lead to a custodial sentence (see, for example, *Hope* (1980) 2 Cr App R (S) 6), merely staying out of trouble does not guarantee the opposite. Thus, in *Smith* (1976) 64 Cr App R 116, where sentence on S for several burglaries was deferred to see if he could (a) work regularly and (b) reduce his alcohol consumption, the Court of Appeal upheld an eventual sentence of 18 months' immediate imprisonment because he had done neither of those things, even though he had avoided further offending. A minor falling short of the deferring court's expectations should not, however, be used as a justification for a custodial sentence (*Smith* (1979) 1 Cr App R (S) 339 – sentence of 15 months' immediate imprisonment for a social security fraud quashed because, when sentence was deferred, S had been told to stay in employment, see a probation officer, behave sensibly and try to repay the money he had dishonestly obtained, and the only way he had failed to comply with those requirements was in not saving money for reparation, for which default he had an exceptionally good excuse). Offences which were allegedly committed during the period of deferment but which are unresolved by the time the period expires should not influence the sentencer in any way unless and until the offender has been convicted of the later alleged offences (*Aquilina* [1990] Crim LR 134).

Sentencing before the End of the Deferment Period

Once sentence has been deferred, the court may not proceed to sentence until the **D17.44** deferment period has expired, unless either it revokes the order for deferment within 28 days by virtue of the Supreme Court Act 1981, s. 47(2) (see **D17.31**), or the PCCA 1973, s. 1(4) or (4A), apply (*McQuaide* (1974) 60 Cr App R 239). The effect of the latter provisions is that, if an offender is convicted of an offence (the subsequent offence) during a deferment period, the court passing sentence on him for the subsequent offence may also sentence for the deferment offence (s. 1(4A)). This does not apply if sentence was deferred by the Crown Court and the sentencing court for the subsequent offence is a magistrates' court (proviso (a) to s. 1(4A)). In the converse case of the Crown Court sentencing for the subsequent offence, sentence having been deferred by a magistrates' court, the Crown Court's powers in respect of the deferment offence are limited to those of a magistrates' court (proviso (b)). Apart from the possibility of the court that sentences an offender for a subsequent offence also sentencing him for the deferment offence, conviction for a subsequent offence during a deferment period always entitles the *deferring* court to sentence forthwith for the deferment offence, even though the deferment period has not expired (s. 1(4)).

Powers of Criminal Courts Act 1973, s. 1

(1) Subject to the provisions of this section, the Crown Court or a magistrates' court may defer passing sentence on an offender for the purpose of enabling the court or any other court to which it falls to deal with him to have regard, in dealing with him, to his conduct after conviction (including, where appropriate, the making by him of reparation for his offence) or to any change in his circumstances.

(2) Any deferment under this section shall be until such date as may be specified by the court, not being more than six months after the date on which deferment is announced by the court; and, subject to subsection (8A) below, where the passing of sentence has been deferred under this section it shall be further deferred thereunder.

(3) The power conferred by this section shall be exercisable only if the offender consents and the court is satisfied, having regard to the nature of the offence and the character and circumstances of the offender, that it would be in the interests of justice to exercise the power.

(4) A court which under this section has deferred passing sentence on an offender may deal with him before the expiration of the period of deferment if during that period he is convicted in Great Britain of any offence.

(4A) If an offender on whom a court under this section deferred passing sentence in respect of one or more offences is during the period of deferment convicted in England or Wales of any offence ('the subsequent offence'), then, without prejudice to subsection (4) above, the court which (whether during that period or not) passes sentence on him for the subsequent offence may also, if this has not already been done, deal with him for the first-mentioned offence or offences:
Provided that—

(a) the power conferred by this subsection shall not be exercised by a magistrates' court if the court which deferred passing sentence was the Crown Court; and

(b) the Crown Court, in exercising that power in a case in which the court which deferred passing sentence was a magistrates' court, shall not pass any sentence which could have not been passed by a magistrates' court in exercising it.

(5) Where a court which under this section has deferred passing sentence on an offender proposes to deal with him, whether on the date originally specified by the court or by virtue of subsection (4) above before that date, or where the offender does not appear on the date specified, the court may issue a summons requiring him to appear before the court, or may issue a warrant for his arrest.

[(6) Powers of magistrates' courts upon non-appearance of the offender upon the deferment date.]

(6A) Notwithstanding any enactment, a court which under this section defers passing sentence on an offender shall not on the same occasion remand him.

ADJOURNMENTS

D17.45   Apart from its power under the PCCA 1973, s. 1, to defer passing sentence for up to six months, the Crown Court has inherent jurisdiction at common law to adjourn before sentencing an offender. In other words, it need not sentence on the occasion on which an offender pleads guilty or is found guilty.

Although there are no express limitations on the grounds for adjourning or the length of the adjournment, it is submitted that the court must exercise its powers judicially and should postpone sentencing only for good and proper reasons. Thus, by analogy with the decision in *Arthur* v *Stringer* (1986) 84 Cr App R 361, it would be improper to adjourn solely because the offender is slightly too young for the form of sentence the court considers desirable in his case and adjourning will allow him to attain the minimum age necessary. In *Arthur v Stringer*, S was found guilty by a magistrates' court on 13 February 1985 of assault. The court adjourned for reports and then sentenced him to four months in a detention centre. At the time of sentence he was 20, and therefore too young for a prison term, whether immediate or suspended (custodial sentences on offenders under 21 cannot be suspended in any event). He appealed against sentence. By the time the appeal was heard he was 21, and the Crown Court replaced the detention centre order with four months' imprisonment suspended for 18 months. The Crown Court justified its decision by arguing that even though its powers on appeal were limited to those that the magistrates had when dealing with S and therefore a prison sentence was prima facie not open to it, nonetheless, had it been dealing with S at first instance, it would have adjourned until he reached the age of 21 and thus secured the power to imprison which it initially lacked. On appeal, the Divisional Court held that, as the Crown Court was determining an appeal from a magistrates' court, its powers of adjournment were no greater than those of the magistrates. Further, it was implicit in the MCA 1980, s. 10(3) (which gives magistrates' courts jurisdiction to adjourn between conviction and sentence), that the discretion vested in the court to adjourn has to be exercised judicially. It cannot be said to have been exercised judicially if the only reason for exercising it was to ensure that the offender had reached the age of 21 by the time he was sentenced, thus clothing the court with power to pass a sentence of imprisonment.

As to the maximum period for an adjournment, it is submitted that the Crown Court should bear in mind the provisions of the MCA 1980, s. 10(3), which restrict an adjournment after conviction to a maximum of three weeks at a time if the offender is remanded in custody, four weeks if he is granted bail. Although the subsection does not directly apply to the Crown Court when dealing with an offender convicted on indictment, it is an indication of the kind of periods Parliament considers appropriate for post-conviction adjournments, at least where the ultimate sentence is likely to be relatively short. Where the Crown Court is dealing with an offender who has appealed against his conviction and/or sentence in the magistrates' court, the higher court is directly bound by the provisions of s. 10(3) since the appeal takes the form of a rehearing, and the Crown Court's powers are therefore no greater than those of the magistrates (see *Arthur v Stringer*).

Common reasons for adjourning prior to sentence are to give the offender the opportunity to apply for legal aid, to obtain reports on him or to await the outcome of the trial of a co-accused who has pleaded not guilty. During the period of the adjournment, the offender may be remanded in custody or granted bail at the court's discretion (see Supreme Court Act 1981, s. 81(1)(c), for the power to grant bail).

A final power possessed by the Crown Court, analogous to adjourning, is to bind the offender over to come up for judgment if called upon to do so. Although in form a postponement of sentence, this is used more as a means of avoiding sentencing an offender if, exceptionally, the court does not want to impose a penalty but the ordinary alternatives to a penalty (such as a conditional discharge or a probation order) are inappropriate to meet the court's concerns in the particular circumstances of the case. The understanding is that, if the offender does not re-offend and complies with any conditions the court imposes when binding him over, then he will not in fact be required to return before the court.

SECTION D18: SUMMARY TRIAL: GENERAL AND PRELIMINARY MATTERS

The subject-matter of this section is the procedure for summary trial, concentrating on those respects in which it differs from that for trial on indictment. It should be read in conjunction with **D4** and **D5** which deal with the proceedings in a magistrates' court prior to the commencement of trial (or committal proceedings), in particular the power of magistrates and justices' clerks to issue summonses or warrants for arrest, the options open to a court upon non-appearance of the accused in response to a summons, and the right to request advance information if the offence charged is triable either way.

THE INFORMATION

Informations Generally

D18.1 At the commencement of a summary trial, the accused is asked to plead guilty or not guilty to a written charge called 'the information'. Depending upon the method by which the prosecution was commenced, the information comes into being either (a) as a result of the prosecutor laying an information before a magistrate or magistrates' clerk in order to obtain the issue of a summons or warrant for arrest, or (b) as a result of the accused being charged at a police station. By convention, a charge sheet completed at the police station is treated as the information.

Informations are not defined by the relevant legislation or rules. However, in *Rubin v DPP* [1990] 2 QB 80, Watkins LJ gave the following brief description of one (at p. 86D):

> It is . . . well established that an information may be oral or in writing. . . . There are no prescribed forms for an information which should . . . identify the informant and also the defendant and give particulars of the offence and any relevant statute or regulation.

In stating the above, his lordship no doubt had in mind the Magistrates' Courts Rules 1981, r. 100(1), which states that:

> Every information, summons, warrant or other document laid, issued or made for the purposes of, or in connection with, any proceedings before a magistrates' court for an offence shall be sufficient if it describes the specific offence with which the accused is charged, or of which he is convicted, in ordinary language avoiding as far as possible the use of technical terms and without necessarily stating all the elements of the offence, and gives such particulars as may be necessary for giving reasonable information of the nature of the charge.

Paragraph (2) of r. 100 further provides that, if the offence is statutory, the 'section of the Act or, as the case may be, rule, order, regulation, by-law or other instrument creating the offence' must be referred to. By r. 4(3) it is not necessary to 'specify or negative an exception, exemption, proviso, excuse or qualification' to liability of which the defendant might possibly take advantage, whether or not that exception etc. accompanies the description of the offence in the statute contravened. This is a procedural corollary of the evidential rule that it is for the accused to prove that he comes within a statutory exception etc., not for the prosecution to show that he falls outside it (see MCA 1980, s. 101).

Beyond the general statement in r. 100(1) that informations should avoid the use of technical terms and give reasonable information about the nature of the charge, there is little guidance on how they should be drafted. For examples of informations for summary offences where the particulars were insufficiently precise or the wrong statutory provision was mentioned, see *Atterton* v *Browne* [1945] KB 122 (wrong and misleading citation of statute) and *Stephenson* v *Johnson* [1954] 1 WLR 375 and *Hunter* v *Coombs* [1962] 1 WLR 573 (insufficient detail about offence). However, reference to a particular statutory provision may cure an apparent defect by making plain what might otherwise be ambiguous (*Karpinski* v *City of Westminster* [1993] Crim LR 606).

Where the offence charged is indictable, a precedent for a count in an indictment may safely be followed. However, there is one major difference between the ways informations and counts are conventionally drafted, namely that the former are *not* split into statement of offence and particulars of offence, but consist merely of what – in a count – would be the particulars of offence with the statute or other instrument contravened added at the end. A further difference is that informations often state the county in which the offence occurred whereas counts do not give the location unless it is an essential element of the offence charged. This difference in practice may derive from the fact that a magistrates' court's jurisdiction to try offences is in some respects geographically restricted whereas the Crown Court's is not. By specifying the venue of the offence, the information makes it clear that proceedings are being taken in a court with jurisdiction. If the information as originally drafted gives insufficient particulars, application for further particulars may be made at any time after the charge being preferred – the defence need not wait until committal proceedings to learn exactly what is being alleged (*Aylesbury Justices, ex parte Wisbey* [1965] 1 WLR 339).

If the information as originally drafted is incomplete or inaccurate, the defect will not necessarily be fatal to a conviction but the prosecution should apply to amend and the defence should be granted an adjournment if they may have been misled by the original error (see MCA 1980, s. 123).

Rule against Duplicity

Like a count in an indictment, an information may allege only one offence. This follows **D18.2** from r. 12(1) of the Magistrates' Courts Rules 1981 which provides that 'Subject to any Act passed after 2nd October 1848, a magistrates' court shall not proceed to the trial of an information that charges more than one offence'. The concept of duplicity and the fine distinctions that have been drawn in deciding whether a count or, as the case may be, information alleges one or several offences have been considered at **D9.16** to **D9.23**. It is unnecessary to repeat that discussion. Extensive quotation of authority is also unlikely to be of much assistance since decided cases turn upon the precise wording of the informations in question and the enactments allegedly contravened. However, the following decisions are illustrative of the approach of the appellate courts.

Whether One or More than One Act Is Being Alleged (a) *Jemmison* v *Priddle* **D18.3** [1972] 1 QB 489. An information alleged that J on 6 February 1971 at . . . unlawfully did take and kill and pursue certain game, to wit two red deer without having a licence as required by the Game Licences Act 1860. It was held not to be bad for duplicity because, although the killing of each of the deer was a potential offence in the absence of the accused having a game licence, the killings – on the evidence – occurred in the same geographical location within a very short time of each other. Thus, what was being alleged was a single activity of shooting deer, not two separate offences.

(b) *Horrix* v *Malam* [1984] RTR 112. Conviction on single information for careless driving upheld where the prosecution case was that the defendant had driven badly on three different roads, the driving complained of being divided into two distinct incidents, witnessed by different police officers and with a 10-minute gap between them.

(c) *Cullen* v *Jardine* [1985] Crim LR 668. Information for felling 90 trees without a licence contrary to the Forestry Act 1967, s. 17(1), held not to be bad for duplicity. Even though the felling had taken place over a three-day period and there might have been separate defences advanced in respect of different trees, it was still possible to regard the felling as one activity. The fact that a number of distinct issues might arise in the course of the trial did not of itself necessitate separate informations. The magistrates were perfectly capable on the information as drafted of determining how many trees the accused had illegally felled and adjusting the penalty accordingly. Whether an information is bad for duplicity is a matter of fact and degree in each case.

(d) *Anderton v Cooper* (1980) 72 Cr App R 232. The information alleged that, on 16 February 1979 *and other days* between that date and 15 March 1979, C managed a brothel contrary to the Sexual Offences Act 1956, s. 33. The evidence showed that the premises in question (of which C was the manager) were being used for purposes of prostitution on three occasions within the specified dates. The justices dismissed the information, agreeing with a defence submission that it was bad for duplicity. The Divisional Court upheld the prosecutor's appeal since the section allegedly contravened referred to 'keeping' and 'managing' a brothel, both of which verbs denoted single transactions which could take a long period of time to complete. Accordingly, although the inclusion of the words 'and other days' in the information was unfortunate, it was in fact alleging a single continuing offence, and so was not bad for duplicity.

(e) *Bristol Crown Court, ex parte Willets* (1985) 149 JP 416. Single information for possessing for publication for gain five different obscene videotapes contrary to the Obscene Publications Act 1959, s. 2(1), not bad for duplicity since all the tapes had been found on the accused's premises as a result of a single search and the information was alleging a single activity (but cf. *Ward* [1988] Crim LR 57 where an information for possessing by way of trade 15 videotaped films in breach of copyright contrary to the Copyright Act 1956, s. 24(1), was held duplicitous).

(f) *Heaton v Costello* (1984) 148 JP 688. Information for stealing a bottle of cider, a pair of trousers and a cardigan from a supermarket held not to be bad for duplicity since all the items were stolen on one visit to the supermarket. The case goes a little beyond the leading authority of *Wilson* (1979) 69 Cr App R 83 since the theft of the cider was effected by switching price labels and the theft of the clothing by walking through the check-outs without paying. Thus, one theft had been completed within the store, while the other remained incomplete until the accused had passed the check-out. Nevertheless, the Divisional Court held that there was but a single activity.

D18.4 ***Whether a Statutory Provision Creates One or More than One Offence***
(a) *Mallon v Allon* [1964] 1 QB 385. Information for admitting and allowing a person apparently under 18 to remain in a licensed betting office contrary to the Betting and Gaming Act 1960, s. 5, held bad because s. 5 prohibits two separate acts, namely (i) admitting an under-age person on to licensed premises and (ii) allowing him to remain after he has got on to the premises. The information was therefore charging two separate offences even though they arose out of one continuing incident.

(b) *Surrey Justices, ex parte Witherick* [1932] 1 KB 450. Information for driving without due care and attention or without reasonable consideration contrary to what is now the Road Traffic Act 1988, s. 3, bad because the section creates two separate offences, one of driving without due care and the other of driving without reasonable consideration. Accordingly, they must be alleged in separate informations, not as alternatives in a single information.

(c) *Ware v Fox* [1967] 1 WLR 379. Conviction on an information alleging that the defendant had permitted the premises he occupied to be used for the purposes of smoking cannabis or dealing in cannabis quashed because the relevant statutory provision created separate offences of (i) allowing premises to be used for smoking cannabis and (ii) allowing them to be used for dealing in it.

(d) *Thomson v Knights* [1947] KB 336. Information alleging driving when unfit through drink or drugs contrary to what is now the Road Traffic Act 1988, s. 4, upheld since the section creates a single offence of driving when in a self-induced state of incapacity, not two separate offences of driving while unfit through drink and driving while unfit through drugs.

(e)   *Amos* v *DPP* [1988] RTR 198. Information alleging that a bus driver, who had had an argument with a passenger about the fare and had then closed the doors so as to trap the passenger in them, was guilty of 'failing to behave in a civil and orderly manner and to take all reasonable precautions to ensure the safety of passengers alighting from the vehicle, contrary to the Public Service Vehicles (Conduct of Drivers) Regulations 1936, reg. 4(a) and (c)', held to be bad for duplicity. The structure of the regulation, with its division of different types of misconduct into separate paragraphs, showed that it was creating a number of separate offences (one per paragraph), not a single compendious offence of misconduct.

Since the insertion of r. 12(3), (4) and (5) in the Magistrates' Court Rules 1981, the prosecution can cure an information bad for duplicity after the trial has started. If such a defect is spotted during the trial, the court must call on the prosecutor to elect on which offence he chooses to proceed. The other offences will be struck out and the court will proceed to try the information afresh, subject to the need to consider an adjournment if the accused requests one and it appears that he has been unfairly prejudiced. If the prosecutor fails to elect, the information must be dismissed.

JURISDICTION TO TRY CASES SUMMARILY

Basis of Jurisdiction

The jurisdiction of a magistrates' court to try cases summarily is set out in the MCA **D18.5** 1980, s. 2. The section should be read in conjunction with s. 1 of the Act, which empowers magistrates to issue process for the purpose of bringing accused persons before the court. The main features of s. 2 are as follows:

(a)   A magistrates' court has jurisdiction to try any summary offence which allegedly occurred within *the county* for which the court acts (s. 2(1)). The offence need not have been within the petty-sessional area of the court, but – as a matter of practice – proceedings are normally taken not only within the county of the offence but within the relevant petty-sessional area. Subject to the exceptions mentioned below, a magistrates' court may *not* try a summary offence occurring outside its county.

(b)   A magistrates' court has jurisdiction to try an offence triable either way provided only that the procedure for determining mode of trial contained in the MCA 1980, ss. 18 to 22, has resulted in a decision for summary trial (s. 2(4)). The venue of the offence is irrelevant to jurisdiction, save in the sense that the English courts as a whole do not claim jurisdiction over offences committed abroad.

(c)   Where an accused charged with a summary offence appears or is brought before a magistrates' court as a result of a summons or warrant for arrest issued under the MCA 1980, s. 1(2)(b), the court has jurisdiction to try the offence irrespective of where it occurred (s. 2(2)). Section 1(2)(b) empowers a magistrate to issue process if one defendant is already being proceeded against within his county and he considers it necessary or expedient in the interests of justice that a second defendant against whom an information is laid should be tried jointly with or in the same place as the first defendant. An example of the possible application of ss. 1(2)(b) and 2(2) is if A1 takes a car without the owner's consent in Clayshire and drives it into Loamshire where it is later driven by A2, and proceedings are taken against A2 in Loamshire for driving the car knowing it to have been taken without authority. A justice acting for Loamshire might issue a summons or warrant for arrest under s. 1(2)(b) in respect of A1's original taking of the car on the basis that, although the offence is summary and occurred outside his county, nonetheless it is expedient for A1 and A2 to be tried in the same place and A2 is already being proceeded against in Loamshire. Further, upon A1 appearing before a court for Loamshire, that court will have jurisdiction to try him by virtue of s. 2(2), again notwithstanding that the offence occurred in Clayshire.

(d)   Where an accused is already being tried by a magistrates' court for an offence (whether summary or indictable), that court has jurisdiction to try him for any summary offence whether committed inside or outside the county (s. 2(6)). There is also power under s. 1(2)(d) to issue process in respect of the summary offence.

(e)   The jurisdiction to try offences conferred by s. 2 is without prejudice to any jurisdiction to try that magistrates' courts may be granted by other enactments. The other jurisdiction-conferring enactments relate chiefly to offences committed outside the UK. They include the Merchant Shipping Act 1995, s. 281 (jurisdiction over offences committed on British ships on the high seas); s. 282 of the same Act (jurisdiction over offences committed abroad if the accused was a member of the crew of a British merchant ship at the time or within the preceding three months); the Territorial Waters Jurisdiction Act 1878, s. 2 (jurisdiction over offences committed on foreign or British ships which are lying off the coast within British territorial waters), and the Civil Aviation Act 1982, s. 92 (jurisdiction over offences on British-controlled aircraft while they are in flight, whether or not within UK airspace).

(f)   Offences committed within 500 yards of a boundary between two or more counties, or in any harbour etc. lying between two or more counties may be treated as having been committed in any one of them (MCA 1980, s. 3(1)). The same applies to offences begun in one county and completed in another or committed on a journey through two or more counties (s. 3(2) and (3)).

Magistrates' Courts Act 1980, ss. 2 and 3

2.—(1)   A magistrates' court for a county, a London commission area or the City of London shall have jurisdiction to try all summary offences committed within the county, the London commission area or the City (as the case may be).

(2)   Where a person charged with a summary offence appears or is brought before a magistrates' court in answer to a summons issued under paragraph (b) of section 1(2) above, or under a warrant issued under that paragraph, the court shall have jurisdiction to try the offence.

(3)   A magistrates' court for a county, a London commission area or the City of London shall have jurisdiction as examining justices over any offence committed by a person who appears or is brought before the court, whether or not the offence was committed within the county, the London commission area or the City (as the case may be).

(4)   Subject to sections 18 to 22 below and any other enactment (wherever contained) relating to the mode of trial of offences triable either way, a magistrates' court shall have jurisdiction to try summarily an offence triable either way in any case in which under subsection (3) above it would have jurisdiction as examining justices.

[(5)   Relates to summary trial of indictable offences alleged against juveniles.]

(6)   A magistrates' court for any area by which a person is tried for an offence shall have jurisdiction to try him for any summary offence for which he could be tried by a magistrates' court for any other area.

(7)   Nothing in this section shall affect any jurisdiction over offences conferred on a magistrates' court by any enactment not contained in this Act.

3.—(1)   Where an offence has been committed on the boundary between two or more areas to which this section applies, or within 500 yards of such a boundary, or in any harbour, river, arm of the sea or other water lying between two or more such areas, the offence may be treated for the purposes of the preceding provisions of this Act as having been committed in any one of those areas.

(2)   An offence begun in one area to which this section applies and completed in another may be treated for the purposes of the preceding provisions of this Act as having been wholly committed in either.

(3)   Where an offence has been committed on any person, or on or in respect of any property, in or on a vehicle or vessel engaged on any journey or voyage through two or more areas to which this section applies, the offence may be treated for the purposes of the

preceding provisions of this Act as having been committed in any one of those areas; and where the side or any part of a road or any water along which the vehicle or vessel passed in the course of the journey or voyage forms the boundary between two or more areas to which this section applies, the offence may be treated for the purposes of the preceding provisions of this Act as having been committed in any of those areas.

(4)   The areas to which this section applies are any county, any London commission area and the City of London.

Transfer of Cases between Magistrates' Courts

Because of the territorial restrictions on the jurisdiction of magistrates' courts and the **D18.6** almost automatic tendency to commence proceedings in the petty-sessional division where the offence occurred even if the rules would have permitted their being brought elsewhere, it not infrequently happens that a defendant has proceedings current against him in two or more different magistrates' courts. The question may then arise (either at the request of the defence or on the court's own initiative) of whether the separate proceedings can be linked up in one or other of the courts in question. The following principles govern the transfer of cases between magistrates' courts:

(a)   If court A is aware that a defendant before it also faces charges or summonses in court B but has not yet entered a plea to the court B matters, it may suggest to the prosecution that – with the consent of court B – the charges or summonses in court B be withdrawn and the defendant be recharged in court A. This could be done, even when the defendant has already pleaded not guilty in court B, if the prosecution gives notice of discontinuance under the Prosecution of Offences Act 1985, s. 23 (see **D2.38**), since it is specifically provided by s. 23(9) that the discontinuance shall not prevent the institution of fresh proceedings in respect of the same offence. Hence the case could then proceed in court A. If the defendant has pleaded guilty in court B, the MCA 1980, s. 39 (see (b) below) may apply.

(b)   By the MCA 1980, s. 39(1), where a magistrates' court has convicted an offender of an offence (the 'instant offence') and is then informed that he also stands convicted in another magistrates' court of some other offence for which he is yet to be sentenced, then it may remit him to that other court to be dealt with for the instant offence. This power of remittal only applies if (i) the offender is aged 18 or over; (ii) the other court agrees to the remittal, and (iii) the instant offence is either imprisonable or punishable with disqualification from driving (s. 39(1) and (6)). The provisions of the MCA 1980, s. 128 (power to remand in custody or on bail and maximum period for remands in custody) apply upon a remittal to another court just as they would apply if the court were adjourning with a view to the offender being brought back before itself (s. 39(3)(a)). In consequence of the remittal, the other court may deal with the case as if all the proceedings before the convicting court had in fact taken place before itself (s. 39(3)(b)). This includes the power to remit the offender to a third magistrates' court (ibid.) or even to remit him back to the original convicting court (s. 39(5)). It will be noted that s. 39 can be of assistance only if the person to be remitted has already been convicted (though not sentenced or committed for sentence) in *both* the courts concerned. Although not expressly stated in the section, the qualifying convictions may clearly be either upon a guilty plea or following a trial.

(c)   To avoid inconveniently long journeys from remand prison to court, a magistrates' court remanding a defendant in custody under the MCA 1980, ss. 5 (remands prior to committal proceedings), 10(1) (remands prior to summary trial of an information) or 18(4) (remands prior to determining mode of trial for an offence triable either way), may order that he be brought up for any subsequent remands before an alternate magistrates' court nearer to the prison where is to be confined while on remand (s. 130(1)). While the order under s. 130(1) is in force, the alternate court exercises all the powers relating to a further remand (whether in custody or on bail) and the granting of legal aid which would otherwise fall to be exercised by the original court (s. 130(3)). The order ceases to have force when either the alternate court – upon making a further remand in custody – orders that the defendant be brought before the original court at the end of the remand, or it grants the accused bail (s. 130(4)). The alternate court would no doubt remand the defendant to be brought back before the original court on the occasion of the last remand before it is anticipated that a substantive step will be taken in the proceedings (e.g., it will ensure that the defendant appears in the original court for the commencement of a summary trial or the determination of mode of trial).

(d)   Over and above the special powers contained in the MCA 1980, s. 130, a magistrates' court before which a defendant first appears charged with an offence may remand him (whether in custody or on bail) to appear before a different court for the same county (*Avon Magistrates' Courts Committee, ex parte Bath Law Society* [1988] QB 409). Moreover, the police are under a duty to bring a person whom they have charged and not released on bail before a court as soon as practicable (see PACE 1984, s. 46), and, if the clerk whom they contact is not prepared to arrange a special Saturday court in the petty-sessional division where a defendant arrested on Friday night or Saturday morning is being held, then they must bring him before whichever court in the county will be sitting (*Avon Magistrates' Courts Committee, ex parte Broome* [1988] 1 WLR 1246). The net effect of the two above decisions was to validate the practice of the courts for the county of Avon of holding a Saturday remand court at the central city court to deal with all the 'overnight charges' throughout the county. The central court would then remand each defendant (in custody or on bail as appropriate), ordering that he thereafter appear before the court for the petty-sessional area where the offence allegedly occurred.

TIME WITHIN WHICH SUMMARY TRIAL SHOULD TAKE PLACE

General Rule

D18.7   A magistrates' court may not try a defendant for a *summary* offence unless the information was laid within six months of the time when the offence was allegedly committed (MCA 1980, s. 127(1), as qualified by s. 127(2)(a)). This is subject to any enactment which expressly permits a longer period. As regards *indictable* offences (including offences triable either way), the rule is that – assuming the other pre-conditions of jurisdiction are satisfied – magistrates may try the offence regardless of when the information was laid, unless it is one of the exceptional offences for which there is statutory limitation on the time for taking proceedings on indictment, in which case that limitation applies equally to summary proceedings (s. 127(2) and (4)).

That there is in general no time limitation on taking proceedings for offences triable either way is confirmed by *Kemp* v *Liebherr (Great Britain) Ltd* [1987] 1 WLR 607. Even where a statute creates an offence triable either way and then appears to impose a time-limit in respect of summary proceedings (but not proceedings on indictment), the limitation is overridden by the MCA 1980, s. 127(2). In *Kemp* v *Liebherr (Great Britain) Ltd*, a prosecution for supplying an unsafe crane contrary to the Health and Safety at Work etc. Act 1974, ss. 6(1)(a) and 33(1)(a), was commenced more than six months after evidence justifying a prosecution had become available to the prosecutor. By s. 34(3) of the Act, summary proceedings for contravening the Act by supplying an article apparently had to be commenced within six months of obtaining the evidence. The Divisional Court held that the proceedings were nonetheless within time since – on a true construction of the Act – the offence charged was triable either way and therefore s. 34(3) was effectively negated by the MCA 1980, s. 127(2). As pointed out at **D3.1**, an offence triable either way is an indictable offence.

The purpose of the six-month limitation on laying informations for summary offences was explained by May J in the course of his judgment in *Newcastle-upon-Tyne Justices, ex parte John Bryce (Contractors) Ltd* [1976] 1 WLR 517. He said that s. 127(1) existed 'to ensure that summary offences are charged and tried as soon as reasonably possible after their alleged commission, so that the recollection of witnesses may still be reasonably clear, and so that there shall be no unnecessary delay in the disposal by magistrates' courts throughout the country of the summary offences brought before them to be tried'. As to the date when an information was laid, any doubt should be resolved in favour of the accused (*Lloyd* v *Young* [1963] Crim LR 703). A written information is, however, treated as laid as soon as it is received in the clerk's office, so the fact that it was not considered by a magistrate or magistrates' clerk until after the six months had expired is not fatal to jurisdiction (see *Manchester Stipendiary Magistrate, ex parte Hill* [1983] 1 AC 328, where, in fact, the information was never put before a magistrate or clerk but was processed solely by an assistant in the clerk's office).

In *Kennet Justices, ex parte Humphrey* [1993] Crim LR 787, the Divisional Court held that an information could be laid by the prosecutor informing the clerk by letter of an intention to charge the defendant at a later date. *Pontypridd Juvenile Court, ex parte B* [1988] Crim LR 842 deals with the position where the information is fed into a computer link. The Divisional Court held that the information was laid at the time when it was fed into the computer link between Pontypridd police station and the magistrates' court. The fact that the information was not printed out at the court until after the time-limit was irrelevant.

For the position where the information is amended after the expiry of the time-limit so as to charge a different offence, see *Scunthorpe Justices, ex parte McPhee* (1998) 162 JP 635 at **D19.7**.

Magistrates' Courts Act 1980, s. 127

    (1)   Except as otherwise expressly provided by any enactment and subject to subsection (2) below, a magistrates' court shall not try an information . . . unless the information was laid . . . within six months from the time when the offence was committed. . . .

    (2)   Nothing in—
        (a)   subsection (1) above; or
        (b)   subject to subsection (4) below, any other enactment (however framed or worded) which, as regards any offence to which it applies, would but for this section impose a time-limit on the power of a magistrates' court to try an information summarily or impose a limitation on the time for taking summary proceedings,
shall apply in relation to any indictable offence.

    (3)   Without prejudice to the generality of paragraph (b) of subsection (2) above, that paragraph includes enactments which impose a time-limit that applies only in certain circumstances (for example, where the proceedings are not instituted by or with the consent of the Director of Public Prosecutions or some other specified authority).

    (4)   Where, as regards any indictable offence, there is imposed by any enactment (however framed or worded, and whether falling within subsection (2)(b) above or not) a limitation on the time for taking proceedings on indictment for that offence no summary proceedings for that offence shall be taken after the latest time for taking proceedings on indictment.

DISCRETION NOT TO PROCEED ON ACCOUNT OF DELAY

Effect of Delay Generally

Even where proceedings were commenced within time, a magistrates' court has a **D18.8** discretion to refuse to try an information and acquit the accused without trial if there has been delay amounting to an abuse of the process of the court (see *Brentford Justices, ex parte Wong* [1981] QB 445). In that case, Donaldson LJ held that the justices erred in holding that they simply had no discretion to refuse to try an information laid within time. Quoting from Lord Widgery CJ in *Fairford Justices, ex parte Brewster* [1976] QB 600 his lordship said (at p. 449G): '. . . where delay is of such an order as to cause the court in justice to refuse to carry on with the hearing, the delay is a matter which goes to jurisdiction, the jurisdiction of the justices'. The principles applied in exercising the discretion are similar to those governing refusal to conduct committal proceedings when there has been delay (as to which, see especially *Grays Justices, ex parte Graham* [1982] QB 1239 and **D7.5**).

According to Bingham LJ in *Willesden Justices, ex parte Clemmings* (1987) 87 Cr App R 280, the decided cases show that the power of magistrates to stop a prosecution arises only when it is an abuse of the process of the court in that either:

(a)   the prosecution have manipulated or misused the process of the court so as to deprive the accused of a protection provided by law or take unfair advantage of a technicality, or

(b)   on a balance of probability, the accused has been or would be prejudiced in the preparation or conduct of his defence by delay on the part of the prosecution which was unjustifiable.

Thus, the cases divide into those concerning deliberate delay for improper reasons and those concerning delay through inefficiency.

Deliberate Delay

D18.9   The leading authority on this is *Brentford Justices, ex parte Wong* [1981] QB 445. An information against W for careless driving was laid one day within the six-month period permitted by the MCA 1980, s. 127. The prosecutor conceded that he had not then reached a firm decision on whether to take proceedings, but had laid the information simply to keep his options open. Having obtained a summons, he retained it for three months before finally deciding that the prosecution ought to go ahead. W was notified of the decision by letter but a further two months elapsed before the summons was actually served. The magistrates indicated sympathy with the defence argument that the prosecution delay was improper but refused an application not to proceed with the trial, since they considered that they were obliged to try a timeously laid information. The Divisional Court held that the lower court did have a discretion to decline jurisdiction if there had been an abuse of process, and what happened in the instant case could properly be regarded as grounds for exercising the discretion in the accused's favour. Donaldson LJ said (at p. 450D–G):

> I think it is open to justices to conclude that it is an abuse of the process of the court for a prosecutor to lay an information when he has not reached a decision to prosecute. The process of laying an information is, I think, assumed by Parliament to be the first stage in a continuous process of bringing a prosecution. [Section 127 of the MCA 1980] is designed to ensure that prosecutions shall be brought within a reasonable time. That purpose is wholly frustrated if it is possible for a prosecutor to obtain summonses and then, in his own good time and at his convenience, serve them. . . .

> Here . . . there was a deliberate attempt to gain further time in which to reach a decision. It is perhaps hard on the prosecutor to characterise that as an abuse of the process of the court because I am sure there was no intention by the prosecutor to abuse the process of the court. He thought he could legitimately do this. . . . I do not think that he can. In such a case I think it is open to the justices to say: 'This is an abuse of the process. We, therefore, decline jurisdiction and we dismiss the summonses.' But I think it is a matter which has to be investigated by the justices.

The principle in *Ex parte Wong* applies also where the prosecution lay an information in time and have decided that they wish to proceed in the sense that they want the accused to stand trial for the offence named in the information, but they are undecided between two possible factual bases on which the case might be advanced. In *Newcastle-upon-Tyne*

Justices, ex parte Hindle [1984] 1 All ER 770, H was charged in two informations, one for driving with excess alcohol, the other for obstructing a police officer in the execution of his duty. The latter information was in general terms, and did not specify the nature of the obstruction alleged. The prosecution might have been alleging either that H had lied to the police when claiming that he had drunk alcohol between driving and being breathalysed, or that he had truly drunk alcohol but had done so with the intent of frustrating the operation of the breathalyser procedure. The defence asked for particulars to resolve the ambiguity but the prosecution refused to give them. The Divisional Court held that the obstruction summons ought not to be heard by the justices because the inference to be drawn from the failure to give particulars was that when the prosecutor laid the information he had not decided on which of the two offences possibly alleged by the information he wished to proceed. That was 'at least as objectionable a course as the laying of an information where no decision has been taken to prosecute, for, if permitted, it would allow a prosecution to postpone, until after the expiry of the six-month period, their decision whether to prosecute for a particular offence' (per Goff LJ at p. 781F). Moreover, prejudice had been caused to the defence because, not knowing how the prosecution intended to put their case, they were unable to make effective representations on the crucial question of whether the obstruction charge should be tried before, after or with the excess alcohol charge (p. 781G).

Inadvertent Delay Causing Prejudice

Where deliberate delay in bringing the case to court cannot be shown, the defence may **D18.10** nonetheless apply for the magistrates to exercise their discretion not to proceed if (a) there has been inordinate or unconscionable delay due to the prosecution's inefficiency, and (b) prejudice to the defence from the delay is either proved or to be inferred (per Lloyd LJ in *Gateshead Justices, ex parte Smith* (1985) 149 JP 681, summarising the effect of earlier decisions). The power to decline to hear an information in such circumstances is, however, to be very strictly confined, and the courts should be careful not to create an artificial limitation period for bringing summary cases to trial when no such period has been prescribed by Parliament (ibid.).

Some further indication of the order of delay which the courts may take as sufficient to justify declining jurisdiction is provided by the following decisions:

(a) *Oxford City Justices, ex parte Smith* (1982) 75 Cr App R 200. An information alleging that S, a student up at Oxford, had driven with excess alcohol in the blood, was laid within time. It being his last term at the university, S gave the police the address of his 'digs' and also his home address. Unfortunately, the summons was sent to the former but not until after he had gone down. The police prosecutions department failed to realise that they also had a home address. Consequently, no further action was taken for over a year, the summons being allowed to remain unserved. Eventually, however, the home address was discovered and the summons was finally served over two years after the alleged offence (about 20 months after the information had been laid). The Divisional Court held that S had been in no way to blame for the delay. Nor was it suggested that the police had deliberately delayed making enquiries about S's whereabouts or been in any way 'malicious' in their behaviour. But they had been 'unobservant, inefficient or both'. The delay was so long as to be 'unconscionable', and it had or would cause prejudice to the defence in that relevant facts (e.g., as to whether there had been compliance with the correct procedure for breathalysing a suspect) might have been forgotten by the defendant or witnesses whom he would otherwise have wished to call. In the circumstances, the justices ought to have acceded to the defence application to dismiss the summons without a hearing.

(b) *Watford Justices, ex parte Outrim* [1983] RTR 26. A summons against O for driving with excess alcohol in the blood was not served for 22 months, the original return date having been one month from date of issue. O was not to blame for the delay. Further, the police could have ascertained his whereabouts for purposes of service at any time during the 22 months. The Divisional Court held that there was a clear inference that something had gone wrong with the prosecutor's process-serving procedures. Moreover, no specific prejudice from the delay was established by the defence, the possibility of prejudice was clear. In the circumstances, the justices could and should have refused to proceed.

(c)   *Gateshead Justices, ex parte Smith* (1985) 149 JP 681. Informations against S for six motoring offences allegedly committed on 14 February 1981 were laid on 9 June 1981 but the summonses were not served until 30 August 1983 (i.e., more than two years after issue). When served they were ineffective as they did not specify a date for S to attend court. Following S's arrest without warrant, the trial was eventually fixed for July 1984. After hearing police evidence as to the reasons for the delay, the justices held (without explanation) that the case should proceed. The Divisional Court reversed their decision. There had been very substantial delay which – although it could not be attributed to fault on either side – was (i) inordinate and (ii) likely to cause prejudice. Grounds for restraining the proceedings were therefore made out.

Two general points about exercise of the discretion to refuse jurisdiction on grounds of delay may be made. First, where there is an element of deliberate delay on the part of the prosecution (as in *Brentford Justices, ex parte Wong* [1981] QB 445: see **D18.9**) the courts are more willing to stay the prosecution than if there has been mere inefficiency. Conversely, if the delay was in part attributable to the defendant's own conduct, an application to stay is unlikely to succeed (see dicta in *Canterbury and St Augustine Justices, ex parte Turner* (1983) 147 JP 193). Secondly, the discretion applies both to proposed trials of summary offences and to summary trials of offences triable either way. However, it is submitted that the discretion is more likely to be exercised in the former class of case since Parliament – by enacting the MCA 1980, s. 127 – has indicated that proceedings for summary offences should take place within a reasonably short period (see May LJ's dictum in *Newcastle-upon-Tyne Justices, ex parte John Bryce (Contractors) Ltd* [1976] 1 WLR 517 quoted at **D18.7**), and delays between information and service of the summons indirectly thwart Parliament's intention.

Thirdly, the discretion is not limited to cases where the delay consists of tardiness in bringing the case before the court. In *Daventry District Council* v *Olins* (1990) 154 JP 478, O was charged with selling food (a pork pie) unfit for human consumption, contrary to the Food Act 1984, s. 8(1). She did not receive advance disclosure of the name of the complainant until 10 months after the alleged offence. The justices dismissed the prosecution on the grounds that it was an abuse of process. The Divisional Court dismissed the prosecutor's appeal by way of case stated. The accused was entitled to know the identity of the complainant, and might be handicapped in preparing the defence until it was known. The justices were entitled to hold that O was prejudiced by the refusal to name the complainant.

PROCEEDING IN ABSENCE OF PARTIES

Failure of Defendant to Appear

D18.11   These paragraphs should be read in conjunction with **D4.13** which deals with the options available to a magistrates' court upon non-appearance in answer to a summons.

A summary trial may take place in the absence of the defendant (MCA 1980, s. 11(1)). However, where proceedings were commenced by summons, then – unless the defendant has appeared on a previous occasion in answer to the summons – it must be proved to the satisfaction of the court that it was served on him a reasonable time before the hearing (s. 11(2)). Proof of service of a summons is governed by r. 99(1) of the Magistrates' Courts Rules 1981, which essentially states that service may be effected by

(a) hand delivery to the defendant, or (b) by leaving the summons with a person at the last known or usual address, or (c) by posting it to that address. This is qualified by r. 99(2), which provides that, in the event of non-appearance in answer to a summons for an indictable offence served otherwise than by hand delivery, service may *not* be treated as proved unless it is further proved that the summons came to the defendant's knowledge. A letter from him to the court may be treated as sufficient indication of knowledge (ibid.). If the summons is for a summary offence, positive proof that it came to the defendant's knowledge is required only if service was affected by sending it to his address by *ordinary* post (so if the summons was left with someone at his address or was sent there by registered letter or recorded delivery and has not been returned by the Post Office undelivered, it is presumed that it came to his knowledge without express proof that it did – see the proviso to r. 99(2)). It is not necessary for the person who delivered the summons or, as the case may be, posted it to the defendant's address to attend court to give oral evidence since proof of those matters may be provided by a signed certificate in the prescribed form in accordance with r. 67, and forms 144 and 145 set out in the Magistrates' Courts (Forms) Rules 1981.

If the defendant does not appear and the conditions for proceeding in his absence described above are satisfied, a not guilty plea is entered on his behalf. The burden is then on the prosecution to prove their case to the normal criminal standard, whether by calling oral evidence or by reading statements served on the accused under the CJA 1967, s. 9. Should the prosecution evidence turn out to be insufficient, the court is obliged to acquit the defendant, notwithstanding his absence. Assuming, however, that the case is proved the court may either proceed immediately to sentence or, in certain circumstances, it may adjourn to give the defendant notice that he should attend for sentencing or issue a warrant for his arrest (see MCA 1980, ss. 10(3) and (4), 11(3) and (4) and 13(5)).

It is rare for the prosecution to have their witnesses at court for the return date specified on the summons. It follows that – unless the defendant appears and pleads guilty or has sent a plea of guilty by post – the case will have to be adjourned for proof. The MCA 1980, s. 10(1), gives magistrates a general discretionary power to adjourn before trial of an information (or the commencement of committal proceedings). However, s. 10(2) provides that the trial shall not be resumed on the date to which it was adjourned unless the court is satisfied that the parties have had adequate notice. Assuming the defendant was not present when the case was adjourned, it will be necessary to send an adjournment notice to him. If the adjournment notice is not served, the prosecution will not be able to proceed to prove their case in his absence, even though there has been proof of service of the summons itself. Rule 15(2) of the Magistrates' Courts Rules 1981 governs service of adjournment notices, and provides essentially that r. 99 (proof of service of a summons) shall apply *mutatis mutandis* to proof of service of adjournment notices. It has also been held by the Family Division in the context of adjourning magistrates' courts' matrimonial proceedings that an adjournment notice in a domestic case should be served with the same degree of solemnity as a summons (*Unitt v Unitt* (1981) FLR 89). Much frustration can be caused by cases where, following good service of the summons and an adjournment, the prosecution arrange to have their witnesses at court for the adjournment date, only to discover on the day that the adjournment notice has not been served.

Although there is some variation between magistrates' courts as to the arrangements for summoning defendants, notifying them of whether and when they should attend court and, if need be, proving the case in their absence, a common sequence of events is as follows:

(a) With the summons is served the additional documentation giving the defendant the opportunity to plead guilty by post. If he enters a plea by post, there is no need either for him to attend or for the prosecution to prove the case, and the matter is disposed of on the papers on the return date named in the summons.

(b)   Whether or not the plea by post procedure is offered, the summons is endorsed to the effect that, if the defendant intends to plead not guilty, he should return a tear-off slip with an indication to that effect. There is then no need for him to appear on the return date but the court, in his absence, adjourns and fixes a date for trial. He is notified of the new date and both parties should be ready to proceed to trial on that date.

(c)   If the defendant neither enters a plea of guilty by post nor indicates a not guilty plea nor appears on the return date, the court must ascertain whether the summons has been served. If it has not, the case will have to be adjourned for a further attempt at service, the summons being reissued with a fresh return date. Usually, a summons is first sent out by ordinary post; if that elicits no response, it is sent by recorded delivery, and, if that also is unsuccessful, there is a further adjournment for personal service (i.e., a police officer goes round with the summons to the address given by the defendant at the time he was spoken to about the alleged offence). Should personal service be abortive (e.g., because the address is a false one), the court generally accepts that the defendant has beaten the system and the case is adjourned *sine die*. Where, however, the summons is for an indictable offence it may be suggested to the prosecutor that he arrange for a police officer to substantiate the information on oath, and it will then be possible for the court to issue a warrant for the defendant's arrest (MCA 1980, s. 1(6): 'Where the offence charged is an indictable offence, a warrant under this section may be issued at any time notwithstanding that a summons has previously been issued').

(d)   If the summons has been served but the defendant has not responded to it, the case is adjourned for proof. The prosecution should have their witnesses at court on the adjournment date (or have served statements under the CJA 1967, s. 9). Provided it can then be shown that the adjournment notice was served on the defendant, it will be open to the prosecution to prove the case in his absence. In fact, there is often difficulty in proving service of an adjournment notice even in cases where the summons was served. If the adjournment notice has not been served, there will have to be a further adjournment and an attempt at serving it by recorded delivery service or hand delivery as seems appropriate.

(e)   Once a case has been proved in the defendant's absence, the court will have to decide whether to proceed to sentence forthwith or to adjourn for his attendance. For the special rules governing sentencing in the offender's absence and the option at that stage of issuing a warrant for his arrest, see **D20.2**.

The power to try an information in the absence of the defendant applies to informations for offences triable either way just as it applies to informations for summary offences. However, if the proceedings are for an either-way matter, it will normally be necessary for the defendant to have attended in person for the determination of mode of trial (see **D3.6**). Assuming he has done so and consented to summary trial, the actual trial may take place in his absence.

If the magistrates decide that it is not appropriate to have the case proved in the defendant's absence (e.g., because the allegations appear relatively serious and they might consider a custodial sentence in the event of conviction), their alternatives are to adjourn or – if either the defendant was bailed to attend or the conditions set out in the MCA 1980, s. 13(1) to (3A), are satisfied – adjourn and issue a warrant for his arrest. In *Dewsbury Magistrates' Court, ex parte K* (1994) *The Times*, 16 March 1994, the Divisional Court quashed the conviction in his absence of a juvenile aged 16, for burglary of a dwelling-house. Their lordships held that the convenience of the court in processing the case could not possibly outweigh the facts that he was 16, on a very serious charge entailing the risk of a custodial sentence if convicted, had no record of non-attendance and had not been put on bail (he had been remanded into the care of the local authority).

In *Bolton Magistrates' Court, ex parte Merna* [1991] 2 WLR 239, the Divisional Court considered the position where the accused is absent, and seeks an adjournment. After M's case had been adjourned on a number of occasions, it was set down for trial, the justices indicating that if, he failed to attend, they would proceed in his absence. He did not attend, but provided a medical certificate and a doctor's letter stating that he was suffering from acute anxiety and depression and was not fit to attend court. The justices refused to adjourn, and proceeded to try and convict him. M sought judicial review, which was granted, and the conviction was quashed. The magistrates should have exercised their discretion judicially; if an accused claimed to be ill with apparently responsible professional support for his claim, the court should not reject that claim without satisfying itself that it was proper to do so.

Declaration that the Defendant Did Not Know of the Proceedings

The provisions as to service of a summons and trial in absence described above make it possible for a defendant to be tried and sentenced when in fact he knew nothing of the proceedings (e.g., if the summons was left for him with someone else at his address who failed to pass it on). The MCA 1980, s. 14, therefore provides a procedure by which a conviction in absence may be set aside. The main points are that, first, the defendant must make a statutory declaration that he did not know of the summons or proceedings until a date after the court had begun to try the information. Secondly, the declaration must specify the date on which he first had knowledge of the proceedings, and must be served on the clerk to the justices within 21 days thereof. Thirdly, the effect of a timeous statutory declaration is to make void the summons and all subsequent proceedings, although the information itself is unaffected. Consequently, the prosecution may serve a fresh summons for the same offence, even though it is summary and more than six months have elapsed since the date of commission. Fourthly, the court may allow a statutory declaration to take effect even though it is served outside time if, in the circumstances, it was not reasonable for the accused to effect service within time. The accused often appears before the court in person to make a statutory declaration. Alternatively, he may send the declaration to the clerk's office by registered letter or recorded delivery (s. 14(2)). **D18.12**

The making of a false statutory declaration is an offence under the Perjury Act 1911, s. 5, punishable with up to two years' imprisonment upon conviction on indictment.

Magistrates' Courts Act 1980, s. 14

(1)   Where a summons has been issued under section 1 above and a magistrates' court has begun to try the information to which the summons relates, then, if—

(a)   the accused, at any time during or after the trial, makes a statutory declaration that he did not know of the summons or the proceedings until a date specified in the declaration, being a date after the court has begun to try the information; and

(b)   within 21 days of that date the declaration is served on the clerk to the justices, without prejudice to the validity of the information, the summons and all subsequent proceedings shall be void.

(2)   For the purposes of subsection (1) above a statutory declaration shall be deemed to be duly served on the clerk to the justices if it is delivered to him, or left at his office, or is sent in a registered letter or by the recorded delivery service addressed to him at his office.

(3)   If on the application of the accused it appears to a magistrates' court (which for this purpose may be composed of a single justice) that it was not reasonable to expect the accused to serve such a statutory declaration as is mentioned in subsection (1) above within the period allowed by that subsection, the court may accept service of such a declaration by the accused after that period has expired; and a statutory declaration accepted under this subsection shall be deemed to have been served as required by that subsection.

(4)   Where any proceedings have become void by virtue of subsection (1) above, the information shall not be tried again by any of the same justices.

Plea of Guilty by Post

D18.13 To avoid the inconvenience of putting the prosecution to proof in cases where the defendant does not wish to contest the charge but is unwilling to attend court to plead guilty, the MCA 1980, s. 12, sets out a procedure allowing the defendant to plead guilty by post.

The procedure applies to proceedings by way of summons in an adult magistrates' court for summary offences carrying no more than three months' imprisonment (s. 12(1)). It also applies to a summons issued in respect of such an offence requiring a person aged 16 or 17 to appear before a youth court (s. 12(2)). Whether to give the defendant the option of pleading by post is at the discretion of the prosecution, there being in practice some variation between different branch offices of the CPS as to the type of offences considered appropriate for the procedure. The main steps in the procedure are:

(a)   With the summons, the prosecutor serves (i) a notice summarising the effect of s. 12 and (ii) a concise statement of the facts of the offence or a copy of the written statements under the CJA 1967, s. 9(2) and (3) (see **D19.5**) (s. 12(3)). Precedents for the notice and statement of facts are set out in the Magistrates' Courts (Forms) Rules 1981, forms 27 and 28. The statement of facts is usually attached to or on the reverse of the summons.

(b)   The prosecutor notifies the clerk of court that the above documents have been served (s. 12(1)(b)).

(c)   Assuming he wishes to take advantage of the procedure, the defendant (or his solicitor) must notify the clerk in writing that he desires to plead guilty without attending court (s. 12(4)). A form is normally enclosed with the summons for the purpose. On the form (or accompanying letter), the defendant may also state any mitigating circumstances that he wants brought to the court's attention. Provided the notification is received before the actual hearing, it does not matter that it arrives after the return date specified in the summons (*Norham and Islandshire Justices, ex parte Sunter Bros Ltd* [1961] 1 WLR 364). If there are several summonses, it is essential that the defendant make it clear that he is pleading guilty to each of them (*Burnham, Bucks, Justices, ex parte Ansorge* [1959] 1 WLR 1041). If the offence is endorsable, he must also send his driving licence, plus a statement of his date of birth and sex (Road Traffic Offenders Act 1988, s. 8).

(d)   If the court is satisfied that all the above has been done, it may proceed to hear and dispose of the case as if the defendant had appeared and pleaded guilty (s. 12(5)). The prosecutor may but need not be present (ibid.). The notification of a guilty plea, the statement of facts served by the prosecution or (unless the court otherwise directs) the written statement or statements under the CJA 1967, s. 9, and any statement submitted in mitigation must be read out by the clerk in open court (s. 12(7) to (7B)). Failure to do so will render the proceedings a nullity – see *Epping and Ongar Justices, ex parte Breach* [1987] RTR 233 where certiorari was granted to quash a company's conviction and sentence for using an overloaded goods vehicle because, although the company had entered a plea of guilty by post, its statement in mitigation had not been read out. The decision followed *Oldham Justices, ex parte Morrissey* [1959] 1 WLR 58 where the statement in mitigation had merely been handed to the magistrates for them to read. Moreover, errors such as occurred in the above cases cannot be remedied by the bench reconsidering its decision within 28 days under the provisions of the MCA 1980, s. 142(2), since that subsection only applies where the defendant has been *found* guilty, not where he has given notice of intention to plead guilty (ibid.). All the prosecution can do is restart the prosecution process by serving a fresh summons (see *Ex parte Breach*). It is also a strict rule that the only statement about the facts of the offence allowed to be given by or on behalf of the prosecution is that which they served on the defendant with the summons (s. 12(8)). Thus, when he pleads guilty by post, the defendant knows exactly how the case against him will be put.

(e)   The court is not obliged to hear and dispose of the case on a plea of guilty by post simply because the parties have chosen to adopt the procedure. The magistrates may, in their discretion, decide that the case is not appropriate for such disposal. If so, they must adjourn so that – at the resumed hearing – the case may be dealt with as if the plea had never been notified (s. 12(9)). The adjournment notice sent to the defendant must state the reason for the adjournment (s. 12(10)). Alternatively, the magistrates may accept the plea, hear the statement of facts and mitigation and then decide that the defendant ought to be given an opportunity to attend before sentence is pronounced. If so they adjourn after convicting. Again the notice of adjournment must specify the reason for it (s. 12(10) and see *Mason* [1965] 2 All ER 308 where a disqualification from driving imposed in the defendant's absence after he had been convicted on a plea of guilty by post at an earlier hearing was quashed because the adjournment notice failed to state that the reason why the magistrates adjourned on the first occasion was because they were considering disqualification).

(f)   At any time before the hearing, the accused may withdraw his plea of guilty by post simply by giving written notice to that effect to the clerk (s. 12(6)). The magistrates have jurisdiction at the hearing itself to allow a change of plea, enabling an accused who earlier pleaded guilty by post to contest the matter (*Bristol Justices, ex parte Sawyers* [1988] Crim LR 754).

(g)   The MCA 1980, s. 12A, enables the court to use the procedure under s. 12 even when the accused is present, provided he consents. In such a case, the accused must be given an opportunity to make an oral submission in mitigation.

Magistrates' Courts Act 1980, s. 12

(1)   This section shall apply where—

(a)   a summons has been issued requiring a person to appear before a magistrates' court, other than a youth court, to answer to an information for a summary offence, not being—

(i)   an offence for which the accused is liable to be sentenced to be imprisoned for a term exceeding 3 months; or

(ii)   an offence specified in an order made by the Secretary of State by statutory instrument; and

(b)   the clerk of the court is notified by or on behalf of the prosecutor that the documents mentioned in subsection (3) below have been served upon the accused with the summons.

(2)   The reference in subsection (1)(a) above to the issue of a summons requiring a person to appear before a magistrates' court other than a youth court includes a reference to the issue of a summons requiring a person who has attained the age of 16 at the time when it is issued to appear before a youth court.

(3)   The documents referred to in subsection (1)(b) above are—

(a)   a notice containing such statement of the effect of this section as may be prescribed;

(b)   either of the following, namely—

(i)   a concise statement of such facts relating to the charge as will be placed before the court by the prosecutor if the accused pleads guilty without appearing before the court, or

(ii)   a copy of such written statement or statements complying with subsections (2)(a) and (b) and (3) of section 9 of the Criminal Justice Act 1967 (proof by written statement) as will be so placed in those circumstances; and

(c)   if any information relating to the accused will or may, in those circumstances, be placed before the court by or on behalf of the prosecutor, a notice containing or describing that information.

(4)   Where the clerk of the court receives a notification in writing purporting to be given by the accused or by a legal representative acting on his behalf that the accused desires to plead guilty without appearing before the court—

(a)   the clerk of the court shall inform the prosecutor of the receipt of the notification; and

(b)   the following provisions of this section shall apply.

(5)   If at the time and place appointed for the trial or adjourned trial of the information—

(a)   the accused does not appear; and

(b)   it is proved to the satisfaction of the court, on oath or in such manner as may be prescribed, that the documents mentioned in subsection (3) above have been served upon the accused with the summons,

the court may, subject to section 11(3) and (4) above and subsections (6) to (8) below, proceed to hear and dispose of the case in the absence of the accused, whether or not the prosecutor is also absent, in like manner as if both parties had appeared and the accused had pleaded guilty.

(6)   If at any time before the hearing the clerk of the court receives an indication in writing purporting to be given by or on behalf of the accused that he wishes to withdraw the notification—

(a)   the clerk of the court shall inform the prosecutor of the withdrawal; and

(b)   the court shall deal with the information as if the notification had not been given.

(7)   Before accepting the plea of guilty and convicting the accused under subsection (5) above, the court shall cause the following to be read out before the court by the clerk of the court, namely—

(a)   in a case where a statement of facts as mentioned in subsection (3)(b)(i) above was served on the accused with the summons, that statement;

(aa)   in a case where a statement or statements as mentioned in subsection (3)(b)(ii) above was served on the accused with the summons and the court does not otherwise direct, that statement or those statement;

(b)   any information contained in a notice so served, and any information described in such a notice and produced by or on behalf of the prosecutor;

(c)   the notification under subsection (4) above; and

(d)   any submission received with the notification which the accused wishes to be brought to the attention of the court with a view to mitigation of sentence.

(7A)   Where the court gives a direction under subsection (7)(aa) above the court shall cause an account to be given orally before the court by the clerk of the court of so much of any statement as is not read aloud.

(7B)   Whether or not a direction under paragraph (aa) of subsection (7) above is given in relation to any statement served as mentioned in that paragraph the court need not cause to be read out the declaration required by section 9(2)(b) of the Criminal Justice Act 1967.

(8)   If the court proceeds under subsection (5) above to hear and dispose of the case in the absence of the accused, the court shall not permit—

(a)   any other statement with respect to any facts relating to the offence charged; or

(b)   any other information relating to the accused,

to be made or placed before the court by or on behalf of the prosecutor except on a resumption of the trial after an adjournment under section 10(3) above.

(9)   If the court decides not to proceed under subsection (5) above to hear and dispose of the case in the absence of the accused, it shall adjourn or further adjourn the trial for the purpose of dealing with the information as if the notification under subsection (4) above had not been given.

(10)   In relation to an adjournment on the occasion of the accused's conviction in his absence under subsection (5) above or to an adjournment required by subsection (9) above, the notice required by section 10(2) above shall include notice of the reason for the adjournment.

(11)   No notice shall be required by section 10(2) above in relation to an adjournment—

(a)   which is for not more than 4 weeks; and

(b)   the purpose of which is to enable the court to proceed under subsection (5) above at a later time.

Failure of Prosecutor to Appear

D18.14   If the prosecutor does not appear for the trial or adjourned trial of an information (but the accused is present), the court may at its discretion either (a) dismiss the information, or (b) adjourn the trial, or (c) proceed in the prosecutor's absence (MCA 1980, s. 15(1)). The third option is available only if the court has received evidence on a previous occasion (i.e. the case was adjourned part-heard after prosecution evidence sufficient to raise a case to answer had been adduced – if that has not been done, the court obviously cannot proceed in the prosecutor's absence because there will be no one with standing to call the evidence). Should the court decide to adjourn, it may not remand the accused in custody unless (a) he has been brought from custody or (b) he cannot be remanded on bail because of his failure to find sureties (s. 15(2)).

The discretion under s. 15(1) to dismiss the information has not been conferred for punitive purposes. The justices must not, therefore, exercise their power to dismiss where they know that a prosecutor is on the way to court, and that the case is otherwise ready to be presented (*Hendon Justices, ex parte DPP* [1994] QB 167; see also *Dudley Justices, ex parte Blatchford* (1992) 156 JP 609).

Failure of Both Parties to Appear

Should neither the prosecutor nor the accused appear for the trial (or adjourned trial) **D18.15** of an information, the court may either dismiss the information or – if evidence has been received on a previous occasion – proceed in their absence (MCA 1980, s. 16).

Appearance by Legal Representative

The parties to proceedings in magistrates' courts may be represented by counsel or **D18.16** solicitor (MCA 1980, s. 122(1)). Alternatively, they may conduct their own case in person (cf. the position in the Crown Court where, although the accused is entitled to represent himself, the prosecution must always appear by legal representative). It is not the practice to grant persons other than the parties or their counsel or solicitor the right of audience, unless statute expressly allows for alternative representation in a particular category of case. (In certain circumstances, the CPS may be represented by a member of staff, designated by the DPP, who is not a barrister or solicitor: see **D2.33**.) However, where a party wishes to have the assistance of a friend, the friend may sit by the party, advise during the course of the hearing, suggest questions or points for argument etc., although he will not be permitted actually to ask questions of witnesses himself or address the court (see *McKenzie* v *McKenzie* [1971] P 33).

The nature of the assistance permitted was examined by the Court of Appeal in *Leicester City Justices, ex parte Barrow* [1991] 2 QB 260. The justices refused to allow the applicants to have the assistance of their adviser in court, during proceedings under the Community Charges (Administration and Enforcement) Regulations 1989. The justices made liability orders against the applicants who then sought judicial review. Their application was refused by the Divisional Court and they appealed to the Court of Appeal. The Court of Appeal emphasised that what was at issue was a party's right to reasonable assistance and held that the justices had erred. The applicants had wanted their friend to assist them in court by taking notes, quietly making suggestions and giving advice. A litigant had the right to present his own case and, in doing so, to arm himself with such assistance as he thought necessary, subject to the right of the court to intervene. It was misleading to refer in this context to a '*McKenzie* friend', since that implied a special status and a right akin to a right of audience. The right at issue was that of a party to the case to arm himself with assistance; he did not have to seek the leave of the court to exercise that right. Nevertheless, the court should be informed of the fact that a party would have his adviser with him; and, if the assistance was unreasonable in manner or degree, was provided for an improper purpose or was in any way inimical to the administration of justice, the court could restrict him in the use of that assistance.

Where a party does not attend court but is represented by counsel or solicitor he is deemed not to be absent (s. 122(2)). The prosecution is customarily conducted by counsel or solicitor without the attendance of the prosecutor himself unless he is required as a witness. If the defendant chooses not to attend but to be legally represented, counsel or solicitor may cross-examine the prosecution witnesses, make submissions and speeches and even call witnesses other than the defendant, exactly as if his client were present. Furthermore, the effect of s. 122(2) is that the presence of the legal representative precludes the issue of a warrant for the defendant's arrest under s. 13 (warrants for arrest where the court adjourns instead of proceeding in the absence of the defendant). However, s. 122(3) limits the effect of the deeming provision to the extent that a represented party is not deemed to be present if his presence was required to 'satisfy any provision of any enactment or any condition of a recognisance expressly requiring his presence'. Consequently, a defendant who fails to surrender to custody in answer to his bail may have a warrant issued for his arrest whether or not he is legally represented in court (see the Bail Act 1976, s. 3(1), which provides that a person granted bail in criminal proceedings shall be under a duty to surrender to custody, and s. 7(1) which empowers the court to issue a bench warrant if he does not do so). Similarly, the terms of the MCA 1980, ss. 4(3) and 23 make it clear that committal proceedings and proceedings to determine mode of trial require the physical presence of the accused save in the exceptional circumstances defined in the sections.

Magistrates' Courts Act 1980, s. 122

(1)   A party to any proceedings before a magistrates' court may be represented by counsel or solicitor.

(2)   Subject to subsection (3) below, an absent party so represented shall be deemed not to be absent.

(3)   Appearance of a party by counsel or solicitor shall not satisfy any provision of any enactment or any condition of a recognisance expressly requiring his presence.

PLEA TO THE INFORMATION

Pleas That May Be Tendered

D18.17   The first stage in a summary trial is for the court (through the clerk) to read the information to the defendant and ask him if he pleads guilty or not guilty (MCA 1980, s. 9(1)). If he pleads guilty, the court may convict him without hearing evidence (s. 9(3)). The recording of a conviction on a guilty plea is without prejudice to the power (indeed duty) of the court to hold a *Newton* hearing if there is a substantial variation between the prosecution and defence versions of the facts of the offence (see *Williams v Another* (1983) 5 Cr App R (S) 134 where it was held that the Crown Court, on an appeal against sentence imposed by a magistrates' court after W had pleaded guilty, should have heard evidence as to the facts of the offence because of the sharp divergence between the prosecution and defence accounts of what occurred – by implication, the magistrates at first instance were under a similar duty). In the absence of a guilty plea, the court is under a duty to hear evidence and either convict the accused or dismiss the information (s. 9(2)).

The only pleas which may be entered to an information are those of guilty or not guilty. A magistrates' court has no power to return a verdict of not guilty as charged in the information but guilty of a lesser offence (see *Lawrence v Same* [1968] 2 QB 93). It follows that a plea to like effect is not an option available to the defendant even if the prosecution would be willing to accept it. However, in a case where a plea to something other than the offence charged would be acceptable to the parties, the procedural difficulty may be overcome by laying a separate information in court specifically for the lesser offence (assuming any relevant time-limit has not expired). The defendant may then plead guilty to the new information in exchange for the prosecution offering no evidence on the original one.

There is no special procedure for pleading autrefois acquit or convict, although the issues may be raised on an ordinary not guilty plea and it is beyond doubt that a previous conviction or acquittal for the offence charged is as much a bar to summary proceedings as to proceedings on indictment (see Lord Morris's second proposition on autrefois in *Connelly* v *DPP* [1964] AC 1254).

Whether the defendant is fit to plead is a question which can be determined *only* on indictment, but magistrates have power under the Mental Health Act 1983, s. 37(3), to make a hospital order without convicting the defendant, which power may be used in cases where the Crown Court would empanel a jury to determine fitness to plead (see **D18.23**).

Magistrates' Courts Act 1980, s. 9

(1)   On the summary trial of an information, the court shall, if the accused appears, state to him the substance of the information and ask him whether he pleads guilty or not guilty.

(2)   The court, after hearing the evidence and the parties, shall convict the accused or dismiss the information.

(3)   If the accused pleads guilty, the court may convict him without hearing evidence.

Plea of Guilty

The same basic principles govern the entry of a guilty plea at summary trial as govern **D18.18** the entry of such a plea at trial on indictment (see **D10.18** *et seq.*). It is essential that the plea be *unequivocal*. If, when the information is put, the defendant does not answer directly or qualifies what purports to be a guilty plea with words suggesting that he is really putting forward a defence, then the court must try to resolve the ambiguity. If the plea remains ambiguous, the court must reject it and hear evidence before convicting or acquitting. The concept of an equivocal plea has been extended to pleas which, although unambiguous when made, are thrown into doubt by something which occurs between plea and sentence (e.g., the presentation of mitigation which is inconsistent with guilt – see *Durham Quarter Sessions, ex parte Virgo* [1952] 2 QB 1). It has also been extended to pleas entered under duress (*Huntingdon Crown Court, ex parte Jordan* [1981] QB 857). One reason why justices must be careful to ensure that a purported plea of guilty is unequivocal is that if they convict and sentence on an equivocal plea the defendant may appeal to the Crown Court against conviction, notwithstanding the general rule that a person who pleads guilty in the magistrates' court may appeal only against sentence. If the Crown Court finds the plea to have been equivocal, it remits the case to the lower court with a direction to hear the evidence on a not guilty plea.

There is little direct authority on the manner in which a guilty plea should be entered before a magistrates' court. If the defendant attends court, the plea must come from him personally and may not be entered by his counsel or solicitor on his behalf (*Wakefield Justices, ex parte Butterworth* [1970] 1 All ER 1181). This accords with the judgment in *Williams* [1978] QB 373 where it was stated (at p. 378G) that 'No qualification of or deviation from the rule that a plea of guilty must come from him who acknowledges guilt is . . . permissible. A departure from the rule in a criminal trial would therefore necessarily be a vitiating factor rendering the whole procedure void and ineffectual.' While that was said in the context of an appeal against conviction on indictment, the Court of Appeal appears to have been laying down a general principle of application to *all* criminal proceedings. However, a special difficulty arises in magistrates' courts when the accused does not appear in person but is deemed to be present because he is legally represented (see MCA 1980, s. 122). Can counsel or solicitor then enter a guilty plea on behalf of his client? It is suggested by the editors of *Stone's Justices' Manual* (see para. 1–461) that he can, and certainly it is manifestly convenient in such cases for the court to be able to proceed straight to sentence, rather than having to hear formal proof of guilt from the prosecution which will not be challenged by the defence lawyer. Unfortunately, no authority is mentioned for the proposition in *Stone*. Moreover, it seems contrary to the dictum from *Williams* quoted above. Therefore, it is submitted that, at the very least, there must be some doubt about the power of an absent accused's legal representative to enter a binding guilty plea.

Where the defendant is a corporation, a duly appointed 'representative' of the corporation may, *inter alia*, enter a plea of guilty or not guilty to the information (MCA 1980, sch. 3, para. 2(c), and see CJA 1925, s. 33(6), for the precise definition of a representative). For the avoidance of doubt, it is advisable that a corporation intending to appear by solicitor should appoint the latter as its representative for purposes of sch. 3 to the MCA 1980 (see *Ascanio Puck & Co. Ltd* (1912) 76 JP 487).

Plea of Not Guilty

D18.19 A not guilty plea to an information will normally be entered by the defendant personally. If, however, he is absent and the court decides to proceed without him, or he remains silent when asked to plead, or enters an ambiguous plea, then the court simply hears the evidence in accordance with the requirement of the MCA 1980, s. 9(2), as if there had been a not guilty plea. By contrast with the procedure at trial on indictment, there is no need to establish that a silent accused is mute of malice before proceeding to summary trial.

The options open to the prosecution (other than proceeding to summary trial) where a defendant does not plead guilty are as follows:

D18.20 *Withdrawal of Summons* Provided the defendant has not actually pleaded to the information, the prosecution may – with the court's leave – withdraw the summons (*Redbridge Justices, ex parte Sainty* [1981] RTR 13). If the prosecution are not in a position to prove guilt on the day appointed for hearing of an information or for any other reason do not wish to proceed forthwith to trial, they may prefer to withdraw the summons (rather than offering no evidence or asking for an adjournment), since such withdrawal avoids there being a verdict of not guilty. Consequently, a fresh summons may later be obtained in respect of the same offence, and the accused will not be able to rely upon autrefois acquit to prevent the trial on that summons proceeding.

That withdrawal of a summons is not equivalent to an acquittal was confirmed in *Grays Justices, ex parte Low* [1990] 1 QB 54. L was summoned to appear before the justices to answer informations alleging that he had assaulted three of his neighbours causing each of them actual bodily harm. The informations were laid by the police. Subsequently, it was agreed between L and the CPS that the case was suitable for disposal by means of a bind-over. Accordingly, on what would have been the day of trial, the CPS representative (with leave of the justices) withdrew the three summonses upon L agreeing to be bound over. Later, Z (one of the persons allegedly assaulted by L) commenced a private prosecution for the offence against her. L asked the justices not to proceed on Z's summons in view of the withdrawal of the police summons in respect of the same offence. The justices refused the application. On an application for judicial review of the justices' decision, Nolan J said (at p. 59A–B):

> I think it must now be regarded as settled law that, despite the dicta to the contrary in *Pickavance* v *Pickavance* [1901] P 60, the withdrawal of a summons with the consent of the justices will not of itself operate as a bar to the issue of a further summons in respect of the same charge where there has been no adjudication upon the merits of the charge in the original summons, and the defendant has not been put in peril of conviction upon it.

Ex parte Low was a case where the withdrawn prosecution was commenced by way of laying an information and obtaining a summons. Presumably, the same principles will apply to prosecutions commenced by way of charge at the police station – i.e. the prosecution can avert a not guilty verdict by withdrawing the charge and then reprosecute.

D18.21 *Offering No Evidence* Once the accused has entered a plea of not guilty to the information, the option of asking for the summons to be withdrawn ceases to be open to the prosecution. Therefore, if they are not ready to proceed on the date that has been fixed for trial, the only course available to them is to ask for an adjournment. If the adjournment is refused, they must either call whatever evidence they do have at court or – if that evidence would plainly be insufficient for a conviction – offer no evidence.

It has been held that, where an accused has been lawfully acquitted by a magistrates' court of competent jurisdiction acting within its jurisdiction, he is *not* to be prosecuted again for the same offence, even if the acquittal resulted from the prosecution being forced to offer no evidence and so did not involve a hearing on the merits (*Pressick* [1978] Crim LR 377). This is merely one aspect of the plea of autrefois acquit. In *Pressick*, P agreed to summary trial of a charge of theft and pleaded not guilty. On the day fixed for trial, the prosecution did not have their witnesses at court. An application for an adjournment was resisted by the defence and refused by the magistrates. Consequently, no evidence was offered and the information dismissed. The prosecution commenced fresh proceedings for the same offence. This time P was committed for trial. The Crown Court (Judge David QC) quashed the indictment, ruling that it was barred by the acquittal in the magistrates' court. Dicta in earlier cases to the effect that the dismissal of an information only prevented further proceedings if there had been a hearing on the merits should be understood as referring to the possible application of issue estoppel in cases where the later proceedings were not for precisely the same offence. Where, as in *Pressick*, the defence were able to rely on autrefois acquit, it mattered not that the acquittal flowed from the prosecution's default in not having their evidence at court. *Pressick* was confirmed by the Divisional Court in *Swansea Justices, ex parte Purvis* (1981) 145 JP 252. Since Judge David's ruling in *Pressick* with its incidental reference to issue estoppel, it has been established that issue estoppel (i.e. the doctrine that a party to proceedings may be bound by a finding of fact on a certain issue made by a court in previous proceedings between the same parties) does not apply to criminal proceedings (*DPP* v *Humphrys* [1977] AC 1). However, it is submitted that the learned judge's reasoning is unaffected by the demise of criminal issue estoppel.

Autrefois in the Context of Summary Proceedings

There is no special procedure for pleading autrefois acquit or autrefois convict at **D18.22** summary trial. However, it is well established that a previous acquittal or conviction for the same matter is as much a bar to summary proceedings as it is to proceedings on indictment (per Lord Morris in *Connelly* v *DPP* [1964] AC 1254). The issue may be raised simply on a not guilty plea. Conversely, an acquittal or conviction by a magistrates' court acting within its jurisdiction is capable of founding a plea of autrefois at proceedings on indictment.

The question most frequently raised by autrefois arising out of summary proceedings is whether there has been a genuine acquittal or, as the case may be, conviction by magistrates acting properly within their jurisdiction. If there has not, the defendant is said never to have been in jeopardy and therefore unable to rely on autrefois. Thus, as explained in **D18.20**, the withdrawal of a summons before a plea is entered does *not* found autrefois, whereas the dismissal of the information following a not guilty plea and the offering of no evidence normally does (see **D18.21** and see also **D10.32** to **D10.38**).

However, a distinction is drawn between cases such as *Pressick* [1978] Crim LR 377 where – for whatever reason – no evidence is offered and those where the proceedings in the magistrates' courts are so flawed that the defendant was never in danger of a valid conviction. In the latter type of case, a purported acquittal (or conviction) does not prevent the magistrates retrying the defendant for the same offence. Thus, in *Marsham, ex parte Pethick Lawrence* [1912] 2 KB 362, PL was convicted of assaulting a police constable upon evidence from the officer which had inadvertently been given unsworn. Later the same day, the stipendiary magistrate was made aware of the error. He simply reheard the case with the officer this time taking the oath. PL's conviction was upheld because the so-called trial resulting in the first verdict was a total mistrial by reason of the fundamental procedural error that had occurred. Similarly, where magistrates purport to acquit without giving the prosecution the opportunity to call their evidence, the 'acquittal' is liable to be quashed by certiorari and the defendant cannot prevent fresh proceedings being taken (see, for example, *Dorking Justices, ex parte Harrington* [1984] AC 743). This is without prejudice to that limited category of cases where justices may properly halt proceedings which are an abuse of the process of their court because of unconscionable delay on the prosecution's part.

An acquittal pronounced by magistrates acting in excess of their jurisdiction does not found autrefois (*West* [1964] 1 QB 15 – magistrates tried W on an information alleging that he had been an accessory after the fact to larceny and found him not guilty following a submission of no case to answer; subsequently, a fresh charge was preferred for the same offence and W was committed for trial and convicted; the conviction was upheld because the offence charged was triable only on indictment and the summary 'acquittal' was therefore a nullity). The same applies *mutatis mutandis* where magistrates convict in excess of jurisdiction (see *Kent Justices, ex parte Machin* [1952] 2 QB 355 – conviction for an either-way offence quashed because the correct procedure for determining mode of trial had not been followed, but the Divisional Court stated that, in the circumstances, there was nothing to prevent M being reprosecuted for the same offence).

Where the prosecution have preferred two informations in the alternative arising out of the same facts and the court puts them to their election as to the one on which they wish to proceed, the immediate dismissal of the information on which they are not proceeding does not enable the accused to rely on autrefois in respect of the other (*Broadbent* v *High* [1985] RTR 359). However, it is wiser in such circumstances for the magistrates to take no action as regards the one information until after the trial of the other (ibid.).

Unfitness to Plead in the Context of Summary Proceedings

D18.23   There is no procedure by which a person's fitness to plead may be determined in the magistrates' court. If the defendant is thought to be suffering from a mental disability such as to render him unable to comprehend the course of the proceedings or make a proper defence to the charge (i.e. he would be found unfit to plead if he were facing trial on indictment), the defence have the following options:

(a)   Assuming the offence is triable either way, they may elect trial on indictment and have the question of fitness determined by a jury in the Crown Court.

(b)   Assuming there is to be a summary trial, they may allow the defendant to plead not guilty (or indicate a not guilty plea if he is incapable even of doing that) and put the prosecution to proof of their case. If the definition of the offence involves the prosecution in proving *mens rea* and especially if it involves a specific intent, the accused's mental condition may make it difficult for the prosecution to discharge their burden. It seems that the common-law defence of insanity is available to a defendant in a summary trial where *mens rea* is in issue (*Horseferry Road Magistrates' Court, ex parte K* [1997] QB 23).

(c)   They may invite the court to make a hospital order under the Mental Health Act 1983, s. 37(3), without convicting the defendant.

The Mental Health Act 1983, s. 37(3), enables magistrates to achieve a result very similar to that which follows upon an accused being found unfit to plead to an indictment. It must be read in conjunction with the MCA 1980, s. 30(1).

Magistrates' Courts Act 1980, s. 30(1)

If, on the trial by a magistrates' court of an offence punishable on summary conviction with imprisonment, the court is satisfied that the accused did the act or made the omission charged but is of opinion that an inquiry ought to be made into his physical or mental condition before the method of dealing with him is determined, the court shall adjourn the case to enable a medical examination and report to be made and shall remand him; but the adjournment shall not be for more than three weeks at a time where the court remands him in custody nor for more than four weeks at a time where it remands him on bail.

Mental Health Act 1983, s. 37(3)

Where a person is charged before a magistrates' court with any act or omission as an offence and the court would have power, on convicting him of that offence, to make a [hospital] order under subsection (1) above in his case as being a person suffering from mental illness or severe mental impairment, then, if the court is satisfied that the accused did the act or made the omission charged, the court may, if it thinks fit, make such an order without convicting him.

It will be noted that the power to order medical reports under the MCA 1980, s. 30(1), and the power to make a hospital order under the Mental Health Act 1983, s. 37(3), both depend merely upon the court being satisfied that the defendant committed the *actus reus* of the offence with which he is charged. Therefore, in a case where the defendant is apparently suffering from mental illness or impairment, the court may cause a not guilty plea to be entered on his behalf and hear the prosecution evidence. Assuming that establishes the *actus reus*, the court may then adjourn for reports. If, on the basis of those reports, the medical criteria for the making of a hospital order are satisfied, the court may forthwith make such an order *without convicting the defendant*. For details about the pre-conditions for a hospital order and, in particular, the need for reports from two medical practitioners (including a Home Office approved psychiatrist) confirming that the accused is suffering from mental illness or severe mental impairment as defined by the Mental Health Act 1983, see **E24.3**.

Where the information is for an offence triable either way an added difficulty arises, namely that the magistrates' court will not have jurisdiction to hear evidence establishing the *actus reus* of the offence unless the accused consents to summary trial. *Ex hypothesi*, he is unlikely to be in a fit state to give his consent. That was the situation in *Lincoln (Kesteven) Justices, ex parte O'Connor* [1983] 1 WLR 335 where O'C was charged with assault occasioning actual bodily harm and there were medical reports before the magistrates recommending an order under what is now the Mental Health Act 1983, s. 37(3). The court agreed to summary trial but O'C, when put to his election, remained silent and plainly did not understand what was being said to him. The magistrates held that they could not make a hospital order unless they were satisfied that O'C did the act or made the omission charged; in the absence of evidence, they could not be so satisfied, and, since the offence was triable either way, they could not hear evidence unless there was consent to summary trial. Therefore, they reluctantly committed O'C for trial. The Divisional Court held that a trial is *not* a necessary pre-condition of the court being satisfied for the purposes of the Mental Health Act 1983, s. 37(3), that the accused committed the *actus reus* of the offence. In an exceptional case such as the instant one, where the accused was legally represented and everybody agreed that he had assaulted the victim, the justices could conclude without evidence that the offence had occurred. Therefore, they had jurisdiction to make a hospital order. It is in any event clear that the magistrates have no jurisdiction under the Mental Health Act 1983, s. 37(3), to make a hospital order in respect of a person charged with an offence triable only upon indictment (*Chippenham Magistrates' Court, ex parte Thompson* (1996) 160 JP 207).

Change of Plea

A magistrates' court may allow an accused to change his plea from guilty to not guilty **D18.24** at any stage before sentence is passed (*S (an infant) v Recorder of Manchester* [1971] AC 481). Whether to accede to an application for a change of plea is in the court's discretion and there is no automatic rule that an accused who was unrepresented when he entered his plea is entitled to change it upon obtaining legal representation during the period of an adjournment before sentence (*South Tameside Magistrates' Court, ex parte Rowland* [1983] 3 All ER 689). The question for the bench is whether the original plea was unequivocal and entered with a proper understanding of what the charge entailed. If it was, then the magistrates are entitled to refuse any application to change. Once the court has passed sentence, it is *functus officio* and the conviction recorded upon the guilty plea can be set aside only by appealing to the Crown Court on the basis that the plea was equivocal. On the other hand, if the court does consent to a change of plea from guilty to not guilty, it should proceed (in the case of an offence triable either way) to allow the defendant to consider afresh whether to consent to summary trial and he should be put to his election again (*Bow Street Magistrates' Court, ex parte Welcombe* (1992) 156 JP 609; see also **D3.16**).

TRIAL OF INFORMATIONS

Discretion Not to Try an Information

D18.25 Save in cases where there has been inordinate delay amounting to an abuse of the process of the court (see **D18.8** to **D18.10**), magistrates are almost always obliged to hear the prosecution evidence, and may not simply dismiss an information because they consider it unfair or oppressive. Thus, in *Brown* (1857) 7 E & B 757, a purported acquittal was quashed and the magistrates ordered to try the case because their original decision to dismiss the information without a hearing was in excess of their powers and a nullity. The reason they acted as they did was because B had been charged with an offence committed in his capacity as the owner and manager of a colliery, and they considered it unfair that the other owners were not also charged. Even if that view were correct, it did not give them power to prevent the prosecution proceeding. Similarly, in *Birmingham Justices, ex parte Lamb* [1983] 1 WLR 339, the Divisional Court held that the justices erred in refusing to try informations for reasons such as the relative triviality of the charge, the apparent frailty of the prosecution evidence insofar as it had been disclosed, and the long period that would elapse before the court would have time to hear the case on the basis of a not guilty plea. McNeill J said (at p. 344D):

> At the end of the day, the law does not permit cases, on grounds of supposed injustice, to be dismissed out of hand without hearing any evidence. The justices can reflect their sense of injustice at the end of the prosecution case if they are not satisfied that the offence has been made out. They can reflect it at the end of the whole of the evidence by acquitting the defendant or, if they feel obliged to convict, they can reflect it by imposing such a penalty as reflects their view of the case.

> In the magistrates' court, there is no power which enables the justices to dismiss a summons simply on the basis that it would be, in the words of one of the chairman, 'unjust to let it continue' and, in the words of the other, 'that the continuation of the proceedings was prejudicial to the defendant'.

It is submitted that this statement may be too wide insofar as it suggests that magistrates may *never* dismiss an information without a hearing. They may do so where there has been unconscionable delay (see **D18.8** to **D18.10**). Furthermore, even in cases where there has not been delay, it would seem that the court may very exceptionally stay a prosecution on the grounds that there has been some other irregularity amounting to an abuse of process (*Grays Justices, ex parte Low* [1990] 1 QB 54). In that case the Divisional Court held that even though the withdrawal of an earlier summons in exchange for L agreeing to be bound over did not enable the defence to rely on autrefois acquit when fresh proceedings were brought for the same offence, the magistrates should have declined to proceed on the second summons because (a) the circumstances of the withdrawal of the first summons had not been brought to the attention of the magistrates issuing the second summons, and (b) that withdrawal, coupled with the bind-over, had involved the concurrence not just of the CPS but of the first court (which had to decide whether the conditions for a bind-over were met) and L himself (who voluntarily took upon himself the risk of having his recognisance estreated if he offended during the relevant period). Apparent bad faith on the part of the prosecutor has also been held sufficient to justify dismissal without hearing (*Sherwood* v *Ross* [1989] Crim LR 576 – private prosecutions for theft, assault and threatening words or behaviour arising out of an incident at the prosecutor's business premises properly stayed because, after the police had declined to prosecute, a period of six months elapsed during which there was correspondence between the solicitors for the parties mentioning only the possibility of civil proceedings; in all the circumstances, it seemed that the prosecutor had decided to institute criminal proceedings merely as a bargaining counter in the negotiations over a civil settlement).

On the other hand, in *Dorchester Justices, ex parte DPP* [1990] RTR 369, the circumstances fell short of what was necessary for the bench to refuse properly to try the information. In that case, an ambulance driver attended court as a defence witness. He was seen talking to police officers, who were witnesses for the prosecution. The defence solicitor submitted that the police officers' evidence could have been tainted. Without hearing any evidence, the bench dismissed the information. The Crown applied for judicial review. The Divisional Court allowed the application, remitting the case to be heard by a different bench. No decision as to whether testimony would be tainted could be reached properly without hearing evidence. In *Watford Justices, ex parte DPP* [1990] RTR 374, a magistrate's court refused to hear evidence and dismissed two charges of burglary. The decision was taken on the basis that the accused had spent time in custody, and the charges were rather trivial. The Divisional Court granted a declaration to the Crown (who decided to proceed no further) that the magistrates had acted contrary to the Magistrates' Court Act 1980, s. 9(2), which required them to hear evidence before convicting an accused or dismissing the information. (See also *DPP* v *Gane* [1991] Crim LR 711 and *Milton Keynes Justices, ex parte DPP* [1991] Crim LR 712.)

Discretion to Try Informations Separately

Where an accused faces several informations or there are several accused charged in **D18.26** separate informations, the decision on whether the informations or accused should be tried together or separately is one for the magistrates (*Chief Constable of Norfolk* v *Clayton* [1983] 2 AC 473). The facts of *Clayton* were that the two defendants (who were husband and wife) were charged in five separate informations with offences contrary to the Post Office Act 1969, s. 78, three informations being against one or other singly and the remaining two against them both. Upon the accused failing to appear for summary trial, the magistrates heard the informations together in their absence and found them both guilty. On appeal to the Divisional Court, the convictions were quashed because neither accused had consented to the joint trial. On a further appeal to the House of Lords, Lord Roskill reviewed the development of the practice in magistrates' courts in respect of trying separate informations jointly, and then stated the practice which should henceforth be followed. His lordship said (at pp. 491G–492E):

> Today I see no compelling reason why your lordships should not say that the practice in magistrates' courts in these matters should henceforth be analogous to the practice prescribed in *Assim* [1966] 2 QB 249 in relation to trials on indictment. Where a defendant is charged on several informations and the facts are connected, for example motoring offences or several charges of shoplifting, I can see no reason why those informations should not, if the justices think fit, be heard together. Similarly, if two or more defendants are charged on separate informations but the facts are connected, I can see no reason why they should not, if the justices think fit, be heard together. In the present cases there were separate informations against the husband and the wife and a joint information against them both. I can see no rational objection to all those informations being heard and determined together. Of course, when this question arises, justices will be well advised to inquire both of the prosecution and of the defence whether either side has any objection to all the informations being heard together. If consent is forthcoming on both sides, there is no problem. If such consent is not

forthcoming, the justices should then consider the rival submissions and . . . rule as they think right in the overall interests of justice. . . . Absence of consent, either express where the defendant is present or represented and objects or necessarily brought about by his absence or the absence of representation, should no longer in practice be regarded as a complete and automatic bar to hearing more than one information at the same time or informations against more than one defendant charged on separate informations at the same time when in the justices' view the facts are sufficiently closely connected to justify this course and there is no risk of injustice to defendants by its adoption. Accordingly, the justices should always ask themselves whether it would be fair and just to the defendant or defendants to allow a joint trial. Only if the answer is clearly in the affirmative should they order joint trial in the absence of consent by or on behalf of the defendant.

The above passage implies that where all parties (including the prosecution) are in favour of a joint trial, the court should automatically agree to that course. In the case of both prosecution and defence being *against* a joint trial, the ultimate decision is still with the magistrates, but they should be slow to exercise their discretion against the parties' wishes (*Highbury Corner Magistrates' Court, ex parte McGinley* (1986) 150 JP 257).

Trial of Successive Informations by Same Bench

D18.27   If the defendant successfully applies for separate trial of a number of informations laid against him, the question then arises whether the bench that decided in favour of separate trials may properly hear any or all of the cases. This is part of the broader question of whether knowledge that the accused faces more than one charge in their court should disqualify magistrates on the ground of possible bias (see also **D2.26**). The following propositions emerge from the cases:

(a)   The test to be applied if magistrates know that the accused has other matters outstanding against him in their court (whether they are matters for which he is yet to be tried or matters in respect of which he has been convicted but awaits sentence) is now that laid down by the House of Lords in *Gough* [1993] AC 646 as being generally 'applicable in all cases of apparent bias, whether concerned with justices or members of other inferior tribunals, or with jurors, or with arbitrators', namely, was there a real danger of bias on the part of the member(s) of the tribunal in question? (see Lord Goff of Chieveley at p. 904).

(b)   Procedurally, there is no objection to the court sheet or sheets put before the magistrates in respect of an accused listing not only the information which they are about to try on a not guilty plea, but also other charges against him which are in the court list for the day (per Mann LJ in *Weston-super-Mare Justices, ex parte Shaw* [1987] QB 640 at pp. 646–8 and Watkins LJ at pp. 648–9). A declaration to the contrary in *Liverpool City Justices, ex parte Topping* [1983] 1 WLR 119 by Ackner LJ was granted upon a misunderstanding of the distinction between the court register (which is completed by the clerk after the relevant adjudication by the magistrates) and the court sheets or court list which are given to the magistrates simply for their information (see per Watkins LJ in *Ex parte Shaw*).

(c)   Notwithstanding proposition (b), if a not guilty plea to an information is expected, court staff do in fact attempt to prevent a bench knowing of other outstanding charges against the accused. Thus, the court sheets for the latter are customarily not handed to the magistrates until after they have adjudicated upon the not guilty plea. At that stage the accused can be asked to enter a plea on the other matters and, if he pleads guilty, the bench will be able conveniently to proceed to sentence him both for those and also – if they have convicted on the original information – for that as well. If the plea to the other charges is also not guilty, it will be in the discretion of the bench whether they proceed to trial or adjourn for trial on a different day (whether by themselves or another bench).

(d)   Applying the above propositions to cases where a bench is asked to order separate trials of informations and does so, it would seem that it may proceed forthwith to trial of one of those informations, notwithstanding that it inevitably knows of the others, provided that there was no real danger of bias. Whether, having tried one case, the same bench can then properly try the others, either on the same day or – more probably – after an adjournment, is again a matter for their discretion (see, on that point, *Sandwich Justices, ex parte Berry* [1982] Crim LR 121, where it was appropriate for one bench to try all the cases as the defence involved allegations that the numerous charges that had been brought against B in a short space of time indicated police harassment).

Informations against Two or More Defendants Jointly

An information may properly charge two or more defendants with having committed an **D18.28** offence jointly (*Lipscombe, ex parte Biggins* (1862) 26 JP 244). The principles governing such informations are analogous to those governing trial of joint counts on indictment. In other words, the justices may convict either or both accused, whether on the basis that they did indeed commit the offence jointly or on the basis that they acted independently of each other. The acquittal of one accused does not prevent the conviction of the other (see, for example, *Barsted v Jones* (1964) 124 JP 400 where, on a joint charge of larceny against J and X, the bench heard the evidence and then announced that there was insufficient on which to convict X but sufficient to convict J; they then accepted a submission by J's solicitor that, as the charge was joint and they were acquitting X, they would have to acquit J also; the Divisional Court allowed the prosecutor's appeal and remitted the case to the magistrates with a direction to convict, Lord Parker CJ saying that J's solicitor's contention had been 'quite unarguable'). As at trial on indictment, there is a discretion to order separate trials of accused who are jointly charged in an information (*Cridland* (1857) 7 E & B 853). However, it is submitted that a joint trial will generally be preferable.

THE ROLE OF THE MAGISTRATES' CLERK

Introduction

The qualifications and appointment of justices' clerks are described at **D2.23**. There is a **D18.29** distinction between clerks in the strict sense of the word (of whom there is normally only one per petty-sessional division) and the deputy and assistant clerks who form part of the staff provided for him by the magistrates' courts committee. Provided an assistant clerk has certain minimum legal qualifications, he may sit as a clerk in court even though he neither has a law degree nor is qualified as a barrister or solicitor. The function of a clerk in court is the same whether he be an assistant clerk or the actual clerk to the justices, although an assistant clerk may and ought to seek assistance from *the* clerk if a point of difficulty arises on which the assistant does not feel qualified to advise the magistrates.

A clerk or other member of the staff of a magistrates' court committee must perform his legal functions independently. He is not subject to the directions of the committee or the justices' chief executive when performing such legal functions, e.g., giving advice to the justices (Justices of the Peace Act 1997, s. 48).

Duties of Clerk with Respect to Questions of Law

Practice Direction (Justices: Clerk to Court) [1981] 1 WLR 1163   D18.30

    1. A justices' clerk is responsible to the justices for the performance of any of the functions set out below by any member of his staff acting as court clerk and may be called in to advise the justices even when he is not personally sitting with the justices as clerk to the court.

    2. It shall be the responsibility of the justices' clerk to advise the justices as follows: (a) on questions of law or of mixed law and fact; (b) as to matters of practice and procedure.

    3. If it appears to him necessary to do so, or he is so requested by the justices, the justices' clerk has the responsibility to (a) refresh the justices' memory as to any matter of evidence and to draw attention to any issues involved in the matters before the court, (b) advise the

justices generally on the range of penalties which the law allows them to impose and on any guidance relevant to the choice of penalty provided by the law, the decisions of the superior courts or other authorities. If no request for advice has been made by the justices, the justices' clerk shall discharge his responsibility in court in the presence of the parties.

4.   The way in which the justices clerk should perform his functions should be stated as follows. (a) The justices are entitled to the advice of their clerk when they retire in order that the clerk may fulfil his responsibility outlined above. (b) Some justices may prefer to take their own notes of evidence. There is, however, no obligation on them to do so. Whether they do so or not, there is nothing to prevent them from enlisting the aid of their clerk and his notes if they are in any doubt as to the evidence which has been given. (c) If the justices wish to consult their clerk solely about the evidence or his notes of it, this should ordinarily, and certainly in simple cases, be done in open court. The object is to avoid any suspicion that the clerk has been involved in deciding issues of fact.

[5.   Confirms that *Practice Note (Justices' Clerks)* [1954] 1 WLR 213 remains in force.]

It will be apparent from para. 2 that the role of the clerk is to *advise* on law, practice and procedure. Since the magistrates are the ultimate arbiters of both law and fact there is no obligation on them to adopt the clerk's advice on law, but it is accepted practice that they do in fact do so. Thus, in *Jones* v *Nicks* [1977] RTR 72 Lord Widgery CJ strongly criticised magistrates for rejecting the clerk's advice that mitigation advanced by a motorist in respect of an offence of speeding could not amount to special reasons for not endorsing his licence. His lordship said: 'Justices really must accept legal advice from their clerk in circumstances like this; if they do not, all that happens is that a great deal of time and money is wasted in bringing the matter up here to be put right.' If the clerk forms the view that the justices are wrong, however, he has no power to ignore their order and treat it as a nullity (*Liverpool Magistrates' Court, ex parte Abiaka* (1999) 163 JP 497). In those circumstances, he should put the matter before the same bench, or another if that constitution is unavailable, so that they can consider his fresh legal advice and alter the original order, or arrange for reconsideration by a superior court.

When a point of law arises during the course of proceedings, the magistrates normally take the initiative and ask the clerk for his advice. It is submitted that the advice should be given publicly in open court. Certainly, should a point arise on which the magistrates do not ask for advice but nonetheless the clerk considers that it is his duty to proffer some, it is expressly stated by para. 3 of the practice direction that he 'shall discharge his responsibility in court in the presence of the parties'. *Ex hypothesi*, when the advice is expressly sought, the parties – and, indeed, the public – should know what the clerk is telling his bench. In *Chichester Justices, ex parte DPP* [1994] RTR 175, a clerk who had not been present in court when legal submissions were made was asked to advise the justices on points of law arising from the case; the Divisional Court stressed that in such a case he should hear submissions from both parties in open court before advising. See also *Moss* v *Jenkins* [1975] RTR 25, where the Divisional Court suggested that magistrates who, in retirement, had taken for themselves a technical point of law relating to a drink-driving charge would have been better advised to have returned to court for the point to be argued before them by the advocates with the clerk openly advising.

Advice on law will certainly include advice on the elements of the offence charged and on questions of admissibility of evidence. The extent to which the clerk may properly advise on sentencing (for example, by reminding the magistrates of a decision of an appellate court indicating that a custodial sentence ought to be imposed for a particular type of offence) is more problematic. There is a danger that, in drawing attention to a 'guidelines' decision of the Court of Appeal, the clerk may seem to be advocating a certain type of disposal and thus interfering with a decision which ought to be for the bench alone. On the other hand, the practice direction does state that the clerk's responsibility is not only to advise on the range of penalties allowed by the law but also to refer to any guidance on choice of penalty given by, *inter alia*, 'the decisions of the superior courts'. *Practice Note (Justices' Clerks)* [1953] 1 WLR 1416 further states that the clerk may inform the magistrates of the level of sentence imposed by their own or neighbouring benches for comparable offences. Most clerks deliver any advice they have on sentence privately after the magistrates have retired, rather than in open court, although the practice is not uniform.

Clerk to Play No Part in Decisions on Questions of Fact

The clerk must not advise on or try to influence the magistrates' decision as to the facts (see **D18.31** *Practice Note (Justices' Clerks)* [1953] 1 WLR 1416, which states that 'In no circumstances . . . may justices consult their clerk as to the guilt or innocence of the accused so far as it is simply a question of fact'). Contravention of the rule may lead to judicial review of the court's decision (see, for example, *Stafford Justices, ex parte Ross* [1962] 1 WLR 456 – conviction quashed because, while R was giving evidence in his own defence, the clerk handed the bench a note which in effect argued that the evidence ought not to be believed.

Retirement of Clerk with Bench

Partly as a corollary of the rule that the clerk must not be a party to factual decisions, he **D18.32** should not retire with the magistrates when they consider their verdict unless either he is asked to do so (whether at the outset of their retirement or later) or he realises while they are in retirement that there is a point of law on which they may need assistance but on which he omitted to advise them in open court (see *Practice Note (Justices' Clerks)* [1953] 1 WLR 1416 for the rule that the clerk should not automatically retire with the bench and *Uxbridge Justices, ex parte Smith* (1985) 149 JP 620 for a case where his joining them uninvited was held to be justified). If the clerk does join the magistrates in their retirement, he should be careful to advise only on the law or other matters within his province. Having advised, he should return to open court. However, in a complicated case where the legal and factual issues are inextricably intertwined, there is no objection to the clerk being with the magistrates throughout virtually the entire period that they are considering their verdict (*Consett Justices, ex parte Postal Bingo Ltd* [1967] 2 QB 9).

In *Eccles Justices, ex parte Farrelly* (1993) 157 JP 77, the clerk to the justices spoke to them as they were about to deliver a verdict and then went with them when they retired to reconsider. No explanation was given. The Divisional Court held that her conduct could give rise to a legitimate inference that she had participated in the decision-making processes of the justices. Although the convictions were quashed, it was made clear that if the clerk had given the parties an explanation her conduct would have been impeccable.

If magistrates ask the clerk to retire with them in a case where there is no colourable reason for their needing his advice on law, the Divisional Court may take the view that they in fact sought his advice on the facts and will therefore quash any conviction (*Guildford Justices, ex parte Harding* (1981) 145 JP 174, where the two reasons suggested by the chairman of the magistrates why he and his colleagues had asked for the clerk – namely, to read them his notes of evidence and to advise on the standard of proof – were dismissed as inadequate because (a) they could have read his notes without having him in the retiring room and (b) if they did not know what the standard of proof was in an ordinary criminal case, then they should not have been sitting as magistrates at all). *Ex parte Harding* and the above-stated principles are without prejudice to the right (indeed responsibility) of the clerk to remind the magistrates of the evidence if the latter are in genuine doubt about what it was (see also *Birmingham Magistrates, ex parte Ahmed* [1995] Crim LR 503).

Running the Court

Routine matters of procedure are conducted by the clerk. These include establishing the **D18.33** identity of the defendant when he comes into the dock; reading the charge or summons to him; asking for representations as to mode of trial; telling the defendant of his right to trial on indictment if the magistrates agree to summary trial on an either-way offence; putting the information to him if there is to be a summary trial, and notifying the court whether the summons or adjournment notice have been properly served in a case where the defendant does not appear.

Noting the Evidence

D18.34 It is implicit in *Practice Direction (Justices: Clerk to the Court)* [1981] 1 WLR 1163 that the clerk should take a note of evidence – see especially para. 3 which states that it is his responsibility to 'refresh the justices' memory as to any matter of evidence and to draw attention to any issues involved in the matters before the court'. Moreover, the magistrates are entitled to 'enlist the aid of their clerk *and his notes* if they are in any doubt as to the evidence which has been given' (para. 4). Additionally, r. 17 of the Magistrates' Courts Rules 1981 requires the clerk to forward to the Crown Court a copy of his notes if an offender is committed for sentence. A similar obligation arises when an offender is remitted for sentence to another magistrates' court (Magistrates' Courts Rules 1981, r. 19(1)). The clerk also has an obligation to take a note of the argument when the court hears full argument as to bail (Magistrates' Courts Rules 1981, r. 90A). As to the desirability of supplying the defence with a copy of the clerk's note if they are appealing against conviction to the Crown Court, see *Clerk to Highbury Corner Justices, ex parte Hussein* [1986] 1 WLR 1266.

It is suggested by the 1981 practice direction that, where the justices do wish to consult the clerk solely about the evidence or his notes of it, they should do so in open court (para. 4, subheading (c)). However, this may seem somewhat impractical in that the justices probably will not realise until after they have retired that their recollection of certain evidence is unclear, and reconvening the court while they are in the middle of considering their verdict merely to look at the clerk's notes is hardly satisfactory.

Role of Clerk where a Defendant Is Unrepresented

D18.35 Although the clerk should not allow himself to become an advocate on behalf of an unrepresented party (per Sachs J in *Hobby* v *Hobby* [1954] 1 WLR 1020), it is accepted that he is entitled to assist such a party to present his own case (*Simms* v *Moore* [1970] 2 QB 327). Thus, it is common practice for clerks to explain to an unrepresented defendant the purpose of cross-examination and, if the defendant himself still seems incapable of doing it properly, to frame suitable questions on his behalf. Under the Magistrates' Courts Rules 1981, r. 13A, the court must explain to an unrepresented defendant the substance of the charge in simple language. The same rule states that if the defendant, instead of asking questions in cross-examination, makes assertions, then the court should put any necessary questions to the witness on behalf of the defendant. Both of these functions are in practice usually discharged by the clerk. At the close of the prosecution case, the clerk will inform the defendant of his right to give and call evidence if he so wishes. It has also been suggested that, where an unrepresented defendant appears in danger of 'throwing away his shield' and exposing himself to cross-examination about previous convictions, the clerk should ask the magistrates to retire briefly so that he and the prosecutor can explain the position to the defendant (*Weston-super-Mare Justices, ex parte Townsend* [1968] 3 All ER 225).

SEEING THE MAGISTRATE IN CHAMBERS

D18.36 The bench (whether lay or stipendiary) has an inherent discretion to hear representations in chambers during the course of a trial (*Nottingham Magistrates' Court, ex parte Furnell* (1996) 160 JP 201). However, the discretion has to be exercised with even greater caution than applies to the analogous procedure of seeing the judge in a trial on indictment (for details of which, see **D12.22**). In any event, all parties should be made aware of the hearing and be represented in chambers (except where there is an issue of public interest immunity to be heard on an *ex parte* basis) and a contemporaneous note should be taken, normally by the clerk.

SECTION D19: SUMMARY TRIAL:
THE COURSE OF THE TRIAL

PROSECUTION CASE

Opening Speech

The prosecution representative has the right to make an opening speech (Magistrates' **D19.1** Courts Rules 1981, r. 13(1): 'On the summary trial of an information, where the accused does not plead guilty, the prosecutor shall call the evidence for the prosecution, and before doing so may address the court'). The opening can usually be kept short and, in very simple cases such as road traffic prosecutions where the evidence comes entirely from police officers, may be dispensed with completely.

In *L and B* v *DPP* [1998] 2 Cr App R 69, the case had been adjourned for a month after the main prosecution witnesses had given evidence. At the resumed hearing, the justices invited and permitted the prosecutor to deliver a second speech in order to remind them of evidence which they were having difficulty in remembering. On appeal to the Divisional Court by way of case stated, the appellants contended that the prosecution should not have been allowed to address the justices again. The Divisional Court dismissed the appeal. There was nothing unfair in the prosecutor being asked to remind the court of evidence which had been given, subject to the safeguard that the defence should invariably be asked to address the court in reply, to correct any errors or draw attention to any differences of recollection.

Advance Warning of the Prosecution Case

Where the offence is triable either way, the defence may learn the nature of the **D19.2** prosecution case by requesting advance information (see the Magistrates' Courts (Advance Information) Rules 1985 (SI 1985 No. 601)). The rules are considered and set out in full at **D4.14**. The main purpose of the information is to assist the defence in determining the mode of trial. Accordingly, the time at which it should be requested and provided is *before* the magistrates consider whether the case is more suitable for summary trial or for trial on indictment (see r. 4(1) of the 1985 rules). If the defence agree to summary trial without the benefit of advance information, it would seem that, strictly speaking, they have lost their right to it, although in practice the prosecution will almost certainly be prepared to give it out of time. Advance information may take the form of copies of the proposed prosecution witnesses' statements (preferably typed) or of a summary of the prosecution case (r. 4(1)(a) and (b)). The former is of much greater assistance to the defence than the latter in the conduct of a summary trial, and it is submitted that – unless there are compelling logistical reasons to the contrary – the prosecution should endeavour to serve copy statements rather than a mere summary.

Where the offence charged is summary, there is no statutory obligation to give advance information. Even so, defence solicitors frequently request it. There is, in practice, a considerable variation in the response of different offices of the CPS to such requests. It is submitted that the better practice is for prosecutors, when faced with a defence request for the statements of witnesses whom the prosecution will call, to comply with that request. This is likely to ensure that the hearing concentrates upon the issues, and that the court's time is not wasted while the defence representative obtains instructions from the accused. It also appears to be within the spirit of the prosecutor's general duty not to 'attempt to obtain a conviction by all means at his command' nor to 'regard himself as appearing for a party' (see the Code of Conduct of the Bar, annexe F).

Prosecution Disclosure of Unused Material

D19.3 The position relating to disclosure in summary trial under the CPIA 1996 is dealt with at **D6.10**. The statutory framework contained in the 1996 Act governs offences in respect of which there was no investigation prior to 1 April 1997. For offences where the investigation commenced prior to that date, reference should be made to the 1997 edition of this work.

Securing the Attendance of Witnesses

D19.4 The attendance of witnesses for purposes of criminal proceedings in magistrates' courts may be secured by the issue of a summons or warrant under the powers given in the MCA 1980, s. 97. The section applies both to witnesses required for committal proceedings and to those required for purposes of summary trial. Moreover, it applies equally to proposed prosecution and proposed defence witnesses.

Section 97 provides, essentially, that, where a magistrate is satisfied that (a) any person within the jurisdiction is likely to be able to give material evidence or produce a material document or thing for purposes of a summary trial to be held in a magistrates' court for the county for which the magistrate acts, and (b) that that person will not voluntarily attend as a witness or, as the case may be, produce the document or thing, then the magistrate may issue a summons requiring the person to attend before the court on the date specified in the summons (s. 97(1)). A similar power is given to justices' clerks by the Justices' Clerks Rules 1999 (SI 1999 No. 2784). If a magistrate (but not a clerk) is further satisfied by evidence on oath that it is probable that a summons issued under s. 97(1) would not procure the witness's attendance, then he may issue a warrant (s. 97(2)). Should a person summoned under s. 97(1) fail to attend as required, the court may issue a warrant (s. 97(3)). It must, however, be satisfied that (a) the witness is indeed likely to be able to give material evidence or produce a material document or thing; (b) that he has been duly served with the summons and been paid or tendered a reasonable sum for costs and expenses, and (c) that there is no just excuse for the failure to attend. Requirement (a) must be established by evidence on oath; requirement (b) may be established either by evidence on oath or in such other manner as is prescribed. By r. 99(6) of the Magistrates' Courts Rules 1981, a witness summons may *not* be served by post. It will therefore be necessary for the party asking for a warrant to show either that the summons was delivered by hand or it was left with a person at the witness's last known or usual address. This may be proved by a certificate signed by the server (r. 67(2)).

The power to issue a witness summons is conditional upon the magistrate being satisfied that the witness will be able to give or produce material evidence (see above). Therefore, a summons should be granted only if the applicant can satisfy the tribunal upon that point (*Peterborough Magistrates' Court, ex parte Willis* (1987) 151 JP 785 – summonses obtained by the defence in respect of two police officers quashed by the Divisional Court because the applicant had not been asked the nature of the officers' anticipated testimony and, indeed, had applied for the summons on the basis that it might turn out that the officers could give material evidence, rather than on the basis that they actually had such evidence). Similarly, where the summons is to produce a document or thing, the applicant must be able to show that the item to be produced would be admissible evidence and not, for example, inadmissible hearsay (*Cheltenham Justices, ex parte Secretary of State for Trade* [1977] 1 WLR 95) or material subject to legal professional privilege (*Derby Magistrates' Court, ex parte B* [1996] AC 487). In the context of prosecutions for drink-driving offences, summonses requiring the police to produce the logbook and service records for the intoximeter machine on which the accused was tested have been quashed (see *Coventry Magistrates' Court, ex parte Perks* [1985] RTR 74 and *Tower Bridge Magistrates' Court, ex parte DPP* [1989] RTR 118). In short, the powers given to magistrates under s. 97 may not be used as a means of conducting a fishing expedition or obtaining discovery from the other side when, in truth, the applicant for a summons cannot show that the person he proposes to summon actually has material evidence, as opposed to hoping that something might turn up if the summons were granted (*Sheffield Justices, ex parte Wrigley* [1985] RTR 78, *Skegness Magistrates' Court, ex parte Cardy* [1985] RTR 49 and *Reading Justices, ex parte Berkshire County Council* [1996] 1 Cr App R 239). Where the conditions in s. 97(1) are satisfied, however, the court has no discretion to refuse the issue of a witness summons (*Highbury Corner Magistrates' Court, ex parte Deering* (1997) 161 JP 138).

Under s. 97(3), on the other hand, the magistrates do have a discretion whether to issue a warrant where they are satisfied as to the necessary conditions. The basis upon which the discretion should be exercised was considered in *Bradford Justices, ex parte Wilkinson* [1990] 1 WLR 692. W was charged with driving with excess alcohol. In September 1988, two witnesses vital to his case failed to attend the trial before justices. Witness summonses were served on them pursuant to s. 97(1), the case being adjourned to November 1988. They again failed to attend at the November hearing. W applied for the justices to issue warrants of arrest in accordance with s. 97(3) to compel their attendance. The justices decided not to do so. W was tried and convicted. He applied to the Divisional Court for judicial review and certiorari to quash his conviction. The Divisional Court held that, despite its customary reluctance to interfere with the justices' discretion, it would grant the application. The decision of the justices was flawed, in that they had a duty to hear the case a defendant wished to advance. The evidence which W sought to adduce was crucial to a proper hearing of his case. The case provides a clear indication that, notwithstanding the discretionary form of s. 97(3), witness warrants definitely ought to be issued if the evidence appears critical.

If a proposed witness attending or brought before a magistrates' court refuses without just excuse to be sworn or give evidence (or to produce a document or thing), he may be imprisoned for up to a month and/or fined up to £2,500 (s. 97(4)). This applies whether the witness attended court entirely voluntarily or in answer to a summons or was brought there following execution of a warrant.

Where a prosecution witness attends court to give evidence in a summary trial, the prosecutor is obliged to call him to give evidence if the defence so requests, or at least tender him for cross-examination (*Wellingborough Magistrates' Court, ex parte Francois* (1994) 158 JP 813). In any event, ultimately the justices have the power to call a witness not called by either party (*Haringey Justices, ex parte DPP* (1990) 160 JP 326).

Magistrates' Courts Act 1980, s. 97

(1)   Where a justice of the peace for any county, any London commission area or the City of London is satisfied that any person in England or Wales is likely to be able to give material evidence, or produce any document or thing likely to be material evidence, at the summary trial of an information or hearing of a complaint by a magistrates' court for that commission area and that that person will not voluntarily attend as a witness or will not voluntarily produce the document or thing, the justice shall issue a summons directed to that person requiring him to attend before the court at the time and place appointed in the summons to give evidence or to produce the document or thing.

(a)   no summons shall be issued by a justice of the peace after the expiry of the period within which a notice of the prosecution case under section 5 above must be served or the service of the notice of the prosecution case, if sooner; and

(b)   the summons shall require the person to whom it is directed to attend before the justice issuing it or another justice for that county, that London commission area or the City of London (as the case may be) to have his evidence taken as a deposition or to produce any document or thing.

(2)   If a justice of the peace is satisfied by evidence on oath of the matters mentioned in subsection (1) above, and also that it is probable that a summons under that subsection would not procure the attendance of the person in question, the justice may instead of issuing a summons issue a warrant to arrest that person and bring him before such a court as aforesaid at a time and place specified in the warrant. . . .

(2A)   A summons may also be issued under subsection (1) above if the justice is satisfied that the person in question is outside the British Islands but no warrant shall be issued under subsection (2) above unless the justice is satisfied by evidence on oath that the person in question is in England or Wales.

(2B)   A justice may refuse to issue a summons under subsection (1) above in relation to the summary trial of an information if he is not satisfied that an application for the summons was made by a party to the case as soon as reasonably practicable after the accused pleaded not guilty.

(2C)   In relation to the summary trial of an information, subsection (2) above shall have effect as if the reference to the matters mentioned in subsection (1) above included a reference to the matter mentioned in subsection (2B) above.

(3)   On the failure of any person to attend before a magistrates' court in answer to a summons under this section, if—

(a)   the court is satisfied by evidence on oath that he is likely to be able to give material evidence or produce any document or thing likely to be material evidence in the proceedings; and

(b)   it is proved on oath, or in such other manner as may be prescribed, that he has been duly served with the summons, and that a reasonable sum has been paid or tendered to him for costs and expenses; and

(c)   it appears to the court that there is no just excuse for the failure,

the court may issue a warrant to arrest him and bring him before the court at a time and place specified in the warrant.

(4)   If any person attending or brought before a magistrates' court refuses without just excuse to be sworn or give evidence, or to produce any document or thing, the court or justice, as the case may be, may commit him to custody until the expiration of such period not exceeding one month as may be specified in the warrant or until he sooner gives evidence or produces the document or thing or impose on him a fine not exceeding £2,500 or both.

(5)   A fine imposed under subsection (4) above shall be deemed, for the purposes of any enactment, to be a sum adjudged to be paid by a conviction.

WRITTEN EVIDENCE AT SUMMARY TRIAL: CRIMINAL JUSTICE ACT 1967, s. 9

D19.5   A party wishing to tender a written statement as evidence at a summary trial rather than calling the maker of the statement may make use of the provisions of the CJA 1967, s. 9. The main points about s. 9 of the CJA 1967 are that:

(a)   The statement it is proposed to use as evidence must be signed by the maker. It must also contain a declaration that it is true to the best of his knowledge and belief, and that he made it knowing that if it were tendered in evidence he might be prosecuted for wilfully stating in it anything he knew to be false or did not believe to be true (s. 9(2)(a) and (b)).

(b)   A copy of the statement (together with a copy of any documentary exhibit referred to therein) must be served on each of the other parties (s. 9(2)(c)). If, within seven days of service, any of them serves a counter-notice objecting to the statement being put in evidence, it may not go in (s. 9(2)(d)). It follows that a party wishing to avail himself of s. 9 should serve the copy statement at least seven days before the proposed hearing date. The onus is then on his opponent to object to the statement within the week. However, the strict requirements of service of the copy statement may be waived by the opposing party (proviso to s. 9(2)). Conversely, even where the copy statement was served more than a week before the hearing and no objection to its being read was indicated, the court may, of its own volition or on the application of a party, require the maker of the statement to attend and give oral evidence (s. 9(4)(b)). In practice, where an s. 9 statement has been served on the defence but by inadvertence no notice objecting it was given within the statutory time, the court is likely to adjourn for the witness to be called rather than insisting upon the strict letter of s. 9(2). This is particularly so where the defendant is unrepresented.

(c)   Form 14 of the Magistrates' Courts (Forms) Rules 1981 sets out a precedent for a notice to be sent to the defendant by the prosecution when they wish to tender a statement in evidence under s. 9. The notice explains the effect of s. 9 and warns that, if the prosecutor is not informed within seven days that the defendant wants the maker of the statement to be called as a witness, the right to insist on his attendance is lost. A reply form is attached to the notice. Service of an s. 9 statement may be effected by any of the methods detailed in s. 9(8). Most conveniently, if the defendant is legally represented, service may be made on his solicitor.

(d)   Where a statement is admitted in evidence under s. 9, it is either read in full to the court or, at the court's discretion, parts of it may be summarised (s. 9(6)). The statement is *not* to be taken conclusively to be true, but is merely 'admissible as evidence to the like extent as oral evidence to the like effect by [the maker]' would be admissible (s. 9(1)). It follows that the defence's having failed to serve notice objecting to the admissibility of the statement does not preclude them at trial from adducing evidence inconsistent with it (*Lister* v *Quaife* [1983] 1 WLR 48). The position is then analogous to that which arises when a prosecution witness is called in person but significant differences between his evidence and the anticipated defence evidence are not put to him in cross-examination as they ought to be. Although the court may then treat the defence case on the disputed areas with some scepticism, they are not entitled to reject it out of hand and – if left in doubt by the combined effect of the defence evidence and the formally unchallenged prosecution evidence – would be obliged to give the benefit of the doubt to the defence. However, the defence should not use the reasoning in *Lister* v *Quaife* as a tactical ploy so as to avoid the necessity of putting the defence case to a prosecution witness in person (per May LJ at p. 55B). If there are differences between the defence case and the contents of a proposed s. 9 statement, then a notice should be served objecting to the statement. In the event of failure to give such notice and defence witnesses then contradicting the statement, the prosecution should ask for an adjournment so that the maker of the statement can be called. The court ought not only to agree to the adjournment but should also consider ordering that the costs thrown away be paid by the defence whatever the eventual outcome of the case (ibid. pp. 54H–55A). In any event, the prosecution should hesitate before making use of the s. 9 procedure in respect of evidence crucial to their case (per Stephen Brown J who said at p. 55E: 'Section 9 of the CJA 1967 is a very valuable provision designed to save expense and trouble in very many instances, but where the evidence which is in written statements, served under the provisions of the notice, is central to the issues in the case, prosecutors should give very careful consideration as to whether or not they should call the actual witness so that the proper impact of that evidence can be made upon the court').

(e)   Where a statement read under s. 9 refers to a person by name (e.g., 'I know Clive Jones') and a defendant accused of the same name is present in court and has answered to his name, the statement is to be treated as prima facie referring to the defendant (*Ellis* v *Jones* [1973] 2 All ER 893). Section 9 statements are also often used to prove cases in the absence of the defendant. In such cases, it is submitted that the statement (in order to identify the defendant) should give both his name and address or other identifying details.

Criminal Justice Act 1967, s. 9

(1)   In any criminal proceedings, other than committal proceedings, a written statement by any person shall, if such of the conditions mentioned in the next following subsection as

are applicable are satisfied, be admissible as evidence to the like extent as oral evidence to the like effect by that person.

(2)   The said conditions are—

(a)   the statement purports to be signed by the person who made it;

(b)   the statement contains a declaration by that person to the effect that it is true to the best of his knowledge and belief and that he made the statement knowing that, if it were tendered in evidence, he would be liable to prosecution if he wilfully stated in it anything which he knew to be false or did not believe to be true;

(c)   before the hearing at which the statement is tendered in evidence, a copy of the statement is served, by or on behalf of the party proposing to tender it, on each of the other parties to the proceedings; and

(d)   none of the other parties or their solicitors, within seven days from the service of the copy of the statement, serves a notice on the party so proposing objecting to the statement being tendered in evidence under this section:

Provided that the conditions mentioned in paragraphs (c) and (d) of this subsection shall not apply if the parties agree before or during the hearing that the statement shall be so tendered.

(3)   The following provisions shall also have effect in relation to any written statement tendered in evidence under this section, that is to say—

(a)   if the statement is made by a person under the age of 18, it shall give his age;

(b)   if it is made by a person who cannot read it, it shall be read to him before he signs it and shall be accompanied by a declaration by the person who so read the statement to the effect that it was so read; and

(c)   if it refers to any other document as an exhibit, the copy served on any other party to the proceedings under paragraph (c) of the last foregoing subsection shall be accompanied by a copy of that document or by such information as may be necessary in order to enable the person on whom it is served to inspect that document or a copy thereof.

(4)   Notwithstanding that a written statement made by any person may be admissible as evidence by virtue of this section—

(a)   the party by whom or on whose behalf a copy of the statement was served may call that person to give evidence; and

(b)   the court may, of its own motion or on the application of any party to the proceedings, require that person to attend before the court and give evidence.

[(5)   Applications before trial under subsection (4)(b) above to courts other than a magistrates' court.]

(6)   So much of any statement as is admitted in evidence by virtue of this section shall, unless the court otherwise directs, be read aloud at the hearing and where the court so directs an account shall be given orally of so much of any statement as is not read aloud.

(7)   Any document or object referred to as an exhibit and identified in a written statement tendered in evidence under this section shall be treated as if it had been produced as an exhibit and identified in court by the maker of the statement.

(8)   A document required by this section to be served on any person may be served—

(a)   by delivering it to him or to his solicitor; or

(b)   by addressing it to him and leaving it at his usual or last known place of abode or place of business or by addressing it to his solicitor and leaving it at his office; or

(c)   by sending it in a registered letter or by the recorded delivery service or by first class post addressed to him at his usual or last known place of abode or place of business or addressed to his solicitor at his office; or

(d)   in the case of a body corporate, by delivering it to the secretary or clerk of the body at its registered or principal office or sending it in a registered letter or by the recorded delivery service or by first class post addressed to the secretary or clerk of that body at that office.

OBJECTIONS TO PROSECUTION EVIDENCE

D19.6   The procedure to be followed where the defence object to proposed prosecution evidence (or have some other preliminary point of law to argue before the magistrates) is a matter of considerable difficulty. The difficulty arises from the magistrates being the judges of both fact and law. Especially if the issue is one of admissibility of evidence, there is a danger that the magistrates will learn the nature of the evidence in the course of the presentation of arguments about its admissibility. Should they then rule it inadmissible, they may nonetheless have difficulty in ignoring it when reaching a verdict. Furthermore, where the objection to the evidence is based upon the manner in which it was obtained (i.e., it is the type of case in which, at a trial on indictment, secondary evidence would be heard and evaluated by the judge on the *voir dire* before he made a ruling on the admissibility of the primary evidence), there is the further difficulty that, if a *voir dire* procedure were to be adopted by the magistrates and they admitted the primary evidence, they might have to hear the secondary evidence they had heard on the *voir dire* all over again in the course of the ordinary defence case, because it would still be relevant to the weight of the primary evidence even though the question of admissibility had been settled. No doubt because of the inherent difficulties in the situation, the guidance given by the High Court on how magistrates should deal with arguments on law and objections to evidence is somewhat confusing. The following propositions emerge from the cases:

(a)   The stage of the trial at which the magistrates rule upon a question of admissibility of evidence (or other incidental issue) is a matter for their discretion (see Lord Lane CJ's judgment in *F* v *Chief Constable of Kent* [1982] Crim LR 682, followed in *Epping and Ongar Justices, ex parte Manby* [1986] Crim LR 555). Even when faced with a preliminary point which would appear to be decisive of the whole case, they are – as judges of both fact and law – entitled to determine their own procedure.

(b)   Notwithstanding this general proposition, delaying the determination of a question of admissibility of a confession until after the conclusion of the prosecution evidence may be unfair to the defence, in that the accused will not be able to give evidence about alleged irregularities in the obtaining of the confession unless he testifies in his own defence, which will expose him to cross-examination about the general issues. Moreover, in taking the decision whether to call evidence at all, the defence advocate ought to know whether evidence as crucial as a confession is to be part of the case against his client. These special considerations were recognised by Lord Lane in the following passage from his judgment in *F* v *Chief Constable of Kent* (quoted at [1986] Crim LR 557), a case which concerned an allegedly involuntary confession:

> It is impossible to lay down any general rule as to when magistrates should announce their decision on this type of point, and indeed when the point itself should be taken. Every case will be different. Some sort of preliminary point, for instance with regard to the admissibility of a document or something like that, can plainly, with the assistance of the clerk, be decided straight away. Other points, such as the one with which we are dealing here, may require a decision at a later stage of the case, possibly after further argument. It may be that in some cases the defendant will be entitled to know what the decision of the justices with regard to the admissibility of a confession is at the close of the prosecution case in order to enable him to know what proper course he should take with regard to giving evidence and calling evidence and so on.

Where the confession is the crucial evidence against the defendant so that without it there might not be a case to answer, the interests of justice clearly dictate that admissibility should be determined as a preliminary issue (per Robert Goff LJ in *ADC* v *Chief Constable of Greater Manchester* (15 March 1983 unreported) although, on the facts of the case, there was other evidence against the defendant as well as his confession, so the justices' decision to postpone determination of its admissibility until the end of the case as a whole was fair).

(c)   The cases referred to above were decided before the enactment of the PACE 1984, ss. 76 and 78. The wording of those two sections has introduced a surprising and scarcely justifiable distinction between the procedure to be adopted where the defence represent that a confession should be excluded because it was obtained by one of the means prohibited by s. 76(2), and that to be adopted where they simply argue that the confession was obtained unfairly (e.g., because of lack of caution, refusal of a solicitor or other breach of Code C) and that therefore its admission would have such an adverse effect on the fairness of the proceedings that it ought to be excluded by virtue of s. 78. In the latter type of case, it is still a matter for the justices' discretion when they determine admissibility (*Vel* v *Chief Constable of North Wales* (1987) 151 JP 510 and *Halawa* v *Federation Against Copyright Theft* [1995] 1 Cr App R 21, dealt with at **F1.25**). Where, however, the objection is based upon s. 76, the terms of the section require that the court shall not admit the confession unless satisfied that it was not obtained by oppression or by words or conduct likely to render it unreliable. It follows that magistrates (just like the Crown Court) are obliged to determine such an issue as soon as it is raised and, if necessary, hear evidence upon the *voir dire* (*Liverpool Juvenile Court, ex parte R* [1988] QB 1). At the conclusion of his judgment in *Ex parte R*, Russell LJ summarised its effect as follows:

1. The effect of section 76(2) of the Police and Criminal Evidence Act 1984 is that in summary proceedings justices must now hold a trial within a trial if it is represented to them by the defence that a confession was or may have been obtained by either of the improper processes appearing in subparagraphs (a) or (b) of section 76(2).

2. In such a trial within a trial the defendant may give evidence confined to the question of admissibility and the justices will not be concerned with the truth or otherwise of the confession.

3. In consequence of paragraphs 1 and 2 above, the defendant is entitled to a ruling upon admissibility of a confession before, or at, the end of the prosecution case.

4. There remains a discretion open to the defendant as to the stage at which an attack is to be made upon an alleged confession. A trial within a trial will only take place before the close of the prosecution case if it is represented to the court that the confession was, or may have been, obtained by one or other of the processes set out in subparagraphs (a) or (b) of section 76(2). If no such representation is made the defendant is at liberty to raise admissibility or weight of the confession at any subsequent stage of the trial. For the avoidance of doubt, I consider that 'representation' is not the same as, nor does it include, cross-examination. Thus the court is not required to embark upon, nor is the defence bound to proceed upon, a *voir dire* merely because of a suggestion in cross-examination that the alleged confession was obtained improperly.

5. It should never be necessary to call the prosecution evidence relating to the obtaining of a confession twice.

Russell LJ's suggestion that the defence at summary trial may at their discretion delay objecting to a confession under the PACE 1984, s. 76(2), until the defence case is at odds with the decisions of the Court of Appeal in connection with challenging confessions at trials on indictment (see **D13.19** and especially *Sat-Bhambra* (1988) 88 Cr App R 55, where it was held that, once a confession had been adduced by the prosecution, it is too late for the defence to represent that it was obtained by oppression or in circumstances likely to render it unreliable). However, whatever may be the position on indictment, it is submitted that forcing the defence to have a *voir dire* before the magistrates may unnecessarily complicate and prolong proceedings.

The reason why prosecution evidence about the obtaining of a confession need only be called once is that, having heard it on the *voir dire*, the magistrates will not need to hear it again even if they rule the confession admissible. They presumably cannot prevent the defence evidence on the point being given twice over, since at the stage of the *voir dire* it goes to the confession's admissibility and at the stage of the defence case it goes to its weight. However, in his fourth paragraph, Russell LJ would seem to be encouraging defence advocates to delay formally objecting to a confession until their own case, at which stage the magistrates may still exclude the confession if the accused's evidence raises a reasonable possibility that there was a breach of s. 76(2).

AMENDMENTS OF INFORMATION

Before or during the course of a summary trial it may become apparent that the **D19.7** information is defective, either in the sense that it does not comply with the Magistrates' Courts Rules 1981, r. 100, on the formal criteria for a valid information (see **D18.1**) or in the sense that there is a discrepancy between the particulars alleged in it and the prosecution evidence adduced at trial. The MCA 1980, s. 123, greatly limits the extent to which any such defect may be used as a ground for objecting to the proceedings, but at the same time requires the court to grant an adjournment if a variation between the information and the evidence may have misled the defence.

Magistrates' Courts Act 1980, s. 123

(1)   No objection shall be allowed to any information or complaint, or to any summons or warrant to procure the presence of the defendant, for any defect in it in substance or in form, or for any variance between it and the evidence adduced on behalf of the prosecutor or complainant at the hearing of the information or complaint.

(2)   If it appears to a magistrates' court that any variance between a summons or warrant and the evidence adduced on behalf of the prosecutor or complainant is such that the defendant has been misled by the variance, the court shall, on the application of the defendant, adjourn the hearing.

If read literally, the wording of s. 123 requires the magistrates to ignore any defect in an information however gross it might be, save to the extent of granting the defence an adjournment in the circumstances set out in s. 123(2). The appellate courts have not, however, allowed the section to have such a sweeping effect. Lord Widgery CJ in *Garfield* v *Maddocks* [1974] QB 7 summarised the modern approach thus:

Those extremely wide words, which on their face seem to legalise almost any discrepancy between the evidence and the information, have in fact always been given a more restricted meaning, and in modern times the section is construed in this way, that if the variance between the evidence and the information is slight and does no injustice to the defence, the information may be allowed to stand notwithstanding the variance which occurred. On the other hand, if the variance is so substantial that it is unjust to the defendant to allow it to be adopted without a proper amendment of the information, then the practice is for the court to require the prosecution to amend in order to bring their information into line. Once they do that, of course, there is provision in [s. 123(2)] whereby an adjournment can be ordered in the interests of the defence.

In fact, the cases appear to recognise three categories of defect in an information. The first category is minor defects which do not require amendment. Thus, in *Sandwell Justices, ex parte West Midlands Passenger Transport Executive* [1979] RTR 17, the Divisional Court held that a variation between the information (which alleged that the Board had put a vehicle on the road with a defective rear nearside tyre) and the evidence (which was that it was a defective rear offside tyre) was so trivial that – even in the absence of the amendment which was in fact made – the conviction would have been upheld. It was clear that the Board was always aware of which tyre was the subject of the complaint, and had in fact brought it to court for inspection at the hearing.

The second category is defects which are substantial enough to require amendment but not so grave as to be incurable. The position here is that, if amendment is sought and allowed, the court must go on to consider whether the defence have been misled by the original error and – if they have – should adjourn in the interests of justice. Failure by the prosecution to ask for the amendment or failure by the court to grant an adjournment may lead to any conviction being reviewed by the Divisional Court and quashed by certiorari. Examples of this second category of defect include:

(a)   *Hunter* v *Coombs* [1962] 1 WLR 573. Justices convicted on an information which failed to state correctly the section under which H was being charged. The information also failed to make it clear that the prosecution case was that, having been disqualified until he passed a driving test, he had failed to display L-plates when driving on the provisional licence that he was still entitled to hold. Fenton Atkinson J stated that, if an appropriate amendment had been made, the justices would have had jurisdiction to convict but, as it was, they had convicted on a bad information and their decision had to be quashed.

(b)   *Meek* v *Powell* [1952] 1 KB 164. Justices convicted on an information setting out an offence under a repealed section of an Act which had later been re-enacted in identical terms: held that they could have amended the information (granting an adjournment if sought), or they could have dismissed it, allowing the prosecution to commence fresh proceedings under the correct Act, but what they could not properly do was to convict on the unamended information.

(c)   *New Southgate Metals Ltd* v *London Borough of Islington* [1996] Crim LR 334. Information based on the Road Traffic Act 1988, s. 41B(1)(b), wrongly referred to the Road Traffic Act 1991. No point was taken before the trial justices, but on appeal to the Crown Court a submission of no case to answer was based on the argument that the summons disclosed no offence known to law. The Divisional Court dismissed the appeal, distinguishing *Hunter* v *Coombes* on the grounds that the full particulars of the offence were accurately set out in the information and the prosecution were not put on notice in the court below.

(d)   *Newcastle-upon-Tyne Justices, ex parte John Bryce (Contractors) Ltd* [1976] 1 WLR 517. Justices amended an information which originally alleged *permitting* the use of an overladen lorry so as to allege actual use of it. It was held that, even though the amendment was more than six months from the date of the alleged offence and even though it substituted a different offence for that originally charged (on a true construction of the legislation 'use' and 'permitting use' were two separate offences), nonetheless the amendment was permissible under what is now the MCA 1980, s. 123. The defence were not misled or taken by surprise, *inter alia*, because the nature of the prosecution case had always been apparent from the statement of facts on the summons.

(e)   *Scunthorpe Justices, ex parte McPhee* (1998) 162 JP 635. The accused had been charged with robbery, but the CPS subsequently agreed to accept pleas of guilty to theft and common assault. The justices granted an application to amend the information to allege theft, but, on the clerk's objection, refused to allow an amendment to charge common assault. The objection was based on the ground that the six-month time-limit for the summary offence of common assault had elapsed. The Divisional Court held that an information could be amended after expiry of the six-month period to allege a different offence or offences provided that (a) such offence(s) alleged the 'same wrongdoing' as the original offence and (b) the amendment could be made in the interests of justice. The phrase 'same wrongdoing' meant that the new offence should arise out of the same, or substantially the same, facts as gave rise to the original offence. Both conditions were met in the instant case, and the information could have been amended accordingly.

(f)   *Wyllie* v *CPS* [1988] Crim LR 753. An information for an offence under the Road Traffic Act 1972, s. 8 (now Road Traffic Act 1988, s. 7), alleged failure to provide a specimen of urine for analysis. The justices correctly allowed it to be amended so as to allege failure to provide a specimen of blood, because, on the facts of the particular case, the evidence would have been the same whichever limb of the section the case was prosecuted under, and the defence had not been misled.

(g)   *Wright* v *Nicholson* [1970] 1 WLR 142. The Crown Court upheld a conviction for inciting a child to commit an act of gross indecency on the basis that, even though the information alleged that the offence occurred on 17 August 1967 and the appellant had provided credible alibi evidence for that date, the child's evidence as to time was vague and the incident he described could have occurred on some other day in August. The Divisional Court quashed the conviction because the variation between the information and the prosecution evidence adduced was so substantial as to mislead the defence. The Divisional Court indicated that, had the information been amended and the defence granted an adjournment to consider the altered basis of the prosecution case, then the conviction could have been upheld. Insofar as *Wright* v *Nicholson* suggests that the Crown Court on appeal may amend an information, it has been overruled by *Garfield* v *Maddocks* [1974] QB 7 but the case remains authority for the proposition stated here. (See also *Norwich Crown Court, ex parte Russell* [1993] Crim LR 518.)

It will be apparent from the decisions summarised above that amendment of an information may be sought and granted in a wide variety of situations. In particular, an amendment may properly be granted even if its effect is to substitute a different offence for that originally charged (see especially *Ex parte John Bryce (Contractors) Ltd* and *Scunthorpe Justices, ex parte McPhee*).

The third category of error in an information comprises those which are so fundamental that they cannot be rescued by amendment. Thus, in *Atterton* v *Browne* [1945] KB 122, the Divisional Court held that an information which appeared to allege that B had sold watered milk to X and Y (with whom she had never had direct contractual dealings) rather than selling it to the Milk Marketing Board who then sold it to X and Y, was so defective and inaccurate that the justices were entitled to dismiss it, rather than being obliged to allow an amendment and adjournment. In that case, Humphreys J said: 'There have been . . . many decisions [under the predecessor of s. 123] which show that the section does not operate to prevent an objection being effective where the error alleged is fundamental, such as, for instance, where one offence is charged in the information and a different offence is found in the conviction recorded by the justices, even though the two matters may seem to be very much the same thing'. Similarly, it has been held that an information laid against the wrong person (e.g., the company secretary when it should have been the company itself) is so flawed that amendment cannot assist (*City of Oxford Tramway Co.* v *Sankey* (1890) 54 JP 564 and compare *Allan* v *Wiseman* [1975] RTR 217 with *Marco (Croydon) Ltd* v *Metropolitan Police* [1984] RTR 24 on the possibly fine distinction between an information which charges the wrong person and one which merely inaccurately describes the correct person).

Where an information is defective because it breaches the rule against duplicity, the procedure under the Magistrates' Courts Rules 1981, r. 12, applies (see **D18.4**).

SUBMISSION OF NO CASE TO ANSWER

At the close of the prosecution evidence the defence may submit that there is no case to **D19.8** answer (see **D7.13** for consideration of the analogous question in committal proceedings and **D13.27** for the position in trial on indictment). The test to be applied when a submission is made was laid down by Lord Parker CJ in *Practice Direction (Submission of No Case)* [1962] 1 WLR 227. As a general rule, the justices should have their attention drawn to this Practice Direction when considering whether to conclude that the case should go no further (*Barking and Dagenham Justices, ex parte DPP* (1995) 159 JP 373).

Practice Direction (Submission of No Case) **[1962] 1 WLR 227**

A submission that there is no case to answer may properly be made and upheld: (a) when there has been no evidence to prove an essential element in the alleged offence; (b) when the evidence adduced by the prosecution has been so discredited as a result of cross-examination or is so manifestly unreliable that no reasonable tribunal could safely convict upon it.

Apart from these two situations a tribunal should not in general be called upon to reach a decision as to conviction or acquittal until the whole of the evidence which either side wishes to tender has been placed before it. If however a submission is made that there is no case to answer, the decision should depend not so much on whether the adjudicating tribunal (if compelled to do so) would at that stage convict or acquit but on whether the evidence is such that a reasonable tribunal might convict. If a reasonable tribunal might convict on the evidence so far laid before it, there is a case to answer.

The test described by Lord Parker is very close to that prescribed in *Galbraith* [1981] 1 WLR 1039 for the determination of submissions at trials on indictment, namely: Is the prosecution evidence so tenuous that, even taken at its highest, a jury properly directed could not properly convict on it? It is arguable that the *Galbraith* test is marginally more restrictive in that it requires the Crown Court judge to 'take the prosecution evidence at its highest', whereas Lord Parker allows for the evidence before justices being so discredited by cross-examination that, in their view, no reasonable tribunal could safely convict on it. Further, the reference to 'safely' convict recalls the practice at trials on indictment which was disapproved in *Galbraith*, namely that of submitting that the jury should be directed to acquit because a conviction on the evidence would be unsafe even though there was a bare sufficiency of evidence as to all elements of the offence. Many clerks in fact advise their justices in terms of *Galbraith* rather than in terms of Lord Parker's practice direction. If, however, there is a significant difference between them, it is submitted that there is no illogicality in allowing the magistrates a slightly broader discretion to accede to a submission of no case than that allowed to a Crown Court judge. Magistrates are judges of both fact and law, and, in borderline cases, it may be thought pedantic to require them to go through the motions of hearing defence evidence if they have found the prosecution evidence so unconvincing that they will not convict on it in any event. Nonetheless, the broad thrust of Lord Parker's practice direction – as of the judgment in *Galbraith* – is that, assuming the necessary minimum amount of prosecution evidence has been adduced so as to raise a case on which a reasonable tribunal *could* convict, the magistrates should allow the trial to run its course rather than acquitting on a submission. When the justices are provisionally minded to uphold the submission of no case to answer, they should first call on the prosecution to address them (*Barking and Dagenham Justices, ex parte DPP*).

DEFENCE CASE AND SPEECHES

D19.9 Paragraphs (2) to (6) of r. 13 of the Magistrates' Courts Rules 1981 entitle the defence to call evidence and to make one speech to the magistrates. The defence speech may, at the advocate's discretion, be made before or after he calls evidence. Almost invariably, he elects to address the bench after the evidence. The prosecution have no right to a closing speech, although they are customarily allowed to reply on any points of law raised in the defence summation. At its discretion, the court may allow either party a second speech. If it grants this benefit to one side, it must allow it to the other also. A second prosecution speech should be made before the defence closing – that is, the defence must always have the last word. Where the defence elect not to call evidence, they may still make a closing speech. This would seem to apply even where an unsuccessful submission of no case was made – that is, the defence advocate may decline to call evidence and, in effect, repeat his submission as a closing speech, making the point that at this stage the magistrates have to be satisfied beyond reasonable doubt by the prosecution evidence rather than simply being satisfied that there is a case to answer. In the event of defence evidence being called, the prosecution may apply to call evidence in rebuttal (r. 13(3)). It is submitted that the same principles should apply as apply at trial on indictment – that is, rebuttal evidence should generally be allowed only if something has arisen *ex improviso* during the course of the defence case which could not reasonably have been foreseen (see **D15.2**). Section 79 of the PACE 1984 (the accused should be the first defence witness unless the court otherwise directs) applies to summary trials just as it does to trials on indictment.

Magistrates' Courts Rules 1981, r. 13

(1)   On the summary trial of an information, where the accused does not plead guilty, the prosecutor shall call the evidence for the prosecution, and before doing so may address the court.

(2)   At the conclusion of the evidence for the prosecution, the accused may address the court, whether or not he afterwards calls evidence.

(3)   At the conclusion of the evidence, if any, for the defence, the prosecutor may call evidence to rebut that evidence.

(4)   At the conclusion of the evidence for the defence and the evidence, if any, in rebuttal, the accused may address the court if he has not already done so.

(5)   Either party may, with the leave of the court, address the court a second time, but where the court grants leave to one party it shall not refuse leave to the other.

(6)   Where both parties address the court twice the prosecutor shall address the court for the second time before the accused does so.

DECISION ON THE ISSUE OF GUILT

Manner of Arriving at and Announcing Decision

In the event of disagreement, a lay bench reaches its decisions (including a decision to **D19.10** acquit or convict) by a majority. It is therefore advisable for an uneven number of justices to sit if that be possible (per Lord Goddard CJ in *Barnsley* v *Marsh* [1947] KB 672 at p. 676). Assuming there is thus the possibility of a majority, justices trying an information are under a duty to reach a decision, and mandamus will lie against them if they do not (*Bridgend Justices, ex parte Randall* [1975] Crim LR 287 and *Bromley Justices, ex parte Haymills (Contractors) Ltd* [1984] Crim LR 235 in both of which cases benches of three pronounced themselves unable to decide on the charge against the defendants and sent the case for rehearing by another bench – the Divisional Court ordered the original justices to reach a decision, saying, in each case, that if two of them were unhappy about convicting then the prosecution had failed to prove its case and the finding would have to be one of not guilty).

Where the bench is even-numbered, the chairman does *not* have a casting vote. Therefore, in the event of the justices being equally divided, it will be necessary for the case to be adjourned for rehearing before a differently constituted court (*Redbridge Justices, ex parte Ram* [1992] QB 384). The practice of one justice retiring or withdrawing his opinion so as to make a majority decision possible was disapproved, *obiter*, in *Barnsley* v *Marsh*, although it was allowed in the earlier case of *Thomas, ex parte O'Hare* [1914] 1 KB 32. Nonetheless, should the justices decline to adjourn for a rehearing by a different bench and simply dismiss an information on the basis that there was no majority in favour of conviction, the dismissal is a bar to a second information for the same offence (*Kinnis* v *Graves* (1898) 67 LJ QB 583). It may be that, in practice, benches that are evenly divided frequently take the view that it would be against the interests of justice for the accused to be put through a second trial, and therefore the opinion of those in favour of acquittal is tacitly allowed to prevail, even though that would appear to be strictly against the guidance given by Lord Goddard in *Barnsley* v *Marsh* in the arguably different circumstances of affiliation proceedings.

The decision is announced in open court by the chairman. He does not state whether it is unanimous or by a majority. Unless the other magistrates demur at the time, it is presumed that the chairman's words accurately communicate the majority view, and the Divisional Court on an appeal or application for judicial review will not go behind the recorded decision (see, for example, *Middlesex Justices* (1877) 2 QBD 516).

Guilty of a Lesser Offence

D19.11 The justices are restricted to reaching a decision of guilty or not guilty on the information actually before them. It follows that they have no power to find an accused not guilty as charged but guilty of a lesser offence (*Lawrence* v *Same* [1968] 2 QB 93). This applies even when a jury, on an equivalently worded count for an offence triable either way, would be entitled under the Criminal Law Act 1967, s. 6(3), to return an alternative verdict. Thus, in *Lawrence* v *Same* a purported summary conviction for common assault on an information charging unlawful wounding was quashed as being in excess of jurisdiction. It would have been otherwise had there been two separate informations, and the court had decided to convict only on the one charging the lesser offence.

There is one major exception to the above rule. By the Road Traffic Offenders Act 1988, s. 24, magistrates may, whenever trying certain driving offences (e.g. dangerous driving) find the accused not guilty of the offence charged, but guilty of another statutorily specified driving offence. The provisions are set out in detail in **C2.15**. The overall effect is to give the magistrates a power to return an alternative verdict of guilty of a lesser offence within these limited categories of offence.

Where an information charges an attempt but the evidence establishes the full offence, the justices may nonetheless convict of the attempt (*Webley* v *Buxton* [1977] QB 481).

Setting aside a Conviction for Rehearing before Differently Constituted Bench

Magistrates' Courts Act 1980, s. 142

D19.12
(2) Where a person is convicted by a magistrates' court and it subsequently appears to the court that it would be in the interests of justice that the case should be heard again by different justices, the court may so direct.

(2A) The power conferred on a magistrates' court by subsection (2) above shall not be exercisable in relation to a conviction if—
  (a) the Crown Court has determined an appeal against—
    (i) the conviction; or
    (ii) any sentence or order imposed or made by the magistrates' court when dealing with the offender in respect of the conviction; or
  (b) the High Court has determined a case stated for the opinion of that court on any question arising in any proceeding leading to or resulting from the conviction.

The effect of a direction is that the conviction and any sentence or other order imposed are of no effect, and the accused may be remanded to appear before the second bench as if the case had had to be adjourned (s. 142(3)). The discretion conferred by s. 142 was considered in *Gwent Magistrates' Court, ex parte Carey* (1996) 160 JP 613. The defendant failed, through his own fault, to attend the trial in the magistrates' court. He later applied to reopen the case under s. 142, but the magistrates refused and he applied for judicial review to the Divisional Court. Henry LJ said, in dismissing the application, that the justices had a broad discretion and were entitled to emphasise the inconvenience to witnesses when defendants, through their own fault, did not attend. They were also entitled to take into account the apparent strength of the prosecution case although little weight should generally be attached to that factor.

SECTION D20: SENTENCING IN THE MAGISTRATES' COURT

The procedures to be followed between a plea or verdict of guilty and the court pronouncing sentence are described in section **D17** with special reference to sentencing in the Crown Court. Sentencing procedure in the magistrates' courts follows the same basic pattern. The following paragraphs, which should be read in conjunction with section **D17** and generally with **part E**, deal with some supplementary topics of relevance only to magistrates' courts.

ADJOURNMENTS PRIOR TO SENTENCE

Magistrates' Courts Act 1980, s. 10(3)

A magistrates' court may, for the purpose of enabling inquiries to be made or of determining **D20.1** the most suitable method of dealing with the case, exercise its power to adjourn after convicting the accused and before sentencing him or otherwise dealing with him; but, if it does so, the adjournment shall not be for more than four weeks at a time unless the court remands the accused in custody and, where it so remands him, the adjournment shall not be for more than three weeks at a time.

It is apparent from the latter half of s. 10(3) that, although the maximum period for adjournment after conviction is four weeks on bail or three weeks in custody, the court is not obliged to sentence at the end of the first such adjournment but may readjourn (e.g., if the reports it needs are still not ready at the end of the first period). However, the power to adjourn must be exercised judicially for the purposes laid down in s. 10(3). Thus, magistrates are not entitled to adjourn simply so that the offender will attain the age of 21 before sentence and thus become eligible for a suspended sentence of imprisonment (*Arthur* v *Stringer* (1986) 84 Cr App R 361). Where an offender is granted bail for a post-conviction adjournment, the court may impose a condition that he make himself available for the purpose of enabling inquiries or a report to be made to assist the court in dealing with him for the offence (Bail Act 1976, s. 3(6)(d)).

Section 10(3) of the MCA 1980 is overlapped by s. 30 which empowers magistrates to adjourn for medical reports once they are satisfied that the accused committed the *actus reus* of the offence. If magistrates have convicted, they must *ex hypothesi* be satisfied as to the *actus reus*, and may therefore adjourn under s. 30. However, the chief value of s. 30 is not so much at the post-conviction stage – since there would seem to be no reason why magistrates should not then adjourn for medical reports under the general powers of s. 10(3) – but before conviction when the obtaining of suitable reports and recommendations may enable the court to make a hospital order without finding the accused guilty. Where the court adjourns under s. 30 and bails the accused it *must* make it a condition of bail that he undergo a medical examination by either one or two duly qualified medical practitioners (s. 30(2)). See **D17.25** for the court's power to remand an accused to hospital for the preparation of full medical reports.

SENTENCING IN ABSENCE OF DEFENDANT

The power in the MCA 1980, s. 11(1), to proceed in the defendant's absence extends **D20.2** to passing sentence without him there once the court has found the case proved. However, this is qualified by s. 11(3) and (4):

(3)   A magistrates' court shall not in a person's absence sentence him to imprisonment or detention in a young offender institution or make a secure training order or an order under section 23 of the Powers of Criminal Courts Act 1973 that a suspended sentence shall take effect.

(4)   A magistrates' court shall not in a person's absence impose any disqualification on him, except on resumption of the hearing after an adjournment under section 10(3) above; and where a trial is adjourned in pursuance of this subsection the notice required by section 10(2) above shall include notice of the reason for the adjournment.

In short, magistrates may not pass a custodial sentence on or disqualify an absent accused save that (in the case of disqualification only) they may do so provided they have adjourned after conviction and given him notice of the reason for the adjournment.

Where an accused is represented by counsel or solicitor, the deeming provision in the MCA 1980, s. 122 (see **D18.16**) presumably has the effect of allowing the normally prohibited sentences to be passed even though the offender is not physically present, but in practice the court would almost certainly prefer to adjourn rather than take such extreme steps *in absentia*. A sentence passed in contravention of s. 11(3) or (4) will be a nullity and liable to be quashed by certiorari (see, for example, *Llandrindod Wells Justices, ex parte Gibson* [1968] 1 WLR 598 – disqualification from driving quashed because, G having pleaded guilty by post, he was disqualified from driving forthwith, no adjournment being granted). Although the prohibition in s. 11(4) will in the majority of cases be relevant to proposed disqualification from driving, it extends to any form of disqualification that a magistrates' court may order.

In the case of an absent offender being sentenced for a summary offence, the court may take account of any previous convictions that he may have, provided notice of intention to cite the convictions was served on him at least seven days prior to the hearing (MCA 1980, s. 104). The section does not apply to sentencing for either-way offences or to sentencing in a youth court. As regards sentencing for endorsable offences, an accused who does not intend to attend court is under a duty to send in his licence before the hearing date, and the court may then take account of any endorsements on the licence when sentencing. If the licence is not duly delivered, the court may adjourn for production of it. Alternatively, if the prosecution have obtained from the Driver and Vehicle Licensing Centre a printout of the details recorded there in respect of the accused, the court may proceed to sentence on the basis of the printout.

Depending on the penalty they have in mind, magistrates may consider it undesirable to proceed to sentence in the offender's absence. If so, they will adjourn. They may also be able to issue a warrant for the offender's arrest. The power to issue a warrant upon adjourning is contained in the MCA 1980, s. 13(1). The same basic conditions apply to issuing a warrant at the post–conviction stage as apply before conviction (i.e. the information must be substantiated on oath; where the proceedings were commenced by way of summons, it must be proved that the summons was served on the accused a reasonable time before the trial or adjourned trial, and the offence must be imprisonable). The recording of a conviction does, however, make two differences to the court's powers. First, its powers are widened in that it may issue a warrant even though the offence is non-imprisonable, provided it is proposing to impose a disqualification on the offender (s. 13(3)(b)). On the other hand, an additional restriction is imposed, namely that it must think it 'undesirable, by reason of the gravity of the offence, to continue the trial in the absence of the accused' (s. 13(5)). In fact, this restriction applies immediately evidence has been adduced for purposes of a not guilty trial (whether or not the court has found the accused guilty by the time of adjournment). In cases where the accused has entered a plea of guilty by post, there is no power to issue a warrant if either the magistrates decide to adjourn rather than accepting the plea, or, having convicted, they adjourn before sentence (e.g., because they are considering disqualification) (s. 13(4)).

However, if the court has adjourned once without issuing a warrant in the circumstances predicated by s. 13(4) and the defendant fails to appear for the adjourned hearing, then (subject to proof that the adjournment notice was served) a warrant may be issued.

RESTRICTIONS ON A MAGISTRATES' COURT'S POWERS OF SENTENCE

The sentences at the disposal of the courts and the restrictions on the imposition of certain types of sentence are considered in **part E**. The following discussion concerns certain special limitations on the sentencing powers of magistrates' courts.

Offences Triable Either Way   D20.3

By the MCA 1980, s. 32(1), the maximum sentence that magistrates may impose upon an offender summarily convicted of an offence triable either way listed in sch. 1 to the Act is six months' imprisonment and a fine of £5,000. Offences listed in sch. 1 are offences which are made triable either way by s. 17 (e.g., the bulk of offences under the Theft Act 1968). Where an offence is made triable either way by the statute creating it, the maximum sentence on summary conviction is six months or the term prescribed by the statute whichever is the less, plus a fine of £5,000 or the amount prescribed by the statute whichever is the greater (MCA 1980, ss. 31(1) and 32(2)).

The six-month ceiling on magistrates' powers of imprisonment contained in s. 31(1) may be expressly excluded by other enactment. Thus, if an offence-creating enactment simply provides that the maximum term on summary conviction for an offence triable either way shall be nine months' imprisonment, the effect of s. 31(1) is to reduce the maximum to six months, but, if it provides that 'notwithstanding anything in section 31(1) of the MCA 1980, the maximum term shall be nine months', then s. 31(1) is overridden and the maximum is indeed nine months.

As to the maximum fine for an offence triable either way always being £5,000, this does not apply if the offence-creating enactment was passed after 1977 (i.e. the maximum fine in such cases is whatever the statute prescribes, whether more or less than £5,000). Nor does the £5,000 maximum apply to fines for continuing offences where the court may impose a penalty for each day on which the offence is continued after a specified date, or to certain specified either-way offences under the Misuse of Drugs Act 1971 (see the MCA 1980, s. 32(4) and (5), qualifying the effect of s. 32(2)).

Summary Offences

The maximum sentence of imprisonment (if any) for a summary offence is six months D20.4 or that prescribed by the statute creating the offence, whichever is the less (MCA 1980, s. 31(1)). Again this is subject to the six-month ceiling in s. 31(1) being expressly overridden by other enactment. The maximum fine for a summary offence is whatever the offence-creating provision specifies. Nearly always, the enactment will fix the fine by reference to a level on the standard scale of fines rather than by reference to a specific sum of money (see **E17.5** for the standard scale of fines). The offence-creating provision will indicate whether a fine may be imposed in addition to any sentence of imprisonment or only as an alternative thereto.

Aggregate Prison Terms

Magistrates may make a sentence of imprisonment run concurrently with or consecu- D20.5 tively to the term of any such sentence that the offender is already serving (MCA 1980, s. 133(1)). Similarly, magistrates sentencing an offender for several offences and imposing imprisonment for two or more of them may make the terms concurrent or consecutive (ibid.). This is subject to the important qualification that the maximum *aggregate* term that a court may impose on one occasion for several offences is six months, unless it is sentencing for two or more offences triable either way, in which case it is 12 months (proviso to s. 133(1) and s. 133(2)). Where magistrates have power to deal with an offender for breach of a suspended sentence, they may – if they choose to activate part or all of the suspended term – make it run consecutively to any term of imprisonment they impose for the offences that put the offender in breach (see PCCA 1973, s. 23). In such a case, the aggregate of the suspended term and the terms for the present offences may exceed the aggregate normally permitted by s. 133(1) and (2) (see *Chamberlain* (1992) 156 JP 440 and *Lamb* [1968] 2 QB 829). An order under the CJA 1991, s. 40 (that an offender should return to custody to serve his original sentence), is to be treated in the same way, i.e. it does not count towards the aggregate permitted by s. 133 of the MCA 1980 (*Worthing Justices, ex parte Varley* [1998] 1 WLR 819).

Aggregate Fines

D20.6 When magistrates are dealing with an offender for several offences (whether summary or triable either way), they may fine him up to the statutory maximum for each offence. In other words, there is no special restriction on the aggregate fine that may be imposed.

Criminal Damage Cases

D20.7 Where magistrates deal with a charge of criminal damage under the special procedure in the MCA 1980, s. 22, as if it were a summary offence (see **D3.12**) and the accused is convicted, their powers of sentencing are restricted to three months' imprisonment or to a fine at level 4 (see **E17.5** for the standard scale). If, on the other hand, they conclude that the value involved in the offence exceeded the relevant sum and therefore adopt the usual procedure for determining mode of trial, the maximum sentence, should there be a decision for summary trial and conviction, is that which may be imposed for any other either-way offence listed in sch. 1 to the MCA 1980 (i.e. six months' imprisonment and/or a fine of £5,000).

Compensation Orders

D20.8 The maximum amount of compensation that a magistrates' court may order in respect of any one offence (whether summary or triable either way) is £5,000 (MCA 1980, s. 40(1)). Where an offender is convicted of several offences there is no special aggregate restriction on the compensation (i.e. he may be ordered to pay £5,000 for each offence). Where he is convicted of one or more offences and also asks for other offences to be taken into consideration, compensation may be ordered for the offences taken into consideration in a sum not exceeding the difference (if any) between the maximum compensation that could be ordered for the conviction offences and the sum actually awarded for those offences.

Other Sentencing Powers

D20.9 Magistrates' powers to sentence young offenders to detention in a young offender institution are limited to the same extent as are their powers to imprison. This flows from the CJA 1982, s. 1A(2), which provides that (subject to certain additional restrictions which apply in the case of juvenile offenders), 'the maximum term of detention in a young offender institution that a court may impose for an offence is the same as the maximum term of imprisonment that it may impose for that offence'. For the provisions relating to secure training orders and detention and training orders, see **E3.16** and **E3.18**.

As to the various non-custodial sentencing options, these are at the disposal of magistrates' courts to the same extent and in the same circumstances as they are at the disposal of the Crown Court. Magistrates are also entitled to suspend a prison sentence, although the term suspended must not exceed that which they could have imposed as a sentence of immediate imprisonment. A consequence of that is that a suspended sentence supervision order is beyond magistrates' powers, since such orders may be made only when the court is passing a suspended sentence for a term of more than six months in respect of one offence (see PCCA 1973, s. 26(1)).

Provisions of the Magistrates' Courts Act 1980 relating to Magistrates' Sentencing Powers

Magistrates' Courts Act 1980, ss. 31 to 33, 40 and 133   **D20.10**

31.—(1) Without prejudice to section 133 below, a magistrates' court shall not have power to impose imprisonment or a sentence of detention in a young offender institution for more than six months in respect of any one offence.

(2) Unless expressly excluded, subsection (1) above shall apply even if the offence in question is one for which a person would otherwise be liable on summary conviction to imprisonment or a sentence of detention in a young offender institution for more than six months.

[(3) and (4) Power to order imprisonment in default of payment of a fine not limited by subsection (1) above.]

32.—(1) On summary conviction of any of the offences triable either way listed in schedule 1 to this Act a person shall be liable to imprisonment for a term not exceeding six months or to a fine not exceeding the prescribed sum or both, except that—

(a) a magistrates' court shall not have power to impose imprisonment for an offence so listed if the Crown Court would not have that power in the case of an adult convicted of it on indictment;

(b) on summary conviction of an offence consisting in the incitement to commit an offence triable either way a person shall not be liable to any greater penalty than he would be liable to on summary conviction of the last-mentioned offence.

(2) For any offence triable either way which is not listed in schedule 1 to this Act, being an offence under a relevant enactment, the maximum fine which may be imposed on summary conviction shall by virtue of this subsection be the prescribed sum unless the offence is one for which by virtue of an enactment other than this subsection a larger fine may be imposed on summary conviction.

(3) Where, by virtue of any relevant enactment, a person summarily convicted of an offence triable either way would, apart from this section, be liable to a maximum fine of one amount in the case of a first conviction and of a different amount in the case of a second or subsequent conviction, subsection (2) above shall apply irrespective of whether the conviction is a first, second or subsequent one.

(4) Subsection (2) above shall not affect so much of any enactment as (in whatever words) makes a person liable on summary conviction to a fine not exceeding a specified amount for each day on which a continuing offence is continued after conviction or the occurrence of any other specified event.

(5) Subsection (2) above shall not apply on summary conviction of any of the following offences:—

(a) offences under section 5(2) of the Misuse of Drugs Act 1971 (having possession of a controlled drug) where the controlled drug in relation to which the offence was committed was a Class B or Class C drug;

(b) offences under the following provisions of that Act, where the controlled drug in relation to which the offence was committed was a Class C drug, namely—

(i) section 4(2) (production, or being concerned in the production, of a controlled drug);

(ii) section 4(3) (supplying or offering a controlled drug or being concerned in the doing of either activity by another);

(iii) section 5(3) (having possession of a controlled drug with intent to supply it to another);

(iv) section 8 (being the occupier, or concerned in the management, of premises and permitting or suffering certain activities to take place there);

(v) section 12(6) (contravention of direction prohibiting practitioner etc. from possessing, supplying etc. controlled drugs); or

(vi) section 13(3) (contravention of direction prohibiting practitioner etc. from prescribing, supplying etc. controlled drugs).

[(6)   Any power by subordinate instrument to restrict the amount of fine which may be imposed on summary conviction for an offence triable either way shall not be affected by subsection (2) above.]

(9)   In this section—

'fine' includes a pecuniary penalty but does not include a pecuniary forfeiture or pecuniary compensation;

'the prescribed sum' means £5,000 or such sum as is for the time being substituted in this definition by an order in force under section 143(3) below;

'relevant enactment' means an enactment contained in the Criminal Law Act 1977 or in any Act passed before, or in the same session as, that Act.

33.—(1)   Where in pursuance of subsection (2) of section 22 above a magistrates' court proceeds to the summary trial of an information, then, if the accused is summarily convicted of the offence—

(a)   the court shall not have power to impose on him in respect of that offence imprisonment for more than three months or a fine on level 4; and

(b)   section 38 below [power to commit for sentence when offender convicted of an offence triable either way] shall not apply as regards that offence.

[(2)   Definition of 'fine' for purposes of subsection (1).]

40.—(1)   The compensation to be paid under a compensation order made by a magistrates' court in respect of any offence of which the court has convicted the offender shall not exceed £5,000; and the compensation or total compensation to be paid under a compensation order or compensation orders made by a magistrates' court in respect of any offence or offences taken into consideration in determining sentence shall not exceed the difference (if any) between the amount or total amount which under the preceding provisions of this subsection is the maximum for the offence or offences of which the offender has been convicted and the amount or total amounts (if any) which are in fact ordered to be paid in respect of that offence or those offences.

(2)   In subsection (1) above 'compensation order' has the meaning assigned to it by section 35(1) of the Powers of Criminal Courts Act 1973.

133.—(1)   Subject to section 102 of the Crime and Disorder Act 1998, a magistrates' court imposing imprisonment or a sentence of detention in a young offender institution on any person may order that the term of imprisonment or detention in a young offender institution shall commence on the expiration of any other term of imprisonment or detention in a young offender institution imposed by that or any other court; but where a magistrates' court imposes two or more terms of imprisonment or detention in a young offender institution to run consecutively the aggregate of such terms shall not, subject to the provisions of this section, exceed six months.

(2)   If two or more of the terms imposed by the court are imposed in respect of an offence triable either way which was tried summarily otherwise than in pursuance of section 22(2) above [criminal damage triable only summarily if the value involved was less than £5,000], the aggregate of the terms so imposed and any other terms imposed by the court may exceed six months but shall not, subject to the following provisions of this section, exceed 12 months.

(2A)   In relation to the imposition of terms of detention in a young offender institution subsection (2) above shall have effect as if the reference to an offence triable either way were a reference to such an offence or an offence triable only on indictment.

(3)   The limitations imposed by the preceding subsections shall not operate to reduce the aggregate of the terms that the court may impose in respect of any offences below the term which the court has power to impose in respect of any one of those offences.

(4)   Where a person has been sentenced by a magistrates' court to imprisonment and a fine for the same offence, a period of imprisonment imposed for non-payment of the fine, or for want of sufficient distress to satisfy the fine, shall not be subject to the limitations imposed by the preceding subsections.

(5)   For the purposes of this section a term of imprisonment shall be deemed to be imposed in respect of an offence if it is imposed as a sentence or in default of payment of a fine adjudged to be paid by the conviction or for want of sufficient distress to satisfy such a sum.

PRESENTING THE FACTS, CHARACTER AND ANTECEDENTS

The procedure before sentence is passed is basically the same as in the Crown Court – **D20.11** the prosecution representative summarises the facts if there has been a guilty plea, reports (if any) are read, and mitigation is presented. In road traffic cases, it is not the practice to provide antecedents or even a list of convictions, although the bench will know of current endorsements from the offender's licence or (failing that) a printout from the Driver and Vehicle Licensing Centre.

ADJUDICATION ON AND PRONOUNCEMENT OF SENTENCE

As with any adjudication of a magistrates' court, the decision as to sentence may be by **D20.12** a majority of those sitting. In the event of an equal division, the court could adjourn under the MCA 1980, s. 10 (adjournments after conviction and before sentence), and reconsider the matter at the resumed hearing. The court passing sentence need not be composed of the justices who convicted the offender (or who sat at an earlier post-conviction hearing when the case was adjourned) (MCA 1980, s. 121(7)).

In announcing sentence, magistrates are obliged to give their reasons in circumstances similar to but slightly wider than those in which the Crown Court is obliged to give reasons (see **D17.34**). In particular, when passing a custodial sentence, the CJA 1991, s. 1(4), requires that they must explain why s. 1(2)(a) or (b) of that Act applies (see **E1.8**). Where they pass a custodial sentence which is for a longer term than is commensurate with the offence, they are also required, by s. 2(4) of the 1991 Act, to explain their reasons (see **E1.13**). A magistrates' court is also required to record the reason for passing a custodial sentence in the warrant of commitment and in the court register. Magistrates must also give reasons for not activating a suspended sentence in full and for not making a compensation order (see PCCA 1973, ss. 23(1) and 35(1) respectively).

The MCA 1980, s. 142(1), allows a magistrates' court to vary or rescind its decision as to sentence. The power is similar to that in respect of setting aside a conviction (see **D19.12**). The power should not, however, be used to punish an offender who has misbehaved in the dock after pronouncement of sentence by increasing what was first announced (*Powell* (1985) 7 Cr App R (S) 247, a case which in fact concerned misbehaviour by an offender at the Crown Court). In *Coles v East Penwith Justices* (1998) 162 JP 687, the Divisional Court held that the power in s. 142(1) was confined to cases where the defendant had been found guilty. Consequently, there was no power to revoke a defendant's costs order under s. 142(1) where the prosecution had withdrawn the charges. For the general principles to be applied when considering whether to vary a sentence by increasing it, see **D17.37**, where the question is considered in relation to the Crown Court. It is submitted that a magistrates' court – like the Crown Court – may use its powers under s. 142(1) to increase sentence, but should do so only in exceptional circumstances.

Magistrates' Courts Act 1980, s. 142

(1) A magistrates' court may vary or rescind a sentence or other order imposed or made by it when dealing with an offender if it appears to the court to be in the interests of justice to do so; and it is hereby declared that this power extends to replacing a sentence or order which for any reason appears to be invalid by another which the court has power to impose or make.

(1A) The power conferred on a magistrates' court by subsection (1) above shall not be exercisable in relation to any sentence or order imposed or made by it when dealing with an offender if—

(a)   the Crown Court has determined an appeal against—
   (i)   that sentence or order;
   (ii)   the conviction in respect of which that sentence or order was imposed or made;
or
   (iii) any other sentence or order imposed or made by the magistrates' court when dealing with the offender in respect of that conviction (including a sentence or order replaced by that sentence or order); or
(b)   the High Court has determined a case stated for the opinion of that court on any question arising in any proceeding leading to or resulting from the imposition or making of the sentence or order.

[(2), (2A) and (3)   Relate to setting aside a conviction: **D19.12.**]

(5)   Where a sentence or order is varied under subsection (1) above, the sentence or other order, as so varied, shall take effect from the beginning of the day on which it was originally imposed or made, unless the court otherwise directs.

COMMITTAL FOR SENTENCE

Powers to Commit for Sentence

D20.13   As an alternative to passing sentence themselves, magistrates may in some circumstances commit the offender to the Crown Court to be sentenced. The major powers to commit for sentence are as follows:

(a)   MCA 1980, s. 38. General power to commit adult offenders summarily convicted of an offence triable either way.

(b)   MCA 1980, s. 37. Power of juvenile court to commit offenders aged 15, 16 or 17 convicted of an indictable offence if six months' detention would be an inadequate penalty. (When the CDA 1998, s. 73 and sch. 8, para. 34, are brought into force, the MCA 1980, s. 37, will be repealed.)

(c)   MCA 1980, s. 38A. Power to commit adult offenders convicted of a triable-either-way offence as a result of a guilty plea indicated before the mode of trial procedure has been embarked upon.

(d)   PCCA 1973, s. 24(2)(a). Power to commit offender in breach of a Crown Court suspended sentence to be dealt with for the breach.

(e)   PCCA 1973, s. 1B(5), and CJA 1991, sch. 2, para. 7(2)(b). Power to commit offender in breach of a Crown Court probation order or conditional discharge to be dealt with for the breach.

(f)   CJA 1991, s. 40(3). Power to commit a prisoner who commits an imprisonable offence between the date of his early release and the expiry of the full term of his sentence. The Crown Court may then order that he be returned to prison.

(g)   CJA 1967, s. 56. Supplementary power to commit offenders who are being committed under one of powers (a) to (e) to be sentenced also for other matters that would otherwise fall to be dealt with by the magistrates.

Of the above powers, (a), (c), and (g) are considered below; (b) is a power possessed by the youth court and is considered at **D21.27**; (d), (e) and (f) relate to specific sentences and are considered at **E2.8, E5.7** and **E1.7**.

Where the defence wish to quash a committal for sentence on the basis that it was in excess of jurisdiction, the remedy is by way of judicial review (see **D25.26**).

Committal under the Magistrates' Courts Act 1980, s. 38

D20.14   **Magistrates' Courts Act 1980, s. 38**

(1)   This section applies where on the summary trial of an offence triable either way (not being an offence as regards which this section is excluded by section 33 above) a person who is not less than 18 years old is convicted of the offence.

(2)   If the court is of opinion—

(a)   that the offence or the combination of the offence and one or more offences associated with it was so serious that greater punishment should be inflicted for the offence than the court has power to impose; or

(b)   in the case of a violent or sexual offence, that a custodial sentence for a term longer than the court has power to impose is necessary to protect the public from serious harm from him,

the court may commit the offender in custody or on bail to the Crown Court for sentence in accordance with the provisions of section 42 of the Powers of Criminal Courts Act 1973.

(2A)   Where the court commits a person under subsection (2) above, section 56 of the Criminal Justice Act 1967 (which enables a magistrates' court, where it commits a person under this section in respect of an offence, also to commit him to the Crown Court to be dealt with in respect of certain other offences) shall apply accordingly.

The PCCA 1973, s. 42, essentially provides that, following a committal for sentence under the MCA 1980, s. 38 or 38A, the Crown Court may deal with the offender as if he had just been convicted on indictment. Therefore, the combined effect of the MCA 1980, s. 38, and the PCCA 1973, s. 42, is to provide a mechanism by which a summarily convicted offender, who merits more than the maximum sentence the magistrates could impose, may be dealt with for his offence with appropriate severity.

Limitations on the Power to Commit under s. 38

Age   The offender must be at least 18 at date of conviction. Although the section is not **D20.15** explicit on the point, it is submitted that it only applies where he was 18 or over when mode of trial was determined. If he was a juvenile when the plea was taken and therefore had no right to elect trial on indictment, it would be unfair to expose him to the greater penalties which the Crown Court could inflict upon committal under the MCA 1980, s. 38, even if he has attained the age of 18 by the date of conviction. For full discussion of the problems raised by defendants who attain the age of 18 during the course of proceedings, see **D21.30** to **D21.32**.

Nature of the Offence   The offender must have been convicted of an offence triable **D20.16** either way, not a summary offence. Furthermore, the MCA 1980, s. 33, provides that the power to commit for sentence contained in s. 38 shall not apply when an offender is convicted of an offence of criminal damage which the magistrates dealt with as if it were summary because the value involved was less than £5,000: see **D3.12** for the special procedure for criminal damage charges.

Reason for Powers of Punishment Being Insufficient   In order to commit to the **D20.17** Crown Court for sentence, the magistrates must be of the opinion:

(a)   that the offence (in combination where appropriate with associated offences) is so serious that the proper punishment exceeds its powers; or

(b)   that, in the case of a violent or sexual offence, a custodial sentence longer than it can impose is necessary to protect the public from serious harm from him.

The grounds for committal mirror the criteria in s. 2(2) of the 1991 Act, which deals with determination of length of sentence, and those criteria are discussed at **E1.13**. The terms 'violent offence' and 'sexual offence' are discussed at **E1.10**.

The usual circumstances which give rise to a committal based upon s. 38(2)(a) are:

(i)   where the accused is revealed as having a record of previous convictions; or
(ii)   he asks for further offences to be taken into consideration.

As far as (i) is concerned, the CJA 1991, s. 29, makes it plain that 'the court may take into account any previous convictions of the offender or any failure of his to respond to previous sentences'. This must apply to a court considering whether to commit, just as it applies to the court which eventually passes sentence (see **E1.8**). As far as (ii) is concerned, the relevance of offences taken into consideration is specifically accepted by the CJA 1991, s. 31(2)(b), which states that 'an offence is associated with another if. . . the offender admits the commission of it . . . and requests the court to take it into consideration in sentencing him'. As far as circumstances outside categories (i) and (ii) above are concerned, the Divisional Court has dealt with a series of cases on the question of whether the magistrates have an unfettered discretion to commit for sentence under s. 38, or are bound (in the absence of new material) by their original acceptance of jurisdiction. In *Manchester Magistrates' Court, ex parte Kaymanesh* (1994) 15 Cr App R (S) 838, K was charged with offences under the Trade Descriptions Act 1968 and the Fair Trading Act 1973. The magistrates accepted jurisdiction, a date was set for trial and K was convicted two months later. He had no previous convictions and there were no offences to be taken into consideration. The magistrates committed him to the Crown Court for sentence. This was a particularly serious decision for K, as the sentencing options on summary trial did not include custody, whereas those available after trial on indictment (and hence on committal for sentence) did. K sought to have the decision quashed. The Divisional Court held that it was wrong to allow K to be committed for sentence after he had given up his right to jury trial in the knowledge that the magistrates had decided that their powers of punishment were adequate. The magistrates' decision was quashed; Balcombe LJ stated that, if nothing further came to light after the decision to try the case summarily had been made, the magistrates should not normally commit for sentence to the Crown Court.

The court took a different view in *Sheffield Crown Court, ex parte DPP* (1994) 15 Cr App R (S) 768 and *Dover Justices, ex parte Pamment* (1994) 15 Cr App R (S) 778. In both of these cases, the Divisional Court held that the power of the magistrates to commit under s. 38 was unfettered. Their lordships held that there was nothing unreasonable or illogical about permitting a court to form one view at the stage of deciding on summary trial, and a different view at the stage of deciding to commit for sentence. In *North Sefton Magistrates' Court, ex parte Marsh* (1995) 16 Cr App R (S) 401, the Divisional Court came down firmly in favour of a broad interpretation of s. 38, and stated that *Ex parte Kaymanesh* was wrongly decided. The magistrates had 'an open textured decision' on whether to commit under s. 38, which was apparently separate from their decision on mode of trial. However, the Divisional Court in both *Ex parte Marsh* and *Ex parte Pamment* did stress that magistrates should think carefully when deciding to accept jurisdiction because normally an accused should be able to conclude that, once jurisdiction had been accepted, he would not on the same facts be committed for sentence.

As far as s. 38(2)(b) is concerned (see (b) above), the position is that committal will be justified where circumstances are revealed which require a longer sentence to protect the public from serious harm. This limb of the power of committal is confined to violent offences and sexual offences.

In *Warley Justices, ex parte DPP* [1999] 1 WLR 216, the Divisional Court dealt with the implications of the plea before venue procedure laid down in MCA 1980, s. 17A (see **D3.4**), for the magistrates deciding whether to commit for sentence, and stated as follows.

(a)   The magistrates must have regard to the discount to be granted on a plea of guilty when deciding whether the punishment which they would have power to inflict would be adequate.

(b)   Where the gravity of the offence was such that even with allowance for the guilty plea and mitigation it was obvious that the punishment should exceed their powers, they should commit to the Crown Court without seeking any pre-sentence report or hearing mitigation.

(c)   The accused should be allowed to make a brief submission in opposition to that course and, if the court was minded to change its mind, the prosecution should also be invited to make submissions.

(d)   If there was a dispute as to the facts which triggered off the need for a *Newton* hearing (see **D17.2**), the magistrates should proceed to hold one if they consider that, whatever the outcome of the hearing, they had adequate powers of sentencing.

(e)   If they considered that, whatever the outcome, the case would have to be committed for sentence, it was clearly preferable to leave the *Newton* hearing to the Crown Court.

(f)   If the decision as to whether to commit for sentence might depend on the outcome of the *Newton* hearing, the magistrates should proceed to conduct it.

In *Rafferty* [1998] 2 Cr App R (S) 449, the Court of Appeal dealt with the question of whether a committal should be on bail or in custody where the defendant indicated a plea of guilty in the plea before venue procedure. They made it clear that, if such a defendant had been on bail, he should normally remain on bail when committed, even if it was anticipated that a custodial sentence would be imposed by the Crown Court, unless there were good reasons for remanding him in custody. If he was already in custody, it would be unusual, if the reasons for refusing bail remained unchanged, to alter the position.

Powers of and Procedure in the Crown Court Following a Committal under the Magistrates' Courts Act 1980, s. 38

Powers of Criminal Courts Act 1973, s. 42(1)   D20.18

> Where an offender is committed by a magistrates' court for sentence under section 38 or 38A of the Magistrates' Courts Act 1980 . . ., the Crown Court shall enquire into the circumstances of the case and shall have power to deal with the offender in any manner in which it could deal with him if he had just been convicted of the offence on indictment before the court.

The Lord Chief Justice's *Practice Direction (Crown Court: Allocation of Business)* [1995] 1 WLR 1083 states that a committal under the MCA 1980, s. 38, shall be to the most convenient location of the Crown Court (para. 8 under the heading 'Classification'). In choosing the most convenient location, magistrates should have regard to the locations specified by a presiding judge of the relevant circuit as being those to which cases should normally be committed from their petty sessions area (para. 9). The Lord Chief Justice's practice direction qualifies the category of professional judge to whom committals for sentence should be allocated by providing that he should be either (a) a resident or designated judge of the Crown Court location in question, or (b) a circuit judge who regularly sits there and has been nominated for the purpose by the resident or designated judge, or (c) an experienced recorder specifically approved by a presiding judge of the circuit, or (d) failing any of the above, a circuit judge or recorder selected by the resident or designated judge to hear a particular case (para. 5 under the heading 'Allocation of business within the Crown Court').

Before proceeding to hear the case, the court should confirm that the person before it has indeed been committed for sentence by the magistrates' court. The usual practice is for the clerk simply to ask him if he admits that fact. In default of such admission, the prosecution must prove the committal by formal evidence (see a note appended by Lord Goddard CJ to his judgment in *Barker* [1951] 1 All ER 479). The evidence might come from a certified copy of the magistrates' court register and a police officer who was present in the lower court on the relevant occasion. Once the committal has been admitted or proved, the procedure before sentence is passed is exactly the same as when there is a guilty plea on indictment. Where the person committed for sentence indicates that he is appealing against his conviction in the lower court, the sentencing proceedings should be adjourned until the conclusion of the appeal (*Faithful* [1950] 2 All ER 1251). If, however, the court inadvertently disposes of the committal for sentence in ignorance of the fact that the offender is appealing against conviction, there is no objection to the appeal subsequently being heard and, if it succeeds, the sentence passed on the committal will simply fall with the conviction (*Croydon Crown Court, ex parte Bernard* [1981] 1 WLR 116). Where the offender asked the lower court to take other offences into consideration, he is not thereby bound to take the same course in the Crown Court (i.e. the normal procedure for taking offences into consideration should be followed in the Crown Court and, in the absence of a request to consider the other matters, they must be ignored: *Davies* (1980) 2 Cr App R (S) 364).

What if there is a dispute between prosecution and defence about the facts of the offence upon which the accused has been committed? Which court ought to hold the *Newton* hearing to determine the factual basis for sentence: the Crown Court or the magistrates? The issue arose in *Munroe v CPS* [1988] Crim LR 823. M was charged with assault occasioning actual bodily harm upon a police officer. In the magistrates' court, he was unrepresented, elected summary trial and pleaded guilty. The magistrates committed him for sentence at the Crown Court under s. 38. The Crown Court was told that M's plea was based on a single blow with an open hand. The officer alleged four punches with a clenched fist. M said he had told the magistrates of his disagreement with the prosecution version. The Crown Court adjourned for inquiries to be made, but the clerk to the justices had no record of M disagreeing with the prosecution version. At the resumed hearing, it was submitted that the case should be remitted to the magistrates for them to determine the factual basis for sentence, and consider in the light of their findings whether to sentence M, or commit him. The Crown Court held (a) that it had no power to remit and (b) even if it had, it would not have exercised it. The factual basis for sentence should be decided in the Crown Court. M appealed by way of case stated. The Divisional Court held that the Crown Court did have power to remit the matter to the magistrates. Equally, it had power to try the issue itself. Whether the discretion to remit should be exercised will depend on the stage at which the dispute about the facts becomes apparent:

(a) Where the matter arises before the magistrates (e.g., after a summary trial) they should hear any evidence necessary to determine the issues and, if they then decide to commit for sentence, must ensure that the Crown Court is informed of any findings of fact. The Crown Court should then sentence upon the facts found by the magistrates, and not allow the dispute to be revived.

(b) If the issue does not arise until the case is before the Crown Court, that court should itself determine the issue, hearing any necessary evidence before proceeding to sentence.

(c) In circumstances such as the present case, where M claimed to have raised the issue before the magistrates but they had not attempted to decide it, the Crown Court must determine the course to follow, taking into account all the circumstances. These would include the facts of the offence as alleged by both parties; whether on the balance of probabilities the accused had raised the issue in the court below; the Crown Court's awareness that the accused's record had been considered serious enough for committal; and the delay which remitting the issue would cause.

If those matters were taken into account the Divisional Court would be slow to interfere with the Crown Court's decision. In this case, there were no grounds for interfering with the Crown Court's decision that, had it power to remit, it would not have exercised it (see also *Warley Justices, ex parte DPP* [1999] 1 WLR 216).

In disposing of the committal the Crown Court is not limited to the sentence that the magistrates' court could have imposed but may deal with the offender as if he had just been convicted on indictment. One consequence of this is that if he has attained an age of relevance to sentencing powers during the period between the magistrates' court and Crown Court proceedings then he is to be sentenced on the basis of his age when he appears in the Crown Court (*Robinson* (1962) CSP L12–3A01). For example, an offender under 21 when committed but aged 21 on appearance in the Crown Court, is liable to imprisonment. The Crown Court on a committal for sentence may itself defer sentence even though the magistrates also deferred sentence before deciding to commit (PCCA 1973, s. 1(8A)). Where the lower court adjourned for reports in circumstances giving rise to a reasonable expectation that the sentence would be non-custodial if the reports should be favourable, the Crown Court on committal for sentence is as much precluded from imposing a custodial sentence as the magistrates would have been (see *Rennes* (1985) 7 Cr App R (S) 343 applying the general principle in *Gillam* (1980) 2 Cr App R (S) 267). Notwithstanding anything prima facie to the contrary in the Road Traffic Act 1988, any power or duty to order endorsement of a driving licence shall be exercised by the Crown Court not the convicting magistrates' court in the event of a committal for sentence (CJA 1967, s. 56).

Committal under the Magistrates' Courts Act 1980, s. 38A

A new s. 38A was inserted in the MCA 1980 by the C(S)A 1997. Its purpose is to deal **D20.19** with the situation where the magistrates' court has committed a person for trial for some offences, but has to deal with him for other related either-way offences. In this context, one offence is related to another if they both be tried on the same indictment (s. 38A(6)). If the person committed for trial has indicated an intention to plead guilty to those related offences, he must, by virtue of the plea before venue procedure (see **D3.4**), be treated as if he had pleaded guilty to them. Section 38A gives the magistrates power to commit the offender to the Crown Court for sentence for the related offences, even if they do not meet the requirements laid down in s. 38, i.e. that the offence is so serious that the magistrates' powers of punishment are inadequate or (in case of a violent or sexual offence) that a sentence longer than they have power to impose is necessary to protect the public from serious harm from him. In s. 38A(2) the power to commit under s. 38A is stated to be 'in accordance with section 56 of the CJA 1967' (see **D20.20**).

The powers of the Crown Court to sentence the offender for the offence committed for sentence under s. 38A depend on whether:

(a) it convicts him of one or more related offences; or
(b) the magistrates' court on committing him for sentence under s. 38A stated that it also had the power to do so under s. 38.

If either of these conditions is fulfilled, then the Crown Court will have the power to impose any sentence which it would have power to impose if the offender had been convicted on indictment. If they are not, the Crown Court's powers to deal with the offender in respect of which he has been committed for sentence are limited to those of the magistrates.

Magistrates' Courts Act 1980, s. 38A

(1) This section applies where—
(a) a person who is 18 or over appears or is brought before a magistrates' court ('the court') on an information charging him with an offence triable either way ('the offence');
(b) he or his representative indicates that he would plead guilty if the offence were to proceed to trial; and
(c) proceeding as if section 9(1) above was complied with and he pleaded guilty under it, the court convicts him of the offence.
(2) If the court has committed the offender to the Crown Court for trial for one or more related offences, that is to say, one or more offences which, in its opinion, are related to the

offence, it may commit him in custody or on bail to the Crown Court to be dealt with in respect of the offence in accordance with the provisions of section 42 of the Powers of Criminal Courts Act 1973.

(3)   If the power conferred by subsection (2) above is not exercisable but the court is still to inquire, as examining justices, into one or more related offences—

(a)   it shall adjourn the proceedings relating to the offence until after the conclusion of its inquiries; and

(b)   if it commits the offender to the Crown Court for trial for one or more related offences, it may then exercise that power.

(4)   Where the court—

(a)   commits the offender to the Crown Court to be dealt with in respect of the offence; and

(b)   does not state that, in its opinion, it also has power so to commit him under section 38(2) above,

the provisions of section 42 of the Powers of Criminal Courts Act 1973 shall not apply unless he is convicted before the Crown Court of one or more of the related offences.

(5)   Where those provisions of that section do not apply, the Crown Court shall have power to deal with the offender in respect of the offence in any manner in which the magistrates' court could deal with him if it had just convicted him of the offence.

(5A)   Where the court commits a person under subsection (2) above, section 56 of the Criminal Justice Act 1967 (which enables a magistrates' court, where it commits a person under this section in respect of an offence, also to commit him to the Crown Court to be dealt with in respect of certain other offences) shall apply accordingly.

(6)   For the purposes of this section one offence is related to another if, where they both to be prosecuted on indictment, the charges for them could be joined in the same indictment.

Committal under the Criminal Justice Act 1967, s. 56

D20.20   The CJA 1967 gives a power to commit for sentence which may be used to supplement a committal under any of the following provisions:

(a)   MCA 1980, s. 38 (see **D20.14** to **D20.18**);

(b)   MCA 1980, s. 37 (power of youth court to commit a person aged 15, 16 or 17 who merits more than six months' detention in a young offender institution for an either-way offence (see **D21.27**);

(c)   CJA 1991, sch. 2, para. 7(2)(b) (power to commit an offender whose summary conviction puts him in breach of a probation order made by the Crown Court);

(d)   PCCA 1973, s. 1B(5) (power to commit an offender whose summary conviction puts him in breach of a conditional discharge imposed by the Crown Court);

(e)   PCCA 1973, s. 24(2) (power to commit an offender whose summary conviction puts him in breach of a suspended sentence passed by the Crown Court);

(f)   CJA 1991, s. 40(3) (power to commit a released prisoner who commits an offence prior to the expiry of the full term of his sentence);

(g)   Vagrancy Act 1824 (power to commit incorrigible rogues).

The above committal powers are referred to below as 'primary powers'.

A similar problem arises in relation to (f) above. Section 56(2) permitted the committal of an offender with a view to revocation of his parole licence under the CJA 1967, s. 62(6), to act as a primary power, triggering off the secondary power to commit under s. 56. Section 62(6) was repealed by the CJA 1991, but s. 56(2) still refers to the repealed section, rather than the section which has replaced it, namely the CJA 1991, s. 40(3)(b). In *Harrow Justices, ex parte Jordan* [1997] 1 WLR 84, the Divisional Court said that the magistrates' court could commit the offender to the Crown Court to be dealt with for both the new offence and the return to custody (see also *Burton on Trent Justices, ex parte Smith* (1997) 161 JP 741).

By the CJA 1967, s. 56(1)(a), when a magistrates' court exercises a primary committal power in respect of an indictable offence, it may also commit the offender to the Crown Court to be dealt with in respect of any other offence of which he stands convicted (whether summary or indictable) that it (the magistrates' court) has jurisdiction to deal with; s. 56(1)(a) expressly states that, provided the committing court would be able to deal with the matter if it were not to commit, the power to commit arises even if the conviction was by a different court. Thus, to take the example of a magistrates' court which has decided to commit an offender under the MCA 1980, s. 38, for one offence triable either way, a committal under the CJA 1967, s. 56(1)(a), may, *inter alia*, relate to:

(a)   another less serious either-way offence of which the magistrates have convicted the offender on the same occasion;

(b)   a summary offence of which they have convicted the offender on the same occasion;

(c)   a suspended sentence, probation order or conditional discharge passed or made by their or another magistrates' court on a previous occasion and of which the offender is in breach by reason of his present conviction (provided, in the case of a probation order or conditional discharge, they have first obtained permission from the convicting court to deal with the breach).

The reason why a committal under the MCA 1980, s. 38, for the secondary offence would be inappropriate in situation (a) is that, the offence not being serious in itself, the magistrates' powers of sentencing for it would be sufficient. In situation (b), a committal under s. 38 would be inappropriate simply because the section does not extend to summary offences. One other frequent occasion for use of the CJA 1967, s. 56, is where a summary conviction puts the offender in breach of a suspended sentence passed by the Crown Court and the magistrates consider that – although the breach must be committed to the Crown Court under the PCCA 1973, s. 24(2) – the offence itself is not serious enough to warrant committal under the MCA 1980, s. 38. The court should then commit the offender under the PCCA 1973, s. 24(2), for possible activation of the suspended sentence and under the CJA 1967, s. 56, for sentence for the present offence.

Where the offence in respect of which the primary power of committal arises is summary, the magistrates' powers under s. 56 are slightly more limited in that they may commit only in respect of (a) any other offence carrying imprisonment or disqualification from driving of which their court has convicted the offender, or (b) breach of a suspended sentence passed on the offender by their or another magistrates' court (s. 56(1)(b)). In fact, the primary power of committal will, in practice, nearly always relate to an indictable offence so s. 56(1)(b) is of little significance.

Following a committal under s. 56(1), the Crown Court may – after inquiring into the circumstances of the case – deal with the offender in any way the magistrates' court might have done had it not committed (s. 56(5)). The Crown Court's powers on a committal under s. 56 are thus identical to the powers of the lower court (cf. the position where there is a committal under the MCA 1980, s. 38). This limitation on the Crown Court's powers reveals the basic purpose of a committal under the CJA 1967, s. 56, namely, to enable one court to deal with an offender for all matters outstanding against him rather than have the sentencing function split between the Crown Court and the magistrates. The purpose is *not* to expose the offender to risk of greater punishment than the lower court could inflict. One oddity of the respective wordings of s. 56(5) and the PCCA 1973, s. 42, is that, on a committal under the former section, the Crown Court's sentencing powers are governed by the offender's age at date of committal (*Wyre Magistrates' Court, ex parte Boardman* (1987) 9 Cr App R (S) 214), whereas on a committal under s. 38 it is age at date of sentence by the Crown Court that is relevant (see above).

SECTION D21: TRIAL OF JUVENILES

INTRODUCTION

D21.1 The normal rules governing mode of trial are much modified in the cases of juveniles. The great majority of juveniles are tried and sentenced in *youth courts*. The term was introduced by the CJA 1991, s. 70. Formerly, of course, such courts were known as juvenile courts. By the CYPA 1933, s. 45, youth courts are courts of *summary* jurisdiction. It follows that trial in the youth court is merely a form of summary trial (for the special rules attaching to the constitution and proceedings of youth courts, see **D21.13**). However, whereas an adult may never be tried summarily for an offence triable only on indictment and always has the right to elect trial on indictment for an offence triable either way, a juvenile may and normally is tried summarily for indictable offences, whatever his wishes as to mode of trial may be. In other words, he has no right of election. If a juvenile is committed to the Crown Court for trial it is because the *magistrates* have decided that they should not accept jurisdiction – the most the juvenile may do is to make representations for or against staying in the lower court.

In determining the court in which a juvenile should be tried, it is necessary to ask, first, whether it is one of the exceptional cases in which juveniles may or must be tried on indictment. If the answer to that is no, the second question is whether it is one of the exceptional cases in which a juvenile may or must be tried in a court of summary jurisdiction other than a youth court (i.e. in an ordinary magistrates' court). In the remainder of this section, magistrates' courts other than youth courts are referred to as 'adult courts'. If the answer to the second question is also no, the juvenile will be tried in a youth court.

Definitions of 'Juvenile', 'Adult', 'Child' and 'Young Person'

D21.2 (a) *Juvenile*. The term is not expressly defined by the relevant legislation. It is, however, convenient to refer to those particularly subject to the jurisdiction of the youth court by a generic term. To call them 'youths' would risk confusion with the more narrowly defined 'young persons' (see (d) below). Moreover, the term 'juvenile' retains some statutory authority in referring to those who have not yet attained their eighteenth birthday. The MCA 1980, s. 29(1)(a), for example, refers to 'a person under the age of 18 ("the juvenile")'. 'Juvenile' is, therefore, used in this sense throughout.

(b) *Adult*. In the context of criminal procedure and mode of trial, the definition of 'adult' is simply a function of the definition of juvenile – i.e., an adult is any person aged 18 or over. In the context of sentencing, however, 'adult' is sometimes used to mean those aged 21 or over, since it is at that age that an offender becomes liable to imprisonment rather than detention in a young offender institution.

(c) *Child*. By the CYPA 1933, s. 107, 'child' (when used in the Act) means a person under the age of 14 years, unless the context otherwise requires. The CYPA 1969, s. 70(1), contains a similar provision in respect of the majority of the provisions of that Act, while the CYPA 1963, s. 65(3), provides that the 1963 Act shall be construed as one with the 1933 Act. It should be noted, however, that in some contexts 'child' is given an extended meaning (e.g., for purposes of children in care where it connotes any person under 18).

(d) *Young person*. The definition sections referred to in (c) above also define 'young person' as a 'person who has attained the age of 14 years and is under the age of 18 years'. Thus, juveniles divide into children and young persons, the former being under 14 and the latter aged 14 to 17 inclusive.

DETERMINING MODE OF TRIAL OF JUVENILES

The limited circumstances in which it is possible for a juvenile to be tried on indictment **D21.3** are set out in the MCA 1980, s. 24.

Magistrates' Courts Act 1980, s. 24

(1) Where a person under the age of 18 appears or is brought before a magistrates' court on an information charging him with an indictable offence other than homicide, he shall be tried summarily unless—

(a) the offence is such as is mentioned in sub-section (2) of section 53 of the Children and Young Persons Act 1933 (under which young persons convicted on indictment of certain grave crimes may be sentenced to be detained for long periods) and the court considers that if he is found guilty of the offence it ought to be possible to sentence him in pursuance of subsection (3) of that section; or

(b) he is charged jointly with a person who has attained the age of 18 and the court considers it necessary in the interests of justice to commit them both for trial;

and accordingly in a case falling within paragraph (a) or (b) of this subsection the court shall commit the accused for trial if either it is of opinion that there is sufficient evidence to put him on trial or it has power under section 6(2) above so to commit him without consideration of the evidence.

(1A) Where a magistrates' court—

(a) commits a person under the age of 18 for trial for an offence of homicide; or

(b) in a case falling within subsection (1)(a) above, commits such a person for trial for an offence,

the court may also commit him for trial for any other indictable offence with which he is charged at the same time if the charges for both offences could be joined in the same indictment.

(2) Where, in a case falling within subsection (1)(b) above, a magistrates' court commits a person under the age of 18 for trial for an offence with which he is charged jointly with a person who has attained that age, the court may also commit him for trial for any other indictable offence with which he is charged at the same time (whether jointly with the person who has attained that age or not) if that other offence arises out of circumstances which are the same as or connected with those giving rise to the first-mentioned offence.

[(3) and (4) concern maximum powers of punishment when a juvenile is tried summarily for an indictable offence.]

The CDA 1998, sch. 8, para. 40(2), amends s. 24(2) so as to substitute for the words 'that other offence' to the end the words 'the charges for both offences could be joined in the same indictment'. The amendment is in force from 4 January 1999 in those pilot areas in which the CDA 1998, s. 51 (no committal proceedings for indictable-only offences) is in force.

It will be apparent from s. 24(1) that there are three categories of case in which a juvenile either must be tried on indictment or the magistrates have a discretion whether to deal with him themselves or commit him for trial. The categories are as follows:

Homicide Cases

The MCA 1980, s. 24(1), applies to 'indictable offences other than homicide'. **D21.4** Homicide is not defined in the subsection. It obviously includes both murder and manslaughter. The editors of *Stone's Justices' Manual*, at note b to para. 1–2053, express the opinion that it also includes causing death by dangerous driving. All three offences are triable only on indictment in the case of an adult. Therefore, since they are excluded from the special rules which otherwise apply to trial of juveniles for indictable offences, the general rule applies, and any juvenile charged with such an offence must (like an adult) be tried on indictment and may not even be offered the option of summary trial.

Cases Falling within the Magistrates' Courts Act 1980, s. 24(1)(a)

D21.5   The MCA 1980, s. 24(1)(a), must be understood in conjunction with the CYPA 1933, s. 53, which provides for the punishment of juveniles convicted on indictment of certain grave crimes. Section 53(2) and (3) states that, in the case of a juvenile convicted on indictment of an offence punishable with 14 years' imprisonment or more, the Crown Court may – if of opinion that no other method of dealing with the offender is suitable – sentence him to be detained in accordance with the Secretary of State's directions for any period up to the maximum prison term imposable. Recent statutory provisions have added certain offences to those subject to s. 53(3), namely, indecent assault on a woman and, in the case of young persons, causing death by dangerous driving and causing death by careless driving while under the influence of drink or drugs (see **E3.12** for details). The power to sentence under s. 53 is conditional upon there having been a conviction on indictment. Where a juvenile offender is summarily convicted (whether in the youth court or adult magistrates' court) and is subsequently committed to the Crown Court for sentence under the MCA 1980, s. 37, the Crown Court may, by virtue of the CJA 1982, s. 1A, sentence him to detention in a young offender institution (to be replaced by the detention and training order: see **E3.18**). However, the maximum term of such a sentence is 24 months in the case of an offender aged 15, 16 or 17. Thus, if the allegations against a young person are of such a nature that – in the event of his being convicted – there ought to be the option of sentencing him to a long term of detention under the CYPA 1933, s. 53(3), rather than to the relatively short terms permitted for persons of his age by the CJA 1982, then it is essential that the magistrates in the youth court be able to decline jurisdiction and commit for trial. The MCA 1980, s. 24(1)(a), simply gives the court that power. As one would expect, the circumstances in which the paragraph applies parallel the circumstances in which the Crown Court may sentence under the CYPA 1933, s. 53(3) (i.e. the accused must be charged either with an offence which would be punishable with 14 years' imprisonment or more in the case of an adult or with one of the other offences to which s. 53(3) applies (see above)).

The procedure to be adopted by the youth court in determining whether to proceed to summary trial or decline jurisdiction in reliance on s. 24(1)(a) is nowhere particularised. In practice, the magistrates tend automatically to accept jurisdiction, even over juveniles charged with offences carrying 14 years' imprisonment or more, unless the possibility that trial on indictment might be more appropriate is positively brought to their attention either by the clerk or the prosecution. It is submitted that the CPS should be alert to the importance of raising the jurisdictional point at an early stage – otherwise juveniles who might merit detention for a lengthy period will escape with 24 months or less simply because (in default of argument to the contrary) they have been tried in the wrong court. Where the propriety of summary trial is canvassed, the court should hear representations from both the prosecution and defence, but *evidence* about the gravity of the offence (as opposed to representations) is not appropriate at this stage (see the observations of the Divisional Court in *South Hackney Juvenile Court, ex parte RB and CB* (1983) 77 Cr App R 294). It has also been held that the justices should not be informed of the accused's criminal record, if any (*Hammersmith Juvenile Court, ex parte O* (1987) 86 Cr App R 343).

Whether jurisdiction should be refused in reliance on the MCA 1980, s. 24(1)(a), in any particular case is obviously bound up with the broader question of which types of offence might merit a sentence under the CYPA 1933, s. 53(3). That question is fully considered in the sentencing section of this work (see **E3.13**). In brief, s. 53(3) sentences are justified if either the offender has committed a serious offence (probably of a violent or sexual nature, or arson) and, because of mental instability, he is likely to be a danger to the public for a lengthy or unpredictable period, or he is an 'ordinary' offender (i.e. not a danger because of mental instability) but the offences he has committed are unusually serious (see especially *Fairhurst* [1986] 1 WLR 1374). Contrary to what was previously thought, the offences need not be absolutely in the first rank of gravity. According to *Inner London Youth Court, ex parte DPP* [1996] Crim LR 834, the magistrates ought to ask themselves whether the Crown Court could properly sentence the defendant to a period of custody exceeding two years; if the answer was 'Yes', then it followed inevitably that he should be committed for trial. Even offences of dishonesty not involving violence can merit committal for trial under the MCA 1980, s. 24(1)(a) (see also *AM* [1998] 1 WLR 363). Thus, in *South Hackney Juvenile Court, ex parte RB and CB* (1983) 77 Cr App R 294, the youth court's decision to hold committal proceedings in respect of RB, CB and six other juveniles charged with conspiracy to burgle was justified because the 'gang' as a whole had allegedly been responsible for some 15 burglaries (even though RB and CB were alleged to have participated in only a few of them); in the course of those burglaries, about £27,000-worth of property had been stolen, and unusual sophistication had been displayed in choosing the premises to burgle and thereafter disposing of the proceeds. These factors took the offences out of the usual run of juvenile crime, and meant that if the accused were to be convicted they could properly be sentenced to long-term detention. In determining whether to accept jurisdiction, the youth court should also take account of any relevant guidelines case from the Court of Appeal (see especially *Billam* [1986] 1 WLR 349 which states, *inter alia*, that a young person charged with rape should never be tried summarily). As to the situation where detention for a period of two years or less under the CYPA 1933, s. 53, would be in the interests of the offender, see *Brown* [1999] 1 Cr App R (S) 132.

Where the youth court commits a juvenile to the Crown Court for trial under s. 24(1)(a), it may also commit him for trial for any other indictable offence with which he is charged at the same time if the charges for both offences could be joined in the same indictment (s. 24(1A)).

Cases Falling within the Magistrates' Courts Act 1980, s. 24(1)(b)

The purpose of the MCA 1980, s. 24(1)(b), is to give the magistrates a discretion to **D21.6** commit a juvenile for trial if (a) he is jointly charged with an adult, and (b) the adult is going to be tried on indictment. The advantage of committing the juvenile for trial is that he and the adult will be tried together in the Crown Court; it being generally desirable that those charged with committing an offence jointly should be jointly tried. The disadvantage is that the Crown Court is not in general considered an appropriate forum for the trial of juveniles, unless the offence is unusually serious. In deciding whether to commit the juvenile, the magistrates should exercise their discretion judicially and should not automatically send him to the Crown Court just because he is jointly charged with an adult (*Newham Justices, ex parte Knight* [1976] Crim LR 323 – application for mandamus to compel the justices to commit a child jointly with her mother on a charge of theft against them both failed because how to proceed in the child's case was a matter of discretion, and the application disclosed no ground for saying that the justices had been wrong). It is submitted that the younger the juvenile and the less grave the charge, the more reluctant the magistrates should be to commit.

If the magistrates decide not to commit the adult co-defendant for trial in the Crown Court then there is no reason on the face of it to commit the juvenile, unless the matter might merit a sentence under the CYPA 1933, s. 53(3). In *Tottenham Youth Court, ex parte Fawzy* [1999] 1 WLR 1350, the Divisional Court provided guidance on the way in which the adult magistrates' court ought to proceed in these circumstances. Once it had discharged the adult in a mixed age case, it should consider, as part of the committal proceedings against the juvenile, whether the case fell under the MCA 1980, s. 24(1)(a), because of the need for the power to sentence under the CYPA 1933, s. 53(3). If it concluded that it did, then it should commit the juvenile. If it determined that it did not, the appropriate mode of trial was summary trial. The adult court should then proceed to summary trial of the information and take a plea. If the juvenile pleaded guilty, he should normally be remitted to the youth court for sentence. If he pleaded not guilty, the adult court had the option whether to send him to the youth court for trial. The adult court had no power, however, to send the case to the youth court for that court to decide upon the mode of trial. The mode of trial question, in these circumstances, is one which must be decided by the adult court.

The power to commit a juvenile under s. 24(1)(b) on a joint charge with an adult is supplemented by the power in s. 24(2) to commit him for any other indictable offence with which he also stands charged (whether by himself or with the adult), provided the circumstances of that offence are linked to the circumstances of the joint offence. It is then possible under the Indictment Rules 1971, r. 9, to have one indictment for all matters (see **D21.3** for the position when the CDA 1998, s. 51 is in force).

Procedure for Determining Mode of Trial of Juvenile

D21.7 Depending on whether the juvenile is jointly charged with an adult, his first appearance will either be in the adult magistrates' court or in the youth court. In the latter event – which presupposes that he is either charged by himself or his co-defendants are all juveniles also – the possibility of trial on indictment will arise only if (a) he is charged with homicide or (b) he is a young person and a sentence of detention under the CYPA 1933, s. 53(3), might be merited in the event of a conviction. The decision to accept summary jurisdiction or to hold committal proceedings will be for the youth court. If it decides that trial on indictment is appropriate, it will also conduct the committal proceedings. Subject to certain special rules governing all proceedings in the youth court (e.g., as to publicity and access of persons not involved in the case), the procedure will be identical to the procedure for an adult. In particular, the last clause of the MCA 1980, s. 24(1), expressly provides that the committal may be with consideration of the evidence or under the MCA 1980, s. 6(2).

Where the juvenile is jointly charged with an adult, he will make his first appearance in the adult magistrates' court, and the decision whether to commit him for trial under s. 24(1)(b) with the adult or to split the proceedings will accordingly be for the adult court. In the event of a decision for joint committal, the proceedings take place in the adult court, and again there are no significant differences in procedure occasioned by the involvement of the juvenile. Should the adult court decide that committal of the juvenile would not be in the interests of justice (or should it turn out that there is no case to answer against the adult accused so that he is discharged), the information should be put to the juvenile. If he pleads not guilty, the adult court has power to remit him to the youth court for trial (MCA 1980, s. 29(2)(b)). It is submitted that, unless there are very strong reasons to the contrary (e.g., the prosecution indicate that they in fact wish to offer no evidence), the adult court should remit rather than trying the juvenile itself. Where the juvenile pleads guilty, the adult court has only limited powers of sentencing, and will probably be obliged to remit to the youth court for a suitable penalty to be imposed.

Varying the Decision on Mode of Trial

D21.8 Apart from the possibility of fresh considerations arising before a plea has even been taken which justify the youth court in reversing its original decision to accept jurisdiction, the court is also given power by the MCA 1980, s. 25(5) to (7), to switch during the course of a hearing from committal proceedings to summary trial or vice versa. Subsections (5) to (7) parallel the earlier part of s. 25 which deals with the same situation in the case of adult accused.

Where a magistrates' court (adult or youth) has begun to try an information against a juvenile on the footing that the case does not fall within either para. (a) or (b) of s. 24(1) (i.e. the accused would not merit a sentence of detention under the CYPA 1933, s. 53(3), if convicted and there is no need in the interests of justice to commit him for trial jointly with an adult), then, by the MCA 1980, s. 25(6), if 'it appears to the court at any time before the conclusion of the evidence for the prosecution that the case is after all one which under [s. 24(1)] ought not to be tried summarily', the court may discontinue the summary trial and hold committal proceedings instead. Before commencing the proceedings it may adjourn either with or without remanding the accused (s. 25(6)). It is submitted that 'evidence for the prosecution' in s. 25(6) connotes evidence adduced to prove guilt following a not guilty plea. Therefore, if the court accepts jurisdiction and the juvenile pleads guilty, it is too late to vary the decision on mode of trial (see *Herefordshire Justices, ex parte J* (1998) *The Times*, 4 May 1998, and also *Dudley Justices, ex parte Gillard* [1986] AC 442 for a decision to that effect in respect of an adult accused).

In (*Newham Juvenile Court, ex parte F* [1986] 1 WLR 939, F was charged with robbery and having an imitation firearm. After full argument, the youth court accepted jurisdiction (although no plea was taken). During the adjournment which followed, F absconded and committed further offences while on bail. After his rearrest, he appeared before a differently constituted bench, who decided that their colleagues had erred in accepting jurisdiction and purported to reverse that decision. The Divisional Court held that the original decision was binding. Stephen Brown LJ said (at p. 946A–B):

> Have [justices] got power to reverse a decision [to accept summary jurisdiction over a juvenile] taken by their colleagues at an earlier hearing? In my judgment, the whole scheme of the Act suggests that they do not have that power before embarking upon the hearing. Once a decision has been made after proper inquiry and consideration of all relevant factors, it cannot be reversed merely by re-examining the case afresh on the same material.

Ironically, the magistrates comprising the second court made it clear in affidavits sworn for the Divisional Court that they had merely taken a different view of the facts placed before the first court – they had deliberately ignored F's absconding and further alleged offences on bail. According to Stephen Brown LJ, however, the latter considerations would have amounted to fresh matters not before the court when it accepted jurisdiction that would have justified a change of mind. Thus, the magistrates on the second occasion had come to the right conclusion but for the wrong reasons, and their ruling had to be quashed. It should be noted that the restriction on the court's power to reverse its acceptance of jurisdiction is without prejudice to its power under the MCA 1980, s. 25(5), to switch from summary trial to committal proceedings once the juvenile has pleaded not guilty and evidence has been called (see **D21.8**).

The implication of the judgment in *Ex parte F* is that, provided fresh considerations have arisen which were not before the court on the first occasion, a decision to accept jurisdiction may subsequently be reversed, even though no evidence has yet been heard for purposes of a summary trial. If that be so, there is a difficult-to-explain distinction between the position in the adult magistrates' courts and in the youth courts, since a decision under the MCA 1980, s. 20, that an either-way offence alleged against an adult is more suitable for summary trial is irreversible unless and until evidence has been called for purposes of a summary trial (see *St Helens Magistrates' Court, ex parte Critchley* (1987) 152 JP 102). In *Liverpool Justices, ex parte CPS* (1990) 90 Cr App R 261, the Divisional Court doubted the validity of the dicta in *Ex parte F* which suggest that there is power in the justices to alter the decision on mode of trial independently of s. 25; in the event, the court did not need to decide the point, since there had been no change of circumstances. In *Fareham Youth Court, ex parte M* [1999] Crim LR 325, the Divisional Court held that there was no power in the MCA 1980, s. 25, permitting a change from summary trial to trial on indictment before a court had begun to try an information summarily. There was clearly no such power where there had been an unequivocal plea of guilty. The court also held that the prosecution could not make use of a notice of transfer in order to reverse a decision by the youth court in favour of summary trial. Where the decision of the justices to try the case summarily was unreasonable, then the remedy was to seek judicial review, and have the decision quashed (as was done by the Divisional Court in *Ex parte M*).

Where magistrates have commenced committal proceedings in respect of a juvenile, they may revert to summary trial at any time before actually deciding to commit (s. 25(7)) and see *Brent Juvenile Court, ex parte S* (1991) *The Times*, 18 June 1991).

TRIAL OF JUVENILES ON INDICTMENT

The procedure for trying a juvenile on indictment is identical to that for trying an adult, subject to the following points.

Reporting Restrictions

D21.9 By the CYPA 1933, s. 39(1), a court may direct that no newspaper report of proceedings before it shall reveal the name, address, or school, or any particulars calculated to lead to the identification of any juvenile concerned in the proceedings. A direction may also be given that no picture of the juvenile shall be published. Section 39 applies to any court – Crown Court, adult magistrates' court or civil courts. It is otiose in respect of youth courts, publicity for such proceedings being governed by s. 49 (see **D21.17**). Under s. 39, the onus is on the court to make an order restricting publicity. If no order is made, the media are at liberty to report the names etc. of juveniles just as they are at liberty to report the names of adults. The protection of the section may be extended not just to a juvenile accused but to any juvenile involved in the proceedings (e.g., as a witness). Section 39 applies to sound and television broadcasts just as it applies to reports in newspapers (CYPA 1963, s. 57(4)). Publication of matter in contravention of a direction given under s. 39(1) is a summary offence punishable with a fine of up to £5,000 (s. 39(2)). As far as the operation of s. 39 is concerned, see **D2.52** and the discussion there of *Leicester Crown Court, ex parte S* [1993] 1 WLR 111.

Attendance of Parent or Guardian

D21.10 Where a juvenile aged under 16 is charged with an offence, the court must require a person who is his parent or guardian to attend all the proceedings in court with him, unless it would be unreasonable to do so (CYPA 1933, s. 34A(1)). Where the juvenile is aged 16 or 17, the court may so require. 'Guardian' is defined as any person who, in the opinion of the court, has for the time being 'the care of the child or young person' (CYPA 1933, s. 107). 'Parent' is not defined in the 1933 Act, but, by the Adoption Act 1976, s. 39, includes the adopter of an adopted child. In cases where the local authority has parental responsibility, their representative, rather than, or in certain cases as well as, the parent must (or may) be required to attend (CYPA 1933, s. 34A(2)).

Less Formality

D21.11 The procedure adopted at trial of a juvenile on indictment may also vary from that for an adult in that the Crown Court may seek to make its proceedings a little less formal (e.g., by not requiring the juvenile to stand in the dock and allowing him to be referred to by his forename). Such variations are, however, a matter of pure practice not law.

Children and Young Persons Act 1933, ss. 34A and 39

34A.—(1) Where a child or young person is charged with an offence or is for any other reason brought before a court, the court—

   (a) may in any case; and

   (b) shall in the case of a child or a young person who is under the age of sixteen years, require a person who is a parent or guardian of his to attend at the court during all the stages of the proceedings, unless and to the extent that the court is satisfied that it would be unreasonable to require such attendance, having regard to the circumstances of the case.

(2)   In relation to a child or young person for whom a local authority have parental responsibility and who—

(a)   is in their care; or

(b)   is provided with accommodation by them in the exercise of any functions (in particular those under the Children Act 1989) which stand referred to their social services committee under the Local Authority Social Services Act 1970,

the reference in subsection (1) above to a person who is a parent or guardian of his shall be construed as a reference to that authority or, where he is allowed to live with such a person, as including such a reference.

In this subsection 'local authority' and 'parental responsibility' have the same meanings as in the Children Act 1989.

39.—(1)   In relation to any proceedings in any court the court may direct that—

(a)   no newspaper report of the proceedings shall reveal the name, address, or school, or include any particulars calculated to lead to the identification, of any child or young person concerned in the proceedings, either as being the person by or against or in respect of whom the proceedings are taken, or as being a witness therein;

(b)   no picture shall be published in any newspaper as being or including a picture of any child or young person so concerned in the proceedings as aforesaid;

except insofar (if at all) as may be permitted by the direction of the court.

(2)   Any person who publishes any matter in contravention of any such direction shall on summary conviction be liable in respect of each offence to a fine not exceeding level 5 on the standard scale.

TRIAL OF JUVENILES IN ADULT MAGISTRATES' COURTS

The exceptional circumstances in which a juvenile who is to be tried summarily is tried **D21.12** in an adult magistrates' court rather than a youth court are set out in the CYPA 1933, s. 46, and the CYPA 1963, s. 18. Their net effect is as follows:

(a)   Where an adult and juvenile are charged jointly with an offence the trial must take place in the adult magistrates' court (first proviso to the CYPA 1933, s. 46(1)). This is subject to the MCA 1980, s. 24(1)(b) (committal for trial of both in the interests of justice: see **D21.6**). It is also subject to the MCA 1980, s. 29(2), which provides that, notwithstanding anything in the CYPA 1933, s. 46(1), where either the adult magistrates' court proceeds to summary trial of the joint charge and the adult pleads guilty or it holds committal proceedings for the adult but decides that summary trial would be more appropriate for the juvenile, then, if the juvenile pleads not guilty, he may be remitted to the youth court for trial. Whether to remit the juvenile in the circumstances predicated by the MCA 1980, s. 29(2), is a matter for the adult court's discretion, but it is submitted that remittal would normally be the appropriate course.

(b)   Where an adult is charged with aiding, abetting, causing, procuring, allowing or permitting a juvenile to commit an offence, and at the same time the juvenile himself is charged with the offence as principal offender, the adult magistrates' court may, in its discretion, hear the charge against the juvenile (second proviso to the CYPA 1933, s. 46(1)). The same applies in the reverse situation (where a juvenile is charged with aiding, abetting etc. an adult: CYPA 1963, s. 18). The normal practice, however, is simply to join aiders and abettors with the principal offender in a single charge, in which event the first proviso to the CYPA 1933, s. 46(1), applies. Thus, the situation envisaged by the second proviso will arise but rarely.

(c)   Where a juvenile is charged separately from but at the same time as an adult, and the charge against the one arises out of circumstances which are the same as or linked with the charge against the other, then the adult court may try the charge against the juvenile (CYPA 1963, s. 18). It is not entirely clear whether, when referring to a juvenile and adult being charged at the same time, the second proviso to the CYPA 1933, s. 46(2), and the CYPA 1963, s. 18, are referring to the moment when proceedings are commenced or to the time when the accused appear before the court. The latter construction of the sections would appear more sensible.

(d)   Where it becomes apparent during the course of proceedings before an adult magistrates' court that an accused who had been thought to be over 18 is in fact a juvenile, the adult court may, if it thinks fit, complete the hearing (third proviso to the CYPA 1933, s. 46(1)). Similarly, the CYPA 1933, s. 46(1A), provides that, where a plea of guilty by post is received from a person who is in fact a juvenile but the court has no reason to be aware of his true age, then he shall be deemed to be an adult.

It will be noted that in situation (a) the adult magistrates' court is obliged to try both the juvenile and adult together unless the MCA 1980, s. 29, comes into play, whereas in situations (b) to (d), whether to try the juvenile or remit him to the youth court is in the court's discretion. It should also be noted that the fact that a juvenile will ultimately have to be tried before the youth court does not prevent him being brought before an adult court for purposes of a bail application and remand (CYPA 1933, s. 46(2)).

The procedure in the adult magistrates' court when a juvenile is being tried is the same as the procedure for trial of an adult, subject to the application of the CYPA 1933, ss. 34A and 39 (attendance of parent or guardian and order restricting divulgence of juvenile's name etc. in the media). Reference should also be made to rr. 4 to 11 of the Magistrates' Courts (Children and Young Persons) Rules 1992 (SI 1992 No. 2071) (see **D21.20**) which apply equally to trial in a youth court and trial of a juvenile in the adult court.

Children and Young Persons Act 1933, s. 46

(1)   Subject as hereinafter provided, no charge against a child or young person, and no application whereof the hearing is by rules made under this section assigned to youth courts, shall be heard by a court of summary jurisdiction which is not a youth court:
Provided that—

(a)   a charge made jointly against a child or young person and a person who has attained the age of 18 years shall be heard by a court of summary jurisdiction other than a youth court, and

(b)   where a child or young person is charged with an offence, the charge may be heard by a court of summary jurisdiction which is not a youth court if a person who has attained the age of 18 years is charged at the same time with aiding, abetting, causing, procuring, allowing or permitting that offence; and

(c)   where in the course of any proceedings before any court of summary jurisdiction other than a youth court it appears that the person to whom the proceedings relate is a child or young person, nothing in this subsection shall be construed as preventing the court, if it thinks fit so to do, from proceeding with the hearing and determination of those proceedings.

(1A)   If a notification that the accused desires to plead guilty without appearing before the court is received by the clerk of a court in pursuance of section 12 of the Magistrates' Courts Act 1980 and the court has no reason to believe that the accused is a child or young person, then, if he is a child or young person he shall be deemed to have attained the age of 18 for the purposes of subsection (1) of this section in its application to the proceedings in question.

(2)   No direction, whether contained in this or any other Act, that a charge shall be brought before a youth court shall be construed as restricting the powers of any justice or justices to entertain an application for bail or for a remand, and to hear such evidence as may be necessary for that purpose.

Children and Young Persons Act 1963, s. 18

Notwithstanding section 46(1) of [the CYPA 1933] . . . a magistrates' court which is not a youth court may hear an information against a child or young person if he is charged—

(a)   with aiding, abetting, causing, procuring, allowing or permitting an offence with which a person who has attained the age of 18 is charged at the same time; or

(b)   with an offence arising out of circumstances which are the same as or connected with those giving rise to an offence with which a person who has attained the age of 18 is charged at the same time.

Magistrates' Courts Act 1980, s. 29

(1)   Where—

(a)   a person under the age of 18 ('the juvenile') appears or is brought before a magistrates' court other than a youth court on an information jointly charging him and one or more other persons with an offence; and

(b)   that other person, or any of those other persons, has attained that age, subsection (2) below shall have effect notwithstanding proviso (a) in section 46(1) of the Children and Young Persons Act 1933 (which would otherwise require the charge against the juvenile to be heard by a magistrates' court other than a youth court).

In the following provisions of this section 'the older accused' means such one or more of the accused as have attained the age of 18.

(2)   If—

(a)   the court proceeds to the summary trial of the information in the case of both or all of the accused, and the older accused or each of the older accused pleads guilty; or

(b)   the court—

(i)   in the case of the older accused or each of the older accused, proceeds to inquire into the information as examining justices and either commits him for trial or discharges him; and

(ii)   in the case of the juvenile, proceeds to the summary trial of the information, then, if in either situation the juvenile pleads not guilty, the court may before any evidence is called in his case remit him for trial to a youth court acting for the same place as the remitting court or for the place where he habitually resides.

(3)   A person remitted to a youth court under subsection (2) above shall be brought before and tried by a youth court accordingly.

(4)   Where a person is so remitted to a youth court—

(a)   he shall have no right of appeal against the order of remission; and

(b)   the remitting court may give such directions as appear to be necessary with respect to his custody or for his release on bail until he can be brought before the youth court.

(5)   The preceding provisions of this section shall apply in relation to a corporation as if it were an individual who has attained the age of 18.

TRIAL OF JUVENILES IN YOUTH COURTS

Constitution and Operation of the Youth Court

The composition and sittings of youth courts are governed by the CYPA 1933, ss. 45   **D21.13** and 47 to 49 and sch. 2, and the Youth Courts (Constitution) Rules 1954 (SI 1954 No. 1711). The main points arising from those provisions are:

The Youth Court Panel   A youth court panel must be formed for every petty sessions   **D21.14** area (CYPA 1933, sch. 2, para. 3). This is subject to the Secretary of State, acting upon a recommendation from the relevant magistrates' courts committee, being empowered to order that a combined youth court panel be formed for two or more areas (paras 4 to 6). By r. 1 of the Youth Courts (Constitution) Rules 1954, the justices for each petty sessions area (or combined area) are required every third year to: 'appoint in accordance with these rules justices specially qualified for dealing with juvenile cases to form a youth court panel for that area'. The persons appointed then serve on the panel for a period of three years running from 1 January next following their appointment (r. 4). Vacancies arising on the panel may be filled as soon as they arise without waiting for the three-yearly meeting (r. 6). Justices elected to the youth court panel are required to undertake training additional to their ordinary training before being permitted to sit in court. For London, see rr. 14 and 15 and the CYPA 1933, sch. 2, part II.

D21.15 ***Composition of Individual Courts*** Justices sitting in the youth court must be drawn from the youth court panel (Youth Courts (Constitution) Rules, r. 11). No more than three may sit (r. 12(1)). Unless unforeseen circumstances have arisen in consequence of which only men or only women are available to form a court, the court must include both a man and a woman (r. 12(1) and (2)). A stipendiary magistrate is a member of the youth court panel ex officio (r. 2) and he may sit alone.

D21.16 ***Special Rules for Youth Courts*** Youth courts are required to sit as often as may be required for the purpose of exercising the jurisdiction conferred upon them by the CYPA 1933 and other relevant legislation (s. 47(1) of the 1933 Act). The only persons allowed to be present during the sitting of a youth court are (a) members and officers of the court; (b) parties in the case, their legal representatives, witnesses after they have given their evidence, and anybody else directly concerned in the matter; (c) representatives of the press, and (d) any other persons the court may specially authorise to be present (s. 47(2)).

D21.17 ***Press Restrictions*** No report of proceedings in a youth court may be published which reveals the name, address or other identifying detail of any juvenile concerned in the proceedings, whether he be concerned as a party or merely as a witness (CYPA 1933, s. 49(1) – for the text, see **D21.20**). The court may, however, lift the ban on publicity to the extent it considers necessary either to avoid injustice to the juvenile himself or, as respects a juvenile to whom s. 49(5)(b) applies, where it is necessary to do so for the purpose of apprehending him and bringing him before a court or returning him to custody (s. 49(5)). Section 49(5)(b) applies to a juvenile charged with or convicted of a violent or sexual offence or an offence punishable in the case of a person aged 21 or over with imprisonment for 14 years or more. Section 49(5) can be employed only when notice has been given by the DPP to the juvenile's legal representative.

In addition, the court may lift the ban on publicity where a juvenile has been convicted of an offence, if it is satisfied that it is in the public interest to do so (s. 49(4A)). Before doing so, it must afford an opportunity to the parties to make representations (s. 49(4B)).

Thus, the rule on publicity in the youth court is the reverse of that which applies in the adult magistrates' court and Crown Court – i.e. the media are permitted to identify a juvenile concerned in proceedings in the latter courts unless an order to the contrary is made under s. 39 of the 1933 Act, whereas in the youth court the juvenile must not be identified unless the court gives permission.

D21.18 ***Attendance of Parent or Guardian*** The CYPA 1933, s. 34A (power of court to order that the juvenile's parent or guardian attend), applies to proceedings in the youth court just as it applies to proceedings in the Crown Court and adult magistrates' court (see **D21.10**).

Course of the Trial in a Youth Court

D21.19 The course of a trial in the youth court is essentially the same as the course of a trial in an adult magistrates' court. The Magistrates' Courts (Children and Young Persons) Rules 1992 (SI 1992 No. 2071), rr. 4 to 9, govern the procedure. By r. 5, if the juvenile is not legally represented, his parent or guardian may assist in the conduct of the defence, even to the extent of cross-examining the prosecution witnesses (and see also r. 8(2) which deals with the clerk asking questions on the juvenile's behalf if he is neither legally represented nor has a parent or guardian present). By r. 6, the court is to explain to the juvenile the substance of the charge in simple language, but that obligation does not extend to giving a detailed elaboration of the elements of the offence (*Blandford Justices, ex parte G* [1967] 1 QB 82 – court not obliged to explain to a juvenile charged with theft that, to be guilty, she had to have been dishonest and to have had the intention permanently to deprive the owner of the property). Having explained the charge, the court asks the juvenile if he pleads guilty or not guilty (r. 7). The former practice of asking whether he 'admits' or 'denies' the charge was found to cause confusion, and was ended by the 1988 Rules. If, after the prosecution evidence, there is a case to answer, an unrepresented juvenile must be told of his right to give evidence and address the court (r. 9). As a matter of terminology, the words 'conviction' and 'sentence' are not to be used in connection with juveniles tried summarily (CYPA 1933, s. 59). They are replaced by, respectively, the terms 'finding of guilt' and 'order made upon finding of guilt'. This applies both to proceedings in the youth court and to proceedings against juveniles in the adult magistrates' court. It does not apply to proceedings on indictment.

Statutes and Rules Relating to Procedure in Youth Court

Children and Young Persons Act 1933, ss. 45 to 49 and 59   D21.20

45. Courts of summary jurisdiction constituted in accordance with the provisions of the second schedule to this Act and sitting for the purpose of hearing any charge against a child or young person or for the purpose of exercising any other jurisdiction conferred on youth courts by or under this or any other Act, shall be known as youth courts and in whatever place sitting shall be deemed to be petty sessional courts.

[**46.** Assignment of cases to youth courts — see **D21.12**.]

47.—(1) Youth courts shall sit as often as may be necessary for the purposes of exercising any jurisdiction conferred on them by or under this or any other Act.

(2) No person shall be present at any sitting of a youth court except—

    (a) members and officers of the court;

    (b) parties to the case before the court, their solicitors and counsel, and witnesses and other persons directly concerned in that case;

    (c) bona fide representatives of newspapers or news agencies;

    (d) such other persons as the court may specially authorise to be present.

[**48.** Miscellaneous provisions concerning powers of youth courts.]

49.—(1) The following prohibitions apply (subject to subsection (5) below) in relation to any proceedings to which this section applies, that is to say—

    (a) no report shall be published which reveals the name, address or school of any child or young person concerned in the proceedings or includes any particulars likely to lead to the identification of any child or young person concerned in the proceedings; and

    (b) no picture shall be published or included in a programme service as being or including a picture of any child or young person concerned in the proceedings.

(2) The proceedings to which this section applies are—

    (a) proceedings in a youth court;

    (b) proceedings on appeal from a youth court (including proceedings by way of case stated);

    (c) proceedings under section 15 or 16 of the Children and Young Persons Act 1969 (proceedings for varying or revoking supervision orders); and

    (d) proceedings on appeal from a magistrates' court arising out of proceedings under section 15 or 16 of that Act (including proceedings by way of case stated).

(3) The reports to which this section applies are reports in a newspaper and reports included in a programme service; and similarly as respects pictures.

(4) For the purposes of this section a child or young person is 'concerned' in any proceedings whether as being the person against or in respect of whom the proceedings are taken or as being a witness in the proceedings.

(4A) If a court is satisfied that it is in the public interest to do so, it may, in relation to a child or young person who has been convicted of an offence, by order dispense to any specified extent with the requirements of this section in relation to any proceedings before it to which this section applies by virtue of subsection (2)(a) or (b) above, being proceedings relating to—

(a)   the prosecution or conviction of the offender for the offence;

(b)   the manner in which he, or his parent or guardian, should be dealt with in respect of the offence;

(c)   the enforcement, amendment, variation, revocation or discharge of any order made in respect of the offence;

(d)   where an attendance centre order is made in respect of the offence, the enforcement of any rules made under section 16(3) of the Criminal Justice Act 1982; or

(e)   where a secure training order is so made, the enforcement of any requirements imposed under section 3(7) of the Criminal Justice and Public Order Act 1994.

(4B)   A court shall not exercise its power under subsection (4A) above without—

(a)   affording the parties to the proceedings an opportunity to make representations; and

(b)   taking into account any representations which are duly made.

(5)   Subject to subsection (7) below, a court may, in relation to proceedings before it to which this section applies, by order dispense to any specified extent with the requirements of this section in relation to a child or young person who is concerned in the proceedings if it is satisfied—

(a)   that it is appropriate to do so for the purpose of avoiding injustice to the child or young person; or

(b)   that, as respects a child or young person to whom this paragraph applies who is unlawfully at large, it is necessary to dispense with those requirements for the purpose of apprehending him and bringing him before a court or returning him to the place in which he was in custody.

(6)   Paragraph (b) of subsection (5) above applies to any child or young person who is charged with or has been convicted of—

(a)   a violent offence,

(b)   a sexual offence, or

(c)   an offence punishable in the case of a person aged 21 or over with imprisonment for fourteen years or more.

(7)   The court shall not exercise its power under subsection (5)(b) above—

(a)   except in pursuance of an application by or on behalf of the Director of Public Prosecutions; and

(b)   unless notice of the application has been given by the Director of Public Prosecutions to any legal representative of the child or young person.

(8)   The court's power under subsection (5) above may be exercised by a single justice.

(9)   If a report or picture is published or included in a programme service in contravention of subsection (1) above, the following persons, that is to say—

(a)   in the case of publication of a written report or a picture as part of a newspaper, any proprietor, editor or publisher of the newspaper;

(b)   in the case of the inclusion of a report or picture in a programme service, any body corporate which provides the service and any person having functions in relation to the programme corresponding to those of an editor of a newspaper,

shall be liable on summary conviction to a fine not exceeding level 5 on the standard scale.

(10)   In any proceedings under section 15 or 16 of the Children and Young Persons Act 1969 (proceedings for varying or revoking supervision orders) before a magistrates' court other than a youth court or on appeal from such a court it shall be the duty of the magistrates' court or the appellate court to announce in the course of the proceedings that this section applies to the proceedings; and if the court fails to do so this section shall not apply to the proceedings.

(11)   In this section—

'legal representative' means an authorised advocate or authorised litigator, as defined by section 119(1) of the Courts and Legal Services Act 1990;

'programme' and 'programme service' have the same meaning as in the Broadcasting Act 1990;

'sexual offence' has the same meaning as in section 31(1) of the Criminal Justice Act 1991;

'specified' means specified in an order under this section;

'violent offence' has the same meaning as in section 31(1) of the Criminal Justice Act 1991;
and a person who, having been granted bail, is liable to arrest (whether with or without a warrant) shall be treated as unlawfully at large.

59.   The words 'conviction' and 'sentence' shall cease to be used in relation to children and young persons dealt with summarily and any reference in any enactment . . . to a person convicted, a conviction or a sentence shall, in the case of a child or young person, be construed as including a reference to a person found guilty of an offence, a finding of guilt or an order made upon such finding, as the case may be.

Children and Young Persons Act 1933, sch. 2

CONSTITUTION OF YOUTH COURTS
PART I   OUTSIDE METROPOLITAN AREA

1.   The following provisions of this part of this schedule shall have effect as respects any area outside the Inner London area and the City of London.

2.   A justice shall not be qualified to sit as a member of a youth court unless he is a member of a youth court panel, that is to say, a panel of justices specially qualified to deal with juvenile cases.

3.   Subject to the following provisions of this part of this schedule, a youth court panel shall be formed for every petty sessions area.

[4. to 10.   Deal with the establishment of combined youth court panels for two or more petty sessions areas].

PART II   METROPOLITAN AREA

[Deals with the special rules governing the composition of the youth court panel for the Inner London area and the City of London.]

Youth Courts (Constitution) Rules 1954 (SI 1954 No. 1711)

1.—(1)   The justices for each petty sessions area shall at their meeting held . . . for the purpose of electing a chairman of the justices, and thereafter at the said meeting in every third year, appoint in accordance with these rules justices specially qualified for dealing with juvenile cases to form a youth court panel for that area.
    (2)   The panel for a petty sessions area shall, except as provided in paragraph (4) of this rule, be appointed from amongst the justices for that area.
    (3)   The number of persons appointed to the panel for a petty sessions area shall be such as the said justices at the time of appointment think sufficient for the youth courts in the area and the said justices may at any time appoint an additional member to the panel.
    [(4)   Justices from another petty-sessional division within the county may be appointed to a panel for a petty sessions area if there would not otherwise be enough suitably qualified justices to form a panel of the required size.]

2.   Where a stipendiary magistrate exercises jurisdiction in a petty sessions area he shall be a member of the panel therefor by virtue of his office.

4.   Subject to rule 7 of these rules the members of a panel shall serve thereon from the first day of January next following the date of appointment for a period of three years.

9.—(1)   The members of the panel for each petty sessions area shall on the occasion of their appointment or as soon as practicable thereafter meet and elect from amongst their number by secret ballot a chairman and as many deputy chairmen as will ensure that each youth court in the area sits under the chairmanship of a person so elected in accordance with paragraph (1) of rule 13 of these rules, and may at any subsequent time elect an additional deputy chairman.
    (2)   If a vacancy occurs in the chairmanship or a deputy chairmanship, the members of the panel shall elect by secret ballot a chairman or, as the case may be, deputy chairman to hold office for the remainder of the period for which the members serve.

11.   The justices to sit in each youth court shall be chosen from the panel, in such manner as the panel determine, so as to ensure that paragraph (1) of rule 12 and paragraph (1) of rule 13 of these rules can be complied with.

12.—(1)   Subject to the following provisions of these rules, each youth court shall consist of either:
    (a)   a stipendiary magistrate sitting alone; or
    (b)   not more than three justices who shall include a man and a woman.
    (2)   If at any sitting of a youth court other than one constituted in accordance with paragraph 1(a) of this rule no man or no woman is available owing to circumstances unforeseen when the justices to sit were chosen under rule 11 of these rules, or if the only man or woman present cannot properly sit as a member of the court, and in any such case the other members of the panel present think it inexpedient in the interests of justice for there to be an adjournment, the court may be constituted without a man or, as the case may be, without a woman.
    (4)   Nothing in paragraph (1) of this rule shall be construed as requiring a youth court to include both a man and a woman in any case in which a single justice has by law jurisdiction to act.

13.—(1)   Except as provided in paragraphs (1A) and (2) of this rule or where the youth court is constituted in accordance with rule 12(1)(a) of these rules, each youth court shall sit under the chairmanship of the chairman or a deputy chairman elected under rule 9 of these rules.
    [(1A) and (2)   Make provision for any magistrate to act as chairman if either the elected chairman present thinks that appropriate or, due to unforeseen circumstances, no elected chairman is present.]

Magistrates' Courts (Children and Young Persons) Rules 1992 (SI 1992 No. 2071), part II (rr. 4 to 9)

PROCEEDINGS IN CRIMINAL MATTERS

4.—(1)   This Part applies, subject to paragraph (3), where proceedings to which paragraph (2) applies are brought in a court in respect of a child or young person ('the relevant minor').
    (2)   This paragraph applies to proceedings in which the relevant minor is charged with an offence, and, where he appears or is brought before the court, to proceedings under—
    (a)   section 15 of the Act of 1969 (variation and discharge of supervision orders),
    (b)   part II, III or IV of schedule 2 to the Criminal Justice Act 1991 (breaches of requirements of, and revocation and amendment of, probation orders, community service orders, combination orders and curfew orders), or
    (c)   section 18 of the Criminal Justice Act 1982 (discharge and variation of attendance centre orders), or
    (d)   schedule 5 to the Crime and Disorder Act 1998 (enforcement etc. of reparation and action plan orders).
    (3)   Where the court is inquiring into an offence as examining justices, only rules 5, 6 and 8(3) apply, and where the proceedings are of a kind mentioned in paragraph (2)(a), (b) or (c) rules 7 and 12 do not apply

5.—(1)   Except where the relevant minor is legally represented, the court shall allow his parent or guardian to assist him in conducting his case.
    (2)   Where the parent or guardian cannot be found or cannot in the opinion of the court reasonably be required to attend, the court may allow any relative or other responsible person to take the place of the parent or guardian for the purposes of this part.

6.—(1)   The court shall explain to the relevant minor the nature of the proceedings and, where he is charged with an offence, the substance of the charge.
    (2)   The explanation shall be given in simple language suitable to his age and understanding.

7.   Where the relevant minor is charged with an offence the court shall, after giving the explanation required by rule 6, ask him whether he pleads guilty or not guilty to the charge.

8.—(1) Where—

(a)   the relevant minor is charged with an offence and does not plead guilty, or

(b)   the proceedings are of a kind mentioned in rule 4(2)(a), (b) or (c),

the court shall hear the witnesses in support of the charge or, as the case may be, the application.

(2)   Except where—

(a)   the proceedings are of a kind mentioned in rule 4(2)(a), (b) or (c), and

(b)   the relevant minor is the applicant,

each witness may at the close of his evidence-in-chief be cross-examined by or on behalf of the relevant minor.

(3)   If in any case where the relevant minor is not legally represented or assisted as provided by rule 5, the relevant minor, instead of asking questions by way of cross-examination, makes assertions, the court shall then put to the witness such questions as it thinks necessary on behalf of the relevant minor and may for this purpose question the relevant minor in order to bring out or clear up any point arising out of any such assertions.

9.   If it appears to the court after hearing the evidence in support of the charge or application that a prima facie case is made out, the relevant minor shall, if he is not the applicant and is not legally represented, be told that he may give evidence or address the court, and the evidence of any witnesses shall be heard.

SENTENCING PROCEDURE AND POWERS IN THE CROWN COURT

Sentencing Powers Generally

All the sentences and other orders provided for by Parliament for use in respect of **D21.21** juvenile offenders are at the disposal of the Crown Court following conviction of a juvenile on indictment (for the more limited powers available to the Crown Court following a committal for sentence under the MCA 1980, s. 37, see **D21.27**). The general nature and limitations on the use of these sentences are discussed in the sentencing part of this work. In brief, the principal sentences are as follows:

(a)   Detention in accordance with the Secretary of State's directions under the CYPA 1933, s. 53(3). Available only in respect of juveniles convicted either of an offence carrying 14 years' imprisonment or of certain other serious offences. The conviction must have been on indictment.

(b)   Detention in a young offender institution under the CJA 1982, s. 1A. Available only in respect of young persons aged 15, 16 or 17. The maximum term which may be imposed, whether or not the offender is being dealt with for several offences, is 24 months.

(c)   A secure training order where the juvenile is aged 12, 13 or 14 under the CJPO 1994, s. 1.

(d)   Fine. Available in respect of juveniles of all ages. There is no limitation on the maximum sum that may be ordered by the Crown Court following conviction on indictment.

(e)   Probation order, combination order, community service order, supervision order, attendance centre order, conditional and absolute discharge. All available to the Crown Court in the same circumstances as they are available to the youth court.

(f)   Action plan orders and reparation orders, introduced by the CDA 1998, are available to certain courts on a pilot basis which is expected to last until March 2000 (see **E11** and **E12** for details).

(g)   When the CDA 1998, ss. 73 to 79, are brought into force, they will create a new custodial sentence for juveniles – the detention and training order. This sentence will replace the sentence of detention in a young offender institution, and the secure training order. These changes are expected to take place in April 2000 (see **E3.18** for details).

Remittal to the Youth Court

D21.22 Save in cases of homicide, where a juvenile has been convicted on indictment, the Crown Court 'shall unless satisfied that it would be undesirable to do so, remit the case to a youth court acting for the place where the offender was committed for trial' (CYPA 1933, s. 56(1)). Upon such remittal, the youth court may deal with the offender as if he had been tried and found guilty by itself (ibid.). There is no appeal against the order of remittal, although the sentence eventually passed by the youth court may be appealed to the Crown Court (or Divisional Court if wrong in law) in the usual way (s. 56(2)). Upon remitting, the Crown Court gives such directions as appear necessary in relation to bail or custody (s. 56(3)).

The obligation imposed on the Crown Court by s. 56(1) to remit a juvenile convicted before it to the youth court for sentence unless satisfied that it would be undesirable to do so might seem to be a major fetter on the power of the higher court to deal with juveniles. However, s. 56(1) has been interpreted so as to give the Crown Court an almost unfettered discretion to retain the sentencing function for itself if it so wishes, and, in practice, the great majority of juveniles convicted in the Crown Court are also sentenced there. Guidance on the application of s. 56(1) was given by Lord Lane CJ in *Lewis* (1984) 79 Cr App R 94. His lordship indicated that sufficient reasons for *not* remitting include:

(a) that, in a case where the juvenile pleaded not guilty and was convicted, the Crown Court judge who presided at the trial will be better informed about the facts of the offence and general nature of the case than the youth court could hope to be;

(b) that, in a case where an adult and juvenile have been jointly tried on indictment and both convicted, sentencing the juvenile in the Crown Court will avoid the risk of unjustifiable disparity in sentencing that would arise if he were to be remitted to the youth court;

(c) that remitting would cause delay, unnecessary duplication of proceedings and extra expense.

It is submitted that, in virtually any case, the Crown Court will be able to justify a decision not to remit on the basis of one or other of the above grounds. Lord Lane's guidance in *Lewis* may be contrasted with the earlier decision in *Holden* [1981] Crim LR 513, where the Court of Appeal held that the Crown Court should remit a juvenile for sentence unless either it had in mind a sentence more severe than the lower court could impose, or, at the opposite extreme, it was considering a very lenient disposition such as a conditional discharge (in which case remitting would merely 'prolong the agony' for the offender); this approach must now be considered as superseded by that in *Lewis*.

Children and Young Persons Act 1933, s. 56

(1) Any court by or before which a child or young person is found guilty of an offence other than homicide, may and, if it is not a youth court, shall unless satisfied that it would be undesirable to do so, remit the case to a youth court acting for the place where the offender was committed for trial or if he was not committed for trial, to a youth court acting either for the same place as the remitting court or for the place where the offender habitually resides; and, where any such case is so remitted, the offender shall be brought before a youth court accordingly, and that court may deal with him in any way in which it might have dealt with him if he had been tried and found guilty by that court.

(2) Where any case is so remitted—

(a) the offender shall have the same right of appeal against any order of the court to which the case is remitted as if he had been found guilty by that court, but shall have no right of appeal against the order of remission.

(3) A court by which an order remitting a case to a youth court is made under this section may give such directions as appear to be necessary with respect to the custody of the

offender or for his release on bail until he can be brought before the youth court, and shall cause to be transmitted to the clerk of the youth court a certificate setting out the nature of the offence and stating that the offender has been found guilty thereof, and that the case has been remitted for the purpose of being dealt with under this section.

SENTENCING PROCEDURE AND POWERS IN THE ADULT MAGISTRATES' COURT

The powers of the adult magistrates' court to deal with a juvenile offender are restricted **D21.23** by the CYPA 1969, s. 7(8).

Children and Young Persons Act 1969, s. 7(8)

Without prejudice to the power to remit any case to a youth court which is conferred on a magistrates' court other than a youth court by section 56(1) of the [CYPA 1933], in a case where such a magistrates' court finds a person guilty of an offence and either he is a [juvenile] or was a [juvenile] when the proceedings in question were begun it shall be the duty of the court to exercise that power unless the court is of the opinion that the case is one which can properly be dealt with by means of—

(a) an order discharging him absolutely or conditionally, or

(b) an order for the payment of a fine, or

(c) an order requiring his parent or guardian to enter into a recognisance to take proper care of him and exercise proper control over him,

with or without any other order that the court has power to make when absolutely or conditionally discharging an offender.

As enacted, s. 7(8) refers to a 'young person' not 'a juvenile'. However, in 1970, the Secretary of State ordered that in s. 7(8), references to a 'young person' should be construed as including a child who has attained the age of 10 (Children and Young Persons (Transitional Modifications of Part I) Order 1970 (SI 1970 No. 1882), art. 4). Hence, the limitation on the sentencing powers of the adult magistrates' court applies to all juveniles who have attained the age of criminal responsibility, not just to young persons.

The maximum fine that an adult magistrates' court may impose on a juvenile is restricted in the same way as is the maximum fine that may be imposed by a youth court (see **D21.24**).

The principal orders which may be made at the same time as ordering a conditional or absolute discharge are disqualification from driving, endorsement of the driving licence and orders ancillary to the sentence proper such as orders to pay compensation or costs. Thus, the effect of s. 7(8) is that – unless the case is trivial enough to be dealt with by fine, discharge or order that the parents enter into a recognisance, whether or not combined with an ancillary order – the adult court *must* remit the juvenile to the youth court to be sentenced. It follows from the terms of s. 7(8) that the adult court cannot even take a decision under the MCA 1980, s. 37, to commit a juvenile to the Crown Court for sentence, although the youth court could take such a course following remittal. The remittal must be either to the youth court acting for the same place as the remitting court or to the court for the place where the juvenile habitually resides (see CYPA 1933, s. 56(1)). The remitting court may grant the juvenile bail or give directions that he be kept in care or in custody (s. 56(3)).

SENTENCING POWERS AND PROCEDURE IN THE YOUTH COURT

Sentencing Powers Generally

The sentencing powers of the youth court in respect of a juvenile found guilty by it of **D21.24** an indictable offence are governed by the MCA 1980, s. 24(3) and (4).

Magistrates' Courts Act 1980, s. 24

(3)   If on trying a person summarily in pursuance of subsection (1) above the court finds him guilty, it may impose a fine of an amount not exceeding £1,000 or may exercise the same powers as it could have exercised if he had been found guilty of an offence for which, but for section 1(1) of the Criminal Justice Act 1982, it could have sentenced him to imprisonment for a term not exceeding—

   (a)   the maximum term of imprisonment for the offence on conviction on indictment; or

   (b)   six months,

whichever is the less.

(4)   In relation to a person under the age of 14 subsection (3) above shall have effect as if for the words '£1,000' there were substituted the words '£250'.

Unless certain exceptional conditions apply, s. 24(1) requires a magistrates' court to proceed to the summary trial of a juvenile charged with any indictable offence other than homicide (see **D21.3** to **D21.8**). The CJA 1982, s. 1(1), prohibits the passing of sentences of imprisonment in respect of offenders under 21. However, the power to pass a sentence of detention in a young offender institution under s. 1A of the 1982 Act is dependent upon the maximum term of imprisonment that could be imposed were the offender over 21. The MCA 1980, s. 24(3), must also be read subject to the CYPA 1969, s. 7(8), which essentially prevents an adult magistrates' court passing any sentence on a juvenile other than a fine or absolute or conditional discharge. Thus, the effect of the MCA 1980, s. 24(3), is that a youth court dealing with a juvenile for one indictable offence may sentence him to a maximum of six months' detention in a young offender institution. By virtue of the MCA 1980, s. 133(1) and (2), a maximum aggregate term of up to 12 months may be imposed for two or more indictable offences. As to the maximum fine that a juvenile summarily convicted of an indictable offence may be ordered to pay, that is £1,000 (whether the finding of guilt is by an adult court or a youth court), unless the juvenile is still a child, in which case the maximum is reduced to £250.

A juvenile found guilty in a youth court of a summary offence may be sentenced to a term of detention in a young offender institution not exceeding the maximum term of imprisonment imposable for the offence in the case of an offender over 21. As with indictable offences, the maximum fine that may be imposed is £1,000 in the cases of young persons and £250 for children (or the maximum fine allowed by the statute creating the offence if that is less) (MCA 1980, s. 36).

All the methods of dealing with juveniles apart from detention in a young offender institution and fine are at the disposal of the youth court to the same extent and in the same circumstances as they are at the disposal of the Crown Court, save that a sentence of detention under the CYPA 1933, s. 53(3), is dependent upon the conviction having been on indictment and therefore can never be passed by the lower court. For the position in relation to the secure training order, see **E3.16**; for the detention and training order (which will be available when the CDA 1998, s. 73, is brought into force), see **E3.18**.

Procedure before Sentence

D21.25   Rules 10 and 11 of the Magistrates' Courts (Children and Young Persons) Rules 1992 make supplementary provisions about the procedure to be followed before a child or young person found guilty of an offence is sentenced by the youth court (or adult magistrates' court). He and his parent or guardian if present must be given an opportunity to make a statement as to sentence, and the court is also obliged to consider any available information about the juvenile's general conduct, home environment, school record and medical history. Information about his general conduct may include the citing of cautions previously administered by the police (Home Office Circular No.

49 of 1978). If the necessary information is not immediately available, the court must consider the desirability of adjourning for inquiries to be made. Reports from probation officers, local authorities, local education authorities, schools or doctors may be considered without being read aloud (although copies should be made available to the juvenile's legal representatives and parent or guardian if present). The juvenile himself should be shown a copy of any report unless the court directs to the contrary on the ground that disclosing the report to him is either impracticable by reason of his age or understanding or undesirable because it might cause him serious harm. If considered necessary in the juvenile's own interests, both he and his parent may be required to withdraw from court during the sentencing process. However, where a report has not been disclosed to an unrepresented juvenile or where the juvenile has been required to leave court, the court is under a duty to disclose to him the gist of information relating to his character or conduct which it considers material to sentence (unless that would be impracticable having regard to his age and understanding). Before finally disposing of the case, the court must inform the juvenile and his parent or guardian (if present) of the way it proposes to deal with him, and give them an opportunity to make final representations. On making its order, the court must explain its nature and effect.

The responsibility for preparing reports on juveniles rests primarily on the local authority in whose area the juvenile resides (CYPA 1969, s. 9), although in the cases of juveniles who have attained the age of 13 the justices or probation and after-care committee for a particular area may direct that the task be undertaken by probation officers (see s. 34(3) of the 1969 Act and SI 1970 No. 1882).

Magistrates' Courts (Children and Young Persons) Rules 1992 (SI 1992 No. 2071), rr. 10 and 11

10.—(1)   This rule applies where—

    (a)   the relevant minor is found guilty of an offence, whether after a plea of guilty or otherwise, or

    (b)   in proceedings of a kind mentioned in rule 4(2)(a), (b) or (c) the court is satisfied that the case for the applicant—

        (i)   if the relevant minor is not the applicant, has been made out, or

        (ii)   if he is the applicant, has not been made out.

    (2)   Where this rule applies—

    (a)   the relevant minor and his parent or guardian, if present, shall be given an opportunity of making a statement,

    (b)   the court shall take into consideration all available information as to the general conduct, home surroundings, school record and medical history of the relevant minor and, in particular, shall take into consideration such information as aforesaid which is provided in pursuance of section 9 of [the CYPA 1969],

    (c)   if such information as aforesaid is not fully available, the court shall consider the desirability of adjourning the proceedings for such inquiry as may be necessary,

    (d)   any written report of a probation officer, local authority, local education authority, educational establishment or registered medical practitioner may be received and considered by the court without being read aloud, and

    (e)   if the court considers it necessary in the interests of the relevant minor, it may require him or his parent or guardian, if present, to withdraw from the court.

    (3)   The court shall arrange for copies of any written report before the court to be made available to—

    (a)   the legal representative, if any, of the relevant minor,

    (b)   any parent or guardian or the relevant minor who is present at the hearing, and

    (c)   the relevant minor, except where the court otherwise directs on the ground that it appears to it impracticable to disclose the report having regard to his age and understanding or undesirable to do so having regard to potential serious harm which might thereby be suffered by him.

    (4)   In any case in which the relevant minor is not legally represented and where a report which has not been made available to him in accordance with a direction under paragraph

(3)(c) has been considered without being read aloud in pursuance of paragraph (2)(d) or where he or his parent or guardian has been required to withdraw from the court in pursuance of paragraph (2)(e), then—

(a)   the relevant minor shall be told the substance of any part of the information given to the court bearing on his character or conduct which the court considers to be material to the manner in which the case should be dealt with unless it appears to it impracticable so to do having regard to his age and understanding, and

(b)   the parent or guardian of the relevant minor, if present, shall be told the substance of any part of such information which the court considers to be material as aforesaid and which has reference to his character or conduct or to the character, conduct, home surroundings or health of the relevant minors and if such a person, having been told the substance of any part of such information, desires to produce further evidence with reference thereto, the court, if it thinks the further evidence would be material, shall adjourn the proceedings for the production thereof and shall, if necessary in the case of a report, require the attendance at the adjourned hearing of the person who made the report.

11.—(1)   Before finally disposing of the case or before remitting the case to another court in pursuance of section 56 of [the CYPA 1933], the court shall inform the relevant minor and his parent or guardian, if present, or any person assisting him in his case, of the manner in which it proposes to deal with the case and allow any of those persons so informed to make representations; but the relevant minor shall not be informed as aforesaid if the court considers it undesirable so to do.

(2)   On making any order, the court shall explain to the relevant minor the general nature and effect of the order unless, in the case of an order requiring his parent or guardian to enter into a recognizance, it appears to it undesirable so to do.

Children and Young Persons Act 1969, s. 9

(1)   Where a local authority or a local education authority bring proceedings for an offence alleged to have been committed by a [juvenile] or are notified that any such proceedings are being brought, it shall be the duty of the authority, unless they are of opinion that it is unnecessary to do so, to make such investigations and provide the court before which the proceedings are heard with such information relating to the home surroundings, school record, health and character of the person in respect of whom the proceedings are brought as appear to the authority likely to assist the court.

(2)   If the court mentioned in subsection (1) of this section requests the authority aforesaid to make investigations and provide information or to make further investigations and provide further information relating to the matters aforesaid, it shall be the duty of the authority to comply with the request.

Children and Young Persons Act 1969, s. 34(3)

In the case of a person who has attained such age as the Secretary of State may by order specify, an authority shall, without prejudice to subsection (2) of section 9 of this Act, not be required by virtue of subsection (1) of that section to make investigations or provide information which it does not already possess with respect to his home surroundings if, by direction of the justices or probation committee acting for any relevant area, arrangements are in force for information with respect to his home surroundings to be furnished to the court in question by a probation officer.

Remittal to Another Youth Court

D21.26   Instead of itself sentencing a juvenile who pleads or is found guilty before it, a youth court may remit him to the youth court for the area where he habitually resides, which court may then deal with him as if it had just convicted him (CYPA 1933, s. 56(1)). The receiving court also has all the powers of jurisdiction that it would have had in the first place. It can, for example, accept a change of plea during the course of proceedings (see **D18.24** for the factors to be taken into account) (*Stratford Youth Court, ex parte Conde* [1997] 1 WLR 113).

Committal for Sentence under the Magistrates' Courts Act 1980, s. 37

Magistrates' Courts Act 1980, s. 37

D21.27

(1)   Where a person who is not less than 15 but under 18 years old is convicted by a magistrates' court of an offence punishable on conviction on indictment with a term of imprisonment exceeding six months, then, if the court is of opinion that he should be sentenced to a greater term of detention in a young offender institution than it has power to impose, the court may commit him in custody or on bail to the Crown Court for sentence.

Powers of Criminal Courts Act 1973, s. 42

(2)   Where an offender is committed by a magistrates' court for sentence under section 37 of the Magistrates' Courts Act 1980 . . ., the Crown Court shall inquire into the circumstances of the case and shall have power—
(a)   to sentence him to a term of detention in a young offender institution not exceeding the maximum term of imprisonment for the offence on conviction on indictment; or
(b)   to deal with him in any manner in which the magistrates' court might have dealt with him.

When the CDA 1998, sch. 8, para. 41, is brought into force, the MCA 1980, s. 37, will be repealed.

Section 1B of the CJA 1982 restricts the maximum term in a young offender institution that may be imposed on a juvenile aged 15, 16 or 17 to 24 months. The maximum applies even if he is being sentenced in the Crown Court, and regardless of whether he is to be dealt with for one or several offences. If, following a committal under s. 37, the Crown Court decides not to impose a sentence of detention in a young offender institution, its powers are limited to those the youth court could have exercised had it not chosen to commit. In particular, the Crown Court will not be able to sentence the juvenile to detention in accordance with the Secretary of State's directions under the CYPA 1933, s. 53(3), since that form of sentence is dependent upon there having been a conviction on indictment.

Further points relevant to committals under the MCA 1980, s. 37, are:

(a)   Although the section itself prima facie allows *any* magistrates' court to make use of the powers therein contained, it must be read in conjunction with the CYPA 1969, s. 7(8), which requires an adult magistrates' court that has convicted a juvenile to remit him to the youth court for sentence unless it can deal with him by fine or discharge. It is submitted that, in the light of s. 7(8), an adult magistrates' court which considers that a juvenile aged 15, 16 or 17 deserves more than six months' detention is nonetheless obliged to remit him to the youth court (rather than committing him direct to the Crown Court). Following remittal, the youth court may decide to send him to the Crown Court.
(b)   Section 37 applies only to juveniles aged 15, 16 or 17. Juveniles under 15 cannot be sentenced to detention in a young offender institution.
(c)   The last clause of s. 37(1) empowers the youth court to commit either in custody or on bail. As to committal in custody see **D5.54**.
(d)   Upon committing a juvenile under s. 37, the court may also commit him under the CJA 1967, s. 56, to be dealt with for any other matters for which the committing court would otherwise have sentenced him. Any power or duty to endorse any driving licence that the juvenile may subsequently obtain or disqualify him from driving must be exercised by the Crown Court, notwithstanding anything in the Road Traffic Offenders Act 1988 which might prima facie require the power to be exercised by the lower court (CJA 1967, s. 56(6)).

MODE OF TRIAL AND PROCEDURE FOR PERSONS AGED 17 OR 18

This section deals with the various provisions relevant to persons whose age at the time of proceedings against them is around 17 or 18. The basic question which arises is whether such persons should be treated as juveniles or adults, in particular with regard to mode of trial and sentencing powers. The decided cases deal generally with the situation where the determining event was the accused's seventeenth birthday. With the coming into force of the CJA 1991, s. 68, the eighteenth birthday became the watershed at which a juvenile is subjected to the adult procedural regime.

Determining Age

D21.28 By the CYPA 1933, s. 99(1), where a person apparently under 18 is brought before a court, the court is to make 'due inquiry' as to his age and must take into account such evidence on the matter as may be forthcoming at the hearing of the case. However, any order or judgment of the court is not to be invalidated by subsequent proof that the person's age was incorrectly stated, and he is deemed for purposes of the 1933 Act to be whatever age he is presumed or declared to be by the court (ibid.). Thus, if an accused who looks like a juvenile is brought before a criminal court, he should be asked his age. The court is entitled to accept what he (or his parent if present) says on the matter, although in cases of doubt it may ask for further inquiries to be undertaken. If, having made the appropriate inquiries, the court proceeds on the assumption that the accused is aged 18 or over, he is deemed to be an adult even if it subsequently turns out that he was under 18, and vice versa. The MCA 1980, s. 150(4), makes similar provision in respect of age-dependent powers granted to magistrates by that Act.

Children and Young Persons Act 1933, s. 99

(1) Where a person, whether charged with an offence or not, is brought before any court otherwise than for the purposes of giving evidence, and it appears to the court that he is a child or young person, the court shall make due inquiry as to the age of that person, and for that purpose shall take such evidence as may be forthcoming at the hearing of the case, but an order or judgment of the court shall not be invalidated by any subsequent proof that the age of that person has not been correctly stated to the court, and the age presumed or declared by the court to be the age of the person so brought before it shall, for the purposes of this Act, be deemed to be the true age of that person, and, where it appears to the court that the person so brought before it has attained the age of 18 years, that person shall for the purposes of this Act be deemed not to be a child or young person.

[(2) to (4) Deal with proof of age of the victim of an offence where the charge alleges that he was a child or young person.]

Magistrates' Courts Act 1980, s. 150(4)

Where the age of any person at any time is material for the purposes of any provision of this Act regulating the powers of a magistrates' court, his age at the material time shall be deemed to be or to have been that which appears to the court after considering any available evidence to be or to have been his age at that time.

Discovery of True Age during Proceedings

D21.29 The statutory presumption (see **D21.28**) that an accused apparently around the age of 17 or 18 is whatever age he is declared to be by the court prevents judgments or orders of the court (in particular, findings of guilt and sentences) being disturbed should it be discovered after the court is *functus officio* that it was misled as to age. The presumption cannot assist where it emerges during the course of the proceedings that the court's initial view about age was erroneous. However, proviso (c) of the CYPA 1933, s. 46(1), gives an adult magistrates' court which has embarked upon the trial of a defendant in the belief that he was an adult a discretion to complete the hearing even if it should appear to the court during the course of the proceedings that he is in fact a juvenile. Conversely, s. 48(1) of the 1933 Act provides that 'A youth court sitting for the purpose of hearing a charge against a person who is believed to be a child or young person may, if it thinks fit to do so, proceed with the hearing and determination of the charge notwithstanding that it is discovered that the person in question is not a child or young person'.

Mode of Trial where the Defendant Attains the Age of 18 during Proceedings

The MCA 1980, s. 18(1), provides that ss. 19 to 23 of the Act which deal with determining **D21.30** mode of trial for an adult) 'shall have effect where a person who has attained the age of 18 appears or is brought before a magistrates' court on an information charging him with an offence triable either way'. The opening clause of s. 24(1) states that 'Where a person under the age of 18 appears or is brought before a magistrates' court on an information charging him with an indictable offence other than homicide, he shall be tried summarily unless . . . .' Plainly the two subsections are interlocking, i.e. where ss. 18(1) and 19 to 23 do not apply the court proceeds under s. 24(1) and vice versa. It is not stated in either provision whether the manner in which the court is to proceed – and hence the right to trial on indictment – depends upon the defendant's age when he first appears or is brought before the court, or upon his age at some subsequent stage of the proceedings. The House of Lords settled the question by holding that it is age at the time when mode of trial falls to be determined that is the determining factor (*Islington North Juvenile Court, ex parte Daley* [1983] 1 AC 347).

In *Ex parte Daley*, D was 16 when arrested and charged with an offence of handling stolen goods. He was still 16 when, having been bailed by the police, he made his first appearance in the juvenile court. On that occasion he was simply remanded to another day. However, by the time he next appeared, he had attained the age of 17 and so had ceased to be a juvenile according to the law at the time. Contrary to the defence argument, the magistrates held that, as D had been a juvenile on the date of his first appearance, they were bound to try him summarily in the juvenile court, notwithstanding that the offence was triable either way in the case of an adult and D wished to elect trial on indictment. D sought judicial review of the magistrates' decision. He was unsuccessful in the Divisional Court, but succeeded on appeal to the House of Lords. Lord Diplock (giving the leading opinion) held that the magistrates had erred because the appearance before the court referred to in both s. 18(1) and s. 24(1) is the appearance on the occasion when mode of trial is determined, not the first appearance. In justification, his lordship mentioned the arbitrary factors that may affect when an accused makes his first appearance (e.g., whether, as in D's case, he is charged at the police station and bailed or, as often happens with juveniles, he is merely told that he will be considered for prosecution but the proceedings are commenced by way of summons, in which case it is standard practice to instruct the defendant not to attend on the return date specified in the summons if he is pleading not guilty but to await notification of a later date for hearing). His lordship also mentioned the fundamental principle that persons who are of a sufficient age to make an informed choice should not be deprived of the advantages of trial on indictment except by exercise of their own free will. His conclusion was that 'reason and justice combine to indicate that the only appropriate date at which to determine whether an accused person has attained an age which entitles him to elect to be tried by jury is the date of his appearance before the court on the occasion when the court makes its decision as to the mode of trial'.

Although *Ex parte Daley* has greatly clarified the interpretation of the MCA 1980, ss. 18(1) and 24(1), the subject is still not totally free of doubt. Lord Diplock makes the question of jurisdiction turn upon age at the moment when the youth court 'makes its decision as to the mode of trial'. But, it is submitted that, where juveniles are concerned, referring to a decision on mode of trial is generally something of a misnomer, since the only situations in which the court has to choose between summary trial and committal proceedings are when either the juvenile is jointly charged with an adult who is being committed or transferred for trial or when a young person is charged with an offence carrying 14 years' imprisonment or more, an indecent assault upon a woman, causing death by dangerous driving or causing death by careless driving while under the influence of drink or drugs and it is suggested that a sentence under the CYPA 1933, s. 53(3), might be appropriate in the event of conviction. In all other cases, there is no choice – the juvenile *must* be tried summarily whether the magistrates like it or not (save when homicide is alleged, in which case he must be tried on indictment). Thus, in the great majority of cases, there is no separate occasion on which mode of trial for a juvenile is determined – he is simply asked to plead guilty or not guilty, and such decision as there is as to mode of trial is implicit in the clerk being allowed to put the charge to him. Therefore, it is submitted that Lord Diplock must be taken as having meant that the right of a person who attains the relevant age during the currency of proceedings against him to be tried on indictment for an indictable offence depends either upon his age when mode of trial is determined, or – if there is no express determination of mode of trial – upon his age when the court is ready for the charge to be put. If he was under that age on the occasion of pleading, he had no right to elect trial on indictment, even if the matter is forthwith adjourned for trial at a later date and he attains the age before any evidence is heard. Partial support for this suggestion is found in *Lewes Juvenile Court, ex parte T* (1984) 149 JP 186. In that case, T pleaded not guilty in the youth court to theft of a pedal cycle. That was on 31 March 1983 when he was still 16. The case was adjourned to 28 April 1983, it being anticipated that summary trial would take place on that date. In fact, both then and on three subsequent occasions, the trial was unable to go ahead for reasons such as non-attendance of prosecution witnesses, non-attendance of T and the justices finding themselves disqualified from adjudicating. Between the last adjournment and the date when the trial could actually have proceeded, T attained the age of 17. It was argued in the Divisional Court that (contrary to the ruling of the justices) T now had the right to elect trial on indictment. The argument failed. Applying *Ex parte Daley*, Stephen Brown LJ said that the significant date was 28 April 1983, the date when the court and parties for the first time assembled in expectation that the case would proceed. Since T was a juvenile on that date, s. 24(1) – not s. 18(1) – was the operative provision. The fact that no evidence was called until after T was 17 was irrelevant. It is submitted that it would have been more logical to put the significant date even further back – to 31 March 1983 when T entered his plea.

The corollary of *Ex parte Daley* is that, where the offence charged is triable only on indictment in the case of an adult, an erstwhile juvenile must go to the Crown Court for trial if he is 18 before a plea is taken. In *Vale of Glamorgan Juvenile Justices, ex parte Beattie* (1985) 82 Cr App R 1 the youth court was held to have no power or discretion to proceed summarily on a charge of robbery because, even though B was 16 when he first appeared and the defence had informally indicated an intention to plead guilty, he had his seventeenth birthday before the court was actually ready to take a plea (and, according to the law at the time, then became an adult). It must also follow that, in cases where the sequence of events is as in *Ex parte Beattie* but the offence is triable either way, the 'juvenile' – if he wants to be dealt with summarily – can only make representations to that effect, the court being entitled to refuse jurisdiction if it considers that the charge is too serious for summary disposal. Moreover, any summary trial would take place in the adult magistrates' court, not the youth court.

In *Nottingham Justices, ex parte Taylor* [1992] QB 557, by contrast, the accused was aged 16 when he pleaded guilty to charges of robbery. He attained the age of 17 (and hence, according to the law at the time, became an adult) before the court was ready to try the case. The justices then ruled that he must be committed to the Crown Court because the charges were triable only on indictment. The Divisional Court held that he should not have been committed, since the material date was that at which the mode of trial was determined, when he was still aged 16.

Sentencing Powers where Defendant Attains the Age of 18 after Finding of Guilt

D21.31   **Children and Young Persons Act 1963, s. 29**

Where proceedings in respect of a young person are begun for an offence and he attains the age of 18 before the conclusion of the proceedings, the court may deal with the case and make any order which it could have made if he had not attained that age.

Prima facie, s. 29 could be interpreted as permitting the youth court to retain jurisdiction to try an indictable offence even where the 'juvenile' attains the age of 18 before mode of trial is determined, provided the proceedings were commenced when he was still 17. In the light of *Islington North Juvenile Court, ex parte Daley* [1983] 1 AC 347 (see **D21.30**), such a broad interpretation is clearly untenable, although Lord Diplock's judgment makes no reference to the section, and its possible relevance does not seem to have been argued before the House. In the absence of any clear authority, the proper scope of s. 29 remains doubtful. It is submitted that it has one clear application, namely, in respect of sentencing. Thus, where an accused pleads or is found guilty when still a juvenile but attains the age of 18 during an adjournment before sentence, the court may deal with him as if he remained under that age (e.g., by making a supervision order, which is not normally available in the cases of 18-year-olds). That the above is the correct interpretation of s. 29 receives some confirmation from *St Albans Juvenile Court, ex parte Goodman* [1981] QB 964, where Skinner J accepted the submissions of both counsel that s. 29 applies only to questions of disposal and not to questions of trial. Skinner J's dictum was referred to with approval by Stephen Brown LJ in *Lewes Juvenile Court, ex parte T* (1984) 149 JP 186 (see **E3.3**). See also *Bruley* [1996] Crim LR 913.

Remittal to Adult Magistrates' Court

Section 47 of the CDA 1998 gives the youth court a discretionary power to remit a **D21.32** juvenile to an adult magistrates' court for trial or sentence once he reaches the age of 18.

Crime and Disorder Act 1998, s. 47

(1) Where a person who appears or is brought before a youth court charged with an offence subsequently attains the age of 18, the youth court may, at any time—
    (a) before the start of the trial; or
    (b) after conviction and before sentence,
remit the person for trial or, as the case may be, for sentence to a magistrates' court (other than a youth court) acting for the same petty sessions area as the youth court.
In this subsection 'the start of the trial' shall be construed in accordance with section 22(11B) of the [Prosecution of Offences Act 1985].

Additional Charges after Defendant Attains the Age of 18

Where an accused against whom proceedings have properly been commenced in the **D21.33** youth court attains the age of 18 and is then charged with an additional matter, the latter charge may not in any circumstances be heard in the youth court (*Chelsea Justices, ex parte DPP* [1963] 1 WLR 1138). That applies regardless of whether the youth court is able to retain jurisdiction over the original charge. Accordingly, in *Chelsea Justices, ex parte DPP*, the Divisional Court issued an order of prohibition preventing the youth court hearing a charge of attempted murder first preferred when the accused was 17 (and hence, at that time, an adult), even though it arose out of the same facts as a charge of wounding with intent preferred when he was 16.

Deliberate Delay Until Defendant Becomes 18

The position where the prosecution deliberately delays the issue of process, so that the **D21.34** accused is no longer a juvenile when he appears in court was considered in *Rotherham Justices, ex parte Brough* [1991] Crim LR 522. B (aged 16) 'glassed' another youth. The prosecution wished him to be tried for an offence under s. 18 of the Offences Against the Person Act 1861, which would be triable only on indictment in the case of an adult. In order to avoid any possibility that the youth court might try him, his court appearance was fixed for a date after his seventeenth birthday, which at that time was the day on which he became an adult. It was argued unsuccessfully on B's behalf before the magistrates that the CPS had abused the process of the court. On appeal, the Divisional Court held that B had not been prejudiced since (a) the delay was under a week, (b) the justices would probably have committed the case to the Crown Court under the Magistrates' Court Act 1980, s. 24(1)(a), in any event, and (c) the trial judge in the Crown Court would no doubt take account of B's age and the circumstances of his committal if he were convicted. Nonetheless, the prosecution's action was said to be 'wrong and undesirable', and the door appears to be open for the defence to argue, in somewhat different circumstances, that usurpation of the youth court's jurisdiction constituted abuse of process.

SECTION D22: APPEAL TO THE COURT OF APPEAL (CRIMINAL DIVISION) FOLLOWING TRIAL ON INDICTMENT

STATUTORY BASES OF JURISDICTION OF COURT OF APPEAL (CRIMINAL DIVISION)

Appeals against conviction on indictment and against sentence passed following **D22.1** conviction on indictment are heard by the Court of Appeal (Criminal Division).

The present legislation on the jurisdiction of the Criminal Division is contained in the Supreme Court Act 1981, supplemented, *inter alia*, by parts I and II of the Criminal Appeal Act 1968, the CJA 1982, s. 36, the CJA 1988, ss. 35 and 36, and the Criminal Appeal Act 1995. The Supreme Court Act 1981, s. 15(2), provides that:

> Subject to the provisions of this Act, there shall be exercisable by the Court of Appeal—
>   (a) all such jurisdiction (whether civil or criminal) as is conferred on it by this or any other Act; and
>   (b) all such other jurisdiction (whether civil or criminal) as was exercisable by it immediately before the commencement of this Act.

In fact, the Supreme Court Act 1981 itself does not directly confer any jurisdiction in criminal matters. The Supreme Court Act 1981, s. 16(1), provides that the Court of Appeal shall have jurisdiction to hear and determine appeals from any judgment or order of the High Court. At first sight this might seem to be conferring a criminal appellate jurisdiction inasmuch as the High Court is empowered to hear appeals by way of case stated and/or entertain applications for judicial review in criminal matters. However, s. 16(1) is subject to s. 18(1)(a) which provides that no appeal shall lie to the Court of Appeal from any judgment of the High Court in any criminal cause or matter. Thus, the nature and extent of the Criminal Division's powers depend upon the other statutes mentioned above. In summary, they provide as follows:

Criminal Appeal Act 1968, ss. 1 and 2	Jurisdiction to determine appeals against conviction on indictment.
Criminal Appeal Act 1968, ss. 9 and 11	Jurisdiction to determine appeals against sentence passed following conviction on indictment.
Criminal Appeal Act 1968, ss. 10 and 11	Jurisdiction to determine appeals against sentence passed on a committal for sentence.
Criminal Justice Act 1982, s. 36	Jurisdiction to give an opinion on a point of law referred to the court by the A-G following an acquittal on indictment.
Criminal Justice Act 1987, s. 9(11) to (14)	Jurisdiction to determine appeals against rulings made at preparatory hearings in serious fraud cases.
Criminal Justice Act 1988, ss. 35 and 36	Jurisdiction to increase sentence on a reference by the A-G following an unduly lenient sentence for an offence triable only on indictment.
Criminal Appeal Act 1995, s. 13	Jurisdiction to determine appeals on a reference by the Criminal Cases Review Commission.

In addition to the above statutory heads of jurisdiction, the Court of Appeal retains the jurisdiction originally exercised by the Court for Crown Cases Reserved to issue a writ of *venire de novo* (see **D22.33**). This is virtually equivalent to a power to order a retrial, and may very occasionally assist an appellant in a case falling outside the ambit of the statutory jurisdiction to quash a conviction conferred by the Criminal Appeal Act 1968, ss. 1 and 2. Although not expressly preserved by the Criminal Appeal Act 1907, it was held in *Crane* v *DPP* [1921] 2 AC 299 that the writ had in fact survived the abolition of the Court for Crown Cases Reserved and was at the disposal of that court's replacement, the Court of Criminal Appeal. The Criminal Appeal Act 1966, upon creating the Criminal Division, provided that it should exercise all jurisdiction belonging to the Court of Criminal Appeal immediately before its abolition, including that of ordering a *venire de novo*. Having regard to the terms of the Supreme Court Act 1981, s. 15(2)(b), it will be apparent that the Court of Appeal continues to enjoy the same power.

Save for the quasi-exception of *venire de novo*, the jurisdiction of the Criminal Division is entirely statutory (see especially *Jefferies* [1969] 1 QB 120). It follows that – save as provided by the CJA 1987, s. 9(11) to (14) – the court has no jurisdiction to hear appeals against interlocutory decisions of the Crown Court relating to a trial on indictment, since each jurisdiction-conferring provision other than the CJA 1987, s. 9, expressly requires that there shall have been a conviction, sentence or, as the case may be, acquittal before the right to appeal arises (see *Collins* [1970] 1 QB 710, where the defence, prior to trial, sought to appeal against the judge's refusal to order the prosecution to serve further particulars of a count which was claimed to be incomprehensible as drafted – the Court of Appeal held that it simply had no jurisdiction in the matter). Similarly, in *Smith* [1975] QB 531, a solicitor who had been ordered by the Crown Court to pay personally the costs thrown away as a result of a last-minute application to adjourn was unable to appeal against the order. Lord Denning MR said (at p. 541D):

> It seems that there is no appeal against an interlocutory order. . . . This may, at first sight, seem surprising, but on consideration there is much to be said for it. The trial judge should have the final word on such matters as adjournments, joint or several trials, bail, particulars and so forth. The only remedy is this: in case a trial judge should make a mistake on an interlocutory matter, such as to cause injustice, the man can appeal against his conviction, and it will be taken into account at that stage. . . . But, save in this way, there is no appeal to the Court of Appeal against an interlocutory order.

Note, however, that in *Holden and Co.* v *CPS* [1990] 2 QB 261 the Court of Appeal *did* hear and allow appeals by a number of solicitors' firms against orders to pay costs thrown away. No point seems to have been taken on the jurisdictional problem – *Smith* was cited in argument but was not referred to in Lord Lane CJ's judgment.

COMPOSITION OF THE COURT OF APPEAL

Judges of the Court

D22.2   The Court of Appeal consists, at present, of up to 32 Lord Justices of Appeal plus a number of ex-officio members (see Supreme Court Act 1981, s. 2). By the Supreme Court Act 1981, s. 3(1), 'There shall be two divisions of the Court of Appeal, namely the Criminal Division and the Civil Division'. The Lord Chief Justice is the president of the Criminal Division (s. 3(2)). He may request any High Court judge to act as a judge of the Division (s. 9(1)) and, upon such request being made, it is the duty of the High Court judge to comply with it (s. 9(3)).

The Lord Chief Justice can request, by virtue of s. 9, any circuit judge who has been approved for the purpose by the Lord Chancellor to act as a judge of the Division. A circuit judge may not, however, act as the single judge for the purposes of s. 31 or 44 of the Criminal Appeal Act 1968. Only one circuit judge may be a member of any particular court, and a circuit judge may not be involved in an appeal where a High Court judge presided over the trial or passed sentence.

The distribution of work between the two Divisions is set out in the Supreme Court Act 1981, s. 53, which provides that the Criminal Division shall exercise (a) the Court of Appeal's jurisdiction under parts I and II of the Criminal Appeal Act 1968; (b) its jurisdiction under the Administration of Justice Act 1960, s. 13 (appeals in cases of contempt of court) where the appeal relates to an order of the Crown Court; (c) such jurisdiction as is expressly conferred on the Division by any Act (see, for example, the CJA 1988, s. 35(2), which provides that the jurisdiction to determine A-G's references of over-lenient sentences shall be exercised by the Criminal Division), and (d) the jurisdiction to issue writs of *venire de novo*. Any other jurisdiction of the Court of Appeal is to be exercised by the Civil Division.

Matters Dealt with by a Full Court

Any number of courts of either Division of the Court of Appeal may sit at the same time **D22.3** (Supreme Court Act 1981, s. 3(5)). A court of the Criminal Division is duly constituted for the purpose of exercising *any* of its jurisdiction if it consists of an uneven number of judges numbering not less than three (s. 55(3)). It is very rare for a court of the Criminal Division to number more than three, but this may occur where the case is of exceptional importance (see *Turnbull* [1977] QB 224 for an example) or where there have previously been apparently conflicting decisions by differently constituted three-judge courts on the point raised by the appeal (see, for example, *Newsome* [1970] 2 QB 711). Although a three-judge court may exercise any part of the Criminal Division's jurisdiction, the effect of the provisions described at **D22.4** and **D22.5** below is that the only matters which *must* be heard by a court so constituted are: (a) the determination of an appeal against conviction, (b) the determination of an appeal against a verdict of not guilty by reason of insanity, (c) the determination of an appeal against a finding of unfitness to plead, (d) the determination of an application for leave to appeal to the House of Lords, and (e) the refusal of an application for leave to appeal to the Court of Appeal in a case where an application has not first been made (unsuccessfully) to a single judge (Supreme Court Act 1981, s. 55(4)).

Matters Dealt with by a Two-Judge Court

The Supreme Court Act 1981, s. 55(4), provides that a court of the Criminal Division **D22.4** consisting of two judges shall be 'duly constituted for every purpose' except those mentioned in **D22.3** above, for which a three-judge court is essential. Thus, a two-judge court may, *inter alia:* (a) determine appeals against sentence; (b) *grant* leave to appeal to the Criminal Division whether or not an application has previously been made to a single judge; (c) *refuse* leave to appeal if – and only if – there has already been an unsuccessful application to a single judge, and (d) deal with any other interlocutory matter relating to an appeal irrespective of whether the matter has previously been considered by a single judge.

Matters Dealt with by a Single Judge

The matters listed in the Criminal Appeal Act 1968, s. 31, may be dealt with by a single **D22.5** judge of the Criminal Division. See **D23.21** for the text of s. 31.

The single judge (who may be – and usually is – a High Court judge requested by the Lord Chief Justice to assist the Criminal Division) usually determines applications upon a private reading of the papers without hearing argument from the parties. Where an appellant makes an unsuccessful application to a single judge (e.g., for leave to appeal), he may renew the application before a court (s. 31(3)).

DECIDING OUTCOME OF APPEAL AND GIVING JUDGMENT

A decision of a court of the Criminal Division may be taken by a majority of its members. **D22.6** If a two-judge court is equally divided, the case must be reargued before and determined by an unevenly numbered court (Supreme Court Act 1981, s. 55(5)). Because of the need for certainty in the criminal law, it is the practice for only one judgment to be given. However, the Supreme Court Act 1981, s. 59, permits a departure from this practice where the judge presiding over the court states that in his opinion the question is one of law on which it is convenient that separate judgments should be pronounced. Assuming only one judgment is given it is delivered by the judge presiding or by such other member of the court as he directs (ibid.).

RIGHT OF APPEAL AGAINST CONVICTION

Statutory Basis of Appeal against Conviction

D22.7   **Criminal Appeal Act 1968, s. 1**

> (1) Subject to subsection (3) below a person convicted of an offence on indictment may appeal to the Court of Appeal against his conviction.
> (2) An appeal under this section lies only—
>   (a) with the leave of the Court of Appeal; or
>   (b) if the judge of the court of trial grants a certificate that the case is fit for appeal.
> [(3) and (4) No appeal to lie against a conviction on indictment for an offence of criminal damage on the ground that the court which committed or transferred the accused for trial was mistaken as to the value involved in the offence and ought to have proceeded as if the offence were triable only summarily.]

The effect of s. 1 is that an accused convicted on indictment may appeal as of right if the Crown Court has granted a certificate that the case is fit for appeal on a ground of fact. In all other cases, he requires leave of the Court of Appeal to appeal.

D22.8 ***Trial Judge's Certificate*** The judge of the court of trial may grant a certificate that the case is fit for appeal (Criminal Appeal Act 1968, s. 1(2) – see **D22.7**). By s. 51(1), 'the court of trial' means the court from which the appeal lies, and 'the judge of the court of trial' means, where the Crown Court consists of a professional judge plus justices, the judge presiding. A certificate may be granted either on the judge's own initiative at the conclusion of the trial or on counsel's application. In the former case, it is suggested that the judge drafts the question which he considers ought to be raised and reads the draft to counsel so that they can comment thereon before it is actually certified. In the latter case, counsel normally drafts the question and the application itself is made in chambers with a shorthand writer present (see *Practice Direction (Crown Court: Bail Pending Appeal)* [1983] 1 WLR 1292, para. 3). A certificate will not be granted merely because counsel asks for it (*Langley* (1923) 17 Cr App R 199) or because the judge is uneasy about the verdict (*Perfect* (1917) 12 Cr App R 273). It must be shown that there is a particular and cogent ground of appeal on which the convicted person (if he chooses to appeal) will have a substantial chance of succeeding (*Parkin* (1928) 20 Cr App R 173, *Bansal* [1999] Crim LR 484, and see also *Practice Direction (Crown Court: Bail Pending Appeal)* [1983] 1 WLR 1292, para. 3).

Disposition of Frivolous and Vexatious Appeals

D22.9 The Criminal Appeal Act 1968, s. 20, provides that:

> If it appears to the Registrar that a notice of appeal or application for leave to appeal does not show any substantial ground of appeal, he may refer the appeal or application for leave to the court for summary determination; and where the case is so referred the court may, if they consider that the appeal or application for leave is frivolous or vexatious, and can be determined without adjourning it for a full hearing, dismiss the appeal or application for leave summarily, without calling on anyone to attend the hearing or to appear for the Crown thereon.

The proper scope of the s. 20 procedure has been considered in a number of cases. A point raised in grounds of appeal may be substantial enough to demand a full hearing even though it is unlikely to succeed (see *Majewski* [1977] AC 443). But, if the ground is so obviously unmeritorious that there is no realistic prospect of it succeeding after full argument, then it comes within the phrase 'frivolous or vexatious' and may properly be dismissed summarily (*Taylor* [1979] Crim LR 649). Thus in *Tejendersingh* (21 March 1975 unreported), which was referred to with approval by Lawton LJ in *Majewski*, T sought to argue that the English courts had had no jurisdiction to try him as he was a foreigner. Since the offence was committed in England, the point was clearly and indisputably bad, and it was properly dismissed by use of the s. 20 procedure.

Directions Concerning Loss of Time

A further way of discouraging frivolous appeals (whether on law alone or on other **D22.10** grounds) is by threat of a direction for loss of time (i.e. a direction that time spent in custody by the appellant or applicant for leave to appeal since the commencement of appeal proceedings shall not count towards service of any custodial sentence that may have been imposed by the Crown Court).

Criminal Appeal Act 1968, s. 29

(1)   The time during which an appellant is in custody pending the determination of his appeal shall, subject to any direction which the Court of Appeal may give to the contrary, be reckoned as part of the term of any sentence to which he is for the time being subject.

(2)   Where the Court of Appeal give a contrary direction under subsection (1) above, they shall state their reasons for doing so; and they shall not give any such direction where—
    (a)   leave to appeal has been granted; or
    (b)   a certificate has been given by the judge of the court of trial under—
        (i)   section 1 or 11(1A) of this Act; or
        (ii)   section 81(1B) of the Supreme Court Act 1981; or
    (c)   the case has been referred to them by the Secretary of State under section 17 of this Act.

[(3)   Any period for which an appellant is bailed under the Criminal Appeal Act 1968, s. 19, is not to count towards service of any sentence to which he is subject.]

[(4)   Concerns the date from which any sentence passed by the Court of Appeal itself is to run.]

Thus, in summary, the effect of s. 29(1) and (2) is that unsuccessful applicants for leave to appeal are at risk of a direction for loss of time. However, if leave to appeal has been granted or if the trial judge has granted a certificate that the case is fit for appeal, no direction may be made, no doubt because the granting of leave or, as the case may be, a certificate shows that the appellant acted reasonably in appealing, even if he was ultimately unsuccessful. By s. 31(2), a single judge may exercise the s. 29 powers.

The approach of the Court of Appeal to exercising its powers under s. 29 is set out in *Practice Direction (Crime: Sentence: Loss of Time)* [1980] 1 WLR 270) given by Lord Lane CJ. In it the Lord Chief Justice first refers to *Practice Note (Crime: Applications for Leave to Appeal)* [1970] 1 WLR 663. That indicated in general terms that the volume of unmeritorious applications for leave to appeal was placing an intolerable burden on the Court of Appeal and on single judges; that any convicted person considering commencing an appeal had been enabled to obtain legal advice on the merits of so doing, and that, therefore, if an application was made which was 'unarguable', the single judge would 'have no reason to refrain from directing that time shall be lost'. The 1980 practice direction then continues:

> In order to accelerate the hearing of those appeals in which there is some merit, single judges will, from 15 April 1980, give special consideration to the giving of a direction for loss of time, whenever an application for leave to appeal is refused. It may be expected that such a direction will normally be made unless the grounds are not only settled and signed by counsel, but also supported by the written opinion of counsel. . . . Counsel should not settle grounds, or support them with written advice, unless he considers that the proposed appeal

is properly arguable. It would, therefore, clearly not be appropriate to penalise the appellant in such a case, even if the single judge considered that the appeal was quite hopeless.

It is also necessary to stress that, if an application is refused by the single judge as being wholly devoid of merit, the full court has power, in the event of renewal, both to order loss of time, if the single judge has not done so, and to increase the amount of time ordered to be lost if the single judge has already made a direction, whether or not grounds have been settled and signed by counsel. It may be expected that this power too will, as from 15 April 1980, normally be exercised.

Thus, the essential effect of the practice direction is that an unsuccessful applicant for leave to appeal is protected from a direction for loss of time if (a) the appeal was advised by counsel in writing and grounds were settled and signed by him, and (b) he does not, following the single judge's rejection of the application, renew it before a court. Commencing an appeal without counsel's advice or renewing an application for leave to appeal (whether or not on counsel's advice) puts the appellant at risk of an s. 29 direction. Since the practice direction there have been two decisions of the Court of Appeal prima facie indicating that, if an application for leave to appeal is totally devoid of merit, loss of time may be ordered even by the single judge, notwithstanding that the grounds were signed by counsel (see *Wanklyn* (1984) *The Times*, 11 November 1984 and *Gayle* (1986) *The Times*, 28 May 1986). However, both cases were in fact renewed applications *to a court* for leave to appeal, and it may be that the comments made were not intended to extend beyond such application. If so, their lordships were merely reiterating what Lord Lane CJ had in any event stated in the practice direction. It is perhaps surprising that neither of the appellants in *Wanklyn* or *Gayle* in fact lost time. This may reflect an understandable reluctance by the court to make directions under s. 29 in practice, even though they periodically remind the profession of the possibility of such directions as a deterrent to frivolous appeals. The difficulty with actually ordering loss of time in a case where the appellant acted on counsel's advice is that the court may appear to be punishing the appellant for counsel's over-optimism. For an unsuccessful challenge to loss of time made to the European Court of Human Rights, and a full discussion of the topic, see *Monnell* v *United Kingdom* (1987) 10 EHRR 205.

Appeal against Conviction with Leave

D22.11 Unless the trial judge has granted a certificate that the case is fit for appeal, a would-be appellant needs leave to appeal. The Court of Appeal's power to grant leave to appeal is one which may be – and, in practice, usually is – exercised by a single judge upon a private reading of the papers without oral argument or even written representations from the parties (see Criminal Appeal Act 1968, s. 31(2)(a)). If leave is refused by the single judge, the applicant is entitled to have the application determined by a court, subject only to serving the appropriate notice upon the Registrar of Criminal Appeals (s. 31(3)). Alternatively, at the discretion of the registrar, an application for leave may be listed for hearing by a court without first going before a single judge. The expectation then is that both parties will be legally represented at the application and, if it is granted, the court can forthwith determine the appeal itself. This expedites the appeal procedure in a case which has obvious prima facie merit. A two-judge court may *refuse* an application for leave to appeal against conviction only if it has already been refused by a single judge; a three-judge court may grant or refuse it even in the absence of prior refusal (see Supreme Court Act 1981, s. 55(4), and **D22.3**).

There is little or no authority on the test to be applied in deciding whether leave to appeal should be granted. It is submitted that, by analogy with the authorities on when appeals not requiring leave may properly be referred to the court for summary determination (see **D22.9**), an application for leave should succeed if the grounds relied upon are reasonably arguable, even if the probability is that the ultimate appeal will fail.

As a matter of pure semantics, it is arguable that a person who needs leave to appeal and is in the process of applying for it should be referred to as an 'applicant' and not as an 'appellant'. However, the Criminal Appeal Act 1968, s. 51(1), provides that, unless the context otherwise requires, the word 'appellant' when used in the Act includes a person who has given notice of application for leave to appeal. Thus, s. 29 of the Act, which empowers the Court of Appeal in certain circumstances to make directions for loss of time in respect of appellants whose appeals are dismissed, applies to unsuccessful applicants for leave as well as to unsuccessful appellants. In the remainder of this section, 'appellant' will be used in the sense it is used in the Act, unless the context requires that a distinction be made between mere applicants and appellants proper.

Appeal against Conviction Following a Plea of Guilty

In conferring a right of appeal, the Criminal Appeal Act 1968, s. 1, does not distinguish **D22.12** between persons convicted following a guilty plea and those convicted by a jury. However, for obvious reasons, the Court of Appeal is rarely prepared to grant leave to appeal if the applicant pleaded guilty in the Crown Court. The *locus classicus* on when an appeal may be entertained notwithstanding a guilty plea is the judgment of Avory J in *Forde* [1923] 2 KB 400. His lordship said (at p. 403):

> A plea of guilty having been recorded, this court can only entertain an appeal against conviction if it appears (1) that the appellant did not appreciate the nature of the charge or did not intend to admit he was guilty of it, or (2) that upon the admitted facts he could not in law have been convicted of the offence charged.

An example of a case falling under heading (1) is provided by *Phillips* [1982] 1 All ER 245. P pleaded guilty to all six counts of an indictment charging him with theft or unlawful taking of cars, even though it had previously been agreed between defence solicitors and the prosecution that not guilty pleas to counts 1 and 6 would be acceptable. In an affidavit, P explained that he had been confused by the length of the indictment, and especially by two counts being in almost identical terms. When arraigned, he thought he was pleading only to those charges which his solicitors had previously agreed he should admit. He had not expected the other two even to be put to him. In the unusual circumstances of the case, the Court of Appeal accepted P's explanation, granted leave to appeal and quashed the convictions on counts 1 and 6. P had not 'appreciated the nature of the charges' or 'intended to admit that he was guilty of them'. Also under heading (1) may be brought cases where the appellant pleaded guilty as a result of improper pressure from the judge rendering the plea a nullity (see *Turner* [1970] 2 QB 321) and cases where a plea of guilty (or change of plea to guilty) flowed from a wrong ruling by the judge on a point of law. Thus, in *Clarke* [1972] 1 All ER 219, C's conviction for shoplifting was quashed, notwithstanding that she ultimately pleaded guilty, because her change of plea during trial was induced by the judge's indication that her claim to have absent-mindedly forgotten to pay for the goods in question amounted to a defence of not guilty by reason of insanity! Similarly in *Hunt* [1986] QB 125, where H changed his plea after the trial judge had rejected a submission of no case to answer, the change did not prevent the Court of Appeal hearing argument that the judge's ruling was wrong in law. As to appeals where the judge makes a preliminary ruling on whether the facts alleged amount to the offence charged either before or immediately after arraignment, see *Vickers* [1975] 1 WLR 811.

As to heading (2), the occasions on which this will be relevant in practice will be rare since it implies that both prosecution and defence at the Crown Court were mistaken as to the true elements of the offence charged. An example is, however, provided by *Whitehouse* [1977] QB 868, where W's conviction on his guilty plea to two counts of inciting his 15-year-old daughter to commit incest with him was quashed because a girl of that age cannot herself commit incest (see Sexual Offences Act 1956, s. 11), and therefore she would not have committed any crime had she acceded to W's invitation to have sexual intercourse. The matter originally came before the Court of Appeal as an appeal against sentence, at which stage it was realised that the indictment as framed might not have disclosed offences known to English law and the court accordingly gave leave to appeal against conviction out of time. In *Boal* [1992] QB 591, the Court of Appeal held that it could entertain an appeal against conviction where the appellant had a potentially successful defence, but he pleaded guilty on the basis of a mistaken understanding of the law by his counsel. This was so even though counsel's error was not a case of 'flagrantly incompetent advocacy' and hence did not satisfy the test in *Ensor* (1989) 89 Cr App R 139 (see **D22.18**). See also *Field* (1943) 29 Cr App R 151 and *Jones* (1948) 33 Cr App R 11 for similar examples.

Although still of major importance, Avory J's dictum quoted above is not an exhaustive statement of when a convicted person may be allowed to appeal notwithstanding a guilty plea (per Ackner LJ in *Lee* [1984] 1 WLR 578 at p. 583E). In exceptional circumstances, leave may be granted even though the appellant knew what he was doing when the indictment was put, intended to make the plea he did, and pleaded guilty without equivocation after receiving expert advice (ibid.). These factors are all highly relevant to whether a conviction is unsafe or unsatisfactory but cannot of themselves deprive the court of jurisdiction to hear an application for leave to appeal. Thus, in *Lee*, convictions for numerous offences of arson and manslaughter were quashed because (a) fresh evidence had come to light strongly suggesting that L could not possibly have committed at least some of the crimes; (b) the reliability of his confessions to the police was doubtful because he was of low intelligence and may have confessed out of a desire for notoriety, and (c) his ultimate decision on the morning of trial to plead guilty was apparently influenced by the knowledge that a place had been found for him in a mental hospital and he was likely to be dealt with under the Mental Health Act 1983, s. 37, if he admitted the offences. Defence counsel and solicitor had been anticipating a not guilty plea and were unhappy about their client's volte-face.

In certain circumstances, a ruling by the judge may result in a plea of guilty which does not shut out the possibility of a subsequent appeal against conviction. In *Sherlock* [1995] Crim LR 799, the two appellants has sought disclosure as to whether a third man (who they alleged was responsible for the offence) was an informer. The Crown resisted the application, but it was granted by Judge M. The prosecution did not comply with the order, but made an application to the resident judge, who referred the matter back to Judge M, who affirmed his earlier ruling following two further *ex parte* applications. The prosecution then made a further application to Judge B, who refused to make the order for disclosure, stating that Judge M had no jurisdiction to make the order, because applications for disclosure were restricted to himself (Judge B) and the resident judge as judges designated to hear such cases under a directive from the Lord Chief Justice. The appellants were than arraigned and pleaded not guilty. The trial later came before a recorder who again heard the prosecution *ex parte* and then both parties in open court. He gave judgment refusing disclosure, framing his decision in terms of whether Judge B's order should be 'interfered with'. Following this final ruling, the appellants changed their pleas to guilty, and subsequently appealed against conviction. The Court of Appeal allowed the appeals. The first decision by Judge M had not been a nullity, and Judge B had no power to review it. The designated judge system was not based on any directive from the Lord Chief Justice, and it was generally more appropriate for the judge trying the case to hear the disclosure application. In any event, the trial judge was entitled to apply his own mind to the question. There had been undesirable forum shopping by the prosecution and the recorder's view had been coloured by the wrongful overriding of Judge M's order by Judge B. Consequently, the appellants' plea of guilty did not prevent the court from considering the appeal against conviction. Their lordships took the view that the refusal of disclosure hampered the defence but had not made it impossible to deny guilt. There was an alternative to pleading guilty, and if there had been a proper ruling on the disclosure point the court would not have entertained the appeal. In view of the irregularities and the flawed nature of the trial judge's ruling, however, the convictions were quashed, notwithstanding that the appellants had pleaded guilty. The Court of Appeal similarly allowed an appeal in *Kenny* [1994] Crim LR 284, where the appellant had changed his plea to guilty after the trial judge decided that his confession (which was the only evidence against him) was admissible. A different conclusion was reached in *Greene* [1997] Crim LR 659, however, where the Court of Appeal reasoned that, notwithstanding the judge's ruling that the appellant's confession was admissible, the truth of its contents remained an issue for the jury. In *Eriemo* [1995] 2 Cr App R 206, E's defence was duress by his co-accused, and he pleaded guilty once the trial judge refused to sever the indictment. E was refused leave to appeal on the basis that his plea of guilty amounted to an admission of the facts which constituted the offence, and that he had therefore lost the right to appeal against conviction. In *Chalkley* [1998] QB 848, the appellants initially pleaded not guilty, on the basis that tape-recorded evidence of conspiracy to commit robberies involving firearms was inadmissible. The judge ruled the evidence admissible, and the appellants accordingly changed their pleas to guilty and appealed. The Court of Appeal distinguished two types of case:

(a)   cases where an incorrect ruling of law on admitted facts left an accused with no legal escape from a verdict of guilty on those facts; and

(b)   cases where an accused was influenced to change his plea to guilty because he recognised that as a result of a ruling to admit strong evidence against him his case was hopeless.

Their lordships considered that a case in category (a) satisfied the test under s. 2(1) of the Criminal Appeal Act 1968, in that the conviction was unsafe, whereas a case in category (b) did not. On the facts, the appellants had by their pleas admitted their guilt, and the convictions were not unsafe, so that the appeals were dismissed. In such cases, said Auld LJ (at p. 162), the accused should maintain their pleas of not guilty, fight the case and, in the event of conviction, seek leave to appeal (see also *Kennedy* [1998] Crim LR 739). In *Rajcoomar* [1999] Crim LR 728, the judge had made a series of rulings relating to disclosure and the admissibility of evidence, culminating in the rejection of an application to stay the indictment on grounds of abuse of process. The accused had changed his plea to guilty and appealed to the Court of Appeal. He was refused leave by the single judge, and renewed his application for leave to the full court. The application was refused without investigating the merits of the judge's ruling that there was no abuse of process. Their lordships placed reliance upon *Chalkley* [1998] QB 848, and considered that the case fell within category (b) above.

Where an appellant pleaded guilty, the Court of Appeal has no power to substitute a verdict of guilty of an alternative offence, since the Criminal Appeal Act 1968, s. 3, applies only where a jury convicted the appellant (see **D22.34**).

Single Right of Appeal

Once an appeal has been dismissed, the unsuccessful appellant is debarred from **D22.13** bringing a second appeal in the same matter (*Grantham* [1969] 2 QB 574; *Pinfold* [1988] QB 462). This applies even if the point it is sought to raise at the second appeal is different from that unsuccessfully relied upon at the first. In *Pinfold*, P's original appeal was on grounds of misdirections in the summing-up and his second proposed appeal would have been in reliance on fresh evidence, namely, affidavits from the prime prosecution witness at trial (one C) that he had in fact given perjured evidence in order to secure P's conviction. The proceedings in *Pinfold* took the form of an application for leave to appeal out of time, but it was accepted that the real point in issue was whether the court would have jurisdiction to determine a second appeal in the light of the dismissal of the earlier one. Lord Lane CJ said:

> . . . there is nothing on the face of [the Criminal Appeal Act 1968, ss. 1(1) and 2(1)] which says in terms that one appeal is all that an appellant is allowed. But, in the view of this court, one must read those provisions against the background of the fact that it is in the interests of the public in general that there should be a limit or a finality to legal proceedings. . . . We have been unable to discover . . . any situation in which a right of appeal couched in similar terms to that, has been construed as a right to pursue more than one appeal in one case.

Moreover, before the Criminal Appeal Act 1968, s. 23 – which requires the court in certain circumstances to receive fresh evidence – can come into operation, the would-be appellant must bring himself within the ambit of s. 1 of the Act. In other words, the fact that, had an appeal lain in *Pinfold*, the court might well have been obliged by statute to receive evidence from the witness C was irrelevant to consideration of whether there was a right of appeal in the first place.

The rule restricting the appellant to a single appeal applies even if the House of Lords restores a quashed conviction. In *Berry* [1991] 1 WLR 125, B was convicted in 1983 of making an explosive substance contrary to s. 4 of the Explosive Substances Act 1883. The Court of Appeal quashed his conviction, but granted the Crown a certificate to appeal to the House of Lords. The House of Lords restored the conviction on the certified point, but B had by then absconded to Spain. In 1989 he was expelled from Spain and returned here. He re-applied to the Court of Appeal seeking to argue grounds of appeal which had originally been raised in the Court of Appeal but had not been dealt with in its judgment or certified for consideration by the House of Lords. The Court of Appeal refused to relist the appeal. The Home Secretary, however, later referred the case to the Court of Appeal, exercising his power under the Criminal Appeal Act 1968, s. 17(1)(b) (see **D24.1**). Their lordships held that they did have power to determine the outstanding grounds of appeal on the basis of such a reference (*Berry* [1994] Crim LR 276). Lord Taylor CJ also laid down guidance as to how such a situation could be avoided in future. If the Court of Appeal allowed an appeal on one of two or more grounds, the Crown should inform the court before judgment if it intended to seek to have the decisive point certified for consideration by the House of Lords. The Court of Appeal could then decide whether, out of caution, to consider the other grounds there and then (see also **D26.1**).

The rule restricting the appellant to a single appeal is subject to two quasi exceptions. First, where he has purported to abandon an appeal (or application for leave to appeal), he may seek to revive the appeal by asking the court to treat the abandonment as a nullity (see **D23.24**). The court will then review the circumstances of the abandonment and may, in very exceptional circumstances, hold it null (see *Medway* [1976] QB 779). Secondly, if the dismissal of the first appeal involved a procedural irregularity on the court's part leading to injustice for the appellant (e.g., he was not notified of the date of hearing or counsel was unable to attend), then again the dismissal may be regarded as null. Both these quasi exceptions were recognised by Lord Lane CJ, *obiter*, in his judgment in *Pinfold* (see p. 464E–F). Save as mentioned above, the 'one appeal only' rule will apply not only when the original proceedings were determined against the appellant after a full hearing, but also when the appeal was effectively determined without a hearing, as when it was abandoned by the appellant himself, or when an application for leave to appeal was rejected by the single judge and not renewed within the appropriate time.

It also appears that, whilst the appellant has the right to one appeal based on the 1968 Act, he has the additional and separate right to appeal on the basis that the proceedings below were a nullity. The residual powers of the Court of Appeal to order *venire de novo* when the proceedings below were a nullity exist independently of ss. 1 and 2(1) of the 1968 Act, and are expressly preserved by the Supreme Court Act 1981, s. 53(2)(d) (see **D22.33**). In *Laming* (1989) 90 Cr App R 450, the Court of Appeal had to consider whether an appeal based on the argument that the trial was a nullity (because the indictment was defective) would shut out a later appeal on other grounds. Watkins LJ said *obiter* that he doubted whether such an appeal would be covered by the *Pinfold* decision, for the reasons outlined above. Nonetheless, the court indicated to counsel for the appellant, for the avoidance of doubt, that if it decided against him on this initial ground, it would adjourn the appeal, granting leave for further grounds to be added.

Right of Appeal Vests only in the Convicted Person

Even where a person other than the person who was convicted has or may have an interest in the outcome of any appeal, the right to appeal vests solely in the person convicted (*Jefferies* [1969] 1 QB 120). This is because the Court of Appeal's powers are purely statutory, and the Criminal Appeal Act 1968, s. 1(1), by its express terms confers a right of appeal only on a person convicted on indictment. Moreover, until the implementation of the Criminal Appeal Act 1995, s. 7(1), there was no procedure whereby, following the death of a convicted person, his estate (or any other interested party) could pursue the appeal. Section 7(1), however, inserted s. 44A in the Criminal Appeal Act 1968, giving the right to begin or continue an appeal to a person approved by the Court of Appeal. It is therefore open to a deceased defendant's estate, for example, to pursue an appeal; in *Whelan* [1997] Crim LR 659, a widow seeking to clear her deceased husband's name was granted leave to pursue the appeal under s. 44A, although the appeal was dismissed on the merits. **D22.14**

Criminal Appeal Act 1968, s. 44A

(1)   Where a person has died—
(a)   any relevant appeal which might have been begun by him had he remained alive may be begun by a person approved by the Court of Appeal; and
(b)   where any relevant appeal was begun by him while he was alive or is begun in relation to his case by virtue of paragraph (a) above or by a reference by the Criminal Cases Review Commission, any further step which might have been taken by him in connection with the appeal if he were alive may be taken by a person so approved.
(2)   In this section 'relevant appeal' means—
(a)   an appeal under section 1, 9, 12 or 15 of this Act; or
(b)   an appeal under section 33 of this Act from any decision of the Court of Appeal on an appeal under any of those sections.
(3)   Approval for the purposes of this section may only be given to—
(a)   the widow or widower of the dead person;
(b)   a person who is the personal representative (within the meaning of section 55(1)(xi) of the Administration of Estates Act 1925) of the dead person; or
(c)   any other person appearing to the Court of Appeal to have, by reason of a family or similar relationship with the dead person, a substantial financial or other interest in the determination of a relevant appeal relating to him.
(4)   Except in the case of an appeal begun by a reference by the Criminal Cases Review Commission, an application for such approval may not be made after the end of the period of one year beginning with the date of death.
(5)   Where this section applies, any reference in this Act to the appellant shall, where appropriate, be construed as being or including a reference to the person approved under this section.
(6)   The power of the Court of Appeal to approve a person under this section may be exercised by a single judge in the same manner as by the Court of Appeal and subject to the same provisions; but if the single judge refuses the application, the applicant shall be entitled to have the application determined by the Court of Appeal.

DETERMINATION OF APPEALS AGAINST CONVICTION

Statutory Basis of Determination of Appeal

D22.15 The Criminal Appeal Act 1968, s. 2(1), was amended by the Criminal Appeal Act 1995, s. 2(1). The amended section reads as follows.

Criminal Appeal Act 1968, s. 2

> (1)   Subject to the provisions of this Act, the Court of Appeal—
>   (a)   shall allow an appeal against conviction if they think that the conviction is unsafe; and
>   (b)   shall dismiss such an appeal in any other case.

Prior to its amendment, s. 2(1) took the following form.

> Except as provided by this Act, the Court of Appeal shall allow an appeal against conviction if they think—
>   (a)   that the conviction should be set aside on the ground that under all the circumstances of the case it is unsafe or unsatisfactory;
>   (b)   that the judgment of the court of trial should be set aside on the ground of a wrong decision of any question of law; or
>   (c)   that there was a material irregularity in the course of the trial,
> and in any other case shall dismiss the appeal:
>   Provided that the court may, notwithstanding that they are of opinion that the point raised in the appeal might be decided in favour of the appellant, dismiss the appeal if they consider that no miscarriage of justice has actually occurred.

For details of the way in which this tripartite test, with its accompanying proviso, was interpreted, reference should be made to the 1995 edition of this book.

The statutory test in its amended form, therefore, is confined to the question: Does the court think that the conviction is unsafe? It is submitted that that was also the effect of the previous version of s. 2(1), since the Court of Appeal, even where there had been a wrong decision in law or a material irregularity, had to dismiss the appeal if they considered there had been no actual miscarriage of justice. Further, the Court of Appeal, in interpreting the previous version of s. 2(1) appeared to take the view that there was no practical difference in meaning, in this context, between 'unsafe' and 'unsatisfactory' (*McIlkenny* (1991) 93 Cr App R 287).

It is clear that the intention of Parliament was that there should be no change in effect despite the simplified wording. In moving the Second Reading of the Criminal Appeal Bill, the then Home Secretary said: 'In substance it restates the existing practice of the Court of Appeal'. It was made clear that this statement followed upon consultation with the Lord Chief Justice (*Hansard*, vol. 256, para. 24, 6 March 1995; and see also Standing Committee B, 21 March 1995, col. 26).

In *Mullen* [1999] 3 WLR 777, an appeal was based upon the circumstances in which the appellant was brought to trial. The English prosecuting authorities, in collusion with Zimbabwean authorities, had procured his deportation from Zimbabwe to England in circumstances which amounted to an abuse of process. The Court of Appeal described the conduct of the British authorities as so unworthy or shameful that it was an affront to the public conscience to allow the prosecution to succeed. Nevertheless, the conduct of the trial itself was not challenged. The real question was whether it was fair to try the accused in view of the way in which he had been brought before the court. In applying the statutory test relating to appeals, did this mean that the conviction was unsafe? The Court of Appeal had recourse to *Hansard*, from which it was apparent that the new form of the Criminal Appeal Act 1968, s. 2, was intended to re-state the existing practice of the Court of Appeal. That practice allowed abuse of process to be a ground for quashing a conviction. Furthermore, for a conviction to be safe, it must be lawful. If the trial should never have taken place, then the conviction could not be regarded as safe.

In *Smith* [1999] 2 Cr App R 238, the ground of appeal was the wrongful rejection of a submission of no case to answer. After the submission had been rejected, the defendant gave evidence and in cross-examination admitted his guilt. Before the unified test for appeals was introduced, the authorities favoured the view that the appeal should succeed since the accused had been deprived, by the wrong ruling, of the absolute certainty of an acquittal upon the judge's direction (see *Cockley* (1984) 79 Cr App R 18, and the other cases cited at **D22.19**). Since the accused had admitted his guilt in court, however, how accurate was it to say, under the new test, that the conviction was 'unsafe'? In *Smith*, the Court of Appeal had no hesitation in doing so. Even in an extreme case such as this one, the wrongful rejection of a submission of no case to answer meant that the appeal must succeed. Again, it would appear that the change in wording in s. 2 had had no practical effect.

It is becoming increasingly clear that the new test is meant to reflect the practice adopted by the Court of Appeal in interpreting the old one. The restrictive reading of the word 'unsafe' anticipated by some commentators has not generally found favour in practice, despite dicta to the contrary in *Chalkley* [1998] QB 848, where the Court of Appeal considered the effect of the changed wording of the test in the context of an appeal against conviction where the appellants had pleaded guilty as a result of an allegedly erroneous ruling on a question of admissibility by the trial judge (see **D22.12** for details). Auld LJ stated:

> This much simpler form is in essence much the same as the intertwined and overlapping provisions of the old test, as was intended by the Royal Commission in recommending it, the Government in promoting it, the senior judiciary in supporting its parliamentary passage and Parliament in enacting it.

Concentrating upon the removal of the word 'unsatisfactory' from the formula, however, his lordship stated:

> The Court has no power under the substituted section 2(1) to allow an appeal if it does not think the conviction unsafe but is dissatisfied in some way with what went on at trial.

He went on to emphasise that this interpretation was subject to the jurisprudence of the European Court of Human Rights in cases such as *Murray* v *United Kingdom* (1996) 22 EHRR 29, *Saunders* v *United Kingdom* (1997) 23 EHRR 313 and *Staines* [1997] 2 Cr App R 426 (see also *MacDonald* [1998] Crim LR 808).

The case of *Cooper* [1969] 1 QB 267 continues to provide guidance on how the word 'unsafe' should be interpreted in determining a criminal appeal. In that case, Lord Widgery CJ explained that if the overall feel of a case left the court with a 'lurking doubt' as to whether an injustice may have been done, then a conviction will be quashed, notwithstanding that the trial was error-free. Lord Widgery said (at p. 271 C–G):

> [This is] a case in which every issue was before the jury and in which the jury was properly instructed, and, accordingly, a case in which this court will be very reluctant indeed to intervene. It has been said over and over again throughout the years that this court must recognise the advantage which a jury has in seeing and hearing the witnesses, and if all the material was before the jury and the summing-up was impeccable, this court should not lightly interfere. Indeed, until the passing of the Criminal Appeal Act 1966 [which somewhat widened the court's powers to quash a conviction] it was almost unheard of for this court to interfere in such a case.
>
> However, now our powers are somewhat different, and we are indeed charged to allow an appeal against conviction if we think that the verdict of the jury should be set aside on the ground that under all the circumstances of the case it is unsafe or unsatisfactory. That means

that in cases of this kind the court must in the end ask itself a subjective question, whether we are content to let the matter stand as it is, or whether there is not some lurking doubt in our minds which makes us wonder whether an injustice has been done. This is a reaction which may not be based strictly on the evidence as such; it is a reaction which can be produced by the general feel of the case as the court experiences it.

Similarly, Lord Kilbrandon in *Stafford* v *DPP* [1974] AC 878 at p. 912 summarised the test to be applied by each member of the appellate court thus: 'Have I a reasonable doubt, or perhaps even a lurking doubt, that this conviction may be unsafe or unsatisfactory?' In *F* [1998] Crim LR 307, the Court of Appeal stated that the phrase 'lurking doubt' was not a proper approach in view of the simple test introduced by the Criminal Appeal Act 1995. It is submitted, however, that *Cooper* retains its authority notwithstanding the amended formula. As is pointed out by Professor Sir John Smith in his commentary on the case ([1999] Crim LR 307), the repealed words 'or unsatisfactory' played no part in the decision in *Cooper*, and that case has not been overruled. The Court of Appeal must still ask itself whether it has a doubt (whether characterised as lurking or not) about the safety of the conviction.

The test is different from that applied by the trial judge on a submission of no case to answer (see *Arobieke* [1988] Crim LR 314, commenting on *Galbraith* [1981] 1 WLR 1039). The supervision of the Court of Appeal extends beyond and operates at a later stage than the decision of the trial judge at the end of the prosecution case. In effect, the Court of Appeal is empowered by s. 2(1) to substitute its own view on the evidence for that of the jury, despite its natural reluctance to do so. In doing so, it is not appropriate for them to consider the views of the trial judge, which are irrelevant to the determination of the Court of Appeal (*Jones* [1998] 2 Cr App R 53 at p. 59).

Further guidance as to the way in which the new single ground of appeal is likely to be interpreted by the Court of Appeal is to be found in the way in which the proviso was applied under the previous version of s. 2(1). Since the crux of the proviso was to eliminate appeals where the conviction was 'safe' (notwithstanding a wrong decision of law or a material irregularity), decisions on its application have a clear relevance to the current form of s. 2(1).

The test commonly applied has been: assuming the wrong decision on law or irregularity had not occurred and the trial had been legally error-free, would the only reasonable and proper verdict have been one of guilty? If the answer to that question is yes (i.e. any reasonable jury would have convicted on the totality of the evidence) then the proviso could be applied. This test was affirmed in *Haddy* [1944] KB 442 (Court of Criminal Appeal), and was adopted by the House of Lords in *Stirland* v *DPP* [1944] AC 315. Essentially, it has been applied ever since, although on occasions the wording is varied (e.g., to ask whether the appellant, by reason of the matters complained of, was deprived of a chance of acquittal which should fairly have been open to him). The nub of the judgment in *Haddy* is the following quotation from *Cohen* (1909) 2 Cr App R 197:

> There is such a miscarriage of justice not only where the court comes to the conclusion that the verdict of guilty was wrong, but also when it is of opinion that the mistake of fact or omission on the part of the judge may reasonably be considered to have brought about that verdict, and when, on the whole facts and with a correct direction, the jury might fairly and reasonably have found the appellant not guilty. Then there has been not only a miscarriage of justice but a substantial one, because the appellant has lost the chance which was fairly open to him of being acquitted. . . . If, however, the court in such a case comes to the conclusion that, on the whole of the facts and with a correct direction, the only reasonable and proper verdict would be one of guilty, there is no miscarriage of justice, or at all events no substantial miscarriage of justice within the meaning of the proviso.

APPROACH OF COURT OF APPEAL TO COMMONLY OCCURRING ERRORS IN THE COURSE OF A TRIAL

It is not proposed to consider exhaustively the various errors in the course of a trial which may lead to a successful appeal. To do so would be to repeat much of what will be found in the evidential and substantive law sections of this work. However, some comment is required on the Court of Appeal's approach in certain commonly occurring types of case.

Wrongful Admission or Exclusion of Evidence

Assuming defence counsel at trial objected to the evidence or, as the case may be, **D22.16** applied unsuccessfully to adduce it, the judge's adverse ruling may amount to a wrong decision on a question of law. Where counsel at trial failed to object to the evidence, an appeal is still possible because it is the judge's duty to prevent inadmissible material being put before the jury even if no objection is taken (see *Stirland* v *DPP* [1944] AC 315). Counsel's failure to object to the evidence at the time may be a factor leading the court to conclude that its admission cannot have been so prejudicial as to render the conviction unsafe. Preventing defence counsel pursuing a proper line of cross-examination with a prosecution witness or allowing prosecuting counsel to ask improper questions of defence witnesses is equally a ground of appeal under s. 2(1)(b) or s. 2(1)(a) (see, for example, *Viola* [1982] 1 WLR 1138 where a conviction for rape was quashed because the defence were refused leave under the Sexual Offences (Amendment) Act 1976, s. 2, to ask the complainant about alleged intercourse with two other men occurring within hours of the alleged offence).

Cases where there has been wrongful admission or exclusion of evidence are governed by the test laid down in *Haddy* [1944] KB 442 (see **D22.15**). However, where evidence of alibi was wrongly excluded at trial, it is unlikely that the appeal will be dismissed (see dicta in *Lewis* [1969] 2 QB 1). Similarly, if the prosecution are wrongly allowed to introduce evidence of the accused's bad character (whether as part of their own case or in cross-examination of the accused), the extreme prejudicial effect makes the success of the appeal probable (*Turner* [1944] KB 463).

Erroneous Exercise of Discretion

The trial judge's exercise (or non-exercise) of a discretionary power in a manner adverse **D22.17** to the interests of the defence is capable of being a ground of appeal. However, such appeals are frequently dismissed on the basis that the discretion is vested in the court below and the Court of Appeal will not interfere save in extreme cases (see *Grondkowski* [1946] KB 369 for a statement of the general principle and *Moghal* (1977) 65 Cr App R 56 for a case where the conviction was upheld even though it was specifically stated that all three appeal judges would, if they had been sitting at first instance, have exercised the discretion in the opposite way to which it was in fact exercised by the trial judge).

In *McCann* (1990) 92 Cr App 239, the Court of Appeal said that while it had to give great weight to the trial judge's exercise of discretion, its power to review was not limited to cases where there had been errors of principle, or a lack of material on which the judge could have arrived at his decision. It must if necessary examine anew the relevant facts and circumstances to exercise a discretion by way of review if it considered that the trial judge's ruling might have resulted in injustice to the appellants.

If, however, the reasons the judge gave for exercising his discretion in the way he did reveal that he approached his decision on an erroneous basis (e.g., he took into account irrelevant factors or ignored relevant ones), the chances of success on appeal are much improved. Thus, in *Sullivan* [1971] 1 QB 253 the judge's refusal of leave for alibi evidence to be called in a case where the notice of particulars had been served out of time resulted in a successful appeal, but only because he had stated that the purpose of the alibi-notice provisions was to prevent the late fabrication of alibis, whereas the Court of Appeal held that their purpose was to give the prosecution time to investigate the defence. The disparate nature of a trial judge's various discretionary powers makes it difficult to generalise about the prospects of a successful appeal in any particular type of case. However, it does appear that there are some areas of discretion where the Court of Appeal is more willing to interfere with the trial judge's decision than it is in others. Thus, appeals based on refusal to sever counts in an indictment or to order separate trials of co-accused are almost invariably dismissed, unless the original joinder was unlawful in which case separate trials would not be a matter of discretion but of law (see *Moghal* and *Grondkowski*). By contrast, in the highly important area of discretionary exclusion of unfairly obtained evidence under the PACE 1984, s. 78, the court has shown a much greater willingness to substitute its own views for those of the judge below (see, for example, *Canale* [1990] 2 All ER 187, where the trial judge admitted evidence of C's admissions to the police despite breaches of the provisions of Code of Practice on the contemporaneous recording of interviews, and the Court of Appeal quashed the conviction saying that 'if the learned judge had appreciated the gravity of the breach of the interview rules in C.11, he would, and should, have acted under [s. 78] to rule out the evidence of admissions'). See **F17.13** *et seq.* for cases involving the discretionary exclusion of confessions.

Errors on the Part of Counsel

D22.18   It is sometimes argued that an error by defence counsel makes the conviction unsafe. The high-water mark of such argument was *Irwin* [1987] 1 WLR 902 where I's conviction was quashed because his counsel took a snap decision not to call I's wife or daughter in support of an alibi. The decision was taken without I's prior approval, while I himself was in the witness-box. The Court of Appeal allowed the appeal. *Irwin* was doubted in *Ensor* [1989] 1 WLR 497, in which it was said that *Irwin* should be regarded as being confined to its own facts. In *Ensor*, E was charged with two counts of rape, said to have been committed on two separate occasions against two different complainants. The counts were properly joined in the same indictment, but E told his solicitor and counsel that he wanted them severed. (It was common ground at the appeal that if such an application had been made, it ought to have succeeded.) E's counsel at trial, however, saw tactical advantages in the two counts being heard together. Accordingly, he decided not to apply to sever. He did not inform E of this decision or the reasons for it. E was in due course convicted on both counts. He appealed, *inter alia*, on the ground that the conduct of his counsel at trial in not applying to sever constituted a material irregularity. The Court of Appeal stated that a conviction should not be set aside on the ground that a decision or action by counsel in the conduct of the trial later appeared to have been mistaken or unwise. This was so even if the decision or action was contrary to the accused's wishes. There was an exception in the case of flagrantly incompetent advocacy on the part of the accused's counsel. In this case, however, counsel's decision not to apply for severance, even if erroneous, could not be described as incompetent, let alone flagrantly incompetent.

The decision, and the reasoning, in *Ensor* are consistent with *Gautam* [1988] Crim LR 109 and *Swain* [1988] Crim LR 109. In *Gautam*, G's complaint was that his counsel at trial had refused to call medical evidence of G's mental state and possible lack of *mens rea* at the time of the offence. Counsel's reason for not doing so was that the defence was a denial of the *actus reus*, so that G's mental state was immaterial. Taylor J said:

> . . . it should be clearly understood that if defending counsel in the course of his conduct of the case makes a decision, or takes a course which later appears to have been mistaken or unwise, that generally speaking has never been regarded as a proper ground for appeal.

In *Swain*, the court held that S's contention that his counsel's cross-examination of prosecution witnesses had done more harm than good was not, on the facts of the case, a basis for quashing the conviction. O'Connor LJ said, however, that if the court had any lurking doubt that an appellant might have suffered some injustice as a result of flagrantly incompetent advocacy by his advocate, then it would quash the conviction. In *Clinton* [1993] 1 WLR 1181, the Court of Appeal approached the question of errors by counsel from a different perspective. C was charged with kidnapping and indecent assault. The complainant gave a description of her attacker which differed in certain crucial respects from the appearance of C. C did not give or call evidence at trial and was convicted. One of his grounds of appeal was that he was not advised to give evidence, and should have been. The appeal was allowed. The absence of strong advice to give or call evidence was a grave error. Exceptionally, where a tactical decision (such as not calling the defendant) is taken without proper instructions or when all the promptings of reason and good sense point the other way, it is open to the appellate court to set aside the verdict. In contrast to the test adopted in *Ensor* and *Swain* their lordships stated that the important feature was not the extent of counsel's alleged ineptitude, but the effect on the trial and verdict in the light of s. 2(1) of the Criminal Appeal Act 1968. It is respectfully submitted that the approach adopted by the Court of Appeal in *Clinton* is to be preferred to the 'flagrant incompetence' test. The court's attention in deciding whether to allow the appeal ought surely to be focused on the safety or otherwise of the conviction, rather than the behaviour of counsel. In *Sankar* v *State of Trinidad and Tobago* [1995] 1 WLR 194, S appealed on the basis that, although he wished to give evidence, his advocate failed to call him as a witness, or even explain the alternatives open to him. The Privy Council allowed the appeal, since the advocate had not fulfilled his duty to his client, so that S had effectively been deprived of his defence.

In *Chatterjee* [1996] Crim LR 801, the Court of Appeal used the approach in *Clinton* to conclude that the defence case had not been properly presented. If there was to be a fair trial, the material available to defence counsel needed to be properly understood and set before the judge and jury. That had not happened in relation to impressive expert medical evidence available to the defendant, and the conviction was set aside as unsafe.

In *Scollan* [1999] Crim LR 566, the Court of Appeal considered a case where counsel had failed to follow her instructions as to the date on which the appellant first knew about the murder with which he was charged. They allowed the appeal, stating that the proper approach to be adopted in such cases was to assess the effect of counsel's alleged ineptitude on the trial and the verdict. This was in accordance with the reasoning in *Clinton*, which is unaffected by the amendment to the test for appeals introduced by the Criminal Appeal Act 1995.

In *Boal* [1992] QB 591, B was the assistant general manager of a bookshop owned by a company and was charged with offences under the Fire Precautions Act 1971. He pleaded guilty at trial on the basis of his counsel's mistaken understanding of the law. On the facts, however, the Court of Appeal considered that he had a defence, which was likely to have succeeded, namely that he was not 'manager of a body corporate'. Whilst their lordships did not think that B's counsel was guilty of 'flagrantly incompetent advocacy', and despite B's unequivocal pleas of guilty, they quashed the conviction, since B 'without fault on his part was deprived of what was in all likelihood a good defence in law'. At the same time, they made it clear that such a course of action would be taken by the court only 'where it believes the defence would quite probably have succeeded and concludes, therefore that a clear injustice has been done'.

In *Doherty* [1997] 2 Cr App R 218, the Court of Appeal set out the procedure to be followed where an appeal involved criticism of former counsel. Judge LJ quoted guidance issued in December 1995 by the Bar Council with the approval of the Lord Chief Justice:

1. Allegations against former counsel may receive substantial publicity whether accepted or rejected by the court. Counsel should not settle or sign grounds of appeal unless he is satisfied that they are reasonable, have some real prospect of success and are such that he is prepared to argue before the court (Guide to proceedings in the Court of Appeal Criminal Division, para. 2.4). When such allegations are properly made however, in accordance with the Code of Conduct counsel newly instructed must promote and protect fearlessly by all proper and lawful means his lay client's best interests without regard to others, including fellow members of the legal profession.

2. When counsel newly instructed is satisfied that such allegations are made, and a waiver of privilege is necessary, he should advise the lay client fully about the consequences of waiver and should obtain a waiver of privilege in writing signed by the lay client relating to communications with, instructions given to and advice given by former counsel. The allegations should be set out in the Grounds of Application for Leave to Appeal. Both waiver and grounds should be lodged without delay; the grounds may be perfected if necessary in due course.

3. On receipt of the waiver and grounds, the Registrar of Criminal Appeals will send both to former counsel with an invitation on behalf of the court to respond to the allegations made.

4. If former counsel wishes to respond and considers the time for doing so insufficient, he should ask the Registrar for further time. The court will be anxious to have full information and to give counsel adequate time to respond.

5. The response should be sent to the Registrar. On receipt, he will send it to counsel newly instructed who may reply to it. The grounds and the responses will go before the single judge.

6. The Registrar may have received grounds of appeal direct from the applicant, and obtained a waiver of privilege before fresh counsel is assigned. In those circumstances, when assigning counsel, the Registrar will provide copies of the waiver, the grounds of appeal and any response from former counsel.

7. This guidance covers the formal procedures to be followed. It is perfectly proper for counsel newly instructed to speak to former counsel as a matter of courtesy before grounds are lodged to inform him of the position.

His lordship added that grounds of appeal based on criticism of trial counsel should not be advanced unless 'it can be demonstrated that in the light of the information available to him at the time no reasonably competent counsel would sensibly have adopted the course taken by him at the time when he took it'. Further, where the allegations against counsel were based on non-compliance with the client's express instructions, unless the client had significant educational impairment, it was difficult to envisage fresh counsel reasonably drafting grounds of appeal without being in possession of a signed statement of facts alleged by the client together with an unequivocal signed waiver of privilege. The client should also be advised that allegations about what had passed between him and trial counsel were unlikely to carry any weight with the court unless they were supported by oral testimony. The precise complaint should be clearly spelt out in the grounds of appeal. The grounds, together with the waiver of privilege and any supporting documentation, should be lodged with the Registrar who should supply all relevant material to trial counsel who should then respond in accordance with the guidance (see also *Hobson* [1998] 1 Cr App R 31 at p. 35 and *Nasser* (1998) *The Times*, 19 February 1998).

Rejection of Submission of No Case to Answer

D22.19 A ruling by the judge at the end of the prosecution case that there is a case to answer is a decision on a question of law and may result in the quashing of the conviction (*Abbott* [1955] 2 QB 497). If the defence stand upon their submission by electing to call no evidence and the jury convict, an appeal may equally well be based on the argument that the conviction is unsafe since there was no evidence on which a reasonable jury properly directed could properly convict. A potential problem arises where, following a submission that ought to have succeeded but did not, the defence call evidence and, in doing so, inadvertently supply that which was lacking in the prosecution's own case. A variation on the same problem is where accused A1 makes an unsuccessful submission and then calls no evidence but his co-accused A2 does testify and implicates A1. Can the Court of Appeal dismiss the appeal on the basis of evidence given after the submission of no case should have been upheld? The earliest case (*Power* [1919] 1 KB 572) states that it may, but subsequent decisions have been to the opposite effect (see *Abbott* [1955] 2 QB 497, *Juett* [1981] Crim LR 113 and *Cockley* (1984) 79 Cr App R 181). It is submitted that the accused whose submission of no case is wrongly rejected has been deprived not merely of the chance of an acquittal that was fairly open to him but of the absolute certainty of an acquittal on the judge's direction. Therefore, applying the test in *Haddy* [1944] KB 442 (see **D22.15**), there was a miscarriage of justice at the Crown Court and the conviction should be quashed. In *Smith* [1999] 2 Cr App R 238, the Court of Appeal decided that, where a submission of no case made at the end of the prosecution case was wrongly rejected, the conviction was unsafe, even though the accused had subsequently admitted his guilt in cross-examination. As a result, it decided that the appeal should be allowed, even under the amended test introduced by the Criminal Appeal Act 1995. Where, however, experienced counsel failed to make a submission in a case which prima facie called for one, the Court of Appeal will presume that he had his reasons for not doing so and will look at the totality of the evidence in deciding whether the conviction is safe (*Juett*).

Defects in the Indictment

Defects in the form of an indictment or in the wording of counts therein are potential **D22.20** grounds of appeal (see *Jones* (1974) 59 Cr App R 120). If the defect was raised at trial by the defence and the judge failed to remedy it, his decision to allow the indictment to stand as drafted will be appealable. If the matter was not canvassed at trial then allowing the case to go to the jury on a defective indictment may be a basis for appeal (see *Power* (1977) 66 Cr App R 159 for that approach). In practice, appeals based on defects in the indictment very rarely succeed. The proper approach to such appeals was stated by the House of Lords in *Ayres* [1984] AC 447 where Lord Bridge of Harwich said (at pp. 460H–461B):

> If the statement and particulars of the offence in an indictment disclose no criminal offence whatever or charge some offence which has been abolished, in which case the indictment could fairly be described as a nullity, it is obvious that a conviction under that indictment cannot stand. But if the statement and particulars of offence can be seen fairly to relate to and to be intended to charge a known and subsisting criminal offence but plead it in terms which are inaccurate, incomplete or otherwise imperfect, then the question whether a conviction on that indictment can properly be affirmed under the proviso must depend on whether, in all the circumstances, it can be said with confidence that the particular error in the pleading cannot in any way have prejudiced or embarrassed the defendant.

A distinction should be drawn between cases such as *Ayres* (where the ground of appeal related to the wording of a count) and cases where the indictment to which the appellant pleaded was unlawful because counts were improperly joined in contravention of the Indictment Rules 1971, r. 9. In the latter type of case, the indictment itself is merely invalid, *not* a nullity, but – unless it is amended before arraignment by deletion of the improperly joined counts – all proceedings flowing from the accused's arraignment on the invalid indictment will themselves be invalid. The Court of Appeal's only option will be to issue a writ of *venire de novo* quashing any convictions and, if appropriate, ordering a retrial (see *Newland* [1988] QB 402 and **D22.33** for writs of *venire de novo*). It might be thought that, where a count is bad on its face for duplicity, the reasoning in *Newland* would apply, with the consequence that all proceedings flowing from the accused's plea to the duplicitous count would be treated as invalid. There is at least one decided case, however, in which an appeal was dismissed in respect of an appellant convicted on a count bad for duplicity (see *Thompson* [1914] 2 KB 99). On the other hand the Court of Appeal made it clear in *Mandair* [1993] Crim LR 679 that an appeal must succeed where the appellant has been convicted of an offence unknown to law. Where the bill of indictment was improperly preferred or where the trial proceeds on an unsigned bill of indictment, the whole proceedings in the Crown Court may be void and the Court of Appeal's only course may be to quash the conviction under its inherent powers (see **D9.2**). For further discussion of defects in the indictment as a ground of appeal, see **D9.40**.

Inconsistent Verdicts

D22.21 Where the jury convict on one count but acquit on another, the Court of Appeal will quash the conviction on the grounds of alleged inconsistency between the two verdicts if, and only if, the conclusion reached by the jury is one at which no reasonable jury who had applied their minds properly to the facts of the case could have arrived. This test was first stated by Devlin J in *Stone* (13 December 1954 unreported) and was formally adopted by the Court of Appeal in *Durante* [1972] 1 WLR 1612 (see the judgment of the court at p. 1617E). In *Stone*, Devlin J said:

> When an appellant seeks to persuade this court as his ground of appeal that the jury has returned a repugnant or inconsistent verdict, the burden is plainly upon him. He must satisfy the court that the two verdicts cannot stand together, meaning thereby that no reasonable jury who had applied their mind properly to the facts in the case could have arrived at the conclusion, and once one assumes that they are an unreasonable jury, or they could not have reasonably come to the conclusion, then the convictions cannot stand. But the burden is upon the defence to establish that.

If, on the other hand, the verdicts reflect a view of the facts and evidence which the jury could reasonably have taken, the appeal will be dismissed, even if the majority of juries faced with the same evidence might have been expected to acquit or, as the case might be, convict on each count rather than return a split verdict (*Hunt* [1968] 2 QB 433). The facts of *Durante* and *Hunt* illustrate the fine distinctions that may have to be drawn in this type of appeal. In *Durante*, D's conviction for handling a stolen cheque was quashed because the jury had also acquitted him of attempting to obtain money on a forged instrument (i.e. the cheque), and his defence had been that – both when he was given the cheque by a third person and when, almost immediately afterwards, he falsely made it out in his own favour – he was too drunk to realise what he was doing or form any criminal intent. Since the evidence of drunkenness was virtually the same on each count, the jury's verdict had to be characterised as 'inexplicable or irrational'. By contrast, the appeal in *Hunt* failed. The prosecution case was that, during the course of one incident, H had assaulted V1 occasioning him actual bodily harm and had also caused grievous bodily harm to V1's companion, V2. There was an alternative count for inflicting grievous bodily harm on V2. The defence was that both offences were committed by one T, who was with H at the relevant time and was called as a prosecution witness. The jury convicted of the assault on V1 but acquitted of both offences in respect of V2. The Court of Appeal held that (contrary to the argument of the appellant's counsel) identity was almost certainly not the sole issue in the case, and the jury might have returned the verdicts they did because they were not satisfied that the injuries to V2 amounted to grievous bodily harm. For further examples of the same principle being applied, see *Drury* (1971) 56 Cr App R 104 (conviction quashed), *Kirby* (1972) 56 Cr App R 758 (appeal dismissed), *Grizzle* [1991] Crim LR 553 (conviction quashed), *McKechnie* (1991) 94 Cr App R 51 (convictions quashed), *Harrison* [1994] Crim LR 859 (conviction quashed), *Cilgram* [1994] Crim LR 861 (conviction quashed), *Aldred* [1995] Crim LR 160 (appeal dismissed), *Diedrich* [1997] 1 Cr App R 361 (conviction quashed), *Malashev* [1997] Crim LR 587 (appeal dismissed) and *G* [1998] Crim LR 483 (appeal dismissed). It has also been held that, where allegedly inconsistent verdicts were returned by different juries in respect of co-accused separately tried and the convicted accused appeals on grounds of the inconsistency between the verdict in his case and the acquittal of the co-accused, the onus thrown on him of establishing inconsistency will be almost impossible to discharge since inevitably there will have been slight differences between the evidence at the two trials (*Andrews-Weatherfoil Ltd* [1972] 1 WLR 118. But see *Ireland* [1985] Crim LR 367, where I's conviction on indictment for driving while disqualified was quashed, *inter alia*, because he was later summarily acquitted of driving with excess alcohol, both prosecutions relating to the same occasion and the defence on each occasion being that I was not the driver. For the linked question of whether the trial judge is entitled to reject the verdicts initially announced on grounds of inconsistency and ask the jury to reconsider, see **D16.10**.

Conduct of the Trial Judge

Excessive intervention by the trial judge is a frequent ground of appeal. In England and **D22.22** Wales, the criminal justice system is essentially adversarial, and the advocates are charged with the proper presentation of the case. In principle, therefore, the judge's interventions ought to be limited to providing the proper framework in which counsel can carry out their duties fairly and efficiently. In *Whybrow* (1994) *The Times*, 14 February 1994, it was argued on appeal that the judge had prevented the appellants from giving their evidence-in-chief properly, and had intervened with such frequency and hostility as to deny them a fair trial. The Court of Appeal quashed their convictions and ordered a retrial. Their lordships stressed that there were occasions on which the judge ought to intervene, e.g., where the answer of a witness was ambiguous or inaudible. The judge ought also to 'curb prolixity and repetition and to exclude irrelevance, discursiveness and oppression of witnesses'. In the instant case, however, the judge's interventions had gone 'far beyond the bounds of legitimate judicial conduct'. One of the cases on which their lordships relied was *Hulusi* (1973) 58 Cr App R 378, in which it was said (per Lawton LJ at 385):

> It is a fundamental principle of an English trial that, if an accused gives evidence, he must be allowed to do so without being badgered and interrupted. Judges should remember that most people go into the witness-box, whether they be witnesses for the Crown or the defence, in a state of nervousness. They are anxious to do their best. They expect to receive a courteous hearing, and when they find, almost as soon as they get into the witness-box and are starting to tell their story, that the judge of all people is intervening in a hostile way, then, human nature being what it is, they are liable to become confused and not to do as well as they would have done had they not been badgered and interrupted.

This passage was cited with approval in *Marsh* (1993) *The Times*, 6 July 1993, the Court of Appeal stating that it was most undesirable that judges should interrupt a witness, particularly a defendant, when giving evidence-in-chief or being cross-examined. See also *Ahmed* (1995) *The Times*, 9 March 1995. In *Alves* [1997] 1 Cr App R 78, the Court of Appeal upheld an appeal based on adverse comments passed by the judge about the defendant's chances of acquittal (in the absence of the jury, but at a point where the defendant was in the middle of giving his evidence); their lordships indicated that the effect upon the defendant may have been equivalent to the handicap of being improperly interrupted by the judge when giving his evidence (see also *Roncoli* [1998] Crim LR 584 and *Frixou* [1998] Crim LR 352).

APPROACH OF THE COURT OF APPEAL TO COMMONLY OCCURRING ERRORS IN SUMMING-UP

Introduction

Errors in and omission from the judge's summing-up are clearly capable of rendering a **D22.23** conviction unsafe. The standard approach of the Court of Appeal is to ask, first, whether there has been a misdirection in the summing-up, and second – if there has – whether the only reasonable and proper verdict would in any event have been one of guilty, in which case the appeal may be dismissed. Summarised below are a few of the many types of defect in a summing-up which may be relied on as a ground of appeal.

Misdirection on Law

D22.24 Misdirections on law may relate, *inter alia*, to the ingredients of the offence charged, the burden or standard of proof or some other evidential matter (such as the need for corroboration, the relevance of the accused's character if that has been given in evidence, or the significance to be attached to his having stayed silent when questioned or having elected not to testify). Whether there is an arguable ground of appeal in such cases is simply a function of the substantive criminal law and the rules of evidence, and multiplication of examples of successful or, as the case may be, unsuccessful appeals is of limited value. Often the real question for the Court of Appeal is whether the admitted error was, in all the circumstances, bad enough to make the conviction unsafe. Thus, in *Edwards* (1983) 77 Cr App R 5, E's appeal on the ground that the judge had failed to direct the jury on the standard of proof was dismissed because the evidence of guilt was overwhelming and the jury had been reminded anyway by both prosecuting and defence counsel of the correct standard. Similarly, in *Donoghue* (1987) 86 Cr App R 267, the Court of Appeal dismissed the appeal despite the fact that the trial judge had given no direction on the burden of proof. Their lordships applied the proviso (which was at that time part of the Criminal Appeal Act 1968, s. 2(1)), saying that the prosecution was a formidable one.

Failure to Give Direction on Law

D22.25 Failure to give a direction on a relevant matter of law is as much a ground of appeal as a positive misdirection (see, for example, *Vickers* [1972] Crim LR 101 where V's conviction was quashed because the judge failed to identify the issues to which evidence of the appellant's previous convictions was relevant, thus leaving the jury with the impression that they went directly to guilt or innocence rather than to his credibility as a witness). It has further been held that a direction as to the ingredients of the offence charged is an essential part of every summing-up (*McVey* [1988] Crim LR 127). In *McVey*, the summing-up which was the subject of the appeal did not define theft for the jury nor, in particular, did it refer to the element of dishonesty. However, since the appellant's defence to a charge that he stole £20 from his employer's till was that he had intended to put two £10 notes back and since, if that story was disbelieved, the jury must inevitably have come to the conclusion that he had been dishonest, it is difficult to see how a fuller direction would have assisted the jury. The position was more clear-cut in *James* [1997] Crim LR 598, where the appellant's conviction for robbery was quashed because the judge had failed to direct the jury that the use of force had to be with the intention of stealing. The Court of Appeal held that it was crucial to direct the jury as to this element, since assault and theft could be separate.

There appears to be a conflict between the Court of Appeal's approach in *McVey* and its approach in earlier cases. For example, in *Mowatt* [1968] 1 QB 421, Diplock LJ said that the function of a summing-up is not to give the jury a general dissertation on some aspect of the criminal law but to tell them what are the issues of fact on which they must make up their minds in order to determine whether the accused is guilty of the particular offence charged.

Wrongful Withdrawal of Issues from the Jury

D22.26 If the judge failed to direct the jury on a vital issue of fact (i.e. one going to an ingredient of the offence as opposed to a peripheral or collateral matter), his failure may be a ground of appeal (*Sheaf* (1925) 19 Cr App R 46 where Avory J said: 'When we once arrive at the conclusion that a vital question of fact has not been left to the jury, the only ground on which we can affirm a conviction is that there has been no miscarriage of justice, on the ground that if the question had been left to the jury, they must necessarily have come to the conclusion that the appellant was guilty'). *Ex hypothesi*, a positive direction to the jury that a certain issue *must*, on the evidence, be decided in favour of the prosecution will normally be a good ground of appeal provided that the resulting conviction is unsafe). However, where the primary facts are not in dispute and the real issue is the conclusions of law to be drawn from those primary facts, it may exceptionally be appropriate to direct the jury that, on the evidence before them, their conclusion must be adverse to the accused (see *Larkin* [1943] KB 174, where, on a charge of murder, the judge directed the jury that they could not acquit and their verdict *must* be either one of guilty as charged or guilty of manslaughter). Similarly, in *Kelly* [1970] 1 WLR 1050 and *Morris* [1972] 1 WLR 228, the Court of Appeal held that it was appropriate to direct the jury that, in the former case, the accused was to be regarded as a person driving and, in the latter case, there had been an accident. Nonetheless, the safer course is usually to leave the issue to the jury, albeit with an indication that the evidence on the issue points all one way (see per Phillips J in *Martin* (1972) 57 Cr App R 279). Moreover, if the judge does not merely withdraw one issue from the jury but withdraws *all* the issues so as effectively to direct them to convict as charged, that is inevitably a misdirection (see *DPP v Stonehouse* [1978] AC 55 and *Thompson* [1984] 1 WLR 962). In such a case, the resulting conviction will usually be considered unsafe. In *Thompson* the issues withdrawn from the jury were (a) whether an obtaining of moneys transferred to T's accounts had taken place inside or outside the jurisdiction, (b) whether letters sent by the accused contained the representations laid in the indictment and (c) whether the letters had been an effective cause of the obtaining. May LJ said (at pp. 969–70):

> [In *Stonehouse's* case, the] majority of their lordships took the view that even where any reasonable jury properly directed on the law must upon the facts reach a verdict of guilty, it is nevertheless incumbent upon the trial judge to leave the issues of fact to the jury.
>
> In those circumstances we are driven to the conclusion that there was an irregularity in the course of this trial in that the three questions of fact were not left to the jury, but that it was in effect directed to convict. . . .
>
> In our opinion, in many cases in which there has been a misdirection of this nature it would not be appropriate to apply the proviso [which was at that time part of the Criminal Appeal Act 1968, s. 2(1)]. On the other hand, in the instant case, as in *DPP v Stonehouse*, we are quite satisfied that had the judge left the questions to the jury, as we have held he was bound to do, no reasonable jury could have come to any other conclusion than did the jury in the present case, namely that this appellant was clearly guilty of the six offences with which he stood charged. . . . No jury, other than a perverse one, could have come to the conclusion that the respective obtainings in this case occurred anywhere else than England. No jury could have come to the conclusion that the letters did anything else than contain the representations pleaded in the indictment. No jury could have come to any other conclusion than that those representations were at least an, if not the, effective cause of [the obtaining].
>
> In those circumstances we have reached the conclusion that this appeal must fail.

Misdirection on Facts

A misstatement in summing-up of the evidence that was actually given or an omission **D22.27** of a significant piece of evidence favourable to the defence may be relied on as a ground of appeal, provided the appellant can establish that the jury may have been misled and may not have returned the verdict they did if the evidence had been correctly stated. Thus, in *Bateson* [1969] 3 All ER 1372, an incorrect suggestion in the summing-up that B's defence had not been mentioned by him until his trial led to his conviction being quashed, since it was at least 'on the cards' that the jury would have acquitted had they been correctly reminded of the evidence. By contrast, in *Wright* (1974) 58 Cr App R 444, the factual errors in the summing-up did not 'loom sufficiently large' for the Court of Appeal to intervene. Scarman LJ said (at p. 452):

> At the end of the day, when the appellant's case is not that the judge erred in law but that the judge erred in his handling of the facts, the question must be, first of all, was there error, and secondly, if there was, was it significant error which might have misled the jury? If this court has a lurking doubt it is its duty to quash the conviction as unsafe, but this court . . . has reached the clear conclusion that this verdict was safe and satisfactory.

As part of the general duty to remind the jury of the evidence, the judge must always remind them of the defence case. Indeed, if there is a defence that could reasonably have been raised on the evidence but defence counsel failed to mention it, the judge is under a duty to repair counsel's omission by pointing the defence out (*Kachikwu* (1968) 52 Cr App R 538). However, the duty to remind the jury of the defence case does not necessarily extend to repeating the *arguments* put forward by defence counsel, as opposed to summarising the evidence on which his arguments were based (*Pountney* [1989] Crim LR 222 – conviction for rape upheld even though the judge failed to refer directly to the prime defence argument that, even accepting the prosecution evidence, the intercourse must have been consensual because the victim voluntarily remained at P's house for an hour after it happened, even though P had left the house and she could have left too had she wanted). The Court of Appeal in *Pountney* distinguished the earlier case of *Anderson* [1972] 1 QB 304 (the *Oz* trial) where the convictions were quashed because the judge both misdirected the jury on the meaning of 'obscene' and failed to remind them of the aversion theory relied on by the defence (i.e. the theory that, however unpleasant the material complained of might be, its effect on a reader would be to instil aversion to what was described and thus not to deprave or corrupt). On the facts of *Anderson*, the jury needed to be told – 'almost as a matter of law' – that if the aversion theory found favour with them it would afford an answer to the charge.

Improper Comment on Facts or Defence Case

D22.28 In directing the jury, it is the judge's duty to – 'state matters impartially, clearly and logically, and not inappropriately to inflate evidence to sarcastic and inappropriate comment' (*Berrada* (1989) 91 Cr App R 131). In *Berrada*, B's conviction for attempted rape was quashed partly because of a failure to deal adequately with the relevance of the appellant's good character (see **D22.30**), and also because the judge referred to defence allegations that the police had fabricated evidence as 'really monstrous and wicked'. Similarly, in *Marr* (1989) 90 Cr App R 154, the judge's dismissive attitude towards a large volume of character evidence tendered on behalf of the accused and her reference to the offence with which he was charged (indecent assault by touching a woman between the thighs) as 'a furtive little crime which is not the kind of thing people tend to tell their friends about' resulted in the conviction being quashed. The latter remark especially might have led to the jury to conclude that the appellant had been in the habit of touching women in the manner alleged but had simply concealed it from his friends. However, *Marr* and *Berrada* are exceptional cases. In general, the judge is given considerable leeway in commenting upon the evidence, even if that be in a manner adverse to the defence (see *O'Donnell* (1917) 12 Cr App R 219 – conviction upheld even though the judge described O'D's story as a 'remarkable one' and contrary to what he had previously told the police). It is only when the judge crosses the line into blatant unfairness and apparent pro-prosecution bias that a conviction is in danger (e.g., *Canny* (1945) 30 Cr App R 143 – conviction quashed because the judge had repeatedly told the jury that the defence case was 'absurd'). See also *Jones* [1987] Crim LR 701.

Comment on Failure of Accused to Testify

D22.29 Where an accused exercises his right not to testify, it is usual for the judge in summing-up to comment on the significance (if any) to be attached to his not going into the witness-box. Comment by the judge on the failure of the accused to testify is dealt with at **F19.11**.

Comment on the Accused's Character

The direction which the judge should give as to any evidence of the defendant's good **D22.30** character is dealt with in detail in **F13**. Where the judge comments erroneously or inadequately on the significance of good character, the prime question for the Court of Appeal will be whether the error makes the conviction unsafe. In *Bryant* [1979] QB 108, the judge implied that B's good character was totally irrelevant because he had not testified and therefore his credibility was not in issue. However, the Court of Appeal held that, having regard to the totality of the evidence, the inadequate direction 'could not possibly have had the effect of rendering the verdict unsafe or unsatisfactory'. The appeal was accordingly dismissed.

In *Vye* [1993] 1 WLR 471, Lord Taylor CJ, after laying down the principles relating to a direction on good character (see further **F13.4 et seq.**) added that what the judge says may vary significantly according to the facts of the case. The Court of Appeal would be 'slow to criticise' any qualifying remarks a judge may add.

Where the accused's *bad* character is revealed in evidence (e.g., as a result of cross-examination permitted under the Criminal Evidence Act 1898, s. 1(f)(ii) or (iii)), the judge must direct the jury that such evidence goes only to the accused's credibility as a witness and is not directly relevant to whether he committed the offence charged. Failure so to direct the jury is likely to lead to the quashing of any conviction (see *Vickers* [1972] Crim LR 101 where V was cross-examined about bad character in a manner suggesting that his previous convictions showed a violent disposition, and the judge merely directed the jury that the convictions did not show that V *must* be guilty of the unlawful wounding alleged, although they could give them such weight as they thought fit – conviction quashed). See generally **F14.18 et seq**. Plainly, different considerations arise where, by way of exception to the general rule, evidence that the accused has previously committed an offence is relevant and admissible because of its striking similarity to the offence charged. See generally **F12.3 et seq**. and **F14.16 et seq**.

EFFECT OF SUCCESSFUL APPEAL AGAINST CONVICTION

Effect of Successful Appeal in Usual Case

The normal consequence of a successful appeal is that the conviction is quashed, and **D22.31** the Crown Court is directed to enter a verdict of acquittal in place of the record of conviction (Criminal Appeal Act 1968, s. 2(2) and (3)). It follows that the successful appellant cannot be retried either for the offence in respect of which the appeal was brought or for any other offence of which he could have been convicted by way of alternative verdict. He may, however, be tried for a different offence based on the same facts and evidence (see *Connelly* v *DPP* [1964] AC 1254 where C's successful appeal against his conviction for murder committed in the course of an armed robbery barred a retrial for either murder or manslaughter but did not prevent his being indicted and tried for robbery, notwithstanding that the evidence relied on by the prosecution at the two trials was identical). The above is subject to the Criminal Appeal Act 1968, s. 7, which gives the Court of Appeal a general discretion to order a retrial. Where that is done, the original conviction is quashed, but a fresh indictment for the same offence is preferred by the direction of the court (see **D22.32**).

Criminal Appeal Act 1968, s. 2

(2) In the case of an appeal against conviction the court shall, if they allow the appeal, quash the conviction.

(3)   An order of the Court of Appeal quashing a conviction shall, except when under section 7 below the appellant is ordered to be retried, operate as a direction to the court of trial to enter, instead of the record of conviction, a judgment and verdict of acquittal.

Power to Order a Retrial

Criminal Appeal Act 1968, s. 7

D22.32   (1)   Where the Court of Appeal allow an appeal against conviction and it appears to the court that the interests of justice so require, they may order the appellant to be retried.

The retrial may not be for any offence other than the one in respect of which the successful appeal was brought (or an offence of which the appellant could have been convicted on the count for that offence by way of alternative verdict, or an offence charged in the alternative in respect of which the jury were discharged from giving a verdict because they had found the appellant guilty on the count in respect of which the appeal was brought) (Criminal Appeal Act 1968, s. 7(2)).

The court will take into account, when deciding whether a retrial is appropriate, both the length of time which has elapsed since the alleged commission of the offence and the strength of the additional evidence. In *Saunders* (1973) 58 Cr App R 248, a retrial was refused because S's appeal was not determined until $3\frac{1}{2}$ years after the offence. In *Grafton* [1993] QB 101, however, the Court of Appeal pointed out, in ordering a retrial, that it was now much more common for trials to take longer to come to court. In *Flower* [1966] 1 QB 146, a retrial was refused because the Court of Appeal was satisfied that the additional evidence conclusively showed F to be innocent. It is submitted that – having regard to the evidential problems inherent in retrials and the strain placed upon an accused by a first trial, an appeal and then a retrial – the Court of Appeal should and will use its powers under s. 7 sparingly, and only when the offence concerned is in the first rank of gravity.

The Criminal Appeal Act 1968, s. 8, contains detailed procedural provisions in respect of retrials. The indictment on which the appellant is to be retried must be one preferred by direction of the Court of Appeal (s. 8(1), and see s. 7(2) for the counts which it is permissible to include therein). A new bill of indictment must be signed in accordance with the formalities laid down in the Administration of Justice (Miscellaneous Provisions) Act 1933, s. 2(1), or the retrial will be invalid (*Jones* [1993] Crim LR 780). Arraignment on the fresh indictment must take place within two months of the order for retrial, unless the Court of Appeal gives leave for late arraignment. At any time after the two months have elapsed the appellant himself may apply to the Court of Appeal to set aside the order for retrial and direct the Crown Court to enter a verdict of acquittal (s. 8(1A)). On applications under s. 8(1) or (1A) the Court of Appeal may either grant leave to arraign or direct an acquittal, but it shall not do the former unless satisfied (a) that the prosecution have acted with all due expedition and (b) that there is good and sufficient cause for a retrial in spite of the lapse of time since the order under s. 7 was made (s. 8(1B)). As far as the requirement of 'due expedition' is concerned, it was stated in *Coleman* (1992) 95 Cr App R 345 that 'expedition' meant promptness or speed; and that 'due' meant reasonable or proper. In *Horne* [1992] Crim LR 304, the prosecution failed to act within the time-limit because papers had gone astray. They were held not to have acted with 'due expedition', despite the fact that an early trial date had, in the event, been set down by the court. When ordering a retrial, the court may make such orders as appear necessary or expedient for (a) the appellant's detention in custody or release on bail, or (b) retention pending the retrial of any property or money forfeited, restored or paid by virtue of the original conviction (or order made on that conviction) (s. 8(2)). Where the appellant was subject to a hospital order under the Mental Health Act 1983, s. 37, immediately before the determination of his appeal, the order is to continue in force until the retrial as if the appeal had not been allowed (s. 8(3) and see also s. 8(3A) for the continuance of interim hospital orders etc.). A transcript of the evidence of a witness at the original trial may be read if either the parties agree, or the judge is satisfied either that the witness is dead or unfit to attend court to give evidence, or that all reasonable efforts have been made to find him or secure his attendance but without success (Criminal Appeal Act 1968, sch. 2, para. 1). If the appellant is convicted at the retrial the court may pass any lawful sentence, provided it is of no greater severity than the sentence passed after the original trial (para. 2(1)). In particular, it may reimpose the sentence passed following the original trial, even if the appellant is now beyond the age at which that sentence would normally be available to the court (para. 2(2)). For purposes of computation of sentence, any custodial sentence passed on retrial is deemed to run from the time when a like sentence passed at the original trial would have begun to run (para. 2(3)).

Writs of *Venire de Novo*

It is convenient at this point to discuss the Court of Appeal's inherent jurisdiction to quash **D22.33** a conviction in cases where there has been a total mistrial. In such cases it has a concomitant power to issue a writ of *venire de novo*. The effect of the writ is that the proceedings are returned to the point they had reached immediately before the error which rendered the original trial abortive. This gives the prosecution the chance to rectify whatever went wrong on the previous occasion. In effect, a retrial is ordered, but it is different from a retrial ordered under the Criminal Appeal Act 1968, s. 7, because the Court of Appeal itself does not direct the preferment of a bill of indictment. The point is illustrated by *Newland* [1988] QB 402 where the Court of Appeal quashed N's convictions because the indictment on which he was arraigned and to which he pleaded guilty was invalid by reason of transgression of the Indictment Rules 1971, r. 9 (joinder of counts in a single indictment). Declining, in its discretion, to order a *venire de novo*, the court said that the consequence of the writ would be that the case would go back to the Crown Court *upon the same defective indictment* (p. 408F). The prosecution would be able to apply to amend the indictment by deletion of the improperly joined counts, but that would still mean further proceedings on a separate indictment in respect of the deleted counts. Having regard to the time N had already spent in custody and the likely sentence were he ultimately to be convicted again on all matters, a writ would cause more trouble than it was worth. Therefore, the court simply quashed N's convictions, not by virtue of the Criminal Appeal Act 1968, s. 2(1) since there had been no trial within the meaning of the paragraph, but under its inherent jurisdiction.

The circumstances in which *venire de novo* may be issued were considered successively by the Court of Appeal and the House of Lords in *Rose* [1982] 1 WLR 614 (CA) and [1982] AC 822 (HL). R's conviction for murder had to be quashed because the trial judge had sent notes to the jury without telling counsel and had come close to applying improper pressure on them to reach a verdict. The prosecution asked for a retrial. Lord Lane CJ (giving the judgment of the Court of Appeal) referred with approval to an article by Sir Robin Cooke (1955) 71 LQR 100. The article identified seven categories of case in which retrials (i.e. by writs of *venire de novo*) had historically been ordered. They were:

(a)   where there was error as to the true plea of the defendant or some doubt about the nature of his plea, whether guilty or not guilty;

(b)   where there was misjoinder of defendants (*Crane* v *DPP* [1921] 2 AC 299);

(c)   where there was failure to take the verdict of the jury on a change of plea from not guilty to guilty (*Hancock* (1931) 23 Cr App R 16);

(d)   where there was some irregularity in the committal proceedings (*Gee* [1936] 2 KB 442);

(e)   where there was personation of a juror (*Wakefield* [1918] 1 KB 216);

(f)   where there was denial of the right to challenge a juror (*Williams* (1925) 19 Cr App R 67); and

(g)   where the judge was unqualified to act as such.

For good measure, the Court of Appeal added an eighth category of its own, namely, where the verdict of the jury was so ambiguous or ill-expressed that no judgment could properly be given on it. Lord Lane CJ then summarised the effect of the above as follows (at p. 622D–E, emphasis added):

> It will be noted that all these examples are matters of procedure, and it has never been held, nor indeed suggested, that a *venire de novo* is appropriate where, for instance, there has been some mistake in the direction to the jury, or some other issue left to the jury which ought not to have been left and so on. The first requirement is irregularity in procedure. Secondly, it seems from this analysis, that the irregular incident may happen at any stage of the proceedings. Thirdly, the defect must be fundamental. *The trial must be marred by an irregularity so serious as to entitle the defendant to a retrial at the least; so serious that it can properly be termed as 'mistrial', or, as some authorities put it, a 'nullity'.*

The irregularity in *Rose* did not render the trial a mistrial or come within any of the categories of case suitable for a *venire de novo*, and accordingly the Court of Appeal was obliged simply to quash the conviction under the Criminal Appeal Act 1968, s. 2(1)(c). There was then no general power to order a retrial when a conviction was quashed in reliance on the statutory powers contained in s. 2(1) rather than under the inherent jurisdiction.

Lord Diplock's speech in the House of Lords (with which the rest of their lordships concurred) also referred with approval to Sir Robin Cooke's article and adopted the same basic reasoning as Lord Lane to arrive at the same conclusion. Lord Diplock said (at p. 833A):

> [The Court of Criminal Appeal could issue a writ of *venire de novo*] if there had been an irregularity of procedure which had resulted in there having been no trial that had been validly commenced. It could do so if the trial had come to an end without a properly constituted jury ever having returned a valid verdict. It could *not* do so because of an irregularity in the course of the trial occurring between the time it had been validly commenced and the discharge of the jury after returning a verdict.

In summary, the effect of the above authorities is that *venire de novo* cases and ordinary appeals are mutually exclusive; if an irregularity is sufficiently fundamental to render the trial a mistrial and thus activate the court's inherent jurisdiction to quash a conviction and issue *venire de novo*, then *ipso facto* no valid trial will have commenced. In both types of case, however, the Court of Appeal now has power to order a retrial. If the appeal is under statute, the power is contained in the Criminal Appeal Act 1968, s. 7, and involves the court itself directing preferment of a bill of indictment (see **D22.32**). If the appeal is under the inherent power, the effect of *venire de novo* is to return the proceedings to the point immediately before the irregularity occurred so that the prosecution can cure the defect and a valid trial may take place. If and only if the appeal is under statute, the court has the additional option of dismissing it, provided that the conviction is safe.

Partially Successful Appeals: Substituting Verdict

D22.34 By the Criminal Appeal Act 1968, s. 3, the Court of Appeal may, in specified circumstances, substitute for the verdict of the jury a verdict of guilty of another offence. This power arises when (a) the jury could, on the indictment, have found the appellant guilty of some offence other than that of which they did in fact convict him (see **D16.18** *et seq.*), and (b) it appears to the Court of Appeal from the actual finding of the jury that they must have been satisfied of the facts proving the appellant guilty of the other offence (s. 3(1)). Upon exercise of the power, the Court of Appeal must itself pass sentence for the other offence, which sentence must not be more severe than the sentence passed at the Crown Court for the offence in respect of which the appellant's conviction has been quashed (s. 3(2)). The power under s. 3 is available only where the jury has given a verdict and not where the appellant has pleaded guilty (*Horsman* [1998] QB 531).

It should be noted that the s. 3 power arises only when the verdict of the jury is sufficient *in itself* to show that they must have been satisfied of facts proving the appellant guilty of the other offence. Therefore, if the ground of appeal relied on by the appellant is an error at trial which must have affected the jury's overall view of the case and thus casts doubt on *all* their findings of fact, s. 3 cannot be invoked, even if the Court of Appeal's opinion of the evidence is that any jury properly directed at an error-free trial would at least have found the appellant guilty of an alternative offence. In *Deacon* [1973] 1 WLR 696, the evidence of D's wife, who was in fact incompetent, was admitted at D's trial for murdering his brother-in-law. The Court of Appeal was therefore obliged to quash the conviction for murder, and was unable to substitute a conviction for manslaughter because, although the jury's actual verdict showed they must have been satisfied that D at least unlawfully killed the victim, that verdict was *entirely* 'coloured' by the fact that they had heard inadmissible evidence. Thus, the appeal in *Deacon* succeeded completely, even though, in the court's opinion, there was enough evidence against the appellant without that of his wife for any reasonable jury properly directed to have convicted him of manslaughter. *Deacon* was distinguished in *Spratt* [1980] 1 WLR 554 where additional evidence which rendered the jury's verdict of guilty of murder unsafe went only to the issue of whether S was suffering from diminished responsibility at the relevant time, not to whether there had been an unlawful killing. Accordingly, the Court of Appeal was able to substitute a verdict of guilty of manslaughter. (See also *Weekes* [1999] Crim LR 907.)

The wording of the Criminal Appeal Act 1968, s. 3, is wide enough to cover two broad categories of case. The first is where the jury could, on a single count of the indictment, have found the appellant not guilty as charged but guilty of some other offence under provisions such as the Criminal Law Act 1967, s. 6(2) to (4). *Spratt* provides one example of that. See also *Reynolds* [1988] Crim LR 679, which is very similar on its facts to *Spratt*, and *Worton* (1989) 154 JP 201, in which W's conviction for violent disorder had to be quashed because the trial judge had failed to direct the jury that if they decided that one of several co-accused charged with violent disorder was not guilty then they would have to acquit the others as well if that reduced the number unlawfully involved in the violence to less than three, but a conviction for affray was substituted as the jury's verdict showed that in the appellant's case they were at least satisfied as to all the ingredients of the latter offence. The fact that the jury were not actually directed about the possibility of an alternative verdict does not deprive the Court of Appeal of its jurisdiction under the Criminal Appeal Act 1968, s. 3 (*Caslin* [1961] 1 WLR 59). Nevertheless, the fact that the jury had no proper direction as to the alternative offence will be a relevant consideration in exercising the jurisdiction (*Caslin* and *Cooke* [1997] Crim LR 436).

The second category of case where s. 3 may be invoked is where there are counts in the alternative and the jury have convicted on the 'wrong' count – i.e. the facts alleged by the prosecution did not amount to the offence of which they actually convicted but did amount to the alternative. In this situation, it is essential that the jury were merely discharged from giving a verdict on the alternative count. If there has been an actual acquittal, the Court of Appeal cannot, under s. 3, set it aside and substitute a conviction (see *Melvin* [1953] 1 QB 481, the headnote to which reads: 'Where an indictment contained two counts, one for larceny and the other for receiving, and the jury acquitted on the larceny count and convicted on the receiving count, although on the evidence the accused were clearly guilty of larceny, the Court of Criminal Appeal had no power . . . to substitute a verdict of guilty of larceny for the incorrect verdict of receiving'). The same point was made by Lord Goddard CJ in *Seymour* [1954] 1 WLR 678:

> In cases where the evidence is as consistent with stealing as with receiving, the indictment ought to contain a count both for stealing and for receiving. . . . if the jury come to the

(1990) 12 Cr App R (S) 88 (following *McCabe* (1988) 10 Cr App R (S) 134), the Court of Appeal held that the Crown Court judge was wrong in principle to pass a suspended sentence of eight months when P had already served while on remand the equivalent of an eight-month term – the sentence should have been immediate, thus allowing for P's instant release without anything further hanging over his head. However, the Court of Appeal itself could not substitute the appropriate sentence (i.e. eight months' immediate imprisonment) because, in theory though not in practice, that was more severe than the Crown Court sentence. Accordingly, the Court of Appeal was obliged to give the appellant a conditional discharge.

(d)   It has been held that a hospital order coupled with a restriction order for an indefinite period is not more severe than a sentence of three years' imprisonment (*Bennett* [1968] 1 WLR 988, cited with approval in *Crozier* (1990) 12 Cr App R (S) 206). It has also been held that an ordinary hospital order may be substituted for a sentence of Borstal training (*Marsden* [1968] 1 WLR 785). The reasoning behind those decisions is that a hospital order – unlike imprisonment or detention in a young offender institution – is not intended as a punishment but as remedial treatment. However, having regard to the long periods for which an offender may find himself compulsorily detained under a hospital order (especially if a restriction order is attached), it may be argued that the Court of Appeal was over-influenced by the theoretical basis of hospital orders while failing to pay due regard to their practical effect as experienced by the offender.

(e)   Where a term of imprisonment is reduced, the appellant may be given a fine in addition. In *Walton* (29 August 1989 unreported), W had been sentenced by the court below to four months' imprisonment. He served 11 days in custody and was then released on bail. At the appeal, such term of imprisonment as would allow immediate release was substituted, with the addition of a fine of £1,000.

(f)   Where sentences of imprisonment have been reduced the Court of Appeal has held itself able to impose or increase an order for disqualification from driving (*Ardani* (1983) 77 Cr App R 302). Conversely, in *McLaren* (1983) 5 Cr App R (S) 332, the appellant's fine was increased but his disqualification reduced. A further variation on the same theme can be found in *Murphy* (1989) 89 Cr App R 176. In that case, M was disqualified for eight years by the court below. On appeal, the term of disqualification was reduced to six years with the addition of an order that at the end of that period M be not permitted to drive until he had passed a driving test.

Criminal Appeal Act 1968, s. 11

(1)   Subject to subsection (1A) below, an appeal against sentence, whether under section 9 or section 10 of this Act, lies only with the leave of the Court of Appeal.

(1A)   If the judge who passed the sentence grants a certificate that the case is fit for appeal under section 9 or 10 of this Act, an appeal lies under this section without the leave of the Court of Appeal.

(2)   Where the Crown Court, in dealing with an offender either on his conviction on indictment or in a proceeding to which section 10(2) of this Act applies, has passed on him two or more sentences in the same proceeding (which expression has the same meaning in this subsection as it has for the purposes of section 10), being sentences against which an appeal lies under section 9(1) or section 10, an appeal or application for leave to appeal against any one of those sentences shall be treated as an appeal or application in respect of both or all of them.

(2A)   Where following conviction on indictment a person has been convicted under section 41 of the Criminal Justice Act 1988 of a summary offence an appeal or application for leave to appeal against any sentence for the offence triable either way shall be treated also as an appeal or application in respect of any sentence for the summary offence and an appeal or application for leave to appeal against any sentence for the summary offence shall be treated also as an appeal or application in respect of the offence triable either way.

(2B)   If the appellant or applicant was convicted on indictment of two or more offences triable either way, the references to the offence triable either way in subsection (2A) above are to be construed, in relation to any summary offence of which he was convicted under section 41 of the Criminal Justice Act 1988 following the conviction on indictment, as references to the offence triable either way specified in the notice relating to that summary offence which was given under subsection (2) of that section.

(3)   On an appeal against sentence the Court of Appeal, if they consider that the appellant should be sentenced differently for an offence for which he was dealt with by the court below may—

(a)   quash any sentence or order which is the subject of the appeal; and

(b)   in place of it pass such sentence or make such order as they think appropriate for the case and as the court below had power to pass or make when dealing with him for the offence;

but the court shall so exercise their powers under this subsection that, taking the case as a whole, the appellant is not more severely dealt with on appeal than he was dealt with by the court below.

(4)   The power of the Court of Appeal under subsection (3) of this section to pass a sentence which the court below had power to pass for an offence shall, notwithstanding that the court below made no order under section 23(1) of the Powers of Criminal Courts Act 1973 or section 47(4) of the Criminal Law Act 1977 in respect of a suspended or partly suspended sentence previously passed on the appellant for another offence, include power to deal with him in respect of that sentence where the court below made no order in respect of it.

[(5) and (6)   Concern respectively the position where the Court of Appeal quashes an interim hospital order but does not replace it with its own sentence, and the position where the court replaces the sentence of the court below with an interim hospital order.]

Approach of the Court of Appeal to Determining Appeals against Sentence

D22.40   Sections 9 to 11 of the Criminal Appeal Act 1968 merely empower the Court of Appeal to hear and determine appeals against sentence. They give no indication of the circumstances in which the court should in practice exercise its powers. However, there emerge from the copious mass of sentencing decisions broad indications of when the court will in practice allow an appeal and reduce sentence. The following paragraphs are intended merely as a guide to the practice of the court.

D22.41   *Sentence Wrong in Law*   This is the most obvious reason for the court to intervene. An example is provided by *Corcoran* (1986) 8 Cr App R (S) 118 where a sentence of three years' detention under the CYPA 1933, s. 53(3), had to be quashed because C (aged 16) had been found guilty of the offences concerned in the juvenile court and committed for sentence to the Crown Court under the MCA 1980, s. 37. Since the power to pass a sentence of s. 53(3) detention arises only if there has been a conviction on indictment, the sentence was unlawful. Even though the original sentence was said to be richly deserved on the facts, it had to be varied to 12 months' youth custody, the maximum which the Crown Court could lawfully have imposed. Similarly, in *Bramble* (1984) 6 Cr App R (S) 80, the Court of Appeal quashed an order depriving B of the car in which he had committed an offence of reckless driving because, under the PCCA 1973, s. 43, as it then stood, forfeiture orders could be made only in respect of property found in possession of the offender at the time of his arrest and B had never been arrested (he was proceeded against by way of summons). Notwithstanding the above examples and the increasing complexity of sentencing law, it is still fairly rare for a sentence to be wrong in law.

D22.42   *Sentence Wrong in Principle or Manifestly Excessive*   This is by far the most frequent basis of an appeal against sentence. Indeed, in a sense, all the remaining examples of situations where appeals are commonly allowed could be regarded merely as instances of sentences which are wrong in principle. The phrase 'wrong in principle or manifestly excessive' has traditionally been accepted as encapsulating the Court of Appeal's general approach. It conveys the idea that the Court of Appeal will not interfere an appeal may be commenced only with the authority of the person convicted, and that authority has to be given *after* conviction, not before. Therefore, the purported notice of application for leave to appeal was a nullity.

Paragraph 1 of the Guide sets out a strict timetable to ensure that notices of appeal or application for leave to appeal are served within time. It recommends that all briefs to counsel to represent a legally aided accused at trial on indictment should include a separate form of instruction to give advice and assistance on appeal in the event of conviction. Counsel should then advise orally on the prospects of an appeal immediately after conviction or sentence. That advice will comprise:

(a) his final view as to the prospects of a successful appeal; or
(b) his provisional view as to its prospects; or
(c) that he requires time to consider its prospects.

If his advice expresses a final view in accordance with (a), then he is not required also to provide written advice to the same effect, and if he does tender such written advice in the absence of a specific request by his client, a claim for fees may be refused by the determining officer as work not reasonably done, unless there are special circumstances (*Lord Chancellor* v *Brennan* (1996) *The Times*, 14 February 1996). Such special circumstances might include the circumstances of the conviction, any particular difficulties at trial, the length and nature of the sentence passed or its effect on the defendant, or the lack of impact which oral advice given immediately after trial might have on the particular defendant's mind (Bar Code of Conduct, annexe F, para. 17.2). If his advice is such that it falls within (b) or (c) above, then he should send to his solicitors within 14 days an advice on appeal and, where appropriate, signed grounds of appeal.

The appellant's solicitors are then responsible for sending copies of the advice to the lay client so as to reach him within a further seven days. If counsel has advised an appeal and the lay client accepts his advice, the completed forms should be lodged with the Crown Court forthwith.

Should an appellant who does not need leave to appeal purport to give notice of application for leave to appeal, the document is treated simply as a notice of appeal (Criminal Appeal Rules 1968, r. 2(7)). The converse also applies (ibid.).

Criminal Appeal Act 1968, s. 18

(1) A person who wishes to appeal under this part of this Act to the Court of Appeal, or to obtain the leave of that court to appeal, shall give notice of appeal or, as the case may be, notice of application for leave to appeal, in such manner as may be directed by rules of court.

(2) Notice of appeal, or of application for leave to appeal, shall be given within 28 days of the conviction, verdict or finding appealed against, or in the case of appeal against sentence, from the date on which sentence was passed or, in the case of an order made or treated as made on conviction, from the date of the making of the order.

(3) The time for giving notice under this section may be extended, either before or after it expires, by the Court of Appeal.

Criminal Appeal Rules 1968, r. 2

(1) Notice of appeal or of an application for leave to appeal under part I of the Act or notice of appeal under section 13 of the Administration of Justice Act 1960 (as required by section 18A of the Act) against an order or decision of the Crown Court shall be given by completing part 1 of form 2 and so much of part 2 thereof as relates to the notice and serving it on the appropriate officer of the Crown Court.

(2) (a) A notice of appeal or of an application for leave to appeal shall be accompanied by a notice in form 3 containing the grounds of the appeal or application.

(b)   If the appellant has been convicted of more than one offence, the notice in form 3 shall specify the convictions or sentences against which the appellant is appealing or applying for leave to appeal.

(c)   The grounds of an appeal or application set out in form 3 may, with the consent of the court, be varied or amplified within such time as the court may allow.

(3)   (a)   Notice of an application to extend the time within which notice of appeal or of an application for leave to appeal may under part I of the Act be given shall be given by completing so much of part 2 of form 2 as relates to the application and by giving notice of appeal or of an application for leave to appeal in accordance with the foregoing provisions of this rule.

(b)   Notice of an application to extend the time within which notice of appeal or of an application for leave to appeal may under part I of the Act be given shall specify the grounds of the application.

(4)   An appellant who is appealing or applying for leave to appeal against conviction shall specify in form 3 any exhibit produced at the trial which he wishes to be kept in custody for the purposes of his appeal.

(5)   Forms 2 and 3 shall be signed by, or on behalf of, the appellant.

[(6)   Copies of forms 2 and 3 to be sent to the appellant if he is in custody and did not sign them personally.]

(7)   Where an appellant does not require leave to appeal, a notice of application for leave to appeal shall be treated as a notice of appeal; and where an appellant requires leave to appeal but serves only a notice of appeal, the notice of appeal shall be treated as an application for leave to appeal.

GROUNDS OF APPEAL

Drafting and Contents of Grounds of Appeal

D23.3   The notice of appeal or application for leave to appeal must be accompanied by the grounds of appeal (Criminal Appeal Rules 1968, r. 2(2)(a)). A notice which merely states, 'Grounds of appeal will follow', or words to that effect, does not comply with the rules, and time will continue to run against the applicant until such time as proper grounds are served (*Wilson* [1973] Crim LR 572). Further, it is stated in the Guide (although without reference to precise authority) that grounds consisting of generalised formulae, such as 'the verdict of the jury was unsafe' or 'the sentence was too severe in all the circumstances of the case', are also insufficient (see para. 2.2). This echoes Lord Parker CJ who, in *Practice Note (Crime: Applications for Leave to Appeal)* [1970] 1 WLR 663, reminded counsel that 'it is useless to appeal without grounds and that the grounds should be substantial and particularised, and not a mere formula.' What degree of particularity is required is obviously not capable of precise definition, but the Guide suggests that they should be detailed enough to enable 'the Registrar and subsequently the court to identify clearly the matters relied upon' (para. 2.2). Authorities upon which the appellant proposes to rely, whether statutory or case law, should be cited (para 2.3). As to appeals based on misdirections or omissions in the summing-up, the words of Du Parcq J in *Fielding* (1938) 26 Cr App R 211 (emphasis added) are still relevant:

> It is most unsatisfactory that grounds of appeal should be drawn with such vagueness as we find in the present case. Ground 4 is in the following terms: 'That the judge failed adequately to direct the jury as to the law and evidence to be considered by them'.

> It has been said many times in this court that particulars must be given in the grounds of appeal. *If misdirection is complained of, it must be stated whether the alleged misdirection is one of law or fact, and its nature must also be stated.* If omission is complained of, it must be stated what it is alleged to have been omitted. It is not only placing an unnecessary burden on the court to ask it to search through the summing-up and the transcript of the evidence to find out what there may be to be complained of, but it is also unfair to the prosecution, who are entitled to know what case they have to meet.

Nicco [1972] Crim LR 420 similarly states that the terms of any misdirection relied upon must be set out in the grounds, while in *Singh* [1973] Crim LR 36 the Court of Appeal drew attention to the danger of extracting sentences from the summing-up out of context when, if they had been quoted in context, they would have been unobjectionable. However, while grounds should be reasonably full, counsel may also be criticised for going to the opposite extreme and overloading them (*Pybus* (1983) *The Times*, 23 February 1983, where the Court of Appeal said that lengthy grounds containing unsubstantiated complaints on points of detail had detracted from their lordships' appreciation of the substantial and genuine points which ultimately led to the quashing of the conviction).

Advice with Grounds

A common practice is for counsel to submit with his grounds of appeal a copy of his **D23.4** advice on whether an appeal should be brought. According to para. 1.6 of the Guide, there is no obligation to do this but in most cases it may be helpful. Although it may be felt anomalous to tender to the court a privileged document intended primarily for counsel's lay and professional clients, the practice has many advantages. In particular, it enables counsel to set out fully the factual and legal basis of the appeal and present his arguments in skeleton form, without overburdening the grounds proper. Trying to incorporate in the grounds all the material that may be useful for the single judge in deciding whether to grant leave may result in a very unwieldy document. An adverse advice should never be included.

Perfection and Variation of Grounds

Rule 2(2)(c) of the Criminal Appeal Rules 1968 states that grounds may, with the **D23.5** consent of the court, be varied or amplified within such time as the court may allow. It is standard practice in the case of appeals against conviction for the Registrar to obtain a transcript of at least the judge's summing-up and send a copy thereof to counsel for the appellant (see **D23.10**). Counsel is then asked to correct and 'perfect' his original grounds in the light of reading the transcript (see para. 4.1 of the Guide). Usually he is given 14 days in which to do so. If he fails to comply, the original grounds may be placed before the judge without further warning (ibid.). The perfected grounds should consist of a fresh document, quoting accurately from the transcript and referring by page number and letter to all relevant passages; authorities upon which counsel relies should be cited, preferably with references to the Criminal Appeal Reports (para. 4.4). Any document mentioned in the grounds should also be clearly identified (e.g., by exhibit number). If each member of the court will require a copy, an indication to that effect should be given. Similarly, if an original exhibit ought to be available for the hearing, counsel should say so in good time (ibid.). Where counsel decides in the light of the transcript that there are not, in fact, good grounds of appeal, he should advise his solicitors accordingly and inform the Registrar that he has done so (para. 4.5). The appellant will be entitled to continue the appeal if he wishes, but may be at risk of a direction for loss of time (ibid. and see **D22.10** for directions for loss of time).

Leaving aside perfection of grounds of appeal in the light of the transcript (which is in effect amendment at the court's request), counsel should not take it for granted that he will be allowed to amend his grounds, but should make a specific application to that effect as soon as he realises the need for amendment. In *Haycraft* (1973) 58 Cr App R 121, the Court of Appeal stressed that grounds should be submitted within the proper time and that, unless the court is asked for permission to file additional grounds, the original ones will stand. Presenting further grounds on the very day of the hearing was described as 'highly unsatisfactory'. The court eventually gave leave for it to be done 'with great reluctance', saying that 'such indulgence could not be granted in the future'. Similarly, in *Upton* [1973] 3 All ER 318, Lawton LJ said:

It is important from the point of view of the proper administration of this court that grounds of appeal should be drafted carefully and accurately.

. . . grounds of appeal mean something and counsel ought not to assume that any ground of appeal which is not set out will be entertained by this court. It follows that having given leave for these grounds of appeal to be varied, the appellants will have to keep to the grounds of appeal now before the court. . . . it is most unlikely that they will be, through their counsel, allowed to argue any point other than those set out in the amended grounds of appeal.

Duty of Counsel with Regard to Grounds of Appeal

D23.6   Counsel have on occasions been criticised for drafting improper grounds of appeal. Thus, in *Morson* (1976) 62 Cr App R 236, where counsel included a ground alleging that the summing-up read as a whole was unfair and amounted to a direction to convict, Scarman LJ said that it was a 'travesty' so to describe the summing-up, and that the Court of Appeal 'deplore the fact that that ground was included in the grounds of appeal' (p. 238). The headnote, reflecting the general tenor of the judgment, reads as follows: 'It is the duty of counsel in drafting and arguing grounds of appeal to act responsibly and not to make sweeping and unjustified attacks on the summing-up of the trial judge unless such attacks can be justified'. More generally, para. 2.4 of the Guide states that: 'Counsel should not settle or sign grounds unless they are reasonable, have some real prospect of success and are such that he is prepared to argue before the court'. If counsel is unable to confirm that his suggested grounds are reasonable within the time for service (e.g., because he needs to look at a transcript of the summing-up before finally making up his mind), then he should settle grounds but accompany them with a note for the Registrar explaining his difficulty. Depending on the information subsequently obtained, it may become necessary to abandon the appeal.

Appellant Drafting Notice and Grounds of Appeal

D23.7   There is nothing to prevent an appellant conducting his appeal in person. If he is in custody, the prescribed forms for notice and grounds of appeal may be obtained by him from the prison etc. in which he is detained; if he is at liberty, they are obtainable from the Crown Court. Where the reason for the appellant acting in person is that he was not legally aided for the Crown Court proceedings, the court may grant him legal aid simply for advice on and preparation of grounds of appeal (see **D27.19**). Where the appellant has had the benefit of legal advice but counsel has advised against appeal, he is not bound by counsel's advice, but he does run an increased risk of a direction for loss of time if he insists on appealing and his application fails (see **D22.10**).

LEAVE TO APPEAL

Procedure for Obtaining Leave to Appeal

D23.8   Leave to appeal may be granted by a single judge (Criminal Appeal Act 1968, s. 31(1)). For purposes of exercising any of his s. 31 powers, the judge may 'sit in such place as he appoints, and may sit otherwise than in open court' (Criminal Appeal Rules 1968, r. 11(1)). A party in proceedings before a single judge may be represented by counsel or solicitor (r. 11(2)).

Once the Registrar has obtained the necessary papers (i.e. the notice and grounds of appeal, the transcript considered necessary and any documentary exhibits from the Crown Court), he normally refers an application for leave to appeal to a single judge (see paras. 5.1 and 5.2 of the Guide). Alternatively, in order to expedite proceedings, he may refer the application direct to a court (ibid.). If he chooses the latter course, he may grant legal aid for the hearing so that, in the event of leave being granted by the court, it can proceed forthwith to determination of the appeal. An application for leave to appeal may not be made to a judge direct but must always go through the Registrar (*Lambert* [1977] Crim LR 736).

Almost invariably, applications for leave referred to a single judge are considered by him privately without the attendance of counsel or solicitors. The judge simply reads through the papers and indicates in writing, with very brief reasons, what his decision is. Notification of the single judge's decision must be served on the applicant by the Registrar as soon as is practicable (Criminal Appeal Rules 1968, r. 15(1)(a)). If the decision is against him, he has the right to have his application determined by the court (Criminal Appeal Act 1968, s. 31(3)). He must, however, serve on the Registrar notice of intention to renew the application within 14 days of himself receiving the Registrar's notification that the single judge refused leave (Criminal Appeal Rules 1968, r. 12(1)). The 14-day period may be extended, either before or after its expiry, by any judge of the court (see r. 12(1) and *Ward* [1971] 1 WLR 1450). However, good reasons will be required if a late renewal of application for leave is to be allowed. The reasons must relate to why the applicant did not give notice within the permitted time, not to the general merits of his case (*Doherty* [1971] 1 WLR 1454 where Lord Widgery CJ said: 'The only issue which arises when an applicant seeks to extend the time is whether he has an excuse for not having renewed within the specified 14 days, and only in cases quite out of the ordinary does this court contemplate that such an excuse will be forthcoming in such circumstances'). A mere change of heart on the applicant's part is insufficient reason. Similarly, lack of additional legal advice after being notified of the single judge's decision is not enough, since the advice the applicant received earlier is considered sufficient to enable him to decide for himself whether he wants to renew his application (*Sullivan* (1972) 56 Cr App R 541). It is otherwise, however, if he received positively misleading advice (*Doherty* [1971] 1 WLR 1454, where the prison governor, according to D, told him that the only course open to him in view of the single judge having refused his application for leave was to petition the Home Secretary). If no notice of application to renew is served on the Registrar within 14 days (or such longer period as is allowed by the court), the application for leave is treated as having been refused by the court and the appeal is consequently at an end (Criminal Appeal Rules 1968, r. 12(4)). In such circumstances, however, the full court is not precluded from determining whether to grant an extension of time for the service of the notice (*Dixon* [1999] 3 All ER 889).

In *Cox* [1999] 2 Cr App R 6, the Court of Appeal considered the position where there are several grounds of appeal against conviction, and the single judge gives leave in respect of one (or more) and does not do so in relation to the remainder. It was confirmed that it was perfectly proper for the single judge to differentiate between grounds in this way. It was not, however, necessary for him to grant or refuse leave on each of the grounds advanced. In other words, it was perfectly in order (and often convenient) for him to identify a good ground (or grounds) of appeal and make no decision in relation to the other(s). The appellant was then entitled to rely on any of the grounds put forward, whether the single judge had approved of the ground in question or not. What the appellant was not entitled to do was to rely upon a ground upon which the single judge had expressly refused leave. In relation to a refused ground, it was necessary for the appellant to renew his application for leave to appeal in front of the full court, notifying the Crown and the Criminal Appeal Office of his intention to do so (on this latter point, see also *Jackson* [1998] Crim LR 835). *Cox* also dealt with appeals against sentence; it was pointed out that it would rarely serve any purpose for the single judge to select a particular ground or grounds for approval or rejection, since the usual appeal against sentence relied upon the cumulative effect of the grounds advanced. If the single judge exceptionally decided to refuse a specific ground, however, then counsel for the appellant would have to renew the application for leave in the same way.

A renewed application for leave to appeal is determined by a court (which may consist of only two judges) sitting in open court. If the applicant is in custody, he is not entitled to be present (see **D23.14**). Moreover, although the Crown Court legal aid will cover advice on whether it is worth renewing an unsuccessful application for leave (*Gibson* [1983] 1 WLR 1038), it will not cover representation at the renewed application itself (*Kearney* [1983] 1 WLR 1046). It follows that, save in the cases of the small minority of applicants able to instruct solicitors and counsel privately, there is no legal representation at a renewed application for leave to appeal (the prosecution would not choose to be represented unless they knew the applicant was going to be). It further follows that the so-called hearing of the renewed application consists merely of their lordships reading the same papers as were before the single judge and then announcing their decision. Thus, apart from the fact that one is in private and the other in public, there is little intrinsic difference between original and renewed applications for leave to appeal – each is decided on the papers without hearing argument.

Leave to Appeal Out of Time

D23.9 The Criminal Appeal Act 1968, s. 18(3), provides that the time for giving notice of appeal or application for leave to appeal may be extended by the court either before or after the normal 28 days has expired; such an extension may be granted on behalf of the court by the single judge or the Registrar (see **D23.25** and **D23.26**). However, the court has expressed itself unwilling to grant extensions (other than very short ones) unless there are very good reasons (see *Rhodes* (1910) 5 Cr App R 35, *Moore* (1923) 17 Cr App R 155, *Ramsden* [1972] Crim LR 547 and *Burley* (1994) *The Times*, 9 November 1994 for examples of the court's approach). In *Dilworth* (1983) 78 Cr App R 182, it was held that a change in parole policy since the applicant was sentenced, which would have the effect that he would serve longer in prison than he anticipated at the time he originally decided against giving notice of appeal, was not sufficient reason for allowing him to appeal 18 months after sentence. Even where there has been a decision of the Court of Appeal after the time for giving notice which indicates that there was a wrong decision on law at the prospective appellant's trial such as would necessitate quashing his conviction had he appealed within time, the court will not necessarily be obliged to give him leave to appeal out of time – it remains a matter of discretion (*Ramsden* [1972] Crim LR 547 and *Hawkins* [1997] 1 Cr App R 234). It is otherwise if an appellant has commenced an appeal against sentence within time and then it becomes apparent that he also has good grounds of appeal against conviction (*Mitchell* [1977] 1 WLR 753). To refuse leave to appeal against conviction in those circumstances would place the court in the impossible position of trying to determine an appeal against sentence knowing that the appellant may have been wrongly convicted in the first place. For a further example of an appeal against conviction being allowed out of time, see *Lee* [1984] 1 WLR 578.

TRANSCRIPTS

D23.10 Section 32 of the Criminal Appeal Act 1968 enables rules of court to provide for (a) the making of a record (whether by shorthand note or mechanical means) of any proceedings in respect of which an appeal lies to the Court of Appeal, and (b) the supply of a transcript of the record to the Registrar or such other persons as may be prescribed. Rules 18 to 20 of the Criminal Appeal Rules 1968 have been made in furtherance of s. 32. Rule 18 provides essentially that the whole of any appealable proceedings shall be recorded apart from the opening and closing speeches of counsel; a breach of r. 18 does not of itself make a conviction unsafe but, according to the circumstances, the absence of a transcript may lead the Court of Appeal to conclude that there may have been a misdirection (*Richards* [1997] Crim LR 48). Rule 19 requires a transcript of the record (or part thereof) to be supplied on request to the Registrar or 'any interested party', subject to payment of such charge as may be fixed by the Treasury. The Registrar may also, at his discretion, supply a copy of any transcript he has obtained to any interested party for purposes of an appeal or application for leave to appeal (r. 19(2)). If the interested party is legally aided, the Registrar must do this free of charge (proviso to r. 19(2)). 'Interested party' means the DPP, or an accused or prosecutor in the proceedings in respect of which the appeal lies, or any other person who is named in or immediately affected by an order made by a Crown Court judge in the proceedings (r. 25(1)).

Assuming the appellant or applicant for leave to appeal is legally aided, the normal procedure for obtaining transcript is that the Registrar, following receipt of the notice and grounds of appeal from the Crown Court, will order as much transcript as he considers necessary for proper disposal of the appeal. In the case of an appeal against conviction, he will almost certainly order a 'short transcript' (i.e. a transcript of the charges, pleas, summing-up and evidence after verdict). If a transcript of the evidence is needed, counsel should so indicate in his grounds of appeal (see para. 3.1 of the Guide). Where counsel and the Registrar cannot agree the extent of transcript necessary, the matter should be referred to a judge (ibid. and see also *Lurie* [1951] 2 All ER 704 at p. 706E–H which indicates that no transcript of evidence should be ordered save with leave of the court or a single judge, unless it be of evidence directly referred to in the notice or grounds). Furthermore, it is counsel's duty not to ask for a transcript unless it is genuinely essential, since provision thereof is expensive and time-consuming (*Flemming* (1987) 86 Cr App R 32). In *Flemming*, Woolf LJ said (at p. 39):

> At considerable public expense, for the purposes of the appeal we were provided with six bundles of transcripts. During the course of the hearing we were referred to only two bundles. On investigating the reasons for such extensive transcripts being prepared it became apparent that a substantial saving could have been achieved if there had been discussion between counsel to try and limit the areas and agree the matters of fact which were not in dispute.

> We would stress it is the duty of counsel to try to avoid public expense being unnecessarily incurred, and that in order to fulfil the duty on an appeal against conviction it is often necessary to confer with counsel for the prosecution to confine the areas of dispute.

Once the Registrar has received the transcript, he supplies a copy to the appellant (and invites counsel to perfect his grounds of appeal in the light of the transcript – see **D23.5**). Provided the appellant is legally aided, this will be done free of charge. It is always open to an appellant to obtain a transcript (even a full transcript including all the evidence) without going through the Registrar (see r. 19(1)). The disadvantage in so doing is that the appellant will initially have to pay for it himself, and the cost will not be allowed on legal aid taxation unless the Registrar considers that what the appellant did was reasonable in all the circumstances (see the Legal Aid in Criminal and Care Proceedings (Costs) Regulations 1989, reg. 7(1)(b)). Thus, the virtually invariable practice is for a legally aided appellant to rely on the Registrar for a transcript. Moreover, even where an appellant is not legally aided, it is generally simpler for him to obtain a transcript via the Registrar, although in such cases the latter is entitled to charge for the service (Criminal Appeal Rules 1968, r. 19(2)).

BAIL PENDING APPEAL

Bail by the Court of Appeal

By the Criminal Appeal Act 1968, s. 19(1)(a), the Court of Appeal may grant an **D23.11** appellant bail pending determination of his appeal, subject to the restrictions placed on the granting of bail by the CJPO 1994, s. 25 (see **D5.10**). By s. 51, 'appellant' includes a person who has given notice of application for leave to appeal. Therefore, the court's power to grant bail arises from the moment notice of appeal has been lodged at the Crown Court in accordance with the Criminal Appeal Rules 1968, r. 2. The power may be exercised either on the application of the appellant or on a reference to the court by the Registrar (Criminal Appeal Act 1968, s. 19(2)). It may be – and, in practice, normally is – exercised by a single judge rather than a court (s. 31(2)(e)). The notice of appeal must be supported by a completed Form B (see para. 16.1 of the Guide). If he so indicates, the matter may conveniently be considered by the single judge at the same time as he considers whether leave to appeal should be granted. Alternatively, if the question needs to be considered urgently (e.g., because the appellant has been given a short custodial sentence by the Crown Court and will have served most or all of it by the time the papers would be ready for a judge to consider leave to appeal) then a separate application for bail may be made and the Registrar requested to lay the application before a single judge at the earliest opportunity. By the Criminal Appeal Rules 1968, r. 3, the reasons for bail should be set out on the prescribed form. In addition, the prosecution must be given at least 24 hours' written notice of the intention to make the application, unless the court or a single judge otherwise directs (r. 3(3)). Where the defence consider that bail should be applied for as a matter of urgency, the application should normally be made first to the Crown Court judge under the Supreme Court Act 1981, s. 81 (see below), and the Court of Appeal may decline to treat the application as urgent if that was not done (see para. 7 of *Practice Direction (Crown Court: Bail Pending Appeal)* [1983] 1 WLR 1292).

Applications for bail are normally considered by a single judge on the papers (see para. 16.1 of the Guide). If the application is refused, the appellant is entitled to have it considered by a court provided he gives notice to the Registrar within 14 days (see Criminal Appeal Act 1968, s. 18(3) and Criminal Appeal Rules 1968, r. 12(1) – the position is the same *mutatis mutandis*, as for renewing applications for leave to appeal). Counsel may appear to argue the application before the single judge if so instructed, but legal aid will not cover his attendance (the Guide, para. 16.1). Oral applications direct to a court are specifically sanctioned by the Criminal Appeal Rules 1968, r. 3(2), and may be appropriate, for example, if the hearing of an appeal has to be adjourned or if the court allows the appeal but orders a retrial.

The approach of the Court of Appeal to applications for bail pending appeal has been consistently cautious. The general principle was stated in *Watton* (1978) 68 Cr App R 293, namely, that bail should be granted only if the court (or single judge) can answer in the affirmative the question: Are there *exceptional circumstances* which would drive the court to the conclusion that justice can only be done by the granting of bail? The fact that the single judge gives the appellant leave to appeal against conviction does not of itself lead to the conclusion that bail should also be granted (*Watton*). If, however, the grounds of appeal are prima facie very strong, that is an argument for the court, in its discretion, allowing bail. Similarly, the time that will elapse before the appeal can be determined coupled with the length of whatever custodial sentence was imposed on the appellant are relevant factors. However, there is no general rule that an appellant given a short custodial sentence should be bailed pending appeal. The better course may be for the judge to contact the listing coordinator for an assessment of when the appeal is likely to be heard and whether it can be expedited (see *Practice Direction (Crown Court: Bail Pending Appeal)* [1983] 1 WLR 1292, para. 6). One reason for the court's reluctance to bail appellants is that, should the appeal ultimately fail, the appellant is likely to be returned to prison to serve the remainder of his sentence, and even a long delay between his release on bail and the determination of the appeal cannot be relied on as a reason for not adopting that course (per Roskill LJ in *Kalia* (1974) 60 Cr App R 200 at p. 209). By contrast, if the appellant remains in custody, the fact that he has had that experience may enable the court – as an act of mercy – to reduce his sentence to allow for his immediate release, even though the appeal would otherwise have failed completely (per Lawton LJ in *Neal* (1986) *The Times*, 29 January 1986).

Rules 4 and 6 of the Criminal Appeal Rules 1968 contain detailed provisions concerning bail subject to sureties, the taking of those sureties and the court's power to estreat their recognisances should the appellant abscond. Paragraphs (b) and (c) of s. 19(1) of the Criminal Appeal Act 1968 additionally give the court power to revoke or vary the terms of bail which had earlier been granted to the appellant either by the Court of Appeal itself or by the Crown Court in exercise of the power given it by the Supreme Court Act 1981, s. 81(1)(f). Obviously any revocation or adverse variation in the terms of bail would be the result of a reference by the registrar rather than an appellant's application.

In certain circumstances, the Registrar has power to vary the conditions of bail granted to an appellant by the Court of Appeal or the Crown Court (see **D23.26** for details).

Criminal Appeal Act 1968, s. 19

    (1)   The Court of Appeal may, subject to section 25 of the CJPO 1994, if they think fit,—
        (a)   grant an appellant bail pending the determination of his appeal; or
        (b)   revoke bail granted to an appellant by the Crown Court under paragraph (f) of section 81(1) of the Supreme Court Act 1981 or paragraph (a) above; or
        (c)   vary the conditions of bail granted to an appellant in the exercise of the power conferred by either of those paragraphs.
    (2)   The powers conferred by subsection (1) above may be exercised—
        (a)   on the application of an appellant; or
        (b)   if it appears to the registrar of criminal appeals of the Court of Appeal . . . that any of them ought to be exercised, on a reference to the court by him.

Bail by the Crown Court

By the Supreme Court Act 1981, s. 81(1)(f), the Crown Court may grant bail to any **D23.12** person 'to whom [it] has granted a certificate under section 1(2) or 11(1A) of the Criminal Appeal Act 1968 or under subsection (1B) below'. Thus, whenever a Crown Court judge grants a certificate that a case is fit for appeal – whether against conviction or sentence – he may also bail the accused pending determination of the appeal. Any time during which he is on bail does not count towards service of his sentence.

Subsections (1C) to (1G) of s. 81 contain supplementary provisions relating to the exercise of the power given by s. 81(1)(f). Where the appeal is under s. 1 or s. 9 of the Criminal Appeal Act 1968 (i.e. is against conviction on indictment or against sentence passed following conviction on indictment), the power is to be exercised by the judge who tried the case; where the appeal is under s. 10 (i.e. is against sentence passed by the Crown Court otherwise than following conviction on indictment), it is to be exercised by the judge who passed the sentence (Supreme Court Act 1981, s. 81(1C)). The time limit for exercise of the power is 28 days from the date of conviction or sentence depending on which the appeal is against (s. 81(1D)). Moreover, an application to the Court of Appeal itself for bail rules out an application to the Crown Court judge (s. 81(1E)). It must be made a condition of bail granted by the Crown Court that (a) a notice of appeal, unless already lodged, shall be lodged within the normal period (see **D23.2** for time for giving notice of appeal), and (b) that, within 14 days of the end of that period, there shall be lodged with the Crown Court a certificate from the Registrar stating that notice has been duly given (s. 81(1F)). The person bailed is directed to appear at such time and place as the Court of Appeal may require (or, if no notice of appeal is given, at such time and place as the Crown Court may require) (s. 81(1G)). The Court of Appeal may revoke or vary the terms of bail granted by a Crown Court judge under s. 81(1)(f) (Criminal Appeal Act 1968, s. 19(1)(b) and (c)).

Practice Direction (Crown Court: Bail Pending Appeal) [1983] 1 WLR 1292 gives guidance both on the granting of certificates that a case is fit for appeal and on the consequent granting of bail. The direction states that the judge 'may well think it right' to hear the application for a certificate in chambers with a shorthand writer present, and also to invite defence counsel to submit in advance of the hearing a draft of the grounds of appeal which he will ask the judge to certify (para. 3). A copy thereof should also preferably be sent to the prosecution (ibid.). The first question for the judge is then whether there are grounds for a certificate (para. 4). The length of the period which might elapse before the hearing of any appeal is not relevant to the answering of that question (para. 5), but – assuming the judge does decide to grant a certificate – it is one factor in the decision whether also to grant bail (para. 6). However, the judge 'may find it advisable' to obtain from the listing officer of the Court of Appeal an accurate and up-to-date assessment of the likely waiting time (para. 6). This will no doubt include advice on whether the hearing of the appeal can be expedited. If the defence fail to apply to the Crown Court judge for a certificate and bail pending appeal, the Court of Appeal may decline to treat as urgent any application to itself for bail (para. 7). The Court of Appeal has warned against the granting of such certificates, save in cases where there is a 'particular and cogent' ground of appeal (see **D22.38**).

Suspension of Other Sentences Pending Appeal

D23.13 In addition to its power to grant bail pending appeal, the Court of Appeal has power to suspend an appellant's disqualification from driving (see Road Traffic Offenders Act 1988, s. 40(2)). Also, by the Criminal Appeal Act 1968, s. 30(1), an order for the restitution of property to a person made by the Crown Court under the Theft Act 1968, s. 28, shall unless the Court of Appeal directs to the contrary in a case in which, in its opinion, title to the property is not in dispute – be suspended until there is no further possibility of an appeal in consequence of which the order could be varied or set aside. In determining whether there is any possibility of an appeal, the power of a court to give leave to appeal out of time is to be disregarded. Thus, a restitution order will take effect 28 days from sentence if no notice of application for leave to appeal is given but, if notice is given, it will be suspended until determination of the appeal unless the Court of Appeal gives a direction to the contrary because title to the property does not appear to be disputed. By the Criminal Appeal Act 1968, s. 30(2), the Court of Appeal may annul or vary the order for restitution even though the conviction is not quashed (s. 30(2)). Compensation orders are treated for the purposes of the Criminal Appeal Act 1968, s. 30, in the same way as restitution orders (PCCA 1973, s. 36(1)). The enforcement of any fine the appellant was ordered to pay is suspended upon notice of appeal or application for leave to appeal being given.

PRESENCE OF THE APPELLANT AT THE APPEAL

Criminal Appeal Act 1968, s. 22

D23.14   (1)   Except as provided by this section, an appellant shall be entitled to be present, if he wishes it, on the hearing of his appeal, although he may be in custody.

      (2)   A person in custody shall not be entitled to be present—
        (a)   where his appeal is on some ground involving a question of law alone; or
        (b)   on an application by him for leave to appeal; or
        (c)   on any proceedings preliminary or incidental to an appeal; or
        [(d)   relates to appeal against findings of not guilty by reason of insanity and findings that the appellant was under a disability],
unless the Court of Appeal give him leave to be present.

      (3)   The power of the Court of Appeal to pass sentence on a person may be exercised although he is for any reason not present.

The upshot of s. 22 is that an appellant who is not in custody has a right to be present at the hearing of his appeal. The Registrar will give him as long notice as possible of the date of hearing. Although not expressly stated, an appellant at liberty must also be entitled to be present at any incidental applications (e.g., for leave to appeal or to call witnesses at the appeal), provided that the application is determined in open court. However, the effect of the Criminal Appeal Rules 1968, r. 11, is that a single judge may – and normally does – determine incidental applications otherwise than in open court and without the attendance of counsel or solicitor. In such cases, since there is effectively no hearing but only a private reading of the papers, the appellant has no right to be present but is simply notified of the decision through the Registrar.

Appellants who are in custody have a right to be present at the actual hearing of the appeal if it is based on fact or mixed law and fact. They have no right to be present at applications for leave to appeal or other incidental applications (even if heard by a court in open court). Nor have they a right to be present at the appeal itself if it is on a ground of pure law. However, in all cases where an appellant or applicant for leave has no right to be present, he may be granted leave to attend by the court. The power to grant leave may be and normally is exercised by a single judge (see Criminal Appeal Act 1968, s. 31). The appellant should indicate on form IA(1) (notice of appeal or application for leave to appeal) that he is also applying for leave to be present, and his reasons should be set out on the prescribed form (form IA(3)) (see Criminal Appeal Rules 1968, r. 3). Where an application for leave to appeal is to be heard by a court and it is anticipated that their lordships may wish to proceed immediately to determine the appeal should they grant leave to bring it, then the Registrar may arrange for the applicant to be brought into the court precincts at the time of the application so that he may forthwith be brought before the court in the event of it succeeding (para. 10.4 of the Guide).

An appellant who is neither in custody nor has been bailed to attend the hearing is under no obligation to be present at his appeal. Assuming he has been given notice of the hearing date, the court will proceed to determine the matter in his absence (*Field* (13 October 1975 unreported)). Where an appellant has escaped from custody during the period between commencement of the appeal and the date fixed for hearing the court will normally either adjourn or summarily dismiss the appeal (*Flower* [1966] 1 QB 146). It may, exceptionally, agree to hear the appeal on its merits (see *Panayi (No. 2)* [1989] 1 WLR 187, where the Court of Appeal adopted this course and went on to quash the conviction). A similar approach may be adopted if an appellant who was bailed to attend the hearing fails to answer to bail (*Carter* (1994) 98 Cr App R 106).

HEARING OF AN APPEAL

Practice in Usual Case

By the Criminal Appeal Act 1968, s. 21(1), the Registrar must take all necessary steps **D23.15** for obtaining a hearing of any appeal or application of which notice is given to him (unless he refers it to a court for summary dismissal under s. 20). He must also obtain and lay before the court all documents, exhibits and other things which appear necessary for the proper determination of the appeal or application (ibid.). By the Criminal Appeal Rules 1968, r. 7(1), the Crown Court must either itself retain for 35 days any exhibit produced at the trial which might be required for purposes of an appeal, or it may give the exhibit into the custody of the person who produced it or any other person for him to retain. If notice of appeal or application for leave to appeal is given, the Registrar informs the Crown Court and gives any necessary directions concerning the future custody of the exhibit (r. 7(2)). Additionally, the Registrar must, on request, supply the parties with copies of documents or other things required for the appeal or make arrangements for them to inspect them (r. 8(1) and (2)). Rule 8 does not apply to transcript of the Crown Court proceedings – for the Registrar's powers and responsibilities in that regard, see **D23.10** and the Criminal Appeal Rules 1968, r. 19.

By the Criminal Appeal Rules 1968, r. 22(2), the Registrar must give as long notice as reasonably possible of the date on which the court will hear any appeal or application.

The notice must be served on (a) the appellant himself, (b) any person having custody of him, and (c) any other interested party (ibid.). 'Any other interested party' will obviously include the prosecution. The duty to give notice of hearing dates does not apply to applications before a single judge (r. 22(3)). However, para. 6(2) of the Guide indicates that the Registrar will in practice go beyond what is required by the rules and inform the appellant's solicitors once he has referred an application for leave to appeal to a single judge. Nor does the rule itself require the Registrar to give notice to the appellant's legal representatives, although he will in practice do so (see para. 10.1 of the Guide). Legal aid for the hearing is normally granted either by the Registrar or by the single judge at the same time as he gives leave to appeal (see **D23.21**). Unless there is a particular need for the services of a solicitor, legal aid will be limited to counsel. The Registrar will forward the necessary papers to counsel and in due course notify counsel's clerk of the hearing date. It is not in general the prosecution's practice to be represented at an appeal against sentence (but see *Dempster* (1987) 85 Cr App R 176 in which Lord Lane CJ said, *obiter*, that the increasing complexity of sentencing law and procedure made it desirable for the prosecution to be in attendance more frequently than heretofore). At an appeal against conviction, the prosecution virtually invariably choose to be represented. The Registrar's staff prepare a summary of each case for the benefit of the judges who will hear it. Such summaries are now disclosed to all counsel in the case unless there is a specific direction to the contrary (*Practice Direction (Criminal Appeals: Summaries)* [1992] 1 WLR 938).

Practice Direction (Criminal Appeals: Skeleton arguments) [1999] 1 WLR 146 lays down the requirements for skeleton arguments in appeals against conviction. The advocate for the appellant must lodge a skeleton argument with the Registrar, and serve it on the prosecuting authority, within 14 days of receipt by the advocate of leave to appeal against conviction (unless a longer period is directed). The prosecutor should lodge a skeleton argument within 14 days of receipt of the appellant's skeleton (unless directed otherwise).

In addressing the court (whether at an appeal against conviction or sentence) counsel should assume that it is familiar with the facts and the grounds as settled (see para. 10.7 of the Guide). In appropriate conviction appeals, counsel should submit at the hearing four copies of a typed note tabulating the propositions on which it is sought to rely (ibid.). In *Miller* (1992) 95 Cr App R 421, the Court of Appeal said that it must be a skeleton argument 'not a fully fleshed body'; and it was stressed that it must be placed before them in good time, not on the morning of the hearing or the previous night. Counsel for the appellant presents his case first and counsel for the prosecution is called upon to reply if required. Save in a small minority of cases (see **D23.16** to **D23.20**), no evidence is received by the court. Thus, the hearing consists entirely of argument based on the grounds of appeal, transcript of the summing-up (plus any transcript of the evidence) and any documentary or other exhibits which are before the court. For the right of the appellant to be present at the hearing, see **D23.14**. For the practice of the court giving a single judgment, and the rule that – in the event of disagreement – decisions may be by a majority, see **D22.6**.

Practice where Evidence is Received by the Court of Appeal

D23.16 The Criminal Appeal Act 1968, s. 23(1), gives the Court of Appeal a discretionary power to receive evidence. Section 23(2) outlines the factors which the court should take into account in deciding whether to receive evidence.

Criminal Appeal Act 1968, s. 23

(1) For purposes of this part of this Act [appeals against conviction and/or sentence and references to the Court of Appeal by the Home Secretary] the Court of Appeal may, if they think it necessary or expedient in the interests of justice—

    (a)   order the production of any document, exhibit or other thing connected with the proceedings, the production of which appears to them necessary for the determination of the case;

    (b)   order any witness who would have been a compellable witness in the proceedings from which the appeal lies to attend for examination and be examined before the court, whether or not he was called in those proceedings; and

    (c)   receive any evidence which was not adduced in the proceedings from which the appeal lies.

    (2)   The Court of Appeal shall, in considering whether to receive any evidence, have regard in particular to—

    (a)   whether the evidence appears to the Court to be capable of belief;

    (b)   whether it appears to the Court that the evidence may afford any ground for allowing the appeal;

    (c)   whether the evidence would have been admissible in the proceedings from which the appeal lies on an issue which is the subject of the appeal; and

    (d)   whether there is a reasonable explanation for the failure to adduce the evidence in those proceedings.

    (3)   Subsection (1)(c) above [power to receive evidence of any witness if tendered] applies to any evidence of a witness (including the appellant) who is competent but not compellable, and applies also to the appellant's husband or wife where the appellant makes an application for that purpose and the evidence of the husband or wife could not have been given in the proceedings from which the appeal lies except on such an application.

    [(4)   Deals with the possibility of having a witness examined before a judge or officer of the court and a deposition taken from him – see **D23.18**.]

Power to Receive Evidence

The discretionary power given to the Court of Appeal by s. 23(1) is unfettered. They **D23.17** may exercise it if it is necessary or expedient in the interests of justice. The factors listed in s. 23(2) are merely factors which the court is to take particularly into account in exercising its discretion; they are not conditions in the sense that each of them must be satisfied before evidence can be heard. Particular care needs to be exercised in this regard when considering the cases decided under the version of s. 23(2) which preceded the coming into force of the Criminal Appeal Act 1995, s. 4(1). In that previous form, s. 23(2) laid down a set of conditions which had to be satisfied in order to trigger off an *obligation* on the part of the Court of Appeal to receive fresh evidence. The cases dealt with in the discussion which follows ought to be considered with this *caveat* in mind.

The factors outlined in s. 23(2) are largely self-explanatory. As to s. 23(2)(a), their lordships have to consider whether the evidence 'appears to the Court to be capable of belief'. They are, of course, making their decision before actually hearing the evidence, and that fact gives some point to the phrase 'appears to the Court to be', which would otherwise be superfluous. At this preliminary stage, they cannot tell whether the evidence *is* capable of belief, merely whether it 'appears to be' such. The previous wording of s. 23(2) was 'likely to be credible' and in *Parks* [1961] 1 WLR 1484 it was said that, in deciding whether evidence met this description, the Court of Appeal should consider the testimony it was anticipated that the witness would give in the context of the case as a whole. It is submitted that this interpretation holds for the slightly different wording now in the statute; relevant factors include the intrinsic credibility of any proof of evidence supplied to the court, and the extent to which it fits with at least some of the evidence adduced at trial.

As to s. 23(2)(c), and the question of whether the proposed evidence would have been admissible at trial, in *Williams* [1995] 1 Cr App R 74, the fresh evidence was the fact that the police officers who had given evidence against the appellant at trial had later been found to have fabricated confessions attributed to suspects in other cases. The Court of Appeal said that it would not shut its eyes to the fact that those officers had been discredited. The criteria for admissibility remained the same.

Section 23(2)(d) raises the issue of 'a reasonable explanation for the failure to adduce the evidence' in the Crown Court. There were a number of cases decided by the Court of Appeal on the import of this phrase in the previous version of s. 23(2). Although the reasoning in some of them may be of assistance in interpreting the statute in its current form, it should be borne in mind that the purpose and context of the new provision is different, in that it deals with one of a series of factors to be considered in exercising a discretion rather than a set of conditions which trigger off a duty. The court has warned against the mischief that would result if it regularly received evidence itself when there was no adequate explanation for failure to adduce it at trial or, indeed, when it was adduced at trial but its significance was apparently not appreciated by the tribunal or parties. Thus, Edmund Davies LJ in *Stafford* [1968] 3 All ER 752 said: '. . . public mischief would ensue and legal process could become indefinitely prolonged were it the case that evidence produced at any time will generally be admitted by this court when verdicts are being reviewed'.

In *Lattimore* (1975) 62 Cr App R 53, the appellants were convicted of murder and arson, the prosecution case being that they had strangled the victim (one C) and then, to cover their tracks, set fire to his home with his body inside it. The case turned largely on confession evidence, which was challenged at trial bcause of the youth of the defendants, their lack of intelligence and the pressure that was brought to bear on them before they admitted the offences. On appeal, the defence successfully applied to adduce medical and scientific evidence to the effect that several hours elapsed between C's death and the firing of his house. That was directly contrary to the terms of the appellants' confessions, which indicated that they had committed the arson almost immediately after committing the murder. The genuineness of the confessions was thus thrown into doubt, and the Court of Appeal quashed the convictions. The court received the above evidence even though (a) some of the witnesses had in fact testified at the trial and (b) all of the evidence could have been adduced before the jury had the defence then realised its importance. Notwithstanding Edmund Davies LJ's strictures (see above), the court adopted the course it did because that was the only way of doing justice in the particular and unusual circumstances of the case. Similarly, in *Lee* [1984] 1 WLR 578 evidence was received under s. 23(1) in a case where L had pleaded guilty at the Crown Court and then appealed because, *inter alia*, subsequent investigative journalism had established that he had an alibi for at least some of the offences he had admitted. Having given leave to appeal against conviction notwithstanding the guilty plea, the Court of Appeal went on to consider whether it should hear evidence. Ackner LJ said (at p. 584E–G emphasis added):

> . . . we have read the *Sunday Times* articles [about the alibi and the circumstances in which L confessed to the offences charged]. . . . We can well appreciate the public concern that those articles must have occasioned: not only on the ground that in respect of some of the arsons it was alleged they could not have been committed by the applicant, but much more serious and sinister, the allegations made as to how his confessions had been obtained. . . .
>
> We are satisfied that *in the wholly unusual circumstances of these applications*, it is both necessary and expedient in the interests of justice that we should, at this stage, hear relevant and admissible evidence called by both the applicant and the Crown as to whether the convictions . . . were either unsafe or unsatisfactory.

In *Ahluwalia* [1992] 4 All ER 889, the Court of Appeal made some important general observations on fresh evidence adduced to promote a line of defence not raised at trial. A killed her husband 'after enduring many years of violence and humiliation' from him, by throwing petrol into his bedroom and setting it alight. She was tried for murder. Her case was that she did not intend to kill him or cause him really serious harm. Provocation was her secondary line of defence. The jury rejected both lines of defence and convicted of murder. She appealed on three grounds. The first two related to the trial judge's directions on provocation and were dismissed. The third ground was that she relied on evidence of diminished responsibility, which had not been raised as a defence at trial. In delivering the judgment of the Court of Appeal, Lord Taylor CJ said:

> There has been put before this court a significant number of reports of a psychiatric and similar nature, most of them obtained only recently. These express the opinion that at the time of the killing, the appellant's mental responsibility for her actions was diminished within the meaning of the Homicide Act 1957.

> Ordinarily, of course, any available defences should be advanced at trial. Accordingly, if medical evidence is available to support a plea of diminished responsibility, it should be adduced at the trial. It cannot be too strongly emphasised that this court would require much persuasion to allow such a defence to be raised for the first time here if the option had been exercised at the trial not to pursue it. Otherwise, as must be clear, defendants might be encouraged to run one defence at trial in the belief that if it fails, this court would allow a different defence to be raised and give the defendant, in effect, two opportunities to run different defences. Nothing could be further from the truth.

> Likewise, if there is no evidence to support diminished responsibility at the time of the trial, this court would view wholly retrospective medical evidence obtained long after the trial with considerable scepticism.

> That said, the present case is most unusual. We have been shown a report which was available before the trial from a recognised medical practitioner for the purposes of the Mental Health Act 1983. That doctor expressed the opinion that the appellant was suffering from endogenous depression at the material time, a condition which, in the opinion of some experts, would be termed 'a major depressive disorder'. It is unclear how this potentially important material came to be overlooked or was not further pursued at the time of the trial. We have been told, we assume correctly, that the appellant herself was not consulted about this report or about the possibility of investigating it further. Although there was opinion available to the Crown to challenge diminished responsibility, and although the appellant herself has not been consistent in her accounts to different consultants, we have concluded that it would be expedient in the interests of justice to admit the fresh evidence under s. 23(1) of the Criminal Appeal Act 1968.

> We have considered that fresh evidence. We have also taken into account the evidence given at trial as to the appellant's strange behaviour after lighting the fire as witnessed by neighbours. We appreciate that the Crown has not had a proper opportunity to consider the fresh evidence and obtain its own advice and evidence on this issue. We make no comment about the cogency of the fresh evidence. Nevertheless, we have been driven to the conclusion that without, it would seem, any fault on the part of the appellant there may well have been an arguable defence which, for reasons unexplained, was not put forward at the trial. In these circumstances, we consider that the verdict must be regarded as unsafe and unsatisfactory. We emphasise that the circumstances we have described and which have led us to this conclusion are wholly exceptional. We consider the proper course here is for us to order a retrial.

See also *Jones* [1997] 1 Cr App R 86, *Hobson* [1998] 1 Cr App R 31, *Borthwick* [1998] Crim LR 274, and *Loughran* [1999] Crim LR 404.

Whether there is a reasonable explanation for failure to call evidence at the Crown Court will always be looked at critically in view of Edmund Davies LJ's comments in *Stafford* about the public mischief that would ensue from the Court of Appeal too readily reopening factual and evidential questions that should have been determined once and for all by the jury. An accused is expected to cooperate with his legal advisers in preparing his defence. Therefore, the fact that defence solicitors did not know the names and addresses of potential alibi witnesses until after trial is not a satisfactory explanation for failure to call them if their client could reasonably have supplied them with information enabling them to trace the witnesses in good time (*Beresford* (1971) 56 Cr App R 143). By contrast, if a witness did not come forward until after trial and could not have been discovered earlier by making reasonable enquiries, there is clearly a good explanation for failure to call him. Similarly, if the matter to which the evidence relates arose after conviction, there is *ex hypothesi* justification for not adducing it at trial (see *Ditch* (1969) 53 Cr App R 627 – Court of Appeal received evidence that D's convicted co-defendant had, after trial, made a confession in which he exculpated D). In *Conway* (1979) 70 Cr App R 4 it was further indicated that, in a case where a prosecution witness has made a statement after trial which is allegedly inconsistent with his testimony at trial, the correct procedure is to call the witness before the Court of Appeal so that the statement can be put to him. If he denies making the statement, it can then be proved under the Criminal Procedure Act 1865, s. 4. In *Davies* [1995] Crim LR 831, D, who was legally aided on a charge of dangerous driving, sought to call an expert witness to challenge the prosecution evidence as to speed. The expert had provided a report after approval by the Legal Aid Board, but declined to attend court unless his quoted fee was paid in full. The Crown Court judge refused to allow the claimed fee in advance of the evidence being given. D was convicted and appealed. The Court of Appeal gave leave for the expert to be called, stating that there was a reasonable explanation for the failure to adduce the evidence in the court below. In *Trevor* [1998] Crim LR 652 it was said that the court should be informed in advance of facts relevant to the explanation for the failure to adduce evidence at trial. Where the explanation was lengthy or complicated, an affidavit or signed statement from the appellant or his solicitor should be supplied.

Procedure for Calling Evidence

D23.18 An appellant who wishes the Court of Appeal to exercise its power to receive evidence should give notice to that effect, using the prescribed form (form 6) (Criminal Appeal Rules 1968, r. 3(1)). If the appellant additionally wishes the witness to be ordered to attend court for examination, he should give notice of that also (ibid.). An order for a witness to attend may be made only if the witness would have been a compellable witness before the Crown Court (see Criminal Appeal Act 1968, s. 23(1)(b)). It may be made by a single judge (Criminal Appeal Act 1968, s. 31(2)). Although a single judge or the Registrar can order a witness to attend the precincts of the court for the purpose of being examined, the decision to receive his evidence is always one for a court, not a single judge. Indeed, even an order under s. 23(4) that the witness be examined by an officer of the court etc. prior to determination of the appeal is one that only a court can make.

Further, by s. 23(4), the court (but not a single judge) may – if they think it necessary or expedient in the interests of justice – order that the examination of any compellable witness be conducted before any judge, officer of the court or other person appointed by the court for the purpose. The examination of such a witness must be conducted by the taking of a deposition in public unless the court otherwise directs (Criminal Appeal Rules 1968, r. 9(2)). A deposition so taken may be admitted as evidence before the Court of Appeal, thus avoiding the necessity for oral evidence (Criminal Appeal Act 1968, s. 23(4)). It should be noted that, although the power to order a witness to attend and to order that his evidence be taken in deposition form before an examiner is exercisable only in respect of compellable witnesses, the discretion and – in certain circumstances – duty to receive evidence tendered by the appellant applies not only to compellable witnesses but also to those who are merely competent (see s. 23(1)(c) and (3), which refers specifically to the tendering of evidence from the appellant himself or his spouse). Where a witness is not formally examined prior to determination of the appeal in the manner described above (either because he was not compellable or because the court simply did not choose to make an order for examination) it is suggested by the Guide that the appellant should serve on the Registrar either an affidavit sworn by the witness or a statement in the form prescribed by the CJA 1967, s. 9 (see para. 14.4). Thus, a statement from the proposed witness (whether taken as a deposition by an examiner or served by the appellant) should always be available to the court from an early stage, and will no doubt assist it at the hearing in deciding whether to receive oral evidence from the witness. Moreover, in some cases, the court may feel able to act on the written statement and there will thus be no need for oral evidence. The rules do not specify the precise manner in which a witness whose oral evidence is received by the court should be taken. It is submitted that, prima facie, the witness should be examined by the party tendering his evidence, cross-examined by the opposite party and then, if need be, questioned directly by the court. Alternatively, the court itself may conduct the initial questioning, leaving the parties to ask such supplementary questions as they see fit. Where the appellant is allowed to tender evidence, the prosecution may be allowed to tender its own evidence in rebuttal (see *Lee* [1984] 1 WLR 578 for a case where the court apparently contemplated hearing virtually the whole of the prosecution and defence cases in order to determine an appeal against conviction where the appellant had pleaded guilty at the Crown Court).

In *Callaghan* [1988] 1 WLR 1, the question arose whether the Court of Appeal, under the terms of s. 23, can inspect material of its own motion. Counsel for the appellants (the 'Birmingham Six') sought to restrict the court's consideration to documents which were put before it by the appellants or the respondents. Their lordships refused to restrict their reading in this way. In principle, they held that they had the right to read any material. If it then proved to be irrelevant or in some other way objectionable, the court would dismiss it from its mind. It therefore appears that the court is prepared to adopt an investigative role in 'fresh evidence' appeals, in sharp contrast to the usual features of the adversarial system of justice.

Approach of the Court of Appeal to 'Evidence' Appeals

Where the Court of Appeal receives evidence under the Criminal Appeal Act 1968, s. 23, **D23.19** the ultimate question for it is whether, in the light of that evidence and all the other circumstances of the case, the conviction is unsafe (*Stafford* v *DPP* [1974] AC 878). In other words, they apply the 'lurking doubt' test. If the individual members of the court are not left with a lurking doubt as to whether an injustice may have been done, they are entitled to dismiss the appeal, even though it is possible that the evidence would have made a difference to the jury's verdict had they heard it. However, gauging the likely effect of the evidence on the jury may often provide the best means of deciding if the conviction is safe (ibid.). That the above is the correct approach to the determination of 'fresh evidence' appeals was confirmed by Ackner LJ in *Lee* [1984] 1 WLR 578. Responding to criticisms (e.g., by Lord Devlin) that the court was usurping the role of the jury, his lordship said (at p. 585C–D):

> . . . in hearing and making our decision in due course on the evidence called before us – which evidence, because of the plea of guilty, has not hitherto been heard by a court – we are not seeking to usurp the functions of a jury; we are carrying out our statutory obligations of either allowing the appeal . . . because we think that the conviction was either unsafe or unsatisfactory or, if we do not so think, of dismissing it.

Nonetheless, the effect of the court carrying out its statutory duty in the peculiar circumstances of appeals where it hears evidence not before the jury is that it may dismiss an appeal because in *its* view the evidence is not worthy of belief or not sufficiently cogent to cast doubt on the remainder of the evidence pointing to guilt, even though it concedes that a reasonable jury, had it heard the evidence, might have taken the opposite view. The anomaly was made starkly apparent in *Lee* because in that case there had not even been a trial. Therefore, if the Court of Appeal had upheld the conviction, it would have been because their lordships thought the evidence showed the appellant guilty, notwithstanding that no jury had ever heard a word of it.

The Court of Appeal had power to order a retrial whenever it allowed an appeal on the basis of evidence heard, or available to be heard, under s. 23. For the approach of the court to possible exercise of the power, see **D22.32** and **D22.36**.

Evidence Heard Informally

D23.20 Apart from exercising its powers under the Criminal Appeal Act 1968, s. 23, the Court of Appeal also receives evidence semi-informally in two other types of case. They are:

(a)   cases where the defence allege an irregularity in the course of the trial, and the court receives accounts as to what occurred from the judge, counsel, the clerk or anybody else who can assist, and

(b)   sentencing cases where the court may receive reports as to how the offender has progressed since he was sentenced.

LEGAL AID AND COSTS OF APPEAL

Legal Aid

D23.21 By the Legal Aid Act 1988, s. 20(2), the Court of Appeal may grant legal aid to any person appealing to it under part I of the Criminal Appeal Act 1968. The subsection itself expressly allows for the power to be exercised even before notice of appeal or notice of application for leave to appeal has been given, but, perhaps strangely, reg. 22(5)(a) of the Legal Aid in Criminal and Care Proceedings (General) Regulations 1989 (SI 1989 No. 344) makes the giving of appeal notice a precondition of a grant of aid. However, a grant once made may be backdated to cover work done at an earlier stage (*Gibson* [1983] 1 WLR 1038 at p. 1043D–F). It would therefore seem that counsel who advises on an appeal and drafts grounds of appeal may be reimbursed through a retrospective grant of aid. In practice, this will only rarely be necessary since, if an accused is legally aided for trial on indictment, that aid will cover both advice on the merits of an appeal and the drafting of grounds of appeal if so advised (Legal Aid Act 1988, s. 2(4)(c), and see **D23.2**). Where an application for leave to appeal is rejected by the single judge, the Crown Court legal aid extends to advising on the merits of renewing the application before a court (*Gibson* [1983] 1 WLR 1038), but it does not extend to representation at the actual hearing of the application, even if counsel advised that it be renewed (*Kearney* [1983] 1 WLR 1046). The court itself could grant aid at that stage but is unlikely to do so.

The power to grant legal aid may be exercised by a single judge (Legal Aid in Criminal and Care Proceedings (General) Regulations 1989, reg. 22(7)). It may also be exercised by the Registrar (ibid.). Unlike the single judge, however, the Registrar may not refuse an application. If not minded to grant it, he must refer it to a court or a single judge (reg. 22(4)). If a single judge refuses an application, the appellant may renew it before a court (reg. 22(3)). An application may be made orally (whether to a court, a judge or the Registrar), or it may be made in writing in such form as the Registrar directs (reg. 22(1)(a) and (b)). Normally, the appellant indicates on his notice of appeal or application for leave to appeal that he is also applying for legal aid. When making an order, the court or Registrar may specify the stage of the proceedings at which the aid shall commence (reg. 22(6)), which may be before the date of the order itself (see *Gibson* above). No order may be made until a statement of means from the applicant has been considered (reg. 22(5)(b)). The provisions about ordering the legally aided person to make contributions to his aid and revoking his aid if he fails to comply with the contribution order apply as much to aid granted by the Court of Appeal as they do to aid granted by magistrates' courts or the Crown Court (see part III of the 1989 Regulations). However, the majority of appellants to the Court of Appeal are in custody as a result of the Crown Court sentence, and will consequently not be required to make any contribution. Where the single judge grants leave to appeal he will almost automatically grant legal aid for the entire appeal proceedings at the same time (see para. 7.1 of the Guide).

Assuming legal aid is granted for an appeal, it may be limited to representation by counsel only (reg. 44(4)). This limitation is usually imposed, since nearly all appeals turn upon legal argument on the papers before the court and the services of a solicitor are therefore unnecessary (see **D23.15**). However, in exceptional cases (such as those turning upon fresh evidence to be adduced before the court), aid will be extended to cover solicitor and counsel. Indeed, the Guide suggests that, whenever work of an exceptionally expensive nature is expected, early application should be made to the Registrar for further legal aid (see paras 11.1 and 14.1). In the normal case where aid is for counsel only, counsel is assigned by the court (or its proper officer) (reg. 46(1)). In selecting counsel, account should be taken of the wishes of the appellant, the identity of counsel who appeared below and the nature of the appeal (reg. 46(2)). The Registrar provides counsel with a brief and papers but does not otherwise act as his solicitor (para. 7.1 of the Guide).

Costs out of Central Funds

By the Prosecution of Offences Act 1985, s. 16(4), the Court of Appeal may make a **D23.22** defendant's costs order in favour of a successful appellant when it:

   (a)   allows an appeal against conviction, or
   (b)   quashes the appellant's conviction but substitutes a verdict of guilty of another offence, or
   (c)   allows an appeal against sentence.

The order may be extended to cover the costs of the proceedings in the magistrates' court and Crown Court (see s. 16(6), which states that a defendant's costs order should prima facie be sufficient to compensate him for expenses properly incurred in 'the proceedings', combined with s. 21 which defines 'proceedings' so as to include 'proceedings in any court below'). Where the prosecution is not conducted by the CPS or other public authority, the respondent's costs may be awarded out of central funds whatever the outcome of the appeal (s. 17).

Costs against an Unsuccessful Appellant

Upon dismissing an appeal or application for leave to appeal, the Court of Appeal may **D23.23** 'make such order as to the costs to be paid by the accused, to such person as may be named in the order, as it considers just and reasonable' (Prosecution of Offences Act 1985, s. 18(2)). The costs thus ordered may include the reasonable cost of any transcript of the Crown Court proceedings (s. 18(6)). It is no doubt to allow for the possibility of an unsuccessful appellant paying for transcript that s. 18(2) gives the court a discretion to order costs in favour of *any* person, not just in favour of the prosecutor or respondent, since the cost of obtaining transcript will initially have been met by the Registrar.

The Court of Appeal's powers in respect of costs may be exercised by a single judge (Criminal Appeal Act 1968, s. 31(1)(c)). In particular, where a single judge rejects an application for leave to appeal, he may also order the applicant to pay costs.

ABANDONING AN APPEAL

Rule 10 of the Criminal Appeal Rules 1968 deals with abandonment of appeals. It **D23.24** provides that an appeal or application for leave to appeal may be abandoned before the hearing by serving on the Registrar notice in the prescribed form (form IA(4)), signed by or on behalf of the appellant or applicant (r. 10(1) and (2)). The appeal or, as the case may be, application for leave to appeal is then treated as having been dismissed or refused by the court (r. 10(4)). Having regard to the terms of r. 10(4) and the Criminal Appeal Act 1968, s. 29(1) and (2) (see **D22.10**), it would seem that a notice of abandonment does not in itself prevent the court or single judge making an order for loss of time. Similarly, there can be an order under the Prosecution of Offences Act 1985, s. 18(2), requiring the appellant to pay any prosecution costs incurred prior to abandonment. However, depending on the stage at which it was given, notice of abandonment will obviously be a powerful factor in persuading a court or single judge not to make any ancillary orders adverse to the appellant. Where the appellant does not give written notice under r. 10, he may nonetheless abandon the appeal orally when it is called on. After the hearing has commenced, however, leave will be required to abandon (*De Courcy* [1964] 1 WLR 1245 and see also *Spicer* (1987) 87 Cr App R 297).

An appellant who has given notice of abandonment may apply to withdraw it and reinstate the appeal (*Medway* [1976] QB 779). However, the court has jurisdiction to permit such withdrawal only if the original abandonment can be treated as a nullity (e.g., because it was brought about by mistake, fraud, wrong advice or misapprehension on the appellant's part). In *Read* (25 January 1990 unreported), the court held that R's decision to abandon had been made under a mistake or misapprehension, and could be treated as a nullity. After R's application for leave to appeal, there had been considerable delay by the shorthand writers in providing the relevant transcript. In the mistaken belief that his eligibility for parole was affected while the appeal was pending, R abandoned his application before consideration by the single judge. The court stressed that only very rarely would someone who had abandoned an appeal be allowed to withdraw that abandonment. This was, however, an exceptional case. The abandonment was treated as a nullity and the court went on to refuse leave to appeal against conviction, but granted leave to appeal against sentence, and reduced R's sentence. Essentially, the question is whether the mind of the appellant went with his act of abandonment. If he cannot show that it did not, there is no jurisdiction to allow withdrawal of the notice, even if there are other special circumstances surrounding the abandonment such as the appellant being a patient in a mental hospital at the relevant time and not able to weigh as well as other appellants might the advantages and disadvantages of abandonment.

APPLICATIONS TO A SINGLE JUDGE

D23.25 At numerous points during the above description of procedure for appealing to the Court of Appeal, reference has been made to the powers of a single judge. The powers which the single judge may exercise are listed in the Criminal Appeal Act 1968, s. 31(1) to (2B) and s. 44. In *Ahmed* [1996] Crim LR 339, the Court of Appeal made it clear that, while s. 31(2)(c) gave power to the single judge to order a witness to attend for examination, that did not decide the question whether the witness should in fact give evidence, which was a matter for the full court at the hearing of the appeal. The discretion of the single judge to determine applications made to him otherwise than in open court and without the attendance of counsel is given by the Criminal Appeal Rules 1968, r. 11. The right of an appellant to renew before a court an application which has been refused by the single judge and the procedure for giving notice of such a renewed application are contained in the Criminal Appeal Act 1968, s. 31(3), and the Criminal Appeal Rules 1968, r. 12, respectively. The procedure for making an application to a single judge is fully described at **D23.8**.

Criminal Appeal Act 1968, ss. 31 and 44

31.—(1) There may be exercised by a single judge in the same manner as by the Court of Appeal and subject to the same provisions—

    (a) the powers of the Court of Appeal under this part of this Act specified in subsection (2) below;

    (b) the power to give directions under section 4(4) of the Sexual Offences (Amendment) Act 1976; and

(c)   the powers to make orders for the payment of costs under sections 16 to 18 of the Prosecution of Offences Act 1985 in proceedings under this part of this Act.

(2)   The powers mentioned in subsection (1)(a) above are the following:—

(a)   to give leave to appeal;

(b)   to extend the time within which notice of appeal or of application for leave to appeal may be given;

(c)   to allow an appellant to be present at any proceedings;

(d)   to order a witness to attend for examination;

(e)   to exercise the powers conferred by section 19 of this Act [bail pending determination of appeal];

(f)   to make orders under section 8(2) of this Act and discharge or vary such orders [orders relating to procedure on a retrial];

[(g)   repealed];

(h)   to give directions under section 29(1) of this Act [directions for loss of time].

(2A)   The power of the Court of Appeal to suspend a person's disqualification under section 40(2) of the Road Traffic Offenders Act 1988 may be exercised by a single judge in the same manner as it may be exercised by the court.

(2B)   The power of the Court of Appeal to grant leave to appeal under section 159 of the CJA 1988 [appeals against orders restricting publicity] may be exercised by a single judge in the same manner as it may be exercised by the court.

(3)   If the single judge refuses an application on the part of an appellant to exercise in his favour any of the powers above specified, the appellant shall be entitled to have the application determined by the Court of Appeal.

44.—(1)   There may be exercised by a single judge—

(a)   the powers of the Court of Appeal under this Part of this Act—

(i)   to extend the time for making an application for leave to appeal;

(ii)   to make an order for or in relation to bail; and

(iii)   to give leave for a person to be present at the hearing of any proceedings preliminary or incidental to an appeal; and

(b)   their powers to make orders for the payment of costs under sections 16 and 17 of the Prosecution of Offences Act 1985 in proceedings under this Part of this Act,

but where the judge refuses an application to exercise any of the said powers the applicant shall be entitled to have the application determined by the Court of Appeal.

(2)   The power of the Court of Appeal to suspend a person's disqualification under section 40(3) of the Road Traffic Offenders Act 1988 may be exercised by a single judge, but where the judge refuses an application to exercise that power the applicant shall be entitled to have the application determined by the Court of Appeal.

By s. 45(2), the references in ss. 31 and 44 to 'a single judge' are references to 'any judge of the Court of Appeal or of the High Court'.

Criminal Appeal Rules 1968, rr. 11 and 12

Hearing by a single judge

11.—(1)   A judge of the court shall, for the purpose of exercising any of the powers referred to in section 31(2) of the Act, . . . sit in such place as he appoints, and may sit otherwise than in open court.

(2)   A party in any proceedings under the said section 31(2) . . . may be represented by counsel or solicitor.

Determination by a full court

12.—(1)   Where a judge of the court has refused an application on the part of an appellant to exercise in his favour any of the powers referred to in section 31(2) of the Act, the appellant may have the application determined by the court by serving a notice in form 15 on the Registrar within 14 days, or such longer period as a judge of the court may fix, from the date on which notice of the refusal was served on him by the Registrar.

(2)   A notice in form 15 shall be signed by, or on behalf of, the appellant.

(3)   If the notice is not signed by the appellant and the appellant is in custody, the Registrar shall, as soon as practicable after receiving the notice, send a copy of it to the appellant.

(4)   If such a notice is not served on the Registrar within the said 14 days or such longer period as a judge of the court may fix, the application shall be treated as having been refused by the court.

APPLICATIONS TO THE REGISTRAR OF CRIMINAL APPEALS

D23.26 The Criminal Appeal Act 1995, s. 6, confers powers upon the Registrar to grant an extension of time for giving notice of appeal, to order witnesses to attend for examination, and to vary bail conditions. These powers are set out in the Criminal Appeal Act 1968, s. 31A.

Criminal Appeal Act 1968, s. 31A

(1)   The powers of the Court of Appeal under this Part of this Act which are specified in subsection (2) below may be exercised by the registrar.

(2)   The powers mentioned in subsection (1) above are the following—

(a)   to extend the time within which notice of appeal or of application for leave to appeal may be given;

(b)   to order a witness to attend for examination; and

(c)   to vary the conditions of bail granted to an appellant by the Court of Appeal or the Crown Court.

(3)   No variation of the conditions of bail granted to an appellant may be made by the registrar unless he is satisfied that the respondent does not object to the variation; but, subject to that, the powers specified in that subsection are to be exercised by the registrar in the same manner as by the Court of Appeal and subject to the same provisions.

(4)   If the registrar refuses an application on the part of an appellant to exercise in his favour any of the powers specified in subsection (2) above, the appellant shall be entitled to have the application determined by a single judge.

SECTION D24: REFERENCE TO THE COURT OF APPEAL (CRIMINAL DIVISION) FOLLOWING TRIAL ON INDICTMENT

REFERENCE BY THE CRIMINAL CASES REVIEW COMMISSION

The Criminal Appeal Act 1995 set up the Criminal Cases Review Commission to **D24.1** investigate and process allegations of miscarriages of justice. Section 3 of the 1995 Act abolished the Home Secretary's power to refer cases to the Court of Appeal. The functions of the Home Secretary were taken over by the Commission. The Commission may refer to the Court of Appeal a conviction of an offence on indictment, or a finding of not guilty by reason of insanity or a finding that a person was under a disability when he did the act or made the omission (s. 9(1), (5) and (6) respectively). The Commission's jurisdiction is, however, wider than that formerly exercised by the Home Secretary. It includes referrals of cases in respect of sentence, as well as conviction, where they were tried on indictment (s. 9(1)). In addition, the Commission may refer to the Crown Court convictions and sentences imposed in the magistrates' court, with the proviso that the Crown Court may not, on a reference, impose any punishment more severe than that of the court whose decision is being referred (s. 11). The Court of Appeal may itself direct that the Commission investigate a particular matter 'in such manner as the Commission think fit'; the Commission must report when they have finished the investigation or are required by the Court of Appeal to do so (s. 15). The Home Secretary may also refer any matter to the Commission for assistance in relation to the prerogative of mercy (s. 16).

The test which the Commission must apply in deciding whether to refer a case is set out in s. 13. The Commission must not refer a case unless they consider that there is 'a real possibility' that the verdict or sentence would not be upheld if the reference were to be made (s. 13(1)(a)). In the case of a conviction, verdict or finding, the 'real possibility' must be judged, save in 'exceptional circumstances', on the strength of an argument or evidence not raised at trial or on appeal or application for leave to appeal. In the case of a sentence, the real possibility must be based on an argument on a point of law or information not raised in the proceedings or on appeal (s. 13(1)(b)). If there are exceptional circumstances, the Commission may make the reference in any event (s. 13(2)).

The Commission's powers to conduct investigations and obtain information are set out in ss. 17 to 21. The Commission may, if it is reasonable, require a person serving in a public body to produce or give access to material in his possession or control which may help them in performing their functions (s. 17). They may require the appointment of an investigating officer (s. 19).

Once a reference has been made, it is to be treated as an appeal for the purposes of the Criminal Appeal Act 1968. The appeal may then be on any ground, whether cited by the Commission as a reason for their reference or not (s. 14(5)).

The Court of Appeal has the discretionary power to adjourn the hearing of an appeal which has been referred to it by the Commission, if practical considerations so require (*Smith* (1999) *The Times*, 20 May 1999).

REFERENCE BY THE ATTORNEY-GENERAL

Introduction

D24.2 Leaving aside the prospect of references by the Criminal Cases Review Commission (see **D24.1**), the function of the Court of Appeal (Criminal Division) is to hear appeals brought by persons who have been convicted and sentenced in Crown Court proceedings. Until recently that was virtually its only function, and the prosecution had no right of redress if they considered that the accused had been wrongly acquitted or sentenced too leniently. It is still true that an accused acquitted on indictment can never have the verdict in his favour overturned. There is, however, a procedure by which the prosecution can test the correctness of a ruling on law given by the Crown Court judge during the course of the trial which culminated in an acquittal, although the accused himself remains acquitted come what may. That procedure was introduced by the CJA 1972, s. 36. More recently, ss. 35 and 36 of the CJA 1988 have empowered the Court of Appeal to increase an offender's sentence where it considers that the sentence imposed by the Crown Court was unduly lenient. Only the A-G has standing to refer either type of case to the Court of Appeal.

Reference on a Point of Law Following Acquittal

D24.3 Section 36 of the CJA 1972 provides that where a person has been tried on indictment and acquitted (whether on the whole indictment or some counts only), the A-G may refer to the Court of Appeal for its opinion any point of law which arose in the case. Before giving its opinion on the point referred, the court must hear argument by or on behalf of the A-G. The person acquitted also has the right to have counsel present argument on his behalf. However, despite his right to be represented at the hearing, the person acquitted is not put in peril by the proceedings. Whatever the opinion expressed by the Court of Appeal — even if it decides that the trial judge was wrong and the facts of the case were such that the accused clearly ought to have been convicted — the acquittal is unaffected (s. 36(7)). By making a reference, the A-G may obtain a ruling which will assist the prosecution in future cases but he cannot ask the court to set aside the acquittal of the particular accused whose case gave rise to the reference.

In *A-G's Ref (No. 1 of 1975)* [1975] QB 773, Lord Widgery CJ stated that references by the A-G should not be confined to cases where 'very heavy questions of law arise', but should also be made when 'short but important points require a quick ruling of [the Court of Appeal] before a potentially false decision of law has too wide a circulation in the courts'.

The procedure to be adopted on making a reference is set out in the Criminal Appeal (Reference of Points of Law) Rules 1973 (SI 1973 No. 1114). Every reference must be in writing and must specify the point of law referred, give any facts of the case necessary for the proper consideration of the point of law, summarise the argument intended to be put to the court and specify the authorities relied on (r. 3). The reference must not mention the proper name of any person or place which is likely to lead to the identification of the person acquitted. The Registrar of Criminal Appeals will serve notice of the reference on the person acquitted, and must inform him that the reference will not affect the outcome of his trial, and that he has a right to be represented and to present argument on the hearing of the reference (r. 4). The person acquitted becomes the respondent to the reference. Rules 5 and 6 provide for withdrawal and amendment of a reference, argument before the Court of Appeal, and the duty of the court to preserve the anonymity of the respondent unless he agrees to the use of his name in the proceedings.

When the Court of Appeal has given its opinion on a point referred under the CJA 1972, s. 36, the court may, of its own motion or in pursuance of an application, refer the point to the House of Lords if it appears to the Court of Appeal that the point ought to be considered by the Law Lords.

Criminal Justice Act 1972, s. 36

(1) Where a person tried on indictment has been acquitted (whether in respect of the whole or part of the indictment) the Attorney-General may, if he desires the opinion of the Court of Appeal on a point of law which has arisen in the case, refer that point to the court, and the court shall, in accordance with this section, consider the point and give their opinion on it.

(2) For the purpose of their consideration of a point referred to them under this section the Court of Appeal shall hear argument—

(a) by, or by counsel on behalf of, the Attorney-General; and

(b) if the acquitted person desires to present any argument to the court, by counsel on his behalf or, with the leave of the court, by the acquitted person himself.

(3) Where the Court of Appeal have given their opinion on a point referred to them under this section, the court may, of their own motion or in pursuance of an application in that behalf, refer the point to the House of Lords if it appears to the court that the point ought to be considered by that House.

(4) If a point is referred to the House of Lords under subsection (3) of this section, the House shall consider the point and give their opinion on it accordingly; and section 35(1) of the Criminal Appeal Act 1968 (composition of House for appeals) shall apply also in relation to any proceedings of the House under this section.

(5) Where, on a point being referred to the Court of Appeal under this section or further referred to the House of Lords, the acquitted person appears by counsel for the purpose of presenting any argument to the court or the House, he shall be entitled to his costs, that is to say to the payment out of central funds of such sums as are reasonably sufficient to compensate him for expenses properly incurred by him for the purpose of being represented on the reference or further reference; and any amount recoverable under this subsection shall be ascertained, as soon as practicable, by the registrar of criminal appeals or, as the case may be, such officer as may be prescribed by order of the House of Lords.

The Criminal Appeal (Reference of Points of Law) Rules 1973 (SI 1973 No. 1114)

1. [Citation and operative date.]

2.—(1) In these rules—

'court' means the Criminal Division of the Court of Appeal;

'reference' means a reference of a point of law to the court in pursuance of section 36 of the Criminal Justice Act 1972;

'the registrar' means the registrar of criminal appeals;

'respondent', in relation to any reference, means the acquitted person in whose case the point of law referred arose.

(2) The Interpretation Act 1889 shall apply for the interpretation of these rules as it applies for the interpretation of an Act of Parliament.

3.—(1) Every reference shall be in writing and shall—

(a) specify the point of law referred and, where appropriate, such facts of the case as are necessary for the proper consideration of the point of law;

(b) summarise the arguments intended to be put to the court; and

(c) specify the authorities intended to be cited:

Provided that no mention shall be made in the reference of the proper name of any person or place which is likely to lead to the identification of the respondent.

(2) A reference shall be entitled 'Reference under section 36 of the Criminal Justice Act 1972' together with the year and number of the reference.

4.—(1) The registrar shall cause to be served on the respondent notice of the reference which shall also—

(a) inform the respondent that the reference will not affect the trial in relation to which it is made or any acquittal in that trial;

(b) invite the respondent, within such period as may be specified in the notice (being not less than 28 days from the date of service of the notice), to inform the registrar if he wishes to present any argument to the court and, if so, whether he wishes to present such argument in person or by counsel on his behalf.

(2) The court shall not hear argument by or on behalf of the Attorney-General until the period specified in the notice has expired unless the respondent agrees or has indicated that he does not wish to present any argument to the court.

5. The Attorney-General may withdraw or amend the reference at any time before the court have begun the hearing, or, after that, and until the court have given their opinion, may withdraw or amend the reference by leave of the court, and notice of such withdrawal or amendment shall be served on the respondent on behalf of the Attorney-General.

6. The court shall ensure that the identity of the respondent is not disclosed during the proceedings on a reference except where the respondent has given his consent to the use of his name in the proceedings.

7. An application under section 36(3) of the Criminal Justice Act 1972 (reference to the House of Lords) may be made orally immediately after the court give their opinion or notice served on the registrar within the 14 days next following.

[**8.** Deals with service of documents.]

Reference for Review of Sentence

D24.4
Criminal Justice Act 1988, part IV (ss. 35 and 36)

PART IV REVIEWS OF SENTENCING

35.—(1) A case to which this part of this Act applies may be referred to the Court of Appeal under section 36 below.

(2) Subject to rules of court, the jurisdiction of the Court of Appeal under section 36 below shall be exercised by the criminal division of the Court, and references to the Court of Appeal in this part of this Act shall be construed as references to that division.

(3) This part of this Act applies to any case—

   (a) of a description specified in an order under this section; or

   (b) in which sentence is passed on a person—

      (i) for an offence triable only on indictment; or

      (ii) for an offence of a description specified in an order under this section.

(4) The Secretary of State may by order made by statutory instrument provide that this part of this Act shall apply to any case of a description specified in the order or to any case in which sentence is passed on a person for an offence triable either way of a description specified in the order.

(5) A statutory instrument containing an order under this section shall be subject to annulment in pursuance of a resolution of either House of Parliament.

(6) In this part of this Act 'sentence' has the same meaning as in the Criminal Appeal Act 1968, except that it does not include an interim hospital order under part III of the Mental Health Act 1983, and 'sentencing' shall be construed accordingly.

36.—(1) If it appears to the Attorney-General—

   (a) that the sentencing of a person in a proceeding in the Crown Court has been unduly lenient; and

   (b) that the case is one to which this part of this Act applies,

he may, with the leave of the Court of Appeal, refer the case to them for them to review the sentencing of that person; and on such a reference the Court of Appeal may—

      (i) quash any sentence passed on him in the proceeding; and

      (ii) in place of it pass such sentence as they think appropriate for the case and as the court below had power to pass when dealing with him.

(2) Without prejudice to the generality of subsection (1) above, the condition specified in paragraph (a) of that subsection may be satisfied if it appears to the Attorney-General that the judge erred in law as to his powers of sentencing or failed to impose a sentence required by section 2(2), 3(2) or 4(2) of the Crime (Sentences) Act 1997.

(3) For the purposes of this part of this Act any two or more sentences are to be treated as passed in the same proceeding if they would be so treated for the purposes of section 10 of the Criminal Appeal Act 1968.

(4) No judge shall sit as a member of the Court of Appeal on the hearing of, or shall determine any application in proceedings incidental or preliminary to, a reference under this section of a sentence passed by himself.

(5) Where the Court of Appeal have concluded their review of a case referred to them under this section the Attorney-General or the person to whose sentencing the reference relates may refer a point of law involved in any sentence passed on that person in the proceeding to the House of Lords for their opinion, and the House shall consider the point and give their opinion on it accordingly, and either remit the case to the Court of Appeal to be dealt with or deal with it themselves; and section 35(1) of the Criminal Appeal Act 1968 (composition of House for appeals) shall apply also in relation to any proceedings of the House under this section.

(6) A reference under subsection (5) above shall be made only with the leave of the Court of Appeal or the House of Lords; and leave shall not be granted unless it is certified by the Court of Appeal that the point of law is of general public importance and it appears to the Court of Appeal or the House of Lords (as the case may be) that the point is one which ought to be considered by that House.

(7) For the purpose of dealing with a case under this section the House of Lords may exercise any powers of the Court of Appeal.

The combined effect of ss. 35 and 36 of the Act is that, where the A-G considers that an offender was sentenced unduly leniently in proceedings in the Crown Court, he may refer the case to the Court of Appeal (Criminal Division) for review of the sentence. This is subject to (a) the Court of Appeal giving leave, and (b) the offence for which sentence was passed being either one which is triable only on indictment, or one which is triable either way and specified in an order made by the Home Secretary by statutory instrument. Upon an A-G's sentencing reference, the Court of Appeal may quash the sentence passed by the Crown Court and replace it with the sentence it thinks appropriate. Although the replacement sentence must be one which the Crown Court had power to pass, it may (and, presumably, normally would) exceed the sentence actually passed at first instance (but see *A-G's Ref (No. 4 of 1989)* [1990] 1 WLR 41 below).

The reference procedure was extended by the Criminal Justice Act 1988 (Reviews of Sentencing) Order 1994 (SI 1994 No. 119) to cover offences of indecent assault, threats to kill, cruelty to a person under 16, and attempts to commit or inciting the commission of those offences. It was further extended by the Criminal Justice Act 1988 (Reviews of Sentencing) Order 1995 (SI 1995 No. 10) to include serious fraud cases (i.e. those tried following notice of transfer under the CJA 1987, part 1: see **D8.6**).

Subsidiary points concerning sentencing references are:

(a) 'Sentence', as used in ss. 35 and 36, includes any order made by a court when dealing with an offender, other than an interim hospital order (s. 35(6)). This broad definition is in line with the definition of sentence given in the Criminal Appeal Act 1968, s. 50, which governs an offender's right to appeal against sentence (see **D22.41**). The definition thus includes, for example, non-punitive orders such as probation or discharges; ancillary orders such as costs or compensation, and also recommendations for deportation. It also includes a decision by the Crown Court to defer sentence (*A-G's Ref (No. 22 of 1992)* [1994] 1 All ER 105).

(b) In determining whether the offence for which sentence was passed is indictable, and hence subject to s. 35(3)(a), the court must focus upon the offence rather than the offender. Thus, although a person under the age of 18 might be tried summarily for rape, rape is an offence triable only on indictment for the purposes of s. 35(3)(a). It can therefore be the subject of a reference by the A-G under s. 36 (*W* (1993) *The Times*, 16 March 1993).

(c) If an offender has been sentenced for two or more matters, the sentences are to be treated as having been passed in the same proceeding if either they are passed on the same day, or they are passed on different days but the court in passing them states that it is treating them as one sentence (see s. 36(3) combined with the Criminal Appeal Act 1968, s. 10(4)). The effect of this is that, where an offender has been sentenced for one offence in respect of which an A-G's reference is permissible and for a second in respect of which a reference could not otherwise be made, the A-G may nonetheless refer the sentencing for both matters to the Court of Appeal and the court may consequently increase the sentence for both, provided that the sentences were either passed on the same day or the sentencing court stated that it was treating them as one sentence.

(d) It is specifically provided that the A-G may refer a sentence to the Court of Appeal if he considers that the judge erred in law as to the extent of his sentencing powers or failed to impose a mandatory or minimum sentence under the C(S)A 1997 (s. 36(2)). However, the power to refer is not limited to such cases and, in practice, most references will simply arise out of the judge having understood his powers correctly but having chosen, in his discretion, to pass a sentence that appears to the A-G too lenient in all the circumstances of the case.

(e) Schedule 3 to the Act deals with the procedure to be followed for sentencing references. It is similar to the procedure for appeals against sentence by an offender. It does not specifically deal with the procedure for obtaining leave to refer but, presumably, it will be analogous to that by which an offender obtains leave to appeal — i.e. the application will initially be made to a single judge under the Criminal Appeal Act 1968, s. 31, and then, if he refuses it, a renewed application will be possible to a court of the Criminal Division.

(f) Following the Court of Appeal's decision on a sentencing reference, either the A-G or the offender may, with leave, further refer the case to the House of Lords for their opinion on any point of law of general public importance involved. The Court of Appeal must certify that there is a suitable point of law, and either they or the House may then grant leave for the further reference to be made (s. 36(5) to (7)).

(g) Further procedural details are dealt with in the Criminal Appeal (Reviews of Sentencing) Rules 1989 (SI 1989 No. 19), which are largely concerned with the supply and service of the various documents involved in a reference.

(h) In *A-G's Ref (No. 4 of 1989)* [1990] 1 WLR 41 the Court of Appeal set out (at pp. 45H–46D) the correct approach to the disposition of references under s. 36:

> The first thing to be observed is that it is implicit in the section that this court may only increase sentences which it concludes were *unduly* lenient. It cannot, we are confident, have been the intention of Parliament to subject defendants to the risk of having their sentences increased — with all the anxiety that this naturally gives rise to — merely because in the opinion of this court the sentence was less than this court would have imposed. A sentence is unduly lenient, we would hold, where it falls outside the range of sentences which the judge, applying his mind to all the relevant factors, could reasonably consider appropriate. In that connection regard must of course be had to reported cases, and in particular to the guidance given by this court from time to time in the so-called guideline cases. However it must always be remembered that sentencing is an art rather than a science; that the trial judge is particularly well placed to assess the weight to be given to various competing considerations; and that leniency is not in itself a vice. That mercy should season justice is a proposition as soundly based in law as it is in literature.
>
> The second thing to be observed about the section is that, even where it considers that the sentence was unduly lenient, this court has a discretion as to whether to exercise its powers. Without attempting an exhaustive definition of the circumstances in which this court might refuse to increase an unduly lenient sentence, we mention one obvious instance: where in the light of events since the trial it appears either that the sentence can be justified or that to increase it would be unfair to the offender or detrimental to others for whose well-being the court ought to be concerned.
>
> Finally, we point to the fact that, where this court grants leave for a reference, its powers are not confined to increasing the sentence.

Having considered the facts presented on the reference, the Court of Appeal quashed a suspended sentence and replaced it with a three-year probation order.

In *A-G's Ref (No. 5 of 1989)* (1990) 90 Cr App R 358, the Court of Appeal said that it would not intervene unless it was shown that there was some error in principle in the judge's sentence, so that public confidence would be damaged if the sentence were not altered.

(i) The Court of Appeal has also made it plain that, in suitable circumstances, the increased sentence which they pass is mitigated by the fact that the offender has had to face the prospect of being sentenced twice over. Thus, in *A-G's Ref (No. 1 of 1991)* [1991] Crim LR 725, the trial judge had imposed a sentence of five years' imprisonment. In the view of the Court of Appeal, a minimum of eight years would have been appropriate but, as the offender had the added anxiety of waiting for the outcome of the reference, some allowance was made and a sentence of seven years substituted.

(j) In *A-G's Ref (No. 40 of 1996)* [1997] 1 Cr App R (S) 357, the Court of Appeal considered the position where the trial judge gave a sentencing indication before plea. The question was whether such an indication bound the Court of Appeal if the A-G referred the judge's sentence as unduly lenient. Their lordships appeared to take the view that, although the trial judge's indication did not bind them, it was relevant to the exercise of their discretion.

Criminal Justice Act 1988, sch. 3

REVIEWS OF SENTENCING — SUPPLEMENTARY

1. Notice of an application for leave to refer a case to the Court of Appeal under section 36 above shall be given within 28 days from the day on which the sentence, or the last of the sentences, in the case was passed.

2. If the registrar of criminal appeals is given notice of a reference or application to the Court of Appeal under section 36 above, he shall—
(a) take all necessary steps for obtaining a hearing of the reference of application; and
(b) obtain and lay before the court in proper form all documents, exhibits and other things which appear necessary for the proper determination of the reference or application.

3. Rules of court may enable a person to whose sentencing such a reference or application relates to obtain from the registrar any documents or things, including copies or reproductions of documents, required for the reference or application and may authorise the registrar to make charges for them in accordance with scales and rates fixed from time to time by the Treasury.

4. An application to the Court of Appeal for leave to refer a case to the House of Lords under section 36(5) above shall be made within the period of 14 days beginning with the date on which the Court of Appeal conclude their review of the case; and an application to the House of Lords for leave shall be made within the period of 14 days beginning with the date on which the Court of Appeal conclude their review or refuse leave to refer the case to the House of Lords.

5. The time during which a person whose case has been referred for review under section 36 above is in custody pending its review and pending any reference to the House of Lords under subsection (5) of that section shall be reckoned as part of the term of any sentence to which he is for the time being subject.

6. Except as provided by paragraphs 7 and 8 below, a person whose sentencing is the subject of a reference to the Court of Appeal under section 36 above shall be entitled to be present, if he wishes it, on the hearing of the reference, although he may be in custody.

7. A person in custody shall not be entitled to be present—
(a) on an application by the Attorney-General for leave to refer a case; or
(b) on any proceedings preliminary or incidental to a reference,
unless the Court of Appeal give him leave to be present.

8. The power of the Court of Appeal to pass sentence on a person may be exercised although he is not present.

9. A person whose sentencing is the subject of a reference to the House of Lords under section 36(5) above and who is detained pending the hearing of that reference shall not be entitled to be present on the hearing of the reference or of any proceeding preliminary or incidental thereto except where an order of the House authorises him to be present, or where the House or the Court of Appeal, as the case may be, give him leave to be present.

10. The term of any sentence passed by the Court of Appeal or House of Lords under section 36 above shall, unless they otherwise direct, begin to run from the time when it would have begun to run if passed in the proceeding in relation to which the reference was made.

11. Where on a reference to the Court of Appeal under section 36 above or a reference to the House of Lords under subsection (5) of that section the person whose sentencing is the subject of the reference appears by counsel for the purpose of presenting any argument to the court or the House, he shall be entitled to his costs, that is to say to the payment out of central funds of such funds as are reasonably sufficient to compensate him for expenses properly incurred by him for the purpose of being represented on the reference; and any amount recoverable under this paragraph shall be ascertained, as soon as practicable, by the registrar of criminal appeals or, as the case may be, such officer as may be prescribed by order of the House of Lords.

SECTION D25: CHALLENGING DECISIONS OF MAGISTRATES' COURTS AND OF THE CROWN COURT IN ITS APPELLATE CAPACITY

METHODS OF CHALLENGING DECISIONS OF MAGISTRATES' COURTS

A decision of a magistrates' court can be challenged in three ways, by: **D25.1**

    (a)   an appeal to the Crown Court, or

    (b)   appeal to the High Court by way of case stated by the magistrates for the High Court's opinion, or

    (c)   on application to the High Court for judicial review of the magistrates' decision, and the issue, as appropriate of the orders of certiorari, mandamus or prohibition.

A person convicted by a magistrates' court following a plea of not guilty may appeal to the Crown Court against his conviction and/or his sentence. There is also a right of appeal against sentence only. The other two procedures (case stated and judicial review) are available to any person aggrieved by a magistrates' court decision, which includes both a convicted accused and an unsuccessful prosecutor. Decisions of the Crown Court, not made in connection with its jurisdiction over trials on indictment, may also be challenged by way of case stated for the opinion of the High Court or an application for review. The jurisdiction of the High Court in all these cases is exercised by a Divisional Court of the Queen's Bench Division.

APPEAL TO THE CROWN COURT

Introduction

Appeals to the Crown Court from a magistrates' court are governed by the MCA 1980, **D25.2** ss. 108 to 110, and rr. 6 to 11 of the Crown Court Rules 1982 (SI 1982 No. 1109). The Crown Court Rules 1982 are set out in **appendix 1**. Youth courts are magistrates' courts and these appeal provisions therefore apply equally to findings of guilt and dispositions made by youth courts.

Appeals against Conviction and Sentence

Magistrates' Courts Act 1980, s. 108   D25.3

    (1)   A person convicted by a magistrates' court may appeal to the Crown Court—
       (a)   if he pleaded guilty, against his sentence;
       (b)   if he did not, against the conviction or sentence.
    (1A)   Section 13 of the Powers of Criminal Courts Act 1973 (under which a conviction of an offence for which a probation order or an order for conditional or absolute discharge is made is deemed not to be a conviction except for certain purposes) shall not prevent an appeal under this section, whether against conviction or otherwise.
    (2)   A person sentenced by a magistrates' court for an offence in respect of which an order for conditional discharge has been previously made may appeal to the Crown Court against the sentence.
    (3)   In this section 'sentence' includes any order made on conviction by a magistrates' court, not being—
       [(a)   repealed by Criminal Justice Act 1982, sch. 16]
       (b)   an order for the payment of costs;
       (c)   an order under section 2 of the Protection of Animals Act 1911 (which enables a court to order the destruction of an animal); or

(d)   an order made in pursuance of any enactment under which the court has no discretion as to the making of the order or its terms.

The expression 'order made on conviction' used in s. 108(3) appears to have the same wide meaning as 'order made when dealing with an offender', which is the phrase used in the Criminal Appeal Act 1968, s. 50, to define 'sentence' in the context of appeals from the Crown Court to the Court of Appeal (see **D22.36**). Thus, there is a right of appeal to the Crown Court against, *inter alia*, a magistrates' court's decision to put an offender on probation, to discharge him conditionally or absolutely, to disqualify him from driving, to recommend him for deportation, or to make a confiscation, compensation or hospital order. However, an order to contribute to one's own legal aid costs would seem to be unappealable for the same reasons as make such an order unappealable if made by the Crown Court (see *Hayden* [1975] 1 WLR 852).

By virtue of the Criminal Appeal Act 1995, s. 11, the Criminal Cases Review Commission is empowered to refer any conviction by a magistrates' court to the Crown Court. Such reference is to be treated for all purposes as an appeal under the MCA 1980, s. 108(1).

Appeal against Conviction Following Plea of Guilty

D25.4   Although a plea of guilty in the magistrates' court is generally a bar to appealing to the Crown Court against conviction, it is sometimes possible to argue that it should not have that consequence because it was not a genuine admission of guilt. If the Crown Court agrees, it remits the case to the magistrates with a direction that a not guilty plea be entered. Non-genuine pleas of guilty before the magistrates are usually referred to as 'equivocal pleas'. For ambiguous and involuntary pleas, and change of plea from guilty to not guilty, see **D18.18 *et seq*.; D18.24**. Three main situations may be distinguished in which the Crown Court will remit for hearing on a not guilty plea following a guilty plea before the magistrates (see (a) to (c) below). Further, where the accused raises autrefois convict or autrefois acquit, the Crown Court may consider his special plea in bar notwithstanding his guilty plea before the magistrates (see (d) below). Finally, it appears from the Criminal Appeal Act 1995, s. 11(2), that any reference of a conviction by the Criminal Cases Review Commission must be treated as if it were an appeal against conviction under the MCA 1980, s. 108(1), even if the defendant pleaded guilty before the magistrates (see (e) below).

(a)   *Pleas equivocal when made.* If the accused says 'Guilty' when the information is put to him but he immediately adds words which show that he might have a defence, the plea is clearly equivocal. An example is the accused charged with assault who pleads, 'Guilty, but I only did it to defend myself'. The magistrates should explain to him the relevant law and then ask the clerk to put the information again. If the accused then unambiguously pleads guilty, the magistrates will properly proceed to sentence, but if the plea remains equivocal they should enter a not guilty plea on the accused's behalf. Failure to do so will, in the event of an appeal, lead to the case being remitted by the Crown Court for hearing on a not guilty plea.

(b)   *Pleas subsequently shown to be equivocal.* A plea which is unequivocally one of guilty when made may be rendered equivocal by information given to the magistrates before they pass sentence. In *Durham Quarter Sessions, ex parte Virgo* [1952] 2 QB 1, for example, the defendant, who was unrepresented, simply answered 'Guilty', when an information for stealing a motor cycle was put to him, but, when later asked if he had anything to say in mitigation, told the magistrates that he had taken the motor cycle by mistake believing that it was his friend's motor cycle and that the friend had given him permission to use it. Thus, his mitigation was inconsistent with the guilty plea. Similarly, in *Blandford Justices, ex parte G* [1967] 1 QB 82, the prosecution brought to the juvenile court's attention, as part of their summary of the facts following G's plea of guilty to stealing jewellery from her employer, a statement to the police made by G in which she claimed that she had merely borrowed the jewellery intending to return it. Neither Virgo nor G were invited to change their pleas. In both cases, the Divisional Court treated the matters subsequently put before the magistrates (Virgo's mitigation and G's written statement) as if they formed part of the plea to the respective informations. Their lordships therefore held that the Crown Court should have remitted the cases to the magistrates for trial since the pleas, although unequivocal when made, were rendered equivocal by the subsequent developments. However, it is important to note that, if a would-be appellant merely tells the Crown Court that he was mistaken about the law when he entered his guilty plea but nothing emerged during the sentencing procedure that could have alerted the magistrates to his error, then he is bound by his plea and cannot have his conviction set aside.

(c) *Pleas entered under duress.* Even if a plea of guilty was unequivocal when made and not put in doubt by any developments prior to the passing of sentence, the accused is not debarred from appealing his conviction to the Crown Court if the plea was entered under duress (*Huntingdon Crown Court, ex parte Jordan* [1981] QB 857). *Ex parte Jordan* concerned a wife, jointly charged with her husband with shoplifting. The defence she would have presented, had she dared, was that her husband forced her to commit the offences by threats of violence. Similar threats (so she alleged) prevented her from pleading not guilty. The Divisional Court held that the Crown Court had jurisdiction to remit to the magistrates for hearing on a not guilty plea. Presumably the same would apply if a plea of guilty in the magistrates' court was induced by any of the forms of pressure which will lead the Court of Appeal to treat a plea of guilty entered on an indictment as a nullity (see **D22.12**).

(d) *Autrefois convict or acquit.* In *Cooper v New Forest DC* [1992] Crim LR 877, the Divisional Court held that the Crown Court had power to consider the accused's special plea in bar even though he had pleaded guilty unequivocally in the magistrates' court. The rule against double jeopardy (see **D10.28** *et seq*.) is so fundamental that it is incumbent upon the Crown Court to enquire into the accused's contention that he has the basis for a plea of autrefois.

(e) *Reference by the Criminal Cases Review Commission.* If the Commission makes use of its powers under the Criminal Appeal Act 1995, s. 11, to refer a conviction in the magistrates' court to the Crown Court, then such a reference 'shall be treated for all purposes as an appeal by the person under s. 108(1) of the MCA 1980 against the conviction *whether or not he pleaded guilty*' (emphasis added). This creates a new exception to the general rule that a guilty plea bars an appeal against conviction to the Crown Court.

Despite the exceptional situations just described, the general rule is that a plea of guilty before the magistrates bars an appeal against conviction to the Crown Court. See, for example, *Birmingham Crown Court, ex parte Sharma* [1988] Crim LR 741, where the applicant sought judicial review of the Crown Court's decision not to extend time for appeal after the applicant had pleaded guilty by post to failing to stop at a red traffic-light and to driving without insurance. He sought to appeal against conviction out of time on the ground that he had not intended to plead guilty to driving without insurance and that he was insured. The Divisional Court said it was impossible for the applicant to bring himself within any of the exceptions to the general rule that a court cannot go behind a plea of guilty. The plea was not equivocal. The mistake was one of fact not law. The Crown Court therefore had no jurisdiction to entertain the appeal.

If a plea was unequivocal when made, was not put into doubt by any subsequent developments prior to sentence and was not entered under duress or oppression, then the MCA 1980, s. 108, permits an appeal against sentence but nothing more. There is no jurisdiction to set aside the conviction or remit to the magistrates simply on the basis that the accused now regrets pleading guilty and thinks that he might have an arguable defence (*Marylebone Justices, ex parte Westminster (City) London Borough Council* [1971] 1 WLR 567). By contrast, if the accused pleaded guilty and was then committed for sentence, the Crown Court has a general discretion to remit to the lower court whenever that appears just (see *Inner London Crown Court, ex parte Sloper* (1978) 69 Cr App R 1). The reason for this apparently anomalous distinction is that committing for sentence does not render the magistrates *functus officio*, whereas convicting and sentencing the accused does. In the former situation, therefore, the accused is not appealing against conviction but merely asking the Crown Court to refrain from sentencing him until proceedings have been properly completed in the lower court.

Crown Court directions that magistrates rehear a case on a not guilty plea can lead to unbecoming inter-court disputes, with the lower court indignantly protesting that the accused's plea was totally unequivocal and therefore refusing to comply with the Crown Court's wishes. Following some contradictory earlier decisions by the Divisional Court, the rights and duties of the respective courts were finally established by Watkins LJ's judgment in *Plymouth Justices, ex parte Hart* [1986] QB 950. Assuming that it conducted a proper inquiry into whether the accused's plea was equivocal and had sufficient evidence before it to come to the conclusion that it was, the Crown Court's direction that a not guilty plea be entered and a summary trial take place is binding on the magistrates and must be obeyed. Furthermore, the magistrates should assist the Crown Court in its inquiry into the equivocality of the plea by supplying affidavits (e.g., from the clerk in court or the chairman of the bench) dealing with what happened when the appellant appeared before them (*Rochdale Justices, ex parte Allwork* [1981] 3 All ER 434, confirmed in *ex parte Hart*). The only situation in which magistrates might be entitled to ignore a direction for a not guilty hearing is if the Crown Court appears to have given the direction without first making proper inquiries. Should the two courts not then be able to resolve their disagreement sensibly and amicably, there would have to be an application to the Divisional Court for judicial review which could then either quash the Crown Court's direction or order the magistrates to comply with it.

Procedure on Appeal to the Crown Court

D25.5   Notice of appeal must be given in writing to the clerk of the relevant magistrates' court and to the prosecutor within 21 days of sentence being passed or the offender being otherwise dealt with by the magistrates, e.g., by committal for sentence (Crown Court Rules 1982, r. 7). The appellant has 21 days from the date of sentence or committal even if that is after the date of conviction and he is only appealing against conviction. No particular form is prescribed for the notice but it must state whether the appeal is against conviction or sentence or both. The grounds of appeal need not be given, although the appellant may choose to state in very general terms why he considers the magistrates' decision was wrong. Provided notice is given within time, no leave to appeal is required. The Crown Court has a discretion to extend the time for giving notice, i.e., to give leave to appeal out of time (r. 7(5). An application for an extension of time must be made in writing specifying the grounds of the application (r. 7(6)). These should include the proposed grounds of appeal as well as any reasons for applying out of time. The court will take into account the merits of the case in deciding whether to extend time or not.

There is no right to an oral hearing in order to make representations for leave to apply out of time though in exceptional circumstances the court has a discretion to grant one. There is no general duty on a judge to give reasons for refusing leave to appeal out of time (see *Croydon Crown Court, ex parte Smith* (1983) 77 Cr App R 277).

If notice of appeal is given by an appellant upon whom the magistrates have passed an immediate custodial sentence, they may bail him to appear at the Crown Court at the time fixed for the hearing of the appeal (MCA 1980, s. 113(1)). If the magistrates refuse to grant bail, application may be made to the Crown Court under the Supreme Court Act 1981, s. 81(1)(b), or to a High Court judge in chambers. Bail pending the appeal is particlarly important because any custodial sentence imposed by a magistrates' court is necessarily short, so if not granted bail the appellant may have served much of his sentence by the time the appeal is heard.

An appeal is listed for hearing by a circuit judge or recorder who must normally sit with two lay magistrates who were not concerned with the original case (*Practice Direction (Crown Court: Allocation of Business)* [1995] 1 WLR 1083 and Supreme Court Act 1981, s. 74). Prior to the hearing, the defence may request a copy of the clerk's notes of evidence of the summary trial (see also **D18.34**). If the appellant is legally aided, the clerk must comply with the request (see Legal Aid in Criminal and Care Proceedings (General) Regulations 1989, especially reg. 42). Rather strangely, a non-legally aided appellant has no legal right to see the notes, but any request he might make for a copy should be 'viewed sympathetically' (per Lord Lane CJ in *Clerk to Highbury Corner Justices, ex parte Hussein* [1986] 1 WLR 1266). The appeal itself takes the form of a rehearing (Supreme Court Act 1981, s. 79(3)), exactly the same steps being gone through as were gone through at the summary trial. Thus, at an appeal against conviction, counsel for the respondent (i.e., the prosecution) makes an opening speech and calls evidence, after which counsel for the appellant may make a submission of no case to answer. If that fails, defence evidence is called, counsel makes a closing speech, and the court announces its decision. The parties are not limited to the evidence called at the summary trial, but may rely on material which has only become available to them since then, or which they simply chose not to use on the earlier occasion. The Crown Court itself, however, may not amend the information on which the appellant was convicted (*Garfield* v *Maddocks* [1974] QB 7; see also *Swansea Crown Court, ex parte Stacey* [1990] RTR 183, in which it was held that the judge was wrong to allow a prosecution application to amend the information with respect to the date of the alleged offences; *Norwich Crown Court, ex parte Russell* [1993] Crim LR 518). Nor can the Crown Court strike out an amendment made by the magistrates (*Fairgrieve* v *Newman* (1985) 82 Cr App R 60). At an appeal against sentence, the prosecution simply outline the facts and call antecedents evidence, reports (if any) on the appellant are read, and defence counsel mitigates. The court will then decide how the appellant ought to be sentenced. If what the court thinks is the appropriate sentence differs significantly from the sentence imposed by the magistrates then the appeal should be allowed and the sentence of the Crown Court substituted for that of the magistrates.

In giving the decision of the Crown Court acting in its appellate capacity, the judge ought to give reasons, stating the main contentious issues in the case and how the court had resolved them. A refusal to give reasons might amount to a denial of natural justice (*Harrow Crown Court, ex parte Dave* [1994] 1 WLR 98).

Powers of the Crown Court on Appeal

The powers of the Crown Court when disposing of an appeal are set out in the Supreme **D25.6** Court Act 1981, s. 48. Those powers are extensive. It may confirm, reverse or vary any part of the decision appealed against; it may remit the matter to the magistrates with its opinion thereon (e.g., where it considers the plea to be equivocal); or it may make such other order in the matter as it thinks just (e.g., in the case of a successful appeal, an order that the costs of the defence in the magistrates' court be paid by the prosecution or out of central funds). Varying the decision appealed against includes increasing the sentence imposed by the magistrates even in a case where the appeal is only against conviction, but the Crown Court sentence must not exceed that which the magistrates could have passed (s. 48(4)). In *Portsmouth Crown Court, ex parte Ballard* (1989) 154 JP 109, it was held that the Crown Court had exceeded its powers when it ordered the sentence which was the subject of the appeal to be consecutive to another sentence passed after the justices had imposed the sentence appealed against. Further, in *Isleworth Crown Court, ex parte Irvin* [1992] RTR 281, the Divisional Court considered the position where the magistrates' court adjourns for inquiries before passing sentence, in such a way that the accused forms the expectation that he will not receive a custodial sentence if the reports are favourable. It held that, where the reports are in fact favourable, it is not open to the Crown Court on an appeal from the magistrates to impose or uphold a custodial sentence as, although the appeal in the Crown Court is a rehearing, that rehearing has to take into account what happened before the justices and it would be unfair to ignore any expectation of the accused which had been created by the justices. In fact, it is unusual for the Crown Court to increase sentence, but the reason it, unlike the Court of Appeal on appeals from the Crown Court, has retained the power to do so may be that leave is never required for appeals to the Crown Court unless they are out of time. The possibility of an increase in sentence may therefore inhibit unmeritorious appeals. Furthermore, whenever an appeal fails, the appellant may be ordered to pay the prosecution's costs (Prosecution of Offences Act 1985, s. 18(1)(b), and see also r. 12 of the Crown Court Rules 1982 which gives the Crown Court a general discretion to make such order for costs between the parties as appears just). A successful appellant may be awarded his costs out of central funds (Prosecution of Offences Act 1985, s. 16(3). This is known as a 'defendant's costs order' and it may include the appellant's costs in the magistrates' court. A publicly funded prosecutor cannot be awarded costs out of central funds, but private prosecutors may have such an order made in their favour whether or not the appeal succeeds, provided it concerned an indictable offence (Prosecution of Offences Act 1985, s. 17(1) and (2)).

Following amendment by the CJA 1988, s. 156, the Supreme Court Act 1981, s. 48, enables the Crown Court to vary (e.g., by increasing sentence) *any part* of the magistrates' decision, even if the appellant has chosen not to appeal against that part. The amended s. 48(2) reads:

> On the termination of the hearing of an appeal [from a magistrates' court] the Crown Court—
>> (a) may confirm, reverse or vary *any part of the decision appealed against, including a determination not to impose a separate penalty in respect of an offence*; or
>> (b) may remit the matter.

In place of the italicised words, the original s. 48(2) simply had 'the decision appealed against'. That wording gave rise to difficult problems of statutory interpretation in *Dutta v Westcott* [1987] QB 291, in which the defendant successfully appealed against a conviction for driving without insurance for which he had been disqualified, and then claimed that the Crown Court was not empowered to order that penalty points should be endorsed on his licence for other lesser offences of which the magistrates had convicted him on the same occasion as they convicted of no insurance but for which they did not order points because of the rule that no points shall be endorsed if the offender is disqualified. By a very strained interpretation of the original s. 48, the Divisional Court was able to hold that the Crown Court had had power to do what it did — indeed, it would have been absurd if the defendant had been able to escape penalty points for offences that would normally incur them simply by getting his conviction and disqualification for something else set aside. The amendment to s. 48 has given the Crown Court a statutory power to do what it did in *Dutta v Westcott*. It also would seem to give the Crown Court power, when a person appeals against his summary conviction for offence A, to quash it and substitute a conviction for offence B of which the magistrates acquitted on the same occasion, since the acquittal is part of the decision against which the appellant is appealing. In theory, indeed, the Crown Court could even dismiss the appeal against conviction for offence A and add a conviction for offence B.

To avoid injustice to appellants, the Crown Court should, it is submitted, use its increased powers under the amended s. 48 sparingly.

Where the Crown Court hears an appeal as a result of a reference by the Criminal Cases Review Commission, however, it is prohibited from increasing sentence (Criminal Appeal Act 1995, s. 11(6): see **D24.1**).

Abandonment of Appeal

The appellant may abandon his appeal by giving notice in writing to that effect to the **D25.7** clerk of the magistrates' court, to the appropriate officer of the Crown Court and to the prosecution (Crown Court Rules 1982, r. 11). The notice should be given at least three days before the hearing of the appeal. Where notice to abandon an appeal has been duly given by the appellant the court against whose decision the appeal was brought may issue process for enforcing that decision, subject to anything already suffered or done under it by the appellant (MCA 1980, s. 109(1)(a)). If notice to abandon an appeal is duly given, the Crown Court is thereby deprived of its power to order the appellant to pay costs but the magistrates may make an order in respect of expenses properly incurred by the prosecutor before he received the notice (s. 109(1)(b)). It follows that, once the judge has given leave for an appeal to be abandoned, he has no power to increase sentence (*Gloucester Crown Court, ex parte Betteridge* (1997) 161 JP 721).

Magistrates' Courts Act 1980, s. 109

(1)   Where notice to abandon an appeal has been duly given by the appellant—
   (a)   the court against whose decision the appeal was brought may issue process for enforcing that decision, subject to anything already suffered or done under it by the appellant; and
   (b)   the said court may, on the application of the other party to the appeal, order the appellant to pay to that party such costs as appear to the court to be just and reasonable in respect of expenses properly incurred by that party in connection with the appeal before notice of the abandonment was given to that party.
(2)   In this section 'appeal' means an appeal from a magistrates' court to the Crown Court, and the reference to a notice to abandon an appeal is a reference to a notice shown to the satisfaction of the magistrates' court to have been given in accordance with Crown Court rules.

In *Knightsbridge Crown Court, ex parte Commissioners of Customs and Excise* [1986] Crim LR 324 it was stated that once notice to abandon an appeal has been given the court is *functus officio* and has no power to reinstate the appeal save in the exceptional circumstances where the abandonment was a nullity. There is no provision in the Crown Court Rules 1982, r. 11, for the reinstatement of an appeal once withdrawn. Therefore once notice of withdrawal has been given the appellate procedure is spent.

Failure of Parties to Attend

What if the appellant fails to attend, but has given no notice of withdrawal? In *Guildford* **D25.8** *Crown Court, ex parte Brewer* (1987) 87 Cr App R 265, B was disqualified by the magistrates for six months and fined £200 for offences of speeding. He gave notice of appeal to the Crown Court and disqualification was suspended pending appeal. On the day fixed for the appeal, B did not appear, and his counsel applied for an adjournment because B was ill. Efforts were unsuccessfully made to reach B during a short adjournment. The court refused a further adjournment and proceeded to hear the appeal. Counsel took no part, his instructions being limited to the application to adjourn. The court increased B's fine to £300 and his disqualification to 12 months, and ordered him to pay £180 costs. B sought judicial review of the decision to proceed in his absence. The Divisional Court dismissed the application. The prosecution were present and able to outline the facts. The court was therefore able to form a judgment as to the sentence, even in the absence of B or his representative.

Where neither party appears, the proper course is to dismiss the appeal (see also *Croydon Crown Court, ex parte Clair* [1986] 1 WLR 746). An applicant cannot give notice to abandon by failing to appear or by failing to instruct his counsel. If no notice in writing in accordance with the Crown Court Rules 1982, r. 11, is given to abandon, an application can be made to the court but would require leave to abandon.

Enforcement of Orders of Crown Court on Appeal

D25.9   **Magistrates' Courts Act 1980, s. 110**

> After the determination by the Crown Court of an appeal from a magistrates' court the decision appealed against as confirmed or varied by the Crown Court, or any decision of the Crown Court substituted for the decision appealed against, may, without prejudice to the powers of the Crown Court to enforce the decision, be enforced—
> (a)   by the issue by the court by which the decision appealed against was given of any process that it could have issued if it had decided the case as the Crown Court decided it;
> (b)   so far as the nature of any process already issued to enforce the decision appealed against permits, by that process;
> and the decision of the Crown Court shall have effect as if it had been made by the magistrates' court against whose decision the appeal is brought.

Appeal against Binding Over to Keep the Peace and Be of Good Behaviour

D25.10 There is also an appeal to the Crown Court from a magistrates' court decision to bind over a defendant to keep the peace and be of good behaviour (Magistrates' Courts (Appeals from Binding Over Orders) Act 1956, s. 1(1)). Such an appeal is by way of rehearing and unless the appellant admits the evidence which was before the magistrates' court, the facts justifying the bind-over must be proved (*Shaw* v *Hamilton* [1982] 1 WLR 1308). In *Lincoln Crown Court, ex parte Jones* (1989) *The Times*, 16 June 1989, it was held that there was no jurisdiction to bind over a person who attended court to give evidence but was not in the event called on to give evidence because there is no jurisdiction to bind over a person not before the court.

Bail Pending Appeal

D25.11 Where magistrates refuse bail or impose conditions when committing to the Crown Court for trial or where they remand in custody and a full bail argument certificate under the Bail Act 1976, s. 5, is issued, an application for bail can be made to the Crown Court. Conversely, the prosecution has the right in certain circumstances to appeal against a decision by magistrates to grant bail (see **D5.38**).

APPEAL TO DIVISIONAL COURT BY WAY OF CASE STATED

D25.12 An appeal by way of case stated is an appeal on a point or points of law, which are identified in a document (the case) drawn up by the clerk of the magistrates' court in conjunction with the magistrates whose decision is being questioned. The appeal is to the High Court which exercises its jurisdiction through a Divisional Court of the Queen's Bench Division. Appeals by case stated are governed by the MCA 1980, s. 111, the Magistrates' Courts Rules 1981, rr. 76 to 81, and the Rules of the Supreme Court 1965, ord. 56.

Right of Appeal to Divisional Court

D25.13 The MCA 1980, s. 111(1), provides that 'Any person who was a party to any proceeding before a magistrates' court or is aggrieved by the conviction, order, determination or other proceeding of the court may question the proceeding on the ground that it is *wrong in law* or is *in excess of jurisdiction* by applying to the [magistrates] to state a case for the opinion of the High Court on the question of law or jurisdiction involved' (emphasis added). The subsection is not as happily worded as it might be since it thrice includes the word 'proceeding', and seems to use it in a slightly different sense on each occasion. Taking the appearances of the word in sequence, it would seem to mean (a) the entire proceedings before the magistrates; (b) a particular decision taken by the magistrates during the course of or in ultimately disposing of those proceedings, and (c) an amalgam of the first two meanings. However, whatever the difficulties raised by a close analysis of s. 111(1), its broad effect is clear.

(a) Appeal by case stated is at the disposal of both the prosecution and the defence.

(b) The appeal must be on one or other of the two grounds mentioned in s. 111(1), namely that the decision complained of was wrong in law or in excess of jurisdiction. In his initial application to the magistrates to state a case, a would-be appellant must specify the question of law or jurisdiction on which the High Court's opinion is sought, and if his application mentions only a question of fact the request for a case would be refused. The kind of issues which may properly be raised for the High Court's consideration are whether the information was bad for duplicity, whether the magistrates had power to try it, whether they were right to find that there was or (as the case may be) was not a case to answer, whether inadmissible evidence was received or admissible evidence excluded, and whether their decision was the correct one in the light of the facts they found proved by the evidence. This last is perhaps the commonest argument put forward on a case stated. Either the prosecution says that the accused's acquittal should be reversed because on their stated view of the facts the magistrates clearly ought to have convicted, or the defence contend that the facts proved to the magistrates' satisfaction did not amount to the offence charged and so the conviction should be set aside. However, the lower court's decision as to what facts were established by the evidence cannot be appealed by case stated, save that a finding of fact which is totally unsupported by evidence or at which no reasonable tribunal properly directing itself could have arrived is treated as revealing an error of law and so may be a proper basis for an appeal to the Divisional Court (*Bracegirdle* v *Oxley* [1947] KB 349). If the defence consider that the magistrates' decision on the facts was merely against the weight of the evidence, their only remedy is to go to the Crown Court for a rehearing of the evidence.

(c) Most appeals by way of case stated are aimed at overturning either a summary conviction or a summary acquittal. They are not aimed at reducing or increasing a sentence passed after summary conviction, simply because it is rare for magistrates to pass a sentence which is wrong in law or in excess of jurisdiction. However, if they should happen to do so, the aggrieved party can ask them to state a case. Thus, on a number of occasions, the prosecution have obtained a ruling that magistrates sentencing for a drink-driving offence should have disqualified the offender since the grounds he advanced for not being disqualified were incapable of being special reasons within the meaning of the Road Traffic Act 1972 (now the Road Traffic Offenders Act 1988) (see *Haime* v *Walklett* [1983] RTR 512 for an example). In exceptional cases, the defence on an appeal by case stated may obtain a reduction in sentence by arguing that, although the magistrates' sentence was within the magistrates' statutory powers of punishment, it was so far outside the normal discretionary limits as to deserve the description 'harsh and oppressive'. The Divisional Court will then presume that the magistrates in passing the sentence must have made some error in law, otherwise they would not have arrived at a decision so grossly out of line with good sentencing practice. As to the test which should be applied where there is an appeal against sentence by way of case stated, it would seem that it is the same as it is on an application for judicial review (see the authorities cited at **D25.21**, *Tucker* v *DPP* [1992] 4 All ER 901 at p. 903, and *Universal Salvage* v *Boothby* (1983) 5 Cr App R (S) 428).

(d) On a correct interpretation of s. 111(1), the right to ask the magistrates to state a case does not arise unless and until the proceedings in their court have resulted in a final determination of the would-be appellant's case (see *Streames* v *Copping* [1985] QB 920 cited with approval in *Loade* v *DPP* [1990] 1 QB 1052, a case dealing with appeals from the Crown Court by way of case stated; see also dicta in *Atkinson* v *United States of America Government* [1971] AC 197). In the context of criminal proceedings, a final determination would be an acquittal, conviction or passing of sentence. It has been held that neither errors of law during committal proceedings nor a decision to commit which was unjustified by the evidence can be challenged by case stated since a committal is not a final determination of a case (*Dewing* v *Cummings* [1971] RTR 295). It follows that the case stated procedure should not be used to challenge errors in relation to committal proceedings. The same reasoning would apply to a decision to commit for sentence, although the conviction which preceded the decision to commit could be appealed. The need for there to have been a final determination also means that if, during the course of a summary trial, the prosecution or defence consider that the magistrates have made a wrong decision in law, they must wait until the decision has been pronounced before asking for a case to be stated — they may not seek an adjournment immediately after the decision complained of with a view to getting a ruling on the matter from the Divisional Court during the period of the adjournment (*Streames* v *Copping* [1985] QB 920). On the other hand, where an objection to prosecution evidence succeeds, the prosecution are not obliged to call their remaining evidence but may close their case, even if that leads inevitably to an acquittal. If the appeal later succeeds, the Divisional Court can remit the case to the justices, so that both the rejected evidence and any additional admissible evidence can be called (*Farrand* v *Galland* [1989] Crim LR 573 — see further **D25.16**).

Procedure on Appeal by Way of Case Stated

D25.14 An application for the magistrates to state a case must be made within 21 days of 'the day on which the court sentences or otherwise deals with the offender' (MCA 1980, s. 111(2) and (3)). This term includes a day on which a decision on costs is made (*Liverpool City Council* v *Worthington* (1998) *The Times*, 16 June 1998). The application, which must be in writing, should identify the question of law or jurisdiction on which the High Court's opinion is sought (Magistrates' Courts Rules 1981, r. 76). If it is suggested that there was no evidence on which the magistrates could reasonably have come to a particular finding of fact, the fact in question should be specified. The application is sent to the clerk of the relevant magistrates' court. Where the magistrates consider that an application to state a case is frivolous they may refuse to comply with the application, but must give the applicant a certificate stating that his application has been refused (MCA 1980, s. 111(5)). The applicant may then apply to the Divisional Court for an order of mandamus compelling the magistrates to state a case. Even if the application cannot be classed as frivolous, the magistrates may still doubt whether the applicant genuinely intends to go through with the appeal. To discourage money and time being wasted over appeals which are not pursued, they may make their agreement to state a case conditional upon the applicant entering into a recognisance that he will 'prosecute the appeal without delay' and pay any costs which are ultimately awarded against him by the High Court (s. 114). If the magistrates refuse to state a case after the applicant has been granted an order of mandamus, they are liable to pay costs (*Huntingdon Magistrates' Court, ex parte Percy* (1994) *The Times*, 4 March 1994).

A statement of case should set out the facts as found by the magistrates, but not the evidence which led them to those findings of fact (*Turtington* v *United Co-operatives Ltd* [1993] Crim LR 376). The only exception to the rule arises when the appellant contends that there was no evidence on which the magistrates could reasonably have reached a finding of fact, in which case a short statement of the relevant evidence must be included. The case also sets out the charge or charges heard by the magistrates, the contentions of the parties on the questions of law or jurisdiction raised, any authorities cited, the magistrates' decision, and the question for the High Court. The clerk to the magistrates is principally responsible for drafting the case. He should, on receipt of a proper application, prepare a draft case immediately. He consults with the magistrates, and takes into account any representations by the parties. The parties have 21 days in which to make representations on the initial draft. After any necessary alterations have been made to the case as initially drafted by the clerk, the final form of the draft is signed by at least two of the magistrates whose decision is being appealed, or by the clerk on their behalf. It is then sent to the appellant or his solicitor (Magistrates' Courts Rules 1981, r. 78), who, within 10 days of receiving it, must lodge it in the Crown Office at the Royal Courts of Justice (Rules of the Supreme Court 1965, ord. 56, r. 6). Unless time for lodging the case is extended by the Divisional Court, failure to lodge it within the 10 days will lead to the appeal being struck out. The appellant must also serve on the respondent to the appeal a notice of entry of the appeal and a copy of the case. This is done within four days of the case being lodged. The appeal is not normally heard until at least eight clear days after the service of the notice.

Where there is a variation between the final version of the case stated and an earlier draft version the court will consider the appeal on the basis of the final case stated and not on the basis of any earlier draft (*Thomas* [1990] Crim LR 269 applying *Tesco Stores Ltd* v *Seabridge* [1988] Crim LR 517).

The 21-day period within which the initial application to the magistrates to state a case must be made is prescribed by statute, and cannot be varied even by the High Court (*Michael* v *Gowland* [1977] 1 WLR 296). Where an application is made within time but it does not comply with the Magistrates' Courts Rules 1981, r. 76, in that it fails to identify the question of law or jurisdiction on which the High Court's opinion is sought, the Divisional Court will still accept jurisdiction if the defect is subsequently remedied, even if that is done out of time (see *Parsons* v *F. W. Woolworth and Co. Ltd* [1980] 1 WLR 1472 and *Croydon Justices, ex parte Lefore Holdings Ltd* [1980] 1 WLR 1465 where, by slightly different reasoning, differently constituted Divisional Courts arrived at substantially the same conclusions). An application is not invalidated by an error in the names of the magistrates to whom it is addressed or if there are no names stated provided it is clearly made to the justices of the court (*Oxford (Bullingdon) Justices, ex parte Bird* [1948] 1 KB 100). In *P and M Supplies (Essex) Ltd* v *Hackney London Borough Council* (1990) 154 JP 814, it was held that an application would comply with the 21-day time-limit if it was written and posted within 21 days even if it had not been received within the time limit. Citing the decision of the Divisional Court in *Brighton Justices, ex parte Bawa* (3 June 1986 unreported), the court stated that this was so provided the application was sent in such circumstances that in the normal course of events it would have arrived on time.

Bail Pending Appeal

Where magistrates have passed on an appellant an immediate custodial sentence, they **D25.15** may grant him bail pending the hearing of his appeal (MCA 1980, s. 113). The terms of bail are that, unless the appeal succeeds, he must appear at the magistrates' court within 10 days of the Divisional Court's judgment being given, the precise date being fixed by the magistrates after the appeal. If the magistrates refuse bail, an application for bail may be made to a High Court judge in chambers.

Disposition by Divisional Court of an Appeal by Way of Case Stated

The appeal is heard by a Divisional Court of the Queen's Bench Division. The court **D25.16** consists of at least two judges of the Division (Supreme Court Act 1981, s. 66(3)), but often three judges sit, including the Lord Chief Justice. The Lord Chancellor may request any Lord Justice of Appeal to sit in a Divisional Court. If a two-judge court is equally divided, the appeal fails (*Flannagan* v *Shaw* [1920] 3 KB 96 per Scrutton LJ at p. 107). No evidence is called before the court. The appeal takes the form of legal argument for the appellant and respondent, based solely upon the facts stated in the case. If those facts give rise to a point of law not taken before the magistrates which might, if it had been taken, have provided the appellant with a good defence to the charge against him, the Divisional Court will consider the point, so long as it does not depend upon any further findings of fact (*Whitehead* v *Haines* [1965] 1 QB 200). In disposing of the appeal, the Divisional Court can 'reverse, affirm or amend' the magistrates' decision, or remit the matter to the magistrates with its opinion thereon, or make any other order it thinks fit in respect of the matter, including an order as to costs (Supreme Court Act 1981, s. 28A). The powers of the Divisional Court thus include both substituting for an appellant's conviction an acquittal, and, where the prosecution appeal following an acquittal, remitting the case to the magistrates with a direction that they convict and proceed to sentence. Alternatively, where it is plain what the sentence should be, the Divisional Court may simply replace the acquittal with a conviction and impose the appropriate penalty themselves. If the appeal concerns a sentence which was allegedly beyond the magistrates' powers or 'harsh and oppressive', the Divisional Court, on allowing the appeal, may pass the sentence it considers right. Costs may be awarded to the accused out of central funds (Prosecution of Offences Act 1985, s. 16(5)). There is also power to order the unsuccessful party to pay his opponent's costs, but there is no power to grant the prosecution their costs out of central funds unless it is a private prosecution (Prosecution of Offences Act 1985, s. 17(2)). See also *Practice Direction (Crime: Costs)* [1991] 1 WLR 498. Where an appellant wishes to withdraw an appeal by way of case stated, he may do so without having to obtain leave of the court (*Collett* v *Bromsgrove District Council* (1996) 160 JP 593).

It had been thought that, despite the wide powers given to the Divisional Court by s. 6 of the Summary Jurisdiction Act 1857 (now the Supreme Court Act 1981, s. 28A), the Divisional Court was not permitted to order a retrial. (See *Rigby* v *Woodward* [1957] 1 WLR 250 and *Maydew* v *Flint* (1984) 80 Cr App R 49). In *Griffith* v *Jenkins* [1992] 2 AC 76, however, the House of Lords held that the Divisional Court *did* have power to order a rehearing, before the same or a different bench. In that case, the justices had dismissed charges of unlawful fishing and theft, acting of their own motion and without inviting representations from the parties. The prosecution appealed, and the Divisional Court held that the justices had erred. Since two of the bench had retired, they could not remit to the same bench. Further, the Divisional Court took the view that they had no power under the Summary Jurisdiction Act 1857, s. 6, to remit the case for rehearing before a different bench. The House of Lords held that there was always power in the Divisional Court, on hearing an appeal by case stated under s. 6, to order a rehearing before the same or a different bench. A rehearing would only be ordered in circumstances where a fair trial was still possible and it was not appropriate to order a rehearing in the instant case.

In *Farrand* v *Galland* [1989] Crim LR 573, the accused were charged with offering to supply a car with a false odometer reading, contrary to the Trade Descriptions Act 1968. The prosecution sought to introduce as evidence, by the PACE 1984, s. 68(2), a card and a mileage slip. The justices ruled that the exhibits were inadmissible because not all the conditions in s. 68 were satisfied. The prosecution then closed their case and inevitably, given the gaps in the evidence, the accused were acquitted. On appeal by way of case stated, the Divisional Court held that the evidence was admissible and remitted the case to the justices so they could admit the documentary evidence. They indicated that the justices would also be expected to exercise their discretion to allow the prosecution to call the extra evidence which they would have called had the documentary evidence been admitted at the original hearing.

In *Jeffrey* v *Black* [1978] QB 490, where the prosecution appealed after the magistrates excluded proposed evidence that the cannabis which was the subject-matter of a possessing drugs charge had been found in B's room — the Divisional Court held that the evidence should have been admitted despite its having been unlawfully obtained, and sent the case back for rehearing by a different bench.

Any order of the Divisional Court made on appeal may be enforced as if it were an order of the magistrates' court from which the appeal was brought (MCA 1980, s. 112).

Loss of Right to Appeal to Crown Court

Upon an application being made to magistrates to state a case for the opinion of the **D25.17** High Court, the applicant loses any right he had to appeal to the Crown Court (MCA 1980, s. 111(4)). This is so even if the application to state a case does not arrive within the statutory 21 days, provided that it was *made* within the prescribed time and would, in the normal course of events, have *arrived* within the prescribed time (*P and M Supplies (Essex) Ltd* v *Hackney London Borough Council* (1990) 154 JP 814). Therefore, if a person convicted by magistrates is dissatisfied both with the view of the facts they apparently took, and with their ruling on any question of law which arose, he is well advised to appeal to the Crown Court against conviction and refrain from asking the magistrates to state a case. At the rehearing in the Crown Court, the evidence is again called, and all questions of both fact and law may be fully ventilated. If the appeal fails, the appellant still has the right to ask the Crown Court to state a case for the High Court's opinion on the question of law (see **D25.29**). Had he appealed on the law direct from the magistrates' court to the Divisional Court, he would have lost the chance of having the evidence reheard in the Crown Court.

Statutory Provisions

Magistrates' Courts Act 1980, ss. 111 to 114   D25.18

111.—(1)   Any person who was a party to any proceeding before a magistrates' court or is aggrieved by the conviction, order, determination or other proceeding of the court may question the proceeding on the ground that it is wrong in law or is in excess of jurisdiction by applying to the justices composing the court to state a case for the opinion of the High Court on the question of law or jurisdiction involved; but a person shall not make an application under this section in respect of a decision against which he has a right of appeal to the High Court or which by virtue of any enactment passed after 31st December 1879 is final.

(2)   An application under subsection (1) above shall be made within 21 days after the day on which the decision of the magistrates' court was given.

(3)   For the purpose of subsection (2) above, the day on which the decision of the magistrates' court is given shall, where the court has adjourned the trial of an information after conviction, be the day on which the court sentences or otherwise deals with the offender.

(4)   On the making of an application under this section in respect of a decision any right of the applicant to appeal against the decision to the Crown Court shall cease.

(5)   If the justices are of opinion that an application under this section is frivolous, they may refuse to state a case, and, if the applicant so requires, shall give him a certificate stating that the application has been refused; but the justices shall not refuse to state a case if the application is made by or under the direction of the Attorney-General.

(6)   Where justices refuse to state a case, the High Court may, on the application of the person who applied for the case to be stated, make an order of mandamus requiring the justices to state a case.

112.   Any conviction, order, determination or other proceeding of a magistrates' court varied by the High Court on an appeal by case stated, and any judgment or order of the High Court on such an appeal, may be enforced as if it were a decision of the magistrates' court from which the appeal was brought.

113.—(1)   Where a person has given notice of appeal to the Crown Court against the decision of a magistrates' court or has applied to a magistrates' court to state a case for the opinion of the High Court, then if he is in custody, the magistrates' court may, subject to section 25 of the Criminal Justice and Public Order Act 1994, grant him bail.

(2)   If a person is granted bail under subsection (1) above, the time and place at which he is to appear (except in the event of the determination in respect of which the case is stated being reversed by the High Court) shall be—

(a)   if he has given notice of appeal, the Crown Court at the time appointed for the hearing of the appeal;

(b)   if he has applied for the statement of a case, the magistrates' court at such time within 10 days after the judgment of the High Court has been given as may be specified by the magistrates' court;

and any recognisance that may be taken from him or from any surety for him shall be conditioned accordingly.

(3)   Subsection (1) above shall not apply where the accused has been committed to the Crown Court for sentence under section 37 or 38 above.

(4)   Section 37(6) of the Criminal Justice Act 1948 (which relates to the currency of a sentence while a person is released on bail by the High Court) shall apply to a person released on bail by a magistrates' court under this section pendng the hearing of a case stated as it applies to a person released on bail by the High Court under section 22 of the Criminal Justice Act 1967.

114.   Justices to whom application has been made to state a case for the opinion of the High Court on any proceeding of a magistrates' court shall not be required to state the case until the applicant has entered into a recognisance, with or without sureties, before the magistrates' court, conditioned to prosecute the appeal without delay and to submit to the judgment of the High Court and pay such costs as that court may award; and (except in any criminal matter) the clerk of a magistrates' court shall not be required to deliver the case to the applicant until the applicant has paid him the fees payable for the case and for the recognisances.

APPLICATION FOR JUDICIAL REVIEW

Prerogative Orders Generally

D25.19   One of the High Court's tasks is to supervise the work of inferior tribunals. The principal way in which it does this is through issuing one or more of the three prerogative orders — namely, certiorari, mandamus and prohibition. An order of certiorari quashes a decision of an inferior tribunal, mandamus compels an inferior tribunal to carry out its duties, and prohibition prevents an inferior tribunal acting unlawfully or in excess of jurisdiction.

The prerogative orders are only issued upon an application being made to the High Court for judicial review of the inferior tribunal's decision. In the field of administrative law, judicial review is of great importance, being used to control the way in which a wide variety of tribunals and other persons under a duty to act judicially exercise their powers. It is also available in respect of decisions by magistrates (whether those decisions were made in the exercise of their civil or criminal jurisdiction), and in respect of decisions by the Crown Court when it is not exercising its jurisdiction in matters relating to trial on indictment (Supreme Court Act 1981, s. 29(3)). It is a useful supplement to appeal by case stated in that a person aggrieved by a decision of a magistrates' court or by a decision of the Crown Court on an appeal from the magistrates may sometimes be able to obtain judicial review when he could not have asked the magistrates or the Crown Court to state a case.

An applicant for judicial review must have a sufficient interest in questioning the decision which it is sought to review. Whatever may be the precise meaning of 'sufficient interest' — and the concept has caused considerable difficulty in cases where the High Court has been asked to review the decision of an inferior tribunal in a civil matter — it is clear that the prosecution and defence each have a sufficient interest to apply for judicial review both of a magistrates' court's decision in a criminal case and of a Crown Court decision upon appeal from the magistrates. The application is made to a Divisional Court of the Queen's Bench Division. The procedure is governed by the Supreme Court Act 1981, ss. 29 to 31, and the Rules of the Supreme Court 1965, ord. 53.

Broadly speaking, the purpose of judicial review is to prevent magistrates' courts and other inferior tribunals exceeding their jurisdiction; to compel them to exercise the jurisdiction which is rightfully theirs, and to control the way they exercise that jurisdiction in the sense of correcting fundamental irregularities in their procedures. Generally, however, the appropriate route from the magistrates to the Divisional Court is by way of case stated, rather than by applying for judicial review. Hence an error of law made by the magistrates when exercising their proper jurisdiction in a proper manner should be questioned by appealing by case stated. As was pointed out by the Divisional Court in *Morpeth Ward Justices, ex parte Ward* (1992) 95 Cr App R 215, it is appropriate to proceed by way of case stated (and not judicial review) where the identification of the facts as found may be critical.

Certiorari Generally

The effect of certiorari is to quash the inferior tribunal's decision. When it grants the **D25.20** remedy, the Divisional Court also has the supplementary powers of (a) remitting the case to the inferior tribunal with a direction to reconsider it and reach a decision in accordance with the Divisional Court's findings, and (b) replacing an unlawful sentence which it has quashed with the sentence it considers fit (Supreme Court Act 1981, ss. 31(5) and 43). See, however, *Leeds Crown Court, ex parte Barlow* [1989] RTR 246, in which the defendant's appeal to the Crown Court against his magistrates' court conviction for speeding had been dismissed. The Divisional Court granted him an order of certiorari in respect of breach of natural justice at the Crown Court but decided that it was not appropriate to remit the case to the Crown Court. The effect was that the defendant's conviction would stand unless and until he reinstated his appeal against conviction to the Crown Court.

The grounds on which the remedy of certiorari is commonly granted are described below. As regards criminal proceedings, its commonest use is to quash a summary conviction. It is also potentially available to quash any of the other orders or decisions which magistrates make in connection with the course of prosecution, such as a decision to commit for trial or sentence, or to withhold legal aid, or to refuse an application to withdraw an election for summary trial. However, the rule against double jeopardy (i.e., an acquitted accused should not be reprosecuted for the same offence) means that certiorari is rarely granted to quash an acquittal. If the magistrates pronounced their decision after a genuine trial at which the accused was at risk of a valid conviction, the acquittal will not be reviewed, even if the prosecution were prejudiced by a gross breach of proper trial procedures which (had it happened in reverse) would have necessitated the quashing of a conviction. This general principle was confirmed by the House of Lords in *Dorking Justices, ex parte Harrington* [1984] AC 743 though their lordships thought it anomalous in view of the fact that summary acquittals can be reversed through appeal by case stated. At the same time, the Law Lords gave a generous interpretation to an exception to the principle. The exception is that, if magistrates purport to acquit when they have no jurisdiction to do so, the trial is treated as a nullity, the accused is regarded as not having been in genuine jeopardy, and certiorari may be issued. Thus, a summary acquittal in respect of an offence triable only on indictment is quashable by certiorari (*West* [1964] 1 QB 15), as is an acquittal for an offence triable either way if the correct procedures for determining mode of trial were not complied with (*Cardiff Magistrates' Court, ex parte Cardiff City Council* (1987) *The Times*, 24 February 1987). Moreover, if magistrates pronounce an acquittal without listening to any prosecution evidence and without having good reason for refusing to hear witnesses whom the prosecution have available at court the decision is similarly liable to be set aside (see *Dorking Justices, ex parte Harrington* [1984] AC 743 and *Hendon Justices, ex parte DPP* [1994] QB 167). If a conviction is quashed by certiorari, it would seem that the rule against double jeopardy does not prevent the accused later being reprosecuted for the same offence (*Kent Justices, ex parte Machin* [1952] 2 QB 355), but that is most unlikely to happen in practice.

Certiorari Where There Is Excess of Jurisdiction

D25.21 An order of certiorari may be issued when the inferior tribunal acts in excess of jurisdiction. *Kent Justices, ex parte Machin* [1952] 2 QB 355 provides an example. The magistrates tried Machin for offences triable either way without first explaining to him the possibility of being committed to Quarter Sessions for sentence. Since the procedure set out in the relevant statute, which alone could give them jurisdiction to try an indictable offence, had not been followed, the magistrates acted in excess of their powers in trying him and certiorari issued to quash his convictions. A sentence passed by magistrates may also be in excess of jurisdiction. In *Llandrindod Wells Justices, ex parte Gibson* [1968] 1 WLR 598, for example, G's disqualification from driving was quashed because, having pleaded guilty by post, he was disqualified in his absence without the magistrates first adjourning and notifying him of the reason for the adjournment. In those circumstances, the court had no power to disqualify him (see MCA 1980, s. 11(4)). In *St Albans Crown Court, ex parte Cinnamond* [1981] QB 480 (which was an appeal by way of case stated against a Crown Court decision), the concept of a sentence in excess of jurisdiction was extended to cover a sentence which was so harsh and oppressive that no reasonable tribunal, properly understanding its powers, could have passed it. There have been attempts to place strict limits upon the effect of *Ex parte Cinnamond*. Thus, in *Croydon Crown Court, ex parte Miller* (1986) 85 Cr App R 152, Watkins LJ said (at p. 155):

> . . . the case of *Ex parte Cinnamond* has to be regarded with circumspection. The reasoning for the decision there can apply only to a very unusual and therefore rare circumstance. . . . for *St Albans Crown Court, ex parte Cinnamond* to be applied the sentence will in all the circumstances need to appear to be, by any acceptable standard, truly astonishing.

In *Truro Crown Court, ex parte Adair* [1997] COD 296, however, Lord Bingham CJ said:

> The court has on previous occasions suggested a test of whether the sentence in question is regarded by any acceptable standard as truly astonishing. I would, for my part, question whether that is an ideal test since some people are more readily astonished than others and it would appear to be a somewhat subjective approach. It would perhaps seem more helpful to ask the question whether the sentence or order in question falls clearly outside the broad area of the lower court's sentencing discretion.

In any event, the Divisional Court clearly does not intend that certiorari should become a regular alternative to appealing against sentence to the Crown Court. An offender who feels that his sentence in the magistrates' court was harsh and oppressive should appeal in the normal way to the Crown Court, and only if that court refuses to reduce the sentence should he apply to the Divisional Court for certiorari (*Battle Justices, ex parte Shepherd* (1983) 5 Cr App R (S) 124). *Ex parte Cinnamond* was a case where the Crown Court, far from reducing sentence, had unreasonably increased it to 18 months' disqualification for an offence of careless driving, so the defendant's only possible remedy was to go to the Divisional Court. (See **D25.13** for the similarly restrictive view taken of appeals against sentence by way of case stated.)

Certiorari Where There Is a Breach of the Rules of Natural Justice

D25.22 Certiorari will issue where the inferior tribunal acted in breach of the rules of natural justice. The modern approach to alleged breaches of the rules of natural justice is to state, simply but vaguely, that a tribunal must act fairly having regard to the nature of the inquiry on which it is engaged. Traditionally, the rules of natural justice have been defined with a little more precision, and are said to involve two main principles – no man may be a judge in his own cause, and the tribunal must hear both sides of the case. Breaches of both so-called rules have led to convictions in the magistrates' courts being quashed by certiorari. Numerous cases have concerned alleged breaches of the first rule through a magistrate or a clerk taking part in a case when he has a pecuniary interest in its outcome, or a non-pecuniary interest which is such as to give rise to a reasonable suspicion of bias. The second rule may be invoked where procedural irregularities have occurred which possibly prejudiced the applicant. Failure to give the accused reasonable time to prepare his defence (*Thames Magistrates' Court, ex parte Polemis* [1974] 1 WLR 1371), failure to allow the defendant an adjournment due to a defence witness being unavailable (*Bracknell Justices, ex parte Hughes* (1989) 154 JP 98) announcing a decision of guilty before hearing a closing speech by counsel on behalf of the accused (*Marylebone Justices, ex parte Farrag* [1981] Crim LR 182), refusing to issue witness warrants (*Bradford Justices, ex parte Wilkinson* [1990] 1 WLR 692), and not notifying the defence of witnesses who could support their case (*Leyland Justices, ex parte Hawthorn* [1979] QB 283) have all been held to be breaches of the rules of natural justice.

Leyland Justices, ex parte Hawthorn is particularly interesting because certiorari issued even though the responsibility for not giving the defence the necessary information lay with the police not the court. Relying on that authority, the Divisional Court has since been prepared to grant certiorari whenever an error by the prosecution seems seriously to have prejudiced the presentation of the defence case. Thus, in *Knightsbridge Crown Court, ex parte Goonatilleke* [1986] QB 1, G's conviction for shoplifting was quashed because the store detective (who was treated by the Divisional Court as being in effect the prosecutor) failed to tell the defence that he had a conviction for wasting police time arising out of his falsely informing the police while a serving officer that his warrant card had been stolen. The information would have been particularly useful as G's defence was that the store detective had planted on him the items allegedly stolen so as to impress his superiors by the number of arrests he was making. Similarly, in *Liverpool Crown Court, ex parte Roberts* [1986] Crim LR 622, failure to tell the defence that a police officer, the alleged victim of an assault by Roberts, had made a statement to a superior officer soon after the event which suggested the incident might have amounted only to an accidental clash of heads was fatal to the conviction. However, in the absence of default by the prosecution, certiorari will not issue merely because fresh evidence favourable to the defence has come to light since the summary trial, unless the appellant can achieve the very difficult task of convincing the Divisional Court that, in the light of the additional evidence, all the crucial evidence on which the magistrates convicted must have been perjured.

In *Ex parte Roberts*, the police officer's failure to carry out his duty was regarded as a failure on the part of 'the total apparatus of the prosecution' (per Glidewell LJ). A similar view was taken in *Bolton Justices, ex parte Scally* [1991] 1 QB 537 where the applicants had pleaded guilty to excess alcohol offences. The level of alcohol in their samples of breath had been within the range giving them the right to have samples of blood tested and they had all exercised that right. Unknown to all concerned, when the blood samples were taken, medical kits were used which included skin-cleansing swabs containing alcohol. The analysis of samples might therefore have produced an artificially high blood/alcohol reading. Charges pending against other defendants in similar circumstances had not been proceeded with when the contamination was discovered. The applicants were granted certiorari, and the convictions were quashed. The Divisional Court held that the police were responsible for issuing the medical kits and the associated lack of ordinary care, and the police were part of the prosecution process, notwithstanding the Prosecution of Offences Act 1985. Although there was no dishonesty, the court held that the prosecutor (a combination of police and CPS) had corrupted the process leading to conviction in a manner which was unfair, since it gave a defendant no proper opportunity to decide whether to plead guilty or not guilty. Certiorari was not limited to quashing proceedings vitiated by fraud, collusion or perjury; other grounds could be relied upon provided they were analogous to such conduct. The overriding principle must be that justice should be done. In *Dolgellau Justices, ex parte Cartledge* [1996] Crim LR 337, by contrast, the Divisional Court dismissed the applications for judicial review because the conduct of the prosecution could not be categorised as analogous to fraud.

Certiorari Where There Is an Error of Law

D25.23 Certiorari will be granted where there is an error of law apparent on the face of the record of the inferior tribunal's proceedings – i.e. just by reading the record, and without receiving evidence on affidavit or otherwise of what occurred in the court below, the Divisional Court can tell that a mistake has been made. Historically, certiorari was developed to correct such patent errors, the effect of the order (or writ as it then was) being to remove the record into the King's Bench where it would be rectified. Today, appeal by way of case stated provides a remedy for errors of law much broader in scope than the remedy provided by certiorari. The problem in relying on certiorari when one wishes to have a magistrates' court decision quashed is that magistrates never give written reasons for their decisions, and such oral reasons as they may choose to give are usually of the briefest. If the magistrates do give oral reasons, it has been held that they may be incorporated into the record of the court's proceedings (*Chertsey Justices, ex parte Franks* [1961] 2 QB 152), but in the absence of such reasons the record will consist only of the charges against the accused, his pleas, the decision and the sentence passed. The only errors likely to be revealed by such basic information are jurisdictional errors such as passing a sentence in excess of the statutory maximum for the offence of which, according to the record, the accused was convicted. One device by which the record can be augmented is illustrated by *Southampton Justices, ex parte Green* [1976] QB 11. Green applied to the Divisional Court to quash a decision by magistrates that she should forfeit the sum of £3,000, that being the amount in which she had stood surety for her husband who had jumped bail. The record of the magistrates' court proceedings simply showed that they had made the order complained of. Since that order was undoubtedly within their powers, no error appeared, and the application for certiorari failed. Green appealed to the Court of Appeal against the Divisional Court's decision. The Court of Appeal had before it affidavits sworn by the chairman of the magistrates and the clerk. They showed that the bench had approached its decision on whether to estreat the recognisance on a basis which was wrong in law. The affidavits were treated as part of the record (see Browne LJ's judgment at p. 22), and therefore an error appeared on the face of the record, which enabled the Court of Appeal to issue certiorari. However, there is no obligation on magistrates to make affidavits explaining the reasoning behind their decisions, and, if they do not, the problem remains that any errors of law they may have made are unlikely to be patent on the face of the record.

Mandamus

D25.24 Mandamus is used to compel an inferior tribunal to carry out its duties. Thus, in *Brown* (1857) 7 E & B 757 magistrates who had refused to try an information on the plainly inadequate ground that, in their view, other persons should have been charged with the offence as well as the accused, were ordered to hear the case. Similarly, magistrates may be ordered to state a case for the opinion of the Divisional Court if one has been properly requested under the MCA 1980, s. 111, and there are no reasons for regarding the application as frivolous. The scope of mandamus is, however, fairly limited. It is appropriate where jurisdiction is wrongly refused, but not where the inferior tribunal accepts jurisdiction and then allegedly makes a mistake in the exercise of that jurisdiction. It follows that if, during the course of a summary trial or committal proceedings, magistrates come to a seemingly erroneous decision (e.g., to exclude certain evidence or disallow a line of cross-examination), the aggrieved party may not there and then obtain an adjournment and go to the Divisional Court for mandamus to compel reversal of the decision. All he can do is wait until the conclusion of the hearing, and then – if the ultimate decision goes against him – challenge that by appeal by case stated or an application for certiorari as appropriate (see *Rochford Justices, ex parte Buck* (1978) 68 Cr App R 114 and *Wells Street Stipendiary Magistrate, ex parte Seillon* [1978] 1 WLR 1002). Broadly similar principles apply when (otherwise than in the actual course of a hearing) magistrates fail or refuse to exercise a discretionary power in favour of a party to criminal proceedings (e.g., they refuse to grant legal aid or to allow a change of plea). If they overlooked the fact that they had the power or applied the wrong principles in deciding whether or not to exercise it, the Divisional Court will grant mandamus to compel them to consider or reconsider the matter, applying the correct principles as stated by their lordships (see *Highgate Justices, ex parte Lewis* [1977] Crim LR 611). However, the magistrates will not be ordered to exercise the power in a certain way, unless it is a clear case where there is only one conclusion to which a reasonable tribunal properly understanding the law could come. In brief, mandamus may be used to compel proper consideration of whether to exercise a discretionary power, but not, generally speaking to compel the actual exercise of it.

Prohibition

The order of prohibition is the reverse of mandamus. It prevents an inferior tribunal **D25.25** acting or continuing to act in excess of jurisdiction. It is, of course, unlikely that a magistrates' court would deliberately want to exceed its jurisdiction and act unlawfully, but occasionally there is genuine doubt about the limits of its powers. In that situation it is convenient to adjourn before the possibly *ultra vires* act is done, thus enabling the party who considers that what the magistrates propose is unlawful to apply to the Divisional Court for prohibition. One example of this happening is *Hatfield Justices, ex parte Castle* [1981] 1 WLR 217, where the magistrates had announced their intention of holding committal proceedings in respect of a charge of criminal damage to a value of £23, believing that the special procedure whereby small-value criminal damage charges must be tried summarily did not apply. The Divisional Court held that the magistrates' understanding of the law was wrong (i.e. the special procedure did apply), and therefore granted prohibition to prevent the committal proceedings taking place.

Discretionary Nature of Prerogative Orders

The ordering of certiorari, mandamus or prohibition is always discretionary. In cases **D25.26** where it is in law open to the Divisional Court to grant the remedy, their lordships may nonetheless refuse it in the broader interests of fairness and the due administration of justice. Thus, in *Battle Justices, ex parte Shepherd* (1983) 5 Cr App R (S) 124, certiorari to quash a sentence was refused because the applicant had ignored the more obvious and convenient remedy of appealing the magistrates' court's sentence to the Crown Court. Similarly, *Birmingham Justices, ex parte Lamb* [1983] 1 WLR 339, an application for mandamus to compel magistrates to try an information which they had wrongly dismissed without hearing any evidence failed on account of the undesirability of having the case heard long after the events in question, albeit that the delay was caused mainly by the prosecution having to make the application for judicial review to correct the magistrates' erroneous original decision.

In *Bradford Justices, ex parte Wilkinson* [1990] 1 WLR 692, on the other hand, the Divisional Court granted certiorari despite the existence of a right to appeal to the Crown Court. At W's trial before the justices, he had applied for warrants to compel the attendance of witnesses vital to his case. The bench had refused to issue the warrants, or to adjourn. On the application for judicial review, counsel for the justices argued that, where there is a right of appeal to the Crown Court, the Divisional Court should not interfere by way of judicial review. Mann LJ said (at p. 695H):

> I believe that a defendant is entitled to have a proper trial and a proper appeal. If he does not have a proper trial, he may, if he wishes, seek leave to come to this court.

Bradford Justices, ex parte Wilkinson was not followed in *Peterborough Justices, ex parte Dowler* [1996] 2 Cr App R 561. The Divisional Court stated that they were entitled to take that course of action as *Ex parte Wilkinson* was in conflict with the earlier decision in *Barnes, ex parte Lord Vernon* [1910] LT 860. Their lordships took the view that a procedurally unfair conviction before the magistrates (which had been flawed by failure to disclose a witness statement potentially helpful to the defence) might be cured by a fair trial on appeal to the Crown Court. Judicial review was a discretionary remedy, and it would be refused to this applicant, who had in train an appeal by way of rehearing before the Crown Court. Exceptional cases could still be brought by way of judicial review where the court considered that such a course would best meet the real justice of the case, as where it might be determinative of the case as a whole. Usually, however, interposing a judicial review hearing would lead to an unnecessary hearing, with consequent costs and delay.

In *Hereford Magistrates' Court, ex parte Rowlands* [1998] QB 110, the Divisional Court distinguished *Ex parte Dowler*, placing clear limits upon its effect. Lord Bingham CJ stated (at p. 125):

> While we do not doubt that *Dowler* was correctly decided, it should not in our view be treated as authority that a party complaining of procedural unfairness or bias in the magistrates' court should be denied leave to move for judicial review and left to whatever rights he may have in the Crown Court. So to hold would be to emasculate the long-established supervisory jurisdiction of this court over magistrates' courts, which has over the years proved an invaluable guarantee of the integrity of proceedings in those courts. The crucial role of the magistrates' courts . . . makes it the more important that that jurisdiction should be retained with a view to ensuring that high standards of procedural fairness and impartiality are maintained.
>
> Two notes of caution should however be sounded. First, leave to move should not be granted unless the applicant advances an apparently plausible complaint which, if made good, might arguably be held to vitiate the proceedings in the magistrates' court. Immaterial and minor deviations from best practice would not have that effect, and the court should be respectful of discretionary decisions of magistrates' courts as of all other courts. This court should be generally slow to intervene, and should do so only where good (or arguably good) grounds for doing so are shown. Secondly, the decision whether or not to grant relief by way of judicial review is always, in the end, a discretionary one. Many factors may properly influence the exercise of discretion, and it would be both foolish and impossible to seek to anticipate them all. The need for an applicant to make full disclosure of all matters relevant to the exercise of discretion should require no emphasis. We do not, however, consider that the existence of a right of appeal to the Crown Court, particularly if unexercised, should ordinarily weigh against the grant of leave to move for judicial review, or the grant of substantive relief, in a proper case.

In appropriate circumstances, certiorari is available to quash a committal for sentence (see, for example, *Tower Bridge Magistrates, ex parte Osman* [1971] 1 WLR 1109 and *Cardiff Magistrates' Court, ex parte Morgan* [1989] Crim LR 503; it is submitted that *London County Quarter Sessions Appeals Committee, ex parte Rogers* [1951] 2 KB 74 no longer represents the law).

Procedure on Application for Judicial Review

D25.27 The procedure for applying for judicial review is contained in the Supreme Court Act 1981, s. 31, and the Rules of the Supreme Court 1965, ord. 53. It falls into two main stages. First, the applicant must obtain leave to apply for review. The application for leave is usually determined by a single judge on the basis of a private perusal of the grounds for review set out in a written statement filed by the applicant at the commencement of the proceedings. If leave to apply is granted, the application itself – the second stage in the procedure – is determined by a Divisional Court, which will hear argument from the applicant and anybody else who appears to have a sufficient interest in the outcome. Evidence may be received by the Divisional Court, but is usually given by affidavit rather than orally.

(a) Notice of application is given by filing in the Crown Office a statement setting out the applicant's name and description, the relief sought and the grounds upon which it is sought, the name and address of the applicant's solicitors, and his address for service. An affidavit expanding upon the grounds of the application and verifying the facts relied upon to establish those grounds must also be filed. The applicant is not limited to asking for just one of the prerogative orders, but can ask for two or more of them cumulatively or in the alternative. For example, an applicant might seek certiorari to quash proceedings in excess of jurisdiction which have already taken place and prohibition to prevent any resumption of them, or might seek certiorari to quash a refusal to make an order and mandamus to compel reconsideration of the matter applying the correct principles. Notice of application should normally be given within three months of the grounds for the application arising and must, in any event, be made without delay.

(b) The application for leave to apply is made *ex parte*. It is made to a High Court judge who may determine it without a hearing unless a request for one is made by the applicant. If a hearing is requested, it need not take place in open court. If there is no hearing the judge considers the applicant's statement and supporting affidavit privately, and decides whether they establish a prima facie case for judicial review which should go before the Divisional Court. The court has inherent jurisdiction in criminal matters, just as in civil, to set aside leave granted ex parte (*Secretary of State for the Home Department, ex parte Chinoy* (1991) *The Times*, 16 April 1991).

(c) A copy of the judge's order is sent from the Crown Office to the applicant. If leave to apply is refused, the applicant may renew his application before a Divisional Court of the Queen's Bench Division. In order to do so the applicant must, within 10 days of being served with notice of the judge's refusal, lodge in the Crown Office a notice of intention to renew the application. The application may be renewed whether or not the judge's refusal followed a hearing.

(d) If leave to apply is granted, the application itself is made by originating motion to a Divisional Court of the Queen's Bench Division. Notice of motion must be served on all persons who will be directly affected by the court's decision. In the context of applications arising out of criminal matters, this simply means that where the prosecution are applying for review they must serve notice on the defence and vice versa. Notice must also be served on the clerk of the court below. The notice should be accompanied by a copy of the statement comprising the initial application for leave to apply for review.

(e) Evidence at the hearing before the Divisional Court, whether it be for the applicant or the respondent, is normally in the form of affidavits. Evidence might be required to show, for example, that a member of the court below was biased or that, through not complying with the proper procedure, the court below was acting in excess of jurisdiction. A party proposing to use an affidavit must, on demand, supply a copy to any other party. Any party may apply by summons to a master for an order that the maker of an affidavit attend at the hearing for cross-examination, or for orders for discovery or interrogatories. Such orders are more likely to be of value where the application for review arises out of civil proceedings than when it arises from a criminal matter.

(f)   The Divisional Court hears argument for the applicant. Unless given leave to amend, he is limited to seeking the relief mentioned in his initial statement. The grounds he relies upon should also be those foreshadowed in the statement. In opposition to the application, the court hears any person who appears to it to be a proper person to be heard. At an application relating to a criminal matter, the only persons likely to wish to be heard are the prosecutor and the accused and, perhaps, the magistrates or judge in the court below.

(g)   The court reaches its decision. The court may make any one or more of the orders sought by the applicant, and also have power when granting certiorari to remit the matter to the lower court for reconsideration (whether or not the applicant expressly asked for that to be done). The granting of a remedy is always discretionary.

Bail Pending Judicial Review

D25.28   Bail pending the hearing of an application for judicial review may be granted by a judge in chambers or, if the application is in respect of one of its decisions, by the Crown Court. Magistrates do not have power to grant bail to a person who is challenging their decision by judicial review, although they do have power to bail somebody who is appealing against their decision by way of case stated.

CHALLENGING DECISIONS OF THE CROWN COURT IN ITS APPELLATE CAPACITY

Appeal by way of Case Stated

D25.29   Appeal by way of case stated may be used not only to question the decisions of magistrates, but also to question the Crown Court's decisions in matters not relating to trial on indictment (Supreme Court Act 1981, s. 28). The precise dividing line between decisions which do and those which do not relate to a trial on indictment is not easy to draw. Since the problem of drawing that line more commonly arises in the context of whether a Crown Court decision is subject to judicial review, detailed consideration of the question will be postponed until **D25.30**. However, it is plain that the allowing or dismissal of an appeal from a magistrates' court is a decision totally unconnected with trial on indictment. Therefore, the unsuccessful party in the Crown Court (whether it be the prosecution who have seen a summary conviction overturned or the defence who have had the same result before the Crown Court as they had in the magistrates' court) may further appeal by case stated to the Divisional Court. Of course, just as with an appeal direct from the magistrates to the Divisional Court, the Crown Court decision may only be questioned on the ground that it was wrong in law or in excess of jurisdiction, not on the ground that it was against the weight of the evidence. Again, as with an appeal from the magistrates, the concept of a sentence which is so harsh that it is in excess of jurisdiction may be prayed in aid. The case of *St Albans Crown Court, ex parte Cinnamond* [1981] QB 480 (see **D25.21**) was, in fact, an appeal by way of case stated against a Crown Court decision (see also **D25.30**).

In line with an application arising from the magistrates' court, the right to ask the Crown Court to state a case does not arise until the Crown Court has reached a final determination of the would-be appellant's case (*Loade* v *DPP* [1990] 1 QB 1052). Put in another way, the word 'decision' in the Supreme Court Act 1981, s. 28, means 'final decision', and the High Court will not entertain an appeal by way of case stated until the Crown Court has reached such a final decision (see **D25.13** point (d)).

An application to the Crown Court to state a case should be made to the appropriate officer of the court within 21 days of the decision challenged being made (Crown Court Rules 1982, r. 26(1)). In *DPP* v *Coleman* [1998] 1 All ER 912, the Divisional Court held that a judge could consider applications for extensions of time, sitting without lay justices. Where the prosecution sought to extend the time in which to apply for a case to be stated following the acquittal of a defendant:

(a)   the defendant should be notified of the application;

(b)   the terms on which the extension was being sought should be disclosed to him, and he should be told of his right to make representations;

(c)   the court should then consider the representations of both parties, and the defendant should be given the opportunity to deal with all the representations made by the prosecution;

(d)   normally the court would consider the application on paper without the necessity for an oral hearing.

In *Coleman*, the judge had failed to consider representations from the defendant. It followed that the procedure was flawed, and the defendant's acquittal on appeal to the Crown Court must stand.

The main difference between the procedure for magistrates stating a case and the procedure for the Crown Court doing so is that an appellant from the Crown Court has the responsibility for drawing up an initial draft case which is put before the judge who presided at the proceedings in which the disputed decision was made (r. 26(8)). The respondent to the appeal is also at liberty to submit a draft case to the judge. Having read the draft(s), the judge states and signs a case (r. 26(12)). It is sent to the appellant, who lodges it in the Crown Office, together with copies of the judgments or orders made both in the Crown Court and the magistrates' court (Rules of the Supreme Court 1965, ord. 56, r. 1). The appeal should normally be entered for hearing within six months of the Crown Court decision. Pending hearing of the appeal, the appellant may be granted bail by either the Crown Court or a High Court judge in chambers (Supreme Court Act 1981, s. 81(1)(d), and CJA 1948, s. 37). On disposing of the appeal, the Divisional Court's powers are identical to those it possesses in disposing of an appeal from the magistrates.

Upon an application being made to magistrates to state a case for the opinion of the High Court, the applicant loses any right he had to appeal to the Crown Court (MCA 1980, s. 111(4)). Therefore, if a person convicted by magistrates is dissatisfied both with the view of the facts they apparently took, and with their ruling on any question of law which arose, he is well advised to appeal to the Crown Court against conviction and refrain from asking the magistrates to state a case. At the rehearing in the Crown Court, the evidence is again called, and all questions of both fact and law may be fully ventilated. If the appeal fails, the appellant still has the right to ask the Crown Court to state a case for the High Court's opinion on the question of law. Had he appealed on the law direct from the magistrates' court to the Divisional Court, he would have lost the chance of having the evidence reheard in the Crown Court (see also **D25.17**).

Supreme Court Act 1981, s. 28

(1)   Subject to subsection (2), any order, judgment or other decision of the Crown Court may be questioned by any party to the proceedings, on the ground that it is wrong in law or is in excess of jurisdiction, by applying to the Crown Court to have a case stated by that court for the opinion of the High Court.

(2)   Subsection (1) shall not apply to—

(a)   a judgment or other decision of the Crown Court relating to trial on indictment; or

(b)   any decision of that court under the Betting, Gaming and Lotteries Act 1963, the Licensing Act 1964, the Gaming Act 1968 or the Local Government (Miscellaneous Provisions) Act 1982 which, by any provision of any of those Acts, is to be final.

(3)   Subject to the provisions of this Act and to rules of court, the High Court shall, in accordance with section 19(2), have jurisdiction to hear and determine—

(a)   any application, or any appeal (whether by way of case stated or otherwise), which it has power to hear and determine under or by virtue of this or any other Act; and

(b)   all such other appeals as it had jurisdicion to hear and determine immediately before the commencement of this Act.

Application for Judicial Review

D25.30   Section 29(3) of the Supreme Court Act 1981 allows a decision of the Crown Court to be challenged through an application for judicial review, provided it was not a decision 'relating to a trial on indictment'. Precisely the same rule applies to appeals by way of case stated from the Crown Court (see **D25.29**). In *Re Smalley* [1985] AC 622, the House of Lords considered what was meant by the phrase 'relating to a trial on indictment'. While not attempting a full definition, Lord Bridge of Harwich said that it extended beyond decisions taken during the actual course of a trial on indictment and covered all decisions 'affecting the conduct of the trial', even if taken at a pre-trial stage. Applying the guidance, it has been held (or suggested in *obiter dicta*) that:

(a)   forfeiting the recognisance of a person who stood surety for an accused who absconded,

(b)   ordering the forfeiture of property belonging to a third party that had been used by an offender in connection with an offence of which he had been convicted, and

(c)   binding over an acquitted accused to keep the peace as a measure of preventative justice,

(d)   discharging a restriction on the publication of details which might lead to the identification of a juvenile,

could all have no bearing on the actual conduct of the accused's trial, and so were open to judicial review (see *Re Smalley*; *Maidstone Crown Court, ex parte Gill* [1986] 1 WLR 1405; *Inner London Crown Court, ex parte Benjamin* (1986) 85 Cr App R 267 and *Leicester Crown Court, ex parte S (A Minor)* [1993] 1 WLR 111 respectively). As to judicial review of the decision to prosecute, see **D1.71**.

On the other hand, in *Re Ashton* [1994] 1 AC 9, the House of Lords held that an order of the Crown Court that the whole or part of an indictment should be stayed as an abuse of process was a decision 'relating to trial on indictment' under the Supreme Court Act 1981, s. 29(3), and was not amenable to judicial review. In the same way an order that counts should lie on the file marked not to be proceeded with without leave relates to the trial and is immune from review (*Central Criminal Court, ex parte Raymond* [1986] 1 WLR 710). In *Southwark Crown Court, ex parte Ward* [1996] Crim LR 123, where the applicant was charged on two indictments, the decision of the Crown Court judge that the trial on one indictment must begin before the trial on the other was said by the Divisional Court to be a matter related to trial on indictment, since it clearly affected the conduct of the trial. In *Lewes Crown Court, ex parte Sinclair* [1992] Crim LR 886, it was held that the Divisional Court had no jurisdiction to hear an appeal on the basis that the sentence had been wrongly entered by the clerk of the Crown Court on the accused's warrant of imprisonment; the correct forum for any such challenge was the Court of Appeal, since it was a matter relating to trial on indictment. It has also been doubted whether the Divisional Court has jurisdiction to review a Crown Court decision that a bill of indictment was properly preferred (see *Liverpool Crown Court, ex parte Bray* [1987] Crim LR 51). In *Chelmsford Crown Court, ex parte Chief Constable of Essex* [1994] 1 WLR 359, the Divisional Court refused judicial review of the decision of a Crown Court judge to order disclosure of certain documents to the defence. The documents were statements taken from police officers during investigations under the Police (Complaints) (Informal Resolution) Regulations 1985 (SI 1985 No. 671). The Chief Constable sought judicial review of the trial judge's decision. The Divisional Court refused on the basis that judicial review was exercisable over inferior courts, not the

Crown Court, which was a superior court of record. Section 29(3) of the Supreme Court Act 1981 did not impose a limitation on the High Court, but granted it powers it would not otherwise have had. Those powers excluded any in relation to the Crown Court's jurisdiction with respect to trial on indictment, which the decision of the trial judge was. Challenges to Crown Court decisions, save those deriving from the original decisions of magistrates, should be made to the Court of Appeal. In *Chester Crown Court, ex parte Cheshire County Council* [1996] Crim LR 336, the Divisional Court confirmed that decisions concerning disclosure relate to the trial and are excluded by s. 29(3). In so doing, their lordships rejected the applicant's argument that the statutory exclusion did not apply where it was alleged that the court did not have jurisdiction to act in the way that it did; they considered that to be a principle applicable to the inferior courts, but not to the Crown Court in relation to trial on indictment. In *Bradford Crown Court, ex parte Bottomley* [1994] Crim LR 753, the Divisional Court held that the decision whether to hold a trial on the issue of fitness to plead related to trial on indictment, and was not susceptible to judicial review.

An application for judicial review can be brought to appeal against a sentence imposed by the Crown Court in its appellate jurisdiction from the magistrates' court. The principles stated in *St Albans Crown Court, ex parte Cinnamond* [1981] QB 480 will apply if this procedure is used, in a similar manner to that where an application is made by way of case stated (see **D25.21** and **D25.29**). In *Swansea Crown Court, ex parte Davies* (1989) *The Times*, 2 May 1989, the sentence imposed by the magistrates was three months' imprisonment, suspended. On appeal to the Crown Court, an application for leave to withdraw the appeal was refused, and the sentence was varied to an immediate sentence of the same length. The Divisional Court held that, on the facts, this was a classic case for a suspended sentence. The court referred to *Ex parte Cinnamond*, in which it had been said that the question for the Divisional Court was whether the sentence was harsh and oppressive. The court ruled that the sentence in the case before it was. It was a quantum leap from that imposed by the magistrates. It so far departed from the norm as to call for the Divisional Court's intervention. In *Oxford Crown Court, ex parte Monaghan* (1999) *Independent*, 12 July 1999, the Crown Court sentenced M to four months' imprisonment for violent disorder. In passing sentence, the court mentioned factors taken into account on her behalf, but failed to mention the major part of her mitigation, which was her role in caring for her children (who were still at school, had learning difficulties and were hyperactive) and her grandchildren. The Divisional Court held that where the Crown Court had passed a sentence without making any reference to the main and decisive mitigating feature put forward by the defendant, and without giving any reasons as to why they had dealt with her in the way in which they did, the sentence was materially flawed and the High Court would have jurisdiction to intervene. The High Court therefore had jurisdiction to impose a sentence which it considered proper; in the instant case that was a conditional discharge for 12 months.

As to the effect of certiorari, see **D25.20** and the reference there to *Leeds Crown Court, ex parte Barlow* [1989] RTR 246.

NO POWER OF JUDICIAL REVIEW OVER DECISIONS OF THE HIGH COURT

There is no power to grant judicial review of any decision of a judge of the High Court. **D25.31** In *McKenzie, ex parte Raymond* (21 April 1989 unreported), it was held that an appellant in the Court of Appeal Criminal Division is not entitled to leave to apply for judicial review in respect of anything which is done by the Registrar of Criminal Appeals. The Divisional Court can exercise no jurisdiction on an application for judicial review in relation to any decision of a judge of the High Court. See also *Manchester Crown Court,* *ex parte Williams* (1990) 154 JP 589, in which it was held that the Divisional Court had no jurisdiction to review the decision of a High Court judge to issue a voluntary bill of indictment under the Administration of Justice (Miscellaneous Provisions) Act 1933.

COMPARISON OF JUDICIAL REVIEW AND CASE STATED

D25.32 The functions of mandamus and prohibition on the one hand, and appeal by case stated on the other are quite distinct. The appellant by case stated argues that the magistrates have made a mistake in exercising jurisdiction. The applicant for mandamus or prohibition argues either that the magistrates have failed to exercise their jurisdiction or that they should be prevented from exercising a jurisdiction which they do not lawfully have. Certiorari and appeal by case stated, on the other hand, serve similar purposes. The effect of both remedies is to set aside the decision of the court below, and counsel advising a person aggrieved by a decision of a magistrates' court or of the Crown Court on appeal from the magistrates may find the choice between the remedies difficult. Most of the points relevant to that choice have already been touched upon, but, in summary, the position is that:

(a) Where the magistrates or Crown Court have acted in excess of jurisdiction both certiorari and appeal by case stated are available.

(b) Where an error of law has been made, but the inferior tribunal was acting within its jurisdiction, appeal by case stated is the obvious remedy. If the error of law is patent on the face of the record of the inferior tribunal's proceedings, certiorari could also be used, but most errors of law are latent rather than patent. Only through the statement of case will the latent error be revealed.

(c) If the rules of natural justice have been broken, the appropriate remedy is certiorari. This is because the procedural irregularities which typically form the basis of an alleged breach of natural justice (e.g., a magistrate had an interest in the outcome of the proceedings or the defence was not given the opportunity to present its case properly) would not emerge from a case stated, which deals essentially with the facts the magistrates found proved and the legal issues arising from those facts.

(d) Certiorari is again the only remedy where the defence wish to quash a committal for trial or sentence. Appeal by case stated will not lie because there has not been a final determination in the case. In fact, an application for certiorari to quash a committal for trial is almost certain to fail but it is at least theoretically available. Applications to quash a committal for sentence on the basis that it was in excess of jurisdiction have a better chance of success.

(e) Where both certiorari and appeal by case stated are available the latter is preferable because it enables the facts as found by the magistrates or the Crown Court to be placed clearly before the Divisional Court, rather than relying on devices such as an affidavit from the chairman of the bench to supplement the court record (see **D25.19** and also *Ipswich Crown Court, ex parte Baldwin* [1981] 1 All ER 596 where McNeill J said of a case which 'bristled with factual difficulties' that the only 'convenient and proper way' to have brought it before the Divisional Court would have been to have appealed by case stated – Baldwin was criticised for applying for judicial review).

Nevertheless, a decision of the magistrates may be challenged on appropriate grounds by way of judicial review, even where an applicant also has the right to apply to the justices to state a case (*Hereford Magistrates' Court, ex parte Rowlands* [1998] QB 110).

SECTION D26: APPEAL TO THE HOUSE OF LORDS, THE EUROPEAN COURT OF JUSTICE, THE EUROPEAN CONVENTION ON HUMAN RIGHTS, FREE PARDON

APPEAL TO THE HOUSE OF LORDS

From the Court of Appeal (Criminal Division)

Either the prosecution or defence may appeal to the House of Lords from a decision of **D26.1** the Criminal Division of the Court of Appeal, but the appeal is subject to:

(a)   the Court of Appeal certifying that the decision which it is sought to appeal involves a point of law of general public importance, and
(b)   either the Court of Appeal or the House of Lords giving leave to appeal because it appears to them that the point of law is one which ought to be considered by the House.

An application to the Court of Appeal for leave to appeal to the House of Lords should either be made orally immediately after the court's decision, or it should be made within 14 days of the decision, notice of the application being served on the Registrar in the prescribed form. There is no appeal against a refusal by the Court of Appeal to certify that a point of law of general public importance is involved (*Gelberg* v *Miller* [1961] 1 WLR 459); nor is it the practice of the court to give reasons for such a refusal (*Cooper* (1975) 61 Cr App R 215). If the Court of Appeal is willing to certify that a point of law of general public importance is involved, but nevertheless refuses leave to appeal, an application may be made to the House of Lords within 14 days of the Court of Appeal's refusal. Such applications are referred to an appeal committee consisting of three Lords of Appeal. If leave to appeal is granted at least three Law Lords must be present for the hearing (Criminal Appeal Act 1968, s. 35) but it is usual to have five deciding the case. In disposing of the appeal, the House of Lords may exercise any powers of the Court of Appeal or remit the case to it (s. 35(3)).

Criminal Appeal Act 1968, ss. 33 and 34

33.—(1)   An appeal lies to the House of Lords, at the instance of the defendant or the prosecutor, from any decision of the Court of Appeal on an appeal to that court under part I of this act or section 9 (preparatory hearings) of the Criminal Justice Act 1987.
(2)   The appeal lies only with the leave of the Court of Appeal or the House of Lords; and leave shall not be granted unless it is certified by the Court of Appeal that a point of law of general public importance is involved in the decision and it appears to the Court of Appeal or the House of Lords (as the case may be) that the point is one which ought to be considered by that House.
(3)   Except as provided by this part of this Act and section 13 of the Administration of Justice Act 1960 (appeal in cases of contempt of court), no appeal shall lie from any decision of the criminal division of the Court of Appeal.

34.—(1)   An application to the Court of Appeal for leave to appeal to the House of Lords shall be made within the period of 14 days beginning with the date of the decision of the court; and an application to the House of Lords for leave shall be made within the period of 14 days beginning with the date on which the application for leave is refused by the Court of Appeal.
(2)   The House of Lords or the Court of Appeal may, upon application made at any time by the defendant, extend the time within which an application may be made by him to that House or the court under subsection (1) above.

(3)   An appeal to the House of Lords shall be treated as pending until any application for leave to appeal is disposed of and, if leave to appeal is granted, until the appeal is disposed of; and for purposes of this part of this Act an application for leave to appeal shall be treated as disposed of at the expiration of the time within which it may be made, if it is not made within that time.

It sometimes happens that a number of grounds of appeal are argued before the Court of Appeal, but that court reaches a clear conclusion upon one ground which determines the case so that it is unnecessary to decide the others. This can give rise to a difficulty if the issue decided by the Court of Appeal is taken to the House of Lords on appeal and the appeal succeeds. What should then happen in relation to those grounds which the Court of Appeal did not consider? In *Mandair* [1995] 1 AC 208, the House of Lords held that it had the power either to remit the matter to the Court of Appeal or itself exercise the powers of the Court of Appeal in relation to the matters which had not been decided. The Lord Chancellor, Lord Mackay, added that, when an appeal was being prepared for the House of Lords, it was necessary that the statement of facts and issues should state plainly whether any grounds of appeal had been undetermined by the Court of Appeal. In their written cases, parties should include submissions on those grounds and on how the House of Lords should dispose of them (see also **D22.13**).

The Court of Appeal may, under the Criminal Appeal Act 1968, s. 36, grant an appellant bail pending determination of his appeal to the House of Lords, subject to the limitations in rape and homicide cases laid down by the CJPO 1994, s. 25 (see **D5.10**). If the prosecution are appealing to the House of Lords against the Court of Appeal's decision to allow an appeal and, but for his successful appeal, the appellant in the Court of Appeal would be liable to be detained in pursuance of a custodial sentence, the Court of Appeal may order that he be detained until the appeal is decided (s. 37). Alternatively, the Court of Appeal may order that he be released on bail instead of being released unconditionally, which would, of course, be the normal consequence of his having his conviction quashed. If the court chooses neither to order continued detention nor to release on bail but allows unconditional release, the appellant is not liable to serve the remainder of his custodial sentence even if the House of Lords restores the conviction.

Directions issued by the House of Lords as to the procedure applicable to criminal appeals are contained in the booklet *House of Lords: Practice Directions Applicable to Criminal Appeals* (March 1995), which should be consulted by any practitioner pursuing an appeal to the House of Lords. It is available from the Judicial Office of the House of Lords (telephone 0171–219 3111). Broadly, it is divided into three sections:

(a)   Directions 1 to 7 deal with Petitions for Leave to Appeal, covering matters such as the certificate of point of law, time limits, lodgment of the petition, the Appeal Committee, costs and fees.

(b)   Directions 8 to 23 deal with various aspects of the appeal itself.

(c)   Directions 24 to 30 deal with miscellaneous matters such as legal aid and bail.

There are Appendices which contain the forms for various petitions and information as to the copies of documents required and authorities provided.

The directions deal with some aspects of procedure in great detail, for example, the precise form in which documentation is to be lodged before the House. There are certain points, however, which are in need of emphasis or comment:

(a)   Before any application for leave to appeal may be lodged, the certificate required by statute (that a point of law of general public importance is involved) must be granted by the court below (see direction 2 and 5(2)(c)).

(b)   The next stage is the petition for leave to appeal. This is, of course, necessary only where leave has been refused by the court below. The application is referred to an

Appeal Committee (three of the Lords of Appeal). That committee will decide whether the petition for leave should be (i) dismissed, (ii) allowed or (iii) referred for an oral hearing. If the Appeal Committee is unanimously of the view that the petition should not be allowed, then it is dismissed. If they are unanimously in favour of granting leave, then the respondent is given an opportunity to make written submissions within 14 days, after which the Appeal Committee will decide on the papers whether to grant leave. If the members of the Appeal Committee are not unanimous, then the petition for leave is referred to an oral hearing. If there is an oral hearing, only one counsel on each side is heard (direction 5).

(c)   If the petition for leave to appeal is granted (or leave was granted by the court below) then the appeal itself will in due course be argued, usually by two counsel on either side. The appeal will be determined according to the test laid down in the Criminal Appeal Act 1968, s. 2. It is not sufficient for the appellant to show that the Court of Appeal has erred in its approach. On an appeal against conviction, for example, the House of Lords must decide whether the conviction was unsafe (*Stafford v DPP* [1974] AC 878 at pp. 893–4). It appears that the appellant can raise matters unrelated to the point of law certified by the court below as being of public importance (*A-G for Northern Ireland v Gallagher* [1963] AC 349 at pp. 365–6, 370 and 383). It seems, however, that where a certificate of appeal on conviction has been given, argument in relation to sentence cannot be heard (*Jones v DPP* [1962] AC 635).

(d)   The House of Lords does not grant bail or legal aid. As far as bail is concerned, that is a matter for the court below. So is legal aid, in respect of appeals from the Court of Appeal. As far as appeals from the Divisional Court (and applications relating thereto) are concerned, application for legal aid should be made to the area office of the Legal Aid Board (directions 24 and 27).

From a Divisional Court of the Queen's Bench Division

The decision of a Divisional Court of the Queen's Bench Division in a criminal cause **D26.2** or matter may be appealed to the House of Lords (Administration of Justice Act 1960, s. 1(1)(a)). The circumstances in which the appeal will lie are analogous to those in which an appeal lies from the Criminal Division of the Court of Appeal to the House of Lords — i.e. the Divisional Court must certify that there is a point of law of general public importance involved, and either the Divisional Court or the House of Lords must grant leave to appeal.

By contrast with the rule governing appeals against their civil decisions, the decision of the Divisional Court in a criminal case may only be appealed to the House of Lords. There is no intermediate right of appeal to the Court of Appeal (Supreme Court Act 1981, s. 18(1)). However, some decisions which are incidentally connected with criminal proceedings are nonetheless classified as being civil in nature so that s. 18(1) does not apply. Thus, in *Southampton Justices, ex parte Green* [1976] QB 11, the Court of Appeal held that it had jurisdiction to entertain an appeal against the Divisional Court's refusal to quash by *certiorari* an order by magistrates forfeiting a surety's recognisance. Although the order against Green would not have been made if there had not been criminal proceedings against the person for whom she was a surety, the order in itself did not and could not result in her being prosecuted for a criminal offence. Therefore, any decisions by the Divisional Court relating to that order were not in a criminal cause.

Where a lower court's order was connected with but not actually made in the course of a criminal trial, it is sometimes difficult to know whether the Divisional Court's decision to grant or not to grant judicial review of that order should be regarded as a decision in a criminal cause or matter (appeal only to the House of Lords) or a 'non-criminal' decision (appeal initially to the Court of Appeal). In *Southampton Justices, ex parte Green*,

Lord Denning MR gave a narrow interpretation of 'criminal decision', restricting the phrase to decisions where the order under review might have led to the prosecution and punishment of the subject thereof. While the actual decision is accepted as being correct, Lord Denning's definition is almost certainly too narrow. Thus, in *Secretary of State for the Home Department, ex parte Dannenberg* [1984] QB 766, the Court of Appeal held that appeal against the Divisional Court's refusal to quash by *certiorari* a recommendation for deportation made by magistrates when dealing with D for offences of theft and fraud lay only to the House of Lords, even though the recommendations could not have entailed the prosecution of D for any offence and so (according to Lord Denning) he should have been able to take the matter to the Court of Appeal. An earlier definition of 'criminal decision', to which the courts now seem to be reverting, was given by Lord Wright in *Amand* v *Home Secretary* [1943] AC 147. Lord Wright said that the Divisional Court's decision is in a criminal cause or matter if the order to which the decision relates was made in the course of criminal proceedings, irrespective of whether it might have entailed criminal sanctions for its subject. In line with this definition, it was held in *Carr* v *Atkins* [1987] QB 963 that refusal of *certiorari* to quash an order for production of special procedure material was a decision in a criminal cause since the original Crown Court order was 'made in a criminal context', albeit that no criminal proceedings were in existence when the order was made and disobedience to the order could only have involved civil proceedings for contempt not criminal sanctions.

THE EUROPEAN COURT OF JUSTICE

D26.3 Any English court, whether civil or criminal, may request a preliminary ruling on a point of European law which arises in proceedings before it. The point is then referred for a preliminary ruling to the European Court of Justice.

Provision for such references is made in Art. 177 of the European Economic Community Treaty (the Treaty of Rome); there are equivalent provisions in Art. 150 of the Euratom Treaty and Art. 41 of the European Coal and Steel Community Treaty. Article 177 gives jurisdiction to the European Court of Justice, for example, to give rulings concerning the interpretation of the treaty itself, and of the validity and interpretation of the acts of its institutions.

The European Court of Justice cannot rule on the facts of the case before the national court, nor can it rule on the validity of national law and its compatibility with Community law. All these are matters for the national court to decide. The question which is referred to the European Court of Justice therefore has to be formulated in an abstract manner.

Article 177 distinguishes between courts which are obliged to refer questions of European law to the European Court of Justice, and those which merely have a discretion so to do. Where it is a court 'against whose decisions there is no judicial remedy under national law', then 'that court . . . *shall* bring the matter before the [European] Court of Justice' (emphasis added). Hence, in a criminal matter, reference of a point of European law would be the obligatory course for the House of Lords. Other criminal courts, however, have a discretion whether to refer a point of Community law: 'Where such a question is raised before any court . . . that court . . . may, if it considers that a decision on the question is necessary to enable it to give judgment, request the [European] Court of Justice to give a ruling thereon'.

Leaving aside the position of the House of Lords, then, an English criminal court has power to refer a point of European law to the European Court of Justice if a preliminary ruling is necessary before it can give judgment in the case before it. In *Plymouth Justices, ex parte Rogers* [1982] QB 863, it was confirmed that magistrates have such a discretion and that the Divisional Court will not interfere with their decision to refer unless they misdirect themselves or act unreasonably. The accused in that case was charged with using a type of fishing net allegedly in contravention of EU regulations. The thrust of his case was that the regulations were invalid as a matter of EU law. His counsel submitted that the effect of the regulations should be referred to the European Court of Justice for a preliminary ruling, and that the proceedings should be adjourned for that purpose. The justices decided to adjourn so that the reference could be made. The prosecution applied to the Divisional Court for judicial review on the ground, *inter alia*, that the justices had erred in law in ordering questions to be referred before all the facts had been determined (the adjournment had been granted after argument at the close of the prosecution case). The Divisional Court dismissed the application. The magistrates had jurisdiction to refer the question of validity to the European Court of Justice even if all the facts had not been admitted. However, the Divisional Court said (at p. 871) that, ordinarily:

> . . . justices should exercise considerable caution before referring [a case to the European Court] even after they have heard all the evidence. If they come to a wrong decision on Community law, a higher court can make the reference and frequently the higher court would be the more suitable forum to do so. The higher court is as a rule in a better position to assess whether any reference is desirable. On references the form of the question referred is of importance and the higher court will normally be in a better position to assess the appropriateness of the question and to assist in formulating it clearly. Leaving it to the higher court will often also avoid delay.

In *Ex parte Rogers*, the Divisional Court was influenced by the consideration that it was only in a technical sense that there was an issue of fact between prosecution and defence. The only real issue before the court was the validity of the regulations. If there had been any live prospect of an acquittal on the facts, then no doubt the decision of the magistrates would have been much more difficult to sustain. On the facts, however, their exercise of the discretion conferred by Art. 177 of the Treaty was upheld.

The exercise of such a discretion by the Crown Court came under scrutiny in *Henn v DPP* [1981] AC 850. H and D imported pornographic articles of Danish origin into England from Holland. They were charged, *inter alia*, with fraudulently evading the prohibition on the importation of indecent or obscene articles, contrary to the Customs Consolidation Act 1876, s. 42, and the Customs and Excise Act 1952, s. 304 (now Customs and Excise Management Act 1979, s. 170). At their trial, it was submitted that the prohibition in question was contrary to Arts. 30 and 36 of the Treaty of Rome. The judge was asked to refer the point to the European Court of Justice for a preliminary ruling but refused. Both were convicted and appealed to the Court of Appeal, which dismissed the appeal. The Court of Appeal refused leave to refer the matter to the European Court of Justice on the ground that the relevant provisions of the Treaty were too plain to raise the need for interpretation. While refusing leave to appeal to the House of Lords, the Court of Appeal certified a point of law of general importance, i.e. whether s. 42 of the 1876 Act was effective to prevent the importation of pornographic articles from Holland, notwithstanding Arts. 30 and 36 of the Treaty of Rome. The House of Lords granted leave to appeal and referred to the European Court of Justice for a preliminary ruling a series of related questions, dealing with the validity of the prohibition in the light of Arts. 30 and 36. In brief, the European Court of Justice held that the terms of Art. 36 meant that a Member State could lawfully impose prohibitions on the importation of goods on grounds of public morality. In line with this ruling, the House of Lords dismissed the appeal. Lord Diplock said ([1981] AC 850 at p. 904):

> . . . in a criminal trial upon indictment it can seldom be a proper exercise of the presiding judge's discretion to seek a preliminary ruling before the facts of the alleged offence have been ascertained, with the result that the proceedings will be held up for nine months or

more in order that at the end of the trial he may give to the jury an accurate instruction as to the relevant law, if the evidence turns out in the event to be as was anticipated at the time the reference was made – which may not always be the case. It is generally better, as the judge himself put it, that the question be decided by him in the first instance and reviewed thereafter if necessary through the hierarchy of the national courts.

Apparently, then, their lordships did not take the view that the trial judge should have sought a preliminary ruling from the European Court of Justice. The case is also instructive for the warning which it issues about an easy assumption that European law on a particular point is obvious. The position generally is that no reference should be made to the European Court of Justice if the European provision in question is clear and obvious, and the court is free from doubt about its meaning. In *Henn,* the Court of Appeal ([1978] 1 WLR 1031) doubted whether an absolute prohibition on a particular import fell within the ambit of Art. 30 at all. Lord Diplock in the House of Lords indicated that he took a view which was diametrically opposed to the Court of Appeal on this point – he was in no doubt that the prohibition *was* within the ambit of Art. 30. This, he said, 'serves as a timely warning to English judges not to be too ready to hold that because the meaning of the English text (which is one of six of equal authority) seems plain to them no question of interpretation can be involved' ([1981] AC 850 at p. 906). In the event, the European Court of Justice held, contrary to the Court of Appeal's view, that the prohibition fell within the scope of Art. 30. Nonetheless, it came to the same conclusion as the Court of Appeal by finding that such a prohibition could be justified on grounds of public morality.

As far as the procedure for a preliminary ruling is concerned:

(a)   the national court makes the reference;
(b)   pending the ruling by the European Court of Justice, the national proceedings are suspended;
(c)   after the ruling is made, the national court applies it to the case and continues to judgment. The procedure is dealt with, so far as the Crown Court is concerned, by the Crown Court Rules 1982, r. 29, and in the Court of Appeal by the Criminal Appeal (References to the European Court) Rules 1972 (SI 1972 No. 1786).

Treaty of Rome, Article 177

The Court of Justice shall have jurisdiction to give preliminary ruling concerning:
(a)   the interpretation of this Treaty;
(b)   the validity and interpretation of acts of the institutions of the Community;
(c)   the interpretation of the statutes of bodies established by an act of the Council, where those statutes so provide.
Where such a question is raised before any court or tribunal of a member State, that court or tribunal may, if it considers that a decision on the question is necessary to enable it to give judgment, request the Court of Justice to give a ruling thereon.
Where any such question is raised in a case pending before a court or tribunal of a member State, against whose decisions there is no judicial remedy under national law, that court or tribunal shall bring the matter before the Court of Justice.

THE EUROPEAN CONVENTION ON HUMAN RIGHTS

D26.4   The Convention for the Protection of Human Rights and Fundamental Freedoms (the European Convention on Human Rights) was signed in 1950, and came into force in 1953. It was produced by the Council of Europe, of which the United Kingdom was one of the original ten members (now considerably expanded), in the aftermath of the Second World War and the Nuremberg Trials. There is of course no direct connection between the Council of Europe and the European Union. Like the European Union, the Council of Europe has a Court, which is based in Strasbourg. The European Court of Justice (see **D26.3**) has at times relied on the European Convention as an influence on the general principles of EU law, but the Convention has no formal role in determining EU law.

The European Convention is an international treaty to which the United Kingdom is a signatory, and it is binding on all its signatories in international law. In some Member States of the Council of Europe, the Convention has been made a directly enforceable part of the domestic legal system, but that has not hitherto been the case in the United Kingdom. The position will, however, change radically once the provisions of the Human Rights Act 1998 are brought into force. Although the legislation received the Royal Assent in November 1998, it is not expected to be implemented until October 2000. Its most important provisions are summarised at the end of this section. Extracts from the Convention and part of the Act's text are reproduced in **appendix** 7. Even without that legislation, however, the Convention may be relied upon in the interpretation of statute law, in line with the general statutory principle that Parliament does not intend to legislate contrary to the country's international treaty obligations. This involves using the Convention as an aid to interpretation, rather than recognising the creation of new rights which appear in it but which Parliament has not intended to implement (see *Secretary of State for the Home Department, ex parte Brind* [1991] 1 AC 696). As far as the common law is concerned, the position would appear to be similar in that, where the law is either unclear or ambiguous, or concerns an issue not yet ruled on, the courts ought to consider the implications of the Convention (*Derby County Council* v *Times Newspapers* [1992] QB 770).

Until the Human Rights Act 1998 is enacted, however, it is not possible for an individual to complain of a breach of the Convention before an English court. In the event of such a breach, the person aggrieved has the right of individual petition — a right which will remain in force once the Human Rights Act 1998 is implemented. Until November 1998, complaints about the breach of the provisions of the Convention were received and examined by the Commission, which acted as a filtering mechanism, referring appropriate cases to the European Court of Human Rights for a decision. Protocol No. 11 to the Convention, which came into effect on 1 November 1998, did away with the part-time Commission and Court, and replaced them with a single Court which sits full-time in Strasbourg.

For a complaint to be admissible, the applicant must have exhausted all domestic remedies and presented the petition within six months of the final decision reached through the pursuit of those remedies. In addition, the petition must raise a matter which is not substantially the same as one already ruled on by the Commission or the Court, and must not have been submitted to 'another procedure of international investigation or settlement' (Art. 27(1)). Further, the Court will rule inadmissible any application 'incompatible with the provisions' of the Convention, 'manifestly ill-founded', or 'an abuse of the right of petition' (Art. 27(2)).

As far as the requirement that the applicant exhaust domestic remedies is concerned, certain remedies may not be regarded as normal, e.g., an application for habeas corpus is not considered as part of the normal appeal procedure (*X* v *UK* (1969) 12 Yearbook 298). Further, there is no obligation to pursue remedies which clearly offer no chance of success. Where an appeal would clearly fail because there is a binding domestic precedent which stands in the way of the applicant, then the case does not have to be pursued all the way to the House of Lords.

The six-month period within which the petition must be brought begins with the date when the final decision is taken (Art. 26). This has been defined as 'the date of a "final decision" taken in the exhaustion of an effective and sufficient domestic remedy, or from the date of the act or decision complained of where such an act or decision finally determines the applicant's position on the domestic level' (*Greenock Ltd* v *UK* (1985) 42 DJR 33 at p. 41). Time will usually cease to run on the date of the first letter to the Court indicating an intention to lodge an application and the nature of the complaint (*Kelly* v *UK* (1985) 42 DR 205), but the Court may look at the circumstances of the case to decide on the relevant date (e.g., where pursuit of the case has been unreasonably delayed). Where the breach of the Convention is a continuing one, then time will not begin to run until the continuing state of affairs ceases to exist (*Temple* v *UK* (1985) 8 EHRR 319).

The procedure is in the main written, affidavits and other documents being filed with the Court in compliance with time limits. A date is fixed for a public oral hearing, in which the applicant, although not strictly a party to the proceedings, is in practice allowed to participate, represented by an advocate. The final judgment of the Court is by a majority, and dissenting judgments are common. It has the power to order a state which is in breach of the Convention to make just compensation (Art. 50). In addition, a judgment finding that a state' s laws are in breach of the Convention imposes a duty on the state in question to rectify the law.

The content of the European Convention is largely concerned with basic personal freedoms. The part most directly relevant to the criminal justice process is Art. 6, which contains a broad statement of the right to a fair trial. Cases in which the United Kingdom has been involved in alleged breaches of this and other articles relevant to criminal practice are detailed in specialist works on the Convention, to which further reference should be made (e.g., *The UK Before the European Court of Human Rights: Case Law and Commentary*, Farran, Blackstone Press, 1996 and *Law of the European Convention on Human Rights*, Harris, O'Boyle and Warbrick, Butterworths, 1995).

The position relating to enforcement of the Convention will alter drastically when the Human Rights Act 1998 is brought into effect, as is expected in October 2000. The Act gives effect to most of the important Articles in the Convention, including Art. 6 and others of relevance to criminal law and procedure. Its implementation will mean that the courts, including the criminal courts, will have to take account of relevant judgments, decisions, declarations and opinions made or given by the Commission or the European Court of Human Rights, or the Committee of Ministers. Any legislation, whether primary or subordinate, will have to be read if possible in a way which is compatible with Convention rights. If that is not possible, the House of Lords, the Court of Appeal or the High Court may make a 'declaration of incompatibility'. The Bill makes it unlawful for a public authority (defined so as to include a court) to act in a way incompatible with the rights under the Convention, unless it is bound to act in the way it did by primary legislation. Where legislation has been declared incompatible or appears to be so, the government may amend it by a remedial order so as to remove incompatibility, using the affirmative resolution procedure.

FREE PARDON

D26.5 The modern practice is to grant pardons after conviction and sentence when it becomes tolerably plain that the convicted person was in fact innocent. In *Secretary of State for the Home Department, ex parte Bentley* [1993] 4 All ER 442, it was stated on behalf of the Home Secretary that the basis for the grant of a free pardon was that the moral as well as the technical innocence of the convicted person could be established. The pardon is granted by the Crown, on the advice of the Home Secretary, in exercise of the royal prerogative of mercy. However, the effect of the pardon is not to quash the conviction or even expressly to acknowledge that the pardoned person did not commit the crime. It merely, to use the words of the pardon itself, releases the recipient from 'all pains penalties and punishments whatsoever that from the said conviction may ensue'. Since he still stands convicted, it is open to a pardoned offender to appeal to the Court of Appeal to have the conviction quashed (*Foster* [1985] QB 115). Indeed, in the eyes of the law, the pardoned person's name is not cleared until that has happened. In view of the establishment of the Criminal Cases Review Commission (see **D24.1**), it may well be that the jurisdiction of that body proves more attractive to those seeking to remedy a perceived miscarriage of justice.

In cases where the Home Secretary is not prepared to recommend a pardon, but the doubts about the offender's conviction are too great for his continued detention to be justified, the intermediate solution of remitting the remainder of his sentence may be adopted.

SECTION D27: LEGAL AID AND COSTS

D27.1　This section deals with the financing of criminal proceedings through orders for legal aid and costs. Subject to one very minor exception, legal aid is available solely for the defence. Orders for costs, depending on the outcome of the proceedings, may be made in favour of either side and may come either out of central funds or from the losing party.

STRUCTURE OF LEGAL AID IN CRIMINAL PROCEEDINGS

Scheme of the Legal Aid Act 1988

The primary source of the law on legal aid is the Legal Aid Act 1988, which is divided into eight parts, as follows:

Part I (ss. 1 and 2)	Introductory, dealing principally with definitions of terms used in the Act.
Part II (ss. 3 to 7)	Creation, powers and duties of the Legal Aid Board.
Part III (ss. 8 to 13)	Legal aid for advice and assistance.
Part IV (ss. 14 to 18)	Legal aid in civil proceedings.
Part V (ss. 19 to 26)	Legal aid in criminal proceedings.
Part VI (ss. 29 and 30)	Legal aid in special cases (i.e. contempt proceedings; ss. 27 and 28 have been repealed).
Part VII and VIII (ss. 31 to 47)	General and supplementary, and miscellaneous.

In numerous respects, the Legal Aid Act 1988 is supplemented by regulations made by the Lord Chancellor in exercise of powers given him by the Act. Any reference in the Act to regulations is to be construed as being a reference to regulations so made (s. 43). Proposed regulations are subject to annulment by resolution of either House of Parliament (s. 36(3)). The regulations of principal relevance to legal aid for criminal proceedings are:

　(a)　The Legal Aid in Criminal and Care Proceedings (General) Regulations 1989 (SI 1989 No. 344), which will be referred to as the 'General Regulations'.

　(b)　The Legal Aid in Criminal and Care Proceedings (Costs) Regulations 1989 (SI 1989 No. 343).

　(c)　The Legal Advice and Assistance Regulations 1989 (SI 1989 No. 340), which will be referred to as the 'Advice and Assistance Regulations'.

　(d)　The Legal Advice and Assistance (Duty Solicitor) (Remuneration) Regulations 1989 (SI 1989 No. 341).

Only part V of the Legal Aid Act 1988 (legal aid in criminal proceedings) will be considered in detail in this work. However, brief mention of the other parts is necessary in order to set part V in context.

The Legal Aid Board (Legal Aid Act 1988, Part II)

D27.2　The Legal Aid Board was created by the Legal Aid Act 1988. It consists of not less than 11 and not more than 17 members appointed by the Lord Chancellor (s. 3(5)). The membership must include at least two solicitors and two barristers (s. 3(7) and (8)). The Board's general function is to oversee the working of the Act and to ensure that 'advice, assistance and representation are available in accordance with' its provisions (s. 3(2)). Insofar as legal aid is not available under the arrangements set out in parts III, IV and V of the Act, the Board, acting under the authority of directions from the Lord Chancellor, may directly arrange for its provision (s. 4(1)). In so doing, it is not limited to providing the necessary aid through counsel or solicitors but may use other persons or bodies suitably qualified or experienced in the particular field of law in question, again subject to directions from the Lord Chancellor (see s. 2(6)). By contrast advice, assistance and representation under the remainder of the Act, in particular, parts III and V which are of primary relevance to criminal proceedings, must be by solicitors and/or counsel.

The broad generality of the Board's role as described above is somewhat restricted by s. 3(4) of the Act. This precludes it from exercising certain functions, including 'functions as respects representation under part V (criminal legal aid), other than determination of the costs of representation for the purposes of proceedings in magistrates' courts' (s. 3(4)(b)). The effect of s. 3(4)(b) is that the granting of legal aid for representation in criminal proceedings (whether in the magistrates' courts, Crown Court or Court of Appeal) remains solely the responsibility of the courts themselves, and is not a matter in which the Board may interfere (save that regs 15 to 17 of the General Regulations provide that, in certain circumstances, a refusal of legal aid by a magistrates' court may be reviewed by an area committee of the Legal Aid Board).

The determination of the costs properly payable out of the legal aid fund is also a matter for the courts (i.e. its authorised officers) where the proceedings for which legal aid was granted were in the Crown Court or Court of Appeal. Where, however, legal aid was granted for magistrates' courts proceedings it is the Board which determines costs.

By reg. 4 of the Civil Legal Aid (General) Regulations 1989 (SI 1989 No. 339), the Board is required to divide the country into 'legal aid areas' and appoint for each area an 'area director' and 'area committee'. The committees and directors exercise the powers conferred on them by the Board. Thus, bills of costs for legally aided work done in the magistrates' courts are submitted to the appropriate committee, which then processes the claim through its administrative and support staff. Area committees are also responsible for the hearing of applications for review where legal aid has been refused for proceedings in a magistrates' court in respect of an indictable offence.

Advice and Assistance (Legal Aid Act 1988, Part III)

Part III of the Legal Aid Act 1988 provides for legal aid under what is commonly known **D27.3** as the 'green form scheme'. Subject to means, a person is entitled to legal aid for 'advice and assistance'. These are defined respectively as:

(a) 'oral or written advice on the application of English law to any particular circumstances that have arisen in relation to the person seeking the advice and as to the steps which that person might appropriately take having regard to the application of English law to those circumstances' (Legal Aid Act 1988, s. 2(2)), and

(b) 'assistance in taking any of the steps which a person might take, including steps with respect to proceedings, having regard to the application of English law to any particular circumstances that have arisen in relation to him, whether by taking such steps on his behalf (including assistance by way of representation) or by assisting him in taking them on his own behalf (Legal Aid Act 1988, s. 2(3)).

Although 'assistance' is thus defined so as to include representation in court, s. 9(3) qualifies that broad definition by providing that 'assistance by way of representation under this part shall not be given without the approval of the Board'. Moreover, s. 8(2) states that part III only applies to assistance by way of representation 'if, and to the extent that, regulations so provide'.

Advice and assistance under the Act must generally be provided by a solicitor or barrister (s. 2(6)). The cost of the advice and assistance must not exceed a prescribed limit, fixed by the Lord Chancellor in regulations (for details, see reg. 4 of the Advice and Assistance Regulations which operates by reference to sch. 1 to the Legal Aid in Criminal and Care Proceedings (Costs) Regulations 1989). The Board has power to approve the exceeding of the normal limit in particular cases. The general purpose of part III is to make available (subject to means) preliminary legal advice and assistance from a solicitor on a broad range of legal questions, including actual or potential criminal proceedings against the person seeking aid. For the operation of the duty solicitor scheme (under which not only advice and assistance but also a limited degree of representation may be provided for accused persons appearing unrepresented in magistrates' courts), see **D27.5**.

Civil Legal Aid (Legal Aid Act 1988, Part IV)

D27.4   Legal aid may be granted by the Legal Aid Board, *inter alia*, for representation at proceedings in or before the House of Lords, Court of Appeal or High Court (Legal Aid Act 1988, s. 14(1) and sch. 2, part I). This does not apply if representation before those courts is available under part V of the Act (the criminal legal aid scheme). Obviously aid for the great bulk of criminal proceedings is catered for under the criminal scheme. However, that scheme does not extend to proceedings in the High Court, even when those proceedings arise out of criminal proceedings in a lower court. Thus, appeals by way of case stated against conviction or sentence in the magistrates' court or against the Crown Court's decision on appeal from the magistrates, applications for judicial review in similar matters, and applications to a High Court judge in chambers for bail are all outside the ambit of part V. The same applies to appeals to the House of Lords against the High Court's decision in the above categories of proceedings. There is also a small minority of matters connected with criminal proceedings which are nonetheless treated as being civil in nature, so that appeal from a High Court decision in such a case goes to the Civil Division of the Court of Appeal, rather than going direct to the House of Lords (e.g., decisions concerning the estreating of a surety's recognisance). Legal aid in the Court of Appeal (Civil Division) cannot be granted under the criminal scheme, even if the cause is loosely linked to criminal proceedings but, in all the above cases, application may be made to the appropriate area committee for the provision of representation under part IV. The procedure for applying, which is the same as for applying in ordinary civil matters, is outside the scope of this work. It should be noted, however, that there is a major limitation on the availability of aid under part IV which does not apply under part V, namely, that the applicant must satisfy the Legal Aid Board that he has reasonable grounds for taking, defending or being a party to the proceedings (s. 15(2)). Thus, it is to the advantage of a person seeking legal aid for criminal proceedings to be able to bring himself within the ordinary criminal legal aid scheme, rather than having to rely on aid under part IV.

The Duty Solicitor Scheme

D27.5   The details of the duty solicitor scheme are beyond the scope of this work. In outline, the purpose of the scheme is to make legal advice and assistance —including a limited degree of assistance by way of representation (ABWOR) – available at magistrates' courts for accused persons who do not have a solicitor to act for them, especially if it is their first appearance in the proceedings in question or they are in custody. By reg. 7 of the Advice and Assistance Regulations, the Board may make arrangements for solicitors designated by the Board to attend at magistrates' courts to provide advice, assistance and representation under a duty solicitor scheme. Solicitors who participate attend at court on a rota basis. The regulations permit them to represent an accused (as opposed to merely advising and assisting him) for the purposes of:

(a)   making a bail application;
(b)   making a plea in mitigation for an accused in custody who wishes to plead guilty and have his case dealt with forthwith, or

(c)   acting as in (b) for an accused who is not in custody but, in the opinion of the solicitor, requires ABWOR.

ABWOR under the duty solicitor scheme may be given only if the client has not previously received it under the scheme and is not otherwise legally represented (i.e. has neither instructed a solicitor privately nor been assigned one under the ordinary criminal legal aid scheme). Moreover, the scheme is subject to the major limitation that it does not extend to (a) committal proceedings; (b) summary trials at which the accused pleads not guilty, or (c) any proceedings for a non-imprisonable offence unless the solicitor considers the circumstances exceptional. Whether or not it is a case in which the duty solicitor will ultimately be able to represent an accused under the scheme, he may – under the scheme – give advice to any accused in custody who asks for it, give advice to an accused not in custody if the solicitor thinks it is required, or assist the accused in making a legal aid application which will enable him to be represented under the ordinary scheme at subsequent hearings. Advice, assistance or ABWOR provided under the duty solicitor scheme is not subject to means and no contribution to the costs of it may be required (regs 7(2) and 8(2) of the Advice and Assistance Regulations). The scope of aid that may be provided is set out in the Legal Advice and Assistance (Scope) Regulations 1989 (SI 1989 No. 550).

In addition to dealing with advice etc. at a magistrates' court, the Advice and Assistance Regulations make provision for the giving of advice and assistance to arrested persons in detention at a police station (see reg. 6). Rota schemes set up by the Board ensure that a solicitor will always be available to attend at a police station should he be summoned (see reg. 6(3)). Provision of aid is not subject to means or a contribution (regs 6(4) and 9(2)).

Jurisdiction to Grant Legal Aid in Criminal Proceedings

Legal aid in criminal proceedings is dealt with in part V (ss. 19 to 26) of the Legal Aid **D27.6** Act 1988. Part V applies to criminal proceedings before a magistrates' court, the Crown Court, the Criminal Division of the Court of Appeal and the House of Lords when hearing appeals from the Criminal Division (Legal Aid Act 1988, s. 19(1)). Unlike civil legal aid (which is granted or withheld by committees set up by the Legal Aid Board), jurisdiction to grant criminal legal aid vests in the courts themselves. Section 20 confers power to grant legal aid as follows:

(a)   The court before which the proceedings take place, or are to take place, is always competent to grant legal aid (save only that legal aid for an appeal to the House of Lords may be granted only by the Court of Appeal and not by the House itself) (s. 20(2)).

(b)   A magistrates' court may grant legal aid for proceedings before the Crown Court when the magistrates' court is (i) transferring or committing for trial or committing for sentence, or (ii) has been given notice of transfer under the CJA 1987, s. 4, in respect of a serious or complex fraud case, or (iii) is having a conviction and/or sentence recorded or imposed by itself appealed to the Crown Court (s. 20(4)).

(c)   A magistrates' court inquiring into an offence as examining justices may grant legal aid for the anticipated Crown Court trial even before it has decided to commit (s. 20(5)). The effect of this is that a magistrates' court dealing with an offence triable only on indictment may make a 'through legal aid order' (i.e. an order that the accused shall have legal aid both for the magistrates' court proceedings and, if he should be committed, for the trial itself). Usually, however, magistrates grant legal aid in two stages, by (i) making an initial order to cover proceedings up to and including committal and (ii) extending that order to cover the Crown Court proceedings immediately after they have decided to commit.

(d)   The Crown Court may grant legal aid for appeals (or applications for leave to appeal) to the Court of Appeal against its own ruling during a preparatory hearing in a serious fraud case (s. 20(6)).

(e)   The Court of Appeal may grant legal aid for an appeal from itself to the House of Lords (s. 20(3)).

(f)   Upon ordering a retrial in the Crown Court, the Court of Appeal or the House of Lords may grant legal aid for the fresh Crown Court proceedings (s. 20(7)).

It will be apparent that the primary responsibility for granting or withholding legal aid in criminal proceedings lies with magistrates since they not only have power – like the other criminal courts – to grant aid for proceedings in their own court, but they may also, when committing an accused to the Crown Court for trial or sentence, extend his aid to cover the Crown Court proceedings.

Legal aid under part V is granted for representation (s. 20(1)) – cf. aid under part III which is basically for advice and assistance, although a limited degree of representation is permitted under the duty solicitor scheme. The primary definition of 'representation' is contained in s. 2(4) of the Act, which states that the term means 'representation for the purposes of proceedings', and includes 'all such assistance as is usually given by a solicitor or counsel in the steps preliminary or incidental to any proceedings', plus 'advice and assistance as to any appeal'. This definition is supplemented in the context of criminal legal aid by s. 19(2), which provides that preliminary or incidental proceedings include bail proceedings (whether before the court granting legal aid or another court, but excluding applications to a High Court judge in chambers). Also, representation for the purposes of proceedings before a magistrates' court includes proceedings before any youth court or other magistrates' court to which the case may be remitted (s. 19(3)).

In order to be granted legal aid under part V, a person must be 'accused' or 'convicted'. This means that it is confined to the defence (Legal Aid Act 1988, s. 21(1)). This is subject to the minor exception that, in a case where a person is appealing to the Crown Court against sentence or conviction in the magistrates' court, a private prosecutor may be granted aid to resist the appeal (s. 21(1)). An appellant who has been found unfit to plead and has been held by the jury to have done the act or made the omission charged is not a person 'accused' or 'convicted' and is not entitled to legal aid under part V (*Egan* [1997] Crim LR 225).

Legal aid under part V is confined to 'criminal proceedings'. The ambit of this phrase was dealt with in *Liverpool Crown Court, ex parte McCann* [1995] RTR 23. The Crown Court refused legal aid to the applicant, who was in the process of applying for the removal of a disqualification from driving for life. The Divisional Court held that he was entitled to have his application considered on the merits, as criminal proceedings were defined, *inter alia*, by s. 19(5) of the Act to include any proceedings in respect of an order made upon a person's conviction for an offence. The order for disqualification had been made upon his conviction for an offence, and his application was in respect of that order. However, proceedings for committal to prison under the Community Charges (Administration and Enforcement) Regulations 1989, reg. 41, have been held to be proceedings other than criminal proceedings, with the result that they do not come under part V (*Ex parte Bold* (1996) *The Times*, 15 July 1996).

Compulsory Legal Aid

D27.7   Subject to means, an accused or, as the case may be, convicted person must be granted legal aid in the following cases (Legal Aid Act 1988, s. 21(3)):

(a)   where he is committed for trial on a charge of murder (or proceedings against him for such a charge are transferred to the Crown Court);

(b)   where the prosecution are appealing (or applying for leave to appeal) to the House of Lords;

(c)   where he is brought before a magistrates' court following an earlier remand in custody when unrepresented, is at risk on this occasion of a further remand in custody (or of being committed to the Crown Court in custody), and is not legally represented but wishes to be; and

(d)   where his case is adjourned for reports prior to sentence and he is to be kept in custody for preparation thereof.

Compulsory aid under (c) and (d) is to be respectively for 'so much of the proceedings as relates to the grant of bail' and 'for the proceedings on sentencing or otherwise dealing with [the offender]'.

Discretionary Legal Aid

In all cases where there is jurisdiction to grant criminal legal aid under part V of the Legal   **D27.8** Aid Act 1988 but its grant is not obligatory by virtue of s. 21(3), the appropriate court has a discretion to grant aid should it appear to the court 'to be desirable to do so in the interests of justice' (s. 21(2)). This is again subject to the applicant's means (s. 21(5)). There is thus, in general, a twofold test for the granting of aid in criminal proceedings. The first question is whether the accused or, as the case may be, offender qualifies for aid having regard to his means (see **D27.13** for details of the assessment of means). Assuming that question is answered affirmatively, the second question is whether, having regard to the circumstances of the particular case, it is in the interests of justice that aid should be granted. Section 22(2) sets out certain factors which must be taken into account in answering the second question with respect to proceedings in the Crown Court and magistrates' courts. They are:

(a)   whether, in the event of conviction, it is likely that the court would impose a sentence which would either deprive the accused of his liberty, or lead to loss of his livelihood, or seriously damage his reputation;

(b)   whether the case may involve consideration of a substantial question of law;

(c)   whether the accused may be unable to understand the proceedings or state his own case, either through lack of knowledge of English or through mental or physical disability;

(d)   whether the nature of the defence is such as to involve the tracing and interviewing of potential defence witnesses or expert cross-examination of the prosecution witnesses, and

(e)   whether it is in the interests of a person other than the accused that the accused should be represented.

Section 22(2) is largely self-explanatory. By their nature, the factors mentioned are not susceptible to a precise objective evaluation. In particular, when assessing whether conviction might lead to deprivation of liberty, loss of livelihood or damage to reputation, the authority asked to grant aid should consider the nature of the facts alleged by the prosecution in the particular case rather than the maximum penalty that might theoretically be imposed (*Highgate Justices, ex parte Lewis* [1977] Crim LR 611). It follows that in the interests of justice, notwithstanding that the offence carries a maximum of five years' imprisonment, the court must make a subjective assessment of the likelihood of loss of liberty etc., having regard, for example, to the nature of the injuries suffered by the victim, whether a weapon was used, whether the accused has previous convictions and whether a conviction would put him in breach of a suspended sentence or other court order (ibid.). In *Liverpool City Magistrates, ex parte McGhee* [1993] Crim LR 609, it was held by the Divisional Court that a community service order was not properly to be regarded as a sentence depriving the accused of his liberty within the terms of s. 22(2)(a). It was, however, conceded that the list of relevant factors in s. 22(2) was not exhaustive, thus leaving open the possibility that, in an appropriate case, a community service order might be a factor to be considered in deciding whether legal aid should be granted. It also follows from the elastic nature of the considerations in s. 22(2) that courts will vary in their willingness to grant aid. Thus, to use the example already given, there are some magistrates' courts which will almost automatically allow aid for an accused charged with assault occasioning actual bodily harm, whereas others will scrutinise each such application with care.

In *Scunthorpe Justices, ex parte* S (1998) *The Times*, 5 March 1998, the Divisional Court considered that refusal of legal aid to an accused aged 16 who sought to challenge whether a police officer had acted in the execution of his duty was irrational. The expertise needed to cross-examine police witnesses, and to find, select and proof defence witnesses was beyond an accused aged 16.

By s. 21(7), any doubt about whether legal aid should be granted under part V must be resolved in favour of the applicant.

CONTRIBUTIONS TO LEGAL AID

Duty to Make Contribution Orders

D27.9   Where a court grants legal aid to a person under part V of the Legal Aid Act 1988 it must also – unless his disposable income and capital are below the prescribed limits – make an order that he contribute a certain amount to the costs which will be expended on his behalf (s. 23(1)). Both the minimum income and capital levels beneath which a person is not required to contribute to his legal aid costs and the amount which he shall be required to contribute if his means are above those levels are set out in sch. 3 and sch. 4 to the General Regulations. Normally the contribution order is simultaneous with the grant of aid, but, in circumstances prescribed by the regulations, it may be made at a later stage (s. 23(3)). The order may require the legally aided person to make his contributions in one sum or by instalments (s. 23(5)). A lump-sum order will be appropriate where the contribution is to be made out of disposable capital, payment by instalments where it will be from disposable income. The contribution period for contributions out of disposable income is six months (see reg. 3 of the General Regulations). Details of the operation of the regulations and the making of contribution orders will be found at **D27.13** *et seq.* The central point to note is that the court granting legal aid has no discretion either as to whether it makes a contribution order or, assuming an order has to be made, as to the amount ordered to be contributed. Those matters are dictated by the regulations. The court's only discretion is in relatively peripheral areas such as whether the grant of legal aid is not to take effect until a certain sum has been paid under the accompanying contribution order, or whether payments by instalments are to be monthly or weekly.

Effect of Non-payment of Contribution on the Grant of Aid

D27.10   If a court granting legal aid with a contribution order directs that a sum is to be paid by way of contribution on the making of the order, it may further direct that the grant of representation shall not take effect until the money has been paid (Legal Aid Act 1988, s. 24(1)). Further, in the event of a legally aided person subject to a contribution order failing to pay any instalment of the contribution when it is due, the court in which the proceedings for the purposes of which he was granted aid are being heard at the time of the default may revoke the grant of aid (s. 24(2)). This applies whether or not the grant of aid was initially made subject to down-payment of a contribution. It will be noted that it is the court in which the proceedings are being heard at the relevant time that has jurisdiction to revoke the legal aid order. Thus, if the magistrates grant aid for a trial on indictment and the accused then fails to make a contribution due from him at a time between his committal and the commencement of the trial, it is the Crown Court which has jurisdiction to revoke the legal aid order, even though it was the magistrates who made it. However, a legal aid order may not be revoked under s. 24(2) unless the appropriate court is satisfied (a) that the legally aided person was able to pay the contribution when it fell due, and (b) that he is still able to pay the whole or part of it but has failed or refused to do so (s. 24(3)). He must be given the opportunity to make representations on the matter (ibid.). He is entitled to re-apply at a later stage under reg. 10 of the General Regulations (*Liverpool Stipendiary Magistrate, ex parte Pender* [1994] 1 WLR 964).

Remission etc. of Outstanding Contributions

The purpose of the power given to the courts by the Legal Aid Act 1988, s. 24(2) (see **D27.11** **D27.10**), is to ensure that contributions are paid as ordered under threat of the legal aid being withdrawn if they are not. There is in any event power under sch. 3 to the Legal Aid Act 1988 for sums required to be paid under a contribution order to be recovered as if they had been adjudged to be paid by an order of a magistrates' court. Enforcement of payment of unpaid contributions under sch. 3 is, however, subject to s. 24(5)(d) of the Act which authorises the making of regulations by virtue of which a court may remit outstanding contribution payments or authorise the repayment of sums already paid.

Regulation 35 of the General Regulations has been made in furtherance of s. 24(5)(d). It provides that the court in which the 'relevant proceedings' are concluded may, at the conclusion of the proceedings, remit any contributions in respect of which the date for payment has still not arrived (reg. 35(1)(a)). That power arises whatever the verdict. In addition, if, and only if, the legally aided person has been acquitted, the court may also remit any sums which are already due but have not been paid and/or order the repayment of sums that have been paid (reg. 35(1)(b)). 'Relevant proceedings' for purposes of reg. 35 means the proceedings for the purposes of which legal aid was granted (including, if it was granted for proceedings in a magistrates' court but those proceedings resulted either in committal to the Crown Court or remittal to the youth court, the proceedings in the Crown Court or, as the case may be, youth court). Thus, if legal aid was granted and contribution ordered by a magistrates' court for purposes of a trial on indictment or other proceedings in the Crown Court, it will be the Crown Court which adjudicates on remission etc. of payments under the order, even though the order itself was by the lower court. Paragraph 11 of *Practice Direction (Crime: Costs)* [1991] 1 WLR 498 states that, where there has been an acquittal, the court should 'normally' both remit unpaid instalments and order repayment of paid ones.

Regulation 35 should also be read in the light of reg. 37 which states, *inter alia,* that the normal contribution period of six months is deemed to be terminated by the legally aided person's receiving an immediate custodial sentence. Upon termination of the contribution period, any liability to make further contributions (other than those which fell due before termination but are still unpaid) obviously ceases.

Where the actual cost of a legally aided person's representation turns out to be less than the contribution he has paid, the surplus must be returned to him (s. 23(7)).

PROCEDURE FOR APPLYING FOR LEGAL AID

Introduction

The system for applying for legal aid and the associated matter of the making of **D27.12** contribution orders are dealt with in part III of the General Regulations. The regulations are detailed and not always easy to follow. Of general importance is the duty of a legal representative to report any abuse of legal aid by a client (reg. 56 of the General Regulations (for the text see **D27.32**)). Summarised below are the main stages of the procedure when an adult applies to a magistrates' court for aid.

Statement of Means

D27.13 In order to assess whether an applicant's means are such as to make him eligible for legal aid, the court must require him to supply a statement of his financial resources in the prescribed form (Legal Aid Act 1988, s. 21(6)). A precedent for a statement of means form is set out in sch. 2 to the General Regulations (see form 5). The statement may be dispensed with if either it appears to the proper officer of the court that the applicant is physically or mentally incapable of supplying one, or he has previously submitted such a statement in connection with a previous application made in the same case and his means have not changed (General Regulations, reg. 23(4)). Thus, where an accused has been granted legal aid for proceedings in a magistrates' court and he is then committed or transferred for Crown Court trial, it is usual to ask for the aid to be extended to cover the Crown Court proceedings, and – provided the defence representative can affirm that his client's means have not changed – there is no need to submit a fresh statement of means.

The Application Itself

D27.14 An application to a magistrates' court for legal aid may be made either in writing to a justices' clerk (or assistant authorised by him to act on his behalf) or orally to the court (reg. 11(1)). If made in writing, the application must be in the prescribed form. The prescribed form requires details of, *inter alia*, the nature of the proceedings, the reasons why legal aid is considered necessary and the solicitor the applicant wishes to act for him. Save where the requirement to furnish a statement of means has been waived under reg. 23(4), aid may not be granted unless and until such a statement has been considered either by the court or by the clerk (reg. 11(3)). In practice, most applications for legal aid are made by submitting both form 1 (the written application) and form 5 (the statement of means) to the clerk's office a few days in advance of the first hearing. Assistants in the clerk's office then process the application. If it is successful, the solicitors are notified in advance of the hearing that aid has been granted. If unsuccessful, it may be renewed in court (see **D27.17**). Where it is not possible to lodge the necessary forms until the day of the hearing, most courts will indicate informally whether the case is suitable for legal aid in the sense that an order would be in the interests of justice. However, the court – unless prepared to consider the applicant's statement of means forthwith – is precluded by reg. 11(3) from actually making an order. Therefore, what happens in such cases is that the statement of means is considered in the clerk's office in due course. Assuming the applicant's means do not render him ineligible for aid, the clerk (or authorised assistant) will grant aid, no doubt having been informed that the court has already stated that the interests of justice test is satisfied. Since the order takes effect from the day that the application was submitted, the costs of representation at the first hearing will be covered even though the decision to grant aid was later. In *Highbury Corner Magistrates' Court, ex parte Sonn and Co.* [1995] 1 WLR 1365, the Divisional Court examined the position where a defendant in the magistrates' court applied for legal aid, but failed to furnish the court with supporting documentary evidence as required by reg. 23. Their lordships held that in such a case reg. 44(7) could be invoked once the supporting documents were received, so as to cover the work earlier undertaken by the defendant's solicitor, provided that the pre-conditions laid down in that regulation were satisfied. The circumstances in which a legal aid order could be retrospective were considered by the Crown Court (Ebsworth J) in *Welsby* [1998] 1 Cr App R 197. It was held that there was no provision for the Crown Court to backdate orders.

Contribution Orders

D27.15 The purpose and outline working of the contribution order system has already been considered at **D27.9**. By regs 26(2) and 27(1) of the General Regulations, the court (or proper officer of the court) is under a duty (a) to consider the applicant's statement of means and determine his disposable income and capital in accordance with sch. 3 to the General Regulations, and (b) make a contribution order in the amount prescribed by sch. 4. The contribution required must be endorsed on the legal aid order itself, and a copy must be sent to the applicant and his solicitor (reg. 27(2)). Where, however, the applicant (or his spouse or a person living with him as if a spouse) is in receipt of income-based jobseeker's allowance, income support, family credit or disability working allowance, no contribution is payable and, indeed, there is no need even to go through the motions of assessing disposable income and capital (reg. 26(3)).

Contributions out of disposable capital are to be for the amount by which the capital exceeds £3,000. If the capital sum ordered is readily available, it is to be paid immediately (reg. 29(2)), and the legal aid order will not take effect until that has been paid (reg. 29(3)). Otherwise, such time as is reasonable must be given for payment.

No upper limit is fixed for the amount of contribution a person granted legal aid may be required to make, whether out of disposable income or out of disposable capital. However, if the contributions that would be required by the application of sch. 3 and sch. 4 clearly exceed the probable cost of the applicant's representation, legal aid will simply be refused on grounds of means. Should a legally aided person pay more by way of contribution than the costs expended on his behalf, the excess must be returned to him (Legal Aid Act 1988, s. 23(7)).

Variation, Revocation etc. of Contribution Orders

By reg. 31 of the General Regulations, a legally assisted person is under a duty to inform **D27.16** the court of any change in his circumstances which might make him liable either to pay a contribution if one was not originally ordered, or, if one was, might affect its amount. Where such information is given (or fresh information about the assisted person's financial resources comes otherwise to the court's attention), the grant of aid may be varied either by the addition of a contribution order or by an alteration (whether up or down) in the contributions originally required (see regs 32 to 34 for details). The effect of reg. 35 (variation and revocation of contribution orders by the court finally disposing of the proceedings for which aid was granted) has already been considered at **D27.11**. Regulation 36 deals with refusal to pay contributions, and requires the court to serve on a legally aided person who has failed to pay as ordered notice that he must comply with his obligations within seven days. If that does not result in payment, a further notice must be served inviting him to make representations as to why he cannot comply with the contribution order. Having considered any representations, the court may then revoke legal aid if the conditions mentioned in the Legal Aid Act 1988, s. 24(3) (see **D27.10**), are satisfied.

Procedure where Legal Aid is Refused

An applicant who is refused aid by a magistrates' court or justices' clerk must be notified **D27.17** by the court of the failure of his application (reg. 12(1) of the General Regulations). The notification must state whether the refusal was on grounds of means or because aid did not appear desirable in the interests of justice (ibid.). A precedent for the notification is contained in sch. 2 to the General Regulations, form 2. A copy should be sent to the applicant's solicitor as well as to the applicant himself (reg. 11(2)). Depending on the circumstances, it may be possible for the unsuccessful applicant to apply to an area committee for review of the decision (see regs 15 to 17). Without prejudice to that possibility, the applicant may renew his application either orally to the court or to the justices' clerk (reg. 14(1)). A clerk to whom a renewed application is made may not himself refuse aid – his options are either to grant the application or refer it to a court or an individual magistrate (reg. 14(3)). A court or magistrate determining a renewed application (whether made direct or referred by the clerk) may grant or refuse the application (or refer it to the clerk) (reg. 14(4)). There thus seems to be a theoretical possibility of applications being endlessly referred from the clerk to the court and back again, although good sense no doubt prevents that from occurring in practice. So that an unsuccessful applicant will know what his contribution would have been had aid been granted, a court or clerk refusing aid must assess the applicant's disposable income and capital in accordance with sch. 3 to the General Regulations and determine the appropriate contribution as specified in sch. 4. Those amounts must be notified to the applicant along with notification of the failure of his application (reg. 13).

Procedure for Application to the Crown Court

D27.18 Regulation 18 of the General Regulations deals with applications for legal aid for proceedings in the Crown Court. Where aid has not been obtained from the lower court, written application may be made to the Crown Court itself using the standard legal aid application form (reg. 18(1)). The application may be determined by an appropriate officer of the Crown Court – i.e. the Court Manager or an officer designated by him to act on his behalf (ibid. and see reg. 3 for the definition of 'appropriate officer'). Alternatively, application may be made orally to the court. The rules regarding supply of a statement of means, assessment of contribution and notification of refusal of aid apply, *mutatis mutandis*, to Crown Court applications just as they apply to applications to magistrates' courts.

Legal Aid in the Court of Appeal

D27.19 The definition of 'representation' in the Legal Aid Act 1988, s. 2(4), means that advice on the merits of an appeal from the Crown Court to the Court of Appeal will be covered by the Crown Court legal aid (assuming the prospective appellant was aided at that stage and within the limits laid down in *Lord Chancellor* v *Brennan* (1996) *The Times*, 14 February 1996 (see **D23.2**)). Aid for the actual proceedings in the Court of Appeal must be sought from the court itself. Normally, the single judge granting leave to appeal will also be asked to grant the appellant aid. Where an appellant did not enjoy aid for the proceedings in the lower court, the Court of Appeal may initially grant him aid limited to advice on the merits of an appeal and assistance in preparing grounds of appeal (Legal Aid Act 1988, s. 21(8)).

Applications for Legal Aid in Respect of Juveniles

D27.20 A juvenile's parent or guardian may apply for legal aid on his behalf, although for purposes of the General Regulations the applicant is still regarded as the juvenile not the parent (see reg. 3). Where the juvenile is under 16, the proper officer of the court may require a statement of means from either the juvenile or an 'appropriate contributor' or both (reg. 23(3)). 'Appropriate contributor' is defined in reg. 3 as the juvenile's father, mother or guardian. The rules as to assessment of disposable income and capital and ordering of contributions upon grant of aid then apply to the appropriate contributor in exactly the same way as they would if he were applying for legal aid for himself (see especially Legal Aid Act 1988, s. 23(2) and General Regulations, reg. 25(1)). Thus, on the assumption that a juvenile under 16 will have no disposable income or capital, whether aid is granted and, if so, the amount of contribution ordered will depend entirely on the parents' means, and it will be the latter who have to make the payments. In the rare case of an under-16 having resources of his own, contribution could be ordered both from him and his parents (see Legal Aid Act 1988, s. 23(2)). However, once the juvenile has attained the age of 16, the liability of the parents to make contribution ceases, and it is only the juvenile's means that are to be considered. This would seem to apply even if he is still receiving full-time education.

REPRESENTATION UNDER A LEGAL AID ORDER

Nature of Representation

The nature of the representation to which a person is entitled under a criminal legal aid **D27.21** order is set out in part V of the General Regulations. The effect of the regulations is that:

(a)   Legal aid for the purposes of proceedings before a magistrates' court must be for solicitor only, unless the offence charged is indictable and the court is of the opinion that the case is unusually grave or difficult so that representation by solicitor and counsel would be desirable (reg. 44(3)).

(b)   Legal aid for proceedings in the Crown Court is normally for both solicitor and counsel (reg. 44(1)). An exception is when the Crown Court itself grants aid as a matter of urgency in a case where there is no time to instruct a solicitor, in which circumstances it may make the aid for counsel only (reg. 44(5)). There is no provision for the Crown Court to make an order for representation by a solicitor alone, even though such representation might assist the court, e.g., where the accused dismissed counsel (*Mills* [1997] 2 Cr App R 206; and *Seale* [1997] Crim LR 898).

(c)   Aid for an appeal to the Court of Appeal may be for counsel and solicitor or for counsel only, at the court's discretion (reg. 44(4)).

The fact that aid is for solicitor only does not, of course, preclude the instruction of counsel in the matter. However, the total remuneration to which the defence lawyers will be entitled is calculated on the basis that only a solicitor needed to attend court.

Selection of Advocates

Whether aid is for solicitor only or for solicitor and counsel, the legally assisted person **D27.22** may select any solicitor who is willing to act for him and such solicitor shall be assigned to him under the order (General Regulations, reg. 45(1)). The legal aid application form contains a box in which the applicant may indicate the name and address of the solicitor he wants. He is also informed that, if he makes no choice, the court will select a solicitor for him. The solicitor assigned may in turn instruct any counsel who is willing to act (reg. 45(2)).

Where aid for an appeal to the Court of Appeal is for counsel only, the court (or a judge of the court or the proper officer of the court) may assign counsel, having regard especially to the wishes of the appellant and the identity of the solicitor and counsel who represented him in the court below (reg. 46). The usual procedure is for the Registrar of Criminal Appeals to select counsel and to send him a brief containing the grounds of appeal, notice of appeal and any necessary transcript of the Crown Court proceedings.

Legal Aid for Two Counsel

Regulation 48 of the General Regulations governs legal aid for Queen's Counsel and **D27.23** more than one counsel. For the various forms which such an order can take, and the courts which have the power to make them, see the text of reg. 48 (reproduced at **D27.32**). The procedure for applying such an order is laid down in *Practice Direction (Crown Court: Counsel)* [1995] 1 WLR 261.

Legal Aid for Two or More Co-accused

One solicitor may be assigned to act for two or more legally aided accused whose cases **D27.24** are to be heard together (General Regulations, reg. 49). This does not apply if the interests of justice require that they be separately represented (ibid.). The obvious case for separate representation and hence the assignment of different solicitors is when there is a conflict between the two accused. Where there is no necessity for separate representation, the initial presumption is that one solicitor will be assigned to act for all the co-accused. However, the matter remains one for the court's discretion. Thus, if one of the accused is already represented in different proceedings by firm X and wishes that firm to represent him in the instant proceedings, whereas the remaining accused wish to be represented by firm Y, the court (or, as the case may be, proper officer of the court) may decide that the extra expense of representation by two different firms is, in all the circumstances, justified. A compromise solution to the above type of problem is for the co-accused to be assigned one solicitor who then instructs separate counsel for the trial.

Exceptional Expenditures

D27.25 Where it appears to the legally aided person's solicitor that the proper conduct of the proceedings requires the taking of certain steps which will incur exceptional costs not normally expected to be covered by legal aid, he may apply to the appropriate area committee for its prior authority before taking the step in question (General Regulations, reg. 54). Particular expenditures for which authorisation is required are listed in reg. 54. They include the obtaining of an expert's report, the bespeaking of shorthand notes or tape recordings of any proceedings (including police interviews with suspects), and the instructing of a Queen's Counsel alone on a legal aid order which provides only for solicitor and counsel. If an application is made unsuccessfully under reg. 54, the solicitor may nonetheless incur the exceptional costs and then – contrary to the general rule that legally aided work is to be paid for solely out of the legal aid fund or from money provided by the Lord Chancellor – may be reimbursed by the legally assisted person privately (see reg. 55).

DETERMINATION OF COSTS PAYABLE UNDER A CRIMINAL LEGAL AID ORDER

Remuneration of Solicitor and Counsel

D27.26 Payment of counsel and solicitors for work done under a criminal legal aid order is governed by the Legal Aid in Criminal and Care Proceedings (Costs) Regulations 1989 (SI 1989 No. 343). Details are beyond the scope of this work.

Judge's Powers in Respect of Legal Aid Costs

D27.27 Paragraph 9 of the Lord Chief Justice's *Practice Direction (Crime: Costs)* [1991] 1 WLR 498 deals with the power of the judge to influence the sums paid to solicitor or counsel for work done under a legal aid order. By para. 9(1), a Crown Court judge or judge of the Court of Appeal sitting in proceedings for which legal aid was granted may make observations to the appropriate authority to the effect that, in his view, work under the order was done incompetently or inefficiently so as to waste money. The matter of complaint should be defined as precisely as possible and the terms of the observation entered in the court record (ibid.). The determining officer may disallow the amount of the order from the amount otherwise payable to solicitors and counsel. He may also deduct a greater amount if appropriate (para. 10.2). Similarly, where standard fees would otherwise be payable for Crown Court work, the judge – if dissatisfied with the solicitor's conduct of the case or otherwise of the view that for exceptional reasons standard fees are inappropriate – may direct that the fees be determined by the appropriate authority (para. 10.3). Before observations are made under para. 10.1 or a direction given under para. 10.3, counsel or solicitor who will be adversely affected thereby must be given the opportunity to make representations to the judge in chambers (para. 10.4). If the judge nonetheless decides to make the observation or, as the case may be, give the direction, that decision may be announced in open court if the judge considers it in the interests of justice to do so. Before disallowing fees, the appropriate authority, like the judge, is obliged to give solicitor or counsel the opportunity to make representations (para. 10.5). Finally, the above is without prejudice to the appropriate authority's general discretionary right to consult the judge as to any matter touching upon the allowance or disallowance of legal aid costs (para. 10.6).

REMEDIES WHERE LEGAL AID IS REFUSED

The options open to a person refused legal aid are as follows.

Renewal of Application

D27.28

If legal aid is refused for proceedings in a magistrates' court following an initial application under reg. 11(1) of the General Regulations, the application may simply be renewed either orally to the court or in writing to the clerk (reg. 14(1)). Renewal of an application will be especially appropriate where either there has been a change in circumstances since the refusal, or the original application was in writing to the clerk and it is hoped that an oral application to the court will prove more persuasive.

Application to the Crown Court

If legal aid for purposes of proceedings in the Crown Court is refused by a magistrates' **D27.29** court, a further application may be made to the higher court which has concurrent jurisdiction to grant aid for proceedings before itself (see Legal Aid Act 1988, s. 20(2) and (4)). The Crown Court will consider the application *de novo*, and the refusal of aid below will not in any way preclude its being granted above.

Application for Judicial Review

Decisions by a magistrates' court (or clerk or single justice) to refuse legal aid are subject **D27.30** to judicial review by the High Court in exactly the same way as are their other decisions. It follows that an unsuccessful applicant may apply to the Divisional Court both for certiorari to quash the refusal of aid and for mandamus requiring the decision to be reconsidered. However, the remedy is of limited value in the context of refusal of legal aid since the granting of aid is usually discretionary and the general rule where an inferior tribunal refuses to exercise a discretionary power in favour of a party to proceedings is that the Divisional Court will intervene only if the decision was apparently arrived at by taking into account irrelevant considerations, or ignoring relevant ones, or was manifestly unreasonable (see *Associated Provincial Picture Houses Ltd* v *Wednesbury Corporation* [1948] 1 KB 223). It will always be difficult to show that a magistrates' court refusing legal aid erred in such a fundamental way, as opposed merely to exercising its proper discretion in a somewhat surprising manner. Thus, in *Highgate Justices, ex parte Lewis* [1977] Crim LR 611 the Divisional Court refused to quash a decision not to grant legal aid for summary trial of an alleged offence of assault occasioning actual bodily harm because it was for the magistrates, having regard to all the circumstances of the individual case and applying the Widgery Committee recommendations, to determine whether legal aid was desirable in the interests of justice. It could not be said that any charge of assault occasioning actual bodily harm was so inherently grave that legal aid ought always to be granted regardless of the individual circumstances, and there was nothing to indicate that the magistrates had taken into account irrelevant considerations or ignored relevant ones. *Ex parte Lewis* may be contrasted with *Derby Justices, ex parte Kooner* [1971] 1 QB 147, in which magistrates refused an application that aid for committal proceedings in respect of a charge of murder be made for solicitor and counsel, not for solicitor only. The refusal was quashed because (a) *any* proceedings for murder had to be regarded as unusually grave (see now reg. 44(3) of the General Regulations, which empowers the court to make aid for proceedings in a magistrates' court cover solicitor and counsel if the case is unusually grave or difficult), and (b) the magistrates had, on their own admission, taken into account the irrelevant factor that, in their view, counsel at an earlier remand hearing had wasted the court's time with irrelevant cross-examination.

Application to an Area Committee for Review

D27.31 Because of the difficulties in remedying a refusal of legal aid for proceedings in a magistrates' court by an application for judicial review, a procedure was introduced in 1982 enabling the unsuccessful applicant to apply to a legal aid committee for review of the magistrates' or clerk's decision. The law on such review is contained in regs 15 to 17 of the General Regulations. An application for review may be made where a legal aid order has been refused after having been considered for the first time by a magistrates' court or justices' clerk provided (reg. 15(2)):

(a) the applicant is charged with an indictable offence, including an offence triable either way (or is to be dealt with in respect of a sentence imposed or other order made for such an offence), and

(b) the application was refused on the ground that aid was not desirable in the interests of justice, as opposed to being refused on grounds of means, and

(c) legal aid was applied for at least 21 days before the date fixed for the trial of the information or, as the case may be, committal proceedings, assuming such a date had been fixed at the time of the application.

Regulation 14(1) provides that the option of renewing an application for legal aid before the magistrates' court (or clerk) by which it has been refused is 'Without prejudice to the provisions of regulation 15'. It would seem, therefore, that – although only the first unsuccessful application for legal aid may be the subject of review – the fact that the applicant chooses to make a further application to the court does not prejudice his right also to have the area committee review the outcome of the first application.

Regulation 15(2) is in identical terms to reg. 6E of the now-revoked Legal Aid in Criminal Proceedings (General) Regulations 1968 (SI 1968 No. 1231). Under the old regulation, it was held that the act of the police in charging a suspect with an offence triable either way and bailing him to appear before a magistrates' court on a certain date did not constitute the fixing of a date for trial or committal proceedings. Therefore, the defence were entitled to have a refusal of aid reviewed even though they did not submit the legal aid application itself until less than three weeks before the date to which the accused had been bailed (*Bury Justices, ex parte N* [1987] QB 284). No doubt the decision in *Ex parte N* applies equally to the interpretation of reg. 15 of the 1989 General Regulations. However, certain difficulties in interpreting the regulation remain, notably whether the specifying of a date in a summons as that on which the accused should attend court to answer the charge amounts to the fixing of a trial date. Moreover, the effect of the regulation can be arbitrary, as where an accused omits to apply for legal aid prior to his first court appearance and the court then fixes a date less than three weeks hence for the effective hearing. Even if he applies for legal aid immediately after the first hearing, the short gap between that and the trial or committal date deprives him of a review should the court refuse his application.

Assuming an unsuccessful applicant for aid is both entitled and wishes to apply for review, the procedure for doing so is for him to give notice to the appropriate area committee within 14 days of receipt of notification that his application to the magistrates has failed (reg. 16(1)). The 'appropriate' area committee is simply the one for the area in which the magistrates' court to which application was made is situated (reg. 3). Copies of the legal aid application form and the notice of refusal should accompany the application (reg. 16(2)). The time-limit of 14 days may be waived or extended by the area committee (reg. 16(3)). Upon review, the area committee may, in its discretion, refuse the application or make a legal aid order (reg. 17(1)). In the latter event, it must make whatever contribution order was notionally fixed by the magistrates' court when it refused aid (see reg. 13 for the obligation to determine what contribution would have been payable notwithstanding that legal aid is refused).

STATUTES AND REGULATIONS RELATING TO LEGAL AID

Legal Aid Act 1988, ss. 2 and 19 to 24   **D27.32**

PART I   PRELIMINARY

2.—(1)   This section has effect for the interpretation of this Act.

(2)   'Advice' means oral or written advice on the application of English law to any particular circumstances that have arisen in relation to the person seeking the advice and as to the steps which that person might appropriately take having regard to the application of English law to those circumstances.

(3)   'Assistance' means assistance in taking any of the steps which a person might take, including steps with respect to proceedings, having regard to the application of English law to any particular circumstances that have arisen in relation to him, whether by taking such steps on his behalf (including assistance by way of representation) or by assisting him in taking them on his own behalf.

(4)   'Representation' means representation for the purposes of proceedings and it includes—

(a)   all such assistance as is usually given by a solicitor or counsel in the steps preliminary or incidental to any proceedings;

(b)   all such assistance as is usually so given in civil proceedings in arriving at or giving effect to a compromise to avoid or bring to an end any proceedings; and

(c)   in the case of criminal proceedings, advice and assistance as to any appeal;

and related expressions have corresponding meanings.

(6)   Advice, assistance and representation under this Act, except when made available under part II, is only by persons who are solicitors or barristers, but in the case of part II, may by by other persons.

(7)   In any particular case, advice, assistance and representation under this Act, except when made available under part II, shall be by solicitor and, so far as necessary counsel; but regulations may prescribe the circumstances in which representation is to be by counsel only or by solicitor only and regulate representation by more than one counsel.

. . .

(11)   In this Act 'legally assisted person' means any person who receives, under this Act, advice, assistance or representation and, in relation to proceedings, any reference to an assisted party or an unassisted party is to be construed accordingly.

PART V   CRIMINAL LEGAL AID

19.—(1)   This part applies to criminal proceedings before any of the following—

(a)   a magistrates' court;

(b)   the Crown Court;

(c)   the Criminal Division of the Court of Appeal or the Courts-Martial Appeal Court; and

(d)   the House of Lords in the exercise of its jurisdiction in relation to appeals from either of those courts;

and representation under this part shall be available to any person subject to and in accordance with sections 21, 22, 23, 24 and 25.

(2)   Representation under this part for the purposes of the proceedings before any court extends to any proceedings preliminary or incidental to the proceedings, including bail proceedings, whether before that or another court.

(3)   Representation under this part for the purposes of the proceedings before a magistrates' court extends to any proceedings before a youth court or other magistrates' court to which the case is remitted.

(4)   In subsection (2) above in its application to bail proceedings, 'court' has the same meaning as in the Bail Act 1976, but that subsection does not extend representation to bail proceedings before a judge of the High Court exercising the jurisdiction of that court.

(5)   In this part—

'competent authority' is to be construed in accordance with section 20;

'Court of Appeal' means the Criminal Division of that court;

'criminal proceedings' includes proceedings for dealing with an offender for an offence or in respect of a sentence or as a fugitive offender and also includes proceedings instituted under section 115 of the Magistrates' Courts Act 1980 (binding over) in respect of an actual or apprehended breach of the peace or other misbehaviour and proceedings for dealing with a person for a failure to comply with a condition of a recognisance to keep the peace or be of good behaviour and also includes proceedings under section 15 of the Children and Young Persons Act 1969 (variation and discharge of supervision orders) and section 16(8) of that Act (appeals in such proceedings);

'proceedings for dealing with an offender as a fugitive offender' means proceedings before a metropolitan stipendiary magistrate under section 9 of the Extradition Act 1870, section 7 of the Fugitive Offenders Act 1967 or section 6 of the Criminal Justice Act 1988; and

'remitted', in relation to a youth court, means remitted under section 56(1) of the Children and Young Persons Act 1933;

and any reference, in relation to representation for the purposes of any proceedings, to the proceedings before a court includes a reference to any proceedings to which representation under this part extends by virtue of subsection (2) or (3) above.

20.—(1)   Subject to any provision made by virtue of subsection (10) below, the following courts are competent to grant representation under this part for the purposes of the following proceedings, on an application made for the purpose.

(2)   The court before which any proceedings take place, or are to take place, is always competent as respects those proceedings, except that this does not apply to the House of Lords; and, in the case of the Court of Appeal and the Courts-Martial Appeal Court, the reference to proceedings which are to take place includes proceedings which may take place if notice of appeal is given or an application for leave to appeal is made.

(3)   The Court of Appeal or, as the case may be, the Courts-Martial Appeal Court is also competent as respects proceedings on appeal from decisions of theirs to the House of Lords.

(4)   The magistrates' court—

(a)   which commits a person for trial or sentence or to be dealt with in respect of a sentence,

(b)   which has been given a notice of transfer under section 4 of the Criminal Justice Act 1987 (transfer of serious fraud cases),

(bb)   which has been given a notice of transfer under part I of the schedule to the War Crimes Act 1991;

(c)   from which a person appeals against his conviction or sentence,

is also competent as respects the proceedings before the Crown Court.

(5)   The magistrates' court inquiring into an offence as examining justices is also competent, before it decides whether or not to commit the person for trial, as respects any proceedings before the Crown Court on his trial.

(6)   The Crown Court is also competent as respects applications for leave to appeal and proceedings on any appeal to the Court of Appeal under section 9(11) of the Criminal Justice Act 1987 (appeals against orders or rulings at preparatory hearings).

(7)   On ordering a retrial under section 7 of the Criminal Appeal Act 1968 (new trials ordered by Court of Appeal or House of Lords on fresh evidence) the court ordering the retrial is also competent as respects the proceedings before the Crown Court.

(8)   Any magistrates' court to which, in accordance with regulations, a person applies for representation when he has been arrested for an offence but has not appeared or been brought before a court is competent as respects the proceedings in relation to the offence in any magistrates' court.

(9)   In the event of the Lord Chancellor making an order under section 3(4) as respects the function of granting representation under this part for the purposes of proceedings before any court, the Board shall be competent as respects those proceedings, on an application made for the purpose.

(10)   An order under section 3(4) may make provision restricting or excluding the competence of any court mentioned in any of subsections (2) to (8) above and may contain such transitional provisions as appear to the Lord Chancellor necessary or expedient.

21.—(1)   Representation under this part for the purposes of any criminal proceedings shall be available in accordance with this section to the accused or convicted person but shall not be available to the prosecution except in the case of an appeal to the Crown Court against conviction or sentence, for the purpose of enabling an individual who is not acting in an official capacity to resist the appeal.

(2)   Subject to subsection (5) below, representation may be granted where it appears to the competent authority to be desirable to do so in the interests of justice; and section 22 applies for the interpretation of this subsection in relation to the proceedings to which that section applies.

(3)   Subject to subsection (5) below, representation must be granted—
    (a)   where a person is committed for trial on a charge of murder, for his trial;
    (b)   where the prosecutor appeals or applies for leave to appeal to the House of Lords, for the proceedings on the appeal;
    (c)   where a person charged with an offence before a magistrates' court—
        (i)   is brought before the court in pursuance of a remand in custody when he may be again remanded or committed in custody, and
        (ii)   is not, but wishes to be, legally represented before the court (not having been legally represented when he was so remanded),
for so much of the proceedings as relates to the grant of bail; and
    (d)   where a person—
        (i)   is to be sentenced or otherwise dealt with for an offence by a magistrates' court or the Crown Court, and
        (ii)   is to be kept in custody to enable enquiries or a report to be made to assist the court,
for the proceedings on sentencing or otherwise dealing with him.

(4)   Subject to any provision made under section 3(4) by virtue of section 20(10), in a case falling within subsection (3)(a) above, it shall be for the magistrates' court which commits the person for trial, and not for the Crown Court, to make the grant of representation for his trial.

(5)   Representation shall not be granted to any person unless it appears to the competent authority that his financial resources are such as, under regulations, make him eligible for representation under this part.

(6)   Before making a determination for the purposes of subsection (5) above in the case of any person, the competent authority shall, except in prescribed cases, require a statement of his financial resources in the prescribed form to be furnished to the authority.

(7)   Where a doubt arises whether representation under this part should be granted to any person, the doubt shall be resolved in that person's favour.

(8)   Where an application for representation for the purposes of an appeal to the Court of Appeal or the Courts-Martial Appeal Court is made to a competent authority before the giving of notice of appeal or the making of an application for leave to appeal, the authority may, in the first instance, exercise its power to grant representation by making a grant consisting of advice on the question whether there appear to be reasonable grounds of appeal and assistance in the preparation of an application for leave to appeal or in the giving of a notice of appeal.

(9)   Representation granted by a competent authority may be amended or withdrawn, whether by that or another authority competent to grant representation under this part.

(10)   Regulations may provide for an appeal to lie to a specified court or body against any refusal by a magistrates' court to grant representation under this part and for that other court or body to make any grant of representation that could have been made by the magistrates' court.

(10A)   Where section 44A of the Criminal Appeal Act 1968 (death of convicted person) applies, the reference in subsection (1) above to the convicted person shall be construed as a reference to the person approved under that section.

(11)   Subsection (3) above shall have effect in its application to a person who has not attained the age of 18 as if the references in paragraphs (c) and (d) to remand in custody and to being remanded or kept in custody included references to being committed under section 23 of the Children and Young Persons Act 1969 to the care of a local authority or a remand centre.

22.—(1)   This section applies to proceedings by way of a trial by or before a magistrates' court or the Crown Court or on an appeal to the Crown Court against a person's conviction.
(2)   The factors to be taken into account by a competent authority in determining

whether it is in the interests of justice that representation be granted for the purposes of proceedings to which this section applies to an accused shall include the following—

(a)   the offence is such that if proved it is likely that the court would impose a sentence which would deprive the accused of his liberty or lead to loss of his livelihood or serious damage to his reputation;

(b)   the determination of the case may involve consideration of a substantial question of law;

(c)   the accused may be unable to understand the proceedings or to state his own case because of his inadequate knowledge of English, mental illness or other mental or physical disability;

(d)   the nature of the defence is such as to involve the tracing and interviewing of witnesses or expert cross-examination of a witness for the prosecution;

(e)   it is in the interests of someone other than the accused that the accused be represented.

(3)   [Power to vary the factors listed in subsection (2).]

23.—(1)   Where representation under this part is granted to any person whose financial resources are such as, under regulations, make him liable to make a contribution, the competent authority shall order him to pay a contribution in respect of the costs of his being represented under this part.

(2)   Where the legally assisted person has not attained the age of 16, the competent authority may, instead of or in addition to ordering him to make a contribution, order any person—

(a)   who is an appropriate contributor in relation to him, and

(b)   whose financial resources are such as, under regulations, make him liable to make a contribution,

to pay a contribution in respect of the costs of the representation granted to the legally assisted person.

(3)   Regulations may authorise the making of a contribution order under subsection (1) or (2) above after the grant of representation in prescribed circumstances.

(4)   The amount of the contribution to be required under subsection (1) or (2) above by the competent authority shall be such as is determined in accordance with the regulations.

(5)   A legally assisted person or appropriate contributor may be required to make his contribution in one sum or by instalments as may be prescribed.

(6)   Regulations may provide that no contribution order shall be made in connection with a grant of representation under this part for the purposes of proceedings in the Crown Court, the Court of Appeal or the House of Lords in a case where a contribution order was made in connection with a grant of such representation to the person in question in respect of proceedings in a lower court.

(7)   Subject to subsection (8) below, if the total contribution made in respect of the costs of representing any person under this part exceeds those costs, the excess shall be repaid—

(a)   where the contribution was made by one person only, to him; and

(b)   where the contribution was made by two or more persons, to them in proportion to the amounts contributed by them.

(8)   Where a contribution has been made in respect of the costs of representing any person under this part in any proceedings and an order for costs is made in favour of that person in respect of those proceedings, then, where sums due under the order for costs are paid to the Board of the Lord Chancellor under section 20(2) of the Prosecution of Offences Act 1985 (recovery regulations)—

(a)   if the costs of the representation do not exceed the sums so paid, subsection (7) above shall not apply and the contribution shall be repaid;

(b)   if the costs of the representation do exceed the sums so paid, subsection (7) above shall apply as if the costs of the representation were equal to the excess.

(9)   References in subsection (8) above to the costs of representation include any charge or fee treated as part of those costs by section 26(2).

(10)   In this part—

'appropriate contributor', means a person of a description prescribed under section 34(2)(c); and

'contribution order' means an order under subsection (1) or (2) above.

24.—(1)   Where a competent authority grants representation under this part and in connection with the grant makes a contribution order under which any sum is required to be paid on the making of the order, it may direct that the grant of representation shall not take effect until that sum is paid.

(2)   Where a legally assisted person fails to pay any relevant contribution when it is due, the court in which the proceedings for the purposes of which he has been granted representation are being heard may, subject to subsection (3) below, revoke the grant.

(3)   A court shall not exercise the power conferred by subsection (2) above unless, after affording the legally assisted person an opportunity of making representations in such manner as may be prescribed, it is satisfied—

(a)   that he was able to pay the relevant contribution when it was due; and

(b)   that he is able to pay the whole or part of it but has failed or refused to do so.

(4)   In subsection (2) above 'relevant contribution', in relation to a legally assisted person, means any sum—

(a)   which he is required to pay by a contribution order made in connection with the grant to him of representation under this part, and

(b)   which falls due after the making of the order and before the conclusion of the proceedings for the purposes of which he has been granted such representation.

(5)   [Power to make regulations.]

Legal Aid in Criminal and Care Proceedings (General) Regulations 1989 (SI 1989 No. 344), excerpts

PART I   GENERAL

Applicants reaching the age of 16
5.   An applicant who attains the age of 16 after the date on which an application for legal aid is made but before the making of a legal aid order shall be treated for the purposes of these regulations as not having attained that age.

Determination in private and in absence of legally assisted person etc.
7.   Where it is provided by these regulations that any matter may be determined otherwise than by a court, it may be determined in private and in the absence of the applicant, the appropriate contributor, the person concerned or the legally assisted person as the case may be.

General power to grant legal aid

10.   Subject to the provisions of section 21(2), (3) and (5) of the Act and to regulation 23, nothing in part II or in regulation 36 shall affect the power of a court, a judge of the court or of the registrar to make a legal aid order, whether an application has been made for legal aid or not, or the right of an applicant whose application has been refused or whose legal aid order has been revoked under section 24(2) to apply to the court at the trial or in other proceedings.

PART II   APPLICATIONS FOR LEGAL AID

Proceedings in magistrates' courts
11.—(1)   An application for a legal aid order (whether or not it will also apply to any proceedings in the Crown Court) in respect of proceedings in a magistrates' court shall be made—

(a)   to the justices' clerk in form 1, or

(b)   orally to the court,

and the justices' clerk or the court may grant or refuse the application.

(2)   Where an application for a legal aid order is made under paragraph (1)(b), the court may refer it to the justices' clerk for determination.

(3)   Except where the applicant is not required to furnish a statement of means under regulation 23(4), a legal aid order shall not be made on an application under paragraph (1) until the court or the justices' clerk has considered the applicant's statement of means.

Notification of refusal of legal aid by a magistrates' court
12.   (1)   Where an application for a legal aid order is refused by a magistrates' court or a justices' clerk, the court or the justices' clerk shall notify the applicant on form 2 that the

application has been refused on one or both of the following grounds, namely that it does not appear to the court or the justices' clerk—

    (a)   desirable to make an order in the interests of justice; or

    (b)   that the applicant's disposable income and disposable capital are such that, in accordance with regulation 26(1), he is eligible for legal aid,

and shall inform him of the circumstances in which he may renew his application or apply to an area committee for the decision to be reviewed.

    (2)   Copies of the following documents shall be sent to the applicant and his solicitor, if any:

    (a)   form 2;

    (b)   if the application was refused on the ground specified in paragraph (1)(a), the record required to be kept by regulation 8(1);

    (c)   where an application for review under regulation 15 may be made, the completed form 1.

Determination of contribution where legal aid is refused by a magistrates' court

13.   Where a magistrates' court or a justices' clerk has refused to make a legal aid order, the court or the justices' clerk shall determine—

    (a)   the applicant's disposable income and disposable capital, and

    (b)   the amount of any contribution which would have been payable and the manner in which it would be payable by the applicant or an appropriate contributor had a legal aid order been made,

and shall notify the applicant of the amounts so determined.

Renewal of application

14.—(1)   Without prejudice to the provisions of regulation 15, an applicant whose application under regulation 11 has been refused may renew his application either orally to the court or to the justices' clerk.

    (2)   Where an application is renewed under paragraph (1), the applicant shall return the notice of refusal which he received under regulation 12 or any such notice received under regulation 17(4).

    (3)   Where an application is renewed to the justices' clerk, he may either grant the application or refer it to the court or to a justice of the peace.

    (4)   Where an application is renewed to the court, the court may grant or refuse the application or refer it to the justices' clerk.

    (5)   The court or a justice of the peace to whom an application is referred under paragraph (3) or (6), may grant or refuse the application.

    (6)   A justices' clerk to whom an application is referred under paragraph (4), may grant the application or refer it either back to the court or to a justice of the peace.

    (7)   Except where the applicant is not required to furnish a statement of means under regulation 23(4), a legal aid order shall not be made where an application is renewed under paragraph (1) until the court, a justice of the peace or the justices' clerk has considered the applicant's statement of means.

    (8)   Regulation 12 shall apply where an application is refused under this regulation with the modification that references to a magistrates' court shall be construed as including references to a justice of the peace.

    (9)   In this regulation, 'a justice of the peace' means a justice of the peace who is entitled to sit as a member of the magistrates' court.

Application for review

15.—(1)   Where an application for a legal aid order has been refused after having been considered for the first time by a magistrates' court or a justices' clerk, the applicant may, subject to paragraphs (2) and (3), apply for review to the appropriate area committee.

    (2)   An application for review shall only lie to an area committee where—

    (a)   the applicant is charged with an indictable offence or an offence which is triable either way or appears or is brought before a magistrates' court to be dealt with in respect of a sentence imposed or an order made in connection with such an offence; and

    (b)   the application for a legal aid order has been refused on the ground specified in regulation 12(1)(a); and

(c)   the application for a legal aid order was made no later than 21 days before the date fixed for the trial of an information or the inquiry into an offence as examining justices, where such a date had been fixed at the time that the application was made.

(3)   An application for review shall not lie to an area committee where the offence is one of those mentioned in schedule 2 to the Magistrates' Courts Act 1980 and by virtue of section 22 of that Act, the offence is triable only summarily.

Procedure on application for review

16.—(1)   An application for review shall be made by giving notice in form 3 to the appropriate area committee within 14 days of the date of notification of the refusal to make a legal aid order and the applicant shall send a copy of form 3 to the justices' clerk of the magistrates' court to which the first application for legal aid was made.

(2)   An application under paragraph (1) shall be accompanied by the following documents—

(a)   a copy of the completed form 1 returned by the court under regulation 12(2); and

(b)   a copy of the notice of refusal received under regulation 12.

(3)   The time-limit within which the application for review is to be made may, for good reason, be waived or extended by the area committee.

(4)   The justices' clerk and the applicant shall supply such further particulars, information and documents as the area committee may require in relation to an application under paragraph (1).

Determination of review

17.—(1)   On a review, the area committee shall consider the application for legal aid and either—

(a)   refuse the application; or

(b)   make a legal aid order.

(2)   Where the area committee makes a legal aid order, it shall make a contribution order in accordance with any determination made under regulation 13.

(3)   Where a magistrates' court or a justices' clerk has determined under regulation 13 that any legal aid order which is made shall not take effect until a contribution from disposable capital is paid, the area committee shall send the legal aid order to the appropriate justices' clerk.

(4)   The area committee shall give notice of its decision and the reasons for it in form 4 to—

(a)   the applicant and his solicitor, if any, and

(b)   the justices' clerk of the magistrates' court to which the application for legal aid was made.

(5)   In the case of proceedings to which section 22 of the Act applies, the statement of reasons required by paragraph (4) shall comply with regulation 8(4).

Proceedings in the Crown Court

18.—(1)   An application for a legal aid order in respect of proceedings in the Crown Court shall be made either to the appropriate officer of the Crown Court in form 1 or

(a)   orally to the Crown Court or to a magistrates' court at the conclusion of any proceedings in that magistrates' court; or

(b)   where a magistrates' court has been given a notice of transfer under section 4 of the Criminal Justice Act 1987 (serious fraud cases), to the justices' clerk of that magistrates' court in form 1; or

(c)   in the case of an appeal to the Crown Court from a magistrates' court, to the justices' clerk of that magistrates' court in form 1; or

(d)   where the applicant was granted legal aid for proceedings in the magistrates' court and was committed for trial in the Crown Court under section 6(2) of the Magistrates' Courts Act 1980, to the justices' clerk of the magistrates' court ordering the committal in such form as may be required; or

(e)   in the case of a retrial ordered under section 7 of the Criminal Appeal Act 1968, orally to the court ordering the retrial,

and the appropriate officer, the court or the justices' clerk may grant or refuse the application.

(2)   Where an application for a legal aid order is made orally to the court, the court may refer it to the proper officer of the court for determination.

(3)   Except where the applicant is not required to furnish a statement of means under regulation 23(4), a legal aid order shall not be made on an application under paragraph (1) until the appropriate officer, the court or the justices' clerk has considered the applicant's statement of means.

[**19 to 21.**   Contain provisions relating to notification of refusal of legal aid, determination of contribution where legal aid is refused and renewal of application to either the court or an appropriate officer of the Crown Court. The regulations are analogous to regulations 12 to 14 which deal with the same matters where legal aid is refused for magistrates' court proceedings.]

[**22.**   Deals with applications for legal aid in respect of proceedings in the Court of Appeal or House of Lords.]

[**22A**   Deals with references for a report on the financial resources of an applicant or assisted person.]

PART III   STATEMENT OF MEANS AND PAYMENT OF CONTRIBUTIONS

[**23 to 39.**   Deal with the applicant's statement of means, the determination, assessment and payment of contributions, the variation and revocation of contribution orders, refusal to pay contributions and the repayment of contributions by the court. The effect of these regulations is summarised in **D27.15** and **D27.16**].

PART IV   LEGAL AID ORDERS

[**40. and 41.**   Deal respectively with the form to be taken by (a) legal aid orders and (b) orders revoking legal aid. They also prescribe the persons to whom copies of the orders are to be sent.]

Withdrawal for abuse of legal aid or for failure to provide information
41A.—(1)   Without prejudice to regulation 41, a legal aid order may be withdrawn where, as a result of information which has been provided under these regulations or otherwise, it appears that the legally assisted person has—

(a)   in relation to any application for a legal aid order, made an untrue statement as to his financial resources or has failed to disclose any material fact concerning them; or

(b)   intentionally failed to comply with any provision of regulations made under the Act by not furnishing any material information concerning any matter other than his financial resources or in furnishing such information has knowingly made a false statement or false representation,

and, in this regulation, 'legally assisted person' includes an appropriate contributor.

(2)   A legal aid order shall not be withdrawn under paragraph (1) where the legally assisted person satisfies the court that he used due care or diligence to avoid such mis-statement or failure.

(3)   A legal aid order may be withdrawn where the court is satisfied that the legally assisted person has failed to attend for an interview or to provide information or documents when required to do so under these regulations.

(4)   Regulation 41(3) and (4) shall apply where a legal aid order is withdrawn under this regulation as it applies where an order is withdrawn under that regulation.

Notes of evidence and depositions
42.   Where a legal aid order is made in respect of an appeal to the Crown Court, the justices' clerk shall supply, on the application of the solicitor assigned to the appellant or respondent on whose application such an order was made, copies of any notes of evidence or depositions taken in the proceedings in the magistrates' court.

[**43.**   Deals with the transfer of documents relating to legal aid between courts when a person is committed for trial or sentence or appeals.]

PART V   LEGAL REPRESENTATION

Nature of representation

44.—(1)   Subject to the following paragraphs of this regulation, a grant of representation shall provide for the services of two legal representatives, whether expressed as such or in equivalent terms, namely solicitor and counsel or authorised litigator and authorised advocate.

(2)   A legal aid order granting representation for the purpose of such part of any proceedings before a magistrates' court as relates to the giving of bail shall not include representation by counsel.

(3)   A legal aid order granting representation for the purposes of proceedings before a magistrates' court shall not include representation by counsel except—

(a)   in the case of any indictable offence, where the court is of the opinion that, because of circumstances which make the case unusually grave or difficult, representation by both solicitor and counsel would be desirable; or

(b)   in the case of proceedings under section 9 of the Extradition Act 1989 or paragraph 6 of schedule 1 to that Act, where the court is of the opinion that, because of circumstances which make the proceedings unusually grave or difficult, representation by both solicitor and counsel would be desirable.

(4)   Where a court grants representation for the purposes of an appeal to the Court of Appeal, the court may order that representation shall be by counsel only.

(5)   Where the Crown Court grants representation for the purposes of—

(a)   an appeal to that court;

(b)   proceedings in which a person is committed to or appears before that court for trial or sentence or appears or is brought before the Crown Court to be dealt with;

the court may, in cases of urgency where it appears to the court that there is no time to instruct a solicitor, order that representation shall be by counsel only.

(6)   Where the Crown Court or a magistrates' court grants representation for the purposes specified in paragraph (5), the court may, if the proceedings are proceedings in which solicitors have a right of audience, order that representation shall be by a solicitor only.

(7)   Where in proceedings in a magistrates' court representation or advice is given before a legal aid order is made, that representation or advice shall be deemed to be representation or advice given under the order if—

(a)   the interests of justice required that the representation or advice be provided as a matter of urgency;

(b)   there was no undue delay in making an application for legal aid; and

(c)   the representation or advice was given by the solicitor who was subsequently assigned under the legal aid order.

Assignment of solicitor and selection of counsel

45.—(1)   Subject to regulations 46 and 49, any person who is granted representation entitling him to the services of a solicitor, may select any solicitor who is willing to act and such solicitor shall be assigned to him.

(2)   Subject to regulations 46 and 49, where a legal aid order is made providing for the services of solicitor and counsel, the solicitor may instruct any counsel who is willing to act.

Assignment of solicitor or counsel for the Court of Appeal or the House of Lords

46.—(1)   In the case of proceedings in the Court of Appeal or the House of Lords, counsel may be assigned by the court, a judge of the court or the proper officer making or amending the legal aid order.

(2)   In assigning counsel or a solicitor to a legally assisted person in respect of an appeal to the Court of Appeal or the House of Lords, the court, a judge of the court or the proper officer shall have regard, as far as is reasonably practicable, to the wishes of the legally assisted person, the identity of the solicitor or counsel, if any, who represented him in any earlier proceedings and the nature of the appeal.

[**47.**   Deals with assignment of counsel where legal aid is for representation by counsel only.]

Assignment of Queen's Counsel and two counsel

48.—(1)   A legal aid order may provide for the services of a Queen's Counsel or of more than one counsel in respect of the whole or any specified part of any proceedings only in the cases specified and in the manner prescribed by the following paragraphs of this regulation.

(2)   The cases specified for the purposes of this regulation are trials in the Crown Court or proceedings in the Court of Appeal or the House of Lords—

(a)   on a charge of murder, or

(b)   where it appears to the court making the order that the case is one of exceptional difficulty, gravity or complexity and that a legal aid order for the provision of services in the terms provided for by paragraph (3)(a) or (b) of this regulation is required in the interests of justice; or

(c)   where the prosecution is being brought by the Serious Fraud Office.

(3)   Subject to paragraphs (4) to (9), a legal aid order may provide for the services of a Queen's Counsel or of more than one counsel in any of the following terms—

(a)   a Queen's Counsel alone;

(b)   where two counsel are required—

(i)   a Queen's Counsel with a junior counsel, or

(ii)   a Queen's Counsel with a noting junior counsel, or

(iii)   two junior counsel, or

(iv)   a junior counsel with a noting junior counsel.

(4)   In proceedings to which paragraph (2)(c) applies, a court making a legal order [*sic*] may, if it considers that three counsel are required, provide for the services of three counsel in any of the terms provided for in paragraph (3)(b) plus an extra junior counsel or noting junior counsel.

(5)   The fact that a Queen's Counsel has been or is proposed to be assigned under this regulation shall not by itself be a reason for making an order in any of the terms provided for by paragraph (3)(b) or (4).

(6)   Where a Queen's Counsel has been or is proposed to be assigned under this regulation, no order in any of the terms provided for by paragraph (3)(b) or (4) shall be made where it appears to the court at the time of making the order that—

(a)   there is reasonable certainty that the indictment wil be disposed of by a guilty plea and there are no special circumstances requiring the provision of the services of more than one counsel, or

(b)   the case relates to an appeal to the Court of Appeal or to the House of Lords and representation can properly be undertaken by a Queen's Counsel alone.

(7)   Unless the court to which the application is made otherwise directs, every application for a legal aid order in any of the terms provided for by paragraph (3) or (4) or for an amendment under paragraph (10) or (11) shall be in writing specifying—

(a)   the terms of the order sought and the grounds of the application; and

(b)   if the order sought is for the provision of services in any terms provided for by paragraph (3)(b) or (4), the reasons why two counsel are required or an extra junior counsel or noting junior counsel is required as the case may be.

(8)   A court may, before making a legal aid order in the terms provided for by paragraph (3) or (4) or amending the order under paragraph (10) or (11), require written advice from any counsel already assigned to the applicant on the question of what representation is needed in the proceedings.

(9)   A magistrates' court which is competent as respects any proceedings by virtue of section 20(4) or (5) of the Act may make a legal aid order providing for the services of a Queen's Counsel with one junior counsel where:—

(a)   the proceedings are a trial for murder and the order is made upon committal or transfer for trial, or

(b)   the prosecution is brought by the Serious Fraud Office and the order is made upon receiving a notice of transfer under section 4 of the Criminal Justice Act 1987 but shall have no other power to make an order under this regulation.

(10)   In proceedings to which paragraph (2)(a) or (b) applies, a legal aid order which provides—

(a)   for one counsel only may be amended to provide for the services of a Queen's Counsel or of more than one counsel in any terms provided for by paragraph (3);

(b)   for two counsel in any terms provided for by paragraph (3)(b) may be amended to provide for the services of the same number of counsel but in other terms provided for by that paragraph, or for a Queen's Counsel alone, or for one counsel only in accordance with regulation 47.

(11)   In proceedings to which paragraph (2)(c) applies, a legal aid order which provides—

(a)   for one counsel only may be amended to provide for the services of a Queen's Counsel or of more than one counsel in any terms provided for by paragraph (3) or (4);

(b)   for two counsel in any terms provided for by paragraph (3)(b) may be amended to provide for the services of three counsel in any terms provided for by paragraph (4), for two counsel but in other terms provided for by paragraph (3)(b), or for a Queen's Counsel alone, or for one counsel only in accordance with regulation 47;

(c)   for three counsel in any terms provided for by paragraph (4) may be amended to provide for the same number of counsel but in other terms provided for by paragraph (4), or for two counsel in any terms provided for by paragraph (3)(b), or for a Queen's Counsel alone, or for one counsel only in accordance with regulation 47.

(12)   In every case in which a legal aid order is made under this regulation for the provision of services in terms provided for by paragraph (3) or (4), it shall be the duty of—

(a)   each legal representative—

(i)   to keep under review the need for more than one counsel to be present in court or otherwise providing services, and

(ii)   to consider whether the legal aid order should be amended as provided for in paragraph (10) or (11);

(b)   Queen's Counsel, where the services of a Queen's Counsel are provided, to keep under review whether he could act alone.

(13)   It shall be the duty of each legal representative, if of the opinion that the legal aid order should be amended as provided for in paragraphs (10) and (11), to notify that opinion in writing:

(a)   to the other legal representatives for the assisted person, and

(b)   to the court;

and the court shall, after considering the opinion and any representations made by any other legal representatives for the assisted person determine whether and in what manner the legal aid order should be amended.

(14)   A decision to make or amend a legal aid order so as to provide for the services of a Queen's Counsel or of more than one counsel may only be made:—

(a)   in the cases specified in paragraph (2)(a) or (b), by a circuit judge or a High Court judge where the proceedings are in the Crown Court, or by a judge of the Court of Appeal or the Registrar where the proceedings are in the Court of Appeal;

(b)   in the case specified in paragraph (2)(c), by the judge expected to try the case or a High Court judge where the proceedings are in the Crown Court, or by a High Court judge or a judge of the Court of Appeal where the proceedings are in the Court of Appeal.

Assignment of one solicitor or counsel to more than one legally assisted person

49.   A solicitor or counsel may be assigned to two or more legally assisted persons whose cases are to be heard together, unless the interests of justice require that such persons be separately represented.

[**50.**   Empowers a court, on application, to amend a legal aid order by assigning different legal representatives from those originally assigned. The court may also withdraw an order if the legal representatives for the time being assigned under the order withdraw from the case, and it appears to the court that because of the legally assisted person's conduct it is not desirable to assign other representatives.]

[**51.**   Procedure on an application to amend a legal aid order and options open to the applicant if the application is refused. The regulation also deals with applications to amend legal aid for proceedings in a magistrates' court so as to make the order cover representation by solicitor and counsel, not just solicitor.]

[**52.**   Circumstances in which an unsuccessful application to the court to amend a legal aid order may be renewed to the area committee, and procedure to be followed on such renewed applications.]

[**53.** Powers of the area committee upon renewed applications to amend under reg. 52.]

PART VI AUTHORITY TO INCUR COSTS AND RESTRICTIONS ON PAYMENT OF LEGAL REPRESENTATIVES

Power of area committee to authorise expenditure

54.—(1)   Where it appears to a legally assisted person's solicitor necessary for the proper conduct of proceedings in a magistrates' court or in the Crown Court for costs to be incurred under the legal aid order by taking any of the following steps—

(a)   obtaining a written report or opinion of one or more experts;

(b)   employing a person to provide a written report or opinion (otherwise than as an expert);

(c)   bespeaking transcripts of shorthand notes or of tape recordings of any proceedings, including police questioning of suspects;

(d)   where a legal aid order provides for the services of solicitor and counsel, instructing a Queen's Counsel alone without junior counsel; or

(e)   performing an act which is either unusual in its nature or involves unusually large expenditure;

he may apply to the appropriate area committee for prior authority so to do.

(2)   Where an area committee authorises the taking of any step specified in paragraph (1)(a), (b), (c) or (e) it shall also authorise the maximum fee to be paid for any such report, opinion, transcript or act.

Prior approval for travelling and accommodation expenses

54A.   A legal representative assigned to a legally assisted person in any proceedings in the Crown Court may apply to the appropriate authority for prior approval for the incurring of travelling and accommodation expenses in order to attend at the trial or other main hearing in those proceedings.

Power to certify for attendance

54B.—(1)   A judge of the Crown Court shall have power to certify that attendance on the authorised advocate instructed in those proceedings is required for the whole or part of any hearing specified in regulation 6(5A) of the Legal Aid in Criminal and Care Proceedings (Costs) Regulations 1989.

(2)   In deciding whether attendance is required for the whole or any part of a hearing, the judge shall have regard to the following factors, in addition to any other factors which he considers to be relevant:—

(a)   on which days if any the attendance of a significant number of defence witnesses is likely to be required;

(b)   where the hearing is a trial, the amount of documentary evidence likely to be adduced on behalf of the defence;

(c)   the likelihood of the legally assisted person disrupting the proceedings if the authorised advocate were to appear alone;

(d)   whether the authorised advocate represents more than one legally assisted person;

(e)   on which days if any the authorised advocate is likely to require notes of the proceedings to be taken for the proper conduct of the defence.

(3)   An application for a certificate under paragraph (1) may be made at or at any time after the pleas and directions hearing or, if there is to be no pleas and directions hearing, at or at any time after the listing of the first hearing of the case; and in either case the application may be made orally or in writing.

[**55.**   Where a legal aid order has been made, the legal representatives assigned are to be paid solely out of the legal aid fund or by the Lord Chancellor, save that – if an application has been made under regulation 54 to incur the exceptional fees or expenses mentioned therein and refused – payment may be made for the step to which the application related from any source, including the legally assisted person privately.]

Duty to report abuse of legal aid

56.   Notwithstanding the relationship between or rights of a legal representative and client or any privilege arising out of such relationship, where the legal representative for an applicant or legally assisted person knows that the person has intentionally failed to comply with any provision of regulations made under the Act concerning the information to be furnished by him or in furnishing such information has knowingly made a false statement or false representation, the legal representative shall forthwith report the fact to the proper officer.

COSTS

Power to Award Costs

The power of the courts to award costs in criminal proceedings is contained in ss. 16 to **D27.33** 21 of the Prosecution of Offences Act 1985, supplemented by the Costs in Criminal Cases (General) Regulations 1986 (SI 1986 No. 1335). The Prosecution of Offences Act 1985, s. 16, deals with costs out of central funds in favour of an acquitted accused, known as 'defendant's costs orders'; s. 17 deals with prosecution costs out of central funds; s. 18 with orders that a convicted accused pay prosecution costs; s. 19 with orders that a party guilty of improper acts or omissions in the course of the proceedings pay any costs thrown away by his opponent in consequence; and s. 19A with awards of costs against legal representatives. Section 20 authorises the Lord Chancellor to make supplemental regulations, and s. 21 contains definitions.

Defendants' Costs Orders

Jurisdiction to Make a Defendant's Costs Order   In any of the situations listed **D27.34** below the appropriate court may make a defendant's costs order in favour of a successful accused or, as the case may be, appellant. The effect of a defendant's costs order is that the defence costs are paid out of central funds. The principal cases in which power to make such an order arises are as follows:

Section of Prosecution of Offences Act 1985	*Nature and result of proceedings*	*Court with power to to make order*
16(1)	An information is not proceeded with, or the magistrates decide not to commit for trial, or the accused is acquitted after a summary trial.	The magistrates' court which refuses to commit or, as the case may be, acquits the accused. The fact that the court would not have tried the case because the information was laid out of time does not prevent the court from making a defendant's costs order (*Patel v Blakey* [1988] RTR 65).
16(2)	An accused is not tried for an offence for which he has been committed for trial (or in respect of which notice of transfer has been given under the Criminal Justice Act 1987, s. 4), or he is tried on indictment and acquitted on any count in the indictment.	The Crown Court
16(3)	An accused convicted in the magistrates' court appeals against conviction and it is set aside by the Crown Court, or he appeals against sentence and is awarded a less severe punishment by the Crown Court.	The Crown Court

In *Liverpool Magistrates' Court, ex parte Abiaka* (1999) 163 JP 497, the Divisional Court held that s. 16(1) gave power to any constitution of the magistrates' court to make a defendant's costs order, and was not confined to the same constitution of justices who had dismissed the case.

Proper Approach to Making of a Defendant's Costs Order

D27.35 The Prosecution of Offences Act 1985, s. 16, merely empowers courts to make defendants' costs orders but gives no guidance on when and how the power should be exercised. Such guidance is, however, provided by the Lord Chief Justice's *Practice Direction (Crime: Costs)* [1991] 1 WLR 498. (The Royal Courts of Justice have published a guide: *A Guide to the Award of Costs in Criminal Proceedings* (RCJ (1991) HMSO), which includes the relevant statutory provisions and the text of the direction, together with an explanatory introduction.)

The practice direction applies whenever the magistrates' court, Crown Court, Divisional Court or Court of Appeal considers an award of costs in criminal proceedings. Paragraph 2.1 makes it clear that magistrates' courts may make defendant's costs orders, whether inquiring into an indictable offence as examining justices (or with a view to transferring the proceedings to the Crown Court for trial), or dealing summarily with an offence. In deciding whether to make an order, magistrates' courts should take into account the same factors as the Crown Court (see below).

By para. 2.2 of the 1991 practice direction, if circumstances have arisen in which the Crown Court has power to make a defendant's costs order in favour of a successful accused (i.e., he has either not been tried for an offence in respect of which he was indicted or committed for trial, or his trial has ended in acquittal), then such an order should normally be made unless there are positive reasons for not doing so. The paragraph then gives two specific examples of reasons for refusing an order, namely, (a) that the accused brought suspicion on himself by his own conduct and thus misled the prosecution into thinking the case against him to be stronger than it really was, and (b) that he was acquitted on a meritless technicality when in fact there was ample evidence to support a conviction. Leaving aside such exceptional circumstances, the general rule is that a successful accused is entitled to his costs. They should not be denied merely because the prosecution acted properly in bringing the case. (See, for example, *Birmingham Juvenile Court, ex parte H* (1992) 156 JP 445, where the defence solicitor admitted that the prosecution was not malicious, but the Divisional Court held that this was no reason for the justices to refuse to make a defendant's costs order). Paragraph 2.3 deals with the problem of an accused being acquitted on some but not all counts. The Prosecution of Offences Act 1985, s. 16(2)(b), expressly allows a defendant's costs order to be made in such cases. However, the presumption in favour of an order created by para. 3.2 of the 1991 practice direction when the accused is acquitted on all counts does not apply if there is a partial acquittal. Instead, the granting or refusal of an order is left completely in the court's discretion, and there is particular reference to the court's power to make an order extending to part only of the costs incurred (see s. 16(7)). No doubt the court's decision will in practice depend on whether the accused was acquitted on the major part of the indictment or only on subsidiary counts. Whether a plea to the matters of which he was ultimately convicted was offered to the prosecution but rejected will also be of importance.

Paragraphs 2.4 to 2.8 of the 1991 practice direction deal with defendants' costs orders on appeal. As regards costs on a successful appeal from a magistrates' court to the Crown Court and costs when a criminal cause or matter is determined in the Divisional Court, the practice direction merely reiterates the provisions of the Prosecution of Offences Act 1985 that the courts in question have power to make an order (see paras 2.4 and 2.5 of the direction respectively). The implication is that the making of an order is entirely discretionary. As regards costs for a successful appellant in the Court of Appeal, it is stated that the court 'will have in mind the principles applied by the Crown Court in relation to acquitted defendants' (para. 2.8).

Costs Payable under a Defendant's Costs Order: the General Rule   Unless the **D27.36** court orders otherwise, the effect of a defendant's costs order is that the accused or appellant is paid out of central funds such amount as the court considers reasonably sufficient to compensate him for any expenses properly incurred by him in the proceedings (Prosecution of Offences Act 1985, s. 16(6)). 'Proceedings' include any there may have been in a court below that making the costs order (see the definition of 'proceedings' in s. 21(1)). Thus, where the Crown Court on trial on indictment or appeal from the magistrates makes a defendant's costs order, the order will (in the absence of express provision to the contrary) cover the costs of the committal proceedings or summary trial. Similarly, an order by the Court of Appeal following a successful appeal from the Crown Court will extend to the costs of the trial on indictment.

If the accused agrees, the amount payable under s. 16(6) may be fixed forthwith and specified in the order (s. 16(9)(a)). Otherwise it is determined in accordance with regulations made by the Lord Chancellor (s. 16(9)(b)). The relevant provisions are part III (regs 4 to 13) of the Costs in Criminal Cases (General) Regulations 1986 (SI 1986 No. 1335). These provide in essence that the 'appropriate authority' (or officers appointed to act on his behalf) shall consider the claim for costs submitted by or on behalf of the defendant, and shall allow reasonable costs in respect of work that appears to have been actually and reasonably done and disbursements that have been actually and reasonably incurred (reg. 7). The 'appropriate authority' is (a) the Registrar in the case of Court of Appeal proceedings; (b) the Master of the Crown Office in the case of Divisional Court proceedings; (c) an officer appointed by the Lord Chancellor in the case of Crown Court proceedings, and (d) the justices' clerk in the case of magistrates' court proceedings (reg. 5). An applicant (i.e. any person in whose favour an order for costs out of central funds has been made) who is dissatisfied with the appropriate authority's decision as to the costs payable may first apply for redetermination by the authority. If the result of that is unsatisfactory, there is an appeal to the Chief Taxing Master of the Supreme Court, and a further appeal from him to the High Court if a point of principle of general importance is involved (regs 9 to 12). The above provisions for redetermination and appeal do not apply where the costs determined are in respect of magistrates' courts proceedings (see reg. 9), although presumably the decision of the justices' clerk may be challenged by judicial review in accordance with the usual principles governing such applications.

The above regulations are complemented by para. 5 of the Lord Chief Justice's *Practice Direction (Crime: Costs)* [1991] 1 WLR 498 which states that, when the Crown Court, Divisional Court or Court of Appeal makes a defendant's costs order, it is under a duty to direct the appropriate authority (a) to disallow any costs which were plainly not properly incurred, and (b) to consider or investigate on taxation any that *may* have been improperly incurred. Costs improperly incurred include those wasted by failure to conduct the proceedings with reasonable competence and expedition (para. 5.1). Either the party whose costs might be affected by a direction under para. 5 or his solicitor should be informed of the precise terms of the direction, and should be given a reasonable opportunity to show cause why no direction should be made (para. 5.2). Paragraphs 5.2 and 5.3 of the practice direction broadly parallel para. 9, which deals with observations by a judge to the effect that legal aid costs should be disallowed.

Orders for Less than the Full Costs Incurred   By the Prosecution of Offences Act **D27.37** 1985, s. 16(7), where the court making a defendant's costs order is of the opinion that there are circumstances making it inappropriate for the defendant to recover the full amount of the costs that would otherwise be assessed payable under s. 16(6), then it shall assess what amount would be just and reasonable and specify it in the order. One obvious situation for fixing the costs at less than the full amount is where an accused is acquitted on some but not all the counts on the indictment. It should be noted that a court acting under s. 16(7) is obliged to specify the sum that shall be paid rather than allowing a percentage of the total costs as assessed by the appropriate authority (see the terms of the subsection).

D27.38 *Order in Favour of a Legally Aided Accused*   By the Prosecution of Offences Act 1985, s. 21(4A)(a) (inserted by the Legal Aid Act 1988), the cost of a legally aided accused shall *not* – for purposes of a defendant's costs order – be taken to include any expenses incurred on his behalf by the Legal Aid Board or the Lord Chancellor. It follows that a defendant's costs order will generally be pointless in the case of such an accused since all the costs properly incurred on his behalf will have been defrayed out of legal aid, and there will be nothing left on which the order can bite. A costs order will, however, be appropriate if, for example, the accused was not aided until a late stage of the proceedings and paid for the costs of his early representation privately, or if there were unusual expenditures incurred on his behalf and an application under reg. 54(1) of the Legal Aid in Criminal and Care Proceedings (General) Regulations 1989 failed to obtain authorisation for the expenditure from the area committee. Similarly, he can, as a result of a defendant's costs order, become entitled to an allowance for travelling and subsistence under reg. 23, as if he had been a witness. Where the accused has made (or is liable to make) a contribution to the costs of his legal aid such contributions again do not count as costs recoverable under a defendant's costs order (last clause of s. 21(4A)(a)). Thus, an argument sometimes advanced under the terms of the Prosecution of Offences Act 1985 as originally drafted – that an accused who was refused remission and/or repayment of contributions under reg. 35 of the General Regulations could nonetheless claim to be reimbursed for those payments out of central funds – is clearly no longer tenable. The upshot of s. 21(4A)(a) is that, save in a minority of exceptional cases, defendants' costs orders are relevant only to accused who have paid for their defences privately.

Prosecution Costs

D27.39 *Power to Make Order for Prosecution Costs*   Subject to what follows, the Prosecution of Offences Act 1985, s. 17(1), provides that the court may award a prosecutor such amount out of central funds as it considers reasonably necessary to compensate him for any expenses properly incurred by him in the proceedings. This applies whether or not the accused is convicted, but applies only to proceedings in respect of an indictable offence (whether tried summarily or on indictment) and proceedings before a Divisional Court in respect of a summary offence (paras (a) and (b) of s. 17(1)). In other words, the prosecution costs of summary trial may never be awarded out of central funds. An even more important restriction on the ambit of s. 17(1) is that no order may be made in favour of a public authority (s. 17(2)), which term is defined by s. 17(3) as comprising a police force, the CPS, local authorities and any other authority appointed by the Crown or financed by money voted by Parliament. Thus, s. 17(1) is of potential value only in that tiny proportion of prosecutions brought by private individuals or organisations. Where the subsection does potentially apply, an order *should* be made unless there is good reason for not doing so – e.g., the proceedings have been instituted or continued without good cause (see para. 3.1 of *Practice Direction (Crime: Costs)* [1991] 1 WLR 498). Even so, an express application must be made, rather than assuming that the court will automatically order costs of its own motion (ibid.). Regulations 4 to 13 of the Costs in Criminal Cases (General) Regulations 1986 apply to assessment of prosecutors' costs out of central funds just as they apply to costs under defendants' costs orders. Under earlier regulations, it was held that a private prosecutor could not claim for the time he had spent in preparation and presentation of the prosecution, although he was entitled to recover travelling and secretarial expenses (*Stockport Magistrates' Court, ex parte Cooper* (1984) 149 JP 261).

Order that the Accused Pay Prosecution Costs Subsections (1) and (2) of the **D27.40**
Prosecution of Offences Act 1985, s. 18, authorise the making of orders that a convicted accused or unsuccessful appellant shall pay costs as indicated in the table below. The first column describes the event giving rise to the liability to a costs order; the second states the court with power to make the order, and the third states the person in whose favour the order is to be made.

Relevant event	*Court*	*Beneficiary of order*
Summary conviction (whether for a summary offence or for one triable either way).	The convicting magistrates' court.	The prosecutor.
Conviction on indictment.	The Crown Court.	The prosecutor.
Dismissal of an appeal to the Crown Court against conviction or sentence by the magistrates.	The Crown Court.	The prosecutor.
Dismissal of an appeal to the Court of Appeal against conviction or sentence (including application for leave to appeal); dismissal of an application for leave to appeal from the Court of Appeal to the House of Lords; dismissal of an appeal to the Court of Appeal in respect of the Crown Court's ruling at a preparatory hearing in a serious fraud case.	The Court of Appeal.	Such person as may be named in the order (not necessarily the prosecutor).

In addition, reg. 14 of the Costs in Criminal Cases (General) Regulations 1986 provides, *inter alia*, that the Prosecution of Offences Act 1985, s. 18, is to apply to proceedings in the Crown Court on committals for sentence (including committals to be dealt with for breach of a suspended sentence, probation order or conditional discharge) just as it applies to trials on indictment. In short, the Crown Court when dealing with the committed offender may order him to pay costs.

Amount of Order for Prosecution Costs When a court makes an order under the **D27.41**
Prosecution of Offences Act 1985, s. 18, for the payment of prosecution costs, it orders the payment of an amount that it considers 'just and reasonable'. That sum must be specified in the order (s. 18(3) – cf. the position under the Costs in Criminal Cases Act 1973 which gave the court the option of either fixing the sum or ordering that the accused pay the whole prosecution costs as subsequently taxed). The court may not delegate (e.g., to a justices' clerk or Crown Court officer) the duty of determining what the accused should pay (*Bunston v Rawlings* [1982] 1 WLR 473 and see also para. 1.8 of *Practice Direction (Crime: Costs)* [1991] 1 WLR 498). Therefore, the prosecution

should if possible be able to inform the court of the costs that have been incurred at each stage of the relevant proceedings, thus enabling the court to make an appropriate order (*Practice Direction (Crime: Costs)*, para. 1.8). Where the prosecution are unable to provide a figure forthwith, the court should adjourn for inquiries to be made by an appropriate officer (ibid.). In *Associated Octel Ltd* [1997] 1 Cr App R (S) 435, the Court of Appeal held that the costs of the prosecution for the purposes of s. 18(1) might include the costs of the prosecuting authority in carrying out investigations. In *Octel*, the offence was both investigated and prosecuted by the Health and Safety Executive. It is submitted that the position would be different where different bodies investigated and prosecuted (e.g., the police and the CPS respectively). It would not seem to be 'just and reasonable' for the court to order the defendant to pay the prosecution in respect of costs for which it was not liable. As to the procedure to be adopted in cases where the prosecution seeks an order requiring the defendant to pay costs, the Court of Appeal observed that:

(a)   the prosecution should serve on the defence, at the earliest time, full details of its costs, so as to give the defence a proper opportunity to consider them and make representations on them, if appropriate;

(b)   if the defendant, once served with a schedule of the prosecution's costs, wished to dispute the whole or any part of the schedule, he should give proper notice to the prosecution of the objections which it was proposed to make and should at least make it clear to the court what the objections were — in some exceptional cases — a full hearing would need to be held for the objections to be resolved, as there was no provision for the taxation of the prosecution's costs in a criminal case.

See also *Maher* [1983] QB 784, although that case was decided under the differently worded provisions of the Costs in Criminal Cases Act 1973. In most cases, precise assessment of prosecution costs will in any event be irrelevant, since the principles discussed below as to the exercise of the court's discretion in the making of orders will result in the amount the accused is required to pay being well below the actual costs, however restrictively interpreted.

Section 18(1) is subject to two specific qualifications. First, where a person is, on summary conviction, fined £5 or less, no order for costs may be made 'unless in the particular circumstances of the case [the court] considers it right to do so'. Secondly, where a juvenile is convicted before a magistrates' court, the amount of any costs he is ordered to pay shall not exceed the amount of any fine imposed on him (s. 18(5)). It is submitted that, where a juvenile is dealt with by means other than a fine, the costs that may be awarded against him are entirely discretionary and not subject to any statutory upper limit.

D27.42   ***Proper Approach to Orders that the Accused Pay Prosecution Costs***   Paragraph 6.4 of *Practice Direction (Crime: Costs)* [1991] 1 WLR 498 states that an order should be made under the Prosecution of Offences Act 1985, s. 18, where the court is satisfied that the offender or appellant has the means and ability to pay. This is the fundamental principle governing costs against the accused and merely confirms pre-existing case law (see, for example, *Mountain* (1978) 68 Cr App R 41 where the Court of Appeal varied orders that M and K pay the entire prosecution costs as assessed – probably £1,000 – to orders that they pay £150 and £250 respectively, Lawton LJ saying that when imposing financial penalties, including costs, the court must have regard to the means of a convicted person). Similarly, in *Nottingham Justices, ex parte Fohmann* (1986) 84 Cr App R 316, the Divisional Court quashed an order by magistrates that F pay a fine of £400 (for offences of obtaining by deception by turning back the odometers on cars he was selling at auction) and prosecution costs of £600, since he was on supplementary benefit and – even if able to maintain the rate of £10 per week ordered by the court –

would have taken two years to pay the combined fine and costs. Glidewell LJ indicated that the amount of costs ordered should not exceed that which the offender can reasonably pay within a year. The case also illustrates that the propriety or otherwise of the decision on costs must be viewed in the light of the overall financial orders made by the court, in particular, any fines or compensation the offender is required to pay. Although *Ex parte Fohmann* remains important for its statement of principle, the suggested time-limit of a year for payment of costs may no longer be appropriate in view of the Court of Appeal having recently held that fines and compensation may now be fixed at amounts requiring payment by instalments over a two or even three-year period (see **E17.13** and **E18.5**). In deciding whether the offender has sufficient means to pay an order for costs, mortgage debts should be taken into account (*Ghadami* [1998] 1 Cr App R (S) 42).

In *Northallerton Magistrates' Court, ex parte Dove* (1999) 163 JP 657, the Divisional Court gave the following series of guidelines on the imposition of costs:

(1)   The order to pay costs should never exceed the sum which the offender was able to pay, and which it was reasonable to expect him to pay, having regard to his means and any other financial order imposed on him.

(2)   Nor should it exceed the sum which the prosecutor had actually and reasonably incurred.

(3)   The purpose of such an order was to compensate the prosecutor and not to punish the offender, e.g., for exercising his constitutional right to defend himself.

(4)   Any costs ordered should not in the ordinary way be grossly disproportionate to any fine imposed. Where the fine and the costs exceeded the sum which the offender could reasonably be ordered to pay, the costs should be reduced, rather than the fine.

(5)   An offender facing a fine or an order as to costs should disclose to the magistrates the data relevant to his financial position, so that they could assess what he could reasonably afford to pay. Failure to make such disclosure could lead the court to draw reasonable inferences as to his means.

(6)   The court should give the offender a fair opportunity to adduce any relevant financial information and make submissions prior to the determination of any financial order.

In addition to these factors, the following matters may influence the court's decisions on costs against him:

(a)   *Plea.* A plea of guilty certainly does not preclude the making of an order for costs. However, combined with other factors such as the offender's limited means, it may persuade the court not to make an order or to make one for considerably less than the actual costs (see O'Connor LJ's judgment in *Maher* [1983] QB 784 at p. 789D–H). The weight to be attached to the plea in this context will depend, *inter alia*, on the stage at which it was entered and the gravity of the case. Thus, in *Maher*, the Court of Appeal (distinguishing the earlier case of *Matthews* (1979) 1 Cr App R (S) 346) ordered that the three appellants should pay a total of £180,000 costs, even though they had all eventually pleaded guilty and one of them had done so at the earliest possible opportunity. The costs orders were justified, *inter alia*, because the offences were exceptionally serious – murder and a major conspiracy to import heroin.

(b)   *Remainder of the sentence.* Where the offender is given an immediate custodial sentence it is unusual to impose an order for costs, if only because he will for the time being have no income out of which to make the required payments. But, again, it is ultimately a matter for the court's discretion. Thus, if there is good reason to suppose that he has substantial capital assets (in particular if they are the proceeds of crime), an order may properly be made (see *Maher* [1983] QB 784 for an example). Where the sentence is non-custodial, one line of authority suggests that any order for costs should not be out of proportion to the penalty proper. This principle was clearly stated by Phillimore LJ in *Whalley* (1972) 56 Cr App R 304:

> This court takes the view that whenever a court is imposing a financial penalty, or making an order in regard to costs, it must have regard to the means of the individual. . . .

The Court of Appeal has considered on a number of occasions the question whether the court should make an order for the payment of prosecution costs which is larger than the fine imposed for the offence itself. For example, in *Whalley*, an order to pay the whole costs of prosecuting a drink-driving offence, for which W had been disqualified and fined £20, was reduced to an order to pay costs not exceeding £50. Similarly, in *Firmston* (1984) 6 Cr App R (S) 189, costs of £400 ordered following F's conviction on indictment for theft from a shop were reduced to £100 because he had been given an absolute discharge for the offence itself. These cases were cited in *Boyle* [1995] Crim LR 514, in which the Court of Appeal nonetheless decided to follow instead the case of *Bushell* (1980) 2 Cr App R (S) 77. Their lordships upheld an order to pay £1,000 prosecution costs where the offender had been fined £250 after electing trial on indictment when the case could conveniently have been tried summarily; in such a case, which was otherwise appropriate for an order for him to pay prosecution costs, the offender could properly be ordered to pay costs on the Crown Court scale.

(c) *Conduct of the defence.* At least in theory, an offender who is found guilty on indictment of an either-way offence should not be punished in costs for having exercised his constitutional right to trial by jury (*Hayden* [1975] 1 WLR 852). However, any order made will inevitably reflect the fact that he has chosen the more expensive method of trial (ibid., and see also *Bushell* (1980) 2 Cr App R (S) 77 where orders to pay £250 costs against each of two accused were upheld because, even though the offence was merely one of obtaining services worth £21 and the fines imposed were only £100, they had elected Crown Court trial in a matter eminently suitable for summary disposition and thus greatly increased the costs incurred by the prosecution). The exercise of the court's discretion may also be affected by the accused having chosen to plead not guilty when the prosecution case against him was manifestly strong and he must have known all along that he was guilty (see dicta in *Singh* (1982) 4 Cr App R (S) 38 where an order of £400 costs against S following his conviction on indictment for a minor assault occasioning actual bodily harm was upheld partly because he had 'extravagantly' elected trial on indictment when there was 'really no need in the circumstances' for him to do so). The relevance of the reasonableness of the defence (albeit disbelieved) to costs was also referred to, *obiter*, by Lawton LJ in *Mountain* (1978) 68 Cr App R 41 (at pp. 43–4 emphasis added):

> In many cases at the trial the accused says, as he is entitled to say and frequently is justified in saying, that there has been some mistake on the part of the prosecution witnesses; that they have confused themselves in thinking that they saw something which they did not see, that their memories have failed them or that the accused has some explanation for what at first sight seems to be criminal conduct. *In that class of case it may be unfair to make an order that the accused should pay the costs of the prosecution.* But there are other kinds of cases which come before the Crown Court where the defence is that everybody except the accused is telling lies and that the prosecution's case is virtually a concocted one. . . .
>
> It is in that kind of case that courts are entitled to make an order that the accused should pay the costs of the prosecution.

(d) *Conduct of the prosecution.* Where a minor case is in the Crown Court through the prosecution's choice, they cannot expect to recover their full costs from the accused. In *Hall* [1989] Crim LR 228, H was willing to plead guilty to careless driving. The case went to the Crown Court because the prosecution insisted on a charge of reckless driving. In the Crown Court, H pleaded guilty to careless driving, and the Crown offered no evidence on the reckless driving charge. H was conditionally discharged and ordered to pay £372 prosecution costs. On appeal, the order was reduced to £25 (the amount appropriate to a guilty plea in the magistrates' court). See also *Clark* (1993) 14 Cr App R (S) 360.

(e) *Apportionment between co-defendants.* Where there is more than one accused, each should be liable only for that portion of the prosecution's costs which is attributable to him. In *Ronson* [1991] Crim LR 794, the appellant and two co-defendants were each ordered to pay a third of the prosecution costs (£440,000 each). The fourth defendant was unable to pay. On appeal, the Court of Appeal held that the right approach was to see what would be a reasonable estimate of the cost of trying each defendant alone. That could not be done here. It was not right that the three defendants who could pay should bear the burden of the fourth. Hence the costs of each defendant were reduced from a third to a quarter.

Orders to Pay Costs Thrown Away

The Prosecution of Offences Act 1985, s. 19(1) and (2), empowered the Lord **D27.43** Chancellor to make regulations by virtue of which a party to criminal proceedings may be ordered to pay costs thrown away as a result of his 'unnecessary or improper act or omission'. Regulation 3 of the Costs in Criminal Cases (General) Regulations 1986 has been made under that power. It provides that, before making such an order, the court shall hear the parties concerned, and shall take into account any other order as to costs (including a legal aid order) which has been made in the proceedings (reg. 3(2)). Conversely, when the time comes to make a general order as to costs, the court shall take into account any order that has already been made under reg. 3 (reg. 3(4)). The amount to be paid by the 'guilty' party must be specified in the order (reg. 3(3)). In the case of a juvenile who has been convicted of an offence, any sum he is ordered to pay by a magistrates' court under reg. 3 shall not exceed the amount of any fine imposed on him (reg. 3(5)). If, during the period of an adjournment, the prosecution serves a notice of discontinuance, the court retains jurisdiction to determine applications for costs (*DPP* v *Denning* [1991] 2 QB 532). For an order as to costs to be made under reg. 3, there must be a causal relationship between the unnecessary or improper act, and the incurring of the costs to be paid under the order (*Wood Green Crown Court, ex parte DPP* [1993] 1 WLR 723).

Regulation 3 is the only provision under which the prosecution may be ordered to pay costs to the accused personally. According to para. 7.4 of *Practice Direction (Crime: Costs)* [1991] 1 WLR 498, an order is appropriate only where the default which has caused costs to be thrown away is that of the defendant or prosecutor personally, not where it is that of the legal representatives. For orders that legal representatives pay costs, see **D27.46**.

Witness Expenses

Section 19(3) of the Prosecution of Offences Act 1985 empowers the Lord Chancellor **D27.44** to make regulations authorising the payment out of central funds of (a) witness expenses, (b) the cost of obtaining medical reports and (c) the fees of an interpreter. Part V of the Costs in Criminal Cases (General) Regulations 1986 (regs 15 to 25) deals with such payments. By reg. 16(1), the expenses properly incurred by the witness or, as the case may be, maker of a medical report or interpreter are to be allowed out of central funds unless the court directs otherwise. This applies whatever the outcome of the proceedings and regardless of whether the witness etc. is required by the prosecution or defence. A non-expert witness (other than police or prison officers) is entitled to travelling expenses, a subsistence allowance and a loss allowance (e.g., for loss of earnings) (see reg. 18). Payment of professional witnesses, experts, suppliers of medical reports and interpreters is dealt with in regs 19 and 20. If a defendant's costs order is made in favour of the accused, he may also be allowed a subsistence allowance and travelling expenses, but he is not entitled to compensation for loss of earnings (reg. 23).

Claw-back by the Lord Chancellor

D27.45 Section 20(2) of the Prosecution of Offences Act 1985 empowers the Lord Chancellor to make regulations enabling sums paid out of the legal aid fund or out of central funds to be recovered from a person who is the beneficiary of an *inter partes* costs order. The Costs in Criminal Cases (General) Regulations 1986, regs 26 and 27, have been made in pursuance of s. 20(2). The effect of the subsection and regulations is that the Lord Chancellor may claw back for the legal aid fund or for central funds money received by:

(a) a defendant who is legally aided where the prosecution are ordered to pay costs under reg. 3 (costs thrown away by a party's default), or

(b) a defendant who is granted costs out of central funds where the prosecution are ordered to pay costs under reg. 3, or

(c) a private prosecutor who is granted costs out of central funds and also obtains an order that the accused pay prosecution costs.

Orders for Costs against Legal Representatives

D27.46 An order to pay costs may be made against a legal representative (as distinct from a party) by virtue of the inherent jurisdiction of the Crown Court (in the case of a solicitor) or under the Prosecution of Offences Act 1985, s. 19A (in respect of a solicitor or a barrister).

The Crown Court, as part of the Supreme Court, has inherent jurisdiction to order that a solicitor pay personally any costs thrown away by his or his staff's improper act or omission (see para. 8.1 of *Practice Direction (Crime: Costs)* [1991] 1 WLR 498). Such an order may not be made unless reasonable notice is given to the solicitor and he has a reasonable opportunity of being heard in reply (para. 8.2). In *Holden and Co.* v *CPS* [1990] 2 QB 261, it was held that mistake, error of judgment or mere negligence were not sufficient to trigger off such an order. The court's jurisdiction arose only where there was a serious dereliction of the solicitor's duty to the court. The primary object of such an order was to reimburse a litigant for costs incurred because of the solicitor's default, but there were also punitive and deterrent elements in the order.

The power to order legal representatives to pay costs has been extended by the Prosecution of Offences Act 1985, s. 19A. This statutory power is an addition to the inherent jurisdiction discussed in the preceding paragraph. A magistrates' court, the Crown Court or the Court of Appeal may disallow costs or order the legal representative concerned to meet the whole or part of the wasted costs. The order can be made against any person exercising a right of audience or a right to conduct litigation. It therefore covers both solicitors and barristers. Wasted costs are costs which are incurred as a result of any improper, unreasonable or negligent act or omission by the representative or his employee, or which the court considers it unreasonable to expect a party to pay in the light of such act or omission occurring after the costs were incurred (s. 19A(3)). The test is therefore extended to cover negligence, in addition to improper or unreasonable acts or omissions. The procedure for the exercise of the new power is laid down in regs 3A to 3D of the Costs in Criminal Cases (General) Regulations 1986. These require the court to specify the amount of the wasted costs order, and allow the representative and any party to the proceedings to make representations. The hearing should normally be in chambers, with a shorthand writer present. The court should give reasons for its order, which it may announce in public.

The procedure was elaborated in *Re a Barrister (Wasted Costs Order) (No. 1 of 1991)* [1993] QB 293, when the Court of Appeal considered an order made against defence counsel in the Crown Court. The trial judge purported to 'disallow such part of the brief fee which would otherwise have been payable on the partial trial as exceeds what would be the proper enhanced refresher for the retrial'. His order was based upon his finding that the barrister was guilty of an 'unreasonable act or omission'. On appeal by the barrister, the Court of Appeal held that the order was *ultra vires* and fatally flawed, since it did not specify the amount of the wasted costs. In any event, the barrister was not, their lordships held, guilty of any unreasonable act or omission such as could found a wasted costs order. They went on to lay down the following guidelines as to the practice to be adopted in deciding upon a wasted costs order:

1 There was a clear need for any judge or court intending to exercise the wasted costs jurisdiction to formulate carefully and concisely the complaint and grounds upon which such an order might be sought. Those measures were draconian, and, as in contempt proceedings, the grounds had to be clear and particular.

2 Where necessary a transcript of the relevant part of the proceedings under discussion should be available. And, in accordance with the rules, a transcript of any wasted costs hearing had to be made.

3 A defendant involved in a case where such proceedings were contemplated should be present if, after discussion with counsel, it was thought that his interests might be affected. And he should certainly be present and represented if the matter might affect the course of his trial. Regulation 3B(2) [of the Costs in Criminal Cases Regulations 1986: see **D27.47**] furthermore required that before a wasted costs order was made 'the court shall allow the legal or other representative and any party to the proceedings to make representations'. There might be cases where it might be appropriate for counsel for the Crown to be present.

4 A three-stage test or approach was recommended when a wasted costs order was contemplated:

(i)   Had there been an improper, unreasonable or negligent act or omission?

(ii) As a result, had any costs been incurred by a party?

(iii) If the answers to (i) and (ii) were yes; should the court exercise its discretion to disallow or order the representative to meet the whole or any part of the relevant costs, and if so what specific sum was involved?

5 It was inappropriate to propose any deal or settlement, such as was suggested in the present case, that the representative might forgo fees. The judge should formally state his complaint, in chambers, and invite the representative to make his own comments.

After any other party had been heard the judge should give his formal ruling. Discursive conversations such as took place in the present case might be unfair and should certainly not take place.

6 As was indicated above the judge had to specify the sum to be disallowed or ordered. Alternatively, the relevant available procedure should be substituted, should it be impossible to fix the sum [see *A Guide to the Award of Costs in Criminal Proceedings* (RCJ (1991) HMSO), para. 6.7].

In *Ridehalgh* v *Horsefield* [1994] Ch 205, the Court of Appeal gave further guidance on the discretion to make a wasted costs order in favour of one party to litigation against the legal representative of the other. Sir Thomas Bingham MR made it clear that the judgment was applicable to criminal as well as civil courts, and made the following points.

(a) 'Improper' covered, but was not confined to, conduct which would ordinarily justify serious professional penalty. It was not limited to significant breach of the relevant code of professional conduct. It included conduct which was improper according to the consensus of professional, including judicial, opinion, whether it violated the letter of a professional code or not.

(b) 'Unreasonable' described conduct which was vexatious, i.e. designed to harass the other side rather than advance the resolution of the dispute. Conduct could not be described as unreasonable simply because it led to an unsuccessful result, or because other more cautious legal representatives would have acted differently. The acid test was whether the conduct permitted of a reasonable explanation. If it did, the course adopted might be regarded as optimistic and reflecting on a practitioner's judgment, but it was not unreasonable.

(c) 'Negligent' should be understood in an untechnical way to denote failure to act with the competence reasonably expected of ordinary members of the profession. It was not a term of art and did not necessarily involve an actionable breach of the legal representative's duty to his own client.

(d) A legal representative was not acting improperly, unreasonably or negligently simply because he acted for a party who pursued a claim or defence which was plainly doomed to fail.

(e) However, a legal representative could not lend his assistance to proceedings which were an abuse of process, and was not entitled to use litigious procedures for purposes for which they were not intended, e.g., by issuing proceedings for reasons unconnected with success in the action, pursuing a case which was known to be dishonest or knowingly conniving at incomplete disclosure of documents.

(f) Any judge considering making a wasted costs order must make full allowance for the fact that an advocate in court often had to make decisions quickly and under pressure.

(g) Legal professional privilege might be relevant. If so, the privilege was the client's which he alone could waive. Judges should make full allowance for the inability of respondent lawyers to tell the whole story. Where there was room for doubt, the respondent lawyers were entitled to the benefit of it. It was only when, with all allowance made, a lawyer's conduct of proceedings was quite plainly unjustifiable that it could be appropriate to make the order.

(h) When a solicitor sought the advice of counsel, he did not abdicate his own professional responsibility. He had to apply his mind to the advice received. But the more specialised the advice, the more reasonable it was likely to be for him to accept it.

(i) A threat to apply for a wasted costs order should not be used as a means of intimidation. However, if one side considered that the conduct of the other was improper, unreasonable or negligent and likely to cause a waste of costs, it was not objectionable to alert the other side to that view.

(j) In the ordinary way, such applications were best left until after the end of the trial.

(k) As to procedure, the respondent lawyer should be told very clearly what he was said to have done wrong. No formal process of discovery would be appropriate. Elaborate pleadings should in general be avoided. The court could not imagine circumstances in which the applicant could interrogate the respondent lawyer or vice versa. The legal representative must have opportunity to show cause why an order should not be made (Rules of the Supreme Court 1965, ord. 62, r. 11(4)), but this did not mean that the burden was on the legal representative to exculpate himself.

In *Re a Barrister (Wasted costs order) (No. 4 of 1992)* (1994) *The Times*, 15 March 1994, the Court of Appeal held that a barrister who practised at home without a clerk must not rely wholly on instructing solicitors to notify him of the dates and times of his cases. He was responsible for keeping abreast of listing details and should have adopted a system which enabled him to do so.

In *Rodney (Wasted Costs Order)* (9 December 1996 unreported), counsel failed to appear before the Court of Appeal due to an error by a junior clerk. A wasted costs order was made although counsel was in no way personally to blame. He was liable for the actions of a clerk in chambers in the same way as a solicitor was vicariously liable on a wasted costs order for the actions of a clerk in his firm.

In *Re A Barrister (Wasted Costs Order No. 4 of 1993)* (1995) *The Times*, 21 April 1995, the Court of Appeal held that a judge should not impose such a Draconian penalty as a wasted costs order without taking into account the daily demands of practice and the difficulties associated with time estimates.

In *Re a Firm of Solicitors (Wasted costs order)* [1999] All ER (D) 728 (unreported in printed form), Q, who was on trial in the Crown Court, was unhappy with his barrister and wished to dispense with her services. Defence counsel suggested that this should be put in writing, and when the court had risen, the experienced solicitor's clerk took a statement from Q to that effect. Whilst the clerk was reading the statement back to Q, the usher brought the jury past them. It was later contended that some of them must have heard what was said, and the jury had to be discharged. The judge made a wasted costs order, which was upheld by the Court of Appeal. The question was whether taking those instructions at a place where he knew the jury was likely to appear and then being oblivious to their appearance constituted negligence on the part of the clerk. In the circumstances, he had been negligent.

The reference to 'criminal proceedings' in the Prosecution of Offences Act 1985, s. 19A(1), is wide enough to include proceedings relating to the issue of a witness summons. A local authority attending to answer an application for disclosure of social services files relating to the complainant in a criminal case is a party to criminal proceedings, and can be the beneficiary of a wasted costs order (*Re A Solicitor (Wasted Costs Order)* [1996] 1 FLR 40).

STATUTES AND REGULATIONS RELATING TO COSTS

Prosecution of Offences Act 1985, ss. 16 to 21 D27.47

PART II COSTS IN CRIMINAL CASES

Award of costs out of central funds

Defence costs
16.—(1) Where—
    (a) an information laid before a justice of the peace for any area, charging any person with an offence, is not proceeded with;
    (b) a magistrates' court inquiring into an indictable offence as examining justices determines not to commit the accused for trial;
    (c) a magistrates' court dealing summarily with an offence dismisses the information;
that court or, in a case falling within paragraph (a) above, a magistrates' court for that area, may make an order in favour of the accused for a payment to be made out of central funds in respect of his costs (a 'defendant's costs order').
    (2) Where—
    (a) any person is not tried for an offence for which he has been indicted or committed for trial; or
    (aa) a notice of transfer is given under a relevant transfer provision but a person in relation to whose case it is given is not tried on a charge to which it relates; or
    (b) any person is tried on indictment and acquitted on any count in the indictment;
the Crown Court may make a defendant's costs order in favour of the accused.
    (3) Where a person convicted of an offence by a magistrates' court appeals to the Crown Court under section 108 of the Magistrates' Courts Act 1980 (right of appeal against conviction or sentence) and, in consequence of the decision on appeal—
    (a) his conviction is set aside; or
    (b) a less severe punishment is awarded;
the Crown Court may make a defendant's costs order in favour of the accused.
    (4) Where the Court of Appeal—
    (a) allows an appeal under part I of the Criminal Appeal Act 1968 against—
        (i) conviction;
        (ii) a verdict of not guilty by reason of insanity; or
        (iii) a finding under section 4 of the Criminal Procedure (Insanity) Act 1964 that the appellant is under disability that he did the act or made the omission charged against him; or
    (aa) directs under section 8(1B) of the Criminal Appeal Act 1968 the entry of a judgment and verdict of acquittal;
    (b) on an appeal under that part against conviction—
        (i) substitutes a verdict of guilty of another offence;

(ii) in a case where a special verdict has been found, orders a different conclusion on the effect of that verdict to be recorded; or

(iii) is of the opinion that the case falls within paragraph (a) or (b) of section 6(1) of that Act (cases where the court substitutes a finding of insanity or unfitness to plead); or

(c) on an appeal under that part against sentence, exercises its powers under section 11(3) of that Act (powers where the court considers that the appellant should be sentenced differently for an offence for which he was dealt with by the court below);
the court may make a defendant's costs order in favour of the accused.

(4A) The court may also make a defendant's costs order in favour of the accused on an appeal under section 9(11) of the Criminal Justice Act 1987 (appeals against orders or rulings at preparatory hearings).

(5) Where—

(a) any proceedings in a criminal cause or matter are determined before a Divisional Court of the Queen's Bench Division;

(b) the House of Lords determines an appeal, or application for leave to appeal, from such a Divisional Court in a criminal cause or matter;

(c) the Court of Appeal determines an application for leave to appeal to the House of Lords under part II of the Criminal Appeal Act 1968; or

(d) the House of Lords determines an appeal, or application for leave to appeal, under part II of that Act;
the court may make a defendant's costs order in favour of the accused.

(6) A defendant's costs order shall, subject to the following provisions of this section, be for the payment out of central funds, to the person in whose favour the order is made, of such amount as the court considers reasonably sufficient to compensate him for any expenses properly incurred by him in the proceedings.

(7) Where a court makes a defendant's costs order but is of the opinion that there are circumstances which make it inappropriate that the person in whose favour the order is made should recover the full amount mentioned in subsection (6) above, the court shall—

(a) assess what amount would, in its opinion, be just and reasonable; and

(b) specify that amount in the order.

[(8) Repealed.]

(9) Subject to subsection (7) above, the amount to be paid out of central funds in pursuance of a defendant's costs order shall—

(a) be specified in the order, in any case where the court considers it appropriate for the amount to be so specified and the person in whose favour the order is made agrees the amount; and

(b) in any other case, be determined in accordance with regulations made by the Lord Chancellor for the purposes of this section.

(10) Subsection (6) above shall have effect, in relation to any case falling within subsection (1)(a) or (2)(a) above, as if for the words 'in the proceedings' there were substituted the words 'in or about the defence'.

(11) Where a person ordered to be retried is acquitted at his retrial, the costs which may be ordered to be paid out of central funds under this section shall include—

(a) any costs which, at the original trial, could have been ordered to be so paid under this section if he had been acquitted; and

(b) if no order was made under this section in respect of his expenses on appeal, any sums for the payment of which such an order could have been made.

(12) In subsection 2(aa) 'relevant transfer provision' means—

(a) section 4 of the Criminal Justice Act 1987, or

(b) section 53 of the Criminal Justice Act 1991.

Prosecution costs

17.—(1) Subject to subsection (2) below, the court may—

(a) in any proceedings in respect of an indictable offence; and

(b) in any proceedings before a Divisional Court of the Queen's Bench Division or the House of Lords in respect of a summary offence;
order the payment out of central funds of such amount as the court considers reasonably sufficient to compensate the prosecutor for any expenses properly incurred by him in the proceedings.

(2)   No order under this section may be made in favour of—
    (a)   a public authority; or
    (b)   a person acting—
        (i)   on behalf of a public authority; or
        (ii)   in his capacity as an official appointed by such an authority.

(3)   Where a court makes an order under this section but is of the opinion that there are circumstances which make it inappropriate that the prosecution should recover the full amount mentioned in subsection (1) above, the court shall—
    (a)   assess what amount would, in its opinion, be just and reasonable; and
    (b)   specify that amount in the order.

(4)   Subject to subsection (3) above, the amount to be paid out of central funds in pursuance of an order under this section shall—
    (a)   be specified in the order, in any case where the court considers it appropriate for the amount to be so specified and the prosecutor agrees the amount; and
    (b)   in any other case, be determined in accordance with regulations made by the Lord Chancellor for the purposes of this section.

(5)   Where the conduct of proceedings to which subsection (1) above applies is taken over by the Crown Prosecution Service, that subsection shall have effect as if it referred to the prosecutor who had the conduct of the proceedings before the intervention of the Service and to expenses incurred by him up to the time of intervention.

(6)   In this section 'public authority' means—
    (a)   a police force within the meaning of section 3 of this Act;
    (b)   the Crown Prosecution Service or any other government department;
    (c)   a local authority or other authority or body constituted for purposes of—
        (i)   the public service or of local government; or
        (ii)   carrying on under national ownership any industry or undertaking or part of an industry or undertaking; or
    (d)   any other authority or body whose members are appointed by Her Majesty or by any Minister of the Crown or government department or whose revenue consist wholly or mainly of money provided by Parliament.

Award of costs against accused

Award of costs against accused
18.—(1)   Where—
    (a)   any person is convicted of an offence before a magistrates' court;
    (b)   the Crown Court dismisses an appeal against such a conviction or against the sentence imposed on that conviction; or
    (c)   any person is convicted of an offence before the Crown Court;
the court may make such order as to the costs to be paid by the accused to the prosecutor as it considers just and reasonable.

(2)   Where the Court of Appeal dismisses—
    (a)   an appeal or application for leave to appeal under part I of the Criminal Appeal Act 1968; or
    (b)   an application by the accused for leave to appeal to the House of Lords under part II of that Act; or
    (c)   an appeal or application for leave to appeal under section 9(11) of the Criminal Justice Act 1987;
it may make such order as to the costs to be paid by the accused, to such person as may be named in the order, as it considers just and reasonable.

(3)   The amount to be paid by the accused in pursuance of an order under this section shall be specified in the order.

(4)   Where any person is convicted of an offence before a magistrates' court and—
    (a)   under the conviction the court orders payment of any sum as a fine, penalty, forfeiture or compensation; and
    (b)   the sum so ordered to be paid does not exceed £5;
the court shall not order the accused to pay any costs under this section unless in the particular circumstances of the case it considers it right to do so.

(5)   Where any person under the age of 18 is convicted of an offence before a magistrates' court, the amount of any costs ordered to be paid by the accused under this section shall not exceed the amount of any fine imposed on him.

(6) Costs ordered to be paid under subsection (2) above may include the reasonable cost of any transcript of a record of proceedings made in accordance with rules of court made for the purposes of section 32 of the Act of 1968.

Other awards

Provision for orders as to costs in other circumstances

19.—(1) The Lord Chancellor may by regulations make provision empowering magistrates' courts, the Crown Court and the Court of Appeal, in any case where the court is satisfied that one party to criminal proceedings has incurred costs as a result of an unnecessary or improper act or omission by, or on behalf of, another party to the proceedings, to make an order as to the payment of those costs.

(2) Regulations made under subsection (1) above may, in particular—

(a) allow the making of such an order at any time during the proceedings;

(b) make provision as to the account to be taken, in making such an order, of any other order as to costs which has been made in respect of the proceedings or any grant of representation for the purposes of the proceedings which has been made under the Legal Aid Act 1988;

(c) make provision as to the account to be taken of any such order in the making of any other order as to costs in respect of the proceedings; and

(d) contain provisions similar to those in section 18(4) and (5) of this Act.

(3) The Lord Chancellor may by regulations make provision for the payment out of central funds, in such circumstances and in relation to such criminal proceedings as may be specified, of such sums as appear to the court to be reasonably necessary—

(a) to compensate any witness in the proceedings, and any other person who in the opinion of the court necessarily attends for the purpose of proceedings otherwise than to give evidence, for the expense, trouble or loss of time properly incurred in or incidental to his attendance;

(b) to cover the proper expenses of an interpreter who is required because of the accused's lack of English;

(c) to compensate a duly qualified medical practitioner who—

(i) makes a report otherwise than in writing for the purpose of section 30 of the Magistrates' Courts Act 1980 (remand for medical examination); or

(ii) makes a written report to a court in pursuance of a request to which section 32(2) of the Criminal Justice Act 1967 (report by medical practitioner on medical condition of offender) applies;

for the expenses properly incurred in or incidental to his reporting to the court.

(d) to cover the proper fee or costs of a person appointed by the Crown Court under section 4A of the Criminal Procedure (Insanity) Act 1964 to put the case for the defence.

(3A) In subsection (3)(a) above 'attendance' means attendance at the court or elsewhere.

(4) The Court of Appeal may order the payment out of central funds of such sums as appear to it to be reasonably sufficient to compensate an appellant who is not in custody and who appears before it on, or in connection with, his appeal under part I of the Criminal Appeal Act 1968.

(5) The Lord Chancellor may by regulations provide that any provision made by or under this part which would not otherwise apply in relation to any category of proceedings in which an offender is before a magistrates' court or the Crown Court shall apply in relation to proceedings of that category, subject to any specified modifications.

19A.—(1) In any criminal proceedings—

(a) the Court of Appeal;

(b) the Crown Court; or

(c) a magistrates' court,

may disallow, or (as the case may be) order the legal or other representative concerned to meet, the whole of any wasted costs or such part of them as may be determined in accordance with regulations.

(2) Regulations shall provide that a legal or other representative against whom action is taken by a magistrates' court under subsection (1) may appeal to the Crown Court and that a legal or other representative against whom action is taken by the Crown Court under subsection (1) may appeal to the Court of Appeal.

(3)   In this section—

'legal or other representative', in relation to any proceedings, means a person who is exercising a right of audience, or a right to conduct litigation, on behalf of any party to the proceedings;

'regulations' means regulations made by the Lord Chancellor; and

'wasted costs' means any costs incurred by a party—

(a)   as a result of any improper, unreasonable or negligent act or omission on the part of any representative or any employee of a representative; or

(b)   which, in the light of any such act or omission occurring after they were incurred, the court considers it is unreasonable to expect that party to pay.

[**20.**   The Lord Chancellor may make regulations for carrying this part of the Act into effect.]

Interpretation, etc.

21.—(1)   In this Part—

'defendant's costs order' has the meaning given in section 16 of this Act;

'legally assisted person', in relation to any proceedings, means a person to whom representation under the Legal Aid Act 1988 has been granted for the purposes of the proceedings;

'proceedings' includes—

(a)   proceedings in any court below; and

(b)   in relation to the determination of an appeal by any court, any application made to that court for leave to bring the appeal; and

'witness' means any person properly attending to give evidence, whether or not he gives evidence or is called at the instance of one of the parties or of the court, but does not include a person attending as a witness to character only unless the court has certified that the interests of justice required his attendance.

(2)   Except as provided by or under this part no costs shall be allowed on the hearing or determination of, or of any proceedings preliminary or incidental to, an appeal to the Court of Appeal under part I of the Criminal Appeal Act 1968.

(3)   Subject to rules of court made under section 53(1) of the Supreme Court Act 1981 (power by rules to distribute business of Court of Appeal between its civil and criminal divisions), the jurisdiction of the Court of Appeal under this part, or under regulations made under this part, shall be exercised by the Criminal Division of that court; and references in this part to the Court of Appeal shall be construed as references to that division.

(4)   For the purposes of sections 16 and 17 of this Act, the costs of any party to proceedings shall be taken to include the expense of compensating any witness for the expenses, trouble or loss of time properly incurred in or incidental to his attendance.

(4A)   Where one party to any proceedings is a legally assisted person then—

(a)   for the purposes of sections 16 and 17 of this Act, his costs shall be taken not to include either the expenses incurred on his behalf by the Legal Aid Board or the Lord Chancellor or, if he is liable to make a contribution under section 23 of the Legal Aid Act 1988, any sum paid or payable by way of contribution; and

(b)   for the purposes of sections 18 and 19 of this Act, his costs shall be taken to include the expenses incurred on his behalf by the Legal Aid Board or the Lord Chancellor (without any deduction on account of any contribution paid or payable under section 23 of the Legal Aid Act 1988) but, if he is liable to make such a contribution, his costs shall be taken not to include any sum paid or payable by way of contribution.

(5)   Where, in any proceedings in a criminal cause or matter or in either of the cases mentioned in subsection (6) below, an interpreter is required because of the accused's lack of English, the expenses properly incurred on his employment shall not be treated as costs of any party to the proceedings.

(6)   The cases are—

(a)   where an information charging the accused with an offence is laid before a justice of the peace for any area but not proceeded with and the expenses are incurred on the employment of the interpreter for the proceedings on the information; and

(b)   where the accused is committed for trial but not tried and the expenses are incurred on the employment of the interpreter for the proceedings in the Crown Court.

Costs in Criminal Cases (General) Regulations 1986 (SI 1986 No. 1335)

PART I PRELIMINARY

1 and 2 Concern citation, commencement and revocations.

PART II COSTS UNNECESSARILY OR IMPROPERLY INCURRED

Unnecessary or improper acts and omissions

3.—(1) Subject to the provisions of this regulation, where at any time during criminal proceedings—

  (a) a magistrates' court,

  (b) the Crown Court, or

  (c) the Court of Appeal

is satisfied that costs have been incurred in respect of the proceedings by one of the parties as a result of an unnecessary or improper act or omission by, or on behalf of, another party to the proceedings, the court may, after hearing the parties, order that all or part of the costs so incurred by that party shall be paid to him by the other party.

  (2) Before making an order under paragraph (1), the court shall take into account any other order as to costs (including any legal aid order) which has been made in respect of the proceedings.

  (3) An order made under paragraph (1) shall specify the amount of costs to be paid in pursuance of the order.

  (4) Where an order under paragraph (1) has been made, the court may take that order into account when making any other order as to costs in respect of the proceedings.

  (5) No order under paragraph (1) shall be made by a magistrates' court which requires a person under the age of 17 who has been convicted of an offence to pay an amount by way of costs which exceeds the amount of any fine imposed on him.

PART IIA WASTED COSTS ORDERS

Application and definitions

3A. This part of these regulations applies to action taken by a court under section 19A of the Act and in this part of these regulations:—

  'wasted costs order' means any action taken by a court under section 19A of the Act; and

  'interested party' means the party benefiting from the wasted costs order and, where he was legally aided, or an order for the payment of costs out of central funds was made in his favour, shall include the authority responsible for determining costs payable in respect of work done under the legal aid order or out of central funds as the case may be.

General

3B.—(1) A wasted costs order may provide for the whole or any part of the wasted costs to be disallowed or ordered to be paid and the court shall specify the amount of such costs.

  (2) Before making a wasted costs order the court shall allow the legal or other representative and any party to the proceedings to make representations.

  (3) When making a wasted costs order the court may take into account any other order as to costs in respect of the proceedings and may take the wasted costs into account when making any other such order.

  (4) Where a wasted costs order has been made the court shall notify any interested party of the order and the amount disallowed or ordered to be paid.

Appeals

3C.—(1) A legal or other representative against whom the wasted costs order is made may appeal—

  (a) in the case of an order made by a magistrates' court, to the Crown Court, and

  (b) in the case of an order made at first instance by the Crown Court, to the Court of Appeal.

  (2) Subject to paragraph (4), an appeal shall be instituted within 21 days of the wasted costs order being made by the appellant's giving notice in writing to the court which made the order, stating the grounds of appeal.

  (3) The appellant shall serve a copy of the notice of appeal and grounds, including any application for an extension of time in which to appeal, on any interested party.

  (4) The time limit within which an appeal may be instituted may, for good reason, be extended before or after it expires—

    (a)   in the case of an appeal to the Crown Court, by a judge of that court;

    (b)   in the case of an appeal to the Court of Appeal, a judge of the High Court or Court of Appeal,

and in each case the court to which the appeal is made shall give notice of the extension to the appellant, the court which made the wasted costs order and any interested party.

    (5)   The court shall give notice of the hearing date to the appellant, the court which made the wasted costs order and any interested party and shall allow the interested party to make representations which may be made orally or in writing.

    (6)   The court may affirm, vary or revoke the order as it thinks fit and shall notify its decision to the appellant, any interested party and the court which made the order.

Recovery of sums due under a wasted costs order

3D.   Where the person required to make a payment in respect of sums due under a wasted costs order fails to do so, the payment may be recovered summarily as a sum adjudged to be paid as a civil debt by order of a magistrates' court by the party benefiting from the order, save that where he was legally aided or an order for the payment of costs out of central funds was made in his favour, the power to recover shall be exercisable by the Lord Chancellor.

PART III   COSTS OUT OF CENTRAL FUNDS

[4 to 13 Prescribe the procedure to be followed by a person in whose favour an order for costs out of central funds has been made; define the 'appropriate authority' to whom the claim for costs should be submitted; prescribe the manner in which the appropriate authority should determine and authorise payment of costs, and provide for redetermination of the costs or an appeal to the taxing master and ultimately the High Court where the applicant for costs is dissatisfied with the appropriate authority's decision.]

PART IV   MISCELLANEOUS APPLICATIONS OF THE ACT

Application of sections 16, 17 and 18 of the Act

14.—(1)   Sections 17 and 18 of the Act [orders for private prosecutors' costs out of central funds and orders that accused pay prosecution costs] shall apply to proceedings in the Crown Court in respect of a person committed by a magistrates' court to that Court—

    (a)   with a view to his being sentenced for an indictable offence in accordance with section 42 of the Powers of Criminal Courts Act 1973 [committals for sentence under the MCA 1980, s. 37 or s. 38]; or

    (b)   with a view to his being sentenced by the Crown Court under section 6(6) or 9(3) of the Bail Act 1976 [committal where magistrates consider that an offence of absconding is too serious to be punished adequately by them etc.]; or

    (c)   with a view to the making of a hospital order with an order restricting his discharge under part III of the Mental Health Act 1983,

as they apply where a person is convicted in proceedings before the Crown Court.

    [(2)   Section 18 of the Act to apply to certain committals and appeals under the Vagrancy Act 1824 – incorrigible rogues etc.]

    [(3)   Section 18 to apply to proceedings in either a magistrates' court or the Crown Court when the proceedings concern (a) breach of conditional discharge, community service order or probation order (CJA 1991, sch. 1, part I, para. 1B and sch. 2, part II, paras 3 and 4); (b) breach of a suspended sentence or a suspended sentence supervision order (s. 23(1) or 27 of the 1973 Act); or (c) breach of an attendance centre order (CJA 1982, s. 19).]

PART V   ALLOWANCES TO WITNESSES

Definitions

15.   In this part of these regulations—

    'expenses' include compensation to a witness for his trouble or loss of time and out of pocket expenses;

    'proceedings in a criminal cause or matter' includes any case in which—

    (a)   an information charging the accused with an offence is laid before a justice of the peace for any area but not proceeded with; or

    (b)   the accused is committed for trial but not tried;

    'professional witness' means a witness practising as a member of the legal or medical profession or as a dentist, veterinary surgeon or accountant who attends to give professional evidence as to matters of fact;

'private prosecutor' means any person in whose favour an order for the payment of costs out of central funds could be made under section 17 of the Act;

'the relevant amount' has the meaning assigned to it by regulation 17;

'witness' means any person properly attending to give evidence, whether or not he gives evidence or is called at the instance of one of the parties or of the court, but does not include—

    (a)   a person attending as a witness to character only unless the court has certified that the interests of justice required his attendance;

    (b)   a member of a police force attending court in his capacity as such;

    (c)   a full-time officer of an institution to which the Prison Act 1952 applies attending court in his capacity as such; or

    (d)   a prisoner in respect of any occasion on which he is conveyed to court in custody.

General

16.—(1) Where, in any proceedings in a criminal cause or matter in a magistrates' court, the Crown Court, a Divisional Court of the Queen's Bench Division, the Court of Appeal or the House of Lords—

    (a)   a witness attends at the instance of the accused, a private prosecutor or the court; or

    (b)   an interpreter is required because of the accused's lack of English; or

    (c)   a medical practitioner makes a report otherwise than in writing,

the expenses properly incurred by that witness, interpreter or medical practitioner shall be allowed out of central funds in accordance with this part of these regulations, unless the court directs that the expenses are not to be allowed out of central funds.

    (2) Subject to paragraph (3), any entitlement to an allowance under this part of these regulations shall be the same whether the witness, interpreter or medical practitioner attends on the same day in one case or more than one case.

    (3) Paragraph (2) shall not apply to allowances under regulation 25.

Determination of rates or scales of allowances payable out of central funds

17. The Lord Chancellor shall, with the consent of the Treasury, determine the rates or scales of allowances payable out of central funds to witnesses, interpreters or medical practitioners and a reference in this part of these regulations to an allowance not exceeding the relevant amount means an amount calculated in accordance with the rates or scales so determined.

[**18.** Witnesses other than professional or expert witnesses may be allowed (a) a loss allowance not exceeding the relevant amount in respect of (i) expenditure to which he would not otherwise have been subject or (ii) any loss of earnings or of State benefit, and (b) a subsistence allowance not exceeding the relevant amount (para. (1)). This also applies to persons who necessarily attend for the purposes of the proceedings but not to give evidence (para. (2)). It does not apply to police officers, prison officers or prisoners conveyed to court in custody (para. (3)).]

Professional witnesses

[**19.** A professional witness may be allowed a professional witness allowance not exceeding the relevant amount.]

Expert witnesses etc.

20.—(1) The court may make an allowance in respect of an expert witness for attending to give expert evidence and for work in connection with its preparation of such an amount as it may consider reasonable having regard to the nature and difficulty of the case and the work necessarily involved.

    (2) Paragraph (1) shall apply, with the necessary modifications, to—

    (a)   an interpreter, or

    (b)   a medical practitioner who makes a report otherwise than in writing for the purpose of section 30 of the Magistrates' Courts Act 1980,

as it applies to an expert witness.

[**21 and 22** Deal respectively with night allowances for professional and expert witnesses, and allowances for seamen detained on shore.]

Prosecutors and defendants

23. A person in whose favour an order is made under section 16, 17 or 19(4) of the Act may be allowed the same subsistence allowance and travelling expenses as if he attended as a witness other than a professional or expert witness.

[**24.** Detailed provisions as to the travelling expenses a witness may be allowed.]

[**25.** Concerns payment for medical reports requested by the court under the MCA 1980, s. 30, or with a view to making a hospital order or a probation order with a condition of treatment.]

PART VI   RECOVERY OF SUMS PAID OUT OF THE LEGAL AID FUND OR CENTRAL FUNDS

Directions by the Lord Chancellor

26.—(1) The Lord Chancellor shall recover in accordance with directions given by him any sums paid out of the legal aid fund or central funds where a costs order has been made against a party to proceedings in favour of—

(a) a legally assisted person, or

(b) a person in whose favour an order for the payment of costs out of central funds has been made.

Insurance etc. Practice.

2C. Any person insured in respect of or made to the provisions of 1(2) or 1(4) (of this Act) may be treated by some surrender and insurance etc. consideration that the insured may require at the time that effect and does not provide.

2D. This section is the transitory provision and where mentioned as different [ ]

[2DA.] Criterion may apply in other cases in respect of the insurance under this Act.

[2E.] Any offence under this Act may be brought under or in respect of a defective practice obligations committee.

PAYMENT OR CREDIT OR COMMAND OUT OF THE FINAL AID FUND
OR CREDIT [Subject] [2]

Some person out of Fund Credit etc.

2A. [2(1)] The Fund Generation shall receive or some matter with appropriate given by a fund any issue period of time of the head of land or control fund where a credit to the fund between a matter in respect of consideration in form or of—

(a) a variation in respect of fund, or a matter or

2(2) No matter in these relevant relation paid to the persons or to other output control which has been subject.

PART E
SENTENCING

Martin Wasik, LLB, MA, Barrister

Professor of Law, Manchester University
Chairman, Sentencing Advisory Panel

E

PART E
SENTENCING

Martin Wasik, LLB, MA

SECTION E1: CUSTODIAL SENTENCES: IMPRISONMENT

SENTENCES OF IMPRISONMENT GENERALLY

Maximum Terms

Maximum prison terms for indictable offences and offences triable either way are almost **E1.1** always laid down by statutes creating those offences. Maximum terms are indicated in respect of each of the offences dealt with in **part B**. Where a person is convicted on indictment and is liable to be sentenced to imprisonment, but the sentence is not limited to a specified term or life by any enactment, the maximum prison sentence available is two years (PCCA 1973, s. 18). This provision does not apply to common-law offences, such as incitement, for which the penalty which may be imposed by the Crown Court is not subject to any limitation except that it must not be disproportionate to the actual offence committed (*Higgins* [1952] 1 KB 7, and see **E1.12**). For sentencing by magistrates' courts, and by the Crown Court when exercising the powers of a magistrates' court, see **E1.2**.

There are special rules in respect of statutory conspiracies and attempts, as to which see **A6.13** and **A6.33** respectively.

The effect of statutory changes to maximum sentences is as follows. Unless there is clear provision to the contrary, where a defendant falls to be sentenced for an offence committed before an increase in the relevant maximum sentence, he should be sentenced on the basis of the old maximum (*Penwith Justices, ex parte Hay* (1979) 1 Cr App R (S) 265). Article 7 of the European Convention on Human Rights states that no heavier penalty shall be imposed than the one applicable at the time the offence was committed (see *Welch* v *UK* (1995) 20 EHRR 247; *Ibbotson* v *UK* [1999] Crim LR 153). When the offence is charged as having been committed on a day unknown between specified dates and the maximum sentence was increased between those dates, the lower maximum applies (*S* (1992) 13 Cr App R (S) 306; *Street* [1997] 2 Cr App R (S) 309; *Cairns* [1998] 1 Cr App R (S) 434). If the maximum penalty is reduced between the time of commission of the offence and the date of conviction then, in the absence of guidance from the relevant provision or commencement order, it seems that the sentencing court should infer the intention of Parliament in a common sense way (see *A-G's Ref (No. 48 of 1994)* (1995) 16 Cr App R (S) 980 and *Shaw* [1996] 2 Cr App R (S) 278).

Limitations on Imposition of Imprisonment

The CJA 1991 provides statutory criteria for determining the imposition and length of **E1.2** custodial sentences. These criteria are considered in detail at **E1.8** and **E1.13**. The criteria apply to sentences of imprisonment (including discretionary life sentences and suspended sentences, but not including a committal or attachment for contempt of court) and to the sentences of detention in a young offender institution, a detention and training order, a secure training order, detention under the CYPA 1933, s. 53 and custody for life under the CJA 1982, s. 8(2).

Offenders aged under 21 at the date of conviction cannot be sentenced to imprisonment (CJA 1982, s. 1(1)). On determining the age of the person before the court, see s. 1(6) and **E3.3**. Those under 21 cannot be committed to prison for any reason, such as non-payment of a fine, but if a person under 21 is remanded in custody, committed in custody for trial or sentence, or sent in custody for trial under the CDA 1998, s. 51, he may be committed to prison for the period before his case is disposed of (s. 1(2)). The custodial sentences which are available for offenders aged under 21 are detention in a young offender institution, a detention and training order, a secure training order, detention under the CYPA 1933, s. 53 and custody for life.

General limits on the power of magistrates' courts to impose imprisonment are specified by the MCA 1980, ss. 31 and 32. The minimum prison sentence which may be imposed is one of five days (s. 132) and the maximum is six months in respect of any one offence (s. 31(1)) unless a shorter maximum term is provided by statute. The six-month limit does not, however, apply to imprisonment for non-payment of a fine (see **E17.6**). The maximum aggregate term which magistrates can impose is six months, unless two of the terms are imposed for offences triable either way, in which case the maximum aggregate term is 12 months (s. 133). These provisions also apply to the sentence of detention in a young offender institution but not to the detention and training order or the secure training order. For more detailed treatment of the sentencing powers of a magistrates' court, see **D20**. Magistrates' courts are, of course, subject to the criteria laid down in the CJA 1991 for determining both the imposition and length of a custodial sentence. These criteria are set out at **E1.8** and **E1.13**.

A magistrates' court having power to imprison a person may instead order him to be detained within the precincts of the court-house or at any police station until such hour, not later than 8 p.m. on the day on which the order is made, as the court directs (MCA 1980, s. 135(1)). Such order shall not operate to deprive the person of a reasonable opportunity of returning home on the same day (s. 135(2)).

Limitation on Imposition of First Prison Sentence

E1.3   The PCCA 1973, s. 21(1), prohibits the imposition of a sentence of imprisonment on an offender who has not previously served such a sentence unless he is legally represented for the purpose of sentence, or has refused to apply for legal aid or has been refused legal aid on the ground that it did not appear that his means were such that he required assistance. 'Legal aid' in this context means legal aid for the purposes of the whole proceedings or the proceedings on or in relation to sentence (s. 21(2)). A sentence passed contrary to the provisions of s. 21(1) is invalid, but may be substituted by a lawful sentence on appeal (see *Hollywood* (1990) 12 Cr App R (S) 325, *Wilson* (1995) 16 Cr App R (S) 997 and **D17.30**).

Mentally Disordered Offenders

E1.4   Before a court forms any opinion as to the desirability of imposing a custodial sentence upon an offender 'who is or appears to be mentally disordered', the court should obtain a medical report before passing a custodial sentence, other than one which is fixed by law or which falls to be imposed under s. 2(2) of the C(S)A 1997 (CJA 1991, s. 4(1)), unless the court is of the opinion that such a report is not necessary (s. 4(2)). Further, before passing a custodial sentence on such a person, the court must consider (s. 4(3)):

>   (a)   any information before it which relates to his mental condition (whether given in a medical report, a pre-sentence report, or otherwise); and
>   (b)   the likely effect of such a sentence on that condition and on any treatment which may be available for it.

The CJA 1991, s. 28(4), also provides that nothing in part I of that Act shall be taken as requiring a court to pass a custodial sentence on a mentally disordered offender, nor as restricting the court's power to deal with a mentally disordered offender in a more appropriate way, whether under the Mental Health Act 1983 or otherwise. See further **E24**.

Concurrent and Consecutive Prison Sentences

E1.5   Where an offender is convicted on more than one count, the court should impose separate sentences on each count. Prison sentences may run concurrently or consecutively, or there may be a mixture of concurrent and consecutive sentences. The court should make it clear which sentence relates to which count and whether the sentences are concurrent or consecutive. If it fails to do so, it is presumed that the sentences are concurrent. Similarly, where a court passes a prison sentence on a person who is already serving one or more sentences of imprisonment, it must make clear whether the fresh sentence is to be served concurrently with or consecutively to the existing sentence or sentences. A court imposing a prison sentence must not direct that the new sentence shall commence on the expiration of any other prison sentence from which the offender has been released under the CJA 1991, part II (CDA 1998, s. 102).

Terms of imprisonment may be ordered to run consecutively even where that results in a total term greater than the maximum which could have been imposed for any of the offences (e.g., *Prime* (1983) 5 Cr App R (S) 127).

A fixed-term prison sentence may not run consecutively to a life sentence (*Foy* [1962] 1 WLR 609) nor vice versa (*Jones* v *DPP* [1962] AC 635, at p. 647). Where a longer-than-normal sentence is passed on an offender under the CJA 1991, s. 2(2)(b), a custodial sentence imposed at the same time for other matters should be ordered to run concurrently rather than consecutively (*King* (1995) 16 Cr App R (S) 987; *Walters* [1997] 2 Cr App R (S) 87). It seems that consecutive longer-than-normal sentences should not be ordered, since it is illogical to require such a sentence to commence at a future date (see *Johnson* [1998] 1 Cr App R (S) 126 and **E1.7**). It is not clear whether concurrent longer-than-normal sentences may lawfully be imposed on an offender.

Generally, where offences arise out of the same transaction, sentences should be concurrent: e.g., driving recklessly and driving while disqualified on the same occasion (*Skinner* (1986) 8 Cr App R (S) 166) or driving while disqualified and taking a conveyance (*Matthews* (1987) 9 Cr App R (S) 1). Exceptionally, however, consecutive sentences may be upheld in this situation (*Lawrence* (1989) 11 Cr App R (S) 580; *Jordan* [1996] 1 Cr App R (S) 181).

Consecutive sentences should normally be imposed where an offender has used violence to resist arrest for another offence (*Wellington* (1988) 10 Cr App R (S) 384) or has used violence to make good his escape (*Bunch* (1971) CSP A5–2C01). Sentences should normally be consecutive where the offender carries a firearm when committing the offence (*French* (1982) 4 Cr App R (S) 57; *McGrath* (1986) 8 Cr App R (S) 372). Consecutive sentences should normally be imposed where the offender commits an offence on bail which was granted in respect of the other offence (*Whittaker* [1998] 1 Cr App R (S) 172, although it is not clear how the principle squares with CJA 1991, s. 29(2): see **E1.16**). A custodial sentence imposed for escape from lawful custody should run consecutively to the sentence being served at the time of the escape (*Clarke* (1994) 15 Cr App R (S) 825) as should a custodial sentence for offences committed within prison by a serving prisoner (*Ali* [1998] 2 Cr App R (S) 123). Where an offender has attempted to interfere with the course of justice in relation to an offence committed by him, sentence for the interference offence should normally be consecutive to the sentence for the other offence (*A-G's Ref (No. 1 of 1990)* (1990) 12 Cr App R (S) 245).

Consecutive sentences are always subject to the totality principle: see **E1.19**.

Effect of Time Spent in Custody on Remand on Length of Sentence

The C(S)A 1997 contains provisions which, if brought into force, will repeal s. 67 of the **E1.6** CJA 1967 and replace it with new arrangements for the crediting of periods of remand in custody under s. 9 of the 1997 Act.

Criminal Justice Act 1967, s. 67

(1) The length of any sentence of imprisonment imposed on an offender by a court shall be treated as reduced by any relevant period, but where he was previously subject to a probation order, a community service order, an order for conditional discharge or a

suspended sentence in respect of that offence, any such period falling before the order was made or suspended sentence passed shall be disregarded for the purposes of this section.

(1A)   In subsection (1) above 'relevant period' means—

(a)   any period during which the offender was in police detention in connection with the offence for which the sentence was passed; or

(b)   any period during which he was in custody—

(i)   by reason only of having been committed to custody by an order of a court made in connection with any proceedings relating to that sentence or the offence for which it was passed or any proceedings from which those proceedings arose; or

(ii)   by reason of his having been so committed and having been concurrently detained otherwise than by order of a court; or

(c)   any period during which, in connection with the offence for which the sentence was passed, he was remanded or committed to local authority accommodation by virtue of an order under section 23 of the Children and Young Persons Act 1969 or section 37 of the Magistrates' Courts Act 1980 and in accommodation provided for the purpose of restricting liberty.

(2)   For the purposes of this section a suspended sentence shall be treated as a sentence of imprisonment when it takes effect under section 23 of the Powers of Criminal Courts Act 1973 and as being imposed by the order under which it takes effect.

Section 67 applies to sentences of detention in a young offender institution, secure training orders and determinate sentences of detention passed under the CYPA 1933, s. 53(3) as it applies to sentences of imprisonment (s. 67(5)). It does not apply to the detention and training order, as to which see **E3.21**. For the effect of s. 67 on arrangements for early release, see CJA 1991, s. 41.

Section 67 does not extend to time spent in custody in a foreign country awaiting extradition to this country in respect of the offence now being dealt with. Section 47 of the CJA 1991 makes it clear that the sentencer may take that period, or part of that period, into account in his discretion when fixing the length of a custodial sentence (see also *Scalise* (1985) 7 Cr App R (S) 395, where it was said by Lawton LJ that such would be the 'normal' approach). In *Stone* (1988) 10 Cr App R (S) 322 the Court of Appeal upheld the judge's decision to take only part of the period into account, in view of the appellant's challenge to extradition proceedings (see also *Vincent* [1996] 2 Cr App R (S) 6). Neither does the provision extend to cases where the accused has been held in custody in respect of an offence subsequently taken into consideration; in *Towers* (1987) 9 Cr App R (S) 333 it was said to be appropriate to make some allowance in those circumstances.

The operation of these provisions has given rise to difficulties of interpretation in respect of both consecutive and concurrent custodial sentences. In *Secretary of State for the Home Department, ex parte Naughton* [1997] 1 WLR 118, the Divisional Court held that, where the defendant had received *consecutive* custodial sentences for two offences and had spent 81 days on remand for the first offence and a further 239 days on remand in respect of both offences, the 'relevant period' for the purposes of the CJA 1991, s. 67(1), was 81 days *plus* 239 days. The overlapping period counted once, not twice. In *Governor of Brockhill Prison, ex parte Evans* [1997] QB 443, the Divisional Court held that where *concurrent* sentences were imposed on a defendant in respect of offences for which he had spent separate periods on remand in custody, the term which he was required to serve would be reduced by the remand time relating to the first offence *plus* the remand time relating to the second offence, provided that these remand periods did not overlap. Again, an overlapping period would count once, not twice. The Court also noted that the effect of the word 'only' in s. 67(1A)(b)(i) was to preclude any account being taken of periods in custody unrelated to the offence or offences for which the relevant sentence or sentences were passed.

As to taking account of time spent in custody when passing a suspended sentence, see **E2.5**.

Effect of Conviction during Currency of Earlier Custodial Sentence

Criminal Justice Act 1991, s. 40

E1.7

(1)   This section applies to a short-term or long-term prisoner who is released under this part if—

(a)   before the date on which he would (but for his release) have served his sentence in full, he commits an offence punishable with imprisonment; and

(b)   whether before or after that date, he is convicted of that offence ('the new offence').

(2)   Subject to subsection (3) below, the court by or before which a person to whom this section applies is convicted of the new offence may, whether or not it passes any other sentence on him, order him to be returned to prison for the whole or any part of the period which—

(a)   begins with the date of the order; and

(b)   is equal in length to the period between the date on which the new offence was committed and the date mentioned in subsection (1) above.

(3)   A magistrates' court—

(a)   shall not have power to order a person to whom this section applies to be returned to prison for a period of more than six months; but

(b)   subject to section 25 of the Criminal Justice and Public Order Act 1994, may commit him in custody or on bail to the Crown Court for sentence to be dealt with under subsection (3A) below and the Crown Court to which he has been so committed may make such an order with regard to him as is mentioned in subsection (2) above.

(3A)   Where a person is committed to the Crown Court under subsection (3) above, the Crown Court may order him to be returned to prison for the whole or any part of the period which—

(a)   begins with the date of the order; and

(b)   is equal in length to the period between the date on which the new offence was committed and the date mentioned in subsection (1) above.

(3B)   Subsection (3)(b) above shall not be taken to confer on the magistrates' court a power to commit the person to the Crown Court for sentence for the new offence, but this is without prejudice to any such power conferred on the magistrates' court by any other enactment.

(4)   The period for which a person to whom this section applies is ordered under subsection (2) or (3A) to be returned to prison—

(a)   shall be taken to be a sentence of imprisonment for the purposes of this part;

(b)   shall, as the court may direct, either be served before and be followed by, or be served concurrently with, the sentence imposed for the new offence; and

(c)   in either case, shall be disregarded in determining the appropriate length of that sentence.

(5)   Where the new offence is found to have been committed over a period of two or more days, or at some time during a period of two or more days, it shall be taken for the purposes of this section to have been committed on the last of those days.

(6)   For the purposes of any enactment conferring rights of appeal in criminal cases, any such order as is mentioned in subsection (2) or (3A) above made with regard to any person shall be treated as a sentence passed on him for the offence for which the sentence referred to in subsection (1) was passed.

A 'short-term' prisoner is a prisoner serving a custodial sentence of less than four years, and a 'long-term' prisoner is a prisoner serving a sentence of four years or more (CJA 1991, s. 33(5)). Section 40 does not apply unless the custodial sentence during the currency of which the new offence has been committed was imposed on or after 1 October 1992 (CJA 1991, sch. 12, para. 8(3)). The original sentence may have been a determinate sentence of imprisonment, a term of detention in a young offender institution, or a term of detention under the CYPA 1933, s. 53(3), but s. 40 is not applicable where the original sentence was life imprisonment, custody for life, detention during Her Majesty's pleasure under the CYPA 1933, s. 53(1) or detention for life under s. 53(3) of that Act. It should be noted that s. 40 applies whether or not the conviction for the new offence takes place after the expiry of the full term of the original sentence; what matters is whether the new offence was committed before that date. The exercise of the power is discretionary, and the court may order the offender to be returned to prison for the full period indicated in the section, a lesser period, or not at all. It is now clear that the court may make an order under s. 40 even though the offender has already been recalled to prison following revocation of his licence by administrative discretion under the CJA 1991, s. 39. In *Sharkey* (1999) *The Times*, 10 November 1999, the Court of Appeal departed from the decision of the Divisional Court in *Governor of Elmley Prison, ex parte Moorton* [1999] 2 Cr App R (S) 165, and held that the two sections provided different regimes. A court making an order under s. 40 in these circumstances should, however, normally make allowance for any time spent in custody by the offender following recall under s. 39, unless that time would in any event be credited against the sentence for the new offence.

The Court of Appeal issued general guidance on the operation of the power under s. 40 in *Taylor* [1998] 1 Cr App R (S) 312. Rose LJ explained that the sentencer should first decide what was the proper sentence for the new offence. The possibility of an order under s. 40 should be disregarded at this stage, as s. 40(4)(c) required. In considering whether an order under s. 40 should be made, it would usually be appropriate to have regard to the nature and extent of any progress made by the defendant since his release and the nature and gravity of the new offence and whether it called for a custodial sentence. It would also be necessary to have regard to the totality, both when determining whether a return to prison should be ordered and whether such a period should be served before or concurrently with the sentence for the new offence, and in determining how long the relevant period should be.

In *Harrow Justices, ex parte Jordan* [1997] 1 WLR 84, it was held that, where an offender who is liable to be returned to custody under s. 40 is convicted in a magistrates' court, the magistrates should deal with both the sentence for the new offence and the order for return to custody under s. 40, or should commit the offender to Crown Court in respect of both matters. Lord Bingham CJ, in the Divisional Court, commented that committal to Crown Court would be the appropriate course for magistrates to adopt where a significant part of the licence period is unexpired and where the new offence is one of any gravity. This would entail in some situations that magistrates would be committing a purely summary offence for sentence by the higher court. The decision in *Harrow Justices* was followed in *Burton-on-Trent Justices, ex parte Smith* [1998] 1 Cr App R (S) 223, where Lord Bingham CJ suggested that the court might at some future date be required to consider the matter further. In *Worthing and District Justices, ex parte Varley* [1998] 1 Cr App R (S) 175, the issue arose whether a magistrates' court could both make an order returning an offender to custody under s. 40 and impose a custodial sentence for a new offence committed during the licence period to run consecutively to it where the aggregate of those two periods exceeded the maximum aggregate term of imprisonment which that court could impose (normally six months: MCA 1980, s. 133). The Divisional Court held that it could do so, since an order that the offender be returned to custody under s. 40 was not, in any ordinary sense, a sentence of imprisonment, but was an order to reactivate custody from which the offender had been prematurely released. Section 40(4)(a), which states that a period of return ordered under s. 40 'shall be taken to be a sentence of imprisonment' was not relevant to the present issue. Its purpose was to deem the reactivated term to be a term of imprisonment for purposes of the early release provisions of the 1991 Act.

If a custodial sentence is imposed for the new offence, that sentence may run concurrently or consecutively to the reinstated period, but the reinstated period cannot run consecutively to the sentence for the new offence (s. 40(4); see *McDonnell* [1997] 1 Cr App R (S) 317 and *Clerkenwell Magistrates' Court, ex parte Feely* [1996] 2 Cr App R

(S) 309). Nothing in CDA 1998, s. 102 (see **E1.5**), prevents the sentence for the new offence from being ordered to run consecutively (*Lowe* [1999] 3 All ER 762). If the sentence imposed for the subsequent offence is a longer-than-normal sentence under the CJA 1991, s. 2(2)(b), any reinstated period required to be served by order made under s. 40 should run concurrently with the sentence passed under s. 2(2)(b). A sentence under s. 2(2)(b) is imposed for the duration considered by the sentencer to be necessary for the protection of the public, and it is illogical to order such a sentence to commence at a future date (*Johnson* [1998] 1 Cr App R (S) 126). An order by the court under s. 40 that the offender be returned to custody is not a relevant consideration in determining the length of the custodial sentence for the subsequent offence (s. 40(4)). In *Foran* [1996] 1 Cr App R (S) 149, the Court of Appeal considered the application of s. 40 in the case of an offender who is aged 15, 16 or 17, for whom the total term of detention in a young offender institution must not exceed 24 months (CJA 1982, s. 1B(2); see **E3.4**). The Court held that, when exercising the power under s. 40 to reinstate part of the original term of detention in a young offender institution, the full duration of the original term and the duration of the term imposed for the new offence must not together constitute a total term in excess of that permitted maximum. The sentence for the new offence was, accordingly, reduced although it would seem to be more consistent with *Ex parte Probyn* to reduce the term under s. 40. Any time spent by the offender in custody on remand will, by virtue of the CJA 1967, s. 67, be deducted from the reinstated term (see **E1.6**).

CUSTODIAL SENTENCES: SENTENCING PRINCIPLES

For Court of Appeal sentencing guideline judgments, Magistrates' Association Sentencing Guidelines, and for indications of general sentencing brackets applicable to particular offences, see the passages relating to the particular substantive offences, set out in **part B** of this work.

Statutory Criteria for the Imposition of Custodial Sentences

Section 1 of the CJA 1991 restricts the powers of the Crown Court and magistrates' courts to impose a custodial sentence.   **E1.8**

Criminal Justice Act 1991, s. 1

(1)   This section applies where a person is convicted of an offence punishable with a custodial sentence other than one fixed by law or falling to be imposed under section 2(2), 3(2) or 4(2) of the Crime (Sentences) Act 1997.

(2)   Subject to subsection (3) below, the court shall not pass a custodial sentence on the offender unless it is of the opinion—

(a)   that the offence, or the combination of the offence and one or more offences associated with it, was so serious that only such a sentence can be justified for the offence; or

(b)   where the offence is a violent or sexual offence, that only such a sentence would be adequate to protect the public from serious harm from him.

(3)   Nothing in subsection (2) above shall prevent the court from passing a custodial sentence on the offender if he fails to express his willingness to comply with—

(a)   a requirement which is proposed by the court to be included in a probation order or supervision order and which requires an expression of such willingness; or

(b)   a requirement which is proposed by the court to be included in a drug treatment and testing order or an order under section 61(6) of the Crime and Disorder Act 1998.

(4)   Where a court passes a custodial sentence, it shall be its duty—

(a)   in a case not falling within subsection (3) above, to state in open court that it is of the opinion that either or both of paragraphs (a) and (b) of subsection (2) above apply and why it is of that opinion; and

(b)   in any case, to explain to the offender in open court and in ordinary language why it is passing a custodial sentence on him.

(5)   A magistrates' court shall cause a reason stated by it under subsection (4) above to be specified in the warrant of commitment and to be entered in the register.

These provisions have general application in the Crown Court and in magistrates' courts and apply to all 'custodial sentences', which expression is defined in the CJA 1991, s. 31. For a person of or over 21 years of age, 'custodial sentence' means 'a sentence of imprisonment', which includes a discretionary life sentence and a suspended sentence, but it does not include a committal or attachment for contempt of court. For a person under 21 years of age, it means a sentence of detention in a young offender institution, detention under the CYPA 1933, s. 53(3), a detention and training order, a secure training order and a sentence of custody for life under the CJA 1982, s. 8(2). Section 1 does not apply where the sentence for the offence is fixed by law or where sentence is imposed under s. 2(2), 3(2) or 4(2) of the C(S)A 1997.

Section 1(3), as amended by the C(S)A 1997, indicates that the stated criteria in s. 1(2) shall not prevent a court from passing a custodial sentence on an offender who fails to express his willingness to comply with a requirement in a probation order or supervision order which requires an expression of willingness to comply. Section 38 of the 1997 Act, which came into effect on 1 October 1997 and which applies to offences committed after that date, abolished pre-existing general requirements of consent in respect of probation orders, community service orders, curfew orders and combination orders, so that the only requirements in such orders to which an offender must express his willingness to comply are now a requirement as to treatment for drug or alcohol dependency, or a requirement of treatment for a mental condition in a probation order (see **E24.1**) and a requirement of treatment for a mental condition in a supervision order imposed on an offender aged 14 or over (see **E24.2**). Section 1(3) was further amended by the CDA 1998 so that, where an offender fails to express his willingness to comply with a proposed drug treatment and testing order (see **E10**), the court is not prevented from passing a custodial sentence on him.

Section 1(4) and (5) of the CJA 1991, together with s. 3 (pre-sentence reports), lay down procedural requirements which must be complied with before any custodial sentence may be imposed under s. 1(2). Since a suspended sentence is a custodial sentence, all these procedural requirements must also be complied with before a suspended sentence is passed (see *Brewer* (1982) 4 Cr App R (S) 380). Any court passing a custodial sentence is obliged by s. 1(4)(a) to explain in open court that either or both of paragraphs (a) and (b) of s. 1(2) apply to the case and to explain why it has formed that view. This is not required where custody is being imposed consequent upon the offender's failure to consent to a community penalty which the court was minded to impose. In all cases, however, the court will be obliged by s. 1(4)(b) to explain to the offender 'in open court and in ordinary language' why it is passing a custodial sentence. Section 1(5) requires that a magistrates' court must also record the reason relied upon for imposing custody in the warrant of commitment and in the court register.

Guidance on these provisions was provided by the Court of Appeal in *Baverstock* [1993] 1 WLR 202. The Court stated that s. 1(4) placed a statutory duty on the sentencer. In their lordships' view a judge should state simply that, in his opinion, either or both subsections (2)(a) or (2)(b) applied, using the words of the subsection. Having stated his opinion in that way the judge was then required to state why he had reached that opinion, and to explain his reasoning to the offender. In general their lordships did not consider that this had to be a two-stage process. In most cases that should be unnecessary, and the judge should be able at one and the same time to explain in ordinary language the reasons for his conclusion and tell the offender why he was passing a custodial sentence. When complying with that second requirement, however, the judge would be addressing the offender directly and if, in complying with s. 1(4)(a), he did not use ordinary language, it would be necessary for him to go on to do so in order to comply with subsection (4)(b). The precise words used by a judge were not critical. The statutory provisions were not to be treated as a verbal tightrope for judges to walk.

Given that the judge's approach accorded with the statutory provisions, the Court of Appeal would not be sympathetic to appeals based on fine linguistic analysis of the sentencing remarks. Sentencing judges had to comply with their sentencing duty but if they erred the Court of Appeal would not interfere with the resultant sentence unless it was wrong in principle or excessive.

Section 3(1) of the CJA 1991 requires that, subject to s. 3(2), for the purpose of determining whether either of the grounds for the imposition of a custodial sentence under s. 1(2) are made out, the court 'shall obtain and consider a pre-sentence report'. Pre-sentence reports are defined in s. 3(5).

Criminal Justice Act 1991, s. 3

(5) . . . 'pre-sentence report' means a report in writing which—
    (a) with a view to assisting the court in determining the most suitable method of dealing with an offender, is made or submitted by—
        (i) a probation officer;
        (ii) a social worker of a local authority social services department; or
        (iii) where the offender is under the age of 18 years, a member of a youth offending team; and
    (b) contains information as to such matters, presented in such manner, as may be prescribed by rules made by the Secretary of State.

It should be noted that a pre-sentence report must be in writing, so that an oral 'stand down' report is not a pre-sentence report.

Criminal Justice Act 1991, s. 3

(1) Subject to subsection (2) below, a court shall obtain and consider a pre-sentence report before forming any such opinion as is mentioned in subsection (2) of section 1 or 2 above.
(2) Subsection (1) does not apply if, in the circumstances of the case, the court is of the opinion that it is unnecessary to obtain a pre-sentence report.
(2A) In the case of an offender under the age of eighteen years, save where the offence or any other offence associated with it is triable only on indictment, the court shall not form such an opinion as is mentioned in subsection (2) above or subsection (4A) below unless there exists a previous pre-sentence report obtained in respect of the offender and the court has had regard to the information contained in that report, or, if there is more than one such report, the most recent report.
(3) In forming any such opinion as is mentioned in subsection (2) of section 1 or 2 above a court—
    (a) shall take into account all such information about the circumstances of the offence or (as the case may be) of the offence and the offence or offences associated with it (including any aggravating or mitigating factors) as is available to it; and
    (b) in the case of any such opinion as is mentioned in paragraph (b) of that subsection, may take into account any information about the offender which is before it.

The normal requirement (as stated in s. 3(1)) is that the court should obtain a pre-sentence report before making a decision to impose a custodial sentence. The court has discretion to dispense with that requirement whenever it appears to the court to be 'unnecessary' to obtain one (s. 3(2)). This discretion is, however, subsequently narrowed (in s. 3(2A)) in respect of offenders who are under the age of 18 and are not convicted of any offence which is triable only on indictment. Section 3(4) provides that no sentence shall be invalidated by failure of the court to comply with s. 3(1), but, on appeal against a custodial sentence passed without the court having obtained and considered a pre-sentence report, the appellate court must obtain and consider one unless, in accordance with s. 3(4A), the appellate court is of opinion that the court below was justified in not calling for a report or that the court below was not so justified but, in the circumstances of the case at the time when it is before the appellate court, it is unnecessary to obtain a pre-sentence report. The appellate court cannot, however, take this line in respect of an offender who is under the age of 18 and is not convicted of any offence which is triable only on indictment. In such a case the appellate court must order a pre-sentence report, or at least have sight of the most recent previous pre-sentence report prepared on the offender (s. 3(2A)).

E1.9   ***Justifying Custody under the Criminal Justice Act 1991, s. 1(2)(a)***   Section 1(2)(a) provides the key justification for the imposition of custody, which is the seriousness of the 'offence, or the combination of the offence and one or more offences associated with it'. The offender must have been convicted of at least one offence, which covers both conviction after a trial and after a guilty plea (*Cole* [1965] 2 QB 388). When a court makes a decision on whether to impose a custodial sentence under s. 1(2)(a), the CJA 1991, s. 3(3)(a), requires that the court 'shall take into account all such information about the circumstances of the offence or (as the case may be) of the offence and the offence or offences associated with it (including any aggravating or mitigating factors) as is available to it'. Additionally, s. 28(1) provides 'Nothing in this Part shall prevent a court from mitigating an offender's sentence by taking into account any such matters as, in the opinion of the court, are relevant in mitigation of sentence'.

These provisions have the effect that the court must have regard to both mitigating and aggravating factors insofar as they impinge upon the seriousness of the offence, and may also take account of any other mitigating (but not aggravating) factors. Their operation is well illustrated by *Cox* [1993] 1 WLR 188. In that case the 18-year-old offender pleaded guilty to reckless driving and theft, and was sentenced to four months' detention in a young offender institution. He had been noticed by police late at night riding a trials motorcycle. When he saw the police car he rode away and was pursued. He rode along a footpath, overtook a car by driving on the pavement and ignored a give way sign, before losing control of the cycle and falling off. He was found to be in possession of electrical goods which had been stolen from a garage earlier in the evening. On appeal against sentence Lord Taylor CJ said that 'on all the known facts of this case, we have reached the conclusion that only a custodial sentence could be justified for this offence'. None the less, having regard to mitigating factors personal to the offender under s. 28(1) (in particular his age and the fact that he had only one previous court appearance), the Court of Appeal quashed the custodial sentence and substituted a probation order. It follows from the reasoning adopted in this case that a later court dealing with a breach of the probation order or with a further offence committed by the same offender could not safely assume that the probation order had been imposed on the basis that the offences were not so serious that only custody could be justified.

In *Cox*, Lord Taylor CJ stated that the meaning of the phrase 'so serious that only such a sentence can be justified for the offence' in the CJA 1991, s. 1(2), meant 'the kind of offence which . . . would make all right thinking members of the public, knowing all the facts, feel that justice had not been done by the passing of any sentence other than a custodial one'. In *Howells* [1999] 1 WLR 307, however, Lord Bingham CJ stated that this test was unhelpful, since a sentencing court had no means of ascertaining the views of such people. In reality, the court was bound to give effect to its own subjective judgment of what justice required in the particular case before it. Criminal sentences were in almost every case intended to protect the public, whether by punishing the offender or reforming him, or by deterring him and others, or all of those things. Courts neither could nor should be unmindful of the important public dimension of sentencing and the importance of maintaining public confidence. While the laying down of prescriptive rules to determine when an offence was so serious that only custody could be justified would be 'dangerous and wrong', his lordship indicated that when dealing with cases which were on or near the custody threshold it would normally be helpful to consider the nature and extent of the defendant's criminal intention and the nature and extent of any injury or damage caused to the victim. Other things being equal, an offence which was deliberate and premeditated would usually be more serious than one which was spontaneous and unpremeditated, or which involved an excessive response to provocation. An offence which inflicted personal injury or mental trauma, particularly if permanent, would usually be more serious than one which inflicted financial loss only. Lord Bingham referred to the CJA 1991, s. 29, on the relevance to offence seriousness of the offender's previous convictions, or of his failure to respond to previous sentences, and of his commission of the offence while on bail (see **E1.16**). Further, in deciding whether to impose a custodial sentence in a borderline case, his lordship explained that the court would ordinarily take account of the following matters:

(a)   the offender's admission of responsibility for the offence, particularly if tendered at the earliest opportunity and accompanied by hard evidence of genuine remorse (see further **E1.18**);

(b)   where offending had been fuelled by an addiction to drink or drugs, a demonstration by the offender of a determination to deal with the addiction;

(c)   the youth and immaturity of the offender, which would often justify a less rigorous penalty than that appropriate for an adult;

(d)   where the offender was positively of good character, or where he had a clean record, some measure of leniency would ordinarily be extended;

(e)   it would sometimes be appropriate to take account of the offender's family responsibilities, or physical or mental disability; and

(f)   while the court would never impose a custodial sentence unless satisfied that it was necessary to do so, there would be even greater reluctance where the offender had not served a custodial sentence before.

In *Cunningham* [1993] 1 WLR 183, Lord Taylor CJ stated that the prevalence of a particular class of offences and public concern about them would be regarded as an aggravating factor, and therefore relevant to offence seriousness, when sentencing for an example of that offence. In *Cunningham* the comment was made in the context of determining the length of a custodial sentence, but it would seem equally relevant to the question whether custody is justified or not, and was apparently so applied in *Cox* [1993] 1 WLR 188 at p. 191.

Where the offender stands convicted of two or more offences the court, in deciding whether custody is justified under s. 1(2)(a) must consider the seriousness of the sum of the offences, provided that these are 'associated' with one other. Section 31(2) of the 1991 Act specifies when one offence is to be regarded as associated with another.

Criminal Justice Act 1991, s. 31

(2)   For the purposes of this part, an offence is associated with another if—

(a)   the offender is convicted of it in the proceedings in which he is convicted of the other offence, or (although convicted of it in earlier proceedings) is sentenced for it at the same time as he is sentenced for that offence; or

(b)   the offender admits the commission of it in the proceedings in which he is sentenced for the other offence and requests the court to take it into consideration in sentencing him for that offence.

In *Baverstock* the offender was dealt with for two offences; the second having been committed while the offender was on bail in respect of the first. The offender was sentenced for the two offences on the same occasion; hence, they were were 'associated' for the purposes of s. 31(2). It seems clear from the case of *Godfrey* (1993) 14 Cr App R (S) 804 that, where a sentencer is sentencing for a new offence and at the same time revokes a community sentence which had earlier been passed on the offender and re-sentences for that offence, or where the sentencer passes a sentence for an offence in respect of which a conditional discharge had earlier been granted, the new offence and the earlier offence are associated offences. In *Godfrey* itself, however, the judge imposed 'no separate penalty' for a breach of conditional discharge. This meant that the earlier offence was not being sentenced on the same occasion as the new offence, and thus the two offences could not be regarded as associated. In *Crawford* (1993) 98 Cr App R 297, it was held that, where the offender had been committed to the Crown Court in respect of an offence of theft which placed him in breach of a suspended sentence imposed for an earlier offence of theft, the two offences were not associated offences. *Crawford* was followed and applied in *Cawley* (1994) 15 Cr App R (S) 25. Where an offender has been convicted in respect of a number of charges which are represented as 'sample counts', offences which are not included in the indictment or formally taken into consideration are not associated offences (*Canavan* [1998] 1 Cr App R (S) 79). See further **D17.33**.

E1.10   ***Justifying Custody under the Criminal Justice Act 1991, s. 1(2)(b)***   Section 1(2)(b) provides a second justification for the imposition of a custodial sentence on an offender, where 'the offence is a violent or sexual offence, that only such a sentence would be adequate to protect the public from serious harm from him'. When making its decision on whether to impose a custodial sentence under s. 1(2)(b), the CJA 1991, s. 3(3)(a), requires that the court 'shall take into account all such information about the circumstances of the offence or (as the case may be) of the offence and the offence or offences associated with it (including any aggravating or mitigating factors) as is available to it' and s. 3(3)(b) states that the court 'may take into account any information about the offender which is before it'. Additionally, s. 28(1) provides that nothing in part I of the 1991 Act 'shall prevent a court from mitigating an offender's sentence by taking into account any such matters as, in the opinion of the court, are relevant in mitigation of sentence'.

The CJA 1991, s. 1(2)(b), must be interpreted in the light of s. 31 of that Act. Section 31(1) provides that a 'violent offence' means an offence:

> which leads, or is intended or likely to lead, to a person's death or to physical injury to a person, and includes an offence which is required to be charged as arson (whether or not it would otherwise fall within this definition).

This definition covers cases which range from those where death or physical injury is actually caused, even where that is not intended or even likely to occur, to cases where no harm at all is occasioned but where such harm was risked by the offender. There is no requirement that the physical injury caused or risked need be 'serious', but an offence which results or is likely to result only in psychological harm is not a violent offence. In respect of many criminal offences, the application of these criteria will be perfectly clear. Other offences, however, will sometimes qualify as 'violent', and sometimes not. The Court of Appeal in *Robinson* [1993] 1 WLR 168 confirmed that whether a particular offence falls within the definition of a 'violent offence', thereby permitting the sentencer to consider the imposition of custody under s. 1(2)(b), depends upon the individual facts of each case. In *Cochrane* (1994) 15 Cr App R (S) 708, the Court of Appeal held that, on the facts before it, the particular robbery at knife point was a 'violent offence', since it had been likely to lead to injury, even though no injury had been inflicted or intended, but in *Bibby* (1995) 16 Cr App R (S) 127 the Court of Appeal doubted whether an offender who had threatened staff in building society branches with a knife, and had demanded cash, had committed a 'violent offence' since the evidence was that Bibby had neither used the knife nor had any intention of doing so. In *Khan* (1995) 16 Cr App R (S) 180, the carrying of an unloaded firearm in the course of a robbery was held not to constitute a violent offence; using an imitation firearm to threaten the victim in the course of a raid on a sub-post office was held not to constitute a violent offence in *Palin* (1995) 16 Cr App R (S) 888. Apart from robbery, another offence giving rise to difficulty in this context is that of threatening to kill. In *Richart* (1995) Cr App R (S) 977, the offender made numerous telephone threats to the victim, threatening to kill her, and also sent her a bullet with her name on it through the post. The Court of Appeal, in finding that there was no 'violent offence', since there was no physical injury nor any evidence that the threats were intended or likely to lead to physical injury, invited Parliament to amend the definition, so as to include cases which on their face would lead to a reasonable apprehension of violence. See, however, *Wilson* [1998] 1 Cr App R (S) 341. Section 31(1) states that 'an offence which is required to be charged as arson' always qualifies as a 'violent offence'. See further **B8.19**. It was held in *Guirke* [1997] 1 Cr App R (S) 170 that all offences of attempted arson are also included. This seems, with respect, doubtful. Since attempted arson is not mentioned in s. 31(1), it appears that such offence may qualify as a violent offence only where it leads, or is intended or likely to lead, to death or physical injury.

It is clear from *Robinson* [1993] 1 WLR 168 that the categories of 'violent offence' and 'sexual offence' are not mutually exclusive.

Section 31(1) provides that 'sexual offence' means:

> (a)   an offence under the Sexual Offences Act 1956, other than an offence under section 30, 31 or 33 to 36 of that Act;
> (b)   an offence under section 128 of the Mental Health Act 1959;
> (c)   an offence under the Indecency with Children Act 1960;
> (d)   an offence under section 9 of the Theft Act 1968 of burglary with intent to commit rape;
> (e)   an offence under section 54 of the Criminal Law Act 1977;
> (f)   an offence under the Protection of Children Act 1978;
> (g)   an offence under section 1 of the Criminal Law Act 1977 of conspiracy to commit any of the offences in paragraphs (a) to (f) above;
> (h)   an offence under section 1 of the Criminal Attempts Act 1981 of attempting to commit any of those offences;
> (i)   an offence of inciting another to commit any of those offences.

In *Dootson* (1995) 16 Cr App R (S) 223, the Court of Appeal noted that the offence of child abduction under the Child Abduction Act 1984 was not a sexual offence within this definition; it remains outside the new version. This was described as 'a grave omission' by Roch LJ in *Wrench* [1996] 1 Cr App R (S) 145. Depending upon the facts of the case, however, the abduction of a child might qualify as a violent offence (see *Newsome* [1997] 2 Cr App R (S) 69).

Reliance upon s. 1(2)(b) requires a judgment by the court that, in the light of the offender's conviction of a violent or sexual offence, only a custodial sentence would be adequate to 'protect the public from serious harm from him'. It is clear from the wording of this provision that the sentencer must consider that the public needs protecting from the particular offender, rather than offenders of the particular type. 'Serious harm' is defined for these purposes by s. 31(3) to mean 'death or serious personal injury, whether physical or psychological, occasioned by further such offences' committed by the offender. Section 3(3)(b) allows the court to take into account any information about the offender when making this prediction. A custodial sentence may therefore be imposed under s. 1(2)(b) in respect of a violent or sexual offence which was not serious enough to justify custody under s. 1(2)(a), provided that the court feels, in the light of all the available evidence, that there is a risk that the offender will commit further such offences. See, further, **E1.15**.

In *Baverstock* [1993] 1 WLR 202 the Court of Appeal said that a sentencer should not pass a sentence in reliance upon s. 1(2)(b) without giving an express indication to counsel that this was being considered.

Prison Sentence to be as Short as Possible to Achieve Purposes for which Imposed

E1.11   In *Bibi* [1980] 1 WLR 1193 Lord Lane CJ said (at p. 1195):

> . . . sentencing courts must be particularly careful to examine each case to ensure, if an immediate custodial sentence is necessary, that the sentence is as short as possible, consistent only with the duty to protect the interests of the public and to punish and deter the criminal.

These remarks must be read in the light of the statutory restrictions on custodial sentence length introduced by the CJA 1991 (see **E1.13**), in particular the prominence given there to the requirement that, except for violent offences and sexual offences, custodial sentence length shall be commensurate with the seriousness of the offence committed. The Court of Appeal in *Ollerenshaw* [1999] 1 Cr App R (S) 65, however, stated that the approach in *Bibi* was no less valid in the light of current prison overcrowding. Rose LJ said that, when a court is considering imposing a custodial sentence of about 12 months or less, it should ask itself (especially where this will be the offender's first prison sentence) whether a shorter period might be equally effective. Six months may be just as effective as nine, or two months may be just as effective as four. *Bibi* was further endorsed in *Howells* [1999] 1 WLR 307.

Length of Prison Sentence to be Proportionate to Harm Caused, Culpability of Offender, Effect of Offence upon the Victim etc.

E1.12   This sentencing principle must be read in the light of the statutory restrictions on custodial sentence length introduced by the CJA 1991 (see **E1.13**), in particular the prominence given there to the requirement that, except for violent offences and sexual offences, custodial sentence length shall be commensurate with the seriousness of the offence committed.

Where two or more offenders are sentenced for participation in the same offence, it is proper that the sentences should reflect relevant differences in their degree of involvement in the offence (*Strutt* (1993) 13 Cr App R (S) 56), their ages, their criminal records (*Walsh* (1980) 2 Cr App R (S) 224), and their respective personal mitigation (*Tremarco* (1979) 1 Cr App R (S) 286). Where there is disparity between sentences imposed on co-accused, the higher sentence may be reduced on appeal where 'right-thinking members of the public, with full knowledge of the facts and circumstances, learning of this sentence [would] consider that something had gone wrong with the administration of justice' (per Lawton LJ in *Fawcett* (1983) 5 Cr App R (S) 158).

There may be objectionable disparity in a case where co-accused have received identical sentences, and where this fails to take account of relevant differences between them. Examples are *Quirke* (1982) 4 Cr App R (S) 187 (where one offender had pleaded guilty and the other had contested the case), *Beard* (1992) 14 Cr App R (S) 302 (where the co-accused had played a lesser role in the offence and had pleaded guilty), and *Belton* [1997] 1 Cr App R (S) 215 (where one offender had played a greater role in the offence and was also being sentenced for an additional offence). In *McClurkin* (1979) 1 Cr App R (S) 67, sentences of three years' imprisonment for importation of cannabis were upheld on both offenders, in a case where the one who played the main role in the offence had pleaded guilty and given considerable help to the authorities and the one who had played a lesser role in the offence had contested the case. In this case the relevant factors cancelled each other out. In *Whitehead* (1995) 16 Cr App R (S) 395, sentences on a 24-year-old offender totalling three years' imprisonment for two burglaries were upheld, notwithstanding that his 19-year-old co-accused received a community service order. The Court of Appeal noted that the older man had five previous convictions and had served two custodial sentences in the past, and had been on bail at the time of the latest offences, while the younger man had only one previous conviction and had not been on bail at the time of the offences.

There is no disparity of sentence where an offender aged 24 receives an appropriate sentence of 18 months' imprisonment but the sentencer is prevented from imposing a similar sentence on his 17-year-old co-accused by restrictions on sentencing powers based on the co-defendant's age (*Harper* (1995) 16 Cr App R (S) 639). There was held to have been no disparity in *Lillie* (1995) 16 Cr App R (S) 534, where the offender received an 'unimpeachable' sentence of five years' imprisonment for an offence of drug trafficking while his co-accused, who was sentenced in Holland, received six months' imprisonment.

A disproportionate sentence should not be imposed on the ground that the offender requires treatment for alcoholism, drug addiction or psychiatric problems (*Roote* (1980) 2 Cr App R (S) 368; *Bassett* (1985) 7 Cr App R (S) 75). The fact that one of the offenders is a woman is not, in itself, a ground for different treatment on sentence (*Okuya* (1984) 6 Cr App R (S) 253).

In *Nunn* [1996] 2 Cr App R (S) 136, a case where the offender pleaded guilty to causing death by dangerous driving, the Court of Appeal said that it was an elementary principle of sentencing that the damaging and distressing effects of a crime upon the victim should be made known to, and taken into account by, the sentencer. This might include the anguish and emotional suffering of the victim (see *Doe* (1995) 16 Cr App R (S) 718) or, in the case of the victim's death, their surviving close family. Information about exceptionally severe effects of a crime upon the victim should be couched in proper evidential form (see *Hobstaff* (1993) 14 Cr App R (S) 605 and **D17.1**). Exceptional cases apart, it is not clear to what extent the sentencer may properly make any assumption about the likely effects of a crime upon its victim without receiving evidence to support that assumption (see *O'S* (1993) 14 Cr App R (S) 632).

The Court of Appeal stated in *Nunn* that the opinions of the victim or members of their family about the appropriate level of punishment for the offender could not provide a sound basis for sentencing; otherwise, cases with identical features would be dealt with in widely different ways. The Court of Appeal in *Hird* [1998] 2 Cr App R (S) 241 received letters from the close relations of the deceased victim, urging that the offender's appeal against sentence for causing death by dangerous driving be rejected; the court stated that it was essential that sentences imposed for the offence be consistent, and accordingly reduced a term of 30 months' detention in a young offender institution to 21 months to bring the sentence into line with other authorities. In a case where the victim has forgiven the offender this is not in itself a sufficient reason for reducing sentence (*Nunn*), but it may indicate that the psychological suffering of the victim has been less severe than would normally result from an offence of that type and an appropriate reduction may therefore be made. An example is *Mills* [1998] 2 Cr App R (S) 252. In the unusual circumstance that a sentence passed by the judge has had the effect of worsening the situation of the victim or his family, the sentence may be reduced on appeal (see *Nunn*, where the offender and the victim had been friends, and relatives of the deceased indicated that the custodial term imposed had made it harder for them to come to terms with the victim's death, and *Roche* [1999] 2 Cr App R (S) 105).

Criminal Justice Act 1991: the Statutory Criteria for the Determination of Custodial Sentence Length

Section 2 of the CJA 1991 lays down criteria for the proper determination of the length **E1.13** of custodial sentences, including discretionary life sentences and suspended sentences, imposed by the Crown Court or by magistrates' courts, whether passed on adults or on young offenders.

Criminal Justice Act 1991, s. 2

(1)   This section applies where a court passes a custodial sentence other than one fixed by law or falling to be imposed under section 2(2) of the Crime (Sentences) Act 1997.

(2)   Subject to section 3(2) and 4(2) of that Act, the custodial sentence shall be—

(a)   for such term (not exceeding the permitted maximum) as in the opinion of the court is commensurate with the seriousness of the offence, or the combination of the offence and one or more offences associated with it; or

(b)   where the offence is a violent or sexual offence, for such longer term (not exceeding that maximum) as in the opinion of the court is necessary to protect the public from serious harm from the offender.

(3)   Where the court passes a custodial sentence for a term longer than is commensurate with the seriousness of the offence, or the combination of the offence and one or more offences associated with it, the court shall—

(a)   state in open court that it is of the opinion that subsection (2)(b) above applies and why it is of that opinion; and

(b)   explain to the offender in open court and in ordinary language why the sentence is for such a term.

(4)   A custodial sentence for an indeterminate period shall be regarded for the purposes of subsections (2) and (3) above as a custodial sentence for a term longer than any actual term.

(5)   Subsection (3) above shall not apply in any case where the court passes a custodial sentence falling to be imposed under subsection (2) of section 3 or 4 of the Crime (Sentences) Act 1997 which is for the minimum term specified in that subsection.

For maximum sentences of imprisonment, see **E1.1**; for maximum custodial sentences for young offenders, see **E3.1**. It will be seen that under this provision a custodial sentence which is more severe than is commensurate with the seriousness of the offence may be justified only under s. 2(2)(b), that is in the case of violent or sexual offences in order to protect the public from serious harm, and cannot otherwise be justified by the court on the grounds of individual prevention or general deterrence. It would seem that deterrence may be pursued as a sentencing aim only to the extent that a deterrent effect may be achieved by passing a commensurate custodial sentence under s. 2(2)(a), or a longer than normal custodial sentence where the circumstances fall within the specific requirements of s. 2(2)(b) (see *Cunningham* [1993] 1 WLR 183, per Lord Taylor CJ at p. 187).

Section 3(1) of the CJA 1991 requires that for the purposes of forming an opinion under s. 2(2)(a) or (2)(b) as to the appropriate length of a custodial sentence, the court 'shall obtain and consider a pre-sentence report' unless the court is of the opinion that this is 'unnecessary'. For pre-sentence reports, see **E1.8** and **D17.19**.

E1.14   *Justifying the Length of a Custodial Sentence under the Criminal Justice Act 1991, s. 2(2)(a)*   Section 2(2)(a) states that the length of a custodial sentence shall be commensurate with the seriousness of the offence. When passing a sentence commensurate with the seriousness of the offence under s. 2(2)(a), the CJA 1991, s. 3(3)(a), requires that the court 'shall take into account all such information about the circumstances of the offence or (as the case may be) of the offence and the offence or offences associated with it (including any aggravating or mitigating factors) as is available to it'. Additionally, s. 28(1) provides that nothing in part I of the 1991 Act 'shall prevent a court from mitigating an offender's sentence by taking into account any such matters as, in the opinion of the court, are relevant in mitigation of sentence'.

The Court of Appeal in *Howells* [1999] 1 WLR 307 set out a number of considerations relevant to the decision whether a particular offence is so serious that only custody can be justified (see **E1.9**). It is clear that most, if not all, of the matters referred to there are also relevant when determining custodial sentence length under s. 2(2)(a). Of the seven linked appeals heard, four resulted in the Court of Appeal adjusting the length of the custodial term originally imposed by the sentencer, while only two resulted in reversal of the decision to impose a custodial sentence. In *Howells*, Lord Bingham stated that when the court was satisfied that only a custodial sentence was justified for the offence, and such a sentence was passed, the custodial term should be for no longer period than was necessary to meet the penal purpose which the court had in mind. In *Cunningham* [1993] 1 WLR 183, Lord Taylor CJ said that the purpose of a custodial sentence had primarily to be to punish and deter, and the phrase 'commensurate with the seriousness of the offence' in s. 2(2)(a) had to mean commensurate with the punishment and deterrence which the seriousness of the offence required. Section 2(2)(a) prohibited adding extra length to the commensurate sentence so as to make a special example of the defendant. Prevalence of the offence was, however, a legitimate factor in determining the length of the custodial sentence to be passed.

Section 2(2)(a) states that the court may have regard to 'the combination of the offence and one or more offences associated with it' when determining the length of a custodial sentence. Section 31(2) defines when one offence may be regarded for these purposes as 'associated with' another, and was considered at **E1.9**.

Where the offender is being sentenced for several offences, this approach could lead to a total sentence which is disproportionate to the overall seriousness of the offending behaviour. The CJA 1991, s. 28(2)(b), in an attempt to avoid this, declares that nothing shall prevent a court 'in a case of an offender who is convicted of one or more other offences, from mitigating his sentence by applying any rule of law as to the totality of sentences'. This provision gives statutory recognition to the totality principle, which has been developed by the Court of Appeal. For discussion of the totality principle, see **E1.19**.

Where a court is dealing with an offender for several offences, one (or more) of which is (or are) so serious that only custody can be justified but the remainder of which are not so serious, the court is not precluded from passing custodial sentences for the lesser offences. However, those sentences should normally be ordered to run concurrently with the sentences for the more serious offences and should not increase the length of the overall term (*Oliver* [1993] 1 WLR 177).

Justifying the Length of a Custodial Sentence under the Criminal Justice Act E1.15
1991, s. 2(2)(b) Section 2(2)(b) deals with the extent to which the Crown Court or (at least in theory) a magistrates' court is permitted to depart from the general principle of commensurability set out in s. 2(2)(a). The court may impose a sentence which is longer than normal but which does not exceed the statutory maximum for the offence, in the case of a custodial sentence passed for a violent or sexual offence, where it is the opinion of the court that a custodial sentence of that length is necessary to protect the public from serious harm from the offender. Definitions of 'violent offence', 'sexual offence' and 'serious harm' are provided in s. 31 of the Act and were considered at **E1.10**. The longer sentence which is imposed in reliance upon s. 2(2)(b) may be a determinate sentence which is longer than could be justified in reliance on s. 2(2)(a), or it may be a discretionary life sentence. The Crown Court may impose a custodial sentence under s. 2(2)(b) upon a defendant convicted in a magistrates' court and committed to the Crown Court for sentence (see MCA 1980, s. 38(2)(b) and *Etchells* [1996] 1 Cr App R (S) 163).

When making its decision on whether to impose a sentence which is longer than normal under s. 2(2)(b), the CJA 1991, s. 3(3)(a), requires that the court 'shall take into account all such information about the circumstances of the offence or (as the case may be) of the offence and the offence or offences associated with it (including any aggravating or mitigating factors) as is available to it', and s. 3(3)(b) states that the court 'may take into account any information about the offender which is before it', including the offender's previous record. Additionally, s. 28(1) provides that nothing in part I of the 1991 Act 'shall prevent a court from mitigating an offender's sentence by taking into account any such matters as, in the opinion of the court, are relevant in mitigation of sentence'.

The court must be sure that it is basing its decision on accurate information about the offender, if necessary by holding a *Newton* inquiry (see **D17.2**) into any important issue (*Oudkerk* (1995) 16 Cr App R (S) 172). In *Baverstock* [1993] 1 WLR 202, the Court of Appeal said that a court should never pass a longer-than-normal sentence without first warning the defendant's lawyer that this was in the offing. This point was re-emphasised in *Bacon* (1995) 16 Cr App R (S) 1031. The evidential basis for imposing a longer-than-normal sentence will normally be found in a psychiatric report prepared on the offender, or in his previous convictions, or both. Normally both elements will be required, but a person with no previous convictions may receive a longer-than-normal sentence provided that the medical evidence is clear (*Crow* (1995) 16 Cr App R (S) 409; *Smith* (1999) *The Times*, 22 June 1999; see also *Thomas* (1995) 16 Cr App R (S) 616, where there were no previous convictions similar to the instant offence). On the other hand, in a case where the previous convictions speak for themselves a longer-than-normal sentence may be passed without receiving a medical report (*Hashi* (1995) 16 Cr App R (S) 121). Where previous convictions are being relied upon, the court must ensure that the information it is relying upon is accurate (*Oudkerk*), and it may be necessary to investigate the circumstances of earlier offences to see whether the offender really does represent a grave risk, or whether he can properly be sentenced on a proportionate basis (*Samuels* (1995) 16 Cr App R (S) 856). It seems that information about the circumstances of the current offence standing alone, without inferences drawn from prior offending and without a psychiatric report, are unlikely to be enough to justify a longer-than-normal sentence (*Ali* (1995) 16 Cr App R (S) 692 and *Khan* (1995) 16 Cr App R (S) 180).

Having decided to impose a longer than normal sentence on the offender, s. 2(3) requires that the sentencer must explain in open court that the court is of the opinion that s. 2(2)(b) applies and why it is of that opinion, and the sentencer must explain to the offender in open court and in ordinary language why the sentence is for such a term. In *Bacon* (1995) 16 Cr App R (S) 1031, the Court of Appeal said that the judge should point out clearly and in straightforward terms what it was that he considered to be the serious harm in question, as was required by s. 2(3). There is, however, no requirement on the judge to indicate the proportionate sentence which he would have imposed had he not invoked s. 2(2)(b) (*Powell* (1996) *The Times*, 9 August 1996).

It is *not* the case that whenever the court is dealing with a violent or sexual offence, it must sentence on the basis of public protection. The general rule in sentencing (violent and sexual cases included) remains that the sentence should be proportionate to the seriousness of the offence but, exceptionally, the court may impose a longer-than-normal sentence on the offender where special risk to the public is made out and where the imposition of a proportionate sentence would not provide adequate protection (*Christie* (1995) 16 Cr App R (S) 469). In *Crow* (1995) 16 Cr App R (S) 409, the Court of Appeal said that if the offence was an isolated example, or there was no good reason to fear a substantial risk of further similar offending, s. 2(2)(b) would not apply. This point is also clear from *Bestwick* (1995) 16 Cr App R (S) 168, where two offenders had been involved in a series of arson offences. One was given a proportionate sentence of 30 months' detention, but the other received 5 years' imprisonment, passed as a longer-than-normal sentence. An appeal on the basis of disparity between the sentences was dismissed, the Court of Appeal noting that the offender who received the longer sentence had a seriously disturbed personality and an obsession with lighting fires and represented a real risk to the public. The other offender had a normal personality and hence fell to be sentenced in accordance with the seriousness of the offending. See also *Ali* (1995) 16 Cr App R (S) 692.

Although the imposition of a longer-than-normal sentence should not, then, be regarded as the normal course for the sentencer to take when dealing with a violent or sexual crime, it has been held that, where a defendant is clearly eligible for a longer-than-normal sentence, the court's decision not to impose one (or its failure to appreciate that it might have done so) may be regarded as the imposition of an unduly lenient sentence. In *A-G's Ref (No. 9 of 1994)* (1995) 16 Cr App R (S) 366, the Court of Appeal upheld a prosecution appeal and said that a longer-than-normal sentence of ten years, rather than a commensurate sentence of six years, should have been passed. The offender had committed a series of sexual offences against young boys, and he represented a real and continuing danger.

Section 2(2)(b) states that a longer-than-normal sentence shall be for such longer term (not exceeding the maximum available for the offence) '. . . as in the opinion of the court is necessary to protect the public from serious harm from the offender'. Three issues arise from this definition.

First, the court must be clear that *the offender* himself poses the risk: the threat must come 'from him'. So, the court cannot employ a longer-than-normal sentence simply to mark disapproval of a particularly unpleasant offence, or to register concern at the prevalence of the type of crime concerned. The court will base its view upon the information it has received relating to the offence and the offender. Thus, in *Walsh* (1995) 16 Cr App R (S) 204, a longer-than-normal sentence was held to be inappropriate in a case where the offender had committed sexual offences on a 13-year-old boy, but where the offence was 'out of character' for the offender and repetition was unlikely.

Second, it must be shown to be necessary to protect *the public* from serious harm from the offender. While normally the risk will be to members of the public generally, it was accepted in *Hashi* (1995) 16 Cr App R (S) 121 and in *Nicholas* (1994) 15 Cr App R (S) 381 that a longer-than-normal sentence might be imposed for the protection of a small group of individuals (in *Hashi* the offender's ex-wife and any male friends the offender might see her with) or a single member of the public, rather than the public at large. In *Nicholas*, however, where the offender had persistently assaulted his wife in the past (but had never assaulted anybody else), it was held that a longer-than-normal sentence for a further assault was not justified since the wife now had a court order restraining the offender from molesting her and the offender had accepted that the marriage was over. Another aspect of this issue arose in *L* (1994) 15 Cr App R (S) 501, where the offender admitted sexually abusing his stepdaughters, aged 10 and 12, over a period of 20 months. The Court of Appeal quashed a longer-than-normal sentence of seven years and substituted a proportionate term of three years on the basis that the offending had been confined within the family and that the offender had no other convictions and would have no future contact with the victims. In the circumstances, the court felt that the defendant did not represent a risk 'to the public'. Similar cases, which reached the same result, are *S* (1995) 16 Cr App R (S) 303 and *Swain* (1994) 15 Cr App R (S) 765.

Third, it must be shown that in the particular case before the court the public requires to be protected from *serious harm*. The 1991 Act states that this phrase should be 'construed as a reference to protecting members of the public from death or serious personal injury, whether physical or psychological, occasioned by further such offences committed by the offender' (s. 31(3)). What matters here is not so much the likelihood of further offences occurring, nor necessarily the seriousness of the current or previous offences committed by the offender (though both of these will weigh with the court), but rather the anticipated seriousness of future offending. Note that the sentencer must anticipate 'further *such* offences' (emphasis added), i.e., further violent or sexual offences, being committed by the offender. In *Creasey* (1994) 15 Cr App R (S) 671, the offender pleaded guilty to indecent assault on a 13-year-old boy, attempting to masturbate him by rubbing his hand on the boy's trousers. Creasey had previous convictions for similar offences, but the Court of Appeal quashed a longer-than-normal sentence of five years and substituted a sentence of 21 months. The offences were 'unpleasant and distressing' but, in the court's view, did not require the protection of the public from serious harm. *Creasey* stands in contrast to *Bowler* (1994) 15 Cr App R (S) 78, where the defendant pleaded guilty to indecent assault, having put his hand up a young girl's skirt and fondled her. He had eight previous convictions for very similar offences, committed on women and girls. In this case a longer-than-normal sentence (of six years) was upheld by the Court of Appeal, on the basis that the court must have in mind the possibility of future victims more vulnerable to such conduct than the average, who might suffer psychological harm. The distinction between these last two cases is not easy to see. *Bowler* was distinguished in *Fishwick* [1996] 1 Cr App R (S) 359, where the defendant had a history of relatively minor physical assaults of a non-sexual nature, and where the Court of Appeal felt that there was no basis to conclude that future victims were likely to suffer serious psychological injury, but was followed in *A-G's Ref (No. 47 of 1998)* [1999] 1 Cr App R (S) 464, where the offender, a man with numerous similar previous convictions, indecently assaulted five different women by pinching the victim's bottom, putting his hand up the victim's skirt and, in two cases, exposing himself to the victim. In the last case a sentence of two years' imprisonment was varied to a longer-than-normal sentence of six years.

There is little specific guidance from the Court of Appeal on the appropriate additional length of sentence to be imposed when a longer-than-normal sentence is passed. In *Mansell* (1994) 15 Cr App R (S) 771 the Court of Appeal said that in each case the sentencer had to try to balance the need to protect the public, on the one hand, with the need to look at the totality of the sentence and see that it was not out of all proportion to the nature of the offending, on the other. It was, the Court of Appeal said, impossible to provide more precise guidance. In *Crow* it was said that, when fixing the length of a longer-than-normal sentence, account should be taken of the age of the offender, in that the risk which the offender represented to the public might be expected to decline over time, that some allowance should normally be made for a guilty plea (even in the worst cases) and that a sentence imposed under s. 2(2)(b) should still bear a 'reasonable relationship' to the offence for which it was imposed, but in *Bowler* the Court of Appeal said that when a sentence was being passed to protect the public matters of personal mitigation, such as a guilty plea, the impulsive nature of the offence and the offender's limited intelligence, would carry less weight than in the case of a proportionate sentence. The decisions in *Campbell* [1997] 1 Cr App R (S) 119 and *Gabbidon* [1997] 2 Cr App R (S) 19 make it clear that, in cases where a very long proportionate sentence imposed under s. 2(2)(a) would in any event be justifiable on the facts of the offence (proportionate custodial terms of 15 years would have been appropriate for rape in the former case and for robbery in the latter case), the court may still pass a longer-than-normal sentence under s. 2(2)(b) where the criteria for such a sentence are made out, even though commensurate sentences of such length would already contain a significant element of public protection. Care should be taken, however, to ensure that the balance referred to in *Mansell* is preserved: the need to protect the public should not produce a sentence which is out of all proportion to the offending behaviour. A total sentence of 20 years was reduced to 17 years in *Campbell*, and 27 years reduced to 20 years in *Gabbidon*. At the other end of the scale, in *Carpenter* [1997] 1 Cr App R (S) 4, where the proportionate sentence for the offence of indecent assault would, in the view of the Court of Appeal, have been no more than two years on a guilty plea but where a longer-than-normal sentence was appropriate in light of the offender's record and the risk which he posed, the addition of a further 12 months was the maximum that could be justified having regard to the offence. See also *Winfield* [1999] 2 Cr App R (S) 116.

In some cases, where there is evidence that the offender is suffering from a psychiatric or personality disorder, the sentencer may have to choose between the imposition of a longer-than-normal sentence under s. 2(2)(b) and a medical disposal. The most likely medical disposal would be a hospital order or a restriction order under the Mental Health Act 1983 (see **E24.3** and **E24.5** respectively). In *Fawcett* (1995) 16 Cr App R (S) 55, the Court of Appeal said that relevant considerations in making this choice would be the seriousness and persistence of the offending, the nature and extent of the disorder, the ability of the offender to appreciate the consequences of his behaviour, evidence of remorse and his willingness or otherwise to undergo treatment.

Another possibility, in cases where the offence with which the offender stands convicted is punishable with life imprisonment, would be to pass a life sentence rather than a longer-than-normal sentence under s. 2(2)(b). For the well established criteria which have to be made out before a discretionary life sentence may be imposed, see *Hodgson* (1967) 52 Cr App R 113 and *Wilkinson* (1983) 5 Cr App R (S) 105, discussed at **E1.23**. It is clear that an offender may qualify for a longer-than-normal sentence without fulfilling all the criteria for the imposition of a life sentence. Thus in *Roche* (1995) 16 Cr App R (S) 849 the offender was convicted of attempted murder and indecent assault, having attacked a woman who was walking on a common and inflicted serious injuries upon her. He had one previous conviction for theft. The Court of Appeal quashed the life sentence imposed by the trial judge and substituted a longer-than-normal sentence of 14 years. The Court accepted medical evidence to the effect that there was nothing to suggest any mental abnormality on the part of the offender, thereby rendering him ineligible for a discretionary life sentence. In *Chapman* (1994) 15 Cr App R (S) 844, the offender had been involved in a robbery in which shots had been fired at a security guard and in the direction of a witness. Chapman was later found in possession of the gun. At the time of the offence he was unlawfully at large from prison. He had numerous previous convictions and had served earlier terms of six, ten and twelve years' imprisonment. It was held by the Court of Appeal that Chapman was *not* mentally unstable (and hence a life sentence was not appropriate) but that he was 'a committed criminal, at war with society . . . he was very dangerous indeed'. A longer-than-normal sentence of 20 years was passed, to protect the public from serious harm from him. It should be noted that Chapman would now attract an automatic life sentence under the provisions of the C(S)A 1997, s. 2 (see **E1.22**).

Relevance of Criminal Record, Offending on Bail and Racial Aggravation

The CJA 1991, s. 29(1), allows a court to take account of the offender's previous **E1.16** convictions where it is gauging issues relevant to offence seriousness. These are, in particular, where the court is considering whether an offence is 'so serious' that only a custodial sentence can be justified for it under s. 1(2)(a), where the court is fixing the length of a custodial sentence as being 'commensurate with the seriousness of the offence' under s. 2(2)(a), where the court is determining whether the offence is 'serious enough' to warrant the passing of a community sentence under s. 6(1) and where the court is determining the restrictions on liberty imposed by a community sentence which are 'commensurate with the seriousness of the offence' under s. 6(2).

Criminal Justice Act 1991, s. 29

(1) In considering the seriousness of any offence, the court may take into account any previous convictions of the offender or any failure of his to respond to previous sentences.

(2) In considering the seriousness of any offence committed while the offender was on bail, the court shall treat the fact that it was committed in those circumstances as an aggravating factor.

Subsections (3) to (6) of s. 29 provide that for the purposes of s. 29 the court may take account of previous convictions of the offender which have been dealt with by way of a probation order, or by the grant of an absolute or conditional discharge. They also provide that the court may take into account any failure of the offender to respond to an earlier probation order, or to any failure of his to respond to the grant of a conditional (but not an absolute) discharge. This is notwithstanding the fact that a conviction which is dealt with by way of a conditional or absolute discharge is deemed, by the PCCA 1973, s. 1C, not to be a conviction for a range of purposes (see **E14.6**). An earlier, similar, provision in respect of probation orders was repealed by the CJA 1991.

It is clear that s. 29(1) confers a discretion on the sentencer, but the subsection gives no indication of when the offender's previous convictions or failure to respond to previous sentences may properly be regarded as relevant to the seriousness of the latest offence. Prior to the coming into force of the CJA 1991, several Court of Appeal decisions had indicated that it was wrong to impose a sentence disproportionate to the seriousness of the offence purely on the basis of the offender's previous convictions (*Galloway* (1979) 1 Cr App R (S) 311; *Queen* (1981) 3 Cr App R (S) 245; *Bailey* (1988) 10 Cr App R (S) 231). Guidance from the Court of Appeal is awaited on whether a similar approach is appropriate in respect of s. 29(1). The Magistrates' Association Guidelines (1997) advise magistrates to 'take care in using previous convictions or any failure to respond to previous sentences in assessing seriousness'. The Guidelines recommend that 'courts should identify any convictions relevant for this purpose and then consider to what extent they affect the seriousness of the present offence'. In any case, a clean record, or a record of few convictions, will often be regarded as a significant mitigating factor and may always be taken into account as personal mitigation under s. 28(1).

Section 29(2), in contrast to s. 29(1), confers a duty on the sentencer to regard the commission of an offence while the offender is on bail as an aggravating feature of that offence. The Court of Appeal in *Baverstock* [1993] 1 WLR 202 stressed that commission of an offence on bail should be regarded as an aggravating factor, those comments being made before the current wording of s. 29 was inserted by the CJA 1993. While s. 29(2) is expressed in mandatory terms, it has to be set against the established sentencing principle that consecutive sentences are appropriate where one offence is committed while the offender is on bail in respect of another (see **E1.5**). Operation of these rules together might well result in a disproportionately severe sentence.

Racial motivation has long been accepted as a serious aggravating factor. For clear statements to this effect by the Court of Appeal see *A-G's Refs (Nos. 29, 30 and 31 of 1994)* (1994) 16 Cr App R (S) 698 (where Lord Taylor CJ said that the racial element in the offence was 'gravely aggravating') and *Craney* [1996] 2 Cr App R (S) 336. Many of the offence guidelines in the Magistrates' Association's *Sentencing Guidelines* (1997) make the same point. Section 82 of the CDA 1998 places this principle on a statutory footing by stating that if an offence was racially aggravated the court shall treat that as a factor which increases the seriousness of the offence. Section 82 further requires that the court shall state in open court that the offence was so aggravated. This provision is of general application in sentencing, except that it does not apply where a court is imposing sentence for one of the offences under the CDA 1998, ss. 29 to 32 (a racially aggravated assault, racially aggravated criminal damage, a racially aggravated public order offence, or racially aggravated harassment). The racially aggravated forms of these offences carry higher maximum penalties than their equivalent non-aggravated form and it is clearly envisaged that they will attract enhanced penalties (see *Miller* [1999] 2 Cr App R (S) 392 for an early example). For the definition of 'racially aggravated', see **B11.154**.

Maximum Sentence to Be Reserved for Gravest Offences

E1.17   In *Carroll* (1995) 16 Cr App R (S) 488, the judge, on imposing the maximum sentence of two years' detention in a young offender institution on an offender who had pleaded guilty to aggravated vehicle-taking, commented that the maximum sentence provided by statute was too low. The Court of Appeal, reducing the sentence to 18 months, said that sentencers must abide loyally by the maximum sentence provided, that the maximum sentence should be reserved for the most serious examples of that offence and that an appropriate discount (such as for a guilty plea) should be made from the sentence which was commensurate with the seriousness of the offence.

In considering whether a particular offence is one of the worst examples of its kind, sentencers should have regard to the range of cases which is actually encountered in practice, 'and ask themselves whether the particular case they are dealing with comes within the broad band of that type' but 'should not use their imaginations to conjure up unlikely worst possible kinds of case' (per Lawton LJ in *Ambler* (1975) CSP A1–4C01). A 'worst case' of dangerous driving was identified in *Hastings* [1996] 1 Cr App R (S) 167; the Court of Appeal upheld the maximum two-year term. The statutory maximum should not normally be imposed where there is substantial mitigation. An example is *Thompson* (1980) 2 Cr App R (S) 244 where a two-year maximum sentence imposed for neglect of the accused's young sons was reduced to allow her immediate release, in the light of personal mitigation.

In general the maximum sentence should not be imposed where the accused has pleaded guilty. In *Greene* (1993) 14 Cr App R (S) 682, the maximum sentence of five years' imprisonment for violent disorder was reduced to three years on the ground that the offender had pleaded guilty; in *Barnes* (1983) 5 Cr App R (S) 368 a maximum sentence imposed for attempted rape was reduced on the grounds of the guilty plea and saving the victim from the ordeal of giving testimony.

Length of Prison Sentence Normally Reduced in Light of Plea of Guilty

Although this principle is very well established, the extent of the appropriate 'discount' **E1.18** has never been fixed. In *Buffery* (1992) 14 Cr App R (S) 511 Lord Taylor CJ indicated that 'something in the order of one-third would very often be an appropriate discount', but much depends on the facts of the case and the timeliness of the plea. In determining the extent of the discount, the court may have regard to the strength of the case against the offender. An offender who voluntarily surrenders to the police and admits a crime which could not otherwise be proved may be entitled to more than the usual discount (*Hoult* (1990) 12 Cr App R (S) 180; *Claydon* (1993) 15 Cr App R (S) 526) and so may an offender who, as well as pleading guilty himself, has given evidence against a co-accused (*Wood* [1997] 1 Cr App R (S) 347) and/or given significant help to the authorities (*Guy* [1999] 2 Cr App R (S) 24). Where an offender has been caught red-handed and a guilty plea is inevitable, any discount may be reduced or lost (*Morris* (1988) 10 Cr App R (S) 216; *Landy* (1995) 16 Cr App R (S) 908). Occasionally the discount may be refused or reduced for other reasons, such as where the accused has delayed his plea in an attempt to secure a tactical advantage (*Hollington* (1985) 82 Cr App R 281; *Okee* [1998] 2 Cr App R (S) 199). Similarly, some or all of the discount may be lost where the offender pleads guilty but adduces a version of facts at odds with that put forward by the prosecution, requiring the court to conduct an enquiry into the facts (*Williams* (1990) 12 Cr App R (S) 415). The leading case in this area is *Costen* (1989) 11 Cr App R (S) 182, where the Court of Appeal confirmed that the discount might be lost in any of the following circumstances: (i) where the protection of the public made it necessary that a long sentence, possibly the maximum sentence, be passed; (ii) cases of 'tactical plea', where the offender delayed his plea until the final moment in a case where he could not hope to put up much of a defence, and (iii) where the offender had been caught red-handed and a plea of guilty was practically certain. It was also established in *Costen* that the discount may be reduced where the accused pleads guilty to specimen counts. In *Byrne* [1997] 1 Cr App R (S) 165 it was held that an offender who had absconded and remained at large for 19 months was not entitled to expect a discount for his guilty plea when he pleaded guilty after being re-arrested.

The Magistrates' Association Guidelines (1997), referred to where appropriate in **part B** of this work, include sentence guides for offences dealt with summarily which are based on a first-time offender pleading not guilty. The Guidelines state that 'A timely guilty plea may attract a sentencing discount of up to one third but the precise amount of discount will depend on the facts of each case and a last-minute plea of guilty may attract only a minimal reduction'.

The CJPO 1994, s. 48, makes specific provision as to reductions in sentences for guilty pleas.

Criminal Justice and Public Order Act 1994, s. 48

(1)   In determining what sentence to pass on an offender who has pleaded guilty to an offence in proceedings before that or another court a court shall take into account—
(a)   the stage in the proceedings for the offence at which the offender indicated his intention to plead guilty, and
(b)   the circumstances in which this indication was given.
(2)   If, as a result of taking into account any matter referred to in subsection (1) above, the court imposes a punishment on the offender which is less severe than the punishment it would otherwise have imposed, it shall state in open court that it has done so.
(3)   In the case of an offence the sentence for which falls to be imposed under subsection (2) of section 3 or 4 of the Crime (Sentences) Act 1997, nothing in that subsection shall prevent the court, after taking into account any matter referred to in subsection (1) above, from imposing any sentence which is not less than 80 per cent of that specified in that subsection.

The references to 'the stage of the proceedings' and the 'circumstances' in which the plea was tendered are sufficiently broad to be regarded as incorporating and re-stating the existing law, as described above. In the important case of *Rafferty* [1998] 2 Cr App R (S) 449 the defendant appeared before a magistrates' court charged with production and possession of cannabis. He indicated that he would plead guilty before venue was determined, in accordance with MCA 1980, s. 17A (see **D3.4**), and was committed to the Crown Court for sentence. At the Crown Court he pleaded guilty to a further charge of possession of cannabis with intent to supply. A total sentence of four months' imprisonment was imposed by the Crown Court judge. In upholding the sentence, the Court of Appeal explained that the discount for the guilty plea tendered at the Crown Court should, in the absence of good reason being shown as to why it was delayed until the Crown Court, be less than if it had been made at the plea before venue. *Rafferty* establishes that a defendant should normally receive less than a full discount if he has not indicated his plea before venue is determined. In *Archer* [1998] 2 Cr App R (S) 76, it was held that appropriate credit should be given to a defendant who was willing to plead guilty to a lesser charge at an early stage in the proceedings, but where the prosecution indicated that such a plea would be acceptable only at a later stage.

While the Court of Appeal authorities are almost all concerned with the extent of the discount on the length of a custodial sentence, a guilty plea may also form the basis for discounting the level of a fine, or reducing the duration of a community sentence. The Magistrates' Association Guidelines (1997) state that 'Discount may be given in respect of the fine or periods of community service' as well as custodial terms. A timely guilty plea, particularly where associated with other mitigation, may also form the basis for passing a community sentence rather than a custodial sentence (see *Howells* [1999] 1 WLR 307 at **E1.9**). A reduction from an immediate prison sentence to a suspended sentence on the basis of plea would not be permissible, however, since even an early guilty plea cannot constitute the 'exceptional circumstances' which must attain before a suspended sentence may be passed (see **E2.6**).

Section 48 imposes a clear duty upon sentencers to state in open court that, in consequence of the guilty plea, the court has imposed a less severe sentence than it would otherwise have done. In *Fearon* [1996] 2 Cr App R (S) 25, the Court of Appeal stressed that the sentencing judge should always make it clear whether or not a reduction for the guilty plea has been made.

Regard to be had to Totality of Offending Conduct

Sentencers must have regard to the total length of sentence passed, particularly where **E1.19** consecutive sentences have been imposed, to ensure that the sentence properly reflects the overall seriousness of the behaviour (*Jones* [1996] 1 Cr App R (S) 153). Overall sentences have been reduced on appeal for this reason in a range of situations, including: where a suspended sentence is activated consecutively to an immediate sentence (*Bocskei* (1970) 54 Cr App R 519); where the offender has committed several offences of moderate gravity (*Holderness* (1974) CSP A5–3B01); where a new custodial sentence is ordered to run consecutively to a custodial sentence which the offender is already serving (*Stevens* [1997] 2 Cr App R (S) 180); and where the offender receives a long sentence together with a short one (consecutive sentences of 11 years and six months adjusted on appeal to run concurrently (*Smith* (1981) 3 Cr App R (S) 201). In *Gorman* (1993) 14 Cr App R (S) 120 it was said to be wrong to add a short consecutive sentence for failure to surrender to bail to a sentence of 12 months for the actual offence.

This principle achieves statutory recognition in the CJA 1991, s. 28(2)(b), which states that nothing shall prevent a court 'in a case of an offender who is convicted of one or more other offences, from mitigating his sentence by applying any rule of law as to the totality of sentences'. This provision applies to the totality of community orders and financial orders as well as to custodial sentences. The Magistrates' Association *Sentencing Guidelines* (1997) state that 'where there are several offences before the court, the totality principle requires a court to consider the total sentence in relation to the totality of the offending and in relation to sentence levels for other crimes'.

Relevance to Sentence of Arrangements for the Early Release of the Offender and of his Allocation to a Particular Prison Regime and Requirement to Explain Practical Effect of Custodial Sentence

In *Practice Statement (Crime: Sentencing)* [1992] 1 WLR 948, issued by Lord Taylor CJ **E1.20** on 1 October 1992, it was stated that:

> It has been an axiomatic principle of sentencing policy until now that the court should decide the appropriate sentence in each case without reference to questions of remission or parole. I have consulted the Lords Justices presiding in the Court of Appeal (Criminal Division) and we have decided that a new approach is essential. Accordingly . . . it will be necessary, when passing a custodial sentence in the Crown Court, to have regard to the actual period likely to be served and, as far as practicable, to the risk of offenders serving substantially longer under the new system than would have been normal under the old. Existing guideline judgments should be applied with these considerations in mind.

The *Practice Statement* was prompted by the fact that, following changes made by the 1991 Act to early release arrangements, the imposition of custodial sentences on or after 1 October 1992 would otherwise result in many offenders serving substantially longer in custody than those given similar sentences before that date. In *Cunningham* [1993] 1 WLR 183, however, Lord Taylor CJ warned that the Court of Appeal would be unmoved 'by nice mathematical comparisons' on the effective length of custodial sentences. The Court of Appeal in *Ensley* [1996] 1 Cr App R (S) 294 held that no disparity arose in a case where one defendant received a sentence of less than four years and the other received four years or more (thus qualifying them as 'short-term' and 'long-term' prisoners respectively and subject to different early release provisions). On the other hand, a sentencer may wish to adjust sentence length to avoid an unusual, adverse effect upon an offender's release date (see *Waite* (1992) 13 Cr App R (S) 26, *Cozens* [1996] 2 Cr App R (S) 321 and *Harrison* [1998] 2 Cr App R (S) 174). In *Cozens* it was said that it may be unjust to impose a short consecutive sentence which has the effect of taking the overall custodial term above four years, since the offender would then qualify as a long-term prisoner and serve a sentence out of all proportion to the additional short term, and this applies whether consecutive sentences are imposed on the same occasion or whether a further custodial sentence is imposed upon an offender already serving such a sentence (*Secretary of State for the Home Department, ex parte Francois* [1998] 2 WLR 530 and *Brown* [1999] 1 Cr App R (S) 47). Nothing in *Practice Statement (Crime: Sentencing)* should be taken to detract from the principle that a sentencer should not increase sentence length merely to bring an offender within a different early release category (*Kenway* (1985) 7 Cr App R (S) 457).

Three specific situations where a sentencer may exercise a direct influence over early release arrangements should also be noted. The first is where, by the Murder (Abolition of Death Penalty) Act 1965, s. 1(2), a sentencer makes a recommendation in respect of the minimum period to be served under a mandatory life sentence for murder (**E1.21**). The second is where, by the C(S)A 1997, s. 28, a sentencer specifies what period of a discretionary life sentence must expire before the case is referred to the Parole Board (see **E1.27**). The third is where, by CDA 1998, s. 58, and CJA 1991, s. 44, the sentencer specifies a change to the normal early release arrangements when imposing a custodial sentence on an offender convicted of a 'violent' or 'sexual' offence committed after 30 September 1998 (see **E1.28**).

The sentencer should not recommend that an offender serve a custodial sentence at a specified prison, such as Grendon Underwood, since it may not always be possible for this to be arranged (*Hook* (1980) 2 Cr App R (S) 353). See, further, *Lancaster* (1995) 16 Cr App R (S) 184. The fact that a prisoner will be required to serve his sentence under rule 43 (in isolation for his own protection) is not a relevant consideration when passing sentence (*Kirby* (1979) 1 Cr App R (S) 214; *Kay* (1980) 2 Cr App R (S) 284; *Parker* [1996] 2 Cr App R (S) 275). An exceptional case is *Holmes* (1979) 1 Cr App R (S) 233.

In *Practice Direction (Custodial Sentences: Explanations)* [1998] 1 WLR 278, the Court of Appeal issued an important requirement to sentencers in the Crown Court to explain in every case the practical effect of any custodial sentence imposed. Lord Bingham CJ indicated that the statutory provisions governing the early release of offenders were not widely understood by the general public, and it was desirable when a custodial sentence was passed that its practical effect should be fully understood by the defendant, any victim, and any member of the public who is present in court or reads a full report of the proceedings. Such explanation of the practical effect of the sentence is to be provided by the sentencer in addition to the need to comply with pre-existing statutory requirements (see **E1.8**). Sentencers should give the explanation in terms of their own choosing, while taking care to ensure that the explanation is clear and accurate. No form of words is prescribed, although annexed to the Practice Direction are short statements which may, adapted as necessary, be of value as models. These statements, set out in full below, are based on the statutory provisions in force on 1 January 1998, and will require modification if those provisions are materially amended.

(1)   Total term less than 12 months

The sentence is [   ] months.
You will serve half that sentence in prison/a young offender institution. After that time the rest of your sentence will be suspended and you will be released. Your release will not bring this sentence to an end. If after your release and before the end of the period covered by the sentence you commit any further offence, you may be ordered to return to custody to serve the balance of the original sentence outstanding at the date of the further offence, as well as being punished for that new offence.

Any time you have spent on remand in custody in connection with the offence[s] for which you are now being sentenced will count as part of the sentence to be served, unless it has already been counted.

(2) Total term of 12 months and less than 4 years

The sentence is [ ] [months/years].
You will serve half that sentence in a prison/a young offender institution. After that time the rest of your sentence will be suspended and you will be released.
Your release will not bring this sentence to an end. If after your release and before the end of the period covered by the sentence you commit any further offence you may be ordered to return to custody to serve the balance of the original sentence outstanding at the date of the further offence, as well as being punished for that new offence.
Any time you have spent on remand in custody in connection with the offence[s] for which you are now being sentenced will count as part of the sentence to be served, unless it has already been counted.
After your release you will also be subject to supervision on licence until the end of three-quarters of the total sentence. [If an order has been made under section 44 of the Criminal Justice Act 1991: After your release you will also be subject to supervision on licence for the remainder of the sentence.]
If you fail to comply with any of the requirements of your licence then again you may be brought before a court which will have power to suspend your licence and order your return to custody.

(3) Total term of 4 years or more

The sentence is [ ] [years/months].
Your case will not be considered by the Parole Board until you have served at least half that period in custody. Unless the Parole Board recommends earlier release, you will not be released until you have served two-thirds of that sentence. Your release will not bring the sentence to an end. Instead, the remainder will be suspended. If after your release and before the end of the period covered by the sentence you commit any further offence you may be ordered to return to custody to serve the balance of the original sentence outstanding at the date of the new offence, as well as being punished for that new offence.
Any time you have spent in custody on remand in connection with the offence[s] for which you are now being sentenced will count as part of the sentence to be served, unless it has already been counted.
After your release you will also be subject to supervision on licence until the end of three-quarters of the total sentence. [If an order has been made under section 44 of the Criminal Justice Act 1991: After your release you will also be subject to supervision on licence for the remainder of the sentence.]
You will be liable to be recalled to prison if your licence is revoked, either on the recommendation of the Parole Board, or, if it is thought expedient in the public interest, by the Secretary of State.

(4) Discretionary life sentence

The sentence of the court is life imprisonment/custody for life/detention for life under section 53(2)(3) of the Children and Young Persons Act 1933. For the purposes of section 28 of the Crime (Sentences) Act 1997 the court specifies a period of [x] years. That means that your case will not be considered by the Parole Board until you have served at least [x] years in custody. After that time the Parole Board will be entitled to consider your release. When it is satisfied that you need no longer be confined in custody for the protection of the public it will be able to direct your release. Until it is so satisfied you will remain in custody. If you are released, it will be on terms that you are subject to a licence for the rest of your life and liable to be recalled to prison at any time if your licence is revoked, either on the recommendation of the Parole Board, or, if it is thought expedient in the public interest, by the Secretary of State.

Sentencers should bear in mind that where an offender is sentenced to terms which are consecutive, or wholly or partly concurrent, they are to be treated as a single term (CJA

1991, s. 51(2)). Also, they should continue to give such explanation as they judge necessary of ancillary orders relating to disqualification, compensation, confiscation, costs and so on.

MANDATORY LIFE SENTENCES

E1.21 An offender aged 21 or over who is convicted of murder (but not related offences such as attempted murder or conspiracy to murder) must be sentenced to imprisonment for life (Murder (Abolition of Death Penalty) Act 1965, s. 1(1)), unless he was under 18 when the offence was committed, in which case the sentence is one of detention during Her Majesty's pleasure (see CYPA 1933, s. 53(1)). Since the sentence is mandatory, there is no right of appeal against it (Criminal Appeal Act 1968, s. 9). For offenders under 21, see **E3.9**.

When passing a sentence of life imprisonment for murder, the court is empowered under the Murder (Abolition of Death Penalty) Act 1965, s. 1(2), to 'declare the period which it recommends to the Secretary of State as the minimum period which in its view should elapse' before the offender is released on licence. It was stated, *obiter*, in *Flemming* [1973] 2 All ER 401 that any such recommendation should not be for a period of less than 12 years. The recommendation is not binding upon the authorities responsible for the early release of the offender. There is no right of appeal against a recommendation (*Aitken* [1966] 1 WLR 1076; *Leaney* [1996] 1 Cr App R (S) 30). Apart from this formal power to make a recommendation, in each case the sentencing judge is required to indicate in writing the 'tariff' period which in his view is necessary to meet the requirements of retribution and deterrence in the case. This report goes to the Lord Chief Justice, who also records his view, and thence to the Home Secretary. These indications do not, however, bind the Home Secretary who may set a higher or lower tariff than is indicated by the judges (*Secretary of State for the Home Department, ex parte Doody* [1994] 1 AC 531). This may, in certain circumstances, include the imposition of a 'whole life' tariff (*Secretary of State for the Home Department, ex parte Hindley* [1999] 2 WLR 1253). The Home Secretary does not have power, apart from wholly exceptional cases, to later increase a tariff period which has already been determined and communicated to the mandatory life sentence prisoner (*Secretary of State for the Home Department, ex parte Pierson* [1998] AC 539). By s. 29 of the C(S)A 1997, where the Secretary of State has referred a case, or a class of case, to the Parole Board and the case is so recommended by the Board, he may, after consultation with the Lord Chief Justice together with the trial judge if available, release on licence a life prisoner who is not one to whom s. 28 of the 1997 Act applies. Section 29 was brought into effect on 1 October 1997 and, apart from the reference to s. 28, reproduces s. 35(2) and (3) of the CJA 1991 (repealed by the 1997 Act). The Home Secretary may refuse to release a mandatory life sentence prisoner who has served the tariff part of his sentence, on the sole ground that there is a risk that he might after release commit serious offences (*Secretary of State for the Home Department, ex parte Stafford* [1999] 2 AC 38). For s. 28 of the 1997 Act, see **E1.27**.

AUTOMATIC LIFE SENTENCES FOR THE SECOND 'SERIOUS OFFENCE'

E1.22 Under the C(S)A 1997, s. 2, the Crown Court is required to impose a life sentence on an offender who is convicted of a 'serious offence' which has been committed after the commencement of s. 2 (1 October 1997) where, at the time when that offence was committed, the offender was aged 18 or over and had already been convicted of another 'serious offence' (s. 2(1)), unless the sentencing court is of the opinion that there are 'exceptional circumstances' relating to either of the offences, or to the offender, which justify its not imposing such a sentence (s. 2(2)). Where the court does not impose a life sentence it must state in open court that there are exceptional circumstances relating to either of the offences, or to the offender, and what those exceptional circumstances are (s. 2(3)). The section provides no assistance as to the meaning of 'exceptional circumstances'. It should be noted that the C(S)A 1997, s. 1, has been repealed by the CDA 1998.

The offences which, when committed within England and Wales, qualify as 'serious offences' for the purposes of s. 2 are, listed in s. 2(5):

(a)   attempted murder, conspiracy to murder or incitement to murder;
(b)   soliciting murder;
(c)   manslaughter;
(d)   wounding or causing grievous bodily harm with intent;
(e)   rape or attempted rape;
(f)   sexual intercourse with a girl under 13;
(g)   an offence under s. 16 (possession of a firearm with intent to injure), s. 17 (use of a firearm to resist arrest) or s. 18 (carrying a firearm with criminal intent) of the Firearms Act 1968; and
(h)   robbery where, at some time during the commission of the offence, the offender had in his possession a firearm or imitation firearm within the meaning of the 1968 Act.

All these offences carry life imprisonment as the maximum penalty. There is no requirement in s. 2 that the 'serious offence' must also qualify as a violent or sexual offence, within the meaning of the CJA 1991, s. 31 (see **E1.10**). In nearly every case an offence falling within categories (a) to (h) above will, in fact, also be a violent or sexual offence as so defined, since those categories are more widely drawn than that of 'serious offence'. One exception might be an offence of robbery using an imitation firearm, which qualifies as a serious offence under s. 2(5)(h) but was held not to amount to a violent offence on the particular facts of *Palin* (1995) 16 Cr App R (S) 888. Specific reference is made in s. 2(5)(e) to attempted rape, as well as to the full offence. It is submitted that since attempts are not referred to in other sub-paragraphs of s. 2(5) it can be inferred, for example, that an attempted wounding, or an attempted armed robbery, is not a 'serious offence' within the meaning of s. 2. It is unclear whether reference to the offences in s. 2(5)(g) should be taken to include 'imitation firearm' as well as 'firearm'. Of the three Firearms Act offences listed, s. 16 does not extend to imitation firearms, but ss. 17 and 18 clearly do (see **B12.50, B12.55** and **B12.63** respectively). The wording of s. 2(5)(g) might be taken to refer to these sections in general terms, or it might be construed to apply to ss. 17 and 18 only where a real firearm was involved. The reference to the offence of robbery in s. 2(5)(h) does make reference to imitation firearms, and it will be seen that unless a firearm or imitation firearm is in the possession of the offender at the time of commission of the offence, robbery does not qualify as a 'serious offence' as such. In *A-G's Ref (No. 71 of 1998)* [1999] Crim LR 587, however, the Court of Appeal held that an offence of robbery qualified as a 'serious offence' within s. 2(5)(h) where the offender did not himself carry a firearm but was aware that a co-defendant did so. The Court doubted whether the offence would so qualify if the offender had no knowledge of the existence of the firearm or imitation firearm. See also *Brownbill* [1999] 2 Cr App R (S) 331, where the offender threatened a shopkeeper with a knife (outside the terms of s. 2(5)(h)) but where the robbery qualified as a 'serious offence' because the offender knew that his co-defendant was carrying a non-working air pistol.

Where the offender is aged 21 or over, the relevant automatic life sentence (specified by s. 2(2)) is life imprisonment; where the offender is aged between 18 and 21, the relevant automatic life sentence is custody for life under the CJA 1982, s. 8(2) (see **E3.9**). The second 'serious offence' which (apart from a case in which exceptional circumstances apply) triggers the sentence of life imprisonment or custody for life is, according to s. 2(4), not to be regarded as an offence the sentence for which is fixed by law. It is clear that, whether the automatic life sentence takes the form of life imprisonment or custody for life, the sentencer may exercise the power under the C(S)A 1997, s. 28, to specify what part of the sentence must expire before the offender is to be considered for early release (see **E1.27**).

It should be noted that the first 'serious offence' may have been committed prior to commencement of s. 2. The age of the offender when he committed the first 'serious offence' is irrelevant. There is no requirement that the two offences be of the same kind, nor is there any restriction on the period of time which has elapsed between the two offences. An offender convicted of two 'serious offences' on the same occasion will not qualify for a life sentence under s. 2 on the basis of those two convictions. Nor will an offender who commits serious offence A, then serious offence B, and is subsequently convicted of A, and then B; the offender must commit the second offence after having been *convicted* of the first. In either of these examples, however, the sentencer might impose a discretionary life sentence where the established criteria in *Hodgson* (1967) 52 Cr App R 113 apply (see **E1.23**). In a case where the first 'serious offence' was dealt with by way of an absolute or conditional discharge (admittedly rather unlikely) or, before 1 October 1992, by way of a probation order, and the offender was not subsequently sentenced for the offence, the conviction for that offence is a conviction for limited purposes only (see PCCA 1973, s. 1C and **E14.6**) and would not count as a qualifying conviction for the purposes of s. 2.

The Court of Appeal considered the imposition of the automatic life sentence under C(S)A 1997, s. 2, in *Kelly* [1999] 2 Cr App R (S) 176. Lord Bingham CJ said that it was clearly Parliament's intention that life sentences were now to be imposed in cases in which, under the pre-existing law (see **E1.23**), discretionary life sentences would not have been passed. The section imposed a duty on the court to impose a life sentence, and it was not relieved of that duty even where the sentencer felt that it would be 'unjust to do so in all the circumstances', a phrase which appears in the C(S)A 1997, ss. 3 and 4 (see **E1.29** and **E1.30**, respectively), but not in s. 2. The sentencing court was relieved of the duty to impose a life sentence under s. 2 only where (i) the court was of the opinion that there were exceptional circumstances relating to either of the relevant offences or the offender, and (ii) that the court of was of the opinion that those exceptional circumstances justified the court in not imposing a life sentence. In his lordship's opinion, 'exceptional' was to be construed as an ordinary, familiar English adjective, and not as a term of art. It described a circumstance which was such as to form an exception, which was out of the ordinary course, or unusual, or special, or uncommon. To be exceptional a circumstance need not be unique, or unprecedented, or very rare; but it could not be one that was regularly, or routinely, or normally encountered. In the case before the court, the circumstances that the offender was only aged 19 when he committed the first 'serious offence', that there was an 18-year gap between the two offences, and that the two offences were different in kind, did not amount to 'exceptional circumstances' either individually or taken together. It was further held in *A-G's Ref (No. 53 of 1998)* [1999] 2 Cr App R (S) 185 that the fact that the sentence imposed for the offender's first 'serious offence' was the relatively short term of 12 months' detention in a young offender institution could not in itself constitute an 'exceptional circumstance'. In *A-G's Ref (No. 71 of 1998)* [1999] Crim LR 587, the Court of Appeal confirmed that the sentencer's own assessment that the imposition of a life sentence would be 'unjust' did not amount to exceptional circumstances within s. 2(2). Nor did the fact that implementation of the automatic life sentence for the second 'serious offence' would create a significant disparity with the sentence received by a co-defendant for whom this was his first 'serious offence'.

The Court of Appeal in *Kelly* declined to address the issue of whether s. 2 was in conformity with the provisions of Arts. 3 and 5 of the European Convention on Human Rights, although it was accepted by Lord Bingham CJ that in due course the matter was likely to come before the court for authoritative decision.

DISCRETIONARY LIFE SENTENCES

A discretionary life sentence may be passed only in respect of an offence for which life **E1.23** imprisonment is provided as the maximum penalty and subject to the application of the C(S)A 1997, s. 2 (automatic life sentence for the second serious offence: see **E1.22**). The statutory criteria in the CJA 1991 for determining whether the imposition of a custodial sentence is justified and, if so, for fixing its length (set out at **E1.8** and **E1.13**) apply to discretionary life sentences. It may be assumed, from the indeterminate nature of this sentence, that while the imposition of a discretionary life sentence may be justified under s. 1(2)(a) or (b), determination of sentence length can only be justified in accordance with s. 2(2)(b) of the Act. This appears to be the meaning of s. 2(4) of the 1991 Act (see **E1.13**), and it follows that a discretionary life sentence can be imposed only in cases of violent or sexual offences, as defined in s. 31 of the 1991 Act (see **E1.10**). This was confirmed in *Robinson* [1997] 2 Cr App R (S) 35, where the offender pleaded guilty to having an imitation firearm with intent to commit burglary. A discretionary life sentence was quashed by the Court of Appeal, and a commensurate sentence of five years' imprisonment substituted, on the basis that the offence was neither a sexual offence within s. 31 nor, on the facts, a violent offence. In *Meek* (1995) 16 Cr App R (S) 1003, the Court of Appeal said that when considering whether to impose a discretionary life sentence on an offender the court must first determine whether the criteria for imposing a longer-than-normal custodial sentence, under s. 2(2)(b) of the 1991 Act, were made out. If not, a discretionary life sentence was inappropriate, and the court should pass a proportionate custodial sentence under s. 2(2)(a) instead.

An offender serving a life sentence may be sentenced to a further life sentence where the criteria for imposition of that sentence are made out (*A-G's Ref (No. 32 of 1996)* [1997] 1 Cr App R (S) 261). A discretionary life sentence and a fixed-term sentence may run concurrently, but the fixed-term sentence should not be made disproportionate to the offence for which it is passed in order to delay the offender's release on licence from the life sentence (*Middleton* (1981) 3 Cr App R (S) 273). Determinate sentences may be ordered to run consecutively to each other and concurrently with a life sentence (*Nugent* (1984) 6 Cr App R (S) 93). A life sentence and a fixed term sentence may not, however, run consecutively.

Several important sentencing principles have been developed by the Court of Appeal to distinguish the use of the discretionary life sentence from the use of proportionate custodial sentences imposed under s. 2(2)(a) of the CJA 1991 and longer-than-normal sentences imposed under s. 2(2)(b). According to Lawton LJ in *Pither* (1979) 1 Cr App R (S) 209, '. . . life sentences for offences other than homicide should not be imposed unless there are exceptional circumstances in the case'. Lord Lane CJ said that:

> . . . life imprisonment . . . must only be passed in the most exceptional circumstances. With a few exceptions . . . it is reserved . . . for offenders who for one reason or another cannot be dealt with under the provisions of the Mental Health Act [1983], yet who are in a mental state which makes them dangerous to the life or limb of members of the public. (*Wilkinson* (1983) 5 Cr App R (S) 105, at p. 108)

According to the leading cases of *Hodgson* (1967) 52 Cr App R 113, *Wilkinson* (1983) 5 Cr App R (S) 105, *De Havilland* (1983) 5 Cr App R (S) 109 and *O'Dwyer* (1986) 86 Cr App R 313, life imprisonment will be justified only where three conditions are satisfied:

(a)   The offence or offences are in themselves grave enough to require a very long sentence.

(b)   It appears from the nature of the offences, or from the accused's history, that he is a person of mental instability who, if at liberty, would probably re-offend and present a grave danger to the public.

(c)   The accused will remain unstable and a potential danger for a long and/or an uncertain period of time.

The continuing relevance of these criteria was confirmed in *J* (1992) 14 Cr App R (S) 500 and in *A-G's Ref (No. 34 of 1992)* (1994) 15 Cr App R (S) 167.

Where the court is considering imposing a life sentence, defence counsel should be informed so that the matter may be addressed by argument (*McDougall* (1983) 5 Cr App R (S) 78; *Morgan* (1987) 9 Cr App R (S) 201). In *Virgo* (1988) 10 Cr App R (S) 427, the judge heard submissions from both counsel.

The Gravity of the Immediate Offence

E1.24   In *Hodgson* (1967) 52 Cr App R 113, it was said that a life sentence was appropriate only where the offence was in itself grave enough to justify a very long sentence, and in *A-G's Ref (No. 32 of 1996)* [1997] 1 Cr App R (S) 261 Lord Bingham CJ stated that unless the offender was convicted of a very serious offence there could be no question of imposing a life sentence. This requirement has not always been strictly applied, however, and even though the instant offence is not in the very first rank of seriousness, it seems that a life sentence may be justified on the grounds of the dangerousness of the offender. In *Ashdown* [1974] Crim LR 130 the accused was convicted of armed robbery when he stole a small sum of money from a man whom he threatened with an air pistol. A life sentence was upheld even though the Court of Appeal observed that the fixed-term sentence proportionate to the gravity of the offence was five years. In *Blogg* (1981) 3 Cr App R (S) 114 the accused set fire to a box in an empty office block. Having regard to the dangerousness of the accused, in the light of a history of arson offences over 30 years, the Court of Appeal upheld the life sentence despite its being 'totally disproportionate to the almost trifling offence of arson which was committed'.

On the other hand, the commission of a very grave offence does not of itself require the imposition of a life sentence (*Owen* (1980) 2 Cr App R (S) 45; *Terence Patrick J* (1993) 14 Cr App R (S) 500), nor does persistence in offending (*Pither* (1979) 1 Cr App R (S) 209; *Wilkinson* (1983) 5 Cr App R (S) 105).

Mental Instability

E1.25   The cases indicate that the mental instability of the accused must be a continuing problem such as to make him a real danger to the public. It is not necessary to show that the offender is suffering from a specific form of mental disorder, and the assessment of mental instability may be based upon criteria which extend beyond those of mental disorder contained in the Mental Health Act 1983. Life sentences have in the past been imposed on the basis of the offender's immaturity and sexual maladjustment in a case of repeated rape (*Thornett* (1979) 1 Cr App R (S) 1), psychopathic disorder not susceptible to treatment (*De Havilland* (1983) 5 Cr App R (S) 109), homosexual paedophilia not susceptible to treatment (*Hatch* [1997] 1 Cr App R (S) 22) and latent schizophrenia with a long history of eccentric and inconsequent behaviour, where no place was available at a secure mental hospital (*Scott* (1981) 3 Cr App R (S) 334). The fact that an offender is of 'borderline subnormal intelligence' is not of itself enough to fulfil the mental instability criterion (*Laycock* (1981) 3 Cr App R (S) 104), nor is the fact that the offender is a chronic alcoholic (*Stewart* (1989) 11 Cr App R (S) 132).

Medical evidence on the question of the offender's mental instability should normally be available to the court (*Pither* (1979) 1 Cr App R (S) 209; *Roche* (1995) 16 Cr App R (S) 849) but such evidence is not essential. In some cases the court has inferred mental instability from the circumstances of the offence and the nature of the criminal record. An example is *Chandler* (1993) 14 Cr App R (S) 586. In *A-G's Reference (No. 76 of 1995)* [1997] 1 Cr App R (S) 81, a case of false imprisonment and repeated rape by an offender with a previous conviction for rape, a longer-than-normal sentence of nine years' imprisonment was increased to a life sentence by the Court of Appeal, without having received any medical evidence.

On the other side of the line are cases such as *Blackburn* (1979) 1 Cr App R (S) 205, where a life sentence for conspiracy to rob was varied to one of eight years' imprisonment. The accused was described in medical reports as having 'a severe personality problem', as 'impulsive' and 'capable of dishonesty', but the evidence did not point to mental instability. In *Wilkinson* (1983) 5 Cr App R (S) 105, the Court of Appeal held that, in the absence of evidence of mental instability, the accused, who had carried out numerous burglaries, sometimes threatening occupants with violence, had to be sentenced like any other 'bad burglar or robber'; an 11-year term was substituted for a life sentence. In *Roche* (1995) 16 Cr App R (S) 849, a case involving attempted murder and indecent assault on a woman, the medical evidence did not disclose any abnormal mental state and the Court of Appeal held that a life sentence could not therefore be justified.

Potential Danger

Usually the potential danger can be ascertained by the court from the facts of the offence, **E1.26** the offender's record and the medical evidence. In *A-G's Ref (No. 34 of 1992)* (1994) 15 Cr App R (S) 167, where the Court of Appeal increased a sentence of eight years' imprisonment for wounding with intent to one of life imprisonment, Lord Taylor CJ said (at p. 171) that 'although fortunately the injury to the girl . . . was not of the most serious, that is not the most important point of this case . . . What is of prime importance here is the unanimous opinion of the doctors that this man represents a high risk to women and one which is not at present treatable and one which therefore is likely to persist for an indefinite period'. The danger will usually be to members of the community generally, though sometimes a threat to a particular person will be sufficient (*Allen* (1987) 9 Cr App R (S) 169). In *A-G's Ref (No. 32 of 1996)* [1997] 1 Cr App R (S) 261, where the offender was convicted of causing grievous bodily harm with intent, the offence was committed the day after he had been released on home leave from a life sentence for murder. A sentence of seven years' imprisonment was increased to a further life sentence by the Court of Appeal. Lord Bingham CJ observed that, while the offender's mental state was often highly relevant in life sentence cases, the crucial point in the case was that the offender was likely to represent a serious danger to the public for an indeterminate period. This test was followed and applied in *McPhee* [1998] 1 Cr App R (S) 201, where the defendant, a man who had difficulty in keeping his anger under control but did not suffer from a personality disorder, pleaded guilty to wounding with intent by stabbing. Notwithstanding the seriousness of the offence itself, the Court of Appeal quashed the life sentence imposed by the trial judge and substituted a commensurate sentence of seven years.

The offender's dangerousness may justify the imposition of a life sentence where there is no real prospect that his condition will improve through treatment or the passage of time (*Stanford* (1972) CSP F3–2D01; *Virgo* (1988) 10 Cr App R (S) 427). However, a life sentence should not be passed where the proportionate determinate sentence would provide sufficient protection for the public, such as where the offender's sexual urges or aggressive tendencies will subside through ageing (*Hercules* (1980) 2 Cr App R (S) 156).

Period Specified under Crime (Sentences) Act 1997, s. 28

E1.27   The C(S)A 1997, s. 28, provides that a sentencer imposing a life sentence on an offender 'for an offence the sentence for which is not fixed by law' may order that 'this section should apply to him as soon as he [has] served a part of his sentence specified in the order' (s. 28(2)). The part of the sentence specified in the order must, by s. 28(3), be:

> such part as the court considers appropriate, taking into account—
> (a)   the seriousness of the offence, or the combination of the offence and other offences associated with it, and
> (b)   the effect of any direction which it would have given under section 9 above [not yet in force] it if had sentenced him to a term of imprisonment and
> (c)   the provisions of this section as compared with those of sections 33(2) and 35(1) of the [CJA 1991].

The imposition of a life sentence is designed to protect the public from the offender, whereas the period specified under s. 28 is meant to reflect the degree of punishment, retribution and deterrence appropriate for the offence, aside from the question of public protection. The effect of specifying part of the sentence under s. 28 is that the life prisoner will not become eligible to be considered for early release until the expiry of that period. If the sentencer does not order that s. 28 shall apply in respect of the life prisoner, 'the Secretary of State shall direct that this section shall apply to him as soon as he has served a part of his sentence specified in the direction' (s. 28(4)). For a person serving more than one discretionary life sentence the court may make an order under s. 28 in respect of each of those sentences, with that person becoming eligible for consideration for early release 'after he has served the relevant part of each of those sentences' (s. 34(1) of the 1997 Act). If the court does not make an order in respect of each of the sentences, s. 28(4) of the 1997 Act will apply.

The power in s. 28 replaces the equivalent power in the CJA 1991, s. 34, which was repealed by the 1997 Act. Section 28 substantially reproduces the effect of s. 34, the main difference being that, as well as applying to a discretionary sentence of life imprisonment, the terms of s. 28 also apply:

(a)   where a court imposes a sentence of custody for life under the CJA 1982, s. 8, on a person aged under 21, whether or not that sentence is imposed as the mandatory life sentence for murder (see **E3.9**);
(b)   where a court passes a sentence of detention for life on a person under the age of 18 pursuant to the CYPA 1933, s. 53(3) (see **E3.12**);
(c)   where the court imposes a sentence of detention during Her Majesty's pleasure (detention of a person convicted of murder who was under 18 at the time of the offence) pursuant to the CYPA 1933, s. 53(1) (see **E3.11**); or
(d)   where a court imposes an automatic life sentence for the second serious offence under the C(S)A 1997, s. 2(2) (see **E1.22**).

It is important to note that s. 28 is applicable in respect of offenders so sentenced on or after 1 October 1997, irrespective of the date on which the offence was committed (s. 34(2) of the 1997 Act).

In *Practice Direction (Crime: Life Sentences)* [1993] 1 WLR 223, Lord Taylor CJ had said that the sentencer should normally specify the relevant period under s. 34, the only exception being the rare case where the sentencer thinks that the offender should never be released, and that if the judge decides not to specify a period he should state this in open court when passing sentence. A decision not to specify might be the subject of an appeal (*Hollies* (1995) 16 Cr App R (S) 463). When specifying the relevant period, the judge should have regard to the specific terms of the section, and should indicate the reasons for the decision. It was also established with respect to s. 34 that, before specifying the relevant period, the sentencer should permit counsel for the defence to address the court on the appropriate length of the relevant part. It was held that an order under s. 34 may be the subject of an appeal (*D* (1995) 16 Cr App R (S) 564). All these points seem equally applicable to s. 28.

Section 28(3)(a) mirrors the former provision in s. 34(2)(a) of the 1991 Act. In *Lundberg* (1995) 16 Cr App R (S) 948, the Court of Appeal emphasised that, when having regard to the seriousness of the offence (or the combination of the offence and other offences associated with it), the section permitted the sentencer to look at the totality of the associated offences, rather than just the offence for which the life sentence was being passed, and to consider whether the sentences for the associated offences would have been consecutive to the main sentence if a life sentence had not been given. See also *Haan* [1996] 1 Cr App R (S) 267.

Section 28(3)(b) makes reference to s. 9 of the 1997 Act. Section 9 is not in force. If it is brought into force, s. 9 will replace the CJA 1967, s. 67 (effect of time spent in custody on remand: see **E1.6**). When fixing the period to be served by a discretionary life sentence prisoner under s. 34 of the 1991 Act, the sentencer was not required to take into account any period spent by the offender in custody on remand which would be deducted from a determinate sentence under the CJA 1967, s. 67 since that time was automatically deducted from the specified period. The C(S)A 1997, sch. 5, para. 5(1), provides as follows:

> In relation to any time before the commencement of section 9 of this Act, section 28 of this Act shall have effect as if, in paragraph (b) of subsection (3), for the words 'of any direction it would have given under section 9 above' there were substituted the words 'which section 67 of the Criminal Justice Act 1967 would have had'.

Therefore, until s. 9 is brought into force, it is important to note that s. 28(3)(b) requires the sentencer to take account of any period spent by the offender in custody on remand since such time will *not* be deducted automatically. According to the Court of Appeal in *M* [1999] 1 WLR 485, the sentencer should normally give full credit for the period spent by the defendant on remand, but there is a discretion in the matter and circumstances might arise where the giving of full credit would not be appropriate. See also *Errington* [1999] 1 Cr App R (S) 403.

Section 28(3)(c) mirrors the equivalent provision in s. 34(2)(b) of the 1991 Act. Its effect is to require a sentencer exercising power under s. 28 to take into account the fact that under ss. 33(2) and 35(1) of the 1991 Act a prisoner who has received a determinate long-term sentence is entitled to be released after serving two-thirds of his term and may be released after serving only a half of his term. The statutory position is, therefore, effectively the same as it was in relation to s. 34 of the 1991 Act. Court of Appeal guidance indicated that the period specified under s. 34 of the 1991 Act should be set at between one-half and two-thirds of the determinate sentence and that when identifying the notional determinate sentence, the judge should make appropriate allowance for any mitigating factors in the case, such as the offender's guilty plea (*Meek* (1995) 16 Cr App R (S) 1003). In *M* [1999] 1 WLR 485, however, the Court of Appeal issued guidance on the setting of the period to be specified under s. 28. Thomas J in *M* stated that henceforth sentencers should make clear what the determinate sentence would have been and should then normally fix the specified period at *one-half* of the notional term. There might be exceptional cases where it would be appropriate to fix a longer period, up to two-thirds of the notional determinate sentence. A specified period equivalent to one-half of the notional term was established as the appropriate period in relation to young offenders in *Secretary of State for the Home Department, ex parte Furber* [1998] 1 Cr App R (S) 208, and the effect of the decision in *M* is to extend that general approach to adult offenders. In the light of this decision, earlier Court of Appeal authorities on the fixing of the specified period under CJA 1991, s. 34, will now be of little assistance to sentencers.

Unlike s. 34 of the 1991 Act, the power conferred by s. 28 of the 1997 Act is not, on the face of it, confined to cases where the discretionary life sentence is imposed as a violent or sexual offence within the meaning of s. 31 of the 1991 Act. A discretionary life sentence can be imposed only for a violent or sexual offence (see **E1.23**) so this change of wording has no effect as far as discretionary life sentences are concerned. However, in the case of an automatic life sentence imposed for the 'second serious offence', under the C(S)A 1997, s. 2, there is no requirement that the second such offence which, subject to exceptional circumstances, will trigger the automatic life sentence need be a violent or sexual offence within the meaning of s. 31 (see **E1.22**).

SEXUAL AND VIOLENT OFFENCES: EXTENDED SENTENCES

E1.28   Sections 58 and 59 of the CDA 1998, which came into force on 30 September 1998, provide new powers to pass 'extended' custodial sentences. An extended sentence is to be imposed by the court in accordance with the provisions of s. 58 of that Act, and s. 59 substitutes a new s. 44 in the CJA 1991, which provides what the effect of such a sentence will be on the offender's supervision arrangements. Section 59 does not apply to offences committed before 30 September 1998, so that where the sexual offence which falls to be sentenced was committed before that date the original version of s. 44 applies (Crime and Disorder Act 1998 (Commencement No. 2 and Transitional Provisions) Order 1998 (SI 1998 No. 2327), para. 8(1)). For the original version of s. 44, see the 1999 edition of this work. The ambit of these provisions is broader than that of the original s. 44, in that they apply to 'violent' as well as 'sexual' offences (both as defined in CJA 1991, s. 31). Section 58(1) of CDA 1998 provides that the court may pass an extended sentence in a case in which it thinks that the offender would otherwise be subject to a licence period which is inadequate for the purposes of (i) preventing the commission by him of further offences and (ii) securing his rehabilitation. The extended sentence will be the sum of the custodial sentence which the court would otherwise have passed for the offence ('the custodial term') and a further period ('the extension period') during which the offender will be subject to a licence and which is itself of a length the court considers necessary to achieve the purposes indicated in (i) and (ii).

It is clear that the power to impose an extended sentence under the CDA 1998, s. 58, is available where the offender would otherwise have received a proportionate sentence under CJA 1991, s. 2(2)(a), or a longer than normal sentence under s. 2(2)(b). Section 58(6) states that the CJA 1991, s. 2(2), 'shall apply as if the term of an extended sentence did not include the extension period', which seems to mean that whether the court is fixing the custodial term in accordance with s. 2(2)(a) or s. 2(2)(b) it should continue to do so in accordance with the relevant subsection and the relevant case law. Only then, if the court considers that the licence period applicable to that custodial term would be inadequate, should it add an extension period to the custodial term, to take account of the purposes specified in s. 58(1). If the offence is a violent offence, the court must not pass an extended sentence the custodial term of which is less than four years, and the extension period must not exceed five years. If the offence is a sexual offence, there is no specified minimum for the length of the custodial term, but the extension period must not exceed 10 years (s. 58(3) and (4)). In no case can the extended sentence exceed the maximum sentence for the offence committed (s. 58(5)).

Section 44 of the CJA 1991, as substituted by the CDA 1998, s. 59, makes the following provision. The question whether the offender qualifies as a short-term or a long-term prisoner is determined by the overall length of the extended sentence (s. 44(7)). If the offender would otherwise have been released unconditionally (i.e. the extended sentence is for less than 12 months), the effect of an order will be that his release will be on licence until the end of the extension period (s. 44(4)). If the offender would otherwise have been released on licence (i.e. the extended period is for 12 months or more), the effect of an order is that the licence period, rather than ending at the three-quarter point of the sentence will last from the date of his release until the end of the extension period (s. 44(3)). If the offender commits a new offence while on licence and the court, in addition to dealing with him for the new offence, decides to order the offender's return to custody under CJA 1991, s. 40 (see **E1.7**) for the whole or part of the period outstanding, it seems from s. 44(2) that the extension period must be included when determining the duration of the period to be reinstated. This means that an order under s. 40 can be made if the new offence is committed at any time within the entire licence period, including the extension period.

CUSTODIAL SENTENCES FOR CLASS A DRUG OFFENCES

Minimum Custodial Sentence of Seven Years for Third Class A Drug Trafficking Offence

E1.29

Section 3 of the C(S)A 1997 provides that where:

(a)   a person is convicted of a Class A drug trafficking offence committed after the commencement of s. 3 (1 October 1997),

(b)   at the time when that offence was committed he was aged 18 or over and had been convicted in any part of the United Kingdom of two other Class A drug trafficking offences, and

(c)   one of those offences was committed after he had been convicted of the other,

the Crown Court shall impose a custodial sentence for a term of at least seven years, unless the court is of the opinion that there are particular circumstances which relate to any of the offences or to the offender which would make it unjust to do so (s. 3(2) and (3)). It should be noted that s. 1 of the 1997 Act has been repealed by the 1998 Act. For an early example of sentencing under this provision, see *Harvey* [1999] Crim LR 849.

For the purposes of s. 3, 'Class A drug trafficking offence' means a drug trafficking offence committed in respect of a Class A drug (see **B20.5**); 'drug trafficking offence' has the same meaning as that in the Drug Trafficking Offences Act 1994 (see **E21.2**) (s. 3(5)); and 'custodial sentence' means imprisonment or detention in a young offender institution (s. 3(6)). Where the court does not impose the prescribed sentence, it shall state in open court that it is of the opinion that to impose such sentence would be unjust and state what the particular circumstances are. Nothing in s. 3 prevents a hospital order being imposed on an offender in an appropriate case (Mental Health Act 1983, s. 37(1A)).

In a case where either of the earlier Class A drug trafficking offences was dealt with by way of an absolute or conditional discharge (admittedly rather unlikely) or, before 1 October 1992, by way of a probation order, and the offender was not subsequently sentenced for the offence, the conviction for that offence is a conviction for limited purposes only (see the PCCA 1973, s. 1C and **E14.6**) and would not count as a qualifying conviction for the purposes of s. 3.

Where the offender has pleaded guilty, the sentencing court is required to take into account the stage at which he indicated his intention to plead guilty and the circumstances in which this indication was given (CJPO 1994, s. 48: see **E1.18**). Section 48(3) states that in the case of an offence coming within s. 3 of the 1997 Act the maximum reduction for a guilty plea shall be 20 per cent of the determinate sentence of at least seven years which would otherwise have been imposed.

CUSTODIAL SENTENCES FOR DOMESTIC BURGLARY

E1.30   **Minimum Custodial Sentence of Three Years for Third Domestic Burglary**

Section 4 of the C(S)A 1997 provides that where:

(a)   a person is convicted of a domestic burglary committed after the commencement of s. 4 (1 December 1999);

(b)   at the time when the domestic burglary was committed he was aged 18 or over and had been convicted in England and Wales of two other domestic burglaries; and

(c)   one of those other burglaries was committed after he had been convicted of the other, and both of them were committed after the commencement of s. 4,

the Crown Court shall impose a custodial term of at least three years except where the court is of the opinion that there are particular circumstances which relate to any of the offences or the offender; and would make it unjust to do so in all the circumstances (s. 4(2), as amended by the CDA 1998). It should be noted that s. 1 of the 1997 Act is repealed by the 1998 Act.

For the purposes of s. 4 'domestic burglary' means a burglary committed in respect of a building or part of a building which is a dwelling (s. 4(5)). The maximum penalty on indictment for such an offence is 14 years' imprisonment (see further **B4.58**). It is unclear whether an attempt to commit a domestic burglary amounts to a qualifying offence, but it is submitted that an attempt should not be regarded as a qualifying offence without clear statutory provision to that effect. 'Custodial sentence' means imprisonment or detention in a young offender institution (s. 3(6), also applicable to s. 4). Where the court does not impose the prescribed sentence, it shall state in open court that to impose such sentence would be unjust and state what the particular circumstances are (s. 4(3)). Nothing in s. 4 prevents a hospital order being imposed on an offender in an appropriate case (Mental Health Act 1983, s. 37(1A)).

In a case where either of the earlier domestic burglaries was dealt with by way of an absolute or conditional discharge (admittedly rather unlikely) or, before 1 October 1992, by way of a probation order, and the offender was not subsequently sentenced for the offence, the conviction for that offence is a conviction for limited purposes only (see the PCCA 1973, s. 1C and **E14.6**), and would not count as a qualifying conviction for the purposes of s. 4. It is unclear whether an earlier spent conviction for domestic burglary counts as a qualifying conviction. It is submitted that such a conviction probably does count, but that the fact that the conviction was spent may be a particular circumstance relating to that offence making the imposition of the prescribed sentence unjust in all the circumstances.

Where the offender has pleaded guilty, the sentencing court is required to take into account the stage at which he indicated his intention to plead guilty and the circumstances in which this indication was given (CJPOA 1994, s. 48: see **E1.18**). Section 48(3) states that in the case of an offence coming within s. 4 of the 1997 Act the maximum reduction for a guilty plea shall be 20 per cent of the determinate sentence of at least three years which would otherwise have been imposed.

SECTION E2: CUSTODIAL SENTENCES: SUSPENDED SENTENCES

SUSPENDED SENTENCES GENERALLY

Power to Impose Suspended Sentences

Powers of Criminal Courts Act 1973, s. 22   E2.1

(1)   Subject to subsection (2) below, a court which passes a sentence of imprisonment for a term of not more than two years for an offence may order that the sentence shall not take effect unless, during a period specified in the order, being not less than one year or more than two years from the date of the order, the offender commits in Great Britain another offence punishable with imprisonment and thereafter a court having power to do so orders under section 23 of this Act that the original sentence shall take effect; and in this Part of this Act 'operational period', in relation to a suspended sentence, means the period so specified.

For s. 23, see **E2.8**. Custodial sentences other than imprisonment, such as a sentence of detention in a young offender institution, may not be suspended. If a sentencer purports to suspend a sentence of imprisonment which he has no power to suspend, such as a sentence of more than two years, the sentence takes effect as an immediate sentence of imprisonment (*Arkle* (1972) 56 Cr App R 722).

Since the longest sentence which may be suspended is two years, and an aggregate of consecutive terms is treated as a single term for these purposes (PCCA 1973, s. 57(2)), if consecutive sentences totalling more than two years are imposed on the same occasion, there is no power to suspend the sentence (*Coleman* [1969] 2 QB 468; *Arkle* (1972) 56 Cr App R 722).

Powers of Criminal Courts Act 1973, s. 22

(2)   A court shall not deal with an offender by means of a suspended sentence unless it is of the opinion—
    (a)   that the case is one in which a sentence of imprisonment would have been appropriate even without the power to suspend the sentence; and
    (b)   that the exercise of that power can be justified by the exceptional circumstances of the case.
    (2A)   A court which passes a suspended sentence on any person for an offence shall consider whether the circumstances of the case are such as to warrant in addition the imposition of a fine or the making of a compensation order.

Section 22(2)(a) contains an important principle of sentencing in relation to the use of suspended sentences. A suspended sentence must not be imposed by a court unless the imposition of an immediate sentence of imprisonment would have been available to the sentencing court, and would have been appropriate for use in the particular case in the absence of the power to suspend. A suspended sentence cannot be ordered unless all the statutory provisions as to the imposition of a sentence of immediate imprisonment have been observed. Before a suspended sentence can be passed the court must take account of the relevant provisions of the CJA 1991, ss. 1 to 3, which must be complied with before any custodial sentence is passed (see **E1.8** and **E1.13**). The court must be clear that it would have passed a sentence of immediate imprisonment in the absence of the power to suspend, and that such sentence would have been for a term of less than two years. The power to impose a suspended sentence in a magistrates' court is limited in the same way in which magistrates' powers to impose prison sentences are limited

(see **E1.2**). The question whether immediate imprisonment would have been appropriate in the particular case in the absence of the power to suspend is discussed further at
E2.3.

Section 22(2)(b) states that there must be 'exceptional circumstances' before a
suspended sentence is appropriate. For the meaning of this phrase, see **E2.6**.

Section 22(2A) encourages the practice of combining a suspended sentence with a fine
(but see **E2.7** for some pitfalls inherent in that approach). It also encourages the making
of a compensation order in addition to a suspended sentence (as to this combination, see
E18.7).

Powers of Criminal Courts Act 1973, s. 22

> (3)   A court which passes a suspended sentence on any person for an offence shall not
> impose a community sentence in his case in respect of that offence or any other offence of
> which he is convicted by or before the court or for which he is dealt with by the court; and
> in this subsection 'community sentence' has the same meaning as in part I of the Criminal
> Justice Act 1991.

This prohibition, which is set out as amended by the CDA 1998, sch. 7, applies when
the sentences are imposed on the same occasion, whether the offences are charged in
the same indictment or in different indictments (*Wright* [1975] Crim LR 728). On the
general question of combining suspended sentences with other sentences or orders, see
E2.7. The effect of combining a suspended sentence with a probation order may be
achieved by passing a suspended sentence supervision order (see **E2.14**).

Section 22(4) provides that on passing a suspended sentence the court shall explain to
the offender in ordinary language his liability under s. 23 if during the operational period
he commits an offence punishable with imprisonment.

Concurrent and Consecutive Suspended Sentences

E2.2   It is wrong in principle to make a suspended sentence consecutive or concurrent to a
sentence actually being served (*Baker* (1971) 55 Cr App R 182).

SUSPENDED SENTENCES: SENTENCING PRINCIPLES

Suspended Sentence May Not Be Imposed Unless Immediate Prison Sentence Proper in Absence of Power to Suspend

E2.3   The PCCA 1973, s. 22(2)(a), precludes the sentencer from imposing a suspended
sentence where an immediate sentence of imprisonment would not be appropriate in
the absence of the power to suspend. The rationale for this rule was provided by Lord
Parker CJ in *O'Keefe* [1969] 2 QB 29 (at p. 32):

> . . . it seems to this court that before one gets to a suspended sentence at all, the court must
> go through the process of eliminating other possible courses such as absolute discharge,
> conditional discharge, probation order, fines, and then say to itself: this is a case for
> imprisonment, and the final question, it being a case for imprisonment, should be: is
> immediate imprisonment required, or can a suspended sentence be given?

The Court of Appeal has on numerous occasions disapproved the imposition of a
suspended sentence with a view to achieving a deterrent effect where it would be
inappropriate to punish that offence with immediate imprisonment. One example is
Watts (1984) 6 Cr App R (S) 61, where a sentence of three months' imprisonment
suspended for two years was reduced on appeal to a conditional discharge for 12
months, in a case where the accused had allowed her premises to be used for smoking
cannabis in circumstances 'not by any means the gravest for this sort of offence'. She
had no previous offences involving cannabis and no convictions at all for 15 years.

It is also contrary to principle to impose a suspended sentence in a case where a fine is the proper sentence, solely because the accused lacks the means to pay. In *Whitehead* (1979) 1 Cr App R (S) 187 a conditional discharge was substituted for a sentence of six weeks' imprisonment suspended for one year, for shoplifting. The suspended sentence was 'quite wrong in principle', the accused being a woman of clean record, beset by personal difficulty and dependent upon social security benefits. Conversely, a suspended sentence should not be imposed for an offence for which a fine would normally be the correct penalty, solely on the ground that the offender is well-off and the fine would have little impact on him (*Hanbury* (1979) 1 Cr App R (S) 243).

Length of Sentence to Be Fixed before Decision to Suspend

In *Mah-Wing* (1983) 5 Cr App R (S) 347 Griffiths LJ said (at p. 348): 'When the court **E2.4** passes a suspended sentence, its first duty is to consider what would be the appropriate immediate custodial sentence, pass that and then go on to consider whether there are grounds for suspending it. What the court must not do is pass a longer custodial sentence than it would otherwise do, because it is suspended.'

Taking Account of Time Spent in Custody

When fixing the duration of the term to be served, the sentencer should take account of **E2.5** any period spent in custody by the offender in respect of that offence (see *Practice Direction (Crime: Suspended Sentence)* [1970] 1 WLR 259). Accordingly, the sentencer activating a suspended sentence should not take account of the period spent in custody by ordering the suspended sentence to take effect with a reduced term (*Williams* (1989) 11 Cr App R (S) 152). In a case where the offender has been in custody on remand for a period equivalent to the appropriate term of immediate imprisonment for the offence, so that the offender has effectively served his sentence on remand, the sentence should be such as to secure his immediate release (*McCabe* (1988) 10 Cr App R (S) 134). It is wrong in these circumstances for the sentencer to pass a suspended sentence at all (*Peppard* (1990) 12 Cr App R (S) 88).

Suspended Sentence Justified only in 'Exceptional Circumstances'

This phrase was inserted into s. 22 by the CJA 1991, and was designed to ensure that **E2.6** the suspended sentence 'should be used far more sparingly than it has been in the past' (*Lowery* (1993) 14 Cr App R (S) 485). The statute gives no indication of what might be regarded as exceptional circumstances and in *Okinikan* [1993] 1 WLR 173 Lord Taylor CJ declined to lay down a definition of the phrase, stating that what amounted to 'exceptional circumstances' would depend on the facts of each case. He did say, however, that 'taken on their own or in combination, good character, youth and an early plea' were *not* exceptional circumstances justifying a suspended sentence, since they were common features of many cases and hence could not be characterised as 'exceptional'. In *Lowery* the court said that 'exceptional circumstances' might be found in the relevant circumstances of the offence or the offender, or in the background circumstances. This comment was cited with approval in *Weston* [1996] 1 Cr App R (S) 297.

In *Sanderson* (1993) 14 Cr App R (S) 361 the offender pleaded guilty to unlawful wounding, and a sentence of six months' imprisonment was upheld by the Court of Appeal. The offender's previous good character, his family circumstances and a measure of provocation on the facts of the offence itself were said to be mitigating factors relevant to the sentence length, but not to suspension of the sentence. Similarly in *Lowery* the offender, a 39-year-old police officer with 20 years' service, pleaded guilty to 11 counts of false accounting, the total sum concerned being just over £1,500. Three months' imprisonment was imposed. The offender's wife had become disabled and the offender had taken the money in order to offset some of the costs of adapting for her needs the police house in which they lived. As a result of the offence the offender had lost his job and his home, and his pension rights had been frozen. He had subsequently made two attempts at suicide. The Court of Appeal stressed the seriousness of the offences and said that the 'catastrophic consequences' did not amount to exceptional circumstances since breach of trust often involved consequences going far beyond the immediate sentence. Other examples are *Frow* (1995) 16 Cr App R (S) 609, where the court declined to suspend a prison term of nine months for dangerous driving despite the fact that the defendant motorcyclist had incurred serious leg injuries in the accident which he had caused, and *Murti* [1996] 2 Cr App R (S) 152, where suspension of a sentence of eight months was inappropriate in the case of a Post Office counter assistant who had permitted other women to cash DSS benefit vouchers which she knew to be stolen, despite the fact that the offender was the mother of two small children, had suffered from post-natal depression at the time of the offence, and had cooperated fully with the prosecuting authorities.

These decisions are, however, very difficult to reconcile with other cases. In *Bowden* [1998] 2 Cr App R (S) 7, a sentence of 12 months' imprisonment for theft in breach of trust was reduced to six months and suspended in light of the fact that the offender was a single mother with four children, each of whom suffered from illness. In *French* (1994) 15 Cr App R 194, 'exceptional circumstances' were found in the offender's financial and emotional difficulties before the offence, which was a conspiracy relating to an insurance fraud, and the fact that she was now under treatment for depression. In *Weston* [1996] 1 Cr App R (S) 297, the 60-year-old offender was convicted of indecent assault on a 13-year-old girl. The sentence of nine months' imprisonment was suspended on the basis that both the offender, a man of hitherto 'unblemished character', and his wife, were suffering from serious illnesses. The 'exceptional circumstances' in *Oliver* [1997] 1 Cr App R (S) 125 were that the offender, who pleaded guilty to possession of amphetamine with intent to supply, had been the victim of a shooting while awaiting trial, in the course of which he had been shot six times. Finally, in *Bellikli* [1998] 1 Cr App R (S) 135, where the offender was convicted of facilitating illegal entry, a sentence of two years' imprisonment was suspended on the basis that the offender's child was very ill and would probably require major surgery in the near future.

Mixing Suspended Sentence with Other Sentences or Orders

E2.7 An immediate prison sentence and a suspended sentence should not be imposed on the same occasion (*Sapiano* (1968) 52 Cr App R 674), nor should a suspended sentence be imposed on an offender currently serving a term of imprisonment (*Butters* (1971) 55 Cr App R 515). For an exceptional situation arising on breach of suspended sentence, see **E2.8**. It is wrong to make a suspended sentence consecutive or concurrent to a sentence actually being served (*Baker* (1971) 55 Cr App R 182, and see **E2.2**).

A suspended sentence and a community sentence may not be imposed by the court on an offender on the same occasion, whether or not the offences are charged in the same indictment (PCCA 1973, s. 22(3)). A suspended sentence cannot be combined with a discharge when sentencing for a single offence (see **E14.4**) but, of course, a discharge could be given for one offence when a suspended sentence was passed in respect of another offence sentenced on the same occasion.

A fine may be combined with a suspended sentence (*Leigh* (1969) 54 Cr App R 169), but it is improper to combine them where a fine standing alone would have been the appropriate sentence. This conclusion follows from the PCCA 1973, s. 22(2)(a) (see **E2.3**). A fine, therefore, may be added to a suspended sentence, but a suspended sentence should not be added to a fine (*Barker* [1980] Crim LR 600). The Court of Appeal explained the correct reasoning as follows:

... if the court decides that there is no other appropriate method of dealing with the offender than imprisonment and imposes a prison sentence, the court can then, in the appropriate case, go on to consider that the sentence should be suspended. ... If the court does go on to consider that the sentence should be suspended ... the court can also consider whether an additional penalty by way of a fine is justified. (*Genese* [1976] 1 WLR 958, at p. 964).

The fine may be imposed as a means of removing an offender's profit from the offending, or as a 'sting in the tail' of the suspension. The court must take into account the offender's means when fixing the level of the fine (*King* [1970] 1 WLR 1016; *Whybrew* (1979) 1 Cr App R (S) 121). The PCCA 1973, s. 22(2A), encourages courts to add either a fine or a compensation order to a suspended sentence.

ACTIVATION OF SUSPENDED SENTENCE

Powers of Court in Dealing with Suspended Sentence

Powers of Criminal Courts Act 1973, s. 23   E2.8

(1) Where an offender is convicted of an offence punishable with imprisonment committed during the operational period of a suspended sentence and either he is so convicted by or before a court having power under section 24 of this Act to deal with him in respect of the suspended sentence or he subsequently appears or is brought before such a court, then, unless the sentence has already taken effect, that court shall consider his case and deal with him by one of the following methods:—
(a) the court may order that the suspended sentence shall take effect with the original term unaltered;
(b) it may order that the sentence shall take effect with the substitution of a lesser term for the original term;
(c) it may by order vary the original order under section 22(1) of this Act by substituting for the period specified therein a period expiring not later than two years from the date of the variation; or
(d) it may make no order with respect to the suspended sentence;
and a court shall make an order under paragraph (a) of this subsection unless the court is of opinion that it would be unjust to do so in view of all the circumstances including the facts of the subsequent offence, and where it is of that opinion the court shall state its reasons.

The sentencing principles governing the choice amongst these options are dealt with below.

There is no power to activate a suspended sentence unless the offender is convicted of an offence punishable with imprisonment which was committed during the operational period of the suspended sentence. In *Melbourne* (1980) 2 Cr App R (S) 116 activation of a suspended sentence was overturned by the Court of Appeal where the defendant was convicted in a magistrates' court during the operational period of the suspended sentence of two offences which were punishable only by fine on summary conviction. It was irrelevant that the offences could have attracted a prison sentence on indictment.

In *Daurge* (1972) CSP A13–2A01 it was held to be wrong to activate a suspended sentence at the time of sentencing the accused to seven years' imprisonment, where the offences which led to the imposition of that sentence were committed prior to those for which the suspended sentence was imposed. If the court takes into consideration the subsequent offence when sentencing the offender for another offence which was not committed during the operational period of the suspended sentence, there is no power to deal with the suspended sentence (*Metcalfe* (1968) CSP A13–2D01).

If a court dealing with the offender in respect of a subsequent offence adopts either of the following courses, there is no power to activate or take any other action in respect of the suspended sentence:

(a)   Where the court imposes an absolute or conditional discharge since, by the PCCA 1973, s. 1C, there is deemed to have been no 'conviction' in respect of that offence (see *Moore* [1995] QB 353), unless the discharge is made in the same proceedings in which the suspended sentence is to be dealt with (see *Barnes* (1986) 8 Cr App R (S) 88).

(b)   Where the court defers sentence, since it remains open to the court to impose an absolute or conditional discharge at the end of the period of deferment (*Salmon* (1973) 57 Cr App R 953).

Where the court chooses to vary the operational period of the suspended sentence under s. 23(1)(c), it may make a suspended sentence supervision order if the conditions of s. 26(10) of the 1973 Act are fulfilled (see **E2.14**). The operational period of the sentence must not be varied so as to reduce it to less than 12 months, which is the minimum operational period for a suspended sentence (*Waite* (1995) 16 Cr App R (S) 110).

Powers of Criminal Courts Act 1973, s. 23

(2)   Where a court orders that a suspended sentence shall take effect, with or without any variation of the original term, the court may order that that sentence shall take effect immediately or that the term thereof shall commence on the expiration of another term of imprisonment passed on the offender by that or another court.

(3)–(5)   [Repealed.]

(6)   In proceedings for dealing with an offender in respect of a suspended sentence which take place before the Crown Court any question whether the offender has been convicted of an offence punishable with imprisonment committed during the operational period of the suspended sentence shall be determined by the court and not by the verdict of a jury.

(7)   Where a court deals with an offender under this section in respect of a suspended sentence the appropriate officer of the court shall notify the appropriate officer of the court which passed the sentence of the method adopted.

(8)   Where on consideration of the case of an offender a court makes no order with respect to a suspended sentence, the appropriate officer of the court shall record that fact.

(9)   For the purposes of any enactment conferring rights of appeal in criminal cases any order made by a court with respect to a suspended sentence shall be treated as a sentence passed on the offender by that court for the offence for which the suspended sentence was passed.

A court activating a suspended sentence is not empowered to suspend part of it (*Gow* (1983) 5 Cr App R (S) 250; *Senior* (1984) 6 Cr App R (S) 15).

Powers of Criminal Courts Act 1973, s. 24

(1)   An offender may be dealt with in respect of a suspended sentence by the Crown Court or, where the sentence was passed by a magistrates' court, by any magistrates' court before which he appears or is brought.

(2)   Where an offender is convicted by a magistrates' court of an offence punishable with imprisonment and the court is satisfied that the offence was committed during the operational period of a suspended sentence passed by the Crown Court—

(a)   the court may, if it thinks fit, commit him in custody or on bail to the Crown Court; and

(b)   if it does not, shall give written notice of the conviction to the appropriate officer of the Crown Court.

(3)   For the purposes of this section and of section 25 of this Act a suspended sentence passed on an offender on appeal shall be treated as having been passed by the court by which he was originally sentenced.

If the magistrates sentence for the new offence, they should not discharge the offender absolutely or conditionally as this makes it impossible for the Crown Court to activate the suspended sentence. It is also inadvisable for magistrates to impose a community service order (*Stewart* (1984) 6 Cr App R (S) 166) or a suspended sentence (*Hamilton* (1984) 6 Cr App R (S) 451) for the new offence, where the offender is in breach of a suspended sentence imposed by the Crown Court. In all these cases the proper course for the magistrates to take is to commit the offender to the Crown Court. If the magistrates have imposed a suspended sentence for an offence committed during the operational period of a suspended sentence imposed by the Crown Court, the Crown Court is not thereby prevented from activating the original suspended sentence (*Hamilton* (1984) 6 Cr App R (S) 451). This is an exception to the general rule considered above, that a sentence of immediate imprisonment and a suspended sentence should not run together.

The PCCA 1973, s. 25, lays down the procedure where a court has convicted an offender of an offence committed during the operational period of a suspended sentence and has not dealt with him in respect of that suspended sentence. The appropriate court may issue a summons or warrant for his arrest requiring him to appear or be brought before the court by which the suspended sentence was passed.

ACTIVATION OF SUSPENDED SENTENCE: SENTENCING PRINCIPLES

Sentencer Should First Impose Sentence Appropriate to Further Offence

In the leading case of *Ithell* [1969] 1 WLR 272, Edmund Davies LJ said (at p. 273): 'the **E2.9** court should first sentence [the offender] in respect of the fresh offence by punishment appropriate to that offence, and thereafter address itself to the question of the suspended sentence'. It should be noted that the further offence and the offence for which the suspended sentence was passed are not 'associated' for the purposes of the CJA 1991, s. 31(2) (see further **E1.9**).

Activation the Normal Consequence of Further Conviction

See the PCCA 1973, s. 23(1), set out at **E2.8**. The Court of Appeal is reluctant to adjust **E2.10** a sentence where the sentencer has complied with this general rule. According to Russell J in *Craine* (1981) 3 Cr App R (S) 198, '. . . it cannot be made too plain that when suspended sentences of imprisonment are imposed they mean what they say. Only in exceptional circumstances, if further offences involving imprisonment are committed, will those suspended sentences not be activated.' Numerous other observations to the same effect may be found. On the question of time spent on remand in custody prior to the imposition of the suspended sentence, see **E2.5**.

Where the court imposes a prison sentence for the new offence, it should normally activate the suspended sentence, rather than extend the operational period, since sentences of immediate and suspended imprisonment should not normally be combined, and the suspended sentence should not still be hanging over the offender's head on release from prison (see *Goodlad* [1973] 1 WLR 1102, applied in several subsequent cases, including *Treays* [1981] Crim LR 511 and *Crawley* (1984) 6 Cr App R (S) 327).

Suspended Sentence Should Normally Run Consecutively to Sentence for Further Offence

In *Ithell* [1969] 1 WLR 272, Edmund Davies LJ said (at pp. 273–4): '. . . unless there **E2.11** are some quite exceptional circumstances, the suspended sentence should be ordered to run consecutively to the sentence given for the current offence'. This general approach is, however, subject to the totality principle (*Bocskei* (1970) 54 Cr App R 519, and see **E1.19**). The sentencer may adjust the length either of the activated suspended sentence or the new sentence to ensure that the total sentence is not excessive. Examples of exceptional circumstances which would justify the activation of the suspended sentence to run concurrently with the prison sentence imposed for the new offence are where the operational period of the suspended sentence has almost expired (*Kilroy* (1979) 1 Cr App R (S) 179; *Carr* (1979) 1 Cr App R (S) 53), or where a very short suspended sentence is activated at the same time as the imposition of a long sentence for the new offence (*Christie* (1979) 1 Cr App R (S) 84).

Activation May Be Unjust if Further Offence Not So Serious that Only Custody Can be Justified

E2.12   In *Moylan* [1970] 1 QB 143, Widgery LJ said (at p. 146) '. . . the court may properly consider as unjust the activation of a suspended sentence where the new offence is a comparatively trivial offence and, particularly, where it is in a different category from that for which the suspended sentence was imposed'. In *Abrahams* (1980) 2 Cr App R (S) 10, the accused was in breach of a suspended sentence of 18 months for burglary. The subsequent offence involved theft of a plastic dinghy whilst on holiday and in a 'drunken frolic'. The Court of Appeal quashed the order activating the suspended sentence. Where the further offence is not so serious that only a custodial sentence could be justified for it, it is generally regarded as inappropriate to activate the suspended sentence. This point was established in *Brooks* (1990) 12 Cr App R (S) 756 and has been applied in several cases since the implementation of the CJA 1991, such as *Burnard* (1994) 15 Cr App R (S) 218. While it will usually be inappropriate to activate the suspended sentence in such a case, there is no absolute prohibition on doing so. Cases where the Court of Appeal has approved the exceptional course include *Calladine* (1994) 15 Cr App R (S) 345 and *Stacey* (1994) 15 Cr App R (S) 585.

In some cases the relative triviality of the later offence seems not in itself to justify a departure from the normal course of activating the suspended sentence, but may provide a reason for activating the sentence with a reduced term (*Cline* (1979) 1 Cr App R (S) 40; *Joshua* (1980) 2 Cr App R (S) 287).

On the other hand, there are several decisions to the effect that the commission of a further offence of a quite different character does not of itself justify a departure from the normal course of activating the suspended sentence. According to Lord Parker CJ in *Saunders* (1970) 54 Cr App R 247, '. . . the mere fact that the current offence is of a different character . . . is no ground whatever for not bringing that suspended sentence into force'. See also *Craine* (1981) 3 Cr App R (S) 198 and *Clitheroe* (1987) 9 Cr App R (S) 159, which disapproved some decisions taking a different line.

While it is not the function of the court dealing with the breach of the suspended sentence to review the propriety of its imposition, the court must be fully aware of the circumstances of the original offence, in order to determine whether it is unjust to activate the suspended sentence (*Munday* (1971) 56 Cr App R 220).

Commission of Further Offence Towards End of Period of Suspension as Ground for Leniency

E2.13   In *Carr* (1979) 1 Cr App R (S) 53 the accused had completed 22 months of the two-year period of suspension before being convicted of a further offence, for which he received two years' immediate imprisonment. The activation of the 12-month suspended sentence in full was disapproved by the Court of Appeal, which ordered that it should run concurrently with the new sentence.

SUSPENDED SENTENCE SUPERVISION ORDERS

E2.14   **Powers of Criminal Courts Act 1973, s. 26**

(1)   Where a court passes on an offender a suspended sentence for a term of more than six months for a single offence, the court may make a suspended sentence supervision order (in this Act referred to as 'a supervision order') placing the offender under the supervision of a supervising officer for a period specified in the order, being a period not exceeding the operational period of the suspended sentence.

(2) [Provides that the Secretary of State may vary the qualifying conditions in subsection (1), but these powers have not been exercised.]

The power to pass a suspended sentence supervision order arises only where a term of imprisonment of 'more than six months' has been imposed and then suspended. In *Seafield* (1988) *The Times*, 21 May 1988, the Court of Appeal stressed that the power was not available where a term of exactly six months had been suspended, and noted that this mistake in sentencing had required correction by the Court of Appeal on several occasions. Nor may a suspended sentence supervision order be passed where two sentences, which are each shorter than six months, are imposed consecutively to make an aggregate sentence of more than six months (*Baker* (1988) 10 Cr App R (S) 409).

The supervision order must specify the petty sessions area in which the offender resides or will reside (s. 26(3)). The court should give copies of the order to the offender and the supervising officer – a probation officer appointed or assigned to the area specified in the order (s. 26(4)) – and, if appropriate, to the clerk to the justices for the petty sessions area specified in the order (s. 26(5), (6) and (7)).

Powers of Criminal Courts Act 1973, s. 26

(4) An offender in respect of whom a supervision order is in force shall keep in touch with the supervising officer in accordance with such instructions as he may from time to time be given by that officer and shall notify him of any change of address.

A failure to comply with these requirements, where it is established that the accused has failed without reasonable cause to comply, may lead to the imposition of a fine under the PCCA 1973, s. 27, of up to £1,000. It is not, however, a ground for activating the suspended sentence. It seems that no other requirements or conditions may be included in a suspended sentence supervision order.

Powers of Criminal Courts Act 1973, s. 26

(8) A supervision order shall cease to have effect if before the end of the period specified in it—
  (a) a court orders under section 23 of this Act that a suspended sentence passed in the proceedings in which the order was made shall have effect; or
  (b) the order is discharged or replaced under the subsequent provisions of this section.

For s. 23 see **E2.8**.

Section 26(9) provides that a supervision order may be discharged on the application of the offender or the supervising officer, either by the relevant magistrates' court or, if it reserved a power of discharging the order to itself, by the Crown Court which made the order. Section 26(10) provides for the possibility of a court making a supervision order when it chooses to deal with an offender under s. 23 of the Act by varying the operational period of the suspended sentence. In such a case, the court may make a supervision order either in place of any such order made when the suspended sentence was passed or where the court which passed the sentence was empowered to make such an order but did not do so.

Section 26(11) provides that: 'On making a supervision order the court shall in ordinary language explain its effect to the offender.'

Suspended Sentence Supervision Order: Sentencing Principle   E2.15

According to the Court of Appeal in *Terry* (1992) *The Times*, 20 March 1992, a suspended sentence supervision order should not be used as an alternative to a probation order, nor should it be regarded as a 'probation order with teeth'. Further, only in the most exceptional circumstances should a suspended sentence supervision order be imposed without the court having regard to a pre-sentence report or to a medical report prepared on the offender.

SECTION E3: CUSTODIAL SENTENCES: DETENTION AND CUSTODY OF YOUNG OFFENDERS

E3.1   The custodial sentences which are available for offenders under the age of 21 are detention in a young offender institution, custody for life, detention during Her Majesty's pleasure, detention under the CYPA 1933, s. 53(3), a secure training order and, when the relevant provisions are brought into force, a detention and training order. Once the detention and training order is available, the secure training order will be abolished and the sentence of detention in a young offender institution will be available only in respect of offenders aged 18, 19 or 20. The detention and training order is now expected to be brought into force in April 2000.

DETENTION IN A YOUNG OFFENDER INSTITUTION

Power to Order Detention

E3.2   **Criminal Justice Act 1982, s. 1A**

(1)   Subject to section 8 below and to section 53 of the Children and Young Persons Act 1933, where—

(a)   an offender under 21 but not less than 15 years of age is convicted of an offence which is punishable with imprisonment in the case of a person aged 21 or over; and

(b)   the court is of the opinion that either or both of paragraphs (a) and (b) of subsection (2) of section 1 of the Criminal Justice Act 1991 apply or the case falls within subsection (3) of that section,

the sentence that the court is to pass is a sentence of detention in a young offender institution.

For the CJA 1982, s. 8, see **E3.9**; for the CYPA 1933, s. 53, see **E3.11**. For detailed discussion of the provisions of the CJA 1991, s. 1, see **E1.8**. It should be noted that the procedural provisions which must be complied with before a custodial sentence may lawfully be imposed upon an adult offender (particularly those relating to pre-sentence reports: see **E1.8**) must also be complied with in respect of an offender aged under 21.

The CJA 1982, s. 3, prohibits the imposition of a sentence of detention in a young offender institution by the Crown Court or a magistrates' court upon an offender who is not represented for the purposes of sentence, unless he has declined to apply for legal aid or his application has been refused on the ground that his means were such that he did not require assistance. The terms of s. 3 are similar to those of s. 21(1) of the PCCA 1973 (see **E1.3**), but note that s. 21 relates solely to the first prison sentence whereas s. 3 applies generally.

In *Danga* [1992] QB 476, where the offender was aged 20 when convicted but aged 21 when sentenced, it was held that the relevant age of the offender for the purposes of s. 1A(1) was the age at the date of conviction.

Time spent in custody on remand counts towards a sentence of detention in a young offender institution (CJA 1967, s. 67(5)). See **E1.6**.

Determining the Age of the Offender

E3.3   **Criminal Justice Act 1982, s. 1**

(6)   For the purposes of any provision of this Act which requires the determination of the age of a person by the court or the Secretary of State his age shall be deemed to be that which it appears to the court or the Secretary of State (as the case may be) to be after considering any available evidence.

When a court imposes a sentence on an assumption of the offender's age made under s. 1(6), the sentence is not rendered unlawful when it is discovered subsequently that the assumption was incorrect (*Brown* (1989) 11 Cr App R (S) 263). If there is a dispute about the offender's age, the best course may be to adjourn until the matter can be resolved (*Steed* (1990) 12 Cr App R (S) 230).

Minimum and Maximum Terms

The CJA 1982, ss. 1A and 1B, provide a scheme of minimum and maximum terms for this sentence. **E3.4**

Criminal Justice Act 1982, ss. 1A and 1B

1A.—(2) Subject to section 1B(2) below, the maximum term of detention in a young offender institution that a court may impose for an offence is the same as the maximum term of imprisonment that it may impose for that offence.

(3) Subject to subsection (4) below, a court shall not pass a sentence for an offender's detention in a young offender institution for less than the minimum period applicable to the offender under subsection (4A) below.

(4) A court may pass a sentence of detention in a young offender institution for less than the minimum period applicable for an offence under section 65(6) of the Criminal Justice Act 1991.

(4A) For the purposes of subsection (3) and (4) above, the minimum period of detention applicable to an offender is—

(a) in the case of an offender under 21 but not less than 18 years of age, the period of 21 days; and

(b) in the case of an offender under 18 years of age, the period of two months.

1B.—(2) In the case of an offender aged 15, 16 or 17 the maximum term of detention in a young offender institution that a court may impose is whichever is the lesser of—

(a) the maximum term of imprisonment the court may impose for the offence; and

(b) 24 months.

The sentence of detention in a young offender institution is available for offenders aged between 15 and 20 inclusive. The maximum term for an offender aged 15, 16 or 17 is 24 months. The normal minimum term is 21 days where the offender is aged 18, 19 or 20, or two months where the offender is aged under 18. In *Dover Youth Court, ex parte K (A Minor)* [1999] 1 WLR 27, the Divisional Court held that, on a proper construction of s. 1A(3) and s. 1A(4A)(b), the word 'sentence' in s. 1A(3) should be taken to refer to the sentence imposed for a particular offence, rather than to the total sentence produced by aggregating more than one custodial term. Thus, the imposition by the sentencer of three one-month sentences ordered to run consecutively to one another did not comply with s. 1A(3). None of the offences was so serious as to require a sentence of at least two months' detention, and so the sentences of detention in a young offender institution were unlawful.

In *Robinson* [1993] 1 WLR 168, it was held that when determining the age of the offender for the purposes of s. 1B(2), the relevant date was the date of conviction rather than sentence.

For s. 1A(5), see **E3.5**. Section 1B(1) and (3) have been repealed. When powers to impose a detention and training order are brought into force, the sentence of detention is a young offender institution will be confined to offenders aged 18, 19 or 20, and the minimum period for a sentence of detention in a young offender institution will be 21 days. Section 1A(4A) and the remainder of s. 1B will be repealed.

Concurrent and Consecutive Sentences of Detention

Criminal Justice Act 1982, s. 1A **E3.5**

(5) Subject to section 1B(4) below, where—

(a) an offender is convicted of more than one offence for which he is liable to a sentence of detention in a young offender institution; or

    (b)   an offender who is serving a sentence of detention in a young offender institution is convicted of one or more further offences for which he is liable to such a sentence,
the court shall have the same power to pass consecutive sentences of detention in a young offender institution as if they were sentences of imprisonment.
    (6)   Subject to section 102 of the Crime and Disorder Act 1998, where an offender who—
        (a)   is serving a sentence of detention in a young offender institution; and
        (b)   is aged over 21 years,
is convicted of one or more further offences for which he is liable to imprisonment, the court shall have the power to pass one or more sentences of imprisonment to run consecutively upon the sentence of detention in a young offender institution.

For concurrent and consecutive sentences of imprisonment, see **E1.5**.

Section 1A(5) is subject to s. 1B(4), which states that a court shall not pass on an offender aged 15, 16 or 17 a sentence of detention in a young offender institution whose effect would be that the offender would be sentenced to a total term which exceeds 24 months. In *Starkey* (1994) 15 Cr App R (S) 576, it was held that, when determining the age of the offender for the purposes of s. 1B(4), the relevant date was the date of conviction rather than sentence. Section 1B(5) further provides that, where the total term of detention in a young offender institution to which such an offender is sentenced exceeds 24 months so much of the term as exceeds that period shall be treated as remitted. For these purposes 'total term' means (s. 1B(6)):

    (a)   in the case of an offender sentenced (whether or not on the same occasion) to two or more terms of detention in a young offender institution which are consecutive or wholly or partly concurrent, the aggregate of those terms; or
    (b)   in the case of any other offender, the term of the sentence of detention in a young offender institution in question.

In *Smithyman* (1993) 14 Cr App R (S) 263 the sentencer purported to pass a sentence of three and a half years' detention on a 16-year-old offender. Since s. 1B(5) automatically takes effect, the Court of Appeal was unable to preserve the effect of the original sentence even though the sentencer could have passed a sentence under the CYPA 1933, s. 53(2), for the longer period. Similar mistakes occurred in *Egdeu* (1994) 15 Cr App R (S) 509, *Venison* (1994) 15 Cr App R (S) 624 and *Read* [1999] 1 Cr App R (S) 456. In *Marriott* (1995) 16 Cr App R (S) 428, the sentencer passed a sentence of 7 years' 'detention' for robbery. The Court of Appeal said that it was clear from the context that the sentencer meant to impose a term under s. 53(2) rather than a sentence of detention in a young offender institution. It followed that s. 1B(5) did not operate. In *AM* [1988] 1 WLR 363, the Court of Appeal reminded sentencers once again of the need to make it clear whether the sentence being imposed was one of detention in a young offender institution or one of long-term detention under s. 53(2).

DETENTION IN A YOUNG OFFENDER INSTITUTION: SENTENCING PRINCIPLES

Mixing Detention with Other Sentences or Orders

E3.6   As to whether it is appropriate to impose a sentence of detention in a young offender institution to run concurrently with, or consecutively to, a sentence of detention under the CYPA 1933, s. 53(2), see **E3.13**.

Length to be Proportionate to Harm Caused, Culpability of Offender etc.

E3.7   The sentence of detention in a young offender institution is subject to the statutory criteria laid down in the CJA 1991, both for determining whether a custodial sentence should be imposed (see **E1.8**) and for determining custodial sentence length (see **E1.13**). Examples of decisions on the appropriate use of the sentence of detention in a young offender institution are given in relation to the particular offences in **part B** of this work.

See also, by analogy, the principles developed in relation to the use of imprisonment for adults at **E1.12**.

Although the statutory criteria in the 1991 Act are equally applicable to sentences of detention in a young offender institution as they are to imprisonment, the authorities suggest that it is often appropriate to pass a shorter custodial sentence on an offender who has not yet attained the age of 21 than the term which would be imposed on an adult who has committed the same offence, although this may be outweighed by other factors in the case. Comment to this effect can be found in *A-G's Ref (No. 42 of 1996)* [1997] 1 Cr App R (S) 388 and in *Howells* [1999] 1 WLR 307. An example of a case where youth, among other factors, saved an offender from a custodial sentence is *Cox* [1993] 1 WLR 188 (see **E1.9**). In *Horney* (1990) 12 Cr App R (S) 20, the offender, aged 20, pleaded guilty to the manslaughter of his baby daughter. A sentence of 18 months' detention in a young offender institution was imposed, but the sentencer indicated that if the offender had been aged 21, a suspended sentence of imprisonment would have been appropriate. The Court of Appeal upheld the sentence, commenting that although the spirit of the legislation which then applied was that a young offender should not be dealt with more harshly than an adult offender, the lack of any power in the courts to suspend a sentence of detention in a young offender institution meant that 'cases of hardship, or apparent hardship, are therefore bound to arise'.

Length of Sentence Normally Reduced Following Guilty Plea

In *George* (1993) 14 Cr App R (S) 12, where the 16-year-old offender pleaded guilty to **E3.8** a 'disgraceful' offence of criminal damage committed in a church at night, the Court of Appeal said that a guilty plea should normally attract a discount, and reduced the maximum available term of 12 months (as it then was) to 10 months. In *Sharkey* (1995) 16 Cr App R (S) 257, the Court of Appeal said that it was 'wrong in principle' to impose the maximum term of detention in a young offender institution on an offender who had pleaded guilty, and the same view was taken in *Carroll* (1995) 16 Cr App R (S) 488. These last two cases involved serious incidents of aggravated vehicle-taking.

There is an exception to this general principle in cases involving young offenders aged 15, 16 or 17 (for whom the maximum sentence of detention in a young offender institution is 24 months), if the offender has pleaded guilty to an offence in respect of which there is power to sentence him under the CYPA 1933, s. 53(3) (see **E3.12**). Where, but for the guilty plea, the sentencer would have imposed a sentence of detention under s. 53(3) in excess of 24 months, the proper sentence (after making appropriate discount for the guilty plea) may be 24 months' detention in a young offender institution. This point was confirmed by the Court of Appeal in *AM* [1988] 1 WLR 363 where, Lord Bingham CJ commented that where the maximum sentence of 24 months was imposed in such circumstances, it was desirable that the sentencer should explain how that sentence had been reached. See further **E3.15**.

The general principle is subject to other exceptions, in parallel to those cases where the discount may be lost in respect of imprisonment on an adult. These were discussed in *Costen* (1989) 11 Cr App R (S) 182. This principle must also be read in the light of the CJA 1991, s. 28, and the CJPO 1994, s. 48 (see further **E1.18**).

CUSTODY FOR LIFE

Power to Sentence to Custody for Life

Criminal Justice Act 1982, s. 8   E3.9

(1) Where a person under the age of 21 is convicted of murder or any other offence the sentence for which is fixed by law as imprisonment for life, the court shall sentence him to

custody for life unless he is liable to be detained under section 53(1) of the Children and Young Persons Act 1933 (detention of persons under 18 convicted of murder).

(2)   Where a person aged 18 years or over but under the age of 21 is convicted of any other offence for which a person aged 21 years or over would be liable to imprisonment for life, the court shall, if it considers that a custodial sentence for life would be appropriate, sentence him to custody for life.

For s. 53(1) of the 1933 Act, see **E3.11**. The criteria for the imposition for the sentence of custody for life, where it is imposed as a discretionary sentence, are those contained in ss. 1 and 2 of the 1991 Act (see **E1.8** and **E1.13**). It may be assumed, from the indeterminate nature of this sentence, that while the imposition of a sentence of custody for life may be justified under s. 1(2)(a) or (b), determination of sentence length can be justified only in accordance with s. 2(2)(b) of the 1991 Act (see **E1.23**). The C(S)A 1997, s. 28, provides that a sentencer imposing a sentence of custody for life, whether as the mandatory sentence for murder under the CJA 1982, s. 8(1), or as a discretionary life sentence under s. 8(2), may specify what part of the sentence must expire before the offender becomes eligible for consideration for early release. The sentencer should start by deciding what determinate sentence would have been appropriate if custody for life had not been imposed, and then specify a period which will normally be one half of that notional sentence as the part to be specified under s. 28 (*M* [1999] 1 WLR 485). Credit should be given for relevant mitigating factors, such as the youth of the offender and for any period spent on remand in custody or in local authority secure accommodation. See further **E1.27**.

Under the C(S)A 1997, s. 2, custody for life may be imposed as the automatic life sentence on an offender under the age of 21 who is convicted for the second time of a 'serious offence' (see **E1.22**).

The CJA 1982, s. 3, prohibits the imposition of a sentence of custody for life against an offender who is not represented for the purposes of sentence, unless he has declined to apply for legal aid or his application has been refused on the ground that his means were such that he did not require assistance. This provision applies both to CJA 1982, s. 8(1) and s. 8(2).

Custody for Life: Sentencing Principle

E3.10   The sentence of custody for life has, in the past, been distinguished from the imposition of a determinate sentence of detention in a young offender institution by the requirement that custody for life should be imposed only in exceptional circumstances and only where the offender displays a degree of mental instability. This is very similar to the requirement for the imposition of a life sentence of imprisonment on an adult (see **E1.23**). The Court of Appeal has stressed that custody for life is reserved for exceptional cases where there is a marked degree of mental instability, and should not be passed on the assumption that it is a more merciful disposal than a fixed-term sentence (*Hall* (1986) 8 Cr App R (S) 458 and *Lynas* (1992) 13 Cr App R (S) 363, following *Pither* (1979) 1 Cr App R (S) 209).

Cases where the Court has quashed sentences of custody for life imposed at trial are: *Hall* (1986) 8 Cr App R (S) 458 (sentence inappropriate after a guilty plea to arson, since 'no real evidence that the offender was suffering from any mental illness or abnormality, although he was immature and a young criminal who had committed many offences'; sentence varied to seven years); and *Powell* (1989) 11 Cr App R (S) 113 (sentence inappropriate after a guilty plea to wounding with intent, taking a conveyance and violent disorder, since the offender had shown a degree of remorse and because there was 'an insufficient degree of mental instability, or dangerousness, to call for the exceptional course which the judge felt obliged to take'; sentence varied to eight years). On the other hand, a sentence of custody for life was upheld in *Silson* (1987) 9 Cr App

R (S) 282, where the accused, who pleaded guilty to two counts of arson, one with intent to endanger life, involving damage of £20,000, was described as not suffering from any psychiatric illness, but as being of dull/normal intelligence, immature and inadequate, and whose behaviour was attributed in part to alcohol and solvent abuse. Such a sentence was similarly upheld in *Busby* (1992) 13 Cr App R (S) 291, where the offender, aged 18, pleaded guilty to buggery of a girl aged three. He was not suffering from any mental illness but was described as 'flat and detached' and showed no remorse. He had committed two earlier assaults on young children and, in the light of that, it was held that the primary responsibility of the court was to protect the public.

DETENTION UNDER THE CHILDREN AND YOUNG PERSONS ACT 1933, S. 53

Detention during Her Majesty's pleasure

Section 53(1) prescribes a mandatory sentence of detention during Her Majesty's **E3.11** pleasure for murder committed by an offender who was under 18 at the time of the offence. It is confined to murder cases (*Abbott* [1964] 1 QB 489). The CJA 1982, s. 3 (restriction on imposing sentence where offender not legally represented), applies. The C(S)A 1997, s. 28, provides that a sentencer imposing a sentence of detention during Her Majesty's pleasure may specify what part of the sentence must expire before the offender becomes eligible for consideration for early release. The sentencer should start by deciding what determinate sentence would have been appropriate if detention during Her Majesty's pleasure had not been imposed, and then specify a period which will normally be one half of the notional determinate sentence as the part to be specified under s. 28. Credit should be given for relevant mitigating factors, such as the youth of the offender and for any period spent on remand in custody or in local authority secure accommodation. See further **E1.27**. The House of Lords has held that the welfare of the child or young person is also highly relevant, and there should be flexibility so as to allow the Home Secretary to reconsider the relevant period in the light of progress during the period of detention (see *Secretary of State for the Home Department, ex parte Venables* [1998] AC 407). A person so sentenced will be detained in such place and under such conditions as the Secretary of State may direct or may arrange.

Detention under s. 53(3)

Children and Young Persons Act 1933, s. 53   **E3.12**

    (2)   Subsection (3) below applies—
      (a)   where a person of at least 10 but not more than 17 years is convicted on indictment of—
         (i)   any offence punishable in the case of an adult with imprisonment for fourteen years or more, not being an offence the sentence for which is fixed by law, or
         (ii)   an offence under section 14 (indecent assault on a woman) or section 15 (indecent assault on a man) of the Sexual Offences Act 1956;
      (b)   where a young person is convicted of—
         (i)   an offence under section 1 of the Road Traffic Act 1988 (causing death by dangerous driving), or
         (ii)   an offence under section 3A of the Road Traffic Act 1988 (causing death by careless driving while under the influence of drink or drugs).
    (3)   Where this subsection applies, then, if the court is of the opinion that none of the other methods in which the case may legally be dealt with is suitable, the court may sentence the offender to be detained for such period not exceeding the maximum term of imprisonment with which the offence is punishable in the case of an adult as may be specified in the sentence; and where such a sentence has been passed the child or young person shall, during that period, be liable to be detained in such place and on such conditions—

(a)   as the Secretary of State may direct, or

(b)   as the Secretary of State may arrange with any person.

(4)   A person detained pursuant to the directions or arrangements made by the Secretary of State under this section shall, while so detained, be deemed to be in legal custody.

By the CYPA 1933, s. 107(1), a 'child' is a person aged 10 or over but under 14 years, and a 'young person' is a person aged 14 or over but under 18. In *Robinson* [1993] 1 WLR 168 it was held, following *Danga* [1992] QB 476 (see **E3.2**), that in determining whether an offender was eligible for a sentence under s. 53(3) the relevant age was the age of the offender at the time of conviction, rather than his age at the time of sentence. If the offence carries imprisonment for life in respect of an adult, then detention for life may be ordered under s. 53(3) of the 1933 Act (*Abbott* [1964] 1 QB 489 and see **E3.14**).

Section 53(3) is available in respect of offenders aged between 10 and 17 inclusive who have been convicted on indictment of an offence punishable in the case of an adult with a term of imprisonment not exceeding 14 years, or convicted on indictment of the offence of indecent assault on a woman or indecent assault on a man (s. 53(2)(a)). The offence of indecent assault on a man was brought within the scope of s. 53(2) by the C(S)A 1997, s. 44, which came into force on 1 October 1997 and applies only to such offences committed after that date. In addition, by s. 53(2)(b), offenders aged between 14 and 17 inclusive convicted on indictment of causing death by dangerous driving or causing death by careless driving while under the influence of drink or drugs may be dealt with under s. 53(3). It should be noted that s. 53(3) is not available in respect of burglary of commercial premises, where the maximum penalty is ten years' imprisonment (*Brown* (1995) 16 Cr App R (S) 932).

Powers under s. 53(3) are limited to conviction in the Crown Court; a youth court may not exercise them, nor may the Crown Court to which a juvenile is committed for sentence after a finding of guilt in a youth court (*McKenna* (1985) 7 Cr App R (S) 348). In a case where the offence merits a greater penalty than is permitted by the scheme of maximum penalties for detention in a young offender institution, provided by the CJA 1982, ss. 1A and 1B (see **E3.4**), the proper course is for the magistrates to commit to the Crown Court for trial to allow for the possibility of an order under s. 53(3) being made. In *Learmonth* (1988) 10 Cr App R (S) 229, the offender, aged under 17, pleaded guilty before a juvenile court to assault with intent to rob. He was committed to the Crown Court for sentence, where three years' detention was ordered under s. 53(3). It was held on appeal that s. 53(3) was not available to the Crown Court, since the defendant had not been convicted on indictment. In *AM* [1998] 1 WLR 363, the Court of Appeal again reminded magistrates of the need to commit for trial any case which might merit detention under s. 53(3).

Time spent in custody (or local authority secure accommodation) on remand counts towards a sentence imposed under s. 53(3) (CJA 1967, s. 67(1A)(c), set out at **E1.6**). For the meaning of 'accommodation provided for the purpose of restricting liberty', see *Collins* (1995) 16 Cr App R (S) 156. The CJA 1982, s. 3 (restriction on imposing sentence where offender not legally represented), applies.

DETENTION UNDER S. 53(3): SENTENCING PRINCIPLES

E3.13   The imposition of a sentence under s. 53(3) is subject to the statutory criteria for determining the imposition of custodial sentences and for determining the length of those sentences which is laid down in the CJA 1991 (see **E1.8** and **E1.13**). It was held in *Fairhurst* [1986] 1 WLR 1374 that a sentence of detention under s. 53(3) should not be imposed consecutively to, or concurrently with, a sentence of detention in a young offender institution. However, in the important case of *AM* [1998] 1 WLR 363, Lord

Bingham CJ noted that statutory changes since that decision meant that there was now no difference in release arrangements between the two forms of detention. Accordingly, when sentencing a young offender for one or more offences which fell within and merited detention under s. 53(3) as well as for other offences which did not fall within that section but which merited a sentence of detention in a young offender institution, the sentencing court might properly and without causing administrative difficulty sentence the offender to a term in a young offender institution consecutively to a term ordered under s. 53(3), unless that order was of an indefinite character. Consecutive sentences should not be imposed in that way on an offender aged 15, however, since such an offender might be detained in secure accommodation and difficulties could result from passing a consecutive sentence of detention in a young offender institution. Lord Bingham stated that it was generally undesirable to impose terms concurrently under both sections. Where some of the offences fell within s. 53(3) and there were associated offences which did not, it would usually be preferable to impose no separate penalty for the lesser offences but to impose a term of detention under s. 53(3) which took them into account. If the court was minded to impose concurrent terms, the administrative difficulties should be borne in mind, especially where a 15-year-old was being sentenced.

Where a young offender has been convicted of more than one offence, and power to sentence the offender under s. 53(3) is available in respect of one of the offences but not the other(s), *Fairhurst* established that it was wrong to pass a sentence under s. 53(3) for an offence which did not warrant such a sentence to compensate for the inability to pass such a sentence for an offence which did justify a longer term of detention but which did not carry power to sentence under s. 53(3). In *Walsh* [1997] 2 Cr App R (S) 210 there were five offenders, all girls aged 14 or 15. They pleaded guilty to false imprisonment and unlawful wounding, committed while carrying out a sustained violent attack on another girl aged 14. Sentences of detention under s. 53(3) were imposed, for terms varying between three and a half years and three years eleven months. It was argued on appeal that the sentences were wrong since the real gravamen of the offending lay in respect of the unlawful wounding, an offence for which s. 53(3) is not available. The Court of Appeal, however, held that the two offences were associated with each other and s. 53(3) was available for the offence of false imprisonment. Sentence lengths were, however, reduced in this case for other reasons. The approach taken in *Walsh* was endorsed in *AM*.

Detention for Life: Requirement that Offender Likely to Remain a Serious Danger to the Public for Indefinite Time

In *Flemming* [1973] 2 All ER 401, the offender was involved in a robbery at a butcher's **E3.14** shop, in the course of which the butcher was stabbed to death by an accomplice. Lawton LJ, commenting that 'this is the very sort of case in which an indeterminate sentence was appropriate', stressed the offender's dangerousness and the uncertainty over whether or at what point the offender would develop signs of 'maturity and social balance'. In *Bryson* (1973) 58 Cr App R 464, a sentence of detention for life was upheld on a 14-year-old who pleaded guilty to arson causing damage worth £20,000 and considerable risk to life, with Lord Widgery CJ pointing out that 'None of the experts give any sort of indication that a particular period of years can in this case be chosen to ensure that the public can be properly protected'. In *Carr* [1996] 1 Cr App R (S) 191, the defendant was a 15-year-old girl who pleaded guilty to causing grievous bodily harm with intent, having stabbed another schoolgirl in the back with a knife. She asked for two other offences, in which she had tried to strangle other schoolgirls, to be taken into consideration. Reports revealed other instances of disturbed and aggressive behaviour and indicated that the defendant was 'exceptionally dangerous'. An indeterminate sentence under s. 53(3) was imposed. See also *Sheldon* [1996] 2 Cr App R (S) 397.

The C(S)A 1997, s. 28, provides that a sentencer imposing a sentence of detention for life may specify what part of the sentence must expire before the offender becomes eligible for consideration for early release. The sentencer should start by deciding what determinate sentence would have been appropriate if detention for life had not been imposed, and then specify a period which will normally be one half of that notional sentence as the part to be specified under s. 28 (*M* [1999] 1 WLR 485). Credit should be given for relevant mitigating factors, and for any period spent on remand in custody or in local authority secure accommodation (see further **E1.27**).

Detention under s. 53(3) for a Fixed Term: Requirement to Balance Punishment, Deterrence, Desirability of Avoiding Long Custodial Terms for Young Offenders etc.

E3.15 General guidance on the use of the CYPA 1933, s. 53(3), was provided by Lord Lane CJ in *Fairhurst* [1986] 1 WLR 1374, in which his lordship commented that it was not necessary, in order to invoke the provisions of s. 53(3), that the crime committed should be one of exceptional gravity, such as attempted murder, manslaughter, wounding with intent, armed robbery or the like but, on the other hand, that it was not good sentencing practice to pass a sentence of detention under s. 53(3) simply because the maximum available sentence of youth custody (now detention in a young offender institution) appeared to be on the low side for the particular offence committed. These comments were endorsed by Lord Bingham CJ in *AM* [1998] 1 WLR 363.

For offenders aged 15, 16 or 17, the maximum sentence of detention in a young offender institution is 24 months (see **E3.4**). The Court of Appeal held in *Wainfur* [1997] 1 Cr App R (S) 43 that, for offenders within this age group, the court should be satisfied before imposing a sentence under s. 53(3) that a sentence 'substantially greater' than 24 months was appropriate. In *AM*, however, the Court of Appeal signalled a change of approach, stating that the effect of the earlier law had been to 'create a sentencing no-man's land' between the maximum sentence of detention in a young offender institution and the shortest term which might appropriately be imposed under s. 53(3). Accordingly, Lord Bingham CJ in *AM* stated that while a Crown Court sentencer should not exceed the 24-month limit without much careful thought, if it was concluded that a longer (even if not much longer) sentence was called for, then the court should impose whatever it considered the appropriate period of detention under s. 53(3) to be. In *Brown* [1999] 1 Cr App R (S) 132, the Court of Appeal, referring to the fact that an offender ordered to be detained under s. 53(3) may be detained in any place that the Secretary of State may direct or arrange, stated that there might be circumstances where the Crown Court would be justified in passing a sentence of detention under s. 53(3) on an offender aged 15, 16 or 17 for a term of less than two years. This might arise where a custodial sentence of less than two years was appropriate for the offence, the court was persuaded that none of the other methods of dealing with the offender (especially detention in a young offender institution) was a 'suitable' method of disposing of the case, there was a place available for the offender in an institution more suitable for his needs than a young offender institution, and that the institution was willing to accept the offender.

In *Bennett* (1995) 16 Cr App R (S) 438, five years' detention was upheld on a boy aged 15, for damaging property being reckless whether life was endangered and for aggravated vehicle-taking. He took a van from a garage and drove it at high speed, starting a police chase during which the van was driven at police vehicles, causing damage to the value of £3,500. The offender had committed over 100 previous offences, and the sentence was justified on punitive and deterrent grounds and having regard to the prevalence of such offending in the area in question. In *Simmons* (1995) 16 Cr App R (S) 801, five years' detention was upheld in the case of a 16-year-old who pleaded guilty to seven counts of burglary and asked for a large number of offences to be taken into consideration, including 67 burglaries and attempted burglaries. It was held that the sentence was appropriate to reflect the gravity and the persistence of the offending and the need for deterrence. In *Taylor* (1995) 16 Cr App R (S) 570, seven years' detention was reduced to six years for robbery in respect of a 17-year-old who, in company with a female offender aged 21, went to the home of a 70-year-old man and attacked him with great violence, punching and kicking him about the head and the body, and stealing £4. The modest reduction in Taylor's sentence was to reflect his youth, the fact that he was under the other offender's influence, his immediate confession and evidence of remorse. A sentence of eight years' detention, passed as a longer-than-normal sentence under s. 2(2)(b) of the CJA 1991 on a boy aged 16 for the rape of his sister aged six, was reduced to six years in *K* (1995) 16 Cr App R (S) 966. The medical report 'gave a disturbing picture of sexual fantasising' and indicated that the defendant would remain a risk for at least the next decade, but the sentence was adjusted to take account of the age of the defendant and the fact that he was cooperating with treatment and coming to terms with his conduct.

SECURE TRAINING ORDERS

The CJPO 1994, s. 1, provides for the secure training order. This order is a custodial **E3.16** sentence for the purposes of the CJA 1991, ss. 1 to 4, so that, in addition to the provisions set out below, the general statutory criteria in the 1991 Act for determining the imposition and length of custodial sentences, and for the obtaining of a pre-sentence report, apply. The CJA 1982, s. 3 (prohibition of imposition of sentence on unrepresented offender) also applies.

Section 1(10) of the CJPO 1994 allows for the bringing into force of these powers in stages, initially applying only to offenders aged 14, but with the extension of the powers thereafter to offenders aged 13, and then to those aged 12. Although these provisions were brought into force on 1 March 1998, they have effect only until such time as the power to pass a detention and training order, introduced by the CDA 1998, s. 73 (see **E3.18**) is brought into force. At that time, the relevant provisions of the CJPO 1994 will be repealed. It is expected that s. 73 will be brought into force in April 2000. The CDA 1998, s. 116 ('transitory provisions') states that, at any time before the commencement of s. 73, a court shall not pass a secure training order unless it has been notified by the Secretary of State that accommodation at a secure training centre, or accommodation provided by a local authority for the purposes of restricting the liberty of children and young persons, is immediately available for the offender, and the notice has not been withdrawn.

Criminal Justice and Public Order Act 1994, s. 1

(1) Subject to section 8(1) of the Criminal Justice Act 1982 and section 53(1) of the Children and Young Persons Act 1933 (sentences of custody for life and long term detention), where—
(a) a person of not less than 12 but under 15 years of age is convicted of an imprisonable offence; and
(b) the court is satisfied of the matters specified in subsection (5) below,
the court may make a secure training order.
(2) A secure training order is an order that the offender in respect of whom it is made shall be subject to a period of detention in a secure training centre followed by a period of supervision.

A secure training order is not available in a case where the young offender has been convicted of murder. A secure training order may be imposed by the Crown Court or by a youth court. For the purposes of s. 1, the age of a person shall be deemed to be that which it appears to the court to be after considering any available evidence (s. 1(9)). For a similarly worded provision, see CJA 1982, s. 1(6), at **E3.3**. A secure training order comprises two parts, the first part being a period of detention, and the second part a period of supervision. The total length of the secure training order must be specified by the court and must be not less than six months and not more than two years (CJPO 1994, s. 1(3)). It was confirmed in *Medway Youth Court, ex parte A* [1999] Crim LR 915 that this maximum is applicable to the youth court as well as to the Crown Court. Restrictions on the imposition by magistrates' courts of sentences of imprisonment and detention in a young offender institution (see **E1.2**) do not apply to secure training orders. The Divisional Court noted that the secure training order provisions were a fresh departure from the previous legislation and were enacted to satisfy public anxiety about offences being repeatedly committed by very young offenders. The period of detention within the secure training order will be half of the total length of the order (s. 1(4)).

Criminal Justice and Public Order Act 1994, s. 1

(5)   The court shall not make a secure training order unless it is satisfied—
   (a)   that the offender was not less than 12 years of age when the offence for which he is to be dealt with by the court was committed;
   (b)   that the offender has been convicted of three or more imprisonable offences; and
   (c)   that the offender, either on this or a previous occasion—
      (i)   has been found by a court to be in breach of a supervision order under the Children and Young Persons Act 1969, or
      (ii)   has been convicted of an imprisonable offence whilst he was subject to such a supervision order.

When a court makes a secure training order, it must state in open court that it is of the opinion that the conditions in s. 1(5) are satisfied (s. 1(7)). It is not clear whether the three or more imprisonable offences referred to in s. 1(5)(b) must be offences for which the offender is being dealt with on the current occasion, or whether they may include previous convictions. For supervision orders, see **E8**.

It is envisaged in the CJPO 1994 that an offender upon whom a secure training order has been imposed will serve the detention part of that sentence in a secure training centre. Section 2(2), taken together with the transitory provisions contained in the CDA 1998, s. 116, state that, until such time as powers to impose a detention and training order under s. 73 of that Act are brought into force and the relevant powers in the 1994 Act to pass secure training orders are repealed, the court, in a case where accommodation at a secure training centre is not immediately available, may commit the young offender to local authority secure accommodation. The period of detention to be served at the secure training centre is reduced by the period spent by the young offender in the secure accommodation provided.

During the supervision part of the secure training order, the offender is supervised by a probation officer appointed to the petty sessions area in which he resides, a social worker of the local authority for the area in which the offender resides, or such other person as the Secretary of State may designate (s. 3(2), (4) and (5)). Before the commencement of the period of supervision, the offender must be given a notice specifying who will be responsible for his supervision and any requirements with which he must comply (s. 3(7) and (8)).

Time spent in custody on remand will count towards a secure training order sentence (CJA 1967, s. 67(5)).

Breach of Supervision Requirement

E3.17   If it appears on information to a justice of the peace acting for a 'relevant petty sessions area' (as defined in the CJPO 1994, s. 4(2)) that an offender subject to a secure training order has failed to comply with, or has contravened, any requirement specified in the supervision part of the order, the justice may issue a summons requiring the offender to appear or, if the information is in writing and on oath, issue a warrant for his arrest (s. 4(1)). If it is proved to the satisfaction of the youth court before which the offender appears that he has failed to comply with, or has contravened, a requirement of the supervision part of the order, the court may (a) order the offender to be detained in a secure training centre (or, where applicable, local authority secure accommodation) for the remainder of the order or for three months, whichever is the shorter, or (b) impose a fine on the offender not exceeding level 3 on the standard scale (s. 4(3)). It appears, though it is not entirely clear from the wording, that if a fine is imposed the supervision part of the order will continue in place.

DETENTION AND TRAINING ORDERS

The CDA 1998, ss. 73 to 79 will, when brought into force, create a new custodial **E3.18** sentence for young offenders — the detention and training order. The order will be available to youth courts and to the Crown Court, in respect of offenders aged under 18 who have been convicted of an offence punishable with imprisonment in the case of an adult. The detention and training order will be a 'custodial sentence' for the purposes of CJA 1991. Section 73(1) states that, subject to the CYPA 1933, s. 53 (detention during Her Majesty's pleasure and sentences of long-term detention in accordance with CYPA 1933, s. 53(3)), and to the CJA 1982, s. 8 (custody for life), where an offender falling within this age group qualifies for a custodial sentence, the 'sentence that the court is to pass' is the detention and training order. The effect of this is that when the powers to impose a detention and training order are brought into force, which is expected to be April 2000, the secure training order (**E3.16**) will be repealed and the sentence of detention in a young offender institution will be available only to offenders aged 18, 19 or 20. Until that time the existing regime for the custodial sentencing of young offenders will remain in place. Section 73(2)(b)(ii) envisages that, even when powers to pass a detention and training order are brought into force, a further order will be required from the Secretary of State to empower courts to impose the sentence on an offender aged under 12.

Crime and Disorder Act 1998, s. 73

(1)   Subject to s. 53 of the 1933 Act [CYPA 1933], s. 8 of the Criminal Justice Act 1982 ('the 1982 Act') and subsection (2) below, where—

(a)   a child or young person ('the offender') is convicted of an offence which is punishable with imprisonment in the case of a person aged 21 or over; and

(b)   the court is of the opinion that either or both of paragraphs (a) or (b) of subsection (2) of section 1 of the [CJA 1991] apply or the case falls within subsection (3) of that section, the sentence that the court is to pass is a detention and training order.

(2)   A court shall not make a detention and training order—

(a)   in the case of an offender under the age of 15 at the time of the conviction, unless it is of the opinion that he is a persistent offender;

(b)   in the case of an offender under the age of 12 at that time, unless—

(i)   it is of the opinion that only a custodial sentence would be adequate to protect the public from further offending by him; and

(ii)   the offence was committed on or after such date as the Secretary of State may by order appoint.

(3)   A detention and training order is an order that the offender in respect of whom it is made shall be subject, for the term specified in the order, to a period of detention and training followed by a period of supervision.

(4)   A detention and training order shall be a custodial sentence for the purposes of part I of the 1991 Act; and the provisions of sections 1 to 4 of that Act shall apply accordingly.

(5)   Subject to subsection (6) below, the term of a detention and training order shall be 4, 6, 8, 10, 12, 18 or 24 months.

(6) The term of a detention and training order may not exceed the maximum term of imprisonment that the Crown Court could (in the case of an offender aged 21 or over) impose for the offence.

For CYPA 1933, s. 53(1) (detention during Her Majesty's pleasure), see **E3.11**; for s. 53(3) (long-term detention), see **E3.12**, and for CJA 1982, s. 8 (custody for life), see **E3.9**. For CJA 1991, s. 1(2)(a) and (b) (general criteria for the imposition of custodial sentences) and (3) (imposition of custodial sentence where the offender fails to express his willingness to comply with a requirement in a community order which requires an expression of such willingness), see **E1.8**.

Anticipated Operation

E3.19   For young offenders aged 15, 16 and 17, the detention and training order will operate in a very similar fashion to the sentence of detention in a young offender institution. For those aged 12, 13 and 14, the detention and training order will operate in a comparable fashion to the secure training order, although it should be noted that power to pass a detention and training order on a young offender aged under 15 at the time of conviction is limited to cases in which the offender qualifies as a 'persistent' offender. This may be compared to the more precisely worded power to pass a secure training order which, in every case, requires proof that the young offender has been convicted of three or more imprisonable offences, has been in breach of a supervision order or has been convicted of an imprisonable offence while subject to a supervision order (CJPO 1994, s. 1(5), set out at **E3.16**). The CDA 1998 offers no equivalent definition of 'persistent' for the purposes of the detention and training order, and presumably it has been left to the sentencing courts to develop their own guidelines. In *Sheffield Youth Justices, ex parte M* (1998) *The Times*, 29 January 1998, Simon Brown LJ observed that, even though powers to pass a secure training order were not in force at the time of that case, counsel might wish to draw the attention of sentencers to the wording of s. 1(5) in any case in which the court was considering imposing a custodial sentence on an offender aged under 15. Section 74(1) of the CDA 1998 states that, where the court makes a detention and training order on an offender aged under 15, it must state in open court that it is of the opinion mentioned in s. 73(2)(a) and, where applicable, (b)(i). This is in addition to the normal obligations on the sentencer under CJA 1991, s. 1(4), to give reasons for imposing a custodial sentence.

Duration of Order and Consecutive Orders

E3.20   By the CDA 1998, s. 73(5), the term of a detention and training order must be for one of the specified periods set out in that subsection, the minimum period being four months and the maximum period 24 months. This subsection is expressed as being 'subject to' s. 73(6), which explains that when imposing such a sentence the court may not exceed the maximum term of imprisonment which the Crown Court could have imposed on an adult for that offence. The intention must be to limit the maximum term of a detention and training order to the period specified in s. 73(5) or the maximum penalty, whichever is the shorter (see the equivalent wording in CJA 1982, s. 1B(2)). The maximum available period of 24 months is applicable to the youth court as well as to the Crown Court, since the restrictions on the imposition of imprisonment and detention in a young offender institution (see **E1.2**) have not been amended by the CDA 1998 to make them applicable to the detention and training order. By analogy, see the decision in *Medway Youth Court, ex parte A* [1999] Crim LR 915, at **E3.16** in relation to secure training orders. Restricting the sentencing courts to the specific terms identified in s. 73(5) is a novel approach, but seems likely to give rise to practical difficulty. If the appropriate duration of a detention and training order would otherwise be, say, 18 months, but the offender enters a timely guilty plea and/or there is other significant mitigation, it is submitted that the court must reduce the term, at least to 12 months, to take that into account. There is no stopping point between 18 and 12 months.

Ordinarily, the period of detention and training shall be one-half of the full term of the order, although the Secretary of State retains a discretion to release a person under such an order at a somewhat earlier date (s. 75). The second half of the order is the period of supervision, although again the Secretary of State retains power to provide by order that the period of supervision shall be curtailed (s. 76). Supervision will be carried out by a probation officer, a social worker of a local authority social services department, or a member of a youth offending team.

Crime and Disorder Act 1998, s. 74

(2) Subject to subsections (3) and (4A) below, a court making a detention and training order may order that its term shall commence on the expiration of the term of any other detention and training order made by that or any other court.

(3) A court shall not make in respect of an offender a detention and training order the effect of which would be that he would be subject to detention and training orders for a term which exceeds 24 months.

(4) Where the term of the detention and training orders to which an offender would otherwise be subject exceeds 24 months, the excess shall be treated as remitted.

(4A) A court making a detention and training order shall not order that its term shall commence on the expiration of the term of a detention and training order under which the period of supervision has already begun (under section 76(1) below).

(4B) Where a detention and training order ('the new order') is made in respect of an offender who is subject to a detention and training order under which the period of supervision has begun ('the old order'), the old order shall be disregarded in determining—

(a) for the purposes of subsection (3) above whether the effect of the new order would be that the offender would be subject to detention and training orders for a term which exceeds 24 months; and

(b) for the purposes of subsection (4) above whether the term of the detention and training orders to which the offender would (apart from that subsection) be subject exceeds 24 months.

This section is printed as amended by the YJCEA 1999, sch. 5, paras. 5 and 6, which are expected to come into force in April 2000.

If a term, or aggregate term, longer than 24 months is imposed by the court, the excess is automatically remitted (s. 74(4)). The period of 24 months has, of course, been the maximum aggregate term of detention in a young offender institution which might be imposed on an offender aged 15, 16 or 17, in which context there has been a similar rule relating to automatic remission of sentence length over 24 months. That rule has frequently caused difficulty for sentencers (see **E3.5**). The maximum duration of a secure training order has also been 24 months.

Requirement to Take Into Account Period Spent on Remand   E3.21

Crime and Disorder Act 1998, s. 74

(5) In determining the term of a detention and training order for an offence, the court shall take account of any period for which the offender has been remanded in custody in connection with the offence, or any other offence the charge for which was founded on the same facts or evidence.

(5A) Where a court proposes to make detention and training orders in respect of an offender for two or more offences—

(a) subsection (5) above shall not apply, but

(b) in determining the total term of the detention and training orders it proposes to make in respect of the offender, the court shall take account of the total period for which he has been remanded in custody in connection with any of those offences, or any other offence the charge for which was founded on the same facts or evidence.

(5B)   Once a period of remand has, under subsection (5) or (5A) above, been taken into account in relation to a detention and training order made in respect of an offender for any offence or offences, it shall not subsequently be taken account of (under either of those subsections) in relation to such an order made in respect of the offender for any other offence or offences.

This section is printed as amended by the YJCEA 1999, sch. 5, paras. 5 and 6. It is important to note that, with respect to the detention and training order, the court must take into account any period for which the offender has been remanded in custody. The detention and training order is the only custodial sentence (apart from where a court imposing a life sentence specifies a period under the C(S)A 1997, s. 28: see **E1.27**) where time spent on remand is not deducted automatically (see CJA 1967, s. 67, set out at **E1.6**). The requirement on the court to make such reduction may cause difficulty in relation to the specified duration of a detention and training order, which must be one of the seven periods set out in s. 73(5). Where the court is minded to impose a detention and training order of, say, 18 months, but the offender has served even a very short period on remand, it seems that the court has no option but to adjust the term of the order from 18 months to 12 months.

Breach of Order

E3.22   Section 77 of the CDA 1998 provides powers in relation to breach of supervision requirements in a detention training order. If it is proved to the satisfaction of a youth court acting for the relevant petty sessions area that the offender has failed to comply with supervision requirements specified in the order, the court may order the offender to be detained in secure accommodation for three months or the remainder of the term of the order (whichever is the shorter), or it may impose on the offender a fine not exceeding level 3. An offender may appeal against such an order to the Crown Court.

Section 78 relates to the commission of a further imprisonable offence by the offender during the currency of a detention and training order. The court, whether or not it passes any other sentence on the offender, may order him to be detained in secure accommodation from the date of the new order for the whole or part of the period between the date of commission of the new offence and the date at which the full term of the original order would have come to an end. Such an order may be made even where the offender is convicted of the new offence after the full term of the original order has come to an end, as long as the offence was committed within the supervision part of the order. The reinstated part of the sentence may be served before any sentence imposed for the new offence, or it may be served concurrently with that sentence, but the reinstated period shall be disregarded in determining the appropriate length of the new sentence.

Section 79 deals with the effect of imposing a detention and training order on a person already subject to a term of detention in a young offender institution, and *vice versa*.

SECTION E4: COMMUNITY SENTENCES: COMMUNITY SERVICE ORDERS

PROVISIONS COMMON TO COMMUNITY ORDERS UNDER THE CRIMINAL JUSTICE ACT 1991

Statutory Criteria for the Imposition of a Community Order

By the CJA 1991, s. 6(4), a 'community order' means any of the following: a community **E4.1** service order, a probation order, a combination order, a curfew order, a supervision order, an attendance centre order, a drug treatment and testing order and an action plan order. Section 6(1) restricts the imposition of community orders.

Criminal Justice Act 1991, s. 6

(1)   A court shall not pass on an offender a community sentence, that is to say, a sentence which consists of or includes one or more community orders, unless it is of the opinion that the offence, or the combination of the offence and one or more offences associated with it, was serious enough to warrant such a sentence.

The requirement in s. 6(1) that the court must consider 'the offence, or the combination of the offence and one or more offences associated with it' mirrors the provision in the CJA 1991, s. 1(2)(a), which relates to justifying the imposition of a custodial sentence (see **E1.8**). A definition of the phrase 'associated with' is provided by s. 31(2) and is considered at **E1.9**. An offence which is taken into consideration may count as an offence to be weighed in accordance with s. 31(2). In contrast with the justification for imposing custody, however, where the offence, or the combination of one or more offences, must be 'so serious that only such a sentence can be justified', a community sentence can be justified whenever the offence, or the combination of one or more offences, 'is serious enough to warrant such a sentence'. In *T* [1999] 2 Cr App R (S) 304 Maurice Kay J said that the phrase 'serious enough' should not be given too exacting an interpretation, since it was often one of the purposes of a community sentence to help the offender. There is no provision in s. 6 equivalent to s. 1(2)(b) (violent or sexual offences). The offender's previous convictions and response to previous sentences are relevant when determining the seriousness of an offence; so is the fact that the offence was committed when the offender was on bail, and the fact that the offence was racially aggravated (see **E1.16**). Section 6 should also be read subject to the provision relating to persistent petty offenders (see **E17.14**).

Criminal Justice Act 1991, s. 6

(2)   Subject to subsection (3) below, where a court passes a community sentence—
(a)   the particular order or orders comprising or forming part of the sentence shall be such as in the opinion of the court is, or taken together are, the most suitable for the offender; and
(b)   the restrictions on liberty imposed by the order or orders shall be such as in the opinion of the court are commensurate with the seriousness of the offence, or the combination of the offence and one or more offences associated with it.

Where an offender is being sentenced for several offences, the court's power to consider the whole pattern of the offending could lead it to pass a total sentence which is disproportionate to the overall seriousness of the offending behaviour. Section 28(2)(b) of the 1991 Act, in an attempt to avoid this, makes reference to the totality principle (see **E1.19**) by stating that the sentencer may mitigate the sentence by 'applying any rule of law as to the totality of sentences'. A difficulty with s. 6(2) is that the twin objectives of 'suitability' and 'seriousness' sometimes conflict, and the statute gives no indication of which objective should then prevail.

In forming its opinion that a community sentence is justified under the Criminal Justice Act 1991, s. 6(1), and in determining the appropriate restrictions on liberty imposed by the community order or orders comprising the community sentence, s. 7(1) of the 1991 Act requires the court to 'take into account all such information about the circumstances of the offence or (as the case may be) of the offence or offences associated with it (including any aggravating or mitigating factors) as is available to it' and, by s. 7(2), in forming an opinion about the suitability of the community order or orders for the offender, the court 'may take into account any information about the offender which is before it'. Further, by s. 28(1) of the 1991 Act, nothing shall prevent a court from 'mitigating an offender's sentence by taking into account any such matters as, in the opinion of the court, are relevant in mitigation of sentence', and, by s. 28(2)(a) and without prejudice to the generality of s. 28(1), the court may mitigate any penalty included in an offender's sentence by taking into account any other penalty included in that sentence. By s. 29(1), the court may take into account any previous convictions of the offender or any failure of his to respond to previous sentences.

Section 7(3) of the CJA 1991 requires that, subject to s. 7(3A), the court 'shall obtain and consider a pre-sentence report' before forming an opinion as to the suitability for the offender of one or more of the following orders:

    (a)   a probation order which includes additional requirements authorised by the PCCA 1973, sch. 1A;
    (b)   a drug treatment and testing order;
    (c)   a community service order;
    (d)   a combination order; or
    (e)   a supervision order which includes requirements imposed under the CYPA 1969, s. 12, 12A, 12AA, 12B or 12C.

For the definition of a pre-sentence report, see CJA 1991, s. 3(5), and **E1.8**. It follows from s. 7(3) that a pre-sentence report is not required by law whenever the court is considering imposing a probation order which does not include additional require-ments, a supervision order which does not include the specified requirements mentioned above, an attendance centre order, or an action plan order. No doubt in many cases, however, it would constitute good sentencing practice to obtain a report. Section 7(3) is subject to s. 7(3A), which states that the court may dispense with a report in any case where the offender is aged 18 or over and the court considers a report to be unnecessary. For offenders who are under the age of 18 years, s. 7(3B) provides that, in a case where the offence or any other offence associated with it is triable only on indictment, the court may dispense with a pre-sentence report if it considers a report to be unnecessary, but that if none of the offences before the court is triable only on indictment, the court must not dispense with obtaining a pre-sentence report 'unless there exists a previous pre-sentence report obtained in respect of the offender and the court has had regard to the information contained in that report or, if there is more than one such report, the most recent report'.

Section 7(4) states that no relevant community sentence shall be invalidated by failure of the court to obtain and consider a pre-sentence report but, on appeal against a relevant community sentence passed without the court having obtained a pre-sentence report, the appellate court must obtain and consider one, unless the court is of the opinion that the court below was justified in not calling for a report or that the court below was not so justified but, in the circumstances of the case at the time it is before the appellate court, it is unnecessary to obtain one.

COMMUNITY SERVICE ORDERS GENERALLY

Powers of Criminal Courts Act 1973, s. 14

E4.2

(1)   Where a person of or over 16 years of age is convicted of an offence punishable with imprisonment (not being an offence the sentence for which is fixed by law or falls to be imposed under section 2(2), 3(2) or 4(2) of the Crime (Sentences) Act 1997), the court by or before which he is convicted may, instead of dealing with him in any other way (but subject to subsection (2) below) make an order (in this Act referred to as 'a community service order') requiring him to perform unpaid work in accordance with the subsequent provisions of this Act.

The reference in this subsection to an offence punishable with imprisonment shall be construed without regard to any prohibition or restriction imposed by or under any enactment on the imprisonment of young offenders; and for the purposes of this subsection a sentence falls to be imposed under section 2(2), 3(2) or 4(2) of the Crime (Sentences) Act 1997 if it is required by that provision and the court is not of the opinion there mentioned.

(1A)   The number of hours which a person may be required to work under a community service order shall be specified in the order and shall be in the aggregate—

(a)   not less than 40; and

(b)   not more than 240.

(2)   A court shall not make a community service order in respect of any offender unless the court, after hearing (if the court thinks it necessary) a probation officer or social worker of a local authority social services department, is satisfied that the offender is a suitable person to perform work under such an order.

(2A)   Subject to paragraphs 3 and 4 of schedule 3 to the Criminal Justice Act 1991 (reciprocal enforcement of certain orders) a court shall not make a community service order in respect of an offender unless it is satisfied that provision for him to perform work under such an order can be made under the arrangements for persons to perform work under such orders which exist in the petty sessions area in which he resides or will reside.

Section 14(1) and (2) is printed as amended by the C(S)A 1997 and by the CDA 1998, sch. 7. The C(S)A 1997, by s. 38(2)(b), abolished the requirement that, before a community service order can be made, the offender must consent. It is at least arguable that the abolition of this requirement contravenes Art. 4(2) of the European Convention on Human Rights: 'No-one shall be required to perform forced or compulsory labour'.

Unless the period during which the community service order is to be performed is extended, by virtue of the CJA 1991, sch. 2, para. 15 (see **E4.9**), the work must be completed during the period of 12 months beginning with the date of the order but, unless revoked, the order remains in force until the offender has completed the number of hours specified in it (PCCA 1973, s. 15(2)).

For the normal requirement to obtain a pre-sentence report, see **E4.1**.

Where a court adjourns for the purpose of obtaining a report to assess the offender's suitability for community service, and if the report shows the offender to be suitable, the court should normally make such an order to avoid feelings of injustice which would otherwise be aroused in the offender (referred to as 'an important principle of sentencing' in *Gillam* (1980) 2 Cr App R (S) 267; followed in *Millwood* (1982) 4 Cr App R (S) 281). For further discussion of this issue, see **D17.27**.

Powers of Criminal Courts Act 1973, s. 14

(3)   Where a court makes community service orders in respect of two or more offences of which the offender has been convicted by or before the court, the court may direct that the hours of work specified in any of those orders shall be concurrent with or additional to those specified in any other of those orders, but so that the total number of hours which are not concurrent shall not exceed the maximum specified in paragraph (b) of subsection (1A) above.

Section 14(3) has direct application to the situation where a court is imposing two community service orders on the same occasion. In such a case, the total number of hours ordered must not exceed 240. In *Evans* [1977] 1 WLR 27, the offender was convicted in a magistrates' court and a sentence of 60 hours' community service was ordered. Three days later he appeared before the Crown Court in respect of a burglary and was given a further 60 hours for that offence, consecutive to the first. The Court of Appeal referred to s. 14(3) and said that nothing in that subsection prevented consecutive community service orders, whether they were imposed on the same or different occasions, provided that 'there should not be orders totalling more than 240 hours in existence at the same time in respect of the same offender'. According to *Anderson* (1989) 11 Cr App R (S) 147, when consecutive community service orders are made, the limitation to 240 hours refers to the total number of hours ordered, rather than to the total which remain to be served. In *Siha* (1992) 13 Cr App R (S) 588, the Court of Appeal said that while s. 14(3) did not actually prevent the imposition of consecutive community service orders on different occasions which together totalled more than 240 hours, sentencers should remember that Parliament had prescribed 240 hours as the maximum to be imposed on a single occasion. Where an offender is made subject to consecutive community service orders, those orders should be regarded 'for all practical purposes' as a single order (*Meredith* (1994) 15 Cr App R (S) 528).

Powers of Criminal Courts Act 1973, s. 14

(4)   A community service order shall specify the petty sessions area in which the offender resides or will reside; and the functions conferred by the subsequent provisions of this Act on the relevant officer shall be discharged by a probation officer appointed for or assigned to the area for the time being specified in the order (whether under this subsection or by virtue of part IV of schedule 2 to the Criminal Justice Act 1991), or by a person appointed for the purposes of those provisions by the probation and after-care committee for that area.

(5)   Before making a community service order the court shall explain to the offender in ordinary language—

(a)   the purpose and effect of the order (and in particular the requirements of the order as specified in section 15 of this Act);

(b)   the consequences which may follow under part II of schedule 2 to the Criminal Justice Act 1991 if he fails to comply with any of those requirements; and

(c)   that the court has under part III and IV of that schedule the power to review the order on the application either of the offender or of a probation officer.

For s. 15 see below. By the CDA 1998, sch. 8, para. 27, references in s. 14(2), (4), (5)(c) and (6) to a 'probation officer' also include reference, where the offender is aged under 18, to a member of a youth offending team; para. 28 is in force in certain pilot areas.

Powers of Criminal Courts Act 1973, s. 14

(6)   The court by which a community service order is made shall forthwith give copies of the order to a probation officer assigned to the court and he shall give a copy to the offender and to the relevant officer, and the court shall, except where it is itself a magistrates' court acting for the petty sessions area specified in the order, send to the clerk to the justices for the petty sessions area specified in the order a copy of the order, together with such documents and information relating to the case as it considers likely to be of assistance to a court acting for that area in exercising its functions in relation to the order.

In *Walsh* v *Barlow* [1985] 1 WLR 90, it was argued by the offender, without success, that a community service order which had been made in respect of him by a magistrates' court was ineffective, as no copy had been delivered to him by the relevant officer, as required by s. 14(6). Stephen Brown LJ held (at pp. 100–1) that such delivery was 'not a prerequisite to the coming into force of the order; the order comes into force as soon as the court has pronounced the sentence . . .'.

Powers of Criminal Courts Act 1973, s. 15

(1)   An offender in respect of whom a community service order is in force shall—
(a)   keep in touch with the relevant officer in accordance with such instructions as he may from time to time be given by that officer and notify him of any change of address; and
(b)   perform for the number of hours specified in the order such work at such times as he may be instructed by the relevant officer.

For the meaning of 'the relevant officer', see s. 14(4), above. The instructions given by the relevant officer under s. 15(1) 'shall, so far as practicable, be such as to avoid any conflict with the offender's religious beliefs, or with the requirements of any other community order to which he may be subject, and any interference with the times, if any, at which he normally works or attends a school or other educational establishment' (s. 15(3)).

COMMUNITY SERVICE ORDERS: SENTENCING PRINCIPLES

Range of Hours in Relation to Sentence Offender Would Otherwise Have Received

The sentencing principles described in this paragraph must be read in the light of the **E4.3** criteria for the imposition of community sentences in general (see **E4.1**). An example of the application of these criteria by the Court of Appeal is *Small* (1993) 14 Cr App R (S) 405. The 20-year-old offender, who was employed as operations manager by a company supplying pizzas, pleaded guilty to three counts of theft. On three occasions he failed to pay into the bank money received in the shop, totalling £1,080. The sentencer considered that the offences were so serious that only a custodial sentence could be justified, and imposed a term of three months' detention in a young offender institution. The Court of Appeal, having regard to the offender's age, good record and information in the pre-sentence report that the offender had been insufficiently mature to cope with the volume of work and degree of responsibility imposed upon him, quashed the custodial sentence but held that the offences were serious enough to warrant a community sentence. The pre-sentence report suggested that the offender did not need supervision, but that a sentence commensurate with the seriousness of the offence would be a 'mid-length term of community service'. The Court of Appeal substituted a community service order for 50 hours, though this sentence made some unspecified allowance for the fact that the offender had already spent one month in custody.

In *Davies* (1984) 6 Cr App R (S) 224, the Court of Appeal imposed a community service order of 60 hours on an offender who was peripherally involved in an attack on another youth, and who pleaded guilty to stealing the victim's jacket, where 'it was wrong in principle to have imposed an immediate custodial sentence'. Sixty hours' community service was held to be appropriate in *Hamilton* (1988) 10 Cr App R (S) 383, where the offender stole property worth £180 and was also approved in *Zaman* (1992) 12 Cr App R (S) 657, where a 19-year-old stole a radio from a car. In *Parkes* (1988) 10 Cr App R (S) 494, the offender pleaded guilty to two counts of handling stolen goods, namely cars: 12 months' imprisonment quashed and 100 hours' community service substituted, to take into account the two months in custody the offender had already served. One hundred and eighty hours' community service was upheld in *Bushell* (1987) 9 Cr App R (S) 537 on a 17-year-old who pleaded guilty in respect of taking a conveyance and crashing it into a van, damaging the car beyond repair. In a case of offenders who were involved in the spraying of paint on carriages at a London Underground depot (*Ferreira* (1988) 10 Cr App R (S) 343), the Court of Appeal replaced custodial sentences with community service orders of 120 hours, Farquharson J commenting that community service was 'designed' for such a case: 'They have done this wanton damage and therefore it behoves them to do some service to the public to put it right.'

Appropriateness with Respect to Serious Offences

E4.4   The sentencing principles described in this paragraph must now be read in the light of the criteria for the imposition of community sentences in general (see **E4.1**).

A community service order may, on occasion, be appropriate in a case involving violence (*McDiarmid* (1980) 2 Cr App R (S) 130, where the offender, aged 18 and of previous good character, in the course of a disturbance in a public house, threw a beer glass at a man, causing a cut lip). However, in a case involving more serious violence (*Heyfron* (1980) 2 Cr App R (S) 230), it was held that community service was 'wholly wrong'. In that case the accused attacked a man who had apparently made sexual advances to his common-law wife, causing severe facial injuries.

Community service may be imposed in cases of burglary, even, on occasion, of dwelling houses. In *Coleman* (1981) 3 Cr App R (S) 178, the Court of Appeal, while agreeing with the trial judge that those who commit burglary in dwellings must expect custodial sentences, varied the sentence to community service in the light of the offender's 'fairly minor' previous convictions. In *Seymour* (1983) 5 Cr App R (S) 85, the offender was 28 and had been sentenced on several previous occasions for burglary, including four custodial sentences. The Court of Appeal varied an 18-month custodial sentence to a community service order, commenting that 'there are other ways of protecting society than merely taking a young criminal out of circulation for what must be a limited period. If one can achieve at any rate some change of heart by some alternative sentence, one may be doing as well for society.' In *Brown* (1981) 3 Cr App R (S) 294, community service was 'tailor-made' for a 19-year-old with no previous convictions, who, in breach of trust, had, together with a co-defendant, committed burglary of his employer's premises, with loss of goods to the value of £2,850. The Court emphasised the offender's clean record (though a 'light' criminal record would, apparently, have produced the same result), his stable home background with wife and young child, good work record, genuine remorse, and only slight chance of re-offending.

Mixing Community Service Orders with Other Sentences or Orders

E4.5   A community service order and a probation order may not be combined together *per se* when sentencing for the same offence (CJA 1991, s. 6(3)) but in a certain mix they form a combination order (see **E6**). Nor can a community service order and a probation order be imposed for separate offences sentenced on the same occasion (*Gilding* v *DPP* (1998) *The Times*, 20 May 1998). It is possible to combine a community service order with a curfew order (see **E7**). A community service order may be combined with an order for costs, a disqualification of any kind imposed upon the offender, a compensation order or a forfeiture order made under the PCCA 1973, s. 43, although specific provision to this effect in the PCCA 1973, s. 14(8), was repealed by the CDA 1998.

A community service order should not be imposed on the same occasion as an immediate sentence of imprisonment (nor, it is submitted, any other custodial sentence), even though the sentences relate to different counts (*Starie* (1979) 69 Cr App R 239). It was held in *Ray* (1984) 6 Cr App R (S) 26 that a community service order and a suspended sentence of imprisonment could not be imposed on the same occasion. A community service order cannot be combined with a discharge when sentencing for a single offence, since a discharge is imposed only where 'it is inexpedient to inflict punishment' (PCCA 1973, s. 1A(1)), but these two measures may, of course, be used for different offences sentenced on the same occasion.

When combining measures on sentence, regard should be had to the CJA 1991, s. 28(2)(a), which states that nothing 'shall prevent a court from mitigating any penalty included in an offender's sentence by taking into account any other penalty included in that sentence'.

ENFORCEMENT OF CERTAIN COMMUNITY ORDERS UNDER THE CRIMINAL JUSTICE ACT 1991

The CJA 1991 contains provisions for breach, revocation and amendment of various **E4.6** community orders. Schedule 2 to the 1991 Act applies to community service orders, probation orders, curfew orders and drug treatment and testing orders; all of these are designated 'community orders' in the CJA 1991, s. 6(4). Schedule 2 also applies to combination orders, since they are treated as a mix between a probation order and a community service order (CJA 1991, s. 11 and sch. 2, para. 1(2)). Although supervision orders, attendance centre orders and action plan orders are also community orders within the meaning of the 1991 Act, sch. 2 does not apply to them. For enforcement provisions in relation to them, see **E8.4**, **E9.3** and **E11.3** respectively. Nor does sch. 2 apply to discharges, which are not community orders within s. 6(4); for breach of conditional discharge, see **E14.5**. Where an offender is convicted of a further offence while a relevant order is in force, the appropriate procedure is revocation (see **E4.8**) and not breach (sch. 2, para. 5(1)).

Breach of Community Order

Schedule 2, para. 2, states that, if at any time while a relevant order is in force in respect **E4.7** of an offender, it appears on information to a justice of the peace acting for the petty sessions area concerned that the offender has failed to comply with any of the requirements of the order, the justice may either issue a summons requiring the offender to appear or, if the information is in writing and on oath, issue a warrant for his arrest. Paragraph 3 deals with the relevant powers of the magistrates' court, para. 4 deals with the powers of the Crown Court.

Criminal Justice Act 1991, sch. 2, paras 3 and 4

3.—(1)   If it is proved to the satisfaction of the magistrates' court before which an offender appears or is brought under paragraph 2 above that he has failed without reasonable excuse to comply with any of the requirements of the relevant order, the court may deal with him in respect of the failure in any one of the following ways, namely—

(a)   it may impose on him a fine not exceeding £1,000;

(b)   subject to paragraph 6(3) to (5) below, it may make a community service order in respect of him;

(c)   where—

(i)   the relevant order is a probation order and the offender is under the age of twenty-one years, or

(ii)   the relevant order is a curfew order and the offender is under the age of sixteen years,

and the court has been notified as required by subsection (1) of section 17 of the [CJA 1982], it may (subject to paragraph 6(6) below) make in respect of him an order under that section (attendance centre orders); or

(d)   where the relevant order was made by a magistrates' court, it may deal with him, for the offence in respect of which the order was made, in any manner in which it could deal with him if he had just been convicted by the court of the offence.

(2)   In dealing with an offender under sub-paragraph (1)(d) above, a magistrates' court—

(a)   shall take into account the extent to which the offender has complied with the requirements of the relevant order; and

(b)   in the case of an offender who has wilfully and persistently failed to comply with those requirements, may impose a custodial sentence notwithstanding anything in section 1(2) of this Act.

(2A)   Where a magistrates' court deals with an offender under sub-paragraph (1)(d) above, it shall revoke the relevant order if it is still in force.

(3)   Where a relevant order was made by the Crown Court and a magistrates' court has power to deal with the offender under sub-paragraph (1)(a), (b) or (c) above, it may instead

commit him to custody or release him on bail until he can be brought or appear before the Crown Court.

(4) A magistrates' court which deals with an offender's case under sub-paragraph (3) above shall send to the Crown Court—

(a) a certificate signed by a justice of the peace certifying that the offender has failed to comply with the requirements of the relevant order in the respect specified in the certificate; and

(b) such other particulars of the case as may be desirable;

and a certificate purporting to be so signed shall be admissible as evidence of the failure before the Crown Court.

(5) A person sentenced under sub-paragraph (1)(d) above for an offence may appeal to the Crown Court against the sentence.

4.—(1) Where under paragraph 2 or by virtue of paragraph 3(3) above an offender is brought or appears before the Crown Court and it is proved to the satisfaction of the court that he has failed without reasonable excuse to comply with any of the requirements of the relevant order, that court may deal with him in respect of the failure in any one of the following ways, namely—

[(a) to (c) identical to sch. 2, para. 3(1)(a) to (c) above]; or

(d) it may deal with him, for the offence in respect of which the order was made, in any manner in which it could deal with him if he had just been convicted before the Crown Court of the offence.

(2) In dealing with the offender under sub-paragraph (1)(d) above, the Crown Court—

[(a) and (b) identical to sch. 2, para. 3(1)(a) and (b) above].

(2A) Where the Crown Court deals with an offender under sub-paragraph (1)(d) above, it shall revoke the relevant order if it is still in force.

Any breach should either be admitted by the offender or be formally proved (*Devine* [1956] 1 WLR 236) and the prosecution should be in a position to put before the court the facts of the original offence, at least in outline, as well as the facts of the breach (*Clarke* [1997] 2 Cr App R (S) 163). If the court employs the option provided by para. 3(1)(b) or 4(1)(b) in respect of an offender who is in breach of a community service order, the total number of hours under both orders must not exceed 240 hours (para. 6(3)(b)). For CJA 1982, s. 17, see **E9.1** (attendance centre orders). The exercise of any of the options in para. 3(1)(a) to (c) or para. 4(1)(a) to (c) is without prejudice to the continuation of the original order. There would appear, in principle, to be no limit to the number of occasions upon which the court might exercise these options in respect of subsequent breaches of the same order by an offender but, if the offender can be said to have 'wilfully and persistently failed to comply' with the order, para. 3(2)(b) or 4(2)(b) may be invoked. By para. 3(2) or 4(2), when choosing to deal with an offender under para. 3(1)(d) or 4(1)(d), the court:

(a) shall take into account the extent to which the offender has complied with the requirements of the relevant order; and

(b) in the case of an offender who has wilfully and persistently failed to comply with those requirements, may imposed a custodial sentence notwithstanding anything in section 1(2) of this Act.

The effect of a court exercising its powers under para. 3(1)(d) or 4(1)(d) is that the original order will cease to have effect. There is perhaps an expectation that, once the court turns to para. 3(1)(d) or 4(1)(d), the offender is facing a custodial sentence, but this is not inevitable, particularly where, having regard to para. 3(2)(a) or 4(2)(a), the offender has completed a substantial portion of the original order. Paragraphs 3(2)(b) and 4(2)(b) deal with the case of an offender who has 'wilfully and persistently failed to comply' with the terms of the community order, and empower the court to substitute a custodial sentence instead, notwithstanding the general restrictions on the imposition of custodial sentences contained in s. 1(2) of the CJA 1991. Custody is not inevitable in such a case; the paragraphs state that the court 'may' impose such a sentence. In *Platts* [1998] 2 Cr App R (S) 34 the offender failed to comply with a condition of his probation order, and subsequently he could not be found. By the time he was arrested and the matter came before the Crown Court dealing with the breach, the term of the probation order had expired. It was argued that the court had no power to revoke an order which had expired, by analogy with *Cousin* (1994) 15 Cr App R (S) 516 (see **E4.8**). The Court of Appeal held, however, that the cases were distinguishable. Where the offender was before the court for breach of the order, rather than for commission of a further offence, it was open to the court where appropriate to revoke the community order and re-sentence for the original offence. Otherwise, the offender could escape the consequences of breach simply by keeping out of the way until the order had expired.

Where a custodial sentence is imposed consequent upon breach of a community sentence, the court must, of course, have regard to the normal limitations upon the imposition of custodial sentences, such as the restriction on the maximum custodial sentence which may be imposed by a magistrates' court. If the court imposes a custodial sentence in place of a community order, it seems that it should also normally observe the statutory restrictions in the CJA 1991 with respect to the imposition and length of custodial sentence (see **E1.8** and **E1.13**). This means that custody should be imposed consequent upon breach only where the original offence was so serious that only custody could be justified for it. It was explained by the Court of Appeal in *Oliver* [1993] 1 WLR 177 that the mere fact that the offender has been dealt with by way of a community sentence need not be inconsistent with a finding that the offence was so serious that only custody could be justified for it, since the court which passed the original sentence may have taken account of matters of personal mitigation which may be less persuasive now, in light of breach of the order. If, however, the court is relying upon para. 3(2)(b) or 4(2)(b), that the offender has 'wilfully and persistently failed to comply' with the requirements of the community order, it is clear that the court is not required to justify the imposition of custody in accordance with s. 1(2) of the 1991 Act.

In *Robinson* (1986) 8 Cr App R (S) 327, the Court of Appeal held that a court should not deal with an offender for breach of a community service order by way of a suspended sentence, where the effect of that would be to place the offender at risk of custody long after the original offence had been committed.

It is clear that where custody is imposed consequent upon breach of a community order, allowance should be made for any period spent by the offender in custody on remand before the community order was passed, since such time will not count as part of that sentence for the purposes of the CJA 1967, s. 67, though the extent of any allowance is a matter for judicial discretion (*McIntyre* (1985) 7 Cr App R (S) 196; *Neville* (1993) 14 Cr App R (S) 768; *Henderson* [1997] 2 Cr App R (S) 266). The extent of the allowance given should be indicated when custody is imposed (*Henderson*).

Where the original community order was made by the Crown Court, a magistrates' court has power to deal with the offender under para. 3(1)(a), (b) or (c) but may not revoke the order. It may, instead of dealing with him, commit the offender to the Crown Court to be dealt with there. The Crown Court has no jurisdiction to deal with the breach of a community order unless the matter has first come to the magistrates' court and the offender is then sent to the Crown Court under para. 3(3). The Crown Court's powers are identical to those of the magistrates' court, except that, under the equivalent power to para. 3(1)(d) (which for the Crown Court is para. 4(1)(d)), it is empowered to deal with the offender in any manner in which it could deal with him if he had just been convicted of that offence before the Crown Court. Schedule 2, para. 4(1)(d) is printed above as amended by the CDA 1998, sch. 7, para. 46, which, by substituting the words 'before the Crown Court' for 'by or before the court', now makes it clear beyond doubt that where the Crown Court is dealing with an offender on breach the Crown Court is not restricted to the sentencing powers of the magistrates' courts.

Where an offender who suffered from arthritis was sentenced to 100 hours' community service, but did not commence the work as required and subsequently produced a medical certificate, the Court of Appeal indicated that the best way of dealing with such a case was to proceed by way of breach under sch. 2, paras 2 and 3, and for the court to determine whether there was 'reasonable excuse' for the failure to comply with the terms of the order or whether the offender had simply tried to 'con' the court (*Booth* [1998] 1 Cr App R (S) 132, following *Jackson* (1984) 6 Cr App R (S) 202 where the offender had claimed that work commitments rendered her unable to comply with the terms of the order). Breach procedure was more appropriate here than making application for revocation of the order, to ensure that the allegations of breach were properly explored and proved (see **E4.8**). See also *Hammon* [1998] 2 Cr App R (S) 202.

Revocation of Community Order

E4.8 The relevant provisions are paras 7 to 11 of sch. 2 to the CJA 1991. Paragraph 7 allows for the revocation of a community order, on application to a magistrates' court acting for the petty sessions area concerned, by the offender or by the responsible officer, on a number of grounds to do with the offender's change of circumstances since the order was imposed. The court may, on such application, revoke the order or (taking account of the extent to which the offender has complied with the order) make an order that the offender should be dealt with in some other manner for the offence in respect of which the order was made (para. 7(2)(a)); if the original order was made by the Crown Court, the court may commit the offender to the Crown Court (para. 7(2)(b)). A common situation in which para. 7 is employed is an application to bring a probation order to an end early, in light of the offender's good progress under para. 7(3).

Criminal Justice Act 1991, sch. 2, para. 8

(1)   This paragraph applies where an offender in respect of whom a relevant order is in force—
(a)   is convicted of an offence before the Crown Court; or
(b)   is committed by a magistrates' court to the Crown Court for sentence and is brought or appears before the Crown Court; or
(c)   by virtue of paragraph 7(2)(b) above is brought or appears before the Crown Court.
(1A)   This paragraph also applies where—
(a)   a drug treatment and testing order made by the Crown Court is in force in respect of an offender; and
(b)   the offender or the responsible officer applies to the Crown Court for the order to be revoked or for the offender to be dealt with in some other manner for the offence in respect of which the order was made.
(2)   If it appears to the Crown Court to be in the interests of justice to do so, having regard to circumstances which have arisen since the order was made, the Crown Court may—
(a)   revoke the order; or
(b)   revoke the order and deal with the offender, for the offence in respect of which the order was made, in any manner in which the court which made the order could deal with him if he had just been convicted of that offence by or before the court which made the order.

The circumstances in which a probation order or drug treatment and testing order may be revoked under para. 8(2)(a) include the offender's making good progress or his responding satisfactorily to supervision or treatment (para. 8(3)). The Crown Court may revoke a community order and sentence the offender for the offence in respect of which the order was made even though there is no application for termination of the order, and no failure by the offender to comply with it (*Williams* (1979) 1 Cr App R (S) 78), but when dealing with an offender under para. 8(2)(b) the Crown Court must take into account the extent to which the offender has complied with the requirements of the order (para. 8(4)). When exercising its powers under para. 8(2)(b) to revoke a community order passed by a magistrates' court and deal with the offender for the original offence, the Crown Court is limited to the powers of the magistrates' court. In *Ogden* [1996] 2 Cr App R (S) 386 the Court of Appeal held that the Crown Court was so limited and the wording of para. 8(2)(b), as substituted by the CDA 1998, sch. 7, para. 46(10), makes the matter clear beyond doubt. It should be noted that it is not necessary for the application of these powers that the new offence must be committed during the period of the community order but, where an offender subject to a community order is convicted by the Crown Court of an offence committed before it was passed, it will seldom be appropriate, if the community order is revoked, to pass a further sentence for the offence in respect of which the community order was made. This is because the offender has not broken the terms of the order by committing a further offence whilst it was current (*Cawley* (1994) 15 Cr App R (S) 209, followed in *Saphier* [1997] 1 Cr App R (S) 235 and *Reid* [1998] 2 Cr App R (S) 40, but see *Kenny* [1996] 1 Cr App R (S) 397 and *Day* [1997] 2 Cr App R (S) 328). Further, the decisions in *Bennett* (1994) 15 Cr App R (S) 213 and *Cousin* (1994) 15 Cr App R (S) 516 establish that, where the offender has committed an offence during the currency of a community order but is convicted by the Crown Court of that offence after the term of the community order to which he was subject has come to an end, the Crown Court has no power to revoke that order and no power to deal with the offender for the original offence.

Where an offender is convicted of a further offence by a magistrates' court while he is subject to a community order imposed by the Crown Court, the Crown Court ordinarily has power to revoke the community order only if there has been an application under para. 7(2)(b) or on a committal for sentence under the MCA 1980, s. 38 (*Adams* (1994) 15 Cr App R (S) 417).

It is clear that where custody is imposed consequent upon revocation of a community order, allowance should be made for any period spent by the offender in custody on remand before the community order was passed, since such time will not count as part of that sentence for the purposes of the CJA 1967, s. 67, though the extent of any allowance is a matter for judicial discretion (*McDonald* (1988) 10 Cr App R (S) 458; *Gyorgy* (1989) 11 Cr App R (S) 1).

Case law indicates that where a community order is revoked and the offender is sentenced for a further offence a separate sentence should normally be passed for the original offence (*Fry* [1955] 1 WLR 28; *Rowsell* (1988) 10 Cr App R (S) 411). It was held in *Anderson* (1982) 4 Cr App R (S) 252 that, where a custodial sentence is imposed for the new offence and a consecutive custodial sentence is imposed for the original offence, this is subject to the totality principle (see **E1.19**). In *Anderson*, the Court of Appeal varied two consecutive sentences of six months' imprisonment, imposed for the offences for which the community order had been made, so as to make them run concurrently with the substantial sentence of imprisonment which had been imposed in respect of the new offences. *Anderson* was followed in *Cook* (1985) 7 Cr App R (S) 249.

Criminal Justice Act 1991, sch. 2, para. 9

(1)   This paragraph applies where—

    (a)   an offender in respect of whom a relevant order is in force is convicted of an offence—

        (i)   by a magistrates' court other than a magistrates' court acting for the petty sessions area concerned; or

        (ii)   where the relevant order is a drug treatment and testing order, by a magistrates' court which is not responsible for the order; and

    (b)   the court imposes a custodial sentence on the offender.

(2)   If it appears to the court, on the application of the offender or the responsible officer, that it would be in the interests of justice to do so having regard to circumstances which have arisen since the order was made, the court may—

    (a)   if the order was made by a magistrates' court, revoke it; and

    (b)   if the order was made by the Crown Court, commit the offender in custody or release him on bail until he can be brought or appear before the Crown Court.

Where, by virtue of para. 9(2)(b), an offender is before the Crown Court that court may revoke the order (para. 10). In such a case the Crown Court may revoke the order but has no power to deal with the original offence by imposing a fresh sentence for it.

Amendment of Community Order

E4.9   Schedule 2 to the CJA 1991 (paras 12 to 18) deals with various powers of amendment of community orders. Paragraph 12 allows for amendments to be made to a community service order, a probation order, a curfew order or a combination order to take account of a change in the offender's place of residence from one petty sessions area to another; para. 13 deals with amendment of the requirements or duration of a probation order or a curfew order; para. 14 relates to probation orders which contain a requirement of mental treatment or treatment for alcohol or drug dependence and provides for variation or cancellation of that requirement; para. 14A regulates the amendment of drug treatment and testing orders; para. 15 allows for the extension of the period of a community service order beyond 12 months for reasons such as the offender's changed work commitments or ill health.

SECTION E5: COMMUNITY SENTENCES: PROBATION ORDERS

PROBATION ORDERS GENERALLY

Power to Make Probation Orders

A probation order is a 'community order' within the meaning of the CJA 1991, s. 6(4), **E5.1** so that the imposition of a probation order requires justification in terms of the seriousness of the offence, or the offence and one or more offences associated with it. The relevant statutory criteria are set out at **E4.1**.

Where the PCCA 1973, s. 2, is set out below, it is set out with the amendments made by the CDA 1998 which were brought into force on 30 September 1998 in pilot areas only. The changes made arise from the creation in certain areas of youth offending teams; where no such teams are in existence for an area, the probation service continues to carry responsibility for supervision.

Powers of Criminal Courts Act 1973, s. 2

(1)   Where a court by or before which a person of or over the age of sixteen years is convicted of an offence (not being an offence for which the sentence is fixed by law or falls to be imposed under section 2(2), 3(2) or 4(2) of the Crime (Sentences) Act 1997) is of the opinion that the supervision of the offender is desirable in the interests of—
  (a)   securing the rehabilitation of the offender; or
  (b)   protecting the public from harm from him or preventing the commission by him of further offences,
the court may make a probation order, that is to say, an order requiring him to be under supervision for a period specified in the order of not less than six months nor more than three years.

(2)   A probation order shall specify the petty sessions area in which the offender resides or will reside; and the offender shall, subject to paragraph 12 of schedule 2 to the Criminal Justice Act 1991 (offenders who change their residence), be required to be under the supervision of—
  (a)   a probation officer appointed for or assigned to that area; or
  (b)   where the offender is under the age of 18 years, a member of a youth offending team as established by the local authority within whose area it appears to the court that the offender resides or will reside.

The minimum qualifying age for a probation order is 16, the same as for community service orders. There is an overlap between probation orders and supervision orders, in that offenders aged 16 and 17 will qualify for either sentence (for supervision orders, see **E8**). For offenders who change their residence, see **E4.9**.

Powers of Criminal Courts Act 1973, s. 2

(3)   Before making a probation order, the court shall explain to the offender in ordinary language—
  (a)   the effect of the order (including any additional requirements proposed to be included in the order in accordance with section 3 below);
  (b)   the consequences which may follow under schedule 2 to the Criminal Justice Act 1991 if he fails to comply with any of the requirements of the order; and
  (c)   that the court has under that schedule power to review the order on the application of either the offender or of the supervising officer.

(4)   The court by which a probation order is made shall forthwith give copies of the order to a probation officer assigned to the court, and he shall give a copy—

(a)   to the offender;
(b)   to the person responsible for the offender's supervision; and
(c)   to the person in charge of any institution in which the offender is required by the order to reside.
(5)   The court by which such an order is made shall also, except where it itself acts for the petty sessions area specified in the order, send to the clerk to the justices for that area—
(a)   a copy of the order; and
(b)   such documents and information relating to the case as it considers likely to be of assistance to a court acting for that area in the exercise of its functions in relation to the order.

For the PCCA 1973, s. 3, see **E5.2**; for sch. 2 to the 1991 Act (breach of community orders), see **E4.7**. It should be noted that, where a requirement as to treatment for drug or alcohol dependency or a requirement as to treatment for a mental condition is to be included in a probation order, the offender must express his willingness to comply with that requirement (see further **E5.5** and **E24.1**). Section 1(3) of the CJA 1991 (see **E1.8**) states that a court may pass a custodial sentence on an offender 'if he fails to express his willingness to comply with a requirement which is proposed by the court to be included in a probation order . . . and which requires an expression of such willingness'. Although s. 2(3) requires 'the court' to explain the effect of the order to the offender in ordinary language, see, by analogy, *Wehner* [1977] 1 WLR 1142, where it was held that explanation of the effect of a conditional discharge might be left to the offender's lawyer. On a failure to give a copy of the order to the probationer, see, by analogy, *Walsh* v *Barlow* [1985] 1 WLR 90, considered at **E4.2**. It was held in *Palmer* (1992) 13 Cr App R (S) 595 that a court dealing with a person for contempt of court has no power to make a probation order.

By the PCCA 1973, s. 12(1), on making a probation order, a court may, 'if it thinks it expedient for the purpose of reformation of the offender, allow any person who consents to do so to give security for the good behaviour of the offender'.

Requirements in Probation Orders

E5.2   **Powers of Criminal Courts Act 1973, s. 2**

(6)   An offender in respect of whom a probation order is made shall keep in touch with the person responsible for his supervision in accordance with such instructions as he may from time to time be given by that person and shall notify him of any change of address.

Powers of Criminal Courts Act 1973, s. 3

(1)   Subject to subsection (2) below, a probation order may in addition require the offender to comply during the whole or any part of the probation period with such requirements as the court, having regard to the circumstances of the case, considers desirable in the interests of—
(a)   securing the rehabilitation of the offender; or
(b)   protecting the public from harm from him or preventing the commission by him of further offences.
(2)   Without prejudice to the power of the court under section 35 of this Act to make a compensation order, the payment of sums by way of damages for injury or compensation for loss shall not be included among the additional requirements of a probation order.
(3)   Without prejudice to the generality of subsection (1) above, the additional requirements which may be included in a probation order shall include the requirements which are authorised by schedule 1A to this Act.

For sch. 1A to the 1973 Act, see below. In *Rogers* v *Cullen* [1982] 1 WLR 729, Lord Bridge indicated that no requirement should be included in a probation order which would 'introduce a custodial or other element', and that any discretion conferred on the probation officer to regulate the probationer's activities should be 'confined within well defined limits'. In *Practice Note* (1952) 35 Cr App R 207, Lord Goddard CJ deprecated 'vague' conditions being written into probation orders. By the Firearms Act 1968, s. 52(1), the court may include a requirement in a probation order that the offender shall not possess, use, or carry a firearm. There is no power to include a condition that the defendant leaves the country and does not return (*McCartan* [1958] 1 WLR 933).

For the normal requirement to obtain a pre-sentence report before imposing a probation order containing any of the additional requirements authorised by sch. 1A, see **E4.1**.

Powers of Criminal Courts Act 1973, sch. 1A, paras. 1 and 2

Requirements as to residence
   1.—(1)   Subject to sub-paragraphs (2) and (3) below, a probation order may include requirements as to the residence of the offender.
   (2)   Before making a probation order containing any such requirement, the court shall consider the home surroundings of the offender.
   (3)   Where a probation order requires the offender to reside in an approved hostel or any other institution, the period for which he is so required to reside shall be specified in the order.

Requirements as to activities etc.
   2.—(1)   Subject to the provisions of this paragraph, a probation order may require the offender—
      (a)   to present himself to a person or persons specified in the order at a place or places so specified;
      (b)   to participate or refrain from participating in activities specified in the order—
      (i)   on a day or days so specified; or
      (ii)   during the probation period or such portion of it as may be so specified.

Before making a requirement under para. 2(1), the court must consult a probation officer and must be satisfied that it is feasible to secure compliance with it (para. 2(2)). A place specified in the order must have been approved by the relevant probation committee as providing facilities suitable for persons subject to probation orders (para. 2(5)). By para. 2(3), no requirement which is mentioned in para. 2(1)(a) or which involves participation in activities may be included in an order if it involves the co-operation of a person other than the probationer and the probation officer, unless that other person consents to its inclusion.

A requirement mentioned in para. 2(1)(a) or involving participation in activities may require the probationer to present himself at a place or participate in activities for not more than a total of 60 days and, while there or so participating, comply with instructions given by, or under the authority of, the person in charge of the place or activities (para. 2(4) and (6)). These arrangements must be such as to avoid, so far as practicable, any conflict with the offender's religious beliefs, with the requirements of any other community order to which he may be subject, or interference with the times, if any, at which the probationer normally works or attends a school or other educational establishment (para. 2(7)). A requirement which involves the probationer from refraining from specified activities (such as attending football matches, where the offence arose out of football-related violence) may be imposed in respect of a day or days specified in the order, or during such portion of the order as may be specified (para. 2(1)(b)).

Powers of Criminal Courts Act 1973, sch. 1A

Requirements as to attendance at probation centre
   3.—(1)   Subject to the provisions of this paragraph, a probation order may require the offender during the probation period to attend at a probation centre specified in the order.
   (2)   A court shall not include such a requirement in a probation order unless—
      (a)   it has consulted a probation officer; and
      (b)   it is satisfied—

    (i)   that arrangements can be made for the offender's attendance at a centre; and
    (ii) that the person in charge of the centre consents to the inclusion of the requirement.

A 'probation centre' is defined in para. 3(7) as premises '(a) at which non-residential facilities are provided for use in connection with the rehabilitation of offenders; and (b) which are for the time being approved by the Secretary of State as providing facilities for persons subject to probation orders.'

A requirement imposed under para. 3(1) may involve attendance at the centre for a maximum of 60 days during the course of the order, during which time the probationer must comply with all the instructions of the staff at the centre (para. 3(3)). The instructions for attendance must, so far as is practicable, avoid any conflict with the offender's religious beliefs, with the requirements of any other community order to which he may be subject, and avoid any interference with the times, if any, when the probationer normally works or attends a school or other educational establishment (para. 3(4)).

E5.3   ***Extension of Requirements for Sexual Offenders***   Paragraph 4(1) of sch. 1A provides that where an offender has been convicted of a sexual offence (as defined in CJA 1991, s. 31(1): see **E1.10**), the normal 60-day limit in relation to being present at a place or required activities (under para. 2) and in relation to attendance at a probation centre (under para. 3) does not apply. The duration may, in the case of a probationer convicted of a sexual offence, be for 'such greater number of days as may be specified in the direction'.

E5.4   ***Requirements as to Treatment for Mental Condition etc.***   Requirements relating to treatment for a mental condition are provided in sch. 1A, para. 5. They are dealt with at **E24.1**.

E5.5   ***Requirements as to Treatment for Drug or Alcohol Dependency***   Schedule 1A, para. 6(1) provides for the insertion of a requirement of treatment for drug or alcohol dependency where:

    a court proposing to make a probation order is satisfied—
      (a)   that the offender is dependent on drugs or alcohol;
      (b)   that his dependency caused or contributed to the offence in respect of which the order is proposed to be made; and
      (c)   that his dependency is such as requires and may be susceptible to treatment.

In these provisions 'dependency' is widely construed and includes cases where the offender has 'a propensity towards the misuse of drugs or alcohol' (para. 6(9)). Treatment for the dependency must be carried out at a place specified in the order (para. 6(3)) and may continue for the whole period of the probation order or for such specific part of it as is required by the court (para. 6(2)). Before such a requirement can be imposed, the court must be satisfied that arrangements have been or can be made for the treatment to be carried out and that the offender has expressed his willingness to comply with the requirement (para. 6(4)). The probation officer's normal supervision duties are relevant only insofar as is necessary for the purpose of revocation or amendment of the order (para. 6(5)).

It would seem from the words 'caused or contributed to the offence' in para. 6(1) that the court is not confined in the use of these powers to cases where the offender has been convicted of an offence which is directly related to drugs or alcohol or committed under the influence of drugs or alcohol. The powers could, for example, be used where an offender had committed theft to obtain money to purchase alcohol or drugs. When the court has been notified that arrangements are in place for implementing drug treatment and testing orders (see **E10**) para. 6(1) shall be construed as being limited only to offenders dependent on alcohol (CDA 1998, sch. 8, para. 34).

MAKING OF PROBATION ORDERS: SENTENCING PRINCIPLES

General Guidance

The PCCA 1973, s. 2(1) provides that the purposes of a probation order are to be either **E5.6**
securing the rehabilitation of the offender or protecting the public from harm from him
or preventing the commission by him of further offences. Additionally, since a probation
order is a 'community order' within the meaning of the CJA 1991, s. 6(4), its imposition
in any case must be justified by the sentencer in terms of the seriousness of the offence,
or the seriousness of the offence and one or more offences associated with it. See **E4.1**.

Mixing Probation Orders with Other Sentences or Orders

It is impermissible to combine a probation order with an immediate custodial sentence, **E5.7**
whether in respect of the same offence or for different offences sentenced on the same
occasion since this is inconsistent with the rationale for s. 2(1). It is also impermissible to
combine a probation order with a suspended sentence of imprisonment (PCCA 1973,
s. 22(3)). The suspended sentence supervision order, however, provides a means of
mixing a suspended sentence with an element of supervision (see **E2.14**). A probation
order may not be combined with a community service order when sentencing for a single
offence (CJA 1991, s. 6(3)), except where imposed in a specified mix to form a
combination order. Nor can a probation order and a community service order be
imposed for separate offences sentenced on the same occasion (*Gilding* v *DPP* (1998)
The Times, 20 May 1998). A probation order may, however, be combined with a fine,
whether imposed in respect of the same or different offences. A probation order may not
be combined with a discharge when sentencing for a single offence, since a discharge is
imposed only where 'it is inexpedient to inflict punishment' (PCCA 1973, s. 1A(1)), but
these two measures may, of course, be used for different offences sentenced on the same
occasion. When combining measures, regard should be had to the CJA 1991,
s. 28(2)(a), which states that nothing 'shall prevent a court from mitigating any penalty
included in an offender's sentence by taking into account any other penalty included in
that sentence'.

A probation order can be combined with an order of disqualification from driving (Road
Traffic Offenders Act 1988, s. 46(1)). Compensation may not be ordered as a
requirement of a probation order (PCCA 1973, s. 3(2)), but a court may make an order
for compensation or for costs, or for restitution of property (Theft Act 1968, s. 28(1))
at the same time as making a probation order. The court may combine with probation
an order for deportation (Immigration Act 1971, s. 6(3), though see **E22.5**), or an
exclusion order in respect of licensed premises (Licensed Premises (Exclusion of
Certain Persons) Act 1980, s. 1(2)). A probation order may be combined with an order
for forfeiture of property under the PCCA 1973, s. 43.

Breach, Revocation and Amendment of Probation Order

A probation order is a 'community order' within the meaning of the CJA 1991, s. 6(4). **E5.8**
For the provisions relating to breach, revocation and amendment of community orders
see **E4.7**, **E4.8** and **E4.9** respectively.

SECTION E6: COMMUNITY SENTENCES: COMBINATION ORDERS

Power to Make Combination Orders

E6.1   Criminal Justice Act 1991, s. 11

(1)   Where a court by or before which a person of or over the age of sixteen years is convicted of an offence punishable with imprisonment (not being an offence for which the sentence is fixed by law or falls to be imposed under section 2(2), 3(2) or 4(2) of the Crime (Sentences) Act 1997) is of the opinion mentioned in subsection (2) below, the court may make a combination order, that is to say, an order requiring him both—
    (a)   to be under supervision for a period specified in the order, being not less than twelve months nor more than three years; and
    (b)   to perform unpaid work for a number of hours so specified, being in the aggregate not less than 40 nor more than 100.
(1A)   The reference in subsection (1) above to an offence punishable with imprisonment shall be construed without regard to any prohibition or restriction imposed by or under any enactment on the imprisonment of young offenders.
(2)   The opinion referred to in subsection (1) above is that the making of a combination order is desirable in the interests of—
    (a)   securing the rehabilitation of the offender; or
    (b)   protecting the public from harm from him or preventing the commission by him of further offences.
(3)   Subject to subsection (1) above, part I of the [PCCA 1973] shall apply in relation to combination orders—
    (a)   in so far as they impose such a requirement as is mentioned in paragraph (a) of that subsection, as if they were probation orders; and
    (b)   in so far as they impose such a requirement as is mentioned in paragraph (b) of that subsection, as if they were community service orders.

A combination order is a 'community order', and in all cases its imposition requires justification by the court in terms of the seriousness of the offence, or the seriousness of the combination of the offence and one or more offences associated with it. These requirements are set out at **E4.2**. Before making a combination order, the court must comply with all the relevant procedural requirements for imposing a community service order and a probation order. For the normal requirement to obtain a pre-sentence report, see **E4.1**.

One effect of s. 11(3) is that the court may insert any of the additional requirements into the probation part of the combination order which are provided for in the PCCA 1973, sch. 1A (see **E5.2 et seq.**), though this must be subject to the proviso that their inclusion is not logically incompatible with the performance of the community service part of the combination order.

Section 6(3) of the CJA 1991 states that 'a community sentence shall not consist of or include both a probation order and a community service order'. Probation and community service can be mixed together only in the form of a combination order. Nor can a probation order and a community service order be imposed for separate offences sentenced on the same occasion. See further **E5.7**.

Enforcement of Combination Orders

E6.2   The relevant enforcement provisions are described at **E4.6 et seq.**

SECTION E7: COMMUNITY SENTENCES: CURFEW ORDERS

Power to Make Curfew Orders

The power to make curfew orders, which is contained in the CJA 1991, s. 12, was **E7.1** brought into force on 9 January 1995. Initially the orders were available only in certain trial areas but they are made available to all courts from 1 December 1999.

Criminal Justice Act 1991, s. 12

(1)   Where a person is convicted of an offence (not being an offence for which the sentence is fixed by law or falls to be imposed under section 2(2), 3(2) or 4(2) of the Crime (Sentences) Act 1997), the court by or before which he is convicted may make a curfew order, that is to say, an order requiring him to remain, for periods specified in the order, at a place so specified.

(2)   A curfew order may specify different places or different periods for different days, but shall not specify—

(a)   periods which fall outside the period of six months beginning with the day on which it is made; or

(b)   periods which amount to less than 2 hours or more than 12 hours in any one day.

(2A)   In relation to an offender who is under the age of sixteen years, subsection (2)(a) above shall have effect as if the reference to six months were a reference to three months.

(3)   The requirements in a curfew order shall, so far as practicable, be such as to avoid—

(a)   any conflict with the offender's religious beliefs or with the requirements of any other community order to which he may be subject; and

(b)   any interference with the times, if any, at which he normally works or attends school or other educational establishment.

(4)   A curfew order shall include provision for making a person responsible for monitoring the offender's whereabouts during the curfew periods specified in the order; and a person who is made so responsible shall be of a description specified in an order made by the Secretary of State.

(4A)   A court shall not make a curfew order unless the court has been notified by the Secretary of State that arrangements for monitoring the offender's whereabouts are available in the area in which the place proposed to be specified in the order is situated and the notice has not been withdrawn.

(5)   Before making a curfew order, the court shall explain to the offender in ordinary language—

(a)   the effect of the order (including any additional requirements proposed to be included in the order in accordance with section 13 below);

(b)   the consequences which may follow under Schedule 2 to this Act if he fails to comply with any of the requirements of the order; and

(c)   that the court has under that Schedule power to review the order on the application either of the offender or of the responsible officer.

(6)   Before making a curfew order, the court shall obtain and consider information about the place proposed to be specified in the order (including information as to the attitude of persons likely to be affected by the enforced presence there of the offender).

(6A)   Before making a curfew order in respect of an offender who is under the age of sixteen years, the court shall obtain and consider information about his family circumstances and the likely effect of such an order on those circumstances.

(6B)   The court by which a curfew order is made shall give a copy of the order to the offender and to the person responsible for monitoring the offender's whereabouts during the curfew periods specified in the order.

(7)   The Secretary of State may by order direct—

(a)   that subsection (2) above shall have effect with the substitution, for any period there specified, of such period as may be specified in the order; or

(b)   that subsection (3) above shall have effect with such additional restrictions as may be so specified.

(8)   References in this section to the offender's being under the age of sixteen years are references to his being under that age on conviction.

Section 12 was amended by the C(S)A 1997 and the CDA 1998. The C(S)A 1997, s. 43(1), removed the words 'of or over the age of 16 years' from s. 12(1), thereby making the curfew order also available for offenders aged between 10 and 15 inclusive. For such offenders, periods of curfew cannot be imposed beyond a period of three months from the date of the order, rather than six months from that date for older offenders (s. 12(2A)), and the court is required to obtain additional information about the young offender's family circumstances (s. 12(6A)). Section 43 came into effect on 1 January 1998 and applies to offences committed on or after that date.

A curfew order is a 'community order', and in all cases its imposition requires justification by the court in terms of the seriousness of the offence, or the seriousness of the combination of the offence and one or more offences associated with it. These requirements are set out at **E4.1**. Although there is no statutory requirement that the court obtain a pre-sentence report before making a curfew order, the court must obtain information in respect of the matters referred to in s. 12(6) and (6A) and, in practice, a pre-sentence report will be required in most cases.

These powers may be compared with powers to include a night restriction order as a requirement of a supervision order made under the CYPA 1969, s. 12A(3)(b) (see **E8.1**). There would appear to be no restrictions arising from s. 12 of the 1991 Act on combining a curfew order with other sentences or orders of the court, although it may safely be assumed that the imposition of a sentence of immediate custody would be incompatible with it. Since a discharge cannot be combined with a punitive measure for the same offence (PCCA 1973, s. 1A: see **E14**), a discharge and a curfew order could not be combined in those circumstances.

Enforcement of Curfew Orders

E7.2   The relevant enforcement provisions are described at **E4.6** *et seq*.

Electronic Monitoring

E7.3   A curfew order imposed under CJA 1991, s. 12, may, and in practice usually will, include requirements for securing the electronic monitoring of the offender's whereabouts during the curfew periods specified in the order in accordance with s. 13. Electronic monitoring is not, therefore, a sentence or order in its own right, but solely a means of regulating a curfew order. Electronic monitoring requirements are made available to all courts from 1 December 1999. Section 13(3) provides for the Secretary of State to enter into 'contracts with other persons' for the electronic monitoring by them of offenders' whereabouts. Private sector contractors are made responsible for installing the monitoring equipment, for monitoring compliance with the curfew and for returning offenders to court when a breach is alleged.

SECTION E8: COMMUNITY SENTENCES: SUPERVISION ORDERS

Power to Make Supervision Orders

A supervision order may be made by a youth court or by the Crown Court, but not by **E8.1** an adult magistrates' court (CYPA 1969, s. 7(8)), where a child (aged 10 to 13 inclusive) or young person (aged 14 to 17 inclusive) is found guilty of any offence (s. 7(7)). This is subject to the CYPA 1933, s. 53(1) (mandatory sentence of detention during Her Majesty's pleasure for murder committed by an offender who was under 18 at the time of the offence: see **E3.11**).

A supervision order will last for three years from the date on which it was made, or for such shorter period as may be specified in the order (CYPA 1969, s. 17(a)). The order places the juvenile under the supervision of either a designated local authority, a probation officer or, where applicable, a member of a youth offending team (s. 11). A local authority shall not be designated as supervisor unless either the person to be supervised resides, or will reside, in that area, or the authority agrees to act (s. 13(1)). Where a probation officer is the supervisor, the officer shall be an officer appointed for or assigned to the petty sessions area named in the order (s. 13(3)). In every case the supervisor's duty is to 'advise, assist and befriend the supervised person' (s. 14). A supervision order does not require the consent of the offender, but the court may not insert a requirement of treatment for a mental condition (see **E24.2**) where the offender has attained the age of 14 and refuses to express his willingness to comply with that requirement. Section 1(3) of the CJA 1991 (see **E1.8**) states that a court may pass a custodial sentence on an offender 'if he fails to express his willingness to comply with a requirement which is proposed by the court to be included in a . . . supervision order and which requires an expression of such willingness'.

Requirements in Supervision Orders

The basic supervision order may be supplemented where appropriate with various **E8.2** requirements. For the normal requirement to obtain a pre-sentence report, see **E4.1**.

Children and Young Persons Act 1969, s. 12

(1) A supervision order may require the supervised person to reside with an individual named in the order who agrees to the requirement, but a requirement imposed by a supervision order in pursuance of this subsection shall be subject to any such requirement of the order as is authorised by the following provisions of this section or by section 12A, 12B or 12C below.

The exceptions relate to cases where a supervised person may from time to time be obliged to reside elsewhere by virtue of a requirement made under one of the other subsections of s. 12.

Intermediate treatment requirements, which allow for the involvement of the juvenile in schemes of constructive and supervised activities, are normally made by the court under s. 12(2).

Children and Young Persons Act 1969, s. 12

(2) Subject to section 19(12) of this Act, a supervision order may require the supervised person to comply with any directions given from time to time by the supervisor and requiring him to do all or any of the following things—

     (a) to live at a place or places specified in the directions for a period or periods so specified;

     (b) to present himself to a person or persons specified in the directions at a place or places and on a day or days so specified;

     (c) to participate in activities specified in the directions on a day or days so specified; but it shall be for the supervisor to decide whether and to what extent he exercises any power to give directions conferred on him by virtue of this subsection and to decide the form of any directions; and a requirement imposed by a supervision order in pursuance of this subsection shall be subject to any such requirement of the order as if authorised by section 12B(1) of this Act.

The CYPA 1969, s. 19(12), makes it the court's duty to ensure that there is such a scheme available in the area where the supervised person resides or will reside. Section 12B deals with a requirement of medical treatment, and is considered at **E24.2**. The number of days in respect of which the supervisor may give directions is fixed by the court, up to a maximum of 90 (s. 12(3)). Intermediate treatment ordered under s. 12(2) leaves the implementation to the discretion of the supervisor, and is sometimes referred to as 'discretionary intermediate treatment'. Directions given by the supervisor under s. 12(2)(b) or (c) should, as far as practicable, avoid conflict with the young offender's religious beliefs, with the requirements of any other community order to which he may be subject, and any interference with the times, if any, at which he normally works or attends school or other educational establishment (s. 12(4)).

Intermediate treatment requirements may also be included by virtue of s. 12A. Under such an arrangement, sometimes referred to as 'stipulated intermediate treatment', the court may itself require the offender to do anything which the supervisor may have required him to do under s. 12(2), and nominate the place where the supervised person is to live or attend, and the activities he is to participate in (s. 12A).

Children and Young Persons Act 1969, s. 12A

     (3) Subject to the following provisions of this section and to section 19(13) of this Act, a supervision order to which subsection (1) of this section applies may require a supervised person—

     (a) to do anything that by virtue of section 12(2) of this Act a supervisor has power, or would but for section 19(12) of this Act have power, to direct a supervised person to do;

     (aa) to make reparation specified in the order to a person or persons so specified or to the community at large;

     (b) to remain for specified periods between 6 pm and 6 am—
       (i) at a place specified in the order; or
       (ii) at one of several places so specified;

     (c) to refrain from participating in activities specified in the order—
       (i) on a specified day or days during the period for which the supervision order is in force; or
       (ii) during the whole of that period or a specified portion of it.

The maximum number of days in respect of which such requirements may be made under s. 12A(3)(a), (aa) or (b) is 90 (s. 12A(5)). Before making any order under s. 12A(3), the court must be satisfied, after consultation with the supervisor as to the offender's circumstances and the feasibility of securing compliance with the requirements, that compliance is feasible (s. 12A(6)(a)); that the requirements are necessary for securing the good conduct of the supervised person or for preventing a repetition by him of the same offence or the commission of other offences (s. 12A(6)(b)); and that, if the supervised person is under the age of 16, it has obtained and considered information about his family circumstances and the likely effect of the requirements on those circumstances (s. 12A(6)(c), as substituted by the C(S)A 1997, s. 38(1)). The court must not by s. 12A(3) include any requirement that would involve the cooperation of any third party without that party's consent (s. 12A(7)(a)), any requirement that the supervised person reside with a specified individual (s. 12A(7)(b)), or a medical treatment requirement (s. 12A(7)(c)). The phrase 'make reparation' in s. 12A(3)(aa) means reparation other than by the payment of compensation (s. 12A(14), inserted by the YJCEA 1999, sch. 5, para. 1).

Where a requirement is made under s. 12A(3)(b), known as a 'night restriction' requirement, the place or one of the places specified in the order must be the place where the supervised person lives (s. 12A(8)). The supervised person shall not be required to remain at a place for longer than 10 hours on any one night (s. 12A(9)). The restriction shall not be imposed in respect of more than 30 separate days in all, and cannot continue in operation for longer than three months from the date of the making of the supervision order (s. 12A(10) and (11)). A supervised person who is required by a night restriction requirement to remain at a place may leave it if he is accompanied by his parent or guardian, his supervisor, or by some other person specified in the supervision order (s. 12A(12)). A night restriction requirement imposed in respect of a period of time beginning in the evening and ending in the morning shall be treated as imposed only in respect of the day upon which the period began (s. 12A(13)).

Children and Young Persons Act 1969, s. 12AA

(1)   Where the conditions mentioned in subsection (6) of this section are satisfied, a supervision order may impose a requirement ('a residence requirement') that a child or young person shall live for a specified period in local authority accommodation.

A residence requirement must designate for these purposes the authority in whose area the child or young person lives (s. 12AA(2)), after consultation with that authority (s. 12AA(3)). The maximum period which may be specified in a residence requirement is six months (s. 12AA(5)). A residence requirement may stipulate that the child or young person shall not live with a named person (s. 12AA(4)).

Children and Young Persons Act 1969, s. 12AA

(6)   The conditions are that—
    (a)   a supervision order has previously been made in respect of the child or young person;
    (b)   that order imposed—
        (i)   a requirement under section 12, 12A or 12C of this Act; or
        (ii)   a residence requirement;
    (c)   fails to comply with that requirement, or is found guilty of an offence while that order was in force; and
    (d)   the court is satisfied that—
        (i)   the failure to comply with the requirement, or the behaviour which constituted the offence, was due to a significant extent to the circumstances in which he was living; and
        (ii)   the imposition of a residence requirement will assist in his rehabilitation;
except that the condition in sub-paragraph (i) of paragraph (d) of this subsection does not apply where the condition in paragraph (b)(ii) is satisfied.

A residence requirement should not be included unless the child or young person was legally represented at the time when the court is considering whether or not to impose such a requirement or, if not so represented, that his application for legal aid was refused on the ground that his resources were such that he did not require assistance or, having been informed of his right to apply for legal aid and having had the opportunity to do so, had nevertheless refused or failed to apply (s. 12AA(9)). A supervision order imposing a residence requirement under s. 12AA may also impose any of the requirements mentioned in s. 12, 12A, 12B or 12C of the Act (s. 12AA(11)).

The CYPA 1969, s. 12B, deals with a requirement of medical treatment, which may be inserted into a supervision order. Such requirements are dealt with in **E24.2**.

Children and Young Persons Act 1969, s. 12C

(1) Subject to subsection (3) below, a supervision order to which section 12A(1) of this Act applies may require a supervised person, if he is of compulsory school age, to comply, for as long as he is of that age and the order remains in force, with such arrangements for his education as may from time to time be made by his parent, being arrangements for the time being approved by the local education authority.

(2) The court shall not include such a requirement in a supervision order unless it has consulted the local education authority with regard to its proposal to include the requirement and is satisfied that in the view of the local education authority arrangements exist for the child or young person to whom the supervision order will relate to receive efficient full-time education suitable to his age, ability and aptitude and to any special educational need he may have.

Expressions used in s. 12C(1) and in the Education Act 1996 have the same meaning as in that Act (s. 12C(3)). The court may not make a requirement under s. 12C(1) unless it has consulted the supervisor about the offender's circumstances, and thereby considers the requirement necessary for securing the good conduct of the supervised person or for preventing a repetition by him of the same offence or the commission of other offences.

Justifying the Imposition of a Supervision Order

E8.3 A supervision order is a 'community order' within the meaning of the CJA 1991, s. 6(4). The imposition of a supervision order requires justification by the court in terms of the seriousness of the offence, or the seriousness of the combination of the offence and one or more offences associated with it. There is a requirement in the 1991 Act, s. 7(3), that the court must obtain a pre-sentence report before making a supervision order which includes requirements imposed under the CYPA 1969, s. 12, 12A, 12AA, 12B or 12C. See further **E4.1**.

Breach of Supervision Order

E8.4 The following provisions are set out as amended by the CDA 1998, s. 72, which came into force on 30 September 1998. The term 'relevant court' means, in the case of a supervised person under the age of 18, a youth court and, in the case of a supervised person who has attained that age, an adult magistrates' court (CYPA 1969, s. 15(11)).

By the CYPA 1969, s. 15(3)(a), where it is proved to the satisfaction of a relevant court, on the application of the supervisor, that a supervised person has failed to comply with any of the requirements of the order included pursuant to the CYPA 1969, s. 12, 12A, 12AA, 12C or 18(2)(b), then, whether or not it also varies or discharges the supervision order (see **E8.5**), the court may order payment of a fine not exceeding £1,000, or, subject to s. 16B, make a curfew order under CJA 1991, s. 12 or, subject to s. 16A(1), may make an attendance centre order. For these purposes, the CJA 1982, s. 17, applies as if its wording were amended to include the making of an attendance centre order in respect of breach of a supervision order as well as a probation order (s. 16A(1)).

By s. 15(3)(b), if the supervision order was made by a relevant court, it may discharge the order and deal with him, for the offence in respect of which the order was made, in any manner in which he could have been dealt with for that offence by the court which made the order if the order had not been made.

By s. 15(3)(c), if the supervision order was made by the Crown Court, the relevant court may commit him in custody or release him on bail until he can be brought or appear before the Crown Court.

Section 15(4) requires that where the original order was made by the Crown Court, the relevant court should send to the Crown Court a certificate giving details of the supervised person's failure to comply with the requirement in question and such other particulars as may be desirable. Section 15(5) states that where the matter comes before the Crown Court pursuant to s. 15(3)(c), and it is proved to the satisfaction of the Crown Court that the offender has failed to comply with the requirement, the Crown Court may deal with him for the offence in respect of which the order was made in any manner in which it could have dealt with him for that offence if it had not made the order. Where the Crown Court deals with a supervised person under s. 15(5), it must also discharge the supervision order (s. 15(6)).

The court dealing with the breach must take account of the extent to which the person supervised has complied with the requirements of the supervision order (s. 15(8)).

Discharge or Variation of Supervision Order

During the currency of a supervision order in respect of a person who has not yet reached the age of 18, a youth court (or in respect of a person who has reached that age, an adult magistrates' court) may, if appropriate, on the application of the supervisor or the supervised person, make an order discharging the supervision order (CYPA 1969, s. 15(1)). The relevant court may also vary the supervision order by cancelling any requirement included in it under s. 12, 12A, 12AA, 12C or 18(2)(b) of the 1969 Act or by inserting any provision which could have been included in the order. The relevant court is not empowered, however, to insert a requirement under s. 12A(3)(b) (night restriction requirement) in respect of any day which falls outside the period of three months beginning with the date the order was made. There are also limitations upon the court's powers to vary a requirement under s. 12B relating to medical treatment (see **E24.2**). **E8.5**

SECTION E9: COMMUNITY SENTENCES: ATTENDANCE CENTRE ORDERS

Power to Make Attendance Centre Orders

E9.1   The CJA 1982, s. 16(2), explains that an attendance centre is 'a place at which offenders under 21 years of age may be required to attend and be given under supervision appropriate occupation or instruction in pursuance of orders made under section 17 below'.

Criminal Justice Act 1982, s. 17

(1)   Where a person under 21 years of age is convicted by or before a court of an offence punishable with imprisonment (not being an offence the sentence for which is fixed by law or falls to be imposed under section 2(2), 3(2) or 4(2) of the Crime (Sentences) Act 1997, or where a court—

(a)   would have power, but for section 1 above, to commit a person under 21 years of age to prison in default of payment of any sum of money or for failing to do or abstain from doing anything required to be done or left undone; or

(b)   has power to deal with a person under 21 years of age under part II of schedule 2 to the Criminal Justice Act 1991 for failure to comply with any of the requirements of a probation order; or

(bb)   has power to deal with a person under 16 years of age under that part of that schedule for failure to comply with any of the requirements of a curfew order; or

(c)   has power to commit to prison for default in payment of any sum of money a person who is under 25 but is not less than 21 years of age,

the court may, if it has been notified by the Secretary of State that an attendance centre is available for the reception of persons of his description, order him to attend at such a centre, to be specified in the order, for such number of hours as may be so specified.

(1A)   For the purposes of subsection (1) above—

(a)   the reference to an offence punishable with imprisonment shall be construed without regard to any prohibition or restriction imposed by or under any enactment on the imprisonment of young offenders; and

(b)   a sentence falls to be imposed under section 2(2), 3(2) or 4(2) of the Crime (Sentences) Act 1997 if it is required by that provision and the court is not of the opinion there mentioned.

(2)   An order under this section is referred to in this Act as an 'attendance centre order'.

Attendance centre orders may be made by a magistrates' court or the Crown Court. Section 1 of the CJA 1982 prohibits a court from passing a sentence of imprisonment on a person under 21.

An attendance centre order can be made by a court only if:

(a)   it has been so notified by the Secretary of State in accordance with s. 17(1); and

(b)   the court is satisfied that the centre to be specified in the order is reasonably accessible to the offender, having regard to his age, the means of access available to him and any other circumstances (s. 17(7)).

An attendance centre order is a 'community order' within the meaning of the CJA 1991, s. 6(4). Section 6(1) of the 1991 Act restricts the imposition of community orders to cases where the court is of the opinion that the offence, or the combination of the offence and one or more offences associated with it, was serious enough to warrant such a sentence. For discussion of this requirement, see **E4.1**.

Sections 17(4) and 17(5) contain important provisions relating to the aggregate number of hours of attendance. First, the aggregate number of hours which form the duration of the order must be specified in the order and must be not less than 12, except where the offender is aged under 14 and in the opinion of the court 12 hours would be excessive, having regard to his age or other circumstances (s. 17(4)). Secondly, the aggregate number of hours must not exceed 12, except where the court is of opinion, having regard to all the circumstances, that 12 hours would be inadequate, in which case it must not exceed 24 hours where the offender is under 16, or 36 hours where the offender is under 21 (or, in the case of s. 17(1)(c), under 25) but not less than 16 (s. 17(5)).

A court may, however, pass a further attendance centre order upon an offender before an earlier one imposed on him has ceased to have effect, without regard to the number of hours specified in the earlier order or to the fact that it is still in effect (s. 17(6)). The order must specify the time at which the offender is first to attend (s. 17(9)), but subsequent times shall be fixed by the officer in charge of the centre (s. 17(10)). In any event, an offender shall not be required to attend a centre on more than one occasion on any day, or for more than three hours on any one occasion (s. 17(11)). The times at which an offender is required to attend at an attendance centre shall, as far as practicable, avoid any conflict with the offender's religious beliefs or with the requirements of any other community order to which he may be subject and interference with the times at which he works, attends school or any other educational establishment (s. 17(8)).

Where the attendance centre order is passed in default of payment of any sum of money (s. 17(1)), payment of the whole sum discharges the order, and payment of a proportion of the sum reduces the number of hours to be served under the order by the same proportion, rounded down to the nearest complete hour (s. 17(13)).

Apart from the powers specified in s. 17, a youth court or the Crown Court may also make an attendance centre order consequent upon the offender's breach of a requirement in a supervision order (CYPA 1969, ss. 15(3)(a) and 16A(1); see also **E8.4**).

Discharge and Variation of Attendance Centre Orders

An attendance centre order may be discharged on application to a court by the offender **E9.2** or the officer in charge of the centre. Such court shall be either a magistrates' court acting for the petty sessions area in which the attendance centre is situated or the court which made the order (CJA 1982, s. 18(3)). The Crown Court may reserve to itself the power to discharge the order (s. 18(4)).

Section 18(4A) of the CJA 1982, as amended by the CDA 1998, sch. 7, para. 37(1), provides that, where a magistrates' court discharges an attendance centre order made by a magistrates' court, or the Crown Court discharges such an order made by the Crown Court, the court has power to deal with the original offence in any manner in which the offender could have been dealt with for that offence by the court which made the order, if the order had not been made. If the attendance centre order was made in consequence of the offender's default etc. under CJA 1982, s. 17(1)(a), rather than in consequence of the commission of an offence, the magistrates' courts and the Crown Court have equivalent powers (s. 18(10), inserted by the CDA 1998, sch. 7, para. 37(3)). For the situation where an attendance centre order is made on appeal, see s. 18(11), also inserted by the CDA 1998, sch. 7, para. 37(3). The amendments to s. 18 made by CDA 1998, sch. 7, para. 37(3) do not have effect in relation to attendance centre orders made before 30 September 1998.

An application for variation may be made by the offender or the officer in charge of the centre, to a magistrates' court acting for the petty sessions area in which the centre is situated (CJA 1982, s. 18(5)). The court may vary the starting day or hour of the order, or may substitute another attendance centre (s. 18(6)).

Breach of Attendance Centre Orders

E9.3 Where it appears on information to a justice acting for the petty sessions area in which the attendance centre is situated, or if the order was made by a magistrates' court, the petty sessions area for which that court was acting (CJA 1982, s. 19(1)), that the offender has failed without reasonable excuse to attend or has committed a breach of the rules for the regulation and management of attendance centres made by the Secretary of State by statutory instrument (under s. 16(3)), which cannot be adequately dealt with under those rules, and it is proved to the satisfaction of the court that he has so failed or has so committed a breach of the rules, the court may, without revoking the order, impose a fine not exceeding £1,000, or, if the order was made by a magistrates' court, the magistrates' court before which the offender is brought has power to revoke the order and deal with the offender for the original offence, in any manner in which he could have been dealt with for that offence by the court which made the order if that order had not been made (s. 19(3)(a)). If the order was made by the Crown Court, the magistrates' court may commit him in custody or release him on bail until he can appear before the Crown Court. The magistrates' court should provide a certificate signed by a justice of the peace giving particulars of the case (s. 19(4)), though this is not conclusive of the failure to attend or breach of the rules, which must be specifically proved before the Crown Court. The Crown Court has powers to revoke the order and deal with the offender for the original offence which are parallel to those of the magistrates' court.

If the court, when dealing with a breach, acts to revoke the order and deal with the offender in respect of which the order was made, it must take into account the extent to which the offender has complied with the requirements of the attendance centre order (s. 19(5A)(a)). This may be compared with the provisions on breach of certain other community orders under CJA 1991, sch. 2, para. 3(2)(a) (see **E4.7**). Further, where the offender has 'wilfully and persistently failed to comply' with the requirements of the order, the court may then deal with the offender by way of a custodial sentence (s. 19(5A)(b)). If the attendance centre order was made in consequence of the offender's default etc. under CJA 1982, s. 17(1)(a), rather than in consequence of the commission of an offence, magistrates' courts and the Crown Court have equivalent powers (s. 19(8), inserted by the CDA 1998, sch. 7, para. 38(3)). For the situation where an attendance centre order is made on appeal, see s. 19(9), also inserted by the CDA 1998, sch. 7, para. 38(3). The amendments made to s. 19 by the CDA 1998, sch. 7, para. 38(3) do not have effect in relation to attendance centre orders made before 30 September 1998.

It seems that where an order for revocation is made, the offender must be dealt with on the basis of his age when the attendance centre order was made (see, by analogy, *Wyre Magistrates' Court, ex parte Boardman* (1987) 9 Cr App R (S) 214). The offender may appeal against the sentence imposed for the original offence after revocation of the order, if the sentence was imposed by a magistrates' court, by virtue of s. 19(6) or, if imposed by the Crown Court, by virtue of the CJA 1982, sch. 14, para. 23.

Mixing Attendance Centre Orders with Other Sentences or Orders

E9.4 It is inappropriate to combine an attendance centre order with a custodial sentence. Since an attendance centre order is one of the methods open to a court where an offender is in breach of a probation order or a supervision order, it seems that a probation order or a supervision order should not be made at the same time as an attendance centre order.

SECTION E10: COMMUNITY SENTENCES: DRUG TREATMENT AND TESTING ORDERS

Under ss. 61 to 64 of the CDA 1998, the Crown Court and magistrates' courts have power to impose a drug treatment and testing order on an offender aged 16 or over who is convicted of any offence. Powers to impose a drug treatment and testing order are made available only to certain courts on a pilot basis (see CDA 1998, s. 61(3)). Such an order cannot be made in respect of an offence committed before the commencement of s. 61 (30 September 1998).

Power to Make Drug Treatment and Testing Order

A drug treatment and testing order is a 'community order' within the meaning of the **E10.1** CJA 1991, s. 6(4), so that the imposition of a drug treatment and testing order requires justification in terms of the seriousness of the offence, or the offence and one or more offences associated with it. The relevant statutory criteria are set out at **E4.1**, and may usefully be compared with the requirement as to treatment for drug or alcohol dependency which may be inserted by the court as a requirement of a probation order (see PCCA 1973, sch. 1A, para. 6(1) at **E5.5**). The main differences between the orders are that the probation requirement extends to alcohol dependency or misuse, which the drug treatment and testing order does not, that the former lacks the 'testing requirement' integral to the latter, and the provisions for the probation requirement state that the offender's dependency should have 'caused or contributed to the offence', while no such causal link is specified for the drug treatment and testing order.

Crime and Disorder Act 1998, s. 61

(1) This section applies where a person aged 16 or over is convicted of an offence other than one for which the sentence—
    (a) is fixed by law; or
    (b) falls to be imposed under section 2(2), 3(2) or 4(2) of the [C(S)A 1997].
(2) Subject to the provisions of this section, the court by or before which the offender is convicted may make an order (a 'drug treatment and testing order') which—
    (a) has effect for a period specified in the order of not less than six months nor more than three years ('the treatment and testing period'); and
    (b) includes the requirements and provisions mentioned in section 62 below.
(3) A court shall not make a drug treatment and testing order unless it has been notified by the Secretary of State that arrangements for implementing such orders are available in the area proposed to be specified in the order and the notice has not been withdrawn.
(4) A drug treatment and testing order shall be a community order for the purposes of part I of the [CJA 1991]; and the provisions of that part, which include provisions with respect to restrictions on imposing, and procedural requirements for, community sentences (sections 6 and 7), shall apply accordingly.
(5) The court shall not make a drug treatment and testing order in respect of the offender unless it is satisfied—
    (a) that he is dependent on or has a propensity to misuse drugs; and
    (b) that his dependency or propensity is such as requires and may be susceptible to treatment.
(6) For the purposes of ascertaining for the purposes of subsection (5) above whether the offender has any drug in his body, the court may by order require him to provide samples of such description as it may specify; but the court shall not make such an order unless the offender expresses his willingness to comply with its requirements.

The requirement in s. 61(6) is one of the occasions on which the court must secure the offender's willingness to comply with the order before it can be imposed. Section 1(3) of the CJA 1991 (see **E1.8**) states that 'nothing shall prevent the court from passing a custodial sentence on the offender if he fails to express his willingness to comply . . .'. One implication of s. 61(4) is that the court should normally obtain a pre-sentence report before imposing a drug treatment and testing order (CJA 1991, s. 7(3), as amended by the CDA 1998, sch. 8, para. 75) unless the court is of the opinion that it is unnecessary to obtain one.

Crime and Disorder Act 1998, s. 62

(1) A drug treatment and testing order shall include a requirement ('the treatment requirement') that the offender shall submit, during the whole of the treatment and testing period, to treatment by or under the direction of a specified person having the necessary qualifications or experience ('the treatment provider') with a view to the reduction or elimination of the offender's dependency on or propensity to misuse drugs.

(2) The required treatment for any period shall be—

(a) treatment as a resident in such institution or place as may be specified in the order; or

(b) treatment as a non-resident in or at such institution or place, and at such intervals, as may be so specified;

but the nature of the treatment shall not be specified in the order except as mentioned in paragraph (a) or (b) above.

(3) A court shall not make a drug treatment and testing order unless it is satisfied that arrangements have been or can be made for the treatment intended to be specified in the order (including arrangements for the reception of the offender where he is to be required to submit to treatment as a resident).

(4) A drug treatment and testing order shall include a requirement ('the testing requirement') that, for the purpose of ascertaining whether he has any drug in his body during the treatment and testing period, the offender shall provide during that period at such times or in such circumstances as may (subject to the provisions of the order) be determined by the treatment provider, samples of such description as may be so determined.

(5) The testing requirement shall specify for each month the minimum number of occasions on which samples are to be provided.

(6) A drug treatment and testing order shall include a provision specifying the petty sessions area in which it appears to the court making the order that the offender resides or will reside.

(7) A drug treatment and testing order shall—

(a) provide that, for the treatment and testing period, the offender shall be under the supervision of a responsible officer, that is to say, a probation officer appointed for or assigned to the petty sessions area specified in the order;

(b) require the offender to keep in touch with the responsible officer in accordance with such instructions as may from time to time be given by that officer, and to notify him of any change of address; and

(c) provide that the results of the tests carried out on the samples provided by the offender in pursuance of the testing requirement shall be communicated to the responsible officer.

(8) Supervision by the responsible officer shall be carried out to such extent only as may be necessary for the purpose of enabling him—

(a) to report on the offender's progress to the court by which the order is made;

(b) to report to that court any failure by the offender to comply with the requirements of the order; and

(c) to determine whether the circumstances are such that he should apply to that court for the revocation or amendment of the order.

Before making a drug treatment and testing order the court must explain to the offender in ordinary language the effect of the order and the requirements proposed to be included in it, the consequences which may follow if he fails to comply with any of those requirements, that the order may be reviewed on application either of the offender or of the responsible officer and that the order will be reviewed periodically by the court making the order (s. 64(1)). The court shall forthwith give copies of the order to a probation officer assigned to the court, and he shall give copies to the offender, to the treatment provider, and to the responsible officer (s. 64(3)). It is unlikely that non-compliance with the provision of the copies of the order would render the drug treatment and testing order invalid, by analogy with *Walsh* v *Barlow* [1985] 1 WLR 90 (see **E4.2**).

Review Hearings

Section 63 provides that periodic reviews of the offender's progress under the terms of **E10.2** the drug treatment and testing order shall be carried out, by the court which made the order, at intervals of not less than one month. These reviews, at least initially, will require the offender's attendance at each 'review hearing' in court, at which the offender's test results, the responsible officer's written report on his progress under the order, and the views of the person providing the treatment will all be considered by the court (s. 63(1)). At a review hearing the court, after considering the report of the responsible officer, may amend any requirement or provision of the order (s. 63(2)), except that the court may not amend the treatment or testing requirement in the order unless the offender expresses his willingness to comply with the amendment, and the court may not reduce the treatment and testing period below the minimum, or increase it above the maximum, specified in s. 61(2). If the offender fails to express his willingness to comply with the treatment or testing requirement as proposed to be amended, the court may revoke the order and deal with him for the offence in respect of which the order was made in any manner in which it could deal with him if he had just been convicted by the court of the offence (s. 63(4)). In so dealing with the offender the court must take into account the extent to which the offender has complied with the order's requirements, and may impose a custodial sentence notwithstanding CJA 1991, s. 1(2) (s. 63(5)). Further, if the drug treatment and testing order was made by a magistrates' court on an offender under the age of 18 for an offence triable only on indictment in the case of an adult, the court's power to re-sentence for the original offence is limited to the imposition of a fine not exceeding £5,000 or to deal with him in any way in which it could deal with him if it had just convicted him of an offence punishable with imprisonment for a term not exceeding six months (s. 63(6)). If, at a review hearing it appears that the offender's progress under the order is satisfactory, subsequent reviews may be carried out by the court without a full review hearing (in the case of the Crown Court, by a judge; in the case of a magistrates' court, by a justice of the peace acting for the relevant commission area) but, if progress subsequently becomes unsatisfactory, a further review hearing in court must be convened (s. 63(8) to (10)).

Breach, Revocation and Amendment of Drug Treatment and Testing Order

A drug treatment and testing order is a 'community order' within the meaning of the **E10.3** CJA 1991, s. 6(4). For the provisions relating to breach, revocation and amendment of community orders, see **E4.7**, **E4.8** and **E4.9** respectively dealing with the relevant provisions of the CJA 1991, sch. 2, as amended by the CDA 1998.

SECTION E11: COMMUNITY SENTENCES: ACTION PLAN ORDERS

Under ss. 69 and 70 of the CDA 1998, the Crown Court and youth courts have power to impose an action plan order on an offender aged under 18 who is convicted of any offence except murder. Powers to impose an action plan order are initially made available only to certain courts on a pilot basis (see CDA 1998, s. 69(3)). Such an order cannot be made in respect of an offence committed before the commencement of ss. 69 and 70 (30 September 1998).

Power to Make an Action Plan Order

E11.1 An action plan order is a 'community order' within the meaning of the CJA 1991, s. 6(4), so that the imposition of an action plan order requires justification in terms of the seriousness of the offence, or the offence and one or more offences associated with it. The relevant statutory criteria are set out at **E4.1**.

Crime and Disorder Act 1998, s. 69

(1) This section applies where a child or young person is convicted of an offence other than one for which the sentence is fixed by law.

(2) Subject to the provisions of this section and section 70 below, the court by or before which the offender is convicted may, if it is of the opinion that it is desirable to do so in the interests of securing his rehabilitation, or of preventing the commission by him of further offences, make an order (an 'action plan order') which—

(a) requires the offender, for a period of three months beginning with the date of the order, to comply with an action plan, that is to say, a series of requirements with respect to his actions and whereabouts during that period;

(b) places the offender under the supervision for that period of the responsible officer; and

(c) requires the offender to comply with any directions given by that officer with a view to the implementation of that plan.

(3) The court shall not make an action plan order unless it has been notified by the Secretary of State that arrangements for implementing such orders are available in the area proposed to be named in the order and the notice has not been withdrawn.

(4) The court shall not make an action plan order in respect of the offender if—

(a) he is already the subject of such an order; or

(b) the court proposes to pass on him a custodial sentence or a sentence under section 53(1) of the [CYPA 1933] or to make in respect of him a probation order, a community service order, a combination order, a supervision order, an attendance centre order or a referral order under part I of the Youth Justice and Criminal Evidence Act 1999.

(5) Requirements included in an action plan order, or directions given by a responsible officer, may require the offender to do all or any of the followings things, namely—

(a) to participate in activities specified in the requirements or directions at a time or times so specified;

(b) to present himself to a person or persons specified in the requirements or directions at a place or places and at a time or times so specified;

(c) to attend at an attendance centre specified in the requirements or directions for a number of hours so specified;

(d) to stay away from a place or places specified in the requirements or directions;

(e) to comply with any arrangements for his education specified in the requirements or directions;

(f) to make reparation specified in the requirements or directions to a person or persons so specified or to the community at large; and

    (g)   to attend any hearing fixed by the court under section 70(3) below.

   (6)   Such requirements and directions shall, as far as practicable, be such as to avoid—

    (a)   any conflict with the offender's religious beliefs or with the requirements of any other community order to which he may be subject; and

    (b)   any interference with the times, if any, at which he normally works or attends school or any other educational establishment.

   (7)   Subsection (5)(c) above does not apply unless the offence committed by the offender is punishable with imprisonment in the case of a person aged 21 or over.

   (8)   A person shall not be specified in requirements or directions under subsection (5)(f) above unless—

    (a)   he is identified by the court or, as the case may be, the responsible officer as a victim of the offence or a person otherwise affected by it; and

    (b)   he consents to the reparation being made.

   (9)   An action plan order shall name the petty sessions area in which it appears to the court making the order, or to the court varying any provision included in the order in pursuance of this subsection, that the offender resides or will reside.

   (10)   In this section 'responsible officer', in relation to an action plan order, means one of the following who is specified in the order, namely—

    (a)   a probation officer;

    (b)   a social worker of a local authority social services department; and

    (c)   a member of a youth offending team.

   (11)   An action plan order shall be a community order for the purposes of part I of the 1991 Act; and the provisions of that part, which include provisions with respect to restrictions on imposing, and procedural requirements for, community sentences (sections 6 and 7), shall apply accordingly.

The requirement of attendance at an attendance centre in s. 69(5)(c) is restricted by s. 69(7) to cases in which the offender has committed an offence punishable with imprisonment in the case of an adult. For attendance centre orders, see **E9**. The requirement to make reparation in s. 69(5)(f) may be compared with the equivalent provision in relation to reparation orders: see **E12**. The wording of s. 69(8) indicates that the court may require reparation to be made to a person who is the victim of the offence or someone 'otherwise affected' by it. Thus the court might require reparation to be made by the offender to the victim of an assault committed by him, and/or to be made to a bystander who suffered shock as a result of witnessing the assault.

The court may pass an action plan order without first obtaining a pre-sentence report, but s. 70(1) requires that before making such an order the court must obtain and consider a written report by a probation officer, a social worker or a member of a youth offending team which indicates the requirements proposed by that person to be included in the order, the benefits to the offender that the proposed requirements are designed to achieve, and the attitude of a parent or guardian of the offender to the proposed requirements. If the offender is aged under 16, the report must also provide information as to the offender's family circumstances and the likely effect of the order on those circumstances. Before making an action plan order the court must explain to the offender in ordinary language the effect of the order and the requirements proposed to be included in it, the consequences which may follow if he fails to comply with any of those requirements, and that the order may be reviewed by the court on the application either of the offender or of the responsible officer (s. 70(2)).

Immediately after making the order the court may fix a further hearing for a date not more than 21 days ahead and direct the officer to make at that hearing a report as to the effectiveness of the order and the extent to which it has been implemented (s. 70(3)); provides the court with a discretion as to whether to order a hearing or further hearings. Section 70(3) in contrast to the requirement of periodic reviews where a drug treatment and testing order has been made by the court (see **E10.2**). At such a hearing, the court, after considering the officer's report may, on the application of the officer or the offender, vary the order by cancelling any provision included in it or by inserting in it any provision which that court could originally have included (s. 70(4)).

Mixing Action Plan Orders with Other Sentences or Orders

E11.2   Section 69(4) makes it clear that an action plan order cannot be imposed where the court also passes on the offender a custodial sentence or one of a range of other community orders. Section 69(4) does not mention drug treatment and testing orders, so presumably an action plan order could be combined with such an order in the case of an offender aged 16 or 17. Nor does s. 69(4) mention curfew orders, so presumably an action plan order could be combined with a curfew order. Although s. 69(4) does not mention reparation orders, the relevant provision on reparation orders (CDA 1998, s. 67(4)) states that reparation orders and action plan orders cannot be combined. There is nothing to prevent an action plan order being combined with a fine, or with ancillary orders such as a compensation order or an order for forfeiture under PCCA 1973, s. 43.

Breach and Revocation of Action Plan Orders and Reparation Orders

E11.3   Arrangements for discharge or variation, and for dealing with the offender's failure to comply with the terms of an action plan order (or reparation order) are set out in the CDA 1998, sch. 5. Where an action plan order or reparation order is in force and it is proved to the satisfaction of the appropriate youth court, on the application of the responsible officer, that the offender has failed to comply with any requirement in the order, the court shall proceed as follows.

Crime and Disorder Act 1998, sch. 5, para. 3

(2)   The court—
(a)   whether or not it also makes an order under paragraph 2 above [to discharge or vary the action plan order or reparation order] may order the offender to pay a fine of an amount not exceeding £1,000, or make an attendance centre order or curfew order in respect of him; or
(b)   if the reparation order or action plan order was made by a magistrates' court, may discharge the order and deal with him, for the offence in respect of which the order was made, in any manner in which he could have been dealt with for that offence by the court which made the order if the order had not been made; or
(c)   if the reparation order or action plan order was made by the Crown Court, may commit him in custody or release him on bail until he can be brought or appear before the Crown Court.

Where the youth court proceeds under para. 3(2)(c), it must send to the Crown Court a certificate detailing the offender's failure to comply, together with such other particulars as may be desirable. Where the offender appears before the Crown Court, and it is proved to the satisfaction of the court that he has failed to comply with the relevant order, that court may deal with him for the offence in respect of which the order was made, in any manner in which it could have dealt with him for the offence if it had not made the order. Where the Crown Court so deals with the offender, it must revoke the action plan order or reparation order, if it is still in force. Whether the offender is dealt with by the youth court or the Crown Court, the court when dealing with the failure to comply must take into account the extent to which the offender has complied with the terms of the order (CDA 1998, sch. 5, para. 3(4) to (8)).

Paragraphs 4 and 5 of sch. 5 deal with further procedural and supplemental matters, including the requirement that the offender shall normally be present before the court which is dealing with his failure to comply with the order.

SECTION E12: REPARATION ORDERS

Under ss. 67 and 68 of the CDA 1998, the Crown Court and youth courts have power to impose a reparation order on an offender aged under 18 who is convicted of any offence except murder. Powers to impose a reparation order are initially made available only to certain courts on a pilot basis (see CDA 1998, s. 67(3)). Such an order cannot be made in respect of an offence committed before the commencement of ss. 67 and 68 (30 September 1998).

Power to Make a Reparation Order

A reparation order is *not* a 'community order' within the meaning of the CJA 1991, **E12.1** s. 6(4).

Crime and Disorder Act 1998, s. 67

(1)   This section applies where a child or young person is convicted of an offence other than one for which the sentence is fixed by law.

(2)   Subject to the provisions of this section and section 68 below, the court by or before which the offender is convicted may make an order (a 'reparation order') which requires the offender to make reparation specified in the order—

(a)   to a person or persons so specified; or

(b)   to the community at large;

and any person so specified must be a person identified by the court as a victim of the offence or a person otherwise affected by it.

(3)   The court shall not make a reparation order unless it has been notified by the Secretary of State that arrangements for implementing such orders are available in the area proposed to be named in the order and the notice has not been withdrawn.

(4)   The court shall not make a reparation order in respect of the offender if it proposes—

(a)   to pass on him a custodial sentence; or

(b)   to make in respect of him a community service order, a combination order, a supervision order which includes requirements imposed in pursuance of sections 12 to 12C of the [CYPA 1969], an action plan order or a referral order under part I of the Youth Justice and Criminal Evidence Act 1999.

(5)   A reparation order shall not require the offender—

(a)   to work for more than 24 hours in aggregate; or

(b)   to make reparation to any person without the consent of that person.

(6)   Subject to subsection (5) above, requirements specified in a reparation order shall be such as in the opinion of the court are commensurate with the seriousness of the offence, or the combination of the offence and one or more offences associated with it.

(7)   Requirements so specified shall, as far as practicable, be such as to avoid—

(a)   any conflict with the offender's religious beliefs or with the requirements of any community order to which he may be subject; and

(b)   any interference with the times, if any, at which the offender normally works or attends school or any other educational establishment.

(8)   Any reparation required by a reparation order—

(a)   shall be made under the supervision of the responsible officer; and

(b)   shall be made within a period of three months from the date of the making of the order.

(9)   A reparation order shall name the petty sessions area in which it appears to the court making the order or to the court varying any provision included in the order in pursuance of this subsection, that the offender resides or will reside.

(10)   In this section 'responsible officer', in relation to a reparation order, means one of the following who is specified in the order, namely—

(a)   a probation officer;

(b)   a social worker of a local authority social services department; and

(c) a member of a youth offending team.

(11) The court shall give reasons if it does not make a reparation order in a case where it has power to do so.

The wording of s. 67(2) indicates that the court may require reparation to be made to a person who is the victim of the offence, or to someone 'otherwise affected' by it. In a case of assault, this might include not just the victim of the assault but, instead or in addition, a bystander who suffered shock as a result of witnessing the assault. Since the reparation order is not a community order, it may be used where the offender has committed an offence which is not serious enough to justify the use of a community sentence although there seems to be no reason why, in an appropriate case, the reparation order could not be used as an alternative to one of the less onerous community orders. Section 67(6) makes it clear that the number of hours of work required of the young offender and, presumably, the nature of that work, must be such as in the opinion of the court are commensurate with the seriousness of the offence committed. A reparation order may be imposed without the court first obtaining a pre-sentence report but, by s. 68(1), before making a reparation order the court must obtain and consider a report from a probation officer, a social worker or a member of a youth offending team indicating the type of work which is suitable for the young offender, and the attitude of the victim, or victims, to the requirements to be included in the order. Before making a reparation order, the court must explain to the offender in ordinary language the effect of the order and of the requirements proposed to be included in it, the consequences which may follow if he fails to comply with any of those requirements, and that the order may be reviewed by the court on the application either of the offender or of the responsible officer (s. 68(2)). Section 67(11) requires the court to give reasons why it has not made a reparation order in a case where it had power to do so. A similar provision exists in relation to compensation orders (see PCCA 1973, s. 35(1), at **E18.1**).

Mixing Reparation Orders with Other Sentences or Orders

E12.2 Section 67(4) makes it clear that a reparation order cannot be imposed where the court also passes on the offender a custodial sentence, or one of a range of community orders. Section 67(4) does not mention drug treatment and testing orders, so presumably a reparation order could be combined with such an order in the case of an offender aged 16 or 17. Nor does s. 67(4) mention fines, probation orders, curfew orders or attendance centre orders, so it appears that such orders could be combined with a reparation order. A reparation order may be combined with a supervision order which does not contain the particular requirements referred to, but it cannot be combined with an action plan order. There is nothing to prevent a reparation order being combined with ancillary orders such as a compensation order or an order for forfeiture under PCCA 1973, s. 43.

Breach and Revocation of Reparation Orders

E12.3 Arrangements for dealing with the offender's failure to comply with the terms of a reparation order are set out in the CDA 1998, sch. 5. The relevant provisions were considered at **E11.3**.

SECTION E13: REFERRAL TO A YOUTH OFFENDER PANEL

Under part I of the YJCEA 1999, a youth court or, exceptionally, an adult magistrates' **E13.1** court, dealing with an offender under the age of 18 for whom this is his first conviction, is in certain circumstances required to sentence the young offender by ordering him to be referred to a youth offender panel. In other circumstances the court has a discretion to deal with the young offender in that way. The youth offender panel is composed of people with an interest or expertise in dealing with young people. The panel will agree a 'contract' with the offender and his family which is aimed at tackling the offending behaviour and its causes. The contract will set out certain requirements, which may include the young offender being required to apologise to, and carry out some form of reparation for, the victim of the offence, or to carry out community work, or to take part in family counselling or drug rehabilitation. These requirements are specified by the youth offender panel rather than the sentencing court, and are not dealt with further here.

Powers to make referral orders are expected to come into force on 1 April 2000. They are initially made available only to certain courts on a pilot basis.

Requirement to Refer, and Power to Refer, Young Offender to a Youth Offender Panel

The circumstances which must exist before the court is *required* to make a referral order **E13.2** are set out in YJCEA 1999, ss. 1 and 2(1). In respect of s. 1, they are as follows:

(a) that the youth court (or other magistrates' court) is dealing with an offender under the age of 18 where neither the offence nor any associated offence is one for which the sentence is fixed by law;

(b) the court is not proposing to pass a custodial sentence or make a hospital order in respect of the offence or any associated offence;

(c) the court is not proposing to grant an absolute discharge in respect of the offence;

(d) the compulsory referral conditions set out in s. 2 are satisfied; and

(e) the court has been notified by the Secretary of State that arrangements for the implementation of referral orders are available in the area in which the young offender resides or will reside.

The compulsory referral conditions referred to are set out in s. 2(1). They are satisfied in relation to an offence if the offender:

(a) pleaded guilty to the offence and to any associated offence;

(b) has never been convicted by or before a court in the United Kingdom of any offence other than the offence and any associated offence; and

(c) has never been bound over in criminal proceedings in England and Wales or Northern Ireland to keep the peace or to be of good behaviour.

The circumstances which must exist before a court has *power* to make a referral order, but is not under a requirement to do so, are set out in YJCEA 1999, ss. 1 and 2(2). The applicable parts of s. 1 (referred to above) are (a) to (c) and (e). The terms of s. 2(2) are satisfied in relation to an offence if:

(a) the offender is being dealt with by the court for the offence and one or more associated offences;

(b)   although he pleaded guilty to at least one of the offences mentioned in paragraph (a), he also pleaded not guilty to at least one of them;
(c)   he has never been convicted by or before a court in the United Kingdom of any offence other than the offences mentioned in paragraph (a); and
(d)   he has never been bound over in criminal proceedings in England and Wales or Northern Ireland to keep the peace or to be of good behaviour.

In relation to s. 2(1)(b) and (2)(c), s. 2(5) makes it clear that an offence in respect of which the offender has previously been conditionally discharged does count as a conviction for these purposes, notwithstanding PCCA 1973, s. 1C (see **E14.6**). It appears that the wording of s. 2(2)(b) is satisfied even if the young offender is acquitted of the offence or offences to which he pleaded not guilty.

Making of Referral Orders

E13.3   The referral order must specify the relevant youth offending team responsible for implementing the order, require the offender to attend each of the appropriate meetings of the panel, and specify the period (the 'compliance period') during which the youth offender contract is to have effect. The minimum compliance period is three months and the maximum period is one year (s. 3(1)). When making the order, the court must explain to the young offender in ordinary language the effect of the order and the consequences which may follow if there is a failure to agree the terms of the contract or if the young offender breaches the terms of the contract (s. 3(3)). Where the court is dealing with the young offender for associated offences and is passing more than one referral order, the court may order that the specified periods of the orders shall run concurrently or consecutively to one another, but the total period shall not exceed 12 months (s. 3(5) to (7)).

In the case of a young offender who is under the age of 16 when the order is made, the court must, and in any other case may, make an order requiring the parent or guardian of the young offender (or a representative of a local authority where that local authority has parental responsibility and the young offender is in the authority's care or is provided by them with accommodation under any statutory provision) to attend the relevant meetings of the youth offender panel (s. 5(1)). Section 5(1) does not apply if the court is satisfied that in the circumstances of the case it would be unreasonable to require such attendance (s. 5(2)).

Mixing Referral Orders with Other Sentences or Orders

E13.4   There are very strict limitations on the mixing of a referral order with other sentences or orders. A referral order cannot be made where the court imposes a custodial sentence or hospital order on the offender for the offence or for any associated offence, or where it grants an absolute discharge for the offence (s. 1(1)). Where the court makes a referral order for an offence, it must not at the same time deal with the offender for that offence in any of the 'prohibited ways', which are to impose any community sentence, fine, reparation order (under CDA 1998, s. 67) or conditional discharge (s. 4(4)). Where the court makes a referral order for an offence, it is required to deal with any associated offence either by making a referral order or by passing an absolute discharge, and it must not deal with any associated offence in any of the 'prohibited ways' (s. 4(3)). Whether in respect of the offence for which the referral order is made or for any associated offence, the court must not make an order binding over the young offender to keep the peace or to be of good behaviour (see **E15.1**) or binding over the parent or guardian of the young offender under the CJA 1991, s. 58 (see **E16.4**) nor may it make a parenting order under CDA 1998, s. 8 (see **E16.1**). Finally, where there is a requirement rather than a power to make a referral order, the court may not defer passing sentence on the young offender under the PCCA 1973, s. 1 (see **D17.40**), although other specified powers of adjournment, remand, remission for sentence and committal for sentence are unaffected (s. 4(7)). Notwithstanding all these restrictions, it would still be permissible for the court, at the same time as making a referral order, in an appropriate case to make a compensation order under PCCA 1973, s. 35, a restitution order under the Theft Act 1968, s. 28 (see **E19**) or a forfeiture order under PCCA 1973, s. 43 (see **E20**).

Breach, Revocation and Amendment of Referral Orders

Provisions for dealing with a young offender who is referred back to court in breach of **E13.5** a referral order, or is convicted while subject to a referral order, are set out in the YJCEA 1999, sch. 1. In the case of a young offender who is under the age of 18 when he appears in court having been referred back, the appropriate court is the youth court acting for the relevant petty sessions area and, if he is 18 or over at that time, it is a magistrates' court acting for that area (para. 1).

If it is proved to the satisfaction of the court that the youth offender panel was entitled to make the finding of breach of the referral order which resulted in the young offender being referred back to court, or that any discretion of the panel in that respect was exercised reasonably, the court may (provided that the young offender is present before it) revoke the referral order and may deal with the young offender in any other manner in which he could have been dealt with for that offence by the court which made the order (para. 5(5)(a)). The court must have regard to the circumstances of his referral back to court and, where a contract has taken effect, the extent of his compliance with it (para. 5(5)(b)). The court may, where appropriate, commit the young offender to the Crown Court for sentence, in which case the Crown Court is not limited to the magistrates' court's powers (para. 5(7)). The court may, on the other hand, decide not to revoke the referral order, either because the court does not endorse the decision of the panel to refer the order back to the court or for any other reason (para. 7).

Where an offender who is subject to a referral order is convicted of an offence, the court dealing with the offence may, if that offence was committed before the referral order was made, sentence the offender for the new offence by extending the compliance period of the referral order (para. 11). The court may adopt a similar course even where the offence was committed after the referral order was made, but only if the court is satisfied that 'exceptional circumstances' exist, and states in open court why it is so satisfied (para. 12). In neither of these situations, however, can the compliance period be extended so as to exceed 12 months. Apart from cases falling within para. 11 or 12, the court will deal with the commission of a further offence under para. 14, which states that, unless the court sentencing for the new offence deals with the case by way of absolute discharge, the effect of dealing with the offender for the further offence is to revoke the referral order. The court may, if it is in the interests of justice, deal with the offender for the original offence in any other manner in which the offender could have been dealt with for that offence by the court which made the referral order (para. 14(3)). The court must have regard, where a contract has taken effect, to the extent to which the young offender has complied with its terms (para. 14(4)). The court may, where appropriate, commit the young offender to the Crown Court for sentence, in which case the Crown Court is limited to the magistrates' court's powers (para. 14(5)).

The court which made the referral order may vary the youth offending team specified in the order because of the young offender's change of residence (s. 6(5)).

SECTION E14: ABSOLUTE AND CONDITIONAL DISCHARGES

Power to Grant Absolute and Conditional Discharges

E14.1   **Powers of Criminal Courts Act 1973, s. 1A**

(1)   Where a court by or before which a person is convicted of an offence (not being an offence the sentence for which is fixed by law or falls to be imposed under section 2(2), 3(2) or 4(2) of the Crime (Sentences) Act 1997) is of opinion, having regard to the circumstances including the nature of the offence and the character of the offender, that it is inexpedient to inflict punishment, the court may make an order either—

(a)   discharging him absolutely; or

(b)   if the court thinks fit, discharging him subject to the condition that he commits no offence during such period, not exceeding three years from the date of the order, as may be specified in the order.

(1A)   Subsection 1(b) above has effect subject to section 66(4) of the Crime and Disorder Act 1998 (effect of reprimands and warnings).

(2)   An order discharging a person subject to such a condition is in this Act referred to as 'an order for conditional discharge', and the period specified in any such order as 'the period of conditional discharge'.

(3)   Before making an order for conditional discharge the court shall explain to the offender in ordinary language that if he commits another offence during the period of conditional discharge he will be liable to be sentenced for the original offence.

(4)   Where, under the following provisions of this part of this Act, a person conditionally discharged under this section is sentenced for the offence in respect of which the order for conditional discharge was made, that order shall cease to have effect.

A discharge is *not* a community order within the meaning of the CJA 1991, s. 6(4).

In *Wehner* [1977] 1 WLR 1143, it was held that while it was 'sound practice' for the court to explain the effect of a conditional discharge to the offender personally, the delegation of the task of explanation to the offender's lawyer is not prohibited, provided that the court is satisfied that the explanation has been made and understood before it makes the order. By the PCCA 1973, s. 12(1), any court may, on making an order for conditional discharge, allow any person who consents to do so to give security for the good behaviour of the offender. Where a conditional discharge has been imposed on appeal, it shall be deemed, if made on appeal from a magistrates' court to have been imposed by that court and, if made on appeal from the Crown Court or the Court of Appeal, to have been made by the Crown Court (s. 12(2)). These subsections are described as amended with effect from 30 September 1998 by the CDA 1998, sch. 7, para. 18.

SENTENCING PRINCIPLES

Use of Absolute Discharge

E14.2   The power to grant an absolute discharge is available to all criminal courts whatever the age of the offender and, with the exception of murder cases or where the C(S)A 1997, s. 2, 3 or 4, applies whatever the offence committed. Its imposition may reflect the triviality of the offence, the circumstances in which it came to be prosecuted, or special factors relating to the offender. Cases in which the Court of Appeal has advocated the use of the absolute discharge include *Smedleys Ltd* v *Breed* [1974] AC 839 and *King* [1977] Crim LR 627.

Use of Conditional Discharge

The power to grant a conditional discharge is available to all criminal courts whatever **E14.3** the age of the offender. The conditional discharge cannot be used in murder cases or where the C(S)A 1997, s. 2, 3 or 4, applies, nor where the offender has been convicted of without reasonable excuse doing something which he is prohibited from doing by an anti-social behaviour order (CDA 1998, s. 1(11)), nor where the offender has been convicted of without reasonable excuse doing anything which he is prohibited from doing by a sex offender order (CDA 1998, s. 2(9)), nor, except where there are 'exceptional circumstances' relating to the offence or the offender which justify its doing so, where the offender is convicted of an offence within two years of receiving a warning from a police officer (CDA 1998, ss. 65 and 66(4)).

When a discharge is conditional, the sole condition is that the offender should commit no further offence during the period of the conditional discharge. No other condition or requirement may be inserted. The period of the conditional discharge is fixed by the court but must not exceed three years. Cases in which the Court of Appeal has advocated the use of the conditional discharge include *Whitehead* (1979) 1 Cr App R (S) 187 and *Watts* (1984) 6 Cr App R (S) 61 (discussed at **E2.3**).

Combining Discharge with Other Sentences or Orders

A discharge cannot be combined with a punitive measure for the same offence (*Savage* **E14.4** (1983) 5 Cr App R (S) 216) except where permitted by statute. Thus a discharge cannot be combined with a custodial sentence, a community sentence or a fine (*Sanck* (1990) 12 Cr App R (S) 155). If, however, an offender is given a discharge for one of a number of offences, the court is free to exercise its normal powers of sentence with respect to his other offences (*Bainbridge* (1979) 1 Cr App R (S) 36). Section 12(4) of the PCCA 1973, as substituted by the CDA 1998, sch. 7, para. 18, states that:

> (4)   Nothing in section 1A of this Act shall be construed as preventing a court, on discharging an offender absolutely or conditionally in respect of any offence, from making an order for costs against the offender or imposing any disqualification on him or from making in respect of the offence an order under section 35 or 43 of this Act or section 28 of the Theft Act 1968.

For the PCCA 1973, s. 35 (compensation orders), see **E18.7**; for s. 43 (forfeiture orders) see **E20.3**; and for s. 28 of the 1968 Act (restitution orders), see **E19.2**. The new wording of s. 12(4) permits the combination of a discharge with 'any disqualification'. Thus, for example, a discharge may be combined with an order for disqualification from driving, whether imposed under the Road Traffic Offenders Act 1988 (see also s. 46 of that Act), or the PCCA 1973, s. 44 (see **E23.4**), or the C(S)A 1997, s. 39 (see **E23.5**). A discharge may also now be combined with an order to disqualify a person from acting as a company director (reversing the decision in *Young* (1990) 12 Cr App R (S) 262).

Breach of Conditional Discharge

A conditional discharge can be breached only by the conviction of the offender of a **E14.5** further offence committed during the period of the discharge (PCCA 1973, s. 1B(1)). A court dealing with the breach (the Crown Court if it made the conditional discharge, or the magistrates' court if it made it) may sentence the offender for the original offence in any manner in which it could have dealt with him if he had just been convicted before the court for that offence (s. 1B(6)), but the Crown Court dealing with a person conditionally discharged by a magistrates' court is limited to the lower court's powers (s. 1B(7)). One magistrates' court may deal with breach of a conditional discharge imposed by a different magistrates' court, but only with the consent of the original magistrates' court (s. 1B(8)). Where an offender aged under 18 has been conditionally discharged by a magistrates' court in respect of an offence triable only on indictment in the case of an adult, and the offender has now attained the age of 18, the powers exercisable by the court under s. 1B(6), (7) or (8) are to impose a fine not exceeding £5,000 for the original offence, or to deal with the offender in any way in which a magistrates' court could deal with him if it had just convicted him of an offence punishable with imprisonment for a term not exceeding six months (s. 1B(9)). Subsection 1B(9) is here described as amended by the CDA 1998, sch. 7, para. 14, which came into force on 30 September 1998. Sentencing for the original offence always terminates the conditional discharge itself, but any order for compensation or costs made at the time of the discharge remains valid (*Evans* [1963] 1 QB 979).

Limited Effect of Conviction on the Grant of Absolute or Conditional Discharge

E14.6   **Powers of Criminal Courts Act 1973, s. 1C**

    (1)   Subject to subsection (2) below and to section 50(1A) of the Criminal Appeal Act 1968 and to section 108(1A) of the Magistrates' Courts Act 1980, a conviction of an offence for which an order is made under this part of this Act discharging the offender absolutely or conditionally shall be deemed not to be a conviction for any purpose other than—

    (a)   the purposes of the proceedings in which the order is made and of any subsequent proceedings which may be taken against the offender under section 1B of this Act

    (b)   [repealed].

    (2)   Where the offender was of or over 18 years of age at the time of his conviction of the offence in question and is subsequently sentenced under this part of this Act for that offence, subsection (1) above shall cease to apply to the conviction.

    (3)   Without prejudice to the preceding provisions of this section, the conviction of an offender who is discharged absolutely or conditionally under this part of this Act shall in any event be disregarded for the purposes of any enactment or instrument which—

    (a)   imposes any disqualification or disability upon convicted persons; or

    (b)   authorises or requires the imposition of any such disqualification or disability.

    (4)   The preceding provisions of this section shall not affect—

    (a)   any right of any offender discharged absolutely or conditionally under this part of this Act to rely on his conviction in bar of any subsequent proceedings for the same offence; or

    (b)   the restoration of any property in consequence of the conviction of any such offender; or

    (c)   . . .

The two statutory provisions mentioned in s. 1C(1) allow an offender who has been discharged by the Crown Court or a magistrates' court to appeal against his conviction, sentence or other ancillary order made in conjunction with the discharge. A conviction in respect of which a discharge is granted does not count for the purpose of putting a suspended sentence into effect (see **E2.8**) nor, it is submitted, does it count as a previous conviction for the purposes of s. 2, 3 or 4 of the C(S)A 1997. The phrase 'subsequently sentenced' in s. 1C(2) refers to the situation where the offender originally granted a discharge is in breach of that order so that he becomes liable to be sentenced for the original offence. Where the court dealing with the breach chooses not to deal with the original offence, therefore, the conviction in respect of it counts for limited purposes only.

By virtue of the CJA 1991, s. 29, a court may, when considering the seriousness of an offence, take into account the offender's previous convictions which were dealt with by way of discharge and any failure of his to respond to previous sentences which were discharges. See **E1.16**.

SECTION E15: BINDING OVER

This section deals with the court's power to bind over a person to keep the peace and the Crown Court's power to bind a person over to come up for judgment. The power to bind over a parent or guardian of an offender aged under 16 is dealt with at **E16.4**.

BINDING OVER TO KEEP THE PEACE

Power to Bind Over to Keep the Peace

Powers of a magistrates' court to bind over a person to keep the peace or to be of good **E15.1** behaviour arise either on complaint (under the MCA 1980, s. 115) or of the court's own motion under common law powers and pursuant to various statutes, most importantly the Justices of the Peace Act 1361. While an order under s. 115 can be made only after a full hearing of the complaint, where the court binds over of its own motion it may do so at any time before the conclusion of criminal proceedings, on withdrawal of the case by the prosecution, on a decision by the prosecution to offer no evidence, on an adjournment, or upon acquittal of the defendant, where a justice considers that the person's conduct is such that there might be a breach of peace in the future, whether committed by him or by others, or where the person's behaviour was *contra bonos mores* (*Hughes* v *Holley* [1987] Crim LR 253). These powers, which are exercisable 'not by reason of any offence having been committed, but as a measure of preventive justice' (*Veater* v *Glennon* [1981] 1 WLR 567), may be used in a wide variety of situations, including as a sentencing option against a convicted offender. A person bound over to keep the peace or to be of good behaviour may be made subject to a condition that he shall not possess, use, or carry a firearm (Firearms Act 1968, s. 52(1)).

The power to bind over is frequently used as a method of disposal in cases involving minor assaults or minor incidents of public disorder, where the prosecution are prepared not to proceed, provided that the defendant agrees to be bound over. The person bound over is required to enter into a recognizance in an amount which will be forfeited if he fails to keep the peace for a specified period.

Justices of the Peace Act 1968, s. 1

> (7)   It is hereby declared that any court of record having a criminal jurisdiction has, as ancillary to that jurisdiction, the power to bind over to be of good behaviour, a person who or whose case is before the court, by requiring him to enter into his own recognisances or to find sureties or both, and committing him to prison if he does not comply.

The Crown Court is a court of record (Supreme Court Act 1981, s. 45), so that both magistrates' courts and the Crown Court have powers to bind over offenders and others who are before the court. The Court of Appeal (Criminal Division) also possesses these powers (*Sharp* [1957] 1 QB 552). Those who may be bound over include an acquitted defendant (*Inner London Crown Court, ex parte Benjamin* (1986) 85 Cr App R 267), a defendant before the court in respect of whom the prosecution has been unable to proceed (*Lincoln Crown Court, ex parte Jude* [1998] 1 WLR 24), a witness before the court (*Sheldon* v *Bromfield Justices* [1964] 2 QB 573), and a complainant (*Wilkins* [1907] 2 KB 380). On the other hand, the victim of an assault who is not a party to the proceedings and has not been called to give evidence against the assailant, who has pleaded guilty, cannot be bound over (*Swindon Crown Court, ex parte Pawitter Singh* [1984] 1 WLR 449), nor can a person who is the subject of an unconditional witness order, but who is in the event not been required to give evidence (*Kingston-upon-Thames Crown Court, ex parte Guarino* [1986] Crim LR 325).

Bind Over: Procedural Requirements

E15.2   Where a court contemplates exercising its power against a person who has not been charged with an offence, it should ensure that the person concerned understands what the court has in mind and give him the opportunity to make representations (*Hendon Justices, ex parte Gorchein* [1973] 1 WLR 1502). It is also good practice to allow an acquitted defendant, upon whom the court proposes to make a bind over, an opportunity to address the court on the matter (*Woking Justices, ex parte Gossage* [1973] QB 448). In *Middlesex Crown Court, ex parte Khan* (1997) 161 JP 240, the Divisional Court stated that before binding over an acquitted defendant the judge should be satisfied beyond reasonable doubt that the defendant posed a potential threat to other persons and was a man of violence. A mere belief that the acquitted person might pose such a threat was not enough. In the case of a disturbance in the face of the court, natural justice does not require that the person concerned be given a warning or a chance to make representations before being bound over (*North London Metropolitan Magistrate, ex parte Haywood* [1973] 1 WLR 965). Where the court proposes to bind over a person who has been convicted, in anything other than a trivial sum, his means and other personal circumstances should be investigated and representations allowed in respect of them (*Central Criminal Court, ex parte Boulding* [1984] QB 813). It was held in *Lincoln Crown Court, ex parte Jude* [1998] 1 WLR 24 that a sum of £500 was not so trivial an amount as to dispense with the requirement of a means inquiry. The court should fix the period of the recognisance and the sum of money to be forfeited upon breach at the time when it orders the bind over. There is no upper limit to the amount, save that it must be reasonable. A person may, therefore, be bound over in a sum which exceeds the maximum fine which could be exacted for the relevant offence (*Sandbach Justices, ex parte Williams* [1935] 2 KB 192).

The period for which the order may run is entirely within the discretion of the court. Although an order to bind over may name a person or persons for whose special protection it is made (e.g., *Wilson* v *Skeock* (1949) 65 TLR 418), there is no power to insert specific conditions in an order binding a person over to keep the peace or to be of good behaviour (*Randall* (1986) 8 Cr App R (S) 433). Under the Magistrates' Courts (Appeals from Binding Over Orders) Act 1956, there is a right of appeal to the Crown Court against an order by a magistrates' court to enter into recognisances to keep the peace or to be of good behaviour. See, further, *Preston Crown Court, ex parte Pamplin* [1981] Crim LR 338. Where the bind over is made by the Crown Court on sentence, an appeal lies to the Court of Appeal by virtue of Criminal Appeal Act 1968, s. 50(1).

Requirement for Additional Penalty

E15.3   It is unclear whether a convicted offender may be bound over to keep the peace or to be of good behaviour without the passing of some other sentence. The wording of the Justices of the Peace Act 1968, s. 1(7) (see **E15.1**), indicates that the bind over is 'ancillary' to the court's criminal jurisdiction, and this may mean that a court should determine the penalty for the offence before the ancillary power of binding over to keep the peace is considered. There is evidence, however, that bind overs are sometimes imposed on sentence without any additional penalty.

Refusal or Failure to Enter into Recognisance

E15.4   The sanction available to a magistrates' court in the case of a failure or a refusal to enter into a recognisance is imprisonment. This may be for a maximum period of six months or until the person complies with the order, if sooner (MCA 1980, s. 115(3)). Imprisonment cannot be imposed on a person who is under the age of 21 (CJA 1982, s. 1). Such a person may properly consent to be bound over even though his refusal to consent could not lead to imprisonment (*Conlan* v *Oxford* (1983) 5 Cr App R (S) 237).

It appears that a person aged between 18 and 20 inclusive who refuses to consent to be bound over by a magistrates' court may be detained under the CJA 1982, s. 9 (see *Howley* v *Oxford* (1985) 81 Cr App R 246 and **E17.2**). There is no power in these circumstances to order the detention of a person who is under the age of 18, but a magistrates' court may order such a person to attend at an attendance centre (see CJA 1982, s. 17(1)(a) and **E9.1**). It seems that the Crown Court may deal with a refusal to be bound over as a contempt of court.

Failure to Comply with Conditions of Order

If a person who has been bound over is adjudged to have failed to comply with the **E15.5** conditions of the order, the court may forfeit the whole or part of the recognisance in its discretion, allow time for payment or direct payment by instalments (PCCA 1973, s. 31(1)), but it is not empowered to impose a prison term (*Finch* (1962) 47 Cr App R 58, *Gilbert* (1974) CSP D10–3A01). The Crown Court, when forfeiting a recognisance, must fix a term of imprisonment or detention, to be served in default (PCCA 1973, s. 31(2), (3) and (3A)). In a magistrates' court, a recognisance can only be declared to be forfeit by way of an order on complaint (MCA 1980, s. 120), by virtue of whichever power the bind over was originally imposed. Such proceedings are civil in character, and require only the civil standard of proof (*Marlow Justices, ex parte O'Sullivan* [1984] QB 381), but the person concerned should be told the nature of the breach alleged and be given opportunity to present evidence, call witnesses or give an explanation (*McGregor* [1945] 2 All ER 180). There is no right of appeal against an adjudication of forfeiture (*Durham Justices, ex parte Laurent* [1945] KB 33).

BINDING OVER TO COME UP FOR JUDGMENT

Powers to Bind Over to Come Up for Judgment

The common-law power (see *Spratling* [1911] 1 KB 77) to bind over to come up for **E15.6** judgment, which can be exercised only by the Crown Court, may be exercised in respect of any offence except one where the penalty is fixed by law. The effect of such an order is that the offender is bound over on recognisance on specified conditions. If he breaks one or more of the conditions, he will be brought back before the court for sentence but, if he does not break any of the conditions during the specified period, he will either not be sentenced for the offence, or will receive a nominal penalty.

A bind over to come up for judgment is in lieu of sentence, and it is therefore wrong to impose it in addition to a sentence for the offence (*Ayu* [1958] 1 WLR 1264). An offender must consent to the making of the order, though consent would not be vitiated by a realistic expectation of a custodial sentence in the alternative (*Williams* [1982] 1 WLR 1398). Where the judge proposes to call an offender to come up for judgment, notice shall be given to him (*David* (1939) 27 Cr App R 50).

If the offender is in breach of the order, he may forfeit the recognisance as well as being sentenced for the original offence. Where a person is brought back before the court on the ground that a recognisance entered into by him has been broken, the facts against him must be proved beyond reasonable doubt (*McGarry* (1945) 30 Cr App R 187). The order is a 'sentence' made on conviction on indictment (*Abrahams* (1952) 36 Cr App R 147) and an appeal lies to the Court of Appeal (Criminal Appeal Act 1968, s. 50(1); *Williams* [1982] 1 WLR 1398).

In *Williams* [1982] 1 WLR 1398, the offender was a youth of 18 who was born in England to Jamaican parents. He was convicted of theft and had a number of previous convictions and findings of guilt. He was bound over to come up for judgment in his own recognisance, on condition that he accompanied his mother to Jamaica and did not return to the United Kingdom for five years. Lord Lane CJ, disapproving the order on the facts of the particular case, commented that the power to keep the offender out of the jurisdiction 'plainly should be used very sparingly' and should normally only be used to ensure that the offender goes to a country of which he is a citizen or in which he is habitually resident. This option may be contrasted with the courts' powers to order an offender's deportation (see **E22**). In the present case no such order could be made since the offender was a British subject. See also *Gonzalez-Baillon* (11 July 1997 unreported), where the Court of Appeal declined leave to appeal in a case where the offender, a Spanish national who had pleaded guilty to assault occasioning actual bodily harm, had been bound over to come up for judgment for five years on condition that he go back to Spain within three weeks and not return to the UK, and that prior to his departure he remain at a specified mental hospital. The offender had consented to this course of action. The Court of Appeal commented that the sentencer had found 'a humane and sensible solution to a difficult sentencing exercise', and declined to consider argument by counsel that exclusion from the UK for such a period contravened the European Convention on Human Rights and the European Community Treaty.

SECTION E16: ORDERS AGAINST PARENTS

PARENTING ORDERS

Under ss. 8 to 10 of the CDA 1998, the Crown Court and youth courts have power to **E16.1**
impose a parenting order on a parent or guardian of a child or young person where, *inter
alia*, that child or young person has been convicted of any offence (s. 8(1)(c)). Powers
to impose parenting orders are initially made available only to certain courts on a pilot
basis. Section 8(1)(a), (b) and (d) allow for the imposing of parenting orders in
consequence of the making of a child safety order in the case of a child, an anti-social
behaviour order or sex offender order in the case of a child or young person, or where a
parent is convicted of an offence involving failure to comply with a school attendance
order or failure to secure the regular attendance at school of a registered pupil. These
provisions are not considered further here.

Power to Make Parenting Order

Crime and Disorder Act 1998, s. 8   E16.2

(4)   A parenting order is an order which requires the parent—
   (a)   to comply, for a period not exceeding twelve months, with such requirements as
are specified in the order; and
   (b)   subject to subsection (5) below, to attend, for a concurrent period not exceeding
three months and not more than once in any week, such counselling or guidance sessions
as may be specified in directions given by the responsible officer;
and in this subsection 'week' means a period of seven days beginning with a Sunday.
(5)   A parenting order may, but need not, include such a requirement as is mentioned
in subsection (4)(b) above in any case where such an order has been made in respect of the
parent on a previous occasion.
(6)   The relevant condition is that the parenting order would be desirable in the interests
of preventing—
      . . .
      (b)   in a case falling within paragraph (c) of that subsection, the commission of any
further offence by the child or young person;
      . . .
(7)   The requirements that may be specified under subsection (4)(a) above are those
which the court considers desirable in the interests of preventing any such repetition or, as
the case may be, the commission of any such further offence.
(8)   In this section and section 9 below 'responsible officer', in relation to a parenting
order, means one of the following who is specified in the order, namely—
   (a)   a probation officer;
   (b)   a social worker of a local authority social services department; and
   (c)   a member of a youth offending team.

Requirements specified in s. 8(4)(a) might commonly include that the parent ensure
that the child is accompanied to and from school each day, and is indoors by a certain
hour in the evening. It is clear from s. 8(4)(b) and (5) that the court has no discretion
to dispense with the requirement of attendance at counselling sessions, unless the parent
has been the subject of a parenting order on a previous occasion. While s. 8 creates a
power to pass a parenting order where the young offender is aged under 18, s. 9 goes
further and places a duty on the court to make a parenting order where the young
offender is aged under 16. If, however, the court is not satisfied that the 'relevant
condition' is fulfilled (i.e. that the making of a parenting order would be desirable in the

interests of preventing the commission of any further offence by the child or young person under 16) then the court must state in open court that it is not so satisfied, and why it is not (s. 9(1)). Before making a parenting order the court need not obtain a pre-sentence report, but, by s. 9(2), before making a parenting order in a case where the young offender is aged under 16, the court must obtain and consider information about the young offender's family circumstances and the likely effect of the order on those circumstances. Section 9(3) requires that before making a parenting order the court must explain to the parent in ordinary language the effect of the order and of the requirements proposed to be included in it, the consequences which may follow if he fails to comply with any of those requirements, and that the court has power to review the order on the application either of the parent or of the responsible officer. Requirements specified in, and directions given under, a parenting order shall, as far as practicable, be such as to avoid any conflict with the parent's religious beliefs and any interference with the times, if any, at which he normally works or attends an educational establishment (s. 9(4)).

It should be noted that a parenting order cannot be made where the young offender has been sentenced by referral order (see **E13**) (CDA 1998, s. 8(2) and 9(1), as amended by YJCEA 1999, sch. 4, paras. 26 and 27).

Variation and Appeal

E16.3   If, while the parenting order is in force, application is made to the court either by the responsible officer or by the parent, the court may, where appropriate, make an order discharging the parenting order or varying it by cancelling any provision included within it or by inserting in it any provision which could have been included in the order if the court had then the power to make it and were exercising that power (s. 9(5)). If an application is made for the discharge of a parenting order and that application is dismissed, no fresh application for discharge can be made without the consent of the court which made the order (s. 9(6)).

A person in respect of whom a parenting order has been made by virtue of s. 8(1)(c) (commission of offence by offender aged under 18) has the same right of appeal against that order as if the offence that led to the making of the order were an offence committed by him and the order were a sentence passed on him for the offence (s. 10(4)).

Breach of Parenting Order

E16.4   If while a parenting order is in force the parent without reasonable excuse fails to comply with any requirement included in the order or specified in directions given by the responsible officer, he shall be liable on summary conviction to a fine not exceeding level 3 on the standard scale (s. 9(7)). It would appear that in the absence of such failure to comply by the parent, commission of a further offence by the child does not constitute a breach of the parenting order.

BINDING OVER OF PARENT OR GUARDIAN OF OFFENDER AGED UNDER 16

E16.5   The CJA 1991, s. 58(1), places an obligation upon magistrates' courts and the Crown Court to bind over the parent or guardian of an offender who is under the age of 16, whenever the court is satisfied that to do so would be desirable in the interests of preventing the commission by the young offender of further offences. If the court is not satisfied of that on the particular facts of the case, it should state in open court that it is not, and give reasons for that view. By virtue of s. 58(1A), inserted by YJCEA 1999, sch. 4, para. 20, such an order cannot be made where the young offender has been dealt with by way of referral order (see **E13**).

By s. 58(2), the court is empowered to order the parent or guardian to enter into a recognisance, in a sum not exceeding £1,000, to take proper care of the offender and exercise proper control over him. The maximum duration of the recognisance is until the offender reaches the age of 18, or for a period of three years, whichever is the shorter period. Entry into the recognisance requires the consent of the parent or guardian, but if consent is refused and the court considers that refusal unreasonable, the parent or guardian may be punished by a fine not exceeding £1,000. A court which has passed a community sentence on the relevant minor may include in the recognisance a provision that the minor's parent or guardian ensure that the minor complies with the requirements of that sentence. In fixing the level of the recognisance, the court shall take into account, among other things, the means of the parent or guardian, whether doing so has the effect of increasing or reducing the level of the recognisance.

As far as forfeiture of the recognisance is concerned, s. 58(3) states that the MCA 1980, s. 120, shall apply in relation to a recognisance under s. 58 as it does to a recognisance to keep the peace (see **E15.5**). The court may order forfeiture of the whole, or part, of the recognisance, together with costs. A right of appeal against an order under s. 58 made by a magistrates' court is created by s. 58(6) and where the order is made by the Crown Court, a similar right applies under s. 58(7).

FINE, COMPENSATION OR COSTS TO BE PAID BY PARENT OR GUARDIAN

The parent or guardian of a juvenile may be ordered by the court to pay the fine, costs **E16.6** or order for compensation imposed upon a juvenile by virtue of the CYPA 1933, s. 55.

Children and Young Persons Act 1933, s. 55

(1) Where—
     (a) a child or young person is convicted or found guilty of any offence for the commission of which a fine or costs may be imposed or a compensation order may be made under section 35 of the Powers of Criminal Courts Act 1973; and
     (b) the court is of opinion that the case would best be met by the imposition of a fine or costs or the making of such an order, whether with or without any other punishment,
it shall be the duty of the court to order that the fine, compensation or costs awarded be paid by the parent or guardian of the child or young person instead of by the child or young person himself, unless the court is satisfied—
     (i) that the parent or guardian cannot be found; or
     (ii) that it would be unreasonable to make an order for payment, having regard to the circumstances of the case.

Section 55(1A) further provides that where a child or young person would otherwise be required to pay a fine in respect of breach of a community order, the court shall order the fine to be paid by the parent or guardian, subject to the same qualifications as appear in s. 55(1). The court may make a financial circumstances order with respect to the parent or guardian (CJA 1991, s. 20(1B)).

Section 55(1B) states that in the case of a young person who has attained the age of 16 years, subsections (1) and (1A) shall have effect as if, instead of imposing a duty, they conferred a power to make such an order.

The court should not make an order under s. 55 against a parent or guardian without first considering the means of that parent or guardian (*Lenihan* v *West Yorkshire Metropolitan Police* (1981) 3 Cr App R (S) 42). It may be 'unreasonable' for the court to make an order under s. 55 in a case where the parent or guardian has done all that he or she reasonably could to prevent the offending (*Sheffield Crown Court, ex parte Clarkson* (1986) 8 Cr App R (S) 454; *TA* v *DPP* [1997] 1 Cr App R (S) 1). It was also made clear in that case that any assessment of the means of the parent or guardian, or any assessment of the extent to which the parent or guardian has been neglectful of the offender, should be made on the basis of properly admissible evidence and not simply assumed from the pre-sentence report prepared upon the offender.

While an order under s. 55 may be made against a parent or guardian who has failed to attend court after having been required to do so, apart from such case no order should be made without giving the parent or guardian an opportunity of being heard (s. 55(2)). An appeal against an order made by a magistrates' court under s. 55 lies to the Crown Court (s. 55(3)) and an appeal against an order made by the Crown Court under s. 55 lies to the Court of Appeal (s. 55(4)).

Section 55(5) provides that where a local authority has parental responsibility for a child or young person, and the child or young person is in the care of a local authority, or is being provided with accommodation by them in the exercise of their functions, references in s. 55 to 'parent or guardian' should be construed as references to that local authority. Section 55(5), which was inserted by the CJA 1991, was apparently overlooked in *Marlowe Child & Family Services* v *DPP* [1998] 2 Cr App R (S) 438. In *D* v *DPP* (1995) 16 Cr App R (S) 1040, the Divisional Court held that a court should not make an order against the local authority in a case where the authority had done all that it reasonably and properly could to protect the public from the young offender and to keep the young offender from criminal ways. Where the local authority so contends, it should be ready to provide evidence to the court of the steps which it has taken. In *Bedfordshire County Council* v *DPP* [1996] 1 Cr App R (S) 322, the Divisional Court further held that before an order under s. 55 could be made a causative link should normally be established between any fault proved on the part of the council and the offences committed. If no such causative fault was shown to the satisfaction of the court, it would be unreasonable to order compensation. 'Local authority' and 'parental responsibility' have the same meaning as in the Children Act 1989.

SECTION E17: FINES

A fine is an order that the offender shall pay a sum of money to the State, and it is the E17.1
most commonly encountered penalty in the courts.

IN THE CROWN COURT

Powers of Crown Court to Impose Fines

Powers of Criminal Courts Act 1973, s. 30

Where a person is convicted on indictment of any offence other than an offence for which
the sentence is fixed by law or falls to be imposed under section 2(2), 3(2) or 4(2) of the
Crime (Sentences) Act 1997, the court, if not precluded from sentencing the offender by
its exercise of some other power, may impose a fine in lieu of or in addition to dealing with
him in any other way in which the court has power to deal with him, subject however to any
enactment requiring the offender to be dealt with in a particular way.

There is no statutory limit to the amount of fine which may be imposed by the Crown
Court (see also Criminal Law Act 1977, s. 32(1)), and this includes a case where an
offender is committed for sentence under the MCA 1980, s. 38, following conviction in
a magistrates' court of an offence triable either way. If, however, the magistrates' court
commits a person to the Crown Court under the CJA 1967, s. 56 (see **D20.19**), the
Crown Court must observe all the limitations on sentencing powers which would have
applied in the magistrates' court with regard, for example, to the limitations on
magistrates' powers to imprison and financial limitations on fines (see **E17.4**) or
compensation orders. These limitations apply even where the offence is triable either
way and the magistrates' court might have committed to the Crown Court under the
MCA 1980, s. 38.

Powers of Criminal Courts Act 1973, s. 31

(1) Subject to the provisions of this section, if the Crown Court imposes a fine on any
person or forfeits his recognisance, the court may make an order—
(a) allowing time for the payment of the amount of the fine or the amount due under
the recognisance;
(b) directing payment of that amount by instalments of such amounts and on such
dates respectively as may be specified in the order;
(c) in the case of a recognisance, discharging the recognisance or reducing the
amount due thereunder.
(2) Subject to the provisions of this section, if the Crown Court imposes a fine on any
person or forfeits his recognisance, the court shall make an order fixing a term of
imprisonment or of detention under section 9 of the Criminal Justice Act 1982 (detention
of persons aged 18 to 20 for default) which he is to undergo if any sum which he is liable to
pay is not duly paid or recovered.

Power and Duty of Court to Fix Term in Default

A term of imprisonment or detention to be served in default must be fixed in every case E17.2
where the Crown Court imposes a fine or forfeits a recognisance (unless the offender is
under 18 years of age), though it seems that a failure to fix such a term does not invalidate
the fine itself (*Hamilton* (1980) 2 Cr App R (S) 1). For the CJA 1982, s. 9, see below,
and for the table of maximum periods of imprisonment or detention in a young offender
institution which may be fixed in default, see **E17.3**. The term which is fixed should
relate to the whole sum, rather than to any instalment (*Power* (1986) 8 Cr App R (S) 8).

Where fines are imposed in respect of more than one offence, the terms to be served in default may be ordered to run concurrently or consecutively (*Savundranayagan* [1968] 1 WLR 1761), and the court may order that the term(s) to be served in default may run concurrently or consecutively to any term of imprisonment or detention in a young offender institution to which the offender is sentenced at that time by the court or which he is currently serving (PCCA 1973, s. 31(4)). A term of imprisonment in default may be imposed consecutively to a maximum prison sentence imposed for the same offence (*Carver* [1955] 1 WLR 181). Consecutive custodial terms are, however, subject to the totality principle (*Savundranayagan* [1968] 1 WLR 1761). See, further, *Benmore* (1983) 5 Cr App R (S) 468.

Where the Crown Court imposes a fine on committal for sentence from a magistrates' court, in circumstances where the powers of the Crown Court are limited to those of the magistrates' court, the Crown Court must specify the term to be served in default (s. 31(6)).

Powers of Criminal Courts Act 1973, s. 31

(3)   No person shall on the occasion when a fine is imposed on him or his recognisance is forfeited by the Crown Court be committed to prison or detained in pursuance of an order under subsection (2) above unless—

(a)   in the case of an offence punishable with imprisonment, he appears to the court to have sufficient means to pay the sum forthwith;

(b)   it appears to the court that he is unlikely to remain long enough at a place of abode in the United Kingdom to enable payment of the sum to be enforced by other methods; or

(c)   on the occasion when the order is made the court sentences him to immediate imprisonment, custody for life, or detention in a young offender institution for that or another offence, or sentences him as aforesaid for an offence in addition to forfeiting his recognisance, or he is already serving a sentence of custody for life or a term—

(i)   of imprisonment

(ii)   of detention in a young offender institution; or

(iii)   of detention under section 9 of the Criminal Justice Act 1982.

Criminal Justice Act 1982, ss. 1 and 9

1.—(5)   No court shall commit a person under 21 years of age to be detained under section 9 below unless it is of the opinion that no other method of dealing with him is appropriate; and in forming any such opinion, the court—

(a)   shall take into account all such information about the circumstances of the default or contempt (including any aggravating or mitigating factors) as is available to it; and

(b)   may take into account any information about that person which is before it.

(5A)   Where a magistrates' court commits a person under 21 years of age to be detained under section 9 below, it shall—

(a)   state in open court the reason for its opinion that no other method of dealing with him is appropriate; and

(b)   cause that reason to be specified in the warrant of commitment and to be entered in the register.

9.—(1)   In any case where, but for section 1(1) above, a court would have power—

(a)   to commit a person under 21 but not less than 18 years of age to prison for default in payment of a fine or any other sum of money; or

(b)   to make an order fixing a term of imprisonment in the event of such a default by such a person; or

(c)   to commit such a person to prison for contempt of court of any kindred offence, the court shall have power, subject to section 1(5) above, to commit him to be detained under this section or, as the case may be, to make an order fixing a term of detention under this section in the event of default, for a term not exceeding the term of imprisonment.

There is no power to fix a term of detention under s. 9 in relation to an offender aged under 18 (*Basid* [1996] 1 Cr App R (S) 421, *Byas* (1995) 16 Cr App R (S) 869). It should be noted that, although s. 1(5) of the 1982 Act states that no court shall commit an offender to be detained unless 'no other method of dealing with him is appropriate', the statutory criteria in the CJA 1991, ss. 1 to 3 (relating to the imposition and length of custodial sentences), and the normal requirement to obtain a pre-sentence report, do not apply to a term of detention in default or for contempt. This is because a sentence of detention under the CJA 1982, s. 9, is not a 'custodial sentence' for the purposes of part I of the 1991 Act. The obligation in the CJA 1982, s. 3 (restriction on imposing custodial sentence on persons under 21 not legally represented), also does not apply in the present context.

Table of Maximum Periods in Default

The periods set out in the following table are the maximum periods of imprisonment or **E17.3** detention to be served in default, applicable to the corresponding fine values (PCCA 1973, s. 31(3A)):

Not exceeding £200	7 days
Over £200, not exceeding £500	14 days
Over £500, not exceeding £1,000	28 days
Over £1,000, not exceeding £2,500	45 days
Over £2,500, not exceeding £5,000	3 months
Over £5,000, not exceeding £10,000	6 months
Over £10,000, not exceeding £20,000	12 months
Over £20,000, not exceeding £50,000	18 months
Over £50,000, not exceeding £100,000	2 years
Over £100,000, not exceeding £250,000	3 years
Over £250,000, not exceeding £1 million	5 years
Over £1 million	10 years

These are maximum periods, and the Crown Court has discretion to fix a shorter term within the appropriate bracket. Where more than one fine is imposed, consecutive terms may be fixed. Where, exceptionally, a magistrates' court is empowered to fix a term in default of payment of a fine, the same periods apply, except that a default term in excess of 12 months canot be exceeded (MCA 1980, sch. 4).

IN THE MAGISTRATES' COURT

Powers of Magistrates' Court to Impose Fines

Where an offender has been summarily convicted of an offence triable either way which **E17.4** is listed in MCA 1980, sch. 1, the magistrates may fine him an amount not exceeding the 'prescribed sum' (MCA 1980, s. 32(1)). By s. 32(9) of that Act, 'the prescribed sum' means £5,000. Where, however, the offender has been summarily convicted of an offence triable either way, and the statute creating the offence prescribes a particular maximum penalty upon summary conviction, the magistrates may fine him an amount not exceeding the maximum penalty indicated in the statute creating the offence or the prescribed sum, whichever is the greater (s. 32(2)), and subject to the exception of certain drug offences listed in s. 32(5). Where the maximum penalty indicated in the statute creating the offence is expressed to be 'the statutory maximum', that maximum shall be the prescribed sum, i.e. £5,000. In the case of an offender under 18 years of age, a lower maximum fine applies (see **E17.6**).

The maximum fine which may be imposed for a summary offence is nearly always prescribed in the statute which creates the offence. If the statute refers only to punishment by means of imprisonment, power to impose a fine at level 3 is nonetheless included (MCA 1980, s. 34(3)).

Standard Scale of Maximum Fines for Summary Offences

E17.5 The 'standard scale' of maximum fines for summary offences is contained in the CJA 1982, s. 37(2). This scale applies to summary offences only; for offences triable either way dealt with summarily, see **E17.4**. For offenders under 18, a special maximum fine applies (see **E17.7**).

Level on the scale	Amount of fine
1	£200
2	£500
3	£1,000
4	£2,500
5	£5,000

Fining Juveniles

E17.6 Under the MCA 1980, s. 36, where a person under 18 years of age is found guilty by a magistrates' court of an offence in respect of which the court would normally be empowered to impose a fine exceeding £1,000, the amount of the fine imposed shall not exceed £1,000. Section 36 also provides that, if the offender is under the age of 14 and the court could otherwise have imposed a fine exceeding £250, the amount of the fine imposed shall not exceed £250.

There is no limit upon the fine which may be imposed by a Crown Court upon a juvenile convicted on indictment.

See **E16.6** for the court's power to order that a fine be paid by a parent or guardian.

Enforcement of Fines

E17.7 Enforcement of all fines is carried out by magistrates' courts, whether the fine was imposed in a magistrates' court or in the Crown Court. The procedure for enforcement of fines is contained in the MCA 1980, ss. 75 to 91. By virtue of the definition of 'fine' in s. 150 of the 1980 Act, the same procedures also apply to the enforcement of compensation orders, the recovery of recognisances which the court has ordered to be forfeited and any other 'sum adjudged to be paid by a conviction or order of a magistrates' court', subject to certain exceptions which are indicated where appropriate below. The magistrates' court which is responsible for enforcement is that court which imposed the fine or, if the fine was imposed by the Crown Court, the court specified in the fine order or, if none was specified, the court which committed the offender for trial or sentence to the Crown Court. If the defendant is now residing in a different petty sessions area, a transfer of fine order may be made (MCA 1980, s. 89). When ordering a fine, the Crown Court must fix a term to be served in default (see **E17.2**) but a magistrates' court should not normally do so (ss. 82(3) and 77(2)).

When a fine is imposed it becomes due for payment immediately. The magistrates' court may, however, instead of requiring immediate payment, allow time for payment or order payment by instalments (s. 75(1)). Subsequently, further time may be given (s. 75(2)). If the court orders payment by instalments, default in any one instalment is taken to be a default in payment of all instalments then unpaid (s. 75(3)). Where the court allows time for payment, it may fix a day on which the offender must appear in person before the court (unless he is serving a custodial sentence) if any part of the sum remains unpaid, to enable an inquiry into his means to be conducted (s. 86). Before the court can impose imprisonment or order detention it must inquire into the means of the defaulter in his presence (s. 82(3)).

The magistrates' court may use the following methods to enforce immediate payment of the sum, without requirement to hold a means inquiry:

(a)   The court may order the offender to be *searched* for money to meet the fine, with any balance being returned to the offender (s. 80(1)). Such money, which includes money found on the offender at the time of his arrest or at the time of his reception into prison or detention (s. 80(2)), must not be used for payment of the fine if the court is satisfied that the money does not belong to the offender or if it is satisfied that 'the loss of the money would be more injurious to his family than would be his detention' (s. 80(3)).

(b)   Where the offence is punishable with imprisonment, the court may order the offender to be *detained* at a police station until 8 am of the following day (s. 136).

(c)   The court, on the occasion of the conviction or on a subsequent occasion, may make a *money payment supervision order* (s. 88) which should specify the terms of the payment. Such order places the defendant under the care of a person, usually a probation officer, whose duty is to 'advise and befriend the offender with a view to inducing him to pay and thereby avoid imprisonment' (Magistrates' Courts Rules 1981, r. 56). There is no requirement that the offender consent to the making of the order. A money payment supervision order may be imposed on a juvenile as well as an adult; in the case of an offender aged under 21 it must be used before committing to detention, unless it is undesirable or impracticable to do so (s. 88(4)). If the court commits an offender aged under 21 to detention without having first issued a money payment supervision order, it must state in the warrant of commitment the reasons for so doing (s. 88(5)). The court must not commit to prison in default a person in respect of whom a money payment supervision order has been made before taking reasonable steps to obtain a report from the supervisor (s. 88(6)).

(d)   The magistrates may issue a *warrant of distress*, authorising the seizure and sale of goods belonging to the offender, using the proceeds to meet the sum outstanding (s. 76). Where there is evidence that the offender has assets available to satisfy the sum outstanding, a distress warrant should be used rather than committal to prison (*Birmingham Justices, ex parte Bennett* [1983] 1 WLR 114). The court may also postpone the issue of a warrant if it thinks it expedient to do so, until such time and on such conditions as the court thinks just (s. 77).

(e)   The court may order the offender's *immediate imprisonment*, (or, in the case of an offender aged 18 or over but under 21, detention under the CJA 1982, s. 9), for the term specified as being the time to be served in default or, if no such time was specified, a term specified by the court having regard to the table in the MCA 1980, sch. 4. This table corresponds to the first seven entries listed in the PCCA 1973, s. 31(3A), which is set out at **E17.3**. It should be noted that the periods specified in the table are the maximum periods which may be ordered, and shorter periods may be ordered in the discretion of the court. The minimum period of imprisonment which can be imposed in any case is five days (1980 Act, s. 132). By s. 82(1), immediate committal to custody cannot be ordered unless:

(i)   in the case of an offence punishable with imprisonment, the offender appears to the court to have sufficient means to pay the sum forthwith,

(ii)   whether the offence is punishable with imprisonment or not, it appears to the court that the offender is unlikely to remain long enough at a place of abode in the United Kingdom to enable payment of the sum to be enforced by other methods, or

(iii)   the offender is being sent to prison or detention on the same or another charge, or the offender is already serving a prison sentence or sentence of detention.

The court should announce its reason(s) for making an immediate committal and the reason(s) should be entered in the court register and on the committal warrant. Failure to specify reasons may result in the committal being challenged successfully by way of judicial review (*Oldham Justices, ex parte Cawley* [1997] QB 1). If, even at this stage, the defendant tenders payment of the fine to court staff or other officials, payment should be received from him, and he is entitled to be released.

The default period can be ordered to be served concurrently with or consecutively to another sentence already being served. If ordered to run consecutively it is not unlawful for the addition of the default period to the custodial term already imposed to exceed the statutory maximum for magistrates' courts (*Green* [1977] 1 All ER 353), but consecutive terms are subject to the totality principle (see **E1.19**). If more than one fine is being enforced, the periods of imprisonment or detention in default may run consecutively to each other, except that the total period to be served must not exceed the maximum stated in the table in sch. 4 to the 1980 Act as being appropriate for the aggregate sum and, again, this is subject to the totality principle (*Southampton Justices, ex parte Davies* [1981] 1 WLR 374).

Where the offender serves the whole of the term in default, this has the effect of expunging the fine. Payment of the sum in default means that the person must be released (MCA 1980, s. 79(1)). Part payment of the sum by the offender will result in a proportionate reduction in the term to be served in default (s. 79(2) and (3)).

Enforcement Pursuant to Means Inquiry

E17.8   If the offender fails to pay the whole or any part of the sum within the time allowed by the court, the magistrates' court may issue a summons or warrant requiring the offender to appear or issue a warrant to arrest him and bring him before the court to conduct a means inquiry to investigate the defendant's ability to pay (MCA 1980, s. 83). The court may require that the defendant produce evidence of his income and outgoings. If the court orders the defendant to produce a statement of means and the defendant fails to do so, such failure is an offence punishable by a fine up to level 3 (s. 84(2)). If the offender knowingly or recklessly furnishes a statement which is false in a material particular, or knowingly fails to disclose any material fact, this is an offence punishable with imprisonment not exceeding four months, a fine not exceeding level 3, or both (s. 84(3)).

In the light of information received by the court at the means inquiry, the magistrates may grant further time to the offender for payment of the fine, or arrange payment by instalments, or reduce the amount of each instalment (s. 75). The court may remit the whole or any part of the fine having regard to any change in the offender's circumstances since his conviction (s. 85(1)). The court may also remit or reduce the fine where the fine was imposed in the absence of adequate information about the offender's means, either because he was convicted in his absence or failed to comply with an order to furnish information concerning his means. If the Crown Court imposed the fine, the magistrates may remit the fine in whole or in part only if they first obtain the consent of the Crown Court. It should be noted that the power to remit is restricted to fines and there is no equivalent power in respect of compensation orders (s. 85(4)).

Pursuant to a means inquiry the magistrates' court may enforce payment by the following methods:

(a)   The four methods set out at paragraphs (a) to (d) of **E17.7**.

(b)   In the case of an offender who is in employment the court may make an *attachment of earnings order*, directing that the employer make deductions from the offender's wages after deduction of tax and remit them to the court. If the magistrates have this option in mind they should first consult with the clerk, who must obtain relevant details about the offender and his employment; the procedure is governed by the Attachment of Earnings Act 1971, s. 14. If the offender changes his employment, he is required to notify the court so that the new employer can make the appropriate deductions (1971 Act, s. 15). An attachment of earnings order may be imposed on a person aged under 18 as well as on a person aged 18 or over.

(c)   In respect of offenders aged 18 or over, the court may make an order for the *deduction from the offender's income support* payments in accordance with the CJA 1991,

s. 24. The court makes application to the appropriate district office of the Department of Social Security for this to be done. Detailed arrangements are set out in the Fines (Deduction from Income Support) Regulations 1992 (SI 1992 No. 2182).

(d)   In respect of offenders under the age of 25, the court may make an *attendance centre order* (CJA 1982, s. 17: see **E9.1**).

(e)   In respect of offenders aged 16 or over, the court may, by the C(S)A 1997, s. 35, make a *community service order*. The minimum number of hours of community service which may be ordered under s. 35 is 20 (s. 35(5)). By s. 35(6), in the case of a sum in default not exceeding £200 the number of hours of community service must not exceed 40, for a sum exceeding £200 but not exceeding £500 the number of hours must not exceed 60, and for a sum exceeding £500 the number of hours must not exceed 100. A magistrates' court may not make an order under s. 35 unless notified by the Secretary of State that arrangements for implementing such orders are available in the relevant area (s. 35(11)). On payment of the whole sum in default the order ceases to have effect and on a payment of part of the sum the number of hours is reduced proportionately (s. 35(13)).

(f)   In respect of an offender aged 16 or over the court may, by the C(S)A 1997, s. 35, make a *curfew order*. By s. 35(9), in the case of a sum in default not exceeding £200 the number of days to which the curfew order may relate must not exceed 20, for a sum exceeding £200 but not exceeding £500 the number of days must not exceed 30, for a sum exceeding £500 but not exceeding £1,000 the number of days must not exceed 60, for a sum exceeding £1,000 but not exceeding £2,500 the number of days must not exceed 90, and for a sum exceeding £2,500 the number of days must not exceed 180. A magistrates' court may not make an order under s. 35 unless notified by the Secretary of State that arrangements for implementing such orders are available in the relevant area (s. 35(11)). On payment of the whole sum in default the order ceases to have effect and on a payment of part of the sum the number of hours or days is reduced proportionately (s. 35(13)).

(g)   By the C(S)A 1997, s. 40, the court may order the person in default to be *disqualified from holding or obtaining a driving licence* for such period, not exceeding 12 months, as the court thinks fit. A magistrates' court may not make an order under s. 40 unless notified by the Secretary of State that the power to make such orders is exercisable by the court (s. 40(3)). On payment of the whole sum in default the disqualification ceases to have effect and on a payment of part of the sum the period of disqualification is reduced proportionately (s. 40(4)).

(h)   The court may order the offender's *immediate imprisonment*, (or, in the case of an offender aged 18 or over but under 21, detention under the CJA 1982, s. 9), for the term originally specified as being the time to be served in default or, if no such time was specified, a term specified by the court having regard to the table in the MCA 1980, sch. 4. This table corresponds to the first seven entries listed in the PCCA 1973, s. 31(3A), which is set out at **E17.3**. An immediate committal to custody can be ordered only where, since the conviction, the court has inquired into the offender's means in his presence on at least one occasion and where:

(i)   in the case of an offence punishable with imprisonment the offender appears to the court to have sufficient means to pay the sum outstanding forthwith, or

(ii)   the court is satisfied that the default is due to the offender's wilful refusal or culpable neglect and has considered or tried all other methods of enforcing payment of the sum but it appears to the court that they are inappropriate or unsuccessful (MCA 1980, s. 82(4)).

Further restrictions on the use of immediate committal to prison are set out in s. 82(5) to (5F) of the 1980 Act. The court must have 'considered or tried' all other methods of enforcement: these words must be complied with and allow no room for the exercise of discretion (*Norwich Magistrates' Court, ex parte Tigger (formerly Lilly)* (1987) 151 JP 689). The warrant of commitment should state the grounds on which the court was satisfied that it was undesirable or impracticable to use the other methods of enforcement (*Oldham Justices, ex parte Cawley* [1997] QB 1). For an offender aged over 18 but under 21, the CJA 1982, s. 1(5A), further requires the justices to specify in the warrant their reasons for concluding that detention is the only appropriate method of dealing with the defaulter (see **E17.2**). 'Wilful refusal', which means a deliberate defiance of the court order, or 'culpable neglect', which means a reckless disregard of the court order, must be established by proof beyond reasonable doubt (*South Tyneside Justices, ex parte Martin* (1995) *The Independent*, 20 September 1995).

FINES: SENTENCING PRINCIPLES

E17.9   Under the CJA 1991, s. 18, the following statutory principles are applicable to the fixing of fines, both in the Crown Court and in magistrates' courts.

Criminal Justice Act 1991, s. 18

(1)   Before fixing the amount of any fine to be imposed on an offender who is an individual, a court shall inquire into his financial circumstances.

(2)   The amount of any fine fixed by a court shall be such as, in the opinion of the court, reflects the seriousness of the offence.

(3)   In fixing the amount of any fine to be imposed on an offender (whether an individual or other person), a court shall take into account the circumstances of the case including, among other things, the financial circumstances of the offender so far as they are known, or appear, to the court.

(4)   Where—

(a)   an offender has been convicted in his absence in pursuance of section 11 or 12 of the Magistrates' Courts Act 1980 (non-appearance of accused),

(b)   an offender—

(i)   has failed to comply with an order under section 20(1) below; or

(ii)   has otherwise failed to cooperate with the court in its inquiry into his financial circumstances, or

(c)   the parent or guardian of an offender who is a child or young person—

(i)   has failed to comply with an order under section 20(1B) below; or

(ii)   has otherwise failed to cooperate with the court in its inquiry into his financial circumstances,

and the court considers that it has insufficient information to make a proper determination of the financial circumstances of the offender, it may make such determination as it thinks fit.

(5)   Subsection (3) above applies whether taking into account the financial circumstances of the offender has the effect of increasing or reducing the amount of the fine.

For the MCA 1980, ss. 11 and 12, see **D4.13** and **D18.13** respectively. For the CJA 1991, s. 20, see **E17.11**.

Proportionality to Gravity of Offence

E17.10   The first principle in relation to the use of the fine, whether in the Crown Court or in magistrates' courts, is that the selection of the fine as a sentence, and the determination of the appropriate level of any fine, should reflect the seriousness of the offence. A fine is an inappropriate penalty where the seriousness of the offence requires an immediate custodial sentence. An example is *A-G's Ref (No. 41 of 1994)* (1995) 16 Cr App R (S) 792, where fines totalling £350 had been imposed on the offender who had pleaded guilty to wounding with intent to cause grievous bodily harm. He had struck the victim on the head with a beer bottle, causing a wound which required stitches, and subsequently threatened him with a knife. The Court of Appeal held that the sentence was 'absurd', and unduly lenient and substituted a custodial term of 30 months. On the other hand, there are cases which are not so serious as to justify a fine. In *Jamieson* (1975) 60 Cr App R 318 the offender, who had a clean record and substantial personal mitigation, was convicted of theft of a half bottle of whisky from a supermarket and fined £300. The Court of Appeal varied the sentence to a conditional discharge.

It is clear from the CJA 1991, s. 18(2), that the level of the fine imposed should reflect the seriousness of the offence. The imposition of the maximum available fine should be reserved for the most serious instances of the offence which are reasonably likely to occur. The existence of significant mitigation, such as the offender's guilty plea, should normally preclude the imposition of the maximum fine. In *Universal Salvage* v *Boothby* (1983) 5 Cr App R (S) 428 a company was fined for breach of regulations requiring it to have in its lorry proper equipment to record the journeys made. It was accepted that, in reliance on a letter from the relevant government department, the company had reasonably believed that the regulations were not applicable to them. Liability for the offence was strict, but the Divisional Court held that the circumstances provided considerable mitigation and that the imposition of the maximum fine on the company by the magistrates' court constituted an error of law. In all cases involving fines it is the 'first duty' of the sentencer to 'measure that fine against the gravity of the offence' (per Kenneth Jones LJ in *Messana* (1981) 3 Cr App R (S) 88), having regard to all relevant matters in aggravation and mitigation. In *Cleminson* (1985) 7 Cr App R (S) 128 the offender pleaded guilty to handling stolen goods, some jewellery which had been stolen in a burglary. The jewellery was recovered, but the offender was fined £1,000. According to Boreham J, 'judged by the gravity of the crime itself, this was a penalty which, in our judgment, was excessive . . . the appropriate fine is £150.' In *F and M Dobson Ltd* (1995) 16 Cr App R (S) 957, a fine of £25,000 was imposed upon a confectionary manufacturer for failing to detect the blade of a Stanley Knife in one of their products. The case was contested in the Crown Court. Lord Taylor CJ, in the Court of Appeal, said that the relevant considerations in determining the appropriate penalty were to reflect the level of culpability involved and an element of deterrence. The level of the fine, however, was manifestly excessive, and it was reduced to £7,000.

The court should not calculate the level of the fine on the basis of the compensation which would have been received if the victim had made application to the Criminal Injuries Compensation Board (*Roberts* (1980) 2 Cr App R (S) 121).

In *Warden* [1996] 2 Cr App (S) 269, the Court of Appeal observed that, where a defendant had spent time on remand in custody but had subsequently received a fine as the appropriate sentence for the offence, some credit should normally be given for the time spent in custody. The amount of the credit was a matter for the discretion of the sentencer.

Important guidance on the proper use of fines, where imposed for several different offences, was issued by the Divisional Court in *Chelmsford Crown Court, ex parte Birchall* (1989) 11 Cr App R (S) 510. The offender, an independent haulage contractor, pleaded guilty before the magistrates to 10 offences of using a goods vehicle whose gross weight exceeded the weight shown on the plating certificate, the degree of overweight varying on these occasions between 15 per cent and 25 per cent. He was fined a total of £7,600, payable at the rate of £300 per month if he was in employment and £25 per month if he was unemployed. The fines were calculated by a formula which took a basic fine of £400 as the starting-point, and added a further £20 for each 1 per cent by which the overweight exceeded the permitted maximum. The offender's appeal to the Crown Court was dismissed, but he then applied for judicial review of the decision of the Crown Court. The Divisional Court found the sentence 'truly astonishing'. It said that the appropriate sentence for the total wrongdoing was a fine of £1,300, allotted between the different offences by imposing a fine of £400 on one and £100 each on the others, the fine to be paid at the rate of £55 per month, whether the offender was employed or not. The court emphasised that the application of a 'rigid formula' was not right, even for a single offence, and it was wrong to apply it to each of 10 offences and add the figures up: the courts had to consider all the circumstances and apply the principles of sentencing which were well known. The main importance of this decision is its clear endorsement of the application to fines of the totality principle (see, in relation to custodial sentences, **E1.19**). When fining in respect of a number of offences, the sentencer must review the total sentence and ensure that it remains proportionate to the totality of the offending, as well as being within the offender's capacity to pay. The CJA 1991, s. 28(2)(b), reinforces this sentencing principle by stating that the court may mitigate the overall sentence 'by applying any rule of law as to the totality of sentences'.

Further guidance on the appropriate level of fines for particular offences may be obtained from the Magistrates' Association Guidelines (1997). Their guideline fines and, where appropriate, other suggested sentences, are set out in **parts B** and **C** of this work in relation to each of the offences dealt with.

Taking into Account Means of Offender

E17.11 Section 18(1) of the CJA 1991 requires the court to inquire into the financial circumstances of the individual offender, and s. 18(3) requires the court to take those circumstances into account when fixing the amount of the fine.

It is well established that while a fine is meant to be a punishment and it is perfectly proper for the offender to have to endure a degree of hardship in paying the fine, since 'one of the objects of the fine is to remind the offender that what he has done is wrong' (per Lord Lane CJ in *Olliver* (1989) 11 Cr App R (S) 10), the imposition of a fine which is quite beyond the means of the offender is wrong in principle.

Where the offender lacks the means to pay the level of fine which is proportionate to the seriousness of the offence, it is contrary to principle to impose a custodial sentence instead. According to Roskill LJ in *Reeves* (1972) 56 Cr App R 366, where the offender had pleaded guilty to obtaining £600 by deception and had received a prison sentence of nine months, the comments made by the sentencer 'must plainly have indicated to the appellant . . . that he was being sent to prison not because the offence itself merited a sentence of immediate imprisonment but because he had not the financial wherewithal to pay a substantial fine. That . . . is, of course, completely wrong'. The same principle applies to the imposition of a suspended sentence rather than a fine in such circumstances (see **E2.3**).

Where the offender is well-off and paying the fine proportionate to the offence would cause him little inconvenience, it is contrary to principle to impose a custodial sentence instead (*Gillies* [1965] Crim LR 64). It is, however, right to raise the level of the fine in such a case, so as to increase its penal impact. It should be noted that CJA 1993, s. 18(5), makes it clear that the level of a fine should be adjusted upwards or downwards to take account of the offender's ability to pay. The Magistrates' Association Guidelines (1997) state that 'the principle behind determining the amount of a fine should be that of equality of hardship rather than equality of monetary penalty. Punishment does not lie in the amount of a fine but in the degree of hardship and inconvenience caused by the need to pay it'. Section 18(5) does not, of course, affect the principle that an offender who is well-off should not be dealt with by financial penalty where the offence itself merits custody and an offender who is less well-off would have gone to prison (*Markwick* (1953) 37 Cr App R 125). The principle that a rich offender must not be permitted to 'buy his way out of prison' is a fundamental one, and it applies equally where the offender has family or friends who are able to meet a substantial fine (*Curtis* (1984) 6 Cr App R (S) 250).

The requirement that the court should adjust the level of the fine in accordance with the offender's means entails that the court should not assume that someone other than the offender will be paying the fine. In *Charambous* (1984) 6 Cr App R (S) 389, where a fine was imposed on a married woman who had limited income of her own, the Court of Appeal stressed that the fine must reflect the offender's means and was not a fine on the family.

Section 18(1) requires the court to inquire into an individual offender's financial circumstanes before fixing the level of the fine. Section 20(1) of the CJA 1991 provides that, where an individual has been convicted of an offence, the court may, before sentencing him, make a 'financial circumstances order' with respect to him. Both magistrates' courts and the Crown Court may make such an order. Where a magistrates' court has been notified in accordance with the MCA 1980, s. 12(4), that an individual wishes to plead guilty without appearing before the court, the court also has power to make a financial circumstances order (CJA 1991, s. 20(1A)). A 'financial circumstances order' is an order requiring the relevent individual 'to give to the court, within such period as may be specified in the order, such a statement of his financial circumstances as the court may require' (s. 20(1C)). An individual who, without reasonable excuse, fails to comply with a financial circumstances order is liable on summary conviction to a fine not exceeding level 3 (s. 20(2)), and if such individual makes, in pursuance of a financial circumstances order, a statement which he knows to be false in a material particular, is reckless as to its falsity or knowingly fails to disclose any material fact he is liable on summary conviction to imprisonment for a term not exceeding three months or a fine not exceeding level 4, or both (s. 20(3)). Section 18(4) provides that, exceptionally, the court may make such determination of the offender's financial circumstances as it thinks fit. This should only be done in a case where the offender has failed to comply with a financial circumstances order, or where one of the other situations specified in s. 18(4)(a) to (c) arises. Section 18 is set out at **E17.9**. If a defendant company wishes to make a submission as to its ability to pay a fine, it should supply copies of its accounts and other financial information to the court. Where such information has been withheld, the court is entitled to assume that the company is able to pay any fine it is minded to impose (*F. Howe and Sons (Engineers) Ltd* [1999] 2 All ER 249).

Instalments should Require Payment within a Reasonable Time

It seems that, apart from exceptional circumstances, where a fine is ordered to be paid **E17.12** by instalments, it should be capable of being paid off by the offender within 12 months (*Knight* (1980) 2 Cr App R (S) 82, *Nunn* (1983) 5 Cr App R (S) 203). In *Olliver* (1989) 11 Cr App R (S) 10, however, it was held by the Court of Appeal that the maximum time is not limited to 12 months. Lord Lane CJ said (at p. 15):

> . . . there is nothing wrong in principle in the period of payment being longer, indeed much longer than one year, providing it is not an undue burden and so too severe a punishment having regard to the nature of the offence and the nature of the offender. Certainly it seems to us that a two-year period will seldom be too long, and in an appropriate case three years will be unassailable, again of course depending on the nature of the offender and the nature of the offence.

The Magistrates' Association Guidelines (1997) state that 'Fines are due to be paid at the time they are imposed. Where time to pay is allowed it should not exceed 12 months: in these circumstances best practice should be to order an amount to be paid immediately and then to set a realistic weekly amount, and a date for a court hearing for compliance with the order to be reviewed'.

There is an exception in relation to corporate defendants, where the fine may be payable over a substantially longer period than for an individual (*Rollco Screw and Rivet Co.* [1999] 2 Cr App R (S) 436).

Combining Fines with Other Sentences or Orders

E17.13   For restrictions imposed by statute on combining a fine with certain custodial sentences see the PCCA 1973, s. 30, at **E17.1**. Apart from those cases, there is no statutory general restriction on combining fines with imprisonment or other custodial sentences, whether in respect of the same offence or different offences sentenced on the same occasion, though this will not often be a desirable combination, since incarceration may well deprive the offender of the means to pay the fine. In any event, a fine and a custodial sentence will be an inappropriate combination where the offender lacks the means to pay the fine, and hence will serve the term fixed in default of payment (*Maund* (1980) 2 Cr App R (S) 289), or where the offender will be saddled with a significant financial burden on his release from prison.

A fine may be combined with an immediate custodial sentence, exceptionally where the custodial term imposed is considered to be inadequate and additional punishment is required (*Garner* [1986] 1 WLR 73, per Hodgson J) but also where the fine is being used as a means of removing an offender's profit from his offending. In *Garner* the Court of Appeal approved the imposition of a fine of £150,000 in addition to the maximum prison term available for the offence of conspiracy to contravene the Finance Act 1972, s. 38(1), relating to payment of VAT. In the 'removal of profit' cases the existence of a 'substantial financial benefit' by the offender must be established (*Forsythe* (1980) 2 Cr App R (S) 15), and the offence which gave rise to the profit must be proved or admitted before a fine may be used in this way (*Ayensu* (1982) 4 Cr App R (S) 248). The imposition of a so-called 'global sentence' has been approved in 'removal of profit' cases on several occasions (particularly *Savundranayagan* [1968] 1 WLR 1761, *Benmore* (1983) 5 Cr App R (S) 468 and *Chatt* (1984) 6 Cr App R (S) 75). In *Garner* Hodgson J described the fine in these cases as 'a rough and ready method of confiscating the profits of crime'. A more sophisticated approach to the removal of substantial proceeds of offending, which was not available to the courts at the time of these decisions, is to make a confiscation order (see **E21**).

A court which imposes a suspended sentence of imprisonment may also impose a fine for the same offence, but the offence must be one which would have been properly dealt with by way of immediate custody in the absence of a power to suspend the sentence: see further, on combining suspended sentence and fine, **E2.7**. The court, as always, must consider the offender's means before fixing the level of the fine (*King* [1970] 1 WLR 1016). The PCCA 1973, s. 22(2A), encourages the combination of a suspended sentence and a fine in the 'exceptional circumstances' in which a suspended sentence may now be imposed (see **E2.1**).

It is possible, whether sentencing for a single offence or for different offences sentenced on the same occasion, to combine a fine with a community sentence of any kind, an action plan order or a reparation order. A fine cannot, however, be combined with a discharge when sentencing for a single offence (*McClelland* [1951] 1 All ER 557, which was based on earlier statutory wording which is preserved: see **E14.1**), although it may be combined with a discharge when sentencing for different offences sentenced on the same occasion. A fine cannot be combined with a hospital order (Mental Health Act 1983, s. 37(8)).

A fine and a compensation order may be combined. The PCCA 1973, s. 35(4A), provides that, where the offender has insufficient means to pay both an appropriate fine and appropriate compensation, the court shall give preference to compensation. In a particular case this will mean that the level of the fine is reduced to enable the full compensation order to stand, or that no fine is ordered and the compensation order stands alone. Fines may be combined with other financial orders, such as an order to pay the costs of the prosecution, though the court must consider the total effect of the orders it is making, and should ensure that the whole sum the offender has to pay is not beyond his means. There is some authority to the effect that a small fine should not be combined with a large order for costs (*Whalley* (1972) 56 Cr App R 304). A fine may also be combined with a restitution order under the Theft Act 1968, s. 28(1), with a forfeiture order under the PCCA 1973, s. 43, and with a disqualification order, where the vehicle was used for the purposes of crime, under the PCCA 1973, s. 44.

Persistent Petty Offenders

By the C(S)A 1997, s. 37(1), where a person is convicted of an offence by a magistrates' **E17.14** court or the Crown Court, the court is satisfied that each of the conditions mentioned in s. 37(2) is fulfilled and, if it were not so satisfied, the court would have imposed a fine in respect of the offence, the court may, instead of fining the offender (and notwithstanding the general restrictions on the imposition of community sentences contained in the CJA 1991, s. 6 (see **E4.1**)), make a community service order or a curfew order. The conditions in s. 37(2) are:

> (a) that one or more fines imposed on the offender in respect of one or more previous offences have not been paid; and
> (b) if a fine were imposed in an amount which was commensurate with the seriousness of the offence, the offender would not have sufficient means to pay it.

Clearly the purpose of this provision is to allow the court to impose a community service order or a curfew order in a case where the seriousness of the offence itself would not justify the use of a community sentence, but where the existence of outstanding fines in the offender's case seems to make the use of the fine unrealistic.

'Community service order' has the same meaning in s. 37 as it has in the PCCA 1973, s. 14 (see **E4**) except as provided for in ss. 35(4) and (5) and 37(3) and (4) of the 1997 Act. If a community service order is made under s. 37, the minimum number of hours which may be ordered is 40 hours, rather than the 20 hours which is the minimum number of hours where community service is imposed in respect of fine default (s. 37(4)). 'Curfew order' has the same meaning here as it has in the CJA 1991, s. 12 (see **E7**) except as provided in ss. 35(7) and (8) and 37(3) and (5) of the 1997 Act. A curfew order under s. 37 cannot be imposed on an offender aged under 16.

A court must not make a community service order or a curfew order under s. 37 unless the court has been notified by the Secretary of State that arrangements for implementing the relevant order are in place in the relevant area (s. 37(6) and (7)).

SECTION E18: COMPENSATION ORDERS

Power to Make Compensation Orders

E18.1   The power of the court to make compensation orders is governed by the PCCA 1973, ss. 35 to 38.

Powers of Criminal Courts Act 1973, s. 35

(1)   Subject to the provisions of this Part of this Act and to section 40 of the Magistrates' Courts Act 1980 (which imposes a monetary limit on the powers of a magistrates' court under this section), a court by or before which a person is convicted of an offence, instead of or in addition to dealing with him in any other way, may, on application or otherwise, make an order (in this Act referred to as 'a compensation order') requiring him to pay compensation for any personal injury, loss or damage resulting from that offence or any other offence which is taken into consideration by the court in determining sentence or to make payments for funeral expenses or bereavement in respect of a death resulting from any such offence, other than a death due to an accident arising out of the presence of a motor vehicle on a road; and a court shall give reasons, on passing sentence, if it does not make such an order in a case where this section empowers it to do so.

(1A)   Compensation under subsection (1) above shall be of such amount as the court considers appropriate, having regard to any evidence and to any representations that are made by or on behalf of the accused or the prosecutor.

The victim does not have to apply to the court before such an order can be made. In *Holt* v *DPP* [1996] 2 Cr App R (S) 314, the Divisional Court held that a compensation order could be made in respect of a victim of theft who had died before sentence was passed. There is no limit to the amount of compensation which the Crown Court may order, though it must have regard to the offender's means (see **E18.4**). In the magistrates' court, the MCA 1980, s. 40(1), provides that the maximum sum which may be ordered by way of compensation for any offence is £5,000. Section 40(1) also places a limit on the total sum which may be ordered by way of compensation in a magistrates' court where the offender asks for offences to be taken into consideration. The total amount ordered must not exceed the maximum which could be ordered for the offences in respect of which the offender has been formally charged and convicted. In *Crutchley* (1994) 15 Cr App R (S) 627, followed in *Hose* (1995) 16 Cr App R (S) 682, the Court of Appeal held that it is not open to a court to make a compensation order in respect of an offence admitted by the offender (as a sample count) but never charged or taken into consideration.

The court should make clear which amounts of compensation relate to which offences: the fixing of a 'global figure' is inappropriate (*Oddy* [1974] 1 WLR 1212), unless the offences were committed against the same victim (*Warton* [1976] Crim LR 520). Where there are competing claimants for available funds, the total compensation available should normally be apportioned on a pro rata basis (*Miller* [1976] Crim LR 694), though in *Amey* [1983] 1 WLR 345 the court selected some claimants for compensation and excluded others. Where there are co-defendants, it is preferable to make separate orders against each of them (*Grundy* [1974] 1 WLR 139).

'Any personal injury, loss or damage': it is not a prerequisite of making a compensation order that the offender would be civilly liable for the loss (*Chappell* (1984) 80 Cr App R 31), though this will generally be the case. The court may compensate distress and anxiety (*Bond* v *Chief Constable of Kent* [1983] 1 WLR 40, *Godfrey* (1994) 15 Cr App R (S) 536). 'Loss' may include a sum by way of interest (*Schofield* [1978] 1 WLR 979).

An award may be made whenever it can fairly be said that a particular loss results from the offence (*Rowlston* v *Kenny* (1982) 4 Cr App R (S) 85), without having regard to technical issues of causation (*Thomson Holidays Ltd* [1974] QB 592). Thus in *Taylor* (1993) 14 Cr App R (S) 276 it was held to be appropriate to require the offender to pay £50 compensation to a man who had been kicked in the course of an affray in which the offender and four others had accosted another group of men and a fight had developed. It could not be established that Taylor had kicked the victim, but it was said to be 'artificial and unjust to look narrowly at the physical acts of each defendant'. A case which fell on the other side of the line was *Derby* (1990) 12 Cr App R (S) 502, where the offender had threatened the victim with a knife and his co-accused had seriously injured the victim by attacking him with a piece of wood. It was held that a compensation order for £4,000 made against the offender was improper, since the offender had clearly not been responsible for inflicting the injuries. This approach was followed in *Denness* [1996] 1 Cr App R (S) 159. See also *Deary* (1994) 14 Cr App R (S) 648.

Where there has been no damage or loss (e.g., where a stolen article is recovered and returned undamaged and is of no less value to the owner), no compensation order can be made (*Hier* (1976) 62 Cr App R 233, *Tyce* (1994) 15 Cr App R (S) 415), since the issue in compensation is the loss to the victim rather than the benefit to the offender. Conversely, where there has been damage or loss to the victim, a compensation order is not precluded by the fact that the offender has made no profit from the offence. The amount of the victim's loss should either be agreed by the defendant or established by evidence. The case of *Vivian* [1979] 1 WLR 291 is clear authority for this point, but the case was decided prior to s. 35(1A) of the Act, which was introduced by the CJA 1982. In *Swann* (1984) 6 Cr App R (S) 22, the Court of Appeal referred to s. 35(1A), Kilner Brown J commenting that its effect was 'slightly to reduce the obligation which was laid down by this court in *Vivian's* case, in which it was said that it had to be proved that the compensation was due. It is however important to appreciate hat there is nothing in these new statutory provisions which indicates that a trial judge, when considering compensation, should simply pluck a figure out of the air.' Further, in *Horsham Justices, ex parte Richards* [1985] 1 WLR 986, Neill LJ said (at p. 993): '. . . in my judgment the court has no jurisdiction to make a compensation order without receiving any evidence where there are real issues raised as to whether the claimants have suffered any, and if so what, loss'. The court should, however, hesitate to embark on a complex inquiry into the scale of loss, since compensation orders are designed to be used only in clear, straightforward cases (see **E18.6**).

In the case of an offence under the Theft Act 1968, where the property in question is recovered, any damage to the property occurring while it was out of the owner's possession is treated as having resulted from the offence, however and by whomsoever it was caused (s. 35(2), applied in *Quigley* v *Stokes* [1977] 1 WLR 434).

A compensation order may only be made in respect of injury, loss or damage (other than loss suffered by a person's dependants in consequence of his death) which was due to an accident arising out of the presence of a motor vehicle on a road, if:

(a)   it is damage which falls within s. 35(2); or
(b)   it is in respect of injury, loss or damage for which the offender is uninsured in relation to the use of the vehicle, and compensation is not payable under any arrangements to which the Secretary of State is a party (i.e. the Motor Insurers' Bureau Agreement) (s. 35(3)).

In the case of property damage, the Agreement does not cover the first £175 of the damage, and a compensation order up to that amount may be made in an appropriate case (*DPP* v *Scott* (1995) 16 Cr App R (S) 292). See further *Austin* [1996] 2 Cr App R (S) 191. If a compensation order is made in respect of such an accident, the compensation can include a sum representing the whole or part of any loss of or reduction in preferential rates of insurance attributable to the accident ('no claims' bonus) (s. 35(3)). A vehicle which is exempted from insurance (see Road Traffic Act 1988, s. 144) is not uninsured for these purposes (s. 35(3A)).

A compensation order in respect of funeral expenses may be made for the benefit of anyone who incurred the expenses (s. 35(3B)). A compensation order in respect of bereavement may only be made for the benefit of a person who could claim damages for bereavement under the Fatal Accidents Act 1976, s. 1A (i.e. the spouse of the deceased or, in the case of a deceased minor, his parents, or mother if the minor is illegitimate), and the amount of that compensation shall not exceed the sum specified in the Fatal Accidents Act 1976, s. 1A(3) (currently £7,500) (s. 35(3C) and (3D)).

In determining whether to make a compensation order, and in determining the amount to be paid, it is the duty of the court to have regard to the offender's means so far as they appear or are known to the court (s. 35(4), and see further, **E18.4**). The court may allow the offender time to pay the sum due under the compensation order, or direct payment of the sum by instalments of such amounts and on such dates as the court may specify (PCCA 1973, s. 34 and MCA 1980, s. 75(1)).

Where a child or young person is convicted of an offence and the court makes an order for compensation, it should, under CYPA 1969, s. 55, normally order the parent or guardian of the child or young person to pay the compensation order (see **E16.6**).

The victim of the offence shall not receive the compensation until there is no further possibility of an appeal on which the order could be varied or set aside (PCCA 1973, s. 36(1)). By s. 37, at any time before the offender has paid into court the whole of the money under the order, the magistrates' court having power to enforce the order may, on the application of the offender, discharge the order or reduce it, on the ground that:

(a)   the injury, loss or damage in respect of which the order was made has been held in civil proceedings to be less than it was taken to be for the purposes of the order;

(b)   that property, the loss of which was the subject of the order, has now been recovered;

(c)   that the means of the offender are insufficient to satisfy both the compensation order and a confiscation order made against him in the same proceedings under the CJA 1988, part IV; or

(d)   that the offender's means have suffered a substantial reduction, which was unexpected at the time of making the order.

Before the magistrates can act to discharge or reduce the order under (c) or (d), they must have the consent of the Crown Court if the Crown Court made the order.

Enforcement of Compensation Orders

E18.2   Enforcement of compensation orders is the function of the magistrates' courts. The maximum terms of imprisonment which a magistrates' court may impose in default of payment of compensation orders are specified in the MCA 1980, sch. 4. These are the same periods which apply in the case of fines, and which are set out in the table at **E17.3**, except that the magistrates have no power to specify a term in default in excess of 12 months. These are maximum terms, and the magistrates have discretion to fix a lower term. The Crown Court is not empowered to make an order fixing the term to be served in default of payment of a compensation order (in contrast to its duty to do so in respect of fines: *Komsta* (1990) 12 Cr App R (S) 63, and see **E17.2**). The maximum terms indicated in sch. 4 will thus normally also apply in default of compensation orders imposed by the Crown Court. Exceptionally, however, if the Crown Court makes a compensation order for an amount in excess of £20,000 and considers that a maximum default term of 12 months is inadequate, the Court may fix a longer period, not exceeding the term specified for the equivalent amount in the PCCA 1973, s. 31(3A). As with fines, part payment of the compensation order will result in a proportionate reduction in the term to be served in default. A court may make an order for sums payable in respect of a compensation order made by a magistrates' court or the Crown Court to be deducted from the offender's income support payments in accordance with the Fines (Deduction from Income Support) Regulations 1992 (SI 1992 No. 2182).

COMPENSATION ORDERS: SENTENCING PRINCIPLES

Compensation Order Not Alternative to Sentence

In *Inwood* (1974) 60 Cr App R 70, Scarman LJ said (at p. 73): 'Compensation orders **E18.3** were not introduced into our law to enable the convicted to buy themselves out of the penalties for crime. Compensation orders were introduced into our law as a convenient and rapid means of avoiding the expense of resort to civil litigation when the criminal clearly has means which would enable the compensation to be paid.' It follows from this important principle that the imposition of a compensation order should not affect the punishment imposed for the offence and, in particular, should not 'permit the offender to buy his way out of a custodial sentence'. In *Dorton* (1987) 9 Cr App R (S) 514, French J commented that 'it is not right, at least in all cases, to regard a compensation order as being an additional punishment. It may indeed be painful for the offender to have to pay compensation, but it would be equally painful if . . . the victim chose to bring civil proceedings.'

This principle is, however, subject to the PCCA 1973, s. 35(4A), which gives priority to the imposition of a compensation order over a fine. This, to some extent, permits the offender to 'buy his way out of the penalties for crime', by reducing the fine in order for compensation to be paid, but s. 35(4A) does not affect sentences other than fines. Some watering down of the principle in *Inwood* (1974) 60 Cr App R 70 may, however, be detected in more recent decisions of the Court of Appeal such as *Huish* (1985) 7 Cr App R (S) 272, but its importance was re-emphasised by Lord Taylor CJ in *A-G's Ref (No. 5 of 1993)* (1994) 15 Cr App R (S) 201.

Taking into Account Means of Offender

It is the responsibility of the offender to inform the court of his resources, and not for **E18.4** the sentencer to initiate inquiries into the matter (*Bolden* (1987) 9 Cr App R (S) 83). It is not the duty of the prosecutor to establish the offender's means (*Johnstone* (1982) 4 Cr App R (S) 141), but where the offender's lawyer advances mitigation on the basis that the offender will pay substantial compensation, the lawyer is under an obligation to ensure that the necessary means exist (*Coughlin* (1984) 6 Cr App R (S) 102, *Huish* (1985) 7 Cr App R (S) 272, *Bond* (1986) 8 Cr App R (S) 11). If the offender misleads the court into believing that he has the means to pay compensation, a subsequent appeal by the offender against the compensation order will not succeed (*Hayes* (1992) 13 Cr App R (S) 454; *Dando* [1996] 1 Cr App R (S) 155). He must pay the compensation, or serve the appropriate term in default of payment.

It is generally wrong to make a compensation order which will require the sale of the offender's home (*Harrison* (1980) 2 Cr App R (S) 313), but it is not unreasonable to expect the offender to sell other items to pay the compensation (*Workman* (1979) 1 Cr App R (S) 335). In such a case the court must ascertain the value of the asset (*Chambers* (1981) 3 Cr App R (S) 318). An order should not be made on the basis of the sale of an asset where it is not certain that the offender will be able to dispose of that asset (*Hackett* (1988) 10 Cr App R (S) 388: family home, in joint names).

Co-defendants may be required to pay different sums by way of compensation if their capacity to pay is different. See *Beddow* (1987) 9 Cr App R (S) 235, where the offender was one of two defendants who pleaded guilty to being carried in a vehicle taken without consent by a third defendant, who had fallen asleep at the wheel, causing the van to crash. The offender was conditionally charged and ordered to pay £300 in compensation. The other two defendants received a suspended sentence and a conditional discharge respectively, but neither was required to pay compensation. The Court of Appeal approved the sentences on the basis that the offender was the only one of the defendants who was in work and could afford to pay. See also *Stapleton* [1977] Crim LR 366. A compensation order should not be imposed on the assumption that persons other than the offender will pay, or contribute to, the order (*Hunt* [1983] Crim LR 270).

Compensation Should be Payable within Reasonable Time

E18.5   In *Webb* (1979) 1 Cr App R (S) 16, Cantley J observed (at p. 18) that: 'It is no use making a compensation order (particularly one with a sentence of imprisonment in default of compliance) if there is no realistic possibility of the compensation order being complied with'. This may be because the offender has very limited means (as in *Webb*) or because the offender is serving a custodial sentence with no immediate prospect of work (e.g., *Grafton* (1979) 1 Cr App R (S) 305). A compensation order should not be made which involves payments by instalment over an unreasonable length of time. In *Bradburn* (1973) 57 Cr App R 948, Lord Widgery CJ said that, in general, compensation orders 'should be sharp in their effect rather than protracted' and that an order which would take four years to complete was 'unreasonably long'. In *Olliver* (1989) 11 Cr App R (S) 10, the Court of Appeal indicated that a fine (or compensation order) might properly be repaid over a period of up to three years. Lord Lane CJ said (at p. 15) that: 'Certainly it seems to us that a two-year period will seldom be too long, and in an appropriate case three years will be unassailable'. See also *Yehou* [1997] 2 Cr App R (S) 48. The Magistrates' Association Guidelines (1997) state that an order for compensation 'should normally be payable within 12 months. In exceptional circumstances it may be payable within a period of up to three years; but courts should always consider whether such an extended order is in the interests of the victim'.

Compensation Order Should be Made Only in Clear Case

E18.6   The offender in *Kneeshaw* [1975] QB 57 pleaded guilty to burglary of a house. Most of the stolen property was recovered, but some items, worth £114, were unaccounted for. The offender claimed that this property either had not been stolen at all or had been taken by someone else. A compensation order for the outstanding sum was quashed by the Court of Appeal, Widgery CJ saying that the 'court should hesitate to embark on any complicated investigation of this kind even at the suit of an applicant making a positive application'. In *Donovan* (1981) 3 Cr App R (S) 192, the offender pleaded guilty to taking a conveyance, having hired a car for two days and failed to return it. The car had suffered no damage. The offender was fined £250, with £100 costs and £1,388 compensation, on the basis of the hire company's loss of use. Eveleigh LJ said that: 'A compensation order is designed for the simple, straightforward case where the amount of the compensation can be readily and easily ascertained'. Since the amount of damages in a civil case of loss of use 'is notoriously open to argument', the compensation order was quashed, and the hire company left to pursue its civil remedy if it wished to do so. In *Hyde* v *Emery* (1984) 6 Cr App R (S) 206 the offender pleaded guilty to three charges of obtaining unemployment benefit by false representation. There was a dispute over whether the sum claimed in compensation by the DHSS should be reduced by the amount of supplementary benefit which he could legitimately have claimed. Watkins LJ said in the Divisional Court that the magistrates should have declined to deal with the matter. See also *Briscoe* (1994) 15 Cr App R (S) 699 and *White* [1996] 2 Cr App R (S) 58.

Combining Compensation Orders with Other Sentences or Orders

Compensation orders may be imposed on an offender 'instead of or in addition to **E18.7** dealing with him in any other way' (PCCA 1973, s. 35(1): see **E18.1**). It is expressly provided that a compensation order may be combined with a discharge (PCCA 1973, s. 12(4)) and a community service order (PCCA 1973, s. 14(8)).

While a compensation order may be combined with a sentence of immediate custody where the offender is clearly able to pay or has good prospects of employment on his release from custody (*Love* [1999] 1 Cr App R (S) 484), it is often inappropriate to impose a compensation order as well as a custodial sentence. It may well be undesirable for a compensation order to be hanging over the offender's head after release, and the order may be 'counterproductive, and force him back into crime to find the money' (*Inwood* (1974) 60 Cr App R 70). See also *Morgan* (1982) 4 Cr App R (S) 358, *Clark* (1992) 13 Cr App R (S) 124 and *Jorge* [1999] 2 Cr App R (S) 1. While it is not wrong to combine a compensation order with a suspended sentence, and, indeed, that combination is positively encouraged by s. 22(2A) of the 1973 Act, regard should be had to the fact that if the offender is in breach of the suspended sentence, its activation may bring to an end any prospect of the payment of compensation (*McGee* [1978] Crim LR 370). It would appear to be contrary to principle to suspend a custodial sentence merely because of the offender's ability to pay compensation.

Where it would be appropriate both to impose a fine and to make a compensation order, but the offender has insufficient means to pay both, the court shall give preference to compensation, though it may impose a fine as well (PCCA 1973, s. 35(4A)). This means that the fine should be reduced or, if necessary, dispensed with altogether, to enable the compensation to be paid. A compensation order may, thus, stand alone on sentence.

Where the court proposes to make a compensation order and a confiscation order under the CJA 1988, part VI, and the offender has insufficient means to pay both, the court shall, by virtue of s. 72(7) of the 1988 Act, order the compensation order to be paid from sums recovered under the confiscation order.

Guidelines for Compensation

The guidelines set out below are provided in Home Office Circular 53/1993 and the **E18.8** Magistrates' Association Guidelines (1997):

Type of Injury		*Suggested Award*
Graze	Depending on size	Up to £50
Bruise	Depending on size	Up to £75
Black eye		£100
Cut (no permanent scarring)	Depending on size and whether stitched	£75–£500
Sprain	Depending on loss of mobility	£100–£1,000
Loss of a non-front tooth	Depending on cosmetic effect and age of victim	£250–£500
Other minor injury	Causing reasonable absence from work (2–3 weeks)	£550–£850
Loss of front tooth		£1,000
Facial scar	However small (resulting in permanent disfigurement)	£750+
Facial scar*	A vicious slash wound from ear to the corner of the mouth or under the chin	£6,000–£9,000+
Jaw	Fractured (wired)	£2,750

Type of Injury		Suggested Award
Nasal	Undisplaced fracture of the nasal bone	£750
Nasal	Displaced fracture of bone requiring manipulation under general anaesthetic	£1,000
Nasal	Not causing fracture but displaced septum requiring sub-mucous resection	£1,750
Wrist	Simple fracture with complete recovery in a few weeks	£1,750–£2,500
Wrist	Displaced fracture (limb in plaster for some six weeks; full recovery 6–12 months)	£2,500+
Finger	Fractured little finger, assuming full recovery after a few weeks	£750
Leg or arm	Simple fracture of tibia, fibula, ulna or radius with full recovery in three months**	£2,500
Laparotomy	Stomach scar 6–8 inches long (resulting from exploratory operation)	£3,500

*Not contained in the Magistrates' Association Guidelines (1997).
**The reference to full recovery in 'three weeks' is an error.

The Home Office Circular emphasises that these suggestions are only guidelines and that there may be factors which could cause any of the awards to be substantially increased (such as the effect of an assault on an elderly or disabled person). The Magistrates' Association Guidelines (1997) state that these figures 'are only a very general guide and may be increased or decreased according to the medical evidence, the victim's sex, age and any other factors which appear to the court to be relevant in the particular case'. It is for the criminal courts to decide what use should be made of the information in this table, but a sentencer certainly cannot be criticised for having had recourse to it (*Broughton* (1986) 8 Cr App R (S) 379).

SECTION E19: RESTITUTION ORDERS

Power to Make Restitution Orders

A restitution order is designed to restore to a person entitled to them, goods which have **E19.1** been stolen or otherwise unlawfully removed from him, or to restore to him a sum of money representing the proceeds of the goods, out of money found in the offender's possession on apprehension. Either the Crown Court or a magistrates' court may make such an order.

Theft Act 1968, s. 28

(1) Where goods have been stolen, and either a person is convicted of any offence with reference to the theft (whether or not stealing is the gist of his offence) or a person is convicted of any other offence but such an offence as aforesaid is taken into consideration in determining his sentence, the court by or before which the offender is convicted may on the conviction (whether or not the passing of sentence is in other respects deferred) exercise any of the following powers—

(a) the court may order anyone having possession or control of the goods to restore them to any person entitled to recover them from him; or

(b) on the application of a person entitled to recover from the person convicted any other goods directly or indirectly representing the first-mentioned goods (as being the proceeds of any disposal or realisation of the whole or part of them or of goods so representing them), the court may order those other goods to be delivered or transferred to the applicant; or

(c) the court may order that a sum not exceeding the value of the first-mentioned goods shall be paid, out of any money of the person convicted which was taken out of his possession on his apprehension, to any person who, if those goods were in the possession of the person convicted, would be entitled to recover them from him.

For the purposes of this section, 'stealing' is very widely construed, to include not just theft and offences where theft is a constituent element, such as robbery and burglary, but also where the goods were obtained by blackmail or deception, or were stolen goods handled following any of these offences (s. 24(4)). A restitution order should not be made unless the evidence on which it is based is clear and has been given before sentence is imposed (s. 28(4); *Church* (1970) 55 Cr App R 65). A restitution order should not be made where the question of title to goods is unclear. According to Woolf J:

> . . . the criminal courts are not the appropriate forum in which to satisfactorily ventilate complex issues as to the ownership of such money or goods. In cases of doubt it is better to leave the victim to pursue his civil remedies or, alternatively, to apply to the magistrates' court under the Police (Property) Act 1897. On the other hand, in appropriate cases where the evidence is clear, it is important that the court should make proper use of the power to order restitution since this can frequently avoid unnecessary expense and delay in the victim receiving the return of his property. (*Calcutt* (1985) 7 Cr App R (S) 385, at p. 390)

For obvious reasons, there is no requirement under these provisions that account should be taken of the offender's means: contrast compensation orders at **E18.4**.

If an order is made under s. 28(1)(a), it will be inappropriate to order restitution under s. 28(1)(b) or (c) in addition, since the person will thereby recover more than the value of the goods (*Parsons* (1976) CSP J3-2F01). Under s. 28(1)(a), the person in 'possession or control' need not be the offender, but may be an innocent purchaser. Where a person has, in good faith, bought the goods from the convicted person, or has, in good faith, lent money to the convicted person on the security of the goods, the court may order payment of compensation to that person out of money taken from the offender under

s. 28(1)(c) (s. 28(3)). Such an order may be made with or without that person's application (CJA 1972, s. 6(2)).

Under s. 28(1)(b), an application must be made by the person claiming, and may not relate to goods held by a third party. Where the offender is no longer in possession of the goods, orders may be made under both s. 28(1)(b) and (c), with reference to the same goods, providing that the person does not thereby recover more than the value of the goods (s. 28(2)).

An order may be made under s. 28(1)(c) with or without an application being made (CJA 1972, s. 6(2)). Where the offender is no longer in possession of the goods, orders may be made under both s. 28(1)(b) and (c), with reference to the same goods, providing that the person does not thereby recover more than the value of the goods (s. 28(2)). Money seized from the offender after he has been arrested may be the subject of an order (*Ferguson* [1970] 1 WLR 1246, where £2,000, taken from the offender's safe deposit box 11 days after his arrest, was held to have been in his possession at the time of his apprehension). But it seems that money seized prior to his arrest may not (*Hinde* (1977) 64 Cr App R 213, a case decided in relation to forfeiture orders but applicable by analogy here). There is no need to show that the money is the proceeds of the relevant offence; all that is necessary is that it be shown that the money belongs to the offender (*Lewis* [1975] Crim LR 353). It was also established in *Lewis* that under s. 28(1)(c), a restitution order may be made against an offender for a greater sum than he received from the offence, provided that it is not for a sum greater than the total loss occasioned by the offence (in contrast to *Grundy* [1974] 1 WLR 139, which established that joint and several liability should not apply in relation to a compensation order).

An offender may appeal against a restitution order as against any other sentence. Such an order is, however, where made on conviction on indictment, subject to an automatic suspension for 28 days from the date of conviction (unless the trial court directs to the contrary on the ground that 'the title to the property is not in dispute': Criminal Appeal Act 1968, s. 30(1)) or, further, until the determination of any appeal, and, where made by a magistrates' court, it is subject to an automatic suspension for 21 days from the date of conviction (unless the court directs to the contrary as above: CJA 1972, s. 6(5)) or, further, until the determination of any appeal (s. 6(5)).

Combining Restitution Orders with Other Sentences or Orders

E19.2   A restitution order may be made in combination with any other sentence passed by the court.

SECTION E20: FORFEITURE ORDERS

Powers to Make Forfeiture Orders under PCCA 1973, s. 43

The main power of the courts to order the forfeiture of property connected with the **E20.1** commission of an offence is created by the PCCA 1973, s. 43(1). Other powers of forfeiture under specific statutes are considered at **E20.4**. The power under s. 43 may be exercised by the Crown Court or a magistrates' court, in respect of any offence.

Powers of Criminal Courts Act 1973, s. 43

(1)   Subject to the following provisions of this section, where a person is convicted of an offence, and—

(a)   the court by or before which he is convicted is satisfied that any property which has been lawfully seized from him or which was in his possession or under his control at the time when he was apprehended for the offence or when a summons in respect of it was issued—

(i)   has been used for the purpose of committing, or facilitating the commission of, any offence; or

(ii)   was intended by him to be used for that purpose; or

(b)   the offence, or an offence which the court has taken into consideration in determining his sentence, consists of unlawful possession of property which—

(i)   has been lawfully seized from him; or

(ii)   was in his possession or under his control at the time when he was apprehended for the offence of which he has been convicted or when a summons in respect of that offence was issued,

the court may make an order under this section in respect of that property, and may do so whether or not it also deals with the offender in respect of the offence in any other way and without regard to any restrictions on forfeiture in an enactment contained in an Act passed before the Criminal Justice Act 1988.

(1A)   In considering whether to make such an order in respect of any property a court shall have regard—

(a)   to the value of the property; and

(b)   to the likely financial and other effects on the offender of the making of the order (taken together with any other order that the court contemplates making).

(1B)   Where a person commits an offence to which this subsection applies by—

(a)   driving, attempting to drive, or being in charge of a vehicle, or

(b)   failing to comply with a requirement made under section 7 of the Road Traffic Act 1988 (failure to provide specimen for analysis or laboratory test) in the course of an investigation into whether the offender had committed an offence while driving, attempting to drive or being in charge of a vehicle, or

(c)   failing, as the driver of a vehicle to comply with subsection (2) or (3) of section 170 of the Road Traffic Act 1988 (duty to stop and give information or report accident),

the vehicle shall be regarded for the purposes of subsection 1(a) above (and subsection 4(b) below) as used for the purpose of committing the offence (and for the purpose of committing any offence of aiding, abetting, counselling or procuring the commission of the offence).

(1C)   Subsection (1B) above applies to—

(a)   an offence under the Road Traffic Act 1988 which is punishable with imprisonment,

(b)   an offence of manslaughter, and

(c)   an offence under section 35 of the Offences Against the Person Act 1861 (wanton and furious driving).

The effect of an order under s. 43 is to deprive the offender of his rights, if any, in the property (s. 43(3)), but it does not affect the rights of any other person, who may apply for recovery of the property (see below). The power does not extend to real property, such as the offender's home (*Khan* (1982) 4 Cr App R (S) 298). Nor should an order be made where the property is subject to joint ownership (*Troth* (1980) 71 Cr App R 1, where it was said that forfeiture orders should be confined to 'simple, uncomplicated cases'). The power does not extend to property which was associated with an offence committed by some person other than the offender: s. 43(1)(a)(i) should be read as if the words 'by him' rather than 'by anyone' appeared after the word 'offence' (*Slater* [1986] 1 WLR 1340, *Neville* (1987) 9 Cr App R (S) 222). The phrase 'facilitating the commission of, any offence' in this section includes the taking of any steps after it has been committed for the purpose of disposing of any property to which it relates or of avoiding apprehension or detection (s. 43(2)). Section 43(1B) and (1C) make it clear that an offender's vehicle *shall* be regarded as having been used for the purpose of any offence specified therein. Subsections 43(1B) and (1C), however, in no way limit the courts' power to order forfeiture of an offender's car in respect of other offences under the general provision in s. 43(1). See also the important sentencing principle at **E20.2**. Where the making of an order for forfeiture is being considered by the court, *Pemberton* (1982) 4 Cr App R (S) 328 requires that evidence be laid before the judge on the issue of forfeiture and that 'full and proper investigation' must be made into the prosecution's application. See also *Richards* [1992] 2 All ER 572.

The property shall be taken into the possession of the police, if not in their possession already, and the Police (Property) Act 1897 shall apply to such property. However, no application can be made by a claimant after six months from the date of the forfeiture order. And no such order can be made unless the claimant satisfies the court either that he had not consented to the offender having possession of the property or, where the order was made under s. 43(1)(a), that he did not know, and had no reason to suspect, that the property was likely to be used for the purpose mentioned in that subsection (s. 43(4)). The police have power under the 1897 Act to dispose of property where its ownership has not been ascertained and no court order has been made in respect of it. In relation to s. 43, the police have similar powers where no application has been made within six months or no such application has succeeded (s. 43(5)).

Powers of Criminal Courts Act 1973, s. 43A

(1)   Where a court makes an order under section 43 above in a case where—
    (a)   the offender has been convicted of an offence which has resulted in a person suffering personal injury, loss or damage; or
    (b)   any such offence is taken into consideration by the court in determining sentence, the court may also make an order that any proceeds which arise from the disposal of the property and which do not exceed a sum specified by the court shall be paid to that person.
    (2)   The court may only make an order under this section if it is satisfied that but for the inadequacy of the means of the offender it would have made a compensation order under which the offender would have been required to pay compensation of an amount not less than the specified amount.

This power to dispose of the property and use the proceeds to compensate the victim was introduced by the CJA 1988. No order can be made under this provision before the expiry of the six-month period mentioned above, or where a successful application has been made under the Police (Property) Act 1897 in respect of the property.

FORFEITURE ORDERS: SENTENCING PRINCIPLES

Forfeiture Order Affects Totality of Sentence

E20.2   See the PCCA 1973, s. 43(1A), at **E20.1**. In *Buddo* (1982) 4 Cr App R (S) 268, the offender pleaded guilty to burglary and assault. In addition to a total prison sentence of two years, the offender was deprived of his rights in a motor caravan in which he had driven to commit the burglary. The Court of Appeal was of the view that such an order could properly be made on the facts but that sentencers were 'not required to make such an order in every case in which a vehicle is used in the commission of a crime'. In this case, according to Park J, the forfeiture order was 'overdoing the punishment', and the order was quashed. See also *Scully* (1985) 7 Cr App R (S) 119 and *Priestley* [1996] 2 Cr App R (S) 144.

Where the order would have a disproportionately severe impact upon the offender, it is also inappropriate. In *Tavernor* [1976] RTR 242, an order depriving the offender of his rights in a car, imposed in addition to a suspended prison sentence and a fine, was quashed in view of the offender's physical disability. See also *Highbury Corner Metropolitan Stipendiary Magistrate, ex parte Di Matteo* [1991] 1 WLR 1374.

In a case where several offenders are equally implicated and receive comparable sentences, it is wrong to impose in addition a forfeiture order upon one of them (*Ottey* (1984) 6 Cr App R (S) 163). This may be contrasted with the principle applicable to compensation orders, the object of which is to compensate the victim, rather than to punish the offender (see **E18.4**).

Combining Forfeiture Orders with Other Sentences or Orders

A forfeiture order may be combined with a compensation order, and provision is made **E20.3** under the PCCA 1973, s. 43A, to allow the sale of property connected with the offence in order to finance compensation for the victim where the means of the offender would otherwise have been inadequate to meet a compensation order. A forfeiture order may be combined with a discharge or a probation order (PCCA 1973, s. 12(4)).

Other Statutory Powers to Make Forfeiture Orders

Certain specific statutes contain their own forfeiture provisions relating to offences **E20.4** committed under those statutes, or to property regulated under those statutes.

Misuse of Drugs Act 1971, s. 27

(1) Subject to subsection (2) below, the court by or before which a person is convicted of an offence under this Act or a drug trafficking offence as defined in s. 1(3) of the Drug Trafficking Act 1994 or an offence to which section 1 of the Proceeds of Crime (Scotland) Act 1995 relates may order anything shown to the satisfaction of the court to relate to the offence, to be forfeited and either destroyed or dealt with in such other manner as the court may order.

(2) The court shall not order anything to be forfeited under this section, where a person claiming to be the owner of or otherwise interested in it applies to be heard by the court, unless an opportunity has been given to him to show cause why the order should not be made.

Any personal property which relates to the offence may be forfeited, including money (*Beard* [1974] 1 WLR 1549), but s. 27 does not extend to intangibles, or to property situated outside the jurisdiction of the English courts (*Cuthbertson* [1981] AC 470). Nor, apparently, does s. 27 permit the forfeiture of real property such as a house (*Pearce* [1996] 2 Cr App R (S) 316). The property must be shown to relate to the offence of which the offender has been convicted; its relation to intended offences is insufficient (*Morgan* [1977] Crim LR 488, *Ribeyre* (1982) 4 Cr App R (S) 165, *Llewellyn* (1985) 7 Cr App R (S) 225 and *Cox* (1986) 8 Cr App R (S) 384). Thus, where the offender was convicted of possession of cocaine, which was hidden in his car, a forfeiture order under s. 27 could not be made in respect of £1,489 also found in his possession and accepted to be the proceeds of drug dealing, since this was the proceeds of drugs other than those to which the conviction related (*Boothe* (1987) 9 Cr App R (S) 8). In *Boothe* an order made under s. 43 of the 1973 Act (see **E20.1**) for forfeiture of the car was upheld. It is clear that an order in relation to the car might have been made under s. 27 of the 1971 Act (*Bowers* (1994) 15 Cr App R (S) 315). If the offender disputes that property is related to the offence of which he has been convicted, he must be permitted to call evidence (*Churcher* (1986) 8 Cr App R (S) 94). Under s. 27(2), it seems that the court may order forfeiture notwithstanding such an application: contrast the position under the PCCA 1973, s. 43 at **E20.1**.

It may be assumed that the sentencing principles listed in relation to the PCCA 1973, s. 43, also apply here. There is, however, under s. 27, no power to sell property to generate compensation.

Firearms Act 1968, s. 52

(1) Where a person—
    (a) is convicted of an offence under this Act (other than an offence under s. 22(3) or an offence relating specifically to air weapons) or is convicted of a crime for which he is sentenced to imprisonment, or detention in a young offender institution or a young offender's institution in Scotland or is subject to a secure training order; or
    (b) has been ordered to enter into a recognisance to keep the peace or to be of good behaviour, a condition of which is that he shall not possess, use or carry a firearm; or
    (c) is subject to a probation order containing a requirement that he shall not possess, use or carry a firearm;
    the court by or before which he is convicted, or by which the order is made, may make such order as to the forfeiture or disposal of any firearm or ammunition found in his possession as the court thinks fit and may cancel any firearm certificate or shot gun certificate held by him.

The wording of s. 52(1) is broad, and does not require the offence to relate in any way to the firearm, or the offender to be in possession of the firearm at any particular time. Firearms forfeited under s. 52 may be disposed of by the court in accordance with s. 52(4) and sch. 6 of the Act.

Prevention of Crime Act 1953, s. 1

(2) Where any person is convicted of an offence under subsection (1) of this section the court may make an order for the forfeiture or disposal of any weapon in respect of which the offence was committed.

The offence relates to having in any public place any offensive weapon without lawful authority or reasonable excuse.

See also the Incitement to Disaffection Act 1934, s. 3(4) (see **B9.94**), the Children and Young Persons (Harmful Publications) Act 1955, s. 3 (see **B19.43**), the Obscene Publications Act 1964, s. 1(4) (articles seized under the Obscene Publications Act 1959, s. 3, where offender convicted under s. 2 of the 1959 Act of having them for publication for gain) (see **B19.27**), the Immigration Act 1971, s. 25(6), the Customs and Excise Management Act 1979, s. 68(5) (see **B17.14**), the Forgery and Counterfeiting Act 1981, s. 7(3) and s. 24(3) (see **B6.91**), the Data Protection Act 1984, s. 19(4) (see **B18.4**), the Public Order Act 1986, s. 25 (see **B11.158**), the Crossbows Act 1987, s. 3 (see **B12.100**) and s. 6 (see **B12.104**), the Prevention of Terrorism (Temporary Provisions) Act 1989, s. 13, s. 16B and sch. 4 (see **B10.20** and **B10.47**), the Dangerous Dogs Act 1991, s. 4 (see **B21.6**), the Trade Marks Act 1994, s. 97 (see **B6.98**) and the Knives Act 1997, s. 6.

SECTION E21: CONFISCATION ORDERS

CONFISCATION ORDERS UNDER THE DRUG TRAFFICKING ACT 1994

The DTA 1994 consolidates the law relating to drug trafficking. It came into force on 3 **E21.1** February 1995 and applies to all cases in which the defendant was charged or the proceedings were otherwise instituted on or after that date, irrespective of when the offence was committed (1994 Act, s. 66). In *Taylor* [1996] 2 Cr App R (S) 96 it was confirmed by the Court of Appeal (construing the provisions of the Drug Trafficking Offences Act 1986) that, when an offender is being dealt with for a drug trafficking offence committed after the commencement of the 1986 Act, the proceeds of drug trafficking arising out of offences which were committed at any time before that Act came into force could be treated as part of the offender's assets for the purposes of a confiscation order. The relevant provisions of the 1986 Act, s. 1(3) and s. 2(1)(a), are reproduced in substantially the same form in s. 2(3) and s. 4(1)(a) of the 1994 Act. Confiscation orders may be made by the Crown Court under the DTA 1994, s. 2; these powers are not available to magistrates' courts. The legislation is designed to allow the court to confiscate the profits of lucrative drug trafficking offences. According to Lord Lane CJ in *Dickens* [1990] 2 QB 102, the law is 'intentionally draconian'.

Summary of the Provisions

The Crown Court is required by the DTA 1994 to follow four basic steps. **E21.2**

(a) Under s. 2 of the Act, the court may determine in respect of a defendant who has been convicted on indictment of one or more drug trafficking offences or who has been committed for sentence under the MCA 1980, s. 38, in relation to such offence or offences whether the defendant has benefited from drug trafficking. The court must so proceed if the prosecution requests it to do so, or the court may itself decide to do so (s. 2(1)(a) and (b)). By s. 2(3), the test of whether a person has so benefited is whether they have 'at any time . . . received payment or other reward in connection with drug trafficking carried on by him or another person'. In making this determination the court may make certain 'required assumptions' set out in s. 4(3). These assumptions must be made unless they are shown to be incorrect in the defendant's case, or if serious injustice would be caused by so doing.

(b) The prosecution is required by s. 11 of the 1994 Act, in every case in which the prosecutor has required the court to proceed under the Act or in any other case in which the court directs the prosecutor to do so, to tender a 'prosecutor's statement' of any matters which are relevant to the determination of whether the defendant has benefited from drug trafficking. Any admission by the defendant of an allegation or allegations in the prosecutor's statement may be treated by the court as conclusive. If he does not admit any allegation, the court may require the defendant to indicate any matters he proposes to rely on, and the court may require the defendant to furnish that information within a specified time. If he fails to comply the court may treat his failure as an acceptance of any allegation in the prosecutor's statement, except an allegation that he has benefited from drug trafficking or an allegation that any payment or other reward has been received by him in connection with drug trafficking.

(c) If the court determines that the defendant has benefited from drug trafficking, it must then determine 'the amount to be recovered' in accordance with the terms of s. 5 of the 1994 Act, as elaborated in ss. 6 to 8. The court must determine the value of the defendant's proceeds of drug trafficking, which sum is prima facie the amount to be recovered under the confiscation order. When the court has determined the value of the defendant's proceeds, it should then make a confiscation order in that amount, unless the court is satisfied that the 'amount that may be realised' in the defendant's case is a lesser figure. In determining the amount that may be realised the court must comply with the provisions of s. 6 of the 1994 Act which defines the 'amount that may be realised' as the total value of all realisable property held by the defendant at the time of the confiscation order, together with the total value of all 'gifts' which are caught by the Act, minus the total value of any obligations having priority at that time.

(d)   A confiscation order in the appropriate sum may then be made. Determination of the sum to be paid should normally be done before sentencing the offender for the offence or offences. The confiscation order should be taken into account before fixing any fine or imposing any other sentence involving forfeiture or deprivation of property, but otherwise the court should leave the confiscation order out of account in determination of sentence (s. 2(5)).

Drug Trafficking Act 1994, s. 2

(1)   Subject to subsection (7) below, where a defendant appears before the Crown Court to be sentenced in respect of one or more drug trafficking offences (and has not previously been sentenced or otherwise dealt with in respect of his conviction for the offence or, as the case may be, any of the offences concerned), then—

(a)   if the prosecutor asks that court to proceed under this section, or

(b)   if the court considers that, even though the prosecutor has not asked it to do so, it is appropriate for it to proceed under this section, it shall act as follows.

(2)   The court shall first determine whether the defendant has benefited from drug trafficking.

(3)   For the purposes of this Act, a person has benefited from drug trafficking if he has at any time (whether before or after the commencement of this Act) received any payment or other reward in connection with drug trafficking carried on by him or another person.

(4)   If the court determines that the defendant has so benefited, the court shall, before sentencing or otherwise dealing with him in respect of the offence or, as the case may be, any of the offences concerned, determine in accordance with section 5 of this Act the amount to be recovered in his case by virtue of this section.

(5)   The court shall then, in respect of the offence or offences concerned—

(a)   order the defendant to pay that amount,

(b)   take account of the order before—

(i)   imposing any fine on him, or

(ii)   making any order involving any payment by him, or

(iii)   making any order under section 27 of the Misuse of Drugs Act 1971 (forfeiture orders) or section 43 of the Powers of Criminal Courts Act 1973 (deprivation orders); and

(c)   subject to paragraph (b) above, leave the order out of account in determining the appropriate sentence or other manner of dealing with him.

(6)   No enactment restricting the power of a court dealing with an offender in a particular way from dealing with him also in any other way shall by reason only of the making of an order under this section restrict the Crown Court from dealing with an offender in any way the court considers appropriate in respect of a drug trafficking offence.

(7)   Subsection 1(1) above does not apply in relation to any offence for which a defendant appears before the Crown Court to be sentenced if—

(a)   he has been committed to the Crown Court for sentence in respect of that offence under section 37(1) of the Magistrates' Courts Act 1980 (committal to Crown Court with a view to sentence of detention in a young offender institution); or

(b)   the powers of the court (apart from this section) to deal with him in respect of that offence are limited to dealing with him in any way in which a magistrates' court might have dealt with him in respect of the offence.

(8)   The standard of proof required to determine any question arising under this Act as to—

(a)   whether a person has benefited from drug trafficking, or

(b)   the amount to be recovered in his case by virtue of this section, shall be that applicable in civil proceedings.

When the CDA 1998, sch. 8, para. 114, is brought into force, s. 2(7)(a) will be repealed.

In *Dickens* [1990] 2 QB 102, Lord Lane CJ said that the object of the legislation was to ensure that the convicted drug trafficker was parted from the proceeds of any drug trafficking which he had carried out. The court should proceed in cases where the defendant might have benefited from drug trafficking, whether or not such benefits are directly related to the drug trafficking offence for which he has just been convicted (*Preston* [1990] Crim LR 528). Where all the conditions of s. 2 are met, and where the prosecutor asks the court to proceed under this section, the wording of s. 2(1) shows that the provisions of the DTA 1994 are mandatory (*Stuart* (1989) 11 Cr App R (S) 89), and all must be fully complied with. The only exception is that provided for in s. 2(1)(b); if the prosecution does not ask the court to proceed under the Act, the court itself still has a discretion whether or not to proceed. Section 2(5) states that while the court's powers to fine etc. are unaffected by the powers of confiscation in the 1994 Act, the issue of confiscation must be resolved first (see further, *Stuart*). Section 2(8) makes it clear that the relevant standard of proof is the civil standard (thereby reversing that part of the decision in *Dickens* which held that the criminal standard of proof was applicable).

'Drug trafficking offences' are defined in s. 1(3) of the 1994 Act to mean offences under the Misuse of Drugs Act 1971, ss. 4(2) and (3), 5(3) and 20 (production, supply and possession for supply of controlled drugs), the Customs and Excise Management Act 1979, ss. 50(2) and (3), 68(2) and 170 (improper importation, exportation, fraudulent evasion of prohibition on importation or exportation of controlled drug), the Criminal Justice (International Co-operation) Act 1990, ss. 12 and 19, and ss. 49 to 51 of the 1994 Act (concealing or transferring proceeds of drug trafficking, assisting another to retain the benefit of drug trafficking and acquisition, possession or use of the proceeds of drug trafficking) together with conspiracy, attempt, incitement and participation in relation to those offences (see **B20.99**).

The meaning of the phrase 'payment or other reward' in s. 2(3) has been considered by the Court of Appeal on a number of occasions. In *Osei* (1988) 10 Cr App R (S) 289, the Court of Appeal rejected an argument that 'payment' meant payment by way of reward, and held that it simply meant any payment. It might, for example, include money given to a drug courier to enable that person to bribe customs officials; 'other reward' might include an air ticket provided for the courier, where that person would receive a free holiday in return for carrying the drugs. In *Smith* (1989) 11 Cr App R (S) 55, it was said that 'any payment in money or kind' is included. Lord Lane CJ also said that the defendant's expenses must not be deducted when making an assessment of the value of the payment or other reward. Thus the court should take account of gross receipts as opposed to actual or net profits. A drug trafficker is not entitled to set against his gross receipts the cost to him of the drugs which he has sold. See also on this point *Comiskey* (1990) 12 Cr App R (S) 562 and *Simons* (1994) 15 Cr App R (S) 126. These decisions were all reached in respect of the Drug Trafficking Offences Act 1986, but their continuing relevance to the Drug Trafficking Offences Act 1994 was confirmed by the Court of Appeal in *Banks* [1997] 2 Cr App R (S) 110, which noted that Parliament had re-enacted the relevant provisions, knowing of the decisions which had been made on them, and therefore intending that they should have continuing effect. In *Simpson* [1998] 2 Cr App R (S) 111, the Court of Appeal said that these principles were as applicable to money laundering offences as to any other drug trafficking offences.

Postponed Determinations

Normally all the provisions of the Act must be fully complied with before the offender **E21.3** is sentenced for the offence(s), but s. 3 allows postponed determinations in certain circumstances. A court may, when it is acting under s. 2 but considers that it requires further information before determining whether the defendant has benefited from drug trafficking or before determining the amount to be recovered in his case, postpone making the determination in order to obtain that information (s. 3(1)). There may be more than one postponement in such a case (s. 3(2)), but such postponement or postponements should not, in the absence of exceptional circumstances, exceed a total period of six months from the date of conviction (s. 3(3)). A postponement may be made on application by the defendant or by the prosecutor, or by the court of its own motion (s. 3(5)). Where the court exercises its power to postpone, it may nevertheless proceed to sentence the defendant (s. 3(7)) but, when sentencing, the court must not impose a fine or make any such order as is specified in s. 2(5)(b)(ii) or (iii) (s. 3(9)).

Determining whether the Offender has Benefited from Drug Trafficking

E21.4   **Drug Trafficking Act 1994, s. 4**

(1)   For the purposes of this Act—
(a)   any payments or other rewards received by a person at any time (whether before or after the commencement of this Act) in connection with drug trafficking carried on by him or another person are his proceeds of drug trafficking, and
(b)   the value of his proceeds of drug trafficking is the aggregate of the values of the payments or other rewards.
(2)   Subject to subsections (4) and (5) below, the Crown Court shall, for the purpose—
(a)   of determining whether the defendant has benefited from drug trafficking, and
(b)   if he has, of assessing the value of his proceeds of drug trafficking,
make the required assumptions.
(3)   The required assumptions are—
(a)   that any property appearing to the court—
(i)   to have been held by the defendant at any time since his conviction, or
(ii)   to have been transferred to him at any time since the beginning of the period of six years ending when the proceedings were instituted against him,
was received by him, at the earliest time at which he appears to the court to have held it, as a payment or reward in connection with drug trafficking carried on by him;
(b)   that any expenditure of his since the beginning of that period was met out of payments received by him in connection with drug trafficking carried on by him; and
(c)   that, for the purpose of valuing any property received or assumed to have been received by him at any time as such a reward, he received the property free of any other interests in it.
(4)   The court shall not make any required assumption in relation to any particular property or expenditure if—
(a)   that assumption is shown to be incorrect in the defendant's case; or
(b)   the court is satisfied that there would be a serious risk of injustice in the defendant's case if the assumption were to be made;
and where, by virtue of this subsection, the court does not make one or more of the required assumptions, it shall state its reasons.
(5)   Subsection (2) above does not apply if the only drug trafficking offence in respect of which the defendant appears before the court to be sentenced is an offence under section 49, 50 or 51 of this Act.
(6)   For the purpose of assessing the value of the defendant's proceeds of drug trafficking in a case where a confiscation order has previously been made against him, the court shall leave out of account any of his proceeds of drug trafficking that are shown to the court to have been taken into account in determining the amount to be recovered under that order.

By s. 4(1), any payments or other rewards received by a person at any time in connection with drug trafficking are the proceeds of his drug trafficking, and the value of his proceeds of drug trafficking is the aggregate of the payments or other rewards. Where there is more than one defendant before the court, a separate assessment of the proceeds of each defendant must normally be made but, in the absence of evidence to the contrary, the sentencer may assume that the proceeds were shared equally. Where only one conspirator in a drug trafficking case is before the court, it may be proper to regard the whole of the proceeds as the proceeds of that person (*Chrastny* [1991] 1 WLR 1381). A confiscation order may not be imposed upon two defendants jointly and severally (*Porter* (1990) 12 Cr App R (S) 377). In assessing the value of the defendant's interest in property which is jointly held with another person, the sentencer should determine the extent of the defendant's own interest. See further *Buckman* [1997] 1 Cr App R (S) 325.

For the meaning of 'payment or other reward' in s. 4(1), see **E21.2**.

Section 4(2) is couched in mandatory terms, but s. 4(4) makes clear that no particular assumption should be made if it can be shown to be unfounded in the particular case (see *Johnson* (1990) 12 Cr App R (S) 182, where the sentencer was entitled to make the prima facie assumption that a particular car was part of the proceeds of drug trafficking but was not entitled to make an assumption of the kind specified in s. 4(3)(a), since the defendant could demonstrate a legitimate source for the funds used to purchase the car). Where the prosecution seeks to rely upon the assumptions under s. 4, a prima facie case must be established by the prosecution to support the facts on the basis of which the assumptions are made (*Dickens* [1990] 2 QB 102). Once this has been done the defence may then rebut any of the assumptions, by showing on a balance of probabilities that the assumption is not justified in respect of that particular item. It is important for the court to indicate which assumptions have been made under s. 4(3), what payments or rewards the court has found the defendant to have received and the aggregate of the values of those payments or rewards (*Johnson*).

Drug Trafficking Act 1994, s. 11

(1)   Where the prosecutor asks the court to proceed under section 2 of this Act he shall give the court, within such period as it may direct, a statement of matters which he considers relevant in connection with—
    (a)   determining whether the defendant has benefited from drug trafficking; or
    (b)   assessing the value of his proceeds of drug trafficking.
(2)   In this section such a statement is referred to as a 'prosecutor's statement'.
(3)   Where the court proceeds under section 2 of this Act without the prosecutor having asked it to do so, it may require him to give it a prosecutor's statement, within such period as it may direct.
(4)   Where the prosecutor has given a prosecutor's statement—
    (a)   he may at any time give the court a further such statement; and
    (b)   the court may at any time require him to give it a further such statement, within such period as it may direct.
(5)   Where any prosecutor's statement has been given and the court is satisfied that a copy of the statement has been served on the defendant, it may require the defendant—
    (a)   to indicate to it, within such period as it may direct, the extent to which he accepts each allegation in the statement; and
    (b)   so far as he does not accept any such allegation, to give particulars of any matters on which he proposes to rely.
(6)   Where the court has given a direction under this section it may at any time vary it by giving a further direction.
(7)   Where the defendant accepts to any extent any allegation in any prosecutor's statement, the court may, for the purposes of—
    (a)   determining whether the defendant has benefited from drug trafficking, or
    (b)   assessing the value of his proceeds of drug trafficking,
treat his acceptance as conclusive of the matters to which it relates.
(8)   If the defendant fails in any respect to comply with a requirement under subsection (5) above he may be treated for the purposes of this section as accepting every allegation in the prosecutor's statement in question apart from—
    (a)   any allegation in respect of which he has complied with the requirement; and
    (b)   any allegation that he has benefited from drug trafficking or that any payment or other reward was received by him in connection with drug trafficking carried on by him or another person.
(9)   Where—

(a)   there is given to the Crown Court by the defendant a statement as to any matters relevant to determining the amount that might be realised at the time the confiscation order is made, and

(b)   the prosecutor accepts to any extent any allegation in the statement,

the court may, for the purposes of that determination, treat the acceptance by the prosecutor as conclusive of the matters to which it relates.

(10)   An allegation may be accepted, or particulars of any matter may be given, for the purposes of this section in such manner as may be prescribed by rules of court or as the court may direct.

(11)   No acceptance by the defendant under this section that any payment or other reward was received by him in connection with drug trafficking carried on by him or another person shall be admissible in evidence in any proceedings for an offence.

In *Emmett* [1998] AC 773 the House of Lords considered the meaning of the phrase 'treat his acceptance as conclusive of the matters to which it relates' in a provision of the Drug Trafficking Offences Act 1986 which is now mirrored in s. 11(7) of the 1994 Act. It was held that this was a procedural provision designed to facilitate proof that a defendant had benefited from drug trafficking but that it should not be construed as ousting the jurisdiction of the Court of Appeal in a case where the defendant had made a fundamental mistake in accepting an allegation in the prosecutor's statement. The comment in *Tredwen* (1994) 99 Cr App R (S) 154 that 'conclusive' meant 'conclusive for all purposes' was incorrect.

Drug Trafficking Act 1994, s. 12

(1)   This section applies where—

(a)   the prosecutor has asked the court to proceed under section 2 of this Act; or

(b)   no such request has been made but the court is nevertheless proceeding, or considering whether to proceed, under section 2.

(2)   For the purpose of obtaining information to assist it in carrying out its functions, the court may at any time order the defendant to give it such information as may be specified in the order.

(3)   An order under subsection (2) above may require all, or any specified part, of the required information to be given to the court in such manner, and before such date, as may be specified in the order.

(4)   Crown Court Rules may make provision as to the maximum or minimum period that may be allowed under subsection (3) above.

(5)   If the defendant fails, without reasonable excuse, to comply with any order under this section, the court may draw such inference from that failure as it considers appropriate.

(6)   Where the prosecutor accepts to any extent any allegation made by the defendant in giving to the court information required by an order under this section, the court may treat that acceptance as conclusive of the matters to which it relates.

(7)   For the purposes of this section, an allegation may be accepted in such manner as may be prescribed by Crown Court rules or as the court may direct.

Sections 13 and 14 allow for questions relating to confiscation orders to be re-opened in the Crown Court in cases where the court did not proceed against the defendant under s. 2, or where it made a determination that the defendant had not benefited from drug trafficking, but where further and contrary evidence comes to light. Section 15 allows for a prosecutor to make application to the court for a fresh determination of the amount which may be recovered in the defendant's case. Sections 19 to 24 make provision for confiscation orders where the defendant has died or absconded.

Determining the Amount to be Recovered

E21.5   ### Drug Trafficking Act 1994, s. 5

(1)   Subject to subsection (3) below, the amount to be recovered in the defendant's case under the confiscation order shall be the amount the Crown Court assesses to be the value of the defendant's proceeds of drug trafficking.

(2)   If the court is satisfied as to any matter relevant for determining the amount that might be realised at the time the confiscation order is made (whether by reason of the acceptance of an allegation under section 11 of this Act or made in the giving of information under section 12 of this Act or otherwise) the court may issue a certificate giving the court's opinion as to the matters concerned, and shall do so if satisfied as mentioned in subsection (3) below.

(3)   If the court is satisfied that the amount that might be realised at the time the confiscation order is made is less than the amount the court assesses to be the value of his proceeds of drug trafficking, the amount to be recovered in the defendant's case under the confiscation order shall be

(a)   the amount appearing to the court to be the amount that might be so realised, or

(b)   a nominal amount, where it appears to the court (on the information available to it at the time) that the amount that might be so realised is nil.

The 'value of the defendant's proceeds of drug trafficking' is the gross value of his aggregate receipts (s. 4(1)(b)). Provisions for the computation of the value of property and for the meaning of gifts are set out in ss. 7 and 8.

The burden of proof is on the defendant to show, on a balance of probability, that the amount that might be realised is less than the value of the proceeds (*Ilsemann* (1990) 12 Cr App R (S) 398; *Carroll* (1992) 13 Cr App R (S) 99). If the defendant fails to do so, the sentencer is entitled to make a confiscation order to the full value of the proceeds. It should be noted that determination of the amount to be recovered is a matter for the court, and may be a sum in excess of that indicated by the prosecutor in any statement made under s. 11 (*Atkinson* (1993) 14 Cr App R (S) 182, confirmed in *Finch* (1993) 14 Cr App R (S) 226). In *Cramer* (1992) 13 Cr App R (S) 390, the Court of Appeal said that when the value of a house was being determined for these purposes a deduction should be made for costs which would be incurred on sale.

Under the DTA 1994, s. 6(1), 'the amount that might be realised' at the time a confiscation order is made is:

(a)   the total of the values at the time of all the realisable property held by the defendant, less

(b)   where there are obligations having priority at that time, the total amount payable in pursuance of such obligations,

together with the total of the values at that time of all gifts caught by this Act.

Section 6(2) defines realisable property, subject to s. 6(3), as 'any property held by the defendant . . . and any property held by a person to whom the defendant has directly or indirectly made a gift caught by this Act'. Section 6(3) excepts property where there is in force in respect of it a forfeiture order or deprivation order under certain other statutory provisions. Property which has been seized from the defendant by the authorities is not property held by the defendant for these purposes (*Thacker* (1995) 16 Cr App R (S) 461; *Akengin* (1995) 16 Cr App R (S) 499).

Enforcing the Confiscation Order

Powers of enforcement are set out in ss. 9 and 25 to 34. The maximum terms of **E21.6** imprisonment, or of detention under the CJA 1982, s. 9, to be served in default of payment of a confiscation order are the same as those applicable to fines, and are set out in the table at **E17.3**. In *Popple* (1992) 14 Cr App R (S) 60, the court stressed that it was a mandatory requirement for a default term to be passed, but in *Szrajber* (1994) 15 Cr App R (S) 821 and in *French* (1995) 16 Cr App R (S) 841 the Court of Appeal stressed that the court, when fixing the term in default, should select an appropriate period from within the band, and not simply impose the maximum term. In *Ellis* [1996] 2 Cr App R (S) 403, it was held that a failure to fix a default term does not invalidate the order itself. By s. 9(5), the serving by the defendant of a term of imprisonment in default of paying an amount due under a confiscation order does not have the effect of wiping out the confiscation order. By s. 10(1), if any sum to be paid under a confiscation order is not paid when required, the defendant is liable to pay interest on the sum for the period for which it remains unpaid.

Confiscation Orders: Effect upon Sentence

E21.7   The seriousness of these offences renders it very likely that an immediate custodial sentence will be imposed on the offender. While the court is obliged to have regard to the general picture of the offender's assets when determining the confiscation order, the sentencer should be careful to relate the custodial sentence only to those offences of which the offender has been convicted (*Bragason* (1988) 10 Cr App R (S) 258). It is an important principle of sentencing that an offender should not normally receive a heavier sentence on the basis of what the sentencer has learned in the course of investigation into the offender's involvement in drug trafficking. In *Saunders* (1990) 12 Cr App R (S) 6, the Court of Appeal said that, while such material could be taken into account in determining the offender's culpability for the offence for which he was being sentenced, the sentencer should be careful not to rely for sentencing purposes on factual matters of which he had not been satisfied beyond reasonable doubt. See also *Callan* (1994) 15 Cr App R (S) 574, where the Court of Appeal held that it was wrong to deny an offender with no previous convictions credit for previous good character where a finding that he had been involved in earlier drug trafficking activities was based on statutory assumptions. In *Harper* (1989) 11 Cr App R (S) 240, it was said that information received in the course of an investigation under the drug trafficking legislation may properly form the basis for rejection of mitigation that the offender was involved in a 'one-off' transaction; *Harper* was approved in *Thompson* [1997] 1 Cr App R (S) 289. In *McNulty* (1994) 15 Cr App R (S) 606, the defendant pleaded guilty to possession of cannabis with intent to supply on the basis that he had been supplying his friends. During the inquiry relating to a confiscation order, evidence emerged that the defendant had in fact been supplying cannabis commercially. The sentencer conducted a *Newton* hearing (where factual matters alleged against the offender must be established beyond reasonable doubt: see **D17.7**), found that the defendant had been supplying commercially, and sentenced accordingly. The Court of Appeal approved this procedure. It seems that in a case where the offender has failed to cooperate fully with the process of investigation of his assets for the purpose of making a confiscation order, this should not have the effect of reducing his discount for pleading guilty (*Nicholson* (1990) 12 Cr App R (S) 58), since the confiscation and sentencing procedures are distinct.

In *Hedley* (1989) 11 Cr App R (S) 298, the Court of Appeal disapproved the imposition of a fine of £5,000 on an offender, where the court had made a confiscation order as well as passing a custodial sentence. The fine was 'not punishment, because that had already been meted out by means of the two years' imprisonment. It was not the removal of ill-gotten gains, because those ill-gotten gains had already been removed by reason of the proceedings under the 1986 Act.' In *Hopes* (1989) 11 Cr App R (S) 38, the Court of Appeal said that it was inappropriate to order the offender (who was made subject to a £12,000 confiscation order and a sentence of 16 years' imprisonment) also to pay prosecution costs of £5,000, unless there was evidence that the offender had means to pay those costs over and above the means required to meet the confiscation order. In *Makanjuola* (1991) 12 Cr App R (S) 643, the court had conducted an inquiry and found that the defendant had not benefited from drug trafficking. The Court of Appeal said that it was wrong in that case to add a fine to the prison sentence imposed for the offence.

CONFISCATION ORDERS UNDER THE CRIMINAL JUSTICE ACT 1988

E21.8   The CJA 1988, ss. 71 to 102, provide the courts with a power (and, in some circumstances, a duty) to investigate the extent to which an offender has benefited from his offence, or more generally from his offending ('relevant criminal conduct') and to order the confiscation of the proceeds of his offences. These provisions do not apply to drug trafficking offences (as to which see the Drug Trafficking Offences Act 1994 at **E21.1**). The powers are available to the Crown Court in respect of all indictable offences and to magistrates' courts in respect of a limited range of summary offences. They are also available to the Crown Court on committal for sentence from a magistrates' court (CJA 1988, s. 71 (9A), inserted by the CDA 1998, s. 83). The 1988 Act provisions were amended by the CJA 1993 and the Proceeds of Crime Act 1995, creating a scheme which is broadly parallel to that in the Drug Trafficking Offences Act 1994, but with some important differences. The amended version, as described below, applies only where all of the offences of which the defendant has been convicted were committed on or after 1 November 1995. The earlier version applies where any of the offences were committed before that date.

Criminal Justice Act 1988, s. 71

(1)   Where an offender is convicted, in any proceedings before the Crown Court or a magistrates' court, of an offence of a relevant description, it shall be the duty of the court—
(a)   if the prosecutor has given written notice to the court that he considers that it would be appropriate for the court to proceed under this section, or
(b)   if the court considers, even though it has not been given such notice, that it would be appropriate for it so to proceed,
to act as follows before sentencing or otherwise dealing with the offender in respect of that offence or any other relevant criminal conduct.
(1A)   The court shall first determine whether the offender has benefited from any relevant criminal conduct.
(1B)   Subject to subsection (1C) below, if the court determines that the offender has benefited from any relevant criminal conduct, it shall then—
(a)   determine in accordance with subsection (6) below the amount to be recovered in his case by virtue of this section, and
(b)   make an order under this section ordering the offender to pay that amount.
(1C)   If, in a case falling within subsection (1B) above, the court is satisfied that a victim of any relevant criminal conduct has instituted, or intends to institute, civil proceedings against the defendant in respect of loss, injury or damage sustained in connection with that conduct—
(a)   the court shall have a power, instead of a duty, to make an order under this section; and
(b)   subsection (6) below shall not apply for determining the amount to be recovered in that case by virtue of this section; and
(c)   where the court makes an order in exercise of that power, the sum required to be paid under that order shall be of such amount, not exceeding the amount which (but for paragraph (b) above) would apply by virtue of subsection (6) below, as the court thinks fit.
(1D)   In this part of this Act 'relevant criminal conduct', in relation to a person convicted of an offence in any proceedings before a court, means (subject to section 72AA(6) below) that offence taken together with any other offences of a relevant description which are either—
(a)   offences of which he is convicted in the same proceedings, or
(b)   offences which the court will be taking into consideration in determining his sentence for the offence in question.
(1E)   For the purposes of this part of this Act an offence is an offence of a relevant description—
(a)   in the case of an offence of which a person is convicted in any proceedings before the Crown Court or which is or will be taken into consideration by the Crown Court in determining any sentence, if it is an offence to which this part of this Act applies; and
(b)   in the case of an offence of which a person is convicted in any proceedings before a magistrates' court or which is or will be taken into consideration by a magistrates' court in determining any sentence, if it is an offence listed in schedule 4 to this Act.
[(2) and (3)   Repealed by 1995 Act.]

(4)   For the purposes of this part of this Act a person benefits from an offence if he obtains property as a result of or in connection with its commission and his benefit is the value of the property so obtained.

(5)   Where a person derives a pecuniary advantage as a result of or in connection with the commission of an offence, he is to be treated for the purposes of this part of this Act as if he had obtained as a result of or in connection with the commission of the offence a sum of money equal to the value of the pecuniary advantage.

(6)   Subject to subsection (1C) above the sum which an order made by a court under this section requires an offender to pay shall be equal to—
  (a)   the benefit in respect of which it is made; or
  (b)   the amount appearing to the court to be the amount that might be realised at the time the order is made,
whichever is the less.

  [(7)   Repealed.]

(7A)   The standard of proof required to determine any question arising under this part of this Act as to—
  (a)   whether a person has benefited from any offence; or
  (b)   [repealed]
  (c)   the amount to be recovered in his case,
shall be that applicable in civil proceedings.

Under s. 71(1) of the Act, the Crown Court or (in certain circumstances) a magistrates' court may determine in respect of a defendant who has been convicted on indictment of an offence of a relevant description (see s. 71(1E)) or has been convicted in a magistrates' court of one of the offences listed in sch. 4 to the 1988 Act whether the defendant has benefited from any relevant criminal conduct. The court must so proceed if the prosecutor has given written notice that he intends to proceed under the section, or it may proceed of its own motion (s. 71(1)(a) and (b)). Prior to the bringing into force of the Proceeds of Crime Act 1995, the courts had power to make such an order but were not under a duty to do so. The legislative purpose is clearly to ensure that more confiscation orders are made by the courts under the 1988 Act than was previously the case. Whether the court is obliged to proceed or itself decides to make a determination under the Act, the court must first decide whether the defendant has 'benefited from any relevant criminal conduct' (s. 71(1A)). This comprises the offences with which he has been convicted together with any offences taken into consideration (s. 71(1D)). By s. 71(4) and (5) a person 'benefits from an offence' if he obtains property (or a pecuniary advantage) as a result of or in connection with the commission of an offence, and his benefit is the value of the property so obtained. Where the court determines that the defendant has benefited from any relevant criminal conduct then it determines the amount to be recovered and makes a confiscation order requiring the defendant to pay that sum (s. 71(1B)) or, if the amount that can be realised is less than the total benefit, the amount which appears to the court to be the amount which can be so realised (s. 71(6)).

Section 71(7A) makes it clear that, since the implementation of the Proceeds of Crime Act 1995, the relevant standard of proof is the civil standard.

Currently, the offences listed in sch. 4 to the 1988 Act are offences under: the Local Government (Miscellaneous Provisions) Act 1982, sch. 3, paras. 20 and 21 (sex establishments); the Video Recordings Act 1984, ss. 9 and 10 (supply of video recordings of unclassified work and possession of such recordings for the purpose of supply); the Cinemas Act 1985, s. 10(1)(a) (use of unlicensed premises for an exhibition which requires a licence); the London Government Act 1963, sch. 12, paras. 10(1) and (2); the Private Places of Entertainment (Licensing) Act 1967, s. 4(1) and (2); the Local Government (Miscellaneous Provisions) Act 1982, sch. 1, paras. 12(1) and (2) (use of places for dancing, music and other entertainment); Copyright, Designs and Patents Act 1988, ss. 107(1), (2) or (3) and 198(1) or (2) (making or dealing with infringing articles etc. and making, dealing with or using illicit recordings); Trade Marks Act 1994, s. 92(1), (2) or (3) (unauthorised use of trade marks etc. in relation to goods); and Social Security Administration Act 1992, s. 114(1) (offences relating to contributions).

Where the court makes a confiscation order against the defendant, it should be taken into account before fixing any fine or imposing any other sentence involving forfeiture or deprivation of property, but otherwise the court should leave the confiscation order out of account in determination of sentence (s. 72(5)).

Criminal Justice Act 1988, s. 72

[(1) to (4) Repealed by the 1995 Act.]
(5) Where a court makes a confiscation order against a defendant in any proceedings, it shall be its duty, in respect of any offence of which he is convicted in those proceedings, to take account of the order before—
(a) imposing any fine on him;
(b) making any order involving payment by him, other than an order under section 35 of the Powers of Criminal Courts Act 1973 (compensation orders); or
(c) making any order under—
(i) section 27 of the Misuse of Drugs Act 1971 (forfeiture orders); or
(ii) section 43 of the Powers of Criminal Courts Act 1973 (deprivation orders), but subject to that shall leave the order out of account in determining the appropriate sentence or other manner of dealing with him.
(6) No enactment restricting the power of a court dealing with an offender in a particular way from dealing with him also in any other way shall by reason only of the making of a confiscation order restrict the court from dealing with an offender in any way it considers appropriate in respect of an offence to which this part of this Act applies.
(7) Where—
(a) a court makes both a confiscation order and an order for the payment of compensation under section 35 of the Powers of Criminal Courts Act 1973 against the same person in the same proceedings; and
(b) it appears to the court that he will not have sufficient means to satisfy both the orders in full,
it shall direct that so much of the compensation as will not in its opinion be recoverable because of the insufficiency of his means shall be paid out of any sums recovered under the confiscation order.

Confiscation relating to a Course of Criminal Conduct

Section 72AA of the CJA 1988 was inserted by the Proceeds of Crime Act 1995, s. 2. **E21.9** This section precedes s. 72A.

Criminal Justice Act 1988, s. 72AA

(1) This section applies in a case where an offender is convicted, in any proceedings before the Crown Court or a magistrates' court, of a qualifying offence which is an offence of a relevant description, if—
(a) the prosecutor gives written notice for the purposes of subsection (1)(a) of section 71 above;
(b) that notice contains a declaration that it is the prosecutor's opinion that the case is one in which it is appropriate for the provisions of this section to be applied; and
(c) the offender—
(i) is convicted in those proceedings of at least two qualifying offences (including the offence in question); or
(ii) has been convicted of a qualifying offence on at least one previous occasion during the relevant period.
(2) In this section 'qualifying offence', in relation to proceedings before the Crown Court or a magistrates' court, means any offence in relation to which all the following conditions are satisfied, that is to say—
(a) it is an offence to which this part of this Act applies;

(b)   it is an offence which was committed after the commencement of section 2 of the Proceeds of Crime Act 1995; and

(c)   that court is satisfied that it is an offence from which the defendant has benefited.

(3)   When proceeding under section 71 above in pursuance of the notice mentioned in subsection (1)(a) above, the court may, if it thinks fit, determine that (subject to subsection (5) below) the assumptions specified in subsection (4) below are to be made for the purpose—

(a)   of determining whether the defendant has benefited from relevant criminal conduct; and

(b)   if he has, of assessing the value of the defendant's benefit from such conduct.

(4)   Those assumptions are—

(a)   that any property appearing to the court—

(i)   to be held by the defendant at the date of conviction or at any time in the period between that date and the determination in question, or

(ii)   to have been transferred to him at any time since the beginning of the relevant period,

was received by him, at the earliest time when he appears to the court to have held it, as a result of or in connection with the commission of offences to which this part of this Act applies;

(b)   that any expenditure of his since the beginning of the relevant period was met out of payments received by him as a result of or in connection with the commission of offences to which this part of this Act applies; and

(c)   that, for the purposes of valuing any benefit which he had or which he is assumed to have had at any time, he received the benefit free of any other interests in it.

(5)   Where the court has determined that the assumptions specified in subsection (4) above are to be made in any case it shall not in that case make any such assumption in relation to any particular property or expenditure if—

(a)   that assumption, so far as it relates to that property or expenditure, is shown to be incorrect in the defendant's case;

(b)   that assumption, so far as it so relates, is shown to be correct in relation to an offence the defendant's benefit from which has been the subject of a previous confiscation order; or

(c)   the court is satisfied that there would (for any other reason) be a serious risk of injustice in the defendant's case if the assumption were to be made in relation to that property or expenditure.

(6)   Where the assumptions specified in subsection (4) above are made in any case, the offences from which, in accordance with those assumptions, the defendant is assumed to have benefited shall be treated as if they were comprised, for the purposes of this part of this Act, in the conduct which is to be treated, in that case, as relevant criminal conduct in relation to the defendant.

(7)   In this section 'the date of conviction' means—

(a)   in a case not falling within paragraph (b) below, the date on which the defendant is convicted of the offence in question, or

(b)   where he is convicted of that offence and one or more other offences in the proceedings in question and those convictions are not all on the same date, the date of the latest of those convictions; and

'the relevant period' means the period of six years ending when the proceedings in question were instituted against the defendant.

Section 72AA extends confiscation powers under the 1988 Act to a range of cases not catered for by s. 71. Confiscation under s. 71 is confined to cases in which the defendant has been convicted of an offence of a relevant description, including offences which have been formally taken into consideration by the court (see s. 71(1E) above). This interpretation of the powers of the court was confirmed by the Court of Appeal in *Crutchley* (1994) 15 Cr App R (S) 627. The purpose of s. 72AA is to extend the reach of the confiscation powers under the 1988 Act to property held by the defendant which is the result of other offending, in respect of which the defendant has not been convicted nor had formally taken into consideration. One effect will be, in a case where the defendant has pleaded guilty to offending on the basis of sample counts, to allow confiscation of the proceeds of all the offending, not just that which relates to the sample counts (see *Crutchley*). Section 72AA may operate only where the prosecutor has served notice to the effect that it should apply (the court may not act of its own motion) and where the defendant is convicted on the present occasion of two 'qualifying offences' (as defined in s. 72AA(2)) or is convicted of one qualifying offence and has a previous conviction for another within the last six years. To qualify, these previous convictions must have been incurred on or after 1 November 1995. Where these conditions are made out, the court may then make the assumptions which are mentioned in s. 72AA(4); these are the same assumptions as may be made by the court under the DTA 1994, s. 4 (see **E21.4**).

Postponed Determinations

The CJA 1988, s. 72A, allows for postponed determinations to be made in certain **E21.10** circumstances. A court may, when it is acting under s. 71 but considers that it requires further information before determining whether the defendant has benefited from any relevant criminal conduct or before determining the amount to be recovered in his case, postpone making that determination in order to obtain that information (s. 72A(1)). There may be more than one postponement in such a case (s. 72A(2)), but such postponement or postponements should not, in the absence of exceptional circumstances, exceed a total period of six months from the date of the postponement (s. 72A(3)). A postponement may be made on application by the defendant or by the prosecutor, or by the court of its own motion (s. 72A(5)). Where the court exercises its power to postpone it may nevertheless proceed to sentence the defendant (s. 72A(7)) but, when sentencing, the court must not impose a fine or make any such order as is specified in s. 72(5)(b) or (c) (s. 72A(9)).

Determining whether the Offender has Benefited and the Amount to be Recovered

The CJA 1988, ss. 73 and 73A deal with determination of whether the offender has **E21.11** benefited and determining the amount that may be recovered. Section 73 requires the prosecutor in a case where he has given written notice to the court under s. 71(1)(a), or where the court has requested the prosecutor to do so under s. 71(1)(b), to provide a statement (and, if necessary, further statements) of any matters relevant to determining whether the defendant has benefited from any relevant criminal conduct or relating to an assessment of the value of the defendant's benefit or, in a case coming within s. 72AA(1)(b), any information relevant for the purposes of subsections (4) and (5)(b) and (c) of s. 72AA. Section 73(1C) states that, where the defendant accepts to any extent any allegation in the prosecutor's statement, the court may treat that acceptance as conclusive. The acceptance is also regarded as conclusive for the purposes of any appeal (*Crutchley* (1994) 15 Cr App R (S) 627), though see *Emmett* [1998] AC 773 (see **E21.4**). Section 73A deals with information provided by the defendant. Where the prosecutor has given written notice to the court under s. 71(1)(a), or where the court is proceeding under s. 71(1)(b), the court may order the defendant to provide it with relevant information. If the defendant fails to do so without reasonable excuse, the court may draw an appropriate inference from that failure (s. 73A(5)). Where the prosecutor accepts to any extent any information so given by the defendant, the court may treat that acceptance as conclusive (s. 73A(6)). These provisions are parallel to those under DTA 1994, ss. 11 and 12 (see **E21.4**).

Section 74 defines a number of terms that are used in the relevant provisions, including 'realisable property' which (subject to s. 74(2)) means '(a) any property held by the defendant; and (b) any property held by a person to whom the defendant has directly or indirectly made a gift caught by this part of this Act', and 'the amount that might be realised' (s. 74(3)). See further *Currey* (1995) 16 App Cr App R (S) 421. The offender's home forms part of his realisable property (*Crutchley*), although in a case where the matrimonial home is jointly owned it may be inappropriate to order the sale of the property (*Taigel* [1998] 1 Cr App R (S) 328; *Lee* [1996] 1 Cr App R (S) 135). By analogy with the drug trafficking legislation, property which has been seized from the defendant by the authorities is not property 'held' by the defendant for these purposes (*Thacker* (1995) 16 Cr App R (S) 461; *Akengin* (1995) 16 Cr App R (S) 499). Further details concerning the assessment of the defendant's assets are also contained in s. 74.

Section 74A allows for the review and revision of a case in which a determination was made not to proceed against the defendant under these powers, within a period not exceeding six years from the date of the conviction, where the prosecutor now has evidence that such determination should have been made. Section 74B allows for the court to make a revised assessment, within a period not exceeding six years from the date of the conviction, in a case where there was an original determination that the defendant had not benefited from any relevant criminal conduct but where the prosecutor now has evidence which was not considered by the court. Section 74C allows for a revision of assessment of the amount to be recovered from the defendant to be made by the court, within a period not exceeding six years from the date of the conviction, where the prosecutor has evidence that the original value of the benefit was underestimated by the court. These powers are equivalent to those in ss. 13 to 15 of the DTA 1994.

Enforcing the Confiscation Order

E21.12 Powers of enforcement are set out in the CJA 1988, ss. 75 to 102. The maximum terms of imprisonment, or of detention under the CJA 1982, s. 9, to be served in default of payment of confiscation orders under the CJA 1988 are the same as in relation to fines, and are set out in the table at **E17.3**. These are maximum terms and the court should select an appropriate default term rather than simply impose the maximum (see, by analogy, *Szrajber* (1994) 15 Cr App R (S) 821). By s. 75(5A) (inserted by s. 8 of the Proceeds of Crime Act 1995), the serving by the defendant of a term of imprisonment in default of paying an amount due under a confiscation order does not have the effect of wiping out the order. By s. 75A, if any sum to be paid under a confiscation order is not paid when required, the defendant is liable to pay interest on the sum for the period for which it remains unpaid.

Confiscation Orders: Effect Upon Sentence

E21.13 In *Andrews* [1997] 1 Cr App R (S) 279, the defendant, who was involved in a family haulage business, was convicted of conspiring to cheat the revenue and of various offences relating to VAT. He was sentenced to five years' imprisonment together with a confiscation order under the 1988 Act in the sum of £543,000, with four years' imprisonment in default. The custodial term was reduced by the Court of Appeal, partly on the basis that the confiscation order would recover nearly all the money but would strip the offender of virtually all of his assets. The case may be criticised as being in conflict with s. 72(5) of the 1988 Act, which requires the sentencer to treat the custodial sentence for the offence and the confiscation order as quite separate exercises (see **E21.8**).

SECTION E22: RECOMMENDATION FOR DEPORTATION

Power to Recommend for Deportation

The Secretary of State is empowered under the Immigration Act 1971 to order the **E22.1** deportation from the United Kingdom of persons who are not British citizens. A court may, on sentencing an offender, make a recommendation that the offender be deported, by virtue of that Act and the British Nationality Act 1981. The final decision on deportation is taken by the Home Secretary, who is able to take account of a wider range of considerations than is the court, such as the political situation in the country to which the offender will go (*Nazari* [1980] 1 WLR 1366). The fact that the offender has overstayed a limited permission to be in the UK is a matter for the Home Secretary, and is not a ground, in itself, for the court to make a recommendation for deportation (*Miller v Lenton* (1981) 3 Cr App R (S) 171). The fact that the offender has refugee status is not a ground, in itself, for not making an order (*Villa* (1992) 14 Cr App R (S) 34).

By the Immigration Act 1971, s. 6(3), a recommendation may be made in respect of any person who is not a British citizen, who is aged 17 or over, and who is convicted of an offence punishable with imprisonment as an adult. A 'British citizen' is a person who has a right of abode in the United Kingdom (see, for the definition, the British Nationality Act 1981, part I), but, in addition, a Commonwealth citizen or a citizen of the Irish Republic shall not be recommended for deportation if that person was resident in the UK when the 1971 Act came into force, and has been ordinarily resident in the UK for at least the five years immediately prior to the date of conviction (s. 7(1)) (for the definition of 'Commonwealth citizen' see the British Nationality Act 1981, s. 37 and sch. 3; the Immigration Act 1971 came into force on 1 January 1973). Periods of six months or more spent in prison or detention do not count towards the five-year period (s. 7(3)). Whether continuity of residence has been broken by periods spent abroad is a matter for the sentencer to decide (*Hussain* (1972) 56 Cr App R 165), but temporary absence on holiday is not relevant (*Edgehill* [1963] 1 QB 593).

Whenever an offender's citizenship is questioned for these purposes, s. 3(8) places the onus on the offender to prove citizenship or entitlement to any exemption under the Act (see further, s. 8 for exemptions in relation to crews of ships and aircraft, military personnel and persons subject to diplomatic immunity). Section 6(2), however, provides that a court shall not make a recommendation for deportation unless the offender has been given at least seven days' written notice. This may require adjournment after conviction. If the court is considering making a recommendation for deportation, the defence should be given an opportunity to address the court on that matter (*Antypas* (1973) 57 Cr App R 207).

A recommendation for deportation may be made against a person protected by the EEC Treaty, Art. 48, if the conditions specified in Arts 3 and 9 of Directive 64/221 are satisfied. These were considered in *Bouchereau* [1978] QB 732, and the principles which emerged have been followed in subsequent cases, particularly *Secretary of State, ex parte Santillo* (1980) 2 Cr App R (S) 274, *Krauss* (1982) 4 Cr App R (S) 113, *Compassi* (1987) 9 Cr App R (S) 270, *Escauriaza* (1987) 87 Cr App R 344 and *Spura* (1988) 10 Cr App R (S) 376. The principles applicable here appear to be the same as those which apply in respect of any other non-British subject who does not come within one of the exceptions in the Immigration Act 1971. In *Escauriaza* (1987) 87 Cr App R 344, it was accepted by the Court of Appeal that EEC law 'simply mirrors the law and practice of this country'. These principles are stated in **E22.2**.

Before making a recommendation for deportation the sentencing court should always give careful consideration to the circumstances of the case, and full reasons for the decision to recommend deportation should always be given, in fairness to the offender and also to provide assistance to the Secretary of State who would have to make the final decision (*Nazari* [1980] 1 WLR 1366; *Rodney* [1996] 2 Cr App R (S) 230). The Court of Appeal in *Bozat* [1997] 1 Cr App R (S) 270, while endorsing these requirements, said that a failure to give reasons did not necessarily mean that a recommendation should be quashed; the Court of Appeal could provide its own reasons if it considered deportation to be appropriate.

The Crown Court's common-law power to bind over an offender to come up for judgment has on occasion been used as a means of requiring an offender to leave the country and not return (see **E16**). Such power is not restricted by the Immigration Act 1971.

RECOMMENDATION FOR DEPORTATION: SENTENCING PRINCIPLES

Whether the Accused's Continued Presence in UK to Detriment of Community

E22.2   In *Nazari* [1980] 1 WLR 1366, Lawton LJ said (at p. 1373):

> This country has no use for criminals of other nationalities, particularly if they have committed serious crimes or have long criminal records. That is self-evident. The more serious the crime and the longer the record the more obvious it is that there should be an order recommending deportation. On the other hand, a minor offence would not merit an order.

In that case Lawton LJ suggested that normally an offence of shoplifting would not justify a recommendation for deportation, but if the offender had been involved in a series of such offences, or if he was a member of an organised shoplifting gang, it might be. A case in which no evidence of community detriment was found is *Ariquat* (1981) 3 Cr App R (S) 83 (offence of indecent assault, where the 19-year-old offender had sexual intercourse with a girl of 15, believing her to be over 16, and so was not guilty of unlawful sexual intercourse). In *David* (1980) 2 Cr App R (S) 362, the offender was convicted of theft of a passport. Although he had previous convictions, they related to offences committed in other countries, and none had occurred since 1972. The recommendation was quashed. In *Tshuma* (1981) 3 Cr App R (S) 97, notwithstanding 'a very serious offence' of arson causing £3,000 worth of damage, the court took account of the fact that it had been committed under emotional stress and that there was very little chance of reoffending. The case of *Serry* (1980) 2 Cr App R (S) 336 decided that the fact that the offender is living on social security is not to the community's detriment and, accordingly, is not a matter to be taken into account when considering whether to make a recommendation for deportation.

A recommendation for deportation should not be made purely on the basis of an offender's criminal record (*Secretary of State, ex parte Santillo* (1980) 2 Cr App R (S) 274), a principle described by Donaldson LJ as 'not only the law in accordance with Article 3 of the Council Directive [but] also only common sense and fairness'. A recommendation may be made, however, if the court considers that the offender's previous record, in the light of the current offence, renders it likely that he will offend again. In *Krauss* (1982) 4 Cr App R (S) 113, the offender, a West German citizen, pleaded guilty to two offences of theft totalling £2,000, in breach of trust. It was argued that a recommendation for deportation was inappropriate since the offender did not constitute a threat to the fundamental interests of society. The court heard, however, that the offender had committed the offences to pay off a blackmailer who had discovered the offender's membership of the Nazi party in Germany, an illegal organisation. Given the offender's membership of that group, together with a reasonable apprehension that he might be subject to further blackmail, the recommendation was upheld.

Harshness of Foreign Regime Not to Be Considered

In *Nazari* [1980] 1 WLR 1366, Lawton LJ said (at p. 1373): '. . . the courts are not **E22.3** concerned with the political systems which operate in other countries. . . . The court has no knowledge of those matters over and above that which is common knowledge; and that may be wrong. . . . It is for the Home Secretary to decide in each case whether an offender's return to his country of origin would have consequences which would make his compulsory return unduly harsh.' This principle was applied in *Antypas* (1972) 57 Cr App R 211, though a different line had been taken in *Thoseby* (1979) 1 Cr App R (S) 280.

A related, though distinct, point is evidence of special hardship to the offender if he is deported: in *Walters* (1977) CSP K1–5II01 the court quashed a recommendation for deportation where its effect would have been to send a 17-year-old back to a country which he hardly knew and which his parents had since left.

Likely Impact on Third Parties

In some cases the courts have been prepared to have regard to the likely impact of the **E22.4** sentence upon third parties. The Court of Appeal in *Nazari* [1980] 1 WLR 1366 said that it had no wish to break up families or impose hardship on innocent people by making a recommendation for deportation. In a case where the offender, a Spanish national, had been convicted of conspiracy to rob and aggravated burglary, but where the offender's wife would be forced to choose whether to go with her husband or stay in the UK to look after the interests of her British-born children, the order was quashed. See also *David* (1980) 2 Cr App R (S) 362, at **E22.2**, where a relevant consideration was the impact upon the offender's daughter if the offender were to be deported. In *Cravioto* (1990) 12 Cr App R (S) 71, the court said that the balance which had to be struck was between the possibility that the offender might commit further crime and the harm that might be done to innocent third parties.

Combining Recommendation with Other Sentences or Orders

A recommendation for deportation is ancillary to sentence. The sentence should be **E22.5** selected first, and should not be mitigated on the ground that the offender is also to be recommended for deportation (*Edgehill* [1963] 1 QB 593). There is no statutory restriction upon combining a recommendation for deportation with any other sentence or order. It may be combined with a sentence of life imprisonment (Immigration Act 1971, s. 6(4)). A recommendation for deportation is most commonly combined with a fine or a custodial sentence. The imposition of a non-custodial penalty would frequently run contrary to the sentencing principle that the continued presence of the accused in the UK would be to the detriment of the community (**E22.2**). In *Akan* [1973] QB 491, however, the Court of Appeal upheld a recommendation for deportation in conjunction with a conditional discharge. Although a conviction followed by a conditional discharge is treated as a conviction for limited purposes only (see **E14.6**), the Immigration Act 1971, s. 6(3), provides that, for the purposes of a recommendation for deportation, a person who has been found to have committed an offence 'shall be regarded as a person convicted of the offence'.

SECTION E23: EXCLUSIONS AND DISQUALIFICATIONS

Exclusion from Licensed Premises

E23.1   **Licensed Premises (Exclusion of Certain Persons) Act 1980, s. 1**

(1)   Where a court by or before which a person is convicted of an offence committed on licensed premises is satisfied that in committing that offence he resorted to violence or offered or threatened to resort to violence, the court may, subject to subsection (2) below, make an order (in this Act referred to as an 'exclusion order') prohibiting him from entering those premises or any other specified premises, without the express consent of the licensee of the premises or his servant or agent.

(2)   An exclusion order may be made either—

(a)   in addition to any sentence which is imposed in respect of the offence of which the person is convicted; or

(b)   where the offence was committed in England or Wales, notwithstanding the provisions of sections 1A and 1C of the Powers of Criminal Courts Act 1973 (cases in which absolute and conditional discharges may be made, and their effect), in addition to an order discharging him absolutely or conditionally;

but not otherwise.

(3)   An exclusion order shall have effect for such period, not less than three months or more than two years, as is specified in the order, unless it is terminated under section 2(2) below.

Such order may be made by the court either of its own motion, on the application of the victim or prosecutor or on the application of an interested third party made by way of representation to the prosecutor (*Penn* [1996] 2 Cr App R (S) 214).

The expression 'licensed premises' means premises in respect of which there is in force a justices' on-licence. In *Grady* (1990) 12 Cr App R (S) 152, the offender pleaded guilty to assault occasioning actual bodily harm, after having been involved in an altercation in a public house, during which she pushed or punched the landlady, causing bruising to her back. The Court of Appeal quashed an order excluding the offender from entering licensed premises within the county of Norfolk for 12 months. It was said that exclusion orders were designed for those who might be described as making a nuisance of themselves in public houses, to the annoyance of other customers and possible danger to the licensee; it was inappropriate to make such an order in the case of a woman of mature years with a clean record. It may also be questioned whether an exclusion order worded to apply generally, rather than to one or more specific premises, is permissible, given the wording of s. 1.

Section 2 of the Act states that anyone who enters premises in breach of an exclusion order shall be guilty of an offence punishable on summary conviction with a fine not exceeding £200, or to imprisonment for one month or both. At the time of such conviction, the court shall consider whether the exclusion order should continue in force, and may terminate it, or vary it by deleting the name of any specified premises, if it thinks fit. There is no power to extend the order. By s. 4, a copy of any exclusion order, or order terminating or varying an exclusion order, shall be sent by the court to the licensee of the premises concerned.

Exclusion from Football Matches

E23.2 Powers contained in the POA 1986 and the Football Spectators Act 1989 to exclude offenders from attendance at football matches have been amended by the Football (Offences and Disorder) Act 1999. The new Act came into force on 27 September 1999 and applies to offences committed on or after that date. For the sentencing powers applicable to offences committed prior to that date see the 1999 edition of this work.

By the POA 1986, s. 30(1), where a person is convicted of an offence to which s. 31 of that Act applies, the court convicting him (or, if a person convicted of such an offence is committed to the Crown Court to be dealt with, the Crown Court dealing with him for the offence) has power to make a 'domestic football banning order' (formerly known as an 'exclusion order') prohibiting him from entering any premises for the purposes of attending any prescribed football match there. By s. 31, the 'relevant offences' are those which are set out in the Football Spectators Act 1989, sch. 1, as amended and expanded by the Football (Offences and Disorder) Act 1999, s. 2. A wide range of offences of violence, drunkenness, public disorder, damage to property and road traffic offences are 'relevant' if committed at or in connection with a football match. Specified offences under the 1989 Act, any offence under the Football (Offences) Act 1991 and the ticket tout offence under the CJPOA 1994, s.166, are also included. The offences listed extend to any attempt, conspiracy or incitement to commit such offence, and to aiding, abetting, counselling or procuring the commission of such an offence. The racially aggravated offences in the CDA 1998, ss. 29 to 32 are not listed, perhaps by oversight.

In respect of a number of the offences listed in the Football Spectators Act 1989, sch. 1, before making a domestic football banning order the court is required to make a 'declaration that the offence related to a particular football match or matches' (formerly known as a 'declaration of relevance'), which ordinarily requires that the prosecutor shall have given notice to the defendant, at least five days before the first day of the trial, that it was proposed to show that the offence charged did relate to a particular football match or matches. Exceptionally, however, the court may make such a declaration in a case where the required notice has not been given, but only if the defendant consents to waive the giving of full notice or if the court is satisfied that the interests of justice do not require further notice to be given (see Football Spectators Act 1989, s. 23). For the definition of a 'prescribed football match' see POA 1986, s. 36 and the Public Order (Domestic Football Banning) Order 1999 (SI 1999 No. 2460).

By the POA 1986, s. 30(2), the court is under a duty to make such a domestic football banning order if it is satisfied that there are reasonable grounds to believe that making the order would help to prevent violence or disorder at or in connection with prescribed football matches. If it is not so satisfied the court should give the reasons why it is not so satisfied in open court (s. 30(3)). The court, on making such an order, must explain its effect to the offender in ordinary language (s. 30(6)).

A domestic football banning order lasts for the period specified in the order, being not less than one year and not more than three years (s. 32(2)).

A domestic football banning order may only be imposed in addition to a sentence imposed on the offender, and that includes a case in which the offender has been discharged absolutely or conditionally for that offence, notwithstanding PCCA 1973, s. 1C (POA 1986, s. 30(4) and (5): see also **E14.6**).

A person who enters premises in breach of a domestic football banning order is guilty of an offence and liable on summary conviction to imprisonment for a term not exceeding six months or a fine not exceeding level 5 or both (s. 32(3)). A person under a domestic football banning order may apply to the court, after a minimum period of one year, to terminate the order under s. 33. If the application is refused, a further application cannot be made for six months.

By the Football Spectators Act 1989, s. 15(1), where a person is convicted of a relevant offence, the court convicting him (or, if a person convicted of such an offence is committed to the Crown Court to be dealt with, the Crown Court dealing with him for the offence) the court has power to make an international football banning order (formerly known as a 'restriction order'). The order requires the person to whom it relates to report to a police station on the occasion of designated football matches. The 'relevant offences' are those which are set out in the Football Spectators Act 1989, sch. 1. A 'designated football match' includes matches played abroad involving the national team of England or Wales or a Premier League or Football League team playing a match abroad (see s. 14(2) and the Football Spectators (Designation of Football Matches Played Outside England and Wales) Order 1990 (SI 1990 No. 732), as amended by the Sports Grounds and Football (Amendment of Various Orders) Order 1992 (SI 1992 No. 1554).

By s. 15(2) of the 1989 Act, the court is under a duty to make such an order if it is satisfied that there are reasonable grounds to believe that making the order would help to prevent violence or disorder at or in connection with designated football matches. If it is not so satisfied the court should give the reasons why it is not so satisfied in open court (s. 15(2A)). The international football banning order must specify the police station in England and Wales at which the person subject to the order is to report initially (s. 15(5)). In addition, the court may under s. 15(5A) to (5C) impose conditions in the order which the offender must comply with, including a requirement that the offender must surrender his passport to the police not more than five days before the date of each designated football match in relation to which he is required to report to the police station. The passport must be returned as soon as reasonably practicable after the match has taken place. The court, on making such an order, shall explain its effect to the offender in ordinary language (s. 15(6)).

An international football banning order lasts for the period specified in the order. In a case where the offender was sentenced for the offence to a period of imprisonment taking immediate effect, the maximum period is ten years and the minimum period is six years. In the case of any other sentence, the maximum period for the order is five years and the minimum period is three years (s. 16(1)).

An international football banning order may only be imposed in addition to a sentence imposed on the offender, and that includes a case in which the offender has been discharged absolutely or conditionally for that offence, notwithstanding PCCA 1973, s. 1C (Football Spectators Act 1989, s. 15(4): see also **E14.6**).

A person who without reasonable excuse fails to comply with the duty to report is guilty of an offence and is liable on summary conviction to imprisonment for a term not exceeding six months or a fine not exceeding level 5 or both (s. 16(5)). A person in relation to whom an international football banning order has had effect for at least two-thirds of the period specified by the court may apply to the court to terminate the order (s. 17(1)). If the application is refused a further application cannot be made for six months.

Disqualification of Company Director

E23.3 By the Company Directors Disqualification Act 1986, ss. 1 and 2, a court may make a disqualification order against an offender, wherever he is convicted of an indictable offence, whether tried on indictment or summarily, in connection with the promotion, formation, management or liquidation of a company (widely construed in *Georgiou* (1988) 87 Cr App R 207 and *Goodman* (1993) 14 Cr App R (S) 147, approving *Corbin* (1984) 6 Cr App R (S) 17), or in connection with the receivership or management of a company's property. This has the effect that the offender must not, without the leave of the court, be a director of a company, a liquidator or administrator of a company, a receiver or manager of a company's property, or in any way, directly or indirectly, be concerned or take part in the promotion, formation or management of a company, for a specified period beginning with the date of the order. The purpose of the order is to protect the public from those who, for reasons of dishonesty, or naivety or incompetence, abuse their role and status as director (*per* Potter LJ in *Edwards* [1998] 2 Cr App R (S) 213).

The maximum period of disqualification which may be imposed by a magistrates' court is five years, and the maximum for the Crown Court is 15 years. There is no minimum period. In *Millard* (1994) 15 Cr App R (S) 445, the Court of Appeal identified an 'upper bracket' or disqualification for more than 10 years, which should be reserved for particularly serious cases (including those where the director has been disqualified previously), and a 'middle bracket' of six to ten years. The decision in *Edwards* appears to recognise a third bracket, of between two and five years, reflecting the distinctions drawn in the civil case of *Re Sevenoaks Stationery (Retail)* [1991] Ch 164, but this may overlook the fact that in a criminal case there is no equivalent to the two-year minimum disqualification period which applies in a civil case.

Disqualification for 15 years was appropriate in *Vanderwell* [1998] 2 Cr App R (S) 439 for a 'thoroughly dishonest fraudster' who pleaded guilty to managing a company while an undischarged bankrupt, obtaining property by deception and failing to keep proper accounts, and who had served an earlier prison sentence for fraud and received an earlier disqualification. See also *Atterbury* [1996] 2 Cr App R (S) 151, when disqualification for 12 years was imposed on the offender who had acted as a company director in contravention of an earlier disqualification order. Disqualification for five years was appropriate in *Theivendran* (1992) 13 Cr App R (S) 601 (managing a company whilst an undischarged bankrupt and obtaining excessive credit contrary to the Insolvency Act 1986) and in *Ashby* [1998] 2 Cr App R (S) 37. In *Edwards* a disqualification for ten years was reduced to one for three years. The offender had played a relatively minor role in a fraud in which a series of small companies were established in rented premises, goods were then obtained on credit and sold cheaply, the companies then ceasing trading with substantial debts. In *Victory* [1999] 2 Cr App R (S) 102, two years' disqualification was reduced to 12 months in the case of a director who was 'careless to the point of incompetence' in keeping accounting records.

A contravention of a disqualification order is, in itself, a criminal offence punishable with up to two years' imprisonment (s. 13). Where a disqualification order is made against a person who is already subject to one, the periods specified shall run concurrently (see *Johnson* [1996] 2 Cr App R (S) 228).

Disqualification from Driving where Motor Vehicle Used for Committing or Facilitating Commission of an Offence

Section 44(1) of the PCCA 1973 provides that the Crown Court may disqualify an E23.4 offender from holding or obtaining a licence to drive a motor vehicle in cases where a motor vehicle has been used for the purpose of committing, or facilitating the commission of, the offence. This power is available:

    (a)   where a person is convicted before the Crown Court of an offence punishable on indictment with imprisonment for a term of two years or more, or where the offender has been convicted by a magistrates' court of such an offence and he is committed under s. 38 of the MCA 1980 to the Crown Court for sentence (s. 44(1)), or

    (b)   where he is convicted before any court of common assault or any other offence involving assault (including an offence of aiding, abetting, counselling or procuring, or inciting the commission of an offence)(s. 44(1A)),

and the Crown Court is satisfied that the motor vehicle was used (whether by the person convicted or by anyone else) for the purpose of committing, or facilitating the commission of the offence in question (s. 44(2)). For the meaning of 'facilitating the commission of an offence', see the PCCA 1973, s. 43(2) at **E20.1**.

In a case falling within s. 44, the Crown Court may order the person convicted to be disqualified, for such period as the court thinks fit, from holding or obtaining a licence (s. 44(2) and (2A)), but there is no power under s. 44 to order the defendant to take an extended driving test on the expiry of the disqualification under the Road Traffic Offenders Act 1988, s. 36.

It should be noted that there is no requirement under s. 44 that the person convicted was the driver of the vehicle (*Matthews* [1975] RTR 32), nor that the vehicle was directly involved in the commission of the offence, although use of the vehicle must at least have facilitated its commission. If there is no causal link at all, an order under s. 44 cannot be made (see *Parrington* (1985) 7 Cr App R (S) 18, although disqualification might now be ordered instead under the C(S)A 1997, s. 39 (see **E23.5**)). In *Patel* (1994) 16 Cr App R (S) 756, the offender had pursued another motorist who had executed a dangerous manoeuvre in front of his car. When both cars stopped at traffic lights the offender got out and seriously assaulted a passenger in the other vehicle. It was held that the use of the car had facilitated the commission of the assault.

Formerly, power to disqualify under s. 44 did not extend to persons who were convicted of an offence but discharged absolutely or conditionally (for the limited effect of 'conviction' on a person so sentenced, see the PCCA 1973, s. 1C, and the 1998 edition of this work at **E19.4**. The restriction has been removed by the PCCA 1973, s. 12(4), as substituted by the CDA 1998, sch. 7, para. 18.

Before disqualifying the offender, the court must warn counsel of the possibility of disqualification under s. 44, and counsel should be given an opportunity to address the court on that matter. Failure to warn may result in the disqualification being quashed on appeal (*Powell* (1984) 6 Cr App R (S) 354).

A court imposing a disqualification under s. 44 should take account of its likely effects on the offender's employment prospects (*Davegun* (1985) 7 Cr App R (S) 110; *Liddey* [1999] 2 Cr App R (S) 122).

Disqualification from Driving on Commission of an Offence

E23.5   By s. 39 of the C(S)A 1997, which came into force on 1 January 1998 in respect of pilot areas only, a court by or before which a person is convicted of an offence may, in addition to dealing with him in any other way, order him to be disqualified, for such period as it thinks fit, from holding or obtaining a driving licence (s. 39(1)). The power is made available to the Crown Court and magistrates' courts and applies in relation to any offence. This very broad power is made subject to s. 39(2), which states that the power to disqualify under s. 39 does not apply to cases where a person is convicted of murder or where the sentence falls to be imposed under the C(S)A 1997, s. 2(2), 3(2) or 4(2). It is also made subject to s. 39(3), which states that disqualification under s. 39 may not be imposed unless the court has been notified by the Secretary of State that the power to make such an order is exercisable by that court.

On a literal reading of s. 39, the section renders redundant all the provisions on disqualification from driving which are contained in the Road Traffic Offenders Act 1988, as well as the power to disqualify from driving contained in the PCCA 1973, s. 44 (see **E23.4**). According to s. 39, conviction for an offence may, without more, attract a period of disqualification from driving for such period as the court thinks fit. Presumably, however, the courts will choose to interpret s. 39 so as to confer an additional power to disqualify offenders who have not committed a driving-related offence (so that the disqualification provisions in the 1988 Act are inapplicable) and who have not otherwise used a vehicle in the commission, or in facilitating the commission, of the offence (so that disqualification under the PCCA 1973, s. 44, is not available). So construed, s. 39 empowers the court to disqualify from driving an offender whose offence is completely unrelated to motor vehicles. The section also allows the court to order that such person may be disqualified from obtaining a driving licence. There is no power under s. 39 to order the defendant to take an extended driving test on the expiry of the disqualification under the Road Traffic Offenders Act 1988, s. 36.

Formerly, power to disqualify under the C(S)A 1997, s. 39, did not extend to persons who were convicted of an offence but discharged absolutely or conditionally (for the limited effect of 'conviction' on a person so sentenced, see PCCA 1973, s. 1C, and the 1998 edition of this work at **E19.5**. The restriction has been removed by the PCCA 1973, s. 12(4), as substituted by the CDA 1998, sch. 7, para. 18.

By analogy with the power under the PCCA 1973, s. 44, it may be desirable for the court, before exercising its powers under s. 39 of the 1997 Act, to give an opportunity to counsel to address the court.

It is unclear whether an order made under s. 39 affects the totality of the sentence (by analogy with the power to order forfeiture of the offender's property under the PCCA 1973, s. 43: see **E20.2**) or whether it should be regarded as an ancillary order (by analogy with compensation orders: see **E18.3**) imposition of which should not affect the punishment imposed for the offence. It is suggested that where disqualification is imposed under s. 39 it is imposed as an additional form of punishment, and so the former view is the preferable one.

For disqualification from driving imposed under the Road Traffic Offenders Act 1988, see **C6** and **C7**.

SECTION E24: MENTALLY DISORDERED OFFENDERS

PROBATION ORDERS WITH REQUIREMENT AS TO TREATMENT FOR MENTAL CONDITION

E24.1   **Powers of Criminal Courts Act 1973, sch. 1A, para. 5**

(1) This paragraph applies where a court proposing to make a probation order is satisfied, on the evidence of a registered medical practitioner approved for the purposes of section 12 of the Mental Health Act 1983, that the mental condition of the offender—

(a) is such as requires and may be susceptible to treatment; but

(b) is not such as to warrant the making of a hospital order or guardianship order within the meaning of that Act.

(2) The probation order may include a requirement that the offender shall submit, during the whole of the probation period or during such part or parts of that period as may be specified in the order, to treatment by or under the direction of a registered medical practitioner or a chartered psychologist (or both, for different parts) with a view to the improvement of the offender's mental condition.

(3) The treatment required by any such order shall be such one of the following kinds of treatment as may be specified in the order, that is to say—

(a) treatment as a resident patient in a mental hospital;

(b) treatment as a non-resident patient at such institution or place as may be specified in the order; and

(c) treatment by or under the direction of such registered medical practitioner or chartered psychologist (or both) as may be so specified;

but the nature of the treatment shall not be specified in the order except as mentioned in paragraph (a), (b) or (c) above.

The probation order may not be for less than six months or more than three years (PCCA 1973, s. 2(1)), but the term of the requirement of treatment need not be co-extensive with the probation period; it may be for less than six months but may not apply for more than three years. The medical practitioner referred to in para. 5(1) must be approved for the purposes of the Mental Health Act 1983, s. 12, as being a person having special experience in the diagnosis and treatment of mental disorder. A chartered psychologist would not come within the terms of para. 5(1).

A probation order with a requirement as to treatment for a mental condition may be made in a case where the offender is not suffering from any of the four forms of mental disorder which justify the making of a hospital order (see **E24.3**). As to proof of an offender's mental condition, see Mental Health Act 1983, s. 54. Treatment may be carried out at a mental hospital, a mental nursing home, but not a special hospital (para. 5(10)). As a precondition to the inclusion of a treatment condition in a probation order, the court must be satisfied that the necessary arrangements have been or can be made relating to the treatment intended to be specified under the order (including arrangements necessary for the reception of the offender) and that the offender has expressed his willingness to comply with the requirement (para. 5(4)). While the probationer is under treatment as a resident patient, the probation officer must carry out his supervision of the offender 'only as may be necessary for the purpose of the revocation or amendment of the order' (para. 5(5)).

Where a probation order with a requirement as to treatment for a mental condition has been made, and the relevant medical practitioner or chartered psychologist takes the view that part of the treatment may be better or more conveniently given in or at an institution not specified in the order (even where the institution is not one which could have been specified in the original order (para. 5(7)), arrangements may be made, with the consent of the probationer, for this to be done (para. 5(6)). Where such a change is made, the probation officer must be notified in writing (para. 5(8)).

If the probationer fails to comply with any of the requirements specified in the probation order, including the requirement as to mental treatment and any breach of a condition inserted under para. 5(6) (provided para. 5(8) was complied with), he may be dealt with for breach of the probation order. A probation order is a community order within the meaning of the CJA 1991, s. 6(4). For provisions relating to breach of community orders, see **E4.7**. If the probationer commits a further offence during the currency of the order, he may be dealt with in respect of the original offence in the usual manner. (For revocation of community orders, see **E4.8**). A probation order with a requirement as to treatment for a mental condition may be amended on application to the court under CJA 1991, sch. 2, paras 13 and 14. Paragraph 13(2)(a) states that the court shall not amend a probation order by inserting a mental treatment condition unless the amending order is made within three months of the original order. Paragraph 14 permits the probation officer, in response to a report in writing from the relevant medical practitioner, to apply to court for a variation or cancellation of the mental treatment requirement.

For powers to make probation orders, see **E5.1** and **E5.2**. Cases on the appropriate use of a probation order with a requirement of treatment for a mental condition should now be read in the light of the changes made by the CJA 1991. Earlier case law indicates that, while a probation order with a condition of psychiatric treatment may sometimes be made in respect of an offender who has committed a serious offence and represents a real risk to the public (e.g., *Hoof* (1980) 2 Cr App R (S) 299, where the offender was convicted of arson with intent to endanger life, and *Nicholls* (1981) CSP F1–2B01, where the offender was convicted of indecent assault on a girl of seven and had a record of sexual offences committed on young girls), it should only be made where there is a reasonable chance that such an order will have a beneficial effect upon the offender and where the risk to the public is thereby outweighed. In *McDonald* (1983) 5 Cr App R (S) 419, the Court of Appeal, without any criticism of the trial judge, varied a sentence of two years' imprisonment, imposed on an offender who pleaded guilty to an indecent assault on a girl aged 11, to a probation order with a condition of psychiatric treatment, on hearing evidence that 'as much has been done as can practically be done to ensure (1) that he will be properly supervised in the community, (2) that he will have a proper place of residence, (3) that that residence will be conveniently sited so that he may attend for treatment, and, finally, that treatment will be available over an extended period of time'.

SUPERVISION ORDERS WITH REQUIREMENT AS TO TREATMENT FOR MENTAL CONDITION

Power to insert a requirement of treatment for a mental condition into a supervision **E24.2** order may be found in the CYPA 1969, s. 12B. The provisions are very similar to those relating to insertion of a treatment requirement into a probation order (**E24.1**). For supervision orders generally, see **E8**.

Children and Young Persons Act 1969, s. 12B

(1) Where a court which proposes to make a supervision order is satisfied, on the evidence of a registered medical practitioner approved for the purposes of section 12 of the Mental Health Act 1983, that the mental condition of a supervised person is such as requires and may be susceptible to treatment but is not such as to warrant the making of a hospital order or guardianship order within the meaning of that Act, the court may include in the supervision order a requirement that the supervised person shall, for a period

specified in the order, submit to treatment of one of the following descriptions so specified, that is to say—

(a)   treatment by or under the direction of a registered medical practitioner specified in the order;

(aa)   treatment by or under the direction of a chartered psychologist specified in the order;

(b)   treatment as a resident or non-resident patient at an institution or place specified in the order; or

(c)   treatment as a resident patient in a hospital or mental nursing home within the meaning of the Mental Health Act 1983, but not a special hospital within the meaning of that Act.

A requirement of treatment for a mental condition cannot be included unless the court is satisfied that arrangements have been made or can be made for the treatment in question. If the offender is aged 14 or over, such a requirement cannot be included by the court unless the offender consents. In no case must such a requirement continue in force after the supervised person has attained the age of 18 (s. 12B(2)).

HOSPITAL ORDERS

E24.3   An admission to a hospital by means of a hospital order has the same effect for most purposes as a compulsory civil commitment under part II of the Mental Health Act 1983. The order lapses after six months, but may be renewed for a further six months and then at yearly intervals thereafter, where the responsible medical officer considers further detention necessary for the protection of the public or in the interests of the patient's health or safety (Mental Health Act 1983, s. 20 and sch. 1). There is no limit to the number of renewals which might subsequently be made, but the patient may be discharged from hospital by way of various powers exercised by the responsible medical officer, the hospital managers, or a mental health review tribunal.

Mental Health Act 1983, s. 37

(1)   Where a person is convicted before the Crown Court of an offence punishable with imprisonment other than an offence the sentence for which is fixed by law or falls to be imposed under section 2(2) of the Crime (Sentences) Act 1997, or is convicted by a magistrates' court of an offence punishable on summary conviction with imprisonment, and the conditions mentioned in subsection (2) below are satisfied, the court may by order authorise his admisson to and detention in such hospital as may be specified in the order or, as the case may be, place him under the guardianship of a local social services authority or of such other person approved by a local social services authority as may be so specified.

(1A)   In the case of an offence the sentence for which would otherwise fall to be imposed under subsection (2) of section 3 of the Crime (Sentences) Act 1997, nothing in that subsection shall prevent a court from making an order under subsection (1) above for the admission of the offender to a hospital.

(2)   The conditions referred to in subsection (1) above are that—

(a)   the court is satisfied, on the written or oral evidence of two registered medical practitioners, that the offender is suffering from mental illness, psychopathic disorder, severe mental impairment or mental impairment and that either—

(i)   the mental disorder from which the offender is suffering is of a nature or degree which makes it appropriate for him to be detained in a hospital for medical treatment and, in the case of psychopathic disorder or mental impairment, that such treatment is likely to alleviate or prevent a deterioration of his condition; or

(ii)   in the case of an offender who has attained the age of 16 years, the mental disorder is of a nature or degree which warrants his reception into guardianship under this Act; and

(b)   the court is of the opinion, having regard to all the circumstances including the nature of the offence and the character and antecedents of the offender, and to the other available methods of dealing with him, that the most suitable method of disposing of the case is by means of an order under this section.

At least one of the two medical practitioners must be approved, for the purposes of s. 12, by the Secretary of State, as having special experience in the diagnosis or treatment of mental disorder (s. 54(1)). Three of the four forms of mental disorder specified in s. 37(2)(a) are defined in s. 1 of the 1983 Act. This section also describes other conditions which do not amount to mental disorder within the Act. Whenever a hospital order (or guardianship order) is made, the court must specify from which of these forms of mental disorder the offender is found by the court to be suffering (s. 37(7)), and an order cannot be made unless the offender is described by each of the medical practitioners as suffering from the same form of mental disorder (s. 37(7)). A hospital order may be appropriate, even though no causal link is established between the offender's mental disorder and the offence in respect of which the order is made (*McBride* (1972) CSP F2–2A01). In *Blackwood* (1974) 59 Cr App R 170, the Court of Appeal said that a court should not normally make a hospital order if the offender was not legally represented. Only a youth court may make a hospital order or guardianship order on a juvenile (CYPA 1969, s. 7(8)).

Section 37(3) of the Mental Health Act 1983 deals with the power of a magistrates' court to make a hospital order, where the court is satisfied that the person did the act or made the omission charged, without proceeding to conviction. This power is to be very sparingly used (see *Lincoln (Kesteven) Justices, ex parte O'Connor* [1983] 1 WLR 335).

A hospital order or guardianship order cannot be made unless the court is satisfied, on the written or oral evidence of the registered medical practitioner who would be in charge of the offender's treatment, or of some other person representing the managers of the hospital, that arrangements have been made for the offender's admission to that hospital within 28 days of the date of the order (s. 37(4)). The health authorities are under no legal obligation to accept offenders from the courts (though see the comment of Lawton LJ in *Harding*, (1983) 5 Cr App R (S) 197 to the effect that those who obstruct the court's wish to make such an order might be guilty of contempt of court). They are, however, under a legal obligation to supply information to the courts about the availability of beds in their regions for the admission of persons under hospital orders (s. 39(1)). In an emergency or other special situation arising within that 28 days, the Secretary of State may give directions for the admission of the offender to a hospital different from that specified in the order (s. 37(5)). Occasionally it may be appropriate to admit an offender to a hospital not situated locally, with a view to subsequent transfer (*Marsden* [1968] 1 WLR 785).

By s. 37(8) of the 1983 Act, when a hospital order or a guardianship order is made, the court shall not pass a sentence of imprisonment, make an order for detention, impose a fine, make a probation order or a supervision order in respect of the offence, or require a parent of a juvenile so dealt with to enter into a recognisance. A hospital order cannot be combined with a referral order (see **E13**). The court may, however, 'make any other order which the court has power to make apart from this section': this would include ancillary orders such as a compensation order.

The Mental Health Act 1983, s. 38, provides for the making of an 'interim hospital order' for the purposes of establishing whether a convicted person is suitable to be the subject of a hospital order. The qualifying conditions are virtually the same as for the making of a hospital order under s. 37, but the interim order is available to the court 'before making a hospital order or dealing with him in some other way'. One difference in the powers is that an interim order can be made only where one of the registered medical practitioners who gives evidence is employed at the hospital where the person is to be detained. An interim hospital order is not a final disposal of the case; such an order may last for up to 12 weeks, renewable for further periods of not more than 28 days at a time, though in no case may it last for more than a total of 12 months (C(S)A

1997, s. 49, increasing the total period specified in s. 38(5) of the 1983 Act from six months). No minimum period is specified. Power to make an interim hospital order under s. 38 may also be exercised for the purposes of determining whether a person should be made subject to a hospital direction or a limitation direction under s. 45A of the Act (s. 45A(8): see **E24.9**). At the end of the interim period the court must make a final disposal of the case, and the interim order comes to an end. In a case where a court renews an interim hospital order, or where it finally disposes of the case by making a hospital order under s. 37, the offender need not appear before the court, provided that he is legally represented and his representative has had an opportunity of being heard (s. 38(2) and (6)).

GUARDIANSHIP ORDERS

E24.4 By the Mental Health Act 1983, s. 40(2), a guardianship order shall confer on the authority or person named in the order as guardian, the same powers as a guardianship application made and accepted under part II of the 1983 Act. These powers, in outline, are to determine place of residence, require attendance for treatment, occupation, education or training, and to require access to the patient in any place of residence for a doctor, social worker or other specified person (Mental Health Act 1983, s. 8).

The relevant statutory provisions are the same as those which relate to the courts' powers to make hospital orders (see **E24.3**), except that there is no requirement in respect of the making of a guardianship order that the mental disorder must be treatable, and see the requirement in s. 37(2)(a)(ii), set out at **E24.3**. In addition, by s. 37(6) of the 1983 Act, a guardianship order cannot be made unless the relevant authority or person is willing to receive the offender into guardianship. Section 39A of the 1983 Act empowers a court which is minded to make a guardianship order to request the local social services authority to inform the court whether it would be willing to comply with the order and, if so, to give information about how it would exercise its powers under s. 40(2). A guardianship order lasts for 12 months, but may be renewed.

RESTRICTION ORDERS

Power to Make Restriction Orders

E24.5 **Mental Health Act 1983, s. 41**

(1) Where a hospital order is made in respect of an offender by the Crown Court, and it appears to the court, having regard to the nature of the offence, the antecedents of the offender and the risk of his committing further offences if set at large, that it is necessary for the protection of the public from serious harm so to do, the court may, subject to the provisions of this section, further order that the offender shall be subject to the special restrictions set out in this section, either without limit of time or during such period as may be specified in the order; and an order under this section shall be known as 'a restriction order'.

(2) A restriction order shall not be made in the case of any person unless at least one of the registered medical practitioners whose evidence is taken into account by the court under section 37(2)(a) above has given evidence orally before the court.

For hospital orders, see **E24.3**. Only the Crown Court may make a restriction order, though magistrates may commit an offender to the Crown Court, provided the offender is aged 14 or over, with a view to such a disposal (s. 43). If the magistrates' court commits the offender to the Crown Court, but the Crown Court decides not to make a restriction order, the Crown Court's powers of sentence are limited to those which the magistrates could have imposed, unless there is also in effect a general committal for sentence.

A restriction order cannot be made unless there is evidence that it is necessary to protect the public from serious harm (*Courtney* (1987) 9 Cr App R (S) 404). A court is not bound to accept medical evidence for or against restricting discharge when a hospital order is made (*Royse* (1981) 3 Cr App R (S) 58, *Birch* (1989) 11 Cr App R (S) 202). There is no requirement for a causal connection between the disorder and the offence (*Hatt* [1962] Crim LR 647, approved in *Birch*).

Unlike a hospital order under s. 37, a restriction order does not lapse in the ordinary way unless renewed, but continues for as long as the restriction order is in place. If the restriction order is for a fixed period, at the end of that period the restrictions no longer apply but the hospital order continues in effect (s. 41(5)). Neither the responsible medical officer nor the hospital managers may discharge the patient without the Secretary of State's consent. The Secretary of State or a mental health review tribunal may release a patient who is subject to a restriction order at any time, either absolutely or conditionally (s. 42(1) and (2)). If the patient is discharged conditionally, the restriction order remains in force and the patient may be recalled to hospital.

RESTRICTION ORDERS: SENTENCING PRINCIPLES

Choice of Disposal

In *Birch* (1989) 11 Cr App R (S) 202, the Court of Appeal gave important guidance **E24.6** upon the selection of sentence for mentally disordered offenders generally, and in particular the appropriate use of restriction orders under the Mental Health Act 1983, s. 41. Earlier cases on the use of restriction orders should be read subject to this decision. The following general points emerge:

(a) In a case involving a degree of mental disorder, the sentencer should consider whether a period of compulsory detention is apposite. If it is not, or may not be, a probation order with a requirement as to treatment for mental condition may be appropriate (see **E24.1**).

(b) If a probation order is inappropriate, the sentencer must consider whether the conditions contained in the Mental Health Act 1983, s. 37, for the making of a hospital order (see **E24.3**), are satisfied. If in doubt, he may wish to make an interim hospital order, giving the court and the doctors further time to decide. If the conditions in s. 37 are satisfied, he will consider whether to make a hospital order or impose a custodial sentence.

(c) The sentencer should then consider whether the conditions of the Mental Health Act 1983, s. 41, are satisfied.

Criteria for Use of Restriction Order

In *Birch* (1989) 11 Cr App R (S) 202, Mustill LJ held that the choice between a hospital **E24.7** order and a restriction order depends on a prognosis which the judge must make (rather than the medical experts). A sentencer should not add a restriction order to a hospital order simply to mark the gravity of the offence, nor as a means of punishment. The words 'from serious harm' in the Mental Health Act 1983, s. 41, mean that the court is required to assess, not the seriousness of the risk that the offender will reoffend, but the risk that if he does so the public will suffer serious harm. His lordship said (at p. 213):

> The harm in question need not, in our view, be limited to personal injury. Nor need it relate to the public in general, for it would in our judgment suffice if a category of persons, or even a single person, were adjudged to be at risk: although the category of person so protected would no doubt exclude the offender himself. Nevertheless the potential harm must be serious, and a high possibility of a recurrence of minor offences will no longer be sufficient.

His lordship also held that it would be a mistake to equate the seriousness of the offence with the likelihood of a restriction order being made. It is only one factor, but the court would have to be very sure of its ground to pass a restriction order where the commission of a serious offence was coupled with a very low risk of reoffending. On the other hand, a relatively minor offence committed by a person who is shown by the medical evidence to be mentally disordered and dangerous may justify the passing of a restriction order. It is not necessary to wait until someone has been seriously injured before a hospital order with restrictions can be made (see *Nwohia* [1996] 1 Cr App R (S) 170).

If the sentencer decides on a restriction order, he must then choose an unlimited order, or one for a fixed term. It is regarded as imprudent in any but the most exceptional circumstances to impose a restriction for a fixed rather than an unlimited period (*Gardiner* [1967] 1 WLR 464, *Birch* (1989) 11 Cr App R (S) 202 and *Nwohia*).

Choice between Restriction Order and Custodial Sentence

E24.8   If the criteria within the Mental Health Act 1983, s. 41, are established, the sentencer may, but is not obliged to, make a restriction order. The decision is that of the judge, and a restriction order may be made even though not recommended by the medical evidence (*Royce* (1981) 3 Cr App R (S) 58). The alternative sentence will be life imprisonment (for which, see **E1.21 *et seq.***), custody for a fixed term or custody for a longer-than-normal sentence under s. 2(2)(b) of the CJA 1991. The cases make it clear that a life sentence is to be preferred to a fixed-term sentence where the offender is subject to a degree of mental instability which makes it probable that he will continue to reoffend unless detained for an indefinite period of time (*Pither* (1979) 1 Cr App R (S) 209). Where the conditions for a restriction order under the Mental Health Act 1983 are made out, and where a bed in an appropriate hospital is available, a restriction order should be imposed in preference to a life sentence (*Howell* (1985) 7 Cr App R (S) 360; *Mbatha* (1985) 7 Cr App R (S) 373; *Moses* [1996] 2 Cr App R (S) 407; *Mitchell* [1997] 1 Cr App R (S) 90; *Hutchinson* [1997] 2 Cr App R (S) 60). Any concern which the sentencer may have that the offender may be released prematurely by a Mental Health Review Tribunal is not sufficient reason for passing a life sentence rather than a restriction order (*Mitchell*, disapproving *Fleming* (1993) 14 Cr App R (S) 151, and pointing out the analogous nature of the composition and powers of the discretionary life panel of the Parole Board and that of the Mental Health Review Tribunal).

Mustill LJ in *Birch* (1989) 11 Cr App R (S) 202, also gave guidance (at p. 215) on the choice between a restriction order and a custodial sentence, suggesting that this choice may arise in two distinct situations:

(a)   'If the offender is dangerous and no suitable secure hospital accommodation is available: here the judge will be driven to impose a prison sentence.' A number of earlier cases indicate that where a determinate custodial sentence is imposed rather than a hospital order, it must be proportionate to the offence committed (*Clarke* (1975) 61 Cr App R 320, *Hook* (1980) 2 Cr App R (S) 353 and *Fisher* (1981) 3 Cr App R (S) 112). In other cases, however, the Court of Appeal has upheld a disproportionate term of custody, on the grounds of the protection of the public, on an offender for whom no place was available in a hospital (*Scanlon* (1979) 1 Cr App R (S) 60, *Gouws* (1981) 3 Cr App R (S) 325).

(b)   'Where the sentencer considers that notwithstanding the offender's mental disorder there was an element of culpability in the offence which merits punishment. This may happen where there is no connection between the mental disorder and the offence, or where the defendant's responsibility for the offence is "diminished" but not wholly extinguished.' In fact, *Mbatha* (1985) 7 Cr App R (S) 373 indicates that in the latter type of case a hospital order is to be preferred.

Hospital and Limitation Directions

E24.9   Sections 45A and 45B of the Mental Health Act 1983 are designed to apply where the court has heard evidence that the offender is suffering from a psychopathic disorder and the making of a hospital order is appropriate, but the court wishes to ensure that the offender (if found not to be capable of responding to treatment for his condition or upon completion of his period of treatment) will thence be transferred to prison for the remainder of the sentence rather than being released from hospital.

Section 45A applies where a person is convicted before the Crown Court of an offence the sentence for which is not fixed by law and, except where the offence is one the sentence for which falls to be imposed under the C(S)A 1997, s. 2 (see **E1.22**), the court considers making a hospital order before deciding to impose a sentence of imprisonment (s. 45A(1)). By s. 45A(2), the court must be satisfied on the written or oral evidence of two registered medical practitioners (at least one of whom must give oral evidence: s. 45A(4)):

    (a)   that the offender is suffering from psychopathic disorder;
    (b)   that the mental disorder from which the offender is suffering is of a nature or degree which makes it appropriate for him to be detained in a hospital for medical treatment; and
    (c)   that such treatment is likely to alleviate or prevent a deterioration of his condition.

In these circumstances the court may make a 'hospital direction', which is a direction that, instead of being detained in prison, the offender be detained in a specified hospital. The court may also make a 'limitation direction', which is a direction that the offender also be made subject to the restrictions set out in s. 41 of the 1983 Act (see **E24.5**). The court must also be satisfied on the written or oral evidence of the registered medical practitioner who would be in charge of the offender's treatment, or of some other person representing the managers of the hospital, that arrangements have been made for the offender's admission to that hospital and for his admission within the period of 28 days from the making of the order. The court may, pending admission within that period, give directions for the offender's detention in a place of safety (s. 45A(5)). A hospital direction and a limitation direction given in respect of an offender have effect not only as regards the sentence of imprisonment imposed but also as regards any other sentence of imprisonment imposed on the same or a previous occasion (s. 45A(9)).

By s. 45A(10), the Secretary of State may by order provide that directions made under s. 45A may apply to offenders suffering from other forms of mental disorder apart from psychopathic disorder. Such an order may apply generally or to certain classes of offenders or offences.

Section 45B provides that with respect to any person a hospital direction shall have effect as a transfer direction and a limitation direction shall have effect as a restriction direction. While a person is subject to a hospital direction and a limitation direction the responsible medical officer must supply to the Secretary of State a report on the offender at least every 12 months.

SECTION E25: REHABILITATION OF OFFENDERS

General Principle

E25.1   Under the Rehabilitation of Offenders Act 1974, after the passage of time convictions may become 'spent' and a convicted person may consider himself 'rehabilitated'. When a conviction is spent the offender is treated for a range of purposes as if he had never been convicted of the offence concerned. While s. 7(2) of the Act excludes from its scope the operation of criminal proceedings, *Practice Direction (Crime: Spent Convictions)* [1975] 1 WLR 1065 nonetheless requires that spent convictions which appear on an offender's record should be marked as such, and that nobody should refer in open court to such spent convictions without the authority of the judge, which should only be given where the interests of justice so require. When passing sentence, the sentencer should make no reference to spent convictions unless it is necessary to do so to explain the sentence being passed. Similar arrangements apply to magistrates' courts, following Home Office Circular No. 98 of 1975. See also the Rehabilitation of Offenders Act 1974 (Exceptions) Order 1975 (SI 1975 No. 1022).

The Act's protection applies to all convictions, except those which result in an excluded sentence (see **E25.2**). 'Conviction' is given a broad meaning in the Act, but would not extend to cover the imposition of a bind over to keep the peace which has been imposed at any time except at sentence. It is unclear whether the Act applies to a recommendation for deportation. Offences in respect of which orders for absolute or conditional discharge are made do not count as convictions for a variety of purposes, but s. 1(4) of the Act provides that these are convictions which may be the subject of rehabilitation.

Sentences Falling outside the Scope of Rehabilitation

E25.2   Certain sentences fall outside the scope of the Rehabilitation of Offenders Act 1974, and an offender who has received such a sentence can never become rehabilitated with respect to that conviction. Those sentences are:

(a)   life imprisonment;
(b)   imprisonment or detention in a young offender institution (or youth custody) for a term exceeding 30 months;
(c)   detention during Her Majesty's pleasure;
(d)   detention under the CYPA 1933, s. 53, for a term exceeding 30 months;
(e)   custody for life.

Rehabilitation Periods

E25.3   Rehabilitation periods in respect of other sentences are set out below. The relevant period runs from the date of conviction, even where sentence is deferred. Some of the rehabilitation periods are, as indicated, reduced where the offender was under 18 years of age at the date of conviction.

Sentence	Rehabilitation period
A sentence of imprisonment or detention in a young offender institution (or youth custody) for more than six months but not more than 30 months	Ten years for an adult, five years for a juvenile

Sentence	Rehabilitation period
A sentence of imprisonment or detention in a young offender institution (or youth custody) of six months or less	Seven years for an adult, three and a half years for a juvenile
A sentence of detention in a detention centre	Three years
A fine	Five years for an adult, two and a half years for a juvenile
A community service order	Five years for an adult, two and a half years for a juvenile
Probation (offenders placed on probation before 3 February 1995), bind over to keep the peace or to be of good behaviour, conditional discharge	The date the order or bind over ceases or one year, whichever is the longer
Probation (offenders placed on probation on or after 3 February 1995)	Five years for an adult, two and a half years for a juvenile
Supervision order	The date the order ceases or one year, whichever is the longer
Attendance centre order	One year after the order expires
Referral order	When the contract ceases to have effect
Secure training order	One year after the order expires
Hospital order	Five years from the date of conviction or two years after the order expires, whichever is the longer
Disqualification and other orders imposing disability, prohibition or other penalty	The date the order ceases to have effect
Absolute discharge	Six months

Some sentences or orders do not appear in this table. For the purposes of the Act, a suspended sentence of imprisonment counts as a sentence of immediate imprisonment of the same length. The relevant length of a partly suspended sentence is the length of the served and suspended parts of the sentence added together. Two consecutive custodial sentences are aggregated for the purposes of the Act (s. 5(9)(b)). Where an offender receives more than one sentence or order in respect of single offence, the relevant rehabilitation period is the longest of those applicable (s. 6(2)).

Effect of Further Conviction

A person who has been convicted can only become rehabilitated under the Rehabilita- **E25.4** tion of Offenders Act 1974 if he is not reconvicted within the relevant rehabilitation period (s. 6(4)). If he is reconvicted of anything other than a summary offence (s. 6(6)), the rehabilitation period for the first offence continues to run until the expiry of the period for the second offence. An exception to the subsequent offence rule is that periods arising from orders of disqualification, disability, prohibition or other penalty are to be disregarded (s. 6(5)), whether such disqualification, etc. relates to the first or the second conviction. If an excluded sentence (see **E25.2** above) is passed for the second offence, then this excludes both convictions permanently from the possibility of rehabilitation.

PART F
EVIDENCE

Diane Birch, LLB

Professor of Criminal Justice and Evidence, University of Nottingham

Peter Fortune, MA, Barrister

Michael Hirst, LLB, LLM

Professor of Criminal Justice, De Montfort University, Leicester

Adrian Keane, LLB, Barrister

Permanent Reader, Inns of Court School of Law
Sometime Lecturer at the School of Law, Hong Kong University

F

SECTION F1: GENERAL PRINCIPLES OF EVIDENCE IN CRIMINAL CASES

FACTS IN ISSUE

The facts in issue comprise: (a) the facts which the prosecution bear the burden of **F1.1** proving or disproving (in order to establish the guilt of the accused) and (b) the facts which, in exceptional cases, the accused bears the burden of proving (in order to succeed in his defence). '[W]henever there is a plea of not guilty, everything is in issue and the prosecution have to prove the whole of their case, including the identity of the accused, the nature of the act and the existence of any necessary knowledge or intent' (*Sims* [1946] KB 531, per Lord Goddard CJ at p. 539). Thus the nature of the facts in issue in any given case is determinable by reference to the legal ingredients of the offence charged and any defence raised. Any fact which is formally admitted under the CJA 1967, s. 10, ceases to be in issue — it must be taken to have been proved and is not open to contradictory proof. Under s. 10(1) of the Act, a formal admission may be made of 'any fact of which oral evidence may be given in any criminal proceedings', words which make it clear that the section cannot be used to admit what would otherwise fall to be excluded because, say, it is inadmissible opinion or hearsay (*Coulson* [1997] Crim LR 886).

FORMAL ADMISSIONS

Criminal Justice Act 1967, s. 10   F1.2

(1) Subject to the provisions of this section, any fact of which oral evidence may be given in any criminal proceedings may be admitted for the purpose of those proceedings by or on behalf of the prosecutor or defendant, and the admission by any party of any such fact under this section shall as against that party be conclusive evidence in those proceedings of the fact admitted.

(2) An admission under this section —

    (a) may be made before or at the proceedings;

    (b) if made otherwise than in court, shall be in writing;

    (c) if made in writing by an individual, shall purport to be signed by the person making it and, if so made by a body corporate, shall purport to be signed by a director or manager, or the secretary or clerk, or some other similar officer of the body corporate;

    (d) if made on behalf of a defendant who is an individual, shall be made by his counsel or solicitor;

    (e) if made at any stage before the trial by a defendant who is an individual, must be approved by his counsel or solicitor (whether at the time it was made or subsequently) before or at the proceedings in question.

(3) An admission under this section for the purpose of proceedings relating to any matter shall be treated as an admission for the purpose of any subsequent criminal proceedings relating to that matter (including any appeal or retrial).

(4) An admission under this section may with the leave of the court be withdrawn in the proceedings for the purpose of which it is made or any subsequent criminal proceedings relating to the same matter.

Following a not guilty plea at a plea and directions hearing, the prosecution and defence are expected to inform the court of facts which are to be admitted and which can be reduced into writing in accordance with s. 10(2)(b) (see *Practice Direction (Crown Court: Plea and Directions Hearings)* [1995] 1 WLR 1318, para. 10(f) at **D12.13**). In court, a formal admission may be made by counsel or a solicitor *orally* (see s. 10(2)(b) and (d), and *Lewis* [1989] Crim LR 61). However, where an admission is made in this way by or on behalf of the prosecutor or accused for the purposes of summary trial or proceedings before magistrates acting as examining justices, the court shall cause the admission to be written down and signed by or on behalf of the party making the admission (Magistrates' Courts Rules 1981, r. 71). Whatever the manner of making a formal admission under s. 10 of the 1967 Act, it should be such that what has been admitted should appear clearly on the shorthand note (*Lennard* [1973] 1 WLR 483). It is also important that the jury are clear as to what has been formally admitted. Thus in *Lewis* (1971) 55 Cr App R 386, in which counsel for the accused formally admitted every fact alleged in the prosecution's opening speech and the prosecution called no evidence, relying solely on admissions, leave to appeal against conviction was refused. The Court added, however, that such a procedure should be adopted only rarely and with caution, because jurors, when considering the opening speech, might find it difficult to distinguish between law, mixed fact and law, and comment.

The CJA 1967, s. 10, has been extended to courts martial (see Armed Forces Act 1976, s. 11 and sch. 5, para. 3).

JUDICIAL NOTICE

Generally speaking, the doctrine of judicial notice allows the tribunal of fact to treat a fact as established, notwithstanding that no evidence has been adduced to establish it. The doctrine, however, takes three distinct forms. The first two, judicial notice without inquiry and judicial notice after inquiry, were defined and distinguished by Lord Sumner in *Commonwealth Shipping Representative* v *Peninsular and Oriental Branch Service* [1923] AC 191, at p. 212: 'Judicial notice refers to facts, which a judge can be called upon to receive and to act upon, either from his general knowledge of them, or from inquiries to be made by himself for his own information from sources to which it is proper for him to refer'. The phrase 'judicial notice' is also used, in a third sense, to refer to the use which may be made by jurors or magistrates of their personal knowledge of facts in issue or relevant to the facts in issue. This has been referred to as jury or magistrate notice. These three forms of judicial notice require separate analysis.

Judicial Notice without Inquiry at Common Law

F1.3 If a fact is sufficiently notorious or of such common knowledge that it requires no proof, the judge, without recourse to any extraneous sources of information, may take judicial notice of it and direct the jury to treat it as established, notwithstanding that it has not been established by evidence. Celebrated examples include: the fact that a fortnight is too short a period for human gestation (*Luffe* (1807) 8 East 193); the fact that the streets of London are full of traffic (*Dennis* v *A.J. White & Co.* [1916] 2 KB 1, at p. 6); and the fact that reconstructed trials with a striking degree of realism are among the popular forms of modern television entertainment (*Yap Chuan Ching* (1976) 63 Cr App R 7). In criminal cases, foreign law, being a question of fact generally calling for the evidence of an appropriately qualified expert, cannot be the subject of judicial notice (*Ofori* (1994) 99 Cr App R 223). There is one exception: the common law of Northern Ireland (*Re Nesbitt* (1844) 14 LJ MC 30 at p. 33).

Judicial Notice without Inquiry Pursuant to Statute

F1.4 Judicial notice of a fact may be required by statute. The most important examples are the Evidence Act 1845, s. 2 and the Interpretation Act 1978, s. 3. Section 2 of the 1845 Act requires judicial notice to be taken of the fact that a judicial or official document purporting to have been signed by a judge of the Supreme Court was signed by that judge. See also the County Courts Act 1984, s. 134(2) (summonses and other documents issuing out of a county court and sealed or stamped with the seal of the court) and the Bankruptcy Act 1914, s. 142 (documents bearing the seal of a court with jurisdiction in bankruptcy or the signature of the judge or registrar of such a court).

Evidence Act 1845, s. 2

All courts, judges, justices, masters in Chancery, masters of courts, commissioners judicially acting, and other judicial officers, shall henceforth take judicial notice of the signature of any of the equity or common law judges of the superior courts at Westminster, provided such signature be attached or appended to any decree, order, certificate, or other judicial or official document.

Section 3 of the Interpretation Act 1978, as supplemented by s. 22(1) and sch. 2, para. 2, requires judicial notice to be taken of statutes of the United Kingdom (whether general, local and personal, or private) passed after 1850.

Interpretation Act 1978, s. 3

Every Act is a public Act to be judicially noticed as such, unless the contrary is expressly provided by the Act.

Thus in the absence of express provision to the contrary, evidence is not required to prove either the contents of an Act passed after 1850 or that such an act has been duly passed by both Houses of Parliament. At common law, the courts are bound to take judicial notice of Public Acts passed before 1850. Private Acts passed before 1850 require to be proved by the production of a Queen's Printer's or Stationery Office copy (see Evidence Act 1845, s. 3 and the Documentary Evidence Act 1882, s. 2).

Statutory instruments may be proved by Queen's Printer's or Stationery Office copies (see *Ashley* (1967) 52 Cr App R 42 and the Documentary Evidence Act 1868, s. 2, at **F8.9**). There is no equivalent to the Interpretation Act 1978, s. 3, for judicial notice to be taken of statutory instruments, although some instruments have acquired such notoriety that judicial notice may be taken of them (*Jones* (1968) 54 Cr App R 63).

Judicial Notice after Inquiry

In a number of cases, judges have taken judicial notice of a fact only after referring to **F1.5** extraneous sources of information, such as certificates from ministers or officials, learned treatises, works of reference and expert witnesses. Such a judicial inquiry is distinct from proof by evidence in the normal way: the rules of evidence are inapplicable; the result of the inquiry is not open to evidence in rebuttal; and the result, except in the case of facts lacking constancy (e.g., the status of a foreign government), constitutes a legal precedent. The justification for judicial notice after inquiry is that some facts, although not sufficiently notorious to be the subject of judicial notice without inquiry, are readily demonstrable by reference to sources of virtually indisputable authority, or arise so frequently that proof in the normal way is undesirable because of the cost and the need for uniformity of decision. Judicial notice after inquiry has been taken of the following three kinds of fact:

(a)   Facts of a political nature, such as relations between the government of the United Kingdom and a foreign state, the status of foreign sovereigns or governments, the membership of diplomatic suites, and the extent of territorial sovereignty. The source of information is usually a minister, whose certificate will be treated as an indisputably accurate source for reasons of public policy, namely the desirability of avoiding conflict between the courts and the executive. In *Bottrill, ex parte Kuechenmeister* [1947] KB 41, the Court of Appeal, treating as conclusive the certificate of the Foreign Secretary that Germany still existed as a State and German nationality as a nationality, and that His Majesty was still in a state of war with Germany, held that the applicant for a writ of *habeas corpus* was still an enemy alien. See also *Duff Development Co. Ltd* v *Government of Kelantan* [1924] AC 797; *Engelke* v *Musmann* [1928] AC 433; and *Carl Zeiss Stiftung* v *Rayner and Keeler Ltd (No. 2)* [1967] 1 AC 853.

(b)   Facts which are readily demonstrable after reference to appropriate authoritative works of reference or learned treatises. Illustrations would be the day of the week on which a certain date fell, after reference to an almanac or diary; the longitude and latitude of a certain place, after reference to an atlas or other geographical work; and the date and location of a well-known historical event, after reference to an appropriate authoritative history. See *Read* v *Bishop of Lincoln* [1892] AC 644.

(c) Customs and professional practices, after consultation with suitably qualified experts. See *Brandao* v *Barnett* (1846) 12 Cl & F 787 (the custom of bankers' lien); *Re Rosher* (1884) 26 ChD 801 (conveyancers' practices); *Davey* v *Harrow Corporation* [1958] 1 QB 60 (ordnance surveyors' practices); and *Heather* v *P-E Consulting Group Ltd* [1973] 1 Ch 189 (accountants' practices).

PERSONAL KNOWLEDGE OF COURT OR JURY

Judges

F1.6   It has been held that a judge may use personal knowledge of matters within the common knowledge of people in the locality, a principle which derives from cases decided under the Workmen's Compensation Acts, under which county court judges sat as arbitrators and took into account, in assessing compensation, personal knowledge of the labour market, conditions of work, and wages (see, e.g., *Keane* v *Mount Vernon Colliery Co. Ltd* [1933] AC 309 and *Reynolds* v *Llanelly Associated Tinplate Co. Ltd* [1948] 1 All ER 140). In *Mullen* v *Hackney London Borough Council* [1997] 1 WLR 1103 it was held that a county court judge, in deciding which penalty to impose on the council for its failure to carry out an undertaking to the court to repair housing, was entitled to take judicial notice of his own knowledge of the council's conduct in relation to previous undertakings. The decision, it is submitted, is difficult to justify. As to judicial notice, the facts were clearly not notorious or of common knowledge, and were not of the kind of which judicial notice has been held to have been properly taken after enquiry. As to personal knowledge, the Court of Appeal has treated the principle established in the cases decided under the Workmen's Compensation Acts as if it were a principle of general application in any county court case: see Christopher Allen, *The International Journal of Evidence and Proof*, 1998 Vol 2, No. 1, 37.

Magistrates

F1.7   In *Wetherall* v *Harrison* [1976] QB 773 the issue was whether the accused had a reasonable excuse for failure to give a blood sample. The accused said that he had had a sort of fit, which the prosecution alleged had been simulated. One of the justices, a practising registered medical practitioner, gave his professional view on the matter to the other justices, who also drew on their own experience of wartime inoculations and the fear that they could create in certain cases. Dismissing the appeal, the Divisional Court held that justices, unlike judges, lack the ability to exclude certain factors from their consideration. In particular, if a magistrate is a specialist, whether doctor, engineer or accountant, it is not possible for him to approach the decision in the case as though he did not have that training, and it would be a very bad thing if he had to. One of the advantages of justices is that they bring a lot of varied experience into the court-room, and use it. Although it would be quite wrong for a justice to give evidence to himself or the other justices in contradiction of that which had been heard in court, he can employ his basic knowledge, for the benefit of himself and the other justices, in considering, weighing up and assessing the evidence given before the court.

'It has always been recognised that justices may and should – after all, they are local justices – take into consideration matters which they know of their own knowledge, and particularly matters in regard to the locality' (*Ingram* v *Percival* [1969] 1 QB 548 per Lord Parker CJ at p. 555). The appellant had been convicted of unlawfully using a net secured by anchors for taking salmon or trout in tidal waters. It was held that the justices were fully entitled to make use of their own knowledge that the place where the net was fixed was in tidal waters. See also *Paul* v *DPP* (1989) 90 Cr App R 173 concerning a charge of soliciting a woman for the purposes of prostitution from a motor vehicle in a street in such manner or in such circumstances as to be likely to cause nuisance to other persons in the neighbourhood, contrary to the Sexual Offences Act 1985, s. 1(1). It was held that the justices, who had no evidence before them that anyone had actually been caused nuisance, were entitled to take into account two matters within their local knowledge: first, that the area in question was often frequented by prostitutes and that there was a constant procession of cars driving around the area at night; and secondly, that it was a heavily populated residential area. In *Field, ex parte White* (1895) 64 LJ MC 158, the issue being whether cocoa necessarily contains foreign ingredients, no evidence was adduced. The justices, relying on their own knowledge of the subject, found for the accused. Although Wills J observed that perhaps in future evidence should be heard on such a matter, the Divisional Court refused to disturb the justices' finding. Local knowledge of the prevalence of a particular kind of offence may be taken into account, but should be applied with care (see generally Stockdale and Devlin, *Sentencing*, 1987, paras 1.69 and 1.70). However, it is submitted that magistrates should exercise extreme caution in using personal knowledge, particularly where the facts are not matters of local notoriety.

Jurors

The doctrine of judicial notice also applies to jurors in relation to matters coming within **F1.8** the sphere of their everyday knowledge and experience (*Rosser* (1836) 7 C & P 648, approved in *Jones* [1970] 1 WLR 16). In *Jones* it was argued that it had not been proved that the accused had been given an opportunity to provide a specimen of breath for a breath test, because there had been no evidence to show that the device used, the Alcotest R80, was 'of a type approved by the Secretary of State' for the purposes of the Road Safety Act, 1967, s. 7. Rejecting this argument, Edmund Davies LJ said, at p. 20: ' . . . the number of decided cases in which it has been proved that the Alcotest R80 device is of an approved type has by now become so large and so widely reported that, in our judgment, a court (including the jury) is entitled to take judicial notice of that fact, and its formal proof is accordingly no longer necessary'.

However, although jurors may use their *general* knowledge, they may not use their *personal* knowledge to supplement or contradict the evidence given in the case. The older authorities suggest that a juror with particular knowledge of a matter should be sworn as a witness and give evidence in the normal way (see *Rosser* (1836) 7 C & P 648; *Manley* v *Shaw* (1840) Car & M 361; *Antrim Justices* [1895] 2 IR 603). A preferable solution, it is submitted, is the course adopted in *Blick* (1966) 50 Cr App R 280. In that case a juror passed a note to the judge to the effect that his own local knowledge contradicted the alibi evidence given by the accused. In consequence the judge allowed the prosecution to call evidence, relating to the matters contained in the note, to rebut the alibi. This decision was upheld by the Court of Criminal Appeal.

RELEVANCE

The cardinal rule of the law of evidence is that, subject to the exclusionary rules, all **F1.9** evidence which is sufficiently relevant to the facts in issue is admissible, and all evidence which is irrelevant or insufficiently relevant to the facts in issue should be excluded. Thus, as to the latter, inasmuch as an offence of strict liability involves no proof of *mens rea*, evidence of motive, intention or knowledge is inadmissible, being irrelevant to what the Crown has to prove and merely prejudicial to the accused (*Sandhu* [1997] Crim LR 288). The classic formulation of relevance is to be found in Article 1 of Stephen's *Digest of the Law of Evidence* (12th ed.), according to which the word signifies that 'any two facts to which it is applied are so related to each other that according to the common course of events one either taken by itself or in connection with other facts proves or renders probable the past, present or future existence or non-existence of the other'. On the question of relevance, Lord Simon of Glaisdale has said:

> Evidence is relevant if it is logically probative or disprobative of some matter which requires proof. I do not pause to analyse what is involved in 'logical probativeness', except to note that the term does not of itself express the element of experience which is so significant of its operation in law, and possibly elsewhere. It is sufficient to say, even at the risk of etymological tautology, that relevant (i.e., logically probative or disprobative) evidence is evidence which makes the matter which requires proof more or less probable. (*DPP* v *Kilbourne* [1973] AC 729, at p. 756)

Some of the more frequently recurring examples of relevant evidence are listed in relation to circumstantial evidence (see **F1.10** to **F1.13**).

The test of 'logical probativeness' is sometimes strictly applied, as it was in *Blastland* [1986] AC 41. The appellant, B, was convicted of the buggery and murder of F, a boy. At the trial, B admitted that he had met F and engaged in homosexual activity with him (including attempted buggery), but said that shortly afterwards he saw another man nearby and, fearing that he had been observed committing a serious offence, panicked and ran away. B's description of the other man corresponded closely to one M. B said that M must have committed both offences charged. There were formal admissions by the prosecution showing M to have been known to engage in the past in homosexual activities with adults but not with children. There were also both formal admissions and evidence relating to M's movements on the evening of F's murder. The defence sought leave to call a number of witnesses to give evidence that before F's body had been found, M had made statements to them that a boy had been murdered. The trial judge ruled that this evidence was inadmissible. Before the House of Lords, the appellant submitted that the statements made by M were admissible as original evidence to show M's state of mind, i.e. his knowledge of the murder before the body had been found. Lord Bridge, giving the judgment of the House, held that such evidence would only have been admissible if M's state of mind had been either directly in issue itself or of direct and immediate relevance to an issue arising at the trial. The evidence had been properly rejected because the issue at the trial was whether B had committed the crimes, and what was relevant to that was not the fact of M's knowledge but how he had come by it; since he might have come by that knowledge in a number of different ways, there was no rational basis on which the jury could be invited to draw an inference as to the source of that knowledge. To do so would have been mere speculation. The evidence of what M said, therefore, could not be put before the jury to support the conclusion that he, rather than B, may have been the criminal. See also *Kearley* [1992] 2 AC 228 at **F15.10**, *Williams* [1998] Crim LR 494 and *Akram* [1995] Crim LR 50. See also, *sed quaere*, *Keast* [1998] Crim LR 748, in which it was held that unless there is some concrete basis for regarding the out-of-court demeanour and state of mind of a victim of sexual abuse as confirming or disproving the occurrence of such abuse, it cannot assist a jury bringing their common-sense to bear on who is telling the truth.

Concerning the offence of possession of drugs with intent to supply, evidence which is arguably relevant to the question of intent may fall to be excluded because of its prejudicial effect in indicating dealing in drugs in the past or generally. Thus evidence of the possession of weights and scales on which there are traces of the drug in question will be admitted (*Batt* [1994] Crim LR 592), but not evidence of past deposits in and withdrawals from savings accounts, because that can only found an inference of past drug dealing (*Gordon* [1995] 2 Cr App R 61). In *Batt* it was also held that evidence of the discovery of £150 in an ornamental kettle in B's house was inadmissible because it had nothing to do with intent to supply in future the drugs found, but had a highly prejudicial effect as evidence of propensity to supply or of past or future supplying generally. *Batt*, however, has not laid down a general principle that evidence of possession of money is never admissible (*Nicholas* [1995] Crim LR 942; *Okusanya* [1995] Crim LR 941). On one view the decision in *Batt* turned on the fact that the trial judge had failed to direct the jury as to how they could properly use the evidence of the money found (*Morris* [1995] 2 Cr App R 69). Alternatively *Batt* should be seen as a case strictly confined to its own facts, bearing in mind that £150 was too small, and its hiding place too unremarkable, to be the hallmark of present drug dealing (*Okusanya*). In *Wright* [1994] Crim LR 55, it was held that drug traders needed to keep by them large sums of cash and therefore evidence of the discovery of £16,000 was capable of giving rise to an inference of dealing and tended to prove that the drugs found were for supply. In *Gordon* [1995] 2 Cr App R 61, it was held that evidence of the discovery of £4,200 was admissible subject to an appropriate direction. Similarly in *Smith* [1995] Crim LR 940, it was held that evidence that in recent months £9,000 had been deposited in S's account, £2,100 of which could not be explained by legitimate transactions, was admissible, subject to an appropriate direction. The jury should be directed that evidence of the discovery of money is relevant only if they reject any innocent explanation for it advanced by the accused, but that, if they conclude that it indicates not merely past dealing but an on-going dealing in drugs, they may take into account the finding of it, together with the drugs, in considering the issue of intent to supply (*Grant* [1996] 1 Cr App R 73). They should be directed not to treat it as evidence of propensity, i.e. not to pursue the line of reasoning that because of the past dealing the accused is likely to be guilty (*Simms* [1995] Crim LR 304 and *Lucas* [1995] Crim LR 400). In *Guney* [1998] 2 Cr App R 242 the Court of Appeal declined to follow earlier authorities to the effect that, where possession of the drugs is in issue, evidence of possession of money or drugs paraphernalia can never be relevant to that issue (see *Halpin* [1996] Crim LR 112 and *Richards* [1997] Crim LR 499). It was held that although evidence of possession of a large sum of cash or enjoyment of a wealthy lifestyle does not, on its own, prove possession, there are numerous sets of circumstances in which it may be relevant to that issue, not least to the issue of knowledge as an ingredient of possession. The real issue in the case was whether G was knowingly in possession of nearly five kilos of heroin or whether it had been 'planted', the defence having conceded that, if possession were to be proved, then it would be open to the jury to infer intent to supply. It was held that, in all the circumstances, evidence of the finding of nearly £25,000 in cash in the wardrobe of G's bedroom and in close proximity to the drugs was relevant to the issue of possession. *Guney* was applied in *Griffiths* [1998] Crim LR 567. See also *Edwards* [1998] Crim LR 207 and *Scott* [1996] Crim LR 652.

Relevance is a question of degree. For example, evidence of facts which supply a motive for an accused to have committed a particular crime is generally admissible to show that it is more likely that he committed that crime (see *Ball* [1911] AC 47, per Lord Atkinson at p. 68; but see also, in the case of offences of strict liability, *Sandhu* [1997] Crim LR 288). However, evidence of motive will be excluded if it is so remote from the offence charged that it can be said to be without any probative value at all (see *Berry* (1986) 83 Cr App R 7). Similarly, on a charge of manslaughter against a doctor, although expert evidence of his skill as shown by his treatment of the case under investigation is admissible, expert evidence as to his skilful treatment of patients on other occasions is inadmissible (*Whitehead* (1848) 3 Car & Kir 202). Evidence of marginal relevance may be excluded on the grounds that it would lead to a multiplicity of subsidiary issues, involving the court in a protracted investigation and distracting it from the main issue (see *A-G v Hitchcock* (1847) 1 Exch 91 per Rolfe B at p. 105 and *Patel* [1951] 2 All ER 29, per Byrne J at p. 30). On occasions, the effect of evidence which is technically admissible is so slight that it is wiser not to adduce it, especially if there is any danger of a contravention of the PACE 1984, s. 78 (see **F2.4**), i.e. where its admission would have such an adverse effect on the fairness of the proceedings that the court ought not to admit it (*Robertson* [1987] QB 920, per Lord Lane CJ at p. 928; and see also *Williams* [1990] Crim LR 409).

Where two trials arise out of the same transaction, evidence of the outcome of the first trial is generally inadmissible at the second trial, because the verdict in the first (whether reached on the same or different evidence) is usually irrelevant, amounting to no more than evidence of the opinion of the jury concerned. Some exceptional feature is needed before it will be considered relevant, such as its effect on the truth of a confession, as in *Hay* (1983) 77 Cr App R 70, or the credibility of a prosecution witness, as in *Cooke* (1986) 84 Cr App R 286 (*Hui Chi-ming* v *The Queen* [1992] 1 AC 34; *Y* [1992] Crim LR 436). Evidence of an acquittal at the first trial following a ruling by the trial judge that there was insufficient evidence to go to the jury, would also appear to be generally inadmissible (*Hudson* [1994] Crim LR 920). As to the relevance (and admissibility) of previous *convictions* as evidence of the facts on which they were based, see PACE 1984, s. 74 (see **F11.2**).

CIRCUMSTANTIAL EVIDENCE

F1.10 Circumstantial evidence is to be contrasted with direct evidence. Direct evidence is evidence of *facts in issue*. In the case of testimonial evidence, it is evidence about facts in issue of which the witness claims to have personal knowledge, for example, 'I saw the accused strike the victim'. Circumstantial evidence is evidence of *relevant facts*, i.e. facts from which the existence or non-existence of facts in issue may be inferred. It does not necessarily follow that the weight to be attached to circumstantial evidence will be less than that to be atttached to direct evidence. For example, the tribunal of fact is likely to attach more weight to a variety of individual items of circumstantial evidence, all of which lead to the same conclusion, than to direct evidence to the contrary coming from witnesses lacking in credibility.

Circumstantial evidence 'works by cumulatively, in geometrical progression, eliminating other possibilities' (*DPP* v *Kilbourne* [1973] AC 729 per Lord Simon at p. 758). Pollock CB, likening circumstantial evidence to a rope comprised of several cords, said:

> One strand of the cord might be insufficient to sustain the weight, but three stranded together may be quite of sufficient strength.
> Thus it may be in circumstantial evidence — there may be a combination of circumstances, no one of which would raise a reasonable conviction, or more than a mere suspicion; but the whole, taken together, may create a strong conclusion of guilt, that is, with as much certainty as human affairs can require or admit of. (*Exall* (1866) 4 F & F 922, at p. 929)

However, although circumstantial evidence may sometimes be conclusive, it must always be narrowly examined, if only because it may be fabricated to cast suspicion on another. For this reason, it has been said that: 'It is also necessary before drawing the inference of the accused's guilt from circumstantial evidence to be sure that there are no other co-existing circumstances which would weaken or destroy the inference' (*Teper* v *The Queen* [1952] AC 480, per Lord Normand at p. 489). Nonetheless, there is no requirement, in cases in which the prosecution's case is based on circumstantial evidence, that the judge direct the jury to acquit unless they are sure that the facts proved are not only consistent with guilt but also inconsistent with any other reasonable conclusion (*McGreevy* v *DPP* [1973] 1 WLR 276).

Certain varieties of circumstantial evidence have arisen so frequently in practice as to attract the label 'presumption of fact'. For the presumption of continuance of life, see **F3.24**; for the presumption of intention, see **F3.25**; and for the presumption of guilty knowledge in cases of handling, theft etc., see **F3.26**. Other frequently recurring examples of circumstantial evidence include evidence of plans and acts preparatory to the commission of an offence (to show intention to commit the offence); evidence of opportunity or lack of opportunity, i.e. alibi evidence (to show presence or absence at the time and place of the crime committed); and evidence of identity, including evidence of physical idiosyncrasy, manner of vocal or written expression, fingerprints and DNA genetic fingerprint tests. Circumstantial evidence of identity can also take the form of evidence that a tracker dog tracked the accused from the scene of the crime (see *Haas* (1962) 35 DLR (2d) 172 (British Columbia) and, for the conditions of admissibility of such evidence, *Pieterson* [1995] 1 WLR 293 and *Sykes* [1997] Crim LR 752). Other typical examples of circumstantial evidence are dealt with below.

Motive

> Surely in an ordinary prosecution for murder you can prove previous acts or words of the **F1.11**
> accused to show that he entertained feelings of enmity towards the deceased, and this is
> evidence not merely of the malicious mind with which he killed the deceased, but of the fact
> that he killed him. . . . it is more probable that men are killed by those who have some motive
> for killing them than by those who have not. (*Ball* [1911] AC 47 per Lord Atkinson (during
> argument) at p. 68, affirmed in *Williams* (1986) 84 Cr App R 299.)

Such evidence may be admissible, notwithstanding that it reveals the accused's criminal disposition. In *Williams* W was charged with making a threat to kill E, intending that she would fear that the threat would be carried out. Evidence was admitted of previous acts of violence by W against E, including an assault in respect of which he had been convicted and sentenced to a term of imprisonment which had come to an end six weeks before the time of the present offence. The prosecution case was that: (a) the threat had been made because of resentment arising from the imprisonment; and (b) the previous acts of violence tended to show that W intended his threat to be taken seriously (cf. *Berry* (1986) 83 Cr App R 7). In the same way, evidence that the accused lacked a motive to commit the crime charged may be admissible to show the comparative improbability of his having committed it (see *Grant* (1865) 4 F & F 322). It does not follow from this, however, that evidence of motive (or its absence) is necessarily relevant to the facts in issue on a particular charge (see for example *Graham-Kerr* (1989) 88 Cr App R 302 (the indecency of a photograph), applied in *Rowley* (1991) 94 Cr App R 95 (an act outraging public decency), and compare *Court* [1989] AC 28 at **B3.84**).

Lies

Lies told by the accused, on their own, do not make a positive case of any crime **F1.12** (*Strudwick* (1994) 99 Cr App R 326 at p. 331). However, they may indicate a consciousness of guilt and in appropriate circumstances may therefore be relied upon by the prosecution as evidence supportive of guilt, as in *Goodway* [1993] 4 All ER 894 where the accused's lies to the police as to his whereabouts at the time of the offence were used in support of the identification evidence adduced by the prosecution. In that case it was held that, whenever a lie told by an accused is relied on by the Crown or may be used by the jury to support evidence of guilt, as opposed merely to reflecting on his credibility (and not only when it is relied on as corroboration or as support for identification evidence), a threefold direction should generally be given to the jury:

(a) The lie must be deliberate and must relate to a material issue.

(b) They must be satisfied that there was no innocent motive for the lie, reminding them that people sometimes lie, for example, in an attempt to bolster up a just cause, or out of shame or a wish to conceal disgraceful behaviour.

(c) The lie must be established by evidence other than that of the witness who is to be corroborated.

See also *Taylor* [1994] Crim LR 680. In *Taylor* [1998] Crim LR 822, a trial for murder in which the only issue was provocation, T admitted that he had lied in saying that he had never had any contact with the victim. The jury were directed that if they were sure that the lies were told to conceal T's guilt in relation to the death, then they might use them as evidence of that guilt. The Court of Appeal held that the jury should also have been told that the lies could support the prosecution case of murder only if they were sure that they were told to conceal the fact that T had murdered the victim, rather than merely to conceal his connection with the death, i.e. to avoid responsibility for deliberate murder rather than a provoked killing.

In *Goodway* it was also held that a direction need not be given where it is otiose as indicated in *Dehar* [1969] NZLR 763, i.e. where the rejection of the explanation given by the accused almost necessarily leaves the jury with no choice but to convict as a matter of logic. For an example, see *Barsoum* [1994] Crim LR 194 and cf. *Wood* [1995] Crim LR 154. See also *Gordon* [1995] Crim LR 306. Nor, it seems, does a judge need to give a *Goodway* direction where the accused has offered an explanation for his lies and the judge has dealt with that explanation fairly in his summing-up (*Saunders* [1996] 1 Cr App R 463 at pp. 518–9).

In *Burge* [1996] 1 Cr App R 163, the Court of Appeal held that a *Goodway* direction is usually required in four situations, which may overlap (Kennedy LJ at p. 173):

1. Where the defence relies on an alibi.
2. Where the judge considers it desirable or necessary to suggest that the jury should look for support or corroboration of one piece of evidence from other evidence in the case, and amongst that other evidence draws attention to lies told, or allegedly told, by the defendant.
3. Where the prosecution seek to show that something said, either in or out of the court, in relation to a separate and distinct issue was a lie, and to rely on that lie as evidence of guilt in relation to the charge which is sought to be proved.
4. Where although the prosecution have not adopted the approach to which we have just referred, the judge reasonably envisages that there is a real danger that the jury may do so.

The Court of Appeal held that the direction (if given) should, so far as possible, be tailored to the circumstances of the case, but that it will normally suffice to make two points: first that the lie must be admitted or proved beyond reasonable doubt, and second that the mere fact that the accused lied is not in itself evidence of guilt since defendants may lie for innocent reasons, so only if the jury is sure that the accused did not lie for an innocent reason can a lie support the prosecution case. The Court also stressed that the need for the direction arises only in cases where the prosecution say, or the judge envisages that the jury may say, that the lie is evidence against the accused, in effect using it as an implied admission of guilt. The direction is not needed in run-of-the-mill cases where the defence case is contradicted by the evidence of prosecution witnesses in such a way as to make it necessary for the prosecution to say that, insofar as the two sides are in conflict, the accused's account is untrue. Equally, a *Goodway* direction is not required simply because the jury may reject the evidence of an accused about a central issue in the case, because that situation is covered by the general direction on the burden and standard of proof (*Hill* [1996] Crim LR 419).

As to the first situation identified in *Burge*, in *Lesley* [1996] 1 Cr App R 39 it was held that where evidence is adduced in support of an alibi, the Judicial Studies Board specimen direction (which ends with the words 'An alibi is sometimes invented to bolster a genuine defence') should routinely be given. It was also held, however, that whether failure to do so renders a conviction unsafe depends on the facts of each case and the strength of the evidence. The accused had served an alibi notice but did not call the person named in it and gave no evidence himself. The prosecution inferentially invited the jury to conclude that the alibi was false and therefore evidence of guilt. Taking account of the fact that the chief prosecution witness was not altogether satisfactory, it was held that failure to give the direction rendered the verdict unsafe (cf. *Drake* [1996] Crim LR 109, in which the proviso was applied). See also *Peacock* [1998] Crim LR 681, in which P, when first interviewed, said that he had spent the evening of the robbery with his girlfriend, but at trial gave evidence that he had spent the evening with his former girlfriend and that what he had said initially was not a lie but a mistake. *Lesley* was distinguished in *Harron* [1996] 2 Cr App R 457, where it was held that the judge had not erred in failing to direct the jury that an alibi is sometimes falsified to bolster a genuine defence because the central issue in the case was whether the prosecution witnesses were lying or whether H was. Lies had not played a part in the way the Crown had put their case nor constituted a matter which the jury might have taken into account separate from their determination of the main issue, which turned upon the truthfulness of the witnesses. If they accepted the evidence for the Crown it necessarily involved a conclusion that the evidence of the accused was untrue, and that he was lying. See also *House* [1994] Crim LR 682.

As to the third situation identified in *Burge*, in *Genus* [1996] Crim LR 502, where the accused claimed to have been acting under duress and the prosecution case was that the accused had told lies to the police and in evidence on collateral issues (i.e. on issues not directly relevant to the question of duress) and that the jury should, by reason of those lies, disbelieve their account of acting under duress, it was held that the case cried out for a *Goodway* direction. In *Robinson* [1996] Crim LR 417, where the judge in his summing-up gave considerable prominence to the issue whether R had lied about when his defence was first made known to the police, it was held that the case fell clearly within the fourth situation identified in *Burge*.

As to the fourth situation identified in *Burge*, the Court of Appeal is unlikely to be persuaded that there was a real danger of the jury treating a particular lie as evidence of guilt if defence counsel at the trial did not alert the judge to that danger and ask him to consider whether a direction should be given to meet it (per Kennedy LJ in *Burge* [1996] 1 Cr App R 163 at p. 174). The failure of defence counsel to raise the matter at the trial may also be taken into account in cases in which both the third and the fourth situations identified in *Burge* arise, and may lead the Court of Appeal to conclude that the matter was not a large or important feature of the case and that the absence of the usual direction did not make the conviction unsafe (*McGuinness* [1999] Crim LR 318).

A *Goodway* direction is required only where lies are directly related in some way to the offence charged, for example a lie which amounts to a false alibi (*Smith* [1995] Crim LR 305), but not a lie concerning some matter which is relevant only to the credibility of the accused (*Landon*) [1995] Crim LR 338). However, even if a lie is relied on merely to attack credibility, a *Goodway* direction is appropriate in exceptional circumstances, for example where the lie figures largely in the case and there is a risk that the jury may think that the accused must be guilty because he lied (*Tucker* [1994] Crim LR 683).

Continuance of Events over Period of Time

Evidence of the speed at which someone was driving at a particular point in time may **F1.13** be admitted to prove the speed at which he was driving a short time earlier or, as the case may be, later (see, respectively, *Dalloz* (1908) 1 Cr App R 258 and *Beresford* v *St Albans Justices* (1905) 22 TLR 1).

MULTIPLE ADMISSIBILITY

Evidence which is admissible in law for one purpose cannot be excluded because it is **F1.14** inadmissible for some other purpose (although if it is tendered by the prosecution it may be excluded as a matter of discretion). '[I]t often happens, both in civil and criminal cases, that evidence is tendered on several alternative grounds, and yet it is never objected that if on any ground it is admissible, that ground must not prevail, because on some other ground it would be inadmissible and prejudicial' (*Bond* [1906] 2 KB 389, per Jelf J at pp. 411–12). The principle has attracted the somewhat misleading label of 'multiple admissibility' (J. H. Wigmore, *Evidence in Trials at Common Law*, vol. 1 (revised by Peter

Tillers) (Boston Mass: Little, Brown & Co. 1983), sect. 13). A typical example would be a case in which the accused, having lost the shield provided by the Criminal Evidence Act 1898, s. 1(f), is cross-examined on his previous convictions. Evidence of the previous convictions may be admitted for the purpose of impugning the credibility of the accused, notwithstanding that it is inadmissible for the purpose of showing that it is more likely that he is guilty of the offence charged (*Jenkins* (1945) 31 Cr App R 1; *Cook* [1959] 2 QB 340). Similarly, a confession which implicates both its maker and a co-accused may be admitted in evidence against its maker, notwithstanding that it is inadmissible evidence against the co-accused.

Where the principle applies, it has been said that 'it is usual for the judge (not always very successfully) to caution the jury against being biased by treating the evidence in the objectionable sense' (*Bond* [1906] 2 KB 389 per Jelf J at p. 412). However, nowadays such a warning is often mandatory (see e.g., *Jenkins* (1945) 31 Cr App R 1 (cross-examination under the second part of s. 1(f)(ii) of the Criminal Evidence Act 1898 for the sole purpose of attacking credibility); *Gunewardene* [1951] KB 600 (a confession admissible for use only against its maker and not against any co-accused); and *Flicker* [1995] Crim LR 493 (statements in which a confession is inextricably linked with material relating to the accused's propensity to offend)). In many cases it may be doubted whether such a warning is capable of preventing the jury from using the evidence in the objectionable sense. If the direction requires the jury to perform difficult feats of intellectual acrobatics which are practically impossible, the trial judge may be justified in exercising his discretion to exclude the evidence (see, in the case of cross-examination under s. 1(f)(ii), *Maxwell* v *DPP* [1935] AC 309, per Viscount Sankey LC at p. 321, and *Watts* [1983] 3 All ER 101, per Lord Lane J at p. 104; and cf. *Burke* (1985) 82 Cr App R 156 and *Powell* [1985] 1 WLR 1364). In the case of a confession tendered by the prosecution and implicating both its maker and his co-accused, one solution is to edit the confession by omitting references to the co-accused or by replacing their names with letters of the alphabet or expressions such as 'another person' (see *Rogers* [1971] Crim LR 413; *Silcott* [1987] Crim LR 765; and generally **F17.41**). Alternatively, but only in exceptional circumstances, the judge may find it necessary to order separate trials for the accused (see *Lake* (1976) 64 Cr App R 172).

CONDITIONAL ADMISSIBILITY

F1.15 The relevance of a particular item of evidence may become apparent only if considered together with other evidence. However, because evidence is given in order and by one witness at a time, it often happens that the other evidence can only be adduced at a later stage. Prima facie, therefore, the first item of evidence is irrelevant, and for that reason inadmissible. In these circumstances, upon an undertaking by counsel to demonstrate the relevance of the first item by introducing the further evidence, the court may allow the first item of evidence to be admitted conditionally or *de bene esse*. If, notwithstanding the introduction of the further evidence, the first item remains irrelevant, the judge will direct the jury to disregard it. For example, in the case of a conspiracy or any crime which, according to the case for the prosecution, was committed in pursuance of a conspiracy, statements of one conspirator which the jury are satisfied were made in the execution or furtherance of the common design are admissible in evidence against any other party to the conspiracy, provided that there is some other evidence of the common design (*Shellard* (1840) 9 C & P 277). Evidence of such statements may be admitted, conditional upon the adduction of some other evidence of the common design. If it transpires that there is no other evidence of the common design, such statements should be disregarded (see *Donat* (1985) 82 Cr App R 173 and generally **F16.48** to **F16.50**). See also the cases on accusations made in the presence of the accused, the relevance of which depends on evidence of the accused's reaction to them (see Lords Atkinson and Reading in *Christie* [1914] AC 545 at pp. 554 and 565 respectively and **F17.49**). In an extreme case, where great prejudice may be caused to an accused, a warning by the judge may be insufficient, and it may be necessary for the judge to discharge the jury.

THE BEST EVIDENCE RULE

As an Inclusionary Rule

The best evidence rule is moribund. In *Omychund* v *Barker* (1745) 1 Atk 21, in which **F1.16** depositions of Hindu witnesses were admitted in evidence, notwithstanding that that they did not accept the authority of the Gospel, Lord Hardwicke said (at p. 49): 'The judges and sages of the law have laid it down that there is but one general rule of evidence, the best that the nature of the case will admit'. This case suggests an inclusionary rule permitting the admission of the best evidence available in the circumstances of the case. Subsequent authorities, however, show that the rule has rarely been used in this way. Under the modern law of evidence, there exists no general rule, of an inclusionary nature, to the effect indicated in *Omychund* v *Barker*.

As an Exclusionary Rule

The best evidence rule, which was used in the 18th and early 19th centuries as an **F1.17** exclusionary principle, i.e. to prevent the admission of certain evidence where better was available, is now all but defunct. In *Francis* (1874) LR 2 CCR 128, in which the accused was indicted for false pretences, in that he falsely represented a ring to be a diamond ring, evidence was admitted of his attempts on other occasions to obtain money on a cluster ring in order to prove guilty knowledge. Rejecting an argument that because the cluster ring itself was not produced in court, evidence of witnesses who saw it and swore to its being false had been improperly admitted, Lord Coleridge CJ said: 'No doubt if there was not admissible evidence that this ring was false it ought not to have been left to the jury; but though the non-production of the article may afford ground for observation more or less weighty, according to circumstances, it only goes to the weight, not to the admissibility, of the evidence'.

However, very occasionally reliance is placed upon the rule. In *Quinn* [1962] 2 QB 245, on a charge of keeping a disorderly house, arising out of the performance of allegedly indecent striptease acts, one of the accused sought to put in evidence a film made three months after the events complained of and purporting to depict the acts performed, together with evidence that the acts depicted in the film were identical to the acts performed. It was held that the evidence had been properly rejected. Ashworth J said (at p. 257): '. . . it was admitted that some of the movements in the film (for instance, that of a snake used in one scene) could not be said with any certainty to be the same movements as were made at the material time. In our judgment, this objection goes not only to weight, as was argued, but to admissibility: it is not the best evidence.' Compare *Thomas* [1986] Crim LR 682, a case of reckless driving in which a video recording of the route taken by the accused was ruled admissible to remove the need for maps and photographs and to convey a more accurate picture of the roads in question. The reasoning in *Quinn* [1962] 2 QB 245 is difficult to reconcile with the clear statement of Lord Denning MR in *Garton* v *Hunter* [1969] 2 QB 37. Referring to the best evidence rule, his lordship said (at p. 44):

> That old rule has gone by the board long ago. The only remaining instance of it that I know is that if an original document is available in your hands, you must produce it. You cannot give secondary evidence by producing a copy. Nowadays we do not confine ourselves to the best evidence. We admit all relevant evidence. The goodness or badness of it goes only to weight, and not to admissibility.

See also Ackner LJ in *Kajala* v *Noble* (1982) 75 Cr App R 149 at p. 152 and *Governor of Pentonville Prison, ex parte Osman* [1990] 1 WLR 277 at p. 308. Proof of the contents of a document on which a party seeks to rely is now governed by the CJA 1988, s. 27.

QUESTIONS OF LAW AND FACT

In a Trial on Indictment: General Principles

F1.18   As a general rule, questions of law (including practice) are for the judge, and questions of fact for the jury. Lay magistrates, when sitting with a judge in the Crown Court, are also judges of the court (see the Supreme Court Act 1981, ss. 8 and 73); they should participate in all questions to be determined by the court, including the factual aspect of any question relating to the admissibility of evidence, but must accept the ruling of the judge on any question of law (*Orpin* [1975] QB 283). In the Crown Court, questions of law for the judge include those relating to:

    (a)   challenges to jurors – see **D11.8** to **D11.12**;
    (b)   the discharge of a juror or the whole jury – see **D11.18** to **D11.23**;
    (c)   the competence of persons to give sworn or unsworn evidence;
    (d)   the admissibility of evidence;
    (e)   the withdrawal of an issue from the jury;
    (f)   submissions of no case to answer – see **D13.26** to **D13.31**;
    (g)   the numerous issues on which the jury should be directed in the summing up, such as the substantive law governing the charge, the burden and standard of proof, the use which the jury is entitled to make of the evidence adduced, the operation of any presumptions, the nature of, and any requirement for, corroboration, etc. – see further **D15.10** to **D15.17** and **F5**; and
    (h)   matters ancillary to the trial itself, such as questions of bail, costs and leave to appeal.

Questions of fact for the jury include:

    (a)   whether the accused stands mute of malice or by visitation of God;
    (b)   whether the accused is fit to plead – see **D10.5** to **D10.11**;
    (c)   the credibility of the witnesses called and the weight of the evidence adduced; and
    (d)   whether, applying the burden and standard of proof applicable to the case, they are satisfied as to the existence or non-existence of the facts in issue.

Questions of fact which fall to be determined by the *judge* are the existence or non-existence of preliminary facts, i.e. facts which must be proved as a condition precedent to the admissibility of certain types of evidence; the sufficiency of evidence (in deciding whether an issue should be withdrawn from the jury); and the evaluation of evidence adduced by the parties (for the purpose of commenting on its weight in his summing up to the jury). There are also a number of special cases, dealt with below, in which questions of fact fall to be determined, either wholly or in part, by the judge.

F1.19   ***Construction of Words***   As a general rule, the construction of ordinary words in a statute is a question for the tribunal of fact (see *Manning* (1871) LR 1 CCR 338, at p. 430 – 'a building' under the Malicious Damage Act 1861, s. 6; *Cozens* v *Brutus* [1973] AC 854 – 'insulting behaviour' under the Public Order Act 1936, s. 5; *Chambers* v *DPP* [1995] Crim LR 896 – 'disorderly behaviour' under the Public Order Act 1986, s. 5; *Feely* [1973] QB 530 – 'dishonestly' under the Theft Act 1968, s. 1(1); *Harris* (1968) 84 Cr App R 75 – 'knowledge or belief' under the Theft Act 1968, s. 22(1); *Jones* [1987] 1 WLR 692 – 'armed' under the Customs and Excise Management Act 1979, s. 86; *Garwood* [1987] 1 WLR 319 – 'menaces' under the Theft Act 1968, s. 21(1); *Goddard* (1990) 92 Cr App R 185 — 'an immoral purpose' under the Sexual Offences Act 1956, s. 32; *Howard* [1993] Crim LR 213 – an 'explosive substance' under the OAPA 1861, s. 29; and *National Rivers Authority* v *Yorkshire Water Services* [1995] 1 AC 444 – 'causes' under the Water Act 1989, s. 107(1)). Thus, although a judge is perfectly at liberty to direct a jury that it is not open to them to give to a word a particular meaning (being a meaning so unreasonable that if it were adopted and the accused convicted, the Court of Appeal would treat the verdict as perverse), normally he should not direct the jury as to the meaning of an ordinary word. The exception to this rule is where the word has been used in a context which indicates that it is being used in an unusual sense or has acquired a special meaning as a result of the authorities, as happened in relation to the word 'fraudulently' under the Larceny Act 1916, s. 1(1) – see Lawton LJ in *Feely* [1973] QB 530. In *Brutus* v *Cozens* [1973] AC 854, Lord Reid said (at p. 861 C–E):

> The meaning of an ordinary word of the English language is not a question of law. The proper construction of a statute is a question of law. If the context shows that a word is used in an unusual sense the court will determine in other words what that unusual sense is. But here there is in my opinion no question of the word 'insulting' being used in any unusual sense. . . . It is for the tribunal which decides the case to consider, not as law but as fact, whether in the whole circumstances the words of the statute do or do not as a matter of ordinary usage of the English language cover or apply to the facts which have been proved. If it is alleged that the tribunal has reached a wrong decision then there can be a question of law but only of a limited character. The question would normally be whether their decision was unreasonable in the sense that no tribunal acquainted with the ordinary use of language could reasonably reach that decision.

When a statutory provision is dealing with a technical subject and can only be understood with the assistance of an expert, then the words used must be given their ordinary and natural meaning to a person qualified to understand them, and evidence as to that meaning may be received from an appropriate expert (*Couzens* [1992] Crim LR 822).

As to the construction of *documents*, this is generally a matter of fact for determination by the jury, with the exception of binding agreements between parties and all forms of parliamentary and local government legislation, which are for the judge to construe as a matter of law. The City Code on Take-overs and Mergers sufficiently resembles legislation as to require construction of its provisions by a judge (*Spens* [1991] 1 WLR 624). In a case of obtaining by deception, arising out of an allegedly false written representation, in which the central question is not as to the legal effect of the document but whether the representation was made and, if so, whether it was false, then both aspects of that question are for the jury (*Adams* [1993] Crim LR 525; and see also *Morris* [1994] Crim LR 596).

Foreign Law   Questions relating to the law of any jurisdiction other than that of **F1.20** England and Wales are questions of fact to be determined, on the evidence adduced, by the judge alone.

Administration of Justice Act 1920, s. 15

> Where for the purpose of disposing of any action or other matter which is being tried by a judge with a jury in any court in England or Wales, it is necessary to ascertain the law of any other country which is applicable to the facts of the case, any question as to the effect of the evidence given with respect to that law shall, instead of being submitted to the jury, be decided by the judge alone.

Section 15 of the 1920 Act applies to criminal proceedings (*Hammer* [1923] 2 KB 786). As to the proof of foreign law, see **F8.13** and **F10.9**.

Autrefois Acquit or Convict   Where an accused pleads autrefois acquit or convict it **F1.21** shall be for the judge, without the presence of a jury, to decide the issue (CJA 1988, s. 122). See also **D10.28** to **D10.38**.

Perjury   The question whether a statement on which perjury is assigned was 'material' **F1.22** in the judicial proceeding in which it was made is a question of law to be determined by the court of trial (Perjury Act 1911, s. 11(6)).

F1.23   **Defamation**   On every trial of an indictment or information for the making or publishing of any libel, it is for the jury to give a verdict of guilty or not guilty upon the whole matter put in issue (see the Libel Act 1792 (Fox's Act), s. 1). However, it is for the judge to determine whether the writing in question is capable of bearing the defamatory meaning ascribed to it by the prosecutor (*Capital and Counties Bank Ltd* v *George Henty and Sons* (1882) 7 App Cas 741). If it can be said that 12 jurors could reasonably come to the conclusion that the writing was defamatory, the question whether the writing does in fact constitute a criminal libel should be left to the jury (*Turner* v *Metro-Goldwyn-Mayer Pictures Ltd* [1950] 1 All ER 449; *Lewis* v *Daily Telegraph Ltd* [1964] AC 334).

In Summary Trials and Trials before Courts Martial

F1.24   In the case of proceedings presided over by lay justices, the justices decide all questions of both law and fact, but on questions of law, including the law of evidence, should seek and accept the advice of the clerk. As to the proper role of the magistrates' clerk in a summary trial, see *Practice Direction (Justices: Clerk to Court)* [1981] 1 WLR 1163, which is set out and discussed in detail at **D18.30** to **D18.35**. In theory, stipendiary magistrates are in the same position as lay justices. In practice, however, the stipendiary magistrate will be the more experienced lawyer, so that the occasions for asking for advice will be quite rare. At courts martial, the tribunal decides all questions of law and fact, but on questions of law must accept the advice of the judge-advocate.

HEARINGS ON THE *VOIR DIRE*

General Principles

F1.25   The hearing on the *voir dire*, or trial within a trial, is the procedure whereby the court determines disputed preliminary facts, i.e. facts which must be established as a condition precedent to the admission of certain items of evidence. The procedure is set out at **D13.16** to **D13.22** (trial on indictment) and **D19.6** (summary trial).

Concerning what evidence is admissible for the purpose of proving or disproving disputed preliminary facts, there is some authority to suggest that the judge is bound by the exclusionary rules of evidence which apply in relation to the admissibility of evidence at the trial proper. Thus it has been held that it is wrong for a judge to determine the admissibility of a confession on the basis of the depositions (*Chadwick* (1934) 24 Cr App R 138). However, most of the decisions concern specific statutory provisions governing the admissibility of evidence. In *O'Loughlin* [1988] 3 All ER 431, a decision on the conditions of admissibility imposed by the CJA 1925, s. 13(3) (now repealed), Kenneth Jones J ruled that in a criminal statute, unless other methods of proof are specified (for example, 'by information or belief'), 'proof' means proof by admissible evidence. Preliminary facts under the CJA 1988, s. 23, also call for proof by admissible evidence (see *Neill* v *North Antrim Magistrates' Court* [1992] 1 WLR 1221, *obiter* but applied in *Belmarsh Magistrates' Court, ex parte Gilligan* [1998] 1 Cr App R 14 and *Wood* [1998] Crim LR 213, at **F16.9**; and *Case* [1991] Crim LR 192 and *Mattey* [1995] 2 Cr App R 409, at **F16.8**). However, it has been held that a written statement may be admitted under the CJA 1988, s. 23(3)(b), on the basis of the *unsworn* evidence of its maker that he is not giving oral evidence through fear (*Greer* [1998] Crim LR 572), although technically he should be sworn (*Jennings* [1995] Crim LR 810). Moreover, it seems that as regards the preliminary facts set out in s. 24(1)(i) and (ii) the CJA 1988, (see **F16.10**), although evidence is often desirable, it is not always essential, because in appropriate circumstances the judge may infer the facts from the document sought to be admitted under s. 24 and the method or route by which it has been produced before the court (*Foxley* [1995] 2 Cr App R 523 and *Ilyas* [1996] Crim LR 810).

In trials on indictment, the various matters which may fall to be determined in ? hearing on the *voir dire* include the following:

(a)   the competence of a witness (see **F4.2, F4.17** and **F4.18**);

(b)   the admissibility of a confession (see **F17.24** to **F17.31**) or some other variety of admissible hearsay, such as a dying declaration or a *res gestae* statement (see, for example, *Jenkins* (1869) LR 1 CCR 187);

(c)   the admissiblity of a tape recording (see *Robson* [1972] 1 WLR 651 and **F8.43**);

(d)   the admissibility of a statement contained in a document produced by a computer (see **F8.31** to **F8.36** and **F8.41**); and

(e)   the admissibility of a plea of guilty against an accused who subsequently changes his plea to not guilty (see *Rimmer* [1972] 1 WLR 268 at **F17.1** and cf. *Hetherington* [1972] Crim LR 703).

Cases in which a Hearing on *Voir Dire* Usually Not Required

A hearing on the *voir dire* is not normally required to determine the admissibility of **F1.26** evidence relating to an identification parade. In *Walshe* (1980) 74 Cr App R 85 Boreham J said (at p. 87):

> . . . those representing the applicant drew some close analogy between the admissibility of evidence of an identification parade and the admissibility of a voluntary statement. But those are very different matters. As soon as a statement is challenged the law places on the Crown the burden of showing that it is admissible by proving that it was voluntarily made. [See now the PACE 1984, s. 76(2).] That is a separate and different matter. Here there was no burden on the Crown to prove the admissibility of the evidence relating to the identification parade and what flowed from it. It was clearly admissible evidence and should have been admitted. Its quality is, of course, another matter, to be considered by the jury.

In *Beveridge* (1987) 85 Cr App R 255, it was argued on appeal that in the light of the PACE 1984, s. 78, *Walshe* could no longer stand. It was held, dismissing the appeal, that where a question arises under s. 78 as to the admissibility of identification parade evidence, although there may be rare occasions when it will be desirable to hold a trial within a trial, in general the judge should decide on the basis of the depositions, statements and submissions of counsel.

In *Flemming* (1987) 86 Cr App R 32, a decision under the law prior to the 1984 Act, the appellant argued that identification evidence was inadmissible on the grounds, *inter alia*, that the identification at the police station was carried out in circumstances which contravened Home Office Circular No. 109 of 1978. It was submitted that the result was that the probative value of the evidence was minimal compared to its prejudicial effect, so that it would be unfair for the evidence to be admitted. The Court of Appeal held that it was quite unnecessary to hold a trial within a trial for this purpose. Woolf LJ (referring to one of the guidelines laid down by Lord Widgery LCJ in *Turnbull* [1977] QB 224, at p. 229, namely that when, in the opinion of the judge, the quality of the identifying evidence is poor, the judge should withdraw the case from the jury unless there is other evidence which goes to support its correctness) said, at pp. 36–7:

> In the normal way the trial judge will make his assessment whether he needs to take the action referred to by the Lord Chief Justice either at the end of the case for the prosecution or after all the evidence in the case has been called. There may be exceptional cases where the position is so clear on the depositions that he can give a ruling at an earlier stage. However, the trial judge should not decide the matter by holding a preliminary trial, as in this case, before the evidence for the prosecution has been placed before the jury.
>
> It is, of course, true that the trial judge has a residual discretion to exclude evidence which is strictly admissible if he comes to the conclusion that its probative value is outweighed by its prejudicial effect, so that its admission would be unfair to the defendant. However, this residual discretion cannot justify the holding of trials within a trial as occurred here. Issues

of this sort can be satisfactorily dealt with by the judge perusing the depositions, together with any facts that are common ground between the prosecution and the defence.

See also *Martin* [1994] Crim LR 218.

Application to Summary Trial

F1.27 There can be no question of a trial within a trial in proceedings before magistrates, because the function of the *voir dire* is to allow the tribunal of law to decide a point of law in the absence of the tribunal of fact, and magistrates are judges of both fact and law. Thus, if the admissibility of a confession is in dispute, and the magistrates decide that matter as a separate issue by hearing evidence as to the preliminary facts and ruling in favour of admissibility, it is unnecessary to repeat the evidence about the confession in the trial proper. See generally, **D19.6**.

It is impossible to lay down any general rule as to when the question of admissibility should be determined by magistrates, or as to when their decision on it should be announced, every case being different (*F v Chief Constable of Kent* [1982] Crim LR 682). These principles, insofar as they relate to confessions, are subject to the statutory constraint of the PACE 1984, s. 76(2), and the decision in *Liverpool Juvenile Court, ex parte R* [1988] QB 1. However, subject to this and other similar statutory constraints, there is still no general rule as to when admissibility should be determined and the decision on it announced. In *Epping and Ongar Justices, ex parte Manby* [1986] Crim LR 555 the applicant, convicted as the proprietor of a firm on whose behalf an overweight vehicle had been driven, contested the admissibility of a certificate of a police officer to the effect that the applicant had admitted responsibility for the vehicle (see **C2.5**), and sought leave to have the question resolved as a preliminary issue. It was held that the justices had not erred in refusing the application and admitting the evidence as providing a prima facie case for the applicant to deal with later, if he saw fit.

If, during the course of a summary trial, the defence challenge the admissibility of a confession under the PACE 1984, s. 76(2) (see **F17.4**), the magistrates are bound by the terms of that subsection to hold a trial within a trial. In *Liverpool Juvenile Court, ex parte R* [1988] QB 1, Russell LJ held as follows:

(a) During the course of a summary trial, if the defence, before the close of the prosecution case, make a representation to the court that a confession made by the defendant was or may have been obtained by either of the improper methods set out in s. 76(2), the magistrates must hold a trial within a trial and make a ruling on the admissibility of the confession during or at the end of the prosecution case. (If the defence make an alternative submission based on the PACE 1984, s. 78, this should be examined at the same trial within a trial at the same time: *Halawa v Federation Against Copyright Theft* [1995] 1 Cr App R 21.)

(b) In such a trial within a trial, the defendant may give evidence confined to the question of admissibility.

(c) At this stage, the magistrates will not be concerned with whether or not the confession is true.

(d) If the defence do not make a representation before the close of the prosecution case, the defendant may raise the question of the admissibility or weight of the confession at any subsequent stage at the trial.

(e) At this later stage, however, although the court retains an inherent jurisdiction to exclude the confession, as well as the power to exclude by virtue of the PACE 1984, s. 78 (see **F2.13**), it is not required to embark on a trial within a trial.

Nothing in the court's judgment was intended to lay down guidance as to the trial of indictable offences in the Crown Court.

Where the defence make a submission that the magistrates should exercise their discretion to exclude evidence under s. 78 of the 1984 Act, they are not entitled to have that issue settled as a preliminary issue in a trial within a trial (*Vel* v *Chief Constable of North Wales* (1987) 151 JP 510). In *Halawa* v *Federation Against Copyright Theft* [1995] 1 Cr App R 21, it was held that the duty of a magistrate, on an application under s. 78, is either to deal with the issue when it arises or to leave the decision until the end of the hearing, the objective being to secure a trial that is fair and just to both parties. Thus in some cases the accused will be given the opportunity to exclude the evidence before giving evidence on the main issues, because if denied that opportunity his right to remain silent on the main issues will be impaired, but in most cases it is better for the whole of the prosecution case, including the disputed evidence, to be heard first, because under s. 78 regard should be had to 'all the circumstances' and fairness to the prosecution requires that the whole of its case, in this regard, be before the court. In deciding, the court may take account of the extent of the issues to be raised by the evidence of the accused in the trial within a trial. A trial within a trial may be appropriate if the issues are limited, but not if it is likely to be protracted and to raise issues which will need to be re-examined in the trial itself.

Application to Committal Proceedings

The effect of s. 76(9) of the PACE 1984 is that in proceedings before a magistrates' court **F1.28** inquiring into an offence as examining justices, a confession made by an accused may be given in evidence insofar as it is relevant to any matter in issue in the proceedings and s.76(2) of the 1984 Act does not apply.

SECTION F2: THE DISCRETION TO EXCLUDE EVIDENCE; EVIDENCE UNLAWFULLY, IMPROPERLY OR UNFAIRLY OBTAINED

THE DISCRETION TO EXCLUDE AT COMMON LAW

General Principles

F2.1 Although there is no authority to suggest that a criminal court has any power to *admit* as a matter of discretion evidence which is inadmissible under an exclusionary rule of law, it is well established that a judge, as part of his inherent power and overriding duty in every case to ensure that the accused receives a fair trial, always has a discretion to *exclude* otherwise admissible prosecution evidence if, in his opinion, its prejudicial effect on the minds of the jury outweighs its true probative value. The classic description of the discretion is that of Lord du Parcq, delivering the reasons of the Board in *Noor Mohamed* v *The King* [1949] AC 182. Referring to cases in which the prosecution seek to admit similar-fact evidence, his lordship said (at p. 192):

> . . . in all such cases the judge ought to consider whether the evidence which it is proposed to adduce is sufficiently substantial, having regard to the purpose to which it is professedly directed, to make it desirable in the interest of justice that it should be admitted. If, so far as that purpose is concerned, it can in the circumstances of the case have only trifling weight, the judge will be right to exclude it. To say this is not to confuse weight with admissibility. The distinction is plain, but cases must occur in which it would be unjust to admit evidence of a character gravely prejudicial to the accused even though there may be some tenuous ground for holding it technically admissible.

The first clear statements as to the existence of this exclusionary discretion are to be found in the speeches of Lord Moulton and Lord Reading CJ in *Christie* [1914] AC 545, at pp. 559 and 564 respectively. Thereafter, the discretion developed on a case-by-case basis in relation to particular and different types of otherwise admissible evidence. In relation to similar fact evidence, for example, see *Harris* v *DPP* [1952] AC 694, at p. 707 (in which Viscount Simon cited and applied the passage from *Noor Mohamed* v *The King* set out above); *DPP* v *Boardman* [1975] AC 421, at pp. 438, 441, 453, and 463; and generally **F12.3** to **F12.17**. In relation to evidence otherwise admissible under the Theft Act 1968, s. 27(3), see *List* [1966] 1 WLR 9; *Herron* [1967] 1 QB 107; *Perry* [1984] Crim LR 680; and generally **F12.24** to **F12.26**. In cases in which the nature or conduct of the defence has been such as to involve imputations on the character of the prosecutor or witnesses for the prosecution, the discretion has also been invoked to prevent the accused from being cross-examined about his previous convictions and bad character under the Criminal Evidence Act 1898, s. 1(f)(ii) (see *Jenkins* (1945) 31 Cr App R 1 at p. 15 and generally **F14.31** to **F14.35**). The discretion may be invoked by a trial judge to exclude statements tendered in committal proceedings (*Blithing* (1983) 77 Cr App R 86), but the judge's power to exclude the sworn deposition of a deceased witness should be exercised with great restraint: see *Scott* v *The Queen* [1989] AC 1242 per Lord Griffiths at pp. 1258–9 and *Neshet* [1990] Crim LR 578. Concerning exercise of the discretion in relation to identification evidence, see **F18.12**. See also *Eatough* [1989] Crim LR 289.

In *Sang* [1980] AC 402, the House of Lords was firmly of the opinion that, notwithstanding its case-by-case development, under the modern law the discretion is a general one. The cases, therefore, are not to be treated as a closed list of the situations in which the discretion may be exercised (see Viscount Dilhorne and Lord Salmon, at pp. 438 and 445 respectively). The cases are nothing more than examples of a single discretion founded on the duty of the judge to ensure that every accused person has a fair trial (per Lords Scarman and Fraser, at pp. 452 and 447 respectively). Lord Salmon said (at p. 445):

> I recognise that there may have been no categories of cases, other than those to which I have referred, in which technically admissible evidence proffered by the Crown has been rejected by the court on the ground that it would make the trial unfair. I cannot, however, accept that a judge's undoubted duty to ensure that the accused has a fair trial is confined to such cases. In my opinion the category of such cases is not and never can be closed except by statute.

The discretion may only be exercised to exclude evidence on which the prosecution, as opposed to any co-accused, proposes to rely. In *Lobban* v *The Queen* [1995] 1 WLR 877 (at p. 887), the Privy Council cited with approval the following description of this principle in Keane, *The Modern Law of Evidence* (3rd edn, 1994) at p. 36:

> There is no discretion to exclude, at the request of one co-accused, evidence tendered by another. Thus although . . . there is a discretion to exclude similar fact evidence tendered by the prosecution, such evidence, when tendered by an accused to show the misconduct on another occasion of a co-accused is, if relevant to the defence of the accused, admissible whether or not it prejudices the co-accused (see per Devlin J in *Miller* [1952] 2 All ER 667 (Winchester Assizes), approved in *Neale* (1977) 65 Cr App R 304). Similarly, there is no discretion to prevent an accused from cross-examining a co-accused about his previous convictions and bad character when, as a matter of law, he becomes entitled to do so under s. 1(f)(iii) Criminal Evidence Act 1898, i.e. where the co-accused has 'given evidence against' the accused, because, it is said, the accused in seeking to defend himself should not be fettered in any way (see *Murdoch* v *Taylor* [1965] AC 574 (HL)).

In *Lobban* v *The Queen* itself, it was held that there is no discretion to exclude the exculpatory part of a 'mixed' statement (see **F6.15**) on which one co-accused wishes to rely on the grounds that it implicates another. R made a statement containing admissions as well as an exculpatory explanation, an integral part of which implicated L, his co-accused. The prosecution tendered the statement against R; it was no evidence against L (see **F17.34**). Counsel for L submitted that the trial judge should have exercised his discretion to edit the statement to exclude the parts implicating L. The Privy Council held that no such discretion existed. The discretionary power applies only to evidence on which the prosecution proposes to rely. Although the prosecution had *tendered* the statement, they could not rely on it as evidence against L and the disputed material supported R's defence. There was therefore no discretionary power to exclude the disputed material. See also, however, per Evans LJ in *Thompson* [1995] 2 Cr App R 589 at pp. 596–7: where evidence is inadmissible against and prejudicial to an accused, but relevant to and therefore admissible for a co-accused, the only safeguard is the cumbersome device of separate trials, and it might be preferable to allow a discretion to exclude where the prejudice to the accused is substantial and the evidence of only limited benefit to the co-accused.

The discretion founded on the duty of the judge to ensure that every accused has a fair trial is not limited to excluding evidence which is likely to have prejudicial value out of proportion to its probative value, but extends to other evidence which might operate unfairly against the accused, namely admissions, confessions and other evidence obtained from the accused after the commission of the offence by improper or unfair means (see *Sang* [1980] AC 402 per Lords Diplock, Fraser and Scarman, at pp. 436, 450 and 456 respectively). The discretion, in its extended form, merits discrete analysis: as to admissions and confessions, see **F2.8**; as to evidence obtained from the accused by improper or unfair means, see generally **F2.6** to **F2.12**.

Exercise of Discretion as Basis of Appeal

F2.2   Exercise of the discretion is a subjective matter, and each case has to be decided in the context of its own particular facts (see *Sang* [1980] AC 402, per Lords Fraser and Scarman, at pp. 450 and 456 respectively). In *Selvey* v *DPP* [1970] AC 304 Lord Guest went so far as to say (at p. 352): 'If it is suggested that the exercise of this discretion may be whimsical and depend on the individual idiosyncrasies of the judge, this is inevitable where it is a question of discretion'. It follows from this that the Court of Appeal will not lightly interfere with judicial exercise of the discretion. In the context of cross-examination under the Criminal Evidence Act 1898, s.1(f)(ii), it has been held that the Court of Appeal will not interfere unless:

(a)   the judge has failed even to consider exercise of the discretion, in which case the appeal court may exercise its own discretion (see *Cook* [1959] 2 QB 340); or

(b)   he has erred in principle, or there is no material on which he could properly have arrived at his decision (*Cook* per Devlin J, at p. 348, approved by Viscount Dilhorne in *Selvey* v *DPP* at p. 342 and applied in *Burke* (1985) 82 Cr App R 156).

In deciding whether a judge has 'erred in principle', a somewhat difficult concept when applied to the exercise of a discretion, it is submitted that regard should be had to the guidelines which the appellate courts have laid down, from time to time, as to the various matters which a trial judge should take into account when exercising the discretion (see, e.g., in relation to the Criminal Evidence Act 1898, s. 1(f)(ii), *Britzman* [1983] 1 WLR 350 per Lawton LJ at p. 355 and *Powell* [1985] 1 WLR 1364). See **F14.31** to **F14.34**.

Application to Summary Trial, Committal and Extradition Proceedings

F2.3   In *Sang* [1980] AC 402, Lord Scarman made the following *obiter* observations (at p. 456):

> The development of the discretion has, of necessity, been largely associated with jury trial. In the result, legal discussion of it is apt to proceed in terms of the distinctive functions of judge and jury. No harm arises from such traditional habits of thought, provided always it be borne in mind that the principles of the criminal law and its administration are the same, whether trial be (as in more than 90 per cent of the cases it is) in the magistrates' court or on indictment before judge and jury. The magistrates are bound, as is the judge in a jury trial, to ensure that the accused has a fair trial according to law; and have the same discretion as he has in the interests of a fair trial to exclude legally admissible evidence. No doubt, it will be rarely exercised. And certainly magistrates would be wise not to rule until the evidence is tendered and objection is taken. . . . They must wait and see what is tendered; and only then, if objection be taken, rule. When asked to rule, they should bear in mind that it is their duty to have regard to legally admissible evidence, unless in their judgment the use of the evidence would make the trial unfair.

This dictum applies to summary *trials*. In the case of *committal proceedings*, at common law examining justices have no discretion to exclude evidence, but must consider all legally admissible evidence tendered in deciding whether there is a case to answer (*Horsham Justices, ex parte Bukhari* (1981) 74 Cr App R 291; *Conway* (1990) 91 Cr App R 143). The position is the same in extradition proceedings (see *Governor of Pentonville Prison, ex parte Voets* [1986] 1 WLR 470).

THE DISCRETION TO EXCLUDE: STATUTORY PROVISIONS

Police and Criminal Evidence Act 1984, s. 78

F2.4   The common-law discretion founded on the duty of the judge or magistrates to ensure that every accused person has a fair trial has now been buttressed by statute. The PACE

1984, s. 78(1), provides that in any criminal proceedings the court may refuse to allow evidence on which the prosecution propose to rely to be given, if it appears to the court that, having regard to all the circumstances, including the circumstances in which the evidence was obtained, the admission of the evidence would have such an adverse effect on the fairness of the proceedings that the court ought not to admit it. Section 78(3) of the 1984 Act provides that s. 78 shall not apply in the case of proceedings before a magistrates' court inquiring into an offence as examining justices. In consequence, s. 78 has probably also ceased to apply to extradition proceedings (per Lord Hoffmann in *Governor of Brixton Prison, ex parte Levin* [1997] AC 741).

Section 78(1) is generally regarded as conferring a discretionary power, but strictly speaking it does not involve an exercise of discretion because if a court decides that admission of the evidence in question would have such an adverse effect on the fairness of the proceedings that it ought not to admit it, it cannot logically exercise a discretion to admit it (per Auld LJ in *Chalkley* [1998] QB 848 at p. 874). Either way, the Court of Appeal has been loath to interfere with the decisions of trial judges under s. 78. It has been said that the Court of Appeal will intervene only if the judge has not exercised his discretion under s. 78 at all or has done so but in a *Wednesbury* unreasonable manner (*Associated Provincial Picture Houses Ltd* v *Wednesbury Corporation* [1948] 1 KB 223) and that where the Court of Appeal does intervene, it will exercise its own discretion (see *O'Leary* (1988) 87 Cr App R 387 per May LJ at p. 391, *Quinn* [1995] 1 Cr App R 480 at p. 498, *Christou* [1992] QB 979, *Khan* [1997] Crim LR 508, and *Dures* [1997] 2 Cr App R 247). However, it is submitted that the true test for the Court of Appeal should be whether the admission of the evidence in question renders the conviction unsafe, since that is now the only ground on which it may allow an appeal against conviction (see the Criminal Appeal Act 1968, s. 2(1) at **D22.15**, and generally Adrian Clarke 'Safety or Supervision' [1999] Crim LR 108).

The subsection may be used to attempt to exclude *any* evidence on which the prosecution propose to rely (see, e.g., *O'Loughlin* [1988] 3 All ER 431 (depositions and documentary records); *Mason* [1988] 1 WLR 139 (confessions); *Beveridge* (1987) 85 Cr App R 255 (identification parades); *Deenik* [1992] Crim LR 578 (voice identifications); and *McGrath* v *Field* [1987] RTR 349 (intoximeter readings)). Thus in the case of (a) any admissible evidence which is likely to have a prejudicial effect out of proportion to its probative value, and (b) admissions, confessions and other evidence obtained from the accused after the commission of the offence by improper or unfair means, and which might operate unfairly against the accused (see *Sang* [1980] AC 402), the court may now exclude *either* under its powers at common law *or* pursuant to s. 78. In *Matto* v *Wolverhampton Crown Court* [1987] RTR 337 Woolf LJ said (at p. 346): 'Whatever is the right interpretation of s. 78, I am quite satisfied that it certainly does not reduce the discretion of the court to exclude unfair evidence which existed at common law. Indeed, in my view in any case where the evidence could properly be excluded at common law, it can certainly be excluded under s. 78.' An example is *O'Connor* (1986) 85 Cr App R 298. A and B were jointly charged with having conspired to commit an offence. A pleaded guilty and B not guilty. At the trial of B the prosecution sought to admit the conviction of A under the PACE 1984, s. 74. The prejudicial effect of this evidence clearly outweighed its probative value, because A's admission of the offence charged might have led the jury to infer that B must have conspired with A, and therefore the common–law discretion to exclude could have been invoked. Instead, the Court of Appeal held that the evidence should have been excluded under s. 78. See also *Kempster* [1989] 1 WLR 1125 and *Mattison* [1990] Crim LR 117, which are considered at **F11.3**.

The primary importance of s. 78, however, is not the degree of overlap with the common law, but the fact that it extends the common-law powers by reason of its potential for the exclusion of evidence obtained by improper or unfair means. Concerning evidence improperly or unfairly obtained, the common-law powers are restricted to admissions, confessions and other evidence obtained from the accused after the commission of the offence (*Sang* [1980] AC 402). In *Sang*, their lordships, despite their apparent unanimity, were neither clear nor in agreement as to the precise meaning of the phrase 'evidence obtained from the accused after the commission of the offence'. Section 78, however, is capable of application to *any* evidence obtained by improper or unfair means and on which the prosecution seek to rely. The application of s. 78 to such evidence is considered separately at **F2.13**.

Criminal Justice Act 1988, s. 25

F2.5   Unlike the PACE 1984, s. 78(1), which is of general application, the CJA 1988, s. 25(1), empowers the court to exclude, in the exercise of its discretion, only two specified varieties of otherwise admissible evidence: the court, if it is of the opinion that, in the interests of justice, a documentary hearsay statement admissible by virtue of s. 23 or s. 24 of the 1988 Act nevertheless ought not to be admitted, may direct that the statement shall not be admitted. In exercising this discretion, the court is under a duty to have regard to the various matters specified in s. 25(2) (see for further details, **F16.14**).

ADMISSIBILITY OF EVIDENCE OBTAINED UNLAWFULLY, IMPROPERLY OR UNFAIRLY

General Rule of Admissibility

F2.6   Except in the case of confessions (see **F17**) and, in appropriate circumstances, privileged documents (see **F2.8** and **F2.9**), evidence obtained unlawfully, improperly or unfairly is admissible as a matter of *law*. (Concerning the existence and extent of the *discretion* to exclude evidence thus obtained, see **F2.10** to **F2.19**). In *Kuruma, Son of Kaniu* v *The Queen* [1955] AC 197, Lord Goddard CJ, on behalf of the Board, said (at p. 203):

> . . . the test to be applied in considering whether evidence is admissible is whether it is relevant to the matters in issue. If it is, it is admissible and the court is not concerned with how the evidence was obtained. While this proposition may not have been stated in so many words in any English case there are decisions which support it, and in their lordships' opinion it is plainly right in principle.

Referring to this pronouncement in *Jeffrey* v *Black* [1978] QB 490, Lord Widgery CJ said (at p. 497): 'I have not the least doubt that we must firmly accept the proposition that an irregularity in obtaining evidence does not render the evidence inadmissible.' Evidence is admissible, therefore, if it has been obtained by any of the following means:

(a)   Theft (see *Leatham* (1861) 8 Cox CC 498 per Crompton J at p. 501).

(b)   Unlawful search of persons (see *Jones* v *Owen* (1870) 34 JP 759 and *Kuruma, Son of Kaniu* v *The Queen* [1955] AC 197).

(c)   Unlawful search of premises (see *Jeffrey* v *Black* [1978] QB 490).

(d)   The use of *agents provocateurs* (*Sang* [1980] AC 402).

(e)   Eavesdropping (see *Stewart* [1970] 1 WLR 907, in which an officer disguised as a prisoner eavesdropped on a conversation in the cells between the appellant and a co-accused; *Keeton* (1970) 54 Cr App R 267, in which an officer listened to a telephone conversation between the accused, who was at the police station, and his wife; and *Maqsud Ali* [1966] 1 QB 688 and *Senat* (1968) 52 Cr App R 282, both of which involved the tape recording of conversations).

(f)   Invasion of privacy (see *Khan* [1997] AC 558, in which evidence of an incriminating conversation was obtained by means of a secret electronic surveillance device).

Procedures for Obtaining Evidence Prescribed by Statute

Although in general the court is not concerned with how evidence is obtained, where it **F2.7** is a necessary step towards procuring a conviction for an offence that the evidence be obtained in accordance with a procedure prescribed by statute, evidence obtained other than in accordance with that procedure will not be admissible. See *Scott* v *Baker* [1969] 1 QB 659 (the procedure for providing a specimen under the Road Safety Act 1967, s. 3, in relation to the offence of driving having consumed alcohol contrary to s. 1 of that Act), approved in *Spicer* v *Holt* [1977] AC 987; and contrast *Trump* (1979) 70 Cr App R 300 (Road Traffic Act 1972, s. 7(1)), *Adams* [1980] QB 575 and *Tunbridge Wells Borough Council* v *Quietlynn Ltd* [1985] Crim LR 594.

Confessions

If it is represented to the court that a confession made by an accused person was or may **F2.8** have been obtained by the means set out in the PACE 1984, s. 76(2), the court shall not allow the confession to be given in evidence against him, except to the extent that the prosecution prove to the court beyond reasonable doubt that the confession was not so obtained. Concerning the admissibility of both confessions and facts discovered in consequence of inadmissible confessions, see generally **F17**.

Privileged Documents

If a document protected by legal professional privilege (or secondary evidence of it) has **F2.9** been obtained by the opponent of the party entitled to assert the privilege, then the document (or secondary evidence of it) will be admissible in evidence. This principle applies whether the document was obtained by the inadvertence of the party entitled to assert the privilege or by the wrongful act of his opponent (see *Calcraft* v *Guest* [1898] 1 QB 759; *Tompkins* (1977) 67 Cr App R 181). In civil proceedings, the party in whom the privilege is vested may apply for an injunction to restrain his opponent from making any use of the confidential information obtained in the document (*Lord Ashburton* v *Pape* [1913] 2 Ch 469). However, the principle of *Lord Ashburton* v *Pape* cannot be used to prevent the prosecution from tendering relevant evidence in a public prosecution (see *Butler* v *Board of Trade* [1971] Ch 680, a decision which is consistent with the general rule that criminal courts are not concerned with the method by which the evidence they consider has been obtained).

In *ITC Film Distributors Ltd* v *Video Exchange Ltd* [1982] Ch 431, one party to civil proceedings obtained by a trick in court privileged documents belonging to the other party. By that stage in the case there were difficulties in the way of granting injunctive relief under the principle established in *Lord Ashburton* v *Pape* [1913] 2 Ch 469. Warner J held that the public interest that litigants should be able to bring their documents into court without fear that they might be filched by their opponents required an exception to the rule in *Calcraft* v *Guest* [1898] 1 QB 759; and he observed that to obtain documents in such circumstances is probably a contempt of court which the court should not countenance by admitting the documents in evidence. It is submitted that if the same facts were to arise in a public prosecution rather than civil proceedings, then, notwithstanding the principles established in *Calcraft* v *Guest* and *Butler* v *Board of Trade* [1971] Ch 680, the result, on the reasoning employed by Warner J, would be the same.

DISCRETIONARY EXCLUSION OF EVIDENCE OBTAINED UNLAWFULLY, IMPROPERLY OR UNFAIRLY

Cases before *Sang*

Prior to *Sang* [1980] AC 402, the cases revealed an unbroken chain of dicta to the effect **F2.10** that in criminal proceedings the court has a general discretion to exclude otherwise admissible prosecution evidence which has been obtained by improper or unfair means:

(a)   In *Kuruma, Son of Kaniu* v *The Queen* [1955] AC 197, Lord Goddard CJ said (at p. 204): 'No doubt in a criminal case the judge always has a discretion to disallow evidence if the strict rules of admissibility would operate unfairly against an accused'. Later, his lordship continued: 'If, for instance, some admission of some piece of evidence, e.g., a document, had been obtained from a defendant by a trick, no doubt the judge might properly rule it out'.

(b)   In *Callis* v *Gunn* [1964] 1 QB 495 Lord Parker CJ, after citing the first part of Lord Goddard CJ's statement set out above, said (at pp. 501–2):

> . . . in considering whether admissibility would operate unfairly against a defendant one would certainly consider whether [the evidence] had been obtained in an oppressive manner by force or against the wishes of an accused person. That is the general principle. . . .
>
> [The overriding discretion] would certainly be exercised by excluding the evidence if there was any suggestion of it having been obtained oppressively, by false representations, by a trick, by threats, by bribes, anything of that sort.

(c)   In *King* v *The Queen* [1969] 1 AC 304, Lord Hodson, giving the judgment of the Judicial Committee, said (at p. 319):

> . . . there is no ground for interfering with the way in which the discretion has been exercised in this case.
>
> This is not in their [lordships'] opinion a case in which evidence has been obtained by conduct of which the Crown ought not to take advantage. If they had thought otherwise they would have excluded the evidence even though tendered for the suppression of crime.

(d)   In *Jeffrey* v *Black* [1978] QB 490, it was held that magistrates had wrongly exercised their discretion to exclude evidence of the possession of drugs, which had been obtained by an illegal search of the accused's room; but Lord Widgery CJ, although stressing that the occasions for exercise of the discretion would be exceptional, said (at p. 498):

> . . . if the case is such that not only have the police officers entered without authority, but they have been guilty of trickery or they have misled someone, or they have been oppressive or they have been unfair, or in other respects they have behaved in a manner which is morally reprehensible, then it is open to the justices to apply their discretion and decline to allow the particular evidence to be let in as part of the trial.

Despite these various dicta as to the existence of a discretion to exclude evidence which has been obtained oppressively, improperly or unfairly, there were very few cases in which such a discretion was in fact exercised. It was exercised in *Ameer* [1977] Crim LR 104 to exclude evidence which had been obtained as a result of the activities of an *agent provocateur*, and a similar course was taken in *Foulder* [1973] Crim LR 45 and in *Burnett* [1973] Crim LR 748; but all three cases were overruled in *Sang* [1980] AC 402. The only other case in which the discretion was exercised was *Payne* [1963] 1 WLR 637. P was charged with drunken driving. He had been induced to submit himself to examination by a doctor to see if he was suffering from any illness or disability, on the understanding that the doctor would not examine him for the purpose of seeing whether he was fit to drive; but at the trial the doctor gave evidence of P's unfitness to drive based on his symptoms and behaviour in the course of that examination. The conviction was quashed on the ground that the judge should have exercised his discretion to exclude the doctor's evidence. In *Sang* [1980] AC 402, however, *Payne* was regarded as analogous to cases in which an accused is unfairly induced to confess to an offence, and the judgment of the Court of Criminal Appeal was therefore seen to be based on the maxim *nemo tenetur se ipsum prodere* (no man is to be compelled to incriminate himself). In *McDonald* [1991] Crim LR 122, a decision under the PACE 1984, s. 78, in which it was held that it was not unfair to adduce evidence of a damaging admission, made by the accused in the course of a psychiatric examination, on a non-medical issue. See also *Gayle* [1994] Crim LR 679.

As to the discretion to exclude otherwise admissible confessions, see generally **F17.13** to **F17.33**.

Sang

In *Sang* [1980] AC 402, the point of law on which the appeal actually turned was **F2.11** whether a judge has a discretion to exclude the prosecution evidence if satisfied that the offence charged was instigated by an *agent provocateur* and, but for this, would not have been committed by the accused. The House of Lords held that, whatever the ambit of the judicial discretion to exclude admissible evidence, it does not extend to excluding evidence of a crime on the grounds that it was instigated by an *agent provocateur*, because if it did so extend it would amount to a procedural device whereby the trial judge could avoid the substantive law, under which it is clearly established that there is no defence of entrapment (see *McEvilly* (1973) 60 Cr App R 150 and *Mealey* (1974) 60 Cr App R 59). The point of law of general importance certified by the Court of Appeal, however, went beyond the issue of *agents provocateurs* and raised a much wider question, namely: 'Does a trial judge have a discretion to refuse to allow evidence, being evidence other than evidence of an admission, to be given in any circumstances in which such evidence is relevant and of more than minimal probative value?' Although it was not strictly necessary for their lordships to answer the certified question in its full breadth, they proceeded to do so, and the primary importance of *Sang* is the *obiter* answer given. Treating the certified question as if it were not confined to trial by jury but concerned the existence of the discretion in any criminal trial, whether in the Crown Court or in a magistrates' court, their lordships, by way of answer, agreed on the following form of words suggested by Viscount Dilhorne (at p. 437):

> (1) A trial judge in a criminal trial has always a discretion to refuse to admit evidence if in his opinion its prejudicial effect outweighs its probative value. (2) Save with regard to admissions and confessions and generally with regard to evidence obtained from the accused after commission of the offence, he has no discretion to refuse to admit relevant admissible evidence on the ground that it was obtained by improper or unfair means. The court is not concerned with how it was obtained. It is no ground for the exercise of discretion to exclude that the evidence was obtained as the result of the activities of an *agent provocateur*.

The first of the above propositions is considered at **F2.1** to **F2.3**. As to the second proposition, despite the apparent unanimity, their lordships expressed various differing views, especially as to the meaning to be ascribed to the words 'and generally with regard to evidence obtained from the accused after commission of the offence', as the following extracts from the speeches illustrate:

(a) Lord Diplock (at p. 436) treated the phrase as referring to 'evidence tantamount to a self-incriminatory admission which was obtained from the defendant, after the offence had been committed, by means which would justify a judge in excluding an actual confession which had the like self-incriminating effect', and cited, by way of illustration, *Barker* [1941] 2 KB 381 (in which fraudulently prepared documents produced to a tax inspector were held to stand on precisely the same footing as an oral or written confession brought into existence as the result of a promise, inducement or threat) and *Payne* [1963] 1 WLR 637 (see **F2.10**). Lord Diplock said (at p. 436):

> The underlying rationale of this branch of the criminal law . . . is . . . now to be found in the maxim *nemo debet prodere se ipsum*. . . . That is why there is no discretion to exclude evidence discovered as the result of an illegal search but there is discretion to exclude evidence which the accused has been induced to produce voluntarily if the method of inducement was unfair.

(b) Viscount Dilhorne was largely in agreement with Lord Diplock. Thus, although he found it unnecessary to decide whether *Payne* [1963] 1 WLR 637 was correctly decided, he sought to explain the statement of Lord Goddard CJ in *Kuruma, Son of Kaniu* v *The Queen* [1955] AC 197 at p. 203 (that a judge might exercise his discretion to exclude a document obtained by a trick: see **F2.10**) on the basis that the Lord Chief Justice was perhaps thinking of admissions, confessions and the decision in *Barker* [1941] 2 KB 381. Viscount Dilhorne was also of the opinion that the observations made by Lord Parker CJ in *Callis* v *Gunn* [1964] 1 QB 495 at p. 501 and by Lord Widgery CJ in *Jeffrey* v *Black* [1978] QB 490 at p. 498 (see **F2.10**) were not correct.

(c)   Lord Salmon, taking a less restrictive view as to the meaning of the phrase, said (at p. 444) 'In my opinion, the decision as to whether evidence may be excluded depends entirely on the particular facts of each case and the circumstances surrounding it — which are infinitely variable'. The category of cases in which evidence may be rejected on the grounds that it would make a trial unfair was not closed and could never be closed except by statute (at p. 445).

(d)   Lord Fraser of Tullybelton, who agreed with Lord Diplock that the decision in *Payne* [1963] 1 WLR 637 was based, at least in part, on the maxim *nemo tenetur se ipsum accusare*, concluded, in apparent reliance on the *obiter dicta* in *Kuruma*, *Callis* v *Gunn* and *Jeffrey* v *Black*, that the phrase under discussion applied 'only to evidence and documents obtained from an accused person or from premises occupied by him' and would 'leave judges with a discretion to be exercised in accordance with their individual views of what is unfair or oppressive or morally reprehensible' (at p. 450).

(e)   Lord Scarman treated the phrase as referring exclusively to the obtaining of evidence from the accused. His lordship said (at pp. 456–7):

> If an accused is misled or tricked into providing evidence (whether it be an admission or the provision of fingerprints or medical evidence or some other evidence), the rule against self-incrimination, – *nemo tenetur se ipsum prodere* – is likely to be infringed. Each case must, of course, depend on its circumstances. All I would say is that the principle of fairness, though concerned exclusively with the use of evidence at trial, is not susceptible to categorisation or classification and is wide enough in some circumstances to embrace the way in which, after the crime, evidence has been obtained from the accused.

Cases after *Sang*

F2.12   Much of the case law subsequent to *Sang* [1980] AC 402 has neither clarified nor refined the principles laid down in that case; see, for example, *Winter* v *Barlow* [1980] RTR 209; *Doyle* v *Leroux* [1981] RTR 438; *Clarke* (1984) 80 Cr App R 344; and *Morris* v *Beardmore* [1981] AC 446, in which Lord Roskill said (at p. 469) that in *Sang* the House had carefully defined the limits of judicial discretion to exclude evidence otherwise clearly admissible, setting at rest many doubts which had previously existed as to its existence and scope, and that it would be a retrograde step to enlarge upon its now narrow limits or to engraft an exception, merely in order to meet the situation under discussion in that case. However, other authorities, such as *Khan* [1997] AC 558, *Trump* (1979) 70 Cr App R 300, *Adams* [1980] QB 575 and *Apicella* (1985) 82 Cr App R 295, are illustrative of what evidence is and is not capable of being treated as 'evidence tantamount to a self-incriminatory admission'; and *Fox* [1986] AC 281 has put a major gloss on the principles established in *Sang* [1980] AC 402, to the effect that where evidence has been unlawfully obtained from the accused after the commission of the offence, the discretion will not be exercised if those who obtained the evidence did so on the basis of a bona fide mistake as to their powers. In this regard, see also *Trump* (1979) 70 Cr App R 300. These cases are considered below.

In *Khan* [1997] AC 558, the House of Lords, relying upon the dictum of Lord Diplock in *Sang* set out at **F2.11**, held that evidence of an incriminating conversation obtained by means of a secret electronic surveillance device was not subject to the discretion recognised in *Sang* to exist in the case of admissions and confessions, because the accused had not been 'induced' to make the admissions recorded.

In *Trump* (1979) 70 Cr App R 300, the appellant was convicted of driving while unfit through drink. He was given a breathalyser test which proved positive. The officer administering the test then arrested him unlawfully. The appellant was taken to the police station and given a statutory warning that he might be prosecuted if he failed to provide a specimen. Under the relevant procedures, no such warning was required. As a result of the warning, the accused consented to the provision of a specimen of blood which was found to contain a proportion of alcohol above the prescribed limit. He appealed on the ground that the specimen of blood had been unlawfully obtained and that the result of its analysis should have been excluded. It was conceded by the appellant that after the breath test had proved positive, the officer had a statutory power of arrest (but not under the statutory provision which the officer purported to use) and that had he exercised that power the result of the analysis of blood would have been admissible as evidence. The Court of Appeal held that:

(a)   the giving of blood by the accused was very close to his making an admission that he had consumed an excessive amount of alcohol, and therefore was subject to the discretion recognised in *Sang* [1980] AC 402 to exist in cases analogous to improperly obtained admissions; but
(b)   the judge would have erred if he had excluded the evidence because, although the blood was given as the result of a threat, the officer was acting in good faith and the evidence could not have undermined the fairness of the trial.

In *Apicella* (1985) 82 Cr App R 295 the appellant was convicted on three counts of rape. Each of the victims had contracted an unusual strain of gonorrhoea. The appellant, whilst held on remand, was suspected by the prison doctor to be suffering from gonorrhoea. The doctor, for solely therapeutic reasons, called in a consultant physician who, on the assumption that the appellant was consenting, took a sample of body fluid in order to make a diagnosis. In fact, the appellant submitted because he had been told by a prison officer that, being a prisoner, he had to submit. The sample showed that the appellant was suffering from the same strain of gonorrhoea as the victims, and the prosecution called evidence to that effect. On appeal, although no reference to *Trump* (1979) 70 Cr App R 300 appears to have been made, the Court of Appeal rejected a submission that the body fluid taken without consent was the physical equivalent of an oral confession. Lawton LJ, giving the judgment of the court, held that the pertinent question was whether the intended use of the evidence was likely to make the trial unfair; that the appellant was not tricked into submitting to the examination in the way which led the court in *Payne* [1963] 1 WLR 637 (see **F2.10**) to exclude evidence; that the prosecution's use of the evidence was not unfair; and that therefore the judge had been right in the exercise of his discretion not to exclude it.

In *Adams* [1980] QB 575 the accused was charged with offences under the Obscene Publications Act 1959, s. 2. On 6 April 1977, the police, acting under a search warrant issued under s. 3(1) of the 1959 Act, entered and searched the accused's bookshop and seized certain articles. On 12 April 1977, officers purporting to act under the same warrant, entered and searched the shop and seized further articles. The Court of Appeal held that since a warrant issued under s. 3(1) authorised only one entry, search and seizure of premises, and was spent once that had been carried out, the entry, search and seizure on 12 April was unlawful. On the question whether the judge should have exercised his discretion to exclude the articles seized on 12 April, it was held that there was no material suggesting that the error of the police as to the continuing validity of the warrant after the search on 6 April was oppressive in the sense that the adjective was used in *Sang* [1980] AC 402. This assumes, contrary to the view of Lord Diplock in *Sang* (see **F2.11**), that evidence discovered as a result of an illegal search *is* subject to the discretion recognised in that case and, in appropriate circumstances, may be excluded.

In *Fox* [1986] AC 281 the appellant was convicted under the Road Traffic Act 1972, s. 6(1), on the basis of the proportion of alcohol in a breath specimen which he had been required to provide at a police station following his wrongful arrest. Officers had entered the appellant's house without his consent and without statutory authority, and required him to provide a specimen of breath. He refused. He was then arrested and taken to the police station where he was required to provide the specimen of breath which was the crucial item of evidence which led to his conviction. The requirement to provide a specimen in the appellant's house was not valid and the appellant had committed no offence by failing to comply with it. Consequently, his arrest for failure to provide a specimen was unlawful. On appeal, it was submitted that the evidence of the specimen obtained at the police station, although relevant and admissible, ought to have been excluded by the justices in the exercise of their discretion. This submission was rejected by both the Divisional Court and the House of Lords. Lord Fraser of Tullybelton, whose reasoning was expressly adopted by Lords Elwyn-Jones, Edmund-Davies, Bridge of Harwich and Brightman, said (at p. 293): 'Of course, if the appellant had been lured to the police station by some trick or deception, or if the police officers had behaved oppressively towards the appellant, the justices' jurisdiction to exclude otherwise admissible evidence recognised in *Sang* might have come into play. But there is nothing of that sort suggested here. The police officers did no more than make a bona fide mistake as to their powers.' This passage was cited and applied by McNeill J in *Gull* v *Scarborough* [1987] RTR 261. See also *DPP* v *Wilson* [1991] RTR 284, a decision under the PACE 1984, s. 78, in which it was held that a police officer, having received information that a person is about to drive whilst under the influence of drink, is under no duty to warn that person of the potential offence, and failure to do so is not 'oppressive'.

Police and Criminal Evidence Act 1984, s. 78

F2.13

(1)   In any proceedings the court may refuse to allow evidence on which the prosecution proposes to rely to be given if it appears to the court that, having regard to all the circumstances, including the circumstances in which the evidence was obtained, the admission of the evidence would have such an adverse effect on the fairness of the proceedings that the court ought not to admit it.

(2)   Nothing in this section shall prejudice any rule of law requiring a court to exclude evidence.

(3)   This section shall not apply in the case of proceedings before a magistrates' court inquiring into an offence as examining justices.

The importance of s. 78(1) is reflected in the large volume of reported cases in which it has arisen for consideration since it came into force. It is important to stress at the outset, however, the salutary warning given by Auld J in *Jelen* (1989) 90 Cr App R 456 at pp. 464–5:

. . . the decision of a judge whether or not to exclude evidence under section 78 of the 1984 Act is made as a result of the exercise by him of a discretion based upon the particular circumstances of the case and upon his assessment of the adverse effect, if any, it would have on the fairness of the proceedings. The circumstances of each case are almost always different, and judges may well take different views in the proper exercise of their discretion even when the circumstances are similar. This is not an apt field for hard case law and well-founded distinctions between cases.

The following paragraphs make a number of general observations about (a) the procedure to be adopted when relying on the subsection, (b) the test for exclusion, (c) the scope of the subsection and (d) the effect of bad faith. The cases concerning confessions and identification evidence are also considered separately and in more detail at **F17.16** to **F17.34** and **F18** respectively.

F2.14   *Procedure*   As to procedure, the issue of unfairness may be raised by counsel for any accused against whom the evidence may be used (by the prosecution). Section 78(1) applies not to evidence which the prosecution have adduced, but to evidence on which the prosecution *propose* to rely. In *Harwood* [1989] Crim LR 285, in which a submission that evidence should be excluded under s. 78 was made *after* the evidence had been given, the Court of Appeal doubted whether s. 78 could in any circumstances entitle the judge to withdraw the evidence or to direct the jury to acquit when the judge had not been invited to refuse to allow the evidence to be given. However, where a judge has excluded evidence on which the prosecution propose to rely but, at some later stage in the trial, in his opinion the balance of fairness shifts, he then has a discretion to reconsider his ruling and admit the evidence (*Allen* [1992] Crim LR 297).

It seems reasonable to suppose that if the court is prepared to entertain a submission that a particular item would have such an adverse effect on the fairness of the proceedings that the court ought not to admit it, argument should take place in the absence of the jury and, in cases in which evidence needs to be called as to the circumstances in which the evidence was obtained (because they are in dispute), there should be a hearing on the *voir dire*. The early indications from the authorities, however, are that such a hearing will not always be necessary. Thus, where a question arises under s. 78(1) as to the admissibility of identification parade evidence, it has been held that, although there may be rare occasions when it will be desirable to hold a trial within a trial, in general the judge should decide on the basis of the depositions, statements and submissions of counsel (*Beveridge* (1987) 85 Cr App R 255). See **F1.26**.

In *Manji* [1990] Crim LR 512 the accused denied that he had made certain damaging admissions in a conversation with police officers and alleged that he had not been cautioned. On a defence application under s. 78 to exclude this evidence as having been obtained in breach of the Codes of Practice under the PACE 1984, the trial judge refused to hold a trial within a trial on the issue of whether the accused had been cautioned. It was held that the judge had erred. He was dealing with a question of admissibility and it would have been of no assistance to the jury if he had admitted the evidence prior to deciding whether it was indeed admissible. It was his task to decide whether the prosecution had proved that a caution had been given, in which case he would have let the conversation in and the matter could have been canvassed again before the jury, or, alternatively, he could have found that the prosecution had failed to prove the caution and then he would have had to address the provisions of s. 78 and decide whether, in those circumstances, it was proper to admit the evidence.

In *Anderson* [1993] Crim LR 447 it was acknowledged, *per curiam*, that it is not entirely clear under s. 78(1) where the burden of proof lies.

As to the procedure in summary trials, see **F1.27**.

The Test for Exclusion Section 78(1) of the PACE 1984 directs the court, in **F2.15** deciding whether to exercise the statutory discretion, to have regard to all the circumstances, including those in which the evidence was obtained. In some cases, of course, the submission to exclude under the subsection will *not* be based on the circumstances in which the evidence was obtained; see, for example, the cases in which an application has been made under s. 78(1) to exclude evidence of the conviction of a person otherwise admissible under s. 74 of the 1984 Act, which are considered at **F11.3**.

In other cases, however, counsel will be fully justified in basing a submission to exclude on the circumstances in which the evidence was obtained, because it is implicit in the subsection that there can be circumstances in which the evidence was obtained which makes it have such an adverse effect on the fairness of the proceedings that the court ought not to admit it (see *Matto* v *Wolverhampton Crown Court* [1987] RTR 337 per Woolf LJ). Thus, the court may have regard to any unlawful, improper or unfair conduct by means of which the evidence was obtained, including, in particular, conduct in breach of the European Convention on Human Rights or the provisions of the 1984 Act (or the codes of practice issued under the Act) relating to such matters as search, seizure, arrest, detention, treatment, questioning and identification. Even where the evidence in question was obtained by someone who is not 'charged with the duty of investigating offences' for the purposes of s. 67(9) of the 1984 Act (see **D1.53**), the principles underlying Code C may be of assistance in considering the discretion to exclude under s. 78(1) (*Smith* [1994] 1 WLR 1396). Regard may also be had to the Cleveland guidelines, which set out what is considered to be the best practice when children are interviewed in connection with sexual abuse, and the Memorandum of Good Practice on Video-Recorded Interviews with Child Witnesses (see *Dunphy* (1993) 98 Cr App R 393). However, breach of the European Convention on Human Rights, the 1984 Act or the PACE codes etc. will not necessarily result in exclusion: every case has to be determined on its own particular facts (see *Parris* (1988) 89 Cr App R 65, per Lord Lane CJ at p. 72, *Khan* [1995] QB 27 (see **F2.17**) and *Keenan* [1990] 2 QB 54 per Hodgson J at p. 69). Equally, the fact that evidence has been obtained by 'oppressive' conduct will not automatically result in exclusion, because oppressive conduct, depending on its degree and actual or possible effect, may or may not affect the fairness of admitting particular evidence (*Chalkley* [1998] QB 848 at p. 874).

In cases in which the court takes the view that there was serious or reprehensible conduct, and this results in exclusion, the decision should not be taken in order to discipline the police (*Mason* [1988] 1 WLR 139 per Watkins LJ and *Delaney* (1988) 88 Cr App R 338 per Lord Lane CJ at p. 341). The critical test under s. 78 is whether any impropriety affects the fairness of the proceedings: the court cannot exclude evidence under the section simply as a mark of its disapproval of the way in which it was obtained (per Auld LJ in *Chalkley*).

Thus if a sample of hair is obtained by an assault and not in accordance with ss. 63 and 65 of the 1984 Act and is then used to prepare a DNA profile which implicates the accused, the evidence will be admitted on the basis that the means used to obtain it have done nothing to cast doubt on its reliability and strength (see *Cooke* [1995] 1 Cr App R 318 and cf. *Nathaniel* [1995] 2 Cr App R 565, but see also s. 64(3B) of the 1984 Act at **F18.28**). The same reasoning may also justify the admission in evidence of the fruits of an improper search (see *Stewart* [1995] Crim LR 500, where the entry involved a number of breaches of Code B; and see also *McCarthy* [1996] Crim LR 818). The evidence should be excluded, however, where there is a real risk that the improper means used to obtain it have affected its reliability, and therefore the fairness of the trial, for example a case involving a complete flouting of Code B in which the accused claims that the property allegedly found must have been planted. (But see *Wright* [1994] Crim LR 55 at **F2.19**.) Equally, where officers are justified in delaying taking a suspect to a police station in order that a search may be conducted with his assistance, but abuse that opportunity to circumvent Code C by asking a series of questions, beyond those necessary to the search, on matters which properly ought to be asked under the rules of the Code applying at a police station, the answers may be excluded on the grounds of unfairness (*Khan* [1993] Crim LR 54, applied in *Raphaie* [1996] Crim LR 812).

In *Quinn* [1990] Crim LR 581 Lord Lane CJ said:

> The function of the judge is therefore *to protect the fairness of the proceedings*, and normally proceedings are fair if a jury hears *all* relevant evidence which either side wishes to place before it, but proceedings may become unfair if, for example, one side is allowed to adduce relevant evidence which, for one reason or another, the other side cannot properly challenge or meet, or where there has been an abuse of process, e.g. because evidence has been obtained in deliberate breach of procedures laid down in an official code of practice.

In *Quinn*, identification evidence had come into existence abroad as a result of arrangements made by a foreign police force. A police officer went to a criminal court in Dublin, where the accused was on trial in respect of other offences committed in the Republic of Ireland, and identified the accused. It was held that, in the circumstances of the case, the judge had to have regard to such factors as (a) the possible cross-examination handicap to the defence; (b) the possibility of mistake being increased because of the way in which the identification was arranged and the fact that both the judge himself and the defence could warn the jury of the disadvantages of the procedure adopted and the consequent danger of relying upon the evidence; (c) the fact that the accused was deprived of the opportunity to stand on an identification parade or to consult a solicitor or to record what happened when the identification was carried out; (d) that the accused was not told of the identification at the time; and (e) the fact that the identification evidence did not stand alone but could be tested by other evidence. The Court of Appeal could find nothing to indicate that the trial judge had misdirected himself, had regard to irrelevant matters or failed to have regard to relevant matters. See also *Konscol* [1993] Crim LR 950, in which the trial judge admitted evidence of an interview with K, containing lies, conducted by a Belgian customs officer. There was no dispute that K had said what was recorded, and the interview was conducted fairly according to Belgian law, but K was neither cautioned nor advised that he could have a lawyer present. The Court of Appeal dismissed the appeal and declined to lay down guidelines as to when a court should admit a statement made overseas according to rules which did not coincide with the provisions of the PACE 1984.

In *Mason* [1988] 1 WLR 139 the accused was convicted of arson. After arrest, the accused and his solicitor were told by police officers that a fingerprint of the accused had been identified on glass from a bottle found at the scene of the crime. This was a deliberate falsehood designed to elicit a confession. The solicitor advised the accused to explain any involvement on his part in the incident, whereupon the accused confessed. There was no other prosecution evidence. Quashing the conviction, the Court of Appeal held that had the judge, in the exercise of the statutory discretion, taken into account the deceit practised on the solicitor, which he had failed to do, he would have been driven to exclude the confession. See also *Samuel* [1988] QB 615. *Mason* was distinguished in *DPP* v *Marshall* [1988] 3 All ER 683. On a charge of selling intoxicating liquor without a licence, evidence was adduced that officers, wearing plain clothes, and without announcing their office, had purchased liquor from the premises in question. It was held that this evidence could not have any effect on the fairness of the trial and therefore was not to be excluded under the PACE 1984, s. 78.

Scope of s. 78(1)   As regards the scope of the PACE 1984, s. 78(1), in *Mason* [1988] **F2.16** 1 WLR 139 Watkins LJ said that it 'does no more than to restate the power which judges had at common law before the 1984 Act was passed'. It is submitted that this view is erroneous in principle and inconsistent with the authorities to date.

  (a)   Concerning the provisions of part VIII of the PACE 1984, s. 82(3) expressly preserves the discretion to exclude which the court possessed at common law prior to the coming into force of the Act, and therefore Parliament, in enacting s. 78, must be taken to have extended the pre-existing discretion.

  (b)   Section 78(1), insofar as it may be used to exclude evidence obtained by improper or unfair means, is not confined, as is the common-law power described in *Sang* [1980] AC 402 (at p. 437), to 'admissions, confessions and generally with regard to evidence obtained from the accused after the commission of the offence', but extends to any evidence on which the prosecution propose to rely.

  (c)   Nor, in relation to evidence obtained improperly or unfairly, is s. 78(1) necessarily confined, in the way that the common-law power apparently is, to cases in which those who obtained the evidence acted *mala fide* (*Fox* [1986] AC 281, see **F2.12**). See further **F2.18**.

Section 78(1) *may* be used to exclude evidence obtained illegally, improperly or unfairly. Insofar as it may be used in this way to exclude admissions, confessions and evidence obtained from the accused after the commission of the offence, it overlaps with the common-law discretion as defined in *Sang*. The subsection, however, has the potential for the exclusion of *any* evidence on which the prosecution propose to rely, whether obtained from the accused, his premises, or from any other source. Thus, in *Gaynor* [1988] Crim LR 242, evidence that a witness had picked out the accused at a group identification was excluded under s. 78 on the basis of a breach of PACE Code D. Under para. 2.3 of Code D, a parade must be held if the suspect asks for one and it is practicable to hold one. An inspector had decided that it was not practicable, on the grounds that there were insufficient volunteers of the same racial origin as the accused. The inspector had not properly exercised his discretion under para. 2.4, because more could have been done to assemble sufficient volunteers. It was held that where a parade is practicable and the accused desires one, the courts should not readily countenance any substitute where the advantages, from the point of view of fairness, are less to the accused.

F2.17 **Police Undercover Operations** Concerning the application of the PACE 1984, s. 78(1), to evidence obtained as a result of police undercover operations, in *Smurthwaite* [1994] 1 All ER 898 it was held that the relevant factors *include* whether the undercover officer was acting as an *agent provocateur*; the nature of any entrapment; whether the evidence consists of admissions to a completed offence or relates to the actual commission of an offence; how active the officer's role was in obtaining the evidence; whether there is an unassailable record of what occurred or whether it is strongly corroborated; and whether the officer abused his role to ask questions which ought properly to have been asked as a police officer and in accordance with the codes (see *Christou* [1992] QB 979 and *Bryce* [1992] 4 All ER 567, below). It was also held that, although s. 78(1) has not altered the substantive rule of law that entrapment or the use of an *agent provocateur* does not *per se* afford a defence to a criminal charge, if in all the circumstances the evidence would have the adverse effect described in s. 78(1), then the judge will exclude it. See also *Gill* [1989] Crim LR 358, doubting *Harwood* [1989] Crim LR 285, and *Edwards* [1991] Crim LR 45. Equally it seems that s. 78(1) cannot be circumvented by the police using, as *agents provocateurs*, informants who will not be called as witnesses. Thus if an informant, acting on police instructions, entraps an accused into committing an offence and the accused is then approached by an undercover police officer in whose presence the offence is committed, a submission may be made under s. 78(1) to exclude the officer's evidence notwithstanding that his behaviour throughout cannot be criticised having regard to the relevant factors in *Smurthwaite* (see *Smith* [1995] Crim LR 658; cf. *Mann* [1995] Crim LR 647). However, entrapment, whether direct or indirect, will not necessarily result in exclusion. In *Governor of Pentonville Prison, ex parte Chinoy* [1992] 1 All ER 317, it was held that, although the fact of entrapment should be taken into account (bearing in mind that entrapment is no defence), the extent to which s. 78(1) has qualified the rule in *Sang* is limited. On the facts, the means used by the undercover agents were appropriate to the situation being investigated and did not require exclusion of the evidence obtained.

In *Smurthwaite*, the two appellants, S and G had been tried for soliciting to murder. In each case the person solicited was an undercover police officer posing as a contract killer, and the prosecution case depended upon secret tape recordings of meetings held between the undercover officer and the accused. In S's case, the Court of Appeal was not persuaded that the officer was an *agent provocateur*. There was an element of entrapment and a trick, but (a) the tapes recorded not admissions about some previous offence but the actual offence being committed, (b) the tapes showed that S made the running and that the officer had taken a minimal role in the planning and had used no persuasion towards S, (c) the tapes were an accurate and unchallenged record and (d) the officer had not abused his role to ask questions which ought properly to have been asked as a police officer. In these circumstances, the judge's decision not to exclude the evidence was upheld. The outcome was the same in G's case: the facts were very similar and, although the first meeting between G and the officer was not recorded and there was a stark conflict of evidence as to what was said at that meeting, the existence of a total record was only one factor, and both the contents of the subsequent taped conversations and statements made by G in her formal police interviews supported the officer's account of the first meeting. In *Latif* [1996] 1 WLR 104, the accused was convicted of being knowingly concerned in the importation of drugs which had been brought into the country by an undercover customs officer. Although the accused had been lured into England by the deceit of an informer and both he and the undercover officer had possibly committed the offence of possessing heroin in Pakistan, the House of Lords upheld the trial judge's refusal to exclude the informer's evidence under s. 78. See also *Pattemore* [1994] Crim LR 836 and *Morley* [1994] Crim LR 919.

As to evidence obtained by undercover operations *after* commission of the offence, although s. 78(1) does apply, each case must be decided on its own facts. In *Jelen* (1989) 90 Cr App R 456, D, J and K were charged with conspiracy to commit false accounting. D pleaded guilty and after he was sentenced gave evidence for the prosecution in the case against J and K. D had been the first to be arrested. He made admissions and implicated J. That was the first that the police had heard of J's involvement and their view was that they would have had to caution J if they had sought to question him then but that they had insufficient evidence upon which they could have arrested and charged him. They accordingly asked D if he would obtain some corroboration of what he had told them by arranging to have a recorded conversation with J without J knowing that it was being recorded. D then held such a conversation with J in the course of which D lied to J, telling him that he had not said anything to the police. During the conversation, J made remarks from which his guilt could have been inferred. At the trial, it was submitted that it would be unfair under s. 78 to admit the tape recording because (a) D had lied to J, (b) it was a confidential discussion and (c) D was acting as an agent of the police who, by using him, had avoided complying with the code of practice governing the questioning of persons by police officers (Code of Practice C). The judge rejected the submission and on an application for leave to appeal, the Court of Appeal held that although there was an element of entrapment, it could see no reason to disagree with the judge's conclusion. Cf. *H* [1987] Crim LR 47, which the court distinguished.

In *Bailey* [1993] 3 All ER 513, two co-accused exercised their right to silence when interviewed by the police. They were charged, remanded in police custody and placed together in a bugged cell by officers who, in order to lull them into a false sense of security, pretended that they had been forced to put them in the same cell by an uncooperative custody officer. It was held that evidence of incriminating conversations between them, obtained by this police subterfuge, was admissible. Although the police were not entitled to question the accused further, they did not have to protect them from any opportunity to hold incriminating conversations, if they chose to do so, and there was nothing in the 1984 Act or Code of Practice C to prohibit them from bugging a cell, even after an accused had been charged and had exercised his right to silence. The judge was therefore entitled, in exercising his discretion under s. 78, to admit the evidence. See also *Shaukat Ali* (1991) *The Times*, 19 February 1991 and *Roberts* [1997] 1 Cr App R 217.

In *Khan* [1997] AC 558 the police made a recording of an incriminating coversation relating to the importation of heroin, by means of a secret electronic surveillance device. The House of Lords held that the fact that evidence has been obtained in apparent or probable breach of the right to privacy set out in Art. 8 of the European Convention on Human Rights, or for that matter the law of a foreign country, is relevant to exercise of the s. 78 power, but the significance of such conduct is its effect, if any, upon the fairness of the proceedings. It therefore upheld the decision of the trial judge that the circumstances in which the evidence had been obtained, even if they constituted a breach of Art. 8, did not require exclusion. An application to the European Court of Human Rights has been declared admissible (see *Khan* v *United Kingdom* [1999] Crim LR 666). See also *Chalkley* [1998] QB 848.

In *Christou* [1992] QB 979, the police set up a shop staffed by two undercover officers who purported to be willing to buy stolen jewellery. Transactions in the shop were recorded (on tape and video) in order to recover stolen property and obtain evidence against thieves and receivers. The accused, charged in consequence of the operation, sought to exclude evidence on the grounds that it had been obtained, without administering a caution in accordance with para. 10.1 of the Code of Practice C, by a trick designed to deprive them of their privilege against self-incrimination. The Court of Appeal, distinguishing *Payne* [1963] 1 WLR 637 (see **F2.10**) and *Mason* [1988] 1 WLR 139 (see **F2.15**), held that the accused had voluntarily applied themselves to the trick and this had resulted in no unfairness. It was further held that although the officers had grounds to suspect the accused of having committed an offence, para. 10.1 of Code of Practice C was not intended to apply to the facts in question. It was designed to protect suspects who are vulnerable to abuse or pressure from officers, or who may believe themselves to be so. Where a suspect, even if not in detention, is being questioned by an officer acting as such, for the purpose of obtaining evidence, the parties are not on equal terms; the officer is perceived to be in a position of authority and the suspect may be intimidated or undermined. The accused, however, were not questioned by officers acting as such, conversation was on equal terms and there was no question of pressure or intimidation. *Christou* was applied in *Maclean* [1993] Crim LR 687, a very similar case in which a person suspected of the illegal importation of drugs 'applied himself to the trick', which was the opportunity of holding a conversation with a car salvage operator, who was in reality a customs officer. In *Cadette* [1995] Crim LR 229 a suspected drug courier, at the request of customs officers, telephoned C, pretended that she had not been arrested and tried to persuade C to come to the airport. Evidence of their conversation was admitted. It was held that although there comes a point when officers may move from following up available lines of inquiry in order to obtain evidence to a stage where they seek in effect to deprive a suspect of the protection afforded by the 1984 Act and Codes, the officers had not crossed the line. See also *Edwards* [1997] Crim LR 348.

In *Christou*, Lord Taylor CJ further held that it *would* be wrong for the police to adopt an undercover pose or disguise to enable them to ask questions about an offence uninhibited by Code of Practice C and with the effect of circumventing it, and a judge could then exclude under s. 78. In that case, however, questions asked by the officers about the origin of the goods formed a part of their undercover pose as receivers — such information would prevent them from reselling the goods in the area from which they were stolen. See also *Lin* [1995] Crim LR 817, where an undercover officer was introduced to the accused not for the purpose of obtaining evidence about a past offence involving a stolen Inland Revenue cheque, but to discover the future plans of the accused in relation to an on-going conspiracy to handle stolen cheques. It was held that a conversation about the Inland Revenue cheque was a necessary part of establishing the officer's credentials as a 'criminal'. The position was different in *Bryce* [1992] 4 All ER 567, where an undercover officer, in conversations with the accused about a car, asked how recently it had been stolen. The accused replied 'two to three days' and added 'we are having two a week away. Would you be interested in any others?'. The Court of Appeal, quashing the conviction for handling, held that the evidence of these conversations should have been excluded. The questions were not necessary to the maintenance of the undercover pose. They went directly to the issue of guilty knowledge, they were disputed, there was no caution and there were no contemporary records.

In *Williams* v *DPP* [1993] 3 All ER 365, plain-clothes officers, as part of a vehicle crime initiative, which was not directed at any specific individual but based on the expectation that someone might act dishonestly, parked an insecure and unattended van, which appeared to contain a valuable load of cigarettes, in a busy street. Concealed officers later observed the accused removing cartons from the van. It was held that magistrates were entitled, in exercising their discretion under s. 78, to admit the police evidence. The officers were not acting as *agents provocateurs* and, following *DPP* v *Marshall* [1988] 3 All ER 683 (see **F2.15**) and the reasoning in *Christou*, the trick was not applied to the accused: they voluntarily applied themselves to the trick. The argument that *Christou* could be distinguished, because in that case the police were seeking to obtain evidence of offences which had already been committed, was rejected. See also *London Borough of Ealing* v *Woolworths plc* [1995] Crim LR 58, where a boy aged 11, acting on the instructions of trading standards officers, had purchased an 18-category video film.

Bad Faith   The common-law discretion to exclude evidence obtained unlawfully will **F2.18** not be exercised if those who obtained the evidence made a *bona fide* mistake as to their powers; but it may be exercised if such persons resorted to trickery, deception or oppression (*Fox* [1986] AC 281). Some of the authorities on the PACE 1984, s. 78, draw the same distinction, laying great stress on whether the police acted *mala fide*, *knowingly* exceeding their powers. In *Matto* v *Wolverhampton Crown Court* [1987] RTR 337, the accused was convicted of driving with excess alcohol. Police officers, when requesting a specimen of breath on the accused's property, realised that they were acting illegally. The specimen proved positive. The accused was then arrested and, at the police station, provided another positive specimen. The appeal was allowed on the grounds that, the officers having acted *mala fide* and oppressively, the Crown Court, had it directed itself properly, could have exercised its discretion under s. 78 to exclude the evidence. See also *Mason* [1988] 1 WLR 139, in which a *deliberate* deceit was practised on both the accused and his solicitor and *Canale* [1990] 2 All ER 187, in which it was held that had the trial judge directed his mind to breaches of the interview rules under Code of Practice C which were 'flagrant', 'deliberate' and 'cynical', he would and should have concluded that the interviews should be excluded under s. 78.

Other authorities, however, adopting an approach designed to protect the suspect from being denied his civil rights, make it clear that the statutory discretion may be exercised even in the absence of *deliberate* or *wilful* misconduct. Thus, in *DPP* v *McGladrigan* [1991] RTR 297, the Divisional Court held that the argument on *mala fides* originated from *Fox*, a case decided before the PACE 1984 came into force, and that s. 78(1) of the 1984 Act gave the courts a new and considerably wider discretion. The court relied upon *Samuel* [1988] QB 615 to reject the argument that *mala fides* had to be established before the statutory discretion could be exercised. The court also pointed out that, insofar as *Matto* v *Wolverhampton Crown Court* suggested that in breathalyser cases *Fox* still applied, it should be noted that the case was not only a successful appeal by the accused, but also preceded *Samuel*. See also *Brine* [1992] Crim LR 123.

In *Foster* [1987] Crim LR 821 a confession was made after caution during an 'exchange' initiated by arresting officers at the police station. Evidence of the confession, based on a note compiled in the absence of the accused, was excluded under s. 78 on the grounds of breach of Code of Practice C: a contemporaneous record should have been made of the 'exchange', which was 'an interview' (para. 11.5(c)); a record should have been made of the reason why no contemporaneous record had been made (para. 11.9); and the accused should have been given the opportunity to read and sign the written record of the interview (para. 11.10). It was ruled that it was irrelevant whether the breaches were wilful or merely ignorant; in the absence of a contemporaneous record at the trial, the accused was deprived of the opportunity to demonstrate that his denial of the offence was not an afterthought but a denial which he made at the time of his arrest.

In *Alladice* (1988) 87 Cr App R 380, a case in which the accused had been improperly denied the right of access to a solicitor pursuant to the PACE 1984, s. 58, Lord Lane CJ, giving the reserved judgment of the Court of Appeal, held that if the police had acted in bad faith, the court would have little difficulty in ruling any confession inadmissible under s. 78; but that if the police, albeit in good faith, had nevertheless fallen foul of s. 58, it was still necessary for the court to decide whether admission of the evidence would adversely affect the fairness of the proceedings to such an extent that the confession ought to be excluded. (On the facts, however, it was held that had the trial judge considered s. 78, he would not have been obliged to exclude the evidence because the accused was well able to cope with the interviews, understood the cautions that he had been given – at times exercising his right to silence – and was aware of his rights. Thus if the solicitor had been present, his advice would have added nothing to the knowledge of his rights which the accused already had.) See also *Dunford* (1990) 91 Cr App R 150; *Parris* (1988) 89 Cr App R 68; *Walsh* (1989) 91 Cr App R 161; and *Anderson* [1993] Crim LR 447. In *Walsh*, Saville J, referring to breaches of s. 58 or the provisions of the Codes of Practice, said (at p. 163):

> . . . although bad faith may make substantial or significant that which might not otherwise be so, the contrary does not follow. Breaches which are themselves significant and substantial are not rendered otherwise by the good faith of the officers concerned.

F2.19 ***Significant and Substantial Breaches*** In *Quinn* [1990] Crim LR 581, *Walsh* (1989) 91 Cr App R 161 and *Keenan* [1990] 2 QB 54 (see **F2.18**) were referred to with approval as authority for the general proposition that a significant and substantial breach of a PACE Code may well result in the exclusion of evidence obtained in consequence, even in the absence of bad faith. Whether a breach is 'significant and substantial' for these purposes is clearly a question of fact and degree. In *Sparks* [1991] Crim LR 128 (in which the proviso to s. 2(1) of the Criminal Appeal Act 1968 was applied), breaches of Code C (failure to caution and failure to keep a proper interview record) were held to be substantial. See also *Okafor* [1994] 3 All ER 741 (failure to caution, to remind of the right to legal advice and to make a contemporaneous record of interview) and *Joseph* [1993] Crim LR 206 (failure to make contemporaneous record of interview). In *Pall* (1992) 156 JP 424, it was held that the absence of a caution was bound to be significant in most circumstances, but see also *Hoyte* [1994] Crim LR 215. See also *Samms* [1991] Crim LR 197, which involved a breach of Code D (identification by confrontation: failure to show that it was impracticable to hold a parade or a group identification). Contrast *Rajakuruna* [1991] Crim LR 458, where a breach of Code C (failure to inform a person not under arrest that he is not obliged to remain with the officer) was held to be not significant or substantial.

It is important to stress, however, that the test for exclusion is not the seriousness of the breach *per se*, but the extent of any unfairness caused thereby (see **F2.15**). In *Ryan* [1992] Crim LR 187, it was argued that the judge's conclusion that there had been a major breach of the identification code (Code of Practice D) should have sufficed to exclude the evidence. Rejecting this argument, the Court of Appeal pointed out that there had been occasions when there had been quite serious breaches but, it being established that this had not caused unjust prejudice to the accused, the judge had quite properly allowed the evidence in. In *Hoyte* [1994] Crim LR 215 a confession was admitted, despite a failure to caution, on the basis that the police had acted in good faith and, in the circumstances, there could have been no unfairness under s. 78. See also *Law-Thompson* [1997] Crim LR 674 (confessions made by a mentally disordered accused in the absence of an appropriate adult).

In *Wright* [1994] Crim LR 55, evidence of a search was admitted notwithstanding that a record of the search had not been made in W's custody record (contrary to s. 18(8) of the 1984 Act) and that there were said to have been breaches of PACE Code B (no communication had been made with W, he was not present at the search and no proper list had been made of the property). Noting that there had been no deliberate breach of Code B, it was held that the judge had taken into account the breach of s. 18(8) and the other matters could not have placed W at any disadvantage. See also *Khan* [1997] Crim LR 508.

SECTION F3: BURDEN AND STANDARD OF PROOF AND PRESUMPTIONS

BURDEN OF PROOF

Legal and Evidential Burdens

F3.1   There are two principal kinds of burden, the legal burden and the evidential burden. The legal burden is a burden of proof, that is a burden imposed on a party to prove a fact or facts in issue. In some cases the legal burden in relation to some of the facts in issue will be on one party, and the legal burden in relation to another (or others) will be on the other party. For example, if insanity is raised by way of defence, the legal burden on that issue is on the defence, whereas the legal burden on the other facts in issue is on the prosecution (*M'Naghten's Case* (1843) 10 Cl & F 200; *Smith* (1910) 6 Cr App R 19). Questions of construction are questions of law in respect of which no burden lies on either party (*Scott* v *Martin* [1987] 1 WLR 841).

The legal burden is sometimes referred to as the persuasive burden or the risk of non-persuasion, phrases which indicate that a party bearing the legal burden on a fact in issue will lose on that issue if the burden is not discharged to the required standard of proof. The standard of proof required to discharge the legal burden varies according to whether the burden is borne by the prosecution or defence. If the legal burden is borne by the prosecution, the standard required is proof beyond reasonable doubt (*Woolmington* v *DPP* [1935] AC 462 – see further **F3.16**). If the legal burden is borne by the accused, the standard required is proof on a balance of probabilities (*Carr-Briant* [1943] KB 607); the accused never bears the heavier burden of proof beyond reasonable doubt – see further **F3.18**). The question whether a party has discharged a legal burden borne by him is decided by the tribunal of fact, whether jury or magistrates, at the end of the trial after all the evidence has been presented.

The evidential burden is not a burden of proof but the burden of adducing evidence or 'the duty of passing the judge', in other words the burden imposed on a party to adduce sufficient evidence on a fact or facts in issue to satisfy the judge that such issue or issues should be left before the tribunal of fact. In some cases, the evidential burden on some of the facts in issue will be on one party and the evidential burden on another (or others) will be on the other party. Very often a party bearing the legal burden on an issue also bears the evidential burden on that issue. However, in the case of many defences (including, for example, provocation and self-defence), the evidential burden in relation to the defence is on the accused and the legal burden in relation to the defence is on the prosecution. Thus, if the evidential burden is not discharged and there is insufficient evidence for that defence to be put before the jury, the issue will be withdrawn from the jury and nothing more will be heard of it; but if the evidential burden is discharged or, whether discharged or not, there is in any event sufficient evidence for that defence to be put before the jury, the legal burden of negativing or disproving that defence will be on the prosecution (see, e.g, *Lobell* [1957] 1 QB 547, and generally **F3.6** to **F3.12**). Although normally a judge will not leave a particular defence to the jury until the conclusion of the evidence, in rare cases in which the precise nature of the evidence to be called is clear it may be appropriate for the judge to indicate at an earlier stage what his ruling is likely to be (*Pommell* [1995] 2 Cr App R 607 at p. 612). If, during a trial, a judge indicates that he will leave a particular defence to the jury, but later changes his view, he should inform the defence, because they may then wish to give more evidence on the matter and defence counsel may wish to seek to persuade the judge not to withdraw the issue (*Wright* [1992] Crim LR 596).

If the evidential burden on a particular issue is borne by the prosecution, it is discharged by the adduction of sufficient evidence to justify as a possibility a finding by the tribunal of fact that the legal burden on the same issue has been discharged, in other words 'such evidence as, if believed and if left uncontradicted and unexplained, could be accepted by the jury as proof' (*Jayasena* v *The Queen* [1970] AC 618, per Lord Devlin at p. 624). If the prosecution bear both the evidential and legal burden on a particular issue and discharge the evidential burden, it does not necessarily follow that they will succeed on that issue – the issue in question will go before the jury for them to determine whether or not the legal burden has been discharged. However, if the prosecution bear both the legal and evidential burden on an issue and fail to discharge the evidential burden, they will necessarily fail on that issue, since the judge will withdraw that issue from the jury. Questions relating to the sufficiency of the evidence adduced by the prosecution may be raised by the judge of his own motion, but usually arise on a defence submission of no case to answer after the prosecution have closed their case. As to submissions of no case to answer more generally, see **D13.26** to **D13.31**.

If the accused bears both the evidential and the legal burden on a particular issue, for example insanity, the evidential burden is discharged by the adduction of such evidence as might satisfy the jury on the probability of that which the accused is called upon to establish (*Carr-Briant* [1943] KB 607, per Humphreys J at p. 612). If the accused bears the evidential but not the legal burden on a particular issue, for example self-defence, the evidential burden is discharged by the adduction of such evidence as 'might leave a jury in reasonable doubt' (*Bratty* v *A-G for Northern Ireland* [1963] AC 386, per Lord Morris at p. 419). In no case is the accused called upon to prove a fact beyond reasonable doubt: the standard of proof is proof on the balance of probabilities (*Carr-Briant*).

Incidence of Legal Burden: General Rule

The general rule is that the prosecution bear the legal burden of proving all the elements in **F3.2** the offence necessary to establish guilt (*Woolmington* v *DPP* [1935] AC 462). See also *Mancini* v *DPP* [1942] AC 1, per Lord Simon at p. 11. In *Woolmington*, W was charged with the murder of his wife, who had left him to return to her mother. He visited her with a sawn-off shotgun concealed under his coat, and when they met she was killed by a shot from the gun. W said that while attempting to induce his wife to return to him by threatening to kill himself, the gun went off accidentally. Swift J directed the jury that, once it was proved that W shot his wife, W bore the burden of disproving malice aforethought. The House of Lords held this to be a misdirection. Viscount Sankey LC said, at pp. 481–2:

> But while the prosecution must prove the guilt of the prisoner, there is no such burden laid on the prisoner to prove his innocence and it is sufficient for him to raise a doubt as to his guilt; he is not bound to satisfy the jury of his innocence. . . .
> Throughout the web of the English criminal law one golden thread is always to be seen, that it is the duty of the prosecution to prove the prisoner's guilt subject to what I have already said as to the defence of insanity and subject also to any statutory exception. . . . No matter what the charge or where the trial, the principle that the prosecution must prove the guilt of the prisoner is part of the common law of England and no attempt to whittle it down can be entertained. . . . It is not the law of England to say, as was said in the summing-up in the present case: 'if the Crown satisfy you that this woman died at the prisoner's hands then he has to show that there are circumstances to be found in the evidence which has been given from the witness-box in this case which alleviate the crime so that it is only manslaughter or which excuse the homicide altogether by showing it was a pure accident'.

The prosecution bear the burden of proving all the elements in the offence, even if this involves proving negative averments. Thus, in a case of rape the prosecution bear the burden of proving that the complainant did not consent (*Horn* (1912) 7 Cr App R 200). Similarly, the prosecution bear the burden of proving absence of consent on a charge of assault (*Donovan* [1934] 2 KB 498). On a charge of obtaining property by deception, the prosecution bear the burden of proving the falsity of the statement, even if that involves proving a negative (*Mandry* [1973] 1 WLR 1232, in which the statement, made by street traders selling scent for £1, was 'You can go down the road and buy it for two guineas in the big stores'). *Mandry* also illustrates that there is a limit to what can reasonably be required of the prosecution when seeking to prove a negative. A constable gave evidence that he had visited four shops in the area and that the scent was not sold at any of them. In cross-examination, he admitted that he had not visited a well-known department store. The judge directed the jury that the police could not be expected to visit every shop in London in order to prove that the scent was not being sold for two guineas in any shop; and that if the accused knew of any shop where it could be bought at that price, they were perfectly entitled to adduce such evidence. The Court of Appeal held that no criticism could be made of this direction. In many cases, however, because of the difficulties of proving a negative proposition, statute may, exceptionally, require the accused to bear the burden of proving certain facts (see **F3.4** and **F3.5**).

There are only three categories of exception to the general rule as laid down in *Woolmington* v *DPP* [1935] AC 462:

    (a)   insanity;
    (b)   express statutory exceptions; and
    (c)   implied statutory exceptions.

F3.3   ***Exception in Case of Defence of Insanity***   If the accused raises the defence of insanity, he will bear the burden of proving it (on a balance of probabilities) (*M 'Naghten's Case* (1843) 10 Cl & F 200; *Smith* (1910) 6 Cr App R 19; *Sodeman* v *The King* [1936] 2 All ER 1138). Under the Criminal Procedure (Insanity) Act 1964, s. 6, if the accused is charged with murder and raises one of two issues, either insanity or diminished responsibility, the court shall allow the prosecution to adduce evidence tending to prove the other of those issues. The burden on the prosecution will be to prove the other of those issues beyond reasonable doubt (*Grant* [1960] Crim LR 424, per Paul J).

Criminal Procedure (Insanity) Act 1964, s. 6

Where on a trial for murder the accused contends —
    (a)   that at the time of the alleged offence he was insane so as not to be responsible according to law for his actions; or
    (b)   that at that time he was suffering from such abnormality of mind as is specified in subsection (1) of section 2 of the Homicide Act 1957 (diminished responsibility),
the court shall allow the prosecution to adduce or elicit evidence tending to prove the other of those contentions, and may give directions as to the stage of the proceedings at which the prosecution may adduce such evidence.

If an accused is alleged to be under a disability rendering him unfit to plead and stand trial on indictment, the issue may be raised by either the prosecution or defence (see the Criminal Procedure (Insanity) Act 1964, s. 4, and generally **D10.5** to **D10.10**). If the prosecution contend that the accused is under such a disability and this is disputed by the defence, the burden of proof is on the prosecution to satisfy the jury beyond reasonable doubt (*Robertson* [1968] 1 WLR 1767). If the defence contend that the accused is under such a disability, the burden is on the defence to satisfy the jury on a balance of probabilities (*Podola* [1960] 1 QB 325).

F3.4   ***Express Statutory Exceptions***   Statute may expressly cast on the accused the burden of proving a particular issue or issues. The legal burden in relation to all other issues in such cases will remain on the prosecution, in accordance with the general rule as laid down in *Woolmington* v *DPP* [1935] AC 462. All of the following statutory provisions put the burden of proving certain specified matters on the accused (emphasis supplied throughout).

Prevention of Corruption Act 1916, s. 2

Where in any proceedings against a person for an offence under the Prevention of Corruption Act 1906, or the Public Bodies Corrupt Practices Act 1889, it is proved that any money, gift, or other consideration has been paid or given to or received by a person in the employment of His Majesty or any Government Department or a public body by or from a person, or agent of a person, holding or seeking to obtain a contract from His Majesty or any Government Department or public body, the money, gift, or consideration shall be deemed to have been paid or given and received corruptly as such inducement or reward as is mentioned in such Act *unless the contrary is proved.*

Where corruption is presumed under s. 2, the onus is on the accused to prove on a balance of probabilities that a payment was not corrupt (*Carr-Briant* [1943] KB 607).

Criminal Justice Act 1925, s. 47

. . . on a charge against a wife for any offence other than treason or murder *it shall be a good defence to prove* that the offence was committed in the presence of and under the coercion of, the husband.

Prevention of Crime Act 1953, s. 1

(1) Any person who without lawful authority or reasonable excuse, *the proof whereof shall lie on him*, has with him in any public place any offensive weapon shall be guilty of an offence . . .

In the case of an offensive weapon *per se*, the prosecution are not required to prove that the accused had it with him with the intention of using it to cause injury to the person; if possession in a public place is proved, the onus is on the accused to prove on a balance of probabilities lawful authority or reasonable excuse for the possession (*Davis* v *Alexander* (1970) 54 Cr App R 398). In the case of an article not made or adapted for use for causing injury to the person, the onus is on the prosecution to prove that the accused carried it with the intention of using it to injure; and if the jury are satisfied as to this, and the issue of lawful authority or reasonable excuse has been raised, the onus is on the accused to prove on a balance of probabilities such authority or excuse (*Petrie* [1961] 1 WLR 358; *Brown* (1971) 55 Cr App R 478).

Sexual Offences Act 1956, s. 30

(2) For the purposes of this section [man living on earnings of prostitution] a man who lives with or is habitually in the company of a prostitute, or who exercises control, direction or influence over a prostitute's movements in a way which shows he is aiding, abetting or compelling her prostitution with others, shall be presumed to be knowingly living on the earnings of prostitution, *unless he proves the contrary.*

Once the presumption arises under s. 30(2), the onus is on the accused to disprove (a) that he is living on immoral earnings, *and* (b) that he is doing so knowingly (*Clarke* [1976] 2 All ER 696).

Sexual Offences Act 1956, s. 47

Where in any of the foregoing sections the description of an offence is expressed to be subject to exceptions mentioned in the section, *proof of the exception is to lie on the person relying on it.*

Homicide Act 1957, s. 2

(2) On a charge of murder, *it shall be for the defence to prove* that the person charged is by virtue of this section [persons suffering from diminished responsibility] not liable to be convicted of murder.

Where the defence of diminished responsibility is raised, the onus is on the defence to prove it on a balance of probabilities (*Dunbar* [1958] 1 QB 1; *Grant* [1960] Crim LR 424). Section 2(2) leaves it to the defence to decide whether the issue of diminished responsibility should be raised; if, therefore, the judge detects evidence of diminished responsibility but the defence do not raise the issue, the judge is not bound to direct the jury to consider the matter, but, at most, should in the absence of the jury draw the matter to the attention of the defence so that they may decide whether they wish the issue to be considered by the jury (*Campbell* (1986) 84 Cr App R 255, per Lord Lane CJ, *obiter*).

Homicide Act 1957, s. 4

(2)   Where it is shown that a person charged with the murder of another killed the other or was a party to his . . . being killed, *it shall be for the defence to prove* that the person charged was acting in pursuance of a suicide pact between him and the other.

Vehicle Excise and Registration Act 1994, s. 53

Where in any proceedings for an offence under section 29, 34, 37 or 45 any question arises as to—
   (a)   the number of vehicles used,
   (b)   the character, weight or cylinder capacity of a vehicle,
   (c)   the seating capacity of a vehicle, or
   (d)   the purpose for which a vehicle has been used,
the burden of proof in respect of the matter lies on the accused.

Misuse of Drugs Act 1971, s. 28

(2)   Subject to subsection (3) below, in any proceedings for an offence to which this section applies [offences under s. 4(2) and (3), s. 5(2) and (3), s. 6(2) and s. 9 of the Act] *it shall be a defence for the accused to prove* that he neither knew of nor suspected nor had reason to suspect the existence of some fact alleged by the prosecution which it is necessary for the prosecution to prove if he is to be convicted of the offence charged.

On a charge of cultivating any plant of the genus *cannabis* contrary to s. 6(2) of the 1971 Act, the onus is on the accused to prove that he did not know that the drug he was cultivating was a plant of the genus *cannabis* (*Champ* (1981) 73 Cr App R 367). However, on a charge of possession of a controlled drug contrary to s. 5(2) of the Act, the onus is on the prosecution to prove that the accused had knowledge of the presence of an article alleged to contain the drug, since proof of such knowledge is an essential prerequisite to proof of its unlawful possession (*Ashton-Rickardt* [1978] 1 WLR 37). See also *McNamara* (1988) 87 Cr App R 246. Under s. 28(3) of the 1971 Act, where in any proceedings for an offence to which the section applies it is necessary, if the accused is to be convicted of the offence charged, for the prosecution to prove that some substance or product was the controlled drug which the prosecution allege, and that is proved, the accused *shall be acquitted if he proves* that he neither believed nor suspected nor had reason to suspect that the substance or product in question was a controlled drug. Thus once the prosecution have proved possession and that the substance in question is the controlled drug alleged, the onus, under s. 28(3), is on the accused (*Rautamaki* [1993] Crim LR 691).

Criminal Justice Act 1988, s. 139

(4)   *It shall be a defence for a person charged* with an offence under this section (having any article which has a blade, or is sharply pointed, in a public place) *to prove* that he had good reason or lawful authority for having the article with him in a public place.

Once the prosecution has discharged the burden of proving the ingredients of the offence, the onus, under s. 139(4), is on the accused (*Godwin* v *DPP* (1992) 96 Cr App R 244).

Implied Statutory Exceptions A statute can place the legal burden of proof on the **F3.5** accused not only expressly but also by implication, i.e. on its true construction. In summary trials, the matter is governed by the MCA 1980, s. 101. Concerning trials on indictment, the leading authorities are *Edwards* [1975] QB 27 and *Hunt* [1987] AC 352; in the latter it was made clear that when, in *Woolmington* v *DPP* [1935] AC 462, Viscount Sankey LC referred to 'any statutory exception' (see **F3.2**), he was referring to statutory exceptions in which Parliament had placed the burden of proof on the accused *either* expressly *or* by implication (per Lords Griffiths and Ackner).

Magistrates' Courts Act 1980, s. 101

Where the defendant to an information or complaint relies for his defence on any exception, exemption, proviso, excuse or qualification, whether or not it accompanies the description of the offence or matter of complaint in the enactment creating the offence or on which the complaint is founded, the burden of proving the exception, exemption, proviso, excuse or qualification shall be on him; and this notwithstanding that the information or complaint contains an allegation negativing the exception, exemption, proviso, excuse or qualification.

Concerning the construction of s. 101, the following matters of general importance should be noted:

(a) On its wording, s. 101 applies to summary trials. However, it is now established that where a statute, on its true construction, places the legal burden of proof on an accused, the burden is on the accused whether the case be tried summarily or on indictment; s. 101 reflects and applies to summary trials the common-law rule relating to the incidence of the burden of proof evolved by judges on trials on indictment (*Hunt* [1987] AC 352).

(b) The section applies where the words of exception etc. amount to a defence.

(c) In *Nimmo* v *Alexander Cowan & Sons Ltd* [1968] AC 107, Lord Pearson gave the following *obiter* guidance (at p. 135) as to the construction of the Scottish equivalent of s. 101. An exemption, exception or proviso is easily recognisable from the wording of the enactment – an exception would naturally begin with the word 'except' and a proviso with the words 'Provided always that'. The addition of the words 'excuse' and 'qualification' showed an intention to widen the provision. There is no usual formula for an 'excuse'. A 'qualification', if understood in a grammatical sense, might cover any adjective, adverb or adjectival or adverbial phrase. More probably it means some qualification, such as a licence, for doing what would otherwise be unlawful. There is no usual formula for 'qualification' in that sense. The court should look at the substance and effect of the enactment in question, as well as its form, in order to ascertain whether it contains an 'excuse or qualification'.

In a case of driving without a licence, it is for the accused driver to prove that he has a current driving licence (*John* v *Humphreys* [1955] 1 WLR 325). Similarly, in cases of driving without insurance, it is for the accused driver to prove that he is insured (*Williams* v *Russell* (1933) 149 LT 190; *Philcox* v *Carberry* [1960] Crim LR 563). In *Gatland* v *Metropolitan Police Commissioner* [1968] 2 QB 279, the accused had left a skip on the road with which a car had collided. They were charged with an offence under the Highways Act 1959, s. 140(1), which provided that 'if a person, without lawful authority or excuse, deposits anything whatsoever on a highway in consequence whereof a user of the highway is injured or endangered, that person shall be guilty of an offence'. The Divisional Court held that it was for the prosecution to prove that a thing had been deposited on the highway and that in consequence a user of the highway had been injured or endangered; but that it was for the accused to prove lawful authority or excuse. Contrast, *Westminster City Council* v *Croyalgrange* [1986] 1 WLR 674.

Nimmo v *Alexander Cowan & Sons Ltd* [1968] AC 107 was a Scottish civil action brought by a workman under the Factories Act 1961, s. 29(1). Section 29(1) provides that every place at which any person has at any time to work 'shall, so far as is reasonably practicable, be made and kept safe for any person working there'. The question before the House of Lords was whether the burden of proving that it was not reasonably practicable to make the working place safe lay on the defendant or the plaintiff. The same question could have arisen in a criminal action: s. 155(1) of the 1961 Act makes a breach of s. 29(1) a summary offence. Both Lord Pearson (at p. 134) and Lord Reid (at p. 115) observed that the incidence of the burden of proof would be the same whether the proceedings were civil or criminal. The House divided on the construction of the section. The majority, Lords Guest, Upjohn and Pearson, held that it was for the plaintiff (or prosecution) to prove that the working place was not safe, and for the defendant (or accused) to excuse himself by proving that it was not reasonably practicable to make it safe. The minority, Lords Reid and Wilberforce, held that it was for the plaintiff (or prosecution) to prove that it was reasonably practicable to make the working place safe. Their lordships were in agreement, however, that if the linguistic construction of a statute does not clearly indicate on whom the burden should lie, the court should look to other considerations to determine the intention of Parliament, such as the mischief at which the Act was aimed and the ease or difficulty that the respective parties would encounter in discharging the burden.

The MCA 1980, s. 101, sets out in statutory form the common-law rule which applies to trials on indictment. This was established in *Edwards* (1975) QB 27. Prior to *Edwards* there was a rule of statutory interpretation that 'if a negative averment be made by one party which is peculiarly within the knowledge of the other, the party within whose knowledge it lies, and who asserts the affirmative, is to prove it and not he who asserts the negative' (*Turner* (1816) 5 M & S 206, per Bayley J at p. 211). This approach was followed in *Oliver* [1944] KB 68, a case of dealing in sugar without a licence, permit or other authority granted by the Ministry of Food, contrary to the Defence Regulations 1939, and *Ewens* [1967] 1 QB 322, a case of possessing drugs without the issue of a prescription by a duly qualified medical practitioner, contrary to the Drugs (Prevention of Misuse) Act 1964.

In *Edwards* [1975] QB 27, the accused was convicted on indictment of selling intoxicating liquor without a licence, contrary to the Licensing Act 1964, s. 160(1)(a). He appealed on the ground that the prosecution had failed to adduce any evidence to show that he was not the holder of a licence. It was submitted that at common law the burden of proving an exception, exemption and the like is borne by the accused only if the facts constituting such exception or exemption are peculiarly within the accused's own knowledge which, in the instant case, they were not, because the police had access to the public register of local licences. The Court of Appeal, dismissing the appeal, held that it was for the accused to prove that he was the holder of a licence. Referring to the common-law exception to the fundamental rule that the prosecution must prove every element of the offence charged, Lawton LJ said, at p. 40:

> It is limited to offences arising under enactments which prohibit the doing of an act save in specified circumstances or by persons of specified classes or with specified qualifications or with the licence or permission of specified authorities. Whenever the prosecution seeks to rely on this exception, the court must construe the enactment under which the charge is laid. If the true construction is that the enactment prohibits the doing of acts, subject to provisos, exemptions and the like, then the prosecution can rely upon the exception.

> In our judgment its application does not depend upon either the fact, or the presumption, that the defendant has peculiar knowledge enabling him to prove the positive of any negative averment.

In *Hunt* [1987] AC 352, the House of Lords held that:

(a)   *Edwards* was decided correctly, subject to one qualification. The formula given by Lawton LJ was 'a helpful approach' and 'an excellent guide to construction' but was not intended to be, and is not, exclusive in its effect – on rare occasions a statute will be construed as imposing the legal burden on the accused although outside the ambit of the formula (see the speech of Lord Griffiths, with which Lords Keith and Mackay agreed, at p. 365 and that of Lord Ackner at p. 379).

(b)   In the final analysis each case must turn on the construction of the particular legislation to determine whether the defence is an exception within the meaning of the MCA 1980, s. 101, which reflects the rule for trials on indictment (per Lord Griffiths at p. 375).

(c)   In construing an enactment in order to ascertain where the burden of proof lies, the court is not restricted to the form or wording of the statutory provision but is entitled to have regard to matters of policy. The court must look at the substance and effect of the enactment and practical considerations affecting the burden of proof, particularly the ease or difficulty that the respective parties would encounter in discharging the burden (per Lord Griffiths at p. 375 and per Lord Ackner at pp. 380 and 382). However, Parliament can never lightly be taken to have intended to impose an onerous duty on an accused to prove his innocence in a criminal case, and a court should be very slow to draw any such inference from the language of a statute (per Lord Griffiths at p. 374).

In *Hunt* [1987] AC 352, the appellant was found to be in possession of a powder containing morphine mixed with two other substances which were not controlled drugs. He was convicted of the unlawful possession of morphine, contrary to the Misuse of Drugs Act 1971, s. 5(2). Under the Misuse of Drugs Regulations 1973, sch. 1, para. 3, any preparation of morphine containing not more that 0.2 per cent of morphine compounded with other ingredients was excepted from the prohibition on possession contained in s. 5 of the 1971 Act. The question, on appeal, was whether it was for the prosecution to prove that the accused did not come within the exception contained in para. 3, or for the accused to prove that he did come within it. Quashing the conviction, the House of Lords held that:

(a)   The case did not come within the formula, laid down by Lawton LJ in *Edwards* [1975] QB 27, as to when the legal burden is on the accused.

(b)   On the true construction of the provisions, it was for the prosecution to prove not only that the powder contained morphine, but also that it was not morphine in the form permitted by para. 3. This would not place an undue burden on the prosecution. In the normal case the substance in question would be analysed for the police, and there would be no difficulty in producing evidence to show that it did not fall within sch. 1 to the 1973 Regulations. However, if the burden were to be placed on the accused, he would be faced with very real difficulties in discharging it, because the suspected substance is usually seized by the police and there is no statutory provision entitling the accused to a portion of it. Often there is very little of the substance, and it may have been destroyed in the process of analysis on behalf of the prosecution.

(c)   Since the question of construction was obviously one of real difficulty, regard should be had to the fact that offences involving the misuse of hard drugs are among the most serious in the criminal calendar, and in these circumstances any ambiguity should be resolved in favour of the accused by placing the burden of proving the nature of the substance involved on the prosecution.

The ruling in *Hunt* that regard may be had to the ease or otherwise that the respective parties will encounter if required to discharge the legal burden, gives an added validity, it is submitted, to a number of cases decided prior to *Edwards* [1975] QB 27 and difficult to reconcile with it. An example is *Curgerwen* (1865) LR 1 CCR 1. The OAPA 1861, s. 57, after defining bigamy, sets out a proviso against its extension 'to any second marriage contracted elsewhere than in England and Ireland by any other than a subject of Her Majesty, or to any person marrying a second time whose husband or wife shall have been continually absent from such person for the space of seven years then last past, and shall not have been known by such person to be living within that time'. Although in *Audley* [1907] 1 KB 383 it was held that it is for the *accused* to prove that he is 'other than a subject of Her Majesty', in *Curgerwen* it was held that it is for the *prosecution* to prove that the accused knew the first spouse to be living within the seven-year period. The latter decision may be justified on the grounds that it would be an undue burden for the accused to prove the negative, i.e. that he did not know the first spouse to be living within that period. See also *Putland* [1946] 1 All ER 85, a case of acquiring rationed goods without surrendering clothing coupons, in which it was held that it was for the prosecution to prove that coupons were not surrendered. The justification for this decision is the utmost difficulty that the accused might encounter in establishing that he had given the appropriate number of coupons for the goods (cf. *Hunt* [1987] AC 352, per Lord Griffiths at p. 375).

Incidence of the Evidential Burden: General Rule

F3.6 Generally speaking, a party bearing the legal burden on a particular issue will also bear the evidential burden on that issue. Thus, as a general rule, the prosecution bear both the legal and evidential burden in relation to all the elements in the offence necessary to establish guilt; and where the defence bear the legal burden of proving insanity or, by virtue of an express or implied statutory exception, some other issue, they will also bear the evidential burden in that regard (although, concerning insanity, in rare and exceptional cases the judge may of his own motion raise the issue and leave it to the jury: *Thomas* [1995] Crim LR 314). In relation to numerous common-law and statutory defences, however, the evidential burden is on the defence, and, if it is discharged so that the defence in question is put before the jury, the legal burden is then on the prosecution to disprove such defence. Although it is said in these cases that the evidential burden is on the defence, that burden will be discharged *whenever* there is sufficient evidence in relation to the defence to leave it to the jury; the evidence may be adduced by the defence (or elicited by them in cross-examination), *or* it may be given by a prosecution witness (or a co-accused) giving his evidence in chief *or* it may be given in any other way (*Bullard* v *The Queen* [1957] AC 635). Where such a defence arises upon the evidence called by any party, then whether or not it has been mentioned by the defence, the judge must leave it to the jury (*Palmer* v *The Queen* [1971] AC 814 at p. 823). See also *Bonnick* (1978) 66 Cr App R 266, *Hopper* [1915] 2 KB 431 at p. 435 and *DPP (Jamaica)* v *Bailey* [1995] 1 Cr App R 257; and *cf Groark* [1999] Crim LR 669, considered at **F3.11**. If there is no evidence to support the defence upon which an accused seeks to rely, the judge is entitled to withdraw the case from the jury (see *Hill* (1988) 89 Cr App R 74 and *Pommell* [1995] 2 Cr App R 607). However it has been said that even if there is no evidence in support of a defence and it is not raised by defence counsel (perhaps for tactical reasons), if there is a reasonable possibility on one interpretation of the evidence adduced that the accused may have that defence, the judge should put it to the jury (*Watson* [1992] Crim LR 434). The defences to which the foregoing principles relate are as follows.

F3.7 ***Provocation*** A judge is under no duty to put before the jury strained and implausible inferences for the purpose of creating a defence of provocation for which, in truth, there is no basis (*Walch* [1993] Crim LR 714; see also *Wellington* [1993] Crim LR 616). The judge is required to leave the defence to the jury only if there is some evidence, from whatever source, suggestive of the reasonable possibility that the accused might have lost his self-control due to provoking words or conduct, because without some evidence of the specific nature of the provocation, the jury cannot decide either the subjective or the objective condition under the Homicide Act 1957, s. 3. If there is no such evidence, but merely the speculative possibility of an act of provocation, the issue does not arise, and suggestions in cross-examination cannot by themselves raise the issue (*Acott* [1997] 1 WLR 306; cf. *Stewart* [1995] 4 All ER 999). If there is sufficient evidence of provocation, whether called by the Crown or the defence, the issue should be put before the jury and the prosecution bear the burden of disproving it beyond reasonable doubt (*Mancini* v *DPP* [1942] AC 1; *Cascoe* [1970] 2 All ER 833; *McPherson* (1957) 41 Cr App R 213). In *Hopper* [1915] 2 KB 431, it was held that provocation should have been left to the jury in a murder trial at which the defence had been accident. See also *Rossiter* [1994] 2 All ER 752 in which the issue of provocation was not raised by the defence, the accused maintaining that she was defending herself. It was held that whenever there is material, on a charge of murder, which is capable of amounting to provocation, however tenuous it may be, the judge should leave that issue to the jury. This principle applies even if the defence do not rely on provocation but rely instead on accident (*Dhillon* [1997] 2 Cr App R 104) or maintain that the accused was not at the scene of the crime or that he was there but that the crime was committed by someone else (*Cambridge* [1994] 1 WLR 971, also explaining that the word 'tenuous', as used in *Rossiter*, described the provocative acts and words, not the evidence of their existence). The principle also applies even if the defence have conveyed to the judge that in their opinion the issue should *not* be left to the jury (*Burgess* [1995] Crim LR 425). However, it is most unsatisfactory that where the defence do not rely on provocation at the trial, the judge's failure to direct the jury on it can found an appeal against conviction. For this reason, in *Cox* [1995] 2 Cr App R 513 it was held that if it appears to *either* counsel that there is evidence on which the jury could find provocation, they should regard it as their duty to point it out to the judge before he sums up. There are compelling grounds, it is submitted, for extending this duty so that it applies in relation to other defences, and not just provocation.

Self-defence   In *Lobell* [1957] 1 QB 547 the appellant was convicted of wounding with   **F3.8**
intent to cause grievous bodily harm. There was some evidence to support his defence of self-defence. The trial judge directed the jury that it was for the defence to establish that plea to their satisfaction. The conviction was quashed on the grounds that this was a misdirection. Although the prosecution are not obliged to give evidence in chief to rebut a suggestion of self-defence before the issue is raised, once there is sufficient evidence to leave the issue before the jury, it is for the prosecution to disprove it beyond reasonable doubt. In *Wheeler* [1967] 3 All ER 829, Winn LJ said (at p. 830) that wherever there has been a killing or the infliction of violence not proving fatal, in circumstances in which the accused puts forward a justification such as self-defence, it is quite essential that the jury should understand that the issue is not properly to be regarded as a defence; and where the judge does slip into the error of referring to such justification as a defence, it is particulary important that he should use language which suffices to make it clear to the jury that it is not a defence in respect of which any onus rests upon the accused, but a matter which the prosecution must disprove as an essential part of their case before a verdict of guilty is justified. See also *Abraham* [1973] 1 WLR 1270, at p. 1273. There may be evidence of self-defence even if the defence of the accused is one of alibi. In *Bonnick* (1978) 66 Cr App R 266, a case of stabbing in which the defence was one of alibi, it was held, rejecting the contention that the evidence of the Crown witnesses had raised the issue of self-defence, that the question whether there was sufficient evidence to leave an issue before the jury was a question for the trial judge to answer by applying common sense to the evidence; but when there was sufficient evidence to raise a prima facie case, the issue should be left to the jury.

Duress   The Crown are not called upon to anticipate a defence of duress and destroy   **F3.9**
it in advance, but if the accused places before the court such material as makes duress a live issue, fit and proper to be left to the jury, it is for the Crown to destroy that defence in such a manner as to leave in the jury's mind no reasonable doubt that the accused cannot be absolved on the grounds of the alleged compulsion (*Gill* [1963] 1 WLR 841, per Edmund Davies J at p. 846). See also *Bone* [1968] 1 WLR 983, per Lord Parker CJ at p. 985. As to duress of circumstances, see also *Pommell* [1995] 2 Cr App R 607.

F3.10 ***Non-insane Automatism*** Although the onus is on the defence to prove insanity on a balance of probabilities, where there is evidence on which a jury could find automatism not due to a disease of the mind, the onus is on the prosecution to disprove such automatism beyond reasonable doubt: the *obiter* view of the majority in *Bratty v A-G for Northern Ireland* [1963] AC 386. See also *Stripp* (1978) 69 Cr App R 318 and *Pullen* [1991] Crim LR 457. Where the defence of automatism is raised by an accused, two questions fall to be decided by the judge before the defence can be left to the jury: (1) whether a proper evidential foundation for the defence has been laid and (2) whether the evidence shows the case to be one of insane automatism, i.e. a case which falls within the M'Naghten Rules, or one of non-insane automatism. If the judge rules that the case is one of insanity, the jury then has to decide, on the basis of the judge's direction, whether the accused is guilty or not guilty by reason of insanity (*Burgess* [1991] 1 QB 92). Where the issues of both insanity and non-insane automatism arise in the same case, the judge should distinguish between them in his summing-up and explain that, whereas it is for the defence to prove insanity, it is not for them to prove automatism; it is for the prosecution to negative it once the defence lay a foundation for it (*Burns* (1973) 58 Cr App R 364, per Stephenson LJ at p. 374).

F3.11 ***Drunkenness*** Insofar as drunkenness may constitute a defence, once there is evidence before the court to support it, the onus of disproof rests on the prosecution (*Kennedy v HM Advocate* 1944 JC 171; *Foote* [1964] Crim LR 405). However, in *Groark* [1999] Crim LR 669 it was held that if, in a case of wounding with intent, there is evidence of drunkenness which might give rise to the issue whether the accused did form the specific intent, but the defence is that the accused knew what was happening but acted in self-defence, defence counsel is not obliged to seek a direction on self-induced intoxication in relation to intent; the judge may ask him if he has any objection to such a direction and, if he does object, then the direction need not be given.

F3.12 ***Alibi*** Although there is no general rule of law that in every case where alibi is raised the judge must specifically direct the jury, quite apart from the general direction on burden and standard of proof, that it is for the prosecution to negative the alibi, it is the clear duty of the judge to give such a direction if there is a danger of the jury thinking that an alibi, because it is called a defence, raises some burden on the defence to establish it (*Wood (No. 2)* (1967) 52 Cr App R 74 per Lord Parker CJ). It is a common and good *practice* to give such a specific and additional direction in any event (*Preece* (1992) 96 Cr App R 264); and ideally it should be given (*Anderson* [1991] Crim LR 361; *Johnson* [1995] Crim LR 242). In *Mussell* [1995] Crim LR 887, it was held that a special direction is necessary if the nature of the alibi is that the accused was at a specific place elsewhere, raising the question why he did not call witnesses in support, but is unnecessary if the evidence amounts to little more than a denial that he committed the crime.

F3.13 ***Mistaken Belief in Consent*** If there is evidence before the court in a rape case that the accused mistakenly believed that the complainant had consented, the onus of disproof lies on the prosecution (*Thomas* (1983) 77 Cr App R 63; *Gardiner* [1994] Crim LR 455).

F3.14 ***Statutory Defences*** The principles set out above also apply in relation to a variety of statutory defences. Thus where an accused puts forward an explanation for his conduct based on the Criminal Law Act 1967, s. 3 (lawful intervention), the jury should be clearly directed that it is for the Crown to destroy the validity of such an explanation and that it is not for the accused to establish it (see *Cameron* [1973] Crim LR 520 and *Khan* [1995] Crim LR 78). See also *Spight* [1986] Crim LR 817: on a charge of procuring the commission by a man of an act of gross indecency contrary to the Sexual Offences Act 1956, s. 13, in which the accused seeks to rely upon the Sexual Offences Act 1967, s. 1(1) (a homosexual act in private shall not be an offence provided that the parties consent thereto and have attained the age of 18 years), there is an evidential burden on the accused to raise the defence of privacy, consent and exempted age; and once the defence is raised, the burden is on the Crown to negative it. Section 1(6) of the Sexual Offences Act 1967 declares that, where it is charged that a homosexual act is an offence, the prosecutor shall have the burden of proving that the act was done otherwise than in private or otherwise than with the consent of the parties, or that any of the parties had not attained the age of 18 years (see **B3.68**).

STANDARD OF PROOF

General Rule

The standard of proof means the degree to which proof must be established by a party **F3.15** bearing a burden of proof. The standard required of the prosecution before the tribunal of fact can find the accused guilty is proof beyond reasonable doubt. Where the legal burden on a particular issue is borne by the accused, the standard required of the defence before the tribunal of fact can find in favour of the accused on that issue is proof on a balance of probabilities. These subjects call for discrete analysis.

Usual Direction Where Legal Burden on Prosecution

It is the duty of the judge in the summing-up to make it clear to the jury what standard **F3.16** of proof the prosecution are required to meet. However, it is not a matter of some precise formula or particular form of words being used (*Allan* [1969] 1 WLR 33, per Fenton Atkinson LJ at p. 36).

> It is not the particular formula that matters: it is the effect of the summing-up. If the jury are made to understand that they have to be satisfied and must not return a verdict against a defendant unless they feel sure, and that the onus is all the time on the prosecution and not on the defence, then whether the judge uses one form of language or another is neither here nor there. (*Kritz* [1950] 1 KB 82, per Lord Goddard CJ at p. 89, *obiter*, but cited with approval in *Walters* v *The Queen* [1969] 2 AC 26.)

However, though the law requires no particular formula, judges are wise, as a general rule, to adopt one; the time-honoured formula is that the jury must be satisfied beyond reasonable doubt (*Ferguson* v *The Queen* [1979] 1 WLR 94 per Lord Scarman). This phrase has been approved by the House of Lords (*Woolmington* v *DPP* [1935] AC 462; *Mancini* v *DPP* [1942] AC 1).

Another well-established formulation of the standard is to direct the jury that in order to find the accused guilty they must be 'sure' or 'satisfied so that they feel sure' (*Kritz* [1950] 1 KB 82, per Lord Goddard CJ at pp. 89–90, approved in *Walters* v *The Queen* [1969] 2 AC 26; and *Summers* [1952] 1 All ER 1059 at p. 1060). Directions using the phrases 'reasonably sure', 'pretty sure' and 'pretty certain' have all been disapproved (see *Head* (1961) 45 Cr App R 225, *Woods* [1961] Crim LR 324, and *Law* [1961] Crim LR 52 respectively). It is inadequate merely to direct the jury that they must be 'satisfied' without any indication of the degree of satisfaction required (*Hepworth* [1955] 2 QB 600; and *Allan* [1969] 1 WLR 33, per Fenton Atkinson LJ). It is proper to direct that 'You, the jury, must be completely satisfied' or 'You must feel sure of the prisoner's guilt' (*Hepworth* [1955] 2 QB 600, per Lord Goddard CJ at p. 603). It is generally sufficient and safe to combine the two classic formulations of the standard and direct that 'You must be satisfied beyond reasonable doubt so that you feel sure of the defendant's guilt' (*Ferguson* v *The Queen* [1979] 1 WLR 94, per Lord Scarman at p. 99).

In *McGreevy* v *DPP* [1973] 1 WLR 276, it was argued on the basis of *Hodge* (1838) 2 Lew CC 227, that if the case against the accused depends wholly or substantially on circumstantial evidence, the judge should direct the jury that not only must they be satisfied that the circumstances are consistent with the accused having committed the offence, but also they must be satisfied that the circumstances are inconsistent with any other rational conclusion than that the accused is the guilty person. The House of Lords held that there is no rule of law requiring such a direction. It suffices, in such a case, to give the usual direction that they, the jury, must be satisfied of the guilt of the accused beyond reasonable doubt.

Cases Requiring Explanation of Usual Direction

F3.17 Judges have used a variety of expressions with a view to explaining to the jury the meaning of 'reasonable doubt', some of which have suggested too low a standard of proof and resulted in a conviction being quashed. For example, in *Gray* (1973) 58 Cr App R 177 the trial judge defined a reasonable doubt as 'a doubt based upon good reason and not a fanciful doubt' and as 'the sort of doubt which might affect you in the conduct of your everyday affairs'. The Court of Appeal, quashing the conviction, held that if the judge had referred to the sort of doubt which may affect the mind of a person in the conduct of important affairs, there could have been no criticism, but the reference to everyday affairs might have suggested too low a standard. See also *Stafford* (1968) 53 Cr App R 1, in which Edmund Davies LJ said (at p. 2): 'We do not . . . agree with the trial judge when, directing the jury upon the standard of proof he told them to "Remember that a reasonable doubt is one for which you could give reasons if you were asked", and we dislike such a description or definition.' It was against a background of cases of this kind that in *Ching* (1976) 63 Cr App R 7 Lawton LJ, delivering the judgment of the Court, said (at p. 11): 'We point out and emphasise that if judges stopped trying to define that which is almost impossible to define there would be fewer appeals. We hope that there will not be any more for some considerable time.' Earlier, his lordship said (at p. 10):

> . . . in most cases . . . judges would be well advised not to attempt any gloss upon what is meant by 'sure' or what is meant by 'reasonable doubt'. In the last two decades there have been numerous cases before this court, some of which have been successful, some of which have not, which have come here because judges have thought it helpful to a jury to comment on what the standard of proof is. Experience in this court has shown that such comments usually create difficulties. They are more likely to confuse than help. But the exceptional case does sometimes arise.

Ching itself illustrates the kind of exceptional case in which a judge should explain to a jury what is meant by reasonable doubt. In that case the judge, in his summing-up, had directed the jury on the standard of proof by using the two classic formulations, 'sure' and 'beyond reasonable doubt', and had explained that these were two ways of saying the same thing. After retirement the jury returned to court, and the judge understood the foreman to ask for a further direction on the standard of proof. The judge said:

> A reasonable doubt . . . is a doubt to which you can give a reason as opposed to a mere fanciful sort of speculation such as 'Well, nothing in this world is certain, nothing in this world can be proved' . . . It is sometimes said the sort of matter which might influence you if you were to consider some business matter. A matter, for example, of a mortgage concerning your house, or something of that nature.

The Court of Appeal held that:

(a) in the light of the foreman's request, the case was an exceptional one, calling for a further direction; and

(b) although it disliked that part of the additional direction in which the judge had defined a reasonable doubt as one to which you can give a reason, taking the effect of both the summing-up and the additional direction together, the judge was right in what he did.

In exceptional cases in which the jury do ask for an explanation of 'reasonable doubt', a suitable form of words is provided by *Walters* v *The Queen* [1969] 2 AC 26. There, the Privy Council, while of the opinion that it is a matter of discretion for the judge to choose the most appropriate set of words to enable the particular jury in question to understand the standard of proof, upheld the following direction of the trial judge: 'A reasonable doubt is that quality and kind of doubt which, when you are dealing with matters of importance in your own affairs, you allow to influence you one way or the other.' The decision was affirmed in *Gray* (1973) 58 Cr App R 177.

Direction Where Legal Burden on Defence

In the exceptional cases in which the legal burden of proving an issue is borne by the **F3.18** defence (see **F3.3** to **F3.5**), it is discharged by proof on a balance of probabilities. See, in the case of insanity, *Sodeman* v *The King* [1936] 2 All ER 1138; in the case of the Prevention of Crime Act 1953, s. 1, an express statutory exception, *Brown* (1971) 55 Cr App R 478; in the case of the Homicide Act 1957, s. 2(2), another express statutory exception, *Dunbar* [1958] 1 QB 1; and in the case of implied statutory exceptions under the MCA 1980, s. 101, *Islington London Borough Council* v *Panico* [1973] 1 WLR 1166. In *Carr-Briant* [1943] KB 607, the accused, who was convicted of an offence under the Prevention of Corruption Acts 1906 and 1916, bore the legal burden of proving that money given or lent to an employee of a Government Department was not paid or given corruptly. The trial judge directed the jury that the burden on the accused was as heavy as that normally resting on the prosecution. Humphreys J, quashing the conviction, said (at p. 612):

> . . . in any case where, either by statute or at common law, some matter is presumed against an accused person 'unless the contrary is proved', the jury should be directed that it is for them to decide whether the contrary is proved, that the burden of proof required is less than that required at the hands of the prosecution in proving the case beyond a reasonable doubt, and that the burden may be discharged by evidence satisfying the jury of the probability of that which the accused is called upon to establish.

The classic definition of proof on a 'balance of probabilities' is that of Denning J in *Miller* v *Minister of Pensions* [1947] 2 All ER 372, at p. 374: 'If the evidence is such that the tribunal can say: "We think it more probable than not", the burden is discharged, but, if the probabilities are equal, it is not.'

BURDEN OF PROOF ON FACTS AFFECTING ADMISSIBILITY OF EVIDENCE

When the admissibility of a particular item of evidence is in dispute, the burden of **F3.19** proving preliminary facts, that is those facts which must be proved as a condition precedent to the admission of the disputed evidence, lies on the party seeking to admit that evidence. Thus, at common law the prosecution bore the burden of proving the facts constituting the condition precedent to the admissibility of confessions, a rule which has now been put on a statutory basis (see *Thompson* [1893] 2 QB 12 and the PACE 1984, s. 76(2)). Likewise, it has been held that the onus of establishing the preliminary facts in relation to a dying declaration is on the party who seeks to admit such a declaration (*Jenkins* (1869) LR 1 CCR 187). The burden of proving the competence of a witness is on the party seeking to call that witness. In *Yacoob* (1981) 72 Cr App R 313 the defence objected to the prosecution calling a woman whom they alleged to be incompetent because she had gone through a ceremony of marriage with the accused. The prosecution alleged that the marriage was bigamous. The trial judge ruled that it was for the defence to prove the validity of the marriage. The Court of Appeal held that this was wrong: it was for the prosecution to prove the woman's competence beyond reasonable doubt. As to the requirement to satisfy the judge of the originality and genuineness of a tape recording, see *Robson* [1972] 1 WLR 651, *Stevenson* [1971] 1 WLR 1, *Rampling* [1987] Crim LR 823, and the Code of Practice for Tape Recording of Police Interviews (Code E).

STANDARD OF PROOF ON FACTS AFFECTING ADMISSIBILITY OF EVIDENCE

F3.20 When the burden of proving the admissibility of a particular item of evidence is borne by the prosecution, the standard to be met is proof beyond reasonable doubt. See, in the case of confessions at common law, *Sartori* [1961] Crim LR 397, *Cave* [1963] Crim LR 371 and *DPP* v *Ping Lin* [1976] AC 574, at p. 580 (a rule now put on a statutory basis by the PACE 1984, s. 76(2)); in the case of dying declarations, *Jenkins* (1869) LR 1 CCR 187; in the case of the competence of a witness, *Yacoob* (1931) 72 Cr App R 313; and on the issue of the genuineness of samples of writing which it is sought to admit under the Criminal Procedure Act 1865, s. 8, for the purposes of comparison with a disputed writing, *Ewing* [1983] QB 1039. In *Ewing*, the Court of Appeal held that since s. 8 of the 1865 Act did not itself deal with the standard of proof required to satisfy the judge as to the genuineness of the sample writing, the matter was governed by the common law, and accordingly, if the prosecution sought to admit such a sample, they should prove genuineness beyond reasonable doubt. The Court was of the opinion that the earlier decision of the Court of Appeal in *Angeli* [1979] 1 WLR 26, that the standard was the civil one, must have been reached *per incuriam*.

Although there is little authority on the point, as a matter of principle, when the burden of proving the admissibility of a particular item of evidence is borne by the defence, the standard to be met should be proof on a balance of probabilities. See, in the case of a defence application under CJA 1988, s. 23, *Mattey* [1995] 2 Cr App R 409.

PRESUMPTIONS

Presumptions without Basic Facts: Generally

F3.21 Presumptions without basic facts come into operation without the need for proof or admission of any basic or primary fact – they are merely rules that a certain conclusion must be drawn by the court in the absence of any evidence in rebuttal. Thus, although referred to as 'presumptions', in fact they are indistinguishable from the other rules relating to the incidence of the legal or evidential burden. Three examples are considered: the presumption of innocence, the presumption of sanity, and the presumption that mechanical and other instruments of a kind that are usually in working order, were in working order at the time of their use.

Presumption of Innocence

F3.22 The phrase 'the presumption of innocence' is often used as a convenient abbreviation of the common-law rule that, generally speaking, the prosecution bears the burden of proving all the elements in the offence necessary to establish guilt (see *Woolmington* v *DPP* [1935] AC 462 and generally **F3.2**).

Presumption of Sanity

F3.23 The presumption of sanity is a convenient abbreviation of the common-law rule that if the accused raises the defence of insanity, he will bear the burden of proving it (on a balance of probabilities) (see *Layton* (1849) 4 Cox CC 149, *M'Naghten's Case* (1843) 10 Cl & F 200, and generally **F3.3**). The phrase is to be distinguished from 'the presumption of mental capacity' which has been used to refer to the common-law rule that the evidential burden in relation to automatism not due to a disease of the mind is borne by the accused (see *Bratty* v *A-G for Northern Ireland* [1963] AC 386 at **F3.10**).

Presumption as to Working of Mechanical and Other Instruments

There is a presumption that mechanical and other instruments of a kind that are usually **F3.24** in working order, were in working order at the time of their use. The party against whom the presumption operates bears an evidential burden to adduce some evidence to the contrary. The presumption has been applied in the case of speedometers: see *Nicholas v Penny* [1950] 2 KB 466, in which it was held that justices were entitled to convict of speeding on the evidence of one officer as to the speedometer reading of a police car driven at an even distance behind the accused's car, notwithstanding that no evidence had been adduced as to the accuracy of the speedometer. Traffic lights have likewise been presumed to be in working order: in *Tingle Jacobs & Co.* v *Kennedy* [1964] 1 WLR 638, Lord Denning MR said (at p. 639) 'when you have a device of this kind set up for public use in active operation . . . the presumption should be that it is in proper working order unless there is evidence to the contrary'.

PRESUMPTIONS OF FACT

General Principles

The phrase 'presumption of fact' has been used to describe certain frequently recurring **F3.25** varieties of circumstantial evidence, i.e. evidence of relevant facts from which the existence of some fact which is in issue *may* be inferred. Thus, presumptions of fact, sometimes referred to as provisional presumptions, operate in the following manner: on the proof or admission of a basic or primary fact, another fact may be presumed in the absence of sufficient evidence to the contrary. The party against whom the presumption operates bears neither a legal nor an evidential burden in relation to the presumed fact; if he adduces no evidence to the contrary, he runs a risk of losing on that issue, but he is not *bound* to lose on that issue. The following examples are considered: the presumption of continuance of life, the presumption of intention, and the presumption of guilty knowledge in cases of handling, theft, etc.

Continuance of Life

On the proof or admission of the basic fact that a person was alive on a certain date, it **F3.26** may be presumed, in the absence of sufficient evidence to the contrary, that he was still alive on some subsequent date (*MacDarmaid* v *A-G* [1950] P 218; *Re Peete* [1952] 2 All ER 599). Whether or not such an inference should be drawn is a question for the jury, and is entirely dependent upon the facts of the case. Thus, if there is proof that a person was in good health on one day, there would be a strong, almost irresistible, inference that he was alive on the next day, and the jury would in all probability find that he was so; if, on the other hand, it were proved that he was in a dying condition on the first day and nothing further was proved, the jury would probably decline to draw the inference that he was alive on the following day (*Lumley* (1869) LR 1 CCR 196, per Lush J at p. 198, on the question of whether a husband was alive at the date of his wife's allegedly bigamous second marriage, approved in *Morrison* (1938) 27 Cr App R 1).

Intention

Criminal Justice Act 1967, s. 8

A court or jury, in determining whether a person has committed an offence — **F3.27**
    (a)   shall not be bound in law to infer that he intended or foresaw a result of his actions by reason only of its being a natural and probable consequence of those actions; but
    (b)   shall decide whether he did intend or foresee that result by reference to all the evidence, drawing such inferences from the evidence as appear proper in the circumstances.

Section 8 of the 1967 Act puts on a statutory basis the common-law presumption of fact that a man intends the natural consequences of his acts, and reverses the decision in

DPP v *Smith* [1961] AC 290 that in certain circumstances the presumption is a presumption of law (see *Wallett* [1968] 2 QB 367 and *Moloney* [1985] AC 905). In *Moloney*, at p. 929, Lord Bridge, approving the judgment of the Court of Criminal Appeal (Lord Goddard CJ, Atkinson and Cassels JJ) delivered by Lord Goddard CJ in *Steane* [1947] KB 997, at p. 1004, held that in the rare cases in which it is necessary to direct a jury by reference to foresight of consequences, the judge need only invite the jury to consider two questions:

(a)   Was the consequence a natural consequence of the defendant's voluntary act?
(b)   Did the defendant foresee that consequence as being a natural consequence of his act?

The jury should then be told that if they answer yes to both questions, it is a proper inference for them to draw that the defendant intended that consequence.

Guilty Knowledge in Cases of Handling, Theft etc.

F3.28   In cases of handling and theft, on proof or admission of the fact that the accused was found in possession of property so shortly after it was stolen that it can fairly be said that he was in recent possession of it, the jury should be directed that such possession calls for explanation, and if none is given, or one is given which they are convinced is untrue, they are entitled to infer, according to the circumstances, that the accused is either the handler or the thief and to convict accordingly (*Schama* (1914) 84 LJ KB 396; *Garth* [1949] 1 All ER 773; *Aves* [1950] 2 All ER 330; *Williams* [1962] Crim LR 54). It is desirable in most cases to direct the jury that the burden of proof remains on the prosecution, and if, therefore, the explanation given by the accused leaves them in doubt as to whether he came by the property honestly, the prosecution have not proved their case and they should acquit (*Aves* and *Hepworth* [1955] 2 QB 600, applied in *Moulding* [1996] Crim LR 440). See also *Aubrey* (1915) 11 Cr App R 182, *Brain* (1918) 13 Cr App R 197 and *Sanders* (1919) 14 Cr App R 11.

The doctrine of recent possession applies not only in the case of 'receiving', but also in the case of a charge under the second limb of the Theft Act 1968, s. 22 (*Ball* [1983] 1 WLR 801). Apart from handling and theft, the doctrine may also apply to other offences with a theft ingredient, as when the accused is charged with burglary contrary to s. 9(1)(b), and it is proved that shortly after the premises were entered and property stolen therefrom, the accused was found in possession of the property (see *Loughlin* (1951) 35 Cr App R 69 and *Seymour* [1954] 1 WLR 678). There is no general rule of law to the effect that the doctrine has no application in cases in which there is some evidence of the circumstances in which the accused came into possession of the stolen goods (see per Stocker LJ in *Raviraj* (1986) 85 Cr App R 93, commenting on *obiter* remarks made in *Bradley* (1979) 70 Cr App R 200). However, the doctrine cannot be relied upon where the accused failed to give an explanation *after* he was cautioned (*Raviraj*).

Whether possession is 'recent' is a question of fact and degree dependent on all the circumstances of the case in question. Relevant factors include the nature of the property, its saleability, and any evidence, other than that of the accused's possession of the goods, connecting him with the offence charged. In *Smythe* (1980) 72 Cr App R 8, Kilner Brown J said (at p. 11): 'Nearly every reported case is merely a decision of fact as an example of what is no more than a rule of evidence'. The precedents, therefore, are of somewhat limited value.

It is instructive, however, to note that in *Cash* [1985] QB 801, in which the goods were found in the possession of the appellant, C, on 25 February 1983, and none of the property was stolen more recently than 16 February 1983, the Court of Appeal, upholding C's conviction for handling, said that it was not properly open to the jury to infer that C was the burglar or thief. In that case two others were charged in the same indictment: A, who was convicted of burglary and handling offences; and E, who pleaded guilty to burglary and obtaining property by deception. The prosecution case was that C handled goods taken, by A, E and other persons unknown, in the course of a number of separate burglaries which took place between July and October 1982 and January and 16 February 1983. Some of the proceeds of the burglaries were recovered from C's flat on 25 February 1983. A was a lodger in the flat. When arrested, C declined to answer questions, and at the trial elected to give no evidence. In *Smythe* (1980) 72 Cr App R 8 the Court of Appeal said that it would be quite unsafe to infer positive proof of participation in a series of burglaries and robberies from the mere fact of possession, between two and three months after the robberies, of articles stolen in the course of them. See also *Marcus* (1923) 17 Cr App R 191: a period of eight months between the theft and the time when the goods were first seen in the possession of the accused was too long a period for the doctrine to apply.

In ordinary cases of handling, the prosecution are not required to adduce affirmative proof that the goods were handled 'otherwise than in the course of the stealing' (see the Theft Act 1968, s. 22(1)). This remains the position in recent possession cases, because if the jury draws the inference that the accused is guilty of handling, this includes the inference that he was not the actual thief. However, where the accused is in possession of stolen goods so recently after they are stolen that the inevitable inference is that he is the thief, as when he is found within a few hundred yards of the scene of the theft and minutes after the theft took place, then if he is only charged with handling, the Crown can prove that offence only if it proves affirmatively that the accused was not the thief, and the judge should direct the jury that they must acquit the accused of handling if they take the view that he was the thief (*Cash* [1985] QB 801, applied in *A-G of Hong Kong v Yip Kai-Foon* [1988] AC 642; *Ryan* v *DPP* (1994) 158 JP 485).

IRREBUTTABLE PRESUMPTIONS OF LAW

General Principles

F3.29 Irrebuttable presumptions of law, or conclusive presumptions, operate in the following way: on the proof or admission of a basic or primary fact another fact must be presumed which no evidence is admissible to rebut. Such presumptions are nothing more than rules of substantive law, as the following example illustrates.

Presumption that Children under 10 Cannot be Guilty of Offence

F3.30 The CYPA 1933, s. 50, provides that: 'It shall be conclusively presumed that no child under the age of 10 years can be guilty of an offence'. It follows from this that a person over the age of 10 who receives property dishonestly acquired by a person under the age of 10 cannot be guilty of receiving stolen property, although if he has the necessary *mens rea*, he may be guilty of theft (*Walters* v *Lunt* [1951] 2 All ER 645; *McGregor* v *Benyon* [1957] Crim LR 608).

REBUTTABLE PRESUMPTIONS OF LAW

General Principles

F3.31 Rebuttable presumptions of law operate in the following manner: on the proof or admission of the basic or primary facts, another fact must be presumed in the absence of sufficient evidence to the contrary. If the defence rely upon a rebuttable presumption of law and adduce prima facie evidence of the basic facts, a legal burden is placed on the prosecution requiring them to disprove or negative the presumed fact beyond reasonable doubt. If the prosecution rely upon a rebuttable presumption of law and adduce prima facie evidence of the basic facts, an evidential burden is placed on the defence which may be discharged by the adduction of such evidence as might leave a jury in reasonable doubt; and if the defence do discharge the evidential burden, the effect is as if the presumption had never come into play – the prosecution are still required to prove the presumed fact beyond reasonable doubt (see *Kay* (1887) 16 Cox CC 292 and *Willshire* (1881) 6 QBD 366 (the presumption of marriage)).

The foregoing relates to common-law presumptions; there are a number of statutory presumptions which operate to place on the defence a legal burden requiring them to disprove or negative a presumed fact by the adduction of such evidence as will satisfy the jury on a balance of probabilities: see, for example, the Prevention of Crime Act 1953, s. 1(1), set out at **F3.4**. As to the statutory presumptions arising under the PACE 1984, s. 74, see **F11.2**. Presumptions relating to the due execution of documents are considered at **F8.29**. The rebuttable presumptions of law that now fall to be considered are the presumptions of regularity, marriage and death.

Presumption of Regularity

F3.32   The presumption of regularity, expressed in the maxim *omnia praesumuntur rite esse acta*, operates as follows: on proof or admission of the basic or primary fact that a person has acted in a public or official capacity, it is presumed, in the absence of sufficient evidence to the contrary, that that person was regularly and properly appointed and that the act was regularly and properly performed. The presumption cannot be rebutted merely by challenging the presumed fact – evidence must be adduced (*Campbell* v *Wallsend Slipway and Engineering Co. Ltd* [1978] ICR 1015). Typical examples concern the validity of an official appointment. Thus, on a charge of assaulting a police officer in the course of his duty, evidence that the officer acted in that capacity is sufficient proof of his due appointment (*Gordon* (1789) 1 Leach 515; and see *Cooper* v *Rowlands* [1971] RTR 291). See also *Borrett* (1833) 6 C & P 124 (a person acting as an officer of the Post Office), *Roberts* (1878) 38 LT 690 (a deputy county court judge), and *Campbell* v *Wallsend Slipway and Engineering Co. Ltd* (an inspector of the Health and Safety Executive). In *Langton* (1876) 2 QBD 296, the presumption operated to establish the due incorporation of a company which had acted as such. In *Cresswell* (1873) 1 QBD 446, evidence that a marriage had been celebrated in a building in which other marriages had also been celebrated was sufficient to establish that the building was duly consecrated.

The presumption must be applied with caution in cases where commission of an offence is dependent upon compliance with formal statutory conditions. Thus, the Divisional Court has held that it is wrong to presume, on the basis of evidence that a breath test device has been issued to the police, that it was officially approved by the Secretary of State (*Scott* v *Baker* [1969] 1 QB 659, approved in *Withecombe* [1969] 1 WLR 84). See also *Swift* v *Barrett* (1940) 163 LT 154, in which the Divisional Court required strict proof that a road sign complied with regulations. Such authorities, it is submitted, are not easily reconciled with *Gibbins* v *Skinner* [1951] 2 KB 379, in which it was held that evidence that speed-limit signs had been erected on a road was sufficient to establish that the local authority had performed its statutory duties pursuant to the Road Traffic Acts and given a direction justifying the erection of the signs.

Presumptions of Marriage

F3.33   The civil authorities, although not explicit on the point, suggest that there are three different presumptions of marriage:

(a)   a presumption of formal validity (i.e. a presumption of compliance with the formal requirements of the *lex loci celebrationis*, e.g., the requirement, in the case of a Church of England marriage under English law, to obtain a common or special licence);

(b)   a presumption of essential validity (i.e. a presumption that each of the parties had the capacity to marry and was not, for example, under the age of 16 or already married); and

(c)   a presumption of marriage arising from cohabitation.

Although there is a dearth of criminal authority, it is submitted that the presumptions of formal and essential validity apply in criminal as well as civil proceedings. The presumption of marriage arising from cohabitation, however, would appear to be of limited utility in criminal proceedings; the authorities show that if the prosecution bear the burden of proving the existence of a marriage, the presumption by itself is insufficient to discharge even the evidential burden. Thus in a case of bigamy, the prosecution, in seeking to prove a valid first marriage which subsisted at the date of the second marriage, must adduce some evidence of the celebration of the first marriage; evidence of acknowledgement, cohabitation or repute will not suffice (*Morris* v *Miller* (1767) 4 Burr 2057). It will suffice, however, if there is not only evidence that the accused had cohabited with a woman and spoken of her as his wife, but also proof from the register of marriages that a person of the same name as the accused married that woman (*Birtles* (1911) 6 Cr App R 177). See also *Umanski* [1961] VR 242.

Presumption of Death

By virtue of a long sequence of judicial statements, which either assert or assume such a **F3.34** rule, it appears accepted that there is a convenient presumption of law applicable to certain cases of seven years' absence where no statute applies. That presumption in its modern shape takes effect (without examining its terms too exactly) substantially as follows. Where as regards 'A.B' there is no acceptable affirmative evidence that he was alive at some time during a continuous period of seven years or more, then if it can be proved first, that there are persons who would be likely to have heard of him over that period, secondly that those persons have not heard of him, and thirdly that all due inquiries have been made appropriate to the circumstances, 'A.B.' will be presumed to have died at some time within that period. (*Chard* v *Chard* [1956] P 259, per Sachs J at p. 272)

The authorities conflict as to the date on which the fact of death may be presumed; it is either the date of the proceedings in question or the date at the end of the period of absence for seven years (see *Lal Chand Marwari* v *Mahant Ranrup Gir* (1925) 42 TLR 159, at p. 160, and contrast *Re Westbrook's Trusts* [1873] WN 167 and *Chipchase* v *Chipchase* [1939] P 31).

Concerning the proviso to the OAPA 1861, s. 57 ('persons [charged with bigamy] marrying a second time whose husband or wife shall have been continually absent for the space of seven years then last past, and shall not have been known by such person to be living within that time'), see **B2.100** and **F3.5**.

CONFLICTING PRESUMPTIONS

There is civil authority that where two presumptions of equal strength apply in a case **F3.35** with the result that two facts are presumed, the one in conflict with the other, the presumptions neutralise each other and the case falls to be determined without the application of either (see *Monckton* v *Tarr* (1930) 23 BWCC 504). *Willshire* (1881) 6 QBD 366 is often cited in support of this proposition, although there was no true conflict in that case, which involved two presumptions of unequal strength, a rebuttable presumption of law and a presumption of fact. W was charged with bigamously marrying D in the lifetime of C. W had gone through four ceremonies of marriage, with A in 1864, with B in 1868, with C in 1879, and with D in 1880. The prosecution relied upon the presumption of essential validity in seeking to establish the validity of the marriage of 1879. W sought to show that the marriage of 1879 was void, and accordingly relied upon his previous conviction, in 1868, for marrying B during the lifetime of A: A was alive in 1868 and under the presumption of continuance of life could be presumed to have been alive in 1879, in which case the marriage of 1879 was void. The trial judge did not leave the issue of whether A was alive in 1879 to the jury, directing them that the onus was on W to adduce evidence of her existence on that date. The conviction was quashed. Lord Coleridge CJ, referring to a 'conflict' of presumptions, held that the accused was not bound to do more than set up A's life in 1868, which would be presumed to continue, and it was then for the prosecution to disprove her existence on that date. It is submitted that there was no real conflict of presumptions in this case. The decision reached was correct. The onus of proving the validity of the 1879 marriage was on the prosecution. Their reliance on the presumption of validity placed nothing more than an evidential burden on W, which he had successfully discharged in reliance upon the presumption of continuance of life. The onus remained on the prosecution to establish the validity of the 1879 marriage.

SECTION F4: COMPETENCE AND COMPELLABILITY OF WITNESSES AND OATHS AND AFFIRMATIONS

Meaning of Competence and Compellability

A witness is competent if he may lawfully be called to testify, and is compellable if, being **F4.1** competent, he may lawfully be compelled by the court to testify. As to securing the attendance of a witness, whether by witness order or witness summons, see **D12.28**, **D12.29** and **D19.4**.

Determining Competence and Compellability

Issues as to the competence or compellability of a witness are decided by the court. **F4.2** According to the circumstances, this may require hearing evidence on a *voir dire*. In the case of prosecution witnesses, the issue should be raised and determined at the beginning of the trial. Once the issue of the competence of such a witness has been raised, it is for the prosecution to prove his competence beyond reasonable doubt (*Yacoob* (1981) 72 Cr App R 313).

An objection to the competence of a witness should normally be made before the witness has been examined in chief (*Wollaston* v *Hakewill* (1841) 3 Man & G 297; *Bartlett* v *Smith* (1843) 11 M & W 483). An exception exists in cases where the incompetence only becomes apparent during the course of examination-in-chief (*Jacobs* v *Layborn* (1843) 11 M & W 685). If it only becomes apparent to a judge during the course of the evidence being given by a sworn witness that the witness is of unsound mind, the judge may rule the witness incompetent, direct the jury to ignore his evidence, and continue with the trial (*Whitehead* (1866) LR 1 CCR 33).

The position at common law will need to be read subject to the YJCEA 1999, s. 54, when it is brought into force. Section 54 is set out at **F4.19**.

Witnessses who Refuse to Take the Oath or Testify

Judges of the Crown Court may exercise their power to punish summarily for contempt **F4.3** of court (Supreme Court Act 1981, s. 45(4)) any compellable witness who refuses to take an oath or make an affirmation (*Hennegal* v *Evance* (1806) 12 Ves Jr 201). Likewise, but subject to public policy or a claim to privilege which the court upholds, a witness who refuses to answer a proper question may be found to be in contempt of court and face the penalty of imprisonment (*Ex parte Fernandez* (1861) 10 CB NS 13). A witness who refuses to testify and runs the risk of committal to prison as a contemnor should be given the opportunity of legal representation (*K* (1984) 78 Cr App R 82). In *Phillips* (1983) 78 Cr App R 88, it was stressed that, on a finding of contempt, sentence need not be passed immediately. The witness may change his mind. It is advisable to sentence at the end of the trial or, at the earliest, at the close of the prosecution case. For the principles to be borne in mind by trial judges, see the observations of Lawton LJ in *Moran* (1985) 81 Cr App R 51 at p. 53 quoted in **B14.64**. For the position in magistrates' courts, see the MCA 1980, s. 97(4), in **B14.63**.

Wards of Court as Witnesses

The leave of the wardship court is not required to call a ward to give evidence at a **F4.4** criminal trial. This is so irrespective of whether (a) the child is interviewed and has made witness statements before or after becoming a ward, (b) it is the prosecution or defence who wish to call the child or (c) the child's failure to give evidence would prevent the prosecution taking place (see *Re K (Minors) (Wardship: Criminal Proceedings)* [1988] Fam 1 and *Re R (A Minor) (Wardship: Criminal Proceedings)* [1991] 2 WLR 912, per Lord Donaldson MR at p. 917). Concerning interviews with wards, see *Practice Direction (Ward: Witness at Trial)* [1987] 1 WLR 1739, *Practice Direction (Ward: Witness at Trial) (No. 2)* [1988] 1 WLR 989, *Re R (Minors)* [1990] 2 All ER 633 and *Re R (A Minor) (Wardship: Criminal Proceedings)* [1991] 2 WLR 912.

General Rule as to Competence and Compellability

F4.5   The general rule relating to the competence and compellability of witnesses has two limbs:

(a)   The first is that any person is a competent witness in any proceedings. The exceptions to this limb relate to the accused, children, and persons of defective intellect.

(b)   The second is that all competent witnesses are compellable. The exceptions to this limb relate to the accused and his or her spouse.

The first limb of the general rule will be put on a statutory basis when the YJCEA 1999, s. 53, is brought into force. Under s. 53(1), which by virtue of s. 53(2) has effect subject to s. 53(3) and (4) (see **F4.8**), 'At every stage in criminal proceedings all persons are (whatever their age) competent to give evidence'.

Deaf and Speech Handicapped Witnesses

F4.6   A deaf mute is competent as a witness, provided that the court is satisfied that he understands the nature of an oath (*Ruston* (1786) 1 Leach 408; *O'Brien* (1845) 1 Cox CC 185). Such a person may take an oath (or make an affirmation) and be examined and cross-examined, through an interpreter, using sign language. The interpreter should also take an oath (or make an affirmation). A witness who cannot speak may be allowed to give his evidence in written form.

No Property in the Evidence of a Witness

F4.7   No party has any property in the evidence of a witness, so that even if there is a contract between a witness and a party, whereby the latter binds himself not to testify on a matter on which the court can compel him to give evidence, such a contract is contrary to public policy and unenforceable (*Harmony Shipping Co. SA v Saudi Europe Line Ltd* [1979] 1 WLR 1380). However, once a witness in a criminal case has testified on behalf of the prosecution, he cannot be compelled to testify on behalf of the defence (*Kelly* (1985) *The Times*, 27 July 1985).

THE ACCUSED

As a Witness for the Prosecution

F4.8   An accused is incompetent as a witness for the prosecution (*Rhodes* [1899] 1 QB 77). An accused charged jointly with another person or persons is also incompetent for the prosecution (*Payne* (1872) LR 1 CCR 349; *Grant* [1944] 2 All ER 311; and *Sharrock* [1948] 1 All ER 145). Where there are separate committal proceedings in respect of two accomplices and one is committed, appears at the Crown Court and pleads guilty, the Crown are permitted, even before he has been sentenced, to call him to give evidence at the committal proceedings in respect of the other; but where both are committed together as co-accused, neither should be called to give evidence for the Crown against the other (*Palmer* (1994) 99 Cr App R 83). However, where a party jointly charged with the accused is improperly allowed to give evidence for the prosecution in the committal proceedings, this will not invalidate the committal (*Norfolk Quarter Sessions, ex parte Brunson* [1953] 1 QB 503).

A co-accused may only give evidence for the prosecution if he has ceased to be a co-accused, as when:

(a)   he pleads guilty, either on arraignment or during the course of the trial (*Tomey* (1909) 2 Cr App R 329; *Gallagher* (1875) 32 LT 406);

(b)   he is acquitted (*Rowland* (1826) Ry & M 401);

(c)   he is tried separately (*Winsor* v *R* (1866) LR 1 QB 390; but see also *Pipe* (1967) 51 Cr App R 17, below); or

(d)   the Attorney-General enters a *nolle prosequi*, putting to an end the proceedings against him (*Sherman* (1736) Cas t Hard 303).

In all of these cases, a former co-accused becomes both competent and compellable for the prosecution.

The foregoing common-law rules will be put on a statutory basis when the YJCEA 1999, s. 53, is brought into force. Under s. 53(4), 'A person charged in criminal proceedings is not competent to give evidence in the proceedings for the prosecution (whether he is the only person, or is one of two or more persons, charged in the proceedings)'. Section 53(5) provides that: 'In subsection (4) the reference to a person charged in criminal proceedings does not include a person who is not, or is no longer, liable to be convicted of any offence in the proceedings (whether as a result of pleading guilty or for any other reason)'.

An accomplice against whom proceedings are pending but who is not an accused in the proceedings in which the prosecution seek to call him, should only be called by the prosecution if they have undertaken to discontinue the proceedings against him. This appears to be a rule of practice rather than of law. In *Pipe* (1967) 51 Cr App R 17, Pipe was charged with housebreaking and larceny. He was alleged to have stolen a safe and its contents. Swan was called to prove that he had helped Pipe to break open the safe. Swan, before the commencement of Pipe's trial, had been charged with complicity in Pipe's crime in relation to the safe. Swan was not indicted with Pipe. It was intended to try him later. The Court of Appeal held that it was 'wholly irregular' to have called Swan in these circumstances.

In *Turner* (1975) 61 Cr App R 67 it was argued that for some time past there had been a practice for judges not to admit the evidence of accomplices who could still be infuenced by continuing inducements, and that in *Pipe* the Court of Appeal had adjudged that this practice had become a rule of law. Rejecting this argument, Lawton LJ said, at p. 78:

> There is nothing in either the arguments [in *Pipe*] or the judgment itself to indicate that the court thought it was changing a rule of law as to the competency of accomplices to give evidence which had been followed ever since the 17th century. The facts of that case must be closely examined. . . .
>
> [*Pipe*'s] *ratio decidendi* is confined to a case in which an accomplice, who has been charged, but not tried, is required to give evidence of his own offence in order to secure the conviction of another accused. *Pipe* on its facts was clearly a right decision. The same result could have been achieved by adjudging that the trial judge should have exercised his discretion to exclude Swan's evidence on the ground that there was an obvious and powerful inducement for him to ingratiate himself with the prosecution and the court and that the existence of this inducement made it desirable in the interests of justice to exclude it. See *Noor Mohamed* v *The King* [1949] AC 182 per Lord du Parcq at p. 192 and followed in *Harris* v *DPP* [1952] AC 694 per Viscount Simon at p. 707. To have reached the decision on this basis would, we think, have been more in line with the earlier authorities. Lord Parker CJ in *Pipe* seems, however, to have viewed the admission of Swan's evidence in the circumstances of that case as more than a wrong exercise of discretion. He described what happened as being 'wholly irregular'. It does not follow, in our judgment, that in all cases calling a witness who can benefit from giving evidence is 'wholly irregular'. To hold so would be absurd.

As a Witness on his Own Behalf

F4.9   Pursuant to the Criminal Evidence Act 1898, s. 1, the accused is a competent but not compellable witness for the defence.

Criminal Evidence Act 1898, s. 1

Every person charged with an offence shall be a competent witness for the defence at every stage of the proceedings, whether the person so charged is charged solely or jointly with any other person. Provided as follows: —

(a)   A person so charged shall not be called as a witness in pursuance of this Act except upon his own application:

(e)–(f)   [See **F14.1**.]

(g)   Every person called as a witness in pursuance of this Act shall, unless otherwise ordered by the court, give his evidence from the witness-box or other place from which the other witnesses give their evidence.

When the relevant provisions of the YJCEA 1999 are brought into force, s. 1 of the 1898 Act will be amended. The section, as opposed to its proviso, will become otiose since, under the YJCEA 1999, s. 53(1), the general rule will be that at every stage in criminal proceedings all persons are competent to give evidence (see **F4.5**). Pursuant to the YJCEA 1999, sch. 4, para. 1, paragraphs (a), (e), (f) and (g) of the proviso shall be respectively numbered as subsections (1), (2), (3) and (4) of the section, and the new subsections (1) and (4) will read as follows:

(1)   A person charged in criminal proceedings shall not be called as a witness in the proceedings except upon his own application.

(4)   Every person charged in criminal proceedings who is called as a witness in the proceedings shall, unless otherwise ordered by the court, give his evidence from the witness-box or other place from which the other witnesses give their evidence.

The words 'at every stage of the proceedings' in s. 1 allow the accused to give evidence not only in the trial itself but also after conviction, in mitigation of sentence (*Wheeler* [1917] 1 KB 283). There is some older authority to the effect that the accused is not entitled as of right to give evidence on the *voir dire* (*Baldwin* (1931) 23 Cr App R 62), and that the court may in its discretion allow the accused to give evidence at this stage if the justice of the case makes this desirable (*Cowell* [1940] 2 KB 49). But given the clear wording of s. 1, it is submitted that these decisions are incorrect. Certainly, the current practice is for the accused to elect whether to testify on the *voir dire*.

The intention of s. 1(g) of the 1898 Act is that the accused 'shall have an opportunity of giving evidence on his own behalf in the same way and from the same place as the witnesses for the prosecution'. Thus the accused should give his evidence from the witness-box unless, for example, he is too infirm to walk there or too violent to be controlled there (*Symonds* (1924) 18 Cr App R 100, per Swift J at p. 101). Section 1(g) does not confer on justices a discretion to direct where evidence should be given from but allows them, in exceptional circumstances of the kind described in *Symonds*, to deny the accused the right he would otherwise have to give evidence from the witness-box. To offer the accused a choice as to whether they wish to give evidence from the dock or the witness stand is also to fetter that right and any such practice should cease (*Farnham Justices, ex parte Gibson* [1991] RTR 309, where the conviction of a defendant required to give evidence from the dock was quashed, applying the principle that justice must not only be done but must also be seen to be done).

If the accused elects to testify, he must give his evidence on oath and will be liable to cross-examination. This is now expressly stated in the CJA 1982, s. 72, which abolished the accused's right to make an unsworn statement from the dock.

Criminal Justice Act 1982, s. 72

(1)   Subject to subsections (2) and (3) below, in any criminal proceedings the accused shall not be entitled to make a statement without being sworn, and accordingly, if he gives evidence he shall do so on oath and be liable to cross-examination; but this section shall not affect the right of the accused, if not represented by counsel or a solicitor, to address the court or jury otherwise than on oath on any matter on which, if he were so represented, counsel or a solicitor could address the court or jury on his behalf.

(2)   Nothing in subsection (1) above shall prevent the accused making a statement without being sworn —
    (a)   if it is one which he is required by law to make personally; or
    (b)   if he makes it by way of mitigation before the court passes sentence upon him.

(3)   Nothing in this section applies —
    (a)   to a trial; or
    (b)   to proceedings before a magistrates' court acting as examining justices,
which began before the commencement of this section.

However, when the YJCEA 1999, sch. 4, para. 10, is brought into force, s. 72(1) will be amended by the insertion, after 'if he gives evidence, he shall do so' of '(subject to sections 55 and 56 of the Youth Justice and Criminal Evidence Act 1999)'. The effect will be that the evidence of an accused who is competent to give evidence but is not permitted to be sworn shall be given unsworn. Section 55 (determining whether a witness should give sworn evidence) and s. 56 (the reception of unsworn evidence) are set out at **F4.19**.

If the accused does testify, he is liable to cross-examination by the prosecution and, whether or not he has given evidence against a co-accused, by counsel for any co-accused (*Hilton* [1972] 1 QB 421). Subject to the remaining provisos to the Criminal Evidence Act 1898, s. 1, he will be treated like any other witness. His evidence will be evidence for all the purposes of the case, including the purpose of being evidence against any co-accused (*Rudd* (1948) 32 Cr App R 138, per Humphreys J at p. 140). In *Paul* [1920] 2 KB 183, in which an accused had confined his evidence in chief to an admission of his own guilt, it was held that the prosecution had properly been allowed to cross-examine him and thereby elicit evidence which undermined the defence of his co-accused.

As a Witness for a Co-accused

An accused is a competent witness for any co-accused (*Macdonell* (1909) 2 Cr App R **F4.10** 322). An accused, however, is not a compellable witness for a co-accused, because, under the Criminal Evidence Act 1898, s. 1(a), 'every person charged with an offence' is a competent witness for the defence but shall not be called 'except upon his own application' (see **F4.9**). An accused who does give evidence for a co-accused may be cross-examined to show his own guilt of the offence charged (*Rowland* [1910] 1 KB 458).

A 'person charged with an offence' means a person charged with an offence within the consideration of the jury at the trial (*Boal* [1965] 1 QB 402, at p. 415). Accordingly, a co-accused who is no longer on trial is both competent and compellable as a witness for any 'co-accused'. This may happen in the following ways:

    (a)   the co-accused pleads guilty (*Boal* [1965] 1 QB 402);
    (b)   the co-accused is discharged at the end of the prosecution case as the result of a successful submission of no case to answer (*Conti* (1973) 58 Cr App R 387); or
    (c)   the co-accused is tried separately as the result of a successful application to sever the indictment (*Richardson* (1967) 51 Cr App R 381).

THE SPOUSE OF THE ACCUSED

F4.11 The competence and compellability of the spouse of an accused is governed by the PACE 1984, s. 80.

Police and Criminal Evidence Act 1984, s. 80

(1) In any proceedings the wife or husband of the accused shall be competent to give evidence —

(a) subject to subsection (4) below, for the prosecution; and

(b) on behalf of the accused or any person jointly charged with the accused.

(2) In any proceedings the wife or husband of the accused shall, subject to subsection (4) below, be compellable to give evidence on behalf of the accused.

(3) In any proceedings the wife or husband of the accused shall, subject to subsection (4) below, be compellable to give evidence for the prosecution or on behalf of any person jointly charged with the accused if and only if —

(a) the offence charged involves an assault on, or injury or a threat of injury to, the wife or husband of the accused or a person who was at the material time under the age of 16; or

(b) the offence charged is a sexual offence alleged to have been committed in respect of a person who was at the material time under that age; or

(c) the offence charged consists of attempting or conspiring to commit, or of aiding, abetting, counselling, procuring or inciting the commission of, an offence falling within paragraph (a) or (b) above.

(4) Where a husband and wife are jointly charged with an offence neither spouse shall at the trial be competent or compellable by virtue of subsection (1)(a), (2) or (3) above to give evidence in respect of that offence unless that spouse is not, or is no longer, liable to be convicted of that offence at the trial as a result of pleading guilty or for any other reason.

(5) In any proceedings a person who has been but is no longer married to the accused shall be competent and compellable to give evidence as if that person and the accused had never been married.

(6) Where in any proceedings the age of any person at any time is material for the purposes of subsection (3) above, his age at the material time shall for the purposes of that provision be deemed to be or to have been that which appears to the court to be or to have been his age at that time.

(7) In subsection (3)(b) above 'sexual offence' means an offence under the Sexual Offences Act 1956, the Indecency with Children Act 1960, the Sexual Offences Act 1967, section 54 of the Criminal Law Act 1977 or the Protection of Children Act 1978.

(8) The failure of the wife or husband of the accused to give evidence shall not be made the subject of any comment by the prosecution.

When the relevant provisions of the YJCEA 1999 are brought into force, s. 80 of the PACE will be amended (see YJCEA 1999, sch. 4, paras 12 to 14). Subsection (1) will be omitted, because otiose (see s. 53(1) at **F4.5**, and s. 53(4) and (5) at **F4.8**). The following will be substituted for s. 80(2) to (4):

(2) In any proceedings the wife or husband of a person charged in the proceedings shall, subject to subsection (4) below, be compellable to give evidence on behalf of that person.

(2A) In any proceedings the wife or husband of a person charged in the proceedings shall, subject to subsection (4) below, be compellable—

(a) to give evidence on behalf of any other person charged in the proceedings but only in respect of any specified offence with which that other person is charged; or

(b) to give evidence for the prosecution but only in respect of any specified offence with which any person is charged in the proceedings.

(3) In relation to the wife or husband of a person charged in any proceedings, an offence is a specified offence for the purposes of subsection (2A) above if—

(a) it involves an assault on, or injury or a threat of injury to, the wife or husband or a person who was at the material time under the age of 16;

(b) it is a sexual offence alleged to have been committed in respect of a person who was at the material time under that age; or

(c) it consists of attempting or conspiring to commit, or of aiding, abetting, counselling, procuring or inciting the commission of, an offence falling within paragraph (a) or (b) above.

(4) No person who is charged in any proceedings shall be compellable by virtue of subsection (2) or (2A) above to give evidence in the proceedings.

(4A) References in this section to a person charged in any proceedings do not include a person who is not, or is no longer, liable to be convicted of any offence in the proceedings (whether as a result of pleading guilty or for any other reason).

In s. 80(5) of the 1984 Act the words 'competent and' will be omitted, but after s. 80 a new s. 80A will be inserted:

80A. The failure of the wife or husband of a person charged in any proceedings to give evidence in the proceedings shall not be made the subject of any comment by the prosecution.

As a Witness for the Prosecution

As to competence, the general rule, subject to only one exception, is that 'the wife or **F4.12** husband of the accused' shall be competent to give evidence 'for the prosecution' (PACE 1984, s. 80(1)(a)).

It is submitted that the words 'wife' and 'husband' used in this and other parts of s. 80, refer to persons whose marriage (wherever celebrated) would be recognised by English law. In *Khan* (1987) 84 Cr App R 44, a decision on the common law before the 1984 Act came into force, it was held that a woman who had gone through a Moslem ceremony of marriage with an accused already married under English law to another woman, was a competent witness for the prosecution. Glidewell LJ said that she was in the same position as a mistress, a woman who had not gone through a ceremony of marriage at all or one who had gone through a ceremony of marriage which was void because bigamous. See also *Yacoob* (1981) 72 Cr App R 313.

The words 'for the prosecution' in s. 80(1) indicate that the spouse is competent irrespective of whether the evidence to be given will be directed against the accused or any co-accused.

The only exception to the general rule is contained in s. 80(4): 'Where a husband and wife are jointly charged with an offence neither spouse shall at the trial be competent . . . to give evidence in respect of that offence unless that spouse is not, or is no longer, liable to be convicted of that offence at the trial as a result of pleading guilty or for any other reason.' The inclusion of the phrase 'with an offence' means, it is submitted, that if the spouses are jointly indicted but charged with separate offences, each is competent to give evidence for the prosecution against the other. Such a case is outside the wording of s. 80(4) and therefore governed by the mandatory language of s. 80(1).

As to compellability, the rule, subject to one exception, is that the wife or husband of the accused shall be compellable to give evidence for the prosecution if, and only if, the offence charged is among those described in s. 80(3)(a),(b) and (c). The exception is where a husband and wife are jointly charged with an offence (see s. 80(4)).

Under s. 80(3)(a), the wife or husband of the accused shall be compellable to give evidence for the prosecution if the offence charged 'involves' an assault on, or injury or a threat of injury to, the wife or husband of the accused or a person who was at the material time under the age of 16. It is unclear, and as yet undecided, whether the 'involvement' must be legal (as a matter of legal definition the offence charged requires an assault on, or injury or a threat of injury to, one of the types of person described in s. 80(3)(a)) or can be factual (as a matter of legal definition the offence charged does not require an assault on or injury or a threat of injury to one of the types of such person but in fact it did involve, or is alleged to have involved, an assault on or injury or a threat of injury to one of the types of such person). See *Lee* [1996] 2 Cr App R 266, construing the similar wording of the CJA 1988, s. 32(2)(a). The phrase 'a threat of injury' may cover not only an uttered threat, but also a threat by conduct, as in *Verolla* [1963] 1 QB 285, where the accused was charged with attempting to murder his wife by poisoning her. A case of that kind, however, is now covered by s. 80(3)(c).

The following propositions, relating to a spouse who is competent but not compellable for the prosecution, derive from *Pitt* [1983] QB 25, at pp. 65–6:

(a) The choice whether to give evidence is that of the spouse, and is not lost because that spouse made a witness statement or gave evidence at the committal proceedings. The spouse retains the right of refusal up to the point when, with full knowledge of that right, he or she takes the oath in the witness-box. Waiver of the right is effective only if made with full knowledge of the right of refusal.

(b) If the spouse waives the right of refusal, he or she becomes an ordinary witness. It follows that if the nature of the evidence then given justifies it, an application may be made to treat the spouse as a hostile witness.

(c) Although not a rule of either law or practice, it is desirable that where a spouse, being competent but not compellable for the prosecution, is called for the prosecution, the judge should explain to the spouse, in the absence of the jury, that before taking the oath, he or she has the right to refuse to give evidence, but that if he or she chooses to give evidence, he or she may be treated like any other witness (but failure to give such an explanation does not necessarily justify interfering with a guilty verdict: *Nelson* [1992] Crim LR 653).

As a Witness for the Accused

F4.13 The spouse of the accused is competent to give evidence for the accused (PACE 1984, s. 80(1)(b)). This remains the case even if they are jointly charged with an offence. Subject to only one exception, the spouse shall be compellable to give evidence for the accused (s. 80(2)). The exception is where the spouses are jointly charged with an offence (s. 80(4)).

As a Witness for a Co-Accused

F4.14 The spouse of the accused is competent to give evidence on behalf of any person 'jointly charged' with the accused (PACE 1984, s. 80(1)(b)). This is so whether or not the accused consents, and even if the spouse and the accused are jointly charged with an offence.

Subject to only one exception, the spouse of the accused is compellable to give evidence on behalf of any person jointly charged with the accused, if, and only if, the offence charged is one which would render her or him compellable to give evidence for the prosecution (s. 80(3)). The exception is where the spouses are jointly charged with an offence (s. 80(4)). In *Woolgar* [1991] Crim LR 545, the Court of Appeal held that the words 'jointly charged' in s. 80(3) mean 'jointly charged with an offence' and not 'jointly indicted' or 'charged in the same indictment'. W and M were jointly indicted, W being charged with criminal damage and M being charged with assault occasioning actual bodily harm. The trial judge ruled that M's wife was not compellable to give evidence on behalf of W. Allowing W's appeal against conviction, it was held that M's wife was a compellable witness because W and M were not jointly charged with anything; if the legislature had meant to say 'jointly indicted' it would have done so. It is submitted that, if the construction adopted by the Court of Appeal is correct, it does not follow that M's wife was competent and compellable. On the construction adopted, the case falls outside s. 80(3) on the question of compellability. It also falls outside s. 80(1)(b) (where the same words are used) on the question of competence. Regard should then be had to the common-law authorities. In *Thompson* (1872) LR 1 CCR 377, where A and B were charged with theft and C with receiving, it was held that C's wife was *not* competent to give evidence on behalf of A and B. (For further discussion of this and other, apparently conflicting, authorities, see [1991] Crim LR 546.)

Competence and Compellability of Former Spouse of the Accused

In any proceedings, a person who has been but is no longer married to the accused shall **F4.15** be competent and compellable to give evidence as if they had never been married (PACE 1984, s. 80(5)). Such a person, therefore, is competent and compellable on behalf of the prosecution, the accused or any co-accused, whether the evidence relates to events which occurred before, during or after the terminated marriage. The phrase 'is no longer married' covers the situation where the parties have been divorced and where a voidable marriage has been annulled; but not the situation where the parties have been judicially separated or are merely not cohabiting (whether or not in consequence of an informal arrangement, formal agreement or non-cohabitation order). If the marriage of the parties was void *ab initio*, there never was a legally valid marriage, and accordingly a party to such a union will be both competent and compellable on behalf of the accused (the other party to that union), any co-accused or the prosecution. The phrase 'in any proceedings' means any proceedings which take place after s. 80(5) came into effect (1 January 1986); and therefore an ex-wife or an ex-husband is competent and compellable to give evidence in such proceedings about any matter, whether it took place before or after that date (*Cruttenden* [1991] 2 QB 66).

OTHER WITNESSES

Children

The competence of children to give evidence in criminal proceedings is governed by the **F4.16** CJA 1988, s. 33A. The YJCEA 1999, ss. 53 to 56 will, when brought into force, replace the CJA 1988, s. 33A. The new provisions are set out at **F4.19**.

Criminal Justice Act 1988, s. 33A

(1)   A child's evidence in criminal proceedings shall be given unsworn.

(2)   A deposition of a child's unsworn evidence may be taken for the purposes of criminal proceedings as if that evidence had been given on oath.

(2A)   A child's evidence shall be received unless it appears to the court that the child is incapable of giving intelligible testimony.

(3)   In this section 'child' means a person under fourteen years of age.

In the case of children aged 14 or over, s. 33A(1) in effect lays down a general rule that they should give sworn evidence. An exception, in relation to examination-in-chief, is provided by s. 32A (see **F16.21**): a video of an interview with a child may be admissible under that section even though at the time of the trial the child is aged 14 or over and therefore must be sworn before giving evidence *viva voce*, whether in chief or in cross-examination and re-examination (see *Day* [1997] 1 Cr App R 181 and *Sharman* [1998] 1 Cr App R 406). Subject to this, it seems that children aged 14 or over should be treated in the same way as adults, i.e. as competent to give sworn evidence unless unable to understand the nature of the oath by reason of unsound mind. Children under 14 years of age, however, must give unsworn evidence (s. 33A(1)), unless it appears to the court that they are incapable of giving intelligible testimony (s. 33A(2A)). There is no duty on the court to enquire whether such children can give sworn evidence.

A child will be capable of giving 'intelligible testimony' if he or she is able to understand questions and to answer them in a manner which is coherent and comprehensible (*DPP v M* [1997] 2 All ER 749). Section 33A(2A) removes the need to determine whether a child knows the difference between truth and a lie and the importance of speaking the truth (*G v DPP* [1997] 2 All ER 755, approving Auld J, *obiter*, in *Hampshire* [1995] 3 WLR 260 at p. 268). However, it is submitted that a child will not be capable of giving 'intelligible testimony' if unable to distinguish between truth and fiction or between fact and fantasy (see *D* (1995) *The Times*, 15 November 1995, which is not an authority on s. 33A(2A)).

In *Hampshire* Auld J expressed the view, *obiter*, that although a judge is no longer bound to investigate a child's competence, unless he has reason to doubt it, he may find it appropriate to remind the child, in the presence of the accused and the jury, of the importance of telling the truth, by saying, for example, 'Tell us all you can remember of what happened. Don't make anything up or leave anything out. This is very important' (at p. 269).

Clearly the younger the child, the more likely it is that he or she will be incapable of giving 'intelligible testimony'. However, a court cannot properly conclude that a child is incapable of giving 'intelligible testimony' on the basis of the child's age alone, because the words of s. 33A(2A) are mandatory. Thus, although care must be taken where a question is raised as to whether a young child is capable of giving intelligible testimony, if the child is so capable then the court does not enjoy some wider discretion to refuse to permit the evidence to be given, subject to rules of evidence (such as PACE 1984, s. 78) which apply to all witnesses (*DPP v M*). The decision in *DPP v M* accords with the views of Lord Lane CJ in *Z* [1990] 2 QB 355. In *Wallwork* (1958) 42 Cr App R 153, it was thought to be most undesirable to call as a witness a child as young as five years old. In *Z* Lord Lane CJ held that that decision had been overtaken by events, in particular by the system of video links and by the repeal of the proviso to s. 38(1) (the requirement of corroboration in the case of the unsworn evidence of children) which indicated a change of attitude by Parliament, reflecting in its turn a change of attitude by the public in general to the acceptability of the evidence of young children and an increasing belief that their testimony, when all precautions have been taken, may be just as reliable as that of their elders.

The fact that a child under 10 years of age cannot be prosecuted for the offence of wilfully giving false evidence contrary to the CYPA 1933, s. 38(2) (see **B14.16**) is not a reason for excluding the unsworn evidence of a competent child witness (*N* (1992) 95 Cr App R 256).

It has become apparent from experience that child victims of sexual offences are sometimes reluctant to give evidence or unable to speak as to the facts. In *X* (1989) 91 Cr App R 36, information had come from the social services that some of the children in that case were likely to be affected in this way if they were confronted in court by seeing those against whom they had to give evidence, particularly their own father and other relations. The Court of Appeal approved the decision of the trial judge to erect a screen in such a way that although the children were prevented from seeing anyone in the dock, counsel and the jury were not prevented from seeing the children. The Court of Appeal agreed with the view of the trial judge that, in the circumstances, the necessity of trying to ensure that the children would be able to give evidence outweighed any possible prejudice to the accused. The trial in this case took place before the CJA 1988, s. 32, made provision for receiving the evidence of a child through a video link (see **D12.30**). However, screens will still serve a useful purpose in courts where no video equipment is available and, it is submitted, in magistrates' courts, to which s. 32 does not apply.

Determining the Competence of Children to Give Evidence

F4.17 If a judge has reason to doubt whether a child is capable of giving intelligible testimony, because the child is very young or has difficulty in expression or comprehension, he will conduct a preliminary investigation. Such an inquiry should be recorded by the shorthand writer so that it appears in the official transcript (*Khan* (1981) 73 Cr App R 190). The leading authority on the procedure to be followed, although not a decision under s. 33A(2A) of the 1988 Act, is *Hampshire* [1995] 3 WLR 260. The court held as follows:

(a)　The issue of competence should be dealt with at the earliest possible moment, not as an act of 'ratification' after the evidence has been given.

(b)　The judge should conduct the investigation. It is a matter of his perception of the child's understanding as demonstrated in ordinary discourse, not an issue to be resolved by him in response to an adversarial examination and cross-examination.

(c)　If there has been an application under the CJA 1988, s. 32A, to use video-recorded evidence, the judge's pre-trial view of the recording, if the interview has been properly conducted, will normally enable him to form a view on competence, but if it leaves him in doubt, he should conduct an investigation.

(d)　The investigation, whether in addition to an earlier view of a video-taped interview or not, should be conducted in open court in the presence of the accused.

(e)　Such an investigation should not be conducted in the presence of the jury. Dicta to the contrary in *Reynolds* [1950] 1 KB 606 were not necessary to that decision and attributed to *Dunne* (1929) 99 LJKB 117 a *ratio* it lacked. The jury's function is to assess the child's evidence on the facts of the case after he or she has been ruled competent. The exercise of determining competence is not a necessary aid to that function.

The test of whether a child is capable of giving 'intelligible testimony' does not require any input from experts such as child psychiatrists, because it is a simple test well within the capability of a judge or magistrate (see *G* v *DPP* [1997] 2 All ER 755, a decision which, it is submitted, should not be taken to prevent the adducing of appropriate expert medical evidence in the case of a mentally handicapped child).

As to the procedure for determining the competence of children to give evidence once the YJCEA 1999, ss. 53 to 56 are in force, see **F4.19**.

Persons of Unsound Mind

If, in the opinion of the judge, a proposed witness does not understand the nature of the　**F4.18** oath, he is incompetent to testify. In *Hill* (1851) 2 Den CC 254, a trial for manslaughter, a patient of a lunatic asylum who laboured under the delusion that he was surrounded by a number of spirits which were continually talking to him, but who nonetheless had a clear apprehension of the obligation of the oath, was held competent to give evidence for the prosecution. The modern test of the competence of a mentally handicapped person is secular; the question is not whether he understands the divine sanction of the oath, but whether he has a sufficient appreciation of the solemnity of the occasion, and the added responsibility to tell the truth, which is involved in taking an oath, over and above the duty to tell the truth which is an ordinary duty of normal social conduct (*Bellamy* (1985) 82 Cr App R 222).

If a judge conducts an inquiry into the competence of a mentally handicapped person, it is not normally necessary to call that person to give evidence on the subject — the proper course is to adduce appropriate expert medical evidence (*Barratt* [1996] Crim LR 495).

The evidence of a psychologist or other expert witness as to the capacity of the proposed witness to tell the truth should be given on the *voir dire* in the absence of the jurors, whom it cannot assist (*Deakin* [1994] 4 All ER 769). In *Deakin* it was also said that where the proposed witness is himself called to give evidence on his competence, the jury should be present because this may assist them in deciding whether to accept his evidence, if subsequently given. However, *Deakin*, in this respect, was based on *Reynolds* [1950] 1 KB 606 upon which, it has been held, reliance should no longer be placed (see *Hampshire* [1995] 3 WLR 260 at **F4.17**).

Where a mentally handicapped person does give evidence, it is left to the jury to attach to his evidence such weight as they see fit. If his evidence is so tainted with insanity as to be unworthy of credit, it is the proper function of the jury to disregard it and not to act upon it (*Hill*). However, a person suffering from a mental illness may be a reliable witness. In *Barratt*, in which the witness was suffering from the psychiatric condition known as fixed belief paranoia and held bizarre beliefs about certain aspects of her private life, the court could see no reason for supposing that on matters not affected by her condition, her evidence was not as reliable as that of any other witness.

The common-law test for determining the competence of a person of unsound mind to give evidence, and the procedure to be followed, will be replaced when the YJCEA 1999, ss. 53 to 56, are brought into force. The new provisions are considered at **F4.19**.

Competence and the Giving of Sworn and Unsworn Evidence under the Youth Justice and Criminal Evidence Act 1999

F4.19   Sections 53 to 57 of the YJCEA 1999 will, when brought into force, introduce changes in the law relating to the competence of witnesses to give evidence in criminal proceedings, determining their competence, determining whether they should be sworn, the reception of unsworn evidence and the penalty for giving false unsworn evidence.

Sections 54 to 57 of the 1999 Act provide as follows.

Youth Justice and Criminal Evidence Act 1999, ss. 53 to 57

53.—(1)   At every stage in criminal proceedings all persons are (whatever their age) competent to give evidence.
    (2)   Subsection (1) has effect subject to subsections (3) and (4).
    (3)   A person is not competent to give evidence in criminal proceedings if it appears to the court that he is not a person who is able to—
        (a)   understand questions put to him as a witness, and
        (b)   give answers to them which can be understood.
    (4)   A person charged in criminal proceedings is not competent to give evidence in the proceedings for the prosecution (whether he is the only person, or is one of two or more persons, charged in the proceedings).
    (5)   In subsection (4) the reference to a person charged in criminal proceedings does not include a person who is not, or is no longer, liable to be convicted of any offence in the proceedings (whether as a result of pleading guilty or for any other reason).

54.—(1)   Any question whether a witness in criminal proceedings is competent to give evidence in the proceedings, whether raised—
        (a)   by a party to the proceedings, or
        (b)   by the court of its own motion,
shall be determined by the court in accordance with this section.
    (2)   It is for the party calling the witness to satisfy the court that, on a balance of probabilities, the witness is competent to give evidence in the proceedings.
    (3)   In determining the question mentioned in subsection (1) the court shall treat the witness as having the benefit of any directions under section 19 [special measures directions in the case of vulnerable and intimidated witnesses] which the court has given, or proposes to give, in relation to the witness.
    (4)   Any proceedings held for the determination of the question shall take place in the absence of the jury (if there is one).
    (5)   Expert evidence may be received on the question.
    (6)   Any questioning of the witness (where the court considers that necessary) shall be conducted by the court in the presence of the parties.

55.—(1)   Any question whether a witness in criminal proceedings may be sworn for the purpose of giving evidence on oath, whether raised—

(a)   by a party to the proceedings, or

(b)   by the court of its own motion,

shall be determined by the court in accordance with this section.

(2)   The witness may not be sworn for that purpose unless—

(a)   he has attained the age of 14, and

(b)   he has a sufficient appreciation of the solemnity of the occasion and of the particular responsibility to tell the truth which is involved in taking an oath.

(3)   The witness shall, if he is able to give intelligible testimony, be presumed to have a sufficient appreciation of those matters if no evidence tending to show the contrary is adduced (by any party).

(4)   If any such evidence is adduced, it is for the party seeking to have the witness sworn to satisfy the court that, on a balance of probabilities, the witness has attained the age of 14 and has a sufficient appreciation of the matters mentioned in subsection (2)(b).

(5)   Any proceedings held for the determination of the question mentioned in subsection (1) shall take place in the absence of the jury (if there is one).

(6)   Expert evidence may be received on the question.

(7)   Any questioning of the witness (where the court considers that necessary) shall be conducted by the court in the presence of the parties.

(8)   For the purposes of this section a person is able to give intelligible testimony if he is able to—

(a)   understand questions put to him as a witness, and

(b)   give answers to them which can be understood.

56.—(1)   Subsections (2) and (3) apply to a person (of any age) who—

(a)   is competent to give evidence in criminal proceedings, but

(b)   (by virtue of section 55(2)) is not permitted to be sworn for the purpose of giving evidence on oath in such proceedings.

(2)   The evidence in criminal proceedings of a person to whom this subsection applies shall be given unsworn.

(3)   A deposition of unsworn evidence given by a person to whom this subsection applies may be taken for the purposes of criminal proceedings as if that evidence had been given on oath.

(4)   A court in criminal proceedings shall accordingly receive in evidence any evidence given unsworn in pursuance of subsection (2) or (3).

(5)   Where a person ('the witness') who is competent to give evidence in criminal proceedings gives evidence in such proceedings unsworn, no conviction, verdict or finding in those proceedings shall be taken to be unsafe for the purposes of any of sections 2(1), 13(1) and 16(1) of the Criminal Appeal Act 1968 (grounds for allowing appeals) by reason only that it appears to the Court of Appeal that the witness was a person falling within section 55(2) (and should accordingly have given his evidence on oath).

57.—(1)   This section applies where a person gives unsworn evidence in criminal proceedings in pursuance of section 56(2) or (3).

(2)   If such a person wilfully gives false evidence in such circumstances that, had the evidence been given on oath, he would have been guilty of perjury, he shall be guilty of an offence and liable on summary conviction to—

(a)   imprisonment for a term not exceeding 6 months, or

(b)   a fine not exceeding £1,000,

or both.

(3)   In relation to a person under the age of 14, subsection (2) shall have effect as if for the words following 'on summary conviction' there were substituted 'to a fine not exceeding £250'.

The Sovereign and Diplomats

The Sovereign is a competent but not a compellable witness. Total or partial immunity **F4.20** from compellability to give evidence is also enjoyed by heads of other sovereign states; diplomatic agents; members of the family of a diplomatic agent forming part of his household; members of the administrative and technical staff of a diplomatic mission and members of their families; persons connected with consular posts; and members of the staff of international organisations. See:

(a) Diplomatic Privileges Act 1964, s. 2(1) and sch. 1, arts 1, 31, 37, 38(2), and 39;
(b) Consular Relations Act 1968, s. 1(1) and sch. 1, arts 1(1), 44 and 58(2);
(c) International Organisations Act 1968;
(d) Diplomatic and Other Privileges Act 1971, s. 4;
(e) State Immunity Act 1978; and
(f) International Organisations Act 1981.

Bankers

F4.21 Subject to a variety of safeguards, a copy of an entry in a banker's book shall in all legal proceedings be received as prima facie evidence of such entry, and of the matters, transactions and accounts therein recorded (Bankers' Books Evidence Act 1879, ss. 3 and 9). Provision is made for proof that the book was one of the ordinary books of the bank, that the entry was made in the usual and ordinary course of business, that the book is in the custody and control of the bank, and that the copy has been examined with the original entry and is correct (ss. 4 and 5 of the 1879 Act). In any legal proceeding to which the bank is not a party, bank personnel cannot be compelled to produce the originals of such books or to give evidence to prove the matters recorded therein, unless specifically ordered to do so by a judge (see Bankers' Books Evidence Act 1879, s. 6 at **F8.27**).

OATHS AND AFFIRMATIONS

General Rule and Exceptions

F4.22 The general rule is that the evidence of any witness must be sworn, that is to say, given by a witness who has taken the oath or made an affirmation. Subject to the exceptions set out below, a conviction based on unsworn evidence may be set aside as a nullity (*Marsham, ex parte Pethick Lawrence* [1912] 2 KB 362). There, the accused was convicted of assault after summary trial, and was then retried by the same magistrates after it was discovered that at the first trial a witness had not given his evidence on oath. The accused argued that the retrial was improper, because it violated the rule that no one should stand in peril twice for the same offence. The Divisional Court held that the retrial was unobjectionable because the accused had never been in peril on the first trial, and therefore on the retrial could not object that the magistrates lacked jurisdiction.

To the general rule there are three exceptions:

(a) Children may give unsworn evidence pursuant to the CJA 1988, s. 33A (see **F4.16**).
(b) At common law a witness called merely for the purpose of producing a document need not be sworn (*Perry* v *Gibson* (1834) 1 A & E 48). Such a person, if not sworn, is not liable to cross-examination. However, if the identity of the document is disputed, and must be established, this must be done by sworn evidence.
(c) At common law, counsel acting for one of two parties who have reached a compromise may give unsworn evidence of its terms from the well of the court (*Hickman* v *Berens* [1895] 2 Ch 638). And in general, counsel is permitted to make factual representations robed in open court. However, the more recent practice of the Court of Appeal, where the court has to establish what happened at trial, is to call for evidence from counsel on affidavit.

Where a video recording of an interview with a child is admitted under the CJA 1988, s. 32A, and the child is then aged 14 or over, the oath should be administered before the start of the cross-examination (*Simmonds* [1996] Crim LR 816). Where the oath is administered at some later stage, the judge should warn the jury that the earlier answers were not evidence until given subsequent ratification. Without such an explanation, an appeal would be unanswerable (*Simmonds,* applying *Lee* [1988] Crim LR 525).

Form and Manner of Oath: Christians and Jews

Oaths Act 1978, s. 1   F4.23

(1)   Any oath may be administered and taken in England, Wales or Northern Ireland in the following form and manner: —

The person taking the oath shall hold the New Testament, or, in the case of a Jew, the Old Testament, in his uplifted hand, and shall say or repeat after the officer administering the oath the words 'I swear by Almighty God that . . .', followed by the words of the oath prescribed by law.

(4)   In this section 'officer' means any person duly authorised to administer oaths.

The words of s. 1 are directive; therefore failure to comply with them will not necessarily invalidate the taking of an oath, because the efficacy of an oath depends upon it being taken in a way binding, and intended to be binding, upon the conscience of the intended witness (*Chapman* [1980] Crim LR 42, where leave to appeal was refused, the witness in question having failed to take the Testament in his hand).

In the case of a witness in the trial proper, 'the words of the oath prescribed by law', approved by a resolution of the judges of the King's Bench Division on 11 January 1927, are 'the evidence which I shall give shall be the truth, the whole truth and nothing but the truth'. When a witness gives evidence in a trial within a trial, the oath is 'I swear by Almighty God that I will true answer make to all such questions as the Court shall demand of me.' In relation to any oath administered to and taken by any person before a youth court, or administered to and taken by any child or young person before any other court, s. 1 of the Oaths Act 1978 shall have effect as if the words 'I promise before Almighty God' were set out instead of the words 'I swear by Almighty God that' (CYPA 1963, s. 28(1)). Where, in any oath otherwise duly administered and taken, either of the forms mentioned in s. 28 of the CYPA 1963 is used instead of the other, the oath shall nevertheless be deemed to have been duly administered and taken (s. 28(2)).

Form and Manner of Oath: Other Religious Beliefs

Oaths Act 1978, s. 1   F4.24

(2)   The officer shall (unless the person about to take the oath voluntarily objects thereto, or is physically incapable of so taking the oath) administer the oath in the form and manner aforesaid without question.

(3)   In the case of a person who is neither a Christian nor a Jew, the oath shall be administered in any lawful manner.

(4)   In this section 'officer' means any person duly authorised to administer oaths.

Section 1(2) makes it clear that it is incumbent upon a person who is neither a Christian nor a Jew to object to the taking of an oath in the form and manner prescribed by s. 1(1). Such a person may affirm or may take the oath upon such holy book as is appropriate to his or her religious belief. Muslims are sworn on the Koran (*Morgan* (1764) 1 Leach 54). Hindus are sworn on the Vedas or other sacred books. Parsees are sworn on the Zendavesta. The modern practice is to inquire what oath a witness accepts as binding and swear him accordingly (Phipson, 13th ed., pp. 31–8).

Whether an oath is administered 'in a lawful manner' for the purposes of s. 1(3) does not depend on what may be the considerable intricacies of the particular religion adhered to by the witness but on (a) whether the oath appears to the court to be binding on the conscience of the witness and (b) whether it is an oath which the witness himself considers to be binding on his conscience (*Kemble* [1990] 1 WLR 1111). In that case a Muslim, who had taken the oath using the New Testament, was held to have been properly sworn because although, according to the strict tenets of Islam no oath taken by a Muslim is valid unless taken on a copy of the Koran in Arabic, the court considered the oath to be binding and the witness himself considered that his conscience was bound by the form of oath that he took.

Swearing with Uplifted Hand

F4.25   **Oaths Act 1978, s. 3**

If any person to whom an oath is administered desires to swear with uplifted hand, in the form and manner in which an oath is usually administered in Scotland, he shall be permitted to do so, and the oath shall be administered to him in such form and manner without further question.

Validity of Oaths

F4.26   **Oaths Act 1978, s. 4**

(1)   In any case in which an oath may lawfully be and has been administered to any person, if it has been administered in a form and manner other than that prescribed by law, he is bound by it if it has been administered in such form and with such ceremonies as he may have declared to be binding.

(2)   Where an oath has been duly administered and taken, the fact that the person to whom it was administered had, at the time of taking it, no religious belief, shall not for any purpose affect the validity of the oath.

Affirmations

F4.27   **Oaths Act 1978, ss. 5 and 6**

5.—(1)   Any person who objects to being sworn shall be permitted to make his solemn affirmation instead of taking an oath.

(2)   Subsection (1) above shall apply in relation to a person to whom it is not reasonably practicable without inconvenience or delay to administer an oath in the manner appropriate to his religious belief as it applies in relation to a person objecting to be sworn.

(3)   A person who may be permitted under subsection (2) above to make his solemn affirmation may also be required to do so.

(4)   A solemn affirmation shall be of the same force and effect as an oath.

6.—(1)   Subject to subsection (2) below, every affirmation shall be as follows: —
'I, [name] do solemnly, sincerely and truly declare and affirm,'
and then proceed with the words of the oath prescribed by law, omitting any words of imprecation or calling to witness.

(2)   Every affirmation in writing shall commence: —
'I, [name] of [address], do solemnly and sincerely affirm,'
and the form in lieu of the jurat shall be 'Affirmed at   this   day of   19   , Before me.'

SECTION F5: CORROBORATION

Sections 32 and 33 of the CJPO 1994, which came into force on 3 February 1995, **F5.1** abolished the rule requiring a corroboration warning to be given in relation to the evidence of accomplices and the evidence of complainants in sexual offences and the requirement for corroboration in offences under the Sexual Offences Act 1956, ss. 2, 3, 4, 22 and 23. The requirement for corroboration will remain for high treason (see **B9**), perjury (see **B14.14**) and offences of speeding (see **C5.81**). For the corroboration rules as they applied before ss. 32 and 33 came into force, see the 1995 edition of this work.

Criminal Justice and Public Order Act 1994, s. 32

32.—(1)   Any requirement whereby at a trial on indictment it is obligatory for the court to give the jury a warning about convicting the accused on the uncorroborated evidence of a person merely because that person is
    (a)   an alleged accomplice of the accused, or
    (b)   where the offence charged is a sexual offence, the person in respect of whom it is alleged to have been commited,
is hereby abrogated.
. . .
   (3)   Any requirement that—
    (a)   is applicable at the summary trial of a person for an offence, and
    (b)   corresponds to the requirement mentioned in subsection (1) above or that mentioned in section 34(2) of the Criminal Justice Act 1988,
is hereby abrogated.
   (4)   Nothing in this section applies in relation to—
    (a)   any trial, or
    (b)   any proceedings before a magistrates' court as examining justices,
which began before the commencement of this section.

Abrogation of the Common-law Rule Concerning the Corroboration Warning

The abrogation of the common law rule concerning the corroboration warning is a result **F5.2** of the recommendation contained in the Report of the Royal Commission on Criminal Justice (the Runciman Commission) (Cm 2263: 1993), which in turn adopted the Law Commission Report, Corroboration of Evidence in Criminal Trials (Law Com No. 202). The Law Commission Report criticised the test in *Baskerville* [1916] 2 KB 658, the common law rule and the statutory requirement relating to procuration offences under the Sexual Offences Act 1956 as having 'proved inflexible, complex, productive of anomalies' and 'inappropriate to the purpose they were intended to serve'. The Runciman Commission, whilst recognising the role of corroborative or supporting evidence in cases of identification, took into account that the general trend in the law had been away from corroboration requirements and that the abolition of the common law rule and the requirement of corroboration in offences of procuring under the Sexual Offences Act 1956 would lead to simplification of the issues in the minds of the jury. However, in such cases, both the Law Commission and the Runciman Commission recognised that there would remain instances in which judicial warnings about unsupported evidence would be both necessary and appropriate. As the Runciman Commission stated (ch. 8, para. 35):

> It may still be necessary for the judge . . . to warn the jury of the dangers of accepting evidence from particular witnesses. We agree, however, with the Law Commission that the approach should be not that the same warning should be applied inflexibly to every case but that, if a warning is required, the judge should tailor it to the particular circumstances of the case.

Confession Evidence and Corroboration

F5.3   In dealing with safeguards against false confessions, in the context of permitting adverse comment at trial on the silence of the accused in the face of police questioning (see **F19.4**), the Runciman Commission devoted considerable attention to the question of whether or not there should be a requirement for supporting evidence or a corroboration warning in cases where there was confession evidence. Whilst the Commission was unable to agree on the proposition that a conviction should never be based on confession evidence alone it recommended the retention of the existing safeguards set out in the PACE 1984, the reversal of *Galbraith* [1981] WLR 1091, (see **D13.27**), the re-introduction of a judicial power to stop any case if the judge takes the view 'that the prosecution evidence is demonstrably unsafe or unsatisfactory or too weak to be allowed to go to the jury' and that the judge should give a strong warning in all cases before relying on confession evidence.

The Runciman Commission envisaged a warning which indicates that great care is needed before convicting on the basis of a confession alone and referring to the possible reasons for persons confessing to crimes which they did not commit. The judge would draw attention to any reasons advanced by the defence as to why the confession may be false and, if appropriate, state 'that cases have been known in which persons have confessed for similar reasons to offences which they did not commit'. In addition:

> The judge would then direct the jury as to what evidence, if any, had been given that was capable of supporting the confession. If there was no such supporting evidence, the judge would so direct the jury. Where the confession had not been tape recorded, the warning would draw attention to this fact and to any possible motive that the person to whom the confession was made might have for fabricating the confession. Finally, since supporting evidence would not be an absolute requirement, the judge would explain that if, after giving full weight to the warning, the jury were nevertheless satisfied that the confession was true, they could convict even in the absence of supporting evidence.

Supporting evidence would be evidence in the sense used to describe evidence supporting identification in *Turnbull* [1977] QB 224; the effect of the evidence would be to make the jury sure that the contents of the confession, once admitted, are credible and that they may safely convict on it despite any dangers to which their attention has been drawn.

Suspect Witnesses

F5.4   The Runciman Commission did not envisage, and there is nothing in the CJPO 1994 to impose, a prohibition on the issuing of appropriate warnings. The difficulty is in establishing when a warning will be appropriate and whether or not a failure to give such a warning will be fatal to a conviction.

Now that the CJPO 1994, ss. 32 and 33, are in force, nearly all the old categories of witness whose evidence needed corroboration or a corroboration warning have been swept away. It seems unlikely that replacement categories will spring up, except, possibly, in relation to confession evidence, but there will remain cases in which the evidence of a witness may be subject to a warning, suitably tailored to the facts of the case, either because that witness is suspect or because his evidence is potentially unreliable. See, for example, the need for a warning in identification cases (see **F18**), and the remarks of Ackner LJ in *Beck* [1982] 1 WLR 461 and *Spencer* [1987] AC 128. Such cases may, perhaps most likely will, involve the evidence of accomplices or complainants in allegations of sexual misconduct. To that extent the existing categories may provide a useful framework for judges in deciding when it is appropriate to give a tailored warning but, it is submitted, it will not be necessary or, indeed, desirable to give a warning unless there is an adequate reason for doing so.

In *Makanjuola* [1995] 1 WLR 1348, the Court of Appeal recognised that a discretion to warn the jury about convicting on the evidence of an unreliable witness remained. Lord Taylor LCJ gave guidelines in respect of the exercise of the discretion (at pp. 1351):

(1) Section 32(1) abrogated the requirement to give a corroboration direction in respect of an alleged accomplice or a complainant of a sexual offence, simply because a witness falls into one of those categories. (2) It is a matter for the judge's discretion what, if any warning, he considers appropriate in respect of such a witness as indeed in respect of any other witness in whatever type of case. Whether he chooses to give a warning and in what terms will depend on the circumstances of the case, the issues raised and the content and quality of the witness's evidence. (3) In some cases, it may be appropriate for the judge to warn the jury to exercise caution before acting upon the unsupported evidence of a witness. This will not be so simply because the witness is a complainant of a sexual offence nor will it necessarily be so because a witness is alleged to be an accomplice. There will need to be an evidential basis for suggesting that the evidence of the witness may be unreliable. An evidential basis does not include mere suggestion by cross-examining counsel. (4) If any question arises as to whether the judge should give a special warning in respect of a witness, it is desirable that the question be resolved by discussion with counsel in the absence of the jury before final speeches. (5) Where the judge does decide to give some warning in respect of a witness, it will be appropriate to do so as part of the judge's review of the evidence and his comments as to how the jury should evaluate it rather than as a set-piece legal direction. (6) Where some warning is required, it will be for the judge to decide the strength and terms of the warning. It does not have to be invested with the whole florid regime of the old corroboration rules. (7) . . . Attempts to re-impose the straitjacket of the old corroboration rules are strongly to be deprecated. (8) Finally, this court will be disinclined to interfere with a trial judge's exercise of his discretion save in a case where that exercise is unreasonable in the *Wednesbury* sense: see *Associated Provincial Picture Houses Ltd* v *Wednesbury Corporation* [1948] 1 KB 223.

It is evident from the guidelines that the traditional warning which follows *Baskerville* [1916] 2 KB 658 does not have to be given and the retention of any discretionary warning in that form is clearly not envisaged by the Court of Appeal. The concept of corroboration or the need for a corroboration warning in its traditional form is firmly denigrated and the exercise of the discretion placed in the context of a 'suspect witness' whose evidence, for one reason or another and with varying degrees of force, the jury should be told to treat with caution. Thus, as was said by the Lord Taylor LCJ in *Makanjuola*:

Where, however, the witness has been shown to be unreliable, [the judge] may consider it necessary to urge caution. In a more extreme case, if the witness is shown to have lied, to have made previous false complaints, or to bear the defendant some grudge, a stronger warning may be thought appropriate and the judge may suggest it would be wise to look for some supporting material before acting on the impugned witness's evidence.

The form of the warning does not have to follow any set or established pattern, although where a warning is to be given it is submitted that it must remain good practice to identify the reason or reasons why the testimony of a witness may need to be treated with caution and, where a stronger warning may be appropriate and the judge recommends to the jury that it would be wise to look for supporting evidence, what that evidence may be and whether or not it is independent or in itself capable of being suspect as it emanates from a witness who is suspect (see *R* [1996] Crim LR 815).

Makanjuola represents a complete retreat from any lingering vestige of the corroboration rules. It was argued in favour of the repeal of those rules that the accused would be adequately protected by the duty of the trial judge to draw attention to actual or potentially unreliable evidence and in certain cases to warn the jury about witnesses who may have interests of their own to serve. This, indeed, appears to be the import of the decision in *Makanjuola*. However it is to be noted that the Court of Appeal adopts language which is not mandatory whilst at the same time stating that they would be disinclined to interfere with any exercise of the discretion which was not *Wednesbury* unreasonable. This approach arguably may reduce the effectiveness of those safeguards which the Law Commission relied upon as being present to ensure that the interests of the accused are adequately safeguarded. If the failure to give a warning is viewed as a decision on a question of law, as it appears may have been the intention behind the decision in *Makanjuola*, the Court of Appeal may still have to consider, it is submitted, whether or not such a failure has rendered the verdict unsafe or unsatisfactory. For consideration of authorities on collusion and propensity, see **F12**.

Previous Authorities on Suspect Witnesses

F5.5   Earlier authorities such as *Prater* [1960] 2 QB 464; *Beck* [1982] 1 WLR 461 and *Spencer* [1987] AC 128 provided some guidance on the sort of case which might, whilst falling outside the established guidelines, have merited a judicial warning. Apart from the (then) established categories of children, accomplices and complainants in sexual cases, the authorities gave consideration to the evidence of co-accused (as witnesses in their own defence: *Prater, Knowlden* (1981) 77 Cr App R 94, *Loveridge* (1982) 76 Cr App R 125 and *Cheema* [1994] 1 WLR 147) mental patients, including those with a 'criminal connection' who were capable of fulfilling an analagous criteria to those witnesses in the accepted categories (*Bagshaw* [1984] 1 WLR 477 and *Spencer*) and witnesses who may be said to have improper motives or interests of their own to serve (*Beck*). Whilst the strength of the warnings to be given varied from case to case (see, for example, *Mills* [1993] Crim LR 210), there emerged, particularly in respect of witnesses who fulfilled analagous criteria in the light of their mental condition and criminal connection, a category of witness whose evidence merited what has been termed a discretionary full warning. The courts were, however, generally unwilling to adopt any general rule requiring a corroboration warning in the case of a witness with an improper motive or an axe to grind. In *Beck* [1982] 1 WLR 461, the authorities were reviewed by the Court of Appeal and it was expressly recognised (per Ackner LJ at p. 469) that there was an obligation 'to advise a jury to proceed with caution when there was material to suggest that a witness's evidence may be tainted by an improper motive', albeit that the strength of such advice should vary according to the facts of the case. However, the suggestion that there was any obligation to give a full corroboration warning in respect of a witness who did not fall within the established categories was expressly rejected.

In *Spencer*, Lord Ackner, having reviewed the earlier authorities, said (at p. 142):

> The certified point of law is in these terms:
>
> 'In a case where the evidence for the Crown is solely that of a witness who is not in one of the accepted categories of suspect witnesses, but who, by reason of his particular mental condition and criminal connection, fulfilled the same criteria, must the judge warn the jury that it is dangerous to convict on his uncorroborated evidence.'
>
> I would amend the question by substituting for the words 'the same criteria' 'analogous criteria'. I would then answer the question in the affirmative, adding, for the sake of clarity, that while it may often be convenient to use the words 'danger' or 'dangerous', the use of such words is not essential to an adequate warning, so long as the jury are made fully aware of the dangers of convicting on such evidence. Again, for the sake of clarity I would further add that *Beck* [1982] 1 WLR 461 was rightly decided and that in a case which does not fall into the three established categories and where there exists potential corroborative material, the extent to which the trial judge should make reference to that material depends upon the facts of each case. The overriding rule is that he must put the defence fairly and adequately.

This question was again considered in *Brown* [1992] Crim LR 178, where the Court of Appeal stated that, in the absence of satisfactory evidence that a witness is an accomplice, a suspect witness warning would be sufficient.

In light of the CJPO 1994, ss. 32 and 33, and *Makanjuola* [1995] 1 WLR 1348, there would seem to be little, if any, room for the retention of a discretionary full corroboration warning and any other warning akin to a corroboration warning is subject to a judicial discretion. However, it is submitted, the previous authorities provide considerable support for the proposition that there is a judicial duty to warn the jury, in appropriate terms, in cases where the evidence of a witness is suspect, as part of the duty to ensure that the defence has been put fairly and adequately by the judge. That duty or obligation is a different one from the requirement which previously existed to give a corroboration warning and as such, it is submitted, survives the enactment of ss. 32 and 33.

Lies of the Accused

The lies of an accused, whether in or out of court, have now only a very limited function F5.6 as corroboration. They may still however be relied upon by the prosecution as supporting evidence of the accused's guilt. For a full discussion of the significance of an accused's lies, see **F1.12**.

Meaning of Corroboration

Although nearly all the old categories of witness whose evidence needed corroboration F5.7 or a corroboration warning have been swept away (see **F5.1**), it may still from time to time be necessary to consider the technical meaning of the term 'corroboration'.

The word connotes support or confirmation, and indicates that certain evidence is confirmed in its tenor and effect by other admissible and independent evidence. In any case where one piece of evidence confirms and supports another, corroboration takes place if both pieces of evidence are accepted by the tribunal of fact.

The classic definition of corroboration is to be found in *Baskerville* [1916] 2 KB 658 (per Lord Reid at p. 667):

> . . . evidence in corroboration must be independent testimony which affects the accused by connecting or tending to connect him with the crime. In other words, it must be evidence which implicates him, that is, which confirms in some material particular not only the evidence that the crime has been committed, but also that the prisoner committed it. The test applicable to determine the nature and extent of the corroboration is thus the same whether the case falls within the rule of practice at common law or within that class of offences for which corroboration is required by statute.

See also *DPP* v *Kilbourne* [1973] AC 729, per Lord Hailsham at p. 741.

Thus in order to satisfy the full technical meaning of the term corroboration, evidence must be:

   (a)   admissible in itself;
   (b)   from a source independent of the evidence required to be corroborated; and
   (c)   such as to tend to show, by confirmation of some material particular, not only that the offence charged was committed, but also that it was committed by the accused.

SECTION F6: EXAMINATION-IN-CHIEF

The object of examination-in-chief (examination of a witness by the party calling him) is to elicit from the witness evidence supportive of the party's case. Examination-in-chief must be conducted in accordance with the exclusionary rules of general application, such as those relating to hearsay, opinion and the character of the accused. This section concerns five other rules governing examination-in-chief:

(a) the rule requiring the prosecution to call all of their evidence before the close of their case; and the rules relating to
(b) leading questions;
(c) refreshing the memory;
(d) previous consistent or self-serving statements; and
(e) impeaching the credit of one's own witness.

RULE REQUIRING PROSECUTION TO CALL ALL THEIR EVIDENCE BEFORE THE CLOSE OF THEIR CASE

General Rule

F6.1   It is a rule of practice, but not law, that all of the evidence which the prosecution intend to rely on as probative of the guilt of the accused should be called before the close of their case (*Rice* [1963] 1 QB 857). The rule applies not only to the adducing of evidence, but also to matters put in cross-examination of the accused (see *Kane* (1977) 65 Cr App R 270). In *Kane*, Scarman LJ said (at p. 274):

> In general, evidence which is capable of forming part of the affirmative case for the prosecution should be tendered and led in the course of that case. If it did not form part of the evidence upon which an accused was committed for trial the practice is to give notice of the additional evidence to the defence before it is tendered.

The rule is confined to evidence probative of guilt, and does not extend to evidence going only to the credit of the accused (*Halford* (1978) 67 Cr App R 318). In that case the trial judge had allowed the prosecution to introduce for the first time in cross-examination of the accused, in order to test his credit, two statements made by him at the investigation stage. There was no suggestion that the statements had been made involuntarily, but the judge, in allowing the cross-examination, said that he would also allow the defence to call evidence to show that the statements were improperly obtained or that their admission would result in injustice.

Where evidence which could have been led as a part of the prosecution case becomes available to the prosecution for the first time after the close of their case, the question of its introduction or exclusion should be referred to and decided by the judge (*Kane* (1977) 65 Cr App R 270). In that case prosecuting counsel first knew of a conversation between the accused and a police officer after the close of the prosecution case. The prosecution, without obtaining the leave of the judge or notifying the defence, cross-examined the accused on the conversation. The Court of Appeal held that the trial judge had wrongly rejected a subsequent defence application for the jury to be discharged.

There are three exceptions to the rule which call for consideration at this stage:

(a) evidence not previously available;
(b) failure to call evidence by reason of inadvertence or oversight; and
(c) evidence in rebuttal of matters arising *ex improviso*.

Evidence in rebuttal is also admissible under the exceptions to the general rule that answers given by a witness under cross-examination to questions concerning collateral matters must be treated as final (see **F7.19** to **F7.24**). As to evidence in rebuttal of evidence of the good character of the accused, see *Rowton* (1855) Le & Ca 520 and **F13**.

Evidence Not Previously Available

The question whether or not evidence available for the first time after the close of the **F6.2** prosecution case should be admitted, is a matter to be determined by the trial judge in his discretion, which should be exercised in such a way and subject to such safeguards as seem to him best suited to achieve justice between the Crown and the defendants, and between the defendants. However, the admission of such evidence will be rare (*Rice* [1963] 1 QB 857, per Winn J). The evidence may be admitted even if not strictly of a rebutting character, but the court must be vigilant in the exercise of its discretion, in case injustice is done to the accused, and should consider whether it is desirable to grant a defence application for an adjournment (*Doran* (1972) 56 Cr App R 429). In *Doran* the prosecution were allowed to call two witnesses after the close of their case. The witnesses, the existence of whom the prosecution had no prior knowledge, were members of the public, present at the trial, who realised that they could give material evidence. See also *Patel* [1992] Crim LR 739, where the judge gave defence counsel the opportunity to seek an adjournment, take further instructions and call evidence. In *Pilcher* (1974) 60 Cr App R 1, the Court of Appeal, having recognised the general rule and the exception in the case of evidence in rebuttal of matters arising *ex improviso*, i.e. evidence which becomes relevant in circumstances which the prosecution could not have foreseen at the time when they presented their case (see **F6.4**), said (at p. 5):

> We do not say that . . . where the matter has not arisen *ex improviso* the judge had no kind of discretion at all, but we are firmly of opinion that in cases where the matter does not arise *ex improviso* the judge's discretion should not be exercised to allow the late introduction of an additional witness called for the prosecution whose evidence was available before the case for the prosecution closed.

As was pointed out in *Scott* (1984) 79 Cr App R 49, however, the judgment in *Pilcher* seems to narrow the circumstances in which evidence can be called in rebuttal in a way which does not agree with *Doran* (1972) 56 Cr App R 429. It is submitted that *Pilcher* should not be treated as restricting either the exception recognised in *Doran* or the exception, considered at **F6.3**, in the case of failure to call evidence of a formal or technical nature by reason of inadvertence or oversight.

Failure to Call Evidence by Reason of Inadvertence or Oversight

The judge has a discretion to admit evidence of a formal, technical or uncontentious **F6.3** nature which, by reason of inadvertence or oversight, has not been adduced by the prosecution before the close of their case. Many of the cases relate to the failure to prove a statutory instrument by production of a Stationery Office copy. In *Palastanga* v *Solman* [1962] Crim LR 334, a case brought under the Motor Vehicles (Construction and Use) Regulations 1955, defence counsel, as a preliminary point, submitted that the burden of proving the regulation in question was on the prosecution, and since a Stationery Office copy had not been produced, the burden had not been discharged. The justices thereupon dismissed the summons. The Divisional Court held that it was a disgraceful point to take. The justices should have adjourned the matter, if the defence had persisted in their submission, to allow the prosecutor to obtain a Stationery Office copy. Failure to produce such a copy did not justify dismissal of the summons. See also *Duffin* v *Markham* (1918) 88 LJ KB 581 and *Royal* v *Prescott-Clarke* [1966] 1 WLR 788, a case of unlawfully driving on a motorway, in which it was held that, after the close of the prosecution case, justices, in the exercise of their discretion, should have allowed the prosecution an adjournment to prove the Special Roads (Notice of Opening) Regulations 1962 and the publication of certain notices of opening thereunder. Compare *Tyrell* v *Cole* (1918) 120 LT 156; and *Ashley* (1967) 52 Cr App R 42: the Prison Rules 1964 require proof by production of a Queen's Printer's Copy. Similarly, evidence may be admitted to make good a failure to prove that leave of the DPP to bring proceedings has been obtained (see *Price* v *Humphries* [1958] 2 QB 353, in which a submission of no case having succeeded on the basis of the failure to prove such consent, the Divisional Court, applying *Waller* [1910] 1 KB 364 and allowing the appeal, held that unless the defence object before the close of the prosecution case, the court should act on the assumption that the clerk had fulfilled his duty, on the application for issue of the summons, to check that the appropriate consent had been given). A further example is *McKenna* (1956) 40 Cr App R 65, a charge of exporting articles made wholly or mainly of iron or steel, in which a submission of no case was made on the basis that no evidence had been adduced that the articles in question, which included steamrollers, lorries, traction engines and concrete mixers, were made of iron or steel. The judge recalled a prosecution witness to give such evidence. It was held that in the circumstances the judge had a complete discretion whether to allow a witness to be recalled; the appellate courts would not interfere with the exercise of that discretion unless it had resulted in an injustice. On the facts, there was no injustice: it required no great leap of the imagination to think that the objects in question were made of iron or steel, and even in the absence of the additional evidence, there was a case to answer.

In appropriate circumstances the prosecution, after the close of their case, may even be permitted to call evidence relating to a matter of substance. Thus, in *Piggott* v *Simms* [1973] RTR 15, in which the prosecution, after the close of their case, were given leave to admit in evidence an analyst's certificate, the Divisional Court held that, although this was a failure to adduce a vital part of their prosecution case, the justices had an absolute discretion to allow the evidence to be admitted. Likewise in *Matthews* v *Morris* [1981] Crim LR 495, it was held that justices had correctly permitted the prosecution to reopen their case to put in evidence a statement, made by the owner of the money allegedly stolen, which, although it had been served on the defence under the CJA 1967, s. 9, was omitted from the prosecution case by reason of simple mistake. According to *Middleton* v *Rowlett* [1954] 1 WLR 831 the court even has a discretion in the case of evidence relating to the identity of the accused. That was a case of dangerous driving, in which the magistrates had refused to allow the prosecution to reopen their case in order to prove the identity of the driver. Although the Divisional Court described the case as 'borderline', it was held that the magistrates were not bound to exercise their discretion in favour of the prosecution.

In *Francis* [1990] 1 WLR 1264, the prosecution called an identification witness to give evidence that at a group identification he had identified the man standing in position number 20 but failed to call any evidence to prove that the man standing at that position was the appellant. The failure was due to a simple misunderstanding between counsel: counsel for the prosecution was under the impression that the name of the person standing at that position was not in issue. After the close of the prosecution case, the trial judge allowed the prosecution to recall the inspector in charge of the identification to say who it was who was standing at position number 20. On appeal, it was held that although the failure was not a mere technicality, but an essential, if minor, link in the chain of identification evidence, the discretion of the judge to admit evidence after the close of the prosecution case is not limited to cases where an issue has arisen *ex improviso* or where what has been omitted is a mere formality. This was one of those rare cases falling outside the two established exceptions and the judge had not erred in the exercise of his discretion. See also, applying *Francis*, *Jackson* [1996] 2 Cr App R 420.

In *Munnery* [1992] Crim LR 215, where the judge allowed the prosecution to call a witness after the close of its case but before the defence case had begun, it was held that the proposition in *Francis*, that the discretion should only rarely be exercised outside the two exceptions, could be expanded to include the words 'especially when the evidence is tendered after the case for the defendant has begun'. An example of the discretion being exercised at this late stage is *James v South Glamorgan County Council* (1994) 99 Cr App R 321. In that case, in which there had not been a submission of no case to answer, the prosecution were allowed to reopen their case, after the accused had given his evidence-in-chief, to call their main witness, who had arrived late because of transport difficulties and genuine confusion as to the whereabouts of the court. Evidence may also be called, at this late stage, by the judge himself. In *Bowles* [1992] Crim LR 726, the defence case had begun when the trial judge, in answer to a question from the jury, decided in the interests of justice to admit further evidence himself, rather than have the prosecution re-open its case. It was held that the judge was justified in calling the evidence; the defence had not yet closed their case, the evidence was non-controversial and did not contradict that of the accused (although it did support the prosecution case) and it is 'undesirable that a jury should decide a case on a factual basis which may be false and the truth or falsity of which has been raised by the jury and can easily and readily be resolved without injustice to the accused'. See also *Aitken* (1991) 94 Cr App R 85, where the jury was provided with a written summary of a tape-recorded interview during which the accused had made an admission. The accused said that the admission was made under pressure and was untrue. During the defence closing speech, the jury asked to listen to the tape and, when the speech was concluded and after hearing submissions, the judge allowed them to do so. The appeal was dismissed. Where the judge is satisfied that no injustice will be done to the accused, the admission of further evidence is a matter of discretion for the judge.

The discretion should not be used to allow the prosecution the opportunity to prove the very matter in issue which it has failed to prove. In *Gainsborough Justices, ex parte Green* (1984) 78 Cr App R 9, the prosecution evidence in support of an allegation of a breach of a community service order revealed no such breach. The justices, rejecting a submission of no case to answer, allowed further evidence to be called to establish the breach. The Divisional Court quashed the conviction.

Evidence in Rebuttal of Matters Arising *Ex Improviso*

There is no doubt that the general rule is that where the Crown begins its case like a plaintiff **F6.4** in a civil suit, they cannot afterwards support their case by calling fresh witnesses, because they are met by certain evidence that contradicts it. They stand or fall by the evidence they have given. They must close their case before the defence begins; but if any matter arises, *ex improviso* which no human ingenuity can foresee, on the part of a defendant in a civil suit, or a prisoner in a criminal case, there seems to me no reason why that matter which so arose *ex improviso* may not be answered by contrary evidence on the part of the Crown. (*Frost* (1839) 4 St Tr NS 85 per Tindal CJ at col. 386)

Lord Goddard CJ, in *Owen* [1952] 2 QB 362, said of this statement (at p. 367) that it was in 'probably wider language than would be applied at the present day'. Under the modern law, it is for the judge, in the exercise of his discretion, to determine whether the relevance of the evidence in question could *reasonably* have been anticipated (*Scott* (1984) 79 Cr App R 49). If the prosecution can reasonably foresee that certain evidence, available *ab initio*, is relevant to their case, it must be adduced as a part of that case and not to remedy defects in the case after it has been closed (*Day* [1940] 1 All ER 402). In *Day*, a charge of forgery and obtaining money by a forged instrument, the prosecution had in their possession from the start of the proceedings, specimens of the accused's admitted handwriting. The prosecution's case depended on the uncorroborated evidence of an accomplice. After the close of the defence case, the judge allowed the prosecution to call a handwriting expert. Quashing the conviction, the Court of Criminal Appeal held that the judge had wrongly exercised his discretion in admitting the additional evidence, which did not relate to any matter that had arisen *ex improviso* but the possible need for which ought to have been foreseen. *Day* may be contrasted with *Milliken* (1969) 53 Cr App R 330, in which the accused, when giving evidence, for the first time accused certain police officers, some of whom gave evidence that they had seen the accused committing the offence, of a conspiracy to fabricate evidence. The trial judge allowed the prosecution to call evidence in rebuttal, on the basis that such evidence became relevant only when the accused gave evidence, a ruling upheld by the Court of Appeal. (The Court of Appeal also held that the evidence in question was not in any sense probative of the guilt of the accused, since it consisted of no more than denials of the accusations of conspiracy and concoction, but cf. *Busby* (1981) 75 Cr App R 79 and *Mendy* (1976) 64 Cr App R 4, which are considered at **F7.19** and **F7.21**.) See also *Flynn* (1957) 42 Cr App R 15, in which the prosecution were allowed to call evidence in rebuttal of an alibi defence, the details of which became known for the first time when the accused gave evidence; and *Blick* (1966) 50 Cr App R 280.

The *ex improviso* principle requires the prosecution to adduce evidence before the close of its case only if it is clearly relevant. Thus, in *Levy* (1966) 50 Cr App R 198, it was held that there was room for the exercise by the judge of his discretion to admit, in rebuttal, evidence in the possession of the prosecution *ab initio*, which was of marginal relevance. The Court of Criminal Appeal said (at p. 202):

> It is quite clear and long established that the judge has a discretion with regard to the admission of evidence in rebuttal; the field in which that discretion can be exercised is limited by the principle that evidence which is clearly relevant – not marginally, minimally or doubtfully relevant, but clearly relevant – to the issues and within the possession of the Crown should be adduced by the prosecution as part of the prosecution's cases and such evidence cannot properly be admitted after evidence for the defence.

Equally, the *ex improviso* principle has to be applied with a recognition that the prosecution are expected to act reasonably to what may be suggested as pre-trial warnings of evidence likely to be given which calls for denial beforehand, and to suggestions put in cross-examination of their witnesses. 'They are not expected to take notice of fanciful and unreal statements no matter from what source they emanate' (*Hutchinson* (1985) 82 Cr App R 51, per Watkins LJ at p. 59). In this case, the accused was convicted of murder. Before the trial he wrote a letter, passed on to the DPP, containing allegations against a journalist. At the trial he alleged that the journalist was the murderer. The Court of Appeal held that the trial judge, at the close of the defence case, had properly given leave to the prosecution to call the journalist to give evidence in rebuttal; although the letter had alerted them to the possibility of what the accused might say in evidence, it contained many other allegations which were so obviously ridiculous and untrue as to justify the prosecution in regarding the whole of it either as a wicked farrago of lying nonsense or the ravings of a deranged mind. It was unreasonable, therefore, to say that the prosecution should have anticipated that anything said in it would be repeated in court.

It seems that the prosecution may rely upon the *ex improviso* principle to adduce evidence not only in rebuttal of defence *evidence*, but also, in appropriate circumstances, in rebuttal of matters unsupported by evidence but arising by implication from the submissions made by counsel for the defence in his closing speech (*O'Hadhmaill* [1996] Crim LR 509).

LEADING QUESTIONS

Leading Questions Generally Impermissible in Chief

F6.5 The general rule is that in examination-in-chief a witness may not be asked leading questions, i.e. questions framed in such a way as to suggest the answer sought or to assume the existence of facts yet to be established. Evidence elicited by such questions is not inadmissible, but the weight to be attached to it may be substantially reduced (*Moor* v *Moor* [1954] 1 WLR 927; *Wilson* (1913) 9 Cr App R 124). 'Leading' is a relative, not an absolute, term (W. M. Best, *The Principles of the Law of Evidence*, 12th ed. by S. L. Phipson (London: Sweet & Maxwell, 1922) at p. 562); and for this reason strict adherence to the rule is not always desirable or possible. Thus leading questions may be allowed, in the interests of justice, at the discretion of the judge. For example, when a magistrate dies in the course of a case in which a witness has given his evidence, the witness, when recalled before a new magistrate, may be asked whether his deposition represents his evidence (*Ex parte Bottomley* [1909] 2 KB 14, at p. 21). It is virtually impossible to ask a witness to identify a person or object in court without the use of leading questions, and accordingly leading questions of this kind are also allowed (see *Watson* (1817) 2 Stark 116, at p. 128). There are two other frequently recurring situations to which the general rule does not apply:

(a) Leading questions may be asked on formal and introductory matters, such as a witness's name, address and occupation; and questions which relate to other relevant facts which are not in dispute, or which are merely introductory to questions about facts which are in dispute, are also generally allowed (*Robinson* (1897) 61 JP 520).

(b) Leading questions may be put to a witness if the party calling him has been given leave to treat him as hostile (see **F6.21**).

REFRESHING THE MEMORY

Refreshing Memory in Court

A witness, in the course of giving his evidence, may refer to a document in order to **F6.6** refresh his memory, provided that the document:

(a) was made or verified by him contemporaneously with the events in question;
(b) is, in certain cases, the original; and
(c) is produced for inspection (if called for by either the court or the opposite party).

These conditions are considered separately below. A witness refreshing his memory in court will normally do so in examination-in-chief but, provided the conditions are met, there is nothing wrong in principle in allowing a witness to refresh his memory during re-examination (*Harman* (1984) 148 JP 289; *Sutton* (1991) 94 Cr App R 70). The rule applies to any witness, including the accused (*Britton* [1987] 1 WLR 539). The application will normally be made by counsel, but it is the proper function of the judge, where the interests of justice demand it, to suggest that a witness, including a prosecution witness, refresh his memory from a document (*Tyagi* (1986) *The Times*, 21 July 1986, per Ralph Gibson LJ). In *Tyagi*, in which the witness was allowed to refresh his memory from a contemporaneous document outside court while the court adjourned, it was held that it would have been preferable for the witness to have remained in court with the document in front of him in the witness-box.

The rule applies not only in the case of 'present recollection revived' (J. H. Wigmore, *Evidence in Trials at Common Law*, vol. 3 (revised by J. H. Chadbourn) (Boston Mass: Little, Brown & Co., 1970), ch. 28), where the witness refreshes his memory by the sight of the document, but also in the case of 'past recollection recorded' (ibid., *loc. cit.*), where the witness has no independent recollection of the facts in question but testifies as to the accuracy of the contents of the document (see, e.g., *Maugham* v *Hubbard* (1828) 8 B & C 14, where a witness with no independent recollection of receiving a certain sum of monaey, was allowed to look at an unstamped receipt bearing his signature, and which was itself inadmissible, and then to give evidence that he had received the sum specified). See also *Topham* v *M'Gregor* (1844) 1 Car & Kir 320 and *Bryant* (1946) 31 Cr App R 146. To say that the witness in such a case has refreshed his memory is to create a fiction. In principle, it is submitted, it would be preferable to treat the out-of-court statement as a variety of admissible hearsay, and admit the document itself as evidence of the truth of its contents. However, it is well established that where the rule operates, then, save in exceptional circumstances, it is what the witness says and not the document itself which constitutes the evidence in the case (*Maugham* v *Hubbard* (1828) 8 B & C 14). See further *Sekhon* (1987) 85 Cr App R 19 and *Virgo* (1978) 67 Cr App R 323.

Making or Verification of Document

F6.7   The witness may refresh his memory from a document prepared either by himself or by another, provided, in the latter case, that he, the witness, verified the document at a time when the facts were still fresh in his memory. In *Langton* (1876) 2 QBD 296, a pay-clerk was allowed to refresh his memory as to the sums paid by him to workmen by reference to entries in a time-book. The entries, which were of days worked and wages due, had been made by another clerk and had been seen by the pay-clerk at pay-time, when the accused had read from the book to enable the pay-clerk to pay wages in accordance with it. Likewise, entries in a ship's log-book, made by the mate and verified by the captain about a week later, could be used to refresh the captain's memory (*Anderson* v *Whalley* (1852) 3 Car & Kir 54). A witness may also refresh his memory from his deposition or from a statement to the police taken down by a police officer and then read over by the maker (see *Mullins* (1848) 3 Cox CC 528; *Gleed* v *Stroud* (1962) 26 JCL 161; and *Lau Pak Ngam* v *R* [1966] Crim LR 443, approved in *Richardson* [1971] 2 QB 484). See also *Sekhon* (1987) 85 Cr App R 19: an observation log compiled by one officer and containing (a) entries based on his own observations, and (b) entries, based on what was reported to him by other officers engaged in the same activity, which were verified by those officers signing such entries at the first convenient opportunity, may be used by the officers to refresh their memories if the usual evidential basis for the application is established (cf. *Eleftheriou* [1993] Crim LR 947). In the case of interpreters, see *Attard* (1958) 43 Cr App R 90: at an interview at which an accused is questioned through an interpreter, in the absence of an independent note made by the interpreter of the questions put and the answers given, the interpreter should initial the interview record so that he may use it to refresh his memory when giving evidence.

Despite the *obiter dictum* of Winn J in *Mills* [1962] 1 WLR 1152, at p. 1156, that the witness should both *see* and *read* a note made by another, in *Kelsey* (1982) 74 Cr App R 213 the Court of Appeal held that where one person dictates a note to another, hears it read back to him, and confirms its accuracy without reading it himself, the first person may use the note to refresh his memory in court, provided that another witness is called to prove that the note used in court is the same one that was dictated and read back. H, a prosecution witness, refreshed his memory as to the registration number of a car from a note dictated to a police officer. H saw the officer making the note but did not read it himself. The officer read the note back aloud and H confirmed that it was correct. At trial the officer gave evidence that the note used by H was the one that he had made. The Court of Appeal dismissed the appeal on the ground that verification could be aural or visual, the important matter being whether the witness satisfied himself, while the matters were fresh in his mind, that the record was made and that it was accurate. The note in this case, since it was made by a person in the course of a 'profession or other occupation', might be admissible itself as evidence of the facts contained in it under the CJA 1988, s. 24 (provided that the court were to give leave under s. 26 of that Act, and subject to the discretion to exclude under s. 25: see generally **F2.5** and **F16.14**). The principle of aural verification, however, continues to assist in cases where the note is not made by someone 'in the course of a trade, business, profession or other occupation, or as the holder of a paid or unpaid office'.

Requirement of Contemporaneity

F6.8   A document, in order to be used for the purposes of refreshing a witness's memory, must have been made or verified contemporaneously, although not necessarily literally so, with the events to which it relates. It has been held that a gap of a fortnight (*Langton* (1876) 2 QBD 296) or three weeks (*Fotheringham* [1975] Crim LR 710) may be acceptable; but that a lapse of 27 days is such as to lead a judge to hesitate before giving a witness leave to refresh his memory (*Graham* [1973] Crim LR 628); and a delay of three months (*Woodcock* [1963] Crim LR 273) or six months (*Jones* v *Stroud* (1825) 2 CP 196) is too long. The precedents, however, are of somewhat limited value, because it has been said that the question of contemporaneity is a matter of fact and degree (*Simmonds* [1969] 1 QB 685). The document must have been written (or verified) either at the time of the transaction or so shortly afterwards that the facts were fresh in the memory, a definition which provides a measure of elasticity and should not be taken to confine witnesses to an over-short period (*Richardson* [1971] 2 QB 484, per Sachs LJ). 'Much will depend on the nature of the evidence to be given. Where, for example, a witness purports to give a verbatim account of a conversation, the note will need to have been made much nearer the time than if he merely purports to give the general effect of a conversation' (*Da Silva* [1990] 1 WLR 31, per Stuart-Smith LJ at p. 32).

In certain circumstances, a witness who has begun to give evidence but who cannot recall the detail of events, because of the lapse of time since they took place, may be permitted by the judge, in the exercise of his discretion and in the interests of justice, to refresh his memory in the witness-box (or out of court) from a statement made near to the time of the events in question, even though it was not made at the time of the events or so shortly thereafter that the facts were fresh in the memory (*Da Silva*). See **F6.12**.

Originals and Copies

A witness may refresh his memory from a document, notwithstanding that it is based on **F6.9** original notes or a tape recording made by him, if, at the time when the document was prepared, the facts were still fresh in his memory. This principle may be justified on the basis that if the document was prepared at a time when the facts were still fresh in the author's memory, it may itself be regarded as the original, or at least quasi-original. In *Cheng* (1976) 63 Cr App R 20, an officer prepared his committal statement in March from his original notes, which had been made after the accused's arrest in February. By the time of the trial, some three years later, the original notebook had been lost. The Court of Appeal held that, although the committal statement was a partial, and therefore not an exact, copy of the earlier notes from which it had been prepared, it substantially reproduced the notes and could be used by the officer to refresh his memory. Similarly, in *A-G's Ref (No. 3 of 1979)* (1979) 69 Cr App R 411, the Court of Appeal held that a police officer could refresh his memory from a notebook, compiled within two hours of an interview when the facts were still fresh in his memory, on the basis of earlier brief jottings made at the interview, notwithstanding that at the trial he could neither decipher the jottings nor recollect fully the questions put and answers given. In *Mills* [1962] 1 WLR 1152 it was held that a police officer who had heard, and made a tape recording of, a conversation between two accused, could refresh his memory by referring to notes written up with the assistance of the tape recording, which was not itself admitted in evidence.

In the case of 'past recollection recorded', as opposed to 'present recollection revived', if the original document is still in existence, a copy of it may not be used (*Doe d Church and Phillips* v *Perkins* (1790) 3 TR 749; *Harvey* (1869) 11 Cox CC 546). However, if the original has been lost or destroyed, a witness may use a copy if it is proved to be an accurate copy either by the witness himself or by some other person. Thus, in *Topham* v *M'Gregor* (1844) 1 Car & Kir 320, the author of an article, written some 14 years earlier, who had no independent recollection of its contents, was allowed to 'refresh his memory' from a copy of the newspaper in which it appeared, evidence having been given by the editor that the original manuscript had been lost and that the newspaper was an accurate copy. *A fortiori*, it is submitted, the result should be the same in cases of present recollection revived, i.e. cases in which the witness does indeed refresh his memory by the sight of the copy. In *Chisnell* [1992] Crim LR 507, an officer was allowed to refresh his memory from a statement, made nine months after an interview and compiled on the basis of a contemporaneous note, since the court was satisfied that the note, which had been lost, had been accurately transcribed into the statement.

Production for Inspection and Cross-examination

F6.10   A witness who has used a document in court to refresh his memory must produce it for the inspection of the opposing party, who may wish to cross-examine on its contents (*Beech* v *Jones* (1848) 5 CB 696; *Sekhon* (1987) 85 Cr App R 19). In the majority of cases, the fact that such cross-examination takes place will not make the record evidence in the case, nor will it be necessary for the jury to inspect the document, and it will be inappropriate for the record to become an exhibit (*Sekhon* at p. 22). However, in five situations the document, at the request of the opposing party, may be shown to the jury:

(a)   In *Senat* v *Senat* [1965] P 172, Sir Jocelyn Simon P said (at p. 177, emphasis added):

> Where a document is used to refresh a witness's memory, cross-examining counsel may inspect that document in order to check it, without making it evidence. Moreover he may cross-examine upon it without making it evidence *provided that* his cross-examination does not go further than the parts which are used for refreshing the memory of the witness.

See also *Gregory* v *Tavernor* (1833) 6 C & P 280 and *Britton* [1987] 1 WLR 539. If cross-examining counsel does go beyond the parts used by the witness to refresh his memory, the document is put in evidence and the jury are allowed to see the document upon which the cross-examination is based. The document, however, is not evidence of the facts stated in it, but evidence of the witness's consistency or inconsistency going only to his credit. Thus in *Virgo* (1978) 67 Cr App R 323, in which the defence cross-examined H, a leading prosecution witness whose evidence required a corroboration warning, on certain diaries used to refresh his memory, and the diaries were put in evidence, an appeal against conviction was allowed on the ground that, although the trial judge had properly directed the jury that the diaries could not corroborate H's evidence, he had referred to the diaries as 'powerful evidence' and failed to further direct the jury that they went only to H's consistency and credibility as a witness. See also *Britton* [1987] 1 WLR 539. In any particular case in which the judge takes the view that the interests of justice so require, he has a discretion to refuse to allow the document to go before the jury if this could give rise to prejudice to the accused (*Virgo*).

(b)   The jury may inspect a memory-refreshing document if it is necessary to their determination of a point in issue. An example is *Bass* [1953] 1 QB 680. In that case the only evidence against the accused was a confession allegedly made to two police officers who, although denying that they had prepared their notes in collaboration, read identical accounts of the interview with the accused. The trial judge rejected a defence application that the jury be allowed to inspect the notebooks. The Court of Criminal Appeal endorsed the practice of officers collaborating in the preparation of their notes after an interview (in order to ensure that they had a correct version of what was said); but, allowing the appeal, held that the jury should have been allowed to inspect the notebooks because it might have assisted them in their evaluation of the credibility and accuracy of the officers. See also *Sekhon* (1986) 85 Cr App R 19, per Woolf LJ at p. 22: where the nature of the cross-examination involves the suggestion that the witness has subsequently fabricated his evidence, which will usually involve, if not expressly at least by implication, the allegation that the record is concocted, the record may be admissible to rebut this suggestion and, if the nature of the record assists as to this, to show whether or not it is genuine, i.e. whether or not it has the appearance of being a contemporaneous record which has not subsequently been altered.

(c) Where the record is inconsistent with the witness's evidence, it can be admitted as evidence of this inconsistency (*Sekhon* at p. 23).

(d) It is appropriate for the record to be put before the jury where it is difficult for the jury to follow the cross-examination of the witness who has refreshed his memory without having the record or, in practice, copies of the record, before them (*Sekhon*).

(e) There may be cases where it is convenient to use the record as an *aide-mémoire* as to the witness's evidence where that evidence is long and involved. However, care should be exercised in adopting this course in cases where the evidence, and therefore the record, is bitterly contested, because of the danger that the use of the document for this purpose could result in the jury misunderstanding its status, and lead to their wrongly regarding the document as being evidence in itself (*Sekhon*).

Use and Treatment of Memory-refreshing Documents

Subject to one exception, if a memory-refreshing document is permitted to go before the **F6.11** jury, it will not be placed before them as evidence of the truth of its contents. Moreover, it can never amount to corroboration of the evidence given by the witness refreshing his memory from the document. It will be before the jury for the more limited purpose of being a tool to assist them in evaluating the truth of the evidence given in the witness-box by the witness. Whether, in these circumstances, it is appropriate to treat the document as an exhibit is of no practical importance. In a case involving a large number of documents, it may be appropriate to give each one an exhibit number just to identify the document. The exception is the case in which the document provides, because of its nature, material by which its authenticity can be judged: in respect of such material, and only for the purpose of assessing the authenticity of the document, it can amount to evidence in the case (*Sekhon* (1986) 85 Cr App R 19; cf. *Fenlon* (1980) 71 Cr App R 307 and *Dillon* (1983) 85 Cr App R 29, both of which related to notes of police interviews which were *not* signed by the accused). In *Sekhon* these cases were distinguished on the ground that, whereas the documents then under consideration could not assist the jury to decide whether they were genuine or not, in the instant case the jury could well obtain some assistance as to whether the document was recorded in the manner described by the police. Woolf LJ said (at p. 26): '[*Fenlon*] does not . . . help with regard to whether or not a record can be admissible for the purpose of assessing consistency or so as to enable the jury to understand the cross-examination of the witnesses which is taking place before them.' Subsequently his lordship said (at p. 27): '. . . in our view the *Fenlon* decision did not purport to lay down that there is any rule of evidence or practice which prohibits a jury being provided with the notes relating to an interview of which there has been evidence given, if this is done merely to save them the inconvenience of making their own notes.'

Refreshing Memory out of Court

The conditions on which a witness may refresh his memory while giving evidence in the **F6.12** witness-box do not apply to a witness who refreshes his memory from a statement before going into the witness-box. In *Richardson* [1971] 2 QB 484 the accused was convicted of burglary offences committed 18 months earlier. Before the trial, four prosecution witnesses were shown their police statements, which they had made some weeks after the alleged offences. On appeal it was argued that the evidence of the four witnesses was, in the circumstances, inadmissible. The appeal was dismissed on the ground that there can be no general rule (which, unlike the rule as to what can be done in the witness-box, would be unenforceable) that witnesses may not before trial see the statements which they made at some period reasonably close to the time of the events which are the subject of the trial. See also, however, *Thomas* [1994] Crim LR 745 where, for reasons that are not disclosed, it was held to be undesirable for a child aged eight to be shown her signed police statement before giving evidence. In *Richardson*, Sachs LJ, giving the judgment of the Court of Appeal, made the following observations:

(a)   It has been recognised in Home Office Circular No. 82–1969 ('Supplies of Copies of Witnesses' Statements'), issued with the approval of the Lord Chief Justice and the judges of the Queen's Bench Division, that witnesses for the prosecution in criminal cases are normally entitled, if they so request, to copies of any statements taken from them by police officers.

(b)   It is the practice, normally, for witnesses for the defence to be allowed to have copies of their statements and to refresh their memories from them before going into the witness-box.

(c)   The Court agreed with the following two observations of the Supreme Court of Hong Kong in *Lau Pak Ngam* v *R* [1966] Crim LR 443: 'Testimony in the witness-box becomes more a test of memory than truthfulness if witnesses are deprived of the opportunity of checking their recollection beforehand by reference to statements or notes made at a time closer to the events in question.' 'Refusal of access to statements would tend to create difficulties for honest witnesses but be likely to do little to hamper dishonest witnesses.'

(d)   Obviously it would be wrong if several witnesses were handed statements in circumstances which enabled one to compare with another what each had said.

Concerning (d), as a general rule discussions between witnesses, particularly just before going into court to give evidence, should not take place, nor should statements or proofs of evidence be read to witnesses in each other's presence (*Skinner* (1994) 99 Cr App R 212). Where such discussions have taken place, each case has to be dealt with on its own facts. If it emerges in cross-examination of the witnesses that the discussion may have led to fabrication, the court may take the view that it would be unsafe to leave any of the evidence of the witnesses concerned to the jury, but in other cases it may suffice to direct the jury on the implications which such conduct might have for the reliability of the evidence of the witnesses concerned (*Arif* (1993) *The Times*, 17 June 1993).

It is also open to the judge, in the exercise of his discretion and in the interests of justice, to permit a witness who has begun to give evidence to refresh his memory from a statement made near to the time of the events in question, even though it is not contemporaneous, provided he is satisfied that:

(a)   the witness indicates that he cannot now recall the details of events because of the lapse of time since they took place;

(b)   the witness made a statement much nearer the time of the events, and that the contents of the statement represented his recollection at the time he made it;

(c)   the witness had not read the statement before coming into the witness-box; and

(d)   the witness wished to have an opportunity to read the statement before he continued to give evidence.

It does not matter whether the witness withdraws from the witness-box and reads the statement, or whether he reads it in the witness-box; but it is important, if the former course is adopted, that no communication be had with the witness other than to see that he can read the statement in peace. If either course is adopted, the statement must be removed from him when he comes to give his evidence, and he should not be permitted to refer to it again, unlike a contemporaneous statement which may be used to refresh memory while giving evidence (per Stuart-Smith LJ, delivering the judgment of the Court of Appeal in *Da Silva* [1990] 1 WLR 31, at p. 35). On the facts of that case, therefore, the Court of Appeal held that the trial judge had properly intervened by inviting a prosecution witness to withdraw and read a statement which was made by him a month after the events to which it related, and which was not treated as a contemporaneous statement.

Da Silva has not laid down as a matter of law that once a witness is in the witness box he can refer to a statement only if all four criteria specified in that case are satisfied, because the court has a real discretion whether to permit a witness to refresh his memory from a non-contemporaneous statement (*South Ribble Magistrates' Court, ex parte Cochrane* [1996] 2 Cr App R 544). In *Ex parte Cochrane*, in which the witness did not satisfy the third criterion ((c) above), because he had read his statement before giving evidence but had not taken it in properly it was held to be proper to allow him to refresh his memory. The Divisional Court could see no logical difference between someone in the position of such a witness and someone who has not read his statement at all.

If prosecution witnesses have refreshed their memories out of court and before entering the witness-box, it is desirable, but not essential, that the defence should be informed of this (*Worley* v *Bentley* [1976] 2 All ER 449, affirmed in *Westwell* [1976] 2 All ER 812). (See also, *sed quaere, H* [1992] Crim LR 516, which suggests that child victims of sexual offences should refresh their memory out of court only *with the consent* of the defence.) In some cases the fact that a witness has read his statement out of court may be relevant to the weight which can properly be attached to his evidence, and injustice might be caused to the accused if the jury were left in ignorance of the fact. Accordingly, if the prosecution are aware that statements have been seen by their witnesses, it will be appropriate to inform the defence, although if for any reason this is not done, the omission cannot of itself be a ground for acquittal (*Westwell*).

If a witness has refreshed his memory out of court and before entering the witness-box, counsel for the other side is entitled not only to inspect the memory-refreshing document, but also to cross-examine the witness upon the relevant matters contained therein. If counsel cross-examines upon material in the document from which the witness has refreshed his memory, the document is not thereby made evidence in the case; but if he cross-examines upon material which has not been referred to by the witness, this entitles the party calling the witness to put the document in evidence so that the tribunal of fact may see the document upon which the cross-examination is based. In this respect, therefore, the rules are the same as those which apply in the case of a witness refreshing his memory in the witness-box (as to which, see *Senat* v *Senat* [1965] P 172, at **F6.10**). See *Owen* v *Edwards* (1983) 77 Cr App R 191.

PREVIOUS CONSISTENT (SELF-SERVING) STATEMENTS

General Rule against Previous Consistent Statements

Under the rule against previous consistent or self-serving statements, sometimes **F6.13** referred to as the rule against narrative, a witness may not be asked about a previous oral or written statement made by him and consistent with his evidence (*Roberts* [1942] 1 All ER 187; *Larkin* [1943] KB 174; *Oyesiku* (1971) 56 Cr App R 240, at pp. 245–7). Equally, evidence of the previous statement may not be given by any other witness (*Roberts*). The previous statement, which may also be inadmissible as evidence of the facts contained in it under the rule against hearsay, is excluded as evidence of the accused's *consistency*. In *Roberts* [1942] 1 All ER 187, the accused was convicted of the murder of a girl by shooting her. His defence was that the gun went off accidentally when he was trying to make up a quarrel with her. The Court of Criminal Appeal held that evidence that two days after the event the accused had told his father that his defence would be accident had been properly excluded. Such evidence is easily manufactured and of no evidential value. The fact that the accused has said the same thing to someone else on a previous occasion does not confirm his evidence (*Roberts*, at p. 191).

The general rule applies in examination-in-chief, cross-examination and re-examination. Thus the credibility of a witness may not be bolstered by evidence of a previous consistent statement merely because his testimony has been impeached in cross-examination, and this remains the case 'even if the impeachment takes the form of contradiction or inconsistency between the evidence given at the trial and something said by the witness on a former occasion' (*Coll* (1889) 24 LR Ir 522, per Holmes J at p. 541. See also *Weekes* [1988] Crim LR 245; *Beattie* (1989) 89 Cr App R 302 per Lord Lane CJ at pp. 306–7; and *P(GR)* [1998] Crim LR 663).

Recent Complaints in Sexual Cases

F6.14   If the complainant, in a case of rape or some other sexual offence, made a voluntary complaint shortly after the alleged offence, the person to whom the complaint was made may give evidence on behalf of the prosecution of the particulars of the complaint, not as evidence of the facts complained of but to show the consistency of the conduct of the complainant with the complainant's evidence and, in cases where consent is in issue, as tending to negative consent (see generally *Lillyman* [1896] 2 QB 167). Evidence of such a complaint is relevant as a matter of common sense to the issue whether the complainant was a victim or not (*per* Evans LJ in *Churchill* [1999] Crim LR 664). The principle applies in the case of written complaints, as well as oral complaints, and will even cover a private note given to someone by mistake (*B* [1997] Crim LR 220). It is for the jury to decide whether a complaint really was made and whether it is consistent with the complainant's evidence (*Lillyman*), but it is essential that they be directed that the complaint is not evidence of the facts complained of, but may be of assistance in assessing the veracity of the complainant. Judges should give the Judicial Studies Board standard direction: '[The evidence] may possibly help you to decide whether she has told you the truth. It cannot be independent confirmation of [the complainant's] evidence since it does not come from a source independent of her' (see per Ognall J in *Wright* (1987) 90 Cr App R 91 at p. 97 and *Islam* [1999] 1 Cr App R 22).

It follows from the foregoing that if the terms of the complaint are not ostensibly consistent with the terms of the complainant's testimony, the introduction of the complaint has no legitimate purpose (*Wright*). Equally, if the complainant does not testify, there will be no evidence with which the complaint may be consistent, and for this reason it should be excluded (*Guttridge* (1840) 9 C & P 471). On this reasoning, in *Wallwork* (1958) 42 Cr App R 153, a charge of incest with a five-year-old, who went into the witness-box but was unable to give evidence, it was held that the child's grandmother had been improperly permitted to give evidence of particulars of a complaint made to her by the child. Lord Goddard CJ was of the opinion that there would have been no objection if the grandmother had given evidence of the bare fact that the girl had made a complaint to her. But see also *Lillyman* [1896] 2 QB 167 per Hawkins J at pp. 178–9 and *Wright* (1987) 90 Cr App R 91 per Ognall J at pp. 96–7. It is submitted that since such evidence could not be admitted, either as evidence of the facts complained of or as evidence of consistency, it would serve only to prejudice the accused and should not be admitted. Insofar as complaints are admitted as tending to negative consent, it is submitted that they are not admitted, as if by way of exception to the hearsay rule, as evidence of lack of consent, but merely as evidence of consistency with the complainant's evidence, if given, as to lack of consent. English authorities are not clear on the point, but see per Barwick CJ, *obiter*, in *Kilby* v *The Queen* (1973) 129 CLR 460.

Originally this exception extended to criminal cases involving personal violence, whether or not of a sexual nature, but it is now confined to sexual offences (*Jarvis* [1991] Crim LR 374). The exception, however, is not confined to cases where consent is in issue. A recent complaint is admissible 'whether non-consent is legally a necessary part of the issue or whether on the other hand it is what may be called a collateral issue of fact' (*Osborne*: indecent assault on a 13-year-old girl, consent therefore being immaterial). The exception also extends to sexual offences against males: see *Camelleri* [1922] 2 KB 122 (gross indecency against a 15-year-old boy); *Wannell* (1922) 17 Cr App R 53 (buggery with a youth of 19).

In *White* v *R* [1999] AC 210, it was held that, if the person to whom the complaint was made does not give evidence, the complainant's evidence that she complained cannot show her consistency or negative consent because, in the absence of independent confirmation, her own evidence takes the jury nowhere in deciding whether she is worthy of belief. Lord Hoffmann held that it did not follow that evidence that the complainant spoke to someone after the incident is inadmissible, but she should not be allowed to say that she had told people 'what had happened', because the jury would be bound to infer that she had made statements in substantially the same terms as her evidence, which would be to infringe the spirit of the rule against previous consistent statements. Lord Hoffmann also held that where evidence is given of the bare fact that the complainant spoke to someone after the incident, the judge must give the jury clear instructions that they are not entitled to treat such evidence as confirming her credibility.

In order to be admissible, a complaint must be made 'at the first opportunity after the offence which reasonably offers itself' (*Osborne* [1905] 1 KB 551, per Ridley J at p. 561). This is a matter to be determined by the court in each case (*Cummings* [1948] 1 All ER 551). Thus, although complaints have been excluded if made after a day (*Rush* (1896) 60 JP 777) or three days (*Ingrey* 1900) 64 JP 106), a complaint made after a week has been admitted (*Hedges* (1909) 3 Cr App R 262). Much turns on the circumstances of the case. Account should be taken of the fact that victims, both male and female, often need time before they can bring themselves to tell what has been done to them. Moreover, whereas some victims find it impossible to complain to anyone other than a parent or member of their family, others may feel it quite impossible to tell their parents or members of their family (*Valentine* [1996] 2 Cr App R 213 at p. 224). A complaint will not be inadmissible merely because there has been an earlier complaint (*Lee* (1912) 7 Cr App R 31 and *Wilbourne* (1917) 12 Cr App R 280). However, the Crown should not be permitted to lead evidence that the same complaint, in substantially the same terms, has been made on several occasions soon after the alleged offence, if that would be prejudicial in that it might incline the jury to regard the complaints as evidence of the truth of their contents (*Valentine*).

A recent complaint, in order to be admissible, must also have been made voluntarily, and not as a result of leading or intimidating questions. However, the mere fact that the statement was made in answer to a question does not make it inadmissible. Questions of a suggestive or leading character, such as 'Did so-and-so (naming the accused) assault you?' or 'Did he do this and that to you?', will have that effect; but not natural questions put by a person in charge, such as 'What is the matter?' or 'Why are you crying?'. In each case the decision on the character of the question put, as well as other circumstances, such as the relationship of the questioner to the complainant, must be left to the discretion of the judge (*Osborne* [1905] 1 KB 551, per Ridley J at p. 556, where a complaint in answer to the questions 'Why are you going home?', 'Why did you not wait until we came back?', was held to be admissible. See also *Norcott* [1917] 1 KB 347).

Self-Serving Statements Made on Accusation

In *Pearce* (1979) 69 Cr App R 365, at pp. 368 and 370, the Court of Appeal could see **F6.15** no reason for casting doubt on the well-established practice, on the part of the prosecution, to admit in evidence all unwritten, and most written, statements made by an accused person to the police, whether they contain admissions or whether they contain denials of guilt. If such a statement is wholly adverse to the accused, it may be admitted as evidence of the truth of the facts contained in it under the PACE 1984, s. 76 (see **F17.4**). If it is a mixed statement, i.e. a statement containing both inculpatory and exculpatory parts, such as 'I killed X. If I had not done so, X would certainly have killed me there and then', the whole statement is admissible (see principle 2(b) in *Pearce*, below), and both parts are admitted as evidence of the truth of the facts they contain (see *Duncan* (1981) 73 Cr App R 359, *Hamand* (1985) 82 Cr App R 65, *Sharp* [1988] 1 WLR 7 and generally at **F17.44**). However, if the statement is purely exculpatory or self-serving, it is not admitted as evidence of the facts stated in it; it 'is evidence in the trial because of its vital relevance as showing the reaction of the accused when first taxed with the incriminating facts' (*Storey* (1968) 52 Cr App R 334, per Widgery LJ at pp. 337–8). The police having found cannabis in the accused's flat, she told them that it belonged to a man who had brought it there against her will. The Court of Appeal upheld the trial judge's rejection of a submission of no case to answer, on the ground that the accused's statement was not evidence of the facts stated but only evidence of her reaction, which was insufficient to negative evidence of possession. Likewise, in a case where the accused gives no evidence, there is no duty on the judge to remind the jury of voluntary statements made by the accused to the police in exonerating himself (*Barbery* (1975) 62 Cr App R 248; *Tooke* (1989) 90 Cr App R 417). In *Barbery* Eveleigh J said (at p. 250): 'In *Storey*, Widgery LJ . . . pointed out that such a statement, while being admissible for the jury's consideration . . . as to the consistency of an accused's defence, was not admissible as evidence of the truth of the contents . . . and it is therefore no part of the judge's duty to put that statement before the jury as being a factor for their consideration in coming to their conclusion'. But contrast *Donaldson* (1976) 64 Cr App R 59 at p. 69; and see also *Squire* [1990] Crim LR 341.

The reference in *Storey* to the reaction of the accused 'when first taxed' must not be read as limiting the principle recognised to statements made on the first encounter with the police (*Pearce* (1979) 69 Cr App R 365). The facts in *Pearce* were as follows. On 6 March the appellant, the manager of a shop, was taxed by his employer's security officer with incriminating facts relating to handling stolen goods, and denied knowledge of them. Two days later he was arrested by the police and made a voluntary statement in the presence of his solicitor. Subsequently, in an interview, he gave certain answers which were relied on by the prosecution. The next day, he made another voluntary statement which was self-serving. The trial judge excluded evidence of all statements made to the police, except those parts of the interview on which the prosecution relied, on the grounds that they were self-serving and therefore inadmissible. On appeal it was argued that the statements had been properly excluded because they were not made when the appellant was first taxed with the incriminating facts on 6 March. Rejecting this argument and quashing the conviction, the Court of Appeal summarised the principles as follows (at p. 369):

(1)   A statement which contains an admission is always admissible as a declaration against interest and is evidence of the facts admitted. With this exception a statement made by an accused person is never evidence of the facts in the statement. [It is now clear, however, that the exception encompasses statements which are either wholly or partially adverse to the accused (see *Sharp* [1988] 1 WLR 7 and generally at **F17.44**)].

(2)   (a) A statement that is not an admission is admissible to show the attitude of the accused at the time when he made it. This however is not to be limited to a statement made on the first encounter with the police. The reference in *Storey* to the reaction of the accused 'when first taxed' should not be read as circumscribing the limits of admissibility. The longer the time that has elapsed after the first encounter the less the weight which will be attached to the denial. The judge is able to direct the jury about the value of such statements. (b) A statement that is not in itself an admission is admissible if it is made in the same context as an admission, whether in the course of an interview, or in the form of a voluntary statement. It would be unfair to admit only the statements against interest while excluding part of the same interview or series of interviews. It is the duty of the prosecution to present the case fairly to the jury; to exclude answers which are favourable to the accused while admitting those unfavourable would be misleading. (c) The prosecution may wish to draw attention to inconsistent denials. A denial does not become an admission because it is inconsistent with another denial. There must be many cases however where convictions have resulted from such inconsistencies between two denials.

(3)   Although in practice most statements are given in evidence even when they are largely self-serving, there may be a rare occasion when an accused produces a carefully prepared written statement to the police, with a view to it being made part of the prosecution evidence. The trial judge would plainly exclude such a statement as inadmissible.

On the facts, the case fell within principles 2(a) and (b). The first statement was relevant to show the attitude of the appellant at the start of the interview: it set the scene, and when it was decided to admit part of the interview, the only fair course was to admit the statement to put the interview in context. The same principle applied to the questions and answers in the interview which were excluded and to the second voluntary statement on the next day. *Pearce* was applied in *McCarthy* (1980) 71 Cr App R 142.

Principle 2(a) above cannot be relied upon to admit in evidence a statement which adds no weight to other evidence already before the jury as to the accused's reaction to the suggestion that he had committed an offence. In *Tooke* (1989) 90 Cr App R 417, a case of unlawful wounding, the attack took place at 9 p.m. and shortly thereafter, at the scene, T made an exculpatory statement. At 9.40 p.m., T went voluntarily to a police station and made a witness statement setting out his version. The trial judge admitted the statement made at the scene but ruled that the defence were not entitled to cross-examine a police constable in order to prove that T had made the exculpatory statement at the station. It was held that the judge had not erred. The fact that the statement made at the station was a witness statement and not a statement in answer to a charge made no difference, because the same test applied. Furthermore, the statement was spontaneous – it was not suggested that T had time to consult a solicitor or had very much time to think about the matter before the witness statement was made. However, the statement was not relevant since it added nothing to the evidence already before the jury about T's reaction to the suggestion that he had committed an assault.

Principle 2(b) above makes it clear, in the case of a 'mixed statement', that, if the prosecution rely on the parts of the statement unfavourable to the accused, they are obliged to put in evidence the other parts of the statement which are favourable to the accused. However, principle 2(a) is not entirely clear: in the case of a statement which is wholly self-serving, are the prosecution *obliged* to adduce such evidence; and are the defence *entitled* to elicit evidence of such statements in cross-examination of the prosecution witnesses? *McCarthy* (1980) 71 Cr App R 142 supports an affirmative answer. In that case the judge had refused to admit details of an alibi given at a police interview. The Court of Appeal held that the evidence had been *improperly excluded* (although the case against the appellant was strong and the proviso was applied), since it did not come within the exception referred to in *Pearce* (i.e. principle 3). Lawton LJ said (at p. 145):

> One of the best pieces of evidence that an innocent man can produce is his reaction to an accusation of a crime. If he has been told, as the appellant was told, that he was suspected of having committed a particular crime at a particular time and place and he says at once, 'That cannot be right, because I was elsewhere', and gives details of where he was, that is something which the jury can take into account.

Principle 3 is designed to prevent an accused from attempting to take unfair advantage of principle 2(a). An example is *Newsome* (1980) 71 Cr App R 325. On a charge of rape, it was held that a self-serving statement, dictated by the accused to the police after consultation with, and in the presence of, his solicitor, some 13 hours after the alleged offence and subsequent to several interviews with the police, was inadmissible under principle 3. See also *Thatcher* [1967] 1 WLR 1278 (a statement drafted by counsel on instructions and submitted to the officer in charge of the case for his signature). In *Hutton* (1988) *The Times*, 27 October 1988, the police, in exercise of their right to do so under the PACE 1984, s. 58, delayed access to a solicitor and interviewed the accused three times. He refused to sign the notes of those interviews. After being charged, he was allowed access to his solicitor, in whose presence he dictated to the police a self-serving statement consistent with the evidence he gave at the trial. Counsel for the defence submitted that this statement should be put before the jury as a part of the prosecution case, or that in any event he was entitled to cross-examine the officers as to its contents. The judge rejected this submission, ruling that if the accused was cross-examined on the contents of the statement, the whole statement could be admitted, but otherwise the defence were only entitled to elicit, in cross-examination of the officers, the bare facts that after being granted access to his solicitor, the accused made a formal statement of his version of events. On appeal, it was argued that the statement should have been admitted, because the police, in exercising their rights under s. 58, had prevented the accused from making known his reaction to the charge. Rejecting the argument, the Court held that exercise of the s. 58 right did not affect the question whether the statement could properly be described as a spontaneous reaction, and therefore admissible under principle 2(a), or a carefully prepared draft following consultation, and therefore inadmissible under principle 3. The trial judge had properly concluded that the statement fell outside principle 2(a).

Statements in Rebuttal of Allegations of Recent Fabrication

F6.16 The previous consistent statement of a witness will not become admissible merely because his evidence is impeached in cross-examination (*Fox* v *General Medical Council* [1960] 1 WLR 1017), even if this takes the form of cross-examination on a previous inconsistent statement (*Coll* (1889) 24 LR Ir 522 at p. 541; *Beattie* (1989) 89 Cr App R 302 per Lord Lane CJ at pp. 306–7 and *P (GR)* [1998] Crim LR 663). However, if in cross-examination it is suggested to a witness that his evidence is a recent fabrication, evidence of a previous consistent statement will be admissible in re-examination, not as evidence of the truth of its contents, but to negative the suggestion and confirm the witness's credibility (*Y* [1995] Crim LR 155). In a trial for a sexual offence in which the previous statement amounts to a complaint, it may be admissible to rebut the allegation of recent fabrication notwithstanding that it is inadmissible as a recent complaint because not made at the first reasonably practicable opportunity (see *Tyndale* [1999] Crim LR 320 and **F6.14**).

In *Oyesiku* (1971) 56 Cr App R 240, Karminski LJ, giving the judgment of the Court of Appeal (at p. 245), approved the following statement of Dixon CJ in *Nominal Defendant* v *Clements* (1960) 104 CLR 476, at pp. 479–80:

> If the credit of a witness is impugned as to some material fact to which he deposes upon the ground that his account is a late invention or has been lately devised or reconstructed, even though not with conscious dishonesty, that makes admissible a statement to the same effect as the account he gave as a witness if it was made by the witness contemporaneously with the event or at a time sufficiently early to be inconsistent with the suggestion that his account is a late invention or reconstruction. But, inasmuch as the rule forms a definite exception to the general principle excluding statements made out of court and admits a possibly self-serving statement made by the witness, great care is called for in applying it. The judge at the trial must determine for himself upon the conduct of the trial before him whether a case for applying the rule of evidence has arisen and, from the nature of the matter, if there be an appeal, great weight should be given to his opinion by the appellate court. It is evident however that the judge at the trial must exercise care in assuring himself not only that the account given by the witness in his testimony is attacked on the ground of recent invention or reconstruction or that a foundation for such an attack has been laid by the party but also that the contents of the statement are in fact to the like effect as his account given in his evidence and that having regard to the time and circumstances in which it was made it rationally tends to answer the attack.

In *Oyesiku* the accused was convicted of assaulting a police officer. His wife, who gave evidence that the officer was the aggressor, was cross-examined on the basis that her evidence was a late invention concocted in order to help her husband. The Court of Appeal held that defence counsel, in re-examination, had been properly allowed to adduce evidence of her prior statement, consistent with her evidence, and made to a solicitor after her husband's arrest but before she had seen him. The conviction was quashed, however, because the trial judge had improperly refused to allow the jury to see the previous statement; by inspection of the statement, the jury would have been in a better position to assess the extent to which it rebutted the attack made on the witness's testimony. See also *Sekhon* (1987) 85 Cr App R 19, at **F6.10**. For earlier authority, see *Benjamin* (1913) 8 Cr App R 146 and *Flanagan* v *Fahy* [1918] 2 IR 361.

Evidence of Previous Identification

> In cases where there has been a considerable lapse of time between the offence and the trial, **F6.17** and where there might be a danger of the witness's recollection of the prisoner's features having become dimmed, no doubt it strengthens the value of the evidence if it can be shown that in the meantime, soon after the commission of the offence, the witness saw and recognised the prisoner. (*Fannon* (1922) 22 SR (NSW) 427, per Ferguson J at pp. 429–30).

It is for reasons of this kind that evidence that a witness identified the accused out of court may be given by the witness himself and by any person who witnessed the identification. In *Christie* [1914] AC 545, a case of indecent assault on a small boy, the boy gave unsworn evidence of the assault and identified the accused, but was not questioned as to a previous identification. The boy's mother and a constable were then allowed to give evidence that, shortly after the offence alleged, they saw the boy approach the accused and identify him by saying, 'That is the man'. The House of Lords, by a majority, held that this evidence had been properly admitted. Viscount Haldane LC (who was of the opinion that this evidence *would have been* admissible if the boy had given evidence of his out-of-court identification) described the evidential value of such evidence as follows (at p. 551): 'Its relevancy is to shew that the boy was able to identify at the time and to exclude the idea that the identification of the prisoner in the dock was an afterthought or mistake.' See also *Fowkes* (1856) *The Times*, 8 March 1856, at **F6.18**.

As a general rule, a 'dock identification', i.e. an identification of the accused for the first time in court, is undesirable and should be avoided (*Cartwright* (1914) 10 Cr App R 219); the usual practice is to elicit evidence of a witness's previous out-of-court identification *before* asking him whether that person is in court. As to dock identifications generally and evidence of previous identification, see **F18**. For the position where the witness fails to identify the accused in court, having previously identified him out of court, see *Osbourne* [1973] QB 678, at **F15.9**.

Statements Forming Part of *Res Gestae*

A previous statement of a witness which was so closely associated in time, place and **F6.18** circumstances with some act or event in issue that it can be said to form a part of the *res gestae*, i.e. the same transaction, is admissible as evidence of consistency to confirm evidence given by the witness to the same effect. Such a statement is also admissible for the truth of its contents (see **F16.31** to **F16.35**). In *Fowkes* (1856) *The Times*, 8 March 1856, the accused, commonly known as 'the butcher', was charged with murder. The victim's son gave evidence that he and a police officer were in a room with his father; that a face appeared at the window through which the fatal shot was then fired; and that he thought the face was that of the accused. He was also allowed to give evidence that on seeing the face, he had shouted, 'There's Butcher'; and the officer, who had not seen the face, was also allowed to give evidence as to this exclamation.

UNFAVOURABLE AND HOSTILE WITNESSES

General Rule against Impeaching Credit of Own Witness

The general rule is that a party is not entitled to impeach the credit of his own witness **F6.19** by asking questions or adducing evidence concerning such matters as the witness's bad character, previous convictions, bias or previous inconsistent statements. In the case of a witness who is 'unfavourable', i.e. a witness who displays no hostile animus to the party calling him but merely fails to come up to proof or gives evidence unfavourable to that party, the general rule prevails: the only remedy available to the party is to call other witnesses, if available, with a view to proving that which the unfavourable witness failed to establish (*Ewer* v *Ambrose* (1825) 3 B & C 746). Insofar as this results in two equally credible witnesses directly contradicting each other upon a major fact in issue, it has been said that the party calling them is not entitled to accredit the one and discredit the other; the testimony of both is to be disregarded (*Sumner and Leivesley* v *John Brown & Co.* (1909) 25 TLR 745, per Hamilton J). However, in *Brent* [1973] Crim LR 295 it was held that this dictum does not apply to criminal proceedings, because of the Crown's duty to call all relevant evidence. In the case of a witness who appears to the judge to be hostile, that is to say not desirous of telling the truth to the court at the instance of the party calling him (Sir James F. Stephen, *A Digest of the Law of Evidence*, 12th ed. by Sir Harry L. Stephen and L. F. Sturge (London: Macmillan, 1936), art. 147), the general rule is modified, but in only two respects:

(a)   under the Criminal Procedure Act 1865, s. 3, that party may, by leave of the judge, prove a previous inconsistent statement of the witness (see **F6.20**); and

(b)   at common law, the party calling the witness may cross-examine him by asking leading questions (see *Thompson* (1976) 64 Cr App R 96, at **F6.21**).

The prosecution may call a person as a witness even if he has shown signs that he is likely to be hostile, e.g. by retracting a statement or by making a second statement prior to the trial. Thus if the evidence of a prosecution witness at committal (or transfer) proceedings represents a substantial departure from his police statement, which implicates the accused, the prosecution are not obliged to treat the witness as hostile at that stage but may wait to see what happens at the trial (*Mann* (1972) 56 Cr App R 750). Equally, the fact that a witness has been treated as hostile before the magistrates is not by itself a reason making it improper for the prosecution to call him at the trial and, if necessary, to apply for leave to treat him as hostile again, although each case turns on its own facts (*Vibert* (21 October 1974 unreported)). However, in cases in which the person indicates that he is no longer in a position to further assist the prosecution or court, or claims to be no longer able to remember anything, it seems that the judge has a discretion to hold a *voir dire* to decide whether to prevent him being called at all (*Honeyghon* [1999] Crim LR 221). The defence are likely to object to the prosecution calling such a person on the basis that it is simply a means to allow the jury to become aware of a previous statement made by him and inconsistent with his testimony. The judge, of course, would direct the jury that the previous statement is not evidence of the facts it contains, but some jurors, at least, would find it difficult to comply with such a direction. *Dat* [1998] Crim LR 488 provides an alternative but only partial solution to the problem: it was held that the prosecution should cross-examine their own witnesses by degrees, so as to limit the damage which might occur as a result of wide-ranging cross-examination on the previous statement.

The application to treat a witness as hostile should be made when the witness first shows unmistakable signs of hostility (*Pestano* [1981] Crim LR 397). If counsel for the prosecution has a statement directly contradicting one of their witnesses who gives evidence that he is unable to identify the accused, he should at once show the statement to the judge and ask for leave to cross-examine the witness (*Fraser* (1956) 40 Cr App R 160). However, although there may be circumstances where a witness is displaying such an excessive degree of hostility that the only appropriate course is to treat him as hostile, if he gives evidence contrary to an earlier statement (or fails to give the evidence expected) the party calling him and the trial judge should first consider inviting him to refresh his memory from material which it is legitimate to use for that purpose and should not immediately proceed to treat him as hostile (*Maw* [1994] Crim LR 841). In *Powell* [1985] Crim LR 592 it was held that the prosecution, during re-examination, had been properly allowed to treat as hostile a witness who had shown no signs of hostility during examination-in-chief. Although such an application is a little unusual, it is a matter for the judge's discretion (ibid.). See also *Little* (1883) 15 Cox CC 319.

The discretion of the judge, however hostile the witness, is absolute (*Rice* v *Howard* (1886) 16 QBD 681; *Price* v *Manning* (1889) 42 ChD 372); and the decision will rarely be open to a successful challenge on appeal (*Manning* [1968] Crim LR 675).

Although the question whether a witness is hostile is for the judge, the jury should not be excluded from the proceedings while the decision is taken. In *Darby* [1989] Crim LR 817, in which an application to treat a witness as hostile was deferred by the judge, who had him questioned further in the absence of the jury before ruling that he was hostile, it was held that the evidence and demeanour of the witness should have been tested in the presence of the jury.

Criminal Procedure Act 1865, s. 3

Criminal Procedure Act 1865, s. 3

> A party producing a witness shall not be allowed to impeach his credit by general evidence **F6.20** of bad character, but he may, in case the witness shall, in the opinion of the judge, prove adverse, contradict him by other evidence, or, by leave of the judge, prove that he has made at other times a statement inconsistent with his present testimony; but before such last mentioned proof can be given the circumstances of the supposed statement, sufficient to designate the particular occasion, must be mentioned to the witness, and he must be asked whether or not he has made such statement.

The first part of this section puts on a statutory basis the common-law rule that a party calling a witness is not entitled to impeach his credit by evidence of bad character, i.e. evidence of previous misconduct, convictions, or other evidence designed to show that the witness is not to be believed on oath. The remaining two rules in the section apply to witnesses who, in the opinion of the judge, prove 'adverse', which means 'hostile' and not merely 'unfavourable' (*Greenough* v *Eccles* (1859) 5 CB NS 786, a decision on the construction of the Common Law Procedure Act 1856, s. 22, which was repealed but re-enacted by s. 3 of the 1865 Act).

The first rule is that a party may 'contradict' a hostile witness, i.e. call other witnesses to prove that which the hostile witness has failed to establish. Although s. 3 suggests that this rule applies only to hostile witnesses, according to Williams and Willes JJ in *Greenough* v *Eccles*, it has not affected the common-law rule to the same effect in the case of unfavourable witnesses (see *Ewer* v *Ambrose* (1825) 3 B & C 746).

The second rule, which does apply only in the case of a witness who is, in the opinion of the judge, hostile, allows the judge to give leave to prove that the witness has made at other times a statement inconsistent with his present testimony. A witness for the defence who is treated as hostile is in the same position as a hostile prosecution witness, and accordingly is open to cross-examination on a previous inconsistent statement (*Booth* (1981) 74 Cr App R 123). The leave of the judge may be given whether the previous inconsistent statement was oral or written (*Prefas* (1986) 86 Cr App R 111). If the witness, when asked, admits that he made the previous statement, this will clearly suffice as proof that he did make it. If the witness does not make such an admission, whether the earlier statement can be used depends on the facts of the particular case. In *Baldwin* [1986] Crim LR 681, where the witness accepted that he had made some parts of a written statement and accepted that the signatures on the statement were his, it was held that this was evidence entitling the judge to conclude that the witness had made the statement, and therefore to rule that cross-examination on it was permissible.

If the nature of the evidence given justifies it, an application may be made to treat as hostile the spouse of an accused who is competent but not compellable for the prosecution, and who has waived his or her right to refuse to testify. However, it is desirable that the judge should explain to the spouse, in the absence of the jury and before the oath is taken, that if the choice is made to give evidence, he or she may be treated like any other witness (*Pitt* [1983] QB 25). See generally, **F4.12**.

Hostile Witnesses at Common Law

F6.21 The Criminal Procedure Act 1865, s. 3, has not destroyed or removed the common-law right of the judge, in the exercise of his discretion, to allow cross-examination of a hostile witness by asking leading questions about a previous statement. In *Thompson* (1976) 64 Cr App R 96 the appellant was convicted of incest with his daughter. She had made a statement to the police implicating her father but, when sworn as a witness at the trial, she refused to give evidence, and leave was given to treat her as hostile. She was asked leading questions, her previous statement was put to her, and she eventually agreed that its contents were true. It was argued, on appeal, that since the girl had initially given no evidence, there was no 'present testimony' with which her previous statement could be said to be inconsistent, and therefore s. 3 did not apply. Lord Parker CJ found it unnecessary to decide whether s. 3 applied to the facts, since the common-law cases prior to the 1865 Act recognised that pressure could be brought to bear upon witnesses who refused to cooperate. Thus, in *Clarke* v *Saffery* (1824) Ry & M 126, in which there does not appear to have been evidence contradicting the earlier statement, Best CJ said (at p. 126): 'If a witness, by his conduct in the box, shows himself decidedly adverse, it is always in the discretion of the judge to allow a cross-examination'. In *Bastin* v *Carew* (1824) cited Ry & M 127, Lord Abbott CJ said: '. . . in each particular case there must be some discretion in the presiding judge as to the mode in which the examination shall be conducted, in order best to answer the purposes of justice'. On this basis, the appeal was dismissed. It is submitted that if the witness in the case had denied making the previous statement and not accepted the truth of its contents, it would not have been open to proof at common law.

Evidential Value of Previous Inconsistent Statement

F6.22 If a hostile witness, on being cross-examined on a previous inconsistent statement, adopts and confirms some of the contents of the statement, then what he says becomes part of his evidence and, subject to the jury assessing his credibility, it is capable of being accepted. However, the evidence is what he says in the witness box, not what he said out of court (*Maw* [1994] Crim LR 841).

If a hostile witness, on being cross-examined on a previous unsworn statement which is inconsistent with his present testimony, admits having made the previous statement but denies the truth of its contents, the statement is admissible to impugn the credit of the witness and not as evidence of the truth of the facts stated therein (*White* (1922) 17 Cr App R 60). Cross-examination upon such previous unsworn assertions is permitted, not for the purpose of substituting them for the witness's sworn testimony, but to show that the sworn testimony, in the light of the unsworn assertions, cannot be regarded as being of importance (*Harris* [1927] 2 KB 587). The position is the same even if the previous inconsistent statement was made on oath (*Birch* (1924) 18 Cr App R 26). Thus, in *Golder* [1960] 1 WLR 1169, where the judge had indicated to the jury that it was open to them to act upon the evidence contained in the previous statement, which was the witness's deposition before the committing magistrates, the Court held that it had no alternative but to quash the convictions. Lord Parker CJ said (at pp. 1172–3):

> . . . when a witness is shown to have made previous statements inconsistent with the evidence given by that witness at the trial, the jury should not merely be directed that the

evidence given at the trial should be regarded as unreliable; they should also be directed that the previous statements, whether sworn or unsworn, do not constitute evidence upon which they can act.

Moreover, since the previous statement is only relevant to the witness's credit, copies of it should not be put before the jury (*Darby* [1989] Crim LR 817).

The dictum in *Golder* was cited with approval in *Oliva* [1965] 1 WLR 1028, at pp. 1036–7. However, Lord Parker's statement that the jury should be directed that 'the evidence given at the trial should be regarded as unreliable' was *obiter*; and in *Driscoll* v *The Queen* (1977) 137 CLR 517, at pp. 535–7, the High Court of Australia refused to accept that it was *always* necessary or even appropriate to direct a jury in this way, a view endorsed by the House of Lords in *Governor of Pentonville Prison, ex parte Alves* [1993] AC 284 (at p. 298) and by the Court of Appeal in *Goodway* [1993] 4 All ER 894 (at p. 899). Thus in *Pestano* [1981] Crim LR 397, where the prosecution cross-examined the witness on his deposition, but nonetheless sought to rely upon his evidence insofar as it supported their case, it was held that the evidence was for the jury to consider, subject to a proper warning from the judge as to the weight which could be attached to it. See also *Nelson* [1992] Crim LR 653, where it was held to be a serious misdirection to fail to warn the jury not to act on the statements of a witness but to suggest instead that the evidence of the witness was unreliable when compared with those statements.

The direction to treat the witness's evidence as 'unreliable' may also be inappropriate in other circumstances, as when a witness gives a rational or convincing explanation for the earlier contradictory statement. See, e.g., *Thomas* [1985] Crim LR 445. Nonetheless, if a witness has been treated as hostile, it is necessary for the jury to consider whether he should be treated as creditworthy at all, and they should be clearly directed on that point before considering which parts of the evidence are worthy of acceptance and which are to be rejected. It is insufficient to tell the jury to approach the evidence with great caution and reservation. The judge should give a clear warning about the dangers involved in a witness who contradicts himself and should direct them to consider whether they can give any credence to such a witness. It is only if they can, that they may then consider which parts of his evidence they can accept (*Maw* [1994] Crim LR 841).

SECTION F7:
CROSS-EXAMINATION AND RE-EXAMINATION

CROSS-EXAMINATION: GENERAL CONSIDERATIONS

Nature and Object of Cross-examination

F7.1 Cross-examination is the questioning of a witness by (a) the opponent of the party calling him or (b) any other party to the proceedings. Thus, as to the latter, an accused has the right to cross-examine a co-accused who has chosen to give evidence (and any witnesses called by the co-accused). This applies not only where the co-accused has given evidence unfavourable to the accused (see *Hadwen* [1902] 1 KB 882 and *Paul* [1920] 2 KB 183), but also if the co-accused has merely given evidence in his own defence (*Hilton* [1972] 1 QB 421, per Fenton Atkinson LJ at pp. 423–4). Usually cross-examination follows immediately after examination-in-chief, but witnesses are sometimes merely tendered by the prosecution for cross-examination. Such a witness is called by the prosecution, sworn, asked no questions in chief other than his name and address, and then cross-examined by the defence (see *Brooke* (1819) 2 Stark 472).

An accused is generally entitled to cross-examine in person any witness called by the prosecution. However, a trial judge is not obliged to give an unrepresented accused his head to ask whatever questions, at whatever length, the accused wishes. It will often be desirable, before any question is asked by the accused in cross-examination of a complainant in a rape trial, for the judge to discuss the course of proceedings with the accused in the absence of the jury. The judge can then elicit the general nature of the defence and identify the specific points in the complainant's evidence with which the accused takes issue, and any points he wishes to put to the complainant. If the accused proposes to call witnesses in his own defence, the substance of their evidence can be elicited so that the complainant's observations on it may, so far as relevant, be invited. It will almost always be desirable in the first instance to allow an accused to put questions to a complainant, but it should be made clear in advance that the accused will be required, having put a point, to move on, and if he fails to do so the judge should intervene and secure compliance. If the accused proves unable or unwilling to comply with the judge's instructions, the judge should, if necessary in order to save the complainant from avoidable distress, stop further questioning by the accused or take over the questioning of the complainant himself. If the accused seeks by his dress, bearing, manner or questions to dominate, intimidate or humiliate the complainant, or if it is reasonably apprehended that he will seek to do so, the judge should not hesitate to order the erection of a screen, in addition to controlling questioning in the way indicated (*Brown* [1998] 2 Cr App R 364).

Concerning cross-examination of alleged child victims, CJA 1988, s. 34A, provides that no person who is charged with an offence to which the CJA 1988, s. 32(2) applies (see **D12.30**) shall cross-examine in person any witness who is alleged to be a person against whom the offence was committed (or to have witnessed the commission of the offence) and who is a child, or who is to be cross-examined following the admission under s. 32A of the 1988 Act of a video recording of testimony from him (see **F16.21**). For these purposes, 'child' means a person who, in the case of an offence falling within s. 32(2)(a) or (b), is under 14 years of age or, in the case of any offence falling within s. 32(2)(c), is under 17 years of age (s. 34A(2)). When an unrepresented defendant is statutorily prohibited from examining a witness, it is generally desirable for the judge to ask such questions as he sees fit to test the reliability and accuracy of the witness's evidence. The judge must not, however, descend into the arena on behalf of the defence. It is also open to the judge to ask the defendant whether there are matters which he would like him to put to the witness, but it is a matter for the judge to decide how to put the questions (*De Oliveira* [1997] Crim LR 600).

When the YJCEA 1999, ss. 34 to 39, are brought into force, they will replace the CJA 1988, s. 34A, and introduce new and wider restrictions on cross-examination by the accused in person. Under the YJCEA 1999, s. 34, no person charged with a sexual offence as defined in s. 62 of the Act (see **F7.18**) will be permitted to cross-examine in person a witness who is the complainant; under s. 35, no person charged with certain specified offences will be permitted to cross-examine in person child complainants or other specified child witnesses; and under s. 36, which applies to cases not covered by ss. 34 and 35, the court will be able to give a direction prohibiting the accused from cross-examining a witness in person if the quality of evidence given by the witness is likely to be diminished by such cross-examination and would be likely to be improved by such a direction. Section 38 makes provision for an accused who is prevented from cross-examining a witness in person to be represented for the purpose of cross-examining the witness, and s. 39 relates to the warning which the judge may need to give to the jury in order to counter any prejudice stemming from the accused being prevented from cross-examining a witness in person.

Youth Justice and Criminal Evidence Act 1999, ss. 34 to 39

    34. No person charged with a sexual offence may in any criminal proceedings cross-examine in person a witness who is the complainant, either—
    (a)   in connection with that offence, or
    (b)   in connection with any other offence (of whatever nature) with which that person is charged in the proceedings.

    35.—(1)   No person charged with an offence to which this section applies may in any criminal proceedings cross-examine in person a protected witness, either—
    (a)   in connection with that offence, or
    (b)   in connection with any other offence (of whatever nature) with which that person is charged in the proceedings.
    (2)   For the purposes of subsection (1) a 'protected witness' is a witness who—
    (a)   either is the complainant or is alleged to have been a witness to the commission of the offence to which this section applies, and
    (b)   either is a child or falls to be cross-examined after giving evidence in chief (whether wholly or in part)—
        (i)   by means of a video recording made (for the purposes of section 27) at a time when the witness was a child, or
        (ii)   in any other way at any such time.
    (3)   The offences to which this section applies are—
    (a)   any offence under—
        (i)   the Sexual Offences Act 1956,
        (ii)   the Indecency with Children Act 1960,
        (iii) the Sexual Offences Act 1967,
        (iv)   section 54 of the Criminal Law Act 1977, or
        (v)   the Protection of Children Act 1978;
    (b)   kidnapping, false imprisonment or an offence under section 1 or 2 of the Child Abduction Act 1984;
    (c)   any offence under section 1 of the Children and Young Persons Act 1933;
    (d)   any offence (not within any of the preceding paragraphs) which involves an assault on, or injury or a threat of injury to, any person.
    (4)   In this section 'child' means—
    (a)   where the offence falls within subsection (3)(a), a person under the age of 17; or
    (b)   where the offence falls within subsection (3)(b), (c) or (d), a person under the age of 14.

(5)   For the purposes of this section 'witness' includes a witness who is charged with an offence in the proceedings.

36.—(1)   This section applies where, in a case where neither of sections 34 and 35 operates to prevent an accused in any criminal proceedings from cross-examining a witness in person—

(a)   the prosecutor makes an application for the court to give a direction under this section in relation to the witness, or

(b)   the court of its own motion raises the issue whether such a direction should be given.

(2)   If it appears to the court—

(a)   that the quality of evidence given by the witness on cross-examination—

(i)   is likely to be diminished if the cross-examination (or further cross-examination) is conducted by the accused in person, and

(ii)   would be likely to be improved if a direction were given under this section, and

(b)   that it would not be contrary to the interests of justice to give such a direction, the court may give a direction prohibiting the accused from cross-examining (or further cross-examining) the witness in person.

(3)   In determining whether subsection (2)(a) applies in the case of a witness the court must have regard, in particular, to—

(a)   any views expressed by the witness as to whether or not the witness is content to be cross-examined by the accused in person;

(b)   the nature of the questions likely to be asked, having regard to the issues in the proceedings and the defence case advanced so far (if any);

(c)   any behaviour on the part of the accused at any stage of the proceedings, both generally and in relation to the witness;

(d)   any relationship (of whatever nature) between the witness and the accused;

(e)   whether any person (other than the accused) is or has at any time been charged in the proceedings with a sexual offence or an offence to which section 35 applies, and (if so) whether section 34 or 35 operates or would have operated to prevent that person from cross-examining the witness in person;

(f)   any direction under section 19 which the court has given, or proposes to give, in relation to the witness.

(4)   For the purposes of this section—

(a)   'witness', in relation to an accused, does not include any other person who is charged with an offence in the proceedings; and

(b)   any reference to the quality of a witness's evidence shall be construed in accordance with section 16(5).

37.—(1)   Subject to subsection (2), a direction has binding effect from the time it is made until the witness to whom it applies is discharged.
In this section 'direction' means a direction under section 36.

(2)   The court may discharge a direction if it appears to the court to be in the interests of justice to do so, and may do so either—

(a)   on an application made by a party to the proceedings, if there has been a material change of circumstances since the relevant time, or

(b)   of its own motion.

(3)   In subsection (2) 'the relevant time' means—

(a)   the time when the direction was given, or

(b)   if a previous application has been made under that subsection, the time when the application (or last application) was made.

(4)   The court must state in open court its reasons for—

(a)   giving, or

(b)   refusing an application for, or for the discharge of, or

(c)   discharging,

a direction and, if it is a magistrates' court, must cause them to be entered in the register of its proceedings.

(5)   [Power to make rules of court.]

38.—(1)   This section applies where an accused is prevented from cross-examining a witness in person by virtue of section 34, 35 or 36.

(2)   Where it appears to the court that this section applies, it must—

(a)   invite the accused to arrange for a legal representative to act for him for the purpose of cross-examining the witness; and

(b)   require the accused to notify the court, by the end of such period as it may specify, whether a legal representative is to act for him for that purpose.

(3)   If by the end of the period mentioned in subsection (2)(b) either—

(a)   the accused has notified the court that no legal representative is to act for him for the purpose of cross-examining the witness, or

(b)   no notification has been received by the court and it appears to the court that no legal representative is to so act,

the court must consider whether it is necessary in the interests of justice for the witness to be cross-examined by a legal representative appointed to represent the interests of the accused.

(4)   If the court decides that it is necessary in the interests of justice for the witness to be so cross-examined, the court must appoint a qualified legal representative (chosen by the court) to cross-examine the witness in the interests of the accused.

(5)   A person so appointed shall not be responsible to the accused.

(6) and (7) [Power to make rules of court.]

(8)   For the purposes of this section—

(a)   any reference to cross-examination includes (in a case where a direction is given under section 36 after the accused has begun cross-examining the witness) a reference to further cross-examination; and

(b)   'qualified legal representative' means a legal representative who has a right of audience (within the meaning of the Courts and Legal Services Act 1990) in relation to the proceedings before the court.

39.—(1)   Where on a trial on indictment an accused is prevented from cross-examining a witness in person by virtue of section 34, 35 or 36, the judge must give the jury such warning (if any) as the judge considers necessary to ensure that the accused is not prejudiced—

(a)   by any inferences that might be drawn from the fact that the accused has been prevented from cross-examining the witness in person;

(b)   where the witness has been cross-examined by a legal representative appointed under section 38(4), by the fact that the cross-examination was carried out by such a legal representative and not by a person acting as the accused's own legal representative.

(2)   Subsection (8)(a) of section 38 applies for the purposes of this section as it applies for the purposes of section 38.

The object of cross-examination is:

(a)   to elicit from the witness evidence supporting the cross-examining party's version of the facts in issue;

(b)   to weaken or cast doubt upon the accuracy of the evidence given by the witness in chief; and

(c)   in appropriate circumstances, to impeach the witness's credibility.

In general, when cross-examination is being conducted by competent counsel, a judge should not intervene, save to clarify matters he does not understand or thinks the jury may not understand. If he wishes to ask questions about matters that have not been touched upon, it is generally better to wait until the end of the examination or cross-examination. A judge should not be criticised for occasional transgressions, but there may come a time, depending on the nature and frequency of the interruptions, that the Court of Appeal is of the opinion that defence counsel was so hampered in the way he properly wished to conduct the cross-examination that the judge's conduct amounts to a material irregularity (*Sharp* [1994] QB 261).

Order of Cross-examination

If there are two or more accused jointly indicted and separately represented by counsel, **F7.2** the order of cross-examination is the order in which the names of the accused appear on the indictment (*Barber* (1844) 1 Car & Kir 434).

Liability to Cross-examination

F7.3   All witnesses are liable to cross-examination, except:

(a)   a witness called merely to produce a document, who is not sworn (*Sumners* v *Moseley* (1834) 2 Cr & M 477) or who is sworn unnecessarily (*Rush* v *Smith* (1834) 1 Cr M & R 94);

(b)   a witness unable to speak as to the matters supposed to be within his knowledge who is called by mistake, provided that the mistake is discovered after the witness has been sworn but before his examination-in-chief (*Wood* v *Mackinson* (1840) 2 Mood & R 273); and

(c)   a witness called by the judge, who may only be cross-examined with the judge's leave, which should be given if the witness is adverse to either party (*Coulson* v *Disborough* [1894] 2 QB 316; *Cliburn* (1898) 62 JP 232).

The evidence in chief of a witness who dies before cross-examination remains admissible, although little weight may attach to it (*Doolin* (1832) 1 Jebb CC 123). Similarly, if a witness, during cross-examination, becomes incapable through illness of answering any further questions, the trial may continue on the basis of the evidence already given (*Stretton* (1986) 86 Cr App R 7). In *Stretton*, the witness was the victim of sexual offences and the judge gave a carefully worded direction to the jury to acquit if they felt that the absence of cross-examination prevented them from judging fairly her credibility. See also *Wyatt* [1990] Crim LR 343 in which a seven-year-old girl, the victim of an indecent assault, was cross-examined through video link for about 20 minutes. She became visibly distressed and the judge adjourned the case for about 20 minutes. After the adjournment, the girl continued to cry and the judge decided that her evidence should proceed no further, even though counsel for the defence still had one important question to ask. The appeal was dismissed: the judge had not erred in the exercise of his discretion to adjourn for the length of time that he did and had directed the jury fairly on the girl's evidence and left it to them to determine her credibility. *Stretton* and *Wyatt* were both distinguished in *Lawless* (1994) 98 Cr App R 342. In that case the only direct evidence on one important part of the prosecution case was given by a witness who, at the end of his examination-in-chief, suffered a heart attack and was unable to give further evidence. It was held at least doubtful whether any direction to the jury, however strongly expressed, could have overcome the powerful prejudice of his evidence going wholly untested by cross-examination.

Effect of Failure to Cross-examine

F7.4   In *Wood Green Crown Court, ex parte Taylor* [1995] Crim LR 879, the Divisional Court approved the following principle as stated in the 1995 edition of this work: a party who fails to cross-examine a witness upon a particular matter in respect of which it is proposed to contradict him or impeach his credit by calling other witnesses, tacitly accepts the truth of the witness's evidence in chief on that matter, and will not thereafter be entitled to invite the jury to disbelieve him in that regard. The proper course is to challenge the witness while he is in the witness-box or, at any rate, to make it plain to him at that stage that his evidence is not accepted (*Hart* (1932) 23 Cr App R 202). Thus in *Bircham* [1972] Crim LR 430, counsel for the accused was not permitted to suggest to the jury in his closing speech that the co-accused and a prosecution witness had committed the offence charged, where the allegation had not been put to either in cross-examination.

. . . nothing would be more absolutely unjust than not to cross-examine witnesses upon evidence which they have given, so as to give them notice, and to give them an opportunity of explanation, and an opportunity very often to defend their own character, and, not having given them such an opportunity, to ask the jury afterwards to disbelieve what they have said, although not one question has been directed either to their credit or to the accuracy of the facts they have deposed to. (*Browne v Dunn* (1893) 6 R 67, per Lord Halsbury at pp. 76–7, followed in *Fenlon* (1980) 71 Cr App R 307.)

See also para. 610(g) of the Code of Conduct of the Bar of England and Wales. Evidence to contradict a witness which was not put to him in cross-examination, may be admitted, provided that the witness is then recalled and cross-examination of him re-opened in order to put the new evidence to him (*Cannan* [1998] Crim LR 284).

The rule under discussion is not hard-and-fast or inflexible. Thus where it is proposed to invite the jury to disbelieve a witness on a particular matter, it will not always be necessary to put to him explicitly that he is lying, provided that the overall tenor of the cross-examination is designed to show that his account is incapable of belief (see *Lovelock* [1997] Crim LR 821). Indeed in some cases it may be that the point upon which the witness is to be impeached is manifest, as when the story he tells is incredible, and it is unnecessary to cross-examine him upon it at all: the most effective cross-examination would be to ask him to leave the box (*Browne v Dunn*, per Lords Herschell LC and Morris). Application of the rule may also be unnecessary in the case of a witness whose evidence is purely corroborative of the evidence of another witness whose evidence-in-chief has already been challenged in cross-examination. It is a sensible practice, however, to secure the assurance of the trial judge, and the agreement of the party calling the witness, that failure to cross-examine in such circumstances will not be taken as a tacit acceptance of the witness's evidence. The rule has also been held to be inapplicable in the case of proceedings in magistrates' courts (*O'Connell v Adams* [1973] RTR 150).

RULES GOVERNING CONDUCT OF CROSS-EXAMINATION

Scope of Cross-examination

Questions in cross-examination are not restricted to matters raised in chief, but may **F7.5** relate to any fact in issue (or relevant fact), or to the credibility of the witness. Cross-examination is governed by the following general rules.

Leading Questions A witness under cross-examination may be asked leading **F7.6** questions. This is so even if he appears to be more favourable to the cross-examining party than to the party calling him (*Parkin v Moon* (1836) 7 C & P 408).

Exclusionary Rules of Evidence The exclusionary rules of evidence relating to **F7.7** hearsay, opinion, privilege etc. apply to cross-examination as they apply to examination-in-chief. Thus in *Thomson* [1912] 3 KB 19, a charge of using an instrument on a woman with intent to procure a miscarriage, it was held that counsel for the defence had properly been prevented from asking a prosecution witness in cross-examination whether the woman (who had died) had told her that she intended to procure her own miscarriage and, later, that she had done so. The evidence was inadmissible hearsay. See also *Windass* (1988) 89 Cr App R 258 (it is improper for counsel for the prosecution, during cross-examination of the accused, to ask him to explain highly damaging statements contained in a document written by a third party and inadmissible against the accused); *Gray* [1998] Crim LR 570 (it is inappropriate to cross-examine an accused on a co-accused's interview that is inadmissible as against the accused, where the effect is to use what the co-accused said as if it were evidence); and *Re P* [1989] Crim LR 897 (it is improper to cross-examine an accused in a sexual case on a complaint which is otherwise inadmissible because not a 'recent' complaint).

In *Treacy* [1944] 2 All ER 229, a charge of murder, it was held that the accused had been cross-examined improperly upon certain inadmissible confessions made on arrest and inconsistent with his evidence. It has been said that the principle established in this case, that an accused cannot be cross-examined by the prosecution in such a way as to reveal that he made an inadmissible confession, also obtains in favour of any co-accused (*Rice* [1963] 1 QB 857, per Winn J at pp. 868–9). However, see also *Rowson* [1986] QB 174 and other authorities considered in **F17.36**.

F7.8   ***Power of Judge to Restrain Unnecessary or Improper Questions***   The trial judge has a discretion to prevent any questions in cross-examination which, in his opinion, are unnecessary, improper or oppressive. Cross-examination is a powerful weapon entrusted to counsel, and should be conducted with restraint and a measure of courtesy and consideration which a witness is entitled to expect in a court of law (*Mechanical & General Inventions Co. Ltd* v *Austin* [1935] AC 346, per Lord Sankey LC at pp. 359–60). Thus, it is no part of the duty of counsel for the defence to embark on lengthy cross-examination on matters which are not really in issue (*Kalia* (1974) 60 Cr App R 200). See also *Simmonds* [1969] 1 QB 685 and *Maynard* (1979) 69 Cr App R 309. Likewise, questions should not be in the nature of comment on the facts; comments should be confined to speeches. Nor should questions be framed in such a way as to invite argument rather than elicit evidence on the facts in issue. Thus counsel should avoid questions such as 'I suggest to you that . . .' and 'Do you ask the jury to believe that . . .'. Cross-examination should be confined to putting questions of fact. Counsel should not state what somebody else has said or is expected to say. The time for statements such as 'The defendant's recollection is . . .' or 'The defendant will say . . .' is the opening speech; such statements should not be made, or put in the form of a question, in cross-examination (*Baldwin* (1925) 18 Cr App R 175, per Lord Hewart CJ at pp. 178–9). The same restrictions apply to questions put by the judge (see *Wilson* [1991] Crim LR 838, where the judge asked the accused 'So this 12-year-old girl has made wicked lies about you?'). See also **F7.10** and **F7.9**.

F7.9   ***Cross-examination as to Credit***   In order to impeach the credibility of a witness, he may be cross-examined about his previous convictions, his bias, any mental or physical disability affecting his reliability, his reputation for untruthfulness, and previous statements made by him relative to the subject-matter of the indictment and inconsistent with his present testimony. If the witness denies any of these matters, the cross-examining party is entitled to prove them (see **F7.20** to **F7.24**). Additionally, the cross-examining party may seek to show that the witness ought not to be believed on oath by asking questions as to his means of knowledge; his opportunities of observation; his powers of perception; the quality of his memory; mistakes, omissions and inconsistencies in his evidence; and his previous misconduct or bad character. However, cross-examination designed to impugn the witness's credibility should comply with the rules contained in the Code of Conduct of the Bar (see **F7.10**). See also *Sweet-Escott* (1971) 55 Cr App R 316. The accused was charged with perjury relating to evidence given by him for the prosecution in committal proceedings in 1970. Under cross-examination in those proceedings, he was asked about his convictions between 1947 and 1950, which he denied but subsequently admitted. From 1950 onwards he had no convictions at all. The jury were directed to acquit of perjury, on the ground that the prosecution had failed to establish that the false statements were 'material' in the committal proceedings. Lawton J posed the question, 'How far back is it permissible for advocates when cross-examining as to credit to delve into a man's past and to drag up such dirt as they can find there?' It was held that the cross-examination in the committal proceedings had offended against the relevant principle, namely that 'Since the purpose of cross-examination as to credit is to show that the witness ought not to be believed on oath, the matters about which he is questioned must relate to his likely standing after cross-examination with the tribunal which is trying him or listening to his evidence' (*Sweet-Escott* at p. 320; cf. *Paraskeva* (1982) 76 Cr App R 162). See also *Hobbs* v *C.T. Tinling & Co. Ltd* [1929] 2 KB 1, per Sankey LJ at p. 51. In *Funderburk* [1990] 1 WLR 587, applying *Sweet-Escott*, it was held that if a witness's testimony is inconsistent with a previous statement made by him, that statement may be put to him in cross-examination to challenge his credibility if the inconsistency relates to his likely standing with the jury after cross-examination, even though evidence of the making of the statement would not be allowed because it was not 'relative to the subject-matter of the indictment' for the purposes of the Criminal Procedure Act 1865, s. 4. See further at **F7.20**.

The extent to which police officers may be cross-examined about their behaviour in previous cases, as throwing light on the reliability of their evidence, was considered in *Edwards* [1991] 1 WLR 207. It was held that, generally speaking, questions may be put to a witness as to any improper conduct of which he may have been guilty, for the purposes of testing his credit, and therefore police officers can be cross-examined as to any relevant criminal offences or disciplinary charges found proved against them. The court also considered (1) complaints by members of the public about the behaviour of the witness not yet adjudicated upon by the Police Complaints Authority; (2) discreditable conduct by *other* officers in the same squad; and (3) other cases in which the witness has given evidence, which have resulted in acquittal of the accused or the quashing of the conviction on appeal. As to these matters, Lord Lane CJ said (at p. 216):

> This is an area where it is impossible and would be unwise to lay down hard and fast rules as to how the court should exercise its discretion. The objective must be to present to the jury as far as possible a fair, balanced picture of the witnesses' reliability, bearing in mind on the one hand the importance of eliciting facts which may show, if it be the case, that the police officer is not the truthful person he represents himself to be, but bearing in mind on the other hand the fact that a multiplicity of complaints may indicate no more than what was described before us as the 'band-wagon' effect.

On the facts, it was held that it would not have been proper to suggest to one officer that he had committed perjury by putting to him that he had been charged with that offence but not yet tried. The matters mentioned at (1) and (2) above were held not to be a proper subject of cross-examination. As to the matter mentioned at (3) above, it was held (at p. 217) applying *Thorne* (1977) 66 Cr App R 6 and *Cooke* (1986) 84 Cr App R 286, that:

> The acquittal of a defendant in case A, where the prosecution case depended largely or entirely upon the evidence of a police officer, does not normally render that officer liable to cross-examination as to credit in case B. But where a police officer who has allegedly fabricated an admission in case B, has also given evidence of an admission in case A, where there was an acquittal by virtue of which his evidence is demonstrated to have been disbelieved, it is proper that the jury in case B should be made aware of that fact. However, where the acquittal in case A does not necessarily indicate that the jury disbelieved the officer, such cross-examination should not be allowed. In such a case the verdict of not guilty may mean no more than that the jury entertained some doubt about the prosecution case, not necessarily that they believed any witness was lying.

See also, applying *Edwards*, *Clancy* [1997] Crim LR 290. In *Y* [1992] Crim LR 436, the accused had been tried on three counts of indecency with a child and acquitted on the third. At a retrial of the first two counts, the acquittal was ruled irrelevant to the credit of the complainant. On appeal, it was held that the test is whether there is an acquittal by virtue of which the witness's evidence can be demonstrated to have been disbelieved, and that it would always be difficult, if not impossible, to come to that conclusion when the jury had been directed as to the danger of convicting on the uncorroborated evidence of the complainant (see also *Scott* [1994] Crim LR 947). Nor can that conclusion be reached when it is possible that the jury may have acquitted either because of the accused's defence or because they did not believe the evidence of a police officer (see *Lucas* [1993] Crim LR 599). See also *Hui Chi-ming* v *The Queen* [1992] 1 AC 34 at **F1.9**, *H* (1990) 90 Cr App R 440, *Gale* [1994] Crim LR 208, *Greer* [1994] Crim LR 745 and *Meads* [1996] Crim LR 519. The fact that the Court of Appeal was not satisfied about aspects of police evidence in case A provides no proper foundation for the cross-examination of individual officers as to their veracity in case B (per Lord Lane CJ in *Edwards* at p. 219, and see also *Guney* [1998] 2 Cr App R 242 at p. 262).

Although in *Edwards* the view was taken that officers should not be cross-examined about unconcluded investigations, it seems that where officers have been under investigation for perjury and other misconduct in similar cases resulting in acquittals in which they have been involved, and in consequence charges against other defendants have been dropped and appeals have gone uncontested, this will constitute grounds for impugning their credibility, even if no formal proceedings have been taken against them (see *Edwards* [1996] 2 Cr App R 345, followed in *Whelan* [1997] Crim LR 353, and cf. *Guney* [1998] 2 Cr App R 242 at p. 262).

As to the limitations on cross-examination in rape cases, see the Sexual Offences (Amendment) Act 1976, s. 2, at **F7.13**. As to cross-examination of the accused to show that he has committed or been convicted of or charged with any offence, or is of bad character, see the Criminal Evidence Act 1898, s. 1(f), and generally **F14**.

F7.10   *The Code of Conduct of the Bar*   The Code of Conduct of the Bar of England and Wales also regulates the conduct of cross-examination.

Concerning cross-examination, see in particular para. 610; annexe F, general standards, paras 5.10 and 5.11; and annexe F, standards applicable to criminal cases, paras 11.1 and 13.5. In *McFaden* (1975) 62 Cr App R 187, the Court of Appeal said that the Bar Council Rules (now superseded by the Code), although they had strong persuasive force, did not bind the courts.

In *O'Neill* (1950) 34 Cr App R 108, it was suggested to police officers, in cross-examination, that they had beaten the accused until they made confessions. The accused elected not to testify. Lord Goddard CJ observed that it was 'entirely wrong' to make the suggestions that were made in cross-examination but not subsequently to call the accused to substantiate what they had instructed their counsel to say. The Court of Appeal in *Callaghan* (1979) 69 Cr App R 88 said that it entirely agreed with these observations. However, the observations in *Callaghan* have since been modified by Waller LJ (see *The Times*, 20 February 1980): if the accused declines to give evidence *because of his very bad record*, counsel should warn him that the judge will probably make a very strong comment on his failure to substantiate his allegations on oath. If the client persists with his instructions, however, counsel must carry them out. See also *Brigden* [1973] Crim LR 579, where the accused's case was that the police had 'planted' certain incriminating articles, but he gave no evidence. The Court of Appeal, *without* criticising the conduct of counsel for the defence, held that the trial judge was justified in making a strong comment on the accused's failure to go into the witness-box. See further, para. 610(h) of annexe F to the Code of Conduct of the Bar.

Inspection of and Cross-examination on Documents

F7.11   As to cross-examination of a witness on a previous inconsistent statement, see the Criminal Procedure Act 1865, ss. 4 and 5, at **F7.20**.

In the case of a document used by a witness to refresh his memory, the cross-examining party may inspect the document without thereby making it evidence (*Gregory* v *Tavernor* (1833) 6 C & P 280; *Senat* v *Senat* [1965] P 172). (As to the cross-examination of a witness on a document used by him to refresh his memory, see **F6.10**.) However, if a party calls for and inspects a document in the possession of another party which has *not* been used to refresh a witness's memory, the other party may require him to put it in evidence (*Wharam* v *Routledge* (1805) 5 Esp 235; and *Calvert* v *Flower* (1836) 7 C & P 386, applied in *Stroud* v *Stroud* (*No. 1*) [1963] 1 WLR 1080). The rule is obscure: it is unclear whether the document is admitted for the truth of its contents or as evidence of the consistency of the witness. In *Stroud* v *Stroud* (*No. 1*) Wrangham J observed that the rule had developed at a time when there was no discovery (whereas nowadays all relevant non-privileged documents are, in civil cases, disclosed), and acknowledged, therefore, that occasions for the practical application of the rule are fewer. Nonetheless, he said (at p. 1082): 'the rule itself has never been abrogated, and it may still be of practical importance, for example in criminal proceedings, where there is no discovery.' The Criminal Law Revision Committee recommended abolition of the rule in criminal proceedings, in which it appears never to have been applied (see 11th Report, Cmnd 4991, para. 223).

A document, the contents of which are inadmissible, is not rendered admissible by being put to a witness in cross-examination (see *Treacy* [1944] 2 All ER 229). However, in cross-examination counsel may produce to the witness a document containing an inadmissible hearsay statement and ask him, *without reading it aloud*, whether he accepts the contents as true. If the witness does accept the contents as true, they become evidence in the case; but if not, the contents remain inadmissible hearsay (*Gillespie* (1967) 51 Cr App R 172; applied in *Cross* (1990) 91 Cr App R 115). In *Cooper* (1985) 82 Cr App R 74, a charge of illegally importing drugs (concealed in a television set delivered to the accused's house), customs officers found letters in the house, written by the accused's wife in his and her names, five days before delivery of the television set, which referred to the 'houses' being 'hashless'. The Court of Appeal, applying *Gillespie* held that the proper procedure would have been for the prosecution to prove the finding of the letters as part of their case in order to give notice to the defence of the use to which they might eventually be put; but at this stage there should have been no indication of the contents of the letters to the jury. Then, in cross-examination of the accused, the letters should have been placed before him, and he should have been asked whether he was aware of their contents. Had he said yes, he should have been asked about the passages relating to the shortage of drugs. Similarly, it has been held that it is improper for counsel, when asking a witness to look at a document (the contents of which are inadmissible) and to say whether he still adheres to his answer, to describe to the jury its nature or contents. The proper course is simply to hand the document to the witness, direct him to look at it, and then to ask whether he still adheres to his answer (*Yousry* (1914) 11 Cr App R 13, per Lord Coleridge CJ at p. 18). See also *Tompkins* (1977) 67 Cr App R 181.

In *Hackney* (1982) 74 Cr App R 194, the Court of Appeal considered the growing practice of the defence, during the trial, to call for, and then cross-examine police officers on, records made during the accused's detention at a police station. Noting that entries in such records are often made by a number of police officers, and therefore that any inquiry into the completeness and accuracy of such records would often entail the questioning of many officers, the Court of Appeal said (at p. 198):

> These records, it should be emphasised, do not prove themselves. The prosecution do not have to produce them without some notice which allows proper opportunity of proving and explaining their contents by the evidence of officers who actually made the records. We think that judges should control the use made of such documents with these factors in mind and also ensure that the use of them is strictly confined to an issue in the case (the credibility of a witness, for example) that time spent exploring them is not inordinate and that indiscriminate use of them is not made either by counsel or by a defendant in person. When deciding what use, if any, should be made of such documents, the judge should take account of whether the defence before the trial began, could have given notice to the prosecution for the production of the documents so that proper steps could have been, at the outset of the trial, taken for the production not only of the documents, but also of witnesses able properly to inform the jury about the contents of them.

PROTECTION OF COMPLAINANTS IN PROCEEDINGS FOR SEXUAL OFFENCES

Rule at Common Law

The position at common law may be summarised as follows. In prosecutions for rape, **F7.12** assault with intent to commit rape, or indecent assault, evidence of previous voluntary acts of sexual intercourse with the *accused* is admissible on the grounds that such evidence renders it more likely that the prosecutrix consented on the occasion under investigation (*Riley* (1887) 18 QBD 481). However, although at common law the prosecutrix may be cross-examined about acts of intercourse with *men other than the accused*, if she denies them, her answer is final (*Holmes* (1871) LR 1 CCR 334). Evidence in rebuttal is admissible only if relevant to a fact in issue. Thus, she may be contradicted if she denies that she is a prostitute, because this is relevant to the issue of consent (*Clay* (1851) 5 Cox CC 146; *Bashir* [1969] 1 WLR 1303). See also *Krausz* (1973) 57 Cr App R 466, where the defence did not seek to suggest that the complainant was a prostitute. The accused alleged that he had met the complainant for the first time and that she had agreed to sleep with him, that after intercourse she had asked for money, which he had refused, and she had complained of rape. Evidence of previous similar conduct by the complainant was held to have been improperly excluded. The Court of Appeal acknowledged that in an age of changing standards of sexual morality it might be hard to say where promiscuity ends and prostitution begins, but was of the opinion that evidence which proved that a woman was in the habit of submitting her body to different men without discrimination, whether for pay or not, should be admissible. The decision in *Riley* (1887) 18 QBD 481 remains the law. The decisions in *Holmes, Clay, Bashir,* and *Krausz*, however, must now be read subject to the Sexual Offences (Amendment) Act 1976, s. 2. When the YJCEA 1999, ss. 41 to 43, are brought into force, they will replace s. 2 of the 1976 Act. The new provisions are set out at **F7.18**.

In *Walker* [1994] Crim LR 763, a case of indecent assault (and therefore not covered by s. 2 of the 1976 Act), it was held that where a young complainant gives details of sexual activities of which a jury might expect her to have no knowledge unless she has participated in such activities, she can be cross-examined as to whether her behaviour with others had made her familiar with such activities; otherwise the jury may think that her knowledge could only have come from the accused. See also *Ahmed* [1994] Crim LR 669, in which the accused admitted buggery of a woman and a count of false imprisonment was tried to determine whether the complainant had consented. The defence sought to cross-examine the complainant as to her previous sexual relations with men other than the accused (which had never included buggery) and to introduce evidence of such behaviour. Noting that buggery of a woman was not covered by s. 2 of the 1976 Act (the case having been decided prior to the amendment of the Sexual Offences Act 1956, s. 1, by the CJPO 1994), it was held that, although leave was not required for the cross-examination, counsel would be bound by her answers and could not call evidence of her previous sexual behaviour because, however promiscuous, it was not relevant to the issue of consent to buggery.

Sexual Offences (Amendment) Act 1976

F7.13

Sexual Offences (Amendment) Act 1976, ss. 2 and 7

2.—(1) If at a trial any person is for the time being charged with a rape offence to which he pleads not guilty, then, except with the leave of the judge, no evidence and no question in cross-examination shall be adduced or asked at the trial, by or on behalf of any defendant at the trial, about any sexual experience of a complainant with a person other than that defendant.

(2) The judge shall not give leave in pursuance of the preceding subsection for any evidence or question except on an application made to him in the absence of the jury by or on behalf of a defendant; and on such an application the judge shall give leave if and only if he is satisfied that it would be unfair to that defendant to refuse to allow the evidence to be adduced or the question to be asked.

(3) In subsection (1) of this section 'complainant' means a woman or man upon whom, in a charge for a rape offence to which the trial in question relates, it is alleged that rape was committed, attempted or proposed.

(4)   Nothing in this section authorises evidence to be adduced or a question to be asked which cannot be adduced or asked apart from this section.

7.—(2)   In this Act—
'a rape offence' means any of the following, namely rape, attempted rape, aiding, abetting, counselling and procuring rape or attempted rape, incitement to rape, conspiracy to rape and burglary with intent to rape.

If a person is charged in one indictment with a 'rape offence' and some other offence, the existence of the other charge does not exclude s. 2(2), although the judge, in deciding whether it is unfair 'to refuse to allow the evidence to be adduced or the questions to be asked' should take the existence of that other charge into account (*C* (1992) 156 JP 649).

Although sexual intercourse with a girl under the age of 16 is not a 'rape offence' within s. 2 of the 1976 Act and therefore the limits on cross-examination as to credit imposed by that Act do not apply in such a case, the courts will not wish to see the mischief sought to be prevented by that Act perpetuated in such a case and will be astute to see that such cross-examination is not abused or extended unnnecessarily (*Funderburk* [1990] 1 WLR 587 per Henry J at p. 593B). See further at **F7.19** and **F7.20**.

Meaning of 'Sexual Experience'

The term 'sexual experience', which is not defined by the Sexual Offences (Amendment)   **F7.14** Act 1976, has been given a wide construction going well beyond acts of sexual intercourse with other men. In *Hinds* [1979] Crim LR 111, Swanwick J held that leave was required to cross-examine the complainant about a *conversation* immediately before the alleged offence, in which she spoke of having sexual intercourse with other men. In *Viola* [1982] 1 WLR 1138, the accused sought to cross-examine the complainant about two matters:

(a)   that she had indicated to certain other men, verbally and by making physical advances, that she would not be averse to sexual intercourse with them; and

(b)   that one morning, another man, naked apart from a pair of slippers, was seen lying on the sofa in the complainant's flat.

The Court of Appeal operated on the assumption that evidence of each of these incidents amounted to evidence of the complainant's 'sexual experience'. See also *Cleland* [1995] Crim LR 742, considered at **F7.15**.

Section 2(1) of the 1976 Act clearly has no application to sexual practices on the part of the complainant not involving any other person and therefore cannot be used, for example, to exclude evidence of the possession of a vibrator, which was otherwise admissible as showing that its use could have caused the ruptured state of the complainant's hymen (*Barnes* [1994] Crim LR 691).

Unfairness to Accused

In *Lawrence* [1977] Crim LR 492, the first reported decision on s. 2 of the Sexual   **F7.15** Offences (Amendment) Act 1976, May J said (at p. 493):

The important part of the statute which I think needs construction are the words 'if and only if he [the judge] is satisfied that it would be unfair to that defendant to refuse to allow the evidence to be adduced or the question to be asked'. And, in my judgment, before a judge is satisfied or may be said to be satisfied that to refuse to allow a particular question or a series of questions in cross-examination would be unfair to a defendant he must take the view that it is more likely than not that the particular question or line of cross-examination, if allowed, might reasonably lead the jury, properly directed in the summing-up, to take a different view of the complainant's evidence from that which they might take if the question or series of questions was or were not allowed.

On the facts, it was ruled that cross-examination designed to form a basis for the unspoken comment, 'Well, there you are, members of the jury, that is the sort of girl she is', was not permissible. A distinction was drawn between cross-examination designed to blacken the complainant's sexual character so as to justify such a comment, and cross-examination as to the trustworthiness of her evidence; and it was ruled that only the latter, going to credit properly so called, was permissible.

In *Mills* (1978) 68 Cr App R 327, the Court of Appeal said that the approach adopted by May J in *Lawrence* was entirely right. In *Mills* the trial judge had refused an application to cross-examine the complainant as to her previous sexual experiences with other men. The application for leave to appeal against conviction was dismissed on the grounds that, the judge having exercised his discretion in accordance with *Lawrence*, it would be entirely wrong for the Court of Appeal to substitute its own discretion for that of the trial judge. However, in the subsequent Court of Appeal decision in *Viola* [1982] 1 WLR 1138, it was held to be wrong to speak of a discretion in this context. The judge has to make a *judgment* as to whether he is satisfied or not in the terms of s. 2, and because the Court of Appeal is in many respects in as good a position as the judge to reach a conclusion, it is entitled to differ from the conclusions of the judge.

The approach adopted by May J in *Lawrence* was approved in *Viola*. The following further guidance derives from the judgment of the Court of Appeal, given by Lord Lane CJ:

(a)   The first question which the judge must ask himself is whether the questions proposed are relevant according to the ordinary common-law rules of evidence, and relevant to the case as it is being put. If they are not so relevant, that is the end of the matter.

(b)   If the questions are relevant, whether they should be allowed or not depends on the terms of s. 2, which limits the admissibility of relevant evidence.

(c)   It is for the judge to apply the dictum of May J in *Lawrence* [1977] Crim LR 492 to the particular facts of the case.

(d)   The 1976 Act was aimed primarily at protecting complainants from cross-examination as to credit, from questions which went merely to credit and no more. The result is that, *generally speaking*, if the proposed questions merely seek to establish that the complainant has had sexual experience with other men to whom she was not married, so as to suggest for that reason she ought not to be believed under oath, the judge will exclude the evidence. On the other hand, if the questions are relevant to an issue in the trial in the light of the way the case is being defended, for instance relevant to the issue of consent, as opposed merely to credit, they are likely to be admitted, because to exclude such a relevant question will usually mean that the jury are being prevented from hearing something which, if they did hear it, might cause them to change their minds about the evidence given by the complainant. (The court stressed that it was very far from laying down any hard and fast rule.)

(e)   There is a grey area between the two types of relevance, relevance to credit and relevance to an issue in the case. On the one hand, evidence of sexual promiscuity may be so strong or so closely contemporaneous in time to the event in issue as to come near to, or indeed to reach the border between, mere credit and an issue in the case. Conversely, the relevance of the evidence to such an issue may be so slight as to lead the judge to conclude that he is not satisfied that its exclusion would be unfair to the accused.

No application for leave to cross-examine under s. 2 can properly be made unless defence counsel has instructions which provide reasonable grounds for making the assertion he wishes to make. The trial judge, therefore, can properly ask what the proposed questions are and what support for them counsel has. However, there is no requirement that the material on which the questions are based must be admissible, as well as relevant, although the question of admissibility is likely to influence the judge's decision. Thus, although there will be cases where supporting grounds exist but admissible evidence cannot be produced, questions which have no foundation in admissible evidence are likely to be excluded because they amount to the kind of roving inquiry or unfounded assertion based on rumour and gossip which s. 2 is intended to exclude (*Howes* [1996] 2 Cr App R 490; and cf. *C* [1996] Crim LR 37).

Although the statutory test is whether it would be 'unfair to the defendant' to refuse to allow the evidence to be adduced or the question to be asked, it has been said that in deciding whether to allow cross-examination under s. 2(2), the court must balance justice to the accused and fairness to and protection of the complainant (*Fenlon* (1980) 71 Cr App R 307, per Lord Lane CJ at p. 314). See also *Hinds* [1979] Crim LR 111, in which Swanwick J, in deciding whether to grant leave, took into account the probable effect of the proposed questions on the complainant, who was only 14 years of age and had attempted to commit suicide. Nonetheless, leave, in that case, was granted. In contrast, in *Bogie* [1992] Crim LR 301, the Court of Appeal stated that the material matter is whether exclusion of the evidence will be unfair to the accused; it matters not that it may be unfortunate for the complainant.

In *Brown* (1988) 89 Cr App R 97, the trial judge refused leave to cross-examine the complainant about her sexual relations with other men on the ground that, since the defence was that the complainant consented, rather than that the accused genuinely believed that she was consenting, the question of promiscuity did not go to the issue in the case. The Court of Appeal held that, by itself, this was not a sufficient ground for rejecting the defence application. May LJ was of the opinion (at p. 99) that it is clearly easier to justify cross-examination under s. 2 when the defence is that the accused, in consequence of his knowledge of the complainant's sexual history, had a genuine or mistaken belief that she was consenting; but that it does not follow that such cross-examination can never be permitted where the defence is that the complainant did consent. See in this regard, *Barton* (1987) 85 Cr App R 5, at **F7.16**.

> The real inquiry is whether on the facts of the particular case the complainant's attitude to sexual relations could be material upon which in these days a jury could reasonably rely to conclude that the complainant may indeed have consented to the sexual intercourse on the material occasion, despite her evidence to the contrary. It is in every case a question of degree. (*Brown* (1988) 89 Cr App R 97 (at p. 101).)

In *Viola* [1982] 1 WLR 1138, the accused was convicted of a rape which allegedly occurred in the complainant's flat shortly before midnight. The only issue was that of consent. The judge refused leave to cross-examine the complainant about two incidents involving other men: the presence of two men in her flat shortly before the alleged rape, and her conduct in 'making up' to them; and the presence of a man lying naked, apart from a pair of slippers, on a sofa in the flat, some eight or nine hours after the alleged rape. The Court of Appeal held that the judge had improperly refused leave, because the two incidents went to the issue of consent and could not be regarded as so trivial or of so little consequence as to allow the judge to say that no injustice would be done to the accused by their exclusion from evidence. In *S.M.S.* [1992] Crim LR 310, the accused, who had only one hand and a false eye, was charged with the rape of a girl aged 14. The issue was consent. The events took place in a grubby flat in circumstances of considerable indecency. The defence sought leave to cross-examine on whether she had had sexual intercourse with anyone prior to the alleged rape, on the basis that the jury may have believed that she was a virgin and may have found it impossible to believe that she would have consented to the loss of her virginity in all the circumstances of the case. On appeal, it was held that leave should have been granted, because the complainant's past experience did go to the issue of consent. See also *Cox* (1986) 84 Cr App R 132, another rape case in which the issue was consent. The conviction was quashed on the grounds that the trial judge had wrongly refused an application to cross-examine the complainant about earlier occasions when she had had consensual sexual intercourse with another man, in circumstances similar to those of the alleged rape, and had subsequently made an allegation of rape, which she eventually admitted to have been false. Compare *Fenlon* (1980) 71 Cr App R 307. In that case, semen having been found on swabs taken following the complainant's allegation of rape, the defence sought leave to cross-examine her on sexual relations with any other person(s) during the five days prior to the night of the alleged rape. The Court of Appeal held that, although other judges might have ruled differently, the trial judge had exercised his discretion properly in ruling that the only question he would allow was as to *when* the complainant had last had sexual intercourse. The defence conceded that any other questions would have amounted to a 'fishing expedition'.

Ellis [1990] Crim LR 717 highlights the difficulty, in this context, of the distinction between relevance to credit and relevance to an issue in the case. C, the complainant, who had known E, the appellant, since their schooldays, invited him to her home where the alleged rape took place. In her evidence, C said that she had bathed more than once afterwards because she felt dirty as a result of being raped. The defence was consent. The defence were granted leave to cross-examine C about alleged previous consensual sexual intercourse with another man, S, after which she was reported to have said to a girlfriend, G, that she 'felt dirty and had a bath'. C denied the alleged sexual encounter with S; and S gave evidence in support of her denial. The defence were then refused leave to call G. Allowing the appeal, it was held that C's evidence that she had bathed more than once was an unusual piece of evidence that the jury might well have thought was very compelling as evidence supporting and lending force to her testimony that she had withheld consent. The impact of that part of her evidence would necessarily have been lessened if it was the case that after consensual intercourse with S she had also felt the need to bathe. The issue went beyond her credit as a witness. It went to a very material part of her evidence, that she did not consent, the sole issue in the case. The judge therefore had erred in declining to allow G to be called. See also *Riley* [1991] Crim LR 460, where evidence in rebuttal of the complainant's denial that she would have consensual intercourse in her bedroom with a child present, was held to be in the same sort of category as the evidence sought to be introduced in *Ellis*. In *Redguard* [1991] Crim LR 213, the accused was charged with raping the complainant in her flat. The issue was consent. The complainant said that she would not have allowed anyone at the time other than her boyfriend to stay at her flat, let alone have a sexual relationship with her. It was held that the defence had been improperly refused permission to cross-examine her about a consensual sexual encounter with another man who stayed the night at her flat some two weeks after the alleged rape, because it was directly relevant both to her credibility and to the issue of consent. In *Cleland* [1995] Crim LR 742, where the issue was also consent, the complainant said that she had become pregnant as a result of the rape and had then had an abortion. She also said that she had not had unprotected sex with her boyfriend. It was held that the defence should have been permitted to cross-examine her about an abortion before the rape and to adduce evidence that she had menstruated after the rape. See also, *sed quaere, Elahee* [1999] Crim LR 399; and *Funderburk* [1990] 1 WLR 587, at **F7.19** and **F7.20**.

Defence of Belief in Consent

F7.16   In *Barton* (1987) 85 Cr App R 5 the appellant was convicted of rape. The only issue at the trial was consent in both of its forms:

(a)   that the complainant consented to intercourse; alternatively
(b)   that the appellant genuinely, but mistakenly, believed that she was consenting to intercourse.

The main ground of appeal was that the trial judge had refused leave to cross-examine the complainant about, and adduce evidence of, her sexual behaviour with other men, including, in particular, the fact that she would scream and bang her head and feet during intercourse, which was consistent with her behaviour during the alleged rape. The following submissions were made:

(a)   An accused is entitled as of right to put before the jury any matter which he said had persuaded him to believe that the complainant was consenting, including his knowledge of her previous promiscuity, because under s. 1(2) of the Sexual Offences (Amendment) Act 1976 it is declared that 'if . . . the jury has to consider whether a man believed that a woman was consenting to sexual intercourse, the presence or absence of reasonable grounds for such a belief is a matter to which the jury is to have regard, in conjunction with any other relevant matters, in considering whether he so believed.' Therefore, if the issue is genuine but mistaken belief in consent, and a ground for such belief was the accused's knowledge of the complainant's previous promiscuity, the prohibition in s. 2(1) did not apply.

(b)   Alternatively, a refusal to permit the accused to tell the jury what his grounds were must be necessarily 'unfair' to him within the meaning in s. 2(2).

Dismissing the appeal, it was held that the wording of s. 1(2) does not permit an accused to circumvent the prohibition in s. 2, because the words 'relevant matters' in s. 1(2) mean 'relevant matters properly before the jury'; and the admissibility of such matters, insofar as they relate to sexual experiences with other men, is controlled by s. 2. O'Connor LJ said (at pp. 12–13) that where both consent and a genuine, but mistaken, belief are in issue, the trial judge has a difficult task. As to the former defence, which necessarily involves an attack upon the credit of the complainant (who has given evidence that she did not consent), the dictum of May J in *Lawrence* [1977] Crim LR 492 is applicable. That dictum, however, is not appropriate in relation to the latter defence, because on that issue the complainant's credit is not being attacked (in the sense, presumably, that it is consistent with the complainant's evidence that she did not consent). When considering the effect of the complainant's past sexual promiscuity upon the accused's belief that she was consenting to intercourse, the judge must decide in the context of the facts of the case. There is a difference between believing that a woman is consenting to intercourse and believing that a woman will consent if advances are made to her. In the end it is the application of common sense to the facts of the individual case. (The last point made, it is submitted, is that only a belief in consent is relevant; and that in each case it must be considered whether evidence of the accused's knowledge has a bearing on that belief, as opposed to a belief that a woman will consent if advances are made.)

The court was satisfied that the trial judge had approached the problem correctly and reached the right decision: nowhere in the course of the lengthy police interview did the appellant suggest that his knowledge of the complainant's previous sexual behaviour had influenced his belief that she was consenting; and the submission that his belief had been influenced by such knowledge was never made to the trial judge, but was raised for the first time on appeal. It was not open to the appellant, therefore, to challenge the judge's decision on material not placed before him.

Committal Proceedings, Summary Trial, Courts Martial

Sexual Offences (Amendment) Act 1976, s. 3   F7.17

(1)   Where a magistrates' court inquires into a rape offence as examining justices, then, except with the consent of the court, no restricted matter shall be raised; and for this purpose a restricted matter is a matter as regards which evidence could not be adduced and a question could not be asked without leave in pursuance of section 2 of this Act if—

(a)   the inquiry were a trial at which a person is charged as mentioned in section 2(1) of this Act, and

(b)   each of the accused at the inquiry were charged at the trial with the offence or offences of which he is accused at the inquiry.

(2)   On an application for consent in pursuance of the preceding subsection for any matter the court shall—

(a)   refuse the consent unless the court is satisfied that leave in respect of the matter would be likely to be given at a relevant trial; and

(b)   give the consent if the court is so satisfied.

(3)   Where a person charged with a rape offence is tried for that offence either by court martial or summarily before a magistrates' court in pursuance of section 6(1) of the Children and Young Persons Act 1969 (which provides for the summary trial in certain cases of persons under the age of 17 who are charged with indictable offences) the preceding section shall have effect in relation to the trial as if—

(a)   the words 'in the absence of the jury' in subsection (2) were omitted; and

(b)   for any reference to the judge there were substituted—

(i)   in the case of a trial by court martial for which a judge advocate is appointed, a reference to the judge advocate, and

(ii)   in any other case, a reference to the court.

Protection under the Youth Justice and Criminal Evidence Act 1999

F7.18   When the YJCEA 1999, ss. 41 to 43, are brought into force, they will replace ss. 2 and 3 of the Sexual Offences (Amendment) Act 1976. Sections 41 to 43 will introduce new restrictions, in proceedings for sexual offences, on evidence or questions about the sexual behaviour of the complainant, whether involving the accused or any person other than the accused. A sexual offence, for theses purposes, is defined more widely than under the 1976 Act, to mean rape or burglary with intent to rape; an offence under any of ss. 2 to 12 and 14 to 17 of the Sexual Offences Act 1956 (unlawful intercourse, indecent assault, forcible abduction etc.); an offence under the Mental Health Act 1959, s. 128 (unlawful intercourse with person receiving treatment for mental disorder by member of hospital staff etc.); an offence under the Indecency with Children Act 1960, s. 1 (indecent conduct towards child under 14); an offence under the Criminal Law Act 1977, s. 54 (incitement of child under 16 to commit incest); and an offence which consists of attempting or conspiring to commit, or of aiding, abetting, counselling, procuring or inciting the commission of, any of the foregoing substantive offences (YJCEA 1999, s. 62).

Youth Justice and Criminal Evidence Act 1999, ss. 41 to 43

41.—(1)   If at a trial a person is charged with a sexual offence, then, except with the leave of the court—

(a)   no evidence may be adduced, and

(b)   no question may be asked in cross-examination,

by or on behalf of any accused at the trial, about any sexual behaviour of the complainant.

(2)   The court may give leave in relation to any evidence or question only on an application made by or on behalf of an accused, and may not give such leave unless it is satisfied—

(a)   that subsection (3) or (5) applies, and

(b)   that a refusal of leave might have the result of rendering unsafe a conclusion of the jury or (as the case may be) the court on any relevant issue in the case.

(3)   This subsection applies if the evidence or question relates to a relevant issue in the case and either—

(a)   that issue is not an issue of consent; or

(b)   it is an issue of consent and the sexual behaviour of the complainant to which the evidence or question relates is alleged to have taken place at or about the same time as the event which is the subject matter of the charge against the accused; or

(c)   it is an issue of consent and the sexual behaviour of the complainant to which the evidence or question relates is alleged to have been, in any respect, so similar—

(i)   to any sexual behaviour of the complainant which (according to evidence adduced or to be adduced by or on behalf of the accused) took place as part of the event which is the subject matter of the charge against the accused, or

(ii)   to any other sexual behaviour of the complainant which (according to such evidence) took place at or about the same time as that event,
that the similarity cannot reasonably be explained as a coincidence.

(4)   For the purposes of subsection (3) no evidence or question shall be regarded as relating to a relevant issue in the case if it appears to the court to be reasonable to assume that the purpose (or main purpose) for which it would be adduced or asked is to establish or elicit material for impugning the credibility of the complainant as a witness.

(5)   This subsection applies if the evidence or question—

(a)   relates to any evidence adduced by the prosecution about any sexual behaviour of the complainant; and

(b)   in the opinion of the court, would go no further than is necessary to enable the evidence adduced by the prosecution to be rebutted or explained by or on behalf of the accused.

(6)   For the purposes of subsections (3) and (5) the evidence or question must relate to a specific instance (or specific instances) of alleged sexual behaviour on the part of the complainant (and accordingly nothing in those subsections is capable of applying in relation to the evidence or question to the extent that it does not so relate).

(7)   Where this section applies in relation to a trial by virtue of the fact that one or more of a number of persons charged in the proceedings is or are charged with a sexual offence—

(a)   it shall cease to apply in relation to the trial if the prosecutor decides not to proceed with the case against that person or those persons in respect of that charge; but

(b)   it shall not cease to do so in the event of that person or those persons pleading guilty to, or being convicted of, that charge.

(8)   Nothing in this section authorises any evidence to be adduced or any question to be asked which cannot be adduced or asked apart from this section.

42.—(1)   In section 41—

(a)   'relevant issue in the case' means any issue falling to be proved by the prosecution or defence in the trial of the accused;

(b)   'issue of consent' means any issue whether the complainant in fact consented to the conduct constituting the offence with which the accused is charged (and accordingly does not include any issue as to the belief of the accused that the complainant so consented);

(c)   'sexual behaviour' means any sexual behaviour or other sexual experience, whether or not involving any accused or other person, but excluding (except in section 41(3)(c)(i) and (5)(a)) anything alleged to have taken place as part of the event which is the subject matter of the charge against the accused; and

(d)   subject to any order made under subsection (2), 'sexual offence' shall be construed in accordance with section 62.

(2)   The Secretary of State may by order make such provision as he considers appropriate for adding or removing, for the purposes of section 41, any offence to or from the offences which are sexual offences for the purposes of this Act by virtue of section 62.

(3)   Section 41 applies in relation to the following proceedings as it applies to a trial, namely—

(a)   proceedings before a magistrates' court inquiring into an offence as examining justices,

(b)   the hearing of an application under paragraph 5(1) of schedule 6 to the Criminal Justice Act 1991 (application to dismiss charge following notice of transfer of case to Crown Court),

(c)   the hearing of an application under paragraph 2(1) of schedule 3 to the Crime and Disorder Act 1998 (application to dismiss charge by person sent for trial under section 51 of that Act),

(d)   any hearing held, between conviction and sentencing, for the purpose of determining matters relevant to the court's decision as to how the accused is to be dealt with, and

(e)   the hearing of an appeal,
and references (in section 41 or this section) to a person charged with an offence accordingly include a person convicted of an offence.

43.—(1)   An application for leave shall be heard in private and in the absence of the complainant.

In this section 'leave' means leave under section 41.

(2)   Where such an application has been determined, the court must state in open court (but in the absence of the jury, if there is one)—

(a)   its reasons for giving, or refusing, leave, and

(b)   if it gives leave, the extent to which evidence may be adduced or questions asked in pursuance of the leave,

and, if it is a magistrates' court, must cause those matters to be entered in the register of its proceedings.

(3)   [Power to make rules of court.]

RULE OF FINALITY OF ANSWERS TO QUESTIONS ON COLLATERAL MATTERS

General Rule

F7.19   The general rule, based on the desirability of avoiding a multiplicity of essentially irrelevant issues, is that evidence is not admissible to contradict answers given by a witness to questions put in cross-examination which concern collateral matters, i.e. matters which go merely to credit but which are otherwise irrelevant to the issues in the case (*Harris* v *Tippett* (1811) 2 Camp 637; *Palmer* v *Trower* (1852) 8 Exch 247). In *A-G* v *Hitchcock* (1847) 1 Exch 91, Pollock CB said (at p. 99): 'The test whether a matter is collateral or not is this: if the answer of a witness is a matter which you would be allowed on your own part to prove in evidence – if it have such a connection with the issues that you would be allowed to give it in evidence – then it is a matter on which you may contradict him.' In that case a maltster was charged with having used a cistern for the making of malt in breach of certain statutory requirements. A prosecution witness, having sworn that the cistern had been used, was asked in cross-examination whether he had not said to one Cook that the Excise officers had offered him £20 to give evidence that the cistern had been used. Upon denial of this allegation, it was held that the defendant was not allowed to call Cook to contradict the witness, because proof that a bribe was offered to the witness and not accepted was irrelevant to the matter in issue. Compare *Phillips* (1936) 26 Cr App R 17, at **F7.21**. Conversely, in *Busby* (1981) 75 Cr App R 79, a prosecution for burglary and handling, police officers were cross-examined to the effect that they had fabricated statements attributed to the accused and indicative of his guilt, and had threatened W, a potential defence witness, to stop him giving evidence. These allegations were denied. The trial judge ruled that the defence could not call W to give evidence that he had been threatened by the officers, because this would go solely to their credit. Allowing the appeal against conviction, the Court of Appeal held that the trial judge had erred: the evidence was relevant to an issue which had to be tried, because, if true, it showed that the police were prepared to go to improper lengths in order to secure a conviction, which would have supported the defence case that the statements attributed to the accused had been fabricated. See also *Marsh* (1985) 83 Cr App R 165.

In *Funderburk* [1990] 1 WLR 587, at p. 591, *Busby* was treated as having created a new *exception* to the rule of finality. However, in *Edwards* [1991] 1 WLR 207, it was held that the fact that the police were allegedly prepared to prevent the potential witness from giving evidence, came within the exception of bias (see **F7.21**); and that if the decision could not be explained on that basis, it was inconsistent with the general rule and inconsistent with the decision in *Harris* v *Tippett* itself (where the facts were not dissimilar to those in *Busby*). In *Edwards* a number of officers involved in the case had given evidence in other trials, which had resulted in acquittal, in circumstances which tended to cast doubt on their reliability. In the other trials, evidence showed that some interview notes were inaccurate and that others had seemingly been rewritten to include admissions which did not exist in the originals. It was held that:

(a) it could be put to the officers in cross-examination that they had given evidence in the previous trials, that in each trial there was an issue as to whether alleged confessions had been fabricated and that each trial had ended in acquittal, because there was a sufficient connection between the evidence given by the officers in those trials and their eventual outcome to entitle such cross-examination on the question of their credibility in the instant case; but

(b) if the officers denied such allegations, they could not be proved by evidence in rebuttal, because the questioning would be as to credit alone, a collateral issue, and would not fall within any of the exceptions to the rule of finality.

Whether a particular item of evidence goes to an issue before the court or is merely collateral can be a question of some nicety. It only adds to the difficulty, it is submitted, to suggest that whether the rule of finality applies may turn on whether the matter which the cross-examining party seeks to prove is a single and distinct fact which is easy of proof rather than a broad and complex issue which is difficult of proof (*S* [1992] Crim LR 307). In *Funderburk* the court urged a flexible approach to the rule, on the basis that a general rule designed to serve the interests of justice should not be used to defeat justice by an over-pedantic approach. Henry J observed (at p. 598D), 'The utility of the test may lie in the fact that the answer is an instinctive one based on the prosecutor's and the court's sense of fair play rather than any philosophic or analytic process' (but *cf* per Evans LJ in *Neale* [1998] Crim LR 737). Accordingly it has been held that the issue of sufficient relevance is one for the trial judge and that the Court of Appeal will only interfere with a decision to exclude evidence as being insufficiently irrelevant if it is either wrong in principle or plainly wrong as being outside that wide ambit (*Somers* [1999] Crim LR 744).

The Court of Appeal in *Funderburk* also agreed with the editors of *Cross on Evidence* (7th ed., 1990, p. 322) that where the disputed issue is a sexual one between two persons in private, the difference between questions going to credit and questions going to the issue is reduced to vanishing-point because sexual intercourse, whether or not consensual, most often takes place in private and leaves few visible traces of having occurred, so that the evidence is often effectively limited to that of the parties, and much is likely to depend upon the balance of credibility between them. See further at **F7.20**.

Previous Inconsistent Statements

If a witness under cross-examination admits to having made a previous oral or written **F7.20** statement inconsistent with his testimony, no further proof of the statement is required or, it seems, allowed (*P (GR)* [1998] Crim LR 663). However, if the witness denies having made such a statement, and the statement is relevant to an issue in the case, then it may be proved. Proof of such a statement is governed by the Criminal Procedure Act 1865, ss. 4 and 5. Section 4 applies to both oral and written statements, but s. 5 applies to written statements only (*Derby Magistrates' Court, ex parte B* [1996] AC 487).

Criminal Procedure Act 1865, s. 4

If a witness, upon cross-examination as to a former statement made by him relative to the subject-matter of the indictment or proceeding, and inconsistent with his present testimony, does not distinctly admit that he has made such statement, proof may be given that he did in fact make it; but before such proof can be given the circumstances of the supposed statement, sufficient to designate the particular occasion, must be mentioned to the witness, and he must be asked whether or not he has made such statement.

Section 4 is not confined to previous statements on oath (*Hart* (1957) 42 Cr App R 47, at p. 50; and *O'Neill* [1969] Crim LR 260 – oral statement made to the police). A witness who 'does not distinctly admit' to the making of the previous statement would include, in addition to a witness who denies such a statement, a witness who claims to have no recollection of it, who is equivocal on the subject, or who declines to answer. However, s. 4 does not apply to a party's own hostile witness. Proof of the previous inconsistent statement of a hostile witness requires the leave of the judge under s. 3 of the 1865 Act (see **F6.20**), a requirement which cannot be circumvented by reliance on s. 4 of the Act (*Booth* (1981) 74 Cr App R 123).

Whether a statement is 'relative to the subject-matter of the indictment or proceeding' is a matter within the discretion of the judge (*Bashir* [1969] 1 WLR 1303 per Veale J at p. 1306; and *Hart* (1957) 42 Cr App R 47 per Devlin J at p. 50). For the difficulties to which the issue may give rise, see *Funderburk* [1990] 1 WLR 587. F was convicted on three counts of sexual intercourse with a girl of 13. In her evidence, the girl gave evidence of a number of acts of intercourse with F, the description of the first act clearly describing the loss of her virginity. The defence was that the child was lying and in order to explain how so young a child could, if she were lying, have given such detailed and varied accounts of the acts of intercourse, wished to show that she was sexually experienced and had either transposed to F experiences which she had had with others and/or fantasised about experience with F. For this purpose, the defence wished to put to her that she had told a potential defence witness, P, that before the first incident complained of she had had sexual intercourse with two named men. The defence then wished to call P to give evidence of the conversation. The trial judge, applying the test in s. 4 of the 1865 Act, ruled that the complainant's previous inconsistent statement could not be put to her, nor could P be called, because the complainant's virginity was immaterial to the question whether F had had sexual intercourse with her and therefore was not 'relative to the subject-matter of the indictment'. On the question whether the previous inconsistent statement could be put in cross-examination *to challenge the complainant's credibility*, it was held that there was nothing in s. 4 to prevent this, even if, under s. 4, evidence of the making of that statement would not be allowed because it was not relative to the subject-matter of the indictment. The test for allowing cross-examination *as to credit* was that suggested by Lawton J in *Sweet-Escott* (1971) 55 Cr App R 316: how might the matters put to the witness affect his or her standing with the jury after cross-examination (see **F7.9**). Applying that test, the cross-examination should have been allowed since the jury might reasonably have wished to reappraise her evidence about the loss of her virginity and her credibility if they had heard of her previous statements regarding her earlier sexual experiences. On the question whether, if the complainant had been cross-examined about the conversation with P and she had denied making the previous statements, the defence would have been entitled to call P to prove the conversation, it was held that the previous statements were relative to the subject-matter of the indictment and therefore P could have been called to prove them under s. 4. Where the disputed issue is a sexual one between two persons in private, the difference between questions going to credit and questions going to the issue is reduced to vanishing-point. On the way the prosecution had presented the evidence, the challenge to the loss of virginity went far beyond a mere question of the complainant's credibility and was sufficiently closely related to the subject-matter of the indictment for justice to require investigation for the basis of such a challenge. (Cf. *Neale* [1998] Crim LR 737 and also, *sed quare, Gibson* [1993] Crim LR 453.) See also *Nagrecha* [1997] 2 Cr App R 401. N was accused of indecently assaulting the complainant. There were no witnesses. Under cross-examination, the complainant denied that she had made allegations of sexual impropriety against other men. It was held that evidence of the making of the other allegations was admissible because it went to the central issue of whether or not there had been any indecent assault.

Criminal Procedure Act 1865, s. 5

A witness may be cross-examined as to previous statements made by him in writing or reduced into writing relative to the subject matter of the indictment or proceeding, without such writing being shown to him; but if it is intended to contradict such witness by the writing, his attention must, before such contradictory proof can be given, be called to those parts of the writing which are to be used for the purpose of so contradicting him: provided always, that it shall be competent for the judge, at any time during the trial, to require the production of the writing for his inspection, and he may thereupon make such use of it for the purposes of the trial as he may think fit.

The first part of s. 5 expressly allows cross-examination on a previous written statement *without* such writing being shown to the witness. However, if counsel proposes to cross-examine in this way, he must have the writing with him, even if he does not intend to *contradict* the witness with it, because under the proviso to s. 5, the judge may require its production for his inspection, and may thereupon make such use of it as he may think fit (*Anderson* (1929) 21 Cr App R 178). If the writing is shown to the witness, this may be done without putting it in evidence. Thus, counsel may hand the document to the witness, direct him to read the relevant part of it to himself, and then ask whether he wishes to adhere to his testimony. If the witness accepts the truth of the former statement, it becomes part of his evidence; if he adheres to his testimony, there is no obligation on the cross-examining party to contradict the witness and put the document in evidence (a course which it may be wise to avoid, especially if the inconsistency relates to some minor matter, and in all other respects the former statement is *consistent* with the witness's evidence). However, if counsel does wish to contradict the witness, he must put the document in evidence by reading out aloud the contradictory statement. The statement may then be inspected to see how far the suggested contradiction exists; whether the absence of a particular statement is explained by the context; and whether the discrepancy is only a minute point so that, taken as a whole, the document is more in the nature of confirmation rather than contradiction (see generally *Riley* (1866) 4 F & F 964 per Channell B; and *Wright* (1866) 4 F & F 967). It is open to the judge to allow the whole of the written statement to go before the jury, because under s. 5 he may 'make such use of it for the purposes of the trial as he may think fit'. However, he has a discretion to allow only part of the statement to go before the jury and therefore, in appropriate circumstances, may permit the jury to see only those parts of the statement upon which the cross-examination was based and not all the other parts relating to other unconnected matters (*Beattie* (1989) 89 Cr App R 302).

If a prior inconsistent statement is put in evidence under s. 4 or s. 5 of the 1865 Act, it is not admitted as evidence of the facts it states, except to the extent that the maker in evidence adopts any part of it as true, but goes to the credit of the witness (*O'Neill* [1969] Crim LR 260); and the judge should warn the jury of the limited evidential use to which it may be put (*Askew* [1981] Crim LR 398; and *Jarvis* [1991] Crim LR 374). In *Birch* (1924) 18 Cr App R 26, Avory J pointed out (at p. 28) that, although s. 5 expressly allows the judge to 'make such use of [the writing] for the purposes of the trial as he may think fit', this does not allow him to treat the statement as evidence of the truth of its contents, but means, for example, that he may call attention to other parts of the statement to which no reference has been made.

The general rule of finality of answers to questions on collateral matters is subject to the following exceptions.

Bias and Partiality

Evidence has always been admissible to contradict a witness's denial of bias or partiality **F7.21** towards one of the parties, and to show that he is prejudicial concerning the case being tried (*Mendy* (1976) 64 Cr App R 4, per Geoffrey Lane LJ at p. 6). For earlier authority, see *Yewin* (1811) cited 2 Camp 638 and *Dunn* v *Aslett* (1838) 2 Mood & R 122. Thus, although evidence is not admissible to contradict a witness's denial that he was *offered* a bribe to give false evidence, because this does not show that he is not a fair and credible witness, evidence is admissible to rebut a witness's denial that he *accepted* such a bribe, because that tends to show his partiality (*A-G* v *Hitchcock* (1847) 1 Exch 91). Pollock CB said: 'A witness may be asked how he stands affected towards one of the parties; and if his relation towards them is such as to prejudice his mind, and fill him with sentiments of revenge and other feelings of a similar kind, and if he denies the fact, evidence may be given to show the state of his mind and feelings.'

Thus, the accused may call evidence to contradict a prosecution witness who, in cross-examination, denies having threatened to be revenged on the accused following a quarrel with him (*Shaw* (1888) 16 Cox CC 503). See also *Whelan* [1996] Crim LR 423. In *Phillips* (1936) 26 Cr App R 17, a case of incest, the principal prosecution witnesses, the accused's two daughters, were cross-examined on the basis that (a) they had been 'schooled' by their mother into giving false evidence, and (b) they had made admissions that evidence given by them in previous criminal proceedings against their father was false. Both allegations were denied. The trial judge refused to allow the defence to call the woman to whom the admissions were alleged to have been made. Quashing the conviction, the Court of Criminal Appeal held that this evidence should have been admitted because the bias that it would have revealed went to the very foundation of the accused's defence.

In *Mendy* (1976) 64 Cr App R 4, the accused was convicted of assault. At her trial, prospective witnesses were kept out of court in accordance with the normal practice. While a police officer was giving evidence, a man in the public gallery was seen taking notes. He was later seen discussing the case with the accused's husband, apparently describing the officer's evidence to him. The husband, under cross-examination, denied this incident. The Court of Appeal held that the trial judge had properly allowed the prosecution to call evidence in rebuttal: the husband was prepared to lend himself to a scheme, designed to defeat the purpose of keeping prospective witnesses out of court, to enable him the more convincingly to describe how he, and not his wife, had caused the injuries alleged.

Previous Convictions

F7.22 If a witness, cross-examined as to a previous conviction, denies it or refuses to answer, it may be proved against him under the Criminal Procedure Act 1865, s. 6.

Criminal Procedure Act 1865, s. 6

A witness may be questioned as to whether he has been convicted of any felony or misdemeanour, and upon being so questioned, if he either denies or does not admit the fact, or refuses to answer, it shall be lawful for the cross-examining party to prove such conviction.

Although on its wording s. 6 operates in relation to any conviction of any witness, irrespective, apparently, of the relevance of the conviction either to the witness's credibility or to the issues in the case, its application is restricted both by statute and, it is submitted, at common law. The following three restrictions are considered at **F14**:

(a) the Criminal Evidence Act 1898, s. 1(f) (cross-examination of an accused about previous convictions);

(b) the CYPA 1963, s. 16(2) (cross-examination of an accused of or over the age of 21 about any offence of which he was found guilty while under the age of 14); and

(c) *Practice Direction (Crime: Spent Convictions)* [1975] 1 WLR 1065 (references in open court to spent convictions under the Rehabilitation of Offenders Act 1974).

It is submitted that cross-examination about a witness's previous convictions under s. 6 of the 1865 Act is also subject to the general discretionary power of the judge to prevent any questions in cross-examination which, in his opinion, are unnecessary, improper or oppressive (see **F7.8** and *Sweet-Escott* (1971) 55 Cr App R 316, at **F7.9**).

Non-compliance with the *Practice Direction* will not necessarily result in a conviction being quashed on appeal (*Smallman* [1982] Crim LR 175). In that case, prosecuting counsel, without seeking the leave of the judge, referred to the spent conviction of a defence witness when cross-examining him. The judge directed the jury to leave out of account the prejudice resulting from the reference. The Court of Appeal held that such a breach of the *Practice Direction* could not be a ground for quashing an otherwise perfectly proper conviction.

Two cases where the charge was wounding and the defence was self-defence can usefully be compared. In *Evans* (1992) 156 JP 539, it was held that the judge should have allowed the defence to cross-examine the victim on her previous but spent convictions for dishonesty and violence because, evidentially, there was a head-on collision between the accused and the victim, and the jury were entitled to know of the victim's criminal record. In *Lawrence* [1995] Crim LR 815, the trial judge refused the defence permission to question the victim in detail on his 20 previous spent convictions, the majority of which were for offences of dishonesty, but only allowed questions on four more recent offences of dishonesty. The Court of Appeal held that the effect of the *Practice Direction* is to give the judge a wide discretion and that although it might have exercised the discretion differently and allowed cross-examination on one of the spent convictions, which involved perverting the course of justice, it was impossible to say that the judge had erred in principle. See also *Whelan* [1996] Crim LR 423.

As to proof of previous convictions, see the PACE 1984, s. 73, at **F11.1**. Where a witness who is cross-examined on a conviction accepts the conviction but claims his innocence, the cross-examining party is not entitled to adduce evidence in rebuttal, such as evidence from the victim of the offence on which the witness stands convicted, because such evidence would go solely to credibility (*Irish* [1995] Crim LR 145, applying *Edwards* [1991] 1 WLR 207, considered at **F7.19**).

Medical Evidence of Disability Affecting Reliability

Medical evidence is admissible to show that a witness suffers from some disease or defect **F7.23** or abnormality of mind that affects the reliability of his evidence. Such evidence is not confined to a general opinion of the unreliability of the witness but may give all the matters necessary to show, not only the foundation of and reasons for the diagnosis, but also the extent to which the credibility of the witness is affected. (*Toohey* v *Metropolitan Police Commissioner* [1965] AC 595, per Lord Pearce at p. 609.)

If the defence adduce such evidence, it may be open to the Crown to call an expert in rebuttal, or even (anticipating the defence expert) as part of the prosecution case. It may even be open to the Crown to rebut by expert evidence a case put only in cross-examination that a prosecution witness is unreliable by reason of mental abnormality. Much may depend on the nature of the abnormality and of the cross-examination. But the rebuttal evidence should be restricted to meeting the specific challenge and should not extend to oath-helping: the Crown cannot call a witness of fact and then, without more, call a psychologist or psychiatrist to give reasons why the jury should regard that witness as reliable (*Robinson* [1994] 3 All ER 346; and see also *Beard* [1998] Crim LR 585).

In *Toohey*, T was charged with others with assaulting M with intent to rob. The defence case was that M had been drinking and that the accused were trying to help him, but that he became hysterical and accused them of assaulting him. The trial judge ruled that the medical evidence of a doctor, who had examined M shortly after the alleged assault, that drink could exacerbate hysteria, and that M was more prone to hysteria than a normal person, was inadmissible. The House of Lords quashed the conviction on the grounds that the evidence was admissible, not only because of its relevance to the facts in issue, but also in order to impeach the credibility of M, *qua* witness. Lord Pearce said (at p. 608):

> If a witness purported to give evidence of something which he believed that he had seen at a distance of 50 yards, it must surely be possible to call the evidence of an oculist to the effect that the witness could not possibly see anything at a greater distance than 20 yards, or the evidence of a surgeon who had removed a cataract from which the witness was suffering at the material time and which would have prevented him from seeing what he thought he saw. So, too, must it be allowable to call medical evidence of mental illness which makes a witness incapable of giving reliable evidence . . .

See also *Eades* [1972] Crim LR 99, a charge of causing death by dangerous driving. In his first statement to the police, one week after the accident, the accused said that he had not suffered from any concussion but was unable to remember any details of the accident itself (although he could remember incidents before and after the accident). Six weeks later, in a second statement to the police, he said that a few days earlier he had driven past the *locus in quo* and, as a result of a car emerging from a side road into his path, he had suddenly remembered the circumstances of the accident. Nield J ruled that if the accused gave evidence, the prosecution would be entitled to call a psychiatrist, who, although he had not examined the accused, had heard the prosecution evidence, to contradict the accused by evidence that his account as to how he had recovered his memory was not consistent with medical knowledge. Such evidence would be admissible because it would be not only relevant to a fact in issue, but also would tend to impugn the reliability of the accused as a witness.

The principle established in *Toohey* v *Metropolitan Police Commissioner* [1965] AC 595, in accordance with the rules governing the use of expert evidence generally, is applicable only in relation to some physical or mental disability calling for expertise, as opposed to matters affecting reliability upon which the jury are capable of forming their own opinion without expert assistance. Thus, expert evidence is generally inadmissible on the issue of an accused's credibility (*Turner* [1975] QB 834, at p. 842). Compare *Lowery* v *The Queen* [1974] AC 85, and see generally **F10**. In *Toohey*, Lord Pearce said (at p. 608):

> Human evidence shares the frailties of those who give it. It is subject to many cross-currents such as partiality, prejudice, self-interest and, above all, imagination and inaccuracy. Those are matters with which the jury, helped by cross-examination and common sense, must do their best. But when a witness through physical (in which I include mental) disease or abnormality is not capable of giving a true or reliable account to the jury, it must surely be allowable for medical science to reveal this vital hidden fact to them.

The distinction drawn, which in the present context is of some nicety, probably provides the best explanation for the decision in *MacKenney* (1980) 72 Cr App R 78; (1981) 76 Cr App R 271 (CA). In that case the accused, charged with murder, alleged that the main prosecution witness had fabricated his evidence. The defence sought to call a *psychologist*, who had not examined the witness but who had watched him as he gave his evidence, to give his opinion that the witness was a psychopath who was likely to be lying. May J held that this evidence was inadmissible: it was for the jury, with warnings from counsel and the court, to decide whether the witness was giving reliable evidence. The conviction was upheld on appeal. A *psychologist*, as opposed to a *psychiatrist*, is not necessarily medically qualified for the purposes of giving expert evidence on diseases and disorders of the mind. *Psychiatric* evidence as to a witness's reliability is admissible if the witness is suffering from a mental illness which makes him *totally incapable* of giving reliable evidence or which *substantially* affects his capacity to give such evidence; but it is not admissible if he is capable of giving reliable evidence but may not be doing so.

Evidence of Reputation for Untruthfulness

F7.24 A party may call a witness to give evidence that a witness called by the opposite party has a reputation for untruthfulness and, on the basis of such knowledge, that he is of the opinion that the witness is not to be believed on his oath (*Mawson* v *Hartsink* (1802) 4 Esp 102). The witness may simply state that he would not believe the oath of the impugned witness (*Watson* (1817) 2 Stark 116; *Brown* (1867) 10 Cox CC 453). (But compare, in cases where the impugned witness is the accused, *Rowton* (1865) Le & Ca 520: see **F13.7** to **F13.11**.) The rule, which has operated for centuries without dispute, is rarely used in modern times. However, in *Toohey* v *Metropolitan Police Commissioner* [1965] AC 595, in which none of the members of the House of Lords could remember being concerned in a case where such evidence was called, it was observed that the rule does not create injustice. In *Richardson* [1969] 1 QB 299, Edmund Davies LJ, giving the judgment of the Court of Appeal, summarised the rule, in its present form (at p. 304):

1.   A witness may be asked whether he has knowledge of the impugned witness's general reputation for veracity and whether (from such knowledge) he would believe the impugned witness's sworn testimony.
2.   The witness called to impeach the credibility of a previous witness may also express his individual opinion (based upon his personal knowledge) as to whether the latter is to be believed upon his oath, and is *not* confined to giving evidence merely of general reputation.
3.   But whether his opinion as to the impugned witness's credibility be based simply upon the latter's general reputation for veracity or upon his personal knowledge, the witness cannot be permitted to indicate during his examination-in-chief the particular facts, circumstances or incidents which formed the basis of his opinion, although he may be cross-examined as to them.

It has been doubted whether a party, as opposed to one of his witnesses, may give evidence of reputation for untruthfulness under the rule (*Beard* [1998] Crim LR 585).

If, in cross-examination, the impeaching witness is asked to give the reasons for his opinion, his answers must be treated as final and cannot be contradicted (*Gunewardene* [1951] 2 KB 600; *Richardson*). However, if evidence of reputation for untruthfulness is given under the rule, it appears that another witness may then be called to give evidence that the impugned witness is worthy of credit or to impeach the credit of the impeaching witness; but the process of recrimination can go no further than that (Pitt Taylor, *A Treatise on the Law of Evidence*, 12th ed. by R. P. Croom-Johnson and G. F. L. Bridgman (London: Sweet & Maxwell, 1931), para. 1473, citing *Viscount Stafford* (1680) 7 St Tr 1293 at col. 1484). Rebuttal evidence is only allowed where *evidence* of reputation for untruthfulness has been given, not where an attack has been made on the impugned witness out of court, e.g. in a police interview (see *Beard* [1998] Crim LR 585).

RE-EXAMINATION

After cross-examination, a witness may be re-examined by the party who called him.   **F7.25** This applies even in the case of a hostile witness, who may be re-examined on any new matters which arose out of cross-examination (*Wong* [1986] Crim LR 683). Leading questions may not be asked in re-examination. The principal rule of re-examination is that, except with the leave of the judge, questions should be confined to matters, including any new matters, arising out of cross-examination. This rule applies not only in the case of a witness who has been examined in chief, but also in the case of a witness whose name is notionally on the back of the indictment and who was called by the prosecution merely to allow the defence to cross-examine him (*Beezley* (1830) 4 C & P 220). Where a witness under cross-examination gives evidence of part of a conversation with him on some previous occasion, questions may not be asked in re-examination about everything else that was said at the same time, but only about so much as can be in some way connected with the statement as to which he was cross-examined, such as other statements which qualify or explain it in any way (*Prince* v *Samo* (1838) 7 A & E 627, per Lord Denman CJ, citing Lord Tenterden in *Queen Caroline's Case* (1820) 2 B & B 284, at p. 297).

A witness may refresh his memory in re-examination: see **F6.6**. As to the admissibility of previous consistent statements in re-examination, see **F6.13** to **F6.18**.

SECTION F8: DOCUMENTARY EVIDENCE AND REAL EVIDENCE

PROOF OF PRIVATE DOCUMENTS

Statements contained in documents are subject to the general rules of evidence on admissibility, including those relating to relevance, hearsay, opinion and privilege. Two additional requirements, concerning documents on the contents of which a party seeks to rely, are: (a) proof of the contents and (b) proof of due execution.

Concerning presumptions relating to documents, see **F8.29**. As to stamped documents, see **F8.30**. As to statements in documents produced by computers, see **F8.31** to **F8.37** and **F8.41**.

PROOF OF CONTENTS: THE BEST EVIDENCE RULE

F8.1   At common law, the general rule, often regarded as the only remaining instance of the best evidence rule, is that a party seeking to rely upon the contents of a document must adduce primary evidence of those contents, i.e. either the original document in question, a copy of an enrolled document, or informal admissions made by parties concerning the contents. Thus if an original document is available in one's hands, one must produce it and one cannot give secondary evidence by producing a copy (*Kajala* v *Noble* (1982) 75 Cr App R 149 at p. 152). A party having a document available in his hands means a party who has the original of the document with him in court, or could have it in court without any difficulty (*Governor of Pentonville Prison, ex parte Osman* [1990] 1 WLR 277 at p. 308). The rule, in criminal cases, is confined to written documents in the strict sense of the term, and has no relevance to tape recordings and films (*Kajala* v *Noble* (1982) 75 Cr App R 149). As to the use of tape recordings, see **F8.43**; as to photographs, video recordings and films, see **F8.44**. The general rule does not apply if:

(a)   it is unnecessary to place reliance upon the contents because the fact or matter in issue, although recorded in a document, can be proved by other evidence (see, e.g., *Holy Trinity, Kingston-upon-Hull (Inhabitants)* (1827) 7 B & C 611: the fact of a tenancy; *Manwaring* (1856) Dears & B 132: proof of a marriage, which may have been registered, by the testimony of a person who had attended the ceremony; and *Seberg* (1870) LR 1 CCR 264: proof by the testimony of eye-witnesses that a ship was British and sailing under the British flag, without production of the register of the vessel); or

(b)   the document is tendered merely for the purpose of identifying it or establishing the bare fact of its existence (see *Boyle* v *Wiseman* (1855) 11 Exch 360, at p. 367 and *Elworthy* (1867) LR 1 CCR 103).

To the general rule there are a number of common-law and statutory exceptions, providing for proof of the contents of documents by secondary evidence. Generally speaking, such secondary evidence may take the form of a copy, a copy of a copy or oral evidence, and 'there are no degrees of secondary evidence' (per Lord Abinger CB in *Doe d Gilbert* v *Ross* (1840) 7 M & W 102). Thus, an inferior copy may be tendered even if a better copy is available (*Lafone* v *Griffin* (1909) 25 TLR 308 and *Collins* (1960) 44 Cr App R 170; but contrast *Everingham* v *Roundell* (1838) 2 Mood & R 138). Likewise, oral evidence of the contents is admissible even if a copy is available (*Brown* v *Woodman* (1834) 6 C & P 206). The exceptions to the rule that there are no degrees of secondary evidence are the contents of:

(a)   a will admitted to probate, which may not be proved by oral evidence if the original or probate copy exists;

(b)   judicial documents and bankers' books (see **F8.7** to **F8.27**), which are generally proved by office copies and examined copies respectively; and

(c)   various public documents (see **F8.7** to **F8.27**), which may be proved by oral evidence only if examined, certified, or other copies are unavailable.

Statutory Provisions

The common-law authorities have been affected by the CJA 1988, s. 27, and the PACE **F8.2** 1984, s. 71.

Criminal Justice Act 1988, s. 27

Where a statement contained in a document is admissible as evidence in criminal proceedings, it may be proved—

(a)   by the production of that document; or

(b)   (whether or not that document is still in existence) by the production of a copy of that document, or of the material part of it,

authenticated in such manner as the court may approve; and it is immaterial for the purposes of this subsection how many removes there are between a copy and the original. This section shall not apply to proceedings before a magistrates' court inquiring into an offence as examining justices.

The words 'statement', 'document' and 'copy' bear the same meaning as under the Civil Evidence Act 1995 (CJA 1988, sch. 2, para. 5, as substituted by the Civil Evidence Act 1995, sch. 1, para. 12). 'Statement' means any representation of fact, however made. 'Document' means anything in which information of any description is recorded. 'Copy', in relation to a document, means anything onto which information recorded in the document has been copied, by whatever means and whether directly or indirectly.

Police and Criminal Evidence Act 1984, s. 71

In any proceedings the contents of a document may (whether or not the document is still in existence) be proved by the production of an enlargement of a microfilm copy of that document or of the material part of it, authenticated in such manner as the court may approve.

For the definition of 'proceedings', see s. 72 of the 1984 Act. In the case of proceedings before a magistrates' court inquiring into an offence as examining justices, s. 71 has effect with the omission of the words 'authenticated in such manner as the court may approve' (CPIA 1996, sch. 1, para. 24).

Two views are possible with regard to the construction of the CJA 1988, s. 27. On one view, it applies only to hearsay statements contained in documents, and not to the proof of the contents of a document as evidence in their own right. On this view, akin to the Civil Evidence Act 1968, s. 6(1), s. 27 does not affect the best evidence rule. On the other view, it is not confined to the various types of documentary hearsay statement admissible under the 1988 Act itself, but applies to any statement contained in a document and admissible in evidence. It is submitted that the first view is to be preferred. In any event s. 27, which on its wording is permissive rather than mandatory as to the means of proof, must be read subject to:

(a)   the exceptions to the general rule at common law, whereby the contents of a document may be proved by secondary evidence which may take the form of *oral* evidence, which is not permitted under s. 27 (see *Nazeer* [1998] Crim LR 750); and, it seems

(b)   statutory exceptions to the general rule at common law, principally relating to public and judicial documents and bankers' books, which, although they allow for proof of the contents of such documents by copies, require those copies to take a particular form (which is not the case under s. 27).

In the cases to which s. 27 does apply, it remains to be seen in what manner the courts will require copies to be 'authenticated'. In the normal case, it is submitted, the court will require the same proof as was necessary when relying upon secondary evidence under one of the common-law exceptions to the general rule, namely proof by the evidence of a person with custody or control of the copy (or some other appropriate person) that it is a true copy of the original. In *Collins* (1960) 44 Cr App R 170, the accused was convicted of obtaining money by false pretences, having cashed a cheque on his bank account which he knew to have been closed. When he failed, after notice to do so, to produce a letter sent to him informing him that the account had been closed, secondary evidence of the contents of the letter became admissible. However, the Court of Criminal Appeal held that a copy of a carbon copy of the letter, produced at the trial by a manager of the bank, had been improperly admitted, there having been no proof that it was a true copy of the carbon copy or that it was in the same terms as the original. Compare *Wayte* (1983) 76 Cr App R 110, another decision reached prior to the 1988 Act: the mere fact that it is easy to construct a false document by photocopying techniques does not render a photocopy inadmissible; the fact that the document was a photocopy went to its weight and not its admissibility. The Court of Appeal in that case also gave guidance on the procedure to be adopted when it is sought to produce in evidence photocopies:

(a) Documents should not normally be handed to the jury until questions of admissibility have been determined.

(b) Prior warning of the intention to produce such copies should be given to opposing counsel so that they may have the chance to consider their admissibility.

(c) If the accused is unrepresented, the guidance of the court should be sought before the document is put before the jury.

(d) On very rare occasions, it may be necessary to hold a trial within a trial on the question of admissibility, although ultimately the issue of the genuineness of the copies should be left to the jury.

Section 27 provides that it is immaterial how many removes there are between a copy and the original. There is no obligation to produce the best copy rather than an inferior copy, even if the best copy, or indeed the original document, is still in existence.

At common law there are four categories of exception to the general rule that a party seeking to rely upon the contents of a document must produce primary evidence of those contents. Since the coming into force of the CJA 1988, s. 27, and on the assumption that the second view of the true construction of that section set forth above is correct, it may only be necessary to rely upon such exceptions if, there being no copy of the document in question, it is sought to adduce *oral* evidence of its contents.

Failure to Produce Original after Notice

F8.3   A party seeking to rely upon the contents of a document may prove them by secondary evidence if the original is in the possession or control of the other party to the proceedings who, having been served with a notice to produce it, fails to do so (*Hunter* (1829) 3 C & P 591, where secondary evidence was admitted as to the contents of an allegedly forged deed, the deed itself being in the custody of the accused who, despite notice, refused to produce it). See also *Collins* (1960) 44 Cr App R 170, at **F8.2**. Service of a notice to produce is unnecessary where the requirement to produce the original can be implied, as when the indictment gives sufficient notice of the subject of inquiry: see *Aickles* (1784) 1 Leach 294, where on a charge of theft of a bill of exchange, parol evidence concerning it was given without service of a notice; *Clube* (1857) 3 Jur NS 698 and *Hunt* (1820) 3 B & Ald 566. Compare *Kitson* (1853) Dears CC 187, where, on a charge of setting fire to property with intent to defraud an insurance company, secondary evidence as to the contents of the policy of insurance was held to be inadmissible. See also *Elworthy* (1867) LR 1 CCR 103, where, on a charge of perjury, it being alleged that the accused had falsely sworn that there was no draft of a statutory declaration prepared by him, it was held that, although the prosecution could properly adduce parol evidence that such a draft existed and was in the possession of the accused, secondary evidence of the contents of the draft, and of certain alterations made in it was inadmissible, the Crown having given no notice to the accused to produce the original. Notice to produce is also excused where the opponent of the party seeking to rely on the document admits that it has been lost (*Haworth* (1830) 4 C & P 254).

Stranger's Lawful Refusal to Produce Original

If a stranger to the proceedings, having been served with a subpoena *duces tecum*, **F8.4** *unlawfully* refuses to produce the document in his possession, its contents cannot be proved by secondary evidence, because the stranger is bound to produce it and is punishable for contempt if he refuses to do so (*Llanfaethly* (*Inhabitants*) (1853) 2 E & B 940). However, the contents may be proved by secondary evidence if the stranger *lawfully* refuses to comply with the subpoena: see *Mills* v *Oddy* (1834) 6 C & P 728 (a claim to privilege); *Kilgour* v *Owen* (1889) 88 LT Jo 7 (stranger outside the jurisdiction); and *Nowaz* [1976] 1 WLR 830, where the Pakistani consulate having refused, on the grounds of diplomatic immunity, to produce a photograph and an application for a passport, a police officer who had seen the documents was allowed to give oral evidence of their contents.

Original Lost or Destroyed

The contents of a document may be proved by secondary evidence if it can be proved **F8.5** that the original has been destroyed or cannot be found after due search: see *Wayte* (1983) 76 Cr App R 110, where, two letters having been lost, a photocopy of the one and a photocopy of a carbon copy of the other were held to be admissible. The quality of evidence required to show the destruction (or loss and due search) varies according to the nature and value of the document in question (*Brewster* v *Sewell* (1820) 3 B & Ald 296). See also *Hall* (1872) 12 Cox CC 159.

Production of Original Impossible or Inconvenient

The contents of a document may be proved by secondary evidence if production of the **F8.6** original is physically or legally impossible. As to the former, see *Mortimer* v *M'Callan* (1840) 6 M & W 58, at p. 72 (inscriptions upon tombstones or on a wall); and *Hunt* (1820) 3 B & Ald 566 (inscriptions on flags or banners). As to the latter, see *Owner* v *Bee Hive Spinning Co. Ltd* [1914] 1 KB 105 (a notice statutorily required to be constantly affixed at a factory or workshop); and *Alivon* v *Furnival* (1834) 1 Cr M & R 277 (a document in the custody of a foreign court). In addition to the statutory provisions governing the proof of the contents of public documents by secondary evidence, at common law secondary evidence may also be used to prove the contents of such documents if production of the originals would entail a high degree of public inconvenience. In *Mortimer* v *M'Callan* (1840) 6 M & W 58, Alderson B said (at p. 72):

> The [books of the Bank of England] are not capable of being produced without so much public inconvenience, that the courts have directed them to remain in the Bank, and copies of them to be received in evidence for the purpose for which the books are receivable. Then, if they are not removable on the ground of public inconvenience, that is upon the same footing in point of principle as in the case of that which is not removable by the physical nature of the thing itself.

PROOF OF PUBLIC AND JUDICIAL DOCUMENTS

Statutory Provisions of General Application

A large number of statutes, the most important of which are considered in the following **F8.7** paragraphs, provide for the proof of the contents of various public and judicial documents by secondary evidence, which, for these purposes, is usually required to take the form of an examined, certified, office, Queen's Printer's or Stationery Office copy. An examined copy is a copy proved by oral evidence to correspond with the original. A certified copy is a copy signed and certified to be accurate by an official who has custody of the original. An office copy is a copy made in the office of the High Court and authenticated, with the seal of the Court, by an officer who has custody of the original and the lawful power to provide copies. Two provisions of general importance are the Evidence Act 1845, s. 1, and the Evidence Act 1851, s. 14. Under s. 1 of the 1845 Act, where a statute provides for proof of a document by a certified, sealed or stamped copy, the copy, provided it purports to be signed, sealed or stamped, is admissible without any proof of the signature, seal or stamp, as the case may be.

Evidence Act 1845, s. 1

Whenever by any Act now in force or hereafter to be in force any certificate, official or public document, or document or proceeding of any corporation or joint-stock or other company, or any certified copy of any document, by-law, entry in any register or other book, or of any other proceeding, shall be receivable in evidence of any particular in any court of justice, or before any legal tribunal, or either House of Parliament, or any committee of either House, or in any judicial proceeding, the same shall respectively be admitted in evidence, provided they respectively purport to be sealed or impressed with a stamp or sealed and signed, or signed alone, as required, or impressed with a stamp and signed, as directed by the respective Acts made or to be hereafter made, without any proof of the seal or stamp, where a seal or stamp is necessary, or of the signature or of the official character of the person appearing to have signed the same, and without any further proof thereof, in every case in which the original record could have been received in evidence.

Under the Evidence Act 1851, s. 14, if no other statute provides for the proof by means of a copy of the contents of a document of such a public nature that it is admissible in evidence on production from proper custody, the contents of such a document may be proved by a certified or examined copy.

Evidence Act 1851, s. 14

Whenever any book or other document is of such a public nature as to be admissible in evidence on its mere production from the proper custody, and no statute exists which renders its contents provable by means of a copy, any copy thereof or extract therefrom shall be admissible in evidence in any court of justice, or before any person now or hereafter having by law or by consent of parties authority to hear, receive, and examine evidence, provided it be proved to be an examined copy or extract, or provided it purport to be signed and certified as a true copy or extract by the officer to whose custody the original is entrusted, and which officer is hereby required to furnish such certified copy or extract to any person applying at a reasonable time for the same, upon payment of a reasonable sum for the same.

Acts of Parliament and Journals of Either House

F8.8   Private and local and personal Acts of Parliament and Journals of either House may be proved by Queen's Printer's or Stationery Office copies.

Evidence Act 1845, s. 3

All copies of private and local and personal Acts of Parliament not public Acts, if purporting to be printed by the Queen's printers, and all copies of the journals of either House of Parliament, and of royal proclamations, purporting to be printed by the printers to the Crown or by the printers to either House of Parliament, or by any or either of them, shall be admitted as evidence thereof by all courts, judges, justices, and others without any proof being given that such copies were so printed.

Documentary Evidence Act 1882, s. 2

Where any enactment, whether passed before or after [19 June 1882] provides that a copy of any Act of Parliament, proclamation, order, regulation, rule, warrant, circular, list, gazette, or document shall be conclusive evidence, or be evidence, or have any other effect, when purporting to be printed by the Government Printer, or the Queen's Printer, or a printer authorised by Her Majesty, or otherwise under Her Majesty's authority, whatever may be the precise expression used, such copy shall also be conclusive evidence, or evidence, or have the said effect (as the case may be) if it purports to be printed under the superintendence or authority of Her Majesty's Stationery Office.

As to public Acts, the Interpretation Act 1978, s. 3, provides that 'Every Act is a public Act to be judicially noticed as such unless the contrary is expressly provided by the Act'. Section 3 applies to all Acts passed after 1850. At common law, judicial notice is taken of earlier enactments, if public. See **F1.4**.

Royal Proclamations and Orders or Regulations issued by Government

These may be proved by Queen's Printer's or Stationery Office copies (see the **F8.9** Documentary Evidence Act 1868, ss. 2 to 6; and the Documentary Evidence Act 1882, s. 2).

Documentary Evidence Act 1868, ss. 2, 3, 5 and 6

2. Prima facie evidence of any proclamation, order, or regulation issued before or after the passing of this Act by Her Majesty or by the Privy Council, also of any proclamation, order, or regulation issued before or after the passing of this Act by or under the authority of any such department of the government or officer as is mentioned in the first column of the schedule hereto, may be given in all courts of justice, and in all legal proceedings whatsoever, in all or any of the modes hereinafter mentioned; that is to say:

(1) By the production of a copy of the Gazette purporting to contain such proclamation, order, or regulation.

(2) By the production of a copy of such proclamation, order, or regulation purporting to be printed by the government printer, or, where the question arises in a court in any British colony or possession, of a copy purporting to be printed under the authority of the legislature of such British colony or possession.

(3) By the production, in the case of any proclamation, order, or regulation issued by Her Majesty or by the Privy Council, of a copy or extract purporting to be certified to be true by the Clerk of the Privy Council, or by any one of the lords or others of the Privy Council, and, in the case of any proclamation, order, or regulation issued by or under the authority of any of the said departments or officers, by the production of a copy or extract purporting to be certified to be true by the person or persons specified in the second column of the said schedule in connection with such department or officer.

Any copy or extract made in pursuance of this Act may be in print or in writing, or partly in print and partly in writing.

No proof shall be required of the handwriting or official position of any person certifying, in pursuance of this Act, to the truth of ant copy of or extract from any proclamation, order, or regulation.

3. Subject to any law that may be from time to time made by the legislature of any British colony or possession, this Act shall be in force in every such colony and possession.

5. The following words shall in this Act have the meaning hereinafter assigned to them, unless there is something in the context repugnant to such construction; (that is to say,)

'British colony and possession' shall for the purposes of this Act include the Channel Islands, the Isle of Man, . . . and all other Her Majesty's dominions.

'Legislature' shall signify any authority other than the Imperial Parliament or Her Majesty in Council competent to make laws for any colony or possession.

'Privy Council' shall include Her Majesty in Council and the Lords and others of Her Majesty's Privy Council, or any of them, and any committee of the Privy Council that is not specially named in the schedule hereto.

'Government printer' shall mean and include the printer to Her Majesty and any printer purporting to be the printer authorised to print the statutes, ordinances, acts of State, or other public Acts of the legislature of any British colony or possession, or otherwise to be the government printer of such colony or possession.

'Gazette' shall include the *London Gazette*, the *Edinburgh Gazette*, and the [*Belfast*] *Gazette*, or any of such gazettes.

6. The provisions of this Act shall be deemed to be in addition to, and not in derogation of, any powers of proving documents given by any existing statute or existing at common law.

In *Clarke* [1969] 2 QB 91, at p. 97, the Court of Appeal said that the word 'order' in the 1868 Act should be given a wide meaning, covering 'any executive act of government performed by the bringing into existence of a public document for the purpose of giving effect to an Act of Parliament'; and held that the Breath Test (Approval) (No. 1) Order 1968 (printed by HMSO), although not a statutory instrument, was an 'order' within s. 2 of the Act. As to statutory instruments, see further **F8.11**.

Proclamations, Treaties and Other Acts of State of Foreign States or British Colonies, and Judgments etc. of Courts in Foreign States or British Colonies

F8.10   These may be proved by examined or authenticated copies (see the Evidence Act 1851, s. 7, below; and the Evidence Act 1845, s. 1, at **F8.7**). As to colonial documents, see also the Documentary Evidence Act 1868, s. 3, at **F8.9**.

Evidence Act 1851, s. 7

All proclamations, treaties, and other acts of State of any foreign State or of any British colony, and all judgments, decrees, orders, and other judicial proceedings of any court of justice in any foreign State or in any British colony, and all affidavits, pleadings, and other legal documents filed or deposited in any such court, may be proved in any court of justice, or before any person having by law or by consent of parties authority to hear, receive, and examine evidence, either by examined copies or by copies authenticated as hereinafter mentioned; that is to say, if the document sought to be proved be a proclamation, treaty, or other act of State, the authenticated copy to be admissible in evidence must purport to be sealed with the seal of the foreign State or British colony to which the original document belongs; and if the document sought to be proved be a judgment, decree, order, or other judicial proceeding of any foreign or colonial court, or an affidavit, pleading, or other legal document filed or deposited in any such court, the authenticated copy to be admissible in evidence must purport either to be sealed with the seal of the foreign or colonial court to which the original document belongs, or, in the event of such court having no seal, to be signed by the judge, or, if there be more than one judge, by any one of the judges of the said court; and such judge shall attach to his signature a statement in writing on the said copy that the court whereof he is a judge has no seal; but if any of the aforesaid authenticated copies shall purport to be sealed or signed as hereinbefore respectively directed, the same shall respectively be admitted in evidence in every case in which the original document could have been received in evidence, without any proof of the seal where a seal is necessary, or of the signature, or of the truth of the statement attached thereto, where such signature and statement are necessary, or of the judicial character of the person appearing to have made such signature and statement.

Statutory Instruments

F8.11   Statutory instruments may be proved by Queen's Printer's or Stationery Office copies (see the Documentary Evidence Act 1868, s. 2, and the Documentary Evidence Act 1882, s. 2). However, where a photocopy from a commercial publication is produced instead, and there is no suggestion of any inaccuracy in the version before the court, the proviso to the Criminal Appeal Act 1968, s. 2, may apply (*Koon Cheung Tang* [1995] Crim LR 813). See also *Ashley* (1967) 52 Cr App R 42 and *Palastanga* v *Solman* [1962] Crim LR 334 (at **F6.3**), and the Statutory Instruments Act 1946, s. 3.

Statutory Instruments Act 1946, s. 3

(1)   Regulations made for the purposes of this Act shall make provision for the publication by His Majesty's Stationery Office of lists showing the date upon which every statutory instrument printed and sold by or under the authority of the King's printer of Acts of Parliament was first issued by or under the authority of that office; and in any legal

proceedings a copy of any list so published shall be received in evidence as a true copy, and an entry therein shall be conclusive evidence of the date on which any statutory instrument was first issued by His Majesty's Stationery Office.

(2)   In any proceedings against any person for an offence consisting of a contravention of any such statutory instrument, it shall be a defence to prove that the instrument had not been issued by or under the authority of His Majesty's Stationery Office at the date of the alleged contravention unless it is proved that at that date reasonable steps had been taken for the purpose of bringing the purport of the instrument to the notice of the public, or of persons likely to be affected by it, or of the person charged.

By-laws

By-laws may be proved by certified printed copies.   F8.12

Local Government Act 1972, s. 238

The production of a printed copy of a by-law purporting to be made by a local authority or a metropolitan county passenger transport authority upon which is endorsed a certificate purporting to be signed by the proper officer of the authority stating—
(a)   that the by-law was made by the authority;
(b)   that the copy is a true copy of the by-law;
(c)   that on a specified date the by-law was confirmed by the authority named in the certificate or, as the case may require, was sent to the Secretary of State and has not been disallowed;
(d)   the date, if any, fixed by the confirming authority for the coming into operation of the by-law;
shall be prima facie evidence of the facts stated in the certificate, and without proof of the handwriting or official position of any person purporting to sign the certificate.

Colonial and Foreign Laws

Colonial statutes may be proved by copies certified by the clerk or other proper officer F8.13
of the colonial legislative body (the Colonial Laws Validity Act 1865, s. 6), or by copies purporting to be printed by the Government printer of that possession (the Evidence (Colonial Statutes) Act 1907, s. 1). Subject to this, and except where ascertained by the British Law Ascertainment Act 1859, colonial and foreign law, including Scots law, even if written, cannot be proved in an English court by production of the documents in which it is recorded, or a copy thereof, but generally requires proof by a suitably qualified expert (*Sussex Peerage Case* (1844) 11 Cl & F 85); *Governor of Brixton Prison, ex parte Shuter* [1960] 2 QB 89). See further, **F10.9**.

Public Records

Public records in the Public Record Office may be proved by copies which have been F8.14
examined, certified and sealed or stamped.

Public Records Act 1958, s. 9

(2)   A copy of or extract from a public record in the Public Record Office purporting to be examined and certified as true and authentic by the proper officer and to be sealed or stamped with the seal of the Public Record Office shall be admissible as evidence in any proceedings without any further or other proof thereof if the original record would have been admissible as evidence in those proceedings.

In this subsection the reference to the proper officer is a reference to the Keeper of Public Records or any other officer of the Public Record Office authorised in that behalf by the Keeper of Public Records, and, in the case of copies and extracts made before the commencement of this Act, the deputy keeper of the records or any assistant record keeper appointed under the Public Record Office Act 1838.

Births, Deaths and Marriages

An entry in the register of births or deaths may be proved by a certified copy purporting F8.15
to be sealed or stamped with the seal of the General Register Office, and is admissible

evidence of the birth or death to which it relates (see the Births and Deaths Registration Act 1953, s. 34). (As to adopted children, see also the Adoption Act 1976, s. 50(2).) Likewise, proof of the celebration of a marriage may be effected by the production of a certified copy of an entry kept at the General Register Office (see the Marriage Act 1949, s. 65(3)). In order to prove a birth or death (or the marriage of persons), it is also necessary to adduce some evidence to identify the person in question with the person named in the certified copy (see *Bellis* (1911) 6 Cr App R 283). The same applies where it is sought to prove a person's age by production of a birth certificate. Thus, although age may be proved by other means, e.g., by the testimony of someone present at the time of the birth, by inference from appearance or by hearsay declarations as to pedigree (see *Cox* [1898] 1 QB 179), if a certificate of birth is produced to prove age, evidence must also be adduced to positively identify the person as the person named in the certificate (*Rogers* (1914) 10 Cr App R 276: proof of the age of the complainant on a charge of unlawful sexual intercourse with a girl under 13). A certified copy of an entry in the register of deaths is prima facie evidence of the fact and date of a death; but information contained in the certificate concerning the cause of death, and based on information supplied by a coroner, is inadmissible as evidence of the cause of death (*Bird* v *Keep* [1918] 2 KB 692, per Swinfen Eady MR, *obiter*).

Births and Deaths Registration Act 1953, s. 34

(1) The following provisions of this section shall have effect in relation to entries in registers under this Act or any enactment repealed by this Act.

(2) An entry or a certified copy of an entry of a birth or death in a register, or in a certified copy of a register, shall not be evidence of the birth or death unless the entry purports to be signed by some person professing to be the informant and to be such a person as might be required or permitted by law at the date of the entry to give to the registrar information concerning that birth or death:

Provided that this subsection shall not apply—

(a) in relation to an entry of a birth which, not being an entry signed by a person professing to be a superintendent registrar, purports to have been made with the authority of the Registrar General; or

(b) in relation to an entry of a death which purports to have been made upon a certificate from a coroner; or

(c) in relation to an entry of a birth or death which purports to have been made in pursuance of the enactments with respect to the registration of births and deaths at sea;

(d) in relation to the re-registration of a birth under section 9(5) of this Act.

(3) Where more than three months have intervened between the date of the birth of any child or the date when any living new-born child or still-born child was found exposed and the date of the registration of the birth of that child, the entry or a certified copy of the entry of the birth of the child in the register, or in a certified copy of the register, shall not be evidence of the birth unless—

(a) if it appears that not more than 12 months have so intervened, the entry purports either to be signed by the superintendent registrar as well as by the registrar or to have been made with the authority of the Registrar General;

(b) if more than 12 months have so intervened, the entry purports to have been made with the authority of the Registrar General:

...

(4) Where more than 12 months have intervened between the date of the death or of the finding of the dead body of any person and the date of the registration of that person's death, the entry or a certified copy of the entry of the death in the register, or in a certified copy of the register, shall not be evidence of the death unless the entry purports to have been made with the authority of the Registrar General:

Provided that this subsection shall not apply in any case where the original entry in the register was made before the first day of January, 1875.

(5) A certified copy of an entry in a register or in a certified copy of a register shall be deemed to be a true copy notwithstanding that it is made on a form different from that on which the original entry was made if any differences in the column headings under which

the particulars appear in the original entry and the copy respectively are differences of form only and not of substance.

(6) The Registrar General shall cause any certified copy of an entry given in the General Register Office to be sealed or stamped with the seal of that Office; and, subject to the foregoing provisions of this section, any certified copy of an entry purporting to be sealed or stamped with the said seal shall be received as evidence of the birth or death to which it relates without any further or other proof of the entry, and no certified copy purporting to have been given in the said Office shall be of any force or effect unless it is sealed or stamped as aforesaid.

Records of marriages, baptisms and burials entered in parish registers may be proved by an examined copy or by a copy certified as a true copy by the incumbent to whose custody the original is entrusted (see the Evidence Act 1851, s. 14, at **F8.7**).

Births, deaths and marriages out of England may be proved by entries properly and regularly recorded in foreign registers kept under the sanction of public authority (see *Lyell* v *Kennedy* (1889) 14 App Cas 437, per Lord Selborne at pp. 448–9, and generally **F16.25**). See also the Registration of Births, Deaths and Marriages (Scotland) Act 1854 and the Registration of Births, Deaths and Marriages (Scotland) Amendment Act 1860. Births, deaths and marriages out of England may also be proved by certified copies of registers kept under the local law in any case where the Evidence (Foreign, Dominion and Colonial Documents) Act 1933 has been applied by an Order in Council. As to proof of records kept in an Army Register in respect of an officer or soldier serving overseas, see the Registration of Births, Deaths and Marriages (Army) Act 1879, s. 3. As to returns of births and deaths on ships registered in the UK, and on ships not registered in the UK but calling at a port in the UK, see the Merchant Shipping Act 1995, s. 108, and the Merchant Shipping (Returns of Births and Deaths) Regulations 1979, SI 1979 No. 1577. Returns or reports under s. 72 of the 1970 Act are admissible in evidence (s. 75). As to births, deaths and marriages on Her Majesty's ships at sea and service aircraft, see the Registration of Births, Deaths and Marriages (Special Provisions) Act 1957, s. 2. Ambassadors' or Consular registers of marriages under British law by British subjects are of such a public nature as to be admissible on mere production from proper custody (Foreign Marriages Act 1892, s. 16).

Minute-Books of Local Authorities

The minutes of the proceedings of local authorities required to be drawn up, entered in **F8.16** a book and signed under the Local Government Act 1972, shall be received in evidence without further proof; and until the contrary is proved, where a minute of such proceedings has been made and signed, the meeting shall be deemed to have been duly convened and held, and all the members present shall be deemed to have been duly qualified (Local Government Act 1972, sch. 12, part VI, para. 41). A document which purports to be a copy of the minutes of the proceedings at a meeting of a local authority (or a committee of a local authority, or a subcommittee of such a committee) or a precursor of a local authority, and which bears a certificate purporting to be signed by the proper officer of the authority and stating that the minutes were signed in accordance with para. 41, shall be evidence in any proceedings of the matters stated in the certificate and of the terms of the minutes in question (Local Government (Miscellaneous Provisions) Act 1976, s. 41(1)).

Professional Lists

Various statutes provide for proof that a person is or is not professionally qualified by **F8.17** production of a list, register or certificate of a registrar. Thus, any list purporting to be published by authority of the Law Society and to contain the names of solicitors who have obtained practising certificates for the current year shall, until the contrary is proved, be evidence that the persons so named are solicitors holding such certificates (the Solicitors Act 1974, s. 18(1)). The absence from any such list of the name of any person shall, until the contrary is proved, be evidence that that person is not qualified to practise as a solicitor under a certificate for the current year, but in the case of any such person an extract from the roll certified as correct by the Society shall be evidence of the facts appearing in the extract. See also the Medical Act 1983, s. 34 (registered medical practitioners); the Nurses, Midwives and Health Visitors Act 1979, s. 10; the Dentists Act 1984, s. 14(6); the Pharmacy Act 1954, s. 6(2) (registered pharmaceutical chemists); and the Veterinary Surgeons Act 1966, ss. 2 and 9.

Documents Relevant to Insolvency

F8.18   In relation to bankruptcy law, any document purporting to be or to contain any order, direction or certificate issued by the Secretary of State shall be received in evidence and be deemed to be (or contain) that order or certificate or those directions without further proof, unless the contrary is shown; and a certificate signed by the Secretary of State or an officer on his behalf and confirming the making of any order, the issuing of any document or the exercise of any discretion, power or obligation arising or imposed under the Insolvency Act 1986 or the Insolvency Rules 1986 (SI 1986 No. 1925) is conclusive evidence of the matter dealt with in the certificate (Insolvency Rules 1986, r. 12.6). A copy of the Gazette containing any notice required by the Act or the Rules to be gazetted is evidence of any facts stated in the notice; and in the case of an order of the court, notice of which is required to be gazetted, a copy of the Gazette containing the notice may be produced in any proceedings as conclusive evidence that the order was made on the date specified in the notice (Insolvency Rules 1986, r. 12.20).

Company Investigations

F8.19   A copy of any report of inspectors appointed under part XIV of the Companies Act 1985, certified by the Secretary of State to be a true copy, is admissible in any legal proceedings as evidence of the opinion of the inspectors in relation to any matter contained in the report; and a document purporting to be such a certificate shall be received in evidence and deemed to be such a certificate unless the contrary is proved (Companies Act 1985, s. 441).

Deposit-Taking Businesses

F8.20   A certificate purporting to be signed on behalf of the Bank of England, and certifying that a particular person is or is not an authorised institution, or was or was not such an institution at a particular time; the date on which an institution became or ceased to be authorised; whether or not an institution's authorisation is or was restricted; the date on which a restricted authorisation expires; or the date on which an institution became or ceased to be a recognised bank or licensed institution under the Banking Act 1979, shall be admissible in evidence; and such a certificate shall be deemed to have been duly signed unless the contrary is shown (Banking Act 1987, s. 101).

Judgments of the House of Lords

F8.21   Such judgments may be proved by Queen's Printer's or Stationery Office copies (see the Evidence Act 1845, s. 3, and the Documentary Evidence Act 1882, s. 2).

Proceedings in Civil Courts

F8.22   Formerly, under RSC ord. 38, r. 10(1), office copies of all writs, records, pleadings and documents filed in the High Court were admissible in evidence in all causes and matters, and between all persons and parties, to the same extent as the originals would be admissible. Under the Civil Procedure Rules 1998, r. 2.6(3), replacing RSC ord. 38, r. 10(2), a document purporting to bear the court's seal shall be admissible in evidence without further proof. See also the Supreme Court Act 1981, s. 132: 'Every document purporting to be sealed or stamped with the seal or stamp of the Supreme Court shall be received in evidence in all parts of the UK without further proof.' As to the proof of affidavits, see **F8.25**. An official copy of the whole or any part of a will may be obtained under the Supreme Court Act 1981, s. 125, and may be proved under s. 132 of that Act. On a prosecution for perjury (or procuring or suborning the commission of perjury) alleged to have been committed on the trial of any indictment, the fact of that former trial shall be sufficiently proved by a certificate signed by the clerk (or his deputy) of the court where the indictment was tried without proof of the signature (Perjury Act 1911, s. 14).

Proceedings in County Courts

Records of county court proceedings may be proved by certified copies.   F8.23

County Courts Act 1984, s. 12

(1) The registrar for every district shall keep or cause to be kept such records of and in relation to proceedings in the court for that district as the Lord Chancellor may by regulations (made by statutory instrument) prescribe.

(2) Any entry in a book or other document required by the said regulations to be kept for the purposes of this section, or a copy of any such entry or document purporting to be signed and certified as a true copy by the registrar, shall at all times without further proof be admitted in any court or place whatsoever as evidence of the entry and of the proceeding referred to by it and of the regularity of that proceeding.

Proceedings in Magistrates' Courts

The Magistrates' Courts Rules 1981, r. 68, provides that the register of a magistrates' F8.24 court, or any document purporting to be an extract from the register and to be certified by the clerk as a true extract, shall be admissible in any legal proceedings as evidence of proceedings of the court entered in the register.

Affidavits

An affidavit filed in the High Court may be proved by office copy (see the Rules of the F8.25 Supreme Court 1965, ord. 38, r. 10(1)). On a prosecution for perjury in an affidavit, the affidavit itself must be produced and proved (*Rees d Howell and Dalton* v *Bowen* (1825) M'Cle & Yo 383), unless it can be proved to have been lost or destroyed, in which case secondary evidence is admissible of its contents and the signature of the accused (*Milnes* (1860) 2 F & F 10, and see **F8.5**).

Convictions and Acquittals

Provision for the proof of convictions and acquittals is made in the PACE 1984, s. 73. F8.26 This is dealt with at **F11.1**.

BANKERS' BOOKS

In order to facilitate the proof of matters recorded in bankers' books, the Bankers' Books F8.27 Evidence Act 1879 provides for proof of the contents of such books by the production of examined copies.

Bankers' Books Evidence Act 1879, s. 3

Subject to the provisions of this Act, a copy of any entry in a banker's book shall in all legal proceedings be received as prima facie evidence of such entry, and of the matters, transactions, and accounts therein recorded.

The expressions 'bank' and 'banker' are defined by s. 9(1) of the Act to mean:

(a) an institution authorised under the Banking Act 1987 or a municipal bank within the meaning of s. 103 of the 1987 Act;

(b)   the National Savings Bank; and

(c)   the Post Office, in the exercise of its powers to provide banking services.

'Bankers' books' were originally defined to include ledgers, daybooks, cash books, account books, and all other books used in the ordinary business of the bank. Section 9(2) of the 1879 Act, as substituted by the Banking Act 1979, has now extended that definition. It provides that expressions in the Act relating to 'bankers' books' include 'ledgers, daybooks, cash books, account books and other records used in the ordinary business of the bank, whether those records are in written form or are kept on microfilm, magnetic tape or any other form of mechanical or electronic data retrieval mechanism'. In *Williams* v *Williams* [1988] QB 161, it was held that paid cheques and paying-in slips retained by a bank after the conclusion of a banking transaction to which they relate are not 'bankers' books', because, even if bundles of such documents can be treated as 'records used in the ordinary business of the bank', the act of adding an individual cheque (paying-in slip) cannot be regarded as the making of an 'entry' in the records. It is submitted that similar reasoning may be used to justify the decision reached in *Dadson* (1983) 77 Cr App R 91 that, prior to the coming into force of the extended definition, copies of letters written by a bank and contained in a file of its correspondence, were not 'bankers' books'. In the case of documents falling outside the statutory definition, use may be made, in appropriate circumstances, of the CJA 1988, ss. 23 or 24, together with s. 27 of that Act (see **F8.2**).

Bankers' Books Evidence Act 1879, ss. 4 to 8 and 10

4.   A copy of an entry in a banker's book shall not be received in evidence under this Act unless it be first proved that the book was at the time of the making of the entry one of the ordinary books of the bank, and that the entry was made in the usual and ordinary course of business, and that the book is in the custody or control of the bank.

Such proof may be given by a partner or officer of the bank, and may be given orally or by an affidavit sworn before any commissioner or person authorised to take affidavits.

Where the proceedings concerned are proceedings before a magistrates' court inquiring into an offence as examining justices, this section shall have effect with the omission of the words 'orally or'.

5.   A copy of an entry in a banker's book shall not be received in evidence under this Act unless it be further proved that the copy has been examined with the original entry and is correct.

Such proof shall be given by some person who has examined the copy with the original entry, and may be given either orally or by an affidavit sworn before any commissioner or person authorised to take affidavits.

Where the proceedings concerned are proceedings before a magistrates' court inquiring into an offence as examining justices, this section shall have effect with the omission of the words 'orally or'.

6.   A banker or officer of a bank shall not, in any legal proceeding to which the bank is not a party, be compellable to produce any banker's book the contents of which can be proved under this Act, or to appear as a witness to prove the matters, transactions, and accounts therein recorded, unless by order of a judge made for special cause.

7.   On the application of any party to a legal proceeding a court or judge may order that such party be at liberty to inspect and take copies of any entries in a banker's book for any of the purposes of such proceedings. An order under this section may be made either with or without summoning the bank or any other party, and shall be served on the bank three clear days before the same is to be obeyed, unless the court or judge otherwise directs.

8.   The costs of any application to a court or judge under or for the purposes of this Act, and the costs of anything done or to be done under an order of a court or judge made under or for the purposes of this Act shall be in the discretion of the court or judge, who may order the same or any part thereof to be paid to any party by the bank, where the same have been occasioned by any default or delay on the part of the bank. Any such order against a bank may be enforced as if the bank was a party to the proceeding.

10.   In this Act—
The expression 'legal proceeding' means any civil or criminal proceeding or inquiry in which evidence is or may be given, and includes an arbitration and an application to, or an inquiry or other proceedings before, the Solicitors Disciplinary Tribunal or any body exercising functions in relation to solicitors in Scotland or Northern Ireland corresponding to the functions of that Tribunal;
The expression 'the court' means the court, judge, arbitrator, persons or person before whom a legal proceeding is held or taken;
The expression 'a judge' means with respect to England a judge of the High Court . . .

'A court', for the purposes of s. 7, includes justices before whom criminal proceedings are pending (*Kinghorn* [1908] 2 KB 949). An application under s. 7 in criminal proceedings will not be refused on the grounds that it incriminates the party against whom it is made; but it is a serious interference with the liberty of the subject, and the court should be satisfied, before making an order, that the application is more than a mere 'fishing expedition' by considering whether the prosecution have other evidence to support the charge. The court should also limit the period of disclosure of the bank account to a period in time which is strictly relevant to the charge (*Williams* v *Summerfield* [1972] 2 QB 512). In *Marlborough Street Stipendiary Magistrate, ex parte Simpson* (1980) 70 Cr App R 290, orders under the Act were quashed on the grounds that they were not limited to a defined period in time. See also *Nottingham City Justices, ex parte Lynn* (1984) 79 Cr App R 238, where, on a charge of drug smuggling, an order for the inspection of accounts over a period of three years was reduced to a period of six months, on the ground that there was insufficient evidence to link the accused with offences during most of the three years.

An order may be made to inspect the accounts of a person who is not a party to the proceedings, even if not compellable as a witness. Thus in *Andover Justices, ex parte Rhodes* [1980] Crim LR 644, the Divisional Court upheld an order in respect of the account of the husband of an accused, charged with the theft of money, who had told the police that the money was in her husband's account. However, in criminal cases, such an order should be made only in exceptional circumstances, and where the private interest in keeping a bank account confidential is outweighed by the public interest in assisting a prosecution (*Grossman* (1981) 73 Cr App R 302, at p. 307). In that case, an application against the Savings and Investment Bank (registered and licensed as a bank under Manx Law) having been refused by the Manx Court, it was held that an order under s. 7 should not have been made in respect of an account held at a branch of Barclays Bank, which was used as a clearing house by the Savings and Investment Bank. In *MacKinnon* v *Donaldson, Lufkin and Jenrette Securities Corpn* [1986] Ch 482, *Grossman* was applied, although it was acknowledged that the decision in that case had been given *per incuriam* since the proceedings were criminal, and under the Supreme Court Act 1981, s. 18(1)(a), the Court of Appeal had no jurisdiction. In *MacKinnon* v *Donaldson, Lufkin and Jenrette Securities Corpn* it was held that, save in exceptional circumstances, an order should not be made against a foreign bank which is not a party to the proceedings, even if it carries on business within the jurisdiction and is a recognised bank under the Banking Act 1979, to produce documents outside the jurisdiction concerning business transacted outside the jurisdiction, because an order under the 1879 Act is an exercise of sovereign authority to assist in the administration of justice, and foreign banks owe their customers a duty of confidence regulated by the law of the country where the documents are kept.

An application under s. 7 of the 1879 Act may be made *ex parte*, but 'there is much to be said for notice being given' (*Marlborough Street Stipendiary Magistrate, ex parte*

Simpson (1980) 70 Cr App R 291, per Widgery LJ at p. 294). See also, in the case of accounts of a person who is not a party to the proceedings, *Grossman* (1981) 73 Cr App R 302, per Oliver LJ at p. 309: either the order should not be made until the person affected has been informed and given an opportunity to be heard, or it should be made in the form of an order *nisi*, allowing a period for that person to show cause why the order should not take effect.

PROOF OF DUE EXECUTION

F8.28   The due execution of a document is established by:

   (a)   proof that it was signed by the person by whom it purports to have been signed; and
   (b)   if attestation is necessary, proof that it was attested.

In the case of public and judicial documents, the statutory provisions which enable their contents to be proved by copies also dispense with the need to prove due execution (see **F8.7** to **F8.26** and **F1.4**). Where a party seeks to rely upon the contents of a private document, due execution may be formally admitted or presumed. A document which is more than 20 years old, produced from proper custody and otherwise free from suspicion, is presumed to have been duly executed. At common law the period was 30 years, but 20 years was substituted by the Evidence Act 1938, s. 4. A document comes from proper custody even if not found in the best and most proper place of deposit, provided that the court is satisfied that the place in which it was found was custody that was reasonable and natural in the circumstances (*Bishop of Meath* v *Marquess of Winchester* (1836) 3 Bing NC 183, per Tindal CJ). Proof of due execution is also unnecessary if the document in question is in the possession of an opponent who refuses to comply with a notice to produce it (*Cooke* v *Tanswell* (1818) 8 Taunt 450). Subject to the foregoing, a party seeking to rely on the contents of a private document must prove its due execution.

Proof that a document was signed or written by the person by whom it purports to have been signed or written may be effected in a variety of ways:

   (a)   by the admission of the person in question (*Waldridge* v *Kennison* (1794) 1 Esp 143);
   (b)   by the testimony (or admissible hearsay assertion) of the signatory identifying his own signature (hand);
   (c)   by the testimony (or admissible hearsay assertion) of a person who witnessed the execution of the document;
   (d)   by the opinion evidence of a person acquainted with the signature or handwriting (*Doe d Mudd* v *Suckermore* (1836) 5 A & E 703, at p. 705, and *Slaney* (1832) 5 C & P 213); or
   (e)   by comparison of the document in question with another document which is admitted or proved to have been signed or written by the person in question under the Criminal Procedure Act 1865, s. 8. See further **F10.7**.

Any of these methods of proof may also be used in the case of a private document which, although not required by law to be attested, was in fact attested. Under the Criminal Procedure Act 1865, s. 7, 'It shall not be necessary to prove by the attesting witness any instrument to the validity of which attestation is not requisite, and such instrument may be proved as if there had been no attesting witness thereto.'

Where a document requires attestation to be formally valid, it is not strictly necessary to prove attestation by calling an attesting witness, except in the case of wills and other testamentary documents. Under the Evidence Act 1938, s. 3, 'an instrument to the validity of which attestation is requisite may, instead of being proved by an attesting witness, be proved in the manner in which it might be proved if no attesting witness were alive: Provided that nothing in this section shall apply to the proof of wills and other testamentary documents.' Thus, the attestation of private documents other than testamentary documents may be proved by the testimony of an attesting witness; or by evidence as to the handwriting of the attesting witness; or by other evidence, such as the testimony of a non-attesting witness to the execution.

PRESUMPTIONS CONCERNING DOCUMENTS

A document which is more than 20 years old and comes from proper custody is **F8.29** presumed to have been duly executed. It is also presumed that:

  (a)   a document was made on the date which it bears (*Re Adamson* (1875) LR 3 P & D 253 at p. 256);
  (b)   a deed was duly sealed (see *Re Sandilands* (1871) LR 6 CP 411); and
  (c)   an alteration or erasure in a deed was made before execution, but that an alteration or erasure in a will was made after execution (*Doe d Tatum* v *Catomore* (1851) 16 QB 745).

STAMPED DOCUMENTS

In criminal proceedings, a document required to be stamped for the purposes of stamp **F8.30** duty is admissible even if not duly stamped.

Stamp Act 1891, s. 14

  (4)   Save as aforesaid, an instrument executed in any part of the United Kingdom, or relating, wheresoever executed, to any property situate, or to any matter or thing done or to be done, in any part of the United Kingdom, shall not, except in criminal proceedings, be given in evidence, or be available for any purpose whatever, unless it is duly stamped in accordance with the law in force at the time when it was first executed.

STATEMENTS IN DOCUMENTS PRODUCED BY COMPUTERS

Whenever a statement in a document produced by a computer is tendered as evidence **F8.31** of any fact stated in it, whether tendered as admissible hearsay or non-hearsay, then the PACE 1984, s. 69, must be complied with. The section does not apply, however, where an expert expresses an opinion derived from an interpretation by him of information contained in a computer printout, if the printout itself is not put in evidence (*Golizadeh* [1995] Crim LR 232, considered at **F10.10**). When the YJCEA 1999, s. 60, is brought into force, the PACE 1984, s. 69, and the supplementary provisions contained in sch. 3 to that Act, will be repealed.

Police and Criminal Evidence Act 1984, s. 69 and sch. 3, pts II and III

  69.—(1)   In any proceedings, a statement in a document produced by a computer shall not be admissible as evidence of any fact stated therein unless it is shown—
    (a)   that there are no reasonable grounds for believing that the statement is inaccurate because of improper use of the computer;
    (b)   that at all material times the computer was operating properly, or if not, that any respect in which it was not operating properly or was out of operation was not such as to affect the production of the document or the accuracy of its contents; and
    (c)   that any relevant conditions specified in rules of court under subsection (2) below are satisfied.

SCHEDULE 3
Part II   Provisions Supplementary to Section 69

  8.   In any proceedings where it is desired to give a statement in evidence in accordance with section 69 above, a certificate—

(a)   identifying the document containing the statement and describing the manner in which it was produced;

(b)   giving such particulars of any device involved in the production of that document as may be appropriate for the purpose of showing that the document was produced by a computer;

(c)   dealing with any of the matters mentioned in subsection (1) of section 69 above; and

(d)   purporting to be signed by a person occupying a responsible position in relation to the operation of the computer,

shall be evidence of anything stated in it; and for the purposes of this paragraph it shall be sufficient for a matter to be stated to the best of the knowledge and belief of the person stating it.

9.   Notwithstanding paragraph 8 above, a court may require oral evidence to be given of anything of which evidence could be given by a certificate under that paragraph; but the preceding provisions of this paragraph shall not apply where the court is a magistrates' court inquiring into an offence as examining justices.

10.   Any person who, in a certificate tendered under paragraph 8 above in a magistrates' court, the Crown Court or the Court of Appeal makes a statement which he knows to be false or does not believe to be true shall be guilty of an offence and liable—

(a)   on conviction on indictment to imprisonment for a term not exceeding two years or to a fine or to both;

(b)   on summary conviction to imprisonment for a term not exceeding six months or to a fine not exceeding the statutory maximum . . .

11.   In estimating the weight, if any, to be attached to a statement regard shall be had to all the circumstances from which any inference can reasonably be drawn as to the accuracy or otherwise of the statement and, in particular—

(a)   to the question whether or not the information which the information contained in the statement reproduces or is derived from was supplied to the relevant computer, or recorded for the purpose of being supplied to it, contemporaneously with the occurrence or existence of the facts dealt with in that information; and

(b)   to the question whether or not any person concerned with the supply of information to that computer, or with the operation of that computer or any equipment by means of which the document containing the statement was produced by it, had any incentive to conceal or misrepresent the facts.

12.   For the purposes of paragraph 11 above information shall be taken to be supplied to a computer whether it is supplied directly or (with or without human intervention) by means of any appropriate equipment.

Part III   Provisions Supplementary to Sections 68 and 69

13.   . . .

14.   For the purpose of deciding whether or not a statement is so admissible the court may draw any reasonable inference—

(a)   from the circumstances in which the statement was made or otherwise came into being; or

(b)   from any other circumstances, including the form and contents of the document in which the statement is contained.

Meaning of 'Computer'

F8.32   There is no statutory definition of 'computer' for the purposes of the PACE 1984, s. 69. In *Shephard* (1991) 93 Cr App R 139, the Court of Appeal noted that the omission was presumably deliberate, and elected to give the word its natural meaning rather than to apply by analogy the definition of 'computer' to be found in s. 5(6) of the Civil Evidence Act 1968. It was considered, *obiter*, that a cash till is not a computer in the ordinary sense of the word. See also *DPP v McKeown* [1997] 1 WLR 295, in which Lord Hoffmann held that a computer was, for the purposes of s. 69, 'a device for storing, processing and retrieving information'. In *Blackburn* (1992) *The Times*, 1 December 1992 it was said, *obiter*, that the mere use of a word processor to produce a document did not render s. 69 applicable, otherwise almost every business document would have to satisfy the section, and this could not have been the intention of Parliament. Section 69 has been applied, however, to a weighbridge printout (*East West Transport Ltd* v *DPP* [1995] Crim LR 642) and to a printout produced by an intoximeter breath-test machine (*DPP* v *McKeown*).

Reason for Regulating Computer Evidence

In *Minors* [1989] 1 WLR 441, Steyn J said that the law of evidence had to adapt to the **F8.33** realities of contemporary business practice, according to which it will often be the case that the only record of a transaction will be stored on a computer. If computer evidence cannot relatively easily be used, therefore, much crime, and notably offences involving dishonesty, will be immune from prosecution. On the other hand, his lordship continued, computer systems occasionally malfunction. Software systems may have 'bugs'. Unauthorised alteration of stored information is possible. A computer system may be vulnerable to attack by a 'virus'. Realistically, therefore, computers must be regarded as imperfect devices, and the safeguards imported by s. 69 are necessary.

Admissibility of Hearsay Computer Evidence

In *Minors* [1989] 1 WLR 441, the Court of Appeal considered and rejected the **F8.34** argument that the PACE 1984, s. 69, constitutes a self-contained code governing the admissibility of computer records in criminal cases. Although, as the court noted, s. 69(2) refers to a statement given in evidence 'by virtue of this section', s. 69 is in fact entirely negative in form, and does not render admissible any evidence which would otherwise be hearsay. Instead it lays down additional requirements for the admissibility of a computer record which has already satisfied the conditions of admissibility laid down by an appropriate exception to the hearsay rule.

At the time when *Minors* was decided, the relevant exception was s. 68 of the 1984 Act, which has since been repealed. The hearsay exception most likely to be used in combination with s. 69 is now the CJA 1988, s. 24. Indeed, the Court of Appeal in *Minors* predicted that 'when section 24 of the 1988 Act comes into operation there will be two hurdles to clear in relation to computer records, viz. the new section 24 and section 69'. This dictum should not be understood as precluding the use of s. 69 in combination with any other hearsay exception within which the computer-produced document in question happens to fit.

Non-hearsay Computer Evidence

In *Minors* [1989] 1 WLR 441, it was said, *obiter*, that the requirements of the PACE **F8.35** 1984, s. 69, do not apply where a printout is tendered as non-hearsay evidence. This dictum was followed in *Spiby* (1990) 91 Cr App R 186, in which a printout produced automatically without any human intervention, and recording details of telephone calls made by hotel guests, was held to be real evidence to which s. 69 was inapplicable. This view of s. 69 has now been held to be erroneous by the House of Lords in *Shephard* [1993] AC 380. In that case (the facts of which are given at **F8.36**) Lord Griffiths reviewed the authorities and concluded that there is no warrant for an interpretation which limits s. 69 to hearsay computer evidence proved under an exception to the hearsay rule. Referring to the facts of *Spiby*, in which the printout was non-hearsay evidence, his lordship pointed out that the prosecution were nevertheless relying upon the facts stated in it as a reliable record of the telephone calls made, and it was thus important to have an assurance that the computer was working properly as required by s. 69.

Conditions of Admissibility

F8.36 The conditions of admissibility of a statement to which s. 69 applies should be determined at trial on indictment by means of a trial within a trial (*Minors* [1989] 1 WLR 441). The party seeking to rely on the statement must prove the matters set out in s. 69(1)(a) and (b). In theory, any conditions laid down in rules of court (made under s. 69(2)) also have to be satisfied, but no such rules have yet been made. The conditions imposed by s. 69 must be established by evidence, and where it is tendered by the prosecution, the criminal standard of proof must be met (*Minors*).

DPP v *McKeown* [1997] 1 WLR 295 involved the admissibility of non-hearsay computer evidence, a printout from an intoximeter breath-test machine. The clock in the intoximeter was displaying a time about an hour and a quarter slow, and this was reflected in the time shown on the printout, but there was evidence that the clock had no bearing on the accuracy of the breath readings. The House of Lords doubted whether the clock was part of the computer, or that the inaccuracy in the clock display showed that the computer was not operating properly, but held that, even assuming that the inaccuracy did mean that the computer was not operating properly, it was not 'such as to affect the production of the document or the accuracy of its contents' for the purposes of s. 69(1)(b), because on the evidence adduced the clock display did not affect the proper functioning of the computer. Section 69 was concerned solely with the proper operation and functioning of a computer and not with the accuracy of the information supplied to it, whether supplied by a computer operator or by some non-human means such as, in the case of the intoximeter, the gas analyser. The purpose of s. 69, it was held, is a relatively modest one. It does not require the prosecution to show that the statement is likely to be true. That is a question of weight for the justices or jury. All that s. 69 requires as a condition of admissibility is positive evidence that the computer has properly processed, stored and reproduced whatever information it received.

Proof that a computer is reliable can be provided in two ways: by calling oral evidence or by tendering a written certificate. Where oral evidence is relied upon, it was held by the House of Lords in *Shephard* [1993] AC 380 that it will only rarely be necessary for the witness to be a computer expert. S was charged with theft of goods from a store, and the main evidence against her consisted of the store's till rolls, from which it could be deduced that the goods had not been the subject of any sale. The tills were linked to a central computer, and a store detective who was familiar with the working of the tills, and who was able to say that the store had had no trouble with the operation of the central computer, was held to be 'fully qualified' to give the evidence required by s. 69. Lord Griffiths said:

> Documents produced by computers are an increasingly common feature of all business and more and more people are becoming familiar with their uses and operation. Computers vary immensely in their complexity and in the operations they perform. The nature of the evidence to discharge the burden of showing that there has been no improper use of the computer and that it was operating properly will inevitably vary from case to case. The evidence must be tailored to suit the needs of the case. I suspect that it will very rarely be necessary to call an expert and that in the vast majority of cases it will be possible to discharge the burden by calling a witness who is familiar with the operation of the computer in the sense of knowing what the computer is required to do and who can say that it is doing it properly.

Because s. 69 imposes an affirmative duty on anyone wishing to introduce computer evidence to prove that the computer was working correctly (a duty expressed in the section by the words 'shall not be admissible . . . unless it is shown'), there is no scope for application of the presumption expressed in the maxim *omnia praesumuntur rite esse acta* (*Shephard*). Suggestions to the contrary in earlier cases (considered in the 1992 edition of this work) must be taken to be incorrect. When the prosecution relies on a printout which appears to have been produced by more than one computer, sufficient evidence of the respective operation of the machines must be produced to enable the court to decide upon the correct application of s. 69 (*Cochrane* [1993] Crim LR 48).

Proof by Certificate

The conditions of admissibility specified in the PACE 1984, s. 69(1), in respect of **F8.37** computer-produced documents, may be proved by a certificate under para. 8 of sch. 3, although para. 9 preserves the power of the court to require instead that oral evidence be given of the matters which could be proved by such a certificate. If a certificate is to be relied upon it should show on its face that it is signed by a person who from his job description can confidently be expected to be in a position to give reliable evidence about the operation of the computer (*Shephard* [1993] AC 380).

In *Minors* [1989] 1 WLR 441 it was noted that the provisions for proof by certificate were of limited utility in relation to hearsay computer evidence unless the conditions of admissibility of the hearsay exception, which also have to be satisfied, could be established in the same manner; yet neither s. 24 of the CJA 1988 nor its predecessor, s. 68 of the 1984 Act, makes sufficient provision for proof by certificate.

REAL EVIDENCE

Tangible Objects

Real evidence is usually some material object, the existence, condition or value of which **F8.38** is in issue or relevant to an issue, produced in court for inspection by the tribunal of fact. (As to inspection out of court, see **F8.42**.) Little if any weight can attach to real evidence in the absence of accompanying testimony identifying the object and connecting it with the facts in issue. In some cases the tribunal of fact must not draw its own unaided conclusion without the assistance of expert testimony: see e.g., *Tilley* [1961] 1 WLR 1309 and *Hipson* [1969] Crim LR 85 (comparison of handwriting).

There is no rule of law that an object must be produced, or its non-production excused, before oral evidence may be given about it. In *Hocking* v *Ahlquist Bros Ltd* [1944] KB 120, proceedings against manufacturers of clothing for non-compliance with restrictions relating to the method of manufacture, in which evidence as to the condition of the garments was received from witnesses who had visited the manufacturer's premises, it was held that the magistrate had been wrong to dismiss the information on the basis that the garments were not produced at the trial. See also *Miller* v *Howe* [1969] 1 WLR 1510: it is not necessary for the police to produce the very breath test device used by them on a particular occasion. Non-production, however, may give rise to an inference adverse to the party failing to produce the object in question (*Armory* v *Delamirie* (1722) 1 Str 505), and may go to the weight of the oral evidence adduced. In *Francis* (1874) LR 2 CCR 128, a trial for attempting to pass off a false ring, at which the ring was not produced but witnesses who had seen it gave evidence as to its falsity, Lord Coleridge CJ said (at p. 133): 'though the production of the article may afford ground for observation more or less weighty, according to the circumstances, it only goes to the weight, not the admissibility of the evidence.'

Once an article has become an exhibit, the court has a responsibility, for the purposes of justice, to preserve and retain it until the trial is concluded, or to arrange for its preservation and retention, the usual course being for the court to entrust the exhibits to the police or to the DPP. The duty of the prosecution, if entrusted with exhibits pending trial and after committal, is:

(a)   to take all proper care to preserve the exhibits safe from loss or damage;

(b)   to cooperate with the defence in order to allow them reasonable access to the exhibits for the purpose of inspection and examination; and

(c)   to produce the exhibits at the trial (*Lambeth Metropolitan Stipendiary Magistrate, ex parte McComb* [1983] QB 551).

See also *Uxbridge Justices, ex parte Sofaer* (1986) 85 Cr App R 367. After the committal of any person for trial, a magistrates' court shall send to the Crown Court documents and articles produced in evidence before the justices or treated as so produced (Magistrates' Courts Rules 1981, r. 11(1)(g) and (h)).

Behaviour, Appearance and Demeanour

F8.39   In addition to material objects, the following may also be regarded as varieties of real evidence:

(a)   a person's behaviour, e.g., his misconduct in court for the purposes of contempt of court;

(b)   a person's physical appearance, e.g., for the purposes of identification or on the question of the existence or causation of personal injuries;

(c)   a person's demeanour or attitude which, in the case of a witness, may be relevant to his credit, the weight to be attached to his evidence, or whether he is to be treated as hostile.

Documents as Real Evidence

F8.40   Documents on the contents of which a party seeks to rely, whether as evidence of their truth, under an exception to the hearsay rule, or as original evidence, are subject to the rules as to proof of contents and due execution, dealt with at **F8.1** to **F8.30**. These rules, however, have no application if:

(a)   the contents are referred to merely for the purposes of identifying the document in question or establishing the bare fact of its existence (see *Boyle* v *Wiseman* (1855) 11 Exch 360, at pp. 367ff); or

(b)   the document is tendered as a material object, regardless of its contents, in order to show, e.g., its appearance, that it bears certain fingerprints, that it is made of a particular substance, or that it is in a particular physical condition.

In such cases, a document may be treated as a tangible object to the extent relevant to do so, and becomes a piece of real evidence.

Statements Produced by Computers and Mechanical Devices

F8.41   Where a computer or mechanical or other device is used as a calculator, i.e. as a tool which does not contribute its own knowledge, but merely performs a sophisticated calculation which could have been done manually, the printout or other reading is not hearsay but an item of real evidence, the proof and relevance of which depends on the evidence of those using the device, such as the computer programmer and other experts involved (see *Wood* (1982) 76 Cr App R 23 (a computer); *Castle* v *Cross* [1984] 1 WLR 1372) (breath-test equipment)). The printout from a computerised machine used to monitor telephone calls and record such information as the numbers from which, and to which, the call was made and the duration of the call is not hearsay but real evidence because it does not depend, in its content, on anything that has passed through a human mind (*Spiby* (1990) 91 Cr App R 186). See also *Governor of Brixton Prison, ex parte Levin* [1997] AC 741; and see further **F15.14**.

There is a rebuttable presumption as to the correct functioning of mechanical and other instruments (see **F3.24**). However, in the case of computer printouts, before the judge can decide whether they are admissible as real evidence or as hearsay (under the CJA 1988, s. 24, in conjunction with the PACE 1984, s. 69), it is necessary for appropriate authoritative evidence to be called to describe the function and operation of the computer (*Cochrane* [1993] Crim LR 48). Furthermore, s. 69 of the 1984 Act imposes a duty on anyone who wishes to admit a statement in a document produced by a computer, whether the statement is or is not hearsay, to produce evidence that will establish that it is safe to rely on the document: the duty cannot be discharged without evidence as there is no scope for application of the presumption as to the correct functioning of mechanical and other instruments. See *Shephard* [1993] AC 380 and generally **F8.31** to **F8.37**. When the YJCEA 1999, s. 60, is brought into force, the PACE 1984, s. 69, will be repealed.

Views

The term 'view' is used to describe: **F8.42**

    (a)   an inspection out of court of some material object which it is inconvenient or impossible to bring to court (see, e.g., *London General Omnibus Co. Ltd* v *Lavell* [1901] 1 Ch 135 (an omnibus)); and
    (b)   an inspection of the *locus in quo*.

A view should not take place after the summing-up: see *Lawrence* [1968] 1 WLR 341, which was distinguished in *Nixon* [1968] 1 WLR 577, where, the inspection having been at the express request of the defence, the Court applied the proviso and affirmed the conviction. A view should be attended by the judge, the tribunal of fact, the parties, their counsel, and the shorthand writer. In the case of magistrates, as a general rule a visit to the *locus in quo* should take place before the conclusion of the evidence and in the presence of the parties or their representatives, so as to afford them the opportunity of commenting on any feature of the locality which has altered since the time of the incident or any feature not previously noticed by the parties which impresses the magistrates (*Parry* v *Boyle* (1987) 83 Cr App R 310). The presence of the accused is important because he may be able to point out some important matter of which his legal adviser is ignorant or about which the magistrates are making a mistake (*Ely Justices, ex parte Burgess* [1992] Crim LR 888).

In a trial by jury, the judge should always be present at a view, whether or not any witness is present for the purposes of a demonstration (*Hunter* [1985] 1 WLR 613). In that case the judge was absent from a view at which a Crown witness answered jurors' questions. The Court of Appeal, quashing the conviction, held that absence of the judge was a fundamental departure from the principle that the whole of the trial must be in the presence of the judge. The judge should take precautions to prevent any witnesses who are present from communicating, except by way of demonstration, with the jury (*Martin* (1872) LR 1 CCR 378; *Karamat* v *The Queen* [1956] AC 256). A witness who has already given evidence at the trial may take part in a view; but witnesses taking part in a view should be recalled to be cross-examined, if desired (*Karamat* v *The Queen*).

It is improper for one juror to attend a view and report back to the others. In *Gurney* [1976] Crim LR 567 the Court of Appeal held that this contravened the principle that the jury should remain together at all times, and quashed the conviction. If the accused declines to attend a view, he cannot afterwards raise the objection that his absence of itself made the view illegal, though he could object if any evidence were given outside the scope of the view as ordered (*Karamat* v *The Queen*).

Tape Recordings and Transcripts

The contents of tape recordings, produced and played over in court, may be admitted as: **F8.43**

    (a)   evidence of their truth, under an exception to the hearsay rule (see, e.g., *Senat* (1968) 52 Cr App R 282: tape recordings of incriminating conversations obtained by telephone tapping; and *Maqsud Ali* [1966] 1 QB 688); or
    (b)   a variety of original evidence, e.g., simply to show that the recording was made.

In either event, the voices recorded must be properly identified (*Maqsud Ali*, at p. 701). At common law, it was held that there is no objection to a properly proved transcript of the recording being put before the jury, provided they are guided by what they *hear* (*Maqsud Ali*, at p. 702). See also *Rampling* [1987] Crim LR 823: the transcript, *not in itself evidence*, may be used as a convenience to the jury. However, a tape recording is a 'document' for the purposes of the CJA 1988, s. 27 (CJA 1988, sch. 2, para. 5: see **F8.2**). Thus, where a statement contained in a tape is admissible as evidence, it may be proved by production of the tape; or (whether or not the original is still in existence) by the production of a copy of the tape, or of the material part of it, authenticated in such manner as the court may approve; and it is immaterial how many removes there are between a copy and the original. A copy, for these purposes, includes a transcript of the sounds embodied in the tape (CJA 1988, sch. 2, para. 5, and Civil Evidence Act 1968, s. 10(1)). As to 'authentification', it is submitted that the courts are likely to require the same kind of proof that was necessary in the case of copies at common law before s. 27 came into force, namely a proper explanation as to why the originals are not available, and proof of the complete accuracy of the copies (*Robson* (June 1973 unreported)).

In the case of tape recordings and transcripts of police interviews, s. 27 of the CJA 1988 must be read in conjunction with the Code of Practice on Tape Recording (PACE Code E: see **appendix 2**), together with Home Office Circular 76/1988, issued on 17 August 1988, and the direction of Lord Lane CJ in *Practice Direction (Crime: Tape Recording Police Interviews)* [1989] 1 WLR 631. The provisions of PACE Code E must be followed in all areas where interviews with suspects are required to be recorded by virtue of the provisions of an order made under s. 60(1)(b) of the PACE 1984. Under s. 67(11) of the 1984 Act, Code E is admissible in evidence, and if any provision thereof appears to the court to be relevant to any question arising in the proceedings, it shall be taken into account in determining that question.

Section 27 of the 1988 Act must also be read, it is submitted, in conjunction with the common-law authorities before it came into force. At common law, if the prosecution seek to adduce a tape recording in evidence, the judge must be satisfied, in the absence of the jury, that the prosecution have made out a prima facie case of originality and authenticity, by evidence which defines and describes the provenance and history of the tape up to the moment of its production in court. If such evidence appears to remain intact after cross-examination, it is not incumbent on the judge to hear and weigh other evidence which might controvert the prima facie case. The judge is required to be satisfied to the civil standard, on a balance of probabilities, because application of the criminal standard would amount to an usurpation by the judge of the function of the jury (*Robson* [1972] 1 WLR 651, per Shaw J, a ruling upheld by the Court of Appeal (unreported); cf. *Stevenson* [1971] 1 WLR 1). A better approach, it is submitted, also involving no usurpation of the jury function, would be for the judge to decide the issue as if the party seeking to adduce the evidence bore an evidential burden. The question for the judge would then be whether sufficient evidence had been adduced to justify, as a possibility, a finding by the jury, on the issues of originality and genuineness, favourable to the party seeking to admit the tape.

In *Rampling* [1987] Crim LR 823, the Court of Appeal gave the following general guidance upon the use in trials of tape recordings and transcripts of police interviews:

(a) The tape can be produced and proved by the interviewing officer or any other officer present when it was taken.

(b) The officer should have listened to the tape before the trial so that he can, if required, deal with any objections to its authenticity or accuracy.

(c) As to authenticity, he can, if required, prove who spoke the recorded words.

(d)   As to accuracy, he can deal with any challenge, e.g., that the recording has been falsified by addition or omission.

(e)   The transcript of the recording can be produced by the officer, who, before the trial, should have checked it against the recording for accuracy. The tape recording is the evidence in the case and can be made an exhibit; the transcript, not in itself evidence, may be used as a convenience to the jury (but see now the CJA 1988, s. 27).

(f)   Use of the transcript is an administrative matter to be decided in his discretion by the trial judge. In many cases the accused will agree to its use and will not require the tape to be played at all, in which case the transcript will be read out by the officer who produced it; however, the accused is entitled, if he so wishes, to have any part of the tape played to the jury.

(g)   If any part of the tape is played, it is for the judge to decide whether the jury should have the transcript, in order to follow the tape, and have it with them when they retire; the use of the transcript is within the judge's discretion and is not dependent on the consent of the parties; a transcript is usually of very considerable value to the jury, but each case has to be decided on its own facts.

Where the tape becomes an exhibit (see (e) above), the jury may take it with them when they retire like any other exhibit in the case, and it makes no difference if the tape has already been heard in open court. In most cases, nothing turns on the tone of voice in which an interview was conducted and therefore it will usually be sufficient for the jury to have a transcript, much of which can and should be summarised; but where the tone of voice is all-important, for example when it is alleged that the interviewing officer spoke in a raised voice or in a brusque and intimidating manner, then subject to editing out any inadmissible material, the jury should be given the original tape (*Emmerson* (1991) 92 Cr App R 284). The Court of Appeal, in that case, also gave the following general guidance (at p. 287):

> (1) If the whole of the tape has been played in open court there is no reason why the jury should not have the tape if either side or the jury want it as well as any transcript. It is the tape, after all, which is the evidence. But in order not to waste time the jury should always be directed to the relevant part of the tape. (2) If only part of the tape has been played in open court but the jury have a transcript of the whole tape, then there is no reason why the jury should not have the whole tape. (3) If only part of the tape has been played in open court and the jury have no transcript, then the tape should be edited so as to ensure that the jury do not have anything that has not been given in evidence. (4) We see no advantage, and some disadvantage, in a court being reassembled in order to enable the jury to re-hear a passage of the tape which they have already heard in open court. This would seem to serve no useful purpose and be productive of unnecessary inconvenience.

If the tape is not played during the course of a trial but, after retirement, the jury ask to hear it rather than rely on the written transcript, they are entitled to hear it because the tape is the exhibit and the transcript merely a convenient method of presenting it (*Riaz* (1991) 94 Cr App R 339). However, where the prosecution opt not to play the tape but to provide the jury with an agreed transcript and agreed expert comment on it, the jury should not be allowed to conduct their own enquiry as to what is on the tape (*Hagan* [1997] 1 Cr App R 464). If the jury are entitled to hear the tape, although it is a matter of judicial discretion, the better practice is to bring the jury back into open court to hear the tape because of the difficulties which might arise if they are permitted free access to the tape, including the risk that they might hear matters inadvertently left on the tape which they should not hear (*Riaz*). Equally, however, where the jury ask to hear a tape, of which there is an agreed transcript, which does not contain inadmissible passages and which *has* already been played in court, the judge may, in his discretion, permit them to listen to it in the privacy of their retiring room (*Tonge* [1993] Crim LR 876). As to a jury request to hear a tape during or after closing speeches, but before retirement, see *Aitken* (1991) 94 Cr App R 85 at **F6.3**).

Photographs, Video Recordings and Films

F8.44 A photograph may be admitted in evidence to enable a witness to identify a person or thing. In *Tolson* (1864) 4 F & F 103, a case of bigamy, a photograph was produced, which was admitted to be a photograph of the first husband, and a witness was allowed to testify that he had seen the man in the photograph alive after the date of the allegedly bigamous marriage. Willes J said (at p. 104): 'The photograph was admissible because it is only a visible representation of the image or impression made upon the minds of the witnesses by the sight of the person or the object it represents; and, therefore is, in reality, only another species of the evidence which persons give of identity, when they speak merely from memory.'

A photograph (or film) the relevance of which can be established by the testimony of someone with personal knowledge of the circumstances in which it was taken (or made), may also be admitted to prove the commission of an offence and the identity of the offender. In *Dodson* [1984] 1 WLR 971, it was held that photographs taken at half-second intervals by security cameras installed at a building society office at which an armed robbery had been attempted, were admissible, on the issue of whether an offence had been committed and, if so, who had committed it, even though no witnesses were called to identify the men in the photographs. However, in a case in which the jury is invited to 'identify' the accused in court from a photograph or video recording of the offender committing the offence, they should be warned of the risk of mistaken identity and of the need to exercise particular care in any identification which they make. They must take into account whether the appearance of the accused has changed since the visual recording was made, but a full *Turnbull* direction (*Turnbull* [1977] QB 224: see **F18.16**) is inappropriate because the process of identifying a person from a photograph is a commonplace event and some things are obvious from the photograph itself. Thus they do not need to be told that the photograph is of good quality or poor, nor whether the person is shown in close-up or was distant from the camera etc. (*Blenkinsop* [1995] 1 Cr App R 7, approving *Downey* [1995] 1 Cr App R 547; cf. *Taylor* v *Chief Constable of Cheshire* [1986] 1 WLR 1479, below). However, it seems that a request by them that the accused stand up and turn around, in order that they may be given a better view of him, does not have to be met, at least not by an accused who has elected not to testify (*McNamara* [1996] Crim LR 750).

In *Roberts* [1998] Crim LR 682, a police constable made a written statement relating to charges of assault and affray. A video camera had recorded the events in question and the constable later provided a commentary on the video to enable prosecuting counsel to explain to the jury, when viewing it, who was who and where the events took place.. The video was then made available to the defence. It was held that it was not wrong in principle that the constable had seen the video. On seeing a video a witness might find that in some respects his recollection had been at fault and might wish to modify earlier evidence. However, nothing should be done which amounted to rehearsing the evidence of a witness or coaching him so as to encourage him to alter the evidence already given. The acid test was whether the procedure adopted was such as to taint the resulting evidence. That was not so in the instant case. The video had been made available to the defence and had been shown to defence witnesses before they gave their evidence, and the constable had been directly challenged on discrepancies between his first statement and his commentary.

In *Thomas* [1986] Crim LR 682, a case of reckless driving, a video recording of the route taken by the accused was admitted to remove the need for maps and still photographs, and to convey a more accurate picture of the roads in question. In *The Statue of Liberty* [1968] 1 WLR 739, a civil action concerning a collision between two ships, Sir Jocelyn Simon P, rejecting a submission that a cinematograph film of radar echoes, recorded by a shore radar station, was inadmissible because produced mechanically without human intervention, said (at p. 740): 'If tape recordings are admissible, it seems that a photograph of radar reception is equally admissible – or indeed, any other type of photograph. It would be an absurd distinction that a photograph should be admissible if the camera were operated manually by a photographer, but not if it were operated by a trip or clock mechanism.' Compare *Wood* (1982) 76 Cr App R 23, at **F8.41**.

The CJA 1988, ss. 23 and 24, provide for the admissibility of statements contained in 'documents', and that term includes photographs and films (1988 Act, sch. 2, para. 5: see **F8.2**). However, even if a photograph or film is treated as containing a 'statement', it would appear to be admissible *at common law* as a variety of real evidence posing no hearsay problem (see *The Statue of Liberty* [1968] 1 WLR 739, where the film, in effect, contained a statement as to the paths taken by the two ships). Moreover, it has been said that a photograph, together with the sketch and the photofit, is in a class of evidence of its own, to which neither the rule against hearsay nor the rule against previous consistent or self-serving statements applies (*Cook* [1987] QB 417 per Watkins LJ; applied in *Constantinou* (1989) 91 Cr App R 74). As to evidence of previous identification of the accused by police photographs, see further at **F18**.

The contents of photographs and films on which a party seeks to rely may be proved by production of the original; or by production of a copy proved to be an authentic copy; or by the parol evidence of witnesses who have seen the photograph or film. In *Kajala* v *Noble* (1982) 75 Cr App R 149, a case of using threatening behaviour likely to occasion a breach of the peace, a prosecution witness who was familiar with the accused gave evidence that he had recognised him on a BBC news programme, and a video cassette recording of the incident, which the court was satisfied was an authentic copy of the original film held by the BBC, was admitted in evidence. Ackner LJ held that the rule, that if an original document is available in a party's hands he must produce it and cannot give secondary evidence of it, was confined to written documents in the strict sense of the term and has no relevance to tapes or films. In *Taylor* v *Chief Constable of Cheshire* [1986] 1 WLR 1479, a video cassette recording, made by a security camera and showing a person in a shop picking up an item and putting it into his jacket, was played to police officers who identified the person as Taylor. The recording, after it had been returned to the shop, was accidentally erased. Evidence by the officers of what they had seen on the video was held to have been properly admitted, on the ground that what they had seen on the video was no different in principle from the evidence of a bystander who had actually witnessed the incident, and the appeal against conviction was dismissed. The Court of Appeal held that the weight and reliability of the evidence had to be assessed carefully and, because identification was in issue, by reference to the guidelines laid down in *Turnbull* [1977] QB 224, which had to be applied in relation to not only the camera, but also the visual display unit or recorded copy and the officers. See also *Constantinou* (1989) 91 Cr App R 74.

Where a video or film has been shown in court and the jury, after retirement, ask to see it again, they may do so, but it is better if they see it again in open court (*Imran* [1997] Crim LR 754, in which the jury had seen a silent video of an attempted robbery). Cf. *Rawlings* [1995] 1 WLR 178 (video recordings of children's evidence), which is considered at **F16.21**.

SECTION F9: PUBLIC POLICY AND PRIVILEGE

EXCLUSION ON GROUNDS OF PUBLIC POLICY

This section concerns the principles of law governing the non-disclosure of material on the grounds of public policy. As to the procedure to be followed on an application to the court that unused material should not be disclosed on such grounds, see also **D6.6** to **D6.8** and **D6.10** and the Crown Court (CPIA 1996) (Disclosure) Rules 1997. Part I of the CPIA 1996 generally disapplies the common-law rules relating to the prosecution duty of disclosure, but s. 21(2) of that Act preserves the rules of common law as to whether disclosure is in the public interest.

General Principles

F9.1   It is in the public interest to withhold material, the disclosure of which would harm the nation or the proper functioning of the public service. It is also in the public interest that justice should be done, and should be publicly seen to be done, by the reception of all relevant evidence. If there is a conflict between these two interests, whether otherwise admissible evidence should be withheld in the public interest is a question of balance, to be decided by the courts and not by the executive (*Conway* v *Rimmer* [1968] AC 910). If the evidence is excluded, it is said to be withheld by reason of public interest immunity: see *Lewes Justices, ex parte Secretary of State for the Home Department* [1973] AC 388, per Lord Reid at p. 400, disapproving use of the expression 'Crown privilege'; but contrast *Science Research Council* v *Nassé* [1980] AC 1028, per Lord Scarman at p. 1087.

In some cases, the relevant minister (or head of department) or the A-G may intervene to claim immunity. Alternatively, the claim to immunity may be made by the party seeking to withhold the evidence, either on its own initiative or at the request of the relevant government department (see, e.g., *Burmah Oil Co. Ltd* v *Bank of England* [1980] AC 1090). If necessary, the judge himself should raise the issue, because if there is a public interest to be protected, that should be done regardless of party advantage (*Duncan* v *Cammell Laird & Co. Ltd* [1942] AC 624, per Viscount Simon LC at p. 642).

A claim to public interest immunity may be supported by affidavit evidence from the relevant minister (or head of department), or by a certificate signed by the minister. However, a minister's affidavit or certificate is not final (except, it seems, in cases concerning national security: see *Balfour* v *Foreign and Commonwealth Office* [1994] 1 WLR 681, considered at **F9.2**). Although an objection by the Crown to the disclosure of material is entitled to the greatest weight, the court may ask for clarification or amplification of the objection, and has the power to inspect documentary evidence privately and to order its production notwithstanding ministerial objection (*Conway* v *Rimmer* [1968] AC 910). In *Conway* v *Rimmer*, it was suggested that certain classes of documents, such as Cabinet papers and Foreign Office despatches should never be disclosed, whatever their contents may be (see per Lords Reid and Upjohn at pp. 952 and 993 respectively). Since then, however, the House of Lords has made it clear that the courts should be prepared to evaluate 'class' claims, even in the case of high-level government papers, and in appropriate circumstances, albeit very rarely, to require their disclosure (see *Burmah Oil Co. Ltd* v *Bank of England* [1980] AC 1090, per Lord Keith at p. 1134, and *Air Canada* v *Secretary of State for Trade (No. 2)* [1983] 2 AC 394, per Lord Fraser at p. 432).

In December 1996 the Lord Chancellor issued a statement that the division into class and contents claims would no longer be applied, and that in future ministers would focus directly on the damage that disclosure of sensitive documents would cause. Under this new approach, ministers claim immunity only when they believe that disclosure of a document will cause real damage or harm to the public interest. Damage will normally have to be in the form of a direct or immediate threat to the safety of an individual or to the nation's economic interests or relations with a foreign state, although in some cases the anticipated damage might be indirect or longer term, such as damage to a regulatory process. In any event the nature of the harm will have to be clearly explained, and ministers will no longer be able to claim immunity for internal advice or national security material merely by pointing to the general nature of the document. It is to be hoped that non-governmental bodies claiming public interest immunity, although not bound by the Lord Chancellor's statement, will in practice adopt the same approach.

Decisions as to what should be withheld from disclosure are for the court and should not be made (without reference to the court) by the prosecution, the police, the DPP or counsel (see *Ward* [1993] 1 WLR 619 and, in the case of co-accused, *Adams* [1997] Crim LR 292). The principles are the same whether the proceedings are summary or on indictment, but when, in the case of an either way offence, it is known that a contested issue as to the disclosure of sensitive material is likely to arise, that consideration may sometimes properly found an application by the Crown for trial on indictment, and magistrates would then be well advised to commit (*Bromley Magistrates' Court, ex parte Smith* [1995] 1 WLR 944, distinguishing *DPP, ex parte Warby* [1994] Crim LR 281). Where a magistrates' court, whatever its composition, hears an application for non-disclosure on the grounds of public interest immunity and rules that the material in question is inadmissible, it should normally proceed to hear the case itself, and should only exercise its discretion to order it to be tried by a different bench in exceptional circumstances, e.g., when material was introduced at the non-disclosure hearing which was prejudicial and irrelevant to the question of admissibility (*Stipendiary Magistrate for Norfolk, ex parte Taylor* (1997) 161 JP 773). See also *Bromley Magistrates, ex parte Smith* and *cf. South Worcestershire Justices, ex parte Lilley* [1995] 1 WLR 1595.

If the prosecution wish to claim immunity for documents which they would otherwise be obliged to disclose to the defence (see **D12.16** to **D12.19**), they are obliged to give notice to the defence of the asserted right so that, if necessary, the court can be asked to rule on the matter. It is incompatible with an accused's absolute right to a fair trial to allow the prosecution to be judge in their own cause on the asserted claim. If they are not prepared to have the issue determined by a court, the result must inevitably be that the prosecution will have to be abandoned (*Ward* [1993] 1 WLR 619). In most cases they should indicate to the defence the category of the material they hold and the defence should be given the opportunity of making representations to the court. However, where to disclose even the category would be to reveal that which the Crown contend should not be revealed, the Crown need not specify the category but should notify the defence that an ex parte application will be made to the court. In rare cases where even notification of the application would defeat the public interest in non-disclosure, the prosecution should make an ex parte application without such notification (*Davis* [1993] 1 WLR 613). The ex parte procedure should only be used, on the application of the Crown, for the specific purpose of enabling the court to test a claim that immunity or sensitivity justifies non-disclosure (*Keane* [1994] 1 WLR 746; and see also *Smith* [1998] 2 Cr App R 1). Defence applications, such as applications for disclosure of details relating to an informer, should not be heard ex parte (*Turner* [1995] 1 WLR 264 and *Tattenhove* [1996] 1 Cr App R 408). The procedures laid down in *Davis* are now, in large measure, reproduced in the Crown Court (Criminal Procedure and Investigations Act 1996) (Disclosure) Rules 1997: see **D6.8**, but see also *Rowe and Davis* v *United Kingdom* [1999] Crim LR 410.

In *Keane* Lord Taylor CJ held that it is for the prosecution to put before the court only those documents which it regards as material but wishes to withhold. It is generally for the prosecution, not the court, to identify the documents and information which are material.

However, if, in an exceptional case, the prosecution are in doubt about the materiality of some documents or information, the court may be asked to rule on that issue. When the court is seized of the material, the judge should perform the balancing exercise, balancing the weight of the public interest in non-disclosure against the importance of the documents to the issues of interest to the defence, present and potential, so far as they have been disclosed to him or he can foresee them. However a ruling made prior to the hearing is not necessarily final, because issues may later emerge whereby the public interest in non-disclosure is eclipsed by the accused's need for access *(Bower* [1994] Crim LR 281). The trial judge is under a continuous duty, in the light of the way in which the trial develops, to keep his initial decision under review, and prosecuting counsel must inform himself fully as to the content of any disputed material so as to be in a position to invite the judge to reassess the situation if the previous denial of the material arguably becomes untenable in the light of developments in the trial *(Brown* [1994] 1 WLR 1599 at p. 1608). See now CPIA 1996, ss. 14 and 15 discussed at **D6.7** and **D6.10**.

The CPS may voluntarily disclose to the defence documents which would otherwise be in a class covered by public interest immunity, without referring the matter to the court for a ruling, subject to the safeguard of first seeking the express written approval of the Treasury Solicitor. The CPS should submit to him copies of the documents in question, identify the public interest immunity class into which they fall and indicate the materiality of the documents to the proceedings in which it is proposed to disclose them. The Treasury Solicitor should consult any other relevant government department and satisfy himself that the balance falls clearly in favour of disclosure. He should be more ready to disclose documents likely to assist the defence than those which the CPS wish to disclose with a view to furthering the interests of the prosecution. Before approving disclosure of documents of a particular class sought to be used by the prosecution, he should consider not only their importance to the prosecution's case, but also the importance of the prosecution itself: it may be preferable to abandon the case rather than damage the integrity of the class claim. He should also maintain a permanent record of all approvals given so that any court ruling on disclosure would know how far immunity for that particular class of documents had been weakened by previous voluntary disclosure *(Horseferry Road Magistrates, ex parte Bennett (No. 2)* [1994] 1 All ER 289).

The principle of public interest immunity is applicable to criminal proceedings, but involves a different balancing exercise to that in civil proceedings. The judge will balance the desirability of preserving the public interest in non-disclosure against the interests of justice. Where the interests of justice arise in a criminal case touching and concerning liberty (or conceivably, on occasion, life), the weight to be attached to the interests of justice is plainly very great; it is a matter of whether the interests of justice outweigh the considerations of public interest as spoken to in the certificate of the Minister. Any prior disclosure of the information in question is a matter to be taken into account in the balance. In assessing the interests of justice, the court must ask whether a document to which the certificate relates is material to the proceedings. Its materiality will depend on the purpose for which it is sought to be deployed. In cases concerning the identity of informers or persons who have allowed their premises to be used for police surveillance (see **F9.5**), there have been observations to the effect that the privilege cannot prevail if the evidence is necessary for the prevention of a miscarriage of justice – no balance is called for *(Governor of Brixton Prison, ex parte Osman* [1991] 1 WLR 281). But see also, in cases concerning the identity of informers, *Keane* [1994] 1 WLR 746, per Lord Taylor CJ (at pp. 751–2):

> We prefer to say that the outcome in the instances given by Lord Esher MR [in *Marks v Beyfus* (1890) 25 QBD 494: see **F9.5**] and Mann LJ [in *Ex parte Osman*] results from performing the balancing exercise, not from dispensing with it. If the disputed material may

prove the defendant's innocence or avoid a miscarriage of justice, then the balance comes down resoundingly in favour of disclosing it.

In *Clowes* [1992] 3 All ER 440, the accused were charged with theft and fraud following the collapse of two deposit-taking companies owing investors over £115 million. The liquidators of the company interviewed a number of people in order to establish whether civil claims could be brought on behalf of the investors. Those interviewed attended voluntarily in circumstances of confidence on assurances, express or implied, that any information given to the liquidators would be used solely for the purposes of the liquidation. At the instance of the accused, a witness summons was issued requiring the liquidators to produce the transcripts. The liquidators applied to the Companies Court for directions that they be at liberty to disclose the transcripts to the accused. The judge held that they should claim public interest immunity and refuse to disclose the transcripts unless ordered to do so by the Crown Court. The liquidators then applied to the Crown Court to discharge the summons on the grounds that the transcripts were not 'likely to be material evidence' or should be protected by reason of public interest immunity. Phillips J held that the transcripts were potentially admissible and material. Concerning the claim to public interest immunity, the question arose whether the court should conduct a balancing exercise between the public interest asserted and the interest of the due administration of criminal justice. After reviewing the authorities relating to informers (see **F9.5**) and the decision in *Ex parte Osman*, Phillips J held that he did not find very easy the concept of a balancing exercise between the nature of the public interest on the one hand and the degree and potential consequences of the risk of a miscarriage of justice on the other, but would not readily accept that proportionality between the two is never of relevance. On the facts, he allowed the summons to stand. It did not seem that the public interest in question should carry greater weight than the public interest in concealing the identity of a police informer. Those interviewed inevitably accepted some risk of dissemination of the information they gave and there would be a relatively limited effect on 'the wells of voluntary information'. On the other hand, the accused were charged with grave offences and it was therefore of particular importance that no unnecessary impediment should be put in the way of presenting their defence in the best light. Another significant factor was the complexity of the evidence and the risk of lapse of memory on the part of witnesses.

Concerning inspection by the judge, it was not suggested that the approach taken in civil cases (see *Air Canada* v *Secretary of State for Trade (No. 2)* [1983] 2 AC 394) was appropriate in a criminal trial. Phillips J could see no reason for not inspecting the transcripts, especially since they contained no sensitive material, and accordingly looked at them to assist in reaching a decision on whether they were likely to contain additional material evidence.

The heads of public interest immunity which have been recognised by the courts relate to national security, diplomatic relations, international comity, the proper functioning of the public service, informers and information for the detection of crime, judges, jurors, and sources of information contained in publications. Each is considered in the following paragraphs.

National Security, Diplomatic Relations and International Comity

Documents falling within this category are those most readily protected against **F9.2** disclosure; in the case of national security, it seems that a ministerial certificate will be conclusive (*Balfour* v *Foreign and Commonwealth Office* [1994] 1 WLR 681). That case concerned material relating to the security and intelligence services. It was held that once there is an actual or potential risk to national security demonstrated by an appropriate ministerial certificate, the court should not exercise its right to inspect. See also *Hennessy* v *Wright* (1888) 21 QBD 509 (communications between the governor of a colony and the colonial secretary); *Chatterton v Secretary of State for India in Council* [1895] 2 QB 189 (communications between the government and the commander-in-chief of forces overseas); *Asiatic Petroleum Co. Ltd v Anglo Persian Oil Co. Ltd* [1916] 1 KB 822 (information relating to the Persian campaign in the First World War); *M. Isaacs & Sons Ltd v Cook* [1925] 2 KB 391 (diplomatic despatches); *Duncan v Cammell Laird & Co. Ltd* [1942] AC 624 (information on the design of a new submarine); and *Buttes Gas and Oil Co. v Hammer (No. 3)* [1981] QB 223 (confidential communications with foreign sovereign states or concerning their interest in international territorial disputes).

Proper Functioning of Public Service

F9.3   Public interest immunity may be claimed for communications to and from ministers and high-level government officials, regarding the formulation of government policy: see, e.g., *Burmah Oil Co. Ltd v Bank of England* [1980] AC 1090 (memoranda of meetings attended by ministers or government officials relating to government policy on economic matters); and *Air Canada v Secretary of State for Trade (No. 2)* [1983] 2 AC 394 (ministerial papers and inter-departmental communications between senior civil servants concerning government policy in relation to the British Airports Authority).

The public also has an interest in the effective working of non-governmental bodies and agencies performing public functions. However, although the categories of public interest are not closed, the courts can only proceed by analogy with interests which have previously been recognised by the authorities: see *D v National Society for the Prevention of Cruelty to Children* [1978] AC 171, per Lords Diplock, Hailsham, and Simon at pp. 219, 226, and 240 respectively, applied in *Science Research Council v Nassé* [1980] AC 1028 (in which the House rejected a claim in respect of confidential reports on employees seeking promotion). Examples include *Re D (Infants)* [1970] 1 WLR 599 (local authorities); *Lewes Justices, ex parte Secretary of State for the Home Department* [1973] AC 388 (the Gaming Board); *D v National Society for the Prevention of Cruelty to Children* [1978] AC 171 (the NSPCC); and *Buckley v Law Society (No. 2)* [1984] 1 WLR 1101 (the Law Society).

Police Communications

F9.4   Public interest immunity also attaches to police communications relating to the investigation of crime, such as documents or information upon the strength of which search warrants have been obtained (*Taylor v Anderton* (1986) *The Times*, 21 October 1986). Reports sent by the police to the DPP, even if the prosecution has been completed, have also attracted immunity, on the ground that there should be freedom of communication with the DPP, without fear that such reports may be inspected, analysed or investigated in subsequent civil proceedings (see *Evans v Chief Constable of Surrey* [1988] QB 588). Immunity also attaches to international communications between police forces or prosecuting authorities (*Horseferry Road Magistrates' Court, ex parte Bennett (No. 2)* [1994] 1 All ER 289), although in that case the balance favoured disclosure, the documents being relevant to the issue of whether B had been unlawfully returned to the jurisdiction. In appropriate circumstances, immunity may also be claimed for internal police communications other than those relating to the investigation of crime, on the ground that the public has an interest in the proper functioning of the police force (*Conway v Rimmer* [1968] AC 910).

Immunity may also be claimed for police complaints and disciplinary files (*Halford v Sharples* [1992] 1 WLR 736). There is no immunity, however, for written complaints against the police prompting investigations under part IX of the PACE 1984 (*Conerney v Jacklin* [1985] Crim LR 234); and there is no class immunity for statements obtained for the purposes of such investigations, although immunity may be claimed in the case of a particular document by reason of its contents (*Chief Constable of the West Midlands Police, ex parte Wiley* [1995] 1 AC 274, overruling *Neilson v Laugharne* [1981] QB 736 and cases in which it was subsequently applied). However, the working papers and reports prepared by the investigating officers do form a class which is entitled to immunity, and therefore production of such material should be ordered only where the public interest in disclosure of their contents outweighs the public interest in preserving confidentiality (*Taylor* v *Anderton* [1995] 1 WLR 447).

Public interest immunity does not attach to statements made during the course of a police grievance procedure, initiated by an officer, alleging either racial or sexual discrimination (*Commissioner of Police of the Metropolis* v *Locker* [1993] 3 All ER 584).

Informers and Information for Detection of Crime

There is a long-established rule of law that in public prosecutions witnesses may not be **F9.5** asked, and should not be allowed to disclose, the names of informers or the nature of the information given (*Hardy* (1794) 24 St Tr 199). The rule applies to public prosecutions brought by the DPP and bodies authorised by statute to bring public prosecutions. It also applies to police prosecutions, but not to other private prosecutions. The rationale of the rule was explained by Lawton LJ in *Hennessey* (1978) 68 Cr App R 419 (at p. 425): 'The courts appreciate the need to protect the identity of informers, not only for their own safety but to ensure that the supply of information about criminal activities does not dry up.' See also *D* v *National Society for the Prevention of Cruelty to Children* [1978] AC 171, per Lord Diplock at p. 218. The judge is obliged to apply the rule even if it is not invoked by the party entitled to object to disclosure (*Marks* v *Beyfus* (1890) 25 QBD 494, per Lord Esher MR at p. 500, and *Rankine* [1986] QB 861, per Mann J at p. 867). See also the Interception of Communications Act 1985, s. 9, which provides that no evidence shall be adduced which tends to suggest that an offence under s. 1 of the 1985 Act has been committed by, *inter alia*, persons holding office under the Crown, or that a warrant has been or is to be issued to any such persons (see *Preston* [1994] 2 AC 130, *Rasool* [1997] 1 WLR 1092, *Owen* [1999] 1 WLR 949 and *Morgans* v *DPP* [1999] 1 WLR 968).

There is an exception to the common-law rule where the judge is of the opinion that disclosure is necessary to establish the innocence of the accused.

> . . . if upon the trial of a prisoner the judge should be of opinion that the disclosure of the name of the informant is necessary or right in order to show the prisoner's innocence, then one public policy is in conflict with another public policy, and that which says that an innocent man is not to be condemned when his innocence can be proved is the policy that must prevail. (*Marks* v *Beyfus* (1890) 25 QBD 494, per Lord Esher MR at p. 498)

This outcome, however, results from performing the balancing exercise, not from dispensing with it (*Keane* [1994] 1 WLR 746 — see **F9.1**). Judges should scrutinise applications for disclosure of details about informants with very great care and should be astute to see whether assertions that knowledge of such details is essential to the running of a defence are justified. In some cases, the informant is an informant and no more; but even when the informant has participated in the events constituting, surrounding or following the crime, the judge must consider whether his role so impinges on an issue of interest to the defence, present or potential, as to make disclosure necessary (*Turner* [1995] 1 WLR 264 per Lord Taylor CJ at p. 268).

In *Agar* [1990] 2 All ER 442, the accused alleged that the police had arranged with an informer to ask the accused to go to the informer's house, where drugs allegedly found on him had been planted by the police. It was held that the disclosure of the identity of the informer was necessary to enable the accused to put forward the tenable defence that he had been set up by the police and the informer acting in concert. Therefore, counsel for the accused should have been permitted to cross-examine police witnesses to elicit the fact that the informer had told the police that the accused was coming to his house. (Compare *Slowcombe* [1991] Crim LR 198, where disclosure of the identity of an informer would have contributed little or nothing to the issue which the jury had to consider, and *Menga* [1998] Crim LR 58.) *Agar* was applied in *Langford* [1990] Crim LR 653. See also *Vaillencourt* [1993] Crim LR 311, *Reilly* [1994] Crim LR 279 and *Baker* [1996] Crim LR 55. It is for the accused to show that there is good reason to expect that disclosure is necessary to show his innocence (*Hennessy* (1978) 68 Cr App R 419, per Lawton LJ, and *Hallett* [1986] Crim LR 462). In *Hennessy*, Lawton LJ said (at p. 426): 'This should normally be done, not in the course of a trial, but in any proceedings which may be started to set aside a subpoena or a witness summons served upon a Crown witness who is alleged to be in possession of, or to have control over, tape recordings, transcripts of such recordings and the like.'

The rule also protects the identity of persons who have allowed their premises to be used for police surveillance, and the identity of their premises (*Rankine* [1986] QB 861). If the accused submits that disclosure of the identification of the premises is necessary in order to show his innocence, the judge may nonetheless exclude the evidence, provided that the prosecution have provided a proper evidential basis for such exclusion. In *Johnson* [1988] 1 WLR 1377, Watkins LJ gave the following guidance as to the minimum evidential requirements in this regard (at pp. 1385–6):

> (a)   The police officer in charge of the observations to be conducted, no one of lower rank than a sergeant should usually be acceptable for this purpose, must be able to testify that beforehand he visited all observation places to be used and ascertained the attitude of occupiers of premises, not only to the use to be made of them, but to the possible disclosure thereafter of the use made and facts which could lead to the identification of the premises thereafter and of the occupiers. He may of course in addition inform the court of difficulties, if any, usually encountered in the particular locality of obtaining assistance from the public.
> (b)   A police officer of no lower rank than a chief inspector must be able to testify that immediately prior to the trial he visited the places used for observations, the results of which it is proposed to give in evidence, and ascertained whether the occupiers are the same as when the observations took place and whether they are or are not, what the attitude of those occupiers is to the possible disclosure of the use previously made of the premises and of facts which could lead at the trial to identification of premises and occupiers.
>
> Such evidence will of course be given in the absence of the jury when the application to exclude the material evidence is made. The judge should explain to the jury, as this judge did, when summing up or at some appropriate time before that, the effect of his ruling to exclude, if he so rules.

In *Johnson*, the appellant was convicted of supplying drugs. The only evidence against him was given by police officers, who testified that, while stationed in private premises in a known drug-dealing locality, they had observed him selling drugs. The defence applied to cross-examine the officers on the exact location of the observation posts, in order to test what they could see, having regard to the layout of the street and the objects in it. In the jury's absence the prosecution called evidence as to the difficulty of obtaining assistance from the public, and the desire of the occupiers, who were also occupiers at the time of the offence, that their names and addresses should not be disclosed because they feared for their safety. The judge ruled that the exact location of the premises need not be revealed. The appeal was dismissed: although the conduct of the defence was to some extent affected by the restraints placed on it, this led to no injustice. The jury were well aware of the restraints, and were most carefully directed about the very special care they had to give to any disadvantage they may have brought to the defence. *Johnson* was applied and approved in *Hewitt* (1992) 95 Cr App R 81. See also *Grimes* [1994] Crim LR 213. The guidelines in *Johnson* do not require a threat of violence before protection can be afforded to the occupier of an observation post; it suffices if the occupier is in fear of harassment (*Blake* v *DPP* (1993) 97 Cr App R 169).

The extension of the rule established in *Rankine* [1986] QB 861 is based on the protection of the owner or occupier of the premises, and not on the identity, *simpliciter*, of the observation post. Thus, where officers have witnessed the commission of an offence as part of a surveillance operation conducted from an unmarked police vehicle, information relating to the surveillance and the colour, make and model of the vehicle should not be withheld (*Brown* (1987) 87 Cr App R 52). Hodgson J said (at pp. 59–60):

> We do not rule out the possibility that with the advent of no doubt sophisticated methods of criminal investigation, there may be cases where the public interest immunity may be successfully invoked in criminal proceedings to justify the exclusion of evidence as to police techniques and methods. But if and when such an argument is to be raised, it must, in the judgment of this court, be done properly. The Crown Prosecution Service must at least ensure that counsel is properly instructed to make the application and to identify with precision the evidence sought to be excluded and the reasons for its exclusion. It would seem clear that if such a contention is put forward the judge must be given as much information as possible and the application will have to be supported, not by the instructions of the junior officer in charge of the case, but by the independent evidence of senior officers.

A further exception to the common-law rule against disclosure of the name of an informer was established in *Savage* v *Chief Constable of Hampshire* [1997] 1 WLR 1061, in which it was held that a police informer who wishes personally to sacrifice his own anonymity will not be precluded from doing so by a claim of immunity, because in such circumstances the primary justification for the claim (that disclosure would endanger the safety of the informer) disappears. The wishes of the informer, however, are not conclusive, and in appropriate cases may be outweighed by other considerations, as when discovery may assist others involved in crime, hamper police operations, or indicate the state of police enquiries into a particular crime.

Judges and Jurors

A judge, including a master of the Supreme Court, cannot be compelled to give evidence **F9.6** of matters of which he became aware relating to, and as a result of, the performance of his judicial functions (as opposed to extraneous matters, such as a crime committed in the face of the court). However, the judge remains competent to give evidence, and if a situation arises where his evidence is vital, the judge should be able to be relied on not to allow his non-compellability to stand in the way of his giving evidence (*Warren* v *Warren* [1997] QB 488, in which the authorities are reviewed).

A jury's verdict cannot be impeached by the testimony of a *juror* as to what happened in the jury room. Thus, in *Thompson* [1962] 1 All ER 65, the Court of Criminal Appeal refused to hear evidence that the majority of the jury had been in favour of acquittal until the foreman had produced a list of the appellant's previous convictions which had not been received in evidence. Likewise in *Roads* [1967] 2 QB 108, the Court of Appeal refused to receive affidavit evidence from a juror that she disagreed with the verdict of guilty. See also *Lalchan Nanan* v *The State* [1986] AC 860 and *Lucas* [1991] Crim LR 844, and compare *Newton* (1912) 7 Cr App R 214, in which a conviction was quashed, where the foreman disclosed to the judge in open court that the jury had decided the case on an impermissible basis. However, misconduct connected with the verdict of a jury may be proved *extrinsically*, for example by the evidence of the officer in charge of the jury or the clerk (*Willmont* (1914) 10 Cr App R 173); and the testimony of a juror may be received as to extraneous matters, i.e. matters extrinsic to the manner in which the verdict was reached and to any occurrence in the jury room (*Hood* [1968] 1 WLR 773).

Sources of Information Contained in Publications

Contempt of Court Act 1981, s. 10   F9.7

> No court may require a person to disclose, nor is any person guilty of contempt of court for refusing to disclose, the source of information contained in a publication for which he is responsible, unless it be established to the satisfaction of the court that disclosure is necessary in the interests of justice or national security or for the prevention of disorder or crime.

Section 10 substitutes for the common-law discretionary protection a rule of law of wide and general application, subject only to the four exceptions specified (*Secretary of State for Defence* v *Guardian Newspapers Ltd* [1985] AC 339, per Lord Scarman). The section applies to information which has been communicated and received for the purposes of publication, even if it is not 'contained in a publication', because the purpose underlying the statutory protection of sources of information is as much applicable before as after publication (*X Ltd* v *Morgan-Grampian (Publishers) Ltd* [1991] 1 AC 1 per Lord Bridge of Harwich). It is sufficient, in order to be protected by s. 10, that an order of the court *may*, and not necessarily *will*, result in disclosure of a source of information (*Secretary of State for Defence* v *Guardian Newspapers Ltd* [1985] AC 339, per Lord Roskill at p. 368). It is a question of fact and not discretion whether an exception applies, and the burden of proof is on the party seeking disclosure (per Lords Diplock and Scarman, at pp. 345 and 364 respectively). Disclosure must be shown to be 'necessary': expediency, however great, will not suffice (per Lord Diplock, at p. 350; *Handmade Films (Productions) Ltd* v *Express Newspapers plc* [1986] FSR 463).

The word 'justice' in s. 10 is not used as the antonym of 'injustice', but in the technical sense of the administration of justice in the course of legal proceedings in a court of law or a tribunal, or a body exercising the judicial powers of the state (*Secretary of State for Defence* v *Guardian Newspapers Ltd* [1985] AC 339, per Lord Diplock at p. 350; see also *X Ltd* v *Morgan-Grampian (Publishers) Ltd* below). In order to decide whether the exception applies, therefore, it is essential first to identify and define the issue in the legal proceedings which requires disclosure, and then to decide whether, looking at the nature of that issue and the circumstances of the case, disclosure is necessary (*Maxwell* v *Pressdram Ltd* [1987] 1 WLR 298, per Kerr LJ at pp. 308–9). The mere fact that the information in question is relevant to the issue is not sufficient: disclosure must be necessary in the interests of justice (*Maxwell* v *Pressdram Ltd*, per Parker LJ, at p. 310). It will not always and inevitably be in the interests of justice to order disclosure of the source of information where the nature of that information suggests that the source has seen material protected by legal professional privilege (see *Saunders* v *Punch Ltd* [1998] 1 WLR 986).

In *X Ltd* v *Morgan-Grampian (Publishers) Ltd*, the House of Lords agreed with the dictum of Lord Diplock in *Secretary of State for Defence* v *Guardian Newspapers Ltd* that the word 'justice' is not used as the antonym of 'injustice', but held that the word should not be confined to the technical sense of the administration of justice in the course of legal proceedings in a court of law. It is 'in the interests of justice' that persons should be enabled to exercise important legal rights and to protect themselves from serious legal wrongs whether or not resort to proceedings in a court of law will be necessary to obtain these objectives. This construction emphasises the importance of the balancing exercise. It will not be sufficient, *per se*, for a party seeking disclosure of a source to show merely that he will be unable without disclosure to exercise the legal right or avert the threatened legal wrong. The judge must always weigh in the scales the importance of enabling the ends of justice to be attained in the circumstances of the particular case on the one hand against the importance of protecting the source on the other. It is only if satisfied that disclosure in the interests of justice is of such preponderating importance as to override the statutory privilege against disclosure that the threshold of necessity will be reached. Many factors will be relevant. Lord Bridge of Harwich gave the following illustrations. If the party seeking disclosure shows that his very livelihood depends on it, the case will be near one end of the spectrum; but if he merely seeks to protect a minor interest in property, the case will be at or near the other end of the spectrum. On the other side, one important factor will be the nature of the information obtained: the greater the legitimate public interest in the information, the greater will be the importance of protecting the source. Another perhaps more significant factor is the manner in which the information was obtained by the source: if the information was obtained legitimately this will enhance the importance of protecting the source. Conversely, if the information was obtained illegally, this will diminish the importance of protecting the source unless this factor is counterbalanced by a clear public interest in publication, as when the source has acted to expose iniquity.

Goodwin v *UK* (1996) 22 EHRR 123, a decision of the European Court of Human Rights, dealt with the same facts as those which were the subject of the decision in *X Ltd* v *Morgan-Grampian (Publishers) Ltd*, but under Article 10 of the European Convention on Human Rights. The tests applied by the European Court and the House of Lords were substantially the same, but the European Court came to a conclusion opposite to that reached by the House of Lords. The explanation may well be that put forward by Thorpe LJ in *Camelot Group plc* v *Centaur Communications Ltd* [1999] QB 124: the making of a value judgment on competing facts is very close to the exercise of a discretion, and the period of time between the decisions in London and Strasbourg was six years, a period during which standards fundamental to the performance of the balancing exercise may change materially.

Concerning the prevention of crime, disclosure will be ordered if shown to be necessary, either for the prevention of crime generally or for the prevention of a particular and identifiable future crime. See *Re an Inquiry under the Company Securities (Insider Dealing) Act 1985* [1988] AC 660. In this case, a journalist who had used confidential price-sensitive information about take-over bids was ordered to disclose his source to inspectors appointed by the Secretary of State to investigate suspected leaks of this kind, on the grounds that they needed the information to expose the leaking of official information and criminal insider trading, and to prevent such behaviour in the future. However, as in the case of the other exceptions, a claim under this head will succeed only if there is clear and specific evidence of 'necessity'. The party seeking disclosure should adduce evidence on matters such as the extent of his inquiries to identify the sources, whether he referred the matter to the police, and whether criminal investigation is the intended or likely outcome (see *X* v *Y* [1988] 2 All ER 648).

CONFIDENTIAL BUT NON-PRIVILEGED RELATIONSHIPS

At common law no privilege attaches to communications made in confidence except in **F9.8** the case of:

    (a) communications between a client and a legal adviser made for the purpose of the obtaining and giving of legal advice; and

    (b) communications between a client or his legal adviser and third parties, the dominant purpose of which was preparation for contemplated or pending litigation (see **F9.15** *et seq*.).

Although the courts have an inherent wish to respect the confidences which arise between doctor and patient, bankers and customers etc., if the question to be put to a witness is relevant and necessary in order that justice be done, the witness will be directed to answer (see, e.g., *A-G* v *Mulholland* [1963] 2 QB 477, per Lord Denning MR at pp. 489–90). Thus, no privilege exists to protect medical records or communications between doctor and patient (*Duchess of Kingston* (1776) 20 St Tr 355; *Gibbons* (1823) 1 C & P 97; *Wheeler* v *Le Marchant* (1881) 17 Ch D 675, at p. 681; *Hunter* v *Mann* [1974] QB 767; *McDonald* [1991] Crim LR 122; *Gayle* [1994] Crim LR 679). This remains the case, notwithstanding that the rule is regarded as unsatisfactory and one which the House of Lords has the power to alter (*D* v *National Society for the Prevention of Cruelty to Children* [1978] AC 171, per Lord Edmund-Davies at pp. 244–5). But see also *K* [1993] Crim LR 281, below. In the case of communications between priest and penitent, there is slender authority in favour of the existence of a privilege:

see *Hay* (1860) 2 F & F 4 (in which it was stressed that the priest was asked about a fact and not a communication) and the *obiter dictum* of Best CJ in *Broad* v *Pitt* (1828) 3 C & P 518: 'I, for one, will never compel a clergyman to disclose communications made to him by a prisoner; but if he chooses to disclose them I shall receive them in evidence.' However, most of such authority as there is, is against the existence of any such privilege (*Normanshaw* v *Normanshaw* (1893) 69 LT 468; *Wheeler* v *Le Marchant* (1881) 17 ChD 675, at p. 681; and the authorities cited in Stephen's *Digest of the Law of Evidence* (12th ed.), at p. 220). Similarly, there is no privilege for confidential communications between friends (*Duchess of Kingston's Case* (1776) 20 St Tr 355); or for documents in the possession of an accountant relating to his client's affairs (*Chantrey Martin & Co.* v *Martin* [1953] 2 QB 286). At common law there is no privilege for journalists who seek to conceal the identities of their sources of information (*A-G* v *Clough* [1963] 1 QB 773; *A-G* v *Mulholland* [1963] 2 QB 477). But see now the Contempt of Court Act 1981, s. 10, above. Concerning a court welfare officer's report, the appropriate court may give leave for it to be used in other proceedings if, after evaluating and balancing the need to maintain the confidentiality of the report against the need for its contents to be put in evidence for there to be a fair trial of the action, the court decides that the interests of justice require the confidentiality of the report to be released (*Brown* v *Matthews* [1990] Ch 662).

Although at common law no privilege attaches to confidential communications *per se*, in appropriate circumstances a party may be able to rely upon some other head of privilege, such as the privilege which attaches to communications made in the course of matrimonial conciliation (which has also been treated as a limb of public interest immunity: see *D* v *National Society for the Prevention of Cruelty to Children* [1978] AC 171, per Lords Hailsham and Simon at p. 226 and pp. 236–7 respectively). Alternatively, a claim to public interest immunity may succeed. Thus an interview with a child victim of a sexual offence, which is conducted on a confidential basis for therapeutic purposes, ought not to be disclosed, unless the interests of justice so require, but where the liberty of the subject is an issue and disclosure might be of assistance to an accused, a claim for disclosure will often be strong (*K (T.D.)* (1993) 97 Cr App R 342). Similarly immunity may be claimed for confidential documents relating to abortions carried out under the Abortion Act 1967 (*Morrow* v *DPP* [1994] Crim LR 58).

In the absence of consent to disclosure by a taxpayer, public interest immunity does attach to documents relating to his tax affairs in the hands of the Inland Revenue, because as a matter of public policy the State should not by compulsory powers obtain information from a citizen for one purpose and then use it for another; but no such immunity attaches to documents held by the taxpayer himself, or his agents, relating to his tax affairs (*Lonrho plc* v *Fayed (No. 4)* [1994] 1 All ER 870). A claim to public interest immunity may also succeed when the person claiming immunity is exercising a statutory function, the effective performance of which would be impaired by disclosure. See, e.g., *Lonrho Ltd* v *Shell Petroleum Co. Ltd* [1980] 1 WLR 627 (immunity granted in subsequent litigation for evidence given in confidence to the Bingham Inquiry into the operation of sanctions against Rhodesia) and contrast *Re Arrows Ltd (No. 4)* [1995] 2 AC 75. See also *Re Barlow Clowes Gilt Managers Ltd* [1992] Ch 208. The liquidators of a company are under no duty to assist directors of the company in defending criminal charges, by providing them with information given to the liquidators by third parties in circumstances of confidentiality and by assurances, express or implied, that it would be used only for the purpose of the liquidation. The provision of such information would jeopardise the proper and efficient functioning of the process of compulsory liquidation because of the danger that professional men would no longer cooperate with liquidators on a voluntary basis. However, whether the information in question constitutes 'material evidence' for the purposes of a witness summons is a question for the Crown

Court (see further *Clowes* [1992] 3 All ER 440 at **F9.1**). It has also been held, in *Umoh* (1986) 84 Cr App R 138, that although no privilege analogous to that between a lawyer and his client can arise to protect confidential communications about the substance of a legal aid application between a prison legal aid officer and a prisoner, such communications should attract public interest immunity, because a prisoner does not have the freedom to go to a solicitor's office, and if he seeks assistance from such an officer he is likely to disclose and discuss matters connected with the alleged offence. It is in the public interest that such discussions, save in exceptional circumstances, should remain confidential, or otherwise prisoners would be reluctant to take advantage of the scheme.

PRIVILEGED RELATIONSHIPS: GENERAL PRINCIPLES

Relevant and otherwise admissible evidence may be excluded on the grounds of either **F9.9** the privilege against self-incrimination (see **F9.10** to **F9.14**) or legal professional privilege (see **F9.15** to **F9.20**). The privilege whereby a married person could refuse to answer questions about communications made to him or her by the spouse during the marriage was abolished for criminal cases by the PACE 1984, s. 80(9) and sch. 7. The privilege whereby, in criminal proceedings, a married person could refuse to answer questions about intercourse with his or her spouse during the marriage, was repealed by s. 80(9) of the 1984 Act.

The following principles are of general application:

(a)   A person entitled to claim privilege may refuse to answer the question put or disclose the document sought. The judge should not balance the claim to privilege against the importance of the evidence in relation to the trial. But see *Rank Film Distributors Ltd* v *Video Information Centre* [1982] AC 380, per Lord Fraser at p. 445.

(b)   If a person entitled to claim privilege fails to do so or waives his privilege, no other person may object. The privilege is that of the witness, and neither party can take advantage from it. Thus, if a judge improperly rejects a claim to privilege made by a witness who is not a party to the proceedings, no appeal will lie, for there has been no infringement of the rights of the parties. In *Kinglake* (1870) 11 Cox CC 499, where a claim to privilege made by a prosecution witness on the basis that his evidence would tend to incriminate himself was overruled by the judge, it was not open to the accused to object that the witness's evidence had been improperly admitted.

(c)   A party seeking to prove a particular matter in relation to which his opponent or a witness claims privilege, is entitled to prove the matter by other evidence, if available (see **F9.20**).

(d)   No adverse inferences may be drawn against a party or witness claiming privilege (*Wentworth* v *Lloyd* (1864) 10 HL Cas 589).

PRIVILEGE AGAINST SELF-INCRIMINATION

Scope of Privilege

No witness is bound to answer questions in court (or to produce documents or things **F9.10** at trial) if to do so would, in the opinion of the judge, have a tendency to expose him to any criminal charge, penalty or forfeiture (of property) which the judge regards as reasonably likely to be preferred or sued for (*Blunt* v *Park Lane Hotel Ltd* [1942] 2 KB 253, per Goddard LJ at p. 257). The courts may substitute a different protection in place of the privilege when requiring a person to comply with a disclosure order, provided adequate protection is available, as when the prosecuting authorities unequivocally agree not to make use of the information (*AT&T Istel* v *Tully* [1993] AC 45). An affidavit sworn by a person in compliance with such an order may then be inadmissible against him in any subsequent criminal trial, but the Crown will not necessarily be prevented from using it to demonstrate his inconsistency and thus to impugn his credit (see *Martin* [1998] 2 Cr App R 385). (Concerning questions in cross-examination of the accused which tend to criminate him as to the offence charged, or to show that he has committed any offence other than that with which he is then charged, see provisos (e) and (f) to the Criminal Evidence Act 1898, s. 1, discussed in **F14**.) Penalties arise mainly under statutes relating to the revenue, and under EC regulations (see, e.g., *Rio Tinto Zinc Corporation* v *Westinghouse Electric Corporation* [1978] AC 547). 'Additional damages', which may be awarded under statutes for breach of copyright, are not penalties (*Rank Film Distributors Ltd* v *Video Information Centre* [1982] AC 380, at p. 425). A witness may not claim privilege on the basis that his answer to the question put would expose him to civil liability (Witnesses Act 1806). Nor does the privilege extend to answers which would expose the witness to criminal liability under foreign law (*King of the Two Sicilies* v *Willcox* (1851) 1 Sim NS 301; *Re Atherton* [1912] 2 KB 251, at p. 255). See also *Arab Monetary Fund* v *Hashim* [1989] 1 WLR 565.

Subject to any statutory exceptions (see **F9.14**), an agent, trustee or other fiduciary of a party may claim the privilege in an action brought against him by that party for breach of that duty (*Bishopsgate Investment Management Ltd* v *Maxwell* [1993] Ch 1).

Requirement of Real and Appreciable Danger

F9.11   If the fact of the witness being in danger be once made to appear, great latitude should be allowed to him in judging for himself the effect of any particular question, for a question which might appear at first sight a very innocent one, may, by affording a link in the chain of evidence, become the means of bringing home an offence to the witness. Subject to this reservation, the court, before acceding to a claim to privilege, should satisfy itself, from the circumstances of the case and the nature of the evidence which the witness is called to give, that there is a reasonable ground to apprehend real and appreciable danger to the witness with reference to the ordinary operation of the law in the ordinary course of things, and not a danger of an imaginary or insubstantial character. See *Boyes* (1861) 1 B & S 311, per Cockburn CJ, where a witness who had been handed a pardon was obliged to answer, notwithstanding the remote possibility of an impeachment by the House of Commons (because technically a pardon may not be pleaded in answer to an impeachment). In refusing protection, it seems that the court may also take into account the triviality of any charge likely to be brought. In *Rank Film Distributors Ltd* v *Video Information Centre* [1982] AC 380, a case concerning the application of the privilege to an *Anton Piller* order, Lord Fraser held (at p. 445) that protection should be refused, partly because the likelihood of prosecution under the Copyright Act 1956, s. 21, was too remote, but also because it would be 'unreasonable to allow the possibility of incrimination of such offences to obstruct disclosure of information which would be of much more value to the owners of the infringed copyright than any protection they might obtain from s. 21.' Protection may also be properly refused if the evidence against the witness is already so strong that, if proceedings are to be taken, they will be taken whether or not the witness answers: see, e.g., *Khan* v *Khan* [1982] 1 WLR 513, where the witness's conduct 'reeked of dishonesty', and evidence as to his use of the proceeds of a stolen cheque did not materially increase the risk of his prosecution for its theft.

Incrimination Must Be of Person Claiming Privilege

F9.12   In criminal cases, the privilege against self-incrimination is restricted to the person claiming it, and does not extend to questions the answers to which would tend to incriminate a spouse: see *Rio Tinto Zinc Corporation* v *Westinghouse Electric Corporation* [1978] AC 547, per Lord Diplock at p. 637, and *Pitt* [1983] QB 25, where the Court of Appeal, in holding that an accused's spouse, if she elects to testify, should be treated like any other witness, surely must have assumed that she cannot then claim privilege against the incrimination of her husband; and contrast *All Saints, Worcester (Inhabitants)* (1817) 6 M & S 194, per Bayley J at p. 201. There is no privilege against incriminating strangers (*Minihane* (1921) 16 Cr App R 38). A company may claim privilege in the same way as an individual (*Triplex Safety Glass Co. Ltd* v *Lancegaye Safety Glass (1934) Ltd* [1939] 2 KB 395). However, the privilege is that of the company and therefore does not extend to incrimination of its office holders (see *Rio Tinto Zinc Corporation* v *Westinghouse Electric Corporation* per Lord Diplock at pp. 637–8; *Sociedade Nacional de Combustiveis de Angola UEE* v *Lundqvist* [1991] 2 QB 310 per Beldam LJ at p. 336; and *Tate Access Floors Inc.* v *Boswell* [1991] Ch 512).

Necessity of Claiming Privilege

A witness may claim the privilege only after he has been sworn and the question put; he **F9.13** is not entitled to refuse to take the oath on the grounds of the privilege (*Boyle* v *Wiseman* (1855) 1 Exch 647). Although in practice a judge will often warn a witness of his right not to answer a question which might expose him to a criminal charge, in the absence of such a warning, the witness must claim the privilege himself (*Thomas* v *Newton* (1827) 2 C & P 606). The witness may claim the privilege at any stage of the proceedings, even if he has already answered, without objection, questions which he was not obliged to answer (*Garbett* (1847) 1 Den CC 236). If the witness answers without seeking the protection of the court, his answers may be used in the proceedings in question and in any subsequent criminal proceedings brought against him (*Sloggett* (1856) Dears CC 656; *Coote* (1873) LR 4 PC 599). However, if a judge wrongly denies a witness the protection of privilege, anything the witness is then compelled to say is treated as having been said involuntarily and will be excluded from the subsequent criminal proceedings (*Garbett* (1847) 1 Den CC 236).

Statutory Provisions Requiring Answers to Questions

Where a statute provides that questions must be answered in certain proceedings **F9.14** notwithstanding that the answers may incriminate the witness, provision may also be made for the answers to be inadmissible in any subsequent criminal proceedings. For example, under the Theft Act 1968, s. 31(1), which requires questions to be answered and orders to be complied with in proceedings for the recovery or administration of any property or dealing with property, notwithstanding that compliance may expose the witness or his spouse to a charge for an offence under the Theft Act 1968, the answers may not be used in proceedings for any such offence. Neither the revocation of the privilege nor the restriction on the use of the answers applies to non-Theft Act offences (*Sociedade Nacional de Combustiveis de Angola UEE* v *Lundqvist* [1991] 2 WLR 280). However, where to answer the question etc. would expose the relevant person to an offence under the Theft Act 1968 and he claims that it would also expose him to a non-Theft Act offence, the test concerning the latter offence is whether to answer the question etc. would create or increase the risk of proceedings for that offence, separate and distinct from its connection with the Theft Act offence. If the answer is no, there is no privilege, but if it is yes, then the privilege subsists in relation to the latter offence (*Renworth* v *Stephansen* [1996] 3 All ER 244). Under the Supreme Court Act 1981, s. 72, whereby the privilege is withdrawn in various proceedings relating to apprehended or actual infringement of rights pertaining to any intellectual property or any apprehended or actual passing off, s. 72(3) provides that answers compelled by reason of such withdrawal of privilege cannot be used in proceedings for certain offences disclosed or for the recovery of certain penalties, liability to which was disclosed. Under the Insolvency Rules 1986 (SI 1986 No. 1925), r. 6.175, a bankrupt at his public examination is required to answer all questions put, and, under the Insolvency Act 1986, s. 433, the written record of that examination may be used in evidence in any proceedings against the bankrupt (*Kansal* [1993] QB 244).

Under the Children Act 1989, s. 98, in any proceedings in which a court is hearing an application relating to the care, supervision or protection of a child, no one shall be excused from giving evidence on any matter or answering any question put in the course of his giving evidence on the grounds that to do so might incriminate him or his spouse of an offence. Under s. 98(2), a statement or admission made in such proceedings shall not be admissible in evidence against the person making it or his spouse in proceedings for an offence other than perjury. A 'statement or admission', for these purposes, includes a filed statement of the evidence which a party intends to adduce at the hearing, an oral admission made by a parent to a guardian ad litem (*Oxfordshire County Council v P* [1995] Fam 161) and, after the proceedings have started, an oral statement to a social worker carrying out the local authority's duties of investigation in a child protection case (*Cleveland County Council v F* [1995] 1 WLR 785). Both of these decisions, however, have since been doubted (see *Re G (A Minor) (Social Worker: Disclosure)* [1996] 1 WLR 1407).

In addition to express statutory removal of the privilege, statute may also abrogate the privilege by necessary implication or on its true construction. See, e.g., the Banking Act 1987, s. 42 (*Bank of England v Riley* [1992] 2 WLR 840), the Companies Act 1985, s. 434 and part XIV (*Re London United Investments plc* [1992] 2 All ER 842), and the Insolvency Act 1986, s. 236 (*Bishopsgate Investment Management Ltd v Maxwell* [1993] Ch 1, *Re Jeffrey S Levitt Ltd* [1992] 2 All ER 509 and *Re Arrows Ltd (No. 4)* [1995] 2 AC 75).

If a statute revokes the privilege without *any* restriction upon the use that may be made of the answers, the answers will not be treated as having been given involuntarily and may be used in any subsequent criminal proceedings (*Scott* (1856) Dears & B 47). It has been suggested that where statutory protection is lacking, evidence obtained from the accused pursuant to statute in the earlier proceedings may be excluded in any subsequent criminal proceedings if, in the court's discretion, its admission would be oppressive to the accused (*Overseas Programming Co. Ltd v Cinematographische Commerz-Anstalt and Induna Film GmbH* (1984) *The Times*, 16 May 1984, per French J). In *Re Arrows Ltd (No. 4)* it was held that documents obtained under the CJA 1987, s. 2(3), from liquidators, such as transcripts of oral examinations conducted under the Insolvency Act 1986, s. 236, may be excluded by the judge at the criminal trial under the PACE 1984, s. 78. Exclusion under s. 78, however, is likely to be rare. In *Staines* [1997] 2 Cr App R 426 answers obtained from the accused by Department of Trade and Industry inspectors, exercising coercive powers of interrogation, were admissible in subsequent criminal proceedings pursuant to the Financial Services Act 1986, s. 177(6). It was held that even if, following the decision of *Saunders v United Kingdom* (1997) 23 EHRR 313, this use of the answers amounted to the denial of a fair trial in breach of Article 6 of the European Convention on Human Rights, the answers should not be excluded under s. 78 of the 1984 Act because s. 177(6) amounted to a statutory presumption that admission of the evidence was fair, in the absence of special features which would make it unfair, and if it were to be excluded on the grounds of unfairness it would be excluded in every case, which would amount to at least a partial repeal by judicial decision of a statutory provision enacted by Parliament. See also *Saunders* [1996] 1 Cr App R 463.

When the YJCEA 1999, s. 59, is brought into force, it will amend a variety of enactments providing for the use of answers and statements given under compulsion so as to restrict, in criminal proceedings, their use in evidence against the persons giving them. The statutory provisions in question (together with the amendments) are set out in sch. 3 to the 1999 Act, and include, *inter alia*, the following provisions to which reference has already been made: the Insolvency Act 1986, s. 433, the Banking Act 1987, s. 42, the Companies Act 1985, s. 434, the CJA 1987, s. 2, and the Financial Services Act 1986, s. 177.

LEGAL PROFESSIONAL PRIVILEGE

Scope of Privilege

A client may, and his legal adviser must (subject to the client's waiver), refuse to give **F9.15** oral evidence or to produce documents relating to two types of confidential communication:

(a)   communications between the client and his legal adviser made for the purpose of enabling the client to obtain or the adviser to give legal advice about any matter, whether or not litigation was contemplated at the time (*Greenough v Gaskell* (1833) 1 My & K 98); and

(b)   communications between the client or his legal adviser and third parties, the sole or dominant purpose of which was to enable the legal adviser to advise or act in relation to litigation that was pending or in the contemplation of the client (*Waugh v British Railways Board* [1980] AC 521).

The privilege also covers items enclosed with or referred to in such communications and brought into existence (i) in connection with the giving of legal advice or (ii) in connection with or in contemplation of legal proceedings and for the purposes of such proceedings: see *R* [1994] 1 WLR 758 and the PACE 1984, s. 10(1)(c). Section 10, which is considered at **F9.17** and **F9.19**, purports to reflect the position at common law.

A legal adviser, for the purposes of legal professional privilege, includes, in addition to a solicitor or a barrister, employed advisers (*Alfred Crompton Amusement Machines Ltd v Customs and Excise Commissioners (No. 2)* [1974] AC 405) and overseas advisers (*Re Duncan* [1968] P 306).

In the case of communications between a client and his legal adviser, the communications must have been made either in the course of that relationship or with a view to its establishment (*Minter v Priest* [1930] AC 558). The privilege extends to instructions given by the client to the solicitor or by the solicitor to the barrister; to counsel's opinion taken by a solicitor (*Bristol Corporation v Cox* (1884) 26 ChD 678); to documents brought into existence for the purpose of instructing the lawyer and obtaining his advice (*Anderson v Bank of British Columbia* (1876) 2 ChD 644, per James LJ at p. 656); and, *arguably*, to copies of documents brought into existence for such a purpose, even if the originals are not privileged (see *The Palermo* (1883) 9 PD 6 and *Board of Inland Revenue, ex parte Goldberg* [1989] QB 267; but contrast *Chadwick v Bowman* (1886) 16 QBD 561 and *Dubai Bank Ltd v Galadari* [1990] Ch 98, in which the Court of Appeal cast doubt upon the judgment in *Ex parte Goldberg*). It seems that the privilege also extends to a selection of pre-existing documents, which are not in themselves privileged but which a solicitor has assembled or copied, where the selection betrays the trend of advice which the solicitor is giving the client (*Lyell v Kennedy (No. 3)* (1884) 27 ChD 1 and *Dubai Bank Ltd v Galadari (No. 7)* [1992] 1 WLR 106). The privilege does not extend, however, to records of time spent with a client on attendance notes, time sheets or fee records, because they are not communications between client and legal adviser, or to records of appointments, because they are not communications made in connection with legal advice (*Manchester Crown Court, ex parte Rogers* [1999] 1 WLR 832). Equally, the privilege does not cover attendance notes made by a solicitor recording what took place in court or in chambers in the presence of the parties on both sides (*Ainsworth v Wilding* [1900] 2 Ch 315); nor does it cover attendance notes recording meetings between the legal advisers of the parties on both sides (with or without their clients in attendance) or attendance notes recording telephone conversations between the parties, because all such notes are not communications between solicitor and client but merely records setting out what passed publicly between the two parties or their advisers (*Parry v News Group Newspapers Ltd* (1990) 140 NLJ 1719). The privilege attaches to communications between the client and his legal adviser for the purposes of obtaining and giving legal advice, and not to *facts* perceived by the legal adviser in the course of that relationship. Thus a solicitor may generally be compelled to give evidence as to his client's identity (*Studdy v Sanders* (1823) 2 Dow & Ry KB 347), handwriting (*Dwyer v Collins* (1852) 7 Exch 639) or mental capacity (*James v Godrich* (1844) 5 Moore PCC 16). See also *Brown v Foster* (1857) 1 H & N 736: a barrister who has seen a book produced at his client's trial may give evidence in subsequent proceedings as to its contents.

In the case of communications with third parties, the privilege can be claimed in respect of a document brought into existence before deciding to instruct a solicitor, provided that litigation was reasonably in prospect and the document was prepared for the sole or dominant purpose of enabling the solicitor to advise whether a claim should be made or resisted (*Re Highgrade Traders Ltd* [1984] BCLC 151). The dominant purpose for which a document was brought into existence should be ascertained by an objective view of all the evidence, taking into account the intention of not only its author, but also the person or authority under whose direction it was procured (*Guinness Peat Properties Ltd v Fitzroy Robinson Partnership* [1987] 1 WLR 1027). However, it should be noted that in *Secretary of State for Trade and Industry v Baker* [1998] Ch 356, Sir Richard Scott V-C doubted the correctness of the decisions in both *Re Highgrade Traders Ltd* and *Guinness Peat Properties Ltd v Fitzroy Robinson Partnership*.

The privilege does not extend to cover original documents, even if obtained by a party to litigation or his legal adviser for purposes of the litigation, if those documents did not come into existence for the purposes of the litigation. The only exception might be where the selection of such documents by the solicitor betrays the trend of the advice which he is giving the client (*Ventouris v Mountain* [1991] 1 WLR 607).

If a client communicates with a lawyer via a third party who is not merely an agent for communication, but someone who also has to make a preliminary decision on whether to refer the matter to the lawyer, no privilege will attach to the information supplied to the third party (*Jones v Great Central Railway Co.* [1910] AC 4).

Legal professional privilege survives the death of a client and vests in his or her personal representative or, once administration is complete, the person entitled to the deceased's estate. Such persons, therefore, are entitled to either claim or waive the privilege (*Molloy (Deceased)* [1997] 2 Cr App R 283).

Effect of Rules Governing Disclosure of Expert Evidence

F9.16   The common-law principles relating to communications with third parties must now be read subject to the Crown Court (Advance Notice of Expert Evidence) Rules 1987 and the Magistrates' Courts (Advance Notice of Expert Evidence) Rules 1997 (see **D12.21**, **D14.8** and **F10.14**). These rules make provision, subject to exceptions, for the disclosure of expert evidence between the parties to Crown Court and summary trials. Under r. 5 of each set of rules, a party who seeks to adduce expert evidence and who fails to comply with the requirements as to disclosure, shall not adduce that evidence in the proceedings without the leave of the court. Rule 5 does not *compel* disclosure: if an expert's report is unhelpful to the party obtaining it, he need not disclose it to his opponent, and the opponent cannot require him, his solicitor or the expert to give evidence as to the instructions given to the expert or the report he prepared. The expert may, however, be called by the opponent to give his opinion on the relevant facts in issue (see *Harmony Shipping Co. SA v Saudi Europe Line Ltd* [1979] 1 WLR 1380, applied in *King* [1983] 1 WLR 411) unless his opinion is based on his examination of an item which is itself privileged because it was brought into existence for the purpose of obtaining legal advice etc. (*R* [1994] 1 WLR 758, at **F9.17**).

Pre-Existing Documents and Items

At common law, a legal adviser (or third party) has no greater privilege than his client. **F9.17** Thus, a document that is not privileged in the hands of the client does not become privileged if given into the custody of a lawyer for the purposes of obtaining legal advice (or if sent by the lawyer to a third party in connection with pending or contemplated litigation). In *Peterborough Justice, ex parte Hicks* [1977] 1 WLR 1371, in which the client had sent a forged document to his solicitor for the purposes of obtaining legal advice, a warrant was ordered under the Forgery Act 1913, s. 16, to search the solicitor's premises and seize the document. On an application for certiorari to quash the search warrant, it was held that the document was not privileged in the hands of the solicitor because it would have been open to seizure in the hands of the client. Eveleigh J said (at p. 1374): '. . . it is the privilege of the client. . . . the solicitor holds the document in the right of his client and can assert in respect of its seizure no greater authority than the client himself . . . possesses.' In *Frank Truman Export Ltd* v *Metropolitan Police Commissioner* [1977] QB 952, Swanwick J expressed views to the contrary, but these dicta were doubted in *King* [1983] 1 WLR 411. In *King*, a case of conspiracy to defraud, an expert instructed by the defence was subpoenaed to produce sample handwriting sent to him by the accused's solicitors for examination (although the instructions sent to him and the report he produced were held to be privileged). But see also *R* [1994] 4 All ER 260, discussed below.

The principle established in *Peterborough Justice, ex parte Hicks* [1977] 1 WLR 1371 must now be read subject to the provisions of the PACE 1984. Section 9(2)(a) of the 1984 Act repeals previous legislation insofar as it authorised, by the issue of a warrant, searches for, *inter alia*, 'items subject to legal privilege' and 'special procedure material'. Section 8 of the 1984 Act provides for the issue of warrants of entry and search if, *inter alia*, a justice of the peace is satisfied that the material sought does not consist of or include 'items subject to legal privilege' or 'special procedure material'. Unless 'special procedure material' has been voluntarily disclosed by the person who acquired or created it (see *Singleton* [1995] 1 Cr App R 431), under s. 9(1), a constable may obtain access to such material for the purposes of a criminal investigation by making an application *inter partes* on notice to a circuit judge. Under s. 14(2), 'special procedure material', includes material, other than items subject to legal privilege, in the possession of a person who acquired or created it in the course of any trade, business, profession etc. and holds it subject to an express or implied undertaking to hold it in confidence. The phrase 'items subject to legal privilege' is defined in s. 10 of the Act, which, it has been held, is intended to reflect the position at common law (see the majority view in *Central Criminal Court, ex parte Francis* [1989] AC 346, at **F9.19**).

Police and Criminal Evidence Act 1984, s. 10

(1) Subject to subsection (2) below, in this Act 'items subject to legal privilege' means—
    (a) communications between a professional legal adviser and his client or any person representing his client made in connection with the giving of legal advice to the client;
    (b) communications between a professional legal adviser and his client or any person representing his client or between such an adviser or his client or any such representative and any other person made in connection with or in contemplation of legal proceedings and for the purposes of such proceedings; and
    (c) items enclosed with or referred to in such communications and made—
        (i) in connection with the giving of legal advice; or
        (ii) in connection with or in contemplation of legal proceedings and for the purposes of such proceedings,
when they are in the possession of a person who is entitled to possession of them.
(2) Items held with the intention of furthering a criminal purpose are not items subject to legal privilege.

In *Guildhall Magistrates' Court, ex parte Primlaks Holdings Co. (Panama) Inc.* [1990] 1 QB 261, it was held that loss of legal privilege by virtue of s. 10(2) does not mean that no express or implied undertaking to hold in confidence can exist. A solicitor's correspondence with his client (and its enclosures) will, if not privileged, fall squarely within s. 14. Thus if, on an application under s. 8, a justice cannot be satisfied that there are reasonable grounds for believing that the material sought does not include any items which are, prima facie, subject to legal privilege or any material which is, prima facie, special procedure material, he should refuse the application and leave the applicant to proceed under s. 9 so that the matter can be fully ventilated before a circuit judge, who will consider the matter *inter partes*. Likewise if the police are aware that what they seek includes items which are, prima facie, the subject of legal privilege, they should proceed under s. 9. It was further observed (at pp. 273–4) that documents of a client sent to a professional legal adviser under cover of privileged correspondence for the purpose of obtaining legal advice would not be within s. 10(1)(c) if they were pre-existing documents and were not made in connection with the giving of legal advice or in connection with or in contemplation of legal proceedings and for the purposes of such proceedings; but such pre-existing documents would be, prima facie, within s. 14(2), and therefore it would be open to the police to make an application under s. 9 of the Act in order to have access to them. However, a document forged by a solicitor or supplied to him by a fraudulent client does not constitute special procedure material because, from its nature, it could not have been acquired or created in the course of the profession of a solicitor (*Leeds Magistrates' Court, ex parte Dumbleton* [1993] Crim LR 866).

In *R* [1994] 1 WLR 758 it was held that the word 'made' in s. 10(1)(c) is used in a general sense and is wide enough to include the meaning 'brought into existence'. It was also held that where an item is protected from production under s. 10(1)(c), oral evidence of opinion based upon the item is also inadmissible. A scientist had carried out DNA tests at the request of the defence solicitors on a blood sample provided by the accused. It was held that s. 10(1)(c) applied not only so as to enable the defence to object to the sample being produced in evidence (because the sample was an item brought into existence for the purposes of legal proceedings), but also so as to prevent the prosecution from calling the scientist to give evidence of opinion based on the sample.

Information Helpful in Establishing Innocence

F9.18 In *Derby Magistrates' Court, ex parte B* [1996] AC 487 the appellant was acquitted of murder. His step-father was subsequently charged with the murder and at his committal proceedings, the appellant was called as a prosecution witness. Counsel for the defence sought to cross-examine the appellant on certain factual instructions that he had given to his solicitors when he had been charged with the offence. The appellant declined to waive his privilege. The magistrates then issued summonses, directing the appellant and his solicitor to produce documentary evidence of the instructions, on the basis that the public interest that all relevant and admissible evidence should be made available to the defence outweighed the public interest which protected confidential communications between a solicitor and a client. An application for judicial review of the decision was refused, but the House of Lords allowed the appeal. It was held that no exception should be allowed to the absolute and permanent nature of 'legal professional privilege' (a phrase used to refer to the privilege attaching to the solicitor-client relationship and not to all other forms of legal professional privilege: see *Re L (A Minor) (Police Investigation: Privilege)* [1997] AC 16) and therefore, overruling *Barton* [1973] 1 WLR 115 and *Ataou* [1988] 2 All ER 321, there could be no question of a balancing exercise of the kind performed by the magistrates. A client must be sure that what he tells his lawyer in confidence will never be revealed without his consent. Once any exception to the general rule is allowed, the client's confidence is necessarily lost. Therefore the documents in question, being protected by legal professional privilege, were immune from production. However, Lord Nicholls, who also rejected any question of a balancing exercise, observed that in cases where the client no longer has any interest in maintaining the privilege, the privilege is spent. His lordship preferred to reserve his final view on the point, being of the opinion that the point did not arise since the appellant had a legitimate interest in not disclosing material which might suggest that he had been improperly acquitted, but in a dictum which, it is submitted, has much to commend it, said (at p. 701):

> I would not expect a law, based explicitly on considerations of the public interest, to protect the right of a client when he has no interest in asserting the right and the enforcement of the right would be seriously prejudicial to another in defending a criminal charge or in some other way.

Communications in Furtherance of Crime or Fraud

Communications in furtherance of crime or fraud are a well-recognised exception to the **F9.19** principle of legal professional privilege (*Derby Magistrates' Court, ex parte B* [1996] AC 487, per Lord Lloyd at p. 509). In *Cox* (1884) 14 QBD 153 a solicitor was compelled to disclose communications with the accused, in which the accused had sought his advice in drawing up a bill of sale alleged to be fraudulent. Stephen J, delivering the judgment of the Court for Crown Cases Reserved, held that if a client applies to a legal adviser for advice intended to facilitate or to guide the client in the commission of a crime or fraud, the legal adviser being ignorant of the purpose for which his advice is sought, the communication between the two is not privileged. See also *Hayward* (1846) 2 Car & Kir 234 and *Smith* (1915) 11 Cr App R 229. The principle can be relied upon only if there is prima facie evidence that it was the client's intention to obtain advice in furtherance of his criminal or fraudulent purpose (*O'Rourke v Darbishire* [1920] AC 581). However, in order to prove the criminal purpose and override the claim to privilege, there is no requirement to produce extraneous evidence, i.e. beyond the communications themselves; if necessary, the court may look at the communications themselves to determine whether they came into existence in furtherance of such a purpose (*Governor of Pentonville Prison, ex parte Osman* [1990] 1 WLR 277 at pp. 309–10). The exception does apply if the legal adviser is aware of or is a party to the crime or fraud, but not if he merely volunteers a warning to his client that certain conduct could result in his being prosecuted (*Butler v Board of Trade* [1971] Ch 680). Fraud, for the purposes of the exception, is not limited to the tort of deceit, and includes all forms of fraud and dishonesty, such as fraudulent breach of trust, fraudulent conspiracy, trickery and sham contrivances, but does not cover the tort of inducing a breach of contract (*Crescent Farm (Sidcup) Sports Ltd v Sterling Offices Ltd* [1972] Ch 553, per Goff J at p. 565) or the torts of trespass and conversion (*Dubai Aluminium Co. Ltd v Al Alawi* [1999] 1 WLR 1964). 'Fraud', in this context, is used in a relatively wide sense. Thus privilege will not attach to legal advice on how to structure a transaction which has been devised to prejudice the interests of a creditor by putting assets beyond his reach (*Barclays Bank Plc v Eustice* [1995] 1 WLR 1238).

The exception is not confined to cases in which solicitors advise on or set up criminal or fraudulent transactions yet to be undertaken, but also covers criminal or fraudulent conduct undertaken for the purposes of acquiring evidence in, or for, litigation. Thus where documents have been generated by, or report on, conduct which constitutes a crime under the data protection legislation, and those documents are relevant to an issue in the proceedings, they will not be protected from disclosure by legal professional privilege (*Dubai Aluminium Co. Ltd v Al Alawi*).

Until recently, there appeared to be no common-law authority to the effect that a criminal intent on the part of a stranger to the relationship of a solicitor and client destroys the privilege of the client (see the speech of Lord Oliver, dissenting, in *Central Criminal Court, ex parte Francis* [1989] AC 346). Such authority as there was suggested the contrary: see, for example, *Banque Keyser Ullman SA v Skandia (UK) Insurance Co. Ltd* [1986] 1 Lloyd's Rep 336, in which it was held that the principle of *Cox* (1884) 14 QBD 153 does not extend to the correspondence between a solicitor and the victim of a fraudster. However, the decision of the majority of the House of Lords in *Ex parte Francis* now provides persuasive authority that the intention of furthering a criminal purpose may be that of the client, the solicitor or any other person. That case concerned the construction of the PACE 1984, s. 10(2), which provides that: 'Items held with the intention of furthering a criminal purpose are not items subject to legal privilege.' In *Snaresbrook Crown Court, ex parte DPP* [1988] QB 532, it was held, giving these words their natural meaning, that what is relevant is the intention of the person holding the items in question. However, in *Ex parte Francis*, a majority of the House, rejecting this construction, held that s. 10(2) was not intended to restrict the principle of *Cox* (1884) 14 QBD 153 to cases in which the legal adviser has the intention of furthering a criminal purpose, but *reflected the position at common law*, and therefore the intention to which it referred could be that of the person holding the document or any other person. On that basis it was held that no privilege attached to documents relating to the purchase of a property by a client and innocently held by a solicitor, because a third party, a relative of the client, intended them to be used to further his criminal purpose in laundering the proceeds of illegal drug trafficking. See also *Leeds Magistrates' Court, ex parte Dumbleton* [1993] Crim LR 866, in which a warrant was issued to search for and seize documents held by a solicitor and allegedly forged by him and another. It was held that the documents were not covered by s. 10(1) because the phrase 'made in connection with . . . legal proceedings' meant lawfully made, and did not extend to forged documents or copies thereof; in any event the items were held with the intention of furthering a criminal purpose — the word 'held' in s. 10(2) relating to the time at which the documents came into the possession of the person holding them.

Waiver of Privilege and the Criminal Justice and Public Order Act 1994, s. 34

F9.20   In *Condron* [1997] 1 WLR 827, the Court of Appeal gave the following guidance relating to legal professional privilege where an accused refuses to answer police questions on the advice of his solicitor. Communications between an accused and his solicitor prior to interviews by the police are subject to the privilege. If an accused gives as a reason for not answering that he has been advised by his solicitor not to do so, that advice does not amount to a waiver of privilege. But if the accused wishes to invite the court not to draw an adverse inference under the CJPO 1994, s. 34 (see **F19.4**), it is necessary to go further and state the basis or reason for the advice. This may well amount to a waiver of privilege so that the accused, or if his solicitor is also called, the solicitor, can be asked whether there were any other reasons for the advice, and the nature of the advice given, so as to explore whether the advice may also have been given for tactical reasons. However, it should be borne in mind that the information which the prosecution seek to draw from failure to mention facts in interview is that they have been subsequently fabricated. It is open to an accused to attempt to rebut this inference by showing that the relevant facts were communicated to a third party, usually the solicitor, at about the time of the interview. This does not involve waiver of privilege if it is the solicitor to whom the fact is communicated.

It is probably desirable that the judge should warn counsel, or the accused, that the privilege may be taken to have been waived if the accused gives evidence of the nature of the advice.

If the defence reveal the basis or reason for the solicitor's advice to the accused not to answer police questions, this will amount to a waiver of privilege whether the revelation is made by the accused or by the solicitor acting within the scope of his authority as agent on behalf of the accused, and whether the revelation is made in the course of pre-trial questioning, in evidence before the jury, or in evidence on the *voir dire* which is *not* repeated before the jury (*Bowden* [1999] 1 WLR 823).

Waiver of Privilege and Use of Secondary Evidence

Legal professional privilege prevents the giving of oral evidence or the production of **F9.21** documents by particular persons, namely the client, the legal adviser (or his clerk or agent) or third parties (in the case of protected communications between the client or his legal adviser and such third parties). If a privilege has been waived, because the contents of a privileged communication have become known to any other person, whether by overhearing a privileged conversation or by obtaining the original or a copy of a privileged document, that person may be compelled to give oral evidence in that regard or to produce the document or copy (see, in the case of copies of privileged documents, *Calcraft v Guest* [1898] 1 QB 759 and, in the case of originals, *Waugh v British Railways Board* [1980] AC 521 per Lord Simon at p. 536 and *Governor of Pentonville Prison, ex parte Osman* [1990] 1 WLR 277 at pp. 309–10). This principle applies not only if the privileged communication was disclosed by accident or error on the part of the client or his legal adviser, but also where it was obtained by improper or even criminal means on the part of his opponent (or some third party). But see also *ITC Film Distributors Ltd v Video Exchange Ltd* [1982] Ch 431, which is considered at **F2.9**. In *Tompkins* (1977) 67 Cr App R 181, a note from the accused to his counsel had been found on the floor of the court and handed to prosecuting counsel by a representative of his instructing solicitor. The contents of the note being in flat contradiction to an answer given by the accused in cross-examination, prosecuting counsel handed the note to the accused, and without referring to its contents asked the accused whether he adhered to the answer he had given. The judge ruled that the cross-examination was proper but that no direct reference should be made to the note. The accused then admitted the opposite of what he had said. The Court of Appeal held that counsel had been properly allowed to put questions in cross-examination on the basis of the contents of the note. In *Cottrill* [1997] Crim LR 56, applying *Tompkins*, it was held that a statement made by the accused to his solicitors, and voluntarily sent by them to the prosecution without his knowledge or consent, could be used in cross-examination, if his evidence did not accord with the account given in the statement, subject to the provisions of the PACE 1984, s. 78. See also the Code of Conduct of the Bar, annexe F, general standards, paras 7.1 to 7.3.2, discussed at **D12.11**.

In civil proceedings, if the contents of a privileged communication have become known to an opponent otherwise than by waiver of the privilege, then although he may prove them in the litigation by secondary evidence, the court may, at the request of the person in whom the privilege is vested, and in the exercise of its discretion, grant an injunction to restrain the opponent from disclosing or making any use of the confidential information contained in the communication (*Lord Ashburton v Pape* [1913] 2 Ch 469; *Goddard v Nationwide Building Society* [1987] QB 670; *Guinness Peat Properties Ltd v Fitzroy Robinson Partnership* [1987] 1 WLR 1027). Although it has been observed that there is much to be said for allowing the spirit of *Lord Ashburton v Pape* to prevail in criminal as well as civil proceedings (see *Goddard v Nationwide Building Society* per Nourse LJ at p. 686), the principle cannot be used in a *public* prosecution to prevent the prosecution from tendering relevant evidence. In *Butler v Board of Trade* [1971] Ch 680 the plaintiff, who was being prosecuted by the Board of Trade for alleged offences under the Companies Act 1948, sought a declaration that the Board was not entitled to produce in evidence at the criminal trial a copy of a letter from the plaintiff's solicitor to the plaintiff, which had been accidentally included in papers handed over to the Official Receiver. It was held that, although the original letter was privileged, the copy was admissible in the criminal proceedings under the rule in *Calcraft v Guest* [1898] 1 QB 759, the principle established in *Lord Ashburton v Pape* being inapplicable. Goff J said (at p. 690):

. . . it would not be a right or permissible exercise of the equitable jurisdiction in confidence to make a declaration at the suit of the accused in a public prosecution in effect restraining the Crown from adducing admissible evidence relevant to the crime with which he is charged. It is not necessary for me to decide whether the same result would obtain in the case of a private prosecution, and I expressly leave that point open.

SECTION F10: OPINION EVIDENCE

GENERAL RULE

The general rule is that witnesses may only give evidence of facts they personally **F10.1** perceived and not evidence of their opinion, i.e. evidence of inferences drawn from such facts. The assumption that it is possible to distinguish fact from inference is arguably false (see Thayer, *A Preliminary Treatise on Evidence at the Common Law* (1898), p. 524), but the distinction has given rise to little case law. In *Meads* [1996] Crim LR 519, it was held that evidence of tests showing the speed at which the handwritten notes of disputed interviews had been made, and whether they could have been written in the time claimed by officers, was no more opinion evidence than evidence of the timing of a given journey in order to test an alibi. The inferences to be drawn from such evidence were for the jury.

There are two exceptions to the general rule:

(a) Non-experts. A statement of opinion on any matter not calling for expertise, if made by a witness as a way of conveying relevant facts personally perceived by him, is admissible as evidence of what he perceived.

(b) Experts. Subject to compliance with the Crown Court (Advance Notice of Expert Evidence) Rules 1987 and the Magistrates' Courts (Advance Notice of Expert Evidence) Rules 1997 (see **D12.21**, **D14.8** and **F10.14**), a statement of opinion on any relevant matter calling for expertise may be made by a witness qualified to give such an expert opinion.

NON-EXPERT OPINION EVIDENCE

A statement of opinion may be given by a witness, on a matter not calling for expertise, as **F10.2** a compendious means of conveying facts perceived by him. Thus an identification witness is not required to give a description of the offender or some other person, leaving it to the tribunal of fact to decide whether that description fits the accused or other person identified, but may express his opinion that the accused (or other person) is the person he saw on the occasion in question. Likewise, a non-expert may give evidence of opinion to identify an object (see *Lucas* v *Williams & Sons* [1892] 2 QB 113: a picture), handwriting with which he is familiar (see *Doe d Mudd* v *Suckermore* (1836) 7 LJ QB 33, *Slaney* (1832) 5 C & P 213, *Rickard* (1918) 13 Cr App R 40) or a voice which he recognises (*Deenik* [1992] Crim LR 578) or with which he is familiar (*Robb* (1991) 93 Cr App R 161). Other examples include evidence of a person's age (*Cox* [1898] 1 QB 179) or the general appearance of his state of health, mind or emotion; the speed of a vehicle (see the Road Traffic Regulation Act 1984, s. 89(2)); the state of the weather; and the passage of time. In *Beckett* (1913) 8 Cr App R 204, in which the value of a plate glass window was in issue, it was held that its value had been established by the evidence of a non-expert, who gave his opinion that it was worth more than five pounds. It is submitted, however, that non-expert opinion evidence should not be received on the value of less commonplace objects or objects such as antiques and works of art, the valuation of which calls for expertise. On a charge of driving when unfit through drink, the fitness of the accused to drive is a matter calling for expertise, though a non-expert may give evidence of his impression as to whether the accused had taken drink, provided he describes the facts on the basis of which he formed that impression (*Davies* [1962] 1 WLR 1111). See also *Neal* [1962] Crim LR 698. Although scientific evidence is not always required to identify a prohibited drug, police officers' descriptions of a drug must be sufficient to justify the inference that it was the drug alleged (*Hill* (1993) 96 Cr App R 456). The evidence of a non-expert is not admissible in support of an accused's plea of insanity (*Loake* (1911) 7 Cr App R 71, per Lord Alverstone CJ).

In *Davies* [1962] 1 WLR 1111, one of the reasons given by Lord Parker CJ as to why the non-expert could not give his opinion on whether the accused, as a result of the drink he had taken, was unfit to drive a car, was that this was 'the very matter which the court itself has to determine'. However, the common-law rule preventing any witness from expressing his opinion on an ultimate issue, i.e. one of the very issues to be determined by the court, appears to be virtually obsolete (see the Eleventh Report of the Criminal Law Revision Committee 1972 (Cmnd 4991, para. 270)). In *Beckett* (1913) 8 Cr App R 204, the value of the window was the very issue to be decided by the court. As to expert opinion evidence on ultimate issues, see **F10.12**.

EXPERT OPINION EVIDENCE

Competence of Expert Witnesses

F10.3   Occasionally statute prescribes the qualifications which a person must possess if he is to give expert opinion evidence on a particular matter. For example, a jury shall not acquit on the ground of insanity, or make a determination of unfitness to plead, except on the evidence of two or more registered medical practitioners, at least one of whom is approved by the Secretary of State as having special experience in the diagnosis or treatment of mental disorder (Criminal Procedure (Insanity and Unfitness to Plead) Act 1991, ss. 1(1) and 2). Subject to provisions of this kind, whether a witness is properly qualified in the subject calling for expertise is a question for the court. Such competence or skill may stem from formal study or training, experience, or both. In *Oakley* (1979) 70 Cr App R 7 a police officer with qualifications and experience in accident investigation was allowed to give evidence, on a charge of causing death by dangerous driving, as to how an accident occurred. Compare, *sed quaere*, *Somers* [1963] 1 WLR 1306, in which a doctor was allowed to prove the conversion of figures in an analyst's certificate into the amount of alcohol consumed by the accused, although not an expert in such conversion, and to prove the rate of bodily destruction of alcohol, having refreshed his memory from a BMA publicaton. See also *Inch* (1989) 91 Cr App R 51, in which it was held that a medical orderly with much experience in the treatment of cuts and lacerations was insufficiently qualified to express an opinion as to whether an inch-long cut to the forehead had been caused by a blunt instrument rather than a head-butt. In *Silverlock* [1894] 2 QB 766 a solicitor, who had for 10 years studied handwriting and on several occasions compared handwriting professionally, was allowed to give expert evidence that an advertisement was in the handwriting of the accused. Affirming the conviction, Lord Russell CJ said (at p. 771):

> There is no decision which requires that the evidence of a man who is skilled in comparing handwriting, and who has formed a reliable opinion from past experience, should be excluded because his experience has not been gained in the way of his business. It is, however, really unnecessary to consider this point; for it seems . . . in the present case that the witness was not only *peritus*, but was *peritus* in the way of his business.

In *Robb* (1991) 93 Cr App R 161, an experienced lecturer in phonetics, who held a PhD in that subject, was allowed to give expert opinion evidence that the voice on two different tapes was the voice of the same person, notwithstanding that his technique, which was to listen to the two tapes for comparisons and to pay close attention to voice quality, pitch and pronunciation, was not generally respected in the field of phonetics because it was not supplemented and verified by acoustic analysis based on physical measurement of resonance and frequency.

As to the competence of a witness to give opinion evidence on a point of foreign law, see **F10.9**.

Matters Calling for Expertise

Expert opinion evidence may only be received on a subject calling for expertise, which a **F10.4** lay person, such as a magistrate or a juror, could not be expected to possess to a degree sufficient to understand the evidence given in the case unaided. If the tribunal of fact can form its own opinion without the assistance of an expert, the matter being within its own experience and knowledge, expert opinion evidence is inadmissible because it is unnecessary (*Turner* [1975] QB 834, per Lawton LJ at p. 841, applied in *Loughran* [1999] Crim LR 404). Thus a psychologist or other medical expert will not be permitted to give an opinion on the likely deterioration of memory of an ordinary witness (*Browning* [1995] Crim LR 227). In some cases, however, it seems that jurors may receive assistance on a matter within their own experience and knowledge if it is provided by someone who has had more time and better facilities to consider that matter than it would be practicable to afford to them (see *Clare* [1995] 2 Cr App R 333, where an officer who had viewed a video-recording about 40 times, examining it in slow motion, and rewinding and replaying it as frequently as was necessary, was permitted to give evidence on whether persons shown on the recording committing violent acts were the accused).

The subjects calling for expertise, which are so diverse as to defy comprehensive classification, include a variety of medical, psychiatric, scientific and technological matters, and questions relating to standards of professional competence. Specific examples include accident investigation; ballistics; blood tests; breath tests and blood-alcohol levels (sometimes including back-calculations thereof, i.e. calculation of the amount of alcohol eliminated in the period between driving and providing a specimen, in order to show that the level was above the prescribed limit at the time of driving: see *Gumbley* v *Cunningham* [1989] AC 281); forgeries; handwriting identification (including the analysis of indented impressions of handwriting, left on one document as a result of writing on another, and revealed by Electrostatic Detection Apparatus (ESDA): see *Wellington* [1991] Crim LR 543); fingerprint identification; voice identification; identification by facial mapping (but only where such evidence would assist the jury: see *Stockwell* (1993) 97 Cr App R 260 and *Hookway* [1999] Crim LR 750); facial identification by video superimposition (see *Clarke* [1995] 2 Cr App R 425); genetic fingerprinting (the technique whereby a human cell taken from a sample of blood, saliva, semen or hair is analysed to reveal a person's DNA or genetic 'fingerprint' — see **F18.26**); insanity; automatism; diminished responsibility; and the competence of a medical practitioner (see *Whitehead* (1848) 3 Car & Kir 202: expert opinion evidence as to the state of knowledge and skill of a physician as shown by his treatment of the case in question).

States of Mind

As to the need for expert evidence to prove insanity, see **A3.12**, **D10.10** and **F10.3**. On **F10.5** the issue of diminished responsibility, the Court of Appeal in *Dix* (1981) 74 Cr App R 306, applying a dictum in *Byrne* [1960] 2 QB 396 at p. 402, said (at p. 311): 'while the Homicide Act 1957, s. 2(1) does not in terms require that medical evidence be adduced in support of a defence of diminished responsibility, it makes it a practical necessity if that defence is to begin to run at all.' As to automatism, see *Smith* [1979] 1 WLR 1445. The accused was convicted of murder by stabbing. The defence was automatism, by sleepwalking. The prosecution, in order to show that this defence was a recently conceived idea, obtained leave to cross-examine the accused about interviews which he had with two psychiatrists while in custody, and to call the psychiatrists to give their views on the defence being run. On appeal it was argued that, since there was no question of insanity or diminished responsibility, the question of automatism should be decided by the jury in the light of their own experience, and unassisted by expert medical evidence. Rejecting this argument, the Court of Appeal held that the type of automatism in question was not something within the realm of the ordinary juror's experience but a matter on which the jury should not be deprived of expert assistance. See also *Hill* v *Baxter* [1958] 1 QB 277, at p. 285. Concerning the defence of duress by threats, expert evidence is admissible for the purposes of the subjective limb of the test, provided that the mental condition or abnormality in question is outside the knowledge and experience of laymen, but inadmissible for the purposes of the objective limb (*Hegarty* [1994] Crim LR 353; cf. *Horne* [1994] Crim LR 584 and *Hurst* [1995] 1 Cr App R 82). Where psychiatric injury is relied on as the basis for an allegation of assault occasioning actual bodily harm, and the matter is not admitted by the defence, the Crown should call expert evidence to prove the injury; in the absence of such evidence the question whether the assault occasioned such injury should not be left to the jury (*Chan-Fook* [1994] 1 WLR 689, applied in *Morris* [1998] 1 Cr App R 386).

In appropriate circumstances, expert medical evidence may be admissible on the question of the effect of a medical abnormality upon intent. Thus in *Toner* (1991) 93 Cr App R 382, a physician gave evidence that the accused had been suffering from a minor hypoglycaemic state caused by the ingestion of food after a prolonged fast. It was held that the defence had been improperly prevented from asking the witness what the effect of that minor degree of hypoglycaemia would be on the ability to make judgments or to form specific intents. The Court of Appeal held that there is no distinction between medical evidence relating to hypoglycaemia and its possible effect upon intent, and medical evidence as to the effect of a drug upon intent: both are matters outside the ordinary experience of jurors who cannot bring to bear their own judgment without the assistance of expert evidence. Subject to cases of this kind, however, and except in the case of an accused who comes into the class of mental defective, expert psychiatric evidence is not admissible on the issue of whether the accused did, or did not, have the required *mens rea*. In *Chard* (1971) 56 Cr App R 268 the Court of Appeal held that the judge, in a murder trial, had properly refused a defence application to call a medical witness to give evidence about the accused's intent to kill or do grievous bodily harm. Roskill LJ, giving the judgment of the court, held (at pp. 270–1) that, had the accused been supposedly abnormal, e.g., suffering from insanity or diminished responsibility, the jury would have been entitled to the benefit of expert evidence; but since the accused was entirely normal, the question of his intention was a matter which the jury were well able, by their ordinary experience, to judge for themselves. See also *Reynolds* [1989] Crim LR 220 and, in the case of adolescents, *Coles* [1995] 1 Cr App R 157. Similarly, in *Masih* [1986] Crim LR 395, a case of rape in which the accused suffered from no psychiatric illness, but had an intelligence quotient of 72, just above the level of subnormality, on the question of whether he knew the complainant was not consenting, or was reckless as to whether she consented, psychiatric evidence as to his state of mind, intelligence and ability to appreciate the situation was held to be inadmissible. Upholding the ruling, the Court of Appeal held that, generally speaking, if an accused comes into the class of mental defective, with an IQ of 69 or below, then insofar as the defectiveness is relevant to an issue, expert evidence may be admitted, provided that it is confined to an assessment of the accused's IQ and an explanation of any relevant abnormal characteristics (in order to enlighten the jury on a matter that is abnormal and outside their experience). However, if an accused is within the scale of normality, albeit at the lower end, as was the appellant, expert evidence should generally be excluded. Compare *Hall* (1987) 86 Cr App R 159, on the question of whether a person is defective within the meaning of the Sexual Offences Act 1956, s. 45 ('a person suffering from a state of arrested or incomplete development of mind which includes severe impairment of intelligence and social functioning'). The appellant was convicted of two offences of indecent assault contrary to s. 14 of the 1956 Act. The victim was said to have a mental age of nine or 10 and an IQ of 53, and the prosecution case was that the victim was a defective and incapable of consent under s. 14(4). The Court of Appeal held that, although expert evidence was admissible to establish the extent of the victim's intelligence, it could not accept that an expert's opinion that a woman of, say, 30, with the intelligence of a girl of five was not severely impaired was of any real weight, if indeed admissible at all. If, having heard such evidence, the jury observed the victim happily playing with toys suitable for a child of five, unable to cope with toys for slightly older girls, and able to converse only like a child of five, the expert's opinion could not be regarded as preferable to the observations of the jury.

In *Wood* [1990] Crim LR 264, the accused, charged with murder, raised the partial defence under Homicide Act 1957, s. 4, of the unsuccessful execution of a suicide pact. In support of this defence, and relying upon an analogy with diminished responsibility, the defence sought unsuccessfully to introduce psychiatric evidence to the effect that the accused suffered from a personality disorder. Refusing leave to appeal, it was held that whereas the defence of diminished responsibility was founded on the existence of some abnormality of mind, in the case of a suicide pact, once the killing had been proved, the questions for the jury are whether there was such a pact and, if so, whether at the time of the killing the accused was acting in pursuance thereof and had the settled intention of dying in pursuance thereof. The Homicide Act 1957, s. 2, introduced no medical or mental tests into the resolution of these questions and therefore psychiatric evidence was no more or less relevant to their solution than it was to the many other questions of fact which juries have to decide. That the applicant had a personality which was to some extent abnormal and liable to give way to excesses of behaviour under stress was not something outside the ordinary experience of the average juror.

Psychiatric evidence is inadmissible in order to establish that the accused was likely to have been provoked. In *Turner* [1975] QB 834 the Court of Appeal upheld the refusal of a trial judge to allow the defence to call a psychiatrist, on the issues of credibility and provocation, to prove that the accused had had a deep emotional relationship with the victim, which was likely to have caused an explosive release of blind rage after her confession of infidelity to him, and that subsequent to the killing he had behaved like someone suffering from profound grief. The court held that these were matters well within ordinary human experience and upon which the jury required no expert assistance. The evidence was not admissible on the issue of provocation, therefore, and the same reasoning prevented its admission on the issue of credibility. *Sed quaere*, whether expert evidence might not be admitted on an issue of provocation, where the accused suffers from some mental abnormality (*Camplin* [1978] AC 705). *Turner* was distinguished in *McDonald* [1991] Crim LR 122. In that case evidence was adduced of an out-of-court statement made by the accused explaining why he had killed the victim, an explanation which was sufficient to lay a foundation for the defence of provocation. Subsequently, in the course of a psychiatric examination, the accused admitted that the explanation was invented. It was held that it was not unfair for the psychiatrist to give evidence of the admission, because it related to a factual matter, not a medical issue.

Psychiatric evidence is also inadmissible on the question of the truth of a confession made by an accused who, although he might have an abnormal personality, such as a histrionic personality disorder characterised by emotional superficiality and impulsive behaviour when under stress, does not suffer from mental illness and is not below normal intelligence. The jury requires no expert assistance to decide such a question (*Weightman* (1990) 92 Cr App R 291). However, the expert evidence of a psychiatrist or psychologist is admissible on the issue of the reliability or truth of a confession if it is to the effect that no reliance can be placed on the confession because the accused was suffering from a personality disorder so severe as properly to be categorised as a mental disorder (*Ward* [1993] 1 WLR 619). See also, as to the admissibility of psychiatric evidence on a *voire dire* to determine the admissibility of a confession, *Everett* [1988] Crim LR 826 and *Raghip* (1991) *The Times*, 9 December 1991 and compare *Heaton* [1993] Crim LR 593.

Credibility

F10.6   Medical evidence is admissible to show that a witness suffers from some disease or defect or abnormality of mind that affects the reliability of his evidence. Such evidence is not confined to a general opinion of the unreliability of the witness but may give all the matters necessary to show, not only the foundation of and reasons for the diagnosis, but also the extent to which the credibility of the witness is affected. (*Toohey* v *Metropolitan Police Commissioner* [1965] AC 595, per Lord Pearce at p. 609)

See further **F7.23**. Subject to this, it is only in exceptional cases that psychologists and psychiatrists may be called to prove the probability of the accused's veracity. A rare example is *Lowery* v *The Queen* [1974] AC 85. L and K were charged with an apparently motiveless murder, the circumstances being that one or both of them must have committed the offence. Each blamed the other for the crime. The Privy Council held that the trial judge had properly permitted K to call a psychologist, who had carried out personality tests on both L and K, to show that K's version of events was more probable than that of L, since, compared to K, L's character and disposition were such that he was more likely to have committed the offence. Commenting upon this decision in *Turner* [1975] QB 834, Lawton LJ said (at p. 842):

> In every case what is relevant and admissible depends on the issues raised in that case. In *Lowery* v *The Queen* the issues were unusual; and the accused to whose disadvantage the psychologist's evidence went had in effect said before it was called that he was not the sort of man to have committed the offence. In giving the judgment of the Board, Lord Morris of Borth-y-Gest said, at p. 103:

>> The only question now arising is whether in the special circumstances above referred to it was open to King in defending himself to call Professor Cox to give the evidence that he gave. The evidence was relevant to and necessary for his case which involved negativing what Lowery had said and put forward; in their lordships' view in agreement with that of the Court of Criminal Appeal [of Victoria] the evidence was admissible.

> We adjudge *Lowery* v *The Queen* to have been decided on its special facts. We do not consider that it is an authority for the proposition that in all cases psychologists and psychiatrists can be called to prove the probability of the accused's veracity. If any such rule was applied in our courts, trial by psychiatrists would be likely to take the place of trial by jury and magistrates. We do not find that prospect attractive and the law does not at present provide for it.

In *Rimmer* [1983] Crim LR 250, the two accused were charged with murder, and each blamed the other. On the basis of a medical report, counsel for B cross-examined R, suggesting to him that he had a history of mental illness and that he had killed the victim in a fit of uncontrollable temper to which he was accustomed. The Court of Appeal upheld the ruling of the trial judge that R was not entitled to call medical evidence to establish that he was not, and never had been, mentally ill. See also *Miller* [1952] 2 All ER 667, *Neale* (1977) 65 Cr App R 304, and *Bracewell* (1978) 68 Cr App R 44.

As a matter of principle, evidence produced by the administration of some mechanical, chemical or hypnotic truth test on a witness is inadmissible to show the veracity or otherwise of that witness (*Fennell* v *Jerome Property Maintenance Ltd* (1986) *The Times*, 26 November 1986). The previous statements of the witness are not only inadmissible hearsay, but insofar as they are consistent with his testimony, inadmissible as evidence of consistency under the rule against previous self-serving statements (see **F6.13**).

Handwriting

F10.7   Handwriting may be identified by a non-expert familiar with the handwriting in question (see *Doe d Mudd* v *Suckermore* (1836) 5 A & E 703, and *Slaney* (1832) 5 C & P 213). The witness's knowledge, however, must not have been acquired for the express purpose of qualifying him to testify at the trial (*Crouch* (1850) 4 Cox CC 163). An expert should be called if there is to be a comparison of the 'disputed writing' with specimen handwriting proved or admitted to have been written by the person in question, under the Criminal Procedure Act 1865, s. 8 (*Tilley* [1961] 1 WLR 1309; *Harden* [1963] 1 QB 8). Such expert evidence is admissible under s. 8 even if the expert has not seen the original 'disputed writing' (e.g., because it is lost), but has made his comparison with a photocopy of the original (*Lockheed-Arabia* v *Owen* [1993] QB 806). See further **F18**. As to the standard of proof required to establish the genuineness of specimen handwriting, see *Ewing* [1983] QB 1039 and *Angeli* [1979] 1 WLR 26.

Obscenity

In the normal case, the issues of indecency or obscenity should be determined by the **F10.8** jury without expert assistance. In *Stamford* [1972] 2 QB 391, a charge of dispatching through the post packets containing indecent articles contrary to the Post Office Act 1953, s. 11, the Court of Appeal held that whether a particular article was 'indecent or obscene' was a matter for the jury, without the assistance of persons who may have views on the matter or might be able to speak as to the effect of the article in question, and the trial judge had properly refused to allow the defence to call evidence to explain the ordinary meaning of those words. Likewise, in *Anderson* [1972] 1 QB 304, Lord Widgery CJ said (at p. 313) that in the ordinary run of the mill cases, the issue 'obscene or no' under the Obscene Publications Act 1959 must be tried without the assistance of expert evidence. His lordship said that *DPP* v *A and BC Chewing Gum Ltd* [1968] 1 QB 159 'should be regarded as highly exceptional and confined to its own circumstances, namely, a case where the alleged obscene matter was directed at very young children, and was of itself of a somewhat unusual kind'. In the latter case the accused were charged with publishing for gain obscene battle cards (which were sold together with packets of bubble gum), contrary to the Obscene Publications Act, s. 2(1) and the Obscene Publications Act 1964, s. 1(1). The Divisional Court held that the magistrates had improperly prevented the prosecution from introducing evidence of experts in child psychiatry as to the likely effect of the cards on children. Lord Parker CJ held that, when considering the effect of something on an adult, an adult jury may be able to judge just as well as an adult witness; but when one is dealing with children of different age groups and children from five upwards, any jury, and any justices, need all the help they can get as to the effect on different children. See also *Skirving* [1985] QB 819, a prosecution arising out of the publication of a book entitled 'Attention Coke Lovers. Free Base. The Greatest Thing Since Sex', which contained explanations, instructions and 'recipes' on how to make use of cocaine to maximum effect. The Court of Appeal held that expert evidence on the characteristics of cocaine and the effects of the various methods of ingesting the drug was admissible, because it was outside the experience of the ordinary person, and only when equipped with such information would the jury be in a position to decide whether the publication had a tendency to deprave and corrupt.

Expert opinion evidence is also admissible on questions of a literary, artistic or scientific nature in relation to the defence of 'public good' under the Obscene Publications Act 1959, s. 4 (see s. 4(2)).

Foreign Law

Points of foreign law of any jurisdiction other than that of England and Wales are **F10.9** questions of fact to be decided on the evidence by the judge (Administration of Justice Act 1920, s. 15: see also **F1.20**). Thus, if there has been an English decision on a point of foreign law and the same point subsequently arises again, it must be decided on new evidence (*M'Cormick* v *Garnett* (1854) 5 De GM & G 278). The general rule is that the law of a foreign country, whether written or not, must be proved by the testimony of a competent expert, by the witnesses statement of such an expert (if admissible), or on the basis of a statement of agreed facts pursuant to CJA 1967, s. 10 (*Ofori* (1994) 99 Cr App R 223). If the expert witnesses agree on a point of foreign law, the court is not entitled to reject their evidence and to conduct its own research by referring to textbooks and foreign law reports (*Bumper Development Corporation Ltd* v *Commissioner of Police of the Metropolis* [1991] 1 WLR 1362). The expert may refresh his memory from foreign law books, but the law itself is proved by his oral evidence (*Sussex Peerage Case* (1844) 11 Cl & F 85). A witness is competent for these purposes if he is a practitioner in the relevant jurisdiction (*Baron de Bode's Case* (1845) 8 QB 208). There is old authority that a practitioner from the jurisdiction in question should always be called (*Bristow* v *Sequeville* (1850) 5 Exch 275). However, a witness has been held to be suitably qualified for these purposes if he is:

(a) a former practitioner in the relevant jurisdiction (*Re Duke of Wellington* [1947] Ch 506);
(b) a person qualified to practise in the relevant jurisdiction, even if he has not done so (*Barford* v *Barford and McLeod* [1918] P 140); or
(c) a person who has acquired the appropriate expertise by academic study (*Brailey* v *Rhodesia Consolidated Ltd* [1910] 2 Ch 95, reader in Roman-Dutch law to the Council of Legal Education); as an embassy official (*In the Goods of Dost Aly Khan* (1889) 6 PD 6); or in the course of a non-legal business such as banking (*De Beéche* v *South American Stores (Gath and Chaves) Ltd* [1935] AC 148).

There are two exceptions to the general rule:

(a) The Evidence (Colonial Statutes) Act 1907, s. 1, and the Colonial Laws Validity Act 1865, s. 6, provide for proof of colonial statutes etc.; and English courts may construe such statutes without accompanying expert evidence (see the authorities cited in *Jasiewicz* v *Jasiewicz* [1962] 1 WLR 1426).
(b) The British Law Ascertainment Act 1859 provides that an English court may state a case on a point of foreign law for the opinion of a superior court in another part of Her Majesty's dominions, and that the opinion thus produced is admissible evidence on the point of law in question.

Competence of Witnesses

F10.10 The test of whether a child is capable of giving 'intelligible testimony' for the purposes of the CJA 1988, s. 33A(2A), does not require any input from an expert (see **F4.17**). The competence of a mentally handicapped person, however, does require appropriate expert medical evidence (see **F4.18**).

Proof of Facts upon which Expert Opinion Evidence Based

F10.11 Before a court can assess the value of an opinion it must know the facts upon which it is based. If the expert has been misinformed about the facts or has taken irrelevant facts into consideration or has omitted to consider relevant ones, the opinion is likely to be valueless. In our judgment, counsel calling an expert should in examination-in-chief ask his witness to state the facts upon which his opinion is based. It is wrong to leave the other side to elicit the facts by cross-examination. (*Turner* [1975] QB 834 at p. 840)

In some cases, some of the relevant facts upon which the opinion is based can be proved by the expert himself, as when he has examined an exhibit or a fingerprint and therefore has personal or first-hand knowledge of those facts. Insofar as he lacks such knowledge, the relevant facts will have to be proved by calling other witnesses (see, for example, *Jackson* [1996] 2 Cr App R 420). In such a case the expert should be asked in examination-in-chief to state the *assumed* facts upon which his opinion is based, and examination-in-chief and cross-examination should take the form of hypothetical questions. Thus, in a trial for murder by stabbing, in which the defence is that the victim's injuries were self-inflicted, a medical witness who has not examined the body may be asked whether, assuming that the facts, described by another medical witness who has examined the body, are true, the wound was inflicted by a person other than the deceased (*Mason* (1911) 7 Cr App R 67).

Where an expert bases his opinion on facts derived from the use of a computer, it seems that there is no obligation to produce the printout (see *Golizadeh* [1995] Crim LR 232, where an expert was allowed to give his opinion that a certain substance was opium on the basis of a printout of a machine used by him to analyse its chemical constituents, the printout itself not having been produced in evidence).

An expert is not subject to the rule against hearsay in the same way as a non-expert or a witness of fact. Thus, although an expert cannot prove facts upon which his opinion is based, but of which he has no personal or first-hand knowledge, because that would be an infringement of the hearsay rule, he may rely upon such facts as a part of the process of forming an opinion. However, if there is no direct evidence to establish such facts, the weight to be attached to the opinion of the expert is likely to be minimal. In *Bradshaw* (1985) 82 Cr App R 79, a murder trial, the only issue was that of diminished responsibility. (The burden of proof was on the defence: Homicide Act 1957, s. 2(2).) Counsel for the defence sought guidance from the judge as to how far the doctors would be permitted to give evidence as to what the accused had told them during interviews, how far they could express opinions based upon such statements, and whether the judge would make adverse comment if the accused were not to give evidence. The judge replied that, if the truth of what the accused had said to the doctors was in question, the only appropriate course was for the accused to prove the facts upon which the expert opinion was based, or for those facts to be proved by other evidence. The accused, who had recovered from any abnormality of mind at the date of the trial, gave evidence and was cross-examined. He appealed against conviction on the grounds that the ruling of the judge was erroneous. The appeal was dismissed. Lord Lane CJ said (at p. 83):

> Although as a concession to the defence doctors are sometimes allowed to base their opinions on what the defendant has told them (i.e. hearsay) without those matters being proved by admissible evidence, yet the strict (and correct) view is that expressed at p. 446 of *Cross on Evidence*, 5th ed., in the following terms: 'A doctor may not state what a patient told him about past symptoms as evidence of the existence of those symptoms because that would infringe the rule against hearsay, but he may give evidence of what the patient told him in order to explain the grounds on which he came to a conclusion with regard to the patient's condition'.

> Thus, if the doctor's opinion is based entirely on hearsay and is not supported by direct evidence, the judge will be justified in telling the jury that the defendant's case (if that is so) is based upon a flimsy or non-existent foundation and that they should reach their conclusion bearing that in mind. In proper cases, for example where, as here, the defendant has completely recovered from any abnormality of mind by the time of the trial, there is no reason why the judge should not comment upon the fact that the defendant could have provided the necessary evidence had he wished to do so, the burden of proof being upon him.

As a part of the process of forming an opinion, expert witnesses may refer not only to their own research, tests and experiments, but also to works of authority, learned articles, research papers, and other similar material written by others and forming part of the general body of knowledge falling within their field of expertise (see generally *Davie* v *Magistrates of Edinburgh* 1953 SC 34; *Seyfang* v *G.D. Searle & Co.* [1973] QB 148, at p. 151; and *H* v *Schering Chemicals Ltd* [1983] 1 WLR 143). In *Abadom* [1983] 1 WLR 126, on the question of whether fragments of glass imbedded in the shoes of the accused had come from a window allegedly broken during a robbery, an expert gave evidence that, based upon his personal analysis of the samples, the glass in the shoes and that from the window bore an identical refractive index; and that, having consulted unpublished statistics compiled by the Home Office Central Research Establishment, which showed that that index occurred in only 4 per cent of all glass samples investigated, in his opinion there was a very strong likelihood that the glass in the shoes came from the window. It was argued, on appeal, that the evidence of the Home Office statistics was inadmissible hearsay, since the expert had no knowledge of the analysis on which the statistics had been based. The appeal was dismissed on the ground that the primary facts, i.e. the refractive indices of the glass samples, had been proved by the expert on the basis of his own analysis; and that once the primary facts upon which an opinion is based have been proved by admissible evidence, an expert is entitled to draw on the work of others as part of the process of arriving at his conclusion, and this involves no breach of the hearsay rule. The Court of Appeal pointed out that part of the experience and expertise of experts lies in their knowledge and evaluation of *unpublished* material; they may draw on such material, provided that they refer to it in their evidence so that the cogency and probative value of their conclusions can be tested and evaluated by reference thereto. Compare *Somers* [1963] 1 WLR 1306.

Opinions on Ultimate Issues

F10.12 In its Eleventh Report (Cmnd 4991, para. 268), the Criminal Law Revision Committee was of the opinion that the old common-law rule that a witness should not express an opinion on an ultimate issue, i.e. one of the very issues to be determined by the court, probably no longer existed. In practice the rule is largely ignored, or treated as being of only semantic effect, so that an expert *is* allowed to express an opinion on an ultimate issue, provided that the actual words he employs are not noticeably the same as those which will be used when the issue falls to be considered by the court. In *DPP* v *A and BC Chewing Gum Ltd* [1968] 1 QB 159, Lord Parker CJ said (at p. 164):

> I think it would be wrong to ask the direct question as to whether any particular cards tended to corrupt or deprave, because that final stage was a matter which was entirely for the justices. No doubt, however, in such a case the defence might well put it to the witness that a particular card or cards could not corrupt, and no doubt, whatever the strict position may be, that question coming from the defence would be allowed, if only to give the defence an opportunity of getting an answer 'No' from the expert.

> . . . I myself would go a little further in that I cannot help feeling that with the advance of science more and more inroads have been made into the old common-law principles. Those who practise in the criminal courts see every day cases of experts being called on the question of diminished responsibility, and although technically the final question 'Do you think he was suffering from diminished responsibility?' is strictly inadmissible, it is allowed time and time again without any objection.

Thus the rule has become 'a matter of form rather than substance' (*Stockwell* (1993) 97 Cr App R 260 at p. 265). For illustrations, see *Mason* 7 Cr App R 67 (whether wounds were self-inflicted), *Holmes* [1953] 1 WLR 686 (insanity), *Silcott* [1987] Crim LR 765 (the unreliability of a confession) and *Hookway* [1999] Crim LR 750 (establishing identity by expert evidence of facial mapping). However, it seems that in a case of possession of drugs with intent to supply, although an officer may give evidence as to the values and prices of drugs in order that the jury may interpret lists found at the accused's premises, the officer should not express an opinion that the lists relate to the sale of drugs, because this amounts to a statement that the accused is guilty as charged (*Jeffries* [1997] Crim LR 819).

Function and Weight of Expert Evidence

F10.13 The duty of the expert witness is 'to furnish the judge or jury with the necessary scientific criteria for testing the accuracy of their conclusions, so as to enable the judge or jury to form their own independent judgment by the application of those criteria to the facts proved in evidence'; and it is a misdirection, therefore, to tell the jury that expert evidence should be accepted if uncontradicted (*Davie Magistrates of* v *Edinburgh* 1953 SC 34, per Lord President Cooper at p. 40). See also *Lanfear* [1968] 2 QB 77: it is wrong to direct the jury that the evidence of an expert should be accepted in the absence of reasons for rejecting it; and *Rivett* (1950) 34 Cr App R 87, in which the Court of Appeal refused to interfere with a conviction despite medical evidence of insanity.

However, it has also been held that it is wrong to direct a jury that they may disregard scientific evidence when the only such evidence adduced on a particular question dictates one answer and only a scientist is qualified to answer that question (*Anderson* v *The Queen* [1972] AC 100). See also *Matheson* [1958] 1 WLR 474 and *Bailey* (1961) 66 Cr App R 31, in both of which the Court of Criminal Appeal substituted verdicts of manslaughter. In *Matheson* it was held that where the medical evidence of diminished responsibility is uncontradicted and the jury return a verdict of guilty of murder, if there are facts entitling the jury to reject or differ from the expert opinion, the Court of Appeal will not interfere with the verdict; but if there are no facts or circumstances to displace or throw a doubt on the unchallenged medical evidence, such a verdict would not be a true verdict in accordance with the evidence. In *Bailey*, where the defence called expert evidence to prove diminished responsibility and the prosecution adduced no evidence in rebuttal, the Court of Criminal Appeal quashed the jury's verdict of guilty of murder on the ground that, although juries are not bound to accept expert medical evidence, they must act on the evidence, and if there is nothing before them to cast doubt on the medical evidence, it is not open to them to reject it. On the other hand, in *Walton* v *The Queen* [1978] AC 788, a conviction for murder was upheld despite uncorroborated medical evidence of diminished responsibility. *Matheson* and *Bailey* were distinguished on the basis of the greater weight and quality of the medical evidence in those cases. *Walton* was followed in *Kiszko* (1978) 68 Cr App R 62. In *Sanders* (1991) 93 Cr App R 245, the Court of Appeal held that two clear principles emerged from the cases, on the issue of diminished responsibility:

(a) if there were no other circumstances to consider, unequivocal, uncontradicted medical evidence favourable to an accused should be accepted by a jury and they should be so directed; and

(b) where there were other circumstances to consider, the medical evidence, though it be unequivocal and uncontradicted, must be assessed in the light of the other circumstances.

In deciding what weight, if any, to attach to the evidence of an expert, the jury are entitled to take into account his qualifications and experience, his credibility, and the extent to which his evidence is based on assumed facts which are or are not established.

Pre-trial Disclosure of Expert Evidence

The Crown Court (Advance Notice of Expert Evidence) Rules 1987 (SI 1987 No. 716), **F10.14** made pursuant to the PACE 1984, s. 81, make provision for the pre-trial disclosure of expert evidence between the parties to Crown Court proceedings (see also **D12.21** and **D14.8**).

Crown Court (Advance Notice of Expert Evidence) Rules 1987, rr. 3 and 4

3.—(1) Following—
  (a) the committal for trial of any person;
  (b) the transfer to the Crown Court of any proceedings for the trial of a person by virtue of a notice of transfer given under section 4 of the Criminal Justice Act 1987;
  (c) the transfer to the Crown Court of any proceedings for the trial of a person by virtue of a notice of transfer served on a magistrates' court under section 53 of the Criminal Justice Act 1991;

(d)   the preferment of a bill of indictment charging a person with an offence under the authority of section 2(2)(b) of the Administration of Justice (Miscellaneous Provisions) Act 1933; or

(e)   the making of an order for the retrial of any person,

if any party to the proceedings proposes to adduce expert evidence (whether of fact or opinion) in the proceedings (otherwise than in relation to sentence) he shall as soon as practicable, unless in relation to the evidence in question he has already done so—

(i)   furnish the other party or parties with a statement in writing of any finding or opinion which he proposes to adduce by way of such evidence; and

(ii)   where a request in writing is made to him in that behalf by any other party, provide that party also with a copy of (or if it appears to the party proposing to adduce the evidence to be more practicable, a reasonable opportunity to examine) the record of any observation, test, calculation or other procedure on which such finding or opinion is based and any document or other thing or substance in respect of which any such procedure has been carried out.

(2)   A party may by notice in writing waive his right to be furnished with any of the matters mentioned in paragraph (1) above and, in particular, may agree that the statement mentioned in subparagraph (a) thereof may be furnished to him orally and not in writing.

(3)   In paragraph (1) above, 'document' means anything in which information of any description is recorded.

4.—(1)   If a party has reasonable grounds for believing that the disclosure of any evidence in compliance with the requirements imposed by rule 3 above might lead to the intimidation, or attempted intimidation, of any person on whose evidence he intends to rely in the proceedings, or otherwise to the course of justice being interfered with, he shall not be obliged to comply with those requirements in relation to that evidence.

(2)   Where, in accordance with paragraph (1) above, a party considers that he is not obliged to comply with the requirements imposed by rule 3 above with regard to any evidence in relation to any other party, he shall give notice in writing to that party to the effect that the evidence is being withheld and the grounds therefor.

5.   A party who seeks to adduce expert evidence in any proceedings and who fails to comply with rule 3 above shall not adduce that evidence in those proceedings without the leave of the court.

The phrase 'expert evidence (whether of fact or opinion)' is sufficiently wide to embrace not only the oral evidence to be given by an expert witness, but also an expert report which it is proposed to adduce under the exception to the hearsay rule contained in the CJA 1988, s. 30(1) (see **F10.15**).

The rules do not supplant or detract from the prosecution's general duty of disclosure in respect of scientific evidence, which exists irrespective of any defence request, extends to anything which may arguably assist the defence, and obliges the prosecution to make full and proper enquiries from forensic scientists in order to ascertain whether there is discoverable material. If an expert has carried out experiments or tests which tend to disprove or cast doubt on the opinion he is expressing (or knows that such experiments or tests have been carried out in his laboratory), he is under a clear obligation to bring the records of such experiments and tests to the attention of the solicitor instructing him (so that it may be disclosed to the other party) or to the expert advising the other party directly (*Ward* [1993] 1 WLR 619).

The Magistrates' Courts (Advance Notice of Expert Evidence) Rules 1997 (SI 1997 No. 705), which are based on the equivalent Crown Court rules of 1987, make provision for the disclosure of expert evidence between the parties to summary trials. Rules 1 to 3 are set out below; rr. 4 and 5 are in identical terms to rr. 4 and 5 of the Crown Court rules.

Magistrates' Courts (Advance Notice of Expert Evidence) Rules 1997, rr. 1 to 3

1.   These Rules may be cited as the Magistrates' Courts (Advance Notice of Expert Evidence) Rules 1997 and shall come into force on 1st April 1997.

2. These Rules shall not have effect in relation to any proceedings which relate to an alleged offence into which a criminal investigation has begun before 1st April 1997.

3.—(1) Where a magistrates' court proceeds to summary trial in respect of an alleged offence and the person charged with that offence pleads not guilty in respect of it, if any party to the proceedings proposes to adduce expert evidence (whether of fact or opinion) in the proceedings (otherwise than in relation to sentence) he shall as soon as practicable after the person charged has so pleaded, unless in relation to the evidence in question he has already done so—

(a)   furnish the other party or parties with a statement in writing of any finding or opinion which he proposes to adduce by way of such evidence; and

(b)   where a request in writing is made to him in that behalf by any other party, provide that party also with a copy of (or if it appears to the party proposing to adduce the evidence to be more practicable, a reasonable opportunity to examine) the record of any observation, test, calculation or other procedure on which such finding or opinion is based and any document or other thing or substance in respect of which any such procedure has been carried out.

(2)   A party may by notice in writing waive his right to be furnished with any of the matters mentioned in paragraph (1) above and, in particular, may agree that the statement mentioned in sub-paragraph (a) thereof may be furnished to him orally and not in writing.

(3)   In paragraph (1) above, 'document' means anything in which information of any description is recorded.

Presentation of Expert and Complicated Evidence

Criminal Justice Act 1988, ss. 30 and 31   F10.15

Expert reports

30.—(1)   An expert report shall be admissible as evidence in criminal proceedings, whether or not the person making it attends to give oral evidence in those proceedings.

(2)   If it is proposed that the person making the report shall not give oral evidence, the report shall only be admissible with the leave of the court.

(3)   For the purpose of determining whether to give leave the court shall have regard—

(a)   to the contents of the report;

(b)   to the reasons why it is proposed that the person making the report shall not give oral evidence;

(c)   to any risk, having regard in particular to whether it is likely to be possible to controvert statements in the report if the person making it does not attend to give oral evidence in the proceedings, that its admission or exclusion will result in unfairness to the accused or, if there is more than one, to any of them; and

(d)   to any other circumstances that appear to the court to be relevant.

(4)   An expert report, when admitted, shall be evidence of any fact or opinion of which the person making it could have given oral evidence.

(4A)   Where the proceedings mentioned in subsection (1) above are proceedings before a magistrates' court inquiring into an offence as examining justices this section shall have effect with the omission of—

(a)   in subsection (1) the words 'whether or not the person making it attends to give oral evidence in those proceedings'; and

(b)   subsections (2) to (4).

(5)   In this section 'expert report' means a written report by a person dealing wholly or mainly with matters on which he is (or would if living be) qualified to give expert evidence.

Form of evidence and glossaries

31.   For the purpose of helping members of juries to understand complicated issues of fact or technical terms Crown Court Rules may make provision—

(a)   as to the furnishing of evidence in any form, notwithstanding the existence of admissible material from which the evidence to be given in that form would be derived; and

(b)   as to the furnishing of glossaries for such purposes as may be specified;
in any case where the court gives leave for, or requires, evidence or a glossary to be so furnished.

SECTION F11: ADMISSIBILITY OF PREVIOUS VERDICTS

PROOF OF CONVICTIONS AND ACQUITTALS

F11.1 The PACE 1984, s. 73, replacing a variety of outdated statutory provisions, provides for the proof of convictions and acquittals in the United Kingdom by a certificate of conviction or acquittal, together with proof that the person named in the certificate is the person whose conviction or acquittal is in issue.

Police and Criminal Evidence Act 1984, ss. 73 and 82

73.—(1) Where in any proceedings the fact that a person has in the United Kingdom been convicted or acquitted of an offence otherwise than by a Service court is admissible in evidence, it may be proved by producing a certificate of conviction or, as the case may be, of acquittal relating to that offence, and proving that the person named in the certificate as having been convicted or acquitted of the offence is the person whose conviction or acquittal of the offence is to be proved.

(2) For the purposes of this section a certificate of conviction or of acquittal—

(a) shall, as regards a conviction or acquittal on indictment, consist of a certificate, signed by the clerk of the court where the conviction or acquittal took place, giving the substance and effect (omitting the formal parts) of the indictment and of the conviction or acquittal; and

(b) shall, as regards a conviction or acquittal on a summary trial, consist of a copy of the conviction or of the dismissal of the information, signed by the clerk of the court where the conviction or acquittal took place or by the clerk of the court, if any, to which a memorandum of the conviction or acquittal was sent;

and a document purporting to be a duly signed certificate of conviction or acquittal under this section shall be taken to be such a certificate unless the contrary is proved.

(3) References in this section to the clerk of a court include references to his deputy and to any other person having the custody of the court record.

(4) The method of proving a conviction or acquittal authorised by this section shall be in addition to and not to the exclusion of any other authorised manner of proving a conviction or acquittal.

Part VIII—interpretation

82.—(1) In this part of this Act— . . .

'court-martial' means a court-martial constituted under the Army Act 1955, the Air Force Act 1955 or the Naval Discipline Act 1957 or a disciplinary court constituted under section 50 of the said Act of 1957;

'proceedings' means criminal proceedings, including—

(a) proceedings in the United Kingdom or elsewhere before a court-martial constituted under the Army Act 1955 or the Air Force Act 1955;

(b) proceedings in the United Kingdom or elsewhere before the Courts-Martial Appeal Court—

(i) on an appeal from a court-martial so constituted or from a court-martial constituted under the Naval Discipline Act 1957; or

(ii) on a reference under section 34 of the Courts-Martial (Appeals) Act 1968; and

(c) proceedings before a Standing Civilian Court; and

'Service court' means a court-martial or a Standing Civilian Court.

(2) In this part of this Act references to conviction before a Service court are references—

(a) as regards a court-martial constituted under the Army Act 1955 or the Air Force Act 1955, to a finding of guilty which is, or falls to be treated as, a finding of the court duly confirmed;

(b) as regards—

(i) a court-martial; or

(ii) a disciplinary court,

constituted under the Naval Discipline Act 1957, to a finding of guilty which is, or falls to be treated as, the finding of the court;

and 'convicted' shall be construed accordingly.

(3)   Nothing in this part of this Act shall prejudice any power of a court to exclude evidence (whether by preventing questions from being put or otherwise) at its discretion.

When the relevant repeal in sch. 6 to the YJCEA 1999 is brought into force, the following words will be deleted from s. 82(1): in the definition of 'proceedings' in paragraph (a), the words after 'court-martial', and in paragraph (b)(i) the words 'so constituted'.

Another 'authorised manner of proving a conviction', for the purposes of s. 73(4), is by fingerprints under the CJA 1948, s. 39.

Criminal Justice Act 1948, s. 39

(1)   A previous conviction may be proved against any person in any criminal proceedings by the production of such evidence of the conviction as is mentioned in this section, and by showing that his fingerprints and those of the person convicted are the fingerprints of the same person.

(2)   A certificate purporting to be signed by or on behalf of the Commissioner of Police of the Metropolis, containing particulars relating to a conviction extracted from the criminal records kept by him, and certifying that the copies of the fingerprints exhibited to the certificate are copies of the fingerprints appearing from the said records to have been taken . . . from the person convicted on the occasion of the conviction, shall be evidence of the conviction and evidence that the copies of the fingerprints exhibited to the certificate are copies of the fingerprints of the person convicted.

(3)   A certificate purporting to be signed by or on behalf of the governor of a prison or remand centre in which any person has been detained in connection with any criminal proceedings, certifying that the fingerprints exhibited thereto were taken from him while he was so detained, shall be evidence in those proceedings that the fingerprints exhibited to the certificate are the fingerprints of that person.

(4)   A certificate, purporting to be signed by or on behalf of the Commissioner of Police of the Metropolis, and certifying that the fingerprints, copies of which are certified as aforesaid by or on behalf of the Commissioner to be copies of the fingerprints of a person previously convicted and the fingerprints certified by or on behalf of the governor as aforesaid, or otherwise shown, to be the fingerprints of the person against whom the previous conviction is sought to be proved are the fingerprints of the same person shall be evidence of the matter so certified.

(5)   The method of proving a previous conviction authorised by this section shall be in addition to any other method of proving the conviction.

The CJA 1967, s. 33, provides that: '. . . in section 39 of the CJA 1948 any reference to fingerprints shall be construed as including a reference to palm prints'.

To overcome the difficulties, at common law, in seeking to prove the previous convictions of a person convicted of a summary offence, if he did not attend the court, the MCA 1980, s. 104, now provides that if the court is satisfied that, not less than seven days before the hearing, a notice, stating the alleged previous convictions which it is proposed to bring to the attention of the court, has been served on the accused, and the accused is not present before the court, the court may take account of the convictions as if the accused had appeared and admitted them. Service of the notice may be effected by delivering it to the accused or by sending it to him by registered letter or recorded delivery (Magistrates' Courts Rules 1981 (SI 1981 No. 552), r. 72). Orders made by magistrates' courts, such as an order disqualifying a person from holding a driving licence, may be proved under the Magistrates' Courts Rules 1981, r. 68, which provides that the register of a magistrates' court, or any document purporting to be an extract from the register and to be certified by the clerk as a true extract, shall be admissible in any legal proceedings as evidence of proceedings of the court entered in the register. Endorsements on a driving licence of the particulars of a conviction or disqualification may be produced as prima facie evidence of the matters endorsed (see the Road Traffic Offenders Act 1988, ss. 31(1) and 44(1)).

For the purposes of extradition proceedings, the fact of a conviction overseas may be proved by a properly certified copy of the court record (see the Extradition Act 1989, sch. 1, para. 12 and *Re Mullin* [1993] Crim LR 390).

CONVICTIONS AS EVIDENCE OF FACTS ON WHICH BASED

F11.2   At common law, the convictions of one person were not admissible as evidence of the facts on which they were based at the subsequent trial of another: see *Turner* (1832) 1 Mood CC 347, at p. 349 (one person's conviction for theft inadmissible as evidence of such theft at the trial of another charged with handling the stolen goods); *Hassan* [1970] QB 423 (a woman's convictions for prostitution inadmissible as evidence of such prostitution at the trial of a man charged with living off her immoral earnings); and *Spinks* [1982] 1 All ER 587 (a principal's conviction of wounding inadmissible as evidence of such wounding at the subsequent trial of an alleged accessory). The PACE 1984, s. 74(1), has now reversed the common-law rule, and s. 74(2) has created a persuasive presumption: the person (other than the accused) convicted of an offence shall be taken to have committed that offence unless the contrary is proved. The legal burden is borne by the party against whom the presumption operates; and if borne by the accused, may be discharged by proof on a balance of probabilities (see *Carr-Briant* [1943] KB 607 and generally **F3.18** and **F3.31**). Section 74(3) creates a similar presumption in the case of the previous convictions of *the accused*, provided that evidence is admissible of the fact that the accused has committed the offence in respect of which he has been convicted.

Police and Criminal Evidence Act 1984, s. 74

(1)   In any proceedings the fact that a person other than the accused has been convicted of an offence by or before any court in the United Kingdom or by a Service court outside the United Kingdom shall be admissible in evidence for the purpose of proving, where to do so is relevant to any issue in those proceedings, that that person committed that offence, whether or not any other evidence of his having committed that offence is given.

(2)   In any proceedings in which by virtue of this section a person other than the accused is proved to have been convicted of an offence by or before any court in the United Kingdom or by a Service court outside the United Kingdom, he shall be taken to have committed that offence unless the contrary is proved.

(3)   In any proceedings where evidence is admissible of the fact that the accused has committed an offence, in so far as that evidence is relevant to any matter in issue in the proceedings for a reason other than a tendency to show in the accused a disposition to commit the kind of offence with which he is charged, if the accused is proved to have been convicted of the offence—

(a)   by or before any court in the United Kingdom; or
(b)   by a Service court outside the United Kingdom,

he shall be taken to have committed that offence unless the contrary is proved.

(4)   Nothing in this section shall prejudice—

(a)   the admissibility in evidence of any conviction which would be admissible apart from this section; or
(b)   the operation of any enactment whereby a conviction or a finding of fact in any proceedings is for the purposes of any other proceedings made conclusive evidence of any fact.

For the definition of 'proceedings', 'Service court' and convictions before a Service court, see s. 82, at **F11.1**.

Police and Criminal Evidence Act 1984, s. 75

(1)   Where evidence that a person has been convicted of an offence is admissible by virtue of section 74 above, then without prejudice to the reception of any other admissible evidence for the purpose of identifying the facts on which the conviction was based—

    (a)   the contents of any document which is admissible as evidence of the conviction; and

    (b)   the contents of the information, complaint, indictment or charge-sheet on which the person in question was convicted,

shall be admissible in evidence for that purpose.

    (2)   Where in any proceedings the contents of any document are admissible in evidence by virtue of subsection (1) above, a copy of that document, or of the material part of it, purporting to be certified or otherwise authenticated by or on behalf of the court or authority having custody of that document shall be admissible in evidence and shall be taken to be a true copy of that document or part unless the contrary is shown.

    (3)   Nothing in any of the following—

    (a)   section 13 of the Powers of Criminal Courts Act 1973 (under which a conviction leading to probation or discharge is to be disregarded except as mentioned in that section);

    (b)   section 247 of the Criminal Procedure (Scotland) Act 1995 (which makes similar provision in respect of convictions on indictment in Scotland); and

    (c)   section 8 of the Probation Act (Northern Ireland) 1950 (which corresponds to section 13 of the Powers of Criminal Courts Act 1973) or any legislation which is in force in Northern Ireland for the time being and corresponds to that section,

shall affect the operation of section 74 above; and for the purposes of that section any order made by a court of summary jurisdiction in Scotland under section 228 or section 246(2) of the said Act of 1995 shall be treated as a conviction.

    (4)   Nothing in section 74 above shall be construed as rendering admissible in any proceedings evidence of any conviction other than a subsisting one.

Under the CJA 1991, the PCCA 1973, s. 13, has been repealed insofar as it applies to offenders placed on probation; its provisions have been replaced by s. 1C of the 1973 Act insofar as they apply to offenders who are discharged.

A 'subsisting' conviction means either a finding of guilt that has not been quashed on appeal or a formal plea of guilt that has not been withdrawn; whether the accused has been sentenced is irrelevant (*Robertson* [1987] QB 920). It seems that one co-accused may rely upon s. 74(1) to adduce evidence of the convictions of another co-accused, provided that they are relevant to an issue in the proceedings (see *Hendrick* [1992] Crim LR 427, where the convictions were held to be irrelevant). It is possible to envisage situations in which a co-accused pleads guilty to a charge even though the evidence is far from conclusive against him, and in such a case it could well be unfair to allow the prosecution to use the conviction as evidence, on that charge, against the remaining accused (see *Lee* [1996] Crim LR 825). Where one co-accused pleads guilty towards or at the end of the prosecution case and the prosecution make an application to reopen their case to adduce evidence of the guilty plea under s. 74(1), the plea, if relevant to an issue in the proceedings, is admissible, subject to exercise of the discretion to exclude under s. 78, as when it would be unfair because, had the guilty plea been entered and admitted in evidence at an earlier stage, cross-examination might have been conducted differently (*Chapman* [1991] Crim LR 44).

Convictions of Persons Other than the Accused

Before convictions can be admitted under the PACE 1984, s. 74, they must be relevant **F11.3** to an 'issue in the proceedings'. In *Hasson* [1997] Crim LR 579 the accused were charged with being concerned in the supply of drugs. It was held that the previous drug-related convictions of six men with whom the accused had socialised had been improperly admitted because it was not the Crown case that the accused were supplying them with drugs and there was no evidence to show that meetings with them were related to the offence charged.

In some cases proof of the commission of an offence by a person other than the accused will establish an essential ingredient of the offence with which the accused is charged, and therefore will be clearly relevant to an 'issue in those proceedings'. In *Pigram* [1995]

Crim LR 808, in which officers had seen H and P transfer goods from H's van to P's lorry and H and P were jointly charged with handling, it was held that H's guilty plea was admissible against P for the purposes of proving that the goods were stolen.

The phrase 'issue in those proceedings', however, is not confined to an issue which is an essential ingredient of the offence charged. In *Robertson* [1987] QB 920, the Court of Appeal held that the phrase also covers less fundamental issues, for example evidential issues arising in the proceedings. The Court also rejected the argument that s. 74(1) applies only to the proof of convictions of offences in which the accused on trial did not participate. Robertson was charged with two co-accused with conspiracy to commit burglary. The co-accused pleaded not guilty to the conspiracy but guilty to some 16 burglaries committed during the period of the conspiracy. Evidence of these convictions was held to be admissible, because it could be inferred from the fact that the co-accused had committed these offences that there was a conspiracy between them, and that was the conspiracy to which, the prosecution alleged, Robertson was a party. In *Golder*, the appeal in which was heard with and is reported with *Robertson* [1987] QB 920, Golder was charged with a robbery committed at garage H. Two of his co-accused pleaded guilty to that robbery, and also to another robbery committed at garage G. The evidence against Golder consisted primarily of a confession statement, which he alleged to have been fabricated by the police, in which he made reference to both robberies. The evidence of the guilty pleas was held to be admissible: proof of the commission of the offences at both garages was relevant, because it showed that the contents of Golder's confession were in accordance with the facts as they were known and the confession was therefore more likely to be true; and proof of the commission of the offence at garage H was relevant, because robbery at that garage was one of the matters which the prosecution had to prove.

The decision in *Robertson* that the phrase 'issue in those proceedings' should be given a wide interpretation so as to include evidentiary matters, was applied in *Castle* [1989] Crim LR 567. C and others, including F, were charged with robbery. The victim, when seeing C and F at the identification parade, said 'yes' in respect of C and 'possibly' in respect of F. F pleaded guilty. It was held that evidence of the guilty plea was admissible because relevant to the issue of the reliability of the identification of C. The evidence, by confirming that the victim was correct in his 'possible' identification of F, tended to corroborate the correctness of his positive identification of C. See also, *sed quaere*, *Buckingham* (1994) 99 Cr App R 303: evidence of W's conviction of conspiracy to pervert the course of justice by obtaining, as the accused in a previous trial, false evidence of defence witnesses, was admissible at the trial of those witnesses for doing acts intended to pervert the course of justice because, although it was not probative that any of the witnesses had given false evidence, it established the conspiracy.

In *O'Connor* (1987) 85 Cr App R 298, B and O'Connor were jointly charged with having conspired together (and with no one else) to obtain property by deception. At the trial of O'Connor, B's plea of guilty was admitted, together with all the detail contained in the conspiracy count (see s. 75(1)(b), at **F11.2**). The Court of Appeal upheld O'Connor's conviction by application of the proviso, but held that the evidence should have been excluded on the ground that it was impossible realistically to exclude the possibility that the jury might infer from B's admission, and the detail contained in the count, that not only had B conspired with O'Connor, but that the converse had also taken place. Furthermore, it was not open to the defence to challenge or test what had been said by B. The court concluded that if it was appropriate within the section to admit the conviction, the judge should have excluded it under s. 78, on the basis that it would have had such an adverse effect on the fairness of the proceedings that it ought not to have been admitted. In *Mattison* [1990] Crim LR 117, M was charged in one count with gross indecency with D. In another count, D was charged with gross indecency with M.

D pleaded guilty and at M's trial evidence of that plea was admitted. The judge directed the jury that the evidence of D's plea did not mean that M was guilty, but was before them to make the background accurate. Allowing the appeal, it was held that although D's guilty plea was relevant in the proceedings against M, the judge, bearing in mind M's defence, which was one of complete denial, should have exercised the discretion under s. 78 to exclude the evidence. See also *Fedrick* [1990] Crim LR 403 and *Turpin* [1990] Crim LR 514, discussed below. It seems that evidence of a conviction, which would otherwise be clearly admissible under s. 74, may also be excluded under s. 78 on the basis that it adds little to an already strong case against the accused (see *Warner* (1993) 96 Cr App R 324).

In *Robertson* [1987] QB 920, counsel for the appellant, relying upon *O'Connor*, submitted that the convictions in that case should also have been excluded under s. 78, because the prosecution, in relying on s. 74, had deprived Robertson of the opportunity to cross-examine the co-accused. The Court of Appeal rejected the argument, distinguishing *O'Connor*. Robertson's name did not appear on any of the burglary counts, and even if the co-accused had given evidence in accordance with their guilty pleas, Robertson's counsel would have been unlikely to cross-examine them (or, if he had done so, he would have seriously prejudiced Robertson). (In this respect, see also *Kempster* [1989] 1 WLR 1125, discussed below.) However, the court added (at p. 928): 'Section 74 is a provision which should be sparingly used. There will be occasions where, although the evidence may be technically admissible its effect is likely to be so slight that it will be wiser not to adduce it. This is particularly so when there is a danger of a contravention of section 78.' It was further observed that where the evidence is admitted, the judge should be careful to explain to the jury its effect and limitations.

In *Turner* [1991] Crim LR 57, T and L, in separate cars, were driving at night down a hill. L overtook T, collided with an oncoming vehicle and killed his (L's) passenger. The prosecution alleged that L and T were racing. L pleaded guilty to causing death by reckless driving. T was tried on the same charge and denied that he was racing. It was held that L's guilty plea was relevant to T's trial because the prosecution case was that L had been the principal and T the secondary party who aided and abetted L. The question was whether the plea should have been excluded under s. 78. Provided that the judge made it clear, as he did, that L's plea did not amount to an admission that he was racing, there was nothing unfair in admitting the evidence. In *Bennett* [1988] Crim LR 686, B was charged with theft. Her co-accused, a supermarket cashier, pleaded guilty to theft, the allegation being that she passed goods to B for less than their true price. Evidence of the guilty plea was admitted against B. The Court held that any decision to the contrary would have bewildered the jury. The evidence was adduced to establish that there had been a theft. The issue of whether B had been a party to the theft had been fairly left with the jury, and the judge had properly exercised his discretion under s. 78. See also *Stewart* [1999] Crim LR 746.

In *Lunnon* [1988] Crim LR 456, in which there were three accused jointly charged with conspiracy, it was held that the guilty plea of one of them had been properly admitted to prove the existence of the conspiracy: the judge had separated two questions for the jury, namely (a) whether there was a conspiracy and (b) who was a party to it, and had made it clear that, despite the evidence of the guilty plea, the jury could acquit the accused. (See also *Garrity* [1994] Crim LR 828; and compare *Humphreys* [1993] Crim LR 288, where it was held that the evidence should have been excluded under s. 78 because there was other prosecution evidence of the conspiracy.) In *Chapman* [1991] Crim LR 44, C and seven others were charged with conspiracy to obtain by deception. The pleas of guilty by one of the others to two specific counts of obtaining by deception, being two incidents in which he was involved with C, were held to be relevant; and since there were others in the conspiracy, and since the other co-accused did not plead guilty to conspiracy but to specific obtainings by deception, the evidence of the conviction did not inevitably import the complicity of C. See also *Hunt* [1994] Crim LR 747 and *cf. Curry* [1988] Crim LR 527. The appellant, Curry, was convicted of conspiracy to obtain property by deception. She was charged with two others, one of whom, H, had pleaded guilty. The prosecution case was that Curry, with H's knowledge, had used H's credit card to obtain goods, and that H then intended to report the card as stolen in order to avoid liability to pay for the goods. The other co-accused, W, had driven the women to the shops. Evidence of H's guilty plea was admitted to establish the existence of an unlawful agreement to deceive. The Court of Appeal, distinguishing *Lunnon* (1988) 88 Cr App R 71, quashed the conviction on the grounds that the evidence of the guilty plea clearly implied as a matter of fact that the appellant had been a party to the conspiracy, even though it did not have that effect as a matter of law, and should have been excluded under s. 78. Section 74, it was said, should be sparingly used, particularly in relation to joint offences such as conspiracy and affray. It should not be used where the evidence, expressly or by necessary inference, suggests the complicity of the accused.

This last observation in *Curry* was reiterated in *Kempster* [1989] 1 WLR 1125, in which the Court of Appeal noted that the effect of admitting a conviction as evidence of the complicity of the accused, is that the prosecution will not have to call the person convicted as a witness and the defence will be deprived of any opportunity to cross-examine him, in particular as to the complicity of the accused. Staughton LJ said (at p. 22):

> No doubt such cross-examination may in itself be unlikely in some cases, or else turn out to be a disaster, as the Lord Chief Justice put it in *Robertson*. But one cannot always assume that.

The Court of Appeal in *Kempster* also stressed (at p. 22) that it is important to ascertain the purpose for which evidence under s. 74 is to be adduced before deciding whether it should be excluded under s. 78; and that if the evidence is admitted, the trial judge should be careful not only to direct the jury about the purpose for which it has been admitted, but also to ensure that counsel do not seek to use it for any other purpose. In that case, evidence of the guilty pleas of a number of co-accused was admitted but not the detailed particulars of the offences committed. At the time of the application to admit, it was unclear whether the prosecution were relying on the evidence in order to prove the guilt of the accused or merely to prevent mystification of the jury, and therefore there was no clear and informed decision by the judge about any adverse effect the evidence might have on the fairness of the proceedings. In the event, the jury were encouraged to rely on the evidence for the purpose of proving the guilt of the accused. The convictions were quashed. In *Mahmood* [1997] 1 Cr App R 414, L, KM and NM were charged with rape. The prosecution case was that the complainant was too drunk to have consented. L pleaded guilty. KM and NM admitted intercourse but alleged consent or alternatively belief in consent. It was held that evidence of L's plea should not have been admitted because, without knowing the basis for it, it was not possible to identify any issue to which it was relevant. There was a real danger that the jury would assume it meant that L knew the complainant could not consent by reason of drink (whereas it is possible that he believed she could consent, but knew she was not consenting or was reckless as to whether she was consenting) and conclude therefore that KM and NM must also have known that she could not consent, an approach which would preclude proper consideration of the state of mind of each accused. Cf. *Skinner* [1995] Crim LR 805. See also *Boyson* [1991] Crim LR 274, where the Court of Appeal held, *per curiam*, that it did not approve of the growing practice of allowing evidence to go before a jury which is irrelevant, inadmissible, prejudicial or unfair simply because it is convenient for the jury to have 'the whole picture', and *Hall* [1993] Crim LR 527.

In *Turpin* [1990] Crim LR 514, T, with three others, was charged with violent disorder. Two of the co-accused pleaded guilty. At the trial of T, counsel for the prosecution, in opening the case, told the jury that the guilty pleas were not probative of the case against T in any way. In his defence, T admitted that there had been violent disorder, but denied being involved in it. In the summing-up, the judge did not refer to the pleas of guilty, nor did he repeat what counsel for the prosecution had said in that regard. Dismissing T's appeal, it was held that although it is desirable to refer to pleas of guilty by co-accused where they necessarily showed complicity with the accused, it is not always necessary for a judge to refer to pleas of guilty by co-accused, and in the present case it was not necessary for the judge to repeat what counsel for the prosecution had said in opening the case. *Turpin* may be compared with *Betterley* [1994] Crim LR 764, where it was held that in a case involving joint enterprise in which one of the co-accused pleads guilty, it is not enough for the judge to direct the jury that they must be sure that each of the accused was a party to the enterprise – they should be told that it is essential that they put the guilty plea out of their minds. See also *Marlow* [1997] Crim LR 457.

Convictions of Accused

There are only three situations, it is submitted, in which reliance may be placed on the **F11.4** PACE 1984, s. 74(3). The first is where the prosecution seek to prove, as an element of the offence with which the accused is charged, the fact that he committed some other offence in respect of which he has been convicted, as when, after the accused's conviction for assault, the victim dies from his injuries, and the accused is then prosecuted for his murder or manslaughter. The second is where an accused, cross-examined on the underlying facts of previous offences under Criminal Evidence Act 1898, s. 1(f)(ii) or (iii), with a view to impugning his credibility (see **F14.35** and **F14.40**), denies those facts or denies having committed the offence at all. The third is where the prosecution seek to admit under the similar fact evidence doctrine, evidence of the accused's commission of an offence in respect of which he has been convicted. There is clear authority that similar fact evidence, in order to be admissible, *must* be relevant for some reason other than the accused's disposition to commit the sort of crime charged (see *Lunt* (1986) 85 Cr App R 241, and **F12**); and on this view *admissible* similar fact evidence is covered by s. 74(3), which, on its wording, makes no changes in the law relating to the admissibility of evidence that the accused has committed an offence (other than that with which he is charged). This view would appear to be supported by *Hendrick* [1992] Crim LR 427, where it was held that the prosecution could not have relied on s. 74 because the only purpose in so doing could have been to show propensity. The difficulty remains, however, that s. 74(3), unlike s. 74(1), does *not* provide that evidence of the previous conviction *shall be admissible*; under s. 74(3), the presumption arises '*if* the accused is proved to have been convicted'. This assumes that the fact of conviction for an offence committed by the accused is itself admissible. In the case of a conviction of an offence admissible as similar fact evidence at common law, there is some authority to the contrary (see *Shepherd* (1980) 71 Cr App R 120). However, *Shepherd* was a case which turned very much on its own facts, and, insofar as it is authority for this proposition, it may be that s. 74(3) should be taken to have overruled it.

RES JUDICATA

The principle underlying the special plea in bar of autrefois acquit (as to which, see **F11.5** generally **D10.28** to **D10.38**), *nemo debet bis puniri pro uno delicto*, has been extended to prohibit the prosecution from adducing evidence, in a trial against an accused person, which is relevant only on the assumption that he is guilty of some other offence of which he has previously been acquitted. Although the doctrine of issue estoppel is inapplicable to criminal cases (*DPP* v *Humphrys* [1977] AC 1, see **D10.38**), a party may nonetheless be prevented from adducing evidence, the effect of which would be to contradict a verdict of acquittal rendered previously by a competent court. In *Sambasivam* v *Public*

Prosecutor of Malaya Federation [1950] AC 458 the prosecution relied upon a statement, alleged to have been made by the appellant, in which he admitted carrying a firearm, the offence for which he was being tried, and being in possession of ammunition, an offence of which he had previously been acquitted. The Privy Council quashed the conviction on the grounds that the judge had failed to direct the two assessors that the accused had been acquitted of being in possession of ammunition, and that the prosecution were bound to accept that the part of the alleged statement relating to the ammunition must be regarded as untrue. Lord MacDermott said (at p. 479):

> The effect of a verdict of acquittal pronounced by a competent court on a lawful charge and after a lawful trial is not completely stated by saying that the person acquitted cannot be tried again for the same offence. To that it must be added that the verdict is binding and conclusive in all subsequent proceedings between the parties to the adjudication. The maxim *res iudicata pro veritate accipitur* is no less applicable to criminal than to civil proceedings.

In *G (an Infant)* v *Coltart* [1967] 1 QB 432, G, a domestic servant, was charged with two offences of theft, one relating to the property of T, her employer, the other relating to the property of D, her employer's guest. No evidence was offered on the charge relating to D's property. On the charge relating to T's property, the prosecution adduced evidence, in order to rebut her defence that she had intended to return the property, that, although she had been told of the departure of D, a day before she had left, she had not returned D's property. The Divisional Court quashed the conviction on the ground that the prosecution, in order to obtain a conviction, had improperly sought to show that the accused was guilty of another offence of which she had been acquitted. The Court distinguished *Ollis* [1900] 2 QB 758. Ollis was acquitted of obtaining a cheque by false pretences. The case against him was that he obtained the cheque from R on 5 July, by falsely pretending that a cheque drawn by him and given to R would be honoured. Ollis was subsequently convicted of obtaining money by cheques that were not valid orders on 24 and 26 June, and on 6 July. At that trial the prosecution called R to give the same evidence that he had given at the first trial, not to prove Ollis's guilt of the first offence, but to show his intent to defraud: if he drew several cheques and knew that some of them were dishonoured, he also knew the state of his account and that subsequent cheques would not be valid orders. The Court for Crown Cases Reserved affirmed the conviction. *Ollis* was applied in *Caceres-Moreira* [1995] Crim LR 489. In *G (an Infant)* v *Coltart* [1967] 1 QB 432, Salmon LJ said (at pp. 439–40):

> I think . . . on general principles that it would be quite wrong to allow the prosecution in order to obtain a conviction in case B to seek to show that the defendant was guilty in case A, after the defendant had been acquitted in case A. I have no doubt that, even although the defendant is acquitted in case A, evidence called against the defendant in case A could be relevant in case B, for example, to show what his intent was in case B.

Sambasivam v *Public Prosecutor of Malaya Federation* [1950] AC 458 and *G (an Infant)* v *Coltart* are not to be regarded as authorities in support of the existence of the doctrine of issue estoppel, which is inapplicable in criminal cases (*DPP* v *Humphrys* [1977] AC 1). See **D10.8**.

SECTION F12: CHARACTER EVIDENCE: ADMISSIBILITY OF EVIDENCE OF BAD CHARACTER

General Exclusion of Evidence of Bad Character

As a general rule, it is not open to the prosecution to adduce evidence of the bad **F12.1** character of the accused in any form. Thus, the previous convictions of the accused may not form part of the case against him, nor may his previous misconduct, his disposition towards wrongdoing or immorality, or his bad reputation in the community in which he lives. If such evidence is to be adduced against an accused, it must be by way of exception to the general rule. The same general observation may be made of evidence of bad character sought to be adduced by one co-accused against another.

Exceptions to Rule of Exclusion

Evidence of the previous misconduct of the accused, and in some cases his disposition, **F12.2** may be admissible at the instance of the prosecution or the defence as similar fact evidence. This is considered at **F12.3** to **F12.20**. Evidence of other misconduct forming part of the same transaction as the offence charged may also be admissible at common law (**F12.21** to **F12.23**). If the accused puts his character in issue, evidence of bad character may be admitted at common law (**F13.15**), and where the accused gives evidence, he may in certain cases face cross-examination on his character under the Criminal Evidence Act 1898 (see **F14**). These are the main cases in which evidence of bad character may be introduced. For the sake of completeness it should be added that various statutes may render evidence of previous convictions admissible in evidence. Of these the most important is the Theft Act 1968, s. 27(3), discussed at **F12.24** to **F12.26**. Certain criminal offences are constructed so that the commission of one offence is a prerequisite to liability for another, such as driving whilst disqualified (Road Traffic Act 1988, s. 103(1)) and offences under s. 21 of the Firearms Act 1968 of possessing a firearm, which can only be committed by a person who has been convicted and has received a sentence of imprisonment (or equivalent) of a certain duration. These offences are considered in the appropriate section of this work. The only point which it is necessary to make here is that in such cases the prosecution are not only permitted to introduce the evidence of the relevant conviction, but must do so in order to prove the offence. This does not, however, permit the prosecution to adduce other evidence of character.

SIMILAR FACT EVIDENCE

Admissibility of Acts Not Covered by Indictment

The general rule of exclusion to which the similar fact doctrine constitutes an exception **F12.3** applies to all criminal acts of the accused which are not covered by the indictment (*Makin* v *A-G for New South Wales* [1894] AC 57). It also precludes proof of the commission of discreditable acts which are not themselves criminal (*Barrington* [1981] 1 WLR 419), of any discreditable propensity which may make the accused more likely to commit the act charged (*Lewis* (1982) 76 Cr App R 33), of facts which have formed the basis of a charge resulting in acquittal (*Caceres-Moreira* [1995] Crim LR 489) and of the possession of incriminating items (*Taylor* (1923) 17 Cr App R 109; *Barner-Rasmussen* [1996] Crim LR 497).

In *DPP* v *Boardman* [1975] AC 421, Lord Hailsham (at p. 451) identified two possible bases for the general rule excluding evidence of bad character. The first is that such evidence is simply irrelevant, because no number of similar offences can connect a person with a particular crime: a view taken by Devlin J in *Miller* [1952] 2 All ER 667. The second is that the prejudice created by such evidence outweighs any probative value it might have; a theory strongly supported by Lord Simon in *DPP v Kilbourne* [1973] AC 729, at p. 757, and approved by Lord Cross in *Boardman*, above, at p. 456. Lord Hailsham's conclusion was that both theories are correct, in the sense that evidence of bad character may be of no probative value if there is nothing to connect the accused with the crime charged, but where there is some evidence to connect him, it may be dangerous to admit evidence of bad character which a jury might invest with a far greater degree of probative value than it actually possesses. Examples of both types of evidence are given below.

In *Rodley* [1913] 3 KB 468, R was charged with breaking into a house with intent to rape. The prosecution case was that he had forced the back door of a house and attempted to rape the female occupant, desisting only when her father appeared on the scene. His defence was that he had entered the house at the woman's invitation and that she was a willing partner to what had happened. At trial, evidence was admitted to show that, an hour after the events in issue, R entered the bedroom of another woman's house via the chimney, and had intercourse with her with her consent. This evidence was rightly adjudged by the Court of Criminal Appeal to be irrelevant to the issues in the case.

A case where the evidence had insufficient probative value was *Noor Mohamed v The King* [1949] AC 183. N was charged with the murder of his mistress, A, who had died from cyanide poisoning. Cyanide was used by N in the course of his business as a goldsmith. The circumstances of A's death were suspicious, but were not inconsistent with the possibility of suicide or accident. Evidence was adduced that N's first wife, G, had died from cyanide poisoning, and there was evidence to suggest that N had tricked G into taking the poison as a cure for toothache. There was no evidence of a similar trick practised on A; indeed, as A was well acquainted with the circumstances of her predecessor's demise such a ploy would have been unlikely to succeed. The Privy Council held that the circumstances of G's death, while deepening the suspicion surrounding N, did not necessarily negative the possible innocent explanations for the death of A. At the same time, there was an obvious risk that the jury might have concluded that N had murdered G (although he had never been charged with such an offence) and was therefore likely to have killed A.

Evidence which tended merely to deepen suspicion was also wrongly admitted in *Harris v DPP* [1952] AC 694. H, a policeman, faced eight counts, each involving theft from an enclosed market. The thefts shared common (though rather commonplace) features, and all occurred while H was on duty in the vicinity. However, it was only in respect of the eighth count that there was any evidence of guilty behaviour on the part of H, in that, after the alarm was raised, he absented himself from the scene, the stolen property being later recovered from a coal-bin in which H would have had time to hide it. It was held that evidence relating to the first seven counts was inadmissible to provide confirmation of H's identity as the thief on the eighth occasion.

Admissibility of Similar Fact Evidence: Relevance the Basic Test

F12.4 It has rightly been said that the principle upon which evidence of similar facts is admissible is easy to state but difficult to apply: see, e.g., *Makin v A-G for New South Wales* [1894] AC 57, per Lord Herschell LC at p. 65; *DPP v Boardman* [1975] AC 421, per Lord Hailsham at p. 446.

The statement of principle is easy, because it rests simply upon the notion of degrees of relevance. Evidence is inadmissible if it does no more than to suggest that the accused is the sort of person who might commit the offence charged, but admissible if it goes further and becomes part of the proof that he did commit it. In *Rowton* (1865) Le & Ca 520 (considered generally at **F13.12**), Willes J, having acknowledged that evidence of the prisoner's antecedents may be admissible for the prosecution in certain cases, explained (at p. 541): 'But these cases only establish the principle that a relevant fact which incidentally casts a slur upon the prisoner is not thereby rendered inadmissible, when it is part of the direct evidence in the case'. The same point was well made in *Thompson* v *The King* [1918] AC 221, by Lord Sumner, who said (at p. 234): 'there is all the difference in the world between evidence proving that the accused is a bad man and evidence proving that he is *the* man.'

A similar observation was made by Lord Herschell LC in *Makin* v *A-G for New South Wales* [1894] AC 57, at p. 67, who contrasted evidence which 'would only shew the prisoner to be a bad man' with evidence which would be 'direct evidence of the fact in issue'. Other early and important references to relevance as the test of admissibility may be found in, e.g., *Ball* [1911] AC 47, per Lord Loreburn LC at p. 71 and in *Bond* [1906] 2 KB 389, per Jelf J at p. 412. The most comprehensive modern statements of the principle that admissibility is governed by relevance are to be found in the judgments of the House of Lords in *DPP* v *Boardman* [1975] AC 421 and *DPP* v *P* [1991] 2 AC 447. The principle itself has never been doubted, however. It is only in the application of it that difficulty has arisen.

In one sense, precedents are of little help in the application of a principle which depends on relevance, for evidence which is directly and sufficiently relevant on one set of facts may be irrelevant, or insufficiently so, if the facts are changed only slightly. Thus, it is often said that other applications of the rule are of little help in deciding admissibility: see, e.g., *Thompson* v *The King* [1918] AC 221, per Lord Atkinson at p. 227; *Harris* v *DPP* [1952] AC 694 per Viscount Simon at p. 711; *Robinson* (1953) 37 Cr App R 95, per Hallett J at p. 103; *Mustafa* (1976) 65 Cr App R 26, per Scarman LJ at p. 31. What can be done, and what the courts have, with some success, attempted to do over the last hundred years, is to proffer some (necessarily general) guidance as to the point at which evidence may be said to become proof positive of the crime charged.

Striking Similarity not a Universal Requirement

The authorities from which the present rule derives are *Makin* v *A-G for New South Wales* **F12.5** [1894] AC 57; *DPP* v *Boardman* [1975] AC 421 and *DPP* v *P* [1991] 2 AC 447. *DPP* v *Boardman* is to be read in the light of the qualifications imposed of the House of Lords in the later case of *DPP* v *P.*

In *Makin* v *A-G for New South Wales*, M and his wife were accused of murdering a child they had taken into their care after receiving payment from its mother for looking after the child. The child's body was found buried at M's home. Evidence that the bodies of other children similarly received into M's care had also been found was held to have been rightly admitted. Lord Herschell LC expressed the rule in the following way (at p. 65):

> It is undoubtedly not competent for the prosecution to adduce evidence tending to show that the accused has been guilty of criminal acts other than those covered by the indictment, for the purpose of leading to the conclusion that the accused is a person likely from his criminal conduct or character to have committed the offence for which he is being tried. On the other hand, the mere fact that the evidence adduced tends to shew the commission of other crimes does not render it inadmissible if it be relevant to an issue before the jury, and it may be so relevant if it bears upon the question whether the acts alleged to constitute the crime charged in the indictment were designed or accidental, or to rebut a defence which would otherwise be open to the accused.

The similar fact evidence in *Makin* v *A-G for New South Wales* was clearly pertinent to the issue of how the child the subject of the indictment had died, but in most cases the facts fall closer to the borderline between Lord Herschell's two categories. In *DPP* v *Boardman* the House of Lords was concerned with accusations of homosexual offences made against B, a schoolmaster, by two boys in his care. The common feature of the allegations which was relied upon at trial to justify admissibility was that B had sought to play the passive role in homosexual acts. It was held that the evidence had been rightly admitted, although some of their Lordships preferred to supplement the 'passive role' similarity with other points of coincidence relating to the unorthodox way in which B was alleged to have approached and entertained the boys. Each member of the House stressed that, in order for the evidence of one boy to be admissible in support of the allegations made by the other, a high degree of probative force was required. Lord Cross put it thus (at p. 457):

> The question must always be whether the similar fact evidence taken together with the other evidence would do no more than raise or strengthen a suspicion that the accused committed the offence with which he is charged or would point so strongly to his guilt that only an ultra-cautious jury, if they accepted it as true, would acquit in the face of it. In the end – although the admissibility of such evidence is a question of law not discretion – the question as I see it must be one of degree.

In ascertaining the point at which the necessary degree of probative force was reached the House of Lords regarded as crucial the presence of 'striking similarity' (an expression taken from *Sims* [1946] KB 531) in the accounts given by the two boys. Lord Morris (at p. 441) said:

> . . . there may be cases where a judge, having both limbs of Lord Herschell LC's famous proposition in mind, considers that the interests of justice (of which the interests of fairness form so fundamental a component) make it proper that he should permit a jury when considering the evidence on a charge concerning one fact or set of facts also to consider the evidence concerning another fact or set of facts if between the two there is such a close or striking similarity or such an underlying unity that probative force could fairly be yielded.

Lords Salmon and Wilberforce also stressed the importance of striking similarity in the type of case with which they were dealing. Lord Salmon said (at p. 462):

> In the case of an alleged homosexual offence, just as in the case of an alleged burglary, evidence which proves merely that the accused has committed crimes in the past and is therefore disposed to commit the crime charged is clearly inadmissible. It has, however, never been doubted that if the crime charged is committed in a uniquely or strikingly similar manner to other crimes committed by the accused the manner in which the other crimes were committed may be evidence on which a jury could reasonably conclude that the accused was guilty of the crime charged. The similarity would have to be so unique or striking that common sense makes it inexplicable on the basis of coincidence.

And Lord Wilberforce expressed himself in similar terms (at p. 444):

> The basic principle must be that the admission of similar fact evidence (of the kind now in question) is exceptional and requires a strong degree of probative force. This probative force is derived, if at all, from the circumstance that the facts testified to by the several witnesses bear to each other such a striking similarity that they must, when judged by experience and common sense, either all be true, or have arisen from a cause common to the witnesses or from pure coincidence. The jury may, therefore, properly be asked to judge whether the right conclusion is that all are true, so that each story is supported by the others.

Subsequently the Court of Appeal, in various decisions including *Scarrott* [1978] QB 1016, expressed concern about the emphasis laid upon the phrase 'striking similarity' in *DPP* v *Boardman* as the acid test for admissibility. In *DPP* v *P*, the House of Lords accepted that 'striking similarity' was not a standard to be reached in all cases. P was charged with rape and incest in respect of each of two of his daughters. There were similarities in the daughters' allegations, involving P's possessive behaviour and his willingness to pay for abortions for both girls, but nothing which was regarded as 'striking' in the sense of going beyond features commonly to be found in such cases. The question of admissibility for the House of Lords was whether the evidence of one victim could be used in support of the allegations of the other in the absence of any striking similarity between the two accounts, and it was held that it could. Lord Mackay LC said:

> . . . I am of opinion that it is not appropriate to single out 'striking similarity' as an essential element in every case in allowing evidence of an offence against one victim to be heard in connection with an allegation against another. Obviously, in cases where the identity of the offender is in issue, evidence of a character sufficiently special reasonably to identify the perpetrator is required, and the discussion which follows in Lord Salmon's speech [in *DPP v Boardman*] indicates that he had that type of case in mind.

> From all that was said by the House in [*DPP v Boardman*] I would deduce the essential feature of evidence which is to be admitted is that its probative force in support of the allegation that an accused person committed a crime is sufficiently great to make it just to admit the evidence, notwithstanding that it is prejudicial to the accused in tending to show that he was guilty of another crime. Such probative force may be derived from striking similarities in the evidence about the manner in which the crime was committed and the authorities provide illustrations of that of which *R v Straffen* [1952] 2 QB 911 [see **F12.7**] and *R v Smith* (1915) [11 Cr App R 229: see **F12.6**] provide notable examples. But restricting the circumstances in which there is sufficient probative force to overcome prejudice of evidence relating to another crime to cases in which there is some striking similarity between them is to restrict the operation of the principle in a way which gives too much effect to a particular manner of stating it, and is not justified in principle.

> . . .

> When a question of the kind raised in this case arises I consider that the judge must first decide whether there is material upon which the jury would be entitled to conclude that the evidence of one victim about what occurred to that victim, is so related to the evidence given by another victim, about what happened to that other victim, that the evidence of the first victim provides strong enough support for the evidence of the second victim to make it just to admit it notwithstanding the prejudicial effect of admitting the evidence. This relationship, from which support is derived, may take many forms and while these forms may include 'striking similarity' in the manner in which the crime was committed, consisting of unusual characteristics in its execution the necessary relationship is by no means confined to such circumstances. Relationships in time and circumstances other than these may well be important relationships in this connection.

The test for admissibility as stated in *DPP v P* may thus be summarised as follows:

(a) The question to be addressed is whether the probative value of the evidence is sufficiently great to justify admissibility notwithstanding its prejudicial effect. Probative value may derive either from striking similarity, or from some other source, such as a relationship in time or circumstance. (It is submitted, and will be assumed in the text which follows, that this general rule is sound and not confined to cases where the evidence of one victim is tendered in support of the evidence of another.)

(b) *DPP v Boardman* may be regarded as correctly stating the *degree* of probative force required of similar fact evidence, but as incorrectly limiting the *manner* in which that force must be demonstrated, insofar as striking similarity was regarded in that case as an essential requirement even though there was no issue as to the identity of B. (For a recent application of this rule see *Groves* [1998] Crim LR 200: possession of drugs at G's home admitted to disprove defence of innocent presence at rendezvous to buy drugs — no striking similarity, but sufficient probative value.)

Comments made by Lord Mackay LC in *DPP v P* suggested that the general rule as stated above was inapplicable to cases where the issue was identification, where striking similarity remained a prerequisite of admissibility. This qualification was strongly criticised both in the last edition of this work and elsewhere, and has since been held not to represent the law in *W (John)* [1998] 2 Cr App R 289. See further **F12.7**.

Striking Similarity providing Probative Value

F12.6 It follows from what has been said above that striking similarity may continue to be a factor conferring admissibility, but only in those cases in which it is asserted that the probative value of the evidence derives, in whole or in part, from striking similarity.

Striking similarity may contribute to probative value in the following way. Where different sets of circumstances share common features, experience may suggest that the best explanation is that there is a common cause or nexus between them. Unusual or 'striking' features surrounding more than one offence may suggest a common perpetrator, in a way that commonplace similarities do not. In its most extreme form, striking similarity can identify the accused as the perpetrator of a crime which bears his 'signature' (see **F12.7**). More commonly, the similarities between a series of occurrences will be used to justify an inference that the accused could not have acted innocently in respect of all of them, so that a defence which might have succeeded with regard to an isolated incident fails when other, similar incidents are brought into account. Alternatively, a series of accusations against an accused person may be shown not to be an unfortunate coincidence by reliance on the similarities between them.

In whatever context it is suggested that 'striking' similarities are present, the following observations hold true:

(a) Offences may be identical without being 'striking'. In *Brown* (1963) 47 Cr App R 204, the commission by S (one of the co-accused) of a burglary a week before the offence charged was insufficient to identify him as the perpetrator of the later offence, as the first offence bore no 'idiosyncratic features' serving to create a nexus with the later crime. The Court of Appeal rightly held that to admit as similar fact evidence a *modus operandi* common to thousands of other offences of burglary would annihilate the general rule prohibiting general evidence of bad character to be given. See also *Wells* (1991) 92 Cr App R 24n.

(b) It follows that 'striking similarity' really means 'striking peculiarity', and the more bizarre the event, the more striking its repetition will be. Every student remembers the illustration adopted by Lord Hailsham in *DPP* v *Boardman* [1975] AC 421 (at p. 454) of the man who commits repeated homosexual offences and whose victims all state that he was attired in 'the ceremonial head-dress of a Red Indian chief or other eccentric garb'. It should not be supposed that all similar fact evidence must reflect this degree of idiosyncrasy. Everything depends on the unlikelihood of repetition being attributable to mere coincidence.

(c) 'Peculiarity' is not 'striking' unless it is also probative of the prosecution case. In *Beggs* (1989) 90 Cr App R 430, B was accused of the murder of a man by cutting his throat. The defence was that B had struck out in self-defence when the victim made unwanted homosexual advances to him. It was decided to try B at the same time on five counts of wounding which were alleged to be relevant to the murder charge, four of which were committed against students occupying the same house as B. Taken together, these incidents strongly suggested that B had a peculiar propensity to cut other people's legs with a sharp instrument while they slept. The Court of Appeal rejected this evidence as probative of the murder, noting that there were, if anything, striking dissimilarities between the murder and the woundings, and that the evidence adduced to prove the woundings, even if it showed that B had acted 'on the offensive' in the past, did not materially assist the prosecution in proving that B had not acted in self-defence in respect of the alleged murder. See also *Mills* [1992] Crim LR 802, but contrast *Seaman* (1978) 67 Cr App R 234, in which the only thing striking about the evidence of previous suspicious conduct introduced to rebut a defence of innocent taking on a charge of shoplifting, was that in each case S had behaved oddly towards a small quantity of bacon (loose or prepacked), and the evidence was admitted. Contrast also *Gurney* [1994] Crim LR 116, in which G entered premises as a trespasser and the issue was whether he had done so with intent to steal (as he claimed) or to rape (as the prosecution alleged). Among the features which the Court of Appeal held justified the use in evidence of a previous incident in which G had been disturbed in the course of an attack on a female householder were that both victims were believed to live alone, that G carried a weapon in both cases, that he did not run away when confronted by the householder and that he had been on the premises for a substantial time without stealing anything before the confrontation took place. Of these, only the first and last appear to have a real bearing on the question of G's specific intent.

(d)   It does not matter whether similar fact evidence displays its relevance by revealing features of a striking similarity with the offence itself, or simply with its surrounding circumstances. In *Scarrott* [1978] QB 1016 the Court of Appeal made it clear (at p. 1025) that the only test was that of relevance:

> Plainly some matters, some circumstances may be so distant in time or place from the commission of an offence as not to be properly considered when deciding whether the subject-matter of similar fact evidence displays striking similarities with the offence charged. On the other hand, equally plainly, one cannot isolate, as a sort of laboratory specimen, the bare bones of a criminal offence from its surrounding circumstances and say that it is only within the confines of that specimen, microscopically considered, that admissibility is to be determined.

The court gave, as a striking example of similarity manifested in surrounding circumstances, *Smith* (1915) 11 Cr App R 229, the 'brides in the bath' case, in which the court had regard to the fact that each of S's victims had been through a ceremony of marriage with him, and that he had insured their lives for substantial sums. *Scarrott* was applied in *Barrington* [1981] 1 WLR 419, where the similarities which were relied on consisted in B's method of approaching young girls to persuade them to take part in various acts of indecency, which included a representation that he was the scriptwriter for a well-known children's television programme.

The case of *Novac* (1976) 65 Cr App R 107 contains observations which may appear to contradict the principle stated above. One similarity which had been relied upon at R's trial for homosexual offences against boys related to his method of picking up his victims in amusement arcades. The Court of Appeal rejected this feature on the ground that it was not a similarity in the commission of the crime, but a similarity in the surrounding circumstances, which was insufficiently proximate to be of assistance in establishing the commission of the offence. It was said in *Scarrott* [1978] QB 1016 that this observation amounted, not to a rule of law, but to a reason for the rejection of the evidence on the facts of the particular case. In other words, the lack of connection between the picking up of the victim and the commission of the offence was the reason why it lacked the requisite probative force.

(e)   Dissimilarities in the evidence, which detract from its probative value, must be taken into account. In *Johnson* [1995] 2 Cr App R 41, J's previous convictions for sexual assault in the course of burglary had in common with the similar offence charged the 'gentleness' of the intruder's approach. However, there were also clear dissimilarities which ought to have been taken into account, and the evidence was wrongly admitted. The same principle was reasserted in the notorious case of *West* [1996] 2 Cr App R 374, where it was said that 'the existence of dissimilarities cannot alone determine the question of admissibility'. Dissimilarity was properly regarded as a feature to which the judge was obliged to have regard when assessing the probative force of the evidence in the light of the purpose for which the prosecution wished to rely on it. Where evidence disclosing striking similarity is properly left to the jury, it is important also to draw the attention of the jury to any attendant dissimilarities (*Tricoglus* (1976) 65 Cr App R 16).

(f)   If the evidence appears to possess 'striking similarity' at the time of its admission, but subsequent evidence reduced the level of similarity to the point where it would not have been judged admissible, it cannot be left to the jury (*Naylor* [1998] Crim LR 662).

Striking Similarity Identifying the Accused

F12.7   In *DPP* v *P* [1991] 2 AC 447 (see F12.5), Lord Mackay LC appeared to state that in cases where the identity of the offender is in issue similar fact evidence must always provide something in the nature of a 'signature or other special feature'. His lordship said:

> Where the identity of the perpetrator is in issue, and evidence of this kind is important in that connection, obviously something in the nature of what has been called in the course of the argument a signature or other special feature will be necessary. To transpose this requirement to other situations where the question is whether a crime has been committed, rather than who did commit it, is to impose an unnecessary and improper restriction upon the application of the principle.

This is not true of all cases, for while there are some circumstances in which the evidence which identifies the accused is indeed equivalent to his signature or hallmark on the deed, it is also possible for an offence to be linked to an accused by a chain of reasoning which does not include this feature. Thus in *Thompson* v *The King* [1918] AC 221 a homosexual pederast had assaulted two young boys and arranged to meet them again. T kept the appointment but denied being the man who had assaulted the boys. Their identification of him was confirmed by evidence of his possession of powder puffs and indecent photographs which were not said to have been used in the offence and did not in any sense constitute T's 'signature'; but it is submitted that the evidence was rightly admitted in the light of the probative value which it possessed to rebut T's claim of mistaken identity. If follows that, despite what was said in *DPP* v *P*, there is no special rule applicable to all cases of identification by evidence of previous misconduct.

What can safely be said about identification cases is that where a feature is relied upon to identify an accused *and* is said to be the equivalent of a signature, it must possess to a very high degree the features associated with 'striking similarity' (in the sense explained at F12.6), and for the very good reason that the logic which permits the identification of a criminal by his 'signature' inevitably requires something almost as personal as a fingerprint before the necessary link to the offence can be forged. Thus in *Johnson* [1995] 2 Cr App R 41 (see F12.6), the only evidence identifying J apart from his previous convictions for sexual offences in the course of similar burglaries was the alleged recognition of his voice by the victims of the offence charged. It was held, applying *DPP* v *P*, that evidence of the previous offences should not have been admitted as there was only one special common feature (all the victims describing the 'gentleness' of the intruder's approach) and too many clear dissimilarities for the offence to be regarded as bearing J's signature.

The approach taken in this work now has the support of the decision of the Court of Appeal in *W (John)* [1998] 2 Cr App R 289. Two offences took place in the same vicinity within two weeks. In both cases the female victim was detained for a short time by the offender. In one case an indecent assault took place, in the other the victim's screams scared the attacker off. The descriptions of the attacker fitted W, who was in the vicinity on both occasions, and whose clothing after the second attack was shown to have torn in a way consistent with an injury suffered by the attacker when escaping. Both the attacker and W were left-handed. From the totality of the evidence the Court of Appeal was able to deduce a 'relationship in time and circumstances' sufficient to satisfy the required degree of probative value. An argument that striking similarity had to be present was rejected. The dictum of Lord Mackay LC in *DPP* v *P* was said to be explicable on the basis that his lordship had in mind only cases where the probative value of the evidence derived from its striking similarity, for example 'where the only evidence of any substance against a defendant on a count was "a signature" or other very striking similarity'. The dictum had no application to cases such as *Thompson* v *The King*. Put in this way Lord Mackay's dictum becomes a harmless truism.

It is submitted that cases decided before *W (John)*, in which the Court of Appeal strove to give effect to what appeared to be Lord Mackay's preference for a special rule in identification cases, should now be read in the light of the principle stated in *W (John)*. Some are 'signature' cases in any event, for example *Ruiz* [1995] Crim LR 151, in which R was charged with murdering X and with administering a stupefying drug to Y in order to rob him. The circumstances of the murder, which had occurred some months after the robbery, were strikingly similar to the earlier offence except that the victim had died. Evidence that R had drugged and robbed Y was admissible to establish the identity of the murderer of X. The case of *West* [1996] 2 Cr App R 374 may require some re-examination. W was convicted of the murders of ten women and girls committed jointly with her husband, who had taken his life before the trial. She denied complicity, and this was taken to be tantamount to raising an issue of identity. Seven murders shared unusual common features, and evidence of four witnesses who had been sexually abused by W and her husband acting together was held to have been rightly admitted to demonstrate that W was an enthusiastic and committed participator in acts of sexual violence, and to show that she derived sexual gratification from them. This evidence was considered to satisfy the requirement of striking similarity to identify W as a participant, but, whether it did or not, it would now seem that the threshold of admissibility can be met on the argument that a person who has participated in acts of serious sexual violence with her husband is unlikely to have been completely unaware that he was also committing murders at their home. (Compare *Groves* [1998] Crim LR 200 at **F12.5**.) *W (John)* also makes it easier to understand the decision in *Downey* [1995] 1 Cr App R 547, in which the Court of Appeal held that evidence identifying D in relation to one offence which is closely connected in time and circumstance with another may be admitted to identify him in relation to that other offence. In effect, this created an exception to the supposed general rule requiring striking similarity, but such an exception is no longer necessary in the light of *W (John)*. (For the facts of *Downey*, see **F12.12**.)

There are many older examples of cases in which 'signature' evidence was admitted. In *Straffen* [1952] 2 QB 911, the murder of a young girl who was found strangled was considered unusual in that no attempt had been made to assault her sexually or to conceal the body. S came under immediate suspicion because he had previously strangled two other girls, each murder having the same peculiar features, and because he was in the neighbourhood at the time, having just escaped from Broadmoor. Under these circumstances, very little other evidence was required to convict S of the third murder: it bore his 'fingerprints'.

In *Butler* (1986) 84 Cr App R 12, B was charged with the rape of two women. His defence was that he had been mistakenly identified. The rapes bore certain features, strongly suggesting that the same man was responsible, including the fact that both victims said that they had been forced to take part in oral intercourse to the point of ejaculation while their abductor was driving them to the scene of the rape in his car. Evidence was given by Mrs U, a former girlfriend of B, who testified that B had done the same peculiar things with her, albeit with her consent. The evidence was held admissible to rebut the defence of mistaken identity. See also *Tricoglus* (1976) 65 Cr App R 16, in which the two rapes with which T was charged were sufficiently peculiar to be regarded as the work of the same man, although T's conviction was quashed because further similar fact evidence which had been used to link him with the crimes was inadmissible. It had been proved that T, who resembled the general description given of the rapist and who drove a car of a similar type, had attempted to pick up two other women in the same city-centre area from which the victims had been taken by the same 'kerb-crawling' method. This evidence proved at most that T had 'unpleasant social habits', without bearing in any way on the material issue in the case, which was whether T was the man who had raped the other two women.

Not all 'signature' cases are of a sexual nature. For example, in *Mullen* [1992] Crim LR 735, it was M's distinctive use of a blow-torch to crack glass in order to enter and burgle premises which provided the link between his crimes.

Evidence of Propensity

F12.8   The 'signature' cases raise the question of whether it is proper to introduce evidence of propensity as similar fact evidence. It is frequently said that the prosecution are not entitled to rely on evidence which would merely be evidence of a propensity to commit crime of a certain type: for recent examples see *A-G of Hong Kong v Siu Yuk-shing* [1989] 1 WLR 236, per Lord Griffiths at p. 239 and *B (R.A.)* [1997] 2 Cr App R 88. The opinion of Lord Herschell LC in the leading case of *Makin v A-G for New South Wales* [1894] AC 57 (see **F12.5**) seeks also to contrast evidence which does no more than show that the accused is the sort of person likely to commit the offence charged, with evidence which goes beyond this general blackening of the accused's character and provides proof that he committed the offence. The view taken in the present work, and supported, it is submitted, by *DPP v P* [1991] 2 AC 447, is that the difference between what is prohibited and what is permitted is best expressed as a matter of degree, i.e. the evidence must be shown to be of very specific significance to the issue before the court. Viewed in this way, 'mere' evidence of propensity is simply another way of describing evidence which does not sufficiently specifically prove guilt. There is, however, another view inconsistent with this, and that is the view taken by Lord Hailsham in *DPP v Boardman* [1975] AC 421 (at p. 453). According to this view, what is prohibited by the *Makin* rule is any chain of reasoning leading from propensity to guilt. Similar fact evidence can only be admissible if some other rational argument can be constructed for admitting it, and if it can, the evidence should be made subject to a warning from the trial judge to the jury that they should 'eschew the forbidden reasoning' (i.e. the reasoning based on propensity) in reaching their conclusions.

The difficulty with this view, pointed out by Lord Cross of Chelsea in *DPP v Boardman* [1975] AC 421 at pp. 456–7, is that evidence of disposition may on occasion have sufficient probative value to merit inclusion. This is particularly true of the 'signature' cases, and Lord Cross himself relied on the example of *Straffen* [1952] 2 QB 911 (see **F12.7**). Under all the circumstances, it would have been an affront to common sense to exclude evidence of the two other murders S had committed, yet they did no more than to show (albeit very convincingly) that S was a person likely from his criminal disposition to have committed the crime charged. No other chain of reasoning enters into it. The same is true of *Butler* (1987) 84 Cr App R 12 (at **F12.7**).

Nor is it only in the 'signature' cases that evidence of propensity may be relied upon: a relevant propensity may also form part of the reason why an otherwise plausible defence becomes incredible, as in *Lewis* (1982) 76 Cr App R 33, where evidence of L's paedophile tendencies rebutted his defence of innocent association with his girlfriend's children, or *Ball* [1911] AC 47, where evidence of a brother and sister's 'guilty passion' was introduced to prove incest. In such cases what is being relied upon is a chain of reasoning based on the likelihood that the disposition in question will affect the behaviour of the individual concerned, making it more likely that the offence was committed. It is submitted that there is no absolute prohibition on the introduction of evidence of propensity.

Whether the prohibition exists or not, however, it has been held that it is certainly not the law that the judge is obliged to warn the jury to 'eschew the forbidden reasoning' in every case where similar fact evidence is admitted (*Rance* (1975) 62 Cr App R 118, at p. 122; see also *Roy* [1992] Crim LR 185 and *Whitehouse* [1996] Crim LR 50).

Rebuttal of Suggestion of Mistake, Innocent Association, Accident etc.

Another function which similar fact evidence may be called upon to perform is to show **F12.9** an event involving an accused person in its true light. It may be, for example, that an incident which the prosecution alleges was designed rather than accidental may be capable of either interpretation, until linked with another incident or incidents, the combined probative value of which rebuts the innocent explanation. In the leading case of *Makin* v *A-G for New South Wales* [1894] AC 57 (see **F12.5**), the discovery of one child's body in the Makins' backyard was not necessarily probative of non-accidental death. It was evidence that many other children had been taken in by the couple and that their bodies too had been discovered in the Makins' gardens, which made the inference of murder irresistible.

How far is 'striking similarity' a relevant consideration in cases of this kind? Three examples will assist in explanation. In *Bond* [1906] 2 KB 389, the prosecution case was that B, a doctor, had operated upon a young woman who was pregnant with his child, with intent to procure her miscarriage. The defence that he was carrying out a lawful medical examination of the girl was held to have been properly rebutted by the evidence of another girl, who claimed that nine months previously B had operated on her when she became pregnant by him, with the intention of terminating her pregnancy, and that he had told her that he had 'put dozens of girls right'. In *Mortimer* (1936) 25 Cr App R 150, M was charged with the murder of a woman cyclist by deliberately driving a motor car at her. To rebut any suggestion that this was a case of manslaughter lacking the element of intention required for murder, evidence was adduced to show that M had, on the evening before the incident, knocked down two other women cyclists in a similar way; that, some hours after the incident he had knocked one other woman off her bicycle, and that he had attempted to avoid capture by driving his car at police officers who tried to apprehend him. Thirdly, in *Smith* (1915) 11 Cr App R 229 (and see also **F12.6**), S was charged with the murder of a woman with whom he had been through a ceremony of marriage, and who was found drowned in her bath. Evidence was given that two other women whom S had induced to 'marry' him had met with the same fate. Each death benefited S, who had taken the precaution of insuring the women's lives.

In each of these three examples, the function of the similar fact evidence was to put a different complexion on what had occurred; in *Bond* by showing a criminal purpose, in *Mortimer* by showing an intention to cause death or injury, and in *Smith* by showing that the deaths had not occurred through natural causes but through the activities of the accused. In *Mortimer* and *Smith* (though not, perhaps, in *Bond*) it could be said that the incidents bore a striking similarity one to another, but to require such similarity in these cases as a precondition of admissibility would be unduly restrictive (and, following *DPP* v *P* [1991] 2 AC 447, unnecessary), for the evidence achieves the necessary degree of probative value the minute it becomes apparent that the link between the events is inexplicable on the basis of coincidence. This point can be achieved, as in *Bond*, without the proof of particularly unusual or striking features in the circumstances surrounding the occurrences. Rather, the probative value derived from the improbability that on one occasion B intended a certain act to procure miscarriage, whereas on a later occasion he performed the same act with an innocent objective: particularly once it was known that he was aware of the benefit to himself from performing the act with a criminal purpose. The degree of improbability depends partly on the number of incidents and partly on other factors which in common experience point to coincidence or lack of it: for example, it is less remarkable to discover a doctor performing a lawful examination such as that described by the defence in *Bond* than it is to find a dentist similarly occupied. Where 'striking similarities' are present, it may be possible to derive the necessary probative value from a shorter series of incidents: two dead brides would surely have been sufficient to convict *Smith*, and (possibly) two injured cyclists would have proved the case against *Mortimer*. *Bond*, on the other hand, shows that the absence of striking similarity may require proof of a greater number of incidents to dispel coincidence, for the majority of the judges regarded it as significant that the similar fact evidence disclosed an admission by B of 'dozens' of other similar incidents. This strengthened the argument that B was unlikely, on the occasion in question, to have departed from his usual method of dealing with young women made pregnant by him.

A still lower level of similarity in terms of circumstances may be required in other cases where, as in *Bond* [1906] 2 KB 389, the accused already has a great deal of explaining to do. In *Rance* (1975) 62 Cr App R 118, evidence of the signing of other, somewhat similar documents by him was introduced to rebut R's defence that he signed a particular document authorising a bribe without knowing what it was: an unlikely explanation in any event, but one made incredible by the introduction of the similar fact evidence. It is noteworthy that it was in this case, where the similarities were not particularly striking, that the Court of Appeal first voiced its doubts about the universal applicability of a test based exclusively upon striking similarity.

If it is right to say that the admissibility of similar fact evidence to rebut an innocent explanation is entirely dependent on the logical capacity of the evidence to refute the explanation in question, then it must follow that in cases where the prosecution allege that similar fact evidence displays a systematic course of conduct by the accused, there can be no fixed rule that two cases cannot constitute a system. This was the view expressed by Lord Cross of Chelsea in *DPP v Boardman* [1975] AC 421 (at p. 460), although his lordship added that it would be right to proceed with great caution in cases where two instances alone are relied upon. On the other hand, in *DPP v Kilbourne* [1973] AC 729, at pp. 750–1, Lord Reid considered two instances insufficient to constitute a system. Both Lord Reid and Lord Cross were speaking of a case where the prosecution are relying on accusations of similar offences by different victims, where there is the added danger of collusion between the witnesses which may account for Lord Reid's reservations (see **F12.13**). It will be contended, however, that even in such cases, the limitation imposed by Lord Reid is unnecessary. If this is so, then *a fortiori* there is no need for such a rule where the court is asked to act on purely circumstantial evidence.

It is rather more obvious that there is no limit to the maximum number of instances which may constitute a system. See, e.g., *Mather* [1991] Crim LR 285, in which the prosecution succeeded in introducing evidence of 79 other offences to establish a system in relation to four offences of theft and false accounting.

Nature of Defence as Factor Affecting Relevance

F12.10   It has already been established that the admissibility of 'similar fact' evidence is governed by the relevance of the evidence to the facts in issue. Evidence which is directed to the proof of some fact which is not in issue cannot be received, not because of the prejudicial effect of such evidence, but simply because it is irrelevant. It is apparent, therefore, that the nature of the defence or defences reasonably open to the accused must have a bearing on the purpose for which the evidence is adduced, on its relevance, and therefore on its admissibility.

That this is so may be demonstrated by the facts of *Butler* (1986) 84 Cr App R 12 (see **F12.7**). B was charged with two rapes which were committed in a bizarre fashion. His suggestion that he had been mistakenly identified was rebutted by the evidence of his former girlfriend that he had done the same things with her, albeit with her consent. This evidence, so relevant to the defence of mistaken identity, would have been inadmissible and irrelevant to the case for the prosecution (and might even have assisted the defence) had B set up the defence of consent.

The nature of the defence may thus be said to be a factor to be taken into account in measuring the probative value of the similar fact evidence. This was recognised by the

Court of Appeal in *Lunt* (1986) 85 Cr App R 241, where it was said that in order to decide whether the evidence is positively probative in relation to the crime charged, it is first necessary to identify the issue to which it relates. *Lunt* was applied in *Wells* (1991) 92 Cr App R 24 n, in which the Court of Appeal referred with approval to the summary of the law in *Phipson on Evidence* (12th ed.), at p. 499 *et seq.*, where it is submitted that 'the nature of the defence or possible defence is one of the factors which the trial judge should take into account in considering whether the probative force of the similar fact evidence outweighs its prejudicial effect.'

In various authorities it is suggested that the raising of a particular defence, such as accident or innocent association, guarantees the admissibility of relevant similar fact evidence, whereas the same evidence would necessarily be inadmissible if the defence were a general denial of the prosecution's case. An example is the decision of the Court of Appeal in *Flack* [1969] 1 WLR 937. F was charged with incest with three of his sisters. It was held that the evidence on each count was inadmissible to prove the other two, since 'no question of identity, intent, system, guilty knowledge, or of rebutting a defence of innocent association ever arose'. The reasoning in *Flack*, and in other cases to the same effect, such as *Chandor* [1959] 1 QB 545, is based on a misunderstanding of the decision of the Privy Council in *Makin v A-G of New South Wales* [1894] AC 57 (see **F12.5** and **F12.9**). It will be remembered that Lord Herschell LC said that similar fact evidence could be admitted where it was relevant to an issue before the jury, and that 'it may be so relevant if it bears upon the question whether the acts alleged to constitute the crime charged in the indictment were designed or accidental, or to rebut a defence which would otherwise be open to the accused.' The error lies in assuming that Lord Herschell had in mind a closed list of defences, to rebut which similar fact evidence could be adduced, and that he intended in particular to prohibit the use of such evidence where the defence of the accused consists of a general denial of the prosecution case. However, the House of Lords has made it abundantly clear that no such closed list exists. Thus, in *Harris v DPP* [1952] AC 694, Lord Simon LC held that it was an error 'to attempt to draw up a closed list of the sort of cases in which the principle operates: such a list only provides instances of its general application, whereas what really matters is the principle itself.' In *DPP v Boardman* [1975] AC 421, Lord Hailsham LC, approving Lord Simon LC's statement, added (at p. 452): 'The rules of logic and common sense are not susceptible to exact codification when applied to the actual facts of life in its infinite variety'.

It follows from Lord Hailsham's premise (which was also endorsed by Lord Morris, at p. 439 and by Lord Cross at p. 457) that there can be no absolute rule that similar fact evidence cannot be used in cases where the defence is a general denial. All depends on the power of the evidence to persuade the jury of the guilt of the accused. In fact, as Lord Hailsham himself pointed out (at p. 452), the possible permutations of fact are so numerous that no clear line can be drawn between all cases of innocent association on the one hand and all cases of general denial on the other. *DPP v Boardman* itself provides an example of a case which cannot be categorised in one way or the other: B, a schoolmaster, in giving an innocent explanation for suspicious conduct towards his pupils, denied all of the acts of indecency imputed to him by his accusers. To have labelled this a general denial so as to avoid the introduction of similar fact evidence would have been illogical. In the same way, it would be improper to dress up every conceivable innocent explanation given by the accused as a 'defence of innocent association', simply in order to found an argument that similar fact evidence must be admissible: a device which Lord Wilberforce rightly regarded as a 'specious manner of outflanking the exclusionary rule' (at p. 443).

Allied to the fallacy that similar fact evidence cannot be used in respect of a defence which involves a complete denial of the prosecution case, is the notion that such evidence may not be used to rebut a defence based on involuntariness. This seems to have been the view taken in *Harrison-Owen* [1951] 2 All ER 726, in which the previous convictions of the accused for housebreaking were held inadmissible to rebut a defence of automatism raised in respect of a similar charge. There can, however, be no absolute rule to this effect. If a man is charged with an indecent assault on a woman, and he claims that he simply tripped and fell against her awkwardly, or blacked out and came round in a compromising position, it may be highly relevant to prove that this is what he says every time he is accused of indecency.

In more recent cases, influenced particularly by *DPP* v *Boardman* and *Scarrott* [1978] QB 1016, the courts have acknowledged that it is unwise to assert an absolute bar to the use of similar fact evidence in rebuttal of a particular kind of defence. Thus, in *Wilmot* (1989) 89 Cr App R 341, the Court of Appeal dealt brusquely with an argument that similar fact evidence could never be used to rebut a defence of consent to a charge of rape, for it was impossible to preclude the possibility that circumstances might arise in which such evidence would be sufficiently germane to be admissible. Similarly, in *Beggs* (1989) 90 Cr App R 430, the Court of Appeal noted that counsel had been unable to discover any case in which similar fact evidence had been used to rebut a defence of self-defence, but (despite being unable to conjure up any circumstances in which such evidence might be of sufficient relevance) the court refrained from saying that in no conceivable circumstances would this be possible. This is, with respect, entirely the correct way to proceed. Many of the difficulties in this area of law in the past were produced by attempts to reduce into fixed and labelled categories those cases where similar fact evidence could be used. In this respect at least, *DPP* v *Boardman* has had a liberating effect upon the attitude of the courts. Nevertheless, isolated instances continue to occur in which the reasoning deprecated in that case appears to have been adopted: see, e.g., *Lewis* (1982) 76 Cr App R 33 (evidence of paedophile tendencies admissible to rebut innocent explanation but not general denial).

Anticipating Defence to be Raised

F12.11 It would not be practicable to require the prosecution to wait and see what defence, if any, is to be relied upon before adducing similar fact evidence. On the other hand, it cannot be right to permit similar fact evidence to be adduced which, in the words of Lord Du Parcq in *Noor Mohamed* v *The King* [1949] AC 182, merely goes to 'strengthen the evidence of a fact which was not denied and, perhaps, could not be the subject of rational dispute'. In deciding whether evidence is relevant to the prosecution's case it is not helpful to rely on the notion that a plea of not guilty technically puts everything in issue. Rather, the test is whether the defence in question may fairly be said to be open to the accused on the facts as they appear from the evidence available to the prosecution. Thus in *Thompson* v *The King* [1918] AC 221, Lord Sumner observed (at p. 232): 'The prosecution cannot credit the accused with fancy defences in order to rebut them at the outset with some damning piece of prejudice'. In *Noor Mohamed* v *The King*, Lord Du Parcq explained this observation (at pp. 191–2):

> An accused person need set up no defence other than a general denial of the crime alleged. The plea of not guilty may be equivalent to saying 'Let the prosecution prove its case, if it can', and having said so much the accused may take refuge in silence. In such a case it may appear (for instance) that the facts and circumstances of the particular offence charged are consistent with innocent intention, whereas further evidence, which incidentally shows that the accused has committed one or more other offences, may tend to prove that they are consistent only with a guilty intent. The prosecution could not be said . . . to be 'crediting the accused with a fancy defence' if they sought to adduce such evidence.

In *Harris* v *DPP* [1952] AC 694, the House of Lords approved the law as stated by Lord Du Parcq, Viscount Simon adding (at p. 707): 'What Lord Sumner meant when he denied the right of the prosecution to 'credit the accused with fancy defences' . . . was that evidence involving the accused ought not to be dragged in to his prejudice without reasonable cause'.

At first sight certain observations of the Court of Appeal in *Sims* [1946] KB 531 may seem to conflict with the approach based on *Thompson* v *The King* [1918] AC 221. In *Sims*, Lord Goddard CJ said (at p. 539) that the admissibility of similar fact evidence could not be allowed to depend on the nature of the defence raised, because a plea of not guilty meant that the prosecution were obliged to prove all the elements of their case, and therefore: 'The accused should not be able, by confining himself at the trial to one issue, to exclude evidence that would be admissible and fatal if he ran two defences; for that would make the astuteness of the accused or his advisers prevail over the interests of justice'. If this is intended to suggest that the prosecution should be permitted to adduce similar fact evidence to prove facts which are not contested, it cannot be accepted. If it is intended to do no more than to say that the prosecution can anticipate any defence which could reasonably be run, it is already catered for by the interpretation placed upon *Thompson* v *The King* in *Noor Mohamed* v *The King* and *Harris* v *DPP*. In the latter case Viscount Simon concluded that the Court of Appeal in *Sims* meant to say no more than that the prosecution were entitled to adduce evidence to prove their case without waiting to see the line adopted by the defence.

If, where a defence is reasonably open to an accused, defence counsel indicates that this line will not in fact be taken, the prosecution ought to accept the indication, for 'no one can know as well as defending counsel what defence is going to be raised' (*Cole* (1941) 28 Cr App R 43). See also *A-G of Hong-Kong* v *Siu Yuk-shing* [1989] 1 WLR 236. S was charged with possession of items relating to a prohibited 'triad' society; the burden of proof being upon the prosecution to show that S knew the significance of the items in his possession. On the indications available to the prosecution at the relevant point of the trial, knowledge seemed to be a live issue, and evidence was admitted which showed that S had previously been convicted of membership of such a society and must therefore have known of the ritual significance of the items. Lord Griffiths said (at p. 240): 'The defence . . . had the opportunity if they so desired to admit knowledge of the triad significance of the articles. If the defence had made this admission knowledge would no longer have been in issue and no proper purpose would have been served by proof of the previous conviction.'

Multiple Charges and Accusations

The principles to be applied to cases of this kind do not differ materially from those **F12.12** applicable where similar fact evidence is used to rebut an explanation otherwise open to the accused: indeed, the function of evidence of multiple accusers is often to rebut such an explanation. Separate exposition is helpful, however, in order to bring out the special problems of collusion which arise under this heading.

Where an accused faces more than one charge of a similar nature or where evidence of similar allegations is tendered in support of one charge, the evidence of one accuser may be admissible to support the evidence of another. In the past, the prosecution has frequently sought to adduce evidence of this kind where corroboration was in issue. In cases of this kind the highest authority appeared to support the application of the 'striking similarity' test (see *DPP* v *Kilbourne* [1973] AC 729; *DPP* v *Boardman* [1975] AC 421), and it was in a case concerning multiple accusations of buggery that the 'striking similarity' test was first formulated (*Sims* [1946] KB 531). In *DPP* v *P* [1991] 2 AC 447 (see **F12.5**), however, the House of Lords held that striking similarity is not a prerequisite of admissibility. The Court of Appeal had with some reluctance quashed the convictions on the ground that, in the absence of any 'striking similarity' between their stories, the allegations of one daughter should not have been admitted to support those of the other. The House of Lords allowed the prosecutor's appeal and in doing so overruled a number of Court of Appeal cases in which it had been held that admissibility could not be based on similar features which were not 'striking' because they were no more than the 'stock in trade' of the child abuser or the incestuous father. The three most important cases affected are *Inder* (1977) 67 Cr App R 143, *Clarke* (1977) 647 Cr App R 398, and *B* (1990) 92 Cr App R 36.

The effect of *DPP* v *P* is that the probative force required of evidence in a case involving a number of accusers may derive *either* from striking similarity *or* from some other relationship between the offence charged and the other evidence, whether in point of time or arising from other relevant circumstances (see **F12.5**). In *DPP* v *P* itself, the evidence was admissible because each girl independently described a 'prolonged course of conduct' involving the general domination of the family by the accused, who seemed obsessed with keeping the girls to himself. The girls' evidence suggested that the younger daughter had taken over the role of the elder when the latter left home. Taken together, these features, together with the fact that the accused had contributed towards the cost of abortions for both girls, gave the evidence sufficient probative force to make it just to admit it, notwithstanding its prejudicial effect.

The outcome of *DPP* v *P* is in fact consistent with the practice of the courts in a number of other cases ostensibly decided under the 'striking similarity' principle. The underlying principle is that the probative value of multiple accusations may depend in part on their similarity, but also on the unlikelihood that the same person would find himself falsely accused on different occasions by different and independent individuals. The making of multiple accusations is a coincidence in itself, which has to be taken into account in deciding admissibility. As Lord Cross of Chelsea put it in *DPP* v *Boardman* [1975] AC 421 (at p. 460):

> ... the point is not whether what the appellant is said to have suggested would be, as coming from a middle-aged active homosexual, in itself particularly unusual but whether it would be unlikely that two youths who were saying untruly that the appellant had made homosexual advances to them would have put such a suggestion into his mouth.

See also *Sims* [1946] KB 531, where Lord Goddard CJ noted (at p. 540) that the probative force of a number of accusations taken together is much greater than one alone, for 'whereas the jury might think one man might be telling an untruth, three or four are hardly likely to tell the same untruth unless they were conspiring together'. These judicial observations, together with the analysis of the evidence in *DPP* v *P*, explain why the level of 'striking similarity' achieved in cases such as *DPP* v *Boardman* [1975] AC 421 and *DPP* v *Kilbourne* [1973] AC 729 and *Sims* appeared to have been pitched rather on the low side: it is because features which would not have been striking in themselves became significant when independent accusers included them in their stories. In *Kilbourne* it was the not uncommon way in which K committed buggery and other indecent acts with boys he had lured to his home. In *DPP* v *Boardman* it was the fact that B, a schoolmaster, offered himself to his pupils as the passive partner in acts of buggery (though it must be said that a majority of their lordships thought this insufficient on its own, bolstering it with other similarities in the accounts given by the boys of the way in which they had been approached by B).

The more permissive approach sanctioned in *DPP* v *P* does not support the conclusion that the mere existence of multiple accusations of similar offences will guarantee admissibility; there must still be some relationship between any given allegations which affords one probative force in relation to the other (*Musquera* [1999] Crim LR 857, where the point is also made that the fact that two or more offences are sexual in nature does not provide a sufficient relationship). There is, however, a risk that the vagueness of the concept of a 'relationship' may result in admissibility on the basis of a very slender nexus, as in *Simpson* (1994) 99 Cr App R 48. In that case *DPP* v *P* was applied and a sufficient relationship held to be present where a series of sexual offences ranging from rape to indecent assault were said to have been committed by S on young girls in his own home. Yet it was acknowledged that there was no nexus in relation to the type of offence or the manner of execution and that the offences were unconnected in point of time; it may be doubted whether the jury would have found any real connection between the offences beyond the fact that the same accused was involved in all of them. See also *Channing* [1994] Crim LR 924. As the Court of Appeal previously noted in *Wilmot* (1989) 89 Cr App R 341, at p. 348, prejudice would result if the jury were to convict on the argument that 'If this many accusations are made, there must be something in each of them'. It is also pertinent that in *Christou* [1996] 2 WLR 620 the appeal to the House of Lords was on the basis that the allegations involving the sexual abuse of C's two young cousins were not capable of being linked as similar fact evidence, yet Lord Griffiths stated that he was firmly of the opinion that the evidence could have been regarded as mutually supportive. Although the principles permitting joinder are different from, and more generous to the prosecution than, the similar fact rule, it appears that the approach in *DPP* v *P* has done much to narrow the gap. See as to joinder **D9.24** *et seq*.

Although the decision in *DPP* v *P* means that many earlier cases turning on striking similarity must now be approached with caution, it does not follow that they must be disregarded. Cases in which evidence was admitted because features were identified which were so bizarre as to amount to striking similarity in the true sense would be decided in precisely the same way after *DPP* v *P*. Thus, for example, in *Lanford* v *General Medical Council* [1990] 1 AC 13, L was accused of misconduct with two female patients. Each allegation involved indecent assault, in one case during a vaginal examination, and in the other during an examination of a sore toe. What was striking was that each patient independently described the use by L of offensive language such as 'screw' and 'pussy', during the assaults, and the strikingness of the evidence was if anything increased by the irrelevance of the language to the case of the patient with the sore toe. The evidence of each patient was rightly admitted to corroborate the allegation of the other.

More caution is required in relation to cases which, while ostensibly turning on the discovery of strikingly similar features, are better explained in the light of the principle stated in *DPP* v *P* as involving evidence possessed of probative value from another source, or from a combination of sources of which similarity is only one. It has already been stated that the cases of *DPP* v *Boardman* [1975] AC 421, *DPP* v *Kilbourne* [1973] AC 729 and *Sims* [1946] KB 531 may require to be interpreted in this way. Two more recent examples are *Shore* (1989) 89 Cr App R 32, and *Bedford* (1991) 93 Cr App R 113. In *Shore* the question was whether a headmaster's relationships with various girl pupils were merely avuncular, or were indecently motivated. In order to justify the admissibility of the evidence the Court of Appeal discovered striking similarity between the girls' accounts by dwelling on a number of features which were not particularly unusual, and it is submitted that the case would now be decided by ascribing probative value to the fact that all of the children independently concluded that there was nothing avuncular in the way that they had been touched. In *Bedford*, described by the Court of Appeal as a 'near borderline case', the principal 'strikingly similar' features linking accusations of sexual assault by one victim to accusations by two other boys in respect of whom guilt was admitted, were that the boys were all teenagers living close by to B, that all the offences happened in B's flat after the victim had been invited to sit on B's knee, and that in each case some money changed hands. It would be unfortunate if cases such as these which accepted a very low level of striking similarity, in all probability so as to get round the restriction improperly imposed by the supposed need to satisfy that test in all cases, were to continue to be regarded as authorities on striking similarity if susceptible instead of explanation on the grounds stated in *DPP* v *P*.

Of a similar kind to cases of multiple accusers is *Robinson* (1953) 37 Cr App R 95, in which it was said to be a remarkable coincidence that R was separately identified by different witnesses as having been involved in two different robberies. Whether such a coincidence is remarkable or not must depend on the facts, but it is submitted that the risk of error inherent in fleeting glimpse identifications is not necessarily counteracted by other purported identifications of the same person. The difficulty is compounded where the facts of the offences are so similar that they appear to be the work of one man, but in each case the evidence identifying the accused as that man lacks conviction. In *McGranaghan* [1992] Crim LR 430, the Court of Appeal held that an identification about which the jury were not sure could not support another identification of which they were also not sure, however similar the facts of the two offences might be. It was held that the jury should be directed that they must be sure on evidence other than similar fact evidence that the accused had committed one offence before considering whether the similarity of the other offences showed that he had committed those also. This precaution goes too far, as there is no logical reason why cumulative evidence of identification should not be relied upon provided that there is other evidence to satisfy the jury that all the offences were committed by the same person. This was accepted in *Downey* [1995] 1 Cr App R 547, in which two filling-station robberies were committed a few minutes apart and the evidence very strongly suggested that the same person committed both offences. It was held that these offences were so 'welded together' that the jury was entitled to combine the identification evidence of the two offences (pictures from a security camera in one case and the evidence of a witness as to the registration number of the getaway car in the other) in order to decide if the robber was D. *Downey* was approved in *Barnes* [1995] 2 Cr App R 491, in which the counts of indecent assault and wounding were sufficiently similar as to be regarded as the work of the same individual, and it was held that the visual identification evidence could be viewed cumulatively. See also *Grant* [1996] 2 Cr App R 272. In each of these authorities *McGranaghan* was confined to the case where the jury are invited to reason that because the accused committed offence B he also committed offence A. This, as Evans LJ pointed out in *Downey* (at p. 552), 'involves proof not only of similarity but that the defendant did in fact commit offence B'. The direction to be given in such a case is frequently described as the 'sequential approach', while the direction when the jury are entitled to consider all the evidence on counts A and B before reaching their verdicts on them is the 'cumulative approach'. In cases where the sequential approach is called for, the trial judge may need to help the jury with guidance as to which count to consider first (*W (John)* [1998] 2 Cr App R 289).

A more difficult application of *Downey* occurred in *Lee* [1996] Crim LR 825 where evidence that two burglaries appeared to bear the hallmark of the same group or gang of individuals was held to justify admissibility, even though there was little evidence to connect L with the second count. The Court of Appeal considered that L was entitled to a consideration of the totality of the evidence against him as an individual upon the making of a submission of no case in relation to count 2, but not at the point at which the evidence was admitted. While this may be a practical solution to the problem of identification where the crime is committed by more than one person, the logic of admitting the evidence in *Downey* is that evidence which identifies the accused in relation to crime A serves also to point to his guilt of crime B. This is not necessarily so in the situation which occurred in *Lee*, however, as it was plausible that the gang had altered in its composition between offences. If such evidence is to be left to a jury, it must surely require a very careful direction as to how to approach it. In *Brown* [1997] Crim LR 502, in which the prosecution relied on cumulative evidence implicating co-accused M in different robberies alleged to have been committed by the same gang, it was held that the issues for the jury, once they were satisfied that the same gang committed both offences, were (1) whether the prosecution had established that M was a gang member, and (2) whether the totality of the evidence established beyond reasonable doubt that M was a member of the gang on each occasion.

If there is no issue as to identity in relation to 'offence B' then the problem identified in *McGranaghan* cannot arise. Thus in *Laidman* [1992] Crim LR 428 L pleaded guilty to one robbery, and it was held that evidence about it was admissible to connect him with other similar robberies, and in *Black* [1995] Crim LR 640, a previous conviction in relation to one offence enabled it to be used as the cornerstone of an argument, based on striking similarity, identifying B as the perpetrator of other offences.

Risk of Collusion between Witnesses

It is obvious that striking similarity between accounts of events given by different **F12.13** witnesses does not prove guilt if it can be accounted for by collusion. Until recently controversy has surrounded the question whether evidence which carries a real risk of collusion should be excluded, or should be left to the jury with a suitable warning. The preponderance of authority appeared to favour exclusion (*DPP* v *Boardman* [1975] AC 421 per Lord Wilberforce at p. 444; *DPP* v *Kilbourne* [1973] AC 729 per Lord Reid at p. 750; *Ananthanarayanan* [1994] 1 WLR 788; *Ryder* [1994] 2 All ER 859). However, in *H* [1995] AC 596, the House of Lords decided that, since the credibility of a witness was a matter for the jury, the risk of collusion should normally go to weight not to admissibility. H was charged with sexual offences against his stepdaughter, A, and his adopted daughter, B. If A's account was true, it was possessed of sufficient probative value to be admissible as similar fact evidence in relation to the offence against B, and to corroborate B's evidence, and vice versa. However the relationship between the girls was such that they could easily have colluded, and the defence contended that they had deliberately conspired to put together a totally false story. The House of Lords unanimously upheld the decision of the trial judge to leave the evidence to the jury, subject to a warning about the risk of collusion.

There are slight differences of emphasis between the views of their lordships on the issue whether a risk of collusion has any part to play in assessing the admissibility of similar fact evidence, but the basic principles which emerge are as follows.

(a) The judge should normally approach the question of admissibility on the basis that the similar facts alleged are true (per Lord Mackay at p. 612, Lord Griffiths at p. 614, Lord Mustill at p. 620 and Lord Nicholls at p. 626).

(b) In exceptional cases, evidence of collusion might be an aspect of the decision whether to admit evidence, i.e. whether the probative force of the evidence is sufficient to justify admitting it despite its prejudicial effect. In such cases, a *voir dire* would be required (per Lord Mackay at p. 612, Lord Mustill at p. 620 and Lord Nicholls at p. 627). However, Lord Griffiths does not appear to have regarded the rule stated in (a) above as subject to any qualification, while Lord Lloyd thought that a risk of collusion appearing on the face of the documents would always be an element in applying the admissibility test (at p. 626).

(c) If, after evidence of similar facts has been admitted, it becomes apparent that no reasonable jury could regard the evidence as free from collusion the judge should direct the jury that they should not rely on the evidence for any purpose adverse to the defence (per Lord Mackay at p. 612, with whom Lord Lloyd concurred, and per Lord Nicholls at p. 627).

(d) Where (c) does not apply but the question of collusion has been raised, the judge must draw the issue to the attention of the jury, telling them that if they are not satisfied that the evidence cannot be relied upon as free of collusion they must not rely upon it for any purpose adverse to the defence (per Lord Mackay at p. 612, with whom Lord Lloyd concurred, and per Lord Nicholls at p. 627).

Attempts to distinguish earlier authorities in *H* are unconvincing: it is submitted that the decision is best seen as embodying a deliberate shift in policy in similar fact cases. It has the strong practical advantage that many cases involving allegations by witnesses who are well known to one another, particularly those within the family circle, would be unprosecutable if the judge was obliged to exclude similar fact evidence as soon as a real risk of collusion presented itself: the prosecution would be faced by what Lord Mustill terms an 'unprovable negative'. Unless there is some reason to suppose that the jury cannot do the job properly, it is a better policy to seek a pronouncement from the jury than from the judge as to whether the true explanation of the similar accounts is that the witnesses have put their heads together, or been unconsciously influenced by one another.

The principles described above apply not only to cases of deliberate conspiracy between witnesses, but also to those where there is a risk that one witness may unconsciously have been influenced by the account of another witness (*H* and *Ryder*). The same considerations would seem in theory also to be applicable where the risk of falsity arises not from collusion between witnesses, but from what Lord Wilberforce (in *DPP* v *Boardman* [1975] AC 421, at p. 444) described as 'a process of infection from media or publicity or simply from fashion'.

No Special Rule in Cases of Homosexual Offences or those Involving Children

F12.14 In *DPP* v *Boardman* [1975] AC 421, the House of Lords laid to rest the theory that homosexual offences fell into a special category such that evidence of similar facts, or even of homosexual disposition, became admissible. The theory was promoted most strongly by Lord Sumner in the earlier decision of the House in *Thompson* v *The King* [1918] AC 221, who said (at p. 235):

> Persons . . . who commit the offences now under consideration seek the habitual gratification of a particular perverted lust, which not only takes them out of the class of ordinary men gone wrong, but stamps them with the hallmark of a specialised and extraordinary class as much as if they carried on their bodies some physical peculiarity.

In *Thompson* v *The King*, the facts of which are considered at **F12.7**, one result of the application of this doctrine was that the prosecution were permitted to introduce evidence of indecent photographs found at the home of T, who was charged with acts of gross indecency against boys, even though there was recognised to be no direct connection between the existence of the photographs and the commission of the offence. Similar evidence was adduced, applying *Thompson* v *The King*, in various cases before 1975, including *Twiss* [1918] 2 KB 853 and *Gillingham* (1939) 27 Cr App R 143, and the 'special category' theory was endorsed unhesitatingly in 1946 by the Court of Appeal in *Sims* [1946] KB 531. Its rejection in *DPP* v *Boardman* [1975] AC 421, which was foreshadowed by dicta in *DPP* v *Kilbourne* [1973] AC 729, is due to changing attitudes. Homosexuality is no longer regarded as an affliction, let alone as a 'hallmark' setting a person in a class apart from the rest of society, so that the theory was termed 'obsolete' by Lord Wilberforce in *DPP* v *Boardman*, who went on to stress that in sexual cases similar fact evidence is received on the same principle as in other cases, and that in applying the rule to given facts judges must be guided by contemporary standards of morality, for: 'What is striking in one age is normal in another; the perversions of yesterday may be the routine or the fashion of tomorrow.'

The note of caution sounded by the House of Lords in *DPP* v *Boardman* extends, it is submitted, beyond the sphere of homosexual offences, and applies to all cases with sexual overtones. Thus, it is no longer correct to assert, as Lord Goddard CJ did in *Sims* [1946] KB 531, that crimes of indecency against children of either sex 'indicate a perverted lust' so as to guarantee admissibility or, as Lord Sands said in *Moorov* v *HM*

Advocate 1930 JC 68, that 'indecency against children is a rare and peculiar offence, and, accordingly, evidence inferring a course of conduct is admitted as relevant'. Lord Sands' dictum was approved by Lord Hailsham LC in *DPP* v *Kilbourne*, but the general tenor of the speeches delivered in that case provide no support for any special rule with regard to sexual offences against children: on the contrary, it is an authority for the application of the general rule to such cases. It is submitted that the law is now as stated by the Court of Appeal in *Clarke* (1977) 67 Cr App R 398, where it was held that there is no special category of offences against children, for to assert that such offences are so rare as to justify admissibility is to ignore the unhappy fact that such offences are nowadays only too common.

Evidence of Homosexuality or Other Specific Sexual Disposition

Whereas evidence of the commission of homosexual offences is necessarily prejudicial **F12.15** to an accused and should not be disclosed unless it has the requisite degree of probative value, it may be argued that modern attitudes to homosexuality are sufficiently tolerant that there is no longer any reason to suppose that a jury would be prejudiced against an accused simply as a result of learning that he is homosexual, with the result that such evidence might be taken out of the rule of exclusion altogether, and admitted in evidence simply on the grounds of relevance. It would seem, however, that the courts remain to be convinced that evidence of this kind would not prejudice a jury (see *Bishop* [1975] QB 274, where it was regarded as an imputation on the character of a prosecution witness to suggest that he was a party to a lawful homosexual relationship). However, it may be symptomatic of a change in thinking, on the part of defence counsel at least, that in *Beggs* (1989) 90 Cr App R 430, evidence of the accused's homosexual tendencies was led by the prosecution without objection. The purpose appears to have been to provide necessary background information to the murder with which B was charged, in which the victim was a homosexual whom B had met at a nightclub and agreed to put up for the night. As the defence was that B killed the other man to repel sexual advances which B found repugnant, however, it was probably the case that the evidence was more than merely relevant, and would have been admissible under the exception to the general rule even if it had been considered to be an essentially prejudicial revelation.

Sometimes it may be relevant to prove a disposition to have sexual relations with a particular individual. For example, in *Ball* [1911] AC 47 the House of Lords held that it was permissible to introduce evidence of a previous sexual relationship between the accused, who were brother and sister, in order to show that sexual relations had taken place in the bedroom which they shared. The evidence in question related to a time when incest was not a criminal offence, but it was held to be highly relevant, and therefore admissible, because (per Lord Loreburn LC, at p. 71):

> The object was to establish that they had a guilty passion towards each other, and that therefore the proper inference from their occupying the same bedroom and the same bed was an inference of guilt, or – which is the same thing in another way – that the defence of innocent living together as brother and sister ought to fail.

To an extent, the readiness of the House of Lords to find the evidence of 'guilty passion' admissible stems from the inevitable difficulty of proving what took place in private between two individuals, both of whom are brought to trial. The difficulty was compounded by the nature of the act alleged, which was unlikely to yield independent evidence, and by the social conditions of the time, under which it was not unusual to find poor families sharing sleeping accommodation (see per Lord Alverstone CJ in *Ball*, at p. 66). The result was that the admission of such evidence was perceived as necessary for the due administration of the Punishment of Incest Act 1908, and it is submitted that the case does not necessarily provide authority for the automatic introduction of evidence of a relevant 'guilty passion', for example, evidence of a previous conviction of incest by a father upon the daughter who is the subject of the present charge. The probative value of such evidence depends entirely on an argument based on propensity, and whereas such reasoning is not necessarily impermissible (see **F12.8**), it requires to be supported by a particularly compelling reason why the propensity should have reasserted itself in the conduct charged. Sexual behaviour towards a particular individual is more likely to provide the foundation for such an inference than is evidence that the accused has sexual feelings towards his own sex, or towards children, at least where the evidence is not 'stale'; but at the same time such evidence is potentially highly prejudicial to the accused, who may be convicted of a second offence simply because he committed a first, and because the jury do not believe that leopards change their spots.

Previous Sexual Conduct and the 'Same Transaction' Rule

F12.16   It is clear that the prosecution may adduce evidence regarding discreditable conduct by the accused where such evidence is part of the transaction under consideration (see **F12.21** to **F12.23**). Under this rule evidence of sexual acts or advances other than those which are the subject of the charge is frequently adduced to show the true nature of the relationship between the parties, a practice which may be regarded as an acceptable and inevitable form of evidence of 'guilty passion' (see, e.g., *Ball* [1911] AC 47, and **F12.15**). In *DPP* v *Boardman* [1975] AC 421, for example, evidence of the accused's previous approaches to a boy with whom he was alleged to have committed buggery was admitted, including evidence of an indecent assault taking place several months before. Similar evidence was given by another complainant of indecent conduct leading over a period of time to incitement to buggery. As Lord Morris observed (at p. 435), no question was raised at the trial as to the admissibility of such evidence. See also, e.g., *Rearden* (1864) 4 F & F 76 (series of rapes on child regarded as one continuing offence); *Flack* [1969] 1 WLR 937 (evidence of previous indecency with alleged victim of incest).

Where a complainant gives evidence of an earlier offence against him which is admissible under the 'same transaction' rule, it has been held that evidence corroborating the earlier offence may go to support the complainant's testimony with regard to the offence charged (*Hartley* [1941] 1 KB 5).

Discretionary Exclusion of Similar Fact Evidence

F12.17   It has been recognised for over 40 years that there is a discretion to exclude evidence which is admissible under the 'similar fact' rule. In *Noor Mohamed* v *The King* [1949] AC 182, Lord Du Parcq observed (at p. 192) that: 'cases must occur in which it would be unjust to admit evidence of a character gravely prejudicial to the accused even though there may be some tenuous ground for holding it technically admissible.' His Lordship's dictum was approved by the House of Lords in *Harris* v *DPP* [1952] AC 694, where Viscount Simon explained (at p. 707) that the proposition stated by Lord Du Parcq 'flows from the duty of the judge when trying a charge of crime to set the essentials of justice above the technical rule if the strict application of the latter would operate unfairly against the accused.' Another commonly-encountered way of stating the ground on which the discretion may be invoked is to say that the prejudicial effect of evidence may be so disproportionate to its probative value that it ought not to be admitted (see, e.g., *Straffen* [1952] 2 QB 911 at p. 917).

A situation in which it is particularly important to consider the exercise of judicial discretion is where evidence is admissible in relation to charge A against an accused person, and inadmissible in relation to charge B. On the assumption that a joint trial of the charges is appropriate, it may be necessary to consider excluding the evidence in order to avoid prejudicing the trial of charge B. This was recognised in *Lewis* (1982) 76 Cr App R 33, in which evidence of the accused's sexual leanings towards children was held admissible to rebut defences of accident and innocent explanation raised in respect of three incidents concerning indecent assault or indecency towards children, but inadmissible in relation to a fourth incident which was completely denied by L. The Court of Appeal acknowledged that the evidence was capable of having an 'unduly prejudicial effect', but it was held sufficient to overcome this risk that the trial judge had given the jury a careful direction as to the use which could be made of the evidence. It follows that, where the judge is not confident that such a direction would work, the evidence should be excluded.

In deciding whether to exercise the discretion, it may be pertinent to consider that evidence which does not disclose the commission of other offences may be less prejudicial than evidence which does have this effect (*Butler* (1987) 84 Cr App R 12).

Where 'similar fact' evidence is tendered by the prosecution, it is immaterial to the outcome whether the governing principles are described as a rule of admissibility to which a discretion is tacked on, or as an open-textured rule of admissibility which requires the assessment of the relative importance of the probative value of the evidence and its prejudicial effect (see *Burns* [1996] Crim LR 323, in which the latter view appears to have been taken but the same result arrived at as if a rule of admissibility had been considered to have been involved). Where such evidence is tendered by a co-accused, however, the respective roles of rule and discretion must be ascertained, because the defence is only bound by the rule, and is not subject to the discretion (*Miller* [1952] 2 All ER 667 per Devlin J, and, as to the rule to be applied in such cases, see **F12.18**). In such cases it appears that the evidence must possess the same degree of probative value as where it is tendered by the prosecution, but that no question of exclusion on the ground of the specific risk of prejudice arises (*Neale* (1977) 65 Cr App R 304, at p. 306).

For discretionary exclusion generally see **F2.4** to **F2.19**.

EVIDENCE OF MISCONDUCT OR DISPOSITION ADDUCED BY ONE ACCUSED AGAINST ANOTHER

Relevance the General Principle

In *Miller* [1952] 2 All ER 667, Devlin J regarded evidence of bad character as being 'no more relevant at the hands of the defence than the prosecution'. Where such evidence was relevant, however, the defence were free to rely upon it, and, unlike the prosecution, could not be restrained in the discretion of the court.   **F12.18**

Evidence of Propensity

In *Miller* [1952] 2 All ER 667, the evidence was relevant for a reason other than its tendency to show the criminal disposition of the co-accused: the case for the defence was that the offences under consideration stopped when the co-accused was in prison. In subsequent cases in which *Miller* has been approved, the argument for the defence has been based on the propensity of the co-accused, but the test of relevance has still been applied. In *Neale* (1977) 65 Cr App R 304, N's defence to arson was that the fire was started by his co-accused, B, and that N was either not there, or not participating when the fire was started. In support of this defence, N sought to adduce evidence that B had a propensity to raise fires. It was said to be clear that 'if this evidence were relevant either to the case against him or to his defence, [N] would be able, as of right, to extract it or adduce it, notwithstanding its prejudicial effect upon [B].' The evidence was held to be inadmissible, however, as B's propensity to start fires on his own did not logically suggest that he had started the fire in question without the help of N. The court interpreted the reference to relevance in *Miller* as a requirement that the evidence be as   **F12.19** cogent for the defence as it would have to be for the prosecution: in other words, as a requirement for a high degree of probative value, applying *Rance* (1975) 62 Cr App R 118 (see **F12.9**). *Miller* and *Neale* were applied in *Knutton* (1993) 97 Cr App R 114, in which K's formidable list of convictions were held to have been of insufficient relevance to be adduced where his co-accused's defence was alibi, and in *Thompson* [1995] 2 Cr App R 589, in which a co-accused, S, was held to have been rightly permitted to cross-examine prosecution witnesses about evidence tending to show that the offence bore the hallmark of T and M. In the latter case the test for admissibility was said to be one of 'relevance strictly applied', by which the court appears to mean that the evidence must be of sufficiently direct relevance, rather than that it should be of the degree of cogency required where such evidence is tendered by the prosecution. Relevance is, however, a concept susceptible of infinite manipulation, and there is probably little to choose between the two formulations.

The accused will be allowed a greater latitude where his co-accused sets up his own good character, or launches an attack on the accused in an attempt to show him in a poor light. In *Bracewell* (1978) 68 Cr App R 44, B and L were jointly charged with the murder of an old man in the course of a burglary. B was prevented from adducing evidence in chief to show L's violent disposition, on the ground of insufficient relevance, but the position changed when it emerged that L's defence was that he was an experienced burglar of a non-violent type, able to keep a cool head, whereas B was inexperienced, nervous, excitable and probably drunk. It was held that by raising this defence L had made an issue of his propensity, and that B should at that stage have been allowed to cross-examine him about his violent nature and to call evidence about it if necessary. In *Douglass* (1989) Cr App R 264, D and P were charged with causing death by reckless driving, the charges arising out of an incident in which the prosecution alleged that D was trying to prevent P from overtaking him, and that in vying for position P lost control and collided head-on with an oncoming vehicle. P cross-examined a prosecution witness with a view to showing that P had not drunk alcohol in the two years that the witness had known him. The purpose of this was to invite the jury to contrast P with D, who, according to the prosecution evidence, had been drinking, so as to cast the blame on him. It was held that P had put his character in issue, and that D was wrongly prevented from introducing relevant evidence of P's bad record for motoring offences including drink-driving.

In both *Bracewell* and *Douglass* the evidence of propensity became sufficiently relevant because the co-accused had put his character in issue. In some cases such evidence might be relevant irrespective of whether this line of defence is adopted. In *Lowery* v *The Queen* [1974] AC 85, L and K were charged with the motiveless and sadistic murder of a young girl. The prosecution case was based on joint enterprise, but each accused blamed the other. In support of his defence, L relied on evidence that he was afraid of K, and that he (L) was a person of good character who was not interested in the sort of behaviour alleged against him. K supported his defence by calling a psychologist who had conducted tests on both accused and who said that, of the two, it was L who had a strong aggressive drive and a basic callousness, and that only L had responded positively to a test designed to show whether sadistic pleasure was taken in the suffering of others. On appeal against conviction, L argued that the evidence of the psychologist ought not to have been admitted. The Privy Council held that the evidence was relevant and therefore admissible for K. There are two difficulties in the way of deducing the principle contended for from the case, however:

(a)   The Privy Council took the view that the evidence was not evidence of the criminal tendencies or propensity of L, but was simply scientific evidence of personality. This can be disputed, as its purpose was clearly to show that L was more likely to be disposed to violent misconduct than K, but the ruling may well have affected the way in which the law was stated.

(b) It is not clear to what extent the putting of L's character in issue affected admissibility. Lord Morris stated the general principle to be that, where the question is which of two men committed a murder, it would be 'unjust to prevent either of them from calling any evidence of probative value which could point to the probability that the perpetrator was the one rather than the other', which suggests that the evidence would have been admissible whatever the defence advanced by L, but his Lordship then went on to state that the admissibility of the evidence was 'placed beyond doubt' by the way in which L had put his character in issue.

Whatever may be the correct analysis of *Lowery* v *The Queen*, it is submitted that there must be cases in which the propensity of one accused may be relied upon by the other, irrespective of whether the other has put his character in issue. If such evidence may, as it may in exceptional cases, be relevant and admissible for the prosecution (see **F12.8**), it must be capable of being relied upon by the defence (see the observations of Devlin J in *Miller* [1952] 2 All ER 667, at **F12.18** and above).

Where evidence is not admissible under the rules stated above, and the provisions of s. 1(f) of the Criminal Evidence Act 1898 (as to which see **F14**) are inapplicable, it is not permissible for one accused to adduce evidence of the bad character of another (*Knutton* (1993) 97 Cr App R 114). In particular, the fact that a defence involves a suggestion that the offence was committed by a co-accused does not automatically trigger the right to attack the character of the accused making that suggestion. In *Parker* (16 November 1992 unreported) an eye-witness to murder testified that Parker was the white-shirted man who had delivered the fatal kick. Parker's counsel suggested to him that Parker was not wearing a white shirt but that Parsons, a co-accused, was. It was held that this did not of itself entitle Parsons to adduce evidence of previous violent misconduct by Parker, unless it was of sufficient relevance to the defence of Parsons that he had left the scene before the kick occurred, which it was not.

Discretion

The judicial discretion by which the prosecution may be restrained from introducing **F12.20** similar fact evidence cannot be exercised in respect of an accused who seeks to introduce such evidence against a co-accused. See generally **F12.17** and **F2.4** to **F2.19**.

EVIDENCE OF MISCONDUCT FORMING PART OF THE BACKGROUND

Same Continuous Transaction

It is permissible for the prosecution to adduce as part of their case evidence of **F12.21** misconduct by the accused which is not strictly part of the offence charged, but which is part of the same continuous transaction. Thus, in *Rearden* (1864) 4 F & F 76, on an indictment for rape of a nine-year-old child, the prosecution were permitted to introduce evidence of subsequent rapes on the same victim in the days following the offence charged, together with threats made by the accused on the first occasion to beat the child if she told her mother. Willes J admitted the evidence on the ground that the acts were 'in substance part of the same transaction'. The same view was taken by Bayley J in *Ellis* (1826) 6 B & C 145, in which E was charged with stealing money from a till, and evidence was given of other thefts by E from the till during the course of the same day, on the ground that it was 'all part of one entire transaction'.

Background to Commission of Offence

Where an offence is alleged it may be necessary to give evidence of the background **F12.22** against which the offence is committed, even though to do so will reveal facts showing the accused in a discreditable light. Such revelations may be incidental to the offence charged, as in *Neale* (1977) 65 Cr App R 304, where the offence charged was arson of a hostel for boys released from Borstal in which N was an inmate; or germane to the inquiry into guilt, as in *Hagan* (1873) 12 Cox CC 357, where evidence was given of statements made by the accused showing animosity towards the child he was alleged to have murdered. In *Kenny* [1992] Crim LR 800, the prosecutor was permitted to adduce evidence of a previous joint trial of K and one, W, in order to prove that K knew of W's criminal propensity and to prove that K's association with W was not an innocent one.

The statement of the law as to the distinction between background evidence and evidence of similar facts in the 1996 edition of this work was approved in *B* [1997] Crim LR 220, in which evidence relating to B's relationship with the girl he was charged with indecently assaulting was admitted, even though it included an allegation of a similar offence committed out of the jurisdiction and in respect of which no criminal proceedings had ensued.

Similar Fact Evidence Distinguished

F12.23 Evidence of the same transaction or of the background to the offence is sometimes objected to on the ground that it is similar fact evidence. Although the two are easily confused (see e.g., *Underwood* [1999] Crim LR 227), it is submitted that rules exist independently of one another, and it appears that the only criterion for admissibility of evidence forming part of the transaction or background to the offence is that it is relevant: the enhanced degree of probative value required for similar fact evidence is not necessary. In *Bond* [1906] 2 KB 389, Kennedy J, speaking of the general rule of exclusion of evidence of bad character, said (at p. 400):

> The general rule cannot be applied where the facts which constitute distinct offences are at the same time part of the transaction which is the subject of the indictment. Evidence is necessarily admissible as to acts which are so closely and inextricably mixed up with the history of the guilty act itself as to form part of one chain of relevant circumstances, and so could not be excluded in the presentment of the case before the jury without the evidence being thereby rendered unintelligible.

Within this category, Kennedy J instanced trials for murder or wounding, where evidence is given to show prior assaults by the accused on the victim, or menaces or threats uttered to him. The same view was taken by Lord Atkinson in *Ball* [1911] AC 47, at p. 68, who regarded evidence of previous acts or words showing enmity as admissible evidence of motive. *Ball* was criticised in *Berry* (1986) 83 Cr App R 7, on the ground that evidence of past incidents should not be regarded as relevant to prove the state of mind with which a particular act (in that case the violent stabbing of B's ex-girlfriend) was done. While this observation may have been correct on the facts of *Berry*, the Court of Appeal in *Williams* (1986) 84 Cr App R 299 reasserted the general rule as stated in *Ball*, and held that evidence of previous threatening and violent conduct of W towards the victim was rightly admitted to establish an intention on the part of W that the victim should fear that the threat to kill, which was the subject of the charge, would be carried out (this being an essential ingredient of the offence under s. 16 of the OAPA 1861). *Ball* and *Williams* were applied in *Fulcher* [1995] 2 Cr App R 251, where the previous non-accidental injuries sustained by the baby F was alleged to have murdered were held to have been relevant to show not only that the child, being in pain, was more likely to be fractious, but also how F was likely to react to the child crying. The court expressly disclaimed the suggestion that the evidence was received as similar fact evidence. In *Giannetto* [1997] 1 Cr App R 1, *Ball* and *Williams* were held to justify the admission of the diary of a deceased woman to show a history of threatening and violent behaviour by G towards her, and to form the basis for an inference that G was more likely to have killed her (although it was recognised that a direction that threats and assaults do not always lead to murder was also required).

Ordinary considerations of relevance appear to have dictated the result in *Sidhu* (1994) 98 Cr App R 59, in which a video showing S apparently leading the activities of a group of armed rebels in Pakistan was admitted to show his object in participating in a conspiracy to possess explosives in England which it was alleged was designed to further the interests of the same group. It was held that provided there was a sufficient nexus in time between S's visit to Pakistan and the offence charged, and provided also that it was necessary to lead the evidence in order to give the jury a complete picture, it was admissible as evidence of a 'continual background of history' relevant to S's part in the conspiracy. To similar effect is *Stevens* [1995] Crim LR 649, in which S was charged with the murder of a woman with whom he had been living, and evidence of previous occasions on which he had assaulted her were admitted as part of the background. The court approved a statement by Purchas LJ in *Pettman* (2 May 1985 unreported) where it was said:

> Where it is necessary to place before the jury evidence of part of a continual background of history relevant to the offence charged in the indictment and without the totality of which the account placed before the jury would be incomplete or incomprehensible, then the fact that the whole account involves including evidence establishing the commission of an offence with which the accused is not charged is not of itself a ground for excluding the evidence.

In *TM* [1999] Crim LR 983 the distinction drawn by the present writer in the Commentary on *Stevens* between background evidence and evidence of similar facts was approved by the Court of Appeal. In that case evidence was admitted of the abuse that TM and his sister S had suffered at the hands of older members of their family, including instances where TM had been forced to abuse his siblings. Without such evidence, the two counts of rape of S could not properly be understood: for example, the jury would inevitably have wondered why S did not turn to other family members for help.

If background evidence shows the accused in a particularly bad light, this may be a factor to be taken into account in deciding whether it should be excluded in the discretion of the court on the ground that the prejudicial effect of the evidence outweighs its probative value. This was confirmed in *TM*. A case in which it is submitted that the discretion ought to have been exercised is *Mackie* (1973) 57 Cr App R 453, in which evidence of earlier misconduct of the accused towards the child whose death he was alleged to have caused was admitted to show the state of mind of the child, who had fled from him and fallen to its death, notwithstanding that the court agreed that 'the prejudicial effect of the evidence admitted was enormous and far outweighed its value'. If this was so, it is submitted that the evidence ought to have been excluded. Where background evidence is admitted, it may be fairest to present it in the form of an agreed statement of facts, for the avoidance of prejudice and to prevent the distraction of the jury (*Butler* [1999] Crim LR 835).

PREVIOUS MISCONDUCT ADMISSIBLE UNDER THEFT ACT 1968, S. 27(3)

Theft Act 1968, s. 27

(3) Where a person is being proceeded against for handling stolen goods (but not for any offence other than handling stolen goods), then at any stage of the proceedings, if evidence has been given of his having or arranging to have in his possession the goods the subject of the charge, or of his undertaking or assisting in, or arranging to undertake or assist in, their retention, removal, disposal or realisation, the following evidence shall be admissible for the purpose of proving that he knew or believed the goods to be stolen goods—

(a) evidence that he has had in his possession, or has undertaken or assisted in the retention, removal, disposal or realisation of, stolen goods from any theft taking place not earlier than 12 months before the offence charged; and

(b) (provided that seven days' notice in writing has been given to him of the intention to prove the conviction) evidence that he has within the five years preceding the date of the offence charged been convicted of theft or of handling stolen goods.

Scope of Provision

F12.24   The Theft Act 1968, s. 27(3), applies to all forms of handling (*Ball* [1983] 1 WLR 801).
It can be relied upon by the prosecution only in a case where handling is the only offence
involved in the proceedings.

The section assists only in the proof of guilty knowledge or belief. It may not assist the
prosecution where an issue arises as to dishonesty (*Duffas* (1994) 158 JP 224), nor may
it be used to prove possession of the goods in question: indeed, the provision cannot be
relied upon unless the prosecution have already adduced evidence of the *actus reus* of
the handling offence. The mere fact that possession is disputed is not of itself a bar to
the use of the section by the prosecution (*List* [1966] 1 WLR 9, per Roskill J, construing
the corresponding provision of the Larceny Act 1916). Where, however, the jury will be
faced with a number of counts, in some of which possession is in issue and in some of
which the issue is guilty knowledge, it was held in *Wilkins* [1975] 2 All ER 734, that:
'very great care should be exercised by the judge first of all before he allows evidence of
the previous convictions to be given at all or, if he does allow that evidence to be
admitted, very great care should be exercised in order to ensure that the jury realise the
issues to which those previous convictions are relevant'. *Wilkins* was decided under
s. 27(3)(b), but it is submitted that precisely the same considerations apply to evidence
adduced under s. 27(3)(a).

Restrictive Construction

F12.25   It has been the practice of the courts to construe both limbs of the Theft Act 1968,
s. 27(3), in a restrictive way. In *Bradley* (1979) 70 Cr App R 200, the Court of Appeal
noted that the section gives the power to introduce evidence which would otherwise not
be regarded as relevant, and would therefore be inadmissible, and concluded that it
should therefore be construed 'with strict regard to its terms'. In particular, it was held
that s. 27(3)(a) does not authorise the giving in evidence of the details of the transaction
by which the earlier stolen property had come into the hands of the accused. *Bradley* was
applied in *Wood* [1987] 1 WLR 779, in which the Court noted a conflict between *Bradley*
and the earlier case of *Smith* [1918] 2 KB 415, the decision in *Bradley* being preferred.
In *Fowler* (1988) 86 Cr App R 219, *Bradley* was applied to s. 27(3)(b), the Court noting
that a 'bare recital of conviction is all that is required, and possibly all that it is
permissible to provide the jury with'. However, in *Hacker* [1994] 1 WLR 1659 it was
held by the House of Lords that s. 27(3)(b) must be read together with s. 73(2) of the
PACE 1984, under which a certificate of conviction of an offence on indictment must
give 'the substance and effect (omitting the formal parts) of the indictment and of the
conviction'. It followed that where H, who was charged with handling the bodyshell of
a car, had a previous conviction for receiving a car, the detail of the subject-matter
of the previous conviction, as it appeared on the certificate, was admissible. A similar
proposition was advanced with regard to a previous summary conviction. The House of
Lords noted that s. 27 had been extensively criticised, but considered that 'not to be able
to show what goods had been stolen or handled on a previous occasion might work in
some cases to the disadvantage of the defendant himself' (per Lord Slynn at p. 1665).

Discretion

F12.26   Where evidence is strictly admissible under the Theft Act 1968, s. 27(3), the court has
a power to exclude it at common law or under the PACE 1984, s. 78 (*Hacker* [1994] 1
WLR 1659; and see also *Herron* [1967] 1 QB 107; *Smith* (1976) 64 Cr App R 217; *Perry*
[1984] Crim LR 680).

SECTION F13: CHARACTER EVIDENCE: ADMISSIBILITY OF EVIDENCE OF GOOD CHARACTER

History

The practice of permitting an accused person to raise evidence of good character as part **F13.1** of his defence has been described as an anomaly (*Rowton* (1865) Le & Ca 520, per Martin B, at p. 537), and so it is, particularly when viewed in the light of the restrictive rules prohibiting the prosecution from introducing evidence of bad character as part of the case against him. Nevertheless, the practice has a long pedigree: the editor of *Cross and Tapper on Evidence* (8th ed., at p. 347) gives as early examples *Turner* (1664) 6 St Tr 565, at p. 613, and *Harris* (1680) 7 St Tr 926, at p. 929. The practice is founded on a notion of indulgence rather than of right: Lord Goddard CJ in *Butterwasser* [1948] KB 4, at p. 6 spoke of a practice, stretching over 200 years, of 'allowing' a prisoner to call evidence of good character. The Privy Council has recently decided, applying *Butterwasser*, that where the issue of good character is not raised by the defence in evidence, the trial judge has no duty to raise the issue himself. The duty of a judge to bring to the attention of the jury a possible defence not relied on by defence counsel is not analogous, because that duty arises only where evidence which gives rise to the defence is before the jury (*Thompson* v *R* [1998] AC 811).

The questions which arise are as to the purpose for which such evidence may be relied upon; the direction which should be given to a jury; the nature of the evidence which may be adduced in support of a claim to good character, and the kind of evidence which may be adduced in rebuttal by the prosecution or, where relevant, by a co-accused.

Purpose of Adducing Evidence of Good Character

The defendant was entitled to adduce evidence of his good character long before the law **F13.2** treated him as a competent witness in his own defence (*Vye* [1993] 1 WLR 471 at p. 474). Such evidence was said by Patteson J in *Stannard* (1837) 7 C & P 673 (at pp. 674–5) to point to the improbability of guilt:

> I cannot in principle make any distinction between evidence of facts, and evidence of character: the latter is equally laid before the jury as the former, as being relevant to the question of guilty or not guilty: the object of laying it before the jury is to induce them to believe, from the improbability that a person of good character should have conducted himself as alleged, that there is some mistake or misrepresentation in the evidence on the part of the prosecution, and it is strictly evidence in the case.

When the defendant became competent to give evidence, evidence of good character acquired the further function of enhancing the credibility of the defendant as a witness. Although historically a subsidiary purpose, evidence of good character came to be regarded as 'primarily a matter which goes to credibility' (*Bellis* [1966] 1 WLR 234). But good character remained relevant to the issue of guilt, and *Stannard* was approved in *Bryant* [1979] QB 108, in which the judge had taken the view that, as B did not give evidence, his character had 'very little if any part to play' in the jury's deliberations. It was held that, insofar as it had been suggested that character was relevant only to the credibility of an accused who has given evidence, there had been a misdirection.

The original function of good character has since reasserted itself, and the tendency now is to lay equal emphasis upon both functions of evidence of good character. In *Aziz* [1996] AC 41 Lord Steyn said (at p. 50):

It has long been recognised that the good character of a defendant is logically relevant to his credibility and to the likelihood that he would commit the offence in question.

The Need for a Jury Direction

F13.3   In *Aziz* [1996] AC 41, Lord Steyn identifies (at p. 50) a 'veritable sea-change in judicial thinking in regard to the proper way in which a judge should direct a jury on the good character of a defendant'. It was at one time thought, following *Smith* [1971] Crim LR 531, that there was no duty to refer to evidence of good character when summing up, the matter being entirely within the discretion of the judge. That this no longer obtains is said by Lord Steyn to derive from the modern view that the defence case must be put before the jury in a fair and balanced way and, as evidence of good character is evidence of probative significance, fairness dictates that the judge should direct on it. Failure to direct is likely to be a material irregularity in every case in which it is appropriate for such a direction to be given (*Fulcher* [1995] 2 Cr App R 251).

The purpose of the direction appears to be to convey to the jury that they ought to take account of relevant evidence of good character, although it would be going too far to suggest that they are bound to give it any weight. In *Miah* [1997] 2 Cr App R 12, the Court of Appeal considered it best to avoid telling a jury that it is 'entitled' to consider such evidence: although not strictly inaccurate, the expression conflates the two stages of the process and risks giving the jury the impression that they may choose not to consider the evidence at all.

Direction on Credibility where Defendant Testifies

F13.4   It has been a settled rule since 1989 that where a defendant testifies the judge must give a direction as to the relevance of good character to the defendant's credibility. In *Berrada* (1989) 91 Cr App R 131, B was convicted of attempted rape. At his trial there was a direct conflict between the evidence of B on the one hand and of the complainant and police witnesses on the other. The trial judge's direction was held to have been defective in that it made no mention of the relevance of evidence of B's previous good character. Waterhouse J said (at p. 134):

> The striking omission . . . is of any reference to the real and primary relevance of the appellant's previous good character. What the learned judge should have said was that it was primarily relevant to the question of the appellant's credibility. . . . In the judgment of this court, the appellant was entitled to have put to the jury from the judge herself a correct direction about the relevance of his previous good character to his credibility. That is a conventional direction and it is regrettable that it did not appear in the summing-up in this case.

Conventionally, the direction on credibility has become known as the 'first limb' of a character direction, with the 'second limb' consisting of a statement as to the relevance of character to the question whether the accused was likely to have committed the offence. The need for a 'first limb' direction has been reaffirmed in numerous decisions since, culminating in *Vye* [1993] 1 WLR 471, where the authorities are reviewed, and *Aziz* [1996] AC 41, in which the House of Lords treats the point as settled by *Vye*. According to *Vye* (at p. 475) however, the authorities since *Berrada* left three important issues unresolved, which were:

    (a)   whether a 'first limb' direction needs to be given in a case where the defendant does not give evidence but has made statements to the police or others;
    (b)   whether the 'second limb' direction should now be regarded as discretionary or obligatory; and
    (c)   what course the judge should take in a joint trial where one defendant is of good character but the other is not.

In *Vye* the court, which was presided over by Lord Taylor CJ, answered each of these questions in favour of giving a direction.

Direction on Credibility where Defendant Does Not Testify

In *Vye* [1993] 1 WLR 471, the Court of Appeal decided that where the defendant has **F13.5** not given evidence at trial but relies on admissible exculpatory statements made to the police or others, the judge should direct the jury to have regard to the defendant's good character when considering the credibility of those statements. The court thought it 'logical' that such evidence should be taken into account, but drew attention also to the judge's entitlement to make observations about the weight to be given to such exculpatory statements in contrast to evidence on oath (see *Duncan* (1981) 73 Cr App R 359 at **F17.45**). In *Aziz* [1996] AC 41, the House of Lords accepted that this 'clear-cut' rule in *Vye* represented the best policy. Where an exculpatory statement was evidence in the case, the credibility of the defendant who had given that account was a matter of evidential significance requiring a direction (see also *Woodward* [1996] Crim LR 207 and *Garrod* [1997] Crim LR 445).

Vye also decides that, where a defendant of good character does not give evidence and has given no pre-trial answers or statements upon which reliance is placed, a 'first limb' direction is not required as no issue as to his credibility arises.

Direction on Propensity

The 'second limb' of a character direction deals with the unlikelihood that a person of **F13.6** previous good character would commit the offence charged. In various authorities, including *Berrada* (1990) 91 Cr App R 131, *Thanki* (1991) 93 Cr App R 12n and *Bainbridge* (1991) 93 Cr App R 32, it has been said that the 'second limb' direction is not obligatory. In other cases, however, the omission of such a direction was said to be inappropriate (see e.g., *Marr* (1990) 90 Cr App R 154 and *Anderson* [1990] Crim LR 862). In *Vye* [1993] 1 WLR 471, the Court of Appeal was 'unable to discern any principle or consistent pattern as to when a 'second limb' direction should be given and when it need not', and in order to resolve the uncertainty surrounding the issue decided that such a direction should be given in all cases where a defendant is of good character, whether he testifies or not. In *Aziz* [1996] AC 41, the House of Lords, while recognising that *Vye* involved a 'policy decision', agreed that the move away from a discretionary system to a settled rule of practice was justified and would reduce the number of appeals.

Vye was applied in *Wren* [1993] Crim LR 952, where it was observed that failure to give a 'second limb' direction might attract the operation of the proviso; see also *Anderson* [1995] Crim LR 430. The obligation is, in any event, subject to the judge's entitlement to make observations qualifying the importance of good character, for example by emphasising that it is not in itself a defence and that in some cases the jury may derive limited assistance from the evidence. The example given in *Vye* is where the defendant, charged with murder, admits manslaughter, so that the argument that he has never stooped to murder before is countered by the fact that he has never committed manslaughter either. Another example is provided by *Hickmet* [1996] Crim LR 588, in which it was said that the absence of relevant convictions over a period of 20 years might provide little assistance to the jury in deciding whether H had raped a woman of good character. In other cases the evidence may be highly relevant, for example where an employee in a position of trust has carried out his duties impeccably for many years but is then charged with theft or fraud.

Where a direction is given about the relevance of good character to guilt it is wrong and unfair to suggest that such evidence comes into play only where the remainder of the evidence leaves the jury in doubt. Evidence of good character is part of the totality of the evidence upon which the jury are to decide whether there is any doubt about guilt (*Handbridge* [1993] Crim LR 287, endorsing the statement of law to this effect in an earlier edition of this work, and see also *Falconer-Atlee* (1973) 58 Cr App R 349 at 357–8). Earlier authorities to the contrary, particularly *Bliss Hill* (1918) 13 Cr App R 125, should, it is submitted, be regarded as wrong on this point.

Where One Defendant is of Good Character but Another is Not

F13.7 The difficulty facing a trial judge in the situation where one defendant is of good character but another is not is that by commenting on the good character of the one he may be taken to be highlighting the bad character of the other. Nevertheless the Court of Appeal in *Vye* [1993] 1 WLR 471 held, disapproving of compromise solutions suggested in earlier authorities such as *Gibson* (1991) 93 Cr App R 9, that the defendant of good character is entitled to the same direction as if he had stood trial alone. This aspect of *Vye* was applied in *Houlden* (1994) 99 Cr App R 244. The possession of disparate characters is said in *Vye* to be a factor to be considered in deciding whether separate trials are needed, but there is no rule in favour of separate trials in such cases (see further **D9.32**). Where no evidence is put in of the record of the defendant with bad character, the judge has a discretion whether to comment about that defendant when summing up (*Shepherd* [1995] Crim LR 153). Where, however, the jury has been told of his previous convictions, the defendant is entitled to an appropriate direction as to the use which may be made of them (*Cain* [1994] 1 WLR 1449).

Meaning of Good Character

F13.8 ***Absence of Previous Convictions*** In *Aziz* [1996] AC 41, the House of Lords held that a defendant could lay claim to a good character, and was entitled to the benefit of a good character direction, not only where he was of positive good character but also where his character was good only in the negative sense that he had no previous convictions. The difficult issue upon which the House was required to rule was whether a defendant who is of good character only in the negative sense might lose his entitlement to directions in accordance with *Vye* [1993] 1 WLR 471 (see **F13.4**) by reason of some other criminal behaviour on his part; for example (in the case of Y, one of the respondents in the case) where he admits to making a false mortgage application in connection with a matter which was not the subject of the indictment. It was held:

(a) In normal circumstances the directions should still be given, with added words of qualification to present a fair and balanced picture to the jury by drawing attention to other proved or possible criminal conduct of the defendant which emerged during the trial. (The misconduct admitted by the respondent Y fell into this category.)

(b) Exceptionally, a residual discretion exists to dispense with the directions where the defendant's claim to good character is 'spurious' and where it would be an insult to common sense to give them. The example given (at p. 52) was of a defendant who is shown to have been guilty of serious criminal conduct similar to the offence charged. The House deduced the existence of the discretion from decisions such as *Zoppola-Barraza* [1994] Crim LR 833, where it was held unnecessary to give the normal directions in the case of Z, who was accused of being involved in the importation of cocaine and who had admitted smuggling gold and jewels into the country. In that case, however, only the propensity limb was withheld. The thrust of *Aziz* would appear to be that in cases of this kind the judge is entitled to withhold both limbs. See also *Akram* [1995] Crim LR 50, in which it was held that revelations about A's use of heroin on previous occasions meant that he should not have been treated as of good character on charges related to the possession of diamorphine. *Zoppola-Barraza* was regarded with some suspicion in *Durbin* [1995] 2 Cr App R 84, where it was said to be a borderline case, and the view which prevailed was that while revelations of misconduct which forms part of the relevant background to the offence charged might cause the *Vye* directions to be qualified, they should not disentitle a defendant to the directions altogether. This seems inconsistent with *Aziz* unless a distinction is taken between misconduct which is similar to, but remote from, the offence charged, and misconduct which is part of the same transaction. While the revelation of related misconduct may be different in that it is an essential element in the defence case (as in *Durbin*, where D admitted involvement in smuggling other goods in order to support his defence that he was unaware that the particular consignment in issue was of drugs), the distinction does not appear material to the question whether the defendant can, in the light of the revelation, lay claim to good character. The situation is comparable to that where the defendant pleads guilty to another offence charged at trial (as to which see *Challenger* [1994] Crim LR 202 at **F13.10**).

(c) Wherever the judge is minded to give a direction which is not likely to be anticipated by counsel, submissions on the proposed direction should first be invited.

Minor or Irrelevant Convictions Where the accused has previous convictions, it **F13.9** does not follow that he cannot be presented as being of good character. If the convictions are 'spent' under the Rehabilitation of Offenders Act 1974 (see **F14.9**), he may, with the leave of the court, be put forward as a person of good character (*Nye* (1982) 75 Cr App R 247; *Bailey* [1989] Crim LR 723). Judicial discretion should, so far as possible, be exercised favourably to the accused, but 'the jury must not be misled and no lie must be told to them about this matter' (*Nye*, per Talbot J, at p. 251). Where the spent convictions of an accused are regarded as immaterial, he should be entitled to the same directions on good character as an unconvicted defendant (*Heath* (1994) *The Times*, 10 February 1994). It is similarly a matter for the judge's discretion whether, and if so to what extent, an unspent conviction prevents a defendant from being treated as of good character; it might well not have that effect, particularly if it is of a different kind from the offence charged (*Timson* [1993] Crim LR 59: drink-driving conviction should have been regarded as irrelevant to charges involving dishonesty; *H* [1994] Crim LR 205: conviction for possessing an offensive weapon irrelevant to charges involving indecent assault on stepdaughter; *Burnham* [1995] Crim LR 491: 'unrelated' offence of criminal damage should have led to a qualified good character direction). Convictions which have been disregarded in this context are frequently of a minor nature in addition to being for unrelated offences. By contrast it may be impossible to disregard a conviction, however ancient, if it bears on an issue of character which is before the jury (*Rackham* [1997] 2 Cr App R 222, where R's sexual preference for young girls was in issue and an old conviction for unlawful sexual intercourse with a 13-year-old was properly regarded as preventing R from presenting himself as of good character). Where a judge has exercised his discretion to allow a defendant to be presented as a person of good character, he should give a form of the good character direction in which the jury are told that, if they form the view that the defendant is a person of good character, they should take this into account in relation both to his credibility and to his propensity (*M (Ian)* [1999] 6 Arch News 3). It appears that the judge is under no obligation to direct the jury that, if they decide that the defendant is not of good character, this cannot count against him (*Aziz* [1999] 3 Arch News 2), though it is unclear from the short report of the case how far this finding goes. If a defendant has no previous convictions then, unless the judge reaches the conclusion that he is clearly not of good character the standard direction should be given; the direction may be balanced, if necessary, by including relevant factors to the defendant's detriment (*Micallef* (1993) *The Times*, 26 November 1993).

In a case where D's previous convictions are not of the sort that would debar him from a good character direction, counsel's failure to seek the leave of the court to treat him as of good character may threaten the safety of the conviction. In *Kamar* (1999) *The Times*, 14 May 1999, K was convicted on little more than his wife's evidence of causing her grievous bodily harm with intent and threatening to kill her, she having jumped out of a window to get away from him. K had convictions for minor driving offences which were of no relevance to either charge. The wife, who was known to have had psychiatric problems, was permitted to testify to other alleged acts of violence within the marriage in order to show that K intended his threats to be taken seriously. In such circumstances it was essential for counsel to apply for the good character direction, and K's conviction was unsafe.

F13.10 ***Effect of Plea of Guilty*** A difficult question arises where a defendant pleads guilty to one or more of the offences charged at trial. In *Challenger* [1994] Crim LR 202, C was charged with simple possession of cannabis, possession with intent to supply and possession of an offensive weapon, and pleaded guilty to simple possession; a week later he was tried for the two other offences. It was held that the plea meant that C was no longer of good character and that the question of what direction, if any, was appropriate fell to be dealt with in the judge's discretion, taking account of such matters as the nature of the offence and its similarity to the offence charged, and whether the jury would be misled if the defendant was treated as of good character in circumstances where they had not heard about the plea. The judge's decision to give no direction was upheld, despite the presentation of the case by counsel as one where C was of good character apart from the admitted offence. However in *Teasdale* [1993] 4 All ER 290 T, who was charged with causing grievous bodily harm with intent, pleaded guilty to assault occasioning actual bodily harm in respect of the same incident. It was held that T was to be treated as of good character and was entitled to the full direction in *Vye* [1993] 1 WLR 471 (see **F13.4**). In *Challenger* the facts in *Teasdale* were regarded as giving rise to an exception to the general rule applicable wherever a conviction for the offence charged would result in the pleas of guilty being vacated. It is hard to see why this should be so, as the vacation of the plea on the facts in *Teasdale* would not have meant that T had not assaulted the victim and that therefore her character was unblemished: the admitted offence would merely have been swallowed up by proof of the more serious allegation. It is submitted that the same rule should govern all cases involving guilty pleas, and that the approach in *Challenger* is to be preferred.

F13.11 ***Other Discreditable Matters*** A defendant who is otherwise of good character may be shown in a poor light by matters emerging at trial, for example, the fact that he has lied to the police at interview or has otherwise behaved dishonestly in relation to the case itself. In such a case the judge has a discretion to qualify the direction on good character by commenting on matters which may adversely affect the jury's impression of the defendant (*Sharp* [1994] QB 261).

F13.12 ***Witnesses to Character*** Since the decision in *Rowton* (1865) Le & Ca 520, it has been the rule that witnesses as to character must testify to the reputation of the accused, and not to specific good acts or individuals' opinions. Lord Cockburn CJ suggested that the true object of the inquiry was in fact the disposition of the accused, but that it was not the practice to inquire into this directly but to arrive at it by 'giving evidence of his general character founded on his general reputation in the neighbourhood in which he lives'. The result was that 'the prisoner cannot give evidence of particular facts, though one fact might weigh more than the opinion of all his friends and neighbours'. Willes J added two further reasons for the exclusion of particular facts: they lack cogency, as even a robber may perform acts of generosity, and they raise issues of which the prosecution have no notice and on which they cannot enter into argument. Although *Rowton* speaks of the accused's reputation within a particular neighbourhood, the concept is capable of an elastic meaning, and it is not uncommon for character witnesses to come from the same workplace as the accused, or the same church or social organisation.

The *Rowton* rule is difficult to apply where character evidence is elicited by the accused in cross-examination of prosecution witnesses, and in cases where evidence of good character is given by the accused himself. Indeed, it may be doubted whether the accused is competent to give evidence of his own reputation. Yet in *Redgrave* (1982) 74 Cr App R 10, it was held that R, charged with importuning for an immoral purpose, was not entitled to raise evidence of his heterosexual disposition to rebut the charge. The effect of *Rowton* was that the accused could 'do no more than say, or call witnesses to prove, that he was not by general repute the kind of young man who would have behaved in the kind of way that the Crown alleged'. The Court noted that a practice had grown up, where allegations of homosexual offences were in issue, of allowing defendants to say that they are happily married and enjoy a normal sexual relationship with their wives, but this was regarded as a special indulgence, both as regards the *Rowton* rule and the fact that such evidence was not necessarily relevant, it being well known that men who commit homosexual acts may also indulge in heterosexual activity.

The good character of the accused cannot be said to be put in issue where a witness for the defence gives an unsolicited testimonial, as in *Redd* [1923] 1 KB 104. At the trial of R for receiving stolen goods, a witness, called by the unrepresented R simply for the purpose of producing a document, blurted out evidence of his good character without being asked to do so. It was held improper for prosecuting counsel to cross-examine the witness by putting to him R's many previous convictions.

Assertions of Good Disposition Despite what has been said at **F13.12** regarding the   **F13.13** introduction of evidence of character following *Rowton* (1865) Le & Ca 520, it is clear from the authorities that an accused may be held to have made an *issue* of his good character without referring to his reputation at all. In the leading case of *Winfield* [1939] 4 All ER 164 for example, W, charged with indecent assault on a woman, put his character in issue by asking for a testimonial from a witness as to his exemplary behaviour towards ladies. In *Douglass* (1989) 89 Cr App R 264, P, D's co-accused, was held to have put his character in issue by cross-examining a prosecution witness with a view to showing that he had not taken a drink for some years, the purpose of such cross-examination being to contrast P's behaviour with that of D, who was alleged to have been drunk at the time of the accident both were charged with having caused. And it is frequently held that an accused who refers to his own stable background, to his lack of previous convictions or to his good disposition, has made an assertion of good character which the prosecution are entitled to rebut. The reason may be that if the court is prepared to indulge the accused by allowing such evidence to be given, it is only right that it should be open to rebuttal if it is misleading.

Good character cannot be said to be put in issue by the mere asking of questions relevant to the issue which may incidentally show the accused in a good light (*Gadbury* (1838) 8 C & P 676). The same rule is applicable under the Criminal Evidence Act 1898, s. 1(f), under which an accused may be cross-examined on his record if he has 'personally or by his advocate asked questions of the witnesses for the prosecution with a view to establish his own good character, or has given evidence of his good character' (as to which see **F14.9**). Decisions under this provision may be of general assistance on the question whether character is in issue for the purposes of the common law.

The accused does not put his character in issue at common law simply because the nature of his defence is such as to involve imputations upon the character of prosecution witnesses (*Butterwasser* [1948] KB 4). However, in such a case he may, if he testifies, be cross-examined on his record under the Criminal Evidence Act 1898, s. 1(f).

Character Indivisible The character of the accused is regarded as indivisible, in the   **F13.14** sense that he cannot pick and choose which aspects of his character should be put before the jury. In *Winfield* [1939] 4 All ER 164, the accused relied upon character evidence as to his good behaviour towards women and it was held that he could not resist the introduction in cross-examination of his previous convictions for dishonesty, as 'there is no such thing known to our procedure as putting half a prisoner's character in issue and leaving out the other half'. By the same token, the accused cannot confine the inquiry to a particular period of his history when his character was good (*Shrimpton* (1851) 2 Den CC 319).

Evidence in Rebuttal

F13.15 Where the accused puts his character in issue the prosecution may respond by calling evidence in rebuttal, by cross-examining witnesses who have testified to the accused's good character, or by cross-examining the accused if he testifies. The accused may be cross-examined on his record only where the provisions of the Criminal Evidence Act 1898 apply (see **F14**), but the cross-examination of character witnesses and the introduction of rebuttal evidence may take place by virtue of the common law, and irrespective of whether the accused testifies or not.

Where the prosecution introduce character evidence in rebuttal, the rule in *Rowton* (1865) Le & Ca 520 (see **F13.12**) applies, with the result that the witnesses must speak to the bad reputation of the accused, not of specific acts done by him which reflect to his discredit.

A witness as to good character may be cross-examined to show that the accused has previously been convicted of offences (*Waldman* (1934) 24 Cr App R 204). He or she may also, it seems, be asked about other offences for which no conviction has taken place (*Rogan* (1846) 1 Cox CC 291; and see also *Hodgkiss* (1836) 7 C&P 298, in which it was said that it is not usual to cross-examine character witnesses 'except you have some definite charge to which to cross-examine them'). A witness should not be asked about suspicions harboured against the accused on another occasion and in respect of which no proceedings were ever brought (*Savory* (1942) 29 Cr App R 1). It is unusual to cross-examine a character witness except upon previous convictions, and it is submitted that judicial discretion ought to be brought to bear to prevent the introduction of specific incidents to the prejudice of the accused.

SECTION F14: CHARACTER EVIDENCE: CROSS-EXAMINATION OF THE ACCUSED; CRIMINAL EVIDENCE ACT 1898

Criminal Evidence Act 1898, s. 1

Criminal Evidence Act 1898, s. 1   F14.1

(e)   A person charged and being a witness in pursuance of this Act may be asked any question in cross-examination notwithstanding that it would tend to criminate him as to the offence charged:

(f)   A person charged and called as a witness in pursuance of this Act shall not be asked, and if asked shall not be required to answer, any question tending to show that he has committed or been convicted of or been charged with any offence other than that wherewith he is then charged, or is of bad character, unless —

(i)   the proof that he has committed or been convicted of such other offence is admissible evidence to show that he is guilty of the offence wherewith he is then charged; or

(ii)   he has personally or by his advocate asked questions of the witnesses for the prosecution with a view to establish his own good character, or has given evidence of his good character, or the nature or conduct of the defence is such as to involve imputations on the character of the prosecutor or the witnesses for the prosecution or the deceased victim of the alleged crime; or

(iii)   he has given evidence against any other person charged in the same proceedings.

The YJCEA 1999, sch. 4, para. 1, amends s. 1 of the 1898 Act so as to make minor updates to the language used and so as to renumber the proviso. These amendments are not expected to come into force until the end of 2000.

General Effect of s. 1

Section 1 of the Criminal Evidence Act 1898 renders the accused a competent witness   F14.2 in his own defence. Provisos (e) and (f) together ensure that, when it comes to cross-examination, the accused is not treated in quite the same way as an ordinary witness. Thus, s. 1(e) removes the privilege against self-incrimination which the accused would otherwise enjoy in respect of the offence with which he is charged: a necessary adjustment if cross-examination is to serve any meaningful purpose. Section 1(f) provides a protection (or shield as it is often called) against cross-examination in relation to various aspects of the past misconduct of the accused, and his bad character generally, a protection which the ordinary rules of evidence would not give him (*Jones* v *DPP* [1962] AC 635, per Lord Reid). If the accused were to receive no special treatment in this respect, it would be a massive disincentive against giving evidence in the proceedings.

Questions Relating Exclusively to Offence Charged

Proviso 1(e) to the Criminal Evidence Act 1898 permits the asking of any question,   F14.3 notwithstanding that it would tend to criminate the accused as to the offence charged. The effectiveness of the prohibition in s. 1(f) would be severely curtailed if s. 1(e) were held to justify not only questions criminating the accused directly by asking him about the offence charged, but also questions incriminating him indirectly via inferences to be drawn from his discreditable past. In *Jones* v *DPP* [1962] AC 635, a majority of the House of Lords held that this was not the proper construction of the section. The correct approach was explained by Lord Morris of Borth-y-Gest, who said (at pp. 682–3):

There is a contrast between proviso (e) and proviso (f). Proviso (e) shows that an accused person who avails himself of his opportunity to give evidence 'may be asked' questions in cross-examination although they would tend 'to criminate him as to the offence charged'. That denotes questions on matters directly relevant to the charge. Then proviso (f) gives the accused person a 'shield'. He 'shall not be asked' certain questions unless certain conditions apply. Proviso (e) permits questions to be asked; the corollary is that they must be answered. Proviso (f) does not say that certain questions may be asked: it says that certain questions may not be asked. This means that even if the questions are relevant and have to do with the issue before the court they cannot be asked unless covered by the permitting provisions of proviso (f).

Lord Reid, who was also of the majority, pointed out the absurdity which would arise if a question was at one and the same time prohibited by proviso (f) but allowed by proviso (e). This conclusion would follow if the words 'tend to criminate' in proviso (e) were to mean 'tend to convince or persuade the jury that the accused is guilty', but could be avoided if the words were given the narrower meaning 'tend to connect him with the commission of the crime charged'. To avoid an insoluble conflict between the two, proviso (e) had to be given the narrower meaning. See also *Maxwell* v *DPP* [1935] AC 309, in which Viscount Sankey LC described the prohibition in proviso (f) as 'universal' and 'absolute' unless the exceptions come into play.

Some uncertainty has since come about as the result of a dictum of Lord Lane CJ in *Anderson* [1988] QB 678; his lordship appears to have regarded a question revealing an offence other than that charged as permissible if the proof of the commission (using the phrase of Lord Reid) 'tended to connect the appellant with the offence charged'. It is submitted that the correct interpretation of the view of the majority in *Jones* v *DPP* is that such a question is permissible only if it falls within the terms of s. 1(f)(i) (see **F14.16** and **F14.17**).

The decision of the House of Lords in *Jones* v *DPP* involved a reappraisal of certain Court of Criminal Appeal decisions which had proceeded on the assumption that questions criminating an accused person indirectly could be asked under proviso (e). These cases, *Chitson* [1909] 2 KB 945 and *Kennaway* [1917] 1 KB 25, were nevertheless said to have been rightly decided, but not for the reason stated. (The correct reason was that in neither case did the cross-examination of the accused tend to reveal anything to the jury of which they were previously unaware: see **F14.4**.)

Questions Relating to Discreditable Matters Already in Evidence

F14.4   Proviso (f) to the Criminal Evidence Act 1898, s. 1, prohibits only questions 'tending to show' that the accused has committed, been convicted of, or been charged with another offence, or is of bad character. If the jury are already aware of the discreditable matter to which the question relates, it follows that cross-examination is permissible, for 'tending to show' means 'tending to make known'. It was so held by a majority of the House of Lords in *Jones* v *DPP* [1962] AC 635. J was charged with murder of a girl guide, having previously been convicted of rape of another girl guide. Only a month separated the offences, which were similar in character, and which would have fallen within the similar fact rule of evidence but for the fact that the prosecution wished to spare the surviving girl from the ordeal of repeating her testimony at the murder trial. J's defence to murder was that he had spent the evening in question with a prostitute, and in support of this he gave evidence of the stormy reception he received upon returning home to his wife. The entire alibi, including the conversation with his wife, was exactly the same as that on which the defence had relied (unsuccessfully) at the rape trial. When first interviewed in connection with the murder, however, J had put forward a different alibi, which fell through when the person with whom he claimed to have spent the evening refused to support him. It was therefore incumbent upon J to explain why he had attempted to fabricate this earlier alibi, which he did by eliciting from various witnesses, and admitting in his own evidence, the fact that he had been 'in trouble' with the police before, and knew that an uncorroborated alibi would be unlikely to be believed.

The question for the House was whether counsel for the prosecution had been right to cross-examine J about the similarity between the alibi eventually relied upon and that used at the previous trial, for though counsel carefully avoided any mention of a previous offence, the detailed note which he had of the earlier alibi suggested (per Lord Reid) a previous charge or (per Lord Morris) that J was of bad character. It was held that the revelation by J that he had been in trouble with the police meant that the cross-examination, in the deliberately vague way it was conducted, made known nothing which the jury had not already been told, and was thus permissible. Questions sought to be put in cross-examination were not to be considered in isolation, but were to be seen against the background of the evidence as it had developed, and having regard to what the jury had already heard. However, if J had not made his revelation, the prosecutor could not have asked questions about the similarity between the alibis, even though his purpose in doing so was not to invite the jury to draw the inference that the accused was guilty because he had been in trouble before, but simply to demonstrate the unlikelihood of the same detailed conversation being repeated between husband and wife at monthly intervals. The reason, (per Lord Morris, at p. 681) is that: 'It is the result of putting the questions that must be regarded and not the purpose which inspired them'. Thus, if the effect had been to show a previous charge or J's bad character, the question would have been disallowed.

Jones v *DPP* was followed in *Anderson* [1988] QB 678. A was charged with conspiracy to cause explosions, and the prosecution case was that she was a member of a team of IRA bombers. A sought to explain certain aspects of the case against her by claiming that her involvement with the IRA was limited to escorting escaped prisoners from Northern Ireland to Scandinavia using false papers; the point of her involvement being that an apparently holidaying couple would attract less attention than a man travelling alone. The prosecution sought to rebut the defence by cross-examining her to show that she was 'wanted' by the police in Ireland, on the ground that a 'wanted' woman would make an unlikely choice of escort for an escaped prisoner. It was held that the cross-examination involved no revelation to the jury, as A had already opened the door by running a defence which necessarily involved the commission of various offences, for any one of which she might have been wanted by the police.

The rulings in *Chitson* [1909] 2 KB 945 and *Kennaway* [1917] 1 KB 25, which can no longer be supported for the reasons given at **F14.3**, were held by the House of Lords in *Jones* v *DPP* to turn instead on the meaning of 'tending to show'. In *Chitson*, C was charged with unlawful sexual intercourse with a girl of 14. In her evidence, the victim said that C had told her that he had previously done the same thing to another young girl. On the assumption that this evidence was admissible to help to corroborate the victim's story, it was clear that C could be cross-examined about it as the jury were already aware of the allegation against him. Similarly, in *Kennaway*, cross-examination was justified because prosecution witnesses had revealed that K, who was charged with forging a will, had told them of a similar offence he had committed some years earlier. The case of *Kurasch* [1915] 2 KB 749, was not discussed in *Jones* v *DPP*, but would appear not to be explicable in the same way as *Chitson* and *Kennaway*. K was convicted of conspiracy to defraud. His defence, which was that he was an innocent employee of the proprietress of the auction room where the fraud was committed, was destroyed when he was asked in cross-examination whether the woman was his mistress. This was something 'made known' to the jury. It may be, however, that the question put to K would be considered permissible today on the simple ground that the possession of a mistress is no longer to be seen as evidence of 'bad character' within the Criminal Evidence Act 1898, s. 1(f).

Revelations Volunteered by Defence in Chief

F14.5   In *Jones* v *DPP* [1962] AC 635, considered at **F14.4**, Lord Reid had this to say about revelations volunteered by the defence (at p. 663):

> It was suggested that [proviso (f)] applies to examination-in-chief as well as to cross-examination. I do not think so. The words 'shall not be required to answer' are quite inappropriate for examination-in-chief. The proviso is obviously intended to protect the accused. It does not prevent him from volunteering evidence, and does not in my view prevent his counsel from asking questions leading to disclosure of a previous conviction or bad character if such disclosure is thought to assist in his defence.

In the same case Lord Devlin (dissenting) expressed the view that the effect of the interpretation contended for by the majority is that counsel for the accused is bound by the Criminal Evidence Act 1898, s. 1, proviso (f). Lord Reid's dictum was approved by Lord Hodson in *Selvey* v *DPP* [1970] AC 304, however, and it is submitted that it is self-evidently correct.

Questions Permitted by the Exceptions To Proviso (f)

The prohibition on questions relating to the accused's discreditable background imposed by the Criminal Evidence Act 1898, s. 1(f), is not absolute, and the accused may lose the protection of the proviso where one of the three exceptions applies.

Proviso (f): The Prohibited Matters

F14.6   The Criminal Evidence Act 1898, s. 1(f), prevents the asking of any question tending to show that the accused 'has committed or been convicted of or been charged with any offence other than that wherewith he is then charged, or is of bad character'. The prohibition on the asking of such questions extends to questions put by the trial judge (*Ratcliffe* (1919) 14 Cr App R 95).

'Committed . . . Any Offence Other Than That Wherewith he Is Then Charged'

F14.7   In most cases where the freedom to cross-examine the accused on his discreditable background is sought, the subject-matter of the intended cross-examination will be his previous convictions, but cross-examination for offences for which no conviction has taken place are equally the subject of the prohibition in the Criminal Evidence Act 1898, s. 1(f). In *Hills* [1980] AC 26, H, charged with causing death by dangerous driving, was wrongly supposed to have lost his shield against cross-examination by virtue of proviso (f)(iii). He was asked, in addition to questions about his previous convictions, whether it was true that he was at the time of the accident in question an unqualified driver driving without L-plates and having no qualified driver in attendance. As he was not on trial for any of these offences, questions relating to them were not covered by proviso (e), and, as the exception contended for was found not to apply, they were prohibited by proviso (f).

The prohibition operates whether the suggestion that the accused has committed an offence is direct or oblique. In *Ratcliffe* (1919) 14 Cr App R 95, the trial judge suggested to R that his answers to questions concerning his whereabouts in 1916 were unsatisfactory for some discreditable reason which was not revealed. It was held that the questioning tended to show the commission of some other offence. See also *Ellis* [1910] 2 KB 746, and *Anderson* [1988] QB 678, in which a suggestion that A was 'wanted' by the police for an unspecified offence was regarded as indicating to the jury that A was 'probably guilty' of that offence.

The most common situation in which the prosecution may wish to introduce evidence of other offences for which no conviction has taken place will be where 'similar fact' evidence is relied upon as evidence of guilt. Provided that such evidence is adduced in chief as part of the prosecution case, the prohibition on cross-examination in proviso (f) will not apply, as the question will not 'tend to show' anything new to the jury. It is not the practice to adduce similar fact evidence for the first time in cross-examination, so that proviso (f) rarely comes into play.

'. . . Or Been Convicted of . . . Any Offence Other Than That Wherewith he Is Then Charged'

The prohibition on questions relating to convictions, and the exceptions thereto, affect **F14.8** all convictions whether prior or subsequent to the offence being tried. In *Coltress* (1978) 68 Cr App R 193, C, who had cast imputations on prosecution witnesses, was properly subjected to cross-examination on convictions which had occurred 10 months after his arrest for the offence charged. The Court of Appeal recognised that the date of the convictions might be a factor affecting the exercise of the trial judge's discretion to prevent cross-examination under the Criminal Evidence Act 1898, s. 1(f)(ii). See also *Wood* [1920] 2 KB 179, in which it was said that an accused person who puts himself forward as of good character may be seeking to mislead the jury if he has, after the date of the offence charged, been convicted of other offences.

The prohibition includes oblique, as well as direct, references to conviction, with the result that it is not permitted to cross-examine the accused as to how he has been employed during a period when, as counsel knows, he has been in prison (*Haslam* (1916) 12 Cr App R 10). What matters is, as Lord Denning stated in *Jones* v *DPP* [1962] AC 635, at p. 667, the impression which the questions would have on the jury. His lordship went on to say that a question which is capable of conveying two impressions — one objectionable and the other not — necessarily 'tends to show' each of them, and should be excluded lest the jury adopt the worse of the two interpretations. Although Lord Denning went on to dissent from the opinion expressed by the majority of the House of Lords as to the proper construction of s. 1(f), it is submitted that on this issue his view accurately states the present law.

Spent Convictions The Rehabilitation of Offenders Act 1974, s. 4(1), lays down a **F14.9** general rule that a person whose conviction is 'spent' under the Act is to be treated as a person who has not committed or been charged with or prosecuted for or convicted of or sentenced for the offence or offences which were the subject of that conviction. Section 7(2)(a) excludes criminal proceedings from the operation of this general rule, although the accused is to an extent protected from the use of spent convictions in cross-examination on his record by *Practice Direction (Crime: Spent Convictions)* [1975] 1 WLR 1065, which directs the court to have regard to the spirit of the 1974 Act by refusing to allow any mention to be made of a spent conviction, except where it is in the interests of justice to do so (see also **F13.13**). In essence this produces the same test as in civil proceedings which *are* covered by s. 4(1), but in respect of which s. 7(3) provides for evidence of spent convictions to be admitted if justice cannot otherwise be done (*Thomas* v *Commissioner of Police of the Metropolis* [1997] QB 813, in which careful consideration is given to the relevant criminal authorities). The *Practice Direction* applies to the use of spent convictions for all purposes, including the discrediting of prosecution witnesses (see *Paraskeva* (1982) 76 Cr App R 162 and *Evans* (1992) 156 JP 539, in both of which it was held to be in the interests of justice for the jury to hear of the witness's spent convictions where there was a head-on collision between the witness's evidence and that of the accused). In *Lawler* [1999] 6 Arch News 2, L argued that the Criminal Procedure Act 1865, s. 6, conferred an absolute right to cross-examine a prosecution witness on his previous convictions, but it was held that the judge retained an overall common-law discretion as to the conduct of cross-examination of witnesses, which the *Practice Direction* sought to set in the context of the 1974 Act. The *Practice Direction* is most likely to be brought to bear where previous convictions of the accused are concerned, and in particular where the shield against cross-examination is lost under s. 1(f)(ii) or (iii) of the Criminal Evidence Act 1898. The provisions of the CYPA 1963, s. 16(2), where they apply, constitute an absolute prohibition on the introduction of the criminal record of the accused in respect of offences committed while under the age of 14, whether spent or not. See **F14.10**.

Rehabilitation of Offenders Act 1974, ss. 1, 4 and 7

1.—(1) Subject to subsection (2) below, where an individual has been convicted, whether before or after the commencement of this Act, of any offence or offences, and the following conditions are satisfied, that is to say—

(a) he did not have imposed on him in respect of that conviction a sentence which is excluded from rehabilitation under this Act; and

(b) he has not had imposed on him in respect of subsequent conviction during the rehabilitation period applicable to the first-mentioned conviction in accordance with section 6 below a sentence which is excluded from rehabilitation under this Act;

then, after the end of the rehabilitation period so applicable (including, where appropriate, any extension under section 6(4) below of the period originally applicable to the first-mentioned conviction) or, where that rehabilitation period ended before the commencement of this Act, after the commencement of this Act, that individual shall for the purposes of this Act be treated as a rehabilitated person in respect of the first-mentioned conviction and that conviction shall for those purposes be treated as spent.

(2) A person shall not become a rehabilitated person for the purposes of this Act in respect of a conviction unless he has served or otherwise undergone or complied with any sentence imposed on him in respect of that conviction; but the following shall not, by virtue of this subsection, prevent a person from becoming a rehabilitated person for those purposes—

(a) failure to pay a fine or other sum adjudged to be paid by or imposed on a conviction, or breach of a condition of a recognisance or of a bond of caution to keep the peace or be of good behaviour;

(b) breach of any condition or requirement applicable in relation to a sentence which renders the person to whom it applies liable to be dealt with for the offence for which the sentence was imposed, or, where the sentence was a suspended sentence of imprisonment, liable to be dealt with in respect of that sentence (whether or not, in any case, he is in fact so dealt with);

(c) failure to comply with any requirement of a suspended sentence supervision order.

(2A) Where in respect of a conviction a person has been sentenced to imprisonment with an order under section 47(1) of the Criminal Law Act 1977, he is to be treated for the purposes of subsection (2) above as having served the sentence as soon as he completes service of so much of the sentence as was by that order required to be served in prison.

(3) In this Act 'sentence' includes any order made by a court in dealing with a person in respect of his conviction of any offence or offences, other than—

(a) an order for committal or any other order made in default of payment of any fine or other sum adjudged to be paid by or imposed on a conviction, or for want of sufficient distress to satisfy any such fine or other sum;

(b) an order dealing with a person in respect of a suspended sentence of imprisonment.

(4) In this Act, references to a conviction, however expressed, include references—

(a) to a conviction by or before a court outside Great Britain; and

(b) to any finding (other than a finding linked with a finding of insanity) in any criminal proceedings that a person has committed an offence or done the act or made the omission charged;

and notwithstanding anything in . . . or section 1C of the Powers of Criminal Courts Act 1973 (conviction of a person discharged to be deemed not to be a conviction) a conviction in respect of which an order is made discharging the person concerned absolutely or conditionally shall be treated as a conviction for the purposes of this Act and the person in question may become a rehabilitated person in respect of that conviction and the conviction a spent conviction for those purposes accordingly.

4.—(1) Subject to sections 7 and 8 below, a person who has become a rehabilitated person for the purposes of this Act in respect of a conviction shall be treated for all purposes in law as a person who has not committed or been charged with or prosecuted for or convicted of or sentenced for the offence or offences which were the subject of that conviction; and notwithstanding the provisions of any other enactment or rule of law to the contrary, but subject as aforesaid—

(a) no evidence shall be admissible in any proceedings before a judicial authority exercising its jurisdiction or functions in Great Britain to prove that any such person has committed or been charged with or prosecuted for or convicted of or sentenced for any offence which was the subject of a spent conviction; and

(b) a person shall not, in any such proceedings, be asked, and, if asked, shall not be required to answer, any question relating to his past which cannot be answered without acknowledging or referring to a spent conviction or spent convictions or any circumstances ancillary thereto.

7.

. . .

(2) Nothing in section 4(1) above shall affect the determination of any issue, or prevent the admission or requirement of any evidence, relating to a person's previous convictions or to circumstances ancillary thereto—

(a) in any criminal proceedings before a court in Great Britain (including any appeal or reference in a criminal matter);

(b) in any service disciplinary proceedings or in any proceedings on appeal from any service disciplinary proceedings;

(bb) in any proceedings on an application for a sex offender order under section 2 or, as the case may be, 20 of the Crime and Disorder Act 1998 or in any appeal against the making of such an order;

(c) and (cc) [apply to proceedings outside the scope of the work];

(d) in any proceedings relating to the variation or discharge of a supervision order under the Children and Young Persons Act 1969, or on appeal from any such proceedings;

(e) [repealed];

(f) [applies to proceedings outside the scope of this work].

. . .

(5) No order made by a court with respect to any person otherwise than on a conviction shall be included in any list or statement of that person's previous convictions given or made to any court which is considering how to deal with him in respect of any offence.

Practice Direction (Crime: Spent Convictions) [1975] 1 WLR 1065

1. The effect of section 4(1) of the Rehabilitation of Offenders Act 1974 is that a person who has become a rehabilitated person for the purpose of the Act in respect of a conviction (known as a 'spent' conviction) shall be treated for all purposes in law as a person who has not committed or been convicted of or sentenced for the offence or offences which were the subject of that conviction.

2. Section 4(1) of the Act does not apply to evidence given in criminal proceedings: section 7(2)(a). Convictions are often disclosed in such criminal proceedings. When the Bill was before the House of Commons on 28 July 1974, the hope was expressed that the Lord Chief Justice would issue a practice direction for the guidance of the Crown Courts with a view to reducing disclosure of spent convictions to a mimimum and securing uniformity of approach.

3. During the trial of a criminal charge reference to previous convictions and therefore to spent convictions, can arise in a number of ways. The most common is when the character of the accused or a witness is sought to be attacked by reference to his criminal record, but there are, of course, cases where previous convictions are relevant and admissible as, for instance, to prove system.

4. It is not possible to give general directions which will govern all these different situations, but it is recommended that both court and counsel should give effect to the general intention of Parliament by never referring to a spent conviction when such reference can be reasonably avoided. If unnecessary references to spent convictions are eliminated much will have been achieved.

5. After a verdict of guilty the court must be provided with a statement of the defendant's record for the purposes of sentence. The record supplied should contain all previous convictions, but those which are spent should, so far as practicable, be marked as such.

6. No one should refer in open court to a spent conviction without the authority of the judge, which authority should not be given unless the interests of justice so require.

7. When passing sentence the judge should make no reference to a spent conviction unless it is necessary to do so for the purpose of explaining the sentence to be passed.

Findings of Guilt of Person under 14

F14.10 **Children and Young Persons Act 1963, s. 16**

(2) In any proceedings for an offence committed or alleged to have been committed by a person of or over the age of 21, any offence of which he was found guilty while under the age of 14 shall be disregarded for the purposes of any evidence relating to his previous convictions; and he shall not be asked, and if asked shall not be required to answer, any question relating to such an offence, notwithstanding that the question would otherwise be admissible under section 1 of the Criminal Evidence Act 1898.

Section 16(3) makes clear that s. 16(2) does not prevent the adduction of evidence of previous convictions for the purposes of establishing the application of any provision of part I of the 1997 Act, which deals with mandatory and minimum custodial sentences.

Whether the introduction of a conviction in breach of s. 16(2) necessitates the discharge of the jury depends on the facts of the case, and in particular upon the degree of prejudice likely to be caused (*Dickerson* [1964] Crim LR 821).

F14.11 ***Disclosure of Previous Convictions to Defence*** Under *Practice Direction (Crime: Antecedents) (No. 2)* [1997] 1 WLR 1482 new arrangements are made for the provision of antecedents following the introduction of computerised information from the police national computer. In the Crown Court, in addition to the antecedents, the police will provide brief details of the circumstances of the last three similar convictions and/or of convictions likely to be of interest to the court, the latter being judged on a case-by-case basis.

The *Practice Direction* is set out at **D17.17**. As to the duty to disclose the previous convictions of prosecution witnesses, see **D12.18**.

'. . . Or Been Charged . . . with any Offence Other Than That Wherewith he Is Then Charged'

F14.12 In *Stirland* v *DPP* [1944] AC 315, the House of Lords held that the word 'charged' in the Criminal Evidence Act 1898, s. 1(f) means 'accused before a criminal court', and not merely 'suspected or accused without prosecution'. The consequence of this was held to be that, where S put his character in issue and said that he had never been 'charged' with an offence, he should have been taken to be using the word in the same sense as the Act, and should not have been cross-examined about an incident in his past in which he had left his employment under suspicion of dishonesty. The incident did not give the lie to what S had said on oath, nor did it supply general evidence of bad character: 'The most virtuous may be suspected, and an unproven accusation proves nothing' (per Viscount Simon LC, at p. 324).

As a result of the decision in *Stirland* v *DPP*, questions about incidents giving rise to suspicion are not covered by the prohibition in proviso (f). It does not follow that such incidents may be the subject of unrestrained cross-examination, however, because of the decision of the House of Lords in *Maxwell* v *DPP* [1935] AC 309 (see **F14.13**), which was approved in *Stirland*, and which stipulates that all questions to be put in cross-examination must satisfy the common-law test of relevance. A question regarding an unproven allegation which is irrelevant both to the charge under consideration and to the issue of good character is, at the same time, potentially prejudicial to the accused, in that it suggests to the jury that he has been in trouble before, and ought not to be allowed.

A question showing that an accused person has been suspected of an offence might be allowed if he has expressly sworn the contrary (*Stirland* v *DPP* [1944] AC 315, per Viscount Simon). Such a question would, however, only have a bearing on the accused's credit if he knew of the suspicion harboured against him.

Acquittals Questioning which reveals a charge which has resulted in an acquittal may **F14.13** be restrained by the doctrine of relevance. In *Maxwell* v *DPP* [1935] AC 309, M was charged with the manslaughter of a girl whose abortion he had attempted to procure. M made an issue of his good character, but it was held that it was nevertheless improper to cross-examine him about a previous charge of manslaughter made in very similar circumstances and upon which he had been acquitted. Acknowledging that the prohibition on questions about previous charges had been lifted by the Criminal Evidence Act 1898, s. 1(f)(ii), Viscount Sankey said (at p. 319):

> ... it does not follow that when the absolute prohibition is superseded by a permission, that the permission is as absolute as the prohibition. When it is sought to justify a question it must not only be brought within the terms of the permission, but also must be capable of justification according to the general rules of evidence and in particular must satisfy the test of relevance.

The unsuccessful charge did not go to show that M was guilty of the crime charged, nor did it affect his credibility as a witness. Questions relating to it therefore ought not to have been put. See also *Meehan* [1978] Crim LR 690, in which M swore that he had only one previous conviction, and it was held that he should not have been cross-examined about proceedings which had resulted in his being bound over without ever having been convicted.

It does not follow that the inclusion of 'charge' in proviso (f) is otiose. In *Maxwell* v *DPP* [1935] AC 309 Viscount Sankey took the view that it was clearly not so as regards the prohibition, and envisaged various cases where cross-examination about an acquittal might be relevant, for example where it is alleged that an accused has uttered threats against another because he was angry with him for bringing a charge which turned out to be unfounded. In *Nicoloudis* (1954) 38 Cr App R 118, it was suggested that questioning about a charge might be relevant if the facts surrounding it gave rise to an inference of knowledge by the accused of facts relevant to the present case. A charge might also, in certain circumstances, be relevant to credit: in *Stirland* v *DPP* [1944] AC 315, Viscount Simon LC said (at p. 323) that a man who has put his character in issue and who swears that he has never been charged in court might be cross-examined to show that this is untrue.

An unsatisfactory authority in this respect is *Waldman* (1934) 24 Cr App R 204. W was charged with receiving stolen property, and put his character in issue. It was held that a previous acquittal for receiving was relevant, both because it suggested that W ought to have been particularly careful about goods in his possession, thus rebutting his claim to be an honest businessman, and also because a previous conviction for receiving was admitted at the same time. It is submitted that neither ground confers upon the acquittal the degree of relevance required by *Maxwell* v *DPP*.

Where the defence involves imputations upon the character of prosecution witnesses, and the accused is cross-examined on his convictions with a view to discrediting his testimony, it may become relevant for him to introduce previous acquittals. In *Doosti* (1985) 82 Cr App R 181, D's defence to a charge of conspiring to supply heroin was that police officers, including M, had fabricated the evidence against him. The prosecution elected to introduce evidence of D's previous conviction for a similar offence, which had been secured chiefly on the evidence of M. It was held that D ought 'in justice' to have been permitted to show that, on the same occasion, he was acquitted of a number of more serious offences, in respect of which evidence had also been given by M. The question which arose, and on which the prosecution had elected to put D's conviction in evidence, was as to the comparative reliability of the testimony of D and M. On this question, D's acquittals were a relevant matter.

F14.14 **Pending Charges** In *Smith* [1989] Crim LR 900, S put her good character in issue and was cross-examined about charges upon which she was awaiting trial. It was held that the questions were improper, as they tended to undermine the accused's right to silence in respect of the offences with which they were concerned. It would appear that the questions were also impermissible for the reasons stated in *Stirland* v *DPP* [1944] AC 315, at **F14.12**.

' . . . Or is of Bad Character'

F14.15 The meaning of 'character' at common law is in theory restricted to evidence of the reputation of the person whose character is in issue (*Rowton* (1865) Le & Ca 320 (see **F13.12**)). But to apply the same meaning to the word where it appears in the Criminal Evidence Act 1898, s. 1(f), would severely limit the scope of the Act, and early interpretations preferred the view that 'character' under the Act includes disposition. In *Dunkley* [1927] 1 KB 323, Lord Hewart CJ considered that it was 'too late in the day' to argue for the application of the common-law rule. See also, e.g., *Stirland* v *DPP* [1944] AC 315, per Viscount Simon LC at p. 324, quoted with apparent approval by Lord Morris in *Malindi* v *The Queen* [1967] AC 439, at p. 451; and *Selvey* v *DPP* [1970] AC 304, per Viscount Dilhorne at p. 333, who noted the above authorities without commenting on their correctness. Lord Devlin, in his dissenting speech in *Jones* v *DPP* [1962] AC 635, at p. 709, considered that the law was not settled and that it was 'inevitable that sooner or later your Lordships will have to consider whether *Dunkley* was rightly decided'. The question was not, however, decided in *Jones* v *DPP*, and is still, in theory, open to argument before the House of Lords. On the assumption that *Dunkley* [1927] 1 KB 323 was correctly decided, proviso (f) protects the accused from allegations of immorality or impropriety falling short of criminal conduct, and proviso (f)(ii) ensures that the shield is lost where the accused makes such allegations against a prosecution witness, or asserts his good disposition. This reading of the statute was recently confirmed in *Carter* (1997) 161 JP 207, in which C was held to have been improperly cross-examined at his trial for fraud about his discreditable behaviour in relation to a civil action. The behaviour in question was highly prejudicial, as it was similar in nature to that alleged against C in the criminal proceedings, but it was assumed at trial that it was only questioning regarding criminal conduct which was caught by proviso (f). The Court of Appeal considered that cross-examination tending to show an accused to be of bad character in the sense either of reputation or disposition, which was based on matters which did not arise from the evidence relating to the indictment, was within the prohibition and should not therefore be embarked upon without the leave of the court.

PROVISO (f)(i): CROSS-EXAMINATION RELEVANT TO GUILT

The Criminal Evidence Act 1898, s. 1(f)(i), applies where:

> the proof that he has committed or been convicted of such other offence is admissible evidence to show that he is guilty of the offence wherewith he is then charged.

'Proof that he Has Committed or Been Convicted of . . .'

Proviso (f) generally prohibits, in addition to questions tending to show that the accused **F14.16** has committed or been convicted of other offences, those questions which show that he has previously been charged with any offence, or is of bad character. Because proviso (f)(i) makes no reference to the previous charges or the bad character of the accused, it has been held that these matters may not be the subject of cross-examination under this exception, except insofar as it may be necessary to refer to a charge as a step on the way to establishing commission or conviction (*Cokar* [1960] 2 QB 207). Thus, it was impermissible for the prosecutor to cross-examine C about a previous charge (which had resulted in his acquittal) with a view to showing that he knew that entering premises merely in order to sleep was a good defence to the offence with which he was charged. So also in *Pommell* [1999] Crim LR 576 it was held impermissible to cross-examine the accused, charged with firearms offences, about a previous successful defence of necessity which was not unlike the defence raised at trial. Any questions about a charge which had led to an acquittal were held to be ruled out by the wording of s. 1(f)(i).

In *G (An Infant)* v *Coltart* [1967] 1 QB 432, it was said that because the effect of *Cokar* was to prevent cross-examination to show a charge which had resulted in an acquittal, even though the correctness of that acquittal was not called into question, then *a fortiori* there could be no such cross-examination if the purpose was to suggest that the accused had committed the offence of which he had been acquitted. It is submitted that the conclusion arrived at is correct, but that it flows, not from *Cokar*, but from the general rule that the prosecution may not lead evidence or ask questions calling into question the accuracy of an acquittal (*Sambasivam* v *Public Prosecutor of Malayan Federation* [1950] AC 458).

Where a previous charge or evidence of bad character has been properly referred to as part of the prosecution case, or by the accused in evidence in chief, then, as in *Jones* v *DPP* [1962] AC 635 (see **F14.4**), cross-examination may be permissible on the grounds that it 'tends to show' nothing of which the jury were previously unaware.

'. . . Is Admissible Evidence to Show that he is Guilty. . .'

In *Cokar* [1960] 2 QB 207, it was said that the Criminal Evidence Act 1898, s. 1(f)(i), **F14.17** is 'directed to the common class of case where evidence of previous convictions is admissible to show system, and matters of that sort'. In other words, the exception allows the accused to be cross-examined on admissible similar fact evidence. Such evidence will, however, generally have been adduced by the prosecution in the course of their evidence in chief, so that, following *Jones* v *DPP* [1962] AC 635 (see **F14.4**), the cross-examination of the accused on the same subject-matter will not 'tend to show' any offence of which the jury were previously unaware. It is therefore unnecessary to invoke proviso (f)(i) in such a case, because the cross-examination does not infringe the general prohibition in proviso (f). Conversely, if the prosecution have withheld the evidence until cross-examination, the court may prevent any questioning of the accused about it, despite proviso (f)(i), on the ground that the evidence ought to have been put in chief (*Coombes* (1960) 45 Cr App R 36). The accused should not be unfairly deprived of an opportunity to cross-examine prosecution witnesses, which might enable him to dispute or explain the similarity of circumstances or pattern of offending alleged by the prosecution (*Jones* v *DPP* [1962] AC 635, per Ashworth J at p. 647). In the House of Lords in the same case, Lord Morris agreed with the Court of Appeal, saying that in general it would be undesirable if such a matter were raised for the first time in cross-examination. Even where the defence raised is not reasonably foreseeable by the prosecution, with the result that evidence of previous convictions or of the commission of other offences is not introduced before the close of the prosecution case, it may be preferable to allow the prosecution to call additional evidence in rebuttal, recalling the accused to deal with the evidence if appropriate, rather than to introduce it for the first time in cross-examination (see *Anderson* [1988] QB 678, at p. 689, in which this course of action was commended).

Subject to the restraints considered in the last paragraph, proviso (f)(i) could be invoked in respect of evidence of previous convictions or the commission of other offences rendered admissible by statute in particular cases, such as the Theft Act 1968, s. 27(3), and the Official Secrets Act 1911, s. 1(2).

PROVISO (f)(ii): ACCUSED INTRODUCING EVIDENCE OF GOOD CHARACTER

The first part of the Criminal Evidence Act 1898, s. 1(f)(ii), applies where the accused:

> has personally or by his advocate asked questions of the witnesses of the prosecution with a view to establish his own good character, or has given evidence of his good character.

Relationship to Common-Law Rules

F14.18   The circumstances in which an accused person may be said to have made an issue of his good character at common law have been considered at **F13.12** to **F13.14**. At common law the accused may call witnesses to his good character, and it is not clear whether the exercise of this prerogative costs him his shield under proviso (f)(ii), as being evidence 'given' by him, or whether the section applies only to evidence given by the accused in person, or elicited under cross-examination from prosecution witnesses. The similarly worded proviso (f)(iii) applies only to evidence 'given' by the accused in person (**F14.37** to **F14.42**). On the other hand, it seems to have been assumed that the calling of character witnesses involves the loss of the shield (see, e.g., *Ellis* [1910] 2 KB 746, at p. 762). As the common law permits character witnesses to be cross-examined in such a way as to bring out the accused's record, however, the point is of no great consequence. Where an accused loses his shield under proviso (f)(ii) as a result of claims made in his evidence, so that the trial judge rules that he may be cross-examined on his record, he cannot avoid the cross-examination by electing to remain mute thereafter, as this would be to frustrate the purpose of the Act. Such an accused may be asked about his convictions and, if he does not reply, they may be proved against him (*Forbes* (1999) 163 JP 629).

Defence Implicitly Involving Good Character

F14.19   The shield against cross-examination is not lost simply because the defence assert facts relevant to the issue which, if believed, show the accused in a favourable light. In *Malindi v The Queen* [1967] AC 439, the issue was whether M was a party to a conspiracy involving the use of violence against property. The prosecution case was that the conspiracy arose out of a meeting at M's house, but M's evidence concerning the meeting was that, when violence was discussed, he had counselled against it and expressed his disapproval. It was held that M had not thereby given evidence of good character, for he did not 'independently of giving his account of what had actually happened, and of what had actually been said, assert that he was a man of good character'. See also *Ellis* [1910] 2 KB 746, in which it was held that a general examination of the circumstances surrounding the allegation was not capable of putting good character in issue, and *Holman* (1992) *The Times*, 9 September 1992 in which it was held that evidence by the accused as to the *res gestae* (in the sense of the circumstances of the commission of the alleged offence) was not given with a view to establishing good character.

Where the accused goes beyond asserting facts relevant to his version of events, his shield may be lost. In *Samuel* (1956) 40 Cr App R 8, S's defence to a charge of theft was that he had found the property and that he intended to return it. He gave evidence of two other occasions on which he had found property and handed it back. It was held that the shield was lost, as the only object of referring to the two previous occasions was to induce the jury to say 'This man is one of those people who, if he finds property, gives it up; in other words he is an honest man.' It follows that where, for example, a man claims to be married with a family and to hold down a regular job, he is putting his character in issue (*Coulman* (1927) 20 Cr App R 106, per Swift J at p. 108).

Samuel was criticised in *Redgrave* (1982) 74 Cr App R 10, on the ground that S's evidence, as it did not bear on his good reputation, was not evidence of his good character at common law, applying *Rowton* (1865) Le & Ca 320. The criticism assumes that the accused is himself subject to the *Rowton* rule when giving evidence in chief of his own good character, but this is unlikely, for the rule was formulated before the accused was generally competent to testify, and it is difficult to imagine the accused ever being in a position to give evidence of his own reputation, because as Lord Denning observed in *Plato Films Ltd* v *Speidel* [1961] AC 1090, at p. 1143, 'he does not know what other people think of him or, at any rate, he cannot give evidence as to what they think of him'.

It is not evidence of good character for the accused to refer to discreditable incidents in his past, unless he is suggesting that in all other respects he has led a good life (*Wattam* (1952) 36 Cr App R 72; *Thompson* [1966] 1 WLR 405). Nor does the accused put his own good character in issue by casting imputations on the character of others. In *Lee* [1976] 1 WLR 71 the accused, in defence to a charge of theft, alleged that there were other people more likely from their criminal records to have committed the offence, including the brother of the victim. It was held that: 'it is not implicit in an accusation of dishonesty that the accuser himself is an honest man'. See also *Butterwasser* [1948] KB 4. A case which is difficult to reconcile with the principles stated above is *Bracewell* (1978) 68 Cr App R 44, in which B and L were charged with murder arising out of a burglary, and L was held to have put his 'disposition' in issue by asserting that, as a mature and experienced burglar, he was less likely to have panicked and resorted to violence than B. As a result, it was held that B would have been entitled to cross-examine L about L's conduct towards his mistress, which displayed a propensity towards uncontrolled violence wholly inconsistent with the image of himself which L was trying to project. The Criminal Evidence Act 1898 is not referred to, and it is submitted that it would be wrong to regard the cross-examination as permissible because of proviso (f)(ii), unless it is supposed that, in referring to his accomplishments as a burglar, L was seeking to mislead the jury as to the true extent of his criminal past (cf. *Wattam* (1952) 36 Cr App R 72). A better view might be that the case was one in which B was entitled to cross-examine by virtue of s. 1(f)(i), on the ground that offences of violence committed by L were relevant to his guilt of the offence charged.

Where an accused is led in cross-examination into giving answers suggestive of good character, it appears that the record may not be brought out, although the authorities are not strong. In *Beecham* (1921) 16 Cr App R 26, B was accused of the manslaughter of a child by driving at excessive speed. He was asked continuously in cross-examination why he had bought that particular car, until the answer was elicited that it was not because he liked to drive at speed. It was held improper for counsel thereupon to cross-examine on B's convictions for speeding, but the judgment seems to proceed as much on the basis that B did not put his character in issue as on the ground that he was improperly driven to do so. In *Punch* (23 April 1996 unreported), however, *Beecham* was said to compel the conclusion that an assertion of good character made under pressure of improper questioning designed to suggest bad character was not to be regarded as sufficient to found cross-examination. The court also relied upon *Baldwin* (1925) 18 Cr App R 175, in which it was held under the other limb of s. 1(f)(ii) that a cross-examination designed to lead an accused to make imputations is impermissible. Answers in cross-examination are prima facie not part of the 'nature and conduct of the defence' for the purposes of the second limb, however, so that the constraints are not identical.

As to the question whether a person whose previous convictions are 'spent' may be presented to the jury as a man of previous good character, and thus preserve his shield, see **F13.9**.

Character Indivisible

F14.20   'An accused who "puts his character in issue" must be regarded as putting the whole of his past record in issue' (*Stirland* v *DPP* [1944] AC 315, per Viscount Simon LC at p. 326). Thus, the accused cannot avoid cross-examination on aspects of his past by dividing up his character and asserting, with truth, that certain parts of it are good. In this respect the rule is the same, whether the prosecution seek to rebut the assertion under the 1898 Act or at common law (see *Winfield* [1939] 4 All ER 164 at **F13.14**).

Purpose of Cross-Examination

F14.21   Where an accused person is cross-examined under the Criminal Evidence Act 1898, s. 1(f)(ii), the jury may treat the evidence thus elicited as relevant to the accused's general credibility in the case, and they should not be directed that evidence of bad character does no more than rebut or cancel out evidence of good character (*Richardson* [1969] 1 QB 299).

A more difficult question is whether evidence admitted in cross-examination by virtue of proviso (f)(ii) may be said to be relevant to the issue of guilt. It is generally accepted that evidence of good character fulfills the dual function of bolstering credibility and supporting a claim of innocence (see **F13.2**), and it has rightly been observed that the distinction between cross-examination to credit and to the issue is, where the evidence of the accused is concerned, of little practical significance (*Samuel* (1956) 40 Cr App R 8, per Lord Goddard CJ at p. 12). Nevertheless, and despite the apparent dictum to the contrary of Lord Sankey in *Maxwell* v *DPP* [1935] AC 309, at p. 319, it is submitted that the function of cross-examination under this limb of proviso (f)(ii) is limited to affecting credibility. This is beyond dispute the purpose of cross-examination under the second limb of (f)(ii) (see **F14.30**), and in *Powell* [1985] 1 WLR 1364, in which P made sure of losing his shield by both setting up his own good character and casting imputations on prosecution witnesses, it was assumed that the function of the resultant cross-examination was to affect credibility, no distinction being drawn between the two limbs of the proviso.

Discretion to Restrain Cross-Examination

F14.22   The judicial discretion to prevent the cross-examination of an accused person who has lost his shield, though more commonly encountered in relation to the second limb of the Criminal Evidence Act 1898, s. 1(f)(ii), is also capable of being exercised in relation to the first limb. However there may be little scope for discretion in practice, for if an accused has laid claim to a character which is better than that which he in fact possesses, it will be necessary in most cases to 'set the record straight', lest the jury be misled. So in *Marsh* [1994] Crim LR 52, M was charged with inflicting grievous bodily harm on another player in the course of an 'off-the-ball' incident in a rugby game. He sought to adduce evidence that he had no previous convictions but the judge ruled that to do so would leave him open to cross-examination about his disciplinary record for violent play on the rugby field. The Court of Appeal held that in the circumstances once M elected to put in his good character the judge was bound to exercise his discretion in favour of allowing cross-examination, otherwise the jury would have been given a seriously misleading impression.

A rare example of a case in which the discretion ought to have been exercised so as to restrain cross-examination is *Davison-Jenkins* [1997] Crim LR 816. D, charged with shoplifting cheap cosmetics, defended herself by asserting that she had acted under the influence of medication and without criminal intention. She put her character in issue by asserting that she was a wealthy woman of good standing who had no use for the items in question. It was held that the needs of s. 1(f)(ii) could have been met by reference in general terms to D's previous convictions for dishonesty, but that to bring out the detail of particular convictions for shoplifting was so overwhelmingly prejudicial as to outweigh any possible marginal relevance to the issue of credibility. The court applied *McLeod* [1994] 1 WLR 1500 (see **F14.35**), which, though primarily concerned with revelation of the detail of previous convictions admitted under the second limb of s. 1(f)(ii), appears to be of equal application to the first limb.

PROVISO (f)(ii): IMPUTATIONS ON CHARACTER OF PROSECUTOR OR WITNESSES FOR PROSECUTION OR DECEASED VICTIM

The second part of the Criminal Evidence Act 1898, s. 1(f)(ii), comes into play where:

> the nature or conduct of the defence is such as to involve imputations on the character of the prosecutor or the witnesses for the prosecution or the deceased victim of the alleged crime.

Nature or Conduct of Defence

The wording of s. 1(f)(ii) is to be contrasted with that of s. 1(f)(iii). Under proviso **F14.23** (f)(iii), it is only the testimony of the accused himself which is relevant to the question whether he has 'given evidence against' his co-accused, but it is necessary to consider his testimony as a whole, including answers given in cross-examination which are part of the 'evidence' he gives (see **F14.37** to **F14.42**). Under proviso (f)(ii), on the other hand, the whole of the defence case must be scrutinised to see whether its 'nature or conduct is such as to involve imputations'. But evidence consisting solely of answers given in cross-examination (by the prosecution or co-accused) are prima facie not to be taken into account, as such answers form part of the cross-examiner's case (*Jones* (1909) 3 Cr App R 67; *Eidinow* (1932) 23 Cr App R 154). In *Britzman* [1983] 1 WLR 350, the Court of Appeal appeared to regard the fact that imputations were made in cross-examination as being relevant to the exercise of judicial discretion in the accused's favour, rather than to the question whether the shield is lost in law. This observation was not essential to the decision, and it is submitted that the earlier authorities remain good law.

Answers given in cross-examination may result in the loss of the shield if, for example, the accused makes a derogatory observation which is not a necessary answer to the question put (*Jones* (1909) 3 Cr App R 67, per Lord Alverstone CJ at p. 69; see also *Courtney* [1995] Crim LR 63, where the response involved a 'voluntary and gratuitous' attack on a witness). Equally (and more obviously), he will lose the shield where his answers in cross-examination do no more than to remove all doubt as to whether the accused was seeking to impugn the character of a prosecution witness (*Selvey* v *DPP* [1970] AC 304). Where, however, a judge thinks that the accused has been trapped into making an imputation by the form of the question put to him, he should not allow cross-examination on the record or character of the accused (*Jones* (1909) 3 Cr App R 67; *Baldwin* (1925) 18 Cr App R 175). It is sometimes said that the imputation implicit in an allegation of consent in a rape trial does not involve the loss of the shield, because the issue arises as part of the prosecution case and not as part of the 'nature and conduct of the defence'. For a discussion of this and other reasons why the shield is not lost in such cases, see **F14.26**.

If the nature or conduct of the defence is such as to involve imputations on a prosecution witness, the accused may avoid cross-examination on his record by declining to give evidence (see *Butterwasser* [1948] KB 4 at **F13.13**). If he elects to give evidence, however, he cannot avoid the revelation of his record by remaining mute when asked about it (*Forbes* (1999) 163 JP 629).

Meaning of 'Imputation'

F14.24   An 'imputation' on the character of another may be made both where there is an attack on his reputation (the restricted common-law meaning of 'character') and where his disposition is impugned by allegations of specific discreditable or disgraceful conduct (*Dunkley* [1927] 1 KB 323). In *Selvey* v *DPP* [1970] AC 304, Lord Hodson pointed out (at p. 343) that to restrict 'character' in this part of the Criminal Evidence Act 1898, s. 1(f)(ii), to its common-law meaning, would make a nonsense of the provision, for 'it would then be possible to argue that someone who swore that a policeman had extracted a confession from him by violence was not casting imputations on the character of a witness for the prosecution'. Lord Pearce (at p. 354) agreed that the common law did not fetter the operation of the section, but for the different reason that the allegation of 'really discreditable matters' necessarily involves an imputation on the general reputation of the person attacked, 'if only as showing how erroneous that reputation must be'. Viscount Dilhorne expressed a similar view to that of Lord Pearce (at p. 337).

What constitutes an 'imputation' may vary from one generation to the next. Having a mistress used to be regarded as evidence of bad character (*Kurasch* [1915] 2 KB 749), but it by no means follows that the courts would so regard it today. In *Bishop* [1975] QB 274, it was argued that it should no longer be regarded as discreditable to suggest that a person has had a lawful homosexual relationship (the allegation being a necessary part of B's defence), but the argument was rejected on the grounds that most people would still find such conduct 'immoral or wrong', and a false allegation of homosexual conduct would still be regarded as defamatory. The fact that the truth of an allegation is not seriously in dispute is of no relevance to whether it is in law an imputation (*Wainwright* [1998] Crim LR 665): a particularly harsh application of the literal rule of construction of the statute.

The mere denial by an accused of knowledge of an incriminating fact, such as the presence in his car of a weapon, does not constitute an imputation (*Goodwin* (1993) *The Times*, 26 November 1993), nor does a suggestion that the alleged victim of a robbery has miscalculated the money in his possession (*Stanton* [1994] Crim LR 834).

'Necessary' Imputations

F14.25   Until the decision of the House of Lords in *Selvey* v *DPP* [1970] AC 304, there was considerable controversy over the position of an accused person whose defence required the making of imputations. A literal interpretation led to the result that the shield was lost in such a case (see, e.g., *Hudson* [1912] 2 KB 464), whereas a benevolent construction based on the presumed intention of Parliament resulted in the accused keeping his shield unless he made imputations going beyond what was necessary in order to elicit the facts relevant to the offence with which he was charged (see, e.g., *Westfall* (1912) 7 Cr App R 176). The House of Lords unanimously endorsed the literal approach, with the proviso that the trial judge has a discretion to prevent any cross-examination of the accused which would be detrimental to the fairness of the trial (see **F14.31**).

As a result of the decision in *Selvey* v *DPP*, it is clear that it is immaterial for the purposes of the Criminal Evidence Act 1898, s. 1(f)(ii), whether the imputation relates directly or indirectly to the issues involved in the proceedings. Thus, it is of direct relevance (but clearly an imputation) to suggest that a prosecution witness himself committed the crime charged (*Hudson* [1912] 2 KB 464); or was an accessory to it (*Manley* (1962) 46 Cr App R 235); or has a particular reason for inventing it (*Selvey* v *DPP*; *Flynn* [1963] 1 QB 729; *Inder* (1977) 67 Cr App R 143). And it is equally an imputation (though it may be of no direct relevance to the issues raised in the case) to suggest that a prosecution witness has lived a promiscuous life, or is homosexual, or has committed unrelated offences.

Rape Cases   Of the cases cited in *Selvey* v *DPP* [1970] AC 304 as authority against a   F14.26
literal interpretation of the wording of the Criminal Evidence Act 1898, s. 1(f)(ii), the most compelling were *Sheean* (1908) 21 Cox CC 561, and *Turner* [1944] KB 463, each of which concerned an allegation of consent made in defence to a charge of rape. In both cases, it was held that the shield was not lost, as the accused had done no more than traverse an allegation which was an essential part of the prosecution case. In the opinion of the House of Lords in *Selvey* v *DPP*, both cases were rightly decided, but were not authority for any general principle permitting the making of an exception in the case of necessary imputations. Three possible justifications for the decisions were advanced:

(a)   rape is a crime which is *sui generis* in this respect (following Devlin J in *Cook* [1959] 2 QB 340);
(b)   the accused is allowed to keep his shield when merely traversing an issue raised by the prosecution as part of their case, as an imputation made in such circumstances is not part of the 'nature and conduct of the defence' within the meaning of the section (relying on statements made by Humphreys J in *Turner* [1944] KB 463);
(c)   an imputation is present in such case, but the discretion to restrain cross-examination should always be exercised in favour of the accused (again following remarks of Devlin J in *Cook* [1959] 2 QB 340).

No clear support emerges in *Selvey* v *DPP* for any one of these three possible reasons, but is submitted that the second or third should be preferred, as the difficulty encountered in *Sheean* and *Turner* is not confined to rape cases. Indeed in *Sheean* (1908) 21 Cox CC 561 Jelf J stated (at p. 562) that the shield remained intact because the imputation was made by an accused 'to clear himself upon a charge to which consent is a defence in law', suggesting that the rule must at least apply, e.g., to the various types of assault to which consent is a defence. However, in *Lasseur* [1991] Crim LR 53 it was said that the rule is a 'special exception concerning rape cases'.

Emphatic Denials   Viscount Dilhorne in *Selvey* v *DPP* [1970] AC 304, stated (at p.   F14.27
339) that a rule had developed whereby: 'If what is said amounts in reality to no more than a denial of the charge, expressed, it may be, in emphatic language, it should not be regarded as coming within the section'. The principle is derived from *Rouse* [1904] 1 KB 184, in which the accused asserted in cross-examination that a prosecution witness's evidence was a lie, and the witness a liar. Lord Alverstone CJ refused to regard this as an imputation, characterising it instead as 'nothing more than a traverse of the truth of an allegation', of the sort which 'is necessary and inevitable in every case where a prisoner goes into the witness-box'. This, though an exaggeration in the sense that it may be possible in some cases for the accused to testify on his own behalf without alleging mendacity on the part of a prosecution witness (for example, in a case where the defence is one of mistaken identity), appears to have been accepted as correct at least by Viscount Dilhorne and Lord Hodson in *Selvey* v *DPP* [1970] AC 304. It is, however, dangerous to rely on *Rouse* as stating an absolute principle, as there are various Court of Appeal decisions in which the accused has lost his shield by challenging the veracity of prosecution witnesses.

In *Rappolt* (1911) 6 Cr App R 156, it was held that R's evidence involved an imputation when he said that a witness was such a horrible liar that even his own brother would not speak to him. The case is distinguishable from *Rouse* [1904] 1 KB 184, because Rappolt had gone beyond what it was necessary to say in order to challenge the veracity of his accuser. Compare *Wignall* [1993] Crim LR 62, in which W, a taxi-driver, was charged with stealing a customer's purse. His counsel cross-examined the complainant on the basis that her evidence was untrue, and suggested that she was making it up as she went along in order to bolster her case. It was held that what counsel said added little to the suggestion that her evidence was untrue and that cross-examination on W's particularly bad record ought not to have been permitted. In *Desmond* [1999] Crim LR 313 it was held, applying *Wignall*, that, where it was alleged that there was a robbery at knife-point, to cross-examine the victim on the basis that he was lying about the knife was not an imputation.

A more difficult problem arises where specific allegations of fabrication of evidence are made. In *Jones* (1923) 17 Cr App R 117, Lord Hewart considered that it was one thing for the accused to deny that he had made a confession upon which the prosecution sought to rely, but quite another for him to allege that a police witness had engaged in an elaborate and deliberate concoction of the confession. See also *Clark* [1955] 2 QB 469. The difficulty with this limitation is that there is no difference in kind (though there may be one of degree) between challenging a witness's evidence on the ground that he is lying, and being specific about the respect in which it is alleged that his testimony is fabricated. Not surprisingly, attempts to apply the rule as stated in *Jones* and *Clark* have led to inconsistent decisions. In *Nelson* (1978) 68 Cr App R 12, the Court of Appeal quashed the conviction for arson of N, who had been cross-examined on his record following an allegation that a police witness had lied when he claimed that N had given him a detailed account of how he started the fire. The court held that the defence involved no imputation because there was no allegation against the prosecution witness independently of the challenge to the evidence he had given. The court distinguished cases where the defence launches an attack on the witness in respect of his conduct on other occasions, e.g., where it is said that a police witness has used threats in order to extricate a statement from the accused. A different view was taken in *Tanner* (1977) 66 Cr App R 56, in which T was held to have been rightly cross-examined on his record where he alleged that police officers had invented confession evidence. It was said to be relevant that T had denied, not merely a single answer or admission, but a 'series of important answers attributed to him by the police'. Similarly, in *McGee* (1979) 70 Cr App R 247, one of the co-accused was held to have lost his shield by asserting that various police witnesses had falsely invented admissions, and had suppressed exculpatory information alleged to have been imparted by him on the same occasion. Whereas it might be possible to reconcile these authorities by regarding an allegation of conspiracy between two or more officers to give false evidence as involving misconduct otherwise than in the witness-box, the distinction thus produced is unsatisfying, depending as it does on the number of persons alleged to have fabricated evidence against the accused.

It is submitted that the best solution, contrary to what was said in *Rouse* [1904] 1 KB 184, is to regard an imputation as having been made in cases where perjury is alleged, and to employ the discretion in order to alleviate the harsher consequences of such a rule. This appears to have been the interpretation favoured by Lord Guest in *Selvey* v *DPP* [1970] AC 304, at 351, and it is supported by the reasoning of Devlin J in *Cook* [1959] 2 QB 340, and by the decision of the Court of Appeal in *Britzman* [1983] 1 WLR 350. In that case, B and H were charged with burglary, and B's evidence involved a denial that certain incriminating conversations, testified to by police witnesses, had taken place. Lawton LJ said (at p. 353):

> A defence to a criminal charge which suggests that prosecution witnesses have deliberately made up false evidence in order to secure a conviction must involve imputations on the

characters of those witnesses with the consequence that the trial judge may, in the exercise of his discretion, allow prosecuting counsel to cross-examine the defendant about offences of which he has been convicted. In our judgment this is what Parliament intended should happen in most cases. When allegations of the fabrication of evidence are made against prosecution witnesses, as they often are these days, juries are entitled to know about the characters of those making them.

See also, to the same effect, *Powell* [1985] 1 WLR 1364 and *Owen* (1986) 83 Cr App R 100.

The Person Subject to the Imputations

The Criminal Evidence Act 1898, s. 1(f)(ii), is not generally infringed when the defence **F14.28** involves imputations upon an individual who is not the prosecutor, and who is not called as a witness for the prosecution. However, the rule that imputations could safely be made against the character of the person whose death the accused is alleged to have caused (see *Biggin* [1920] 1 KB 213) no longer applies.

In *Miller* [1997] 2 Cr App R 178 it was held that a person who did not give oral evidence, but whose statement was read by the prosecution at trial pursuant to the CJA 1988, s. 23 (see **F16.3**), was a 'witness' for the purposes of s. 1(f)(ii). This, though a desirable outcome, invests the word 'witness' with a very wide meaning, and it is submitted that the result would have been more elegantly procured by amendment of the 1898 Act.

Duty of Judge to Warn

In *Selvey* v *DPP* [1970] AC 304, Viscount Dilhorne suggested that the judge should give **F14.29** a warning when it became apparent that the defence was taking a course which might expose the accused to cross-examination on his record, although the failure to give such a warning was not necessarily to be regarded as grounds for an appeal. However, in *McGee* (1979) 70 Cr App R 247, Eveleigh LJ considered that it was not always the responsibility of the judge to alert counsel to the dangerous path he is pursuing. The reason given lacks some of its urgency today, for Eveleigh LJ was concerned that if a warning were to be obligatory, counsel could 'cross-examine as pointedly as may be until a warning was received from the judge', whereupon he could choose between desisting and calling his client at a later stage, or persisting and letting his client make a dock statement upon which he could not be cross-examined. Dock statements having been abolished since *McGee* was decided, counsel who 'pushes his luck' in the manner described would now be in a much less advantageous position. In *Stanton* [1994] Crim LR 834 the current position was stated to be that a warning is desirable 'in many if not most cases', though not obligatory.

The argument against giving a warning in all cases is that, where a defendant is represented, counsel should be able to judge for himself how far to go. The counter-argument is that judges may legitimately take different views, in the light of authorities discussed in this section, both as to the point at which the shield is lost in law and as to the extent of the protection which judicial discretion should afford to the defendant once his shield is down, so that a warning serves a useful purpose when discharging a function once described by the Court of Appeal as being 'like walking through a legal minefield' (*Britzman* [1983] 1 WLR 350, and see the remarks of Devlin J in *Cook* [1959] 2 QB 340, at p. 349).

Warnings are particularly important where an accused is unrepresented (*Cook* [1959] 2 QB 340, per Devlin J at p. 349). In summary trial of an unrepresented defendant, it has been held that a warning should be given by the clerk and the prosecutor together in the absence of the bench. It is the obligation of the prosecutor to ask for an adjournment so that this can be done (*Weston-Super-Mare Justices, ex parte Townsend* [1968] 3 All ER 225).

Purpose of Cross-Examination

F14.30 The purpose of cross-examining the accused under the Criminal Evidence Act 1898, s. 1(f)(ii), is to diminish the credit to be given to his testimony.

> If the accused is seeking to cast discredit on the prosecution, then the prosecution should be allowed to do likewise. If the accused is seeking to persuade the jury that the prosecutor behaved like a knave, then the jury should know the character of the man who makes these accusations, so that it may judge fairly between them instead of being in the dark as to one of them. (*Selvey v DPP* [1970] AC 304, per Lord Pearce at p. 353.)

As a consequence of this so-called 'tit for tat' argument, the jury must be told that they must not treat the information about the accused's record as having a direct bearing on his guilt see, e.g., *McLeod* [1994] 1 WLR 1500: considered further at **F14.32**). In *Watts* [1983] 3 All ER 101, Lord Lane CJ rightly observed that 'This in many cases requires the jury to perform difficult feats of intellectual acrobatics'. It follows that, when exercising the discretion to exclude evidence, the prejudicial effect of which outweighs its probative value, the risk of the jury being misled into thinking that the record is an indicator of guilt is a factor to be weighed in the 'prejudicial' side of the equation. As will be seen, however (at **F14.31** to **F14.36**), it is unlikely that evidence will be excluded on this basis alone. Instead, great faith is placed in the direction to the jury and in their ability to perform 'intellectual acrobatics', as Lord Lane CJ subsequently stated when revising much of what he had said in *Watts* in *Powell* [1985] 1 WLR 1364.

Does prosecuting counsel have a duty to take advantage of s. 1(f)(ii)? In *Chinn* (1996) 160 JP 765 the trial judge put pressure on counsel by suggesting that such a duty existed. The Court of Appeal did not censure this approach, commenting only that it was not wrong for the trial judge to 'initiate discussion' about invoking the provision if counsel failed to do so. While this may be so, there is a difference between initiating discussion and seeking to place counsel under a duty, and it is submitted that the true position is that ultimately counsel has a choice in the matter.

Discretion to Restrain Cross-Examination

F14.31 In *Selvey v DPP* [1970] AC 304, the House of Lords held, following a long line of authorities, that there is a discretion to restrain the prosecution from unfairly cross-examining an accused who has forfeited his shield by making imputations. What constitutes unfairness will vary according to the circumstances in the case, and the House of Lords considered it inadvisable to lay down detailed rules for the exercise of the discretion. As Lord Pearce put it (at p. 360): 'the question is whether *this* attack on the prosecution ought to let in *these* convictions on the particular facts of the case, and rules are no substitute for a discretion in producing a fair trial'.

What can be safely stated, it is submitted, is that there are certain factors to be taken into account in deciding whether to exercise the discretion. Taking irrelevant considerations into account may lead to a conviction being quashed on appeal (*Showers* [1996] Crim LR 739). In *Selvey v DPP* the House of Lords approved of the guidance given by the Court of Appeal in *Jenkins* (1945) 31 Cr App R 1, and in *Cook* [1959] 2 QB 340. The principles laid down in these cases and approved by the House were conveniently summarised by Ackner LJ in *Burke* (1985) 82 Cr App R 156, as follows (at p. 161):

> 1. The trial judge must weigh the prejudicial effect of the questions against the damage done by the attack on the prosecution's witnesses, and must generally exercise his discretion so as to secure a trial that is fair both to the prosecution and the defence (thus approving the observations of Devlin J, as he then was, when giving the judgment of the full court (five judges) of the Court of Criminal Appeal in *Cook* [1959] 2 QB 340 at p. 348).

> 2. Cases must occur in which it would be unjust to admit evidence of a character gravely prejudicial to the accused, even though there may be some tenuous grounds for holding it

technically admissible (thus approving the observation made by Lord du Parcq, giving the opinion of the Privy Council in *Noor Mohammed* v *The King* [1949] AC 182 at p. 192). Thus, although the position is established in law, still the putting of the questions as to character of the accused person may be fraught with results which immeasurably outweigh the result of questions put by the defence and which make a fair trial of the accused almost impossible (thus approving the observations of Singleton J in *Jenkins* (1945) 31 Cr App R 1 at p. 15).

3. In the ordinary and normal case the trial judge may feel that if the credit of the prosecutor or his witnesses has been attacked, it is only fair that the jury should have before them material on which they can form their judgment whether the accused person is any more worthy to be believed than those he has attacked. It is obviously unfair that the jury should be left in the dark about an accused person's character if the conduct of his defence has attacked the character of the prosecutor or the witnesses for the prosecution within the meaning of the section (thus approving the observations of Singleton J in *Jenkins* (*supra*) again at p. 15).

4. In order to see if the conviction should be quashed, it is not enough that the court think it would have exercised its discretion differently. The court will not interfere with the exercise of a discretion by a judge below unless he has erred in principle, or there is no material on which he could properly have arrived at his decision (per Lord Dilhorne [in *Selvey* v *DPP* [1970] AC 340 at p. 342], quoting Pickford J in *Watson* (1913) 8 Cr App R 249 at p. 254 and Devlin J in *Cook* (*supra*) at p. 147).

The following considerations, though relevant, do not compel the exercise of the discretion in the accused's favour.

Discretion: Similarity of Offences Where the offences which will be revealed to the F14.32 jury if the cross-examination takes place are of a similar nature to the offence charged, there is inevitably a risk that the jury will wrongly perceive the convictions as being relevant to guilt rather than to credit. In *Maxwell* v *DPP* [1935] AC 309, Viscount Sankey suggested (*obiter*) that the discretion should be exercised in favour of the accused in such a case, but in *Powell* [1985] 1 WLR 1364, the Court of Appeal held that there is no absolute rule to this effect. Reliance was placed on *Selvey* v *DPP* [1970] AC 304, in which the accused's convictions for homosexual offences were put to him after S had lost his shield by alleging that the man with whom he was alleged to have committed buggery was in effect a male prostitute who had invented the allegation out of spite because S declined his services. Had this been an incorrect exercise of the discretion, the House of Lords might have been expected to say so, but no adverse comment was made.

It is pertinent to consider the nature of the dispute which the jury will be asked to resolve by using the accused's record. In *Selvey* v *DPP* the vital issue was whether the accused or the prosecution witness was lying, and it was perhaps particularly important to balance S's discreditable background against what he had said about the complainant. Similar conclusions were reached in *Burke* (1985) 82 Cr App R 156, and in *Powell* [1985] 1 WLR 1364. In *Burke*, B, charged with drugs offences, alleged that all of the prosecution evidence had been fabricated by the police officers who had raided his premises. It was considered that, in the circumstances, the probative value of revealing to the jury that he was a convicted criminal outweighed the prejudice that necessarily resulted from the revelation that he had a record for drug-related offences. In *Powell*, P was charged with living on the earnings of prostitution, and he not only put his character in issue, but also launched a thoroughgoing attack upon the veracity of police witnesses, and it was held to be a proper exercise of the judge's discretion to permit P to be cross-examined about previous offences relating to prostitution. Indeed, Lord Lane CJ went further, and said that a defendant with previous convictions for similar offences may have a very great incentive to make false allegations against witnesses for fear of greater punishment on conviction.

Watts [1983] 3 All ER 101 constitutes, it is submitted, an example of a case where the prejudicial effect of the accused's previous similar convictions outweighed their probative value. W, a man of limited intelligence, was charged with indecent assault against an adult woman. He lost his shield by asserting that the confession which he was said by police witnesses to have made had been fabricated by them, and he was then cross-examined so as to reveal his record for serious sexual offences against young girls. The Court of Appeal held that the trial judge should have prevented the cross-examination, on the ground that similar offences ought not to be revealed to the jury, applying the dictum of Viscount Selvey in *Maxwell* v *DPP* [1935] AC 309. *Watts* can no longer be supported on this ground alone, following the subsequent decision of the Court of Appeal in *Powell* [1985] 1 WLR 1364, but it is submitted that the result was correct, as (a) the record was particularly likely to inflame the jury against W, and (b) the issue regarding the confession, and therefore of W's credibility in respect of his allegations, was not as central to the case against W as was the evidence in respect of which the shield was lost in *Selvey* v *DPP*, *Burke*, and *Powell*. (In *McLeod* [1994] 1 WLR 1500 it was considered that the likely reason for excluding cross-examination on the offences in *Watts* was the likelihood of prejudice arising from the detail of those offences.) The dictum in *Maxwell* v *DPP* appears to have formed the basis for the quashing of the conviction in *Lawrence* [1995] Crim LR 815 where, however, the previous offences seem to have been adduced because of their tendency to show a propensity to violence rather than for their relevance to credibility.

F14.33 ***Discretion: Offences Not Involving Dishonesty*** In *Watts* [1983] 3 All ER 101 the Court of Appeal gave as one reason for excluding the criminal record of W for sexual offences that the previous offences did not involve dishonesty. Insofar as this dictum implied that cross-examination should be limited to offences of dishonesty it cannot be supported, for it follows from the 'tit for tat' principle which underlies the right to cross-examine the accused whose defence involves imputations that the jury is entitled to know in general terms the character of the person making the imputation. It is significant that in *Powell* [1985] 1 WLR 1364 the Court of Appeal criticised *Watts* for 'paying too much attention . . . to the question whether the previous offences did or did not involve dishonesty'. *Powell* was approved on this point in *Owen* (1985) 83 Cr App R 100. In *Wheeler* [1995] Crim LR 312, it was held that there is no authority for a different approach to the exercise of discretion by reference to the character of the offences in play.

F14.34 ***Discretion: Defence Necessarily Involving Imputations*** Before the decision of the House of Lords in *Selvey* v *DPP* [1970] AC 304, it was thought that the discretion should be exercised in favour of the accused in any case where the very nature of the defence necessarily involved an imputation against a prosecution witness. Thus, in *Flynn* [1963] 1 QB 729, it was held that F ought not to have been cross-examined on his record simply because his defence to a charge of robbery was that the money had been willingly handed over by the victim to buy F's silence about indecent overtures which the victim had made to him. In *Selvey* v *DPP*, however, there was held to be no general rule to this effect, for the reason that such a rule would amount, under the guise of discretion, to a rewriting of the Act so as to permit necessary imputations to be made: a rewriting which the House had declared to be impermissible (see **F14.25**).

The fact that the imputation was necessary to the proper development of the defence is at best, according to Lord Pearce in *Selvey* v *DPP*, 'a consideration which will no doubt be taken into account' by the trial judge when exercising his discretion. In a number of recent cases it has become apparent that this consideration is easily outweighed by other factors. In *Tanner* (1977) 66 Cr App R 56, T lost his shield by denying that he had confessed to the crimes with which he was charged: a denial which called into question the veracity of police witnesses. It would be hard to imagine a more 'necessary' imputation, but the Court of Appeal held that it was impossible to say that the trial judge had exercised his discretion wrongly in permitting T to be cross-examined on his record. See also, e.g., *Burke* (1985) 82 Cr App R 156, and *Powell* [1985] 1 WLR 1364, considered at **F14.32**. In *Britzman* [1983] 1 WLR 350, the Court of Appeal gave the following guidelines (at p. 355) for the exercise of discretion where the conduct of the defence necessarily involves an allegation that prosecution witnesses have deliberately made up false evidence in order to secure a conviction:

> First, [the discretion] should be used if there is nothing more than a denial, however emphatic or offensively made, of an act or even a short series of acts amounting to one incident or in what was said to have been a short interview. Examples are provided by the kind of evidence given in pickpocket cases and where the defendant is alleged to have said: 'Who grassed on me this time?' The position would be different however if there were a denial of evidence of a long period of detailed observation extending over hours and just as in this case and in *Tanner* (1977) 66 Cr App R 56 where there were denials of long conversations.
>
> Secondly, cross-examination should only be allowed if the judge is sure that there is no possibility of mistake, misunderstanding or confusion and that the jury will inevitably have to decide whether the prosecution witnesses have fabricated evidence. Defendants sometimes make wild allegations when giving evidence. Allowance should be made for the strain of being in the witness-box and the exaggerated use of language which sometimes results from such strain or lack of education or mental instability. Particular care should be used when a defendant is led into making allegations during cross-examination. The defendant who, during cross-examination, is driven to explaining away the evidence by saying it has been made up or planted on him usually convicts himself without having his previous convictions brought out. Finally, there is no need for the prosecution to rely upon section 1(f)(ii) if the evidence against a defendant is overwhelming.

The suggestion in the guidelines that the shield is lost where the accused is driven into making imputations in cross-examination is controversial, and is discussed at **F14.23**. What is clear is that once the shield is down the accused will be lucky to attract the exercise of judicial discretion in his favour, where his defence involves a sustained attack on the veracity of a witness whose testimony is perceived as crucial to the prosecution case. This point has recently been emphasised in *Powell* [1985] 1 WLR 1364, in which the Court of Appeal approved a dictum of Devlin J in *Cook* [1959] 2 QB 340, who said (at pp. 347–8):

> The cases on this subject-matter . . . indicate the factors to be borne in mind and the sort of question that a judge should ask himself. Is a deliberate attack being made upon the conduct of the police officer calculated to discredit him wholly as a witness? If there is, a judge might well feel that he must withdraw the protection which he would desire to extend as far as possible to an accused who was endeavouring only to develop a line of defence. If there is a real issue about the conduct of an important witness which the jury will inevitably have to settle in order to arrive at their verdict, then . . . the jury is entitled to know the credit of the man on whose word the witness's character is being impugned.

Details of Previous Convictions

The extent to which the details of the accused's previous offences may be given in **F14.35** evidence under the Criminal Evidence Act 1898, s. 1(f)(ii), was considered in *McLeod* [1994] 1 WLR 1500. M, who was alleged to have taken part in an armed robbery, set up an alibi and claimed that the case against him had been fabricated by police officers. M had a long record for offences of dishonesty including robbery, and was questioned as to the details of what had occurred, and how he had pleaded. He was also asked about a previous unsuccessful defence of alibi, and whether he had given evidence in support of it which was disbelieved. No objection was taken at the time. The Court of Appeal held that the questions were permissible. The applicable principles may be summarised as follows:

(a) The primary purpose of the cross-examination as to previous convictions and bad character of the accused is to show that he is not worthy of belief, not to show disposition (see, e.g., *Vickers* [1972] Crim LR 101, *Khan* [1991] Crim LR 51 and *Barsoum* [1994] Crim LR 194). But the mere fact that offences are similar in type, or have a tendency to suggest a propensity to commit the offence charged, does not preclude their use (see, e.g., *Selvey* v *DPP* [1970] AC 304, *Powell* [1985] 1 WLR 1364 (see **F14.32**) and *Owen* (1985) 83 Cr App R 100 (see **F14.33**).

(b)   Prolonged or extensive cross-examination about previous offences is undesirable and diverts the jury's attention from the instant offence. Unless earlier offences are admissible under the similar fact rule (see **F12.3**), counsel should not probe or emphasise similarities between the underlying facts of earlier offences and the instant offence.

(c)   Similarities of defences rejected by juries on previous occasions, such as false alibis and accusations of 'planting', together with information about the plea and whether the accused was disbelieved having testified on oath, may be a legitimate matter for cross-examination since they are relevant to credibility.

(d)   Underlying facts showing particularly bad character over and above the bare facts of the case are not necessarily to be excluded. The judge has to balance the gravity of the attack on the prosecution witness with the prejudice the revelation will cause. Details of sexual offences on children, such as those in issue in *Watts* [1983] 3 All ER 101 (see **F14.30**) may be particularly prejudicial in the eyes of a jury.

(e)   If objection is to be taken to a line of questioning about underlying facts it should be taken as soon as defence counsel realises that it is danger of going too far. If taken subsequently it will not normally be a ground for discharging the jury. While it is the judge's duty to keep cross-examination within proper bounds, it will be difficult to contend that there has been an improper exercise of discretion if no objection is taken at the time.

(f)   In every case where cross-examination on character and previous offences has taken place, the judge must tell the jury that the purpose of the questioning goes only to credit, and they should not regard it as showing a propensity to commit the offence charged.

Cross-Examination by Co-Accused under Proviso (f)(ii)

F14.36   In *Lovett* [1973] 1 WLR 241, the Court of Appeal considered that there were cases where it might be appropriate for a co-accused to cross-examine the accused on his record on the strength of a breach by him of the Criminal Evidence Act 1898, s. 1(f)(ii). Such cross-examination could not be undertaken as of right, but was subject to the discretion of the court in the same way as cross-examination by the prosecution. *Lovett* has since been explained in *Rowson* [1986] QB 174 as turning on the form which proviso (f)(iii) took before the Criminal Evidence Act 1979, for it was at that time impossible for a co-accused to avail himself of proviso (f)(iii) unless charged with the same offence (see **F14.39**). There was thus no automatic right of redress for a co-accused such as Lovett, who was charged in the same proceedings with a different offence, unless (as happened) L's co-accused attacked, not only L, but also a witness for the prosecution. The inference from *Rowson* would seem to be that *Lovett* would be decided differently today.

PROVISO (f)(iii): ACCUSED GIVING EVIDENCE AGAINST A PERSON CHARGED IN THE SAME PROCEEDINGS

The Criminal Evidence Act 1898, s. 1(f)(iii), is satisfied where an accused 'has given evidence against any other person charged in the same proceedings'.

'Has Given Evidence'

F14.37   The Criminal Evidence Act 1898, s. 1(f)(iii), appears to apply only where the evidence of the accused himself is 'against' a co-accused, with the result that the calling by A1 of a witness who implicates A2 does not render A1 liable to cross-examination on his record. However, in *Bircham* [1972] Crim LR 430, it was suggested that where counsel for A1 cross-examines A2 with a view to showing A2's guilt of the offence charged, then A1 will, if he testifies, be liable to cross-examination on his record. It is submitted that this consequence only follows if A1 makes allegations against A2 on oath, for only then is there an issue as to the credit to be given to A1 as against A2, and it is on the issue of credit alone that the record is admissible under (f)(iii).

It does not matter whether the evidence A1 gives which is 'against' A2 emerges in chief or in cross-examination. (Contrast s. 1(f)(ii), at **F14.23**.) In *Murdoch v Taylor* [1965] AC 574, M and L were charged with handling stolen goods, and M was pressed, in the course of cross-examination by counsel for L, to assert that his defence was that he had nothing to do with the goods, which were in the exclusive possession of L. It was held that M was rightly cross-examined on his previous convictions. Lord Morris said (at p. 583): 'If an accused person becomes a witness his sworn testimony, if admissible, becomes a part of the evidence in the case. What he says in cross-examination is just as much a part of that evidence as what he says in examination-in-chief'. The same view was expressed by Lord Donovan (at p. 590), who noted that the effect on the co-accused in the minds of the jury was exactly the same whether the evidence was given in chief or under cross-examination.

Later in his speech (at p. 584) Lord Morris considered the difficult position of A1 who wishes only to give evidence exonerating himself, and who is cross-examined by A2 with a view to showing his (A1's) guilt. In such a case it might be easy for A1 to be cajoled into saying 'more than it was ever his plan or wish or intention to say', but Lord Morris considered that the judge should be alert to prevent this. In some cases, however, a forceful cross-examination may be necessary in order to bring out the true nature of the evidence given by A1. In *Davis* [1975] 1 WLR 345, D avoided making any express assertions that his co-accused, O, had committed the offence with which they were both charged until he was cross-examined by counsel for O who 'made him do so'. But the assertion was necessarily implicit in D's evidence in chief, for the circumstances were such that either D or O, or both of them, must have committed the offence.

'. . . Against Any Other Person'

' "Evidence against" means evidence which supports the prosecution case in a material **F14.38** respect or which undermines the defence of a co-accused'(*Murdoch v Taylor* [1965] AC 574, per Lord Donovan at p. 592). His lordship qualified the earlier definition proffered by the Court of Criminal Appeal in *Stannard* [1965] 2 QB 1, in which it was said that the question was whether the evidence 'tended to' support the prosecution case or undermine the defence. This was wrong insofar as it suggested that evidence given by A1 might be evidence against A2 simply because it differed from evidence given by A2.

Undermining a defence should, it is submitted, cost the accused his shield only where his evidence, if accepted, implicates his co-accused. It should not be enough that the credibility of the co-accused is damaged. In *Kirkpatrick* [1998] Crim LR 63, K's defence to indecent assault was that he had been intervening to prevent B and another committing the offence. B's defence was that he was asleep and took no part in the events. It was held that B had not given evidence against K: he gave no support to the prosecution case, neither did he, merely by providing an inconsistent account, undermine K's defence. It is submitted that the decision is correct, even though a jury which believed B's account could not at the same time believe K's. The loss of the shield for giving evidence against another is such a high price to pay that it should be demanded only if the words of the statute are clearly satisfied. A fortiori if the evidence of A1, if believed, would result in the acquittal of A2, even though it is fundamentally inconsistent with the defence put forward by A2. Thus, in *Bruce* [1975] 1 WLR 1252,

B, M and others were charged with robbery, and convicted of stealing cash from a foreigner. M's defence was that there had been a preconceived plan to rob, but he maintained that he was not a party to it, whereas B claimed that there had been no preconceived plan, and indeed that neither he nor M had received any money from the victim. It was held that the inconsistency between their defences did not entitle counsel for M to cross-examine B on his record, because acceptance of B's evidence would have led to the acquittal of M, not his conviction, and: 'The fact that [B's] evidence undermined [M's] defence by supplying him with another does not make it evidence given against him' (per Stephenson LJ, at p. 1259). In a situation where A1 provides an alternative explanation, however, it should be noted that the prosecution's case needs only to be supported 'in a material respect' for A1 to lose his shield. It may not take much to persuade a court that A1 has, on balance, not only undermined A2's credit but has implicated him in the offence. Thus, in *Hatton* (1976) 64 Cr App R 88, Hatton's evidence was found on balance to be against that of Hildon who, together with Hatton and Ripley, was charged with theft of scrap metal. Hatton claimed that all three accused acted in pursuance of a plan to take the scrap, but that their intention was not dishonest, because a relation of Hildon had assured them that he had permission to take it. Hildon, on the other hand, claimed that he had happened by the site while Hatton and Ripley were collecting the metal, and had been persuaded to help on the understanding that they had paid for it. Hatton's evidence was held to support 'a material part of the prosecution case' (i.e. a preconceived plan between the three to collect the scrap), and 'although it provided Hildon with another defence, it not merely undermined his credit but on balance did more to undermine his defence than to undermine the prosecution's case' (per Stephenson LJ, at p. 91).

Where evidence given by A1 wholly supports the prosecution case, it is unnecessary to consider whether it also undermines any defence advanced by A2 (*Adair* [1990] Crim LR 571).

It may happen that the only way an accused can assert his innocence is by placing the blame on a co-accused. In this unfortunate situation the shield against cross-examination is lost. In *Varley* [1982] 2 All ER 519, V and D were charged with robbery, and D's defence was that he took part in the robbery only because V was present and made threats against D's life. V gave evidence in which he completely denied that he had taken any part in the offence: evidence which clearly undermined D's account, because 'it amounted to saying that not only was [D] telling lies but that [D] would be left as a participant on his own and not acting under duress'. The Court of Appeal summarised the position in the following way (at p. 522):

> Mere denial of participation in a joint venture is not of itself sufficient to rank as evidence against the co-defendant. For the proviso to apply, such denial must lead to the conclusion that if the witness did not participate then it must have been the other who did. . . . Where the one defendant asserts or in due course would assert one view of the joint venture which is directly contradicted by the other such contradiction may be evidence against the co-defendant.

The same result was reached in *Davis* [1975] 1 WLR 345, in which D, under cross-examination, was driven to accuse O, his co-accused, of stealing a gold cross and chain which had disappeared from a house in circumstances such that either D or O must have taken it. Any denial by D in the circumstances necessarily involved undermining the chance of acquittal of O, and was thus evidence against him. A similar case is *Crawford* [1997] 1 WLR 1329. The prosecution contended that three women entered a public lavatory and robbed the victim. A's defence was that she had been present, along with C and the third woman, but had taken no part in the robbery. C's defence was that she had left the lavatory by the time the robbery occurred. C's account of events was held to be a 'direct contradiction' of A's so as to undermine A's defence and to permit A to cross-examine C on her previous convictions. In *Hendrick* [1992] Crim LR 427, by contrast, co-accused, F and H, were alleged to have been involved in a joint venture to steal a handbag. F's denial of participation did not lead to the loss of his shield against cross-examination as the innocence of F was not incompatible with the innocence of H.

Where evidence is 'against' a co-accused in the sense described above, it does not matter that the co-accused's defence is already a lost cause, for example because he has admitted his guilt in evidence in chief. In *Mir* [1989] Crim LR 894, a co-accused's (A's) defence to importing heroin was that he was an innocent dupe of M, whereas M began by alleging that the offence was committed by A alone. In the course of his evidence in chief, however, M admitted a degree of involvement in the offence which, if believed, was conclusive of his guilt, but refused to change his plea. It was held that M remained a co-accused of A, and that the evidence given by A in support of his defence was evidence against M within the meaning of the Criminal Evidence Act 1898, s. 1(f)(iii).

It is not necessary that the evidence of A1 be given with any hostile intent against A2, for 'it is the effect of the evidence upon the minds of the jury which matters, not the state of mind of the person who gives it' (*Murdoch* v *Taylor* [1965] AC 574, per Lord Donovan at p. 591). Applying this objective test, it is obvious that damaging evidence 'would be just as damaging whether given with regret or whether given with relish' (per Lord Morris, at p. 584).

If it is discovered after A1 has been cross-examined on his record that his evidence was not evidence 'against' A2, the judge should accede to A1's application for a retrial (*Tyrer* (1988) *The Times*, 13 October 1988, discussed by Munday [1990] Crim LR 92)). See also *Ellis* [1961] 1 WLR 1064.

'. . . Charged in the Same Proceedings'

As originally enacted, this condition of the Criminal Evidence Act 1898, s. 1(f)(iii), was **F14.39** satisfied only where the evidence was given against a person charged 'with the same offence'; a provision the meaning of which gave rise to so much difficulty that the wording was changed by the Criminal Evidence Act 1979, s. 1. (See *Hills* [1980] AC 26.) As amended by the 1979 Act, the proviso (f)(iii) requires only that both accused are before the court on the same occasion.

Purpose of Cross-Examination

The purpose of cross-examination under the Criminal Evidence Act 1898, s. 1(f)(iii), is **F14.40** to enable an accused person 'to discredit someone who has given evidence against him' (*Murdoch* v *Taylor* [1965] AC 574, per Lord Morris at p. 585). It follows that evidence designed *only* to show the guilt of the person who has given such evidence, and having no bearing on his credit as a witness, is irrelevant and therefore inadmissible under the section. It will, however, be rare for evidence tendered under s. 1(f)(iii) to have no relevance to the issue of credibility, and, provided it has some relevance, the judge has no discretion to exclude it on the ground that it is primarily relevant to the issue of guilt (see **F14.41**). In *Reid* [1989] Crim LR 719, R was alleged to have been one of four passengers who robbed a minicab-driver at knifepoint. His defence was that he got into the cab only after the robbery had occurred, and it was held that he could be cross-examined about a previous conviction for robbery of a taxi-driver in which he had raised the defence that he had left the car before the robbery took place. The revelation that R had unsuccessfully employed the same defence before was suggestive of guilt, but the cross-examination was said to be relevant also to the issue of credibility, in that it showed that the accused was prepared to lie so as to incriminate others. In such a case it will be incumbent upon the trial judge to make clear to the jury that the evidence adduced is not evidence of guilt.

No Discretion to Restrain Cross-Examination by Co-Accused

F14.41   In *Murdoch* v *Taylor* [1965] AC 574, it was argued that the trial judge has a discretion to restrain cross-examination by a co-accused against whom evidence is given. A majority of the House of Lords (Lord Pearce dissenting) held that no such discretion exists. Lord Donovan acknowledged the existence of a discretion where it is the prosecution who seek to cross-examine, for in such a case it is part of the judge's duty to secure a fair trial to prevent evidence being heard, the prejudicial effect of which outweighs its probative value. By contrast, however, the co-accused against whom evidence is given has a statutory right to defend himself and to support that assertion by evidence of bad character, which right cannot be fettered by discretion. The principle thus established in *Murdoch* v *Taylor* formed part of the guidance given to trial judges by the Court of Appeal in *Varley* [1982] 2 All ER 519 (considered at **F14.38**), and was held to be of general application in *Rowson* [1986] QB 174, where it was held that R had an unfettered right to cross-examine his co-accused, K, on a statement which K had made to the police, notwithstanding that the statement had been excluded as part of the prosecution case owing to breaches of the Judges' Rules. See also *Lui Mei Lin* v *The Queen* [1989] AC 288.

It does not follow from the principle stated above that there is no discretion to restrain the prosecution from cross-examining under s. 1(f)(iii) in the rare cases where such a course is appropriate (as to which see *Seigley* (1911) 6 Cr App R 106). On the contrary, in *Murdoch* v *Taylor* [1965] AC 574, Lord Donovan expressly recognised the existence of such a discretion. It would also appear that a co-accused seeking permission to cross-examine under s. 1(f)(ii), which he has no statutory right to do, may be restrained in the discretion of the court (*Lovett* [1973] 1 WLR 241, see **F14.36**). It is submitted that a discretion also exists to prevent a second co-accused (A3) cross-examining A1 as of right, on the ground that A1 has given evidence against A2. Section 1(f), though couched in terms wide enough to permit such cross-examination, is intended to aid the accused against whom the evidence is given to defend himself by undermining the credit to be given to that testimony; not as a general permission to attack the character of A1.

Procedure

F14.42   The absence of any judicial discretion to restrain cross-examination by a co-accused does not mean that the trial judge has no function to discharge. According to Lord Morris of Borth-y-Gest in *Murdoch* v *Taylor* [1965] AC 574, at pp. 584–6:

> In the first place it will be for him to rule as a matter of law whether a witness has or has not given evidence against any other person. . . . In the second place, it is always for a judge to rule in regard to the relevance of any evidence and therefore in regard to the propriety of any question which it is desired to ask.
> . . . The result, in my judgment, is that where it is claimed that an accused person has given evidence against another person [charged in the same proceedings] and it is desired to put questions of the kind denoted in section 1(f), intimation of this desire should (in such a way as may be appropriate) be given to the court and to counsel concerned. The temporary withdrawal of the jury might become desirable. It will then be for the judge to rule in regard to the matters to which I have referred.

This passage was applied in *McGregor* (1992) 95 Cr App R 240. Counsel, without informing the judge of his intentions, cross-examined M on the basis that proceedings against her in the USA had resulted in a conviction. This was based on a misunderstanding of M's plea in those proceedings, and it was held that, had counsel advised the judge that he intended to embark on such a cross-examination, it might have been possible to ascertain the true purport of M's plea and to have avoided the flawed cross-examination which followed.

SECTION F15: THE RULE AGAINST HEARSAY: GENERAL PRINCIPLES

Definition of Hearsay Evidence

In *Sharp* [1988] 1 WLR 7 Lord Havers adopted the statement in *Cross on Evidence* (6th **F15.1** ed.) that 'an assertion other than one made by a person while giving oral evidence in the proceedings is inadmissible as evidence of any fact asserted'. This formulation of the rule was also approved by Lord Ackner in *Kearley* [1992] 2 AC 228.

'An Assertion. . .'   Whereas most hearsay statements are made (whether orally or in **F15.2** writing) in words, hearsay may also occur in the form of conduct. In *Chandrasekera* v *The King* [1937] AC 220, a woman's throat had been cut, depriving her of the power of speech. She described C as her attacker using sign language, and nodded when asked whether C had caused her injuries. These communications were likened to the language of a deaf person able to converse only by means of a finger alphabet, and the 'conversation' was admitted under an exception to the hearsay rule.

A difficult question arises as to whether a statement is hearsay when tendered to prove the truth of a fact which the maker did not intend to assert. This question, which was the subject of the decision of the House of Lords in *Kearley* [1992] 2 AC 228, is dealt with separately at **F15.10**.

'. . . Other than One Made by a Person while Giving Oral Evidence in the **F15.3** *Proceedings'*   A statement made on oath in other proceedings is hearsay, and may only be received as evidence of its truth under an exception to the rule (*Berkeley Peerage Case* (1811) 4 Camp 401). Even statements made in committal proceedings may only be admitted at trial by way of exception to the hearsay rule. In *O'Loughlin* [1988] 3 All ER 431, for example, depositions made in committal proceedings by witnesses who were said to be too frightened to give evidence at trial were excluded, because the prosecution failed to prove that any relevant hearsay exception applied.

The out-of-court statements of witnesses who give evidence in the proceedings may be introduced as evidence of consistency or inconsistency without infringing the hearsay rule. (See as to the circumstances in which statements may be used for this purpose **F6.13** to **F6.18** and **F7.19**.) Such statements may not, however, be given in evidence to prove the truth of what was said, unless an exception to the hearsay rule applies. Thus a prompt complaint in a case of rape or indecent assault is generally admissible only to show the consistency of the complainant, and not to prove that what was said was true (*Lillyman* [1896] 2 QB 167, see **F6.14**). If, however, the complaint formed part of the *res gestae*, it would be evidence of its truth by way of exception to the hearsay rule (see *Sparks* v *The Queen* [1964] AC 964, in which this possibility was recognised but rejected on the facts, and *Shickle* (30 July 1997 unreported)). As to the *res gestae* exception, see **F16.31** to **F16.37**.

'. . . Inadmissible as Evidence of Any Fact Asserted'   Evidence is hearsay where **F15.4** the purpose of the party adducing it is to prove the truth of some fact asserted. Thus, where it is sought to establish the registration number of a car involved in an incident, and an eye-witness, A, who has seen the incident, relates the number to B, who has not, it is hearsay for B to tell the court what the number was for the purpose of proving the identity of the car (*McLean* (1967) 52 Cr App R 80; *Jones* v *Metcalfe* [1967] 1 WLR 1286). (Where B makes a note of the number which A verifies, A may give evidence of

the number by refreshing his memory from B's note: *Jones* v *Metcalfe*; *Kelsey* (1982) 74 Cr App R 213. As to refreshing memory, see **F6.6** to **F6.12**.)

Where goods are imported in bags marked 'Produce of Morocco', the marks are hearsay evidence of the country of origin of the goods (*Patel* v *Comptroller of Customs* [1966] AC 356). The same result follows even where the information is indelibly stamped into the goods (*Comptroller of Customs* v *Western Lectric Co. Ltd* [1966] AC 367). Similarly, information stamped on to a document is hearsay evidence of the matters stated, for example of a date: see *Cook* (1980) 71 Cr App R 205, in which is was assumed that such information was admissible only where there was an applicable exception to the hearsay rule. Compare, however, *Miller* v *Howe* [1969] 1 WLR 1510, in which a police officer was allowed to give evidence identifying a particular device although he had derived his knowledge from the label on the box.

A car's vehicle registration document provides only hearsay evidence of its engine number (*Sealby* [1965] 1 All ER 701), as do records compiled in the course of the manufacture of the car (*Myers* v *DPP* [1965] AC 1001). A person who relates his own date and place of birth necessarily gives hearsay evidence (*Inhabitants of Rishworth* (1842) 2 QB 476, see also *Day* (1841) 9 C & P 722). A party to a conversation which has been conducted through an interpreter infringes the hearsay rule if he seeks to prove what the other party said by relating to the court what the interpreter told him (*Attard* (1958) 43 Cr App R 90). Similarly, where a police officer testifies that a person receiving a commodity alleged to be heroin from the defendant is a 'known heroin user', he is giving hearsay evidence if the basis of his knowledge is information supplied to him by others, including the recipient in question (*Rothwell* (1994) 99 Cr App R 388).

Rationale of Hearsay Rule

F15.5   In *Sharp* [1988] 1 WLR 7, Lord Havers said (at p. 11) that the hearsay rule is 'so firmly entrenched that the reasons for its adoption are of little more than historical interest', but his lordship suspected that 'the principal reason that led the judges to adopt it many years ago was the fear that juries might give undue weight to evidence the truth of which could not be tested by cross-examination, and possibly also the risk of an account becoming distorted as it was passed from one person to another'. Similarly, in *Blastland* [1986] AC 41, Lord Bridge of Harwich said (at p. 54): 'The rationale of excluding [hearsay] as inadmissible, rooted as it is in the system of trial by jury, is a recognition of the great difficulty, even more acute for a juror than for a trained judicial mind, of assessing what, if any, weight can properly be given to a statement by a person whom the jury have not seen or heard and which has not been subject to any test of reliability by cross-examination'. An additional reason was given by Lord Normand in *Teper* v *The Queen* [1952] AC 480, who said (at p. 486) that '[Hearsay] is not the best evidence and it is not delivered on oath'.

The various reasons for the rule might be thought to lead to the conclusion that hearsay evidence which is the best evidence available, and which is of undoubted probative value, should not be excluded, but this is not the case. In *Myers* v *DPP* [1965] AC 1001, the prosecution sought to show that M had bought various cars in a wrecked condition, and had then stolen and disguised other cars in order to sell them as rebuilt wrecks. Records, compiled by the manufacturers from information supplied by the unidentifiable workmen who had made the cars, clearly showed that the vehicles sold by M were the stolen cars. The method of record-keeping strongly suggested that the records were accurate, but because the records consisted of no more than the out-of-court assertions of the workmen that certain identifying numbers had been given to the cars, the records were held to be hearsay when tendered to prove the truth of the facts asserted. Once classified as hearsay, the admissibility of evidence was held to depend, not on its cogency, but simply upon whether it fell within a recognised exception to the rule. No such exception being available to the prosecution, the records were inadmissible. (The records in *Myers* v *DPP* could now be received under the CJA 1988, s. 24, see **F16.7**.)

In *Pieterson* [1995] 1 WLR 293, the Court of Appeal held that the 'evidence' of a police tracker dog was not subject to the hearsay rule, although it was subject to safeguards to ensure the reliability of the individual dog. This, it is submitted, is the correct approach, as the desirability of receiving evidence on oath and subject to cross-examination, which underlies the hearsay rule, has no bearing on evidence of this type.

Hearsay Not Rendered Admissible When Tendered by Defence

In *Turner* (1975) 61 Cr App R 67 the Court of Appeal rejected an argument that an **F15.6** accused person should be entitled to rely on hearsay evidence to show that a third party who has not been called as a witness has admitted committing the offence charged. Milmo J added (at p. 88): 'The idea, which may be gaining prevalence in some quarters, that in a criminal trial the defence is entitled to adduce hearsay evidence to establish facts, which if proved would be relevant and would assist the defence, is wholly erroneous.' The existence of any exception in favour of third-party admissions was also denied, *obiter*, by the House of Lords in *Blastland* [1986] AC 41, although where a joint trial takes place it appears that the confession of one co-accused may, by way of exception to the rule, be relied upon by the other (*Myers* [1998] AC 124: see **F17.12**).

In *Sparks* v *The Queen* [1964] AC 964, a statement made by a child, who was too young to testify, in which she alleged that she had been attacked by a coloured boy, was held inadmissible on behalf of S, a white man. It was argued that it was 'unjust' to leave the jury with the impression that the child had given no clue as to the identity of her attacker, but it was held that the cause of justice was best served by adherence to settled rules, and that, just as the prosecution could not rely on inadmissible hearsay evidence to prove the guilt of S, so also S was unable to rely on such evidence to establish his innocence.

Statements Tendered for Purpose Other Than as Evidence of Facts Asserted

The hearsay rule is not infringed where a statement is tendered for some reason other **F15.7** than to establish the truth of what was said. In *Subramaniam* v *Public Prosecutor* [1956] 1 WLR 965, S was charged with the capital offence of possession of ammunition. His defence was that he acted under duress. At his trial, he sought to give evidence of threats made to him by certain terrorists who were not called to give evidence, and was prevented from doing so on the ground that such evidence was hearsay. The Privy Council held that this was not the case (at p. 970):

> Evidence of a statement made to a witness by a person who is not himself called as a witness may or may not be hearsay. It is hearsay and inadmissible where the object of the evidence is to establish the truth of what is contained in the statement. It is not hearsay and is admissible where it is proposed to establish by the evidence, not the truth of the statement, but the fact that it was made. The fact that the statement was made, quite apart from its truth, is frequently relevant in considering the mental state and conduct thereafter of the witness or of some other person in whose presence the statement was made.

On the facts of *Subramaniam* v *Public Prosecutor* itself, it was held that the purpose of proving that S had been subjected to threats was to establish, not that the threats were true, but rather that, if they had been believed by S, they might have induced in him an apprehension of instant death if he failed to conform to the terrorists' wishes. The evidence was thus original, non-hearsay evidence, which had been wrongly excluded at trial. See also *Blastland* [1986] AC 41, in which it was held that a statement made to a witness by a third party is not hearsay when put in evidence solely to prove the state of mind of the maker of the statement or the person to whom it was made. Such evidence was, it seems, considered to be first-hand hearsay admissible by way of exception to the rule in *Neill* v *North Antrim Magistrates' Court* [1992] 1 WLR 1221, considered further at **F16.6** and **F16.36**, but the preponderance of authority suggests that it is not hearsay in the first place. (See, for example, *Kearley* [1992] 2 AC 228, considered at **F15.10**.) The inconsistency in the authorities was considered in *Gilfoyle* [1996] 1 Cr App R 302. G was convicted of the murder of his wife, P. Notes written by P in which she expressed an intention to take her own life were admitted to support the defence of suicide. The Court of Appeal considered that evidence of further statements made by P showing that she was not in a suicidal frame of mind, and that she had written the notes in the belief that they were required to help G, a nurse, with a project at work was also admissible. It was said (at p. 321) that 'strictly speaking' such evidence fell outside the hearsay rule, but 'in any event, hearsay evidence to prove the declarant's "state of mind" is an exception to the rule which has been accepted by the common law for many years'. Whether hearsay or not, then, such evidence is clearly admissible.

Another illustration of this principle is *Willis* [1960] 1 WLR 55, in which evidence of a statement made to W by his employee, N, in which N denied stealing a drum of cable, was held admissible. The purpose of introducing the statement was to explain the subsequent conduct of W on the basis that W had formed a belief as to N's innocence as a consequence of what he had been told.

A recent illustration of significant practical importance is *Davis* [1998] Crim LR 659. D, on being interviewed in connection with theft, failed to reveal facts upon which he afterwards sought to rely in his defence. At trial he wished to give evidence of what his solicitor had said to him prior to the interview, but was prevented from doing so on the grounds that it would infringe the hearsay rule. The Court of Appeal pointed out, correctly, that this was not necessarily the case. It was material for the jury to consider D's reasons for failing to disclose the relevant facts in deciding whether to draw an inference against him under the CJPOA 1994, s. 34 (see **F19.4**). If D's purpose in repeating the solicitor's words was simply to show the impact on him of the advice given, the hearsay rule would not have been infringed. It would have been otherwise if D had sought to demonstrate the truth of anything said.

In the above cases the statements relied upon were relevant as tending to establish facts in issue. Original evidence may also be relied upon where the making of the statement is itself a fact in issue. Thus, in *Chapman* [1969] 2 QB 436, the Road Safety Act 1967, s. 2(2), provided that C could not be required to take a breath test while at a hospital unless the medical practitioner in charge of his case had been notified and did not object to the provision of a specimen. It was held that the officer who notified the medical practitioner was entitled to give evidence of the fact that no objection was made, and that it was unnecessary for the doctor to give evidence in person. Similarly, in *Woodhouse* v *Hall* (1980) 72 Cr App R 39, the question to be decided was whether a massage parlour was being run as a brothel. Having defined a brothel as 'an establishment at which two or more women were offering sexual services', the Divisional Court held that it was open to police officers who had attended the premises posing as customers to prove that the women employed there had offered them various sexual services. There was no question of hearsay: the relevant issue was simply whether the offers had been made.

Further illustrations of the use of statements as original evidence are an admission of bankruptcy tendered to prove, not the truth of the assertion (which was proved by other means), but the maker's knowledge of his insolvency (*Thomas* v *Connell* (1838) 4 M & W 267); an allegation of forgery made against A tendered to show why A had been arrested (*Perkins* v *Vaughan* (1842) 4 Man & G 988); a cry of 'murder' by the alleged victim of a rape, tendered to prove lack of consent, and a subsequent request by her for money, tendered to prove the contrary (*Guttridges* (1840) 9 C & P 471). A statement which is demonstrably false may show a consciousness of guilt (*Mawaz Khan* v *The Queen* [1967] 1 AC 454; *A-G* v *Good* (1825) M'Cle & Yo 286; *Binham* [1991] Crim LR

774), but see *Malcherek* [1981] 1 WLR 690, in which the telling of lies was thought (*obiter*) to be hearsay evidence of guilt. Where negligence by omission is alleged, a promise made by a third party to take action on behalf of D may show why D took no action (*The Douglas* (1882) 7 PD 151). Where D denied knowledge that certain premises were being used as a brothel, an advertisement which he had sought to place, referring to the premises and containing a reference to 'many stunning masseuses', was admissible to show that he did know (*Roberts* v *DPP* [1994] Crim LR 926).

Upon application of the test described above, it is perfectly possible that evidence may be admissible, original evidence for one purpose, and inadmissible hearsay for another. Such cases require a very careful judicial direction as to the use to which the evidence may properly be put. Where it happens that the evidence is admissible in relation to one count in an indictment but not another, the inadmissibility is relevant to whether the counts should be tried together (*Watson* [1997] Crim LR 680).

Inferences Founded on Statements

Where evidence is inadmissible as hearsay, it is not possible to evade the difficulty by **F15.8** adducing evidence from which it can be inferred that the inadmissible statement was made and that it was true. In *Glinski* v *McIver* [1962] AC 726, Lord Devlin described the 'customary devices' employed where the hearsay rule is sought to be evaded in this way (at pp. 780–1):

> The first consists in not asking what was said in a conversation or written in a document but in asking what the conversation or document was about; it is apparently thought that what would be objectionable if fully exposed is permissible if decently veiled. . . . The other device is to ask by means of 'Yes' or 'No' questions what was done. (Just answer 'Yes' or 'No': Did you go to see counsel? Do not tell us what he said but as a result of it did you do something? What did you do?) This device is commonly defended on the ground that counsel is asking only about what was done and not about what was said. But in truth what was done is relevant only because from it there can be inferred something about what was said. Such evidence seems to me to be clearly objectionable. If there is nothing in it, it is irrelevant; if there is something in it, what there is in it is inadmissible.

See also *Saunders* [1899] 1 QB 490.

It is submitted that the same criticism can be made of an attempt to draw a circumstantial inference from a hearsay statement in a document. This occurred in *Rice* [1963] 1 QB 857, where the prosecution relied on an airline ticket in the names of 'Rice and Moore', produced by an airline official whose job it was to deal with used tickets, to give rise to a circumstantial inference that R had travelled on the flight in question. Although the Court of Appeal was agreed that the ticket 'must not be treated as speaking its contents for what it might say could only be hearsay', it was held (at p. 872) that 'the production of the ticket from the place where used tickets would properly be kept was a fact from which the jury might infer that probably two people had flown on the particular flight and that it might or might not seem to them by applying their common knowledge of such matters that the passengers bore the surnames which were written on the ticket'. It is submitted, however, that the production of the ticket proved that the traveller was R only if reliance were placed on its 'contents', i.e. on the statement it bore which showed that it had been issued to one Rice.

Rice has never been overruled, but it has been seriously discredited. In *Myers* v *DPP* [1965] AC 1001, the Court of Appeal relied on its own previous decision in *Rice* to infer, from the efficient manner in which records were compiled by the manufacturers of motor vehicles, that what was stated in the records was inherently likely to be true. In the House of Lords, however, it was held that the records were hearsay if tendered to prove the truth of the matters recorded in them. Of the argument advanced by the Court of Appeal, Lord Reid agreed that it was undeniable as a matter of common sense, but held that it could not be reconciled with the existing law. Lord Morris also disagreed with the reasoning. He said (at p. 1027): 'The circumstances referred to show that evidence of the nature now being considered might with advantage be admitted because there would be every expectation that figures would be correctly recorded. This, however, does not change the character of the evidence. It remains hearsay evidence . . .'

In *Lydon* (1986) 85 Cr App R 221, the Court of Appeal said that there was 'some justification' for the view, expressed by Cox J in *Romeo* (1982) 30 SASR 243, that the airline ticket in *Rice* [1963] 1 QB 857 was being put forward as proof of the truth of the statement implicit in it, and that the decision was therefore contrary to the principle established in *Myers* v *DPP*. A distinction should, however, be drawn between the permissible use of a statement as an original and independent fact, and the impermissible use of it as evidence of the facts stated. In *Lydon*, the prosecution were permitted to tender in evidence a piece of paper found near a weapon believed to have been used in a robbery, and bearing ink of a similar kind to that staining the weapon. On the paper, someone had written 'Sean rules' and 'Sean rules 85'. It was held that the words on the paper created an inferential link with L, whose first name was Sean. *Rice* [1963] 1 QB 857 was distinguished, because 'The reference to Sean could be regarded as no more than a statement of fact involving no assertion as to the truth of the contents of the document' (per Woolf LJ, at p. 224). *Lydon* was applied in *McIntosh* [1992] Crim LR 651, in which a piece of paper bearing calculations as to the profit and loss made from buying and selling a substance (inferentially a drug) was found on M's premises. The document was not in M's handwriting, but this was immaterial as it was admitted not as evidence of its truth but as purely circumstantial evidence suggesting M's involvement with drug-related offences.

Statements Inextricably Linked to Relevant Acts

F15.9 Where an issue arises as to the doing of a composite act made up of physical actions and words, the admissibility of the words may be regarded in a different light from the same words standing alone. In *Ratten* v *The Queen* [1972] AC 378, R was charged with the murder of his wife, and the defence was that she had been shot by accident as R cleaned his gun. The prosecution relied on the evidence of a telephone operator to show that, shortly before she was shot, the victim had telephoned the exchange in a state of hysteria and asked for the police. R denied that any such call had been made. The Privy Council held that, because the making of the call was itself a relevant act, the words used and the state of emotion in which they were spoken were 'relevant and necessary evidence in order to explain and complete the fact of the call being made', and were not hearsay. See also *Blastland* [1986] AC 41, in which it was said (at p. 59) that *Ratten* was authority for the proposition that the admissibility of the telephone call in that case had to be considered as a whole. In *Kearley* [1992] AC 228, however, the majority of the House of Lords appears to have considered that the request for the police, insofar as it implied an assertion that the maker of the request was being attacked, was hearsay and capable of being received only under the exception governing the admission of spontaneous statements (see **F16.31**). For further detail as to implied assertions, see **F15.10**.

According to the civil case of *Howe* v *Malkin* (1878) 40 LT 196, a statement may be admitted in evidence where it accompanies a relevant act done by the speaker, and it is so mixed up with the act to which it relates as to be part of the *res gestae*. *Howe* v *Malkin* was applied by the Court of Appeal in *McCay* [1990] 1 WLR 645 to the statement of a witness who said, while picking out M from an identification parade, 'It's number 8'. The witness was subsequently unable to remember, when giving evidence at trial, the number of the man he had identified, and a police officer who had been present when the identification had been made was permitted to tell the court what the witness had said. See also *Osbourne* [1973] 1 QB 678, in which a police officer was allowed to prove identifications made in the course of identification parades by witnesses who, in varying degrees, failed to come up to proof, but the hearsay point was not taken.

Implied Statements as Hearsay

In cases where the maker of a statement seeks to use it to convey information, the **F15.10** statement is hearsay evidence of the information intended to be conveyed, whether the communication is express or implicit. Thus, in *Teper* v *The Queen* [1952] AC 480, T was charged with setting fire to his own business premises with intent to defraud his insurers. It was held to be inadmissible hearsay for a police officer who was on duty near the fire to testify that he heard an unknown woman shout 'Your place burning and you going away from the fire', as a man resembling T drove past. Similarly, in *Gibson* (1887) 18 QBD 537 it was held to be inadmissible evidence of identification of G to prove that an unidentified person gestured at G's house and shouted, 'The man who threw the stone went in there'.

It is a more difficult question whether the hearsay rule applies to statements, not intended to be assertive, from which the belief of the maker of the statement as to the truth of the fact to be established can be deduced. In *Wright* v *Doe d. Tatham* (1837) 7 A & E 313, the Court of Exchequer Chamber decided that letters written to a deceased testator, being such as one would write to a sane person, were inadmissible as evidence of the testator's sanity. Parke B said (at p. 384): 'For this purpose they are mere hearsay evidence, statements of the writers, not on oath, of the truth of the matter in question'. Parke B considered that the hearsay rule would also have been infringed by evidence of conduct tendered to prove the truth of some belief exhibited by the conduct, as where the family of a person takes the same precautions in respect of him as if he were a lunatic.

Wright v *Doe d. Tatham* was approved by the House of Lords in *Kearley* [1992] 2 AC 228. K was charged with possession of a controlled drug with intent to supply. The amount found in K's possession being of itself inadequate to warrant an inference of such an intent, the prosecution relied upon evidence that, after K's arrest, a number of telephone calls had been made to his home in which the callers asked for K by his nickname and sought to buy drugs, and that a number of individuals had visited the house and asked to be supplied with drugs. None of these persons was called to give evidence at the trial. The House of Lords by a majority held that the hearsay rule precluded the use of the callers' requests as implied assertions by them that K was a supplier of drugs. Lord Bridge stated (at p. 665) that the English authorities were both 'clear and unequivocal' in holding that the hearsay rule applies equally to express and to implied assertions. Lord Ackner (whose preferred view was that the evidence was simply irrelevant in that it proved no more than the state of mind of the callers, which was not in issue) considered that just as a request for drugs containing an express statement that K was a supplier would clearly have been objectionable as hearsay, so a request containing an implied assertion to the same effect would break the hearsay rule. His lordship said (at p. 676):

> If . . . the simple request or requests for drugs to be supplied by the appellant, as recounted by the police, contains in substance, but only by implication, the same assertion, then I can find neither authority nor principle to suggest that the hearsay rule should not be equally applicable and exclude such evidence. What is sought to be done is to use the oral assertion, even though it may be an implied assertion, as evidence of the truth of the proposition asserted. That the proposition is asserted by way of necessary implication rather than expressly cannot, to my mind, make any difference.

Lord Oliver (at p. 686) considered that the 'general soundness of the views expressed by the Court of Exchequer Chamber in *Wright* v *Doe d. Tatham* . . . has not . . . been challenged in or affected by subsequent authority during the past 150 years'. It follows that where a statement or conduct is only of value insofar as it contains an implied assertion of relevant facts, it is hearsay and inadmissible unless an exception to the rule can be found. If the statement or conduct is relevant for some other purpose, however, there is no objection to it being received for that purpose. Thus, for example, in *Kearley* the House of Lords confirmed that evidence of the making of a statement may be used as evidence of the state of mind of the maker where that state of mind is in issue or relevant to an issue in the proceedings (as to which see **F15.7**). The state of mind of the callers was, however, of no relevance on the facts of that case. A further non-hearsay purpose for adducing the evidence in *Kearley* was thought by the dissenting minority (Lords Griffiths and Browne-Wilkinson) to exist in that the conduct of the callers pointed towards the existence of a 'market' for the supply of drugs, but this argument was thought by the majority to be unsound on the basis that the conduct itself was not relevant except as an implied assertion as to the caller's beliefs, which were hearsay.

Admissions Based on Hearsay

F15.11 Where a person admits something, his own knowledge of which is based on hearsay, the admission does not prove the fact. In *Comptroller of Customs* v *Western Lectric Co. Ltd* [1966] AC 367, it was held that admissions as to the country of origin of goods, which were based on markings on the goods themselves, were inadmissible. Lord Hodson further described such admissions as being of no real value. See also *Surujpaul* v *The Queen* [1958] 1 WLR 1050.

The same problem frequently arises in handling cases, where there is a dearth of direct evidence to prove that the goods are stolen. In *Hulbert* (1979) 69 Cr App R 243, H admitted that she bought certain goods at very low prices from unnamed sellers in various public houses, and that, in some cases, the sellers told her that the goods were stolen. It was held that H's admission as to facts within her own knowledge (e.g., the price paid, and the circumstances in which the goods were offered for sale) was admissible evidence that the goods might have been stolen, but that her admission as to what she had been told could not be evidence that the goods were stolen. What she had been told would, however, be admissible to prove the state of her knowledge or belief at the time. See also *Sbarra* (1918) 87 LJ KB 1003; *Korniak* (1982) 76 Cr App R 145; *Overington* [1978] Crim LR 692; and see **F15.7**.

In cases involving the possession of drugs, the accused's admission that the substance in question was a controlled drug would be inadmissible if based on hearsay, and of limited evidential value if based on his own opinion. In some cases the admissions of experienced drug users have been held to be prima facie evidence of the nature of a substance (see *Chatwood* [1980] 1 WLR 874; *Bird* v *Adams* [1972] Crim LR 174; *Wells* [1976] Crim LR 518). *Mieras* v *Rees* [1975] Crim LR 224, which appears to be authority to the contrary, is misreported. The charge was one of attempt, where it was accepted that there was no proof as to the nature of the substance (*Chatwood* [1980] 1 WLR 874).

Statements Tendered to Prove Non-existence of Alleged Facts

F15.12 A statement which is hearsay when tendered to prove the truth of a fact asserted in it, is equally hearsay when tendered as circumstantial evidence of the non-existence of facts which might have been expected to have been asserted in it if they had been true. Thus, Home Office records listing the names of legal immigrants are hearsay if tendered to prove that X, who is named in the record, is a legal immigrant, and are likewise hearsay if tendered to show that Y, whose name does not appear, is therefore an illegal immigrant. This was accepted in *Patel* [1981] 3 All ER 94.

It follows that a statement introduced to prove a negative ought only to be admissible if it satisfies an exception to the hearsay rule. However, in *Patel* it was suggested, *obiter*, that this is not the case. The Home Office record relied upon in that case to prove that one Ashraf was an illegal immigrant would not, at the time, have been admissible by way of exception to the hearsay rule (see now the CJA 1988, s. 24, at **F16.10**). Yet the Court of Appeal stated that a negative inference could have been drawn from the records if 'an officer responsible for their compilation and custody [had] been called to give evidence that the method of compilation and custody is such that, if Ashraf's name is not there, he must be an illegal entrant'.

Patel [1981] 3 All ER 94 was followed in *Shone* (1982) 76 Cr App R 72. The records in question in *Shone* were the stock records of a company which was alleged to have been the victim of theft. They showed that the goods in question had been received into stock and had not been sold; the inference being that they had been stolen. Two witnesses were called to give an account of the manner in which goods were checked in and out of stock, in order to support the inference. The Court of Appeal took the view that the record was not itself admissible by way of exception to the hearsay rule, because the Criminal Evidence Act 1965, which was relied upon by the prosecution, postulated a 'person' who 'supplied' the information: a state of affairs which cannot by definition be established in relation to non-existent or negative information. (The 1965 Act has been repealed, but the CJA 1988, s. 24, imposes a similar condition of admissibility.) It was, however, possible, following *Patel*, for the two witnesses, each of whom had personal knowledge of the way in which the relevant records were kept, to give evidence from which the inference could be drawn that the goods had been stolen. Such evidence was not to be regarded as hearsay, but as direct evidence from which such an inference could be drawn. It is submitted that two criticisms are to be made of *Shone*.

(a) Where a record is admissible only where information contained in it is supplied by a person with personal knowledge of it, it does not follow that the record, once admitted, cannot form the basis for a negative, as well as a positive, inference. The records in *Patel* and in *Shone* would now be admissible under the CJA 1988, s. 24, and that it would be open to the court to use them as evidence from which the non-existence of non-recorded facts could be drawn.

(b) If a record *is* inadmissible hearsay, it should not be possible to call witnesses to give evidence that, from the manner in which the records were maintained, a negative inference can properly be drawn: unless, of course, the record is that of the witness himself who is using it to refresh his memory. To hold otherwise is inconsistent with *Myers* v *DPP* [1965] AC 1001.

When dealing with such 'negative hearsay', considerable inconvenience may be encountered if the rule is applied in all strictness, and some relaxation may occur. This, it is submitted, is the best explanation of *Muir* (1983) 79 Cr App R 153. M was charged with theft of a video recorder, hired to him by G Ltd. M's defence was that the video had been taken away by two men who had called at his house. To rebut the suggestion that G Ltd had repossessed the video, S, the district manager of G Ltd, gave evidence that there had been no repossession by the local showroom: a fact within his own knowledge. He was asked in cross-examination about the possibility of repossession by the company's head office, and was allowed to say in response that he had telephoned head office and had been told that they had not ordered the repossession of the video. The Court of Appeal held that, '[I]n the way in which the evidence came out', it was not hearsay, on the ground that S 'was the best person to give the relevant evidence', including informing the court that a check had been made with head office. This analysis ignores the fact that what S had been told during the check was hearsay. On the facts of the case, the only option open to the prosecution if the rule had been strictly applied would have been to call a further witness from head office, and it may have been that expediency dictated the result. However, the decision is hardly satisfactory and was noted to have attracted adverse comment in *Coventry Justices, ex parte Bullard* (1992) 95 Cr App R 175.

Mechanically Produced Evidence as Hearsay

F15.13   The production in evidence of mechanically produced evidence, such as photographs, tapes and the like, does not constitute an infringement of the hearsay rule. Thus, juries may be allowed to see still photographs taken by a security camera during an armed robbery (*Dodson* [1984] 1 WLR 971), or a video recording of an incident (*Fowden* [1982] Crim LR 588; *Grimer* [1982] Crim LR 674), and they may hear a tape recording of a relevant conversation (*Maqsud Ali* [1966] 1 QB 688). Futhermore, just as a video recording of the commission of an offence is admissible, so also a witness who has seen the recording may give evidence of what he saw, as he is in effect in the same position as a witness with a 'direct view of the action' (*Taylor* v *Chief Constable of Cheshire* [1986] 1 WLR 1479). See also as to computer-produced evidence, **F15.14** and **F8.31** *et seq*.

In *Cook* [1987] QB 417, the Court of Appeal considered that sketches and photofit likenesses made under the direction of identifying witnesses were analogous to photographs, in that they were not subject to the hearsay rule. The court distinguished between the production of a sketch or photofit, which is not hearsay, and the recital by a witness of the distinguishing features of the person to be identified, which is. There is, however, a difficulty with the analogy preferred by the court, in that photofit likenesses, despite the resemblance of the finished product to a photograph, are compiled at the instigation of a human mind, and are subject to the same dangers as other out-of-court statements. Photographs, on the other hand, are mechanically produced likenesses which are not in any sense the assertions of a person. It should be noted that the ruling in *Cook* was made on the basis that evidence of the kind dealt with was *sui generis*. It should not, it is submitted, be extended to cover other types of hearsay evidence. *Cook* was applied in *Constantinou* (1989) 91 Cr App R 74.

Computer Evidence and the Hearsay Rule

F15.14   Computer evidence may or may not be hearsay. To the extent to which a computer is used merely to perform functions of calculation, no question of hearsay is involved in receiving evidence of what the computer 'said' (*Minors* [1989] 1 WLR 441, per Steyn J at p. 446). The reason, it is submitted, is that the court, when acting on such information, is not being asked to accept the truth of an assertion made by any person. Thus, in *Wood* (1982) 76 Cr App R 23, the prosecution alleged that metal found at W's premises was stolen. Chemists performed tests on samples of the metal, and used a computer as a tool to perform complicated calculations based on the data they had obtained. At trial, the chemists gave evidence of the outcome of the tests, and produced the computer printout to prove the results of the calculations. It was held that the printout was admissible for this purpose and did not constitute hearsay evidence, being instead real evidence analogous to the reaction of litmus paper as evidence of the acidity of a solution. See also *Golizadeh* [1995] Crim LR 232. In the same way, the printout of an Intoximeter which has performed an analysis of specimens of breath is admissible non-hearsay evidence (*Castle* v *Cross* [1984] 1 WLR 1372, where the rule regarding admissibility of computer evidence was said to be the same in this respect as in respect of less sophisticated machines; *Castle* v *Cross* was affirmed by the House of Lords in *DPP* v *McKeown* [1997] 1 WLR 295). See *The Statue of Liberty* [1968] 1 WLR 739 (automatic record made by radar set at a shore radio station admissible), and see also the rule as it applies to photographs etc. at **F15.13**.

An authority which cannot be reconciled with the view stated above is *Pettigrew* (1980) 71 Cr App R 39, in which an issue was raised as to the admissibility of a printout under an exception to the hearsay rule and it was assumed that the printout was hearsay. As the machine was programmed simply to sort bank notes and to record the serial numbers of the notes sorted, it is submitted that no question of hearsay was involved and that *Pettigrew* was decided *per incuriam*. In *Wood*, it was said that *Pettigrew* 'did not assist' on the question whether the printout was hearsay at common law.

Where a computer is used to record information which is supplied by a person, the hearsay rule will come into play if it is sought to use a printout from the computer to prove that what the person said was true. Thus, documentary records stored on computer are hearsay (*Minors*), and see *Coventry Justices, ex parte Bullard* (1992) 95 Cr App R 175, in which it was held that the crucial distinction was between 'computer printouts containing information implanted by a human, and printouts containing records produced without human intervention'. Similarly, in *Wood*, it was necessary for the chemists who tested the metal to give evidence of the facts on which the tests were based: the computer printout could not have been used to prove that the information fed into the computer was accurate, only that the calculations performed by the computer itself were correct.

A more difficult problem of classification arose in *Governor of Brixton Prison, ex parte Levin* [1997] AC 741. L was alleged to have initiated unauthorised payment instructions from his computer terminal in Russia, as a result of which the computerised fund transfer service of an American bank was induced to transfer funds from clients' accounts into accounts controlled by L. The transaction occurred automatically upon receipt of the instruction by L, and was duly copied to the American computer's historical records. L objected to the production of printouts showing the transactions on the grounds that they were hearsay, but the House of Lords held that they were not. Lord Woolf said:

> The printouts are tendered to prove the transfers of funds which they record. They do not assert that such transfers took place. They record the transfers themselves, created by the interaction between whoever purported to request the transfers and the computer program in Parsipanny [New Jersey]. The evidential status of the printouts is no different from that of a photocopy of a forged cheque.

In other words the printout proved the thing done because it *was* the thing done, or at least a copy of the thing done (commentary by Professor Sir John Smith on *Ewing* [1983] Crim LR 472 at p. 473).

Where a computer-produced document is tendered in evidence to prove any fact stated in it, the provisions of the PACE 1984 s. 69 (see **F8.31**), must be complied with, although that provision is prospectively repealed by the YJCEA 1999, s. 60.

SECTION F16: EXCEPTIONS TO THE RULE AGAINST HEARSAY (EXCLUDING CONFESSIONS)

Hearsay Exceptions and the Role of the Courts

F16.1 In *Myers* v *DPP* [1965] AC 1001, Lord Reid noted (at p. 1020) that the hearsay rule has never been absolute. Various common-law and statutory exceptions exist in criminal cases, and these are dealt with in the following sections. In *Myers* v *DPP*, a majority of the House of Lords declined to extend the common-law exception for public records so as to allow reliable private records to be proved. Lord Hodson (at p. 1034) said that this would be 'judicial legislation with a vengeance in an attempt to introduce reform of the law of evidence which if needed can properly be dealt with only by the legislature'. Lord Reid, whilst agreeing that the common law 'must be developed to meet changing economic conditions and habits of thought', nevertheless concluded (at p. 1021): 'If we are to extend the law it must be by the development and application of fundamental principles. We cannot introduce arbitrary conditions or limitations; that must be left to legislation. And if we do in effect change the law, we ought in my opinion only to do that in cases where our decision will produce some finality or certainty'. In *Blastland* [1986] AC 41, Lord Bridge regarded *Myers* v *DPP* as establishing 'the principle, never since challenged, that it is for the legislature, not the judiciary, to create new exceptions to the hearsay rule'.

This section deals with the more important of the various exceptions to the hearsay rule which operate in criminal cases, with the exception of confessions, which are dealt with at **F17**.

Of the exceptions dealt with in this section, some exist by virtue of the common law, while others have been created from time to time by statute. As no attempt has been made to codify the law in this area, it frequently happens that the exceptions overlap to a perplexing extent, and that safeguards applicable to one exception are absent from related exceptions dealing with similar subject-matter. Thus, for example, a record made by a person, since deceased, acting under a duty imposed by his employment, might be admissible at common law, but only if, *inter alia*, the statement relates to an act done by the person concerned, and is made more or less contemporaneously with the act to which it relates. Yet under the more general provisions of the CJA 1988, s. 24, a document created or received in the course of a trade, business etc. may be admitted, notwithstanding that there is no specific duty to make it, and irrespective of whether it is made by a person with personal knowledge of the matters dealt with and of whether it was made contemporaneously with the facts recorded in it. The result is that the conditions of admissibility imposed by the common-law rule can in practice be circumvented by using the Act instead. Many other cases exist where it will be necessary for the advocate to be aware that there is more than one possible avenue for the admission of evidence by way of exception to the hearsay rule, and frequent cross-references are provided in an effort to facilitate this.

CRIMINAL JUSTICE ACT 1988

Scope and Effect of Act

F16.2 The provisions of part II of the CJA 1988 contain two wide exceptions to the hearsay rule as it affects documentary evidence. Section 23 allows any 'first-hand' hearsay statement in a document to be admitted, provided that the maker is unavailable to give evidence for one of the reasons stated in the section. Section 24 allows a statement in any 'business etc. document' to be admitted, whether first-hand or otherwise. There is no requirement concerning the unavailability of the maker, unless the document is one prepared for criminal proceedings or a criminal investigation, in which case the maker must be unavailable for one of the reasons stated. As may be seen, these exceptions overlap, and it may be necessary to consider whether an advantage is to be gained from invoking one rather than the other.

Part II of the 1988 Act replaced the PACE 1984, s. 68, under which documentary records compiled under a duty were admissible. All other statutory and common-law exceptions to the hearsay rule are unaffected (see s. 28(1)(a) of the 1988 Act). Thus, it remains possible, for example, to prove a written dying declaration at common law, although such a statement might also be given in evidence under s. 23. Again, a choice may have to be made as to which exception it is preferable to invoke.

It does not follow from the satisfaction of the conditions of admissibility under s. 23 or s. 24 that a statement will in practice be admitted in evidence under the 1988 Act. Both sections are subject to the provisions of s. 25 (see **F16.14**), which confers a general discretion upon the court to exclude evidence which is otherwise admissible, and s. 26 (see **F16.14**), which requires that the leave of the court be obtained before certain documents prepared for the purposes of criminal proceedings or investigations are admitted.

Where the prosecution wishes to rely on a statement as original evidence, and the defence as evidence of its truth, or vice versa, it will clearly be for the party relying on the evidence as hearsay to establish admissibility under s. 23 or s. 24, as the case may be, and to comply with the relevant provisions of s. 25 and s. 26 *(Dyer* [1997] Crim LR 442).

First-hand Hearsay: s. 23

Criminal Justice Act 1988, s. 23 F16.3

(1) Subject—
     (a) to subsection (4) below;
     (b) to paragraph 1A of schedule 2 to the Criminal Appeal Act 1968 (evidence given orally at original trial to be given orally at retrial); and
     (c) to section 69 of the Police and Criminal Evidence Act 1984 (evidence from computer records),
a statement made by a person in a document shall be admissible in criminal proceedings as evidence of any fact of which direct oral evidence by him would be admissible if—
     (i)   the requirements of one of the paragraphs of subsection (2) below are satisfied; or
     (ii) the requirements of subsection (3) below are satisfied.
(2) The requirements mentioned in subsection (1)(i) above are—
     (a) that the person who made the statement is dead or by reason of his bodily or mental condition unfit to attend as a witness;
     (b) that—
     (i)   the person who made the statement is outside the United Kingdom; and
     (ii) it is not reasonably practicable to secure his attendance; or
     (c) that all reasonable steps have been taken to find the person who made the statement, but that he cannot be found.
(3) The requirements mentioned in subsection (1)(c)(ii) above are—
     (a) that the statement was made to a police officer or some other person charged with the duty of investigating offences or charging offenders; and
     (b) that the person who made it does not give oral evidence through fear or because he is kept out of the way.
(4) Subsection (1) above does not render admissible a confession made by an accused person that would not be admissible under section 76 of the Police and Criminal Evidence Act 1984.

(5)   This section shall not apply to proceedings before a magistrates' court inquiring into an offence as examining justices.

For the position in committal proceedings, see **F16.19**. The YJCEA 1999, sch. 4, para. 16 and sch. 6, amend s. 23; these amendments relate to, and will take effect on the implementation of, the prospective repeal of the PACE 1984, s. 69.

F16.4   ***A Statement Made by a Person in a Document***   'Statement' includes any representation of fact, however made and 'Document' means anything in which information of any description is recorded (CJA 1988, sch. 2, para. 5). Thus, for example, a video recording of an interview with the alleged victim of a rape, in which she gives an account of what happened, is a statement made by her in a document, as is a witness statement dictated by her and signed in her own handwriting. But the notes which a solicitor takes of an interview with a client, but which the client does not see or sign, do not constitute a statement *made by the client* in a document (see *Re D (A Minor)* [1986] 2 FLR 189, decided under the Civil Evidence Act 1968). In *Jones v Metcalfe* [1967] 1 WLR 1286, Lord Parker CJ said that where an eye-witness supplied information to a police officer, and saw him write it down, then albeit that the note was not in the witness's handwriting 'it was in effect his note', with the result that the witness could refresh his memory from it when testifying. (See generally as to refreshing memory, **F6.6** to **F6.12**.) The same result follows if the witness is unavailable and his statement is tendered under s. 23. In *MacGillivray* (1993) 97 Cr App R 232, M was convicted of the murder of a man to whom he had set fire. The victim made a statement which was contemporaneously recorded and read back to him by a police officer in the presence of a hospital nurse, but the victim was too badly injured to sign the record. It was held that the statement was admissible under s. 23, the court holding that the section applied where a person 'had clearly indicated by speech or otherwise that the record was accurate'. A statement made orally and surreptitiously tape-recorded by another without the maker's knowledge was held not to be made 'in a document' for the purposes of the Civil Evidence Act 1968 (see *Ventouris v Mountain (No. 2)* [1992] 1 WLR 817). In *Duffy* [1998] 3 WLR 1060 a more difficult question arose. D was convicted of the robbery and manslaughter of an elderly man. Her defence, which was that she was present under duress and took no part in the killing, was supported by a statement made by the victim's disabled son, C. C was unfit to attend the trial, and subsequently died. Although C's mental faculties were unimpaired by his various disabilities, his speech was so difficult to understand that only a particular social worker, E, was able to comprehend him. The interview with C was video-recorded, and E subsequently provided a transcript setting out his understanding of what C had told the police. It was held that the video recording was a document falling within the meaning of s. 23, although the transcript was not. E's account had not been signed or acknowledged in any way by C so that it could not be said to be a statement by C in a document. The Court of Appeal held that the trial judge, who had excluded the recording, should have admitted it, incomprehensible though it was in itself, and allowed the evidence of E to act in effect as a translation. This would have been tantamount to C giving evidence through an interpreter.

There is no restriction on the kind of document which may be adduced. Under the repealed PACE 1984, s. 68, the only type of document which could be adduced was a 'record' compiled under a 'duty'; it was held to apply only to those records which had come into existence independently of the issues raised in the proceedings in which it was sought to admit the document, with the result that witness statements and depositions prepared for the proceedings could not be admitted under the section (*Martin* [1988] 1 WLR 655). Such statements are clearly admissible under the 1988 Act, provided that s. 26 is satisfied (i.e. the court is of the opinion that, in the interests of justice, the statement ought to be admitted). It is not a valid objection to the use of a statement under s. 23 that it would not be admissible under some other exception to the hearsay rule (*Millen* [1995] Crim LR 568; *James* [1996] 2 Cr App R 39).

Admissible . . . As Evidence of Any Fact of Which Direct Oral Evidence . . . F16.5
Admissible The CJA 1988, s. 23, is supposed to be limited to first hand hearsay by the requirement that the statement be as to a fact of which the maker could have given 'direct oral evidence'. Where a person makes a statement in a document, but it is not clear whether the statement relates to her own knowledge or to something she has been told, the statement cannot be admitted under s. 23 (*JP* [1999] Crim LR 401). An exception might occur where the person could have given oral evidence of a particular matter, but only under another exception to the hearsay rule, for example where a written statement made by W, since deceased, includes a claim that the accused confessed her guilt to W, and the confession satisfies the conditions of admissibility appertaining to such evidence. It is implicit in *Lockley* [1995] 2 Cr App R 554 that such evidence may be admitted. C, L's co-accused, allegedly confessed to F, a witness who gave evidence when L and C were first tried but who was unavailable at a retrial. The transcript of F's evidence was held admissible under s. 23, although the double hearsay point was not taken, but excluded under the discretion and leave provisions (see **F16.4**). The admissibility of double hearsay was considered and accepted in relation to a similar provision in the Civil Evidence Act 1968 in *Compagnie Générale Maritime* v *Diakan Spirit SA* [1981] 1 Lloyd's Rep 550.

In *Irish* [1994] Crim LR 922 the Court of Appeal doubted whether s. 23 applied where a statement by an elderly victim of fraud was tendered to prove that he was senile and in no fit state to conduct his affairs. The court's objection was concerned with the words 'of which direct oral evidence would be admissible', and it is true that the man could not have given evidence of his own senility. However, the court missed the point that the statement was tendered to show the confusion of its maker, not as evidence of its truth. Hence is was admissible, non-hearsay evidence to which s. 23 had no relevance.

Proof of Unavailability of Maker The statutory reasons for not calling the maker F16.6
of a statement are disjunctive: provided that the party seeking to rely on the statement can establish that one of the reasons exists, it does not matter that other reasons cannot be made out (*Farrand* v *Galland* [1989] Crim LR 573, decided under the PACE 1984, s. 68; and see to the same effect *Rasool* v *West Midlands Passenger Transport Executive* [1974] 3 All ER 638, and *Piermay Shipping Co. SA* v *Chester* [1978] 1 WLR 411, decided under the Civil Evidence Act 1968).

In *Minors* [1989] 1 WLR 441, the Court of Appeal held that the admissibility of evidence adduced by the prosecution under the PACE 1984, s. 68, had to be established to the criminal standard of proof beyond reasonable doubt. (See also *Nicholls* (1976) 63 Cr App R 187, decided under the Criminal Evidence Act 1965.) The same result follows in respect of evidence adduced under the CJA 1988 (*Acton Justices, ex parte McMullen* (1990) 92 Cr App R 98, in which Watkins LJ said that he was 'in no doubt that the criminal standard of proof must be applied to subsections (2) and (3) [of s. 23]'; see also *Case* [1991] Crim LR 192 – discussed below). The standard of proof to be achieved by the defence is the ordinary civil standard of proof on a balance of probability (*Mattey* [1995] 2 Cr App R 409).

Unfitness to Attend The CJA 1988, s. 23(2)(a), applies not only to the physical act of F16.7
attending at court, but also to the capacity of the witness when there to give evidence, and includes unfitness through any mental condition. Where, therefore, a witness was unable to recollect relevant events, and medical evidence established that the cause was a mental disorder giving rise to great anxiety and failure of recall when under stress, the conditions of the section were satisfied (*Setz-Dempsey* (1994) 98 Cr App R 23). The effect of the witness's mental condition at the time the statement was made is, of course, a factor relevant to whether it should be excluded under s. 25 or s. 26 (see **F16.14**).

F16.8 ***Outside the United Kingdom and Not Reasonably Practicable to Secure Attendance or Cannot be Found after Reasonable Steps*** In *Castillo* [1996] 1 Cr App R 438 the Court of Appeal held that there were three considerations involved in the issue whether it is reasonably practicable for a witness to attend. The mere fact that it is possible for a witness to come does not answer the question. The court has to consider the importance of the evidence the witness could give, the expense and inconvenience of securing attendance and the weight to be given to the reasons put forward for non-attendance. The court also suggested a consideration of the prejudice to the defence which might arise if prosecution evidence were to be admitted under s. 23(2)(b), but this would appear more naturally to be a consideration relevant to the discretion and leave requirements of ss. 25 and 26 (see **F16.4**). In *French* (1993) 97 Cr App R 421 it was stressed that in a case where there was a long history of attempts by the prosecution to secure the attendance of the witness it was not helpful to ask when, if ever, the witness's attendance might be secured; the matter should be considered as it stood at the date of the application. In *Hurst* [1995] 1 Cr App R 82, the words 'reasonably practicable' were said to involve a consideration of the normal steps which would be taken to secure the attendance of a witness, and that cost was a relevant factor. As to the steps it may be reasonably practicable to take see also *Maloney* [1994] Crim LR 525; *Gonzalez de Orango* [1992] Crim LR 180 (a case decided under the PACE 1984, s. 68); and *Holman* [1995] Crim LR 80, in which Bank of Ireland employees declined to attend the trial without an order of the Irish court and it was held that the statutory conditions were plainly made out. The provision is not intended for use where the prosecution have failed to monitor the witness's availability prior to trial and are then taken by surprise by absence abroad of which they should have been aware (*Bray* (1988) 88 Cr App R 354, decided under the PACE 1984, s. 68). In such cases the question of what is reasonably practicable must be considered over a longer period than what was practicable on the day of the trial.

The need for the prosecution to satisfy the criminal standard of proof was stressed in *Case* [1991] Crim LR 192, where the only 'evidence' to support the contention that the maker of the statement the admissibility of which was in issue was out of the country was the statement itself (which was, of course, inadmissible hearsay until proved otherwise), and there was no evidence at all on the issue of whether it would have been practicable to secure the attendance of the maker at the trial. Holding that the statement ought not to have been admitted, the Court of Appeal pointed out that, had the matter been approached properly and with the criminal standard of proof in mind, it was likely that evidence could have been found which would have secured the admissibility of the statement. In *Mattey* [1995] 2 Cr App R 409, where the statement, which was tendered by the defence, had only to satisfy the condition on a balance of probabilities, it was held inadmissible in part because hearsay was relied on in support of it, but the hearsay may have been admissible evidence of the state of mind of the maker, so that *Case* was distinguishable. In any event, it should be noted that there is no bar to the use of a statement by one witness which is itself admissible under s. 23 to prove the inability of *another* witness to attend the trial (*Castillo* [1996] 1 Cr App R 438).

A letter written by a diplomat who is within the United Kingdom does not fall within s. 23(2)(b) of the 1988 Act even though the writer enjoys diplomatic immunity from compulsion to testify (*Jiminez-Paez* (1994) 98 Cr App R 239).

In *Coughlan* [1999] 5 Arch News 2 the court was concerned with the interpretation of s. 23(3)(c), when a witness cannot be found after taking all reasonable steps. As with the witness who is outside the country, it was said that it was relevant to consider the importance of the evidence and the cost implications, although the seriousness of the offence was said not to be relevant. In reality, of course, the resources devoted to tracing witnesses will necessarily take account of offence-seriousness.

Fear   In *Bird* (1997) 161 JP 96, the Court of Appeal emphasised the importance of   **F16.9**
considering the application of the CJA 1988, s. 23(3), in cases where witnesses to
incidents of domestic violence prefer to be held in contempt rather than to give evidence
at trial. Attention was drawn to the policy document *CPS Policy for Prosecuting Cases of
Domestic Violence* (1995). It is also important to note, however, that the subsection is not
limited to cases of domestic violence, but applies regardless of the context in which the
'fear' arises.

Section 23(3), contains conditions which were not included in the 1984 Act, and raises
difficult questions of interpretation. In *Ashford Magistrates' Court, ex parte Hilden* [1993]
2 WLR 529, it was held that the words 'does not give oral evidence through fear' include
a witness who takes the oath but who, through fear, is unable to complete her evidence.
McCowan LJ held that s. 23 applies only where the witness has given 'evidence of no
significant relevance to the case' at the point where she is deterred by fear, but
Popplewell J held that s. 23 applies no matter what the point at which the witness is
prevented by fear from giving further oral evidence. In *Waters* (1997) 161 JP 249, the
Court of Appeal preferred the approach of Popplewell J, adding:

> In our judgment, what matters is whether or not there is, at the time when the section is
> invoked, any relevant evidence which the witness is still expected to give, because, if there
> is such evidence, then it can properly be said that the witness is in the position where he
> does not give oral evidence.

It follows that a hostile prosecution witness who is motivated by fear may fall within
s. 23(3), so that the section will provide a mechanism for allowing the witness's
out-of-court statement to be evidence of the truth of the facts stated, and not merely of
inconsistency (see, as to hostile witnesses generally, **F6.19** to **F6.22**). A hostile
prosecution witness who is motivated simply by the desire to protect the accused
remains outside the purview of the section.

The words 'through fear' do not connote any objective requirement that the fear be
reasonable, nor that it must be caused by something said or done after the crime (*Acton
Justices, ex parte McMullen* (1990) 92 Cr App R 98). In that case Watkins LJ suggested
that it would be sufficient to show that the witness was in fear as a result of the crime
itself or of something said or done afterwards in relation to the offence and the possibility
of the witness testifying as to it. Even this limitation was rejected, however, in *Martin*
[1996] Crim LR 589, on the basis that as the statutory words were unrestricted no
limitation should be imposed by the court, particularly given that witness intimidation
is a subject of grave concern. In that case a witness refused to give evidence, having been
put in fear by the appearance of a silent stranger outside his door. There was no evidence
of anything said or done by the stranger: the witness had simply interpreted the man's
appearance as a threat. If no restriction at all is placed on the statutory words, then
arguably the fear could be completely unconnected with the crime, as where the witness
fears arrest in connection with some other matter. If it is thought desirable to exclude
such cases it would seem that this must henceforth be achieved under the discretion and
leave requirements in ss. 25 and 26. Whatever meaning is given to 'through fear',
however:

(a)   the maker's fear must be established by evidence to the appropriate standard of
proof, and such evidence must itself be admissible; and

(b)   evidence which satisfies the conditions of admissibility under the 1988 Act may
nevertheless fall to be excluded under s. 25 or s. 26 of the Act, under which provisions
the court is directed to consider where the interests of justice lie with regard to the
admission of the evidence.

Both of these points arose for consideration in *Neill* v *North Antrim Magistrates' Court*
[1992] 1 WLR 1221. Two boys made statements to the police in which they claimed to

have witnessed an assault and to have identified one of the perpetrators. However they did not attend committal proceedings, and evidence was given by a police officer that the boys' mothers had told him that the boys were too afraid to attend. The resident magistrate admitted the boys' statements under art. 3(3)(b) of the Criminal Justice (Evidence, Etc.) (Northern Ireland) Order 1988 (SI 1988 No. 1847), which corresponds to s. 23 of the CJA 1988. The House of Lords held that the statements should not have been received because the evidence of the officer was hearsay, being based on what he had been told by the mothers of the boys and not by the boys themselves. If the boys had communicated their fears to him directly he could have given evidence of what they had told him under the 'long-established law that a person's declaration of his contemporaneous state of mind is admissible to prove the existence of that state of mind', per Lord Mustill at p. 1228 following *Blastland* [1986] AC 41 (see **F15.7**). However the point was also made that, even had such evidence been available, a court would be cautious about whether it was in the interests of justice under s. 26 or its equivalent provision to admit documentary evidence of identification or recognition which formed the principal element in the prosecution's case. (See further **F16.14**.) The need for proof of fear was also accepted in *Waters* (1997) 161 JP 249, in which it was rightly said that the demeanour of the witness (who testified at a *voir dire* after giving incomplete evidence at trial) was a material factor to which the trial judge rightly had regard. The Court of Appeal also regarded as significant a medical report on the witness's condition, despite the fact that the report contained hearsay in that it repeated the witness's assertions as to the cause of the fear. This seems to be correct in the light of the decision in *Martin* that the cause of the fear is irrelevant. If *Martin* be wrong, however, and the source of the fear is a material consideration, a report such as that relied on in *Waters* could not prove it. The difficulties of proof which arise if *Martin* is wrong may provide a cogent reason for following that decision.

In many cases the court will be able to receive oral evidence as to the fear of the witness, either because the witness himself is prepared to testify on the *voir dire* (as in *Waters*) or because a person such as a police officer who has first-hand knowledge of the fear will be available to testify (cf. the procedure recommended in *Neill* v *North Antrim Magistrates' Court*. In some cases a statement by the fearful person has been received by the court (see, e.g., *Rutherford* [1998] Crim LR 490, in which the Court of Appeal approved the decision of the trial judge to admit the evidence). In *Belmarsh Magistrates' Court, ex parte Gilligan* [1998] 1 Cr App R 14, however, the Divisional Court on application for judicial review held that it was necessary for a court to hear oral evidence as to fear in order to satisfy the requirements of s. 23. This would seem to be going too far, as documentary evidence should be permitted provided it is admissible. The evidence in *Gilligan* was said to be inadmissible because there was no authority to support the submission that this statement could prove itself. Indeed it could not: it would have to be proved that the document was that which it purported to be, which is presumably what occurred in *Rutherford*. In *Greer* [1998] Crim LR 572, the Court of Appeal appears to have dispensed with the requirement for strict proof by allowing the judge to act on the unsworn evidence of two eye-witnesses to a serious assault who attended court to explain why they were not prepared to give evidence. Technically, however, it would seem that witnesses should be sworn (*Jennings* [1995] Crim LR 810). Furthermore, it has been held that the defence should be entitled to cross-examine witnesses called by the prosecution to establish the conditions in s. 23 (*Wood* [1998] Crim LR 213). If this degree of formality is required, it might be enough to frighten away the truly intimidated witness but, if it is not, there is a risk that hearsay evidence which is likely to be crucial to the outcome of the trial will be too readily admitted. The authorities considered in this paragraph are, to say the least, not entirely consistent, and some further guidance as to the true principles to be followed would be welcomed.

Where evidence has been admitted on the ground that the maker's absence is attributable to threats made by the accused, it was noted in *Ricketts* [1991] Crim LR

915, that this may exercise a powerful influence over the trial. In that case, the maker of the statement presented himself in court after the jury had retired, and explained his absence on grounds unrelated to any fear of the accused, and it was held that the jury ought to have been discharged as it had become apparent that the trial had proceeded on a false basis, though it is not apparent why it was necessary to have informed the jury of the reason for the absence of the witness. In *Churchill* [1993] Crim LR 285 the jury asked why B, an alleged accomplice whose statement was admitted under s. 23(3)(b), had not given evidence. It was held wrong for the judge to say that the reason 'involved nothing to B's detriment', as this was tantamount to giving B a 'pat on the back', and it would have been better to say nothing. In most cases it ought to be possible for the judge, assisted by counsel, to arrive at a form of words which, while not giving the jury a false impression, creates no prejudice either. See also *Jennings* [1995] Crim LR 810.

As to proof of fear by hearsay evidence forming part of the *res gestae*, see **F16.36**.

It is not clear whether the prosecution may claim that a witness is 'kept out of the way' under s. 23(3)(b) only where the person against whom the proceedings are being taken, or someone acting in his interests, is doing the keeping, or whether the condition may also be satisfied where the police have decided to keep the witness out of the way for his own protection. It seems highly questionable that the prosecution should be permitted to make use of the provisions of s. 23(3)(b) in the latter case.

Business and Similar Documents: s. 24

Criminal Justice Act 1988, s. 24   F16.10

(1)   Subject—
    (a)   to subsections (3) and (4) below;
    (b)   to paragraph 1A of Schedule 2 to the Criminal Appeal Act 1968; and
    (c)   to section 69 of the Police and Criminal Evidence Act 1984,
a statement in a document shall be admissible in criminal proceedings as evidence of any fact of which direct oral evidence would be admissible, if the following conditions are satisfied—
    (i)   the document was created or received by a person in the course of a trade, business, profession or other occupation or as the holder of a paid or unpaid office; and
    (ii)   the information contained in the document was supplied by a person (whether or not the maker of the statement) who had, or who may reasonably be supposed to have had, personal knowledge of the matters dealt with.
(2)   Subsection (1) above applies whether the information contained in the document was supplied directly or indirectly but, if it was supplied indirectly, only if each person through whom it was supplied received it—
    (a)   in the course of a trade, business, profession or other occupation; or
    (b)   as the holder of a paid or unpaid office.
(3)   Subsection (1) above does not render admissible a confession made by an accused person that would not be admissible under section 76 of the Police and Criminal Evidence Act 1984.
(4)   A statement prepared otherwise than in accordance with section 3 of the Criminal Justice (International Co-operation) Act 1990 or an order under paragraph 6 of Schedule 13 to this Act or under section 30 or 31 below for the purposes —
    (a)   of pending or contemplated criminal proceedings; or
    (b)   of a criminal investigation,
shall not be admissible by virtue of subsection (1) above unless—
    (i)   the requirements of one of the paragraphs of subsection (2) of section 23 above are satisfied; or
    (ii)   the requirements of subsection (3) of that section are satisfied; or
    (iii)   the person who made the statement cannot reasonably be expected (having regard to the time which has elapsed since he made the statement and to all the circumstances) to have any recollection of the matters dealt with in the statement.
(5)   This section shall not apply to proceedings before a magistrates' court inquiring into an offence as examining justices.

For the position in committal proceedings, see **F16.19**. The YJCEA 1999, sch. 4, para. 16 and sch. 6, amend s. 24; the amendments relate to, and will take effect from the implementation of, the prospective repeal of the PACE 1984, s. 69.

F16.11 ***Document Created or Received*** The marginal note of the CJA 1988, s. 24, refers to 'Business etc. documents', but the term does not appear in the section itself, which refers only to a document created or received by a person in the course of a trade, business, profession or other occupation, or as the holder of a paid or unpaid office. In *Clowes* [1992] 3 All ER 440, transcripts of interviews between the liquidators of companies and persons involved with the companies were held to have been 'received' by the liquidators in the course of their profession and as holders of the office of liquidator. As any such document may be admissible (subject to the requirement of 'personal knowledge' in s. 24(1)(ii)), the section is considerably wider than any of its predecessors. Records previously admitted under the PACE 1984, s. 68, remain admissible under s. 24, together with many documents which would have been inadmissible under the 1984 Act because they were not records or were not compiled under a duty, such as individual letters or items submitted for publication to learned journals.

Under the Criminal Evidence Act 1965, the term 'business' was said to be confined to activities of a commercial nature (*Crayden* [1978] 1 WLR 604). At the time, the effect of the ruling was to render inadmissible a National Health Service hospital's records of examinations conducted by a doctor and a radiologist. Such records would now be admissible under s. 24 as documents created in the course of the profession or occupation of the makers. Indeed the transcript of the evidence given by a witness at an earlier trial may be admitted at a retrial under s. 23 or under s. 24, even though the court is plainly not a business in any sense (*Lockley* [1995] 2 Cr App R 554). Similarly, a police custody record was admitted under s. 24 in *Hogan* [1997] Crim LR 349.

Because s. 24 applies only to documentary evidence, the compiler of documents for use in criminal proceedings who leaves out important details of information he has gathered from others who do not give evidence cannot supplement his record with oral hearsay testimony (*Hinds* [1993] Crim LR 528).

In *Foxley* [1995] 2 Cr App R 523, the documents in question were copies of credit notes and payments allegedly made by overseas companies to F, who was accused of receiving them corruptly. They had been obtained by letters of request to the authorities in the relevant countries. It was objected, *inter alia*, that no evidence was available from the creator as to whether these documents had come into existence in the course of a business etc., but it was held to be the intention of the statute that the court be allowed to draw relevant inferences from the documents themselves and from the way in which they had been placed before the court. As Professor Sir John Smith points out in his commentary at [1995] Crim LR 637, the court failed to note that the documents in question were not hearsay evidence, so that recourse to s. 24 was not necessary. However, the point made would have been valid in relation to true hearsay evidence.

F16.12 ***Personal Knowledge*** The 'supplier' of the information (who must have, etc., personal knowledge of the matters dealt with under the CJA 1988, s. 24 (1)(ii)) may also be the person who 'creates' the document under s. 24(1)(i). Thus, e.g., a note made by an operator working for a paging company that messages have been left for a customer would be admissible under s. 24 (as in *Rock* [1994] Crim LR 843), and also under s. 23 as a first hand hearsay statement. Where such a document is received in evidence under s. 24, it is not necessary, as it is under s. 23, to prove the unavailability of the maker of the statement.

Section 24 may also be invoked where several degrees of hearsay are involved. Provided each of the persons through whom the information was supplied received it in the course of a trade etc. (s. 24(2)), the facts stated in the document are admissible. A document produced by a computer without any human intervention cannot be said to contain information 'supplied by a person' with 'personal knowledge' (*Pettigrew* (1980) 71 Cr App R 39). However, as such a document is unlikely to constitute hearsay evidence, it will not matter that the conditions of the s. 24 exception cannot be satisfied (see *Wood* (1982) 76 Cr App R 23, considered at **F15.14**).

The only facts which may be proved are those of which 'direct oral evidence' would be admissible, and it is submitted that the intention is:

(a)   to limit the applicability of the section to those matters of which the supplier (and any intermediaries by whom the information has been transmitted) would have been competent to give evidence; and

(b)   to prevent the introduction of evidence which contravenes a rule of admissibility, e.g., the similar-fact evidence rule.

It cannot be a valid objection to the admissibility of evidence under the section that an intermediary through whom the information was 'indirectly supplied' under s. 24(2) could not have given evidence of the fact without contravening the hearsay rule, otherwise the section could not be made to apply to second hand hearsay, and it is clearly meant to do so.

Unavailability of Maker of Statement Prepared for Purposes of Criminal F16.13
Proceedings or Investigation   It is not generally necessary to show grounds why the maker of a statement should not be called before tendering his statement in evidence under the CJA 1988, s. 24. The only exception is a statement prepared for the purposes of pending or contemplated criminal proceedings, or of a criminal investigation, to which s. 24(4) applies (*Murphy* [1992] Crim LR 883). In such a case it is necessary to establish either:

(a)   one of the reasons for not calling the maker which apply in the case of a s. 23 statement (see **F16.3** and **F16.6** to **F16.9**); or

(b)   that the maker cannot reasonably be expected (having regard to the time which has elapsed since he made the statement and to all the circumstances) to have any recollection of the matters dealt with in the statement (s. 24(4)(iii)).

In *Bedi* (1992) 95 Cr App R 21 the 'lost and stolen' reports maintained by a bank in respect of credit cards it had issued were held not to fall within s. 24(4). An examination of the reports disclosed that they were kept for the proper conduct of the bank's business, not for criminal proceedings. In *Hogan* [1997] Crim LR 349 it was assumed, surely rightly, that a police custody record fell within s. 24(4).

Section 24(4)(iii) may apply where a witness is unable to recollect one part of a longer statement but is able to give evidence as to the rest (*Carrington* [1994] Crim LR 438, in which the witness's recollection was supplemented by the section in relation to a car registration number which she had forgotten, in circumstances where she was not entitled to refresh her memory from the statement). See as to the evidence which may satisfy the condition contained in s. 24(4)(iii), *Crayden* [1978] 1 WLR 604 at p. 608, decided under the Criminal Evidence Act 1965, and *Feest* [1987] Crim LR 766, decided under the PACE 1984.

A difficulty in the construction of s. 24(4) arises because s. 24(1)(ii) appears to envisage a case where the person who supplied the information contained in the document is not the same individual as the person who made the statement. Where this division of roles occurs, the literal interpretation of the section suggests that it is the creator of the document who must be unavailable to give evidence when applying s. 24(4), and that the availability or otherwise of the supplier is immaterial, though whether this is a desirable result seems highly questionable. Thus in *Bedi* it appears to have been accepted that reports of the loss or theft of credit cards compiled by a bank employee from information supplied by the owners of the cards were 'made' by the employee rather than by the owners of the cards, and in *Carrington* it was accepted by the parties that, where S had reported a car registration number to B, who made a note of it, it was B's ability or otherwise to recollect the facts stated in the document which was in issue for the purposes of admitting the note in evidence under s. 24(4)(iii), not S's. A different interpretation was placed on the provision in *Derodra* (1999) *The Times*, 16 July 1999. B gave information about a burglary to G, a police officer, who made a record of the incident. Buxton LJ held that what is admitted under s. 24 is the 'statement', rather than the 'document', and that the various conditions attached by Parliament to the 'maker' are intended to apply to the maker of the statement and not (where the two are different) the maker of the document. The person whose ability to recollect the facts was pertinent for the purposes of s. 24(4)(iii) was therefore G, and not B. This achieves a very much more desirable practical outcome than was achieved in, say, *Carrington*.

Discretion and Leave Requirements: ss. 25 and 26

F16.14 **Criminal Justice Act 1988, ss. 25 and 26**

25.—(1)   If, having regard to all the circumstances—
  (a)   the Crown Court—
    (i)   on a trial on indictment;
    (ii)   on an appeal from a magistrates' court;
    (iii)   on the hearing of an application under section 6 of the Criminal Justice Act 1987 (applications for dismissal of charges of fraud transferred from magistrates' court to Crown Court); or
    (iv)   on the hearing of an application under paragraph 5 of schedule 6 to the Criminal Justice Act 1991 (applications for dismissal of charges in certain cases involving children transferred from magistrates' court to Crown Court); or
  (b)   the criminal division of the Court of Appeal; or
  (c)   a magistrates' court on a trial of an information,
is of the opinion that in the interests of justice a statement which is admissible by virtue of section 23 or 24 above nevertheless ought not to be admitted, it may direct that the statement shall not be admitted.

  (2)   Without prejudice to the generality of subsection (1) above, it shall be the duty of the court to have regard—
  (a)   to the nature and source of the document containing the statement and to whether or not, having regard to its nature and source and to any other circumstances that appear to the court to be relevant, it is likely that the document is authentic;
  (b)   to the extent to which the statement appears to supply evidence which would otherwise not be readily available;
  (c)   to the relevance of the evidence that it appears to supply to any issue which is likely to have to be determined in the proceedings; and
  (d)   to any risk, having regard in particular to whether it is likely to be possible to controvert the statement if the person making it does not attend to give oral evidence in the proceedings, that its admission or exclusion will result in unfairness to the accused or, if there is more than one, to any of them.

26.   Where a statement which is admissible in criminal proceedings by virtue of section 23 or 24 above appears to the court to have been prepared, otherwise than in accordance with section 29 below or an order under paragraph 6 of Schedule 13 to this Act or under section 30 or 31 below, for the purposes—
  (a)   of pending or contemplated criminal proceedings; or
  (b)   of a criminal investigation,
the statement shall not be given in evidence in any criminal proceedings without the leave of the court, and the court shall not give leave unless it is of the opinion that the statement ought to be admitted in the interests of justice; and in considering whether its admission would be in the interests of justice, it shall be the duty of the court to have regard—

     (i)   to the contents of the statement;

     (ii)   to any risk, having regard in particular to whether it is likely to be possible to controvert the statement if the person making it does not attend to give oral evidence in the proceedings, that its admission or exclusion will result in unfairness to the accused or, if there is more than one, to any of them; and

     (iii)   to any other circumstances that appear to the court to be relevant.

This section shall not apply to proceedings before a magistrates' court inquiring into an offence as examining justices.

For the position in committal proceedings, see **F16.19**.

As to the factors to be taken into account in exercising the discretion conferred by s. 25 in relation to letters of request, see the Criminal Justice (International Co-operation) Act 1990, s. 3(8).

Relationship between s. 25 and s. 26   In *Cole* [1990] 1 WLR 866, the Court of   **F16.15** Appeal noted the similarities between ss. 25 and 26 of the CJA 1988, but contrasted them in the following way. When considering the question posed by s. 25, 'the court must be made to hold the opinion that the statement ought not to be admitted'; whereas under s. 26 'the court is not to admit the statement unless made to hold the opinion that in the interests of justice it ought to be admitted. The emphasis is the other way round.' It would seem to follow from this that, although there is no provision excluding the application of s. 25 to the class of documents to which s. 26 applies, there is no point in applying the two provisions cumulatively in such cases (*Grafton* [1995] Crim LR 60). In some cases, however, the two provisions appear to have been treated as applying cumulatively (see, e.g., *Batt* [1995] Crim LR 240, *Holman* [1995] Crim LR 80, *Lockley* [1995] 2 Cr App R 554 and *Gokal* [1997] 2 Cr App R 266). This may be overkill but cannot be wrong in the light of the statutory wording. However, it is clearly a material error, entitling the Court of Appeal to review the exercise of discretion, if a trial judge mistakenly applies s. 25 instead of s. 26 (*Setz-Dempsey* (1994) 98 Cr App R 23; *Jennings* [1995] Crim LR 810).

It would also be wrong, and unduly favourable to the defence, to insist that the judge approach the question whether to admit a murder victim's diary under s. 25 with the same 'bias in favour of exclusion' as is required under s. 26 (*Giannetto* [1997] 1 Cr App R 1).

Relationship with other Discretionary Powers   The CJA 1988, s. 28(1)(b), makes   **F16.16** it clear that the courts retain their existing powers to exclude at their discretion evidence admissible under s. 23 or s. 24 of the Act. Such powers may overlap with the discretion and leave requirements in ss. 25 and 26. The most obvious contender was the discretion which the courts had developed in respect of depositions admissible under the CJA 1925, s. 13(3) (*Blithing* (1983) 77 Cr App R 86) but recent changes to the rules on committal proceedings and the repeal of s. 13(3) will, over time, relieve the courts of the necessity to reconcile the two powers. (Section 13(3) and the relationship between the discretionary powers is considered in the 1997 edition of this work.)

The general common-law powers of a court to exclude evidence at its discretion, and the statutory power under the PACE 1984, s. 78, to exclude evidence which would operate unfairly in the proceedings, are considered at **F2.1** to **F2.5**. A significant difference between these discretionary powers and those contained in the 1988 Act is that the latter's provisions apply to evidence tendered by either side, whereas the other discretionary powers can be brought to bear on prosecution evidence only.

Exercise of Powers under s. 25 and s. 26   **F16.17**

    The overall purpose of the provisions [of the CJA 1988, ss. 25 and 26] was to widen the power of the court to admit documentary hearsay evidence while ensuring that the accused receives a fair trial. In judging how to achieve the fairness of the trial a balance must on occasions be struck between the interests of the public in enabling the prosecution case to be properly presented and the interest of a particular defendant in not being put in a disadvantageous position, for example by the death or illness of a witness. The public of course also has a direct interest in the proper protection of the individual accused. The point of balance, as directed by Parliament, is set out in the sections. (*Cole* [1990] 1 WLR 866, at 875D–E)

In *Gokal* [1997] 2 Cr App R 266, one of the grounds of challenge to the admission of evidence from a witness who was abroad was that the admission of such evidence under the statutory scheme in the CJA 1988, ss. 23 to 26, ran counter to the 'fair trial' provisions of the European Convention on Human Rights. After careful consideration of decisions under the Convention the Court of Appeal concluded: 'Since the whole basis of the discretion conferred by section 26 is to assess the interests of justice by reference to the risk of unfairness to the accused, our procedures appear to us to accord fully with our treaty obligations'. This observation, which reflects what was said in *Cole* in relation to the whole statutory scheme and not just s. 26, appears a sufficient answer to the challenge based on the Convention, provided that the most anxious consideration is always given (as it was in these two authorities) to achieving the right balance after consideration of all relevant matters. Because ss. 23 and 24 are cast in such wide terms, it is under the discretion and leave provisions of ss. 25 and 26 that the accused's right to a fair trial must be vindicated. The Convention was more recently invoked by way of challenge to the exercise of the s. 26 discretion in *Thomas* [1998] Crim LR 887. T was convicted of offences including conspiracy to supply heroin and causing grievous bodily harm to C, an addict whom it was alleged M had employed as a courier. C was too afraid to give evidence at trial, and his original statement and committal deposition were read. On appeal it was argued that the court in *Gokal* had misinterpreted the jurisprudence of the European Court of Human Rights: a contention categorically rejected by the Court of Appeal. The court referred to *Kostovski* v *Netherlands* (1990) 12 EHRR 434 as establishing the following principles.

(a)   Admissibility of evidence is primarily a matter of national law.

(b)   The role of the European Court of Human Rights is not to express a view as to whether statements were correctly admitted but rather as to whether the proceedings considered as a whole, including the way in which evidence was taken, were fair.

(c)   To admit statements in evidence which have been obtained at the pre-trial stage and which are not made by the witness at a public hearing in the presence of the accused is not necessarily inconsistent with Art. 6. As a rule, however, the accused should be given an adequate and proper opportunity to challenge and question a witness against him, either at the time the statement was made or at some later stage of proceedings.

In *Thomas* the court considered that there could properly be exceptions to the third principle, and that the words 'as a rule', used by the court in *Kostovski*, supported this view. The balancing act required by the domestic 'interests of justice' test ensured that the statutory scheme did not itself infringe Art. 6. In support of its conclusion the court noted the decision of the Commission in *Trivedi* v *United Kingdom* (1997) No. 31700/96, 89DRI36 (27 May 1997). In that case T, a doctor, was charged with false accounting by claiming for patient visits which had not occurred. The evidence against him included the s. 23 statement of one elderly patient who was too ill to attend. Factors which influenced the Commission's decision that T's application in respect of this matter was manifestly unfounded were (i) the statement was not the only evidence; (ii) the judge in summing up had given a warning about the secondary nature of the evidence; and (iii) counsel for T had been given full opportunity to comment on the statement with a view to impugning the credit and reliability of the maker. The same could be said of the evidence in *Thomas,* indeed the court observed that it was possible to go further and say that the evidence of C had been subjected to some (albeit limited) cross-examination in the magistrates' court. It may be that the Convention is most likely to pose a difficulty in cases where the statement is the only evidence on an essential aspect of the case.

Where the statement is one to which s. 26 applies, it was held in *Cole* that an important factor to be considered is the quality of the evidence contained in the statement (citing with approval the observations of Lord Griffiths in *Scott* v *The Queen* [1989] AC 1242). Thus, 'the weight to be attached to the inability to cross-examine and the magnitude of any consequential risk that the admission of the statement will result in unfairness to the accused will depend in part upon the court's assessment of the quality of the evidence shown in the statement.' *Cole* further requires the court to consider whether any potential unfairness may be effectively counterbalanced by a warning to the jury pointing out that the evidence had not been tested by cross-examination and drawing attention to its possible limitations. (In *Cole* the trial judge went even further and commented that the written statement could not possibly have been worth as much as the evidence of other witnesses, but this elaboration was rightly held to be unnecessary in *Greer* [1988] Crim LR 572.) This aspect of *Cole* was applied in *Kennedy* [1992] Crim LR 64, where the issue was whether K, by fighting with his co-accused, H, was guilty of affray or was acting in self-defence. It was held that a statement by one M, who was the only independent witness to the fight and who had since died, was rightly admitted. It had been contended that M's evidence was flawed in that it was inconsistent with the testimony of both K and H, but, as the Court of Appeal rightly pointed out, such inconsistency is not unusual in such cases, and it was sufficient for the trial judge to give the jury a warning of the disadvantages of not having M as a witness in the case. See also *Samuel* [1992] Crim LR 189 (considered further below) and *Kennedy* [1994] Crim LR 50, in which a statement made by W, the victim of an assault (who subsequently died of other causes), was held on balance to have been rightly admitted, notwithstanding that W was very drunk at the time of the incident and there were important inconsistencies between his version of events and that of other witnesses. However K's appeal was allowed because the judge had failed to stress these weaknesses when warning the jury how to approach W's statement. Compare *Thompson* [1999] Crim LR 747, in which it was held proper to admit, subject to a warning, the statement of the victim of a robbery notwithstanding that he was awaiting discharge from a hospital to which he had been admitted for drink-related mental problems. It is perhaps significant that there was substantial prosecution evidence apart from the victim's statement.

There is however no general rule that a statement which is 'crucial' to the case of the party tendering it must be excluded (*Patel* (1993) 97 Cr App R 294 (statement tendered by defence); *Setz-Dempsey* (1994) 98 Cr App R 23 (statement tendered by prosecution)); on the contrary, the significance of the evidence is a factor which may tell in its favour (*Batt* [1995] Crim LR 240). Where identification or recognition evidence is tendered in documentary form, and such evidence forms the principal element in the prosecution case, a court will be very reluctant to receive the evidence, even in committal proceedings (*Neill* v *North Antrim Magistrates' Court* [1992] 1 WLR 1221 at p. 1229 per Lord Mustill). *Dragic* [1996] 2 Cr App R 232, in which a statement identifying the accused was admitted, should not be regarded as providing strong authority against Lord Mustill's view both because *Neill's* case was not considered and because the statement was made by a person who knew D well, and it was to be challenged not on the basis of mistake (which is the likely defect of eye-witness identification), but of deliberate fabrication.

Section 25(2)(d) and s. 26(ii) direct the court to have regard to any risk of unfairness to the accused if the statement is admitted or excluded, having regard in particular to whether it is likely to be possible to controvert the statement if the maker does not give evidence in person. Although the trial judge must consider the stipulated 'risk of unfairness to the accused', it does not follow that, where the defence seeks to admit the evidence, he should not also consider, and in an appropriate case be more influenced by, the risk of an unfair result if the evidence is admitted (*W* [1997] Crim LR 678). In *Cole* the Court of Appeal considered the meaning of 'controvert' when applying s. 26(ii) to a deposition of one L, who had witnessed the assault with which C was charged, but who had died before the trial. L was not the only witness to the incident, but he had the best view of it. It was held that the trial judge, in deciding to admit L's statement, had been right to take into account:

(a)   the availability for cross-examination of other prosecution witnesses;
(b)   the availability of witnesses for the defence;
(c)   the availability of C himself to give evidence in support of the defence raised, which was self-defence.

Although the court cannot require to be told whether the accused intends to give evidence or call witnesses, it is not bound to assess the possibility of controverting the statement upon the basis that the accused will do neither of these things. The Court considered that if Parliament had intended the question to be considered on the basis that the accused has no obligation to give or call evidence, express words would have been used to make that intention clear. The effect of ss. 25 and 26 on the right to silence was further considered, and *Cole* approved, in *Gokal* [1997] 2 Cr App R 266. It was held that the provisions of the 1988 Act did not, as G contended, abrogate the accused's right to silence, although it was accepted that it was more difficult for him to exercise the choice to remain silent in circumstances where the most obvious way to 'controvert' admissible prosecution evidence was to testify. *Cole* was also applied in *Price* [1991] Crim LR 707, where the issue concerned the contents of a conversation which took place between P and a bank manager, and to which there were no independent witnesses. It was held to be no bar to the admission under s. 23 or s. 24 of a note of the conversation made by the manager that the only way in which P could 'controvert' its contents was to give evidence. In *Samuel* [1992] Crim LR 189, the statement of D, the ailing 80-year-old victim of a deception offence, was held to have been rightly admitted given that it was possible for S and his co-accused to give evidence to controvert the statement and the trial judge had warned the jury that S had had no opportunity to cross-examine D. In *Moore* [1992] Crim LR 882 it was held that there is no general principle against admitting a statement the effect of which will be to force an accused to testify. See also *Grafton* [1995] Crim LR 61.

If the witness has been shown to be absent through fear, and it is proper to infer that the fear was caused by threats made by, or on behalf of, the accused, it does not 'lie in the mouth' of that accused to protest that the witness is not available for cross-examination (*Harvey* [1998] 10 Arch News 2).

In *Dyer* [1997] Crim LR 442, it was held that the reference in s. 25 to the likelihood of a document being 'authentic' involved the court in a consideration of the reliability of its contents, but this is surely wrong. It is submitted that a better approach is that of Buxton J at first instance in *Gokal*, who held a written statement by C to be authentic 'in the sense that it is what it purported to be, namely, [C's] statement, not a forgery'.

In *French* (1993) 97 Cr App R 421, it was held that the court's obligation to have regard to 'any other circumstances' appearing to be relevant in s. 26(iii) was wide enough to include the conduct of the prosecutor in making an application to sever which delayed proceedings at a time when the victim of one of the offences, a Mexican, had travelled to this country to give evidence. Subsequently, the victim returned home and the prosecution, having failed to persuade him to return, sought to adduce his witness statement in reliance on s. 23(2)(b) (see **F16.8**). The statement contained an identification which was central to the proceedings and the Court of Appeal, holding that the statement should have been excluded, commented that the prosecution should have proceeded when the witness was available. To similar effect is *Radak* [1999] 1 Cr App R 187. The defence in this case would have suffered a significant degree of unfairness if they had been deprived of the opportunity to cross-examine the absent witness. The prosecution proceeded with an application to admit the evidence under s. 23 even though it would have been possible, had appropriate arrangements been made in time, to have taken the witness's evidence on commission in the United States; a procedure which would have afforded opportunity for cross-examination. It was held that the failure of the prosecution timeously to explore this alternative was a factor to be taken into account under s. 26, and should have led to the conclusion that the evidence should not have been admitted. It was considered that Art. 6 of the European Convention on Human Rights (considered above: see **appendix** 7 for text) pointed to the same conclusion.

Another factor which may be relevant in deciding where the interests of justice lie with regard to the admission of a statement, is the extent to which the party against whom the evidence is tendered has had an opportunity to investigate it prior to the trial. In *Iqbal* [1990] 1 WLR 756, decided under the PACE 1984, s. 68, the accused had disclosed the existence of the statements on which he wished to rely some six months before the trial, thus giving the prosecution ample opportunity to investigate the circumstances and gather evidence to challenge the consistency and credibility of the information, which, if believed, was wholly exculpatory of the accused. It was held that there was no reason why the trial judge should have exercised his discretion to exclude the statement.

A court considering where the interests of justice lie as between two or more accused may be faced with a particularly difficult task. In *Gregory* [1995] Crim LR 507, G and M were convicted of murder on the basis of joint enterprise. G argued that a statement made by the sister of M, who had died before the trial, should have been admitted. The court upheld the 'balancing act' performed by the judge in the exercise of his discretion in which he had taken account of the fact that the damage done to M by admitting the statement would have outweighed the advantage to G. The contrast with the general rule that admissible evidence tendered by one accused cannot be excluded to protect another from unfairness is at its starkest here, and it may be that severance should be more readily resorted to in consequence.

Where a statement tendered in evidence under s. 24 is not a deposition or other statement prepared for the purpose of criminal proceedings, the absence of any opportunity to cross-examine the maker is likely to be of less importance, even where the statement relied upon is crucial to the case for the prosecution. Thus, in *Schreiber* [1988] Crim LR 112, decided under the Criminal Evidence Act 1965, it was held that customs documents compiled abroad could be given in evidence without calling the maker, even though the documents were the most cogent evidence of fraud by the accused.

Credit of Maker of Statement: Schedule 2

Criminal Justice Act 1988, sch. 2　　　　　　　　　　　　　　　　**F16.18**

Documentary Evidence – Supplementary

　　1.　Where a statement is admitted as evidence in criminal proceedings by virtue of part II of this Act—
　　　　(a)　any evidence which, if the person making the statement had been called as a witness, would have been admissible as relevant to his credibility as a witness shall be admissible for that purpose in those proceedings;
　　　　(b)　evidence may, with the leave of the court, be given of any matter which, if that person had been called as a witness, could have been put to him in cross-examination as

relevant to his credibility as a witness but of which evidence could not have been adduced by the cross-examining party; and

(c)   evidence tending to prove that that person, whether before or after making the statement, made (whether oraly or not) some other statement which is inconsistent with it shall be admissible for the purpose of showing that he had contradicted himself.

2.   A statement which is given in evidence by virtue of part II of this Act shall not be capable of corroborating evidence given by the person making it.

3.   In estimating the weight, if any, to be attached to such a statement regard shall be had to all the circumstances from which any inference can reasonably be drawn as to its accuracy or otherwise.

See, as to the evidence which is admissible under para. 1(a) as relevant to the credibility of a person called as a witness and as to the evidence which, under para. 1(b), may be put in cross-examination to a witness, **F7.9** and **F7.19** to **F7.24** and, as to the admissibility of previous inconsistent statements, under para. 1(c), **F7.20**. Note that an imputation against a person whose statement is relied on by the prosecution under the 1988 Act may lead to the loss of the accused's shield under the Criminal Evidence Act 1898, s. 1(f) (*Miller* [1997] 2 Cr App R 178: see **F14.28**).

PRE-TRIAL STATEMENTS OF WITNESSES

Statements made for the purpose of criminal proceedings and are the subject of various common-law and statutory exceptions to the hearsay rule, but may also be admissible under the CJA 1988, s. 23 or s. 24 (see **F16.3** to **F16.13**).

Committal Statements Admissible at Trial

F16.19   The CPIA 1996 makes far-reaching provision for the admissibility of statements at committal (see **D7.9** *et seq*.). One consequence of that provision is that ss. 23 and 24 of the CJA 1988 cease to apply in committal proceedings (CPIA 1996, sch. 1, paras 28 and 29). Under sch. 2 to the 1996 Act (set out at **D7.17**), statements and depositions which have been admitted at committal are automatically admissible at trial, except that the court has a discretion to exclude the evidence and a party to the proceedings may object to its admission, although the court has a statutory power to order that the objection be of no effect if it is in the interests of justice so to order.

Transcript Admissible at Retrial

F16.20   **Criminal Appeal Act 1968, sch. 2, paras 1 and 1A**

1.   On a retrial, paragraphs 1 and 2 of schedule 2 to the Criminal Procedure and Investigations Act 1996 (use of written statements and depositions) shall not apply to any written statement or deposition read as evidence at the original trial; but a transcript of the record of the evidence given by any witness at the original trial may, with the leave of the judge, be read as evidence—
(a)   by agreement between the prosecution and the defence; or
(b)   if the judge is satisfied that the witness is dead or unfit to give evidence or to attend for that purpose, or that all reasonable efforts to find him or to secure his attendance have been made without success,
and in either case may be so read without further proof, if verified in accordance with rules of court.
1A.   Subject to paragraph 1 above, evidence given orally at the original trial must be given orally at the retrial.

For the provisions of sch. 2 to the 1996 Act, see **D7.17**. The provisions of sch. 2 reaffirm and clarify a wider common-law rule: see *Thompson* [1982] QB 647, in which it was held that the transcript of evidence of a witness might be read out at a retrial upon proof that she was too ill to travel, notwithstanding that the retrial was not ordered by the Court of Appeal under the 1968 Act. Similarly, in *Hall* [1973] 1 QB 496, it was held that a transcript of evidence is admissible at common law at a retrial if the witness has since died, provided it is authenticated in appropriate manner, e.g., by calling the shorthand writer who took the original note. The trial judge has a discretion to exclude such evidence if it would be unfair to the accused to admit it, and a 'powerful factor' in deciding whether to exercise the discretion is the lack of opportunity on the part of the second jury to observe the demeanour of the witness. In *Lockley* [1995] 2 Cr App R 554, a transcript of evidence was also held to be admissible under the CJA 1988, ss. 23 and 24 (considered at **F16.2** to **F16.17**).

Video Recordings of Children's Evidence

The provisions considered below will be replaced upon the coming into force of chapter **F16.21** I of part II of the YJCEA 1999. The Act brings together a number of special measures for protecting vulnerable witnesses when giving their evidence. The possibility of video-recording evidence in chief is retained (s. 27) and extended to a wider range of witnesses, including adult victims of distressing offences such as rape, and adults suffering from physical or mental incapacity. The Act also introduces for the first time the possibility of pre-recorded cross-examination (s. 28) where video-recording is the medium by which evidence in chief is to be given. This should enable some witnesses to be spared altogether from the experience of participation in the trial proper. The evidence of children in sexual cases and cases involving violence is most likely to be received in this way, unless the child wishes otherwise (ss. 19(7)(b) and 22). These provisions are unlikely to be brought into force before the end of 2000. Detailed consideration of the provisions described above will be found in the next edition of this work.

The CJA 1991, s. 54, made a significant change in the admissibility of hearsay evidence from child witnesses by adding s. 32A to the CJA 1988. It provides that, in trials on indictment and in youth courts for the offences to which s. 32 of that Act applies (see **D12.30** and *Lee* [1996] 2 Cr App R 266 and *McAndrew-Bingham* [1999] 1 WLR 1897) and in appeals from such proceedings, a pre-recorded interview between an adult and a child (as defined by s. 32A(7)) who is not the accused is admissible as evidence of anything of which the child could have given evidence in chief. (As to the competence of very young children, see **F4.17**.) The admissibility of recordings under other rules of evidence, e.g., under the CJA 1988, s. 23 (see **F16.3**), is not prejudiced (s. 32A(12)).

The object of the new provision is to reduce the trauma associated with the giving of evidence by the very young, and it is envisaged that in time this will become the normal method by which children give their evidence. Where a pre-recorded interview is admitted, the child will be called as a witness by the party tendering the recording in evidence but will not be examined in chief on any matter which has been adequately dealt with in the recorded testimony. The child will, however, be cross-examined 'live' at the trial. (As to the adminstering of an oath to witnesses over the age of 14, see **F4.22**.) An amendment to s. 32 of the 1988 Act (see **D12.30**) ensures that the live-link apparatus will be available in respect of any witness who is to be cross-examined following the admission under s. 32A of a video recording of testimony from him (CJA 1991, s. 55(2)).

Although a video recording tendered under s. 32A is admissible only with leave of the court, s. 32A(3) provides that leave should be given unless the child is not available for cross-examination, or rules of court requiring disclosure of the circumstances in which the recording was made have not been satisfactorily complied with, or in the interests of justice the recording ought not to be admitted. The same subsection empowers the court to exclude any part of the recording, but s. 32A(4) operates as a disincentive to do this except in the case where the prejudice created by the admission of the whole outweighs the desirability of showing the whole recording.

Under the CPIA 1996, s. 62, a pre-trial ruling giving leave to admit a video recording will be binding in that the child may not then be called to give evidence-in-chief in any other form, unless the court subsequently considers it to be in the interests of justice that he should do so. If a child has been prepared for trial on the basis that the recording will be shown, it is unfortunate for the child to be faced with the ordeal of giving evidence in a different way. An example of a case in which a change may be in the interests of justice may be derived from *Parker* [1995] Crim LR 511, in which the child was known to have retracted the allegation made on the recording, and it was held that the trial judge should not have allowed it to be shown but should instead have directed that the child give evidence in court or via the live-link so that the jury were not affected by seeing the retracted evidence.

The provisions of s. 32A are supplemented by the *Memorandum of Good Practice on Video Recorded Interviews with Child Witnesses for Criminal Proceedings*, a non-statutory code of practice. Part 3B of the memorandum is particularly relevant in that it deals with the legal constraints on an interview, and in particular with the use of leading questions and the inclusion of references to previous statements or the bad character of the accused. The memorandum is voluntary and non-compliance does not render an interview inadmissible unless it would be contrary to the interests of justice to admit it under s. 32A(3). In *G* v *DPP* [1998] QB 919 the Divisional Court held that whether failure to comply with the memorandum should lead to the exclusion of video evidence was not necessarily a question which could be answered simply by considering the nature and extent of the breaches which had occurred. Amongst other factors on which the decision to admit might depend were the extent to which passages in the evidence affected by the breaches were supported by other passages which were not so affected, and the presence or absence of other corroborating evidence. The defence had submitted that the 'substantial and significant' breaches which had allegedly occurred were enough to require exclusion, and the court's rejection of this approach signals a clear (and, it is submitted, correct) distinction between the memorandum on the one hand, and on the other the PACE Codes of Practice, under which such breaches may well lead to discretionary exclusion. In *G* the breaches went only to the weight to be given to the evidence.

Where a jury has seen a recording as evidence in chief, the judge has a discretion to accede to their request to see it again by permitting it to be replayed in court (*Rawlings* [1995] 1 WLR 178), provided that a warning is given that other evidence cannot be replayed, and the jury are reminded of what the child said in cross-examination and in re-examination (safeguards not observed in *M* [1995] Crim LR 336 and *B* [1996] Crim LR 499). A replay may be desirable because the jury requires to be reminded of how the witness gave evidence, rather than of what was said: in the latter case the judge can remind them from his own note. It is only in exceptional circumstances that a video should be replayed otherwise than at the request of the jury (*M* [1996] 2 Cr App R 56). A transcript may be a valuable tool to allow the jury to follow what is said on the tape, provided that it is made clear that the transcript itself is not evidence (*Welstead* [1996] 1 Cr App R 59; *Morris* [1998] Crim LR 416). Similar considerations may affect the replaying of tapes in the magistrates' court. In *L and B* v *DPP* [1998] 2 Cr App R 69 the Divisional Court declined to lay down the precise procedure to be followed if the tape is to be replayed, but *Rawlings* was cited with approval. It is submitted that the same guidelines should apply, and in particular that nothing should be done which might give the impression that the court has received a double measure of the taped evidence whilst hearing the other side only once. (As to the replaying of a tape which was initially used by the defence to show inconsistencies in the witness's taped evidence in chief, see *Eldridge* [1999] Crim LR 166.)

Where a video recording is admitted in evidence, a particularly careful direction may be required concerning any specific problems alleged by the defence to exist in relation to the quality of the evidence (*Springer* [1996] Crim LR 903, where the child's account was alleged to be based on hearsay).

Criminal Justice Act 1988, s. 32A

(1)   This section applies in relation to the following proceedings, namely—

(a)   trials on indictment for any offence to which section 32(2) above applies;

(b)   appeals to the criminal division of the Court of Appeal and hearings of references under section 17 of the Criminal Appeal Act 1968 in respect of any such offence; and

(c)   proceedings in youth courts for any such offence and appeals to the Crown Court arising out of such proceedings.

(2)   In any such proceedings a video recording of an interview which—

(a)   is conducted between an adult and a child who is not the accused or one of the accused ('the child witness'); and

(b)   relates to any matter in issue in the proceedings,

may, with the leave of the court, be given in evidence in so far as it is not excluded by the court under subsection (3) below.

(3)   Where a video recording is tendered in evidence under this section, the court shall (subject to the exercise of any power of the court to exclude evidence which is otherwise admissible) give leave under subsection (2) above unless—

(a)   it appears that the child witness will not be available for cross-examination;

(b)   any rules of court requiring disclosure of the circumstances in which the recording was made have not been complied with to the satisfaction of the court; or

(c)   the court is of the opinion, having regard to all the circumstances of the case, that in the interests of justice the recording ought not to be admitted;

and where the court gives such leave it may, if it is of the opinion that in the interests of justice any part of the recording ought not to be admitted, direct that that part shall be excluded.

(4)   In considering whether any part of a recording ought to be excluded under subsection (3) above, the court shall consider whether any prejudice to the accused, or one of the accused, which might result from the admission of that part is outweighed by the desirability of showing the whole, or substantially the whole, of the recorded interview.

(5)   Where a video recording is admitted under this section—

(a)   the child witness shall be called by the party who tendered it in evidence;

(b)   that witness shall not be examined in chief on any matter which, in the opinion of the court, has been adequately dealt with in his recorded testimony.

(6)   Where a video recording is given in evidence under this section, any statement made by the child witness which is disclosed by the recording shall be treated as if given by that witness in direct oral testimony; and accordingly—

(a)   any such statement shall be admissible evidence of any fact of which such testimony from him would be admissible;

(b)   no such statement shall be capable of corroborating any other evidence given by him;

and in estimating the weight, if any, to be attached to such a statement, regard shall be had to all the circumstances from which an inference can reasonably be drawn (as to its accuracy or otherwise).

(6A)   Where the court gives leave under subsection (2) above the child witness shall not give relevant evidence (within the meaning given by subsection (6D) below) otherwise than by means of the video recording; but this is subject to subsection (6B) below.

(6B)   In a case falling within subsection (6A) above the court may give permission for the child witness to give relevant evidence (within the meaning given by subsection (6D) below) otherwise than by means of the video recording if it appears to the court to be in the interests of justice to give such permission.

(6C)   Permission may be given under subsection (6B) above—

(a)   on an application by a party to the case, or

(b)   of the court's own motion;

but no application may be made under paragraph (a) above unless there has been a material change of circumstances since the leave was given under subsection (2) above.

(6D)   For the purposes of subsections (6A) and (6B) above evidence is relevant evidence if—

(a)   it is evidence in chief on behalf of the party who tendered the video recording, and

(b)   it relates to matter which, in the opinion of the court, is dealt with in the recording and which the court has not directed to be excluded under subsection (3) above.

(7)   In this section 'child' means a person who—

(a)   in the case of an offence falling within section 32(2)(a) or (b) above, is under fourteen years of age or, if he was under that age when the video recording was made, is under fifteen years of age; or

(b)   in the case of an offence falling within section 32(2)(c) above, is under seventeen years of age or, if he was under that age when the video recording was made, is under eighteen years of age.

(8)   Any reference in subsection (7) above to an offence falling within paragraph (a), (b) or (c) of section 32(2) above includes a reference to an offence which consists of attempting or conspiring to commit, or of aiding, abetting, counselling, procuring or inciting the commission of, an offence falling within that paragraph.

(9)   In this section—

'statement' includes any representation of fact, whether made in words or otherwise;

'video recording' means any recording, on any medium, from which a moving image may by any means be produced and includes the accompanying sound track.

(10)   A magistrates' court inquiring into an offence as examining justices under section 6 of the Magistrates' Courts Act 1980 may consider any video recording as respects which leave under subsection (2) above is to be sought at the trial.

(11)   [Power to make rules of court.]

(12)   Nothing in this section shall prejudice the admissibility of any video recording which would be admissible apart from this section.

Practice Direction (Crime: Child's Video Evidence) [1992] 1 WLR 839

1.   The procedure for making application for leave to adduce a video recording of testimony from a child witness under s. 32A of the Criminal Justice Act 1988, as inserted by s. 54 of the Criminal Justice Act 1991, is laid down in r. 23C of the Crown Court Rules 1982 (SI 1982 No. 1109), as inserted by the Crown Court (Amendment) Rules 1992 (SI 1992 No. 1847).

2.   Where a court grants leave to admit a video recording in evidence under s. 32A(2) of the 1988 Act it may direct that any part of the recording be excluded (s. 32A(3)). When such a direction is given, the party who made the application to admit the video recording must edit the recording in accordance with the judge's directions and send a copy of the edited recording to the appropriate officer of the Crown Court and to every other party to the proceedings.

3.   Where a video recording is to be adduced during proceedings before the Crown Court, it should be produced and proved by the interviewer, or any other person who was present at the interview with the child at which the recording was made. The applicant should ensure that such a person will be available for this purpose, unless the parties have agreed to accept a written statement in lieu of attendance by that person.

4.   It is for the party adducing the video recording to make arrangements for the operation of the video playing equipment in court during the trial.

5.   Once a trial has begun, if by reason of faulty or inadequate preparation or for some other cause the procedures set out above have not been properly complied with, and an application is made to edit the video recording, thereby making necessary an adjournment for the work to be carried out, the court may make at its discretion an appropriate award of costs.

Deposition of Child or Young Person

F16.22   **Children and Young Persons Act 1933, s. 43**

Where, in any proceedings in respect of any of the offences mentioned in the first schedule to this Act, the court is satisfied by the evidence of a duly qualified medical practitioner that the attendance before the court of any child or young person in respect of whom the offence is alleged to have been committed would involve serious danger to his life or health, any deposition of the child or young person taken under the Indictable Offences Act 1848, or this part of this Act, shall be admissible in evidence either for or against the accused person without further proof thereof if it purports to be signed by the justice by or before whom it purports to be taken:

> Provided that the deposition shall not be admissible in evidence against the accused person unless it is proved that reasonable notice of the intention to take the deposition has been served upon him and that he or his counsel or solicitor had, or might have had if he had chosen to be present, an opportunity of cross-examining the child or young person making the deposition.

The offences to which the provision relates are:

(a)   the murder or manslaughter of a child or young person, including (by the Suicide Act 1961, sch. 1) aiding, abetting, counselling or procuring the suicide of a child or young person, and infanticide;

(b)   any offence under the OAPA 1861, s. 27 or s. 56, and any offence against a child or young person under s. 5 of that Act;

(c)   common assault or battery;

(d)   any offence under ss. 1, 3, 4, 11, or 23 of the 1933 Act itself;

(e)   any offence against a child or young person under the Sexual Offences Act 1956, ss. 2 to 7, 10 to 16, 19, 20, 22 to 26 and 28, and attempts to commit offences under ss. 2, 5, 6, 7, 10, 11, 12, 22, or 23 of that Act against a child or young person; and

(f)   any other offence involving bodily injury to a child or young person.

See also the Indecency with Children Act 1960, s. 1(3), incorporating offences under s. 1 of that Act, the Protection of Children Act 1978, s. 1(5), incorporating offences under s. 1(1)(a) of that Act, and the CJA 1988, sch. 15, incorporating offences under the Child Abduction Act 1984, part I.

Written Statements Admissible under Criminal Justice Act 1967, s. 9

F16.23 For an account of the provisions of the CJA 1967, s. 9, which deal with the admissibility of written statements, see **D19.5**.

Statements Admissible under Miscellaneous Statutory Provisions

F16.24 Various statutes make provision for the admission of hearsay statements. The following are the most commonly invoked.

Under the CJA 1988, s. 30 (see **F10.14**), the report of an expert witness on matters of which he would have been competent to give oral evidence is admissible as evidence of the facts and opinions stated therein. This provision applies only to 'written' reports so that the admissibility of, say, a tape-recorded report may be in doubt.

Under the CJA 1972, s. 46(1), written statements made in Scotland or Northern Ireland may be admitted as evidence in other criminal proceedings on the same terms as statements made in England and Wales (see **D19.5**).

PUBLIC DOCUMENTS

Admissibility of Public Documents at Common Law

F16.25 A document compiled by a public officer acting under a public duty to inquire and report facts of public interest, which is maintained in order that interested members of the public may have access to the information contained in it, is admissible at common law by way of exception to the hearsay rule as evidence of the facts stated (*Sturla* v *Freccia* (1880) 5 App Cas 623). Thus, for example, registers of baptisms, marriages and funerals are public documents, as are surveys of Crown Lands, and university records may prove the granting of degrees (*Collins* v *Carnegie* (1834) 1 A & E 695). Foreign registers may be public documents if the relevant conditions are satisfied (*Lyell* v *Kennedy* (1889) 14

App Cas 437; *Sturla* v *Freccia*). See also the Evidence (Foreign Dominion and Colonial Documents) Act 1933, s. 1 of which confers a power to declare that certain foreign registers are public documents.

One reason for the rule is the presumption that entries in such documents made by public officers are to be relied upon (*Irish Society* v *Bishop of Derry* (1846) 12 Cl & F 641, per Parke B). However, it is also the case that the rule is based on necessity: were it not for the admissibility of public documents, many facts occurring in the distant past would be incapable of proof.

In modern times the importance of the common-law rule is overshadowed (a) by various statutes rendering particular documents admissible, and (more importantly) (b) by the CJA 1988, s. 24 (see **F16.10**), under which virtually all of the documents which were receivable under the common-law rule, and many that were not, are admissible. Whereas it may continue to be convenient (if only for the sake of convention) to rely on the public documents exception in respect of documents admissible both under the common law and s. 24, it must be remembered that many documents, inadmissible at common law, are now covered by the Act, so that the conditions of admissibility imposed by the common law are of limited importance.

Public Duty

F16.26 The document must have been made in pursuance of what Lord Blackburn termed 'a judicial, or quasi-judicial, duty to inquire' (*Sturla* v *Freccia* (1880) 5 App Cas 623, at p. 643). The duty must be imposed by virtue of a public office: thus, parish registers of baptisms, marriages and burials are public documents, whereas similar records compiled by other religious groups such as the Quakers are not (*Re Woodward* [1913] 1 Ch 392. Older authority strongly supports the view that the document must be made by the very officer whose duty it is to inquire into the facts, and who would therefore have satisfied himself of the truth of the facts stated (see e.g., *Sturla* v *Freccia*), and *Daniel* v *Wilkin* (1852) 7 Exch 429). However, in *Halpin* [1975] QB 907 it was held that the functions of inquirer and recorder could be divided, with the result that the statutory returns of a company kept in the Companies Register were admissible where it appeared that the officer making the return had a duty to inquire, and the Registrar of Companies had the duty to record the results of the inquiry. Geoffrey Lane LJ said (at p. 95): 'The common law should move with the times and should recognise the fact that the official charged with recording matters of public import can no longer in this highly complicated world . . . have personal knowledge of their accuracy.' The decision has been criticised on the grounds that the House of Lords in *Myers* v *DPP* [1965] AC 1001 prohibited further judicial extension of the rules admitting hearsay evidence, but, whatever the merits of the criticism, the evidence would now be admissible by virtue of the CJA 1988, s. 24.

Where a record is kept by a public officer not for the benefit of others, but simply as a check upon himself, it is not a public document (*Merrick* v *Wakley* (1838) 8 A & E 170).

Public Matter

F16.27 The subject-matter of the document need not concern the public as a whole. In *Sturla* v *Freccia* (1880) 5 App Cas 623, Lord Blackburn said (at p. 643): 'I do not think that "public" . . . is to be taken in the sense of meaning the whole world. I think an entry in the books of a manor is public in the sense that it concerns all the people interested in the manor. And an entry probably in a corporation book concerning a corporate matter, or something in which all the corporation is concerned, would be "public" within that sense.' Whether a document deals with a matter of public concern inevitably raises a question of degree, and entries in a corporation's book are not necessarily admissible, despite Lord Blackburn's dictum (see, e.g., *Hill* v *Manchester & Salford Waterworks Co.* (1833) 5 B & Ad 866). Documents which do not comply with this condition are likely to be admissible under the CJA 1988, s. 24.

Public Reference

Documents which are not maintained for the use of such members of the public as may **F16.28** need to refer to them are not admissible under this exception. In *Lilley* v *Pettit* [1946] KB 401, P was prosecuted for falsely stating that her husband was the father of her child. It was held that regimental records showing that the husband was a prisoner of war abroad when the child was conceived were inadmissible because they were not intended for the use of the public. See also *Ioannou* v *Demetriou* [1952] AC 84.

For the same reason, a record which is maintained for a temporary purpose cannot be received under this exception (*Mercer* v *Denne* [1905] 2 Ch 538; *Heyne* v *Fischel & Co.* (1913) 30 TLR 190), although there would be no such objection to its reception in evidence under the CJA 1988, s. 24.

Other Registers etc. Admissible by Statute

Some entries in registers are admissible as public documents (see **F16.25**). In many **F16.29** cases, however, statute makes express provision for the admissibility of particular registers. Detailed consideration of such provisions is beyond the scope of this work, and readers are referred to the comprehensive account in Chapter 31 of *Phipson on Evidence*, 14th. ed.

Of particular importance are the provisions of the Births and Deaths Registration Act 1953, s. 34, the text of which is set out at **F8.15**. See also the Non-Parochial Registers Act 1840, s. 6, under which certain records and registers deposited in the General Register Office in accordance with that Act are admissible, and the Births and Deaths Registration Act 1858.

An entry in a register showing that a person has died is admissible evidence of the fact and date of death, but not of the cause of death (*Bird* v *Keep* [1918] 2 KB 692). Where a birth certificate is relied upon to prove some fact contained in it, the evidence may be of no use unless it can be proved that the person named in it is the same individual with whom the court is concerned. This is difficult to establish without breaking the hearsay rule, for the person named cannot himself give evidence that the certificate appertains to him. A person who was present at the birth may establish identity (*Weaver* (1873) LR 2 CCR 85), though such proof may be hard to come by. It is not surprising that, in some cases, hearsay evidence has been admitted: see, e.g., *Bellis* (1911) 6 Cr App R 283, in which the court admitted evidence of inquiries made about the girl whose age was in issue, which had led the inquirer to be satisfied as to her identity.

BANKERS' BOOKS

Section 3 of the Bankers' Books Evidence Act 1879 (see **F8.27**) was designed to **F16.30** facilitate proof of bankers' records without bringing the original document to court. As the provision is confined to copies, nothing in s. 3 renders the original banker's book admissible: in most cases, however, the original would now be admissible under the CJA 1988, s. 24, and a copy would be admissible by virtue of s. 27 of that Act. Before a copy can be given in evidence under s. 3 of the 1879 Act, s. 4 of that Act requires proof to be given that the banker's book was at the time of the relevant entry one of the ordinary books of the bank, that the entry was made in the usual and ordinary course of business, and that the book is in the custody or control of the bank. If s. 24 of the CJA 1988 is relied upon, no such conditions need be satisfied. It should also be noted that the 1879

Act confines itself to the various books and records of a bank. In *Dadson* (1983) 77 Cr App R 91, which concerned events which occurred before the 1879 Act was amended to include records, it was held that a file of correspondence was inadmissible under s. 3 as not being a 'book'. The correspondence would now be admissible under the 1879 Act only if it is held to constitute a 'record', whereas the 1988 Act imposes no such constraint.

As to the practice surrounding inspection of bankers' books and their relationship to the best evidence rule, see generally **F8.27**.

STATEMENTS FORMING PART OF *RES GESTAE*

Spontaneous Statements in Response to Exciting Events

F16.31 '*Res gestae*' is an inappropriate label for this common-law exception to the hearsay rule, in which admissibility depends on proof of what Lord Ackner in *Andrews* [1987] AC 281 called the 'close and intimate connection' between the exciting events in issue and the making of the statement, the theory being that the spontaneity of the utterance is some guarantee against concoction. The nomenclature has in the past led to confusion and to incorrect decisions, but *Andrews* clarified the law by approving the test for admissibility adopted by the Privy Council in *Ratten* v *The Queen* [1972] AC 378. In *Mills* v *The Queen* [1995] 1 WLR 511, the Privy Council praised the changes effected by these decisions, regarding *res gestae* as a modernised exception to the hearsay rule under which the focus was on the probative value of evidence rather than on the question whether it falls within some artificial and rigid category.

In *Ratten* v *The Queen*, Lord Wilberforce described the rule under which spontaneous statements are admitted in the following way (at p. 389–90):

> A hearsay statement is made either by the victim of an attack or by a bystander – indicating directly or indirectly the identity of the attacker. The admissibility of the statement is then said to depend on whether it was made as part of the *res gestae*. A classical instance of this is the much-debated case of *Bedingfield* (1879) 14 Cox CC 341, and there are other instances of its application in reported cases. These tend to apply different standards, and some of them carry less than conviction. The reason why this is so, is that concentration tends to be focused upon the opaque or at least imprecise Latin phrase rather than upon the basic reason for excluding the type of evidence which this group of cases is concerned with. There is no doubt what this reason is: it is twofold. The first is that there may be uncertainty as to the exact words used because of their transmission through the evidence of another person than the speaker. The second is because of the risk of concoction of false evidence by persons who have been victims of assault or accident. The first matter goes to weight. The person testifying to the words used is liable to cross-examination: the accused person (as he could not at the time when earlier reported cases were decided) can give his own account if different. There is no such difference in kind or substance between evidence of what was said and evidence of what was done (for example between evidence of what the victim said as to an attack and evidence that he (or she) was seen in a terrified state or was heard to shriek) as to require a total rejection of one and admission of the other.
>
> The possibility of concoction, or fabrication, where it exists, is on the other hand an entirely valid reason for exclusion, and is probably the real test which judges in fact apply. In their lordships' opinion this should be recognised and applied directly as the relevant test: the test should be not the uncertain one whether the making of the statement was in some sense part of the event or transaction. This may often be difficult to establish: such external matters as the time which elapses between the events and the speaking of the words (or vice versa), and differences in location being relevant factors but not, taken by themselves, decisive criteria. As regards statements made after the event it must be for the judge, by preliminary ruling, to satisfy himself that the statement was so clearly made in circumstances of spontaneity or involvement in the event that the possibility of concoction can

be disregarded. Conversely, if he considers that the statement was made by way of narrative of a detached prior event so that the speaker was so disengaged from it as to be able to construct or adapt his account, he should exclude it. And the same must in principle be true of statements made before the event. The test should be not the uncertain one, whether the making of the statement should be regarded as part of the event or transaction. This may often be difficult to show. But if the drama, leading up to the climax, has commenced and assumed such intensity and pressure that the utterance can safely be regarded as a true reflection of what was unrolling or actually happening, it ought to be received. The expression '*res gestae*' may conveniently sum up these criteria, but the reality of them must always be kept in mind: it is this that lies behind the best reasoned of the judges' rulings.

Lord Wilberforce's reasoning led him to doubt the correctness of the decision in *Bedingfield* (1879) 14 Cox CC 341, in which the statement of a woman whose throat had been cut a few moments before was rejected, on the ground that it was made after the act to which it related was done. Of this, Lord Wilberforce said (at p. 390) that 'there could hardly be a case where the speaker's words carried more clearly the mark of spontaneity and intense involvement'. In *Andrews* [1987] AC 281, the House of Lords overruled *Bedingfield*, on the ground that it was inconsistent with the true principle as laid down by Lord Wilberforce in *Ratten v The Queen* [1972] AC 378. *Bedingfield* had previously been approved by the Privy Council in *Teper v The Queen* [1952] AC 480. See also *Christie* [1914] AC 545, per Lord Reading, and *Gibson* (1887) 18 QBD 537. These and other statements of the law involving the application of the discredited test must also be regarded as no longer authoritative.

In *Andrews* [1987] AC 281, the House of Lords accepted and applied the law as stated in *Ratten v The Queen*. A was charged with the murder by stabbing of M, who was attacked by two men in his own home. Within minutes neighbours called the police, who arrived promptly, whereupon M made a statement identifying his attackers. The trial judge admitted the statement and, in a ruling regarded as 'impeccable' both by the Court of Appeal and the House of Lords, he held that there was no possibility in the circumstances of concoction or fabrication of the identification, and that the injuries sustained by M were of such a nature as to drive out any possibility of his being actuated by malice. He also took account of the fact that M correctly identified the other attacker as O, who had subsequently pleaded guilty to manslaughter. Lord Ackner summarised the position which confronts a trial judge when faced in a criminal case with an application under the *res gestae* doctrine to admit evidence of statements, with a view to establishing the truth of some fact thus narrated. He said (at pp. 300–301):

1. The primary question which the judge must ask himself is – can the possibility of concoction or distortion be disregarded?
2. To answer that question the judge must first consider the circumstances in which the particular statement was made, in order to satisfy himself that the event was so unusual or startling or dramatic as to dominate the thoughts of the victim, so that his utterance was an instinctive reaction to that event, thus giving no real opportunity for reasoned reflection. In such a situation the judge would be entitled to conclude that the involvement or the pressure of the event would exclude the possibility of concoction or distortion, providing that the statement was made in conditions of approximate but not exact contemporaneity.
3. In order for the statement to be sufficiently 'spontaneous' it must be so closely associated with the event which has excited the statement, that it can be fairly stated that the mind of the declarant was still dominated by the event. Thus the judge must be satisfied that the event which provided the trigger mechanism for the statement, was still operative. The fact that the statement was made in answer to a question is but one factor to consider under this heading.
4. Quite apart from the time factor, there may be special features in the case, which relate to the possibility of concoction or distortion. In the instant appeal the defence relied on evidence to support the contention that the deceased had a motive of his own to fabricate or concoct, namely, a malice which resided in him against O'Neill and the appellant

because, so he believed, O'Neill had attacked and damaged his house and was accompanied by the appellant, who ran away on a previous occasion. The judge must be satisfied that the circumstances were such that having regard to the special feature of malice, there was no possibility of any concoction or distortion to the advantage of the maker or the disadvantage of the accused.

5.   As to the possibility of error in the facts narrated in the statement, if only the ordinary fallibility of human recollection is relied upon, this goes to the weight to be attached to and not the admissibility of the statement and is therefore a matter for the jury. However, here again there may be special features that may give rise to the possibility of error. In the instant case there was evidence that the deceased had drunk to excess, well over double the permitted limit for driving a motor car. Another example would be where the identification was made in circumstances of particular difficulty or where the declarant suffered from defective eyesight. In such circumstances the trial judge must consider whether he can exclude the possibility of error.

Some of the difficulties surrounding identification referred to by Lord Ackner arose and were considered in *Turnbull* (1984) 80 Cr App R 104 (see **F16.33**).

Prior to the decision in *Andrews*, it had been held, in *Nye* (1977) 66 Cr App R 252, that the possibility of error by the maker of the statement was an 'additional factor to be taken into consideration' when determining admissibility. It is now clear from the extract from the speech of Lord Ackner in *Andrews* set out above, that the risk of error bears on the question of admissibility only in cases having 'special features', e.g., an identification in difficult circumstances or by a person with defective eyesight, or by someone who had been drinking. In *Nye*, one Lucas was driving his car when it was struck from behind by another vehicle in which the accused, N and L, were travelling. One of the accused then got out and punched Lucas in the face, while the other tried to put a stop to the assault. Shortly afterwards, when the police arrived, Lucas spontaneously identified L as the man who had hit him. It was argued that Lucas might have made a mistake as to which of the accused had attacked him. On these facts the Court of Appeal considered that there was no chance of an error, stressing in particular that: 'anyone who has been assaulted usually has good reason for remembering what his assailant's face looks like'. It is therefore unlikely that, applying the test in *Andrews*, special circumstances such as the great stress immediately after a motor accident, will be held to affect the admissibility of evidence. The fact that the maker of the statement had been drinking, though capable of being a 'special feature', does not necessarily lead to exclusion. In *Andrews* the deceased had 'drunk to excess', and in *Edwards* [1992] Crim LR 576 the Divisional Court held that a spontaneous allegation of theft of a wallet made against E by A, who was drunk, was admissible.

The event which generates the statement admitted under the rule stated above, must be the commission of the offence in question. This is implicit in both *Ratten* v *The Queen* and *Andrews*, and is expressly stated by Lord Normand in *Teper* v *The Queen* [1952] AC 480, who said (at p. 488): 'for identification purposes in a criminal trial the event with which the words sought to be proved must be so connected as to form part of the *res gestae*, is the commission of the crime itself, the throwing of the stone, the striking of the blow, the setting fire to the building or whatever the criminal act might be'.

A *res gestae* statement will typically have been made by the victim of the offence, or a bystander, but may also, if the conditions of admissibility are satisfied, be made by the accused himself (*Glover* [1991] Crim LR 48).

F16.32   ***Statement Not to be Used as Substitute for Available Witness***   In *Andrews* [1987] AC 281, Lord Ackner observed (at p. 302): 'I would, however, strongly deprecate any attempt in criminal prosecutions to use the doctrine as a device to avoid calling, where he is available, the maker of the statement. Thus to deprive the defence of the opportunity to cross-examine him, would not be consistent with the fundamental duty of the prosecution to place all the relevant material facts before the court, so as to ensure that justice is done'. Lord Ackner's dictum was applied in *Tobi* v *Nicholas* [1988] RTR 343, considered at **F16.33**.

It does not follow from this rule that the *res gestae* exception has no application where the witness is available to give evidence. In *Shickle* (30 July 1997 unreported), S was charged with murder and evidence was given by his teenage son, A, who had witnessed the event. It was held that A's evidence was properly supplemented by spontaneous statements he made at the time, such as 'Mummy's putting needles in the old boy' and 'Hurry up, we've got to stop Mummy'. Although spontaneous statements are often introduced under this exception because the declarant is dead, or is for some other reason unable to give first-hand evidence, the court could find no reason of principle why the evidence should be withheld when the declarant is available. It was further held that the statement, when admitted, goes not only to the truth of the matter but to the consistency of the maker, on the basis that the greater purpose includes the lesser; the court endorsed a passage to this effect in *Cross and Tapper on Evidence* (8th ed., p. 295). It is submitted that the court's approach is entirely correct.

Illustrations of Application of Rule In *Turnbull* (1984) 80 Cr App R 104, a man who **F16.33** had been mortally wounded staggered into the bar of a public house. In the minutes before an ambulance arrived, and in the ambulance on the way to hospital, various witnesses thought that they heard the victim state, in answer to the question who had stabbed him, that it was 'Ronnie Tommo'. The deceased had a strong Scottish accent and the prosecution case was that he in fact said 'Turnbull'. The statements were admitted, and it was held to be irrelevant that the deceased went on to mutter other words which the witnesses were unable to understand, for: 'If a man is asked a straight question . . . and he gives an answer . . . the fact that he mumbles something afterwards, or is trying to say something when he loses consciousness cannot make the completeness of what he has just said incomplete so that it cannot be used in evidence' (per O'Connor LJ, at p. 111). (Compare the rule with regard to dying declarations, at **F16.38** to **F16.43**).

In *O'Shea* (24 July 1986 unreported), which was considered in *Andrews* [1987] AC 281, the elderly occupier of a second-floor flat into which O was trying to break, slipped while trying to escape through a window and sustained injuries which eventually resulted in his death. He was found lying where he had fallen an hour or so after the incident, and the statement which he then made, in which he stated the reason for his injuries, was admitted in evidence. By contrast, in *Newport* [1998] Crim LR 581 a telephone call made by N's wife 20 minutes before he inflicted fatal injuries on her, in which she arranged to take sanctuary in a friend's house if she had to flee in a hurry, was held to have been wrongly admitted. On the facts there was an insufficient connection between the incident and the wife's request: the call was not a spontaneous and unconsidered reaction to an immediately impending emergency. In all probability the evidence might have been admitted if restricted to an account of the wife's contemporaneous state of emotion and agitation, either because such evidence is not within the hearsay rule at all or because, if it is, it falls within the exception for statements of contemporaneous feelings (see **F15.7** and **F16.36**).

In *Tobi* v *Nicholas* [1988] RTR 343, a collision occurred between a car and a stationary motor coach. Some 20 minutes later the driver of the coach, who had summoned the police, identified T as the driver of the car involved. The coach driver was not called to give evidence at the trial, and the Divisional Court held, applying *Andrews* [1987] AC 281, that there were three reasons why his statement should not have been admitted as part of the *res gestae*:

(a)   The event which had occurred was not so unusual or dramatic as to dominate the thoughts of the victim. 'Of course anybody whose vehicle has been damaged is annoyed about it, but there is a world of difference between such an unfortunately commonplace situation and the thoughts of somebody who has been assaulted and stabbed' (per Glidewell LJ, at p. 356).

(b)   The statement was not sufficiently contemporaneous with the event.

(c)   The *res gestae* doctrine should not be used as a device to avoid calling the maker of the statement where he is available, as the coach driver was, to give evidence.

F16.34   ***Use of Statement itself to Determine Admissibility***   In *Ratten* v *The Queen* [1972] AC 378, Lord Wilberforce said (at p. 391) that in principle it would not be right for the involvement of the speaker in the pressure of the drama surrounding the event to be proved only by the statement itself, 'otherwise the statement would be lifting itself into the area of admissibility'. However, it was difficult to imagine a case where there was no other evidence to connect the speaker to the event, and it would not be wrong in principle for the judge to take the statement into account, together with other things, in reaching his decision.

F16.35   ***Direction to Jury***   In *Andrews* [1987] AC 281, Lord Ackner said that where a 'spontaneous' statement has been admitted in evidence as part of the *res gestae*, the judge must make it clear to the jury:

(a)   that it is for them to decide what was said and to be sure that the witnesses were not mistaken in what they believed had been said to them;

(b)   that they must be satisfied that the declarant did not concoct or distort to his advantage or to the disadvantage of the accused the statement relied on, and where there is material to raise the issue, that he was not activated by any malice or ill-will;

(c)   where there are special features that bear on the possibility of mistake, then the jury's attention must be invited to those matters.

In *Mills* v *The Queen* [1995] 1 WLR 511, the Privy Council rejected an argument that a specific direction must always be given as to the risk of mistaken identification by a dying man in a *res gestae* statement. The jury in that case had been adequately directed about the risks of mistaken identification in relation to the evidence of other witnesses, and fairness did not require a repetition.

Statements of Contemporaneous Bodily or Mental Feelings

F16.36   The statements of a person in which he relates his contemporaneous bodily feelings are admissible to prove the feelings, but not their cause. Thus, in *Nicholas* (1846) 2 Car & Kir 246, Pollock CB said (at p. 248):

> If a man says to his surgeon, 'I have a pain in the head', or in such a part of the body, that is evidence; but, if he says to his surgeon, 'I have a wound'; and was to add, 'I met John Thomas, who had a sword, and ran me through the body with it', that would be no evidence against John Thomas.

Similarly, in *Gloster* (1888) 16 Cox CC 471, statements by a woman who was dying from the effects of an illegal operation, naming the person responsible for her bodily condition, were held inadmissible under this exception. Charles J held (at p. 473) that 'the statements must be confined to contemporaneous symptoms, and nothing in the nature of a narrative is admissible as to who caused them, or how they were caused'. *Gloster* was followed in *Thomson* [1912] 3 KB 19, in which the statements of a woman who had recently suffered a miscarriage and who claimed to have operated upon herself were excluded.

What is contemporaneous is a question of fact. In *Black* (1922) 16 Cr App R 118, B was convicted of the murder by poisoning of his wife. It was held on appeal that her descriptions of symptoms she had suffered after taking medicine given to her by B were admissible only because they were made in B's presence in such a way as to demand an answer from him. (See, as to statements made in the presence of the accused, **F17.48** to **F17.50**.) Had the statements been made behind his back it would, per Avory J, have required 'grave consideration whether they could have been admitted', because they concerned her past, rather than her contemporaneous, feelings. However, Salter J in the course of argument said (at p. 119):

> . . . 'contemporaneous' cannot be confined to feelings experienced at the actual moment when the patient is speaking; it must include such a statement as 'Yesterday I had a pain after meals'.

In the civil case of *Aveson* v *Lord Kinnaird* (1805) 6 East 188, statements made by a woman concerning symptoms from which she claimed to have been suffering for some time were admitted, not only to establish her feelings when the statement was made, but also to establish that she had had the same symptoms when seen by a doctor some days previously.

Where a doctor gives expert evidence as to the condition of a patient, he may not give evidence of past symptoms as they have been narrated to him in order to prove that the symptoms existed, although he may be allowed to state what he was told simply in order to explain the conclusion to which he has come. If the existence of past symptoms is in issue, they must be proved by admissible evidence (*Bradshaw* (1985) 82 Cr App R 79).

In some cases statements indicating contemporaneous feelings may be admissible as original evidence. In *Conde* (1867) 10 Cox CC 547, evidence was admitted that a child who died from starvation had begged a neighbour to give him bread. Of this request Channell B is reported as having said that 'it was not so much a statement as an act. A complaint of hunger was an act; although the particulars of the statement might not be receivable, the fact of the complaint was clearly so'. It is also permissible to prove a contemporaneous statement in which the maker claims to be in a particular mental state, such as fear. In *Vincent* (1840) 9 C & P 275, a policeman was allowed to prove statements made by bystanders at a public meeting who claimed that they were frightened by what took place. In *Edwards* (1872) 12 Cox CC 230, E was charged with the murder of his wife, R, and a neighbour testified that a week before R died she came to the neighbour's house bearing a carving knife and a large axe. Quain J allowed the neighbour to state that R had asked her to take care of the implements as 'my husband always threatens me with these and when they're out of the way I feel safer'. In the light of the authorities stated above, it would seem that R's statement should not have been admitted to prove the cause of her fear, but only (if it were relevant to do so) that she was in a state of trepidation when delivering the weapons.

Evidence of state of mind may also be used to negate inferences which might otherwise be drawn from conduct. In *Gilfoyle* [1996] 1 Cr App R 302, P died by hanging, leaving suicide notes. Evidence that she was not in a suicidal frame of mind was admissible in order to support the prosecution's contention that P had been tricked by her killer into writing the notes.

In recent times there has been a division of opinion as to whether a statement revealing the maker's state of mind is admissible as non-hearsay evidence from which the state of mind may be inferred (*Blastland* [1986] AC 41; *Kearley* [1992] 2 AC 228) or hearsay admissible under an exception to the rule (*Neill* v *North Antrim Magistrates' Court* [1992] 1 WLR 1221; *Gilfoyle* [1996] 1 Cr App R 302). Both views are tenable although the preponderance of modern authority favours the former.

Statements of Present Intention

In various criminal cases statements indicating the present intention of the speaker have **F16.37** been received in evidence, apparently by way of exception to the hearsay rule. In *Buckley*

(1873) 13 Cox CC 293, an inspector of police was permitted to narrate a statement made to him by G, a constable, who said that he intended to go that evening to keep watch on B, whom he suspected of theft. G was later found stabbed to death at some distance from B's cottage, and the statement was relied upon as circumstantial evidence that G had carried out his intention, with fatal consequences. No reason was given for the decision to admit the statement, and it may be that the case is best viewed as involving a declaration made by the deceased G in the course of his duty (as to which see **F16.45**).

In *Moghal* (1977) 65 Cr App R 56, M was charged with the murder of R, and his defence was that the crime was committed by S. It was held that a statement made by S six months before, in which S declared her intention to murder R, was admissible. However, statements which S made to the police after R had been killed, in which she described her state of mind and feelings before and at the time of the killing, were rejected as inadmissible hearsay on the ground that 'the condition precedent to the admissibility of such statements is that they should relate to the maker's contemporaneous state of mind or emotion'. What is contemporaneous was said to be a question of degree, but what was said in the course of police investigations occurred far too long after the event to be admitted. Where non-contemporaneous declarations are self-serving there is an additional reason for excluding them, for such declarations might otherwise be used to construct a fraudulent defence (*Petcherini* (1855) 7 Cox CC 79).

Moghal was doubted by the House of Lords in *Blastland* [1986] AC 41, but only on the ground that the isolated declaration of intention made six months before the murder was insufficiently relevant to be admitted. See also *Wainwright* (1875) 13 Cox CC 171, in which W was charged with the murder of a girl, and the prosecution were not allowed to prove that the victim had announced her intention of going to W's premises on the night she died. Cockburn CJ said that the girl's statement was 'only a statement of intention which might or might not be carried out'.

The existence of a hearsay exception for statements of intention seems to have been overlooked in *Thomson* [1912] 3 KB 19, in which the statement of a woman made before she suffered a miscarriage, and in which she declared her intention to operate upon herself, was rejected as inadmissible hearsay. The statement was said not to form part of the *res gestae*, in the sense that it was not a spontaneous statement connected with the operation itself. The possibility that it might be admissible as a declaration of intention does not appear to have been canvassed.

More recently, in *Callender* [1998] Crim LR 337, the Court of Appeal refused to admit statements made by C two weeks before his arrest for conspiring to commit arson, in which he told an acquaintance that his intention was limited to making dummy devices, resembling explosives, which could be used to attract publicity to the cause of animal rights without actually causing damage to property. This mirrored his defence at trial and, if true, was an answer to the charge. C did not give evidence, however, and the court appears to have been concerned that his statement, if admitted, would have permitted C to raise a reasonable doubt about the prosecution case in a manner contrary to the principles of s. 35 of the CJPOA 1994 (see **F19.12**). But the adverse inferences which the statute permits if an accused fails to testify could still be drawn where his *res gestae* statement is admissible. The reason given for rejection was that the *res gestae* rule was in fact a single principle governed by the decisions in *Andrews* [1987] AC 281 and *Ratten* v *The Queen* [1972] AC 378 (see **F16.31**). C's statement was thus ruled inadmissible because it was not made in circumstances whereby the possibility of concoction or distortion could be disregarded. It is submitted that this is not the case. The true reason for admitting evidence of a statement revealing the maker's intention or other state of mind, or bodily feelings, is the difficulty of proving the matter by other means. Although C's statement was self-serving, and there was a possibility that he was setting up a defence for himself, it was made when he had no inkling that he was about to be arrested, and might be thought to have had some probative value in relation to his state of mind at the relevant time. Whether it was concocted or not should, under this exception, have been a question for the jury.

STATEMENTS BY DECEASED PERSONS ADMISSIBLE AT COMMON LAW

Of the various exceptions to the hearsay rule recognised at common law, several turned on the unavailability through death of the declarant. Death alone was never a sufficient reason for admitting a statement, however: some further condition, designed to promote reliability, was always attached. In *Bedingfield* (1879) 14 Cox CC 341, Cockburn CJ said (at p. 342): 'I regret that according to the law of England, any statement made by the deceased should not be admissible'. The law of England has now been changed by statute so that the *documentary* hearsay statements of deceased persons are generally available as evidence (see the CJA 1988, part II, at **F16.2** to **F16.18**). Existing exceptions to the hearsay rule are unaffected by the 1988 Act (see s. 28), but it will generally be more convenient to admit evidence under the Act wherever it is possible to do so, rather than to become embroiled with the conditions of admissibility laid down by the common law. As the Act is concerned exclusively with documentary evidence, however, the common law remains of importance with regard to oral statements.

Dying Declarations

A statement made by a person who expects to die is admissible where his death is the **F16.38** subject of the charge, and the circumstances of the death the subject of the dying declaration. The exception is most frequently invoked by the prosecution but applies equally to the defence (see, e.g., *Scaife* (1836) 2 Lew CC 150). In *Mills* v *The Queen* [1995] 1 WLR 511, the Privy Council regarded the exception as in need of re-examination, possibly by reformulation along the lines of the *res gestae* exception (see **F16.31**), with the focus on probative value so as to permit the introduction of a wider range of statements by persons since deceased. In that case, however, the deceased's statement was clearly part of the *res gestae*, so that it was unnecessary to change the exception for dying declarations. (The two rules frequently overlap; the traditional distinctions between them being recently reaffirmed in *Lawson* [1998] Crim LR 883.)

The rule exists because 'it is presumed that no person, who is immediately going into the presence of his Maker, will do so with a lie on his lips' (*Osman* (1881) 15 Cox CC 1, per Lush LJ at p. 3). In *Woodcock* (1789) 1 Leach 500, Eyre CB concluded (at p. 502) that 'a situation so solemn, and so awful, is considered by the law as creating an obligation equal to that which is imposed by a positive oath administered in a court of justice'. There are nevertheless obvious practical differences between dying declarations and statements under oath in court. In *Ashton* (1837) 2 Lew CC 147, Alderson B said: 'though the sanction is the same, the opportunity of investigating the truth is very different, and therefore the accused is entitled to every allowance and benefit that he may have lost by the absence of the opportunity of more full investigation by the means of cross-examination.' In *Nembhard* v *The Queen* [1981] 1 WLR 1515, Sir Owen Woodhouse added (at p. 1518) a further reason for the admission of dying declarations, i.e. 'that it is important in the interests of justice that a person implicated in a killing should be obliged to meet in court the dying accusation of his victim'. (As to the direction to be given to the jury when such evidence is admitted, see **F16.43**.) The onus is on the party tendering the declaration to prove that it is admissible (*Spilsbury* (1835) 7 C & P 187; *Jenkins* (1869) LR 1 CCR 187).

F16.39 ***Requirement of Settled, Hopeless Expectation of Death*** In *Gloster* (1888) 16 Cox CC 471, Charles J summed up the authorities in the following way (at p. 476):

> The result of the decisions upon this subject is this: that there must be an unqualified belief in the nearness of death; there must be a belief without hope in the declarant that he is about to die. The language of the learned judges in the different cases has varied, but that is the result. In one case, for instance, it was laid down that 'every hope of this world must be gone' (Eyre CB, *Woodcock* (1789) 1 Leach 500 at p. 502). In another (*Peel* (1860) 2 F & F 21) Willes J says: 'It must be proved that the man was dying, and there must be a settled hopeless expectation of death in the declarant'.

The important question concerns the state of mind of the declarant. Thus in *Peel* (1860) 2 F & F 21, a declaration was admitted where the declarant had given up hope, even though the surgeons did not consider death to be inevitable; and in *Mosley* (1825) 1 Mood CC 97, a declaration made before the surgeon informed the declarant that he was bound to die was admitted.

If any vestige of hope remains, the statement is inadmissible (*Errington* (1838) 2 Lew CC 148; *Jenkins* (1869) LR 1 CCR 187). An expectation of death may be inferred from the declarant's knowledge of the dire state of his or her condition (*Woodcock* (1789) 1 Leach 500), but the courts have been reluctant to infer an expectation simply because the injury was likely to prove fatal (*Cleary* (1862) 2 F & F 850; *Morgan* (1875) 14 Cox CC 337; *Bedingfield* (1879) 14 Cox CC 341).

Other circumstantial evidence may be relevant. In *Spilsbury* (1835) 7 C & P 187, the declarant's failure to give directions as to his affairs, or to arrange his funeral, or to take leave of his wife was evidence suggesting that he did not believe that death was approaching.

It is not the case that the declarant must expect to die immediately, provided that all hope of life is abandoned (*Austin* (1912) 8 Cr App R 27; *Jenkins* (1869) 11 Cox CC 250; *Perry* [1909] 2 KB 697: *Gloster* (1881) 15 Cox CC 1, which is to the contrary, must be regarded as wrongly decided). Although it was so held in *Osman* (1881) 15 Cox CC 1, the true principle was stated in *Austin* (1912) 8 Cr App R 27, in which Darling J approved of the following statement by the trial judge, Avory J (at p. 28): 'it must be an expectation of death not necessarily immediate, but within a short time. My own opinion is that the last qualification was necessary because it is involved in the hopeless expectation under which alone a statement can be admitted. If a statement is made when all hope of life is abandoned it is immaterial whether the declarant anticipates death within an hour or within a day.'

Provided that the conditions of admissibility are established, it does not matter that the declarant lingers for some time before dying: see, e.g., *Bernadotti* (1869) 11 Cox CC 316, in which the declarant lived for nearly three weeks after making the declaration. Similarly, it does not matter if, after making the statement, the declarant's hopes revive (*Austin* (1912) 8 Cr App R 27, per Darling J).

F16.40 ***Requirement that Death be Subject of Both Charge and Declaration*** In *Mead* (1824) 2 B & C 605, Abbott CJ rejected the dying declaration of a man killed by M because it related only to the charge of perjury for which M was on trial. *Mead* was followed in *Hind* (1860) 8 Cox CC 300, in which Pollock CB rejected a dying declaration on a charge of using instruments with intent to procure miscarriage, saying (at p. 302): 'the reception of this kind of evidence is clearly an anomalous exception in the law of England, which I think ought not to be extended'. In *Newton* (1859) 1 F & F 641, the dying declaration of a woman who killed herself after being raped was rejected on the same ground. See also *Lloyd* (1830) 4 C & P 233 (robbery); *Hutchinson* (1822) 2 B & C 608n (administering savin to procure abortion).

In *Baker* (1837) 2 Mood & R 53, a dying declaration by a person who was not the subject of the charge against B was admitted. The declaration was that of a maid who had baked a cake which contained a poison which killed both her and her master, in which she stated that she had not poisoned the cake, but that B had had the opportunity to do so. B was tried for poisoning the master, and the declaration was admitted by Coltman J on the ground that what had happened 'was all one transaction'.

Competence of Declarant   In *Pike* (1829) 3 C & P 598 the dying declaration of a   F16.41
four-year-old child was ruled inadmissible on the ground that a child of such tender years could not have had that idea of a future state which is necessary to make such a declaration admissible. It might be an alternative ground for objection that the child would, at that time, have been incompetent to testify, but it seems that it is not. In *Perkins* (1840) 9 C & P 395, the declaration of a boy between 10 and 11 was received, the child having stated that he believed he would go to hell if he lied.

Form of Statement   In *Mitchell* (1892) 17 Cox CC 503, Cave J rejected a statement   F16.42
which related the substance of questions put to a dying woman and answers given by her, *inter alia*, because:

(a)   it was not taken down in the exact words the woman had used; and
(b)   there was no record of the form of the questions.

A declaration elicited in response to leading questions might have to be excluded.

It appears that the court must be able to infer that the declaration was complete, or at least substantially so. In *Waugh* v *The King* [1950] AC 203 the declarant fell into a coma while making the statement, and died without regaining consciousness. The declaration was held to be inadmissible on the ground that it was incomplete, 'and no one can tell what the deceased was about to add'. In this case, however, it was clear that the deceased had intended to add something further of significance, since his last word was 'because'.

Direction to Jury   In *Waugh* v *The King* [1950] AC 203 it was held that a jury must   F16.43
be directed to bear in mind that a dying declaration has not been subjected to cross-examination. See also *Jenkins* (1869) LR 1 CCR 187, in which Kelly CB noted the particular risk that the makers of such statements may be very liable to the influences of misrepresentation or error.

In *Nembhard* v *The Queen* [1981] 1 WLR 1515 the Privy Council rejected an argument that a jury should be instructed to look for corroboration of a dying declaration, but stressed (at p. 1518) that the jury must be warned 'to scrutinise with care the necessarily hearsay evidence of what the deceased was alleged to have said both because they have the problem of deciding whether the deponent who has provided the evidence can be relied upon and also because they will have been denied the opportunity of forming a direct impression against the test of cross-examination of the deceased's own reliability'.

In *Lawson* [1998] Crim LR 883 the trial judge (rightly according to the Court of Appeal) acceded to counsel's request to direct the jury to consider whether the declarant was indeed under a settled, hopeless expectation of death when the declaration was made. This would seem to add an unnecessary layer of complexity to the jury's task. Are the deceased's devotional habits also to be regarded as relevant to be put before the jury?

Declarations against Interest

A statement by a deceased person which is, and which is known by him to be, against   F16.44
his pecuniary or proprietary interest at the time it is made is admissible to prove the facts stated. The reason is that a person is unlikely to make such a statement unless it be true (see, e.g., *Ward* v *H.S. Pitt & Co.* [1913] 2 KB 130). Thus, for example, an acknowledgement that money due to the declarant under a bond was not his own, but

was to be held on trust for another, is admissible (*Gleadow* v *Atkin* (1833) 1 Cr & M 410), and so is an acknowledgement of a moral obligation to pay money to another, even though the obligation was not legally enforceable (*Coward* v *Motor Insurers' Bureau* [1963] 1 QB 259). But an acknowledgement of the existence of a contract or similar obligation which is for the mutual benefit of the speaker and the other party is not admissible, as it is not to the declarant's disadvantage to make the statement (*Inhabitants of Worth* (1843) 4 QB 132). By the same token, the statement is inadmissible where the prospect of disadvantage is too remote to provide any guarantee of the reliability of the statement (*Smith* v *Blakey* (1867) LR 2 QB 326).

This exception to the hearsay rule has largely developed in civil cases but applies in criminal proceedings too (*Rogers* [1995] 1 Cr App R 374). R argued that a statement made shortly before he died by L, in which he asserted that he, and not R, was the owner of heroin and a firearm, was admissible evidence of the facts contained in it because it was made at the same time as a statement by L that 'a number of guys were after him for the money for the heroin that the police had found'. The argument failed first because the declaration was not against L's proprietary interest in that it was not equivalent to an acknowledgment of indebtedness, and second because, even if it was, the comments about the ownership of the heroin and the firearm were collateral matters and as such could only have been admissible to the extent that they were necessary to explain the nature of the transaction to which the declaration relates. As there was no doubt about the identity of the heroin in question, the collateral declarations were inadmissible.

Rogers illustrates the narrow scope of the exception. It may well be unnecessary to rely upon it in criminal cases in respect of statements in documents to which the CJA 1988, ss. 23 or 24, apply. It may, however, be useful to invoke the common law in respect of oral declarations.

The rationale of the rule suggests that statements known by the maker to render him liable to criminal prosecution ought also to be admissible, but this is not the case. In the *Sussex Peerage Case* (1844) 11 Cl & F 85 the House of Lords declined to extend the rule to declarations against penal interest, partly on the ground that to do so would render an accused person liable to be tried on the strength of incriminating statements by a deceased accomplice. The exception is thus of limited usefulness in criminal cases, though it might be employed, for example, in a case of theft where the defence is that the property belonged to the accused, to prove that the deceased predecessor in title of the victim admitted that he had given the property to the accused.

Where a declaration is admissible as being against the pecuniary or proprietary interest of the maker, it may be used to prove certain collateral matters stated in it. So, for example, in *Higham* v *Ridgeway* (1808) 10 East 109, a statement made by a midwife to the effect that he had received payment due for delivering a child was received in evidence to prove a collateral statement concerning the date on which the child was born. See also, as to the extent to which collateral matters may be proved, *Rogers* (above).

Statements in Course of Duty

F16.45 A statement made in fulfilment of a deceased person's duty to report on, or to record his actions, is admissible at common law to prove, by way of exception to the hearsay rule, so much of the statement as it was his duty to make, provided:

(a) the statement was made contemporaneously with the act;

(b) the statement deals with the maker's own acts; and

(c)   the maker of the statement had no motive to misrepresent the facts stated.

In *McGuire* (1985) 81 Cr App R 323, the Court of Appeal approved a statement in *Cross on Evidence* (5th ed.), at p. 561, in which it was said:

> The grounds of the exception appear to be that, in many cases, it would be impossible to obtain other evidence of a servant's acts after his death, and in most cases, the likelihood of detection if errors were made together with the sanction of dismissal if the duty were unfulfilled afford some guarantee of the trustworthiness of the statement.

Where, as will usually be the case, the statement is presented to the court in documentary form, it is likely to be admissible by virtue of the CJA 1988, ss. 23 or 24, under which Act there is no need to satisfy the complex conditions attaching to the common-law exception. Where the statement is oral, the 1988 Act does not apply, and it will be necessary to resort to the common law.

The duty must be to do the very thing to which the statement relates, and then to record it (*Smith* v *Blakey* (1867) LR 2 QB 326, per Blackburn J). The duty must be proved by evidence (*Mercer* v *Denne* [1905] 2 Ch 538), and only acts falling precisely within the proven duty are admissible. Thus, in *Chambers* v *Bernasconi* (1834) 1 Cr M & R 347 the record of a police officer showing the location at which he had made an arrest was rejected on the ground that his duty did not extend beyond the recording of the fact of the arrest and the time at which it had occurred.

The statement must relate to the acts of the deceased. A statement cannot be received under this exception if it records the acts of others (*The Henry Coxon* (1878) 3 PD 156; *Brain* v *Preece* (1843) 11 M & W 773). It is not clear whether the statement must relate to past acts: in *Rowlands* v *De Vecchi* (1882) Cab & El 10, a note made of letters which the deceased intended to post was held to provide insufficient evidence that he had subsequently posted them, but this is not to say that the note was inadmissible, and in *Buckley* (1873) 13 Cox CC 293 the statement of a police officer that he was going to keep watch on B was admitted as circumstantial evidence that he had met his death at B's hands, following proof from the officer's superior that the report was one which he was obliged to make. See also **F16.37**.

The absence of a motive to misrepresent the facts stated is sometimes to be found included in statements of the rule. See, e.g., *Poole* v *Dicas* (1835) 1 Bing NC 649; *The Henry Coxon* (1878) 3 PD 156; *Chambers* v *Bernasconi* (1834) 1 Cr M & R 347. It does not appear, however, that evidence has ever been excluded on this ground alone, though in *The Henry Coxon* it was one of three grounds stated for excluding the evidence.

Requirement of Contemporaneity   The report need not be made in circumstances **F16.46** of exact contemporaneity with the doing of the act. A record made later on the same day as the act in question has been admitted (*Price* v *Torrington* (1703) 1 Salk 285), and it may be that a record made on the following day can be received (*Re Djambi (Sumatra) Rubber Estates Ltd* (1912) 107 LT 631, per Cozens Hardy MR at p. 634). A lapse of two days has, however, been held to be too great (*The Henry Coxon* (1878) 3 PD 156).

Statements of Opinion

It is not possible under this exception to prove a statement of opinion as distinct from a **F16.47** statement of fact. Thus, in *McGuire* (1985) 81 Cr App R 323, the report of a forensic scientist which, had he lived, would have formed the basis of his testimony to the court regarding the probable seat of a fire, was inadmissible after his death to prove the accuracy of his opinion, although admissible to prove the facts recorded by him and on which his opinion was based. See now the CJA 1988, s. 30, at **F10.14**, under which an 'expert report' may be admitted without calling the maker to give evidence.

MISCELLANEOUS COMMON-LAW EXCEPTIONS

Statements in Furtherance of Common Purpose

F16.48   The rule that the acts and statements of one party to a common purpose may be evidence against another is particularly associated with charges of conspiracy. However, it is not confined to such cases, and applies to other offences where complicity is alleged. Thus, in *Jessop* (1877) 16 Cox CC 204, for example, J was charged with the murder of A, with whom he had entered into a suicide pact to die by taking poison. The plan miscarried and J survived. Field J held that evidence of the purchase of poison by A, being an act done in furtherance of the common purpose, was admissible against J. A more modern illustration is *Jones* [1997] 2 Cr App R 119, in which it was held that the rule applied to a joint enterprise to evade the prohibition on the importation of drugs, despite the fact that no charge of conspiracy was brought.

The limits of the doctrine were recently considered in *Gray* [1995] 2 Cr App R 100. G and others were each convicted of offences relating to insider dealing. Although there was alleged to be a 'network' between them for the passing of information, each allegation related only to an offence committed by one of them alone. The prosecution case consisted mainly of telephone conversations between the defendants, and the judge told the jury that a statement made in the course of such a conversation, though a particular defendant was not party to it, could nevertheless be evidence against that defendant if there was a joint enterprise between them for the unlawful dissemination of 'inside' information and the statement was made in furtherance of that joint enterprise. The Court of Appeal was inclined to the view that this stated the principle too widely: the acts and declarations of a person engaged in a joint enterprise and made in pursuance of that enterprise might be admissible against another, but only where the evidence shows the complicity of that other in a common offence or series of offences. As none of the offences was alleged to have been committed jointly, the rule did not apply. If, contrary to that view, the principle could be stated in the wider form, the prosecution would have to make clear the limits of the alleged agreement in pursuit of which the specific offences were said to have been committed; as this had not been done the appeals were allowed. Thus it appears that the case for a wider principle could still be made. In *Murray* [1997] 2 Cr App R 136, the Court of Appeal adopted the interpretation of *Gray* in the 1996 edition of this work (which is the same as that set out above) and added that that case is authority primarily for the proposition that the common-law exception cannot be extended to cases where individual defendants are charged with a number of separate substantive offences and the terms of a common enterprise are not provided or are ill-defined. An argument, based on dicta in the case, the *Gray* in fact narrows the scope of the common-law exception was rejected.

The rule permits the actions and declarations of one party, A, to be used in evidence against the other, B, and is thus an exception to the general rule that B is not to be prejudiced by the acts or statements of another, and an exception to the hearsay rule insofar as it may involve reliance on A's statements as evidence of their truth. As an exception to the hearsay rule it defies classification, some writers regarding it as appertaining to the *res gestae* (see *Andrews & Hirst on Criminal Evidence*, 3rd ed., at 20–027), others as based on implied agency (see *Cross and Tapper on Evidence*, 8th ed., at p. 655), and others as an independent exception, the justification for which is that such evidence must be used if the 'secret' crime of conspiracy is ever to be proved at all (Gilles, *The Law of Criminal Conspiracy* (1981)).

In order for the act or statement of A to be admissible against B, the rule requires:

(a)   that the act or statement of A must be in the course and furtherance of the common purpose; and

(b)   that independent evidence be adduced of the existence of the conspiracy and the involvement in it of B.

Meaning of Course and Furtherance of Common Purpose   In the leading case of   **F16.49**
Blake (1844) 6 QB 126, B and T were charged with conspiring to avoid payment of duty on imported goods. B, in the course of his employment at the Customs House, certified that the amount of goods imported by T as an agent was less than was in fact the case. T then charged his principal duty on the full amount, recording the charge in his own day book, and split the proceeds with B. It was held that the entry in T's day book was admissible against B, as being evidence of something done in the course of the transaction, but that the counterfoil of the cheque by which B received his share of the proceeds was not, for it was an act done after the common purpose was effected which had nothing to do with the carrying out of the conspiracy. It will be apparent from *Blake* that it may be difficult to distinguish precisely where a transaction begins and ends, and whether acts are done in furtherance of it or not. A clearer case of inadmissibility owing to the termination of the criminal purpose is that of the confession of one conspirator made after his apprehension, which is evidence only against the maker (see, e.g., *Walters* (1979) 69 Cr App R 115, at p. 120). And a more obvious example of a statement which cannot be said to be in furtherance of any criminal purpose occurred in *Steward* [1963] Crim LR 697, where one conspirator simply recited to another the various acts of B which had been done in execution of the common purpose, and the statement was held inadmissible against B. See also *Hardy* (1794) 24 St Tr 199, in which a similar recital by a conspirator of his own past acts was held not to be in furtherance of the conspiracy.

In *Devonport* [1996] 1 Cr App R 221, a statement was admitted which may not, in the strict sense, have furthered the conspiracy. The court was concerned with a document drawn up by D concerning the proposed division of spoils between himself and others involved. This was regarded by Judge J as a document in furtherance of the conspiracy, distinguishing *Blake* on the ground that the document was not a record of distribution after the conspiracy but an indication of the intended or prospective distribution of the proceeds of the conspiracy when it has been fulfilled. Even so, as there was no evidence that the document served any purpose other than D's own convenience the decision seems to go further than previous authority. So also does *Ilyas* [1996] Crim LR 810, in which a diary was admitted which was a record of the receipt of stolen car parts by some of the parties to the conspiracy. Nothing was made of the argument that the document was a mere record of what had already occurred and not in furtherance of the enterprise. Latham J, however, asserted that it was 'a document created *in the course of, or furtherance, of* the conspiracy' (emphasis added). This would seem to be a new and alternative ground of admissibility, as a document such as the diary can be said to be created in the course of a conspiracy without being in any way in furtherance of it. It would seem that the rule is in the course of being broadened by the courts. See also *Reeves* [1999] 3 Arch News 2, in which an *aide-memoire* by one conspirator for his own assistance appears to have been regarded as potentially admissible against co-conspirators under this exception.

Where the hearsay statements of co-conspirators in furtherance of the conspiracy implicate an accused, the trial judge must give a careful direction to the jury that the statements cannot be used to provide the link between that accused and the conspiracy (*Blake* (1993) Cr App R 169).

Requirement of Independent Evidence of Common Purpose   In *Blake* (1844) 6   **F16.50**
QB 126, a case involving conspiracy, Patteson J stated the principle to be that 'you must establish the fact of a conspiracy before you can make the act of one the act of all'. This does not mean that such evidence must be brought forward and accepted before the act or statement in question can be proved, for: 'from the nature of this charge [conspiracy]

the evidence must necessarily grow up as it proceeds. The acts of the one party must be given in evidence and then the acts of the other, and it may then be shown that those acts fully prove a conspiracy between them' (*Murphy* (1837) 8 C & P 297, per Coleridge J at pp. 302–3). See also *Governor of Pentonville Prison, ex parte Osman* [1990] 1 WLR 277 in which Lloyd LJ said (at p. 316): '. . . there must always be some evidence other than the hearsay evidence of a fellow conspirator to prove that a particular defendant is party to a conspiracy. Provided there is some other evidence, it does not matter in what order the evidence is adduced.' The principle is thus one of conditional admissibility, in that if, after the evidence has been heard, it transpires that there is no independent evidence of common purpose, the act or statement of A will have to be excluded from the case against B (*Donat* (1985) 82 Cr App R 173, approving the statement of the law in *Cross on Evidence* (6th ed., at p. 527). It is submitted that there is no difference in practice between this view and that expressed in *Whittaker* [1914] 3 KB 1283, in which it was said that the act or statement of A, though it may be proved as evidence against him, remains inadmissible against B until the necessary foundation is laid. Insofar as there is a difference, it is submitted that the correct practice is as stated in *Donat*. Failure by the prosecution to satisfy the requirement after evidence of a statement has been admitted *de bene esse* will require a careful direction to the jury, and may require the discharge of the jury and a retrial if the evidence admitted was prejudicial. Where evidence is admitted under the rule it is not necessary for the jury to be directed to convict only if they find evidence against B other than the statement of A. It is for the judge alone to satisfy himself that such evidence exists: if it does, the jury is permitted to look at all the evidence in order to decide guilt. If, however, there is a danger that the jury will rely on the statement by A as primary evidence of B's involvement, 'sweeping away' the other evidence which has led the judge to admit the statement in the first place, the judge should direct the jury as to the shortcomings in the evidence of A, including (if such be the case) the absence of any opportunity to cross-examine A, and the absence of corroborative evidence (*Jones* [1997] 2 Cr App R 119).

Admissions by Agents and Referees

F16.51 An admission made by the agent of an accused person, such as his legal adviser, may be admissible against him (*Turner* (1975) 61 Cr App R 67). Although at first sight such an admission may appear to be a confession, and thus to be governed by the rules of admissibility in the PACE 1984, s. 76 (see **F17**), it is submitted that this is not the case, for the section applies only to a confession made 'by an accused person', and, by s. 82(1), 'confession' includes any statement adverse to 'the person who made it'. It would seem to follow that vicarious admissions continue to be governed by common-law principles.

A statement made by his agent is admissible against the accused only where it is shown that the statement was made within the scope of the agent's authority. The majority of cases dealing with the proof of such authority are civil, and of limited assistance in criminal proceedings, as the few criminal authorities which exist take a more restrictive view as to the extent to which an agent's admissions affect his principal. Thus, in civil cases, admissions made by a solicitor in correspondence on his client's behalf will generally be evidence against the client (see, e.g., *Ellis* v *Allen* [1914] 1 Ch 904), whereas in criminal cases a client is not bound by statements in letters written by his solicitor in the absence of proof of specific instructions from him (*Downer* (1880) 43 LT 445). Agency may be inferred from the circumstances: thus, in *Turner* (1975) 61 Cr App R 67, it was held that it is permissible to infer from the fact that a barrister makes an admission in court on behalf of and in the presence of his client, that he was authorised to make it. The strength of the inference depends on the circumstances, however, and in *Evans* [1981] Crim LR 699, it was held that agency was not to be inferred simply from the fact that the admission was made by E's solicitor's clerk. An inference of agency will yield to express evidence to the contrary: in *Turner*, the barrister who had made the admissions in previous proceedings against T, gave evidence that he had exceeded his authority in doing so, and the statement was ruled inadmissible.

Evidence of agency must, of course, be admissible in its own right. In *Evans* [1981] Crim LR 699, statements made by the solicitor's clerk indicating that he was acting with E's authority were inadmissible to prove agency, being hearsay.

The rule as stated above is qualified by statute in the case of an alibi notice which purports to be given on behalf of an accused by his solicitor, as the CJA 1967, s. 11(5), provides that such notice is deemed to have been given with the accused's authority, unless the contrary is proved. See, as to the circumstances in which the prosecution may lead evidence of an alibi notice which adversely affects the defence at trial, *Rossborough* (1985) 81 Cr App R 139, and **D14.8**, and as to the reasons of policy for excluding statements made on behalf of an accused in the course of a pre-trial review, *Hutchinson* (1985) 82 Cr App R 51, and **D12.13** to **D12.16**.

A statement made by a person to whom the accused refers another for information on a particular matter may be evidence against him. Thus, in *Williams v Innes* (1808) 1 Camp 364, an executor referred the plaintiff to a particular individual for information pertaining to the assets of the estate, and it was held that what the referee said was admissible against the executor. Similarly, in *Mallory* (1884) 13 QBD 33, where M told a police officer that his wife would supply a list showing where certain items, suspected of being stolen, were purchased, the list handed over by the wife in M's presence was admissible against him. Coleridge CJ refrained from stating what the outcome would have been had M been absent when the list was handed over, but it is submitted that it would have made no difference.

SECTION F17: THE RULE AGAINST HEARSAY: CONFESSIONS

Definition

F17.1   **Police and Criminal Evidence Act 1984, s. 82**

(1) In this part of this Act—
'confession', includes any statement wholly or partly adverse to the person who made it, whether made to a person in authority or not and whether made in words or otherwise.

The admissibility of confession evidence is governed by provisions to be found in the PACE 1984, part VII, from which the above definition is taken. At common law, the test for admissibility of confessions was that of voluntariness, and a statement obtained by fear of prejudice or hope of advantage excited or held out by a person in authority was regarded as having been made involuntarily (see, e.g., *Baldry* (1852) 2 Den CC 430, per Baron Parke at p. 444; *Ibrahim* v *The King* [1914] AC 599; *DPP* v *Ping Lin* [1976] AC 574). The 1984 Act introduced a new test for admissibility (as to which see **F17.4**) and redefines 'confession'. Section 82(1) makes it clear that the law is no longer concerned with whether the confession was made to a person in authority, such as a police or customs officer, and that the statutory test for admissibility is equally applicable to, for example, an informal admission to a friend or colleague. Dissatisfaction with the common law had been expressed in *Deokinanan* v *The Queen* [1969] 1 AC 20, in which it was noted that a person who is not in authority may induce an unreliable confession by, for example, offering a bribe. Most confessions will, however, continue to be made to persons in authority such as the police, and the observation made in *Deokinanan* v *The Queen* that, 'The fact that an inducement is made by a person in authority may make it more likely to operate on the accused's mind and lead him to confess', continues to be true.

A plea of guilty is a confession for the purposes of the PACE 1984, s. 82(1), and as such is admissible in evidence provided that the provisions of s. 76(2) are complied with. At common law a plea of guilty was regarded as an admission of fact and was admissible in evidence against an accused who subsequently changed his plea to 'not guilty', provided that:

(a)   the plea had some probative value; and
(b)   the probative value exceeded the prejudicial effect that might be imported by referring to it (*Rimmer* [1972] 1 WLR 268, and see also *Hetherington* [1972] Crim LR 703).

In the vast majority of cases such evidence would not be admitted. Any admission of a guilty plea in evidence would have to be followed by a very careful direction by the trial judge as to exactly how it should be looked at by the jury (*Rimmer*, at p. 272).

An admission made by an accused in other proceedings would similarly constitute a confession for the purposes of the 1984 Act, and could be relied upon provided, as is likely, that it complies with the provisions of s. 76(2). At common law, in *McGregor* [1968] 1 QB 371 there had been a previous trial of M, and at his retrial the prosecution adduced evidence of admissions made at the earlier trial. The Court of Appeal could 'conceive of no ground upon which it could be said that this evidence was inadmissible'.

A plea in mitigation made by counsel on behalf of a client who has been convicted on his plea of 'not guilty' should not be understood as a confession by the convicted person through his counsel. So to regard mitigation would be both unjust and unrealistic, as it is counsel's duty to accept the verdict and seek to mitigate the consequences (*Wu Chun-Piu* v *The Queen* [1996] 1 WLR 1113). It is submitted that the same must be true if the convicted person advances his mitigation in person.

Confessions Otherwise than in Words

There is no statutory definition of 'statement' for the purposes of part VII of the PACE F17.2
1984, but the inclusion in s. 82(1) of the expression 'whether made in words or otherwise' suggests that 'confession' may, in addition to admissions in oral or written form, include conduct such as a nod of acceptance of an accusation or a 'thumbs-up' sign which may be properly regarded as a 'statement' in sign language. In *Li Shu-Ling* v *The Queen* [1989] AC 270, L, who had previously made a full confession to the police, agreed to take part in a filmed re-enactment of the crime with which he was charged, which was the murder of a woman by strangulation. He gave a running commentary explaining his movements, which he demonstrated on a woman police officer who played the part of the victim. At trial, his account of the killing was entirely different. It was held by the Privy Council (applying common-law principles) that the re-enactment was to be regarded as a confession, and the point was made that it is very much more difficult for an accused to escape from the visual record of his confession than to challenge an oral statement, with the result that a film may constitute most valuable evidence of guilt. Such a film would, it is submitted, constitute a confession under s. 82(1), and may be given in evidence, provided that the conditions of admissibility under the 1984 Act are satisfied. (See, to the same effect, *Lam Chi-ming* v *The Queen* [1991] 2 AC 212.)

It is submitted that conduct which is not intended to convey guilt, but which may be interpreted as doing so, is not a 'statement' and hence not a confession. Thus, for example, driving away at speed from the scene of an accident is not a confession to which the 1984 Act applies, though evidence of such conduct would be relevant and admissible.

Partly and Wholly Exculpatory Statements

A confession may be 'wholly or partly adverse' to the maker, with the result that a so- F17.3
called 'mixed statement', which is part confession and part exculpation, is a confession for the purposes of the PACE 1984. (See to the same effect at common law, *Customs and Excise Commissioners* v *Harz* [1967] 1 AC 760, per Lord Reid at p. 818, and see further as to the use of mixed statements in evidence **F17.44** to **F17.48**). However, a statement which, when made, is purely self-serving, but which comes to be adverse to the interest of the accused at trial (e.g., because it is inconsistent with the defence being put forward), has been said not to be a confession within the meaning of the Act (*Sat-Bhambra* (1988) 88 Cr App R 55, approving a dictum of Lord Widgery CJ in *Pearce* (1979) 69 Cr App R 365 at p. 370). The view expressed in *Sat-Bhambra* was technically *obiter*, as the appeal was disposed of on other grounds, and in *Ismail* [1990] Crim LR 109, the Court of Appeal appears to have regarded s. 76 of the 1984 Act as applicable to a purely exculpatory statement made at interview, which will only be the case if such a statement is a confession. However, in *Jelen* (1989) 90 Cr App R 456 at p. 464, the Court of Appeal doubted (*obiter*) whether J's 'potentially incriminating remarks' were confessions within s. 82(1) and in *Park* (1994) 99 Cr App R 270 exculpatory statements which were inconsistent with P's evidence at trial and demonstrably false were held not to be confessions, on the ground that s. 82(1) was not aimed at such statements. An exculpatory statement, whether or not it is a confession, may be excluded in the discretion of the court under s. 78 of the 1984 Act (see **F17.16** to **F17.22**) where the prosecution propose to rely on the statement as part of their case. Thus in *Jelen*, the Court of Appeal was able to consider whether the 'potentially incriminating remarks' J had made ought to have been excluded in the discretion of the court on the grounds that

he had been trapped into making them, and that they had been tape-recorded without his knowledge. It was held that the evidence was properly admitted.

Principles of Admissibility under PACE 1984, s. 76

F17.4 **Police and Criminal Evidence Act 1984, s. 76**

(1)   In any proceedings a confession made by an accused person may be given in evidence against him insofar as it is relevant to any matter in issue in the proceedings and is not excluded by the court in pursuance of this section.

(2)   If, in any proceedings where the prosecution proposes to give in evidence a confession made by an accused person, it is represented to the court that the confession was or may have been obtained—

(a)   by oppression of the person who made it; or

(b)   in consequence of anything said or done which was likely, in the circumstances existing at the time, to render unreliable any confession which might be made by him in consequence thereof,

the court shall not allow the confession to be given in evidence against him except insofar as the prosecution proves to the court beyond reasonable doubt that the confession (notwithstanding that it may be true) was not obtained as aforesaid.

(3)   In any proceedings where the prosecution proposes to give in evidence a confession made by an accused person, the court may of its own motion require the prosecution, as a condition of allowing it to do so, to prove that the confession was not obtained as mentioned in subsection (2) above.

The CPIA 1996, sch. 1, para. 25, inserted s. 76(9), which provides that, in the case of proceedings before a magistrates' court inquiring into an offence as examining justices, the section shall have effect with the omission in s. 76(1) of the words 'and is not excluded by the court in pursuance of this section' and subsections (2) to (6) and (8).

It is unclear whether s. 76 is intended as a mechanism for regulating the admissibility of a confession made by one co-accused as evidence for another. In *Myers* [1998] AC 124, the House of Lords declined to decide whether s. 76(1) applied to defence evidence, but resolved the issue of admissibility by reference to principles analogous to those enshrined in s. 76(2) (see **F17.12**). For ease of exposition the position with regard to prosecution evidence will be explained first.

The prosecution do not have to prove the admissibility of a confession upon which they rely unless either (a) the defence 'represents' that it is inadmissible under s. 76(2), or (b) the court of its own motion requires proof of admissibility under s. 76(3). If in either case the prosecution are unable to prove admissibility beyond reasonable doubt, the confession must be excluded, notwithstanding that it may be true: the court has no discretion in the matter (*Paris* (1993) 97 Cr App R 99). A confession may be excluded in part (cf. s. 76(4) and (6) at **F17.37** *et seq.*). As to procedure, see **F17.13** *et seq*.

A confession which is inadmissible in criminal proceedings in consequence of s. 76 should not be used as the basis for a formal caution (*Metropolitan Police Commissioner, ex parte Thompson* [1997] 1 WLR 1519).

EXCLUSION FOR OPPRESSION: S. 76(2)(a)

Definition of Oppression

F17.5 **Police and Criminal Evidence Act 1984, s. 76**

(8)   In this section 'oppression' includes torture, inhuman or degrading treatment, and the use or threat of violence (whether or not amounting to torture).

The reference to 'torture' may be interpreted in the light of the offence of torture contained in the CJA 1988, s. 134. 'Torture and inhuman or degrading treatment' is also prohibited by Art. 3 of the European Convention on Human Rights, and reference may be made to case law under the article (see, e.g., *Republic of Ireland* v *United Kingdom* (1978) 2 EHRR 25). See also the Northern Ireland (Emergency Provisions) Act 1996, s. 12, which prohibits the reception in evidence of statements obtained after the maker has been subjected 'to torture, to inhuman or degrading treatment, or to any violence or threat of violence (whether or not amounting to torture), in order to induce him to make the statement'. Cases decided under this provision may provide useful guidance in the interpretation of s. 76(2)(a).

Oppression at Common Law

At common law, a confession obtained by oppression was regarded as involuntary and therefore inadmissible (see, e.g., *Callis* v *Gunn* [1964] 1 QB 495; *Prager* [1972] 1 WLR 260). 'Oppression' was understood not only to include physical oppression (*Burut* v *Public Prosecutor* [1995] 2 AC 579, in which the Privy Council held that the manacling and hooding of suspects under interrogation in Brunei was 'plainly oppressive') but carried a wider sense; it was described by Sachs J in *Priestley* (1965) 51 Cr App R 1 at p. 1 as 'something which tends to sap, and has sapped, that free will which must exist before a confession is voluntary'. This, and other common-law definitions of the term, do not, however, provide reliable indications of the meaning of the word in its present statutory context. In *Fulling* [1987] QB 426 the court held (without referring to the PACE 1984, s. 76(8)) that the 1984 Act does not follow the wording of earlier rules or decisions, nor is it expressed to be a consolidating Act. It is a codifying Act, in the interpretation of which the proper course is to start by ascertaining the natural meaning of the language used, uninfluenced by any considerations derived from the previous state of the law (applying the principles set out by Lord Herschell in *Bank of England* v *Vagliano Brothers* [1891] AC 107, at pp. 144–5). It was further stated that much of the sort of treatment which would have fallen within the definition of oppression at common law will now fall to be dealt with under the 'reliability' head of exclusion.

F17.6

Ambit of Oppression

In *Fulling* [1987] QB 426 the prosecution tendered a confession by F in which she admitted her part in an insurance fraud initiated by her boyfriend, D. F claimed that the confession was made in order to secure her release from custody after a police officer had revealed, to F's great distress, not only that D had been unfaithful to her, but also that the 'other woman' was being held in the cell next to F's. On the assumption that these revelations were made, the trial judge ruled that there was no oppression in the sense of 'something above and beyond that which is inherently oppressive in police custody . . . [importing] some impropriety . . . actively applied in an improper manner by the police'. The Court of Appeal upheld the ruling of the trial judge. 'Oppression' was to be given its 'ordinary dictionary meaning' of: 'Exercise of authority or power in a burdensome, harsh or wrongful manner; unjust or cruel treatment of subjects, inferiors etc., the imposition of unreasonable or unjust burdens'.

F17.7

Oppression almost inevitably involves some impropriety on the part of the interrogator (*Fulling* at p. 432). It does not follow that all impropriety necessarily involves oppression; otherwise all wrongful acts, including breaches of the PACE Codes of Practice, could be termed oppressive, which is clearly not so (*Parker* [1995] Crim LR 233). In *Fulling*, the Court drew attention to a quotation which exemplifies the meaning of the term: 'There is not a word in our language that expresses more detestable wickedness than oppression.' In *Emmerson* (1991) 92 Cr App R 284, a police officer had given way to impatience during an interview and had raised his voice and used bad language to the accused. The Court of Appeal ruled that to regard such conduct as oppressive would be to give the word a completely false meaning. Unduly hostile questioning may, however, be oppressive: it is a question of degree. In *Paris* (1993) 97 Cr App R 99 a tape recording of an interview with M revealed that he had been 'bullied and hectored'. The Court of Appeal commented that, short of physical violence, it was hard to conceive of a more hostile and intimidating approach by officers to a suspect. The interview was oppressive and M's later confession ought to have been excluded. However, in *L* [1994] Crim LR 839, tactics similar to those employed in *Paris* appear to have been regarded as acceptable provided the reliability of the confession was not compromised.

A degree of impropriety which is insufficient for oppression may serve to support an argument that a confession should be excluded under the PACE 1984, s. 76(2)(b) or s. 78, considered at **F17.9** *et seq*. and **F17.16** *et seq*. respectively. Thus, in *Samuel* [1988] QB 615, the Court of Appeal, while acknowledging the possibility that oppression might be present where access to legal advice is improperly denied, preferred to quash S's conviction by reference to s. 78. Exclusion for oppression is likely to be reserved for those rare cases where an accused has been subjected to misconduct of a deliberate and serious nature, and even then it will almost inevitably be the case that the confession could have been excluded under one of the other provisions. See, for example, the ruling of the trial judge in *Beales* [1991] Crim LR 118, who was in 'no doubt whatsoever' that a confession, excluded on grounds of oppression after the accused had been deliberately hectored and bullied in interview, would also have been inadmissible under s. 76(2)(b).

Where a confession made in the course of an interview is excluded on grounds of oppression, it may be necessary to consider whether the effect on the accused was such that the repetition by him of the same information at a later, properly conducted interview ought also to be excluded (*Ismail* [1990] Crim LR 109, in which it was held that to accede to the prosecution's submission that misconduct in earlier interviews could be 'cured' by a properly conducted interview would be to condone flouting of the provisions of the Act and codes designed to protect against false confessions).

Relevance of Character and Attributes of Accused

F17.8   At common law it was held that the nature of oppression varied according to the character and attributes of the accused. Thus, an 'experienced professional criminal' might expect a vigorous interrogation (*Gowan* [1982] Crim LR 821), and in *Dodd* (1981) 74 Cr App 50, O'Connor LJ said (at p. 56) that the trial judge 'was entitled to consider the type of men he was dealing with', all of whom were experienced criminals. O'Connor LJ contrasted the case with that of *Hudson* (1980) 72 Cr App R 163, in which a middle-aged man of previous good character had been subjected to a lengthy, and in certain respects unlawful, interrogation, which was subsequently held to have been oppressive. At the other end of the spectrum, in *Miller* [1986] 1 WLR 1191 Watkins LJ said that it might be oppressive to put questions to an accused who is known to be mentally ill so as 'skilfully and deliberately' to induce a delusionary state in him. Despite the rejection in *Fulling* [1987] QB 426 of common-law rulings on oppression, these cases may still be good law, for the Court of Appeal in *Fulling* was concerned to reject the 'artificially wide' common-law definition of oppression, while the above cases appear to proceed on a meaning which is consistent with the ordinary meaning of oppression as adopted in *Fulling*. This view appears to have been confirmed by *Seelig* [1992] 1 WLR 148, in which Henry J, in a ruling described by the Court of Appeal as 'entirely right', took account of the fact that the person being questioned was 'an experienced merchant banker' and 'intelligent and sophisticated', in determining whether he had been questioned in an oppressive way, and in *Smith* [1994] 1 WLR 1396 the Court of Appeal regarded it as relevant that S, who was questioned by a person in authority within a bank, was himself a chairman and managing director of a substantial financial organisation. Similarly in *Paris* (1993) 97 Cr App R 99 (**F17.7**) the court, although of the opinion that the bullying and hectoring of M in interview would have been oppressive even with a suspect of normal intelligence, went out of its way to stress that M was on the borderline of mental handicap.

EXCLUSION FOR UNRELIABILITY: S. 76(2)(b)

Unreliability at Common Law

At common law, a confession was regarded as involuntary, and therefore inadmissible, if **F17.9** it was obtained by fear of prejudice or hope of advantage held out or excited by a person in authority (*DPP* v *Ping Lin* [1976] AC 574). According to a majority of the House of Lords in that case, it did not matter whether the person who induced the confession was behaving improperly or not. Many cases occurred where confessions had to be excluded, notwithstanding that there was no reason to suppose that the threat or inducement concerned had caused the accused to provide an unreliable statement (see, e.g., *Northam* (1967) 52 Cr App R 97, *Zaveckas* [1970] 1 WLR 516). The Criminal Law Revision Committee, in its 11th Report, *Evidence* (1972) Cmnd 4991, proposed that a confession obtained in consequence of a threat or inducement should not be excluded unless the circumstances were such that any confession made by the accused would be likely to be unreliable. This proposal became the PACE 1984, s. 76(2)(b), though the term 'threat or inducement' was replaced by the wider notion of 'anything said or done'.

Application of Statutory Test

The PACE 1984 requires the trial judge to consider a hypothetical question: not **F17.10** whether *this* confession is unreliable, but whether *any* confession which the accused might make in consequence of what was said or done was likely to be rendered unreliable. In *Cox* [1991] Crim LR 276, a mentally handicapped accused gave evidence at the *voir dire* in the course of which he admitted one of the offences with which he was charged. The trial judge based his decision to admit C's out of court confession, which had been obtained in the absence of an 'appropriate adult' and thus in breach of the relevant code of practice, on the reliability of the actual confession as admitted by C. The Court of Appeal held that the question was not whether the actual confession was reliable, but whether it was made in consequence of something said or done which was likely to give rise to unreliability. The same point was made in *Crampton* (1991) 92 Cr App R 372, where it was said that, if acts are done or words spoken which are likely to induce unreliable confessions, then, whether or not the confession is true, it is inadmissible. Although the judge may not be influenced by evidence that the confession is true in deciding admissibility, he is not precluded from taking into account any other relevant evidence given at trial before the *voir dire* begins which assists him to determine the questions posed by s. 76(2)(b) (*Tyrer* (1989) 90 Cr App R 446 at pp. 449–50).

Section 76(2) obliges the judge to consider everything said or done by the police, and not to confine himself to a narrow analysis analogous to offer and acceptance in the law of contract (*Barry* (1992) 95 Cr App R 384). The use of the phrase 'anything said or done', and the inclusion of all the surrounding circumstances, are indications that the new test follows the common law in acknowledging that a confession may be inadmissible, notwithstanding that the police have not behaved improperly. In *Fulling* [1987] QB 426 the Court of Appeal stated, *obiter*, that it was 'abundantly clear' that a confession may be excluded under s. 76(2)(b) where there is no suspicion of any impropriety. Dicta in *Brine* [1992] Crim LR 123, stating that s. 76(2) is 'primarily concerned' with police misconduct, should not be understood to qualify this statement of principle. See also *Harvey* [1988] Crim LR 241, in which a psychopathically disordered woman of low normal intelligence heard her lover confess to a murder. As this experience may have led her to make a false confession out of a child-like desire to protect her lover, her statement was excluded under s. 76(2)(b). *Harvey* was cited with approval in *Raghip* (1991) *The Times*, 9 December 1991. Such a confession might also be excluded under s. 78 (see **F17.16**).

It has been held that a confession cannot be rendered inadmissible under s. 76(2)(b) by reason only of something said or done by the accused himself (*Goldenberg* (1988) 88 Cr App R 285). In this case G was interviewed on suspicion of conspiracy to supply controlled drugs. The admissions which he made were alleged by the defence to be (a) an attempt by him to get bail, and (b) tainted by the fact that he was a heroin addict who, having been in custody for some time, would have said or done anything, however false, to gain his release so as to feed his addiction. The Court of Appeal considered that this argument was founded entirely 'on what was said or done by the appellant himself and on his state of mind', and that this was beyond the scope of the provision. The wording of the section, and in particular the words 'in consequence' in s. 76(2)(b), imported a causal link between what was said or done and the subsequent confession. It followed that the provision was looking to something external to the person making the confession and which was likely to have some effect on him. *Goldenberg* was considered in *Crampton* (1991) 92 Cr App R 372, in which police officers interviewed C, a heroin addict, who it subsequently transpired was suffering from withdrawal symptoms. It was noted that in *Goldenberg* it was G himself who had requested the interview, but this was thought not to provide a ground for distinguishing the case, for it was doubtful whether the requirement for something external to be 'said or done' could be satisfied by the mere holding of an interview with an addict in withdrawal. The words of the statute contemplated some words spoken or acts done by the police which were likely to induce unreliable confessions. More recently, in *Walker* [1998] Crim LR 211, the Court of Appeal appears to have considered that the issue of whether W had taken cocaine before confessing had a material bearing on admissibility, but this appears to have been achieved by regarding the impairment of the accused as one of the 'circumstances' referred to in s. 76(2)(b).

The accused's own mental state may be part of the 'circumstances' for the purposes of s. 76(2)(b). It does not matter whether these circumstances were known to the interrogator at the time. In *Everett* [1988] Crim LR 826, E was discovered in a compromising position with a five-year-old boy. On the way to the police station, and while he was there, he admitted indecently assaulting the child. E was a 42-year-old man with a mental age of eight, and was regarded by a medical witness as being in the bottom 2 per cent of the population. The trial judge regarded the medical evidence as irrelevant provided that he was satisfied (as he was) from listening to the tape recording of the police station interview that E's replies were rational and showed understanding of the questions. The Court of Appeal ruled against this approach, and held that the circumstances to be taken into account 'obviously include' the mental condition of a suspect at the time the confession came into being. The test to be applied was an objective one, i.e. not what the police officers thought (if they thought anything) about the mental condition of the suspect, but instead the actual condition of the suspect as subsequently ascertained from a doctor. The confession ought to have been excluded because the prosecution 'most certainly had not' discharged the burden of proving it admissible. Similarly, in *McGovern* (1991) 92 Cr App R 228, it was said that the physical condition and particular vulnerability of M (she was six months pregnant and of limited intelligence), while not being 'anything said or done' to M, were part of the background against which the submission that she had been wrongly denied access to legal advice had to be judged. The combination of circumstances had the far-reaching result that it was appropriate to exclude both the confession made as a direct consequence of the denial of access and a subsequent confession made in the presence of a solicitor which was tarnished as a result of the earlier confession. In *Souter* [1995] Crim LR 729, a confession was held to be inadmissible where it was made by a soldier who was in a state of extreme emotion and distress to an officer who had been sent to calm him down; other relevant factors were that the conversation between the two had an appearance of confidentiality, and the officer had a very partial recollection of the rest of what had been said. The kind of mental condition which may be taken into account under s. 76(2)(b) is not limited to what might be termed 'impairment of intelligence or social functioning', still less to 'mental impairment' (*Walker* [1998] Crim LR 211). In cases where the mental condition of the accused is a relevant factor, medical evidence should be admitted if it is required to resolve the question arising under s. 76(2)(b), even where the accused's IQ is outside the range of mental defective. The judicial approach is not governed by which side of an arbitrary line, whether at 69/70 or elsewhere, the IQ falls (*Raghip* (1991) *The Times*, 9 December 1991). Expert evidence may also help to determine whether the accused is suffering from a personality disorder which is relevant to the reliability of the confession (*Walker*).

It is common for the defence to allege that the 'something said or done' includes a breach by the police of an obligation under the PACE 1984 or the Code of Practice for the Detention, Treatment and Questioning of Persons by Police Officers (PACE Code C). Such a breach will not lead to automatic exclusion of a confession obtained in consequence (*Delaney* (1988) 88 Cr App R 338), though it may, on its own or together with other factors, provide evidence that s. 76(2)(b) has not been complied with. In *Delaney*, D, whose psychological make-up was such that he was likely to feel unusual pressure to escape from interrogation, alleged that he had been induced to confess by a suggestion that the serious indecent assault of which he was suspected was more deserving of treatment than punishment. The interview was not recorded until the following day, in breach of Code C, and the Court of Appeal held that the absence of a reliable record of what occurred 'deprived the court of what was, in all likelihood, the most cogent evidence as to what did indeed happen during those interviews and what did induce the appellant to confess'. The breach was therefore significant, in that, the burden of proof being on the prosecution, the speculation necessarily engendered by the breach was sufficient to tip the scale in favour of the defence. For other cases where confessions were excluded, see, e.g., *Doolan* [1988] Crim LR 747 (failure to caution and to maintain a proper interview record or to show it to D); *Chung* (1991) 92 Cr App R 314 (questioning before allowing access to a solicitor and failure to show note to C or subsequently to his solicitor); *Waters* [1989] Crim LR 62 (improper questioning after charge resulting in ambiguous and potentially unreliable answer); *DPP* v *Blake* [1989] 1 WLR 432 (the 'spirit of the Code' was broken when a juvenile's estranged father was insisted on by police as the appropriate adult to attend her interview); *Morse* [1991] Crim LR 195 (juvenile's father acting as 'appropriate adult' and subsequently discovered to have low IQ and to be incapable of appreciating the gravity of the situation in which M found himself); *Moss* (1990) 91 Cr App R 371 (suspect of low intelligence interviewed nine times during a lengthy period of detention; access to legal advice improperly denied and no independent person present at interview).

Delaney and *Doolan* serve also to illustrate that 'something said or done' may consist of an omission to fulfil the requirements of the Code, although such an omission might always be described in more positive terms, for example, as interviewing the accused without having cautioned him as the Code requires.

Where a breach of the Act or codes has occurred which renders a confession inadmissible under s. 76(2)(b), it may be necessary to consider whether a repetition of the confession at a subsequent, properly conducted interview is also inadmissible. In *McGovern* (1991) 92 Cr App R 228, a subsequent interview was held inadmissible as it had been tainted by the matters which had led to the exclusion of an earlier interview, namely breaches of s. 58 and the interviewing provisions of Code C. It was further stated that the very fact that admissions were made at an earlier stage was likely to have an effect on the suspect thereafter, with adverse consequences for the admissibility of any repetition of the confession. In *Glaves* [1993] Crim LR 685 the Court of Appeal, whilst denying that there must necessarily be a 'continuing blight' on confessions obtained subsequent to a confession which is excluded under s. 76(2), nevertheless held that the breaches in the case (which included giving C, a juvenile, the impression that he was bound to answer questions) were not cured by a change of police officers and a caution, particularly as C had received no legal advice between the two interviews.

Section 76 and Causation

F17.11   At common law a confession which had been obtained following an inducement was admissible provided the prosecution could establish that the inducement was not the cause of the obtaining (*DPP* v *Ping Lin* [1976] AC 574, per Lord Hailsham of St Marylebone at p. 601: '. . . what excludes evidence is a chain of causation resulting from words or conduct on the part of the person in authority . . . giving rise to a decision by the accused actuated by fear of prejudice or hope of reward'). The PACE 1984, s. 76(2)(a) and (b), imports the same causal link by reason of the words '*by* oppression' and '*in consequence of* anything said or done'. It follows that it may be helpful to consider decisions at common law such as *Rennie* [1982] 1 WLR 64, in which Lord Lane CJ held that the judge should avoid any 'refined analysis of the concept of causation' and 'should approach it much as would a jury. . . . In other words, he should understand the principle and the spirit behind it, and apply his common sense.' See also *Tyrer* (1989) 90 Cr App R 446 and *Barry* (1992) 95 Cr App R 384, in both of which it was accepted that the prosecution may discharge the onus of proof under s. 76(2) by showing that there is no causal link between the confession and things said or done by police officers which might have been conducive to unreliability, and *Crampton* (1991) 92 Cr App R 369 in which *Rennie* was cited in support of the proposition that a confession will not have been caused by anything said or done by an interviewer if a suspect is motived to confess because he perceives in his own mind that there may be an advantage from doing so. The demeanour of the accused when giving evidence on the *voir dire* may assist the prosecution in showing that he was not affected by threats allegedly made at interview (*Weeks* [1995] Crim LR 52).

Confession Tendered by Co-accused

F17.12   In *Myers* [1998] AC 124, M and Q were charged with murder. Q's defence was that M alone committed the offence, and he sought to rely upon a confession to that effect which M had made. The statement was not relied upon in evidence by the prosecution, in consequence of breaches of the Codes of Practice. However there was no suggestion that the confession was not freely made by M. The House of Lords held that the statement was admissible for Q, although the reasoning behind the decision is somewhat obscure. The following principles appear to emerge from the speeches of Lord Slynn (with whom Lords Steyn and Hutton agreed) and Lord Hope (with whom Lord Mustill agreed).

(a)   Where the circumstances are such that proving the guilt of co-accused A assists accused B to establish his defence, a confession by A is clearly relevant evidence for B.

(b)   B ought to be allowed to make use of such evidence in support of his defence unless the confession was obtained in a manner which would have made it inadmissible for the prosecution under the PACE 1984, s. 76(2).

(c)   The fact that the prosecution are prevented from relying on the confession by operation of s. 78 (see **F17.13**) does not prevent B from adducing it in evidence, as s. 78 applies only to evidence on which the prosecution seeks to rely.

Myers leaves many questions unanswered. In particular, it is not clear how, as evidence of A's confession is (as Lord Hope explicitly accepts) hearsay, B can be permitted to rely on it unless an exception to that rule applies. Such a rule could be either statutory or common-law, but the rule of analogy with s. 76(2) advanced in *Myers* seems to be neither. Both Lord Slynn and Lord Hope, however, appear to equate the proposition (accepted by the Court of Appeal) that M's confession was 'voluntary', with the notion that it would have been admissible for the prosecution under s. 76(2). Thus it may be that the hearsay exception relied upon by Q is of common-law origin, but for ease of application the test to be applied is to be taken as that stated in the 1984 Act. If this be so, it is difficult to ascertain with any certainty what burden of proof is to be applied, as the prosecution must establish admissibility beyond reasonable doubt under the Act, but it is not at common law regarded as proper to expect the defence to do more than establish admissibility on a balance of probabilities. Lord Hope creates (so it is submitted) further confusion when he states that evidence obtained in breach of s. 76(2) is 'worthless' and, though not thereby rendered irrelevant when tendered by the defence, could properly be excluded by the trial judge in the 'exercise of his discretion'. The source of such a discretion cannot easily be found. Section 78 is (as already stated) of no application, and Lord Hope accepts that at common law there is no general discretion for a trial judge, as between co-defendants, 'to exclude relevant evidence on the ground that he is choosing the course which involves the least injustice as between the defendants' (a point affirmed in *Lobban* v *R* [1995] 1 WLR 877: see **F2.1**). If such a power of exclusion exists then it would appear to be *sui generis*, but it is submitted that it is without foundation and that evidence of the sort admitted in *Myers* is admitted as of right by way of common-law exception to the hearsay rule, and not subject to the discretion of the court.

What is clear is that nothing in *Myers* changes the rule that an accused person may not rely on the out-of-court confession of a third party to the offence charged. Such evidence, though it may be relevant, is hearsay and no special exception applies, whether the confession is voluntary or not (*Blastland* [1986] AC 41: see **F15.6**). *Myers* applies only where the maker of the confession is a party to the proceedings.

THE DISCRETION TO EXCLUDE CONFESSION EVIDENCE

At Common Law

The common-law power of a court to exclude evidence in its discretion is considered in **F17.13** general at **F2.1** *et seq*. The following section is concerned only with the application of the discretion to exclude confession evidence.

Police and Criminal Evidence Act 1984, s. 82

(3) Nothing in this part of this Act shall prejudice any power of a court to exclude evidence (whether by preventing questions from being put or otherwise) at its discretion.

Section 82 applies to part VIII of the 1984 Act, which includes ss. 76 and 78. Prior to the enactment of the Act and the codes of practice made under it, exclusion of confession evidence at common law was recognised in two contexts:

(a) the exclusion of unreliable confessions, the prejudicial effect of which could be said to outweigh their true probative value; and
(b) the exclusion of confession evidence, the admission of which might operate unfairly against the accused.

Exclusion for Unreliability In *Miller* [1986] 1 WLR 1191 the Court of Appeal **F17.14** acknowledged the existence of a discretion to refuse to admit 'a confession which came from a mind which at the time was possibly irrational and [where] what the defendant said may have been the product of delusions and hallucinations'. In *Isequilla* [1975] 1

WLR 716, the court accepted the statement in *Cross on Evidence* (3rd ed., 1967) that 'it would be in accordance with principle to exclude a confession made by someone whose mental state was such as to render his utterances completely unreliable'. See also *Stewart* (1972) 56 Cr App R 272.

F17.15 ***Exclusion for Unfairness*** In *Sang* [1980] AC 402, Lord Diplock said (at p. 437 emphasis added): '*save with regard to admissions and confessions* and generally with regard to evidence obtained from the accused after commission of the offence, he [the trial judge] has no discretion to refuse to admit relevant admissible evidence on the ground that it was obtained by improper or unfair means'. The unfairness discretion was well established at common law with regard to confession evidence. In *Houghton* (1978) 68 Cr App R 197, Lawton LJ held (at p. 206) that evidence 'would operate unfairly against an accused if it had been obtained in an oppressive manner by force or against the wishes of an accused person or by a trick or by conduct of which the Crown ought not to take advantage', and said that trial judges enjoyed a discretion to disallow such evidence. The discretion was recognised to exist, although it was infrequently exercised, with regard to breaches of the Judges' Rules (see, e.g., *Voisin* [1918] 1 KB 531; *Lemsatef* [1977] 1 WLR 812) and where a confession had been extracted following a period of unlawful detention (*Hudson* (1980) 72 Cr App R 163).

The common-law powers, though preserved by the PACE 1984, s. 82(3), are unlikely to be resorted to in practice given the wide ambit of s. 78 (see **F17.16**). The situation in which they are most likely to be used is where a judge becomes aware, after a confession has been admitted in evidence, of circumstances suggesting that it should not have been. Neither s. 76 nor s. 78 applies to this situation (*Sat-Bhambra* (1988) 88 Cr App R 55, discussed in detail at **F17.32**), so the court is thrown back on its common-law powers.

Exclusion under Police and Criminal Evidence Act 1984, s. 78

F17.16 **Police and Criminal Evidence Act 1984, s. 78**

(1) In any proceedings the court may refuse to allow evidence on which the prosecution proposes to rely to be given if it appears to the court that, having regard to all the circumstances, including the circumstances in which the evidence was obtained, the admission of the evidence would have such an adverse effect on the fairness of the proceedings that the court ought not to admit it.

(2) Nothing in this section shall prejudice any rule of law requiring a court to exclude evidence.

(3) This section shall not apply in the case of proceedings before a magistrates' court inquiring into an offence as examining justices.

Section 78(3) was added by the CPIA 1996, sch. 1, para. 26. It is likely that the effect of this provision is to exclude the application of s. 78 in extradition proceedings too: see Extradition Act 1989, s. 9(2) and sch. 1, para. 6(1), considered in *Governor of Brixton Prison, ex parte Levin* [1997] AC 741.

For the meaning of 'proceedings', see s. 82(1). The power may be used in respect of confession evidence tendered by the prosecution (*Mason* [1988] 1 WLR 139), and numerous instances of its use for this purpose exist. In practice, if not in law, the common-law discretion appears to have been superseded.

The Court of Appeal will not interfere with the exercise of a trial judge's discretion to admit evidence under s. 78 unless satisfied that the decision was perverse (*Dures* [1997] 2 Cr App R 247, applying the general principle stated in *Quinn* [1995] 1 Cr App R 480). It follows that cases in which the discretion is said to have been wrongly exercised are comparatively rare. A recent example is *Miller* [1998] Crim LR 209, in which the judge adverted to an out-of-date version of the PACE Codes of Practice and thereby reached an incorrect conclusion through failure to note serious breaches of the applicable Code.

Section 78 and the PACE Codes of Practice

Codes of practice issued under the PACE 1984, s. 66, are admissible in evidence in both **F17.17** criminal and civil proceedings, and any provision of such a code appearing to the court or tribunal conducting the proceedings to be relevant to any question arising in the proceedings, must be taken into account in determining that question by virtue of s. 67(11). Breach of a relevant code provision does not lead to the automatic exclusion of a confession obtained in consequence (see, e.g., *Delaney* (1988) 88 Cr App R 338, where the Court of Appeal heard submissions on ss. 76 and 78, and it was held that '. . . the mere fact that there has been a breach of the PACE Codes does not of itself mean that evidence has to be rejected'; *Parris* (1988) 89 Cr App R 68 at p. 72, where the same point was made). The question is whether the admission of the evidence would have such an adverse effect on the fairness of the proceedings that the court ought not to admit it. Even a plain and admitted breach, though it is to be deplored, may fail to trigger exclusion if it does not operate in a way prejudicial to the accused (*Canale* [1990] 2 All ER 187). See further **F17.18**. In *Roberts* [1997] 1 Cr App R 217, it was held that breach of a PACE Code C provision designed to protect another suspect, could not be prayed in aid by the accused R. This was because there was no causal link between the breaches and R's admission. On the facts, however, had the Code been complied with, it might have resulted in a record which would have supported R's contention that the other accused, to whom R subsequently confessed, was acting in the role of police agent in soliciting the confession. It is submitted that the issue is not whether the breach against the other accused caused the confession by R (as plainly it did not) but whether the breach affected the fairness of using R's confession (which it may have done).

Breach of a code of practice is in many cases an important factor in considering whether to exclude evidence. Where confession evidence is concerned, the code most likely to be involved is Code C, dealing with the detention, treatment and questioning of persons by police officers. Certain of the rights guaranteed by Code C, such as the right of access to legal advice, are also to be found in the body of the 1984 Act itself (see PACE Code C, section 6 and s. 58). In *Keenan* [1990] 2 QB 54, the Court of Appeal declined to express a view as to whether a court should differentiate between breaches of the Act and of the codes. It is submitted that, whereas the location of such a right in the body of the Act may be an indication of its importance, the principles to be followed when considering the application of s. 78 are no different.

In *Samuel* [1988] QB 615 the Court of Appeal stated that it was undesirable to give any general guidance on the way in which a judge's discretion under s. 78 or under his inherent powers should be exercised, because circumstances may vary infinitely. Without seeking to give any such general guidance, it is submitted that the following considerations have proved to be of importance where s. 78 is concerned.

Nature and Extent of Breach In *Walsh* (1989) 91 Cr App R 161, W was denied **F17.18** access to legal advice, and it was common ground that there had been a breach of the PACE 1984, s. 58 (see **D1.38**). The Court of Appeal observed (at p. 163):

> The main object of section 58 of the Act and indeed of the codes of practice is to achieve fairness – to an accused or suspected person so as, among other things, to preserve and protect his legal rights; but also fairness for the Crown and its officers so that again, among other things, there might be reduced the incidence or effectiveness of unfounded allegations of malpractice.

> To our minds it follows that if there are significant and substantial breaches of section 58 or the provisions of the code, then prima facie at least the standards of fairness set by Parliament have not been met. So far as a defendant is concerned, it seems to us also to follow that to admit evidence against him which has been obtained in circumstances where these standards have not been met, cannot but have an adverse effect on the fairness of the proceedings. This does not mean, of course, that in every case of a significant or substantial

breach of section 58 or the code of practice the evidence concerned will automatically be excluded. Section 78 does not so provide. The task of the court is not merely to consider whether there would be an adverse effect on the fairness of the proceedings, but such an adverse effect that justice requires the evidence to be excluded.

In assessing the effect on the fairness of the proceedings of a breach of s. 58, it is relevant to note that it has frequently been stressed that the right of access to legal advice is 'fundamental' (see, e.g., *Samuel* [1988] QB 615) and that it is regarded as of great importance in the jurisprudence of the European Court of Human Rights (*Murray* v *UK* (1996) 22 EHRR 29, considered in *Aspinall* [1999] 2 Cr App R 115. However, it does not follow that a breach of s. 58 or the provisions of the code relating to access to legal advice will always be regarded as sufficiently significant or substantial to result in exclusion of evidence. In *Alladice* (1988) 87 Cr App R 380, A was denied access to legal advice by officers who had genuinely misconstrued the provisions of s. 58. A admitted in evidence that he was able to cope with being interviewed, that he had been given and understood the caution, and that he was aware of his legal rights. However, he had requested legal advice in order to have a check on the conduct of the police during interview. The trial judge found that the interviews were properly conducted, and that the only function of legal advice would have been to remind A of rights of which he was already well aware. On these facts, the Court of Appeal held that there was no obligation to exclude the confession. See also *Dunford* (1990) 91 Cr App R 150, *Oliphant* [1992] Crim LR 40 and, by way of contrast, *Sanusi* [1992] Crim LR 43, in which the failure to inform S, a foreigner, of his right to advice was particularly significant in the light of his lack of familiarity with police procedures and meant that his confession ought to have been excluded.

Breaches of the various provisions of Code C regarding the procedures to be followed when interviewing suspects have also tended to lead to the exclusion of evidence under s. 78, for reasons similar to those stated in *Walsh*. In *Keenan* [1990] 2 QB 54, it was said to be desirable that the provisions of Code C which are designed to ensure that interviews are fully recorded and the suspect afforded an opportunity to contest the record be 'strictly complied with', and that the courts would not be slow to exclude evidence obtained following 'substantial breaches' by the interrogator. Other provisions which have been held capable of requiring or contributing to the exclusion of evidence are those relating to cautioning, and to the right to have an appropriate adult present at interview. In *Aspinall* it was noted that the denial of the right to an appropriate adult might lead to the failure of the accused to recognise the need for legal advice. A waiver in these circumstances would be worthless. (As to the content of the provisions of Code C regarding interrogation, see **D1.53** to **D1.56**.)

The failure of the interrogator to appreciate that he is conducting an 'interview' within the meaning of that term in Code C by questioning a suspect about his involvement in an offence has proved an important peg on which to hang arguments for exclusion, as such failure frequently leads to a multiplicity of relevant breaches of Code C. The leading authorities are *Absolam* (1988) 88 Cr App R 332 (breaches including failure to caution, to record, and to offer legal advice prior to impromptu questioning by custody officer: confession should have been excluded); *Cox* (1993) 96 Cr App R 464 (informal questioning in C's own home amounting to interview which ought to have taken place only in a police station, inadequate recording and late caution: confession should have been excluded); *Weekes* (1993) 97 Cr App R 222 (inadequate recording and failure to ensure presence of appropriate adult at conversation in police car amounting to interview: confession should have been excluded); *Okafor* (1994) 99 Cr App R 97 (questioning by customs officer during search of O's bag conducted without caution or other incidents of an interview in order not to excite O's suspicion that the drugs in his luggage had been detected: questioning still an interview and confession should have been excluded for breaches); and *Weedersteyn* [1995] 1 Cr App R 405 (W believed he was assisting officers to find drugs importers and was not aware of the significance of his own incriminating statement, taken without caution, until two months later: statement should have been excluded as arising out of an interview not under caution, and because no record was shown to W). The frequent appearance of cases of this type in applications to exclude under s. 78 may in part be accounted for by the difficulty of applying the definition of interview provided by the first revision of Code C which has now been superseded by the second revision (1995) (see *Cox*, in which the authorities are reviewed). The recent decision in *Miller* [1998] Crim LR 209, in which a confession made in interview without caution was said to have been wrongly admitted, came to appeal only because the judge mistakenly applied the pre-1995 definition.

Although the provisions regarding the conduct of interviews are of great importance, breaches may nevertheless occur which are insufficiently significant or substantial to trigger s. 78. For example, in *Matthews* (1989) 91 Cr App R 43, the decision of the trial judge not to exclude evidence of a confession was upheld where the breach concerned the failure of a police officer to show the suspect a note of a conversation which the suspect had asked to be kept 'off the record'. See also *Courtney* [1995] Crim LR 63 (where the provisions of Code C were 'largely followed'), *RSPCA* v *Eager* [1995] Crim LR 60 (to similar effect), and *Blackwell* [1995] 2 Cr App R 641 (in which the court's decision that the trial judge was 'perfectly entitled' to admit the evidence was said to be 'highlighted by the technicality of the breaches'. Alternatively, a breach may be more than technical, but in the particular circumstances of the case no unfairness results from admitting the evidence. In *Dunn* (1990) 91 Cr App R 150, the failure of the interviewer to observe the provisions designed to prevent fabrication of the interview record would have been regarded as sufficient to require exclusion but for the fact that D's solicitor's clerk was present during the alleged conversation. It was held that it was legitimate for the trial judge to take account of this factor in exercising his discretion to admit the confession, as the presence of the clerk would have been likely to inhibit fabrication, and provided the accused with a witness as to what was actually said. In *Findlay* [1992] Crim LR 372, two suspects had wrongly been held incommunicado but it was held that the fact that one of them had subsequently had access to a solicitor for half an hour before signing the notes of his interview justified the admission of his confession.

Where the defence relies on breaches of PACE Code C in constructing a challenge to a confession under s. 78, but the court decides that no breach occurred, it follows that it is most unlikely that the discretion will be exercised. For examples see *Hughes* [1988] Crim LR 519 (provisions regarding interviewing in the absence of a solicitor not infringed); *Maguire* (1989) 90 Cr App R 115 (exchange between police officer and M not an 'interview'); *Menard* (1994) *The Times*, 23 March 1994 (meeting sought by M in order to volunteer information not an 'interview').

Where the provisions of Code C have changed in the accused's favour since his interrogation, the court may take account of the new provision as the Code reflects what is considered to be fair (*Ward* (1994) 98 Cr App R 337).

Bad Faith   It is not the function of the court to use the PACE 1984, s. 78, to discipline **F17.19** the police (*Mason* [1988] 1 WLR 139; *Canale* [1990] 2 All ER 187). However, the presence of bad faith where the police have acted in breach of the Act or Code is a factor making it more likely that evidence will be excluded. In *Alladice* (1988) 87 Cr App R 380, the facts of which are stated at **F17.18**, the Court of Appeal held that there is a distinction to be drawn between cases where the police have acted in bad faith, and cases where the police, albeit in good faith, have fallen foul of s. 58. In the former case, a court would have 'little difficulty in ruling any confession inadmissible under s. 78'. In the latter, the evidence would still fall to be excluded in many cases, so that it behoves the police to use their powers of delaying access to a solicitor only with great circumspection, but it was not possible 'to say in advance what would or would not be fair'. A similar distinction was drawn in *Walsh* (1989) 91 Cr App R 160 where it was said (at p. 163) that: 'although bad faith may make substantial or significant that which might not otherwise be so, the contrary does not follow. Breaches which are in themselves significant and substantial are not rendered otherwise by the good faith of the officers concerned.' See also *Samuel* [1988] QB 615, in which a submission was made that, in the absence of impropriety, the discretion should never be exercised to exclude admissible evidence. The Court of Appeal had 'no hesitation in rejecting that submission, although the propriety or otherwise of the way in which the evidence was obtained is something which a court is, in terms, enjoined by the section to take into account'.

Information on which Discretion is to be Exercised

F17.20 The discretion does not fall to be exercised because the judge of his own motion recognises that a serious breach such as might trigger exclusion has taken place: if the accused is represented by an advocate who appears competent, and a particular part of the evidence might be the subject of a tactical or strategic plan on the part of the defence, the judge should not take it upon himself to exclude evidence, though he might consider it appropriate to make pertinent inquiry of counsel in the absence of the jury (*Raphaie* [1996] Crim LR 812).

When the defence seek to exclude evidence obtained by or in circumstances alleged to amount to breaches of the PACE 1984 or codes, the Court of Appeal in *Keenan* [1990] 2 QB 54 noted that a number of different situations may face the judge:

(a) One or more breaches of a code may be apparent in the custody record itself or from the witness statements.

(b) There may be a prima facie breach which, if objection is taken, must be justified by evidence adduced by the prosecution.

(c) There may be alleged breaches which can probably only be established by the evidence of the accused himself.

Cases under (c) are likely to be rare, and it is likely that in cases under (a) and (b) the trial judge will have no means of knowing what will ensue after he has made his ruling. If he rules against admissibility, it may be that the accused will exercise his right not to give evidence. To permit the evidence to be given may therefore effectively deprive the accused of a right which he would otherwise have had. If the evidence is admitted, the judge does not know what the response to it may be. The accused may testify that the interview in question never took place at all, or that, though it took place, the questions and answers were fabricated, or that what was said was inaccurately recorded, or he might accept the accuracy of the record. Despite these difficulties, the judge must make his ruling on the information available to him at the time. In *Keenan* itself, the trial judge had wrongly assumed that any unfairness which might have been present could be cured by K giving evidence at the trial. Failure to give evidence at the *voir dire* is a different matter, and, in considering whether an accused has been prejudiced by a breach, the trial judge is entitled to take account of his failure to give evidence at the *voir dire* (*Oni* [1992] Crim LR 183).

The record of interview and the contents of the confession itself may assist on the question whether the admission of the evidence would affect the fairness of the proceedings (*Dunford* (1990) 91 Cr App R 150 at p. 155). However, it was also said that it may be necessary to avoid reference to such material in cases where there is a 'root and branch' challenge by the defence to the contents of the statement.

Unfairness not Arising from Breach of Codes of Practice

F17.21 In various authorities the significance of conduct not amounting to a breach of a code of practice or of the PACE 1984 has been considered, and it is clear that s. 78 may be invoked in such cases, though instances of the exercise of the discretion are rarer. The principles which have developed in relation to confessions apply also to other forms of prosecution evidence, and reference should be made also to **F2.15** to **F2.17**.

The provisions of Code of Practice C do not apply to conversations between suspects and undercover investigators, unless the undercover pose is deliberately abused as a means of circumventing the code (*Christou* [1992] QB 979; *Bryce* [1992] 4 All ER 569; *Edwards* [1997] Crim LR 348). Where genuine undercover operations yield evidence, including incriminating statements, the use of subterfuge does not of itself entail a finding of unfairness. Relevant considerations in *Christou* (where undercover police set up as 'shady' jewellers in order to recover stolen property and gather evidence againt the thieves and handlers) were that the public interest favoured the operation, that the offences had already been committed and that there was no incitement to crime on the part of the police, and that the suspects had 'applied themselves to the trick' without pressure from the officers. See also *Maclean* [1993] Crim LR 687, a similar operation concerning illegally imported drugs.

In *Bailey* [1993] 3 All ER 513 subterfuge in the interrogation process was considered. B and S were arrested and charged with robbery, but maintained their right to silence at interview. They were placed together in a bugged police cell, their suspicions being allayed by play-acting on the part of the police, who pretended to be reluctant to leave them alone together. Their resultant incriminating conversation was admitted, and it was held that the fact that B and S could not, under Code of Practice C, properly have been subjected to further questioning did not mean that they had to be protected from the opportunity to speak incriminatingly to one another if they chose to do so. It was acknowledged to appear odd that, alongside the 'rigorously controlled legislative regime' for questioning it should be considered acceptable for 'parallel covert investigations' legitimately to continue, but, provided such stratagems were used only in grave cases and that there was no suggestion of oppression or unreliability, there was nothing unfair about admitting the evidence obtained in consequence. The court distinguished as improper the subterfuge employed in *Mason* [1988] 1 WLR 139 in which a police officer told deliberate lies to M and to M's solicitor regarding the availability of fingerprint evidence connecting M with the offence of which he was suspected, in order to extract a confession from him. The trial judge admitted the confession, but the Court of Appeal held that he had failed to take into account one vital factor, 'namely the deceit practised upon the appellant's solicitor. If he had included that in his consideration . . . he would have been driven to an opposite conclusion.' *Mason* is not, it is submitted, authority for the proposition that lies may safely be told to an accused person provided his legal adviser is not hoodwinked; on the contrary, both aspects of the deception were regarded as equally serious and 'most reprehensible' by the Court of Appeal. The trial judge's failure to take account of the lie told to the solicitor merely provided the ground on which the court was able to review the exercise of his discretion. *Bailey* was applied in *Roberts* [1997] 1 Cr App R 217, in which R was induced to confess by a fellow suspect, C (with whom he had been placed in a bugged cell), to one robbery with which R had already been charged and to another with which he was subsequently charged. The trial judge's conclusion that C was not a police agent and had not been told what to ask R was regarded as 'unassailable', despite breaches of the Code in relation to C which made it hard to determine what precisely had been said to him (see **F17.17**). On the facts as found, the test was said to be whether the conduct of the police, either wittingly or unwittingly, led to unfairness or injustice, and the judge's decision to admit the evidence was upheld. The only difference between this case and *Bailey* was said to be that the police 'had perhaps a rather firmer basis for their expectations' of a confession than in *Bailey*.

Unfairness may arise from misunderstanding as well as from subterfuge. In *Smith* [1994] 1 WLR 1396, S was under the impression that R, the bank manager questioning him, was concerned only to obtain information about the impact of a transaction on the market, and not about S's criminal involvement. Although R was guilty of no impropriety, the Court of Appeal held that S's statements should not have been admitted. In *Hayter* v *L* [1998] 1 WLR 854 the issue was whether it was an abuse of process for a private prosecution to proceed after an offender had been cautioned by the police (a procedure which necessarily involves an admission of guilt). Holding that it was not, the Divisional Court said that any unfairness arising from the use of the cautioned party's admission in the subsequent proceedings could be met by the s. 78 discretion. As a prerequisite of a caution, a party should be made aware that there is the possibility of a private prosecution, but it might still be thought unfair to permit a confession made in hope of escaping a prosecution to be used in order to found one.

The discretion may, it seems, be used in respect of evidence which is unreliable as the result of the physical condition of the suspect, whether or not the interview in which he participates is conducted in breach of the code (see, e.g., *Effik* (1992) 95 Cr App R 427, in which the trial judge, in a ruling endorsed by the Court of Appeal, made it clear that he would have excluded the confession of M, a heroin addict, had it been made at a time when he was suffering acute withdrawal symptoms).

In exercising the discretion under s. 78, a trial judge is entitled to have regard to relevant provisions of the European Convention on Human Rights (*Law-Thompson* [1977] Crim LR 674, applying the general principle stated in *Khan* [1997] AC 558 (see **F2.12**) to confession evidence). However his focus when dealing with confession evidence must be on ss. 76 and 78 and any applicable provisions of the Code of Practice. Under those provisions, the absence of an appropriate adult at the interview of a mentally disordered suspect did not render the interview evidence automatically inadmissible; thus even if the treatment of L involved a prima facie breach of the Convention, it did not follow that the evidence was necessarily to be excluded.

Exclusion of Subsequent Confession

F17.22 Where a confession is excluded, either under s. 76 or under s. 78, for breach of a code, the question may arise as to whether it would be unfair to admit a subsequent confession which has itself been obtained without breaking the rules. In *Gillard* (1991) 92 Cr App R 61, it was held, upholding the admission of subsequent statements by two accused, that there is no universal rule requiring the exclusion of such a subsequent confession. The question is whether, on the facts of a particular case, there is a sufficient nexus between the circumstances in which the two statements were made to render it unfair to admit the subsequent statement, so that, for example, the accused is still affected by some impropriety which took place during the first, excluded interview. Important considerations are whether the objections leading to the exclusion of the first interview were of a fundamental and continuing nature, and whether the arrangements for the subsequent interview gave the accused a sufficient opportunity to exercise an informed and independent choice as to whether he should repeat or retract what he said, or say nothing (*Neil* [1994] Crim LR 441; *Nelson* [1998] 2 Cr App R 399). See also *Canale* (1990) 91 Cr App R 1, in which a subsequent interview was held to have been tainted by an earlier one in which promises were alleged to have been made; *Y* v *DPP* [1991] Crim LR 917, in which earlier confessions, despite their spontaneous nature, were excluded because of breaches of the code, but a subsequent, properly conducted interview was held to have been rightly admitted; *Wood* [1994] Crim LR 222, in which a multiplicity of breaches at the first interview of a mentally handicapped suspect tainted a later interview; and *Prouse* v *DPP* [1999] All ER (D) 748, unreported in printed form, in which the provision of legal advice before the later interview rendered it admissible.

Confessions by Mentally Handicapped Persons

F17.23 A confession made by a mentally handicapped person may be admitted in evidence, provided it satisfies the conditions imposed by the PACE 1984, s. 76, (see **F17.4**), and provided also that it is not excluded by the court in the exercise of its discretion to exclude prosecution evidence under s. 78 of the Act. Where such a confession is received in evidence, the provisions of s. 77 come into play and must be complied with.

Police and Criminal Evidence Act 1984, s. 77

(1)   Without prejudice to the general duty of the court at a trial on indictment to direct the jury on any matter on which it appears to the court appropriate to do so, where at such a trial—
    (a)   the case against the accused depends wholly or substantially on a confession by him; and
    (b)   the court is satisfied—
        (i)   that he is mentally handicapped; and
        (ii)   that the confession was not made in the presence of an independent person,
the court shall warn the jury that there is special need for caution before convicting the accused in reliance on the confession, and shall explain that the need arises because of the circumstances mentioned in paragraphs (a) and (b) above.

(2)   In any case where at the summary trial of a person for an offence it appears to the court that a warning under subsection (1) above would be required if the trial were on indictment, the court shall treat the case as one in which there is a special need for caution before convicting the accused on his confession.

(3)   In this section—
    'independent person' does not include a police officer or a person employed for, or engaged on, police purposes;
    'mentally handicapped' in relation to a person, means that he is in a state of arrested or incomplete development of mind which includes significant impairment of intelligence and social functioning; and
    'police purposes' has the meaning assigned to it by section 101(2) of the Police Act 1996.

In its application to Customs and Excise, s. 77(3) is modified to the extent that the definition of 'independent person' includes, in addition to the persons mentioned therein, an officer or any other person acting under the authority of the Commissioners of Customs and Excise (Police and Criminal Evidence Act 1984) (Application to Customs and Excise) Order 1985 (SI 1985 No. 1800)).

There is no need to give a warning in accordance with s. 77 unless the case for the Crown would be 'substantially less strong' without the confession (*Campbell* [1995] Crim LR 157).

PACE Code C requires (para. 11.14) the presence at interview of an 'appropriate adult' when the interviewee is a person at risk by reason, *inter alia*, of mental handicap, unless the interview is conducted on an emergency basis (annexe C of the code). The concept of an 'appropriate adult' is substantially the same as, though not identical to, the 'independent person' mentioned in s. 77. In particular, a solicitor attending the suspect would be an 'independent person', but would be unlikely to be the 'appropriate adult', who would normally be a relative or someone with experience of caring for the suspect (*Lewis* [1996] Crim LR 260). The warning required by s. 77 serves to draw the magistrates' or jury's attention to the potential unreliability of a confession obtained without this safeguard and should be tailored to any specific evidence of unreliability relating to the accused himself (*Campbell*). In *Bailey* [1995] 2 Cr App R 262, it was held to be necessary to give the warning in respect of informal admissions made to members of the public in the absence of an independent third party, but this does not appear to be the mischief at which s. 77 was aimed.

In *Lamont* [1989] Crim LR 813, L was convicted of the attempted murder of his baby son. The only evidence of L's intention came from a confession made in an interview at which no independent person was present. Expert defence evidence indicated mental retardation and impairment of intelligence and social functioning, but the trial judge concluded that L was not mentally handicapped and therefore did not warn the jury in accordance with s. 77. Quashing the conviction, the Court of Appeal held that the required direction under s. 77 was an essential ingredient of a fair summing-up, yet the trial judge had neither suggested to nor directed the jury that if they accepted the expert evidence they should exercise the caution called for by the section. The decision of the Court may, however, be open to doubt in part, in that it is the function of the judge, not the jury, to decide whether the accused is mentally handicapped. In establishing whether a defendant is mentally handicapped within the meaning of s. 77(3) it is not appropriate to take figures produced by intelligence tests in one case and to apply them slavishly in another in order to produce a rigid definition: every case has its individual features (*Kenny* [1994] Crim LR 284).

In the present climate of opinion, a confession made by a mentally handicapped person otherwise than in the presence of an independent person would be likely to be excluded at trial under either s. 76 or s. 78 of the 1984 Act. It follows that there will be few cases where a court is called on to follow the procedure laid down in s. 77. In *Moss* (1990) 91 Cr App R 371 it was thought that the section was aimed at two possible cases: (a) where a confession has been properly obtained from a mentally handicapped person in the absence of an independent person in the course of an 'urgent interview' as permitted by Code C, Annexe C; (b) where the interview was in breach of Code C but there was only 'one interview during a comparatively short period of custody'. In *Moss*, confessions obtained in the course of nine interviews over a lengthy period of detention were held to have been wrongly admitted despite the s. 77 direction given by the trial judge: the statements ought to have been excluded under s. 76(2)(b) (see **F17.10**).

The decision of the Court of Appeal to limit the circumstances in which a case depending on confession evidence of this type should be left to the jury further restricts the ambit of s. 77. In *MacKenzie* (1992) 96 Cr App R 98, the Court of Appeal considered the application of the rule in *Galbraith* [1981] 1 WLR 1039 (see **D13.26**) to the case where the confession of a mentally handicapped person had been admitted at trial, but was unsupported by other evidence. The court laid down the following rules:

> (1) Where the prosecution case depends wholly upon confessions; (2) the defendant suffers from a significant degree of mental handicap; and (3) the confessions are unconvincing to a point where a jury properly directed could not properly convict upon them, then the judge, assuming that he has not excluded the confessions earlier, should withdraw the case from the jury. The confessions may be unconvincing, for example, because they lack the incriminating details to be expected of a guilty and willing confessor, or because they are inconsistent with other evidence, or because they are otherwise inherently improbable.

M, a mentally handicapped man with a personality disorder, was convicted of two offences of manslaughter and two of arson. The prosecution case in respect of the killings depended entirely on unsupported confessions, whereas the proof of arson, though largely dependent on confessions, was supported by other independent evidence. During questioning M had also confessed to twelve other killings, none of which, in the end, the Crown believed he had committed. At the point in the trial when the confessions to the killings were admitted, it was thought that they contained details which only the killer could have known. On a careful review of the confessions, however, the Court of Appeal considered that the knowledge of the basic circumstances of the killings which they contained were of the sort that would not have been confined to the killer, and that they also contained some striking errors and omissions. Bearing in mind that M's credibility was diminished by his false confessions to other killings, and that he may well have been motivated by a desire to stay in the secure hospital at which he had been detained, the court was left with at least a lurking doubt as to whether the verdicts of manslaughter were safe and satisfactory. The convictions for arson, however, were allowed to stand. *MacKenzie* was applied in *Wood* [1994] Crim LR 222, in which the only blow which W had confessed to striking was proved by medical evidence not to have caused the death of the victim.

A confession which falls within the first two limbs of the *MacKenzie* test, but which is admitted because it falls outside the third, may require a very careful judicial direction (*Bailey* [1995] 2 Cr App R 262, where it was held that the judge was obliged, in addition to giving the s. 77 warning, to give the jury a 'full and proper statement' of the defendant's case against the confession being accepted by the jury as true).

DETERMINING THE ADMISSIBILITY OF CONFESSIONS: THE *VOIR DIRE*

The general rules regarding the holding of a *voir dire*, or trial within a trial, in order to determine disputed issues regarding preliminary facts on which the admissibility of evidence depends, are dealt with in detail at **D13.20**. The principles considered in this section are those which have particular significance with regard to confessions, or are relevant solely to the reception of confession evidence.

The *Voir Dire* and the Police and Criminal Evidence Act 1984, s. 76

At common law, where the admissibility of a confession statement was to be challenged **F17.24** in a trial on indictment, the following practice was followed:

(a)   Defending counsel would notify prosecuting counsel that an objection to admissibility was to be raised.
(b)   Prosecuting counsel would then refrain from mentioning the statement in his opening to the jury.
(c)   At the appropriate time the judge would conduct a trial on the *voir dire* to decide on the admissibility of the statement (*Ajodha* v *The State* [1982] AC 204).

The *voir dire* was normally held in the absence of the jury, but only at the request or with the consent of the defence (*Ajodha*, citing *Anderson* (1929) 21 Cr App R 178). See further, as to the obligations of counsel, *Cole* (1941) 28 Cr App R 43, *Patel* [1951] 2 All ER 29 and *Mitchell* v *The Queen* [1998] AC 695 at p. 704.

The PACE 1984, s. 76(2), follows the common law by providing that where the defence represent that a confession on which the prosecution propose to rely was, or may have been, obtained in such a way as to render it inadmissible in evidence, the court shall not allow the confession to be given in evidence except insofar as the prosecution prove to the court beyond reasonable doubt that the confession was not so obtained. Section 76(3) provides in addition that the court may of its own motion require the prosecution, as a condition of allowing them to give a confession in evidence, to prove that it was not obtained in such a way as to render it inadmissible. Both provisions strongly indicate that a *voir dire* is the correct procedure for determining whether the confession may be given, and the common-law procedure set out above continues to be followed in practice. However it has now been established that the court may require the jury to withdraw whether the defence consents or not (*Davis* [1990] Crim LR 860, and see also *Hendry* [1988] Crim LR 766).

In *Liverpool Juvenile Court, ex parte R* [1988] QB 1, it was held that s. 76 requires magistrates conducting a summary trial to hold a *voir dire* to determine admissibility where the defence, before the close of the prosecution case, represent to the court that the confession was obtained in breach of s. 76(2). The decision represents a significant departure from the common law, which regarded the *voir dire* as inappropriate in summary trials (see further as to summary trials, **D19.6**). As magistrates are judges of both fact and law, a ruling that a confession is to be excluded will mean that they have to put the objectionable material out of their minds when considering guilt; this is a task with which it has recently been said 'they are well capable of coping both by training and by disposition' (*Hayter* v *L* [1998] 1 WLR 854, commenting on the comparable situation which arises after the s. 78 discretion to exclude has been exercised).

F17.25 ***Unrepresented Accused*** In *Ajodha* v *The State* [1982] AC 204 Lord Bridge said (at p. 223):

> Particular difficulties may arise in the trial of an unrepresented defendant, when the judge must, of course, be especially vigilant to ensure a fair trial. No rules can be laid down, but it may be prudent, if the judge has any reason to suppose that the voluntary character of a statement proposed to be put in evidence by the prosecution is likely to be in issue, that he should speak to the defendant before the trial begins and explain his rights in the matter.

The position appears to be unaltered under the 1984 Act, if for 'voluntary character' is read 'admissibility'. The court also enjoys the power under s. 76(3) to put the prosecutor to his proof on the issue of admissibility, and it is submitted that it would generally be appropriate to exercise that power in the case of an unrepresented accused.

Challenging Admissibility at Trial

F17.26 The position at common law was stated in *Ajodha* v *The State* [1982] AC 204 by Lord Bridge, who said (at p. 223):

> Though the case for the defence raises an issue as to the voluntariness of a statement . . . , defending counsel may for tactical reasons prefer that the evidence bearing on that issue be heard before the jury, with a single cross-examination of the witnesses on both sides, even though this means that the jury hear the impugned statement whether admissible or not. If the defence adopts this tactic, it will be open to defending counsel to submit at the close of the evidence that, if the judge doubts the voluntariness of the statement, he should direct the jury to disregard it, or, if the statement is essential to sustain the prosecution case, direct an acquittal. Even in the absence of such a submission, if the judge himself forms the view that the voluntariness of the statement is in doubt, he should take the like action *proprio motu*.

In *Liverpool Juvenile Court, ex parte R* [1988] QB 1, at p. 10 it was considered that the defence retained this option:

> There remains a discretion open to the defendant as to the stage at which an attack is to be made upon an alleged confession. A trial within a trial will only take place before the close of the prosecution case if it is represented to the court that the confession was, or may have been, obtained by one or other of the processes set out in subparagraph (a) or (b) of section 76(2). If no such representation is made the defendant is at liberty to raise admissibility or weight of the confession at any subsequent stage of the trial.

It may be argued that this view overlooks the power of the court under the PACE 1984, s. 76(3), to compel the holding of a *voir dire*, apparently irrespective of the defendant's wishes. This power may, however, be intended primarily to enable a court to assist an unrepresented defendant to vindicate his rights, rather than to overrule the wishes of defence counsel where the accused is legally represented. A more fundamental objection to the view taken in *Ex parte R* may be found in *Sat-Bhambra* (1988) 88 Cr App R 55. Certain statements by S had been ruled admissible at the *voir dire*, because there was no evidence to suggest that the statements were likely to be unreliable as a result of the accused's ill health at the time. At the trial, medical evidence was adduced by the defence which came down more strongly in favour of S's contention that he was suffering from hypoglycaemia when he was interviewed. When asked to reconsider his decision on admissibility, the trial judge ruled that the terms of s. 76 prevented him from taking this course. The Court of Appeal agreed, holding (at p. 62):

The words of section 76 are crucial: 'proposes to be given in evidence' and 'shall not allow the confession to be given' are not, in our judgment, appropriate to describe something which has happened in the past. They are directed solely to the situation before the statement goes before the jury. Once the judge has ruled that it should do so, section 76 (and section 78, for the same reasons) ceases to have effect.

The court went on to consider the powers which the judge may, by virtue of the common law, exercise in this situation, (at p. 62) before concluding: 'If a defendant wishes under section 76 to exclude a confession, the time to make his submission to that effect is before the confession is put in evidence and not afterwards.' It has been noted (see **F17.3**) that the statements in issue in *Sat-Bhambra* were self-serving, and were therefore regarded as not being confessions to which s. 76 applied. However, the Court of Appeal was careful to state that its views on that subsidiary matter were *obiter*, so that the *ratio* of the case appears to be that the admissibility of a confession may not be challenged under s. 76 once the confession has been given in evidence. The contrary view, stated by the Divisional Court in *Liverpool Juvenile Court, ex parte R* [1988] QB 1, was expressed to apply to summary proceedings only, but it is difficult to see why the interpretation of the Act should vary according to the nature of the trial. Thus, the law, whatever the mode of trial, would appear to be as stated in *Sat-Bhambra*. See also *Davis* [1990] Crim LR 860, in which the Court of Appeal inclined to the view (but without deciding the point) that the language of the section anticipated a *voir dire* taking place before the challenged evidence was heard by the jury.

The *Voir Dire* and the Police and Criminal Evidence Act 1984, s. 78

Section 78 is set out at **F17.17**. The view taken, *obiter*, by the Court of Appeal in *Sat-Bhambra* (1988) 88 Cr App R 55 was that the wording of the section suggested that defence objections should be made before the confession is given in evidence. The relevant words are 'the court may refuse to allow evidence *on which the prosecution proposes to rely* to be given'. It does not necessarily follow from this that a *voir dire* should always be held; indeed, it has been said that in a summary trial the defence have no right to a *voir dire* simply in order to determine a preliminary issue under s. 78 (*Vel v Chief Constable of North Wales* (1987) 151 JP 510 and see **D19.6**). However, in many cases it will be convenient to investigate the submission in this way, particularly where the defence also challenge the confession under s. 76, and in *Halawa v Federation Against Copyright Theft* [1995] 1 Cr App R 21 it was said, *obiter*, that if, in connection with an application to exclude evidence under s. 78 alone, the accused wished to proceed by way of a trial within a trial, magistrates might find it necessary to proceed in that way in order to allow the accused to give evidence in relation to the evidential issue without prejudicing his right to silence at trial.

F17.27

Disputes as to Making of Confession

At common law the *voir dire* was inappropriate in trials on indictment where the defence case was simply that no confession was made (*Ajodha v The State* [1982] AC 204). The Board gave as examples cases where the defence allege that an interview never took place, or that no incriminating answers were given, or, in the case of a written statement, that it is a forgery. The issue of fact whether or not the statement was made by the accused is purely for the jury. In the same case, however, the Privy Council recognised that issues of voluntariness might be intertwined with disputes as to the making of the confession, and that it is a fallacy to suppose that the two grounds of challenge are mutually exclusive. Such a case may arise where the accused claims that he was not the author of a written statement which bears his name, and alleges that his signature at the end of the statement was procured by force or by deception. Such cases required the holding of a *voir dire* to determine the issue of voluntariness at common law, leaving the jury to determine the value and weight of the statement if it is admitted. Issues as to

F17.28

admissibility under the PACE 1984, s. 76, are equally capable of arising in combination with disputes as to the making of the statement, and it is submitted that the principles stated in *Ajodha* continue to represent the law.

Where the defence in a trial on indictment challenge the confession under s. 78, they may ultimately wish to assert at the trial that no confession was made. At the point at which the challenge is made, however, the judge may be unaware of the line the defence intend to take at trial, and the defence are under no obligation to disclose their case in this respect (*Keenan* [1990] 2 QB 54). The issue at the *voir dire* is simply whether the introduction of the confession would have such an adverse effect on the fairness of the proceedings that the court ought not to admit it. It is not the function of the judge to decide whether the confession was made (*Keenan*). See, however, *Alladice* (1988) 87 Cr App R 380, in which the trial judge reached such a decision before deciding to admit the statement.

Truth of Confession as Issue on *Voir Dire*

F17.29 It is not the function of the judge or magistrates at a *voir dire* to determine whether a confession is true, but simply whether it should be admitted. The PACE 1984, s. 76, underlines this limitation by providing that the court shall not allow the confession to be admitted 'except insofar as the prosecution proves beyond reasonable doubt that the confession (notwithstanding that it may be true) was not obtained [in breach of s. 76(2)]'.

It does not necessarily follow from this that the truth of the statement is irrelevant to the question whether it should be admitted. At common law there was a conflict of authority on the point. In *Hammond* [1941] 3 All ER 318, H was charged with murder. He gave evidence on the *voir dire*, claiming that he had been knocked about and brutally ill-treated in order to induce a confession. It was held that he was properly cross-examined as to whether his confession was true, as it was relevant to the credit to be given to his assertions, on the basis that: 'If a man says, "I was forced to tell the story . . ." it must be relevant to know whether he was made to tell the truth, or whether he was made to say a number of things which were untrue' (per Humphreys J at p. 321).

In *Wong Kam-ming* v *The Queen* [1980] AC 247, a majority of the Privy Council disapproved of *Hammond*, and held that it should no longer be followed in Hong Kong. W gave evidence at the *voir dire*, claiming that his confession had been extracted by force. He was cross-examined in detail as to the truth of the statement, which was subsequently excluded. At the trial, prosecuting counsel called evidence to prove that, at the *voir dire*, W had admitted that he was present at the scene of the crime. It was held that the cross-examination was impermissible and that it did not affect the credit of the accused as a witness. Lord Edmund-Davies said (at p. 256) 'If the defendant denies the truth of the confession or some self-incriminating admission contained in it, the question whether his denial is itself true or false cannot be ascertained until after the *voir dire* is over and the defendant's guilt or innocence has been determined by the jury'. If the defendant admits the truth, this tends to show that he is a truthful witness and goes to support his allegations rather than, as *Hammond* supposes, to undermine them. Lord Hailsham of St Marylebone, dissenting on this issue, considered (at p. 262C) that 'the only general limitations on what may be asked or tendered ought to be relevance to the issue to be tried' and concluded that it was not possible 'to say *a priori* that in no circumstances is the truth or falsity of the alleged confession relevant to the question at issue on the *voir dire* or admissible as to credibility of either the prosecution or defence witnesses'. He instanced, *inter alia*, cases in which the defence argue that, because a confession is demonstrably false, it must have been obtained by improper means. It must then be relevant for the prosecution to cross-examine on the truth of the statement.

It is submitted that Lord Hailsham's dissent in *Wong Kam-ming* v *The Queen* has logic on its side, but that the view of the majority has a sure foundation in policy, being consistent with the rule under which the accused is protected from the consequences of damaging admissions which further his case at the *voir dire* (see **F17.30**).

Precisely the same questions may fall to be considered under s. 76 or s. 78 of the 1984 Act. Although *Hammond* has never been overruled as far as English courts are concerned, in *Liverpool Juvenile Court, ex parte R* [1988] QB 1 the Divisional Court relied on the authority of *Wong Kam-ming* v *The Queen* for the proposition that a defendant cannot be asked about the truth of a confession during an inquiry as to its admissibility. It should be noted, however, that:

(a)   the judgment in that case expressly confined itself to summary proceedings (where it may be thought particularly important that the justices do not confuse the functions of the *voir dire* and the trial); and, more importantly,

(b)   the court was not concerned directly with the question under discussion, but was instead engaged in enumerating the advantages to the defendant of the *voir dire* procedure.

In *Davis* [1990] Crim LR 860 the Court of Appeal referred to *Wong Kam-ming* v *The Queen* as 'strong persuasive authority' for the view that D could not be cross-examined as to the truth of his confession when giving evidence on the *voir dire*, but the point was not decided as the trial judge's ruling to the contrary had had no bearing upon the outcome of the trial.

Admissibility of Evidence Given on *Voir Dire*

In *Wong Kam-ming* v *The Queen* [1980] AC 247 the Privy Council was unanimously of   **F17.30** the opinion that the prosecution could not lead at the trial evidence regarding the testimony given by the defendant at the *voir dire*. Such a rule was necessary (per Lord Hailsham), so that 'the defendant should be able and feel free either by his own testimony or by other means to challenge the voluntary character of the tendered statement'. The rule applies even where the confession is admitted (per Lord Edmund-Davies), because 'it is preferable to maintain a clear distinction between the issue of voluntariness, which is alone relevant to the *voir dire*, and the issue of guilt falling to be decided in the main trial'.

Wong Kam-ming v *The Queen* was applied in *Brophy* [1982] AC 476. B was tried in Northern Ireland for a large number of offences, including murder, and for being a member of the IRA, a proscribed organisation. At the *voir dire* he succeeded in challenging the admissibility of confessions tendered by the prosecution, on the ground that the statements were extracted from him by extreme misconduct on the part of his interrogators. In support of his case he admitted to membership of the IRA, in order to found an inference that his interrogators would have known of his allegiance and treated him brutally because of it. It was held that the accused's admission, being relevant to the issue at the *voir dire*, was inadmissible for the prosecution at the trial. Furthermore according to Lord Fraser of Tullybelton (at p. 481): 'Where . . . evidence is given at the *voir dire* by an accused person in answer to questions by his counsel, and without objection by counsel for the Crown, his evidence ought . . . to be treated as relevant to the issue at the *voir dire*, unless it is clearly and obviously irrelevant', for example, the accused 'goes out of his way to boast' of his guilt.

Some commentators have argued (see, e.g., *Andrews and Hirst on Criminal Evidence*, 1st ed., at 19.61, in a passage omitted from later editions) that the law has altered as a result of the PACE 1984, s. 76, the effect of which is to render such a confession admissible, there being no question of it having been obtained by oppression or in circumstances conducive to unreliability. Even if this is the case, however, the policy behind *Wong Kam-ming* v *The Queen* and *Brophy* can be preserved and the same result achieved by invoking s. 78 of the 1984 Act to prevent unfairness in the proceedings. It is submitted that the policy is worth preserving, and that the accused would derive no protection from the statutory rules prohibiting the reception of confessions obtained in certain circumstances if the accused could only invoke the rule at the cost of admitting afresh that what he said was true.

Cross-examination on Statements Made on *Voir Dire*

F17.31 In *Wong Kam-ming* v *The Queen* [1980] AC 247 W gave evidence at trial and was cross-examined in detail as to statements made on the *voir dire* which were inconsistent with his testimony. The Privy Council held that where, as in the instant case, the confession had been excluded at the *voir dire*, it was not open to the prosecution to conduct such a cross-examination: 'Once a statement has been excluded . . . to adopt the words of Humphreys J in *Treacy* [1944] 2 All ER 229, nothing more should be heard of the *voir dire* unless it gives rise to a prosecution for perjury' (per Lord Hailsham at pp. 260–1).

The rule was otherwise where the confession which was the subject of the *voir dire* was admitted in evidence. In such a case (per Lord Hailsham, at p. 261). '. . . the whole evidence relating to the statement will have to be rehearsed once more . . . in front of the jury', and '. . . the statements on oath by the defendant on the *voir dire* as material for cross-examination do not, from the point of view of public policy, stand in any other situation than any other statements made by him, including the statement which has been admitted'.

The reasons of policy underlying the law as stated in *Wong Kam-ming* v *The Queen* have not altered since the coming into force of the PACE 1984, and it is submitted that the law remains as stated.

CONFESSION ADMISSIBLE AT TRIAL

Reconsidering Admissibility

F17.32 It has already been noted (**F17.27**) that in *Sat-Bhambra* (1988) 88 Cr App R 55, the Court of Appeal held that, once a confession has been ruled admissible on the *voir dire*, the trial judge has no power under the PACE 1984, s. 76 or s. 78, to reconsider his decision if the evidence given at trial convinces him that he was wrong. To this extent the Act reverses the decision in *Watson* [1980] 1 WLR 991, where it was said that the judge had the power to reconsider the question of admissibility of evidence on which he had already ruled, and had the duty to exclude from the jury's consideration evidence which was inadmissible. However, the court in *Sat-Bhambra* noted that s. 82(3) of the 1984 Act preserved the common-law powers of a court to exclude evidence in its discretion. It followed that the trial judge retained the power, if only under the common law, to take such steps as were necessary to prevent injustice. He might, if he thought that the matter was not capable of remedy by a direction, discharge the jury; he might direct the jury to disregard the statement; or he might by way of direction point out to the jury matters which affect the weight of the confession and leave the matter in their hands. He was not, however, under any obligation to discharge the jury. The change brought about by the Act would seem therefore to be mainly technical, and it is submitted that in any event there is still force in the dictum of the Court of Appeal in *Watson* [1980] 1 WLR 991 that, 'the occasions on which a judge should allow counsel to invite him to reconsider a ruling already made are likely to be extremely rare'.

The problem is perhaps most likely to arise where a decision has been made on the basis that the confession was not obtained pursuant to a breach of the Code of Practice, but it then emerges that a breach may have occurred. In *Hassan* [1995] Crim LR 404, a concession to this effect by a police officer in cross-examination led the trial judge to use his common law powers to reconsider his decision to admit H's confession, although he quite properly did not regard the concession as decisive of whether there had been a breach, and concluded that there had not. It is also possible to reconsider a decision to exclude a statement. In *Allen* [1992] Crim LR 297 the defence sought to cross-examine a police witness to elicit their version of a conversation, the prosecution version of which had been excluded under s. 78. It was held that the judge had correctly exercised his discretion to admit the prosecution version of what had been said.

Role of Jury

The PACE 1984 has, it is submitted, left untouched the rules of the common law F17.33 regarding the role of the jury where confession evidence is admitted. At common law the admissibility of a confession was a matter for the judge alone, so that, if the confession was admitted, it was unnecessary to leave the same matters to the jury. The proper instruction to be given to the jury was that what weight they attached to the confession depended on all the circumstances in which it was taken, and that it was their right to give it such weight as they thought fit (*Burgess* [1968] 2 QB 112, approving *Chan Wei Keung* v *The Queen* [1967] 2 AC 16). There were previous authorities to the contrary, particularly *Bass* [1953] 1 QB 680, where it was held that the jury were to be directed to consider the application of the rule of admissibility when estimating the weight to be given to a confession; and *Francis* (1959) 43 Cr App R 174, where it was held that the onus was on the prosecution to satisfy the jury that the confession was voluntary. Both decisions were disapproved in *Chan Wei Keung* v *The Queen*. Nor should dicta in the subsequent case of *McCarthy* (1980) 70 Cr App R 270 be understood as requiring the jury to reconsider admissibility; the true position is that the jury should take into account all the circumstances in which a confession was made, including such matters as allegations of force, if they think they may be true, in assessing the probative value of a confession (*Ragho Prasad* v *The Queen* [1981] 1 WLR 469).

Because the jury were entitled at common law to consider all the circumstances in which a confession was made before deciding whether to act on it, it was held in *Murray* [1951] 1 KB 391 to be 'the right of counsel for the defence to cross-examine again the witnesses who have already given evidence in the absence of the jury; for if he can induce the jury to think that the confession was obtained through some threat or promise, its value will be enormously weakened'. This rule also would appear to be unchanged as a result of the enactment of the PACE 1984.

If the jury were to be told that the judge had ruled the confession admissible, it is possible that they might be influenced by the judge's view on admissibility in deciding the issues which are for them alone: i.e. whether the confession was made, and if it was, whether it is true. Thus it has been the practice in England, both before and after the PACE 1984, for this information to be withheld from them (*Mitchell* v *The Queen* [1998] AC 695; *Thompson* v *R* [1998] AC 811).

If a confession is voluntary, the inference that it is also true follows naturally in most cases. On rare occasions, however, the mental condition of the accused may give rise to doubts as to the reliability of his confession. In such a case, expert medical evidence may be admitted to assist the jury in evaluating the reliability of the confession (*Ward* [1993] 1 WLR 619 (severe personality disorder amounting to mental disorder); *MacKenzie* (1992) 96 Cr App R 98 (mentally handicapped accused also suffering personality disorder: Crown conceded jury entitled to the assistance of expert testimony to evaluate confessions: see also **F17.23**).

Confession Implicating Co-accused

A confession made by an accused person which is admitted in evidence is evidence against F17.34 him (PACE 1984, s. 76(1)). It is not, however, evidence against any other person implicated in it (*Rhodes* (1959) 44 Cr App R 23), unless it is made in the presence of that person and he acknowledges the incriminating parts so as to make them, in effect, his own. In this it is to be contrasted with the evidence on oath of a co-accused in a joint trial, which is evidence for all purposes, including the purpose of being evidence against the accused (*Rudd* (1948) 32 Cr App R 138). At common law the plea of guilty of a co-accused was not evidence against the accused (*Moore* (1956) 40 Cr App R 50). See now, however, the PACE 1984, s. 74, at **F11.3**.

In cases where a jury hear a confession which implicates a co-accused, 'it is the duty of the judge to impress on the jury that the statement of one prisoner not made on oath in the course of the trial is not evidence against the other and must be entirely disregarded' (*Gunewardene* [1951] 2 KB 600, at p. 610). For the circumstances in which a confession may be edited so as to remove incriminating references to a co-accused, see **F17.42**. In exceptional circumstances the existence of a confession by one accused which seriously prejudices another may be grounds for ordering separate trials (*Gunewardene*). Joint offences should generally be tried jointly, however, even though this may involve evidence which is inadmissible in respect of a particular accused being given. The fact that there is some risk of prejudice is not enough, though 'if a case is strong enough, if the prejudice is dangerous enough, if the circumstances are particular enough, all rules of this kind must go in the interests of justice' (*Lake* (1976) 64 Cr App R 172, at p. 175).

CONFESSION EXCLUDED AT TRIAL

Effect of Exclusion on Prosecution

F17.35 In *Treacy* [1944] 2 All ER 229, the prosecution had not sought to put in evidence, as part of their case, a statement made by T to a police officer following T's arrest for murder. Instead it was used in cross-examination of T as a previous inconsistent statement. The statement was assumed by the Court of Appeal to have been inadmissible as part of the prosecution case, and, that being so, it was held that 'nothing more ought to be heard of it, and it is quite a mistake to think that a document can be made admissible in evidence which is otherwise inadmissible simply because it is put to a person in cross-examination'. In *Rice* [1963] 1 QB 857 it was held that the same principle obtains in favour of a co-accused of the maker of the inadmissible statement. The rule prohibits the revelation that the accused has made a statement, 'since evidence of, or revelation of that fact tends in common sense to lend weight to the subsequent evidence'. It does not preclude the use of information derived from the statement as the basis of cross-examination (*Rice*).

Effect of Exclusion on Co-Accused

F17.36 A confession which is inadmissible under the PACE 1984, s. 76(2)(b), on behalf of the prosecution may not be relied upon by a co-accused as evidence of its truth (*Myers* [1998] AC 124: see **F17.12**). It may, however, be put to the maker in cross-examination, in which case the only limitation is relevancy (*Lui Mei Lin* v *The Queen* [1989] AC 288). It follows that a co-accused cannot be restrained from cross-examining the accused on the content of any previous statement made by him which is relevant, notwithstanding that that statement may have been ruled inadmissible as part of the prosecution case (*Lui Mei Lin* v *The Queen*, approving *Rowson* [1986] QB 174). Where evidence of an otherwise inadmissible previous statement is elicited by a co-accused in cross-examination, the judge should explain to the jury why the statement has previously been excluded and cannot be relied on by the prosecution to prove their case. It should also be remembered that in cross-examination as to credit the cross-examiner is bound by the answers which he receives, and that it is not legitimate to reopen all the circumstances in which the excluded statement was taken. The trial judge should insist that irrelevant material contained in the statement is not referred to, and that such material is, where necessary, excised from any copies which the jury might see (*Lui Mei Lin* v *The Queen*).

EVIDENCE YIELDED BY INADMISSIBLE CONFESSIONS

Police and Criminal Evidence Act 1984, s. 76

(4)   The fact that a confession is wholly or partly excluded in pursuance of this section shall not affect the admissibility in evidence—

(a)   of any facts discovered as a result of the confession; or

(b)   where the confession is relevant as showing that the accused speaks, writes or expresses himself in a particular way, of so much of the confession as is necessary to show that he does so.

(5)   Evidence that a fact to which this subsection applies was discovered as a result of a statement made by an accused person shall not be admissible unless evidence of how it was discovered is given by him or on his behalf.

(6)   Subsection (5) above applies—

(a)   to any fact discovered as a result of a confession which is wholly excluded in pursuance of this section; and

(b)   to any fact discovered as a result of a confession which is partly so excluded, if the fact is discovered as a result of the excluded part of the confession.

Discovery of Facts

The PACE 1984, s. 76(4)(a), follows the common-law rule as stated in *Warickshall* **F17.37** (1783) 1 Leach 263. W made a full confession to receiving stolen goods, in consequence of which the goods were found concealed in her bed. The confession was ruled inadmissible, but the prosecution were allowed to prove the discovery of the stolen property. It was held that the principle requiring the rejection of certain confessions in evidence 'has no application whatever as to the admission or rejection of facts, whether the knowledge of them be obtained in consequence of an extorted confession, or whether it arises from any other source; for a fact, if it exists at all, must exist invariably in the same manner, whether the confession from which it is derived be in other respects true or false'.

Some difficulty may arise as to where the 'confession' ends and 'facts discovered as a result of it' begin. At common law, in *Barker* [1941] 2 KB 381 documents delivered up by B as a direct result of an inducement were treated as the equivalent of confession evidence, and excluded accordingly. Section 82(1) of the 1984 Act now provides a definition of 'confession' as including 'any statement wholly or partly adverse to the person who made it . . . whether made in words or otherwise'. Words, documents or conduct which come within this definition and which fall foul of the exclusionary rule in s. 76(2) cannot be treated as 'facts' for the purpose of s. 76(4)(a). Thus, for example, a filmed re-enactment of a murder, in which a defendant is shown disposing of the murder weapon, should be regarded as a confession statement rather than as independent facts (*Lam Chi-ming* v *The Queen* [1991] 2 AC 212). However, it does not seem entirely satisfactory to regard conduct such as that in *Barker* as the equivalent of a 'statement' by him 'in consequence of anything said or done' under s. 76(2)(b) for the purposes of the 1984 Act, and such evidence would seem to be more correctly considered as admissible evidence of facts which, like all prosecution evidence, may in appropriate circumstances be excluded under s. 78 of the 1984 Act.

Confession Relevant to Show Speech, Writing or Expression

Section 76(4)(b) of the 1984 Act embodies a principle stated in argument by Lush J in **F17.38** *Voisin* [1918] 1 KB 531. V was charged with the murder of a woman, part of whose body was found in a parcel together with a handwritten note bearing the legend 'Bladie Belgiam'. V, who had not been cautioned, was asked by the police to write the words 'Bloody Belgian', which he did, misspelling them in precisely the same fashion as the writer of the note. The case did not concern an inadmissible confession, but the principle involved in the reception of the note in evidence was said by Lush J to be that 'it cannot make any difference to the admissibility of handwriting whether it is written voluntarily or under compulsion of threats'. Section 76(4)(b) might be used, for example, in a case of rape, where a tape-recorded confession is ruled inadmissible, but the voice of the accused can be heard speaking with an unusual speech impediment which was also described by the victim, or with a particular local accent. Care must be taken to avoid prejudice to the accused when adducing such evidence; s. 76(4)(b) permits the prosecution to adduce only 'so much of the confession as is necessary to show' the relevant feature, but even this may in some cases be impossible without the jury becoming aware that a confession has been made. In such cases it will have to be considered whether the risk of prejudice can be overcome by a direction as to the purpose for which the evidence has been adduced, or whether the discretion of the court to exclude prosecution evidence, either under s. 78 of the 1984 Act or at common law, should be exercised.

Linking Facts to Confession

F17.39 At common law there was some controversy as to the extent to which it was permissible to show that certain facts had come to light as the result of an inadmissible confession by the accused. Section 76(5) and (6) of the 1984 Act confirms the view taken in *Warickshall* (1783) 1 Leach 263, and *Berryman* (1854) 6 Cox CC 388 that no such link can be proved. The only exception is where the defence choose to give evidence of how the facts came to be discovered, in which case, presumably, the prosecution may challenge the account given by the defence, even if to do so involves making reference to the excluded statement.

Evidence Yielded by Confession Excluded under s. 78

F17.40 The PACE 1984, s. 76(4), applies only to matters coming to light as a result of a confession excluded under s. 76 itself. Where the confession is excluded in the discretion of the court under s. 78, no statutory rule applies, but the common-law principles suggest that evidence discovered in consequence is admissible.

As to the linking of the discovery with the confession, it may be that a court dealing with an application under s. 78 will not feel compelled to follow the principle laid down in s. 76(5), given that the common law on the point was unclear (see, e.g., *Griffin* (1809) Russ & Ry 151; *Gould* (1840) 9 C & P 364, and the views expressed by a majority of the Criminal Law Revision Committee in their 11th Report, *Evidence* (1972) Cmnd 4991, para. 69). It should also be noted that the reasons which led the court to exercise its discretion in respect of the confession may extend also to the subsequently discovered facts, as where an accused discloses information in a confession made after he has been denied access to legal advice by a police officer acting in deliberate and flagrant disregard of s. 58 of the 1984 Act.

Another possibility is that the court will take into account the confirmation of a confession by the discovery of incontrovertible facts in deciding whether to exercise its discretion to exclude the confession statement. Nothing in s. 78 appears to prevent such reasoning, indeed the court is enjoined to have regard to 'all the circumstances' in reaching its conclusion. (Contrast s. 76(2), in which it is clear that the truth of the confession is not a factor to be taken into account in determining admissibility.) The argument is particularly attractive where the defence rely on breach of a provision of a code of practice, the function of which is thought by the court to be to guard against the production of unreliable confession statements, such as the obligation to maintain records of interviews.

EDITING OF CONFESSIONS

Editing at Trial to Protect Accused

Where the confession of an accused person is admitted in evidence against him, the **F17.41**
whole confession is admissible, notwithstanding that it includes matter prejudicial to the
accused. In *Turner* v *Underwood* [1948] 2 KB 284 the response of the accused when
charged with an offence of indecency was to say 'I have done time for this before', and
it was held that the whole confession was admissible in evidence before the magistrates.
However, Lord Goddard noted (at p. 286) that: 'It is the practice as a rule in cases which
are tried before juries that where the court knows there is something said by a man in
his statement which admits a previous conviction, or shows other matter reflecting on
his character, the court sees that that is not read out to the jury.'

Similarly, in *Weaver* [1968] 1 QB 353 Sachs LJ said that a statement by an accused ought
to be edited at trial to avoid prejudicing him and to eliminate matters which 'it would
be better that the jury should not know'. In *Knight* (1946) 31 Cr App R 52 portions of
the accused's confessions which related to other offences which were irrelevant to the
offence charged were held to have been improperly received in evidence. Quashing the
convictions, Lewis J regarded it as 'contrary to the rules of evidence' to admit what was
in effect evidence of the bad character of the accused, who had not put their characters
in issue. In some cases the material edited out is irrelevant, in others it has a prejudicial
effect exceeding its probative value. See also *Hall* [1971] Crim LR 480.

When a statement is to be edited in this way, the proper procedure was said in *Weaver*
[1968] 1 QB 353 to be that the statement should not be edited until the trial, at which
stage, according to Sachs LJ (at p. 358) 'counsel can confer, and the judge can, if
necessary, take his part in ensuring that any "editing" is done, if it is done at all, in the
right way and to the right degree'.

Where the matter concerned is relevant and admissible in the trial there is no reason to
omit it, even if the jury are made aware of other offences (*Evans* [1950] 1 All ER 601).

In *Pearce* (1979) Cr App R 365, it was said that the rule of practice whereby the courts
'admit in evidence all unwritten and most written statements made by an accused person
to the police whether they contain admissions or whether they contain denials of guilt,'
was subject to the limitation that any admission of a previous conviction would be
excluded.

Editing at Trial to Protect Co-Accused

Where the confession of an accused person is admitted, it is not, as a general rule, **F17.42**
admissible in evidence against a co-accused (see **F17.34**). Where an accused has laid
blame, perhaps the greater blame, on his co-accused, the risk of prejudice to the co-
accused if the whole statement is heard is obvious. The rule, however, is that the
prosecution ought to present the accused's confession as a whole (*Pearce* (1979) 69 Cr
App R 365) and the accused could, with good reason, complain if the prosecution picked
out certain passages and left out others (*Gunewardene* [1951] 2 KB 600). In
Gunewardene, G was charged as an accessory to manslaughter arising out of an abortion
performed by H, his co-accused. H's confession was read to the jury, including those
parts of it which implicated G, the trial judge warning the jury that the statement was
not evidence against G. Lord Goddard CJ said (at p. 611) that 'although in many cases
counsel do refrain from reading passages which implicate another prisoner and have no
real bearing on the case against the prisoner making the statement, we cannot say that
anything has been admitted . . . which was not admissible'.

Gunewardene was applied in *Lobban* v *R* [1995] 1 WLR 877, where the issue before
the Privy Council was whether the exculpatory part of a mixed statement made by L's

co-accused, R, which incriminated L in a murder, could be excluded or edited in the exercise of the court's discretion to protect L from prejudice, given that the statement was hearsay and inadmissible as against him. The answer was that it could not; the prosecution had placed reliance upon the mixed statement as against R, and the exculpatory parts were therefore admissible evidence for R (see **F17.44**). There was no discretion to restrain a co-accused from defending himself by adducing admissible evidence, and nothing to support the suggestion made in earlier cases that the judge had a discretion to edit a confession so as to deprive one defendant of relevant defence evidence in order to minimise injustice to another (see, e.g., *Rogers* [1971] Crim LR 413). This, while a correct application of principle, may remove what has been an attractive option in some cases (see, e.g., the discussion of earlier authorities in *Jefferson* (1994) 99 Cr App R 14 at p. 26), but it would seem still to leave open the possibility of editing out information irrelevant to the co-accused's case, or of editing with the co-accused's consent.

Pre-trial Editing of Written Statement Made by Suspect

F17.43   *Practice Direction (Crime: Evidence by Written Statements)* **[1986] 1 WLR 805**

> 5.   (b)   When a suspect is interviewed about more offences than are eventually made the subject of committal charges, a fresh statement should be prepared and signed omitting all questions and answers about the uncharged offences unless either they might appropriately be taken into consideration or evidence about those offences is admissible on the charges preferred, such as evidence of system. It may however be desirable to replace the omitted questions and answers with a phrase such as: 'After referring to some other matters, I then said . . .' so as to make it clear that part of the interview has been omitted.

> 7.   None of the above principles applies, in respect of committal proceedings, to statements which are exhibited (including statements under caution and signed contemporaneous notes). Nor do they apply to oral statements of a defendant which are recorded in the witness statements of interviewing police officers, except in the circumstances referred to in para. 5(b) above. All this material should remain in its original state in the committal bundles, any editing being left to prosecuting counsel at the Crown Court (after discussion with defence counsel and, if appropriate, the trial judge).

Where the prosecution tender written statements in evidence, it will frequently be necessary to edit, *inter alia*, statements which contain inadmissible, irrelevant or prejudicial material. The *Practice Direction (Crime: Evidence by Written Statements)* [1986] 1 WLR 805 recognises that, whereas other written statements may be satisfactorily dealt with by editing, it is preferable in the circumstances identified in para. 5(b), where an interview ranges over more offences than are eventually charged, to prepare a fresh statement. In summary proceedings particularly, there may be a greater need to prepare fresh statements rather than using the method of striking out or bracketing those parts on which no reliance is to be placed by the prosecution in the proceedings (ibid., para. 6). See also **D7.11**.

MIXED STATEMENTS

Admissibility of Mixed Statements

F17.44   The expression 'mixed statement' is used to refer to a statement made by an accused which is in part comprised of admissions and in part of exculpatory or self-serving statements (*Hamand* (1985) 82 Cr App R 65 at p. 67). An example would be 'I admit I hit him, but he was trying to kill me'. Such a statement is admissible for the prosecution as a confession, provided that the requirements of the PACE 1984, s. 76, are complied with.

Where an admission is made which is qualified by an explanation or excuse, all the authorities agree that it would be unfair to admit the admission without admitting the explanation (*Sharp* [1988] 1 WLR 7 per Lord Havers at p. 12). In *Jones* (1827) 2 C & P 629, the rule was said to be that 'if a prosecutor uses the declaration of a prisoner, he must take the whole of it together, and cannot select one part and leave another'. In *Pearce* (1979) 69 Cr App R 365, it was said that to exclude answers at interview which are favourable to the accused, while admitting those which are unfavourable, would be misleading, and a breach of duty on the part of the prosecutor, whose obligation is to present the case fairly to the jury. See also *McGregor* [1968] 1 QB 371 and *Duncan* (1981) 73 Cr App R 359, at p. 363.

It will be a question for the court in each case to determine whether an excuse or explanation so accompanies an admission as to be part of a mixed statement for the purposes of this rule. In *Pearce* (1979) 69 Cr App R 365, the principle was said to be that a statement which is not an admission is admissible if it is made 'in the same context as an admission', and the Court of Appeal accepted that the two parts of the mixed statement may occur at different places in 'the same interview or series of interviews'.

In many cases, the mixed statement will have been made in the course of questioning of the accused by the police, no distinction being taken in this respect between a written statement and a record of questions and answers at interview (*Polin* [1991] Crim LR 293). It is not, however, a condition of admissibility that the statement was made to a police officer – a point taken by Lord Havers in *Sharp*. Thus, for example, mixed statements have been received which were made by the accused when giving evidence at a previous trial (*McGregor*; *Higgins* (1829) 3 C & P 603).

Evidential Value of Self-serving Parts of Mixed Statements

In *Sharp* [1988] 1 WLR 7, Lord Havers identified two views which had emerged as to F17.45 the evidential value of the self-serving parts of a mixed statement. The view which the House of Lords accepted is that the whole statement is admissible by way of exception to the hearsay rule, and is thus evidence of the truth of all the facts stated in it. The House expressed approval of the law as stated in *Duncan* (1981) 73 Cr App R 359 by Lord Lane CJ, who said (at p. 365):

> Where a 'mixed' statement is under consideration by the jury in a case where the defendant has not given evidence, it seems to us that the simplest, and, therefore, the method most likely to produce a just result, is for the jury to be told that the whole statement, both the incriminating parts and the excuses or explanations, must be considered by them in deciding where the truth lies. It is, to say the least, not helpful to try to explain to the jury that the exculpatory parts of the statement are something less than evidence of the facts they state.

For examples of earlier decisions to the same effect, see *Clewes* (1830) 4 C & P 221; *McGregor* [1968] 1 QB 371; *Hamand* (1985) 82 Cr App R 65. *Sharp* has recently been approved by the House of Lords in *Aziz* [1996] AC 41 and by the Privy Council in *Lobban* v *R* [1995] 1 WLR 877.

The other view which has from time to time been taken, is that the self-serving parts of the statement are not evidence of their truth, but form material which may be of use to the jury in evaluating the admissions. This was said to be the law in, for example, *Sparrow* [1973] 1 WLR 488 and in *Leung Kam-Kwok* v *The Queen* (1984) 81 Cr App R 83. The House of Lords in *Sharp* [1988] 1 WLR 7 rejected this 'purist' approach:

(a) because the weight of authority supported the contrary view; and

(b) because common sense suggested that the only way in which a jury could use the self-serving parts of the statement to 'evaluate the facts in the admission' would be if they first reached a conclusion as to the truth of the explanation given by the accused.

The question of the evidential value of a mixed statement arises most acutely in cases where the accused does not testify. In both *Duncan* (1981) 73 Cr App R 359 and *Sharp*

[1988] 1 WLR 7 the accused gave no evidence, and the statement of Lord Lane CJ which was approved in *Sharp* concerns the direction to be given to a jury in such a case; indeed it incorporates the right to comment on the failure of the accused to repeat the exculpatory statement on oath (*Downes* (1993) *The Independent*, 25 October 1993). Despite this, there is no logical reason why the status of the statement should be any different if the accused testifies.

Weight to be Attached to Self-serving Parts of Mixed Statements

F17.46 In *Sharp* [1988] 1 WLR 7 the House of Lords approved of the following statement of Lord Lane CJ in *Duncan* (1981) 73 Cr App R 359 at p. 365:

> . . . where appropriate, as it usually will be, the judge may, and should, point out that the incriminating parts are likely to be true (otherwise why say them?), whereas the excuses do not have the same weight. Nor is there any reason why, again where appropriate, the judge should not comment in relation to the exculpatory remarks upon the election of the accused not to give evidence.

In *Donaldson* (1976) 64 Cr App R 59 it was said that the jury, when deciding what weight, if any, to give to those parts of the statement which are favourable to an accused who has elected not to give evidence, should take into account that it was not made on oath and has not been tested by cross-examination. See also *McGregor* [1968] 1 QB 371.

Mixed Statements and the Evidential Burden

F17.47 Where the accused bears the evidential burden of establishing a sufficient foundation so that a defence such as self-defence or provocation may be left to the jury, he may rely on the self-serving part of a mixed statement which is admitted in evidence under the principles stated above. In *Hamand* (1985) 82 Cr App R 65, H made a statement to the police in which he admitted that he had struck a man in the face, but claimed that the man had acted in such a way as to lead H to believe that he was about to be attacked. The statement was proved in evidence as part of the prosecution case. The Court of Appeal held that the trial judge had been wrong to rule that H's mixed statement was not evidence of self-defence, thus forcing H to testify in his own defence. In assessing the weight to be given to such a statement where it is not supported by any evidence from the accused himself, the comments of Lord Lane CJ in *Duncan* (1981) 73 Cr App R 359 (see **F17.46**) should be borne in mind.

Prosecution Placing No Reliance on Admission Contained in Mixed Statement

F17.48 The derivation of the rule as stated at **F17.44** and **F17.45** suggests that a mixed statement becomes evidence of the truth of its self-serving parts only where the prosecution elect to rely on it as containing an admission. Some difficulty may arise in cases where the prosecution adduces a mixed statement simply as evidence showing the reaction of the accused when taxed with the offence, and not as evidence of its truth. That this may be done is well established (see, e.g., *Storey* (1968) 52 Cr App R 334; *Donaldson* (1976) 64 Cr App R 59; *Pearce* (1979) 69 Cr App R 365), and may benefit the prosecution by enabling them to draw attention to any inconsistencies between the explanation advanced in the statement and any defence put forward at trial. It seems unlikely that, in such cases, the self-serving passages become evidence of their truth.

For the same reason, it is submitted, a mixed statement which is not relied on by the prosecution for any purpose ought not to be regarded as admissible evidence for the defence of any excuse or explanation asserted in it. This was accepted by the House of Lords in *Aziz* [1996] AC 41 (at p. 50), where the statement to this effect in the 1995 edition of this work was approved. It should, however, be noted that in *Sharp* [1988] 1 WLR 7 the question certified for decision by the House (as amended by Lord Havers) was: 'Where a statement made to a person out of court by a defendant contains both admissions and self-exculpatory parts do the exculpatory parts constitute evidence of the truth of the facts alleged therein?' The question does not confine itself to cases where the prosecution seek to rely on the admissions contained in the statement. It is submitted, however, in the light of *Aziz*, that the answering of this question in the affirmative by the House of Lords does not provide any warrant for qualifying the law as it is stated above.

Recent decisions of lower courts have suggested a wider approach. In *Garrod* [1997] Crim LR 445, the Court of Appeal considered that a statement was properly regarded as 'mixed' if it contained an admission of fact which was capable of adding some degree of weight to the prosecution case, regardless (apparently) of whether the prosecution were relying on it or not. However the statement in that case was purely exculpatory, whichever test was applied. In *Western v DPP* [1997] 1 Cr App R 474, W appealed against conviction for a public order offence on the grounds that the magistrates had wrongly treated as purely self-serving an interview in which W admitted fighting with the victim but claimed to have acted in self-defence. The prosecution resisted the appeal precisely on the grounds that the interview was not a mixed statement unless the prosecution relied on the admission. The appeal was allowed because there was nothing within the stated case to suggest that the prosecution had *not* relied on the admission: on the contrary the circumstances suggested it was highly likely that they had. Butterfield J nevertheless expressed 'grave doubts' about the proposition relied on by the prosecutor, advancing instead the view that whether a statement is mixed should be determined by an examination of its contents, not by the use to which it is put. *Aziz* was not considered. The view of Butterfield J has practical advantages for trial judges, who would not be obliged to draw fine distinctions between apparently similar statements. It is submitted, however, that the current law requires these distinctions to be drawn.

STATEMENTS IN PRESENCE OF ACCUSED

General Rule

> . . . the rule of law undoubtedly is that a statement made in the presence of an accused **F17.49** person, even upon an occasion which should be expected reasonably to call for some explanation or denial from him, is not evidence against him of the facts stated save so far as he accepts the statement, so as to make it, in effect, his own. (*Christie* [1914] AC 545, per Lord Atkinson at p. 554)

Although it is a salutary rule of practice, there is no rule of law requiring the production, before the content of the statement is given in evidence, of some proof of the accused's acceptance of the statement (*Christie*, modifying the stricter rule suggested by the Court of Criminal Appeal in *Norton* [1910] 2 KB 496). Lord Atkinson considered that the procedure suggested by Pickford J in *Norton* was unobjectionable, provided that it was workable. According to that procedure, in a trial on indictment the judge, where it is possible to do so, decides by considering the depositions whether there is any evidence of acknowledgement of the statement. Where acknowledgement cannot be deduced by this method, the fact of a statement having been made in the accused's presence may be given in evidence, but not the contents, and the question asked, what the accused said or did on such a statement being made. If the answer is such that acknowledgement may properly be inferred, the contents of the statement become admissible.

If the statement is admitted, the question whether the accused's conduct amounted to an acknowledgement is a question for the jury. If they find that the statement was acknowledged, in whole or in part, then they may take the statement or the relevant part of it into consideration. If they do not so find, they should be directed to disregard the statement altogether (*Norton*). In *Christie*, Lord Atkinson said (at p. 554) that, if the trial judge is of the view that no evidence has been given on which the jury could reasonably find that the accused had accepted the statement, he should direct the jury to disregard it.

Where the acknowledgement takes the form of a statement by the accused which is wholly or partly adverse to him, he will by virtue of the PACE 1984, s. 82(1), have made a confession for the purposes of part VIII of that Act, and accordingly the conditions of s. 76 must be complied with.

The jury should be given a clear direction as to the inferences to which the accused's conduct may give rise (*Horne* [1990] Crim LR 188; *Chandler* [1976] 1 All ER 585; but see *Black* (1922) 16 Cr App R 118).

Evidence of Acknowledgement

F17.50 In *Christie* [1914] AC 545, Lord Atkinson considered the various ways in which an accused person might accept an accusation put to him (at p. 554):

> He may accept the statement by word or conduct, action or demeanour, and it is the function of the jury which tries the case to determine whether his words, action, conduct or demeanour at the time when the statement was made amounts to an acceptance of it in whole or in part. It by no means follows, I think, that a mere denial by the accused of the facts mentioned in the statement necessarily renders the statement inadmissible, because he may deny his statement in such a manner and under such circumstances as may lead a jury to disbelieve him, and constitute evidence from which an acknowledgement can be inferred.

See also *Norton* [1910] 2 KB 496. In *Christie*, C was charged with indecent assault on a young boy who, shortly after the alleged offence and in the presence of his mother and of a police officer who was on the spot, confronted C with the words 'That is the man,' and gave details of the assault. C replied 'I am innocent'. Although in the form of a denial, the response was regarded as one from which it was open to the jury to draw an inference of acceptance. Lord Moulton said (at p. 559):

> Going back to first principles . . . the deciding question is whether the evidence of the whole occurrence is relevant or not. If the prisoner admits the charges the evidence is obviously relevant. If he denies it, it may or may not be relevant. For instance, if he is charged with a violent assault and denies that he committed it, that fact might be distinctly relevant if at the trial his defence was that he did commit the act, but that it was in self-defence.

Where the accused denies the accusation, it must, however, be asked whether the effect on the jury of hearing that an accusation has been made might be to create prejudice on their part which is out of all proportion to the evidential value of the accused's behaviour. If the evidence would have very little or no value, the judge ought to exercise his discretion to exclude it (*Christie*, per Lord Moulton at p. 560).

Accused Confronted with Statement by Co-accused

F17.51 The principles set out at **F17.49** are of equal application where the accused is confronted with an accusation made by his co-accused. Difficulties may, however, arise if the police show the accused a statement made by a co-accused implicating him, ostensibly to gauge the accused's reaction, but intending also to profit by getting the statement before the court in circumstances where the maker of the statement cannot be called as a witness. The practice was condemned in *Gardner* (1915) 11 Cr App R 265, and although the court was not prepared to say that admissions obtained in this way were inadmissible, it appears to have been regarded as within the discretion of the trial judge to exclude statements put to the accused for the purpose of extracting a confession. See also *Taylor* [1978] Crim LR 92, in which it was said that the prejudicial effect of a co-accused's accusation vastly outweighed its probative value as evidence introducing T's reaction, though it does not appear what the reaction of T was alleged to have been. In *Mills*

[1947] KB 297 the Court of Appeal considered that the co-accused's statement ought not to be given in evidence in such circumstances, and the reaction of the accused ought likewise to be excluded unless it could be understood without reference to what the co-accused had said (e.g., where the accused went on to make a full confession).

The practice of the police is now regulated by PACE Code C, para. 16.4 of which provides that, where, after a person has been charged or informed that he may be prosecuted, a police officer wishes to bring to his notice a statement made by, or the content of an interview with, another person, he must give him a true copy of the statement or bring to his attention the content of the interview record whilst doing nothing to invite any reply or comment save to caution him. This should ensure that the only evidence of reaction on which a court is asked to rely will be a voluntary statement under caution. If the co-accused's statement is improperly read, it is likely that the statement will be excluded under the PACE 1984, s. 78, together with the accused's reaction to it, particularly if the latter cannot be made sense of without reference to the statement.

SECTION F18: EVIDENCE OF IDENTIFICATION

Introduction

F18.1 Evidence of identification may take several different forms. Difficulties most often arise in respect of visual identification by witnesses, but consideration must also be given to fingerprint evidence, body samples (including those used for DNA profiling), voice identification, video film, photographs, photofits and artist's sketches.

VISUAL IDENTIFICATION

F18.2 The visual identification of suspects or defendants by witnesses has for many years been recognised as problematic and potentially unreliable. It is easy for an honest witness to make a confident, but false, identification of a suspect, even in some cases where the suspect is well known to him. There are several possible reasons for errors of this kind. Some persons may have difficulty in distinguishing between different subjects of only moderately similar appearance, and many witnesses to crimes are able to see the perpetrators only fleetingly, often in stressful circumstances. Visual memory may fade with the passage of time, and may become confused or distorted by suggestive influences from photographs or other sources of contamination. There is evidence that false identification can sometimes be caused by a process known as unconscious transference, in which the witness confuses a face he recognises from the scene of the crime (perhaps that of an innocent bystander) with that of the offender. Such problems may then be compounded by the understandable, but often misguided, eagerness of many witnesses to help the police by making a positive identification.

The Criminal Law Revision Committee asserted in its Eleventh Report, Evidence (General) 1972, (Cmnd 4991) 'that cases of mistaken identification constituted by far the greatest cause of actual or possible wrong convictions'. Much has been done since then to reduce the dangers posed by such errors, and to ensure that courts and juries are made aware of them. In particular, the Court of Appeal in *Turnbull* [1977] QB 224 laid down important rules for the guidance of trial courts faced with contested identification evidence, and PACE Code D (set out at **appendix 2**) attempts to ensure that pre-trial identification procedures are conducted as fairly as possible.

Recognition, Lies and Mistaken Identification

F18.3 If the accuracy of a purported identification (as opposed to the truthfulness of the accusing witness) is not in issue, then neither the *Turnbull* guidelines nor the provisions of Code D will need to be considered; but care should be taken before either of those safeguards are ignored. Identification issues may still arise, even where the witness claims to have recognised the suspect or accused as someone already well known to him, and they are not necessarily excluded where the principal line of defence involves an attack on the honesty or truthfulness of the witness.

This can be seen in *Conway* (1990) 91 Cr App R 143. Two witnesses claimed to have recognised C as the man responsible for a stabbing and he was arrested. He denied that he knew either of the witnesses and asked to be put on an identification parade, but the police took the view that this was unnecessary, as C was a 'named person'. The Court of Appeal held this to be wrong: identification became an issue as soon as C questioned the witnesses' ability to recognise him and Code D provides that a parade should be held, where practicable, in any case where the suspect disputes an identification. See also **F18.10**.

In *Beckford* v *The Queen* (1993) 97 Cr App R 409, the identifying witness claimed to have recognised the offenders as persons well known to him. The defence alleged that his evidence was wilfully false, but the Privy Council nevertheless held that there was also a possibility of genuine mistake. The alleged crime had been viewed by the witness at a distance of some 500 feet and the closest he had come to the perpetrators was some 120 feet. Mistakes can obviously be made at such distances, even where known acquaintances are involved, and it was held that a *Turnbull* direction should have been given.

Much will depend on the precise circumstances and on the stance adopted by the defence. In cases such as *Beckford* or *Reid* [1994] Crim LR 442 (see **F18.12**), where the witness clearly does know the suspect but may not have seen the offender properly, identification parades will be of little if any real value. A mistake made from 500 feet away, or in a moment of sudden confusion, is not likely to be repeated during an identification parade. See **F18.10**.

There will also be cases in which any attempt to apply the *Turnbull* guidelines would merely serve to confuse the jury by focusing their attention on the wrong issue (*Courtnell* [1990] Crim LR 115; *Cape* [1996] 1 Cr App R 191). If, for example, the witness claims to have known the defendant for many years and to have conversed with him for half an hour in the same room, mistaken identification cannot be an issue. According to the Privy Council in *Beckford*, such clearcut cases will be 'rare and exceptional'. The general rule is that an appropriate *Turnbull* warning should be given, even in cases of alleged recognition. See also *Bentley* [1991] Crim LR 620; *Bowden* [1993] Crim LR 379 (discussed in greater detail at **F18.16**).

Pre-Trial Identification Procedures: PACE Code D

Where the ability of a witness to make a positive identification of the suspect is in issue, **F18.4** this should generally be tested as soon as possible, in accordance with the procedures laid down in PACE Code D (see **appendix 2**). Code D, para. 2.0 states that a record must first be made of the description of the suspect as first given by the witness. This record must be disclosed to the suspect or to his solicitor before any identification procedures are undertaken, and any discrepancies between the original description and the actual appearance of any person identified will be a matter for judicial comment under the *Turnbull* guidelines (see **F18.15**). As to the advanced disclosure of media material (i.e. film of incidents etc. previously circulated through national or local media), see Code D, paras. 2.21A and 2.21B. A dock identification in which the witness makes his identification for the first time in court is not strictly inadmissible but is not ordinarily considered to be a fair or acceptable procedure and will rarely be allowed (see **F18.12**).

Although Code D refers only to cases 'which involve disputed identification evidence', the Court of Appeal has held that its procedures may also need to be followed in cases where such a dispute might reasonably be anticipated (*Rutherford* (1993) 98 Cr App R 191). If, for example, the police have arrested a suspect on the basis of other evidence, and there are witnesses who indicate that they might be able to make an identification, then an identification parade (or group identification etc.) should be arranged. A positive identification would strengthen the case for the prosecution; moreover defendants should not be deprived of the opportunity to have witnesses to the crime declare that the offender seen by them is not on the parade. The position may be different if the witness has already stated that he would not be able to identify the offender (*Montgomery* [1996] Crim LR 507 and *Nicholson* (1999) *The Times*, 7 September 1999).

Breaches of Code D: General Principles

As with the other codes of practice issued under the PACE 1984, breaches of Code D **F18.5** need not inevitably lead to the exclusion of evidence (*Khan* [1997] Crim LR 584;

McEvoy [1997] Crim LR 887). It is however essential that the trial court or judge determines whether any alleged breaches have occurred, and whether they may have caused any prejudice to the accused (*Grannell* (1989) 90 Cr App R 149; see also *Ryan* [1992] Crim LR 187; *Quinn* [1995] 1 Cr App R 480; and *Hickin* [1996] Crim LR 584 at **F18.6**). If it is clear that no prejudice resulted, then there will be no case for excluding the evidence. If, on the other hand, some prejudice may have been caused, it will be necessary to determine, under the PACE 1984, s. 78, whether the adverse effect would be such that justice requires the evidence to be excluded. Cases will, to a large extent, turn on their own facts. A trial court or judge should nevertheless give reasons for any decision to admit identification evidence obtained in breach of Code D (*Allen* [1995] Crim LR 643). In *Beveridge* (1987) 85 Cr App R 255, the Court of Appeal stated that the determination of such facts can usually be accomplished without the need for a trial within a trial, but this cannot be an absolute rule. The holding of a trial within a trial was not questioned in *Willoughby* [1999] 2 Cr App R 82. See further **F1.27**.

Identification of Known Suspects

F18.6 Where the identity of a suspect is known, Code D provides for four possible methods of identification by witnesses, namely identification parades, group identification, video film identification and, as a last resort, confrontation. There is a hierarchy to be observed: a parade will ordinarily be the first choice, and should be held if the suspect disputes an identification, unless the suspect refuses his consent or holding a parade would be unfair, impracticable or unsatisfactory for one or more of the reasons specified in Code D, paras. 2.4, 2.7 and 2.10. Group identification procedures may however be acceptable in some cases, especially where the suspect is uncooperative, and it is recognised that a group identification may sometimes be a more practicable or satisfactory procedure than a parade. Fear on the part of the witness may be a factor here (see para. 2.7), but it is unlikely to be relevant where facilities exist for witnesses to view a parade without themselves being seen by the suspect. Paragraph 2.10 of Code D anticipates that video film may be resorted to because of the suspect's refusal to co-operate with a parade or group identification, but it may also be used in other (unspecified) cases where it is considered to be the most satisfactory method available. In contrast, confrontation 'may not take place unless none of the other procedures are practicable' (para. 2.13).

In *Hickin* [1996] Crim LR 584, a group of 14 defendants were charged following an incident in which two men had been beaten up by a gang. The suspects had all been arrested a few minutes later, and witnesses to the incident had been confronted with them, for the purposes of making identifications. The Court of Appeal recognised that it would not have been practicable to arrange 14 identification parades that night, and that delay might have weakened witnesses' powers of recollection, but it was stressed that there were several procedures which ought to be followed in such a case. Initial descriptions of the alleged offender should, if possible, be recorded before inviting the witness to make an identification, detailed records should be taken of anything said at the identification, and if there are several possible witnesses, some should be kept back for a later identification parade. None of this was done in *Hickin,* and this led the court to conclude that, even if there had not been breaches of Code D, the evidence had been unfairly prejudicial and ought not to have been admitted (see also *El-Hannachi* [1998] 2 Cr App R 226).

Identification Parades and Group Identification

F18.7 Identification parades should be conducted in accordance with the procedures set out in Annexe A to PACE Code D (see **appendix 2**). Group identifications should be conducted in accordance with the newly introduced Annexe E, which expressly permits the procedure to be undertaken with or without the consent or knowledge of the suspect (see Annexe E, para. 2), but covert identification is permissible only where the suspect has already refused to cooperate or has failed to attend a parade or group identification. It is recognised that the suspect's solicitor cannot be expected to be present during a covert identification (Annexe E, para. 34).

Problems may arise at trial where there have allegedly been irregularities in the conduct of a parade or group identification, or where the defence disputes a police assertion that it was impracticable to hold a parade. Irregularities which tend significantly to weaken the protection afforded to suspects under Code D are likely to be dealt with by the exclusion of the offending evidence; although this is ultimately a matter of judicial discretion, the appellate courts have usually adopted an exclusionary approach in cases where important provisions have been flouted. In *Nagah* [1991] Crim LR 55, the appellant's conviction was quashed after evidence had been admitted at his trial of a deliberately staged encounter outside the police station, in which he had been confronted by the identifying witness as he left, after having being told that there was insufficient evidence to charge him. He had previously agreed to stand on an identity parade, which was never held.

In *Finley* [1993] Crim LR 50, the Court of Appeal again held that identification evidence should have been excluded following serious and deliberate breaches of Code D. Witnesses to a robbery had been shown photographs of the appellant, contrary to para. 2.18, which forbids this where there is a known suspect available to stand on a parade. Nothing was done to prevent witnesses from discussing the case between themselves whilst waiting for the parade, and the parade contained nobody, save for the appellant, who resembled descriptions of the robber. See also *Gall* (1989) 90 Cr App R 64.

Although Code D lays down strict rules to prevent contact between witnesses, or between witnesses and investigating officers, during the parade or immediately before it, it says nothing about the propriety of such contact once the witnesses in question have viewed the parade. Lord Bingham CJ nevertheless observed in *Willoughby* [1999] 2 Cr App R 82 that:

> There . . . would be the utmost ground for concern if there were any question of the police nudging, prompting or encouraging any witness . . . to make a more positive identification of a suspect. . . . It would seem to us important that a witness should not be told whether an identification is right or wrong until after the witness has made any further statement that the witness may wish.

If the police fail to hold a parade when the suspect requests one, this is clearly a decision they may have to justify at the trial. Some of the earlier first instance decisions seemed to suggest that the courts would be very slow to accept excuses such as the difficulty of finding volunteers of the right racial group or appearance. For example, in *Gaynor* [1988] Crim LR 242, the trial judge took the view that the police could have made a greater effort to find volunteers of G's racial group, and he excluded evidence from a group identification that had been held in lieu. Whilst *Gaynor* may have been a perfectly valid decision on its own facts, the Court of Appeal in *Jamel* [1993] Crim LR 52 appears to have taken a softer line, holding that the defence could not object to the holding of a group identification if the holding of a parade (made up with mixed-race volunteers) might, in the circumstances, have taken weeks to arrange; in other words, 'impracticable' may mean impracticable within a reasonable timescale.

If a fair and satisfactory alternative to a parade is for some reason impossible to arrange, the prosecution may be left without any identification evidence at all. Judicial rejection of weak confrontation evidence, for example, may not necessarily imply any criticism of the police for not holding a parade or group identification. The confrontation may merely have been considered inadequate evidence on which to base a conviction. (See *Joseph* [1994] Crim LR 48, where it was held that such evidence should have been excluded even though the appellant asked for the confrontation himself.)

Video Identification

F18.8   Video identification should be carried out in accordance with the procedures set out in Annexe B to Code D (see **appendix 2**). Code D does not apply to cases in which suspects are identified from closed circuit security videotapes or from any other scene-of-crime recordings which may be made before the emergence of a suspect (*Jones (MA)* (1995) 159 JP 293). There may however be some analogy between the showing of such videos to witnesses and the showing of photographs (as to which, see **F18.11**).

Confrontation

F18.9   A confrontation must generally be carried out, if at all, in accordance with Annexe C to Code D (see **appendix 2**). The procedure has the advantage of not requiring the suspect's consent or co-operation (Code D, para. 2.13). Code D does not state whether physical force may be used to make a suspect reveal himself at a confrontation, but in *Jones* (1999) *The Times*, 21 April 1999 the Court of Appeal refused to sanction the use of any such force. No specific sanction is provided where non-co-operation makes lawful identification impossible. In particular, there is no express provision permitting adverse inferences to be drawn by courts or juries (cf. the PACE 1984, s. 62(10): see **F18.25**).

Confrontation is in some respects little better than a dock identification, and the courts may well exclude such evidence where the limited safeguards required under Annexe C have not been provided. See, for example, *Powell* v *DPP* [1992] RTR 270, where the identifying officer had apparently arranged his own confrontation in breach of Code D and the conviction was quashed. See also *Samms* [1991] Crim LR 197.

Judicial mistrust of confrontation can most clearly be seen in *Joseph* [1994] Crim LR 48, where the police had done their best to arrange for a parade, group identification or video identification, but without success (the appellant was tall, black and bearded, with shoulder length dreadlocks). The prosecution sought to proceed on the basis of other evidence, but the appellant demanded a confrontation immediately before the trial, in the hope that the witnesses would fail to identify him. This did not work out as he had hoped, as he was identified by two of the witnesses, and the trial judge admitted that evidence, on the basis that the defence had asked for the confrontation. The Court of Appeal took the view that, on balance, the weakness of such evidence still pointed to exclusion under the PACE 1984, s. 78, as the better course of action.

Cases in which a Parade, etc., may not be Necessary

F18.10   The formal identification procedures prescribed by PACE Code D may not always be applicable to cases in which alleged offenders are identified close to the time and scene of the crime. The courts have recognised this on a number of occasions. In *Oscar* [1991] Crim LR 778, the appellant was allegedly seen by a witness attempting to break into premises opposite her house, and was subsequently arrested nearby on the basis of the distinctive clothing he was wearing, which matched the verbal description of the clothing given by the witness. No identification parade was held: instead, the appellant was confronted there and then by the witness, and identified by her. In dismissing his appeal against conviction, Lord Lane CJ distinguished between cases involving confrontation near to the time and place of the incident and cases where the suspect has been arrested some time afterwards. He also observed that, where identification is made on the basis of clothing, a parade with different clothing would be valueless. See also *Rogers* [1993] Crim LR 386.

Where a suspect has already been identified at or close to the crime scene, the question arises as to whether he should be entitled to an identity parade (or group identification, etc.) if he disputes that identification. On a literal interpretation of Code D, para. 2.3, a parade etc. would still have to be held, but in some such cases such a procedure would appear to be futile. Arresting officers, or witnesses to the arrest, are unlikely to identify anyone on a parade other than the person who has been arrested, even if the original arrest was indeed mistaken. Similarly, if a witness to a crime purports to have recognised his next door neighbour as the offender, perhaps under difficult viewing conditions, the holding of a parade would do nothing to address the real issue, which is not whether the witness is capable of identifying his neighbour, but whether he identified him correctly under the particular conditions prevailing at the relevant time. In *Popat* [1998] 2 Cr App R 208, the Court of Appeal considered a number of earlier authorities and concluded that the mandatory obligation to hold a parade etc. under para. 2.3 applies only 'where the police produce a suspect to the witness'. It does not arise 'where the witness produces the suspect to the police'. If an 'actual and complete' identification has already been made by the witness, a parade etc. need be held only 'if it would be useful under all the circumstances'. It does not become mandatory merely because the suspect continues to dispute the original identification. See also *El Hannachi* [1998] 2 Cr App R 226 and *Bell* [1998] Crim LR 879. *Popat* was doubted in *Forbes* (1999) 163 JP 629, where the Court of Appeal preferred a literal reading of para. 2.3, but *Forbes* was itself rejected as 'misguided' in *Popat (No. 2)* (1999) *The Times*, 7 September 1999, where it was stated that *Popat* should be followed unless the House of Lords ruled otherwise.

No Identified Suspect

Where there is no identified suspect who is available to stand on an identity parade, **F18.11** Code D allows witnesses to be shown photographs, or to be taken to a particular neighbourhood or place, in the hope that they will recognise the offender (see paras 2.17 and 2.18 and *Kitchen* [1994] Crim LR 684). The showing of photographs should be done in accordance with Annexe D to the Code (see **appendix 2**). Once one witness has made a positive identification from photographs then, unless the person identified can be eliminated from the enquiry, no further witnesses should be shown photographs; if identity remains in dispute, a parade etc. should be arranged as soon as possible. As to the need for advance disclosure of media material (i.e. film of incidents etc. previously circulated through national or local media), see Code D, paras. 2.21A and 2.21B.

Identification from police photographs indicates that the defendant must have a criminal record, or be known to the police, and the prosecution should not ordinarily reveal this fact (*Lamb* (1979) 71 Cr App R 198), unless the defendant's record is already before the jury (*Allen* [1996] Crim LR 426). If, however, the defence choose to make an issue of the witness's ability to make an identification at that time, it may be necessary to admit such evidence to prevent the jury being misled. In *Bleakley* [1993] Crim LR 203, B had been identified by a witness, first from photographs and subsequently at a parade. The defence suggested that the witness identified B at the parade only because B had visited his premises the night before. Evidence of the earlier identification by photographs was held to have been properly admitted to rebut this suggestion. This does not mean that the jury should be told all about the defendant's criminal record. Care should be taken to minimise any prejudice to him (*Campbell* [1994] Crim LR 357).

The showing of a security videotape to witnesses is not covered by Annexe D (*Crabtree* [1992] Crim LR 65; *Caldwell* (1994) 99 Cr App R 73), but the Court of Appeal in *Caldwell* thought it desirable that viewing procedures should be regulated (as under Annexe D) so as to minimise the risk of contamination between witnesses. The Court of Appeal's view is now addressed in para. 2.12A of the revised Code D.

Videotape showing the commission of a crime would ordinarily be kept as evidence at trial (see **F18.23**). If the tape should accidentally be lost or erased, testimony from those who viewed it may be admissible in lieu, although such testimony it would tend to carry less weight than the video itself, and it might in some cases be proper to exclude the viewer's evidence under the PACE 1984, s. 78. In *Taylor* v *Chief Constable of Cheshire* [1986] 1 WLR 1479, Ralph Gibson LJ said:

> The weight and reliability of the evidence will depend upon assessment of all relevant considerations, including the clarity of the recording, its length and . . . the witness's prior knowledge of the person said to be identified.

A *Turnbull* warning would be needed in such a case.

Dock Identification

F18.12　Identification of a defendant for the first time at committal proceedings, or at the trial itself, is recognised to be an unreliable method of proof. The A-G and the DPP undertook in 1976 as follows:

> The [prosecution] at committal proceedings, or Crown Counsel at any subsequent trial, will not invite a witness to identity, who has not previously identified the accused at an identity parade, to make a dock identification unless the witness's attendance at a parade was unnecessary or impracticable, or there are exceptional circumstances.

This is a statement of policy, rather than a rule of law. Dock identification remains legally admissible, subject however to judicial powers of discretionary exclusion under the PACE 1984, s. 78 or at common law. At trial on indictment, this discretion would usually be exercised by a trial judge so as to exclude evidence of a dock identification (see *Fergus* (1993) 98 Cr App R 313), but different considerations may apply in respect of summary offences where the holding of an identity parade etc. will often be quite impracticable (*Barnes* v *Chief Constable of Durham* [1997] 2 Cr App R 505). The discretion to exclude such evidence does not appear to have been exercisable by justices in committal proceedings (*Horsham Justices, ex parte Bukhari* (1982) 74 Cr App R 291; *Reid* [1994] Crim LR 442). A trial judge might nevertheless have little option but to exclude identification evidence from a witness who first identified the accused in committal proceedings (ibid).

There is a danger that a witness may sometimes make a dock identification even where none has been solicited by the prosecution. If that happens (as for example in *Thomas* [1994] Crim LR 128), it may be necessary for the trial judge to warn the jury against giving it any weight or credence. It would not suffice merely to observe (as did the trial judge in *Thomas*) that an identification of that sort would not ordinarily take place.

There is a risk, if the defendant is not in custody and no identification has previously been arranged, that a witness will identify him as he arrives or waits outside the court. In *Tiplady* (1995) 159 JP 548, the prosecution actually arranged for a group identification in the foyer of the court building as the defendant arrived and this evidence was properly admitted at trial. It is unlikely, however, that the circumstances of such an identification would be wholly satisfactory (especially where a considerable time has elapsed since the alleged offence), and it may prove necessary in some cases to exclude such evidence (*Martin* [1994] Crim LR 218, but cf. *Campbell* [1996] Crim LR 500).

Recognition cases, such as *Reid*, appear to be different. The Court of Appeal in *Reid* were anxious not to encourage dock identification, but saw no reason to interfere with the trial judge's decision to admit recognition evidence in that case, notwithstanding that no identification parade or group identification had been held. A *Turnbull* direction was still needed; but, as explained at **F18.3**, it was not a case in which the witness's ability to make a leisurely identification was in doubt.

Pre-Trial Identification: Admissibility

F18.13　Since dock identification is considered unsatisfactory, it might be thought that evidence of pre-trial identification in accordance with Code D would be admissible in its place, but the position is not straightforward, and has been obfuscated by some very doubtful decisions of the Court of Appeal.

In the ordinary course of events, where the identifying witness testifies adequately against the accused at trial, the pre-trial identification serves to prove his consistency and his ability to make an identification under fair and objective circumstances. It is admissible, in other words, by way of an exception to the rule against previous consistent statements (*Christie* [1914] AC 545). If the police officer who supervised the identification parade is called to testify as to the identification, he can do so only in support of the identifying witness. His testimony cannot go to the issue of the accused's guilt, because he has no first-hand knowledge of it. Without the evidence of the original witness, his testimony would be hearsay, and there is no special rule making hearsay admissible in identification cases (*Sparks* v *The Queen* [1964] AC 964).

This basic principle was unfortunately overlooked by the Court of Appeal in *Osbourne* [1973] QB 678, where witnesses to a robbery identified the appellants at a parade but failed to come up to proof at the trial some months later. One witness could not remember identifying anyone and the other's evidence was so confused as to be worthless. This left the prosecution without any real identification evidence, but the trial judge allowed the gap to be filled by testimony from a police officer, who asserted that the witnesses had each identified one or other of the appellants.

Upholding the convictions in the Court of Appeal, Lawton LJ cited *Christie* as authority for admitting evidence of identification 'other than identification in the witness box'. This was, with respect, erroneous. *Christie* is authority only for admitting pre-trial identification as evidence of the identifying witness's consistency. If that witness fails to come up to proof, as in *Osbourne*, pre-trial identification is not a substitute for the evidence he fails to give. *Osbourne* is arguably a decision *per incuriam* on this issue, and conflicts with the Court of Appeal's more recent decision in *Smith* (1987) 85 Cr App R 197, where similar evidence was held to be 'clearly inadmissible'.

In *Smith*, an elderly witness originally picked out the second appellant (D) at a group identification, and afterwards said of S: 'That was like him, but I am afraid to say'. At the trial, however, she proved to be an ineffective witness, and was unable to distinguish between the two men in the dock. The judge allowed a video recording of the group identification to be shown to the jury and also allowed a police officer to recount the tentative identification of S, but the Court of Appeal had no hesitation in quashing the convictions. *Osbourne* was not referred to in *Smith*, but the latter decision is clearly to be preferred.

Pre-trial Identification and the *Res Gestae* Principle

A witness may recall making an identification, and be positive that it was correct, but be **F18.14** unable for some reason to swear that the accused is the person he identified. (One possible explanation would be a change in the accused's appearance in the intervening period; another would be the fading of visual memory in the months between identification and trial.) In such a case, an officer who conducted or witnessed the parade would undoubtedly be permitted to testify that the person identified was the accused.

The Court of Appeal in *McCay* [1990] 1 WLR 645 (**F15.9**) reached this conclusion on comparable facts by reasoning that evidence of what the witness says at the parade is admissible hearsay under the *res gestae* principle, as a statement inextricably linked to a relevant act, namely the act of identification. This, with respect, is highly questionable, and manifestly inconsistent with the narrower view that was taken of the *res gestae* principle in *Kearley* [1992] 2 AC 228, according to which acts cannot merely be treated as pegs on which to hang statements.

The better view is that the police officer's evidence need not be hearsay at all. In contrast to *Osbourne* [1973] QB 678 or *Smith* (1987) 85 Cr App R 197 (**F18.13**), the officer need testify only that the witness pointed to the accused (a fact directly perceived by him); he need not say why the witness did this or what the witness claimed to have seen, because the witness can do so himself.

The *Turnbull* Guidelines

F18.15   In response to widespread concern over the problems posed by cases of mistaken identification, the Court of Appeal in *Turnbull* [1977] QB 224 laid down important guidelines for judges in trials that involve disputed identification evidence. The guidelines are also applicable, *mutatis mutandis,* in summary trials, and are reproduced (with slight abridgement) below:

> First, whenever the case against an accused depends wholly or substantially on the correctness of one or more identifications of the accused which the defence alleges to be mistaken, the judge should warn the jury of the special need for caution before convicting the accused in reliance on the correctness of the identification or identifications. In addition he should instruct them as to the reason for the need for such a warning and should make some reference to the possibility that a mistaken witness can be a convincing one and that a number of such witnesses can all be mistaken. Provided this is done in clear terms the judge need not use any particular form of words.

> Secondly, the judge should direct the jury to examine closely the circumstances in which the identification by each witness came to be made. How long did the witness have the accused under observation? At what distance? In what light? Was the observation impeded in any way, as for example, by passing traffic or a press of people? Had the witness ever seen the accused before? How often? If only occasionally, had he any special reason for remembering the accused? How long elapsed between the original observation and the subsequent identification to the police? Was there any material discrepancy between the description of the accused given to the police by the witness when first seen by them and his actual appearance? If in any case, whether it is being dealt with summarily or on indictment, the prosecution have reason to believe that there is such a material discrepancy they should supply the accused or his legal advisers with particulars of the description the police were first given. In all cases if the accused asks to be given particulars of such descriptions, the prosecution should supply them. Finally, he should remind the jury of any specific weaknesses which had appeared in the identification evidence.

> Recognition may be more reliable than identification of a stranger; but even when the witness is purporting to recognise someone whom he knows, the jury should be reminded that mistakes in recognition of close relatives and friends are sometimes made.

> All these matters go to the quality of the identification evidence. If the quality is good and remains good at the close of the accused's case, the danger of a mistaken identification is lessened; but the poorer the quality, the greater the danger.

> In our judgment when the quality is good, as for example when the identification is made after a long period of observation, or in satisfactory conditions by a relative, a neighbour, a close friend, a workmate and the like, the jury can safely be left to assess the value of the identifying evidence even though there is no other evidence to support it; provided always, however, that an adequate warning has been given about the special need for caution. Were the Courts to adjudge otherwise, affronts to justice would frequently occur. . . .

> When, in the judgment of the trial judge, the quality of the identifying evidence is poor, as for example when it depends solely on a fleeting glance or on a longer observation made in difficult conditions, the situation is very different. The judge should then withdraw the case from the jury and direct an acquittal unless there is other evidence which goes to support the correctness of the identification. This may be corroboration in the sense lawyers use that word; but it need not be so if its effect is to make the jury sure that there has been no mistaken identification. . . .

> The trial judge should identify to the jury the evidence which he adjudges is capable of supporting the evidence of identification. If there is any evidence or circumstances which

the jury might think was supporting when it did not have this quality, the judge should say so.

Scope of the *Turnbull* Guidelines

The *Turnbull* guidelines should be followed in all cases where the possible mistaken **F18.16** identification of the defendant is in issue (see **F18.3**). The absence of an adequate *Turnbull* direction, tailored to the facts of the particular case, will usually require a conviction to be quashed as unsafe (*Beckford* v *The Queen* (1993) 97 Cr App R 409; *Bowden* [1993] Crim LR 379; *Farquharson* v *The Queen* (1993) 98 Cr App R 398) although it may be condonable if the other evidence is overwhelming (see *Freemantle* v *The Queen* [1994] 1 WLR 437). Paying lip service to the guidelines will not be enough (*Graham* [1994] Crim LR 212), nor will it suffice to give a general warning without detailed references to any particular circumstances that may have affected the accuracy of the witness's observation (*Reid* v *The Queen* [1990] 1 AC 363). See for example *Keane* (1977) 65 Cr App R 247, where the Court of Appeal criticised the trial judge for failing to identify possible supporting evidence or specific weaknesses, and for appearing 'more anxious to reassure the jury than to warn them'. On the other hand, the guidelines do not require the slavish use of a rigid form of words in every case (*Mills* v *The Queen* [1995] 1 WLR 511; *Qadir* [1998] Crim LR 828) and a judge may properly point out that a mistaken identification (as where a witness has identified a volunteer at a parade) does not necessarily prove that the accused is innocent or that the witness is untrustworthy in other respects, especially if his view of the crime was imperfect (*Trew* [1996] Crim LR 441).

The guidelines may also need to be followed in cases involving the disputed identification of an alleged accomplice (*Bath* (1990) 154 JP 849) and an inadequate direction in respect of the evidence against one defendant may render unsafe the conviction of another (*Elliott* (1986) *The Times*, 8 August 1986), although this will depend on the circumstances of the particular case.

The guidelines are not applicable to cases involving the identification of motor vehicles. The reliability of a vehicle identification may however depend, *inter alia*, on the witness having had a satisfactory opportunity to see the vehicle and on his ability to distinguish between one model and another. This should be drawn to the jury's attention (*Browning* (1991) 94 Cr App R 109).

It was held in *Oakwell* [1978] 1 All ER 1223 that the guidelines were 'intended primarily to deal with the ghastly risk run in cases of fleeting encounters' and were not applicable to a case in which the witness may merely have been mistaken as to which person in a well identified group had struck him. In that case the judge had drawn the jury's attention to the possibility that the witness may have been momentarily unsighted, and this was held to be sufficient. *Oakwell* was followed in *Curry* [1983] Crim LR 737 and *Beckles* [1999] Crim LR 148; but in *Bowden* the Court of Appeal held that this principle was applicable only to situations in which the defendant's presence at the scene of the crime is admitted. A *Turnbull* warning was accordingly held to have been necessary in *Bowden*, even though a police officer claimed to have had a long and careful look at the offender.

It does not follow from *Oakwell* that no *Turnbull* direction would ever be necessary if the defendant's presence at the scene is admitted. There will be some circumstances in which it will be appropriate to give such a direction and some in which it will not (contrast *Thornton* [1995] 1 Cr App R 578 with *Slater* [1995] 1 Cr App R 584 and see also *Pattinson* [1996] 1 Cr App R 51).

The applicability of the *Turnbull* guidelines to cases of alleged recognition is discussed at **F18.3**. As the guidelines themselves explain, recognition evidence will often be more reliable than identification of a stranger, but may still be erroneous. Lord Lane CJ elaborated on this point in *Bentley* [1991] Crim LR 620:

> Many people have experienced seeing someone in the street whom they knew, only to discover that they were wrong. The expression, 'I could have sworn it was you' indicated the sort of warning which a judge should give, because that was exactly what a testifying witness did — he swore that it was the person he thought it was. But he may have been mistaken . . .

Supporting Evidence

F18.17 Evidence capable of supporting a disputed identification may take any admissible form, including self-incrimination by the defendant, similar fact evidence and other evidence of identification. The judge must identify evidence that is capable of providing such support and warn the jury against reliance on anything that might appear supportive without really having that capability.

F18.18 ***Mutually Supportive Identifications*** It is permissible in appropriate cases for two or more disputed identifications of the defendant to be treated as mutually supportive (*Weeder* (1980) 71 Cr App R 228; *Shelton* [1981] Crim LR 776). This is permissible only if the identifications are 'of a quality that a jury can safely be left to assess' (*Weeder*); but it does not matter that both witnesses may have made their identifications from the same spot (*Tyler* (1992) 96 Cr App R 332) and in some cases the identifications may relate to separate incidents (see *Barnes* [1995] 2 Cr App R 491).

F18.19 ***Self-incrimination*** Disputed identification evidence can clearly be supported by an admissible confession, but careful consideration must be given to cases in which the defendant is alleged to have incriminated himself by lies or false alibis. In *Turnbull* [1977] QB 224, Lord Widgery CJ said (at p. 230):

> Care should be taken by the judge when directing the jury about the support for an identification which may be derived from the fact that they have rejected an alibi. False alibis may be put forward for many reasons; an accused, for example, who has only his own truthful evidence to rely on may stupidly fabricate an alibi and get lying witnesses to support it out of fear that his own evidence will not be enough. Further, alibi witnesses can make genuine mistakes about dates and occasions like any other witnesses can. It is only when the jury is satisfied that the sole reason for the fabrication was to deceive them and there is no other explanation for its being put forward can fabrication provide any support for identification evidence. The jury should be reminded that proving the accused has told lies about where he was at the material time does not by itself prove that he was where the identifying witness says he was.

This guidance remains valid, but the governing principles in relation to self-incrimination by false alibis or other lies, as set out by the Court of Appeal in *Lucas* [1981] QB 720, have now been held applicable in identification cases (*Goodway* [1993] 4 All ER 894). Before such lies can be regarded as supporting an identification, they must accordingly be shown to be deliberate and material; the court or jury must be able to discount any possible innocent motive for the lies and they must be proved to be lies by evidence other than the identification(s) that they are to support.

F18.20 ***The Defendant's Silence*** Lord Widgery CJ warned in *Turnbull* [1977] QB 277 that a defendant's failure to testify must not be viewed as capable of supporting the evidence against him. This must now be reconsidered in the light of recent legislation. Under the CJPO 1994, ss. 34 to 38, the failure of a defendant:

(a) to mention facts when questioned or charged which are later relied upon in his defence;

(b) to account for objects in his possession or substances or marks on his body or clothing;

(c)   to account for his presence at a particular place; or

(d)   to testify at his trial,

may each, in appropriate cases, entitle the court or jury to 'draw such inferences as appear proper'. They do not, in themselves, constitute evidence of guilt and should not be seen as a substitute for satisfactory identification evidence, but the absence of testimony or explanation from the defendant may legitimately enable a court or jury to infer, in appropriate cases, that the prosecution evidence is correct and that the defendant has no answer to it. See generally, **F19**.

The Quality of the Witness

There is no doubt that some witnesses may be capable of providing more reliable **F18.21** identification evidence than others in the same position. A witness with perfect vision may clearly be expected to do better than a myopic witness who has lost his spectacles. More controversial is the suggestion that police officers may, by virtue of their training, be more observant than ordinary witnesses, or at least better at noting features or details that may be significant. That suggestion was rejected by the Privy Council in *Reid* v *The Queen* [1990] AC 363, but was subsequently held to be quite proper by the Court of Appeal in *Ramsden* [1991] Crim LR 295, where Lord Lane CJ opined that it would be wrong for a trial judge not to direct the jury as to the potentially greater reliability of police identification. See also *Tyler* (1992) 96 Cr App R 332; *Williams* (1994) *The Times*, 7 October 1994.

Stopping a Trial Based on Inadequate Identification

The *Turnbull* guidelines require the trial judge to direct an acquittal in cases where **F18.22** identification evidence is both deficient and unsupported by alternative evidence. If necessary, the trial judge should invite the defence to make submissions to that effect (*Fergus* (1993) 98 Cr App R 313). In such cases, the Court of Appeal may quash a conviction, even though the judge's direction on the evidence was otherwise impeccable (see for example *Pope* (1986) 85 Cr App R 201).

This does not involve any conflict with the principles laid down by the Court of Appeal in *Galbraith* [1981] 1 WLR 1039 (**D13.32**) because, in stopping the trial, the judge does not purport to determine whether prosecution witnesses are telling the truth. He merely decides that there is insufficient evidence on which a jury could properly convict (*Daley* v *The Queen* [1994] 1 AC 117; *Macmath* [1997] Crim LR 586).

PHOTOGRAPHS, PHOTOFITS AND VIDEOTAPE

The use of photographs or video footage in order to help witnesses identify possible **F18.23** offenders is dealt with at **F18.11**. What follows is concerned with the use of visual images as evidence at trial.

Photographs and videotape are relatively unproblematic. Originals or copies can be shown as real evidence and may provide the court with the equivalent of a direct view of the incident in question. A full *Turnbull* warning would not be appropriate in such cases, but the jury should still be warned of the dangers of mistaken identification, and should be reminded of the need to exercise great care when attempting to make an identification from photographs or video recordings (*Blenkinsop* [1995] 1 Cr App R 7). In many cases, however, the quality of security videos is so poor that juries may need expert assistance in interpreting them. Facial mapping may, for example, enhance the value of poor quality images; expert evidence on that subject was held admissible in *Stockwell* (1993) 97 Cr App R 260 and in *Clarke* (1994) *The Times*, 26 December 1994.

In *Hookway* [1999] Crim LR 750, security video footage showed a robbery being committed by a group of stocking-masked men, one of whom was alleged to be H. There was no way in which the jury itself could be expected to identify H under such conditions, but evidence was admitted from two experts in facial mapping, who had studied the masked video images and compared them with photographs of H, so as to establish whether key facial features, such as the distance between the eyes, corresponded. They were satisfied that these features did indeed correspond, and opined that this provided 'very powerful support for the assertion that the offender was the appellant'. On the other hand, they 'could not be 100% certain' that H was one of the raiders. Notwithstanding the total absence of any other incriminating evidence, the jury convicted H, and his conviction was upheld on appeal.

With respect, the expert evidence seems to have established only that H could have been one of the robbers. As the Court of Appeal admitted, there was no statistical evidence as to the significance of such similarities as were identified, because without an apporopriate database it is impossible to know how many persons share the same features. How then could a jury properly convict on such evidence alone?

In *Clare* (1995) 159 JP 142, it was held that a police officer who had spent many hours studying a video recording of crowd violence could act as an *ad hoc* expert, interpreting and explaining the action for the benefit of the jury.

Sketches or photofits (including the computer-enhanced E-FIT or CD-FIT systems) are fundamentally different in principle, in that they depend on the fallible (and potentially mendacious) assertions of the witnesses who help to compile them. A photofit showing a bald or bearded suspect is manifestly a product of a witness's assertion that the suspect was bald or bearded, and should logically be categorised as a kind of statement, albeit one in visual form. In *Cook* [1987] QB 417, the Court of Appeal nevertheless held that such images should be regarded not as statements but as analogous to photographs, and thus free from the limitations which would otherwise be imposed on them under the hearsay rule. *Cook* is, with respect, a demonstrably flawed decision, but it was followed in *Constantinou* (1989) 91 Cr App R 74, in which a photofit picture compiled by the victim of a robbery was admitted in evidence against the appellant. Although the victim could have had only a partially obscured view of the robber through the sunroof of his car, no *Turnbull* warning was deemed necessary. This seems most unsatisfactory.

If a witness purports to identify the defendant, after having previously helped produce a photofit bearing no resemblance to him, this should presumably be treated as the equivalent of a previous inconsistent statement by him, although it might be difficult to reconcile this with the reasoning in *Cook,* according to which it cannot be regarded as a statement at all.

VOICE IDENTIFICATION

F18.24　At trial, evidence may properly be admitted from persons who claim to have recognised the defendant's voice (*Robb* (1991) 93 Cr App R 161; *Hersey* [1998] Crim LR 281). There are few guidelines, however, as to the procedures which should be followed in voice-identification cases. The only reference to voice identification in Code D is to be found in Annexe A, para. 17, which provides that a witness may ask any member of a normal visual identity parade to speak. The witness should first be asked if he can make a purely visual identification, and must be reminded that participants will have been chosen on the basis of their appearance only (see **appendix 2**). Code D makes no direct provision for cases in which the attempted identification is to be made on the basis of voice alone, but one possible approach is to adapt the usual Code D procedures, so as to hold what is in effect a 'voice identification parade'. In *Hersey*, the Court of Appeal upheld a conviction based largely on evidence derived from such a parade. The victim of a masked robbery claimed that he had recognised the voice of one of the robbers as being that of H, and was then able to identify H's voice on a 'parade' in which H and 11 volunteers each read out a passage from an earlier interview with H himself. It will clearly be necessary in such cases for the 'parade' to be composed of persons with broadly similar accents to that of the suspect, but it may not be helpful or realistic to assemble an entire parade of similarly-pitched voices. In *Hersey* the trial judge refused to admit expert evidence from the defence, to the effect that most of the volunteers on the parade had higher pitched voices than H.

It was acknowledged in *Hersey* that voice identification shares many of the dangers of visual identification, and should be subject at trial to analogous warnings derived or adapted from the *Turnbull* guidelines. See also *Gummerson* [1999] Crim LR 680.

If there are taped recordings of the offender's voice, expert evidence may also be admissible on the question of whether this matches the voice of the defendant. Most phoneticians use acoustic analysis techniques for this purpose, but an expert who uses only auditory techniques may still be competent to testify, even though the rejection of such methods by other phoneticians might mean that a jury would possibly give his views less weight (*Robb* (1991) 93 Cr App R 161). The jury should be allowed to hear any such recordings for themselves, so that they may form their own judgment of the opinions expressed (*Bentum* (1989) 153 JP 538).

IDENTIFICATION BY DENTAL IMPRESSIONS OR BODY SAMPLES

The obtaining of samples and dental impressions is governed by the PACE 1984, ss. 62 **F18.25** to 63A, and by Code D, paras 5.1 to 5.12 (see **appendix 2**). A distinction is made between intimate and non-intimate samples, as defined in the PACE 1984, s. 65(2) and (3). Intimate samples are defined as meaning blood, semen or tissue fluid; urine; pubic hair; dental impressions and swabs from orifices other than the mouth. Non-intimate samples are defined as samples of hair, other than pubic hair; samples taken from or from under a nail; mouth swabs and swabs which are not taken from body orifices; saliva; footprints and bodily impressions other than those of the hand. Hair samples may be plucked with roots (for the purpose of DNA testing) without becoming intimate samples (s. 63A(2): cf. *Cooke* [1995] 1 Cr App R 318).

Under the PACE 1984, s. 62, intimate samples may be taken only on the authority of an officer of at least the rank of superintendent and with the 'appropriate consent' (i.e. the consent in writing of the suspect, if he has reached 17; that of his parent or guardian if he is a child aged under 14; and the consent of both suspect and parent or guardian where the suspect is aged between 14 and 17: PACE 1984, s. 65). The authorising officer must have reasonable grounds for suspecting involvement in a recordable offence, as presently defined in the National Police Records (Recordable Offences) Regulations 1985 (SI 1985 No. 1941) and for believing that the sample will tend to confirm or disprove the suspect's involvement.

Under the PACE 1984, s. 63, non-intimate samples must usually be taken with the appropriate consent (as defined in s. 65), but may be taken without consent where the suspect is in custody or detention and an officer of at least the rank of superintendent so authorises. This authorisation may be given where the officer has reasonable grounds for suspecting the subject's involvement in a recordable offence and for believing that the sample will tend to confirm or disprove his involvement. Alternatively, under s. 63(3A), a non-intimate sample may be taken without consent from a person who has been charged with a recordable offence or informed that he will be reported for such an offence and has not already provided such a sample or has provided one which proved unsuitable or insufficient. Under s. 63(3B), a non-intimate sample may also be taken without consent after conviction for a recordable offence on or after 10 April 1995 or, regardless of the date of conviction, in the case of a person serving a sentence of detention or imprisonment for an offence listed in the Criminal Evidence (Amendment) Act 1997, sch. 1. Section 63(3C) makes similar provision in respect of persons found insane or unfit to plead.

Intimate or non-intimate samples (or fingerprints) may be used for 'speculative searches' (as to which see **F18.28**). Suspects must be told of this possibility before samples are taken (ss. 62(7A) and 63(8B)).

Dental impressions may be taken only by a registered dentist; other intimate samples (except urine) may be taken only by a registered medical practitioner (s. 62(9)).

Under s. 62(10), a refusal, without good cause, to consent to the taking of an intimate sample may entitle a court or jury to draw 'such inferences as appear proper'. (The suspect should be warned of this in accordance with PACE Code D, para. 5(2).) A court or jury might not necessarily draw any such inferences, but would be entitled to do so if they thought fit. See also **F19.18**.

The taking of samples from terrorist suspects is governed by modified rules: see the Prevention of Terrorism (Temporary Provisions) Act 1989, s. 15 and sch. 5.

Evaluation of DNA Evidence

F18.26 DNA profiling is an extremely complex procedure and, despite the popular analogy with fingerprint evidence, the two methods of identification are not entirely comparable. The unique characteristics of a fingerprint can be identified by relatively well understood procedures, but this can rarely be emulated by DNA profiling. DNA profiling is also, by reason of its complexity, very difficult to explain to a court or jury, and it is easy for juries to be given the impression that DNA evidence is conclusive, when it may not be.

DNA extracted from blood or semen stains found at the scene of the crime, or on the victim, is compared with samples taken from the suspect. The process is described by Lord Taylor CJ in *Deen* (1994) *The Times*, 10 January 1994 and *Gordon* [1995] 1 Cr App R 290. It is not necessary that a court or jury fully understands the technicalities of the process, but it is vital that they understand the significance of matches or mismatches between DNA profiles taken from the crime stain and the defendant. Some margin of error must be allowed for in the process, but a clear mismatch between specific bands will prove that the samples came from different persons, and will in many cases be conclusive of innocence.

A positive match between the two profiles does not provide comparable proof of guilt. Assuming that the matching process was accurate (which may be a matter for conflicting expert opinion), there remains the problem of evaluating the significance of the match. As Lord Taylor explained in *Deen,* this partly depends on the number of matching bands and on the frequency of such matches amongst the relevant population. Some matches may be more significant than others. It is essential that the jury are not confused between the 'match probability' (or random occurrence ratio) on the one hand and the 'likelihood ratio' on the other. The odds against an innocent individual, chosen at random, matching the DNA profile of the crime stain might be estimated in a given case at a million to one; but if the *only* evidence against a given suspect is a match between his DNA profile and that of the crime stain, one cannot possibly deduce, on that evidence alone, that the odds against him being innocent (the likelihood ratio) are a million to one. On the contrary, there may be several unrelated individuals in the United Kingdom with similar profiles. In *Deen*, the prosecution misled the jury by confusing the two questions, and the appellant's conviction was quashed.

The procedure to be followed in respect of the disclosure and presentation of DNA evidence has more recently been laid down by the Court of Appeal in *Doheny* [1997] 1

Cr App R 369. Prosecution experts should adduce the evidence of the DNA comparisons together with their calculations of the random occurrence ratio. The Crown should serve upon the defence details as to how the calculations have been carried out, sufficient for the defence to scrutinise the basis of the calculations; and the forensic science service should make available to a defence expert, if requested, the databases upon which the calculations are based. An expert witness should not express opinions as to the likelihood of the accused being the source of a crime stain, because this requires consideration of factors other than those within his area of expertise. Phillips LJ suggested in *Doheny* that juries be directed along the following lines:

> If you accept the scientific evidence called by the Crown, that indicates that there are probably only four or five white males in the United Kingdom from whom that semen stain could have come. The defendant is one of them. The decision you have to reach, on all the evidence, is whether you are sure that it was the defendant who left that stain or whether it is possible that it was one of that other small group of men who share the same DNA characteristics.

In practice, there will usually be more evidence against a defendant than the results of DNA profiling. If it can be proved, not only that the defendant's DNA matches that of the crime stain, but also that his fingerprints were found on a weapon used in the crime, his involvement in it may be difficult to deny. Conversely, evidence derived from DNA profiling may be contradicted by an alibi or other 'non-scientific' defence evidence. When evaluating DNA evidence alongside other such evidence, juries should use their common sense knowledge of the world. They should not (at least in the absence of special features or circumstances) be invited to use complex mathematical formulae, such as Bayes' Theorem, in doing so (*Doheny*; and see also *Adams* [1996] 2 Cr App R 467). Such an approach would be a 'recipe for confusion, misunderstanding and misjudgment' (*Adams (No. 2)* [1998] 1 Cr App R 377 at p. 384).

FINGERPRINTS AND PALM-PRINTS

F18.27 The taking of fingerprints (which are defined so as to include palm prints) is governed by the PACE 1984, ss. 27, 61 and 63A, and by PACE Code D, paras 3.1 to 3.8 (see **appendix 2**).

The PACE 1984, s. 27, enables the police to require a person convicted of a recordable offence to attend a police station within one month of conviction for the purpose of providing his fingerprints, if he has not at any time been in police custody for that offence and has not already provided them in the course of the investigation of that offence.

The principal provision governing the taking of fingerprints is s. 61.

Police and Criminal Evidence Act 1984, s. 61

(1) Except as provided by this section no person's fingerprints may be taken without the appropriate consent.

(2) Consent to the taking of a person's fingerprints must be in writing if it is given at a time when he is at a police station.

(3) The fingerprints of a person detained at a police station may be taken without the appropriate consent—

(a) if an officer of at least the rank of superintendent authorises them to be taken; or

(b) if—

(i) he has been charged with a recordable offence or informed that he will be reported for such an offence; and

(ii) he has not had his fingerprints taken in the course of the investigation of the offence by the police.

(4) An officer may only give an authorisation under subsection (3)(a) above if he has reasonable grounds—

    (a) for suspecting the involvement of the person whose fingerprints are to be taken in a criminal offence; and

    (b) for believing that his fingerprints will tend to confirm or disprove his involvement.

    (5) An officer may give an authorisation under subsection (3)(a) above orally or in writing but, if he gives it orally, he shall confirm it in writing as soon as is practicable.

    (6) Any person's fingerprints may be taken without the appropriate consent if he has been convicted of a recordable offence.

    (7) In a case where by virtue of subsection (3) or (6) above a person's fingerprints are taken without the appropriate consent—

    (a) he shall be told the reason before his fingerprints are taken; and

    (b) the reason shall be recorded as soon as is practicable after the fingerprints are taken.

    (7A) If a person's fingerprints are taken at a police station, whether with or without the appropriate consent—

    (a) before the fingerprints are taken, an officer shall inform him that they may be the subject of a speculative search; and

    (b) the fact that the person has been informed of this possibility shall be recorded as soon as is practicable after the fingerprints have been taken.

    (8) If he is detained at a police station when the fingerprints are taken, the reason for taking them and, in the case falling within subsection 7A above, the fact referred to in paragraph (b) of that subsection shall be recorded on his custody record.

    (9) Nothing in this section—

    (a) affects any power conferred by paragraph 18(2) of schedule 2 to the Immigration Act 1971; or

    (b) except as provided in section 15(10) of, and paragraph 7(6) of Schedule 5 to, the Prevention of Terrorism (Temporary Provisions) Act 1989, applies to a person arrested or detained under the terrorism provisions.

For the meaning of 'appropriate consent' see **F18.25**.

Fingerprint evidence should be presented by a qualified expert, with at least five years' experience in the examination and comparison of such evidence. Properly presented fingerprint evidence has long been accepted as capable of providing sufficient identification, but, in a case which depends wholly on such evidence, it is clearly essential that the defendant is linked to the relevant prints by admissible evidence (*Chappell* v *DPP* (1988) 89 Cr App R 82). Fingerprint experts used to seek at least 16 matching ridge characteristics between the suspect's print and the crime print before asserting that the prints come from the same person, but this has never been a strict legal requirement, and courts have a discretion to admit evidence based on fewer matching characteristics. See for example *Buckley* (1999) 163 JP 561, in which the Court of Appeal upheld a robbery conviction following a trial at which the appellant was identified on the basis of a mere nine-point match. Rose LJ said:

> Fingerprint evidence, like any other evidence, is admissible . . . if it tends to prove the guilt of the accused. It may so tend, even if there are only a few similar ridge characteristics, but it may, in such a case, have little weight. It may be excluded in the exercise of judicial discretion, if its prejudicial effect outweighs its probative value. . . .

He added that courts or judges would have to consider, before exercising this discretion, the experience and expertise of the witness presenting it, the number of similar ridge characteristics identified, the presence of any dissimilar characteristics, the size of the crime print (because a given number of matches in a fragment of a print may be more compelling than a similar number in a complete print) and the quality and clarity of that print (including any evidence of injury to the person who left the print, and any smearing or contamination of the print). Rose LJ still considered it 'highly unlikely' that anything less than an eight-point match could be acceptable, in the absence of exceptional circumstances.

The old '16-point standard' will be abandoned in April 2000, to be replaced by guidelines which will emphasise the primacy of subjective evaluation over any mere numerical count of matching ridge characteristics.

Speculative Searches

'Speculative searches' are dealt with in the PACE 1984, s. 63A, which provides that **F18.28** fingerprints, samples or the information derived from samples taken under the 1984 Act from a person arrested on suspicion of involvement in a recordable offence, or who has been charged with or informed that he will be reported for such an offence, may be checked against other fingerprints or samples contained in records held by or on behalf of the police, or in connection with or as a result of an investigation of an offence.

Under s. 64, if the person from whom the fingerprints or samples are taken is cleared of the original offence, or if it is decided that he shall not be prosecuted for it (unless he admits the offence and has been cautioned by a constable), then they must ordinarily be destroyed as soon as is practicable. Prior to the enactment of the CJPO 1994, it was held in *Kelt* [1994] 1 WLR 765 that this need not necessarily preclude the use, in other criminal proceedings against that person, of information already legitimately derived from such samples. In *Kelt*, a blood sample taken during an investigation into a suspected murder had been found to implicate the suspect in an otherwise unrelated robbery, prior to his being eventually cleared of the murder. The CJPO 1994, s. 57(3), appears to reverse the effect of *Kelt*, as far as samples are concerned, by inserting a new subsection (3B) into s. 64. This provides that information derived from samples subject to destruction under s. 64 cannot be used in evidence against the person concerned, or for the purpose of any criminal investigation. On facts such as those in *Kelt*, it may now be prudent for the police to obtain or request separate samples in relation to each further offence in which the suspect appears to have been implicated by the original sample (cf. *Cooke* [1995] 1 Cr App R 318). An acquittal on the original charge need not then have adverse consequences in relation to any subsequent proceedings.

Section 64(3B) does not appear to apply to fingerprints or palm prints, but the courts are unlikely to tolerate deliberate violations of rules requiring the destruction of such prints following acquittal or the dropping of charges. *Kelt*, in which the police acted in good faith, can in this respect be contrasted with *Nathaniel* [1995] 2 Cr App R 565.

OTHER EVIDENCE OF IDENTIFICATION

The identification of disputed handwriting is dealt with at **F10.7**. As to the possession of **F18.29** potentially incriminating items, such as weapons or housebreaking implements, admissibility depends to some extent on whether there is evidence linking those items to the alleged crime. Thus, whilst possession of the proven murder weapon may be admissible to identify the defendant as the offender, possession of a weapon that has not been used in the crime (or perhaps seen by witnesses in the possession of the offender) merely constitutes evidence of criminal disposition, and is prima facie inadmissible under the similar fact rule. Admissibility would depend on the prosecution establishing it as having a clear and positive probative value that outweighs any corresponding risk of prejudice. As to the admissibility of similar fact evidence, see **F12**.

SECTION F19: INFERENCES FROM SILENCE AND THE NON-PRODUCTION OF EVIDENCE

THE RIGHT TO SILENCE

F19.1 An accused person in a criminal trial has traditionally been accorded a 'right to silence', sometimes termed a privilege against self-incrimination. The right embraces the idea that the accused is under no legal obligation to assist police with their inquiries (*Rice* v *Connolly* [1966] 2 QB 414) and is not a compellable witness at trial (Criminal Evidence Act 1898, s. 1, **F4.9**). At common law it is supplemented by a further right: the failure to assist the police or to give evidence at trial is not evidence against the accused, with the result that it is wrong to invite a jury to draw adverse inferences from silence. (A possible exception is considered at **F19.3**.)

Under the CJPO 1994, ss. 34 to 38, the accused remains at liberty to maintain silence under interrogation and at trial. However, the supplementary right to be free from adverse inferences is removed and replaced by provisions specifying the circumstances in which 'proper' inferences may be drawn against him. Although these changes have been controversial, the European Court of Human Rights has held that similar provisions in force in Northern Ireland do not of themselves contravene the accused's right to a fair trial guaranteed by Art. 6 of the European Convention on Human Rights and Fundamental Freedoms (*Murray* v *United Kingdom* (1996) 22 EHRR 29). Some changes have, however, been made to bring the Act into line with the Court's judgment in *Murray* (see **F19.4** and **F19.8**). A revised Code of Practice for the Detention, Treatment and Questioning of Persons by Police Officers (Code C) was promulgated to amplify the Act's provisions. The provisions, their relationship with the common law and with other provisions concerning silence or the non-production of evidence is the subject of this section.

OUT-OF-COURT SILENCE AT COMMON LAW

Accused and Accuser on 'even terms'

F19.2 It has been seen that the conduct of the accused when an accusation is made against him may form the basis of an inference that he accepts the accusation (see **F17.48**). In the authorities which follow, it was the silence of the accused which was relied upon as the basis for such an inference. The CJPO 1994, s. 34(5) (see **F19.4**), makes it clear that insofar as these authorities permit inferences to be drawn they remain good law. Even if none of the statutory inferences is in play, therefore, the trial judge needs to have the possibility of a common-law inference in mind before resorting to the standard direction (in accordance with *McGarry* [1999] 1 WLR 1500: see **F19.7**) that no inference should be drawn.

In *Norton* [1910] 2 KB 496 it was accepted that the silence of the accused 'on an occasion which demanded an answer' might be conduct from which an inference of acknowledgement might be drawn. In *Mitchell* (1892) 17 Cox CC 503, Cave J described more fully the circumstances in which silence in the face of an accusation might be tantamount to an admission of guilt. He said (at p. 508):

> Now the whole admissibility of statements of this kind rests upon the consideration that if a charge is made against a person in that person's presence it is reasonable to expect that he or she will immediately deny it, and that the absence of such a denial is some evidence of an admission on the part of the person charged, and of the truth of the charge. Undoubtedly, when persons are speaking on even terms, and a charge is made, and the

> person charged says nothing, and expresses no indignation, and does nothing to repel the charge, that is some evidence to show that he admits the charge to be true.

It follows that silence does not constitute an acknowledgement of guilt if the circumstances are such that a reasonable person would not be expected to counter the allegation. In *Mitchell* the accusation was made by a woman on her deathbed. M and her solicitor were present to hear the statement, which was recorded by a magistrate for use at M's trial for manslaughter. The statement proved to be inadmissible either as a dying declaration or a deposition, and the prosecution sought instead to admit the accusation as a statement made in M's presence. Cave J refused the application, holding that it would be 'monstrous' to say that, because M had not 'started up and denied' the charge, she must have accepted it. In all the circumstances, including the woman's condition, the formality of the proceedings, and the presence of a solicitor to represent M's interests, it was unreasonable to expect any response from M.

Mitchell was approved by the Privy Council in *Parkes* v *The Queen* [1976] 1 WLR 1251. A girl was stabbed to death, and P was charged with her murder. The girl's mother gave evidence that, on finding her daughter injured, she immediately accused P, who made no reply. When she threatened to detain him until the police arrived, he tried to stab her. It was held that P's reactions to the accusations, including his silence, were matters to be taken into account by the jury in deciding whether P had committed the offence charged. It is not entirely clear whether the outcome would have been the same had silence alone been relied on as evidence of guilt, for the Board made a particular point of noting that P's reaction was 'not one of mere silence', but it is submitted that the difference is that mere silence might be entitled to less weight than silence coupled with positive conduct, depending on the circumstances.

Accusations by or in the Presence of Police Officers

It is not clear whether the principles stated above apply to accusations by or in the **F19.3** presence of police officers. In *Hall* v *The Queen* [1971] 1 WLR 298, H was charged jointly with T and G with unlawful possession of drugs. Premises occupied by the three had been searched by the police in H's absence and a quantity of drugs found in a bag which T said belonged to H. Shortly afterwards the police brought H to the premises, where he was told of the allegation made by T. H, who had not been cautioned, said nothing. It was held that the principle that a person is entitled to refrain from answering a question put to him for the purpose of discovering whether he has committed a crime meant that, 'exceptional circumstances' apart, 'silence alone on being informed by a police officer that someone else has made an accusation against him cannot give rise to an inference that the person to whom this information is communicated accepts the truth of the accusation'. The fact that H was not under caution was irrelevant as the 'caution merely serves to remind the accused of a right which he already possesses at common law. The fact that in a particular case he has not been reminded of it is no ground for inferring that his silence was not in exercise of that right, but was an acknowledgement of the truth of the accusation'.

The law stated in *Hall* must now be read subject to the CJPO 1994, ss. 34, 36 and 37 (see **F19.4** *et seq*.). Silence in the face of the sort of questioning to which those provisions apply may clearly give rise to specific adverse inferences arising out of the failure to mention facts subsequently relied upon (s. 34) or to account for various matters including the possession of incriminating material and presence at the scene of an offence (ss. 36 and 37); the caution and warnings to be given to suspects makes this clear (see PACE Code C, paras 10.4, 10.5A and 10.5B).

The decision in *Hall*, however, would seem still to be authority for the principle that a suspect, whether cautioned or not, should not be regarded as accepting the truth of a charge which he does not deny. In *Chandler* [1976] 1 WLR 585, however, the Court of Appeal expressed reservations about the correctness of the law as stated in *Hall*, regarding it as in conflict with the general rule laid down in *Christie* [1914] AC 545 (see **F17.49**), a criticism reiterated in *Raviraj* (1986) 85 Cr App R 93. The right of a person not to incriminate himself was well accepted, but it 'does not follow that a failure to answer an accusation or question when an answer could reasonably be expected may not provide some evidence in support of an accusation' (*Chandler,* at p. 589). If *Chandler* is right about this, and *Hall* is wrong, the inferences which may be drawn from silence under police questioning may, subject to what is said below, go beyond what is expressly permitted by the 1994 Act. *Chandler* does, however, accept two important limitations: an inference of acceptance cannot be drawn (a) where the parties are not on even terms and (b) where the suspect has been cautioned that he does not have to say anything.

In *Parkes* v *The Queen* [1976] 1 WLR 1251 the decision in *Hall* was distinguished on the ground that the person by whom the accusation was communicated to the accused was a police officer whom he knew was investigating an offence, whereas in *Parkes* the accusation was made spontaneously by a mother about an injury done to her daughter. In other words, in *Parkes* the parties were, while in *Hall* they were not, on even terms. In *Chandler* C was interviewed in connection with a fraud involving rented television sets. His solicitor was present. In the early stages of questioning, and before he had been cautioned, C refused to answer certain questions, including one which concerned his acquaintance with a man, A, who later stood trial with C. The Court of Appeal regarded *Mitchell* (1892) 17 Cox CC 503 as the applicable authority: the presence of C's solicitor meant that the parties were on 'even terms'. On the facts, however, the trial judge was wrong to suggest that an inference of guilt might be drawn directly from C's failure to answer the questions put, for the most that could be concluded, for example from C's silence when asked if he knew A, was that he did indeed know A. Had the trial judge not 'short-circuited the proper intellectual processes' required, but gone on instead to invite the jury to consider whether guilt could reasonably have been inferred from C's acknowledgement, the direction would have been correct. *Chandler* was applied in *Horne* [1990] Crim LR 188, in which police officers brought about a confrontation between H and a man he was suspected of having wounded. The man, still bleeding from his wounds, accused H of having caused them, and H refrained from making any reply. As in *Chandler,* the jury were not given a sufficiently full direction with regard to the use which could be made of the accused's silence, as nothing was said by the trial judge as to the circumstances in which silence might constitute an acknowledgement, or as to how the jury should approach the question of whether those circumstances existed in the case before them.

It was accepted in *Chandler* that the drawing of inferences after a suspect has been cautioned that he need say nothing is inappropriate. Since the coming into force of the PACE 1984 and its Codes of Practice, the questioning of a suspect otherwise than under caution which occurred in *Chandler* would rarely be permissible. For this reason the decision has been of limited effect in recent years, but it is arguable that the caution and warnings relating to the inferences which may be drawn under the 1994 Act will, because they put the accused on notice that specific inferences may be drawn, open the door to an argument that wider inferences are also possible, at least where the suspect's legal adviser is also present. However the caution before interview continues to include the words 'You do not have to say anything'. This being so, it is submitted that the appropriate inference from failure to deny an accusation under caution is still that the suspect is relying on his right to silence.

OUT-OF-COURT SILENCE UNDER THE 1994 ACT

Failure to Reveal Facts Afterwards Relied upon in Court

F19.4 A strong argument for drawing an adverse inference from silence occurs where the accused withholds his defence under interrogation but presents it at trial when it may be too late for it to be countered. At common law it was improper to invite the jury to draw an adverse inference. In *Gilbert* (1977) 66 Cr App R 237, G, who was suspected of murdering a colleague, declined to answer questions put to him under caution, but on the following day proffered a statement which dealt only with his business relationship with the deceased and not with the circumstances surrounding the killing. At trial, G relied on self-defence. The trial judge correctly directed the jury that no inferences could be drawn from G's refusal to answer questions, but went on to suggest that, so far as the statement was concerned, it was 'remarkable' that nothing was said about self-defence. This was held to be misdirection. The authorities (some of which were considered to be in conflict) established that the jury should not be invited to form an adverse opinion against an accused on account of his exercise of the right to silence. The court regarded the law as unsatisfactory, as did a later Court of Appeal in *Alladice* (1988) 87 Cr App R 380, where Lord Lane CJ considered that the quid pro quo for the right to have access to legal advice while in custody, conferred by s. 58 of the PACE 1984, was that proper comment on the late production of defences or explanations should be permitted.

Section 34 of the CJPO 1994 addresses this problem. It follows the recommendations of the Criminal Law Revision Committee *11th Report: Evidence* (Cmnd 4991, 1972), previously implemented in Northern Ireland (Criminal Evidence (Northern Ireland) Order 1988). In so doing it disregards the recommendations of a majority of the Royal Commission on Criminal Justice (the Runciman Commission) (Cm 2263, 1993), who considered that no inferences should be drawn from silence at the police station, and that it was when and only when the prosecution case had been fully disclosed that defendants should be required to offer an answer to the charges or risk adverse comment at trial on any new line of defence.

Criminal Justice and Public Order Act 1994, s. 34

(1) Where, in any proceedings against a person for an offence, evidence is given that the accused—

(a) at any time before he was charged with the offence, on being questioned under caution by a constable trying to discover whether or by whom the offence had been committed, failed to mention any fact relied on in his defence in those proceedings; or

(b) on being charged with the offence or officially informed that he might be prosecuted for it, failed to mention any such fact,

being a fact which in the circumstances existing at the time the accused could reasonably have been expected to mention when so questioned, charged or informed, as the case may be, subsection (2) below applies.

(2) Where this subsection applies—

(a) a magistrates' court, in deciding whether to grant an application for dismissal made by the accused under section 6 of the Magistrates' Courts Act 1980 (application for dismissal of charge in course of proceedings with a view to transfer for trial);

(b) a judge, in deciding whether to grant an application made by the accused under—

(i) section 6 of the Criminal Justice Act 1987 (application for dismissal of charge of serious fraud in respect of which notice of transfer has been given under section 4 of that Act); or

(ii) paragraph 5 of schedule 6 to the Criminal Justice Act 1991 (application for dismissal of charge of violent or sexual offence involving child in respect of which notice of transfer has been given under section 53 of that Act);

(c) the court, in determining whether there is a case to answer; and

(d) the court or jury, in determining whether the accused is guilty of the offence charged,

may draw such inferences from the failure as appear proper.

(2A) Where the accused was at an authorised place of detention at the time of the failure, subsections (1) and (2) above do not apply if he had not been allowed an opportunity to consult a solicitor prior to being questioned, charged or informed as mentioned in subsection (1) above.

(3)   Subject to any directions by the court, evidence tending to establish the failure may be given before or after evidence tending to establish the fact which the accused is alleged to have failed to mention.

(4)   This section applies in relation to questioning by persons (other than constables) charged with the duty of investigating offences or charging offenders as it applies in relation to questioning by constables; and in subsection (1) above 'officially informed' means informed by a constable or any such person.

(5)   This section does not—

(a)   prejudice the admissibility in evidence of the silence or other reaction of the accused in the face of anything said in his presence relating to the conduct in respect of which he is charged, in so far as evidence thereof would be admissible apart from this section; or

(b)   preclude the drawing of any inference from any such silence or other reaction of the accused which could properly be drawn apart from this section.

(6)   This section does not apply in relation to a failure to mention a fact if the failure occurred before the commencement of this section.

Section 34(2A) was added by the YJCEA 1999, s. 58, which is expected to come into force in April 2000. It is designed to bring the law into line with the judgment of the European Court of Human Rights in *Murray* v *United Kingdom* (1996) 22 EHRR 29. An 'authorised place of detention' is defined by s. 38(2A) to include police stations and any other place prescribed by order.

The function of this provision is to permit the tribunal of fact to draw 'such inferences as appear proper' (s. 34(2)) from the accused's silence, provided that the various conditions set forth in s. 34(1) are made out and any questions of fact arising thereunder are resolved against the accused (*Argent* [1997] 2 Cr App R 27). The provision applies only where a particular fact is advanced by the defence which is suspicious by reason of not being put forward at an early opportunity. Thus *Gilbert* (1977) 66 Cr App R 237 is reversed. It appears to have become accepted that the 'proper' inference which may be drawn in such circumstances (as to which the Act itself is silent) includes a general inference of guilt. Under the current Judicial Studies Board direction, the jury are told that they may take the failure to mention the fact into account as 'some additional support' for the prosecution case. This is contrary to the view propounded in earlier editions of this work where it was argued that the only permissible inference was a specific one as to the credit to be attached to the fact in question. But the section has no function if the accused makes no attempt to put previously undisclosed facts forward at trial (e.g., he simply contends that the prosecution has failed to prove its case). In *Moshaid* [1998] Crim LR 420, M, acting on legal advice, declined to answer any questions. At trial he did not give or call any evidence. It was held that in these circumstances s. 34 did not bite. It goes too far, however, to suggest that s. 34 applies only where the accused gives evidence: a fact relied on may be established by a witness called by the accused, or elicited from a prosecution witness (*Bowers* [1998] Crim LR 817).

No Conviction etc. on Silence Alone

F19.5

Criminal Justice and Public Order Act 1994, s. 38

(3)   A person shall not have the proceedings against him transferred to the Crown Court for trial, have a case to answer or be convicted of an offence solely on an inference drawn from such a failure or refusal as is mentioned in section 34(2), 35(3), 36(2) or 37(2).

(4)   A judge shall not refuse to grant such an application as is mentioned in section 34(2)(b), 36(2)(b) and 37(2)(b) solely on an inference drawn from such a failure as is mentioned in section 34(2), 36(2) or 37(2).

Section 38(3) applies to all four of the provisions of the 1994 Act which operate to permit the drawing of inferences from silence, and s. 38(4) to the three appertaining to out-of-court silence. It is hard to see that they confer any tangible benefits in relation to inferences drawn under s. 34, which, as they go only to the credit to be given to a fact relied on in defence, could hardly in any event form the *sole* reason for any of the outcomes referred to in s. 38(3) or (4). A further difficulty with the application of s. 34 was identified in *Hart* (23 April 1998 unreported). H declined in interview to respond to questions about his involvement in the importation of cannabis. A submission of no case to answer was made but rejected by the trial judge, apparently on the basis that the provisions of s. 34 tipped the scales against H. However there was nothing on which s. 34 could bite, as the defence had done nothing at that stage to amount to placing reliance on any particular fact. This will commonly be the case before the defence case has begun. The suggestion that s. 34 might be triggered by a defence argument, advanced in support of the submission of no case, that there might be an innocent explanation for the circumstantial evidence relied upon by the prosecution was dismissed by the Court of Appeal as 'fanciful'. It was suggested that the sort of case in which s. 34 might have a bearing on a submission of no case was where the accused has chosen to remain silent in interview, but has later produced a prepared statement. The question whether a defence statement prepared in compliance with the provisions of the CPIA 1996, s. 5 (see **D6.4**), could also be relevant in this context was not considered. In both of the above examples, however, it may be doubted whether the accused has relied on the facts in the statement within the meaning of s. 34 at the time when the submission falls to be considered.

Where the prosecution rely on an inference to be drawn under s. 34, it is essential that the jury be directed that such an inference alone cannot prove guilt (*Abdullah* [1999] 3 Arch News 3). The same presumably holds good for ss. 36 and 37 (and see, as to the direction where s. 35 is invoked, *Cowan* [1996] QB 373 at **F19.3**).

Under Caution

Inferences before a suspect is charged under s. 34 may not be drawn except 'on being   **F19.6** questioned under caution by a constable' (s. 34(1)(a)). (The reference to 'constable' includes others charged with investigating offences: s. 34(4)). The caution requirement formed an important amendment to the original Bill, and the caution makes clear the risks that attend the failure to mention facts which later form part of the defence. It is set out in Code C, para. 10.4 and runs as follows:

> You do not have to say anything. But it may harm your defence if you do not mention when questioned something which you later rely on in court. Anything you do say may be given in evidence.

Minor deviations from the formula are not a breach of the code as long as the sense is preserved (para. 10.5), and an officer is permitted to paraphrase if it appears that the person with whom he is dealing does not understand what the caution means (Note for Guidance 10C). A suspect who has been arrested should not normally be questioned about his involvement in an offence except in an interview at a police station, and it is envisaged that questioning to which s. 34 applies should occur in the course of such an interview which, being properly recorded, will then allow the court to make reliable deductions about the nature and extent of any silence. Clearly, if the accused alleges that he did mention the relevant fact when questioned, the prosecution will have to prove the contrary before any adverse inference can be drawn. Where it is alleged that a 'significant silence' (i.e. one which appears capable of being used in evidence against the suspect) has occurred before his arrival at a police station, then at the beginning of an interview at the station the interviewing officer should put the matter to the suspect, under caution, and ask him whether he confirms or denies that earlier silence and whether he wishes to add anything (para. 11.2A). The consequence of failing to go through this procedure (which applies to evidentially significant statements as it does to silences) must be to increase significantly the likelihood that the evidence in question will be excluded under s. 78 if the suspect denies that the earlier statement was made or that the silence occurred. Furthermore if the suspect is questioned improperly in circumstances prohibited by Code C, e.g., where there already exists sufficient evidence for the accused to be charged, s. 34 should not be brought to bear on the suspect's failure to respond (*Pointer* [1997] Crim LR 676; *Gayle* [1999] Crim LR 502). There is a lack of consistency in the authorities on when there is sufficient evidence for this purpose (see *McGuinness* [1999] Crim LR 318; *Ioannou* [1999] Crim LR 586), but no doubt about the principle.

Facts which Should Have Been Mentioned

F19.7   Inferences may be drawn from facts subsequently relied upon in defence only if 'in the circumstances existing at the time the accused could reasonably have been expected to mention them'. This must make allowance:

(a)   for the personal characteristics of the accused (e.g., mental handicap/illness) to be taken into account in deciding what he could reasonably be expected to have mentioned;
(b)   for the extent of the accused's knowledge of the case against him (e.g., if he is not told when an offence is supposed to have occurred he cannot reasonably be expected to mention an alibi).

As to (a), the Court of Appeal in *Argent* [1997] 2 Cr App R 27 confirmed that courts should not construe the expression 'in the circumstances' restrictively, and that amongst the personal factors which might be relevant to an assessment of what an individual could reasonably have been expected to mention were age, experience, mental capacity, state of health, sobriety, tiredness and personality.

As to (b), the failure of the police to disclose relevant information when asked to do so by the accused or his legal adviser must be a factor capable of affecting the propriety of drawing an inference. If little information is forthcoming a legal adviser may well counsel silence until a better assessment of the case to answer can be made. In this situation it is likely to be particularly difficult to draw adverse inferences from non-disclosure by the defence.

The difficult issue of what use, if any, can be made of a 'no comment' interview in which the accused remains silent on legal advice was considered by the Court of Appeal in *Condron* [1997] 1 WLR 827. C and his wife, admitted heroin addicts, were convicted of offences relating to the supply of the drug. At interview, both remained silent on the advice of their solicitor who (despite medical advice to the contrary) considered that their drug withdrawal symptoms rendered them unfit to be interviewed. At trial, the defence relied upon detailed innocent explanations of incriminating evidence which, if true, would have been available to them at the time of the interview.

Two grounds of appeal were considered. On the first, the Court of Appeal held that the trial judge had rightly declined to exclude evidence of the interview. Only in exceptional circumstances would it be appropriate to exclude such an interview before the conclusion of all the evidence, as it would not at that stage be apparent what material facts were not disclosed, or the reason for non-disclosure. The example given of a possible exceptional case was that of an accused of low intelligence who is advised to remain silent (compare the CJPO 1994, s. 35(1) (at **F19.12**), where specific provision is made for the physical or mental condition of an accused which makes it undesirable for him to give evidence).

On the second ground, it was held that the trial judge's direction to the jury that it was for them to decide whether to draw an adverse inference was correct, although it would have been desirable to add a further direction based on *Cowan* [1996] QB 373 (see **F19.13**) that such an inference should be drawn only if the jury concluded that the failure to answer questions at interview could only sensibly be attributed to C's having no answer, or none that would stand up to questioning. The fact that C's silence followed legal advice did not of itself preclude the drawing of inferences. Much depended on the reasons for the advice and, while an accused would not be held to have waived his legal professional privilege merely by asserting that he had been advised to be silent, such a bare assertion was unlikely to carry much weight. Investigation of the reasons for the advice would involve waiver of privilege, and both the accused and, if he testified, his solicitor could be questioned on whether there were any further reasons for the advice, such as the desire to gain a tactical advantage. The same point was made in *Roble* [1997] Crim LR 449, in which Rose LJ also noted that the advice to remain silent might readily be understood where, for example, the interviewing officer had disclosed too little of the case for the solicitor usefully to advise his client, or where the nature of the offence, or the material in the hands of the police, was so complex or related to matters so long ago that no sensible immediate response was feasible. In *Bowden* [1999] 1 WLR 823 a waiver was held to have occurred where B called evidence in his defence of a statement made by his solicitor at interview, namely that he had advised B to remain silent because of the lack of evidence against him. B was held to have been properly cross-examined about the extent to which he had disclosed to the solicitor the facts that subsequently formed the basis of his defence. Lord Bingham CJ stated, *obiter*, that the giving of evidence at a *voir dire* as to the reasons for legal advice for silence would operate as a waiver of privilege at trial even if the evidence was not repeated before the jury: the accused cannot 'have his cake and eat it' where privilege is concerned.

In *Condron* C's solicitor had a plausible reason for the advice he gave, which might have influenced the jury against drawing an inference. It must follow from *Condron*, however, that an accused is theoretically at risk of an adverse inference being drawn from silence consequent upon legal advice, even where he is given advice which is plainly bad (for example, where he is told to keep to himself facts which provide a complete defence). This might be thought unfair to the accused who puts his faith in his adviser's judgment. In such a case, however, the jury might find it difficult to conclude that the failure to answer questions could 'only sensibly be attributed' to the non-existence of any sustainable answer. Where the accused's solicitor, following a consultation with his client, makes a statement to the officers conducting the interview with regard to the accused's reasons for silence (in the presence of the accused who says nothing in dissent), the statement may be given in evidence and may form the basis of an adverse inference (*Fitzgerald* [1998] 4 Arch News 2). It would appear that the Court of Appeal had in mind by way of exception to the hearsay rule either the doctrine of admission by an agent, or implied admission by silence where a statement is made in the presence of the accused (see **F16.51** and **F19.2** respectively). In *Bowden* the Court of Appeal expressed a preference for the explanation based on agency, which it is submitted is correct. In this connection it is relevant to note that privilege should not be regarded as waived if the accused merely seeks to demonstrate the fact that he communicated relevant exculpatory facts to his legal adviser prior to the interview (cf. *Wilmot* (1988) 89 Cr App R 341). Nor is it hearsay for the accused to tell the court what advice the solicitor gave him, provided that his purpose in doing so is not to establish the truth of any fact narrated by the solicitor. It is the accused's reason for withholding facts that is in issue, so provided that, for example, he merely wishes to explain the impact upon him of the advice given, there is no hearsay problem (*Davis* [1998] Crim LR 659).

Where the fact is one which the accused could reasonably have been expected to mention it will be permissible to draw 'such inferences from the failure as appear proper' (s. 34(2)) in a variety of contexts including the determination of guilt (s. 34(2)(d), and whether there is a case to answer (s. 34(2)(c)), bearing in mind always that an inference drawn under the subsection is not by itself sufficient to sustain either determination (s. 38(3): see **F19.5**). It has been said by the Privy Council, in the context of Singaporean legislation permitting inferences to be drawn from refusal to testify, that 'what inferences are proper to be drawn . . . depend on the circumstances of the particular case, and is a question to be decided by applying ordinary commonsense' (*Haw Tua Tau* v *Public Prosecutor* [1982] AC 136, per Lord Diplock at p. 153).

Although the most common inference from failure to reveal facts which are subsequently relied on is that the facts have been invented after the interview, it may equally appear to the jury that the accused had the facts in mind at the time of interview, but was unwilling to expose his account to critical questioning which he feared would demonstrate its falsity (*Randall* [1998] 5 Arch News 1). Similarly, the jury may deduce that the accused was faced with a choice between on the one hand silence, and on the other either lying or incriminating himself further with the truth. Again, this is a permissible inference under s. 34 (*Daniel* [1998] 2 Cr App R 373). It follows that, even if it is common ground that an accused spoke to his solicitor about a proposed defence of alibi before any interview took place, his failure to reveal the alibi in interview was still a matter from which inferences could be drawn if the jury were unconvinced by the accused's explanation (*Taylor* [1999] Crim LR 77). Nothing in *Condron* or *Cowan* should be read as indicating that the only adverse inference to be drawn is one of recent fabrication (*Beckles* [1999] Crim LR 148).

In some cases an inference cannot logically be drawn without first concluding that the accused is guilty, and in such cases, s. 34 is of no assistance. Such a case was *Mountford* [1999] Crim LR 575. M, charged with possession of heroin with intent to supply, put forward the defence that the actual dealer was W, the main prosecution witness, while he was merely a customer. M gave as his explanation for failing to reveal this defence at interview his reluctance to expose W to prosecution. The Court of Appeal held that the jury could not properly reject M's reason for not mentioning this fact without first concluding that the fact was untrue: the very issue on which M's guilt turned. In these (somewhat unusual) circumstances the judge should not have left s. 34 to the jury.

Where the judge concludes that the requirements of s. 34 have not been met, but the jury have been made aware of the accused's failure to answer questions, it was held in *McGarry* [1999] 1 WLR 1500 that a direction should be given to the jury that they should not hold the accused's silence against him. If that were not done, the jury would be left in 'no-man's land' between the common law rule and the statutory exception, without any guidance as to how to regard the accused's silence.

In all cases where s. 34 is to be relied upon, it is submitted that a clear judicial direction will be required as to the nature of the inference that may properly be drawn. Where prosecution counsel had not sought to rely upon s. 34, and had not raised the matter with the accused in cross-examination, the Court of Appeal in *Khan* [1999] 2 Arch News 2 rightly 'deprecated' the decision of the trial judge to direct the jury that they might draw an inference under s. 34 without first raising the matter with counsel. It was held, however, that (as there would have been no basis upon which the judge could have been deterred from giving the direction had the matter been argued) K had suffered no disadvantage. It is submitted that this is a dangerous approach. A trial judge ought not, in fairness, to leave it open to the jury to make use of silence which, because the defence did not expect to have to explain it away, has not been the subject of any comment by the accused or the defence witnesses. If the judge thinks that s. 34 might come into play, the matter should be raised in time for it to be the subject of evidence not speculation.

A direction may be called for where there is more than one accused. If A has failed to mention a relevant fact so as to attract a s. 34 direction, it is desirable in the case of co-accused B whose case stands or falls with A's to give a direction not to draw any inference against B.

As to the 'unfair' use of silence, see **F19.10**.

Failure to Account for Objects, Substances, Marks and Presence

Criminal Justice and Public Order Act 1994, ss. 36 and 37   **F19.8**

36.—(1) Where—
    (a) a person is arrested by a constable, and there is—
        (i) on his person; or
        (ii) in or on his clothing or footwear; or
        (iii) otherwise in his possession; or
        (iv) in any place in which he is at the time of his arrest,
any object, substance or mark, or there is any mark on any such object; and
    (b) that or another constable investigating the case reasonably believes that the presence of the object, substance or mark may be attributable to the participation of the person arrested in the commission of an offence specified by the constable; and
    (c) the constable informs the person arrested that he so believes, and requests him to account for the presence of the object, substance or mark; and
    (d) the person fails or refuses to do so,
then if, in any proceedings against the person for the offence so specified, evidence of those matters is given, subsection (2) below applies.
    (2) Where this subsection applies—
    (a) a magistrates' court, in deciding whether to grant an application for dismissal made by the accused under section 6 of the Magistrates' Courts Act 1980 (application for dismissal of charge in course of proceedings with a view to transfer for trial);
    (b) a judge, in deciding whether to grant an application made by the accused under—
        (i) section 6 of the Criminal Justice Act 1987 (application for dismissal of charge of serious fraud in respect of which notice of transfer has been given under section 4 of that Act); or
        (ii) paragraph 5 of schedule 6 to the Criminal Justice Act 1991 (application for dismissal of charge of violent or sexual offence involving child in respect of which notice of transfer has been given under section 53 of that Act);
    (c) the court, in determining whether there is a case to answer; and
    (d) the court or jury, in determining whether the accused is guilty of the offence charged,
may draw such inferences from the failure or refusal as appear proper.
    (3) Subsections (1) and (2) above apply to the condition of clothing or footwear as they apply to a substance or mark thereon.
    (4) Subsections (1) and (2) above do not apply unless the accused was told in ordinary language by the constable when making the request mentioned in subsection (1)(c) above what the effect of this section would be if he failed or refused to comply with the request.
    (4A) Where the accused was at an authorised place of detention at the time of the failure or refusal, subsections (1) and (2) do not apply if he had not been allowed an opportunity to consult a solicitor prior to the request being made.
    (5) This section applies in relation to officers of customs and excise as it applies in relation to constables.
    (6) This section does not preclude the drawing of any inference from a failure or refusal of the accused to account for the presence of an object, substance or mark or from the condition of clothing or footwear which could properly be drawn apart from this section.
    (7) This section does not apply in relation to a failure or refusal which occurred before the commencement of this section.
37.—(1) Where—
    (a) a person arrested by a constable was found by him at a place at or about the time the offence for which he was arrested is alleged to have been committed; and
    (b) that or another constable investigating the offence reasonably believes that the presence of the person at that place and at that time may be attributable to his participation in the commission of the offence; and

(c)   the constable informs the person that he so believes, and requests him to account for that presence; and

(d)   the person fails or refuses to do so,

then if, in any proceedings against the person for the offence, evidence of those matters is given, subsection (2) below applies.

(2)   Where this subsection applies—

(a)   a magistrates' court, in deciding whether to grant an application for dismissal made by the accused under section 6 of the Magistrates' Courts Act 1980 (application for dismissal of charge in course of proceedings with a view to transfer for trial);

(b)   a judge, in deciding whether to grant an application made by the accused under—

(i)   section 6 of the Criminal Justice Act 1987 (application for dismissal of charge of serious fraud in respect of which notice of transfer has been given under section 4 of that Act); or

(ii)   paragraph 5 of schedule 6 to the Criminal Justice Act 1991 (application for dismissal of charge of violent or sexual offence involving child in respect of which notice of transfer has been given under section 53 of that Act);

(c)   the court, in determining whether there is a case to answer; and

(d)   the court or jury, in determining whether the accused is guilty of the offence charged,

may draw such inferences from the failure or refusal as appear proper.

(3)   Subsections (1) and (2) do not apply unless the accused was told in ordinary language by the constable when making the request mentioned in subsection (1)(c) above what the effect of this section would be if he failed or refused to comply with the request.

(3A)   Where the accused was at an authorised place of detention at the time of the failure or refusal, subsection (1) and (2) do not apply if he had not been allowed an opportunity to consult a solicitor prior to the request being made.

(4)   This section applies in relation to officers of customs and excise as it applies in relation to constables.

(5)   This section does not preclude the drawing of any inference from a failure or refusal of the accused to account for his presence at a place which could properly be drawn apart from this section.

(6)   This section does not apply in relation to a failure or refusal which occurred before the commencement of this section.

Sections 36(4A) and 37(3A) were added by the YJCEA 1999, s. 58, which is expected to come into force in April 2000. They are designed to bring the law into line with the judgment of the European Court of Human Rights in *Murray* v *United Kingdom* (1996) 22 EHRR 29. An 'authorised place of detention' is defined by s. 38(2A) to include police stations and any other place prescribed by order.

These two provisions are based on the Irish Criminal Justice Act 1984. They go further than s. 34, which relates to the weight to be given to D's defence, and amount to positive evidence to support the prosecution case.

Basis for Inference

F19.9   Neither s. 36 nor s. 37 of the CJPO 1994 permits an inference to be drawn unless four conditions are satisfied:

(a)   the accused is arrested;

(b)   a constable (not necessarily the arresting officer) reasonably believes that the object, substance or mark, or the presence of the accused at the relevant place, may be attributable to the accused's participation in a crime (in s. 36 an offence 'specified by the constable'; in s. 37 the offence for which he was arrested);

(c)   the constable informs the accused of his belief and requests an explanation of the matter in question;

(d)   the constable tells the suspect in ordinary language the effect of a failure or refusal to comply with the request.

The four conditions may, on their face, be satisfied where an arrested person is confronted with incriminating circumstances before he is taken to the police station for interview. However, a request for information under the two sections would appear to be a form of questioning, and because an arrested suspect should not normally be questioned about his involvement in an offence except in interview at a police station (PACE Code C, para. 11.1) the tendering in evidence of an unproductive request for information 'on the beat' should be the exception rather than the norm. If such a request is made and is alleged to have yielded a silence from which inferences can properly be drawn, the procedure for putting the silence to the suspect in a subsequent interview at the police station will apply (para. 11.2A: see **F19.6**). The 'special warnings' to be given at interview in connection with ss. 36 and 37 are dealt with in PACE Code C, paras. 10.5A and 10.5B).

As with s. 34 (see **F19.4**), only 'proper' inferences may be drawn. Clearly the strength of the inference increases with the suspicious nature of the circumstances, so that if the accused is arrested when in possession of a car with explosive devices in full view on the back seat, his failure to give an account is more suggestive of guilt than if he refuses to account for a dirty mark on his clothing following a fight in which he is alleged to have fallen to the ground. In some cases a strong inference is proper. In *Connolly* (10 June 1994 unreported), C had been given an opportunity to account for an incriminating receipt found in his pocket, and his presence near the scene of the crime, but had maintained complete silence. The Court of Appeal for Northern Ireland accepted the trial judge's inference, drawn under provisions equivalent to ss. 36 and 37, that C was determined to sit out interrogation, assess the strength of the case against him and, if charged, to present a version of his activities unembarrassed by any statements to which he might have committed himself during interview.

Sections 36 and 37 are somewhat restrictively drawn. Section 36 is concerned with the state of the suspect at the time of his arrest, and not with his state at other relevant times, e.g., when seen by an eye-witness at the time of the crime. Section 37 is similarly concerned only with the suspect's location at the time of arrest, and applies only when he was found at the location of the crime at or about the relevant time. No mention is made of his presence at the scene at other relevant times: what if he gave the police the slip at the scene and was arrested elsewhere? If the intention is to build upon already suspicious circumstances by allowing an additional guilty inference if the accused fails to explain them, it is not clear why the provisions are so restrictive: a suspected rapist may have inferences drawn for failing to explain away stains on his trousers, but not for refusing to explain why he is not wearing any (unless he has discarded them nearby).

Section 38(3) (see **F19.5**) provides that an inference drawn under these provisions may, *inter alia*, form part of the case to answer or contribute to a verdict of guilty, though neither outcome may be based 'solely' upon such an inference. It is not clear what this means. An inference drawn under ss. 36 and 37 can never exist 'solely', in the sense of independently of the proof of the suspicious circumstances for which the accused refuses to account. In some cases, such circumstances may be sufficient to convict, as in the case of the man arrested with two bombs on the back seat of his car. The fact that the accused gave no explanation cannot prevent the circumstances having this effect: on the contrary, it strengthens the inference to be drawn from them. Perhaps the intention behind the provision is to prompt the judge to tell the jury not to convict just because the accused has been unhelpful.

It is not clear how frequently these two provisions will function independently of ss. 34 and 35. If D goes on to present a defence relying on facts he could have mentioned earlier, as in *Connolly*, it is likely that s. 34 will also apply. If he gives no evidence, then s. 35 (see **F19.11**) may come into play.

Unfair Use of Pre-trial Silence

F19.10   Failure or refusal to respond to questioning relevant to ss. 34, 36 and 37 seems unlikely to be regarded as a 'statement', and is thus incapable of being a confession within s. 82 of the PACE 1984 for the purposes of s. 76 of that Act (see **F17.4**). Silence obtained by oppression or in circumstances conducive to unreliability would not therefore be automatically inadmissible, as would a confession similarly obtained. It would however be subject to exclusion under the discretion conferred by the PACE 1984, s. 78, in respect of all prosecution evidence, to the extent that it would be unfair to make use of it.

Extensive use has also been made of s. 78 in rejecting confession evidence which, while admissible under s. 76, has been obtained in breach of the 1984 Act or Codes of Practice, or by other unfair means (see **F17.13**). These authorities would seem to apply also to silence, with the result that, e.g., failure to make proper records of an interrogation, may lead to exclusion.

FAILURE OF ACCUSED TO TESTIFY

F19.11   The CJPO 1994 repealed the Criminal Evidence Act 1898, s. 1(b). The 1898 Act provided that the failure of the accused to testify was not to be made the subject of any comment by the prosecution. Comment by the judge was permissible but the scope for it was limited, and it had always to be accompanied with a reminder that the accused was not bound to give evidence and that, while the jury had been deprived of the opportunity of hearing his story tested in cross-examination, they were not to assume that he was guilty because he had not gone into the witness-box (*Bathurst* [1968] 2 QB 99). Stronger comment was permitted where the defence case involved the assertion of facts which were at variance with the prosecution evidence, or additional to it and exculpatory, and which, if true, would have been within the accused's own knowledge (*Martinez-Tobon* [1994] 1 WLR 388).

Failure to Testify following the 1994 Act

F19.12   Under the CJPO 1994, s. 35, it is submitted that the common-law authorities will continue to provide useful guidance as to the type of case in which the strongest inferences are permissible. (See further **F19.13** to **F19.16**.) However it is also submitted that a careful direction will be required, probably in all cases where the accused does not testify, in order to make the jury aware of the inferences which may properly be drawn.

Criminal Justice and Public Order Act 1994, s. 35

(1)   At the trial of any person for an offence, subsections (2) and (3) below apply unless—
   (a)   the accused's guilt is not in issue; or
   (b)   it appears to the court that the physical or mental condition of the accused makes it undesirable for him to give evidence;
but subsection (2) below does not apply if, at the conclusion of the evidence for the prosecution, his legal representative informs the court that the accused will give evidence or, where he is unrepresented, the court ascertains from him that he will give evidence.
(2)   Where this subsection applies, the court shall, at the conclusion of the evidence for the prosecution, satisfy itself (in the case of proceedings on indictment, in the presence of the jury) that the accused is aware that the stage has been reached at which evidence can be given for the defence and that he can, if he wishes, give evidence and that, if he chooses not to give evidence, or having been sworn, without good cause refuses to answer any question, it will be permissible for the court or jury to draw such inferences as appear proper from his failure to give evidence or his refusal, without good cause, to answer any question.
(3)   Where this subsection applies, the court or jury, in determining whether the accused is guilty of the offence charged, may draw such inferences as appear proper from the failure of the accused to give evidence or his refusal, without good cause, to answer any question.

(4)   This section does not render the accused compellable to give evidence on his own behalf, and he shall accordingly not be guilty of contempt of court by reason of a failure to do so.

(5)   For the purposes of this section a person who, having been sworn, refuses to answer any question shall be taken to do so without good cause unless—

(a)   he is entitled to refuse to answer the question by virtue of any enactment, whenever passed or made, or on the ground of privilege; or

(b)   the court in the exercise of its general discretion excuses him from answering it.

(6)   [Repealed by CDA 1998, s. 35.]

(7)   This section applies—

(a)   in relation to proceedings on indictment for an offence, only if the person charged with the offence is arraigned on or after the commencement of this section;

(b)   in relation to proceedings in a magistrates' court, only if the time when the court begins to receive evidence in the proceedings falls after the commencement of this section.

Practice Direction (Crown Court: Defendant's Evidence)
[1995] 1 WLR 657

Form of words to be used pursuant to section 35 of the Criminal Justice and Public Order Act 1994

1.   At the conclusion of the evidence for the prosecution, section 35(2) requires the court to satisfy itself that the accused is aware that the stage has been reached at which evidence can be given for the defence and that he can, if he wishes, give evidence and that, if he chooses not to give evidence or, having been sworn, without good cause refuses to answer any question, it will be permissible for the jury to draw such inferences as appear proper from his failure to give evidence of his refusal, without good cause, to answer any question.

If the accused is legally represented

2.   Section 35(1) provides that section 35(2) does NOT apply if at the conclusion of the evidence for the prosecution the accused's legal representative informs the court that the accused will give evidence. This should be done in the presence of the jury. If the representative indicates that the accused will give evidence, the case should proceed in the usual way.

3.   If the court is not so informed, or if the court is informed that the accused does NOT intend to give evidence, the judge should in the presence of the jury inquire of the representative in these terms:

'Have you advised your client that the stage has now been reached at which he may give evidence and, if he chooses not to do so or, having been sworn, without good cause refuses to answer any question, the jury may draw such inferences as appear proper from his failure to do so?'

4.   If the representative replies to the judge that the accused has been so advised, then the case shall proceed. If counsel replies that the accused has not been so advised then the judge shall direct the representative to advise his client of the consequences set out in paragraph 3 hereof and should adjourn briefly for this purpose before proceeding further.

If the accused is not legally represented

5.   If the accused is not represented the judge shall at the conclusion of the evidence for the prosecution and in the presence of the jury say to the accused:

'You have heard the evidence against you. Now is the time for you to make your defence. You may give evidence on oath, and be cross-examined like any other witness. If you do not give evidence or, having been sworn, without good cause refuse to answer any question the jury may draw such inferences as appear proper. That means they may hold it against you. You may also call any witness or witnesses whom you have arranged to attend court. Afterwards you may also, if you wish, address the jury by arguing your case from the dock. But you cannot at that stage give evidence. Do you now intend to give evidence?'

'Proper' Inferences of Guilt

Under the CJPO 1994, s. 35, the 'proper' inferences come about as a result of the failure **F19.13** of the accused to give evidence or his refusal without good cause to answer any question

(s. 35(3)). Defendants whose 'physical or mental condition make it undesirable' for them to give evidence are excluded from the operation of the section, together with those whose 'guilt is not in issue' (s. 35(1)). Until 30 September 1998 (when s. 35 of the CDA 1998 came into force) defendants under the age of 14 enjoyed equivalent protection, but now stand on the same footing as adults. By virtue of s. 35(5), privilege remains a valid ground for refusing to answer, as does a statutory entitlement such as the Criminal Evidence Act 1898, s. 1(f) (see **F14.1**). Subject to these exceptions, the accused must answer all proper questions or risk the drawing of inferences, and a judge may remind him of his duty in this regard, though he should avoid doing so in an oppressive way (*Ackinclose* [1996] Crim LR 747). The court is obliged to satisfy itself that defendants who have not indicated that they intend to give evidence understand the consequences of declining to do so (s. 35(2) and (3) and the *Practice Direction (Crown Court: Defendant's Evidence)* [1995] 1 WLR 657). The *Practice Direction* makes clear that the burden of explaining the option to testify and the consequences of failing to do so to the defendant rests, in the case of a legally represented defendant, with the legal representative. This accords with the position at common law (cf. *Sankar* v *State of Trinidad and Tobago* [1995] 1 WLR 194).

The meaning of s. 35(1)(b) was considered in *Friend* [1997] 1 WLR 1433. F was tried for murder. He had a physical age of 15, a mental age of 9, and an IQ of 63. Expert evidence suggested that, although not suggestible, his powers of comprehension were limited and he might find it difficult to do justice to himself in the witness box. Nevertheless F had given a clear account of his defence at various stages prior to trial. Taking all of these matters into account, the trial judge ruled that F's mental condition did not make it 'undesirable' for him to give evidence, so that his failure to do so led to the jury being directed that they might draw inferences under s. 35(3). The Court of Appeal agreed, noting that it would only be in a rare case that the judge would be called upon to arrive at a decision under s. 35(1)(b); generally an accused who was unable to comprehend proceedings so as to make a proper defence would be unfit to plead, so the issue would not arise. Section 35(1)(b) was intended to mitigate any injustice to a person whose physical or mental handicap was less severe, and it gave a wide discretion to a trial judge which did not require to be circumscribed by any further judicial test. The trial judge had been right not to base his conclusion on the mental age of F: a person with a mental age of less than 14 did not automatically qualify for the protection which before 1998 applied to a person of that physical age. Nor was he bound to determine the issue on the expert evidence alone, but was entitled to take account of the behaviour of F before and after the commission of the offence including the way in which he had put his defence in interview. (The conduct of F at the time of the offence, which was hotly disputed, was rightly not considered by the judge.) The trial judge in *Friend* seems to have been much influenced by the fact that young children regularly appear as witnesses in criminal cases, and that measures can be taken by which they and other vulnerable witnesses can, if their needs are correctly assessed, be protected from unfair or oppressive cross-examination. Thus, as the main reason for questioning the desirability of F testifying was that he might give a poor account of himself unless care were taken to ensure that he understood and had time to respond to questions, the fact that the court itself could respond sensitively to F's needs was a factor militating against the defence argument. The outcome suggests that the discretion will be exercised against the background of an assumption that it is generally desirable for an accused to testify, so that cases in which it can be said to be 'undesirable' will be rare indeed.

Both *Friend* and the later decision in *A* [1997] Crim LR 883 require there to be an evidential basis for a ruling that s. 35(1)(b) applies. A *voir dire* may be required to determine the issue, although the judge is, according to *A*, under no obligation to initiate the procedure if defence counsel does not seek to do so.

The adverse inference which it may be proper to draw under s. 35(3) is that the accused 'is guilty of the offence charged'. As s. 35 does not come into play until after the close of the evidence for the prosecution, it presupposes that a prima facie case has already been established against the accused. In *Murray v DPP* [1994] 1 WLR 1, a decision concerning the equivalent provision in the Criminal Evidence (Northern Ireland) Order 1988, M was convicted of attempted murder and possession of a firearm with intent to endanger life. Scientific evidence linked M with a car used in the attack: the situation was one calling for 'confession and avoidance'. M advanced various explanations during interrogation, but gave no evidence at trial, from which failure the trial judge drew a strong adverse inference. The House of Lords considered that the inference was justified. The 1988 Order was intended to change the law and practice and to lay down new rules as to the comments which could be made and inferences which could be drawn. The accused is not compellable to testify, but he must risk the consequences if he does not do so. These consequences are not simply that specific inferences may be drawn from specific facts, but include in a proper case the inference that the accused is guilty. As to what is proper, Lord Slynn said (at p. 11):

> If there is no prima facie case shown by the prosecution there is no case to answer. Equally, if parts of the prosecution case had so little evidential value that they called for no answer, a failure to deal with those specific matters cannot justify an inference of guilt.

> On the other hand, if aspects of the evidence taken alone or in combination with other facts clearly call for an explanation which the accused ought to be in a position to give, if an explanation exists, then a failure to give any explanation may as a matter of common sense allow the drawing of an inference that there is no explanation and that the accused is guilty.

As with ss. 34, 36 and 37, the accused cannot be convicted solely on an inference drawn from a failure or refusal (s. 38(3)). Again it is not clear what effect the provision has. If a case to answer has been established a jury would by definition be entitled to convict (see **D13.26** to **D13.32**). Presumably the provision means no more than that the judge must tell the jury not to convict just because the accused has not given evidence.

In *Cowan* [1996] QB 373, the Court of Appeal rejected an argument that s. 35 should be permitted to operate in exceptional cases only. The argument was based first on the extent to which the section breached a long-established principle by inhibiting the exercise of the right to silence, and secondly on the effect it was alleged to have of 'watering down' the burden of proof. The court held that even before the 1994 Act the accused had been in certain respects inhibited from exercising the right to silence (for example out of fear that the jury might draw adverse inferences even where the classic direction in *Bathurst* was given) and that the burden of proof, far from being altered or watered down, remained on the prosecution. The effect of s. 35 was simply to add a further evidential factor in support of the prosecution case. The Court of Appeal emphasised that silence cannot be the only factor on which a conviction is based (s. 38(3); see **F19.5**) and that the prosecution remains under an obligation to establish a prima facie case before any question of the defendant testifying is raised. Their lordships took this to mean not only that the case should be fit to be left to the jury, but also that the judge should make clear to the jury that *they* must be convinced of the existence of a prima facie case before drawing an adverse inference from silence. (This last point seems to go beyond the requirements of s. 35 or of s. 38(3).)

Having rejected both limbs of the argument, the court also stressed that the plain wording of s. 35 indicated that it was not limited to exceptional cases: on the contrary, the exceptional cases were those dealt with in s. 35(1) in which the provisions were *not* to be invoked. However, it was open to a court in any case to which the exceptions in s. 35(1) did not apply to decline to draw an inference from silence, though for a judge to advise a jury against drawing such an inference would require either 'some evidential basis for doing so or some exceptional factors in the case making that a fair course to take'. The Court of Appeal gave no example of the situation in which it would be improper to draw an inference from silence.

Cowan was applied in *Napper* (1997) 161 JP 16. N claimed that the failure of the police to interview him while the frauds with which he was charged were reasonably fresh in his mind should have led the judge to direct the jury to draw no adverse inferences from his silence at trial. It was held that this was not, under *Cowan*, an exceptional case where such a direction would have been justified in the interests of justice. Nothing prevented N from making his own record from which to refresh his memory, and the crucial issues were in any case sufficiently memorable to present him with no difficulty of recollection.

Weak Prosecution Case

F19.14 It seems from the observations of Lord Slynn in *Murray* v *DPP* [1994] 1 WLR 1 (see **F19.13**) that inferences of guilt should not be drawn from failure to give evidence to contradict a prosecution case of 'little evidential value'. This accords with the position at common law, where it was considered improper for a judge to bolster up a weak prosecution case by making comments on an accused's failure to give evidence (*Waugh* v *The King* [1950] AC 203). W had been convicted of murder on very weak evidence. The only evidence of any strength was a statement made by the deceased shortly before his death. The police accepted the appellant's explanation as to what had happened, but a coroner ordered his prosecution. At the trial the appellant did not testify. In his summing-up the trial judge commented nine times on the fact. The Privy Council disapproved of these comments. Lord Oaksey said (at pp. 211–12):

> . . . in the present case their lordships think that the prisoner's counsel was fully justified in not calling the prisoner, and that the judge, if he made any comment on the matter at all, ought at least have pointed out to the jury that the prisoner was not bound to give evidence and that it was for the prosecution to make out the case beyond reasonable doubt.

Burden on Defendant

F19.15 A different form of comment was required at common law in cases in which the accused bears the burden of proof, namely 'that he is not bound to go into the witness box, nobody can force him to go into the witness box, but the burden is upon him, and if he does not, he runs the risk of not being able to prove his case' (*Bathurst* [1968] 2 QB 99: see **F19.11**). The same situation under the CJPO 1994 would seem to justify a strong adverse inference if the defence is one which, if true, could be proved by the accused's own evidence (e.g., that his possession of an offensive weapon was lawful: Prevention of Crime Act 1953, s. 1(1), see **B12.94**).

In cases in which there is a defence of diminished responsibility, only rarely was it proper for a comment to be made (*Bathurst*). A defence such as diminished responsibility or insanity can be made out without the accused's contribution. Under the 1994 Act the position appears to be the same: s. 35(1)(b) provides that no inference may be drawn if the mental condition of the accused makes it undesirable for him to give evidence.

Confession and Avoidance and Facts within Accused's Knowledge

F19.16 In *Mutch* [1973] 1 All ER 178, the Court of Appeal identified exceptional cases at common law in which stronger comment was justified. They were those in which an inference could be drawn from uncontested or clearly established facts which point so strongly to guilt as to call for an explanation. *Corrie* (1904) 20 TLR 365 and *Bernard* (1908) 1 Cr App R 218 are cited in *Mutch* as exceptional examples of the kind of case in which such an inference may properly be drawn. So also is *Brigden* [1973] Crim LR 579. The accused gave no evidence, but alleged that the police had planted incriminating evidence on him and cross-examined a prosecution witness on a conviction. It is submitted that such a case would support a strong inference under the

CJPO 1994 that the defence was untrue. The same may be said of other cases concerning facts within the accused's own knowledge which were said to justify strong comment at common law in *Martinez-Tobon* [1994] 1 WLR 388 (see **F19.11**).

OTHER STATUTORY INCURSIONS ON THE RIGHT TO SILENCE

Other existing statutory incursions on the right to silence include the obligation to make **F19.17** pre-trial disclosure in fraud cases under the CJA 1987, s. 2 (see **D1.59**) and the obligation to give notice of the intended use of expert evidence under the PACE 1984, s. 81 (see **F10.3**).

ACCUSED FAILING TO PROVIDE SAMPLES ETC.

At common law, adverse inference could be drawn from unhelpful conduct other than **F19.18** silence while under interrogation. In *Smith* (1985) 81 Cr App R 286, S was asked in the presence of his solicitor if he was willing to provide a sample of hair. When he asked why, S was told that it was for comparison with hairs found at the scene of the robbery of which he was suspected. He replied 'In that case, no I am not'. It was held that the fact that, at that time, such samples could not lawfully be taken without S's consent did not mean that no inferences could be drawn from his refusal. Leonard J considered that it would be 'contrary to good sense' to prohibit the drawing of inferences and that the case was 'in a wholly different category' from evidence of a failure to answer questions under caution. Nevertheless the court borrowed from the rules regarding silence when it stressed the fact that the presence of S's solicitor rendered the parties 'on even terms' (see **F19.2**). (See also *McVeigh* v *Beattie* [1988] Fam 69, in which it was held that the refusal of the respondent in affiliation proceedings to submit to a blood test which might have excluded the possibility that he had fathered the child in question could, in the absence of a reasonable explanation, amount to corroboration of the evidence of the complainant.)

Under the PACE 1984, s. 63, a sample of hair can now be taken from a suspect without his consent. The taking of intimate samples continues to require consent (s. 62), and the rule in *Smith* has found statutory expression in s. 62(10), which permits 'such inferences as appear proper' to be drawn 'where the appropriate consent to the taking of an intimate sample from a person was refused without good cause'.

Police and Criminal Evidence Act 1984, s. 62

(10)   Where the appropriate consent to the taking of an intimate sample from a person was refused without good cause, in any proceedings against that person for an offence—
   (a)   the court in determining—
      (i)   whether to commit that person for trial; or
      (ii)   whether there is a case to answer; and
   (b)   the court or jury, in determining whether that person is guilty of the offence charged,
may draw such inferences from the refusal as appear proper.

FAILURE TO CALL WITNESSES OR PROVIDE EVIDENCE

If the accused fails to call a particular person as a witness, then, if appropriate, as when **F19.19** the prosecution had no possible means of knowing that that person had any relevant evidence to give until the accused himself gave evidence at the trial, the judge may direct the jury that they may take into account the fact that the potential witness was not called, but should exercise a degree of care. In particular he should avoid the suggestion that the failure is something of importance where there may be a valid reason for not calling the witness (Megaw LJ in *Gallagher* [1974] 1 WLR 1204, affirmed in *Couzens* [1992] Crim

LR 822). Comment may also be justified if there is a very strong case for suggesting that an account which an accused is giving has recently been fabricated and where, if it has not, there would be another witness or other witnesses of any description who could substantiate the accused's story if it were true (*Wilmot* (1988) 89 Cr App R 341 per Glidewell LJ at p. 352). However, comment in this area has to be made with circumspection and reserve (*Weller* [1994] Crim LR 856). In *Weller* the Court of Appeal held that it could not envisage any case in which it would be appropriate to make a comment to the effect that if there were any truth in the accused's story, he would have been expected to have called a particular witness. In the somewhat extreme case of *Forsyth* [1997] 2 Cr App R 299, the witness, J, was not one whom the defence might have been expected to call in the light of the issues raised by prosecution or defence at trial, but his absence was the subject of comment by prosecuting counsel in his closing address, and the jury subsequently asked the judge for guidance. It was held that the judge should have made it clear to the jury that they should draw no inference from the absence of J, and that they should decide the case on the evidence and without speculating on what J might have said.

Comment on Failure of Spouse of Accused to Testify

F19.20 The failure of the spouse of the accused to give evidence shall not be made the subject of any comment by the prosecution (PACE 1984, s. 80(8), formerly part of proviso (b) to the Criminal Evidence Act 1898, s. 1). In *Brown* [1983] Crim LR 38, it was held that the wording of s. 1(b) of the 1898 Act was mandatory, and that breach of the prohibition would amount to a material irregularity in the course of the trial. However, whether a breach of s. 1(b) would lead to a conviction being quashed depended upon all the circumstances, and in particular whether the trial judge corrected the breach in his summing-up. In *Dickman* (1910) 5 Cr App R 135, in which counsel inadvertently commented upon the failure of the spouse of the accused to testify but the jury were told to dismiss the comment from their minds, the appeal against conviction was dismissed. Likewise in *Hunter* [1969] Crim LR 262, where a comment was made in breach of s. 1(b) but the judge, refusing to discharge the jury, warned them about the comment, the conviction was upheld. These cases may be contrasted with *Naudeer* [1984] 3 All ER 1036. N, a man of good character, was convicted of theft. At the trial, counsel for the prosecution suggested that the failure of N's wife to give evidence had deprived the jury of what would probably have been material evidence, and the judge failed in his summing-up to give any direction to repair the breach of s. 1(b). The Court of Appeal quashed the conviction on the grounds that the breach was central to the overall justice of the case, particularly since the accused was a man of good character (which he had put before the jury), and the question of his bona fides was central to the offence itself. It was the duty of the judge, depending upon the circumstances of each case, to remedy a breach of s. 1(b) in his summing-up.

Section 80(8) of the PACE 1984 does not prevent comment by the judge on the failure of the spouse of the accused to testify. In *Naudeer*, Purchas LJ said (at p. 1039) that 'if a judge in the exercise of his discretion decides to comment upon the failure of the accused to call his spouse or to give evidence himself he must, except in exceptional circumstances, do this with a great deal of circumspection'. The same degree of circumspection would also appear to be required in the case of failure to call cohabitees, who are not covered by s. 80(8) (see *Weller* [1994] Crim LR 856). In *Whitton* [1998] Crim LR 492, prosecuting counsel commented on the failure of W's husband, who had been present when she allegedly assaulted a neighbour, to give evidence. This clear breach of s. 80(8) was, however, held to have been subsumed in the summing-up in which the trial judge quite properly elected to make a comment of his own. It was not possible in the circumstances to argue that counsel's comment undermined the safety of W's conviction, though this should clearly not be read as an invitation to counsel to disregard the statutory provision, however strong the case for judicial comment.

APPENDIX 1 CROWN COURT RULES 1982 (SI 1982 NO. 1109)

PART I INTRODUCTION

Citation, commencement, revocations and transitionals
1.—(1)   These rules may be cited as the Crown Court Rules 1982 and shall come into operation on 1st October 1982.
 [(2)   Revocations.]
 [(3)   Transitional provisions.]

Interpretation
2.—(1)   In these rules, unless the context otherwise requires, any reference to a judge is a reference to a judge of the High Court or a circuit judge or a recorder; 'justice' means a justice of the peace; and 'Taxing Master' means a Master of the Supreme Court (Taxing Office).
 (2)   In these rules any reference to a rule or schedule shall be construed as a reference to a rule contained in these rules or, as the case may be, to a schedule thereto; and any reference in a rule to a paragraph shall be construed as a reference to a paragraph of that rule.

PART II JUSTICES AS JUDGES OF CROWN COURT

Number and qualification of justices
3.—(1)   Subject to the provisions of rule 4 and to any directions under section 74(4) of the Supreme Court Act 1981, on any proceedings to which a subsequent paragraph of this rule applies, the number of justices sitting to hear the proceedings and the qualification of those justices shall be as specified in that paragraph.
 [(2)   Relates to liquor licensing.]
 [(3)   Relates to gaming licensing.]
 (4)   On the hearing of an appeal from a juvenile court, the Crown Court shall consist of a judge sitting with two justices each of whom is a member of a youth court panel and who are chosen so that the court shall include a man and a woman.
 [(5)   Relates to affiliation proceedings (now abolished).]

Dispensations for special circumstances
4.—(1)   The Crown Court may enter on any appeal notwithstanding that the court is not constituted as required by section 74(1) of the Supreme Court Act 1981 or rule 3 if it appears to the judge that the court could not be so constituted without unreasonable delay and the court includes—
 [(a)   relates to liquor licensing];
 [(b)   relates to gaming licensing];
 (c)   in a case to which paragraph (4) of that rule applies, one justice who is a member of a youth court panel;
 [(d)   relates to affiliation proceedings (now abolished)];
 (e)   in any other case, one justice:
[Proviso relates to liquor and gaming licensing.]
 (2)   [omitted]
 (3)   The Crown Court may at any stage continue with any proceedings with a court from which any one or more of the justices initially comprising the court has withdrawn, or is absent for any reason.

Disqualifications
5.   A justice of the peace shall not sit in the Crown Court on the hearing of an appeal in a matter on which he adjudicated.

PART III APPEALS TO THE CROWN COURT

Application of Part III
6.—(1)   Subject to the following provisions of this rule, this part of these rules shall apply to every appeal which by or under any enactment lies to the Crown Court from any court, tribunal or

person except any appeal against a decision of a magistrates' court under section 22(7) or (8) of the Prosecution of Offences Act 1985 or under section 1 of the Bail (Amendment) Act 1993.

[(2) Relates to proceedings outside the scope of this work.]

Notice of appeal

7.—(1) An appeal shall be commenced by the appellant's giving notice of appeal in accordance with the following provisions of this rule.

(2) The notice required by the preceding paragraph shall be in writing and shall be given—

  (a) in a case where the appeal is against a decision of a magistrates' court, to the clerk of the magistrates' court;

  [(b) relates to liquor licensing];

  (c) in any other case, to the appropriate officer of the Crown Court;

  (d) [relates to care proceedings: now spent];

  (e) in any case, to any other party to the appeal.

(3) Notice of appeal shall be given not later than 21 days after the day on which the decision appealed against is given and, for this purpose, where the court has adjourned the trial of an information after conviction, that day shall be the day on which the court sentences or otherwise deals with the offender:

Provided that, where a court exercises its power to defer sentence under section 1(1) of the Powers of Criminal Courts Act 1973, that day shall, for the purposes of an appeal against conviction, be the day on which the court exercises that power.

(4) A notice of appeal shall state—

  (a) in the case of an appeal arising out of a conviction by a magistrates' court, whether the appeal is against conviction or sentence or both; and

  [(b) relates to proceedings outside the scope of this work].

(5) The time for giving notice of appeal (whether prescribed under paragraph (3), or under an enactment listed in part I of schedule 3) may be extended, either before or after it expires, by the Crown Court, on an application made in accordance with paragraph (6).

(6) An application for an extention of time shall be made in writing, specifying the grounds of the application and sent to the appropriate officer of the Crown Court.

(7) Where the Crown Court extends the time for giving notice of appeal, the appropriate officer of the Crown Court shall give notice of the extension to—

  (a) the appellant;

  (b) in the case of an appeal from a decision of a magistrates' court, to the clerk of that court;

  [(c) relates to liquor licensing],

and the appellant shall give notice of the extension to any other party to the appeal [further provision relating to care proceedings: now spent].

Entry of appeal and notice of hearing

8. On receiving notice of appeal, the appropriate officer of the Crown Court shall enter the appeal and give notice of the time and place of the hearing to—

  (a) the appellant;

  (b) any other party to the appeal;

  (c) in the case of an appeal from a decision of a magistrates' court, to the clerk of that court;

  [(d) relates to liquor licensing],

and [relates to care proceedings: now spent].

[Rules 9 to 10B are concerned with care proceedings and related matters.]

Abandonment of appeal

11.—(1) Without prejudice to the power of the Crown Court to give leave for an appeal to be abandoned, an appellant may abandon an appeal by giving notice in writing, in accordance with the following provisions of this rule, not later than the third day before the day fixed for hearing the appeal.

(2) The notice required by the preceding paragraph shall be given—

  (a) in a case where the appeal is against a decision of a magistrates' court, to the clerk of the magistrates' court;

  [(b) relates to liquor licensing]

  (c) in any other case, to the appropriate officer of the Crown Court; and

  (d) in any case, to any other party to the appeal and to any other person to whom notice of appeal was required to be given by rule 7(2)(d);

and, in the case of an appeal mentioned in subparagraph (a) or (b), the appellant shall send a copy of the notice to the appropriate officer of the Crown Court.

(3)   For the purposes of determining whether notice of abandonment was given in time there shall be disregarded any Saturday, Sunday and any day which is specified to be a bank holiday in England and Wales under section 1(1) of the Banking and Financial Dealings Act 1971.

PART IIIA   APPEALS UNDER THE BAIL (AMENDMENT) ACT 1993

11A.—(1)   This rule shall apply where the prosecution appeals under section 1 of the Bail (Amendment) Act 1993 against a decision of a magistrates' court granting bail and in this rule, 'the 1993 Act' means that Act and 'the person concerned' has the same meaning as in that Act.

(2)   The written notice of appeal required by section 1(5) of the 1993 Act shall be in the form prescribed in schedule 9 or a form to the like effect and shall be served on—
   (a)   the clerk of the magistrates' court
   (b)   the person concerned.

(3)   The appropriate officer of the Crown Court shall enter the appeal and give notice of the time and place of the hearing to—
   (a)   the prosecution
   (b)   the person concerned or his legal representative
   (c)   the clerk of the magistrates' court.

(4)   The person concerned shall not be entitled to be present at the hearing of the appeal unless he is acting in person or, in any other case of an exceptional nature, a judge of the Crown Court is of the opinion that the interests of justice require him to be present and gives him leave to be so.

(5)   Where a person concerned has not been able to instruct a solicitor to represent him at the appeal, he may give notice to the Crown Court requesting that the Official Solicitor shall represent him at the appeal, and the court may, if it thinks fit, assign the Official Solicitor to act for the person concerned accordingly.

(6)   At any time after the service of written notice of appeal under paragraph (2) above, the prosecution may abandon the appeal by giving notice in writing in the form prescribed in schedule 10 or a form to the like effect.

(7)   The notice of abandonment required by the preceding paragraph shall be served on—
   (a)   the person concerned or his legal representative
   (b)   the clerk of the magistrates' court
   (c)   the appropriate officer of the Crown Court.

(8)   Any record required by section 5 of the Bail Act 1976 (together with any note of reasons required by subsection (4) of that section to be included) shall be made by way of an entry in the file relating to the case in question and the record shall include the following particulars, namely—
   (a)   the effect of the decision;
   (b)   a statement of any condition imposed in respect of bail, indicating whether it is to be complied with before or after release on bail;
   (c)   where bail is withheld, a statement of the relevant exception to the right to bail (as provided in schedule 1 to the said Act of 1976) on which the decision is based.

(9)   The appropriate officer of the Crown Court shall, as soon as practicable after the hearing of the appeal, give notice of the decision and of the matters required by the preceding paragraph to be recorded to—
   (a)   the person concerned or his legal representative
   (b)   the prosecution
   (c)   the police
   (d)   the clerk of the magistrates' court
   (e)   the governor of the prison or person responsible for the establishment where the person concerned is being held.

(10)   Where the judge hearing the appeal grants bail to the person concerned, the provisions of rule 20 shall apply as if that person had applied to the Crown Court for bail.

(11)   In addition to the methods of service permitted by rule 28, the notices required by paragraphs (3), (5), (7) and (9) of this rule may be sent by way of facsimile transmission and the notice required by paragraph (3) may be given by telephone.

PART IV   COSTS BETWEEN PARTIES IN CROWN COURT

Jurisdiction to award costs
12.—(1)   Subject to the provisions of section 109(1) of the Magistrates' Courts Act 1980 (power of magistrates' courts to award costs on abandonment of appeal from magistrates' courts), . . . no

party shall be entitled to recover any costs of any proceedings in the Crown Court from any other party to the proceedings except under an order of the court.

(2) Subject to section 4 of the Costs in Criminal Cases Act 1973 and to the following provisions of this rule, the Crown Court may make such order for costs as it thinks just.

[(3) and (4) Relate to liquor licensings.]

(5) No order for costs shall be made on the abandonment of an appeal from a magistrates' court by giving notice under rule 11.

(6) Without prejudice to the generality of paragraph (2), the Crown Court may make an order for costs on dismissing an appeal where the appellant has failed to proceed with the appeal or on the abandonment of an appeal not being an appeal to which paragraph (3), (4) or (5) applies.

Costs in proceedings from which appeal is brought
13. Where an appeal is brought to the Crown Court from the decision of a magistrates' court or a tribunal and the appeal is successful, the Crown Court may make any order as to the costs of the proceedings in the magistrates' court or tribunal which that court or tribunal had power to make.

Taxation
14.—(1) Where under these rules the Crown Court has made an order for the costs of any proceedings to be paid by a party and the court has not fixed a sum, the amount of the costs to be paid shall be ascertained as soon as practicable by the appropriate officer of the Crown Court (hereinafter referred to as the taxing authority).

(2) On a taxation under the preceding paragraph or under section 4(2) of the Costs in Criminal Cases Act 1973, there shall be allowed the costs reasonably incurred in or about the prosecution and conviction or the defence, as the case may be.

Review by taxing authority
15.—(1) Any party dissatisfied with the taxation of any costs by the taxing authority under section 4(2) of the Costs in Criminal Cases Act 1973 or rule 14 may apply to the taxing authority to review his decision.

(2) The application shall be made by giving notice to the taxing authority and to any other party to the taxation within 14 days of the taxation, specifying the items in respect of which the application is made and the grounds of objection.

(3) Any party to whom notice is given under the preceding paragraph may within 14 days of the service of the notice deliver to the taxing authority answers in writing to the objections specified in that notice to the taxing authority and, if he does, shall send copies to the applicant for the review and to any other party to the taxation.

(4) The taxing authority shall reconsider his taxation in the light of the objections and answers, if any, of the parties and any oral representations made by or on their behalf and shall notify them of the result of his review.

Futher review by Taxing Master
16.—(1) Any party dissatisfied with the result of a review of taxation under rule 15 may, within 14 days of receiving notification thereof, request the taxing authority to supply him with reasons in writing for his decision and may within 14 days of the receipt of such reasons apply to the Chief Taxing Master for a further review and shall, in that case, give notice of the application of the taxing authority and to any other party to the taxation, to whom he shall also give a copy of the reasons given by the taxing authority.

(2) Such application shall state whether the applicant wishes to appear or be represented, or whether he will accept a decision given in his absence and shall be accompanied by a copy of the notice given under rule 15, of any answer which may have been given under paragraph (3) thereof and of the reasons given by the taxing authority for his decision, together with the bill of costs and full supporting documents.

(3) A party to the taxation who receives notice of an application under this rule shall inform the Chief Taxing Master whether he wishes to appear or be represented at a further review, or whether he will accept a decision given in his absence.

(4) The further review shall be conducted by a Taxing Master and if the applicant or any other party to the taxation has given notice of his intention to appear or be represented, the Taxing Master shall inform the parties (or their agents) of the date on which the further review will take place.

(5)   Before reaching his decision the Taxing Master may consult the judge who made the order for costs and the taxing authority and, unless the Taxing Master otherwise directs, no further evidence shall be received on the hearing of the further review; and no ground of objection shall be valid which was not raised on the review under rule 15.

(6)   In making his review, the Taxing Master may alter the assessment of the taxing authority in respect of any sum allowed, whether by increase or decrease.

(7)   The Taxing Master shall communicate the result of the further review to the parties and to the taxing authority.

Appeal to High Court judge
17.—(1)   Any party dissatisfied with the result of a further review under rule 16 may, within 14 days of receiving notification thereof, appeal by originating summons to a judge of the Queen's Bench Division of the High Court if, and only if, the Taxing Master certifies that the question to be decided involves a point of principle of general importance.

(2)   On the hearing of the appeal the judge may reverse, affirm or amend the decision appealed against or make such other order as he thinks appropriate.

Supplementary provisions
18.—(1)   On a further review or an appeal to a judge of the High Court the Taxing Master or judge may make such order as he thinks just in respect of the costs of the hearing of the further review or the appeal, as the case may be.

(2)   The time prescribed by rule 15, 16 or 17 may be extended by the taxing authority, Taxing Master or judge of the High Court on such terms as he thinks just.

PART V   MISCELLANEOUS

Applications to Crown Court relating to bail
19.—(1)   This rule applies where an application to the Crown Court relating to bail is made otherwise than during the hearing of proceedings in the Crown Court.

(2)   Subject to paragraph (7), notice in writing of intention to make such an application to the Crown Court shall, at least 24 hours before it is made, be given to the prosecutor and, if the prosecution is being carried on by the Crown Prosecution Service, to the appropriate Crown Prosecutor or, if the application is to be made by the prosecutor or a constable under section 3(8) of the Bail Act 1976, to the person to whom bail was granted.

(3)   On receiving notice under paragraph (2), the prosecutor or appropriate Crown Prosecutor or, as the case may be, the person to whom bail was granted shall—
    (a)   notify the appropriate officer of the Crown Court and the applicant that he wishes to be represented at the hearing of the application; or
    (b)   notify the appropriate officer and the applicant that he does not oppose the application; or
    (c)   give to the appropriate officer, for the consideration of the Crown Court, a written statement of his reasons for opposing the application, at the same time sending a copy of the statement to the applicant.

(4)   A notice under pragraph (2) shall be in the form prescribed in schedule 4 or a form to the like effect, and the applicant shall give a copy of the notice to the appropriate officer of the Crown Court.

(5)   Except in the case of an application made by the prosecutor or a constable under section 3(8) of the Bail Act 1976, the applicant shall not be entitled to be present on the hearing of his application unless the Crown Court gives him leave to be present.

(6)   Where a person who is in custody or has been released on bail desires to make an application relating to bail and has not been able to instruct a solicitor to apply on his behalf under the preceding paragraphs of this rule, he may give notice in writing to the Crown Court of his desire to make an application relating to bail, requesting that the Official Solicitor shall act for him in the application, and the court may, if it thinks fit, assign the Official Solicitor to act for the applicant accordingly.

(7)   Where the Official Solicitor has been so assigned the Crown Court may, if it thinks fit, dispense with the requirements of paragraph (2) and deal with the application in a summary manner.

(8)   Any record required by section 5 of the Bail Act 1976 (together with any note of reasons required by subsection (4) of that section to be included) shall be made by way of an entry in the file relating to the case in question and the record shall include the following particulars, namely—

    (a)   the effect of the decision;

    (b)   a statement of any condition imposed in respect of bail, indicating whether it is to be complied with before or after release on bail;

    (c)   where conditions of bail are varied, a statement of the conditions as varied;

    (d)   where bail is withheld, a statement of the relevant exception to the right to bail (as provided in schedule 1 to the said Act of 1976) on which the decision is based.

Supplementary provisions about bail

20.—(1) Every person who makes an application to the Crown Court relating to bail shall inform the court of any earlier application to the High Court or the Crown Court relating to bail in the course of the same proceedings.

    (2) Where the Crown Court grants bail in criminal proceedings, the recognisance of any surety required as a condition of bail may be entered into before an officer of the Crown Court or, where the person who has been granted bail is in a prison or other place of detention, before the governor or keeper of the prison or place as well as before the persons specified in section 8(4) of the Bail Act 1976.

    (3) Where the Crown Court under section 3(5) or (6) of the Bail Act 1976 imposes a requirement to be complied with before a person's release on bail, the court may give directions as to the manner in which and the person or persons before whom the requirement may be complied with.

    (4) On hearing an application for bail (other than bail in criminal proceedings) the Crown Court may order that the applicant shall be released from custody on entering into a recognisance, with or without sureties, or giving other security before—

    (a)   an officer of the Crown Court; or

    (b)   any other person authorised by virtue of section 119(1) of the Magistrates' Courts Act 1980 to take a recognisance where a magistrates' court having power to take the recognisance has, instead of taking it, fixed the amount in which the principal and his sureties, if any, are to be bound.

    (5) A person who, in pursuance of an order made by the Crown Court for the grant of bail in criminal proceedings, proposes to enter into a recognisance or give security must, unless the Crown Court otherwise directs, give notice to the prosecutor at least 24 hours before he enters into the recognisance or gives security as aforesaid.

    (6) Where, in pursuance of an order of the Crown Court, a recognisance is entered into or any requirement imposed under section 3(5) or (6) is complied with (being a requirement to be complied with before a person's release on bail) before any person, it shall be his duty to cause the recognisance or, as the case may be, a statement of the requirement to be transmitted forthwith to the appropriate officer of the Crown Court; and a copy of the recognisance or statement shall at the same time be sent to the governor or keeper of the prison or other place of detention in which the person named in the order is detained, unless the recognisance was entered into or the requirement was complied with before such governor or keeper.

    (7) Where, in pursuance of section 3(5) of the Bail Act 1976, security has been given in respect of a person granted bail with a duty to surrender to the custody of the Crown Court and either—

    (a)   that person surrenders to the custody of the court; or

    (b)   that person having failed to surrender to the custody of the court, the court decides not to order the forfeiture of the security,

the appropriate officer of the court shall as soon as practicable give notice of the surrender to custody or, as the case may be, of the decision not to forfeit the security to the person before whom the security was given.

    (8) In this rule 'bail in criminal proceedings' has the same meaning as in the Bail Act 1976.

Estreat of recognisances

21.—(1) Where a recognisance has been entered into in respect of a person granted bail to appear before the Crown Court and it appears to the court that a default has been made in performing the conditions of the recognisance, other than by failing to appear before the Court in accordance with any such condition, the court my order the recognisance to be estreated.

    (2) Where the Crown Court is to consider making an order under paragraph (1) for a recognisance to be estreated, the appropriate officer of the court shall give notice to that effect to the person by whom the recognisance was entered into indicating the time and place at which the matter will be considered; and no such order shall be made before the expiry of seven days after the notice required by this paragraph has been given.

21A.—(1)   Where a recognizance is conditioned for the appearance of an accused before the Crown Court and the accused fails to appear in accordance with the condition, the court shall declare the recognizance to be forfeited.

(2)   Where the Crown Court declares a recognizance to be forfeited under paragraph (1) above, the appropriate officer of the court shall issue a summons to the person by whom the recognizance was entered into requring him to appear before the court at a time and place specified in the summons to show cause why the court should not order the recognizance to be estreated.

(3)   At the time specified in the summons the court may proceed in the absence of the person by whom the recognizance was entered into if it is satisfied that he has been served with the summons.

Conditional witness order
22.   Any objection under paragraph 1(3)(c) or paragraph 2(3)(c) of schedule 2 to the Criminal Procedure and Investigations Act 1996 to the reading out at the trial of a statement or deposition without further evidence shall be made in writing to the prosecutor and the Crown Court within 14 days of the accused being committed for trial unless the court at its discretion permits such an objection to be made outside that period.

[Note: the version of r. 20 set out above has effect from 1 April 1997 in the same way as the Criminal Procedure and Investigations Act 1996, schs 1 and 2 have effect (see **D6.1**).]

Application for witness summons
23.—(1)   This rule applies to an application under section 2 of the 1965 Act for the issue of a witness summons and in this rule references to 'the application' and 'the applicant' shall be construed accordingly.

(2)   Subject to paragraphs (8) to (10), the application shall be made in writing to the appropriate officer of the Crown Court and shall—

(a)   contain a brief description of the stipulated evidence, document or thing;

(b)   set out the reasons why the applicant considers that the stipulated evidence, document or thing is likely to be material evidence;

(c)   set out the reason why the applicant considers that the directed person will not voluntarily attend as a witness or produce the document or thing; and

(d)   if the witness summons is proposed to require the directed person to produce a document or thing—

(i)   inform the directed person of his right to make representations in writing and at a hearing, under paragraph (5); and

(ii)   state whether the applicant seeks a requirement also to be imposed under section 2A of the 1965 Act (advance production) and, if such a requirement is sought, specify the place and time at which the applicant wishes the document or thing to be produced.

(3)   The application shall be supported by an affidavit—

(a)   setting out any charge on which the proceedings concerned are based;

(b)   specifying the stipulated evidence, document or thing in such a way as to enable the directed person to identify it;

(c)   specifying grounds for believing that the directed person is likely to be able to give the stipulated evidence or to produce the stipulated evidence or thing;

(d)   specifying grounds for believing that the stipulated evidence is likely to be material evidence or, as the case may be, that the stipulated document or thing is likely to be material evidence.

(4)   A copy of the application and the supporting affidavit shall be served on the directed person at the same time as it is served on the appropriate officer of the Crown Court.

(5)   The directed person may, within 7 days of receiving a copy of the application under paragraph (4), inform the appropriate officer of the Crown Court whether or not he wishes to make representations, concerning the issue of the witness summons proposed to be directed to him, at a hearing and may also make written representations to that officer.

(6)   The appropriate officer of the Crown Court shall—

(a)   if the directed person indicates that he wishes to have the application considered at a hearing, fix a time, date and place for the hearing;

(b)   if the directed person does not indicate in accordance with paragraph (5) that he wishes to make representations at a hearing, refer the application to a judge of the Crown Court for determination with or without a hearing; and

(c)   notify the applicant and, where sub-paragraph (a) applies, the directed person of the time, date and place fixed for any hearing of the application.

(7)   Any hearing under this rule shall, unless the judge directs otherwise, take place in private and the proceedings at the hearing shall be recorded.

(8)   In the case of an application for a witness summons which it is proposed shall require the directed person to give evidence but not to produce any document or thing, that application may be made orally to a judge or in writing and, in such a case—

(a)   paragraphs (3) to (7) shall not have effect; and

(b)   the application shall, in addition to the matters set out in sub-paragraphs (a) to (c) of paragraph (2), specify—

(i)   any charge on which the proceedings concerned are based; and

(ii)   the grounds for believing that the directed person is likely to be able to give the stipulated evidence.

(9)   Subject to paragraph (10), in the case of an application for a witness summons which it is proposed shall require the directed person to produce any document or thing and which is made within 7 days of the date fixed for trial, the appropriate officer shall refer the notice of application to the trial judge, or such other judge as may be available, to determine the application or to give such directions as the judge to whom the notice is referred considers appropriate, and paragraphs (2)(d)(i) and (4) to (6) shall not have effect.

(10)   In the case of an application for a witness summons which it is proposed shall require the directed person to produce any document or thing and which is made during the trial, such application shall be made orally to the trial judge, to determine the application or to give such directions as he considers appropriate, and in such a case—

(a)   paragraphs (3) to (7) shall not have effect; and

(b)   the application shall, in addition to the matters set out in sub-paragraphs (a) to (c) of paragraph (2), specify the grounds for believing that the directed person is likely to be able to produce the document or thing.

(11)   In this rule and rules 23ZA, 23ZB and 23ZC—

'the 1965 Act' means the Criminal Procedure (Attendance of Witnesses) Act 1965;

references to 'the directed person' and 'the stipulated evidence, document or thing' shall be construed in accordance with section 2(10) of the 1965 Act.

Application that summons be of no further effect

23ZA.—(1)   This rule applies to an application under section 2B of the 1965 Act and references in this rule to 'the applicant' and 'the application' shall be construed accordingly.

(2)   The application shall be made in writing to the appropriate officer of the Crown Court as soon as reasonably practicable after the document or thing has been produced for inspection in pursuance of a requirement imposed by the witness summons under section 2A of the 1965 Act.

(3)   The application shall state that the applicant concludes that the requirement imposed by the witness summons under section 2(2) of the 1965 Act is no longer needed.

(4)   If a direction is given under section 2B of the 1965 Act following the application, the appropriate officer of the court shall notify the person to whom the witness summons is directed as to the effect of the direction.

Application to make summons issued on application ineffective

23ZB.—(1)   This rule applies to an application under section 2C of the 1965 Act and in this rule references to 'the application' and 'the applicant' shall, unless the contrary intention appears, be construed accordingly.

(2)   The application shall be made in writing to the appropriate officer of the Crown Court and shall—

(a)   state that the applicant was not served with notice of the application to issue the summons and that he was neither present nor represented at any hearing of that application; and

(b)   set out the reasons why the applicant considers that he cannot give any evidence likely to be material evidence or, as the case may be, produce any document or thing likely to be material evidence.

(3)   On receiving the application, the appropriate officer of the court shall serve notice of the application on the person on whose application the witness summons was issued.

(4)   The court shall not grant or, as the case may be, refuse the application unless the applicant and the person on whose application the witness summons has been issued have been given an

opportunity of making representations, whether at a hearing or (where they agree to do so) in writing without a hearing.

(5) In a case where the witness summons to which the application relates imposed a requirement to produce any document or thing, then if—

(a) the applicant can produce that document or thing, but

(b) he seeks to satisfy the court that the document or thing is not likely to be material evidence, the applicant must, unless the judge directs otherwise, arrange for the document or thing to be available at the hearing of the application.

(6) Any hearing under this rule shall, unless the judge directs otherwise, take place in private and the proceedings at the hearing shall be recorded.

(7) The appropriate officer of the court shall notify the applicant and the person on whose application the witness summons was issued of the decision of the court in relation to the application.

Application to make summons issued of court's own motion ineffective

23ZC.—(1) Rule 23ZB shall apply to an application under section 2E of the 1965 Act as it applies to an application under section 2C of that Act, subject to the following modifications.

(2) Paragraphs (2)(a) and (3) shall be omitted.

(3) In paragraphs (4) and (7), the words 'and the person on whose application the witness summons was issued' shall be omitted.

(4) In paragraph (4), for the words '(where they agree to do so)', there shall be substituted the words '(where he agrees to do so)'.

Evidence through television link where witness is a child or is to be cross-examined after admission of a video recording

23A.—(1) Any party may apply for leave under section 32(1)(b) of the Criminal Justice Act 1988 for evidence to be given through a live television link where—

(a) the offence charged is one to which section 32(2) applies; and

(b) the evidence is to be given by a witness who is either—

(i) in the case of an offence falling within section 32(2)(a) or (b), under the age of 14; or

(ii) in the case of an offence falling within section 32(2)(c), under the age of 17; or

(iii) a person who is to be cross-examined following the admission under section 32A of that Act of a video recording of testimony from him;

and references in this rule to an offence include references to attempting or conspiring to commit, or aiding, abetting, counselling, procuring or inciting the commission of, that offence.

(2) An application under paragraph (1) shall be made by giving notice in writing, which shall be in the form prescribed in schedule 5 or a form to the like effect.

(3) An application under paragraph (1) shall be made within 28 days after the date of the committal of the defendant, or of the consent to the preferment of a bill of indictment in relation to the case, or of the service of notice of transfer under section 53 of the Criminal Justice Act 1991, or of the service of Notice of Appeal from a decision of a youth court or magistrates' court, as the case may be.

(4) The notice under paragraph (2) shall be sent to the appropriate officer of the Crown Court and at the same time a copy thereof shall be sent by the applicant to every other party to the proceedings.

(5) A party who receives a copy of a notice under paragraph (2) and who wishes to oppose the application shall within 14 days notify the applicant and the appropriate officer of the Crown Court, in writing, of his opposition, giving the reasons therefor.

(6) An application under paragraph (1) shall be determined by a judge of the Crown Court without a hearing, unless the judge otherwise directs, and the appropriate officer of the Crown Court shall notify the parties of the time and place of any such hearing.

(7) The appropriate officer of the Crown Court shall notify all the parties and any person who is to accompany the witness (if known) of the decision of the Crown Court in relation to an application under paragraph (1). Where leave is granted, the notification shall state—

(a) where the witness is to give evidence on behalf of the prosecutor, the name of the witness, and, if known, the name, occupation and relationship (if any) to the witness of any person who is to accompany the witness, and

(b) the location of the Crown Court at which the trial should take place.

(8) The period specified in paragraph (3) may be extended, either before or after it expires, on an application made in writing, specifying the grounds of the application and sent to the

appropriate officer of the Crown Court, and a copy of the application shall be sent by the applicant to every other party to the proceedings. The appropriate officer of the Crown Court shall notify all the parties of the decision of the Crown Court.

(9)   An application for extension of time under paragraph (8) shall be determined by a judge of the Crown Court without a hearing unless the judge otherwise directs.

(10)   A witness giving evidence through a television link pursuant to leave granted under paragraph (7) shall be accompanied by a person acceptable to a judge of the Crown Court and, unless the judge otherwise directs, by no other person.

[Note: By virtue of the Crown Court (Modification) Rules 1998 (SI 1998 No. 3047), this rule is modified in respect of persons sent for trial under the CDA 1998, s. 51, so that after the words 'under section 53 of the Criminal Justice Act 1991' in r. 23A(3) there is inserted 'or of the service of copies of the documents containing the evidence on which the charge or charges are based under paragraph 1 of Schedule 3 to the Crime Disorder Act 1998'.]

Evidence through television link where witness is outside United Kingdom

23B.—(1)   Any party may apply for leave under section 32(1) of the Criminal Justice Act 1988 for evidence to be given through a live television link by a witness who is outside the United Kingdom.

(2)   An application under paragraph (1), and any matter relating thereto which, by virtue of the following provisions of this rule, falls to be determined by the Crown Court, may be dealt with in chambers by any judge of the Crown Court.

(3)   An application under paragraph (1) shall be made by giving notice in writing, which shall be in the form pescribed in schedule 6 or a form to the like effect.

(4)   An application under paragraph (1) shall be made within 28 days after the date of the committal of the defendant or, as the case may be, of the giving of a notice of transfer under section 4(1)(c) of the Criminal Justice Act 1987, or of the preferral of a bill of indictment in relation to the case.

(5)   The period of 28 days in paragraph (4) may be extended by the Crown Court, either before or after it expires, on an application made in writing, specifying the grounds of the application. The appropriate officer of the Crown Court shall notify all the parties of the decision of the Crown Court.

(6)   The notice under paragraph (3) or any application under paragraph (5) shall be sent to the appropriate officer of the Crown Court and at the same time a copy thereof shall be sent by the applicant to every other party to the proceedings.

(7)   A party who receives a copy of a notice under paragraph (3) shall, within 28 days of the date of the notice, notify the applicant and the appropriate officer of the Crown Court, in writing—

(a)   whether or not he opposes the application, giving his reasons for any such opposition, and

(b)   whether or not he wishes to be represented at any hearing of the application.

(8)   After the expiry of the period referred to in paragraph (7), the Crown Court shall determine whether an application under paragraph (1) is to be dealt with—

(a)   without a hearing, or

(b)   at a hearing at which the applicant and such other party or parties as the court may direct may be represented,

and the appropriate officer of the Crown Court shall notify the applicant and, where necessary, the other party or parties, of the time and place of any such hearing.

(9)   The appropriate officer of the Crown Court shall notify all the parties of the decision of the Crown Court in relation to an application under paragraph (1) and, where leave is granted, the notification shall state—

(a)   the country in which the witness will give evidence,

(b)   if known, the place where the witness will give evidence,

(c)   where the witness is to give evidence on behalf of the prosecutor, or where disclosure is required by section 11 of the Criminal Justice Act 1967 (alibi) or by rules under section 81 of the Police and Criminal Evidence Act 1984 (expert evidence), the name of the witness,

(d)   the location of the Crown Court at which the trial should take place, and

(e)   any conditions specified by the Crown Court in accordance with paragraph (10).

(10)   The Crown Court dealing with an application under pragraph (1) may specify that as a condition of the grant of leave the witness should give the evidence in the presence of a specified person who is able and willing to answer under oath or affirmation any questions the trial judge

may put as to the circumstances in which the evidence is given, including questions about any persons who are present when the evidence is given and any matters which may affect the giving of the evidence.

[Note: By virtue of the Crown Court (Modification) Rules 1998, this rule is modified in respect of persons sent for trial under the CDA 1998, s. 51. In r. 23B(4), after 'Criminal Justice Act 1987', the same words are inserted as are referred to in the note to r. 23A.]

Video recordings of testimony from child winesses

23C.—(1) Any party may apply for leave under section 32A of the Criminal Justice Act 1988 to tender in evidence a video recording of testimony from a witness where—

(a) the offence charged is one to which section 32(2) of that Act applies;

(b) in the case of an offence falling within section 32(2)(a) or (b), the proposed witness is under the age of 14 or, if he was under 14 when the video recording was made, is under the age of 15;

(c) in the case of an offence falling within section 32(2)(c), the proposed witness is under the age of 17 or, if he was under 17 when the video recording was made, is under the age of 18; and

(d) the video recording is of an interview conducted between an adult and a person coming within sub-paragraph (b) or (c) above (not being the accused or one of the accused) which relates to any matter in issue in the proceedings;

and references in this rule to an offence include references to attempting or conspiring to commit, or aiding, abetting, counselling, procuring or inciting the commission of, that offence.

(2) An application under paragraph (1) shall be made by giving notice in writing, which shall be in the form prescribed in schedule 7 or a form to the like effect. The application shall be accompanied by the video recording which it is proposed to tender in evidence and shall include the following, namely—

(a) the name of the defendant and the offence or offences charged;

(b) the name and date of birth of the witness in respect of whom the application is made;

(c) the date on which the video recording was made;

(d) a statement that in the opinion of the applicant the witness is willing and able to attend the trial for cross-examination;

(e) a statement of the circumstances in which the video recording was made which complies with paragraph (4) below;

(f) the date on which the video recording was disclosed to the other party or parties.

(3) Where it is proposed to tender part only of a video recording of an interview with the witness, an application under paragraph (1) must specify that part and be accompanied by a video recording of the entire interview, including those parts which it is not proposed to tender in evidence, and by a statement of the circumstances in which the video recording of the entire interview was made which complies with paragraph (4) below.

(4) The statement of the circumstances in which the video recording was made referred to in paragraphs (2)(e) and (3) above shall include the following information, except in so far as it is contained in the recording itself, namely—

(a) the times at which the recording commenced and finished, including details of any interruptions;

(b) the location at which the recording was made and the usual function of the premises;

(c) the name, age and occupation of any person present at any point during the recording; the time for which he was present; his relationship (if any) to the witness and to the defendant;

(d) a description of the equipment used including the number of cameras used and whether they were fixed or mobile; the number and location of microphones; the video format used and whether there were single or multiple recording facilities;

(e) the location of the mastertape if the video recording is a copy and details of when and by whom the copy was made.

(5) An application under paragraph (1) shall be made within 28 days after the date of the committal for trial of the defendant, or of the giving of a notice of transfer under section 53 of the Criminal Justice Act 1991, or of consent to the preferment of a bill of indictment in relation to the case, or of the service of Notice of Appeal from a decision of a youth court or magistrates' court, as the case may be.

(6) The period of 28 days in paragraph (5) may be extended by a judge of the Crown Court, either before or after it expires, on an application made in writing, specifying the grounds of the application. The appropriate officer of the Crown Court shall notify all the parties of the decision of the Crown Court.

(7)   The notice under paragraph (2) or (6) shall be sent to the appropriate officer of the Crown Court and at the same time, copies thereof shall be sent by the applicant to every other party to the proceedings. Copies of any video recording required by paragraph (2) or (3) to accompany the notice shall at the same time be sent to the court and to any other party who has not already been served with a copy or in the case of a defendant acting in person, shall be made available for viewing by him.

(8)   A party who receives a copy of a notice under paragraph (2) shall, within 14 days of service of the notice, notify the applicant and the appropriate officer of the Crown Court, in writing—

(a)   whether he objects to the admission of any part of the video recording or recordings disclosed, giving his reasons why it would not be in the interests of justice for it to be admitted; and

(b)   whether he would agree to the admission of part of the video recording or recordings disclosed and if so, which part or parts; and

(c)   whether he wishes to be represented at any hearing of the application.

(9)   After the expiry of the period referred to in paragraph (8), a judge of the Crown Court shall determine whether an application under paragraph (1) is to be dealt with—

(a)   without a hearing, or

(b)   where any party notifies the appropriate officer of the Crown Court pursuant to paragraph (8) that he objects to the admission of any part of the video recording and that he wishes to be represented at any hearing, or in any other case where the judge so directs, at a hearing at which the applicant and such other party or parties as the judge may direct may be represented, and the appropriate officer of the Crown Court shall notify the applicant and, where necessary, the other party or parties, of the time and place of any such hearing.

(10)   The appropriate officer of the Crown Court shall within 3 days of the decision of the Crown Court in relation to an application under paragraph (1) being made, notify all the parties of it in the Form prescribed in Schedule 8 or a form to the like effect, and, where leave is granted, the notification shall state whether the whole or specified parts only of the video recording or recordings disclosed are to be admitted in evidence.

[Note: By virtue of the Crown Court (Modification) Rues 1998, this rule is modified in respect of persons sent for trial under the CDA 1998, s. 51. In r. 23C(5), after 'under section 53 of the Criminal Justice Act 1991', the same words are inserted as are referred to in the note to r. 23A.]

Time-limits for beginning of trials

24.   The periods prescribed for the purposes of paragraphs (a) and (b) of section 77(2) of the Supreme Court Act 1981 shall be 14 days and eight weeks respectively and accordingly the trial of a person committed by a magistrates' court—

(a)   shall not begin until the expiration of 14 days beginning with the date of his committal, except with his consent and the consent of the prosecution, and

(b)   shall, unless the Crown Court has otherwise ordered, begin not later than the expiration of eight weeks beginning with the date of his committal.

[Note: By virtue of the Crown Court (Modification) Rules 1998, an additional rule (r. 24ZA) applies where a person is sent for trial under the CDA 1998, s. 51:

24ZA.   The appropriate officer of the Crown Court sitting at a place to which notice has been given under *section 51(7)* of the Crime and Disorder Act 1998, shall list the first Crown Court appearance of the person to whom the notice relates so that it shall be no later than 28 days after the date on which the Crown Court received the notice or, in the case of a person committed to custody under section 52(1)(a) of that Act, 8 days after that date.]

Hearings in camera

24A.—(1)   Where a prosecutor or a defendant intends to apply for an order that all or part of a trial be held in camera for reasons of national security or for the protection of the identity of a witness or any other person, he shall not less than 7 days before the date on which the trial is expected to begin serve a notice in writing to that effect on the appropriate officer of the Crown Court and the prosecutor or the defendant as the case may be.

(2)   On receiving such notice, the appropriate officer shall forthwith cause a copy thereof to be displayed in a prominent place within the precincts of the Court.

(3)   An application by a prosecutor or a defendant who has served such a notice for an order that all or part of a trial be heard in camera shall, unless the Court orders otherwise, be made in camera, after the defendant has been arraigned but before the jury has been sworn and, if such an order is made, the trial shall be adjourned until whichever of the following shall be appropriate—

(a) 24 hours after the making of the order, where no application for leave to appeal from the order is made, or

(b) after the determination of an application for leave to appeal, where the application is dismissed, or

(c) after the determination of the appeal, where leave to appeal is granted.

Appeal against refusal to excuse from jury service or to defer attendance
25.—(1) A person summoned under the Juries Act 1974 for jury service may appeal in accordance with the provisions of this rule against any refusal of the appropriate officer to excuse him under section 9(2), or to defer his attendance under section 9A(1), of that Act.

(2) Subject to paragraph (3), an appeal under this rule shall be heard by the Crown Court.

(3) Where the appellant is summoned under the Juries Act 1974 to attend before the High Court in Greater London the appeal shall be heard by a judge of the High Court and where the appellant is summoned under that Act to attend before the High Court outside Greater London or before a county court and the appeal has not been decided by the Crown Court before the day on which the appellant is required by the summons to attend, the appeal shall be heard by the court before which he is summoned to attend.

(4) An appeal under this rule shall be commenced by the appellant's giving notice of appeal to the appropriate officer of the Crown Court or the High Court in Greater London, as the case may be, and such notice shall be in writing and shall specify the matters upon which the appellant relies as providing good reason why he should be excused from attending in pursuance of the summons or why his attendance should be deferred.

(5) The court shall not dismiss an appeal under this rule unless the appellant has been given an opportunity of making representations.

(6) Where an appeal under this rule is decided in the absence of the appellant, the appropriate officer of the Crown Court or the High Court in Greater London, as the case may be, shall notify him of the decision without delay.

Statements etc. in connection with confiscation orders
25A.—(1) Where, in any proceedings in respect of a drug trafficking offence or in respect of an offence to which part VI of the Criminal Justice Act 1988 applies, the prosecutor or the defendant proposes to tender to the Crown Court any statement or other document under section 11 of the Drug Trafficking Act 1994 or section 73 of the Criminal Justice Act 1988, he must serve a copy thereof as soon as practicable to the defendant or the prosecutor, as the case may be.

(2) Any statement tendered to the Crown Court by the prosecutor under section 11(1) of the said Act of 1994 or section 73(1A) of the said Act of 1988 shall include the following particulars, namely—

(a) the name of the defendant;

(b) the name of the person by whom the statement is tendered and the date on which it was made;

(c) where the statement is not tendered immediately after the defendant has been convicted, the date on which and the place where the relevant conviction occurred;

(d) such information known to the prosecutor as is relevant to the determination as to whether or not the defendant has benefitted from drug trafficking or relevant criminal conduct and to the assessment of the value of his proceeds of drug trafficking or, as the case may be, benefit from relevant criminal conduct.

(3) Where, in accordance with section 11(7) of the said Act of 1994 or section 73(1C) of the said Act of 1988, the defendant indicates in writing the extent to which he accepts any allegation contained within the prosecutor's statement, he must indicate the same to the prosecutor, and serve a copy of that reply on the appropriate officer of the Crown Court.

(4) Expressions used in this rule shall have the same meanings as in the said Act of 1994 or, where appropriate, the said Act of 1988.

Statements etc. relevant to making confiscation orders under the Criminal Justice Act 1988
25AA.—(1) Where a defendant has been convicted of an offence to which part VI of the Criminal Justice Act 1988 applies and the prosecutor or the defendant proposes to tender to the Crown Court any statement or other document under s. 73 of that Act (statements, etc. relevant to making confiscation orders) he shall serve it within such time as the court may require on the appropriate officer of the Crown Court, and at the same time serve a copy thereof on the defendant or the prosecutor, as the case may be.

(2)   Any statement tendered to the Crown Court by the prosecutor or the defendant under s. 73 of the said Act of 1988 shall include the following particulars, namely—

(a)   the name of the defendant and the indictment number;

(b)   the name of the person by whom the statement is tendered and, if different, the name of the person by whom it is made;

(c)   the date on which and the place where the conviction for the offence occurred;

(d)   the facts relied on in support of any allegation or matter indicated.

Investigation into drug trafficking or into the proceeds of criminal conduct

25B.—(1)   Where an order under section 55 of the Drug Trafficking Act 1994 or section 93H of the Criminal Justice Act 1988 has been made, the person required to comply with it may apply in writing to the appropriate officer of the Crown Court for the order to be discharged or varied, and on hearing such an application a circuit judge may discharge the order or make such variations to it as he thinks fit.

(2)   Subject to paragraph (3) below, where a person proposes to make an application under paragraph (1) above for the discharge or variation of an order, he shall give a copy of the application, not later than 48 hours before the making of the application, to a constable at the police station from which the application for the order was made, together with a notice indicating the time and place at which the application for discharge or variation is to be made.

(3)   A circuit judge may direct that paragraph (2) above need not be complied with if he is satisfied that the person making the application has good reason to seek a discharge or variation of the order as soon as possible and it is not practicable to comply with that paragraph.

(4)   In this rule—

'constable' includes a person commissioned by the Commissioners of Customs and Excise;

'police station' includes a place for the time being occupied by Her Majesty's Customs and Excise.

Application to Crown Court to state case

26.—(1)   An application under section 28 of the Supreme Court Act 1981 to the Crown Court to state a case for the opinion of the High Court shall be made in writing to the appropriate officer of the Crown Court within 21 days after the date of the decision in respect of which the application is made.

(2)   The application shall state the ground on which the decision of the Crown Court is questioned.

(3)   After making the application, the applicant shall forthwith send a copy of it to the parties to the proceedings in the Crown Court.

(4)   On receipt of the application, the appropriate officer of the Crown Court shall forthwith send it to the judge who presided at the proceedings in which the decision was made.

(5)   On receipt of the application, the judge shall inform the appropriate officer of the Crown Court as to whether or not he has decided to state a case and that officer shall give notice in writing to the applicant of the judge's decision.

(6)   If the judge considers that the application is frivolous, he may refuse to state a case and shall in that case, if the applicant so requires, cause a certificate stating the reasons for the refusal to be given to him.

(7)   If the judge decides to state a case, the procedures to be followed shall, unless the judge in a particular case otherwise directs, be the procedure set out in paragraphs (8) to (12).

(8)   The applicant shall, within 21 days of receiving the notice referred to in paragraph (5), draft a case and send a copy of it to the appropriate officer of the Crown Court and to the parties to the proceedings in the Crown Court.

(9)   Each party to the proceedings in the Crown Court shall, within 21 days of receiving a copy of the draft case under paragraph (8), either—

(a)   give notice in writing to the applicant and the appropriate officer of the Crown Court that he does not intend to take part in the proceedings before the High Court; or

(b)   indicate in writing on the copy of the draft case that he agrees with it and send the copy to the appropriate officer of the Crown Court; or

(c)   draft an alternative case and send it, together with the copy of the applicant's case, to the appropriate officer of the Crown Court.

(10)   The judge shall consider the applicant's draft case and any alternative draft case sent to the appropriate officer of the Crown Court under paragraph (9)(c).

(11)   If the Crown Court so orders, the applicant shall, before the case is stated and delivered to him, enter before an officer of the Crown Court into a recognisance, with or without sureties and in such sum as the Crown Court considers proper, having regard to the means of the applicant, conditioned to prosecute the appeal without delay.

(12)   The judge shall state and sign a case within 14 days after either—

(a)   the receipt of all the documents required to be sent to the appropriate officer of the Crown Court under paragraph (9); or

(b)   the expiration of the period of 21 days referred to in that paragraph,

whichever is the sooner.

(13)   A case state by the Crown Court shall state the facts found by the Crown Court, the submissions of the parties (including any authorities relied on by the parties during the course of those submissions), the decision of the Crown Court in respect of which the application is made and the question on which the opinion of the High Court is sought.

(14)   Any time-limit referred to in this rule may be extended either before or after it expires by the Crown Court.

(15)   If the judge decides not to state a case but the stating of a case is subsequently required by the High Court by order of mandamus, paragraphs (7) to (14) shall apply to the stating of the case save that—

(a)   in paragraph (7) the words 'If the judge decides to state a case' shall be omitted; and

(b)   in paragraph (8) for the words 'receiving the notice referred to in paragraph (5)' there shall be substituted the words 'the day on which the order of mandamus was made'.

Business in chambers

27.—(1)   The jurisdiction of the Crown Court specified in the following paragraph may be exercised by a judge of the Crown Court sitting in chambers.

(2)   The said jurisdiction is—

(a)   hearing applications for bail;

(b)   issuing a summons or warrant;

(c)   hearing any application relating to procedural matters preliminary or incidental to proceedings in the Crown Court, including applications relating to legal aid but not including an application under section 76(3) of the Supreme Court Act 1981 (application for direction varying the place of trial on indictment);

(d)   jurisdiction under rule 7(7), 9, 23, 25 or 26.

(e)   hearing applications under subsection (3) of section 22 of the Prosecution of Offences Act 1985 for the extension or further extension of a time-limit imposed by regulations made under subsection (1) of that section;

(f)   hearing an appeal brought by an accused under subsection (7) of the said section 22 against a decision of a magistrates' court to extend, or further extend, such a time-limit or brought by the prosecution under subsection (8) thereof against a decision of a magistrates' court to refuse to extend, or further extend, such a time-limit;

(g)   hearing appeals under section 1 of the Bail (Amendment) Act 1993.

[Note: By virtue of the Crown Court (Modification) Rules 1998, an additional provision (r. 27(2)(h)) applies where a person is sent for trial under the CDA 1998, s. 51, namely '(h) jurisdiction under rule 24ZA'.]

Appeals relating to time-limits

27A.—(1)   This rule applies—

(a)   to any appeal brought by an accused, under subsection (7) of section 22 of thie Prosecution of Offences Act 1985, against a decision of a magistrates' court to extend, or further extend, a time-limit imposed by regulations made under subsection (1) of that section; and

(b)   to any appeal brought by the prosecution, under subsection (8) of the said section 22, against a decision of a magistrates' court to refuse to extend, or further extend, such a time-limit.

(2)   An appeal to which this rule applies shall be commenced by the appellant's giving notice in writing of appeal—

(a)   to the clerk to the magistrates' court which took the decision;

(b)   if the appeal is brought by the accused, to the prosecutor and, if the prosecution is to be carried on by the Crown Prosecution Service, to the appropriate Crown Prosecutor;

(c)   if the appeal is brought by the prosecution, to the accused; and

(d)   to the appropriate officer of the Crown Court.

(3)   The notice of an appeal to which this rule applies shall state the date on which the time-limit applicable to the case is due to expire and, if the appeal is brought by the accused under section 22(7) of the Prosecution of Offences Act 1985, the date on which the time-limit would have expired had the court decided not to extend or further extend the time-limit.

(4)   On receiving notice of an appeal to which this rule applies, the appropriate officer of the Crown Court shall enter the appeal and give notice of the time and place of the hearing to—

  (a)   the appellant;
  (b)   the other party to the appeal; and
  (c)   the clerk to the magistrates' court which took the decision.

(5)   Without prejudice to the power of the Crown Court to give leave for an appeal to be abandoned, an appellant may abandon an appeal to which this rule applied by giving notice in writing to any person to whom notice of the appeal was required to be given by paragraph (2) not later than the third day preceding the day fixed for the hearing of the appeal:

Provided that, for the purpose of determining whether notice was properly given in accordance with this paragraph, there shall be disregarded any Saturday and Sunday and any day which is specified to be a bank holiday in England and Wales under section 1(1) of the Banking and Financial Dealings Act 1971.

Service of documents
28.   Any notice or other document which is required by these rules to be given to any person may be served personally on that person or sent to him by post at his usual or last known residence or place of business in England or Wales or, in the case of a company, at the company's registered office in England or Wales.

References to the European Court
29.—(1)   In this rule 'order' means an order referring a question to the European Court for a preliminary ruling under Article 177 of the Treaty establishing the Economic Community, Article 150 of the Treaty establishing Euratom or Article 41 of the Treaty establishing the Coal and Steel Community.

(2)   An order may be made by the Crown Court of its own motion or on application by a party to proceedings in the Crown Court.

(3)   An order shall set out in a schedule the request for the preliminary ruling of the European Court, and the Crown Court may give directions as to the manner and form in which the schedule is to be prepared.

(4)   When an order has been made, a copy shall be sent to the senior master of the Supreme Court (Queen's Bench Division) for transmission to the Registrar of the European Court.

(5)   The proceedings in which an order is made shall, unless the Crown Court otherwise determines, be adjourned until the European Court has given a preliminary ruling on the question referred to it.

(6)   Nothing in paragraph (5) shall be taken as preventing the Crown Court from deciding any preliminary or incidental question which may arise in the proceedings after an order is made and before a preliminary ruling is given by the European Court.

Service of summons or order outside the United Kingdom
30.   Where a witness summons or order is issued or made by the Crown Court in accordance with section 2(1) of the Criminal Justice (International Co-operation) Act 1990 for service outside the United Kingdom it shall be sent forthwith by the appropriate officer of the Crown Court to the Secretary of State with a view to its being served there in accordance with arrangements made by the Secretary of State.

Application for letters of request
31.—(1)   Notice of an application under section 3(1) of the Criminal Justice (International Co-operation) Act 1990 (overseas evidence for use in the United Kingdom) shall be given to the appropriate officer of the Crown Court and shall—

  (a)   be made in writing, save that the court may in exceptional circumstances dispense with the need for notice;
  (b)   state the particulars of the offence which it is alleged has been committed or the grounds upon which it is suspected that an offence has been committed;
  (c)   state whether proceedings in respect of the offence have been instituted or the offence is being investigated;
  (d)   include particulars of the assistance requested in the form of a draft letter of request.

(2)   The application may be heard *ex parte*.

(3)   When hearing the application the court may, if it thinks it necessary in the interests of justice, direct that the public be excluded from the court.

(4)   The powers conferred on the Crown Court by paragraph (3) above shall be in addition and without prejudice to any other powers of the court to hear proceedings in camera.

(5)   Where in a case of urgency the Crown Court sends a letter of request direct to any court or tribunal in accordance with section 3(5) of the Criminal Justice (International Co-operation) Act 1990, the appropriate officer of the Crown Court shall forthwith notify the State of this and send with the notification a copy of the letter of request.

Proceedings before a nominated court

32.—(1)   Where the Crown Court receives evidence in proceedings before a nominated court in pursuance of a notice under section 4(2) of the Criminal Justice (International Co-operation) Act 1990 the court may, if it thinks it necessary in the interests of justice, direct that the public be excluded from the court.

(2)   The powers conferred on the Crown Court by paragraph (1) above shall be in addition and without prejudice to any other powers of the court to hear proceedings in camera.

(3)   Where the Crown Court receives evidence in proceedings mentioned in paragraph (1) above the appropriate officer of the Crown Court shall make a record of—

    (a)   which persons with an interest in the proceedings were present;

    (b)   which of the said persons were represented and by whom;

    (c)   whether any of the said persons were denied the opportunity of cross-examining a witness as to any part of his testimony and the reasons for any such denial.

(4)   When so requested by the Secretary of State, the appropriate officer of the Crown Court shall send to him a copy of the record as mentioned in paragraph (3) above.

Application for increase in term of imprisonment in default of payment of a confiscation order

33.—(1)   The following provisions of this rule shall have effect for the purposes of applications under subsection (2) of section 15 of the Criminal Justice (International Co-operation) Act 1990 (which provides for interest on sums unpaid under confiscation orders in drug trafficking cases) or under section 75A of the Criminal Justice Act 1988.

(2)   Notice of application under subsection (2) of the said section 15 of the said Act of 1990 or under subsection 2 of section 75A of the said Act of 1988 to increase the term of imprisonment or detention fixed in default of payment of a confiscation order by a person ('the defendant') shall be made by the prosecutor in writing to the appropriate officer of the Crown Court.

(3)   A notice under paragraph (2) above shall—

    (a)   state the name and address of the defendant;

    (b)   specify the grounds for the application;

    (c)   give details of the enforcement measures taken, if any; and

    (d)   include a copy of the confiscation order.

(4)   On receiving a notice under paragraph (2) above, the appropriate officers of the Crown Court shall—

    (a)   forthwith send to the defendant and the magistrates' court required to enforce payment of the confiscation order under section 32(1) of the Powers of Criminal Courts Act 1973, a copy of the said notice; and

    (b)   notify in writing the applicant and the defendant of the date, time and place appointed for the hearing of the application.

(5)   Where the Crown Court makes an order pursuant to an application mentioned in paragraph (1) above, the appropriate officer of the Crown Court shall send forthwith a copy of the order—

    (a)   to the applicant;

    (b)   to the defendant;

    (c)   where the defendant is at the time of the making of the order in custody, to the person having custody of him; and

    (d)   to the magistrates' court mentioned in paragraph (4)(a) above.

Postponed determinations

34.—(1)   Where an application to the Crown Court is made by the defendant or the prosecutor under section 3(5)(a) of the Drug Trafficking Act 1994 asking the Court to exercise its powers under section 3(4) of that Act, or under section 72A(5)(a) of the Criminal Justice Act 1988 asking the court to exercise its powers under section 72A(4) of that Act, such an application must be made in writing and a copy thereof must be served on the prosecutor or the defendant, as the case may be.

(2)   A party which is served with a copy of an application under paragraph (1) shall, within 28 days of the date of service, notify the applicant and the appropriate officer of the Crown Court, in writing, whether or not it proposes to oppose the application, giving its reasons for any such opposition.

(3)   After the expiry of the period referred to in paragraph (2), the Crown Court shall determine whether an application under paragraph (1) is to be dealt with—

(a)   without a hearing, or

(b)   at a hearing at which the parties may be represented.

Confiscation – revised assessments

35.—(1)   Where the prosecutor makes an application under section 13, 14 or 15 of the Drug Trafficking Act 1994 or under section 74A, 74B or 74C of the Criminal Justice Act 1988, such an application must be in writing and a copy thereof must be served on the defendant.

(2)   The application must include the following particulars, namely—

(a)   the name of the defendant;

(b)   the date on which and the place where any relevant conviction occurred;

(c)   the date on which and the place where any relevant confiscation order was made or, as the case may be, varied;

(d)   the grounds on which the application is made;

(e)   an indication of the evidence available to support the application.

Drug trafficking – compensation

36.   Where a Crown Court cancels a confiscation order under section 22(2) of the Drug Trafficking Act 1994, the appropriate officer of the Crown Court shall serve notice to that effect on the High Court and on the magistrates' court which has responsibility for enforcing the order.

[Schedule 1 is concerned with revocations of earlier rules. Schedule 2 is concerned with transitional provisions. Schedule 3 relates to proceedings outside the scope of this work.]

SCHEDULE 4 FORM OF NOTICE OF APPLICATION RELATING TO BAIL IN THE CROWN COURT

Take notice that an application relating to bail will be made to the Crown Court
at
on   at   a.m./p.m.
on behalf of the defendant/appellant/prosecutor/respondent.

Name of defendant/appellant: (Block letters)	Crown Court No.
Solicitor for the *Applicant:* Address:	
If defendant/appellant is in custody: state place of detention and give Prison No. if applicable	
State particulars of proceedings during which defendant/appellant was committed to custody or bailed [un]conditionally:	
Enter details of any relevant previous applications for bail or variation of conditions of bail:	
Nature and grounds of application: (State fully facts relied on and list previous convictions (if any). Give details of any proposed sureties and answer any objections raised previously):	

Notes

The appropriate officer of the Crown Court should be consulted about the time and place of the hearing before this notice is sent to the other party to the application.

A copy of this notice should be sent to the Crown Court.

[Schedule 5 sets out the form of a notice of application for leave to use television link under s. 32(1)(b) of the Criminal Justice Act 1988. Schedule 6 sets out the form of a notice of application for leave to use television link where witness is outside the United Kingdom. Schedule 7 sets out the form of a notice of application for leave to tender in evidence a video recording under s. 32A of the Criminal Justice Act 1988; sch. 8 sets out the form of notice of decision on such an application. Schedule 9 sets out the form of notice of appeal under the Bail (Amendment) Act 1993; sch. 10 sets out the form of notice of abandonment of such an appeal.]

APPENDIX 2   CODES OF PRACTICE UNDER THE POLICE AND CRIMINAL EVIDENCE ACT 1984

PACE CODE A: THE EXERCISE BY POLICE OFFICERS OF STATUTORY POWERS OF STOP AND SEARCH

1.   General

1.1   This code of practice must be readily available at all police stations for consultation by police officers, detained persons and members of the public.

1.2   The notes for guidance included are not provisions of this code, but are guidance to police officers and others about its application and interpretation. Provisions in the annexes to the code are provisions of this code.

1.3   This code governs the exercise by police officers of statutory powers to search a person without first arresting him or to search a vehicle without making an arrest. The main stop and search powers to which this code applies at the time the code was prepared are set out in Annex A, but that list should not be regarded as definitive.

1.4   This code does not apply to the following powers of stop and search:
    (i)   Aviation Security Act 1982, s. 27(2);
    (ii)   Police and Criminal Evidence Act 1984, s. 6(1) (which relates specifically to powers of constables employed by statutory undertakers on the premises of the statutory undertakers).

1.5   This code applies to stops and searches under powers:
    (a)   requiring reasonable grounds for suspicion that articles unlawfully obtained or possessed are being carried;
    (b)   authorised under section 60 of the Criminal Justice and Public Order Act 1994, (as amended by section 8 of the Knives Act 1997), based upon a reasonable belief that incidents involving serious violence may take place or that people are carrying dangerous instruments or offensive weapons within any locality in the police area [See Note 1A];
    (c)   authorised under section 13A of the Prevention of Terrorism (Temporary Provisions) Act 1989, (as amended by section 81 of the Criminal Justice and Public Order Act 1994 and section 1 of the Prevention of Terrorism (Additional Powers) Act 1996);
    (d)   authorised under section 13B of the Prevention of Terrorism (Temporary Provisions) Act 1989, (as inserted by section 1 of the Prevention of Terrorism (Additional Powers) Act 1996);
    (e)   exercised under paragraph 4(2) of Schedule 5 to the Prevention of Terrorism (Temporary Provisions) Act 1989.
[See Note 1AA]

(a)   Powers requiring reasonable suspicion

1.6   Whether a reasonable ground for suspicion exists will depend on the circumstances in each case, but there must be some objective basis for it. An officer will need to consider the nature of the article suspected of being carried in the context of other factors such as the time and the place, and the behaviour of the person concerned or those with him. Reasonable suspicion may exist, for example, where information has been received such as a description of an article being carried or of a suspected offender; a person is seen acting covertly or warily or attempting to hide something; or a person is carrying a certain type of article at an unusual time or in a place where a number of burglaries or thefts are known to have taken place recently. But the decision to stop and search must be based on all the facts which bear on the likelihood that an article of a certain kind will be found.

1.6A   For example, reasonable suspicion may be based upon reliable information or intelligence which indicates that members of a particular group or gang, or their associates, habitually carry knives unlawfully or weapons or controlled drugs.

1.7   Subject to the provision in paragraph 1.7AA below, reasonable suspicion can never be supported on the basis of personal factors alone without supporting intelligence or information.

For example, a person's colour, age, hairstyle or manner of dress, or the fact that he is known to have a previous conviction for possession of an unlawful article, cannot be used alone or in combination with each other as the sole basis on which to search that person. Nor may it be founded on the basis of stereotyped images of certain persons or groups as more likely to be committing offences.

1.7AA   However, where there is reliable information or intelligence that members of a group or gang who habitually carry knives unlawfully or weapons or controlled drugs, and wear a distinctive item of clothing or other means of identification to indicate membership of it, the members may be identified by means of that distinctive item of clothing or other means of identification. [See Note 1H]

1.7A   Where a police officer has reasonable grounds to suspect that a person is in innocent possession of a stolen or prohibited article or other item for which he is empowered to search, the power of stop and search exists notwithstanding that there would be no power of arrest. However every effort should be made to secure the person's co-operation in the production of the article before resorting to the use of force.

(b)   Authorisation under section 60 of the Criminal Justice and Public Order Act 1994, as amended by section 8 of the Knives Act 1997

1.8   Authority to exercise the powers of stop and search under section 60 of the Criminal Justice and Public Order Act 1994, as amended by section 8 of the Knives Act 1997, may be given where it is reasonably believed that incidents involving serious violence may take place in any locality in the police area, and it is expedient to use these powers to prevent their occurrence, or that persons are carrying dangerous instruments or offensive weapons without good reason in any locality in any police area. Authorisation may only be given by an officer of the rank of inspector or above, in writing, specifying the grounds on which it was given, the locality in which the powers may be exercised and the period of time for which they are in force. The period authorised shall be no longer than appears reasonably necessary to prevent, or try to prevent incidents of serious violence, or to deal with the problem of carrying dangerous instruments or offensive weapons and it may not exceed 24 hours. If an inspector gives an authorisation, he must, as soon as practicable, inform an officer of or above the rank of superintendent. An officer of or above the rank of superintendent may direct that the period shall be extended for a further 24 hours if violence or the carrying of dangerous instruments or offensive weapons has occurred or is suspected to have occurred and the continued use of the powers is considered necessary to prevent or deal with further such activity. That direction must also be given in writing at the time or as soon as practicable afterwards. [See Notes 1A, 1F and 1G]

(c)   Authorisation under section 13A of the Prevention of Terrorism (Temporary Provisions) Act 1989, as inserted by section 81 of the Criminal Justice and Public Order Act 1994 and amended by the Prevention of Terrorism (Additional Powers) Act 1996

1.8A   (Removed)

1.9   An authorisation given under section 13A of the Prevention of Terrorism (Temporary Provisions) Act 1989 gives a constable in uniform the power to stop and search any vehicle, its driver and any passengers for articles which could be used for terrorist purposes. A constable may exercise the power whether or not he has any grounds for suspecting the presence of such articles.

1.10   Authority for the use of the power may be given where it appears expedient to do so to prevent acts of terrorism. The authorisation must:
    (i)   be given by an officer of the rank of assistant chief constable (or equivalent or above);
    (ii)   be in writing (it may be given orally at first but should be confirmed in writing by the officer who gave it as soon as reasonably practicable);
    (iii)   be signed, dated and timed by the officer giving the authorisation;
    (iv)   state the geographical area in which the power may be used (i.e. whether it applies to the whole or only a specific part of his force area); and
    (v)   specify the time and date that the authorisation starts and ends (up to a, maximum of 28 days from the time the authorisation was given).

1.11   Further use of the power requires a new authorisation.

[See Notes 1F, 1G and 1I]

(d) Authorisation under section 13B of the Prevention of Terrorism (Temporary Provisions) Act 1989, as inserted by section 1 of the Prevention of Terrorism (Additional Powers) Act 1996

1.12   An authorisation given under section 13B of the Prevention of Terrorism (Temporary Provisions) Act 1989 gives a constable in uniform the power to stop a pedestrian and search him, or anything carried by him, for articles which could be used for terrorist purposes. A constable may exercise the power whether or not he has any grounds for suspecting the presence of such articles.

1.13   Authority for the use of the power may be given where it appears expedient to do so to prevent acts of terrorism. The authorisation must be given in exactly the same way as explained in paragraph 1.10 (and may in fact be combined with a section 13A authorisation). However, the officer giving an authorisation under section 13B must cause the Secretary of State to be informed, as soon as reasonably practicable, that such an authorisation has been given. The authorisation may take effect before the Secretary of State has decided whether to confirm it. But it ceases to have effect if it is not confirmed by the Secretary of State within 48 hours of its having been given.

1.14   Following notification of the authorisation, the Secretary of State may:
(i)   cancel the authorisation with immediate effect or with effect from such other time as he may direct;
(ii)   confirm it but for a shorter period than that specified in the authorisation (which may not be more than 28 days); or
(iii)   confirm the authorisation as given.

1.15   Further use of the power requires a new authorisation.

1.16   The selection of persons stopped under sections 13A and 13B of the Prevention of Terrorism (Temporary Provision) Act 1989 should reflect an objective assessment of the threat posed by the various terrorist groups active in Great Britain. The powers should not be used to stop and search for reasons unconnected with terrorism. Officers should take particular care not to discriminate against members of ethnic minorities in the exercise of these powers. There may be circumstances, however, where it is appropriate for officers to take account of a person's ethnic origin in selecting persons to be stopped in response to a specific terrorist threat (for example, some international terrorist groups are associated with particular ethnic identities).

[See Notes 1F, 1G and 1I]

Notes for Guidance

1A   Section 60 is amended by section 25 of the Crime and Disorder Act 1998 to provide a power to demand the removal of face coverings where an authority referred to in paragraph 1.8 above is given. The officer exercising the power must reasonably believe that someone is wearing the face covering wholly or mainly for the purpose of concealing identity. There is also a power to seize face coverings where the officer believes that a person intends to wear them for this purpose. **There is not a power to stop and search for face coverings**. An officer may seize any face covering which he comes across when exercising a power of search for something else, or which he sees being carried, and which he reasonably believes is intended to be used for concealing anyone's identity.

1AA   It is important to ensure that powers of stop and search are used responsibly by those who exercise them and those who authorise their use. An officer should bear in mind that he may be required to justify the authorisation or use of the powers to a senior officer and in court, and that misuse of the powers is likely to be harmful to the police effort in the long term and can lead to mistrust of the police by the community. Regardless of the power exercised, all police officers should be careful to ensure that the selection and treatment of those questioned or searched is based upon objective factors and not upon personal prejudice. It is also particularly important to ensure that any person searched is treated courteously and considerately. Where there may be religious sensitivities about asking someone to remove a face covering using the powers in section 25 of the Crime and Disorder Act 1998, for example in the case of a Muslim woman wearing a face covering for religious purposes, the officer should permit the item to be removed out of public view. Where practicable, the item should be removed in the presence of an officer of the same sex as the person and out of sight of anyone of the opposite sex. In all cases, the officer must reasonably believe that the person is wearing the item in question *wholly or mainly* to conceal his or her identity.

1B   This code does not affect the ability of an officer to speak to or question a person in the ordinary course of his duties (and in the absence of reasonable suspicion) without detaining him or exercising any element of compulsion. It is not the purpose of the code to prohibit such encounters between the police and the community with the co-operation of the person concerned and neither does it affect the principle that all citizens have a duty to help police officers to prevent crime and discover offenders.

1C   (Not Used)

1D   Nothing in this code affects

(a)   the routine searching of persons entering sports grounds or other premises with their consent, or as a condition of entry; or

(b)   the ability of an officer to search a person in the street with his consent where no search power exists. In these circumstances, an officer should always make it clear that he is seeking the consent of the person concerned to the search being carried out by telling the person that he need not consent and that without his consent he will not be searched.

1E   If an officer acts in an improper manner this will invalidate a voluntary search. Juveniles, people suffering from a mental handicap or mental disorder and others who appear not to be capable of giving an informed consent should not be subject to a voluntary search.

1F   It is for the authorising officer to determine the period of time during which the powers mentioned in paragraph 1.5(b), (c) and (d) may be exercised. The officer should set the minimum period he considers necessary to deal with the risk of violence, the carrying of knives or offensive weapons, or terrorism. A direction to extend the period authorised under the powers mentioned in paragraph 1.5(b) may be given only once. Thereafter further use of the powers requires a new authorisation. There is no provision to extend an authorisation of the powers mentioned in paragraph 1.5(c) and (d); further use of the powers requires a new authorisation.

1G   It is for the authorising officer to determine the geographical area in which the use of the powers are to be authorised. In doing so he may wish to take into account factors such as the nature and venue of the anticipated incident, the numbers of people who may be in the immediate area of any possible incident, their access to surrounding areas and the anticipated level of violence. The officer should not set a geographical area which is wider than that he believes necessary for the purpose of preventing anticipated violence, the carrying of knives or offensive weapons, or terrorism. It is particularly important to ensure that constables exercising such powers are fully aware of where they may be used. If the area specified is smaller than the whole force area, the officer giving the authorisation should specify either the streets which form the boundary of the area or a divisional boundary within the force area. If the power is to be used in response to a threat or incident that straddles police force areas, an officer from each of the forces concerned will need to give an authorisation.

1H   Other means of identification might include jewellery, insignias, tattoos or other features which are known to identify members of the particular gang or group.

1I   An officer who has authorised the use of powers under section 13B of the Prevention of Terrorism (Temporary Provisions) Act 1989 must take immediate steps to send a copy of the authorisation to the National Joint Unit, Metropolitan Police Special Branch, who will forward it to the Secretary of State. The Secretary of State should be informed of the reasons for the authorisation. The National Joint Unit will inform the force concerned, within 48 hours of the authorisation being made, whether the Secretary of State has confirmed or cancelled or altered the authorisation. The National Joint Unit should also be sent a copy of all section 13A authorisations for national monitoring purposes.

2.   Action before a search is carried out

(a)   Searches requiring reasonable suspicion

2.1   Where an officer has the reasonable grounds for suspicion necessary to exercise a power of stop and search, he may detain the person concerned for the purposes of and with a view to searching him. There is no power to stop or detain a person against his will in order to find grounds for a search.

2.2   Before carrying out a search the officer may question the person about his behaviour or his presence in circumstances which gave rise to the suspicion, since he may have a satisfactory explanation which will make a search unnecessary. If, as a result of any questioning preparatory to a search, or other circumstances which come to the attention of the officer, there cease to be reasonable grounds for suspecting that an article is being carried of a kind for which there is a power of stop and search, no search may take place. [See Note 2A]

2.3   The reasonable grounds for suspicion which are necessary for the exercise of the initial power to detain may be confirmed or eliminated as a result of the questioning of a person detained for the purposes of a search (or such questioning may reveal reasonable grounds to suspect the possession of a different kind of unlawful article from that originally suspected); but the reasonable grounds for suspicion without which any search or detention for the purposes of a search is unlawful cannot be retrospectively provided by such questioning during his detention or by his refusal to answer any question put to him.

(b)   All searches

2.4   Before any search of a detained person or attended vehicle takes place the officer must take reasonable steps to give the person to be searched or in charge of the vehicle the following information:

     (i)   his name (except in the case of enquiries linked to the investigation of terrorism, in which case he shall give his warrant or other identification number) and the name of the police station to which he is attached;
     (ii)   the object of the search; and
     (iii)   his grounds or authorisation for undertaking it.

2.5   If the officer is not in uniform he must show his warrant card. In doing so in the case of enquiries linked to the investigation of terrorism, the officer need not reveal his name. Stops and searches under the powers mentioned in paragraphs 1.5 (b) and (c) may be undertaken only by a constable in uniform.

2.6   Unless it appears to the officer that it will not be practicable to make a record of the search, he must also inform the person to be searched (or the owner or person in charge of a vehicle that is to be searched, as the case may be) that he is entitled to a copy of the record of the search if he asks for it within a year. If the person wishes to have a copy and is not given one on the spot, he shall be advised to which police station he should apply.

2.7   If the person to be searched, or in charge of a vehicle to be searched, does not appear to understand what is being said, or there is any doubt about his ability to understand English, the officer must take reasonable steps to bring the information in paragraphs 2.4 and 2.6 to his attention. If the person is deaf or cannot understand English and has someone with him then the officer must try to establish whether the person can interpret or otherwise help him to give the required information.

Note for Guidance

2A   In some circumstances preparatory questioning may be unnecessary, but in general a brief conversation or exchange will be desirable, not only as a means of avoiding unsuccessful searches but to explain the grounds for the stop/search, to gain co-operation and reduce any tension there might be surrounding the stop/search. Where a person is lawfully detained for the purpose of a search, but no search in the event takes place, the detention will not thereby have been rendered unlawful.

3.   Conduct of the search

3.1   Every reasonable effort must be made to reduce to the minimum the embarrassment that a person being searched may experience.

3.2   The co-operation of the person to be searched shall be sought in every case, even if he initially objects to the search. A forcible search may be made only if it has been established that the person is unwilling to co-operate (e.g. by opening a bag) or resists. Although force may only be used as a last resort, reasonable force may be used if necessary to conduct a search or to detain a person or vehicle for the purposes of a search.

3.3 The length of time for which a person or vehicle may be detained will depend on the circumstances, but must in all circumstances, be reasonable and not extend beyond the time taken for the search. Where the exercise of the power requires reasonable suspicion, the thoroughness and extent of a search must depend on what is suspected of being carried, and by whom. If the suspicion relates to a particular article which is seen to be slipped into a person's pocket, then, in the absence of other grounds for suspicion or an opportunity for the article to be moved elsewhere, the search must be confined to that pocket. In the case of a small article which can readily be concealed, such as a drug, and which might be concealed anywhere on the person, a more extensive search may be necessary. In the case of searches mentioned in paragraph 1.5(b), (c), (d) and (e), which do not require reasonable grounds for suspicion, the officer may make any reasonable search to find what he is empowered to search for. [See Note 3B]

3.4 The search must be conducted at or nearby the place where the person or vehicle was first detained.

3.5 Searches in public must be restricted to superficial examination of outer clothing. There is no power to require a person to remove any clothing in public other than an outer coat, jacket or gloves (other than under sections 13A and 13B of the Prevention of Terrorism (Temporary Provisions) Act 1989, which grant a constable in addition the power to require a person to remove in public any headgear and footwear, or under section 60 of the Criminal Justice and Public Order Act 1994 as amended by the Crime and Disorder Act 1998, which grants a constable power to require the removal of any item worn to conceal identity). Where on reasonable grounds it is considered necessary to conduct a more thorough search (e.g. by requiring a person to take off a T-shirt), this shall be done out of public view for example, in a police van or police station if there is one nearby. Any search involving the removal of more than an outer coat, jacket, gloves, headgear or footwear, or any other item concealing identity, may only be made by an officer of the same sex as the person searched and may not be made in the presence of anyone of the opposite sex unless the person being searched specifically requests it. [See Note 3A and 3C]. No search involving exposure of intimate parts of the body may take place in a police van. All searches involving exposure of intimate parts of the body shall be conducted in accordance with paragraph 11 of Annex A to Code C. The other provisions of Code C do not apply to persons at police stations for the purposes of searches under stop and search powers.

3.5A The powers under sections 13A and 13B of the Prevention of Terrorism (Temporary Provisions) Act 1989 allow a constable to search only for articles which could be used for terrorist purposes. The powers must not be used for any other purpose (for example to search for drugs in the absence of reasonable grounds for suspicion). However, this would not prevent a search being carried out under other powers if, in course of exercising powers under sections 13A or 13B, the police officer formed reasonable grounds for suspicion.

Notes for Guidance

3A A search in the street itself should be regarded as being in public for the purposes of paragraph 3.5 above, even though it may be empty at the time a search begins. Although there is no power to require a person to do so, there is nothing to prevent an officer from asking a person to voluntarily remove more than an outer coat, jacket or gloves (and headgear or footwear under section 13A and 13B of the Prevention of Terrorism (Temporary Provisions) Act 1989) in public.

3B As a search of a person in public should be superficial examination of outer clothing, such searches should be completed as soon as possible.

3C Where there may be religious sensitivities about asking someone to remove headgear using a power under section 13A or 13B of the Prevention of Terrorism (Temporary Provisions) Act 1989, the police officer should offer to carry out the search out of public view (for example, in a police van or police station if there is one nearby).

4. Action after a search is carried out

(a) General

4.1 An officer who has carried out a search must make a written record unless it is not practicable to do so, on account of the numbers to be searched or for some other operational reason, e.g. in situations involving public disorder.

4.2   The records must be completed as soon as practicable – on the spot unless circumstances (e.g. other immediate duties or very bad weather) make this impracticable.

4.3   The record must be made on the form provided for this purpose (the national search record).

4.4   In order to complete the search record the officer shall normally seek the name, address and date of birth of the person searched, but under the search procedures there is no obligation on a person to provide these details and no power to detain him if he is unwilling to do so.

4.5   The following information must always be included in the record of a search even if the person does not wish to identify himself or give his date of birth:
    (i)   the name of the person searched, or (if he withholds it) a description of him;
    (ii)   a note of the person's ethnic origin; [See Note 4DA]
    (iii)   when a vehicle is searched, a description of it, including its registration number;
[See Note 4B]
    (iv)   the object of the search;
    (v)   the grounds for making it;
    (vi)   the date and time it was made;
    (vii)   the place where it was made;
    (viii) its results;
    (ix)   a note of any injury or damage to property resulting from it;
    (x)   the identity of the officer making it (except in the case of enquiries linked to the investigation of terrorism, in which case the record shall state the officer's warrant or other identification number and duty station). [See Note 4A]

4.6   A record is required for each person and each vehicle searched. However, if a person is in a vehicle and both are searched, and the object and grounds of the search are the same, only one record need be completed.

4.7   The record of the grounds for making a search must, briefly but informatively, explain the reason for suspecting the person concerned, whether by reference to his behaviour or other circumstances; or in the case of those searches mentioned in paragraph 1.5 (b), (c), (d) and (e) by stating the authority provided to carry out such a search. [See Note 4D]

4.7A   The driver of a vehicle which is stopped in accordance with the powers mentioned in paragraphs 1.5 (b) and (c) may obtain a written statement to that effect within twelve months from the day the vehicle was stopped. A written statement may be similarly obtained by any person if he is searched in accordance with the powers mentioned in paragraph 1.5 (b) and (d) (see paragraph 2.6). The statement may form part of the national search record or be supplied on a separate document. [See Note 4C]

(b)   Unattended vehicles

4.8   After searching an unattended vehicle, or anything in or on it, an officer must leave a notice in it (or on it, if things in or on it have been searched without opening it) recording the fact that it has been searched.

4.9   The notice should include the name of the police station to which the officer concerned is attached and state where a copy of the record of the search may be obtained and where any application for compensation should be directed.

4.10   The vehicle must if practicable be left secure.

Notes for Guidance

4A   Where a search is conducted by more than one officer the identity of all the officers engaged in the search must be recorded on the search record.

4B   Where a vehicle has not been allocated a registration number (e.g. a rally car or a trials motorbike) that part of the requirements under 4.5 (iii) does not apply.

4C   In paragraph 4.7A, a written statement means a record that a person or vehicle was stopped under the powers contained in paragraph 1.5 (b), (c) or (d) of this code.

4D   It is important for national monitoring purposes to specify in the record whether a stop and search under the Prevention of Terrorism (Temporary Provisions) Act 1989 were made under section 13A or section 13B powers.

4DA   Supervising officers, in monitoring the exercise of officers' stop and search powers, should consider in particular whether there is any evidence that officers are exercising their discretion on the basis of stereotyped images of certain persons or groups contrary to the provisions of this code. It is important that any such evidence should be addressed. Supervising officers should take account of the information about the ethnic origin of those stopped and searched which is collected and published under section 95 of the Criminal Justice Act 1991.

ANNEX A

SUMMARY OF MAIN STOP AND SEARCH POWERS [See paragraph 1.3]

POWER	OBJECT OF SEARCH	EXTENT OF SEARCH	WHERE EXERCISABLE
Unlawful articles general			
1. Public Stores Act 1875, s. 6	HM Stores stolen or unlawfully obtained	Persons, vehicles and vessels	Anywhere where the constabulary powers are exercisable
2. Firearms Act 1968, s. 47	Firearms	Persons and vehicles	A public place, or anywhere in the case of reasonable suspicion of offences of carrying firearms with criminal intent or trespassing with firearms
3. Misuse of Drugs Act 1971, s. 23	Controlled drugs	Persons and vehicles	Anywhere
4. Customs and Excise Management Act 1979, s. 163	Goods: (a) on which duty has not been paid; (b) being unlawfully removed, imported or exported; (c) otherwise liable to forfeiture to HM Customs and Excise	Vehicles and vessels only	Anywhere
5. Aviation Security Act 1982, s. 27(1)	Stolen or unlawfully obtained goods	Airport employees and vehicles carrying airport employees or aircraft or any vehicle in a cargo area whether or not carrying an employee	Any designated airport
6. Police and Criminal Evidence Act 1984, s. 1	Stolen goods; articles for use in certain Theft Act offences; offensive weapons, including bladed or sharply-pointed articles (except folding pocket knives with a bladed cutting edge not exceeding 3 inches)	Persons and vehicles	Where there is public access
Police and Criminal Evidence Act 1984, s. 6(3) (by a constable of the United Kingdom Atomic Energy Authority Constabulary in respect of property owned or controlled by British Nuclear Fuels plc)	HM Stores (in the form of goods and chattels belonging to British Nuclear Fuels plc)	Persons, vehicles and vessels	Anywhere where the constabulary powers are exercisable

POWER	OBJECT OF SEARCH	EXTENT OF SEARCH	WHERE EXERCISABLE
7. Sporting Events (Control of Alcohol etc.) Act 1985, s. 7	Intoxicating liquor	Persons, coaches and trains	Designated sports grounds or coaches and trains travelling to or from a designated sporting event
8. Crossbows Act 1987, s. 4	Crossbows or parts of crossbows (except crossbows with a draw weight of less than 1.4 kilograms)	Persons and vehicles	Anywhere except dwellings
Evidence of game and wildlife offences			
9. Poaching Prevention Act 1862, s. 2	Game or poaching equipment	Persons and vehicles	A public place
10. Deer Act 1991, s. 12	Evidence of offences under the Act	Persons and vehicles	Anywhere except dwellings
11. Conservation of Seals Act 1970, s. 4	Seals or hunting equipment	Vehicles only	Anywhere
12. Badgers Act 1992, s. 11	Evidence of offences under the Act	Persons and vehicles	Anywhere
13. Wildlife and Countryside Act 1981, s. 19	Evidence of wildlife offences	Persons and vehicles	Anywhere except dwellings
Other			
14. Prevention of Terrorism (Temporary Provisions) Act 1989, s. 15(3)	Evidence of liability to arrest under section 14 of the Act	Persons	Anywhere
15. Section 13A of the Prevention of Terrorism (Temporary Provisions) Act 1989	Articles which could be used for a purpose connected with the commission, preparation or instigation of acts of terrorism	Vehicles, drivers and passengers	Anywhere within the area or locality authorised under subsection (1)
16. Section 13B of the Prevention of Terrorism (Temporary Provisions) Act 1989	Articles which could be used for a purpose connected with the commission, preparation or instigation of acts of terrorism	Pedestrians	Anywhere within the area of locality authorised
17. Paragraph 4.2 of Schedule 5 to the Prevention of Terrorism (Temporary Provisions) Act 1989	Anything relevant to determining if a person being examined falls within paragraph 2(1)(a) to (c) of Schedule 5	Persons, vehicles, vessels etc	Ports and airports
18. Section 60 Criminal Justice and Public Order Act 1994, as amended by s.8 of the Knives Act 1997	Offensive weapons or dangerous instruments to prevent incidents of serious violence or to deal with the carrying of such items	Persons and vehicles	Anywhere within a locality authorised under subsection (1)

PACE CODE B: THE SEARCHING OF PREMISES BY POLICE OFFICERS AND THE SEIZURE OF PROPERTY FOUND BY POLICE OFFICERS ON PERSONS OR PREMISES

1. General

1.1 This code of practice must be readily available at all police stations for consultation by police officers, detained persons and members of the public.

1.2 The notes for guidance included are not provisions of this code, but are guidance to police officers and others about its application and interpretation.

1.3 This code applies to searches of premises:
    (a) undertaken for the purposes of an investigation into an alleged offence, with the occupier's consent, other than searches made in the following circumstances:
    – routine scenes of crime searches
    – calls to a fire or a burglary made by or on behalf of an occupier or searches following the activation of fire or burglar alarms
    – searches to which paragraph 4.4 applies
    – bomb threat calls;
    (b) under powers conferred by sections 17, 18 and 32 of the Police and Criminal Evidence Act 1984;
    (c) undertaken in pursuance of a search warrant issued in accordance with section 15 of, or schedule 1 to the Police and Criminal Evidence Act 1984, or section 15 of, or schedule 7 to the Prevention of Terrorism (Temporary Provisions) Act 1989.
'Premises' for the purpose of this code is defined in section 23 of the Police and Criminal Evidence Act 1984. It includes any place and, in particular, any vehicle, vessel, aircraft, hovercraft, tent or movable structure. It also includes any offshore installation as defined in section 1 of the Mineral Workings (Offshore Installations) Act 1971.

1.3A Any search of a person who has not been arrested which is carried out during a search of premises shall be carried out in accordance with Code A.

1.3B This code does not apply to the exercise of a statutory power to enter premises or to inspect goods, equipment or procedures if the exercise of that power is not dependent on the existence of grounds for suspecting that an offence may have been committed and the person exercising the power has no reasonable grounds for such suspicion.

2. Search warrants and production orders

(a) Action to be taken before an application is made

2.1 Where information is received which appears to justify an application, the officer concerned must take reasonable steps to check that the information is accurate, recent and has not been provided maliciously or irresponsibly. An application may not be made on the basis of information from an anonymous source where corroboration has not been sought. [See Note 2A]

2.2 The officer shall ascertain as specifically as is possible in the circumstances the nature of the articles concerned and their location.

2.3 The officer shall also make reasonable enquiries to establish what, if anything, is known about the likely occupier of the premises and the nature of the premises themselves; and whether they have been previously searched and if so how recently; and to obtain any other information relevant to the application.

2.4 No application for a search warrant may be made without the authority of an officer of at least the rank of inspector (or, in the case of urgency where no officer of this rank is readily available, the senior officer on duty). No application for a production order or warrant under schedule 7 to the Prevention of Terrorism (Temporary Provisions) Act 1989, may be made without the authority of an officer of at least the rank of superintendent.

2.5 Except in a case of urgency, if there is reason to believe that a search might have an adverse effect on relations between the police and the community then the local police/community liaison officer shall be consulted before it takes place. In urgent cases, the local police/community liaison officer should be informed of the search as soon as practicable after it has been made. [See Note 2B]

(b) Making an application

2.6 An application for a search warrant must be supported by an information in writing, specifying:

(i) the enactment under which the application is made;

(ii) the premises to be searched and the object of the search; and

(iii) the grounds on which the application is made (including, where the purpose of the proposed search is to find evidence of an alleged offence, an indication of how the evidence relates to the investigation).

2.7 An application for a search warrant under paragraph 12(a) of Schedule 1 to the Police and Criminal Evidence Act 1984, or under Schedule 7 to the Prevention of Terrorism (Temporary Provisions) Act 1989, shall also, where appropriate, indicate why it is believed that service of notice of an application for a production order may seriously prejudice the investigation.

2.8 If an application is refused, no further application may be made for a warrant to search those premises unless supported by additional grounds.

Notes for Guidance

2A The identity of an informant need not be disclosed when making an application, but the officer concerned should be prepared to deal with any questions the magistrate or judge may have about the accuracy of previous information provided by that source or other related matters.

2B The local police/community consultative group, where it exists, or its equivalent, should be informed as soon as practicable after a search has taken place where there is reason to believe that it might have had an adverse effect on relations between the police and the community.

3. Entry without warrant

(a) Making an arrest etc.

3.1 The conditions under which an officer may enter and search premises without a warrant are set out in section 17 of the Police and Criminal Evidence Act 1984.

(b) Search after arrest of premises in which arrest takes place or in which the arrested person was present immediately prior to arrest

3.2 The powers of an officer to search premises in which he has arrested a person or where the person was immediately before he was arrested are as set out in section 32 of the Police and Criminal Evidence Act 1984.

(c) Search after arrest of premises other than those in which arrest takes place

3.3 The specific powers of an officer to search premises occupied or controlled by a person who has been arrested for an arrestable offence are as set out in section 18 of the Police and Criminal Evidence Act 1984. They may not (unless subsection (5) of section 18 applies) be exercised unless an officer of the rank of inspector or above has given authority in writing. That authority shall (unless wholly impracticable) be given on the Notice of Powers and Rights (see paragraph 5.7(i)). The record of the search required by section 18(7) of the Act shall be made in the custody record, where there is one. In the case of enquiries linked to the investigation of terrorism, the authorising officer shall use his warrant or other identification number.

4. Search with consent

4.1 Subject to paragraph 4.4 below, if it is proposed to search premises with the consent of a person entitled to grant entry to the premises the consent must, if practicable, be given in writing on the Notice of Powers and Rights before the search takes place. The officer must make enquiries to satisfy himself that the person is in a position to give such consent. [See Notes 4A and 4B and paragraph 5.7(i)]

4.2 Before seeking consent the officer in charge of the search shall state the purpose of the proposed search and inform the person concerned that he is not obliged to consent and that anything seized may be produced in evidence. If at the time the person is not suspected of an offence, the officer shall tell him so when stating the purpose of the search.

4.3 An officer cannot enter and search premises or continue to search premises under 4.1 above if the consent has been given under duress or is withdrawn before the search is completed.

4.4   It is unnecessary to seek consent under paragraphs 4.1 and 4.2 above where in the circumstances this would cause disproportionate inconvenience to the person concerned. [Note 4C]

Notes for Guidance

4A   In the case of a lodging house or similar accommodation a search should not be made on the basis solely of the landlord's consent unless the tenant, lodger or occupier is unavailable and the matter is urgent.

4B   Where it is intended to search premises under the authority of a warrant or a power of entry and search without warrant, and the co-operation of the occupier of the premises is obtained in accordance with paragraph 5.4 below, there is no additional requirement to obtain written consent as at paragraph 4.1 above.

4C   Paragraph 4.4 is intended in particular to apply to circumstances where it is reasonable to assume that innocent occupiers would agree to, and expect that, police should take the proposed action. Examples are where a suspect has fled from the scene of a crime or to evade arrest and it is necessary quickly to check surrounding gardens and readily accessible places to see whether he is hiding; or where police have arrested someone in the night after a pursuit and it is necessary to make a brief check of gardens along the route of the pursuit to see whether stolen or incriminating articles have been discarded.

5.   Searching of premises: general considerations

(a)   Time of searches

5.1   Searches made under warrant must be made within one calendar month from the date of issue of the warrant.

5.2   Searches must be made at a reasonable hour unless this might frustrate the purpose of the search. [See Note 5A]

5.3   A warrant authorises an entry on one occasion only.

(b)   Entry other than with consent

5.4   The officer in charge shall first attempt to communicate with the occupier or any other person entitled to grant access to the premises by explaining the authority under which he seeks entry to the premises and ask the occupier to allow him to enter, unless:
   (i)   the premises to be searched are known to be unoccupied;
   (ii)   the occupier and any other person entitled to grant access are known to be absent; or
   (iii)   there are reasonable grounds for believing that to alert the occupier or any other person entitled to grant access by attempting to communicate with him would frustrate the object of the search or endanger the officers concerned or other people.

5.5   Where the premises are occupied the officer shall identify himself (by warrant or other identification number in the case of inquiries linked to the investigation of terrorism) and, if not in uniform, show his warrant card (but in so doing in the case of enquiries linked to the investigation of terrorism, the officer need not reveal his name); and state the purpose of the search and the grounds for undertaking it, before a search begins, unless sub-paragraph 5.4 (iii) applies.

5.6   Reasonable force may be used if necessary to enter premises if the officer in charge is satisfied that the premises are those specified in any warrant, or in exercise of the powers described in 3.1 to 3.3 above, and where:
   (i)   the occupier or any other person entitled to grant access has refused a request to allow entry to his premises;
   (ii)   it is impossible to communicate with the occupier or any other person entitled to grant access; or
   (iii)   any of the provisions of 5.4(i) to (iii) apply.

(c)   Notice of powers and rights

5.7   If an officer conducts a search to which this code applies he shall, unless it is impracticable to do so, provide the occupier with a copy of a notice in a standard format:

     (i)   specifying whether the search is made under warrant, or with consent, or in the exercise of the powers described in 3.1 to 3.3 above (the format of the notice shall provide for authority or consent to be indicated where appropriate – see 3.3 and 4.1 above);

     (ii)   summarising the extent of the powers of search and seizure conferred in the Act;

     (iii)   explaining the rights of the occupier, and of the owner of property seized in accordance with the provisions of 6.1 to 6.5 below, set out in the Act and in this code;

     (iv)   explaining that compensation may be payable in appropriate cases for damages caused in entering and searching premises, and giving the address to which an application for compensation should be directed; and

     (v)   stating that a copy of this code is available to be consulted at any police station.

5.8   If the occupier is present, copies of the notice mentioned above, and of the warrant (if the search is made under warrant) should if practicable be given to the occupier before the search begins, unless the officer in charge of the search reasonably believes that to do so would frustrate the object of the search or endanger the officers concerned or other people. If the occupier is not present, copies of the notice, and of the warrant where appropriate, should be left in a prominent place on the premises or appropriate part of the premises and endorsed with the name of the officer in charge of the search (except in the case of inquiries linked to the investigation of terrorism, in which case the officer's warrant or other identification number shall be given), the name of the police station to which he is attached and the date and time of the search. The warrant itself shall be endorsed to show that this has been done.

(d)   Conduct of searches

5.9   Premises may be searched only to the extent necessary to achieve the object of the search, having regard to the size and nature of whatever is sought. A search under warrant may not continue under the authority of that warrant once all the things specified in it have been found, or the officer in charge of the search is satisfied that they are not on the premises.

5.10   Searches must be conducted with due consideration for the property and privacy of the occupier of the premises searched, and with no more disturbance than necessary. Reasonable force may be used only where this is necessary because the co-operation of the occupier cannot be obtained or is insufficient for the purpose.

5.11   If the occupier wishes to ask a friend, neighbour or other person to witness the search then he must be allowed to do so, unless the officer in charge has reasonable grounds for believing that this would seriously hinder the investigation or endanger the officers concerned or other people. A search need not be unreasonably delayed for this purpose.

(e)   Leaving premises

5.12   If premises have been entered by force the officer in charge shall before leaving them, satisfy himself that they are secure either by arranging for the occupier or his agent to be present or by any other appropriate means.

(f)   Search under Schedule 1 to the Police and Criminal Evidence Act 1984

5.13   An officer of the rank of inspector or above shall take charge of and be present at any search made under a warrant issued under schedule 1 to the Police and Criminal Evidence Act 1984 or under schedule 7 to the Prevention of Terrorism (Temporary Provisions) Act 1989. He is responsible for ensuring that the search is conducted with discretion and in such a manner as to cause the least possible disruption to any business or other activities carried on in the premises.

5.14   After satisfying himself that material may not be taken from the premises without his knowledge, the officer in charge of the search shall ask for the documents or other records concerned to be produced. He may also, if he considers it to be necessary, ask to see the index to files held on the premises, if there is one; and the officers conducting the search may inspect any files which, according to the index, appear to contain any of the material sought. A more extensive search of the premises may be made only if the person responsible for them refuses to produce the material sought, or to allow access to the index; if it appears that the index is inaccurate or incomplete; or if for any other reason the officer in charge has reasonable grounds for believing that such a search is necessary in order to find the material sought. [See Note 5B]

Notes for Guidance

5A   In determining at what time to make a search, the officer in charge should have regard, among other considerations, to the time of day at which the occupier of the premises is likely to be present, and should not search at a time when he, or any other person on the premises, is likely to be asleep unless not doing so is likely to frustrate the purpose of the search.

5B   In asking for documents to be produced in accordance with paragraph 5.14 above, officers should direct the request to a person in authority and with responsibility for the documents.

5C   If the wrong premises are searched by mistake, everything possible should be done at the earliest opportunity to allay any sense of grievance. In appropriate cases assistance should be given to obtain compensation.

6.   Seizure and retention of property

(a)   Seizure

6.1   Subject to paragraph 6.2 below, an officer who is searching any premises under any statutory power or with the consent of the occupier may seize:
   (a)   anything covered by a warrant; and
   (b)   anything which he has reasonable grounds for believing is evidence of an offence or has been obtained in consequence of the commission of an offence.
Items under (b) may only be seized where this is necessary to prevent their concealment, alteration, loss, damage or destruction.

6.2   No item may be seized which is subject to legal privilege (as defined in section 10 of the Police and Criminal Evidence Act 1984).

6.3   An officer who decides that it is not appropriate to seize property because of an explanation given by the person holding it, but who has reasonable grounds for believing that it has been obtained in consequence of the commission of an offence by some person, shall inform the holder of his suspicions and shall explain that, if he disposes of the property, he may be liable to civil or criminal proceedings.

6.4   An officer may photograph or copy, or have photographed or copied, any document or other article which he has power to seize in accordance with paragraph 6.1 above.

6.5   Where an officer considers that a computer may contain information which could be used in evidence, he may require the information to be produced in a form which can be taken away and in which it is visible and legible.

(b)   Retention

6.6   Subject to paragraph 6.7 below, anything which has been seized in accordance with the above provisions may be retained only for as long as is necessary in the circumstances. It may be retained, among other purposes:
   (i)   for use as evidence at a trial for an offence;
   (ii)   for forensic examination or for other investigation in connection with an offence; or
   (iii)   where there are reasonable grounds for believing that it has been stolen or obtained by the commission of an offence, in order to establish its lawful owner.

6.7   Property shall not be retained in accordance with 6.6(i) and (ii) (i.e. for use as evidence or for the purposes of investigation) if a photograph or copy would suffice for those purposes.

(c)   Rights of owners etc.

6.8   If property is retained the person who had custody or control of it immediately prior to its seizure must on request be provided with a list or description of the property within a reasonable time.

6.9   He or his representative must be allowed supervised access to the property to examine it or have it photographed or copied, or must be provided with a photograph or copy, in either case within a reasonable time of any request and at his own expense, unless the officer in charge of an investigation has reasonable grounds for believing that this would prejudice the investigation of an offence or any criminal proceedings. In this case a record of the grounds must be made.

Note for Guidance

6A   Any person claiming property seized by the police may apply to a magistrates' court under the Police (Property) Act 1897 for its possession, and should, where appropriate, be advised of this procedure.

7.   Action to be taken after searches

7.1   Where premises have been searched in circumstances to which this code applies, other than in the circumstances covered by the exceptions to paragraph 1.3(a), the officer in charge of the search shall, on arrival at a police station, make or have made a record of the search. The record shall include:

(i)   the address of the premises searched;

(ii)   the date, time and duration of the search;

(iii)   the authority under which the search was made. Where the search was made in the exercise of a statutory power to search premises without warrant, the record shall include the power under which the search was made; and where the search was made under warrant, or with written consent, a copy of the warrant or consent shall be appended to the record or kept in a place identified in the record;

(iv)   the names of all the officers who conducted the search (except in the case of enquiries linked to the investigation of terrorism, in which case the record shall state the warrant or other identification number and duty station of each officer concerned);

(v)   the names of any people on the premises if they are known;

(vi)   either a list of any articles seized or a note of where such a list is kept and, if not covered by a warrant, the reason for their seizure;

(vii)   whether force was used, and, if so, the reason why it was used;

(viii)   details of any damage caused during the search, and the circumstances in which it was caused.

7.2   Where premises have been searched under warrant, the warrant shall be endorsed to show:

(i)   whether any articles specified in the warrant were found;

(ii)   whether any other articles were seized;

(iii)   the date and time at which it was executed;

(iv)   the names of the officers who executed it (except in the case of enquiries linked to the investigation of terrorism, in which case the warrant or other identification number and duty station of each officer concerned shall be shown);

(v)   whether a copy, together with a copy of the Notice of Powers and Rights was handed to the occupier; or whether it was endorsed as requested by paragraph 5.8, and left on the premises together with the copy notice and, if so, where.

7.3   Any warrant which has been executed or which has not been executed within one calendar month of its issue shall be returned, if it was issued by a justice of the peace, to the clerk to the justices for the petty sessions area concerned or, if issued by a judge, to the appropriate officer of the court from which he issued it.

8.   Search registers

8.1   A search register shall be maintained at each sub-divisional police station. All records which are required to be made by this code shall be made, copied, or referred to in the register.

PACE CODE C: THE DETENTION, TREATMENT AND QUESTIONING OF PERSONS BY POLICE OFFICERS

1.   General

1.1   All persons in custody must be dealt with expeditiously, and released as soon as the need for detention has ceased to apply.

1.1A   A custody officer is required to perform the functions specified in this code as soon as is practicable. A custody officer shall not be in breach of this code in the event of delay provided that the delay is justifiable and that every reasonable step is taken to prevent unnecessary delay. The custody record shall indicate where a delay has occurred and the reason why. [See Note 1H]

1.2   This code of practice must be readily available at all police stations for consultation by police officers, detained persons and members of the public.

1.3   The notes for guidance included are not provisions of this code, but are guidance to police officers and others about its application and interpretation. Provisions in the annexes to this code are provisions of this code.

1.4   If an officer has any suspicion, or is told in good faith, that a person of any age may be mentally disordered or mentally handicapped, or mentally incapable of understanding the significance of questions put to him or his replies, then that person shall be treated as a mentally disordered or mentally handicapped person for the purposes of this code. [See Note 1G]

1.5   If anyone appears to be under the age of 17 then he shall be treated as a juvenile for the purposes of this code in the absence of clear evidence to show that he is older.

1.6   If a person appears to be blind or seriously visually handicapped, deaf, unable to read, unable to speak or has difficulty orally because of a speech impediment, he should be treated as such for the purposes of this code in the absence of clear evidence to the contrary.

1.7   In this code 'the appropriate adult' means:
    (a)   in the case of a juvenile:
        (i)   his parent or guardian (or, if he is in care, the care authority or voluntary organisation. The term 'in care' is used in this code to cover all cases in which a juvenile is 'looked after' by a local authority under the terms of the Children Act 1989);
        (ii)   a social worker;
        (iii)   failing either of the above, another responsible adult aged 18 or over who is not a police officer or employed by the police.
    (b)   in the case of a person who is mentally disordered or mentally handicapped:
        (i)   a relative, guardian or other person responsible for his care or custody;
        (ii)   someone who has experience of dealing with mentally disordered or mentally handicapped people but is not a police officer or employed by the police (such as an approved social worker as defined by the Mental Health Act 1983 or a specialist social worker); or
        (iii)   failing either of the above, some other responsible adult aged 18 or over who is not a police officer or employed by the police.
[See Note 1E]

1.8   Whenever this code requires a person to be given certain information he does not have to be given it if he is incapable at the time of understanding what is said to him or is violent or likely to become violent or is in urgent need of medical attention, but he must be given it as soon as practicable.

1.9   Any reference to a custody officer in this code includes an officer who is performing the functions of a custody officer.

1.10   Subject to paragraph 1.12, this code applies to people who are in custody at police stations in England and Wales whether or not they have been arrested for an offence and to those who have been removed to a police station as a place of safety under sections 135 and 136 of the Mental Health Act 1983. Section 15 (reviews and extensions of detention) however applies solely to people in police detention, for example those who have been brought to a police station under arrest for an offence or have been arrested at a police station for an offence after attending there voluntarily.

1.11   People in police detention include anyone taken to a police station after being arrested under section 14 of the Prevention of Terrorism (Temporary Provisions) Act 1989 or under paragraph 6 of schedule 5 to that Act by an examining officer who is a constable.

1.12   This code does not apply to the following groups of people in custody:
        (i)   people who have been arrested by officers from a police force in Scotland exercising their powers of detention under section 137(2) of the Criminal Justice and Public Order Act 1994 (cross border powers of arrest etc.);
        (ii)   people arrested under section 3(5) of the Asylum and Immigration Appeals Act 1993 for the purpose of having their fingerprints taken;
        (iii)   people who have been served a notice advising them of their detention under powers contained in the Immigration Act 1971;
        (iv)   convicted or remanded prisoners held in police cells on behalf of the Prison Service under the Imprisonment (Temporary Provisions) Act 1980;

but the provisions on conditions of detention and treatment in sections 8 and 9 of this code must be considered as the minimum standards of treatment for such detainees.

Notes for Guidance

1A   Although certain sections of this code (e.g. section 9 – treatment of detained persons) apply specifically to people in custody at police stations, those there voluntarily to assist with an investigation should be treated with no less consideration (e.g. offered refreshments at appropriate times) and enjoy an absolute right to obtain legal advice or communicate with anyone outside the police station.

1B   This code does not affect the principle that all citizens have a duty to help police officers to prevent crime and discover offenders. This is a civic rather than a legal duty; but when a police officer is trying to discover whether, or by whom, an offence has been committed he is entitled to question any person from whom he thinks useful information can be obtained, subject to the restrictions imposed by this code. A person's declaration that he is unwilling to reply does not alter this entitlement.

1C   A person, including a parent or guardian, should not be an appropriate adult if he is suspected of involvement in the offence in question, is the victim, is a witness, is involved in the investigation or has received admissions prior to attending to act as the appropriate adult. If the parent of a juvenile is estranged from the juvenile, he should not be asked to act as the appropriate adult if the juvenile expressly and specifically objects to his presence.

1D   If a juvenile admits an offence to or in the presence of a social worker other than during the time that the social worker is acting as the appropriate adult for that juvenile, another social worker should be the appropriate adult in the interest of fairness.

1E   In the case of people who are mentally disordered or mentally handicapped, it may in certain circumstances be more satisfactory for all concerned if the appropriate adult is someone who has experience or training in their care rather than a relative lacking such qualifications. But if the person himself prefers a relative to a better qualified stranger or objects to a particular person as the appropriate adult, his wishes should if practicable be respected.

1EE   A person should always be given an opportunity, when an appropriate adult is called to the police station, to consult privately with a solicitor in the absence of the appropriate adult if they wish to do so.

1F   A solicitor or lay visitor who is present at the police station in that capacity may not act as the appropriate adult.

1G   The generic term 'mental disorder' is used throughout this code. 'Mental disorder' is defined in section 1(2) of the Mental Health Act 1983 as 'mental illness, arrested or incomplete development of mind, psychopathic disorder and any other disorder or disability of mind'. It should be noted that 'mental disorder' is different from 'mental handicap' although the two are dealt with similarly throughout this code. Where the custody officer has any doubt as to the mental state or capacity of a person detained an appropriate adult should be called.

1H   Paragraph 1.1A is intended to cover the kinds of delays which may occur in the processing of detained persons because, for example, a large number of suspects are brought into the police station simultaneously to be placed in custody, or interview rooms are all being used, or where there are difficulties in contacting an appropriate adult, solicitor or interpreter.

1I   It is important that the custody officer reminds the appropriate adult and the detained person of the right to legal advice and records any reasons for waiving it in accordance with section 6 of this code.

2.   Custody records

2.1   A separate custody record must be opened as soon as practicable for each person who is brought to a police station under arrest or is arrested at the police station having attended there voluntarily. All information which has to be recorded under this code must be recorded as soon as practicable in the custody record unless otherwise specified. Any audio or video recording made in the custody area is not part of the custody record.

2.2   In the case of any action requiring the authority of an officer of a specified rank, his name and rank must be noted in the custody record. The recording of names does not apply to officers dealing with people detained under the Prevention of Terrorism (Temporary Provisions) Act 1989. Instead the record shall state the warrant or other identification number and duty station of such officers.

2.3   The custody officer is responsible for the accuracy and completeness of the custody record and for ensuring that the record or a copy of the record accompanies a detained person if he is transferred to another police station. The record shall show the time of and reason for transfer and the time a person is released from detention.

2.4   A solicitor or appropriate adult must be permitted to consult the custody record of a person detained as soon as practicable after their arrival at the police station. When a person leaves police detention or is taken before a court, he or his legal representative or his appropriate adult shall be supplied on request with a copy of the custody record as soon as practicable. This entitlement lasts for 12 months after his release.

2.5   The person who has been detained, the appropriate adult, or the legal representative shall be permitted to inspect the original custody record after the person has left police detention provided they give reasonable notice of their request. A note of any such inspection shall be made in the custody record.

2.6   All entries in custody records must be timed and signed by the maker. In the case of a record entered on a computer this shall be timed and contain the operator's identification. Warrant or other identification numbers shall be used rather than names in the case of detention under the Prevention of Terrorism (Temporary Provisions) Act 1989.

2.7   The fact and time of any refusal by a person to sign a custody record when asked to do so in accordance with the provisions of this code must itself be recorded.

3.   Initial action

(a)   Detained persons: normal procedure

3.1   When a person is brought to a police station under arrest or is arrested at the police station having attended there voluntarily, the custody officer must tell him clearly of the following rights and of the fact that they are continuing rights which may be exercised at any stage during the period in custody.

(i)   the right to have someone informed of his arrest in accordance with section 5 below;

(ii)   the right to consult privately with a solicitor and the fact that independent legal advice is available free of charge; and

(iii)   the right to consult these codes of practice.

[See Note 3E]

3.2   In addition the custody officer must give the person a written notice setting out the above three rights, the right to a copy of the custody record in accordance with paragraph 2.4 above and the caution in the terms prescribed in section 10 below. The notice must also explain the arrangements for obtaining legal advice. The custody officer must also give the person an additional written notice briefly setting out his entitlements while in custody. [See Notes 3A and 3B] The custody officer shall ask the person to sign the custody record to acknowledge receipt of these notices and any refusal to sign must be recorded on the custody record.

3.3   A citizen of an independent Commonwealth country or a national of a foreign country (including the Republic of Ireland) must be informed as soon as practicable of his rights of communication with his High Commission, Embassy or Consulate. [See Section 7]

3.4   The custody officer shall note on the custody record any comment the person may make in relation to the arresting officer's account but shall not invite comment. If the custody officer authorises a person's detention he must inform him of the grounds as soon as practicable and in any case before that person is then questioned about any offence. The custody officer shall note any comment the person may make in respect of the decision to detain him but, again, shall not invite comment. The custody officer shall not put specific questions to the person regarding his involvement in any offence, nor in respect of any comments he may make in response to the arresting officer's account or the decision to place him in detention. Such an exchange is likely to constitute an interview as defined by paragraph 11.1A and would require the associated safeguards included in section 11. [See also paragraph 11.13 in respect of unsolicited comments.]

3.5   The custody officer shall ask the detained person whether at this time he would like legal advice (see paragraph 6.5). The person shall be asked to sign the custody record to confirm his decision. The custody officer is responsible for ensuring that in confirming any decision the person signs in the correct place.

3.5A   If video cameras are installed in the custody area, notices which indicate that cameras are in use shall be prominently displayed. Any request by a detained person or other person to have video cameras switched off shall be refused.

(b)   Detained persons: special groups

3.6   If the person appears to be deaf or there is doubt about his hearing or speaking ability or ability to understand English, and the custody officer cannot establish effective communication, the custody officer must as soon as practicable call an interpreter and ask him to provide the information required above. [See Section 13]

3.7   If the person is a juvenile, the custody officer must, if it is practicable, ascertain the identity of a person responsible for his welfare. That person may be his parent or guardian (or, if he is in care, the care authority or voluntary organisation) or any other person who has, for the time being, assumed responsibility for his welfare. That person must be informed as soon as practicable that the juvenile has been arrested, why he has been arrested and where he is detained. This right is in addition to the juvenile's right in section 5 of the code not to be held incommunicado. [See Note 3C]

3.8   In the case of a juvenile who is known to be subject to a supervision order, reasonable steps must also be taken to notify the person supervising him.

3.9   If the person is a juvenile, is mentally handicapped or appears to be suffering from a mental disorder, then the custody officer must, as soon as practicable, inform the appropriate adult (who in the case of a juvenile may or may not be a person responsible for his welfare, in accordance with paragraph 3.7 above) of the grounds for his detention and his whereabouts, and ask the adult to come to the police station to see the person.

3.10   It is imperative that a mentally disordered or mentally handicapped person who has been detained under section 136 of the Mental Health Act 1983 shall be assessed as soon as possible. If that assessment is to take place at the police station, an approved social worker and a registered medical practitioner shall be called to the police station as soon as possible in order to interview and examine the person. Once the person has been interviewed and examined and suitable arrangements have been made for his treatment or care, he can no longer be detained under section 136. The person should not be released until he has been seen by both the approved social worker and the registered medical practitioner.

3.11   If the appropriate adult is already at the police station, then the provisions of paragraphs 3.1 to 3.5 above must be complied with in his presence. If the appropriate adult is not at the police station when the provisions of paragraphs 3.1 to 3.5 above are complied with, then these provisions must be complied with again in the presence of the appropriate adult once that person arrives.

3.12   The person shall be advised by the custody officer that the appropriate adult (where applicable) is there to assist and advise him and that he can consult privately with the appropriate adult at any time.

3.13   If, having been informed of the right to legal advice under paragraph 3.11 above, either the appropriate adult or the person detained wishes legal advice to be taken, then the provisions of section 6 of this code apply. [See Note 3G]

3.14   If the person is blind or seriously visually handicapped or is unable to read, the custody officer should ensure that his solicitor, relative, the appropriate adult or some other person likely to take an interest in him (and not involved in the investigation) is available to help in checking any documentation. Where this code requires written consent or signification then the person who is assisting may be asked to sign instead if the detained person so wishes. [See Note 3F]

(c)   Persons attending a police station voluntarily

3.15   Any person attending a police station voluntarily for the purpose of assisting with an investigation may leave at will unless placed under arrest. If it is decided that he should not be allowed to leave then he must be informed at once that he is under arrest and brought before the custody officer, who is responsible for ensuring that he is notified of his rights in the same way as other detained persons. If he is not placed under arrest but is cautioned in accordance with section 10 below, the officer who gives the caution must at the same time inform him that he is not under arrest, that he is not obliged to remain at the police station but that if he remains at the police station he may obtain free and independent legal advice if he wishes. The officer shall point out that the right to legal advice includes the right to speak with a solicitor on the telephone and ask him if he wishes to do so.

3.16   If a person who is attending the police station voluntarily (in accordance with paragraph 3.15) asks about his entitlement to legal advice, he shall be given a copy of the notice explaining the arrangements for obtaining legal advice. [See paragraph 3.2]

(d)   Documentation

3.17   The grounds for a person's detention shall be recorded, in his presence if practicable.

3.18   Action taken under paragraphs 3.6 to 3.14 shall be recorded.

Notes for Guidance

3A   The notice of entitlements is intended to provide detained persons with brief details of their entitlements over and above the statutory rights which are set out in the notice of rights. The notice of entitlements should list the entitlements contained in this code, including visits and contact with outside parties (including special provisions for Commonwealth citizens and foreign nationals), reasonable standards of physical comfort, adequate food and drink, access to toilets and washing facilities, clothing, medical attention, and exercise where practicable. It should also mention the provisions relating to the conduct of interviews, the circumstances in which an appropriate adult should be available to assist the detained person and his statutory rights to make representation whenever the period of his detention is reviewed.

3B   In addition to the notices in English, translations should be available in Welsh, the main ethnic minority languages and the principal European languages whenever they are likely to be helpful.

3C   If the juvenile is in the care of a local authority or voluntary organisation but is living with his parents or other adults responsible for his welfare then, although there is no legal obligation on the police to inform them, they as well as the authority or organisation should normally be contacted unless suspected of involvement in the offence concerned. Even if a juvenile in care is not living with his parents, consideration should be given to informing them as well.

3D   Most local authority Social Services Departments can supply a list of interpreters who have the necessary skills and experience to interpret for the deaf at police interviews. The local Community Relations Council may be able to provide similar information in cases where the person concerned does not understand English. [See Section 13]

3E   The right to consult the codes of practice under paragraph 3.1 above does not entitle the person concerned to delay unreasonably any necessary investigative or administrative action while he does so. Procedures requiring the provision of breath, blood or urine specimens under the terms of the Road Traffic Act 1988 need not be delayed.

3F   Blind or seriously visually handicapped persons may be unwilling to sign police documents. The alternative of their representative signing on their behalf seeks to protect the interests of both police and detained people.

3G   The purpose of paragraph 3.13 is to protect the rights of a juvenile, mentally disordered or mentally handicapped person who may not understand the significance of what is being said to him. If such a person wishes to exercise the right to legal advice the appropriate action should be taken straightaway and not delayed until the appropriate adult arrives.

4.   Detained persons' property

(a)   Action

4.1   The custody officer is responsible for:
  (a)   ascertaining:

(i)   what property a detained person has with him when he comes to the police station (whether on arrest, re-detention on answering to bail, commitment to prison custody on the order or sentence of a court, lodgement at the police station with a view to his production in court from such custody, arrival at a police station on transfer from detention at another police station or from hospital or on detention under section 135 or 136 of the Mental Health Act 1983);

(ii)   what property he might have acquired for an unlawful or harmful purpose while in custody;

(b)   the safekeeping of any property which is taken from him and which remains at the police station.

To these ends the custody officer may search him or authorise his being searched to the extent that he considers necessary (provided that a search of intimate parts of the body or involving the removal of more than outer clothing may only be made in accordance with Annex A to this code). A search may only be carried out by an officer of the same sex as the person searched. [See Note 4A]

4.2   A detained person may retain clothing and personal effects at his own risk unless the custody officer considers that he may use them to cause harm to himself or others, interfere with evidence, damage property or effect an escape or they are needed as evidence. In this event the custody officer may withhold such articles as he considers necessary. If he does so he must tell the person why.

4.3   Personal effects are those items which a person may lawfully need or use or refer to while in detention but do not include cash and other items of value.

(b)   Documentation

4.4   The custody officer is responsible for recording all property brought to the police station which a detained person had with him, or had taken from him on arrest. The detained person shall be allowed to check and sign the record of property as correct. Any refusal to sign should be recorded.

4.5   If a detained person is not allowed to keep any article of clothing or personal effects the reason must be recorded.

Notes for Guidance

4A   Section 54(1) of PACE and paragraph 4.1 require a detained person to be searched where it is clear that the custody officer will have continuing duties in relation to that person or where that person's behaviour or offence makes an inventory appropriate. They do not require *every* detained person to be searched. Where, for example, it is clear that a person will only be detained for a short period and is not to be placed in a cell, the custody officer may decide not to search him. In such a case the custody record will be endorsed 'not searched', paragraph 4.4 will not apply, and the person will be invited to sign the entry. Where the person detained refuses to sign, the custody officer will be obliged to ascertain what property he has on him in accordance with paragraph 4.1.

4B   Paragraph 4.4 does not require the custody officer to record on the custody record property in the possession of the person on arrest, if by virtue of its nature, quantity or size, it is not practicable to remove it to the police station.

4C   Paragraph 4.4 above is not to be taken as requiring that items of clothing worn by the person be recorded unless withheld by the custody officer in accordance with paragraph 4.2.

5.   Right not to be held incommunicado

(a)   Action

5.1   Any person arrested and held in custody at a police station or other premises may on request have one person known to him or who is likely to take an interest in his welfare informed at public expense of his whereabouts as soon as practicable. If the person cannot be contacted the person who has made the request may choose up to two alternatives. If they too cannot be contacted the person in charge of detention or of the investigation has discretion to allow further attempts until the information has been conveyed. [See Notes 5C and 5D]

5.2   The exercise of the above right in respect of each of the persons nominated may be delayed only in accordance with Annex B to this code.

5.3   The above right may be exercised on each occasion that a person is taken to another police station.

5.4   The person may receive visits at the custody officer's discretion. [See Note 5B]

5.5   Where an enquiry as to the whereabouts of the person is made by a friend, relative or person with an interest in his welfare, this information shall be given, if he agrees and if Annex B does not apply. [See Note 5D]

5.6   Subject to the following condition, the person shall be supplied with writing materials on request and allowed to speak on the telephone for a reasonable time to one person [See Notes 5A and 5E]. Where an officer of the rank of inspector or above considers that the sending of a letter or the making of a telephone call may result in:

    (a)   any of the consequences set out in the first and second paragraphs of Annex B and the person is detained in connection with an arrestable or a serious arrestable offence, for which purpose, any reference to a serious arrestable offence in Annex B includes an arrestable offence; or

    (b)   either of the consequences set out in paragraph 8 of Annex B and the person is detained under the Prevention of Terrorism (Temporary Provisions) Act 1989;

that officer can deny or delay the exercise of either or both these privileges. However, nothing in this section permits the restriction or denial of the rights set out in paragraphs 5.1 and 6.1.

5.7   Before any letter or message is sent, or telephone call made, the person shall be informed that what he says in any letter, call or message (other than in the case of a communication to a solicitor) may be read or listened to as appropriate and may be given in evidence. A telephone call may be terminated if it is being abused. The costs can be at public expense at the discretion of the custody officer.

(b)   Documentation

5.8   A record must be kept of:
    (a)   any request made under this section and the action taken on it;
    (b)   any letters, messages or telephone calls made or received or visits received; and
    (c)   any refusal on the part of the person to have information about himself or his whereabouts given to an outside enquirer. The person must be asked to countersign the record accordingly and any refusal to sign shall be recorded.

Notes for Guidance

5A   An interpreter may make a telephone call or write a letter on a person's behalf.

5B   In the exercise of his discretion the custody officer should allow visits where possible in the light of the availability of sufficient manpower to supervise a visit and any possible hindrance to the investigation.

5C   If the person does not know of anyone to contact for advice or support or cannot contact a friend or relative, the custody officer should bear in mind any local voluntary bodies or other organisations who might be able to offer help in such cases. But if it is specifically legal advice that is wanted, then paragraph 6.1 below will apply.

5D   In some circumstances it may not be appropriate to use the telephone to disclose information under paragraphs 5.1 and 5.5 above.

5E   The telephone call at paragraph 5.6 is in addition to any communication under paragraphs 5.1 and 6.1.

6.   Right to legal advice

(a)   Action

6.1   Subject to the provisos in Annex B all people in police detention must be informed that they may at any time consult and communicate privately, whether in person, in writing or by telephone with a solicitor, and that independent legal advice is available free of charge from the duty solicitor. [See paragraph 3.1 and Note 6B and Note 6J]

6.2   [Not Used]

6.3   A poster advertising the right to have legal advice must be prominently displayed in the charging area of every police station. [See Note 6H]

6.4   No police officer shall at any time do or say anything with the intention of dissuading a person in detention from obtaining legal advice.

6.5   The exercise of the right of access to legal advice may be delayed only in accordance with Annex B to this code. Whenever legal advice is requested (and unless Annex B applies) the custody officer must act without delay to secure the provision of such advice to the person concerned. If, on being informed or reminded of the right to legal advice, the person declines to speak to a solicitor in person, the officer shall point out that the right to legal advice includes the right to speak with a solicitor on the telephone and ask him if he wishes to do so. If the person continues to waive his right to legal advice the officer shall ask him the reasons for doing so, and any reasons shall be recorded on the custody record or the interview record as appropriate. Reminders of the right to legal advice must be given in accordance with paragraphs 3.5, 11.2, 15.3, 16.4 and 16.5 of this code and paragraphs 2.15(ii) and 5.2 of Code D. Once it is clear that a person neither wishes to speak to a solicitor in person nor by telephone he should cease to be asked his reasons. [See Note 6K]

6.6   A person who wants legal advice may not be interviewed or continue to be interviewed until he has received it unless:
   (a)   Annex B applies; or
   (b)   an officer of the rank of superintendent or above has reasonable grounds for believing that:
      (i)   delay will involve an immediate risk of harm to persons or serious loss of, or damage to, property; or
      (ii)   where a solicitor, including a duty solicitor, has been contacted and has agreed to attend, awaiting his arrival would cause unreasonable delay to the process of investigation; or
   (c)   the solicitor nominated by the person, or selected by him from a list:
      (i)   cannot be contacted; or
      (ii)   has previously indicated that he does not wish to be contacted; or
      (iii)   having been contacted, has declined to attend;
and the person has been advised of the Duty Solicitor Scheme but has declined to ask for the duty solicitor, or the duty solicitor is unavailable. (In these circumstances the interview may be started or continued without further delay provided that an officer of the rank of Inspector or above has given agreement for the interview to proceed in those circumstances – See Note 6B).
   (d)   the person who wanted legal advice changes his mind.
In these circumstances the interview may be started or continued without further delay provided that the person has given his agreement in writing or on tape to being interviewed without receiving legal advice and that an officer of the rank of inspector or above, having inquired into the person's reasons for his change of mind, has given authority for the interview to proceed. Confirmation of the person's agreement, his change of mind, his reasons where given and the name of the authorising officer shall be recorded in the taped or written interview record at the beginning or re-commencement of interview. [See Note 6I]

6.7   Where 6.6(b)(i) applies, once sufficient information to avert the risk has been obtained, questioning must cease until the person has received legal advice unless 6.6(a), (b)(ii), (c) or (d) apply.

6.8   Where a person has been permitted to consult a solicitor and the solicitor is available (i.e. present at the station or on his way to the station or easily contactable by telephone) at the time the interview begins or is in progress, the solicitor must be allowed to be present while he is interviewed.

6.9   The solicitor may only be required to leave the interview if his conduct is such that the investigating officer is unable properly to put questions to the suspect. [See Notes 6D and 6E]

6.10   If the investigating officer considers that a solicitor is acting in such a way, he will stop the interview and consult an officer not below the rank of superintendent, if one is readily available, and otherwise an officer not below the rank of inspector who is not connected with the investigation. After speaking to the solicitor, the officer who has been consulted will decide whether or not the interview should continue in the presence of that solicitor. If he decides that it should not, the suspect will be given the opportunity to consult another solicitor before the interview continues and that solicitor will be given an opportunity to be present at the interview.

6.11   The removal of a solicitor from an interview is a serious step and, if it occurs, the officer of superintendent rank or above who took the decision will consider whether the incident should be reported to the Law Society. If the decision to remove the solicitor has been taken by an officer below the rank of superintendent, the facts must be reported to an officer of superintendent rank or above who will similarly consider whether a report to the Law Society would be appropriate. Where the solicitor concerned is a duty solicitor, the report should be both to the Law Society and to the Legal Aid Board.

6.12   In Codes of Practice issued under the Police and Criminal Evidence Act 1984, 'solicitor' means a solicitor who holds a current practising certificate, a trainee solicitor, a duty solicitor representative or an accredited representative included on the register of representatives maintained by the Legal Aid Board. If a solicitor wishes to send a non-accredited or probationary representative to provide advice on his behalf, then that person shall be admitted to the police station for this purpose unless an officer of the rank of inspector or above considers that such a visit will hinder the investigation of crime and directs otherwise. (Hindering the investigation of a crime does not include giving proper legal advice to a detained person in accordance with Note 6D.) Once admitted to the police station, the provisions of paragraphs 6.6 to 6.10 apply.

6.13   In exercising his discretion under paragraph 6.12, the officer should take into account in particular whether the identity and status of the non-accredited or probationary representative have been [satisfactorily] established; whether he is of suitable character to provide legal advice (a person with a criminal record is unlikely to be suitable unless the conviction was for a minor offence and is not of recent date); and any other matters in any written letter of authorisation provided by the solicitor on whose behalf the clerk or legal executive is attending the police station. [See Note 6F]

6.14   If the inspector refuses access to a non-accredited or probationary representative or a decision is taken that such a person should not be permitted to remain at an interview, he must forthwith notify a solicitor on whose behalf the non-accredited or probationary representative was to have acted or was acting, and give him an opportunity to make alternative arrangements. The detained person must also be informed and the custody record noted.

6.15   If a solicitor arrives at the station to see a particular person, that person must (unless Annex B applies) be informed of the solicitor's arrival whether or not he is being interviewed and asked whether he would like to see him. This applies even if the person concerned has already declined legal advice or having requested it, subsequently agreed to be interviewed without having received advice. The solicitor's attendance and the detained person's decision must be noted in the custody record.

(b)   Documentation

6.16   Any request for legal advice and the action taken on it shall be recorded.

6.17   If a person has asked for legal advice and an interview is begun in the absence of a solicitor or his representative (or the solicitor or his representative has been required to leave an interview), a record shall be made in the interview record.

Notes for Guidance

6A   In considering whether paragraph 6.6(b) applies, the officer should where practicable ask the solicitor for an estimate of the time that he is likely to take in coming to the station, and relate this information to the time for which detention is permitted, the time of day (i.e. whether the period of rest required by paragraph 12.2 is imminent) and the requirements of other investigations in progress. If the solicitor says that he is on his way to the station or that he will set off immediately, it will not normally be appropriate to begin an interview before he arrives. If it appears that it will be necessary to begin an interview before the solicitor's arrival he should be given an indication of how long the police would be able to wait before paragraph 6.6(b) applies so that he has an opportunity to make arrangements for legal advice to be provided by someone else.

6B   A person who asks for legal advice should be given an opportunity to consult a specific solicitor or another solicitor from that solicitor's firm or the duty solicitor. If advice is not available by these means, or he does not wish to consult the duty solicitor, the person should be given an opportunity to choose a solicitor from a list of those willing to provide legal advice. If this solicitor is unavailable, he may choose up [to] two alternatives. If these attempts to secure legal advice are unsuccessful, the custody officer has discretion to allow further attempts until a solicitor has been contacted and agrees to provide legal advice. Apart from carrying out his duties under Note 6B, a police officer must not advise the suspect about any particular firm of solicitors.

6C   [Not Used]

6D   A detained person has a right to free legal advice and to be represented by a solicitor. The solicitor's only role in the police station is to protect and advance the legal rights of his client. On occasions this may require the solicitor to give advice which has the effect of his client avoiding giving evidence which strengthens a prosecution case. The solicitor may intervene in order to seek clarification or to challenge an improper question to his client or the manner in which it is put, or to advise his client not to reply to particular questions, or if he wishes to give his client further legal advice. Paragraph 6.9 will only apply if the solicitor's approach or conduct prevents or unreasonably obstructs proper questions being put to the suspect or his response being recorded. Examples of unacceptable conduct include answering questions on a suspect's behalf or providing written replies for him to quote.

6E   In a case where an officer takes the decision to exclude a solicitor, he must be in a position to satisfy the court that the decision was properly made. In order to do this he may need to witness what is happening himself.

6F   If an officer of at least the rank of inspector considers that a particular solicitor or firm of solicitors is persistently sending non-accredited or probationary representatives who are unsuited to provide legal advice, he should inform an officer of at least the rank of superintendent, who may wish to take the matter up with the Law Society.

6G   Subject to the constraints of Annex B, a solicitor may advise more than one client in an investigation if he wishes. Any question of a conflict of interest is for the solicitor under his professional code of conduct. If, however, waiting for a solicitor to give advice to one client may lead to unreasonable delay to the interview with another, the provisions of paragraph 6.6(b) may apply.

6H   In addition to the poster in English advertising the right to legal advice, a poster or posters containing translations into Welsh, the main ethnic minority languages and the principal European languages should be displayed wherever they are likely to be helpful and it is practicable to do so.

6I   Paragraph 6.6(d) requires the authorisation of an officer of the rank of inspector or above, to the continuation of an interview, where a person who wanted legal advice changes his mind. It is permissible for such authorisation to be given over the telephone, if the authorising officer is able to satisfy himself as to the reason for the person's change of mind and is satisfied that it is proper to continue the interview in those circumstances.

6J   Where a person chooses to speak to a solicitor on the telephone, he should be allowed to do so in private unless this is impractical because of the design and layout of the custody area or the location of telephones.

6K   A person is not obliged to give reasons for declining legal advice and should not be pressed if he does not wish to do so.

7.   Citizens of Independent Commonwealth countries or foreign nationals

(a)   Action

7.1   Any citizen of an independent Commonwealth country or a national of a foreign country (including the Republic of Ireland) may communicate at any time with his High Commission, Embassy or Consulate. He must be informed of this right as soon as practicable. He must also be informed as soon as practicable of his right, upon request to have his High Commission, Embassy or Consulate told of his whereabouts and the grounds for his detention. Such a request should be acted upon as soon as practicable.

7.2   If a person is detained who is a citizen of an independent Commonwealth or foreign country with which a bilateral consular convention or agreement is in force requiring notification of arrest, the appropriate High Commission, Embassy or Consulate shall be informed as soon as practicable, subject to paragraph 7.4 below. The countries to which this applies as at 1 January 1995 are listed in Annex F.

7.3   Consular officers may visit one of their nationals who is in police detention to talk to him and, if required, to arrange for legal advice. Such visits shall take place out of the hearing of a police officer.

7.4   Notwithstanding the provisions of consular conventions, where the person is a political refugee (whether for reasons of race, nationality, political opinion or religion) or is seeking political asylum, a consular officer shall not be informed of the arrest of one of his nationals or given access or information about him except at the person's express request.

(b)   Documentation

7.5   A record shall be made when a person is informed of his rights under this section and of any communications with a High Commission, Embassy or Consulate.

Note for Guidance

7A   The exercise of the rights in this section may not be interfered with even though Annex B applies.

8.   Conditions of Detention

(a)   Action

8.1   So far as is practicable, not more than one person shall be detained in each cell.

8.2   Cells in use must be adequately heated, cleaned and ventilated. They must be adequately lit, subject to such dimming as is compatible with safety and security to allow people detained overnight to sleep. No additional restraints shall be used within a locked cell unless absolutely necessary, and then only suitable handcuffs. In the case of a mentally handicapped or mentally disordered person, particular care must be taken when deciding whether to use handcuffs. [See Annex E paragraph 13]

8.3   Blankets, mattresses, pillows and other bedding supplied shall be of a reasonable standard and in a clean and sanitary condition. [See Note 8B]

8.4   Access to toilet and washing facilities must be provided.

8.5   If it is necessary to remove a person's clothes for the purposes of investigation, for hygiene or health reasons or for cleaning, replacement clothing of a reasonable standard of comfort and cleanliness shall be provided. A person may not be interviewed unless adequate clothing has been offered to him.

8.6   At least two light meals and one main meal shall be offered in any period of 24 hours. [See Note 8C] Drinks should be provided at meal times and upon reasonable request between meal times. Whenever necessary, advice shall be sought from the police surgeon on medical or dietary matters. As far as practicable, meals provided shall offer a varied diet and meet any special dietary needs or religious beliefs that the person may have; he may also have meals supplied by his family or friends at his or their own expense. [See Note 8B]

8.7   Brief outdoor exercise shall be offered daily if practicable.

8.8   A juvenile shall not be placed in a police cell unless no other secure accommodation is available and the custody officer considers that it is not practicable to supervise him if he is not placed in a cell or the custody officer considers that a cell provides more comfortable accommodation than other secure accommodation in the police station. He may not be placed in a cell with a detained adult.

8.9   Reasonable force may be used if necessary for the following purposes:
      (i)   to secure compliance with reasonable instructions, including instructions given in pursuance of the provisions of a code of practice; or
      (ii)   to prevent escape, injury, damage to property or the destruction of evidence.

8.10   People detained shall be visited every hour, and those who are drunk, at least every half hour. A person who is drunk shall be roused and spoken to on each visit. [See Note 8A] Should the custody officer feel in any way concerned about the person's condition, for example because he fails to respond adequately when roused, then the officer shall arrange for medical treatment in accordance with paragraph 9.2 of this code.

(b) Documentation

8.11 A record must be kept of replacement clothing and meals offered.

8.12 If a juvenile is placed in a cell, the reason must be recorded.

Notes for Guidance

8A Whenever possible juveniles and other persons at risk should be visited more frequently.

8B The provisions in paragraphs 8.3 and 8.6 respectively regarding bedding and a varied diet are of particular importance in the case of a person detained under the Prevention of Terrorism (Temporary Provisions) Act 1989, immigration detainees and others who are likely to be detained for an extended period.

8C Meals should so far as practicable be offered at recognised meal times.

9. Treatment of Detained Persons

(a) General

9.1 If a complaint is made by or on behalf of a detained person about his treatment since his arrest, or it comes to the notice of any officer that he may have been treated improperly, a report must be made as soon as practicable to an officer of the rank of inspector or above who is not connected with the investigation. If the matter concerns a possible assault or the possibility of the unnecessary or unreasonable use of force then the police surgeon must also be called as soon as practicable.

(b) Medical Treatment

9.2 The custody officer must immediately call the police surgeon (or, in urgent cases, – for example, where a person does not show signs of sensibility or awareness, – must send the person to hospital or call the nearest available medical practitioner) if a person brought to a police station or already detained there:
    (a) appears to be suffering from physical illness or a mental disorder; or
    (b) is injured; or
    (c) [Not Used]
    (d) fails to respond normally to questions or conversation (other than through drunkenness alone); or
    (e) otherwise appears to need medical attention.
This applies even if the person makes no request for medical attention and whether or not he has already had medical treatment elsewhere (unless brought to the police station direct from hospital). It is not intended that the contents of this paragraph should delay the transfer of a person to a place of safety under section 136 of the Mental Health Act 1983 where that is applicable. Where an assessment under that Act is to take place at the police station, the custody officer has discretion not to call the police surgeon so long as he believes that the assessment by a registered medical practitioner can be undertaken without undue delay. [See Note 9A]

9.3 If it appears to the custody officer, or he is told, that a person brought to the police station under arrest may be suffering from an infectious disease of any significance he must take steps to isolate the person and his property until he has obtained medical directions as to where the person should be taken, whether fumigation should take place and what precautions should be taken by officers who have been or will be in contact with him.

9.4 If a detained person requests a medical examination the police surgeon must be called as soon as practicable. He may in addition be examined by a medical practitioner of his own choice at his own expense.

9.5 If a person is required to take or apply any medication in compliance with medical directions, but prescribed before the person's detention, the custody officer should consult the police surgeon prior to the use of the medication. The custody officer is responsible for the safekeeping of any medication and for ensuring that the person is given the opportunity to take or apply medication which the police surgeon has approved. However no police officer may administer medicines which are also controlled drugs subject to the Misuse of Drugs Act 1971 for this purpose. A person may administer a controlled drug to himself only under the personal supervision of the police surgeon. The requirement for personal supervision will have been satisfied if the custody officer consults the police surgeon (this may be done by telephone) and both the police surgeon and the custody officer are satisfied that, in all the circumstances, self administration of the controlled drug will not expose the detained person, police officers or anyone to the risk of harm or injury. If so satisfied, the police surgeon may authorise the custody officer to permit the detained person to administer the controlled drug. If the custody officer is in any doubt, the police surgeon should be asked to attend. Such consultation should be noted in the custody record.

9.6   If a detained person has in his possession or claims to need medication relating to a heart condition, diabetes, epilepsy or a condition of comparable potential seriousness then, even though paragraph 9.2 may not apply, the advice of the police surgeon must be obtained.

(c)   Documentation

9.7   A record must be made of any arrangements made for an examination by a police surgeon under paragraph 9.1 above and of any complaint reported under that paragraph together with any relevant remarks by the custody officer.

9.8   A record must be kept of any request for a medical examination under paragraph 9.4, of the arrangements for any examination made, and of any medical directions to the police.

9.9   Subject to the requirements of section 4 above the custody record shall include not only a record of all medication that a detained person has in his possession on arrival at the police station but also a note of any such medication he claims he needs but does not have with him.

Notes for Guidance

9A   The need to call a police surgeon need not apply to minor ailments or injuries which do not need attention. However, all such ailments or injuries must be recorded in the custody record and any doubt must be resolved in favour of calling the police surgeon.

9B   It is important to remember that a person who appears to be drunk or behaving abnormally may be suffering from illness or the effects of drugs or may have sustained injury (particularly head injury) which is not apparent, and that someone needing or addicted to certain drugs may experience harmful effects within a short time of being deprived of their supply. Police should therefore always call the police surgeon when in any doubt, and act with all due speed.

9C   If a medical practitioner does not record his clinical findings in the custody record, the record must show where they are recorded.

10.   Cautions

(a)   When a caution must be given

10.1   A person whom there are grounds to suspect of an offence must be cautioned before any questions about it (or further questions if it is his answers to previous questions which provide the grounds for suspicion) are put to him regarding his involvement or suspected involvement in that offence if his answers or his silence (i.e. failure or refusal to answer a question or to answer satisfactorily) may be given in evidence to a court in a prosecution. He therefore need not be cautioned if questions are put for other purposes, for example, solely to establish his identity or his ownership of any vehicle or to obtain information in accordance with any relevant statutory requirement (see paragraph 10.5C) or in furtherance of the proper and effective conduct of a search (for example to determine the need to search in the exercise of powers of stop and search or to seek cooperation while carrying out a search), or to seek verification of a written record in accordance with paragraph 11.13.

10.2   Whenever a person who is not under arrest is initially cautioned or is reminded that he is under caution (see paragraph 10.5) he must at the same time be told that he is not under arrest and is not obliged to remain with the officer (see paragraph 3.15).

10.3   A person must be cautioned upon arrest for an offence unless:
    (a)   it is impracticable to do so by reason of his condition or behaviour at the time; or
    (b)   he has already been cautioned immediately prior to arrest in accordance with paragraph 10.1 above.

(b) Action: general

10.4   The caution shall be in the following terms:

> 'You do not have to say anything. But it may harm your defence if you do not mention when questioned something which you later rely on in court. Anything you do say may be given in evidence.'

Minor deviations do not constitute a breach of this requirement provided that the sense of the caution is preserved. [See Note 10C]

10.5   When there is a break in questioning under caution the interviewing officer must ensure that the person being questioned is aware that he remains under caution. If there is any doubt the caution should be given again in full when the interview resumes. [See Note 10A]

Special warnings under sections 36 and 37 of the Criminal Justice and Public Order Act 1994

10.5A   When a suspect who is interviewed after arrest fails or refuses to answer certain questions, or to answer them satisfactorily, after due warning, a court or jury may draw such inferences as appear proper under sections 36 and 37 of the Criminal Justice and Public Order Act 1994. This applies when:

(a)   a suspect is arrested by a constable and there is found on his person, or in or on his clothing or footwear, or otherwise in his possession, or in the place where he was arrested, any objects, marks or substances, or marks on such objects, and the person fails or refuses to account for the objects, marks or substances found; or

(b)   an arrested person was found by a constable at a place at or about the time the offence for which he was arrested, is alleged to have been committed, and the person fails or refuses to account for his presence at that place.

10.5B   For an inference to be drawn from a suspect's failure or refusal to answer a question about one of these matters or to answer it satisfactorily, the interviewing officer must first tell him in ordinary language:

(a)   what offence he is investigating;

(b)   what fact he is asking the suspect to account for;

(c)   that he believes this fact may be due to the suspect's taking part in the commission of the offence in question;

(d)   that a court may draw a proper inference if he fails or refuses to account for the fact about which he is being questioned;

(e)   that a record is being made of the interview and that it may be given in evidence if he is brought to trial.

10.5C   Where, despite the fact that a person has been cautioned, failure to cooperate may have an effect on his immediate treatment, he should be informed of any relevant consequences and that they are not affected by the caution. Examples are when his refusal to provide his name and address when charged may render him liable to detention, or when his refusal to provide particulars and information in accordance with a statutory requirement, for example, under the Road Traffic Act 1988, may amount to an offence or may make him liable to arrest.

(c) Juveniles, the mentally disordered and the mentally handicapped

10.6   If a juvenile or a person who is mentally disordered or mentally handicapped is cautioned in the absence of the appropriate adult, the caution must be repeated in the adult's presence.

(d) Documentation

10.7   A record shall be made when a caution is given under this section, either in the officer's pocket book or in the interview record as appropriate.

Notes for Guidance

10A   In considering whether or not to caution again after a break, the officer should bear in mind that he may have to satisfy a court that the person understood that he was still under caution when the interview resumed.

10B   [Not Used]

10C   If it appears that a person does not understand what the caution means, the officer who has given it should go on to explain it in his own words.

10D   [Not Used]

11.   Interviews: general

(a)   Action

11.1A   An interview is the questioning of a person regarding his involvement or suspected involvement in a criminal offence or offences which, by virtue of paragraph 10.1 of Code C, is required to be carried out under caution. Procedures undertaken under section 7 of the Road Traffic Act 1988 do not constitute interviewing for the purpose of this code.

11.1   Following a decision to arrest a suspect he must not be interviewed about the relevant offence except at a police station or other authorised place of detention unless the consequent delay would be likely:
   (a)   to lead to interference with or harm to evidence connected with an offence or interference with or physical harm to other people; or
   (b)   to lead to the alerting of other people suspected of having committed an offence but not yet arrested for it; or
   (c)   to hinder the recovery of property obtained in consequence of the commission of an offence.
Interviewing in any of these circumstances shall cease once the relevant risk has been averted or the necessary questions have been put in order to attempt to avert that risk.

11.2   Immediately prior to the commencement or re-commencement of any interview at a police station or other authorised place of detention, the interviewing officer shall remind the suspect of his entitlement to free legal advice and that the interview can be delayed for him to obtain legal advice (unless the exceptions in paragraph 6.6 or Annex C apply). It is the responsibility of the interviewing officer to ensure that all such reminders are noted in the record of interview.

11.2A   At the beginning of an interview carried out in a police station, the interviewing officer, after cautioning the suspect, shall put to him any significant statement or silence which occurred before his arrival at the police station, and shall ask him whether he confirms or denies that earlier statement or silence and whether he wishes to add anything. A 'significant' statement or silence is one which appears capable of being used in evidence against the suspect, in particular a direct admission of guilt, or failure or refusal to answer a question or to answer it satisfactorily, which might give rise to an inference under part III of the Criminal Justice and Public Order Act 1994.

11.3   No police officer may try to obtain answers to questions or to elicit a statement by the use of oppression. Except as provided for in paragraph 10.5C, no police officer shall indicate, except in answer to a direct question, what action will be taken on the part of the police if the person being interviewed answers questions, makes a statement or refuses to do either. If the person asks the officer directly what action will be taken in the event of his answering questions, making a statement or refusing to do either, then the officer may inform the person what action the police propose to take in that event provided that action is itself proper and warranted.

11.4   As soon as a police officer who is making enquiries of any person about an offence believes that a prosecution should be brought against him and that there is sufficient evidence for it to succeed, he should ask the person if he has anything further to say. If the person indicates that he has nothing more to say the officer shall without delay cease to question him about that offence. This should not, however, be taken to prevent officers in revenue cases or acting under the confiscation provisions of the Criminal Justice Act 1988 or the Drug Trafficking [Act 1994] from inviting suspects to complete a formal question and answer record after the interview is concluded.

(b)   Interview records

11.5   (a)   An accurate record must be made of each interview with a person suspected of an offence, whether or not the interview takes place at a police station.
   (b)   The record must state the place of the interview, the time it begins and ends, the time the record is made (if different), any breaks in the interview and the names of all those present; and must be made on the forms provided for this purpose or in the officer's pocket-book or in accordance with the code of practice for the tape-recording of police interviews with suspects (Code E).
   (c)   The record must be made during the course of the interview, unless in the investigating officer's view this would not be practicable or would interfere with the conduct of the interview,

and must constitute either a verbatim record of what has been said or, failing this, an account of the interview which adequately and accurately summarises it.

11.6 The requirement to record the names of all those present at an interview does not apply to police officers interviewing people detained under the Prevention of Terrorism (Temporary Provisions) Act 1989. Instead the record shall state the warrant or other identification number and duty station of such officers.

11.7 If an interview record is not made during the course of the interview it must be made as soon as practicable after its completion.

11.8 Written interview records must be timed and signed by the maker.

11.9 If an interview record is not completed in the course of the interview the reason must be recorded in the officer's pocket book.

11.10 Unless it is impracticable the person interviewed shall be given the opportunity to read the interview record and to sign it as correct or to indicate the respects in which he considers it inaccurate. If the interview is tape-recorded the arrangements set out in Code E apply. If the person concerned cannot read or refuses to read the record or to sign it, the senior police officer present shall read it over to him and ask him whether he would like to sign it as correct (or make his mark) or to indicate the respects in which he considers it inaccurate. The police officer shall then certify on the interview record itself what has occurred. [See Note 11D]

11.11 If the appropriate adult or the person's solicitor is present during the interview, he shall also be given an opportunity to read and sign the interview record (or any written statement taken down by a police officer).

11.12 Any refusal by a person to sign an interview record when asked to do so in accordance with the provisions of the code must itself be recorded.

11.13 A written record shall also be made of any comments made by a suspected person, including unsolicited comments, which are outside the context of an interview but which might be relevant to the offence. Any such record must be timed and signed by the maker. Where practicable the person shall be given the opportunity to read that record and to sign it as correct or to indicate the respects in which he considers it inaccurate. Any refusal to sign shall be recorded. [See Note 11D]

(c) Juveniles, mentally disordered people and mentally handicapped people

11.14 A juvenile or a person who is mentally disordered or mentally handicapped, whether suspected or not, must not be interviewed or asked to provide or sign a written statement in the absence of the appropriate adult unless paragraph 11.1 or Annex C applies.

11.15 Juveniles may only be interviewed at their places of education in exceptional circumstances and then only where the principal or his nominee agrees. Every effort should be made to notify both the parent(s) or other person responsible for the juvenile's welfare and the appropriate adult (if this is a different person) that the police want to interview the juvenile and reasonable time should be allowed to enable the appropriate adult to be present at the interview. Where awaiting the appropriate adult would cause unreasonable delay and unless the interviewee is suspected of an offence against the educational establishment, the principal or his nominee can act as the appropriate adult for the purposes of the interview.

11.16 Where the appropriate adult is present at an interview, he should be informed that he is not expected to act simply as an observer; and also that the purposes of his presence are, first, to advise the person being questioned and to observe whether or not the interview is being conducted properly and fairly, and secondly, to facilitate communication with the person being interviewed.

Notes for Guidance

11A [Not Used]

11B It is important to bear in mind that, although juveniles or people who are mentally disordered or mentally handicapped are often capable of providing reliable evidence, they may, without knowing or wishing to do so, be particularly prone in certain circumstances to provide information which is unreliable, misleading or self-incriminating. Special care should therefore always be exercised in questioning such a person, and the appropriate adult should be involved, if there is any doubt about a person's age, mental state or capacity. Because of the risk of unreliable evidence it is also important to obtain corroboration of any facts admitted whenever possible.

11C   It is preferable that a juvenile is not arrested at his place of education unless this is unavoidable. Where a juvenile is arrested at his place of education, the principal or his nominee must be informed.

11D   When a suspect agrees to read records of interviews and of other comments and to sign them as correct, he should be asked to endorse the record with words such as 'I agree that this is a correct record of what was said' and add his signature. Where the suspect does not agree with the record, the officer should record the details of any disagreement and then ask the suspect to read these details and then sign them to the effect that they accurately reflect his disagreement. Any refusal to sign when asked to do so shall be recorded.

12. Interviews in police stations

(a) Action

12.1   If a police officer wishes to interview, or conduct enquiries which require the presence of a detained person, the custody officer is responsible for deciding whether to deliver him into his custody.

12.2   In any period of 24 hours a detained person must be allowed a continuous period of at least 8 hours for rest, free from questioning, travel or any interruption by police officers in connection with the investigation concerned. This period should normally be at night. The period of rest may not be interrupted or delayed, except at the request of the person, his appropriate adult or his legal representative, unless there are reasonable grounds for believing that it would:

     (i)   involve a risk of harm to persons or serious loss of, or damage to, property; or

     (ii)   delay unnecessarily the person's release from custody; or

     (iii)   otherwise prejudice the outcome of the investigation.

If a person is arrested at a police station after going there voluntarily, the period of 24 hours runs from the time of his arrest and not the time of arrival at the police station. Any action which is required to be taken in accordance with section 8 of this code, or in accordance with medical advice or at the request of the detained person, his appropriate adult or his legal representative, does not constitute an interruption to the rest period such that a fresh period must be allowed.

12.3   A detained person may not be supplied with intoxicating liquor except on medical directions. No person, who is unfit through drink or drugs to the extent that he is unable to appreciate the significance of questions put to him and his answers, may be questioned about an alleged offence in that condition except in accordance with Annex C. [See Note 12B]

12.4   As far as practicable interviews shall take place in interview rooms which must be adequately heated, lit and ventilated.

12.5   People being questioned or making statements shall not be required to stand.

12.6   Before the commencement of an interview each interviewing officer shall identify himself and any other officers present by name and rank to the person being interviewed, except in the case of persons detained under the Prevention of Terrorism (Temporary Provisions) Act 1989 when each officer shall identify himself by his warrant or other identification number and rank rather than his name.

12.7   Breaks from interviewing shall be made at recognised meal times. Short breaks for refreshment shall also be provided at intervals of approximately two hours, subject to the interviewing officer's discretion to delay a break if there are reasonable grounds for believing that it would:

     (i)   involve a risk of harm to people or serious loss of, or damage to, property;

     (ii)   delay unnecessarily the person's release from custody; or

     (iii)   otherwise prejudice the outcome of the investigation.

[See Note 12C]

12.8   If in the course of the interview a complaint is made by the person being questioned or on his behalf concerning the provisions of this code then the interviewing officer shall:

(i)   record it in the interview record; and

(ii)   inform the custody officer, who is then responsible for dealing with it in accordance with section 9 of this code.

(b)   Documentation

12.9   A record must be made of the time at which a detained person is not in the custody of the custody officer, and why; and of the reason for any refusal to deliver him out of that custody.

12.10   A record must be made of any intoxicating liquor supplied to a detained person, in accordance with paragraph 12.3 above.

12.11   Any decision to delay a break in an interview must be recorded, with grounds, in the interview record.

12.12   All written statements made at police stations under caution shall be written on the forms provided for the purpose.

12.13   All written statements made under caution shall be taken in accordance with Annex D to this code.

Notes for Guidance

12A   If the interview has been contemporaneously recorded and the record signed by the person interviewed in accordance with paragraph 11.10 above, or has been tape recorded, it is normally unnecessary to ask for a written statement. Statements under caution should normally be taken in these circumstances only at the person's express wish. An officer may, however, ask him whether or not he wants to make such a statement.

12B   The police surgeon can give advice about whether or not a person is fit to be interviewed in accordance with paragraph 12.3 above.

12C   Meal breaks should normally last at least 45 minutes and shorter breaks after two hours should last at least 15 minutes. If the interviewing officer delays a break in accordance with paragraph 12.7 of this code and prolongs the interview, a longer break should then be provided. If there is a short interview, and a subsequent short interview is contemplated, the length of the break may be reduced if there are reasonable grounds to believe that this is necessary to avoid any of the consequences in paragraph 12.7(i) to (iii).

13.   Interpreters

(a)   General

13.1   Information on obtaining the services of a suitably qualified interpreter for the deaf or for people who do not understand English is given in Note for Guidance 3D.

(b)   Foreign languages

13.2   Except in accordance with paragraph 11.1 or unless Annex C applies, a person must not be interviewed in the absence of a person capable of acting as interpreter if:
(a)   he has difficulty in understanding English;
(b)   the interviewing officer cannot himself speak the person's own language; and
(c)   the person wishes an interpreter to be present.

13.3   The interviewing officer shall ensure that the interpreter makes a note of the interview at the time in the language of the person being interviewed for use in the event of his being called to give evidence, and certifies its accuracy. He shall allow sufficient time for the interpreter to make a note of each question and answer after each has been put or given and interpreted. The person shall be given an opportunity to read it or have it read to him and sign it as correct or to indicate the respects in which he considers it inaccurate. If the interview is tape-recorded the arrangements set out in Code E apply.

13.4   In the case of a person making a statement in a language other than English:
(a)   the interpreter shall take down the statement in the language in which it is made;
(b)   the person making the statement shall be invited to sign it; and
(c)   an official English translation shall be made in due course.

(c) Deaf people and people with a speech handicap

13.5   If a person appears to be deaf or there is doubt about his hearing or speaking ability, he must not be interviewed in the absence of an interpreter unless he agrees in writing to be interviewed without one or paragraph 11.1 or Annex C applies.

13.6   An interpreter shall also be called if a juvenile is interviewed and the parent or guardian present as the appropriate adult appears to be deaf or there is doubt about his hearing or speaking ability, unless he agrees in writing that the interview should proceed without one or paragraph 11.1 or Annex C applies.

13.7   The interviewing officer shall ensure that the interpreter is given an opportunity to read the record of the interview and to certify its accuracy in the event of his being called to give evidence.

(d) Additional rules for detained persons

13.8   All reasonable attempts should be made to make clear to the detained person that interpreters will be provided at public expense.

13.9   Where paragraph 6.1 applies and the person concerned cannot communicate with the solicitor, whether because of language, hearing or speech difficulties, an interpreter must be called. The interpreter may not be a police officer when interpretation is needed for the purposes of obtaining legal advice. In all other cases a police officer may only interpret if he first obtains the detained person's (or the appropriate adult's) agreement in writing or if the interview is tape-recorded in accordance with Code E.

13.10   When a person is charged with an offence who appears to be deaf or there is doubt about his hearing or speaking ability or ability to understand English, and the custody officer cannot establish effective communication, arrangements must be made for an interpreter to explain as soon as practicable the offence concerned and any other information given by the custody officer.

(e) Documentation

13.11   Action taken to call an interpreter under this section and any agreement to be interviewed in the absence of an interpreter must be recorded.

Note for Guidance

13A   If the interpreter is needed as a prosecution witness at the person's trial, a second interpreter must act as the court interpreter.

14.   Questioning: special restrictions

14.1   If a person has been arrested by one police force on behalf of another and the lawful period of detention in respect of that offence has not yet commenced in accordance with section 41 of the Police and Criminal Evidence Act 1984 no questions may be put to him about the offence while he is in transit between the forces except in order to clarify any voluntary statement made by him.

14.2   If a person is in police detention at a hospital he may not be questioned without the agreement of a responsible doctor. [See Note 14A]

Note for Guidance

14A   If questioning takes place at a hospital under paragraph 14.2 (or on the way to or from a hospital) the period concerned counts towards the total period of detention permitted.

15.   Reviews and extensions of detention

(a) Action

15.1   The review officer is responsible under section 40 of the Police and Criminal Evidence Act 1984 (or, in terrorist cases, under Schedule 3 to the Prevention of Terrorism (Temporary Provisions) Act 1989) for determining whether or not a person's detention continues to be necessary. In reaching a decision he shall provide an opportunity to the detained person himself to make representations (unless he is unfit to do so because of his condition or behaviour) or to his solicitor or the appropriate adult if available at the time. Other people having an interest in the person's welfare may make representations at the review officer's discretion.

15.2   The same people may make representations to the officer determining whether further detention should be authorised under section 42 of the Act or under Schedule 3 to the 1989 Act. [See Note 15A]

15.2A   After hearing any representations, the review officer or officer determining whether further detention should be authorised shall note any comment the person may make if the decision is to keep him in detention. The officer shall not put specific questions to the suspect regarding his involvement in any offence, nor in respect of any comments he may make in response to the decision to keep him in detention. Such an exchange is likely to constitute an interview as defined by paragraph 11.1A and would require the associated safeguards included in section 11. [See also paragraph 11.13]

(b)   Documentation

15.3   Before conducting a review the review officer must ensure that the detained person is reminded of his entitlement to free legal advice (see paragraph 6.5). It is the responsibility of the review officer to ensure that all such reminders are noted in the custody record.

15.4   The grounds for and extent of any delay in conducting a review shall be recorded.

15.5   Any written representations shall be retained.

15.6   A record shall be made as soon as practicable of the outcome of each review and application for a warrant of further detention or its extension.

Notes for Guidance

15A   If the detained person is likely to be asleep at the latest time when a review of detention or an authorisation of continued detention may take place, the appropriate officer should bring it forward so that the detained person may make representations without being woken up.

15B   An application for a warrant of further detention or its extension should be made between 10am and 9pm, and if possible during normal court hours. It will not be practicable to arrange for a court to sit specially outside the hours of 10am to 9pm. If it appears possible that a special sitting may be needed (either at a weekend, Bank/Public Holiday or on a weekday outside normal court hours but between 10am and 9pm) then the clerk to the justices should be given notice and informed of this possibility, while the court is sitting if possible.

15C   If in the circumstances the only practicable way of conducting a review is over the telephone then this is permissible, provided that the requirements of section 40 of the Police and Criminal Evidence Act 1984 or of schedule 3 to the Prevention of Terrorism (Temporary Provisions) Act 1989 are observed. However, a review to decide whether to authorise a person's continued detention under section 42 of the 1984 Act must be done in person rather than over the telephone.

16.   Charging of detained persons

(a)   Action

16.1   When an officer considers that there is sufficient evidence to prosecute a detained person, and that there is sufficient evidence for a prosecution to succeed, and that the person has said all that he wishes to say about the offence, he shall without delay (and subject to the following qualification) bring him before the custody officer who shall then be responsible for considering whether or not he should be charged. When a person is detained in respect of more than one offence it is permissible to delay bringing him before the custody officer until the above conditions are satisfied in respect of all the offences (but see paragraph 11.4). Any resulting action should be taken in the presence of the appropriate adult if the person is a juvenile or mentally disordered or mentally handicapped.

16.2   When a detained person is charged with or informed that he may be prosecuted for an offence he shall be cautioned in the following terms:

'You do not have to say anything. But it may harm your defence if you do not mention now something which you later rely on in court. Anything you do say may be given in evidence.'

16.3   At the time a person is charged he shall be given a written notice showing particulars of the offence with which he is charged and including the name of the officer in the case (in terrorist cases, the officer's warrant or other identification number instead), his police station and the reference number for the case. So far as possible the particulars of the charge shall be stated in simple terms, but they shall also show the precise offence in law with which he is charged. The notice shall begin with the following words:

'You are charged with the offence(s) shown below. You do not have to say anything. But it may harm your defence if you do not mention now something which you later rely on in court. Anything you do say may be given in evidence.'

If the person is a juvenile or is mentally disordered or mentally handicapped the notice shall be given to the appropriate adult.

16.4   If at any time after a person has been charged with or informed that he may be prosecuted for an offence, a police officer wishes to bring to the notice of that person any written statement made by another person or the content of an interview with another person, he shall hand to that person a true copy of any such written statement or bring to his attention the content of the interview record, but shall say or do nothing to invite any reply or comment save to warn him that he does not have to say anything but that anything he does say may be given in evidence and to remind him of his right to legal advice in accordance with paragraph 6.5 above. If the person cannot read then the officer may read it to him. If the person is a juvenile or mentally disordered or mentally handicapped the copy shall also be given to, or the interview record brought to the attention of, the appropriate adult.

16.5   Questions relating to an offence may not be put to a person after he has been charged with that offence, or informed that he may be prosecuted for it, unless they are necessary for the purpose of preventing or minimising harm or loss to some other person or to the public or for clearing up an ambiguity in a previous answer or statement, or where it is in the interests of justice that the person should have put to him and have an opportunity to comment on information concerning the offence which has come to light since he was charged or informed that he might be prosecuted. Before any such questions are put to him, he shall be warned that he does not have to say anything but that anything he does say may be given in evidence and reminded of his right to legal advice in accordance with paragraph 6.5 above. [See Note 16A]

16.6   Where a juvenile is charged with an offence and the custody officer authorises his continued detention he must try to make arrangements for the juvenile to be taken into the care of a local authority to be detained pending appearance in court unless he certifies that it is impracticable to do so, or, in the case of a juvenile of at least 12 years of age, no secure accommodation is available and there is a risk to the public of serious harm from that juvenile, in accordance with section 38(6) of the Police and Criminal Evidence Act 1984, as amended by section 59 of the Criminal Justice Act 1991 and section 24 of the Criminal Justice and Public Order Act 1994. [See Note 16B]

(b)   Documentation

16.7   A record shall be made of anything a detained person says when charged.

16.8   Any questions put after charge and answers given relating to the offence shall be contemporaneously recorded in full on the forms provided and the record signed by that person or, if he refuses, by the interviewing officer and any third parties present. If the questions are tape-recorded the arrangements set out in Code E apply.

16.9   If it is not practicable to make arrangements for the transfer of a juvenile into local authority care in accordance with paragraph 16.6 above the custody officer must record the reasons and make out a certificate to be produced before the court together with the juvenile.

Notes for Guidance

16A   The service of the Notice of Intended Prosecution under sections 1 and 2 of the Road Traffic Offenders Act 1988 does not amount to informing a person that he may be prosecuted for an offence and so does not preclude further questioning in relation to that offence.

16B   Except as provided for in 16.6 above, neither a juvenile's behaviour nor the nature of the offence with which he is charged provides grounds for the custody officer to decide that it is impracticable to seek to arrange for his transfer to the care of the local authority. Similarly, the lack of secure local authority accommodation shall not make it impracticable for the custody officer to transfer him. The availability of secure accommodation is only a factor in relation to a juvenile aged 12 or over when the local authority accommodation would not be adequate to protect the public from serious harm from the juvenile. The obligation to transfer a juvenile to local authority accommodation applies as much to a juvenile charged during the daytime as it does to a juvenile to be held overnight, subject to a requirement to bring the juvenile before a court under section 46 of the Police and Criminal Evidence Act 1984.

ANNEX A
INTIMATE AND STRIP SEARCHES [SEE PARAGRAPH 4.1]

A. INTIMATE SEARCH

1.   An 'intimate search' is a search which consists of the physical examination of a person's body orifices other than the mouth.

(a)   Action

2.   Body orifices other than the mouth may be searched only if an officer of the rank of superintendent or above has reasonable grounds for believing:

(a)   that an article which could cause physical injury to the detained person or others at the police station has been concealed; or

(b)   that the person has concealed a Class A drug which he intended to supply to another or to export; and

(c)   that in either case an intimate search is the only practicable means of removing it.

The reasons why an intimate search is considered necessary shall be explained to the person before the search takes place.

3.   An intimate search may only be carried out by a registered medical practitioner or registered nurse, unless an officer of at least the rank of superintendent considers that this is not practicable and the search is to take place under sub-paragraph 2(a) above.

4.   An intimate search under sub-paragraph 2(a) above may take place only at a hospital, surgery, other medical premises or police station. A search under sub-paragraph 2(b) may take place only at a hospital, surgery or other medical premises.

5.   An intimate search at a police station of a juvenile or a mentally disordered or mentally handicapped person may take place only in the presence of an appropriate adult of the same sex (unless the person specifically requests the presence of a particular adult of the opposite sex who is readily available). In the case of a juvenile the search may take place in the absence of the appropriate adult only if the juvenile signifies in the presence of the appropriate adult that he prefers the search to be done in his absence and the appropriate adult agrees. A record shall be made of the juvenile's decision and signed by the appropriate adult.

6.   Where an intimate search under sub-paragraph 2(a) above is carried out by a police officer, the officer must be of the same sex as the person searched. Subject to paragraph 5 above, no person of the opposite sex who is not a medical practitioner or nurse shall be present, nor shall anyone whose presence is unnecessary but a minimum of two people, other than the person searched, must be present during the search. The search shall be conducted with proper regard to the sensitivity and vulnerability of the person in these circumstances.

(b)   Documentation

7.   In the case of an intimate search the custody officer shall as soon as practicable record which parts of the person's body were searched, who carried out the search, who was present, the reasons for the search and its result.

8.   If an intimate search is carried out by a police officer, the reason why it was impracticable for a suitably qualified person to conduct it must be recorded.

B. STRIP SEARCH

9.   A strip search is a search involving the removal of more than outer clothing.

(a)   Action

10.   A strip search may take place only if it is considered necessary to remove an article which a person would not be allowed to keep, and the officer reasonably considers that the person might

have concealed such an article. Strip searches shall not be routinely carried out where there is no reason to consider that articles have been concealed.

The conduct of strip searches

11.   The following procedures shall be observed when strip searches are conducted:

(a)   a police officer carrying out a strip search must be of the same sex as the person searched;

(b)   the search shall take place in an area where the person being searched cannot be seen by anyone who does not need to be present, nor by a member of the opposite sex (except an appropriate adult who has been specifically requested by the person being searched);

(c)   except in cases of urgency, where there is a risk of serious harm to the person detained or to others, whenever a strip search involves exposure of intimate parts of the body, there must be at least two people present other than the person searched, and if the search is of a juvenile or a mentally disordered or mentally handicapped person, one of the people must be the appropriate adult. Except in urgent cases as above, a search of a juvenile may take place in the absence of the appropriate adult only if the juvenile signifies in the presence of the appropriate adult that he prefers the search to be done in his absence and the appropriate adult agrees. A record shall be made of the juvenile's decision and signed by the appropriate adult. The presence of more than two people, other than an appropriate adult, shall be permitted only in the most exceptional circumstances;

(d)   the search shall be conducted with proper regard to the sensitivity and vulnerability of the person in these circumstances and every reasonable effort shall be made to secure the person's co-operation and minimise embarrassment. People who are searched should not normally be required to have all their clothes removed at the same time, for example, a man shall be allowed to put on his shirt before removing his trousers, and a woman shall be allowed to put on her blouse and upper garments before further clothing is removed;

(e)   where necessary to assist the search, the person may be required to hold his or her arms in the air or to stand with his or her legs apart and to bend forward so that a visual examination may be made of the genital and anal areas provided that no physical contact is made with any body orifice;

(f)   if, during a search, articles are found, the person shall be asked to hand them over. If articles are found within any body orifice other than the mouth, and the person refuses to hand them over, their removal would constitute an intimate search, which must be carried out in accordance with the provisions of part A of this Annex;

(g)   a strip search shall be conducted as quickly as possible, and the person searched allowed to dress as soon as the procedure is complete.

(b)   Documentation

12.   A record shall be made on the custody record of a strip search including the reason it was considered necessary to undertake it, those present and any result.

ANNEX B
DELAY IN NOTIFYING ARREST OR ALLOWING ACCESS TO LEGAL ADVICE

A.   Persons detained under the Police and Criminal Evidence Act 1984

(a)   Action

1.   The rights set out in sections 5 or 6 of the code or both may be delayed if the person is in police detention in connection with a serious arrestable offence, has not yet been charged with an offence and an officer of the rank of superintendent or above has reasonable grounds for believing that the exercise of either right:

(i)   will lead to interference with or harm to evidence connected with a serious arrestable offence or interference with or physical injury to other people; or

(ii)   will lead to the alerting of other people suspected of having committed such an offence but not yet arrested for it; or

(iii)   will hinder the recovery of property obtained as a result of such an offence. [See Note B3]

2.   These rights may also be delayed where the serious arrestable offence is either:

    (i)   a drug trafficking offence and the officer has reasonable grounds for believing that the detained person has benefited from drug trafficking, and that the recovery of the value of that person's proceeds of drug trafficking will be hindered by the exercise of either right or;

    (ii)   an offence to which part VI of the Criminal Justice Act 1988 (covering confiscation orders) applies and the officer has reasonable grounds for believing that the detained person has benefited from the offence, and that the recovery of the value of the property obtained by that person from or in connection with the offence, or if the pecuniary advantage derived by him from or in connection with it, will be hindered by the exercise of either right.

3.   Access to a solicitor may not be delayed on the grounds that he might advise the person not to answer any questions or that the solicitor was initially asked to attend the police station by someone else, provided that the person himself then wishes to see the solicitor. In the latter case the detained person must be told that the solicitor has come to the police station at another person's request, and must be asked to sign the custody record to signify whether or not he wishes to see the solicitor.

4.   These rights may be delayed only for as long as is necessary and, subject to paragraph 9 below, in no case beyond 36 hours after the relevant time as defined in section 41 of the Police and Criminal Evidence Act 1984. If the above grounds cease to apply within this time, the person must as soon as practicable be asked if he wishes to exercise either right, the custody record must be noted accordingly, and action must be taken in accordance with the relevant section of the code.

5.   A detained person must be permitted to consult a solicitor for a reasonable time before any court hearing.

(b)   Documentation

6.   The grounds for action under this Annex shall be recorded and the person informed of them as soon as practicable.

7.   Any reply given by a person under paragraphs 4 or 9 must be recorded and the person asked to endorse the record in relation to whether he wishes to receive legal advice at this point.

B.   Persons detained under the Prevention of Terrorism (Temporary Provisions) Act 1989

(a)   Action

8.   The rights set out in sections 5 or 6 of this code or both may be delayed if paragraph 1 above applies or if an officer of the rank of superintendent or above has reasonable grounds for believing that the exercise of either right:

    (a)   will lead to interference with the gathering of information about the commission, preparation or instigation of acts of terrorism; or

    (b)   by alerting any person, will make it more difficult to prevent an act of terrorism or to secure the apprehension, prosecution or conviction of any person in connection with the commission, preparation or instigation of an act of terrorism.

9.   These rights may be delayed only for as long as is necessary and in no case beyond 48 hours from the time of arrest. If the above grounds cease to apply within this time, the person must as soon as practicable be asked if he wishes to exercise either right, the custody record must be noted accordingly, and action must be taken in accordance with the relevant section of this code.

10.   Paragraphs 3 and 5 above apply.

(b)   Documentation

11.   Paragraphs 6 and 7 above apply.

Notes for Guidance

B1   Even if Annex B applies in the case of a juvenile, or a person who is mentally disordered or mentally handicapped, action to inform the appropriate adult (and the person responsible for a juvenile's welfare, if that is a different person) must nevertheless be taken in accordance with paragraph 3.7 and 3.9 of this code.

B2   In the case of Commonwealth citizens and foreign nationals see Note 7A.

B3   Police detention is defined in section 118(2) of the Police and Criminal Evidence Act 1984.

B4   The effect of paragraph 1 above is that the officer may authorise delaying access to a specific solicitor only if he has reasonable grounds to believe that that specific solicitor will, inadvertently or otherwise, pass on a message from the detained person or act in some other way which will lead to any of the three results in paragraph 1 coming about. In these circumstances the officer should offer the detained person access to a solicitor (who is not the specific solicitor referred to above) on the Duty Solicitor Scheme.

B5   The fact that the grounds for delaying notification of arrest under paragraph 1 above may be satisfied does not automatically mean that the grounds for delaying access to legal advice will also be satisfied.

ANNEX C
VULNERABLE SUSPECTS: URGENT INTERVIEWS AT
POLICE STATIONS

1.   When an interview is to take place in a police station or other authorised place of detention if, and only if, an officer of the rank of superintendent or above considers that delay will lead to the consequences set out in paragraph 11.1(a) to (c) of this Code:
    (a)   a person heavily under the influence of drink or drugs may be interviewed in that state; or
    (b)   a juvenile or a person who is mentally disordered or mentally handicapped may be interviewed in the absence of the appropriate adult; or
    (c)   a person who has difficulty in understanding English or who has a hearing disability may be interviewed in the absence of an interpreter.

2.   Questioning in these circumstances may not continue once sufficient information to avert the immediate risk has been obtained.

3.   A record shall be made of the grounds for any decision to interview a person under paragraph 1 above.

Note for Guidance

C1   The special groups referred to in this Annex are all particularly vulnerable. The provisions of the Annex, which override safeguards designed to protect them and to minimise the risk of interviews producing unreliable evidence, should be applied only in exceptional cases of need.

ANNEX D
WRITTEN STATEMENTS UNDER CAUTION [SEE PARAGRAPH 12.13]

(a)   Written by a person under caution

1.   A person shall always be invited to write down himself what he wants to say.

2.   Where the person wishes to write it himself, he shall be asked to write out and sign, before writing what he wants to say, the following:

    I make this statement of my own free will. I understand that I do not have to say anything but that it may harm my defence if I do not mention when questioned something which I later rely on in court. This statement may be given in evidence.

3.   Any person writing his own statement shall be allowed to do so without any prompting except that a police officer may indicate to him which matters are material or question any ambiguity in the statement.

(b)   Written by a police officer

4.   If a person says that he would like someone to write it for him, a police officer shall write the statement, but, before starting, he must ask him to sign, or make his mark, to the following:

    'I, ..., wish to make a statement. I want someone to write down what I say. I understand that I need not say anything but that it may harm my defence if I do not mention when questioned something which I later rely on in court. This statement may be given in evidence.'

5.   Where a police officer writes the statement, he must take down the exact words spoken by the person making it and he must not edit or paraphrase it. Any questions that are necessary (e.g. to make it more intelligible) and the answers given must be recorded contemporaneously on the statement form.

6.   When the writing of a statement by a police officer is finished the person making it shall be asked to read it and to make any corrections, alterations or additions he wishes. When he has finished reading it he shall be asked to write and sign or make his mark on the following certificate at the end of the statement:

'I have read the above statement, and I have been able to correct, alter or add anything I wish. This statement is true. I have made it of my own free will.'

7.   If the person making the statement cannot read, or refuses to read it, or to write the above mentioned certificate at the end of it or to sign it, the senior police officer present shall read it to him and ask him whether he would like to correct, alter or add anything and to put his signature or make his mark at the end. The police officer shall then certify on the statement itself what has occurred.

ANNEX E
SUMMARY OF PROVISIONS RELATING TO MENTALLY DISORDERED AND MENTALLY HANDICAPPED PEOPLE

1.   If an officer has any suspicion, or is told in good faith, that a person of any age may be mentally disordered or mentally handicapped, or mentally incapable of understanding the significance of questions put to him or his replies, then that person shall be treated as mentally disordered or mentally handicapped for the purposes of this code. [See paragraph 1.4]

2.   In the case of a person who is mentally disordered or mentally handicapped, 'the appropriate adult' means:
    (a)   a relative, guardian or some other person responsible for his care or custody;
    (b)   someone who has experience of dealing with mentally disordered or mentally handicapped people but is not a police officer or employed by the police; or
    (c)   failing either of the above, some other responsible adult aged 18 or over who is not a police officer or employed by the police.
[See paragraph 1.7(b)]

3.   If the custody officer authorises the detention of a person who is mentally handicapped or appears to be suffering from a mental disorder he must as soon as practicable inform the appropriate adult of the grounds for the person's detention and his whereabouts, and ask the adult to come to the police station to see the person. If the appropriate adult is already at the police station when information is given as required in paragraphs 3.1 to 3.5 the information must be given to the detained person in the appropriate adult's presence. If the appropriate adult is not at the police station when the provisions of 3.1 to 3.5 are complied with then these provisions must be complied with again in the presence of the appropriate adult once that person arrives. [See paragraphs 3.9 and 3.11]

4.   If the appropriate adult, having been informed of the right to legal advice, considers that legal advice should be taken, the provisions of section 6 of the code apply as if the mentally disordered or mentally handicapped person had requested access to legal advice. [See paragraph 3.13 and Note E2]

5.   If a person brought to a police station appears to be suffering from mental disorder or is incoherent other than through drunkenness alone, or if a detained person subsequently appears to be mentally disordered, the custody officer must immediately call the police surgeon or, in urgent cases, send the person to hospital or call the nearest available medical practitioner. It is not intended that these provisions should delay the transfer of a person to a place of safety under section 136 of the Mental Health Act 1983 where that is applicable. Where an assessment under that Act is to take place at the police station, the custody officer has discretion not to call the police surgeon so long as he believes that the assessment by a registered medical practitioner can be undertaken without undue delay. [See paragraph 9.2]

6.   It is imperative that a mentally disordered or mentally handicapped person who has been detained under section 136 of the Mental Health Act 1983 should be assessed as soon as possible.

If that assessment is to take place at the police station, an approved social worker and a registered medical practitioner should be called to the police station as soon as possible in order to interview and examine the person. Once the person has been interviewed and examined and suitable arrangements have been made for his treatment or care, he can no longer be detained under section 136. The person shall not be released until he has been seen by both the approved social worker and the registered medical practitioner. [See paragraph 3.10]

7.   If a mentally disordered or mentally handicapped person is cautioned in the absence of the appropriate adult, the caution must be repeated in the appropriate adult's presence. [See paragraph 10.6]

8.   A mentally disordered or mentally handicapped person must not be interviewed or asked to provide or sign a written statement in the absence of the appropriate adult unless the provisions of paragraph 11.1 or Annex C of this code apply. Questioning in these circumstances may not continue in the absence of the appropriate adult once sufficient information to avert the risk has been obtained. A record shall be made of the grounds for any decision to begin an interview in these circumstances. [See paragraphs 11.1 and 11.14 and Annex C]

9.   Where the appropriate adult is present at an interview, he should be informed that he is not expected to act simply as an observer; and also that the purposes of his presence are, first, to advise the person being interviewed and to observe whether or not the interview is being conducted properly and fairly, and, secondly to facilitate communication with the person being interviewed. [See paragraph 11.16]

10.   If the detention of a mentally disordered or mentally handicapped person is reviewed by a review officer or a superintendent, the appropriate adult must, if available at the time, be given an opportunity to make representations to the officer about the need for continuing detention. [See paragraphs 15.1 and 15.2]

11.   If the custody officer charges a mentally disordered or mentally handicapped person with an offence or takes such other action as is appropriate when there is sufficient evidence for a prosecution this must be done in the presence of the appropriate adult. The written notice embodying any charge must be given to the appropriate adult. [See paragraphs 16.1 to 16.3]

12.   An intimate or strip search of a mentally disordered or mentally handicapped person may take place only in the presence of the appropriate adult of the same sex, unless the person specifically requests the presence of a particular adult of the opposite sex. A strip search may take place in the absence of an appropriate adult only in cases of urgency where there is a risk of serious harm to the person detained or to others. [See Annex A, paragraphs 5 and 11(c)]

13.   Particular care must be taken when deciding whether to use handcuffs to restrain a mentally disordered or mentally handicapped person in a locked cell. [See paragraph 8.2]

Notes for Guidance

E1   In the case of mentally disordered or mentally handicapped people, it may in certain circumstances be more satisfactory for all concerned if the appropriate adult is someone who has experience or training in their care rather than a relative lacking such qualifications. But if the person himself prefers a relative to a better qualified stranger or objects to a particular person as the appropriate adult, his wishes should if practicable be respected. [See Note 1E]

E2   The purpose of the provision at paragraph 3.13 is to protect the rights of a mentally disordered or mentally handicapped person who does not understand the significance of what is being said to him. If the person wishes to exercise the right to legal advice, the appropriate action should be taken and not delayed until the appropriate adult arrives. [See Note 3G] A mentally disordered or mentally handicapped person should always be given an opportunity, when an appropriate adult is called to the police station, to consult privately with a solicitor in the absence of the appropriate adult if he wishes to do so. [See Note 1EE].

E3   It is important to bear in mind that although mentally disordered or mentally handicapped [people are] often capable of providing reliable evidence, they may, without knowing or wishing to do so, be particularly prone in certain circumstances to provide information which is unreliable, misleading or self-incriminating. Special care should therefore always be exercised in questioning such a person, and the appropriate adult involved, if there is any doubt about a person's mental state or capacity. Because of the risk of unreliable evidence, it is important to obtain corroboration of any facts admitted whenever possible. [See Note 11B]

E4   Because of the risks referred to in Note E3, which the presence of the appropriate adult is intended to minimise, officers of superintendent rank or above should exercise their discretion to authorise the commencement of an interview in the adult's absence only in exceptional cases, where it is necessary to avert an immediate risk of serious harm. [See paragraph 11.1 and Annex C and Note C1]

ANNEX F
COUNTRIES WITH WHICH BILATERAL CONSULAR CONVENTIONS OR AGREEMENTS REQUIRING NOTIFICATION OF THE ARREST AND DETENTION OF THEIR NATIONALS ARE IN FORCE AS AT 1 JANUARY 1995

Armenia	Kyrgyzstan
Austria	Macedonia
Azerbaijan	Mexico
Belarus	Moldova
Belgium	Mongolia
Bosnia-Hercegovina	Norway
Bulgaria	Poland
China*	Romania
Croatia	Russia
Cuba	Slovak Republic
Czech Republic	Slovenia
Denmark	Spain
Egypt	Sweden
France	Tajikistan
Georgia	Turkmenistan
German Federal Republic	Ukraine
Greece	USA
Hungary	Uzbekistan
Kazakhstan	Yugoslavia

*Police are required to inform Chinese officials of arrest/detention in the Manchester consular district only. This comprises Derbyshire, Durham, Greater Manchester, Lancashire, Merseyside, North, South and West Yorkshire, and Tyne and Wear.

PACE CODE D: THE IDENTIFICATION OF PERSONS BY POLICE OFFICERS

1.   General

1.1   This code of practice must be readily available at all police stations for consultation by police officers, detained persons and members of the public.

1.2   The notes for guidance included are not provisions of this code, but are guidance to police officers and others about its application and interpretation. Provisions in the Annexes to the code are provisions of this code.

1.3   If an officer has any suspicion, or is told in good faith, that a person of any age may be mentally disordered or mentally handicapped, or mentally incapable of understanding the significance of questions put to him or his replies, then that person shall be treated as a mentally disordered or mentally handicapped person for the purposes of this code.

1.4   If anyone appears to be under the age of 17 then he shall be treated as a juvenile for the purposes of this code in the absence of clear evidence to show that he is older.

1.5   If a person appears to be blind or seriously visually handicapped, deaf, unable to read, unable to speak or has difficulty orally because of a speech impediment, he shall be treated as such for the purposes of this code in the absence of clear evidence to the contrary.

1.6 In this code the term 'appropriate adult' has the same meaning as in paragraph 1.7 of Code C, and the term 'solicitor' has the same meaning as in paragraph 6.12 of Code C.

1.7 Any reference to a custody officer in this code includes an officer who is performing the functions of a custody officer.

1.8 Where a record is made under this code of any action requiring the authority of an officer of a specified rank, his name (except in the case of enquiries linked to the investigation of terrorism, in which case the officer's warrant or other identification number shall be given) and rank must be included in the record.

1.9 All records must be timed and signed by the maker. Warrant or other identification numbers shall be used rather than names in the case of detention under the Prevention of Terrorism (Temporary Provisions) Act 1989.

1.10 In the case of a detained person records are to be made in his custody record unless otherwise specified.

1.11 In the case of any procedure requiring a suspect's consent, the consent of a person who is mentally disordered or mentally handicapped is only valid if given in the presence of the appropriate adult; and in the case of a juvenile the consent of his parent or guardian is required as well as his own (unless he is under 14, in which case the consent of his parent or guardian is sufficient in its own right). [See Note 1E]

1.12 In the case of a person who is blind or seriously visually handicapped or unable to read, the custody officer shall ensure that his solicitor, relative, the appropriate adult or some other person likely to take an interest in him (and not involved in the investigation) is available to help in checking any documentation. Where this code requires written consent or signification, then the person who is assisting may be asked to sign instead if the detained person so wishes. [See Note 1F]

1.13 In the case of any procedure requiring information to be given to or sought from a suspect, it must be given or sought in the presence of the appropriate adult if the suspect is mentally disordered, mentally handicapped or a juvenile. If the appropriate adult is not present when the information is first given or sought, the procedure must be repeated in his presence when he arrives. If the suspect appears to be deaf or there is doubt about his hearing or speaking ability or ability to understand English, and the officer cannot establish effective communication, the information must be given or sought through an interpreter.

1.14 Any procedure in this code involving the participation of a person (whether as a suspect or a witness) who is mentally disordered, mentally handicapped or a juvenile must take place in the presence of the appropriate adult; but the adult must not be allowed to prompt any identification of a suspect by a witness.

1.15 Subject to paragraph 1.16 below, nothing in this code affects any procedure under:
    (i) Sections 4 to 11 of the Road Traffic Act 1988 or sections 15 and 16 of the Road Traffic Offenders Act 1988; or
    (ii) paragraph 18 of schedule 2 to the Immigration Act 1971; or
    (iii) the Prevention of Terrorism (Temporary Provisions) Act 1989, section 15(9), paragraph 8(5) of schedule 2, and paragraph 7(5) of schedule 5.

1.16 Notwithstanding paragraph 1.15, the provisions of section 3 below on the taking of fingerprints, and of section 5 below on the taking of body samples, do apply to people detained under section 14 of, or paragraph 6 of schedule 5 to, the Prevention of Terrorism (Temporary Provisions) Act 1989. (In the case of fingerprints, section 61 of PACE is modified by section 15(10) of, and paragraph 7(6) of schedule 5 to, the 1989 Act.) In the case of samples, sections 62 and 63 of PACE are modified by section 15(11) of and paragraph 7(6A) of Schedule 5 to the 1989 Act. The effect of both of these modifications is to allow fingerprints and samples to be taken in terrorist cases to help determine whether a person is or has been involved in terrorism, as well as where there are reasonable grounds for suspecting that person's involvement in a particular offence. There is, however, no statutory requirement (and, therefore, no requirement under paragraph 3.4 below) to destroy fingerprints or body samples taken in terrorist cases, no requirement to tell the people from whom these were taken that they will be destroyed, and no statutory requirement to offer such people an opportunity to witness the destruction of their fingerprints.

1.17   In this code, references to photographs, negatives and copies include reference to images stored or reproduced through any medium.

1.18   The code does not apply to those groups of people listed in paragraph 1.12 of Code C.

Notes for Guidance

1A   A person, including a parent or guardian, should not be the appropriate adult if he is suspected of involvement in the offence, is the victim, is a witness, is involved in the investigation or has received admissions prior to attending to act as the appropriate adult. If the parent of a juvenile is estranged from the juvenile, he should not be asked to act as the appropriate adult if the juvenile expressly and specifically objects to his presence.

1B   If a juvenile admits an offence to or in the presence of, a social worker other than during the time that the social worker is acting as the appropriate adult for that juvenile, another social worker should be the appropriate adult in the interest of fairness.

1C   In the case of people who are mentally disordered or mentally handicapped, it may in certain circumstances be more satisfactory for all concerned if the appropriate adult is someone who has experience or training in their care rather than a relative lacking such qualifications. But if the person himself prefers a relative to a better-qualified stranger, or objects to a particular person as the appropriate adult, his wishes should if practicable be respected.

1D   A solicitor or lay visitor who is present at the station in that capacity may not act as the appropriate adult.

1E   For the purposes of paragraph 1.11 above, the consent required to be given by a parent or guardian may be given, in the case of a juvenile in the care of a local authority or voluntary organisation, by that authority or organisation.

1F   Persons who are blind, seriously visually handicapped or unable to read may be unwilling to sign police documents. The alternative of their representative signing on their behalf seeks to protect the interests of both police and suspects.

1G   Further guidance about fingerprints and body samples is given in Home Office circulars.

1H   The generic term 'mental disorder' is used throughout this code. 'Mental disorder' is defined in section 1(2) of the Mental Health Act 1983 as 'mental illness, arrested or incomplete development of mind, psychopathic disorder and any other disorder or disability of mind'. It should be noted that 'mental disorder' is different from 'mental handicap' although the two are dealt with similarly throughout this code. Where the custody officer has any doubt as to the mental state or capacity of a person detained an appropriate adult should be called.

2.   Identification by witnesses

2.0   A record shall be made of the description of the suspect as first given by a potential witness. This must be done before the witness takes part in the forms of identification listed in paragraph 2.1 or Annex D of this code. The record may be made or kept in any form provided that details of the description as first given by the witness can accurately be produced from it in a written form which can be provided to the suspect or his solicitor in accordance with this code. A copy shall be provided to the suspect or his solicitor before any procedures under paragraph 2.1 of this code are carried out. [See Note 2D]

(a) Cases where the suspect is known

2.1   In a case which involves disputed identification evidence, and where the identity of the suspect is known to the police and he is available (See Note 2E), the methods of identification by witnesses which may be used are:
    (i)   a parade;
    (ii)   a group identification;
    (iii) a video film;
    (iv) a confrontation.

2.2   The arrangements for, and conduct of, these types of identification shall be the responsibility of an officer in uniform not below the rank of inspector who is not involved with the investigation ('the identification officer'). No officer involved with the investigation of the case against the suspect may take any part in these procedures.

Identification Parade

2.3 Whenever a suspect disputes an identification, an identification parade shall be held if the suspect consents unless paragraphs 2.4 or 2.7 or 2.10 apply. A parade may also be held if the officer in charge of the investigation considers that it would be useful, and the suspect consents.

2.4 A parade need not be held if the identification officer considers that, whether by reason of the unusual appearance of the suspect or for some other reason, it would not be practicable to assemble sufficient people who resembled him to make a parade fair.

2.5 Any parade must be carried out in accordance with Annex A. A video recording or colour photograph shall be taken of the parade.

2.6 If a suspect refuses or, having agreed, fails to attend an identification parade or the holding of a parade is impracticable, arrangements must if practicable be made to allow the witnesses an opportunity of seeing him in a group identification, a video identification, or a confrontation (see below).

Group Identification

2.7 A group identification takes place where the suspect is viewed by a witness amongst an informal group of people. The procedure may take place with the consent and co-operation of a suspect or covertly where a suspect has refused to co-operate with an identification parade or a group identification or has failed to attend. A group identification may also be arranged if the officer in charge of the investigation considers, whether because of fear on the part of the witness or for some other reason, that it is, in the circumstances, more satisfactory than a parade.

2.8 The suspect should be asked for his consent to a group identification and advised in accordance with paragraphs 2.15 and 2.16 of this code. However, where consent is refused the identification officer has the discretion to proceed with a group identification if it is practicable to do so.

2.9 A group identification shall be carried out in accordance with Annex E. A video recording or colour photograph shall be taken of the group identification in accordance with Annex E.

Video Film Identification

2.10 The identification officer may show a witness a video film of a suspect if the investigating officer considers, whether because of the refusal of the suspect to take part in an identification parade or group identification or other reasons, that this would in the circumstances be the most satisfactory course of action.

2.11 The suspect should be asked for his consent to a video identification and advised in accordance with paragraphs 2.15 and 2.16. However, where such consent is refused the identification officer has the discretion to proceed with a video identification if it is practicable to do so.

2.12 A video identification must be carried out in accordance with Annex B.

Confrontation

2.13 If neither a parade, a group identification nor a video identification procedure is arranged, the suspect may be confronted by the witness. Such a confrontation does not require the suspect's consent, but may not take place unless none of the other procedures are practicable.

2.14 A confrontation must be carried out in accordance with Annex C.

Notice to Suspect

2.15 Before a parade takes place or a group identification or video identification is arranged, the identification officer shall explain to the suspect:

    (i)   the purposes of the parade or group identification or video identification;

    (ii)   that he is entitled to free legal advice (see paragraph 6.5 of Code C);

    (iii)   the procedures for holding it (including his right to have a solicitor or friend present);

    (iv)   where appropriate the special arrangements for juveniles;

    (v)   where appropriate the special arrangements for mentally disordered and mentally handicapped people;

    (vi)   that he does not have to take part in a parade, or co-operate in a group identification, or with the making of a video film and, if it is proposed to hold a group identification or video identification, his entitlement to a parade if this can practically be arranged;

(vii)   if he does not consent to take part in a parade or co-operate in a group identification or with the making of a video film, his refusal may be given in evidence in any subsequent trial and police may proceed covertly without his consent or make other arrangements to test whether a witness identifies him;

(vii)a   that if he should significantly alter his appearance between the taking of any photograph at the time of his arrest or after charge and any attempt to hold an identification procedure, this may be given in evidence if the case comes to trial; and the officer may then consider other forms of identification;

(vii)b   that a video or photograph may be taken of him when he attends for any identification procedure;

(viii)   whether the witness had been shown photographs, photofit, identikit or similar pictures by the police during the investigation before the identity of the suspect became known; [See Note 2B]

(ix)   that if he changes his appearance before a parade it may not be practicable to arrange one on the day in question or subsequently and, because of his change of appearance, the identification officer may then consider alternative methods of identification;

(x)   that he or his solicitor will be provided with details of the description of the suspect as first given by any witnesses who are to attend the parade, group identification, video identification or confrontation.

2.16   This information must also be contained in a written notice which must be handed to the suspect. The identification officer shall give the suspect a reasonable opportunity to read the notice, after which he shall be asked to sign a second copy of the notice to indicate whether or not he is willing to take part in the parade or group identification or co-operate with the making of a video film. The signed copy shall be retained by the identification officer.

(b)   Cases where the identity of the suspect is not known

2.17   A police officer may take a witness to a particular neighbourhood or place to see whether he can identify the person whom he said he saw on the relevant occasion. Before doing so, where practicable a record shall be made of any description given by the witness of the suspect. Care should be taken not to direct the witness's attention to any individual.

2.18   A witness must not be shown photographs, photofit, identikit or similar pictures if the identity of the suspect is known to the police and he is available to stand on an identification parade. If the identity of the suspect is not known, the showing of such pictures to a witness must be done in accordance with Annex D. [See paragraph 2.15(viii) and Note 2E]

(c)   Documentation

2.19   The identification officer shall make a record of the parade, group identification or video identification on the forms provided.

2.20   If the identification officer considers that it is not practicable to hold a parade, he shall tell the suspect why and record the reason.

2.21   A record shall be made of a person's refusal to co-operate in a parade, group identification or video identification.

(d)   Showing films and photographs of incidents

2.21A   Nothing in this code inhibits an investigating officer from showing a video film or photographs of an incident to the public at large through the national, or local media, or to police officers, for the purposes of recognition and tracing suspects. However when such material is shown to potential witnesses (including police officers [see Note 2A] for the purpose of obtaining identification evidence, it shall be shown on an individual basis so as to avoid any possibility of collusion, and the showing shall, as far as possible, follow the principles for Video Film Identification (see paragraph 2.10) or Identification by Photographs (see paragraph 2.18) as appropriate).

2.21B   Where such a broadcast or publication is made a copy of the material released by the police to the media for the purposes of recognising or tracing the suspect shall be kept and the suspect or his solicitor should be allowed to view such material before any procedures under paragraph 2.1 of this code are carried out [see Notes 2D and 2E] provided it is practicable to do so and would not unreasonably delay the investigation. Each witness who is involved in the procedure shall be asked by the investigating officer after they have taken part whether they have seen any broadcast or published films or photographs relating to the offence and their replies shall be recorded.

Notes for Guidance

2A   Except for the provision of Annex D paragraph 1, a police officer who is a witness for the purposes of this part of the code is subject to the same principles and procedures as a civilian witness.

2B   Where a witness attending an identification parade has previously been shown photographs or photofit, identikit or similar pictures, it is the responsibility of the officer in charge of the investigation to make the identification officer aware that this is the case.

2C   [Not Used]

2D   Where it is proposed to show photographs to a witness in accordance with Annex D, it is the responsibility of the officer in charge of the investigation to confirm to the officer responsible for supervising and directing the showing that the first description of the suspect given by that witness has been recorded. If this description has not been recorded, the procedure under Annex D must be postponed. (See Annex D paragraph 1A)

2E   References in this section to a suspect being 'known' means there is sufficient information known to the police to justify the arrest of a particular person for suspected involvement in the offence. A suspect being 'available' means that he is immediately available to take part in the procedure or he will become available within a reasonably short time.

3.   Identification by fingerprints

(a)   Action

3.1   A person's fingerprints may be taken only with his consent or if paragraph 3.2 applies. If he is at a police station consent must be in writing. In either case the person must be informed of the reason before they are taken and that they will be destroyed as soon as practicable if paragraph 3.4 applies. He must be told that he may witness their destruction if he asks to do so within five days of being cleared or informed that he will not be prosecuted.

3.2   Powers to take fingerprints without consent from any person over the age of ten years are provided by sections 27 and 61 of the Police and Criminal Evidence Act 1984. These provide that fingerprints may be taken without consent:

(a)   from a person detained at a police station if an officer of at least the rank of superintendent has reasonable grounds for suspecting that the fingerprints will tend to confirm or disprove his involvement in a criminal offence and the officer authorises the fingerprints to be taken;

(b)   from a person detained at a police station who has been charged with a recordable offence or informed that he will be reported for such an offence and he has not previously had his fingerprints taken in relation to that offence;

(c)   from a person convicted of a recordable offence. Section 27 of the Police and Criminal Evidence Act 1984 provides power to require such a person to attend a police station for the purposes of having his fingerprints taken if he has not been in police detention for the offence nor had his fingerprints taken in the course of the investigation of the offence or since conviction. Reasonable force may be used if necessary to take a person's fingerprints without his consent.

3.2A   A person whose fingerprints are to be taken with or without consent shall be informed beforehand that his prints may be subject of a speculative search against other fingerprints. [See Note 3B]

3.3   [Not Used]

3.4   The fingerprints of a person and all copies of them taken in that case must be destroyed as soon as practicable if:

(a)   he is prosecuted for the offence concerned and cleared; or

(b)   he is not prosecuted (unless he admits the offence and is cautioned for it).

An opportunity of witnessing the destruction must be given to him if he wishes and if, in accordance with paragraph 3.1, he applies within five days of being cleared or informed that he will not be prosecuted.

3.5   When fingerprints are destroyed, access to relevant computer data shall be made impossible as soon as it is practicable to do so.

3.6   References to fingerprints include palm prints.

(b)   Documentation

3.7   A record must be made as soon as possible of the reason for taking a person's fingerprints without consent and of their destruction. If force is used a record shall be made of the circumstances and those present.

3.8   A record shall be made when a person has been informed under the terms of paragraph 3.2A that his fingerprints may be subject of a speculative search.

Notes for Guidance

3A   References to recordable offences in this code relate to those offences for which convictions may be recorded in national police records. (See section 27(4) of the Police and Criminal Evidence Act 1984.) The recordable offences to which this code applies at the time when the code was prepared, are any offences which carry a sentence of imprisonment on conviction (irrespective of the period, or the age of the offender or actual sentence passed) and non-imprisonable offences under section 1 of the Street Offences Act 1959 (loitering or soliciting for purposes of prostitution), section 43 of the Telecommunications Act 1984 (improper use of public telecommunications system), section 25 of the Road Traffic Act 1988 (tampering with motor vehicles), section 1 of the Malicious Communications Act 1988 (sending letters etc. with intent to cause distress or anxiety) and section 139(1) of the Criminal Justice Act 1988 (having article with a blade or point in a public place).

3B   A speculative search means that a check may be made against other fingerprints contained in records held by or on behalf of the police or held in connection with or as a result of an investigation of an offence.

4.   Photographs

(a)   Action

4.1   The photograph of a person who has been arrested may be taken at a police station only with his written consent or if paragraph 4.2 applies. In either case he must be informed of the reason for taking it and that the photograph will be destroyed if paragraph 4.4 applies. He must be told that if he should significantly alter his appearance between the taking of the photograph and any attempt to hold an identification procedure this may be given in evidence if the case comes to trial. He must be told that he may witness the destruction of the photograph or be provided with a certificate confirming its destruction if he applies within five days of being cleared or informed that he will not be prosecuted.

4.2   The photograph of a person who has been arrested may be taken without consent if:

(i)   he is arrested at the same time as other people, or at a time when it is likely that other people will be arrested, and a photograph is necessary to establish who was arrested, at what time and at what place; or

(ii)   he has been charged with, or reported for a recordable offence and has not yet been released or brought before a court [see Note 3A]; or

(iii)   he is convicted of such an offence and his photograph is not already on record as a result of (i) or (ii). There is no power of arrest to take a photograph in pursuance of this provision which applies only where the person is in custody as a result of the exercise of another power (e.g. arrest for fingerprinting under section 27 of the Police and Criminal Evidence Act 1984); or

(iv)   an officer of at least the rank of superintendent authorises it, having reasonable grounds for suspecting the involvement of the person in a criminal offence and where there is identification evidence in relation to that offence.

4.3   Force may not be used to take a photograph.

4.4   Where a person's photograph has been taken in accordance with this section, the photograph, negatives and all copies taken in that particular case must be destroyed if:

(a)   he is prosecuted for the offence and cleared unless he has a previous conviction for a recordable offence; or

(b)   he has been charged but not prosecuted (unless he admits the offence and is cautioned for it or he has a previous conviction for a recordable offence).

An opportunity of witnessing the destruction or a certificate confirming the destruction must be given to him if he so requests, provided that, in accordance with paragraph 4.1, he applies within five days of being cleared or informed that he will not be prosecuted. [See Note 4B]

(b)   Documentation

4.5   A record must be made as soon as possible of the reason for taking a person's photograph under this section without consent and of the destruction of any photographs.

Notes for Guidance

4A   The admissibility and value of identification evidence may be compromised if a potential witness in an identification procedure views any photographs of the suspect otherwise than in accordance with the provisions of this code.

4B   This paragraph is not intended to require the destruction of copies of a police gazette in cases where, for example, a remand prisoner has escaped from custody, or a person in custody is suspected of having committed offences in other force areas, and a photograph of the person concerned is circulated in a police gazette for information.

5.   Identification by body samples and impressions

(a)   Action

Intimate samples
5.1   Intimate samples may be taken from a person in police detention only:
    (i)   if an officer of the rank of superintendent or above has reasonable grounds to believe that such an impression or sample will tend to confirm or disprove the suspect's involvement in a recordable offence and gives authorisation for a sample to be taken; and
    (ii)   with the suspect's written consent.

5.1A   Where two or more non-intimate samples have been taken from a person in the course of an investigation of an offence and the samples have proved unsuitable or insufficient for a particular form of analysis and that person is not in police detention, an intimate sample may be taken from him if a police officer of at least the rank of superintendent authorises it to be taken, and the person concerned gives his written consent. [See Note 5B and Note 5E]

5.2   Before a person is asked to provide an intimate sample he must be warned that if he refuses without good cause, his refusal may harm his case if it comes to trial. [See Note 5A] If he is in police detention and not legally represented, he must also be reminded of his entitlement to have free legal advice (see paragraph 6.5 of Code C) and the reminder must be noted in the custody record. If paragraph 5.1A above applies and the person is attending a police station voluntarily, the officer shall explain the entitlement to free legal advice as provided for in accordance with paragraph 3.15 of Code C.

5.3   Except for samples of urine, intimate samples or dental impressions may be taken only by a registered medical or dental practitioner as appropriate.

Non-intimate samples
5.4   A non-intimate sample may be taken from a detained person only with his written consent or if paragraph 5.5 applies.

5.5   A non-intimate sample may be taken from a person without consent in accordance with the provisions of section 63 of the Police and Criminal Evidence Act 1984, as amended by section 55 of the Criminal Justice and Public Order Act 1994. The principal circumstances provided for are as follows:
    (i)   if an officer of the rank of superintendent or above has reasonable grounds to believe that the sample will tend to confirm or disprove the person's involvement in a recordable offence and gives authorisation for a sample to be taken; or
    (ii)   where the person has been charged with a recordable offence or informed that he will be reported for such an offence; and he has not had a non-intimate sample taken from him in the course of the investigation or if he has had a sample taken from him, it has proved unsuitable or insufficient for the same form of analysis [See Note 5B]; or

(iii)   if the person has been convicted of a recordable offence after the date on which this code comes into effect. Section 63A of the Police and Criminal Evidence Act 1984, as amended by section 56 of the Criminal Justice and Public Order Act 1994, describes the circumstances in which a constable may require a person convicted of a recordable offence to attend a police station in order that a non-intimate sample may be taken.

5.6   Where paragraph 5.5 applies, reasonable force may be used if necessary to take non-intimate samples.

(b)   Destruction

5.7   [Not Used]

5.8   Except in accordance with paragraph 5.8A below, where a sample or impression has been taken in accordance with this section it must be destroyed as soon as practicable if:
(a)   the suspect is prosecuted for the offence concerned and cleared; or
(b)   he is not prosecuted (unless he admits the offence and is cautioned for it).

5.8A   In accordance with section 64 of the Police and Criminal Evidence Act 1984 as amended by section 57 of the Criminal Justice and Public Order Act 1994 samples need not be destroyed if they were taken for the purpose of an investigation of an offence for which someone has been convicted, and from whom a sample was also taken. [See Note 5F]

(c)   Documentation

5.9   A record must be made as soon as practicable of the reasons for taking a sample or impression and of its destruction. If force is used a record shall be made of the circumstances and those present. If written consent is given to the taking of a sample or impression, the fact must be recorded in writing.

5.10   A record must be made of the giving of a warning required by paragraph 5.2 above. A record shall be made of the fact that a person has been informed under the terms of paragraph 5.11A below that samples may be subject of a speculative search.

(d)   General

5.11   The terms intimate and non-intimate samples are defined in section 65 of the Police and Criminal Evidence Act 1984, as amended by section 58 of the Criminal Justice and Public Order Act 1994, as follows:
(a)   'intimate sample' means a dental impression or a sample of blood, semen or any other tissue fluid, urine, or pubic hair, or a swab taken from a person's body orifice other than the mouth;
(b)   'non-intimate sample' means:
(i)   a sample of hair (other than pubic hair) which includes hair plucked with the root [See Note 5C];
(ii)   a sample taken from a nail or from under a nail;
(iii)   a swab taken from any part of a person's body including the mouth but not any other body orifice;
(iv)   saliva;
(v)   a footprint or similar impression of any part of a person's body other than a part of his hand.

5.11A   A person from whom an intimate or non-intimate sample is to be taken shall be informed beforehand that any sample taken may be the subject of a speculative search. [See Note 5D]

5.11B   The suspect must be informed, before an intimate or non-intimate sample is taken, of the grounds on which the relevant authority has been given, including where appropriate the nature of the suspected offence.

5.12   Where clothing needs to be removed in circumstances likely to cause embarrassment to the person, no person of the opposite sex who is not a medical practitioner or nurse shall be present, (unless in the case of a juvenile or a mentally disordered or mentally handicapped person, that person specifically requests the presence of an appropriate adult of the opposite sex who is readily available) nor shall anyone whose presence is unnecessary. However, in the case of a juvenile this is subject to the overriding proviso that such a removal of clothing may take place in the absence of the appropriate adult only if the person signifies in the presence of the appropriate adult that he prefers the search to be done in his absence and the appropriate adult agrees.

Notes for Guidance

5A   In warning a person who is asked to provide an intimate sample in accordance with paragraph 5.2, the following form of words may be used:

> 'You do not have to [provide this sample] [allow this swab or impression to be taken], but I must warn you that if you refuse without good cause, your refusal may harm your case if it comes to trial.'

5B   An insufficient sample is one which is not sufficient either in quantity or quality for the purpose of enabling information to be provided for the purpose of a particular form of analysis such as DNA analysis. An unsuitable sample is one which, by its nature, is not suitable for a particular form of analysis.

5C   Where hair samples are taken for the purpose of DNA analysis (rather than for other purposes such as making a visual match) the suspect should be permitted a reasonable choice as to what part of the body he wishes the hairs to be taken from. When hairs are plucked they should be plucked individually unless the suspect prefers otherwise and no more should be plucked than the person taking them reasonably considers necessary for a sufficient sample.

5D   A speculative search means that a check may be made against other samples and information derived from other samples contained in records or held by or on behalf of the police or held in connection with or as a result of an investigation of an offence.

5E   Nothing in paragraph 5.1A prevents intimate samples being taken for elimination purposes with the consent of the person concerned but the provisions of paragraph 1.11, relating to the role of the appropriate adult, should be applied.

5F   The provisions for the retention of samples in 5.8A allow for all samples in a case to be available for any subsequent miscarriage of justice investigation. But such samples – and the information derived from them – may not be used in the investigation of any offence or in evidence against the person who would otherwise be entitled to their destruction.

ANNEX A
IDENTIFICATION PARADES

(a)   General

1.   A suspect must be given a reasonable opportunity to have a solicitor or friend present, and the identification officer shall ask him to indicate on a second copy of the notice whether or not he so wishes.

2.   A parade may take place either in a normal room or in one equipped with a screen permitting witnesses to see members of the parade without being seen. The procedures for the composition and conduct of the parade are the same in both cases, subject to paragraph 7 below (except that a parade involving a screen may take place only when the suspect's solicitor, friend or appropriate adult is present or the parade is recorded on video).

2A   Before the parade takes place the suspect or his solicitor shall be provided with details of the first description of the suspect by any witnesses who are to attend the parade. The suspect or his solicitor should also be allowed to view any material released to the media by the police for the purpose of recognising or tracing the suspect, provided it is practicable to do so and would not unreasonably delay the investigation.

(b)   Parades involving prison inmates

3.   If an inmate is required for identification, and there are no security problems about his leaving the establishment, he may be asked to participate in a parade or video identification.

4.   A parade may be held in a Prison Department establishment, but shall be conducted as far as practicable under normal parade rules. Members of the public shall make up the parade unless there are serious security or control objections to their admission to the establishment. In such cases, or if a group or video identification is arranged within the establishment, other inmates may participate. If an inmate is the suspect, he shall not be required to wear prison uniform for the parade unless the other people taking part are other inmates in uniform or are members of the public who are prepared to wear prison uniform for the occasion.

(c)   Conduct of the parade

5.   Immediately before the parade, the identification officer must remind the suspect of the procedures governing its conduct and caution him in the terms of paragraph 10.4 of Code C.

6.   All unauthorised people must be excluded from the place where the parade is held.

7.   Once the parade has been formed, everything afterwards in respect of it shall take place in the presence and hearing of the suspect and of any interpreter, solicitor, friend or appropriate adult who is present (unless the parade involves a screen, in which case everything said to or by any witness at the place where the parade is held must be said in the hearing and presence of the suspect's solicitor, friend or appropriate adult or be recorded on video).

8.   The parade shall consist of at least eight people (in addition to the suspect) who so far as possible resemble the suspect in age, height, general appearance and position in life. One suspect only shall be included in a parade unless there are two suspects of roughly similar appearance in which case they may be paraded together with at least twelve other people. In no circumstances shall more than two suspects be included in one parade and where there are separate parades they shall be made up of different people.

9.   Where all members of a similar group are possible suspects, separate parades shall be held for each member of the group unless there are two suspects of similar appearance when they may appear on the same parade with at least twelve other members of the group who are not suspects. Where police officers in uniform form an identification parade, any numerals or other identifying badges shall be concealed.

10.   When the suspect is brought to the place where the parade is to be held, he shall be asked by the identification officer whether he has any objection to the arrangements for the parade or to any of the other participants in it. The suspect may obtain advice from his solicitor or friend, if present, before the parade proceeds. Where practicable, steps shall be taken to remove the grounds for objection. Where it is not practicable to do so, the officer shall explain to the suspect why his objections cannot be met.

11.   The suspect may select his own position in the line. Where there is more than one witness, the identification officer must tell the suspect, after each witness has left the room, that he can if he wishes change position in the line. Each position in the line must be clearly numbered, whether by means of a numeral laid on the floor in front of each parade member or by other means.

12.   The identification officer is responsible for ensuring that, before they attend the parade, witnesses are not able to:
    (i)   communicate with each other about the case or overhear a witness who has already seen the parade;
    (ii)   see any member of the parade;
    (iii) on that occasion see or be reminded of any photograph or description of the suspect or be given any other indication of his identity; or
    (iv) on that occasion, see the suspect either before or after the parade.

13.   The officer conducting a witness to a parade must not discuss with him the composition of the parade, and in particular he must not disclose whether a previous witness has made any identification.

14.   Witnesses shall be brought in one at a time. Immediately before the witness inspects the parade, the identification officer shall tell him that the person he saw may or may not be on the parade and if he cannot make a positive identification he should say so but that he should not make a decision before looking at each member of the parade at least twice. The officer shall then ask him to look at each member of the parade at least twice, taking as much care and time as he wishes. When the officer is satisfied that the witness has properly looked at each member of the parade, he shall ask him whether the person he himself saw on an earlier relevant occasion is on the parade.

15.   The witness should make an identification by indicating the number of the person concerned.

16.   If the witness makes an identification after the parade has ended the suspect and, if present, his solicitor, interpreter or friend shall be informed. Where this occurs, consideration should be given to allowing the witness a second opportunity to identify the suspect.

17. If a witness wishes to hear any parade member speak, adopt any specified posture or see him move, the identification officer shall first ask whether he can identify any persons on the parade on the basis of appearance only. When the request is to hear members of the parade speak, the witness shall be reminded that the participants in the parade have been chosen on the basis of physical appearance only. Members of the parade may then be asked to comply with the witness's request to hear them speak, to see them move or to adopt any specified posture.

17A. Where video films or photographs have been released to the media by the police for the purpose of recognising or tracing the suspect, the investigating officer shall ask each witness after the parade whether he has seen any broadcast or published films or photographs relating to the offence and shall record his reply.

18. When the last witness has left, the identification officer shall ask the suspect whether he wishes to make any comments on the conduct of the parade.

(d) Documentation

19. A colour photograph or a video film of the parade shall be taken. A copy of the photograph or video film shall be supplied on request to the suspect or his solicitor within a reasonable time.

20. The photograph or video film taken in accordance with paragraph 19 and held by the police shall be destroyed or wiped clean at the conclusion of the proceedings unless the person concerned is convicted or admits the offence and is cautioned for it.

21. If the identification officer asks any person to leave a parade because he is interfering with its conduct the circumstances shall be recorded.

22. A record must be made of all those present at a parade whose names are known to the police.

23. If prison inmates make up a parade the circumstances must be recorded.

24. A record of the conduct of any parade must be made on the forms provided.

ANNEX B
VIDEO IDENTIFICATION

(a) General

1. Where a video parade is to be arranged the following procedures must be followed.

2. Arranging, supervising and directing the making and showing of a video film to be used in a video identification must be the responsibility of an identification officer or identification officers who have no direct involvement with the relevant case.

3. The film must include the suspect and at least eight other people who so far as possible resemble the suspect in age, height, general appearance and position in life. Only one suspect shall appear on any film unless there are two suspects of roughly similar appearance in which case they may be shown together with at least twelve other people.

4. The suspect and other people shall as far as possible be filmed in the same positions or carrying out the same activity and under identical conditions.

5. Provisions must be made for each person filmed to be identified by number.

6. If police officers are filmed, any numerals or other identifying badges must be concealed. If a prison inmate is filmed either as a suspect or not, then either all or none of the people filmed should be in prison uniform.

7. The suspect and his solicitor, friend, or appropriate adult must be given a reasonable opportunity to see the complete film before it is shown to witnesses. If he has a reasonable objection to the video film or any of its participants, steps shall, if practicable be taken to remove the grounds for objection. If this is not practicable the identification officer shall explain to the suspect and/or his representative why his objections cannot be met and record both the objection and the reason on the forms provided.

8. The suspect's solicitor, or where one is not instructed the suspect himself, where practicable shall be given reasonable notification of the time and place that it is intended to conduct the video identification in order that a representative may attend on behalf of the suspect. The suspect himself may not be present when the film is shown to the witness(es). In the absence of a person representing the suspect the viewing itself shall be recorded on video. No unauthorised people may be present.

8A. Before the video identification takes place the suspect or his solicitor shall be provided with details of the first description of the suspect by any witnesses who are to attend the parade. The suspect or his solicitor should also be allowed to view any material released to the media by the police for the purpose of recognising or tracing the suspect, provided it is practicable to do so and would not unreasonably delay the investigation.

(b) Conducting the Video Identification

9. The identification officer is responsible for ensuring that, before they see the film, witnesses are not able to communicate with each other about the case or overhear a witness who has seen the film. He must not discuss with the witness the composition of the film and must not disclose whether a previous witness has made any identification.

10. Only one witness may see the film at a time. Immediately before the video identification takes place the identification officer shall tell the witness that the person he saw may or may not be on the video film. The witness should be advised that at any point he may ask to see a particular part of the tape again or to have a particular picture frozen for him to study. Furthermore, it should be pointed out that there is no limit on how many times he can view the whole tape or any part of it. However, he should be asked to refrain from making a positive identification or saying that he cannot make a positive identification until he has seen the entire film at least twice.

11. Once the witness has seen the whole film at least twice and has indicated that he does not want to view it or any part of it again, the identification officer shall ask the witness to say whether the individual he saw in person on an earlier occasion has been shown on the film and, if so, to identify him by number. The identification officer will then show the film of the person identified again to confirm the identification with the witness.

12. The identification officer must take care not to direct the witness's attention to any one individual on the video film, or give any other indication of the suspect's identity. Where a witness has previously made an identification by photographs, or a photofit, identikit or similar picture has been made, the witness must not be reminded of such a photograph or picture once a suspect is available for identification by other means in accordance with this code. Neither must he be reminded of any description of the suspect.

12A Where video films or photographs have been released to the media by the police for the purpose of recognising or tracing the suspect, the investigating officer shall ask each witness after the parade whether he has seen any broadcast or published films or photographs relating to the offence and shall record his reply.

(c) Tape Security and Destruction

13. It shall be the responsibility of the identification officer to ensure that all relevant tapes are kept securely and their movements accounted for. In particular, no officer involved in the investigation against the suspect shall be permitted to view the video film prior to it being shown to any witness.

14. Where a video film has been made in accordance with this section all copies of it held by the police must be destroyed if the suspect:
    (a) is prosecuted for the offence and cleared; or
    (b) is not prosecuted (unless he admits the offence and is cautioned for it).
An opportunity of witnessing the destruction must be given to him if he so requests within five days of being cleared or informed that he will not be prosecuted.

(d) Documentation

15. A record must be made of all those participating in or seeing the video whose names are known to the police.

16. A record of the conduct of the video identification must be made on the forms provided.

ANNEX C
CONFRONTATION BY A WITNESS

1.   The identification officer is responsible for the conduct of any confrontation of a suspect by a witness.

2.   Before the confrontation takes place, the identification officer must tell the witness that the person he saw may or may not be the person he is to confront and that if he cannot make a positive identification he should say so.

2A   Before the confrontation takes place, the suspect or his solicitor shall be provided with details of the first description of the suspect given by any witness who is to attend the confrontation. The suspect or his solicitor should also be allowed to view any material released by the police to the media for the purposes of recognising or tracing the suspect provided that it is practicable to do so and would not unreasonably delay the investigation.

3.   The suspect shall be confronted independently by each witness, who shall be asked 'Is this the person?' Confrontation must take place in the presence of the suspect's solicitor, interpreter or friend, unless this would cause unreasonable delay.

4.   The confrontation should normally take place in the police station, either in a normal room or in one equipped with a screen permitting a witness to see the suspect without being seen. In both cases the procedures are the same except that a room equipped with a screen may be used only when the suspect's solicitor, friend or appropriate adult is present or the confrontation is recorded on video.

5.   Where video films or photographs have been released to the media by the police for the purposes of recognising or tracing the suspect, the investigating officer shall ask each witness after the procedure whether he has seen any broadcast or published films or photographs relating to the offence and shall record his reply.

ANNEX D
SHOWING OF PHOTOGRAPHS

(a)   Action

1.   An officer of the rank of sergeant or above shall be responsible for supervising and directing the showing of photographs. The actual showing may be done by a constable or a civilian police employee.

1A   The officer must confirm that the first description of the suspect given by the witness has been recorded before the witness is shown the photographs. If he is unable to confirm that the description has been recorded, he shall postpone the showing.

2.   Only one witness shall be shown photographs at any one time. He shall be given as much privacy as practicable and shall not be allowed to communicate with any other witness in the case.

3.   The witness shall be shown not less than twelve photographs at a time, which shall, as far as possible, all be of a similar type.

4.   When the witness is shown the photographs, he shall be told that the photograph of the person he saw may or may not be amongst them. He shall not be prompted or guided in any way but shall be left to make any selection without help.

5.   If a witness makes a positive identification from photographs, then, unless the person identified is otherwise eliminated from enquiries, other witnesses shall not be shown photographs. But both they and the witness who has made the identification shall be asked to attend an identification parade or group or video identification if practicable unless there is no dispute about the identification of the suspect.

6.   Where the use of a photofit, identikit or similar picture has led to there being a suspect available who can be asked to appear on a parade, or participate in a group or video group identification, the picture shall not be shown to other potential witnesses.

7.   Where a witness attending an identification parade has previously been shown photographs or photofit, identikit or similar pictures (and it is the responsibility of the officer in charge of the

investigation to make the identification officer aware that this is the case) then the suspect and his solicitor must be informed of this fact before the identity parade takes place.

8.   None of the photographs used shall be destroyed, whether or not an identification is made, since they may be required for production in court. The photographs shall be numbered and a separate photograph taken of the frame or part of the album from which the witness made an identification as an aid to reconstituting it.

(b)   Documentation

9.   Whether or not an identification is made, a record shall be kept of the showing of photographs and of any comment made by the witness.

ANNEX E
GROUP IDENTIFICATION

(a)   General

1.   The purpose of the provisions of this Annex is to ensure that as far as possible, group identifications follow the principles and procedures for identification parades so that the conditions are fair to the suspect in the way they test the witness's ability to make an identification.

2.   Group identifications may take place either with the suspect's consent and co-operation or covertly without his consent.

3.   The location of the group identification is a matter for the identification officer, although he may take into account any representations made by the suspect, appropriate adult, his solicitor or friend. The place where the group identification is held should be one where other people are either passing by, or waiting around informally, in groups such that the suspect is able to join them and be capable of being seen by the witness at the same time as others in the group. Examples include people leaving an escalator, pedestrians walking through a shopping centre, passengers on railway and bus stations waiting in queues or groups or where people are standing or sitting in groups in other public places.

4.   If the group identification is to be held covertly, the choice of locations will be limited by the places where the suspect can be found and the number of other people present at that time. In these cases, suitable locations might be along regular routes travelled by the suspect, including buses or trains, or public places he frequents.

5.   Although the number, age, sex, race and general description and style of clothing of other people present at the location cannot be controlled by the identification officer, in selecting the location he must consider the general appearance and number of people likely to be present. In particular, he must reasonably expect that over the period the witness observes the group, he will be able to see, from time to time, a number of others (in addition to the suspect) whose appearance is broadly similar to that of the suspect.

6.   A group identification need not be held if the identification officer believes that because of the unusual appearance of the suspect, none of the locations which it would be practicable to use satisfy the requirements of paragraph 5 necessary to make the identification fair.

7.   Immediately after a group identification procedure has taken place (with or without the suspect's consent), a colour photograph or a video should be taken of the general scene, where this is practicable, so as to give a general impression of the scene and the number of people present. Alternatively, if it is practicable, the group identification may be video recorded.

8.   If it is not practicable to take the photograph or video film in accordance with paragraph 7, a photograph or film of the scene should be taken later at a time determined by the identification officer, if he considers that it is practicable to do so.

9.   An identification carried out in accordance with this code remains a group identification notwithstanding that at the time of being seen by the witness the suspect was on his own rather than in a group.

10.   The identification officer need not be in uniform when conducting a group identification.

11.   Before the group identification takes place the suspect or his solicitor should be provided with details of the first description of the suspect by any witnesses who are to attend the

identification. The suspect or his solicitor should also be allowed to view any material released by the police to the media for the purposes of recognising or tracing the suspect provided that it is practicable to do so and would not unreasonably delay the investigation.

12.   Where video films or photographs have been released to the media by the police for the purposes of recognising or tracing the suspect, the investigating officer shall ask each witness after the procedure whether he has seen any broadcast or published films or photographs relating to the offence and shall record his reply.

(b)   Identification with the consent of the suspect

13.   A suspect must be given a reasonable opportunity to have a solicitor or friend present. The identification officer shall ask him to indicate on a second copy of the notice whether or not he so wishes.

14.   The witness, identification officer and suspect's solicitor, appropriate adult, friend or any interpreter for the witness, if present may be concealed from the sight of the persons in the group which they are observing if the identification officer considers that this facilitates the conduct of the identification.

15.   The officer conducting a witness to a group identification must not discuss with the witness the forthcoming group identification and in particular he must not disclose whether a previous witness has made any identification.

16.   Anything said to or by the witness during the procedure regarding the identification should be said in the presence and hearing of the identification officer and, if present, the suspect's solicitor, appropriate adult, friend or any interpreter for the witness.

17.   The identification officer is responsible for ensuring that before they attend the group identification witnesses are not able to:
>   (i)   communicate with each other about the case or overhear a witness who has already been given an opportunity to see the suspect in the group;
>   (ii)   on that occasion see the suspect; or
>   (iii)   on that occasion see or be reminded of any photographs or description of the suspect or be given any other indication of his identity.

18.   Witnesses shall be brought to the place where they are to observe the group one at a time. Immediately before the witness is asked to look at the group, the identification officer shall tell him that the person he saw may or may not be in the group and if he cannot make a positive identification he should say so. The witness shall then be asked to observe the group in which the suspect is to appear. The way in which the witness should do this will depend on whether the group is moving or stationary.

Moving group
19.   When the group in which the suspect is to appear is moving, for example, leaving an escalator, the provisions of paragraphs 20 to 23 below should be followed.

20.   If two or more suspects consent to a group identification, each should be the subject of separate identification procedures. These may however be conducted consecutively on the same occasion.

21.   The identification officer shall tell the witness to observe the group and ask him to point out any person he thinks he saw on the earlier relevant occasion. When the witness makes such an indication the officer shall, if it is practicable, arrange for the witness to take a closer look at the person he has indicated and ask him whether he can make a positive identification. If this is not practicable, the officer shall ask the witness how sure he is that the person he has indicated is the relevant person.

22.   The witness should continue to observe the group for the period which the identification officer reasonably believes is necessary in the circumstances for the witness to be able to make comparisons between the suspect and other persons of broadly similar appearance to the suspect in accordance with paragraph 5.

23.   Once the identification officer has informed the witness in accordance with paragraph 21, the suspect should be allowed to take any position in the group he wishes.

Stationary groups

24. When the group in which the suspect is to appear is stationary, for example, people waiting in a queue, the provisions of paragraphs 25 to 28 below should be followed.

25. If two or more suspects consent to a group identification, each should be the subject of separate identification procedures unless they are of broadly similar appearance when they may appear in the same group. Where separate group identifications are held, the groups must be made up of different persons.

26. The suspect may take any position in the group he wishes. Where there is more than one witness, the identification officer must tell the suspect, out of the sight and hearing of any witness, that he can if he wishes change his position in the group.

27. The identification officer shall ask the witness to pass along or amongst the group and to look at each person in the group at least twice, taking as much care and time as is possible according to the circumstances, before making an identification. When he has done this, the officer shall ask him whether the person he saw on an earlier relevant occasion is in the group and to indicate any such person by whatever means the identification officer considers appropriate in the circumstances. If this is not practicable, the officer shall ask the witness to point out any person he thinks he saw on the earlier relevant occasion.

28. When the witness makes an indication in accordance with paragraph 27, the officer shall, if it is practicable, arrange for the witness to take a closer look at the person he has indicated and ask him whether he can make a positive identification. If this is not practicable, the officer shall ask the witness how sure he is that the person he has indicated is the relevant person.

All Cases

29. If the suspect unreasonably delays joining the group, or having joined the group, deliberately conceals himself from the sight of the witness, the identification officer may treat this as a refusal to co-operate in a group identification.

30. If the witness identifies a person other than the suspect, an officer should inform that person what has happened and ask if they are prepared to give their name and address. There is no obligation upon any member of the public to give these details. There shall be no duty to record any details of any other member of the public present in the group or at the place where the procedure is conducted.

31. When the group identification has been completed, the identification officer shall ask the suspect whether he wishes to make any comments on the conduct of the procedure.

32. If he has not been previously informed the identification officer shall tell the suspect of any identifications made by the witnesses.

(c) Identification without suspect's consent

33. Group identifications held covertly without the suspect's consent should so far as is practicable follow the rules for conduct of group identification by consent.

34. A suspect has no right to have a solicitor, appropriate adult or friend present as the identification will, of necessity, take place without the knoweldge of the suspect.

35. Any number of suspects may be identified at the same time.

(d) Identifications in police stations

36. Group identifications should only take place in police stations for reasons of safety, security, or because it is impracticable to hold them elsewhere.

37. The group identification may take place either in a room equipped with a screen permitting witnesses to see members of the group without being seen, or anywhere else in the police station that the identification officer considers appropriate.

38. Any of the additional safeguards applicable to identification parades should be followed if the identification officer consider it is practicable to do so in the circumstances.

(e) Identifications involving prison inmates

39. A group identification involving a prison inmate may only be arranged in the prison or at a police station.

40.   Where a group identification takes place involving a prison inmate, whether in a prison or in a police station, the arrangements should follow those in paragraphs 36 to 38 of this Annex. If a group identification takes place within a prison other inmates may participate. If an inmate is the suspect he should not be required to wear prison uniform for the group identification unless the other persons taking part are wearing the same uniform.

(f)   Documentation

41.   Where a photograph or video film is taken in accordance with paragraph 7 or 8, a copy of the photograph or video film shall be supplied on request to the suspect or his solicitor within a reasonable time.

42.   If the photograph or film includes the suspect, it and all copies held by the police shall be destroyed or wiped clean at the conclusion of the proceedings unless the person is convicted or admits the offence and is cautioned for it.

43.   A record of the conduct of any group identification must be made on the forms provided. This shall include anything said by the witness or the suspect about any identifications or the conduct of the procedure and any reasons why it was not practicable to comply with any of the provisions of this code governing the conduct of group identifications.

PACE CODE E: TAPE RECORDING OF INTERVIEWS WITH SUSPECTS

1.   General

1.1   This code of practice must be readily available for consultation by police officers, detained persons and members of the public at every police station to which an order made under section 60(1)(b) of the Police and Criminal Evidence Act 1984 applies.

1.2   The notes for guidance included are not provisions of this code. They form guidance to police officers and others about its application and interpretation.

1.3   Nothing in this code shall be taken as detracting in any way from the requirements of the Code of Practice for the Detention, Treatment and Questioning of Persons by Police Officers (Code C). [See Note 1A]

1.4   This code does not apply to those groups of people listed in paragraph 1.12 of Code C.

1.5   In this code the term 'appropriate adult' has the same meaning as in paragraph 1.7 of Code C; and the term 'solicitor' has the same meaning as in paragraph 6.12 of Code C.

Notes for Guidance

1A   As in Code C, references to custody officers include those carrying out the functions of a custody officer.

2.   Recording and the sealing of master tapes

2.1   Tape recording of interviews shall be carried out openly to instil confidence in its reliability as an impartial and accurate record of the interview. [See Note 2A]

2.2   One tape, referred to in this code as the master tape, will be sealed before it leaves the presence of the suspect. A second tape will be used as a working copy. The master tape is either one of the two tapes used in a twin deck machine or the only tape used in a single deck machine. The working copy is either the second tape used in a twin deck machine or a copy of the master tape made by a single deck machine. [See Notes 2B and 2C]

Notes for Guidance

2A   Police Officers will wish to arrange that, as far as possible, tape recording arrangements are unobtrusive. It must be clear to the suspect, however, that there is no opportunity to interfere with the tape recording equipment or the tapes.

2B   The purpose of sealing the master tape before it leaves the presence of the suspect is to establish his confidence that the integrity of the tape is preserved. Where a single deck machine is used the working copy of the master tape must be made in the presence of the suspect and without the master tape having left his sight. The working copy shall be used for making further copies where the need arises. The recorder will normally be capable of recording voices and have a time coding or other security device.

2C   Throughout this code any reference to 'tapes' shall be construed as 'tape', as appropriate, where a single deck machine is used.

3.   Interviews to be tape recorded

3.1   Subject to paragraph 3.2 below, tape recording shall be used at police stations for any interview:

    (a)   with a person who has been cautioned in accordance with section 10 of Code C in respect of an indictable offence (including an offence triable either way) [see Notes 3A and 3B];

    (b)   which takes place as a result of a police officer exceptionally putting further questions to a suspect about an offence described in sub-paragraph (a) above after he has been charged with, or informed he may be prosecuted for, that offence [see Note 3C]; or

    (c)   in which a police officer wishes to bring to the notice of a person, after he has been charged with, or informed he may be prosecuted for an offence described in sub-paragraph (a) above, any written statement made by another person, or the content of an interview with another person [see Note 3D].

3.2   Tape recording is not required in respect of the following:

    (a)   an interview with a person arrested under section 14(1)(a) or schedule 5 paragraph 6 of the Prevention of Terrorism (Temporary Provisions) Act 1989 or an interview with a person being questioned in respect of an offence where there are reasonable grounds for suspecting that it is connected to terrorism or was committed in furtherance of the objectives of an organisation engaged in terrorism. This sub-paragraph applies only where the terrorism is connected with the affairs of Northern Ireland or is terrorism of any other description except terrorism connected solely with the affairs of the United Kingdom or any part of the United Kingdom other than Northern Ireland. 'Terrorism' has the meaning given by section 20(1) of the Prevention of Terrorism (Temporary Provisions) Act 1989 [see Notes 3E, 3F, 3G and 3H];

    (b)   an interview with a person suspected on reasonable grounds of an offence under section 1 of the Official Secrets Act 1911 [see Note 3H].

3.3   The custody officer may authorise the interviewing officer not to tape record the interview:

    (a)   where it is not reasonably practicable to do so because of failure of the equipment or the non-availability of a suitable interview room or recorder and the authorising officer considers on reasonable grounds that the interview should not be delayed until the failure has been rectified or a suitable room or recorder becomes available [see Note 3J]; or

    (b)   where it is clear from the outset that no prosecution will ensue.

In such cases the interview shall be recorded in writing and in accordance with section 11 of Code C. In all cases the custody officer shall make a note in specified terms of the reasons for not tape recording. [See Note 3K]

3.4   Where an interview takes place with a person voluntarily attending the police station and the police officer has grounds to believe that person has become a suspect (i.e. the point at which he should be cautioned in accordance with paragraph 10.1 of Code C) the continuation of the interview shall be tape recorded, unless the custody officer gives authority in accordance with the provisions of paragraph 3.3 above for the continuation of the interview not to be recorded.

3.5   The whole of each interview shall be tape recorded, including the taking and reading back of any statement.

Notes for Guidance

3A   Nothing in this code is intended to preclude tape recording at police discretion of interviews at police stations with persons cautioned in respect of offences not covered by paragraph 3.1, or responses made by interviewees after they have been charged with, or informed they may be prosecuted for, an offence, provided that this code is complied with.

3B   Attention is drawn to the restrictions in paragraph 12.3 of Code C on the questioning of persons unfit through drink or drugs to the extent that they are unable to appreciate the significance of questions put to them or of their answers.

3C Circumstances in which a suspect may be questioned about an offence after being charged with it are set out in paragraph 16.5 of Code C.

3D Procedures to be followed when a person's attention is drawn after charge to a statement made by another person are set out in paragraph 16.4 of Code C. One method of bringing the content of an interview with another person to the notice of a suspect may be to play him a tape recording of that interview.

3E Section 14(1)(a) of the Prevention of Terrorism (Temporary Provisions) Act 1989, permits the arrest without warrant of a person reasonably suspected to be guilty of an offence under section 2, 8, 10 or 11 of the Act.

3F Section 20(1) of the Prevention of Terrorism (Temporary Provisions) Act 1989 says 'terrorism means the use of violence for political ends, and includes any use of violence for the purpose of putting the public or any section of the public in fear'.

3G It should be noted that the provisions of paragraph 3.2 apply only to those suspected of offences connected with terrorism connected with Northern Ireland, or with terrorism of any other description other than terrorism connected solely with the affairs of the United Kingdom or any part of the United Kingdom other than Northern Ireland, or offences committed in furtherance of such terrorism. Any interviews with those suspected of offences connected with terrorism of any other description or in furtherance of the objectives of an organisation engaged in such terrorism should be carried out in compliance with the rest of this code.

3H When it only becomes clear during the course of an interview which is being tape recorded that the interviewee may have committed an offence to which paragraph 3.2 applies the interviewing officer should turn off the tape recorder.

3J Where practicable, priority should be given to tape recording interviews with persons who are suspected of more serious offences.

3K A decision not to tape record an interview for any reason may be the subject of comment in court. The authorising officer should therefore be prepared to justify his decision in each case.

4. The interview

(a) Commencement of interviews

4.1 When the suspect is brought into the interview room the police officer shall without delay, but in the sight of the suspect, load the tape recorder with clean tapes and set it to record. The tapes must be unwrapped or otherwise opened in the presence of the suspect. [See Note 4A]

4.2 The police officer shall then tell the suspect formally about the tape recording. He shall say:
    (a) that the interview is being tape recorded;
    (b) his name and rank and the name and rank of any other police officer present except in the case of enquiries linked to the investigation of terrorism where warrant or other identification numbers shall be stated rather than names;
    (c) the name of the suspect and any other party present (e.g. a solicitor);
    (d) the date, time of commencement and place of the interview; and
    (e) that the suspect will be given a notice about what will happen to the tapes.
[See Note 4B]

4.3 The police officer shall then caution the suspect in the following terms:

You do not have to say anything. But it may harm your defence if you do not mention when questioned something which you later rely on in court. Anything you do say may be given in evidence.

Minor deviations do not constitute a breach of this requirement provided that the sense of the caution is preserved. [See Note 4C].

4.3A The police officer shall remind the suspect of his right to free and independent legal advice and that he can speak to a solicitor on the telephone in accordance with paragraph 6.5 of Code C.

4.3B The police officer shall then put to the suspect any significant statement or silence (i.e. failure or refusal to answer a question or to answer it satisfactorily) which occurred before the start of the tape-recorded interview, and shall ask him whether he confirms or denies that earlier statement or silence or whether he wishes to add anything. A 'significant' statement or silence means one which appears capable of being used in evidence against the suspect, in particular a direct admission of guilt, or failure or refusal to answer a question or to answer it satisfactorily, which might give rise to an inference under Part III of the Criminal Justice and Public Order Act 1994.

Special warnings under Sections 36 and 37 of the Criminal Justice and Public Order Act 1994
4.3C   When a suspect who is interviewed after arrest fails or refuses to answer certain questions, or to answer them satisfactorily, after due warning, a court or jury may draw a proper inference from this silence under sections 36 and 37 of the Criminal Justice and Public Order Act 1994. This applies when:

(a)   a suspect is arrested by a constable and there is found on his person, or in or on his clothing or footwear, or otherwise in his possession, or in the place where he was arrested, any objects, marks or substances, or marks on such objects, and the person fails or refuses to account for the objects, marks or substances found; or

(b)   an arrested person was found by a constable at a place at or about the time the offence for which he was arrested, is alleged to have been committed, and the person fails or refuses to account for his presence at that place.

4.3D   For an inference to be drawn from a suspect's failure or refusal to answer a question about one of these matters or to answer it satisfactorily, the interviewing officer must first tell him in ordinary language:

(a)   what offence he is investigating;
(b)   what fact he is asking the suspect to account for;
(c)   that he believes this fact may be due to the suspect's taking part in the commission of the offence in question;
(d)   that a court may draw a proper inference from his silence if he fails or refuses to account for the fact about which he is being questioned;
(e)   that a record is being made of the interview and may be given in evidence if he is brought to trial.

4.3E   Where, despite the fact that a person has been cautioned, failure to co-operate may have an effect on his immediate treatment, he should be informed of any relevant consequences and that they are not affected by the caution. Examples are when his refusal to provide his name and address when charged may render him liable to detention, or when his refusal to provide particulars and information in accordance with a statutory requirement, for example, under the Road Traffic Act 1988, may amount to an offence or may make him liable to arrest.

(b)   Interviews with the deaf

4.4   If the suspect is deaf or there is doubt about his hearing ability, the police officer shall take a contemporaneous note of the interview in accordance with the requirements of Code C, as well as tape record it in accordance with the provisions of this code. [See Notes 4E and 4F]

(c)   Objections and complaints by the suspect

4.5   If the suspect raises objections to the interview being tape recorded either at the outset or during the interview or during a break in the interview, the police officer shall explain the fact that the interview is being tape recorded and that the provisions of this code require that the suspect's objections should be recorded on tape. When any objections have been recorded on tape or the suspect has refused to have his objections recorded, the police officer may turn off the recorder. In this eventuality he shall say that he is turning off the recorder and give his reasons for doing so and then turn it off. The police officer shall then make a written record of the interview in accordance with section 11 of Code C. If, however, the police officer reasonably considers that he may proceed to put questions to the suspect with the tape recorder still on, he may do so. [See Note 4G]

4.6   If in the course of an interview a complaint is made by the person being questioned, or on his behalf, concerning the provisions of this code or of Code C, then the officer shall act in accordance with paragraph 12.8 of Code C. [See Notes 4H and 4J]

4.7   If the suspect indicates that he wishes to tell the police officer about matters not directly connected with the offence of which he is suspected and that he is unwilling for these matters to be recorded on tape, he shall be given the opportunity to tell the police officer about these matters after the conclusion of the formal interview.

(d)   Changing tapes

4.8   When the recorder indicates that the tapes have only a short time left to run, the police officer shall tell the suspect that the tapes are coming to an end and round off that part of the interview. If the police officer wishes to continue the interview but does not already have a second set of tapes, he shall obtain a set. The suspect shall not be left unattended in the interview room. The police officer will remove the tapes from the tape recorder and insert the new tapes which shall be unwrapped or otherwise opened in the suspect's presence. The tape recorder shall then be set to record on the new tapes. Care must be taken, particularly when a number of sets of tapes have been used, to ensure that there is no confusion between the tapes. This may be done by marking the tapes with an identification number immediately they are removed from the tape recorder.

(e)   Taking a break during interview

4.9   When a break is to be taken during the course of an interview and the interview room is to be vacated by the suspect, the fact that a break is to be taken, the reason for it and the time shall be recorded on tape. The tapes shall then be removed from the tape recorder and the procedures for the conclusion of an interview set out in paragraph 4.14 below followed.

4.10   When a break is to be a short one and both the suspect and a police officer are to remain in the interview room the fact that a break is to be taken, the reasons for it and the time shall be recorded on tape. The tape recorder may be turned off; there is, however, no need to remove the tapes and when the interview is recommenced the tape recording shall be continued on the same tapes. The time at which the interview recommences shall be recorded on tape.

4.11   When there is a break in questioning under caution the interviewing officer must ensure that the person being questioned is aware that he remains under caution and of his right to legal advice. If there is any doubt the caution must be given again in full when the interview resumes. [See Notes 4K and 4L]

(f)   Failure of recording equipment

4.12   If there is a failure of equipment which can be rectified quickly, for example by inserting new tapes, the appropriate procedures set out in paragraph 4.8 shall be followed, and when the recording is resumed the officer shall explain what has happened and record the time the interview recommences. If, however, it will not be possible to continue recording on that particular tape recorder and no replacement recorder or recorder in another interview room is readily available, the interview may continue without being tape recorded. In such circumstances the procedures in paragraphs 3.3 above for seeking the authority of the custody officer will be followed. [See Note 4M]

(g)   Removing tapes from the recorder

4.13   Where tapes are removed from the recorder in the course of an interview, they shall be retained and the procedures set out in paragraph 4.15 below followed.

(h)   Conclusion of interview

4.14   At the conclusion of the interview, the suspect shall be offered the opportunity to clarify anything he has said and to add anything he may wish.

4.15   At the conclusion of the interview, including the taking and reading back of any written statement, the time shall be recorded and the tape recorder switched off. The master tape shall be sealed with a master tape label and treated as an exhibit in accordance with the force standing orders. The police officer shall sign the label and ask the suspect and any third party present to sign it also. If the suspect or third party refuses to sign the label, an officer of at least the rank of inspector, or if one is not available the custody officer, shall be called into the interview room and asked to sign it. In the case of enquiries linked to the investigation of terrorism, an officer who signs the label shall use his warrant or other identification number.

4.16   The suspect shall be handed a notice which explains the use which will be made of the tape recording and the arrangements for access to it and that a copy of the tape shall be supplied as soon as practicable if the person is charged or informed that he will be prosecuted.

Notes for Guidance

4A   The police officer should attempt to estimate the likely length of the interview and ensure that the appropriate number of clean tapes and labels with which to seal the master copies are available in the interview room.

4B   It will be helpful for the purpose of voice identification if the officer asks the suspect and any other people present to identify themselves.

4C   If it appears that a person does not understand what the caution means, the officer who has given it should go on to explain it in his own words.

4D   [Not Used]

4E   This provision is intended to give the deaf equivalent rights of first hand access to the full interview record as other suspects.

4F   The provisions of paragraphs 13.2, 13.5 and 13.9 of Code C on interpreters for the deaf or for interviews with suspects who have difficulty in understanding English continue to apply. In a tape recorded interview there is no requirement on the interviewing officer to ensure that the interpreter makes a separate note of interview as prescribed in section 13 of Code C.

4G   The officer should bear in mind that a decision to continue recording against the wishes of the suspect may be the subject of comment in court.

4H   Where the custody officer is called immediately to deal with the complaint, wherever possible the tape recorder should be left to run until the custody officer has entered the interview room and spoken to the person being interviewed. Continuation or termination of the interview should be at the discretion of the interviewing officer pending action by an inspector under paragraph 9.1 of Code C.

4I   [Not Used]

4J   Where the complaint is about a matter not connected with this code of practice or Code C, the decision to continue with the interview is at the discretion of the interviewing officer. Where the interviewing officer decides to continue with the interview the person being interviewed shall be told that the complaint will be brought to the attention of the custody officer at the conclusion of the interview. When the interview is concluded the interviewing officer must, as soon as practicable, inform the custody officer of the existence and nature of the complaint made.

4K   In considering whether to caution again after a break, the officer should bear in mind that he may have to satisfy a court that the person understood that he was still under caution when the interview resumed.

4L   The officer should bear in mind that it may be necessary to show to the court that nothing occurred during a break in an interview or between interviews which influenced the suspect's recorded evidence. The officer should consider, therefore, after a break in an interview or at the beginning of a subsequent interview summarising on tape the reason for the break and confirming this with the suspect.

4M   If one of the tapes breaks during the interview it should be sealed as a master tape in the presence of the suspect and the interview resumed where it left off. The unbroken tape should be copied and the original sealed as a master tape in the suspect's presence, if necessary after the interview. If equipment for copying the unbroken tape is not readily available, both tapes should be sealed in the suspect's presence and the interview begun again. If the tape breaks when a single deck machine is being used and the machine is one where a broken tape cannot be copied on available equipment, the tape should be sealed as a master tape in the suspect's presence and the interview begun again.

5.   After the interview

5.1   The police officer shall make a note in his notebook of the fact that the interview has taken place and has been recorded on tape, its time, duration and date and the identification number of the master tape.

5.2   Where no proceedings follow in respect of the person whose interview was recorded the tapes must nevertheless be kept securely in accordance with paragraph 6.1 and Note 6A.

Note for Guidance

5A   Any written record of a tape recorded interview shall be made in accordance with national guidelines approved by the Secretary of State.

6.   Tape security

6.1   The officer in charge of each police station at which interviews with suspects are recorded shall make arrangements for master tapes to be kept securely and their movements accounted for on the same basis as other material which may be used for evidential purposes, in accordance with force standing orders. [See Note 6A]

6.2   A police officer has no authority to break the seal on a master tape which is required for criminal proceedings. If it is necessary to gain access to the master tape, the police officer shall arrange for its seal to be broken in the presence of a representative of the Crown Prosecution Service. The defendant or his legal adviser shall be informed and given a reasonable opportunity to be present. If the defendant or his legal representative is present he shall be invited to reseal and sign the master tape. If either refuses or neither is present this shall be done by the representative of the Crown Prosecution Service. [See Notes 6B and 6C]

6.3   Where no criminal proceedings result it is the responsibility of the chief officer of police to establish arrangements for the breaking of the seal on the master tape, where this becomes necessary.

Notes for Guidance

6A   This section is concerned with the security of the master tape which will have been sealed at the conclusion of the interview. Care should, however, be taken of working copies of tapes since their loss or destruction may lead unnecessarily to the need to have access to master tapes.

6B   If the tape has been delivered to the Crown Court for their keeping after committal for trial the crown prosecutor will apply to the chief clerk of the Crown Court centre for the release of the tape for unsealing by the crown prosecutor.

6C   Reference to the Crown Prosecution Service or to the crown prosecutor in this part of the code shall be taken to include any other body or person with a statutory responsibility for prosecution for whom the police conduct any tape recorded interviews.

APPENDIX 3   ATTORNEY-GENERAL'S GUIDELINES

EXERCISE BY THE CROWN OF ITS RIGHT OF STAND-BY

1.   Although the law has long recognised the right of the Crown to exclude a member of a jury panel from sitting as a juror by the exercise in open court of the right to request a stand-by or, if necessary, by challenge for cause, it has been customary for those instructed to prosecute on behalf of the Crown to assert that right only sparingly and in exceptional circumstances. It is generally accepted that the prosecution should not use its right in order to influence the overall composition of a jury or with a view to tactical advantage.

2.   The approach outlined above is founded on the principles that (a) the members of a jury should be selected at random from the panel subject to any rule of law as to right of challenge by the defence, and (b) the Juries Act 1974 together with the Juries (Disqualification) Act 1984 identified those classes of persons who alone are disqualified from or ineligible for service on a jury. No other class of person may be treated as disqualified or ineligible.

3.   The enactment by Parliament of s. 118 of the Criminal Justice Act 1988 abolishing the right of defendants to remove jurors by means of peremptory challenge makes it appropriate that the Crown should assert its right to stand by only on the basis of clearly defined and restrictive criteria. Derogation from the principle that members of a jury should be selected at random should be permitted only where it is essential.

4.   Primary responsibility for ensuring that an individual does not serve on a jury if he is not competent to discharge properly the duties of a juror rests with the appropriate court officer and, ultimately, the trial judge. Current legislation provides, in ss. 9 and 10 of the Juries Act 1974, fairly wide discretions to excuse or discharge jurors either at the person's own request, where he offers 'good reason why he should be excused', or where the judge determines that 'on account of physical disability or insufficient understanding of English there is doubt as to his capacity to act effectively as a juror'.

5.   The circumstances in which it would be proper for the Crown to exercise its right to stand by a member of a jury panel are: (a) where a jury check authorised in accordance with the Attorney-General's guidelines on jury checks reveals information justifying exercise of the right to stand by in accordance with para. 9 of the guidelines and the Attorney-General personally authorises the exercise of the right to stand by; or (b) where a person is about to be sworn as a juror who is manifestly unsuitable and the defence agree that, accordingly, the exercise by the prosecution of the right to stand by would be appropriate. An example of the sort of *exceptional* circumstances which might justify stand-by is where it becomes apparent that, despite the provisions mentioned in para. 4 above, a juror selected for service to try a complex case is in fact illiterate.

JURY CHECKS

1.   The principles which are generally to be observed are (a) that members of a jury should be selected at random from the panel, (b) the Juries Act 1974 together with the Juries (Disqualification) Act 1984 identified those classes of persons who alone are either disqualified from or ineligible for service on a jury; no other class of person may be treated as disqualified or ineligible, and (c) the correct way for the Crown to seek to exclude a member of the panel from sitting as a juror is by the exercise in open court of the right to request a stand-by or, if necessary, to challenge for cause.

2.   Parliament has provided safeguards against jurors who may be corrupt or biased. In addition to the provision for majority verdicts, there is the sanction of a criminal offence for a disqualified person to serve on a jury. The omission of a disqualified person from the panel is a matter for court officials but any search of criminal records for the purpose of ascertaining whether or not a jury panel includes any disqualified person is a matter for the police as the only authority able to carry out such a search and as part of their usual function of preventing the commission of offences. The recommendations of the Association of Chief Police Officers respecting checks on criminal records for disqualified persons are annexed to these guidelines.

3.   There are, however, certain exceptional types of case of public importance for which the provisions as to majority verdicts and the disqualification of jurors may not be sufficient to ensure the proper administration of justice. In such cases it is in the interests of both justice and the public that there should be further safeguards against the possibility of bias and in such cases checks which go beyond the investigation of criminal records may be necessary.

4.   These classes of case may be defined broadly as (a) cases in which national security is involved and part of the evidence is likely to be heard in camera, and (b) terrorist cases.

5.   The particular aspects of these cases which may make it desirable to seek extra precautions are (a) in security cases a danger that a juror, either voluntarily or under pressure, may make an improper use of evidence which, because of its sensitivity, has been given in camera, (b) in both security and terrorist cases the danger that a juror's political beliefs are so biased as to go beyond normally reflecting the broad spectrum of views and interests in the community to reflect the extreme views of sectarian interest or pressure group to a degree which might interfere with his fair assessment of the facts of the case or lead him to exert improper pressure on his fellow jurors.

6.   In order to ascertain whether in exceptional circumstances of the above nature either of these factors might seriously influence a potential juror's impartial performance of his duties or his respecting the secrecy of evidence given in camera, it may be necessary to conduct a limited investigation of the panel. In general, such further investigation beyond one of criminal records made for disqualifications may only be made with the records of police Special Branches. However, in cases falling under para. 4(a) above (security cases), the investigation may, additionally, involve the security services. No checks other than on these sources and no general inquiries are to be made save to the limited extent that they may be needed to confirm the identity of a juror about whom the initial check has raised serious doubts.

7.   No further investigation, as described in para. 6 above, should be made save with the personal authority of the Attorney-General on the application of the Director of Public Prosecutions and such checks are hereafter referred to as 'authorised checks'. When a chief officer of police has reason to believe that it is likely that an authorised check may be desirable and proper in accordance with these guidelines he should refer the matter to the Director of Public Prosecutions with a view to his having the conduct of the prosecution from an early stage. The Director will make any appropriate application to the Attorney-General.

8.   The result of any authorised check will be sent to the Director of Public Prosecutions. The Director will then decide, having regard to the matters set out in para. 5 above, what information ought to be brought to the attention of prosecuting counsel.

9.   No right of stand-by should be exercised by counsel for the Crown on the basis of information obtained as a result of an authorised check save with the personal authority of the Attorney-General and unless the information is such as, having regard to the facts of the case and the offences charged, to afford strong reason for believing that a particular juror might be a security risk, be susceptible to improper approaches or be influenced in arriving at a verdict for the reasons given above.

10.   Where a potential juror is asked to stand by for the Crown, there is no duty to disclose to the defence the information on which it was founded; but counsel may use his discretion to disclose it if its nature and source permit it.

11.   When information revealed in the course of an authorised check is not such as to cause counsel for the Crown to ask for a juror to stand by but does give reason to believe that he may be biased against the accused, the defence should be given, at least, an indication of why that potential juror may be inimical to their interests; but because of its nature and source it may not be possible to give the defence more than a general indication.

12.   A record is to be kept by the Director of Public Prosecutions of the use made by counsel of the information passed to him and of the jurors stood by or challenged by the parties to the proceedings. A copy of this record is to be forwarded to the Attorney-General for the sole purpose of enabling him to monitor the operation of these guidelines.

13.   No use of the information obtained as a result of an authorised check is to be made except as may be necessary in direct relation to or arising out of the trial for which the check was authorised.

Annexe: Recommendations of the Association of Chief Police Officers

1.   The Association of Chief Police Officers recommends that in the light of observations made in *Mason* [1981] QB 881 the police should undertake a check of the names of potential jurors against records of previous convictions in any case when the Director of Public Prosecutions or a chief constable considers that in all the circumstances it would be in the interests of justice so to do, namely (i) in any case in which there is reason to believe that attempts are being made to circumvent the statutory provisions excluding disqualified persons from service on a jury, including any case when there is reason to believe that a particular juror may be disqualified, (ii) in any case in which it is believed that in a previous related abortive trial an attempt was made to interfere with a juror or jurors, and (iii) in any other case in which in the opinion of the Director of Public Prosecutions or the chief constable it is particularly important to ensure that no disqualified person serves on the jury.

2.   The association also recommends that no further checks should be made unless authorised by the Attorney-General under his guidelines and no inquiries carried out save to the limited extent that they may be needed to confirm the identity of a juror about whom the initial check has raised serious doubts.

3.   The association further recommends that chief constables should agree to undertake checks of jurors on behalf of the defence only if requested to do so by the Director of Public Prosecutions acting on behalf of the Attorney-General. Accordingly if the police are approached directly with such a request they will refer it to the Director.

4.   When, as a result of any checks of criminal records, information is obtained which suggests that, although not disqualified under the terms of the Juries Act 1974, a person may be unsuitable to sit as a member of a particular jury the police or the Director may pass the relevant information to prosecuting counsel, who will decide what use to make of it.

APPENDIX 4   THE CODE FOR CROWN PROSECUTORS

1   Introduction

1.1   The decision to prosecute an individual is a serious step. Fair and effective prosecution is essential to the maintenance of law and order. But even in a small case, a prosecution has serious implications for all involved – the victim, a witness and a defendant. The Crown Prosecution Service applies the Code for Crown Prosecutors so that it can make fair and consistent decisions about prosecutions.

1.2   The Code contains information that is important to police officers, to others who work in the criminal justice system and to the general public. It helps the Crown Prosecution Service to play its part in making sure that justice is done.

2   General Principles

2.1   Each case is unique and must be considered on its own, but there are general principles that apply in all cases.

2.2   The duty of the Crown Prosecution Service is to make sure that the right person is prosecuted for the right offence and that all relevant facts are given to the court.

2.3   Crown Prosecutors must be fair, independent and objective. They must not let their personal views of the ethnic or national origin, sex, religious beliefs, political views or sexual preference of the offender, victim or witness influence their decisions. They must also not be affected by improper or undue pressure from any source.

3   Review

3.1   Proceedings are usually started by the police. Sometimes they may consult the Crown Prosecution Service before charging a defendant. Each case that the police send to the Crown Prosecution Service is reviewed by a Crown Prosecutor to make sure that it meets the tests set out in this Code. Crown Prosecutors may decide to continue with the original charges, to change the charges or sometimes to stop the proceedings.

3.2   Review, however, is a continuing process so that Crown Prosecutors can take into account any change in circumstances. Wherever possible, they talk to the police first if they are thinking about changing the charges or stopping the proceedings. This gives the police the chance to provide more information that may affect the decision. The Crown Prosecution Service and the police work closely together to reach the right decision, but the final responsibility for the decision rests with the Crown Prosecution Service.

4   The Code Tests

4.1   There are two stages in the decision to prosecute. The first stage is *the evidential test*. If the case does not pass the evidential test, it must not go ahead, no matter how important or serious it may be. If the case does pass the evidential test, Crown Prosecutors must decide if a prosecution is needed in the public interest.

4.2   This second stage is *the public interest test*. The Crown Prosecution Service will only start or continue a prosecution when the case has passed both tests. The evidential test is explained in section 5 and the public interest test is explained in section 6.

5   The Evidential Test

5.1   Crown Prosecutors must be satisfied that there is enough evidence to provide a 'realistic prospect of conviction' against each defendant on each charge. They must consider what the defence case may be and how that is likely to affect the prosecution case.

5.2   A realistic prospect of conviction is an objective test. It means that a jury or bench of magistrates, properly directed in accordance with the law, is more likely than not to convict the defendant of the charge alleged.

5.3   When deciding whether there is enough evidence to prosecute, Crown Prosecutors must consider whether the evidence can be used and is reliable. There will be many cases in which the evidence does not give any cause for concern. But there will also be cases in which the evidence may not be as strong as it first appears. Crown Prosecutors must ask themselves the following questions:

Can the evidence be used in court?

(a)   Is it likely that the evidence will be excluded by the court? There are certain legal rules which might mean that evidence which seems relevant cannot be given at a trial. For example, is it likely that the evidence will be excluded because of the way in which it was gathered or because of the rule against using hearsay as evidence? If so, is there enough other evidence for a realistic prospect of conviction?

Is the evidence reliable?

(b)   Is it likely that a confession is unreliable, for example, because of the defendant's age, intelligence or lack of understanding?
(c)   Is the witness's background likely to weaken the prosecution case? For example, does the witness have any dubious motive that may affect his or her attitude to the case or a relevant previous conviction?
(d)   If the identity of the defendant is likely to be questioned, is the evidence about this strong enough?

5.4   Crown Prosecutors should not ignore evidence because they are not sure that it can be used or is reliable. But they should look closely at it when deciding if there is a realistic prospect of conviction.

6   The Public Interest Test

6.1   In 1951, Lord Shawcross, who was Attorney-General, made the classic statement on public interest, which has been supported by Attorneys-General ever since: 'It has never been the rule in this country – I hope it never will be – that suspected criminal offences must automatically be the subject of prosecution'. (House of Commons Debates, Vol. 483, col. 681, 29 January 1951.)

6.2   The public interest must be considered in each case where there is enough evidence to provide a realistic prospect of conviction. In cases of any seriousness, a prosecution will usually take place unless there are public interest factors tending against prosecution which clearly outweigh those tending in favour. Although there may be public interest factors against prosecution in a particular case, often the prosecution should go ahead and those factors should be put to the court for consideration when sentence is being passed.

6.3   Crown Prosecutors must balance factors for and against prosecution carefully and fairly. Public interest factors that can affect the decision to prosecute usually depend on the seriousness of the offence or the circumstances of the offender. Some factors may increase the need to prosecute but others may suggest that another course of action would be better.

The following lists of some common public interest factors, both for and against prosecution, are not exhaustive. The factors that apply will depend on the facts in each case.

Some common public interest factors in favour of prosecution

6.4   The more serious the offence, the more likely it is that a prosecution will be needed in the public interest. A prosecution is likely to be needed if:

(a)   a conviction is likely to result in a significant sentence;
(b)   a weapon was used or violence was threatened during the commission of the offence;
(c)   the offence was committed against a person serving the public (for example, a police or prison officer, or a nurse);
(d)   the defendant was in a position of authority or trust;
(e)   the evidence shows that the defendant was a ringleader or an organiser of the offence;
(f)   there is evidence that the offence was premeditated;
(g)   there is evidence that the offence was carried out by a group;
(h)   the victim of the offence was vulnerable, has been put in considerable fear, or suffered personal attack, damage or disturbance;
(i)   the offence was motivated by any form of discrimination against the victim's ethnic or national origin, sex, religious beliefs, political views or sexual preference;

(j) there is a marked difference between the actual or mental ages of the defendant and the victim, or if there is any element of corruption;

(k) the defendant's previous convictions or cautions are relevant to the present offence;

(l) the defendant is alleged to have committed the offence whilst under an order of the court;

(m) there are grounds for believing that the offence is likely to be continued or repeated, for example, by a history of recurring conduct; or

(n) the offence, although not serious in itself, is widespread in the area where it was committed.

Some common public interest factors against prosecution

6.5 A prosecution is less likely to be needed if:

(a) the court is likely to impose a very small or nominal penalty;

(b) the offence was committed as a result of a genuine mistake or misunderstanding (these factors must be balanced against the seriousness of the offence);

(c) the loss or harm can be described as minor and was the result of a single incident, particularly if it was caused by a misjudgment;

(d) there has been a long delay between the offence taking place and the date of the trial, unless:
- the offence is serious;
- the delay has been caused in part by the defendant;
- the offence has only recently come to light; or
- the complexity of the offence has meant that there has been a long investigation;

(e) a prosecution is likely to have a very bad effect on the victim's physical or mental health, always bearing in mind the seriousness of the offence;

(f) the defendant is elderly or is, or was at the time of the offence, suffering from significant mental or physical ill health, unless the offence is serious or there is a real possibility that it may be repeated. The Crown Prosecution Service, where necessary, applies Home Office guidelines about how to deal with mentally disordered offenders. Crown Prosecutors must balance the desirability of diverting a defendant who is suffering from significant mental or physical ill health with the need to safeguard the general public;

(g) the defendant has put right the loss or harm that was caused (but defendants must not avoid prosecution simply because they can pay compensation); or

(h) details may be made public that could harm sources of information, international relations or national security.

6.6 Deciding on the public interest is not simply a matter of adding up the number of factors on each side. Crown Prosecutors must decide how important each factor is in the circumstances of each case and go on to make an overall assessment.

The relationship between the victim and the public interest

6.7 The Crown Prosecution Service acts in the public interest, not just in the interests of any one individual. But Crown Prosecutors must always think very carefully about the interests of the victim, which are an important factor, when deciding where the public interest lies.

Youth offenders

6.8 Crown Prosecutors must consider the interests of a youth when deciding whether it is in the public interest to prosecute. The stigma of a conviction can cause very serious harm to the prospects of a youth offender or a young adult. Young offenders can sometimes be dealt with without going to court. But Crown Prosecutors should not avoid prosecuting simply because of the defendant's age. The seriousness of the offence or the offender's past behaviour may make prosecution necessary.

Police cautions

6.9 The police make the decision to caution an offender in accordance with Home Office guidelines. If the defendant admits the offence, cautioning is the most common alternative to a court appearance. Crown Prosecutors, where necessary, apply the same guidelines and should look at the alternatives to prosecution when they consider the public interest. Crown Prosecutors should tell the police if they think that a caution would be more suitable than a prosecution.

7 Charges

7.1 Crown Prosecutors should select charges which:

(a) reflect the seriousness of the offending;

(b)   give the court adequate sentencing powers; and

(c)   enable the case to be presented in a clear and simple way.

This means that Crown Prosecutors may not always continue with the most serious charge where there is a choice. Further, Crown Prosecutors should not continue with more charges than are necessary.

7.2   Crown Prosecutors should never go ahead with more charges than are necessary just to encourage a defendant to plead guilty to a few. In the same way, they should never go ahead with a more serious charge just to encourage a defendant to plead guilty to a less serious one.

7.3   Crown Prosecutors should not change the charge simply because of the decision made by the court or the defendant about where the case will be heard.

8   Mode of Trial

8.1   The Crown Prosecution Service applies the current guidelines for magistrates who have to decide whether cases should be tried in the Crown Court when the offence gives the option. (See the 'National Mode of Trial Guidelines' issued by the Lord Chief Justice.) Crown Prosecutors should recommend Crown Court trial when they are satisfied that the guidelines require them to do so.

8.2   Speed must never be the only reason for asking for a case to stay in the magistrates' courts. But Crown Prosecutors should consider the effect of any likely delay if they send a case to the Crown Court, and any possible stress on victims and witnesses if the case is delayed.

9   Accepting Guilty Pleas

9.1   Defendants may want to plead guilty to some, but not all, of the charges. Or they may want to plead guilty to a different, possibly less serious, charge because they are admitting only part of the crime. Crown Prosecutors should only accept the defendant's plea if they think the court is able to pass a sentence that matches the seriousness of the offending. Crown Prosecutors must never accept a guilty plea just because it is convenient.

10   Re-starting a Prosecution

10.1   People should be able to rely on decisions taken by the Crown Prosecution Service. Normally, if the Crown Prosecution Service tells a suspect or defendant that there will not be a prosecution, or that the prosecution has been stopped, that is the end of the matter and the case will not start again. But occasionally there are special reasons why the Crown Prosecution Service will re-start the prosecution, particularly if the case is serious.

10.2   These reasons include:

(a)   rare cases where a new look at the original decision shows that it was clearly wrong and should not be allowed to stand;

(b)   cases which are stopped so that more evidence which is likely to become available in the fairly near future can be collected and prepared. In these cases, the Crown Prosecutor will tell the defendant that the prosecution may well start again;

(c)   cases which are stopped because of a lack of evidence but where more significant evidence is discovered later.

11   Conclusion

11.1   The Crown Prosecution Service is a public service headed by the Director of Public Prosecutions. It is answerable to Parliament through the Attorney-General. The Code for Crown Prosecutors is issued under section 10 of the Prosecution of Offences Act 1985 and is a public document. This is the third edition and it replaces all earlier versions. Changes to the Code are made from time to time and these are also published.

11.2   The Code is designed to make sure that everyone knows the principles that the Crown Prosecution Service applies when carrying out its work. Police officers should take account of the principles of the Code when they are deciding whether to charge a defendant with an offence. By applying the same principles, everyone involved in the criminal justice system is helping the system to treat victims fairly, and to prosecute defendants fairly but effectively.

APPENDIX 5   PLEA AND DIRECTIONS HEARING: JUDGE'S QUESTIONNAIRE

Plea and Directions Hearing

Judge's Questionnaire
(In accordance with the practice rules issued by the Lord
Chief Justice)

*A copy of this questionnaire, completed as far as possible with the
agreement of both advocates, is to be handed in to the court prior to
the commencement of the Plea and Directions Hearing.*

The Crown Court at

Case No. T
PTI URN
R v

Date of PDH
Name of Prosecution Advocate at PDH

Name of Defence Advocate at PDH

1	a	Are the actual/proposed not guilty pleas definitely to be maintained through to a jury trial?	Yes ☐ No ☐
	b	Has the defence advocate advised his client of section 48 of CJPOA 1994? *(Reductions in sentence for guilty pleas)*	Yes ☐ No ☐
	c	Will the prosecution accept part guilty or alternative pleas?	Yes ☐ No ☐
2		How long is the trial likely to take?	
3		What are the issues in the case?	
4		Issues as to the mental or medical condition of any defendant or witness.	
5		Prosecution witnesses whose evidence will be given.	To be read (number) ☐
		Can any statement be read instead of calling the witnesses?	To be called (number) ☐ Names:
6	a	Number of Defence witnesses whose evidence will be placed before the Court.	Defendant + ☐
	b	Any whose statements have been served which can be agreed and accepted in writing.	
7		Is the prosecution intending to serve any further evidence?	Yes ☐ No ☐
		If Yes, what area(s) will it cover?	
		What are the witnesses' names?	
8		Facts which are admitted and can be reduced into writing. (s. 10(2)(b) CJA 1967)	
9		Exhibits and schedules which are to be admitted.	
10		Is the order and pagination of the prosecution papers agreed?	
11		Any alibi which should have been disclosed in accordance with CJA 1967?	Yes ☐ No ☐

12	a	Any points of law likely to arise at trial?	
	b	Any questions of admissibility of evidence together with any authorities it is intended to rely upon.	
13	a	Has the defence notified the prosecution of any issue arising out of the record of interview? (*Practice Direction (Crime: Tape Recording Police Interview*) [1989] 1 WLR 631)	Yes ☐ No ☐
	b	What efforts have been made to agree verbatim records or summaries and have they been successful?	
14		Any applications granted/pending for:	
		(i) evidence to be given through live television links?	Yes ☐ No ☐
		(ii) evidence to be given by pre-recorded video interviews with children?	Yes ☐ No ☐
		(iii) screens?	Yes ☐ No ☐
		(iv) the use of video equipment during the trial?	Yes ☐ No ☐
		(v) use of tape playback equipment?	Yes ☐ No ☐
15		Any other significant matter which might affect the proper and convenient trial of the case? (e.g. expert witnesses or other cases outstanding against the defendant)	
16		Any other work which needs to be done. Orders of the Court with time limits should be noted [under 'other directions, orders, comments' below].	Prosecution _____ Defence _____
17	a	Witness availability and approximate length of witness evidence.	Prosecution _____ Defence _____
	b	Can any witness attendance be staggered?	Yes ☐ No ☐
	c	If Yes, have any arrangements been agreed?	Yes ☐ No ☐
18		Advocates' availability?	Prosecution _____ Defence _____

Case listing arrangements

Name of Trial Judge:

Custody Cases *Fixed or warned list within 16 weeks of committal*

Fixed for trial on

Place in a warned list for trial   for week beginning

Further directions fixed for

Not fixed or put in warned list within
16 weeks because:

Bail Cases

Further directions fixed for

Fixed for trial on

Fixed as a floater/backer on

Place in a reserve/warned list   for week beginning
for trial

List officer to allocate   ☐ within   [   ] days/weeks

☐ before

Sentence

Adjourned for sentence on

(to follow trial of R v

Other directions, orders, comments

Signed: *Judge*   Date:

APPENDIX 6   DISCLOSURE: CRIMINAL PROCEDURE AND INVESTIGATIONS ACT 1996: CODE OF PRACTICE UNDER PART II

Introduction

1.1   This code of practice is issued under part II of the Criminal Procedure and Investigations Act 1996 ('the Act'). It applies in respect of criminal investigations conducted by police officers which begin on or after the day on which this code comes into effect. Persons other than police officers who are charged with the duty of conducting an investigation as defined in the Act are to have regard to the relevant provisions of the code, and should take these into account in applying their own operating procedures.

1.2   This code does not apply to persons who are not charged with the duty of conducting an investigation as defined in the Act.

1.3   Nothing in this code applies to material intercepted in obedience to a warrant issued under section 2 of the Interception of Communications Act 1985, or to any copy of that material as defined in section 10 of that Act.

1.4   This code extends only to England and Wales.

Definitions

2.1   In this code:

- a *criminal investigation* is an investigation conducted by police officers with a view to it being ascertained whether a person should be charged with an offence, or whether a person charged with an offence is guilty of it. This will include

  - investigations into crimes that have been committed;

  - investigations whose purpose is to ascertain whether a crime has been committed, with a view to the possible institution of criminal proceedings; and

  - investigations which begin in the belief that a crime may be committed, for example when the police keep premises or individuals under observation for a period of time, with a view to the possible institution of criminal proceedings;

- charging a person with an offence includes prosecution by way of summons;

- an *investigator* is any police officer involved in the conduct of a criminal investigation. All investigators have a responsibility for carrying out the duties imposed on them under this code, including in particular recording information, and retaining records of information and other material;

- the *officer in charge of an investigation* is the police officer responsible for directing a criminal investigation. He is also responsible for ensuring that proper procedures are in place for recording information, and retaining records of information and other material, in the investigation;

- the *disclosure officer* is the person responsible for examining material retained by the police during the investigation; revealing material to the prosecutor during the investigation and any criminal proceedings resulting from it, and certifying that he has done this; and disclosing material to the accused at the request of the prosecutor;

- the *prosecutor* is the authority responsible for the conduct of criminal proceedings on behalf of the Crown. Particular duties may in practice fall to individuals acting on behalf of the prosecuting authority;

- *material* is material of any kind, including information and objects, which is obtained in the course of a criminal investigation and which may be relevant to the investigation;

-   material may be *relevant to an investigation* if it appears to an investigator, or to the officer in charge of an investigation, or to the disclosure officer, that it has some bearing on any offence under investigation or any person being investigated, or on the surrounding circumstances of the case, unless it is incapable of having any impact on the case;

-   *sensitive material* is material which the disclosure officer believes, after consulting the officer in charge of the investigation, it is not in the public interest to disclose;

-   references to *primary prosecution disclosure* are to the duty of the prosecutor under section 3 of the Act to disclose material which is in his possession or which he has inspected in pursuance of this code, and which in his opinion might undermine the case against the accused;

-   references to *secondary prosecution disclosure* are to the duty of the prosecutor under section 7 of the Act to disclose material which is in his possession or which he has inspected in pursuance of this code, and which might reasonably be expected to assist the defence disclosed by the accused in a defence statement given under the Act;

-   references to the disclosure of material to a person accused of an offence include references to the disclosure of material to his legal representative;

-   references to police officers and to the chief officer of police include those employed in a police force as defined in section 3(3) of the Prosecution of Offences Act 1985.

General responsibilities

3.1   The functions of the investigator, the officer in charge of an investigation and the disclosure officer are separate. Whether they are undertaken by one, two or more persons will depend on the complexity of the case and the administrative arrangements within each police force. Where they are undertaken by more than one person, close consultation between them is essential to the effective performance of the duties imposed by this code.

3.2   The chief officer of police for each police force is responsible for putting in place arrangements to ensure that in every investigation the identity of the officer in charge of an investigation and the disclosure officer is recorded.

3.3   The officer in charge of an investigation may delegate tasks to another investigator or to civilians employed by the police force, but he remains responsible for ensuring that these have been carried out and for accounting for any general policies followed in the investigation. In particular, it is an essential part of his duties to ensure that all material which may be relevant to an investigation is retained, and either made available to the disclosure officer or (in exceptional circumstances) revealed directly to the prosecutor.

3.4   In conducting an investigation, the investigator should pursue all reasonable lines of inquiry, whether these point towards or away from the suspect. What is reasonable in each case will depend on the particular circumstances.

3.5   If the officer in charge of an investigation believes that other persons may be in possession of material that may be relevant to the investigation, and if this has not been obtained under paragraph 3.4 above, he should ask the disclosure officer to inform them of the existence of the investigation and to invite them to retain the material in case they receive a request for its disclosure. The disclosure officer should inform the prosecutor that they may have such material. However, the officer in charge of an investigation is not required to make speculative enquiries of other persons: there must be some reason to believe that they may have relevant material. That reason may come from information provided to the police by the accused or from other inquiries made or from some other source.

3.6   If, during a criminal investigation, the officer in charge of an investigation or disclosure officer for any reason no longer has responsibility for the functions falling to him, either his supervisor or the police officer in charge of criminal investigations for the police force concerned must assign someone else to assume that responsibility. That person's identity must be recorded, as with those initially responsible for these functions in each investigation.

Recording of information

4.1   If material which may be relevant to the investigation consists of information which is not recorded in any form, the officer in charge of an investigation must ensure that it is recorded in a durable or retrievable form (whether in writing, on video or audio tape, or on computer disk).

4.2   Where it is not practicable to retain the initial record of information because it forms part of a larger record which is to be destroyed, its contents should be transferred as a true record to a durable and more easily-stored form before that happens.

4.3   Negative information is often relevant to an investigation. If it may be relevant it must be recorded. An example might be a number of people present in a particular place at a particular time who state that they saw nothing unusual.

4.4   Where information which may be relevant is obtained, it must be recorded at the time it is obtained or as soon as practicable after that time. This includes, for example, information obtained in house-to-house enquiries, although the requirement to record information promptly does not require an investigator to take a statement from a potential witness where it would not otherwise be taken.

Retention of material

(a)   Duty to retain material

5.1   The investigator must retain material obtained in a criminal investigation which may be relevant to the investigation. This includes not only material coming into the possession of the investigator (such as documents seized in the course of searching premises) but also material generated by him (such as interview records). Material may be photographed, or retained in the form of a copy rather than the original, if the original is perishable, or was supplied to the investigator rather than generated by him and is to be returned to its owner.

5.2   Where material has been seized in the exercise of the powers of seizure conferred by the Police and Criminal Evidence Act 1984, the duty to retain it under this code is subject to the provisions on the retention of seized material in section 22 of that Act.

5.3   If the officer in charge of an investigation becomes aware as a result of developments in the case that material previously examined but not retained (because it was not thought to be relevant) may now be relevant to the investigation, he should, wherever practicable, take steps to obtain it or ensure that it is retained for further inspection or for production in court if required.

5.4   The duty to retain material includes in particular the duty to retain material falling into the following categories, where it may be relevant to the investigation:

- crime reports (including crime report forms, relevant parts of incident report books or police officers' notebooks);

- custody records;

- records which are derived from tapes of telephone messages (for example, 999 calls) containing descriptions of an alleged offence or offender;

- final versions of witness statements (and draft versions where their content differs from the final version), including any exhibits mentioned (unless these have been returned to their owner on the understanding that they will be produced in court if required);

- interview records (written records, or audio or video tapes, of interviews with actual or potential witnesses or suspects);

- communications between the police and experts such as forensic scientists, reports of work carried out by experts, and schedules of scientific material prepared by the expert for the investigator, for the purposes of criminal proceedings;

- any material casting doubt on the reliability of a confession;

- any material casting doubt on the reliability of a witness;

- any other material which may fall within the test for primary prosecution disclosure in the Act.

5.5 The duty to retain material falling into these categories does not extend to items which are purely ancillary to such material and possess no independent significance (for example, duplicate copies of records or reports).

(b) Length of time for which material is to be retained

5.6 All material which may be relevant to the investigation must be retained until a decision is taken whether to institute proceedings against a person for an offence.

5.7 If a criminal investigation results in proceedings being instituted, all material which may be relevant must be retained at least until the accused is acquitted or convicted or the prosecutor decides not to proceed with the case.

5.8 Where the accused is convicted, all material which may be relevant must be retained at least until:

- the convicted person is released from custody, or discharged from hospital, in cases where the court imposes a custodial sentence or a hospital order;

- six months from the date of conviction, in all other cases.

If the court imposes a custodial sentence or hospital order and the convicted person is released from custody or is discharged from hospital earlier than six months from the date of conviction, all material which may be relevant must be retained at least until six months from the date of conviction.

5.9 If an appeal against conviction is in progress when the release or discharge occurs, or at the end of the period of six months specified in paragraph 5.8, all material which may be relevant must be retained until the appeal is determined. Similarly, if the Criminal Cases Review Commission is considering an application at that point in time, all material which may be relevant must be retained at least until the Commission decides not to refer the case to the Court of Appeal, or until the Court determines the appeal resulting from the reference by the Commission.

5.10 Material need not be retained by the police as required in paragraph 5.8 if it was seized and is to be returned to its owner.

Preparation of material for prosecutor

(a) Introduction

6.1 The officer in charge of the investigation, the disclosure officer or an investigator may seek advice from the prosecutor about whether any particular item of material may be relevant to the investigation.

6.2 Material which may be relevant to an investigation, which has been retained in accordance with this code, and which the disclosure officer believes will not form part of the prosecution case, must be listed on a schedule.

6.3 Material which the disclosure officer does not believe is sensitive must be listed on a schedule of non-sensitive material. The schedule must include a statement that the disclosure officer does not believe the material is sensitive.

6.4 Any material which is believed to be sensitive must be either listed on a schedule of sensitive material or, in exceptional circumstances, revealed to the prosecutor separately.

6.5 Paragraphs 6.6 to 6.11 below apply to both sensitive and non-sensitive material. Paragraphs 6.12 to 6.14 apply to sensitive material only.

(b) Circumstances in which a schedule is to be prepared

6.6 The disclosure officer must ensure that a schedule is prepared in the following circumstances:

- the accused is charged with an offence which is triable only on indictment;

- the accused is charged with an offence which is triable either way, and it is considered either that the case is likely to be tried on indictment or that the accused is likely to plead not guilty at a summary trial;

- the accused is charged with a summary offence, and it is considered that he is likely to plead not guilty.

6.7   In respect of either way and summary offences, a schedule may not be needed if a person has admitted the offence, or if a police officer witnessed the offence and that person has not denied it.

6.8   If it is believed that the accused is likely to plead guilty at a summary trial, it is not necessary to prepare a schedule in advance. If, contrary to this belief, the accused pleads not guilty at a summary trial, or the offence is to be tried on indictment, the disclosure officer must ensure that a schedule is prepared as soon as is reasonably practicable after that happens.

(c)   Way in which material is to be listed on schedule

6.9   The disclosure officer should ensure that each item of material is listed separately on the schedule, and is numbered consecutively. The description of each item should make clear the nature of the item and should contain sufficient detail to enable the prosecutor to decide whether he needs to inspect the material before deciding whether or not it should be disclosed.

6.10   In some enquiries it may not be practicable to list each item of material separately. For example, there may be many items of a similar or repetitive nature. These may be listed in a block and described by quantity and generic title.

6.11   Even if some material is listed in a block, the disclosure officer must ensure that any items among that material which might meet the test for primary prosecution disclosure are listed and described individually.

(d)   Treatment of sensitive material

6.12   Subject to paragraph 6.13 below, the disclosure officer must list on a sensitive schedule any material which he believes it is not in the public interest to disclose, and the reason for that belief. The schedule must include a statement that the disclosure officer believes the material is sensitive. Depending on the circumstances, examples of such material may include the following among others:

- material relating to national security;
- material received from the intelligence and security agencies;
- material relating to intelligence from foreign sources which reveals sensitive intelligence gathering methods;
- material given in confidence;
- material which relates to the use of a telephone system and which is supplied to an investigator for intelligence purposes only;
- material relating to the identity or activities of informants, or under-cover police officers, or other persons supplying information to the police who may be in danger if their identities are revealed;
- material revealing the location of any premises or other place used for police surveillance, or the identity of any person allowing a police officer to use them for surveillance;
- material revealing, either directly or indirectly, techniques and methods relied upon by a police officer in the course of a criminal investigation, for example covert surveillance techniques, or other methods of detecting crime;
- material whose disclosure might facilitate the commission of other offences or hinder the prevention and detection of crime;
- internal police communications such as management minutes;
- material upon the strength of which search warrants were obtained;
- material containing details of persons taking part in identification parades;

- material supplied to an investigator during a criminal investigation which has been generated by an official of a body concerned with the regulation or supervision of bodies corporate or of persons engaged in financial activities, or which has been generated by a person retained by such a body;

- material supplied to an investigator during a criminal investigation which relates to a child or young person and which has been generated by a local authority social services department, an Area Child Protection Committee or other party contacted by an investigator during the investigation.

6.13   In exceptional circumstances, where an investigator considers that material is so sensitive that its revelation to the prosecutor by means of an entry on the sensitive schedule is inappropriate, the existence of the material must be revealed to the prosecutor separately. This will apply where compromising the material would be likely to lead directly to the loss of life, or directly threaten national security.

6.14   In such circumstances, the responsibility for informing the prosecutor lies with the investigator who knows the detail of the sensitive material. The investigator should act as soon as is reasonably practicable after the file containing the prosecution case is sent to the prosecutor. The investigator must also ensure that the prosecutor is able to inspect the material so that he can assess whether it needs to be brought before a court for a ruling on disclosure.

Revelation of material to prosecutor

7.1   The disclosure officer must give the schedules to the prosecutor. Wherever practicable this should be at the same time as he gives him the file containing the material for the prosecution case (or as soon as is reasonably practicable after the decision on mode of trial or the plea, in cases to which paragraph 6.8 applies).

7.2   The disclosure officer should draw the attention of the prosecutor to any material an investigator has retained (whether or not listed on a schedule) which may fall within the test for primary prosecution disclosure in the Act, and should explain why he has come to that view.

7.3   At the same time as complying with the duties in paragraphs 7.1 and 7.2, the disclosure officer must give the prosecutor a copy of any material which falls into the following categories (unless such material has already been given to the prosecutor as part of the file containing the material for the prosecution case):

- records of the first description of a suspect given to the police by a potential witness, whether or not the description differs from that of the alleged offender;

- information provided by an accused person which indicates an explanation for the offence with which he has been charged;

- any material casting doubt on the reliability of a confession;

- any material casting doubt on the reliability of a witness;

- any other material which the investigator believes may fall within the test for primary prosecution disclosure in the Act.

7.4   If the prosecutor asks to inspect material which has not already been copied to him, the disclosure officer must allow him to inspect it. If the prosecutor asks for a copy of material which has not already been copied to him, the disclosure officer must give him a copy. However, this does not apply where the disclosure officer believes, having consulted the officer in charge of the investigation, that the material is too sensitive to be copied and can only be inspected.

7.5   If material consists of information which is recorded other than in writing, whether it should be given to the prosecutor in its original form as a whole, or by way of relevant extracts recorded in the same form, or in the form of a transcript, is a matter for agreement between the disclosure officer and the prosecutor.

Subsequent action by disclosure officer

8.1   At the time a schedule of non-sensitive material is prepared, the disclosure officer may not know exactly what material will form the case against the accused, and the prosecutor may not have given advice about the likely relevance of particular items of material. Once these matters have been determined, the disclosure officer must give the prosecutor, where necessary, an amended schedule listing any additional material:

- which may be relevant to the investigation,
- which does not form part of the case against the accused,
- which is not already listed on the schedule, and
- which he believes is not sensitive,

unless he is informed in writing by the prosecutor that the prosecutor intends to disclose the material to the defence.

8.2   After a defence statement has been given, the disclosure officer must look again at the material which has been retained and must draw the attention of the prosecutor to any material which might reasonably be expected to assist the defence disclosed by the accused; and he must reveal it to him in accordance with paragraphs 7.4 and 7.5 above.

8.3   Section 9 of the Act imposes a continuing duty on the prosecutor, for the duration of criminal proceedings against the accused, to disclose material which meets the tests for disclosure (subject to public interest considerations). To enable him to do this, any new material coming to light should be treated in the same way as the earlier material.

Certification by disclosure officer

9.1   The disclosure officer must certify to the prosecutor that, to the best of his knowledge and belief, all material which has been retained and made available to him has been revealed to the prosecutor in accordance with this code. He must sign and date the certificate. It will be necessary to certify not only at the time when the schedule and accompanying material is submitted to the prosecutor, but also when material which has been retained is reconsidered after the accused has given a defence statement.

Disclosure of material to accused

10.1   If material has not already been copied to the prosecutor, and he requests its disclosure to the accused on the ground that:

- it falls within the test for primary or secondary prosecution disclosure, or
- the court has ordered its disclosure after considering an application from the accused,

the disclosure officer must disclose it to the accused.

10.2   If material has been copied to the prosecutor, and it is to be disclosed, whether it is disclosed by the prosecutor or the disclosure officer is a matter for agreement between the two of them.

10.3   The disclosure officer must disclose material to the accused either by giving him a copy or by allowing him to inspect it. If the accused person asks for a copy of any material which he has been allowed to inspect, the disclosure officer must give it to him, unless in the opinion of the disclosure officer that is either not practicable (for example because the material consists of an object which cannot be copied, or because the volume of material is so great), or not desirable (for example because the material is a statement by a child witness in relation to a sexual offence).

10.4   If material which the accused has been allowed to inspect consists of information which is recorded other than in writing, whether it should be given to the accused in its original form or in the form of a transcript is a matter for the discretion of the disclosure officer. If the material is transcribed, the disclosure officer must ensure that the transcript is certified to the accused as a true record of the material which has been transcribed.

10.5   If a court concludes that it is in the public interest that an item of sensitive material must be disclosed to the accused, it will be necessary to disclose the material if the case is to proceed. This does not mean that sensitive documents must always be disclosed in their original form: for example, the court may agree that sensitive details still requiring protection should be blocked out, or that documents may be summarised, or that the prosecutor may make an admission about the substance of the material under section 10 of the Criminal Justice Act 1967.

APPENDIX 7   HUMAN RIGHTS

Convention for the Protection of Human Rights and Fundamental Freedoms, Arts 5 to 7

Article 5

Right to liberty and security

1.   Everyone has the right to liberty and security of the person. No one shall be deprived of his liberty save in the following cases and in accordance with a procedure prescribed by law:

(a)   the lawful detention of a person after conviction by a competent court;

(b)   the lawful arrest or detention of a person for non-compliance with the lawful order of a court or in order to secure the fulfilment of any obligation prescribed by law;

(c)   the lawful arrest or detention of a person effected for the purpose of bringing him before the competent legal authority on reasonable suspicion of having committed an offence or when it is reasonably considered necessary to prevent his committing an offence or fleeing after having done so;

(d)   the detention of a minor by lawful order for the purpose of educational supervision or his lawful detention for the purpose of bringing him before the competent legal authority;

(e)   the lawful detention of persons for the prevention of spreading of infectious diseases, of persons of unsound mind, alcoholics or drug addicts or vagrants;

(f)   the lawful arrest or detention of a person to prevent his effecting an unauthorised entry into the country or of a person against whom action is being taken with a view to deportation or extradition.

2.   Everyone who is arrested shall be informed promptly, in a language which he understands, of the reasons for his arrest and of any charge against him.

3.   Everyone arrested or detained in accordance with the provisions of paragraph (1)(c) of this Article shall be brought promptly before a judge or other officer authorised by law to exercise judicial power and shall be entitled to trial within a reasonable time or to release pending trial. Release may be conditioned by guarantees to appear for trial.

4.   Everyone who is deprived of his liberty by arrest or detention shall be entitled to take proceedings by which the lawfulness of his detention shall be decided speedily by a court and his release ordered if the detention is not lawful.

5.   Everyone who has been the victim of arrest or detention in contravention of the provisions of this Article shall have an enforceable right to compensation.

Article 6

Right to a fair trial

1.   In the determination of his civil rights and obligations or of any criminal charge against him, everyone is entitled to a fair and public hearing within a reasonable time by an independent and impartial tribunal established by law. Judgment shall be pronounced publicly but the press and public may be excluded from all or part of the trial in the interests of morals, public order or national security in a democratic society, where the interests of juveniles or the protection of the private life of the parties so require, or to the extent strictly necessary in the opinion of the court in special circumstances where publicity would prejudice the interests of justice.

2.   Everyone charged with a criminal offence shall be presumed innocent until proved guilty according to law.

3.   Everyone charged with a criminal offence has the following minimum rights:

(a)   to be informed promptly, in a language which he understands and in detail, of the nature and cause of the accusation against him;

(b)   to have adequate time and facilities for the preparation of his defence;

(c)   to defend himself in person or through legal assistance of his own choosing or, if he has not sufficient means to pay for legal assistance, to be given it free when the interests of justice so require;

(d)   to examine or have examined witnesses against him and to obtain the attendance and examination of witnesses on his behalf under the same conditions as witnesses against him;

(e)   to have the free assistance of an interpreter if he cannot understand or speak the language used in court.

Article 7

No punishment without law

1.   No one shall be held guilty of any criminal offence on account of any act or omission which did not constitute a criminal offence under national or international law at the time when it was committed. Nor shall a heavier penalty be imposed than the one that was applicable at the time the criminal offence was committed.

2.   This Article shall not prejudice the trial and punishment of any person for any act or omission which, at the time when it was committed, was criminal according to the general principles of law recognised by civilised nations.

Human Rights Act 1998, ss. 2 to 4, 6 and 10

2.—(1)   A court or tribunal determining a question which has arisen under this Act in connection with a Convention right must take into account any—

(a)   judgment, decision, declaration or advisory opinion of the European Court of Human Rights,

(b)   opinion of the Commission given in a report adopted under Article 31 of the Convention,

(c)   decision of the Commission in connection with Article 26 or 27(2) of the Convention, or

(d)   decision of the Committee of Ministers taken under Article 46 of the Convention, whenever made or given, so far as, in the opinion of the court or tribunal, it is relevant to the proceedings in which that question has arisen.

(2)   Evidence of any judgment, decision, declaration or opinion of which account may have to be taken under this section is to be given in proceedings before any court or tribunal in such manner as may be provided by rules.

(3)   In this section 'rules' means rules of court or, in the case of proceedings before a tribunal, rules made for the purposes of this section—

(a)   by the Lord Advocate or Secretary of State, in relation to proceedings in Scotland; or

(b)   by the Lord Chancellor or Secretary of State, in relation to any other proceedings.

(4)   Where a court or tribunal is determining a question which has arisen under this Act in connection with a Convention right it shall be a defence for a person to show that he has acted in pursuance of a manifestation of religious belief in accordance with the historic teaching and practices of a christian or other principal religious tradition represented in Great Britain.

(5)   For the avoidance of doubt, the teaching and practices referred to in subsection (4) above do not include any teaching or practice which contravenes the criminal law.

(6)   Subject to subsection (5) above, the teaching and practices referred to in subsection (4) above shall include teaching or practice in accordance with a relevant historic creed, canon, confession of faith, catechism or formulary.

(7)   In this section 'manifestation of religious belief' shall be taken to include actions such as worship, observance, conformity to a moral or ethical principle, practice, teaching and employment policies.

3.—(1)   So far as it is possible to do so, primary legislation and subordinate legislation must be read and given effect in a way which is compatible with the Convention rights.

(2)   This section—

(a)   applies to primary legislation and subordinate legislation whenever enacted;

(b)   does not affect the validity, continuing operation or enforcement of any incompatible primary legislation; and

(c)   does not affect the validity, continuing operation or enforcement of any incompatible subordinate legislation if (disregarding any possibility of revocation) primary legislation prevents removal of the incompatibility.

4.—(1)   Subsection (2) applies in any proceedings in which a court determines whether a provision of primary legislation is compatible with a Convention right.

(2)   If the court is satisfied that the provision is incompatible with a Convention right, it may make a declaration of that incompatibility.

(3)   Subsection (4) applies in any proceedings in which a court determines whether a provision of subordinate legislation, made in the exercise of a power conferred by primary legislation, is compatible with a Convention right.

(4)   If the court is satisfied—

(a)   that the provision is incompatible with a Convention right, and

(b)   that (disregarding any possibility of revocation) the primary legislation concerned prevents removal of the incompatibility,

it may make a declaration of that incompatibility.

(5)   In this section 'court' means—

(a)   the House of Lords;

(b)   the Judicial Committee of the Privy Council;

(c)   the Courts-Martial Appeal Court;

(d)   in Scotland, the High Court of Justiciary sitting otherwise than as a trial court or the Court of Session;

(e)   in England and Wales or Northern Ireland, the High Court or the Court of Appeal.

(6)   A declaration under this section ('a declaration of incompatibility')—

(a)   does not affect the validity, continuing operation or enforcement of the provision in respect of which it is given; and

(b)   is not binding on the parties to the proceedings in which it is made.

6.—(1)   It is unlawful for a public authority to act in a way which is incompatible with a Convention right.

(2)   Subsection (1) does not apply to an act if—

(a)   as the result of one or more provisions of primary legislation, the authority could not have acted differently; or

(b)   in the case of one or more provisions of, or made under, primary legislation which cannot be read or given effect in a way which is compatible with the Convention rights, the authority was acting so as to give effect to or enforce those provisions.

(3)   In this section 'public authority' includes—

(a)   a court or tribunal, and

(b)   any person certain of whose functions are functions of a public nature, but does not include either House of Parliament or a person exercising functions in connection with proceedings in Parliament.

10.—(1)   This section applies if—

(a)   a provision of legislation has been declared under section 4 to be incompatible with a Convention right and, if an appeal lies—

(i)   all persons who may appeal have stated in writing that they do not intend to do so;

(ii)   the time for bringing an appeal has expired and no appeal has been brought within that time; or

(iii)   an appeal brought within that time has been determined or abandoned; or

(b)   it appears to a Minister of the Crown or Her Majesty in Council that, having regard to a finding of the European Court of Human Rights made after the coming into force of this section in proceedings against the United Kingdom, a provision of legislation is incompatible with an obligation of the United Kingdom arising from the Convention.

(2)   If a Minister of the Crown considers that there are compelling reasons for proceeding under this section, he may by order make such amendments to the legislation as he considers necessary to remove the incompatibility.

(3)   If, in the case of subordinate legislation, a Minister of the Crown considers—

(a)   that it is necessary to amend the primary legislation under which the subordinate legislation in question was made, in order to enable the incompatibility to be removed, and

(b)   that there are compelling reasons for proceeding under this section, he may by order make such amendments to the primary legislation as he considers necessary.

INDEX